EIGHTH EDITION

FOOD CHEMICALS CODEX

FCC 8

By authority of the United States Pharmacopeial Convention. Prepared by the Council of Experts and published by the Board of Trustees

THE UNITED STATES PHARMACOPEIAL CONVENTION
12601 Twinbrook Parkway, Rockville, MD 20852

NOTICE AND WARNING

Compliance with Federal Statues and Other Laws
The fact that an article appears in the *Food Chemicals Codex* or its supplements does not exempt it from compliance with requirements of acts of Congress, with regulations and rulings issued by agencies of the United States Government under authority of these acts, or with requirements and regulations of governments in other countries as relevant.

Concerning U.S. Patent or Trademark Rights
The inclusion in *Food Chemical Codex* of a monograph on any article in respect to which patent or trademark rights may exist shall not be deemed, and is not intended as, a grant of, or authority to exercise, any right or privilege protected by such patent or trademark. All such rights and privileges are vested in the patent or trademark owner, and no other person may exercise the same without express permission, authority, or license secured from such patent or trademark owner.

Concerning Use of FCC Text
Attention is called to the fact that *FCC* text is fully copyrighted. Authors and others wishing to use portions of the text should request permission to do so from the Legal Department of the United States Pharmacopeial Convention.

Copyright © 2012 The United States Pharmacopeial Convention
12601 Twinbrook Parkway, Rockville, MD 20852

All rights reserved.

ISBN 978-1-936424-05-4
ISSN 2153-1412 (print)
ISSN 2153-1455 (online)

Printed in the United States by United Book Press, Inc., Baltimore, MD

Contents

PREFACE v

PEOPLE xi

ADMISSIONS xviii

ANNOTATED xix

GENERAL PROVISIONS AND REQUIREMENTS APPLYING TO SPECIFICATIONS, TESTS, AND ASSAYS OF THE *FOOD CHEMICALS CODEX* 1

MONOGRAPH SPECIFICATIONS 9

PROVISIONAL MONOGRAPH SPECIFICATIONS 1209

GENERAL TESTS AND ASSAYS 1213
    Appendix I: Apparatus for Test and Assays 1217
    Appendix II: Physical Tests and Determinations 1221
        A. Chromatograhy 1221
        B. Physicochemical Properties 1230
        C. Others 1242
    Appendix III: Chemical Tests and Determinations 1262
        A. Identification Tests 1262
        B. Limit Tests 1264
        C. Others 1279
    Appendix IV: Chewing Gum Base 1298
    Appendix V: Enzyme Assays 1303
    Appendix VI: Essential Oils and Flavors 1336
    Appendix VII: Fats and Related Substances 1341
    Appendix VIII: Oleoresins 1357
    Appendix IX: Rosins and Related Substances 1360
    Appendix X: Carbohydrates (Starches, Sugars, and Related Substances) 1364
    Appendix XI: Flavor Chemicals (Other Than Essential Oils) 1375
    Appendix XII: Microbiological Tests 1381
    Appendix XIII: Adulterants and Contaminants in Food Ingredients 1384
    Appendix XIV: Markers for Authenticity Testing 1388

SOLUTIONS AND INDICATORS 1393

GENERAL INFORMATION 1409

INDEX 1613

Preface

FCC 8

This section provides general information about the Eighth Edition of the *Food Chemicals Codex* (*FCC*) and background information on the United States Pharmacopeial Convention (USP). Additional information about the specific uses of this compendium is provided in the *General Provisions and Requirements* section (page 1).

MISSION

FCC is published in continuing pursuit of the mission of USP: To improve the health of people around the world through public standards and related programs that help ensure the quality, safety, and benefit of medicines and foods.

HISTORY

FCC began after the passage of the 1958 Food Additives Amendment to the United States (U.S.) Federal Food, Drug, and Cosmetic Act. Although the U.S. Food and Drug Administration (FDA) had, by regulations and informal statements, defined in general terms the quality requirements for food additives, food colors, substances generally recognized as safe for use in foods (GRAS) and other food chemicals in the US market prior to 1958 (prior-sanctioned articles), these requirements were not sufficiently specific to serve as release, procurement, and acceptance specifications for manufacturers and users of food chemicals. Therefore, regulators, industry and other interested parties recognized the need for a compendium of standards designed especially for food chemicals, comparable to the *United States Pharmacopeia* for drugs and the *National Formulary* for excipients, which would define the quality of food-grade chemicals in terms of identity, strength, and purity. The National Academy of Sciences (NAS) was requested to develop this compendium and published the first edition of the *FCC* in 1966. Subsequent editions were published by the NAS in 1972, 1981, 1996, and 2003, through the Food and Nutrition Board of the Institute of Medicine (IOM), which formed a Committee on Food Chemicals Codex to elaborate the *FCC*.

The scope of *FCC* has expanded with each new edition. Substances included in the first edition were limited to chemicals added directly to foods to achieve a desired function. Subsequent editions added: (a) processing aids such as enzymes, extraction solvents, filter media, and boiler water additives; (b) foods, such as fructose and dextrose; and (c) functional ingredients that affect not the foods to which they are added, but the human body when the food is consumed. Over the years, *FCC* has become a comprehensive compendium of standards for these articles, collectively termed food ingredients. The introduction of new food ingredients as well as constant changes in manufacturing processes and advances in analytical and metrological sciences lead to a need for continuous revision of the *FCC*. Because of its regulatory status in countries other than the United States, and its worldwide use, the *FCC* contains monographs for ingredients that may not be currently marketed in the United States.

USP acquired *FCC* from the NAS in 2006 and assumed responsibility for its ongoing development and publication. To continue the work of the Food and Nutrition Board of IOM, USP formed a Food Ingredients Expert Committee within its Council of Experts. This Expert Committee is responsible for approving all new and revised standards in *FCC*.

FCC 8

The Eighth Edition of *FCC* (*FCC 8*) includes more than 1,100 monographs. It also contains more than 150 *General Tests* and *Assays*, providing procedures frequently cited in monographs, sometimes with acceptance criteria, in order to avoid repetition of this text. Additionally, *FCC 8* offers a chapter with up-to-date relevant informational materials on method validation and various analytical techniques, reference tables and information on current Good Manufacturing Practices. Additions, deletions, and other revisions of text from the *FCC* Seventh Edition are indicated on page xix in the *Admissions* section. The *FCC* and its *Supplements* become effective 90 days from the official date of publication, unless otherwise noted.

Monograph Elements

Each *FCC 8* monograph represents the documentary standard for an article, manifested by specifications that speak to the quality and safety of the food ingredient. Each monograph includes, when available, the following: empirical formula, structural formula, and formula weight; description of the substance, including physical form, odor (flavoring agents only), and solubility (see the descriptive terms for solubility in the *General Provisions and Requirements* section); function; packaging and storage; labeling; identification; assay (or a quantitative test to serve as an assay); impurities (inorganic and organic); specific tests; and other requirements. The specifications provided, taken together, represent a compositional understanding of the substance.

PUBLICATION OF FCC REVISIONS

FCC revisions are published biennially in new editions, in *Supplements* published in intervening years and, when circumstances warrant, as *Expedited Standards* or *Immediate Standards*.

Supplements

The *First Supplement* to *FCC 8* will be published in September 2012 and will become effective 90 days from the official date of publication, unless otherwise noted. The Index in each *Supplement* is cumulative and includes citations to the biennial revision. The contents of the *Supplement* are integrated into the following edition of *FCC*, along with new revisions that have been adopted since the *Supplement* to the previous compendium.

Expedited Standards

Expedited Standards are revisions that the Food Ingredients Expert Committee determines, for public health or other reasons, should become effective prior to publication of the next edition of the *FCC* or *Supplement*. Proposed expedited standards are posted on the *FCC Forum* website for a comment period of 90 days. If there are no significant comments, they become effective on the date posted on the USP website, unless otherwise noted. These revisions will be incorporated into the next published edition of the *FCC* or *Supplement*.

Immediate Standards

Immediate Standards are revisions that the Food Ingredients Expert Committee determines should be made available immediately because of an urgent public health need. These standards are posted as final on the USP website without prior public notice and comment and are effective upon website publication unless a delayed effective date is specified. These standards will be incorporated into the next published edition of the *FCC* or *Supplement*.

Errata

Errata are text published in the *FCC* or its *Supplements* that do not accurately reflect the intended standards as approved by the Food Ingredients Expert Committee. A list of errata and corresponding corrections to an edition of the *FCC* or to a *Supplement* are published on USP's website, and incorporated into the next published edition of the *FCC* or *Supplement*. Errata shall not be subject to public notice and comment.

Print and Electronic Presentations

The *FCC* and its *Supplements* are available in print form and in an Internet version that allows individual registered users to access the *FCC* online. The Internet format provides access to *FCC* content, along with extensive search options. It is continuously and cumulatively updated to integrate the content of *Supplements*. For users of the print edition, the *Supplements* are included with the purchase of the *FCC*. Users of the *FCC* print edition must retain the *Supplements* and review the *FCC* portion of the USP website in order to have up-to-date information.

Symbols

Indicating change to effective text, symbols identify the beginning and end of each revision. The following table summarizes the types of symbols and the associated subscripts used in FCC publications:

Revision Type	Symbol	Subscript
Text Deletion Adopted as an Expedited or Immediate Standard	• •	Effective Date
Text Deletion Adopted in a *Supplement*	■ ■	1S, 2S, 3S (*FCC* biennial edition)
Text Deletion Adopted in *FCC*	▲ ▲	*FCC* biennial edition
New Text Adopted as an Expedited or Immediate Standard	•new text•	Effective Date
New Text Adopted in a *Supplement*	■new text■	1S, 2S, 3S (*FCC* biennial edition)
New Text Adopted in *FCC*	▲new text▲	*FCC* biennial edition

The following table shows symbols and effective dates for *FCC* 8 and its *Supplements*:

Supplement	Effective Date	Symbols
FCC 8	June 1, 2012	▲and▲$_{FCC8}$
1	December 1, 2012	■and■$_{1S(FCC8)}$
2	June 1, 2013	■and■$_{2S(FCC8)}$
3	December 1, 2013	■and■$_{3S(FCC8)}$

FCC REVISION PROCESS

The *FCC* is revised on an ongoing basis in accordance with USP Policies and Rules and Procedures. Users of the *FCC* are requested and encouraged to submit suggestions for updating and improving the specifications and general analytical methods, and to review and comment upon proposed revisions through the processes discussed below.

Food Ingredients Expert Committee

The Food Ingredient Expert Committee (FIEC) is part of USP's Council of Experts and is the scientific decision-making body for the *FCC*. Its principal functions include the following:

- To propose means by which *FCC* standards may be kept current in reflecting food-grade quality on the basis of ingredient safety, good manufacturing practices, and advances in analytical capabilities.
- To provide information on issues relating to standards for particular substances and analytical test procedures.
- To recommend the establishment of Expert Panels consisting of a committee member and other experts or specialists to address specific issues relevant to monograph development and to report their findings and advisory recommendations to the full committee.
- To evaluate comments submitted by interested parties on any aspect of proposed *FCC* standards.
- To approve final standards before their publication in the *FCC* or its *Supplements*.
- To consider and act on any other issues concerning the development and publication of standards for new and existing food-grade ingredients.

The FIEC meets regularly to discuss food ingredients topics, including technical and policy issues relevant to the FCC.

Public Participation in FCC Revisions

Although the FIEC is the ultimate decision-making body for *FCC* standards, these standards are developed by an exceptional process of public involvement and substantial interaction between USP and its stakeholders, both domestically and internationally. Participation in the revision process results from the support of many individuals and groups and also from scientific, technical, and trade organizations.

Public Review and Comment Process for FCC Standards Development

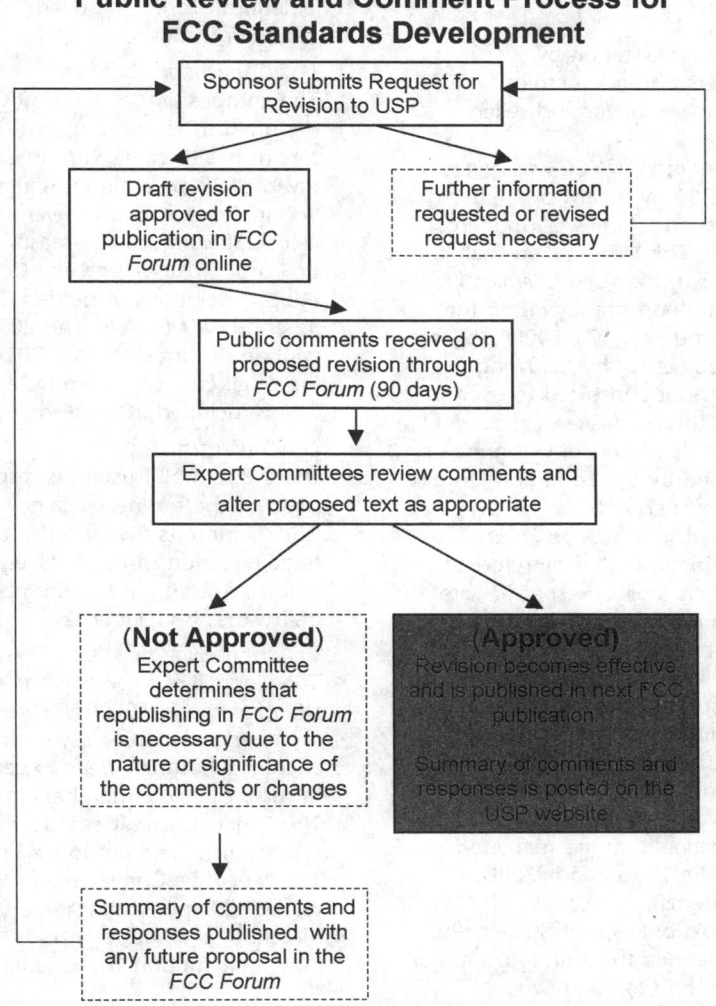

Figure 1. Public Review Process

Requests for revision of monographs, either new monographs or those needing updating, contain information submitted voluntarily by manufacturers and other interested parties. At times, USP staff may develop information to support a monograph through a *Request for Revision*. USP has developed a document titled *Guideline for Submitting Requests for Revision to FCC*, which is available at www.usp.org. To facilitate the continuous revision of *FCC* and ensure an open, transparent, and participatory revision process, USP solicits and encourages public comment on *FCC* monographs, *General Tests and Assays*, and other draft documents via the *FCC Forum*. The *Forum* is available free of charge. For more information, visit www.usp.org/fcc.

Comments received are considered by the FIEC, who determine whether changes should be made to the proposed revisions based on those comments. Proposed standards are finalized when the FIEC votes to make them effective text in *FCC*. Thus, the USP standards-setting process gives those who manufacture, regulate, and use food ingredients the opportunity to comment on the development and revision of *FCC* standards. All proposals will have a 90-day comment period. *Figure 1* shows the public review and comment process and its relationship to standards development.

Working with Government Agencies

USP works in many ways with government agencies in the United States and abroad, including the FDA, to promote good communications and optimal interactions. The USP Government Liaison Program allows government representatives to participate in FIEC meetings, enabling continuing interactions between the regulators' scientific staff and Expert Committee activities. Staff in the FDA Centers, who are responsible for review of USP compendial activities, provide specific links and opportunities for exchange of comments. The Center for Food Safety and Applied Nutrition is the center that links FDA and USP in the areas of food ingredients and *FCC*.

LEGAL RECOGNITION OF FCC STANDARDS

The *FCC* has earned international recognition by manufacturers, vendors, and users of food chemicals. *FCC* standards serve as the basis for many buyer and seller contractual agreements.

In the United States, the first edition of *FCC* was given quasi-legal recognition in July 1966 by means of a letter of endorsement from FDA Commissioner James L. Goddard, which was reprinted in the book. The letter stated that "the FDA will regard the specifications in the *Food Chemicals Codex* as defining an 'appropriate food grade' within the meaning of Sec. 121.101(b)(3) and Sec. 121.1000(a)(2) of the food additive regulations, subject to the following qualification: this endorsement is not construed to exempt any food chemical appearing in the *Food Chemicals Codex* from compliance with requirements of Acts of Congress or with regulations and rulings issued by the Food and Drug Administration under authority of such Acts."

Subsequently, various additional specifications from previous *FCC* editions were also incorporated by reference in the U.S. *Code of Federal Regulations* to define specific safe ingredients under Title 21, in various parts of Sections 172, 173, and 184. It is anticipated that FDA will from time to time continue to update its regulatory references to the *FCC*.

USP will work diligently to assure that the *FCC* contains monographs for all substances added to foods in the United States, including all ingredients that are marketed as food additives and color additives under an FDA regulation following a successful petition of FDA, ingredients that are affirmed to be GRAS, and ingredients that are marketed under approvals issued prior to the 1958 Food Additive Amendments (prior-sanctioned items).

In Canada, in the absence of national specifications, the Fourth edition of the *FCC*, as amended from time to time, is officially recognized in the *Canadian Food and Drug Regulations* under Section B.01.045(b) as the reference for specifications for food additives.

For Australia and New Zealand, the Food Standards Australia New Zealand recognizes the Seventh Edition of the *FCC* as a primary source of identity and purity specifications for substances added to food in Standard 1.3.4 Identity and Purity of its Food Standards Code.

In Israel, the Public Health Regulations state that those who produce, import, market, or store a food additive must comply with the requirements established in the latest edition of *FCC* or in the latest edition of the *Compendium of Food Additive Specifications* published by the Joint FAO/WHO Expert Committee on Food Additives (JECFA).

GENERAL INFORMATION REGARDING USP

USP GOVERNANCE, STANDARDS-SETTING, AND ADVISORY BODIES

USP's governing, standards-setting, and advisory bodies include the USP Convention, the Board of Trustees, the Council of Experts and its Expert Committees, Expert Panels (formerly known as Advisory Panels), and staff. Additional volunteer bodies include Stakeholder Forums, Project Teams, and Advisory Groups, which act in an advisory capacity to provide input to USP's governing, standards-setting, and management bodies.

USP Convention
The composition of the USP Convention membership is designed to ensure a global representation from all sectors of health care, with an emphasis on practitioners, given USP's practitioner heritage (see the *History* section). Voting Delegates of Convention member organizations elect USP's President, Treasurer, other members of the Board of Trustees, and the Council of Experts. They also adopt resolutions to guide USP's strategic direction and amend USP's Bylaws. The 2010 meeting of the USP Convention occurred in April 2010 in Washington, DC. A listing of all current Voting Delegates of the USP Convention is included in the *People* section.

Board of Trustees
USP's Board of Trustees is responsible for the management of the business affairs, finances, and property of USP. During its 5-year term, the Board defines USP's strategic direction through its key policy and operational decisions. A listing of the members of the 2010–2015 Board of Trustees is included in the *People* section.

Council of Experts
The Council of Experts is the standards-setting body of USP. For the 2010–2015 cycle it is composed of 21 members, elected to 5-year terms by USP's Convention, each of whom chairs an Expert Committee. These Chairs, in turn, elect the members of their Expert Committees. The Expert Committees are responsible for the content of USP's official and authorized publications (see *Figure 2*). The Executive Committee of the Council of Experts includes all Expert Committee Chairs and provides overall direction, is an appeals body, and performs other functions that support the Council of Experts' operations.

Expert Panels to the Council of Experts
The Chair of the Council of Experts may appoint Expert Panels to assist the Council of Experts by providing advisory recommendations to particular Expert Committees in response to a specific charge consistent with the Expert Committee's Work Plan. Expert Panels are continuously formed; their topics and membership appear in the *People* section.

Stakeholder Forums and Project Teams
USP may form several domestic and international Stakeholder Forums and Project Teams during the 2010–2015 cycle, including the Food Ingredients and Dietary Supplements Stakeholder Forums, to exchange information and receive comments on USP's standards-setting activities. Depending on the topic, a Stakeholder Forum may create Project Teams to work on selected topics. USP also holds Standards and Science Symposia in various regions throughout the world to promote scientific exchanges on topics relating to USP compendia.

International Standards and Science Symposia
- North America
- India/West Asia
- China/East Asia
- Latin America

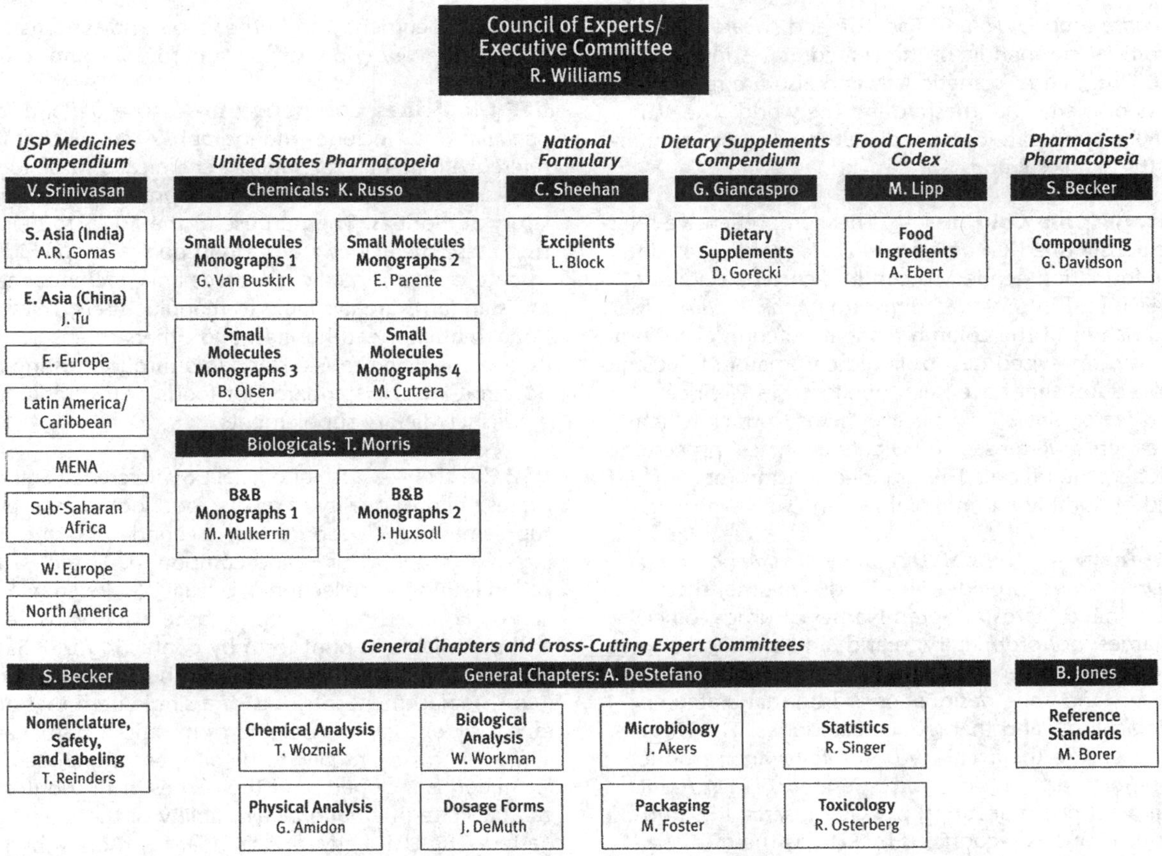

```
                          Council of Experts/
                          Executive Committee
                              R. Williams
```

USP Medicines Compendium	**United States Pharmacopeia**	**National Formulary**	**Dietary Supplements Compendium**	**Food Chemicals Codex**	**Pharmacists' Pharmacopeia**
V. Srinivasan	Chemicals: K. Russo	C. Sheehan	G. Giancaspro	M. Lipp	S. Becker

- S. Asia (India) — A.R. Gomas
- E. Asia (China) — J. Tu
- E. Europe
- Latin America/Caribbean
- MENA
- Sub-Saharan Africa
- W. Europe
- North America

United States Pharmacopeia — Chemicals: K. Russo
- Small Molecules Monographs 1 — G. Van Buskirk
- Small Molecules Monographs 2 — E. Parente
- Small Molecules Monographs 3 — B. Olsen
- Small Molecules Monographs 4 — M. Cutrera

Biologicals: T. Morris
- B&B Monographs 1 — M. Mulkerrin
- B&B Monographs 2 — J. Huxsoll

National Formulary: Excipients — L. Block
Dietary Supplements Compendium: Dietary Supplements — D. Gorecki
Food Chemicals Codex: Food Ingredients — A. Ebert
Pharmacists' Pharmacopeia: Compounding — G. Davidson

General Chapters and Cross-Cutting Expert Committees

S. Becker — Nomenclature, Safety, and Labeling — T. Reinders

General Chapters: A. DeStefano
- Chemical Analysis — T. Wozniak
- Biological Analysis — W. Workman
- Microbiology — J. Akers
- Statistics — R. Singer
- Physical Analysis — G. Amidon
- Dosage Forms — J. DeMuth
- Packaging — M. Foster
- Toxicology — R. Osterberg

B. Jones — Reference Standards — M. Borer

Figure 2. 2010–2015 USP Council of Experts

- Europe
- Middle East/North Africa

Staff
USP maintains a staff of over 700 scientists, professionals, and administrative personnel at its Rockville, Maryland headquarters and throughout the world, including an account management office in Basel, Switzerland, and laboratory facilities in Hyderabad, India; Shanghai, China; and São Paulo, Brazil.

USP POLICIES, RULES, AND PROCEDURES

Governing Documents
USP's Articles of Incorporation, its Constitution and Bylaws, and the Rules and Procedures of the 2010–2015 Council of Experts are available on USP's website (www.usp.org). Collectively, these documents serve USP volunteers and staff as the governing principles for USP's standards-setting activities.

Conflicts of Interest
USP's Conflict of Interest provisions require all members of the Council of Experts, its Expert Committees, Expert Panels, Board of Trustees, and key staff to disclose financial or other interests that may interfere with their duties as USP volunteers. Members of the Board of Trustees, Council of Experts, and its Expert Committees are not allowed to take part in the final discussion or vote on any matter in which they have a conflict of interest or there is the appearance of a conflict of interest. Members of Expert Panels may participate and vote, so long as any conflicts have been adequately and promptly disclosed and are communicated to the relevant Expert Committee along with any Expert Panel recommendations.

Confidentiality and Document Disclosure
Members of the Council of Experts, Expert Committees, and Expert Panels sign confidentiality agreements, in keeping with USP's Confidentiality Policy and the confidentiality provisions of the *Rules and Procedures* of the Council of Experts. The USP Document Disclosure Policy, available on USP's website, contributes to the transparency of the standards-setting process by making information available to the public, yet provides protection to manufacturers and others who submit confidential information to USP.

OTHER USP PUBLICATIONS

United States Pharmacopeia and the National Formulary— The *United States Pharmacopeia (USP)* and *National Formulary (NF)* are compendia of science-based standards for drug and biologic dosage forms, drug substances, excipients, medical devices, and dietary supplements. These standards are set by Expert Committees following public notice and opportunity for comment through publication in the free *Pharmacopeial Forum*. The *USP* and *NF* are recognized as official compendia of the United States in the Federal Food, Drug, and Cosmetic Act, and also are recognized in the laws of many countries around the world. The *USP* and the *NF* are separate compendia although they are published in the same volume.

Chromatographic Columns— This comprehensive reference, previously titled *Chromatographic Reagents*, provides detailed information needed to conduct chromatographic procedures found in *USP–NF*. *Chromatographic Columns* lists the brand names of the column reagents cited in every proposal for new or revised gas- or liquid-chromatographic analytical procedures that have been published in *PF* since 1980. *Chromatographic Columns* also helps to track which column reagents were used to validate analytical procedures that have become official. The branded column reagents list is updated bimonthly and maintained on USP's website.

USP Dictionary— The *USP Dictionary of USAN and International Drug Names* provides, in a single volume, the most up-to-date United States Adopted Names of drugs; official *USP–NF* names; nonproprietary, brand, and chemical names; graphic formulas; molecular formulas and weights; CAS registry numbers and code designations; drug manufacturers; and pharmacologic and therapeutic categories. The *Dictionary* helps to ensure the accuracy of the following: product labeling; reports, articles, and correspondence; FDA regulatory filings; and pharmaceutical package inserts. It is published annually and is recognized by FDA as the official source for established drug names. (See *Nomenclature*.)

USP Dietary Supplements Compendium— The *Dietary Supplements Compendium* combines, in a single volume, *USP–NF* standards for dietary supplements, standards and information from the *Food Chemicals Codex*, regulatory and industry documents, and other tools and resources. It is published every two years, as a hardcover print edition.

USP Medicines Compendium— The *USP Medicines Compendium (MC)* includes monographs, general chapters, and reference materials for suitable chemical and biological medicines and their ingredients approved by national regulatory authorities. The purpose of the *MC* is to help ensure that these medicines are of good quality by providing up-to-date, relevant public standards and reference materials. *MC* standards are available to manufacturers, purchasers, national regulatory authorities, and others to ensure conformity of a medicine to *MC* standards through testing. The *MC* does not include standards for foods or for traditional medicines/dietary supplements.

USP Catalog— Use of official USP Reference Standards promotes uniform quality of drugs, food ingredients, and dietary supplements and supports first-, second-, and third-party testing of all manufactured and compounded articles. The publication listing the collection of official USP Reference Standards can be accessed on the USP website at www.usp.org and is available in print form by contacting USP Sales and Marketing staff at 301-816-8237. The listing identifies new items, replacement lots, lots of a single item that are simultaneously official, lots deleted from official status, and a preview of items eventually to be adopted. Purchase order information is included, and the names of distributors who can facilitate international availability of these items are suggested. The USP Reference Standards program benefits from the widespread voluntary contribution of suitable materials and test data from manufacturers. USP advances this unofficial material to official status via careful characterization studies and collaborative testing, followed by review and approval by the appropriate Expert Committee.

People
2010–2015 Revision Cycle

Officers of the USP Convention, Board of Trustees, and the Council of Experts, Expert Committees, Expert Panels, and Advisory Groups

Officers (2010–2015)

Timothy R. Franson, B.S. Pharm., M.D.
President
Washington, DC

René H. Bravo, M.D., F.A.A.P.
Past President
San Luis Obispo, CA

John E. Courtney, Ph.D.
Treasurer
Bethesda, MD

Susan S. de Mars, J.D.
Secretary
Rockville, MD

Board of Trustees (2010–2015)

Duane M. Kirking, Pharm.D., Ph.D.
Chair
Trustee Representing the Pharmaceutical Sciences
Ann Arbor, MI

Carolyn H. Asbury, Ph.D., Sc.M.P.H.
Trustee Representing the Public
New York, NY

Robert L. Buchanan, Ph.D.
Trustee At-Large
College Park, MD

Michael Maves, M.D., M.B.A.
Trustee Representing the Medical Sciences
Millwood, VA

Thomas Menighan, B.S. Pharm., M.B.A., Sc.D., F.A.Ph.A.
Trustee At-Large
Washington, DC

Robert M. Russell, M.D.
Trustee Representing the Medical Sciences
Arlington, MA

Marilyn K. Speedie, Ph.D.
Trustee Representing the Pharmaceutical Sciences
Minneapolis, MN

Jeffrey L. Sturchio, Ph.D.
Trustee At-Large
New York, NY

Thomas R. Temple, R.Ph., M.S.
Trustee At-Large
Des Moines, IA

Gail Wilensky, Ph.D.
Trustee At-Large
Bethesda, MD

Roger L. Williams, M.D.
Chief Executive Officer
(ex-officio)
Rockville, MD

Council of Experts (2010–2015)

Roger L. Williams, M.D.
Chair, Council of Experts
Rockville, MD

James E. Akers, Ph.D.
Chair, General Chapters—Microbiology
Leawood, KS

Gregory E. Amidon, Ph.D.
Chair, General Chapters—Physical Analysis
Ann Arbor, MI

Lawrence H. Block, Ph.D.
Chair, Monographs—Excipients
Pittsburgh, PA

Matthew W. Borer, Ph.D.
Chair, Reference Standards
Indianapolis, IN

Michael A. Cutrera, M.Sc.
Chair, Monographs—Small Molecules 4
Langhorne, PA

Gigi S. Davidson, B.S.Pharm., DICVP
Chair, Compounding
Raleigh, NC

James E. DeMuth, Ph.D.
Chair, General Chapters—Dosage Forms
Madison, WI

Andrew G. Ebert, Ph.D.,
Chair, Monographs—Food Ingredients
Sandy Springs, GA

Mary G. Foster, Pharm.D., BFA
Chair, General Chapters—Packaging, Storage, and Distribution
Philadelphia, PA

Antony Raj Gomas, Ph.D.
Chair, USP Medicines Compendium
Hyderabad, India

Dennis K.J. Gorecki, B.S.P., Ph.D.
Chair, Monographs—Dietary Supplements
Saskatoon, SK, Canada

Jean F. Huxsoll, Ph.D.
Chair, Monographs—Biologics & Biotechnology 2
Emeryville, CA

Michael G. Mulkerrin, Ph.D.
Chair, Monographs—Biologics & Biotechnology 1
Redwood City, CA

Bernard A. Olsen, Ph.D.
Chair, Monographs—Small Molecules 3
West Lafayette, IN

Robert E. Osterberg, Ph.D.
Chair, Toxicology
Vienna, VA

Ernest Parente, Ph.D.
Chair, Monographs—Small Molecules 2
Overland Park, KS

Thomas P. Reinders, Pharm.D.
Chair, Nomenclature, Safety, and Labeling
Richmond, VA

Robert Singer, M.Sc.
Chair, Statistics
Union City, CA

Glenn A. Van Buskirk, Ph.D.
Chair, Monographs—Small Molecules 1
Basking Ridge, NJ

Wesley E. Workman, Ph.D.
Chair, General Chapters—Biological Analysis
Chesterfield, MO

Timothy J. Wozniak, Ph.D.
Chair, General Chapters—Chemical Analysis
Indianapolis, IN

Expert Committees (2010–2015)

[NOTE—The following listing of Expert Committees includes the Expert Panels that serve in an advisory capacity to the specific Expert Committee. The listing of Expert Panels and their membership represents those that have been fully formed and approved as of October 2011. Expert Panels are continuously formed and concluded throughout the USP revision cycle, and other membership listings will appear in the future.]

Expert Panels for the Council of Experts Executive Committee

Spanish Translation Expert Panel
ENRIQUE FEFER, PH.D., *Chair*
Peggy Casanova, M.Sc.; Ofelia Espejo, Ph.D.; Lidiette Fonseca González, M.Sc.; José Juárez Eyzaguirre, Ph.D.; José María Parisi, M.Sc.; Regina Pezoa, Ph.D.; Luisa Fernanda Ponce D'León Quiroga, Ph.D.; Oscar Quattrocchi, M.Sc.; Doris Rivera, M.Sc.

Expert Committees for the *United States Pharmacopeia*

Nomenclature, Safety, and Labeling
THOMAS P. REINDERS, PHARM.D., *Chair*
Loyd V. Allen, Ph.D.; Mary B. Baker, M.B.A., Pharm.D.; Lawrence H. Block, Ph.D.; Dawn M. Boothe, D.V.M., Ph.D.; David H. Campen, M.D.; Mrunal S. Chapekar, Ph.D.; Stephanie Y. Crawford, Ph.D., M.P.H.; Steven J. Dentali, Ph.D.; Dennis E. Doherty, M.D.; Abraham G. Hartzema, Pharm.D., Ph.D., MSPH; Kent T. Johnson, M.S.; Donald S. MacLean, Ph.D.; Joan C. May, Ph.D.; Ginette A. Pepper, R.N., Ph.D., FAAN; Ping Wang, M.S.; Joanne G. Schwartzberg, M.D.; Debora J. Simmons, R.N., M.S.N.; R. William Soller, Ph.D.; Theodore G. Tong, Pharm.D.; Jeanne Tuttle, B.S.Pharm.; Anthony Wong, M.D., Ph.D.

Medicare Model Guidelines Expert Panel — CONCLUDED
DAVID H. CAMPEN, M.D., *Chair*
Nancy Jo Braden, M.D.; Chester B. Good, M.D., MPH; Roy Guharoy, Pharm.D., MBA; Raymond Hohl, M.D., Ph.D.; Arthur I. Jacknowitz, Pharm.D.; Ronald P. Jordan, R.Ph., APhA; Rice C. Leach, M.D., MSHSA; David B. Lorber, M.D., FCCP; Raymond C. Love, Pharm.D., FASHP; Philip Marcus, M.D., MPH; Gary Matzke; Joel S. Mindel, M.D.; Mark Noga, Pharm.D.; Charles D. Ponte, Pharm.D.; N. Lee Rucker, MSPH; Melody Ryan, Pharm.D., MPH; Joanne G. Schwartzberg, M.D.; Brian K. Solow, M.D.; Robert L. Talbert, Pharm. D.; Dennis P. West, Ph.D.

Prescription Container Labeling Expert Panel
JOANNE G. SCHWARTZBERG, M.D., *Chair*
Cindy Brach, MPP; Joan E. Kapusnik-Uner, Pharm.D.; Sandra Leal, Pharm.D.; Linda L. Lloyd, M.Ed.; Melissa A. Madigan, Pharm.D.; Gerald McEvoy, Pharm.D.; Daniel G. Morrow, Ph.D.; Ruth M. Parker, M.D.; Cynthia L. Raehl, Pharm.D.; Thomas P. Reinders, Pharm.D.; William H. Shrank, M.D.; Patricia E. Sokol, R.N., J.D.; Darren K. Townzen, MBA; Jeanne Tuttle, Pharm.D.; Michelle D. Wiest, Pharm.D.; Michael S. Wolf, Ph.D., MPH

Monographs—Small Molecules 1
GLENN A. VAN BUSKIRK, PH.D., *Chair*
Elizabeth B. Cariello; David A. Fay, Ph.D.; Rupa Iyer, M.S.; Amy J. Karren, N.R.C.M.; Assad J. Kazeminy, Ph.D.; Huiyi Li, Ph.D.; Raphael M. Ornaf, Ph.D.; Jeffrey S. Rohrer, Ph.D.; David F. Schuck, Ph.D.; Nhan L. Tran, Ph.D.; Danny L. Tuck, Ph.D.; Patricia C. Tway, Ph.D.

Monographs—Small Molecules 2
ERNEST PARENTE, PH.D., *Chair*
Mahmoud M. H. Al Omari, Ph.D.; Allan D. Bokser, Ph.D.; Shrikant N. Dhumal, Ph.D.; Tina M. Engel, Ph.D.; Maria Ines R. M. Santoro, Ph.D.; Dennis A. Stephens, Ph.D.; Luciano Virgili, Ph.D.; Yuwen Wang, Ph.D.; Bo Wen, Ph.D.; Joseph E. Yakupkovic, Ph.D.; Patrick N. Yat, Ph.D.; Louis W. Yu, Ph.D.

Acetaminophen Expert Panel
DAVID A. FAY, PH.D., *Chair*
Greg J. Davies; Tina M. Engel, Ph.D.; Saulius A. Gylys; Clifford J. Herman, Ph.D.; Poonam Pall, M.S.; Greg A. Roberts, M.A.; David H. Rogers, Ph.D.; Gregory K. Webster, Ph.D.; Kylen W. Whitaker, Ph.D.

Monographs—Small Molecules 3
BERNARD A. OLSEN, PH.D., *Chair*
Richard A. Blessing, M.S.; Thomas A. Broadbent, Ph.D.; Nicholas Cappuccino, Ph.D., M.B.A.; Ian Chung, Ph.D.; John E. Daniels, M.S., M.B.A.; Jeffrey S. Fleitman, Ph.D.; Yuri Goldberg, Ph.D., D.Sc.; Pauline M. Lacroix, M.Sc.; Julie K. Lorenz, Ph.D.; Mark G. Papich, D.V.M, M.S.; Donald M. Parsons, Ph.D.; David G. Reed, M.B.A.; Thomas W. Rosanske, Ph.D.; Joseph G. Stowell, Ph.D.; Cathy L. Wood

Monographs—Small Molecules 4
MICHAEL A. CUTRERA, M.SC., *Chair*
Richard C. Adams, M.Sc., M.B.A.; Lakshmi Prasad Alaparthi, Ph.D.; Mark S. Bailey; Josep M. de Ciurana; Alain Duguet, Ph.D.; Quanyin Gao, Ph.D.; Jerome M. Lewis, M.B.A., Ph.D.; Oscar Liu, Ph.D.; Eugene J. McGonigle, Ph.D.; Marian L. Meyer, M.B.A., Ph.D.; Colin Minchom, Ph.D.; Patrick A. Noland, M.S.; Vijaya Ramesh, B.Pharm.; Hemant Kumar Sharma, Ph.D.; Michael J. Skibic, M.S.; William J. Taraszewski, Ph.D.; Michiel M. Van Oort, Ph.D.; Martin J. Williamson, Ph.D.; Steve S. Zigler, Ph.D.

Monographs—Biologics & Biotechnology 1
MICHAEL G. MULKERRIN, PH.D., *Chair*
Jan Amstrup, Ph.D.; Parastoo Azadi, Ph.D.; Frederic Carriere, Ph.D.; Charles S. Craik, Ph.D.; Helene Gazzano-Santoro, Ph.D.; Anne Munk Jespersen; Kristian Johansen, Ph.D.; Ned Mozier, Ph.D.; Barbara Mulloy, Ph.D.; Harold N. Rode, Ph.D.; Martin Schiestl, Ph.D.; Yeowon Sohn, Ph.D.

Glucagon Expert Panel
HAROLD RODE, PH.D., *Chair*
Jan Amstrup, Ph.D.; Matthew W. Borer, Ph.D.; Adrian F. Bristow, Ph.D.; Anne M. Jespersen; Elizabeth Clark Kramer, Ph.D.

Insulin Expert Panel
HAROLD RODE, PH.D., *Chair*
Jan Amstrup, Ph.D.; Wilfried P. Arz, Ph.D.; Matthew W. Borer, Ph.D.; Chris J. Burns, Ph.D.; Helene Gazzano-Santoro, Ph.D.; Morten Hach, M.S.; Anne M. Jespersen; Elizabeth Clark Kramer, Ph.D.; Martin Schiestl, Ph.D.

Low Molecular Weight Heparins Expert Panel
ELAINE GRAY, PH.D., and EDWARD K. CHESS, PH.D., *Co-Chairs*
Soby M. Abraham; Christopher P. Bryant, Ph.D.; Ishan Capila, Ph.D.; Venkatesan S. Chidambaram, Ph.D.; Barry T. Giles, Ph.D.; Gyongyi S. Gratzl, Ph.D.; Kristian Johansen, Ph.D.; Barbara Mulloy, Ph.D.; Anna K. Y.

Nordin; Bruna Parma, M.Sc.; Zachary Shriver, Ph.D.; Christian Viskov, Ph.D.

Pharmaceutical Enzymatic Preparation Expert Panel
FREDERIC CARRIERE, PH.D., Chair
Anisha Akula, Ph.D.; Gregory M. Beck, Ph.D.; Charles S. Craik, Ph.D.; Luigi Ghidorsi; Andreas Koerner; Thomas Langdon; Claus Middelberg, Ph.D.; Henry Francis Motkowski, M.A.; Tibor Sipos, Ph.D.

Unfractionated Heparin Expert Panel
WESLEY E. WORKMAN, PH.D., Chair
Edward K. Chess, Ph.D.; Huihong Fan, Ph.D.; Gyongyi S. Gratzl, Ph.D.; Elaine Gray, Ph.D.; Kristian Johansen, Ph.D.; Jian Liu, Ph.D.; Barbara Mulloy, Ph.D.; Zachary Shriver, Ph.D.; Pearle Torralba, Ph.D.; Christian Viskov, Ph.D.

Monographs—Biologics & Biotechnology 2
JEAN F. HUXSOLL, PH.D., Chair
Merry L. Bain, M.S.; Barbara E. Blum, Ph.D., M.P.H.; Pamela Clark, M.D., J.D.; Elaine Gray, Ph.D.; Deepak Jain, Ph.D.; Christopher Mason, Ph.D., FRCS; Brian K. Nunnally, Ph.D.; Nicole M. Provost, Ph.D.; William E. Tente, M.S.; Darin J. Weber, Ph.D.; Earl K. Zablackis, Ph.D.

Plasma Protein Analytical Expert Panel
TIMOTHY K. HAYES, PH.D., Chair
Mehrshid Alai, Ph.D.; Joseph Bertolini, Ph.D.; Elaine Gray, Ph.D.; Steven Herring, Ph.D.; Dorothea Sesardic, Ph.D.; Peter J. Vandeberg, Ph.D.

Plasma-Derived and Recombinant Coagulation Factors Expert Panel
JEAN F. HUXSOLL, PH.D., Chair
Mehrshid Alai, Ph.D.; Gretchen A. Elliott, M.S.; Elaine Gray, Ph.D.; Steven Herring, Ph.D.; Michael Jankowski

Tissue and Tissue-Based Products Expert Panel
DEEPAK JAIN, PH.D., and WILLIAM E. TENTE, M.S. Co-Chairs
Merry L. Bain, M.S.; Barbara E. Blum, Ph.D., M.P.H.; Robert Buehler, Ph.D.; Frederick Cahn, Ph.D.; Shannon L.M. Dahl, Ph.D.; John E. Kemnitzer, Ph.D.; Alyce Linthurst Jones, Ph.D.; Timoty Neja, M.B.A; Darin J. Weber, Ph.D.; Wesley E. Workman, Ph.D.

General Chapters—Chemical Analysis
TIMOTHY J. WOZNIAK, PH.D., Chair
Anthony C. Bevilacqua, Ph.D.; Christopher Burgess, Ph.D.; Geoffrey P. R. Carr, Ph.D., FRSC; Pei Chen, Ph.D.; Thomas J. DiFeo, Ph.D.; John W. Dolan, Ph.D.; Edward J. Fletcher; John P. Hammond, FRSC; Ravi Harapanhalli, Ph.D.; John V. Hinshaw, Ph.D.; Paul R. Keller, Ph.D.; Nancy Lewen; Todd D. Maloney, Ph.D.; Nuno Matos; Ganapathy Mohan, Ph.D.; Greg A. Pennyroyal; Melissa M. Phillips, Ph.D.; Oscar A. Quattrocchi, M.Sc.; Mark C. Roman, Ph.D.; Timothy L. Shelbourn, M.S., M.B.A.; Teri C. Soli, Ph.D.; Daniel D. Traficante, Ph.D.; Bruno A.R. Vrebos, Ph.D.

⟨761⟩ **Nuclear Magnetic Resonance Expert Panel**
DANIEL D. TRAFICANTE, PH.D., Chair
Andreas Kaerner, Ph.D.; Andrew C. Kolbert, Ph.D., M.T.M.; Yue Luo, Ph.D.; Joseph Ray, Ph.D.; Susan Reutzel-Edens, Ph.D.; Timothy L. Shelbourn, M.B.A., M.S.; Christina Szabo, Ph.D.; Fred Xi, Ph.D.

Mass Spectrometry Expert Panel
PAUL R. KELLER, PH.D., Chair
Parastoo Azadi, Ph.D.; Timothy R. Baker, Ph.D.; Geoffrey P. R. Carr, Ph.D., FRSC; Roy Dobson, Ph.D.; Kenneth D. Greis, Ph.D.; Douglas E. Kiehl, M.S.; Mike S. Lee, Ph.D.; Jun Wheeler

Metal Impurities Expert Panel
NANCY LEWEN, Chair
Charles Barton, Ph.D., DABT; Courtney M. Callis, MPH, DABT; Steven J. Dentali, Ph.D.; Anna M. Fan, Ph.D., DABT; Bruce A. Fowler, Ph.D., A.T.S.; Roland Frotschl; Assad J. Kazeminy, Ph.D.; Richard Ko, Pharm.D., Ph.D.; Timothy L. Shelbourn, M.B.A., M.S.; Gregory C. Turk, Ph.D.; Robert Wiens, M.S.

Sterile Packaged Water Attributes Expert Panel
ANTHONY C. BEVILACQUA, PH.D., Chair
Dennis R. Jenke, Ph.D., M.B.A.; Max S. Lazar; Timothy J. McGovern, Ph.D.; Rostyslaw O. Slabicky; Teri C. Soli, Ph.D.

Water for Analytical Purposes Expert Panel
TERI C. SOLI, PH.D., Chair
Anthony C. Bevilacqua, Ph.D.; Lucia Clontz, D.H.Sc., M.Sc.; Max S. Lazar; Nancy Lewen; Bruno Rossi, M.S.

Water for Pharmaceutical Purposes Expert Panel
TERI C. SOLI, PH.D., Chair
Anthony C. Bevilacqua, Ph.D.; Lucia Clontz, D.H.Sc., M.Sc.; Max S. Lazar; Rostyslaw O. Slabicky

XRF Spectrometry Expert Panel
TIMOTHY L. SHELBOURN, M.B.A., M.S., Chair
Lora L. Brehm; W. Tim Elam; George J. Havrilla; Andrew J. Jensen; Riitta Kaijansaari, M.Sc.; John I.H. Patterson, Ph.D.; Rene E. Van Grieken, Ph.D.; Bruno A. R. Vrebos, Ph.D.

General Chapters—Physical Analysis
GREGORY E. AMIDON, PH.D., Chair
Shaukat Ali, Ph.D.; Abdullah M. Al-Mohizea, Ph.D.; Graham Buckton, Ph.D., D.SC., FRSC; David J. Goldfarb, Ph.D.; Bruno C. Hancock, Ph.D.; Xiaorong He, M.B.A.; Stephen W. Hoag, Ph.D.; Ronald G. Iacocca, Ph.D.; Ravi Harapanhalli, Ph.D.; Gregory P. Martin, M.S.; Richard Meury; Prabu Nambiar, M.B.A., Ph.D.; James A. Ponto, M.S.; Sally W. Schwarz, M.S.; Changquan C. Sun, Ph.D.; Kevin A. Swiss, Ph.D.; Allen C. Templeton, Ph.D.; Dale Eric Wurster, Ph.D.; Geoff G. Z. Zhang, Ph.D.

⟨1059⟩ **Excipient Performance Expert Panel**
GREGORY E. AMIDON, PH.D., Chair
Shaukat Ali, Ph.D.; Abdullah M. Al-Mohizea, Ph.D.; Lawrence H. Block, Ph.D.; Carl Frey, M.S.; Xiaorong He, Ph.D., M.B.A.; Stephen W. Hoag, Ph.D.; M. Sherry Ku, Ph.D.; Michelle A. Long, Ph.D.; Richard C. Moreton, Ph.D.; Prabu Nambiar, Ph.D., M.B.A.; James A. Ponto, M.S.; Eric A. Schmitt, Ph.D.; Kevin A. Swiss, Ph.D.; Sean V. Taylor, Ph.D.

⟨1197⟩ **Good Distribution Practices for Bulk Pharmaceutical Excipients Expert Panel**
GREGORY E. AMIDON, PH.D. AND RICHARD C. MORETON, PH.D., Co-Chairs
Loyd V. Allen, Ph.D.; Lawrence H. Block, Ph.D.; William Dale Carter, M.S.; Zak T. Chowhan, Ph.D.; Marc Fages; Elizabeth Ferguson-Brown; Mary G. Foster, Pharm.D., BFA; Rick Green; Linda A. Herzog, M.B.A.; Ashok V. Katdare, Ph.D.; Zakiya Kurdi, Ph.D.; Edward G. Malawer, Ph.D., CQA; Frank Milek, Ph.D.; Becca Mitchell; Dwight Mutchler; Garnet E. Peck, Ph.D.; Mike Schultz, R.Ph.; Alexa Smith, M.S.; Glenn Sokoloski; Kelly Taylor; Jiasheng Tu, Ph. D.; Ranga Velagaleti, Ph.D.

Drugs for Positron Emission Tomography—Compounding Expert Panel
STEVEN S. ZIGLER, PH.D., Chair
Samuel C. Augustine, PharmD, FAPhA; Marc Berridge, Ph.D.; Joseph C. Hung, Ph.D., BCNP; Donald R. Kinney; Maxim Kiselev, Ph.D.; Neale Scott Mason, Ph.D.; Steve Mattmuller, M.S., R.Ph.; Sally W. Schwarz, M.S.; Jean-Luc Vanderheyden, Ph.D.

Impurities in Drug Products Expert Panel
PRABU NAMBIAR, PH.D., M.B.A., Chair
Shaukat Ali, Ph.D.; Abdullah M. Al-Mohizea, Ph.D.; Steven W. Baertschi, Ph.D.; Judy P. Boehlert, Ph.D.; Robert G. Buice, Ph.D.; Greg J. Davies; Xiaorong He, Ph.D., M.B.A.; Michael Koberda, Ph.D.; Ernest Parente, Ph.D.; David H. Rogers, Ph.D.; Mary W. Seibel; Kevin A. Swiss, Ph.D.

Weights and Balances Expert Panel
GREGORY P. MARTIN, M.S., Chair
Dirk Ahlbrecht; Cesar D. Bautista, Jr., Ph.D.; Klaus Fritsch, Ph.D.; Robert Mielke; David Sebastian Pattavina,

M.S.; Arthur Reichmuth, M.S.; Allen C. Templeton, Ph.D.

General Chapters—Biological Analysis
WESLEY E. WORKMAN, PH.D., *Chair*
Robert G. Bell, Ph.D.; Jill A. Crouse-Zeineddini, Ph.D.; Gary C. du Moulin, Ph.D.; Barry D. Garfinkle, Ph.D.; Timothy K. Hayes, Ph.D.; Christopher Jones, Ph.D.; Kenneth R. Miller, Ph.D.; Anthony R. Mire-Sluis, Ph.D.; Elizabeth I. Read, M.D.; Anthony A.G. Ridgway, Ph.D.; John A. Saldanha, Ph.D.; Junzhi Wang, Ph.D.; Teruhide Yamaguchi, Ph.D.; Lynn C. Yeoman, Ph.D.

⟨1050⟩ Viral Safety Evaluation of Biotechnology Products Derived from Cell Lines of Human or Animal Origin Expert Panel
ROBERT G. BELL, PH.D., *Chair*
Johannes Bluemel, Ph.D.; Mark Plavsic, Ph.D.; Michael Rubino, Ph.D.; Raymond Nims, Ph.D.; Jeri Ann Boose, Ph.D.; Yuling L. Li, Ph.D.; Houman Dehghani, Ph.D.

⟨1102–1105⟩ Immunological Test Methods Expert Panel
KENNETH R. MILLER, PH.D., *Chair*
Ralph Abraham, Ph.D.; Jan Amstrup, Ph.D., JoAnne Bruno, Ph.D.; Shalini Gupta; Yadira Hernandez Rodriguez, Ph.D.; John S. Ivancic, Ph.D.; Rakesh Kakkar, Ph.D.; David M. Lansky, Ph.D.; Kelledy Manson; Hersh Mehta, Ph.D.; Patrick Niven; Robert J. Strouse, Ph.D.; Steven J. Swanson, Ph.D.; Mohammed Yousef, Ph.D.

⟨1240⟩ Viral Testing for Human Plasma Designated for Further Manufacturing Expert Panel
JOHN A. SALDANHA, PH.D., *Chair*
Albrecht Groener, Ph.D.; Mary Gustafson, Ph.D.; Thomas S. Jones, Ph.D.; Douglas C. Lee, Ph.D.; Hannelore M. Willkommen, Ph.D.; Mey-Ying W. Yu, Ph.D.

Cryopreservation Expert Panel
JAMES MOLDENHAUER, M.S., *Chair*
Allison Hubel, Ph.D.; Elizabeth I. Read, M.D.; Yvonne A. Reid, Ph.D.; Glyn Stacey, Ph.D.

Glycoconjugate Vaccines Expert Panel
CHRISTOPHER JONES, PH.D., *Chair*
Paolo Costantino; Didier A. Giffroy, Ph.D.; Suresh Karupothula, Ph.D.; Jeremy P. Kunkel, Ph.D.; SureshBabu Rajan, M.Pharm; Neil Ravenscroft, Ph.D.; Mary L. Retzlaff, Ph.D.; Marsha Richmond, Ph.D.; Philippe Talaga, Ph.D.

Glycoproteins and Glycan Analysis Expert Panel
CHRISTOPHER JONES, PH.D., *Chair*
Parastoo Azadi, Ph.D.; Michael R. DeFelippis, Ph.D.; Gary Rogers, Ph.D.; Jeffrey S. Rohrer, Ph.D.; Martin Schiestl, Ph.D.; Jihong Wang, Ph.D.; Zhuchun Wu, Ph.D.; Rebecca A. Zangmeister, Ph.D.

Immunogenicity Expert Panel
ANTHONY R. MIRE-SLUIS, PH.D., *Chair*
Viswanath Devanarayan, Ph.D.; Eugene Koren, M.D., Ph.D.; Valerie Quarmby, Ph.D.; Gopi Shankar, Ph.D.; Meena Subramanyam, Ph.D.; Steven J. Swanson, Ph.D.

Measurement of Residual DNA in Biotechnology-Derived Products Expert Panel
WESLEY E. WORKMAN, PH.D., *Chair*
Pascal R. Anger; Jon R. Borman; Audrey Chang, Ph.D.; Zhongping Guo; Thomas E. Haemmerle, Ph.D.; Scott Kuhns, Ph.D.; Austin J. Power, M.S.; Junzhi Wang, Ph.D.; Weihong Wang, Ph.D.; Judith Zhu-Shimoni, Ph.D.

Recombinant Therapeutic Monoclonal Antibodies Expert Panel
ANTHONY R. MIRE-SLUIS, PH.D., *Chair*
Michel P. Byrne, Ph.D.; Mary E.M. Cromwell, Ph.D.; Jill A. Crouse-Zeineddini, Ph.D.; Michael R. DeFelippis, Ph.D.; Siegfried Giess, Ph.D.; Steffen Gross, Ph.D.; Alka Kamra, Ph.D.; Joseph Kutza, Ph.D.; Kenneth R. Miller, Ph.D.; Michael G. Mulkerrin, Ph.D.; Martin Schiestl, Ph.D.; Dieter Schmalzing, Ph.D.; Yeowon Sohn, Ph.D.; Robin Christopher Thorpe, Ph.D.; Ziping Wei, Ph.D.; David C. Wylie, Ph.D.

Total Protein Measurement Expert Panel
WESLEY E. WORKMAN, PH.D., *Chair*
Methal Albarghouthi, Ph.D.; Matthew W. Borer, Ph.D.; Olivier C. Germay, Ph.D.; Susan Janes, Ph.D.; Anne M. Jespersen, Ph.D.; Lars Nygaard, M.S.; Brian K. O'Connor, M.S.; Wendy R. Safell-Clemmer, M.S.; Martin Schiestl, Ph.D.; William M. Skea, Ph.D.; Lynn C. Yeoman, Ph.D.

Vaccines for Human Use — Viral Vaccines Expert Panel
BARRY D. GARFINKLE, PH.D., *Chair*
John G. Aunins, Ph.D.; Francesco Berti, Ph.D.; Mark Galinski; Lucy Gisonni-Lex; John D. Grabenstein, Ph.D.; Joan C. May, Ph.D.; Brian K. Nunnally, Ph.D.; Cecile Maria Ponsar, Ph.D.; Silke M. Schepelmann, Ph.D.; Earl K. Zablackis, Ph.D.

General Chapters—Dosage Forms
JAMES E. DEMUTH, PH.D., *Chair*
Dale S. Aldrich; Paul D. Curry, Jr., Ph.D.; Russell P. Elliott, Ph.D.; Gordon L. Flynn, Ph.D.; Mario A. Gonzalez, Ph.D.; Vivian A. Gray; Ralph A. Heasley, Ph.D.; Anthony J. Hickey, Ph.D., D.Sc.; Michael E. Houghton, Ph.D.; Munir A. Hussain, Ph.D.; Johannes Kraemer, Ph.D.; David F. Long, Ph.D.; Jolyon P. Mitchell, Ph.D., FRSC; Alan F. Parr, Pharm.D., Ph.D.; Guirag Poochikian, Ph.D.; Galen W. Radebaugh, Ph.D., R.Ph.; John G. Shabushnig, Ph.D.; Raymond D. Skwierczynski, Ph.D.; Jason A. Suggett, Ph.D., M.B.A.; Thomas R. Tice, Ph.D.; Terrence P. Tougas, Ph.D.

⟨1⟩ Injections Expert Panel
JOHN G. SHABUSHNIG, PH.D., *Chair*
Dale S. Aldrich; Lori Alquier, M.S.; Diane J. Burgess, Ph.D.; David F. Driscoll, Ph.D.; David F. Long, Ph.D.; Thomas R. Tice, Ph.D.; Martin Woodle, Ph.D.

⟨787⟩ Particulate Matter in Biopharmaceutical Injections Expert Panel
DALE S. ALDRICH, *Chair*
Mary E.M. Cromwell, Ph.D.; Paul D. Curry, Ph.D.; Jolyon P. Mitchell, Ph.D., FRSC; Linda O. Narhi, Ph.D.; Melissa D. Perkins, Ph.D.; Alla Polozova, Ph.D.; John G. Shabushnig, Ph.D.; Satish K. Singh, Ph.D.; Terrence P. Tougas, Ph.D.; Lisa A. Wenzler, Ph.D.

Liquid-Filled Capsules Expert Panel Expert Panel
VIVIAN A. GRAY, *Chair*
Ewart Cole, Ph.D.; Jean-Luc Colin, Ph.D.; Michael A. Cutrera, M.Sc.; Joe Fotso, Ph.D.; Munir A. Hussain, Ph.D.; Vi N. Schmidt, M.S.; Stephen C. Tindal

Solubility Criteria for Veterinary Drugs Expert Panel
MARIO A. GONZALEZ, PH.D., *Chair*
Mike Apley, DVM, Ph.D.; Bryan Crist; Robert P. Hunter, M.S., Ph.D.; Mark G. Papich, M.S., D.V.M.; Alan F. Parr, Pharm.D., Ph.D.; Jim E. Riviere, DVM, Ph.D., D.Sc.

Use of Enzymes in the Dissolution Testing of Gelatin Capsules Expert Panel
VIVIAN A. GRAY, *Chair*
Ewart Cole, Ph.D.; Jean-Luc Colin, Ph.D.; Jian-Hwa Guo, Ph.D.; Feixue Han, Ph.D.; Jian-Hwa Han, Ph.D.; Teresa R. Henry, Ph.D.; Jianmei D. Kochling, Ph.D.; Johannes Kraemer, Ph.D.; Thomas Langdon; Steven R. Leinbach; Gregroy P. Martin, M.S.; Richard C. Moreton, Ph.D.; Krishnaswamy S. Raghavan, Ph.D.; Ed Shneyvas, Ph.D.; Stephen C. Tindal; Hu Wang, M.S.

Visual Inspection of Parenterals Expert Panel
RUSSELL E. MADSEN, M.S., *Chair*
Dale S. Aldrich; Roy Cherris; John G. Shabushnig, Ph.D.; Deborah Shnek, Ph.D.

General Chapters—Microbiology
JAMES E. AKERS, PH.D., *Chair*
James P. Agalloco, M.S., M.B.A.; Dilip Ashtekar, Ph.D.; Anthony M. Cundell, Ph.D.; Russell E. Madsen, M.S.; Karen Z. McCullough, M.S.; Jianghong Meng, Ph.D.; Leonard W. Mestrandrea, Ph.D.; Rainer F. Newman, M.S.; Donald C. Singer, M.S.; Scott V.W. Sutton, Ph.D.; Edward C. Tidswell, Ph.D.

⟨81⟩ **Antibiotics—Microbial Assays Expert Panel — CONCLUDED**
THOMAS B. MAY, PH.D., *Chair*
David L. Gibbs, Ph.D.; Amy J. Karren, RM/SM; Nilesh Prabhakar Shinde, M.S.; Brenda Sullivan

General Chapters—Packaging, Storage, and Distribution
MARY G. FOSTER, PHARM.D., BFA, *Chair*
Chris Chandler, Pharm.D.; Michael N. Eakins, Ph.D.; Shirley A. Feld, M.Sc.; Dana M. Guazzo, Ph.D.; Ian Holloway, M.Sc.; Dennis R. Jenke, M.B.A., Ph.D.; Daniel J. Malinowski; Daniel L. Norwood, M.S.P.H., Ph.D.; Kevin E. O'Donnell; Devinder Pal, M.Pharm.; Diane M. Paskiet; Michael A. Ruberto, Ph.D.; Marv D. Shepherd, Ph.D.; Sarah Skuce; Kola Stucker, M.S.; Li Xiong, Ph.D.

⟨671⟩ **Containers—Performance Testing Expert Panel**
DAN J. MALINOWSKI, *Chair*
Yisheng Chen, Ph.D.; Michael N. Eakins, Ph.D.; Mary G. Foster, Pharm.D., BFA; Hugh E. Lockhart, Ph.D.; Dennis P. O'Reilly; Frank D. Witulski, M.S.

⟨1207⟩ **Sterile Product Packaging Expert Panel**
DANA M. GUAZZO, PH.D., *Chair*
James P. Agalloco, M.S., M.B.A.; James E. Akers, Ph.D.; Peter Buus; Shu-chen Chen; Ronald Forster, Ph.D.; Lee E. Kirsch, Ph.D.; Ronald Mueller; Donald C. Singer, M.S.; David Walker

⟨1664⟩ **Leachables, Threshold and Best Practices Expert Panel**
DANIEL L. NORWOOD, PH.D., *Chair*
Michael N. Eakins, Ph.D.; Dennis R. Jenke, Ph.D., M.B.A.; Timothy J. McGovern, Ph.D.; James O. Mullis, M.S.; Lee M. Nagao, Ph.D.; Diane M. Paskiet; Michael A. Ruberto, Ph.D.; Cheryl Stults, Ph.D.

Reference Standards
MATTHEW W. BORER, PH.D., *Chair*
Bianca Avramovitch, Ph.D.; Adrian F. Bristow, Ph.D.; Antony Raj Gomes, Ph.D.; Shaohong Jin; Catherine A. Rimmer, Ph.D.; Iffaaz M. Salahudeen, Ph.D.; Ralph E. Sturgeon, Ph.D.; Robert L. Watters, Ph.D.; M. L. Jane Weitzel

Statistics
ROBERT R. SINGER, M.SC., *Chair*
Bruno Boulanger, Ph.D.; Richard K. Burdick, Ph.D.; J. David Christopher, M.S.; David J. LeBlond, Ph.D.; Anthony G. Okinczyc, M.P.H., M.B.A.; Dennis Sandell, Ph.D.; Timothy Schofield, M.A.; Charles Y. Tan, Ph.D.; Harry Yang, Ph.D.

Bioassay General Chapters Expert Panel
ROBERT R. SINGER, M.SC., *Chair*
Janice D. Callahan, Ph.D.; Jill A. Crouse-Zeineddini, Ph.D.; David M. Lansky, Ph.D.; David J. LeBlond, Ph.D.; Karen J. Roberts, R.Ph.; Timothy Schofield, M.A.

Toxicology
ROBERT E. OSTERBERG, PH.D., *Chair*
Charles Barton, Ph.D.; Li Bo, Ph.D.; Joseph F. Borzelleca, Ph.D.; John Doull, Ph.D., M.D.; Marion Ehrich, Ph.D.; Gregory L. Erexson, Ph.D., DABT; Bruce A. Fowler, Ph.D., ATS; Bo Li, Ph.D.; Timothy J. McGovern, Ph.D.; Michel Mikhail, Ph.D.; Jeffrey P. Smith, Ph.D.

Expert Committees for the *National Formulary*

Monographs—Excipients
LAWRENCE H. BLOCK, PH.D., *Chair*
Kenneth S. Alexander, Ph.D., Ed.Sp.; Fernando A. Alvarez-Nunez, Ph.D.; Shireesh P. Apte, Ph.D.; Tim D. Cabelka, Ph.D.; Brian A.C. Carlin, Ph.D.; Richard N. Cawthorne, Ph.D.; Arthur J. Falk, M.B.A., Ph.D.; Jian-Hwa Guo, Ph.D.; Felicitas Guth, Ph.D.; Mary C. Houck, Ph.D.; M. Sherry Ku, Ph.D.; William J. Lambert, Ph.D.; Philip H. Merrell, Ph.D.; Richard C. Moreton, Ph.D.; Eric J. Munson, Ph.D.; Paul B. Myrdal, Ph.D.; Franz K. Penz, Ph.D.; Yihong Qiu, Ph.D.; Venkatramana Rao, Ph.D.; Sibichen J. Thekveli, Ph.D., P.Eng.; Jiasheng Tu, Ph.D.; Richard H. Wendt, Ph.D.

Talc Expert Panel
LAWRENCE H. BLOCK, PH.D., *Chair*
Detlef Beckers, Ph.D.; Jocelyne Ferret, Ph.D.; Gregory P. Meeker, M.S.; Aubrey Miller, M.D., M.P.H.; Robert E. Osterberg, Ph.D.; Dilip M. Patil, M.S.; Julie W. Pier, M.S.; Steve Riseman, Ph.D.; Gary P. Tomaino; Drew Van Orden, M.S., M.A.; James S. Webber, Ph.D.

Expert Committee for the *USP* and the *Dietary Supplements Compendium*

Monographs—Dietary Supplements
DENNIS K.J. GORECKI, B.S.P., PH.D., *Chair*
Marilyn L. Barrett, Ph.D.; Joseph M. Betz, Ph.D.; Michael S. Bradley, M.S.; Josef A. Brinckmann; James R. Brooks, Ph.D.; Robert L. Chapman, Ph.D.; De-an Guo, Ph.D.; Bill J. Gurley, Ph.D.; Sukhdev Swami Handa, Ph.D.; David C. Hopp, Ph.D.; Scott A. Jordan, Ph.D.; Joy A. Joseph, M.S.; A. Douglas Kinghorn, Ph.D., D.Sc.; Richard Ko, Pharm.D., Ph.D.; Raimar Löbenberg, Ph.D.; Tieraona Low Dog, M.D.; Gail B. Mahady, Ph.D.; Robin J. Marles, Ph.D.; Guido F. Pauli, M.D., Ph.D.; Zhongzhi Qian, M.S.; Eike Reich, Ph.D.; Paul L. Schiff, Jr., Ph.D.; Fabio M. B. Soldati, Ph.D.; Edward H. Waysek, Ph.D.; Wayne R. Wolf, Ph.D.

Beta-Alanine Review Expert Panel
RICHARD KO, PHARM.D., PH.D., *Chair*
Louis Cantilena, M.D., Ph.D.; Rebecca B. Costello, Ph.D.; William J. Evans, Ph.D.; Mary L. Hardy, M.D.; Scott A. Jordan, Ph.D.; Ronald J. Maughan, Ph.D.; Janet W. Rankin, Ph.D.; Abbie E. Smith, Ph.D.

USP Evidence-Based Reviews Expert Panel
TIERAONA LOW DOG, M.D., *Chair*
Louis Cantilena, M.D., Ph.D.; Stephanie Chang, M.D., M.P.H.; Rebecca B. Costello, Ph.D.; Dennis K. J. Gorecki, Ph.D.; Donnamaria R. Jones, Pharm.D.; Scott A. Jordan, Ph.D.

Expert Committee for the *Food Chemicals Codex*

Monographs—Food Ingredients
ANDREW G. EBERT, PH.D., *Chair*
Michael H. Auerbach, Ph.D.; Hans K. Biesalski, M.D., Ph.D.; Simon Brooke-Taylor, Ph.D.; Robert G. Bursey, Ph.D.; Richard C. Cantrill, Ph.D.; Junshi Chen, M.D.; Grady W. Chism, Ph.D.; Roger A. Clemens, Dr.P.H.; Jonathan W. DeVries, Ph.D.; John W. Finley, Ph.D.; Carl Frey, M.S.; Einat Haleva, Ph.D.; Lori L. Klopf, Ph.D.; Diane B. McColl, J.D.; Richard A. Myers, Ph.D.; Fereidoon Shahidi, Ph.D.; Karina R. Vega-Villa, Ph.D.; Ranga Velagaleti, Ph.D.; Liangli Yu, Ph.D.

Food Ingredients Intentional Adulterants Expert Panel
JONATHAN W. DEVRIES, PH.D., *Chair*
Susan M. Brown, M.E.A.; Henry Chin, Ph.D.; Kevin O. Gillies; Shaun Kennedy; Richard Lane, Ph.D.; Petra Lutter, Ph.D.; Richard A. Myers, Ph.D.; John Spink, Ph.D.; Richard Stadler, Ph.D.; Carl Winter, Ph.D.; Liangli Yu, Ph.D.

Expert Committee for the *USP* and the *Pharmacists' Pharmacopeia*

Compounding
GIGI S. DAVIDSON, B.S.PHARM., DICVP, *Chair*
Loyd V. Allen, Ph.D.; Lisa D. Ashworth, R.Ph.; Gus S. Bassani, Pharm.D.; Edmund J. Elder, Jr., Ph.D.; Maria do Carmo M. Garcez, B.S.Pharm.; Deborah R. Houston, Pharm.D.; Ken Hughes, R.Ph.; Eric S. Kastango, B.S.Pharm., M.B.A.; Patricia C. Kienle, M.P.A.; Keisha D. Lovoi, B.S.Pharm.; Linda F. McElhiney, Pharm.D.; William A. Mixon, M.S.; David W. Newton, Ph.D.; Alan F. Parr, Pharm.D., Ph.D.; Regina F. Peacock, Ph.D.; Robert P. Shrewsbury, Ph.D.

Expert Committee for the *USP Medicines Compendium*

USP Medicines Compendium
ANTONY RAJ GOMAS, PH.D., *Chair*
Dale M. Adkisson, M.S.; Mahesh K. Bhalgat, Ph.D.; Pramod N. Dalvi, Ph.D.; Rajeev A. Desai, Ph.D.; Manish G. Gangrade, Ph.D.; Sushil S. Gangwal, Ph.D.; Sridevi Khambhampati, Ph.D.; Rustom S. Mody, Ph.D.; Petla Y. Naidu, Ph.D.; Vikram M. Paradkar, Ph.D.; Dhananjay B. Patankar, Ph.D.; Akundi V. Sriram, Ph.D.

Therapeutic Proteins Expert Panel
RUSTOM S. MODY, PH.D., *Chair*
Susobhan Das, Ph.D.; Jaby Jacob, Ph.D.; Venkata Ramanna, Ph.D.; M. K. Sahib, Ph.D.; Alok Sarma, Ph.D.; Utpal Tatu, Ph.D.; Meenu Wadhwa, Ph.D.

Vaccines Expert Panel
MAHESH K. BHALGAT, PH.D., *Chair*
H. G. Bramhne, Ph.D.; Sunil Gairola, Ph.D.; Mei Mei Ho, Ph.D.; K. Anand Kumar, Ph.D.; K. R. Mani, Ph.D.; Ashok Panwar, Ph.D.; Y. U. B. Rao, Ph.D.

FDA Liaisons
Rajiv Agarwal, Ph.D.; Ali Al-Hakim, Ph.D.; Om Anand, Ph.D.; Howard A. Anderson, Ph.D.; Juan Arciniega, D.Sc.; Anamitro Banerjee, Ph.D.; Shastri Bhamidipati, Ph.D.; John H. Callahan, Ph.D.; Steven Casper, Ph.D.; Jane Chang, Ph.D.; Barry Cherney, Ph.D.; John F. Cipollo, Ph.D.; Carolyn Cohran, Ph.D.; Thomas Colatsky, Ph.D.; Jerry Cott, Ph.D.; Mike Darj, Ph.D.; Mamata De, Ph.D.; Ian DeVeau, Ph.D.; William Doub, Ph.D.; Patrick Faustino, Ph.D.; Daniel Folmer, Ph.D.; Michael Scott Furness, Ph.D.; Zongming Gao, Ph.D.; Tapash Ghosh, Ph.D.; Devinder S. Gill, Ph.D.; Lillie D. Golson, Pharm.D.; Edisa Gozun; Dennis Guilfoyle, Ph.D.; Yin Guo, Ph.D.; Rajesh Gupta, Ph.D.; Abhay Gupta, Ph.D.; Michael Hadwiger, Ph.D.; Martine Hartogensis, DVM; William Hess; CAPT Carol Holquist, R.Ph; David Hussong, Ph.D.; Robert Iser, M.S.; Joseph E. Jablonski, Ph.D.; Lauren Jackson, Ph.D.; John F. Kauffman, Ph.D., M.B.A.; Mansoor A. Khan, R.Ph., Ph.D.; Bogdan Kurtyka, Ph.D.; Stephen E. Langille, Ph.D.; Carla S.R. Lankford, M.D., Ph.D.; Sau L. Lee, Ph.D.; Robin Levis, Ph.D.; Tsai-lien Lin, Ph.D.; Richard Lostritto, Ph.D.; Ragine Maheswaran, Ph.D.; Frederic J. Marsik, Ph.D.; Ewa Marszal, Ph.D.; Marilyn N. Martinez Pelsor, Ph.D.; Dorota Matecka, Ph.D.; Judith McMeekin, Pharm.D.; Jeffrey B. Medwid, Ph.D.; Randa Melhem, Ph.D.; John Metcalfe, Ph.D.; Yana Mille, R.Ph.; Tahseen Mirza, Ph.D.; Amit K. Mitra, Ph.D.; Sanja Modric, D.V.M.; Magdi M. Mossoba, Ph.D.; Laxma Nagavelli, Ph.D.; Terrance W. Ocheltree, Ph.D., R.Ph.; Mickey Parish, Ph.D.; Suhas Patankar, Ph.D.; S. Prasad Peri, Ph.D.; Vaikunth Prabhu, Ph.D.; CAPT Kimberly Rains, Pharm.D.; Rahdika Rajagopalan, Ph.D.; Brian D. Rogers, Ph.D.; Barry Rothman; Allen Rudman, Ph.D.; R. Duane Satzger, Ph.D.; Peter Scholl, Ph.D.; Paul Schwartz, Ph.D.; Paul Seo, Ph.D.; Rakhi Shah, Ph.D.; Glen Jon Smith, M.S., M.A.S.; Aloka Srinivasan, Ph.D.; Jannavi Srinivasan, Ph.D.; Marla Stevens-Riley, Ph.D.; Yichun Sun, Ph.D.; Patrick G. Swann, Ph.D.; Neeru Takiar, M.S.; Paula R. Trumbo, Ph.D.; Lisa Tung, Pharm.D.; Saleh A. Turujman, Ph.D.; Luis Valerio, Ph.D.; Willie F. Vann; Perry Wang, Ph.D.; Russell Wesdyk, M.B.A.; Karen L. Wheless, M.S.; Steven Wolfgang, Ph.D.; Keith Wonnacott, Ph.D.; Li Xia, Ph.D.; Pei Zhang, M.D.; Jinglin Zhong, Ph.D.; Susan Zuk

Advisory Groups

Note—The CEO may appoint advisory bodies to advance the work of the Council of Experts and the Convention and provide advice to staff on policy matters. The following listing of USP Advisory Groups and their membership represents those that have been fully formed and approved as of May 2011. Advisory Groups are continuously formed and concluded throughout the USP revision cycle, and other membership listings will appear in the future.

ChP-USP Advisory Group on Monographs for Traditional Chinese Medicine Ingredients and Products
ZHONGZHI QIAN, M.S., *Chair*
ShiLin Chen, Ph.D.; De-an Guo, Ph.D.; Brad WC Lau, M.S., Ph.D.; Clara Bik San Lau, Ph.D., MRPharmS; Rui Chao Lin, Ph.D.; Ruihua Tian, Ph.D.; Ji Shen, Ph.D.; Shangmei Shi, B.S.; Zheng-Tao Wang, Ph.D.; Pengfei Tu, Ph.D.; Zhao Zhonzhen, Ph.D.; Zuguang Ye, M.S.

Monograph Naming Advisory Group
Robert S. Beardsley, R.Ph., Ph.D.; Michael Cohen, R.Ph.; Marjorie Coppinger; Mary Jo Goolsby, Ed.D., M.S.N., C.A.E.; Chandraprakash Kasireddy, Ph.D.; Barbara Kochanowski, Ph.D.; Murray Kopelow, M.D., F.R.C.P.C.; Linda F. McElhiney, Pharm.D., R.Ph.; Gary Matzke, Pharm.D.; David Newton, Ph.D.; Annette Perschke, R.N., M.S.N.; Marjorie Phillips, M.S.; Peter H. Rheinstein, J.D., M.S.; Elliott M. Sogol, Ph.D., R.Ph.; Vaiyapuri Subramaniam, Pharm.D., M.S.; Philip Travis; Mark Wiggins, M.S.

Skim Milk Powder Advisory Group
Robert Magaletta, Ph.D., *Chair*
Keller Barnhardt, Ph.D.; Marti Bergana, Ph.D.; Sneh Bhandari, Ph.D.; Ludovic Canelle, Ph.D.; Jack Cappozzo, M.S.; Jonathan DeVries, Ph.D.; George Greene; James M. Harnly, Ph.D.; Steven Holroyd, Ph.D.; William J. Hurst; Moon S. Kim, Ph.D.; Nam-Cheol Kim, Ph.D.; Petra Lutter, Ph.D.; Carmen Martin-Hernandez; Anitra Payne; Paul Wehling; Zhuohong Xie; Steven Zbylut, Ph.D.; Carol Zyrbko, Ph.D.

Admissions

New Articles Admitted to *FCC 8* from Supplement 1 of *FCC 7*

FCC Appendices
Appendix XII—Microbiological Tests

FCC Monographs
5′-Adenylic Acid
Betaine
Calcium Lignosulfonate (40–65)
5′-Cytidylic Acid
DHA from Algal (*Crypthecodinium*) Oil
DHA from Algal (*Schizochytrium*) Oil
Disodium 5′-Uridylate
Alpha-Lactalbumin
Propylene Oxide

FCC Provisional Monographs
Meso-Zeaxanthin

New Articles Admitted to *FCC 8* from Supplement 2 of *FCC 7*

FCC Appendices
Appendix XIII—Adulterants and Contaminants in Food Ingredients

FCC Monographs
Calcium Benzoate
Lycopene from *Blakeslea trispora*
Lycopene Extract from Tomato
Magnesium Ammonium Potassium Chloride, Hydrate
Magnesium Phosphate, Monobasic
Maritime Pine Extract
Mineral Oil, High Viscosity
Patent Blue V
L-Selenomethionine

New Articles Admitted to *FCC 8* from Supplement 3 of *FCC 7*

FCC Appendices
Appendix XIV—Markers for Authenticity Testing

FCC Monographs
ARA from Fungal (*Mortierella alpina*) Oil
Astaxanthin Esters from *Haemotococcus pluvialis*
Brown HT
Calcium Cyclamate
Citric and Fatty Acid Esters of Glycerol
Ethyl Lauroyl Arginate
Ferrous Ammonium Phosphate
Beta Glucan from Baker's Yeast (*Saccharomyces cerevisiae*)
Monk Fruit Extract
1,3-Propanediol
Sodium Cyclamate
Sucromalt
L-Theanine

New Articles Appearing in *FCC 8*

FCC Monographs
Amaranth
Azorubine
Cyclamic Acid
DHA from Algal *(Ulkenia)* Oil
Neohesperidine Dihydrochalcone
Ponceau 4R
Sodium Molybdate Dihydrate
Stearyl Alcohol

ANNOTATED LIST

Appendices and Monographs Affected by Changes Appearing in This Publication

Note—In the table below, if a section is new or if a subsection is added to or deleted from an existing section, it is labeled as such in parentheses after the section or subsection name. Items on this list that appear without the designation "new," "added," or "deleted," are items in which changes have been made to existing effective text.

[NOTE—The articles included in this list are noted in the book with the following symbols ▲ ▲*FCC8*. This applies to new articles as well as sections of existing items that have been revised.]

Appendices

Appendix III: Chemical Tests and Determinations
  B. LIMIT TESTS
    Lead Limit Test (subsection *Atomic Absorption Spectrophotometric Graphite Furnace Method*)
    Selenium Limit Test (subsection *Reagents and Solutions*)

Monographs

Amaranth (new)
Azorubine (new)
BHA
  DESCRIPTION
    Packaging and Storage
  IDENTIFICATION
    Test A
    Test B (added)
  ASSAY
Cassia Oil
  SPECIFIC TESTS
    Rosin or Rosin Oils (subsections *Analysis* and *Acceptance criteria*)
Cyclamic Acid (new)
DHA from Algal (*Crypthecodinium*) Oil
  IDENTIFICATION
    Fatty Acid Composition (subsection *Acceptance criteria*)
  ASSAY
    DHA, Fatty Acid Composition (subsection *Acceptance criteria*)
DHA from Algal (*Ulkenia*) Oil (new)
Ferrous Citrate
  ASSAY
    Ferrous Iron Content (subsection *Acceptance criteria*)
Gellan Gum
  DESCRIPTION
  ADDITIONAL REQUIREMENTS (added)
(+)-Limonene
  OTHER REQUIREMENTS
    Angular Rotation (subsection *Acceptance criteria*)
Neohesperidine Dihydrochalcone (new)
Ponceau 4R (new)
Sodium Molybdate Dihydrate (new)
Sodium Phosphate, Dibasic
  SPECIFIC TESTS
    Pyrophosphate (added)
Stearyl Alcohol (new)
Xanthan Gum
  DESCRIPTION
  IMPURITIES
    Organic Impurities (subsection *Ethanol and Isopropyl Alcohol*)

General Provisions and Requirements Applying to Specifications, Tests, and Assays of the *Food Chemicals Codex*

The General Provisions provide, in summary form, guidelines for the interpretation and application of the standards, tests and assays, and other specifications of the *Food Chemicals Codex* and make it unnecessary to repeat throughout the book those requirements that are pertinent in numerous instances. Where exceptions to the General Provisions are made, the wording in the individual monograph or general test chapter takes precedence and specifically indicates the directions or the intent.

TITLE OF BOOK

The title of this book, including its supplements, is the *Food Chemicals Codex*, Eighth Edition. It may be abbreviated to *FCC 8*. Where the term *FCC* is used without further qualification in the text of this book, it applies to the *Food Chemicals Codex*, Eighth Edition.

APPROPRIATE USE OF THE *FOOD CHEMICALS CODEX*

As a compendium that addresses known food ingredients used in food products either in the United States or internationally, the *FCC* has many practical applications in industry, research, and academia. The *FCC* does not, however, provide information on the regulatory status or safety of food chemicals, nor does the presence or absence of standards for a particular food ingredient indicate in any way USP's endorsement (or lack thereof) of that item for use in foods or food processing. It is the responsibility of the user to determine the safety and regulatory status of a particular food ingredient for any specific application.

FCC standards have been developed in cooperation with regulatory authorities and industry in the United States and elsewhere both under the stewardship of the Institute of Medicine and, more recently, USP. While USP makes great efforts to dialog with the U.S. Food and Drug Administration (FDA) regarding creating or revising monograph standards in the *FCC*, USP has no official legislative authority to establish legal requirements for food ingredients in the United States.[1] The *FCC* serves as a resource for companies that manufacture, process, purchase, or use food ingredients and seek to determine appropriate minimum standards for components of their food products.

The structure and format of the *FCC* monographs and informational chapters allow users to quickly access the following types of information:
- General information about food ingredients
- Chemical information specific to food ingredients
- Information regarding laboratory method validation components
- Guidance for establishing and using Good Manufacturing Practices
- Validated testing methods (including enzyme assays and methods that use highly-characterized reference standards)
- Minimum standards for identity, purity, and quality of food ingredients

Food ingredient manufacturers, processors, and purchasers often use the *FCC*'s standards as the basis for establishing minimum requirements for identity, purity, and quality of their ingredients. *FCC* standards are also used to define these parameters within commercial purchase agreements between buyers and sellers of ingredients and food and, thus, help to promote food quality and food safety programs in industry. The validated test methods included in the *FCC* can be used to demonstrate the identity, quality, and purity of food ingredients, or they can be a starting point in developing new test methods. Manufacturers, processors, and purchasers of food ingredients will find these validated test methods useful, as will regulatory agency labs, contract labs, and students of chemistry or food science. In addition to being a resource for purchasing and quality control operations, portions of the *FCC* are useful to quality assurance groups and can serve as references for internal Standard Operating Procedures (SOPs) and quality manuals used by the food industry. The *FCC* is an excellent resource that may be used to provide important information in order to ascertain identity, quality, and purity of ingredients. In addition, the *FCC* can be an important part of a food manufacturer or purchaser's comprehensive food quality program and it provides a common basis for evaluations of food ingredients in all aspects of food research and the food industry.

FCC SPECIFICATIONS

FCC specifications are presented in monograph form for each substance or group of related substances. They are designed to ensure that food ingredients have the specified identity and a sufficiently high level of quality to be safe under usual conditions of intended use in foods or in food processing. Thus, *FCC* specifications generally represent acceptable levels of quality and purity of food-grade ingredients available in the United States (or in other countries or instances in which *FCC* specifications are recognized).

Manufacturers, vendors, and users of *FCC* substances are expected to exercise good manufacturing practices (GMPs) (see *General Information*). They are also expected to establish food safety assurance systems such as Hazard Analysis and Critical Control Points (HACCP) to ensure that *FCC* substances are safe and otherwise suitable for their intended use. *FCC* substances must meet applicable

---
[1] For further information about the legal status of *FCC*, see *Legal Recognition of FCC Standards*, in the Preface.

regulatory requirements, including microbiological criteria, for safety and quality.

The name of the substance on a container label, plus the designation "Food Chemicals Codex Grade," "FCC Grade," or simply "FCC," is a representation by the manufacturer, vendor, or user of the substance that at the time of shipment, the substance conforms to the specifications in *FCC 8*, including any *Supplement* that is current at that time. When an *FCC* substance is available commercially in solution form as a component of a mixture and there is no provision in the *FCC* for such solution or mixture, the manufacturer, vendor, or user may indicate on the label that the product contains substances meeting *FCC* specifications by use of the initials "FCC" after the name of those components that meet the *FCC* specifications. For the labeling of *FCC* substances in which added substances are permitted, see *Added Substances*.

Added Substances *FCC* specifications are intended for application to individual substances and not to proprietary blends or other mixtures. Some specifications, however, allow "added substances" (i.e., functional secondary ingredients such as anti-caking agents, antioxidants, diluents, emulsifiers, and preservatives) intentionally added when necessary to ensure the integrity, stability, utility, or functionality of the primary substance in commercial use.

If an *FCC* monograph allows such additions, each added substance must meet the following requirements: (1) it is approved for use in foods by the FDA or by the responsible government agency in other countries; (2) it is of appropriate food-grade quality and meets the requirements of the *FCC*, if listed therein; (3) it is used in an amount not to exceed the minimum required to impart its intended technical effect or function in the primary substance; (4) its use will not result in concentrations of contaminants exceeding permitted levels in any food as a consequence of the affected *FCC* primary substance's being used in food; and (5) it does not interfere with the tests and assays prescribed for determining compliance with the *FCC* requirements for the primary substance, unless the monograph for the primary substance has provided for such interferences. Where added substances are specifically permitted in an *FCC* substance, the label shall state the name(s) of any added substance(s).

Adding substances not specifically provided for and mentioned by name or function in the monograph of an *FCC* substance will cause the substance to no longer be designated as an *FCC* substance. Such a combination is a mixture to be described by disclosure of its ingredients, including any that are not *FCC* substances.

Title of Monograph The titles of *FCC* monographs are in most instances the common or usual names. *FCC* specifications apply equally to substances bearing the main titles, synonyms listed under the main titles, and names derived by transposition of definitive words in main titles. The nomenclature used for flavoring agents may not be consistent with other authoritative sources.

Molecular Structures and Chemical Formulas Molecular structures, chemical formulas, and formula weights immediately following titles are included for the purpose of information and are not to be considered an indication of the purity of the substance. Molecular formulas given in specifications, tests, and assays, however, denote the pure chemical entity.

CAS Number If available, Chemical Abstracts Service (CAS) registry numbers are included for informational purposes. Additional *CAS numbers* may be relevant.

INS Numbers If available, numbers adopted by the Codex Alimentarius Commission under the International Numbering System for Food Additives are included for informational purposes.

FEMA Numbers If available, numbers assigned by the Flavor and Extract Manufacturers Association of the United States (FEMA) are included for informational purposes.

UNII The Unique Ingredient Identifier (UNII) is a nonproprietary, free, unique, unambiguous, nonsemantic, alphanumeric identifier based on a substance's molecular structure and/or descriptive information issued through the joint FDA/USP Substance Registration System (SRS) to support health information technology initiatives for substances in drugs, biologics, foods, and devices.

Alternative Analytical Procedures Although the tests and assays described constitute procedures upon which the specifications of the *FCC* depend, analysts are not prevented from applying alternative procedures if supporting data shows that the procedures used will produce results of equal or greater accuracy. In the event of the doubt or disagreement concerning a substance purported to comply with the specifications of the *FCC*, only the methods described herein are applicable and authoritative.

Labeling For purpose of compliance with *FCC* monographs, "labeling" means all labels and other written, printed, or graphic matter (1) on any article of any of its containers or wrappers or (2) accompanying such article, or otherwise provided by vendors to purchasers for purposes of product identification.

Sulfiting agents If an *FCC* substance contains 10 mg/kg or more of any sulfiting agent, the presence of such sulfiting agent shall be indicated on the labeling.

Requirements for Listing Substances in the FCC

The *FCC* is intended to be an international compendium of food ingredient standards. The requirements for listing substances in the *FCC* are as follows: (1) the substance is approved for use in food or in food processing in the United States or in other countries, (2) it is commercially available, and (3) suitable specifications and analytical test procedures are available to determine its identity and purity.

GENERAL SPECIFICATIONS AND STATEMENTS

Certain specifications and statements in the monographs of the *FCC* are not amenable to precise description and accurate determination within narrow limiting ranges.

Because of the subjective or general nature of these specifications, good judgment, based on experience, must be used in interpreting and attaching significance to them.

Description Characteristics described and statements made in the *Description* section of a monograph are not requirements, but are provided as information that may assist with the overall evaluation of a food ingredient. The section includes a description of physical characteristics such as color and form and information on stability under certain conditions of exposure to air and light. It may also include odor terms that are general descriptors and do not necessarily indicate the source of the material. Statements in this section may also cover approximate indications of properties such as solubility (see below) in various solvents, pH, melting point, and boiling point, with numerical values modified by "about," "approximately," "usually," "~," and other comparable nonspecific terms.

Function A statement of function is provided to indicate the technical effect(s) of the substance in foods or in food processing or a principle application such as "Nutrient". The statement is not intended to limit in any way the choice or use of the substance or to indicate that it has no other utility. The term "Source of..." is used to describe the function of materials that may, following ingestion, exhibit a functional effect on the human body, in a manner similar to that of some nutrients. These substances are products of an emerging science, and a comprehensive understanding of their beneficial effects has yet to be developed. The inclusion of monographs for these materials should not be interpreted as implying an endorsement of the claimed potential health or other benefits.

Odorless This term, when used in describing a flavoring material, applies to the examination, after exposure to air for 15 min, of about 25 g of the material that has been transferred from the original container to an open evaporating dish of about 100-mL capacity. If the package contains 25 g or less, the entire contents should be examined.

Packaging and Storage Statements in monographs relating to packaging and storage are advisory in character and are intended only as general information to emphasize instances where deterioration may be accelerated under adverse packaging and storage conditions, such as exposure to air, light, or temperature extremes, or where safety hazards are involved. Additionally, to reduce the risk of intentional or accidental introduction of undesirable materials into food substances, containers should be equipped with tamper-resistant closures.

Cool Place A cool place is one where the temperature is between 8° and 15° (46° and 59°F). Alternatively, it may be a refrigerator, unless otherwise specified in the monograph.

Excessive Heat Any temperature above 40° (104°F).

Storage under Nonspecific Conditions Where no specific storage directions or limitations are provided in the individual monograph, the conditions of storage and distribution include protection from moisture, freezing, and excessive heat. Containers should be stored in secure areas when not in use to reduce the possibility of tampering.

Containers The container is the device that holds the substance and that is or may be in direct contact with it. The immediate container is in direct contact with the substance at all times. The closure is a part of the container. Closures should be tamper-resistant and tamper-evident. The container should not interact physically or chemically with the material that it holds so as to alter its strength, quality, or purity. The food ingredient contact surface of the container should comply with relevant regulations promulgated under the Federal Food, Drug, and Cosmetic Act (or with applicable laws and regulations in other countries). Polyunsaturated fats and oils are particularly susceptible to oxidation when stored in metal containers, at elevated temperatures, and/or in open containers. Oxidation can be minimized by storing them in closed, nonmetal containers with minimal headspace or flushed with nitrogen gas.

Light-Resistant Container A light-resistant container is designed to prevent deterioration of the contents beyond the prescribed limits of strength, quality, or purity under the ordinary or customary conditions of handling, shipments, storage, and sale. A colorless container may be made light resistant by enclosing it in an opaque carton or wrapper (see also *Apparatus*, below).

Well-Closed Container A well-closed container protects the contents from extraneous solids and from loss of the chemical under the ordinary or customary conditions of handling, shipment, storage, and sale.

Tight Container A tight container protects the contents from contamination of extraneous liquids, solids, or vapors; from loss of the chemical; and from efflorescence, deliquescence, or evaporation under the ordinary or customary conditions of handling, shipment, storage, and sale, and is capable of tight reclosure.

Product Security Tamper-evident packaging closures and security tags should be used. Containers that appear to have been opened or otherwise altered by unauthorized persons should not be used until the purity of the substance has been confirmed.

Solubility Statements included in a monograph under a heading such as *Solubility in Alcohol* express exact requirements and constitute quality specifications. Statements relating to solubility given in the *Description*, however, are intended as information regarding approximate solubilities only and are not to be considered as exact *FCC*-quality specifications. Such statements are considered to be of minor significance as a means of identification or determination of purity. For those purposes, dependence must be placed upon other *FCC* specifications.

Approximate solubilities given in the *Description* are indicated by the following descriptive terms:

Descriptive Term	Parts of Solvent Required for 1 part of Solute
Very Soluble	less than 1
Freely Soluble	from 1 to 10
Soluble	from 10 to 30
Sparingly Soluble	from 30 to 100
Slightly Soluble	from 100 to 1000
Very Slightly Soluble	from 1000 to 10,000
Practically Insoluble or Insoluble	more than 10,000

Soluble substances, when brought into solution, may show slight physical impurities, such as fragments of filter paper, fibers, and dust particles unless excluded by definite tests or other requirements. Significant amounts of black specks, metallic chips, glass fragments, or other insoluble matter are not permitted.

TESTS AND ASSAYS

Every substance in commerce that claims or purports to conform to *FCC*, when tested in accordance with its tests and assays, meets all of the requirements in the *FCC* monograph defining it.

The methods and analytical procedures described in the *FCC* are designed for use by properly trained personnel in a suitably equipped laboratory. In common with many laboratory procedures, test methods in the *FCC* frequently involve hazardous materials. In performing the test procedures and assays in the *FCC*, safe laboratory practices must be followed. This includes the use of precautionary measures, protective equipment, and work practices consistent with the chemicals and procedures used. Before undertaking any assay or procedures described in the *FCC*, the individual should be aware of the hazards associated with the chemicals and of the procedures and means of protecting against them. Material Safety Data Sheets, which contain precautionary information related to safety and health concerns, are available from manufacturers and distributors of chemicals such as USP and should provide helpful information about the safe use of such chemicals. Certain chemical reagents specified in *FCC* test procedures may be considered to be hazardous or toxic by the Occupational Safety and Health Administration, by the Environmental Protection Agency (under provisions of the Toxic Substances Control Act), or by health authorities in other countries. Where such reagents are specified, the analyst is encouraged to investigate the use of suitable substitute reagents, as appropriate, and to inform the *USP FCC* Liaison (fcc@usp.org) of the results so obtained.

Analytical Samples In the description of tests and assays, the approximate quantity of the analytical sample to be used is usually indicated. The quantity actually used, however, should not deviate by more than 10% from the stated amount. Tests or assays sometimes call for a sample taken to be "previously dried." Where a test for *Loss on Drying* or *Loss on Ignition* is included in a monograph, the conditions specified for these procedures are to be used to dry the sample prior to performing the test procedure or assay, unless otherwise specified. Often, the results of tests or assays that do not call for use of a "previously dried" sample are expressed as calculated on the dried, anhydrous, or ignited basis. In such cases, a test for *Loss on Drying*, *Water*, or *Loss on Ignition* is included in the monograph and the result of such a test is used for the calculation on the dried, anhydrous, or ignited basis, provided that any moisture or other volatile matter in the undried sample does not interfere with the specified test procedures and assays.

In editions of the *FCC* prior to the *Seventh* edition, the terms "exactly," "accurately weighed," and "accurately measured" are used in connection with gravimetric or volumetric measurements and linked directly to a sample weight or volume. These terms indicate that an operation should be carried out within the limits of error prescribed under *Volumetric Apparatus* or *Weights and Balances*, Appendix I. In the *Seventh* edition and each subsequent edition, these terms have been removed from most monographs, to be more concise. Nonetheless, it shall be understood that all quantitative measurements are to be performed "accurately" and in conformance with the provisions in *Volumetric Apparatus* or *Weights and Balances*, Appendix I, unless otherwise indicated by qualifiers such as "about" or by the particular nature of the test procedure.

The word "transfer," when used in describing tests and assays, means that the procedure should be carried out quantitatively.

Apparatus With the exception of volumetric flasks and other exact measuring or weighing devices, directions to use a definite size or type of container or other laboratory apparatus are intended only as recommendations, unless otherwise specified. Where an instrument for physical measurement, such as a thermometer, spectrophotometer, or gas chromatograph, is designated by its distinctive name or trade name in a test or assay, a similar instrument of equivalent or greater sensitivity of accuracy may be employed. An instrument may be substituted for the specified instrument if the substitute uses the same fundamental principles of operation and is of equivalent or greater sensitivity and accuracy. These characteristics must be validated as appropriate. Where low-actinic or light-resistant containers are specified, clear glass containers that have been rendered opaque by application of a suitable coating or wrapping may be used. Where a particular brand or source of a material, instrument, or piece of equipment, or the name and address of the manufacturer, or distributor, is mentioned (ordinarily in a footnote), this identification is furnished solely for informational purposes as a matter of convenience, without implication of approval, endorsement, or certification.

Atomic Weights The atomic weights used in computing formula weights and volumetric and gravimetric factors stated in tests and assays are those recommended in 1991 by the IUPAC Commission on Isotopic Abundances and Atomic Weights.

Blank Tests Where a blank determination is specified in a test or assay, it is to be conducted using the same quantities of the same reagents and by the same procedure repeated in every detail except that the substance being tested is omitted.

A residual blank titration may be stipulated in tests and assays involving a back titration in which a volume of a volumetric solution larger than is required to react with the sample is added, and the excess of this solution is then titrated with a second volumetric solution. Where a residual blank titration is specified or where the procedure involves such a titration, a blank is run as directed in the preceding paragraph. The volume of the titrant consumed in the back titration is then subtracted from the volume required for the blank. The difference between the two, equivalent to the actual volume consumed by the sample, is the corrected volume of the volumetric solution to be used in calculating the quantity of the substance being determined.

Centrifuge Where the use of a centrifuge is indicated, unless otherwise specified, the directions are predicated on the use of the apparatus having an effective radius of about 20 cm (8 in) and driven at a speed sufficient to clarify the supernatant layer within 15 min. If necessary, determine the gravity by using the equation $g = \{[(rpm \times 2 \times \pi)/60] \times r_m\}/980$, in which rpm is the rotor speed and r_m is the mean radius, in cm, of the tube holding the sample in the rotor.

Desiccators and Desiccants The expression "in a desiccator" means using a tightly closed container of appropriate design in which a low moisture content can be maintained by means of a suitable desiccant. Preferred desiccants include anhydrous calcium sulfate, magnesium perchlorate, phosphorus pentoxide, and silica gel.

Filtration Where it is directed to "filter," without further qualification, the intent is that the liquid be filtered through suitable filter paper or an equivalent device until the filtrate is clear.

Identification The tests described under this heading in monographs are designed for application to substances taken from labeled containers and are provided only as an aid to substantiate identification. These tests, regardless of their specificity, are not necessarily sufficient to establish proof of identity, but failure of a substance taken from a labeled container to meet the requirements of a prescribed identification test means that it does not conform to the requirements of the monograph.

Indicators The quantity of an indicator solution used should be 0.2 mL (approximately 3 drops) unless otherwise directed in a test or assay.

mg/kg and Percent The term "mg/kg" is used in expressing the concentrations of trace amounts of substances, such as impurities, up to 10 mg/kg. Above 10 mg/kg, percent (by weight) is used. For example, a monograph requirement equivalent to 20 mg/kg is expressed as 0.002%, or 0.0020%, depending on the number of significant figures justified by the test specified for use in conjunction with the requirement.

Microbial Limit Tests The *FCC* directly references the procedures in the *FDA Bacteriological Analytical Manual* (BAM) (http://www.fda.gov/Food/default.htm) for its microbial limit tests. Where the sample size is not defined in the limit, the results are based on the sampling procedures described in BAM.

Negligible The term "negligible," as used in some *Residue on Ignition* specifications, indicates a quantity not exceeding 0.5 mg.

Pressure Measurements The term "mm Hg" used with respect to pressure within an apparatus, or atmospheric pressure, refers to the use of a suitable manometer or barometer calibrated in terms of the pressure exerted by a column of mercury of the stated height.

Reagents Specifications for reagents are not included in the *FCC*. Unless otherwise specified, reagents required in tests and assays should conform to the specifications of the current editions of *Reagent Chemicals – American Chemical Society Specifications* or in the section on *Reagent Specifications* in the *United States Pharmacopeia*. Reagents not covered by any of these specifications should be of a grade suitable to the proper performance of the method of test or assay involved.

Acids and Ammonium Hydroxide When ammonium hydroxide, glacial acetic acid, hydrochloric acid, hydrofluoric acid, nitric acid, phosphoric acid, or sulfuric acid is called for in tests and assays, reagents of ACS grade and strengths are to be used. (These reagents sometimes are called "concentrated," but this term is not used in the *FCC*.)

Alcohol, Ethyl Alcohol, Ethanol When one of these substances is called for in tests and assays, use ACS-grade *Ethyl Alcohol* (95%) or USP-grade *Alcohol*.

Alcohol Absolute, Anhydrous Alcohol, Dehydrated Alcohol When one of these substances is called for in tests and assays, use ACS-grade *Ethyl alcohol, Absolute* or USP-grade *Dehydrated alcohol*.

Water When water is called for in tests and assays or in the preparation of solutions, it shall have been prepared by distillation, ion-exchange treatment, or reverse osmosis.

Water, Carbon Dioxide-Free When this type of water is called for, it shall have been boiled vigorously for 5 min or more, and allowed to cool while protected from absorption of carbon dioxide from the atmosphere.

"Deaerated water" or *"degassed water"* is water that has been treated to reduce the content of dissolved air by suitable means, such as by boiling vigorously for 5 min and cooling while protected from air or by the application of ultrasonic vibration.

Reference Standards Test and assay results are determined on the basis of comparison of the test sample with a reference standard that has been freed from or corrected for volatile residues or water content, as instructed on the reference standard label. The requirements for any new *FCC* standards, tests, or assays for which a new USP or *FCC* Reference Standard or Authentic Substance is specified are not in effect until the specified Reference Standard or Authentic Substance is available. If a reference standard is required to be dried before use, transfer a sufficient amount to a clean, dry vessel. Do not use the original container as the drying vessel, and do not dry a reference standard repeatedly at temperatures above 25°. Where the titrimetric determination of water is required at the time a reference standard is to be used, proceed as directed in the *Karl Fischer Titrimetric Method* under *Water Determination*, Appendix IIB. Unless a reference standard label bears a specific potency or content, assume that the reference standard is 100.0% pure. [Directions for use printed on the label text of USP and *FCC* reference standards are lot-specific, and they take precedence over any other indication listed in the *FCC*.]

Significant Figures When tolerance limits are expressed numerically, the values are significant to the number of digits indicated. Record the observed or calculated analytical result with only one digit included in the decimal place to the right of the last place in the limit expression. If this digit is smaller than 5, eliminate it and leave the preceding digit unchanged. If this digit is greater than 5, eliminate it and increase the preceding digit by one. If this digit equals 5, eliminate it and increase the preceding digit by one. For example, a requirement of not less than 96.0% would not be met by a result of 95.94%, but would be met by results of 95.96% or 95.95%, both of which would be rounded to 96.0%. When a range is stated, the upper and lower limits are inclusive so that the range consists of the two values themselves, properly rounded, and all values between them.

Solutions Prepare all solutions, unless otherwise specified, with water prepared by distillation, ion-exchange treatment, reverse osmosis, or as otherwise indicated in the monograph. Expressions such as "1:10" or "10%" mean that *1 part by volume* of a liquid or *1 part by weight* of a solid is to be dissolved in a volume of the diluent or solvent sufficient to make the finished solution 10 parts by volume. Directions for the preparation of colorimetric solutions (CS), test solutions (TS), and volumetric solutions (VS), are provided in the section on *Solutions and Indicators*. Prepare a volumetric solution to have a normality (molarity) within 10% of the stated value and to be standardized to four significant figures. When volumetric equivalence factors are provided in tests and assays, the term "0.X N(M)" is understood to mean a VS having a normality (molarity) of exactly 0.X000 N(M). If the normality (molarity) of the VS employed in a particular procedure differs from 0.X000, apply an appropriate correction factor.

Specific Gravity Numerical values for specific gravity, unless otherwise noted, refer to the ratio of the weight of a substance in air at 25° to that of an equal volume of water at the same temperature. Determine specific gravity by any reliable method, unless otherwise specified.

Temperatures Unless otherwise specified, temperatures are expressed in Celsius (centigrade) degrees, and all measurements are to be made at 25°, unless otherwise directed.

Time Limits Unless otherwise specified, allow 5 minutes for a reaction to take place when conducting limit tests for trace impurities such as chloride or iron. Expressions such as "exactly 5 min" mean that the stated period should be accurately timed.

Tolerances Minimum purity tolerance limits presented in monographs neither bar the use of lots of articles that more nearly approach 100% purity nor constitute a basis for a claim that such lots exceed the quality prescribed by the *FCC*. When no maximum assay tolerance is given, the assay should show the equivalent of not more than 100.5%.

Trace Impurities Tests for inherent trace impurities are provided to limit such substances to levels that are consistent with good manufacturing practice and that are safe and otherwise unobjectionable under conditions in which the food additive or ingredient is customarily employed. It is impossible for *FCC* to provide limits and tests in each monograph for the detection of all possible unusual or unexpected impurities, the presence of which would be inconsistent with good manufacturing practice. The limits and tests provided in *FCC* are those considered to be necessary according to currently recognized methods of manufacture and are based on information available to or provided to the Food Ingredients Expert Committee. If other methods of manufacture or other than the usual raw materials are used, or if other possible impurities may be present, additional tests may be required and should be applied, as necessary, by the manufacturer, vendor, or user to demonstrate that the substance is suitable for its intended application. Such tests should be submitted to the USP *FCC* Liaison (fcc@usp.org) for consideration for inclusion in the *FCC*.

Vacuum The unqualified use of the term "in vacuum" means a pressure at least as low as that obtainable by an efficient aspirating water pump (not higher than 20 mm Hg).

Water and Loss on Drying In general, for compounds containing water of crystallization or adsorbed water, a limit test, to be determined by the *Karl Fischer Titrimetric Method*, is provided under the heading *Water*. For compounds in which the *Loss on Drying* may not necessarily be attributable to water, a limit test, to be determined by other methods, is provided under the heading *Loss on Drying*.

Weighing Practices

Constant Weight A direction that a substance is to be "dried to constant weight" means that the drying should continue until two consecutive weighings differ by not more than 0.5 mg/g of the sample taken, the second weighing to follow an additional hour of drying. The direction "ignite to constant weight" means that the ignition should be continued at 800° ± 25°, unless otherwise specified, until two consecutive weighings do not differ by more than 0.5 mg/g of the sample taken, the second weighing to follow an additional 15 min of ignition.

Tared Container When a tared container, such as a gloss filtering crucible, a porcelain crucible, or a platinum dish, is called for in an analytical procedure, it shall be treated as is specified in the procedure, e.g., dried or ignited for a specified time or to constant weight, cooled in a desiccator as necessary, and weighed accurately.

Weights and Measures, Symbols and Abbreviations The International System of Units (SI), to the extent possible, is used in most specifications, tests, and assays in this edition of *FCC*. The SI metric units, and other units and abbreviations commonly employed, are as follows:

° = degrees Celsius
kg = kilogram
g = gram
mg = milligram
µg = microgram
ng = nanogram
pg = picogram
L = liter
mL = milliliter

μL = microliter
m = meter
cm = centimeter
dm = decimeter
mm = millimeter
μm = micrometer (0.001 mm)
nm = nanometer
~ = approximately
C = coulomb
A = ampere
V = volt
mV = millivolt
W = watt
dc = direct current
ft = foot
in = inch
in³ = cubic inch
gal = gallon
lb = pound
oz = ounce
mEq = milliequivalents
mg/kg = parts per million (by weight)
μg/kg = parts per billion (by weight)
ng/kg = parts per trillion (by weight)
psi = pounds per square inch
psia = pounds per square inch absolute
kPa = kilopascal
sp. gr. = specific gravity
b.p. = boiling point
m.p. = melting point

id = inside diameter
od = outside diameter
h = hour
min = minute
s = second
N = normality
M = molarity
mM = millimolar
mmol = millimole
μM = micromolar
μmol = micromole
CFU = colony-forming unit(s)
ACS = American Chemical Society
AOAC = AOAC International
AOCS = American Oil Chemists Society
ASTM = ASTM (American Society for Testing and Materials) International
CAS = Chemical Abstracts Service
CFR = Code of Federal Regulations (U.S.)
FDA = United States Food and Drug Administration
FEMA = Flavor and Extract Manufacturers Association of the United States
INS = International Numbering System of the Codex Alimentarius
IUPAC = International Union of Pure and Applied Chemistry
NIST = National Institute of Standards and Technology
UNII = Unique Ingredient Identifier (as defined by US FDA)

Monographs

Acesulfame Potassium
First Published: Prior to FCC 6
Last Revision: FCC 7

Acesulfame K
6-Methyl-1,2,3-oxathiazine-4(3H)-one-2,2 Dioxide Potassium Salt

$C_4H_4KNO_4S$ Formula wt 201.24
INS: 950   CAS: [55589-62-3]
UNII: 23OV73Q5G9 [acesulfame potassium]

DESCRIPTION
Acesulfame Potassium occurs as a white, free-flowing crystalline powder. It is freely soluble in water and very slightly soluble in ethanol.
Function: Non-nutritive sweetener; flavor enhancer
Packaging and Storage: Store in well-closed containers in a cool, dry place.

IDENTIFICATION
- **A. PROCEDURE**
  Sample solution: 0.3 g in 1 mL of glacial acetic acid and 5 mL of water
  Analysis: Add a few drops of sodium cobaltinitrite TS to the *Sample solution*.
  Acceptance criteria: A yellow precipitate forms.
- **B. ULTRAVIOLET ABSORPTION**
  Sample solution: 0.01 mg/mL
  Acceptance criteria: The *Sample solution* shows an absorption maximum at 227 ± 2 nm.
- **C. INFRARED ABSORPTION**, *Spectrophotometric Identification Tests*, Appendix IIIC
  Reference standard: USP Acesulfame Potassium RS
  Sample and standard preparation: *K*
  Acceptance criteria: The spectrum of the sample exhibits maxima at the same wavelengths as those in the spectrum of the *Reference standard*.

ASSAY
- **PROCEDURE**
  Sample: 200–300 mg, previously dried at 105° for 2 h
  Analysis: Dissolve the *Sample* in 50 mL of glacial acetic acid in a 250-mL flask. [NOTE—Dissolution may be slow.] Add 2 or 3 drops of crystal violet TS, and titrate with 0.1 N perchloric acid to a blue-green endpoint that persists for at least 30 s. [**CAUTION**—Handle perchloric acid in an appropriate fume hood.] Perform a blank determination (see *General Provisions*), and make any necessary correction. Each mL of 0.1 N perchloric acid is equivalent to 20.12 mg of $C_4H_4KNO_4S$.
  Acceptance criteria: 99.0%–101.0% of $C_4H_4KNO_4S$, on the dried basis

IMPURITIES
Inorganic Impurities
- **FLUORIDE**, *Fluoride Limit Test, Method III*, Appendix IIIB
  Sample: 4 g
  Acceptance criteria: NMT 3 mg/kg
- **LEAD**, *Lead Limit Test*, Appendix IIIB
  Sample solution: 2 g in 20 mL of water
  Control: 2 µg Pb (2 mL of *Diluted Standard Lead Solution*)
  Acceptance criteria: NMT 1 mg/kg

Organic Impurities
- **ORGANIC IMPURITIES**
  Mobile phase: Acetonitrile and 0.01 M tetrabutyl ammonium hydrogen sulfate (40:60, v/v)
  Standard: 4-hydroxybenzoic acid ethyl ester
  Sample solution: 10 mg/mL
  Dilute sample solution: 0.2 mg/L
  Chromatographic system, Appendix IIA
    Mode: High-performance liquid chromatography
    Detector: UV or diode array (227 nm)
    Column: 25-cm × 4.6-mm (id) stainless steel, or equivalent, packed with 3- to 5-µm reversed phase C18 silica gel, or equivalent
    Flow rate: About 1 mL/min
    Injection volume: 20 µL
    Elution: Isocratic
  System suitability
    Suitability requirements: The resolution, R, between acesulfame potassium and 4-hydroxybenzoic acid ethyl ester is NLT 2.
  Analysis: Inject the *Sample solution* into the chromatograph and obtain the chromatogram. If peaks other than that caused by acesulfame potassium appear within three times the elution time of acesulfame potassium, carry out a second analysis using the *Dilute sample solution*.
  Acceptance criteria: The sum of the areas of all peaks eluted in the analysis of the *Sample solution* within three times the elution time of acesulfame potassium, except for the acesulfame potassium peak, does not exceed the peak area of acesulfame potassium in the analysis of the *Dilute sample solution* (NMT 20 µg/g of UV-active compounds).

SPECIFIC TESTS
- **LOSS ON DRYING**, Appendix IIC: 105° for 2 h
  Acceptance criteria: NMT 1.0%
- **PH**, *pH Determination*, Appendix IIB
  Sample solution: 10 mg/mL
  Acceptance criteria: Between 5.5 and 7.5

Acetaldehyde Diethyl Acetal

First Published: Prior to FCC 6

Acetal

C$_6$H$_{14}$O$_2$ Formula wt 118.17
FEMA: 2002
UNII: 5G14F9E2HB [acetal]

DESCRIPTION
Acetaldehyde Diethyl Acetal occurs as a colorless to pale yellow liquid.
Odor: Ethereal, fruity
Solubility: Soluble in propylene glycol, vegetable oils; slightly soluble in water
Boiling Point: ~102°
Solubility in Alcohol, Appendix VI: One mL dissolves in 1 mL of 95% ethanol.
Function: Flavoring agent

IDENTIFICATION
- **INFRARED SPECTRA,** Spectrophotometric Identification Tests, Appendix IIIC
  Acceptance criteria: The spectrum of the sample exhibits relative maxima at the same wavelengths as those of the spectrum below.

ASSAY
- **PROCEDURE:** Proceed as directed under M-1b, Appendix XI.
  Acceptance criteria: NLT 97.0% of C$_6$H$_{14}$O$_2$

SPECIFIC TESTS
- **REFRACTIVE INDEX,** Appendix II: At 20°
  Acceptance criteria: Between 1.379 and 1.384
- **SPECIFIC GRAVITY:** Determine at 25° by any reliable method (see General Provisions).
  Acceptance criteria: Between 0.821 and 0.827

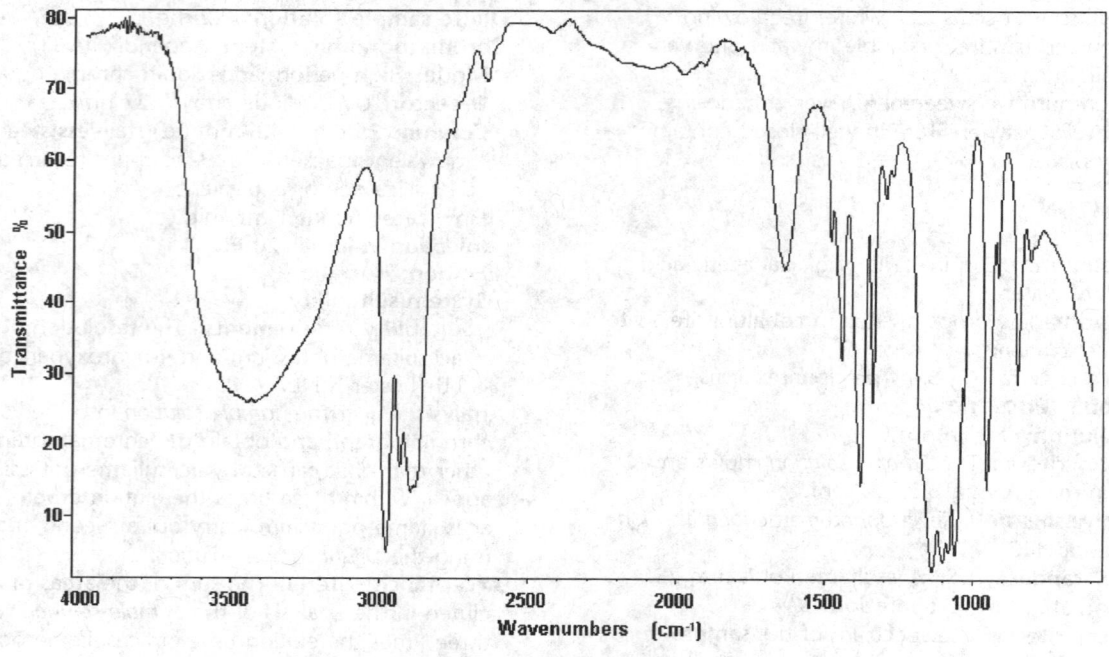

Acetaldehyde Diethyl Acetal

Acetaldehyde

First Published: Prior to FCC 6
Last Revision: First Supplement, FCC 6

Acetic Aldehyde
Ethanal

C$_2$H$_4$O Formula wt 44.05
FEMA: 2003
UNII: GO1N1ZPR3B [acetaldehyde]

DESCRIPTION
Acetaldehyde occurs as a flammable, colorless liquid. It may contain a suitable antioxidant.
Odor: Pungent, ethereal
Solubility: Miscible in alcohol, organic solvents, water
Boiling Point: ~21°
Function: Flavoring agent

FCC 8   Monographs / Acetanisole / 11

IDENTIFICATION

- **INFRARED SPECTRA,** *Spectrophotometric Identification Tests,* Appendix IIIC
  Acceptance criteria: The spectrum of the sample exhibits relative maxima at the same wavelengths as those of the spectrum below.

ASSAY

- **PROCEDURE:** Proceed as directed under *M-2b,* Appendix XI.
  Acceptance criteria: NLT 99.0% of C_2H_4O

SPECIFIC TESTS

- **ACID VALUE, FLAVOR CHEMICALS (OTHER THAN ESSENTIAL OILS),** *M-15,* Appendix XI
  Acceptance criteria: NMT 5.0
- **SPECIFIC GRAVITY:** Determine at 0° ± 0.05° by means of a hydrometer calibrated to give the apparent specific gravity at 0°/20° (see *General Provisions*).
  Acceptance criteria: Between 0.804 and 0.811

OTHER REQUIREMENTS

- **RESIDUE ON EVAPORATION,** *M-16,* Appendix XI
  Acceptance criteria: 0.006%

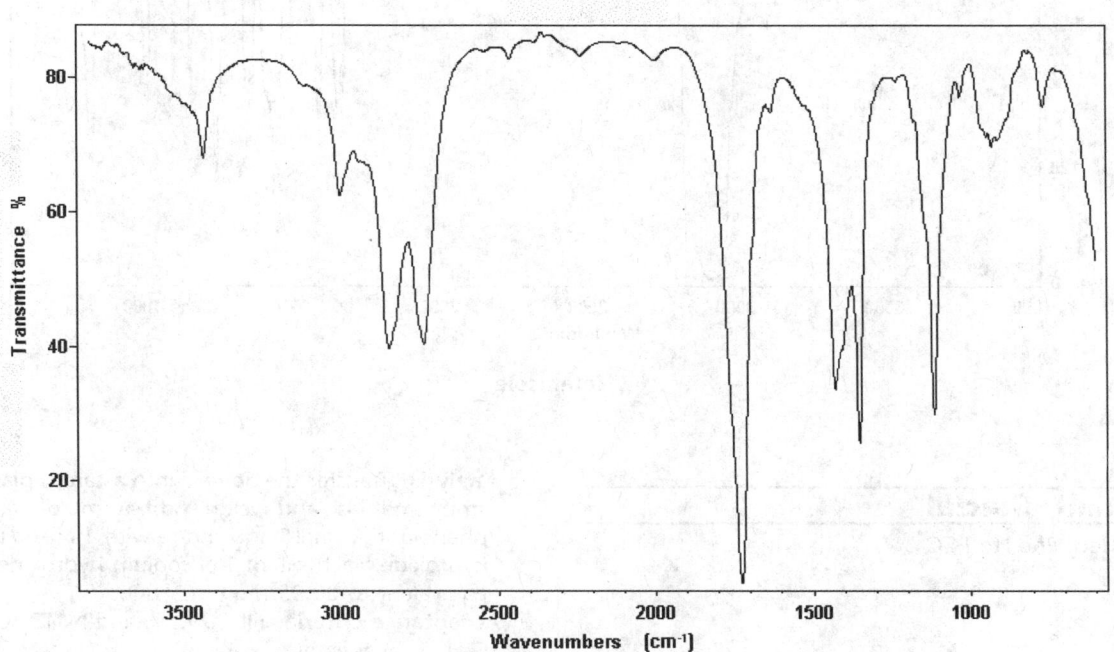

Acetaldehyde

Acetanisole

First Published: Prior to FCC 6

4-Acetylanisole
p-Methoxyacetophenone

$C_9H_{10}O_2$ Formula wt 150.18
FEMA: 2005
UNII: 0IRH2BR587 [4-acetylanisole]

DESCRIPTION

Acetanisole occurs as a colorless to pale yellow fused solid.
Odor: Hawthorn
Solubility: Soluble in most fixed oils, propylene glycol; insoluble or practically insoluble in glycerin
Boiling Point: ~153° (26 mm Hg)
Solubility in Alcohol, Appendix VI: One g dissolves in 5 mL of 50% alcohol.
Function: Flavoring agent

IDENTIFICATION

- **INFRARED SPECTRA,** *Spectrophotometric Identification Tests,* Appendix IIIC
  Acceptance criteria: The spectrum of the sample exhibits relative maxima at the same wavelengths as those of the spectrum below.

ASSAY

- **PROCEDURE:** Proceed as directed under *M-1b,* Appendix XI.
  Acceptance criteria: NLT 98.0% of $C_9H_{10}O_2$

OTHER REQUIREMENTS

- **CHLORINATED COMPOUNDS,** Appendix VI
  Acceptance criteria: Passes test

- **LEAD,** *M-9,* Appendix XI
    Acceptance criteria: 10 mg/kg

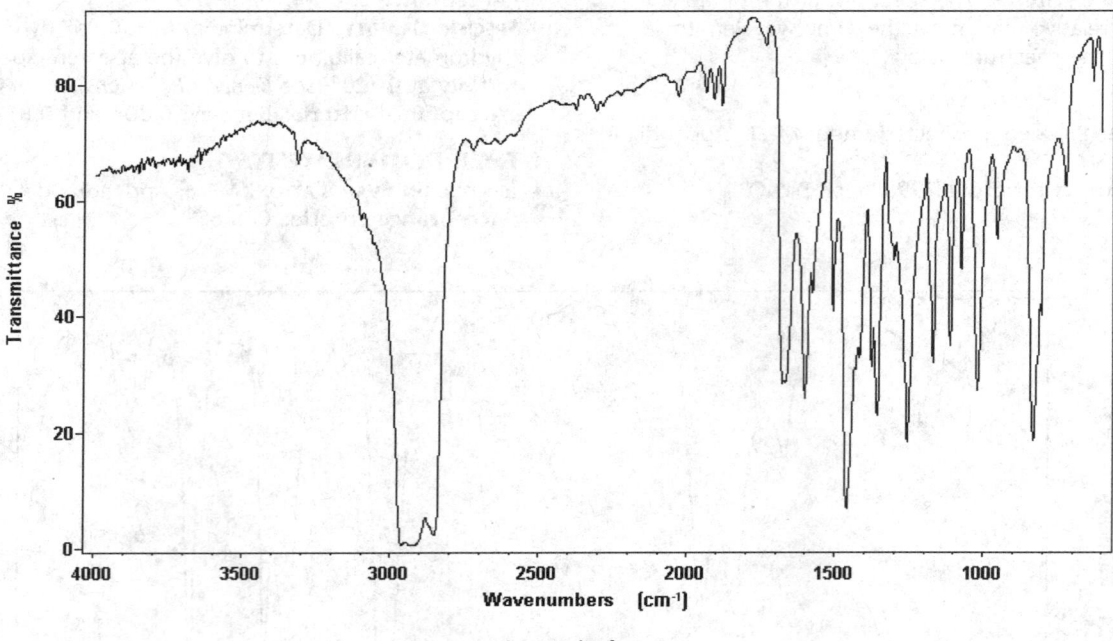

Acetanisole

Acetic Acid, Glacial

First Published: Prior to FCC 6

C₂H₄O₂   Formula wt 60.05
INS: 260
FEMA: 2006

CAS: [64-19-7]

UNII: Q40Q9N063P [acetic acid]

DESCRIPTION
Acetic Acid, Glacial, occurs as a clear, colorless liquid. It boils at about 118°. When well-diluted with water (e.g., 1:100), it has a vinegar odor and taste. It is miscible with water, with alcohol, and with glycerin.
Function: Acidifier; flavoring agent
Packaging and Storage: Store in tightly closed containers.

IDENTIFICATION
- **ACETATE,** Appendix IIIA
    Sample solution: 333 mg/mL
    Acceptance criteria: Passes tests

ASSAY
- **PROCEDURE**
    Sample: 2 mL
    Analysis: Transfer the *Sample* into a tared, glass-stoppered flask and weigh. Add 40 mL of water and phenolphthalein TS and titrate with 1 N sodium hydroxide. Each mL of 1 N sodium hydroxide is equivalent to 60.05 mg of C₂H₄O₂.
    Acceptance criteria: NLT 99.5% and NMT 100.5% C₂H₄O₂ by weight

IMPURITIES
Inorganic Impurities
- **LEAD,** Lead Limit Test, Atomic Absorption Spectrophotometric Graphite Furnace Method, *Method I,* Appendix IIIB
    Acceptance criteria: NMT 0.5 mg/kg

SPECIFIC TESTS
- **NONVOLATILE RESIDUE**
    Sample: 19 mL (20 g)
    Analysis: Evaporate the *Sample* in a tared dish on a steam bath and dry at 105° for 1 h.
    Acceptance criteria: NMT 0.005%
- **READILY OXIDIZABLE SUBSTANCES**
    Sample: 2 mL
    Analysis: Dilute the *Sample* with 10 mL of water in a glass-stoppered container and add 0.1 mL of 0.1 N potassium permanganate.
    Acceptance criteria: The pink color does not change to brown within 2 h.
- **SOLIDIFICATION POINT,** Appendix IIB
    Acceptance criteria: NLT 15.6°

Acetoin Dimer

First Published: Prior to FCC 6

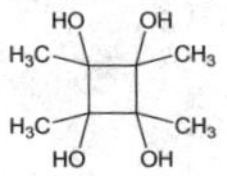

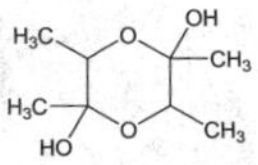

C₈H₁₆O₄   Formula wt 176.21
FEMA: 2008
UNII: BG4D34CO2H [acetoin]

DESCRIPTION
Acetoin Dimer occurs as a white to pale yellow powder.
Odor: Odorless
Solubility: Soluble in hot propylene glycol; slightly soluble in weak alkali; insoluble or practically insoluble in most solvents
Function: Flavoring agent

ASSAY
- **PROCEDURE:** Proceed as directed under *M-1b*, Appendix XI.
  Acceptance criteria: NLT 96.0% of C₄H₈O₂

Acetoin Monomer

First Published: FCC 6
Last Revision: Second Supplement, FCC 7

Acetyl Methyl Carbinol
Dimethylketol
3-Hydroxy-2-butanone

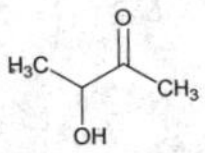

C₄H₈O₂   Formula wt 88.11
FEMA: 2008
UNII: BG4D34CO2H [acetoin]

DESCRIPTION
Acetoin Monomer occurs as a colorless to pale yellow liquid. It can contain some variable amount of its dimer.
Odor: Buttery
Solubility: Miscible in alcohol, propylene glycol, water; insoluble or practically insoluble in vegetable oils
Boiling Point: ~148°
Function: Flavoring agent

IDENTIFICATION
- **INFRARED SPECTRA,** *Spectrophotometric Identification Tests,* Appendix IIIC
  Acceptance criteria: The spectrum of the sample exhibits relative maxima at the same wavelengths as those of the spectrum below.

ASSAY
- **PROCEDURE:** Proceed as directed under *M-1b*, Appendix XI.
  Acceptance criteria: NLT 96.0% of C₄H₈O₂

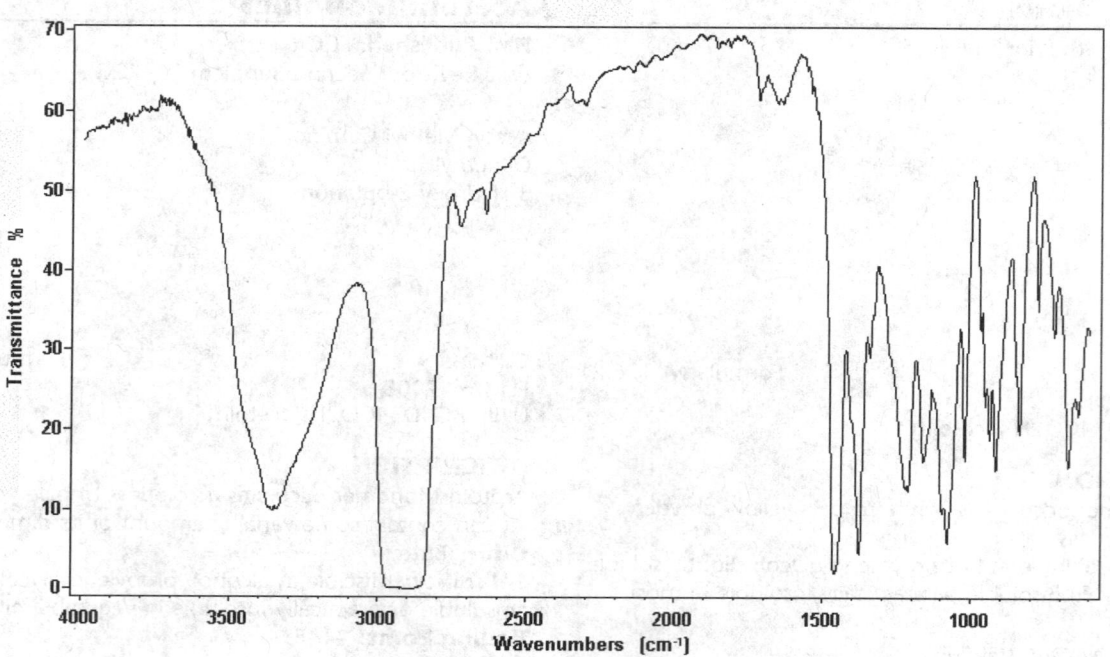

Acetoin Monomer

Acetone

First Published: Prior to FCC 6

2-Propanone
Dimethyl Ketone

C₃H₆O
Formula wt 58.08
CAS: [67-64-1]

UNII: 1364PS73AF [acetone]

DESCRIPTION
Acetone occurs as a clear, colorless, volatile liquid. It is miscible with water, with alcohol, with ether, with chloroform, and with most volatile oils.

Function: Extraction solvent

Packaging and Storage: Store in tight containers remote from fire.

[CAUTION—Acetone is highly flammable.]

IDENTIFICATION
- **PROCEDURE**
  Sample: 0.1 mL
  Analysis: Mix the *Sample* with 10 mL of water, add 5 mL of 1 N sodium hydroxide, warm, and add 5 mL of iodine TS.
  Acceptance criteria: A yellow precipitate of iodoform forms.

ASSAY
- **PROCEDURE**
  Sample solution: 1 mg/mL
  Analysis: Place 10 mL of the *Sample solution* into a glass-stoppered flask, add 25 mL of sodium hydroxide TS, and allow the mixture to stand for 5 min. Add 25 mL of 0.1 N iodine, stopper the flask, allow the contents to stand in a cold, dark place for 10 min, and add 30 mL of 1 N sulfuric acid. Titrate the excess iodine with 0.1 N sodium thiosulfate, using starch TS as the indicator. Perform a blank determination (see *General Provisions*) and make any necessary correction. Each mL of 0.1 N iodine is equivalent to 0.9675 mg of C₃H₆O.
  Acceptance criteria: NLT 99.5% and NMT 100.5% C₃H₆O, by weight

IMPURITIES
Inorganic Impurities
- **LEAD,** *Lead Limit Test, Atomic Absorption Spectrophotometric Graphite Furnace Method, Method I,* Appendix IIIB
  Acceptance criteria: NMT 1 mg/kg

Organic Impurities
- **ALDEHYDES (AS FORMALDEHYDE)**
  Sample solution: 2.5 mL of sample and 7.5 mL of water
  Standard solution: 40 µg formaldehyde in 10 mL of water
  Analysis: To both the *Sample solution* and 10 mL of the *Standard solution,* add 0.15 mL of a 5% solution of 5,5-dimethyl-1,3-cyclohexanedione in alcohol, and evaporate on a steam bath until the Acetone is volatilized. Dilute both to 10 mL with water and cool quickly in an ice bath while stirring vigorously.

Acceptance criteria: Any turbidity produced by the *Sample solution* does not exceed that produced by the *Standard solution* (NMT 0.002%).

- **METHANOL**
  Sample solution: 100 μL/mL
  Control solution: 40 μg/mL methanol
  Analysis: Add 0.2 mL of 10% phosphoric acid and 0.25 mL of 50 mg/mL potassium permanganate solution to 1 mL of each *Control solution* and *Sample solution*. Allow the mixtures to stand for 15 min, then add 0.3 mL of 100 mg/mL sodium bisulfite solution to each, and shake until colorless. Slowly add 5 mL of ice-cold 80% sulfuric acid, keeping the mixtures cold during the addition. Add 0.1 mL of 10 mg/mL chromotropic acid solution, mix, and digest on a steam bath for 20 min.
  Acceptance criteria: Any violet color produced by the *Sample solution* does not exceed that produced by the *Control solution* (NMT 0.05%).
- **PHENOLS**
  Sample: 3 mL
  Analysis: Evaporate the *Sample* to dryness at 60°. Add 3 drops of a solution of 100 mg of sodium nitrite in 5 mL of sulfuric acid to the residue, allow the mixture to stand for about 3 min, and then carefully add 3 mL of 2 N sodium hydroxide.
  Acceptance criteria: No color appears.

SPECIFIC TESTS

- **ACIDITY (AS ACETIC ACID)**
  Sample: 38 mL
  Analysis: Mix the *Sample* with an equal volume of carbon dioxide-free water, add 0.1 mL of phenolphthalein TS, and titrate with 0.1 N sodium hydroxide.
  Acceptance criteria: NMT 0.1 mL is required to produce a pink color (NMT 0.002%)
- **ALKALINITY (AS AMMONIA)**
  Sample: 23 mL
  Analysis: Add 1 drop of methyl red TS to 25 mL of water, add 0.1 N sulfuric acid until a red color just appears, then add the *Sample*, and mix.
  Acceptance criteria: NMT 0.1 mL of 0.1 N sulfuric acid is required to restore the red color (NMT 10 mg/kg)
- **DISTILLATION RANGE,** Appendix IIB
  Acceptance criteria: Within a range of 1°, including 56.1°
- **NONVOLATILE RESIDUE**
  Sample: 125 mL (~100 g)
  Analysis: Evaporate the *Sample* to dryness in a tared dish on a steam bath, dry the residue at 105° for 30 min, cool, and weigh.
  Acceptance criteria: NMT 10 mg/kg
- **REFRACTIVE INDEX,** Appendix IIB
  [NOTE—Use an Abbé or other refractometer of equal or greater accuracy.]
  Acceptance criteria: Between 1.358 and 1.360 at 20°
- **SOLUBILITY IN WATER**
  Sample: 38 mL
  Analysis: Mix the *Sample* with an equal volume of carbon dioxide-free water.
  Acceptance criteria: The solution remains clear for at least 30 min.
- **SPECIFIC GRAVITY:** Determine by any reliable method (see *General Provisions*).
  Acceptance criteria: NMT 0.7880 at 25°/25° (equivalent to 0.7930 at 20°/20°)
- **SUBSTANCES REDUCING PERMANGANATE**
  Sample: 10 mL
  Analysis: Transfer the *Sample* into a glass-stoppered cylinder, add 0.05 mL of 0.1 N potassium permanganate, mix, and allow to stand for 15 min.
  Acceptance criteria: The pink color does not entirely disappear.
- **WATER,** *Water Determination,* Appendix IIB
  Analysis: Use freshly distilled pyridine instead of methanol as the solvent.
  Acceptance criteria: NMT 0.5%

Acetone Peroxides

First Published: Prior to FCC 6

INS: 929 CAS: [1336-17-0]
UNII: 3O959710YK [acetone peroxide]

DESCRIPTION

Acetone Peroxides, usually mixed with an edible carrier such as cornstarch, occur as a fine, white, free-flowing powder. They are a mixture of monomeric and linear dimeric acetone peroxides (mainly 2,2-hydroperoxypropane), with minor proportions of higher polymers.

Function: Bleaching agent; maturing agent; dough conditioner

Packaging and Storage: Store in tightly closed containers in a cool, dry place, preferably below 24°.
[CAUTION—Acetone Peroxides are strong oxidizing agents. Avoid exposure to the skin and eyes.]

IDENTIFICATION

- **PROCEDURE**
  Analysis: Dissolve 20 mg of sample in 5 mL of 1:10 sulfuric acid, allow to stand for a few minutes, and add a drop of potassium permanganate TS.
  Acceptance criteria: The pink color disappears.

ASSAY

- **PROCEDURE**
  Sample: 200 mg
  Analysis: Transfer the *Sample* into a 250-mL beaker, add 50 mL of 10% sulfuric acid, allow to stand for at least 3 min, stirring occasionally, and titrate with 0.1 N potassium permanganate to a light pink color that persists for at least 20 s. Calculate the total peroxides, P, as g of hydrogen peroxide equivalents per 100 g of the sample, by the equation:

$$P = V \times N \times 0.017 \times 100/W$$

V = volume of the potassium permanganate (mL)

N = normality of the potassium permanganate
0.017 = milliequivalent weight of hydrogen peroxide
W = weight of the sample (g) taken

Multiply the value P so obtained by 1.6 to convert to percent acetone peroxides.

Acceptance criteria: A sample yields an amount of hydrogen peroxide equivalent to NLT 16.0% of acetone peroxides.

IMPURITIES
Inorganic Impurities
- **LEAD**, *Lead Limit Test*, Appendix IIIB
  Sample solution: Prepare as directed for organic compounds.
  Control: 4 µg Pb (4 mL of *Diluted Standard Lead Solution*)
  Acceptance criteria: NMT 4 mg/kg

Acetophenone
First Published: Prior to FCC 6

Acetylbenzene
Methyl Phenyl Ketone

C_8H_8O Formula wt 120.15
FEMA: 2009
UNII: RK493WHV10 [acetophenone]

DESCRIPTION
Acetophenone occurs as a practically colorless liquid above 20°.

Odor: Very sweet, pungent
Solubility: Very soluble in most fixed oils, propylene glycol; soluble in alcohol, chloroform, ether; slightly soluble in water; insoluble or practically insoluble in glycerin
Boiling Point: ~202°
Solubility in Alcohol, Appendix VI: One mL dissolves in 5 mL of 50% alcohol.
Function: Flavoring agent

IDENTIFICATION
- **INFRARED SPECTRA**, *Spectrophotometric Identification Tests*, Appendix IIIC
  Acceptance criteria: The spectrum of the sample exhibits relative maxima at the same wavelengths as those of the spectrum below.

ASSAY
- **PROCEDURE:** Proceed as directed under *M-1b*, Appendix XI.
  Acceptance criteria: NLT 98.0% of C_8H_8O

SPECIFIC TESTS
- **REFRACTIVE INDEX**, Appendix II: At 20°
  Acceptance criteria: Between 1.533 and 1.535
- **SPECIFIC GRAVITY:** Determine at 25° by any reliable method (see *General Provisions*).
  Acceptance criteria: Between 1.025 and 1.028

OTHER REQUIREMENTS
- **CHLORINATED COMPOUNDS**, Appendix VI
  Acceptance criteria: Passes test
- **SOLIDIFICATION POINT**, Appendix IIB
  Acceptance criteria: NLT 19°

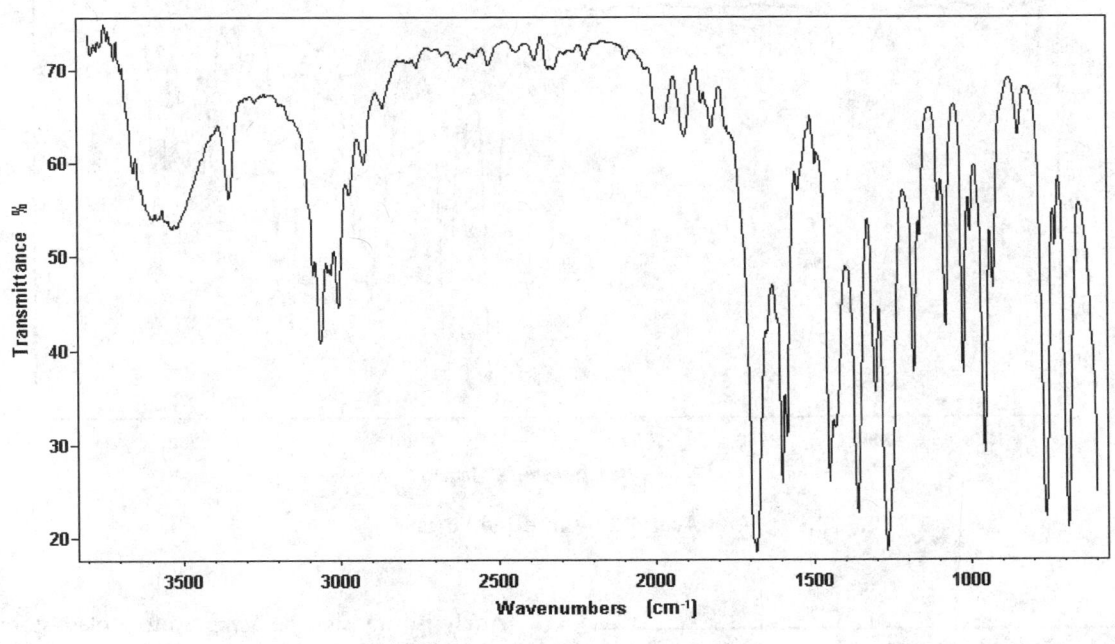

Acetophenone

3-Acetyl-2,5-dimethyl Furan

First Published: Prior to FCC 6

2,5-Dimethyl-3-acetylfuran

$C_8H_{10}O_2$
FEMA: 3391
UNII: 798V2T7ZBV [3-acetyl-2,5-dimethylfuran]

Formula wt 138.17

DESCRIPTION
3-Acetyl-2,5-dimethyl Furan occurs as a yellow liquid.
Odor: Powerful, slightly roasted, nutty
Solubility: Soluble in alcohol, most fixed oils, propylene glycol; slightly soluble in water
Boiling Point: ~83° (11 mm Hg)

Function: Flavoring agent

IDENTIFICATION
- **INFRARED SPECTRA,** *Spectrophotometric Identification Tests,* Appendix IIIC
  Acceptance criteria: The spectrum of the sample exhibits relative maxima at the same wavelengths as those of the spectrum below.

ASSAY
- **PROCEDURE:** Proceed as directed under *M-1a,* Appendix XI.
  Acceptance criteria: NLT 99.0% of $C_8H_{10}O_2$

SPECIFIC TESTS
- **REFRACTIVE INDEX,** Appendix II: At 20°
  Acceptance criteria: Between 1.484 and 1.492
- **SPECIFIC GRAVITY:** Determine at 25° by any reliable method (see *General Provisions*).
  Acceptance criteria: Between 1.027 and 1.048

18 / 3-Acetyl-2,5-dimethyl Furan / *Monographs*

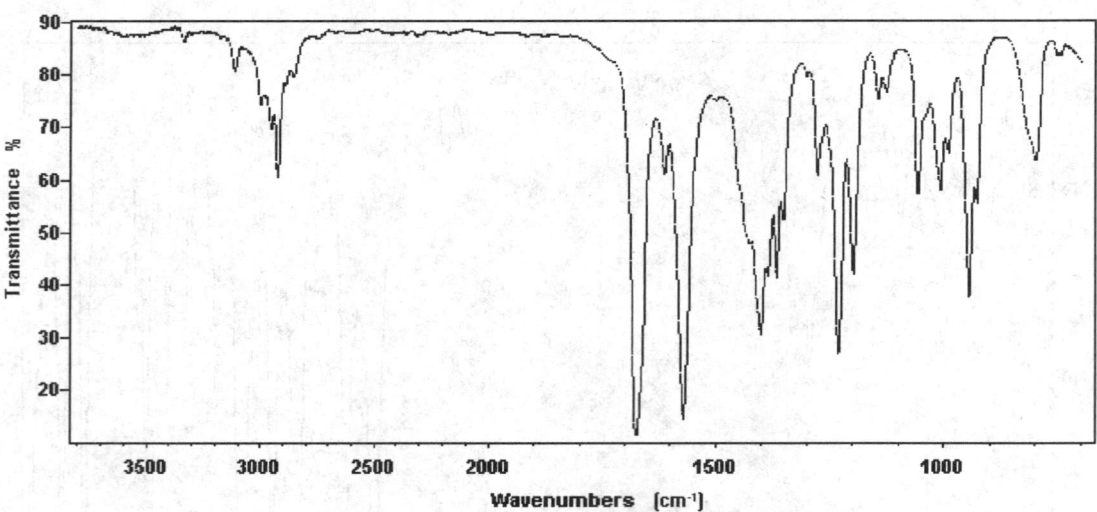

3-Acetyl-2,5-dimethyl Furan

N-Acetyl-L-Methionine

First Published: Prior to FCC 6

N-Acetyl-L-2-amino-4-(methylthio)butyric Acid

$C_7H_{13}NO_3S$ Formula wt 191.25
CAS: [65-82-7]
UNII: 9J12WX5B6A [n-acetylmethionine]

DESCRIPTION
N-Acetyl-L-Methionine occurs as a colorless or lustrous, white, crystalline solid or a white powder. It is soluble in water, in alcohol, in alkali solutions, and in dilute mineral acids, but practically insoluble in ether.
Function: Nutrient
Packaging and Storage: Store in tightly closed, light-resistant containers.

IDENTIFICATION
- **INFRARED ABSORPTION,** *Spectrophotometric Identification Tests,* Appendix IIIC
  Sample preparation: Mineral oil mull
  Acceptance criteria: The spectrum of the sample exhibits relative maxima at the same wavelengths as those of the spectrum below.

ASSAY
- **PROCEDURE**
  Sample: 250 mg
  Analysis: Transfer the *Sample* into a glass-stoppered flask and add 100 mL of water, 5 g of dibasic potassium phosphate, 2 g of monobasic potassium phosphate, and 2 g of potassium iodide. Mix well to dissolve, add 50.0 mL of 0.1 N iodine, stopper the flask, and mix. Allow to stand for 30 min, add starch TS indicator, and then titrate the excess iodine with 0.1 N sodium thiosulfate. Perform a residual blank titration. Each mL of 0.1 N iodine is equivalent to 9.563 mg $C_7H_{13}NO_3S$.
  Acceptance criteria: NLT 98.5% and NMT 101.5% $C_7H_{13}NO_3S$, calculated on the dried basis

IMPURITIES
Inorganic Impurities
- **LEAD,** *Lead Limit Test,* Appendix IIIB
  Sample Solution: Prepare as directed for organic compounds.
  Control: 5 µg Pb (5 mL of *Diluted Standard Lead Solution*)
  Acceptance criteria: NMT 5 mg/kg

SPECIFIC TESTS
- **LOSS ON DRYING,** Appendix IIC: 105° for 2 h
  Acceptance criteria: NMT 0.5%
- **OPTICAL (SPECIFIC) ROTATION,** Appendix IIB
  Sample: 20 mg/mL (sample previously dried), made to 100 mL
  Acceptance criteria: $[\alpha]_D^{20}$ between −18.0° and −22.0°, on the dried basis
- **RESIDUE ON IGNITION (SULFATED ASH),** Appendix IIC
  Sample: 1 g
  Acceptance criteria: NMT 0.1%

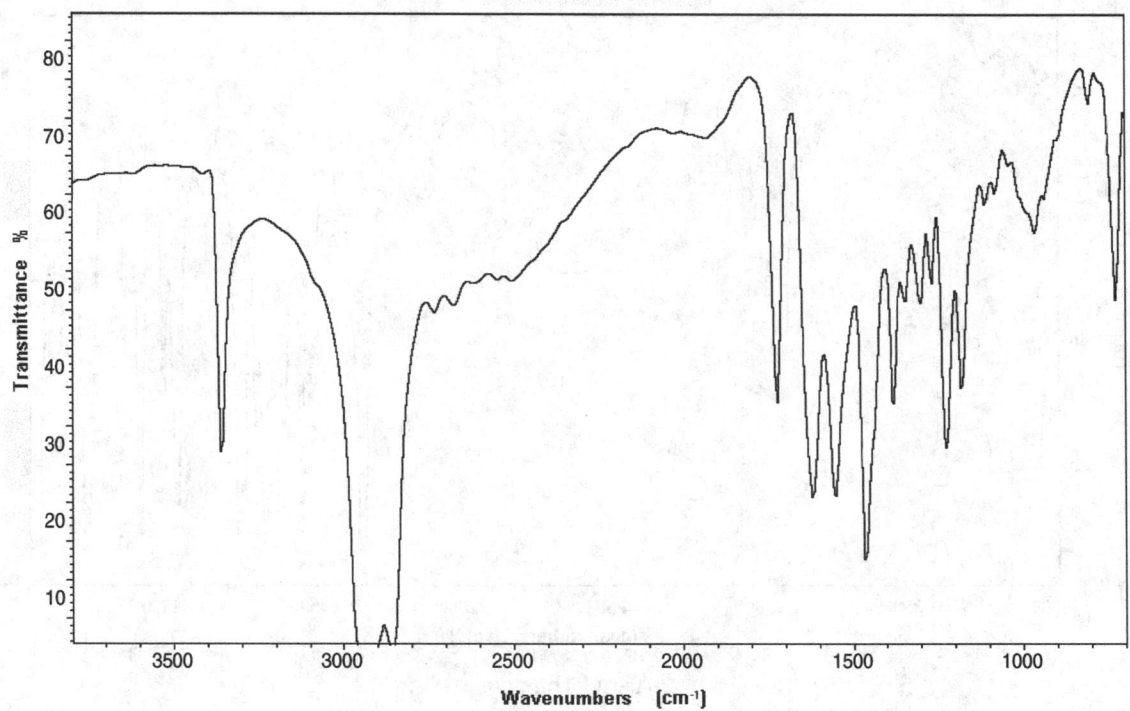

N-Acetyl-L-Methionine (Mineral Oil Mull)

2-Acetyl Thiazole

First Published: Prior to FCC 6

C_5H_5NOS Formula wt 127.17
FEMA: 3328
UNII: 16IGS52681 [2-acetylthiazole]

DESCRIPTION
2-Acetyl Thiazole occurs as a colorless to pale yellow liquid.
Odor: Popcorn
Solubility: Soluble in propylene glycol, vegetable oils; insoluble or practically insoluble in water
Boiling Point: ~89° (12 mm Hg); ~91° (1 mm Hg)
Solubility in Alcohol, Appendix VI: One mL dissolves in 1 mL of 95% ethanol.

Function: Flavoring agent

IDENTIFICATION
- **INFRARED SPECTRA,** Spectrophotometric Identification Tests, Appendix IIIC
  Acceptance criteria: The spectrum of the sample exhibits relative maxima at the same wavelengths as those of the spectrum below.

ASSAY
- **PROCEDURE:** Proceed as directed under M-1b, Appendix XI.
  Acceptance criteria: NLT 98.0% of C_5H_5NOS

SPECIFIC TESTS
- **REFRACTIVE INDEX,** Appendix II: At 20°
  Acceptance criteria: Between 1.542 and 1.552
- **SPECIFIC GRAVITY:** Determine at 25° by any reliable method (see General Provisions).
  Acceptance criteria: Between 1.219 and 1.226

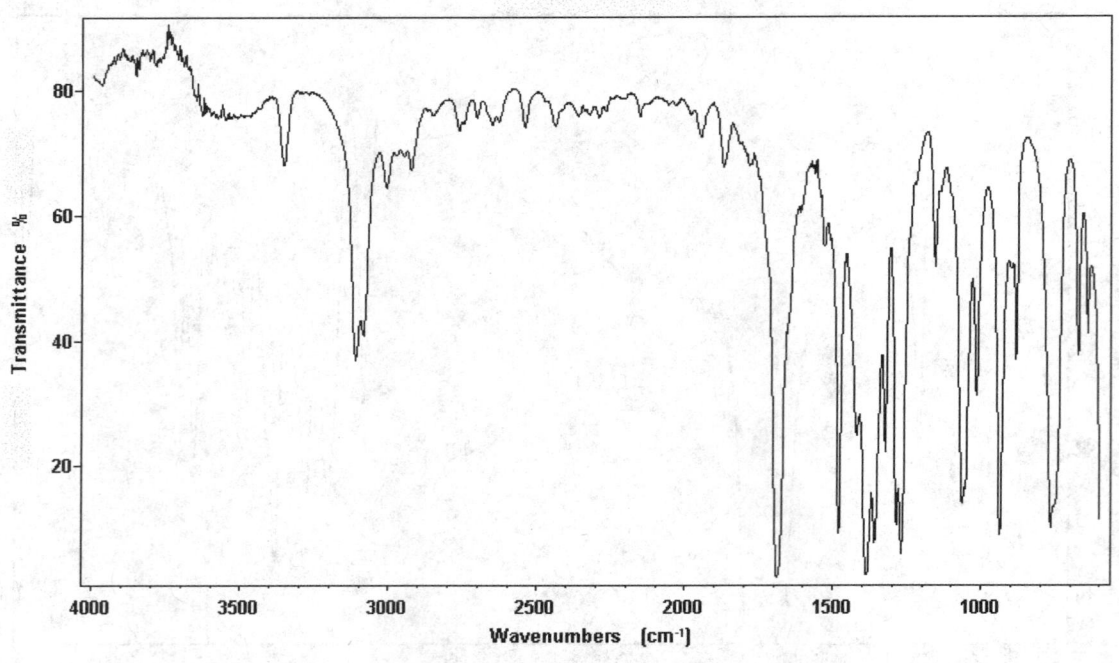

2-Acetyl Thiazole

Acetylated Monoglycerides

First Published: Prior to FCC 6

Acetylated Mono- and Diglycerides
Acetic and Fatty Acid Esters of Glycerol
Acetoglycerides

R1, R2, R3 = H or fatty acid or acetyl (CH₃CO)

INS: 472a
UNII: 5Z17386USF [diacetylated monoglycerides]

DESCRIPTION
Acetylated Monoglycerides occur as clear, thin liquids or solids, ranging in color from white to pale yellow. They consist of partial or complete esters of glycerin with a mixture of acetic acid and edible fat-forming fatty acids. They may be manufactured by the interesterification of edible fats with triacetin and glycerin in the presence of catalytic agents, followed by molecular distillation, or by the direct acetylation of edible monoglycerides with acetic anhydride and without the use of a catalyst or molecular distillation. They are insoluble in water, but are soluble in alcohol, in acetone, and in other organic solvents, the extent of solubility depending on the degree of esterification and the melting range.

Function: Emulsifier; coating agent; texture-modifying agent; solvent; lubricant
Packaging and Storage: Store in well-closed containers.

IMPURITIES
Inorganic Impurities
- **Lead,** *Lead Limit Test, Flame Atomic Absorption Spectrophotometric Method,* Appendix IIIB
  Sample: 10 g
  Acceptance criteria: NMT 2 mg/kg

SPECIFIC TESTS
- **Acid Value,** *Method II,* Appendix VII
  Acceptance criteria: NMT 6
- **Free Glycerin,** *Free Glycerin or Propylene Glycol,* Appendix VII
  Acceptance criteria: The result should conform to the representations of the vendor.
- **Iodine Value,** Appendix VII
  Acceptance criteria: The result should conform to the representations of the vendor.
- **Reichert-Meissl Value,** Appendix VII
  Acceptance criteria: Between 75 and 200
- **Saponification Value,** Appendix VII
  Acceptance criteria: The result should conform to the representations of the vendor.

3-Acetylpyridine

First Published: Prior to FCC 6

Methyl Pyridyl Ketone

C_7H_7NO Formula wt 121.14
FEMA: 3424
UNII: 00QT8FX306 [3-acetylpyridine]

DESCRIPTION
3-Acetylpyridine occurs as a colorless to yellow liquid.
Odor: Sweet, nutty, popcorn
Solubility: Soluble in acids, alcohol, ether, water
Boiling Point: ~230°
Function: Flavoring agent

IDENTIFICATION
- **INFRARED SPECTRA,** *Spectrophotometric Identification Tests,* Appendix IIIC
  Acceptance criteria: The spectrum of the sample exhibits relative maxima at the same wavelengths as those of the spectrum below.

ASSAY
- **PROCEDURE:** Proceed as directed under *M-1a,* Appendix XI.
  Acceptance criteria: NLT 98.0% of C_7H_7NO

SPECIFIC TESTS
- **REFRACTIVE INDEX,** Appendix II: At 20°
  Acceptance criteria: Between 1.530 and 1.540
- **SPECIFIC GRAVITY:** Determine at 25° by any reliable method (see *General Provisions*).
  Acceptance criteria: Between 1.100 and 1.115

OTHER REQUIREMENTS
- **WATER,** *Water Determination, Method I,* Appendix IIB
  Acceptance criteria: 0.5%

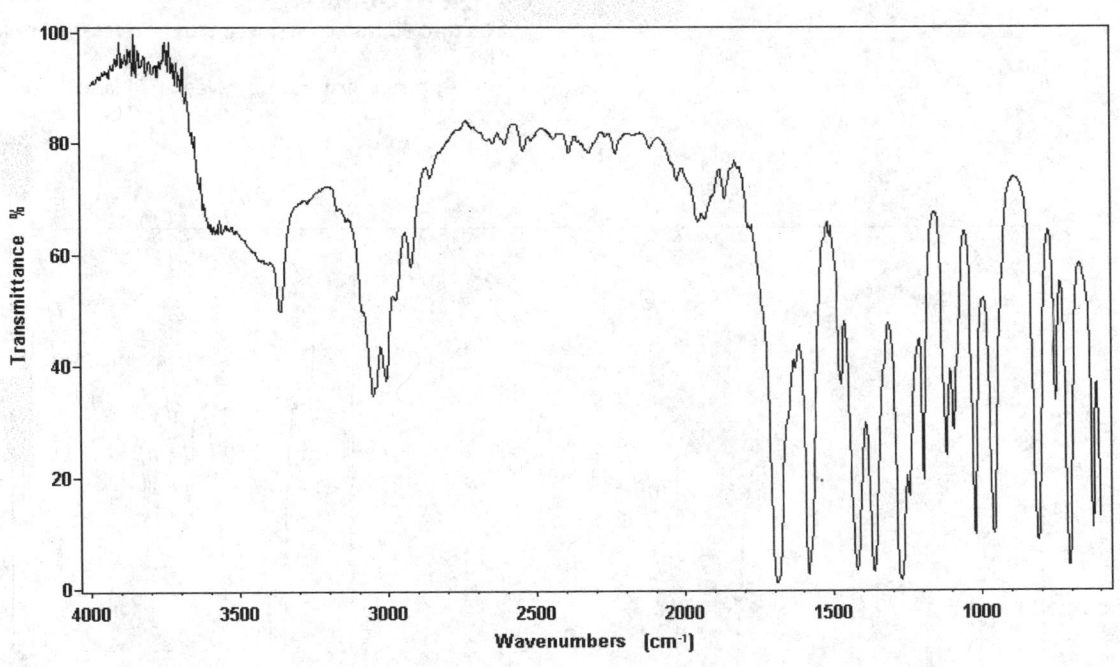

3-Acetylpyridine

2-Acetylpyrrole

First Published: Prior to FCC 6

Methyl 2-Pyrrolyl Ketone

C_6H_7NO Formula wt 109.13

FEMA: 3202
UNII: 9K28W7PM6N [2-acetylpyrrole]

DESCRIPTION
2-Acetylpyrrole occurs as a white to pale brown fine crystal.
Odor: Bready
Solubility: Insoluble or practically insoluble in propylene glycol, vegetable oils, water
Boiling Point: ~220°

Solubility in Alcohol, Appendix VI: One g dissolves in 6 mL of ethanol.
Function: Flavoring agent

ASSAY
- **Procedure:** Proceed as directed under *M-1a,* Appendix XI.
  Acceptance criteria: NLT 98.0% of C_6H_7NO

OTHER REQUIREMENTS
- **Melting Range or Temperature Determination,** Appendix IIB
  Acceptance criteria: Between 88° and 92°
- **Residue on Ignition (Sulfated Ash),** Appendix IIC
  Acceptance criteria: NMT 0.3%

2-Acetylpyrazine

First Published: Prior to FCC 6

Methyl Pyrazinyl Ketone

$C_6H_6N_2O$ Formula wt 122.13

FEMA: 3126
UNII: GR391IBU5C [2-acetylpyrazine]

DESCRIPTION
2-Acetylpyrazine occurs as colorless to pale yellow crystals.
Odor: Popcorn
Solubility in Alcohol, Appendix VI: One g dissolves in 20 mL of 95% alcohol.
Function: Flavoring agent

IDENTIFICATION
- **Infrared Spectra,** *Spectrophotometric Identification Tests,* Appendix IIIC
  Sample preparation: Mineral oil mull
  Acceptance criteria: The spectrum of the sample exhibits relative maxima at the same wavelengths as those of the spectrum below.

ASSAY
- **Procedure:** Proceed as directed under *M-1a,* Appendix XI.
  Acceptance criteria: NLT 99.0% of $C_6H_6N_2O$

OTHER REQUIREMENTS
- **Melting Range or Temperature Determination,** Appendix IIB
  Acceptance criteria: Between 75° and 78°

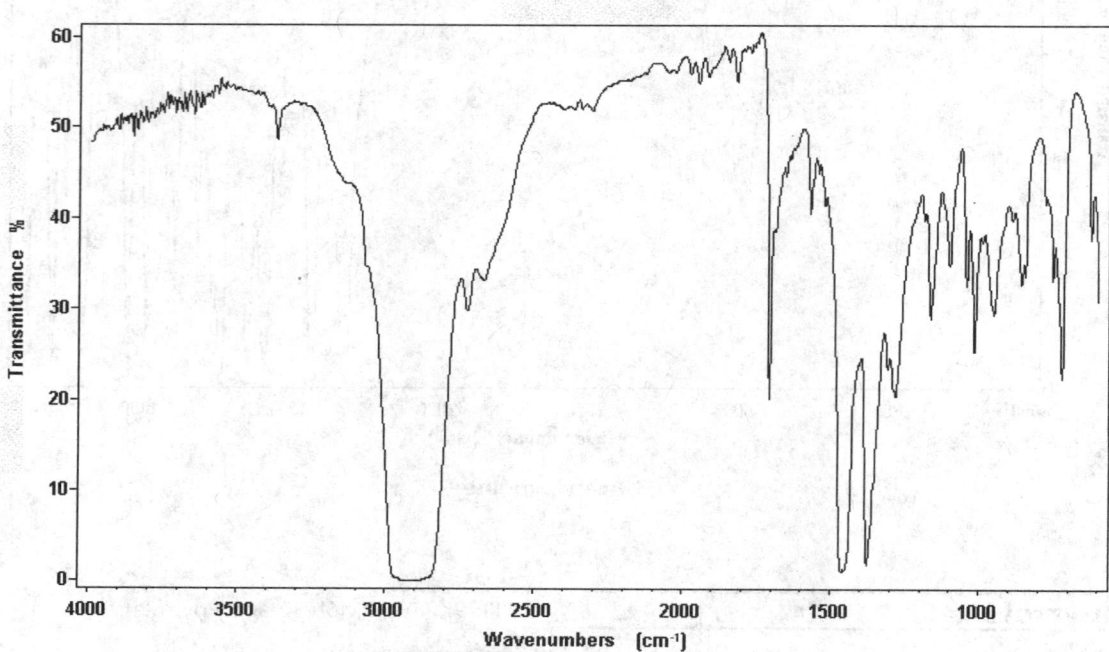

2-Acetylpyrazine (Mineral Oil Mull)

Acid Hydrolysates of Proteins

First Published: Prior to FCC 6
Last Revision: Second Supplement, FCC 7

Acid-Hydrolyzed Proteins
Hydrolyzed Vegetable Protein (HVP)
Hydrolyzed Plant Protein (HPP)
Hydrolyzed (Source) Protein Extract
Acid-Hydrolyzed Milk Protein

DESCRIPTION

Acid Hydrolysates of Proteins occur as liquids, pastes, powders, or granules. They are composed primarily of amino acids, small peptides (peptide chains of five or fewer amino acids), and salts resulting from the essentially complete hydrolysis of peptide bonds in edible proteinaceous materials, catalyzed by food-grade acids and/or heat. Cleavage of peptide bonds typically ranges from a low of 85% to essentially 100%. In processing, the protein hydrolysates may be treated with safe and suitable alkaline materials. The edible proteinaceous materials used as raw materials are derived from corn, soy, wheat, yeast, peanuts, rice, or other safe and suitable vegetable or plant sources, or from milk.

Function: Flavoring agent; flavor enhancer
Packaging and Storage: Store in well-closed containers. [NOTE—Perform all tests on the dried basis. Evaporate liquid and paste samples to dryness in a suitable tared container; then, as for the powdered and granular forms, dry to constant weight at 105°. (See *General Provisions*.)]

ASSAY

- **TOTAL NITROGEN,** *Nitrogen Determination,* Appendix IIIC
  Acceptance criteria: NLT 4.0%

IMPURITIES

Inorganic Impurities

- **LEAD,** *Lead Limit Test,* Appendix IIIB
  Sample solution: Prepare as directed for organic compounds.
  Control: 3 µg Pb (3 mL of *Diluted Standard Lead Solution*)
  Acceptance criteria: NMT 3 mg/kg, on the dried basis

Organic Impurities

- **3-CHLOROPROPANE-1,2-DIOL (3-MCPD)**
  Standard stock solution: 125 µg/mL of reagent-grade 3-chloropropane-1,2-diol (3-MCPD) in ethyl acetate
  Diluted standard solution: 6.25 µg/mL of 3-MCPD in ethyl acetate from the *Standard stock solution*
  Internal standard solution: 10 µg/mL of 1-chlorotetradecane in ethyl acetate
  Standard solution A: 2 mL of *Diluted standard solution* and 2.5 mL of *Internal standard solution* diluted to 25 mL with ethyl acetate (contains 0.5 µg/mL 3-MCPD)
  Standard solution B: 8 mL of *Diluted standard solution* and 2.5 mL of *Internal standard solution* diluted to 25 mL with ethyl acetate (contains 2.0 µg/mL 3-MCPD)
  Standard solution C: 16 mL of *Diluted standard solution* and 2.5 mL of *Internal standard solution* diluted to 25 mL with ethyl acetate (contains 4.0 µg/mL 3-MCPD)
  Sample stock solution: Dissolve sample, as needed with 20% aqueous sodium chloride, to obtain a solution with a solids content of 36%.
  Sample preparation: Transfer a 20-g aliquot of the *Sample stock solution* into a 20-mL Extrelut NT column (EM Science, Gibbstown, NJ), or equivalent, and allow it to equilibrate for 15 min. Elute the column with 150 mL of ethyl acetate, collecting the eluent in a 250-mL short-neck, round-bottom flask with a 24/40 joint. Using a rotary evaporator at 50°, concentrate the eluent to a volume of approximately 3 mL. Add 0.5 mL of *Internal standard solution* to the eluent, transfer this mixture to a 4-dram screw-cap vial, and dilute to a volume of 5.0 mL.
  Chromatographic system, Appendix IIA
    Mode: Gas chromatography
    Detector: Electrolytic conductivity detector. [NOTE—Operate the detector in the halogen mode.]
    Column: 30-m × 0.53-mm (id), fused-silica column, or equivalent, coated with 1-µm Supelcowax 10 or an equivalent bonded carbowax column fitted with a 50-cm retention gap of 0.53-mm, deactivated, fused silica, or equivalent
    Temperature
      Column: Hold at 170° for 5 min, then increase at 5°/min to 250°, hold at 250° for 10 min
      Injector: 225°
      Detector reactor: 900°
      Detector base: 275°
    Carrier gas: Helium
    Reactant gas: Hydrogen
    Solvent: 1-Propanol
    Flow rate
      Helium: 8 mL/min
      Hydrogen: 30 mL/min
      1-Propanol: 0.5 mL/min through the cell or at the manufacturer's specified flow rate for the optimum operation of the detector
    Injection volume: 1.0 µL
    Injection type: Use a capillary injector operated in the splitless mode or a purged, packed injector with a glass insert.
    [NOTE—Minimize contamination of the reaction tube by venting flow from the column at all times, except for the time during which compounds of interest elute.]
  Analysis: Separately inject *Standard solution A, Standard solution B, Standard solution C,* and the *Sample preparation* into the chromatograph and record the resulting chromatograms. Calculate the area ratios of 3-MCPD to the *Internal standard solution* for each *Standard solution*. Plot the area ratios versus the µg of 3-MCPD in each *Standard solution* to obtain the standard curve. From the chromatogram of the *Sample preparation,* measure the area ratio of 3-MCPD to the *Internal standard solution* and, using the standard curve, determine the amount of 3-MCPD, in µg, in the 20-g aliquot of *Sample stock solution* taken.
  Acceptance criteria: NMT 1 mg/kg, on the dried basis

- **1,3-DICHLORO-2-PROPANOL (DCP)**
  Diluent: Pentane and diethyl ether (85:15) (v/v)
  Stock solution: 1 mg/mL of reagent-grade 1,3-dichloro-2-propanol (DCP) in *Diluent*
  Diluted standard solution: 1 µg/mL of DCP in *Diluent* made from the *Stock solution*
  Internal standard solution: 1 µg/mL of trichlorobenzene in *Diluent*
  Standard solutions: Pipet 1, 2, 3, and 4 mL portions of *Diluted standard solution*, into separate 50-mL volumetric flasks. Add 1.0 mL of *Internal standard solution* to each and dilute with *Diluent* to volume.
  Sample solution: Dissolve 5.0 g of the sample in a minimal volume of 20% aqueous sodium chloride solution. Quantitatively transfer this solution to an Extrelut NT column (EM Science, Gibbstown, NJ), or equivalent. After 15 min, elute the column with three 20-mL portions of *Diluent*, and collect all of the eluate. Carefully evaporate the eluate to less than 4 mL. Add 1.0 mL of *Internal standard solution*, and dilute with *Diluent*, as necessary, to bring the final volume to 5.0 mL.
  Chromatographic system, Appendix IIA
    Mode: Gas chromatography with a split injector
    Detector: Electrolytic conductivity detector
    Column: 50-m × 0.2-mm (id), fused-silica column (Carbowax 20M, or equivalent) coated with dimethylpolysiloxane, or equivalent
    Temperature
      Column: Hold at 115° for 10 min, then increase at 30°/min to 200°, hold at 200° for 12 min
      Injector: 250°
      Detector: 300°
      [NOTE—Precondition the column by heating it at 200° and the detector at 300° for 24 h.]
    Carrier gas: Nitrogen
    Flow rate: 8 mL/min
    Injection size: 1.0 µL
  Analysis: Separately inject each of the *Standard solutions* and the *Sample solution* into the chromatograph and record the resulting chromatograms. Calculate the area ratios of DCP to *Internal standard solution* for each *Standard solution*. Plot the area ratios versus the µg of DCP in each *Standard solution* to obtain the standard curve. From the chromatograph of the *Sample solution*, measure the area ratio of DCP to the *Internal standard solution* and, using the standard curve, determine the amount of DCP, in µg, in the sample taken.
  Acceptance criteria: NMT 0.05 mg/kg, on the dried basis

SPECIFIC TESTS
- **α-AMINO NITROGEN,** Appendix IIIC
  Acceptance criteria: NLT 3.0%, on the dried basis
- **α-AMINO NITROGEN/TOTAL NITROGEN PERCENT RATIO**
  Analysis: Calculate by the formula:

  $$\text{Result} = 100[(AN - P)/(TN - P)]$$

  AN = percentage of *α-Amino Nitrogen*, determined above
  P = percentage of *Ammonia Nitrogen*, determined below
  TN = percentage of *Total Nitrogen*, determined above
  Acceptance criteria: 62.0%–85.0%, when calculated on an ammonia nitrogen-free basis
- **AMMONIA NITROGEN,** Appendix IIIC
  Acceptance criteria: NMT 1.5%, on the dried basis
- **GLUTAMIC ACID,** Appendix IIIC
  Acceptance criteria: NMT 20.0% as glutamic acid ($C_5H_9NO_4$) and NMT 35.0% of the total protein, both on the dried basis
- **INSOLUBLE MATTER**
  Sample: 5 g
  Analysis: Transfer the *Sample* into a 250-mL Erlenmeyer flask, add 75 mL of water, cover the flask with a watch glass, and boil gently for 2 min. Filter the solution through a tared filtering crucible, dry at 105° for 1 h, cool, and weigh.
  Acceptance criteria: NMT 0.5%, on the dried basis
- **POTASSIUM**
  Standard solution: 1.91 µg/mL of potassium chloride (corresponds to 1.0 µg/mL of potassium ion)
  Sample stock solution: Transfer 1.00 ± 0.05 g of previously dried sample into a silica or porcelain dish. Ash in a muffle furnace at 550° for 2–4 h. Allow the ash to cool, and dissolve in 5 mL of 20% hydrochloric acid, warming the solution if necessary to complete solution of the residue. Filter the solution through acid-washed filter paper into a 1000-mL volumetric flask. Wash the filter paper with hot water, dilute to volume, and mix.
  Sample solution: 1:300 (v/v) dilution of the *Sample stock solution*
  Analysis: Using a suitable atomic absorption spectrophotometer, determine the absorbance of the *Standard solution* and the *Sample solution* at 766.5.
  Acceptance criteria: The absorbance of the *Sample solution* does not exceed that of the *Standard solution*. (NMT 30.0%, on the dried basis)
- **SODIUM**
  Standard stock solution: 254.2 µg/mL of sodium chloride
  Standard solution: 12.71 ng/mL of sodium chloride made from the *Standard stock solution* (corresponds to 5 ng/mL of sodium ion)
  Sample stock solution: Transfer 1.00 ± 0.05 g of previously dried sample into a silica or porcelain dish. Ash in a muffle furnace at 550° for 2–4 h. Allow the ash to cool, and dissolve in 5 mL of 20% hydrochloric acid, warming the solution if necessary to complete solution of the residue. Filter the solution through acid-washed filter paper into a 100-mL volumetric flask. Wash the filter paper with hot water, dilute to volume, and mix.
  Sample solution: 1:4000 (v/v) dilution of the *Sample stock solution*
  Analysis: Using a suitable atomic absorption spectrophotometer, determine the absorbance of the *Standard solution* and the *Sample solution* at 589.0.

Acceptance criteria: The absorbance of the *Sample solution* does not exceed that of the *Standard solution*. (NMT 20.0%, on the dried basis)

Acidified Sodium Chlorite Solutions

First Published: Prior to FCC 6

DESCRIPTION

Acidified Sodium Chlorite (ASC) Solutions occur as clear, colorless to pale yellow liquids. The ASC Solutions are equilibrium mixtures of sodium chlorite ($NaClO_2$) and chlorous acid ($HClO_2$). ASC Solutions are produced by lowering the pH of a sodium chlorite solution with a safe and suitable acid to achieve a pH within the range 2.3 to 3.9 depending on the intended use.

Function: Antimicrobial agent in processing water used to spray, dip, rinse, or store food before processing, to be followed by rinsing in potable water or by blanching, cooking, or canning; sanitizer for hard surfaces; broad-spectrum bactericide, virucide, fungicide, and sporicide

Packaging and Storage: Store in closed, opaque containers. Avoid exposure to sun or ultraviolet light because chlorine dioxide gas will generate in the solution.

IMPURITIES

Inorganic Impurities

- **LEAD,** *Lead Limit Test,* Appendix IIIB
  Sample solution: 1.0 mL of sample mixed with 5 mL of water and 11 mL of 2.7 N hydrochloric acid
  Control: 10 μg of Pb (10 mL of *Diluted Standard Lead Solution*)
  Acceptance criteria: NMT 1 mg/kg
- **MERCURY,** *Mercury Limit Test,* Appendix IIIB
  Sample preparation: Transfer 2.0 mL of sample into a 50-mL beaker; add 10 mL of water, 1 mL of 20% sulfuric acid, and 1 mL of a 40 mg/mL potassium permanganate solution. Cover the beaker with a watch glass, boil for a few seconds, and cool.
  Acceptance criteria: NMT 1 mg/kg

SPECIFIC TESTS

- **PH,** *pH Determination,* Appendix IIB
  [**CAUTION**—To minimize the evolution of hazardous chlorine dioxide gas, do not adjust the pH below 2.3.]
  Acceptance criteria: Between 2.3 and 3.9
  [NOTE—The pH is chosen depending on the application. It controls the concentration of metastable chlorous acid, which rapidly breaks down into chlorine dioxide, chloride, and in some applications, chlorate]
- **SODIUM CHLORITE**
  [NOTE—See 21 CFR 173.325; "Determination of Sodium Chlorite: 50 ppm to 1500 ppm," Alcide Corporation.]
  Sample: For solutions containing 40 to 250 ppm, use a 100-g sample; for those containing 250 to 500 ppm, use a 50-g sample; for those containing 500 to 1100 ppm, use a 20-g sample; for those containing 1100 to 1500 ppm, use a 15-g sample.

Analysis: Transfer the appropriate *Sample* into a tared 250-mL Erlenmeyer flask, and record the weight to the nearest 0.1 mg. Add a magnetic stirring bar. Add approximately 2 g of potassium iodide, place the flask over a magnetic stirrer, and stir until the potassium iodide crystals dissolve (about 1 min). Add 1 mL of 6 N hydrochloric acid, and stir for 30 s. While continuously stirring, titrate the liberated iodine with standardized 0.025 N sodium thiosulfate ($Na_2S_2O_3$). When most of the brown iodine color has faded, add 2 mL of starch indicator solution, and titrate to a clear endpoint, allowing adequate mixing time between additions of titrant near the endpoint. Record the volume of titrant, V, in mL. Calculate the amount of Sodium Chlorite, in ppm, by the formula:

$$\text{Result} = (V \times N \times M_r \times F)/(W \times F_E)$$

V = volume of titrant (mL)
N = normality of the sodium thiosulfate titrant
M_r = molecular weight of sodium chlorite, 90.44
F = conversion factor for mg/g to ppm, 1000
W = weight of the sample taken (g)
F_E = mEq of sodium thiosulfate/mEq of sodium chlorite, 4

[NOTE—The concentration of sodium chlorite also can alternatively be determined using ion chromatography by following U.S. Environmental Protection Agency Method 300.1[1] or amperometrically by following American Public Health Association Method 4500-ClO_2.[2]]

Acceptance criteria: Between 40 and 1200 ppm, depending on the application

Aconitic Acid

First Published: Prior to FCC 6

Equisetic Acid
Citridic Acid
Achilleic Acid
1-Propene-1,2,3-tricarboxylic Acid

$C_6H_6O_6$ Formula wt 174.11
FEMA: 2010
         CAS: [499-12-7]
UNII: 93371T1BXP [aconitic acid]

---

[1] Hautman, Daniel P. and Munch, David J. "Method 300.1: Determination of inorganic anions in drinking water by ion chromatography, Revision 1.0." U.S. Environmental Protection Agency, Office of Ground Water and Drinking Water. 1997. Online Available: http://www.epa.gov/OGWDW/methods/sourcalt.html [accessed October 19, 2007].

[2] Franson, MA, ed. 1998. Standard methods 4500-ClO_2, amperometric method II. In: *Standard Methods for the Examination of Water and Wastewater*, 20th Ed. Baltimore, MD: APHA/AWWA/WEF. Pp. 4-73 and 4-79.

Aconitic Acid

DESCRIPTION
Aconitic Acid occurs in the leaves and tubers of *Aconitum napellus* L. (Fam. Ranunculaceae) and various species of *Achillea* and *Equisetum*, in beet root, and in sugar cane. It may be synthesized by the dehydration of citric acid by sulfuric or methanesulfonic acid. Aconitic Acid from the above sources has the "*trans*" configuration. It has a melting point of 195° to 200° with decomposition. It is practically odorless and has a winy taste. It is soluble in water and in alcohol and is slightly soluble in ether.
Function: Flavoring substance; adjuvant
Packaging and Storage: Store in tightly closed containers.

IDENTIFICATION
- **INFRARED ABSORPTION SPECTRUM**
  Sample preparation: Neat as a potassium bromide dispersion
  Acceptance criteria: The *Sample preparation* exhibits infrared absorption bands at 3030, 2630, and 1720 cm^{-1}.
- **VISIBLE ABSORPTION SPECTRUM**
  Sample solution: Aqueous solution
  Acceptance criteria: The *Sample solution* exhibits major absorption peaks at 411 and 432 nm, with little or no absorption at 389 nm.

ASSAY
- **PROCEDURE**
  Sample solution: 3 g
  Analysis: Dissolve the *Sample* in 40 mL of water, add phenolphthalein TS, and titrate with 1 N sodium hydroxide. Each mL of 1 N sodium hydroxide is equivalent to 58.04 mg of $C_6H_6O_6$.
  Acceptance criteria: NLT 98.0% and NMT 100.5% of $C_6H_6O_6$, calculated on the anhydrous basis

IMPURITIES
Inorganic Impurities
- **LEAD,** *Lead Limit Test, Atomic Absorption Spectrophotometric Graphite Furnace, Method I,* Appendix IIIB
  Sample: 10 g
  Acceptance criteria: NMT 0.5 mg/kg

SPECIFIC TESTS
- **OXALATE**
  Sample solution: 100 mg/mL
  Analysis: Neutralize 10 mL of *Sample solution* with 6 N ammonium hydroxide, add 5 drops of 2.7 N hydrochloric acid, cool, and add 2 mL of calcium chloride TS.
  Acceptance criteria: No turbidity develops.
- **READILY CARBONIZABLE SUBSTANCES,** Appendix IIB
  Sample: 1.0 g, finely powdered
  Control: *Matching Fluid K*
  Analysis: Transfer the *Sample* into a 22- × 175-mm test tube previously rinsed with 10 mL of 95% sulfuric acid and allowed to drain for 10 min. Add 10 mL of 95% sulfuric acid, agitate the tube until solution is complete, and immerse the tube in a water bath at 90° ± 1° for 60 ± 0.5 min, keeping the level of the acid below the level of the water during the heating period. Cool the tube in a stream of water and transfer the acid solution into a color comparison tube. View the tube vertically against a white background and compare to the same volume of the *Control* in a similar matching tube.
  Acceptance criteria: The color of the *Sample* solution is not darker than that of the *Control*.
- **RESIDUE ON IGNITION (SULFATED ASH),** *Method I,* Appendix IIC
  Sample: 4 g
  Acceptance criteria: NMT 0.1%
- **WATER,** *Water Determination,* Appendix IIB
  Acceptance criteria: NMT 0.5%

5′-Adenylic Acid

First Published: First Supplement, FCC 7

Adenosine 5′-monophosphate
Adenylic acid
AMP
Adenosine 5′-phosphoric acid

$C_{10}H_{14}N_5O_7P$ Formula wt 347.23
CAS: [61-19-8]
UNII: 415SHH325A [adenosine phosphate]

DESCRIPTION
5′-Adenylic Acid occurs as colorless or white crystals, or as a white, crystalline powder. It is very slightly soluble in water, and practically insoluble in alcohol. It is produced by enzymatic cleavage of yeast ribonucleic acid (RNA) with a 5′-phosphodiesterase followed by heat treatment, further purification steps, and washing of crystals with ethanol.
Function: Source of 5′-Adenylic Acid
Packaging and Storage: Store in tight containers protected from light and moisture.

IDENTIFICATION
- **A. INFRARED ABSORPTION,** *Spectrophotometric Identification Tests,* Appendix IIIC
  Reference standard: USP 5′-Adenylic Acid RS
  Sample and standard preparation: A
  Acceptance criteria: The spectrum of the sample exhibits maxima at the same wavelengths as those in the spectrum of the *Reference standard*.
- **B. PROCEDURE**
  Acceptance criteria: The retention time of the major peak (excluding the solvent peak) in the chromatogram of the *Sample solution* corresponds to that of the *Standard solution* in the *Assay*.

ASSAY
- **PROCEDURE**
  Mobile phase: 0.1 M potassium dihydrogen phosphate (KH_2PO_4) in degassed water, adjusted with 0.1 M

dipotassium hydrogen phosphate (K$_2$HPO$_4$) to a pH of 5.6

Standard solution: 0.02 mg/mL of USP 5′-Adenylic Acid RS in *Mobile phase*. [NOTE—Ultra-sonication for 15 min at 30° may be necessary to aid in complete dissolution.]

Sample solution: 0.02 mg/mL in *Mobile phase*. [NOTE—Ultra-sonication for 15 min at 30° may be necessary to aid in complete dissolution.]

Chromatographic system, *Appendix IIA*
  Mode: High-performance liquid chromatography
  Detector: UV 254 nm
  Column: 25 cm × 4.6-mm; packed with 5-μm reversed phase C18 silica gel[1]
  Column temperature: Ambient
  Flow rate: About 1.0 mL/min
  Injection size: 50 μL
  System suitability
    Sample: *Standard solution*
    Suitability requirements
      Suitability requirement 1: The relative standard deviation of the 5′-adenylic acid area responses from replicate injections is NMT 2.0%.
      Suitability requirement 2: The resolution, *R*, between the 5′-adenylic acid peak and all other peaks is NLT 2.0.

Analysis: Separately inject equal volumes of the *Standard solution* and *Sample solution* into the chromatograph, and measure the responses for the major peaks on the resulting chromatograms. [NOTE—The approximate retention time for 5′-adenylic acid is 27.5 min.] Calculate the percentage of 5′-adenylic acid, C$_{10}$H$_{14}$N$_5$O$_7$P, in the sample taken:

$$\text{Result} = (r_U/r_S) \times (C_S/C_U) \times 100$$

  r_U = peak area response for 5′-adenylic acid in the *Sample solution*
  r_S = peak area response for 5′-adenylic acid in the *Standard solution*
  C_S = concentration of 5′-adenylic acid in the *Standard solution* (mg/mL)
  C_U = concentration of the sample in the *Sample solution* (mg/mL)

Acceptance criteria: 98.0%–103.0%, calculated on the anhydrous basis

IMPURITIES
Inorganic Impurities
- **ARSENIC**
  [NOTE—When water is specified as a diluent, use deionized ultra-filtered water. When nitric acid is specified, use nitric acid of a grade suitable for trace element analysis with as low a content of arsenic as practical.]
  Diluent: 4% nitric acid in water
  Standard stock solution: 100 μg/mL of arsenic prepared by diluting a commercially available 1000 mg/kg arsenic ICP standard solution
  Standard solutions: 0.05, 0.1, 0.2, 0.5, 1, and 2 μg/mL of arsenic, from the *Standard stock solution* diluted with *Diluent*
  Sample: 5 g
  Sample solution: Dissolve the *Sample* in 40 mL of 10% nitric acid in a 100-mL volumetric flask, and dilute with water to volume.
  Spectrophotometric system, *Plasma Spectrochemistry, Appendix IIC*
    Mode: Inductively coupled plasma–optical emission spectroscopy (ICP–OES)
    Setup: Use a suitable ICP–OES configured in a radial optical alignment. [NOTE—This method was developed using a Varian Vista MPX ICP–OES unit.] The instrument parameters are as follows: Set the ultra-violet detector to scan arsenic at 188.980 nm. Set the sample read time to 20 s. Set the forward power from the RF generator to 1150 watts. Use an argon plasma feed gas flow of 13.5 L/min with the auxiliary gas set to flow at 2.25 L/min. The sample is delivered to the spray chamber by a multi-channel peristaltic pump set to deliver the sample at a rate of 20 rpm. Samples are flushed through the system for 20 s prior to analysis. A 40-s read delay is also programmed into the sampling routine to allow for fluid flow equilibration after the high-speed flush, prior to the first analytical read of the sample. Between samples, the pumping system is washed by flushing the *Diluent* for 20 s.
  Analysis: Generate a standard curve using *Diluent* as a blank and the *Standard solutions*. [NOTE—The correlation coefficient for the best-fit line should not be less than 0.999.]
  Similarly, analyze the *Sample solution* on the ICP. Calculate the concentration (mg/kg) of arsenic in the *Sample* taken:

  $$\text{Result} = (C/W) \times F$$

  C = concentration of arsenic in the *Sample solution* determined from the standard curve (μg/mL)
  W = weight of the *Sample* taken (g)
  F = final volume of the *Sample solution*, 100 mL

  Acceptance criteria: NMT 2 mg/kg

- **CADMIUM**
  [NOTE—When water is specified as a diluent, use deionized ultra-filtered water. When nitric acid is specified, use nitric acid of a grade suitable for trace element analysis with as low a content of cadmium as practical.]
  Diluent: 4% nitric acid in water
  Standard stock solution: 100 μg/mL of cadmium prepared by diluting a commercially available 1000 mg/kg cadmium ICP standard solution
  Standard solutions: 0.005, 0.05, 0.1, 0.2, 0.5, 1, and 2 μg/mL of cadmium, from the *Standard stock solution* diluted with *Diluent*
  Sample: 5 g
  Sample solution: Dissolve the *Sample* in 40 mL of 10% nitric acid in a 100-mL volumetric flask, and dilute with water to volume.

---
[1] YMC-Pack ODS-AQ (YMC Europe GmbH, Dinslaken, Germany), or equivalent.

Spectrophotometric system, *Plasma Spectrochemistry,* Appendix IIC
  Mode: ICP–OES
  Setup: Same as that described in the test for *Arsenic*, but set to scan for cadmium at 228.802 nm
Analysis: Generate a standard curve using *Diluent* as a blank and the *Standard solutions*. [NOTE—The correlation coefficient for the best-fit line should not be less than 0.999.]
Similarly, analyze the *Sample solution* on the ICP. Calculate the concentration (mg/kg) of cadmium in the *Sample* taken:

$$\text{Result} = (C/W) \times F$$

C = concentration of cadmium in the *Sample solution* determined from the standard curve (µg/mL)
W = weight of the *Sample* taken (g)
F = final volume of the *Sample solution*, 100 mL
Acceptance criteria: NMT 0.1 mg/kg

- **LEAD**
  [NOTE—When water is specified as a diluent, use deionized ultra-filtered water. When nitric acid is specified, use nitric acid of a grade suitable for trace element analysis with as low a content of lead as practical.]
  Diluent: 4% nitric acid in water
  Standard stock solution: 100 µg/mL of lead prepared by diluting a commercially available 1000 mg/kg lead ICP standard solution
  Standard solutions: 0.05, 0.1, 0.2, 0.5, 1, and 2 µg/mL of lead, from the *Standard stock solution* diluted with *Diluent*
  Sample: 5 g
  Sample solution: Dissolve the *Sample* in 40 mL of 10% nitric acid in a 100-mL volumetric flask, and dilute with water to volume.
  Spectrophotometric system, *Plasma Spectrochemistry,* Appendix IIC
    Mode: ICP–OES
    Setup: Same as that described in the test for *Arsenic*, but set to scan for lead at 220.353 nm
  Analysis: Generate a standard curve using *Diluent* as a blank and the *Standard solutions*. [NOTE—The correlation coefficient for the best-fit line should not be less than 0.999.]
  Similarly, analyze the *Sample solution* on the ICP. Calculate the concentration (mg/kg) of lead in the *Sample* taken:

$$\text{Result} = (C/W) \times F$$

  C = concentration of lead in the *Sample solution* determined from the standard curve (µg/mL)
  W = weight of the *Sample* taken (g)
  F = final volume of the *Sample solution*, 100 mL
  Acceptance criteria: NMT 1 mg/kg

- **MERCURY**
  [NOTE—When water is specified as a diluent, use deionized ultra-filtered water. When nitric acid is specified, use nitric acid of a grade suitable for trace element analysis with as low a content of mercury as practical.]
  Diluent: 4% nitric acid in water
  Standard stock solution: 100 µg/mL of mercury prepared by diluting a commercially available 1000 mg/kg mercury ICP standard solution
  Standard solutions: 0.025, 0.05, 0.1, 0.2, 0.5, 1, and 2 µg/mL of mercury, from the *Standard stock solution* diluted with *Diluent*
  Sample: 5 g
  Sample solution: Dissolve the *Sample* in 40 mL of 10% nitric acid in a 100-mL volumetric flask, and dilute with water to volume.
  Spectrophotometric system, *Plasma Spectrochemistry,* Appendix IIC
    Mode: ICP–OES
    Setup: Same as that described in the test for *Arsenic*, but set to scan for mercury at 194.164 nm
  Analysis: Generate a standard curve using *Diluent* as a blank and the *Standard solutions*. [NOTE—The correlation coefficient for the best-fit line should not be less than 0.999.]
  Similarly, analyze the *Sample solution* on the ICP. Calculate the concentration (mg/kg) of mercury in the *Sample* taken:

$$\text{Result} = (C/W) \times F$$

  C = concentration of mercury in the *Sample solution* determined from the standard curve (µg/mL)
  W = weight of the *Sample* taken (g)
  F = final volume of the *Sample solution*, 100 mL
  Acceptance criteria: NMT 0.5 mg/kg

Organic Impurities
- **ETHANOL**
  Standard solution: 10 mg/kg of ethanol in 1 N sodium hydroxide. Add 10 mL of this solution to a 20-mL headspace vial, and cap tightly.
  Sample solution: 100 mg/g in 1 N sodium hydroxide. Add 10 mL of this solution to a 20-mL headspace vial, and cap tightly.
  Chromatographic system, Appendix IIA
    Mode: Gas chromatography equipped with pressure-loop headspace autosampler
    Detector: Flame ionization
    Column: 30-m × 0.53-mm (id) capillary column with a 6% cyanopropylphenyl–94% dimethylpolysiloxane stationary phase and a 3.00-µm film thickness[2]
    Column temperature: 20 min at 40°; increase to 240° at 10°/min; maintain at 240° for 10 min
    Injection port temperature: 140°
    Detector temperature: 250°
    Carrier gas: Nitrogen
    Flow rate: 2.5 mL/min
    Headspace unit: 2.5 mL/min
      Equilibration temperature: 80°
      Equilibration time: 60 min
      Loop temperature: 85°

---
[2] CP-Select 624 CB (Varian-Chrompack, Palo Alto, CA), or equivalent.

Transfer temperature: 90°
Pressurization time: 0.5 min
Loop fill time: 0.1 min
Injection time: 1 min
Injection size: 1 mL of headspace
System suitability
Sample: *Standard solution*
Suitability requirement: The relative standard deviation of the ethanol peak area responses from replicate injections is NMT 5.0%.
Analysis: Separately inject equal volumes of the *Standard solution* and *Sample solution* into the chromatograph, record the chromatograms, and measure the peak responses. [NOTE—The approximate retention time for ethanol is 11 min.]
Acceptance criteria: The peak area from the *Sample solution* does not exceed that from the *Standard solution* (NMT 100 mg/kg).

- **OTHER RIBONUCLEOTIDES**
  Mobile phase and Chromatographic system: Prepare as directed in the *Assay*.
  Sample solution: 1.0 mg/mL. [NOTE—Ultra-sonication for 15 min at 30° may be necessary to aid in complete dissolution.]
  Standard solution: Mixture of USP Disodium 5'-Uridylate RS, USP 5'-Adenylic Acid RS, USP 5'-Cytidylic Acid RS, USP Disodium Guanylate RS, and USP Disodium Inosinate RS, each at 0.02 mg/mL in *Mobile phase*
  Suitability requirements
    Sample: *Standard solution*
    Suitability requirement 1: The relative standard deviation of the 5'-adenylic acid peak area responses from replicate injections is NMT 2.0%.
    Suitability requirement 2: The resolution, R, between the 5'-adenylic acid peak and all other nucleotide peaks is NLT 2.0.
  Analysis: Separately inject equal volumes of the *Standard solution* and *Sample solution* into the chromatograph, and measure the responses for all nucleotide peaks on the resulting chromatograms, except the peak from 5'-adenylic acid. [NOTE—The approximate retention times are 4.6 min (5'-cytidylic acid), 6.2 min (5'-uridylic acid), 10.3 min (5'-guanylic acid), 11.5 min (5'-inosinic acid), and 27.5 min (5'-adenylic acid).] Separately calculate the percentage of each analyte (5'-cytidylic acid, 5'-guanylic acid, 5'-inosinic acid, and 5'-uridylic acid) in the sample taken:

  Result = $(r_U/r_S) \times (C_S/C_U) \times 100$

  r_U = peak area of the analyte from the *Sample solution*
  r_S = peak area of the analyte from the *Standard solution*
  C_S = concentration of analyte in the *Standard solution* (mg/mL)
  C_U = concentration of analyte in the *Sample solution* (mg/mL)
  Acceptance criteria: The sum of the percentages for all nucleotide impurities is NMT 0.5%, calculated on the anhydrous basis.

SPECIFIC TESTS
- **pH**, *pH Determination*, Appendix IIB
  Sample solution: 0.05 mg/mL
  Acceptance criteria: 3.3–4.3
- **WATER**, *Water Determination, Method I*, Appendix IIB
  Acceptance criteria: NMT 6.0%
- **BILE-TOLERANT GRAM-NEGATIVE BACTERIA**, Appendix XIIC
  Sample preparation: Proceed as directed using a 10-g sample and incubating at 30–35° for 18–24 h.
  Acceptance criteria: Negative in 10 g
- **ENTEROBACTER SAKAZAKII** (*Cronobacter Spp.*), Appendix XIIC
  Sample preparation: Proceed as directed using a 10-g sample and incubating at 30–35° for 18–24 h.
  Acceptance criteria: Negative in 10 g
- **SALMONELLA SPP.**, Appendix XIIC
  Sample preparation: Dissolve 25 g of the sample at a sample/broth ratio of 1/8, and proceed as directed.
  Acceptance criteria: Negative in 25 g
- **TOTAL AEROBIC MICROBIAL COUNT**, *Method I (Plate Count Method)*, Appendix XIIB
  Acceptance criteria: NMT 1,000 cfu/g
- **TOTAL YEASTS AND MOLDS COUNT**, *Method I (Plate Count Method)*, Appendix XIIB
  Acceptance criteria: NMT 100 cfu/g

Adipic Acid
First Published: Prior to FCC 6
Last Revision: FCC 7

Hexanedioic Acid
1,4-Butanedicarboxylic Acid

$C_6H_{10}O_4$ Formula wt 146.14
INS: 355   CAS: 124-04-9
UNII: 76A0JE0FKJ [adipic acid]

DESCRIPTION
Adipic Acid occurs as white crystals or a crystalline powder. It is not hygroscopic. It is freely soluble in alcohol, soluble in acetone, and slightly soluble in water.
Function: Buffer; neutralizing agent
Packaging and Storage: Store in well-closed containers.

IDENTIFICATION
- **INFRARED ABSORPTION**, *Spectrophotometric Identification Tests*, Appendix IIIC
  Reference standard: USP Adipic Acid RS
  Sample and standard preparation: K
  Acceptance criteria: The spectrum of the sample exhibits maxima at the same wavelengths as those in the spectrum of the *Reference standard*.

ASSAY
- **PROCEDURE**
  Sample: 1.5 g

Analysis: Mix the *Sample* with 75 mL of recently boiled and cooled water contained in a 250-mL glass-stoppered Erlenmeyer flask, add phenolphthalein TS, and titrate with 0.5 N sodium hydroxide to the first appearance of a faint pink endpoint that persists for at least 30 s, shaking the flask as the endpoint is approached. Each mL of 0.5 N sodium hydroxide is equivalent to 36.54 mg of $C_6H_{10}O_4$.

Acceptance criteria: 99.6%–101.0% of $C_6H_{10}O_4$, calculated on the anhydrous basis

IMPURITIES
Inorganic Impurities
- **LEAD**, *Lead Limit Test, Flame Atomic Absorption Spectrophotometric Method,* Appendix IIIB
  Sample: 5 g
  Acceptance criteria: NMT 2 mg/kg

SPECIFIC TESTS
- **MELTING RANGE OR TEMPERATURE DETERMINATION**, Appendix IIB
  Acceptance criteria: Between 151.5° and 154°
- **RESIDUE ON IGNITION**
  Sample: 100.0 g
  Analysis: Transfer the *Sample* into a tared 125-mL platinum dish that has been previously cleaned by fusing with 5 g of potassium pyrosulfate or bisulfate, followed by boiling in 2 N sulfuric acid and rinsing with water. Melt the sample completely over a gas burner, then ignite the melt with the burner. After ignition starts, lower or remove the flame to prevent the sample from boiling and to keep it burning slowly until it is completely carbonized. Ignite at 850° in a muffle furnace for 30 min or until the carbon is completely removed, then cool and weigh.
  Acceptance criteria: NMT 0.002%
- **WATER**, *Water Determination*, Appendix IIB
  Acceptance criteria: NMT 0.2%

Agar
First Published: Prior to FCC 6

INS: 406 CAS: [9002-18-0]
UNII: 89T13OHQ2B [agar, unspecified]

DESCRIPTION
Agar is commercially available as white to pale yellow bundles consisting of thin, membranous agglutinated strips, or in cut, flaked, granulated, or powdered forms. Agar is a generic name given to a group of related molecules with a repeating unit of agarobiose formed basically by D- and L-galactose units interlinked with α-1,3 and β-1,4 linkages. Approximately every tenth D-galactopyranose unit contains a sulfate ester group. It is extracted from the cellular walls of agarophyte seaweed, considering as such the red seaweed from phylum Rodophyta, which belong to the Gelidiceae, Gracilariaceae, and Ahnpheltiaceae families. It is insoluble in cold water, but it is soluble in boiling water.

Function: Stabilizer; emulsifier; thickener
Packaging and Storage: Store in well-closed containers.

IDENTIFICATION
- **A. PROCEDURE**
  Analysis: Place a few fragments of unground sample or a small amount of the powder on a slide, add a few drops of water, and examine microscopically.
  Acceptance criteria: The sample appears granular and somewhat filamentous. A few fragments of the spicules of sponges and a few frustules of diatoms may be present.
- **B. PROCEDURE**
  Sample: 1 g
  Analysis: While stirring continuously, boil the *Sample* with 65 mL of water for 10 min, and adjust to a concentration of 1.5%, by weight, with hot water.
  Acceptance criteria: A clear liquid results that congeals between 32° and 39° to form a firm, resilient gel that does not liquefy below 85°.

IMPURITIES
Inorganic Impurities
- **ARSENIC**, *Arsenic Limit Test*, Appendix IIIB
  Sample solution: Prepare as directed for organic compounds.
  Acceptance criteria: NMT 3 mg/kg
- **LEAD**, *Lead Limit Test*, Appendix IIIB
  Sample solution: Prepare as directed for organic compounds.
  Control: 5 µg Pb (5 mL of *Diluted Standard Lead Solution*)
  Acceptance criteria: NMT 5 mg/kg

SPECIFIC TESTS
- **ASH (ACID-INSOLUBLE)**, Appendix IIC
  Acceptance criteria: NMT 0.5%, calculated on the dried basis
- **ASH (TOTAL)**, Appendix IIC
  Acceptance criteria: NMT 6.5%, calculated on the dried basis
- **GELATIN**
  Analysis: Dissolve 1 g of sample in 100 mL of boiling water and cool to 50°. Add 5 mL of trinitrophenol TS to 5 mL of the solution.
  Acceptance criteria: No turbidity forms within 10 min.
- **INSOLUBLE MATTER**
  Sample: 7.5 g
  Analysis: Add sufficient water to the *Sample* to make 500 g, boil for 15 min, and readjust to the original weight. Add hot water to 100 g of the mixture to make 200 mL, heat almost to boiling, filter while hot through a tared filtering crucible, rinse the container with several portions of hot water, and pass the rinsings through the crucible. Dry the crucible and its contents at 105° to constant weight, cool, and weigh.
  Acceptance criteria: The weight of the residue does not exceed 15 mg. (NMT 1.0%)
- **LOSS ON DRYING**, Appendix IIC: 105° for 5 h
  Sample preparation: Cut unground sample into 2- to 5-mm pieces before drying.
  Acceptance criteria: NMT 20.0%

- **STARCH**
  Analysis: Boil 100 mg of sample in 100 mL of water, cool, and add a few drops of iodine TS.
  Acceptance criteria: No blue color appears.
- **WATER ABSORPTION**
  Sample: 5 g
  Analysis: Place the *Sample* in a 100-mL graduated cylinder, fill to volume with water, mix, and allow to stand at about 25° for 24 h. Pour the contents of the cylinder through moistened glass wool, allowing the water to drain into another 100-mL graduated cylinder.
  Acceptance criteria: NMT 75 mL of water is obtained.

DL-Alanine

First Published: Prior to FCC 6

DL-2-Aminopropanoic Acid

$C_3H_7NO_2$
UNII: 1FU7983T0U [alanine, dl-]
Formula wt 89.09
CAS: [302-72-7]

DESCRIPTION
DL-Alanine occurs as a white crystalline powder. It is freely soluble in water, but sparingly soluble in alcohol. The pH of a 1:20 aqueous solution is between 5.5 and 7.0. It melts with decomposition at about 198°. It is optically inactive.
Function: Nutrient
Packaging and Storage: Store in well-closed, light-resistant containers.

IDENTIFICATION
- **INFRARED ABSORPTION,** *Spectrophotometric Identification Tests,* Appendix IIIC
  Sample preparation: Mineral oil mull
  Acceptance criteria: The spectrum of the sample exhibits relative maxima at the same wavelengths as those of the spectrum below.

ASSAY
- **PROCEDURE**
  Sample: 200 mg
  Analysis: Dissolve the *Sample* in 3 mL of formic acid and 50 mL of glacial acetic acid. Add 2 drops of crystal violet TS and titrate with 0.1 N perchloric acid to a blue-green endpoint. Perform a blank determination (see *General Provisions*), and make any necessary correction. Each mL of 0.1 N perchloric acid is equivalent to 8.909 mg of $C_3H_7NO_2$.
  [**CAUTION**—Handle perchloric acid in an appropriate fume hood.]
  Acceptance criteria: NLT 98.5% and NMT 101.5% of $C_3H_7NO_2$, calculated on the dried basis

IMPURITIES
Inorganic Impurities
- **LEAD,** *Lead Limit Test,* Appendix IIIB
  Sample preparation: Prepare as directed for organic compounds.
  Control: 5 µg Pb (5 mL of *Diluted Standard Lead Solution*)
  Acceptance criteria: NMT 5 mg/kg

SPECIFIC TESTS
- **LOSS ON DRYING,** Appendix IIC: 105° for 3 h
  Acceptance criteria: NMT 0.3%
- **RESIDUE ON IGNITION (SULFATED ASH),** Appendix IIC
  Sample: 1 g
  Acceptance criteria: NMT 0.2%

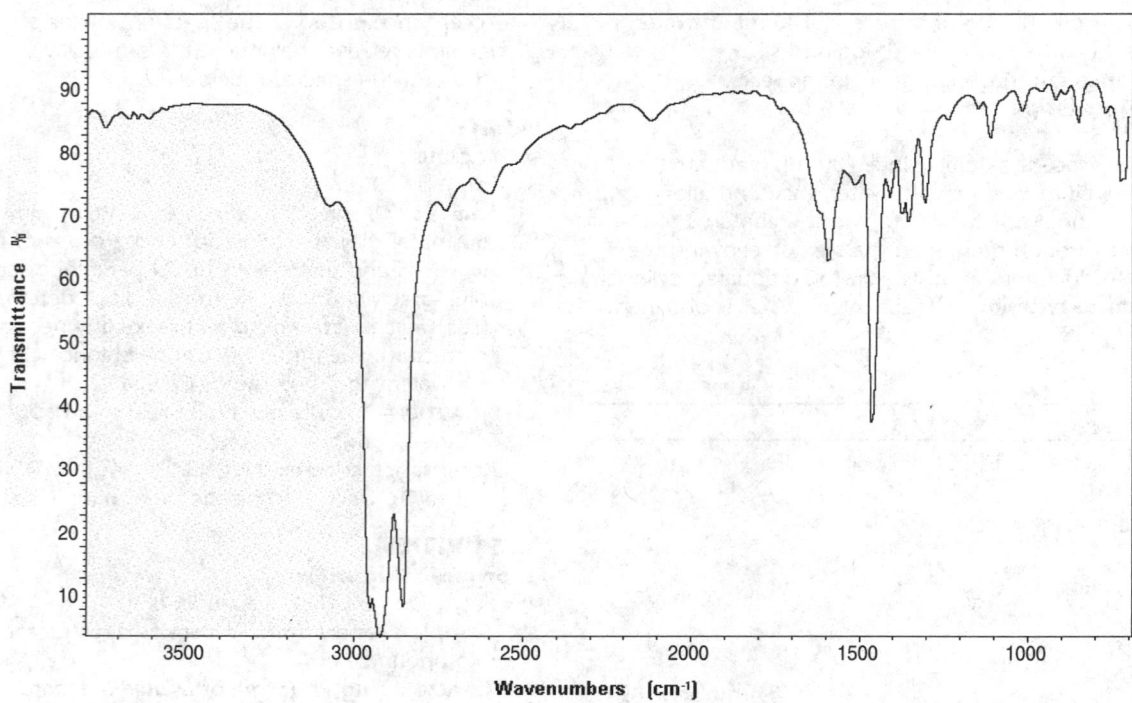

DL-Alanine (Mineral Oil Mull)

L-Alanine

First Published: Prior to FCC 6
Last Revision: FCC 6

L-2-Aminopropanoic Acid

$C_3H_7NO_2$

UNII: OF5P57N2ZX [alanine]

Formula wt 89.09
CAS: [56-41-7]

DESCRIPTION

L-Alanine occurs as a white crystalline powder. It is freely soluble in water, sparingly soluble in alcohol, and insoluble in ether. The pH of a 1:20 aqueous solution is between 5.5 and 7.0.

Function: Nutrient
Packaging and Storage: Store in well-closed, light-resistant containers.

IDENTIFICATION

- **INFRARED ABSORPTION,** *Spectrophotometric Identification Tests,* Appendix IIIC
  Reference standard: USP L-Alanine RS
  Sample and Standard preparation: *K*
  Acceptance criteria: The spectrum of the sample exhibits maxima at the same wavelengths as those in the spectrum of the *Reference standard.*

ASSAY

- **PROCEDURE**
  Sample: 200 mg
  Analysis: Dissolve the *Sample* in 3 mL of formic acid and 50 mL of glacial acetic acid. Add 2 drops of crystal violet TS and titrate with 0.1 N perchloric acid to a blue-green endpoint. Perform a blank determination (see *General Provisions*), and make any necessary correction. Each mL of 0.1 N perchloric acid is equivalent to 8.909 mg of $C_3H_7NO_2$. [**CAUTION**—Handle perchloric acid in an appropriate fume hood.]
  Acceptance criteria: NLT 98.5% and NMT 101.5% of $C_3H_7NO_2$, calculated on the dried basis

IMPURITIES

Inorganic Impurities

- **LEAD,** *Lead Limit Test,* Appendix IIIB
  Sample solution: Prepare as directed for organic compounds.
  Control: 5 µg Pb (5 mL of *Diluted Standard Lead Solution*)
  Acceptance criteria: NMT 5 mg/kg

SPECIFIC TESTS

- **LOSS ON DRYING,** Appendix IIC: 105° for 3 h
  Acceptance criteria: NMT 0.3%
- **OPTICAL (SPECIFIC) ROTATION,** Appendix IIB
  Sample: 10 g, previously dried
  Analysis: Dissolve the *Sample* in sufficient 6 N hydrochloric acid to make 100 mL.
  Acceptance criteria
  $[\alpha]_D^{20}$ between +13.5° and +15.5°, on the dried basis; or

$[\alpha]_D^{25}$ between +13.2° and +15.2°, on the dried basis
- **RESIDUE ON IGNITION (SULFATED ASH),** Appendix IIC
  Sample: 1 g
  Acceptance criteria: NMT 0.2%

Alginic Acid

First Published: Prior to FCC 6

$(C_6H_8O_6)_n$ Formula wt, calculated 176.13
                        Formula wt, actual (avg.) 200.00
INS: 400   CAS: [9005-32-7]
UNII: 8C3Z4148WZ [alginic acid]

DESCRIPTION
Alginic Acid occurs as a white to yellow-white, fibrous powder. It is a hydrophilic colloidal carbohydrate extracted from various species of brown seaweeds (*phaeophyceae*) with dilute alkali. It may be described chemically as a linear glycuronoglycan consisting mainly of β-1,4 linked D-mannuronic and L-guluronic acid units in the pyranose ring form. Alginic Acid is insoluble in water, readily soluble in alkaline solutions, and insoluble in organic solvents. The pH of a 3:100 suspension in water is between 2.0 and 3.4.
Function: Stabilizer; thickener; emulsifier
Packaging and Storage: Store in well-closed containers.

IDENTIFICATION
- **A. PROCEDURE**
  Sample solution: 1:150 in 0.1 N sodium hydroxide
  Analysis: Add 1 mL of calcium chloride TS to 5 mL of *Sample solution*.
  Acceptance criteria: A voluminous gelatinous precipitate forms.
- **B. PROCEDURE**
  Sample solution: 1:150 in 0.1 N sodium hydroxide
  Analysis: Add 1 mL of 2 N sulfuric acid to 5 mL of *Sample solution*.
  Acceptance criteria: A heavy gelatinous precipitate forms
- **C. PROCEDURE**
  Sample: 5 mg
  Analysis: Place the *Sample* in a test tube. Add 5 mL of water, 1 mL of a freshly prepared 1:100 solution of naphtholresorcinol:ethanol, and 5 mL of hydrochloric acid. Heat the mixture to boiling, boil gently for about 3 min, and then cool to about 15°. Transfer the contents of the test tube into a 30-mL separatory funnel with the aid of 5 mL of water, and extract with 15 mL of isopropyl ether. Perform a blank determination (see *General Provisions*).
  Acceptance criteria: The isopropyl ether extract from the *Sample* exhibits a deeper purple hue than that from the blank.

ASSAY
- **ALGINATES ASSAY,** Appendix IIIC
  Analysis: Each mL of 0.25 N sodium hydroxide consumed in the assay is equivalent to 25 mg of $(C_6H_8O_6)_n$ (equiv wt 200.00).

Acceptance criteria: NLT 20% and NMT 23% of carbon dioxide (CO_2), corresponding to between 91.0% and 104.5% of $(C_6H_8O_6)_n$ (equiv wt 200.00), calculated on the dried basis.

IMPURITIES
Inorganic Impurities
- **ARSENIC,** *Arsenic Limit Test,* Appendix IIIB
  Sample solution: Prepare as directed for organic compounds.
  Acceptance criteria: NMT 3 mg/kg
- **LEAD,** *Lead Limit Test,* Appendix IIIB
  Sample solution: Prepare as directed for organic compounds.
  Control: 5 µg Pb (5 mL of *Diluted Standard Lead Solution*)
  Acceptance criteria: NMT 5 mg/kg

SPECIFIC TESTS
- **LOSS ON DRYING,** Appendix IIC: 105° for 4 h
  Acceptance criteria: NMT 15.0%
- **RESIDUE ON IGNITION (SULFATED ASH),** Appendix IIC
  Sample: 3 g
  Acceptance criteria: NMT 8.0%, calculated on the dried basis

Alitame

First Published: FCC 7
Last Revision: Third Supplement, FCC 7

L-α-Aspartyl-*N*-(2,2,4,4-tetramethyl-3-thietanyl)-D-alaninamide, hydrated

$C_{14}H_{25}N_3O_4S \cdot 2.5\ H_2O$ Formula wt hydrated 376.5
INS: 956   CAS: hydrated [99016-42-9]
UNII: 6KI9M51JOG [alitame]

DESCRIPTION
Alitame occurs as a white, odorless, crystalline powder having an intensely sweet taste. One method of production is through a multi-step synthesis involving the reaction between two intermediates, (*S*)-[2,5-dioxo-(4-thiazolidine)] acetic acid and (*R*)-2-amino-*N*-(2,2,4,4-tetramethyl-3-thietanyl)propanamide. The final product is isolated and purified through crystallization of an alitame/4-methylbenzenesulfonic acid adduct followed by additional purification steps, and finally recrystallization from water as the 2.5 hydrate. It is freely soluble in water and alcohol, and the pH of a 5% solution is between 5.0 and 6.0.
Function: Sweetener; flavor enhancer
Packaging and Storage: Store in tight containers in a cool place.

IDENTIFICATION

- **A. INFRARED ABSORPTION,** *Spectrophotometric Identification Tests,* Appendix IIIC
  Reference standard: USP Alitame RS
  Sample and standard preparation: *K*
  Acceptance criteria: The spectrum of the sample exhibits maxima at the same wavelengths as those in the spectrum of the *Reference standard.*
- **B. PROCEDURE**
  Sample: 10 mg
  Analysis: To 5 mL of a solution containing 300 mg of ninhydrin in 100 mL of *n*-butanol and 2 mL of glacial acetic acid, add the *Sample*, and heat to gentle reflux.
  Acceptance criteria: An intense blue-violet color is formed.
- **C. PROCEDURE**
  Sample: 10 mg
  Analysis: To 5 mL of a freshly prepared 0.001 M potassium permanganate solution, add the *Sample*, and mix thoroughly.
  Acceptance criteria: The purple solution changes to brown.

ASSAY

- **PROCEDURE**
  [NOTE—In this procedure, alitame and its impurities, alanine amide (*N*-(2,2,4,4-tetramethyl-3-thietanyl)-D-alaninamide) and beta-isomer (L-β-aspartyl-*N*-(2,2,4,4-tetramethyl-3-thietanyl)-D-alaninamide hydrate) [2:5]), are measured by reverse-phase ion-pair high performance liquid chromatography.]
  Solution A: Dissolve 0.69 g of sodium phosphate monobasic monohydrate and 4.32 g of 1-octanesulfonate, sodium in 200 mL of water. Adjust with 85% phosphoric acid to a pH of 2.5, then dilute with water to 1000 mL. Pass through a 0.22-μm Millipore filter, or equivalent.
  Mobile phase: Acetonitrile and *Solution A* (1:4). [NOTE—Degas by sonication under aspirator vacuum for 2 min.]
  Standard solution A: Transfer 25 mg each of a suitable alanine amide reference standard and a suitable beta-isomer reference standard to a 500-mL volumetric flask, using 50 mL of methanol to aid in dissolution. Dilute with water to volume. [NOTE—Store in a refrigerator.]
  Dilute standard solution A: Transfer 15.0 mL of *Standard solution A* to a 50-mL volumetric flask, and dilute with water to volume.
  Standard solution B: Transfer 50 mg of USP Alitame RS to a 10-mL volumetric flask. Add 3 mL of water to dissolve, then add 5 mL of *Dilute standard solution A*, and dilute with water to volume.
  Dilute standard solution B: Transfer 5 mL of *Standard solution B* to a 50-mL volumetric flask, and dilute with water to volume.
  Sample solution: 5 mg/mL
  Dilute sample solution: 0.5 mg/mL from the *Sample solution*
  Chromatographic system, Appendix IIA
   Mode: High-performance liquid chromatography
   Detector: UV 217 nm
   Column: 15-cm × 0.39-cm NovaPak C18 reverse phase ion-pair (Waters, or equivalent)
   Flow rate: 1.0 mL/min. [NOTE—Maintain the *Mobile phase* at a pressure and flow rate capable of giving the elution times listed under *Analysis*.]
   Injection size: 100 μL
  System suitability
   Sample: *Dilute standard solution B* (three replicates)
   Suitability requirement: The relative standard deviation is NMT 2% for the alitame peak area.
  Analysis: [NOTE—All injections should be done in triplicate. The retention times for the beta-isomer, alitame, and alanine amide should be approximately 6, 10, and 15 min, respectively. If a column of a different make or length is used, the retention times may vary proportionally to the times listed.]
  Equilibrate the column by pumping *Mobile phase* through it until a drift-free baseline is obtained. Inject the *Dilute sample solution* and *Dilute standard solution B* into the chromatograph, and record the chromatograms. Calculate the average peak areas for alitame from both chromatograms.
  Calculate the weight percentage for alitame in the sample taken:

  $$\text{Result} = (r_{DU}/r_{DS}) \times (C_{DS}/C_{DU}) \times 100$$

  r_{DU} = peak response for alitame from the *Dilute sample solution*
  r_{DS} = peak response for alitame from *Dilute standard solution B*
  C_{DS} = concentration of alitame in *Dilute standard solution B*, corrected for water content and purity (mg/mL)
  C_{DU} = concentration of the *Dilute sample solution*, corrected for water (mg/mL)

  Acceptance criteria: 98.0%–101.0% of alitame, on the anhydrous basis

IMPURITIES
Inorganic Impurities
- **LEAD,** *Lead Limit Test, Atomic Absorption Spectrophotometric Graphite Furnace Method,* Appendix IIIB
  Sample: 5 g
  Acceptance criteria: NMT 1 mg/kg

Organic Impurities
- **ALANINE AMIDE AND BETA-ISOMER**
  Solution A, **Mobile phase**, **Standard solution A**, **Dilute standard solution A**, **Standard solution B**, **Dilute standard solution B**, **Sample solution**, **Dilute sample solution**, and **Chromatographic system:** Proceed as directed in the *Assay*.
  Analysis: Proceed as directed in the *Assay*. Inject the *Sample solution* and *Standard solution B* into the chromatograph, and record the chromatograms. Calculate the average peak areas for the beta-isomer and alanine amide from both chromatograms.
  Calculate the weight percentage of alanine amide and beta-isomer in the sample taken:

  $$\text{Result} = (r_U/r_S) \times (C_S/C_U) \times 100$$

  r_U = peak response for the analyte from the *Sample solution*
  r_S = peak response for the analyte from *Standard solution B*
  C_S = concentration of the analyte in *Standard solution B*, corrected for water content and purity (mg/mL)
  C_U = concentration of the *Sample solution*, corrected for water (mg/mL)
  Acceptance criteria
  Alanine amide: NMT 0.2% on the anhydrous basis
  Beta-isomer: NMT 0.3% on the anhydrous basis

SPECIFIC TESTS
- **RESIDUE ON IGNITION (SULFATED ASH)**, Appendix IIC
  Sample: 1 g
  Acceptance criteria: NMT 1.0%
- **OPTICAL (SPECIFIC) ROTATION**, Appendix IIB
  Sample solution: 10 mg/mL, on the as-is (undried) basis
  Acceptance criteria: $[\alpha]_D^{25}$ between +40° and +50°
- **WATER**, *Water Determination*, Appendix IIB
  Acceptance criteria: 11%–13%

Allura Red[1]

First Published: Prior to FCC 6

Allura Red AC
CI 16035
Class: Monoazo

$C_{18}H_{14}N_2O_8S_2Na_2$ Formula wt 496.43
INS: 129   CAS: [25956-17-6]
UNII: WZB9127XOA [fd&c red no. 40]

DESCRIPTION
Allura Red occurs as a red-brown powder or granule. It is principally the disodium salt of 6-hydroxy-5-[(2-methoxy-5-methyl-4-sulfophenyl)azo]-2-naphthalenesulfonic acid. It dissolves in water to give a solution red at neutrality and in acid and dark red in base. It is insoluble in ethanol.
Function: Color
Packaging and Storage: Store in well-closed containers.

IDENTIFICATION
- **PROCEDURE**
  Sample solution: 16.4 µg/mL
  Analysis: Adjust the pH of three aliquots of the *Sample solution* to pH 1, pH 7, and pH 13. Measure the absorbance intensities (*A*) and wavelength maxima of these solutions with a suitable UV-visible spectrophotometer.
  Acceptance criteria
  pH 1: *A* = 0.83 at 490 nm (Both neutral and acid solutions exhibit a shoulder at about 410 nm.)
  pH 7: *A* = 0.87 at 500 nm
  pH 13: *A* = 0.37 at 500 nm and *A* = 0.41 at 450 nm

ASSAY
- **TOTAL COLOR,** *Color Determination, Methods I and II*, Appendix IIIC: Both methods must be used.
  Method I Spectrophotometric
  Sample: 175 to 225 mg
  Analysis: Transfer the *Sample* into a 1-L volumetric flask; dissolve in and dilute to volume with water. Determine as directed at 502 nm using 0.052 L/(mg·cm) for the absorptivity (*a*) for Allura Red.
  Method II TiCl₃ Titration
  Sample: 0.2 g
  Analysis: Determine as directed using 8.06 as the stoichiometric factor (F_s) for Allura Red.
  Acceptance criteria: The average of results obtained from *Methods I and II* is NLT 85.0% total coloring matters.

IMPURITIES
Inorganic Impurities
- **ARSENIC**, Appendix IIIB
  Sample solution: Prepare as directed for organic compounds.
  Acceptance criteria: NMT 3 mg/kg
- **LEAD**, *Lead Limit Test*, Appendix IIIB
  Sample solution: Prepare as directed for organic compounds.
  Control: 10 µg Pb (10 mL of *Diluted Standard Lead Solution*)
  Acceptance criteria: NMT 10 mg/kg

---

[1] To be used or sold for use to color food that is marketed in the United States, this color additive must be from a batch that has been certified by the U.S. Food and Drug Administration (FDA). If it is not from an FDA-certified batch, it is not a permitted color additive for food use in the United States, even if it is compositionally equivalent. The name FD&C Red No. 40 can be applied only to FDA-certified batches of this color additive. Allura Red is a common name given to the uncertified colorant. See the monograph entitled *FD&C Red No. 40* for directions for producing an FDA-certified batch.

Organic Impurities
- **UNCOMBINED INTERMEDIATES AND PRODUCTS OF SIDE REACTIONS,** *Color Determination, Method II,* Appendix IIIC
  Sample solution: 250 mg/mL in 0.1 M disodium borate ($Na_2B_4O_7$)
  Analysis: Use an injection volume of 20 µL for the *Sample solution.*
  Acceptance criteria
    4-Amino-5-methoxy-o-toluenesulfonic acid: NMT 0.2%
    6,6'-Oxybis(2-naphthalenesulfonic acid), Disodium salt: NMT 1.0%;
    6-Hydroxy-2-naphthalenesulfonic acid, Sodium salt: NMT 0.3%

SPECIFIC TESTS
- **COMBINED TESTS**
  Tests
  - **LOSS ON DRYING (VOLATILE MATTER),** *Color Determination,* Appendix IIIC
  - **CHLORIDE,** *Sodium Chloride, Color Determination,* Appendix IIIC
  - **SULFATES (AS SODIUM SALTS),** *Sodium Sulfate, Color Determination,* Appendix IIIC
  Acceptance criteria: NMT 15.0% in combination
- **ETHER EXTRACTS,** *Color Determination,* Appendix IIIC
  Acceptance criteria: NMT 0.2%
- **SUBSIDIARY COLORS,** *Thin-Layer Chromatography,* Appendix IIA
  Adsorbent: Silica Gel G
  Developing solvent system: Acetonitrile, ethyl acetate, isoamyl alcohol, water and ammonium hydroxide (5:5:5:5:1)
  Standard solution: 20 mg/mL of purified Allura Red (free of subsidiary colors) and 1 mg/mL each of lower and higher sulfonated subsidiary colors. [NOTE—Store in the dark.]
  Sample solution: 20 mg/mL
  Application volume: 3 µL
  Analysis: Prepare a 20- × 20-cm glass plate coated with a 0.25-mm layer of *Adsorbent.* Spot aliquots of the *Sample solution* and the *Standard solution* side-by-side 3 cm from the bottom. [NOTE—Up to seven samples and standards may be run simultaneously.] When the plate has air dried for 15 min, develop it in an unlined tank equilibrated with the *Developing solvent system* for at least 20 min. Allow the solvent front to reach to within 3 cm from the top of the plate. Allow the plate to dry in a fume hood, and by visual inspection, compare the intensities of the lower and higher sulfonated subsidiary colors with those in the *Standard solution.* If the subsidiary colors in the *Sample solution* appear more concentrated than those in the *Standard solution,* determine the quantity of each, using a densitometer set to monitor the absorbance maximum of each. Calculate the percentage of each of the subsidiary colors, if present above 0.1%, by the formula:

$$\text{Result} = (A \times p)/A_s$$

  A = area of the densitometer curve
  p = percent of subsidiary color in the *Standard solution*
  A_s = area of the densitometer curve for the subsidiary color in the *Standard solution*
  Acceptance criteria
    6-Hydroxy-5-[(2-methoxy-5-methyl-4-sulfophenyl)azo]-8-(2-methoxy-5-methyl-4-sulfophenoxy)-2-naphthalenesulfonic acid, Disodium salt: NMT 1.0%
    Higher and Lower Sulfonated Subsidiary Colors (as sodium salts): NMT 1.0% each
- **WATER-INSOLUBLE MATTER,** *Color Determination,* Appendix IIIC
  Acceptance criteria: NMT 0.2%

Allyl α-Ionone
First Published: Prior to FCC 6

Allyl Ionone

$C_{16}H_{24}O$ Formula wt 232.37
FEMA: 2033
UNII: 8IP66F9ODG [allyl α-ionone]

DESCRIPTION
Allyl α-Ionone occurs as a colorless to yellow liquid.
Odor: Fruity, woody
Solubility: Soluble in alcohol; insoluble or practically insoluble in water
Boiling Point: ~265°
Solubility in Alcohol, Appendix VI: One mL dissolves in 1 mL of 90% alcohol to give a clear solution.
Function: Flavoring agent

IDENTIFICATION
- **INFRARED SPECTRA,** *Spectrophotometric Identification Tests,* Appendix IIIC
  Acceptance criteria: The spectrum of the sample exhibits relative maxima at the same wavelengths as those of the spectrum below.

ASSAY
- **PROCEDURE:** Proceed as directed under *M-1b,* Appendix XI.
  Acceptance criteria: NLT 88.0% of $C_{16}H_{24}O$

SPECIFIC TESTS
- **REFRACTIVE INDEX,** Appendix II: At 20°
  Acceptance criteria: Between 1.502 and 1.507
- **SPECIFIC GRAVITY:** Determine at 25° by any reliable method (see *General Provisions*).
  Acceptance criteria: Between 0.926 and 0.932

OTHER REQUIREMENTS
- ALLYL ALCOHOL, *M-1b,* Appendix XI
  Acceptance criteria: NMT 0.1%

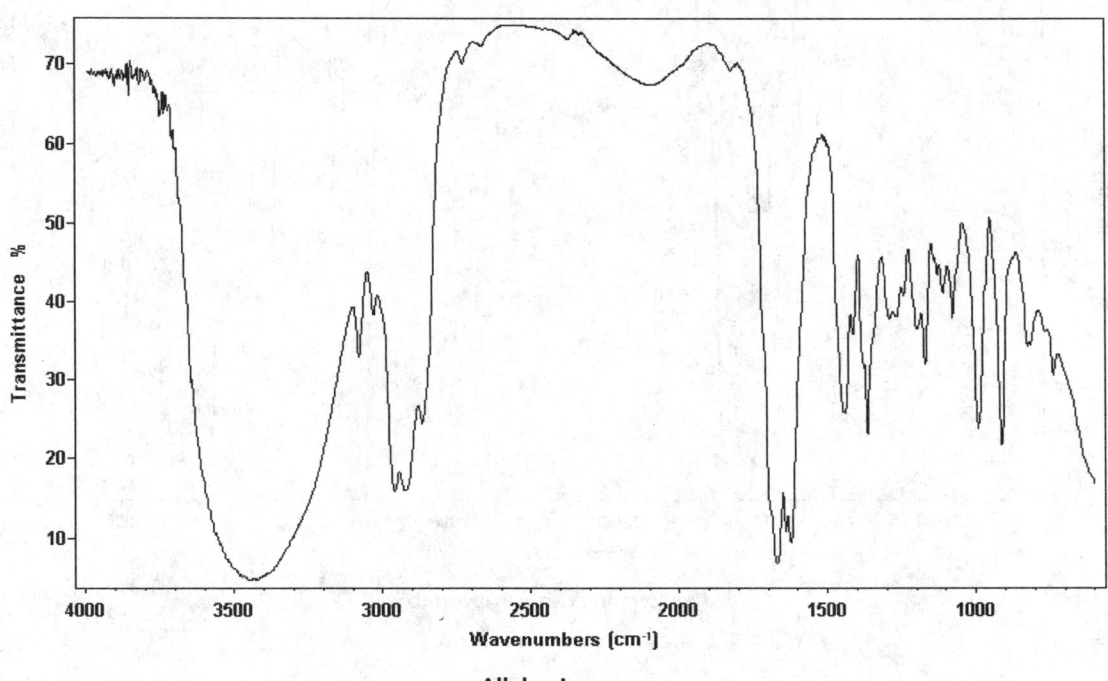

Allyl α-Ionone

Allyl Cyclohexanepropionate
First Published: Prior to FCC 6

Allyl-3-cyclohexanepropionate

$C_{12}H_{20}O_2$ Formula wt 196.29
FEMA: 2026
UNII: H4W9H3L241 [allyl cyclohexanepropionate]

DESCRIPTION
Allyl Cyclohexanepropionate occurs as a colorless liquid.
Odor: Pineapple
Solubility: Miscible in alcohol, chloroform, ether; insoluble or practically insoluble in glycerin, water
Solubility in Alcohol, Appendix VI: One mL dissolves in 4 mL of 80% alcohol.
Function: Flavoring agent

IDENTIFICATION
- INFRARED SPECTRA, *Spectrophotometric Identification Tests,* Appendix IIIC
  Acceptance criteria: The spectrum of the sample exhibits relative maxima at the same wavelengths as those of the spectrum below.

ASSAY
- PROCEDURE: Proceed as directed under *M-1b,* Appendix XI.
  Acceptance criteria: NLT 98.0% of $C_{12}H_{20}O_2$

SPECIFIC TESTS
- ACID VALUE, FLAVOR CHEMICALS (OTHER THAN ESSENTIAL OILS), *M-15,* Appendix XI
  Acceptance criteria: NMT 5.0
- REFRACTIVE INDEX, Appendix II: At 20°
  Acceptance criteria: Between 1.457 and 1.462
- SPECIFIC GRAVITY: Determine at 25° by any reliable method (see *General Provisions*).
  Acceptance criteria: Between 0.945 and 0.950

OTHER REQUIREMENTS
- ALLYL ALCOHOL, *M-1b,* Appendix XI
  Acceptance criteria: NMT 0.1%

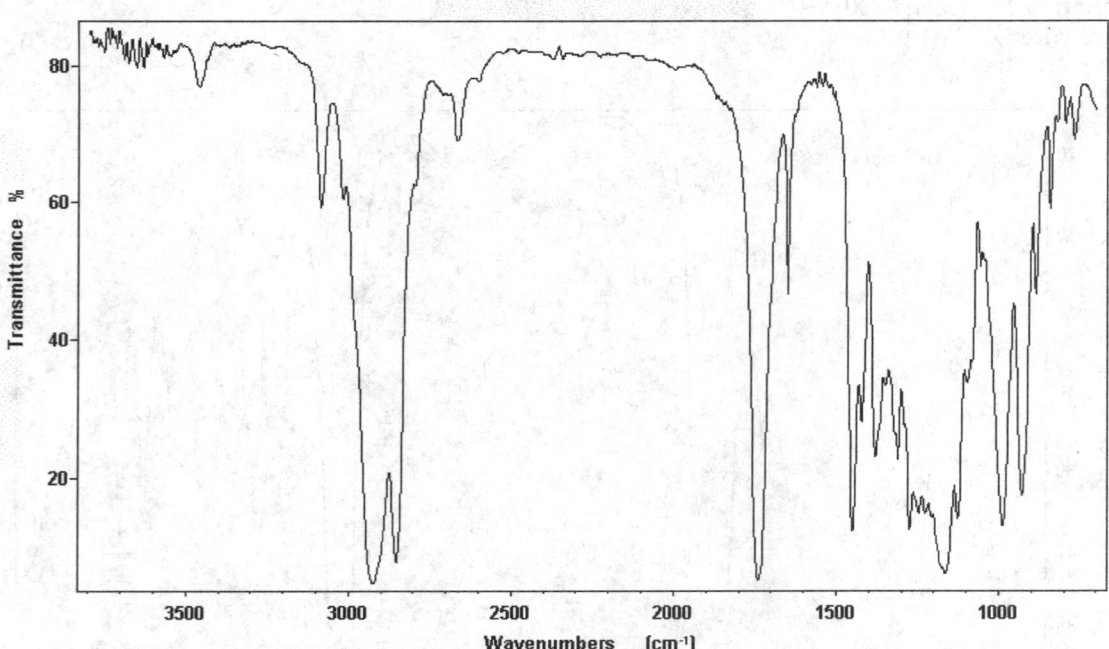

Allyl Cyclohexanepropionate

Allyl Heptanoate

First Published: Prior to FCC 6

Allyl Heptoate

C₁₀H₁₈O₂   Formula wt 170.25
FEMA: 2031
UNII: AU4CYG9V68 [allyl heptanoate]

DESCRIPTION
Allyl Heptanoate occurs as a colorless to pale yellow liquid.
Odor: Sweet, pineapple
Boiling Point: ~210°
Solubility in Alcohol, Appendix VI: One mL dissolves in 1 mL of 95% alcohol.
Function: Flavoring agent

IDENTIFICATION
- **INFRARED SPECTRA,** *Spectrophotometric Identification Tests,* Appendix IIIC

  Acceptance criteria: The spectrum of the sample exhibits relative maxima at the same wavelengths as those of the spectrum below.

ASSAY
- **PROCEDURE:** Proceed as directed under *M-1b,* Appendix XI.
  Acceptance criteria: NLT 97.0% of C₁₀H₁₈O₂

SPECIFIC TESTS
- **ACID VALUE, FLAVOR CHEMICALS (OTHER THAN ESSENTIAL OILS),** *M-15,* Appendix XI
  Acceptance criteria: NMT 1.0
- **REFRACTIVE INDEX,** Appendix II: At 20°
  Acceptance criteria: Between 1.426 and 1.430
- **SPECIFIC GRAVITY:** Determine at 25° by any reliable method (see *General Provisions*).
  Acceptance criteria: Between 0.880 and 0.885

OTHER REQUIREMENTS
- **ALLYL ALCOHOL,** *M-1b,* Appendix XI
  Acceptance criteria: NMT 0.1%

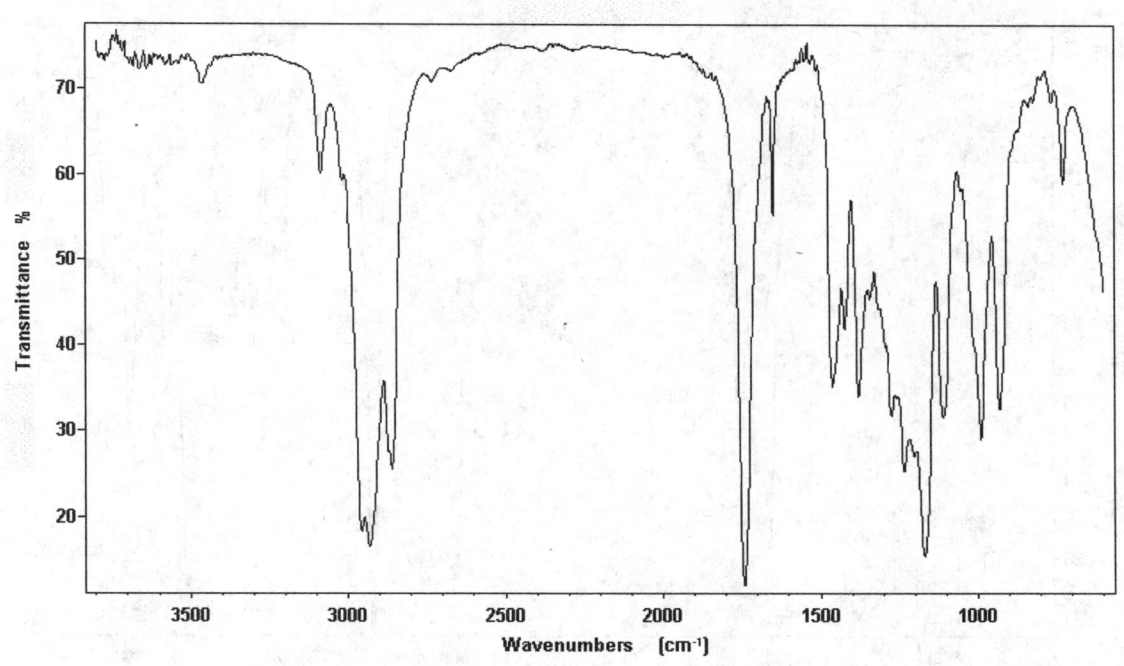

Allyl Heptanoate

Allyl Hexanoate

First Published: Prior to FCC 6

Allyl Caproate

$C_9H_{16}O_2$ Formula wt 156.22
FEMA: 2032
UNII: 3VH84A363D [allyl hexanoate]

DESCRIPTION
Allyl Hexanoate occurs as a colorless to light yellow liquid.
Odor: Strong, pineapple
Solubility: Miscible in alcohol, most fixed oils; insoluble or practically insoluble in propylene glycol, water
Boiling Point: ~185°
Solubility in Alcohol, Appendix VI: One mL dissolves in 6 mL of 70% alcohol.
Function: Flavoring agent

IDENTIFICATION
- **INFRARED SPECTRA,** Spectrophotometric Identification Tests, Appendix IIIC
  Acceptance criteria: The spectrum of the sample exhibits relative maxima at the same wavelengths as those of the spectrum below.

ASSAY
- **PROCEDURE:** Proceed as directed under *M-1b,* Appendix XI.
  Acceptance criteria: NLT 98.0% of $C_9H_{16}O_2$

SPECIFIC TESTS
- **ACID VALUE, FLAVOR CHEMICALS (OTHER THAN ESSENTIAL OILS),** *M-15,* Appendix XI
  Acceptance criteria: NMT 1.0
- **REFRACTIVE INDEX,** Appendix II: At 20°
  Acceptance criteria: Between 1.422 and 1.426
- **SPECIFIC GRAVITY:** Determine at 25° by any reliable method (see *General Provisions*).
  Acceptance criteria: Between 0.884 and 0.890

OTHER REQUIREMENTS
- **ALLYL ALCOHOL,** *M-1b,* Appendix XI
  Acceptance criteria: NMT 0.1%

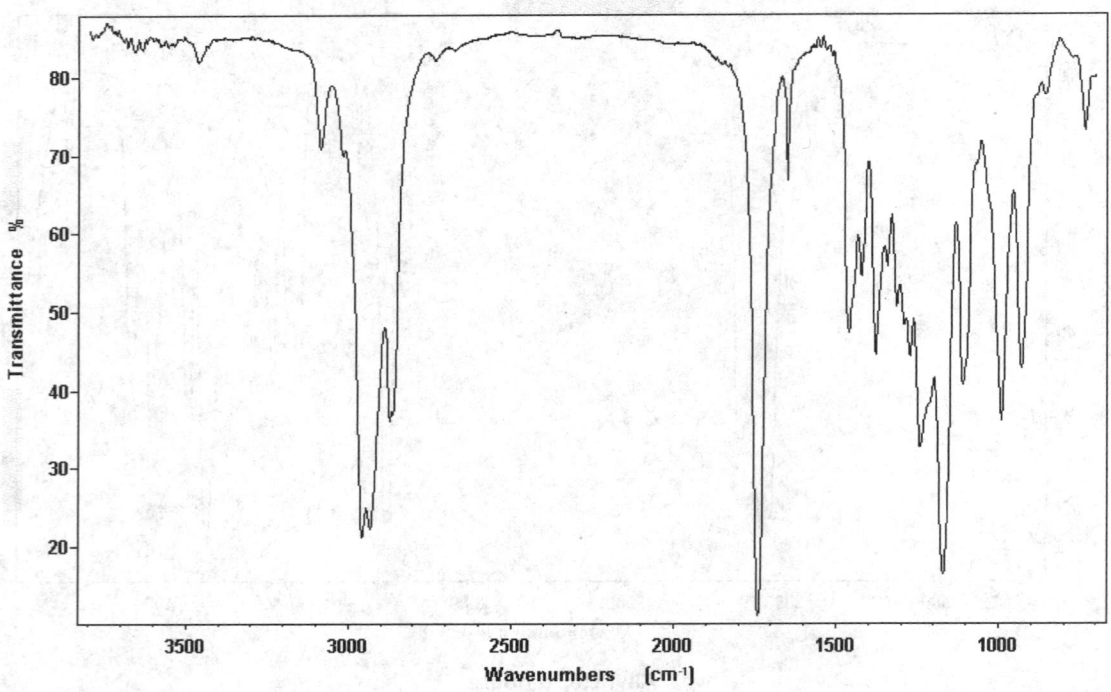

Allyl Hexanoate

Allyl Isothiocyanate

First Published: Prior to FCC 6

C₄H₅NS Formula wt 99.16
FEMA: 2034
UNII: BN34FX42G3 [allyl isothiocyanate]

DESCRIPTION
Allyl Isothiocyanate occurs as a colorless to pale yellow, strongly refractive liquid.
Odor: Irritating, acrid taste, mustard [**Caution**—lachrymator]
Solubility: Miscible in alcohol, carbon disulfide, ether
Boiling Point: ~150°
Function: Flavoring agent

IDENTIFICATION
- **Infrared Spectra,** *Spectrophotometric Identification Tests,* Appendix IIIC
  Acceptance criteria: The spectrum of the sample exhibits relative maxima at the same wavelengths as those of the spectrum below.

ASSAY
- **Procedure:** Proceed as directed under *M-1a,* Appendix XI.
  Acceptance criteria: NLT 93.0% of C₄H₅NS

SPECIFIC TESTS
- **Refractive Index,** Appendix II: At 20°
  Acceptance criteria: Between 1.527 and 1.531
- **Specific Gravity:** Determine at 25° by any reliable method (see *General Provisions*).
  Acceptance criteria: Between 1.013 and 1.020

OTHER REQUIREMENTS
- **Allyl Alcohol,** *M-1b,* Appendix XI
  Acceptance criteria: NMT 0.1%
- **Distillation Range,** Appendix IIB
  Acceptance criteria: Between 148° and 154°
- **Phenols,** *M-17,* Appendix XI
  Acceptance criteria: Passes test

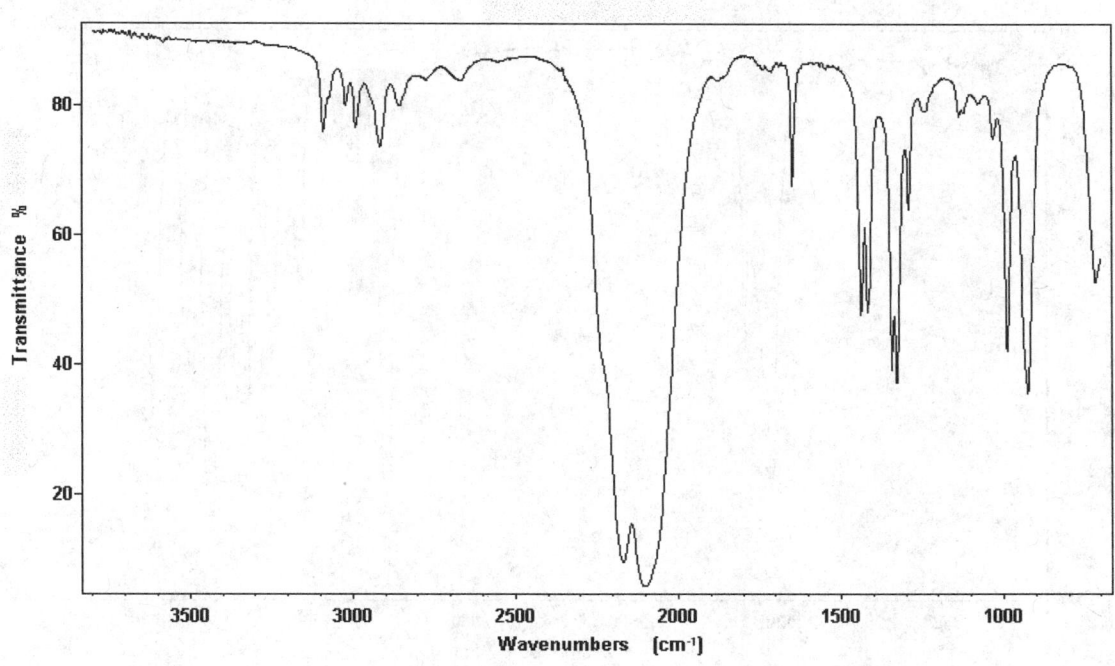

Allyl Isothiocyanate

Allyl Isovalerate

First Published: Prior to FCC 6

Allyl Isopentanoate

C₈H₁₄O₂ Formula wt 142.20
FEMA: 2045
UNII: 3551Z86V7T [allyl isovalerate]

DESCRIPTION
Allyl Isovalerate occurs as a colorless to pale yellow liquid.
Odor: Fruity, apple
Boiling Point: ~155°
Solubility in Alcohol, Appendix VI: One mL dissolves in 1 mL of 95% alcohol.
Function: Flavoring agent

IDENTIFICATION
- **INFRARED SPECTRA,** *Spectrophotometric Identification Tests,* Appendix IIIC

  Acceptance criteria: The spectrum of the sample exhibits relative maxima at the same wavelengths as those of the spectrum below.

ASSAY
- **PROCEDURE:** Proceed as directed under *M-1b,* Appendix XI.
  Acceptance criteria: NLT 98.0% of C₈H₁₄O₂ (one isomer)

SPECIFIC TESTS
- **ACID VALUE, FLAVOR CHEMICALS (OTHER THAN ESSENTIAL OILS),** *M-15,* Appendix XI
  Acceptance criteria: NMT 1.0
- **REFRACTIVE INDEX,** Appendix II: At 20°
  Acceptance criteria: Between 1.413 and 1.418
- **SPECIFIC GRAVITY:** Determine at 25° by any reliable method (see *General Provisions*).
  Acceptance criteria: Between 0.879 and 0.884

OTHER REQUIREMENTS
- **ALLYL ALCOHOL,** *M-1b,* Appendix XI
  Acceptance criteria: NMT 0.1%

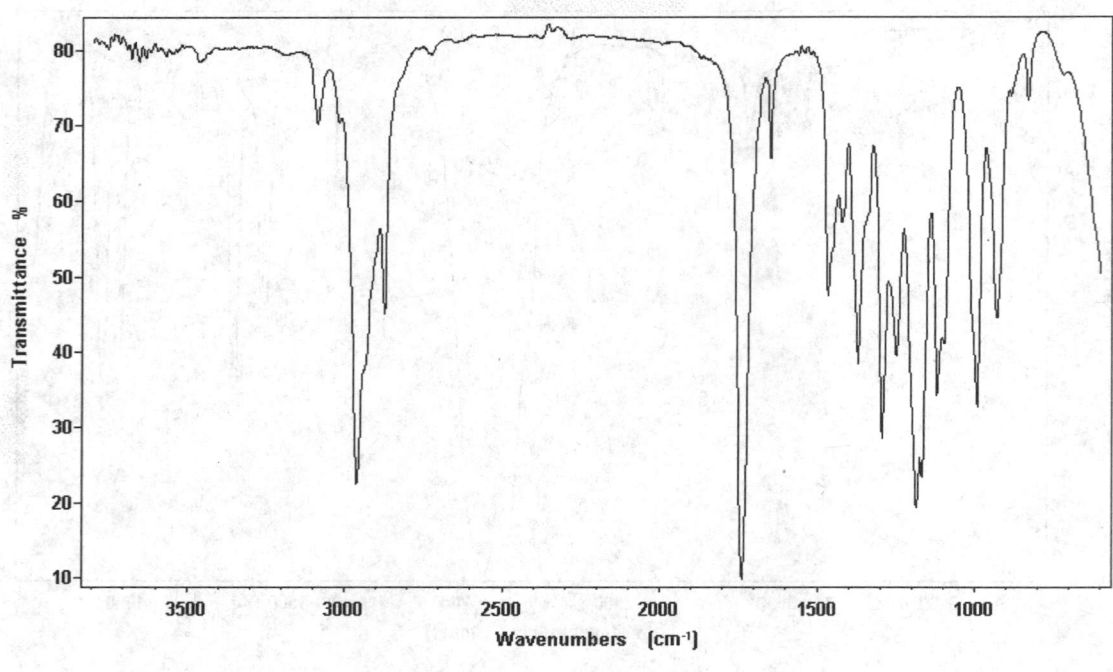

Allyl Isovalerate

Allyl Phenoxy Acetate
First Published: Prior to FCC 6

C₁₁H₁₂O₃ Formula wt 192.21
FEMA: 2038
UNII: Q3P8UAF9WE [allyl phenoxyacetate]

DESCRIPTION
Allyl Phenoxy Acetate occurs as a colorless to pale yellow liquid.
Odor: Honey, pineapple
Solubility: Slightly soluble in propylene glycol; very slightly soluble in water; insoluble or practically insoluble in vegetable oils
Boiling Point: ~265°
Solubility in Alcohol, Appendix VI: One mL dissolves in 1 mL of 95% ethanol.

Function: Flavoring agent

IDENTIFICATION
- **INFRARED SPECTRA,** Spectrophotometric Identification Tests, Appendix IIIC
  Acceptance criteria: The spectrum of the sample exhibits relative maxima at the same wavelengths as those of the spectrum below.

ASSAY
- **PROCEDURE:** Proceed as directed under M-1b, Appendix XI.
  Acceptance criteria: NLT 97.0% of C₁₁H₁₂O₃

SPECIFIC TESTS
- **ACID VALUE, FLAVOR CHEMICALS (OTHER THAN ESSENTIAL OILS),** M-15, Appendix XI
  Acceptance criteria: NMT 1.0
- **REFRACTIVE INDEX,** Appendix II: At 20°
  Acceptance criteria: Between 1.513 and 1.518
- **SPECIFIC GRAVITY:** Determine at 25° by any reliable method (see General Provisions).
  Acceptance criteria: Between 1.100 and 1.105

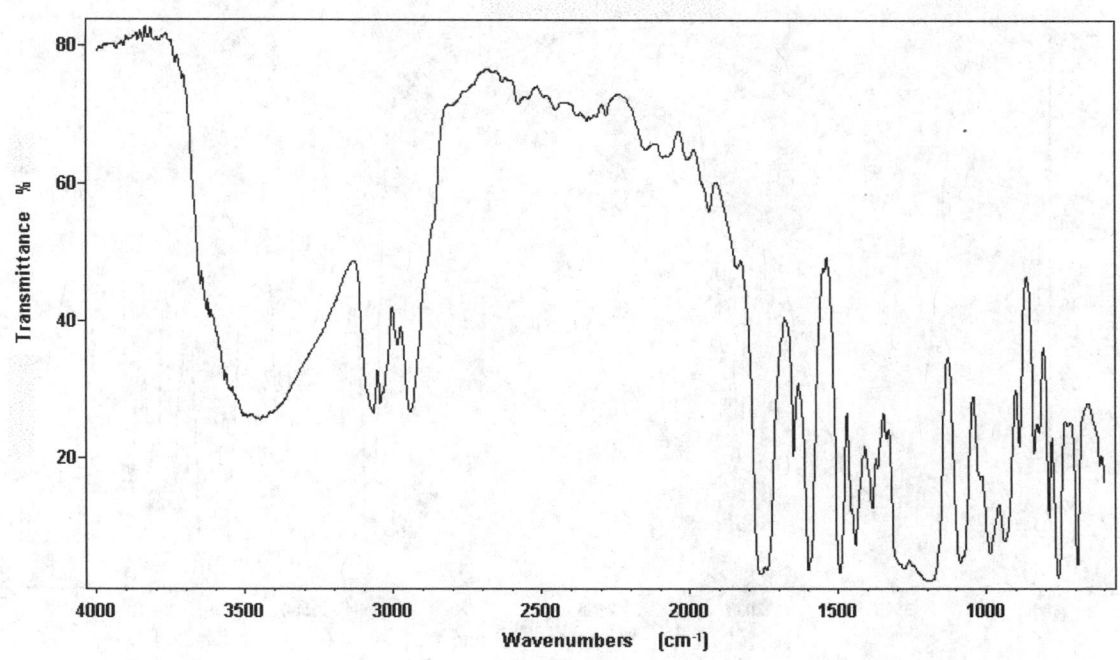

Allyl Phenoxy Acetate

Allyl Propionate

First Published: Prior to FCC 6

$C_6H_{10}O_2$ Formula wt 114.15
FEMA: 2040
UNII: 0OYW8C5029 [allyl propionate]

DESCRIPTION
Allyl Propionate occurs as a colorless to pale yellow liquid.
Odor: Ethereal, fruity
Solubility: Soluble in propylene glycol, vegetable oils; insoluble or practically insoluble in water
Boiling Point: ~124°
Solubility in Alcohol, Appendix VI
 One mL dissolves in 1 mL of 95% ethanol.
Function: Flavoring agent

IDENTIFICATION
- **INFRARED SPECTRA,** *Spectrophotometric Identification Tests,* Appendix IIIC
  Acceptance criteria: The spectrum of the sample exhibits relative maxima at the same wavelengths as those of the spectrum below.

ASSAY
- **PROCEDURE:** Proceed as directed under *M-1b,* Appendix XI.
  Acceptance criteria: NLT 97.0% of $C_6H_{10}O_2$

SPECIFIC TESTS
- **ACID VALUE, FLAVOR CHEMICALS (OTHER THAN ESSENTIAL OILS),** *M-15,* Appendix XI
  Acceptance criteria: NMT 2.0
- **REFRACTIVE INDEX,** Appendix II: At 20°
  Acceptance criteria: Between 1.408 and 1.413
- **SPECIFIC GRAVITY:** Determine at 25° by any reliable method (see *General Provisions*).
  Acceptance criteria: Between 0.912 and 0.917

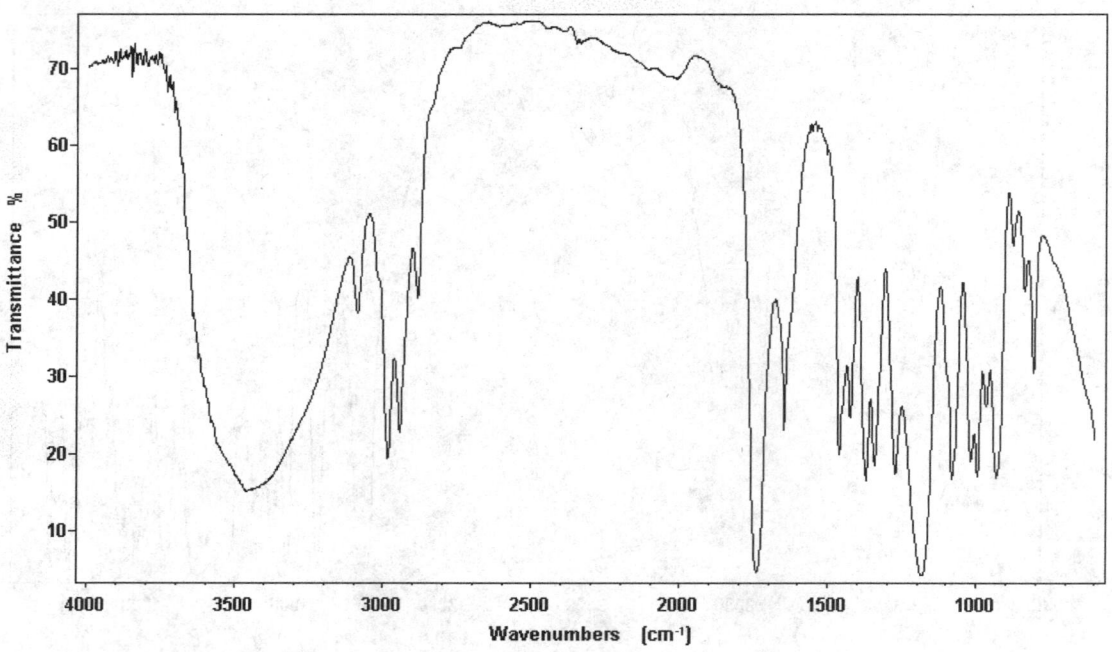

Allyl Propionate

Almond Oil, Bitter, FFPA

First Published: Prior to FCC 6
Last Revision: FCC 6

Bitter Almond Oil Free from Prussic Acid
CAS: [8013-76-1]
UNII: 6TQK77W0EX [bitter almond oil]

DESCRIPTION
Almond Oil, Bitter, FFPA, occurs as a colorless to slightly yellow liquid with a strong almond aroma and a slightly astringent, mild taste. It is a volatile oil obtained from the nuts of the bitter almond tree, *Prunus amygdalus* Batsch var. *amara* (De Candolle) Focke (Fam. Rosaceae), apricot kernel (*Prunus armeniaca* L.), and other fruit kernels containing amygdalin. It is prepared by steam distillation of a water-macerated, powdered, and pressed cake that has been specially treated and redistilled to remove hydrocyanic acid. It is soluble in most fixed oils and in propylene glycol, slightly soluble in mineral oil, and insoluble in glycerin.
Function: Flavoring agent
Packaging and Storage: Store in a cool place protected from light in full, tight containers that are made from steel or aluminum and that are suitably lined.

IDENTIFICATION
- **INFRARED SPECTRA,** *Spectrophotometric Identification Tests,* Appendix IIIC
  Acceptance criteria: The spectrum of the sample exhibits relative maxima at the same wavelengths as those of the spectrum below.

ASSAY
- **ALDEHYDES,** Appendix VI
  Sample: 1 mL
  Analysis: Use 53.05 for the equivalence factor (*e*) in the calculation.
  Acceptance criteria: NLT 95.0% of aldehydes, calculated as benzaldehyde (C_7H_6O)

SPECIFIC TESTS
- **ACID VALUE (ESSENTIAL OILS AND FLAVORS),** Appendix VI
  Acceptance criteria: NMT 8.0
- **CHLORINATED COMPOUNDS,** Appendix VI
  Acceptance criteria: Passes test
- **HYDROCYANIC ACID**
  Sample: 1 mL
  Analysis: Transfer the *Sample* into a test tube and add 1 mL of water, 5 drops of a 100 mg/mL sodium hydroxide solution, and 5 drops of a 100 mg/mL solution of ferrous sulfate solution. Shake the test tube thoroughly, and acidify with 0.5 N hydrochloric acid.
  Acceptance criteria: No blue precipitate or color appears. (about 0.015%)
- **OPTICAL (SPECIFIC) ROTATION,** Appendix IIB: Use a 100 mm tube.
  Acceptance criteria: Optically inactive, or NMT ±0.15°
- **REFRACTIVE INDEX,** Appendix IIB
  [NOTE—Use an Abbé or other refractometer of equal or greater accuracy.]
  Acceptance criteria: Between 1.541 and 1.546 at 20°
- **SOLUBILITY IN ALCOHOL,** Appendix VI
  Acceptance criteria: One mL of sample dissolves in 2 mL of 70% alcohol to form a clear solution.

- **SPECIFIC GRAVITY:** Determine by any reliable method (see *General Provisions*).

Acceptance criteria: Between 1.040 and 1.050

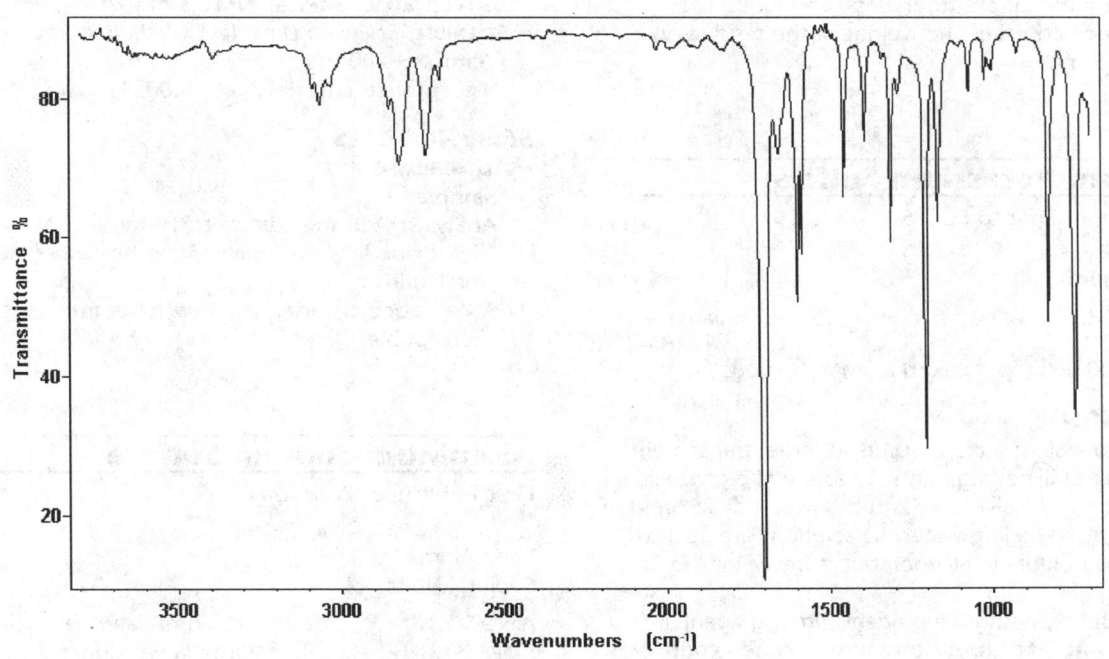

Almond Oil, Bitter, FFPA

Aluminum Ammonium Sulfate
First Published: Prior to FCC 6

Ammonium Alum

AlNH₄(SO₄)₂·12H₂O
INS: 523
UNII: 5C36DRL9ZN [ammonium alum]

Formula wt 453.32
CAS: [7784-25-0]

DESCRIPTION
Aluminum Ammonium Sulfate occurs as large, colorless crystals, white granules, or a powder. One g dissolves in 7 mL of water at 25° and in about 0.3 mL of boiling water. Its solutions are acid to litmus. It is insoluble in alcohol, and is freely, but slowly, soluble in glycerin.
Function: Buffer; neutralizing agent
Packaging and Storage: Store in well-closed containers.

IDENTIFICATION
- **ALUMINUM,** Appendix IIIA
  Sample solution: 50 mg/mL
  Acceptance criteria: Passes tests
- **AMMONIUM,** Appendix IIIA
  Sample solution: 50 mg/mL
  Acceptance criteria: Passes test
- **SULFATE,** Appendix IIIA
  Sample solution: 50 mg/mL
  Acceptance criteria: Passes tests

ASSAY
- **PROCEDURE**
  Sample: 1 g
  pH 4.5 Buffer solution: 77.1 g of ammonium acetate and 57 mL of glacial acetic acid diluted to 1000 mL
  Analysis: Dissolve the *Sample* in 50 mL of water, add 50.0 mL of 0.05 M disodium EDTA and 20 mL of *pH 4.5 Buffer solution,* and boil gently for 5 min. Cool and add 50 mL of alcohol and 2 mL of dithizone TS. Back titrate with 0.05 M zinc sulfate to a bright rose-pink color. Perform a blank determination (see *General Provisions*) and make any necessary correction. The volume of 0.05 M disodium EDTA consumed (in mL) is equivalent to 50 minus the mL of 0.05 M zinc sulfate used. Each mL of 0.05 M disodium EDTA consumed is equivalent to 22.67 mg of AlNH₄(SO₄)₂·12H₂O.
  Acceptance criteria: NLT 99.5% and NMT 100.5% of AlNH₄(SO₄)₂·12H₂O

IMPURITIES
Inorganic Impurities
- **FLUORIDE,** *Fluoride Limit Test, Method V,* Appendix IIIB
  Acceptance criteria: NMT 0.003%
- **LEAD,** *Lead Limit Test, APDC Extraction Method,* Appendix IIIB
  Acceptance criteria: NMT 3 mg/kg
- **SELENIUM,** *Selenium Limit Test, Method II,* Appendix IIIB
  Sample: 200 mg
  Acceptance criteria: NMT 0.003%

SPECIFIC TESTS
- **ALKALIES AND ALKALINE EARTHS**
  Sample: 1 g
  Analysis: Completely precipitate the aluminum from a boiling solution of the *Sample* in 100 mL of water by

46 / Aluminum Ammonium Sulfate / *Monographs*

adding enough 6 N ammonium hydroxide to render the solution distinctly alkaline to methyl red TS. Filter, evaporate the filtrate to dryness, and ignite.
Acceptance criteria: The weight of the residue does not exceed 5 mg.

Aluminum Potassium Sulfate

First Published: Prior to FCC 6

Potassium Alum

AlK(SO$_4$)$_2$·12H$_2$O Formula wt 474.38
INS: 522 CAS: [7784-24-9]
UNII: 09OXB01F3O [potassium alum anhydrous]

DESCRIPTION
Aluminum Potassium Sulfate occurs as large, transparent crystals or crystalline fragments, or as a white crystalline powder. One g dissolves in 7.5 mL of water at 25° and in about 0.3 mL of boiling water. Its solutions are acid to litmus. It is insoluble in alcohol, but is freely soluble in glycerin.
Function: Buffer; neutralizing agent; firming agent
Packaging and Storage: Store in well-closed containers.

IDENTIFICATION
- **ALUMINUM,** Appendix IIIA
  Sample solution: 50 mg/mL
  Acceptance criteria: Passes test
- **POTASSIUM,** Appendix IIIA
  Sample solution: 50 mg/mL
  Acceptance criteria: Passes tests
- **SULFATE,** Appendix IIIA
  Sample solution: 50 mg/mL
  Acceptance criteria: Passes tests

ASSAY
- **PROCEDURE**
  Sample: 1 g
  pH 4.5 Buffer solution: 77.1 g of ammonium acetate and 57 mL of glacial acetic acid diluted to 1000 mL.
  Analysis: Dissolve the *Sample* in 50 mL of water, add 50.0 mL of 0.05 M disodium EDTA and 20 mL of *pH 4.5 Buffer solution* and boil gently for 5 min. Cool and add 50 mL of alcohol and 2 mL of dithizone TS. Back titrate with 0.05 M zinc sulfate to a bright rose-pink color. Perform a blank determination (see *General Provisions*) and make any necessary correction. The volume of 0.05 M disodium EDTA consumed (in mL) is equivalent to 50 minus the mL of 0.05 M zinc sulfate used. Each mL of 0.05 M disodium EDTA consumed is equivalent to 23.72 mg of AlK(SO$_4$)$_2$·12H$_2$O.
  Acceptance criteria: NLT 99.5% and NMT 100.5% of AlK(SO$_4$)$_2$·12H$_2$O

IMPURITIES
Inorganic Impurities
- **FLUORIDE,** *Fluoride Limit Test, Method V,* Appendix IIIB
  Acceptance criteria: NMT 0.003%

- **LEAD,** *Lead Limit Test, APDC Extraction Method,* Appendix IIIB
  Acceptance criteria: NMT 3 mg/kg
- **SELENIUM,** *Selenium Limit Test, Method II,* Appendix IIIB
  Sample: 200 mg
  Acceptance criteria: NMT 0.003%

SPECIFIC TESTS
- **AMMONIUM SALTS**
  Sample: 1 g
  Analysis: Add the *Sample* to 10 mL of 1 N sodium hydroxide in a small baker, and heat on a steam bath for 1 min.
  Acceptance criteria: The odor of ammonia is not perceptible.

Aluminum Sodium Sulfate

First Published: Prior to FCC 6

Soda Alum
Sodium Alum

AlNa(SO$_4$)$_2$ Formula wt, anhydrous 242.09
AlNa(SO$_4$)$_2$·12H$_2$O Formula wt, dodecahydrate 458.29
INS: 521 CAS: anhydrous [10102-71-3]
  dodecahydrate [7784-28-3]
UNII: 0CM6A697VV [aluminum sodium sulfate]

DESCRIPTION
Aluminum Sodium Sulfate occurs as colorless crystals, white granules, or a powder. It is anhydrous or may contain up to 12 molecules of water of hydration. The anhydrous form is slowly soluble in water. The dodecahydrate is freely soluble in water, and it effloresces in air. Both forms are insoluble in alcohol.
Function: Buffer; neutralizing agent; firming agent
Packaging and Storage: Store in tight containers.

IDENTIFICATION
- **SODIUM,** Appendix IIIA
  Acceptance criteria: A sample passes the flame test.
- **ALUMINUM,** Appendix IIIA
  Acceptance criteria: Passes test
- **SULFATE,** Appendix IIIA
  Acceptance criteria: Passes tests

ASSAY
- **PROCEDURE**
  Sample: 500 mg, previously dried
  pH 4.5 Buffer solution: 77.1 g of ammonium acetate and 57 mL of glacial acetic acid diluted to 1000 mL
  Analysis: Moisten the *Sample* with 1 mL of glacial acetic acid and dissolve in 50 mL of water, warming gently on a steam bath until dissolution is complete. Cool, neutralize with 6 N ammonium hydroxide, add 50.0 mL of 0.05 M disodium EDTA and 20 mL of *pH 4.5 Buffer solution,* and boil gently for 5 min. Cool, and add 50 mL of alcohol and 2 mL of dithizone TS. Back titrate with 0.05 M zinc sulfate to a bright rose-pink color. Perform a blank determination (see *General Provisions*)

and make any necessary correction. The volume of 0.05 M disodium EDTA consumed (in mL) is equivalent to 50 minus the mL of 0.05 M zinc sulfate used. Each mL of 0.05 M disodium EDTA consumed is equivalent to 12.10 mg of $AlNa(SO_4)_2$.

Acceptance criteria
Anhydrous: NLT 99.0% and NMT 104.0% of $AlNa(SO_4)_2$, on the dried basis
Dodecahydrate: NLT 99.5% of $AlNa(SO_4)_2$, on the dried basis

IMPURITIES
Inorganic Impurities
- **FLUORIDE,** *Fluoride Limit Test, Method V,* Appendix IIIB
  Sample: 1.76 g
  Acceptance criteria: NMT 0.003%
- **LEAD,** *Lead Limit Test, APDC Extraction Method,* Appendix IIIB
  Acceptance criteria: NMT 3 mg/kg
- **SELENIUM,** *Selenium Limit Test, Method II,* Appendix IIIB
  Sample: 200 mg
  Acceptance criteria: NMT 0.003%

SPECIFIC TESTS
- **AMMONIUM SALTS**
  Sample: 1 g
  Analysis: Heat the *Sample* with 10 mL of 1 N sodium hydroxide on a steam bath for 1 min.
  Acceptance criteria: The odor of ammonia is not perceptible.
- **LOSS ON DRYING,** Appendix IIC Anhydrous: 200° for 16 h; Dodecahydrate: 50° to 55° for 1 h, then 200° for 16 h
  Acceptance criteria
  Anhydrous: NMT 10%
  Dodecahydrate: NMT 47.2%
- **NEUTRALIZING VALUE**
  Sample: 500 mg (anhydrous)
  Analysis: Transfer the *Sample* into a 200-mL Erlenmeyer flask, add 30 mL of water and 4 drops of phenolphthalein TS, and boil until the *Sample* dissolves. Add 13.0 mL of 0.5 N sodium hydroxide, boil for a few seconds, and titrate with 0.5 N hydrochloric acid to the disappearance of the pink color, adding the acid dropwise and agitating vigorously after each addition. Calculate the neutralizing value, as parts of $NaHCO_3$ equivalent to 100 parts of the *Sample* by the formula:

  $$Result = 8.4V$$

  V = volume (mL) of 0.5 N sodium hydroxide consumed by the sample
  Acceptance criteria
  Anhydrous: Between 104 and 108

Aluminum Sulfate
First Published: Prior to FCC 6

$Al_2(SO_4)_3$ Formula wt, anhydrous 342.14
$Al_2(SO_4)_3 \cdot 18H_2O$ Formula wt, octadecahydrate 666.41
INS: 520   CAS: anhydrous [10043-01-3]
    octadecahydrate [7784-31-8]
UNII: 34S289N54E [aluminum sulfate]

DESCRIPTION
Aluminum Sulfate occurs as a white powder, as shining plates, or as crystalline fragments. It is anhydrous or contains 18 molecules of water of crystallization. Because of efflorescence, the hydrate may have a composition approximating the formula $Al_2(SO_4)_3 \cdot 14H_2O$. One g of the hydrate dissolves in about 2 mL of water. The anhydrous approaches the same solubility, but the rate of solution is so slow that it initially appears to be relatively insoluble. The pH of a 1 : 20 aqueous solution is 2.9 or above.
Function: Firming agent
Packaging and Storage: Store in well-closed containers.

IDENTIFICATION
- **ALUMINUM,** Appendix IIIA
  Sample solution: 100 mg/mL
  Acceptance criteria: Passes test
- **SULFATE,** Appendix IIIA
  Sample solution: 100 mg/mL
  Acceptance criteria: Passes tests

ASSAY
- **PROCEDURE**
  Sample solution: Transfer an amount of sample equivalent to 4 g of $Al_2(SO_4)_3$ into a 250-mL volumetric flask, dissolve in and dilute to volume with water, and mix.
  pH 4.5 Buffer solution: 77.1 g of ammonium acetate and 57 mL of glacial acetic acid diluted to 1000 mL
  Analysis: Pipet 10 mL of the *Sample solution* into a 250-mL beaker, add 25.0 mL of 0.05 M disodium EDTA and 20 mL of *pH 4.5 Buffer solution,* and boil gently for 5 min. Cool and add 50 mL of alcohol and 2 mL of dithizone TS. Back titrate with 0.05 M zinc sulfate to a bright rose-pink color. Perform a blank determination (see *General Provisions*) and make any necessary correction. The volume of 0.05 M disodium EDTA consumed (in mL) is equivalent to 50 minus the mL of 0.05 M zinc sulfate used. Each mL of 0.05 M disodium EDTA consumed is equivalent to 8.5540 mg of $Al_2(SO_4)_3$ or to 16.66 mg of $Al_2(SO_4)_3 \cdot 18H_2O$.
  Acceptance criteria
  Anhydrous: NLT 99.5% of $Al_2(SO_4)_3$, calculated on the ignited basis
  Octadecahydrate: NLT 99.5% and NMT 114.0% of $Al_2(SO_4)_3 \cdot 18H_2O$, corresponding to NMT approximately 101.7% of $Al_2(SO_4)_3 \cdot 14H_2O$

IMPURITIES
Inorganic Impurities
- **FLUORIDE,** *Fluoride Limit Test, Method V,* Appendix IIIB
  Sample: 1.67 g

48 / Aluminum Sulfate / *Monographs*

  Acceptance criteria: NMT 0.003%
- **LEAD**, *Lead Limit Test, APDC Extraction Method,* Appendix IIIB
  Acceptance criteria: NMT 3 mg/kg
- **SELENIUM**, *Selenium Limit Test, Method II,* Appendix IIIB
  Sample: 200 mg
  Acceptance criteria: NMT 0.003%

SPECIFIC TESTS
- **ALKALIES AND ALKALINE EARTHS**
  Sample: 2 g
  Analysis: Add a few drops of methyl red TS to a boiling solution of the *Sample* in 150 mL of water, then add 6 N ammonium hydroxide until the color of the solution just changes to a distinct yellow. Add hot water to restore the original volume and filter while hot. Evaporate 75 mL of the filtrate to dryness and ignite to constant weight.
  Acceptance criteria: The weight of the residue does not exceed 4 mg. (NMT about 0.4%)
- **AMMONIUM SALTS**
  Sample: 1 g
  Analysis: Heat the *Sample* with 10 mL of 1 N sodium hydroxide on a steam bath for 1 min.
  Acceptance criteria: The odor of ammonia is not perceptible.
- **LOSS ON IGNITION**
  [NOTE—This test does not apply to $Al_2(SO_4)_3 \cdot 18H_2O$.]
  Sample: 2 g
  Analysis: Ignite the *Sample,* preferably in a muffle furnace, at about 500° for 3 h.
  Acceptance criteria
  Anhydrous: NMT 5%

Add the following:

▲Amaranth[1]
First Published: FCC 8

CI Food Red 9
Naphthol Rot S
CI No. 16185
Class: Mono-Azo
Trisodium 3-hydroxy-4-(4-sulfonato-1-naphthylazo)-2,7-naphthalenedisulfonate

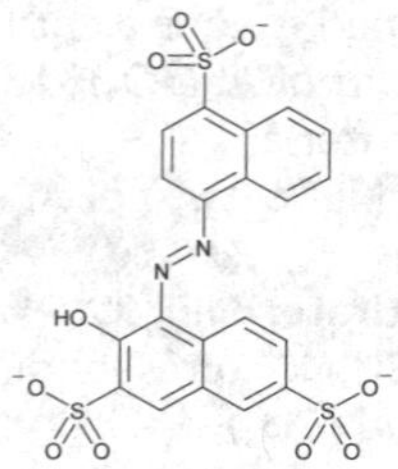

$C_{20}H_{11}N_2Na_3O_{10}S_3$ Formula wt 604.48

---
[1] Amaranth is approved for use in some countries but banned in others, such as the United States.

INS: 123   CAS: [915-67-3]
UNII: 7RBV3X49K [amaranth]

DESCRIPTION
Amaranth occurs as reddish brown to dark reddish brown powder or granules. It is principally the trisodium salt of 3-hydroxy-4-(4-sulfonato-1-naphthylazo)-2,7-naphthalenedisulfonate and subsidiary coloring matters together with sodium chloride and/or sodium sulfate as the principal uncolored components. It is soluble in water and sparingly soluble in ethanol.
Function: Color
Packaging and Storage: Store in well-closed containers.

IDENTIFICATION
- **VISIBLE ABSORPTION SPECTRUM**
  Sample solution: Dissolve a sample in water, and dilute appropriately.
  Analysis: Measure the absorption spectrum of the *Sample solution* using a suitable UV-visible spectrophotometer.
  Acceptance criteria: The *Sample solution* exhibits a wavelength maximum at 520 nm.

ASSAY
- **TOTAL COLOR**, *Color Determination, Methods I and II,* Appendix IIIC: Both methods must be used.
  Method I: (Spectrophotometric)
  Sample solution: 10 mg/mL
  Analysis: Determine as directed at 520 nm using 0.044 L/(mg · cm) for the absorptivity (*a*) for amaranth.
  Method II: ($TiCl_3$ Titration)
  Sample: 0.7–0.8 g
  Analysis: Determine as directed, except in the *Procedure* use 10 g of sodium citrate instead of 21–22 g of *Sodium Bitartrate* and use 150 mL of water instead of 275 mL. For the calculation, use 6.618 as the stoichiometric factor (F_S) for the trisodium salt of Amaranth.
  Acceptance criteria: The average of results obtained from *Method I* and *Method II* is NLT 85% total coloring matters.

IMPURITIES
Inorganic Impurities
- **LEAD**, *Lead Limit Test,* Appendix IIIB
  Sample solution: Prepare as directed for organic compounds.
  Control: 2 μg Pb (2 mL of *Diluted Standard Lead Solution*)
  Acceptance criteria: NMT 2 mg/kg

Organic Impurities
- **UNCOMBINED INTERMEDIATES AND PRODUCTS OF SIDE REACTIONS**
  Solution A: 0.2 N ammonium acetate
  Solution B: Methanol
  Mobile phase: See the gradient table below.

Time (min)	Solution A (%)	Solution B (%)	Comments
0	98	2	Analysis
24.5	0	100	Wash

Time (min)	Solution A (%)	Solution B (%)	Comments
30.5	0	100	Return to initial gradient and column equilibration
44.5	100	0	

Sample solution: 5 mg/mL in 0.02 M ammonium acetate

Standard solution: 25 μg/mL 4-amino-1-naphthalenesulfonic acid, 25 μg/mL 7-hydroxy-1,3-naphthalenedisulfonic acid, 25 μg/mL 3-hydroxy-2,7-naphthalenedisulfonic acid, 25 μg/mL 6-hydroxy-2-naphthalenesulfonic acid, 25 μg/mL 7-hydroxy-1,3,6-naphthalenetrisulfonic acid in 0.02 M ammonium acetate

Chromatographic system, Appendix IIA
 Mode: High-performance liquid chromatography
 Detector: UV-Vis
 Column: 25-cm × 4.6-mm C18 analytical column (5-μm), with a 15-mm × 4.6-mm C18 guard column (5-μm)
 Column temperature: Ambient
 Flow rate: 1.0 mL/min
 Injection volume: 20 μL

Analysis: Separately inject equal volumes of the *Standard solution* and *Sample solution* into the chromatograph, and measure the responses for the major peaks on the resulting chromatograms.

Calculate the percentages of all impurities (4-amino-1-naphthalenesulfonic acid, 7-hydroxy-1,3-naphthalenedisulfonic acid, 3-hydroxy-2,7-naphthalenedisulfonic acid, 6-hydroxy-2-naphthalenesulfonic acid, and 7-hydroxy-1,3,6-naphthalenetrisulfonic acid) in the sample taken:

$$\text{Result} = (r_U/r_S) \times (C_S/C_U) \times F \times 100$$

r_U = peak area for analyte in the *Sample solution*
r_S = peak area for analyte in the *Standard solution*
C_S = concentration of analyte in the *Standard solution* (μg/mL)
C_U = concentration of sample in the *Sample solution* (mg/mL)
F = mg-to-μg conversion factor, 1000

Acceptance criteria: NMT 0.5% for all five impurities combined

SPECIFIC TESTS

- **COMBINED TESTS**
  Tests
  - LOSS ON DRYING (VOLATILE MATTER), *Color Determination*, Appendix IIIC
  - CHLORIDE, *Sodium Chloride, Color Determination*, Appendix IIIC
  - SULFATES (AS SODIUM SALTS), *Sodium Sulfate, Color Determination*, Appendix IIIC

  Acceptance criteria: NMT 15%, combined as the sum of all three tests

- **ETHER EXTRACTS**, *Color Determination*, Appendix IIIC
  Acceptance criteria: NMT 0.2%

- **SUBSIDIARY COLORING MATTERS**
  [NOTE—In this method, subsidiary coloring matters are separated from the main coloring matter of Amaranth by ascending paper chromatography (see *Paper Chromatography*, Appendix IIA), and extracted separately from the chromatographic paper. The absorbance of each extract is measured at the wavelength of maximum absorption for Amaranth (520 nm) by visible spectrophotometry. Because it is impractical to identify each subsidiary coloring matter using this procedure, and because the subsidiary coloring matters are usually minor components of food colors, the method assumes that the maximum absorbance of each subsidiary coloring matter is the same as that of the total coloring matters. The subsidiary color matters content is calculated by adding together the absorbances of the extracts in conjunction with the total coloring matters content of the sample.]

  Chromatographic apparatus: The chromatography tank (*Figures 1* and *2*) is comprised of a glass tank (A) and cover (B); frame to support chromatography paper (C); solvent tray (D); secondary frame (E) for supporting "drapes" of the filter paper; and 20-cm × 20-cm chromatography grade paper.[2] Mark out the chromatography paper as shown in *Figure 3*.

---

[2] Whatman No 1, or equivalent.

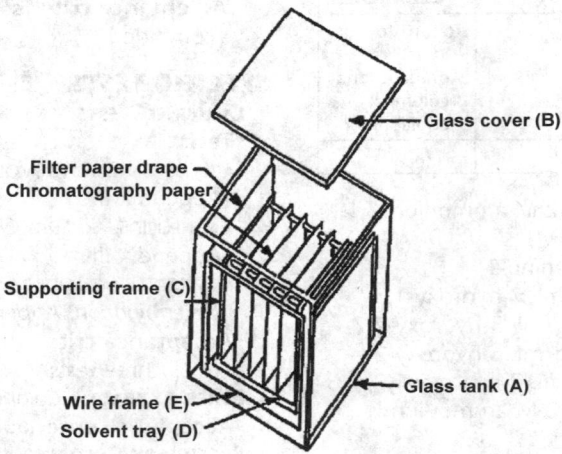

Figure 1. Assembly of the Chromatographic Apparatus

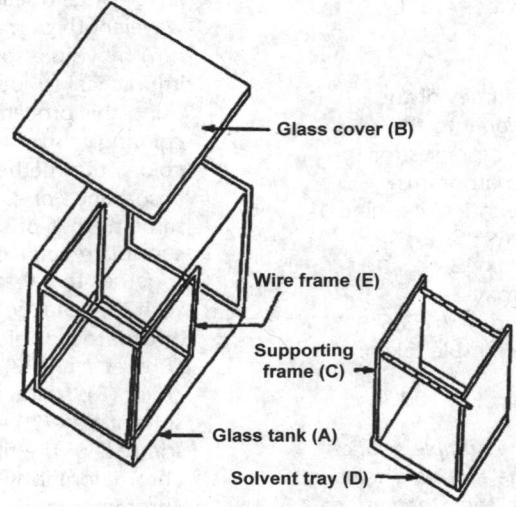

Figure 2. Components of the Chromatographic Apparatus

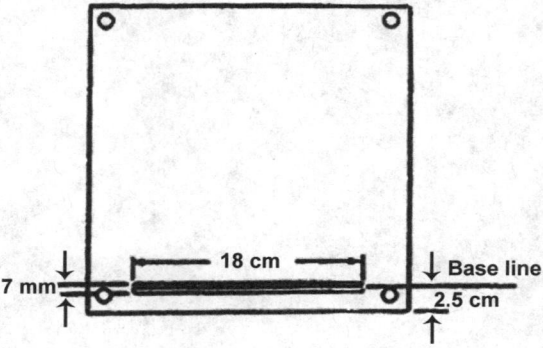

Figure 3. Method for Marking the Chromatographic Paper

Chromatographic solvent: Prepare a mixture of 2-butanone, acetone, and water (7:3:3). Shake for 2 min, allow the layers to separate, and use the upper layer as the chromatographic solvent.
Sample solution: 10 mg/mL sample
Standard solution: 0.3 mg/mL sample prepared by diluting the *Sample solution*
Application volume: 0.10 mL
Analysis: NLT 2 h before analysis, arrange the filter-paper drapes in the glass tank, and pour sufficient *Chromatographic solvent* over the drapes and into the bottom of the tank to cover the bottom of the tank to a depth of 1 cm. Place the solvent tray in position, and fit the cover to the tank. Using a microsyringe capable of delivering 0.1 mL with a tolerance of ±0.002 mL, apply to separate chromatography sheets 0.1-mL aliquots of the *Sample solution* and *Standard solution*, as uniformly as possible within the confines of the 18-cm × 7-mm rectangle, holding the nozzle of the microsyringe steadily in contact with the paper. Allow the papers to dry at room temperature for 1–2 h or at 50° in a drying cabinet for 5 min followed by 15 min at room temperature. Mount the dried sheets, together with two plain sheets to act as blanks on the supporting frame. [NOTE—If required, several dried sheets may be developed simultaneously.]

Pour sufficient *Chromatographic solvent* into the solvent tray to bring the surface of the solvent about 1 cm below the base line of the chromatography sheets. The volume necessary will depend on the dimensions of the apparatus and should be predetermined. Put the supporting frame into position, and replace the cover. Allow the solvent front to ascend approximately 17 cm above baseline, and then allow for 1 h of further development. Remove the supporting frame and transfer it to a drying cabinet at 50°–60° for 10–15 min. Remove the sheets from the frame.

For the *Sample solution* sheets, cut each subsidiary band from each chromatogram sheet as a strip, and cut an equivalent strip from the corresponding position of the plain (blank) sheet. For the *Standard solution* sheet, cut the entire band from the sheet, and cut an equivalent strip from the corresponding position of the plain (blank) sheet. Place each strip, subdivided into a suitable number of approximately equal portions, in a separate test tube. Add 5.0 mL of a mixture of water and acetone (1:1 by vol) to each test tube, swirl for 2–3 min, add 15.0 mL of 0.05 N sodium hydrogen carbonate solution, and shake the tube to ensure mixing. Filter the colored extracts and blanks through 9-cm coarse porosity filter papers into clean test tubes, and determine the absorbances of the colored extracts at 520 nm using a suitable spectrophotometer with 40-mm closed cells against a filtered mixture of 5.0 mL of a mixture of water and acetone (1:1 by vol) and 15.0 mL of the 0.05 N sodium hydrogen carbonate solution. Measure the absorbances of the extracts of the blank strips at 520 nm, and correct the absorbances of the colored extracts with the blank values. Calculate the percent subsidiary coloring matter in the portion of the sample taken:

$$\text{Result} = 0.03 \times D \times [(A_a + A_b + A_c \ldots A_n)/A_s] \times 100$$

0.03 = dilution factor for the *Standard solution*
D = total coloring matter content of the sample, determined from the *Total Color* test above and expressed as a decimal
A_s = absorbance from the *Standard solution*

$A_a + A_b + A_c \ldots A_n$ = sum of the absorbances of the subsidiary coloring matters from the *Sample solution*, corrected for the blank values

Acceptance criteria: NMT 3%

- **UNSULFONATED PRIMARY AROMATIC AMINES**
[NOTE—Under the conditions of this test, unsulfonated primary aromatic amines are extracted into toluene from an alkaline solution of the sample, re-extracted into acid, and then determined spectrophotometrically after diazotization and coupling.]
R salt solution: 0.05 N 2-naphthol-3,6-disulfonic acid, disodium salt
Sodium carbonate solution: 2 N sodium carbonate
Standard stock solution: Weigh 0.100 g of redistilled aniline into a small beaker, and transfer to a 100-mL volumetric flask, rinsing the beaker several times with water. Add 30 mL of 3 N hydrochloric acid, and dilute to the mark with water at room temperature. Dilute 10.0 mL of this solution with water to 100 mL, and mix well; 1 mL of this solution is equivalent to 0.0001 g of aniline. [NOTE—Prepare the *Standard stock solution* fresh.]
Standard solutions: Separately dilute 5-, 10-, 15-, 20-, and 25-mL aliquots of the *Standard stock solution* with 1 N hydrochloric acid to 100 mL.
Standard blank solution: In a 25-mL volumetric flask mix 10.0 mL of 1 N hydrochloric acid, 10.0 mL of *Sodium carbonate solution*, 2.0 mL of *R salt solution*, and dilute with water to volume.
Sample solution: Add 2.0 g of the sample into a separatory funnel containing 100 mL of water, rinse down the sides of the funnel with 50 mL of water, swirling to dissolve the sample, and add 5 mL of 1 N sodium hydroxide. Extract with two 50-mL portions of toluene, and wash the combined toluene extracts with 10-mL portions of 0.1 N sodium hydroxide to remove traces of color. Extract the washed toluene with three 10-mL portions of 3 N hydrochloric acid, and dilute the combined extract with water to 100 mL.
Sample blank solution: In a 25-mL volumetric flask mix 10.0 mL of the *Sample solution*, 10 mL of *Sodium carbonate solution*, and 2.0 mL of *R salt solution*, and dilute with water to volume.
Analysis: Pipet 10-mL aliquots of the *Sample solution* and each of the *Standard solutions* into separate, clean dry test tubes. Cool the tubes for 10 min by immersion in a beaker of ice water, add 1 mL of 50% potassium bromide solution and 0.05 mL of 0.5 N sodium nitrite

solution. Mix, and allow the tubes to stand for 10 min in the ice water bath while the aniline is diazotized. Into each of five 25-mL volumetric flasks, measure 1 mL of *R salt solution* and 10 mL of *Sodium carbonate solution*. Separately pour each diazotized aniline solution into a 25-mL volumetric flask containing *R salt solution* and *Sodium carbonate solution*; rinse each test tube with a small volume of water to allow for a quantitative transfer. Dilute to the mark with water, stopper the flasks, mix the contents well, and allow them to stand for 15 min in the dark.

Measure the absorbance of each of the solutions containing the coupled *Standard solutions* at 510 nm using a suitable spectrophotometer with 40-mm cells against the *Standard blank solution*. Plot a standard curve relating absorbance to weight (g) of aniline in each 100 mL of the *Standard solutions*.

Measure the absorbance of the solutions containing the coupled *Sample solution* at 510 nm using a suitable spectrophotometer with 40-mm cells against the *Sample blank solution*. From the standard curve, determine the weight (g) of aniline in each 100 mL of the *Sample solution*.

Calculate the percent unsulfonated primary aromatic amine (as aniline) in the portion of the sample taken:

$$\text{Result} = W_A/W \times 100$$

W_A = weight of aniline in the *Sample solution* calculated from the standard curve (g/100 mL)

W = weight of sample used to prepare the *Sample solution* (g)

Acceptance criteria: NMT 0.01%, calculated as aniline
- **WATER-INSOLUBLE MATTER**, *Color Determination*, Appendix IIIC
  Acceptance criteria: NMT 0.2%▲FCC8

Ambrette Seed Oil

First Published: Prior to FCC 6

Ambrette Seed Liquid

CAS: [8015-62-1]

UNII: YC79BB3F4Y [ambrette seed oil]

DESCRIPTION
Ambrette Seed Oil occurs as a clear yellow to amber liquid with the strong, musky odor of ambrettolide. It is a volatile oil obtained by steam distillation from the partially dried and crushed seeds of the plant *Abelmoschus moschatus* Moench, syn. *Hibiscus abelmoschus* L. (Fam. Malvaceae). It is refined by solvent extraction to remove fatty acids or by precipitation of the fatty acid salts. It is soluble in most fixed oils and in mineral oil, often with cloudiness, but it is relatively insoluble in glycerin and in propylene glycol.

Function: Flavoring agent

Packaging and Storage: Store in a cool place protected from light in full, tight containers that are made from steel or aluminum and that are suitably lined.

IDENTIFICATION
- **INFRARED SPECTRA**, *Spectrophotometric Identification Tests*, Appendix IIIC
  Acceptance criteria: The spectrum of the sample exhibits relative maxima at the same wavelengths as those of the spectrum below.

SPECIFIC TESTS
- **ACID VALUE (ESSENTIAL OILS AND FLAVORS)**, Appendix VI
  Acceptance criteria: NMT 3.0
- **OPTICAL (SPECIFIC) ROTATION**, Appendix IIB: Use a 100-mm tube.
  Acceptance criteria: Between −2.5° and +3°
- **REFRACTIVE INDEX**, Appendix IIB
  [NOTE—Use an Abbé or other refractometer of equal or greater accuracy.]
  Acceptance criteria: Between 1.468 and 1.485 at 20°
- **SAPONIFICATION VALUE**, *Esters*, Appendix VI
  Sample: 1 g
  Acceptance criteria: Between 140 and 200
- **SPECIFIC GRAVITY**: Determine by any reliable method (see *General Provisions*).
  Acceptance criteria: Between 0.898 and 0.920

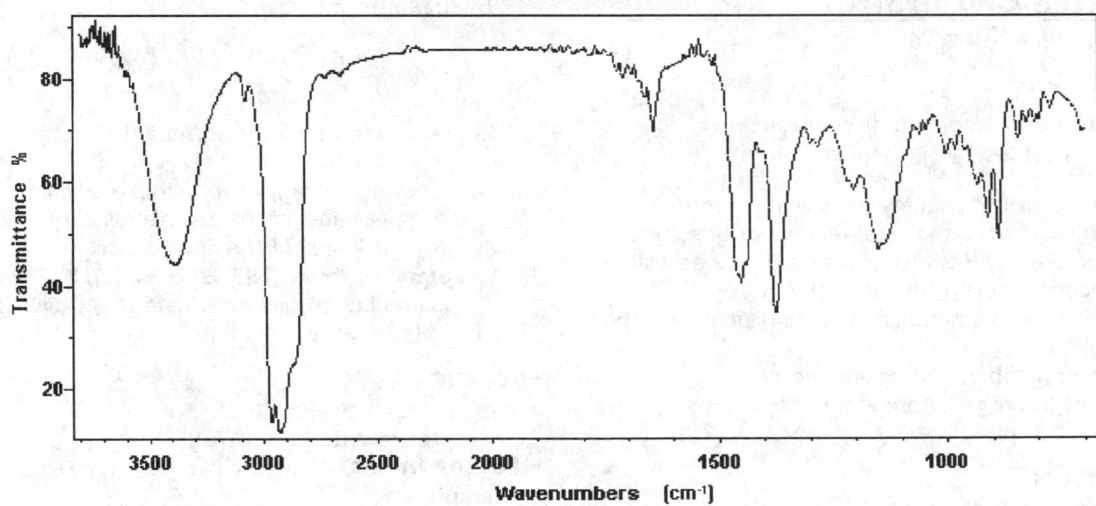

Ambrette Seed Oil

Ammonia Solution

First Published: Prior to FCC 6

Ammonium Hydroxide
Stronger Ammonia Water

NH₃ Formula wt 17.03
INS: 527 CAS: [7664-41-7]
UNII: 5138Q19F1X [ammonia]

DESCRIPTION
Ammonia Solution occurs as a clear, colorless liquid. Upon exposure to air it loses ammonia rapidly. Its specific gravity is about 0.90.
Function: pH control agent; surface finishing agent; boiler water additive
Packaging and Storage: Store in tight containers at a temperature not exceeding 25°.
[CAUTION—Ammonia Solution is irritating to the oral mucosa and respiratory tract. Perform tests in a well-ventilated fume hood.]

IDENTIFICATION
- **PROCEDURE**
  Analysis: Hold a glass rod wet with hydrochloric acid near the surface of the sample liquid.
  Acceptance criteria: Dense, white fumes evolve.

ASSAY
- **PROCEDURE**
  Sample preparation: Accurately tare a 125-mL glass-stoppered Erlenmeyer flask containing 35.0 mL of 1 N sulfuric acid. Cool a sample, contained in the original bottle, to 10° or cooler. Partially fill a 10-mL graduated pipet from near the bottom of this sample. [NOTE—Do not use vacuum to draw up the sample.] Wipe off any liquid adhering to the outside of the pipet, and discard the first mL of sample. Hold the pipet just above the surface of the acid, and transfer 2 mL into the flask, leaving at least 1 mL in the pipet. Stopper the flask, mix, and weigh again to obtain the weight of the sample.
  Analysis: To the Sample preparation, add methyl red TS, and titrate the excess acid with 1 N sodium hydroxide. Each mL of 1 N sulfuric acid is equivalent to 17.03 mg of NH₃.
  Acceptance criteria: NLT 27.0% and NMT 30.0%, by weight, of NH₃

IMPURITIES
Inorganic Impurities
- **LEAD**, Lead Limit Test, Atomic Absorption Spectrophotometric Graphite Furnace Method, Method I, Appendix IIIB
  Acceptance criteria: NMT 0.5 mg/kg

SPECIFIC TESTS
- **NONVOLATILE RESIDUE**
  Sample: 11 mL (10 g)
  Analysis: Evaporate the Sample in a tared platinum or porcelain dish to dryness, dry at 105° for 1 h, cool, and weigh.
  Acceptance criteria: NMT 0.02%
- **READILY OXIDIZABLE SUBSTANCES**
  Sample: 4 mL
  Analysis: Dilute the Sample with 6 mL of water and add a slight excess of 2 N sulfuric acid and 0.1 mL of 0.1 N potassium permanganate.
  Acceptance criteria: The pink color does not completely disappear within 10 min.

Ammoniated Glycyrrhizin

First Published: Prior to FCC 6

CAS: [1407-03-0]
UNII: 3VRD35U26C [ammonium glycyrrhizate]

DESCRIPTION
Ammoniated Glycyrrhizin occurs as a brown powder. It is precipitated by acid from the water extract of dried and ground rhizomes and roots of *Glycyrrhiza glabra* or related *Glycyrrhiza* (licorice root) (Fam. Leguminosae) and neutralized with dilute ammonia. Suitable diluents may be added.

Function: Flavoring agent; flavor enhancer

Packaging and Storage: Store in a tightly closed container in a cool, dry place.

IDENTIFICATION
- **Ammonium**, Appendix IIIA
  Acceptance criteria: Passes test

ASSAY
- **Procedure**
  [NOTE—The Assay is based on AOAC method 982.19.]
  Mobile phase: Acetonitrile, glacial acetic acid, and water (38:1:61), mixed and degassed. [NOTE—The water should be glass-distilled and filtered through a 0.45-μm filter (Millipore, or equivalent).]
  Standard solution: Amount equivalent to 10 mg (on the dried basis using its labeled loss on drying percentage) of monoammonium glycyrrhizinate standard for analytical use (Sigma, or equivalent) dissolved in 20 mL of a 1:1 (v/v) solution of acetonitrile:water. Filter the solution through a 0.45-μm filter (Millipore, or equivalent). Prepare fresh daily.
  Sample solution: 40 g in 20 mL of water, filtered through a 0.45-μm filter (Millipore, or equivalent)
  Chromatographic system, Appendix IIA
  Mode: High-performance liquid chromatography
  Detector: UV at 254 nm (0.2 to 0.1 AUFS range)
  Column: 30-cm × 4-mm (id), C18 reverse-phase column (μBondapak C18 column, Waters Corp., 34-T Maple Street, Milford, MA 01757, or equivalent) with 10-μm particle size
  Flow rate: About 2 mL/min
  Injection volume: 10 μL
  System suitability
  Sample: *Standard solution*
  Suitability requirements
    Mean standard deviation: NMT 2.0% for replicate injections. [NOTE—The retention time of monoammonium glycyrrhizinate is ~6 min.]
  Analysis: Separately inject, in duplicate, equal volumes of the *Standard solution* and *Sample solution* into the chromatograph, record the chromatograms, and determine the mean peak area for each solution. Calculate the percent monoammonium glycyrrhizinate (%MG), equivalent to $C_{42}H_{65}NO_{16}$ in the sample taken by the formula below:

$$\%MG = 100 \times (20C_S/W_U) \times (A_U/A_S)$$

C_S = concentration (mg/mL) of the *Standard solution*
W_U = weight (mg) of the sample taken
A_U = peak area of the *Sample solution*
A_S = peak area of the *Standard solution*

  Acceptance criteria: NLT 22.0% and NMT 32.0% of monoammonium glycyrrhizinate ($C_{42}H_{65}NO_{16}$), calculated on the dried basis

SPECIFIC TESTS
- **Ash (Total)**, Appendix IIC
  Acceptance criteria: NMT 2.5%
- **Loss on Drying**, Appendix IIC: 105° for 1 h
  Sample: 1 g
  Acceptance criteria: NMT 6.0%

Ammonium Alginate

First Published: Prior to FCC 6

Algin

$(C_6H_7O_6NH_4)n$ Formula wt, calculated 193.16
          Formula wt, actual (avg.) 217.00
INS: 403   CAS: [9005-34-9]
UNII: Q9QKJ39Q3X [ammonium alginate]

DESCRIPTION
Ammonium Alginate occurs as a white to yellow, fibrous or granular powder. It is the ammonium salt of alginic acid (see the monograph for *Alginic Acid*). It dissolves in water to form a viscous, colloidal solution. It is insoluble in alcohol and in hydroalcoholic solutions in which the alcohol content is greater than about 30% by weight. It is insoluble in chloroform, in ether, and in acids having a pH lower than about 3.

Function: Stabilizer; thickener; emulsifier

Packaging and Storage: Store in well-closed containers.

IDENTIFICATION
- **A. Procedure**
  Sample solution: 10 mg/mL
  Analysis: To 5 mL of the *Sample solution*, add 1 mL of calcium chloride TS.
  Acceptance criteria: A voluminous, gelatinous precipitate forms.
- **B. Procedure**
  Sample solution: 10 mg/mL
  Analysis: To 10 mL of the *Sample solution*, add 1 mL of 2.7 N sulfuric acid.
  Acceptance criteria: A heavy, gelatinous precipitate forms.
- **C. Procedure**
  Sample: 5 mg

Analysis: Place the *Sample* into a test tube. Add 5 mL of water, 1 mL of a freshly prepared 1% solution of naphtholresorcinol in ethanol, and 5 mL of hydrochloric acid. Heat the mixture to boiling, boil gently for about 3 min, and then cool to about 15°. Transfer the contents of the test tube to a 30-mL separatory funnel with the aid of 5 mL of water, and extract with 15 mL of isopropyl ether. Perform a blank determination (see *General Provisions*), and make any necessary correction.
Acceptance criteria: The isopropyl ether extract from the *Sample* exhibits a deeper purple hue than that from the blank.
- **D. PROCEDURE**
  Sample: 1 g
  Analysis: Add 5 mL of 1 N sodium hydroxide to the *Sample* contained in a test tube, and shake the mixture briefly.
  Acceptance criteria: The odor of ammonia is evident.

ASSAY
- **ALGINATES ASSAY,** Appendix IIIC
  Analysis: Each mL of 0.25 N sodium hydroxide consumed in the assay is equivalent to 27.12 mg of ammonium alginate (equiv wt 217.00).
  Acceptance criteria: NLT 18% and NMT 21% of carbon dioxide (CO_2), corresponding to between 88.7% and 103.6% of ammonium alginate (equiv wt 217.00), calculated on the dried basis

IMPURITIES
Inorganic Impurities
- **ARSENIC,** *Arsenic Limit Test,* Appendix IIIB
  Sample solution: Prepare as directed for organic compounds.
  Acceptance criteria: NMT 3 mg/kg
- **LEAD,** *Lead Limit Test,* Appendix IIIB
  Sample solution: Prepare as directed for organic compounds.
  Control: 5 µg Pb (5 mL of *Diluted Standard Lead Solution*)
  Acceptance criteria: NMT 5 mg/kg

SPECIFIC TESTS
- **LOSS ON DRYING,** Appendix IIC: 105° for 4 h
  Acceptance criteria: NMT 15.0%
- **RESIDUE ON IGNITION (SULFATED ASH),** *Method I,* Appendix IIC
  Sample: 3 g
  Acceptance criteria: NMT 7.0%, calculated on the dried basis

---

Ammonium Bicarbonate
First Published: Prior to FCC 6

NH_4HCO_3 Formula wt 79.06
INS: 503(ii)   CAS: [1066-33-7]
UNII: 45JP4345C9 [ammonium bicarbonate]

DESCRIPTION
Ammonium Bicarbonate occurs as white crystals or as a crystalline powder. It volatilizes rapidly at 60°, dissociating into ammonia, carbon dioxide, and water, but it is quite stable at room temperature. One g dissolves in about 6 mL of water. It is insoluble in alcohol.
Function: Alkali; leavening agent
Packaging and Storage: Store in well-closed containers.

IDENTIFICATION
- **A. AMMONIUM,** Appendix IIIA
  Acceptance criteria: Passes tests
- **B. BICARBONATE,** Appendix IIIA
  Acceptance criteria: Passes tests

ASSAY
- **PROCEDURE**
  Sample: 3 g
  Analysis: Dissolve the *Sample* in 40 mL of water. Add 2 drops of methyl red TS, and while constantly stirring, titrate with 1 N hydrochloric acid, adding the acid slowly, until the solution becomes faintly pink. Heat the solution to boiling, cool, and continue the titration until the faint pink color no longer fades after boiling. Each mL of 1 N hydrochloric acid is equivalent to 79.06 mg of NH_4HCO_3.
  Acceptance criteria: NLT 99.0% and NMT 100.5% of NH_4HCO_3

IMPURITIES
Inorganic Impurities
- **CHLORIDE,** *Chloride and Sulfate Limit Tests, Chloride Limit Test,* Appendix IIIB
  Sample: 500 mg
  Control: 15 µg of chloride (1.5 mL of *Standard Chloride Solution*)
  Acceptance criteria: Any turbidity produced by the *Sample* does not exceed that shown in the *Control* (NMT 0.003%).
- **LEAD,** *Lead Limit Test, APDC Extraction Method,* Appendix IIIB
  Acceptance criteria: NMT 3 mg/kg
- **SULFATE,** *Chloride and Sulfate Limit Tests, Chloride Limit Test,* Appendix IIIB
  Sample preparation: Dissolve 4 g of sample in 40 mL of water, add about 10 mg of sodium carbonate and 1 mL of 30% hydrogen peroxide, and evaporate the solution to dryness on a steam bath.
  Control: 280 µg of sulfate (28.0 mL of *Standard Sulfate Solution*)
  Acceptance criteria: Any turbidity produced by the *Sample preparation* does not exceed that in the *Control* (NMT 0.007%).

SPECIFIC TESTS
- **NONVOLATILE RESIDUE**
  Sample: 4 g
  Analysis: Transfer the *Sample* into a tared dish, add 10 mL of water, and evaporate to dryness on a steam bath. Heat the dish at 105° for 1 h, cool in a desiccator, and weigh.

Acceptance criteria: NMT 0.05% (0.55% for products containing a suitable anticaking agent)

Ammonium Carbonate
First Published: Prior to FCC 6

INS: 503(i) CAS: [10361-29-2]
UNII: NJ5VT0FKLJ [ammonium carbonate]

DESCRIPTION
Ammonium Carbonate occurs as a white powder or as hard, white or translucent masses. It consists of ammonium bicarbonate (NH_4HCO_3) and ammonium carbamate ($NH_2 \cdot COONH_4$) in varying proportions. On exposure to air it becomes opaque and is finally converted into porous lumps or a white powder of ammonium bicarbonate because of the loss of ammonia and carbon dioxide. One g dissolves slowly in about 4 mL of water. Its solutions are alkaline to litmus.
Function: Buffer; leavening agent; neutralizing agent
Packaging and Storage: Store in tight, light-resistant containers, preferably at a temperature not exceeding 30°.

IDENTIFICATION
- **A. PROCEDURE**
  Acceptance criteria: When heated, a sample volatilizes without charring, and the vapor is alkaline to moistened litmus paper.
- **B. PROCEDURE**
  Sample solution: 50 mg/mL
  Analysis: Add acid to the *Sample solution*.
  Acceptance criteria: The solution effervesces.

ASSAY
- **PROCEDURE**
  Sample: 2 g
  Analysis: Place about 10 mL of water in a weighing bottle, tare the bottle and its contents, then add the *Sample* and accurately weigh. Transfer the contents of the bottle to a 250-mL flask and, while mixing, slowly add 50.0 mL of 1 N sulfuric acid, allowing for the release of carbon dioxide. When dissolution is complete, wash down the sides of the flask with a few mL of water, add a few drops of methyl orange TS, and titrate the excess acid with 1 N sodium hydroxide. Each mL of 1 N sulfuric acid is equivalent to 17.03 mg of NH_3.
  Acceptance criteria: NLT 30.0% and NMT 34.0% of NH_3

IMPURITIES
Inorganic Impurities
- **CHLORIDE,** *Chloride and Sulfate Limit Tests, Chloride Limit Test,* Appendix IIIB
  Sample preparation: Dissolve 500 mg of sample in 10 mL of hot water, add about 5 mg of sodium carbonate, and evaporate to dryness on a steam bath.
  Control: 15 µg of chloride (1.5 mL of *Standard Chloride Solution*)
  Acceptance criteria: Any turbidity produced by the *Sample preparation* does not exceed that shown in the *Control* (NMT 0.003%).
- **LEAD,** *Lead Limit Test, APDC Extraction Method,* Appendix IIIB
  Acceptance criteria: NMT 3 mg/kg
- **SULFATE,** *Chloride and Sulfate Limit Tests, Chloride Limit Test,* Appendix IIIB
  Sample preparation: Dissolve 4 g of sample in 40 mL of water, add about 10 mg of sodium carbonate and 1 mL of 30% hydrogen peroxide, and evaporate the solution to dryness on a steam bath.
  Control: 200 µg sulfate (20.0 mL of *Standard Sulfate Solution*)
  Acceptance criteria: Any turbidity produced by the *Sample preparation* does not exceed that in the *Control* (NMT 0.005%).

SPECIFIC TESTS
- **NONVOLATILE RESIDUE**
  Sample preparation: 4 g in 10 mL of water
  Analysis: Transfer the *Sample preparation* into a tared dish and evaporate to dryness on a steam bath. Heat the dish at 105° for 1 h, cool in a desiccator, and weigh.
  Acceptance criteria: NMT 0.05%

Ammonium Chloride
First Published: Prior to FCC 6

NH_4Cl Formula wt 53.49
INS: 510 CAS: [12125-02-9]
UNII: 01Q9PC255D [ammonium chloride]

DESCRIPTION
Ammonium Chloride occurs as colorless crystals or as a white, fine or coarse, crystalline powder. It is somewhat hygroscopic. One g dissolves in 2.6 mL of water at 25°, in 1.4 mL of boiling water, in about 100 mL of alcohol, and in about 8 mL of glycerin. The pH of a 1:20 solution is between 4.5 and 6.0.
Function: Yeast food; dough conditioner
Packaging and Storage: Store in tight containers.

IDENTIFICATION
- **AMMONIUM,** Appendix IIIA
  Sample solution: 100 mg/mL
  Acceptance criteria: Passes test
- **CHLORIDE,** Appendix IIIA
  Sample solution: 100 mg/mL
  Acceptance criteria: Passes test

ASSAY
- **PROCEDURE**
  Sample solution: 200 mg, previously dried
  Analysis: Dissolve the *Sample* in 40 mL of water contained in a glass-stoppered flask. While agitating the mixture, add 3 mL of nitric acid, 5 mL of nitrobenzene, and 50.0 mL of 0.1 N silver nitrate. Shake vigorously and add 2 mL of ferric ammonium sulfate TS. Titrate

the excess silver nitrate with 0.1 N ammonium thiocyanate. Each mL of 0.1 N silver nitrate is equivalent to 5.349 mg of NH₄Cl.
Acceptance criteria: NLT 99.0% of NH₄Cl, on the dried basis

IMPURITIES
Inorganic Impurities
- **LEAD,** Lead Limit Test, Appendix IIIB
  Control: 4 µg Pb (4 mL of Diluted Standard Lead Solution)
  Acceptance criteria: NMT 4 mg/kg

SPECIFIC TESTS
- **LOSS ON DRYING,** Appendix IIC: Over silica gel for 4 h
  Acceptance criteria: NMT 0.5%

Ammonium Citrate, Dibasic

First Published: FCC 6

Diammonium Hydrogen Citrate

(NH₄)₂HC₆H₅O₇   Formula wt 226.19
                       CAS: [3012-65-5]
UNII: N9BUG430K8 [ammonium citrate, dibasic]

DESCRIPTION
Ammonium Citrate occurs as white to off-white crystals. It is soluble in water, but insoluble in alcohol.
Function: pH control agent
Packaging and Storage: Store in well-closed containers.

IDENTIFICATION
- **AMMONIUM,** Appendix IIIA
  Sample solution: 100 mg/mL
  Acceptance criteria: Passes test
- **CITRATE,** Appendix IIIA
  Sample solution: 100 mg/mL
  Acceptance criteria: Passes test

ASSAY
- **PROCEDURE**
  Sample: 1 g
  Analysis: Transfer the Sample into a 250-mL flask and dissolve in 100 mL of water. Add 40 mL of a mixture of equal volumes of formalin and water, previously neutralized to phenolphthalein TS with 1 N sodium hydroxide. Mix, allow to stand for 30 min, and titrate the mixture with 1 N sodium hydroxide to a pink endpoint that persists for 5 min. Each mL of 1 N sodium hydroxide is equivalent to 75.40 mg of (NH₄)₂HC₆H₅O₇.
  Acceptance criteria: NLT 98.0% and NMT 103.0% of (NH₄)₂HC₆H₅O₇

IMPURITIES
Inorganic Impurities
- **CHLORIDE,** Chloride and Sulfate Limit Tests, Chloride Limit Test, Appendix IIIB
  Sample solution: 1 g of sample mixed with 25 mL of water and 2 mL of nitric acid, heated until dissolution is complete. Cool and dilute to 30 to 40 mL with water
  Analysis: Proceed as directed beginning with "... add 1 mL of silver nitrate TS ..."
  Control: 10 µg of chloride (1 mL of Standard Chloride Solution)
  Acceptance criteria: Any turbidity produced by the Sample solution does not exceed that in the Control (NMT 0.001%).
- **IRON**
  Sample solution: 20 mg/mL
  Control: 20 µg Fe (2.0 mL of Iron Standard Solution, see Standard Solutions for the Preparation of Controls and Standards, Iron Standard Solution, Solutions and Indicators)
  Analysis: Add 2 mL of a 200 mg/mL solution of citric acid and 0.1 mL of thioglycollic acid to 10 mL of the Sample solution. Mix, make alkaline with ammonia (18%), and dilute to 20 mL with water. Repeat the preceding using the Control in place of the 10 mL of Sample solution.
  Acceptance criteria: Any red color produced by the Sample solution does not exceed that show by the Control (NMT 0.001%).
- **LEAD,** Lead Limit Test, Flame Atomic Absorption Spectrophotometric Method, Appendix IIIB
  Sample: 1 g
  Acceptance criteria: NMT 2 mg/kg
- **SULFATE,** Chloride and Sulfate Limit Tests, Chloride Limit Test, Appendix IIIB
  Sample solution: 1 g in 1 mL of 2.7 N hydrochloric acid, diluted to 30 to 40 mL with water
  Control: 50 µg sulfate (5 mL of Standard Sulfate Solution)
  Analysis: Proceed as directed, beginning with "... add 3 mL of barium chloride TS... "
  Acceptance criteria: Any turbidity produced by the Sample solution does not exceed that produced by the Control (NMT 0.005%).

SPECIFIC TESTS
- **PH,** pH Determination, Appendix IIB
  Sample solution: 50 mg/mL
  Analysis: Use the Potentiometric Method (pH Meter)
  Acceptance criteria: Between 4.5 and 5.5

Ammonium Citrate, Tribasic

First Published: Second Supplement, FCC 6

Triammonium Citrate
Citric Acid Triammonium Salt

C₆H₁₇N₃O₇   Formula wt 243.22
INS: 380   CAS: [3458-72-8]
UNII: J90A52459R [ammonium citrate, tribasic]

DESCRIPTION
Ammonium Citrate, Tribasic occurs as white crystals or crystalline powder. It is freely soluble in water.

Function: pH control agent
Packaging and Storage: Store in well-closed containers.

IDENTIFICATION
- **A. Ammonium,** Appendix IIIA
  Sample solution: 100 mg/mL
  Acceptance criteria: Passes test
- **B. Citrate,** Appendix IIIA
  Sample solution: 100 mg/mL
  Acceptance criteria: Passes test

ASSAY
- **Procedure**
  Phenolphthalein solution: Dissolve 0.2 g of phenolphthalein in 60 mL of 90% ethanol, and dilute with water to 100 mL.
  Sample: 3.5 g
  Analysis: Dissolve the *Sample* in 50 mL of water, add 50 mL of 1 N sodium hydroxide, boil for 15 min or until ammonia ceases to be evolved, and add sufficient 1 N sulfuric acid to make the solution acid to the *Phenolphthalein solution*. Boil the solution for 5 min, cool, and titrate with 1 N sodium hydroxide, using the *Phenolphthalein solution* as the indicator. Each mL of 1 N sodium hydroxide is equivalent to 81.07 mg of $C_6H_{17}N_3O_7$.
  Acceptance criteria: NLT 97.0% of $C_6H_{17}N_3O_7$

IMPURITIES
Inorganic Impurities
- **Lead,** *Lead Limit Test, Flame Atomic Absorption Spectrophotometric Method,* Appendix IIIB
  Sample: 1 g
  Acceptance criteria: NMT 2 mg/kg

SPECIFIC TESTS
- **Oxalate**
  Sample: 0.5 g
  Analysis: Dissolve the *Sample* in 4 mL of water, add 3 mL of concentrated hydrochloric acid, and then 1 g of granulated zinc. Heat for 1 min in a boiling water bath. Let stand for 2 min at room temperature, then decant the supernatant solution into a test tube containing 0.25 mL of a 1% solution of phenylhydrazine hydrochloride. Mix, heat to boiling, and cool immediately. Transfer the solution into a glass cylinder with a ground-glass stopper, and add an equal volume of concentrated hydrochloric acid. Add 0.25 mL of a 5% solution of potassium hexacyanoferrate (III), mix well, and let stand for 30 min.
  Acceptance criteria: The color of the solution so obtained is not more intense than that of a standard solution prepared in the same manner and containing 4.0 mL of a solution of 0.005% oxalic acid in water.

Ammonium Phosphate, Dibasic
First Published: Prior to FCC 6

Diammonium Hydrogen Phosphate
Diammonium Phosphate

$(NH_4)_2HPO_4$ Formula wt 132.06
INS: 342(ii) CAS: [7783-28-0]
UNII: 10LGE70FSU [ammonium phosphate, dibasic]

DESCRIPTION
Ammonium Phosphate, Dibasic occurs as white crystals, a crystalline powder, or granules. It is freely soluble in water. The pH of a 1:100 aqueous solution is between 7.6 and 8.2.
Function: Buffer; dough conditioner; leavening agent; yeast food
Packaging and Storage: Store in tightly closed containers.

IDENTIFICATION
- **Ammonium,** Appendix IIIA
  Sample solution: 50 mg/mL
  Acceptance criteria: Passes tests
- **Phosphate,** Appendix IIIA
  Sample solution: 50 mg/mL
  Acceptance criteria: Passes tests

ASSAY
- **Procedure**
  Sample: 600 mg
  Analysis: Dissolve the *Sample* in 40 mL of water, and titrate to a pH of 4.6 with 0.1 N sulfuric acid. Each mL of 0.1 N sulfuric acid is equivalent to 13.21 mg of $(NH_4)_2HPO_4$.
  Acceptance criteria: NLT 96.0% and NMT 102.0% of $(NH_4)_2HPO_4$

IMPURITIES
Inorganic Impurities
- **Arsenic,** *Arsenic Limit Test,* Appendix IIIB
  Sample solution: 1 g in 35 mL of water
  Acceptance criteria: NMT 3 mg/kg
- **Fluoride,** *Fluoride Limit Test, Method IV,* Appendix IIIB
  Buffer solution: [Note—Use the following buffer solution preparation in place of the one specified under *Method IV*.] Add two volumes of 6 N acetic acid to 1 volume of water, and adjust the pH to 5.0 with 50% potassium hydroxide solution.
  Sample: 2 g
  Acceptance criteria: NMT 10 mg/kg
- **Lead,** *Lead Limit Test, APDC Extraction Method,* Appendix IIIB
  Acceptance criteria: NMT 4 mg/kg

Ammonium Phosphate, Monobasic

First Published: Prior to FCC 6

Ammonium Dihydrogen Phosphate
Monoammonium Phosphate

$NH_4H_2PO_4$ Formula wt 115.03
INS: 342(i)   CAS: [7722-76-1]
UNII: 09254QB17T [ammonium phosphate, monobasic]

DESCRIPTION
Ammonium Phosphate, Monobasic, occurs as white crystals, a crystalline powder, or granules. It is freely soluble in water. The pH of a 1:100 aqueous solution is between 4.3 and 5.0.
Function: Buffer; dough conditioner; leavening agent; yeast food
Packaging and Storage: Store in tightly closed containers.

IDENTIFICATION
- **AMMONIUM,** Appendix IIIA
  Sample solution: 50 mg/mL
  Acceptance criteria: Passes test
- **PHOSPHATE,** Appendix IIIA
  Sample solution: 50 mg/mL
  Acceptance criteria: Passes tests

ASSAY
- **PROCEDURE**
  Sample: 500 mg
  Analysis: Dissolve the Sample in 50 mL of water, and titrate to a pH of 8.0 with 0.1 N sodium hydroxide. Each mL of 0.1 N sodium hydroxide is equivalent to 11.50 mg of $NH_4H_2PO_4$.
  Acceptance criteria: NLT 96.0% and NMT 102.0% of $NH_4H_2PO_4$

IMPURITIES
Inorganic Impurities
- **ARSENIC,** Arsenic Limit Test, Appendix IIIB
  Sample solution: 1 g in 35 mL of water
  Acceptance criteria: NMT 3 mg/kg
- **FLUORIDE,** Fluoride Limit Test, Method IV, Appendix IIIB
  Buffer solution: [NOTE—Use the following buffer solution preparation in place of the one specified under Method IV.] Add two volumes of 6 N acetic acid to 1 volume of water, and adjust the pH to 5.0 with 50% potassium hydroxide solution.
  Sample: 2 g
  Acceptance criteria: NMT 10 mg/kg
- **LEAD,** Lead Limit Test, APDC Extraction Method, Appendix IIIB
  Acceptance criteria: NMT 4 mg/kg

Ammonium Saccharin

First Published: Prior to FCC 6

1,2-Benzisothiazolin-3-one 1,1-Dioxide Ammonium Salt

$C_7H_8N_2O_3S$ Formula wt 200.21
UNII: 63Q3BCF15A [ammonium saccharin]

DESCRIPTION
Ammonium Saccharin occurs as white crystals or as white, crystalline powder. It is freely soluble in water. The pH of a 1:3 aqueous solution is between 5 and 6.
Function: Nonnutritive sweetener
Packaging and Storage: Store in well-closed containers.

IDENTIFICATION
- **A. PROCEDURE**
  Sample: 100 mg
  Analysis: Dissolve the Sample in 5 mL of a 50 mg/mL solution of sodium hydroxide, evaporate to dryness, and gently fuse the residue over a small flame until ammonia no longer evolves. After the residue has cooled, dissolve it in 20 mL of water, neutralize the solution with 2.7 N hydrochloric acid, and filter. Add 1 drop of ferric chloride TS to the filtrate.
  Acceptance criteria: A violet color appears.
- **B. PROCEDURE**
  Sample: 20 mg
  Analysis: Mix the Sample with 40 mg of resorcinol, cautiously add 10 drops of sulfuric acid, and heat the mixture in a liquid bath at 200° for 3 min. After cooling, add 10 mL of water and an excess of 1 N sodium hydroxide.
  Acceptance criteria: A fluorescent green liquid is produced.
- **C. AMMONIUM,** Appendix IIIA
  Sample solution: 100 mg/mL
  Acceptance criteria: Passes test
- **D. MELTING RANGE OR TEMPERATURE DETERMINATION,** Appendix IIB
  Sample solution: 100 mg/mL
  Analysis: Add 1 mL of hydrochloric acid to 10 mL of the Sample solution. A crystalline precipitate of saccharin forms. Wash the precipitate well with cold water, and dry at 105° for 2 h.
  Acceptance criteria: The saccharin thus obtained melts between 226° and 230°.

ASSAY
- **PROCEDURE**
  Sample: 500 mg
  Analysis: With the aid of 10 mL of water, quantitatively transfer the Sample into a separatory funnel. Add 2 mL of 2.7 N hydrochloric acid, and extract the precipitated saccharin, first with 30 mL, then with five 20-mL portions, of solvent comprising 9:1 (v/v)

chloroform:alcohol. Filter each extract through a small filter paper moistened with the solvent mixture, and evaporate the combined filtrates to dryness on a steam bath with the aid of a current of air. Dissolve the residue in 75 mL of hot water, cool, add phenolphthalein TS, and titrate with 0.1 N sodium hydroxide. Perform a blank determination (see *General Provisions*), and make any necessary correction. Each mL of 0.1 N sodium hydroxide is equivalent to 20.02 mg of $C_7H_8N_2O_3S$.

Acceptance criteria: NLT 98.0% and NMT 101.0% of $C_7H_8N_2O_3S$, calculated on the anhydrous basis

IMPURITIES
Inorganic Impurities
- **LEAD,** *Lead Limit Test, Flame Atomic Absorption Spectrophotometric Method,* Appendix IIIB
  Sample: 10 g
  Acceptance criteria: NMT 2 mg/kg
- **SELENIUM,** *Selenium Limit Test, Method I,* Appendix IIIB
  Sample: 200 mg
  Acceptance criteria: NMT 0.003%

Organic Impurities
- **BENZOATE AND SALICYLATE**
  Sample: 50 mg/mL
  Analysis: Add 3 drops of ferric chloride TS to 10 mL of *Sample solution* previously acidified with 5 drops of glacial acetic acid.
  Acceptance criteria: No precipitate or violet color appears.
- **TOLUENESULFONAMIDES**
  [NOTE—For all solutions requiring methylene chloride, use a suitable grade (such as that obtainable from Burdick & Jackson Laboratories, Inc.) equivalent to the product obtained by distillation in an all-glass apparatus.]
  Internal standard stock solution: 10 mg/mL 95% *n*-tricosane (obtainable from Chemical Samples Co.) in *n*-heptane, made to 10 mL
  Standard stock solution: 2 mg/mL each of reagent-grade *o*-toluenesulfonamide and *p*-toluenesulfonamide in methylene chloride, made to 10 mL
  Standard solutions: Pipet 0.1, 0.25, 1.0, 2.5, and 5.0 mL, respectively, of the *Standard stock solution* into five 10-mL volumetric flasks. Pipet 0.25 mL of the *Internal standard stock solution* into each flask, dilute each to volume with methylene chloride, and mix. These solutions contain, respectively, 20, 50, 200, 500, and 1000 µg/mL of each toluenesulfonamide, in addition to 250 µg of *n*-tricosane.
  Sample solution: Dissolve 2.00 g of sample in 8.0 mL of 5% sodium bicarbonate solution, and mix the solution thoroughly with 10.0 g of chromatographic siliceous earth (Celite 545, Johns-Manville, or equivalent). Transfer the mixture into a 250-mm × 25-mm chromatographic tube, or equivalent, having a fritted-glass disk and a Teflon stopcock at the bottom and a reservoir at the top. Pack the contents of the tube by tapping the column on a padded surface, and then by tamping firmly from the top. Place 100 mL of methylene chloride in the reservoir, and adjust the stopcock so that 50 mL of eluate is collected in 20 to 30 min. Add 25 µL of *Internal standard stock solution* to the eluate, mix, and then concentrate the solution to a volume of 1.0 mL in a suitable concentrator tube fitted with a modified Snyder column, using a Kontes tube heater maintained at 90°.
  Chromatographic system, Appendix IIA
    Mode: Gas chromatography
    Detector: Flame-ionization detector
    Column: 3-m × 2-mm (id) glass column, or equivalent, packed with 3% phenylmethyl silicone (OV-17, Applied Science Laboratories, Inc., or equivalent) on 100- to 120-mesh, silanized and calcined diatomaceous silica (Gas-Chrom Q, Applied Science, or equivalent). [CAUTION—The glass column should extend into the injector for on-column injection and into the detector base to avoid contact with metal.]
    Oven temperature: 180°
    Injection port temperature: 225°
    Detector temperature: 250°
    Carrier gas: Helium
    Flow rate: 30 mL/minute
    Injection volume: 2.5 µL
  Analysis: Set the instrument attenuation so that 2.5 µL of the *Standard solution* that contains 200 µg/mL of each toluenesulfonamide gives a response of 40% to 80% of full-scale deflection. [NOTE—The retention times for *o*-toluenesulfonamide, *p*-toluenesulfonamide, and *n*-tricosane are about 5, 6, and 15 min, respectively.] Separately inject each of the five *Standard solutions* and the *Sample solution* into the chromatograph, record the chromatograms, and, for each solution, determine the areas of the *o*-toluenesulfonamide, *p*-toluenesulfonamide, and *n*-tricosane peaks. From the values thus obtained from the *Standard solutions*, prepare standard curves by plotting the concentration of each toluenesulfonamide (µg/mL) versus the ratio of the respective toluenesulfonamide peak area to that of *n*-tricosane. From the standard curve, determine the concentration (µg/mL) of each toluenesulfonamide in the *Sample solution*. Divide each value by 2 to convert the result to mg/kg of the toluenesulfonamide in the 2 g sample taken for analysis.
  [NOTE—If the toluenesulfonamide content of the sample is greater than about 500 mg/kg, the impurity may crystallize out of the methylene chloride concentrate (see *Sample solution*). Although this level of impurity exceeds that permitted by the specification, the analysis may be completed by diluting the concentrate with methylene chloride containing 250 µg/mL of *n*-tricosane, and by applying appropriate dilution factors in the calculation. Care must be taken to redissolve completely any crystalline toluenesulfonamide to give a homogeneous solution.]
  Acceptance criteria: NMT 0.0025%

SPECIFIC TESTS
- **READILY CARBONIZABLE SUBSTANCES,** Appendix IIB
  Sample: 200 mg

Sample solution: Dissolve the *Sample* in 5 mL of 95% sulfuric acid and hold at 48° to 50° for 10 min.
Acceptance criteria: The color of the resulting solution is no darker than that of *Matching Fluid A*.
- **WATER,** *Water Determination,* Appendix IIB
Acceptance criteria: NMT 0.3%

Ammonium Sulfate

First Published: Prior to FCC 6

(NH$_4$)$_2$SO$_4$ Formula wt 132.14
INS: 517   CAS: [7783-20-2]
UNII: SU46BAM238 [ammonium sulfate]

DESCRIPTION
Ammonium Sulfate occurs as colorless or white crystals or granules that decompose at temperatures above 280°. One gram is soluble in about 1.5 mL of water. It is insoluble in alcohol. The pH of a 0.1 M solution is between 4.5 and 6.0.
Function: Dough conditioner; yeast nutrient
Packaging and Storage: Store in well-closed containers.

IDENTIFICATION
- **AMMONIUM,** Appendix IIIA
Acceptance criteria: Passes test
- **SULFATE,** Appendix IIIA
Acceptance criteria: Passes tests

ASSAY
- **PROCEDURE**
Sample: 2 g
Analysis: Transfer the *Sample* into a 250-mL flask, and dissolve in 100 mL of water. Add 40 mL of a mixture of equal volumes of formaldehyde and water, previously neutralized to phenolphthalein TS with 1 N sodium hydroxide. Mix, allow to stand for 30 min, and titrate the mixture with 1 N sodium hydroxide to a pink endpoint that persists for 5 min. Each mL of 1 N sodium hydroxide is equivalent to 66.06 mg of (NH$_4$)$_2$SO$_4$.
Acceptance criteria: NLT 99.0% and NMT 100.5% of (NH$_4$)$_2$SO$_4$

IMPURITIES
Inorganic Impurities
- **LEAD,** *Lead Limit Test, APDC Extraction Method,* Appendix IIIB
Acceptance criteria: NMT 3 mg/kg
- **SELENIUM,** *Selenium Limit Test, Method II,* Appendix IIIB
Sample: 200 mg
Acceptance criteria: NMT 0.003%

SPECIFIC TESTS
- **RESIDUE ON IGNITION (SULFATED ASH),** Appendix IIC
Sample: 1 g
Acceptance criteria: NMT 0.25%

1-Amyl Alcohol

First Published: Prior to FCC 6

1-Pentanol

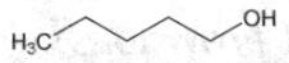

C$_5$H$_{12}$O   Formula wt 88.15
FEMA: 2056
UNII: M9L931X26Y [1-pentanol]

DESCRIPTION
1-Amyl Alcohol occurs as a colorless to pale yellow liquid.
Odor: Fusel, winey
Solubility: Soluble in propylene glycol, vegetable oils; sparingly soluble in water
Boiling Point: ~136°
Function: Flavoring agent

ASSAY
- **PROCEDURE:** Proceed as directed under *M-1b,* Appendix XI.
Acceptance criteria: NLT 98.0% of C$_5$H$_{12}$O

SPECIFIC TESTS
- **REFRACTIVE INDEX,** Appendix II: At 20°
Acceptance criteria: Between 1.407 and 1.412
- **SPECIFIC GRAVITY:** Determine at 25° by any reliable method (see *General Provisions*).
Acceptance criteria: Between 0.810 and 0.816

Amyl Butyrate

First Published: Prior to FCC 6

1-Pentyl Butyrate

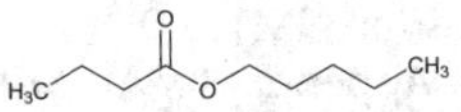

C$_9$H$_{18}$O$_2$ Formula wt 158.23
FEMA: 2059
UNII: 3Q2JP0VD8J [amyl butyrate]

DESCRIPTION
Amyl Butyrate occurs as a colorless to pale yellow liquid.
Odor: Fruity, banana
Solubility: Soluble in propylene glycol, vegetable oils; slightly soluble in water
Boiling Point: ~184° to 188°
Solubility in Alcohol, Appendix VI: One mL dissolves in 1 mL of 95% ethanol.
Function: Flavoring agent

ASSAY
- **PROCEDURE:** Proceed as directed under *M-1b,* Appendix XI.
Acceptance criteria: NLT 98.0% of C$_9$H$_{18}$O$_2$ (sum of main isomers)

62 / Amyl Butyrate / *Monographs*

SPECIFIC TESTS
- **ACID VALUE, FLAVOR CHEMICALS (OTHER THAN ESSENTIAL OILS),** *M-15,* Appendix XI
  Acceptance criteria: NMT 1.0
- **REFRACTIVE INDEX,** Appendix II: At 20°
  Acceptance criteria: Between 1.409 and 1.414
- **SPECIFIC GRAVITY:** Determine at 25° by any reliable method (see *General Provisions*).
  Acceptance criteria: Between 0.863 and 0.866

Amyl Formate

First Published: Prior to FCC 6

1-Pentyl Formate

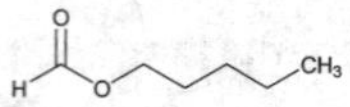

$C_6H_{12}O_2$ Formula wt 116.16
FEMA: 2068
UNII: P46O2510D8 [amyl formate]

DESCRIPTION
Amyl Formate occurs as a colorless to pale yellow liquid.
Odor: Fruity
Solubility: Miscible in alcohol
Boiling Point: ~128° to 130°
Function: Flavoring agent

ASSAY
- **PROCEDURE:** Proceed as directed under *M-1b,* Appendix XI.
  Acceptance criteria: NLT 92.0% of $C_6H_{12}O_2$ (sum of *n-*, 2-methyl butyl, and 3-methyl butyl isomers)

SPECIFIC TESTS
- **ACID VALUE, FLAVOR CHEMICALS (OTHER THAN ESSENTIAL OILS),** *M-15,* Appendix XI: Add ice to solution.
  Acceptance criteria: NMT 5.0
- **REFRACTIVE INDEX,** Appendix II: At 20°
  Acceptance criteria: Between 1.396 and 1.402
- **SPECIFIC GRAVITY:** Determine at 25° by any reliable method (see *General Provisions*).
  Acceptance criteria: Between 0.881 and 0.887

Amyl Heptanoate

First Published: Prior to FCC 6

Pentyl Heptanoate

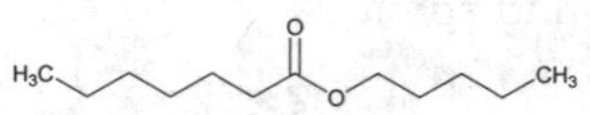

$C_{12}H_{24}O_2$ Formula wt 200.32
FEMA: 2073
UNII: I91PDA80HT [amyl heptanoate]

DESCRIPTION
Amyl Heptanoate occurs as a colorless to pale yellow liquid.
Odor: Fruity
Boiling Point: ~245°
Solubility in Alcohol, Appendix VI: One mL dissolves in 1 mL of 95% alcohol.
Function: Flavoring agent

ASSAY
- **PROCEDURE:** Proceed as directed under *M-1a,* Appendix XI.
  Acceptance criteria: NLT 93.0% of $C_{12}H_{24}O_2$ (sum of *n-*, 2-methyl butyl, and 3-methyl butyl isomers)

SPECIFIC TESTS
- **ACID VALUE, FLAVOR CHEMICALS (OTHER THAN ESSENTIAL OILS),** *M-15,* Appendix XI
  Acceptance criteria: NMT 1.0
- **REFRACTIVE INDEX,** Appendix II: At 20°
  Acceptance criteria: Between 1.422 and 1.426
- **SPECIFIC GRAVITY:** Determine at 25° by any reliable method (see *General Provisions*).
  Acceptance criteria: Between 0.859 and 0.863

Amyl Octanoate

First Published: Prior to FCC 6

Amyl Caprylate
Isoamyl Caprylate
Isoamyl Octanoate

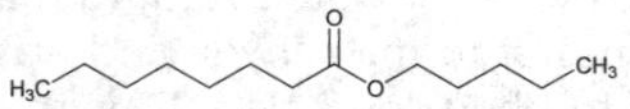

$C_{13}H_{26}O_2$ Formula wt 214.35
FEMA: 2079
UNII: 1KWP15429R [amyl octanoate]

DESCRIPTION
Amyl Octanoate occurs as a colorless liquid.
Odor: Fruity
Solubility: Soluble in alcohol, most fixed oils; slightly soluble in propylene glycol; insoluble or practically insoluble in glycerin, water
Boiling Point: ~260°
Solubility in Alcohol, Appendix VI: One mL dissolves in 7 mL of 80% alcohol, and remains in solution on dilution to 10 mL.
Function: Flavoring agent

IDENTIFICATION
- **INFRARED SPECTRA,** *Spectrophotometric Identification Tests,* Appendix IIIC
  Acceptance criteria: The spectrum of the sample exhibits relative maxima at the same wavelengths as those of the spectrum below.

ASSAY
- **PROCEDURE:** Proceed as directed under *M-1b*, Appendix XI.
  Acceptance criteria: NLT 98.0% of $C_{13}H_{26}O_2$ (sum of n-, 2-methyl butyl, and 3-methyl butyl isomers)

SPECIFIC TESTS
- **ACID VALUE, FLAVOR CHEMICALS (OTHER THAN ESSENTIAL OILS),** *M-15,* Appendix XI
  Acceptance criteria: NMT 1.0
- **REFRACTIVE INDEX,** Appendix II: At 20°
  Acceptance criteria: Between 1.425 and 1.429
- **SPECIFIC GRAVITY:** Determine at 25° by any reliable method (see *General Provisions*).
  Acceptance criteria: Between 0.855 and 0.861

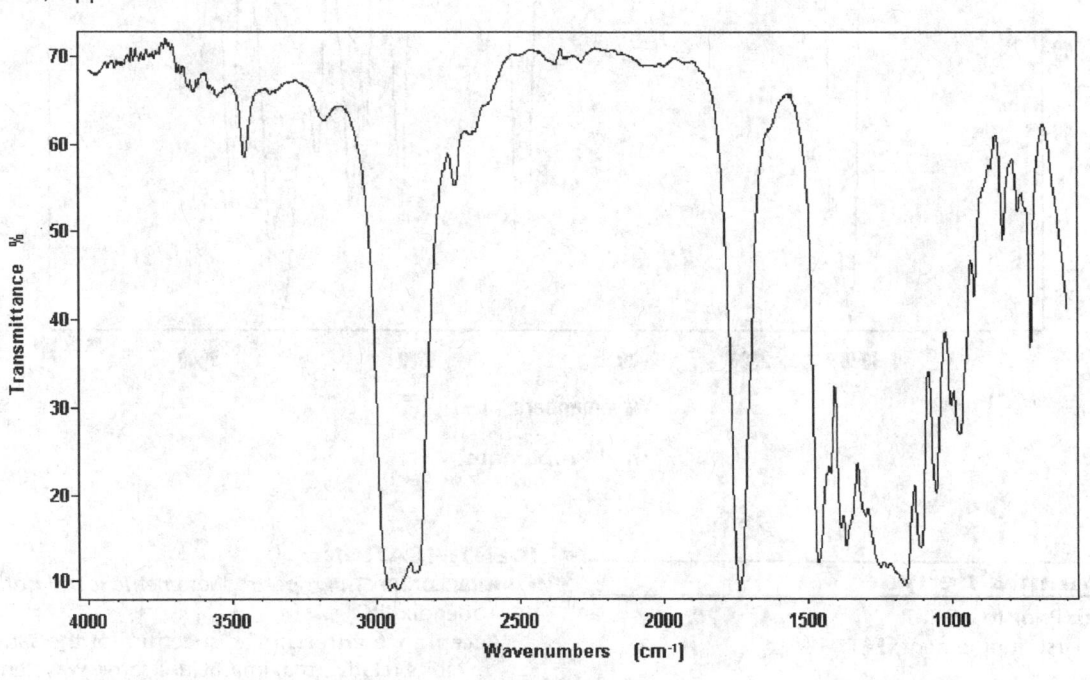

Amyl Octanoate

Amyl Propionate

First Published: Prior to FCC 6

Isoamyl Propionate

$C_8H_{16}O_2$ Formula wt 144.21
FEMA: 2082
UNII: 2A8739M82Z [isoamyl propionate]

DESCRIPTION
Amyl Propionate occurs as a colorless liquid.
Odor: Fruity, apricot-pineapple
Solubility: Soluble in alcohol, most fixed oils; insoluble or practically insoluble in glycerin, propylene glycol, water
Boiling Point: ~160°
Solubility in Alcohol, Appendix VI: One mL dissolves in 3 mL of 70% alcohol.
Function: Flavoring agent

IDENTIFICATION
- **INFRARED SPECTRA,** *Spectrophotometric Identification Tests,* Appendix IIIC
  Acceptance criteria: The spectrum of the sample exhibits relative maxima at the same wavelengths as those of the spectrum below.

ASSAY
- **PROCEDURE:** Proceed as directed under *M-1b,* Appendix XI.
  Acceptance criteria: NLT 98.0% of $C_8H_{16}O_2$ (sum of n-, 2-methyl butyl, and 3-methyl butyl isomers)

SPECIFIC TESTS
- **ACID VALUE, FLAVOR CHEMICALS (OTHER THAN ESSENTIAL OILS),** *M-15,* Appendix XI
  Acceptance criteria: NMT 1.0
- **REFRACTIVE INDEX,** Appendix II: At 20°
  Acceptance criteria: Between 1.405 and 1.409
- **SPECIFIC GRAVITY:** Determine at 25° by any reliable method (see *General Provisions*).
  Acceptance criteria: Between 0.866 and 0.871

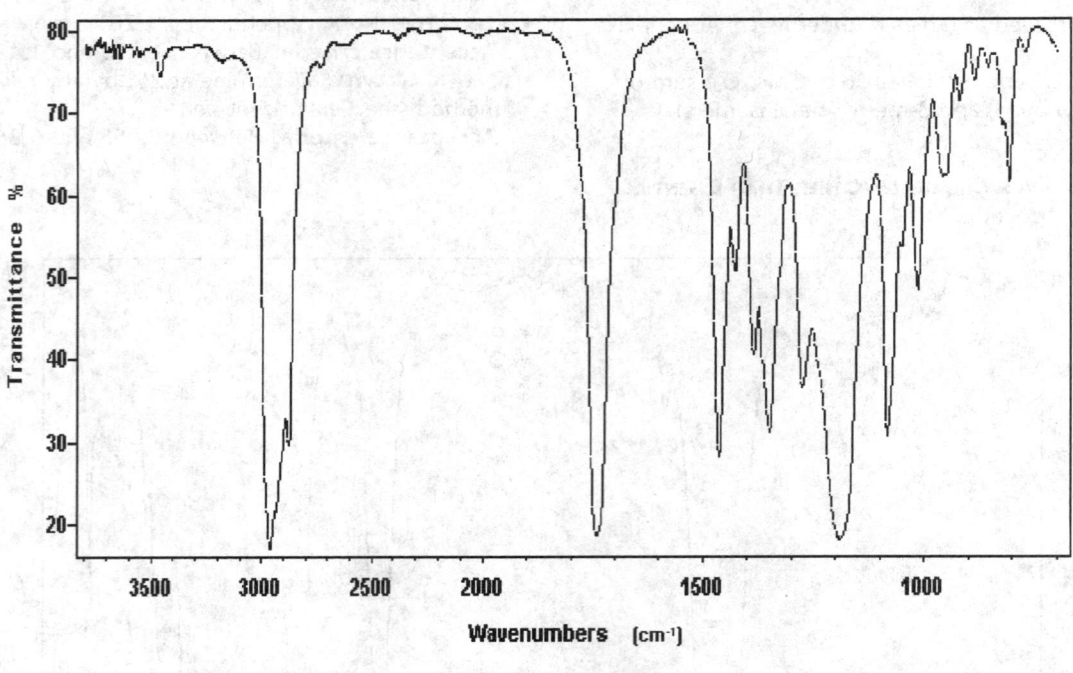

Amyl Propionate

α-Amylcinnamaldehyde

First Published: Prior to FCC 6
Last Revision: First Supplement, FCC 6

Amylcinnamaldehyde

$C_{14}H_{18}O$ Formula wt 202.30
FEMA: 2061
UNII: WC51CA3418 [α-amylcinnamaldehyde]

DESCRIPTION
α-Amylcinnamaldehyde occurs as a yellow liquid. It may contain a suitable antioxidant.
Odor: Strong, floral, jasmine on dilution, spicy
Solubility: Soluble in most fixed oils; insoluble or practically insoluble in glycerin, propylene glycol
Boiling Point: ~285°
Solubility in Alcohol, Appendix VI: One mL dissolves in 5 mL of 80% alcohol.
Function: Flavoring agent

IDENTIFICATION
- **INFRARED SPECTRA,** *Spectrophotometric Identification Tests,* Appendix IIIC
  Acceptance criteria: The spectrum of the sample exhibits relative maxima at the same wavelengths as those of the spectrum below.

ASSAY
- **PROCEDURE:** Proceed as directed under *M-1b,* Appendix XI.
  Acceptance criteria: NLT 97.0% of $C_{14}H_{18}O$ (sum of two isomers) and NLT 90% of the main isomer

SPECIFIC TESTS
- **ACID VALUE, FLAVOR CHEMICALS (OTHER THAN ESSENTIAL OILS),** *M-15,* Appendix XI
  Acceptance criteria: NMT 5.0
- **REFRACTIVE INDEX,** Appendix II: At 20°
  Acceptance criteria: Between 1.554 and 1.559
- **SPECIFIC GRAVITY:** Determine at 25° by any reliable method (see *General Provisions*).
  Acceptance criteria: Between 0.963 and 0.968

OTHER REQUIREMENTS
- **CHLORINATED COMPOUNDS,** Appendix VI
  Acceptance criteria: Passes test

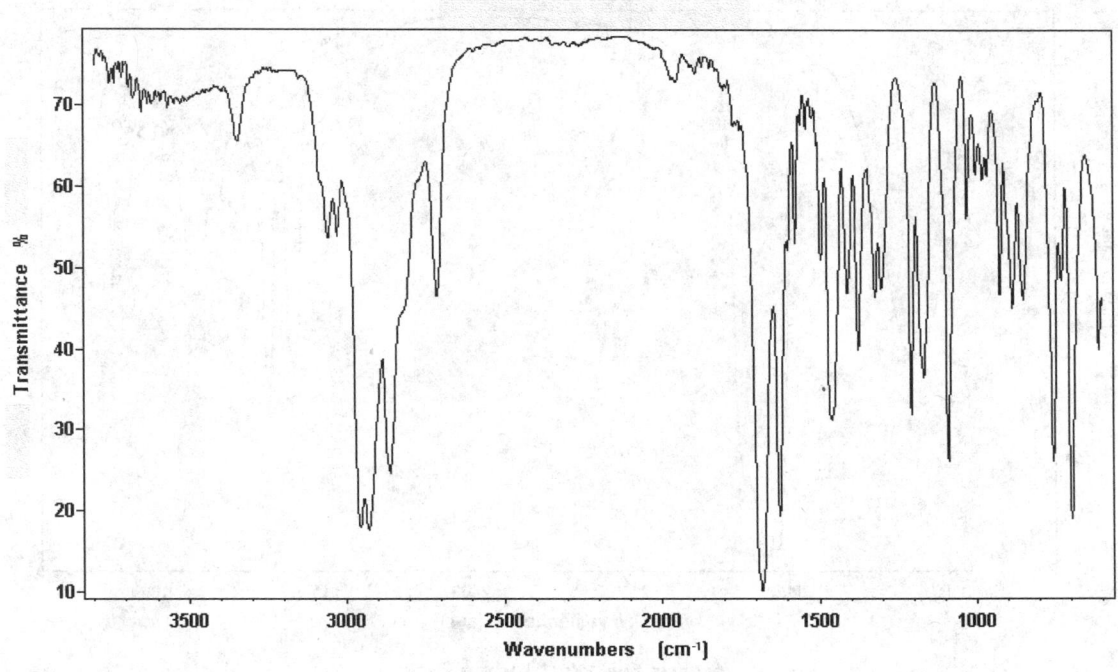

α-Amylcinnamaldehyde

Amyris Oil, West Indian Type
First Published: Prior to FCC 6

Sandalwood Oil, West Indian Type
UNII: I1BJ961J2E [amyris balsamifera oil]

DESCRIPTION
Amyris Oil, West Indian Type, occurs as a clear, pale yellow, viscous liquid having a distinct odor suggestive of sandalwood. It is the volatile oil obtained by steam distillation from the wood of *Amyris balsamifera* L. (Fam. Rutaceae). It is soluble in most fixed oils and usually in mineral oil. It is soluble in an equal volume of propylene glycol, the solution often becoming opalescent on further dilution. It is practically insoluble in glycerin.
Function: Flavoring agent
Packaging and Storage: Store in a cool place protected from light in full, tight containers that are made of aluminum or glass or that are lined with tin.

IDENTIFICATION
- **INFRARED SPECTRA,** *Spectrophotometric Identification Tests,* Appendix IIIC
  Acceptance criteria: The spectrum of the sample exhibits relative maxima at the same wavelengths as those of the spectrum below.

SPECIFIC TESTS
- **ACID VALUE (ESSENTIAL OILS AND FLAVORS),** Appendix VI
  Acceptance criteria: NMT 3.0
- **ANGULAR ROTATION,** *Optical (Specific) Rotation,* Appendix IIB: Use a 100-mm tube.
  Acceptance criteria: Between +10° and +53°
- **ESTER VALUE,** *Esters,* Appendix VI
  Sample: 5 g
  Acceptance criteria: NMT 7
- **ESTER VALUE AFTER ACETYLATION,** *Total Alcohols,* Appendix VI
  Sample: 2 g of the dried acetylated oil
  Analysis: Modify the reflux time for the acetylation to 2 h, instead of 1 h. Calculate the *Ester Value after Acetylation* by the formula:

  $$\text{Result} = A \times 28.05/B$$

  A = amount (mL) of 0.5 N alcoholic potassium hydroxide consumed in the saponification
  B = weight (g) of the acetylated oil used
  Acceptance criteria: Between 115 and 165
- **REFRACTIVE INDEX,** Appendix IIB
  [NOTE—Use an Abbé or other refractometer of equal or greater accuracy.]
  Acceptance criteria: Between 1.503 and 1.512 at 20°
- **SOLUBILITY IN ALCOHOL,** Appendix VI
  Acceptance criteria: One mL of sample dissolves in 3 mL of 80% alcohol, often with opalescence.
- **SPECIFIC GRAVITY,** Appendix VII
  Acceptance criteria: Between 0.943 and 0.976

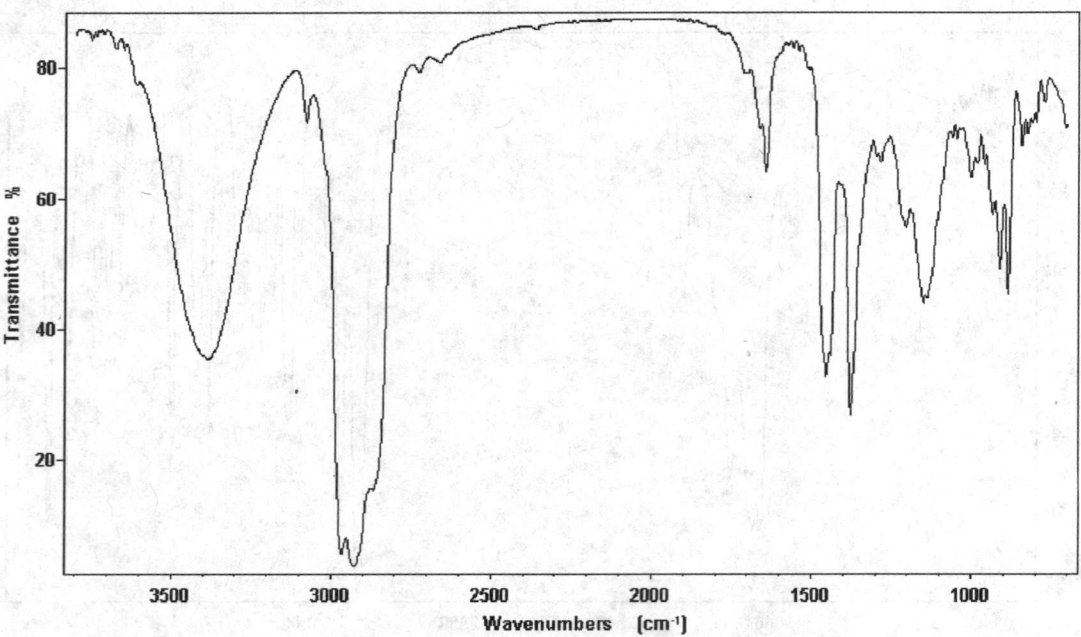

Amyris Oil, West Indian Type

Anethole

First Published: Prior to FCC 6
Last Revision: FCC 6

trans-Anethole
Isoestragole
p-Propenylanisole

$C_{10}H_{12}O$ Formula wt 148.20
FEMA: 2086
UNII: Q3JEK5DO4K [anethole]

DESCRIPTION
Anethole occurs as a colorless to faintly yellow liquid at or above 23°; sweet taste.
Odor: Anise
Solubility: Slightly soluble in water; miscible in chloroform, ether
Boiling Point: ~234°
Solubility in Alcohol, Appendix VI: One mL dissolves in 2 mL of alcohol.
Function: Flavoring agent

IDENTIFICATION
- **INFRARED ABSORPTION,** *Spectrophotometric Identification Tests,* Appendix IIIC
  Reference standard: USP Anethole AS
  Sample and standard preparation: *F*
  Acceptance criteria: The spectrum of the sample exhibits maxima at the same wavelengths as those in the spectrum of the *Reference standard*.

ASSAY
- **PROCEDURE:** Proceed as directed under *M-1b*, Appendix XI.
  Acceptance criteria: NLT 99.0% of $C_{10}H_{12}O$

SPECIFIC TESTS
- **REFRACTIVE INDEX,** Appendix II: At 20°
  Acceptance criteria: Between 1.557 and 1.562
- **SPECIFIC GRAVITY:** Determine at 25° by any reliable method (see *General Provisions*).
  Acceptance criteria: Between 0.983 and 0.988

OTHER REQUIREMENTS
- **ANGULAR ROTATION,** *Optical (Specific) Rotation,* Appendix IIB: Use a 100-mm tube.
  Acceptance criteria: Between −0.15° and +0.15°
- **DISTILLATION RANGE,** Appendix IIB
  Acceptance criteria: Between 231° and 237°
- **PHENOLS,** *M-17,* Appendix XI
  Acceptance criteria: Passes test
- **SOLIDIFICATION POINT,** Appendix IIB
  Acceptance criteria: NLT 20°

Angelica Root Oil

First Published: Prior to FCC 6

CAS: [8015-64-3]

UNII: B25G881UOX [angelica root oil]

DESCRIPTION
Angelica Root Oil occurs as a pale yellow to deep amber liquid with a warm, pungent odor and bittersweet taste. It is obtained by steam distillation of the dried slender rootlets of *Angelica archangelica* L. (Fam. Umbelliferae). It is soluble in most fixed oils, slightly soluble in mineral oil, but relatively insoluble in glycerin and in propylene glycol. The oil increases in specific gravity and viscosity during storage.
Function: Flavoring agent
Packaging and Storage: Store in a cool place protected from light in full, tight containers that are made from steel or aluminum and that are suitably lined.

IDENTIFICATION
- **INFRARED SPECTRA,** *Spectrophotometric Identification Tests,* Appendix IIIC
  Acceptance criteria: The spectrum of the sample exhibits relative maxima at the same wavelengths as those of the spectrum below.

SPECIFIC TESTS
- **ACID VALUE (ESSENTIAL OILS AND FLAVORS),** Appendix VI
  Acceptance criteria: NMT 7.0
- **ANGULAR ROTATION,** *Optical (Specific) Rotation,* Appendix IIB: Use a 100-mm tube.
  Acceptance criteria: Between 0° and +46°
- **ESTERS,** *Ester Value,* Appendix VI
  Sample: 5 g
  Acceptance criteria: Between 10 and 65
- **REFRACTIVE INDEX,** Appendix IIB
  [NOTE—Use an Abbé or other refractometer of equal or greater accuracy.]
  Acceptance criteria: Between 1.473 and 1.487 at 20°
- **SOLUBILITY IN ALCOHOL,** Appendix VI
  Acceptance criteria: One mL of sample dissolves in 1 mL of 90% alcohol, often with turbidity, and remains in solution on further addition of alcohol to a total of 10 mL.
- **SPECIFIC GRAVITY:** Determine by any reliable method (see *General Provisions*.)
  Acceptance criteria: Between 0.850 and 0.880

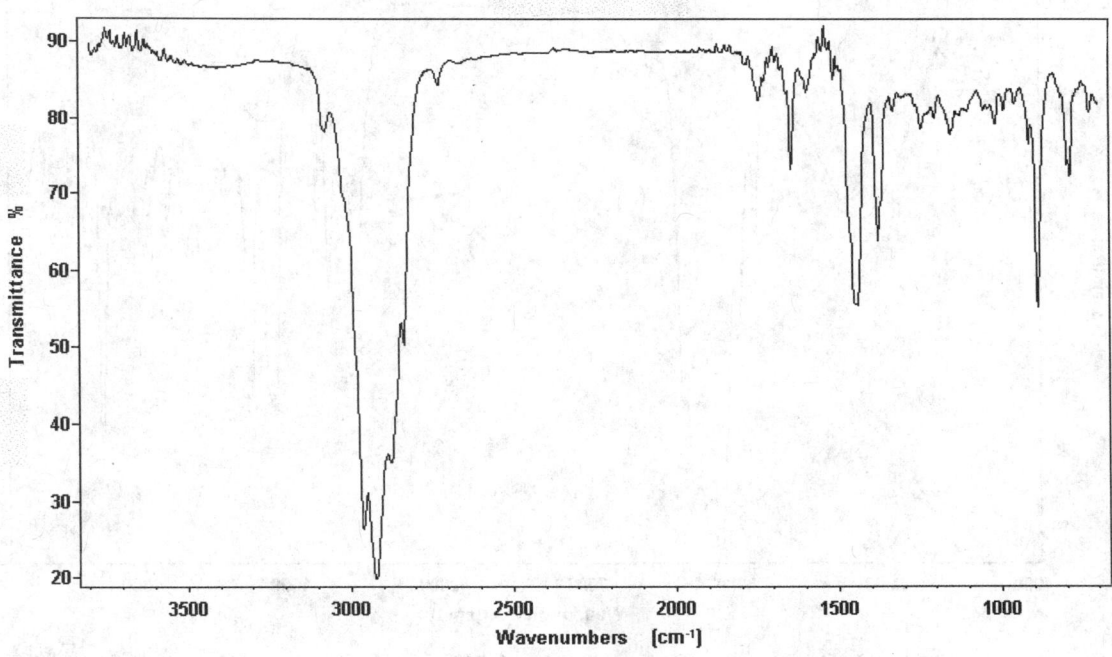

Angelica Root Oil

Angelica Seed Oil

First Published: Prior to FCC 6

UNII: 67IO7RRV7A [angelica seed oil]

DESCRIPTION
Angelica Seed Oil occurs as a light yellow liquid having a sweeter and more delicate aroma than the root oil. It is obtained by steam distillation of the fresh seeds of *Angelica archangelica* L. (Fam. Umbelliferae). It is soluble in most fixed oils, slightly soluble in mineral oil, but relatively insoluble in glycerin and in propylene glycol.

Function: Flavoring agent

Packaging and Storage: Store in a cool place protected from light in full, tight containers that are made from steel or aluminum and that are suitably lined.

IDENTIFICATION
- **INFRARED SPECTRA,** *Spectrophotometric Identification Tests,* Appendix IIIC
  Acceptance criteria: The spectrum of the sample exhibits relative maxima at the same wavelengths as those of the spectrum below.

SPECIFIC TESTS
- **ACID VALUE (ESSENTIAL OILS AND FLAVORS),** Appendix VI
  Acceptance criteria: NMT 3.0
- **ANGULAR ROTATION,** *Optical (Specific) Rotation,* Appendix IIB: Use a 100-mm tube.
  Acceptance criteria: Between +4° and +16°
- **ESTERS,** *Ester Value,* Appendix VI
  Sample: 5 g
  Acceptance criteria: Between 14.0 and 32.0
- **REFRACTIVE INDEX,** Appendix IIB
  [NOTE—Use an Abbé or other refractometer of equal or greater accuracy.]
  Acceptance criteria: Between 1.480 and 1.488 at 20°
- **SOLUBILITY IN ALCOHOL,** Appendix VI
  Acceptance criteria: One mL of sample dissolves in 4 mL of 90% alcohol, often with considerable turbidity, and it remains in solution on further addition of alcohol to a total of 10 mL.
- **SPECIFIC GRAVITY:** Determine by any reliable method (see *General Provisions*).
  Acceptance criteria: Between 0.853 and 0.876

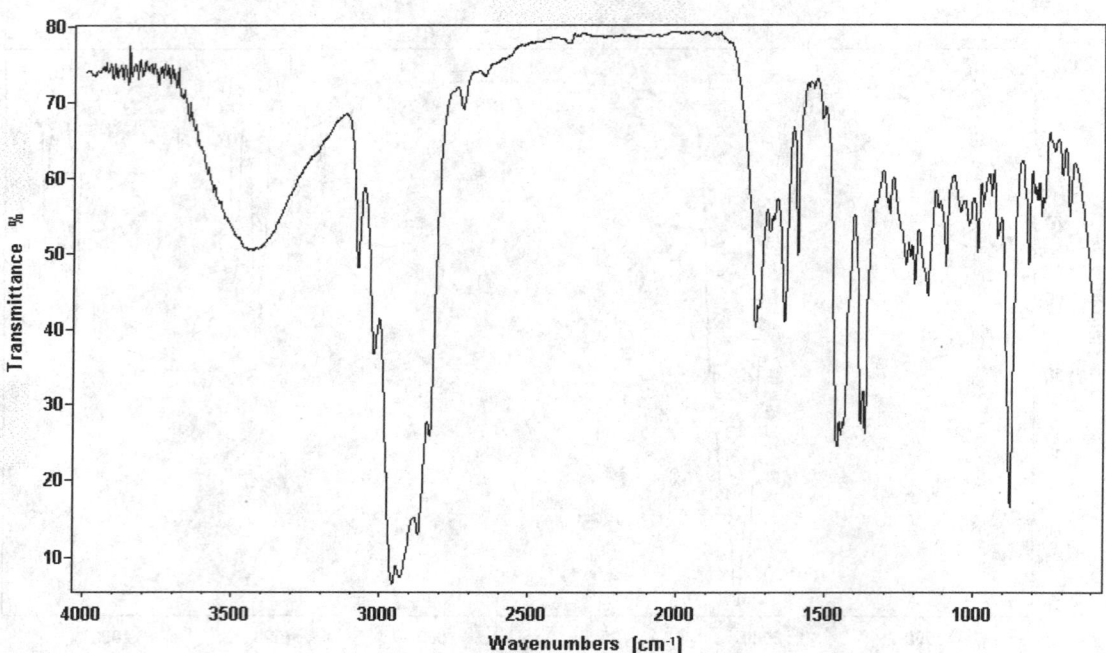

Angelica Seed Oil

Anise Oil

First Published: Prior to FCC 6

CAS: [8007-70-3]

UNII: 6Y89129C8H [anise oil]

DESCRIPTION
Anise Oil occurs as a colorless to pale yellow, strongly refractive liquid with the characteristic odor and taste of anise. It is obtained by steam distillation of the dried ripe fruit of *Pimpinella anisum* L. (Fam. Umbelliferae) or *Illicium verum* Hooker filius (Fam. Magnoliaceae).

[NOTE—If solid material has separated, carefully warm the sample until it is completely liquefied, and mix before using it.]

Function: Flavoring agent

Packaging and Storage: Store in a cool place protected from light in full, tight containers that are made from steel or aluminum and that are suitably lined.

IDENTIFICATION
- **INFRARED SPECTRA,** *Spectrophotometric Identification Tests,* Appendix IIIC
  Acceptance criteria: The spectrum of the sample exhibits relative maxima at the same wavelengths as those of the spectrum below.

SPECIFIC TESTS
- **ANGULAR ROTATION,** *Optical (Specific) Rotation,* Appendix IIB: Use a 100-mm tube.
  Acceptance criteria: Between −2° and +1°
- **PHENOLS**
  Sample solution: 1 : 3 in 90% alcohol, using a recently distilled sample
  Analysis: Test the *Sample solution* with moistened litmus paper. Then, add 1 drop of ferric chloride TS to 5 mL of the *Sample solution.*
  Acceptance criteria: The *Sample solution* is neutral to litmus and no blue or brown color is produced by the addition of ferric chloride TS.
- **REFRACTIVE INDEX,** Appendix IIB
  [NOTE—Use an Abbé or other refractometer of equal or greater accuracy.]
  Acceptance criteria: Between 1.553 and 1.560 at 20°
- **SOLIDIFICATION POINT,** Appendix IIB
  Acceptance criteria: NLT 15°
- **SOLUBILITY IN ALCOHOL,** Appendix VI
  Analysis: Use 3 mL of 90% alcohol.
  Acceptance criteria: Passes test
- **SPECIFIC GRAVITY:** Determine by any reliable method (see *General Provisions*).
  Acceptance criteria: Between 0.978 and 0.988

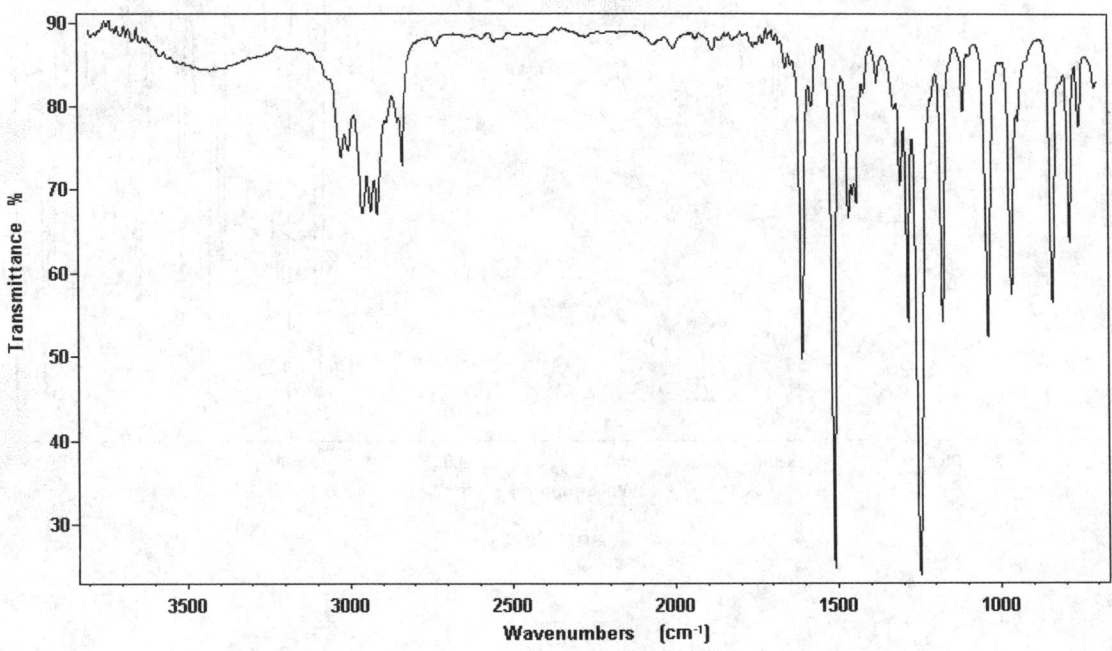

Anise Oil

Anisole

First Published: Prior to FCC 6

Methylphenyl Ether

C₇H₈O   Formula wt 108.14
FEMA: 2097
UNII: B3W693GAZH [anisole]

DESCRIPTION
Anisole occurs as a colorless liquid.
Odor: Phenolic, anise
Solubility: Soluble in alcohol, ether; insoluble or practically insoluble in water
Boiling Point: ~154°
Function: Flavoring agent

IDENTIFICATION
- **INFRARED SPECTRA,** *Spectrophotometric Identification Tests,* Appendix IIIC
  Acceptance criteria: The spectrum of the sample exhibits relative maxima at the same wavelengths as those of the spectrum below.

ASSAY
- **PROCEDURE:** Proceed as directed under *M-1b,* Appendix XI.
  Acceptance criteria: NLT 97.0% of C₇H₈O

SPECIFIC TESTS
- **REFRACTIVE INDEX,** Appendix II: At 20°
  Acceptance criteria: Between 1.515 and 1.518
- **SPECIFIC GRAVITY:** Determine at 25° by any reliable method (see *General Provisions*).
  Acceptance criteria: Between 0.990 and 0.993

OTHER REQUIREMENTS
- **DISTILLATION RANGE,** Appendix IIB
  Acceptance criteria: Within a 2° range
- **PHENOLS,** *M-17,* Appendix XI
  Acceptance criteria: Passes test

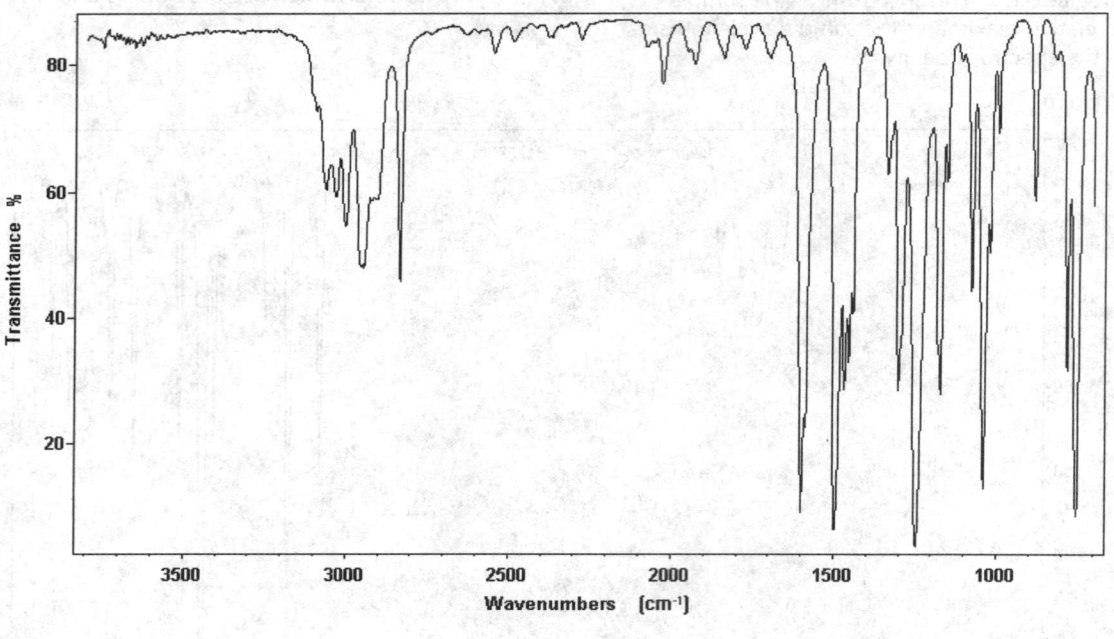

Anisole

Anisyl Acetate

First Published: Prior to FCC 6

p-Methoxybenzyl Acetate

C₁₀H₁₂O₃ Formula wt 180.20
FEMA: 2098
UNII: 2GEC7KBO31 [anisyl acetate]

DESCRIPTION
Anisyl Acetate occurs as a colorless to slightly yellow liquid.
Odor: Floral, fruity, balsamic
Solubility: Soluble in alcohol, most fixed oils; insoluble or practically insoluble in glycerin, propylene glycol
Boiling Point: ~235°
Solubility in Alcohol, Appendix VI: One mL dissolves in 6 mL of 60% alcohol, and remains in solution to 10 mL.

Function: Flavoring agent

IDENTIFICATION
- **INFRARED SPECTRA,** *Spectrophotometric Identification Tests,* Appendix IIIC
  Acceptance criteria: The spectrum of the sample exhibits relative maxima at the same wavelengths as those of the spectrum below.

ASSAY
- **PROCEDURE:** Proceed as directed under *M-1b,* Appendix XI.
  Acceptance criteria: NLT 97.0% of C₁₀H₁₂O₃

SPECIFIC TESTS
- **ACID VALUE, FLAVOR CHEMICALS (OTHER THAN ESSENTIAL OILS),** *M-15,* Appendix XI
  Acceptance criteria: NMT 1.0
- **REFRACTIVE INDEX,** Appendix II: At 20°
  Acceptance criteria: Between 1.511 and 1.516
- **SPECIFIC GRAVITY:** Determine at 25° by any reliable method (see *General Provisions*).
  Acceptance criteria: Between 1.104 and 1.111

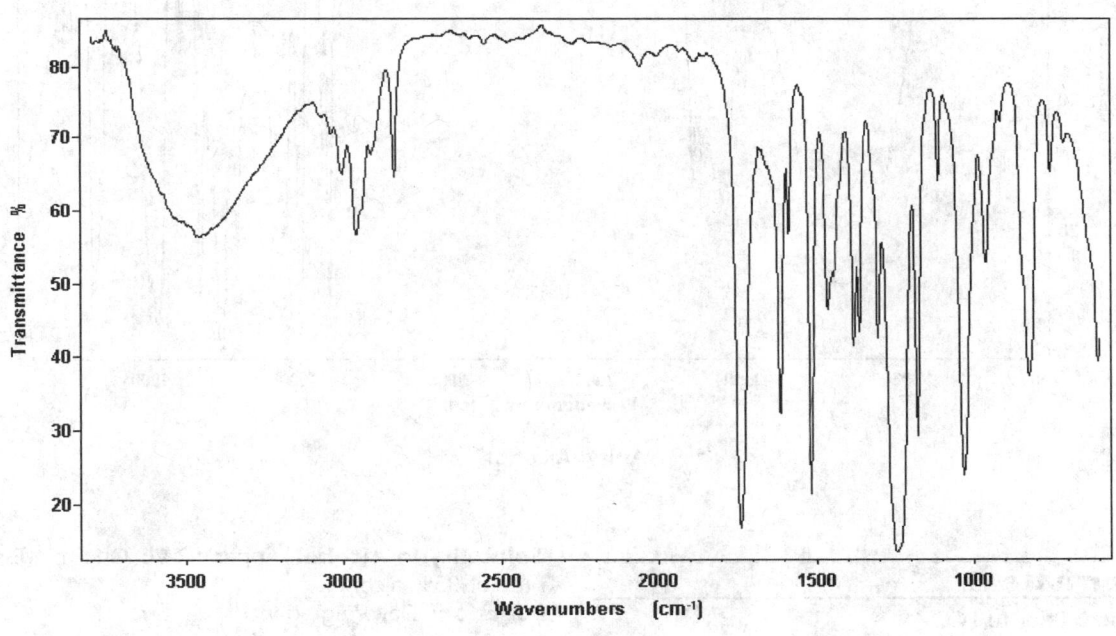

Anisyl Acetate

Anisyl Alcohol

First Published: Prior to FCC 6

Anisic Alcohol
p-Methoxybenzyl Alcohol

C₈H₁₀O₂ Formula wt 138.17
FEMA: 2099
UNII: 7N6XGV3U49 [anisyl alcohol]

DESCRIPTION
Anisyl Alcohol occurs as a colorless to slightly yellow liquid.
Odor: Floral
Solubility: Soluble in most fixed oils; slightly soluble in glycerin
Boiling Point: ~259°

72 / Anisyl Alcohol / *Monographs*

Solubility in Alcohol, Appendix VI: One mL dissolves in 1 mL of 50% alcohol, and remains in solution on dilution to 10 mL.
Function: Flavoring agent

IDENTIFICATION
- **INFRARED SPECTRA,** *Spectrophotometric Identification Tests,* Appendix IIIC
  Acceptance criteria: The spectrum of the sample exhibits relative maxima at the same wavelengths as those of the spectrum below.

ASSAY
- **PROCEDURE:** Proceed as directed under *M-1b,* Appendix XI.
  Acceptance criteria: NLT 97.0% of $C_8H_{10}O_2$

SPECIFIC TESTS
- **ACID VALUE, FLAVOR CHEMICALS (OTHER THAN ESSENTIAL OILS),** *M-15,* Appendix XI
  Acceptance criteria: NMT 1.0
- **REFRACTIVE INDEX,** Appendix II: At 20°
  Acceptance criteria: Between 1.542 and 1.547
- **SPECIFIC GRAVITY:** Determine at 25° by any reliable method (see *General Provisions*).
  Acceptance criteria: Between 1.110 and 1.115

OTHER REQUIREMENTS
- **ALDEHYDES,** *M-1b,* Appendix XI
  Acceptance criteria: NMT 1.0% as anisaldehyde
- **SOLIDIFICATION POINT,** Appendix IIB
  Acceptance criteria: NLT 23.5°

Anisyl Alcohol (IR spectrum)

Anisyl Formate

First Published: Prior to FCC 6

p-Methoxybenzyl Formate

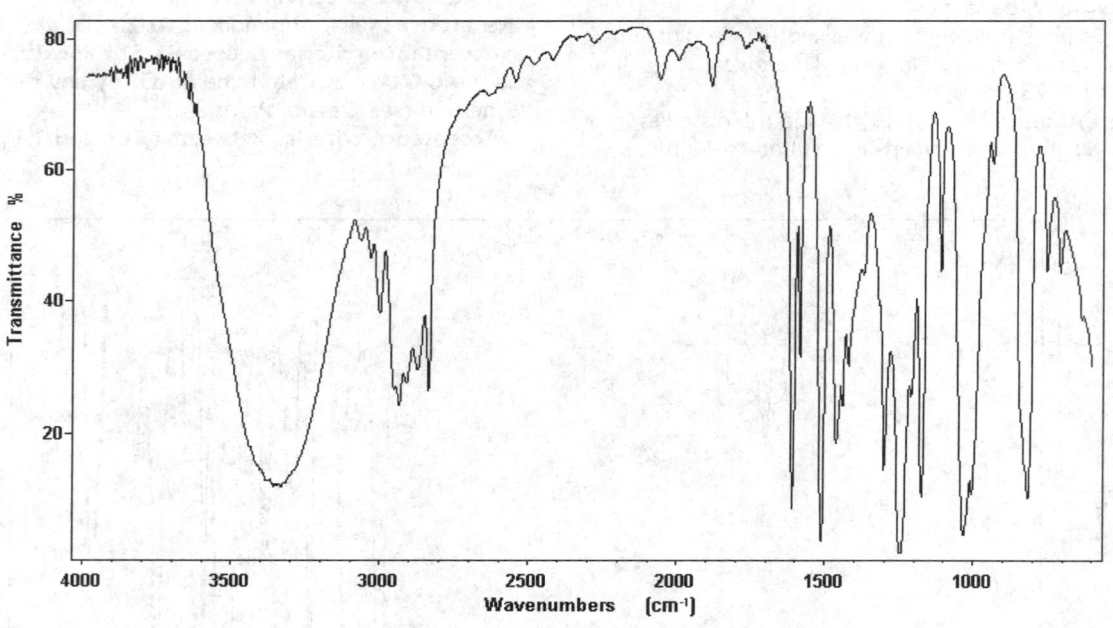

$C_9H_{10}O_3$ Formula wt 166.18
FEMA: 2101
UNII: 7N0AD05BXI [anisyl formate]

DESCRIPTION
Anisyl Formate occurs as a colorless to pale yellow liquid.
Odor: Sweet, floral, tonka
Boiling Point: ~100°

Solubility in Alcohol, Appendix VI: One mL dissolves in 1 mL of 95% alcohol.
Function: Flavoring agent

IDENTIFICATION
- **INFRARED SPECTRA,** *Spectrophotometric Identification Tests,* Appendix IIIC
  Acceptance criteria: The spectrum of the sample exhibits relative maxima at the same wavelengths as those of the spectrum below.

ASSAY
- **PROCEDURE:** Proceed as directed under *M-1b,* Appendix XI.
  Acceptance criteria: NLT 90.0% of $C_9H_{10}O_3$

SPECIFIC TESTS
- **ACID VALUE, FLAVOR CHEMICALS (OTHER THAN ESSENTIAL OILS),** *M-15,* Appendix XI

Acceptance criteria: NMT 3.0
- **REFRACTIVE INDEX**, Appendix II: At 20°
  Acceptance criteria: Between 1.521 and 1.525

- **SPECIFIC GRAVITY**: Determine at 25° by any reliable method (see *General Provisions*).
  Acceptance criteria: Between 1.138 and 1.142

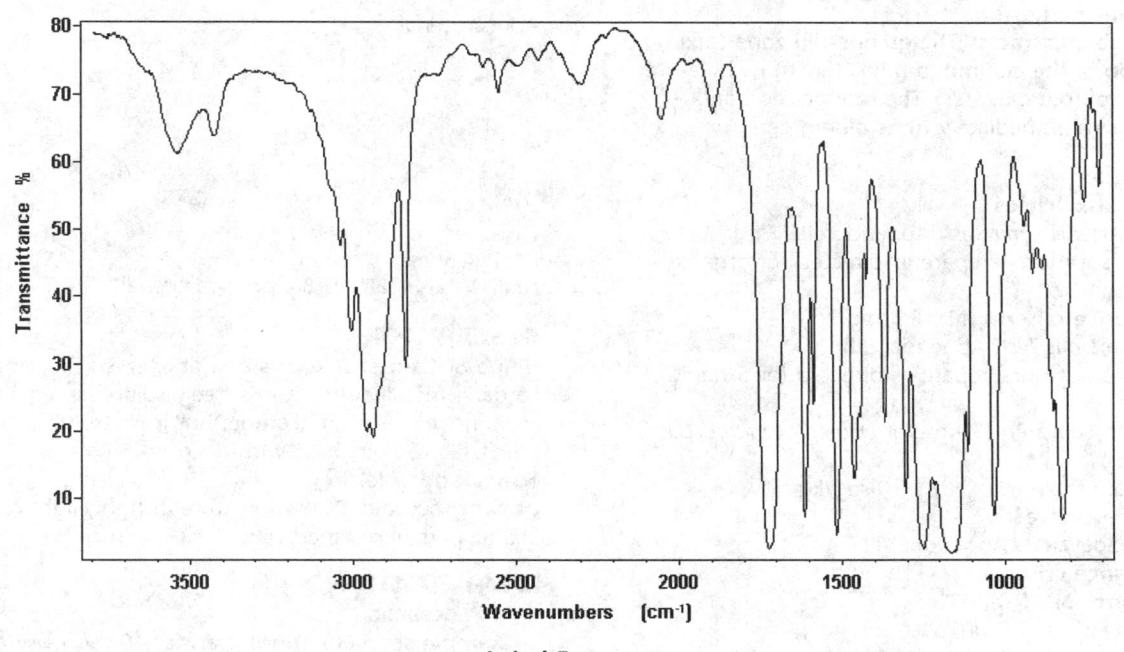

Anisyl Formate

Annatto Extracts

First Published: Prior to FCC 6

INS: 160b
UNII: 6PQP1V1B6O [annatto]
CAS: [1393-63-1]

DESCRIPTION
Annatto Extracts occur as dark red solutions, emulsions, or suspensions in water or oil or as dark red powders. The extract is prepared from annatto seeds, *Bixa orellana* L. (Fam. Bixaceae), using a food-grade extraction solvent. Bixin is the principal pigment of oil-soluble Annatto Extracts. Norbixin is the principal pigment of alkaline water-soluble Annatto Extracts. Commercial preparations are usually mixtures of bixin, norbixin, and other carotenoids.

Function: Color

Packaging and Storage: Store under refrigeration in full, well-closed containers that are made from steel or aluminum and that are suitably lined.

IDENTIFICATION
- **VISIBLE ABSORPTION SPECTRUM**
  Sample preparation
    Oil-soluble extracts: Dilute a sample with acetone.
    Water-soluble extracts: Dilute a sample with water.
  Acceptance criteria
    Oil-soluble extracts: The solution exhibits absorbance maxima at 439, 470, and 501 nm.
    Water-soluble extracts: The solution exhibits absorbance maxima at 451 to 455 nm and 480 to 484 nm.
- **CARR-PRICE REACTION,** *Column Chromatography*, Appendix IIA
  Column: Fill a 200- × 7-mm glass tube, stoppered with glass wool, with alumina (80- to 200-mesh) slurried in toluene so that the settled alumina fills about 2/3 of the tube. Use a rubber outlet tube and clamp to adjust the flow rate to about 30 drops/min.
  Analysis
    Oil-soluble extracts: Add to the top of the *Column* 3 mL of a solution containing sufficient sample, in toluene, to impart a color equivalent to a solution of 0.1% potassium dichromate. Elute with toluene until a pale yellow fraction is washed from the column. Wash the column with three 10-mL volumes of dry acetone and follow with 5 mL of *Carr-Price Reagent* (see *Test Solutions (TS) and Other Reagents,* Solutions and Indicators), added to the top of the column.
    Water-soluble extracts: Transfer 2 mL or 2 g of sample into a 50-mL separatory funnel, and add sufficient 2 N sulfuric acid to make the solution acidic to pH test paper (pH 1 to 2). Dissolve the red precipitate of norbixin by mixing the solution with 50 mL of toluene. Discard the water layer, and wash the toluene phase with water until it no longer gives an acid reaction. Remove any undissolved norbixin by centrifugation or filtration, and dry the solution over anhydrous sodium sulfate. Transfer 3 to 5 mL of the dry solution to the top of the *Column* and elute with

toluene, three 10-mL volumes of dry acetone, and 5 mL of *Carr-Price Reagent* (see *Test Solutions (TS) and Other Reagents,* Solutions and Indicators,) added to the top of the column.

Acceptance criteria
Oil-soluble extracts: The orange-red zone (bixin) at the top of the column immediately turns blue-green.
Water-soluble extracts: The orange-red band (norbixin) immediately turns blue-green.

IMPURITIES
Inorganic Impurities
- **Arsenic,** *Arsenic Limit Test,* Appendix IIIB
  Sample solution: Prepare as directed for organic compounds.
  Acceptance criteria: NMT 3 mg/kg
- **Lead,** *Lead Limit Test,* Appendix IIIB
  Sample solution: Prepare as directed for organic compounds.
  Control: 10 μg Pb (10 mL of *Diluted Standard Lead Solution*)
  Acceptance criteria: NMT 10 mg/kg

Organic Impurities
- **Residual Solvents,** Appendix VIII
  Acceptance criteria
  Acetone: NMT 0.003%
  Hexanes: NMT 0.0025%
  Isopropyl alcohol: NMT 0.005%
  Methyl alcohol: NMT 0.005%
  Trichloroethylene and Dichloromethane: NMT 0.003%, individually or in combination

SPECIFIC TESTS
- **Color Intensity**
  Analysis
  Oil-soluble extracts: Transfer a sample, accurately weighed, into a solution of 1% glacial acetic acid in acetone, and dilute to a suitable volume (absorbance of 0.5 to 1.0). Filter the sample to clarify it if necessary. Measure the absorbance at 454 nm, and calculate the color intensity by the formula:

  $$\text{Result} = A/(b \times c)$$

  A = absorbance of the sample solution
  b = pathlength of the cell (cm)
  c = concentration of the sample solution (g/L)

  Water-soluble extracts: Proceed as directed for *Oil-soluble extracts,* but dissolve the sample in 0.1 M sodium hydroxide, and measure the absorbance at 453 nm.
  Acceptance criteria: The sample meets the representations of the vendor.

β-Apo-8'-Carotenal
First Published: Prior to FCC 6

Apocarotenal
APO

$C_{30}H_{40}O$ Formula wt 416.65
INS: 160e CAS: [1107-26-2]
UNII: V22N3E2U32 [8'-apo-β-carotenal]

DESCRIPTION
β-Apo-8'-Carotenal occurs as a fine, crystalline powder with a dark, metallic sheen. It is freely soluble in chloroform and sparingly soluble in acetone, but it is insoluble in water. It melts at 136° to 140° with decomposition.
Function: Color
Packaging and Storage: Store in tight, light-resistant containers under inert gas.

IDENTIFICATION
- **A. Procedure**
  Sample stock solution: Transfer 40 mg of sample into a 100-mL volumetric flask, add 10 mL of acid-free chloroform to dissolve the sample, dilute to volume with cyclohexane, and mix. Pipet 2 mL of this solution into a 50-mL volumetric flask, dilute to volume with cyclohexane, and mix.
  Sample solution: Pipet 5 mL of *Sample stock solution* into a 50-mL volumetric flask, dilute to volume with cyclohexane, and mix.
  Analysis: Determine the absorbance (A) of the *Sample solution* at 488 nm and at 460 nm.
  Acceptance criteria: The ratio A_{488}/A_{460} is between 0.77 and 0.85.
- **B. Procedure**
  Sample stock solution: Prepared as directed above under *Identification* test A
  Sample solution: Prepared as directed above under *Identification* test A
  Analysis: Determine the absorbance (A) of the *Sample stock solution* at 332 nm and of the *Sample solution* at 460 nm.
  Acceptance criteria: The ratio A_{332}/A_{460} is between 0.63 and 0.75.

ASSAY
- **Procedure:** [Note—Carry out all work in low-actinic glassware and in subdued light.]
  Sample stock solution: Prepared as directed above under *Identification* test A.
  Sample solution: Prepared as directed above under *Identification* test A.
  Analysis: Using a suitable spectrophotometer and a 1-cm cell, measure the absorbance at 460 nm of the *Sample solution*; use cyclohexane for the blank.

Calculate the weight (mg) of $C_{30}H_{40}O$ in the sample taken by the formula:

$$Result = 25{,}000 \times A/a$$

A = absorbance of Sample solution B
a = absorptivity (264) of pure β-Apo-8'-Carotenal

Acceptance criteria: NLT 96.0% and NMT 101.0% of $C_{30}H_{40}O$

IMPURITIES
Inorganic Impurities
- **ARSENIC,** Arsenic Limit Test, Appendix IIIB
  Sample solution: Prepare as directed for organic compounds.
  Acceptance criteria: NMT 1 mg/kg
- **LEAD,** Lead Limit Test, Appendix IIIB
  Sample solution: Prepare as directed for organic compounds.
  Control: 10 μg Pb (10 mL of Diluted Standard Lead Solution)
  Acceptance criteria: NMT 10 mg/kg

SPECIFIC TESTS
- **RESIDUE ON IGNITION (SULFATED ASH),** Appendix IIC
  Sample: 2 g
  Acceptance criteria: NMT 0.2%

ARA from Fungal (*Mortierella alpina*) Oil

First Published: Third Supplement, FCC 7

Arachidonic Acid-Rich Oil
ARA Fungal Oil
ARA-Rich Oil
ARA-Rich Single Cell Oil
Mortierella alpina Oil
Refined Arachidonic Acid-Rich Oil (RAO)

DESCRIPTION
ARA from Fungal (*Mortierella alpina*) Oil occurs as a clear, yellow-colored oil providing a source of arachidonic acid (ARA, $C_{20}H_{32}O_2$) (C20:4 n-6), an omega-6 long-chain polyunsaturated fatty acid. It is obtained from fermentation of the species of fungus *Mortierella alpina* usually followed by solvent extraction. The oil may be winterized, bleached, and deodorized to substantially remove free fatty acids, phospholipids, odor and flavor components, and other material. Arachidonic acid is the main polyunsaturated fatty acid present; ARA content may be standardized with other oils. Suitable antioxidants may be added.

Function: Source of ARA
Packaging and Storage: Store in tight, light-resistant containers. Avoid exposure to excessive heat.

IDENTIFICATION
- **FATTY ACID COMPOSITION,** Fatty Acid Composition (Saturated, cis-Monounsaturated, and cis-Polyunsaturated) in Oils Containing Long Chain Polyunsaturated Fatty Acids, Appendix VII
  Acceptance criteria: The retention times of the peaks of the arachidonic acid methyl ester from the Sample Preparation correspond to those from the Standard Solution. The percentage of the fatty acids (calculated using the results from the corresponding methyl esters) from the Sample Preparation, determined as the percentage of total fat, meet the requirements for each fatty acid indicated in the table below.

Fatty Acid	Shorthand Notation	Lower Limit (Area %)	Upper Limit (Area %)
Myristic acid	14:0	0.1	0.5
Palmitic acid	16:0	4.3	8.1
Palmitoleic acid	16:1 n-9	0	0.4
Stearic acid	18:0	4.2	7.6
Oleic acid	18:1 n-9	3.4	9.5
Linoleic acid	18:2 n-6	3.8	15.2
gamma-Linolenic acid	18:3 n-6	1.7	2.7
Arachidic acid	20:0	0.6	1.0
Dihomo-gamma-linolenic acid	20:3 n-6	3.0	5.0
Arachidonic acid	20:4 n-6	38.0	48.5
Behenic acid	22:0	2.5	4.1
Lignoceric acid	24:0	7.8	12.6

ASSAY
- **ARA,** Fatty Acid Composition (Saturated, cis-Monounsaturated, and cis-Polyunsaturated) in Oils Containing Long Chain Polyunsaturated Fatty Acids, Appendix VII
  Analysis: Proceed as directed. Calculate the percentage of ARA (w/w, as a percentage of total fatty acids) in the portion of the sample taken:

$$Result = (W_{FAMEx} \times F_{FAx})/\Sigma W_{TAG}$$

  [NOTE—Use the definitions provided for W_{FAMEx}, F_{FAx}, and ΣW_{TAG} in the method referenced, where x is arachidonic acid.]
  Acceptance criteria: NLT 38.0% arachidonic acid (ARA)

IMPURITIES
Inorganic Impurities
- **ARSENIC,** Elemental Impurities by ICP, Appendix IIIC
  [NOTE—Alternatively, the arsenic content may be determined by the following method.]
  Apparatus
  Sample digestion: Use a microwave oven[1] equipped with advanced composite vessels with 100-mL Teflon liners. Use rupture membranes to vent vessels should the pressure exceed 125 psi. The vessels fit into a turntable, and each vessel can be vented into an overflow container. Equip the microwave oven with an exhaust tube to ventilate fumes.

---
[1] CEM Model MDS-2100, or equivalent.

Sample analysis: Use a suitable graphite furnace atomic absorption spectrophotometer (GFAAS) equipped with an autosampler, pyrolytically coated graphite tubes, solid pyrolytic graphite platforms, and an adequate means of background correction.[2] An electrodeless discharge lamp serves as the source, argon as the purge gas, and air as the alternate gas. Set up the instrument according to the manufacturer's specifications, with consideration of current good GFAAS practices. The instrument parameters are as follows:
Wavelength: 193.7 nm
Lamp current: 300 (EDL) modulated
Pyrolysis: 1000°
Atomization: 2400°
Slit: 0.7
Characteristic mass: 15 pg
Glassware: Acid wash all glass, Teflon, and plastic vessels by soaking them in a nitric acid bath containing a 4:1 solution of water and nitric acid. [**Caution**—Wear a full face shield, protective clothing, and gloves at all times when working with acid baths.] After acid soaking, rinse the acid-washed items in deionized water, dry them, and store them in clean, covered cabinets.
Calibration standard stock solution: 100 µg/L. Prepare from a suitable standard, which may be purchased [accuracy certified against National Institute of Standards and Technology (NIST) spectrometric standard solutions].
Calibration standard solutions: 2.0 µg/L, 5.0 µg/L, 10.0 µg/L, 25.0 µg/L, and 50.0 µg/L in 2% nitric acid from the *Calibration standard stock solution*
1% Palladium stock solution: Mix 1 g of ultrapure palladium metal with 20 mL of water and 10 mL of nitric acid in a Teflon beaker, and warm the solution on a hot plate to dissolve the palladium. Allow the solution to cool to room temperature, transfer it into a 100-mL volumetric flask, and dilute with deionized water to volume.
1% Magnesium nitrate stock solution: Mix 1 g of ultrapure magnesium nitrate with 40 mL of water and 1 mL of nitric acid in a Teflon beaker, and warm the solution on a hot plate to dissolve. Allow the solution to cool to room temperature, transfer it into a 100-mL volumetric flask, and dilute with deionized water to volume.
[Note—Because of the difficulty in preparing matrix modifier stock solutions with the required purity, purchasing modifier stock solutions and using them to prepare modifier working solutions is recommended.[3]]
Modifier working solution: Transfer 3 mL of *1% Palladium stock solution* and 2 mL of *1% Magnesium nitrate stock solution* to a 10-mL volumetric flask, and dilute with 2% nitric acid to volume. A volume of 5 µL provides 0.015 mg of palladium and 0.01 mg of magnesium nitrate.
Sample solution: [**Caution**—Wear proper eye protection, protective clothing, and gloves during sample preparation. Closely follow the manufacturer's safety instructions for use of the microwave digestion apparatus.] Transfer 500 mg of sample into a Teflon digestion vessel liner. Prepare samples in duplicate. Add 15 mL of nitric acid, and swirl gently. Cover the vessels with lids, leaving the vent fitting off. Predigest overnight under a hood. Place the rupture membrane in the vent fitting, and tighten the lid. Place all vessels on the microwave oven turntable. Connect the vent tubes to the vent trap, and connect the pressure-sensing line to the appropriate vessel. Initiate a two-stage digestion procedure by heating the microwave at 15% power for 15 min followed by 25% power for 45 min. Remove the turntable of vessels from the oven, and allow the vessels to cool to room temperature (a cool water bath may be used to speed the cooling process). Vent the vessels when they reach room temperature. Remove the lids, and slowly add 2 mL of 30% hydrogen peroxide to each. Allow the reactions to subside, and seal the vessels. Return the vessels on the turntable to the microwave oven, and heat for an additional 15 min at 30% power. Remove the vessels from the oven, and allow them to cool to room temperature. Transfer the cooled digests into 25-mL volumetric flasks, and dilute with deionized water to volume.
Analysis: The graphite furnace program is as follows:
1. Dry at 115° using a 1-s ramp, a 65-s hold, and a 300-mL/min argon flow.
2. Char the sample at 1000° using a 1-s ramp, a 20-s hold, and a 300-mL/min air flow.
3. Cool down and purge the air from the furnace for 10 s using a 20° set temperature and a 300-mL/min argon flow.
4. Atomize at 2400° using a 0-s ramp and a 5-s hold with the argon flow stopped.
5. Clean out at 2600° with a 1-s ramp and a 5-s hold.

Use the autosampler to inject 20-µL aliquots of blanks, *Calibration standard solutions*, *Sample solution*, and 5 µL of *Modifier working solution*. Inject each solution in duplicate, and average the results. Use peak area measurement for all quantitations. After ensuring that the furnace is clean by running a 5% nitric acid blank, check the instrument's sensitivity by running a 20-µL aliquot of the 25.0-µg *Calibration standard solution*. Compare the results obtained with the expected results for the equipment used, and take the necessary steps to correct any problems.
Calculate the characteristic mass. Record and track the integrated absorbance and characteristic mass for reference and quality assurance.
Inject each *Calibration standard solution* in duplicate. Use the algorithms provided in the instrument software to establish calibration curves. Recheck calibration periodically, and recalibrate if the recheck differs from the original calibration by more than 10%.

---

[2] This method was developed using a Perkin-Elmer Model 5100, HGA-600 furnace, and an AS-60 autosampler with Zeeman effect background correction.

[3] A palladium (0.3%) and magnesium nitrate (0.2%) solution may be purchased from High Purity Standards, or equivalent.

Inject the *Sample solution* in duplicate, and record the integrated absorbance. If the instrument response exceeds that of the calibration curve, dilute with 5% nitric acid to bring the sample's response into the working range, and note the dilution factor (DF). All sample analyses should be blank corrected using a sample solution blank.

If a computer-based instrument is used, the data output is reported as µg/L.

Calculate the concentration of arsenic, in µg/g (equivalent to mg/kg), in the original sample taken:

$$\text{Result} = (C \times DF \times V)/W$$

C = concentration of arsenic in the sample aliquot injected (µg/L)
DF = dilution factor of the *Sample solution*
V = final volume of the *Sample solution* (L)
W = weight of the sample taken to prepare the *Sample solution* (g)

[NOTE—To monitor recovery and ensure analytical accuracy for proper quality assurance, analyze blanks, spiked blanks, and a spiked oil with each digestion set.]

Acceptance criteria: NMT 0.1 mg/kg

- **CADMIUM,** *Elemental Impurities by ICP,* Appendix IIIC
  Acceptance criteria: NMT 0.1 mg/kg
- **LEAD,** *Elemental Impurities by ICP,* Appendix IIIC
  [NOTE—Alternatively, the lead content may be determined by the following method.]

  Apparatus
  Sample digestion: Use a microwave oven[1] equipped with advanced composite vessels with 100-mL Teflon liners. Use rupture membranes to vent vessels should the pressure exceed 125 psi. The vessels fit into a turntable, and each vessel can be vented into an overflow container. Equip the microwave oven with an exhaust tube to ventilate fumes.
  Sample analysis: See *Apparatus* in Lead Limit Test, Atomic Absorption Spectrophotometric Graphite Furnace Method, Method I, Appendix IIIB

  Calibration standard stock solution: 100 µg/L. Prepare from a suitable standard, which may be purchased (accuracy certified against NIST spectrometric standard solutions).

  Calibration standard solutions: 2.0 µg/L, 5.0 µg/L, 10.0 µg/L, 25.0 µg/L, and 50.0 µg/L in 2% nitric acid, from the *Calibration standard stock solution*

  10% Ammonium dihydrogen phosphate stock solution: Mix 10 g of ultrapure ammonium dihydrogen phosphate with 40 mL of water and 1 mL of nitric acid to dissolve the phosphate. Dilute with deionized water to 100 mL.

  1% Magnesium nitrate stock solution: Mix 1 g of ultrapure magnesium nitrate with 40 mL of water and 1 mL of nitric acid in a Teflon beaker, and warm on a hot plate to dissolve the solids. Allow the solution to cool to room temperature, transfer it into a 100-mL volumetric flask, and dilute with deionized water to volume.

  [NOTE—Because of the difficulty in preparing matrix modifier stock solutions with the required purity, purchasing modifier stock solutions and using them to prepare modifier working solutions is recommended.[4]]

  Modifier working solution: Transfer 4 mL of *10% Ammonium dihydrogen phosphate stock solution* and 2 mL of *1% Magnesium nitrate stock solution* to a 10-mL volumetric flask, and dilute with 2% nitric acid to volume. A volume of 5 µL provides 0.2 mg of phosphate plus 0.01 mg of magnesium nitrate.

  Sample solution: Prepare as directed for *Sample solution* in the test for *Arsenic*. [**CAUTION**—Wear proper eye protection, protective clothing, and gloves during sample preparation. Closely follow the manufacturer's safety instructions for use of the microwave digestion apparatus.]

  Analysis: The graphite furnace program is as follows:
  1. Dry at 120° using a 1-s ramp, a 55-s hold, and a 300-mL/min argon flow.
  2. Char the sample at 850° using a 1-s ramp, a 30-s hold, and a 300-mL/min air flow.
  3. Cool down and purge the air from the furnace for 10 s using a 20° set temperature and a 300-mL/min argon flow.
  4. Atomize at 2100° using a 0-s ramp and a 5-s hold with the argon flow stopped.
  5. Clean out at 2600° with a 1-s ramp and a 5-s hold.

  Use the autosampler to inject 20-µL aliquots of blanks, *Calibration standard solutions*, *Sample solution*, and 5 µL of *Modifier working solution*. Inject each solution in duplicate, and average the results. Use peak-area measurement for all quantitation. After ensuring that the furnace is clean by running a 5% nitric acid blank, check instrument sensitivity by running an aliquot of the 25.0-µg *Calibration standard solution*. Compare the results obtained with the expected results for the equipment used, and take the necessary steps to correct any problems.

  Calculate the characteristic mass, and record and track the integrated absorbance and characteristic mass for reference and quality assurance.

  Inject each *Calibration standard solution* in duplicate. Use the algorithms provided in the instrument software to establish calibration curves. Recheck the calibration periodically, and recalibrate if recheck differs from the original calibration by more than 10%.

  Inject the *Sample solution* in duplicate, and record the integrated absorbance. If the instrument response exceeds that of the calibration curve, dilute with 5% nitric acid to bring the sample response into the working range, and note the dilution factor (DF). All sample analyses should be blank corrected using a sample solution blank.

---

[4] An ammonium dihydrogen phosphate (4%) and magnesium nitrate (0.2%) solution may be purchased from High Purity Standards, or equivalent.

If a computer-based instrument is used, the data output is reported as µg/L. Calculate the concentration, in µg/g (equivalent to mg/kg), of lead in the original sample:

$$\text{Result} = (C \times DF \times V)/W$$

C = concentration of lead in the sample aliquot injected (µg/L)
DF = dilution factor of the *Sample solution*
V = final volume of the *Sample solution* (L)
W = weight of the sample taken to prepare the *Sample solution* (g)

[NOTE—To monitor recovery and ensure analytical accuracy for proper quality assurance, analyze blanks, spiked blanks, and a spiked oil with each digestion set.]

Acceptance criteria: NMT 0.1 mg/kg

- **MERCURY**
  Apparatus
  Sample digestion: Use a microwave oven[1] equipped with advanced composite vessels with 100-mL Teflon liners. Use rupture membranes to vent vessels should the pressure exceed 125 psi. The vessels fit into a turntable, and each vessel can be vented into an overflow container. Equip the microwave oven with an exhaust tube to ventilate fumes.
  Sample analysis: Use a suitable atomic absorption spectrophotometer equipped with an atomic vapor assembly.[5] An electrodeless discharge lamp serves as the source, with an inert gas such as argon or nitrogen as the purge gas. Set up the instrument according to the manufacturer's specifications. Instrument parameters are as follows:
  Wavelength: 253.6 nm
  Slit: 0.7
  Reagent setting: 5
  Gas flow: 5–6 L/min
  Reaction time: 0.5 min
  Glassware: Acid wash all glass, Teflon, and plastic vessels by soaking them in a nitric acid bath containing a 4:1 solution of water and nitric acid. [CAUTION—Wear a full face shield, protective clothing, and gloves at all times when working with acid baths.] After acid soaking, rinse the acid-washed items in deionized water, dry, and store them in clean, covered cabinets.
  Calibration standard stock solution: 200 ng/g of mercury. Prepare from a suitable standard, which may be purchased (accuracy certified against NIST spectrometric standard solutions).
  Calibration standard solutions: 20 ng, 60 ng, 100 ng, 200 ng, and 400 ng of mercury in 1 N hydrochloric acid from the *Calibration standard stock solution*
  Reducing reagent: 5% Stannous chloride in 25% hydrochloric acid (trace-metal grade). [NOTE—Prepare daily.]
  Sample solution: Prepare as directed for the *Sample solution* in the test for *Arsenic*. [CAUTION—Wear proper eye protection, protective clothing, and gloves during sample preparation. Closely follow the manufacturer's safety instructions for use of the microwave digestion apparatus.]
  Analysis: Optimize the instrument settings for the spectrophotometer as described in the instrument manual. The instrument parameters for cold vapor generation are as follows:
  Wavelength: 253.6 nm
  Slit: 0.70 nm
  Reagent setting: 5
  Gas flow: 5–6 L/min
  Reaction time: 0.5 min
  Use a peak height integration method with a 40-s integration time and a 20-s read delay in an unheated absorption cell. Zero the instrument as follows: Place a Fleaker containing 50 mL of 1 N hydrochloric acid in the sample well of the hydride generator. Press "start" on the vapor generator and "read" on the atomic absorption spectrophotometer. The instrument will automatically flush the sample container with nitrogen, dispense the designated amount of reagent, stir the sample for a designated reaction time, and purge the head volume again with nitrogen, sweeping any vapor into the quartz cell for determination of absorption. The atomic absorption spectrophotometer will automatically zero on this sample when "autozero" is selected from the calibration menu.
  Generate a standard curve of concentration versus absorption by analyzing the five *Calibration standard solutions* prepared as described for daily standards under *Calibration standard solutions*. Analyze each solution in duplicate, generate the calibration curve, and store, using procedures specific for the instrumentation.
  Transfer an appropriate aliquot of *Sample solution* (usually 2 mL) in a Fleaker containing 50 mL of 1 N hydrochloric acid. Analyze solutions in duplicate using the procedure specified in the instrument manual. Using the calibration algorithm provided in the instrument software, calculate and report the mercury concentration in ng of mercury in the aliquot analyzed.
  Calculate the level of mercury, as µg/g (equivalent to mg/kg), in the original sample:

  $$\text{Result} = (A \times DF)/(W \times 1000)$$

  A = amount of mercury in the aliquot analyzed (ng)
  DF = dilution factor (final volume of *Sample solution*/volume taken for analysis)
  W = weight of the sample taken to prepare the *Sample solution* (g)

  [NOTE—To monitor recovery and ensure analytical accuracy for proper quality assurance, analyze blanks, spiked blanks, and a spiked oil with each digestion set.]
  Acceptance criteria: NMT 0.1 mg/kg

---
[5] This method was developed using a Perkin-Elmer Model 5100 and IL 440 Thermo Jarrell Ash atomic vapor assembly.

Organic Impurities

- **HEXANE RESIDUES**[6]

  Vegetable oil: Use solvent-free vegetable oil that is similar in nature to the sample. Deodorization of the oil in the laboratory may be used to reduce the amount of extraction solvent present in the oil.

  Internal standard: *n*-Heptane

  Calibration solutions: Prepare a series of solutions by adding 0 µL, 20 µL, 40 µL, 60 µL, 80 µL, and 100 µL of *n*-hexane, separately, to a series of vials, each containing 25 g of *Vegetable oil*. Close the vials, then mechanically shake them vigorously for 1 h at room temperature. After shaking the vials, add 5 µL of the *Internal standard* to each vial, using a syringe. [NOTE—The vial with 0 µL of *n*-hexane added is the blank.]

  Sample solution: Weigh 25.00 g of the sample into a septum vial. Close the vial and, using a syringe, add 25 µL of the *Internal standard* to the sample. Shake the vial vigorously for about 1 min before proceeding with the *Analysis*.

  Chromatographic system, Appendix IIA
  - **Mode:** Headspace gas chromatography
  - **Detector:** Flame ionization
  - **Column:** 30-m × 0.3-mm fused silica or glass capillary column coated with methyl polysiloxane (0.2-µm thickness)[7]
  - **Temperature**
    - **Oven:** 40°
    - **Injection port:** 120°
    - **Detector:** 120°
  - **Headspace sampling conditions**
    - **Sample heating temperature:** 60°
    - **Sample heating time:** 30 min
    - **Syringe temperature:** 60°
  - **Carrier gas:** Helium
  - **Flow rate:** Optimize accordingly
  - **Injection volume:** 1000 µL

  Determination of calibration factors: Warm a 1000-µL gas-tight syringe to 60°. Temper each *Calibration solution* in a water bath maintained at 60° for exactly 30 min, then, without removing the vial from the bath, use the gas-tight syringe and withdraw 1000 µL of the headspace above the oil. Inject immediately into the gas chromatograph, record the chromatograms from each *Calibration solution*, and determine the peak areas. For each of the *Calibration solutions* containing *n*-hexane (not including the blank solution) calculate the calibration factor, F:

  $$F = (C_S \times A_I) / [(A_H - A_B - A_I) \times C_I]$$

  C_S = concentration of *n*-hexane in the *Calibration solution* of interest (mg/kg)

  A_I = peak area corresponding to the *Internal standard* in the chromatogram of the *Calibration solution*

  A_H = total peak area of solvent hydrocarbons in the chromatogram of the *Calibration solution*, including the area of the *Internal standard*, not including peaks due to the oxidation products

  A_B = peak area of the solvent hydrocarbons present in the blank solution, minus the peak area of the *Internal standard*

  C_I = quantity of the *Internal standard* added to the *Calibration solution*, in mg/kg of oil (680 mg)

  [NOTE—Calculate calibration factors to three decimal points. The mean calibration factor will be used in the *Analysis*.]

  Analysis: Warm a 1000-µL gas-tight syringe to 60°. Temper the *Sample solution* in a water bath maintained at 60° for exactly 30 min, then, without removing the vial from the bath, use the gas-tight syringe and withdraw 1000 µL of the headspace above the oil. Inject immediately into the gas chromatograph, record the chromatogram, and determine the peak areas. Determine the residual solvent content, in mg/kg of hexane:

  $$\text{Result} = (A_H - A_I) \times F \times C_I \times (1/A_I)$$

  A_H = total peak area of solvent hydrocarbons in the chromatogram of the *Sample solution*, including the area of the *Internal standard* (do not include peaks due to oxidation products)

  A_I = peak area corresponding to the *Internal standard* in the chromatogram of the *Sample solution*

  F = mean calibration factor determined above

  C_I = quantity of the *Internal standard* added to the *Sample solution*, in mg/kg of sample (680 mg)

  Acceptance criteria: NMT 1.0 mg/kg

SPECIFIC TESTS

- **ACID VALUE (FATS AND RELATED SUBSTANCES),** Appendix VII
  Acceptance criteria: NMT 1.0
- **ANISIDINE VALUE,** Appendix VII
  Acceptance criteria: NMT 20
- **FREE FATTY ACIDS (AS OLEIC ACID),** Appendix VII
  Analysis: Use 28.2 for the equivalence factor (e) in the formula given in the procedure.
  Acceptance criteria: NMT 0.2%
- **PEROXIDE VALUE,** Appendix VII
  Acceptance criteria: NMT 2.0 mEq/kg
- **UNSAPONIFIABLE MATTER,** Method II, Appendix VII
  Acceptance criteria: NMT 3.0%

OTHER REQUIREMENTS

- **LABELING:** Label to indicate the content of arachidonic acid in mg/g (%). Indicate the name of any added antioxidant and the presence of any other oil(s) used to standardize the arachidonic acid content.

---

[6] Adapted from AOCS Method Ca 3b-87 (1997). The original method is available from the American Oil Chemists' Society (AOCS) at *www.aocs.org*.
[7] HP-1 (Agilent Technologies), or equivalent.

Arabinogalactan

First Published: Prior to FCC 6

Larch Fiber
Larch Gum
INS: 409
CAS: [9036-66-2]

DESCRIPTION
Arabinogalactan occurs as a white to yellow-white, coarse or fine powder. It is the dried water extract from the wood of the larch trees *Larix occidentalis* and *Larix laricina* (Fam. Pinaceae). It is a highly branched polysaccharide that has a molecular weight of 15,000 to 60,000 daltons and is composed of galactose units and arabinose units in the approximate ratio of 6 : 1. It is freely dispersible in hot or cold water. It is insoluble in alcohol.
Function: Dietary fiber; humectant; stabilizer
Packaging and Storage: Store in well-closed containers.

IDENTIFICATION
- **A. PROCEDURE**
  Sample: 20 g
  Sample solution: Add the *Sample* to 20 mL of water and stir until completely dissolved. Pour the solution into a 500 mL beaker and add 100 mL of water.
  Analysis: Transfer 7 mL of the *Sample solution* into a 250-mL beaker and add 0.2 mL of diluted lead subacetate TS. [NOTE—Retain the remaining *Sample solution* for *Identification* test *B* (below).]
  Acceptance criteria: No precipitate forms.
- **B. PROCEDURE**
  Sample solution: Retained *Sample solution* from *Identification* test *A* (above)
  Analysis: To the *Sample solution*, add 280 mL of 95% ethyl alcohol.
  Acceptance criteria: No precipitate forms.

ASSAY
- **TOTAL CARBOHYDRATES**
  Analysis: Determine the difference between 100% and the sum of the percent *Ash (Total)*, *Loss on Drying*, and *Protein*.
  Acceptance criteria: NLT 80% (as arabinogalactan)

IMPURITIES
Inorganic Impurities
- **LEAD,** Lead Limit Test, Atomic Absorption Spectrophotometric Graphite Furnace, Method I, Appendix IIIB
  Acceptance criteria: NMT 0.1 mg/kg

SPECIFIC TESTS
- **ASH (TOTAL),** Appendix IIC
  Acceptance criteria: 10.0%
- **INSOLUBLE MATTER**
  Sample: 5 g
  Analysis: Dissolve the *Sample* in about 100 mL of water contained in a 250-mL Erlenmeyer flask, add 10 mL of 2.7 N hydrochloric acid, and boil gently for 15 min. Filter the hot solution by suction through a tared filtering crucible and wash the residue thoroughly with hot water. Dry the residue at 105° for 2 h, and weigh.
  Acceptance criteria: NMT 0.1%
- **LOSS ON DRYING,** Appendix IIC: 105° for 5 h
  Acceptance criteria: NMT 8%
- **PROTEIN,** Nitrogen Determination, Method I, Appendix IIIC
  Sample: 3.5 g
  Analysis: Transfer the *Sample* into a 500-mL Kjeldahl flask. Multiply the percentage of nitrogen determined by 6.25.
  Acceptance criteria: NMT 1.0%
- **STARCH**
  Sample solution: 100 mg/mL
  Analysis: Add a few drops of iodine TS to the *Sample solution*.
  Acceptance criteria: No blue or red color appears.

L-Arginine

First Published: Prior to FCC 6
Last Revision: FCC 6

L-2-Amino-5-guanidinovaleric Acid

$C_6H_{14}N_4O_2$
UNII: 94ZLA3W45F [arginine]
Formula wt 174.20
CAS: [74-79-3]

DESCRIPTION
L-Arginine occurs as white crystals or as a white crystalline powder. It is soluble in water, insoluble in ether, and sparingly soluble in alcohol. It is strongly alkaline, and its water solutions absorb carbon dioxide from the air.
Function: Nutrient
Packaging and Storage: Store in well-closed, light-resistant containers.

IDENTIFICATION
- **INFRARED ABSORPTION,** Spectrophotometric Identification Tests, Appendix IIIC
  Reference standard: USP L-Arginine RS
  Sample and Standard preparation: *K*
  Acceptance criteria: The spectrum of the sample exhibits maxima at the same wavelengths as those in the spectrum of the *Reference standard*.

ASSAY
- **PROCEDURE**
  Sample: 200 mg
  Analysis: Dissolve the *Sample* in 3 mL of formic acid and 50 mL of glacial acetic acid. Add 2 drops of crystal violet TS, and titrate with 0.1 N perchloric acid to a green endpoint or until the blue color disappears completely. Each mL of 0.1 N perchloric acid consumed in the assay is equivalent to 8.710 mg of $C_6H_{14}N_4O_2$.
  [CAUTION—Handle perchloric acid in an appropriate fume hood.]

Acceptance criteria: NLT 98.5% and NMT 101.5% of $C_6H_{14}N_4O_2$, calculated on the dried basis

IMPURITIES
Inorganic Impurities
- **LEAD,** *Lead Limit Test,* Appendix IIIB
  Sample solution: Prepare as directed for organic compounds.
  Control: 5 µg Pb (5 mL of *Diluted Standard Lead Solution*)
  Acceptance criteria: NMT 5 mg/kg

SPECIFIC TESTS
- **LOSS ON DRYING,** Appendix IIC: 105° for 3 h
  Acceptance criteria: NMT 1.0%
- **OPTICAL (SPECIFIC) ROTATION,** Appendix IIB
  Sample: 8 g, previously dried
  Analysis: Dissolve the *Sample* in sufficient 6 N hydrochloric acid to make 100 mL.
  Acceptance criteria
  $[\alpha]_D^{20}$ between +26.0° and +27.9°, on the dried basis; or
  $[\alpha]_D^{25}$ between +25.8° and +27.7°, on the dried basis
- **RESIDUE ON IGNITION (SULFATED ASH),** Appendix IIC
  Sample: 1 g
  Acceptance criteria: NMT 0.2%

L-Arginine Monohydrochloride

First Published: Prior to FCC 6
Last Revision: FCC 6

L-2-Amino-5-guanidinovaleric Acid Monohydrochloride

$C_6H_{14}N_4O_2 \cdot HCl$ Formula wt 210.66
CAS: [1119-34-12]
UNII: F7LTH1E20Y [arginine hydrochloride]

DESCRIPTION
L-Arginine Monohydrochloride occurs as a white or nearly white crystalline powder. It is soluble in water, slightly soluble in hot alcohol, and insoluble in ether. It is acidic and melts with decomposition at about 235°.
Function: Nutrient
Packaging and Storage: Store in well-closed, light-resistant containers.

IDENTIFICATION
- **INFRARED ABSORPTION,** *Spectrophotometric Identification Tests,* Appendix IIIC
  Reference standard: USP Arginine Hydrochloride RS
  Sample and **Standard preparation:** K
  Acceptance criteria: The spectrum of the sample exhibits maxima at the same wavelengths as those in the spectrum of the *Reference standard.*

ASSAY
- **PROCEDURE**
  Sample: 100 mg, previously dried
  Analysis: Dissolve the *Sample* in 2 mL of formic acid, add exactly 15.0 mL of 0.1 N perchloric acid, and heat on a water bath for 30 min. [**CAUTION**—Handle perchloric acid in an appropriate fume hood.] After cooling, add 45 mL of glacial acetic acid, and titrate the excess perchloric acid with 0.1 N sodium acetate, determining the endpoint potentiometrically. Perform a blank determination (see *General Provisions*), and make any necessary correction. Each mL of 0.1 N perchloric acid is equivalent to 10.53 mg of $C_6H_{14}N_4O_2 \cdot HCl$.
  Acceptance criteria: NLT 98.5% and NMT 101.5% of $C_6H_{14}N_4O_2 \cdot HCl$ on the dried basis

IMPURITIES
Inorganic Impurities
- **LEAD,** *Lead Limit Test,* Appendix IIIB
  Sample solution: Prepare as directed for organic compounds.
  Control: 5 µg Pb (5 mL of *Diluted Standard Lead Solution*)
  Acceptance criteria: NMT 5 mg/kg

SPECIFIC TESTS
- **LOSS ON DRYING,** Appendix IIC: 105° for 3 h
  Acceptance criteria: NMT 0.3%
- **OPTICAL (SPECIFIC) ROTATION,** Appendix IIB
  Sample: 8 g, previously dried
  Analysis: Dissolve the *Sample* in sufficient 6 N hydrochloric acid to make 100 mL.
  Acceptance criteria
  $[\alpha]_D^{20}$ between +21.3° and +23.5°, on the dried basis; or
  $[\alpha]_D^{25}$ between +21.3° and +23.4°, on the dried basis.
- **RESIDUE ON IGNITION (SULFATED ASH),** Appendix IIC
  Sample: 1 g
  Acceptance criteria: NMT 0.1%

Ascorbic Acid
First Published: Prior to FCC 6

Vitamin C
L-Ascorbic Acid

$C_6H_8O_6$ Formula wt 176.13
INS: 300 CAS: [50-81-7]
UNII: PQ6CK8PD0R [ascorbic acid]

DESCRIPTION
Ascorbic Acid occurs as white or slightly yellow crystals or as powder. It melts at about 190°. It gradually darkens on exposure to light, is reasonably stable in air when dry, but rapidly deteriorates in solution in the presence of air. One

82 / Ascorbic Acid / Monographs

g is soluble in about 3 mL of water and in about 30 mL of alcohol. It is insoluble in chloroform and in ether.

Function: Antioxidant; meat-curing aid; nutrient

Packaging and Storage: Store in tight, light-resistant containers.

IDENTIFICATION
- **A. Procedure**
  Sample solution: 20 mg/mL
  Acceptance criteria: The *Sample solution* slowly reduces alkaline cupric tartrate TS at 25°, but more readily upon heating.
- **B. Infrared Absorption,** *Spectrophotometric Identification Tests,* Appendix IIIC
  Reference standard: USP Ascorbic Acid RS
  Sample and Standard preparation: *K*
  Acceptance criteria: The spectrum of the sample exhibits maxima at the same wavelengths as those in the spectrum of the *Reference Standard*.

ASSAY
- **Procedure**
  Sample: 400 mg
  Analysis: Dissolve the *Sample* in a mixture of 100 mL of water, recently boiled and cooled, and 25 mL of 2 N sulfuric acid. Titrate the solution immediately with 0.1 N iodine, adding starch TS near the endpoint. Each mL of 0.1 N iodine is equivalent to 8.806 mg of $C_6H_8O_6$.
  Acceptance criteria: NLT 99.0% and NMT 100.5% of $C_6H_8O_6$

IMPURITIES
Inorganic Impurities
- **Lead,** *Lead Limit Test, Flame Atomic Absorption Spectrophotometric Method,* Appendix IIIB
  Sample: 10 g
  Acceptance criteria: NMT 2 mg/kg

SPECIFIC TESTS
- **Optical (Specific) Rotation,** Appendix IIB
  Sample solution: 1 g in 10 mL of carbon dioxide-free water
  Acceptance criteria: $[\alpha]_D^{25}$ between +20.5° and +21.5°
- **Residue on Ignition (Sulfated Ash),** Appendix IIC
  Sample: 2 g
  Acceptance criteria: NMT 0.1%

Ascorbyl Palmitate
First Published: Prior to FCC 6
Last Revision: First Supplement, FCC 7

Palmitoyl L-Ascorbic Acid

$C_{22}H_{38}O_7$ Formula wt 414.54
INS: 304 CAS: [137-66-6]
UNII: QN83US2B0N [ascorbyl palmitate]

DESCRIPTION
Ascorbyl Palmitate occurs as a white or yellow-white powder. It is very slightly soluble in water and in vegetable oils. One gram dissolves in about 4.5 mL of alcohol.

Function: Antioxidant

Packaging and Storage: Store in tightly closed containers, preferably in a cool, dry place.

IDENTIFICATION
- **A. Infrared Absorption,** *Spectrophotometric Identification Tests,* Appendix IIIC
  Reference standard: USP Ascorbyl Palmitate RS
  Sample and standard preparation: *K*
  Acceptance criteria: The spectrum of the sample exhibits maxima at the same wavelengths as those in the spectrum of the *Reference standard*.
- **B. Procedure**
  Sample solution: 100 mg/mL in alcohol
  Acceptance criteria: The *Sample solution* decolorizes dichlorophenol–indophenol TS.

ASSAY
- **Procedure**
  Sample: 300 mg
  Analysis: Dissolve the *Sample* in 50 mL of alcohol in a 250-mL Erlenmeyer flask. Add 30 mL of water and immediately titrate with 0.1 N iodine to a yellow color that persists for at least 30 s. Each mL of 0.1 N iodine is equivalent to 20.73 mg of $C_{22}H_{38}O_7$.
  Acceptance criteria: NLT 95.0% of $C_{22}H_{38}O_7$, calculated on the dried basis

IMPURITIES
Inorganic Impurities
- **Lead,** *Lead Limit Test, Flame Atomic Absorption Spectrophotometric Method,* Appendix IIIB
  Sample: 10 g
  Acceptance criteria: NMT 2 mg/kg

SPECIFIC TESTS
- **Loss on Drying,** Appendix IIC: Vacuum oven at 56° to 60° for 1 h
  Acceptance criteria: NMT 2%
- **Melting Range or Temperature Determination,** Appendix IIB
  Analysis: Determine as directed in *Procedure for Class Ia*
  Acceptance criteria: Between 107° and 117°
- **Optical (Specific) Rotation,** Appendix IIB
  Sample solution: 1 g in 10 mL of methanol
  Acceptance criteria: $[\alpha]_D^{25}$ between +21° and +24°, calculated on the dried basis
- **Residue on Ignition (Sulfated Ash),** Method I, Appendix IIC
  Sample: 2 g
  Acceptance criteria: NMT 0.1%

L-Asparagine

First Published: Prior to FCC 6

L-α-Aminosuccinamic Acid

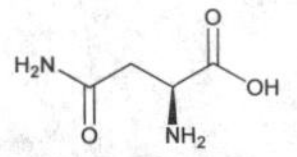

C₄H₈N₂O₃
C₄H₈N₂O₃·H₂O
Formula wt, anhydrous 132.12
Formula wt, monohydrate 150.13
CAS: anhydrous [70-47-3]
CAS: monohydrate [5794-13-8]
UNII: 7NG0A2TUHQ [asparagine anhydrous]

DESCRIPTION
L-Asparagine occurs as white crystals or as a crystalline powder. It is soluble in water and practically insoluble in alcohol and in ether. Its solutions are acid to litmus. It melts at about 234°.

Function: Nutrient

Packaging and Storage: Store in well-closed, light-resistant containers.

IDENTIFICATION
- **INFRARED SPECTRA,** *Spectrophotometric Identification Tests,* Appendix IIIC
  Sample preparation: Mineral oil mull
  Acceptance criteria: The spectrum of the sample exhibits relative maxima at the same wavelengths as those of the spectrum below.

ASSAY
- **PROCEDURE**
  Sample: 130 mg, previously dried
  Analysis: Dissolve the *Sample* in 3 mL of formic acid and 50 mL of glacial acetic acid, and titrate with 0.1 N perchloric acid, determining the endpoint potentiometrically. [**CAUTION**—Handle perchloric acid in an appropriate fume hood.] Perform a blank determination (see *General Provisions*), and make any necessary correction. Each mL of 0.1 N perchloric acid is equivalent to 13.21 mg of $C_4H_8N_2O_3$.
  Acceptance criteria: NLT 98.0% and NMT 101.5% of $C_4H_8N_2O_3$, on the dried basis

IMPURITIES
Inorganic Impurities
- **LEAD,** *Lead Limit Test,* Appendix IIIB
  Sample solution: Prepare as directed for organic compounds.
  Control: 5 µg Pb (5 mL of *Diluted Standard Lead Solution*)
  Acceptance criteria: NMT 5 mg/kg

SPECIFIC TESTS
- **LOSS ON DRYING,** Appendix IIC: 130° for 3 h
  Acceptance criteria: Between 11.5% and 12.5%
- **OPTICAL (SPECIFIC) ROTATION,** Appendix IIB
  Sample solution: 10 g of a previously dried sample in sufficient 6 N hydrochloric acid to make 100 mL
  Acceptance criteria
  $[\alpha]_D^{20}$ between +33.0° and +36.5°, on the dried basis
- **RESIDUE ON IGNITION (SULFATED ASH),** Appendix IIC
  Sample: 1 g
  Acceptance criteria: NMT 0.1%

84 / L-Asparagine / Monographs

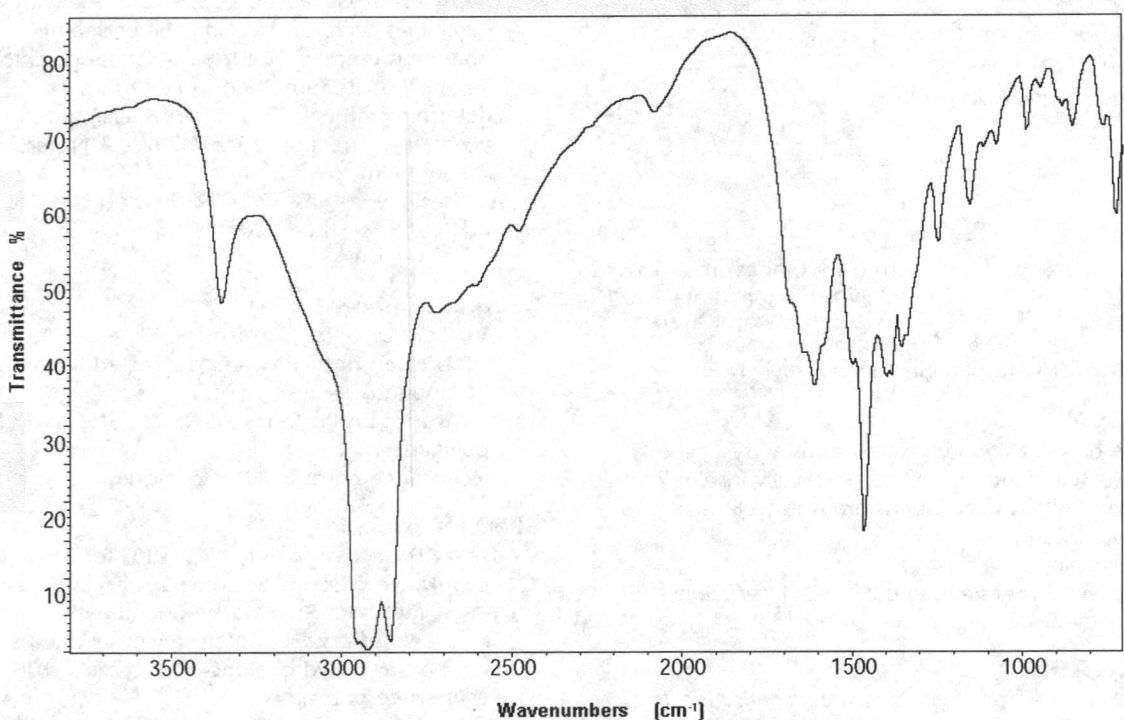

L-Asparagine (Mineral Oil Mull)

Aspartame

First Published: Prior to FCC 6

N-L-α-Aspartyl-L-phenylalanine 1-Methyl Ester
APM

$C_{14}H_{18}N_2O_5$
INS: 951
UNII: Z0H242BBR1 [aspartame]

Formula wt 294.31
CAS: [22839-47-0]

DESCRIPTION
Aspartame occurs as a white, crystalline powder. It is sparingly soluble in water and slightly soluble in alcohol. The pH of a 0.8% solution is between about 4.5 and 6.0.
Function: Sweetener; sugar substitute; flavor enhancer
Packaging and Storage: Store in well-closed containers in a cool, dry place.

IDENTIFICATION
- **INFRARED ABSORPTION,** *Spectrophotometric Identification Tests,* Appendix IIIC
  Reference standard: USP Aspartame RS
  Sample and Standard preparation: K

  Acceptance criteria: The spectrum of the sample exhibits maxima at the same wavelengths as those in the spectrum of the *Reference standard.*

ASSAY
- **PROCEDURE**
  Sample: 300 mg
  Analysis: Transfer the *Sample* to a 150-mL beaker, dissolve in 1.5 mL of 96% formic acid, and add 60 mL of glacial acetic acid. Add crystal violet TS, and titrate immediately with 0.1 N perchloric acid to a green endpoint. [**CAUTION**—Handle perchloric acid in an appropriate fume hood.] [NOTE—Use 0.1 N perchloric acid previously standardized to a green endpoint. A blank titration exceeding 0.1 mL may be due to excessive water content and may cause loss of visual endpoint sensitivity.] Perform a blank determination (see *General Provisions*) and make any necessary correction. Each mL of 0.1 N perchloric acid is equivalent to 29.43 mg of $C_{14}H_{18}N_2O_5$.
  Acceptance criteria: NLT 98.0% and NMT 102.0% of $C_{14}H_{18}N_2O_5$, calculated on the dried basis

IMPURITIES
Inorganic Impurities
- **LEAD,** *Lead Limit Test, Atomic Absorption Spectrophotometric Graphite Furnace Method, Method II,* Appendix IIIB
  Sample: 1 g
  Acceptance criteria: NMT 1 mg/kg

Organic Impurities
- **5-BENZYL-3,6-DIOXO-2-PIPERAZINEACETIC ACID**
  Mobile phase: Dissolve 5.6 g of potassium phosphate monobasic in 820 mL of water contained in a 1-L flask. Use phosphoric acid to adjust the pH to 4.3, add 180 mL of methanol, and mix.
  Diluent: Add 200 mL of methanol to 1800 mL of water, and mix.
  Standard stock solution: Dissolve 25 mg USP 5-Benzyl-3,6-dioxo-2-piperazineacetic Acid RS in 10 mL of methanol and dilute to 100 mL with water.
  Standard solution: Pipet 15 mL of the *Standard stock solution* into a 50-mL volumetric flask, dilute to volume with *Diluent*, and mix. [NOTE—This solution should be freshly prepared on the day of use.]
  Sample solution: 5 mg/mL in *Diluent*. [NOTE—This solution should be freshly prepared on the day of use. Save the unused portion of this solution for use in the test for *Related Impurities* (below).]
  Chromatographic system, Appendix IIA
   Mode: High-performance liquid chromatography
   Detector: UV 210 nm
   Column: 250-mm × 4.6-mm (id) or equivalent, packed with octadecyl silanized silica (10-μm Partisil ODS-3, or equivalent)
   Column temperature: 40°
   Flow rate: About 2 mL/min
   Injection volume: 20 μL
   System suitability
    Sample: *Standard solution*
    Suitability requirement: The area responses for three replicate injections show a relative standard deviation of NMT 2.0%.
  Analysis: Separately inject the *Standard solution* and the *Sample solution* into the chromatograph, record the chromatograms, and measure all the peak area responses. [NOTE—The approximate retention times of 5-benzyl-3,6-dioxo-2-piperazineacetic acid and aspartame are 4 min and 11 min, respectively.]
  Calculate the percentage of 5-benzyl-3,6-dioxo-2-piperazineacetic acid in the sample taken by the formula:

  $$\text{Result} = (r_U/r_S) \times (C_S/C_U) \times 100\%$$

  r_U = peak area response of 5-benzyl-3,6-dioxo-2-piperazineacetic acid in the *Sample solution*
  r_S = peak area response of 5-benzyl-3,6-dioxo-2-piperazineacetic acid in the *Standard solution*
  C_S = concentration (mg/mL) of 5-benzyl-3,6-dioxo-2-piperazineacetic acid in the *Standard solution*
  C_U = concentration (mg/mL) of the *Sample solution*

  Acceptance criteria: NMT 1.5%
- **OTHER RELATED IMPURITIES**
  Mobile phase: Dissolve 5.6 g of potassium phosphate monobasic in 820 mL of water contained in a 1-L flask. Use phosphoric acid to adjust the pH to 4.3, add 180 mL of methanol, and mix.
  Diluent: Add 200 mL of methanol to 1800 mL of water, and mix.
  Standard stock solution: Dissolve 25 mg USP 5-Benzyl-3,6-dioxo-2-piperazineacetic Acid RS in 10 mL of methanol and dilute to 100 mL with water.
  Standard solution: Pipet 15 mL of the *Standard stock solution* into a 50-mL volumetric flask, dilute to volume with *Diluent*, and mix. [NOTE—This solution should be freshly prepared on the day of use.]
  Sample solution: 5 mg/mL in *Diluent*. [NOTE—This solution should be freshly prepared on the day of use.]
  Related substances solution: Pipet 2 mL of the *Sample solution* from the test for *5-Benzyl-3,6-dioxo-2-piperazineacetic Acid* into a 100-mL volumetric flask, dilute to volume with the *Diluent*, and mix.
  Chromatographic system, Appendix IIA
   Mode: High-performance liquid chromatography
   Detector: UV 210 nm
   Column: 250-mm × 4.6-mm (id) or equivalent, packed with octadecyl silanized silica (10-μm Partisil ODS-3, or equivalent)
   Column temperature: 40°
   Flow rate: About 2 mL/min
   Injection volume: 20 μL
   System suitability
    Sample: *Standard solution*
    Suitability requirement: The area responses for three replicate injections show a relative standard deviation of NMT 2.0%.
  Analysis: Separately inject the *Related substances solution* and the *Sample solution* into the chromatograph, and record the chromatograms for a time equal to twice the retention time of aspartame.
  Acceptance criteria: In the chromatogram obtained from the *Sample solution*, the sum of the responses of all secondary peaks, other than those for 5-benzyl-3,6-dioxo-2-piperazineacetic acid, is not more than the response of the aspartame peak obtained in the chromatogram from the *Related substances solution*. (NMT 2.0%)

SPECIFIC TESTS
- **LOSS ON DRYING,** Appendix IIC: 105° for 4 h
  Acceptance criteria: NMT 4.5%
- **OPTICAL (SPECIFIC) ROTATION,** Appendix IIB
  Sample solution: Dissolve 4 g of sample in sufficient 15 N formic acid to make 100 mL.
  Analysis: Make the determination within 30 min of preparation of the *Sample solution*.
  Acceptance criteria: $[\alpha]_D^{20}$ between +14.5° and +16.5°, calculated on the dried basis
- **RESIDUE ON IGNITION (SULFATED ASH),** Appendix IIC
  Sample: 1 g
  Acceptance criteria: NMT 0.2%

Aspartame–Acesulfame Salt

First Published: Prior to FCC 6
Last Revision: FCC 6

APM-Ace
[2-carboxy-β-(N-(b-methoxycarbonyl-2
   phenyl)ethylcarbamoyl)] ethanaminium 6-methyl-4-oxo-1,
   2,3-oxathiazin-3-ide-2,2-dioxide
L-Phenylalanine, L-α-aspartyl-2-methyl ester compound with
   6-methyl-1,2,3-oxathiazin-4(3H)-one 2,2-dioxide (1:1)

$C_{18}H_{23}O_9N_3S$ Formula wt 457.45
INS: 962   CAS: [106372-55-8]
UNII: IFE6C6BS24 [aspartame acesulfame]

DESCRIPTION
Aspartame–Acesulfame Salt occurs as a white, crystalline powder. It is sparingly soluble in water and slightly soluble in alcohol.
Function: Sweetener
Packaging and Storage: Store in well-closed containers in a cool, dry place.

IDENTIFICATION
- **INFRARED ABSORPTION,** *Spectrophotometric Identification Tests,* Appendix IIIC
   Reference standard: USP Aspartame–Acesulfame RS
   Sample and **Standard preparation:** K
   Acceptance criteria: The spectrum of the sample exhibits maxima at the same wavelengths as those in the spectrum of the *Reference standard*.

ASSAY
- **PROCEDURE**
   Sample: 0.100 to 0.150 g
   Analysis: [NOTE—Use a combination pH-electrode for all titrations.] Dissolve the *Sample* in 50 mL of ethanol. Under a flow of nitrogen, titrate the solution with standardized 0.1 N tetrabutylammonium hydroxide in methanol or 2-propanol. Determine the volume of titrant needed to reach the first equivalence point and the second equivalence point. Perform a blank titration with 50 mL of ethanol. Calculate the percentages of acesulfame and aspartame, respectively, taken by the formulas:

   $$\text{Result} = [(V_1 - V_B) \times N \times M_{r1}]/(W \times F)$$

   $$\text{Result} = [(V_2 - V_B) \times N \times M_{r2}]/(W \times F)$$

   V_1 = volume of titrant used to reach the first equivalence point for the *Sample* (mL)
   V_2 = volume of titrant used to reach the second equivalence point for the *Sample* (mL)
   V_B = volume of titrant used for the blank (mL)
   N = exact normality of the tetrabutylammonium hydroxide used
   M_{r1} = formula weight of acesulfame, 163
   M_{r2} = formula weight of aspartame, 294
   W = weight of the sample taken (g)
   F = factor, 10

   Acceptance criteria
   Aspartame: NLT 63.0% and NMT 66.0%, calculated on the dried basis
   Acesulfame: NLT 34.0% and NMT 37.0%, calculated as acid formed on the dried basis

IMPURITIES
Inorganic Impurities
- **LEAD,** *Lead Limit Test, Atomic Absorption Spectrophotometric Graphite Furnace Method, Method II,* Appendix IIIB
   Acceptance criteria: NMT 1 mg/kg
- **POTASSIUM**
   Standard stock solution: 19.07 μg/mL potassium chloride (previously dried at 105° for 2 h), made to 1000 mL. This solution contains 10 μg/mL of potassium.
   Standard solutions: Pipet 10.0-, 15.0-, and 20.0-mL aliquots of the *Standard stock solution* into separate 100-mL volumetric flasks; add 2.0 mL of a 200 mg/mL solution of sodium chloride and 1.0 mL of hydrochloric acid to each flask, dilute to volume, and mix. These *Standard solutions* contain, respectively, 1.0, 1.5, and 2.0 μg/mL of potassium.
   Sample solution: Transfer 3.0 g of sample into a 500-mL volumetric flask, dilute to volume, and mix. Transfer 10 mL of this solution into a 100-mL volumetric flask and add 2.0 mL of a 200 mg/mL sodium chloride solution and 1.0 mL of hydrochloric acid, dilute to volume, and mix. Filter the solution.
   Analysis: Using a suitable atomic absorption spectrophotometer equipped with a potassium hollow-cathode lamp and an air–acetylene flame with water as the blank, concomitantly determine the absorbances of the *Standard solutions* and the *Sample solution* at the potassium emission line of 766.5 nm. Plot the absorbance of the *Standard solutions* versus concentration, in μg/mL, of potassium and draw the straight line best fitting the plotted points. From the graph, determine the potassium concentration, C, in μg/mL, in the *Sample solution*. Calculate the percent potassium in the sample by the formula:

   $$\text{Result} = 500C/W$$

   C = potassium concentration in the *Sample solution*, calculated from the standard curve (μg/mL)
   W = weight of sample taken to prepare the *Sample solution* (mg)

   Acceptance criteria: NMT 0.5%

Organic Impurities
- **5-BENZYL-3,6-DIOXO-2-PIPERAZINEACETIC ACID**
   Mobile phase: Dissolve 5.6 g of potassium phosphate monobasic in 820 mL of water contained in a 1-L flask.

Use phosphoric acid to adjust the pH to 4.3, add 180 mL of methanol, and mix. Filter through a 0.45-μm disk, and degas.
Diluent: Add 200 mL of methanol to 1800 mL of water, and mix.
Standard stock solution: Dissolve 25 mg of USP 5-Benzyl-3,6-dioxo-2-piperazineacetic Acid RS in 10 mL of methanol contained in a 100-mL volumetric flask, and dilute to volume with water.
Standard solution: Pipet 15 mL of the *Standard stock solution* into a 50-mL volumetric flask, dilute to volume with *Diluent*, and mix. [NOTE—This solution should be freshly prepared on the day of use.]
Sample solution: 5 mg/mL in *Diluent*. [NOTE—This solution should be freshly prepared on the day of use. Save the unused portion of this solution for use in the test for *Related Impurities* (below).]
Chromatographic system, Appendix IIA
  Mode: High-performance liquid chromatography
  Detector: UV 210 nm
  Column: 250-mm × 4.6-mm (id) or equivalent, packed with octadecyl silanized silica (10-μm Partisil ODS-3, or equivalent)
  Column temperature: 40°
  Flow rate: About 2 mL/min
  Injection volume: 20 μL
  System suitability
    Sample: *Standard solution*
    Suitability requirement: The area responses for replicate injections show a relative standard deviation of NMT 2.0%.
Analysis: Separately inject the *Standard solution* and the *Sample solution* into the chromatograph, record the chromatograms, and measure all the peak area responses. [NOTE—The approximate retention times of 5-benzyl-3,6-dioxo-2-piperazineacetic acid and aspartame are 4 min and 11 min, respectively.]
Calculate the percentage of 5-benzyl-3,6-dioxo-2-piperazineacetic acid in the sample taken by the formula:

$$\text{Result} = (r_U/r_S) \times (C_S/C_U) \times 100$$

r_U	= peak area response of 5-benzyl-3,6-dioxo-2-piperazineacetic acid in the *Sample solution*
r_S	= peak area response of 5-benzyl-3,6-dioxo-2-piperazineacetic acid in the *Standard solution*
C_S	= concentration of 5-benzyl-3,6-dioxo-2-piperazineacetic acid in the *Standard solution* (mg/mL)
C_U	= concentration of the *Sample solution* (mg/mL)

Acceptance criteria: NMT 0.5%
- **RELATED IMPURITIES**
  [NOTE—Determine as directed in the test for *5-Benzyl-3,6-dioxo-2-piperazineacetic Acid* (above), using the following *Standard solution* and *Analysis*.]
  Standard solution: Pipet 1.5 mL of the *Sample solution* from the test for *5-Benzyl-3,6-dioxo-2-piperazineacetic Acid* into a 100-mL volumetric flask, dilute to volume with the *Diluent*, and mix.
  Analysis: Separately inject equal 20-μL portions of the *Standard solution* and the *Sample solution* into the chromatograph, and record the chromatograms for a time equal to twice the retention time of aspartame.
  Acceptance criteria: In the chromatogram obtained from the *Sample solution*, the sum of the responses of all secondary peaks, other than those for 5-benzyl-3,6-dioxo-2-piperazineacetic acid and acesulfame, is not more than the response of the aspartame peak obtained in the chromatogram from the *Standard solution*. (NMT 1.0%)

SPECIFIC TESTS
- **LOSS ON DRYING,** Appendix IIC: 105° for 4 h
  Acceptance criteria: NMT 0.5%
- **OPTICAL (SPECIFIC) ROTATION,** Appendix IIB
  Sample: 6.2 g, previously dried
  Analysis: Dissolve the *Sample* in sufficient 15 N formic acid, made to 100 mL. Make the determination within 30 min of preparation of the *Sample*. Divide the calculated specific rotation by 0.646 to correct for the aspartame content in aspartame–acesulfame salt.
  Acceptance criteria: $[\alpha]_D^{20}$ between +14.5° and +16.5°, on the dried basis

DL-Aspartic Acid

First Published: Prior to FCC 6

DL-Aminosuccinic Acid

$C_4H_7NO_4$ Formula wt 133.10
CAS: [617-45-8]
UNII: 28XF4669EP [aspartic acid, dl-]

DESCRIPTION
DL-Aspartic Acid occurs as colorless or white crystals. It is slightly soluble in water, but insoluble in alcohol and in ether. It is optically inactive and melts with decomposition at about 280°.
Function: Nutrient
Packaging and Storage: Store in well-closed, light-resistant containers.

IDENTIFICATION
- **INFRARED SPECTRA,** *Spectrophotometric Identification Tests*, Appendix IIIC
  Sample preparation: Mineral oil mull
  Acceptance criteria: The spectrum of the sample exhibits relative maxima at the same wavelengths as those of the spectrum below.

ASSAY
- **PROCEDURE**
  Sample: 200 mg

88 / DL-Aspartic Acid / Monographs

Analysis: Dissolve the *Sample* in 3 mL of formic acid and 50 mL of glacial acetic acid. Add 2 drops of crystal violet TS and titrate with 0.1 N perchloric acid to a green endpoint or until the blue color disappears completely. [**Caution**—Handle perchloric acid in an appropriate fume hood.] Perform a blank determination (see *General Provisions*) and make any necessary correction. Each mL of 0.1 N perchloric acid is equivalent to 13.31 mg of $C_4H_7NO_4$.
Acceptance criteria: NLT 98.5% and NMT 101.5% of $C_4H_7NO_4$, calculated on the dried basis

IMPURITIES
Inorganic Impurities
- **Lead,** *Lead Limit Test,* Appendix IIIB: Using a *Sample Solution* prepared as directed for organic compounds
  Control: 5 µg Pb (5 mL of *Diluted Standard Lead Solution*)
  Acceptance criteria: NMT 5 mg/kg

SPECIFIC TESTS
- **Loss on Drying,** Appendix IIC: 105° for 3 h
  Acceptance criteria: NMT 0.3%
- **Residue on Ignition (Sulfated Ash),** Appendix IIC
  Sample: 1 g
  Acceptance criteria: NMT 0.1%

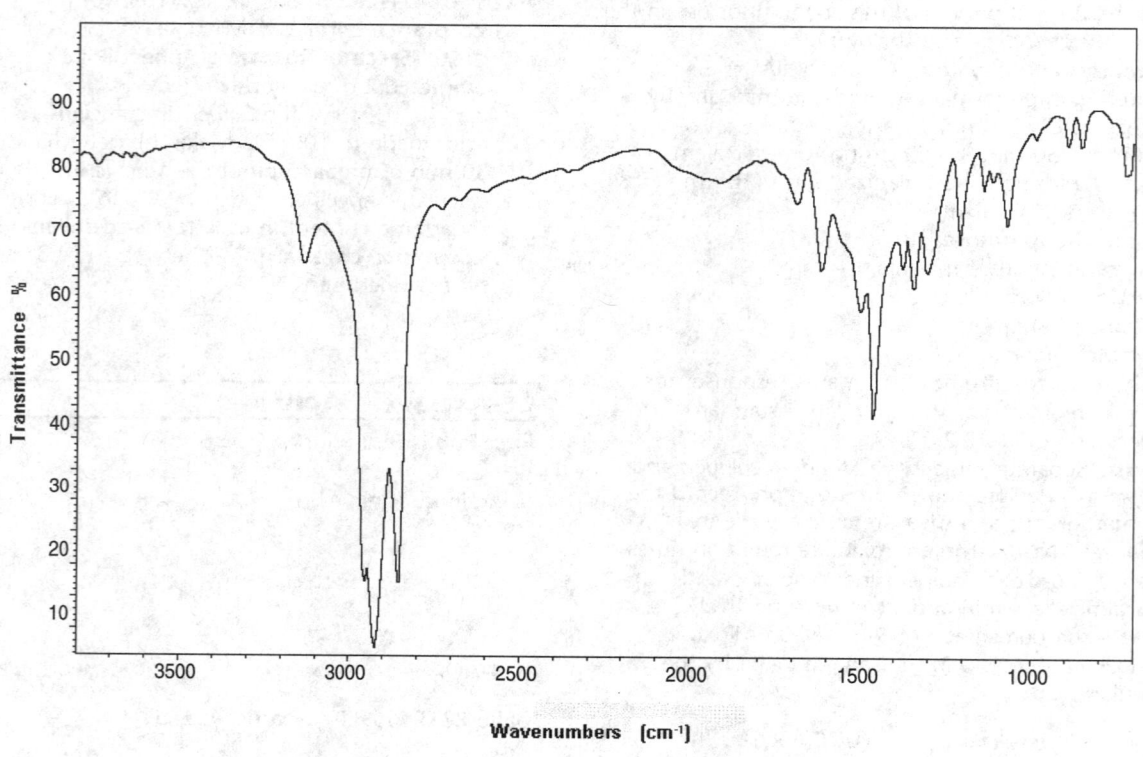

DL-Aspartic Acid (Mineral Oil Mull)

L-Aspartic Acid
First Published: Prior to FCC 6
Last Revision: FCC 6

L-Aminosuccinic Acid

$C_4H_7NO_4$

Formula wt 133.10
CAS: [56-84-8]

UNII: 30KYC7MIAI [aspartic acid]

DESCRIPTION
L-Aspartic Acid occurs as white crystals or as a crystalline powder. It is slightly soluble in water, but insoluble in alcohol and in ether. It melts at about 270°.
Function: Nutrient
Packaging and Storage: Store in well-closed, light-resistant containers.

IDENTIFICATION
- **Infrared Absorption,** *Spectrophotometric Identification Tests,* Appendix IIIC
  Reference standard: USP Aspartic Acid RS
  Sample and **Standard preparation:** K

Acceptance criteria: The spectrum of the sample exhibits maxima at the same wavelengths as those in the spectrum of the *Reference standard*.

ASSAY
- **PROCEDURE**
  Sample: 200 mg
  Analysis: Dissolve the *Sample* in 3 mL of formic acid and 50 mL of glacial acetic acid. Add 2 drops of crystal violet TS, and titrate with 0.1 N perchloric acid to a green endpoint or until the blue color disappears completely. [**CAUTION**—Handle perchloric acid in an appropriate fume hood.] Perform a blank determination (see *General Provisions*), and make any necessary correction. Each mL of 0.1 N perchloric acid is equivalent to 13.31 mg of $C_4H_7NO_4$.
  Acceptance criteria: NLT 98.5% and NMT 101.5% of $C_4H_7NO_4$, calculated on the dried basis

IMPURITIES
Inorganic Impurities
- **LEAD,** *Lead Limit Test,* Appendix IIIB
  Sample solution: Prepare as directed for organic compounds.
  Control: 5 µg Pb (5 mL of *Diluted Standard Lead Solution*)
  Acceptance criteria: NMT 5 mg/kg

SPECIFIC TESTS
- **LOSS ON DRYING,** Appendix IIC: 105° for 3 h
  Acceptance criteria: NMT 0.25%
- **OPTICAL (SPECIFIC) ROTATION,** Appendix IIB
  Sample: 8 g, previously dried
  Analysis: Dissolve the *Sample* in sufficient 6 N hydrochloric acid to make 100 mL.
  Acceptance criteria: $[\alpha]_D^{20}$ between +24.5° and +26.0°, on the dried basis
- **RESIDUE ON IGNITION (SULFATED ASH),** Appendix IIC
  Sample: 1 g
  Acceptance criteria: NMT 0.1%

Astaxanthin Esters from *Haematococcus pluvialis*

First Published: Third Supplement, FCC 7

Astaxanthin[1]
Astaxanthin Esters
Astaxanthin Fatty Acid Esters
(3*S*,3'*S*)-3,3'-dihydroxy-β,β-carotene-4,4'-dione

DESCRIPTION
Astaxanthin Esters from *Haematococcus pluvialis* occurs as a dark red, viscous oil. It is the product of the fermentation of *Haematococcus pluvialis*, extracted with either super critical CO_2 or acetone. It is a complex mixture, primarily composed of lipids, with astaxanthin esterified with common edible fatty acids to form both mono- and diesters. Esterified astaxanthin is the primary carotenoid present and the approximate astaxanthin composition is: 75% monoester, 20% diester, and 5% free form astaxanthin. Astaxanthin Esters from *Haematococcus pluvialis* is soluble in *n*-hexane, acetone, and ether; partially soluble in alcohol; practically insoluble in water and hot water. Suitable antioxidants may be added.

Function: Source of astaxanthin
Packaging and Storage: Store in tight, light-resistant containers in a cool place.

IDENTIFICATION
- **EPA CONTENT,** *Fatty Acid Composition (Saturated, cis-Monounsaturated, and cis-Polyunsaturated) in Oils Containing Long Chain Polyunsaturated Fatty Acids,* Appendix VII
  Analysis: Proceed as directed, then calculate the amount of EPA (eicosapentaenoic acid; C20:5 n-3) present as the percentage of total fatty acids.
  Acceptance criteria: NMT 1.0%
- **THIN-LAYER CHROMATOGRAPHY,** Appendix IIA
  Sample solution: 10 mg/mL in acetone
  Standard solution: 10 mg/mL of USP Astaxanthin Esters from *Haematococcus pluvialis* RS in acetone
  Adsorbent: 0.25-mm layer of chromatographic silica gel. [NOTE—Dry silica gel at 110° for 1 h before use.]
  Developing solvent system: Hexane and acetone [70:30]
  Application volume: 5 µL
  Analysis: Develop the chromatogram in the *Developing solvent system* until the solvent front has moved about three-fourths of the length of the plate. Remove the plate from the chamber and dry in a current of air.
  Acceptance criteria: The principal spots obtained from the *Sample solution* correspond in color, size, and R_F value to those obtained from the *Standard solution*.

ASSAY
- **ASTAXANTHIN (TOTAL)** [NOTE—Astaxanthin measured by this method is total astaxanthin, including free astaxanthin and both mono- and diesters.]
  Buffer solution: Dissolve 6.06 g of tris(hydroxymethyl)aminomethane in 750 mL of water, adjust with 1 M hydrochloric acid to a pH of 7.0, and dilute with water to 1000 mL.
  Solution A: 4 U/mL of cholesterol esterase[2] in *Buffer solution*. [NOTE—Prepare fresh daily.]
  Internal standard solution: 37.5 µg/mL of USP Apocarotenal RS in acetone
  Standard stock solution: Transfer 30 mg of USP Astaxanthin Esters from *Haematococcus pluvialis* RS to a 100-mL volumetric flask. Dissolve in 30 mL of acetone, shake by mechanical means, and dilute with acetone to volume.
  Standard solution: Combine 2.0 mL of the *Standard stock solution* and 1.0 mL of the *Internal standard solution* in a glass centrifuge tube. Add 3.0 mL of *Solution A* to the tube, and mix gently by inversion. Place the tube in a block heater set to 37° and allow

---

[1] Commercial products marketed as astaxanthin are actually often mixtures of free and esterified astaxanthin or primarily esterified astaxanthin.

[2] Use Wako Pure Chemicals catalog no. 037-11221, available from www.wakousa.com; Sigma catalog no. C9281, available from www.sigmaaldrich.com; or equivalent.

the reaction to continue for 45 min, gently and slowly inverting the tube every 10 min. After 45 min, add 1 g of sodium sulfate decahydrate and 2 mL of petroleum ether to the tube. Vortex the tube for 30 s, then centrifuge at 3000 rpm for 3 min. Carefully transfer the petroleum ether layer to a 10-mL glass centrifuge tube containing 1 g of sodium sulfate anhydrate. Be careful to avoid pipetting the intermediate emulsive layer. Evaporate the petroleum ether layer using a vacuum or a stream of inert gas at room temperature, add 3 mL of acetone, sonicate, and filter the mixture. The filtered solution is the *Standard solution*.

Sample stock solution: Warm a quantity of the sample in a water bath at 50°–60° for 30 min. Shake the sample well at 10-min intervals. After 30 min, transfer 30 mg of the sample to a 100-mL volumetric flask. Dissolve in 30 mL of acetone, shake by mechanical means, and dilute with acetone to volume. [NOTE—Prepare in triplicate.]

Sample solution: Combine 2.0 mL of the *Sample stock solution* and 1.0 mL of the *Internal standard solution* in a glass centrifuge tube. Add 3.0 mL of *Solution A* to the tube, and mix gently by inversion. Place the tube in a block heater set to 37° and allow the reaction to continue for 45 min, gently and slowly inverting the tube every 10 min. After 45 min, add 1 g of sodium sulfate decahydrate and 2 mL of petroleum ether to the tube. Vortex the tube for 30 s, then centrifuge at 3000 rpm for 3 min. Carefully transfer the petroleum ether layer to a 10-mL glass centrifuge tube containing 1 g of sodium sulfate anhydrate. Be careful to avoid pipetting the intermediate emulsive layer. Evaporate the petroleum ether layer using a vacuum or a stream of inert gas at room temperature, add 3 mL of acetone, sonicate, and filter the mixture. The filtered solution is the *Sample solution*.

Chromatographic system, Appendix IIA
Mode: High-performance liquid chromatography
Detector: 474 nm
Column: 4.6-mm × 250-mm column with a C30 silane bonded stationary phase on fully porous spherical silica, 5-μm in diameter[3]
Column temperature: 25°
Flow rate: 1.0 mL/min
Injection size: 20 μL
Mobile phase: See the gradient table below.

Time (min)	Methanol (%)	t-Butyl-methylether (%)	Phosphoric acid, 1% aqueous (%)
0	81	15	4
15	66	30	4
23	16	80	4
27	16	80	4
27.1	81	15	4
35	81	15	4

---
[3] YMC-Carotenoid™ S 5-μm column, available at www.ymc.co.jp/en, or equivalent.

Analysis: Separately inject the *Standard solution* and the *Sample solution* into the chromatograph. Record the chromatograms, and identify the peaks by comparison to the Reference Chromatograms supplied with the USP Apocarotenal RS (internal standard) and with the USP Astaxanthin Esters from *Haematococcus pluvialis* RS. [NOTE—The approximate retention times for 13-*cis*-astaxanthin, *trans*-astaxanthin, 9-*cis*-astaxanthin, and the internal standard apocarotenal (*trans*-beta-apo-8'-carotenal) are 9 min, 10 min, 14 min, and 17 min, respectively.]

For the *Standard solution* and the *Sample solution*, separately calculate the ratios of the peak responses of total astaxanthin to the internal standard obtained from the individual analysis:

$$\text{Result} = (F_1 P_{13\text{-}cis} + P_{trans} + F_2 P_{9\text{-}cis})/P_{IS}$$

F_1 = relative response coefficient of 13-*cis*-astaxanthin to *trans*-astaxanthin (1.3)
$P_{13\text{-}cis}$ = peak response for 13-*cis*-astaxanthin obtained from the chromatogram
P_{trans} = peak response for *trans*-astaxanthin obtained from the chromatogram
F_2 = relative response coefficient of 9-*cis*-astaxanthin to *trans*-astaxanthin (1.1)
$P_{9\text{-}cis}$ = peak response for 9-*cis*-astaxanthin obtained from the chromatogram
P_{IS} = peak response for the internal standard, apocarotenal

Calculate the percentage of astaxanthin (w/w) in the portion of the sample taken:

$$\text{Result} = (R_U/R_S) \times (C_S/C_U) \times 100$$

R_U = ratio of peak responses of total astaxanthin to the internal standard obtained from the *Sample solution*
R_S = ratio of peak responses of total astaxanthin to the internal standard obtained from the *Standard solution*
C_S = concentration of astaxanthin in the *Standard solution* (mg/mL)
C_U = concentration of the *Sample solution* (mg/mL)

Acceptance criteria: 5.0%–15.0%

IMPURITIES
Inorganic Impurities
- **ARSENIC,** *Elemental Impurities by ICP,* Appendix IIIC [NOTE—Alternatively, the arsenic content may be determined by the following method.]
  Apparatus
  Sample digestion: Use a microwave oven[4] equipped with advanced composite vessels with 100-mL Teflon liners. Use rupture membranes to vent vessels should the pressure exceed 125 psi. The vessels fit into a turntable, and each vessel can be vented into an overflow container. Equip the microwave oven with an exhaust tube to ventilate fumes.

---
[4] CEM Model MDS-2100, or equivalent.

Sample analysis: Use a suitable graphite furnace atomic absorption spectrophotometer (GFAAS) equipped with an autosampler, pyrolytically coated graphite tubes, solid pyrolytic graphite platforms, and an adequate means of background correction.[5] An electrodeless discharge lamp serves as the source, argon as the purge gas, and air as the alternate gas. Set up the instrument according to manufacturer's specifications, with consideration of current good GFAAS practices. The instrument parameters are as follows:
Wavelength: 193.7 nm
Lamp current: 300 (EDL) modulated
Pyrolysis: 1000°
Atomization: 2400°
Slit: 0.7
Characteristic mass: 15 pg

Glassware: Acid wash all glass, Teflon, and plastic vessels by soaking them in a nitric acid bath containing a 4:1 solution of water and nitric acid. [**CAUTION**—Wear a full face shield and protective clothing and gloves at all times when working with acid baths.] After acid soaking, rinse acid-washed items in deionized water, dry them, and store them in clean, covered cabinets.

Calibration standard stock solution: 100 µg/L Prepare from a suitable standard, which may be purchased [accuracy certified against National Institute of Standards and Technology (NIST) spectrometric standard solutions].

Calibration standard solutions: 2.0 µg/L, 5.0 µg/L, 10.0 µg/L, 25.0 µg/L, and 50.0 µg/L in 2% nitric acid from the *Calibration standard stock solution*

1% Palladium stock solution: Mix 1 g of ultrapure palladium metal, with 20 mL of water and 10 mL of nitric acid in a Teflon beaker, and warm the solution on a hot plate to dissolve the palladium. Allow the solution to cool to room temperature, transfer it into a 100-mL volumetric flask, and dilute with deionized water to volume.

1% Magnesium nitrate stock solution: Mix 1 g of ultrapure magnesium nitrate, with 40 mL of water and 1 mL of nitric acid in a Teflon beaker, and warm the solution on a hot plate to dissolve. Allow the solution to cool to room temperature, transfer it into a 100-mL volumetric flask, and dilute with deionized water to volume.

[NOTE—Because of the difficulty in preparing matrix modifier stock solutions with the required purity, purchasing modifier stock solutions and using them to prepare working modifier solutions is recommended. A palladium (0.3%) and magnesium nitrate (0.2%) solution may be purchased from High Purity Standards, or equivalent.]

Modifier working solution: Transfer 3 mL of *1% Palladium stock solution* and 2 mL of *1% Magnesium nitrate stock solution* to a 10-mL volumetric flask, and dilute with 2% nitric acid to volume. A volume of 5 µL provides 0.015 mg of palladium and 0.01 mg of magnesium nitrate.

Sample solution: [**CAUTION**—Wear proper eye protection and protective clothing and gloves during sample preparation. Closely follow the manufacturer's safety instructions for use of the microwave digestion apparatus.]

Transfer 500 mg of the sample into a Teflon digestion vessel liner. Prepare samples in duplicate. Add 15 mL of nitric acid, and swirl gently. Cover the vessels with lids, leaving the vent fitting off. Predigest overnight under a hood. Place the rupture membrane in the vent fitting, and tighten the lid. Place all vessels on the microwave oven turntable. Connect the vent tubes to the vent trap, and connect the pressure-sensing line to the appropriate vessel. Initiate a two-stage digestion procedure by heating the microwave at 15% power for 15 min followed by 25% power for 45 min. Remove the turntable of vessels from the oven, and allow the vessels to cool to room temperature (a cool water bath may be used to speed the cooling process). Vent the vessels when they reach room temperature. Remove the lids, and slowly add 2 mL of 30% hydrogen peroxide to each. Allow the reactions to subside, and seal the vessels. Return the vessels on the turntable to the microwave oven, and heat for an additional 15 min at 30% power. Remove the vessels from the oven, and allow them to cool to room temperature. Transfer the cooled digests into 25-mL volumetric flasks, and dilute with deionized water to volume.

Analysis: The graphite furnace program is as follows:
1. Dry at 115° using a 1-s ramp, a 65-s hold, and a 300-mL/min argon flow.
2. Char the sample at 1000° using a 1-s ramp, a 20-s hold, and a 300-mL/min air flow.
3. Cool down and purge the air from the furnace for 10 s using a 20° set temperature and a 300-mL/min argon flow.
4. Atomize at 2400° using a 0-s ramp and a 5-s hold with the argon flow stopped.
5. Clean out at 2600° with a 1-s ramp and a 5-s hold.

Use the autosampler to inject 20-µL aliquots of blanks, *Calibration standard solutions*, and *Sample solutions* and 5 µL of *Modifier working solution*. Inject each solution in duplicate, and average the results. Use peak area measurement for all quantitations. After ensuring that the furnace is clean by running a 5% nitric acid blank, check the instrument's sensitivity by running a 20-µL aliquot of the 25-µg *Calibration standard solution*. Compare the results obtained with the expected results for the equipment used, and take the necessary steps to correct any problems.

Calculate the characteristic mass. Record and track the integrated absorbance and characteristic mass for reference and quality assurance.

Inject each *Calibration standard solution* in duplicate. Use the algorithms provided in the instrument software to establish calibration curves. Recheck calibration periodically, and recalibrate if the recheck differs from the original calibration by more than 10%.

---

[5] This method was developed using a Perkin-Elmer Model 5100, HGA-600 furnace, and an AS-60 autosampler with Zeeman effect background correction.

Inject the *Sample solution* in duplicate, and record the integrated absorbance. If the instrument response exceeds that of the calibration curve, dilute with 5% nitric acid to bring the sample's response into the working range, and note the dilution factor (DF). All sample analyses should be blank corrected using a sample solution blank.

If a computer-based instrument is used, the data output is reported as µg/L. Calculate the concentration of arsenic, in µg/g (equivalent to mg/kg), in the original sample taken:

$$\text{Result} = (C \times DF \times V)/W$$

- C = concentration of arsenic in the sample aliquot injected (µg/L)
- DF = dilution factor of the *Sample solution*
- V = final volume of the *Sample solution* (L)
- W = weight of the sample taken to prepare the *Sample solution* (g)

[NOTE—To monitor recovery and ensure analytical accuracy for proper quality assurance, analyze blanks, spiked blanks, and a spiked oil with each digestion set.]

Acceptance criteria: NMT 2.0 mg/kg

- **CADMIUM,** *Elemental Impurities by ICP,* Appendix IIIC
Acceptance criteria: NMT 1.0 mg/kg
- **LEAD,** *Elemental Impurities by ICP,* Appendix IIIC

[NOTE—Alternatively, the lead content may be determined by the following method.]

Apparatus

Sample digestion: Use a microwave oven[4] equipped with advanced composite vessels with 100-mL Teflon liners. Use rupture membranes to vent vessels should the pressure exceed 125 psi. The vessels fit into a turntable, and each vessel can be vented into an overflow container. Equip the microwave oven with an exhaust tube to ventilate fumes.

Sample analysis: See *Apparatus* in *Lead Limit Test, Atomic Absorption Spectrophotometric Graphite Furnace Method, Method I,* Appendix IIIB.

Calibration standard stock solution: 100 µg/L
Prepare from a suitable standard, which may be purchased [accuracy certified against National Institute of Standards and Technology (NIST) spectrometric standard solutions].

Calibration standard solutions: 2.0 µg/L, 5.0 µg/L, 10.0 µg/L, 25.0 µg/L, and 50.0 µg/L in 2% nitric acid from the *Calibration standard stock solution*

10% Ammonium dihydrogen phosphate stock solution: Mix 10 g of ultrapure ammonium dihydrogen phosphate, with 40 mL of water and 1 mL of nitric acid to dissolve the phosphate. Dilute with deionized water to 100 mL.

1% Magnesium nitrate stock solution: Mix 1 g of ultrapure magnesium nitrate, with 40 mL of water and 1 mL of nitric acid in a Teflon beaker, and warm on a hot plate to dissolve the solids. Allow the solution to cool to room temperature, transfer it into a 100-mL volumetric flask, and dilute with deionized water to volume.

[NOTE—Because of the difficulty in preparing matrix modifier stock solutions with the required purity, purchasing modifier stock solutions and using them to prepare working solutions is recommended. An ammonium dihydrogen phosphate (4%) and magnesium nitrate (0.2%) solution may be purchased from High Purity Standards, or equivalent.]

Modifier working solution: Transfer 4 mL of *10% Ammonium dihydrogen phosphate stock solution* and 2 mL of *1% Magnesium nitrate stock solution* to a 10-mL volumetric flask, and dilute with 2% nitric acid to volume. A volume of 5 µL provides 0.2 mg of phosphate plus 0.01 mg of magnesium nitrate.

Sample solution: Prepare as directed for the *Sample solution* in the *Arsenic* test.

[CAUTION—Wear proper eye protection and protective clothing and gloves during sample preparation. Closely follow the manufacturer's safety instructions for use of the microwave digestion apparatus.]

Analysis: The graphite furnace program is as follows:

1. Dry at 120° using a 1-s ramp, a 55-s hold, and a 300-mL/min argon flow.
2. Char the sample at 850° using a 1-s ramp, a 30-s hold, and a 300-mL/min air flow.
3. Cool down and purge the air from the furnace for 10 s using a 20° set temperature and a 300-mL/min argon flow.
4. Atomize at 2100° using a 0-s ramp and a 5-s hold with the argon flow stopped.
5. Clean out at 2600° with a 1-s ramp and a 5-s hold.

Use the autosampler to inject 20-µL aliquots of blanks, *Calibration standard solutions, Sample solutions,* and 5 µL of *Modifier working solution.* Inject each solution in duplicate, and average the results. Use peak-area measurement for all quantitation. After ensuring that the furnace is clean by running a 5% nitric acid blank, check instrument sensitivity by running an aliquot of the 25-µg *Calibration standard solution.* Compare the results obtained with the expected results for the equipment used, and take the necessary steps to correct any problems.

Calculate the characteristic mass, and record and track the integrated absorbance and characteristic mass for reference and quality assurance.

Inject each *Calibration standard solution* in duplicate. Use the algorithms provided in the instrument software to establish calibration curves. Recheck the calibration periodically and recalibrate if recheck differs from the original calibration by more than 10%.

Inject the *Sample solution* in duplicate, and record the integrated absorbance. If the instrument response exceeds that of the calibration curve, dilute with 5% nitric acid to bring the sample response into the working range, and note the dilution factor (DF). All sample analyses should be blank corrected using a sample solution blank.

If a computer-based instrument is used, the data output is reported as micrograms per liter.

Calculate the concentration, in µg/g (equivalent to mg/kg), of lead in the original sample taken:

$$\text{Result} = (C \times DF \times V)/W$$

C = concentration of lead in the sample aliquot injected (µg/L)
DF = dilution factor of the *Sample solution*
V = final volume of the *Sample solution* (L)
W = weight of the sample taken to prepare the *Sample solution* (g)

[NOTE—To monitor recovery and ensure analytical accuracy for proper quality assurance, analyze blanks, spiked blanks, and a spiked oil with each digestion set.]

Acceptance criteria: NMT 1.0 mg/kg

- **MERCURY**
  Apparatus
    Sample digestion: Use a microwave oven (CEM Model MDS-2100, or equivalent) equipped with advanced composite vessels with 100-mL Teflon liners. Use rupture membranes to vent vessels should the pressure exceed 125 psi. The vessels fit into a turntable, and each vessel can be vented into an overflow container. Equip the microwave oven with an exhaust tube to ventilate fumes.
    Sample analysis: Use a suitable atomic absorption spectrophotometer equipped with an atomic vapor assembly. This method was developed using a Perkin-Elmer Model 5100 and IL 440 Thermo Jarrell Ash atomic vapor assembly. An electrodeless discharge lamp serves as the source, with an inert gas such as argon or nitrogen as the purge gas. Set up the instrument according to manufacturer's specifications. Instrument parameters are as follows:
    Wavelength: 253.6 nm
    Slit: 0.7
    Reagent setting: 5
    Gas flow: 5–6 L/min
    Reaction time: 0.5 min
    Glassware: Acid wash all glass, Teflon, and plastic vessels by soaking them in a nitric acid bath containing a 4:1 solution of water and nitric acid. [CAUTION—Wear a full face shield and protective clothing and gloves at all times when working with acid baths.] After acid soaking, rinse acid-washed items in deionized water, dry, and store them in clean, covered cabinets.
    Calibration standard stock solution: 200 ng/g of mercury. Prepare from a suitable standard, which may be purchased [accuracy certified against National Institute of Standards and Technology (NIST) spectrometric standard solutions].
    Calibration standard solutions: 20 ng, 60 ng, 100 ng, 200 ng, and 400 ng of mercury in 1 N hydrochloric acid from the *Calibration standard stock solution*
    Reducing reagent: 5% stannous chloride in 25% hydrochloric acid (trace-metal grade). [NOTE—Prepare daily.]
    Sample solution: Prepare as directed for the *Sample solution* in the *Arsenic* test.
    [CAUTION—Wear proper eye protection and protective clothing and gloves during sample preparation. Closely follow the manufacturer's safety instructions for use of the microwave digestion apparatus.]
  Analysis: Optimize the instrument settings for the spectrophotometer as described in the instrument manual. The instrument parameters for cold vapor generation are as follows:
  Wavelength: 253.6 nm
  Slit: 0.70 nm
  Reagent setting: 5
  Gas flow: 5–6 L/min
  Reaction time: 0.5 min
  Use a peak height integration method with a 40-s integration time and a 20-s read delay in an unheated absorption cell. Zero the instrument as follows: Place a Fleaker containing 50 mL of 1 N hydrochloric acid in the sample well of the hydride generator. Press "start" on the vapor generator and "read" on the atomic absorption spectrophotometer. The instrument will automatically flush the sample container with nitrogen, dispense the designated amount of reagent, stir the sample for a designated reaction time, and purge the head volume again with nitrogen, sweeping any vapor into the quartz cell for determination of absorption. The atomic absorption spectrophotometer will automatically zero on this sample when "autozero" is selected from the calibration menu.
  Generate a standard curve of concentration versus absorption by analyzing the five *Calibration standard solutions* prepared as described for daily standards under *Calibration standard solutions*. Analyze each solution in duplicate, generate the calibration curve, and store, using procedures specific for the instrumentation.
  Transfer an appropriate aliquot of the *Sample solution* (usually 2 mL) in a Fleaker containing 50 mL of 1 N hydrochloric acid. Analyze solutions in duplicate using the procedure specified in the instrument manual. Using the calibration algorithm provided in the instrument software, calculate and report the mercury concentration in nanograms of mercury in the aliquot analyzed.
  Calculate the level of mercury as µg/g (equivalent to mg/kg), in the original sample taken:

  $$\text{Result} = (A \times DF)/(W \times 1000)$$

  A = amount of mercury in the aliquot analyzed (ng)
  DF = dilution factor (final volume of *Sample solution*/volume taken for analysis)
  W = weight of the sample taken to prepare the *Sample solution* (g)

  [NOTE—To monitor recovery and ensure analytical accuracy for proper quality assurance, analyze blanks, spiked blanks, and a spiked oil with each digestion set.]
  Acceptance criteria: NMT 1.0 mg/kg

Organic Impurities
- **PHEOPHORBIDE CONTENT**
    Solution A: 50 mg/mL of sodium sulfate
    Solution B: Saturated solution of sodium sulfate
    Sample stock solution: Transfer 100 mg of the sample to a 10-mL test tube, add 10 mL of acetone, and dissolve with sonication. Quantitatively transfer this solution to a separatory funnel, rinsing the test tube three times with 10-mL portions of acetone and adding the rinsings to the funnel. Add 30 mL of ethyl ether to the separatory funnel, followed by 50 mL of *Solution A*. Mix the contents of the separatory funnel by shaking gently, then draw off and discard the lower layer. Repeat washing with *Solution A* three times. Dehydrate the remaining extract with sodium sulfate anhydrate, then transfer the extract to a 50-mL volumetric flask. Dilute with ethyl ether to volume.
    Sample solution: Transfer 20 mL of the *Sample stock solution* to a small beaker. Add 20 mL of 17% hydrochloric acid, and mix the solution vigorously. Transfer the hydrochloric acid layer to a separatory funnel and repeat the extraction with a second 10-mL portion of 17% hydrochloric acid, adding the hydrochloric acid layer to the separatory funnel. Add 150 mL of *Solution B*, 20 mL of ethyl ether, and mix the contents of the separatory funnel by shaking. Transfer the ethyl ether layer to a 20-mL volumetric flask, and dilute with ethyl ether to volume.
    Analysis: Using a suitable spectrophotometer, determine the absorbance of the *Sample solution* at 667 nm in a 1-cm cuvette, using ethyl ether as the blank. If necessary, the *Sample solution* may be further diluted with ethyl ether to obtain an absorbance within the linear operating range of the instrument.
    Calculate the percentage of pheophorbide in the portion of the sample taken:

    $$\text{Result} = A_U/(C_U \times E) \times 100$$

    A_U = absorbance of the *Sample solution*
    C_U = concentration of the *Sample solution* (mg/mL)
    E = absorption constant for 1 mg/mL pheophorbide in ethyl ether at 667 nm in a 1-cm cuvette (70.2 mL/mg^{-1}cm^{-1})
    Acceptance criteria: NMT 0.02%

SPECIFIC TESTS
- **WATER,** *Water Determination,* Appendix IIB
    Acceptance criteria: NMT 1.0%

OTHER REQUIREMENTS
- **LABELING** Label to indicate the name of any added antioxidant.

Azodicarbonamide
First Published: Prior to FCC 6

Azodicarboxylic Acid Diamide

$C_2H_4N_4O_2$
INS: 927a
UNII: 56Z28B9C8O [azodicarbonamide]
Formula wt 116.08
CAS: [123-77-3]

DESCRIPTION
Azodicarbonamide occurs as a yellow to orange-red, crystalline powder. It is practically insoluble in water and in most organic solvents. It is slightly soluble in dimethyl sulfoxide. It melts above 180° with decomposition.
Function: Maturing agent for flour
Packaging and Storage: Store in well-closed, light-resistant containers.

IDENTIFICATION
- **ULTRAVIOLET ABSORPTION**
    Sample solution: 35 µg/mL
    Acceptance criteria: The *Sample solution* exhibits an ultraviolet absorption maximum at about 245 nm.

ASSAY
- **PROCEDURE**
    Sample: 225 mg, previously dried
    Analysis: Transfer the *Sample* into a 250-mL glass-stoppered iodine flask. Add about 23 mL of dimethyl sulfoxide to the flask, washing any adhered sample down with the solvent, then stopper the flask and place about 2 mL of the solvent in the cup or lip of the flask. Swirl occasionally, until dissolution of the *Sample* is complete, and then loosen the stopper to drain the remainder of solvent into the flask and to rinse down any dissolved sample into the solution. Add 5.0 g of potassium iodide followed by 15 mL of water, then immediately pipet 10 mL of 0.5 N hydrochloric acid into the flask, and rapidly stopper. Swirl until the potassium iodide dissolves, and allow to stand for 20 to 25 min protected from light. Titrate the liberated iodine with 0.1 N sodium thiosulfate to the disappearance of the yellow color. Titrate with additional thiosulfate if any yellow color appears within 15 min. Perform a blank determination (see *General Provisions*) on a solution consisting of 25 mL of dimethyl sulfoxide, 5.0 g of potassium iodide, 15 mL of water, and 5 mL of 0.5 N hydrochloric acid, and make any necessary correction. Each mL of 0.1 N sodium thiosulfate is equivalent to 5.804 mg of $C_2H_4N_4O_2$.
    Acceptance criteria: NLT 98.6% and NMT 100.5% of $C_2H_4N_4O_2$, on the dried basis

IMPURITIES
Inorganic Impurities
- **LEAD,** *Lead Limit Test,* Appendix IIIB

Sample solution: Prepare as directed for organic compounds.
Control: 5 µg Pb (5 mL of *Diluted Standard Lead Solution*)
Acceptance criteria: NMT 5 mg/kg

SPECIFIC TESTS
- **LOSS ON DRYING,** Appendix IIC: Vacuum oven at 50° for 2 h
  Acceptance criteria: NMT 0.5%
- **NITROGEN,** Appendix IIIC
  Sample: 50 mg
  Analysis: Transfer the *Sample* into a 100-mL Kjeldahl flask, add 3 mL of concentrated hydriodic acid solution (57% freshly assayed), and digest the mixture with gentle heating for 1.25 h, adding sufficient water, when necessary, to maintain the original volume. Increase the heat at the end of the digestion period, and continue heating until the volume is reduced by about one-half. Cool to room temperature, add 1.5 g of potassium sulfate, 3 mL of water, and 4.5 mL of sulfuric acid, and heat until iodine fumes no longer evolve. Allow the mixture to cool, wash down the sides of the flask with water, heat until charring occurs, and again cool to room temperature. Add 40 mg of mercuric oxide to the charred material, heat until the color of the solution is pale yellow, then cool, wash down the sides of the flask with a few mL of water, and digest the mixture for an additional 3 h. Cool the digest, add 20 mL of ammonia-free water, 16 mL of a 50% sodium hydroxide solution, and 5 mL of a 44% sodium thiosulfate solution. Immediately connect the flask to a distillation apparatus and distill, collecting the distillate in 10 mL of a 4% boric acid solution. Add a few drops of methyl red-methylene blue TS to the distillate, and titrate with 0.05 N sulfuric acid. Perform a blank determination (see *General Provisions*), and make any necessary correction. Each mL of 0.05 N sulfuric acid is equivalent to 0.7004 mg of nitrogen.
  Acceptance criteria: Between 47.2% and 48.7%
- **PH,** *pH Determination,* Appendix IIB
  Sample preparation: 2 g in 100 mL of water, agitated with a power stirrer for 5 min
  Acceptance criteria: NLT 5.0
- **RESIDUE ON IGNITION (SULFATED ASH),** Appendix IIC
  Sample: 1.5 g
  Acceptance criteria: NMT 0.15%

Add the following:

▲Azorubine[1]
First Published: FCC 8

Carmoisine
CI Food Red 3
CI No. 14720
Class: Mono-Azo

Disodium 4-hydroxy-3-(4-sulfonato-1-naphthylazo)-1-naphthalenesulfonate

$C_{20}H_{12}N_2Na_2O_7S_2$ Formula wt 502.44
INS: 122
UNII: DR4641L47F [azorubine] CAS: [3567-69-9]

DESCRIPTION
Azorubine occurs as red powder or granules. It is principally the disodium salt of 4-hydroxy-3-(4-sulfonato-1-naphthylazo)-1-naphthalenesulfonate and subsidiary coloring matters, with sodium chloride and/or sodium sulfate as the principal uncolored components. It is soluble in water and sparingly soluble in ethanol.
Function: Color
Packaging and Storage: Store in well-closed containers.

IDENTIFICATION
- **VISIBLE ABSORPTION SPECTRUM**
  Sample solution: Dissolve a sample in water, and dilute appropriately.
  Analysis: Measure the absorption spectrum of the *Sample solution*, using a suitable UV-visible spectrophotometer.
  Acceptance criteria: The *Sample solution* exhibits a wavelength maximum at 516 nm.

ASSAY
- **TOTAL COLOR,** *Color Determination, Methods I and II,* Appendix IIIC: Both methods must be used.
  Method I: (Spectrophotometric)
  Sample solution: 10 mg/mL
  Analysis: Determine as directed at 516 nm, using 0.051 L/(mg · cm) for the absorptivity (*a*) for Azorubine.
  Method II: (TiCl₃ Titration)
  Sample: 0.5–0.6 g
  Analysis: Determine as directed, except under *Procedure*, use 15 g of *Sodium Bitartrate* instead of 21–22 g, and use 150 mL of water instead of 275 mL. For the calculation, use 7.962 as the stoichiometric factor (F_S) for the disodium salt of Azorubine.
  Acceptance criteria: The average of the results obtained from *Method I* and *Method II* is NLT 85% total coloring matters.

IMPURITIES
Inorganic Impurities
- **LEAD,** *Lead Limit Test,* Appendix IIIB
  Sample solution: Prepare as directed for organic compounds.
  Control: 2 µg Pb (2 mL of *Diluted Standard Lead Solution*)
  Acceptance criteria: NMT 2 mg/kg

---
[1] Azorubine is approved for use in some countries but banned in others, such as the United States.

Organic Impurities

- **UNCOMBINED INTERMEDIATES AND PRODUCTS OF SIDE REACTIONS**

  Solution A: 0.2 N ammonium acetate
  Solution B: Methanol
  Mobile phase: Exponential gradient program from (99% A and 1% B) to (0% A and 100% B) at a rate of 2% per min, followed by 6 min of 100% B to wash the column, and (0% A and 100% B) to (99% A and 1% B) in 14 min to return to the initial gradient composition and equilibrate column.
  Standard solution: 25 µg/mL of 4-amino-1-naphthalenesulfonic acid and 25 µg/mL of 4-hydroxy-1-naphthalenesulfonic acid in 0.02 M ammonium acetate
  Sample solution: 5 mg/mL in 0.02 M ammonium acetate
  Chromatographic system, Appendix IIA
   Mode: High-performance liquid chromatography
   Detector: UV
   Column
    Guard column: 15-mm × 4.6-mm; 5-µm C18 column
    Analytical column: 25-cm × 4.6-mm; 5-µm C18 column
   Column temperature: Ambient
   Flow rate: 1.0 mL/min
   Injection volume: 20 µL
  Analysis: Separately inject equal volumes of the *Standard solution* and *Sample solution* into the chromatograph, and measure the responses for the major peaks on the resulting chromatograms.
  Calculate the percentage of both impurities (4-amino-1-naphthalenesulfonic acid and 4-hydroxy-1-naphthalenesulfonic acid) in the portion of the sample taken:

  $$\text{Result} = (r_U/r_S) \times (C_S/C_U) \times F \times 100$$

  r_U = peak area for analyte in the *Sample solution*
  r_S = peak area for analyte in the *Standard solution*
  C_S = concentration of analyte in the *Standard solution* (µg/mL)
  C_U = concentration of sample in the *Sample solution* (mg/mL)
  F = mg-to-µg conversion factor, 1000

  Acceptance criteria: 4-amino-1-naphthalenesulfonic acid and 4-hydroxy-1-naphthalenesulfonic acid: NMT 0.5% combined

SPECIFIC TESTS

- **COMBINED TESTS**
  Tests
  - LOSS ON DRYING (VOLATILE MATTER), *Color Determination,* Appendix IIIC
  - CHLORIDE, *Sodium Chloride, Color Determination,* Appendix IIIC
  - SULFATES (AS SODIUM SALTS), *Sodium Sulfate, Color Determination,* Appendix IIIC

  Acceptance criteria: NMT 15%, combined as the sum of all three tests

- **ETHER EXTRACTS,** *Color Determination,* Appendix IIIC
  Acceptance criteria: NMT 0.2%

- **SUBSIDIARY COLORING MATTERS**
  [NOTE—In this method, subsidiary coloring matters are separated from the main coloring matter of Azorubine by ascending paper chromatography (see *Paper Chromatography,* Appendix IIA), and extracted separately from the chromatographic paper. The absorbance of each extract is measured at the wavelength of maximum absorption for Azorubine (516 nm) by visible spectrophotometry. Because it is impractical to identify each subsidiary coloring matter using this procedure, and because the subsidiary coloring matters are usually minor components of food colors, the method assumes that the maximum absorbance of each subsidiary coloring matter is the same as that of the total coloring matters. The subsidiary coloring matters content is calculated by adding together the absorbances of the extracts in conjunction with the total coloring matters content of the sample.]

  Chromatographic apparatus: The chromatography tank (*Figures 1* and *2*) is composed of a glass tank (A) and cover (B); frame to support chromatography paper (C); solvent tray (D); wire secondary frame (E) for supporting "drapes" of the filter paper; and 20-cm × 20-cm chromatography grade paper.[2] Mark out the chromatography paper as shown in *Figure 3*.

---

[2] Whatman No 1, or equivalent.

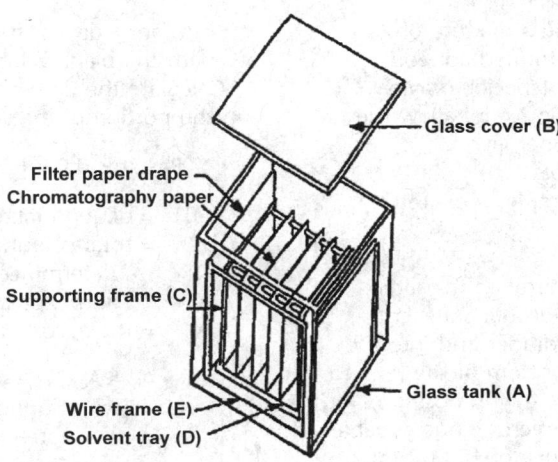

Figure 1. Assembly of the Chromatographic Apparatus

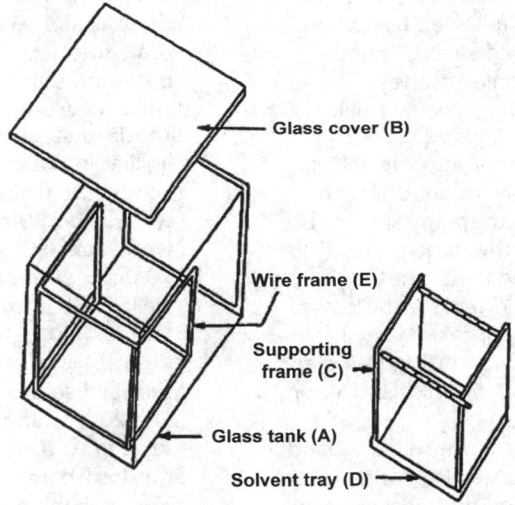

Figure 2. Components of the Chromatographic Apparatus

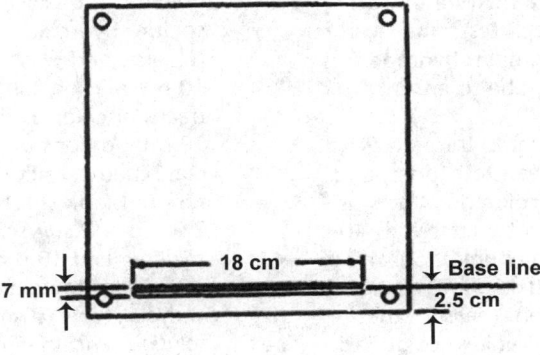

Figure 3. Method for Marking the Chromatographic Paper

Chromatographic solvent: Prepare a mixture of 2-butanone, acetone, water, and saturated aqueous solution of ammonium hydroxide (specific gravity of 0.880), (700:300:300:2). Shake for 2 min, allow the layers to separate, and use the upper layer.

Sample solution: 10 mg/mL sample

Standard solution: 0.1 mg/mL sample, prepared by diluting the *Sample solution*

Application volume: 0.10 mL

Analysis: NLT 2 h before analysis, arrange the filter-paper drapes in the glass tank, and pour sufficient *Chromatographic solvent* over the drapes and into the bottom of the tank to cover the bottom of the tank to a depth of 1 cm. Place the solvent tray in position, and fit the cover to the tank. Using a microsyringe capable of delivering 0.1 mL with a tolerance of ±0.002 mL, apply to separate chromatography sheets 0.1-mL aliquots of the *Sample solution* and *Standard solution*, as uniformly as possible within the confines of the 18-cm × 7-mm rectangle, holding the nozzle of the microsyringe steadily in contact with the paper. Allow the papers to dry at room temperature for 1–2 h or at 50° in a drying cabinet for 5 min followed by 15 min at room temperature. Mount the dried sheets, together with two plain sheets to act as blanks on the supporting frame. [NOTE—If required, several dried sheets may be developed simultaneously.]

Pour sufficient *Chromatographic solvent* into the solvent tray to bring the surface of the solvent about 1 cm below the base line of the chromatography sheets. The volume necessary will depend on the dimensions of the apparatus and should be predetermined. Put the supporting frame into position, and replace the cover. Allow the solvent front to ascend approximately 17 cm above base line, then remove the supporting frame and transfer it to a drying cabinet at 50–60° for 10–15 min. Remove the sheets from the frame.

For the *Sample solution* sheets, cut each subsidiary band from each chromatography sheet as a strip, and cut an equivalent strip from the corresponding position of the plain (blank) sheet. For the *Standard solution* sheet, cut the entire band from the sheet, and cut an equivalent strip from the corresponding position of the plain (blank) sheet. Place each strip, subdivided into a suitable number of approximately equal portions, in a separate test tube. Add 5.0 mL of a mixture of water and acetone (1:1 by volume) to each test tube, swirl for 2–3 min, add 15.0 mL of 0.05 N sodium hydrogen carbonate solution, and shake the tube to ensure mixing.

Filter the colored extracts and the blanks through 9-cm coarse-porosity filter papers into clean test tubes, and determine the absorbances of the colored extracts at 516 nm, using a suitable spectrophotometer with 40-mm closed cells against a filtered mixture of 5.0 mL of water and acetone (1:1 by vol) and 15.0 mL of 0.05 N sodium hydrogen carbonate solution. Measure the absorbances of the extracts of the blank strips at 516 nm, and correct the absorbances of the colored extracts with the blank values.

Calculate the percentage of subsidiary coloring matter in the portion of the sample taken:

$$\text{Result} = 0.01 \times D \times [(A_a + A_b + A_c \ldots A_n)/A_s] \times 100$$

0.01 = dilution factor for the *Standard solution*

D = total coloring matter content of the sample, determined from the *Total Color* test above and expressed as a decimal

A_s = the absorbance from the *Standard solution*

$A_a + A_b + A_c \ldots A_n$ = the sum of the absorbances of the subsidiary coloring matters from the *Sample solution*, corrected for the blank values

Acceptance criteria: NMT 1%

- **UNSULFONATED PRIMARY AROMATIC AMINES**

[NOTE—Under the conditions of this test, unsulfonated primary aromatic amines are extracted into toluene from an alkaline solution of the sample, reextracted into acid, then determined spectrophotometrically after diazotization and coupling.]

R salt solution: 0.05 N 2-naphthol-3,6-disulfonic acid, disodium salt

Sodium carbonate solution: 2 N sodium carbonate

Standard stock solution: Weigh 0.100 g of redistilled aniline into a small beaker, and transfer to a 100-mL volumetric flask, rinsing the beaker several times with water. Add 30 mL of 3 N hydrochloric acid, and dilute with water at room temperature to the mark. Dilute 10.0 mL of this solution to 100 mL with water, and mix well; 1 mL of this solution is equivalent to 0.0001 g of aniline. [NOTE—Prepare the *Standard stock solution* fresh.]

Standard solutions: Separately dilute 5-mL, 10-mL, 15-mL, 20-mL, and 25-mL aliquots of the *Standard stock solution* with 1 N hydrochloric acid to 100 mL.

Standard blank solution: In a 25-mL volumetric flask mix 10.0 mL of 1 N hydrochloric acid, 10.0 mL of the *Sodium carbonate solution*, and 2.0 mL of the *R salt solution*, and dilute with water to volume.

Sample solution: Add 2.0 g of the sample to a separatory funnel containing 100 mL of water; rinse down the sides of the funnel with 50 mL of water, swirling to dissolve the sample; and add 5 mL of 1 N sodium hydroxide. Extract with two 50-mL portions of toluene, and wash the combined toluene extracts with 10-mL portions of 0.1 N sodium hydroxide to remove traces of color. Extract the washed toluene with three 10-mL portions of 3 N hydrochloric acid, and dilute the combined extract with water to 100 mL.

Sample blank solution: In a 25-mL volumetric flask mix 2.0 mL of *R salt solution*, 10 mL of *Sodium carbonate solution*, and 10.0 mL of the *Sample solution*, and dilute with water to volume.

Analysis: Pipet 10-mL aliquots of each of the *Standard solutions* and the *Sample solution* into separate clean, dry test tubes. Cool the tubes for 10 min by immersion in a beaker of ice water, and add 1 mL of 50% potassium bromide solution and 0.05 mL of 0.5 N sodium nitrite solution. Mix and allow the tubes to stand for 10 min in the ice water bath while the aniline is diazotized. Into each of five 25-mL volumetric flasks, measure 1 mL of the *R salt solution* and 10 mL of the *Sodium carbonate solution*. Separately pour each diazotized aniline solution into a 25-mL volumetric flask containing *R salt solution* and *Sodium carbonate solution*; rinse each test tube with a small volume of water to allow for a quantitative transfer. Dilute with water to the mark, stopper the flasks, mix the contents well, and allow them to stand for 15 min in the dark.

Measure the absorbance of each of the solutions containing the coupled *Standard solutions* at 510 nm, using a suitable spectrophotometer with 40-mm cells, against the *Standard blank solution*. Plot a standard curve relating absorbance to weight (g) of aniline in each 100 mL of the *Standard solutions*.

Measure the absorbance of the solutions containing the coupled *Sample solution* at 510 nm, using a suitable spectrophotometer with 40-mm cells, against the *Sample blank solution*. From the standard curve, determine the weight (g) of aniline in each 100 mL of the *Sample solution*.

Calculate the percentage of unsulfonated primary aromatic amine (as aniline) in the portion of the sample taken:

$$\text{Result} = W_A/W \times 100$$

W_A = weight of aniline in the *Sample solution*, calculated from the standard curve (g/100 mL)

W = weight of sample used to prepare the *Sample solution* (g)

Acceptance criteria: NMT 0.01%, calculated as aniline

- **WATER-INSOLUBLE MATTER**, *Color Determination*, Appendix IIIC

  Acceptance criteria: NMT 0.2%▲$_{FCC8}$

Balsam Peru Oil

First Published: Prior to FCC 6
Last Revision: Third Supplement, FCC 7

CAS: [8007-00-9]

UNII: DIK0395679 [balsam peru oil]

DESCRIPTION
Balsam Peru Oil occurs as a yellow to pale brown, slightly viscous liquid having a sweet, balsamic odor. It is obtained by extraction or distillation of Peruvian Balsam obtained from *Myroxylon pereirae* Royle Klotzsche (Fam. Leguminosae). Occasionally, crystals may occur within the liquid. It is soluble in most fixed oils, and is soluble, with turbidity, in mineral oil. It is partly soluble in propylene glycol, but it is practically insoluble in glycerin.

Function: Flavoring agent

Packaging and Storage: Store in a cool place protected from light in full, tight containers that are made from steel or aluminum and that are suitably lined.

IDENTIFICATION
- **INFRARED SPECTRA,** *Spectrophotometric Identification Tests,* Appendix IIIC
  Acceptance criteria: The spectrum of the sample exhibits relative maxima at the same wavelengths as those of the spectrum below.

SPECIFIC TESTS
- **ACID VALUE (ESSENTIAL OILS AND FLAVORS),** Appendix VI
  Acceptance criteria: 30–60
- **ANGULAR ROTATION,** *Optical (Specific) Rotation,* Appendix IIB: Use a 100-mm tube.
  Acceptance criteria: Between −1° and +2°
- **ESTERS,** *Ester Value,* Appendix VI
  Sample: 1 g
  Acceptance criteria: 200–225
- **REFRACTIVE INDEX,** Appendix IIB
  [NOTE—Use an Abbé or other refractometer of equal or greater accuracy.]
  Acceptance criteria: 1.567–1.579 at 20°
- **SOLUBILITY IN ALCOHOL,** Appendix VI
  Acceptance criteria: One mL of the sample dissolves in 0.5 mL of 90% alcohol, and remains in solution on further dilution to 10 mL.
- **SPECIFIC GRAVITY:** Determine by any reliable method (see *General Provisions*).
  Acceptance criteria: 1.110–1.120

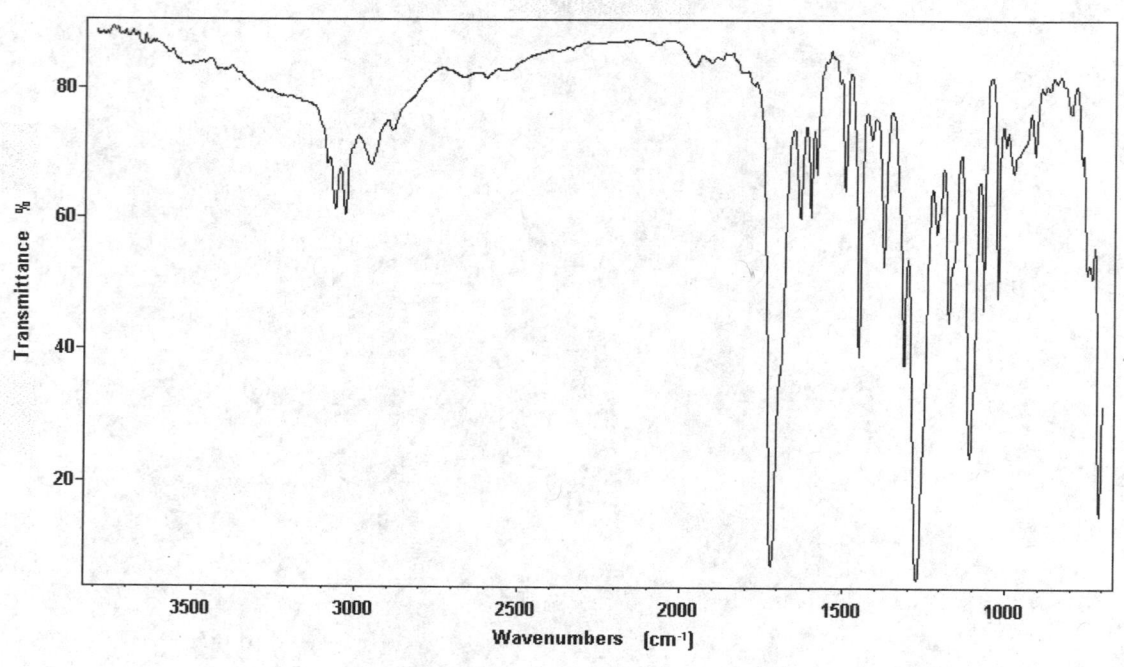

Balsam Peru Oil

Basil Oil, Comoros Type

First Published: Prior to FCC 6

Basil Oil Exotic
Basil Oil, Réunion Type
UNII: Z129UMU8LE [basil oil]

DESCRIPTION
Basil Oil, Comoros Type occurs as a light yellow liquid with a spicy odor. It is obtained by steam distillation of the flowering tops or the entire plant of *Ocimum basilicum* L. (Fam. Lamiaceae). It may be distinguished from other types, such as basil oil, European type, by its camphoraceous odor and physicochemical constants. It is soluble in most fixed oils and, with turbidity, in mineral oil.

One mL is soluble in 20 mL of propylene glycol with slight haziness, but it is insoluble in glycerin.

Function: Flavoring agent

Packaging and Storage: Store in a cool place protected from light in full, tight containers that are made from steel or aluminum and that are suitably lined.

IDENTIFICATION

- **INFRARED SPECTRA,** *Spectrophotometric Identification Tests,* Appendix IIIC
  Acceptance criteria: The spectrum of the sample exhibits relative maxima at the same wavelengths as those of the spectrum below.

SPECIFIC TESTS

- **ACID VALUE (ESSENTIAL OILS AND FLAVORS),** Appendix VI
  Acceptance criteria: NMT 1.0
- **ANGULAR ROTATION,** *Optical (Specific) Rotation,* Appendix IIB: Use a 100 mm tube.
  Acceptance criteria: Between −2° and +2°
- **ESTER VALUE AFTER ACETYLATION,** *Linalool Determination,* Appendix VI
  Sample: 2.5 g of the dry acetylated oil
  Analysis: Calculate the *Ester value after acetylation* by the formula:

  $$\text{Result} = A \times 28.05/B$$

  A = amount (mL) of 0.5 N alcoholic potassium hydroxide consumed in the saponification
  B = weight (g) of acetylated sample oil taken
  Acceptance criteria: Between 25 and 45
- **REFRACTIVE INDEX,** Appendix IIB
  [NOTE—Use an Abbé or other refractometer of equal or greater accuracy.]
  Acceptance criteria: Between 1.512 and 1.520 at 20°
- **SAPONIFICATION VALUE,** *Esters,* Appendix VI
  Sample: 5 g
  Acceptance criteria: Between 4 and 10
- **SOLUBILITY IN ALCOHOL,** Appendix VI
  Acceptance criteria: One mL of the sample dissolves in 4 mL of 80% alcohol.
- **SPECIFIC GRAVITY:** Determine by any reliable method (see *General Provisions*).
  Acceptance criteria: Between 0.952 and 0.973

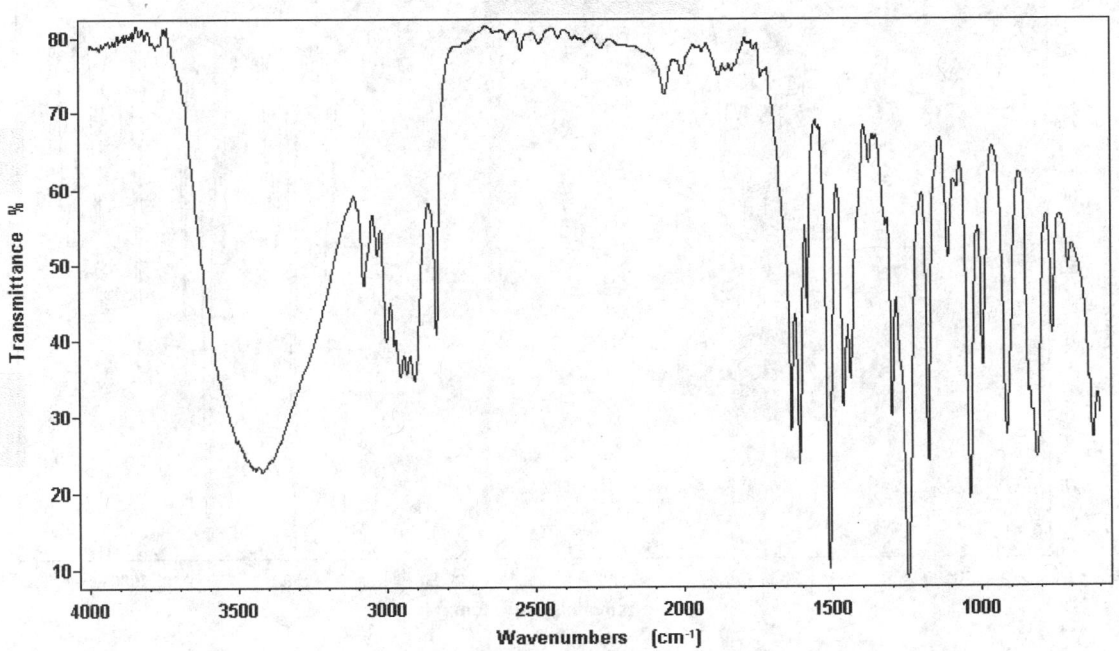

Basil Oil, Comoros Type

Basil Oil, European Type

First Published: Prior to FCC 6

Basil Oil, Italian Type
Sweet Basil Oil

CAS: [8015-73-4]

UNII: Z129UMU8LE [basil oil]

DESCRIPTION

Basil Oil, European Type occurs as a pale yellow to yellow liquid with a floral-spicy odor. It is obtained by the steam distillation of the flowering tops or the entire plant of *Ocimum basilicum* L. It may be distinguished from other types, such as basil oil, Comoros type, or basil oil, Réunion type, by its more floral odor and its physicochemical constants. It is soluble in most fixed oils and, with turbidity, in mineral oil. One mL is soluble in 20 mL of

propylene glycol with slight haziness, but it is insoluble in glycerin.
Function: Flavoring agent
Packaging and Storage: Store in a cool place protected from light in full, tight containers that are made from steel or aluminum and that are suitably lined.

IDENTIFICATION
- **INFRARED SPECTRA,** *Spectrophotometric Identification Tests,* Appendix IIIC
  Acceptance criteria: The spectrum of the sample exhibits relative maxima at the same wavelengths as those of the spectrum below.

SPECIFIC TESTS
- **ACID VALUE (ESSENTIAL OILS AND FLAVORS),** Appendix VI
  Acceptance criteria: NMT 2.5
- **ANGULAR ROTATION,** *Optical (Specific) Rotation,* Appendix IIB: Use a 100-mm tube.
  Acceptance criteria: Between $-5°$ and $-15°$
- **ESTER VALUE AFTER ACETYLATION,** *Linalool Determination,* Appendix VI
  Sample: 2.5 g of the dry acetylated oil
  Analysis: Calculate the *Ester value after acetylation* by the formula:

  $$\text{Result} = A \times 28.05/B$$

  A = amount (mL) of 0.5 N alcoholic potassium hydroxide consumed in the saponification
  B = weight (g) of acetylated sample oil taken
  Acceptance criteria: Between 140 and 180
- **REFRACTIVE INDEX,** Appendix IIB
  [NOTE—Use an Abbé or other refractometer of equal or greater accuracy.]
  Acceptance criteria: Between 1.483 and 1.493 at 20°
- **SOLUBILITY IN ALCOHOL,** Appendix VI
  Analysis: Use 4 mL of 80% alcohol.
  Acceptance criteria: Passes test
- **SPECIFIC GRAVITY:** Determine by any reliable method (see *General Provisions*).
  Acceptance criteria: Between 0.900 and 0.920

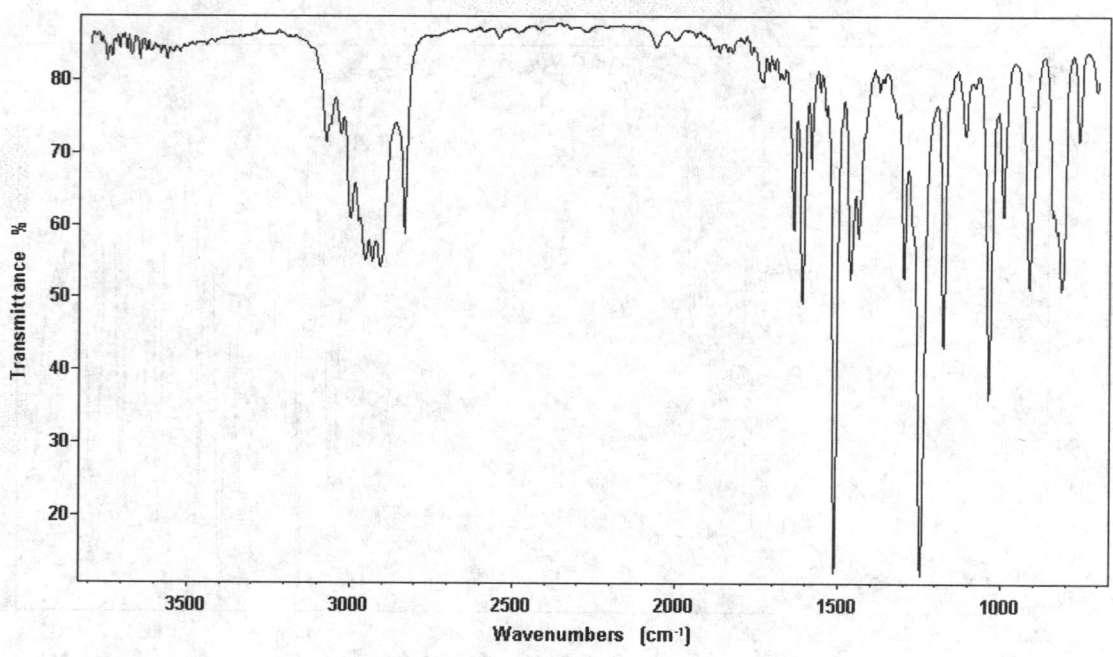

Basil Oil, European Type

Bay Oil

First Published: Prior to FCC 6

Myrcia Oil
UNII: 3T5GC5CQ33 [bay oil (pimenta racemosa)]

DESCRIPTION
Bay Oil occurs as a yellow or brown-yellow liquid with a pleasant, aromatic odor and a pungent, spicy taste. It is the volatile oil distilled from the leaves of *Pimenta acris* Kostel (Fam. Myrtaceae). It is soluble in alcohol and in glacial acetic acid. Its solutions in alcohol are acid to litmus.
Function: Flavoring agent
Packaging and Storage: Store in full, tight containers in a cool place protected from light.

IDENTIFICATION
- **A. INFRARED SPECTRA,** *Spectrophotometric Identification Tests,* Appendix IIIC

Acceptance criteria: The spectrum of the sample exhibits relative maxima at the same wavelengths as those of the spectrum below.
- **B. PROCEDURE**
  Sample: 1 mL
  Analysis: Shake the *Sample* with 20 mL of hot water, and filter. Test the filtrate with litmus, and then add 1 drop of ferric chloride TS.
  Acceptance criteria: The filtrate is acid to litmus and, after addition of ferric chloride TS, yields only a transient gray-green, not a blue or purple, color.

ASSAY
- **PHENOLS,** Appendix VI
  Acceptance criteria: NLT 50% and NMT 65%, by volume, of phenols.

SPECIFIC TESTS
- **ANGULAR ROTATION,** *Optical (Specific) Rotation,* Appendix IIB: Use a 100-mm tube.
  Acceptance criteria: Levorotatory (not more levorotatory than −3°)
- **REFRACTIVE INDEX,** Appendix IIB
  [NOTE—Use an Abbé or other refractometer of equal or greater accuracy.]
  Acceptance criteria: Between 1.507 and 1.516 at 20°
- **SPECIFIC GRAVITY:** Determine by any reliable method (see *General Provisions*).
  Acceptance criteria: Between 0.950 and 0.990

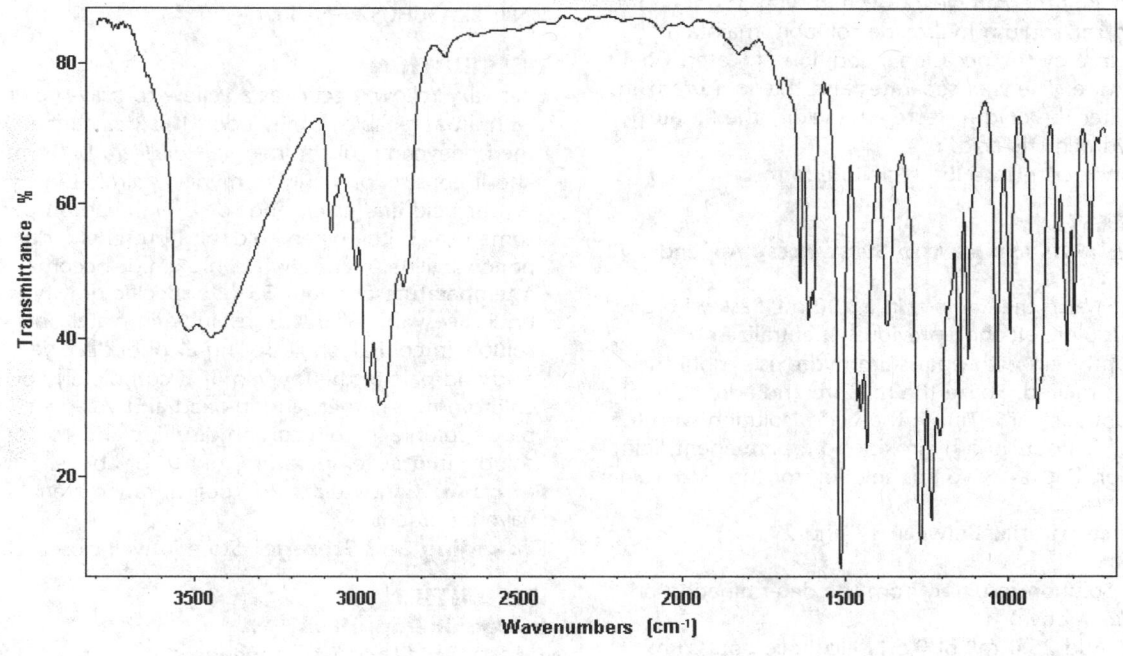

Bay Oil

Beeswax, White

First Published: Prior to FCC 6

White Wax
INS: 901
UNII: 7G1J5DA97F [white wax]

DESCRIPTION
Beeswax, White, occurs as a yellow-white solid, somewhat translucent in thin layers, with a faint, characteristic odor, free from rancidity. It is the bleached, purified wax from the honeycomb of the bee *Apis mellifera* L. (Fam. Apidae), and it consists primarily of myricyl palmitate (myricin), cerotic acid and ester, and some high-carbon paraffins. Its specific gravity is about 0.95. Beeswax, White, is insoluble in water and sparingly soluble in cold alcohol. Boiling alcohol dissolves cerotic acid and part of the myricin. It is completely soluble in chloroform, in ether, and in fixed and volatile oils. It is partly soluble in cold carbon disulfide and is completely soluble in it at temperatures of 30° or above.

Function: Surface-finishing (glazing) agent; release agent; raw material for flavoring agent
Packaging and Storage: Store in well-closed containers.

IMPURITIES
Inorganic Impurities
- **LEAD,** *Lead Limit Test,* Appendix IIIB
  Sample solution: Prepare as directed for organic compounds.
  Control: 5 µg Pb (5 mL of *Diluted Standard Lead Solution*)

Acceptance criteria: NMT 5 mg/kg

Organic Impurities
- **CARNAUBA WAX**
  Sample: 100 mg
  Analysis: Place the *Sample* in a test tube, and add 20 mL of *n*-butanol. Immerse the test tube in boiling water, and shake the mixture gently until dissolution is complete. Transfer the test tube into a beaker of water at 60°, and allow it to cool to room temperature. A loose mass of fine, needlelike crystals separate from a clear mother liquor.
  Acceptance criteria: Under the microscope, the crystals appear as loose needles or stellate clusters, and no amorphous masses are observed, indicating the absence of carnauba wax.
- **FATS, JAPAN WAX, ROSIN, AND SOAP**
  Sample: 1 g
  Analysis: Boil the *Sample* for 30 min with 35 ml of a 143 mg/mL sodium hydroxide solution, maintaining the volume by the occasional addition of water. Cool the mixture. The wax separates and the liquid remains clear. Filter the cold mixture and acidify the filtrate with hydrochloric acid.
  Acceptance criteria: No precipitate forms.

SPECIFIC TESTS
- **ACID VALUE (FATS AND RELATED SUBSTANCES)**, Appendix VII
  Sample: 3 g
  Analysis: Warm the *Sample*, in a 200-mL flask with 25 mL of absolute alcohol, previously neutralized to phenolphthalein with potassium hydroxide, until the sample is melted. Shake the mixture and add 1 mL of phenolphthalein TS. Titrate the warm solution with 0.5 N alcoholic potassium hydroxide to a permanent, faint pink color. [NOTE—Save this solution for the *Ester Value* test.]
  Acceptance criteria: Between 17 and 24
- **ESTER VALUE**
  Sample: Solution resulting from the determination of *Acid Value* (above).
  Analysis: Add 25.0 mL of 0.5 N alcoholic potassium hydroxide and 50 mL of alcohol to *Sample solution*, heat the mixture under a reflux condenser for 4 h, and titrate the excess alkali with 0.5 N hydrochloric acid. Perform a residual blank titration, and calculate the *Ester Value* as the number of mg of potassium hydroxide required for each g of the sample taken for the test.
  Acceptance criteria: Between 72 and 79
- **MELTING RANGE OR TEMPERATURE DETERMINATION**, *Procedure for Class II*, Appendix IIB
  Acceptance criteria: Between 62° and 65°
- **SAPONIFICATION CLOUD TEST**
  Saponifying solution: Dissolve 40 g of potassium hydroxide in about 900 mL of aldehyde-free alcohol maintained at a temperature of 15° until solution is complete. Warm to room temperature, and add sufficient aldehyde-free alcohol to make 1000 mL.
  Sample: 3.00 g
  Analysis: Transfer the *Sample* into a round-bottom, 100-mL boiling flask provided with a ground-glass joint, add 30 mL of the *Saponifying solution*, attach a reflux condenser to the flask, and heat the mixture gently on a steam bath for 2 h. At the end of this period, remove the reflux condenser, insert a thermometer into the solution, and place the flask in an 80° water bath. Rotate the flask while both the bath and the solution cool to 65°.
  Acceptance criteria: The solution shows no cloudiness or globule formation before the solution reaches 65°.

Beeswax, Yellow
First Published: Prior to FCC 6

Yellow Wax
INS: 901
UNII: 2ZA36H0S2V [yellow wax]
CAS: [8012-89-3]

DESCRIPTION
Beeswax, Yellow, occurs as a yellow to gray-brown solid with an agreeable, honey odor. It is the purified wax from the honeycomb of the bee *Apis mellifera* L. (Fam. Apidae), and it consists primarily of myricyl palmitate (myricin), cerotic acid and ester, and some high-carbon paraffins. It is somewhat brittle when cold, and presents a dull, granular, noncrystalline fracture when broken. It becomes pliable at a temperature of about 35°. Its specific gravity is about 0.95. Beeswax, Yellow, is insoluble in water and sparingly soluble in cold alcohol. Boiling alcohol dissolves cerotic acid and part of the myricin. It is completely soluble in chloroform, in ether, and in fixed and volatile oils. It is partly soluble in cold carbon disulfide and completely soluble in it at temperatures of 30° or above.

Function: Candy glaze and polish; raw material for flavoring agent

Packaging and Storage: Store in well-closed containers.

IMPURITIES
Inorganic Impurities
- **LEAD**, *Lead Limit Test*, Appendix IIIB
  Sample solution: Prepare as directed for organic compounds.
  Control: 5 μg Pb (5 mL of *Diluted Standard Lead Solution*)
  Acceptance criteria: NMT 5 mg/kg

Organic Impurities
- **CARNAUBA WAX**
  Sample: 100 mg
  Analysis: Place the *Sample* in a test tube, and add 20 mL of *n*-butanol. Immerse the test tube in boiling water, and shake the mixture gently until dissolution is complete. Transfer the test tube into a beaker of water at 60°, and allow it to cool to room temperature. A loose mass of fine, needlelike crystals separate from a clear mother liquor.
  Acceptance criteria: Under the microscope, the crystals appear as loose needles or stellate clusters, and no amorphous masses are observed, indicating the absence of carnauba wax.

- **FATS, JAPAN WAX, ROSIN, AND SOAP**
  Sample: 1 g
  Analysis: Boil the *Sample* for 30 min with 35 ml of a 143 mg/mL sodium hydroxide solution, maintaining the volume by the occasional addition of water. Cool the mixture. The wax separates and the liquid remains clear. Filter the cold mixture and acidify the filtrate with hydrochloric acid.
  Acceptance criteria: No precipitate forms.

SPECIFIC TESTS
- **ACID VALUE (FATS AND RELATED SUBSTANCES),** Appendix VII
  Sample: 3 g
  Analysis: Warm the *Sample*, in a 200-mL flask with 25 mL of absolute alcohol, previously neutralized to phenolphthalein with potassium hydroxide, until the sample is melted. Shake the mixture and add 1 mL of phenolphthalein TS. Titrate the warm solution with 0.5 N alcoholic potassium hydroxide to a permanent, faint pink color. [NOTE—Save this solution for the *Ester Value* test]
  Acceptance criteria: Between 18 and 24
- **ESTER VALUE**
  Sample: Solution resulting from the determination of *Acid Value* (above)
  Analysis: Add 25.0 mL of 0.5 N alcoholic potassium hydroxide and 50 mL of alcohol to *Sample solution*, heat the mixture under a reflux condenser for 4 h, and titrate the excess alkali with 0.5 N hydrochloric acid. Perform a residual blank titration, and calculate the *Ester Value* as the number of mg of potassium hydroxide required for each g of the sample taken for the test.
  Acceptance criteria: Between 72 and 77
- **MELTING RANGE OR TEMPERATURE DETERMINATION,** *Procedure for Class II,* Appendix IIB
  Acceptance criteria: Between 62° and 65°
- **SAPONIFICATION CLOUD TEST**
  Saponifying solution: Dissolve 40 g of potassium hydroxide in about 900 mL of aldehyde-free alcohol maintained at a temperature of 15° until solution is complete. Warm to room temperature, and add sufficient aldehyde-free alcohol to make 1000 mL.
  Sample: 3.00 g
  Analysis: Transfer the *Sample* into a round-bottom, 100-mL boiling flask provided with a ground-glass joint, add 30 mL of the *Saponifying solution*, attach a reflux condenser to the flask, and heat the mixture gently on a steam bath for 2 h. At the end of this period, remove the reflux condenser, insert a thermometer into the solution, and place the flask in an 80° water bath. Rotate the flask while both the bath and the solution cool to 65°.
  Acceptance criteria: The solution shows no cloudiness or globule formation before the solution reaches 65°.

Bentonite
First Published: Prior to FCC 6
Last Revision: Third Supplement, FCC 7

Smectite
Aluminum Silicate
INS: 558   CAS: [1302-78-9]
UNII: A3N5ZCN45C [bentonite]

DESCRIPTION
Bentonite occurs commercially as powders ranging in colors and tints from off white to pale brown to gray depending on the cations present in natural deposits. It comprises natural smectite clays consisting primarily of colloidal hydrated aluminum silicates of the montmorillonite or hectorite type of minerals with varying quantities of alkalies, alkaline earths, and iron. It is insoluble in water, in alcohol, in dilute acids, and in alkalies. The pH of a 2% suspension of Bentonite is typically in the range of 4.5–10.5.
Function: Clarifying, filter agent
Packaging and Storage: Store in tight containers.

IDENTIFICATION
- **A. X-RAY DIFFRACTION**
  Sample preparation A: With intense agitation, add 2 g of sample, in small portions, to 100 mL of water. Allow the mixture to stand for 12 h to ensure complete hydration. Place 2 mL of the mixture so obtained on a suitable glass slide, and allow it to air dry at room temperature to produce an oriented film. Place the slide in a vacuum desiccator over a free surface of ethylene glycol. Evacuate the desiccator, and close the stopcock so that ethylene glycol saturates the desiccator chamber. Allow the slide to stand for 12 h.
  Sample preparation B: Prepare a random powder specimen of the sample.
  Analysis: Record the X-ray diffraction pattern using a copper source, and calculate the *d* values. [NOTE—For *Sample preparation B*, determine the *d* value between the range of 1.48 and 1.54 Å.]
  Acceptance criteria: For *Sample preparation A*, the largest peak corresponds to a *d* value between 15.0 and 17.2 Å. For *Sample preparation B*, the peak is between 1.492 and 1.504 Å or between 1.510 and 1.540 Å.
- **B. PROCEDURE**
  Sample: 0.5 g
  Analysis: Add 1 g of potassium nitrate and 3 g of anhydrous sodium carbonate to the *Sample* contained in a metal crucible, heat until the mixture has melted, and allow it to cool. Add 20 mL of boiling water to the residue, mix, filter, and wash the residue with 50 mL of water. Add 1 mL of hydrochloric acid and 5 mL of water to the residue, and filter. Add 1 mL of 10 N sodium hydroxide to the filtrate, filter, and add 3 mL of 2 M ammonium chloride.
  Acceptance criteria: A gelatinous, white precipitate forms.

IMPURITIES
Inorganic Impurities
- **ARSENIC**, *Arsenic Limit Test,* Appendix IIIB
  Sample solution: Transfer 8.0 g of dried sample into a 250-mL beaker containing 100 mL of 1:25 hydrochloric acid, mix, cover with a watch glass, and boil gently, stirring occasionally, for 15 min without allowing excessive foaming. Filter the hot supernatant liquid through a rapid-flow filter paper into a 200-mL volumetric flask, and wash the filter with four 25-mL portions of hot 4% hydrochloric acid, collecting the washings in the volumetric flask. Cool the combined filtrates to room temperature, add 4% hydrochloric acid to volume, and mix.
  Control: 5 µg As (5 mL of *Standard Arsenic Solution*)
  Analysis: Proceed as directed using a 25-mL aliquot of the *Sample solution*.
  Acceptance criteria: NMT 5 mg/kg
- **LEAD**
  [NOTE—The *Standard solution* and the *Sample solution* may be modified, if necessary, to obtain solutions of suitable concentrations, adaptable to the linear or working range of the spectrophotometer used.]
  Sample preparation: Transfer 3.75 g of dried sample into a 250-mL beaker containing 100 mL of 1:25 hydrochloric acid, stir, cover with a watch glass, and boil for 15 min. Cool to room temperature, and allow the insoluble matter to settle. Decant the supernatant through a rapid-flow filter paper into a 400-mL beaker. Wash the filter with four 25-mL portions of hot water, collecting the filtrate in the 400-mL beaker. Concentrate the combined extracts by gentle boiling to approximately 20 mL. If a precipitate forms, add 2–3 drops of nitric acid, heat to boiling, and cool to room temperature. Filter the concentrated extracts through a rapid-flow filter paper into a 50-mL volumetric flask. Transfer the remaining contents of the 400-mL beaker through the filter paper and into the flask with water. Dilute with water to volume, and mix.
  Standard solution: 3 µg/mL Pb: from *Lead Nitrate Stock Solution, Lead Limit Test, Flame Atomic Absorption Method,* Appendix IIIB. [NOTE—Prepare this solution on the day of use.]
  Analysis: Using a suitable atomic absorption spectrophotometer equipped with a lead hollow-cathode lamp, deuterium arc background correction, a single-slot burner, and using an oxidizing air–acetylene flame, determine the absorbances of the *Sample preparation* and the *Standard solution* at 284 nm.
  Acceptance criteria: The absorbance of the *Sample preparation* is not greater than that of the *Standard solution* (NMT 4 mg/kg).

SPECIFIC TESTS
- **COARSE PARTICLES**
  Sample preparation: 20 g in 100 mL of water, mixed for 15 min at NLT 5000 rpm
  Analysis: Transfer the *Sample preparation* to a wet sieve of nominal mesh aperture (75 µm), previously dried at 100°–105° and weighed, and wash with three 500-mL volumes of water, ensuring that any agglomerates are dispersed. Dry at 100°–105°, and weigh. The difference in weight corresponds to the measure of coarse particles.
  Acceptance criteria: NMT 0.5% of sample is retained on a 75-µm sieve
- **GEL FORMATION**
  Sample: 6 g
  Analysis: Mix the *Sample* with 300 mg of magnesium oxide. Add the mixture, in several divided portions, to 200 mL of water contained in a blender jar with an approximately 500-mL capacity. Blend thoroughly for 5 min at high speed, transfer 100 mL of the mixture into a 100-mL graduated cylinder, and leave undisturbed for 24 h.
  Acceptance criteria: NMT 2 mL of supernatant appears on the surface.
- **LOSS ON DRYING**, Appendix IIC (105° for 2 h)
  Acceptance criteria: NMT 12.0%
- **MICROBIAL LIMITS**
  [NOTE—Current methods for the following tests may be found by accessing the Food and Drug Administration's Bacteriological Analytical Manual (BAM) online at www.cfsan.fda.gov.]
  Acceptance criteria
  Aerobic plate count: NMT 1000 cfu/g
  E. coli: Negative in 25 g

Benzaldehyde
First Published: Prior to FCC 6
Last Revision: FCC 7

C_7H_6O Formula wt 106.12
FEMA: 2127
UNII: TA269SD04T [benzaldehyde]

DESCRIPTION
Benzaldehyde occurs as a colorless liquid with a burning taste. It may contain a suitable antioxidant.
Odor: Bitter almond oil
Solubility: Slightly soluble in water; miscible in alcohol, ether, most fixed oils, volatile oils
Boiling Point: ~178°
Function: Flavoring agent

IDENTIFICATION
- **INFRARED ABSORPTION**, *Spectrophotometric Identification Tests,* Appendix IIIC
  Reference standard: USP Benzaldehyde RS
  Sample and standard preparation: F
  Acceptance criteria: The spectrum of the sample exhibits maxima at the same wavelengths as those in the spectrum of the *Reference standard*.

ASSAY

- **PROCEDURE:** Proceed as directed under *M-1b*, Appendix XI.
  Acceptance criteria: NLT 98.0% of C_7H_6O

SPECIFIC TESTS

- **REFRACTIVE INDEX,** Appendix II: At 20°
  Acceptance criteria: Between 1.544 and 1.547
- **SPECIFIC GRAVITY:** Determine at 25° by any reliable method (see *General Provisions*).
  Acceptance criteria: Between 1.041 and 1.046

OTHER REQUIREMENTS

- **CHLORINATED COMPOUNDS,** Appendix VI
  Acceptance criteria: Passes test
- **HYDROCYANIC ACID**, *M-8*, Appendix XI
  Acceptance criteria: Passes test

Benzaldehyde Glyceryl Acetal

First Published: Prior to FCC 6

Mixture of 1,2- and 1,3-Benzaldehyde Cyclic Acetals of Glycerin

$C_{10}H_{12}O_3$ Formula wt 180.20
FEMA: 2129
UNII: DTD5NUE52Q [benzaldehyde glyceryl acetal]

DESCRIPTION

Benzaldehyde Glyceryl Acetal occurs as a colorless to pale yellow liquid.
Odor: Mild almond
Boiling Point: ~185°
Solubility in Alcohol, Appendix VI: One mL dissolves in 1 mL of 95% alcohol.
Function: Flavoring agent

IDENTIFICATION

- **INFRARED SPECTRA,** *Spectrophotometric Identification Tests,* Appendix IIIC
  Acceptance criteria: The spectrum of the sample exhibits relative maxima at the same wavelengths as those of the spectrum below.

ASSAY

- **PROCEDURE:** Proceed as directed under *M-1a*, Appendix XI.
  Acceptance criteria: NLT 95.0% of $C_{10}H_{12}O_3$ (sum of four isomers; each isomer between 5% and 40%)

SPECIFIC TESTS

- **ACID VALUE, FLAVOR CHEMICALS (OTHER THAN ESSENTIAL OILS),** *M-15,* Appendix XI
  Acceptance criteria: NMT 2.0
- **REFRACTIVE INDEX,** Appendix II: At 20°
  Acceptance criteria: Between 1.535 and 1.541
- **SPECIFIC GRAVITY:** Determine at 25° by any reliable method (see *General Provisions*).
  Acceptance criteria: Between 1.181 and 1.191

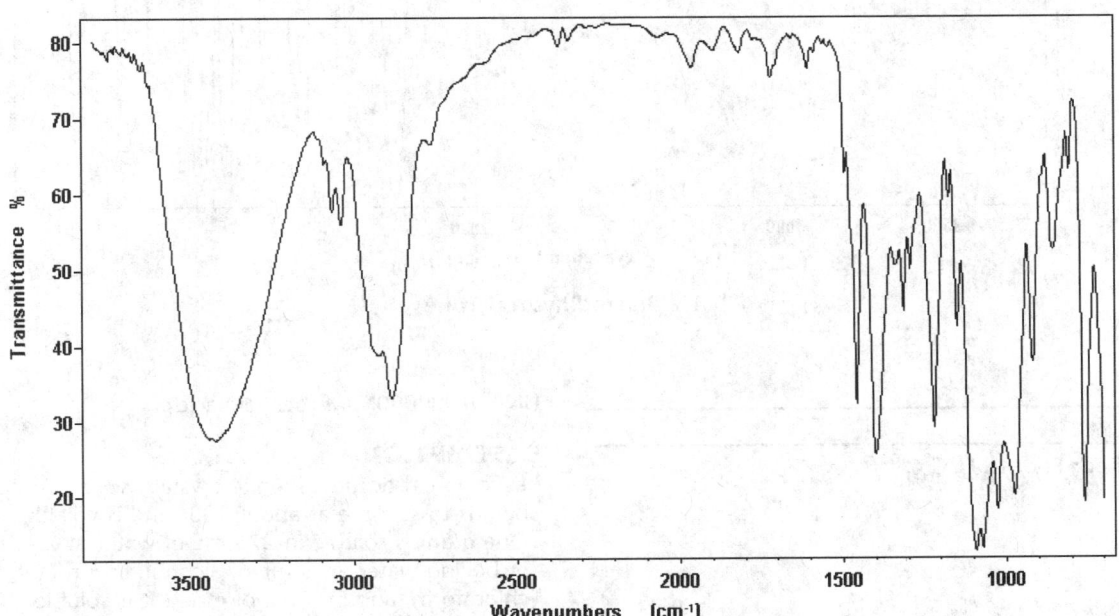

Benzaldehyde Glyceryl Acetal

1,2-Benzodihydropyrone

First Published: Prior to FCC 6

Dihydrocoumarin

C₉H₈O₂
FEMA: 2381
UNII: NM5K1Y1BT2 [benzodihydropyrone]

Formula wt 148.16

DESCRIPTION
1,2-Benzodihydropyrone occurs as a colorless to pale yellow liquid.
Odor: Coconut
Boiling Point: ~272°
Solubility in Alcohol, Appendix VI: One mL dissolves in 1 mL of 95% alcohol.
Function: Flavoring agent

IDENTIFICATION
- **INFRARED SPECTRA,** *Spectrophotometric Identification Tests,* Appendix IIIC
  Acceptance criteria: The spectrum of the sample exhibits relative maxima at the same wavelengths as those of the spectrum below.

ASSAY
- **PROCEDURE:** Proceed as directed under *M-1b,* Appendix XI.
  Acceptance criteria: NLT 99.0% of C₉H₈O₂

SPECIFIC TESTS
- **REFRACTIVE INDEX,** Appendix II: At 20°
  Acceptance criteria: Between 1.555 and 1.559
- **SPECIFIC GRAVITY:** Determine at 25° by any reliable method (see *General Provisions*).
  Acceptance criteria: Between 1.186 and 1.192

OTHER REQUIREMENTS
- **SOLIDIFICATION POINT,** Appendix IIB
  Acceptance criteria: NLT 22°

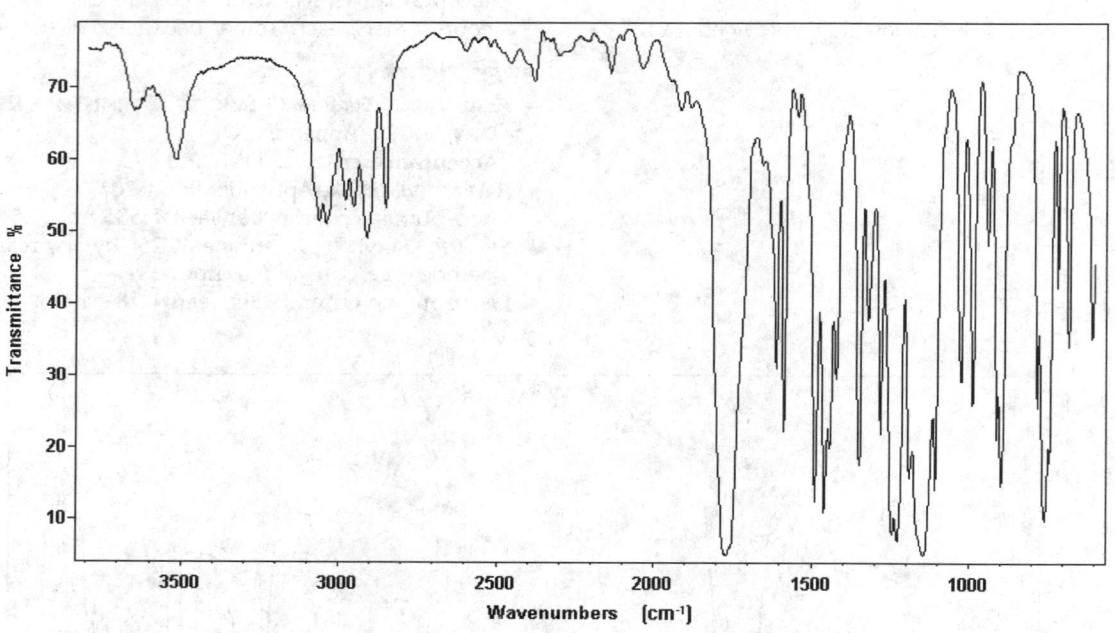

1,2-Benzodihydropyrone

Benzoic Acid

First Published: Prior to FCC 6

C₇H₆O₂
INS: 210

Formula wt 122.12
CAS: [65-85-0]

UNII: 8SKN0B0MIM [benzoic acid]

DESCRIPTION
Benzoic Acid occurs as white crystals, scales, or needles. It begins to sublime at about 100° and is volatile with steam. One gram is soluble in 275 mL of water at 25°, in 20 mL of boiling water, in 3 mL of alcohol, in 5 mL of chloroform, and in 3 mL of ether. It is soluble in fixed and in volatile oils and is sparingly soluble in hexane.
Function: Preservative; antimicrobial agent
Packaging and Storage: Store in well-closed containers.

IDENTIFICATION
- **PROCEDURE**
  Sample solution: 1 g in a 20:1 (v/v) mixture of water and 1 N sodium hydroxide
  Analysis: Filter the *Sample solution* and add about 1 mL of ferric chloride TS.
  Acceptance criteria: A buff-colored precipitate forms.

ASSAY
- **PROCEDURE**
  Sample: 500 mg
  Analysis: Dissolve the *Sample* in 25 mL of 50% alcohol, previously neutralized with 0.1 N sodium hydroxide, add phenolphthalein TS, and titrate with 0.1 N sodium hydroxide. Each mL of 0.1 N sodium hydroxide is equivalent to 12.21 mg of $C_7H_6O_2$.
  Acceptance criteria: NLT 99.5% and NMT 100.5% of $C_7H_6O_2$, calculated on the anhydrous basis

IMPURITIES
Inorganic Impurities
- **LEAD**, *Lead Limit Test, Flame Atomic Absorption Spectrophotometric Method,* Appendix IIIB
  Sample: 10 g
  Acceptance criteria: NMT 2.0 mg/kg
- **WATER**, *Water Determination, Method I,* Appendix IIB
  [NOTE—Use methanol:pyridine (1:2) as the solvent.]
  Acceptance criteria: NMT 0.7%

SPECIFIC TESTS
- **READILY CARBONIZABLE SUBSTANCES**, Appendix IIB
  Sample solution: Dissolve 500 mg of sample in 5 mL of 95% sulfuric acid.
  Acceptance criteria: The color resulting from treatment of the *Sample solution* is no darker than *Matching Fluid Q*.
- **READILY OXIDIZABLE SUBSTANCES**
  Sample: 1 g
  Analysis: Add 0.1 N potassium permanganate, drop wise, to a mixture of 100 mL of water and 1.5 mL of sulfuric acid heated to 100°, until a pink color persists for 30 s. Dissolve the *Sample* in the hot solution. Titrate with 0.1 N potassium permanganate to a pink color that persists for 15 s.
  Acceptance criteria: The volume of 0.1 N potassium permanganate consumed in the titration does not exceed 0.5 mL.
- **RESIDUE ON IGNITION (SULFATED ASH)**, *Method I,* Appendix IIC
  Sample: 2 g
  Acceptance criteria: NMT 0.05%

- **SOLIDIFICATION POINT**, Appendix IIB
  Acceptance criteria: Between 121° and 123°

Benzophenone
First Published: Prior to FCC 6

Benzoylbenzene
Diphenyl Ketone

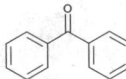

$C_{13}H_{10}O$ Formula wt 182.22
FEMA: 2134
UNII: 701M4TTV9O [benzophenone]

DESCRIPTION
Benzophenone occurs as a white rhombic crystal or flaky solid.
Odor: Delicate, persistent, rose
Solubility: Soluble in most fixed oils; slightly soluble in propylene glycol; insoluble or practically insoluble in glycerin
Boiling Point: ~305°
Solubility in Alcohol, Appendix VI: One g dissolves in 10 mL of 80% alcohol.
Function: Flavoring agent

IDENTIFICATION
- **INFRARED SPECTRA**, *Spectrophotometric Identification Tests,* Appendix IIIC
  Acceptance criteria: The spectrum of the sample exhibits relative maxima at the same wavelengths as those of the spectrum below.

ASSAY
- **PROCEDURE:** Proceed as directed under *M-1a,* Appendix XI.
  Acceptance criteria: NLT 98.0% of $C_{13}H_{10}O$

OTHER REQUIREMENTS
- **CHLORINATED COMPOUNDS**, Appendix VI
  Acceptance criteria: Passes test
- **LEAD**, *M-9,* Appendix XI
  Acceptance criteria: NMT 10 mg/kg
- **SOLIDIFICATION POINT**, Appendix IIB
  Acceptance criteria: NLT 47°

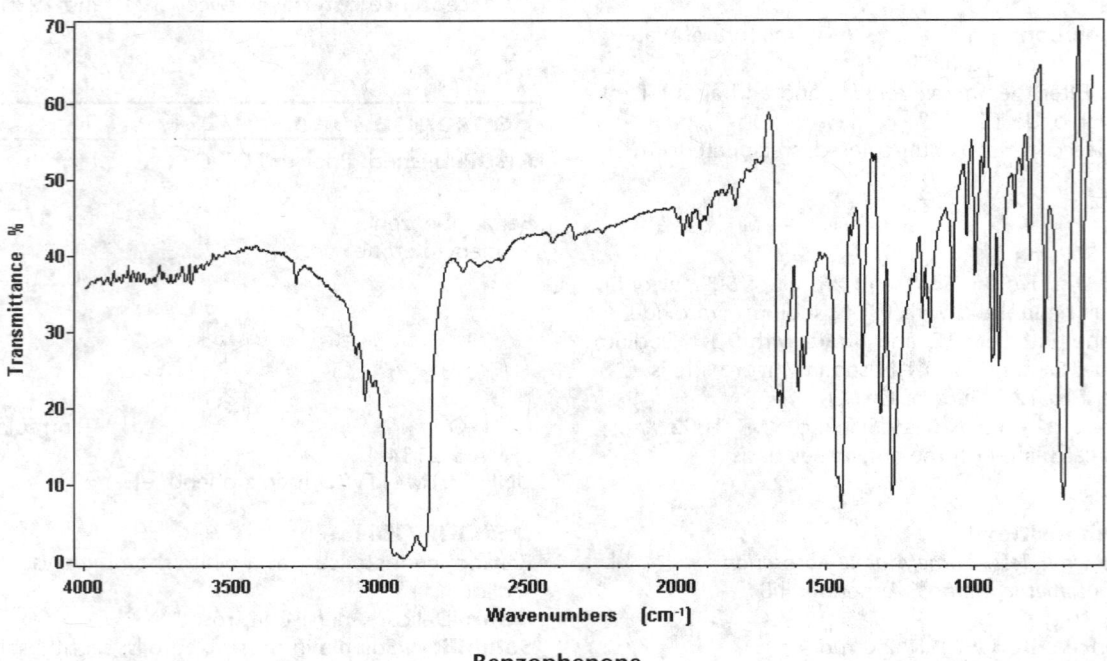
Benzophenone

Benzoyl Peroxide

First Published: Prior to FCC 6

$C_{14}H_{10}O_4$ Formula wt 242.23
INS: 928 CAS: [94-36-0]
UNII: W9WZN9A0GM [benzoyl peroxide]

DESCRIPTION
Benzoyl Peroxide occurs as a colorless, crystalline solid. It is insoluble in water, slightly soluble in alcohol, and soluble in chloroform and in ether. It melts between 103° and 106° with decomposition.
Function: Bleaching agent
Packaging and Storage: Store in the original container and observe the safety precautions printed on the label.
[CAUTION—Benzoyl Peroxide, especially in the dry form, is a dangerous, highly reactive oxidizing material and has been known to explode spontaneously. Observe safety precautions printed on the label of the container.]

IDENTIFICATION
- MELTING RANGE OR TEMPERATURE DETERMINATION, Appendix IIB
  Sample preparation: Add 50 mL of 0.5 N alcoholic potassium hydroxide to 500 mg of sample, heat gradually to boiling, and continue boiling for 15 min.

Cool, dilute to 200 mL with water, and make the solution strongly acid with 0.5 N hydrochloric acid. Extract with ether, dry the extract with anhydrous sodium sulfate, and then evaporate to dryness on a steam bath.
  Acceptance criteria: The residue of benzoic acid so obtained melts between 121° and 123°.

ASSAY
- PROCEDURE
  Sample: 250 mg
  Analysis: Dissolve the *Sample* in 15 mL of acetone contained in a 100-mL glass-stoppered bottle and add 3 mL of a 500 mg/mL solution of potassium iodide. Swirl for 1 min and immediately titrate with 0.1 N sodium thiosulfate (without the addition of starch TS). Each mL of 0.1 N sodium thiosulfate is equivalent to 12.11 mg of $C_{14}H_{10}O_4$.
  Acceptance criteria: NLT 96.0% of $C_{14}H_{10}O4$

IMPURITIES
Inorganic Impurities
- LEAD, *Lead Limit Test,* Appendix IIIB
  Sample solution: Prepare as directed for organic compounds from the residue of a mixture prepared by mixing 1 g of sample with 10 mL of 1 N sodium hydroxide, slowly evaporating to dryness on a steam bath, and cooling.
  Control: 4 µg Pb (4 mL of *Diluted Standard Lead Solution*)
  Acceptance criteria: NMT 4 mg/kg

Benzyl Acetate

First Published: Prior to FCC 6

$C_9H_{10}O_2$ Formula wt 150.18
FEMA: 2135
UNII: 0ECG3V79ZJ [benzyl acetate]

DESCRIPTION
Benzyl Acetate occurs as a colorless liquid.
Odor: Sweet, floral, fruity
Solubility: Soluble in alcohol, most fixed oils, propylene glycol; insoluble or practically insoluble in glycerin, water
Boiling Point: ~214°
Solubility in Alcohol, Appendix VI: One mL dissolves in 5 mL of 60% alcohol.
Function: Flavoring agent

IDENTIFICATION
- **INFRARED SPECTRA,** Spectrophotometric Identification Tests, Appendix IIIC
  Acceptance criteria: The spectrum of the sample exhibits relative maxima at the same wavelengths as those of the spectrum below.

ASSAY
- **PROCEDURE:** Proceed as directed under M-1b, Appendix XI.
  Acceptance criteria: NLT 98.0% of $C_9H_{10}O_2$

SPECIFIC TESTS
- **ACID VALUE, FLAVOR CHEMICALS (OTHER THAN ESSENTIAL OILS),** M-15, Appendix XI [NOTE—Use phenol red TS as the indicator.]
  Acceptance criteria: NMT 1.0
- **REFRACTIVE INDEX,** Appendix II: At 20°
  Acceptance criteria: Between 1.501 and 1.504
- **SPECIFIC GRAVITY:** Determine at 25° by any reliable method (see General Provisions).
  Acceptance criteria: Between 1.052 and 1.056

OTHER REQUIREMENTS
- **CHLORINATED COMPOUNDS,** Appendix VI
  Acceptance criteria: Passes test

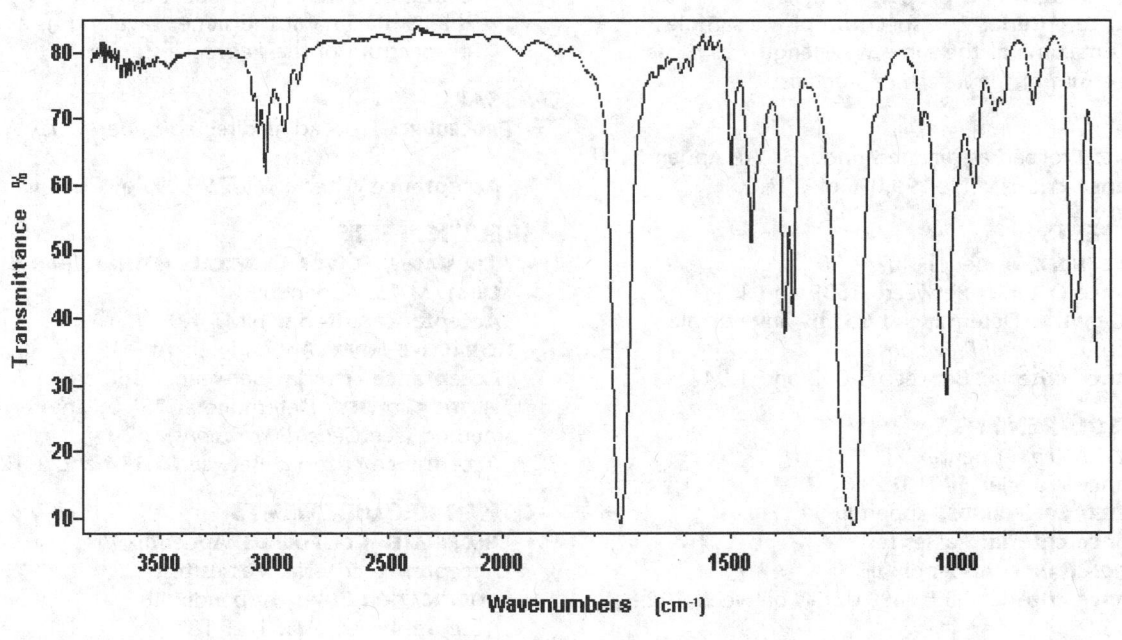

Benzyl Acetate

Benzyl Alcohol

First Published: Prior to FCC 6
Last Revision: FCC 6

Phenyl Carbinol

C_7H_8O Formula wt 108.14
FEMA: 2137
UNII: LKG8494WBH [benzyl alcohol]

DESCRIPTION
Benzyl Alcohol occurs as a colorless liquid with a sharp burning taste.
Odor: Faint, aromatic
Solubility: Miscible in alcohol, chloroform, ether; 1 mL dissolves in 30 mL of water
Boiling Point: ~206° (decomp)
Function: Flavoring agent

IDENTIFICATION
- **INFRARED ABSORPTION,** *Spectrophotometric Identification Tests,* Appendix IIIC
  Reference standard: USP Benzyl Alcohol RS
  Sample and **Standard preparation:** *F*
  Acceptance criteria: The spectrum of the sample exhibits maxima at the same wavelengths as those in the spectrum of the *Reference standard.*

ASSAY
- **PROCEDURE:** Proceed as directed under *M-1a,* Appendix XI
  Acceptance criteria: NLT 99.0% of C_7H_8O

SPECIFIC TESTS
- **REFRACTIVE INDEX,** Appendix II: At 20°
  Acceptance criteria: Between 1.539 and 1.541
- **SPECIFIC GRAVITY:** Determine at 25° by any reliable method (see *General Provisions*).
  Acceptance criteria: Between 1.042 and 1.047

OTHER REQUIREMENTS
- **ALDEHYDES,** *M-1b,* Appendix XI
  Acceptance criteria: NMT 0.2%
- **CHLORINATED COMPOUNDS,** Appendix VI
  Acceptance criteria: Passes test
- **DISTILLATION RANGE,** Appendix IIB
  Acceptance criteria: NLT 95% distills between 202.5° and 206.5°

Benzyl Benzoate

First Published: Prior to FCC 6
Last Revision: FCC 6

$C_{14}H_{12}O_2$ Formula wt 212.25
FEMA: 2138
UNII: N863NB338G [benzyl benzoate]

DESCRIPTION
Benzyl Benzoate is a colorless, oily liquid.
Odor: Slight, balsamic
Solubility: Miscible in alcohol, chloroform, ether; insoluble or practically insoluble in glycerin, water
Boiling Point: ~323°
Function: Flavoring agent

IDENTIFICATION
- **INFRARED ABSORPTION,** *Spectrophotometric Identification Tests,* Appendix IIIC
  Reference standard: USP Benzyl Benzoate RS
  Sample and **Standard preparation:** *F*
  Acceptance criteria: The spectrum of the sample exhibits maxima at the same wavelengths as those in the spectrum of the *Reference standard.*

ASSAY
- **PROCEDURE:** Proceed as directed under *M-1b,* Appendix XI.
  Acceptance criteria: NLT 99.0% of $C_{14}H_{12}O_2$.

SPECIFIC TESTS
- **ACID VALUE, FLAVOR CHEMICALS (OTHER THAN ESSENTIAL OILS),** *M-15,* Appendix XI
  Acceptance criteria: NMT 1.0
- **REFRACTIVE INDEX,** Appendix II: At 20°
  Acceptance criteria: Between 1.568 and 1.570
- **SPECIFIC GRAVITY,** Determine at 25° by any reliable method (see *General Provisions*).
  Acceptance criteria: Between 1.116 and 1.120

OTHER REQUIREMENTS
- **CHLORINATED COMPOUNDS,** Appendix VI
  Acceptance criteria: Passes test
- **SOLIDIFICATION POINT,** Appendix IIB
  Acceptance criteria: NLT 18°

Benzyl Butyrate

First Published: Prior to FCC 6

Benzyl *n*-Butyrate

$C_{11}H_{14}O_2$ Formula wt 178.23
FEMA: 2140
UNII: 84L0NDE31F [benzyl butyrate]

DESCRIPTION
Benzyl Butyrate occurs as a colorless liquid.
Odor: Floral, fruity, plum
Solubility: Soluble in alcohol, most fixed oils; insoluble or practically insoluble in glycerin, propylene glycol, water
Boiling Point: ~239°
Solubility in Alcohol, Appendix VI: One mL dissolves in 2 mL of 80% alcohol.
Function: Flavoring agent

IDENTIFICATION
- **INFRARED SPECTRA,** *Spectrophotometric Identification Tests,* Appendix IIIC
  Acceptance criteria: The spectrum of the sample exhibits relative maxima at the same wavelengths as those of the spectrum below.

ASSAY
- **PROCEDURE:** Proceed as directed under *M-1b,* Appendix XI.
  Acceptance criteria: NLT 98.0% of $C_{11}H_{14}O_2$

SPECIFIC TESTS
- **ACID VALUE, FLAVOR CHEMICALS (OTHER THAN ESSENTIAL OILS),** *M-15,* Appendix XI
  Acceptance criteria: NMT 1.0
- **REFRACTIVE INDEX,** Appendix II: At 20°
  Acceptance criteria: Between 1.492 and 1.496
- **SPECIFIC GRAVITY:** Determine at 25° by any reliable method (see *General Provisions*).
  Acceptance criteria: Between 1.006 and 1.009

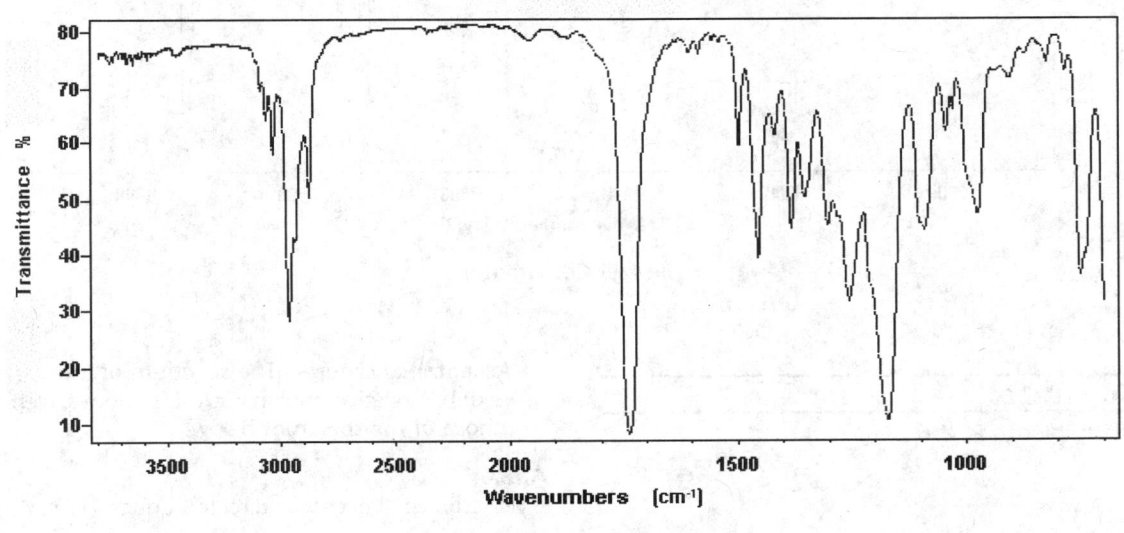

Benzyl Butyrate

Benzyl Cinnamate

First Published: Prior to FCC 6

$C_{16}H_{14}O_2$ Formula wt 238.29
FEMA: 2142
UNII: V67O3RO97U [benzyl cinnamate]

DESCRIPTION
Benzyl Cinnamate occurs as a white to pale yellow solid.
Odor: Sweet, balsamic
Solubility: Soluble in most fixed oils; insoluble or practically insoluble in glycerin, propylene glycol
Boiling Point: ~195° (5 mm Hg)
SOLUBILITY IN ALCOHOL, Appendix VI: One g dissolves in 8 mL of 90% alcohol.
Function: Flavoring agent

IDENTIFICATION
- **INFRARED SPECTRA,** *Spectrophotometric Identification Tests,* Appendix IIIC
  Acceptance criteria: The spectrum of the sample exhibits relative maxima at the same wavelengths as those of the spectrum below.

114 / Benzyl Cinnamate / *Monographs*   FCC 8

ASSAY
- **Procedure:** Proceed as directed under *M-1b*, Appendix XI.
  Acceptance criteria: NLT 98.0% of $C_{16}H_{14}O_2$

SPECIFIC TESTS
- **Acid Value, Flavor Chemicals (Other Than Essential Oils),** *M-15*, Appendix XI
  Acceptance criteria: NMT 1.0

OTHER REQUIREMENTS
- **Chlorinated Compounds,** Appendix VI
  Acceptance criteria: Passes test
- **Solidification Point,** Appendix IIB
  Acceptance criteria: Between 33.0° and 35.0°

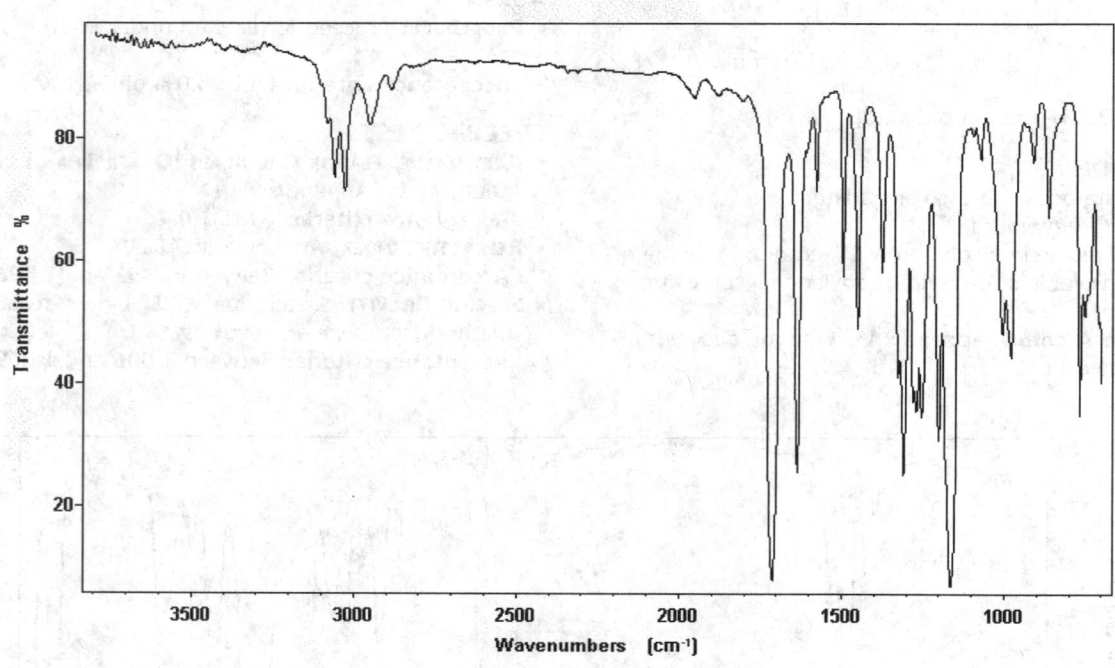

Benzyl Cinnamate

Benzyl Formate

First Published: Prior to FCC 6

$C_8H_8O_2$ Formula wt 136.15
FEMA: 2145
UNII: 79GJF97O0Y [benzyl formate]

DESCRIPTION
Benzyl Formate occurs as a colorless to pale yellow liquid.
Odor: Sweet, balsamic, floral
Boiling Point: ~203°
Solubility in Alcohol, Appendix VI: One mL dissolves in 1 mL of 95% alcohol.
Function: Flavoring agent

IDENTIFICATION
- **Infrared Spectra,** *Spectrophotometric Identification Tests*, Appendix IIIC
  Acceptance criteria: The spectrum of the sample exhibits relative maxima at the same wavelengths as those of the spectrum below.

ASSAY
- **Procedure:** Proceed as directed under *M-1b*, Appendix XI.
  Acceptance criteria: NLT 95.0% of $C_8H_8O_2$

SPECIFIC TESTS
- **Acid Value, Flavor Chemicals (Other Than Essential Oils),** *M-15*, Appendix XI
  Acceptance criteria: NMT 3.0
- **Refractive Index,** Appendix II: At 20°
  Acceptance criteria: Between 1.508 and 1.515
- **Specific Gravity:** Determine at 25° by any reliable method (see *General Provisions*).
  Acceptance criteria: Between 1.082 and 1.092

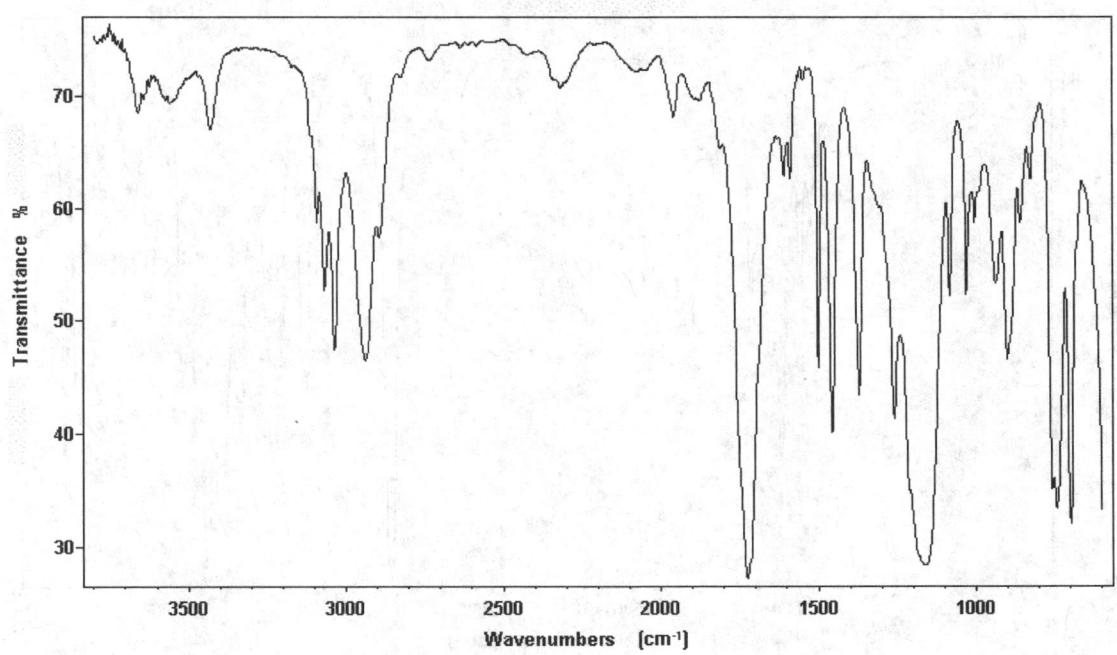

Benzyl Formate

Benzyl Isobutyrate

First Published: Prior to FCC 6

Benzyl 2-Methyl Propionate

$C_{11}H_{14}O_2$ Formula wt 178.23
FEMA: 2141
UNII: P98PE45V9M [benzyl isobutyrate]

DESCRIPTION
Benzyl Isobutyrate occurs as a colorless liquid.
Odor: Floral, fruity, jasmine
Solubility: Soluble in alcohol, most fixed oils; slightly soluble in propylene glycol; insoluble or practically insoluble in glycerin
Boiling Point: ~229°
SOLUBILITY IN ALCOHOL, Appendix VI: One mL dissolves in 6 mL of 70% alcohol.

Function: Flavoring agent

IDENTIFICATION
- **INFRARED SPECTRA,** Spectrophotometric Identification Tests, Appendix IIIC
  Acceptance criteria: The spectrum of the sample exhibits relative maxima at the same wavelengths as those of the spectrum below.

ASSAY
- **PROCEDURE:** Proceed as directed under M-1b, Appendix XI.
  Acceptance criteria: NLT 97.0% of $C_{11}H_{14}O_2$

SPECIFIC TESTS
- **ACID VALUE, FLAVOR CHEMICALS (OTHER THAN ESSENTIAL OILS),** M-15, Appendix XI
  Acceptance criteria: NMT 1.0
- **REFRACTIVE INDEX,** Appendix II: At 20°
  Acceptance criteria: Between 1.488 and 1.492
- **SPECIFIC GRAVITY:** Determine at 25° by any reliable method (see General Provisions).
  Acceptance criteria: Between 1.000 and 1.005

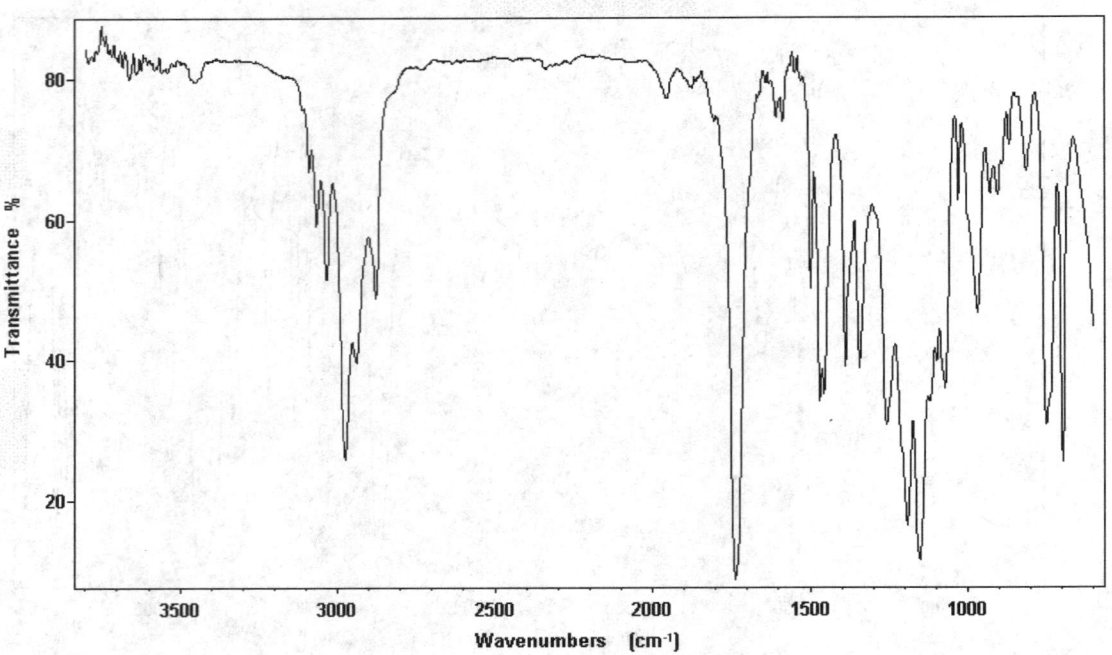

Benzyl Isobutyrate

Benzyl Isovalerate

First Published: Prior to FCC 6

Benzyl 3-Methyl Butyrate

$C_{12}H_{16}O_2$ Formula wt 192.26
FEMA: 2152
UNII: 87UKH01DMA [benzyl isovalerate]

DESCRIPTION
Benzyl Isovalerate occurs as a colorless liquid.
Odor: Fruity, herbaceous, apple
Solubility: Soluble in alcohol, most fixed oils; slightly soluble in propylene glycol; insoluble or practically insoluble in glycerin, water
Boiling Point: ~246°
Solubility in Alcohol, Appendix VI: One mL dissolves in 3 mL of 80% alcohol, and remains in solution on dilution.

Function: Flavoring agent

IDENTIFICATION
- **INFRARED SPECTRA,** *Spectrophotometric Identification Tests,* Appendix IIIC
  Acceptance criteria: The spectrum of the sample exhibits relative maxima at the same wavelengths as those of the spectrum below.

ASSAY
- **PROCEDURE:** Proceed as directed under *M-1b,* Appendix XI.
  Acceptance criteria: NLT 98.0% of $C_{12}H_{16}O_2$ (one isomer)

SPECIFIC TESTS
- **ACID VALUE, FLAVOR CHEMICALS (OTHER THAN ESSENTIAL OILS),** *M-15,* Appendix XI
  Acceptance criteria: NMT 1.0
- **REFRACTIVE INDEX,** Appendix II: At 20°
  Acceptance criteria: Between 1.486 and 1.490
- **SPECIFIC GRAVITY:** Determine at 25° by any reliable method (see *General Provisions*).
  Acceptance criteria: Between 0.983 and 0.989

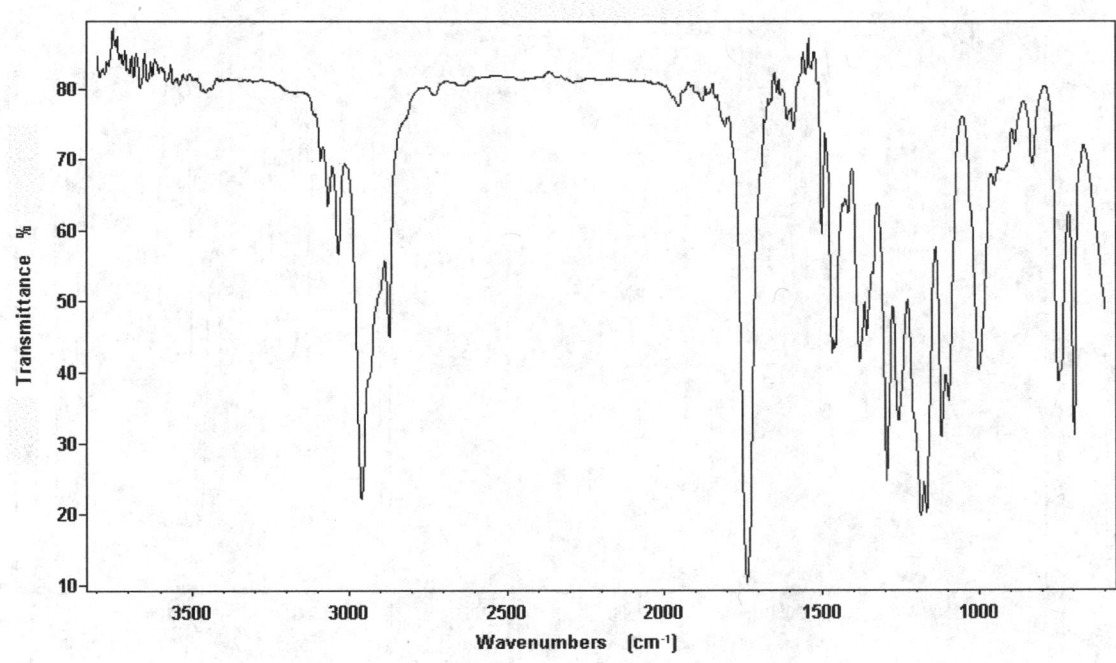

Benzyl Isovalerate

Benzyl Phenylacetate

First Published: Prior to FCC 6

$C_{15}H_{14}O_2$ Formula wt 226.27
FEMA: 2149
UNII: A7LDA0CIWF [benzyl phenylacetate]

DESCRIPTION
Benzyl Phenylacetate occurs as a colorless liquid.
Odor: Sweet, floral, honey undertone
Solubility: Miscible in alcohol, chloroform, ether
Boiling Point: ~317°
Solubility in Alcohol, Appendix VI: One mL dissolves in 3 mL of 90% alcohol to give a clear solution.
Function: Flavoring agent

IDENTIFICATION
- **INFRARED SPECTRA,** *Spectrophotometric Identification Tests,* Appendix IIIC
  Acceptance criteria: The spectrum of the sample exhibits relative maxima at the same wavelengths as those of the spectrum below.

ASSAY
- **PROCEDURE:** Proceed as directed under *M-1b,* Appendix XI.
  Acceptance criteria: NLT 98.0% of $C_{15}H_{14}O_2$

SPECIFIC TESTS
- **ACID VALUE, FLAVOR CHEMICALS (OTHER THAN ESSENTIAL OILS),** *M-15,* Appendix XI
  Acceptance criteria: NMT 1.0
- **REFRACTIVE INDEX,** Appendix II: At 20°
  Acceptance criteria: Between 1.553 and 1.558
- **SPECIFIC GRAVITY:** Determine at 25° by any reliable method (see *General Provisions*).
  Acceptance criteria: Between 1.095 and 1.099

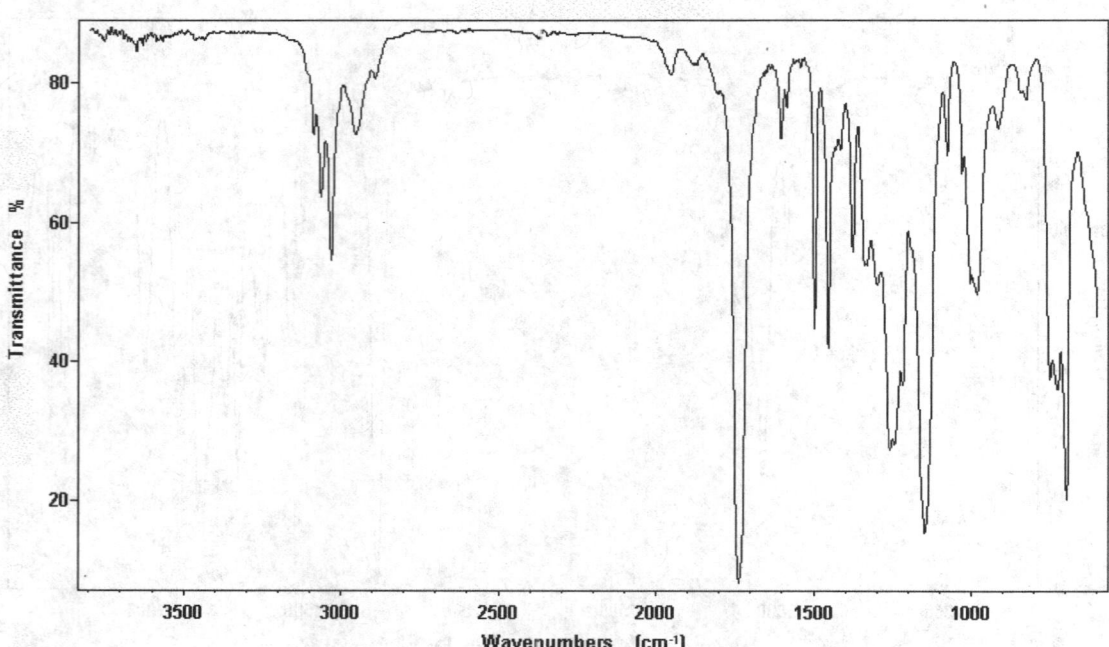

Benzyl Phenylacetate

Benzyl Propionate

First Published: Prior to FCC 6

Benzyl Propanoate

$C_{10}H_{12}O_2$ Formula wt 164.20
FEMA: 2150
UNII: 307DN1208L [benzyl propionate]

DESCRIPTION
Benzyl Propionate occurs as a colorless liquid.
Odor: Sweet, floral, fruity
Solubility: Soluble in alcohol, most fixed oils; slightly soluble in propylene glycol; insoluble or practically insoluble in glycerin, water
Boiling Point: ~222°
Solubility in Alcohol, Appendix VI: One mL dissolves in 3 mL of 70% alcohol, and remains in solution on dilution to 10 mL.

Function: Flavoring agent

IDENTIFICATION
- **INFRARED SPECTRA,** Spectrophotometric Identification Tests, Appendix IIIC
  Acceptance criteria: The spectrum of the sample exhibits relative maxima at the same wavelengths as those of the spectrum below.

ASSAY
- **PROCEDURE:** Proceed as directed under M-1b, Appendix XI.
  Acceptance criteria: NLT 98.0% of $C_{10}H_{12}O_2$

SPECIFIC TESTS
- **ACID VALUE, FLAVOR CHEMICALS (OTHER THAN ESSENTIAL OILS),** M-15, Appendix XI
  Acceptance criteria: NMT 1.0
- **REFRACTIVE INDEX,** Appendix II: At 20°
  Acceptance criteria: Between 1.496 and 1.500
- **SPECIFIC GRAVITY:** Determine at 25° by any reliable method (see General Provisions).
  Acceptance criteria: Between 1.028 and 1.032

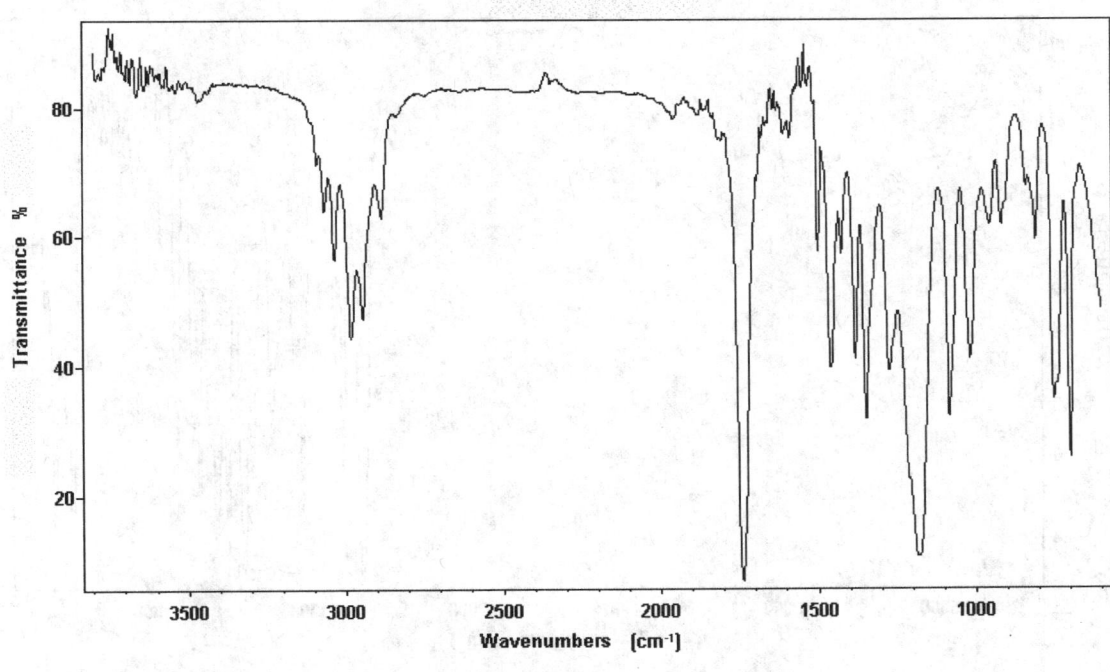

Benzyl Propionate

Benzyl Salicylate

First Published: Prior to FCC 6

$C_{14}H_{12}O_3$ Formula wt 228.25
FEMA: 2151
UNII: WAO5MNK9TU [benzyl salicylate]

DESCRIPTION
Benzyl Salicylate occurs as an almost colorless liquid.
Odor: Faint, sweet
Solubility: Soluble in most fixed oils; insoluble or practically insoluble in glycerin, propylene glycol
Boiling Point: ~300°
Solubility in Alcohol, Appendix VI: One mL dissolves in 5 mL of 95% alcohol.
Function: Flavoring agent

IDENTIFICATION
- **INFRARED SPECTRA,** Spectrophotometric Identification Tests, Appendix IIIC
  Acceptance criteria: The spectrum of the sample exhibits relative maxima at the same wavelengths as those of the spectrum below.

ASSAY
- **PROCEDURE:** Proceed as directed under M-1b, Appendix XI.
  Acceptance criteria: NLT 98.0% of $C_{14}H_{12}O_3$

SPECIFIC TESTS
- **ACID VALUE, FLAVOR CHEMICALS (OTHER THAN ESSENTIAL OILS),** M-15, Appendix XI
  [NOTE—Use phenol red TS as the indicator.]
  Acceptance criteria: NMT 1.0
- **REFRACTIVE INDEX,** Appendix II: At 20°
  Acceptance criteria: Between 1.573 and 1.582
- **SPECIFIC GRAVITY:** Determine at 25° by any reliable method (see General Provisions).
  Acceptance criteria: Between 1.176 and 1.180

OTHER REQUIREMENTS
- **SOLIDIFICATION POINT,** Appendix IIB
  Acceptance criteria: NLT 23.5°

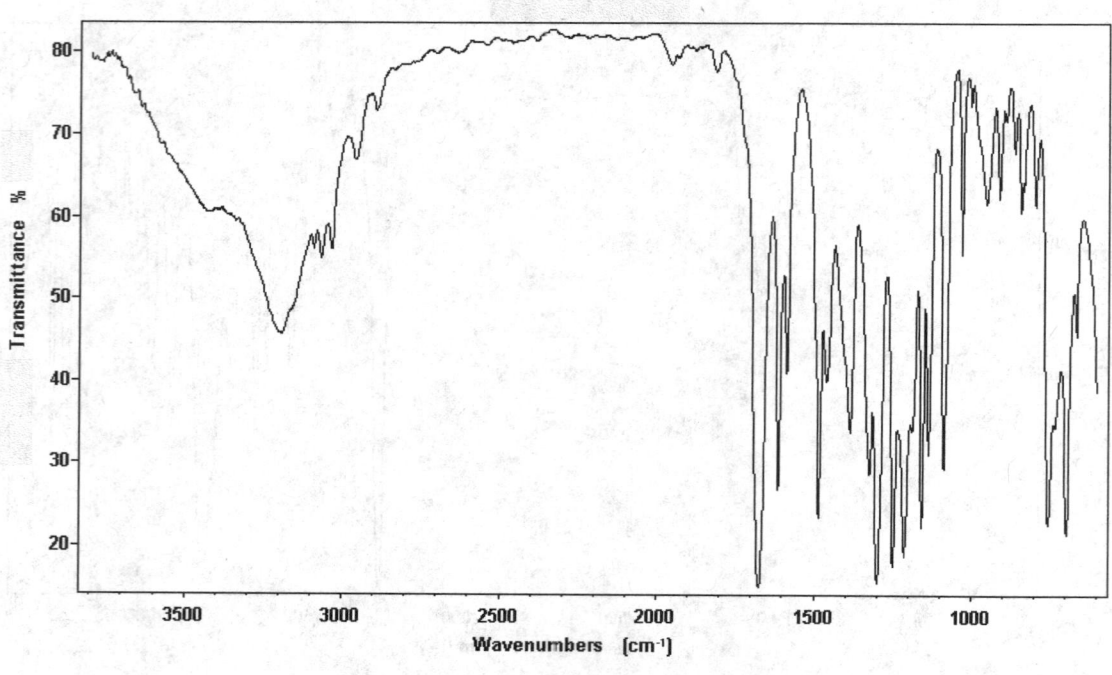

Benzyl Salicylate

Bergamot Oil, Coldpressed

First Published: Prior to FCC 6
Last Revision: Second Supplement, FCC 7

FEMA: 2153

CAS: [8007-75-8]

UNII: 39W1PKE3JI [bergamot oil]

DESCRIPTION
Bergamot Oil, Coldpressed occurs as a green to yellow-green or yellow-brown liquid with a fragrant, sweet-fruity odor. It is a volatile oil obtained by pressing, without the aid of heat, the fresh peel of the fruit of *Citrus bergamia* Risso et Poiteau (Fam. Rutaceae). It is miscible with alcohol and with glacial acetic acid. It is soluble in most fixed oils, but is insoluble in glycerin and in propylene glycol. It may contain a suitable antioxidant.
Function: Flavoring agent
Packaging and Storage: Store in a cool place protected from light in full, tight containers that are made from steel or aluminum and that are suitably lined.

IDENTIFICATION
- **INFRARED SPECTRA,** *Spectrophotometric Identification Tests,* Appendix IIIC
  Acceptance criteria: The spectrum of the sample exhibits relative maxima at the same wavelengths as those of the spectrum below.

ASSAY
- **ESTERS,** *Ester Determination,* Appendix VI
  Sample: 2 g
  Analysis: Heat the mixture for 30 min on a steam bath, rather than for 1 h. Use 98.15 as the equivalence factor (e) in the calculation.
  Acceptance criteria: NLT 36.0% of esters, calculated as linalyl acetate ($C_{12}H_{20}O_2$).

SPECIFIC TESTS
- **ANGULAR ROTATION,** *Optical (Specific) Rotation,* Appendix IIB: Use a 100-mm tube.
  Acceptance criteria: Between +12° and +30°
- **REFRACTIVE INDEX,** Appendix IIB
  [NOTE—Use an Abbé or other refractometer of equal or greater accuracy.]
  Acceptance criteria: Between 1.465 and 1.468 at 20°
- **RESIDUE ON EVAPORATION,** Appendix VI: Heat sample for 5 h.
  Acceptance criteria: NMT 6.0%
- **SOLUBILITY IN ALCOHOL,** Appendix VI
  Acceptance criteria: One mL of the sample dissolves in 2 mL of 90% alcohol.
- **SPECIFIC GRAVITY:** Determine by any reliable method (see *General Provisions*).
  Acceptance criteria: 0.871–0.879
- **ULTRAVIOLET ABSORBANCE,** *Ultraviolet Absorbance of Citrus Oils,* Appendix VI
  Sample: 50 mg
  Acceptance criteria: The absorbance difference is NLT 0.32. [NOTE—The absorbance maximum occurs at 315 ± 3 nm.]

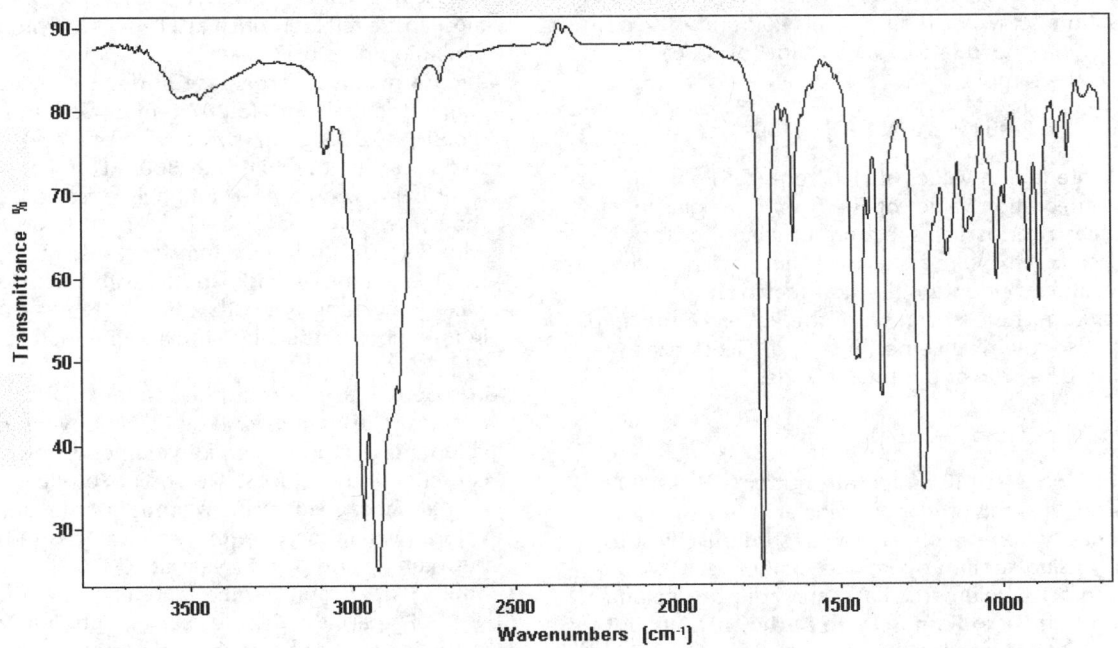

Bergamot Oil, Coldpressed

Beta Glucan from Baker's Yeast (*Saccharomyces cerevisiae*)

First Published: Third Supplement, FCC 7

Baker's Yeast Beta Glucan
(1-3), (1-6)-β-d-glucan, Poly-(1-6)-β-d-glucopyranosyl-(1,3)-β-d glucopyranose

DESCRIPTION
Beta Glucan from Baker's Yeast (*Saccharomyces cerevisiae*) is a light beige to tan fine powder. This ingredient is the result of the fermentation of food-grade baker's yeast (*Saccharomyces cerevisiae*) and later lysis through a thermal process. The cell wall component is separated from the yeast extract using centrifugation. Then, the cell wall isolate undergoes a caustic treatment to strip the mannosylated cell wall proteins that are linked to the cell wall and to remove the residual cellular lipids. After that, the isolate undergoes an acid treatment, which results in the removal of most of the chitin. Lastly, the yeast wall slurry undergoes flash sterilization, followed by pH adjustment steps, which results in the final dry product. It is comprised mainly of β-(1,3)/(1,6) branched glucan polymers, and trace amounts of protein and lipid. Small amounts of β-(1,6)-glucan and chitin are also expected to be present in the final product.

Function: Nutrient

Packaging and Storage: Store in closed, sealed packages in a dry controlled environment (21° and 50% RH).

IDENTIFICATION
- **¹HNMR Spectroscopy,** *Nuclear Magnetic Resonance Spectroscopy,* Appendix IIC

  Reference standard solution: Dissolve 10 mg of USP Beta Glucan RS in 0.6 mL of dimethyl sulfoxide–d_6 at 100° for 1 h. After incubation time, add 0.1 mL of D_2O, mix the solution, and transfer to an NMR tube.

  Sample solution: Dissolve 10 mg of sample in 0.6 mL of dimethyl sulfoxide–d_6 at 100° for 1 h. After incubation time, add 0.1 mL of D_2O, mix the solution, and transfer to an NMR tube.

  Analysis: Collect ¹HNMR spectra at 80°, and compare individual resonances from the *Sample solution* to those from the *Reference standard solution*. The major signals associated with this ingredient are shown in the table below. The relative area of the resonance corresponding to the ¹H signal of (1,6) linked beta glucan with respect to the ¹H signal of (1,3) linked beta glucan is also measured and compared to the range shown in the table.

¹HNMR Major Signals	USP Beta Glucan RS
H-1 (1,3-glucan)	4.52, d, J = 7.5 Hz, 1H
H-2, 4, and 5 (1,3-)	3.27–3.33, m, 3H
H-3 and 6b (1,3-)	3.45–3.48, m, 2H
H-6a (1,3-)	3.71, d, J = 11 Hz, 1H
H-1 (1,6-glucan)	4.27, d, J = 7.7 Hz, 1H
Relative % of 1,6	10%–18%

Integrate the area under the peaks five times for each sample, and average. Integration values are then used in the equation below for the peaks at 4.52 and 4.27 ppm to determine the relative percentage of (1,6) linked glucan in the sample.

$$\text{Result} = \{A/(A + B)\} \times 100$$

A = integration values of H-1 from (1,6) glucan
B = integration values of H-1 from (1,3) glucan

Acceptance criteria: The spectrum obtained for the *Sample solution* exhibits a chemical shift pattern with signal locations and intensities that match those obtained from the preparation of the *Reference standard solution*. Also, the relative percentage of (1,6) linked glucan is 10%–18% of the total linkages.

ASSAY

- **PROCEDURE**

  Buffer solution A (sodium acetate buffer, pH 5, 200 mM): Add 11.6 mL of glacial acetic acid to approximately 900 mL of water with stirring. Adjust to a pH of 5 using sodium hydroxide solution (4 M). Transfer to a 1-L volumetric flask, and adjust to volume.

  Buffer solution B (sodium acetate buffer, pH 3.8, 1.2 M): Add 69.6 mL of glacial acetic acid to approximately 800 mL of water with stirring. Adjust to a pH of 3.8 using sodium hydroxide solution (4 M). Transfer to a 1-L volumetric flask, and adjust to volume.

  10 X TES buffer (10 X (hydroxymethyl)aminomethane (TRIS)/EDTA/Saline): Dissolve 12.12 g of TRIS, 11.69 g of NaCl, and 4.16 g of EDTA tetrasodium dihydrate salt in approximately 900 mL of purified water with stirring. Adjust to a pH of 7.5 with concentrated HCl or 4 M NaOH. Transfer the solution to a 1-L volumetric flask, and dilute with water to volume. [NOTE—Buffer can be stored for 1 year at 2°–8°.]

  Lyticase solution (10 U/µL in 1 X TES buffer): Prepare the required volume of lyticase from *Arthrobacter luteus*[1] at a concentration of 10 U/µL by dissolving the quantity stated by the manufacturer (U/mg) in a solution containing 10% *10 X TES buffer* (v/v). [NOTE—Unused solution can be stored at NMT –15° with an expiration date of 1 year. Every time a different lot of lyticase is used, the concentration of lyticase solution required needs to be qualified.]

  (1,6)-Glucanase solution: Dissolve lyophilized (1,6)-glucanase[2] in *Buffer solution A* in amounts that yield 1U/300 µL solution. [NOTE—Solids may not fully dissolve. So, this solution should be handled as a homogeneous suspension. Solution is stable for at least 60 days at NMT –15°.]

  Polishing enzyme mix: For 100 mL total volume, mix 2000 U of exo-beta-glucanase[3] and 400 U of beta-glucosidase[4] with *Buffer solution A* in a 100-mL volumetric flask. A pre-mix of the enzymes may be used as an alternative[5]. Mix well by inverting at least 10 times. [NOTE—Store on ice during the procedure, and for use in a same-day assay. Unused *Polishing enzyme mix* can be refrozen once at NMT –15° with an expiration date of 2 years.]

  Glucose oxidase/peroxidase buffer[6]**:** In a 1-L volumetric flask add 45.287 g of potassium phosphate dibasic, 30.382 g of *p*-hydroxybenzoic acid, and 4 g of sodium azide. Carefully add 800 mL of water. Mix with a stir bar and mild heat until fully dissolved. Transfer the contents to a large beaker. Adjust to a pH of 7.4 with 2 M KOH solution. Transfer the solution back to the 1-L volumetric flask, and fill with water to volume. Mix by inverting at least six times. [NOTE—Store buffer in an amber bottle with an expiration date of 3 years at 4°.]

  Glucose oxidase/peroxidase reagent: Dissolve 50 mL of *Glucose oxidase/peroxidase buffer* in water to a total volume of 1 L. In this entire volume, dissolve the contents of the Glucose Determination Reagent[7]. [NOTE—Store reagent in an amber bottle, and label with an expiration date of 3 months at a temperature between 2° and 8° or 1 year at NMT –17°. Minimize time spent at room temperature.]

  [NOTE—Prepare the *Sample solution* and *Standard solution* in triplicate. It is critical for the success of the assay that the sample is well dispersed.]

  Sample solution: Accurately weigh 15–20 mg of sample into a 16-mm × 100-mm glass vial. Place the vial in an ice bath. Add 0.4 mL of cold KOH solution (2 M) all in one aliquot while vortexing to disperse the powder. Return the vial to the ice bath. Continue cycling through vortexing and placing the vials in the ice bath as much as possible for 20 min. The mixture should turn into a homogenous, translucent dispersion.

  Standard solution: Repeat the *Sample solution* steps with USP Beta Glucan RS (15–20 mg).

  Lyticase digestion: Upon removal of all vials containing *Sample solution* or *Standard solution* from the ice bath, add 1.6 mL of *Buffer solution B* and 600 µL of *Lyticase solution* to each vial. Incubate the mixture at 50° for 12–18 h, and cool to room temperature.

  (1,6)-Glucanase digestion: After cooling of all vials, remove a 130-µL aliquot of each vial and digest further by adding 25 µL of KOH solution (2 M) and 300 µL of *(1,6)-Glucanase solution*. Incubate vials at 80° for 15 min, and cool to room temperature.

  Beta glucanase/glucosidase digestion: After cooling of all vials, add 390 µL of the *Polishing enzyme mix* to each vial, and incubate the vials at 40° for 1 h. Cool them to room temperature, centrifuge, and transfer the 50-µL aliquots (in duplicate) to new vials.

  Enzyme blank solution: Prepare enzyme blanks in triplicate by combining all the reagents used during the digestion steps except the *Sample solution* or *Standard solution*.

  Analysis: Dilute the 50-µL aliquots obtained after the *Beta glucanase/glucosidase digestion* with 50 µL of water,

---

[1] Lyticase from *Arthrobacter luteus*, Sigma L4025, or equivalent.
[2] Commercially available as Pustulanase, Cel136, Prokazyme, or equivalent.
[3] E-EXBGL 200 U/mL, 200 U/bottle, Megazyme, or equivalent.
[4] 200 U/bottle, Megazyme, or equivalent.
[5] E-EXBGOS, Megazyme, or equivalent.

[6] This buffer is also available as Bottle #3 of the K-YBGL kit (Megazyme), or Bottle #1 of the GOPOD kit (Megazyme).
[7] Bottle #4 of K-YBGL kit, or Bottle #2 of GOPOD kit, Megazyme, or equivalent.

and then add 3 mL of *Glucose oxidase/peroxidase reagent*. Incubate the vials for 20 min at 40°. Using a suitable spectrophotometer, determine the absorbance of each vial with *Sample solution* or *Standard solution* at 510 nm against the *Enzyme blank solution*. Prepare a standard curve using the absorbance of similarly treated series of glucose standards (0 mg/mL, 0.1 mg/mL, 0.25 mg/mL, 0.5 mg/mL, and 1.0 mg/mL). From the slope of the standard curve and the absorbance of the digested *Sample solution* and *Standard solution*, determine the concentration of liberated glucose in the cuvette (C), in mg/mL:

$$C = (Abs_S - Abs_B)/slope$$

Abs_S = average absorbance of sample or USP Beta Glucan RS
Abs_B = average absorbance of *Enzyme blank solution*
Calculate the percentage of beta glucan as glucose in the sample:

$$Result = 100 \times C/\{[(WT_S/F1) \times (F2/F3)]/2\}$$

C = concentration of liberated glucose in the cuvette (mg/mL)
WT_S = original weight of the sample or USP Beta Glucan RS (mg)
F1 = total volume in the vial during *Lyticase digestion*, 2.6 mL
F2 = volume of the sample or USP Beta Glucan RS transferred to a new vial during *(1,6)-glucanase digestion*, 0.130 mL
F3 = total volume during *Beta glucanase/glucosidase digestion*, 0.845 mL

Acceptance criteria: NLT 70% beta glucan as glucose, calculated on the dried basis

IMPURITIES
Inorganic Impurities
- **ARSENIC**, *Elemental Impurities by ICP, Method I: ICP-OES*, Appendix IIIC
  Acceptance criteria: NMT 0.5 ppm
- **CADMIUM**, *Elemental Impurities by ICP, Method I: ICP-OES*, Appendix IIIC
  Acceptance criteria: NMT 0.5 ppm
- **LEAD**, *Elemental Impurities by ICP, Method I: ICP-OES*, Appendix IIIC
  Acceptance criteria: NMT 0.5 ppm
- **MERCURY**, *Elemental Impurities by ICP, Method I: ICP-OES*, Appendix IIIC
  Acceptance criteria: NMT 0.1 ppm

Organic Impurities
- **GLYCOGEN**
  Amyloglucosidase/invertase solution[8]: Dissolve amyloglucosidase and invertase in 20 mL of glycerol solution (50% v/v) to obtain a solution containing 1630 U/mL of amyloglucosidase and 500 U/mL of invertase.
  Analysis: Weigh 100 mg of sample in triplicate into individual 16-mm × 150-mm glass screw cap vials. Place the vials in an ice bath, and add to each vial 2 mL of cold 2 M KOH (in one aliquot) while vortexing to disperse the powder. Return the vial to the ice bath. Continue cycling through vortexing and placing vials in the ice bath as much as possible for 20 min. The mixture should turn into a homogenous, translucent dispersion. Add 8 mL of *Buffer solution B*. Vortex thoroughly, and immediately add 200 µL of *Amyloglucosidase/invertase solution* and vortex again. Incubate the mixture at 40° for 30–35 min. Cool to room temperature. Vortex again, transfer to a suitable centrifuge tube, and centrifuge until a clear supernatant is obtained. Transfer duplicate 50-µL aliquots of supernatant into new vials, and proceed with the *Analysis* as outlined in the *Assay* section.
  Acceptance criteria: NMT 1.0%

- **MANNOSE**
  Mobile phase A: 100% Purified Water
  Mobile phase B: 956 mM NaOH
  Internal standard solution: Dissolve USP Inositol RS, or equivalent, in water (0.8 mg/mL).
  Sample solution: Weigh 2.0–4.0 mg of sample in duplicate into vials with stir bars. Add 500 µL of pure trifluoroacetic acid (TFA), and allow the mixture to form a uniform dispersion by stirring for 1 h at room temperature. Incubate in an 80° water bath for 2 h with stirring, and then cool to room temperature. Add 100 µL of *Internal standard solution* to each vial, and incubate with stirring in a boiling water bath for 15 min. Cool again to room temperature, then add 1.07 mL of water to each vial, and incubate with stirring in a boiling water bath for 1 h. Cool the solutions to room temperature, and dry overnight on a SpeedVac, or equivalent, at low heat with the cryopumping system off. Dissolve the dried preparation in 2.5 mL of deionized water, and filter through a 0.2-µm PTFE syringe filter. Dilute with an equal volume of water before injection.
  Standard solutions: Dissolve USP Dextrose RS or equivalent, and USP Mannose RS or equivalent, in water, aliquot them in duplicate as shown in the table below, and freeze dry them. Continue preparation as directed in the *Sample solution*, beginning with "Add 500 µL of pure trifluoroacetic acid".

Standard Identification Number	µL/vial of 4.0 µg/mL Glucose	µL/vial of 80 µg/mL Mannose
0	0	0
1	100	25
2	200	50
3	300	100
4	500	200
5	1000	400

Chromatographic system, Appendix IIA
  Mode: High-performance liquid chromatography
  Column: Strong anion-exchange column 4.0-mm × 250-mm (CarboPac MA-1, with CarboPac MA-1 4.0-mm × 50-mm guard column, Dionex, or equivalent)

---
[8] Alternatively, Bottle #2 of K-YBGL kit (Megazyme, or equivalent) could be used directly.

Column temperature: 30°
Flow rate: 0.4 mL/min
Injection volume: 10 µL
Gradient program: See the gradient table below.

Time (min)	Mobile phase A (%)	Mobile phase B (%)
0	36.0	64.0
15.0	36.0	64.0
35.0 (sample injection)	59.4	40.6
80.0	59.4	40.6

[NOTE—The run time typically required is 80 min.]
Detector mode: Integrated amperometry
Detector range: 3000 µC (may be modified if needed)
Working electrode: Gold
Reference electrode: pH, Ag/AgCl
Electrochemical waveform: See the table below.

Time (s)	Potential (V)	Integration
0.00	0.10	—
0.20	0.10	Start
0.40	0.10	End
0.41	−2.00	—
0.42	−2.00	—
0.43	0.60	—
0.44	−0.10	—
0.50	−0.10	—

Analysis: Separately inject equal volumes of the Standard solutions and Sample solution into the chromatograph, and measure the responses for the major peaks on the resulting chromatograms. For each injection, calculate the ratios of the area of the glucose and mannose peaks to the area of the internal standard inositol peak. Make two standard curves of the peak area ratio versus the concentration for the glucose and mannose standards, and calculate their linear regression. The glucose and mannose concentration of the sample is then calculated from their peak area ratio using the respective slope and intercept of the standards regression lines.
Calculate the percentage of mannose present in the sample:

$$\text{Result} = [C_M/(C_M + C_G)] \times 100$$

C_M = mannose concentration in the sample (µL/mL)
C_G = glucose concentration in the sample (µL/mL)
Acceptance criteria: NMT 1.0% mannose, as a function of total hexose recovered (glucose and mannose)

SPECIFIC TESTS
- **LOSS ON DRYING**, Appendix IIC: 105°, 3 h
  Sample: 0.9–1.2 g
  Acceptance criteria: NMT 8.0%

- **RESIDUE ON IGNITION (SULFATED ASH)**, Appendix IIC
  Sample: 2.0 g
  Acceptance criteria: NMT 2.5%

Betaine
First Published: First Supplement, FCC 7

Trimethylglycine
2-Trimethylammonioacetate
TMG
Glycine betaine
FEMA: 4223

$C_5H_{11}O_2N$ Formula wt, anhydrous 117.15
$C_5H_{11}O_2N \cdot H_2O$ Formula wt, monohydrate 135.16
   CAS: anhydrous [107-43-7]
    monohydrate [590-47-6]
UNII: 3SCV180C9W [betaine]

DESCRIPTION
Betaine occurs as a white, very hygroscopic powder. It is recovered and purified from the aqueous liquor (molasses) remaining from the production of sucrose from sugar beets. It is very soluble in water, freely soluble in methanol, and soluble in ethanol.
Function: Source of betaine, flavoring agent
Packaging and Storage: Store in well-closed containers.

IDENTIFICATION
- **INFRARED ABSORPTION**, Spectrophotometric Identification Tests, Appendix IIIC
  Reference standard: USP Betaine RS
  Sample and standard preparation: K
  Acceptance criteria: The spectrum of the sample exhibits absorption bands at approximately the following wavelengths, which correspond in intensity and wavelength to those in the spectrum of the Reference standard (s = strong, m = medium): 1415 cm^{-1} (s), 1393 cm^{-1} (s), 1333 cm^{-1} (s), 932 cm^{-1} (s), 892 cm^{-1} (s), 625 cm^{-1} (s), and 604 cm^{-1} (m).

ASSAY
- **PROCEDURE**
  [NOTE—Betaine is very hygroscopic and should be handled accordingly for appropriate test procedures.]
  Mobile phase: 0.142 g/L anhydrous sodium sulfate. Adjust with sodium hydroxide solution to a pH of 9.
  Standard solution: 7.0 mg/mL USP Betaine RS, filtered through a 0.2-µm filter
  Sample solution: 10 mg/mL, filtered through a 0.2-µm filter
  Chromatographic system, Appendix IIA
   Mode: High-performance liquid chromatography
   Detector: Refractive index

Analytical column: 7.8-mm × 300-mm column packed with a strong cation-exchange sodium form resin[1], and a 4.6-mm × 30-mm guard column[2]
Flow rate: 0.6 mL/min
Injection volume: 10 µL
Elution: Isocratic
Column temperature: 75°
System suitability
　Sample: *Standard solution*
　Relative standard deviation: Peak heights NMT 1.0% for replicate injections
Analysis: Separately inject equal volumes of the *Standard solutions* and *Sample solution* into the chromatograph, record the chromatograms, and measure the peak responses. Calculate the percent betaine in the sample taken by the equation:

$$\text{Result} = (r_U/r_S) \times (C_S/C_U) \times 100$$

r_U = peak response from the *Sample solution*
r_S = peak response from the *Standard solution*
C_S = concentration of the *Standard solution* (mg/mL)
C_U = concentration of the *Sample solution* (mg/mL)

Acceptance criteria: NLT 99.0% of betaine ($C_5H_{11}O_2N$), calculated on the anhydrous basis

IMPURITIES
Inorganic Impurities
- **ARSENIC**, *Arsenic Limit Test*, Appendix IIIB
　Sample: 1 g
　Acceptance criteria: NMT 1 mg/kg, calculated on the anhydrous basis
- **LEAD**, *Lead Limit Test, Atomic Absorption Spectrophotometric Graphite Furnace Method, Method I*, Appendix IIIB
　Sample: 5 g
　Acceptance criteria: NMT 1 mg/kg, calculated on the anhydrous basis
- **SULFATE**, *Chloride and Sulfate Limit Tests, Sulfate Limit Test*, Appendix IIIB
　Sample: Equivalent to 4.0 g on the anhydrous basis
　Control: 400 µg sulfate (40 mL of *Standard Sulfate Solution*)
　Acceptance criteria: Any turbidity produced by the *Sample solution* does not exceed that produced by the *Control* (NMT 0.01%).

SPECIFIC TESTS
- **COLOR**
　Sample: Equivalent to 5 g on the anhydrous basis
　Sample solution: Transfer the *Sample* into a 100-mL volumetric flask, and dissolve in and dilute with water to volume. Pass through a 0.45-µm filter.
　Analysis: Measure the absorbance of the *Sample solution* in a suitable cuvette at 420 nm against water using a suitable spectrophotometer. Calculate the color using the following formula:

$$\text{Color} = (A_U \times 10{,}000)/(C_U \times L)$$

A_U = absorbance of the *Sample solution*
C_U = concentration of the *Sample solution* on the anhydrous basis (g/100 mL)
L = pathlength (cm)

Acceptance criteria: NMT 20
- **PH**, *pH Determination*, Appendix IIB
　Sample solution: 5 g/100 mL
　Acceptance criteria: 5–7
- **RESIDUE ON IGNITION (SULFATED ASH)**, Appendix IIC
　Sample: 1 g
　Acceptance criteria: NMT 0.1%, calculated on the anhydrous basis
- **WATER**, *Water Determination, Method I*, Appendix IIB
　Acceptance criteria
　　Anhydrous: NMT 2%
　　Monohydrate: NMT 15%

OTHER REQUIREMENTS
- **LABELING:** Indicate whether the material is anhydrous or monohydrate.

BHA

First Published: Prior to FCC 6
Last Revision: FCC 8

Butylated Hydroxyanisole

$C_{11}H_{16}O_2$　　　　　　　　　Formula wt 180.25
INS: 320　　　　　　　　　　　CAS: [25013-16-5]
UNII: REK4960K2U [butylated hydroxyanisole]

DESCRIPTION
BHA occurs as a white or slightly yellow, waxy solid. It is predominantly 3-*tert*-butyl-4-hydroxyanisole (3-BHA), with varying amounts of 2-*tert*-butyl-4-hydroxyanisole (2-BHA). It melts between 48° and 63°. It is freely soluble in alcohol and in propylene glycol, and insoluble in water.
Function: Antioxidant

Change to read:

Packaging and Storage: Store in well-closed containers ▲protected from light and heat.▲*FCC8*

IDENTIFICATION

Change to read:

- ▲**A. PROCEDURE**▲*FCC8*
　Sample solution: 100 µg/mL in 72% alcohol
　Analysis: Add 2 mL of sodium borate TS and 1 mL of a 100 µg/mL solution of 2,6-dichloroquinone chlorimide

---
[1] Transgenomic Coregel 87N, or equivalent
[2] Bio-Rad 125-0508, or equivalent

in absolute alcohol to 5 mL of the *Sample solution* and mix.
Acceptance criteria: A blue color appears.

Add the following:

- ▲**B. Procedure**
  Acceptance criteria: The retention times of 3-*tert*-butyl-4-hydroxyanisole and 2-*tert*-butyl-4-hydroxyanisole from the *Sample solution* correspond to those from the *Standard solution*, as obtained in the *Assay*.▲*FCC8*

ASSAY

Change to read:

- **Procedure**
  ▲**Solution A:** 5% Acetic acid
  Mobile phase: Acetonitrile and *Solution A* (45:55)
  Standard solution: 90 µg/mL of USP 3-*tert*-Butyl-4-hydroxyanisole RS and 10 µg/mL of USP 2-*tert*-Butyl-4-hydroxyanisole RS in *Mobile phase*
  Sample solution: 100 µg/mL in *Mobile phase*
  Chromatographic system, Appendix IIA
    Mode: HPLC
    Detector: UV 290 nm
    Column: 4.6-mm × 75-mm; packed with 3.5-µm octadecylsilane chemically bonded to porous silica or ceramic micro-particles packing[1]
    Column temperature: 30°
    Flow rate: 1.2 mL/min
    Injection size: 20 µL
  System suitability
    Sample: *Standard solution*
    [Note—The retention times of 3-*tert*-butyl-4-hydroxyanisole and 2-*tert*-butyl-4-hydroxyanisole are about 4.2 and 4.6 min, respectively.]
    Suitability requirements
      Resolution: NLT 1.5 between the 3-*tert*-butyl-4-hydroxyanisole isomer and 2-*tert*-butyl-4-hydroxyanisole isomer peaks
      Tailing factor: NMT 1.5
      Relative standard deviation: NMT 2.0% for the 3-*tert*-butyl-4-hydroxyanisole isomer and 2-*tert*-butyl-4-hydroxyanisole isomer peaks
  Analysis: Separately inject equal volumes of the *Standard solution* and *Sample solution* into the chromatograph, and measure the responses for the major peaks on the resulting chromatograms.
  Calculate the percentage of each isomer (3-*tert*-butyl-4-hydroxyanisole and 2-*tert*-butyl-4-hydroxyanisole) in the portion of the sample taken:

  $$\text{Result} = (r_U/r_S) \times (C_S/C_U) \times 100$$

  r_U = peak area response for the analyte in the *Sample solution*
  r_S = peak area response for the analyte in the *Standard solution*
  C_S = concentration of the analyte in the *Standard solution* (µg/mL)
  C_U = concentration of the sample in the *Sample solution* (µg/mL)

---

[1] Symmetry C18 (Waters), or equivalent.

Calculate the percentage of $C_{11}H_{16}O_2$ in the sample taken by adding the percentages of the two isomers.▲*FCC8*
Acceptance criteria: NLT 98.5% $C_{11}H_{16}O_2$

SPECIFIC TESTS

- **Residue on Ignition (Sulfated Ash),** *Method I*, Appendix IIC
  Sample: 10 g
  Acceptance criteria: NMT 0.05%

BHT

First Published: Prior to FCC 6

Butylated Hydroxytoluene
2,6-Di-*tert*-butyl-*p*-cresol

$C_{15}H_{24}O$ Formula wt 220.35
INS: 321   CAS: 128-37-0
UNII: 1P9D0Z171K [butylated hydroxytoluene]

DESCRIPTION

BHT occurs as a white, crystalline solid. It is freely soluble in alcohol, and insoluble in water and in propylene glycol.
Function: Antioxidant
Packaging and Storage: Store in well-closed containers.

IDENTIFICATION

- **Procedure**
  Sample solution: 100 µg/mL in methanol
  Analysis: Dissolve 200 mg of 3,3'-dimethoxy-benzidine dihydrochloride in a mixture of 40 mL of methanol and 60 mL of 1 N hydrochloric acid. Add 5 mL of the resulting dianisidine solution to 10 mL of water and 2 mL of a 30 mg/mL solution of sodium nitrite. Add this solution to 10 mL of the *Sample solution*. An orange-red color appears within 3 min. Add 5 mL of chloroform, and shake.
  Acceptance criteria: The chloroform layer exhibits a purple or magenta color that fades when exposed to light.

ASSAY

- **Solidification Point,** Appendix IIB
  Acceptance criteria: NLT 69.2° (indicating a purity of NLT 99.0% $C_{15}H_{24}O$).

SPECIFIC TESTS

- **Residue on Ignition (Sulfated Ash),** Appendix IIC
  Sample: 50 g
  Analysis: Transfer the *Sample* into a tared crucible, ignite until thoroughly charred, and cool. Moisten the ash with 1 mL of sulfuric acid, and complete the ignition by heating for 15-min periods at 800° ± 25° to constant weight.

Acceptance criteria: NMT 0.002%

Biotin

First Published: Prior to FCC 6

cis-Hexahydro-2-oxo-1H-thieno[3,4]imidazole-4-valeric Acid
d-Biotin

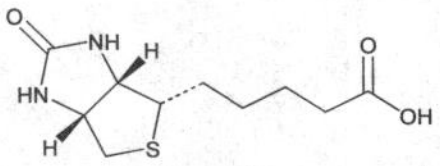

$C_{10}H_{16}N_2O_3S$
Formula wt 244.31
CAS: [58-85-5]
UNII: 6SO6U10H04 [biotin]

DESCRIPTION
Biotin occurs as a practically white, crystalline powder. It is stable to air and heat. One g dissolves in about 5000 mL of water at 25° and in about 1300 mL of alcohol; it is more soluble in hot water and in dilute alkali, and it is insoluble in other common organic solvents.
Function: Nutrient
Packaging and Storage: Store in tight containers.

IDENTIFICATION
- **A. INFRARED ABSORPTION,** *Spectrophotometric Identification Tests,* Appendix IIIC
  Reference standard: USP Biotin RS
  Sample and Standard preparation: *K*
  Acceptance criteria: The spectrum of the sample exhibits maxima at the same wavelengths as those in the spectrum of the *Reference standard.*
- **B. PROCEDURE**
  Sample solution: Saturated solution in warm water
  Acceptance criteria: The *Sample solution* decolorizes bromine TS, added dropwise.

ASSAY
- **PROCEDURE**
  Sample: 500 mg
  Analysis: Mix the *Sample* with 100 mL of water, add phenolphthalein TS and, while heating and stirring continuously, slowly titrate the suspension with 0.1 N sodium hydroxide to a pink color. Each mL of 0.1 N sodium hydroxide is equivalent to 24.43 mg of $C_{10}H_{16}N_2O_3S$.
  Acceptance criteria: NLT 97.5% and NMT 100.5% $C_{10}H_{16}N_2O_3S$

IMPURITIES
Inorganic Impurities
- **LEAD,** *Lead Limit Test, Flame Atomic Absorption Spectrophotometric Method,* Appendix IIIB
  Sample: 10 g
  Acceptance criteria: NMT 2 mg/kg

SPECIFIC TESTS
- **MELTING RANGE OR TEMPERATURE DETERMINATION,** Appendix IIB
  Acceptance criteria: Between 229° and 232°, with decomposition
- **OPTICAL (SPECIFIC) ROTATION,** Appendix IIB
  Sample solution: 20 mg/mL in 0.1 N sodium hydroxide
  Acceptance criteria: $[\alpha]_D^{20}$ between +89° and +93°

Birch Tar Oil, Rectified

First Published: Prior to FCC 6

UNII: 7JK2RXJ8G7 [betula pendula tar oil]

DESCRIPTION
Birch Tar Oil, Rectified occurs as a clear, dark brown liquid with a strong leather odor. It is the pyroligneous oil obtained by dry distillation of the bark and the wood of *Betula pendula* Roth and related species of *Betula* (Fam. Betulaceae) and rectified by steam distillation. It is soluble in most fixed oils, but it is insoluble in glycerin, in mineral oil, and in propylene glycol.
Function: Flavoring agent
Packaging and Storage: Store in a cool place protected from light in full, tight containers that are made from steel or aluminum and that are suitably lined.

IDENTIFICATION
- **INFRARED SPECTRA,** *Spectrophotometric Identification Tests,* Appendix IIIC
  Acceptance criteria: The spectrum of the sample exhibits relative maxima (that may vary in intensity) at the same wavelengths as those of the spectrum below.

SPECIFIC TESTS
- **SOLUBILITY IN ALCOHOL,** Appendix VI
  Acceptance criteria: One mL of sample dissolves in 3 mL of absolute alcohol.
- **SPECIFIC GRAVITY:** Determine by any reliable method (see *General Provisions*).
  Acceptance criteria: Between 0.886 and 0.950

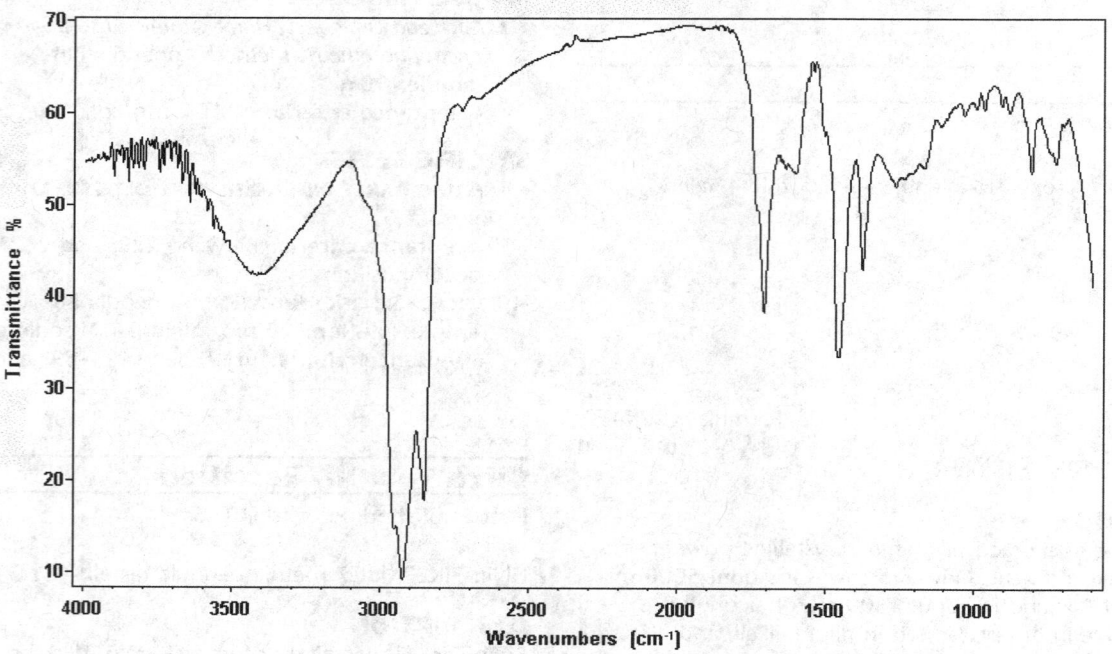

Birch Tar Oil, Rectified

Black Pepper Oil

First Published: Prior to FCC 6

CAS: [8006-82-4]

UNII: U17J84S19Z [black pepper oil]

DESCRIPTION
Black Pepper Oil occurs as an almost colorless to slightly green liquid with the characteristic odor of pepper and a relatively mild taste. It is the volatile oil obtained by steam distillation from the dried, unripened fruit of the plant *Piper nigrum* L. (Fam. Piperaceae). It is soluble in most fixed oils, in mineral oil, and in propylene glycol. It is sparingly soluble in glycerin.

Function: Flavoring agent

Packaging and Storage: Store in a cool place protected from light in full, tight containers that are made from steel or aluminum and that are suitably lined.

IDENTIFICATION
- **INFRARED SPECTRA,** *Spectrophotometric Identification Tests,* Appendix IIIC

  Acceptance criteria: The spectrum of the sample exhibits relative maxima (that may vary in intensity) at the same wavelengths as those of the spectrum below.

SPECIFIC TESTS
- **ANGULAR ROTATION,** *Optical (Specific) Rotation,* Appendix IIB: Use a 100-mm tube.
  Acceptance criteria: Between −1° and −23°
- **REFRACTIVE INDEX,** Appendix IIB
  [NOTE—Use an Abbé or other refractometer of equal or greater accuracy.]
  Acceptance criteria: Between 1.479 and 1.488 at 20°
- **SOLUBILITY IN ALCOHOL,** Appendix VI
  Acceptance criteria: One mL of sample dissolves in 3 mL of 95% alcohol.
- **SPECIFIC GRAVITY:** Determine by any reliable method (see *General Provisions*).
  Acceptance criteria: Between 0.864 and 0.884

Black Pepper Oil

Bohenin

First Published: Prior to FCC 6

1,3-Behenic-2-oleic Glyceride

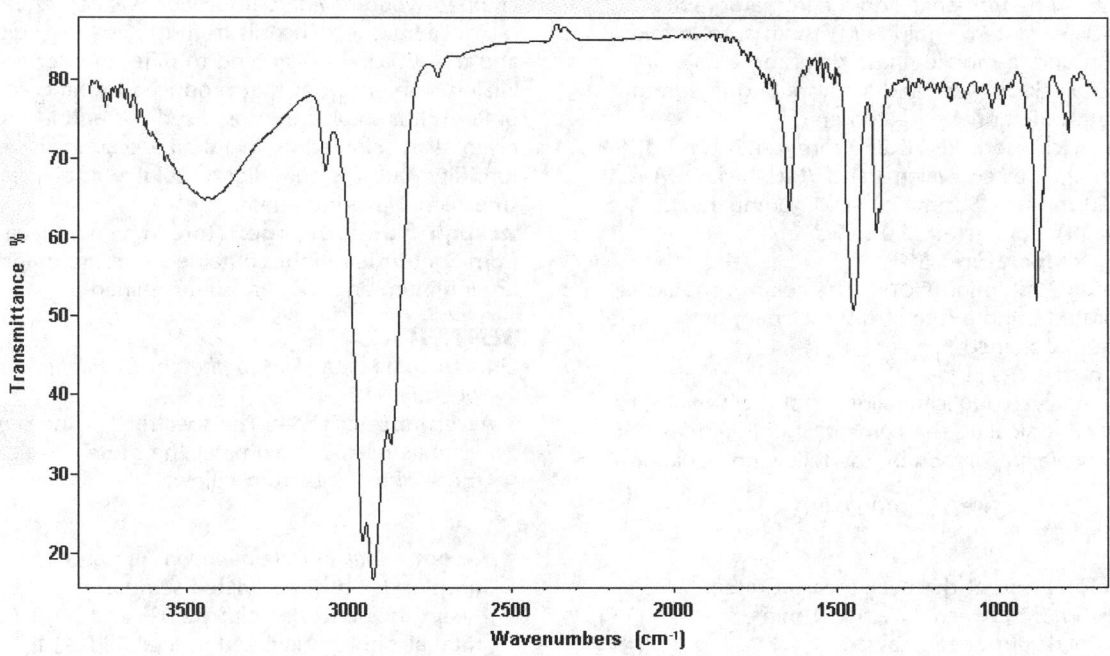

UNII: 1E62B2M7C5 [bohenin]

DESCRIPTION
Bohenin occurs as a white to light tan, waxy solid. It is a triglyceride containing behenic acid at the 1- and 3- positions and oleic acid at the 2-position. Behenic acid is a saturated fatty acid that occurs naturally in peanuts, most seed fats, animal milk fat, and marine oils. It is produced by the interesterification of triolein and ethyl behenate in the presence of a suitable lipase enzyme preparation. It melts at approximately 52°. It is insoluble in water; soluble in hexane, in chloroform, and in acetone; and slightly soluble in hot ethanol.

Function: Tempering aid and antibloom agent in the manufacture of chocolate and chocolate coatings

Packaging and Storage: Store in closed containers away from excessive heat.

IDENTIFICATION
- **FATTY ACID COMPOSITION,** Appendix VII
  Acceptance criteria: A sample exhibits the following fatty acid composition profile:

Fatty Acid	Weight % (Range)
16:0	<1.5
18:0	<3.0
18:1	>25.0
20:0	<7.0
22:0	>58.0
24:0	<3.0

IMPURITIES
Inorganic Impurities
- **LEAD,** *Lead Limit Test, Atomic Absorption Spectrophotometric Method II,* Appendix IIIB
  Acceptance criteria: NMT 0.5 mg/kg

SPECIFIC TESTS
- **ACID VALUE (FATS AND RELATED SUBSTANCES),** Appendix VII
  Acceptance criteria: NMT 0.3
- **DIGLYCERIDES AND TRIGLYCERIDES**
  Mobile phase: Acetone, acetonitrile [80:20]
  Sample preparation: Transfer 5 g of sample into a 50-mL beaker and warm at 80° to melt. Transfer 300 µL of melted sample into a 10-mL volumetric flask, add 9 mL of acetone, and swirl to dissolve. If crystals of bohenin form, warm the flask to 40° in a water bath. After complete dissolution, dilute to volume with acetone.

Chromatographic system, Appendix IIA
  Mode: High-performance liquid chromatography
    [NOTE—Use a system equipped with an autosampler injection unit, a mobile-phase degasser, a column heating block or oven, and a computing integrator.]
  Detector: Differential refractometer
  Column: Lichrosorb RP-18 250 mm × 4.5 mm (id) (GL Science, Inc., or equivalent) and YMC-Pack ODA-A A-303 250 mm × 4.5 mm (id) (YMC Company, Ltd., or equivalent), connected in a series, or equivalent
  Column temperature: 50°
  Flow rate: 2 mL/min. [NOTE—The column should be equilibrated using a rate of 0.9 mL/ min, until a stable baseline is obtained.]
  Injection size: 30 µL
  Analysis: Analyze duplicate aliquots of the *Sample preparation*. Calculate the percent of diglycerides (%D) in the *Sample preparation* by the following equation:

$$\%D = 100(D_G/S_A)$$

  D_G = total sum of the peak areas at retention times between 11 and 14 min
  S_A = total sum of all peak areas
  Calculate the percent of triglycerides (%T) in the *Sample preparation* by the following equation:

$$\%T = 100\,[(S_A - D_G)\,/\,S_A]$$

  Acceptance criteria
    Diglycerides: NMT 5.0%
    Triglycerides: NLT 95.0%
- **IODINE VALUE,** Appendix VII
  Acceptance criteria: Between 24 and 30
- **PEROXIDE VALUE,** Appendix VII
  Acceptance criteria: NMT 0.3 mEq/kg
- **SAPONIFICATION VALUE,** Appendix VII
  Acceptance criteria: Between 162 and 172

Bois de Rose Oil

First Published: Prior to FCC 6

UNII: F2522O5L7B [rosewood oil]

DESCRIPTION
Bois de Rose Oil occurs as a colorless to pale yellow liquid with a slightly camphoraceous, pleasant, floral odor. It is the volatile oil obtained by steam distillation from the chipped wood of *Aniba rosaeodora* var. *amazonica* Ducke (Fam. Lauraceae). The oils from the coastal region of Brazil and the Amazon valley tend to differ in odor and in linalool content from that produced in the Loreto province of Peru. It is soluble in most fixed oils and in propylene glycol. It is soluble in mineral oil, occasionally with turbidity, but it is only slightly soluble in glycerin.
Function: Flavoring agent
Packaging and Storage: Store in a cool place protected from light in full, tight containers that are made from steel or aluminum and that are suitably lined.

IDENTIFICATION
- **INFRARED SPECTRA,** *Spectrophotometric Identification Tests,* Appendix IIIC
  Acceptance criteria: The spectrum of the sample exhibits relative maxima at the same wavelengths as those of the spectrum below.

ASSAY
- **LINALOOL,** *Linalool Determination,* Appendix VI
  Sample: 1.2 g of acetylated sample
  Acceptance criteria: NLT 82.0% and NMT 92.0% of total alcohols, calculated as linalool ($C_{10}H_{18}O$).

SPECIFIC TESTS
- **ANGULAR ROTATION,** *Optical (Specific) Rotation,* Appendix IIB: Use a 100-mm tube.
  Acceptance criteria: Between −4° and +6°
- **DISTILLATION RANGE,** Appendix IIB: Use a 125-mL distillation flask.
  Sample: 50 mL, previously dried over anhydrous sodium sulfate
  Acceptance criteria: NLT 70% distills between 195° and 205°.
- **REFRACTIVE INDEX,** Appendix IIB
  [NOTE—Use an Abbé or other refractometer of equal or greater accuracy.]
  Acceptance criteria: Between 1.462 and 1.470 at 20°
- **SOLUBILITY IN ALCOHOL,** Appendix VI
  Acceptance criteria: One mL of sample dissolves in 6 mL of 60% alcohol.
- **SPECIFIC GRAVITY:** Determine by any reliable method (see *General Provisions*).
  Acceptance criteria: Between 0.868 and 0.889

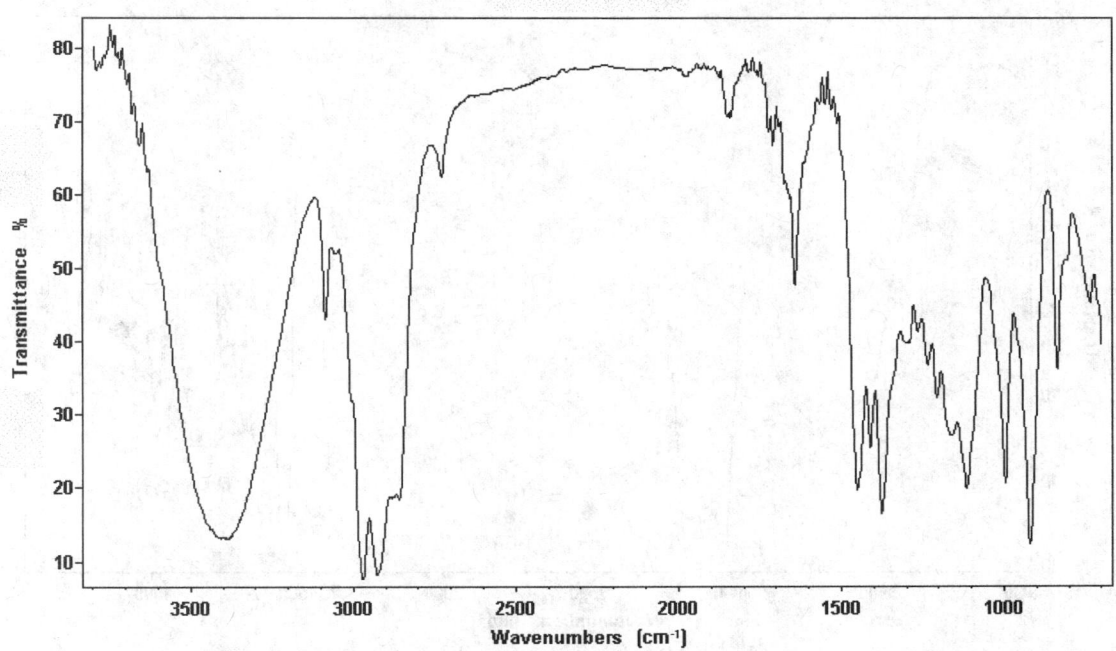

Bois de Rose Oil

Borneol

First Published: Prior to FCC 6

$C_{10}H_{18}O$ Formula wt 154.25
FEMA: 2157
UNII: M89NIB437X [borneol]

DESCRIPTION
Borneol occurs as a white to off-white crystal.
Odor: Piney, camphoraceous
Solubility: Slightly soluble in propylene glycol; very slightly soluble in water; insoluble or practically insoluble in vegetable oils
Boiling Point: ~210°

Solubility in Alcohol, Appendix VI: One g dissolves in 2 mL of 95% ethanol.
Function: Flavoring agent

IDENTIFICATION
- **INFRARED SPECTRA,** *Spectrophotometric Identification Tests,* Appendix IIIC
  Acceptance criteria: The spectrum of the sample exhibits relative maxima at the same wavelengths as those of the spectrum below.

ASSAY
- **PROCEDURE:** Proceed as directed under *M-1b,* Appendix XI.
  Acceptance criteria: NLT 97.0% of $C_{10}H_{18}O$

OTHER REQUIREMENTS
- **MELTING RANGE OR TEMPERATURE DETERMINATION,** Appendix IIB
  Acceptance criteria: NLT 202°

132 / Borneol / *Monographs*

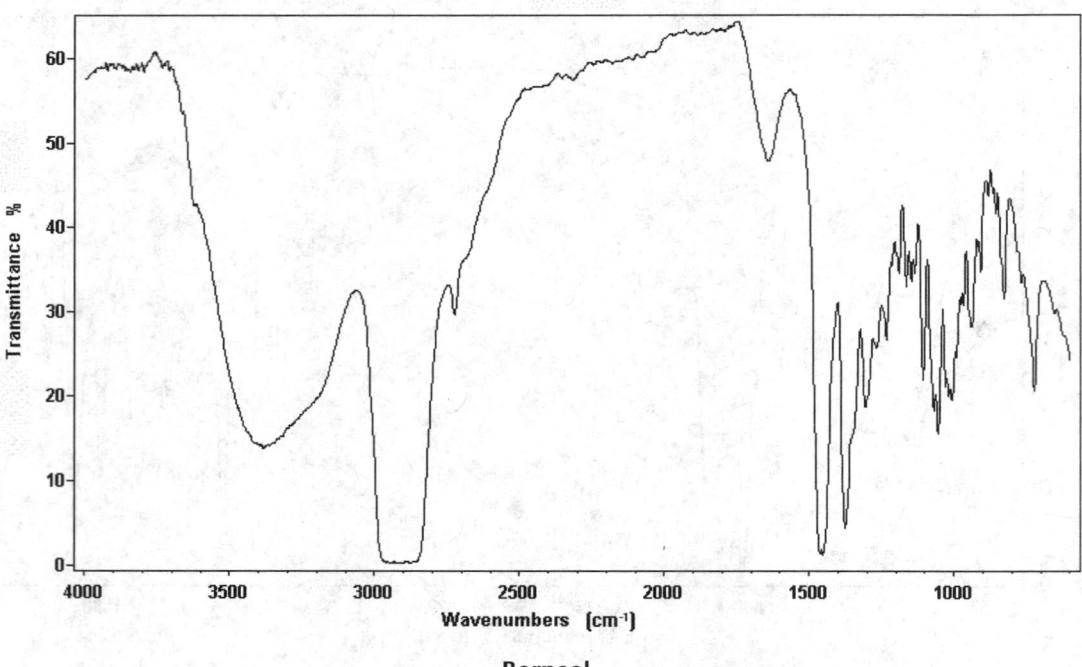

Borneol

Bornyl Acetate

First Published: Prior to FCC 6

L-Bornyl Acetate

$C_{12}H_{20}O_2$ Formula wt 196.29
FEMA: 2159
UNII: 213431586X [bornyl acetate]

DESCRIPTION
Bornyl Acetate occurs as a colorless liquid, semicrystalline mass, or white crystalline solid.
Odor: Sweet, herbaceous, piney
Solubility: Soluble in alcohol, most fixed oils; slightly soluble in water; insoluble or practically insoluble in glycerin, propylene glycol
Boiling Point: ~226°
Solubility in Alcohol, Appendix VI: One mL dissolves in 3 mL of 70% alcohol, and remains in solution on dilution to 10 mL.
Function: Flavoring agent

IDENTIFICATION
- **INFRARED SPECTRA,** *Spectrophotometric Identification Tests,* Appendix IIIC
  Acceptance criteria: The spectrum of the sample exhibits relative maxima at the same wavelengths as those of the spectrum below.

ASSAY
- **PROCEDURE:** Proceed as directed under *M-1b,* Appendix XI.
  Acceptance criteria: NLT 98.0% of $C_{12}H_{20}O_2$

SPECIFIC TESTS
- **ACID VALUE, FLAVOR CHEMICALS (OTHER THAN ESSENTIAL OILS),** *M-15,* Appendix XI
  Acceptance criteria: NMT 1.0
- **REFRACTIVE INDEX,** Appendix II: At 20°
  Acceptance criteria: Between 1.462 and 1.466
- **SPECIFIC GRAVITY:** Determine at 25° by any reliable method (see *General Provisions*).
  Acceptance criteria: Between 0.981 and 0.985

OTHER REQUIREMENTS
- **ANGULAR ROTATION,** *Optical (Specific) Rotation,* Appendix IIB: Use a 100-mm tube.
  Acceptance criteria: Between −39.5° and −45.0°
- **SOLIDIFICATION POINT,** Appendix IIB
  Acceptance criteria: NLT 25°

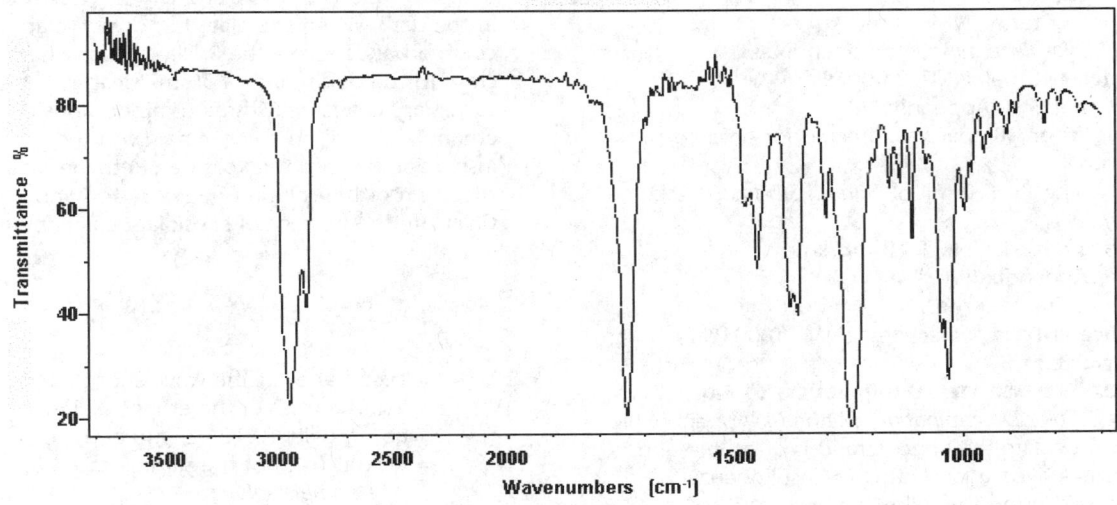

Bornyl Acetate

Brilliant Blue[1]

First Published: Prior to FCC 6

Brilliant Blue FCF
CI 42090
Class: Triphenylmethane

$C_{37}H_{34}N_2O_9S_3Na_2$
INS: 133
UNII: H3R47K3TBD [fd&c blue no. 1]

Formula wt 792.86
CAS: [3844-45-9]

DESCRIPTION
Brilliant Blue occurs as a dark purple to bronze powder or granules. It is principally the disodium salt of ethyl[4-[p-[ethyl(m-sulfobenzyl)amino]-α-(o-sulfophenyl)-benzylidene]-2,5-cyclohexadien-1-ylidene](m-sulfobenzyl)ammonium hydroxide inner salt. It dissolves in water to give a solution green-blue at neutrality, green in weak acid, and yellow in stronger acid. Addition of base to its neutral solution produces a violet color only on boiling. When dissolved in concentrated sulfuric acid, it yields a yellow solution that turns green when diluted with water. It is slightly soluble in ethanol.

Function: Color
Packaging and Storage: Store in well-closed containers.

IDENTIFICATION
- **Procedure**
  Sample solution: 10 μg/mL, freshly prepared
  Analysis: Adjust the pH of three aliquots of the *Sample solution* to pH 1, pH 7, and pH 13. Measure the absorbance intensities (A) and wavelength maxima of these solutions with a suitable UV-visible spectrophotometer.
  Acceptance criteria
  pH 1: A = 0.95 at 629 nm and A = 0.2 at 410 nm
  pH 7: A = 1.11 at 630 nm
  pH 13: A = 1.29 at 630 nm and A = 0.15 at 408 nm

ASSAY
- **Total Color,** *Color Determination, Methods I and II,* Appendix IIIC (Both methods must be used)
  Method I (Spectrophotometric)
  Sample: 50 to 75 mg
  Analysis: Transfer the *Sample* into a 1-L volumetric flask; dissolve in and dilute to volume with water. Determine as directed at 630 nm using 0.164 L/(mg·cm) for the absorptivity (a) for Brilliant Blue.
  Method II (TiCl₃ Titration)
  Sample: 0.5 g
  Analysis: Determine as directed using 2.52 as the stoichiometric factor (F_s) for Brilliant Blue.
  Acceptance criteria: The average of results obtained from *Methods I* and *II* is NLT 85.0% coloring matters

IMPURITIES
Inorganic Impurities
- **Arsenic,** Appendix IIIB

---

[1] To be used or sold for use to color food that is marketed in the United States, this color additive must be from a batch that has been certified by the U.S. Food and Drug Administration (FDA). If it is not from an FDA-certified batch, it is not a permitted color additive for food use in the United States, even if it is compositionally equivalent. The name FD&C Blue No. 1 can be applied only to FDA-certified batches of this color additive. Brilliant Blue is a common name given to the uncertified colorant. See the monograph entitled *FD&C Blue No. 1* for directions for producing an FDA-certified batch.

Sample solution: Prepare as directed for organic compounds.
Acceptance criteria: NMT 3 mg/kg
- **Chromium,** Color Determination, Appendix IIIC
Acceptance criteria: NMT 0.0005%
- **Lead,** Lead Limit Test, Appendix IIIB
Sample solution: Prepare as directed for organic compounds.
Control: 10 μg Pb (10 mL of Diluted Standard Lead Solution)
Acceptance criteria: NMT 10 mg/kg
- **Manganese,** Appendix IIIA
Sample solution: 50 mg/mL
Acceptance criteria: Passes test (NMT 0.001%)

Organic Impurities
- **Uncombined Intermediates and Products of Side Reactions,** Color Determination, Method I, Appendix IIIC
Analysis: Calculate the concentrations of o-, m-, and p-sulfobenzaldehyde and N-ethyl-N-(3-sulfobenzyl)-sulfanilic acid using the following absorptivities: a = 0.0495 L/(mg·cm) at 246 nm (acid solution) for o-, m-, and p-sulfobenzaldehyde and a = 0.078 L/(mg·cm) at 277 nm (alkaline solution) for N-ethyl-N-(3-sulfobenzyl)-sulfanilic acid.
Acceptance criteria
o-, m-, and p-Sulfobenzaldehydes: NMT 1.5%, combined
N-Ethyl-N-(3-sulfobenzyl)-sulfanilic acid: NMT 0.3%

SPECIFIC TESTS
- **Combined Tests**
Tests
- Loss on Drying (Volatile Matter), Color Determination, Appendix IIIC
- Chloride, Sodium Chloride, Color Determination, Appendix IIIC
- Sulfates (as sodium salts), Sodium Sulfate, Color Determination, Appendix IIIC
Acceptance criteria: NMT 15.0% in combination
- **Ether Extracts,** Color Determination, Appendix IIIC
Acceptance criteria: NMT 0.2%
- **Leuco Base,** Color Determination, Appendix IIIC
Sample solution: 120 μg/mL
Acceptance criteria: NMT 5.0%
- **Subsidiary Colors,** Thin-Layer Chromatography, Appendix IIA
Adsorbent: Silica Gel G
Developing solvent system: Acetonitrile, isoamyl alcohol, 2-butanone, water, and ammonium hydroxide (10:10:3:1:1).
Sample solution: Transfer 1 g of sample into a 100-mL volumetric flask. Fill the flask about 3/4 full with water, place it in the dark for 1 h, dilute to volume with water, and mix well.
Application volume: 0.1 mL
Analysis: Prepare a 20- × 20-cm glass plate coated with a 0.25-mm layer of Adsorbent. Spot the Sample solution 3 cm from the bottom edge. Allow the plate to dry for about 20 min in the dark, then develop with the Developing solvent system in an unlined tank equilibrated for at least 20 min before the plate is inserted. Allow the solvent front to reach within about 3 cm of the top of the plate. Dry the developed plate in the dark. When the plate has dried, scrape off all the colored bands above the Brilliant Blue, which remains close to the origin, into a 30-mL beaker. Extract the subsidiary colors with three 6-mL portions of 95% ethanol, or until no color remains on the gel by visual inspection. Record the volume of ethanol used and the spectrum of the solution between 400 and 700 nm. Calculate the percent of subsidiary colors by the formula:

$$\text{Result} = (A \times V \times 100)/(a \times W \times b)$$

A = absorbance at the wavelength maximum
V = volume (mL) of the ethanol solution
a = absorptivity (0.126 L/(mg·cm))
W = weight (mg) of the sample taken to prepare the Sample solution
b = cell pathlength (cm)

Acceptance criteria
Ethyl[4-[p-[ethyl(p-sulfobenzyl)amino]-1-(o-sulfophenyl)benzylidene]-2,5-cyclohexadien-1-ylidene](p-sulfobenzyl) ammonium hydroxide inner salt, Isomeric disodium salts
and
Ethyl[4-[p-[ethyl(o-sulfobenzyl)amino]-α-(o-sulfophenyl)benzylidene]-2,5-cyclohexadien-1-ylidene](o-sulfobenzyl) ammonium hydroxide inner salt, Isomeric disodium salts: NMT 6.0%, combined
- **Water-Insoluble Matter,** Color Determination, Appendix IIIC
Acceptance criteria: NMT 0.2%

Brominated Vegetable Oil

First Published: Prior to FCC 6

DESCRIPTION
Brominated Vegetable Oil occurs as a pale yellow to dark brown, viscous, oily liquid. It is a bromine addition product of vegetable oil or oils. It is soluble in chloroform, in ether, in hexane, and in fixed oils, and is insoluble in water.
Function: Flavoring agent; beverage stabilizer
Packaging and Storage: Store in well-closed containers.

IDENTIFICATION
- **Procedure**
Sample: 0.2 mL
Analysis: Mix the Sample with 1 g of anhydrous sodium carbonate in a suitable crucible, cover the mixture with an additional 1 g of sodium carbonate; compact the mixture by gentle tapping; and heat the crucible over an open flame until the crucible turns red. Cool the crucible and its contents, dissolve the residue in 20 mL of hot water, and filter. Add 1.7 N nitric acid to the filtrate until effervescence ceases, then add 1 mL of silver nitrate TS. A curdy, yellow precipitate forms.

Acceptance criteria: The yellow precipitate is insoluble in nitric acid but soluble in an excess of stronger ammonia water.

SPECIFIC TESTS
- **FREE BROMINE**
  Sample: 1 g
  Analysis: Dissolve the *Sample* in 20 mL of acetone, add 1 g of sodium iodide, and allow the mixture to stand in a stoppered flask in the dark for 30 min; shake the flask occasionally. Add 25 mL of water and 1 mL of starch TS.
  Acceptance criteria: No blue color appears.
- **FREE FATTY ACIDS (AS OLEIC ACID)**, Appendix VII
  Sample: See Table in Appendix VII
  Analysis: Titrate with the appropriate normality of sodium hydroxide solution, shaking the flask vigorously, to the first permanent pink color of the same intensity as that of the neutralized alcohol (if the sample color interferes, titrate to a pH of 8.5, determined with a suitable instrument). Use 28.2 as the equivalence factor (e) in the calculation for oleic acid.
  Acceptance criteria: NMT 2.5%
- **IODINE VALUE**, Appendix VII
  Acceptance criteria: NMT 16
- **SPECIFIC GRAVITY:** Determine by any reliable method (see *General Provisions*) at the temperature specified by the vendor.
  Acceptance criteria: Within the range specified by the vendor

Brown HT[1]

First Published: Third Supplement, FCC 7

Chocolate Brown HT
CI Food Brown 3
CI No. 20285
Class: Bis-azo
Disodium 4,4'-(2,4-dihydroxy-5-hydroxymethyl-1,3-phenylene-bisazo) di-1-naphthalene-sulfonate

$C_{27}H_{18}N_4Na_2O_9S_2$
INS: 155
Formula wt 652.57
CAS: [4553-89-3]

DESCRIPTION
Brown HT occurs as a brown powder or granules. It is principally the disodium salt of 4,4'-(2,4-dihydroxy-5-hydroxymethyl-1,3-phenylene-bisazo) di-1-naphthalene-sulfonate and subsidiary coloring matters with sodium chloride and/or sodium sulfate as the principal uncolored components. It is soluble in water and insoluble in ethanol.
Function: Color
Packaging and Storage: Store in well-closed containers.

IDENTIFICATION
- **VISIBLE ABSORPTION SPECTRUM**
  Sample solution: Dissolve a sample in water and adjust the pH to 7.
  Analysis: Measure the absorption spectrum of the *Sample solution* using a suitable UV-visible spectrophotometer.
  Acceptance criteria: The *Sample solution* exhibits a wavelength maximum at 460 nm.

ASSAY
- **TOTAL COLOR**, *Color Determination, Method I*, Appendix IIIC
  Diluent: Phosphate buffer, pH 7, prepared by combining 50 mL of 0.2 M potassium dihydrogen phosphate and 29.54 mL of 0.2 M sodium hydroxide, and diluting with water to 200 mL
  Sample stock solution: 250 mg/L in diluent
  Sample solution: 10 mg/L prepared by diluting the *Sample stock solution* with diluent
  Analysis: Determine the absorbance of the *Sample solution* (instead of the directed sample preparation) at 460 nm. Calculate the total color as directed using 0.0403 L/(mg·cm) for the absorptivity (*a*) for Brown HT.
  Acceptance criteria: NLT 70.0% total coloring matters

IMPURITIES
Inorganic Impurities
- **LEAD**, *Lead Limit Test*, Appendix IIIB
  Sample solution: Prepare as directed for organic compounds.
  Control: 2 µg Pb (2 mL of *Diluted Standard Lead Solution*)
  Acceptance criteria: NMT 2 mg/kg

Organic Impurities
- **4-AMINONAPHTHALENE-1-SULFONIC ACID**
  Solution A: 0.2 N ammonium acetate
  Solution B: Methanol
  Mobile phase: Exponential gradient program from (99% A and 1% B) to (0% A and 100% B) at a rate of 2% per min
  Sample solution: 5 mg/mL in 0.02 M ammonium acetate
  Standard solution: 35 µg/mL of 4-aminonaphthalene-1-sulfonic acid
  Chromatographic system, Appendix IIA
  Mode: High-performance liquid chromatography
  Detector: UV
  Column: 25-cm × 4.6-mm C18 analytical column (5-µm), with a 15-mm × 4.6-mm C18 guard column (5-µm)
  Column temperature: Ambient
  Flow rate: 1.0 mL/min
  Injection volume: 20 µL
  Analysis: Separately inject equal volumes of the *Standard solution* and *Sample solution* into the

---
[1] Brown HT is approved for use in some countries but banned in others, such as the United States.

chromatograph, and measure the responses for the major peaks on the resulting chromatograms.

Calculate the percentage of 4-aminonaphthalene-1-sulfonic acid in the sample taken:

$$\text{Result} = (r_U/r_S) \times (C_S/C_U) \times 1000 \times 100$$

- r_U = peak area for 4-aminonaphthalene-1-sulfonic acid in the *Sample solution*
- r_S = peak area for 4-aminonaphthalene-1-sulfonic acid in the *Standard solution*
- C_S = concentration of 4-aminonaphthalene-1-sulfonic acid in the *Standard solution* (µg/mL)
- C_U = concentration of sample in the *Sample solution* (mg/mL)
- 1000 = mg-to-µg conversion factor

Acceptance criteria: NMT 0.7%

SPECIFIC TESTS

- **COMBINED TESTS**
  Tests
  - LOSS ON DRYING (VOLATILE MATTER), *Color Determination*, Appendix IIIC
  - CHLORIDE, *Sodium Chloride, Color Determination*, Appendix IIIC
  - SULFATES (AS SODIUM SALTS), *Sodium Sulfate, Color Determination*, Appendix IIIC

  Acceptance criteria: NMT 30%, combined as the sum of all three tests

- **ETHER EXTRACTS**, *Color Determination*, Appendix IIIC
  Acceptance criteria: NMT 0.2%

- **SUBSIDIARY COLORING MATTERS**
  [NOTE—In this method, subsidiary coloring matters are separated from the main coloring matter of Brown HT by ascending paper chromatography (see *Paper Chromatography*, Appendix IIA), and extracted separately from the chromatographic paper. The absorbance of each extract is measured at the wavelength of maximum absorption for Brown HT (460 nm) by visible spectrophotometry. Because it is impractical to identify each subsidiary coloring matter using this procedure, and because the subsidiary coloring matters are usually minor components of food colors, the method assumes that the maximum absorbance of each subsidiary coloring matter is the same as that of the total coloring matters. The subsidiary coloring matters content is calculated by adding together the absorbances of the extracts in conjunction with the total coloring matters content of the sample.]

  Chromatographic apparatus: The chromatography tank (*Figures 1* and *2*) is comprised of a glass tank (A) and cover (B); frame to support chromatography paper (C); solvent tray (D); secondary frame (E) for supporting "drapes" of the filter paper; and 20-cm × 20-cm chromatography grade paper[2]. Mark out the chromatography paper as shown in *Figure 3*.

  Chromatographic solvent: Prepare a mixture of *n*-butanol, glacial acetic acid, and water (4:1:5). Shake for 2 min, allow the layers to separate, and use the upper layer as the chromatographic solvent.

  Sample solution: 10 mg/mL sample

  Standard solution: Dilute 1.0 mL of the *Sample solution* with water to 100 mL, and mix. Transfer 0.1 mL of this solution to a test tube. Add 5.0 mL of a water and acetone mixture (1:1 v/v), and then add 14.9 mL of 0.05 N sodium carbonate solution, and shake the tube to ensure mixing.

  Application volume: 0.10 mL

  Analysis: NLT 2 h before analysis, arrange the filter-paper drapes in the glass tank and pour a sufficient amount of the *Chromatographic solvent* over the drapes and into the bottom of the tank to cover the bottom of the tank to a depth of 1 cm. Place the solvent tray in position and fit the cover to the tank. Using a microsyringe capable of delivering 0.1 mL with a tolerance of ±0.002 mL, apply a 0.1-mL aliquot of the *Sample solution* to a chromatograph sheet as uniformly as possible within the confines of the 18-cm × 7-mm rectangle, holding the nozzle of the microsyringe steadily in contact with the paper. Allow the papers to dry at room temperature for 1–2 h or at 50° in a drying cabinet for 5 min followed by 15 min at room temperature. Mount the dried sheet together with a plain sheet to act as a blank on the supporting frame. [NOTE—If required, several dried sheets may be developed simultaneously.] Pour a sufficient amount of the *Chromatographic solvent* into the solvent tray to bring the surface of the solvent about 1 cm below the base line of the chromatography sheets. The volume necessary will depend on the dimensions of the apparatus and should be predetermined. Put the supporting frame into position and replace the cover. Allow the system to develop for approximately 14 h, then remove the supporting frame and transfer it to a drying cabinet at 50–60° for 10–15 min. Remove the sheets from the frame. Cut each subsidiary band from each chromatogram sheet as a strip, and cut an equivalent strip from the corresponding position of the plain (blank) sheet. Add 5.0 mL of water and acetone (1:1 by vol) to each test tube, swirl for 2–3 min, add 15.0 mL of 0.05 N sodium hydrogen carbonate solution, and shake the tube to ensure mixing. Filter the colored extracts and blanks through 9-cm coarse porosity filter papers into clean test tubes and determine the absorbances of the colored extracts at 460 nm using a suitable spectrophotometer with 40-mm closed cells against a filtered mixture of 5.0 mL of water and acetone (1:1 by vol) and 15.0 mL of the 0.05 N sodium hydrogen carbonate solution. Measure the absorbances of the extracts of the blank strips at 460 nm, and correct the absorbances of the colored extracts with the blank values.

---

[2] Whatman No 1, or equivalent.

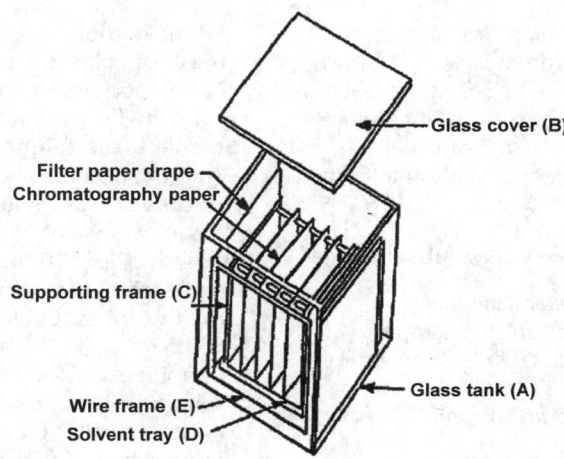

Figure 1. Assembly of the Chromatographic Apparatus.

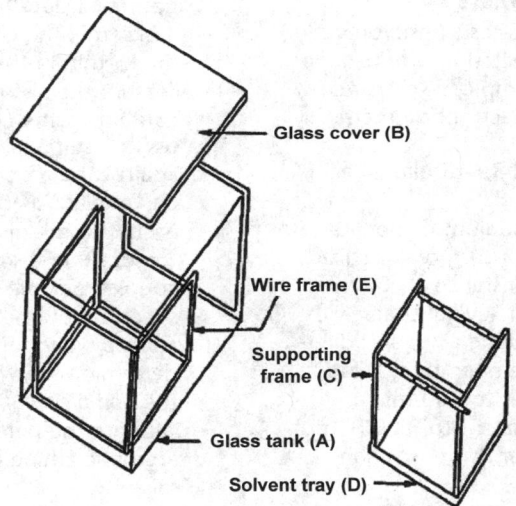

Figure 2. Components of the Chromatographic Apparatus.

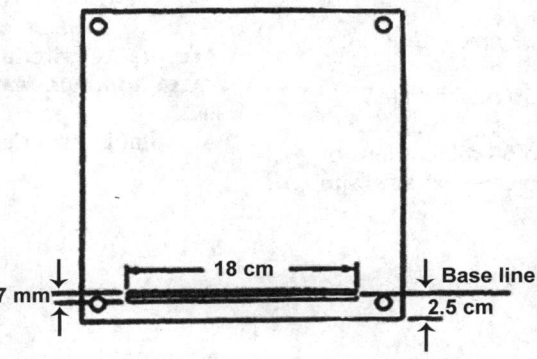

Figure 3. Method for Marking the Chromatographic Paper.

Measure the absorbance of the *Standard solution* at 460 nm using a suitable spectrophotometer with 40-mm closed cells against a filtered mixture of 5.0 mL of water and acetone (1:1 by vol), 14.9 mL of the 0.05 N sodium hydrogen carbonate solution, and 0.1 mL of water. Calculate the percentage of subsidiary coloring matter in the portion of the sample taken:

$$\text{Result} = 0.01 \times D \times [(A_A + A_B + A_C ... A_N)/A_S] \times 100$$

0.01 = dilution factor for the *Standard solution*
D = total coloring matter content of the sample, determined from the *Total Color* test above, expressed as a decimal
A_S = absorbance from the *Standard solution* corrected for the blank

$A_A + A_B + A_C ... A_N$ = sum of the absorbances of the subsidiary coloring matters from the *Sample solution*, corrected for the blank values

Acceptance criteria: NMT 10%

- **UNSULFONATED PRIMARY AROMATIC AMINES**
[NOTE—Under the conditions of this test, unsulfonated primary aromatic amines are extracted into toluene from an alkaline solution of the sample, re-extracted into acid, and then determined spectrophotometrically after diazotization and coupling.]
R salt solution: 0.05 N 2-naphthol-3,6-disulfonic acid, disodium salt
Sodium carbonate solution: 2 N sodium carbonate
Standard stock solution: Weigh 0.100 g of redistilled aniline into a small beaker and transfer to a 100-mL volumetric flask, rinsing the beaker several times with water. Add 30 mL of 3 N hydrochloric acid, and dilute to the mark with water at room temperature. Dilute 10.0 mL of this solution with water to 100 mL, and mix well; 1 mL of this solution is equivalent to 0.0001 g of aniline. [NOTE—Prepare the *Standard stock solution* fresh.]
Standard solutions: Separately dilute 5-mL, 10-mL, 15-mL, 20-mL, and 25-mL aliquots of the *Standard stock solution* with 1 N hydrochloric acid to 100 mL.
Standard blank solution: In a 25-mL volumetric flask mix 10.0 mL of 1 N hydrochloric acid, 10.0 mL of *Sodium carbonate solution*, 2.0 mL of *R salt solution*, and dilute with water to volume.
Sample solution: Add 2.0 g of the sample into a separatory funnel containing 100 mL of water, rinse down the sides of the funnel with 50 mL of water, swirling to dissolve the sample, and add 5 mL of 1 N sodium hydroxide. Extract with two 50-mL portions of toluene, and wash the combined toluene extracts with 10-mL portions of 0.1 N sodium hydroxide to remove traces of color. Extract the washed toluene with three 10-mL portions of 3 N hydrochloric acid, and dilute the combined extract with water to 100 mL.
Sample blank solution: In a 25-mL volumetric flask mix 10.0 mL of the *Sample solution*, 10 mL of *Sodium carbonate solution*, and 2.0 mL of *R salt solution*, and dilute with water to volume.
Analysis: Pipet 10-mL aliquots of the *Sample solution* and each of the *Standard solutions* into separate, clean dry test tubes. Cool the tubes for 10 min by immersion in a beaker of ice water, add 1 mL of 50% potassium bromide solution and 0.05 mL of 0.5 N sodium nitrite solution. Mix, and allow the tubes to stand for 10 min in the ice water bath while the aniline is diazotized. Into each of five 25-mL volumetric flasks, measure 1 mL of *R salt solution* and 10 mL of *Sodium carbonate solution*. Separately pour each diazotized aniline solution into a 25-mL volumetric flask containing *R salt solution* and *Sodium carbonate solution*, and rinse each test tube with a small volume of water to allow for a quantitative transfer. Dilute to the mark with water, stopper the flasks, mix the contents well, and allow them to stand for 15 min in the dark.
Measure the absorbance of each of the solutions containing the coupled *Standard solutions* at 510 nm using a suitable spectrophotometer with 40-mm cells against the *Standard blank solution*. Plot a standard curve relating absorbance to weight (g) of aniline in each 100 mL of the *Standard solutions*.
Measure the absorbance of the solutions containing the coupled *Sample solution* at 510 nm using a suitable spectrophotometer with 40-mm cells against the *Sample blank solution*. From the standard curve, determine the weight (g) of aniline in each 100 mL of the *Sample solution*.
Calculate the percentage of unsulfonated primary aromatic amine (as aniline) in the portion of the sample taken:

$$\text{Result} = W_A/W \times 100$$

W_A = weight of aniline in the *Sample solution* calculated from the standard curve (g/100 mL)
W = weight of sample used to prepare the *Sample solution* (g)

Acceptance criteria: NMT 0.01%, calculated as aniline
- **WATER-INSOLUBLE MATTER**, *Color Determination*, Appendix IIIC
Acceptance criteria: NMT 0.2%

Butadiene-Styrene Rubber

First Published: Prior to FCC 6

DESCRIPTION

Butadiene-Styrene Rubber occurs as a synthetic liquid latex or solid rubber produced by the emulsion polymerization of butadiene and styrene, using fatty acid soaps as emulsifiers, and a suitable catalyst, molecular weight regulator (if required), and shortstop. It also occurs as a solid rubber produced by the solution copolymerization of butadiene and styrene in a hexane solution, using butyl lithium as a catalyst. Solvents and volatiles are removed by processing with hot water or by drum drying.

The latex, which has a pH between 9.5 and 11.0 and a solids content between 26% and 63%, is coagulated with or without other food-grade ingredients in a heated kettle. The coagulated mass is squeezed to drain off sera, and the coagulum is washed with hot water (with or without alkali), and it is rinsed with water until the batch is neutral. Finally, the coagulum is dried to remove residual volatiles. When butadiene-styrene rubber is purchased in the latex form, it must be washed by the preceding or an equivalent procedure. In the case of the solvent-polymerized product, solvent and volatiles are removed by processing in hot water or by drum drying.

Both of the solid forms are supplied by the manufacturer either as a slab or as a uniform, free-flowing crumb and may contain a suitable food-grade antioxidant. The crumb form, in addition, may contain a suitable food-grade partitioning agent.

Function: Masticatory substance in chewing gum base
Packaging and Storage: Store in well-closed containers.

[NOTE—The following requirements apply to the solid rubber as supplied by the manufacturer or to the washed and dried coagulum obtained from the latex as described above.]

IDENTIFICATION
- **INFRARED SPECTRA,** *Spectrophotometric Identification Tests,* Appendix IIIC
  Sample preparation (latex): Dry a sample at 105° for 4 h, then dissolve it in hot toluene and evaporate the solution on a potassium bromide plate.
  Sample preparation (solid): Dissolve a sample in hot toluene and evaporate the solution on a potassium bromide plate.
  Acceptance criteria: The spectrum of the sample exhibits relative maxima at the same wavelengths as those of the appropriate spectrum below.

IMPURITIES
Inorganic Impurities
- **CADMIUM,** *Cadmium Limit Test,* Appendix IIIB

[NOTE—Alternatively, the cadmium content may be determined by the following method]
[NOTE—For this assay, use reagent-grade chemicals with the lowest practicable Sb, As, Bi, Cd, Cu, Pb, Hg, Ag, and Sn levels, and use only high-purity water and gases. Rinse all glass- and plastic-ware twice with 10% nitric acid and twice with 10% hydrochloric acid, and then rinse thoroughly with *High-purity water*.]

High-purity water: Obtain from a mixed-bed strong-acid, strong-base ion exchange apparatus capable of producing water of more than 15-megohm resistivity.
10% nitric acid solution: 1:10 (v/v) nitric acid in *High-purity water*
10% hydrochloric acid solution: 1:10 (v/v) hydrochloric acid in *High-purity water*
Cadmium stock solution: Use any commercially available NIST traceable 1000 ppm (1000 mg/kg) plasma-grade standard stock solution of cadmium.
Cadmium calibration standards: Tare three clean, dry 4-oz polyethylene bottles (or equivalent). Add approximately 50 g of *High-purity water* to each. Slowly add 28 ± 1 g of concentrated nitric acid, mix thoroughly, slowly add 12 ± 1 g of concentrated hydrochloric acid, and mix thoroughly again. Using a precision micropipet, add 10, 50, and 500 µL, respectively, of *Cadmium stock solution* to one of each of the bottles. Dilute each solution to 100.0 ± 0.1 g with *High-purity water*, and mix thoroughly to obtain calibration standards with 0.1, 0.5, and 5.0 mg/kg, respectively.

- **CALIBRATION BLANK SOLUTION:** Prepare one solution as directed under *Cadmium calibration standards*, omitting the addition of *Cadmium stock solution*.

[NOTE—For the solutions listed below, use a Parr Closed Digestion Vessel (catalog number 4748) with polyethylene vessel liners. Any equivalent apparatus may be used if the predigestion fortification recoveries are within the specifications noted below.]

Fortification solution: Use any commercially available NIST traceable 1000 ppm (1000 mg/kg) plasma-grade standard stock solution of cadmium.
Sample digestion preparation: Weigh a representative sample on a balance with 0.1-mg precision (see *Apparatus for Tests and Assays, Weights and Balances,* Appendix I). Transfer the sample to a digestion vessel that has been cleaned according to the manufacturer's specifications. Slowly add 5.0 mL of concentrated nitric acid to the digestion vessel, seal, and heat the vessel for 8 to 16 h at 210° ± 5°. Allow the vessel to cool to room temperature, and quantitatively transfer its contents into a clean, dry, tared 1-oz polyethylene bottle. Slowly add concentrated hydrochloric acid to achieve a final concentration of 10% (w/w), and dilute to an appropriate final mass with *High-purity water*.
Digestion blank preparation: Prepare as directed under *Sample digestion preparation*, omitting the addition of the sample.
Digestion fortification preparation: Prepare as directed under *Sample digestion preparation*, except immediately before heating the sample, add 25 µL of the *Fortification*

solution. Determine the recovery of the *Digestion fortification preparation* by analyzing the *Sample digestion preparation* for cadmium. Calculate the percent recovery for cadmium by subtracting the unfortified assay result from the fortified assay result and multiplying the difference, in mg/kg, by 100. The fortification level for cadmium is 1 mg/kg. Acceptable recoveries are in the 85% to 110% range.

Analysis: Use an Inductively Coupled Plasma Atomic Emission Spectrometer (ICP-AES), or equivalent instrumentation with similar capabilities. Follow the instrument manufacturer's instructions for setting instrument parameters for assay of cadmium. Select appropriate background correction points for the cadmium analyte according to the recommendations of the instrument manufacturer. Select analytical wavelengths to yield adequate sensitivity and freedom from interference.

Analyze the *Calibration blank solution*. Results for cadmium should indicate a concentration of less than 0.01 mg/kg. If the results are NLT 0.01 mg/kg, repeat the analysis. In the event that reanalysis is unsuccessful, take steps consistent with the manufacturer's recommendations to identify and remediate the sources of contamination or interference. Do not proceed with the analysis until the sources of contamination or interference have been identified and corrected.

Subsequently analyze all three *Cadmium calibration standards*, from lowest concentration to highest. Results for each of the *Cadmium calibration standards* should indicate concentrations of 100 ± 5 mg/kg, 500 ± 25 mg/kg, and 5000 ± 250 mg/kg, respectively. If the results are not as indicated, repeat the analysis. In the event that reanalysis is unsuccessful, take steps consistent with the manufacturer's recommendations to identify and remediate the sources of contamination or interference. Do not proceed with the analysis until the sources of contamination or interference have been identified and addressed. After successful calibration of the instrument for cadmium, reanalyze the *Calibration blank solution* to demonstrate that there is no carryover of the cadmium.

Next, analyze the *Sample digestion preparation*, *Digestion blank preparation* (2 replicates), and the *Digestion fortification preparation* in groups of no more than 10. [NOTE—At a minimum, each group should contain a digestion blank, a prepared digestion sample, a second replicate of the prepared digestion sample, and that same digestion sample prepared as a fortification sample.] Analyze the *Calibration blank solution* followed by any of the *Cadmium calibration standards* between each group of ten samples.

To determine the calibration curve, aspirate the *Cadmium calibration standards* and the *Calibration blank solution*. If possible, use the calibration function incorporated in the ICP-AES instrument's software or firmware. If necessary, plot instrument response versus concentration of cadmium. Fit this line with a linear equation of the form $y = mx + b$, in which y is instrument response, m is the slope of the best-fit line, x is concentration, and b is the y intercept of the best-fit line. The correlation coefficient for the best-fit line should be ≥ 0.99. Concentrations of cadmium in the *Calibration blanks*, *Cadmium calibration standards*, *Digestion blank preparations*, *Sample digestion preparations*, and *Digestion fortification preparations* can be directly read from the ICP-AES when using its software or firmware, or they can be calculated from the best-fit equation.

Acceptance criteria: NMT 1 mg/kg

- **LEAD,** Appendix IIIB

    Lead stock solution: Use any commercially available NIST traceable 1000 mg/kg plasma-grade standard stock solution of lead.

    Lead calibration standards: Tare three clean, dry 4-oz polyethylene bottles (or equivalent). Add approximately 50 g of *High-purity water* to each. Slowly add 28 ± 1 g of concentrated nitric acid, mix thoroughly, slowly add 12 ± 1 g of concentrated hydrochloric acid, and mix thoroughly again. Using a precision micropipet, add 10, 50, and 500 µL, respectively, of *Lead stock solution* to one of each of the bottles. Dilute each solution to 100.0 ± 0.1 g with *High-purity water*, and mix thoroughly to obtain calibration standards with 0.1, 0.5, and 5.0 mg/kg, respectively.

    Analysis: Determine as directed in the alternate procedure for *Cadmium* (above) using the *Lead stock solution* and *Lead calibration standards* in place of the *Cadmium stock solution* and *Cadmium calibration standards*. Substitute the word "lead" for "cadmium" throughout the test.

    Acceptance criteria: NMT 3 mg/kg

- **LITHIUM**

    Standard solution: Transfer 399.3 mg of reagent-grade lithium carbonate to a 1000-mL volumetric flask, dissolve in a minimal amount of 1:1 hydrochloric acid:water, dilute to volume with water, and mix. Transfer 10.0 mL of this solution to a 100-mL volumetric flask, dilute to volume with water, and mix. Finally, transfer 10.0 mL of this solution to a second 100-mL volumetric flask, add 1.0 mL of hydrochloric acid, dilute to volume with water, and mix. This solution contains 75 µg of lithium per 100 mL.

    Sample solution: Weigh 1 g of a solid-rubber sample, wrap it tightly in ashless filter paper, and place it in a tared platinum crucible. Heat in an oven at 100° for 15 min, and then transfer to a muffle furnace programmed to reach 500° within 1 to 3 h after introduction of the sample. Remove the crucible from the furnace 15 to 20 min after 500° has been reached, and cool in a desiccator. Quantitatively transfer the contents of the crucible to a 100-mL volumetric flask, using 1 mL of hydrochloric acid and water, dilute to volume with water, and mix.

    Analysis: Use a suitable atomic absorption spectrophotometer equipped with a lithium hollow-cathode lamp, capable of measuring the radiation absorbed by lithium in the 670-nm spectral band. Following the manufacturer's instructions for operating the instrument, aspirate a suitable portion of the *Standard solution* through the flame. In a similar

manner, aspirate a suitable portion of the *Sample solution*.
  Acceptance criteria: Any absorbance produced by the *Sample solution* should not exceed that produced by the *Standard solution*. (NMT 0.0075%)
- **Mercury,** Appendix IIIB
  Mercury stock solution: Use any commercially available NIST traceable 1000 ppm (1000 mg/kg) plasma-grade standard stock solution of mercury.
  Mercury calibration standards: Tare three clean, dry 4-oz polyethylene bottles (or equivalent). Add approximately 50 g of *High-purity water* to each. Slowly add 28 ± 1 g of concentrated nitric acid, mix thoroughly, slowly add 12 ± 1 g of concentrated hydrochloric acid, and mix thoroughly again. Using a precision micropipet, add 10, 50, and 500 μL, respectively, of *Mercury stock solution* to one of each of the bottles. Dilute each solution to 100.0 ± 0.1 g with *High-purity water*, and mix thoroughly to obtain calibration standards with 0.1, 0.5, and 5.0 mg/kg, respectively.
  Analysis: Determine as directed in the alternate procedure for *Cadmium* (above) using the *Mercury stock solution* and *Mercury calibration standards* in place of the *Cadmium stock solution* and *Cadmium calibration standards*. Substitute the word "mercury" for "cadmium" throughout the test.
  Acceptance criteria: NMT 3 mg/kg

Organic Impurities
- **Quinones,** Appendix IV
  Acceptance criteria: NMT 0.002%
- **Residual Hexane**
  [Note—The isooctane (also called 2,2,4-trimethylpentane) used in this test should be of chromatographic-grade quality.]
  Internal standard stock solution: 3.0 mg/mL of *n*-nonane, in isooctane
  Internal standard solution: 6 μg/mL of *n*-nonane in isooctane: made from *Internal standard stock solution*
  Standard stock solution: 30 μg/mL of *n*-hexane in isooctane
  Standard solution: Pipet 10.0 mL of *Standard stock solution* and 10.0 mL of *Internal standard stock solution* into a 50-mL volumetric flask, dilute to volume with isooctane, and mix.
  Sample preparation: Transfer 1.5 g of a solid-rubber sample into a 4-oz bottle and pipet 25.0 mL of the *Internal standard solution* into the bottle. Stopper the bottle, and shake mechanically overnight to dissolve the rubber. Add 50 mL of methanol to precipitate the polymer, and shake vigorously for 15 min. Allow the mixture to settle, and decant the liquid phase into a 250-mL separatory funnel. Wash the polymer with 25 mL of methanol, and add the wash to the separatory funnel. Add 50 to 75 mL of cold water to the separatory funnel, and shake vigorously for 1 min, venting periodically to release any pressure. Allow the phases to separate, drain off the bottom (aqueous) phase, and rewash the isooctane phase with a second 50-mL portion of cold water. Shake again, allow to separate, and drain off the bottom layer. Transfer 10 mL of the isooctane phase to a 20-mL vial for the analysis.
  Chromatographic system, Appendix IIA
    Mode: Gas chromatography
    Detector: Flame-ionization
    Column: 3-m × 3-mm stainless steel column, or equivalent, packed with 60-to 80-mesh Chromosorb P containing 15% didecyl phthalate and capable of separating hexane, isooctane, and *n*-nonane, or equivalent
    Temperature
      Column: 120° (isothermal)
      Injection port: 240°
      Detector: 250°
    Carrier gas: Helium
    Flow rate: 30 mL/min.
    Injection volume: 5 μL
  Analysis: Separately inject the *Standard solution* and the *Sample preparation* into the chromatograph (duplicate injections for each) and record the resulting chromatograms. Measure the areas under the hexane and *n*-nonane peaks on the resulting chromatograms.
  Acceptance criteria: The peak area ratio of hexane to *n*-nonane (i.e., sum of hexane areas divided by sum of *n*-nonane areas) produced by the *Sample preparation* does not exceed that produced by the *Standard solution*. (NMT 0.01%)
- **Residual Styrene,** Appendix IV
  Acceptance criteria: NMT 0.003%

SPECIFIC TESTS
- **Bound Styrene,** Appendix IV
  Acceptance criteria: Between 1.0% and 50.0%

142 / Butadiene-Styrene Rubber / *Monographs*

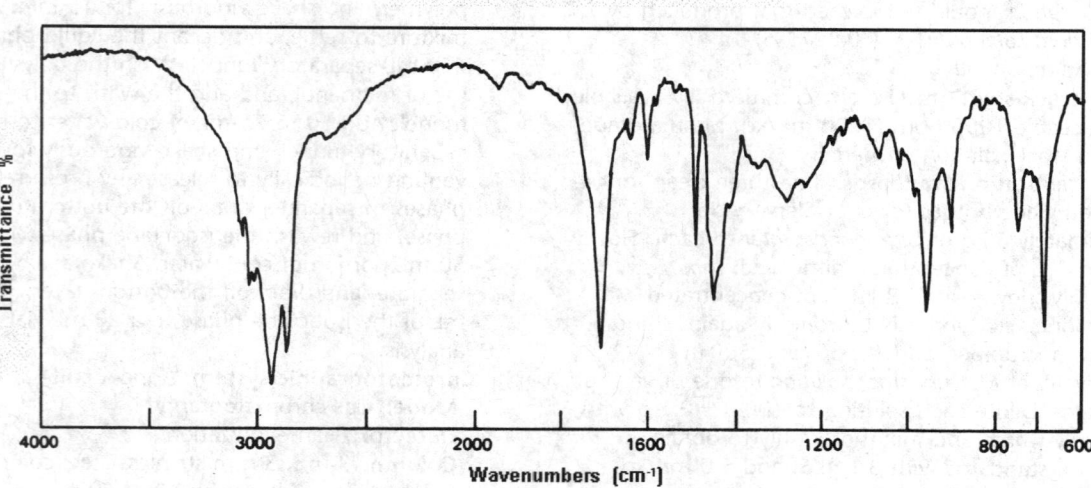

Butadiene-Styrene 50/50 Rubber (Solid)

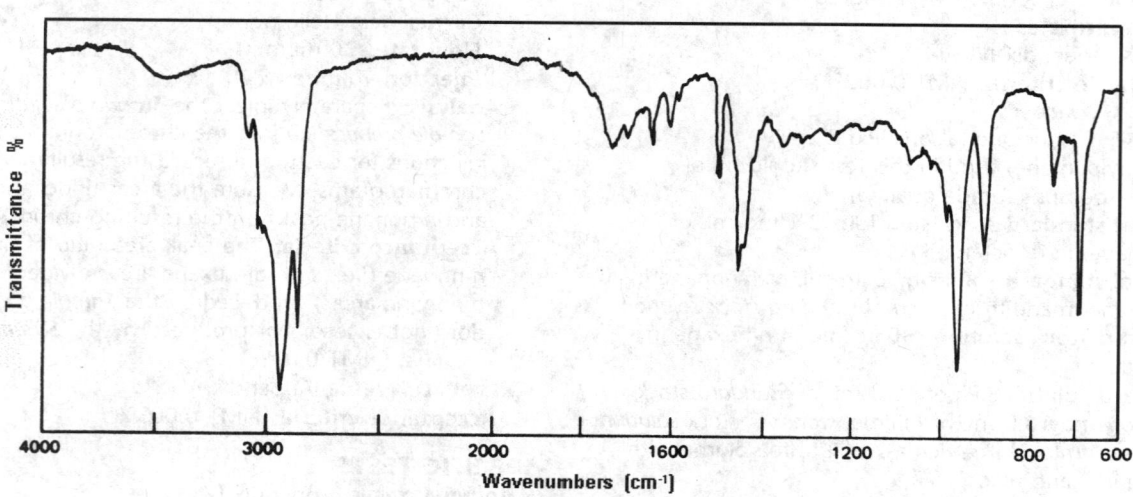

Butadiene-Styrene 75/25 Rubber (Emulsion-Polymerized Latex)

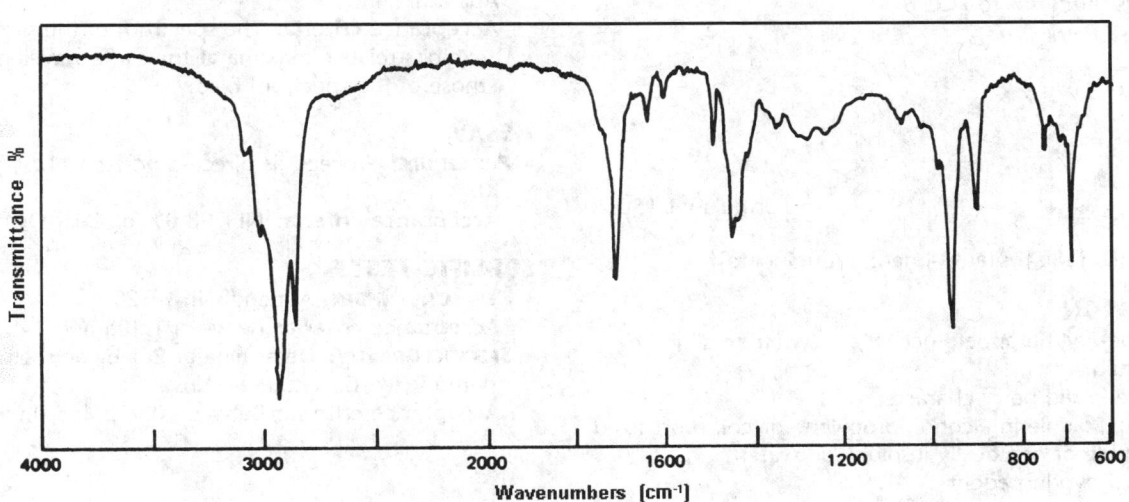

Butadiene-Styrene 75/25 Rubber (Emulsion-Polymerized Solid)

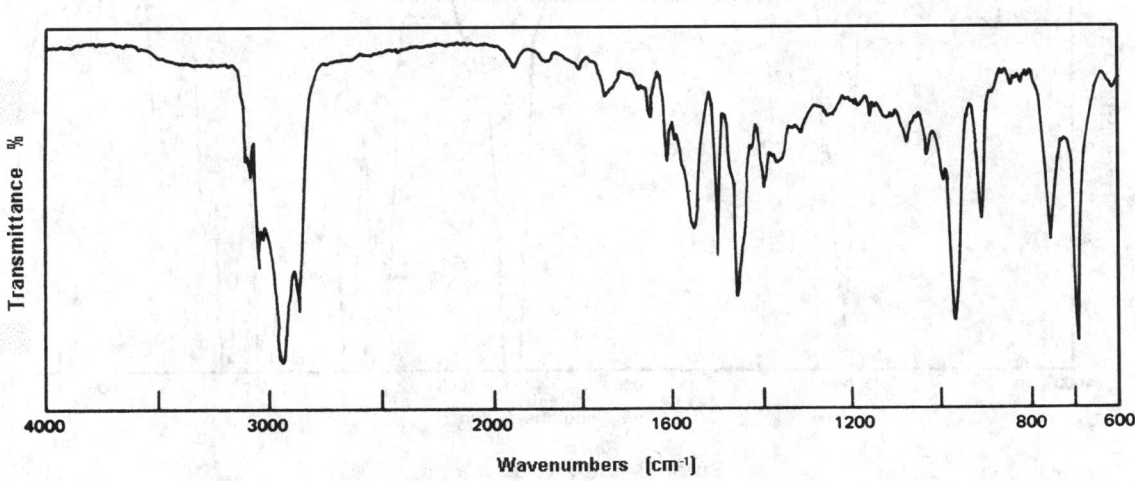

Butadiene-Styrene 50/50 Rubber (Latex)

Butan-3-one-2-yl Butanoate

First Published: Prior to FCC 6

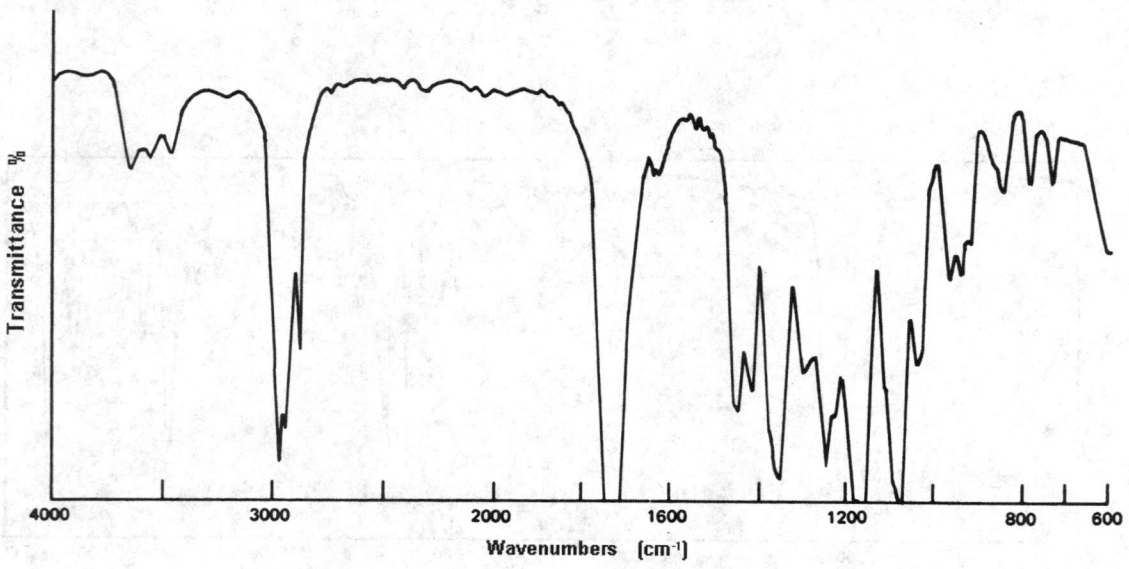

C₈H₁₄O₃   Formula wt 158.20
FEMA: 3332
UNII: SEN8DCI58L [butan-3-one-2-yl butanoate]

DESCRIPTION
Butan-3-one-2-yl Butanoate occurs as a white to slightly yellow liquid.
Odor: Sweet, red berry character
Solubility: Soluble in alcohol, propylene glycol, most fixed oils; insoluble or practically insoluble in water
Function: Flavoring agent

IDENTIFICATION
- **INFRARED SPECTRA,** *Spectrophotometric Identification Tests,* Appendix IIIC
  Acceptance criteria: The spectrum of the sample exhibits relative maxima at the same wavelengths as those of the spectrum below.

ASSAY
- **PROCEDURE:** Proceed as directed under *M-1a,* Appendix XI.
  Acceptance criteria: NLT 98.0% of C₈H₁₄O₃

SPECIFIC TESTS
- **REFRACTIVE INDEX,** Appendix II: At 20°
  Acceptance criteria: Between 1.408 and 1.429
- **SPECIFIC GRAVITY:** Determine at 25° by any reliable method (see *General Provisions*).
  Acceptance criteria: Between 0.972 and 0.992

Butan-3-one-2-yl Butanoate

Butane

First Published: Prior to FCC 6
Last Revision: FCC 6

n-Butane

C_4H_{10}
INS: 943a
UNII: 6LV4FOR43R [butane]
Formula wt 58.12
CAS: [106-97-8]

DESCRIPTION
Butane occurs as a colorless, flammable gas. One volume of water dissolves 0.15 volume; 1 volume of alcohol dissolves 18 volumes; 1 volume of ether dissolves 25 volumes, at 17° and 770 mm Hg. Its boiling temperature is −0.5°.
Function: Propellant; aerating agent
Packaging and Storage: Store in tight cylinders protected from heat.
[CAUTION—Butane is highly flammable and explosive. Observe precautions and perform sampling and analytical operations in a well-ventilated fume hood.]

[NOTE—For obtaining a test sample of gas, use a stainless steel specimen cylinder equipped with a stainless steel valve and having a capacity of not less than 200 mL and a pressure rating of 240 psi or more. Dry the cylinder with the valve open at 110° for 2 h, and evacuate the hot cylinder to less than 1 mm Hg. Close the valve, and cool and weigh the cylinder. Tightly connect one end of a charging line to the sample cylinder, and loosely connect the other end to the specimen cylinder. Carefully open the sample cylinder, and allow the sample gas to flush out the charging line through the loose connection. Avoid excessive flushing that causes moisture to freeze in the charging line and connections. Tighten the fitting on the specimen cylinder, and open its valve, allowing the sample gas to flow into the evacuated cylinder. Continue until the desired amount of sample gas is obtained, then close the sample cylinder valve, and finally, close the specimen cylinder valve. Weigh the charged specimen cylinder again, and calculate the sample gas weight.]
[CAUTION—Do not overload the specimen cylinder.]

IDENTIFICATION
- **INFRARED ABSORPTION SPECTRUM**
  Acceptance criteria: The spectrum of a sample exhibits absorptions, among others, at approximately 3.4 μm (vs), 6.8 μm (s), 7.2 μm (m), and 10.4 μm (m).
- **VAPOR PRESSURE**
  Analysis: Determine the vapor pressure of the sample gas at 21° by means of a suitable pressure gauge.
  Acceptance criteria: Approximately 213 kPa absolute (31 psia)

ASSAY
- **PROCEDURE**
  Chromatographic system, Appendix IIA
  Mode: Gas chromatography
  Detector: Thermal conductivity
  Column: 6-m × 3-mm aluminum column, or equivalent, packed with 10 weight percent tetraethylene glycol dimethyl ether liquid phase on a support of crushed firebrick (GasChrom R, or equivalent), which has been calcined or burned with a clay binder above 900° and silanized, or equivalent
  Column temperature: 33°
  Carrier gas: Helium
  Flow rate: 50 mL/min
  Injection volume: 2 μL
  System suitability
    Sample: Sample gas
    Suitability requirement: The peak responses obtained for the sample gas in the chromatograms from duplicate determinations agree within 1%.
  Analysis: Connect one sample cylinder to the chromatograph through a suitable sampling valve and a flow control valve downstream from the sampling valve. Flush the liquid sample through the sampling valve, taking care to avoid trapping gas or air in the valve. Inject a sample and record the chromatogram. Calculate the purity of the sample using the following formula:

  $$\text{Result} = 100S/\Sigma s$$

  S = sample peak response
  Σs = sum of all of the peak responses in the chromatogram
  Acceptance criteria: NLT 97.0% of C_4H_{10}

IMPURITIES
Inorganic Impurities
- **WATER,** *Water Determination,* Appendix IIB
  Sample: 100 g (see *Note* above on sampling)
  Analysis: Proceed as directed using the following modifications: (a) Provide the closed-system titrating vessel with an opening and pass through it a coarse-porosity gas dispersion tube connected to a sampling cylinder. (b) Dilute the reagent with anhydrous methanol to give a water equivalence factor of between 0.2 and 1.0 mg/mL; age this diluted solution for not less than 16h before standardization. (c) Introduce the gas *Sample* into the titration vessel through the gas dispersion tube at a rate of about 100 mL/min; if necessary, heat the sampling cylinder gently to maintain this flow rate.
  Acceptance criteria: NMT 10 mg/kg

Organic Impurities
- **HIGH-BOILING RESIDUE**
  Analysis: Prepare a cooling coil from copper tubing (about 6.1 m × 6 mm (od)) to fit into a suitable vacuum-jacketed flask. Immerse the cooling coil in a mixture of Dry Ice and acetone in a vacuum-jacketed flask, and connect one end of the tubing to the sample cylinder (see *Note* above on sampling). Carefully open the sample cylinder valve, flush the cooling coil with about 50 mL of the liquified sample, and discard this portion of liquid. Continue delivering liquid from the cooling coil, and collect it in a previously chilled 1000-

mL sedimentation cone until the cone is filled to the 1000-mL mark (approximately 600 g). Using a warm water bath maintained at about 40° to reduce evaporating time, allow the liquid to evaporate. When all of the liquid has evaporated, rinse the sedimentation cone with two 50-mL portions of pentane, and combine the rinsings in a tared 150-mL evaporating dish. Transfer 100 mL of the pentane solvent to a second, tared 150-mL evaporating dish, place both evaporating dishes on a water bath, evaporate to dryness, and heat the dishes in an oven at 100° for 60 min. Cool the dishes in a desiccator, and weigh them. Repeat the heating for 15-min periods until successive weighings are within 0.1 mg. [NOTE—Retain the residue for the test for *Acidity of Residue* (below).] The weight of the residue obtained from the sample is the difference between the weights of the residues in the two evaporating dishes. Calculate the mg/kg of high-boiling residue based on a sample weight of 600 g.
Acceptance criteria: NMT 5 mg/kg
- **SULFUR COMPOUNDS**
Analysis: Carefully open the container valve to produce a moderate flow of gas. Do not direct the gas stream toward the face, but deflect a portion of the stream toward the nose.
Acceptance criteria: The gas is free from the characteristic odor of sulfur compounds.

SPECIFIC TESTS
- **ACIDITY OF RESIDUE**
Sample: The residue obtained in the test for *High-Boiling Residue* (above)
Analysis: Add 10 mL of water to the *Sample*, mix by swirling for about 30 s, add 2 drops of methyl orange TS, insert the stopper in the tube, and shake the tube vigorously.
Acceptance criteria: No pink or red color appears in the aqueous layer.

2-Butanone

First Published: Prior to FCC 6

Methyl Ethyl Ketone

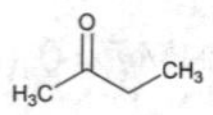

C_4H_8O Formula wt 72.11

FEMA: 2170
UNII: 6PT9KLV9IO [methyl ethyl ketone]

DESCRIPTION
2-Butanone occurs as a colorless, mobile liquid.
Odor: Ethereal, nauseating
Solubility: One mL dissolves in 4 mL of water; miscible in alcohol, ether, and most fixed oils
Boiling Point: ~78.6° to 80°
Function: Flavoring agent

IDENTIFICATION
- **INFRARED SPECTRA,** *Spectrophotometric Identification Tests,* Appendix IIIC
Acceptance criteria: The spectrum of the sample exhibits relative maxima at the same wavelengths as those of the spectrum below.

ASSAY
- **PROCEDURE:** Proceed as directed under *M-1b*, Appendix XI.
Acceptance criteria: NLT 99.5% of C_4H_8O

SPECIFIC TESTS
- **ACID VALUE, FLAVOR CHEMICALS (OTHER THAN ESSENTIAL OILS),** *M-15,* Appendix XI
Acceptance criteria: NMT 2.0
- **REFRACTIVE INDEX,** Appendix II: At 20°
Acceptance criteria: Between 1.375 and 1.384
- **SPECIFIC GRAVITY:** Determine at 25° by any reliable method (see *General Provisions*).
Acceptance criteria: Between 0.801 and 0.803

OTHER REQUIREMENTS
- **DISTILLATION RANGE,** Appendix IIB
Acceptance criteria: Within 1.5°
- **WATER,** *Water Determination, Method I,* Appendix IIB: [NOTE—Use freshly distilled pyridine as solvent.]
Acceptance criteria: NMT 0.2%

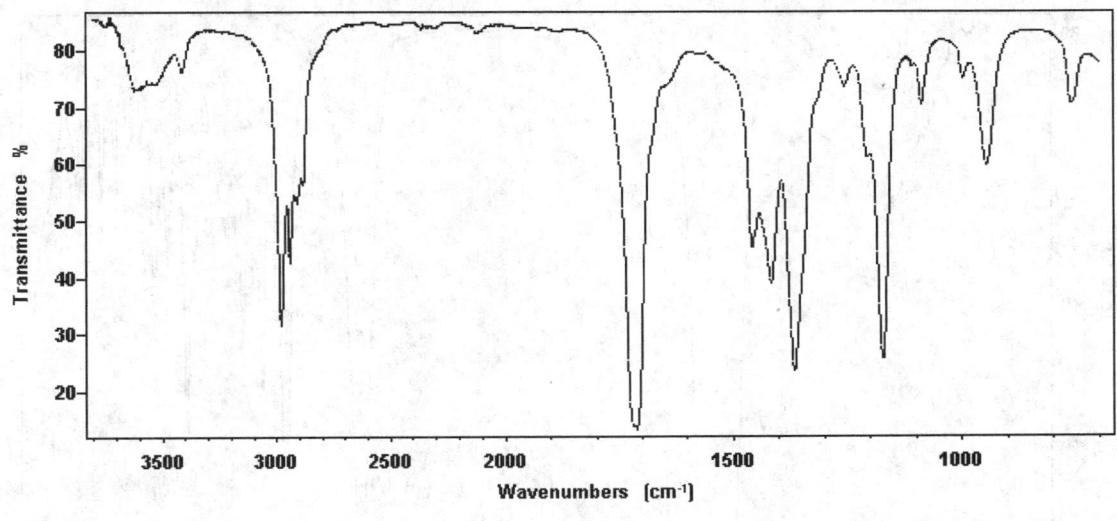

2-Butanone

2-sec-Butyl Cyclohexanone

First Published: Prior to FCC 6

Freskomenthe

$C_{10}H_{18}O$ Formula wt 154.25
FEMA: 3261
UNII: 5WA6R1KL5J [2-sec-butyl cyclohexanone]

DESCRIPTION
2-sec-Butyl Cyclohexanone occurs as a colorless to pale yellow liquid.
Odor: Camphoraceous
Solubility: Soluble in propylene glycol, vegetable oils; insoluble or practically insoluble in water
Boiling Point: ~76° (8 mm Hg)
Solubility in Alcohol, Appendix VI: One mL dissolves in 1 mL of 95% ethanol.

Function: Flavoring agent

IDENTIFICATION
- **INFRARED SPECTRA,** Spectrophotometric Identification Tests, Appendix IIIC
  Acceptance criteria: The spectrum of the sample exhibits relative maxima at the same wavelengths as those of the spectrum below.

ASSAY
- **PROCEDURE:** Proceed as directed under M-1b, Appendix XI.
  Acceptance criteria: NLT 97.0% of $C_{10}H_{18}O$ (sum of two isomers)

SPECIFIC TESTS
- **REFRACTIVE INDEX,** Appendix II: At 20°
  Acceptance criteria: Between 1.456 and 1.462
- **SPECIFIC GRAVITY:** Determine at 25° by any reliable method (see General Provisions).
  Acceptance criteria: Between 0.910 and 0.915

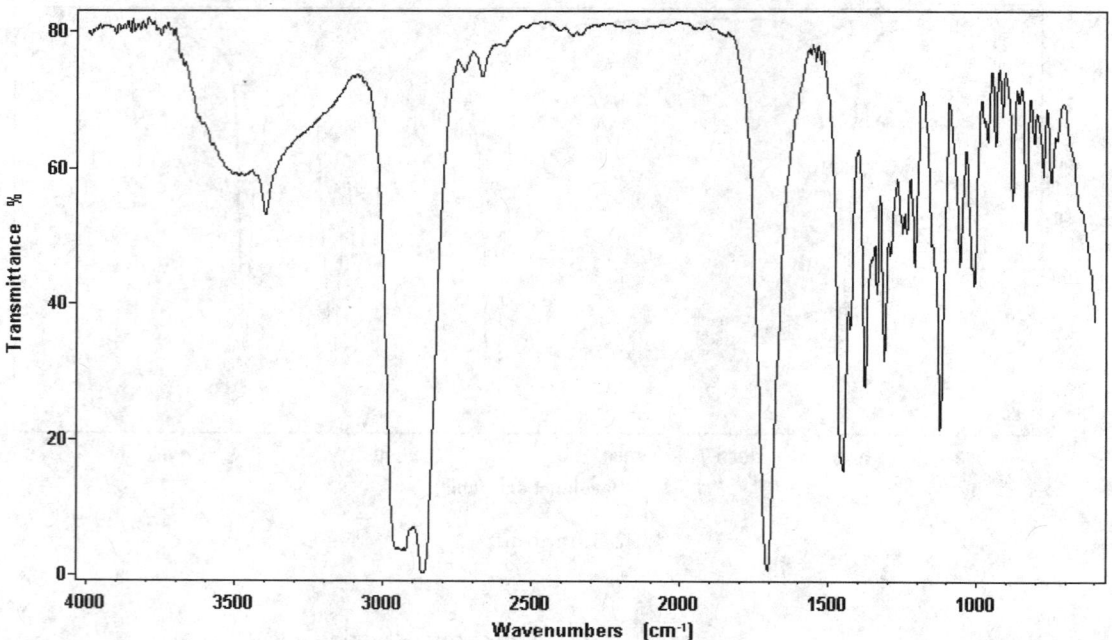

2-sec-Butyl Cyclohexanone

Butyl 2-Methyl Butyrate

First Published: Prior to FCC 6

$C_9H_{18}O_2$ Formula wt 158.24
FEMA: 3393
UNII: W313K2V7PG [butyl 2-methyl butyrate]

DESCRIPTION
Butyl 2-Methyl Butyrate occurs as a colorless to pale yellow liquid.
Odor: Fruity
Solubility: Soluble in propylene glycol, vegetable oils; insoluble or practically insoluble in water
Boiling Point: ~173° (730 mm Hg)
Solubility in Alcohol, Appendix VI: One mL dissolves in 1 mL of 95% ethanol.

Function: Flavoring agent

IDENTIFICATION
- **INFRARED SPECTRA,** *Spectrophotometric Identification Tests,* Appendix IIIC
  Acceptance criteria: The spectrum of the sample exhibits relative maxima at the same wavelengths as those of the spectrum below.

ASSAY
- **PROCEDURE:** Proceed as directed under *M-1b,* Appendix XI.
  Acceptance criteria: NLT 98.0% of $C_9H_{18}O_2$

SPECIFIC TESTS
- **ACID VALUE, FLAVOR CHEMICALS (OTHER THAN ESSENTIAL OILS),** *M-15,* Appendix XI
  Acceptance criteria: NMT 1.0
- **REFRACTIVE INDEX,** Appendix II: At 20°
  Acceptance criteria: Between 1.407 and 1.413
- **SPECIFIC GRAVITY:** Determine at 25° by any reliable method (see *General Provisions*).
  Acceptance criteria: Between 0.858 and 0.863

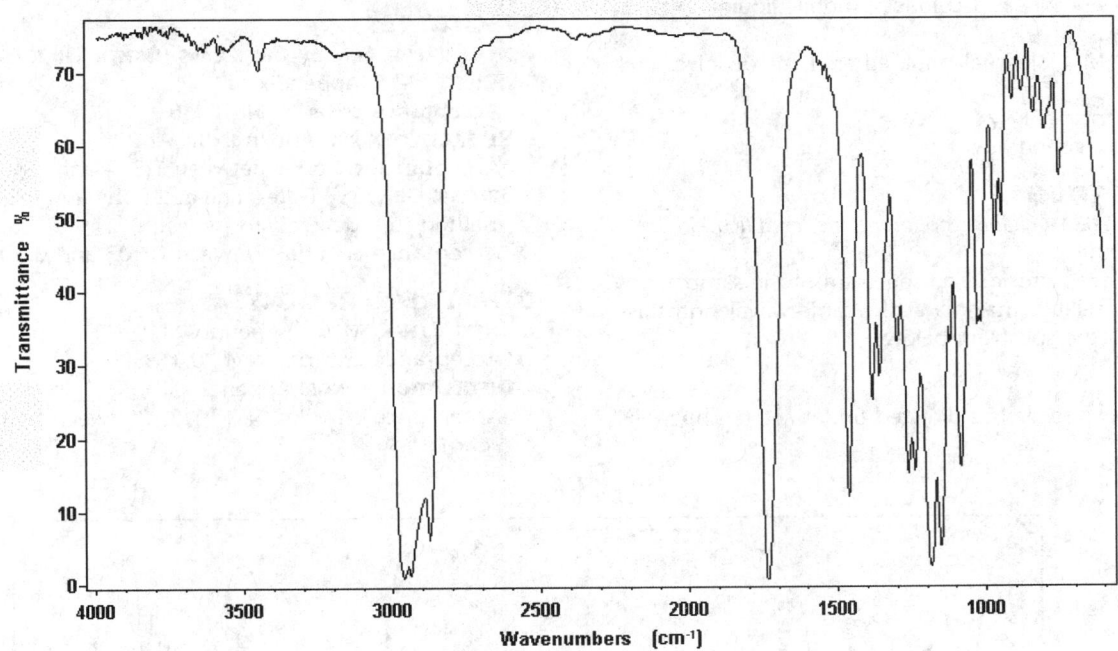

Butyl 2-Methyl Butyrate

Butyl Acetate

First Published: Prior to FCC 6
Last Revision: FCC 7

n-Butyl Acetate

C₆H₁₂O₂   Formula wt 116.16
FEMA: 2174
UNII: 464P5N1905 [butyl acetate]

DESCRIPTION
Butyl Acetate occurs as a colorless, mobile liquid.
Odor: Strong, fruity
Solubility: Miscible in alcohol, ether, propylene glycol; one mL in 145 mL water
Boiling Point: ~126°
Function: Flavoring agent

IDENTIFICATION
- **INFRARED ABSORPTION**, *Spectrophotometric Identification Tests*, Appendix IIIC
  Reference standard: USP Butyl Acetate RS
  Sample and standard preparation: *F*
  Acceptance criteria: The spectrum of the sample exhibits maxima at the same wavelengths as those in the spectrum of the *Reference standard*.

ASSAY
- **PROCEDURE:** Proceed as directed under *M-1b*, Appendix XI.
  Acceptance criteria: NLT 98.0% of C₆H₁₂O₂

SPECIFIC TESTS
- **ACID VALUE, FLAVOR CHEMICALS (OTHER THAN ESSENTIAL OILS)**, *M-15*, Appendix XI
  Acceptance criteria: NMT 2.0
- **REFRACTIVE INDEX**, Appendix II: At 20°
  Acceptance criteria: Between 1.393 and 1.396
- **SPECIFIC GRAVITY:** Determine at 25° by any reliable method (see *General Provisions*).
  Acceptance criteria: Between 0.876 and 0.880

OTHER REQUIREMENTS
- **DISTILLATION RANGE**, Appendix IIB
  Acceptance criteria: Between 120° and 128°

Butyl Alcohol

First Published: Prior to FCC 6

1-Butanol

C₄H₁₀O   Formula wt 74.12
FEMA: 2178
UNII: 8PJ61P6TS3 [butyl alcohol]

150 / Butyl Alcohol / *Monographs*

Butyl Alcohol

DESCRIPTION
Butyl Alcohol occurs as a colorless, mobile liquid.
Odor: Vinous
Solubility: Miscible in alcohol, ether; 1 mL dissolves in 15 mL water
Boiling Point: ~117.7°
Function: Flavoring agent

IDENTIFICATION
- **INFRARED SPECTRA,** *Spectrophotometric Identification Tests,* Appendix IIIC
  Acceptance criteria: The spectrum of the sample exhibits relative maxima at the same wavelengths as those of the spectrum below.

ASSAY
- **PROCEDURE:** Proceed as directed under *M-1b,* Appendix XI.
  Acceptance criteria: NLT 99.5% of $C_4H_{10}O$

SPECIFIC TESTS
- **ACID VALUE, FLAVOR CHEMICALS (OTHER THAN ESSENTIAL OILS),** *M-15,* Appendix XI
  Acceptance criteria: NMT 2.0
- **REFRACTIVE INDEX,** Appendix II: At 20°
  Acceptance criteria: Between 1.397 and 1.402
- **SPECIFIC GRAVITY:** Determine at 25° by any reliable method (see *General Provisions*).
  Acceptance criteria: Between 0.807 and 0.809

OTHER REQUIREMENTS
- **BUTYL ETHER,** *M-1b,* Appendix XI
  Acceptance criteria: NMT 0.15%
- **DISTILLATION RANGE,** Appendix IIB
  Acceptance criteria: NMT 1.5° (between beginning and end)

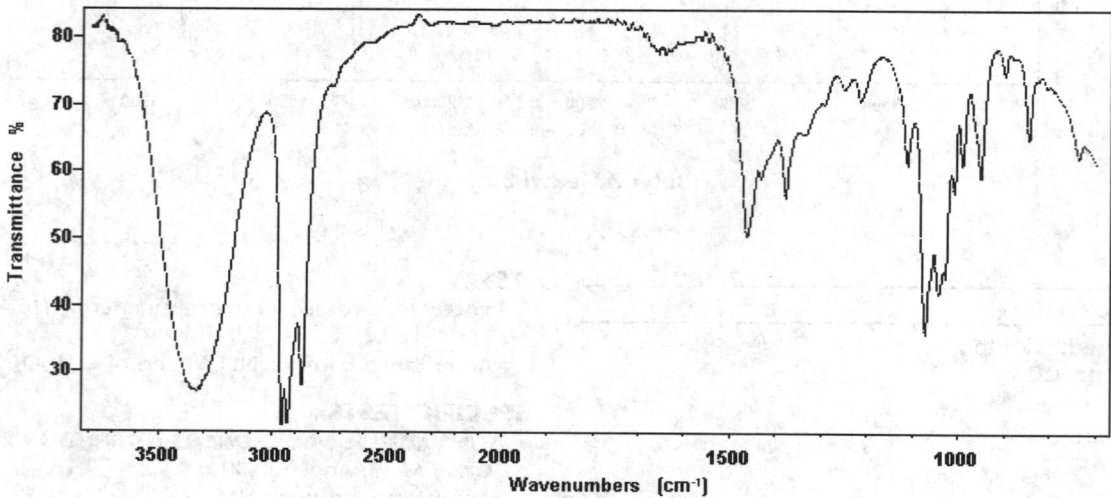

Butyl Alcohol

Butyl Butyrate

First Published: Prior to FCC 6

n-Butyl *n*-Butyrate

$C_8H_{16}O_2$ Formula wt 144.21
FEMA: 2186
UNII: 1BHV00T1M4 [butyl butyrate]

DESCRIPTION
Butyl Butyrate occurs as a colorless liquid.
Odor: Fruity, pineapple on dilution
Solubility: Slightly soluble in propylene glycol, water; miscible in alcohol, ether, most vegetable oils; 1 mL dissolves in 3 mL 70% alcohol
Boiling Point: ~165°
Function: Flavoring agent

IDENTIFICATION
- **INFRARED SPECTRA,** *Spectrophotometric Identification Tests,* Appendix IIIC
  Acceptance criteria: The spectrum of the sample exhibits relative maxima at the same wavelengths as those of the spectrum below.

ASSAY
- **PROCEDURE:** Proceed as directed under *M-1b,* Appendix XI.
  Acceptance criteria: NLT 98.0% of $C_8H_{16}O_2$

SPECIFIC TESTS
- **ACID VALUE, FLAVOR CHEMICALS (OTHER THAN ESSENTIAL OILS),** *M-15,* Appendix XI
  Acceptance criteria: NMT 1.0
- **REFRACTIVE INDEX,** Appendix II: At 20°
  Acceptance criteria: Between 1.405 and 1.407
- **SPECIFIC GRAVITY:** Determine at 25° by any reliable method (see *General Provisions*).
  Acceptance criteria: Between 0.867 and 0.871

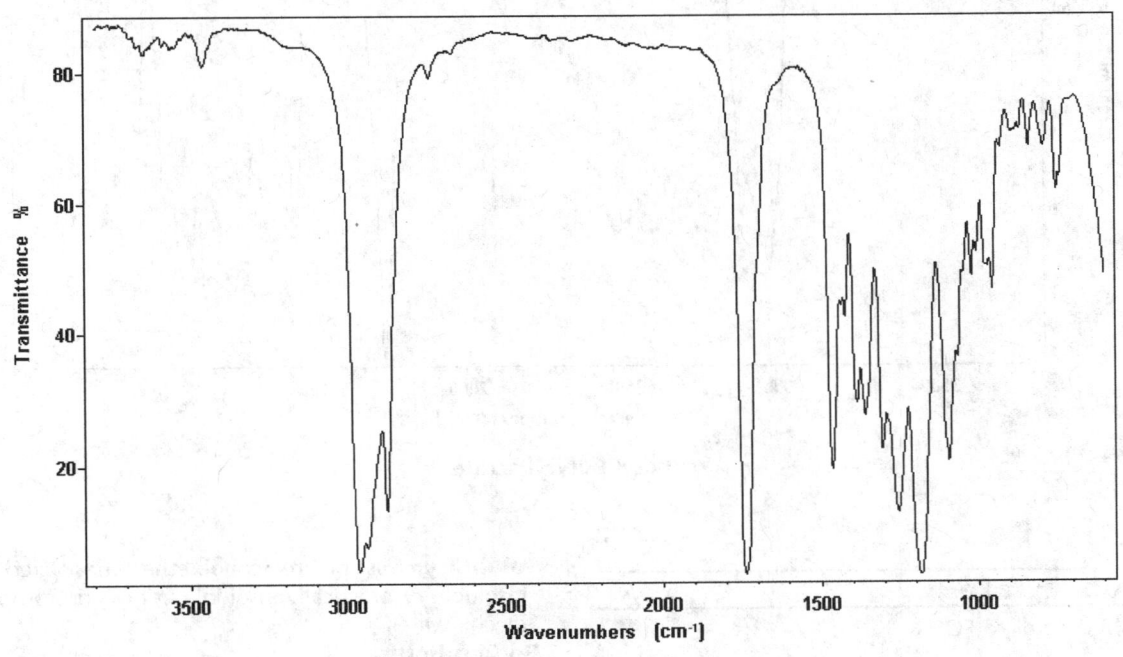

Butyl Butyrate

Butyl Butyryllactate

First Published: Prior to FCC 6

Butyl Ester
Butyrate
Butyryllactic Acid
Lactic Acid

$C_{11}H_{20}O_4$ Formula wt 216.28
FEMA: 2190
UNII: OCR0ONT89C [butyl butyryllactate]

DESCRIPTION
Butyl Butyryllactate occurs as a colorless liquid.
Odor: Mild, buttery, cream

152 / Butyl Butyryllactate / *Monographs*

Solubility: Soluble in propylene glycol; miscible in alcohol, most fixed oils; insoluble or practically insoluble in water
Solubility in Alcohol, Appendix VI: One mL dissolves in 3 mL of 70% alcohol.
Function: Flavoring agent

IDENTIFICATION

- **INFRARED SPECTRA,** *Spectrophotometric Identification Tests,* Appendix IIIC
  Acceptance criteria: The spectrum of the sample exhibits relative maxima at the same wavelengths as those of the spectrum below.

ASSAY

- **PROCEDURE:** Proceed as directed under *M-1b,* Appendix XI.
  Acceptance criteria: NLT 95.0% of $C_{11}H_{20}O_4$

SPECIFIC TESTS

- **ACID VALUE, FLAVOR CHEMICALS (OTHER THAN ESSENTIAL OILS),** *M-15,* Appendix XI
  Acceptance criteria: NMT 1.0
- **REFRACTIVE INDEX,** Appendix II: At 20°
  Acceptance criteria: Between 1.420 and 1.423
- **SPECIFIC GRAVITY:** Determine at 25° by any reliable method (see *General Provisions*).
  Acceptance criteria: Between 0.970 and 0.974

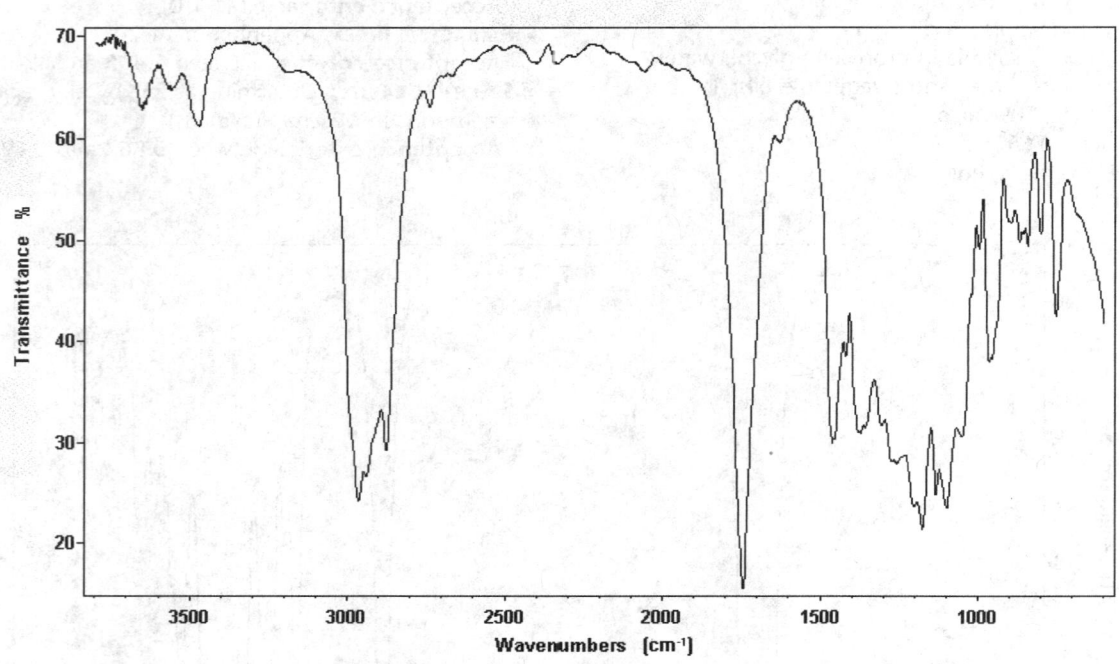

Butyl Butyryllactate

Butyl Isobutyrate

First Published: Prior to FCC 6

$C_8H_{16}O_2$ Formula wt 144.21
FEMA: 2188
UNII: PW9UJ5C0F3 [butyl isobutyrate]

DESCRIPTION

Butyl Isobutyrate occurs as a colorless liquid.
Odor: Fresh, fruity, apple-pineapple

Solubility: Miscible in alcohol, ether, most fixed oils; insoluble or practically insoluble in glycerin, propylene glycol, water
Boiling Point: ~166°
Solubility in Alcohol, Appendix VI: One mL dissolves in 7 mL of 60% alcohol.
Function: Flavoring agent

IDENTIFICATION

- **INFRARED SPECTRA,** *Spectrophotometric Identification Tests,* Appendix IIIC
  Acceptance criteria: The spectrum of the sample exhibits relative maxima at the same wavelengths as those of the spectrum below.

ASSAY

- **PROCEDURE:** Proceed as directed under *M-1b,* Appendix XI.

Acceptance criteria: NLT 97.0% of $C_8H_{16}O_2$ (one isomer)

SPECIFIC TESTS
- **ACID VALUE, FLAVOR CHEMICALS (OTHER THAN ESSENTIAL OILS),** *M-15,* Appendix XI
  Acceptance criteria: NMT 1.0
- **REFRACTIVE INDEX,** Appendix II: At 20°
  Acceptance criteria: Between 1.401 and 1.404
- **SPECIFIC GRAVITY:** Determine at 25° by any reliable method (see *General Provisions*).
  Acceptance criteria: Between 0.859 and 0.864

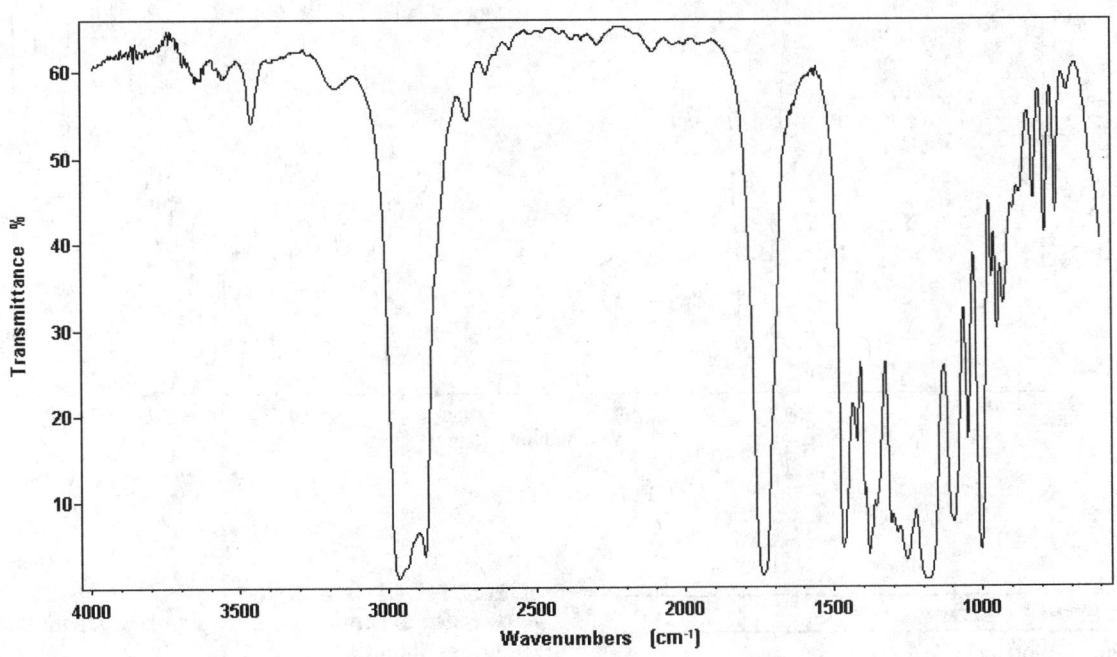

Butyl Isobutyrate

Butyl Isovalerate
First Published: Prior to FCC 6

$C_9H_{18}O_2$
FEMA: 2218
UNII: 4UX6V9QM2J [butyl isovalerate]

Formula wt 158.24

DESCRIPTION
Butyl Isovalerate occurs as a colorless to pale yellow liquid.
Odor: Fruity
Solubility: Soluble in alcohol, most fixed oils; insoluble or practically insoluble in propylene glycol, water
Boiling Point: ~175°
Solubility in Alcohol, Appendix VI: One mL dissolves in 1 mL of 95% alcohol.
Function: Flavoring agent

IDENTIFICATION
- **INFRARED SPECTRA,** *Spectrophotometric Identification Tests,* Appendix IIIC
  Acceptance criteria: The spectrum of the sample exhibits relative maxima at the same wavelengths as those of the spectrum below.

ASSAY
- **PROCEDURE:** Proceed as directed under *M-1b,* Appendix XI
  Acceptance criteria: NLT 97.0% of $C_9H_{18}O_2$ (one isomer)

SPECIFIC TESTS
- **ACID VALUE, FLAVOR CHEMICALS (OTHER THAN ESSENTIAL OILS),** *M-15,* Appendix XI
  Acceptance criteria: NMT 1.0
- **REFRACTIVE INDEX,** Appendix II: At 20°
  Acceptance criteria: Between 1.407 and 1.411
- **SPECIFIC GRAVITY:** Determine at 25° by any reliable method (see *General Provisions*).
  Acceptance criteria: Between 0.856 and 0.859

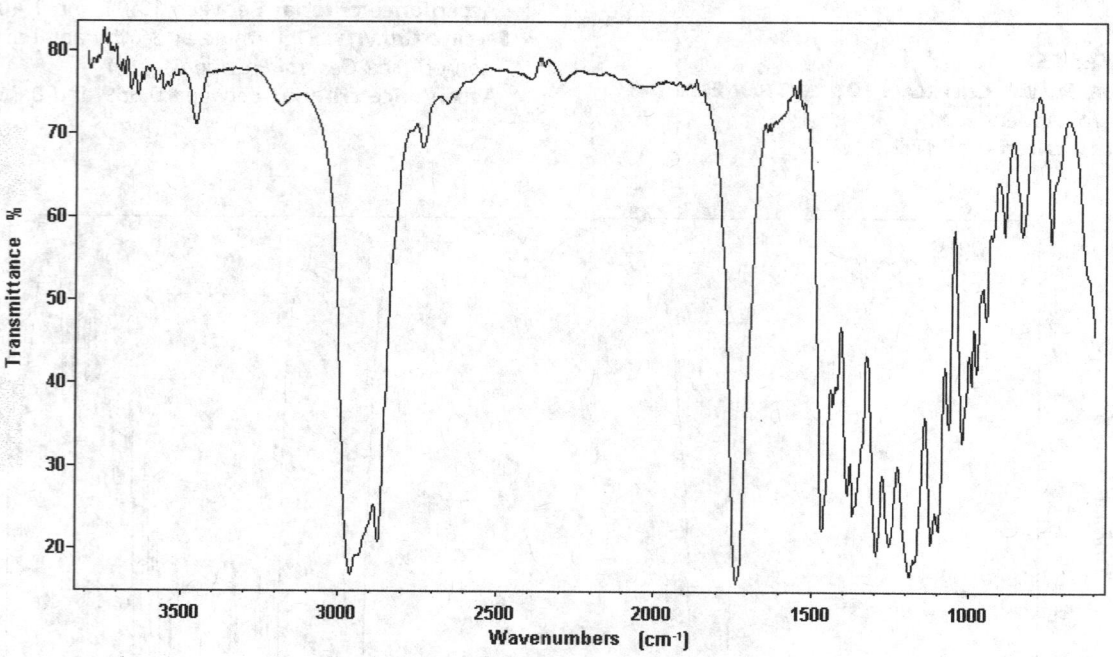
Butyl Isovalerate

Butyl Phenylacetate

First Published: Prior to FCC 6

$C_{12}H_{16}O_2$ Formula wt 196.26
FEMA: 2209
UNII: TR6RZ109SI [butyl phenylacetate]

DESCRIPTION
Butyl Phenylacetate occurs as a colorless to pale yellow liquid.
Odor: Honey, rose
Boiling Point: ~260°
Solubility in Alcohol, Appendix VI: One mL dissolving in 1 mL of 95% alcohol.
Function: Flavoring agent

IDENTIFICATION
- **INFRARED SPECTRA,** *Spectrophotometric Identification Tests,* Appendix IIIC
  Acceptance criteria: The spectrum of the sample exhibits relative maxima at the same wavelengths as those of the spectrum below.

ASSAY
- **PROCEDURE:** Proceed as directed under *M-1a,* Appendix XI.
  Acceptance criteria: NLT 98.0% of $C_{12}H_{16}O_2$

SPECIFIC TESTS
- **ACID VALUE, FLAVOR CHEMICALS (OTHER THAN ESSENTIAL OILS),** *M-15,* Appendix XI
  Acceptance criteria: NMT 1.0
- **REFRACTIVE INDEX,** Appendix II: At 20°
  Acceptance criteria: Between 1.488 and 1.492
- **SPECIFIC GRAVITY:** Determine at 25° by any reliable method (see *General Provisions*).
  Acceptance criteria: Between 0.990 and 0.997

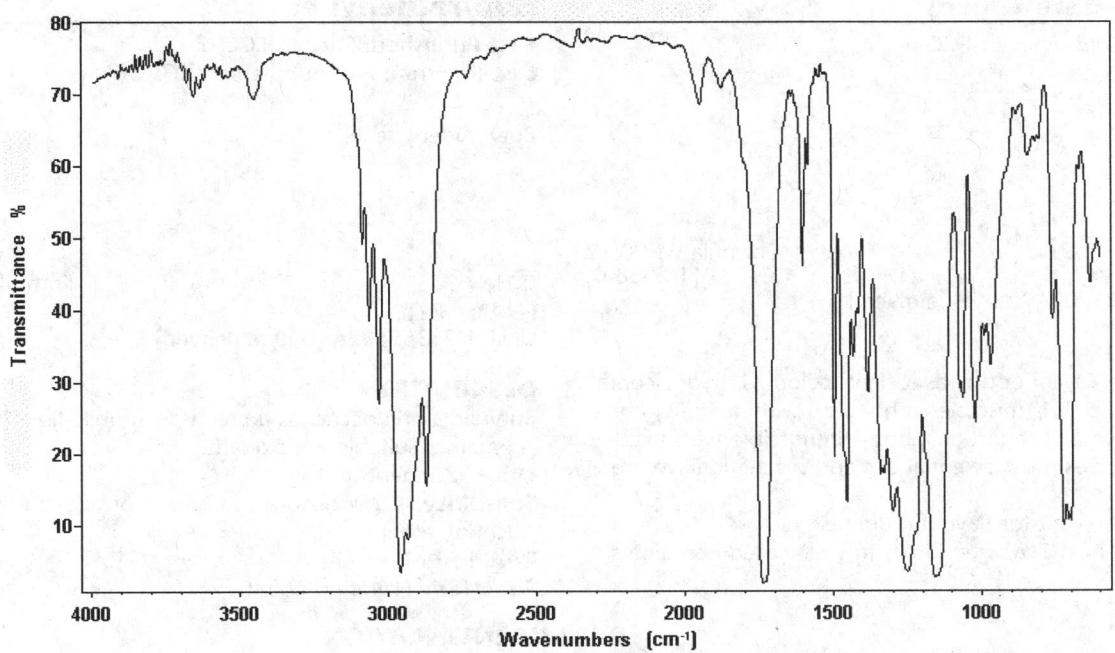

Butyl Phenylacetate

Butyl Stearate

First Published: Prior to FCC 6

Butyl Octadecanoate

$C_{22}H_{44}O_2$ Formula wt 340.59
FEMA: 2214
UNII: 6Y0AI5605C [butyl stearate]

DESCRIPTION
Butyl Stearate occurs as a colorless, waxy solid.
Odor: Odorless to faintly fatty
Solubility: Soluble in alcohol, most fixed oils; insoluble or practically insoluble in propylene glycol, water
Boiling Point: ~223°
Solubility in Alcohol, Appendix VI: One mL dissolves in 6 mL of 95% alcohol.
Function: Flavoring agent

OTHER REQUIREMENTS
- **IODINE VALUE,** Appendix VII
  Acceptance criteria: NMT 1
- **MELTING RANGE OR TEMPERATURE DETERMINATION,** Appendix IIB
  Acceptance criteria: Between 17° and 21°
- **SAPONIFICATION VALUE,** Appendix VI
  Acceptance criteria: Between 165 and 180

Butylated Hydroxymethylphenol

First Published: Prior to FCC 6

$C_{15}H_{24}O_2$ Formula wt 236.35
UNII: 46ND6GQI48 [butylated hydroxymethylphenol]

DESCRIPTION
Butylated Hydroxymethylphenol occurs as a nearly white, crystalline solid. It is freely soluble in alcohol, and insoluble in water and in propylene glycol.
Function: Antioxidant
Packaging and Storage: Store in well-closed containers.

IDENTIFICATION
- **PROCEDURE**
  Analysis: Butylated Hydroxymethylphenol may be identified by its solidification point, as determined in the *Assay* (below).
  Acceptance criteria: Passes test

ASSAY
- **SOLIDIFICATION POINT,** Appendix IIB
  Acceptance criteria: The solidification point is NLT 140° (indicating a purity of NLT 98.0%, by weight of $C_{15}H_{24}O_2$).

1,3-Butylene Glycol

First Published: Prior to FCC 6

Butane-1,3-diol

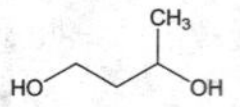

C$_4$H$_{10}$O$_2$　　　　　　　　　　Formula wt 90.12
　　　　　　　　　　　　　　　CAS: [107-88-0]
UNII: 3XUS85K0RA [butylene glycol]

DESCRIPTION
1,3-Butylene Glycol occurs as a clear, colorless, hygroscopic, viscous liquid. It is miscible with water, with acetone, and with ether in all proportions, but is immiscible with fixed oils. It dissolves most essential oils and synthetic flavoring substances.
Function: Solvent for flavoring agents
Packaging and Storage: Store in well-closed containers.

ASSAY
- **PROCEDURE**
  Acetylating reagent: Prepare within one week of use, by mixing 3.4 mL of water and 130 mL of acetic anhydride with 1000 mL of anhydrous pyridine.
  Sample: 1 g
  Analysis: Pipet 20 mL of *Acetylating reagent* into a 250-mL iodine flask and add the *Sample*. Attach a dry reflux condenser to the flask, and reflux for 1 h. Allow the flask to cool to room temperature, then rinse the condenser with 50 mL of chilled (10°) carbon dioxide-free water, allowing the water to drain into the flask. Stopper the flask, cool to below 20°, and add phenolphthalein TS. Titrate with 0.5 N sodium hydroxide, swirling the contents of the flask continuously during the titration. Perform a blank determination (see *General Provisions*), and make any necessary correction. Each mL of 0.5 N sodium hydroxide is equivalent to 22.53 mg of C$_4$H$_{10}$O$_2$.
  Acceptance criteria: NLT 99.0% of C$_4$H$_{10}$O$_2$

IMPURITIES
Inorganic Impurities
- **LEAD,** *Lead Limit Test, Atomic Absorption Spectrophotometric Graphite Furnace Method, Method I,* Appendix IIIB
  Acceptance criteria: NMT 2 mg/kg

SPECIFIC TESTS
- **DISTILLATION RANGE,** Appendix IIB
  Acceptance criteria: Between 200° and 215°
- **SPECIFIC GRAVITY:** Determine by any reliable method (see *General Provisions*).
  Acceptance criteria: Between 1.004 and 1.006 at 20°

Butyraldehyde

First Published: Prior to FCC 6
Last Revision: First Supplement, FCC 6

Butyl Aldehyde

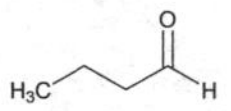

C$_4$H$_8$O　　　　　　　　　　　　Formula wt 72.11
FEMA: 2219
UNII: H21352682A [butyraldehyde]

DESCRIPTION
Butyraldehyde occurs as a colorless, mobile liquid. It may contain a suitable antioxidant.
Odor: Pungent, nutty
Solubility: 1 mL dissolves in 15 mL of water; miscible in alcohol, ether
Boiling Point: ~74.8°
Function: Flavoring agent

IDENTIFICATION
- **INFRARED SPECTRA, INFRARED SPECTRA,** *Spectrophotometric Identification Tests,* Appendix IIIC
  Acceptance criteria: The spectrum of the sample exhibits relative maxima at the same wavelengths as those of the spectrum below.

ASSAY
- **PROCEDURE:** Proceed as directed under *M-2c,* Appendix XI.
  Acceptance criteria: NLT 98.0% of C$_4$H$_8$O

SPECIFIC TESTS
- **ACID VALUE, FLAVOR CHEMICALS (OTHER THAN ESSENTIAL OILS),** *M-15,* Appendix XI: Use methyl red TS as the indicator.
  Acceptance criteria: NMT 5.0
- **REFRACTIVE INDEX,** Appendix II: At 20°
  Acceptance criteria: Between 1.381 and 1.387
- **SPECIFIC GRAVITY:** Determine at 25° by any reliable method (see *General Provisions*).
  Acceptance criteria: Between 0.797 and 0.802

OTHER REQUIREMENTS
- **DISTILLATION RANGE,** Appendix IIB
  Acceptance criteria: Between 72° and 80° (first 95%)
- ***para*-BUTYRALDEHYDE,** *M-1b,* Appendix XI
  Acceptance criteria: NMT 2.5%
- **WATER,** *Water Determination, Method I,* Appendix IIB
  Acceptance criteria: NMT 0.5%

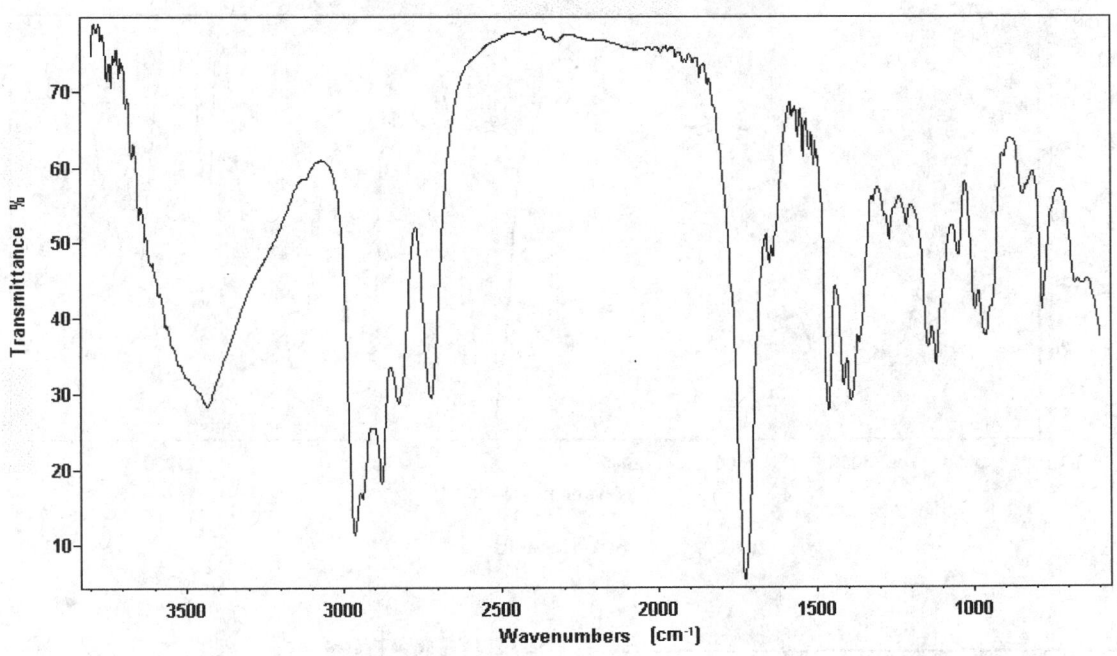

Butyraldehyde

Butyric Acid

First Published: Prior to FCC 6

C$_4$H$_8$O$_2$ Formula wt 88.11
FEMA: 2221
UNII: 4OUIR9Q29H [butyric acid]

DESCRIPTION
Butyric Acid occurs as a colorless liquid.
Odor: Strong, rancid, buttery
Solubility: Miscible in alcohol, most fixed oils, propylene glycol, water
Boiling Point: ~164°
Function: Flavoring agent

IDENTIFICATION
- **INFRARED SPECTRA,** Spectrophotometric Identification Tests, Appendix IIIC

Acceptance criteria: The spectrum of the sample exhibits relative maxima at the same wavelengths as those of the spectrum below.

ASSAY
- **PROCEDURE:** Proceed as directed under M-3a, Appendix XI.
  Acceptance criteria: NLT 99.0% of C$_4$H$_8$O$_2$

SPECIFIC TESTS
- **REFRACTIVE INDEX,** Appendix II: At 20°
  Acceptance criteria: Between 1.397 and 1.399
- **SPECIFIC GRAVITY:** Determine at 25° by any reliable method (see General Provisions).
  Acceptance criteria: Between 0.953 and 0.957

OTHER REQUIREMENTS
- **REDUCING SUBSTANCES,** M-14, Appendix XI
  Acceptance criteria: Passes test

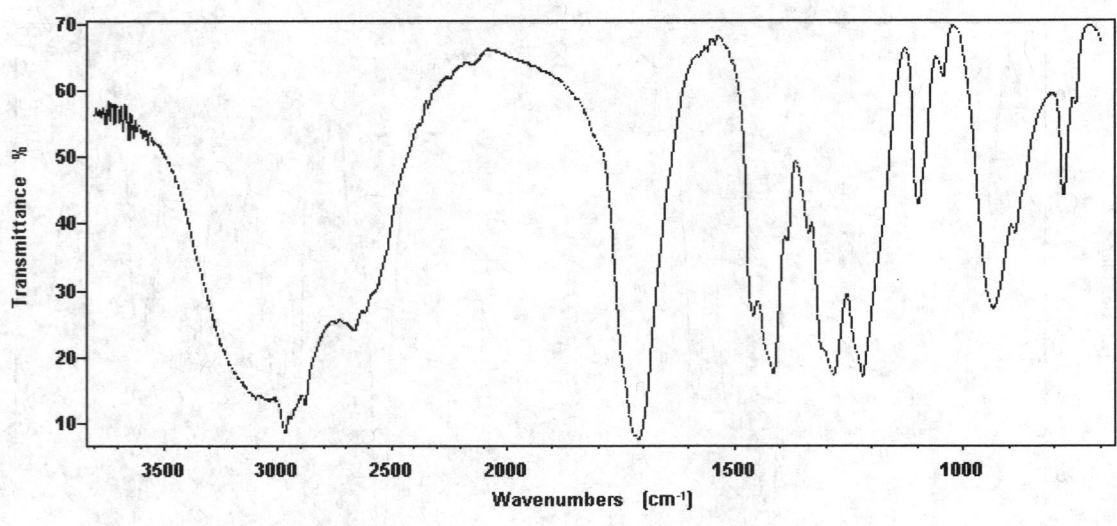

Butyric Acid

γ-Butyrolactone

First Published: Prior to FCC 6

C₄H₆O₂
FEMA: 3291
UNII: OL659KIY4X [butyrolactone]

Formula wt 86.09

DESCRIPTION
γ-Butyrolactone occurs as a colorless to slightly yellow liquid.
Odor: Faint, sweet, caramel
Solubility: Soluble in water; miscible in alcohol
Boiling Point: ~204°
Function: Flavoring agent

IDENTIFICATION
- **INFRARED SPECTRA,** Spectrophotometric Identification Tests, Appendix IIIC
  Acceptance criteria: The spectrum of the sample exhibits relative maxima at the same wavelengths as those of the spectrum below.

ASSAY
- **PROCEDURE:** Proceed as directed under M-1a, Appendix XI.
  Acceptance criteria: NLT 98.0% of C₄H₆O₂

SPECIFIC TESTS
- **REFRACTIVE INDEX,** Appendix II: At 20°
  Acceptance criteria: Between 1.430 and 1.440
- **SPECIFIC GRAVITY:** Determine at 25° by any reliable method (see General Provisions).
  Acceptance criteria: Between 1.120 and 1.130

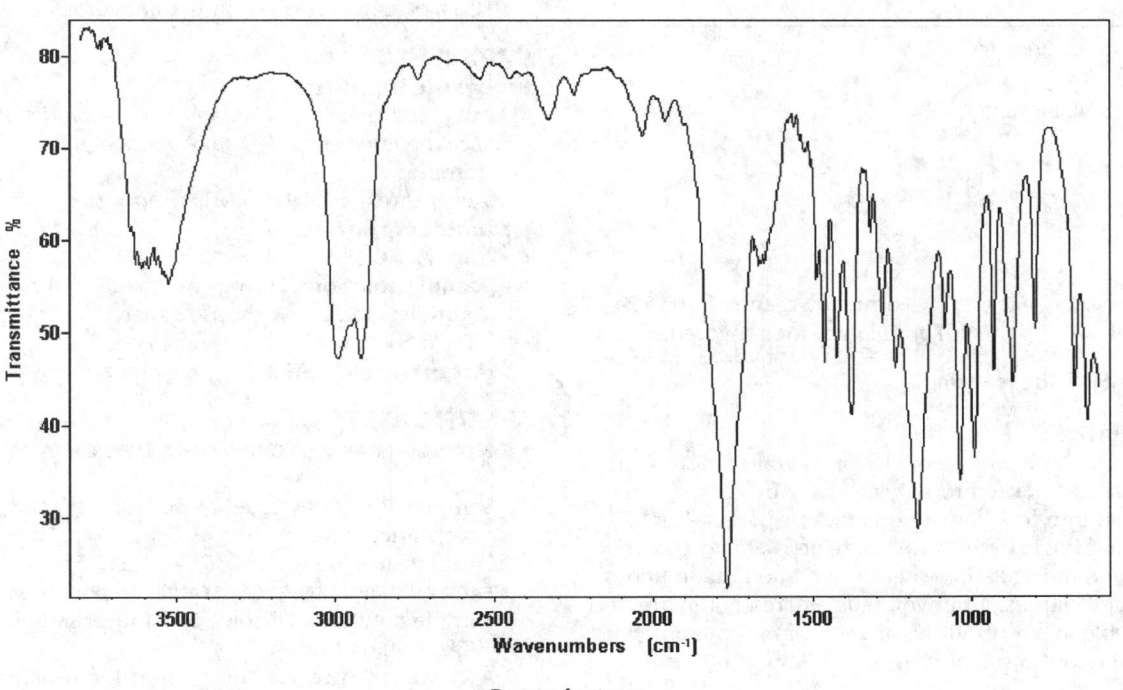

γ-Butyrolactone

Caffeine

First Published: Prior to FCC 6

1,3,7-Trimethylxanthine

$C_8H_{10}N_4O_2$ Formula wt, anhydrous 194.19
$C_8H_{10}N_4O_2 \cdot H_2O$ Formula wt, monohydrate 212.21
            CAS: anhydrous [58-08-2]
UNII: 3G6A5W338E [caffeine]

DESCRIPTION
Caffeine occurs as a white powder or as white, glistening needles, usually matted together. It may be compacted or compressed into free-flowing granules or pellets. It is odorless and has a bitter taste. Caffeine is anhydrous or contains one molecule of water of hydration. Its solutions are neutral to litmus. The hydrate is efflorescent in air, and 1 g is soluble in about 50 mL of water, in 75 mL of alcohol, in about 6 mL of chloroform, and in 600 mL of ether.

Function: Flavoring agent
Packaging and Storage: Store hydrous caffeine in tight containers and anhydrous caffeine in well-closed containers.

IDENTIFICATION
- **A. PROCEDURE**
  Sample: 5 mg
  Analysis: Dissolve the *Sample* in 1 mL of hydrochloric acid contained in a porcelain dish, add 50 mg of potassium chlorate, and evaporate on a steam bath to dryness. Invert the dish over a vessel containing a few drops of 6 N ammonium hydroxide.
  Acceptance criteria: The residue acquires a purple color, which disappears on the addition of a solution of a fixed alkali.
- **B. INFRARED ABSORPTION**, *Spectrophotometric Identification Tests*, Appendix IIIC
  Reference standard: USP Caffeine RS
  Sample and standard preparation: *M* (previously dried at 80° for 4 h)
  Acceptance criteria: The spectrum of the sample exhibits maxima at the same wavelengths as those in the spectrum of the *Reference standard*.

ASSAY
- **PROCEDURE**
  Sample: 170 mg, finely powdered
  Analysis: Dissolve the *Sample* in 5 mL of glacial acetic acid with warming. Cool, add 10 mL of acetic anhydride and 20 mL of toluene. Titrate with 0.1 N perchloric acid, determining the endpoint potentiometrically. [**CAUTION**—Handle perchloric acid in an appropriate fume hood.] Each mL of 0.1 N perchloric acid is equivalent to 19.42 mg of $C_8H_{10}N_4O_2$.
  Acceptance criteria: NLT 98.5% and NMT 101.0% of $C_8H_{10}N_4O_2$, calculated on the anhydrous basis

IMPURITIES
Inorganic Impurities
- **LEAD**, *Lead Limit Test, Flame Atomic Absorption Spectrophotometric Method*, Appendix IIIB
  Sample: 3 g
  Acceptance criteria: NMT 1 mg/kg

Organic Impurities
- **OTHER ALKALOIDS**
  Sample solution: 20 mg/mL, made to 5 mL
  Analysis: Add a few drops of mercuric–potassium iodide TS to 5 mL of the *Sample solution*.
  Acceptance criteria: No precipitate forms.

SPECIFIC TESTS
- **MELTING RANGE OR TEMPERATURE DETERMINATION**, Appendix IIB
  Sample: Previously dried at 80° for 4 h
  Acceptance criteria
    Anhydrous: Between 235° and 237.5°
- **READILY CARBONIZABLE SUBSTANCES**, Appendix IIB
  Sample solution: Dissolve 500 mg of sample in 5 mL of 95% sulfuric acid.
  Acceptance criteria: The color of the resulting *Sample solution* is no darker than that of *Matching Fluid D*.
- **RESIDUE ON IGNITION (SULFATED ASH)**, Appendix IIC
  Sample: 2 g
  Acceptance criteria: NMT 0.1%
- **WATER**, *Water Determination*, Appendix IIB
  Acceptance criteria
    Anhydrous: NMT 0.5%
    Hydrous: NMT 8.5%

OTHER REQUIREMENTS
- **LABELING:** Indicate whether it is anhydrous or hydrous.

Calcium Acetate

First Published: Prior to FCC 6

$Ca(C_2H_3O_2)_2$ Formula wt 158.17
INS: 263   CAS: [62-54-4]
UNII: Y882YXF34X [calcium acetate]

DESCRIPTION
Calcium Acetate occurs as a fine, white, bulky powder. It is freely soluble in water and slightly soluble in alcohol.
Function: Buffer; stabilizer; firming agent
Packaging and Storage: Store in well-closed containers.

IDENTIFICATION
- **ACETATE**, Appendix IIIA
  Sample solution: 100 mg/mL
  Acceptance criteria: Passes tests
- **CALCIUM**, Appendix IIIA
  Sample solution: 100 mg/mL
  Acceptance criteria: Passes tests

ASSAY
- **PROCEDURE**
  Sample: 300 mg
  Analysis: Dissolve the *Sample* in 150 mL of water containing 2 mL of 2.7 N hydrochloric acid. While stirring, preferably with a magnetic stirrer, add about 30 mL of 0.05 M disodium EDTA from a 50-mL buret. Then add 15 mL of 1 N sodium hydroxide and 300 mg of hydroxy naphthol blue indicator and continue the titration to a blue endpoint. Each mL of 0.05 M disodium EDTA is equivalent to 7.909 mg of $Ca(C_2H_3O_2)_2$.
  Acceptance criteria: NLT 99.0% and NMT 100.5% of $Ca(C_2H_3O_2)_2$, calculated on the anhydrous basis

IMPURITIES
Inorganic Impurities
- **CHLORIDE,** *Chloride and Sulfate Limit Tests*, *Chloride Limit Test*, Appendix IIIB
  Sample: 40 mg
  Control: 20 µg chloride (2 mL of *Standard Chloride Solution*)
  Acceptance criteria: Any turbidity produced by the *Sample* does not exceed that produced by the *Control*. (NMT 0.05%)
- **FLUORIDE,** *Fluoride Limit Test*, *Method III*, Appendix IIIB
  Analysis: Use 10 mL of 1 N hydrochloric acid instead of water to dissolve the sample.
  Acceptance criteria: NMT 0.005%
- **LEAD,** *Lead Limit Test*, *Flame Atomic Absorption Spectrophotometric Method*, Appendix IIIB
  Sample: 10 g
  Acceptance criteria: NMT 2 mg/kg
- **SULFATE,** *Chloride and Sulfate Limit Tests*, *Sulfate Limit Test*, Appendix IIIB
  Sample: 200 mg
  Control: 200 µg sulfate (20 mL of *Standard Sulfate Solution*)
  Acceptance criteria: Any turbidity produced by the *Sample* does not exceed that by the *Control*. (NMT 0.1%)

SPECIFIC TESTS
- **WATER,** *Water Determination*, Appendix IIB
  Acceptance criteria: NMT 7.0%

Calcium Acid Pyrophosphate
First Published: Prior to FCC 6

$CaH_2P_2O_7$ Formula wt 216.04
                   CAS: [14866-19-4]
UNII: A7X6BBX98K [calcium acid pyrophosphate]

DESCRIPTION
Calcium Acid Pyrophosphate occurs as a fine, white, acidic powder. It is insoluble in water, but it is soluble in dilute hydrochloric and nitric acids.
Function: Leavening agent; nutrient
Packaging and Storage: Store in well-closed containers.

IDENTIFICATION
- **A. PROCEDURE**
  Sample: 100 mg
  Analysis: Dissolve the *Sample* by warming it in a mixture of 5 mL of 2.7 N hydrochloric acid and 5 mL of water. Add dropwise, while shaking, 2.5 mL of 6 N ammonium hydroxide and then add 5 mL of ammonium oxalate TS.
  Acceptance criteria: A white precipitate forms.
- **B. PRODEDURE**
  Sample solution: Dissolve 100 mg of sample in 100 mL of 1.7 N nitric acid.
  Analysis:
  Mixture A: Add 0.5 mL of the *Sample solution* to 30 mL of quimociac TS.
  Mixture B: Heat the remaining portion of the *Sample solution* for 10 min at 95°, and then add 0.5 mL of the heated solution to 30 mL of quimociac TS.
  Acceptance criteria: A yellow precipitate does not form with *Mixture A*, but forms immediately with *Mixture B*.

ASSAY
- **PROCEDURE**
  Sample solution: Dissolve 300 mg of sample in 10 mL of 2.7 N hydrochloric acid.
  Analysis: To the *Sample solution*, add about 120 mL of water and a few drops of methyl orange TS and boil for 30 min. Keep the volume and pH of the solution constant during the boiling period by adding hydrochloric acid or water if necessary. Add 2 drops of methyl red TS and 30 mL of ammonium oxalate TS. Then, add, dropwise, with constant stirring, a mixture of equal volumes of 6 N ammonium hydroxide and water until the pink color of the indicator just disappears. Digest on a steam bath for 30 min, cool to room temperature, allow the precipitate to settle, and filter the supernatant liquid through a sintered-glass filter crucible using gentle suction. Wash the precipitate in the beaker with about 30 mL of cold (below 20°) wash solution, prepared by diluting 10 mL of ammonium oxalate TS to 1000 mL with water. Allow the precipitate to settle and pour the supernatant liquid through the filter. Repeat this washing by decantation three more times. Using the wash solution, transfer the precipitate as completely as possible to the filter. Finally, wash the beaker and the filter with two 10-mL portions of cold (below 20°) water. Place the sintered-glass filter crucible in the beaker and add 10 mL of water and 50 mL of cold, 1:6 sulfuric acid. Add 35 mL of 0.1 N potassium permanganate from a buret and stir until the color disappears. Heat to about 70° and complete the titration with 0.1 N potassium

162 / Calcium Acid Pyrophosphate / *Monographs*

permanganate. Each mL of 0.1 N potassium permanganate is equivalent to 5.40 mg of $CaH_2P_2O_7$.
Acceptance criteria: NLT 95.0% and NMT 100.5% of $CaH_2P_2O_7$

IMPURITIES
Inorganic Impurities
- **ARSENIC,** *Arsenic Limit Test,* Appendix IIIB
  Sample solution: 1 g in 5 mL of 2.7 N hydrochloric acid
  Acceptance criteria: NMT 3 mg/kg
- **FLUORIDE,** *Fluoride Limit Test,* Appendix IIIB
  Sample: 1.0 g
  Acceptance criteria: NMT 0.005%
- **LEAD,** *Lead Limit Test, APDC Extraction Method,* Appendix IIIB
  Acceptance criteria: NMT 2 mg/kg

SPECIFIC TESTS
- **LOSS ON IGNITION**
  Sample: 1 g
  Analysis: Transfer the *Sample* into a suitable tared crucible, ignite at 800° ± 25° for 30 min, cool in a desiccator, and weigh.
  Acceptance criteria: NMT 10.0%

Calcium Alginate

First Published: Prior to FCC 6

Algin

$[(C_6H_7O_6)_2Ca]_n$ Formula wt, calculated 195.16
                          Formula wt, actual (avg) 219.00
INS: 404   CAS: [9005-35-0]
UNII: 8P20S56HZI [calcium alginate]

DESCRIPTION
Calcium Alginate occurs as a white to yellow, fibrous or granular powder. It is the calcium salt of alginic acid. (See the monograph for *Alginic Acid*.) It is insoluble in water, but it is soluble in alkaline solutions or in solutions of substances that combine with the calcium. It is insoluble in organic solvents.
Function: Stabilizer; thickener; emulsifier
Packaging and Storage: Store in well-closed containers.

IDENTIFICATION
- **PROCEDURE**
  Sample: 5 mg
  Analysis: Place the *Sample* in a test tube, add 5 mL of water, 1 mL of a freshly prepared 1:100 solution of naphtholresorcinol:ethanol, and 5 mL of hydrochloric acid. Heat the mixture to boiling, boil gently for about 3 min, and then cool to about 15°. Transfer the contents of the test tube into a 30-mL separatory funnel with the aid of 5 mL of water, and extract with 15 mL of isopropyl ether. Perform a blank determination (see *General Provisions*).
  Acceptance criteria: The isopropyl ether extract from the *Sample* exhibits a deeper purple hue than that from the blank.

ASSAY
- **ALGINATES ASSAY,** Appendix IIIC
  Analysis: Each mL of 0.25 N sodium hydroxide consumed in the assay is equivalent to 27.38 mg of calcium alginate (equiv wt 219.00).
  Acceptance criteria: A sample yields NLT 18% and NMT 21% of carbon dioxide (CO_2), corresponding to between 89.6% and 104.5% of calcium alginate (equiv wt 219.00), calculated on the dried basis.

IMPURITIES
Inorganic Impurities
- **ARSENIC,** *Arsenic Limit Test,* Appendix IIIB
  Sample solution: Prepare as directed for organic compounds.
  Acceptance criteria: NMT 3 mg/kg
- **LEAD,** *Lead Limit Test,* Appendix IIIB
  Sample solution: Prepare as directed for organic compounds.
  Control: 5 µg Pb (5 mL of *Diluted Standard Lead Solution*)
  Acceptance criteria: NMT 5 mg/kg

SPECIFIC TESTS
- **LOSS ON DRYING,** Appendix IIC: 105° for 4 h
  Acceptance criteria: NMT 15.0%

Calcium Ascorbate

First Published: Prior to FCC 6

$C_{12}H_{14}CaO_{12} \cdot 2H_2O$ Formula wt 426.34
INS: 302   CAS: [5743-27-1]
UNII: 183E4W213W [calcium ascorbate]

DESCRIPTION
Calcium Ascorbate occurs as a white to slightly yellow, crystalline powder. It is soluble in water, slightly soluble in alcohol, and insoluble in ether. The pH of a 1:10 aqueous solution is between 6.8 and 7.4.
Function: Antioxidant
Packaging and Storage: Store in tight containers, preferably in a cool, dry place.

IDENTIFICATION
- **A. CALCIUM,** Appendix IIIA
  Sample solution: 100 mg/mL
  Acceptance criteria: Passes tests
- **B. PROCEDURE**
  Sample solution: 100 mg/mL

Acceptance criteria: The Sample solution decolorizes dichlorophenol-indophenol TS.

ASSAY
- **PROCEDURE**
  Sample: 300 mg
  Analysis: Dissolve the Sample in 50 mL of water in a 250-mL Erlenmeyer flask and immediately titrate with 0.1 N iodine to a pale yellow color that persists for at least 30 s. Each mL of 0.1 N iodine is equivalent to 10.66 mg of $C_{12}H_{14}CaO_{12} \cdot 2H_2O$.
  Acceptance criteria: NLT 98.0% and NMT 100.5% of $C_{12}H_{14}CaO_{12} \cdot 2H_2O$

IMPURITIES
Inorganic Impurities
- **LEAD**, Lead Limit Test, Flame Atomic Absorption Spectrophotometric Method, Appendix IIIB
  Sample: 10 g
  Acceptance criteria: NMT 2 mg/kg

SPECIFIC TESTS
- **OPTICAL (SPECIFIC) ROTATION**, Appendix IIB
  Sample solution: 50 mg/mL
  Acceptance criteria: $[\alpha]_D^{25}$ between +95° and +97°
- **OXALATE**
  Sample solution: 1 g in 10 mL of water
  Analysis: Add 2 drops of glacial acetic acid and 5 mL of a 100 mg/mL calcium acetate solution to the Sample solution.
  Acceptance criteria: The solution remains clear after standing for 5 min.

Calcium Benzoate

First Published: Second Supplement, FCC 7

Monocalcium Benzoate

$n = 0, 1, \text{or } 3$

$C_{14}H_{10}CaO_4 \cdot xH_2O$ Formula wt, anhydrous 282.31
INS: 213   CAS: [2090-05-3]
UNII: 3QDE968MKD [calcium benzoate]

DESCRIPTION
Calcium Benzoate occurs as white or colorless crystals, or as a white powder. It contains up to three molecules of water of hydration. It is sparingly soluble in water.
Function: Preservative; antimicrobial agent
Packaging and Storage: Store in well-closed containers.

IDENTIFICATION
- **BENZOATE**, Appendix IIIA
  Acceptance criteria: Passes test
- **CALCIUM**, Appendix IIIA
  Acceptance criteria: Passes tests
- **INFRARED ABSORPTION**, Spectrophotometric Identification Tests, Appendix IIIC
  Reference standard: USP Calcium Benzoate RS
  Sample and standard preparation: K
  Acceptance criteria: The spectrum of the sample exhibits maxima at the same wavelengths as those in the spectrum of the Reference standard.

ASSAY
- **PROCEDURE**
  Sample: 600 mg
  Analysis: Dissolve the Sample in a mixture of 20 mL of water and 2 mL of dilute hydrochloric acid TS, and dilute with water to 100 mL. While stirring (preferably with a magnetic stirrer), add about 30 mL of 0.05 M disodium ethylenediaminetetraacetate from a 50-mL buret, then add 15 mL of sodium hydroxide TS, 40 mg of murexide indicator preparation, and 3 mL of naphthol green TS (250 mg of hydroxynaphthol blue may be used as an indicator preparation in place of murexide and naphthol green TS), and continue the titration until the solution is deep blue in color. Each mL of 0.05 M disodium ethylenediaminetetraacetate is equivalent to 14.116 mg of $C_{14}H_{10}CaO_4$.
  Acceptance criteria: NLT 99.0% on the dried basis

IMPURITIES
Inorganic Impurities
- **FLUORIDE**, Fluoride Limit Test, Method I or III, Appendix IIIB
  Analysis: Proceed as directed using a 5-g sample.
  Acceptance criteria: NMT 10 mg/kg
- **LEAD**, Lead Limit Test, Flame Atomic Absorption Spectrophotometric Method, Appendix IIIB
  Sample: 10 g
  Acceptance criteria: NMT 2 mg/kg

SPECIFIC TESTS
- **CHLORINATED COMPOUNDS**
  Sample: 0.25 g
  Control: Mix 0.5 mL of 0.1 N silver nitrate with 20 mL of dilute nitric acid TS containing 0.5 mL of 0.01 N hydrochloric acid.
  Analysis: Dissolve the Sample in 10 mL of water. Acidify with nitric acid and filter off the precipitate. Mix the precipitate with 0.5 g of calcium carbonate, dry the mixture, and then ignite. Take up the ignition residue in 20 mL of dilute nitric acid TS and filter. Mix the filtrate with 0.5 mL of 0.1 N silver nitrate.
  Acceptance criteria: Any turbidity produced by the Sample does not exceed that produced by the Control. (NMT 0.07% as Cl_2)
- **LOSS ON DRYING**, Appendix IIC: 105° for 4 h
  Acceptance criteria: NMT 17.5%
- **READILY OXIDIZABLE SUBSTANCES**
  Sample: 1 g
  Analysis: Add 0.1 N potassium permanganate, dropwise, to a mixture of 100 mL of water and 1.5 mL of sulfuric acid heated to boiling, until a pink color persists for 30 s. Dissolve the Sample in the hot solution. Titrate with 0.1 N potassium permanganate to a pink color that persists for 15 s.

Acceptance criteria: The volume of 0.1 N potassium permanganate consumed in the titration does not exceed 0.5 mL.
- WATER-INSOLUBLE MATTER
  Sample: 10 g
  Analysis: Dissolve the Sample in 100 mL of hot water. Filter through a tared Gooch crucible, and wash any residue with hot water. Dry the crucible for 2 h at 105°. Cool, weigh, and calculate the percentage of water-insoluble matter.
  Acceptance criteria: NMT 0.3%

Calcium Bromate
First Published: Prior to FCC 6

$Ca(BrO_3)_2 \cdot H_2O$ Formula wt 313.90
INS: 924b   CAS: [10102-75-7]
UNII: QJ2S78C3RO [calcium bromate]

DESCRIPTION
Calcium Bromate occurs as a white, crystalline powder. It is very soluble in water.
Function: Maturing agent; oxidizing agent
Packaging and Storage: Store in well-closed containers.

IDENTIFICATION
- A. PROCEDURE
  Sample solution: 50 mg/mL in 2.7 N hydrochloric acid
  Acceptance criteria: The Sample solution imparts a transient yellow-red color to a nonluminous flame.
- B. PROCEDURE
  Sample solution: 50 mg/mL
  Analysis: Add sulfurous acid dropwise to the Sample solution.
  Acceptance criteria: A yellow color develops that disappears upon the addition of an excess of sulfurous acid.

ASSAY
- PROCEDURE
  Sample: 900 mg
  Analysis: Dissolve the Sample in 50 mL of water in a 250-mL glass-stoppered Erlenmeyer flask. To the flask, add 3 g of potassium iodide followed by 3 mL of hydrochloric acid. Allow the mixture to stand for 5 min and then add 100 mL of cold water. Titrate the liberated iodine with 0.1 N sodium thiosulfate, adding starch TS near the endpoint. Perform a blank determination (see General Provisions), and make any necessary correction. Each mL of 0.1 N sodium thiosulfate is equivalent to 26.16 mg of $Ca(BrO_3)_2 \cdot H_2O$.
  Acceptance criteria: NLT 99.8% and NMT 100.5% of $Ca(BrO_3)_2 \cdot H_2O$

IMPURITIES
Inorganic Impurities
- LEAD, Lead Limit Test, Appendix IIIB
  Sample solution: Dissolve 2 g of sample in 10 mL of water, 10 mL of hydrochloric acid, and evaporate to dryness on a steam bath. Dissolve the residue in 5 mL of hydrochloric acid, again evaporate to dryness, and then dissolve the residue in 40 mL of water.
  Control: 4 μg Pb (4 mL of Diluted Standard Lead Solution)
  Analysis: Use 20 mL of the Sample solution.
  Acceptance criteria: NMT 4 mg/kg

Calcium Carbonate
First Published: Prior to FCC 6

$CaCO_3$ Formula wt 100.09
INS: 170(i)   CAS: [471-34-1]
UNII: H0G9379FGK [calcium carbonate]

DESCRIPTION
Calcium Carbonate occurs as a fine, white or colorless, microcrystalline powder. It is stable in air, and it is practically insoluble in water and in alcohol. The presence of any ammonium salt or carbon dioxide increases its solubility in water, but the presence of any alkali hydroxide reduces the solubility.
Function: pH control agent; nutrient; dough conditioner; firming agent; yeast nutrient
Packaging and Storage: Store in well-closed containers.

IDENTIFICATION
- A. PROCEDURE
  Analysis: Add a sample to 1 N acetic acid, 2.7 N hydrochloric acid, and 1.7 N nitric acid.
  Acceptance criteria: The sample dissolves with effervescence in each case.
- B. CALCIUM, Appendix IIIA
  Sample solutions: The three resulting solutions from Identification Test A
  Analysis: Boil the solutions and perform the test for Calcium on each.
  Acceptance criteria: Each solution passes tests.

ASSAY
- PROCEDURE
  Sample: 200 mg, previously dried
  Analysis: Transfer the Sample into a 400-mL beaker, add 10 mL of water, and swirl to form a slurry. Cover the beaker with a watch glass and introduce 2 mL of 2 N hydrochloric acid from a pipet inserted between the lip of the beaker and the edge of the watch glass. Swirl the contents of the beaker to dissolve the sample. Wash down the sides of the beaker, the outer surface of the pipet, and the watch glass, and dilute the contents to about 100 mL with water. While stirring, preferably with a magnetic stirrer, add about 30 mL of 0.05 M disodium EDTA from a 50-mL buret, then add 15 mL of 1 N sodium hydroxide and 300 mg of hydroxy naphthol blue indicator. Continue the titration to a blue endpoint. Each mL of 0.05 M disodium EDTA is equivalent to 5.004 mg of $CaCO_3$.
  Acceptance criteria: NLT 98.0% and NMT 100.5% of $CaCO_3$, on the dried basis

IMPURITIES
Inorganic Impurities
- **ACID-INSOLUBLE SUBSTANCES**
  Sample: 5 g
  Analysis: Suspend the *Sample* in 25 mL of water and agitate the suspension while cautiously adding 25 mL of 1:2 hydrochloric acid. Add water to make a volume of about 200 mL. Heat the solution to boiling, cover, digest on a steam bath for 1 h, cool, and filter. Wash the precipitate with water until the last washing shows no chloride with silver nitrate TS, and then ignite it.
  Acceptance criteria: The weight of the residue does not exceed 10 mg. (NMT 0.2%)
- **ARSENIC,** *Arsenic Limit Test,* Appendix IIIB
  Sample solution: 1 g in 10 mL of 2.7 N hydrochloric acid
  Acceptance criteria: NMT 3 mg/kg
- **FLUORIDE,** *Fluoride Limit Test, Method III,* Appendix IIIB
  Acceptance criteria: NMT 0.005%
- **LEAD,** *Lead Limit Test,* Appendix IIIB
  Sample solution: Cautiously dissolve 5 g of sample in 25 mL of 1:2 hydrochloric acid and evaporate the solution to dryness on a steam bath. Dissolve the residue in about 15 mL of water and dilute to 25 mL (200 mg/mL).
  Control: 12 µg Pb (12 mL of *Diluted Standard Lead Solution*)
  Analysis: Use 20 mL of *Sample solution*.
  [NOTE—As an alternative to the above test, determine as directed in the *Lead Limit Test, APDC Extraction Method,* Appendix IIIB.]
  Acceptance criteria: NMT 3 mg/kg
- **MAGNESIUM AND ALKALI SALTS**
  Sample: 1 g
  Analysis: Mix the *Sample* with 40 mL of water, carefully add 5 mL of hydrochloric acid, mix, and boil for 1 min. Rapidly add 40 mL of oxalic acid TS and stir vigorously until precipitation is well established. Immediately add 2 drops of methyl red TS. Then, add 6 N ammonium hydroxide, dropwise, until the mixture is just alkaline, and cool. Transfer the mixture to a 100-mL graduated cylinder, dilute to 100 mL with water, and let stand for 4 h or overnight. Decant the clear, supernatant liquid through a dry filter paper and place 50 mL of the clear filtrate in a platinum dish. Add 0.5 mL of sulfuric acid, and evaporate the mixture on a steam bath to a small volume. Carefully evaporate the remaining liquid to dryness over a free flame and continue heating until the ammonium salts have been completely decomposed and volatilized. Finally, ignite the residue to constant weight.
  Acceptance criteria: The weight of the residue does not exceed 5 mg. (NMT 1%)

SPECIFIC TESTS
- **LOSS ON DRYING,** Appendix IIC : 200° for 4 h
  Acceptance criteria: NMT 2%

Calcium Chloride
First Published: Prior to FCC 6

$CaCl_2$ — Formula wt, anhydrous 110.98
$CaCl_2 \cdot 2H_2O$ — Formula wt, dihydrate 147.01
INS: 509
CAS: anhydrous [10043-52-4]
CAS: dihydrate [10035-04-8]
UNII: M4I0D6VV5M [calcium chloride]

DESCRIPTION
Calcium Chloride occurs as white, hard fragments, granules, or powder. It is anhydrous or contains two molecules of water of hydration. It is deliquescent. It is soluble in water and slightly soluble in alcohol. The pH of a 1:20 aqueous solution is between 4.5 and 11.0.
Function: Firming agent
Packaging and Storage: Store in tight containers.

IDENTIFICATION
- **CALCIUM,** Appendix IIIA
  Sample solution: 100 mg/mL
  Acceptance criteria: Passes test
- **CHLORIDE,** Appendix IIIA
  Sample solution: 100 mg/mL
  Acceptance criteria: Passes test

ASSAY
- **PROCEDURE**
  Sample: 1.5 g
  Analysis: Transfer the *Sample* into a 250-mL volumetric flask, dissolve it in a mixture of 100 mL of water and 5 mL of 2.7 N hydrochloric acid, dilute to volume with water, and mix. Transfer 50 mL of this solution into a suitable container and add 50 mL of water. While stirring, preferably with a magnetic stirrer, add about 30 mL of 0.05 M disodium EDTA from a 50-mL buret. Then, add 15 mL of 1 N sodium hydroxide and 300 mg of hydroxy naphthol blue indicator. Continue the titration to a blue endpoint. Each mL of 0.05 M disodium EDTA is equivalent to 5.55 mg of $CaCl_2$ or 7.35 mg of $CaCl_2 \cdot 2H_2O$.
  Acceptance criteria
  Anhydrous: NLT 93.0% and NMT 100.5% of $CaCl_2$
  Dihydrate: NLT 99.0% and NMT 107.0% of $CaCl_2 \cdot 2H_2O$

IMPURITIES
Inorganic Impurities
- **ACID-INSOLUBLE MATTER (ANHYDROUS SALT)**
  Filter assembly: Place a 32-mm (od) lintine disk filter[1] in a suitable filter assembly comprised of a 2.5-L screw-cap bottle cut in half horizontally and fitted with a rubber washer (35-mm od and 25-mm id), followed by the lintine disk, a 20-mesh stainless steel screen (35-mm od), and a bottle cap with a 25-mm hole in the top.
  Sample solution: Dissolve 1 kg sample in 3 L of water containing 10 mL of glacial acetic acid. Allow the solution to cool.

---
[1] Available from Filter Fabrics, Inc., 814 E. Jefferson, Goshen, IN 46526; 219-533-3114

Analysis: Wash the *Filter assembly,* with the filter at the bottom, with 100 mL of 1:300 acetic acid, followed by 100 mL of water. Remove the disk from the assembly, place it on a watch glass, dry the combination at 105° for 2 h, let cool and weigh. Filter the *Sample solution* through the lintine disk. Rinse the walls of the *Filter assembly* so that all insoluble matter is transferred to the disk, and wash with 100 mL of water. Place the disk on the same watch glass mentioned above, dry at 105° for 2 h, let cool and weigh the combination, being careful at all times not to lose any particles that may be on the disk. The difference in the two weights is the weight of the acid-insoluble matter. Place the disk under a low-power magnifier (4× to 10× magnification). Using a millimeter rule, measure the largest dimension of each particle (or as many as may be necessary) on the disk.

Acceptance criteria
 Anhydrous: NMT 0.02% and; no particles of sample greater than 2 mm in any dimension are present.

- **ARSENIC,** *Arsenic Limit Test,* Appendix IIIB
  Sample solution: 1 g in 10 mL
  Acceptance criteria: NMT 3 mg/kg
- **FLUORIDE,** *Fluoride Limit Test, Method III,* Appendix IIIB
  Acceptance criteria: NMT 0.004%
- **LEAD,** *Lead Limit Test,* Appendix IIIB
  Sample solution: 1 g in 20 mL
  Control: 5 µg Pb (5 mL of *Diluted Standard Lead Solution*)
  Acceptance criteria: NMT 5 mg/kg
- **MAGNESIUM AND ALKALI SALTS**
  Sample: 1 g
  Analysis: Dissolve the *Sample* in 50 mL of water, add 500 mg of ammonium chloride, mix, and boil for 1 min. Rapidly add 40 mL of oxalic acid TS and stir vigorously until precipitation is well established. Immediately add 2 drops of methyl red TS. Then add 6 N ammonium hydroxide, dropwise, until the mixture is just alkaline, and cool. Transfer the mixture to a 100-mL cylinder, dilute to 100 mL with water, and let it stand for 4 h or overnight. Decant the clear, supernatant liquid through a dry filter paper, and transfer 50 mL of the clear filtrate to a platinum dish. Add 0.5 mL of sulfuric acid to the dish and evaporate the mixture on a steam bath to a small volume. Carefully evaporate the remaining liquid to dryness over a free flame and continue heating until the ammonium salts have been completely decomposed and volatilized. Finally, ignite the residue to constant weight.
  Acceptance criteria
   Anhydrous: NMT 25 mg of residue (NMT 5.0%)
   Dihydrate: NMT 20 mg of residue (NMT 4.0%)

OTHER REQUIREMENTS
- **LABELING:** Indicate whether the salt is anhydrous or the dihydrate.

Calcium Chloride Solution
First Published: Prior to FCC 6

UNII: OFM21057LP [calcium chloride anhydrous]

DESCRIPTION
Calcium Chloride Solution occurs as a clear to slightly turbid, colorless or slightly colored liquid at room temperature. It is nominally available in a concentration range of about 35% to 45% of $CaCl_2$.
Function: Sequestrant; firming agent
Packaging and Storage: Store in tight containers.

IDENTIFICATION
- **CALCIUM,** Appendix IIIA
  Sample solution: 100 mg/mL ($CaCl_2$ basis)
  Acceptance criteria: Passes tests
- **CHLORIDE,** Appendix IIIA
  Sample solution: 100 mg/mL ($CaCl_2$ basis)
  Acceptance criteria: Passes test

ASSAY
- **PROCEDURE**
  Sample: Quantity equivalent to 1 g of $CaCl_2$
  Analysis: Transfer the *Sample* into a 250-mL volumetric flask, add 5 mL of 2.7 N hydrochloric acid and 100 mL of water to dissolve; dilute to volume with water, and mix. Transfer 50.0 mL of this solution into a suitable container and add 50 mL of water. While stirring, preferably with a magnetic stirrer, add about 30 mL of 0.05 M disodium EDTA from a 50-mL buret. Then add 15 mL of 1 N sodium hydroxide and 300 mg of hydroxy naphthol blue indicator. Continue the titration to a blue endpoint. Each mL of 0.05 M disodium EDTA is equivalent to 5.55 mg of $CaCl_2$.
  Acceptance criteria: NLT 90.0% and NMT 110.0%, by weight, of the labeled amount of calcium chloride, expressed as $CaCl_2$

IMPURITIES
Inorganic Impurities
- **FLUORIDE,** *Fluoride Limit Test, Method III,* Appendix IIIB
  Sample: Quantity equivalent to 1 g of $CaCl_2$
  Acceptance criteria: NMT 0.004%, calculated on the amount of $CaCl_2$ as determined in the *Assay*
- **LEAD,** *Lead Limit Test,* Appendix IIIB
  Sample solution: Quantity of sample equivalent to 1 g of $CaCl_2$, diluted to 10 mL
  Control: 4 µg Pb (4 mL of *Diluted Standard Lead Solution*)
  Acceptance criteria: NMT 4 mg/kg, calculated on the amount of $CaCl_2$ as determined in the *Assay*
- **MAGNESIUM AND ALKALI SALTS**
  Sample solution: Quantity of sample equivalent to 1 g of $CaCl_2$, diluted to 50 mL
  Analysis: To the *Sample solution*, add 500 mg of ammonium chloride, mix, and boil for 1 min. Rapidly add 40 mL of oxalic acid TS and stir vigorously until precipitation is well established. Immediately add 2 drops of methyl red TS, then add 6 N ammonium hydroxide, dropwise, until the mixture is just alkaline,

and cool. Transfer the mixture to a 100-mL cylinder, dilute to 100 mL with water, and let it stand for 4 h or overnight. Decant the clear, supernatant liquid through a dry filter paper and transfer 50 mL of the clear filtrate to a platinum dish. Add 0.5 mL of sulfuric acid to the dish and evaporate the mixture on a steam bath to a small volume. Carefully evaporate the remaining liquid to dryness over a free flame, and continue heating until the ammonium salts have been completely decomposed and volatilized. Finally, ignite the residue to constant weight.
Acceptance criteria: The weight of the residue does not exceed 25 mg, calculated on the amount of $CaCl_2$ as determined in the Assay (NMT 5.0%).

SPECIFIC TESTS

- **ALKALINITY (AS $Ca(OH)_2$)**
  Sample solution: Quantity of sample equivalent to 5 g of $CaCl_2$ diluted to 50 mL
  Analysis: Add phenolphthalein TS to the Sample solution and titrate with 0.1 N hydrochloric acid. Each mL of 0.1 N hydrochloric acid is equivalent to 3.71 mg of $Ca(OH)_2$.
  Acceptance criteria: NMT 0.3%

Calcium Citrate

First Published: Prior to FCC 6

Tricalcium Citrate

$Ca_3(C_6H_5O_7)_2 \cdot 4H_2O$ Formula wt 570.50
INS: 333   CAS: [5785-44-4]
UNII: MLM29U2X85 [calcium citrate]

DESCRIPTION
Calcium Citrate occurs as a fine, white powder. It is very slightly soluble in water, but it is insoluble in alcohol.
Function: Sequestrant; buffer; firming agent
Packaging and Storage: Store in well-closed containers.

IDENTIFICATION

- **A. PROCEDURE**
  Sample: 500 mg
  Analysis: Dissolve the Sample in 10 mL of water and 2.5 mL of 1.7 N nitric acid. Add 1 mL of mercuric sulfate TS, heat to boiling, and then add potassium permanganate TS.
  Acceptance criteria: A white precipitate forms.
- **B. PROCEDURE**
  Sample: 500 mg
  Analysis: Completely ignite the Sample at as low a temperature as possible. Cool the residue and dissolve it in a mixture of 10 mL of water and 1 mL of glacial acetic acid. Filter and add 10 mL of ammonium oxalate TS to the filtrate.
  Acceptance criteria: A voluminous, white precipitate forms that is soluble in hydrochloric acid.

ASSAY

- **PROCEDURE**
  Sample: 350 mg, previously dried
  Analysis: Dissolve the Sample, in a mixture of 10 mL of water and 2 mL of 2.7 N hydrochloric acid, and dilute to about 100 mL with water. While stirring, preferably with a magnetic stirrer, add about 30 mL of 0.05 M disodium EDTA from a 50-mL buret. Add 15 mL of 1 N sodium hydroxide and 300 mg of hydroxy naphthol blue indicator, and continue the titration to a blue endpoint. Each mL of 0.05 M disodium EDTA is equivalent to 8.300 mg of $Ca_3(C_6H_5O_7)_2$.
  Acceptance criteria: NLT 97.5% and NMT 100.5% of $Ca_3(C_6H_5O_7)_2$, on the dried basis

IMPURITIES
Inorganic Impurities

- **FLUORIDE**, Fluoride Limit Test, Method III, Appendix IIIB
  Sample solution: Prepare as directed using 10 mL of hydrochloric acid instead of 20 mL.
  Analysis: Prepare a calibration curve as directed using 1.0, 5.0, and 10.0 mL of the Sodium Fluoride Solution (equivalent to 5.0, 25.0, and 50.0 mg/kg of fluoride, respectively).
  Acceptance criteria: NMT 0.003%
- **LEAD**, Lead Limit Test, Flame Atomic Absorption Spectrophotometric Method, Appendix IIIB
  Sample: 10 g
  Acceptance criteria: NMT 2 mg/kg

SPECIFIC TESTS
- **LOSS ON DRYING**, Appendix IIC: 150° for 4 h
  Acceptance criteria: Between 10.0% and 14.0%

Calcium Cyclamate

First Published: Third Supplement, FCC 7

Calcium Cyclohexanesulfamate
Calcium Cyclohexylsulfamate

$C_{12}H_{24}CaN_2O_6S_2 \cdot 2H_2O$ Formula wt, anhydrous 396.53
                                          Formula wt, dihydrate 432.57
INS: 952(ii)   CAS: anhydrous [139-06-0]
                                               dihydrate [5897-16-5]

DESCRIPTION
Calcium Cyclamate occurs as colorless to white crystals or crystalline powder. It is soluble in water and sparingly soluble in ethanol.
Function: Sweetener

168 / Calcium Cyclamate / Monographs

Packaging and Storage: Store in tight containers in a cool, dry place.

IDENTIFICATION
- **CALCIUM,** Appendix IIIA
  Sample solution: 50 mg/mL
  Acceptance criteria: Passes test
- **INFRARED ABSORPTION,** *Spectrophotometric Identification Tests,* Appendix IIIC
  Reference standard: USP Calcium Cyclamate RS
  Sample and standard preparation: *K*
  Acceptance criteria: The spectrum of the sample exhibits maxima at the same wavelengths as those in the spectrum of the *Reference standard*.

ASSAY
- **PROCEDURE**
  Sample: 0.4 g
  Analysis: Dissolve the *Sample* in a mixture of 50 mL of water and 5 mL of hydrochloric acid TS, diluted. Titrate the solution with 0.1 M sodium nitrite. Add the last mL of titrant dropwise until a blue color is produced immediately when a glass rod dipped into the titrated solution is streaked on a piece of starch iodide test paper. Alternatively, the endpoint may be determined potentiometrically. When the titration is complete, the endpoint is reproducible after the mixture has been allowed to stand for 1 min. Each mL of 0.1 M sodium nitrite is equivalent to 19.83 mg of $C_{12}H_{24}CaN_2O_6S_2$.
  Acceptance criteria: 98.0%–102.0%, calculated on the anhydrous basis

IMPURITIES
Inorganic Impurities
- **LEAD,** *Lead Limit Test, Flame Atomic Absorption Spectrophotometric Method,* Appendix IIIB
  Sample: 5 g
  Acceptance criteria: NMT 1.0 mg/kg

Organic Impurities
- **CYCLOHEXANAMINE, ANILINE, AND *N*-CYCLOHEXYLCYCLOHEXANAMINE**
  Internal standard solution: Dissolve 0.02 µL/mL of tetradecane in methylene chloride.
  Solution A: Dissolve 10 mg of cyclohexanamine, 1 mg of *N*-cyclohexylcyclohexanamine, and 1 mg of aniline in water, then dilute with the same solvent to 1000 mL. Dilute 10 mL of this solution with water to 100 mL.
  Solution B: 42% w/v sodium hydroxide solution
  Standard solution: To 20 mL of *Solution A*, add 0.5 mL of *Solution B*, and extract with 30 mL of toluene. Shake 20 mL of the upper layer with 4 mL of a mixture of equal volumes of water and an acetic acid solution (12% w/v). Separate the lower layer, add 0.5 mL of *Solution B* and 0.5 mL of the *Internal standard solution*, and shake. Use the lower layer immediately after separation.
  Sample solution: Dissolve 2 g of sample in 20 mL of water, add 0.5 mL of *Solution B*, and shake with 30 mL of toluene. Shake 20 mL of the upper layer with 4 mL of a mixture of equal volumes of an acetic acid solution (12% w/v) and water. Separate the lower layer, add 0.5 mL of *Solution B* and 0.5 mL of the *Internal standard solution*, and shake. Use the lower layer immediately after separation.
  Chromatographic system, Appendix IIA
    Mode: Gas chromatography
    Detector: Flame ionization
    Column: 25-m × 0.32-mm (i.d.) fused-silica column with poly(dimethyl)(diphenyl)siloxane containing 95% of methyl groups and 5% of phenyl groups (DB-5, SE52) as stationary phase (film thickness 0.51 µm)
    Carrier gas: Helium
    Flow rate: 1.8 mL/min
    Temperature
      Injection port: 250°
      Detector: 270°
      Column: See the temperature program in the table below.

Time (min)	Temperature (°)
0–1	85
1–9	85–150
9–13	150

  Injection volume: 1.5 µL. Use a split vent at a flow rate of 20 mL/min.
  Analysis: Separately inject equal volumes of the *Standard solution* and *Sample solution* into the chromatograph, record the chromatograms, and measure the responses. [NOTE—The approximate retention times (relative to cyclohexanamine, which has a retention time of about 2.3 min) for aniline, tetradecane, and *N*-cyclohexylcyclohexanamine are about 1.4 min, 4.3 min, and 4.5 min, respectively.]
  Acceptance criteria
    Cyclohexanamine: NMT 10.0 mg/kg
    Aniline: NMT 1.0 mg/kg
    ***N*-Cyclohexylcyclohexanamine:** NMT 1.0 mg/kg

SPECIFIC TESTS
- **LOSS ON DRYING,** Appendix IIC: 140° for 2 h
  Acceptance criteria: 6.0%–9.0%

Calcium Disodium EDTA

First Published: Prior to FCC 6

Calcium Disodium Ethylenediaminetetraacetate
Calcium Disodium (Ethylenedinitrilo)tetraacetate
Calcium Disodium Edetate

$C_{10}H_{12}CaN_2Na_2O_8 \cdot 2H_2O$ Formula wt 410.30
INS: 385   CAS: [23411-34-9]
UNII: 25IH6R4SGF [edetate calcium disodium]

DESCRIPTION
Calcium Disodium EDTA occurs as white, crystalline granules or as a white to off-white powder. It is slightly hygroscopic and is stable in air. It is freely soluble in water.
Function: Preservative; sequestrant
Packaging and Storage: Store in well-closed containers.

IDENTIFICATION
- **A. Calcium,** Appendix IIIA
  Sample solution: 50 mg/mL
  Acceptance criteria: Passes oxalate test
- **B. Infrared Absorption,** *Spectrophotometric Identification Tests,* Appendix IIIC
  Reference standard: USP Edetate Calcium Disodium RS
  Sample and standard preparation: *M*
  Acceptance criteria: The spectrum of the *Sample* exhibits maxima at the same wavelengths as those in the spectrum of the *Reference standard.*
- **C. Sodium,** Appendix IIIA
  Sample solution: 50 mg/mL
  Acceptance criteria: Passes flame test
- **D. Procedure**
  Sample: 50 mg
  Analysis: Add 2 drops of ammonium thiocyanate TS and 2 drops of ferric chloride TS to 5 mL of water contained in a test tube. Add the *Sample* to the deep red solution so obtained and mix.
  Acceptance criteria: The deep red color disappears.

ASSAY
- **Procedure**
  Sample: 1.2 g
  Analysis: Transfer the *Sample* to a 250-mL beaker and dissolve in 75 mL of water. Add 25 mL of 1 N acetic acid and 1.0 mL of diphenylcarbazone TS and titrate slowly with 0.1 M mercuric nitrate to the first appearance of a purple color. Each mL of 0.1 M mercuric nitrate is equivalent to 37.43 mg of $C_{10}H_{12}CaN_2Na_2O_8$.
  Acceptance criteria: NLT 97.0% and NMT 102.0% of $C_{10}H_{12}CaN_2Na_2O_8$, calculated on the anhydrous basis

IMPURITIES
Inorganic Impurities
- **Lead,** *Lead Limit Test,* Appendix IIIB
  Sample solution: Prepare as directed for organic compounds, using 70% perchloric acid instead of 30% hydrogen peroxide to decompose the sample.
  [**Caution**—Handle perchloric acid in an appropriate fume hood.]
  Control: 4 µg Pb (4 mL of *Diluted Standard Lead Solution*)
  Acceptance criteria: NMT 4 mg/kg

Organic Impurities
- **Nitrilotriacetic Acid**
  Mobile phase: Add 10 mL of a 1:4 solution of tetrabutylammonium hydroxide in methanol to 200 mL of water, and adjust with 1 M phosphoric acid to a pH of 7.5 ± 0.1. Transfer the solution into a 1000-mL volumetric flask, add 90 mL of methanol, dilute to volume with water, mix, filter through a membrane filter (0.5-µm or finer porosity), and de-gas.
  Cupric nitrate solution: 10 mg/mL
  Standard stock solution: Transfer 100 mg of nitrilotriacetic acid into a 10-mL volumetric flask; add 0.5 mL of ammonium hydroxide, and mix. Dilute to volume with water, and mix.
  Standard solution: Transfer 1.0 g of sample into a 100-mL volumetric flask. Add 100 µL of *Standard stock solution*, dilute to volume with *Cupric nitrate solution*, and mix. Sonicate, if necessary, to aid in dissolution.
  Sample solution: Transfer 1.0 g of sample into a 100-mL volumetric flask, dilute to volume with *Cupric nitrate solution*, and mix. Sonicate, if necessary, to aid in dissolution.
  Chromatographic system, Appendix IIA
  Mode: High-performance liquid chromatography
  Detector: UV 254 nm
  Column: 15-cm × 4.6-mm column that contains 5- to 10-mm porous microparticles of silica bonded to octylsilane (Zorbax 8, or equivalent)
  Flow rate: about 2 mL/min
  Injection volume: about 50 µL
  System suitability
  Sample: *Standard solution*
  Suitability requirement 1: The resolution between nitrilotriacetic acid and calcium disodium EDTA is NLT 4.0.
  Suitability requirement 2: The relative standard deviation is NMT 2.0% for three replicate injections.
  Analysis: Separately inject equal volumes of the *Standard solution* and the *Sample solution* into the chromatograph, record the chromatograms, and measure the responses for the major peaks. [Note—The retention times are about 3.5 min for nitrilotriacetic acid and 9 min for calcium disodium EDTA.]
  Acceptance criteria: The response of the nitrilotriacetic acid peak of the *Sample solution* does not exceed the difference between the nitrilotriacetic acid peak responses obtained from the *Standard solution* and the *Sample solution*. (NMT 0.1%)

SPECIFIC TESTS
- **Magnesium-Chelating Substances**
  Buffer solution: Dissolve 67.5 g of ammonium chloride in 200 mL of water. Add 570 mL of ammonium hydroxide and dilute to 1000 mL with water.
  Sample solution: 1 g of sample in 5 mL of water and 5 mL of *Buffer solution*
  Analysis: Add 5 drops of eriochrome black TS to the *Sample solution* and titrate with 0.1 M magnesium acetate to the appearance of a deep wine red color.
  Acceptance criteria: NMT 2.0 mL of 0.1 M magnesium acetate titrant is required
- **pH,** *pH Determination,* Appendix IIB
  Sample solution: 10 mg/mL
  Acceptance criteria: Between 6.5 and 7.5
- **Water,** *Water Determination,* Appendix IIB
  Acceptance criteria: NMT 13.0%

Calcium Gluconate

First Published: Prior to FCC 6

$C_{12}H_{22}CaO_{14}$ — Formula wt, anhydrous 430.38
$C_{12}H_{22}CaO_{14} \cdot H_2O$ — Formula wt, monohydrate 448.39
INS: 578 CAS: anhydrous [299-28-5]
UNII: SQE6VB453K [calcium gluconate]

DESCRIPTION
Calcium Gluconate occurs as white, crystalline granules or powder. It is anhydrous or contains one molecule of water of hydration. It is stable in air. One g dissolves slowly in about 30 mL of water at 25° and in about 5 mL of boiling water. It is insoluble in alcohol and in many other organic solvents. Its solutions are neutral to litmus.
Function: Firming agent; stabilizer; texturizer
Packaging and Storage: Store in well-closed containers.

IDENTIFICATION
- **CALCIUM,** Appendix IIIA
  Sample: 20 mg/mL
  Acceptance criteria: Passes tests
- **THIN-LAYER CHROMATOGRAPHY,** Appendix IIA
  Sample solution: 10 mg/mL (Heat in a water bath at 60°, if necessary, to dissolve the sample.)
  Standard solution: 10 mg/mL of USP Potassium Gluconate RS
  Adsorbent: 0.25-mm layer of chromatographic silica gel
  Developing solvent system: Alcohol, water, ammonium hydroxide, and ethyl acetate [50:30:10:10]
  Spray reagent: Dissolve 2.5 g of ammonium molybdate in 50 mL of 2 N sulfuric acid in a 100-mL volumetric flask. Add 1.0 g of ceric sulfate, swirl to dissolve, dilute to volume with 2 N sulfuric acid, and mix.
  Application volume: 5 μL
  Analysis: Develop the chromatogram in the Developing solvent system until the solvent front has moved about three-fourths of the length of the plate. Remove the plate from the chamber and dry at 110° for 20 min. Allow to cool and spray with Spray reagent. After spraying, heat the plate at 110° for about 10 min.
  Acceptance criteria: The principal spot obtained from the Sample solution corresponds in color, size, and R_F value to that obtained from the Standard solution.

ASSAY
- **PROCEDURE**
  Sample: 800 mg
  Analysis: Dissolve the Sample in 100 mL of water containing 2 mL of 2.7 N hydrochloric acid. While stirring, preferably with a magnetic stirrer, add about 30 mL of 0.05 M disodium EDTA from a 50-mL buret. Then, add 15 mL of 1 N sodium hydroxide and 300 mg of hydroxy naphthol blue indicator and continue the titration to a blue endpoint. Each mL of 0.05 M disodium EDTA is equivalent to 21.52 mg of $C_{12}H_{22}CaO_{14}$ or 22.42 mg of $C_{12}H_{22}CaO_{14} \cdot H_2O$.
  Acceptance criteria
    Anhydrous: NLT 98.0% and NMT 102.0% of $C_{12}H_{22}CaO_{14}$, calculated on the dried basis
    Monohydrate: NLT 98.0% and NMT 102.0% of $C_{12}H_{22}CaO_{14} \cdot H_2O$, calculated on the as-is basis

IMPURITIES
Inorganic Impurities
- **LEAD,** Lead Limit Test, Flame Atomic Absorption Spectrophotometric Method, Appendix IIIB
  Sample: 10 g
  Acceptance criteria: NMT 2 mg/kg

Organic Impurities
- **SUCROSE AND REDUCING SUGARS**
  Sample: 1.0 g
  Analysis: Transfer the Sample into a 250-mL conical flask and add 20 mL of hot water to dissolve the sample. Cool the flask, add 25 mL of alkaline cupric citrate TS, cover the flask, and boil gently for 5 min, accurately timed. Cool the flask rapidly to room temperature, add 25 mL of 0.6 N acetic acid, 10.0 mL of 0.1 N iodine, and 10 mL of 2.7 N hydrochloric acid. Immediately titrate with 0.1 N sodium thiosulfate, using starch TS as the indicator. Perform a blank determination (See General Provisions) and make any necessary correction. Each mL of 0.1 N sodium thiosulfate consumed is equivalent to 2.7 mg of reducing substances (as dextrose).
  Acceptance criteria: NMT 1.0%

SPECIFIC TESTS
- **LOSS ON DRYING,** Appendix IIC: 105° for 16 h
  Acceptance criteria:
    Anhydrous: NMT 3.0%
    Monohydrate: NMT 2.0%

OTHER REQUIREMENTS
- **LABELING:** Indicate whether the material is anhydrous or the monohydrate.

Calcium Glycerophosphate

First Published: Prior to FCC 6

$C_3H_7CaO_6P$ — Formula wt 210.14
INS: 383 CAS: [27214-00-2]
UNII: XWV9Z12C1C [calcium glycerophosphate]

DESCRIPTION
Calcium Glycerophosphate occurs as a fine, white powder. It is somewhat hygroscopic. One g dissolves in about 50 mL of water at 25°. It is more soluble in water at a lower temperature, and citric acid increases its solubility in water. It is insoluble in alcohol.
Function: Nutrient
Packaging and Storage: Store in tight containers.

IDENTIFICATION
- **CALCIUM,** Appendix IIIA
  Sample solution: Saturated solution
  Acceptance criteria: Passes tests

ASSAY
- **PROCEDURE**
  Sample: 2 g, previously dried
  Analysis: Dissolve the *Sample* in 100 mL of water and 5 mL of 2.7 N hydrochloric acid. Transfer the solution into a 250-mL volumetric flask, dilute to volume with water, and mix well. Pipet 50.0 mL of this solution into a suitable container and add 50 mL of water. While stirring, preferably with a magnetic stirrer, add about 30 mL of 0.05 M disodium EDTA from a 50-mL buret. Then, add 15 mL of 1 N sodium hydroxide and 300 mg of hydroxy naphthol blue indicator. Continue the titration to a blue endpoint. Each mL of 0.05 M disodium EDTA is equivalent to 10.51 mg of $C_3H_7CaO_6P$.
  Acceptance criteria: NLT 98.0% and NMT 100.5% $C_3H_7CaO_6P$, on the dried basis

IMPURITIES
Inorganic Impurities
- **LEAD,** *Lead Limit Test, APDC Extraction Method,* Appendix IIIB
  Acceptance criteria: NMT 4 mg/kg

SPECIFIC TESTS
- **ALKALINITY**
  Sample: 1 g
  Analysis: Dissolve the *Sample* in 60 mL of water. Titrate the solution with 0.1 N sulfuric acid to neutralization, using 3 drops of phenolphthalein TS as indicator.
  Acceptance criteria: Not more than 1.5 mL of acid is required.
- **LOSS ON DRYING,** Appendix IIC: 150° for 4 h
  Acceptance criteria: NMT 12.0%

Calcium Hydroxide

First Published: Prior to FCC 6

Slaked Lime

$Ca(OH)_2$ Formula wt 74.10
INS: 526   CAS: [1305-62-0]
UNII: PF5DZW74VN [calcium hydroxide]

DESCRIPTION
Calcium Hydroxide occurs as a white powder. One g dissolves in 630 mL of water at 25°, and in 1300 mL of boiling water. It is soluble in glycerin and in a saturated solution of sucrose but insoluble in alcohol.
Function: Buffer; neutralizing agent; firming agent
Packaging and Storage: Store in tight containers.

IDENTIFICATION
- **ALKALINITY**
  Sample solution: Mix a sample with from 3 to 4 times its weight of water. The sample forms a smooth magma. Test the clear supernatant liquid from the magma with litmus.
  Acceptance criteria: Alkaline to litmus
- **CALCIUM,** Appendix IIIA
  Sample solution: Mix 1 g of sample with 20 mL of water and add sufficient glacial acetic acid to aid in dissolution.
  Acceptance criteria: Passes tests

ASSAY
- **PROCEDURE**
  Sample solution: Transfer 1.5 g of sample into a beaker and gradually add 30 mL of 2.7 N hydrochloric acid. When the sample has completely dissolved, transfer the solution into a 500-mL volumetric flask. Rinse the beaker thoroughly and add the rinsings to the flask. Dilute to volume with water and mix.
  Analysis: Transfer 50.0 mL of the *Sample solution* into a suitable container and add 50 mL of water. While stirring, preferably with a magnetic stirrer, add about 30 mL of 0.05 M disodium EDTA from a 50-mL buret. Then, add 15 mL of 1 N sodium hydroxide and 300 mg of hydroxy naphthol blue indicator. Continue the titration to a blue endpoint. Each mL of 0.05 M disodium EDTA is equivalent to 3.705 mg of $Ca(OH)_2$.
  Acceptance criteria: NLT 95.0% and NMT 100.5% of $Ca(OH)_2$

IMPURITIES
Inorganic Impurities
- **ARSENIC,** *Arsenic Limit Test,* Appendix IIIB
  Sample solution: 1 g in 15 mL of 2.7 N hydrochloric acid
  Acceptance criteria: NMT 3 mg/kg
- **CARBONATE**
  Sample solution: To 2 g of sample in 50 mL of water, add an excess of 2.7 N hydrochloric acid.
  Acceptance criteria: No more than a slight effervescence is observed.
- **FLUORIDE,** *Fluoride Limit Test,* Appendix IIIB
  Sample: 1.0 g
  Acceptance criteria: NMT 0.005%
- **LEAD,** *Lead Limit Test,* Appendix IIIB
  Sample solution: 1 g in 15 mL of 2.7 N hydrochloric acid
  Control: 5 µg Pb (5 mL of *Diluted Standard Lead Solution*)
  Acceptance criteria: NMT 2 mg/kg
- **MAGNESIUM AND ALKALI SALTS**
  Sample solution: Dissolve 500 mg of sample in a mixture of 30 mL of water and 10 mL of 2.7 N hydrochloric acid.
  Analysis: Boil the *Sample solution* for 1 min, rapidly add 40 mL of oxalic acid TS, and stir vigorously until precipitation is well established. Immediately add 2 drops of methyl red TS; then add 6 N ammonium hydroxide, dropwise, until the mixture is just alkaline.

Cool the mixture and transfer it into a 100-mL graduated cylinder, dilute to 100 mL with water, and let it stand for 4 h or overnight. Then decant the clear, supernatant liquid through a dry filter paper. Add 0.5 mL of sulfuric acid to 50 mL of the clear filtrate contained in a tared platinum dish, and evaporate the mixture on a steam bath to a small volume. Carefully evaporate the remaining liquid to dryness over a free flame and continue heating until the ammonium salts have been completely decomposed and volatilized. Finally, ignite the residue at 800° ± 25° to constant weight.
Acceptance criteria: NMT 4.8%

SPECIFIC TESTS
- **ACID-INSOLUBLE SUBSTANCES**
  Sample: 2 g
  Analysis: Dissolve the *Sample* in 30 mL of 1:3 hydrochloric acid, and heat to boiling. Filter the mixture through a suitable tared, porous-bottom porcelain crucible, and wash the residue with hot water until the last washing is free from chloride. Ignite the residue at 800° ± 25° for 45 min, cool and weigh the residue. [NOTE—Avoid exposing the crucible to sudden temperature changes.]
  Acceptance criteria: NMT 0.5%

Calcium Iodate

First Published: Prior to FCC 6

$Ca(IO_3)_2 \cdot H_2O$ Formula wt 407.90
INS: 916 CAS: [7789-80-2]
UNII: L8MN4Y57BR [calcium iodate]

DESCRIPTION
Calcium Iodate occurs as a white powder. It is slightly soluble in water and insoluble in alcohol.
Function: Maturing agent; dough conditioner
Packaging and Storage: Store in well-closed containers.

IDENTIFICATION
- **PROCEDURE**
  Sample: Saturated solution of the sample
  Analysis: Add 1 drop of starch TS and a few drops of 20% hypophosphorous acid to 5 mL of the *Sample*.
  Acceptance criteria: A transient blue color appears.

ASSAY
- **PROCEDURE**
  Sample solution: Dissolve 600 mg of sample, in 10 mL of 70% perchloric acid and 10 mL of water, heating gently if necessary, and dilute with water to 250.0 mL. [CAUTION—Handle perchloric acid in an appropriate fume hood.]
  Analysis: Transfer 50.0 mL of the *Sample solution* to a 250-mL glass-stoppered Erlenmeyer flask, add 1 mL of 70% perchloric acid and 5 g of potassium iodide, stopper the flask, and swirl briefly. Let the solution stand for 5 min. Titrate with 0.1 N sodium thiosulfate, adding starch TS just before the endpoint is reached. Each mL of 0.1 N sodium thiosulfate is equivalent to 3.398 mg of $Ca(IO_3)_2 \cdot H_2O$.
  Acceptance criteria: NLT 99.0% and NMT 101.0% of $Ca(IO_3)_2 \cdot H_2O$

IMPURITIES
Inorganic Impurities
- **LEAD,** *Lead Limit Test, Flame Atomic Absorption Spectrophotometric Method,* Appendix IIIB
  Sample: 10 g
  Acceptance criteria: NMT 4 mg/kg

Calcium Lactate

First Published: Prior to FCC 6

2-Hydroxypropanoic Acid, Calcium Salt

$C_6H_{10}CaO_6 \cdot xH_2O$ Formula wt, anhydrous 218.22
INS: 327 CAS: [814-80-2]
UNII: 2URQ2N32W3 [calcium lactate]

DESCRIPTION
Calcium Lactate occurs as a white to cream-colored, crystalline powder or granules. It contains up to five molecules of water of crystallization. The pentahydrate is somewhat efflorescent and at 120° becomes anhydrous. It is soluble in water and practically insoluble in alcohol.
Function: Buffer; dough conditioner; yeast nutrient
Packaging and Storage: Store in tight containers.

IDENTIFICATION
- **CALCIUM,** Appendix IIIA
  Sample solution: 50 mg/mL
  Acceptance criteria: Passes tests
- **LACTATE,** Appendix IIIA
  Sample solution: 50 mg/mL
  Acceptance criteria: Passes test

ASSAY
- **PROCEDURE**
  Sample: Amount equivalent to 350 mg of $C_6H_{10}CaO_6$
  Analysis: Dissolve the *Sample* in 150 mL of water containing 2 mL of 2.7 N hydrochloric acid. While stirring, preferably with a magnetic stirrer, add about 30 mL of 0.05 M disodium EDTA from a 50-mL buret. Then, add 15 mL of 1 N sodium hydroxide and 300 mg of hydroxy naphthol blue indicator. Continue the titration with the disodium EDTA to a blue endpoint. Each mL of 0.05 M disodium EDTA is equivalent to 10.91 mg of $C_6H_{10}CaO_6$.
  Acceptance criteria: NLT 98.0% and NMT 101.0% of $C_6H_{10}CaO_6$, calculated on the dried basis

IMPURITIES
Inorganic Impurities
- **FLUORIDE**, *Fluoride Limit Test, Method I or Method III,* Appendix IIIB
  Sample: 3.3 g for *Method I* or 1.0 g for *Method III*
  Acceptance criteria: NMT 0.0015%
- **LEAD**, *Lead Limit Test, Flame Atomic Absorption Spectrophotometric Method,* Appendix IIIB
  Sample: 3 g
  Acceptance criteria: NMT 2 mg/kg
- **MAGNESIUM AND ALKALI SALTS**
  Sample: 1 g
  Analysis: Mix the *Sample* with 40 mL of water and carefully add 1 mL of hydrochloric acid. Boil the solution for 1 min and rapidly add 40 mL of oxalic acid TS, followed immediately by 2 drops of methyl red TS. Then add 6 N ammonium hydroxide, dropwise from a buret, until the mixture is just alkaline. Cool the mixture to room temperature and transfer it into a 100-mL graduate cylinder. Dilute with water to 100 mL, mix, and allow the mixture to stand for 4 h or overnight. Decant the clear, supernatant liquid through a dry filter paper, transfer 50 mL of the clear filtrate to a tared platinum dish, and add 0.5 mL of sulfuric acid. Evaporate the contents of the dish to a small volume on a steam bath; then carefully heat over a free flame to dryness, and continue heating to complete decomposition and volatilization of the ammonium salts. Finally, ignite the residue to constant weight.
  Acceptance criteria: The weight of the residue does not exceed 5 mg. (NMT 1%)

SPECIFIC TESTS
- **ACIDITY (AS LACTIC ACID)**
  Sample solution: 1 g in 20 mL of water
  Analysis: Add 3 drops of phenolphthalein TS to the *Sample solution* and titrate with 0.1 N sodium hydroxide.
  Acceptance criteria: NMT 0.5 mL of titrant is required. (About 0.45%, as lactic acid)
- **LOSS ON DRYING**, Appendix IIC: 120° for 4 h
  Sample: 1.5 g
  Acceptance criteria
  Pentahydrate: Between 22.0% and 27.0%
  Trihydrate: Between 15.0% and 20.0%
  Monohydrate: Between 5.0% and 8.0%
  Dried Form: NMT 3.0%

Calcium Lactobionate
First Published: Prior to FCC 6

Calcium 4-(β,D-Galactosido)-D-gluconate

$C_{24}H_{42}CaO_{24}$ Formula wt, anhydrous 754.66
INS: 399   CAS: [5001-51-4]
UNII: 7D8YVA497F [calcium lactobionate]

DESCRIPTION
Calcium Lactobionate occurs as a white to cream-colored, free-flowing powder. It readily forms double salts, such as the chloride, bromide, and gluconate. It is anhydrous when obtained by spray-drying, or the dihydrate when obtained by crystallization. It is freely soluble in water, but insoluble in alcohol and in ether. It decomposes at about 120°. The pH of a 1:10 aqueous solution is between 6.5 and 7.5.
Function: Firming agent in dry pudding mixes; nutrient
Packaging and Storage: Store in well-closed containers.

IDENTIFICATION
- **CALCIUM**, Appendix IIIA
  Acceptance criteria: Passes tests
- **INFRARED ABSORPTION**, *Spectrophotometric Identification Tests,* Appendix IIIC
  Reference standard: USP Calcium Lactobionate RS
  Sample and Standard preparation: *K* (Sample previously dried at 105° for 8 h)
  Acceptance criteria: The spectrum of the sample exhibits maxima at the same wavelengths as those in the spectrum of the *Reference standard*.

IMPURITIES
Inorganic Impurities
- **HALIDES**, *Chloride and Sulfate Limit Tests, Chloride Limit Test,* Appendix IIIB
  Sample: 1.2 g
  Control: 0.7 mL of 0.020 N hydrochloric acid
  Acceptance criteria: The *Sample* shows no more turbidity than the *Control* (NMT 0.04%).
- **LEAD**, *Lead Limit Test, Flame Atomic Absorption Spectrophotometric Method,* Appendix IIIB
  Sample: 3 g
  Acceptance criteria: NMT 2 mg/kg
- **SULFATE**
  Sample: 25 g

Analysis: Transfer the *Sample* to a 600-mL beaker, dissolve it in 200 mL of water, adjust the solution to a pH between 4.5 and 6.5 with 2.7 N hydrochloric acid, and filter, if necessary. Heat the filtrate or clear solution to just below the boiling point. Then, while stirring vigorously, add 10 mL of barium chloride TS, boil gently for 5 min, and allow the solution to stand for at least 2 h, or, preferably, overnight. Collect the precipitate of barium sulfate on a suitable, tared crucible, wash until free from chloride, dry, and ignite at 600° to constant weight. The weight of barium sulfate so obtained, multiplied by 0.412, represents the weight of sulfate (SO_4) in the sample taken.
Acceptance criteria: NMT 0.7%

Organic Impurities
- **REDUCING SUBSTANCES (AS DEXTROSE)**
Sample: 1.0 g
Analysis: Transfer the *Sample* to a 250-mL conical flask, dissolve it in 20 mL of water, and add 25 mL of alkaline cupric citrate TS. Cover the flask, boil the contents gently for 5 min, accurately timed, and cool the flask rapidly to room temperature. Add 25 mL of 0.6 N acetic acid, 10.0 mL of 0.1 N iodine, and 10 mL of 3 N hydrochloric acid. Titrate with 0.1 N sodium thiosulfate, adding 3 mL of starch TS as the endpoint is approached. Perform a blank determination (see *General Provisions*), make any necessary correction. Each mL of 0.1 N sodium thiosulfate consumed is equivalent to 2.7 mg of reducing substances (as dextrose).
Acceptance criteria: NMT 1.0%

SPECIFIC TESTS
- **CALCIUM CONTENT**
Sample: 1.5 g
Analysis: Dissolve the *Sample* in 100 mL of water containing 2 mL of 2.7 N hydrochloric acid. While stirring, preferably with a magnetic stirrer, add about 30 mL of 0.05 M disodium EDTA from a 50-mL buret. Then, add 15 mL of 1 N sodium hydroxide and 300 mg of hydroxy naphthol blue indicator. Continue the titration with disodium EDTA to a blue endpoint. Each mL of 0.05 M disodium EDTA is equivalent to 2.004 mg of calcium (Ca).
Acceptance criteria: NLT 5.05% and NMT 5.55%, calculated on the dried basis
- **LOSS ON DRYING,** Appendix IIC: 105° for 8 h
Acceptance criteria: NMT 8.0%
- **OPTICAL (SPECIFIC) ROTATION,** Appendix IIB
Sample solution: 50 mg/mL (on the anhydrous basis)
Acceptance criteria: $[\alpha]_D^{25}$ between +23° and +25°

OTHER REQUIREMENTS
- **LABELING:** Indicate whether the product has been obtained through spray-drying or from crystallization.

Calcium Lignosulfonate
First Published: Prior to FCC 6
Last Revision: First Supplement, FCC 6

CAS: [8061-52-7]
UNII: 33T2H9O73P [calcium lignosulfonate (20000 mw)]

DESCRIPTION
Calcium Lignosulfonate occurs as a brown, amorphous polymer. It is obtained from the spent sulfite and sulfate pulping liquor of wood or from the sulfate (Kraft) pulping process. It may contain up to 30% reducing sugars. It is soluble in water, but not in any of the common organic solvents. The pH of a 1:100 aqueous solution is between approximately 3 and 11.
Function: Binder; dispersant
Packaging and Storage: Store in well-closed containers.

IDENTIFICATION
- **A. CALCIUM,** Appendix IIIA
Sample solution: 0.15 mg/mL
Acceptance criteria: Passes tests
- **B. PROCEDURE**
Sample: 100 mg
Analysis: Dissolve the *Sample* in 50 mL of water. Add 1 mL each of 10% acetic acid and 10% sodium nitrite solution, and mix by swirling. Allow the solution to stand for 15 min at room temperature.
Acceptance criteria: A brown color appears.
- **C. ULTRAVIOLET ABSORPTION**
Sample solution: 0.1 mg/mL (pH 5)
Acceptance criteria: A peak is observed between 275 and 280 nm.

ASSAY
- **SULFONATE SULFUR**
Sample: 1.0 g
Analysis: Dissolve the *Sample* in 400 mL of water in a beaker. Direct a gentle stream of nitrogen gas over the liquid's surface. Add 10 mL of nitric acid, and swirl the solution thoroughly until the reaction subsides. Add 10 mL of 70% perchloric acid, and swirl thoroughly again. [**CAUTION**—Handle perchloric acid in an appropriate fume hood.] Place the uncovered beaker on a hot plate, and heat the contents vigorously until the center of the bottom of the beaker becomes clear. Remove the beaker, and cool it to room temperature. Add 5 mL of hydrochloric acid, and heat it again until white fumes evolve. After cooling the beaker, dilute the solution to approximately 100 mL with water, adjust to pH 6 ± 0.2 with 10% sodium hydroxide, and heat the solution to boiling. Add 15 mL of 10% barium chloride solution, and leave the solution overnight in a fresh beaker in a steam bath at 90° to 95°. Pass through ashless filter paper (Whatman No. 42, or equivalent), and wash the precipitate with 200 mL of warm water. Transfer the paper and precipitate into a tared crucible. Heat the crucible slowly on a Bunsen burner to expel moisture. Place the crucible and contents in a muffle furnace at 850° for 1 h. Let the crucible cool in a desiccator, and

then weigh the residue to the nearest 0.0001 g. Calculate the percent sulfonate sulfur by the formula:

$$\text{Result} = (R/S) \times 13.7$$

R = weight of the residue (g)
S = weight of the sample taken (g)

Acceptance criteria: NLT 5.0% sulfonate sulfur

IMPURITIES
Inorganic Impurities
- **LEAD,** *Lead Limit Test, Atomic Absorption Spectrophotometric Graphite Furnace, Method I,* Appendix IIIB
  Acceptance criteria: NMT 1 mg/kg

SPECIFIC TESTS
- **CALCIUM**
  Strontium chloride solution: While stirring, add 164.7 g of 60% perchloric acid to 500 mL of water contained in a 1-L beaker. [**CAUTION**—Handle perchloric acid in an appropriate fume hood.] Then, while stirring, add 15.2 g of strontium chloride hexahydrate, stirring until solution is complete. Transfer the solution into a 1-L volumetric flask, and dilute to volume at room temperature with water. Mix thoroughly.
  Standard solution: 0.7 mg/mL of calcium, prepared from a certified Calcium Standard Solution (NIST, or equivalent). [NOTE—Store the *Standard solution* in polyethylene bottles because of its instability in glass.]
  Sample: 1 g, previously dried
  Sample solution: Dilute the *Sample* to 10 mL, and mix. If the solution is not particle-free, pass through a 0.45-μm disposable Millipore filter, discarding the first few mL of filtrate. Pipet 5 mL of *Strontium chloride solution* into a 50-mL volumetric flask, and add 5.0 mL of the filtrate or clear solution. Dilute with water to volume, and mix well.
  Analysis: Using a suitably calibrated atomic absorption spectrophotometer, determine the absorbance of the *Standard solution* and the *Sample solution* at 422.7 nm.
  Acceptance criteria: The absorbance of the *Sample solution* is not greater than that of the *Standard solution*. (NMT 7.0%)
- **LOSS ON DRYING,** Appendix IIC: 105° for 24 h
  Acceptance criteria: NMT 10.0%
- **REDUCING SUGARS**
  Copper reagent solution: [NOTE—Solution must be prepared several days in advance of use.] Dissolve 28 g of anhydrous dibasic sodium phosphate and 40 g of potassium sodium tartrate tetrahydrate in 700 mL of water. Add 100 mL of 1 N sodium hydroxide and 8 g of copper sulfate pentahydrate, followed by 180 g of anhydrous sodium sulfate. Add 0.7134 g of potassium iodate, and dilute to 1 L. Allow to stand for several days, then filter the clear top part of the solution through a medium-porosity, sintered-glass funnel.
  Lead subacetate solution: Dissolve 80 g of lead subacetate in 220 mL of water. Stir overnight, and pass through Whatman No. 42 filter paper, or equivalent. Dilute the supernatant solution to a specific gravity of 1.254 with freshly boiled water.
  Dibasic sodium phosphate solution: 190 mg/mL dibasic sodium phosphate heptahydrate, made to 100 mL
  Standard solution: 280 μg/mL dried dextrose, made to 500 mL
  Sample solution: Dissolve 1 g of sample in 150 mL of water, and adjust the pH to between 6.9 and 7.2 with sodium hydroxide solution or acetic acid.
  Analysis: To the *Sample solution*, add *Lead subacetate solution* in increments until no further precipitation is observed. Bring the volume to 250.0 mL with water, and mix well. Centrifuge the mixture, pipet 10 mL of the supernatant into a 50-mL volumetric flask, and dilute with water to about 35 mL. Add 2 mL or more of *Dibasic sodium phosphate solution* until no further precipitation forms. Dilute with water to 50 mL, and mix. Centrifuge at 2100× gravity for 10 min. Pipet 5 mL of supernatant solution into a test tube containing exactly 5 mL of *Copper reagent solution*, and mix. Loosely plug the tube, and place it in a boiling water bath for 40 min ± 10 s. At the end of the heating period, cool the tube immediately in cold water. Add 2 mL of 2.5% potassium iodide solution and 1.5 mL of 2 N sulfuric acid. Mix well, and titrate with 0.005 N sodium thiosulfate, using starch as the indicator, and note the volume of 0.005 N sodium thiosulfate consumed as V_S. Perform a corresponding blank titration using 5 mL of water and 5 mL of *Copper reagent solution*, and record the volume of 0.005 N sodium thiosulfate consumed as V_B.
  Repeat the entire procedure using 5 mL of *Standard solution* and 5 mL of *Copper reagent solution*, noting the volume of 0.005 N sodium thiosulfate consumed as V_D. Perform a corresponding blank titration using 5 mL of water and 5 mL of *Copper reagent solution*; record the volume of 0.005 N sodium thiosulfate consumed as V_B. Calculate the percent reducing sugars by the formula:

  $$\text{Result} = (A \times F)/B$$

  A = volume of 0.005 N sodium thiosulfate consumed by the 5-mL aliquot of *Sample solution*, determined by $V_B - V_S$ (mL)
  F = factor, 35
  B = volume of 0.005 N sodium thiosulfate consumed by 5 mL of the *Standard solution*, determined by $V_B - V_D$ (mL)

  Acceptance criteria: NMT 30.0%
- **RESIDUE ON IGNITION (SULFATED ASH),** Appendix IIC
  Sample: 1 g
  Acceptance criteria: NMT 20.0%
- **VISCOSITY OF A 50% SOLUTION**
  Sample: 200 g, on the dried basis
  Analysis: Dissolve the *Sample* in 200 mL of water contained in a 500-mL beaker. Equilibrate the solution at 25°, and measure its relative viscosity with a Brookfield viscometer (Model RVT, or equivalent), using a number 2 spindle at 20 rpm.
  Acceptance criteria: NMT 3000 centipoises

Calcium Lignosulfonate (40–65)

First Published: First Supplement, FCC 7

Lignosulfonic Acid, Calcium Salt (40–65)
INS: 1522
UNII: 6HPP8U6S23 [calcium lignosulfonate (50000 mw)]

DESCRIPTION

Calcium Lignosulfonate (40–65) occurs as a light yellow-brown to brown powder. It is an amorphous material obtained from the sulfite pulping of softwood. The lignin framework is a sulfonated random polymer of three aromatic alcohols: coniferyl alcohol, *p*-coumaryl alcohol, and sinapyl alcohol, of which coniferyl alcohol is the principal unit. After completion of the pulping, the water-soluble calcium lignosulfonate is separated from the cellulose, purified (ultrafiltration), and acidified. The recovered material is evaporated and spray dried. It is distinguished from Calcium Lignosulfonate by its characteristic weight average molecular weight, its low degree of sulfonation, and its low level of reducing sugars. It is soluble in water and practically insoluble in organic solvents.

Function: Carrier, encapsulating agent
Packaging and Storage: Store in well-closed containers.

IDENTIFICATION

- **DEGREE OF SULFONATION:** [NOTE—The degree of sulfonation is determined as the content ratio of organic sulfur to methoxyl. The organic sulfur content is determined indirectly as the difference between the total sulfur content (determined by elemental analysis) and inorganic sulfur content (determined by ion-exchange chromatography).]

  Total sulfur determination
  Calibration standards: Add approximately 0.2 mg of vanadium pentoxide into each of four tin capsules. Accurately weigh 0.5, 1.0, 1.5, and 2.0 mg of BBOT (2,5-(bis(5-*tert*-butyl-2-benzo-oxazol-2-yl) thiophene)) into the four capsules.
  System suitability standard: Add approximately 0.2 mg of vanadium pentoxide and 0.5–2.0 mg of BBOT into a tin capsule.
  Samples: Add approximately 0.2 mg of vanadium pentoxide into each of two tin capsules. Accurately weigh 1–2 mg of sample, previously dried, into each capsule.
  Equipment: Elemental analyzer capable of analyzing for sulfur[1]
  Equipment parameters
  Carrier gas: Helium, 120 mL/min
  Combustion furnace temperature: 1000°
  Oven temperature: 70°
  Helium pressure: 150 kPa
  Oxygen pressure: 150 kPa
  Oxygen loop: 5 mL
  Run time: 300 s
  System suitability
  [NOTE—A system suitability check should be performed after every fourth sample.]
  Sample: System suitability standard
  Suitability requirement 1: The chromatogram contains a sulfur peak.
  Suitability requirement 2: The standard deviation for triplicate analyses is NMT 0.20.
  Analysis: Run the four calibration standards and construct a calibration curve. [NOTE—The correlation coefficient should be at least 0.999.] Run the Samples. Obtain the weight (mg) of total sulfur in the Sample using the calibration curve. Calculate the percentage of total sulfur in the portion of the sample taken:

  $$\text{Result} = W_U/W_{SMP} \times 100$$

  W_U = weight of total sulfur calculated from the standard curve (mg)
  W_{SMP} = weight of the sample taken, on the dried basis (mg)

  Inorganic sulfur determination
  Mobile phase: 0.1 N sodium hydroxide and water (10:90)
  Standard stock solution: 1 mg/mL of sulfate, prepared by dissolving 0.1479 g of sodium sulfate in 100 mL of water
  Standard solutions: 2.0, 5.0, 20.0, and 40.0 mg/L of sulfate, prepared by pipetting 0.1, 0.25, 1.0, and 2.0 mL of Standard stock solution into separate 50-mL volumetric flasks, adding 1 mL of 3% H_2O_2 to each, and diluting with water to volume.
  Sample solution: Transfer 30 mg of previously dried sample into a 50-mL volumetric flask, and dissolve in 10 mL of 10 mg/mL of NaOH. Add 5 mL of 3% H_2O_2, and allow to stand overnight, then dilute with water to volume.
  Chromatographic system, Appendix IIA
  Mode: High-performance liquid chromatography[2]
  Detector: Ion detector with anion self-regenerating conductivity suppressor[3]
  Column: 25-cm × 4-mm, anion-exchange analytical column[4], and 5-cm × 4-mm anion-exchange guard column[5]
  Flow rate: 0.7 mL/min
  Injection size: 10 µL
  System suitability
  Sample: Sample solution
  Relative standard deviation: NMT 3.0%
  Analysis: Separately inject equal volumes of the Standard solutions and Sample solution (previously filtered using a 0.2-µm syringe filter) into the chromatograph, and measure the responses for the major peaks on the resulting chromatograms. [NOTE—The approximate retention time for sulfate is 7 min.] Prepare a standard curve for sulfate by plotting sulfate peak areas versus concentrations in mg/L. From the standard curve, calculate the concentration (C_U) of

---

[1] Thermo Fisher Scientific, or equivalent.
[2] Dionex Corporation (Sunnyvale, CA) ion exchange chromatograph, or equivalent.
[3] ASRS-300 4mm (Dionex Corporation, Sunnyvale, CA), or equivalent.
[4] IonPac AS11 (Dionex Corporation, Sunnyvale, CA), or equivalent.
[5] IonPac AG11 (Dionex Corporation, Sunnyvale, CA), or equivalent.

sulfate in the *Sample solution* in mg/L. Calculate the percentage of inorganic sulfur in the portion of the sample taken:

$$\text{Result} = C_U/C_{SMP} \times F_1/F_2 \times 100$$

C_U = concentration of sulfate in the *Sample solution* determined from the standard curve (mg/L)
C_{SMP} = concentration of the sample, on the dried basis, in the *Sample solution* (mg/L)
F_1 = formula weight of sulfur, 32
F_2 = formula weight of sulfate, 96

Methoxyl (–OCH3) determination
Sample: 15–20 mg, previously dried and weighed onto a small piece of aluminum foil
0.025 N sodium thiosulfate: Dilute 0.1 N sodium thiosulfate VS with water (1:3).
Analysis See *Figure 1* for apparatus setup. Wrap the foil around the *Sample* and put it into the reaction flask (A) to which 5 mL of hydroiodic acid (min. 57%), approximately 2 g of phenol, and a few glass beads have been added. Add 5 mL of 50 mg/mL cadmium sulfate solution containing about 0.3 mg of red phosphorus into the washer (G). Add 10 mL of glacial acetic acid (saturated with sodium acetate) and 10 droplets of bromine to the receiver (D). Finally, fill the U-trap (E) with sodium hydroxide or other suitable absorbant that will prevent bromine from leaving the system. Pass nitrogen gas through a 30 mg/mL Na_2CO_3 solution and into the system through the side arm (I) of the air condenser (B). Heat the reaction flask (A) to 140°–145° for 1 h in a glycerin bath. Wash the contents of the receiver (D) into a 250-mL Erlenmeyer flask containing 10 mL of acetic acid (saturated with sodium acetate). Rotate the flask and add formic acid dropwise until the color disappears. Add 5 mL of 10% potassium iodide solution, and mix. Then add 10 mL of 1 M sulfuric acid and let the flask stand for 3 min. Titrate the solution with *0.025 N sodium thiosulfate* until the color changes from yellowish to colorless. Calculate the percentage of methoxyl:

$$\text{Result} = V \times F_1 \times F_2/(W \times F_3 \times F_4) \times 100$$

V = volume of *0.025 N sodium thiosulfate* used in the titration (mL)
F_1 = concentration of the *0.025 N sodium thiosulfate*, 0.025
F_2 = formula weight of methoxyl, 31
W = weight of the sample taken on the dried basis (mg)
F_3 = stoichiometric conversion factor from titrant to methoxyl moiety, 6
F_4 = mL-to-L conversion factor for the *0.025 N sodium thiosulfate*, 1000

Degree of sulfonation calculation: Calculate the degree of sulfonation:

$$\text{Result} = (\%OS)/(\%M)$$

%OS = % organic sulfur, as (% total sulfur) – (% inorganic sulfur), determined above in the *Total sulfur determination* and *Inorganic sulfur determination* test procedures
%M = % methoxyl, determined above in the *Methoxyl (–OCH3) determination* test procedure

Acceptance criteria: 0.3–0.7, on the dried basis

- **INFRARED ABSORPTION**, *Spectrophotometric Identification Tests,* Appendix IIIC
  Reference standard: USP Calcium Lignosulfonate (40-65) RS
  Sample and standard preparation: *K*
  Acceptance criteria: The spectrum of the sample exhibits maxima at the same wavelengths as those in the spectrum of the *Reference standard*.

- **ULTRAVIOLET ABSORPTION**
  Sample stock solution: 500 µg/mL
  Sample solution: 50 µg/mL made from *Sample stock solution*, and adjusted to a pH of 2.0–2.2 with 5 M hydrochloric acid.
  Acceptance criteria: The *Sample solution* exhibits an absorption maximum at 280 nm.

- **WEIGHT-AVERAGE MOLECULAR WEIGHT**
  Mobile phase: Combine 1600 g of water with 161.8 g of dimethyl sulfoxide in a 2-L flask. Add 21.44 g of dibasic sodium phosphate heptahydrate, and adjust the pH to 10.5 with NaOH. Add 1.6 g of sodium dodecylsulfate and pass through a 0.22-µm filter.
  Standard solutions: Prepare two lignosulfonate calibration standard[6] solutions, each at 2 mg/mL in *Mobile phase*. One should be prepared using a lignosulfonate standard with a weight-average molecular weight from 30,000–60,000 g/mol, and the other using a lignosulfonate standard with a weight-average molecular weight from 5,000–10,000 g/mol. Filter each solution into a vial using a 0.2-µm syringe filter.
  Sample solution: 2 mg/mL using a previously dried sample. Filter into vial using a 0.2-µm syringe filter.
  Chromatographic system, Appendix IIA
  Mode: High-performance liquid chromatography
  Detector: UV 280 nm
  Column: 50-cm × 10-mm glucose divinylbenzene (DVB), 5-µm, 10^4 Å analytical column[7], and 4-cm × 6-mm, 7-µm, 300 Å guard column[8]
  Oven temperature: 60°
  Flow rate: 1.0 mL/min
  Injection size: 200 µL

---

[6] Lignosulfonate calibration standards available from Borregaard Industries Limited, Borregaard LignoTech Research and Development, P.O. Box 162, NO-1701 Sarpsborg, Norway. Phone no: +47 69118000; e-mail: borregaard@borregaard.com.
[7] Jordi Gel DVB Glucose (Jordi Labs, Bellingham, MA), or equivalent.
[8] TSK-Gel PWXL (TOSOH Bioscience, Montgomeryville, PA), or equivalent.

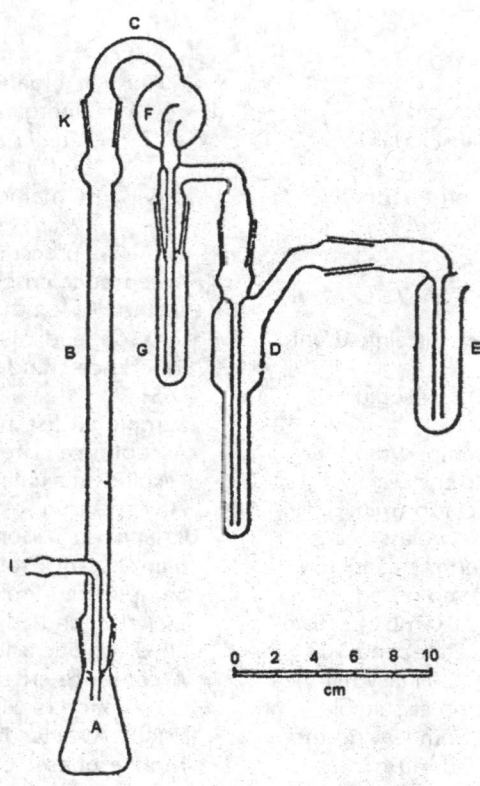

Figure 1. (Reprinted from Analytica Chimica Acta, Vol 15, P.O. Bethge and O.T. Carlson, On the Semimicro Determination of Methoxyl, Pages No. 279–283 (Fig. 1), Copyright (1956), with permission from Elsevier.)

System suitability
  Sample: The *Standard solution* with the highest weight-average molecular weight.
  Suitability requirement: The relative standard deviation of the lignosulfonate peak retention time for three injections is NMT 0.5%.
  Analysis: Run *Mobile phase* through the system for NLT 2 h. [NOTE—Pressure should not exceed 1000 psi.] Inject the *Standards solutions*, then the *Sample solution* followed by another set of *Standard solutions*. Generate a calibration curve using the *Standard solutions*. Calculate the weight-average molecular weight from the chromatogram of the *Sample solution* using suitable software.[9]
  Acceptance criteria: Between 40,000 and 65,000 with >90% of the sample ranging from 1,000–250,000

IMPURITIES
Inorganic Impurities
• **ARSENIC**, *Arsenic Limit Test*, Appendix IIIB: Prepare as directed for organic compounds.

[NOTE—Alternatively, the arsenic content may be determined by the following graphite furnace atomic absorption spectrophotometric method.]
  Standard solutions: 0–15 ng/mL of arsenic; prepared from a commercially available 1000 mg/kg arsenic standard solution. [NOTE—Store this solution in polyethylene bottles due to instability in glass.]
  Sample solution: [**CAUTION**—Wear proper eye protection, protective clothing, and gloves during sample preparation. Closely follow the manufacturer's safety instructions for use of the microwave digestion apparatus.] Transfer 200 mg of sample into a Teflon digestion vessel liner. Add 3 mL of 65% nitric acid, 2 mL of 30% hydrogen peroxide, and cover. Heat for 20 min in a microwave oven, and allow the vessel to cool to room temperature (a cool water bath may be used to speed the cooling process), and carefully open in a ventilation hood. Dilute the cooled digest with water to 12 mL.
  Reagent blank: Use the same quantities of reagents as used to prepare the *Sample solution*, but omitting the sample.

---
[9] Empower (Waters, Milford, MA), or equivalent.

Analysis: Use any suitable graphite furnace atomic absorption spectrophotometer. Optimize the instrument according to the manufacturer's instructions. Determine the absorbance of each of the *Standard solutions*, of the *Sample solution*, and of the *Reagent blank* at 193.7 nm. Determine the corrected absorbance values by subtracting the *Reagent blank* absorbance from each of the *Standard solutions* and from the *Sample solution* absorbances. Prepare a standard curve by plotting the corrected absorbance of the *Standard solutions* versus the concentration of arsenic (ng/mL). Calculate the concentration (mg/kg) of arsenic in the sample taken:

$$\text{Result} = C/W \times F_1$$

C = concentration of arsenic in the *Sample solution* determined from the standard curve (ng/mL)
W = weight of the sample taken to prepare the *Sample solution* (g)
F_1 = sample dilution factor, 12 mL

Acceptance criteria: NMT 1 mg/kg

- **LEAD**, *Lead Limit Test, Atomic Absorption Spectrophotometric Graphite Furnace Method, Method II*, Appendix IIIB
  Acceptance criteria: NMT 2 mg/kg

- **SULFITE**
  Mobile phase: 0.1 M sodium hydroxide and water (10:90)
  Diluent: Dilute 0.5 mL of 37% formaldehyde with water to 1000 mL.
  Standard stock solution: 1 mg/mL of sulfite in *Diluent*, prepared by dissolving 0.1574 g of sodium sulfite in and diluting with *Diluent* to 100 mL
  Standard solutions: 2.0, 5.0, 10.0, and 20.0 mg/L of sulfite in *Diluent*, made from *Standard stock solution*
  Sample solution: 3.0 mg/mL in *Diluent*
  Chromatographic system, Appendix IIA
    Mode: High-performance liquid chromatography[2]
    Detector: Ion detector with anion self-regenerating conductivity suppressor[3]
    Column: 25-cm × 4-mm, anion-exchange analytical column[4], and 5-cm × 4-mm anion-exchange guard column[5]
    Flow rate: 0.7 mL/min
    Injection size: 10 μL
  System suitability
    Sample: *Sample solution*
    Relative standard deviation: NMT 3.0% for the sulfite peak area
  Analysis: Separately inject equal volumes of the *Standard solutions* and *Sample solution* (previously filtered using a 0.2-μm syringe filter) into the chromatograph, and measure the responses for the major peaks on the resulting chromatograms. [NOTE—The approximate retention time for sulfite is 6 min.] Prepare a standard curve for sulfite by plotting sulfite peak areas versus concentrations in mg/L. From the standard curve, calculate the concentration (C_U) of sulfite in the *Sample solution* in mg/L. Calculate the percentage of sulfite in the portion of the sample taken:

$$\text{Result} = C_U/(C_{SMP} \times F_1) \times 100$$

C_U = concentration of sulfite in the *Sample solution* determined from the standard curve (mg/L)
C_{SMP} = concentration of the sample, on the dried basis, in the *Sample solution* (mg/mL)
F_1 = mL-to-L conversion factor, 1000

Acceptance criteria: NMT 0.5%, on the dried basis

Organic Impurities
- **REDUCING SUGARS**
  Standard solutions: 0.10, 1.0, and 2.0 mg/mL of glucose
  Sample solution: 10 mg/mL
  Equipment: Flow injection analyzer[10] with flow set to "low" position on both pumps, and heater set at 90°. [NOTE—The signal should be less than ± 1000 microabsorbance units before starting analysis.]
  Analysis: Introduce 100 μL each of the *Sample solution* and the *Standard solutions* into the analyzer. For each analysis, air is introduced followed by addition of 2 mg/mL of Brij-35 (polyoxyethyleneclycol dodecyl ether[11]), at a continuous flow of 0.287 mL/min. The solutions are then dialyzed through a cellulose membrane[12]. After dialysis add 1 M NaOH at 0.385 mL/min, and $CaCl_2$ and PHBH (*p*-hydroxylbenzoichydrazide), both at 0.074 mL/min, into the mixing chamber of the analyzer. The mixture then enters the heater (previously set at 90°) where bubbles are eliminated, after which it reaches the detector (set at 410 nm). Run duplicate injections of every *Sample solution*. Construct a calibration curve from the *Standard solutions*. Calculate the percentage of reducing sugars in the portion of the sample taken:

$$\text{Result} = C_U/C_{SMP} \times 100$$

C_U = concentration of reducing sugars, as glucose, in the *Sample solution* determined from the standard curve (mg/mL)
C_{SMP} = concentration of the sample, on the dried basis, in the *Sample solution* (mg/mL)

Acceptance criteria: NMT 5.0% (as glucose), on the dried basis

SPECIFIC TESTS
- **ASH (TOTAL)**, Appendix IIC
  Sample: 0.5–1 g, previously dried
  Analysis: Proceed as directed, but igniting at 550° for 1 h and then 900° for 10 min until all dark particles have disappeared and the ash is white.
  Acceptance criteria: NMT 14%, on the dried basis
- **CALCIUM**
  Standard stock solution: 3.00 μg/mL of calcium, prepared from a certified Calcium Standard Solution[13]. [NOTE—Store in polyethylene bottles because of its instability in glass.]

---
[10] O.I. Analytical (College Station, TX), or equivalent.
[11] Ultra grade, O.I. Analytical (College Station, TX), or equivalent.
[12] Type C 25 MM (Astoria-Pacific, Inc, Clackamas, OR), or equivalent.
[13] NIST or equivalent.

Standard solutions: 0.750, 1.50, 2.25, and 3.00 µg/mL of calcium, made from *Standard stock solution*. [NOTE—Store in polyethylene bottles because of its instability in glass.]

Sample stock solution: 4000 µg/mL prepared as follows. Transfer 0.2 g of a previously dried sample into a graduated flask. Add 5 mL of 65% nitric acid and 2 mL of 30% hydrogen peroxide. Boil for 1 h in a microwave oven. Dilute with water to 50 mL.

Sample solution: 40 µg/mL from *Sample stock solution*

Analysis: Using a suitably calibrated atomic absorption spectrophotometer, determine the absorbance of the *Standard solutions* and *Sample solution* at 422.7 nm. Prepare a standard curve for calcium by plotting calcium peak areas versus concentrations in mg/L. From the standard curve, determine the concentration (C_U) of calcium in the *Sample solution* in µg/mL. Calculate the percentage of calcium in the portion of the sample taken:

$$Result = C_U/C_{SMP} \times 100$$

C_U = concentration of calcium in the *Sample solution* determined from the standard curve (µg/mL)

C_{SMP} = concentration of the sample in the *Sample solution* (µg/mL)

Acceptance criteria: NMT 5.0%, on the dried basis

- **LOSS ON DRYING**, Appendix IIC: 105° for 24 h

  Acceptance criteria: NMT 8.0%

Calcium Oxide

First Published: Prior to FCC 6

Lime

CaO Formula wt 56.08
INS: 529 CAS: [1305-78-8]
UNII: C7X2M0VVNH [lime (cao)]

DESCRIPTION

Calcium Oxide occurs as hard, white or gray-white masses or granules or as a white to gray-white powder. One g dissolves in about 840 mL of water at 25° and in about 1740 mL of boiling water. It is soluble in glycerin but insoluble in alcohol.

Function: pH control agent; nutrient; dough conditioner; yeast food

Packaging and Storage: Store in tight containers.

IDENTIFICATION

- **CALCIUM**, Appendix IIIA

  Sample solution: Slake 1 g of sample with 20 ml of water and add glacial acetic acid until the sample is dissolved.

  Acceptance criteria: Passes tests

ASSAY

- **PROCEDURE**

  Sample: 1 g of sample ignited to a constant weight (See *Loss on Ignition* below.)

  Analysis: Dissolve the *Sample* in 20 mL of 2.7 N hydrochloric acid. Cool the solution, dilute to 500.0 mL with water, and mix. Pipet 50.0 mL of this solution into a suitable container, and add 50 mL of water. While stirring, preferably with a magnetic stirrer, add about 30 mL of 0.05 M disodium EDTA from a 50-mL buret. Then, add 15 mL of 1 N sodium hydroxide and 300 mg of hydroxy naphthol blue indicator. Continue the titration with disodium EDTA to a blue endpoint. Each mL of 0.05 M disodium EDTA is equivalent to 2.804 mg of CaO.

  Acceptance criteria: NLT 95.0% and NMT 100.5% of CaO, on the ignited basis

IMPURITIES

Inorganic Impurities

- **ALKALIES OR MAGNESIUM**

  Sample: 500 mg

  Analysis: Dissolve the *Sample* in 30 mL of water and 15 mL of 2.7 N hydrochloric acid. Heat the solution, boil for 1 min, and rapidly add 40 mL of oxalic acid TS, and stir vigorously. Add 2 drops of methyl red TS, and neutralize the solution with 6 N ammonium hydroxide to precipitate the calcium completely. Heat the mixture on a steam bath for 1 h and allow it to cool. Dilute the mixture to 100 mL with water, mix well, and filter. Add 0.5 mL of sulfuric acid to 50 mL of the filtrate. Then evaporate to dryness and ignite to constant weight in a tared platinum crucible at 800° ± 25°.

  Acceptance criteria: NMT 3.6%

- **ARSENIC**, *Arsenic Limit Test*, Appendix IIIB

  Sample solution: 1 g in 15 mL of 2.7 N hydrochloric acid

  Acceptance criteria: NMT 3 mg/kg

- **FLUORIDE**, *Fluoride Limit Test*, Appendix IIIB

  Sample: 1.0 g

  Acceptance criteria: NMT 0.015%

- **LEAD**, *Lead Limit Test*, Appendix IIIB

  Sample solution: 1 g in 15 mL of 2.7 N hydrochloric acid

  Control: 5 µg Pb (5 mL of *Diluted Standard Lead Solution*)

  Acceptance criteria: NMT 2 mg/kg

SPECIFIC TESTS

- **ACID-INSOLUBLE SUBSTANCES**

  Sample solution: Slake 5 g of sample, and then mix it with 100 mL of water and sufficient hydrochloric acid, added dropwise, to dissolve it.

  Analysis: Boil the *Sample solution*, cool, add hydrochloric acid, if necessary, to make the solution distinctly acid, and filter through a tared glass filter crucible. Wash the residue with water until free of chlorides, dry at 105° for 1 h, cool, and weigh.

  Acceptance criteria: NMT 1%

- **LOSS ON IGNITION**

  Sample: 1 g

Calcium Pantothenate

First Published: Prior to FCC 6

D-Calcium Pantothenate
Dextro Calcium Pantothenate

$C_{18}H_{32}CaN_2O_{10}$ Formula wt 476.54
                                           CAS: [137-08-6]
UNII: 568ET80C3D [calcium pantothenate]

DESCRIPTION
Calcium Pantothenate occurs as a slightly hygroscopic, white powder. It is the calcium salt of the dextrorotatory isomer of pantothenic acid. It is stable in air. One g dissolves in about 3 mL of water. It is soluble in glycerin, but is practically insoluble in alcohol, in chloroform, and in ether.

Function: Nutrient
Packaging and Storage: Store in tight containers.

IDENTIFICATION
- **A. CALCIUM,** Appendix IIIA
  Sample: 50 mg/mL
  Acceptance criteria: Passes tests
- **B. INFRARED ABSORPTION,** *Spectrophotometric Identification Tests,* Appendix IIIC
  Reference standard: USP Calcium Pantothenate RS
  Sample and standard preparation: K (Sample previously dried at 105° for 3 h)
  Acceptance criteria: The spectrum of the sample exhibits maxima at the same wavelengths as those in the spectrum of the *Reference standard.*
- **C. PROCEDURE**
  Sample: 50 mg
  Analysis: Boil the *Sample* in 5 mL of 1 N sodium hydroxide for 1 min, and allow the solution to cool. Then add 5 mL of 1 N hydrochloric acid and 2 drops of ferric chloride TS.
  Acceptance criteria: A strong yellow color appears

ASSAY
- **PROCEDURE**
  [NOTE—Use low-actinic glassware throughout this procedure.]
  Mobile phase: Transfer 2.0 mL phosphoric acid into a 2–L volumetric flask and dilute to volume with water. Filter the solution through a 0.45-μm pore-size disk.
  Internal standard solution: Transfer 80 mg of *p*-hydroxybenzoic acid into a 1–L volumetric flask, dissolve in 5 mL of alcohol, dilute to volume with *Mobile phase,* and mix.
  Standard solution: Transfer 15 mg of USP Calcium Pantothenate RS, previously dried, into a 25-mL volumetric flask, dilute to volume with *Internal standard solution,* and mix.
  Sample solution: Transfer 15 mg of sample, previously dried, into a 25-mL volumetric flask, dilute to volume with *Internal standard solution,* and mix.
  Chromatographic system, Appendix IIA
    Mode: High-performance liquid chromatography
    Detector: UV 210 nm
    Column: 15-cm × 3.9-mm (id) column packed with octadecylsilanized silica (10-μm μBondapak C 18, or equivalent)
    Flow rate: About 1.5 mL/min
    Injection volume: About 10 μL
  System Suitability
    Analysis: Chromatograph 3 replicate injections of the *Standard solution* and record the peak responses. [NOTE—The relative retention times are 0.5 for calcium pantothenate and 1.0 for *p*-hydroxybenzoic acid.]
    Suitability requirement: The relative standard deviation is NMT 2.0%.
  Analysis: Separately inject equal volumes of the *Standard solution* and the *Sample solution* into the chromatograph, record the chromatograms, and measure the peak responses obtained for each solution. [NOTE—The relative retention times are 0.5 for calcium pantothenate and 1.0 for *p*-hydroxybenzoic acid.] Calculate the quantity (mg), of $C_{18}H_{32}CaN_2O_{10}$ in the sample taken by the formula:

$$\text{Result} = 25C(R_U/R_S)$$

  C = concentration (mg/mL) of USP Calcium Pantothenate RS in the *Standard solution*
  R_U = ratio of the peak responses obtained for calcium pantothenate and *p*-hydroxybenzoic acid from the *Sample solution*
  R_S = ratio of the peak responses obtained for calcium pantothenate and p-hydroxybenzoic acid from the *Standard solution*

  Acceptance criteria: NLT 97.0% and NMT 103.0% of calcium pantothenate ($C_{18}H_{32}CaN_2O_{10}$), on the dried basis

IMPURITIES
Inorganic Impurities
- **LEAD,** *Lead Limit Test, Flame Atomic Absorption Spectrophotometric Method,* Appendix IIIB
  Sample: 10 g
  Acceptance criteria: NMT 2 mg/kg
- **ORGANIC IMPURITIES**
- **ALKALOIDS**
  Sample: 200 mg
  Analysis: Dissolve the *Sample* in 5 mL of water, add 1 mL of 2.7 N hydrochloric acid and 2 drops of mercuric–potassium iodide TS.

Analysis: Ignite the *Sample* to constant weight in a tared platinum crucible at 1100° ± 50°.
Acceptance criteria: NMT 10.0%

Acceptance criteria: No turbidity develops within 1 min.

SPECIFIC TESTS
- **ALKALINITY**
  Sample: 1 g
  Analysis: Dissolve the *Sample* in 15 mL of recently boiled and cooled water in a small flask. As soon as the *Sample* is completely dissolved, add 1.6 mL of 0.1 N hydrochloric acid to the *Sample solution*, then add 0.05 mL of phenolphthalein TS, and mix.
  Acceptance criteria: No pink color appears within 5 s.
- **CALCIUM CONTENT**
  Sample: 950 mg, previously dried
  Analysis: Dissolve the *Sample* in 100 mL of water containing 2 mL of 2.7 N hydrochloric acid. While stirring, preferably with a magnetic stirrer, add about 30 mL of 0.05 M disodium EDTA from a 50-mL buret. Then, add 15 mL of 1 N sodium hydroxide and 300 mg of hydroxy naphthol blue indicator. Continue the titration with disodium EDTA to a blue endpoint. Each mL of 0.05 M disodium EDTA is equivalent to 2.004 mg of calcium (Ca).
  Acceptance criteria: NLT 8.2% and NMT 8.6% of calcium (Ca), on the dried basis
- **LOSS ON DRYING,** Appendix IIC: 105° for 3 h
  Acceptance criteria: NMT 5.0%
- **OPTICAL (SPECIFIC) ROTATION,** Appendix IIB
  Sample: 50 mg/mL, prepared using a previously dried sample
  Acceptance criteria: $[\alpha]_D^{25}$ between +25.0° and +27.5°, on the dried basis

Calcium Pantothenate, Calcium Chloride Double Salt

First Published: Prior to FCC 6

Calcium Chloride Double Salt of DL- or D-Calcium Pantothenate

$C_{18}H_{32}CaN_2O_{10} \cdot CaCl_2$ Formula wt 587.52
CAS: [6363-38-8]
UNII: 43A575C21D [calcium pantothenate chloride]

DESCRIPTION
Calcium Pantothenate, Calcium Chloride Double Salt occurs as a white, free-flowing, fine powder. It is a chemical complex composed of approximately equimolar quantities of dextrorotatory (D) or racemic (DL) calcium pantothenate and calcium chloride. It is freely soluble in water, but insoluble in alcohol. Its solutions in water are alkaline to litmus.
Function: Nutrient
Packaging and Storage: Store in tight containers.

IDENTIFICATION
- **A. CALCIUM,** Appendix IIIA
  Sample solution: 50 mg/mL
  Acceptance criteria: Passes tests
- **B. PROCEDURE**
  Sample: 50 mg
  Analysis: Dissolve the *Sample* in 5 mL of 1 N sodium hydroxide, and filter. Add 1 drop of cupric sulfate TS to the filtrate.
  Acceptance criteria: A deep blue color appears.
- **C. UNCOMPLEXED MATERIAL**
  Sample: 1.0 g, previously dried
  Analysis: Stir the *Sample* with 15 mL of dimethylformamide for 5 min. Centrifuge the mixture, transfer 2.0 mL of the clear supernatant liquid to a weighing dish, evaporate the liquid under vacuum on a steam bath, and dry the residue in an oven at 105° for 1 h. The weight (g) of the residue (composed of uncombined calcium pantothenate and calcium chloride) multiplied by 750 equals the percentage of uncomplexed material in the sample.
  Acceptance criteria: NMT 10.0%

ASSAY
- **PROCEDURE**
  [NOTE—Use low-actinic glassware throughout this procedure.]
  Mobile phase: Transfer 2.0 mL phosphoric acid into a 2-L volumetric flask and dilute to volume with water. Filter the solution through a 0.45 μm pore-size disk.
  Internal standard solution: Transfer 80 mg of *p*-hydroxybenzoic acid into a 1-L volumetric flask, dissolve in 5 mL of alcohol, dilute to volume with *Mobile phase*, and mix.
  Standard solution: Transfer 15 mg of USP Calcium Pantothenate RS, previously dried, into a 25-mL volumetric flask, dilute to volume with *Internal standard solution*, and mix.
  Sample solution: Transfer 15 mg of sample, previously dried, into a 25-mL volumetric flask, dilute to volume with *Internal standard solution*, and mix.
  Chromatographic system, Appendix IIA
    Mode: High-performance liquid chromatography
    Detector: UV 210 nm
    Column: 15-cm × 3.9-mm (id) column packed with octadecylsilanized silica (10-μm μBondapak C 18, or equivalent)
    Flow rate: About 1.5 mL/min
    Injection volume: About 10 μL
  System Suitability
    Sample: *Standard solution*
    Suitability requirement: The relative standard deviation is NMT 2.0% for replicate injections.
  Analysis: Separately inject equal volumes of the *Standard solution* and the *Sample solution* into the chromatograph, record the chromatograms, and measure the peak responses obtained for each solution. [NOTE—The relative retention times are 0.5 for Calcium Pantothenate and 1.0 for *p*-hydroxybenzoic acid.] Calculate the quantity (mg), of $C_{18}H_{32}CaN_2O_{10}$ in the sample taken by the formula:

$$\text{Result} = 25C(R_U/R_S)$$

C = concentration (mg/mL) of USP Calcium Pantothenate RS in the *Standard solution*
R_U = ratio of the peak responses obtained for calcium pantothenate and *p*-hydroxybenzoic acid from the *Sample solution*
R_S = ratio of the peak responses obtained for calcium pantothenate and p-hydroxybenzoic acid from the *Standard solution*

Acceptance criteria: NLT 45.0% and NMT 55.0% of calcium pantothenate ($C_{18}H_{32}CaN_2O_{10}$), on the dried basis

IMPURITIES
Inorganic Impurities
- **ARSENIC**, *Arsenic Limit Test*, Appendix IIIB
  Sample solution: 1 g in 25 mL
  Acceptance criteria: NMT 3 mg/kg
- **LEAD**, *Lead Limit Test, APDC Extraction Method*, Appendix IIIB
  Acceptance criteria: NMT 2 mg/kg

SPECIFIC TESTS
- **CALCIUM CONTENT**
  Sample: 950 mg, previously dried
  Analysis: Dissolve the *Sample* in 100 mL of water containing 2 mL of 2.7 N hydrochloric acid. While stirring, preferably with a magnetic stirrer, add about 30 mL of 0.05 M disodium EDTA from a 50-mL buret. Then, add 15 mL of 1 N sodium hydroxide and 300 mg of hydroxy naphthol blue indicator. Continue the titration with disodium EDTA to a blue endpoint. Each mL of 0.05 M disodium EDTA is equivalent to 2.004 mg of calcium (Ca).
  Acceptance criteria: NLT 12.4% and NMT 13.6% of calcium (Ca), on the dried basis
- **CHLORIDE CONTENT** (as Cl)
  Sample: 1 g, previously dried
  Analysis: Transfer the *Sample* to a 250-mL beaker, and add sufficient water to make 100 mL. Equip a pH meter with glass and silver electrodes, and set it on the + millivolt scale. Insert the electrodes and a motor-driven glass stirring rod into the sample beaker. Add 1 to 2 drops of methyl orange TS, stir, and add, dropwise, 10% nitric acid until a pink color appears; then add 10 mL in excess. Titrate the solution with 0.1 N silver nitrate to a reading of +1.0 millivolt. Each mL of 0.1 N silver nitrate is equivalent to 3.545 mg of chloride.
  Acceptance criteria: Between 10.5% and 12.1% of chloride, on the dried basis
- **LOSS ON DRYING**, Appendix IIC: in vacuum, 100° for 1 h
  Acceptance criteria: NMT 5.0%

Calcium Pantothenate, Racemic
First Published: Prior to FCC 6

$C_{18}H_{32}CaN_2O_{10}$ Formula wt 476.54
CAS: [6381-63-1]
UNII: 2KC899R47Q [calcium pantothenate, racemic]

DESCRIPTION
Calcium Pantothenate, Racemic occurs as a white, slightly hygroscopic powder. It is a mixture of the calcium salts of the dextrorotatory (D) and levorotatory (L) isomers of pantothenic acid. It is optically inactive. It is stable in air and freely soluble in water. It is soluble in glycerin, and is practically insoluble in alcohol, in chloroform, and in ether. Its solutions are neutral or alkaline to litmus. [NOTE—The physiological activity of racemic Calcium Pantothenate is approximately one-half that of the dextrorotatory isomer.]
Function: Nutrient
Packaging and Storage: Store in tight containers.

IDENTIFICATION
- **A. CALCIUM**, Appendix IIIA
  Sample: 50 mg/mL
  Acceptance criteria: Passes tests
- **B. INFRARED ABSORPTION**, *Spectrophotometric Identification Tests*, Appendix IIIC
  Reference standard: USP Calcium Pantothenate RS
  Sample and Standard preparation: *K* (Sample previously dried at 105° for 3 h)
  Acceptance criteria: The spectrum of the sample exhibits maxima at the same wavelengths as those in the spectrum of the *Reference Standard*.
- **C. PROCEDURE**
  Sample: 50 mg
  Analysis: Boil the *Sample* in 5 mL 1 N sodium hydroxide for 1 min, cool, and add 5 mL of 1 N hydrochloric acid and 2 drops of ferric chloride TS.
  Acceptance criteria: A strong yellow color appears.

ASSAY
- **PROCEDURE**
  [NOTE—Use low-actinic glassware throughout this procedure.]
  Mobile phase: Transfer 2.0 mL phosphoric acid into a 2-L volumetric flask and dilute to volume with water. Filter the solution through a 0.45-µm pore-size disk.
  Internal standard solution: Transfer 80 mg of *p*-hydroxybenzoic acid into a 1-L volumetric flask, dissolve in 5 mL of alcohol, dilute to volume with *Mobile phase*, and mix.
  Standard solution: Transfer 15 mg of USP Calcium Pantothenate RS, previously dried, into a 25-mL volumetric flask, dilute to volume with *Internal standard solution*, and mix.
  Sample solution: Transfer 15 mg of sample, previously dried, into a 25-mL volumetric flask, dilute to volume with *Internal standard solution*, and mix.
  Chromatographic system, Appendix IIA
  Mode: High-performance liquid chromatography
  Detector: UV 210 nm

Column: 15-cm × 3.9-mm (id) column packed with octadecylsilanized silica (10-μm μBondapak C 18, or equivalent)
Flow rate: About 1.5 mL/min
Injection volume: About 10 μL
System suitability
  Sample: *Standard solution*
  Suitability requirement: The relative standard deviation for three replicate injections is NMT 2.0%.
Analysis: Separately inject equal volumes of the *Standard solution* and the *Sample solution* into the chromatograph, record the chromatograms, and measure the peak responses obtained for each solution. [NOTE—The relative retention times are 0.5 for calcium pantothenate and 1.0 for *p*-hydroxybenzoic acid.] Calculate the quantity (mg), of $C_{18}H_{32}CaN_2O_{10}$ in the sample taken by the formula:

$$\text{Result} = 25C(R_U/R_S)$$

C = concentration (mg/mL) of USP Calcium Pantothenate RS in the *Standard solution*
R_U = ratio of the peak responses obtained for calcium pantothenate and *p*-hydroxybenzoic acid from the *Sample solution*
R_S = ratio of the peak responses obtained for calcium pantothenate and *p*-hydroxybenzoic acid from the *Standard solution*

Acceptance criteria: NLT 97.0% and NMT 103.0% of calcium pantothenate, on the dried basis

IMPURITIES
Inorganic Impurities
- **LEAD,** *Lead Limit Test, Flame Atomic Absorption Spectrophotometric Method,* Appendix IIIB
  Sample: 10 g
  Acceptance criteria: NMT 2 mg/kg

Organic Impurities
- **ALKALOIDS**
  Sample: 200 mg
  Analysis: Dissolve the *Sample* in 5 mL of water, add 1 mL of 2.7 N hydrochloric acid and 2 drops of mercuric-potassium iodide TS.
  Acceptance criteria: No turbidity develops within 1 min.

SPECIFIC TESTS
- **ALKALINITY**
  Sample: 1 g
  Analysis: Dissolve the *Sample* in 15 mL of recently boiled and cooled water in a small flask. As soon as the *Sample* is completely dissolved, add 1.6 mL of 0.1 N hydrochloric acid to the *Sample solution*, then add 0.05 mL of phenolphthalein TS, and mix.
  Acceptance criteria: No pink color appears within 5 s.
- **CALCIUM CONTENT**
  Sample: 950 mg, previously dried
  Analysis: Dissolve the *Sample* in 100 mL of water containing 2 mL of 2.7 N hydrochloric acid. While stirring, preferably with a magnetic stirrer, add about 30 mL of 0.05 M disodium EDTA from a 50-mL buret. Then, add 15 mL of 1 N sodium hydroxide and 300 mg of hydroxy naphthol blue indicator. Continue the titration with disodium EDTA to a blue endpoint. Each mL of 0.05 M disodium EDTA is equivalent to 2.004 mg of calcium (Ca).
  Acceptance criteria: NLT 8.2% and NMT 8.6% of calcium (Ca), on the dried basis
- **LOSS ON DRYING,** Appendix IIC: 105° for 3 h
  Acceptance criteria: NMT 5.0%
- **OPTICAL (SPECIFIC) ROTATION,** Appendix IIB
  Sample solution: 50 mg/mL, prepared using a previously dried sample
  Acceptance criteria: $[\alpha]_D^{25}$ between −0.05° and +0.05°, on the dried basis

Calcium Peroxide
First Published: Prior to FCC 6

CaO_2 Formula wt 72.08
INS: 930 CAS: [1305-79-9]
UNII: 7FRO2ENO91 [calcium peroxide]

DESCRIPTION
Calcium Peroxide occurs as a white or yellow powder or granular material. It decomposes in moist air, is practically insoluble in water, and dissolves in acids, forming hydrogen peroxide. A 1:100 aqueous slurry has a pH of about 12.
Function: Dough conditioner; oxidizing agent
Packaging and Storage: Store in tight containers, and avoid contact with readily oxidizable materials. Observe the safety precautions printed on the label of the original container.

IDENTIFICATION
- **CALCIUM,** Appendix IIIA
  Sample solution: Cautiously dissolve 250 mg of sample in 5 mL of glacial acetic acid and add a few drops of a saturated solution of potassium iodide. Iodine is liberated. Add 20 mL of water and sufficient sodium thiosulfate TS to remove the iodine color.
  Acceptance criteria: Passes tests

ASSAY
- **PROCEDURE**
  Sample: 1 g
  Analysis: Transfer the *Sample* into an Erlenmeyer flask, add 30 mL of water and 30 mL of 1:1 (v/v) 85% phosphoric acid:water, and titrate immediately with 0.5 N potassium permanganate to the first faint pink color that persists for 1 min. Each mL of 0.5 N potassium permanganate is equivalent to 18.02 mg of CaO_2.
  Acceptance criteria: NLT 60.0% of CaO_2

IMPURITIES
Inorganic Impurities
- **FLUORIDE,** *Fluoride Limit Test,* Appendix IIIB
  Sample: 1.0 g

Acceptance criteria: NMT 0.005%
- **LEAD,** *Lead Limit Test,* Appendix IIIB
  Sample solution: Transfer 4.0 g of sample, into a 250-mL beaker, cautiously add 50 mL of nitric acid, and evaporate just to dryness on a steam bath. Add 20 mL of nitric acid, repeat the evaporation, cool, and dissolve the residue in sufficient water containing 4 drops of nitric acid to make 40.0 mL.
  Control: 4 µg of Pb (4 mL of *Diluted Standard Lead Solution*)
  Analysis: Use 10 mL of the *Sample solution.*
  Acceptance criteria: NMT 4 mg/kg

Calcium Phosphate, Dibasic

First Published: Prior to FCC 6

Dicalcium Phosphate

$CaHPO_4$	Formula wt, anhydrous 136.06
$CaHPO_4 \cdot 2H_2O$	Formula wt, dihydrate 172.09
INS: 341(ii)	CAS: anhydrous [7757-93-9]
	dihydrate [7789-77-7]

UNII: L11K75P92J [calcium phosphate, dibasic, anhydrous]
UNII: O7TSZ97GEP [calcium phosphate, dibasic, dihydrate]

DESCRIPTION
Calcium Phosphate, Dibasic occurs as a white powder. It is anhydrous or contains two molecules of water of hydration. It is stable in air. It is insoluble in alcohol, is practically insoluble in water, but is readily soluble in dilute hydrochloric and nitric acids.
Function: Leavening agent; dough conditioner; nutrient; yeast food
Packaging and Storage: Store in tightly closed containers.

IDENTIFICATION
- **A. PROCEDURE**
  Sample: 100 mg
  Analysis: Dissolve the *Sample* by warming it with 5 mL of 2.7 N hydrochloric acid and 5 mL of water. While shaking the solution, add 2.5 mL of 6 N ammonium hydroxide, dropwise, and then add 5 mL of ammonium oxalate TS.
  Acceptance criteria: A white precipitate forms.
- **B. PROCEDURE**
  Sample solution: 10 mg/mL
  Analysis: Add 10 mL ammonium molybdate TS to 10 mL of warm *Sample solution* in a slight excess of nitric acid.
  Acceptance criteria: A yellow precipitate of ammonium phosphomolybdate forms.

ASSAY
- **PROCEDURE**
  Sample: 250 mg
  Analysis: Dissolve the *Sample*, with the aid of gentle heat if necessary, in a mixture of 5 mL of hydrochloric acid and 3 mL of water contained in a 250-mL beaker equipped with a magnetic stirrer, and cautiously add 125 mL of water. With constant stirring, add, in the order named, 0.5 mL of triethanolamine, 300 mg of hydroxy naphthol blue indicator, and, from a 50-mL buret, about 23 mL of 0.05 M disodium EDTA. Then, add a 45:100 sodium hydroxide solution until the initial red color changes to clear blue and continue to add it dropwise until the color changes to violet; then, add an additional 0.5 mL. The pH is between 12.3 and 12.5. Continue the titration, dropwise, with the disodium EDTA to the appearance of a clear blue endpoint that persists for NLT 60 s. Each mL of 0.05 M disodium EDTA is equivalent to 6.803 mg of $CaHPO_4$ or to 8.604 mg of $CaHPO_4 \cdot 2H_2O$.
  Acceptance criteria: NLT 97.0% and NMT 105.0% (Anhydrous or dihydrate)

IMPURITIES
Inorganic Impurities
- **ARSENIC,** Appendix IIIB
  Sample solution: 1 g in 5 mL 2.7 N hydrochloric acid
  Acceptance criteria: NMT 3 mg/kg
- **FLUORIDE**
  [NOTE—Prepare and store all solutions in plastic containers.]
  Buffer solution: Dissolve 73.5 g sodium citrate in water, made to 250 mL.
  Standard stock solution: 1.1052 mg/mL USP Sodium Fluoride RS
  Standard solution: Transfer 20.0 mL of the *Standard stock solution* to a 100-mL volumetric flask containing 50 mL of *Buffer solution*, dilute to volume with water, and mix. (100 µg/mL fluoride ion)
  Sample solution: Transfer 2.0 g of sample to a beaker containing a plastic-coated stirring bar, add 20 mL of water and 2.0 mL of hydrochloric acid, and stir until the sample is dissolved. Add 50.0 mL of *Buffer solution* and sufficient water to make 100 mL.
  Electrode system: Use a fluoride-specific, ion-indicating electrode and a silver-silver chloride reference electrode connected to a pH meter capable of measuring potentials with a minimum reproducibility of ±0.2 mV.
  Standard response line: Transfer 50.0 mL of *Buffer solution* and 2.0 mL of hydrochloric acid into a beaker and add water to make 100 mL. Add a plastic-coated stirring bar, insert the electrodes into the solution, stir for 15 min, and read the potential (mV). Continue stirring, and at 5-min intervals, add 100 µL, 100 µL, 300 µL, and 500 µL of *Standard solution*, reading the potential 5 min after each addition. Plot the logarithms of the cumulative fluoride ion concentrations (0.1, 0.2, 0.5, and 1.0 µg/mL) versus potential, in mV.
  Analysis: Rinse and dry the electrodes, insert them into the *Sample solution*, stir for 5 min, and read the potential (mV). From the measured potential and the *Standard response line*, determine the concentration, C (µg/mL), of fluoride ion in the *Sample solution*. Calculate the percentage of fluoride in the sample taken by the formula:

$$\text{Result} = C \times 0.005$$

  Acceptance criteria: NMT 0.005%

- **LEAD,** *Lead Limit Test, APDC Extraction Method,* Appendix IIIB
  Acceptance criteria: NMT 2 mg/kg

SPECIFIC TESTS
- **LOSS ON IGNITION**
  Sample: 3 g
  Analysis: Ignite the *Sample*, preferably in a muffle furnace, at 800° to 825° to constant weight.
  Acceptance criteria
   Anhydrous: Between 7.0% and 8.5%
   Dihydrate: Between 24.5% and 26.5%

OTHER REQUIREMENTS
- **LABELING:** Indicate whether the product is anhydrous or the dihydrate.

Calcium Phosphate, Monobasic
First Published: Prior to FCC 6

Monocalcium Phosphate
Calcium Biphosphate
Acid Calcium Phosphate

Ca(H$_2$PO$_4$)$_2$ Formula wt anhydrous 234.05
Ca(H$_2$PO$_4$)$_2$·H$_2$O   Formula wt monohydrate 252.07
INS: 341(i)   CAS: anhydrous [7758-23-8]
                              monohydrate [10031-30-8]
UNII: 0N4E6L5449 [calcium phosphate, monobasic, monohydrate]
UNII: 701EKV9RMN [calcium phosphate, monobasic, anhydrous]

DESCRIPTION
Calcium Phosphate, Monobasic, occurs as white crystals or granules or as a granular powder. It is anhydrous or contains one molecule of water of hydration, but because of its deliquescent nature, more than the calculated amount of water may be present. It is sparingly soluble in water and is insoluble in alcohol.
Function: Buffer; dough conditioner; firming agent; leavening agent; nutrient; yeast food; sequestrant
Packaging and Storage: Store in well-closed containers.

IDENTIFICATION
- **A. PROCEDURE**
  Sample: 100 mg
  Analysis: Dissolve the *Sample* by warming it in a mixture of 2 mL of 2.7 N hydrochloric acid and 8 mL of water. Add 5 mL of ammonium oxalate TS.
  Acceptance criteria: A white precipitate forms.
- **B. PROCEDURE**
  Analysis: Add ammonium molybdate TS to a warm solution of sample in a slight excess of nitric acid.
  Acceptance criteria: A yellow precipitate of ammonium phosphomolybdate forms.

ASSAY
- **CALCIUM**
  Sample: Amount equivalent to 475 mg of Calcium Phosphate, Monobasic, Anhydrous [Ca(H$_2$PO$_4$)$_2$]
  Wash solution: Dilute 10 mL of ammonium oxalate TS to 1000 mL with water.
  Analysis: Dissolve the *Sample* in 10 mL of 2.7 N hydrochloric acid, add a few drops of methyl orange TS, and boil for 5 min, keeping the volume and pH of the solution constant during the boiling period by adding hydrochloric acid or water as necessary. Add 2 drops of methyl red TS and 30 mL of ammonium oxalate TS. Then, while constantly stirring, add, dropwise, a mixture of equal volumes of 6 N ammonium hydroxide and water until the pink color of the indicator just disappears. Digest on a steam bath for 30 min, cool to room temperature, allow the precipitate to settle, and filter the supernatant liquid through a sintered-glass crucible, using gentle suction. Wash the precipitate in the beaker with about 30 mL of cold (below 20°) *Wash solution*. Allow the precipitate to settle, and pour the supernatant liquid through the filter. Repeat this washing by decantation three more times. Using the *Wash solution*, transfer the precipitate as completely as possible to the filter. Finally, wash the beaker and the filter with two 10-mL portions of cold (below 20°) water. Place the sintered-glass crucible in the beaker, and add 100 mL of water and 50 mL of cold 1:6 sulfuric acid. Add 35 mL of 0.1 N potassium permanganate from a buret and stir until the color disappears. Heat to about 70°, and complete the titration with 0.1 N potassium permanganate. Each mL of 0.1 N potassium permanganate is equivalent to 2.004 mg of Ca.
  Acceptance criteria
   Anhydrous: NLT 16.8% and NMT 18.3% of Ca
   Monohydrate: NLT 15.9% and NMT 17.7% of Ca

IMPURITIES
Inorganic Impurities
- **ARSENIC,** *Arsenic Limit Test,* Appendix IIIB
  Sample solution: 1 g in 5 mL of 2.7 N hydrochloric acid
  Acceptance criteria: NMT 3 mg/kg
- **FLUORIDE**
  [NOTE—Prepare and store all solutions in plastic containers.]
  Anhydrous material: *Fluoride Limit Test, Method II,* Appendix IIIB
  Monohydrate:
   Buffer solution: Dissolve 73.5 g sodium citrate in water, made to 250 mL.
   Standard stock solution: 1.1052 mg/mL USP Sodium Fluoride RS
   Standard solution: Transfer 20.0 mL of the *Standard stock solution* to a 100-mL volumetric flask containing 50 mL of *Buffer solution*, dilute to volume with water, and mix. (100 µg/mL fluoride ion)
   Sample solution: Transfer 2.0 g of sample to a beaker containing a plastic-coated stirring bar, add 20 mL of water and 2.0 mL of hydrochloric acid, and stir until

the sample is dissolved. Add 50.0 mL of *Buffer solution* and sufficient water to make 100 mL.

Electrode system: Use a fluoride-specific, ion-indicating electrode and a silver-silver chloride reference electrode connected to a pH meter capable of measuring potentials with a minimum reproducibility of ±0.2 mV.

Standard response line: Transfer 50.0 mL of *Buffer solution* and 2.0 mL of hydrochloric acid into a beaker and add water to make 100 mL. Add a plastic-coated stirring bar, insert the electrodes into the solution, stir for 15 min, and read the potential (mV). Continue stirring, and at 5-min intervals, add 100 µL, 100 µL, 300 µL, and 500 µL of *Standard solution*, reading the potential 5 min after each addition. Plot the logarithms of the cumulative fluoride ion concentrations (0.1, 0.2, 0.5, and 1.0 µg/mL) versus potential, in mV.

Analysis: Rinse and dry the electrodes, insert them into the *Sample solution*, stir for 5 min, and read the potential (mV). From the measured potential and the *Standard response line*, determine the concentration, C (µg/mL), of fluoride ion in the *Sample solution*. Calculate the percentage of fluoride in the sample taken by the formula:

$$\text{Result} = C \times 0.005$$

Acceptance criteria: NMT 0.005%

- **LEAD,** *Lead Limit Test, APDC Extraction Method,* Appendix IIIB

  Acceptance criteria: NMT 2 mg/kg

SPECIFIC TESTS

- **LOSS ON DRYING,** Appendix IIC: 60° for 3 h
  [NOTE—Monohydrate only.]
  Acceptance criteria: NMT 1%
- **LOSS ON IGNITION**
  [NOTE—Anhydrous material only.]
  Sample: 3 g
  Analysis: Ignite the *Sample*, preferably in a muffle furnace, at 800° for 30 min.
  Acceptance criteria: Between 14.0% and 15.5%

OTHER REQUIREMENTS

- **LABELING:** Indicate the state of hydration.

Calcium Phosphate, Tribasic

First Published: Prior to FCC 6

Tricalcium Phosphate
Precipitated Calcium Phosphate
Calcium Hydroxyapatite

$Ca_3(PO_4)_2$ Formula wt 310.18
$Ca_5OH(PO_4)_3$ Formula wt 502.31
$Ca_{10}(OH)_2(PO_4)_6$ Formula wt 1004.61
INS: 341(iii)   CAS: [7758-87-4]
                                       [1306-06-5]
                                       [62974-97-4]

UNII: 91D9GV0Z28 [tribasic calcium phosphate]
UNII: K4C08XP666 [tricalcium phosphate]

DESCRIPTION

Calcium Phosphate, Tribasic occurs as a white powder that is stable in air. It consists of a variable mixture of calcium phosphates. It is insoluble in alcohol and almost insoluble in water, but it dissolves readily in dilute hydrochloric and nitric acids.

Function: Anticaking agent; buffer; nutrient; clouding agent

Packaging and Storage: Store in well-closed containers.

IDENTIFICATION

- **A. PROCEDURE**
  Analysis: Add ammonium molybdate TS to a warm solution of sample in a slight excess of nitric acid.
  Acceptance criteria: A yellow precipitate of ammonium phosphomolybdate forms.
- **B. PROCEDURE**
  Sample: 100 mg
  Analysis: Dissolve the *Sample* by warming it with 5 mL of 2.7 N hydrochloric acid and 5 mL of water. While shaking the solution, add 1 mL of 6 N ammonium hydroxide, dropwise; then add 5 mL of ammonium oxalate TS.
  Acceptance criteria: A white precipitate forms.

ASSAY

- **CALCIUM**
  Sample: 150 mg
  Analysis: Dissolve the *Sample*, with the aid of gentle heat if necessary, in a mixture of 5 mL of hydrochloric acid and 3 mL of water contained in a 250-mL beaker equipped with a magnetic stirrer, and cautiously add 125 mL of water. With constant stirring, add, in the order named, 0.5 mL of triethanolamine, 300 mg of hydroxy naphthol blue indicator, and, from a 50-mL buret, about 23 mL of 0.05 M disodium EDTA. Then, add a 45:100 sodium hydroxide solution until the initial red color changes to clear blue and continue to add it dropwise until the color changes to violet; then, add an additional 0.5 mL. The pH is between 12.3 and 12.5. Continue the titration, dropwise, with the disodium EDTA to the appearance of a clear blue endpoint that persists for not less than 60 s. Each mL of 0.05 M disodium EDTA is equivalent to 2.004 mg of Ca.
  Acceptance criteria: NLT 34.0% and NMT 40.0% of Ca

IMPURITIES

Inorganic Impurities

- **ARSENIC,** *Arsenic Limit Test,* Appendix IIIB
  Sample solution: 1 g in 5 mL of 2.7 N hydrochloric acid
  Acceptance criteria: NMT 3 mg/kg
- **FLUORIDE**
  [NOTE—Prepare and store all solutions in plastic containers.]
  Buffer solution: Dissolve 73.5 g sodium citrate in water, made to 250 mL.
  Standard stock solution: 1.1052 mg/mL USP Sodium Fluoride RS

Standard solution: Transfer 20.0 mL of the *Standard stock solution* to a 100-mL volumetric flask containing 50 mL of *Buffer solution*, dilute to volume with water, and mix. (100 µg/mL fluoride ion)

Sample solution: Transfer 2.0 g of sample to a beaker containing a plastic-coated stirring bar, add 20 mL of water and 3.0 mL of hydrochloric acid, and stir until the sample is dissolved. Add 50.0 mL of *Buffer solution* and sufficient water to make 100 mL.

Electrode system: Use a fluoride-specific, ion-indicating electrode and a silver-silver chloride reference electrode connected to a pH meter capable of measuring potentials with a minimum reproducibility of ±0.2 mV.

Standard response line: Transfer 50.0 mL of *Buffer solution* and 3.0 mL of hydrochloric acid into a beaker and add water to make 100 mL. Add a plastic-coated stirring bar, insert the electrodes into the solution, stir for 15 min, and read the potential (mV). Continue stirring, and at 5-min intervals, add 100 µL, 100 µL, 300 µL, and 500 µL of *Standard solution*, reading the potential 5 min after each addition. Plot the logarithms of the cumulative fluoride ion concentrations (0.1, 0.2, 0.5, and 1.0 µg/mL) versus potential, in mV.

Analysis: Rinse and dry the electrodes, insert them into the *Sample solution*, stir for 5 min, and read the potential (mV). From the measured potential and the *Standard response line*, determine the concentration, C (µg/mL), of fluoride ion in the *Sample solution*. Calculate the percentage of fluoride in the sample taken by the formula:

$$\text{Result} = C \times 0.005$$

Acceptance criteria: NMT 0.0075%

- **LEAD**, *Lead Limit Test, APDC Extraction Method*, Appendix IIIB

  Acceptance criteria: NMT 2 mg/kg

SPECIFIC TESTS
- **LOSS ON IGNITION**

  Sample: 3 g

  Analysis: Ignite the *Sample*, preferably in a muffle furnace, at 800° to 825° to constant weight.

  Acceptance criteria: NMT 10.0%

Calcium Propionate

First Published: Prior to FCC 6
Last Revision: Second Supplement, FCC 6

Calcium Propanoate

$C_6H_{10}CaO_4$
INS: 282
UNII: 8AI80040KW [calcium propionate]

Formula wt 186.22
CAS: [4075-81-4]

DESCRIPTION
Calcium Propionate occurs as white crystals or as a crystalline solid. It is produced by reacting calcium hydroxide (lime) with propionic acid. The pH of a 1:10 aqueous solution is between 7.5 and 10.5. One g dissolves in about 3 mL of water.

Function: Preservative; mold inhibitor
Packaging and Storage: Store in tightly closed containers.

IDENTIFICATION
- **A. CALCIUM,** Appendix IIIA

  Sample solution: 50 mg/mL

  Acceptance criteria: Passes tests
- **B. PROCEDURE**

  Analysis: Ignite a sample at a relatively low temperature.

  Acceptance criteria: An alkaline residue that effervesces with acids is formed.

ASSAY
- **PROCEDURE**

  Sample solution: Dissolve 400 mg of sample in 75 mL of hot water (>82°) and filter through a 30 medium filtering crucible; wash the filtering crucible with 25 mL of hot water (>82°). Combine all collected filtrate and use as the *Sample solution*.

  Analysis: While stirring the *Sample solution*, preferably with a magnetic stirrer, add about 30 mL of 0.05 M disodium EDTA from a 50-mL buret. Then, add 15 mL of 1 N sodium hydroxide and 300 mg of hydroxy naphthol blue indicator. Continue the titration with the disodium EDTA to a blue endpoint. Each mL of 0.05 M disodium EDTA is equivalent to 9.311 mg of $C_6H_{10}CaO_4$.

  Acceptance criteria: NLT 98.0% and NMT 100.5% of $C_6H_{10}CaO_4$, calculated on the anhydrous basis

IMPURITIES
Inorganic Impurities
- **FLUORIDE,** *Fluoride Limit Test, Method III*, Appendix IIIB

  Sample: 1.0 g

  Acceptance criteria: NMT 0.003%
- **LEAD,** *Lead Limit Test, Flame Atomic Absorption Spectrophotometric Method*, Appendix IIIB

  Sample: 10 g

  Acceptance criteria: NMT 2 mg/kg
- **MAGNESIUM (as MgO)**

  Sample: 400.0 mg

  Magnesium standard solution: 50 µg/mL (see *Standard Solutions for the Preparation of Controls and Standards, Solutions and Indicators*)

  Analysis: Place the *Sample*, 5 mL of 2.7 N hydrochloric acid, and about 10 mL of water in a small beaker, and dissolve the sample by heating it on a hot plate. Evaporate the solution to a volume of about 2 mL, and cool. Transfer the residual liquid into a 100-mL volumetric flask, dilute with water to volume, and mix. Dilute 7.5 mL of this solution with water to 20 mL, add 2 mL of 1 N sodium hydroxide and 0.05 mL of a 1:1000 solution of Titan yellow (Clayton yellow), mix, allow the mixture to stand for 10 min, and shake. Note any color produced, and repeat the preceding using 1.0 mL of the *Magnesium standard solution* in the same volume as that of a control solution containing 2.5 mL of the sample solution (corresponding to 10 mg of sample) and the quantities of the reagents used in the test.

Acceptance criteria: Any color produced by the *Sample* does not exceed that produced by the control solution (about 0.4%).

SPECIFIC TESTS
- **ACID-INSOLUBLE SUBSTANCES**
  Sample: 2 g
  Analysis: Dissolve the *Sample* in 30 mL of 1:3 hydrochloric acid, and heat to boiling. Filter the mixture through a suitable tared, porous-bottom porcelain crucible, and wash the residue with hot water until the last washing is free from chloride. Ignite the residue at 800° ± 25° for 45 min, cool, and weigh the residue. [NOTE—Avoid exposing the crucible to sudden temperature changes.]
  Acceptance criteria: NMT 0.2%
- **WATER,** *Water Determination,* Appendix IIB
  Acceptance criteria: NMT 5.0%

Calcium Pyrophosphate

First Published: Prior to FCC 6

$Ca_2P_2O_7$ Formula wt 254.10
INS: 450(vi)   CAS: [7790-76-3]
UNII: X69NU20D19 [calcium pyrophosphate]

DESCRIPTION
Calcium Pyrophosphate occurs as a fine, white powder. It is insoluble in water, but is soluble in dilute hydrochloric and nitric acids.
Function: Buffer; neutralizing agent; nutrient
Packaging and Storage: Store in well-closed containers.

IDENTIFICATION
- **A. PROCEDURE**
  Sample: 100 mg
  Analysis: Dissolve the *Sample* by warming it with a mixture of 5 mL of 2.7 N hydrochloric acid and 5 mL of water. While shaking the solution, add 2.5 mL of 6 N ammonium hydroxide, dropwise. Then add 5 mL of ammonium oxalate TS.
  Acceptance criteria: A white precipitate forms.
- **B. PROCEDURE**
  Sample: 100 mg
  Analysis: Dissolve the *Sample* in 100 mL of 1.7 N nitric acid and add 0.5 mL of this solution (reserving the remainder for *Identification* test C) to 30 mL of quimociac TS.
  Acceptance criteria: A yellow precipitate does not form.
- **C. PROCEDURE**
  Sample: Reserved solution from *Procedure B*
  Analysis: Heat the *Sample* for 10 min at 95°, and then add 0.5 mL of the solution to 30 mL of quimociac TS.

  Acceptance criteria: A yellow precipitate forms immediately.

ASSAY
- **PROCEDURE**
  Sample: 300 mg
  Wash solution: Dilute 10 mL of ammonium oxalate TS to 1000 mL with water.
  Analysis: Dissolve the *Sample* in 10 mL of 2.7 N hydrochloric acid, add about 120 mL of water and a few drops of methyl orange TS and boil for 30 min. Keep the volume and pH of the solution constant during the boiling period by adding hydrochloric acid or water if necessary. Add 2 drops of methyl red TS and 30 mL of ammonium oxalate TS. Then add, dropwise, with constant stirring, a mixture of equal volumes of 6 N ammonium hydroxide and water until the pink color of the indicator just disappears. Digest the solution on a steam bath for 30 min, cool it to room temperature, allow the precipitate to settle, and filter the supernatant liquid through a sintered-glass filter crucible using gentle suction. Wash the precipitate in the beaker with about 30 mL of cold (below 20°) *Wash solution.* Allow the precipitate to settle and pour the supernatant liquid through the filter. Repeat this washing by decantation three more times. Using the *Wash solution,* transfer the precipitate as completely as possible to the filter. Finally, wash the beaker and the filter with two 10-mL portions of cold (below 20°) water. Place the sintered-glass filter crucible in the beaker and add 100 mL of water and 50 mL of cold, 1:6 sulfuric acid. Add 35 mL of 0.1 N potassium permanganate from a buret and stir until the color disappears. Heat to about 70°, and complete the titration with 0.1 N potassium permanganate. Each mL of 0.1 N potassium permanganate is equivalent to 6.35 mg of $Ca_2P_2O_7$.
  Acceptance criteria: NLT 96.0% of $Ca_2P_2O_7$

IMPURITIES
Inorganic Impurities
- **ARSENIC,** *Arsenic Limit Test,* Appendix IIIB
  Sample: 1 g in 5 mL of 2.7 N hydrochloric acid
  Acceptance criteria: NMT 3 mg/kg
- **FLUORIDE,** *Fluoride Limit Test,* Appendix IIIB
  Sample: 1 g
  Acceptance criteria: NMT 0.005%
- **LEAD,** *Lead Limit Test, APDC Extraction Method,* Appendix IIIB
  Acceptance criteria: NMT 2 mg/kg

SPECIFIC TESTS
- **LOSS ON IGNITION**
  Sample: 1 g
  Analysis: Ignite the *Sample,* preferably in a muffle furnace, at 800° to 825° for 30 min.
  Acceptance criteria: NMT 1.0%

Calcium Saccharin

First Published: Prior to FCC 6

1,2-Benzisothiazolin-3-one-1,1-Dioxide, Calcium Salt

$C_{14}H_8CaN_2O_6S_2 \cdot 3^{1}/_{2}H_2O$　　　Formula wt 467.48
INS: 954　　　CAS: [6485-34-3]
UNII: 5101OP7P2I [saccharin calcium]

DESCRIPTION
Calcium Saccharin occurs as white crystals or as a white, crystalline powder. One g is soluble in 1.5 mL of water.
Function: Non-nutritive sweetener
Packaging and Storage: Store in well-closed containers.

IDENTIFICATION
- **A. Procedure**
  Sample: 100 mg
  Analysis: Dissolve the *Sample* in 5 mL of a 50 mg/mL solution of sodium hydroxide, evaporate to dryness, and gently fuse the residue over a small flame until ammonia no longer evolves. After the residue has cooled, dissolve it in 20 mL of water, neutralize the solution with 2.7 N hydrochloric acid, and filter. Add 1 drop of ferric chloride TS to the filtrate.
  Acceptance criteria: A violet color appears.
- **B. Procedure**
  Sample: 20 mg
  Analysis: Mix the *Sample* with 40 mg of resorcinol, cautiously add 10 drops of sulfuric acid, and heat the mixture in a liquid bath at 200° for 3 min. After cooling, add 10 mL of water and an excess of 1 N sodium hydroxide.
  Acceptance criteria: A fluorescent green liquid is produced.
- **C. Calcium,** Appendix IIIA
  Sample solution: 100 mg/mL
  Acceptance criteria: Passes tests
- **D. Melting Range or Temperature Determination,** Appendix IIB
  Sample solution: 100 mg/mL
  Analysis: Add 1 mL of hydrochloric acid to 10 mL of the *Sample solution*. A crystalline precipitate of saccharin forms. Wash the precipitate well with cold water, and dry it at 105° for 2 h.
  Acceptance criteria: The saccharin thus obtained melts between 226° and 230°.

ASSAY
- **Procedure**
  Sample: 500 mg
  Analysis: With the aid of 10 mL of water, quantitatively transfer the *Sample* into a separatory funnel. Add 2 mL of 2.7 N hydrochloric acid, and extract the precipitated saccharin, first with 30 mL, then with five 20-mL portions, of solvent comprising 9:1 (v/v) chloroform:alcohol. Filter each extract through a small filter paper moistened with the solvent mixture, and evaporate the combined filtrates to dryness on a steam bath with the aid of a current of air. Dissolve the residue in 75 mL of hot water, cool, add phenolphthalein TS, and titrate with 0.1 N sodium hydroxide. Perform a blank determination (see *General Provisions*), and make any necessary correction. Each mL of 0.1 N sodium hydroxide is equivalent to 20.22 mg of $C_{14}H_8CaN_2O_6S_2$.
  Acceptance criteria: NLT 98.0% and NMT 101.0% of $C_{14}H_8CaN_2O_6S_2$, calculated on the anhydrous basis.

IMPURITIES
Inorganic Impurities
- **Lead,** *Lead Limit Test, Flame Atomic Absorption Spectrophotometric Method,* Appendix IIIB
  Sample: 10 g
  Acceptance criteria: NMT 2 mg/kg
- **Selenium,** *Selenium Limit Test, Method I,* Appendix IIIB
  Sample: 200 mg
  Acceptance criteria: NMT 0.003%

Organic Impurities
- **Benzoate and Salicylate**
  Sample solution: 50 mg/mL
  Analysis: Add 3 drops of ferric chloride TS to 10 mL of *Sample solution* previously acidified with 5 drops of glacial acetic acid.
  Acceptance criteria: No precipitate or violet color appears.
- **Toluenesulfonamides**
  [Note—For all solutions requiring methylene chloride, use a suitable grade (such as that obtainable from Burdick & Jackson Laboratories, Inc.) equivalent to the product obtained by distillation in an all-glass apparatus.]
  Internal standard stock solution: 10 mg/mL 95% *n*-tricosane (obtainable from Chemical Samples Co.) in *n*-heptane, made to 10 mL
  Standard stock solution: 2 mg/mL each of reagent-grade *o*-toluenesulfonamide and *p*-toluenesulfonamide in methylene chloride, made to 10 mL
  Standard solutions: Pipet 0.1, 0.25, 1.0, 2.5, and 5.0 mL, respectively, of the *Standard stock solution* into five 10-mL separate volumetric flasks. Pipet 0.25 mL of the *Internal standard stock solution* into each flask, dilute each to volume with methylene chloride, and mix. These solutions contain, respectively, 20, 50, 200, 500, and 1000 µg/mL of each toluenesulfonamide, in addition to 250 µg of *n*-tricosane.
  Sample solution: Dissolve 2.00 g of sample in 8.0 mL of 5% sodium bicarbonate solution, and mix the solution thoroughly with 10.0 g of chromatographic siliceous earth (Celite 545, Johns-Manville, or equivalent). Transfer the mixture into a 250-mm × 25-mm chromatographic tube, or equivalent, having a fritted-glass disk and a Teflon stopcock at the bottom and a reservoir at the top. Pack the contents of the tube by tapping the column on a padded surface, and then by tamping firmly from the top. Place 100 mL of

methylene chloride in the reservoir, and adjust the stopcock so that 50 mL of eluate is collected in 20 to 30 min. Add 25 µL of *Internal standard stock solution* to the eluate, mix, and then concentrate the solution to a volume of 1.0 mL in a suitable concentrator tube fitted with a modified Snyder column, using a Kontes tube heater maintained at 90°.

Chromatographic system, Appendix IIA
  Mode: Gas chromatography
  Detector: Flame-ionization detector
  Column: 3-m × 2-mm (id) glass column, or equivalent, packed with 3% phenylmethyl silicone (OV-17, Applied Science Laboratories, Inc., or equivalent) on 100- to 120-mesh, silanized and calcined diatomaceous silica (Gas-Chrom Q, Applied Science, or equivalent). [CAUTION—The glass column should extend into the injector for on-column injection and into the detector base to avoid contact with metal.]
  Oven temperature: 180°
  Injection port temperature: 225°
  Detector temperature: 250°
  Carrier gas: Helium
  Flow rate: 30 mL/minute
  Injection volume: 2.5 µL

Analysis: Set the instrument attenuation so that 2.5 µL of the *Standard solution* that contains 200 µg/mL of each toluenesulfonamide gives a response of 40% to 80% of full-scale deflection. [NOTE—The retention times for *o*-toluenesulfonamide, *p*-toluenesulfonamide, and *n*-tricosane are about 5, 6, and 15 min, respectively.] Separately inject each of the five *Standard solutions* and the *Sample solution* into the chromatograph, record the chromatograms, and, for each solution, determine the areas of the *o*-toluenesulfonamide, *p*-toluenesulfonamide, and *n*-tricosane peaks. From the values thus obtained from the *Standard solutions*, prepare standard curves by plotting the concentration of each toluene-sulfonamide (µg/mL) versus the ratio of the respective toluenesulfonamide peak area to that of *n*-tricosane. From the standard curve, determine the concentration (µg/mL) of each toluenesulfonamide in the *Sample solution*. Divide each value by 2 to convert the result to mg/kg of the toluenesulfonamide in the 2 g sample taken for analysis. [NOTE—If the toluenesulfonamide content of the sample is greater than about 500 mg/kg, the impurity may crystallize out of the methylene chloride concentrate (see *Sample solution*). Although this level of impurity exceeds that permitted by the specification, the analysis may be completed by diluting the concentrate with methylene chloride containing 250 µg/mL of *n*-tricosane, and by applying appropriate dilution factors in the calculation. Care must be taken to redissolve completely any crystalline toluenesulfonamide to give a homogeneous solution.]

Acceptance criteria: NMT 0.0025%

SPECIFIC TESTS
- **READILY CARBONIZABLE SUBSTANCES,** Appendix IIB
  Sample: 200 mg
  Analysis: Dissolve the *Sample* in 5 mL of 95% sulfuric acid and hold the solution at 48° to 50° for 10 min.
  Acceptance criteria: The color of the resulting solution is no darker than that of *Matching Fluid A*.
- **WATER,** *Water Determination,* Appendix IIB
  Acceptance criteria: NMT 15.0%

Calcium Silicate

First Published: Prior to FCC 6
Last Revision: First Supplement, FCC 6

INS: 552   CAS: [1344-95-2]
UNII: S4255P4G5M [calcium silicate]

DESCRIPTION
Calcium Silicate occurs as a white to off-white, free-flowing powder that remains so after absorbing relatively large amounts of water or other liquids. It is a hydrous or anhydrous silicate with varying proportions of CaO and SiO$_2$. It is manufactured by two distinct processes identified by the form of silica used, either diatomaceous earth or precipitated silica. *Diatomaceous earth-based products* are produced through hydrothermal reaction processes, which combine natural, or flux-calcined diatomaceous earth with hydrated lime to produce synthetic mineral forms of gyrolite and tobermorite. *Precipitated or other silica-based products* are produced by reacting sodium silicate and calcium oxide. It is insoluble in water, but it forms a gel with mineral acids. The pH of 1:20 aqueous slurry is between 8.4 and 12.5.

Function: Anticaking agent; filter aid
Packaging and Storage: Store in well-closed containers.

IDENTIFICATION
- **CALCIUM,** Appendix IIIA
  Sample solution: Mix 500 mg of sample with 10 mL of 2.7 N hydrochloric acid, filter, and neutralize the filtrate to litmus paper with 6 N ammonium hydroxide.
  Acceptance criteria: Passes tests
- **SILICA**
  Analysis: Prepare a bead by fusing a few crystals of sodium ammonium phosphate on a platinum loop in the flame of a Bunsen burner. Place the hot, transparent bead in contact with a sample, and again fuse.
  Acceptance criteria: Silica floats about in the bead, producing, upon cooling, an opaque bead with a weblike structure.

ASSAY
- **SILICON DIOXIDE**
  Sample: 400 mg
  Analysis: Transfer the *Sample* into a beaker, add 5 mL of water and 10 mL of perchloric acid, and heat until dense, white fumes of perchloric acid evolve. [CAUTION—Handle perchloric acid in an appropriate fume hood.] Cover the beaker with a watch glass, and continue to heat for 15 min longer. Allow to cool, add 30 mL of water, filter, and wash the precipitate with

200 mL of hot water. Retain the combined filtrate and washings for use in the *Assay* for *Calcium Oxide*. Transfer the filter paper and its contents into a platinum crucible, heat slowly to dryness, and then heat sufficiently to char the filter paper. After cooling, add a few drops of sulfuric acid, and then ignite at about 1300° to constant weight. Moisten the residue with 5 drops of sulfuric acid, add 15 mL of hydrofluoric acid, heat cautiously on a hot plate until all of the acid is driven off, and ignite to constant weight at a temperature not lower than 1000°. [CAUTION—Handle hydrofluoric acid in an appropriate fume hood.] Cool in a desiccator, and weigh. The loss in weight is equivalent to the amount of SiO_2 in the *Sample* taken.

Acceptance criteria: The result should conform to the representations of the vendor.

- **CALCIUM OXIDE**

  Sample solution: The retained combined filtrate and washings from the *Assay* for *Silicon Dioxide* above

  Analysis: Using 1 N sodium hydroxide, neutralize the *Sample solution* to litmus and add, while stirring, about 30 mL of 0.05 M disodium EDTA from a 50-mL buret. Add 15 mL of 1 N sodium hydroxide and 300 mg of hydroxy naphthol blue indicator. Continue the titration with the disodium EDTA to a blue endpoint. Each mL of 0.05 M disodium EDTA is equivalent to 2.804 mg of CaO.

  Acceptance criteria: The result should conform to the representations of the vendor.

IMPURITIES
Inorganic Impurities

- **FLUORIDE**

  [NOTE—Store all fluoride solutions in plastic containers.]

  0.2 N EDTA/0.2 N TRIS solution: Transfer 18.6 g of disodium ethylenediaminetetraacetate (EDTA) and 6.05 g of tris-(hydroxymethyl)aminomethane (TRIS), into a single 250-mL beaker. Add 200 mL of hot, deionized water, and stir until dissolved. Adjust the pH to 7.5 to 7.6 by adding 5 N sodium hydroxide. Cool the solution, and adjust the pH to 8.0 with 5 N sodium hydroxide. Transfer the solution into a 250-mL volumetric flask, and dilute with deionized water to volume. Mix well, and store in a plastic container.

  Standard stock solution: (1000 mg/kg fluoride) Dissolve 2.210 g of sodium fluoride in 50 mL of deionized water. Transfer the solution into a 1-L volumetric flask, and dilute to volume.

  Standard solutions: (1 mg/kg and 10 mg/kg fluoride) [NOTE—Prepare on the day of use.] Pipet 10 mL of the *Standard stock solution* into a 100-mL volumetric flask, dilute with deionized water to volume, and mix. Pipet 10 mL and 1 mL of this solution into separate 100-mL volumetric flasks, and dilute each with deionized water to volume.

  Sample solution

  Precipitated or other silica-based product: Transfer 5 g of sample into a 150-mL Teflon beaker. Add 40 mL of deionized water and 20 mL of 1 N hydrochloric acid. Heat to near boiling for 1 min while stirring continuously. Cool the beaker in an ice bath, transfer its contents into a 100-mL volumetric flask, and dilute with deionized water to volume. [NOTE—The sample does not dissolve completely.]

  Diatomaceous earth-based product: Transfer 5 g of sample into a 150-mL Teflon beaker. Add 60 mL of deionized water and stir for 1 min. Transfer the beaker contents into a 100-mL volumetric flask, and dilute with deionized water to volume. [NOTE—The sample does not dissolve completely.] Decant the supernatant into two 50-mL centrifuge tubes and centrifuge until the solution is clear, usually less than 30 min.

  Calibration curve: Pipet 20 mL of each of the two *Standard solutions* into separate 100-mL plastic beakers. Add 10 mL of *0.2 N EDTA/0.2 N TRIS solution* to each beaker. Measure the potential (mV) of each solution with a suitable fluoride-selective, ion-indicating electrode and a calomel reference electrode connected to a pH meter capable of measuring potentials with a reproducibility of ±0.2 mV (Orion model 96-09 combination fluoride electrode, or equivalent). Generate a standard curve by plotting the logarithms of the fluoride ion concentrations (mg/kg) of the *Standard solutions* versus the potential (mV) or calibrate an Orion Expandable Ion Analyzer EA-940 (or an equivalent instrument) for a direct concentration reading.

  Analysis: Pipet a 20-mL aliquot of *Sample solution* into a 100-mL plastic beaker, add 10 mL of *0.2 N EDTA/0.2 N TRIS solution*, and measure the solution potential as described for the *Calibration curve* (above). From the measured potential of the *Sample solution*, calculate the concentration (mg/kg) of fluoride ion using the *Calibration curve*.

  Acceptance criteria: NMT 10 mg/kg

- **LEAD**

  Standard stock solution: (100 µg/mL lead ion) [NOTE—Prepare and store this solution in glass containers that are free from lead salts.] Dissolve 159.8 mg of ACS reagent-grade lead nitrate in 100 mL of water containing 1 mL of nitric acid. Dilute with water to 1000.0 mL, and mix.

  Standard solution: 0.25 µg/mL of lead, prepared on the day of use from the *Standard stock solution*

  Sample solution: Transfer 5.0 g of sample into a 250-mL beaker, add 50 mL of 0.5 N hydrochloric acid, cover with a watch glass, and heat slowly to boiling. Boil gently for 15 min, cool, and let the undissolved material settle. Decant the supernatant through Whatman No. 4, or equivalent, filter paper into a 100-mL volumetric flask, retaining as much as possible of the insoluble material in the beaker. Wash the slurry and beaker with three 10-mL portions of hot water, decanting each washing through the filter paper into the flask. Finally, wash the filter paper with 15 mL of hot water, cool the filtrate to room temperature, dilute with water to volume, and mix.

  Analysis: Using a suitable atomic absorption spectrophotometer set at 217 nm, separately aspirate and read the absorbances of the *Standard solution* and *Sample solution* which has been zeroed with water.

Acceptance criteria: The absorbance of the *Sample solution* is not more than that of the *Standard solution*. (NMT 5 mg/kg)

SPECIFIC TESTS
- LOSS ON DRYING, Appendix IIC: 105° for 2 h
  Acceptance criteria: The result should conform to the representations of the vendor.
- LOSS ON IGNITION
  Sample: 1 g, previously dried at 105° for 2 h
  Analysis: Transfer the *Sample* into a suitable tared crucible, and ignite at 900° to constant weight.
  Acceptance criteria: The result should conform to the representations of the vendor.

OTHER REQUIREMENTS
- LABELING: If it is the *Diatomaceous earth-based product*, it is so labeled.

Calcium Sorbate

First Published: Prior to FCC 6

2,4-Hexadienoic Acid, Calcium Salt

$C_{12}H_{14}CaO_4$ Formula wt 262.32
INS: 203   CAS: [7492-55-9]
UNII: 2P47R6817F [calcium sorbate]

DESCRIPTION
Calcium Sorbate occurs as a fine, white crystalline powder. It decomposes at about 400°. It is sparingly soluble in water and practically insoluble in organic solvents, in fats, and in oils.
Function: Antimicrobial agent; preservative
Packaging and Storage: Store in tight containers.

IDENTIFICATION
- A. CALCIUM, Appendix IIIA
  Sample: 1 g
  Analysis: Ignite the *Sample* at 800°. Cool, and slake with 10 mL of water. Add glacial acetic acid until the sample is dissolved, and filter if necessary.
  Acceptance criteria: Passes tests
- B. PROCEDURE
  Sample: 200 mg
  Analysis: Place the *Sample* in 5 mL of methanol. Add 0.1 mL of 1 N sodium hydroxide, and dissolve in 95 mL of water. Add a few drops of bromine TS.
  Acceptance criteria: The color disappears.

ASSAY
- PROCEDURE
  Sample: 150 mg
  Analysis: Dissolve the *Sample* in 50 mL of glacial acetic acid in a 250-mL glass-stoppered Erlenmeyer flask, warming if necessary to dissolve the *Sample*. Cool the flask to room temperature, add 2 drops of crystal violet TS, and titrate with 0.1 N perchloric acid in glacial acetic acid to a blue-green endpoint that persists for at least 30 s. [CAUTION—Handle perchloric acid in an appropriate fume hood.] Perform a blank determination (see *General Provisions*) and make any necessary correction. Two mL of 0.1 N perchloric acid is equivalent to 26.23 mg of $C_{12}H_{14}CaO_4$.
  Acceptance criteria: NLT 98.0% and NMT 101.0% $C_{12}H_{14}CaO_4$, calculated on the dried basis

IMPURITIES
Inorganic Impurities
- LEAD, *Lead Limit Test, Flame Atomic Absorption Spectrophotometric Method*, Appendix IIIB
  Sample: 10 g
  Acceptance criteria: NMT 2 mg/kg

SPECIFIC TESTS
- ACIDITY OR ALKALINITY
  Sample: 1 g
  Analysis: Add some drops of methanol, 30 mL of water, and several drops of phenolphthalein TS to the *Sample*. If the mixture is colorless, titrate with 0.1 N sodium hydroxide to a pink color that persists for 15 s. If the mixture is pink, titrate with 0.1 N hydrochloric acid until pink color is discharged.
  Acceptance criteria
    Acidity (as sorbic acid): NMT 1.0 mL of 0.1 N sodium hydroxide is required to reach a persistent pink color (~1%).
    Alkalinity (as Ca(OH)$_2$): NMT 1.35 mL of hydrochloric acid is required to discharge the pink color (~0.5%).
- LOSS ON DRYING, Appendix IIC: 105° for 3 h
  Acceptance criteria: NMT 1.0%

Calcium Stearate

First Published: Prior to FCC 6

CAS: [1592-23-0]
UNII: 776XM7047L [calcium stearate]

DESCRIPTION
Calcium Stearate occurs as a fine, white to yellow-white, bulky powder. It is a compound of calcium with a mixture of solid organic acids obtained from edible sources and consists chiefly of variable proportions of calcium stearate and calcium palmitate. It is unctuous and free from grittiness. It is insoluble in water, in alcohol, and in ether.
Function: Anticaking agent; binder; emulsifier
Packaging and Storage: Store in well-closed containers.

IDENTIFICATION
- CALCIUM, Appendix IIIA
  Sample: 1 g
  Sample solution: The water layer on which floats an oily layer of fatty acids that are liberated by heating the *Sample* with a mixture of 25 mL of water and 5 mL of hydrochloric acid
  Acceptance criteria: The water layer passes tests.

194 / Calcium Stearate / Monographs

- **SOLIDIFICATION POINT,** Appendix IIB
  Sample: 25 g
  Analysis: Mix the *Sample* with 200 mL of hot water, add 60 mL of 2 N sulfuric acid, and heat the mixture, while stirring frequently, until the fatty acids separate cleanly as a transparent layer. Wash the fatty acids with boiling water until free from sulfate, collect them in a small beaker, and warm them on a steam bath until the water has separated and the fatty acids are clear. Allow the acids to cool, pour off the water layer, then melt the acids, filter into a dry beaker, and dry at 105° for 20 min.
  Acceptance criteria: The solidification point of the fatty acids so obtained is not below 54°.

ASSAY
- **PROCEDURE**
  Sample: 1.2 g
  Analysis: Boil the *Sample* with 50 mL of 0.1 N hydrochloric acid for 10 min or until the fatty acid layer is clear, adding water if necessary to maintain the original volume. Cool the mixture, filter, and wash the filter and flask thoroughly with water until the last washing is not acid to litmus. Neutralize the filtrate to litmus with 1 N sodium hydroxide. While stirring, preferably with a magnetic stirrer, add about 30 mL of 0.05 M disodium EDTA from a 50-mL buret. Then, add 15 mL of 1 N sodium hydroxide and 300 mg of hydroxy naphthol blue indicator. Continue the titration with the disodium EDTA to a blue endpoint. Each mL of 0.05 M disodium EDTA is equivalent to 2.804 mg of CaO.
  Acceptance criteria: NLT 9.0% and NMT 10.5% of CaO, calculated on the dried basis

IMPURITIES
Inorganic Impurities
- **LEAD,** *Lead Limit Test, Flame Atomic Absorption Spectrophotometric Method,* Appendix IIIB
  Sample: 10 g
  Acceptance criteria: NMT 2 mg/kg

SPECIFIC TESTS
- **FREE FATTY ACIDS (AS STEARIC ACID)**
  Sample: 2g
  Analysis: Transfer the *Sample* into a dry 125-mL Erlenmeyer flask containing 50 mL of acetone, fit an air-cooled reflux condenser onto the neck of the flask, boil the mixture on a steam bath for 10 min, and cool. Filter through two layers of Whatman No. 42, or equivalent, filter paper and wash the flask, residue, and filter with 50 mL of acetone. Add phenolphthalein TS and 5 mL of water to the filtrate, and titrate with 0.1 N sodium hydroxide. Perform a blank determination (see *General Provisions*) using 100 mL of acetone and 5 mL of water, and make any necessary correction. Each mL of 0.1 N sodium hydroxide is equivalent to 28.45 mg of stearic acid ($C_{18}H_{36}O_2$).
  Acceptance criteria: NMT 3.0%
- **LOSS ON DRYING,** Appendix IIC: 105° using 2 h increments of heating, to constant weight
  Acceptance criteria: NMT 4.0%

Calcium Stearoyl Lactylate
First Published: Prior to FCC 6

Calcium Stearoyl-2-Lactylate
Calcium Stearoyl Lactate
INS: 482(i)   CAS: [5793-94-2]
UNII: 30MXH4012A [calcium stearoyl lactylate]

DESCRIPTION
Calcium Stearoyl Lactylate occurs as a cream-colored powder. It is a mixture of calcium salts of stearoyl lactic acid, with minor proportions of other salts of related acids. It is slightly soluble in hot water.
Function: Dough conditioner; stabilizer; whipping agent
Packaging and Storage: Store in tight containers in a cool, dry place.

IDENTIFICATION
- **CALCIUM,** Appendix IIIA
  Sample: 1 g
  Sample solution: The water layer on which floats an oily layer of fatty acids that are liberated by heating the *Sample* with a mixture of 25 mL of water and 5 mL of hydrochloric acid.
  Acceptance criteria: The water layer passes tests.
- **SOLIDIFICATION POINT,** Appendix IIB
  Sample: 25 g
  Analysis: Mix the *Sample* with 200 mL of hot water, add 60 mL of 2 N sulfuric acid, and heat the mixture, while stirring frequently, until the fatty acids separate cleanly as a transparent layer. Wash the fatty acids with boiling water until free from sulfate, collect them in a small beaker, and warm them on a steam bath until the water has separated and the fatty acids are clear. Allow the acids to cool, pour off the water layer, then melt the acids, filter into a dry beaker, and dry at 105° for 20 min.
  Acceptance criteria: The solidification point of the fatty acids so obtained is not below 54°.

IMPURITIES
Inorganic Impurities
- **LEAD,** *Lead Limit Test, Flame Atomic Absorption Spectrophotometric Method,* Appendix IIIB
  Sample: 10 g
  Acceptance criteria: NMT 2 mg/kg

SPECIFIC TESTS
- **ACID VALUE**
  Sample: 1 g
  Analysis: Transfer the *Sample* into a 125-mL conical flask, add 25 mL of alcohol, previously neutralized in phenolphthalein TS, and heat on a hot plate until the sample is dissolved. Cool the flask, add 5 drops of phenolphthalein TS, and titrate rapidly with 0.1 N sodium hydroxide to the appearance of the first pink color that persists for at least 30 s. [NOTE—Retain the

neutralized solution for the determination of *Ester Value* below.] Calculate the *Acid value* by the formula:

$$\text{Result} = 56.1V \times N/W$$

V = volume (mL) of 0.1 N sodium hydroxide used in the titration
N = normality of the sodium hydroxide used in the titration
W = weight (g) of the sample taken

Acceptance criteria: Between 50 and 86

- **CALCIUM CONTENT**

  Lanthanum stock solution: Transfer 5.86 g of lanthanum oxide (La_2O_3) into a 100-mL volumetric flask, wet with a few mL of water, slowly add 25 mL of hydrochloric acid, and swirl until the lanthanum oxide is completely dissolved. Dilute to volume with water and mix.

  Calcium stock solution: Transfer 124.8 mg of calcium carbonate, previously dried at 200° for 2 h, into a 100-mL volumetric flask, carefully dissolve in 2 mL of 2.7 N hydrochloric acid, dilute to volume with water, and mix. [NOTE—This 500-mg/kg calcium solution is commercially available.]

  Standard solutions: Transfer 10.0 mL of the *Lanthanum stock solution* into each of three 50-mL volumetric flasks. Using a microliter syringe, transfer 0.20 mL of *Calcium stock solution* into the first flask, 0.40 mL into the second flask, and 0.50 into the third flask. Dilute the contents of each flask with water to volume and mix. The flasks contain, respectively, 2.0, 4.0, and 5.0 µg/mL of Ca. [NOTE—Prepare these solutions fresh daily.]

  Sample solution: Transfer 250 mg of sample, into a 30-mL beaker. While heating, dissolve the sample in 10 mL of alcohol, and quantitatively transfer the solution into a 25-mL volumetric flask. Wash the beaker with two 5-mL portions of alcohol, adding the washings to the flask, dilute to volume with alcohol, and mix. To a second 25-mL volumetric flask, transfer 5.0 mL of the *Lanthanum stock solution* and, using a microliter syringe, 0.25 mL of the alcoholic solution of the sample, dilute to volume, and mix.

  Analysis: Determine the absorbance of each *Standard solution* and of the *Sample solution* at 422.7 nm using a suitable atomic absorption spectrophotometer. Plot the absorbance of the *Standard solutions* versus concentration of calcium (µg/mL). From the curve so obtained, determine the concentration, C (µg/mL), of calcium in the *Sample solution*. Calculate the quantity (mg) of calcium in the sample taken by the formula:

  $$\text{Result} = 2.5C$$

  C = concentration (µg/mL) of Ca in the *Sample solution*

  Acceptance criteria: Between 4.2% and 5.2%

- **ESTER VALUE**

  Alcoholic potassium hydroxide solution: Dissolve 11.2 g of potassium hydroxide in 250 mL of alcohol, diluting with 25 mL of water.

  Sample solution: Neutralized solution retained from determination of *Acid Value* above

  Analysis: Add 10.0 mL of the *Alcoholic potassium hydroxide solution* to the *Sample solution*. Add 5 drops of phenolphthalein TS, connect a suitable condenser, and reflux for 2 h. Cool the flask, add 5 additional drops of phenolphthalein TS, and titrate the excess alkali with 0.1 N sulfuric acid. Perform a blank determination (see *General Provisions*) using 10.0 mL of the *Alcoholic potassium hydroxide solution*, and make any necessary correction. Calculate the ester value by the formula:

  $$\text{Result} = 56.1(B - S) \times (N/W)$$

  B = volume (mL) of 0.1 N sulfuric acid used in the titration of the blank
  S = volume (mL) of 0.1 N sulfuric acid used in the titration of the *Sample solution*
  N = normality of the sulfuric acid used in this titration
  W = weight (g) of the sample taken

  Acceptance criteria: Between 125 and 164

- **TOTAL LACTIC ACID**

  Sample stock solution: Transfer 200 mg of sample into a 125-mL Erlenmeyer flask, add 10 mL of 0.5 N alcoholic potassium hydroxide and 10 mL of water, attach an air condenser, and reflux gently for 45 min. Wash the sides of the flask and the condenser with about 40 mL of water, and heat on a steam bath until no odor of alcohol remains. Add 6 mL of 1:2 sulfuric acid, heat until the fatty acids are melted, then cool to about 60°, and add 25 mL of petroleum ether. Swirl the mixture gently, and transfer quantitatively to a separatory funnel. Collect the water layer in a 100-mL volumetric flask, and wash the petroleum ether layer with two 20-mL portions of water, adding the washings to the volumetric flask. Dilute to volume with water, and mix.

  Sample solution: Transfer 1.0 mL of the *Sample stock solution* into a 100-mL volumetric flask, dilute to volume with water, and mix.

  Standard stock solution: 1.067 mg/mL of lithium lactate ($LiC_3H_5O_3$), made to 1000.0 mL

  Standard solutions: 1, 2, 4, 6, and 8 µg/mL of lactic acid prepared by first transferring 10.0 mL of the *Standard stock solution* into a 100-mL volumetric flask, diluting to volume and mixing, and then transferring 1.0, 2.0, 4.0, 6.0, and 8.0 mL of this solution into separate 100-mL volumetric flasks, and diluting each flask to volume and mixing.

  Analysis: Transfer 1.0 mL of each *Standard solution* and the *Sample solution* into separate test tubes. Similarly transfer 1.0 mL of water to a test tube to serve as the blank. Treat each tube as follows: Add 1 drop of cupric sulfate TS, swirl gently, and then rapidly add 9.0 mL of sulfuric acid from a buret. Loosely stopper the tube, and heat in a water bath at 90° for exactly 5 min. Cool immediately to below 20° in an ice bath for 5 min, add 3 drops of *p*-phenylphenol TS, shake the tube immediately, and heat in a water bath at 30° for 30 min, shaking the tube twice during this time to disperse

the reagent. Heat the tube in a water bath at 90° for exactly 90 s, and then cool immediately to room temperature in an ice water bath. Using a suitable spectrophotometer set at 570 nm and the blank to zero the instrument, determine the absorbance of each solution in a 1-cm cell. Construct a standard curve by plotting the absorbance values for the *Standard solutions* versus the amount of lactic acid (μg) in each solution. Use the curve so obtained to obtain the weight (μg) of lactic acid in the portion of the *Sample solution* used in this *Analysis*.
  Acceptance criteria: Between 32.0% and 38.0%

Calcium Sulfate

First Published: Prior to FCC 6

$CaSO_4$ — Formula wt, anhydrous 136.14
$CaSO_4 \cdot 2H_2O$ — Formula wt, dihydrate 172.18
INS: 516
CAS: anhydrous [7778-18-9]
dihydrate [10101-41-4]
UNII: 4846Q921YM [calcium sulfate dihydrate]
UNII: E934B3V59H [calcium sulfate anhydrous]

DESCRIPTION
Calcium Sulfate occurs as a fine, white to slightly yellow-white powder. It is anhydrous or contains two molecules of water of hydration.
Function: Nutrient; yeast food; dough conditioner; firming agent; sequestrant
Packaging and Storage: Store in well-closed containers.

IDENTIFICATION
- **A. Procedure**
  Sample solution: Dissolve 200 mg of sample by warming it with a mixture of 4 mL of 2.7 N hydrochloric acid and 16 mL of water.
  Analysis: Add 5 mL of ammonium oxalate TS to 10 mL of the *Sample solution*. Retain the remainder of the solution for Identification Procedure B below.
  Acceptance criteria: A white precipitate forms.
- **B. Procedure**
  Analysis: Add barium chloride TS to the retained 10 mL of *Sample solution* prepared for *Procedure A* above.
  Acceptance criteria: A white precipitate forms that is insoluble in hydrochloric and nitric acids.

ASSAY
- **Procedure**
  Sample solution: Disperse 250 mg of sample in 100 mL of water and 4 mL of 2.7 N hydrochloric acid. Boil to dissolve the sample and cool the solution.
  Analysis: While stirring the *Sample solution*, preferably with a magnetic stirrer, add about 30 mL of 0.05 M disodium EDTA from a 50-mL buret. Then, add 25 mL of 1 N sodium hydroxide and 300 mg of hydroxy naphthol blue indicator. Continue the titration with disodium EDTA to a blue endpoint. Each mL of 0.05 M disodium EDTA is equivalent to 6.807 mg of $CaSO_4$.
  Acceptance criteria: NLT 98.0% of $CaSO_4$, calculated on the dried basis

IMPURITIES
Inorganic Impurities
- **Fluoride**, *Fluoride Limit Test*, Appendix IIIB
  Sample: 1.67 g
  Acceptance criteria: NMT 0.003%
- **Lead**, *Lead Limit Test, APDC Extraction Method*, Appendix IIIB
  Acceptance criteria: NMT 2 mg/kg
- **Selenium**, *Selenium Limit Test, Method II*, Appendix IIIB
  Sample: 200 mg
  Acceptance criteria: NMT 0.003%

SPECIFIC TESTS
- **Loss on Drying**, Appendix IIC: 250° to constant weight
  Acceptance criteria
  Anhydrous: NMT 1.5%
  Dihydrate: Between 19.0% and 23.0%

Camphene

First Published: Prior to FCC 6
Last Revision: First Supplement, FCC 6

$C_{10}H_{16}$ — Formula wt 136.24
FEMA: 2229
UNII: G3VG94Z26E [camphene]

DESCRIPTION
Camphene occurs as a colorless crystalline mass. It may contain a suitable antioxidant.
Odor: Camphoraceous-oily
Solubility: Soluble in alcohol; miscible in most fixed oils; insoluble or practically insoluble in water
Boiling Point: ~159°
Function: Flavoring agent

ASSAY
- **Procedure:** Proceed as directed under *M-1a*, Appendix XI.
  Acceptance criteria: NLT 80.0% of $C_{10}H_{16}$

OTHER REQUIREMENTS
- **Solidification Point**, Appendix IIB
  Acceptance criteria: NLT 40°

(+)-Camphor

First Published: Prior to FCC 6
Last Revision: First Supplement, FCC 7

d-Camphor

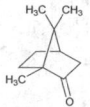

C₁₀H₁₆O Formula wt 152.24
FEMA: 2230
UNII: N20HL7Q941 [camphor (natural)]

DESCRIPTION
(+)-Camphor occurs as a white to gray translucent crystalline or fused mass.
Odor: Minty, ethereal
Solubility: Soluble in alcohol; insoluble or practically insoluble in most fixed oils, propylene glycol, water
Boiling Point: ~204°
Solubility in Alcohol, Appendix VI: One mL dissolves in 1 mL of 95% alcohol.
Function: Flavoring agent

IDENTIFICATION
- **INFRARED ABSORPTION**, *Spectrophotometric Identification Tests*, Appendix IIIC
  Reference standard: USP Camphor RS
  Sample and standard preparation: *M*
  Acceptance criteria: The spectrum of the sample exhibits maxima at the same wavelengths as those in the spectrum of the *Reference standard*.

OTHER REQUIREMENTS
- **MELTING RANGE OR TEMPERATURE DETERMINATION**, Appendix IIB
  Acceptance criteria: Between 174° and 179°
- **ANGULAR ROTATION**, *Optical (Specific) Rotation*, Appendix IIB
  Acceptance criteria: Between +41° and +43°

Cananga Oil

First Published: Prior to FCC 6

CAS: [68606-83-7]
UNII: 8YOY78GNNX [cananga oil]

DESCRIPTION
Cananga Oil occurs as a light to deep yellow liquid with a harsh, floral odor suggestive of ylang ylang. It is the oil obtained by distillation from the flowers of the tree *Cananga odorata* Hook f. et Thoms (Fam. Anonaceae). It is soluble in most fixed oils and in mineral oil, but it is practically insoluble in glycerin and in propylene glycol.
Function: Flavoring agent
Packaging and Storage: Store in a cool place protected from light in full, tight containers that are made from steel or aluminum and that are suitably lined.

IDENTIFICATION
- **INFRARED SPECTRA**, *Spectrophotometric Identification Tests*, Appendix IIIC
  Acceptance criteria: The spectrum of the sample exhibits relative maxima at the same wavelengths as those of the spectrum below.

SPECIFIC TESTS
- **ANGULAR ROTATION**, *Optical (Specific) Rotation*, Appendix IIB: Use 100 mm tube.
  Acceptance criteria: Between −15° and −30°
- **REFRACTIVE INDEX**, Appendix IIB
  [NOTE—Use an Abbé or other refractometer of equal or greater accuracy.]
  Acceptance criteria: Between 1.495 and 1.505 at 20°
- **SOLUBILITY IN ALCOHOL**, Appendix VI
  Acceptance criteria: One mL of sample dissolves in 0.5 mL of 95% alcohol, usually becoming cloudy on further dilution.
- **SPECIFIC GRAVITY:** Determine by any reliable method (see *General Provisions*).
  Acceptance criteria: Between 0.904 and 0.920

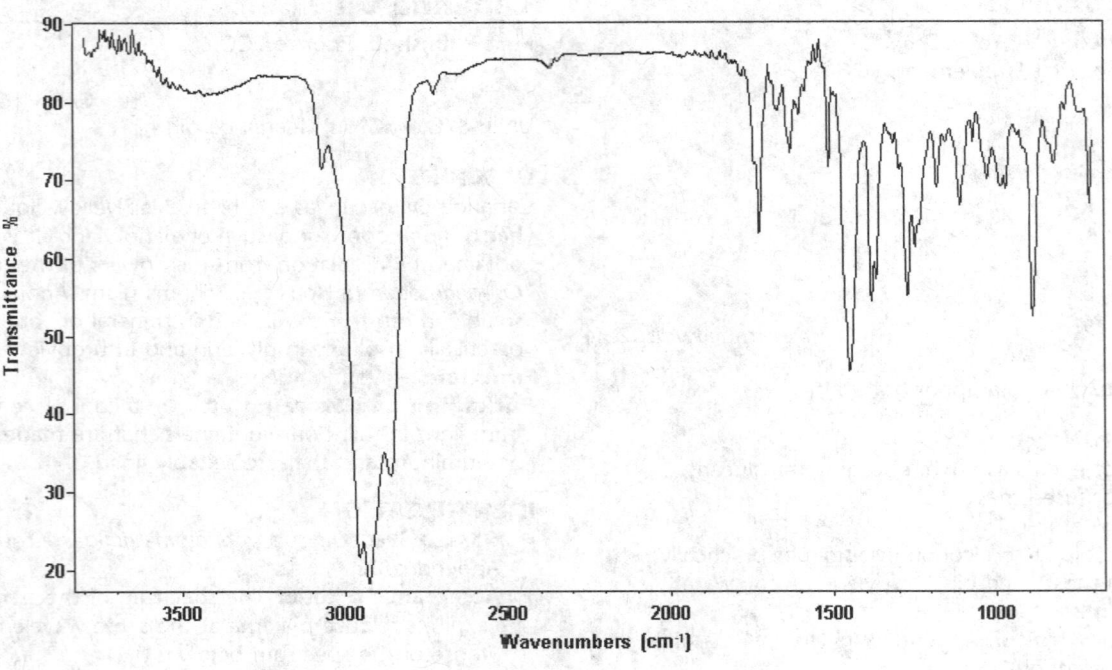

Cananga Oil

Candelilla Wax

First Published: Prior to FCC 6

INS: 902
UNII: WL0328HX19 [candelilla wax]
CAS: [8006-44-8]

DESCRIPTION
Candelilla Wax occurs as a hard, yellow-brown, opaque to translucent wax. It is a purified wax obtained from the leaves of the candelilla plant, *Euphorbia antisyphilitica* (Fam. Euphorbiaceae). Its specific gravity is about 0.983. It is soluble in chloroform and in toluene, but insoluble in water.

Function: Masticatory substance in chewing gum base; surface-finishing agent

Packaging and Storage: Store in well-closed containers.

IDENTIFICATION
- INFRARED SPECTRA, *Spectrophotometric Identification Tests,* Appendix IIIC
  Sample preparation: Melted sample on a potassium bromide plate
  Acceptance criteria: The spectrum of the sample exhibits relative maxima at the same wavelengths as those of the spectrum below.

IMPURITIES
Inorganic Impurities
- LEAD, *Sample Solution for Lead Limit Test,* Appendix IV
  Control: 10 µg Pb (10 mL of *Diluted Standard Lead Solution*)
  Acceptance criteria: NMT 3 mg/kg

SPECIFIC TESTS
- ACID VALUE [FATS AND RELATED SUBSTANCES], *Method I,* Appendix VII
  Acceptance criteria: Between 12 and 22
- MELTING RANGE OR TEMPERATURE DETERMINATION, *Procedure for Class II,* Appendix IIB
  Acceptance criteria: Between 68.5° and 72.5°
- SAPONIFICATION VALUE, Appendix VII
  Acceptance criteria: Between 43 and 65

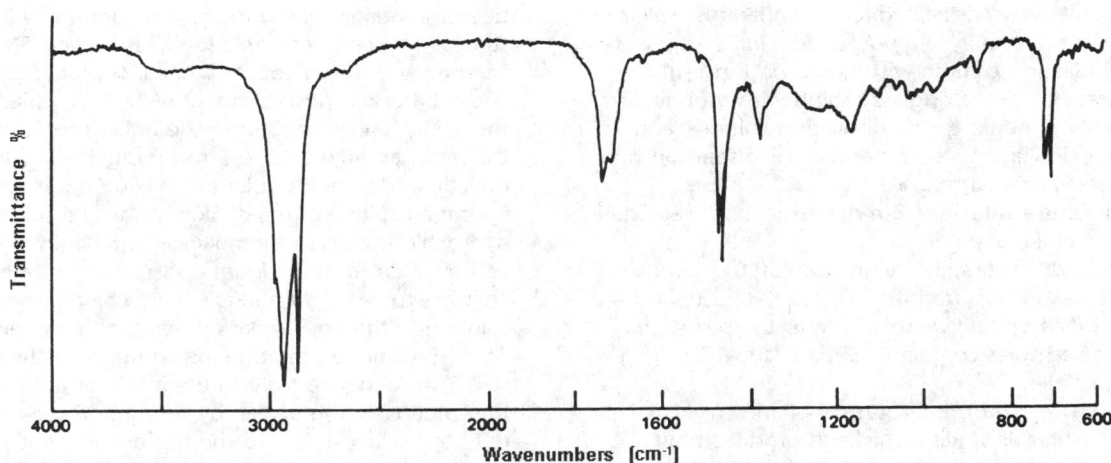

Candelilla Wax

Canola Oil

First Published: Prior to FCC 6

Low Erucic Acid Rapeseed Oil
LEAR Oil

CAS: [120962-03-0]

UNII: 331KBJ17RK [canola oil]

DESCRIPTION
Canola Oil occurs as a light yellow oil. It is typically obtained by a combination of mechanical expression followed by n-hexane extraction, from the seed of the plant Brassica juncea, Brassica napus, or Brassica rapa (Fam. Cruciferae). The plant varieties are those producing oil-bearing seeds with a low erucic acid ($C_{22:1}$) content. It is a mixture of triglycerides composed of both saturated and unsaturated fatty acids. It is refined, bleached, and deodorized to substantially remove free fatty acids, phospholipids, color, odor and flavor components, and miscellaneous, other non-oil materials. It can be hydrogenated to reduce the level of unsaturated fatty acids for functional purposes in foods. It is a liquid at 0° and above.

Function: Cooking or salad oil; component of margarine or shortening; coating agent; texturizer

Packaging and Storage: Store in tightly closed containers, ensuring no contact with metals, filled to the top or flushed with nitrogen gas.

IDENTIFICATION
- **FATTY ACID COMPOSITION,** Appendix VII
  Acceptance criteria: A sample exhibits the following composition profile of fatty acids:

Fatty Acid	Weight % (Range)
<14	<0.1
14:0	<0.2
16:0	<6.0
16:1	<1.0
18:0	<2.5
18:1	>50
18:2	<40.0
18:3	<14
20:0	<1.0
20:1	<2.0
22:0	<0.5
22:1	<2.0
24:0	<0.2
24:1	<0.2

IMPURITIES
Inorganic Impurities
- **LEAD,** Lead Limit Test, Atomic Absorption Spectrophotometric Graphite Furnace Method, Method II, Appendix IIIB
  Acceptance criteria: NMT 0.1 mg/kg

Organic Impurities
- **SULFUR COMPOUNDS**
  [NOTE—Organosulfur compounds present in the sample react with Raney nickel to produce nickel sulfides. Nickel sulfides are treated with a strong acid to produce hydrogen sulfide, which is trapped and titrated with mercuric acetate using a dithizone indicator.]
  [CAUTION—This test requires the use of the following hazardous substances: mercuric acetate, spongy nickel, and dibenzyl disulfide. Conduct the test in a fume hood.]

Apparatus: Fit a 125-mL, round-bottom boiling flask with a cylindrical filling funnel (20 mL with open top), an ST PTFE metering valve stopcock, and a gas inlet tube [see the figure for Raney Nickel Reduction Apparatus, *Sulfur (by Oxidative Microcoulometry)*, Appendix IIIC]. Fit a water-jacketed distillation column with hooks on top of the boiling flask. Fit a piece of glass tubing with ground ST inner joints with hooks to the distillation column, and connect the distillation column and a gas dispersion tube with ST outer joints with hooks.

Dibenzyl disulfide solution: 3 mg/mL dibenzyl disulfide in methyl isobutyl ketone

Sulfur standard: Accurately weigh five 250.0-g samples of food-grade peanut oil. Transfer 0.0, 1.0, 2.0, 3.0, and 4.0 mL of the *Dibenzyl disulfide solution* into the peanut oil samples; the samples contain 0, 3, 6, 9, and 12 mg/kg of sulfur, respectively.

Raney nickel preparation: [CAUTION—Raney nickel is pyrophoric when dry.] Raney nickel is produced by reacting nickel–aluminum alloy with sodium hydroxide. Each Raney nickel pellet is prepared individually, and each is enough catalyst for one determination. To produce one Raney nickel pellet, accurately weigh 1 g of nickel–aluminum alloy powder (50% Ni, 50% Al), place it in a 50-mL centrifuge tube, and chill it in an ice bath. Slowly add 5 mL of water to the tube, and let it stand for 10 min. Then, slowly add 10 mL of 2.5 N sodium hydroxide, and allow the mixture to react for 30 min. Cap the tube, and place it in a 50° water bath for 2 h. Centrifuge the mixture at 1000 rpm for 10 min, and discard the supernatant liquid. Wash the pellet twice with 15 mL of water and twice with 15 mL of isopropanol, centrifuging between each wash. Store the catalyst under isopropanol for no longer than 2 weeks. [NOTE—Properly dispose of unused *Raney nickel preparation* by transferring it to a 250-mL Erlenmeyer flask, and placing it in a fume hood. Add 20 mL of 60% (w/v) hydrochloric acid, and allow complete digestion of the catalyst.] [CAUTION—Hydrogen gas evolves during the digestion process.]

Dithizone indicator solution: 1 mg/mL of dithizone (diphenylthiocarbazone) in acetone

Mercuric acetate titrant: [CAUTION—Mercuric acetate is a strong irritant when ingested or inhaled or upon dermal exposure.] Transfer 3.82 g of mercuric acetate into a 1000-mL volumetric flask containing 950 mL of water. Add 12.2 mL of glacial acetic acid, dilute to volume with water, and mix. Transfer 10.0 mL of this solution into a 100-mL volumetric flask, dilute to volume with water, and mix. The titrant solution contains 0.0012 M mercuric acetate.

Titration reagent blank: Add 50.0 mL of 1 N sodium hydroxide and 50.0 mL of acetone to a 250-mL beaker, and mix. Add 0.5 mL of the *Dithizone indicator solution*, and titrate with *Mercuric acetate titrant* until the color changes from bright amber to red. Record the volume of titrant used.

Sample: 15 to 20 g

Analysis: Place the *Sample* on the bottom of the boiling flask. Discard the isopropanol from the *Raney nickel preparation*, add 10 mL of 95% isopropanol, mix, and add the mixture to the sample. Attach the water condenser and the nitrogen line to the boiling flask, and adjust the gas flow through the sample to 4 psi. Place a heating mantle under the flask. Immerse the bubbler in a 250-mL beaker containing 50.0 mL of 1 N sodium hydroxide, and stir slowly. Boil the sample for 90 min. Add 50 mL of acetone and 0.5 mL of *Dithizone indicator solution* to the 250-mL beaker. Add 20 mL of 60% hydrochloric acid into the filling funnel fitted onto the boiling flask, and adjust the nitrogen flow to 2 to 3 psi. Position the stir bar directly under the bubbler for maximum dispersion of the hydrogen sulfide bubbles. Slowly add the solution of 60% hydrochloric acid to the boiling flask. Begin the titration with *Mercuric acetate titrant* until the bright amber color changes to red. Add enough hydrochloric acid to turn the solution in the boiling flask green, and then let it boil for 15 min. Continue the titration throughout the boiling stage, making sure to rinse the inside of the bubbler with the solution in the beaker by turning off the nitrogen flow until the solution rises to the top of the vertical tube (the solution usually returns to amber during the first rinse). Rinse the tube a second time. Continue the titration, and record the volume of titrant used to the nearest 0.01 mL. Calculate the concentration of sulfur in the sample, in mg/kg, by the following formula:

$$\text{Result} = (V_U - V_B) \times K / W$$

V_U = volume (mL) of titrant to the endpoint for the Sample
V_B = volume (mL) of titrant to the endpoint for the blank (usually about 0.10 mL)
K = constant determined (below) from the calibration of the *Sulfur standard* (μg of sulfur per mL of titrant)
W = weight of the sample (g) taken

Analyze the *Sulfur standards*, in duplicate, to determine the constant, K, using the following formula:

$$K = W \times C/(V_S - V_{RB})$$

W = weight of the *Sulfur standard* (g)
C = concentration of the *Sulfur standard* (mg/kg)
V_S = volume of titrant for the *Sulfur standard* (mL)
V_{RB} = volume of titrant for the *Titration reagent blank*

Acceptance criteria: NMT 10 mg/kg

SPECIFIC TESTS

- **ACID VALUE [FATS AND RELATED SUBSTANCES],** *Method II,* Appendix VII
  Acceptance criteria: NMT 6
- **COLD TEST,** Appendix VII
  Acceptance criteria: Passes test
- **COLOR (FATS AND RELATED SUBSTANCES),** Appendix VII: Use a 133.4-mm cell.
  Acceptance criteria: NMT 1.5 red/15 yellow
- **ERUCIC ACID,** *Fatty Acid Composition,* Appendix VII
  Acceptance criteria: NMT 2.0%

- **FREE FATTY ACIDS (AS OLEIC ACID),** Appendix VII
  Analysis: Use 28.2 for the equivalence factor (e).
  Acceptance criteria: NMT 0.05%
- **IODINE VALUE,** Appendix VII
  Acceptance criteria: Between 110 and 126
- **LINOLENIC ACID,** *Fatty Acid Composition,* Appendix VII
  Acceptance criteria: NMT 14.0%
- **PEROXIDE VALUE**
  Sample: 10 g
  Analysis: To the *Sample,* add 30 mL of a 3:2 mixture of glacial acetic acid: chloroform, and mix. Add 1 mL of a saturated solution of potassium iodide, and mix for 1 min. Add 100 mL of water, begin titrating with 0.05 N sodium thiosulfate, adding starch TS as the endpoint is approached, and continue the titration until the blue starch color has just disappeared. Perform a blank determination (see *General Provisions*), and make any necessary correction. Calculate the peroxide value, as mEq of peroxide per kg of sample, by the formula:

  $$\text{Result} = S \times N \times 1000/W$$

  S = net volume of sodium thiosulfate solution required for the sample (mL)
  N = exact normality of the sodium thiosulfate solution
  W = weight of the sample taken (g)
  Acceptance criteria: NMT 10 mEq/kg
- **REFRACTIVE INDEX,** Appendix IIB
  [NOTE—Use an Abbé or other refractometer of equal or greater accuracy.]
  Acceptance criteria: Between 1.465 and 1.467 at 40°
- **SAPONIFIABLE VALUE,** *Saponification Value,* Appendix VII
  Acceptance criteria: Between 178 and 193
- **STABILITY,** Appendix VII
  Acceptance criteria: NLT 7 h
- **UNSAPONIFIABLE MATTER,** Appendix VII
  Acceptance criteria: NMT 1.5%
- **WATER,** *Water Determination,* Appendix IIB
  Analysis: In place of 35 to 40 mL of methanol, use 50 mL of 1:1 chloroform:methanol mixture to dissolve the sample.
  Acceptance criteria: NMT 0.1%

OTHER REQUIREMENTS
- **LABELING:** Hydrogenated Canola Oil less than fully hydrogenated must be labeled as Partially Hydrogenated Canola Oil.

Canthaxanthin
First Published: Prior to FCC 6

4,4′-Diketo-β-carotene
Cantha
β-Carotene-4,4′-dione

$C_{40}H_{52}O_2$ Formula wt 564.85
INS: 161g   CAS: [514-78-3]
UNII: 4C3C6403MU [canthaxanthin]

DESCRIPTION
Canthaxanthin occurs as a dark, crystalline powder. It is soluble in chloroform, very slightly soluble in acetone, but insoluble in water. It melts at about 207° to 212° with decomposition.
Function: Color
Packaging and Storage: Store in tight, light-resistant containers under inert gas.

IDENTIFICATION
- **PROCEDURE**
  Acceptance criteria: The *Sample solution* (prepared below under *Assay*) exhibits a maximum absorbance near 470 nm.

ASSAY
- **PROCEDURE:** [NOTE—Carry out all work in low-actinic glassware and in subdued light.]
  Sample stock solution: Transfer 50 mg of sample into a 100-mL volumetric flask, add 10 mL of acid-free chloroform to dissolve the sample, dilute to volume with cyclohexane, and mix. Pipet 5 mL of this solution into a second 100-mL volumetric flask, dilute to volume with cyclohexane, and mix.
  Sample solution: Pipet 5 mL of *Sample stock solution* into a 50-mL volumetric flask, dilute to volume with cyclohexane, and mix.
  Analysis: Using a suitable spectrophotometer and a 1-cm cell, measure the absorbance of the *Sample solution* at the wavelength maximum of about 470 nm; use cyclohexane for the blank. Calculate the weight (mg) of $C_{40}H_{52}O_2$ in the sample taken by the formula:

  $$\text{Result} = 20{,}000\, A/a$$

  A = absorbance of *Sample solution*
  a = absorptivity (220) of pure canthaxanthin
  Acceptance criteria: NLT 96.0% and NMT 101.0% of $C_{40}H_{52}O_2$

IMPURITIES
Inorganic Impurities
- **ARSENIC,** *Arsenic Limit Test,* Appendix IIIB
  Sample solution: Prepare as directed for organic compounds.
  Acceptance criteria: NMT 3 mg/kg
- **LEAD,** *Lead Limit Test,* Appendix IIIB
  Sample solution: Prepare as directed for organic compounds.
  Control: 10 µg Pb (10 mL of *Diluted Standard Lead Solution*)
  Acceptance criteria: NMT 10 mg/kg

- **MERCURY**, *Mercury Limit Test,* Appendix IIIB
  Acceptance criteria: NMT 1 mg/kg

SPECIFIC TESTS
- **RESIDUE ON IGNITION (SULFATED ASH)**, Appendix IIC
  Sample: 1 g
  Analysis: Proceed as directed, using a silica crucible and moistening the residue with 2 mL of nitric acid and 1 mL of sulfuric acid.
  Acceptance criteria: NMT 0.2%

Caramel
First Published: Prior to FCC 6

Caramel Color
INS: 150
UNII: T9D99G2B1R [caramel]
CAS: [8028-89-5]

DESCRIPTION
Caramel usually occurs as a dark brown to black liquid or solid. It is a complex mixture of compounds, some of which are in the form of colloidal aggregates. Caramel is manufactured by heating carbohydrates, either alone or in the presence of food-grade acids, alkalies, and/or salts. Caramel is produced from commercially available food-grade nutritive sweeteners consisting of fructose, dextrose (glucose), invert sugar, sucrose, malt syrup, molasses, and starch hydrolysates and fractions thereof. The acids that may be used are food-grade sulfuric, sulfurous, phosphoric, acetic, and citric acids; the alkalies are ammonium, sodium, potassium, and calcium hydroxides; and the salts are ammonium, sodium, and potassium carbonate, bicarbonate, phosphate (including mono- and dibasic), sulfate, and bisulfite. Food-grade antifoaming agents, such as polyglycerol esters of fatty acids, may be used as processing aids during its manufacture. Caramel is soluble in water.

Four distinct classes of Caramel can be distinguished by the reactants used in their manufacture and by specific identification tests:

Class I (Plain Caramel, Caustic Caramel): Prepared by heating carbohydrates with or without acids or alkalis; no ammonium or sulfite compounds are used.
Class II (Caustic Sulfite Caramel): Prepared by heating carbohydrates with or without acids or alkalis in the presence of sulfite compounds; no ammonium compounds are used.
Class III (Ammonia Caramel): Prepared by heating carbohydrates with or without acids or alkalis in the presence of ammonium compounds; no sulfite compounds are used.
Class IV (Sulfite Ammonia Caramel): Prepared by heating carbohydrates with or without acids or alkalis in the presence of both sulfite and ammonium compounds.

All of these Caramels shall meet the criteria established for Caramel in this monograph.
Function: Color

Packaging and Storage: Store in well-closed containers and avoid exposure to excessive heating and, for solid products, excessive humidity.

IMPURITIES
Inorganic Impurities
- **ARSENIC**, *Arsenic Limit Test,* Appendix IIIB
  Sample solution: Prepare as directed for organic compounds.
  Control: 1 µg As (1.0 mL of *Standard Arsenic Solution*)
  Acceptance criteria: NMT 1 mg/kg
- **LEAD**

  [NOTE—Use reagent-grade chemicals with as low a lead content as is practicable as well as high-purity water and gases. Before use, rinse all glassware and plasticware twice with 10% nitric acid and twice with 10% hydrochloric acid. Then rinse them thoroughly with high-purity water, preferably obtained from a mixed-bed, strong-acid, strong-base ion-exchange cartridge capable of producing water with an electrical resistivity of 12 to 15 megohms.]

  Lead nitrate solution: 100 µg Pb/mL, prepared by transferring 159.8 mg of ACS reagent-grade lead nitrate, $Pb(NO_3)_2$, into a 1000-mL volumetric flask, adding 100 mL of water containing 1 mL of nitric acid to dissolve the lead nitrate, diluting to volume with water, and mixing. [NOTE—Prepare and store this solution in glass containers that are free from lead salts.]

  Standard stock solution: 10 µg Pb/mL prepared by transferring 50.0 mL of *Lead nitrate solution* into a 500-mL volumetric flask containing 50 mL of water, adding 5 mL of nitric acid, diluting to volume with water, and mixing. [NOTE—Prepare on the day of use.]

  Standard solutions: 0.20, 0.50, 1.00 and 2.00 µg Pb/mL, prepared by pipeting 2, 5, 10, and 20 mL of *Standard stock solution* into separate 100-mL volumetric flasks, adding 1 mL of nitric acid to each, diluting to volume with water, and mixing.

  Sample solution: Transfer 25 g of sample into an ashing vessel. [NOTE—Suitable ashing vessels have approximately a 100-mL capacity and are flat-bottomed platinum crucibles or dishes, Vycor or quartz tall-form beakers, or Vycor evaporating dishes (Corning Glass Works No. 13180, or equivalent). Discard Vycor vessels when the inner surfaces become etched.] Dry the sample overnight at 120° in a forced draft oven. [NOTE—The sample must be absolutely dry to prevent flowing or spattering in the furnace.] Place the sample in a furnace equipped with a pyrometer to control the temperature over a range of 260° to 600°, with a variation of less than 10° and set the temperature at 250°. Slowly, in 50° increments, raise the temperature to 350°, and hold at this temperature until smoking ceases. Increase the temperature to 500° in approximately 75° increments; the sample must not ignite. Ash for 16 h or overnight at 500°. Remove the sample from the furnace and allow it to cool. The ash should be white and essentially carbon free. If the ash still contains excess carbon particles (i.e., the ash is gray rather than white), proceed as follows: Wet the ash with a minimal amount of water followed by the dropwise addition of 0.5 to 3 mL of nitric acid. Dry on a hot plate. Transfer the ash to a furnace set at 250°, slowly increase the temperature to 500°, and continue heating for 1 to 2 h. Repeat the nitric acid treatment and ashing, if necessary, to obtain a carbon-free residue. [NOTE—Local overheating or deflagration may result if the sample still contains much intermingled carbon and especially if much potassium is present in the ash.]

Dissolve the residue in 5 mL of 1 N nitric acid, warming on a steam bath or hot plate for 2 to 3 min to aid solution. Filter, if necessary, and decant through S&S 589 Black Ribbon paper, or equivalent, into a 50-mL volumetric flask. Repeat with two 5-mL portions of 1 N nitric acid, filter, and add the washings to the original filtrate. Dilute to volume with 1 N nitric acid and mix to prepare the *Sample solution*.

Reagent blanks: Prepare duplicate blanks for each *Standard solution* and for the *Sample solution*, including any additional water and nitric acid if used for sample ashing. [NOTE—Do not ash nitric acid in a furnace because the lead contaminant will be lost.] Evaporate nitric acid to dryness in an ashing vessel on a steam bath or hot plate. Dissolve the residue in 5 mL of 1 N nitric acid, warming on a steam bath or hot plate for 2 to 3 min to aid solution. Filter, if necessary, and decant through S&S 589 Black Ribbon paper, or equivalent, into a 50-mL volumetric flask. Repeat with two 5-mL portions of 1 N nitric acid, filter, and add the washings to the original filtrate. Dilute to volume with 1 N nitric acid, and mix to prepare each reagent blank.

[NOTE—Complete the sample preparation (above) and the analysis (below) on the same day.]

Aqueous butyl acetate: Use spectral-grade butyl acetate and saturate it with water.

APDC solution: 20 mg/mL of APDC (ammonium 1-pyrrolidinedithiocarbamate, Aldrich Chemical, or equivalent) made to 100 mL. Remove insoluble free acid and other impurities normally present by two to three extractions with 10-mL portions of *Aqueous butyl acetate*.

Citric acid solution, lead-free: Dissolve 10 g of citric acid in 30 mL of water. While stirring, slowly add ammonium hydroxide until the pH is between 8.0 and 8.5, using short-range pH paper as an external indicator. Transfer the solution into a separatory funnel, and extract with 10-mL portions of *Dithizone Extraction Solution* (see *Lead Limit Test*, Appendix IIIB), until the dithizone solution retains its green color or remains unchanged. Drain the final dithizone layer, plus about 1 mL of the aqueous layer, into a beaker and, while stirring, slowly add 1:1 nitric acid until the pH is between 3.5 and 4, again using short-range pH paper as an external indicator. Transfer this solution into a 100-mL volumetric flask (through a filter, if necessary), dilute to volume with water, and mix thoroughly.

Test solutions: Pipet 20 mL each of the *Standard solutions*, the *Sample solution*, and the appropriate *Reagent blanks* into separate 60-mL separatory funnels. Treat each solution as follows: Add 4 mL of *Citric acid solution, lead-free* and 2 to 3 drops of bromocresol green TS. The solution should be yellow. Adjust the pH to about 5.4, using ammonium hydroxide initially and then ammonium hydroxide diluted with 4 volumes of water in the vicinity of the color change (the first permanent appearance of light blue). Add 4 mL of *APDC solution*, stopper, and shake the funnel for 30 to 60 s. Pipet 5.0 mL of *Aqueous butyl acetate*, stopper the funnel, and shake the funnel vigorously for 30 to 60 s. Let stand until the layers separate clearly, drain, and discard the lower aqueous phase. If an emulsion forms or the solvent layer is cloudy, drain the solvent layer into a 15-mL centrifuge tube, cover the tube with aluminum foil or Parafilm (or equivalent), and centrifuge it for about 1 min at 2000 rpm.

Analysis: Use an atomic absorption spectrophotometer equipped with a 4-in., single-slot burner head. Set the instrument to previously determined optimum conditions for organic solvent aspiration (3 to 5 mL/min) and at a wavelength of 283.3 nm. Use an air–acetylene flame adjusted for maximum lead absorption with a fuel-lean flame. Aspirate each of the *Test solutions*, flushing with water and then with *Aqueous butyl acetate* between measurements and record their absorbance. Correct the absorbances of the *Test solutions* prepared from the *Standard solutions*, and the *Sample solution*, with the readings of the *Test solutions* prepared from the *Reagent blanks*. Prepare a standard curve by plotting the absorbance of each of the *Test solutions* prepared from the *Standard solutions* against their concentrations (μg Pb/mL). (These concentrations, in butyl acetate, are four times those in the aqueous standard.) From the standard curve, determine the concentration, C, (μg/mL), of the *Sample solution*. Calculate the quantity, in mg/kg, of lead in the sample by the formula:

$$\text{Result} = 12.5 \times C/W$$

W = weight of the sample taken (g)

Acceptance criteria: NMT 2 mg/kg

- **MERCURY,** *Mercury Limit Test, Method I,* Appendix IIIB

Standard preparation: Prepare as directed transferring 1.0 mL of the stock solution (1 μg Hg) into a 50-mL beaker rather than the specified 2.0 mL.

Sample preparation: Transfer 5 g of sample into a 250-mL Erlenmeyer flask and add 5 mL of sulfuric acid and a few glass beads. Digest the mixture at a temperature not exceeding 120° until charring begins, preferably using a hot plate in a fume hood. [NOTE—Additional sulfuric acid may be necessary to completely wet some samples, but the total volume added should not exceed about 10 mL.] After the acid has initially decomposed the sample, cautiously add, dropwise, hydrogen peroxide (30%), allowing the reaction to subside and reheating the sample between drops. Add the first few drops very slowly with sufficient mixing to prevent a rapid reaction and discontinue heating if foaming becomes excessive. Swirl the solution in the flask to prevent unreacted substance from caking on the walls or bottom of the flask during digestion. [NOTE—Maintain oxidizing conditions at all times during the digestion by adding small quantities of the peroxide whenever the mixture turns brown or darkens.] Continue the digestion until the organic matter is destroyed, gradually raising the temperature of the hot plate to 250° to 300° until fumes of sulfur trioxide are copiously evolved and the solution becomes colorless or retains only a light straw color. Cool the flask, cautiously add 10 mL of water, heat again to strong fuming, and cool. Cautiously add 10 mL of water, mix, wash the sides of the flask with a few milliliters of water, and dilute to 35 mL. Add 1 mL of a 1:25 solution of potassium permanganate, and mix.

Analysis: Continue as directed in the *Procedure*, using a suitable atomic absorption spectrophotometer.

Acceptance criteria: Any absorbance produced by the *Sample preparation* is not more than half that produced by the *Standard preparation*, indicating NMT 0.1 mg/kg.

- **SULFUR DIOXIDE,** *Sulfur Dioxide Determination,* Appendix X

  Sample: 0.5 g

  Analysis: Determine as directed, and calculate on an equivalent color basis expressed in terms of a caramel having a *Color Intensity* of 0.1 a.u. (absorbance unit).

  Acceptance criteria: NMT 0.2%, calculated on the equivalent color basis

Organic Impurities

- **4-METHYLIMIDAZOLE**

  4-Methylimidazole stock solution: Purify reagent-grade 4-methylimidazole (Aldrich, or equivalent) by redistillation (b.p. 92° to 93°, 0.05 mm Hg). Transfer 50 mg of the distillate, into a 50-mL volumetric flask, dilute to volume with tetrahydrofuran (acetone is also acceptable), and mix thoroughly. Store in a refrigerator until ready for use.

  Standard solutions: 100, 150, 200, 250, 300, 350, 400, and 500 µg/mL prepared by pipetting, respectively 1.0-, 1.5-, 2.0-, 2.5-, 3.0-, 3.5-, 4.0-, and 5.0-mL portions of *4-Methylimidazole stock solution* into separate 10-mL volumetric flasks, diluting each to volume with the same solvent used to prepare the stock solution, and mixing. Store the solutions in a refrigerator; use them within 1 month.

  Sample solution: Transfer 10.0 g of sample into a 250-mL polypropylene beaker, and mix thoroughly with 5.0 g of 3 N sodium hydroxide; the pH of the mixture should exceed 12. Add 20.0 g of chromatographic siliceous earth (Johns-Manville Celite 545, or equivalent) to the beaker and thoroughly mix with a wide-blade, stainless steel spatula until a homogeneous, semidry mixture is obtained. Homogeneity is obtained when the color is uniform and no dark clumps are seen. Place a plug of fine glass wool in the base of a 300-× 22-mm (id) chromatography tube having a Teflon stopcock. Quantitatively transfer the mixture into the column. The column bed, approximately 150 mm tall, should be of uniform consistency, yet open enough to allow elution to occur readily. Place a plug of glass wool on top of the column, and then allow the column to fall a short distance vertically to help settle the contents. Rinse the sample beaker with methylene chloride and pour the contents into the column with the stopcock open. Allow the methylene chloride to pass down the column until it reaches the stopcock. Close the stopcock and allow the methylene chloride to remain in contact with the column bed for 5 min. Open the stopcock and pass methylene chloride through the column at a rate of 5 mL/min. Collect 200 mL of eluate in a 300-mL round-bottom flask. While maintaining the flask at 35° in a water bath, remove the bulk of the solvent from the eluate by rotary vacuum evaporation (350 to 390 mm Hg). Reduce the volume to about 1 mL. During the concentration step, watch the flask carefully to ensure that no loss of sample occurs by bumping. Use a disposable Pasteur pipet to quantitatively transfer the extract residue to a 5-mL volumetric flask, rinsing the flask several times with small (approximately 0.7 mL) portions of the same solvent used to prepare the original solutions (tetrahydrofuran or acetone); transfer the rinsings to the volumetric flask until the 5-mL dilution mark is reached. Mix thoroughly.

Chromatographic system, Appendix IIA

  Mode: Gas chromatography

  Detector: Hydrogen flame-ionization

  Column: 1-m × 4-mm (id) silanized glass column, or equivalent, packed with 90- to 100-mesh Anakrom ABS, or equivalent, containing 7.5% Carbowax 20M and 2% potassium hydroxide, or equivalent

  Column temperature: 190°

  Injection port temperature: 200°

  Detector temperature: 250°

  Carrier gas: Nitrogen

  Flow rate: 50 mL/min

  Injection volume: 5.0 µL

Analysis: [NOTE—Preferably, use an autosampler to inject the *Standard solutions*. If using manual injections, avoid fractionation in the syringe needle, and ensure that 5.0 µL is injected by using the solvent-flush technique with the solvent used to prepare the *Standard solutions*.]

Inject the *Standard solutions* into the chromatograph and obtain the chromatograms. From each chromatogram, obtain the corrected peak area. If not using an integrator, calculate the corrected peak area by multiplying the peak height (mm) by the peak width at one-half height (mm), and by the proper attenuation and range factors, depending on the particular apparatus and operating parameters used. Plot each corrected peak area versus its respective concentration of 4-methylimidazole to obtain the standard curve. In the same manner, chromatograph a 5.0-µL portion of the *Sample solution*, calculate the peak area corresponding to any 4-methylimidazole contained in the sample, and, by reference to the standard curve, obtain the content of the 4-methylimidazole in the sample. Calculate the percent 4-methylimidazole on an equivalent color basis

expressed in terms of a Caramel having a *Color Intensity* of 0.1 a.u.
Acceptance criteria: NMT 0.025%, calculated on the equivalent color basis

SPECIFIC TESTS
• **AMMONIACAL NITROGEN**
Sample: 2 g
Analysis: Transfer 25.0 mL of 0.1 N sulfuric acid into a 500-mL receiving flask. Connect the flask to a distillation apparatus consisting of a Kjeldahl connecting bulb and a condenser, making certain that the condenser delivery tube is immersed beneath the surface of the acid solution in the receiving flask. Transfer the *Sample* into an 800-mL long-neck Kjeldahl digestion flask and add 2 g of carbonate-free magnesium oxide, 200 mL of water, and several boiling chips to the flask. Swirl the digestion flask to mix the contents, and quickly connect it to the distillation apparatus. Heat the contents of the flask to boiling and collect about 100 mL of distillate in the receiving flask. Wash the tip of the delivery tube with a few milliliters of water, collecting the washings in the receiving flask. Add 4 or 5 drops of methyl red TS, titrate with 0.1 N sodium hydroxide, and record the volume (mL) as S. Conduct a blank determination (see *General Provisions*) and record the mL of 0.1 N sodium hydroxide required as B. Calculate the percent *Ammoniacal Nitrogen* (on an equivalent color basis) by the formula:

$$\text{Result} = [(B - S) \times W_N \times 100/W] \times F/A_{610}$$

W_N = the mEq weight of nitrogen for 0.1 N sodium hydroxide, 0.0014
W = weight of sample taken (g)
F = the basis of color equivalency, 0.1
A_{610} = absorbance of the 0.1% solution prepared for the determination of *Color intensity* (below)

[NOTE—The above formula gives the result on an equivalent color basis that permits expression in terms of a caramel having a color intensity standardized to 1 a.u.]
Acceptance criteria: NMT 0.6%, calculated on the equivalent color basis

• **COLOR INTENSITY**
Sample solution: 1 mg/mL (0.1%) [NOTE—Centrifuge if the solution is cloudy.]
Analysis: Using a suitable spectrophotometer and a 1-cm cell, determine the absorbance (A_{610}) of the clear *Sample solution* at 610 nm; use water as the blank. Calculate the *Color intensity* by the formula:

$$\text{Result} = (A_{610} \times 100)/S$$

S = the percent *Total solids* (see test below)
Acceptance criteria: Between 0.01 and 0.6 absorbance units (a.u.)

• **TOTAL NITROGEN,** *Nitrogen Determination, Method II,* Appendix IIIC

Analysis: Determine as directed and calculate on an equivalent color basis expressed in terms of a caramel having a *Color Intensity* of 0.1 a.u.
Acceptance criteria: NMT 3.3%, calculated on the equivalent color basis

• **TOTAL SOLIDS**
Liquid samples
Sample: 1.5-2.0 g
Analysis: Mix the *Sample* with 30.0 g of fine quartz sand that passes a No. 40, but not a No. 60 sieve, and that has been digested with hydrochloric acid, washed acid-free, dried, and ignited. Dry the mixture to constant weight at 60° under reduced pressure (50 mm Hg). Record the final weight of the sand plus the sample solids and calculate the percent solids as follows:

$$\text{Result} = [(W_F - W_S)/W_C] \times 100$$

W_F = weight of the sand and sample solids (g)
W_S = weight of the prepared sand taken (g)
W_C = weight of the sample taken (g)

Use the calculated percent *Total solids* in the calculation for *Color intensity* (see above).

Solid samples (powdered or granular)
Analysis: Determine as directed under *Loss on Drying,* Appendix IIC, drying a sample at 60° under reduced pressure (50 mm Hg) to constant weight. Calculate the percent solids as follows:

$$\text{Result} = [(W_D - W_B)/(W_S - W_B)] \times 100$$

W_D = weight of the bottle and sample after drying (g)
W_B = weight of the empty bottle (g)
W_S = weight of the bottle and sample before drying (g)

Use the calculated percent *Total solids* in the calculation for *Color intensity* (see above).

• **TOTAL SULFUR**
Sample: 5 g when the expected amount of sulfur is 2.5% or less; or 1 g when the expected amount of sulfur is greater than 2.5%
Analysis: Into the largest casserole available that fits in an electric muffle furnace, place: 1 to 3 g of magnesium oxide or an equivalent quantity of magnesium nitrate, hexahydrate (6.4 to 19.2 g); 1 g of powdered sucrose; and 50 mL of nitric acid. Transfer the *Sample* into the casserole. Place the same quantities of reagents in another casserole for the blank and carry through the following procedure for both the *Sample* and the blank: Evaporate the casserole contents on a steam bath to the consistency of paste. Place the casserole in a cold electric muffle furnace, gradually heat to 525°, and hold at that temperature until all nitrogen dioxide fumes are driven off. Cool the casserole, add 100 mL of water (the sample should dissolve), and neutralize to pH 7 with hydrochloric acid, using short-range pH indicator paper as an external indicator. Add an additional 2 mL of hydrochloric acid, filter the solution

into a suitable beaker, heat to boiling, and while stirring, slowly add 20 mL of barium chloride TS to the hot solution. Boil the contents of the beaker for 5 min, and allow it to stand overnight. Filter the contents of the beaker through a tight, ashless filter paper and quantitatively transfer the precipitate to the paper. Thoroughly wash the paper and the precipitate with hot water and transfer the paper to a tared crucible previously ignited for 1 h at 800° in a muffle furnace. Dry the paper in the crucible for 1 h at 105°. Then carefully char it, with free access to air, at low heat over a burner. Gradually increase the heat to burn away the paper and ignite the crucible and contents for 1 h at 800°. Cool and weigh it and calculate the percent sulfur by the formula:

$$\text{Result} = [(W_S - W_B)/S] \times 13.74 \times F/A_{610}$$

W_S = weight of the ignited residue of barium sulfate from the sample determination (g)
W_B = weight of the ignited residue from the blank determination (g)
S = weight of the sample taken (g)
F = the basis of color equivalency, 0.1
A_{610} = absorbance of the 0.1% solution prepared for the determination of *Color intensity* (above)

[NOTE—The above formula gives the result on an equivalent color basis that permits expression in terms of a caramel having a color intensity standardized to 1 a.u.]

Acceptance criteria: NMT 3.5%, calculated on the equivalent color basis

ADDITIONAL INFORMATION

- **IDENTIFICATION OF CLASSES**
  [NOTE—The four classes of Caramel may be distinguished from each other by the methods below.]
  Class I: Not more than 50% of the color is bound by DEAE (diethylaminoethyl) cellulose, and not more than 50% of the color is bound by phosphoryl cellulose.
  Class II: More than 50% of the color is bound by DEAE cellulose and it exhibits an *Absorbance Ratio* (see below) of more than 50.
  Class III: Not more than 50% of the color is bound by DEAE cellulose, and more than 50% of the color is bound by phosphoryl cellulose.
  Class IV: More than 50% of the color is bound by DEAE cellulose and it exhibits an *Absorbance Ratio* (see below) of not more than 50.

- **IDENTIFICATION TESTS FOR CLASSES**
  Tests
  - ABSORBANCE RATIO
    Sample solution: 1 mg/mL [NOTE—Any cloudiness appearing can be eliminated by centrifuging the solution.]
    Dilute sample solution: 50 µg/mL: made from *Sample solution*
    Analysis: Use a spectrophotometer equipped with a monochromator to provide a band width of 2 nm or less and of such quality that the stray-light characteristic is 0.5% or less. With water as a reference, measure the absorbance of the *Sample solution* solution in a 1-cm cell at 560 nm and that of the *Dilute sample solution* at 280 nm. Calculate the *Absorbance Ratio* of the sample by the formula:

    $$\text{Result} = (A_{280} \times 20)/A_{560}$$

    A_{280} = absorbance at 280 nm for the *Dilute sample solution*
    A_{560} = absorbance at 560 nm for the *Sample solution*
    20 = dilution factor

- COLOR BOUND BY DEAE CELLULOSE
  [NOTE—*Color Bound by DEAE Cellulose* is defined here as the percent decrease in absorbance of a caramel solution at 560 nm after treatment with DEAE cellulose.]
  DEAE cellulose: Use material with a capacity of 1.0 mEq/g. *DEAE cellulose* of higher or lower capacities may be used in proportionately higher or lower quantities.
  Sample solution: Prepare a *Sample solution* of approximately 0.5 absorbance unit at 560 nm by transferring an appropriate amount of sample into a 100-mL volumetric flask with the aid of 0.025 N hydrochloric acid. Dilute to volume with 0.025 N hydrochloric acid, and centrifuge or filter if the solution is cloudy.
  Supernatant: To a 20-mL aliquot of the *Sample solution*, add 140 mg of *DEAE cellulose*, mix thoroughly for several minutes, centrifuge or filter, and collect the clear supernatant liquid.
  Analysis: Using a suitable spectrophotometer previously standardized with 0.025 N hydrochloric acid, measure the absorbance of the *Sample solution* and of the *Supernatant* in a 1-cm cell at 560 nm. Calculate the percent of color bound by *DEAE cellulose* by the formula:

  $$\text{Result} = 100[(X_1 - X_2)/X_1]$$

  X_1 = absorbance of the *Sample solution* at 560 nm
  X_2 = absorbance of the *Supernatant* at 560 nm

- COLOR BOUND BY PHOSPHORYL CELLULOSE
  [NOTE—*Color Bound by Phosphoryl Cellulose* is defined here as the percent decrease in absorbance of a caramel solution at 560 nm after treatment with phosphoryl cellulose.]
  Phosphoryl cellulose: Use material with a capacity of 1.2 mEq/g. *Phosphoryl cellulose* (cellulose phosphate) of higher or lower capacities may be used in proportionately higher or lower quantities.
  Sample solution: Transfer 200 to 300 mg of sample into a 100-mL volumetric flask, dilute to volume with 0.025 N hydrochloric acid; centrifuge or filter if the solution is cloudy.
  Supernatant: To a 40-mL aliquot of the *Sample solution*, add 1.42 g of *Phosphoryl cellulose*, mix

thoroughly for several minutes, centrifuge or filter, and collect the clear supernatant liquid.

Analysis: Using a suitable spectrophotometer previously standardized with 0.025 N hydrochloric acid, measure the absorbance of the *Sample solution* and of the *Supernatant* in a 1-cm cell at 560 nm. Calculate the percent of color bound by *Phosphoryl cellulose* by the formula:

$$\text{Result} = 100[(X_1 - X_2)/X_1]$$

X_1 = absorbance of the *Sample solution* at 560 nm
X_2 = absorbance of the *Supernatant* at 560 nm

- **2-ACETYL-4(5)-TETRAHYDROXYBUTYLIMIDAZOLE (THI)**
[NOTE—Class III (Ammonia Caramel) is the only class of caramel color found to contain THI. Because some countries have a THI limit of 25 mg/kg on an equivalent color basis (on the basis of a product with *Color intensity* standardized to 0.1 absorbance units), the following method for determining THI is provided.]

2,4-Dinitrophenylhydrazine-hydrochloride (DNPH-HCl): Add 5 g of reagent-grade 2,4-dinitrophenylhydrazine (DNPH) to 10 mL of hydrochloric acid contained in a 100-mL Erlenmeyer flask, and gently shake the latter until the free base (red) is converted to the hydrochloride (yellow). Add 100 mL of ethanol and heat the mixture on a steam bath until all of the solids have dissolved. Cool to room temperature and, after the solution has crystallized, filter off the hydrochloride. Wash the hydrochloride with ether, dry it at room temperature, and store it in a desiccator. Upon storage, the hydrochloride slowly converts to the free base. The latter can be removed by washing with purified (peroxide-free) dimethoxyethane.

DNPH-HCl reagent: Mix 0.5 g of *DNPH–HCl* with 15 mL of 5% methanol in dimethoxyethane for 30 min. Store in a refrigerator at 4°. When properly prepared and stored, this reagent is stable for at least 3 months.

THI-DNPH standard: Add 0.5 g of *DNPH–HCl* to 1 mL of hydrochloric acid, followed by 10 mL of ethyl alcohol, and heat on a steam bath until the hydrochloride dissolves. Add 100 mg of 2-acetyl-4(5)-tetrahydroxybutylimidazole (THI) to the hot solution. Crystallization begins in a few minutes. Filter off the THI-DNPH when the suspension reaches room temperature. Recrystallize the THI-DNPH with a hydrochloric acid-ethyl alcohol mixture (1 drop of hydrochloric acid per 5 mL of ethyl alcohol). The yield is 70% to 80% based on the THI used. When stored in the refrigerator, the *THI–DNPH standard* is stable for at least 1 year.

Stock THI-DNPH solution: Dissolve 10 mg of *THI–DNPH standard* in a 100-mL volumetric flask and dilute to volume with absolute *Carbonyl-free methanol* (see below). Dilute a portion of this solution tenfold with the methanol. The THI concentration (mg/L) of the *Stock THI–DNPH solution* is 0.47 times that of *THI–DNPH standard*. When stored in the refrigerator, the *Stock THI–DNPH solution* is stable for at least 20 weeks.

Cation-exchange resin (Strong): Dowex 50 AG × 8, proton form, 100- to 200-mesh

Cation-exchange resin (Weak): Amberlite CG AG 50 I, proton form, 100- to 200-mesh [NOTE—Sediment two or three times before use.]

Carbonyl-free methanol: Add 5 g of Girard's Reagent P (Aldrich, or equivalent) and 0.2 mL of hydrochloric acid to 500 mL of methanol and reflux for 2 h. Distill the refluxed methanol through a short Vigreux column, and store in tightly closed bottles.

Purified dimethoxyethane: Distill dimethoxyethane from DNPH in the presence of acid and redistill it from sodium hydroxide. Immediately before use, pass it through a column of neutral alumina to remove peroxides.

Combination column
  Dropping funnel: 100-mL, equipped with a Teflon stopcock and fitted with a 14.5-mm standard ground-glass joint, as the solvent reservoir
  Upper column: Glass, 150 × 12.5 mm (id), filling height: max 9 cm and bed height: 50 to 60 mm; or 200 × 10 mm (id), filling height: max 14 cm and bed height 80 to 90 mm, equipped with a 1-mm (id) capillary outlet and fitted with 14.5-mm standard ground-glass joints
  Lower column: Glass, 175 mm × 10 mm (id), bed height 60 mm, equipped with a 1-mm (id) capillary outlet and a Teflon stopcock and fitted with a 14.5-mm standard ground-glass joint
  Assembly: Fill the *Upper column* with *Cation-exchange resin (Weak)*. Fill the *Lower column* with *Cation-exchange resin (Strong)*. Connect the *Dropping funnel* and the two columns, one fitted above the other.

Sample solution: Dissolve 200 to 250 mg of sample in 3 mL of water. Quantitatively transfer the solution to the upper part of the *Combination column*. Elute with water until a total of about 100 mL of water has passed through the column. Disconnect the *Upper column* and elute the *Lower column* with 0.5 N hydrochloric acid. Discard the first 10.0 mL of eluate and subsequently collect a volume of 35 mL. Concentrate the solution to dryness at 40° (15 mm Hg). Then, dissolve the syrupy residue in 250 μL of *Carbonyl-free methanol* and add 250 μL of *DNPH–HCl reagent*. Transfer the reaction mixture (*Sample solution*) to a septum-capped vial, and store the vial for 5 h at room temperature.

Mobile phase: 50:50 (v/v) methanol:0.1 M phosphoric acid

THI–DNPH standard solutions: Pipet 1, 2, and 5 mL of the *Stock THI-DNPH solution* into separate 10-mL volumetric flasks and dilute to volume with absolute *Carbonyl-free methanol*.

Chromatographic system, Appendix IIA
  Mode: High-performance liquid chromatography
  Detector: UV 385 nm
  Column: 250-mm × 4-mm (id), 10-1m LiChrosorb RP-8 HPLC column (Alltech Associates, Inc., or equivalent)

Injection volume: 5 µL
Flow rate: 2 mL/min
Analysis: Prepare a standard curve by injecting the *Stock THI–DNPH solution*, and the serially diluted *THI–DNPH standard solutions*, recording the chromatograms, and measuring the peak areas for THI-DNPH. Inject the *Sample solution* and measure the peak response. [NOTE—THI-DNPH elutes at about 6.3±0.1 min.] Calculate the amount of THI in the sample from the standard curve. [NOTE—For THI limits greater than 25 mg/kg, prepare a series of *THI–DNPH standard solutions* in a range encompassing the expected THI concentration in the sample.]

Caraway Oil
First Published: Prior to FCC 6

CAS: [8000-42-8]

UNII: C2J9B08Q3I [caraway oil]

DESCRIPTION
Caraway Oil occurs as a colorless to pale yellow liquid with the characteristic odor and taste of caraway. It is a volatile oil distilled from the dried, ripe fruit of *Carum carvi* L. (Fam. Umbelliferae).
Function: Flavoring agent

Packaging and Storage: Store in full, tight containers in a cool place protected from light.

IDENTIFICATION
- **INFRARED SPECTRA,** *Spectrophotometric Identification Tests,* Appendix IIIC
  Acceptance criteria: The spectrum of the sample exhibits relative maxima at the same wavelengths as those of the spectrum below.

ASSAY
- **KETONES,** *Aldehydes and Ketones, Neutral Sulfite Method,* Appendix VI
  Acceptance criteria: NLT 50.0%, by volume, of ketones as carvone

SPECIFIC TESTS
- **ANGULAR ROTATION,** *Optical (Specific) Rotation,* Appendix IIB
  Acceptance criteria: Between +70° and +80°
- **REFRACTIVE INDEX,** Appendix IIB
  [NOTE—Use an Abbé or other refractometer of equal or greater accuracy.]
  Acceptance criteria: Between 1.484 and 1.488 at 20°
- **SOLUBILITY IN ALCOHOL,** Appendix VI
  Acceptance criteria: One mL of the sample dissolves in 8 mL of 80% alcohol.
- **SPECIFIC GRAVITY:** Determine by any reliable method (see *General Provisions*).
  Acceptance criteria: Between 0.900 and 0.910

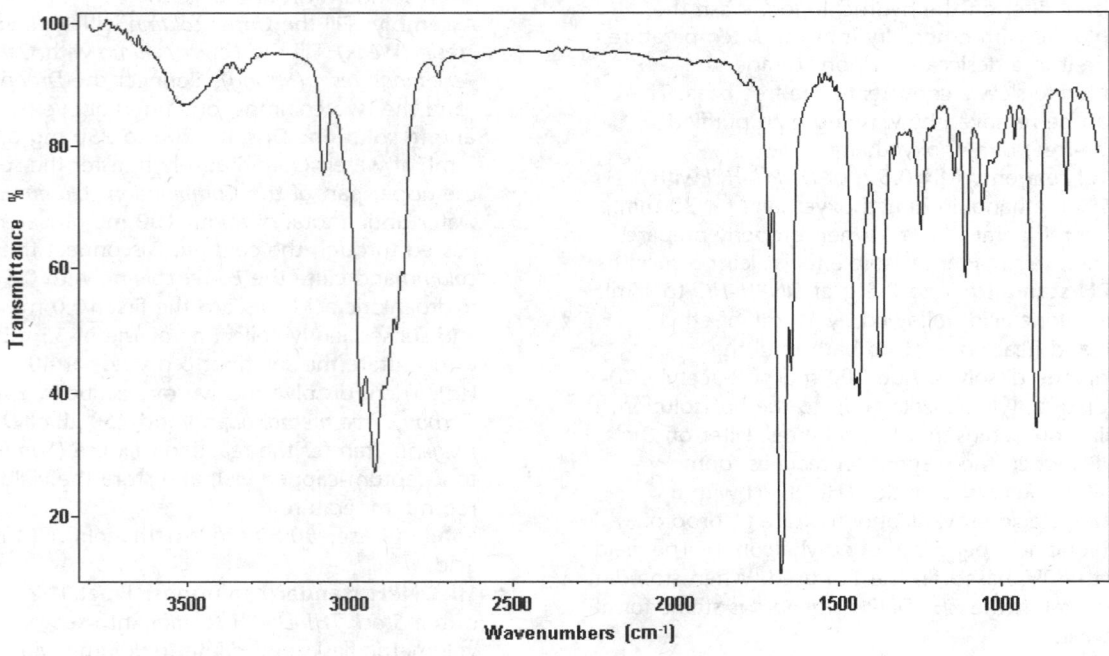

Caraway Oil

Carbon, Activated

First Published: Prior to FCC 6
Last Revision: First Supplement, FCC 7

UNII: 2P3VWU3H10 [activated charcoal]

DESCRIPTION
Carbon, Activated occurs as a black substance, varying in particle size from coarse granules to a fine powder. It is a solid, porous, carbonaceous material prepared by carbonizing and activating organic substances. The raw materials, which include sawdust, peat, lignite, coal, cellulose residues, coconut shells, and petroleum coke, may be carbonized and activated at a high temperature with or without the addition of inorganic salts in a stream of activating gases such as steam or carbon dioxide. Alternatively, carbonaceous matter may be treated with a chemical activating agent such as phosphoric acid or zinc chloride, and the mixture carbonized at an elevated temperature, followed by removal of the chemical activating agent by water washing. Activated Carbon is insoluble in water and in organic solvents.
Function: Decolorizing agent; taste- and odor-removing agent; purification agent in food processing
Packaging and Storage: Store in well-closed containers.

IDENTIFICATION
- **A. Procedure**
  Sample: 3 g, powdered
  Control: Dilute 10 mL of iodine TS with water to 50 mL.
  Analysis: Place the *Sample* in a glass-stoppered Erlenmeyer flask containing 10 mL of dilute hydrochloric acid (5%), boil for 30 s, and cool to room temperature. Add 100 mL of iodine TS, stopper, and shake vigorously for 30 s. Filter through Whatman No. 2 filter paper, or equivalent, discarding the first portion of filtrate. Compare 50 mL of the subsequent filtrate with the *Control*.
  Acceptance criteria: The color of the carbon-treated iodine solution is no darker than that of the *Control*, indicating the adsorptivity of the sample.
- **B. Procedure**
  Analysis: Ignite a sample in air.
  Acceptance criteria: Carbon monoxide and carbon dioxide are produced, and an ash remains.

IMPURITIES
Inorganic Impurities
- **Arsenic,** *Arsenic Limit Test,* Appendix IIIB
  Sample solution: Use a 20-mL portion of the filtrate obtained in the test for *Water Extractables*, diluted to 35 mL.
  Acceptance criteria: NMT 3 mg/kg
- **Lead,** *Lead Limit Test,* Appendix IIIB
  Sample solution: Use a 20-mL portion of the filtrate obtained in the test for *Water Extractables*.
  Control: 10 µg Pb (10 mL of *Diluted Standard Lead Solution*)
  Acceptance criteria: NMT 10 mg/kg

- **Heavy Metals (as Pb)**
  Method I
  [NOTE—This test is designed to limit the content of common metallic impurities colored by sulfide ion (Ag, As, Bi, Cd, Cu, Hg, Pb, Sb, Sn) by comparing the color with a standard containing lead (Pb) ion under the specified test conditions. It demonstrates that the test substance is not grossly contaminated by such heavy metals, and within the precision of the test, that it does not exceed the *Heavy Metals* limit given as determined by concomitant visual comparison with a control solution. In the specified pH range, the optimum concentration of lead (Pb) ion for matching purposes by this method is 20 µg in 50 mL of solution.
  The most common limitation of the *Heavy Metals* test is that the color the sulfide ion produces in the *Sample solution* depends on the metals present and may not match the color in the dilution of the *Standard lead solution* used for matching purposes. Lead sulfide is brown, as are Ag, Bi, Cu, Hg, and Sn sulfides. While it is possible that ions not mentioned here may also yield nonmatching colors, among the nine common metallic impurities listed above, the sulfides with different colors are those of As and Cd, which are yellow, and that of Sb, which is orange. If these criteria are met, Cd may be a contributor to the yellow color, so the Cd content should be determined. If an orange color is observed, the Sb content should be determined. These additional tests are in accord with the section on *Trace Impurities* in the *General Provisions*, as follows: "if other possible impurities may be present, additional tests may be required, and should be applied, as necessary, by the manufacturer, vendor, or user to demonstrate that the substance is suitable for its intended application."
  Determine the amount of heavy metals by *Method I* for substances that yield clear, colorless solutions before adding sulfide ion. Use *Method II* for those substances that do not yield clear, colorless solutions under the test conditions specified for *Method I* or for substances that by virtue of their complex nature, interfere with the precipitation of metals by sulfide ion.]

  [NOTE—In the following tests, failure to accurately adjust the pH of the solution within the specified limits may result in a significant loss of test sensitivity.]
  Lead nitrate stock solution: Dissolve 159.8 mg of Reagent-Grade ACS Lead Nitrate [Pb(NO$_3$)$_2$] in 100 mL of water containing 1 mL of nitric acid, dilute to 1000.0 mL, and mix. [NOTE—Prepare and store this solution in glass containers that are free from lead salts.]
  Standard lead solution: Dilute 10.0 mL of *Lead nitrate stock solution* with water to 100.0 mL. Each mL is equivalent to 10 µg of lead (Pb) ion. [NOTE—Prepare on the day of use.]
  Sample solution: Use the filtrate obtained in the test for *Water Extractables*.
  Solution A: Pipet 2.0 mL of *Standard lead solution* (20 µg of Pb) into a 50-mL color-comparison tube, and add water to make 25 mL. Adjust the pH to between

3.0 and 4.0 (using short-range pH indicator paper) by adding 1 N acetic acid or 6 N ammonia, dilute with water to 40 mL, and mix.

Solution B: Transfer 10 mL of the *Sample solution* into a 50-mL color-comparison tube that matches the one used for *Solution A*, adjust the pH to between 3.0 and 4.0 (using short-range pH indicator paper) by adding 1 N acetic acid or 6 N ammonia, dilute with water to 40 mL, and mix.

Solution C: Transfer 10 mL of the *Sample solution* into a third color-comparison tube that matches those used for *Solutions A* and *B*, and add 2.0 mL of *Standard lead solution*. Adjust the pH to between 3.0 and 4.0 (using short-range pH indicator paper) by adding 1 N acetic acid or 6 N ammonia, dilute with water to 40 mL, and mix.

Analysis: Add 10 mL of freshly prepared hydrogen sulfide TS to each tube, mix, allow to stand for 5 min, and view downward over a white surface. [NOTE—If the color of *Solution C* is lighter than that of *Solution A*, the sample is interfering with the test procedure and *Method II* must be used.]

Acceptance criteria: The color of *Solution B* is not darker than that of *Solution A*, and the intensity of the color of *Solution C* is equal to or greater than that of *Solution A* (NMT 0.004%).

Method II

Solution A: Prepare as directed in *Method I*.

Solution B: Place 0.5 g of sample into a suitable crucible, add sufficient sulfuric acid to wet the sample, and carefully ignite at a low temperature until thoroughly charred, covering the crucible loosely with a suitable lid during the ignition. After the sample is thoroughly carbonized, add 2 mL of nitric acid and 5 drops of sulfuric acid, cautiously heat until white fumes no longer evolve, then ignite, preferably in a muffle furnace, at 500°–600° until all of the carbon is burned off. Cool, add 4 mL of 1:2 hydrochloric acid, cover, and digest on a steam bath for 10–15 min. Uncover, and slowly evaporate on a steam bath to dryness. Moisten the residue with 1 drop of hydrochloric acid, add 10 mL of hot water, and digest for 2 min. Add 6 N ammonia dropwise until the solution is just alkaline to litmus paper, dilute with water to 25 mL, and adjust the pH to between 3.0 and 4.0 (using short-range pH indicator paper) by adding 1 N acetic acid. Filter if necessary, rinse the crucible and the filter with 10 mL of water, transfer the solution and rinsings into a 50-mL color-comparison tube, dilute with water to 40 mL, and mix.

Analysis: Add 10 mL of freshly prepared hydrogen sulfide TS to each tube, mix, allow to stand for 5 min, and view downward over a white surface.

Acceptance criteria: The color of *Solution B* is not darker than that of *Solution A* (NMT 0.004%).

Organic Impurities
- **CYANOGEN COMPOUNDS**
    Sample: 5 g
    Analysis: Mix the *Sample* with 50 mL of water and 2 g of tartaric acid and distill the mixture, collecting 25 mL of distillate below the surface of a mixture of 2 mL of 1 N sodium hydroxide and 10 mL of water contained in a small flask placed in an ice bath. Dilute the distillate with water to 50 mL and mix. Add 12 drops of ferrous sulfate TS to 25 mL of the diluted distillate, heat almost to boiling, cool, and add 1 mL of hydrochloric acid.
    Acceptance criteria: No blue color is produced.
- **HIGHER AROMATIC HYDROCARBONS**
    Sample solution: Extract 1 g of sample with 12 mL of cyclohexane in a continuous-extraction apparatus for 2 h. Place the extract in a Nessler tube.
    Control solution: Dissolve 100 μg of quinine sulfate in 1000 mL of 0.1 N sulfuric, and transfer into a matching Nessler tube.
    Acceptance criteria: The *Sample solution* shows no more color or fluorescence than the *Control solution* when observed under ultraviolet light.

SPECIFIC TESTS
- **IODINE NUMBER**[1]
    Hydrochloric acid solution (5% by weight): Add 70 mL of concentrated hydrochloric acid to 550 mL of water, and mix well.
    Potassium iodate solution (0.1000 N): Dry 4 or more g of primary standard-grade potassium iodate (KIO_3) at 110° ± 5° for 2 h, and cool to room temperature in a desiccator. Dissolve 3.5667 g ± 0.1 mg of the dry potassium iodate in about 100 mL of water. Quantitatively transfer to a 1-L volumetric flask, dilute with water to volume, and mix thoroughly. Store in a glass-stoppered bottle.
    Starch solution: Mix 1.0 ± 0.5 g of starch with 5–10 mL of cold water to make a paste. Continue to stir while adding an additional 25 ± 5 mL of water to the starch paste. Pour the mixture, while stirring, into 1 L of boiling water, and boil for 4–5 min. [NOTE—Make this solution fresh daily.]
    Sodium thiosulfate solution (0.100 N): Dissolve 24.820 g of sodium thiosulfate in approximately 75 ± 25 mL of freshly boiled water, and add 0.10 ± 0.01 g of sodium carbonate. Quantitatively transfer the mixture to a 1-L volumetric flask, and dilute with water to volume. Allow the solution to stand for a minimum of 4 days before standardizing. Store the solution in an amber bottle. To standardize the solution, perform the following in triplicate: Pipet 25.0 mL of 0.1000 N *Potassium iodate solution* into a wide-mouthed Erlenmeyer flask. Add 2.00 ± 0.01 g of potassium iodide, and shake the flask to dissolve the potassium iodide crystals. Pipet 5.0 mL of concentrated hydrochloric acid into the flask, and titrate the free iodine with *Sodium thiosulfate solution* to a light yellow color. Add a few drops of *Starch solution*, and continue the titration until 1 drop produces a

---
[1] Portions of this test are adapted from "ASTM D 4607-94(1999)—Standard Test Method for Determination of Iodine Number of Activated Carbon." The original ASTM method is available in its entirety from ASTM, 100 Barr Harbor Drive, West Conshohocken, PA 19428; phone: 610-832-9585; fax: 610-832-9555; email: service@astm.org; website: <www.astm.org>.

colorless solution. Determine the *Sodium thiosulfate solution* normality using the following formula:

$$\text{Result} = (P \times R)/S$$

P = volume of 0.1000 N *Potassium iodate solution* (mL)
R = normality of the 0.1000 N *Potassium iodate solution*
S = volume of *Sodium thiosulfate solution* (mL)

Average the three normality results. Repeat the test if the range of values exceeds 0.003 N.

Iodine solution (0.100 ± 0.001 N): Transfer 12.700 g of iodine and 19.100 g of potassium iodide (KI), accurately weighed, into a beaker, and mix. Add 2–5 mL of water, and stir well. While stirring, continue to add small increments, approximately 5 mL each, of water until the total volume is 50–60 mL. Allow the solution to stand a minimum of 4 h to ensure crystal dissolution, stirring occasionally. Quantitatively transfer the solution to a 1-L volumetric flask, and dilute with water to volume. The iodide-to-iodine weight ratio must be 1.5:1. Store the solution in an amber bottle. [NOTE—Standardize this solution just before use.]

To standardize this solution, perform the following in triplicate. Pipet 25.0 mL into a 250-mL wide-mouthed Erlenmeyer flask. Titrate with the standardized *Sodium thiosulfate solution* until a light yellow color develops. Add a few drops of *Starch solution*, and continue the titration until 1 drop produces a colorless solution. Determine the *Iodine solution* normality using the following formula:

$$\text{Result} = (S \times N_1)/I$$

S = volume of the standardized *Sodium thiosulfate solution* (mL)
N_1 = normality of the standardized *Sodium thiosulfate solution*, determined above
I = volume of *Iodine solution* (mL)

Average the three normality results. Repeat the test if the range of values exceeds 0.003 N. The standardized *Iodine solution* concentration must be 0.100 ± 0.001 N.

Sample preparation: Grind a representative sample until 60 wt % (or more) passes through a 325-mesh screen and 95 wt % (or more) passes through a 100-mesh screen. Dry the ground sample, and cool to room temperature in a desiccator.

Analysis: Three dosages of *Sample preparation* must be estimated to determine the iodine number. Weigh the three dosages (M) of dry carbon to the nearest mg. Transfer each to one of three clean, dry 250-mL Erlenmeyer flasks equipped with ground-glass stoppers. Pipet 10.0 mL of *Hydrochloric acid solution* into each flask, stopper each flask, and swirl gently until the carbon is completely wetted. Loosen the stoppers to vent the flasks, place on a hot plate in a fume hood, and bring the contents to a boil. Allow to boil gently for 30 ± 2 s to remove any sulfur (which may interfere with the test results). Remove the flasks from the hot plate and cool to room temperature. Standardize and then pipet 100.0 mL of the standardized *Iodine solution* into each flask. [NOTE—Stagger the addition of standardized *Iodine solution* to the three flasks so that no delays are encountered in handling.]

Immediately stopper the flasks, and shake the contents vigorously for 30 ± 1 s. Quickly filter each mixture by gravity through one sheet of folded filter paper (Whatman No. 2V, or equivalent) into one of three beakers. [NOTE—Prepare the filtration equipment in advance to avoid delays in filtering the samples.]

For each filtrate, use the first 20–30 mL to rinse a pipet, and discard the rinse portions. Use clean beakers to collect the remaining filtrates. Mix each filtrate by swirling the beaker, and pipet 50.0 mL of each filtrate into one of three clean 250-mL Erlenmeyer flasks. Titrate each filtrate with standardized *Sodium thiosulfate solution* until a pale yellow color develops. Add 2 mL of *Starch solution*, and continue the titration with standardized *Sodium thiosulfate solution* until 1 drop produces a colorless solution. Record the volume (S) of standardized *Sodium thiosulfate solution* used.

Calculations: The capacity of a carbon for any adsorbate depends on the concentration of the adsorbate. The concentrations of the standardized *Iodine solution* and filtrate must be known to determine an appropriate carbon weight to produce final concentrations agreeing with the definition of iodine number. The amount of sample to be used in the determination is governed by the activity of the sample. If filtrate normalities (C) are not within the range of 0.008–0.040 N, repeat the procedure using different sample weights. Once filtrate normalities are set within the specified range, perform the following calculations for each carbon dosage:

$$A = N_2 \times 12693.0$$

N_2 = normality of the standardized *Iodine solution*

$$B = N_1 \times 126.93$$

N_1 = normality of the standardized *Sodium thiosulfate solution*

Calculate the dilution factor (DF) using the equation:

$$DF = (I + H)/F$$

I = volume of standardized *Iodine solution* used in the standardization procedure (mL)
H = volume of *Hydrochloric acid solution* used (mL)
F = volume of filtrate (mL)

Calculate the weight, in mg, of iodine adsorbed per g of sample (X/M) by the equation:

$$X/M = [A - (DF) \times (B) \times (S)]/M$$

S = volume of standardized *Sodium thiosulfate solution* (mL)
M = weight of the *Sample* taken (g)

Calculate the normality of the residual filtrate (C):

$$C = (N_1 \times S)/F$$

Using logarithmic paper, plot X/M (as the ordinate) versus C (as the abscissa) for each of the three carbon dosages. Calculate the least squares fit for the three points, and plot. The iodine number is the X/M value at a residual iodine concentration (C) of 0.02 N. The regression coefficient for the least squares fit should be greater than 0.995. Carbon dosages may be estimated initially by using three values of C (usually 0.01, 0.02, and 0.03):

$$M = [A - (DF) \times (C) \times (126.93) \times (50)]/E$$

M = weight of the carbon dosage (g)
E = nominal iodine number of the *Sample*

If new carbon dosages have been determined, repeat the *Analysis* and *Calculations*.
Acceptance criteria: NLT 400

- **LOSS ON DRYING,** Appendix IIC: 120° for 4 h
  Acceptance criteria: Results conform to the representations of the vendor.
- **RESIDUE ON IGNITION (SULFATED ASH),** Appendix IIC
  Sample: 500 mg
  Acceptance criteria: Results conform to the representations of the vendor.
- **WATER EXTRACTABLES**
  Sample: 5 g
  Analysis: Transfer the *Sample* into a 250-mL flask provided with a reflux condenser and a Bunsen valve. Add 100 mL of water and several glass beads, and reflux for 1 h. Cool slightly, and filter through Whatman No. 2, or equivalent, filter paper, discarding the first 10 mL of filtrate. Cool the subsequent filtrate to room temperature, and pipet 25.0 mL into a tared crystallization dish. [NOTE—Retain the remainder of the filtrate for the *Arsenic* and *Lead* tests.] Evaporate the filtrate in the dish to incipient dryness on a hot plate, never allowing the solution to boil. Dry for 1 h at 100° in a vacuum oven, cool, and weigh.
  Acceptance criteria: NMT 4.0%

Carbon Dioxide

First Published: Prior to FCC 6

CO_2 Formula wt 44.01
INS: 290 CAS: [124-38-9]
UNII: 142M471B3J [carbon dioxide]

DESCRIPTION
Carbon Dioxide occurs as a colorless gas. One L of Carbon Dioxide weighs about 1.98 g at 0° and a pressure of 760 mm Hg. Under a pressure of about 59 atmospheres, it may be condensed to a liquid, a portion of which forms a white solid ("Dry Ice") upon rapid vaporization. Solid Carbon Dioxide evaporates without melting upon exposure to air. One volume of the gas dissolves in about 1 volume of water, forming a solution that is acid to litmus.
Function: Propellant and aerating agent; carbonating agent; direct-contact freezing agent
Packaging and Storage: Store in metal cylinders.

[NOTE—The following tests are designed to reflect the quality of Carbon Dioxide in both its vapor and its liquid phases, which are present in previously unopened cylinders. Reduce the container pressure by means of a regulator. Withdraw the samples for the tests with the least possible release of gas, consistent with proper purging of the sampling apparatus. Measure the gases with a gas volume meter downstream from the detector tubes to minimize contamination of or changes to the samples. The various detector tubes called for in the respective tests are listed under *Detector Tubes,* Solutions and Indicators.]

IDENTIFICATION
- **A. CARBON DIOXIDE**
  Sample: 100 ± 5 mL (Released from the vapor phase of the contents of the container)
  Analysis: Pass the *Sample* through a carbon dioxide detector tube (see *Detector Tubes,* Solutions and Indicators) at the rate specified for the tube. Note the indicator change.
  Acceptance criteria: The indicator change extends throughout the entire indicating range of the tube.
- **B. PROCEDURE**
  Analysis: Pass a sample through barium hydroxide TS.
  Acceptance criteria: A precipitate is formed that dissolves with effervescence in acetic acid.

[NOTE—Perform the *Assay* and the tests under *Inorganic Impurities* and *Organic Impurities* in the following order: *Assay, Carbonyl sulfide, Hydrogen sulfide, Nitric Oxide (NO) and Nitrogen Dioxide (NO_2), Nonvolatile hydrocarbons, Sulfur dioxide, Volatile hydrocarbons,* and *Water.*]

ASSAY
- **PROCEDURE**
  [NOTE—Sampling for this *Assay* may be done from the vapor phase for convenience, but this results in more residual volume than sampling from the liquid phase. If the specification of 0.5 mL is exceeded from a vapor phase sample, a liquid sample may be taken.]
  Sample: 100.0 mL taken from the liquid phase as directed in the test for *Nitric Oxide and Nitrogen Dioxide* (below)
  Analysis: Assemble a 100-mL gas buret provided with a leveling bulb and a two-way stopcock to a gas absorption pipet of suitable capacity by connecting the pipet to one of the buret outlets. Fill the buret with slightly acidified water (turned pink with methyl orange), and fill the pipet with potassium hydroxide solution (1:2). By manipulating the leveling bulb and leveling water, draw the potassium hydroxide solution to fill the pipet and capillary connection up to the stopcock, and then fill the buret with the leveling water, and draw it through the other stopcock, opening it in such a manner that all gas bubbles are eliminated

from the system. Draw the *Sample* into the buret. By raising the leveling bottle, force the measured *Sample* into the pipet. The absorption may be facilitated by rocking the pipet or by flowing the *Sample* between pipet and buret. Draw any residual gas into the buret, and measure its volume.

Acceptance criteria: NMT 0.5 mL of gas remains (NLT 99.5% of CO_2, by volume)

IMPURITIES
Inorganic Impurities
- **CARBONYL SULFIDE**
    Standard: Gas mixture of 50 ppm carbonyl sulfide in helium (obtain from a specialty gas supplier)
    Chromatographic system, Appendix IIA
        Mode: Gas chromatography
        Detector: Sievers 350 (or equivalent)[1] Chemiluminescence Detector (SCD) [NOTE—Operate the SCD with 190 mL/min of hydrogen and 396 mL/min of air, and optimize the gas flows and probe position of the SCD for maximum sensitivity.]
        Column: 30-m × 0.53-mm (id), 5 mm DB-5 capillary column (J&W Scientific Company, or equivalent)
        Column temperature: 30°
        Injection port temperature: 100°
        Carrier gas: Helium, 5 psig head-pressure
        Split ratio: 1:1
        Injection volume: 5.00 mL
        System suitability
        [NOTE—The retention time for carbonyl sulfide is approximately 3 min.]
            Suitability requirement: The peak areas resulting from triplicate injections of the *Standard* give a relative standard deviation of NMT 5.0%.
    Analysis: Inject the sample, in triplicate, average the peak area responses, and calculate the concentration, C (ppm), of carbonyl sulfide in the sample by the equation:

    $$C\ (ppm) = S(A_U / A_S)$$

    S = the calculated concentration (ppm) of carbonyl sulfide in the *Standard* (approximately 50 ppm)
    A_U = average of the peak area responses for the sample
    A_S = average of the peak area responses for the *Standard*

    Acceptance criteria: NMT 0.5 ppm, by volume

- **HYDROGEN SULFIDE**
    Sample: 50 mL, released from the vapor phase
    Analysis: Pass the *Sample* through a hydrogen sulfide detector tube (Dräger #672804, 0.5 to 15 ppm, or equivalent) at the rate specified for the tube. Note the indicator change.
    Acceptance criteria: NMT 0.5 ppm, by volume, for the volume of *Sample* specified in this test

- **NITRIC OXIDE (NO) AND NITROGEN DIOXIDE (NO_2)**
    Sample: 500 mL of liquid sample
    Analysis: Position the sample container so that when its valve is opened, the liquid phase can be sampled; generally this requires that the cylinder be inverted. Attach a section of tubing long enough to act as a vaporizer for the small quantity of liquid to be sampled. Connect one end of a nitric oxide–nitrogen dioxide detector tube (*Detector Tubes,* Solutions and Indicators) to the tubing and the other end to a gas flow meter. Pass the *Sample* through the tube at a suitable rate. No frost should reach the tube inlet from the expanding sample. Note the indicator change.
    Acceptance criteria: NMT 5 ppm total, by volume

- **SULFUR DIOXIDE**
    Sample: 1050 ± 50 mL from the liquid phase (see *Nitric Oxide and Nitrogen Dioxide,* above)
    Analysis: Pass the *Sample* through a sulfur dioxide detector tube (see *Detector Tubes,* Solutions and Indicators) at the rate specified for the tube. Note the indicator change.
    Acceptance criteria: NMT 5 ppm, by volume

- **WATER**
    Sample: 24,000 mL of gas
    Analysis: Pass the *Sample* through a suitable water-absorption tube (see *Detector Tubes,* Solutions and Indicators), NLT 100 mm long, which previously has been flushed with about 500 mL of sample and weighed. Regulate the flow so that about 60 min will be required for passage of the *Sample.* Then weigh the absorption tube and calculate the weight gain.
    Acceptance criteria: NMT 1.0 mg

Organic Impurities
- **NONVOLATILE HYDROCARBONS**
    Sample: 500 g solid, prepared by passing liquid sample from a storage container or sample cylinder through a commercial carbon dioxide snow horn directly into an open, clean container.
    Analysis: Weigh the specified amount of *Sample* collected and transfer it into a clean beaker. Allow the solid sample to sublime completely; place a watch glass placed over the beaker to prevent ambient contamination. Wash the beaker with a residue-free solvent, and transfer the solvent from the beaker to a clean, tared watch glass or petri dish with two additional rinses of the beaker with the solvent. Allow the solvent to evaporate, by heating to 104°, until the watch glass or petri dish is at a constant weight. Determine the weight of the residue by difference.
    Acceptance criteria: The weight of the residue is NMT 5 mg. (NMT 10 mg/kg)

- **VOLATILE HYDROCARBONS (AS METHANE)**
    Standard: Standard gas mixture of 50 ppm methane in helium (obtain from a specialty gas supplier)
    Chromatographic system, Appendix IIA
        Mode: Gas chromatography
        Detector: Flame ionization with a sensitivity range of 10^{-12} A/mV and an attenuation of 32
        Column: 1.8-m × 3-mm (od) metal column, or equivalent, packed with 80- to 100-mesh HayeSep Q (or equivalent)

---
[1] Any sulfur-selective detector may be used; e.g., electrolytic conductivity, flame photometric, or sulfur chemiluminescence. The detector must be capable of detecting less than 0.1 ppm v/v of carbonyl sulfide with a signal-to-noise ratio of 10:1.

Column temperature: 70° for 1 min, increase to 200° at a rate of 20°/min, hold at 200° for 10 min
Injection port temperature: 230°
Detector: 230°
Carrier gas: Helium
Flow rate: 30 mL/min
Injection volume: 1.00 mL
System suitability
  Sample: *Standard* [NOTE—The typical retention time for methane is 0.4 min.]
  Suitability requirement: The peak areas resulting from triplicate injections give a relative standard deviation of NMT 5.0%
Analysis: Inject the sample, in triplicate. [NOTE—The composition of hydrocarbons present will vary from sample to sample.] Sum the averages of the individual peak areas for the individual hydrocarbons (Do not include the peak areas for carbon dioxide.). [NOTE—The typical retention times for methane, carbon dioxide, and hexane are 0.4, 0.8, and 14.4 min, respectively.] Calculate the total concentration, C (ppm), of *Volatile Hydrocarbons* in the sample by the equation:

$$C\ (ppm) = S(A_U/A_S)$$

S = calculated concentration (ppm) of methane in the *Standard* (approximately 50 ppm)
A_U = sum of the averages of the individual peak area responses in the sample
A_S = average of the peak area responses for the *Standard*

Acceptance criteria: NMT 0.005%, by volume (as methane)

Cardamom Oil

First Published: Prior to FCC 6

CAS: [8000-66-6]
UNII: JM0KJ091HZ [cardamom oil]

DESCRIPTION
Cardamom Oil occurs as a colorless or very pale yellow liquid with the aromatic, penetrating, and somewhat camphoraceous odor of cardamom and a pungent, strongly aromatic taste. It is the volatile oil distilled from the seed of *Elettaria cardamomum* (L.) Maton (Fam. Zingiberaceae). It is affected by light. It is miscible with alcohol.
Function: Flavoring agent
Packaging and Storage: Store in full, tight containers in a cool place protected from light.

IDENTIFICATION
- **INFRARED SPECTRA,** *Spectrophotometric Identification Tests,* Appendix IIIC
  Acceptance criteria: The spectrum of the sample exhibits relative maxima at the same wavelengths as those of the spectrum below.

SPECIFIC TESTS
- **ANGULAR ROTATION,** *Optical (Specific) Rotation,* Appendix IIB: Use a 100 mm tube.
  Acceptance criteria: Between +22° and +44°
- **REFRACTIVE INDEX,** Appendix IIB
  [NOTE—Use an Abbé or other refractometer of equal or greater accuracy.]
  Acceptance criteria: Between 1.462 and 1.466 at 20°
- **SOLUBILITY IN ALCOHOL,** Appendix VI
  Acceptance criteria: One mL of the sample dissolves in 5 mL of 70% alcohol. The solution can be clear or hazy.
- **SPECIFIC GRAVITY:** Determine by any reliable method (see *General Provisions*).
  Acceptance criteria: Between 0.917 and 0.947

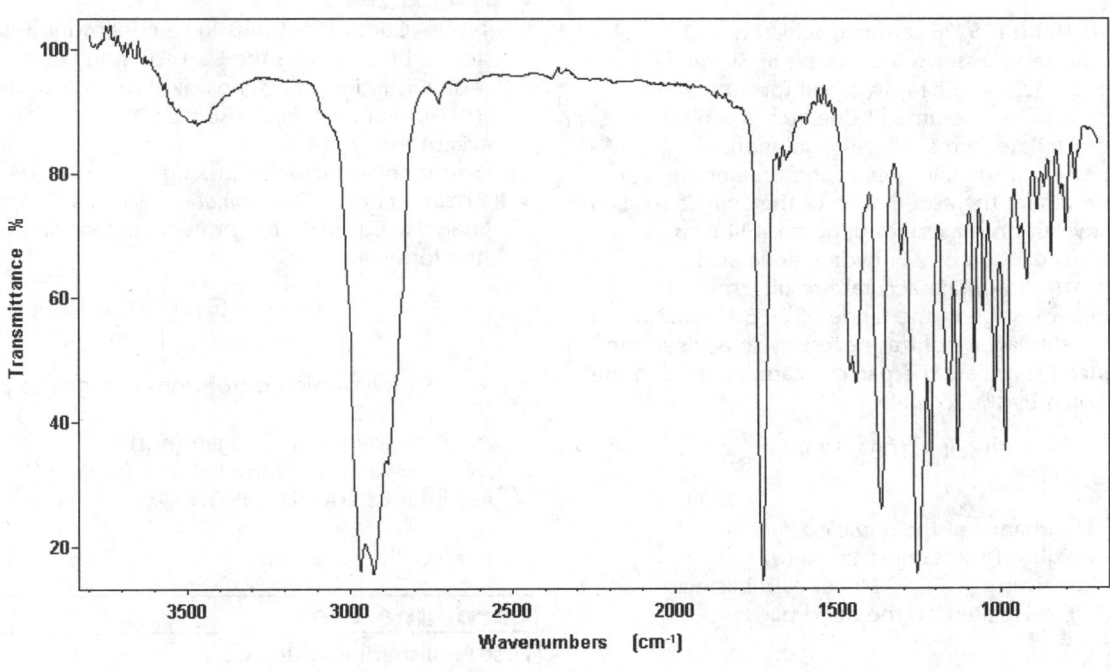

Cardamom Oil

Carmine

First Published: Prior to FCC 6

Carminic Acid

C$_{22}$H$_{20}$O$_{13}$
INS: 120
UNII: TZ8Z31B35M [cochineal]

Formula wt 492.39
CAS: [1390-65-4]

DESCRIPTION

Carmine occurs as bright red, friable pieces or as a dark red powder. It is the aluminum or the calcium-aluminum lake, on an aluminum hydroxide substrate, of the coloring principles obtained by an aqueous extraction of cochineal. Cochineal consists of the dried female insects *Dactylopius coccus costa* (*Coccus cacti* L.), enclosing young larvae; the coloring principles thus derived consist mainly of carminic acid (C$_{22}$H$_{20}$O$_{13}$). It is soluble in alkali solutions, slightly soluble in hot water, and practically insoluble in cold water and in dilute acids.

Carminic acid crystallizes from water as bright red crystals that darken at 130° and decompose at 250°; it is freely soluble in water, in alcohol, in ether, in concentrated sulfuric acid, and in solutions of alkali hydroxides; it is insoluble in petroleum ether and in chloroform. Its aqueous solutions at pH 4.8 are red-orange to yellow, and at 6.2 are dark red to violet.

[NOTE—Before use in food, Carmine must be pasteurized or otherwise treated to destroy all viable *Salmonella* microorganisms. According to the pertinent U.S. color additive regulation (21 CFR 73.100(b)(2)), "… pasteurization or such other treatment is deemed to permit the adding of safe and suitable substances (other than chemical preservatives) that are essential to the method of pasteurization or other treatment used."]

[NOTE—The specifications and tests in this monograph refer to Carmine without any added substances for pasteurization or any other such treatment.]

Function: Color

Packaging and Storage: Store in well-closed containers in a cool, dry place.

IDENTIFICATION
- **PROCEDURE**

  Sample solution: Mix 333 mg of sample with 44 mL of water, 0.15 mL of a 1:10 sodium hydroxide solution, and 0.2 mL of ammonium hydroxide in a 500-mL volumetric flask. Warm the mixture to dissolve the sample, allow the solution to cool, dilute to volume with water, and mix. Pipet 10.0 mL of this solution into a 250-mL volumetric flask, dilute to volume with water, and mix.

  Analysis: Using a suitable spectrophotometer and a 1-cm cell, measure the absorbance of the *Sample solution*; use water as a blank.

  Acceptance criteria: The *Sample solution* exhibits absorption maxima at 520 nm and 550 nm and the absorbance at 520 nm is not less than 0.30.

ASSAY
- **PROCEDURE**
  Sample: 0.100 g (~52% carminic acid content)
  Sample solution: Dissolve the *Sample* in 30 mL of 2 N hydrochloric acid and heat to a boil for 30 s. After cooling, dilute to a volume of one liter. If a black or brown precipitate forms, filter the solution.
  Analysis: Using a suitable spectrophotometer and a 1-cm cell, measure the absorbance of the *Sample solution* at the wavelength maximum of about 494 nm; use a 1:3 aqueous dilution of 2 N hydrochloric acid as the blank. [NOTE—To obtain accurate results, the absorbance must be in the range of 0.650 to 0.750. Adjust the starting weight as necessary to achieve this absorbance.] Calculate the percent carminic acid in the sample taken by the formula:

  $$\text{Result} = 100A/13.9W$$

  A = absorbance of the *Sample solution*
  W = weight of the sample taken (g)
  Acceptance criteria: NLT 50.0% of carminic acid ($C_{22}H_{20}O_{13}$), calculated on the dried basis

IMPURITIES
Inorganic Impurities
- **ARSENIC,** *Arsenic Limit Test,* Appendix IIIB
  Sample: 3.0 g
  Sample solution: Transfer the *Sample* into a 500-mL Kjeldahl flask equipped with a steam trap, add 5 g of ferrous sulfate and 75 mL of hydrochloric acid, and mix. Connect the flask with the steam trap and with a condenser, the delivery tube of which consists of a large-sized straight adapter and extends to slightly above the bottom of a 500-mL Erlenmeyer flask containing 100 mL of water. Begin heating the Kjeldahl flask and collect about 40 mL of distillate in the Erlenmeyer flask. Pour the distillate mixture into a 600-mL beaker add 20 mL of bromine water, and heat on a hot plate until the volume is reduced to about 2 mL. Transfer the residual liquid into a 125-mL arsine generator flask (see Figure 11) with the aid of 35 mL of water, and continue as directed in the *Procedure* beginning with "Add 20 mL of 1:5 sulfuric acid..."
  Acceptance criteria: NMT 1 mg/kg
- **LEAD,** *Lead Limit Test,* Appendix IIIB
  Sample solution: Prepare as directed for organic compounds.
  Control: 10 µg Pb (10 mL of *Diluted Standard Lead Solution*)
  Acceptance criteria: NMT 2 mg/kg

SPECIFIC TESTS
- **ASH**
  Sample: 1 g
  Analysis: Transfer the *Sample* into a tared, previously ignited and cooled porcelain crucible, and ignite red-hot with a Meker burner to constant weight.
  Acceptance criteria: NMT 12.0%
- **LOSS ON DRYING,** Appendix IIC: 135° for 3 h
  Sample: 1 g
  Acceptance criteria: NMT 20.0%
- **MICROBIAL LIMITS**
  [NOTE—Current methods for the following tests may be found by accessing the US Food and Drug Administration's Bacteriological Analytical Manual (BAM) online at www.cfsan.fda.gov.]
  Acceptance criteria
  Salmonella: Negative in 25 g
- **PROTEIN,** *Nitrogen Determination,* Method II, Appendix IIIC
  Analysis: Calculate the protein content, in percent, by the formula:

  $$\text{Result} = (F \times N/W) \times 100$$

  F = conversion factor from nitrogen to protein, 6.25
  N = weight of nitrogen (mg)
  W = weight of sample taken (mg)
  Acceptance criteria: NMT 25%

Carnauba Wax
First Published: Prior to FCC 6

INS: 903 CAS: [8015-86-9]
UNII: R12CBM0EIZ [carnauba wax]

DESCRIPTION
Carnauba Wax occurs as a hard, brittle substance with a resinous fracture and a color ranging from light brown to pale yellow. It is a purified wax obtained from the leaf buds and leaves of the Brazilian wax palm *Copernicia cereferia* (Arruda) Mart. [synonym *C. prunifera* (Muell.)]. Its specific gravity is about 0.997. It is partially soluble in boiling alcohol, is soluble in chloroform and in ether, but is insoluble in water.
Function: Anticaking agent; surface-finishing (glazing) agent; release agent; carrier for flavors
Packaging and Storage: Store in well-closed containers.

IMPURITIES
Inorganic Impurities
- **LEAD,** Appendix IIIB
  Sample solution: Prepare as directed for organic compounds.
  Control: 5 µg Pb (5 mL of *Diluted Standard Lead Solution*)
  Acceptance criteria: NMT 5 mg/kg

SPECIFIC TESTS
- **ACID VALUE [FATS AND RELATED SUBSTANCES],** *Method I,* Appendix VII
  Acceptance criteria: Between 2 and 7
- **ESTER VALUE**
  Analysis: Subtract the *Acid Value* (above) from the *Saponification Value* (below) to obtain this value.
  Acceptance criteria: Between 71 and 88
- **MELTING RANGE OR TEMPERATURE DETERMINATION,** *Procedure for Class II,* Appendix IIB
  Acceptance criteria: Between 80° and 86°

- **RESIDUE ON IGNITION (SULFATED ASH),** Appendix IIC
  Sample: 2 g
  Analysis: Heat the *Sample* in a tared, open, porcelain or platinum dish over an open flame. It volatilizes without emitting an acrid odor. Ignite as directed.
  Acceptance criteria: NMT 0.25%
- **SAPONIFICATION VALUE,** Appendix VII
  Sample: 5 g
  Acceptance criteria: Between 78 and 95
- **UNSAPONIFIABLE MATTER,** Appendix VII
  Acceptance criteria: Between 50.0% and 55.0%

L-Carnitine

First Published: Prior to FCC 6

4-Amino-3-hydroxybutyric Acid Trimethylbetaine
Levocarnitine
4-Trimethylamino-3-hydroxybutyrate
(R)-3-Carboxy-2-hydroxy-N,N,N-trimethyl-1-propanaminium Hydroxide, Inner Salt

$C_7H_{15}NO_3$ Formula wt 161.20
              CAS: [541-15-1]
UNII: 0G389FZZ9M [levocarnitine]

DESCRIPTION
L-Carnitine occurs as white crystals or as a white, crystalline, hygroscopic powder. It is freely soluble in water, in alcohol, in alkaline solutions, and in dilute mineral acids. It is practically insoluble in acetone and in ethyl acetate. It decomposes without melting at about 185° to 195°.
Function: Nutrient
Packaging and Storage: Store in tight containers.

IDENTIFICATION
- **A. PROCEDURE**
  Analysis: Dissolve 1 g of sample in 10 mL of water and 10 mL of 1 N hydrochloric acid, and add 5 mL of sodium tetraphenylborate TS.
  Acceptance criteria: A white precipitate forms.
- **B. INFRARED ABSORPTION,** *Spectrophotometric Identification Tests,* Appendix IIIC
  Reference standard: USP Levocarnitine RS
  Sample and standard preparation: K (previously dried in vacuum at 60° for 5 h)
  Acceptance criteria: The spectrum of the sample exhibits maxima at the same wavelengths as those in the spectrum of the *Reference standard*.

ASSAY
- **PROCEDURE**
  Sample: 1.0 g [NOTE—Avoid atmospheric moisture uptake during weighing.]
  Analysis: Dissolve the *Sample* in water contained in a 250-mL flask. Titrate with 1.0 N hydrochloric acid to a potentiometric endpoint. Perform a blank determination (see *General Provisions*), and make any necessary correction. Each mL of 1.0 N hydrochloric acid is equivalent to 161.2 mg of $C_7H_{15}NO_3$.
  Acceptance criteria: NLT 97.0% and NMT 103.0% of $C_7H_{15}NO_3$, calculated on the anhydrous basis

IMPURITIES
Inorganic Impurities
- **CHLORIDE**
  Sample solution: Add 100 mg of sample in 30 to 40 mL of water in a 50-mL flask, and mix. Add 10% nitric acid dropwise until the solution is neutral to litmus. Add an additional 1 mL of 10% nitric acid and dilute with water to a total volume of 50 mL.
  Control: Add 0.56 mL of 0.02 N hydrochloric acid solution to 30 to 40 mL of water in a 50-mL flask. Add 1 mL of 10% nitric acid and dilute to volume with water.
  Analysis: Add 1 mL of 0.1 N silver nitrate to both the *Sample solution* and the *Control*. Mix, allow to stand for 5 min protected from direct sunlight, and visually compare the two solutions.
  Acceptance criteria: Any turbidity produced by the *Sample solution* does not exceed that shown in the *Control* (NMT 0.4%).
- **LEAD,** *Lead Limit Test, Flame Atomic Absorption Spectrophotometric Method,* Appendix IIIB
  Sample: 10 g
  Acceptance criteria: NMT 1 mg/kg
- **POTASSIUM**
  [NOTE—The *Standard solution* and the *Sample solutions* may be modified, if necessary, to obtain solutions of suitable concentrations adaptable to the linear or working range of the spectrophotometer.]
  Standard stock solution: 12.5 mg/mL potassium, made by transferring 5.959 g of potassium chloride, previously dried at 105° for 2 h, into a 250-mL volumetric flask, dilute to volume with water, and mix.
  Standard solution: 31.25 µg/mL potassium: from *Standard stock solution*
  Sample: 62.5 mg
  Sample stock solution: Transfer the *Sample* into a 100-mL volumetric flask, dissolve in and dilute to volume with water, and mix.
  Sample solutions: Add 0, 2.0, and 4.0 mL of the *Standard solution* to three separate 25-mL volumetric flasks. Add 20.0 mL of the *Sample stock solution* to each flask, dilute to volume with water, and mix. These solutions contain 0 (*Sample solution A*), 2.5 (*Sample solution B*), and 5.0 (*Sample solution C*) µg/mL of potassium.
  Analysis: Using a suitable atomic absorption spectrophotometer equipped with an air-acetylene flame and using water as the blank, concomitantly determine the absorbance values of the *Sample solutions* at the potassium emission line at 766.7 nm. Plot the absorbance values of the *Sample solutions* versus their contents of potassium, in µg/mL; draw the straight line best fitting the three points and extrapolate the line until it intersects with the concentration axis. From the intercept, determine the

amount, in μg, of potassium in each mL of *Sample solution A*. Calculate the percent potassium in the portion of *Sample* taken by multiplying the concentration, in μg/mL, of potassium found in *Sample solution A* by 0.2.
Acceptance criteria: NMT 0.2%

- **SODIUM**
  [NOTE—The *Standard solution* and the *Sample solutions* may be modified, if necessary, to obtain solutions of suitable concentrations adaptable to the linear or working range of the spectrophotometer.]
  Standard stock solution: 10.0 mg/mL sodium, made by transferring 6.355 g of sodium chloride, previously dried at 105° for 2 h, into a 250-mL volumetric flask, dilute to volume with water, and mix.
  Standard solution: 250 μg/mL sodium: from *Standard stock solution*
  Sample: 4 g
  Sample stock solution: Transfer the *Sample* into a 100-mL volumetric flask, dissolve in and dilute to volume with water, and mix.
  Sample solutions: Add 0, 2.0, and 4.0 mL of the *Standard solution* to three separate 25-mL volumetric flasks. Add 20.0 mL of the *Sample stock solution* to each flask, dilute to volume with water, and mix. These solutions contain 0 (*Sample solution A*), 20.0 (*Sample solution B*), and 40.0 (*Sample solution C*) μg/mL of sodium.
  Analysis: Using a suitable atomic absorption spectrophotometer equipped with an air-acetylene flame and using water as the blank, concomitantly determine the absorbance values of the *Sample solutions* at the sodium emission line at 589.0 nm. Plot the absorbance values of the *Sample solutions* versus their contents of sodium, in μg/mL; draw the straight line best fitting the three points and extrapolate the line until it intersects with the concentration axis. From the intercept, determine the amount, in μg, of sodium in each mL of *Sample solution A*. Calculate the percent sodium in the portion of *Sample* taken by multiplying the concentration, in μg/mL, of sodium found in *Sample solution A* by 0.003125.
  Acceptance criteria: NMT 0.1%

SPECIFIC TESTS
- **OPTICAL (SPECIFIC) ROTATION,** Appendix IIB
  Sample solution: 100 mg/mL (using a previously dried sample)
  Acceptance criteria: $[\alpha]_D^{20}$ between −29.0° and −32.0°, calculated on the anhydrous basis
- **PH,** *pH Determination*, Appendix IIB
  Sample solution: 50 mg/mL
  Acceptance criteria: Between 5.5 and 9.5
- **RESIDUE ON IGNITION (SULFATED ASH),** Appendix IIC
  Sample: 2 g
  Acceptance criteria: NMT 0.5%
- **WATER,** *Water Determination*, Appendix IIB
  Acceptance criteria: NMT 4.0%

β-Carotene

First Published: Prior to FCC 6

Carotene

$C_{40}H_{56}$ Formula wt 536.88
INS: 160a(i)
UNII: 01YAE03M7J [β-carotene]   CAS: [7235-40-7]

DESCRIPTION
β-Carotene occurs as red crystals or as crystalline powder. It is insoluble in water and in acids and alkalies, but is soluble in carbon disulfide and in chloroform. It is sparingly soluble in ether, in solvent hexane, and in vegetable oils, and is practically insoluble in methanol and in ethanol. It melts between 176° and 182°, with decomposition.
Function: Nutrient; color
Packaging and Storage: Store in a cool place in tight, light-resistant containers under inert gas.

[NOTE—Carry out all work in low-actinic glassware and in subdued light]

IDENTIFICATION
- **VISIBLE ABSORPTION SPECTRUM**
  Sample solution: Use *Sample solution B* prepared for the *Assay* (below).
  Analysis: Using a suitable spectrophotometer, determine the absorbance of *Sample solution B* at 455 nm and at 483 nm.
  Acceptance criteria: The ratio of absorbance values obtained, A_{455}/A_{483}, is between 1.14 and 1.18.
- **VISIBLE ABSORPTION SPECTRUM**
  Sample solutions: Use *Sample solution A* and *Sample solution B* prepared for the *Assay* (below).
  Analysis: Using a suitable spectrophotometer, determine the absorbance of *Sample solution B* at 455 nm and that of *Sample solution A* at 340 nm.
  Acceptance criteria: The ratio of absorbance values obtained, A_{455}/A_{340}, is NLT 1.5.

ASSAY
- **PROCEDURE**
  Sample stock solution: Transfer 50 mg of sample into a 100-mL volumetric flask, dissolve it in 10 mL of acid-free chloroform, immediately dilute to volume with cyclohexane, and mix.
  Sample solution A: 5 mL of *Sample stock solution* diluted to 100 mL with cyclohexane
  Sample solution B: 5 mL of *Sample solution A* diluted to 50 ml with cyclohexane
  Analysis: Determine the absorbance of *Sample solution B* using a suitable atomic absorption spectrophotometer with a 1-cm cell, set to the wavelength of maximum absorption at about 455 nm, using cyclohexane as the

blank. Calculate the quantity, in mg, of $C_{40}H_{56}$ in the sample taken by the formula:

$$Result = 20{,}000\ A/250$$

A = absorbance of the solution
250 = absorptivity of pure β-carotene

Acceptance criteria: NLT 96.0% and NMT 101.0% of $C_{40}H_{56}$, calculated on the dried basis

IMPURITIES
Inorganic Impurities
- **LEAD**, *Lead Limit Test, Flame Atomic Absorption Spectrophotometric Method*, Appendix IIIB
  Sample: 5 g
  Acceptance criteria: NMT 5 mg/kg

SPECIFIC TESTS
- **LOSS ON DRYING**, Appendix IIC: In a vacuum over phosphorus pentoxide at 40° for 4 h
  Acceptance criteria: NMT 0.2%
- **RESIDUE ON IGNITION (SULFATED ASH)**, Appendix IIC
  Sample: 2 g
  Acceptance criteria: NMT 0.2%

Carrageenan

First Published: First Supplement, FCC 6

Irish moss (from *Chondrus spp.*)
Eucheuman (from *Eucheuma spp.*)
Iridophycan (from *Iridaea spp.*)
Hypnean (from *Hypnea spp.*)
Processed Eucheuma Seaweed, PES, PNG-carrageenan, and Semi-refined carrageenan (from *E. spinosum* or *E. cottonii*)
INS: 407   CAS: [9000-07-1]
UNII: 5C69YCD2YJ [carrageenan]

DESCRIPTION
Carrageenan occurs as a yellow or tan to white, coarse to fine powder. It is obtained from certain members of the class Rhodophyceae (red seaweeds). The principal commercial sources of carrageenans are the following families and genera of the class Rhodophyceae[1]:

Furcellariaceae such as *Furcellaria*;
Gigartinaceae such as *Chondrus, Gigartina, Iridaea*;
Hypnaeceae such as *Hypnea*;
Phyllophoraceae such as *Phyllophora, Gynmogongrus, Ahnfeltia*;
Solieriaceae such as *Eucheuma, Anatheca, Meristotheca*.

Carrageenan is a hydrocolloid consisting mainly of the ammonium, calcium, magnesium, potassium, and sodium sulfate esters of galactose and 3,6-anhydrogalactose polysaccharides. These hexoses are alternately linked α-(1→3) and β-(1→4) in the copolymer. The relative proportions of cations existing in carrageenan may be changed during processing to the extent that one may become predominant.

The prevalent polysaccharides in carrageenan are designated as *kappa-, iota-,* and *lambda*-carrageenan. *Kappa*-carrageenan is mostly the alternating polymer of D-galactose-4-sulfate and 3,6-anhydro-D-galactose; *iota*-carrageenan is similar except that the 3,6-anhydrogalactose is sulfated at carbon 2. Between *kappa*-carrageenan and *iota*-carrageenan, there is a continuum of intermediate compositions differing in degree of sulfation at carbon 2. In *lambda*-carrageenan, the alternating monomeric units are mostly D-galactose-2-sulfate (1→3-linked) and D-galactose-2,6-disulfate (1→4-linked).

Carrageenan may be obtained from any of the cited seaweeds by extraction into water or aqueous dilute alkali. It may be recovered by alcohol precipitation, by drum drying, or by precipitation in aqueous potassium chloride and subsequent freezing. Additionally, carrageenan may be obtained by extracting the cleaned seaweed with alkali for a short time at elevated temperatures. The material is then thoroughly washed with water to remove residual salts followed by purification, drying and milling to a powder. Carrageenan obtained by this method contains a higher percentage of algal cellulose. The alcohols used during recovery and purification of carrageenan are restricted to methanol, ethanol, and isopropanol.

Carrageenan is insoluble in ethanol but it is soluble in water at 80°, forming a viscous clear or cloudy and slightly opalescent solution that flows readily. Some samples form a cloudy viscous suspension in water. Carrageenan disperses in water more readily if first moistened with alcohol, glycerol, or a saturated solution of glucose or sucrose in water.

Articles of commerce may include sugars for standardization purposes, salts to obtain specific gelling or thickening characteristics, or emulsifiers carried over from drum-drying processes.

Function: Thickener, gelling agent, stabilizer, emulsifier
Packaging and Storage: Store in well-closed containers.
[NOTE—Carrageenan must be well dispersed in water in many of the following tests so dispersion technique must be kept in mind throughout this monograph. Carrageenan is best dispersed by slowly sprinkling the powder into cold water with continuous vigorous stirring. This allows the carrageenan particles to wet and hydrate effectively prior to dissolving. Adding carrageenan directly to hot water, or too rapidly to cold water, or not stirring vigorously will cause the carrageenan particles to form lumps which are very difficult to break down and solubilize. If appropriate, carrageenan disperses more readily in cold water if first moistened with alcohol, glycerol, or saturated solutions of glucose/sucrose/salt. Alternatively, for improved dispersion, carrageenan powder may be pre-blended with other water soluble solids before adding to cold water.]

IDENTIFICATION
- **GUM CONSTITUENTS**, *Thin-Layer Chromatography*, Appendix IIA
  Absorbent: Silica Gel G

---
[1] In the United States, only the following seaweed species from the families Gigartinaceae and Solieriaceae are authorized as sources of carrageenan intended for use in foods (Title 21 US Code of Federal Regulations Part 172, section 620 (21 CFR 172.620)): *Chondrus crispus, C. ocellatus, Eucheuma cottonii, E. spinosum, Gigartina acicularis, G. pistillata, G. radula,* and *G. stellata.*

Standards: Galactose, rhamnose, galacturonic acid, 3,6-anhydrogalactose, mannose, arabinose, and xylose

Developing solvent systems
  A: Formic acid, methyl ethyl ketone, tertiary butanol and water (3:6:8:3)
  B: Glacial acetic acid, chloroform, water (74:65:11)

Sample solution: Boil a mixture of 200 mg of sample and 20 mL of 10% sulfuric acid for 3 h. Allow the mixture to cool and add excess barium carbonate, mixing with a magnetic stirrer until the solution reaches pH 7; filter the solution. Evaporate the filtrate in a rotary evaporator at 30 - 50° under vacuum until a crystalline or syrupy residue is obtained. Dissolve this hydrolysate in 10 mL of 40% methanol.

Standard solution: Separately, dissolve each of the *Standards* in 10 mL of 40% methanol.

Spray reagent: Dissolve 1.23 g of anisidine and 1.66 g of phthalic acid in 100 mL ethanol.

Application volumes: 1-5 μL *Sample solution* and 1-10 μL of the *Standard solutions*

Analysis: Apply the *Sample solution* on the starting lines of two Silica Gel G plates. On the same plates apply the *Standard solutions*. Develop one plate in *Developing solvent system A* and the other in *Developing solvent system B*. After developing the two plates, remove the plates from the chambers and dry them at 110° for 20 min. Allow the plates to cool and spray with *Spray reagent*. After spraying, heat the plates at 100° for 10 min. [NOTE—A greenish yellow color is produced with hexoses, a red color with pentoses and a brown color with uronic acids.]

Acceptance criteria: Spots corresponding in color and R_F with galactose and 3,6-anhydrogalactose from the *Standard solutions* are obtained from the *Sample solution*.

- **INFRARED SPECTRA,** *Spectrophotometric Identification Tests,* Appendix IIIC

  Sample preparation
  [NOTE—If the carrageenan sample does not contain standardizing salts or sugars, the following purification step is not necessary.] Disperse 1 g of carrageenan in 250 mL of cold water, heat the mixture at 90° for 10 min, cool it to 60°, and dissolve 1 g of potassium chloride into the solution. Coagulate the mixture with 2 volumes of isopropyl alcohol, then recover, wash, and dry the purified carrageenan. Disperse 0.5 g of the purified carrageenan sample in 250 mL of cold water, heat the mixture at 90° for 10 min, and cool it to 60°. Cast films 0.5 mm thick (when dry) on a suitable non-stick surface such as Teflon or a plastic petri dish. Alternatively, use films cast on a potassium bromide plate, care being taken to avoid moisture.

  Acceptance criteria
  All types: The spectrum of the sample exhibits strong, broad absorption bands, typical of all polysaccharides, in the 1000 cm^{-1} to 1100 cm^{-1} region. Maxima are at 1065 cm^{-1} and 1020 cm^{-1} for gelling and non-gelling types, respectively.

  Kappa-type (see appropriate spectrum below):
    Low ester sulfate absorbance at 1220–1260 cm^{-1}
    Strong 3,6-AG absorbance at 930–935 cm^{-1}
    Strong galactose-4-sulfate absorbance at 840–850 cm^{-1}
    No 3,6-AG-2-sulfate absorbance at 800–805 cm^{-1}

  Iota-type (see appropriate spectrum below):
    Same as *kappa*-type except strong ester sulfate absorbance at 1220–1260 cm^{-1} and strong 3,6-AG-2-sulfate absorbance at 800–805 cm^{-1}

  Lambda-type (see appropriate spectrum below):
    Strong ester sulfate absorbance 1220–1260 cm^{-1}
    Weak to no 3,6AG absorbance at 930–935 cm^{-1}
    Strong galactose-2-sulfate absorbance at 825–830 cm^{-1}
    Strong galactose-6-sulfate absorbance at 810–820 cm^{-1}

- **PREDOMINANT POLYSACCHARIDES**

  Sample: 4 g

  Analysis: Transfer the *Sample* to a flask containing 200 mL of water and heat the mixture in a water bath at 80°, with constant stirring, until dissolved. Replace any water lost by evaporation and allow the solution to cool to room temperature. [NOTE—The solution becomes viscous and may form a gel.] To 50 mL of the solution or gel, add 200 mg of potassium chloride; then reheat, mix well, and cool.

  Acceptance criteria
    kappa type: A short-textured "brittle" gel forms.
    iota type: A compliant "elastic" gel forms.
    lambda type: The solution does not gel.

IMPURITIES

Inorganic Impurities

- **ARSENIC,** *Arsenic Limit Test,* Appendix IIIB

  Sample solution: Prepare as directed for organic compounds.

  Acceptance criteria: NMT 3 mg/kg

- **CADMIUM**

  [NOTE—Throughout this test, use distilled, deionized water.]

  Standard stock solution: 10 μg/mL cadmium prepared by diluting a commercially available standard solution

  Standard solutions: 0.05, 0.1, 0.2, 0.4, and 0.6 μg/mL of cadmium: from *Standard stock solution*

  Sample: 7.5 g [NOTE—The sample should be powdered and dry.]

  Sample solution: [CAUTION—Handle perchloric acid in an appropriate fume hood.] Transfer the *Sample* to a 250-mL Erlenmeyer flask and wet it with 10 mL of water; add 25 mL of nitric acid. As soon as any initial reaction subsides, heat gently on a hot plate set at 100–150° for about 1 h or until most of the dark fumes that form are evolved. Swirl the flask occasionally. Cool the flask and add 5 mL of perchloric acid. Salt-like particles are visible at this stage. Resume heating the flask on the hot plate at 100–150° until the digest is yellow or colorless; this takes about 1 h. Do not allow the solution to dry; if necessary add 2–3 mL of nitric acid. Cool the digest and wash the insides of the flask with 5 mL of water and swirl the flask. Add 2 mL of hydrochloric acid to complete the digestion. Resume heating the solution on the hot plate at 100–150° until brown fumes are no longer visible and the solution is white to yellowish in color. Again, do not allow the solution to dry; if necessary add 2–3 mL of nitric acid. Cool the solution. It will become slightly viscous and salt-like particles will be visible. Add 10 mL of water to the flask, while washing the sides. Transfer the viscous solution to a 50-mL volumetric flask, dilute to volume with water, and mix. Filter the salt-like particles from the solution using two layers of Whatman no. 5 filter paper (or equivalent).

Reagent blank: Use the same quantities of reagents as used to prepare the *Sample solution,* but omitting the *Sample.*

Analysis: Use any suitable atomic absorption spectrophotometer equipped with a Boling-type burner, an air–acetylene flame, and a hollow-cathode cadmium lamp. Optimize the instrument according to the manufacturer's instructions. Determine the absorbance of each of the *Standard solutions,* of the *Sample solution,* and of the *Reagent blank* at 228.8 nm. Determine the corrected absorbance values by subtracting the *Reagent blank* absorbance from each of the *Standard solutions* and from the *Sample solution* absorbances. Prepare a standard curve by plotting the corrected absorbance of the *Standard solutions* versus concentration of lead (µg/mL). Calculate the concentration (mg/kg) of cadmium in the *Sample* using the following formula:

$$\text{Result} = C/W \times 50$$

C = the concentration (µg/mL) of cadmium in the *Sample solution* determined from the standard curve
W = the weight of *Sample* taken (g)
50 = the sample dilution factor

Acceptance criteria: NMT 2 mg/kg

- **LEAD**
[NOTE—Throughout this test, use distilled, deionized water.]

Standard stock solution: 100 µg/mL of lead prepared by diluting a commercially available standard solution

Standard solutions: 0.1, 0.2, 0.4, 0.8, and 1.6 µg/mL of lead: from *Standard stock solution*

Sample: 7.5 g [NOTE—The sample should be powdered and dry.]

Sample solution: [CAUTION—Handle perchloric acid in an appropriate fume hood.] Transfer the *Sample* to a 250-mL Erlenmeyer flask and wet it with 10 mL of water; add 25 mL of nitric acid. As soon as any initial reaction subsides, heat gently on a hot plate set at 100–150° for about 1 h or until most of the dark fumes that form are evolved. Swirl the flask occasionally. Cool the flask and add 5 mL of perchloric acid. Salt-like particles are visible at this stage. Resume heating the flask on the hot plate at 100–150° until the digest is yellowish or colorless; this takes about 1 h. Do not allow the solution to dry; if necessary add 2–3 mL of nitric acid. Cool the digest and wash the insides of the flask with 5 mL of water and swirl the flask. Add 2 mL of hydrochloric acid to complete the digestion. Resume heating the solution on the hot plate at 100–150° until brown fumes are no longer visible and the solution is white to yellowish in color. Again, do not allow the solution to dry; if necessary add 2–3 mL of nitric acid. Cool the solution. It will become slightly viscous and salt-like particles will be visible. Add 10 mL of water to the flask, while washing the sides. Transfer the viscous solution to a 50-mL volumetric flask, dilute to volume with water, and mix. Filter the salt-like particles from the solution using two layers of Whatman no. 5 filter paper (or equivalent).

Reagent blank: Use the same quantities of reagents as used to prepare the *Sample solution,* but omitting the *Sample.*

Analysis: Use any suitable atomic absorption spectrophotometer equipped with a lead electrodeless discharge lamp (EDL) and an air–acetylene flame. Optimize the instrument according to the manufacturer's instructions. Determine the absorbance of each of the *Standard solutions,* of the *Sample solution,* and of the *Reagent blank* at 283.3 nm. Determine the corrected absorbance values by subtracting the *Reagent blank* absorbance from each of the *Standard solutions* and from the *Sample solution* absorbances. Prepare a standard curve by plotting the corrected absorbance of the *Standard solutions* versus concentration of lead (µg/mL). Calculate the concentration (mg/kg) of lead in the *Sample* using the following formula:

$$\text{Result} = C/W \times 50$$

C = the concentration (µg/mL) of lead in the *Sample solution* determined from the standard curve.
W = the weight of *Sample* taken (g)
50 = the sample dilution factor

Acceptance criteria: NMT 5 mg/kg

- **MERCURY**
[NOTE—Throughout this test, use distilled, deionized water.]
[CAUTION—Handle perchloric acid in an appropriate fume hood.]

Reagent solutions
Sodium borohydride solution: 0.4% solution prepared by first dissolving 2.5 g of sodium hydroxide in water and then adding and dissolving 2.0 g of sodium borohydride (>98%) followed by dilution with water to 500 mL. [NOTE—Prepare immediately before use.]
5 M Hydrochloric acid: Dilute 417 mL of hydrochloric acid to 1 L.

Standard stock solution: 1 mg/mL mercury prepared by diluting a commercially available standard solution.

Standard solutions: 10, 25, 50, 100, and 200 ng/mL of mercury, from *Standard stock solution*

Sample: 2 g [NOTE—The sample should be powdered and dry.]

Sample solution: Transfer the *Sample* to a 250-mL Erlenmeyer flask and wet it with 5 mL of water; add 10 mL of nitric acid–perchloric acid (1:1) solution. As soon as any initial reaction subsides, heat gently on a hot plate set at 100–150° for about 1 h until all of the dark fumes that form are evolved and the solution turns yellowish or colorless. Swirl the flask occasionally. Salt-like particles are visible at this stage. Do not allow the solution to dry. Cool the solution. It will become slightly viscous and salt-like particles will be visible. Rinse down the sides of the flask with 5 mL of water and allow the solution to stand overnight to facilitate elimination of dissolved gas. Transfer the viscous solution to a 200-mL volumetric flask, dilute to volume with water, and mix. Filter the salt-like particles from the solution using two layers of Whatman no. 5 filter paper (or equivalent). Transfer the filtrate to a 500-mL Erlenmeyer flask and, in an ultrasonic bath, sonicate the flask for 10 min or until bubbles no longer form on the surface; this indicates that all dissolved gas has been removed.

Reagent blank: Use the same quantities of reagents as used to prepare the *Sample solution*.

Cold-Vapor Atomic Absorption Method
  Instrument: Use any suitable atomic absorption spectrophotometer equipped with a hydride vapor generator (e.g., Shimadzu Model 6601F or equivalent) or atomic vapor assembly. [NOTE—Integral to the hydride generator is a reactor tube or coil and a peristaltic pump with dual tubing channels: one channel for the *Sample solution* and one for the two *Reagent solutions*. Flow control is determined by tubing size and tubing clamps. Flow rates are measured at the exit of the hydride generator. The hydride generator manifold is where the three solutions are mixed and pass into the reactor coil to generate atomic mercury, which is carried into the absorbance cell of the instrument.]
  Lamp: Mercury at 253.7 nm
  Purge gas: Argon
  Pump calibration: Calibrate (using water) the peristaltic pump so that it will provide a flow rate of the *Sample solution* of 8 mL/min and a combined flow rate for the two *Reagent solutions* of 2 mL/min. [NOTE—The combined flow rate is achieved with a single pump setting.]
  Analysis: Set the spectrophotometer to previously established optimum conditions at 253.7 nm. Transfer suitable quantities of the two *Reagent solutions* into separate graduated cylinders. Insert separate aspirator tubing leading from the peristaltic pump into each of the *Reagent solutions* and into the *Sample solution* contained in the 100-mL Erlenmeyer flask. Start the flow of argon gas (tank outlet pressure: 3.2 ± 0.2 kg/cm^2) through the hydride vapor generator of the spectrophotometer. Start the pump to initiate flow of the three solutions into the hydride generator manifold. Measure the absorbance for the *Sample solution*. Repeat for the *Reagent blank* and for each of the *Standard solutions*.

Determine the corrected absorbance values by subtracting the *Reagent blank* absorbance from each of the *Standard solutions* and from the *Sample solution* absorbances. Prepare a standard curve by plotting the corrected absorbance of the *Standard solutions* versus concentration of mercury (ng/mL). Calculate the concentration (mg/kg) of mercury in the *Sample* using the following formula:

$$\text{Result} = (C/W) \times (50/1000)$$

C = the concentration (ng/mL) of mercury in the *Sample solution* determined from the standard curve
W = the weight of *Sample* taken (g)
50 = the sample dilution factor
1000 = ng/g to mg/kg conversion factor

Acceptance criteria: NMT 1 mg/kg

Organic Impurities
- **RESIDUAL SOLVENTS**
  Internal standard solution: Add 50.0 mL of water to a 50 mL injection vial and seal. Weigh and inject 15 µL of 3-methyl-2-pentanone through the septum and reweigh to within 0.01 mg.
  Blank: A sample with very low solvent content [NOTE—Depending on the solvent or solvents used in the purification and recovery of the *Sample*, more than one solvent may be present.]
  Blank solution: Weigh 0.20 g of the *Blank* into an injection vial. Add 5.0 mL of water and 1.0 mL of the *Internal standard solution*. Heat the vial at 60° for 10 min and shake it vigorously for 10 s.
  Standard solution: Weigh 0.20 g of the *Blank* into an injection vial. Add 5.0 mL of water and 1.0 mL of the *Internal standard solution*. Weigh the vial to within 0.01 mg. Inject 4 µL each of ethanol, isopropanol, and methanol through the septum, reweighing the vial between the addition of each solvent. Heat the vial at 60° for 10 min and shake it vigorously for 10 s.
  Sample: 5 g
  Sample solution: Disperse 1 mL of a suitable antifoam emulsion, such as Dow-Corning G-10 or equivalent, in 200 mL of water contained in a 1000-mL 24/40 round-bottom distilling flask. Add the *Sample* and shake the flask for 1 h on a wrist-action mechanical shaker. Connect the flask to a fractionating column and distill about 100 mL, adjusting the heat so that the foam does not enter the column. Quantitatively transfer the distillate to a 200-mL volumetric flask, fill to the mark with water, and shake the flask to mix. Weigh 8.0 g of this solution into an injection vial. Add 1.0 mL of the *Internal standard solution*. Heat the vial at 60° for 10 min and shake it vigorously for 10 s.
  Chromatographic system, Appendix IIA
    Mode: Head space gas chromatography
    Detector: Flame-ionization detector
    Column: Fused silica, (0.8 m × 0.53 mm id) coated with DB-wax (1-µm thickness) coupled with fused silica column, (30 m × 0.53 mm id) coated with DB-1 (5-µm thickness)
    Temperature
      Oven: 35° for 5 min; 5°/min to 90°; 6 min at 90°
      Injection port: 140°
      Detector: 300°
    Headspace sampling conditions
      Sample heating temperature: 60°
      Sample heating time: 10 min
      Syringe temperature: 70°

Transfer temperature: 80°
Carrier gas: Helium
Flow rate: 5 mL/min (208 kPa)
Injection volume: 1.0 mL
Analysis: Inject equal volumes from the *Sample solution*, *Blank solution*, and *Standard solution* into the chromatograph, record the chromatograms, and determine the peak areas. [NOTE—The approximate retention times for ethanol, methanol, isopropanol, and 3-methyl-2-pentanone are 2.81, 2.93, 5.23, and 16.90 min, respectively.]
Calculations: For each solvent being analyzed, determine the calibration factor, C, from the following equation:

$$C = 50D/(E(F - G))$$

D = the weight (mg) of solvent in the *Standard solution*
E = the weight (mg) of internal standard in the *Standard solution*
F = the relative peak area for the solvent in the *Standard solution*
G = the relative peak area for the same solvent in the *Blank solution*

For each solvent being analyzed, its weight (mg) in the *Sample solution* is given by the formula:

$$Result = ABC/50$$

A = the relative peak area of the solvent
B = the weight (mg) of internal standard
C = the calibration factor for the solvent

For each solvent being analyzed, its percentage in the *Sample* is given by the formula:

$$Result = 0.1 w/W$$

w = the weight (mg) of the solvent in the *Sample solution*
W = the weight (g) of the sample taken
Acceptance criteria: NMT 0.1% of ethanol, isopropanol, or methanol, singly or in combination

SPECIFIC TESTS
- **ASH** (Total)
  Sample: 2 g of *Sample 1* from the procedure for determination of *Sulfate* (below).
  Analysis: Transfer the *Sample* to a previously ignited, tared silica or platinum crucible. Heat the *Sample* with a suitable infrared lamp, increasing the intensity gradually, until the *Sample* is completely charred; continue heating for an additional 30 min. Transfer the crucible with the charred *Sample* into a muffle furnace and ignite at about 550° for 1 h. Cool in a desiccator and weigh. Repeat the ignition in the muffle furnace until a constant weight is obtained. If a carbon-free ash is not obtained after the first ignition, moisten the charred spot with a 10% solution of ammonium nitrate and dry under an infrared lamp. Repeat the ignition step. Calculate the percentage of total ash of the sample using the formula:

  $$Result = W_2/W_1 \times 100\%$$

  W_1 = the weight of *Sample* (g)
  W_2 = the weight of ash determined (g)
  [NOTE—Retain the ash for the *Acid-Insoluble Ash* test.]
  Acceptance criteria: NLT 15% and NMT 40%, on the dried basis
- **ACID-INSOLUBLE ASH,** Appendix IIC
  Sample: Use the ash from the test for *Ash (Total)*
  Analysis: Ignite to constant weight at 800° ± 25°
  Acceptance criteria: NMT 1%
- **ACID-INSOLUBLE MATTER**
  Sample: 2 g of *Sample 1* obtained from the procedure for determination of *Sulfate* (below).
  Analysis: Transfer the *Sample* into a 250-mL beaker containing 150 mL of water and 1.5 mL of sulfuric acid TS. Cover the beaker with a watch glass and heat the mixture on a steam bath for 6 h, rubbing down the wall of the beaker frequently with a rubber-tipped stirring rod and replacing any water lost by evaporation. Weigh 500 mg of a suitable acid-washed filter aid, pre-dried at 105° for 1 h, to the nearest 0.1 mg, add the filter aid to the sample solution, and filter it through a tared sintered-glass filter crucible. Wash the residue several times with hot water, dry the crucible and its contents at 105° for 3 h, cool in a desiccator, and weigh. The difference between the total weight and the weight of the filter aid plus crucible is the weight of the *Acid-Insoluble Matter*. Calculate as a percentage.
  Acceptance criteria: NMT 15%
- **LOSS ON DRYING,** Appendix IIC: 105° to constant weight
  Acceptance criteria: NMT 12%
- **PH,** *pH Determination,* Appendix IIB
  Sample solution: 1:100 suspension
  Acceptance criteria: Between 8 and 11
- **SULFATE**
  Sample 1: Disperse 15 g of a sample of product in 500 mL of 60% w/w isopropanol/water at room temperature. Stir gently for 4 h. Filter through ash-free filter paper and discard the filtrate. Wash the material remaining on the filter paper with two 15-mL portions of 60% isopropanol/water. Dry the material at 105° to constant weight.
  Sample 2: 1 g of *Sample 1* [NOTE—Retain the remainder of *Sample 1* for determination of *Ash (Total), Acid-insoluble matter,* and *Viscosity of a 1.5% solution.*]
  Sample solution: Transfer *Sample 2* to a 100-mL long-necked round-bottom flask. Add 50 mL of 0.2 N hydrochloric acid. Fit a condenser, preferably one with at least five condensing bulbs, to the flask and reflux for 1 h. Add 25 mL of a 10% (by volume) hydrogen peroxide solution and resume refluxing for about 5 h or until the solution becomes completely clear.
  Analysis: Transfer the *Sample solution* to a 600-mL beaker, bring to a boil, and add dropwise 10 mL of a 10% barium chloride solution. Heat the reaction mixture for 2 h on a boiling water bath. Filter the

mixture through ash-free slow-filtration filter paper. Wash with boiling distilled water until the filtrate is free from chloride. Dry the filter paper and contents in a drying oven. Gently burn and ash the paper at 800° in a tared porcelain or silica crucible until the ash is white. Cool in a desiccator. Weigh the cooled crucible containing the ash. Calculate the percentage ester sulfate, %ES, in the sample taken using the following equation:

$$\%ES = (W_2/W_1) \times 0.4116 \times 100\%$$

W_1 = the weight (g) of *Sample 2* taken
W_2 = the weight (g) of the ash (barium sulfate)

Calculate the acid-insoluble matter corrected percentage of ester sulfate, %ES$_C$, in the sample taken using the following equation:

$$\%ES_C = \%ES/[1 - (\%AIM/100)]$$

%AIM = the percent *Acid-Insoluble Matter* (determined above).

Acceptance criteria: NLT 20% and NMT 40% (as ester sulfate), on the washed, dried, and acid-insoluble matter corrected basis

- **VISCOSITY OF A 1.5% SOLUTION**

  Sample: 7.5 g of *Sample 1* obtained from the procedure for determination of *Sulfate* (above)

  Sample solution: Transfer the *Sample* into a tared, 600-mL tall-form (Berzelius) beaker, and disperse it with agitation for 10 to 20 min in 450 mL of deionized water. Add sufficient water to bring the final weight to 500 g and heat in a water bath with continuous agitation, until a temperature of 80° is reached (20–30 min). Add water to adjust for loss by evaporation, cool to 76–77°, and heat in a constant temperature bath at 75°.

  Analysis: Pre-heat the bob and guard of a Brookfield LVF or LVT viscometer to approximately 75° in water. Dry the bob and guard and attach them to the viscometer, which should be equipped with a No.1 spindle (19 mm in diameter, approximately 65 mm in length) and capable of rotating at 30 rpm. Adjust the height of the bob in the *Sample solution,* start the viscometer rotating at 30 rpm and, after six complete revolutions of the viscometer, take the viscometer reading on the 0–100 scale. Record the result in centipoises, obtained by multiplying the reading on the scale by the factor given by the Brookfield manufacturer. [NOTE—If the viscosity is very low, increased precision may be obtained by using the Brookfield UL (ultra low) adapter or equivalent, in which case the viscometer reading on the 0–100 scale should be multiplied by 0.2 to obtain the viscosity in centipoises. On the other hand, samples of some types of carrageenan may be too viscous to read when a No. 1 spindle is used. Such samples obviously pass the specification, but if a viscosity reading is desired for other reasons, use a No. 2 spindle and take the reading on the 0–100 scale or on the 0–500 scale.]

  Acceptance criteria: NLT 5 cP at 75°

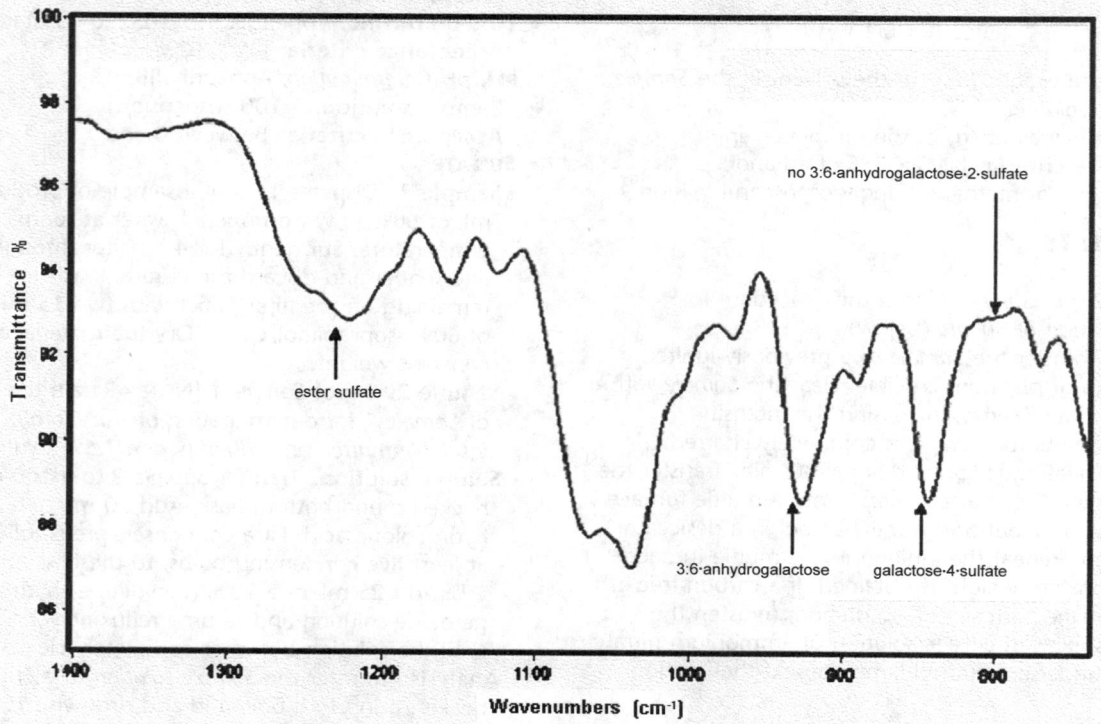

Kappa-Carrageenan

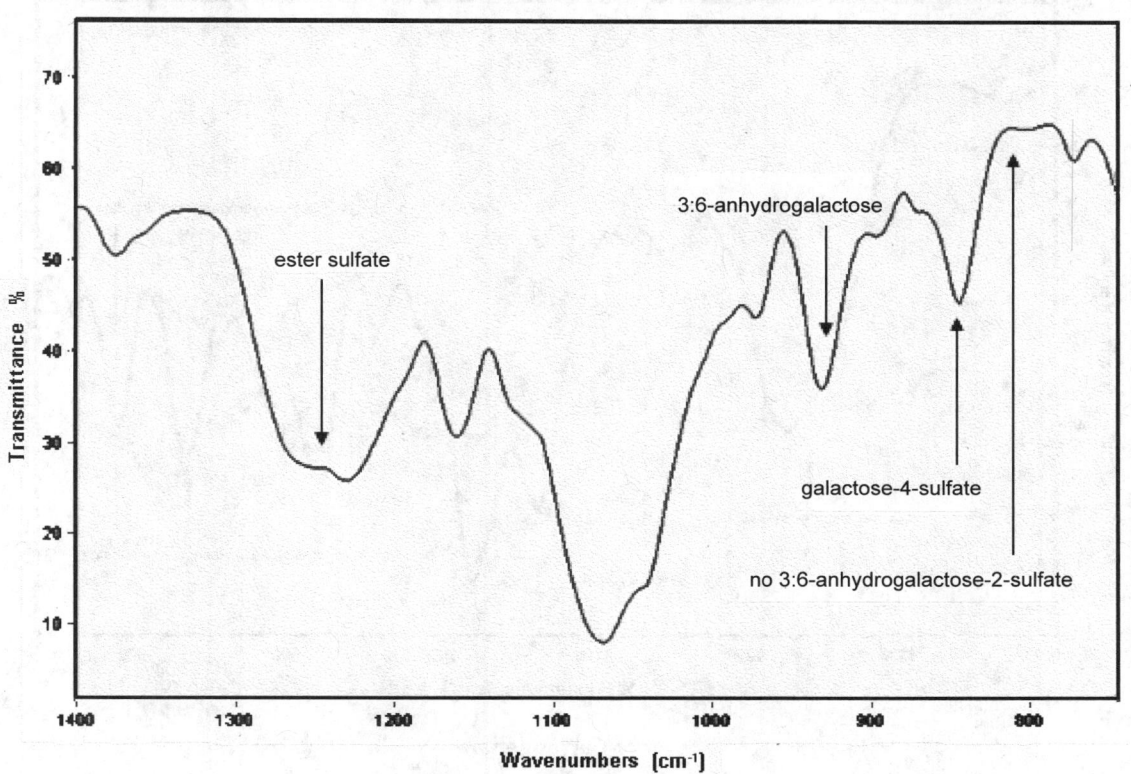

Kappa-PES-Carrageenan

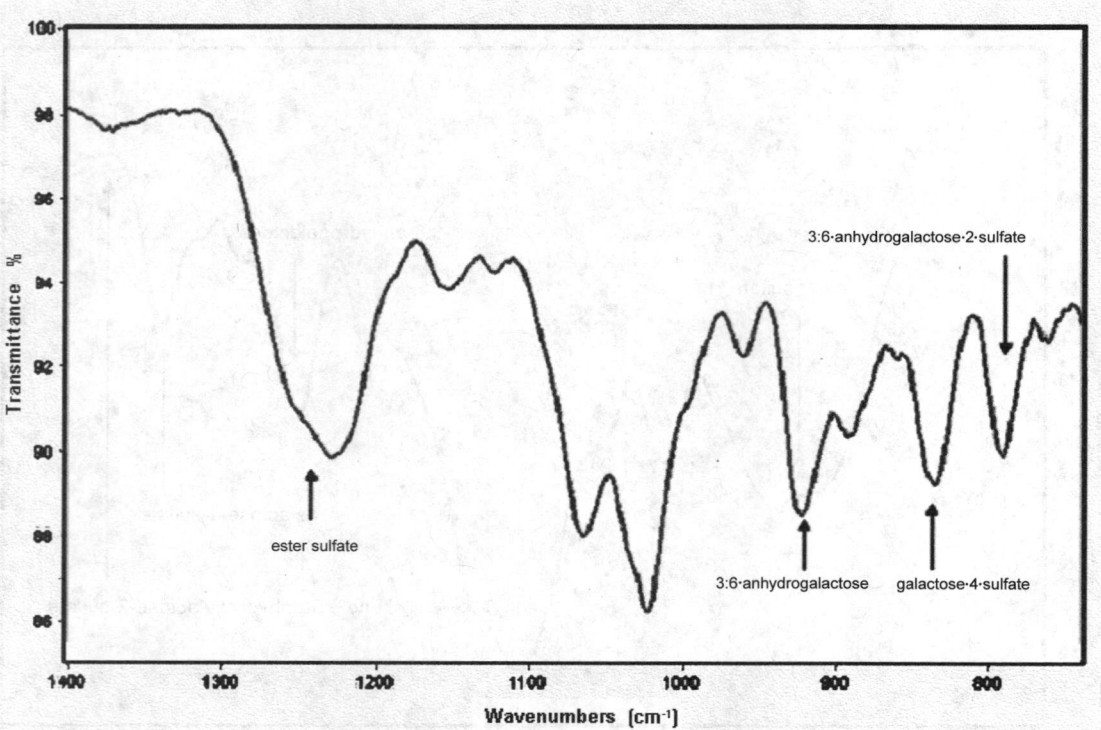

Iota-Carrageenan

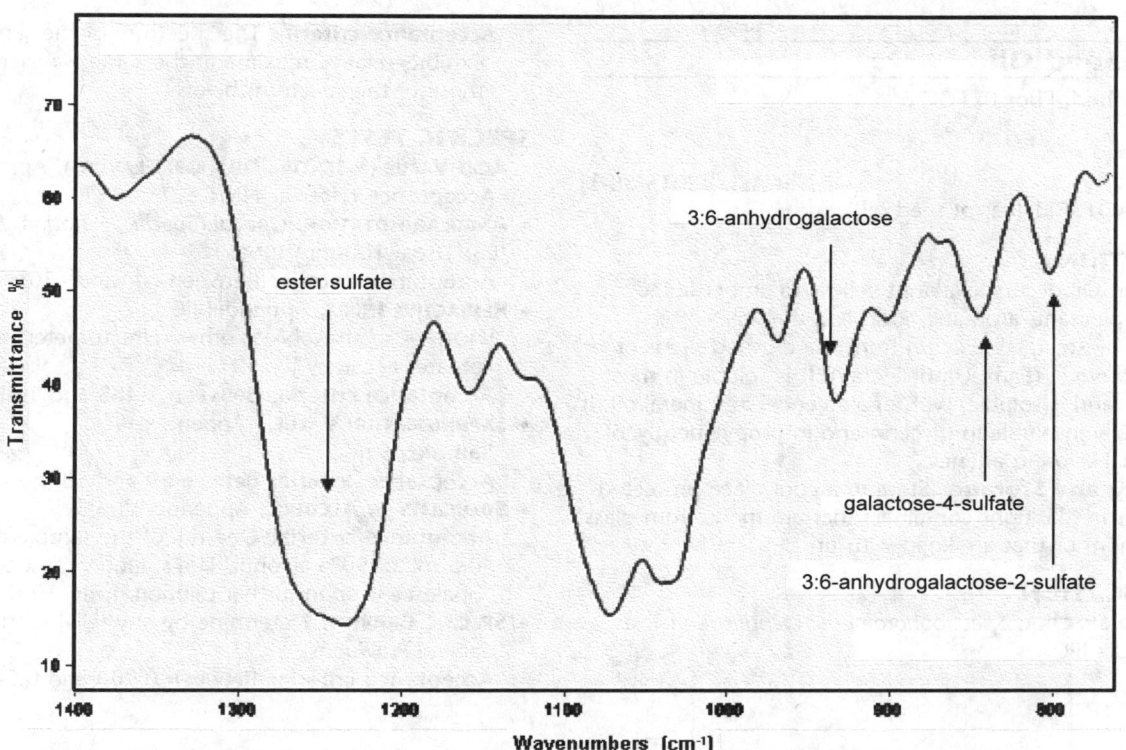

Iota-PES-Carrageenan

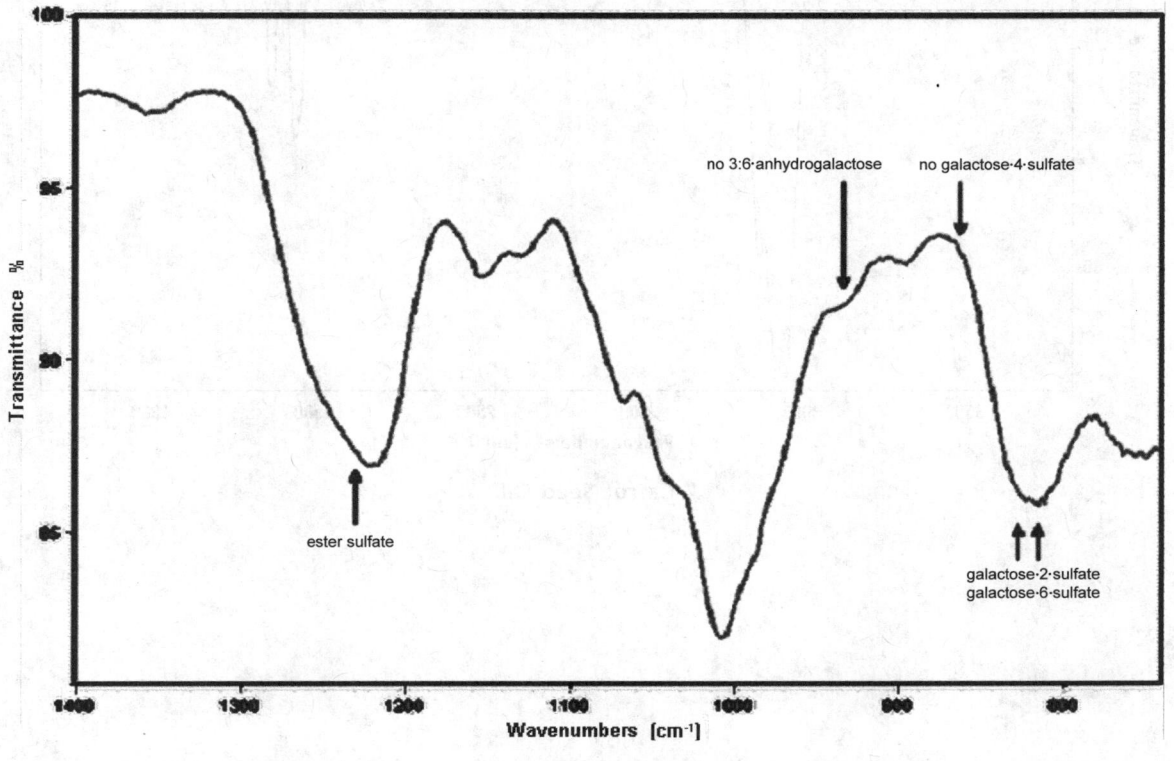

Lambda-Carrageenan

Carrot Seed Oil

First Published: Prior to FCC 6

FEMA: 2244

CAS: [8015-88-1]

UNII: 595AO13F11 [carrot seed oil]

DESCRIPTION
Carrot Seed Oil occurs as a light yellow to amber liquid having a pleasant, aromatic odor. It is the volatile oil obtained by steam distillation from the crushed seeds of *Daucus carota* L. (Fam. Umbelliferae). It is soluble in most fixed oils, and is soluble, with opalescence, in mineral oil. It is practically insoluble in glycerin and in propylene glycol.

Function: Flavoring agent

Packaging and Storage: Store in a cool place protected from light in full, tight containers that are made from glass or aluminum or that are lined with tin.

IDENTIFICATION
- **INFRARED SPECTRA,** *Spectrophotometric Identification Tests,* Appendix IIIC

Acceptance criteria: The spectrum of the sample exhibits relative maxima at the same wavelengths as those of the spectrum below.

SPECIFIC TESTS
- **ACID VALUE (ESSENTIAL OILS AND FLAVORS),** Appendix VI
  Acceptance criteria: NMT 5.0
- **ANGULAR ROTATION,** *Optical (Specific) Rotation,* Appendix IIB: Use a 100-mm tube.
  Acceptance criteria: Between −4° and −30°
- **REFRACTIVE INDEX,** Appendix IIB
  [NOTE—Use an Abbé or other refractometer of equal or greater accuracy.]
  Acceptance criteria: Between 1.483 and 1.493 at 20°
- **SAPONIFICATION VALUE,** Appendix VI
  Sample: 5 g
  Acceptance criteria: Between 9 and 58
- **SOLUBILITY IN ALCOHOL,** Appendix VI
  Acceptance criteria: One mL of the sample dissolves in 0.5 mL of 90% alcohol. The solution can become opalescent upon further dilution up to 10 mL.
- **SPECIFIC GRAVITY:** Determine by any reliable method (see *General Provisions*).
  Acceptance criteria: Between 0.900 and 0.943

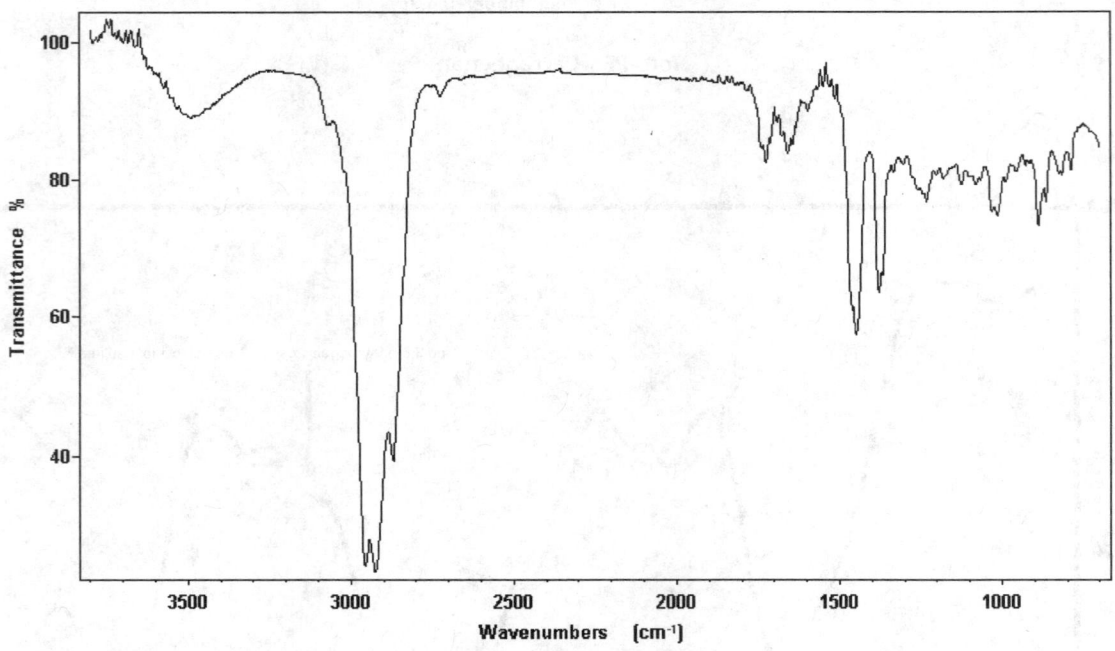

Carrot Seed Oil

Carvacrol

First Published: Prior to FCC 6

$C_{10}H_{14}O$ Formula wt 150.22
FEMA: 2245
UNII: 9B1J4V995Q [carvacrol]

DESCRIPTION
Carvacrol occurs as a colorless to pale yellow liquid.
Odor: Pungent, spicy, thymol
Solubility: Soluble in alcohol, ether; insoluble or practically insoluble in water
Boiling Point: ~238°
Solubility in Alcohol, Appendix VI: One mL dissolves in 4 mL of 60% alcohol to give a clear solution.

Function: Flavoring agent

IDENTIFICATION
- **INFRARED SPECTRA,** *Spectrophotometric Identification Tests,* Appendix IIIC
  Acceptance criteria: The spectrum of the sample exhibits relative maxima at the same wavelengths as those of the spectrum below.

ASSAY
- **PROCEDURE:** Proceed as directed under *M-1b,* Appendix XI.
  Acceptance criteria: NLT 98.0% of $C_{10}H_{14}O$

SPECIFIC TESTS
- **REFRACTIVE INDEX,** Appendix II: At 20°
  Acceptance criteria: Between 1.521 and 1.526
- **SPECIFIC GRAVITY:** Determine at 25° by any reliable method (see *General Provisions*).
  Acceptance criteria: Between 0.974 and 0.980

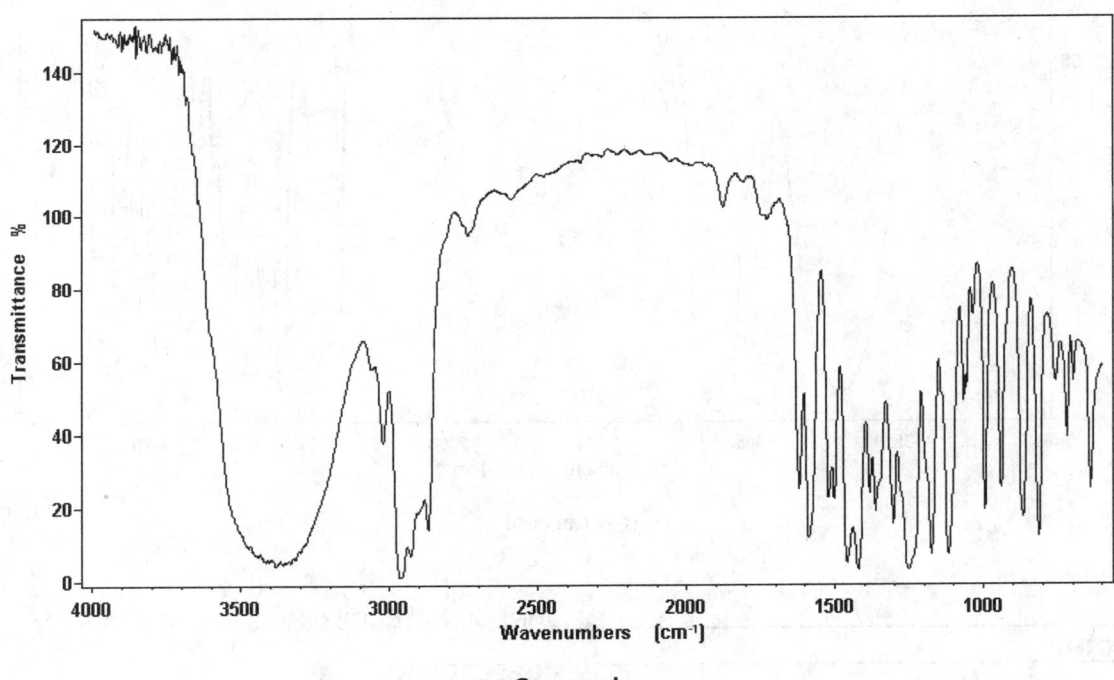

Carvacrol

(–)-Carveol

First Published: Prior to FCC 6
Last Revision: First Supplement, FCC 7

l-Carveol
p-Mentha-6,8-dien-2-ol

$C_{10}H_{16}O$ Formula wt 152.24
FEMA: 2247
UNII: 1L9KXT85R9 [carveol, (–)-]

230 / (−)-Carveol / Monographs

DESCRIPTION
(−)-Carveol occurs as a colorless to pale yellow liquid.
Odor: Spearminty
Solubility: Soluble in propylene glycol, vegetable oils; insoluble or practically insoluble in water
Boiling Point: ~226° to 227° (751 mm Hg)
Solubility in Alcohol, Appendix VI: One mL dissolves in 1 mL of 95% alcohol.
Function: Flavoring agent

IDENTIFICATION
- **INFRARED SPECTRA,** *Spectrophotometric Identification Tests,* Appendix IIIC
  Acceptance criteria: The spectrum of the sample exhibits relative maxima at the same wavelengths as those of the spectrum below.

ASSAY
- **PROCEDURE:** Proceed as directed under *M-1b,* Appendix XI.
  Acceptance criteria: NLT 96.0% of $C_{10}H_{16}O$

SPECIFIC TESTS
- **REFRACTIVE INDEX,** Appendix II: At 20°
  Acceptance criteria: Between 1.493 and 1.497
- **SPECIFIC GRAVITY:** Determine at 25° by any reliable method (see *General Provisions*).
  Acceptance criteria: Between 0.947 and 0.953

OTHER REQUIREMENTS
- **ANGULAR ROTATION,** *Optical (Specific) Rotation,* Appendix IIB
  Acceptance criteria: Between −117° and −130°

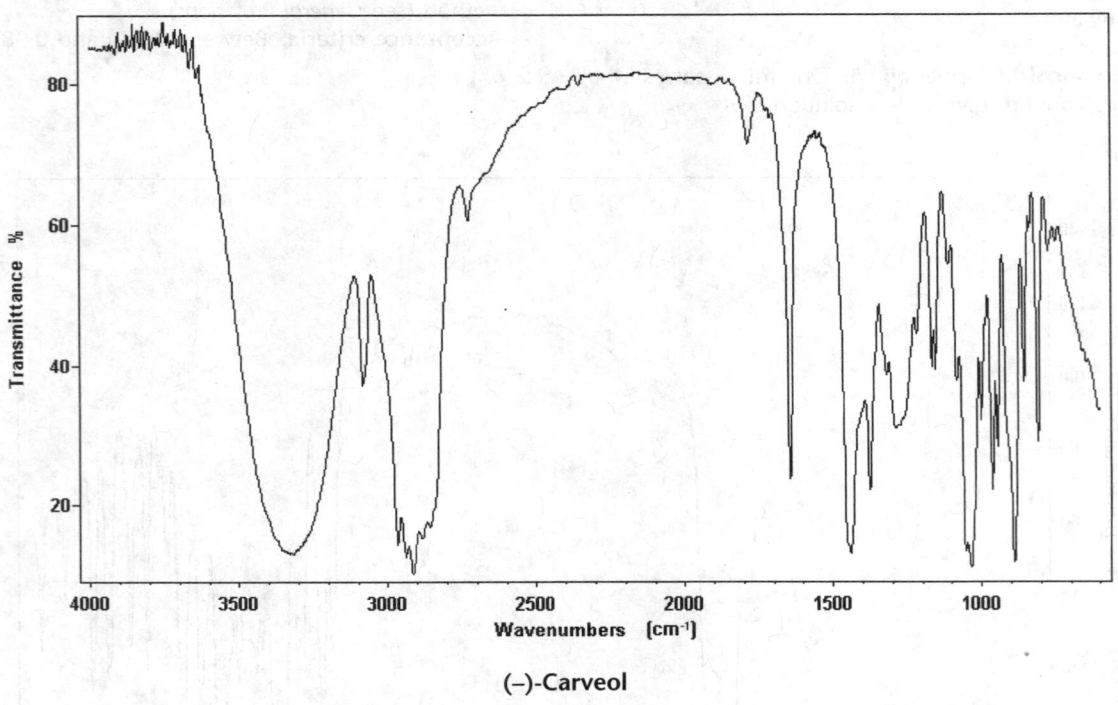

(−)-Carveol

(+)-Carvone

First Published: Prior to FCC 6
Last Revision: First Supplement, FCC 7

d-Carvone
dextro-Carvone
d-1-Methyl-4-isopropenyl-6-cyclohexen-2-one

$C_{10}H_{14}O$ Formula wt 150.22
FEMA: 2249

UNII: 4RWC1CMS3X [carvone, (+)-]

DESCRIPTION
(+)-Carvone occurs as a colorless to light yellow liquid.
Odor: Caraway
Solubility: Soluble in propylene glycol, most fixed oils; miscible in alcohol; insoluble or practically insoluble in glycerin
Boiling Point: ~230°
Solubility in Alcohol, Appendix VI: One mL dissolves in 5 mL of 60% alcohol.
Function: Flavoring agent

IDENTIFICATION
- **INFRARED SPECTRA,** *Spectrophotometric Identification Tests,* Appendix IIIC

Acceptance criteria: The spectrum of the sample exhibits relative maxima at the same wavelengths as those of the spectrum below.

ASSAY
- **PROCEDURE:** Proceed as directed under *M-1b,* Appendix XI.
  Acceptance criteria: NLT 95.0% of $C_{10}H_{14}O$

SPECIFIC TESTS
- **REFRACTIVE INDEX,** Appendix II: At 20°
  Acceptance criteria: Between 1.496 and 1.499

- **SPECIFIC GRAVITY:** Determine at 25° by any reliable method (see *General Provisions*).
  Acceptance criteria: Between 0.955 and 0.960

OTHER REQUIREMENTS
- **ANGULAR ROTATION,** *Optical (Specific) Rotation,* Appendix IIB: Use a 100-mm tube.
  Acceptance criteria: Between +50° and +60°

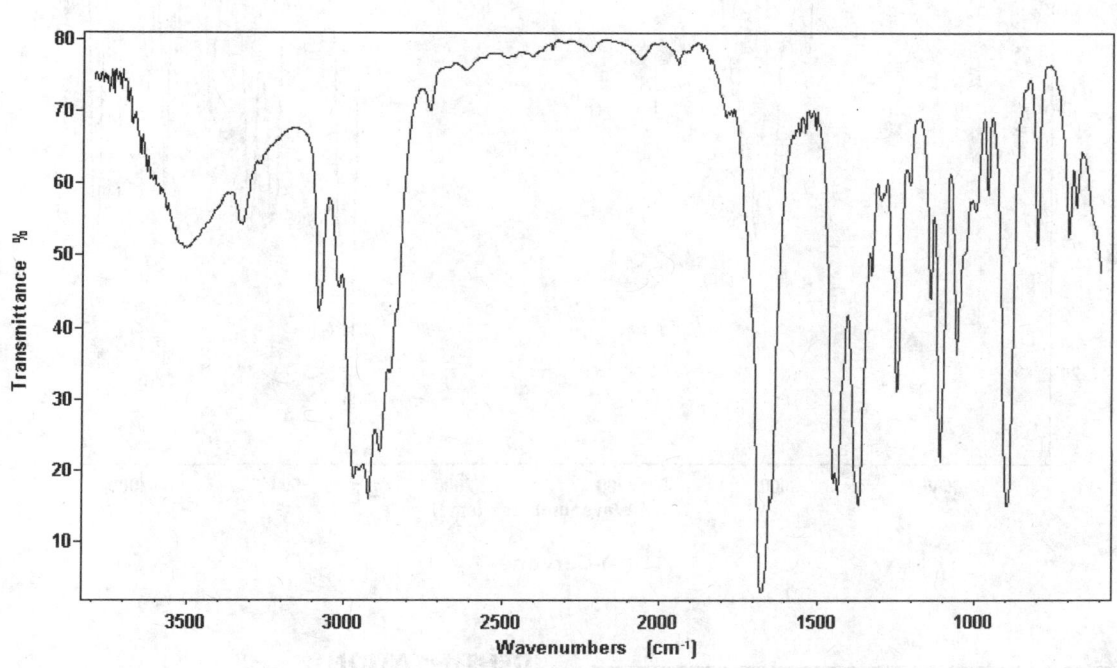

(+)-Carvone

(−)-Carvone

First Published: Prior to FCC 6
Last Revision: First Supplement, FCC 7

l-Carvone
levo-Carvone
1-1-Methyl-4-isopropenyl-6-cyclohexen-2-one

Formula wt 150.22

$C_{10}H_{14}O$
FEMA: 2249
UNII: 5TO7X34D3D [carvone, (−)-]

DESCRIPTION
(−)-Carvone occurs as a colorless to pale strawberry colored liquid.
Odor: Spearminty
Solubility: Soluble in propylene glycol, most fixed oils; miscible in alcohol; insoluble or practically insoluble in glycerin
Boiling Point: ~231°
SOLUBILITY IN ALCOHOL, Appendix VI: One mL dissolves in 2 mL of 70% alcohol.
Function: Flavoring agent

IDENTIFICATION
- **INFRARED SPECTRA,** *Spectrophotometric Identification Tests,* Appendix IIIC
  Acceptance criteria: The spectrum of the sample exhibits relative maxima at the same wavelengths as those of the spectrum below.

ASSAY
- **Procedure:** Proceed as directed under *M-1b*, Appendix XI.
  Acceptance criteria: NLT 97.0% of $C_{10}H_{14}O$

SPECIFIC TESTS
- **Refractive Index**, Appendix II: At 20°
  Acceptance criteria: Between 1.495 and 1.502
- **Specific Gravity:** Determine at 25° by any reliable method (see *General Provisions*).
  Acceptance criteria: Between 0.956 and 0.960

OTHER REQUIREMENTS
- **Angular Rotation**, *Optical (Specific) Rotation*, Appendix IIB: Use a 100-mm tube.
  Acceptance criteria: Between −57° and −62°

(−)-Carvone

(−)-Carvyl Acetate

First Published: Prior to FCC 6
Last Revision: First Supplement, FCC 7

l-Carvyl Acetate
p-Mentha-6,8-dien-2-yl Acetate

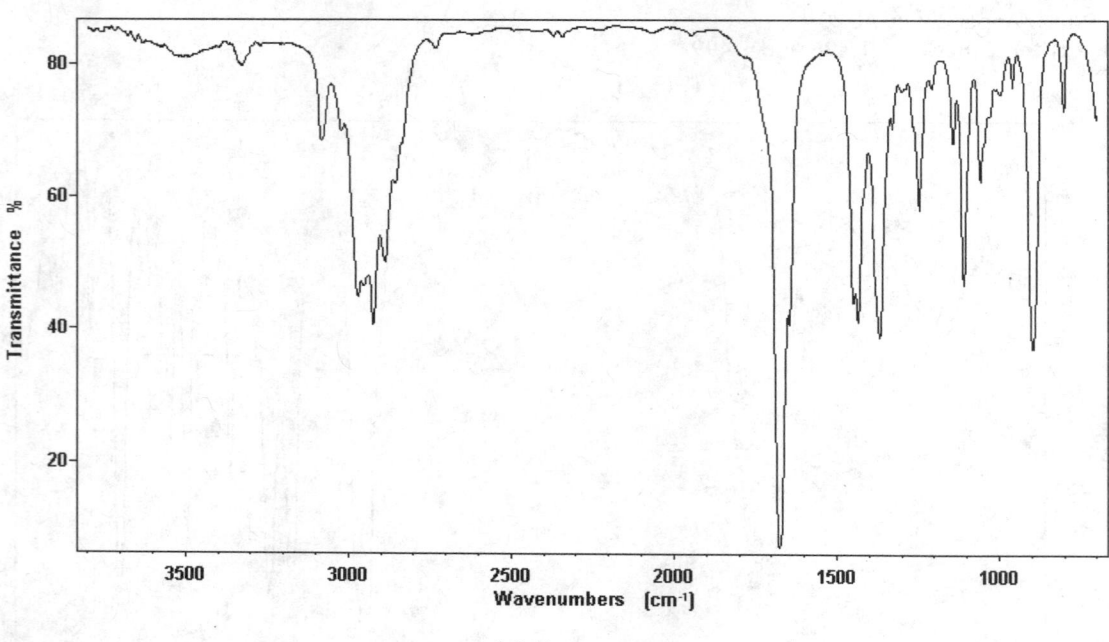

$C_{12}H_{18}O_2$ Formula wt 194.27
FEMA: 2250
UNII: IJM42H65AV [carvyl acetate, (-)-]

DESCRIPTION
(−)-Carvyl Acetate occurs as a colorless to pale yellow liquid.
Odor: Spearminty
Solubility: Soluble in alcohol
Boiling Point: ~77° to 79° (0.1 mm Hg)
Function: Flavoring agent

IDENTIFICATION
- **Infrared Spectra**, *Spectrophotometric Identification Tests*, Appendix IIIC
  Acceptance criteria: The spectrum of the sample exhibits relative maxima at the same wavelengths as those of the spectrum below.

ASSAY
- **Procedure:** Proceed as directed under *M-1b*, Appendix XI.
  Acceptance criteria: NLT 98.0% of $C_{12}H_{18}O_2$

SPECIFIC TESTS
- **Acid Value, Flavor Chemicals (Other Than Essential Oils)**, *M-15*, Appendix XI
  Acceptance criteria: NMT 1.0
- **Refractive Index**, Appendix II: At 20°
  Acceptance criteria: Between 1.473 and 1.479
- **Specific Gravity:** Determine at 25° by any reliable method (see *General Provisions*).
  Acceptance criteria: Between 0.964 and 0.970

OTHER REQUIREMENTS
- **Angular Rotation**, *Optical (Specific) Rotation*, Appendix IIB
  Acceptance criteria: Between −90° and −120°

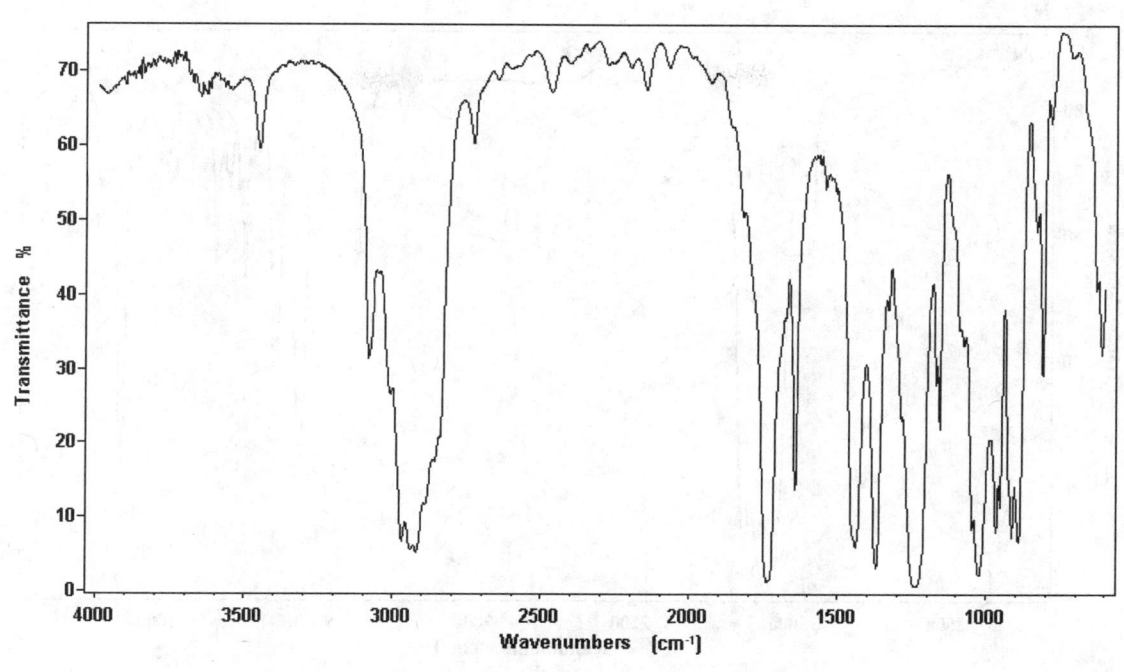

(–)-Carvyl Acetate

β-Caryophyllene

First Published: Prior to FCC 6
Last Revision: First Supplement, FCC 6

C₁₅H₂₄ Formula wt 204.36
FEMA: 2252
UNII: BHW853AU9H [caryophyllene]

DESCRIPTION
β-Caryophyllene occurs as a colorless to slightly yellow, oily liquid. It may contain a suitable antioxidant.
Odor: Woody, spicy
Solubility: Soluble in alcohol, ether; insoluble or practically insoluble in water
Boiling Point: ~256°
Solubility in Alcohol, Appendix VI: One mL dissolves in 6 mL of 95% alcohol to give a clear solution.
Function: Flavoring agent

IDENTIFICATION
- **INFRARED SPECTRA,** *Spectrophotometric Identification Tests,* Appendix IIIC
  Acceptance criteria: The spectrum of the sample exhibits relative maxima at the same wavelengths as those of the spectrum below.

ASSAY
- **PROCEDURE:** Proceed as directed under *M-1a,* Appendix XI.
  Acceptance criteria: NLT 80.0% of C₁₅H₂₄

SPECIFIC TESTS
- **REFRACTIVE INDEX,** Appendix II: At 20°
  Acceptance criteria: Between 1.498 and 1.504
- **SPECIFIC GRAVITY:** Determine at 25° by any reliable method (see *General Provisions*).
  Acceptance criteria: Between 0.897 and 0.910

OTHER REQUIREMENTS
- **ANGULAR ROTATION,** *Optical (Specific) Rotation,* Appendix IIB: Use a 100-mm tube.
  Acceptance criteria: Between −5° and −10°
- **PHENOLS,** *M-1b,* Appendix XI
  Acceptance criteria: NMT 3.0%

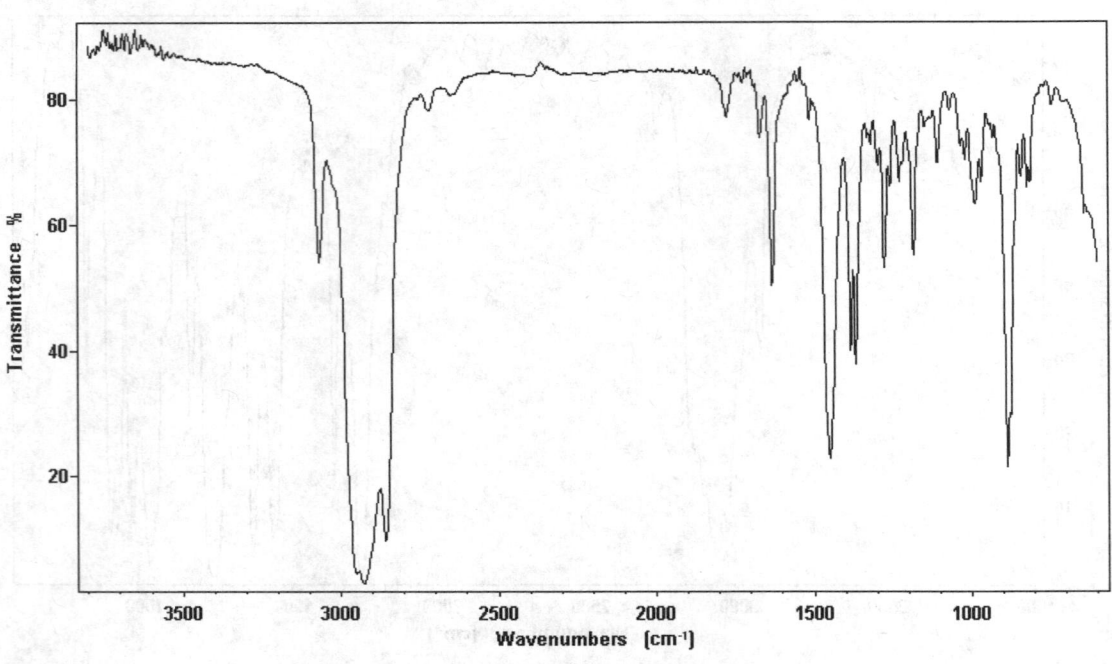

β-Caryophyllene

Cascarilla Oil

First Published: Prior to FCC 6

Sweetwood Bark Oil

CAS: [8007-06-5]

UNII: N81EA2A6NP [cascarilla oil]

DESCRIPTION
Cascarilla Oil occurs as a light yellow to brown amber liquid with a pleasant, spicy odor. It is the volatile oil obtained by steam distillation of the dried bark of *Croton cascarilla* Benn. and of *Croton eluteria* Benn. (Fam. Euphorbiaceae). It is soluble in most fixed oils and in mineral oil, but it is practically insoluble in glycerin and in propylene glycol.

Function: Flavoring agent

Packaging and Storage: Store in a cool place protected from light in full, tight containers that are made from steel or aluminum and that are suitably lined.

IDENTIFICATION
- **INFRARED SPECTRA,** *Spectrophotometric Identification Tests,* Appendix IIIC
  Acceptance criteria: The spectrum of the sample exhibits relative maxima at the same wavelengths as those of the spectrum below.

SPECIFIC TESTS
- **ACID VALUE (ESSENTIAL OILS AND FLAVORS),** Appendix VI
  Acceptance criteria: Between 3 and 10
- **ANGULAR ROTATION,** *Optical (Specific) Rotation,* Appendix IIB: Use a 100-mm tube.
  Acceptance criteria: Between −1° and +8°
- **ESTER VALUE AFTER ACETYLATION,** *Total Alcohols,* Appendix VI
  Sample: 2 g of the dried, acetylated sample oil
  Analysis: Calculate the *Ester Value after Acetylation* by the formula:

  $$\text{Result} = A \times 28.05 / B$$

  A = amount (mL) of 0.5 N alcoholic potassium hydroxide consumed in the saponification
  B = weight (g) of acetylated sample oil taken
  Acceptance criteria: Between 62 and 88
- **REFRACTIVE INDEX,** Appendix IIB
  [NOTE—Use an Abbé or other refractometer of equal or greater accuracy.]
  Acceptance criteria: Between 1.488 and 1.494 at 20°
- **SAPONIFICATION VALUE,** Appendix VI
  Sample: 5 g
  Acceptance criteria: Between 8 and 20
- **SOLUBILITY IN ALCOHOL,** Appendix VI
  Acceptance criteria: One mL of the sample dissolves in 0.5 mL of 90% alcohol and remains in solution on dilution to 10 mL.
- **SPECIFIC GRAVITY:** Determine by any reliable method (see *General Provisions*).
  Acceptance criteria: Between 0.892 and 0.914

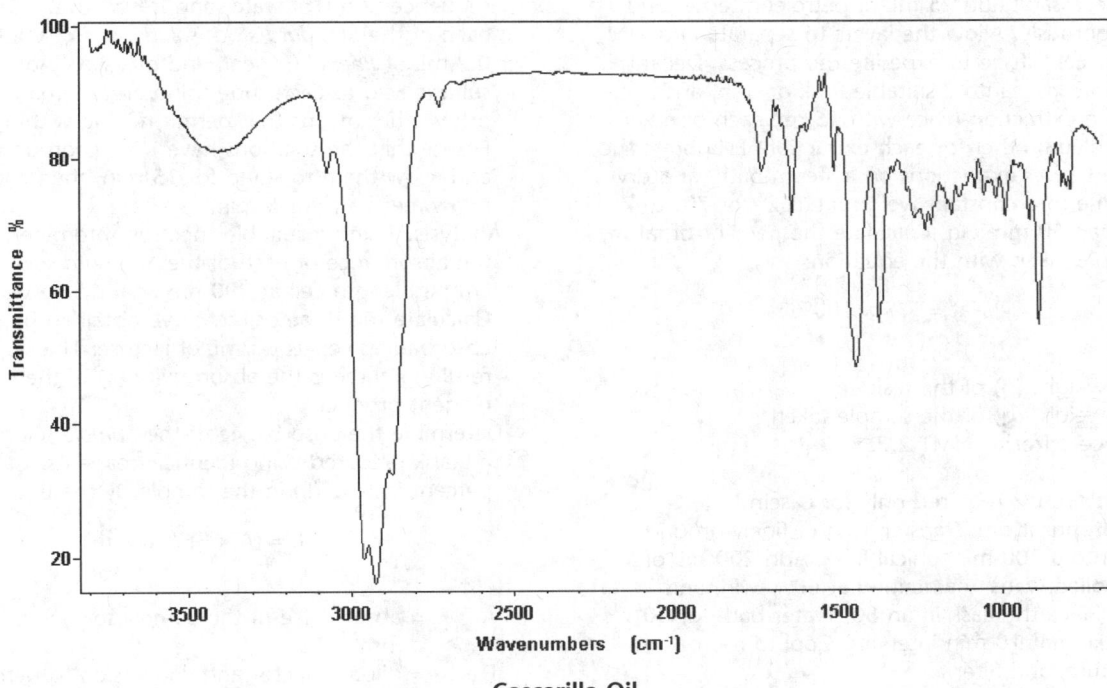

Cascarilla Oil

Casein and Caseinate Salts

First Published: Prior to FCC 6

CAS: [9000-71-9]
UNII: 48268V50D5 [casein]

DESCRIPTION
Casein occurs as an off-white to cream-colored, granular or fine powder. It is derived from the coagulum formed by treating skim milk with a food-grade acid (*Acid Casein*), enzyme (*Rennet Casein*), or other food-grade precipitating agent. After the precipitation, Casein is separated from the soluble milk fraction, washed, and dried. Chemically, Casein is a mixture of at least 20 electrophoretically distinct phosphoproteins. The main fractions—designated α-casein, β-casein, and κ-casein—are known to be mixtures, rather than single proteins. Casein contains all the amino acids known to be essential for human nutrition. It is insoluble in water and alcohol, but it can be dissolved by aqueous alkalies to form Caseinate Salts.

Caseinate Salts occur as white to cream-colored granules or powders. They are soluble or dispersible in water. They are prepared by treatment of Casein with food-grade alkalies, neutralizing agents, enzymes, buffers, or sequestrants. Common counter-ions are NH_4^+, Ca^{++}, Mg^{++}, K^+, and Na^+.

Function: Binder; extender; clarifying agent; emulsifier; stabilizer

Packaging and Storage: Store in well-closed containers.

ASSAY
- **PROTEIN,** *Nitrogen Determination,* Appendix IIIC
  Analysis: Calculate the percent protein (P) by the equation:

$$P = N \times 6.38$$

  N = percent nitrogen
  Acceptance criteria
    Acid casein: NLT 90.0% protein, calculated on the dried basis
    Rennet casein: NLT 86.0% protein, calculated on the dried basis
    Caseinate salts: NLT 84.0% protein, calculated on the dried basis

IMPURITIES
Inorganic Impurities
- **LEAD,** *Lead Limit Test, Flame Atomic Absorption Spectrophotometric Method,* Appendix IIIB
  Sample: 10 g
  Acceptance criteria: NMT 1 mg/kg

SPECIFIC TESTS
- **FAT**
  Sample: 1 g
  Analysis: Transfer the *Sample* to a fat-extraction flask, add 10 mL of water, and shake until homogeneous (warm if necessary). Add approximately 1 mL of ammonium hydroxide and heat in a water bath for 15 min at 60° to 70°, shaking occasionally. Add 10 mL of alcohol, and mix well. Add 25 mL of peroxide-free

ether, stopper, and shake vigorously for 1 min. Allow to cool if necessary, add 25 mL of petroleum ether and shake vigorously. Allow the layers to separate and clarify, or centrifuge to expedite the process. Decant the organic layer into a suitable flask or dish, and repeat the extraction twice with 15 mL each of ether and petroleum ether for each extraction. Evaporate the combined ether extractions on a steam bath, and dry the residue to a constant weight at 102°, or 70° to 75° at less than 50 mm Hg. Calculate the percent of fat in the sample taken with the equation:

$$\%Fat = R/S \times 100\%$$

R = weight (g) of the residue
S = weight (g) of the sample taken
Acceptance criteria: NMT 2.25%

- **FREE ACID**
[NOTE—This test is required only for casein.]
Sample preparation: Transfer 10 g of finely-ground sample into a 500-mL conical flask. Add 200 mL of freshly boiled water maintained at 60°, swirl, and stopper. Place the flask in an 80° water bath for 30 min, shaking at 10-min intervals. Cool to room temperature, and filter.
Analysis: Transfer a 100.0-mL portion of the clear filtrate from the *Sample preparation* into a 250-mL conical flask, add 0.5 mL of phenolphthalein TS, and titrate with 0.1 N sodium hydroxide to a pink endpoint that persists for 30 s.
Acceptance criteria
Casein: NMT 2.7 mL of 0.1 N sodium hydroxide is consumed

- **LACTOSE**
Phenol reagent: Heat a mixture of 8 g of phenol and 2 g of water until the crystals dissolve.
Sample solution: Transfer 1 g of sample into a 150-mL beaker. If the sample is *Acid Casein*, add 0.10 g of sodium hydrogen carbonate to the beaker. If the sample is *Rennet Casein*, add 0.10 g of sodium tripolyphosphate. Add 25 mL of water, and dissolve the sample by gently swirling while warming to 60° to 70° on a hot plate. Cool the solution to ambient temperature, and add 15 mL of water, 8 mL of 0.1 N hydrochloric acid, and 1 mL of a 10% solution of acetic acid. Mix well by swirling and, after 5 min, add 1 mL of 1 M sodium acetate, and mix well.
After the precipitate has settled, filter and discard the first 5 mL of filtrate. Pipet 2 mL of the remaining filtrate into a test tube, add 0.2 mL of *Phenol reagent*, and mix well. Add 5 mL of sulfuric acid using an automatic dispenser or by other means that permit mixing within 1 to 2 s. Ensure that the solution has been thoroughly mixed, and allow it to stand for 15 min, then cool to 20° in a water bath for 5 min.
Lactose solution: 2 mg/mL lactose monohydrate
Standard stock solutions: Transfer, respectively, 1, 2, 3, and 4 mL of *Lactose solution* into four separate 500-mL volumetric flasks and dilute to volume with water. These dilutions contain 20, 40, 60, and 80 μg/mL of lactose, respectively.
Standard solutions: Into each of five test tubes add, in sequence, 2 mL of water and, respectively, 3 mL of each of the *Standard stock solutions*. To each tube, add 0.2 mL of *Phenol reagent*, and mix well. Add 5 mL of sulfuric acid to each tube using an automatic dispenser or by other means that permit mixing within 1 to 2 s. Ensure that the solutions have been thoroughly mixed, and allow them to stand for 15 min, then cool to 20° in a water bath for 5 min.
Analysis: Using a suitable spectrophotometer, determine the absorbance of each of the *Standard solutions* in a 1-cm pathlength cell at 490 nm against the water blank. Calculate the slope of the curve obtained by plotting absorbances versus μg/mL of lactose. The slope of the resulting curve is the absorptivity (a) of the lactose-reagent product.
Determine the absorbance of the *Sample solution* against a blank prepared using identical reagents. Calculate the percent lactose (L) in the sample by the equation:

$$L = (A \times F) / (a \times m)$$

A = absorbance of the *Sample solution* at 490 nm
F = dilution factor and conversion to percent from μg/mL, 0.00475
a = absorptivity of the lactose-reagent product calculated above
m = weight of the sample (g) taken
Acceptance criteria: NMT 2.0%

- **LOSS ON DRYING**, Appendix IIC: 102° for 3 h
Acceptance criteria: NMT 12.0%

Cassia Oil

First Published: Prior to FCC 6
Last Revision: FCC 8

Cinnamon Oil
FEMA: 2258
CAS: [8007-80-5]
UNII: A4WO0626T5 [chinese cinnamon oil]

DESCRIPTION
Cassia Oil occurs as a yellow or brown liquid having the characteristic odor and taste of cassia cinnamon. It is the volatile oil obtained by steam distillation from the leaves and twigs of *Cinnamomum cassia* Blume (Fam. Lauraceae), rectified by distillation, and consisting mainly of cinnamic aldehyde. Upon aging or exposure to air it darkens and thickens. It is soluble in glacial acetic acid and in alcohol.
Function: Flavoring agent
Packaging and Storage: Store in full, tight, light-resistant containers. Avoid exposure to excessive heat.

IDENTIFICATION
- **INFRARED SPECTRA**, *Spectrophotometric Identification Tests*, Appendix IIIC

Acceptance criteria: The spectrum of the sample exhibits relative maxima at the same wavelengths as those of the spectrum below.

ASSAY
- **ALDEHYDES**, *Aldehydes and Ketones, Neutral Sulfite Method*, Appendix VI
  Acceptance criteria: NLT 80.0%, by volume, of total aldehydes

SPECIFIC TESTS
- **ANGULAR ROTATION**, *Optical (Specific) Rotation*, Appendix IIB: Use a 100-mm tube.
  Acceptance criteria: Between −1° and +1°
- **CHLORINATED COMPOUNDS**, Appendix VI
  Acceptance criteria: Passes test
- **REFRACTIVE INDEX**, Appendix IIB
  [NOTE—Use an Abbé or other refractometer of equal or greater accuracy.]
  Acceptance criteria: 1.602–1.614 at 20°

Change to read:
- **ROSIN OR ROSIN OILS**
  Sample: 2 mL
  Analysis: Shake the *Sample* in a test tube with 5–10 mL of solvent hexane, and allow the liquids to separate. Decant the hexane layer, which is just slightly colored, into another test tube, shake it with an equal volume of 1:1000 cupric acetate solution, ▲and allow the phases to separate.▲FCC8
  Acceptance criteria: The ▲hexane layer▲FCC8 does not turn green.
- **SOLUBILITY IN ALCOHOL**, Appendix VI
  Acceptance criteria: One mL of sample dissolves in 2 mL of 70% alcohol.
- **SPECIFIC GRAVITY**: Determine by any reliable method (see *General Provisions*).
  Acceptance criteria: 1.045–1.063

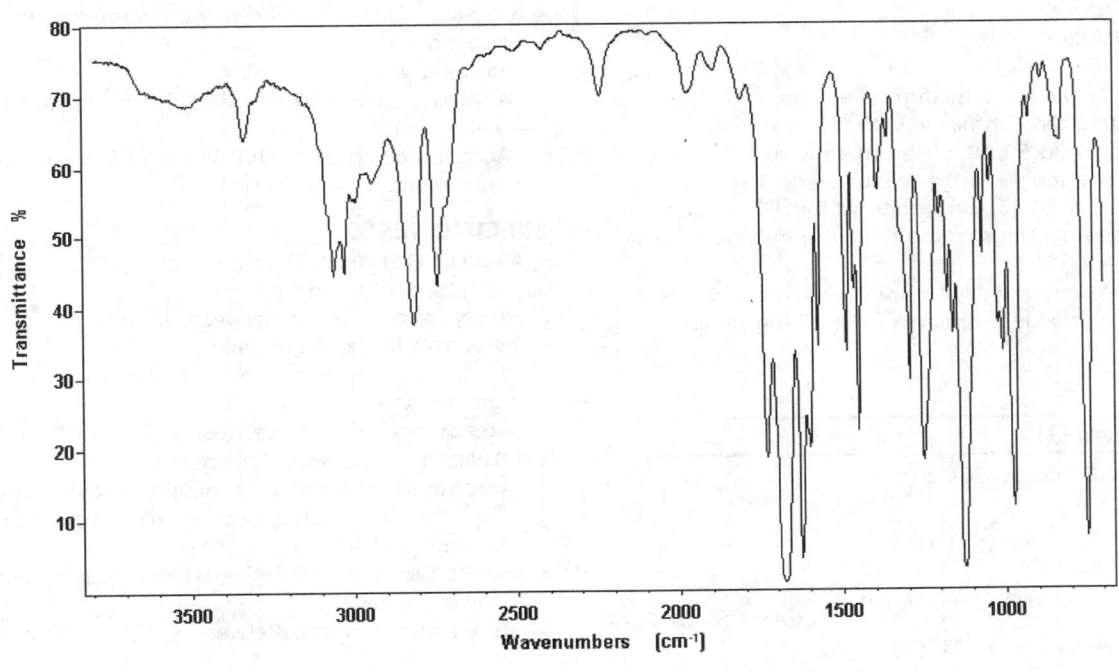

Cassia Oil

Castor Oil
First Published: Prior to FCC 6

Ricinus Oil
INS: 1503   CAS: [8001-79-4]
UNII: D5340Y2I9G [castor oil]

DESCRIPTION
Castor Oil occurs as a pale yellow or almost colorless, transparent, viscous liquid. It is the fixed oil obtained from the seed of *Ricinus communis* L. (Fam. Euphorbiaceae) and consists mainly of the triglyceride of ricinoleic acid. It is soluble in alcohol, and is miscible with absolute alcohol, with glacial acetic acid, with chloroform, and with ether.
Function: Antisticking agent; release agent; component of protective coatings
Packaging and Storage: Store in tight containers, and avoid exposure to excessive heat.

IDENTIFICATION
- **A. PROCEDURE**
  Acceptance criteria: A sample is only partly soluble in solvent hexane (distinction from *most other fixed oils*), but it yields a clear liquid with an equal volume of alcohol (*foreign fixed oils*).

- **B. Fatty Acid Composition,** Appendix VII
  Acceptance criteria: Castor oil exhibits the following composition profile of fatty acids:

Fatty Acid	Weight % (Range)
16:0	0.9–1.6
18:0	1.0–1.8
18:1	3.7–6.7
18:3	0.2–0.6
18:0 di-OH	0.4–1.3
18:1 -OH	83.6–89.0
20:0	0.2–0.5

IMPURITIES
Inorganic Impurities
- **Lead,** *Lead Limit Test, Atomic Absorption Spectrophotometric Graphite Furnace Method II,* Appendix IIIB
  Acceptance criteria: NMT 0.1 mg/kg

SPECIFIC TESTS
- **Free Fatty Acids**
  Sample: 10 g
  Analysis: Neutralize a mixture of alcohol and ether (50:50) to phenolphthalein with 0.1 N sodium hydroxide. Add 50 mL of this mixture to a flask and dissolve the *Sample* in the mixture. Add 1 mL of phenolphthalein TS, and titrate with 0.1 N sodium hydroxide until the solution remains pink after shaking the flask for 30 s.
  Acceptance criteria: Not more than 7 mL of 0.1 N sodium hydroxide is required for a 10.0-g sample.

Cedar Leaf Oil
First Published: Prior to FCC 6

Thuja Oil
White Cedar Leaf Oil
FEMA: 2267

CAS: [8007-20-3]

UNII: BJ169U4NLG [cedar leaf oil]

DESCRIPTION
Cedar Leaf Oil occurs as a colorless to yellow liquid having a strong camphoraceous and sage odor. It is the volatile oil obtained by steam distillation from the fresh leaves and branch ends of the eastern arborvitae, *Thuja occidentalis* L. (Fam. Cupressaceae). It is soluble in most fixed oils, in mineral oil, and in propylene glycol. It is practically insoluble in glycerin.
Function: Flavoring agent
Packaging and Storage: Store in a cool place protected from light in full, tight containers that are made from glass or that are lined with tin.

IDENTIFICATION
- **Infrared Spectra,** *Spectrophotometric Identification Tests,* Appendix IIIC
  Acceptance criteria: The spectrum of the sample exhibits relative maxima at the same wavelengths as those of the spectrum below.

ASSAY
- **Ketones,** *Aldehydes and Ketones, Hydroxylamine Method,* Appendix VI
  Sample: 1 g
  Analysis: Use 76.10 as the equivalence factor (e) in the calculation.
  Acceptance criteria: NLT 60.0% of ketones, calculated as thujone ($C_{10}H_{16}O$)

SPECIFIC TESTS
- **Angular Rotation,** *Optical (Specific) Rotation* Appendix IIB: Use a 100-mm tube.
  Acceptance criteria: Between −7° and −14°
- **Refractive Index,** Appendix IIB
  [Note—Use an Abbé or other refractometer of equal or greater accuracy.]
  Acceptance criteria: Between 1.456 and 1.460 at 20°
- **Solubility in Alcohol,** Appendix VI
  Acceptance criteria: One mL of the sample dissolves in 3 mL of 70% alcohol, occasionally becoming cloudy on dilution to 10 mL.
- **Specific Gravity:** Determine by any reliable method (see *General Provisions*).
  Acceptance criteria: Between 0.906 and 0.916

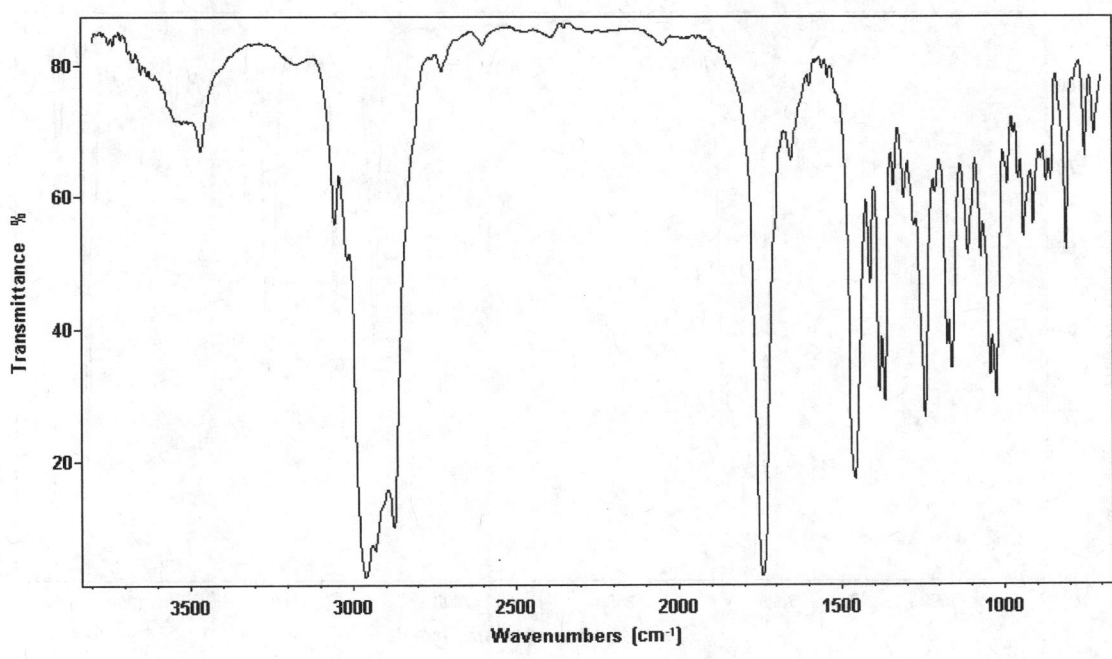

Cedar Leaf Oil

Celery Seed Oil

First Published: Prior to FCC 6

UNII: 8MBL58728K [celery seed oil]

DESCRIPTION
Celery Seed Oil occurs as a yellow to green-brown liquid with a pleasant, aromatic odor. It is the volatile oil obtained by steam distillation of the fruit or seed of *Apium graveolens* L. It is soluble in most fixed oils with the formation of a flocculent precipitate, and in mineral oil with turbidity. It is partly soluble in propylene glycol, but it is insoluble in glycerin.
Function: Flavoring agent
Packaging and Storage: Store in a cool place protected from light in full, tight containers that are made from steel or aluminum and that are suitably lined.

IDENTIFICATION
- **INFRARED SPECTRA,** *Spectrophotometric Identification Tests,* Appendix IIIC
  Acceptance criteria: The spectrum of the sample exhibits relative maxima at the same wavelengths as those of the spectrum below.

SPECIFIC TESTS
- **ACID VALUE (ESSENTIAL OILS AND FLAVORS),** Appendix VI
  Acceptance criteria: NMT 4.5
- **ANGULAR ROTATION,** *Optical (Specific) Rotation,* Appendix IIB: Use a 100-mm tube.
  Acceptance criteria: Between +48° and +78°
- **REFRACTIVE INDEX,** *Appendix IIB*
  [NOTE—Use an Abbé or other refractometer of equal or greater accuracy.]
  Acceptance criteria: Between 1.480 and 1.490 at 20°
- **SAPONIFICATION VALUE,** Appendix VI
  Sample: 5 g
  Acceptance criteria: Between 25 and 65
- **SOLUBILITY IN ALCOHOL,** Appendix VI
  Acceptance criteria: One mL of sample dissolves in 8 mL of 90% alcohol, usually with turbidity.
- **SPECIFIC GRAVITY:** Determine by any reliable method (see *General Provisions*).
  Acceptance criteria: Between 0.870 and 0.910

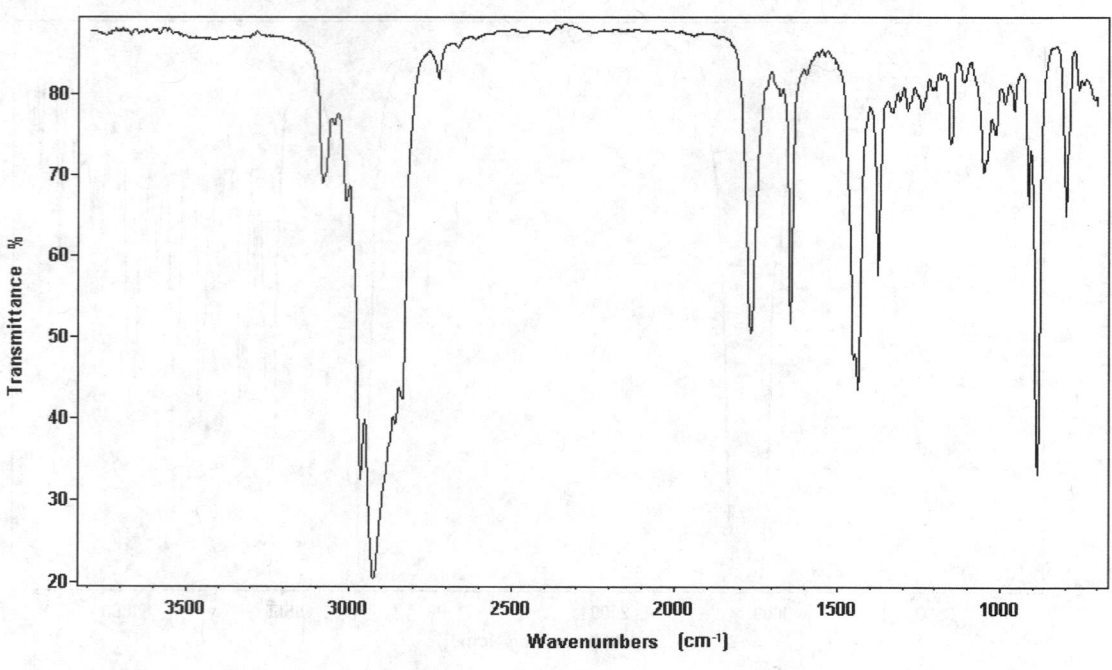

Celery Seed Oil

Cellulose Gel

First Published: Prior to FCC 6

Cellulose, Microcrystalline
INS: 460   CAS: [9004-34-6]
UNII: OP1R32D61U [cellulose, microcrystalline]

DESCRIPTION
Cellulose Gel occurs as a fine, white or almost white powder. It is purified, partially depolymerized cellulose prepared by treating *alpha*-cellulose, obtained as a pulp from fibrous plant material, with mineral acids. It consists of free-flowing, nonfibrous particles that may be compressed into self-binding tablets that disintegrate rapidly in water. It is insoluble in water, in dilute acids, in dilute sodium hydroxide solutions, and in most organic solvents.

Function: Anticaking agent; binding agent; dispersing agent

Packaging and Storage: Store in well-closed containers.

IDENTIFICATION
- **A. PROCEDURE**
  Sample preparation: Sift 20 g of sample for 5 min on an air-jet sieve equipped with a screen having 38-µm openings. If more than 5% is retained on the screen, mix 30 g of sample with 270 mL of water; otherwise, mix 45 g of sample with 255 mL of water.
  Blender setup: Use a single-speed, high-speed (equal to or greater than 18,000 rpm) power blender (Waring Blender, Model 700G, or equivalent) that has a clover-shaped jar design. The jar and blades meet the following specifications: the jar has a 7.0-cm id at the bottom and a 9.2-cm id at the top and an overall height of 21.9 cm, and the four blades are arranged so that two of the blades are pointed up and two are pointed down.
  Analysis: Mix the *Sample preparation* for 5 min with the *Blender setup*. Transfer 100 mL of the dispersion into a 100-mL graduated cylinder, and allow it to stand for 3 h.
  Acceptance criteria: A white, opaque, bubble-free dispersion that does not form a supernatant liquid at the surface is obtained. [NOTE—Save this dispersion for use in *Identification* test *B* (below).]
- **B. PROCEDURE**
  Sample: Use the dispersion obtained from *Identification* test *A* (above).
  Analysis: Add a few drops of iodine TS to a 20-mL aliquot of the *Sample* and mix.
  Acceptance criteria: No purple to blue or blue color appears.

ASSAY
- **PROCEDURE**
  Sample: 125 mg
  Analysis: With the aid of about 25 mL of water, transfer the *Sample* into a 300-mL Erlenmeyer flask. Add 50.0 mL of 0.5 N potassium dichromate, mix, then carefully add 100 mL of sulfuric acid, and heat to boiling. Remove the mixture from the heat, allow it to stand at room temperature for 15 min, cool it in a water bath, and transfer it into a 250-mL volumetric flask. Dilute almost to volume with water, cool to 25°, then dilute to volume with water, and mix. Titrate a 50.0-mL

aliquot with 0.1 N ferrous ammonium sulfate, using 2 or 3 drops of orthophenanthroline TS as the indicator, and record the volume required (S), in mL. Perform a blank determination (see *General Provisions*), and record the volume of 0.1 N ferrous ammonium sulfate required (B), in mL. Calculate the percent cellulose in the sample by the formula:

$$\text{Result} = (B - S) \times 338/W$$

W = weight of sample (mg), on the dried basis
Acceptance criteria: NLT 97.0% and NMT 102.0% of carbohydrate, calculated as cellulose on the dried basis

IMPURITIES
Inorganic Impurities
- **LEAD,** *Lead Limit Test, Flame Atomic Absorption Spectrophotometric Method,* Appendix IIIB
  Sample: 10 g
  Acceptance criteria: NMT 2 mg/kg

SPECIFIC TESTS
- **LOSS ON DRYING,** Appendix IIC: 105° to constant weight
  Acceptance criteria: NMT 7.0%
- **PH,** *pH Determination,* Appendix IIB
  Sample mixture: Shake 5 g of sample with 40 mL of water for 20 min and centrifuge.
  Analysis: Determine the pH of the supernatant liquid from the *Sample mixture*.
  Acceptance criteria: Between 5.0 and 7.5
- **RESIDUE ON IGNITION (SULFATED ASH),** Appendix IIC
  Sample: 2 g
  Acceptance criteria: NMT 0.05%
- **WATER-SOLUBLE SUBSTANCES**
  Sample mixture: 5 g of sample with 80 mL of water
  Analysis: Shake the *Sample mixture* for 10 min. Filter the mixture through Whatman No. 42, or equivalent, filter paper into a tared beaker, evaporate the filtrate to dryness on a steam bath, dry at 105° for 1 h, cool, and weigh.
  Acceptance criteria: NMT 0.24%

Cellulose Gum
First Published: Prior to FCC 6

Sodium Carboxymethylcellulose
CMC
Modified Cellulose

INS: 466   CAS: [9004-32-4]
UNII: K679OBS311 [carboxymethylcellulose sodium]

DESCRIPTION
Cellulose Gum occurs as a white to cream colored powder or as granules. The powder is hygroscopic. It readily disperses in water to form colloidal solutions. It is insoluble in most solvents. A 1:100 aqueous suspension has a pH between 6.5 and 8.5.
Function: Thickener; stabilizer
Packaging and Storage: Store in well-closed containers.

IDENTIFICATION
- **A. PROCEDURE**
  Sample: 1 g, powdered
  Sample dispersion: Add the *Sample* to 50 mL of warm water while stirring to produce a uniform dispersion. Continue stirring until a colloidal solution is produced, then cool to room temperature.
  Analysis: Add 10 mL of cupric sulfate TS to 10 mL of *Sample dispersion*. [NOTE—Save the remainder of the *Sample dispersion* for *Identification* test B (below).]
  Acceptance criteria: A fluffy, blue-white precipitate forms.
- **B. SODIUM,** Appendix IIIA
  Sample: Use a portion of the *Sample dispersion* prepared in *Identification* test A (above).
  Acceptance criteria: Passes tests

ASSAY
- **PROCEDURE**
  Calculation: Calculate the *Percent Cellulose Gum* by subtracting from 100 the *Percent Sodium Chloride* and *Percent Sodium Glycolate* determined using the procedures below.
  Acceptance criteria: NLT 99.5% and NMT 100.5% of cellulose gum, calculated on the dried basis
- **PERCENT SODIUM CHLORIDE**
  Sample: 5 g
  Analysis: Transfer the *Sample* into a 250-mL beaker, add 50 mL of water and 5 mL of 30% hydrogen peroxide, and heat on a steam bath for 20 min, stirring occasionally to ensure complete dissolution. Cool, add 100 mL of water and 10 mL of nitric acid, and titrate with 0.05 N silver nitrate to a potentiometric endpoint, using a silver/calomel (AgCl) electrode set, and stirring constantly. Calculate the percent sodium chloride in the sample by the formula:

$$\text{Result} = (V \times N \times F_E)/[(100 - b) \times W]$$

V = volume of the silver nitrate (mL)
N = normality of the silver nitrate
F_E = equivalence factor for sodium chloride, 584.4
b = percent *Loss on Drying* (determined separately, below)
W = weight of the sample taken (g)

- **PERCENT SODIUM GLYCOLATE**
  Standard stock solution: 1 mg/mL of glycolic acid (using glycolic acid previously dried in a desiccator at room temperature overnight) [NOTE—Use this solution within 30 days.]
  Standard solutions: Transfer 1.0, 2.0, 3.0, and 4.0 mL, respectively, of the *Standard solution* into separate 100-

mL volumetric flasks, add sufficient water to each flask to make 5 mL, then add 5 mL of glacial acetic acid, and dilute to volume with acetone.

Sample solution: Transfer 500 mg of sample into a 100-mL beaker; moisten thoroughly with 5 mL glacial acetic acid followed by 5 mL of water, and stir with a glass rod until dissolution is complete (usually about 15 min). While stirring, slowly add 50 mL of acetone, then add 1 g of sodium chloride, and stir for several minutes to ensure complete precipitation of the cellulose gum. Filter through a soft, open-textured paper, previously wetted with a small amount of acetone, and collect the filtrate in a 100-mL volumetric flask. Use an additional 30 mL of acetone to facilitate transfer of the solids and to wash the filter cake, then dilute to volume with acetone, and mix.

Blank solution: 5% each of glacial acetic acid and water in acetone

Analysis: Transfer 2.0 mL of the *Sample solution*, 2.0 mL of each of the *Standard solutions*, and 2.0 mL of the *Blank solution* into separate 25-mL volumetric flasks. Place the uncovered flasks in a boiling water bath for exactly 20 min to remove the acetone, remove from the bath, and cool. Add to each flask 5.0 mL of 2,7-dihydroxynaphthalene TS, mix thoroughly, add an additional 15 mL, and again mix thoroughly. Cover the mouth of each flask with a small piece of aluminum foil. Place the flasks upright in a boiling water bath for 20 min, then remove from the bath, cool, dilute to volume with sulfuric acid, and mix. Using a suitable spectrophotometer, determine the absorbance of the solutions prepared from the *Sample solution* and from the *Standard solutions* at 540 nm against the solution prepared from the *Blank solution*. Prepare a standard curve using the absorbance obtained from each of the *Standard solutions*. From the standard curve and the absorbance of the *Sample solution*, determine the weight (w), in mg, of glycolic acid in the sample taken, and calculate the percent sodium glycolate in the sample by the formula:

$$\text{Result} = (w \times F)/[(100 - b) \times W]$$

w = weight of glycolic acid in the *Sample*, as determined from the standard curve
F = factor converting glycolic acid to sodium glycolate, 12.9
b = percent *Loss on Drying*, determined separately (below)
W = weight of the sample taken (g)

IMPURITIES
Inorganic Impurities
- **LEAD,** *Lead Limit Test,* Appendix IIIB
  Sample solution: Prepare as directed for organic compounds using 2 g of sample.
  Control: 6 µg Pb (6 mL of *Diluted Standard Lead Solution*)

  Acceptance criteria: NMT 3 mg/kg

SPECIFIC TESTS
- **DEGREE OF SUBSTITUTION**
  Electrode system: Use a standard glass electrode and a calomel electrode modified as follows: Discard the aqueous potassium chloride solution contained in the electrode, rinse and fill with the supernatant liquid obtained by shaking thoroughly 2 g each of potassium chloride and silver chloride (or silver oxide) with 100 mL of methanol, then add a few crystals of potassium chloride and silver chloride (or silver oxide) to the electrode.
  Sample: 200 mg, previously dried
  Analysis: Add 75 mL of glacial acetic acid to the *Sample* contained in a 250-mL glass stoppered Erlenmeyer flask, connect the flask with a water-cooled condenser, and reflux gently on a hot plate for 2 h. Cool, transfer the solution to a 250-mL beaker with the aid of 50 mL of glacial acetic acid, and titrate with 0.1 N perchloric acid in dioxane while stirring with a magnetic stirrer.
  [**CAUTION**—Handle perchloric acid in an appropriate fume hood.] Determine the endpoint potentiometrically with a pH meter equipped with the *Electrode system* described. Record the mL of 0.1 N perchloric acid versus mV (0- to 700-mV range), and continue the titration to a few mL beyond the endpoint. Plot the titration curve and read the volume (A), in mL, of 0.1 N perchloric acid at the inflection point. Calculate the degree of substitution by the formula:

  $$\text{Result} = [F_1 V/W]/[1.000 - (F_2 V/W)]$$

  F_1 = 1/10th of the molecular weight of 1 anhydroglucose unit, 16.2
  V = volume of 0.1 N perchloric acid (mL)
  W = weight of the sample taken (mg)
  F_2 = 1/10th of the molecular weight of 1 sodium carboxymethyl group, 8.0

  Acceptance criteria: NLT 0.2 and NMT 1.50 carboxymethyl groups (–CH$_2$COOH) per anhydroglucose unit on the dried basis

- **LOSS ON DRYING,** Appendix IIC: 105° to constant weight
  Acceptance criteria: NMT 10.0%

- **SODIUM**
  Analysis: From the weight of the sample taken and the number of mL of 0.1 N perchloric acid consumed in the determination of *Degree of Substitution* (above), calculate the percent sodium. Each mL of 0.1 N perchloric acid is equivalent to 2.299 mg of sodium (Na).
  Acceptance criteria: NMT 12.4%, on the dried basis

- **VISCOSITY DETERMINATION,** *Viscosity of Cellulose Gum,* Appendix IIB
  Sample solution: 2% (w/w)
  Acceptance criteria: NLT 25 cP

Cellulose, Powdered
First Published: Prior to FCC 6

INS: 460(ii) CAS: [9004-34-6]
UNII: SMD1X3XO9M [powdered cellulose]

DESCRIPTION
Cellulose, Powdered, occurs as a white substance and consists of fibrous particles that may be compressed into self-binding tablets that disintegrate rapidly in water. It exists in various grades, exhibiting degrees of fineness ranging from a dense, free-flowing powder to a coarse, fluffy, nonflowing material. It is purified, mechanically disintegrated cellulose prepared by processing bleached cellulose obtained as a pulp from such fibrous materials as wood or cotton. It is insoluble in water, in dilute acids, and in nearly all organic solvents. It is slightly soluble in 1 N sodium hydroxide.

Function: Anticaking agent; binding agent; bulking agent; dispersing agent; filter aid; texturizing agent; thickening agent

Packaging and Storage: Store in well-closed containers.

IDENTIFICATION
- **A. Procedure**
  Sample mixture: Mix the 30 g of sample with 270 mL of water in a high-speed (approximately 12,000 rpm) power blender for 5 min.
  Analysis: If the *Sample mixture* is a free-flowing suspension, transfer 100 mL of it (saving the remainder for *Identification* tests D and E (below)), into a 100-mL graduated cylinder, and allow it to settle for 1 h.
  Acceptance criteria: The *Sample mixture* will be either a free-flowing suspension or a heavy, lumpy suspension that flows poorly (if at all), settles only slightly, and contains many trapped air bubbles. The mixture is not slimy. If the *Analysis* is carried out, a supernatant liquid appears above the layer of sample.
- **B. Procedure**
  Sample mixture: 10 g in 90 mL of water
  Analysis: Boil the *Sample mixture* for 5 min, filter while hot through ashless, fine quantitative paper (S & S 589 Blue Ribbon, or equivalent), and add 2 drops of iodine TS to the filtrate.
  Acceptance criteria: The color does not change from yellow-red.
- **C. Procedure**
  Sample: 2 to 5 mg
  Analysis: Add the *Sample* to 20 mL of a 0.1% solution of anthrone in 75% sulfuric acid, and heat on a steam bath.
  Acceptance criteria: The solution turns blue-green within 5 min.
- **D. Microscopy**
  Sample: Use the mixture obtained from *Identification* test A.
  Analysis: Place a few drops of the stirred *Sample* on a microscope slide, and insert a cover glass. Observe at 100 magnifications with a microscope.
  Acceptance criteria: Fibers and fiber fragments are visible, regardless of the degree of fineness of the sample.
- **E. Procedure**
  Sample: Use the mixture obtained from *Identification* test A.
  Analysis: Dilute 10 mL of the stirred *Sample* to 1000 mL with water, and filter 125 mL of the dilution through a Büchner funnel using Whatman No. 4 filter paper, or equivalent. Rinse the pad with 25 mL of acetone, and dry (paper included) at 105°. Transfer the powder to a tared weighing bottle, weigh, then transfer to a 50-mL Erlenmeyer flask, and seal with a rubber stopper. Record the weight of the sample (w), in mg, of the sample. Prepare 0.167 M and 1.0 M solutions of cupriethylenediamine (CED), determining the necessary volumes of each as follows: $0.12 \times w$ equals the mL of 0.167 M CED to use, and $0.08 \times w$ equals the mL of 1.0 M CED to use. Add a few 3-mm glass beads and the calculated volume of 0.167 M CED, blow nitrogen over the surface of the solution, and shake for 2 min. Add the calculated volume of 1.0 M CED, again introduce the nitrogen, and shake vigorously for at least 3 min.
  Acceptance criteria: A dark blue solution, clear under microscopic examination, appears.

ASSAY
- **Procedure**
  Sample: 125 mg
  Analysis: With the aid of about 25 mL of water, transfer the *Sample* into a 300-mL Erlenmeyer flask. Add 50.0 mL of 0.5 N potassium dichromate, mix, then carefully add 100 mL of sulfuric acid and heat to boiling. Remove the flask from the heat, allow the solution to stand at room temperature for 15 min, cool it in a water bath, and transfer the solution to a 250-mL volumetric flask. Dilute with water almost to volume, cool to 25°, dilute to volume with water, and mix. Titrate a 50-mL aliquot with 0.1 N ferrous ammonium sulfate, using 2 or 3 drops of orthophenanthroline TS. Perform a blank determination (see *General Provisions*), and make any necessary correction. Calculate the normality, N, of the ferrous ammonium sulfate solution by the formula:

  $$\text{Result} = (0.1 \times 50)/B$$

  B = volume of ferrous ammonium sulfate solution required in the blank titration (mL)

Calculate the percent cellulose in the *Sample* by the formula:

$$\text{Result} = 6.75(B - S) \times N/2W$$

- S = volume (mL) of ferrous ammonium sulfate solution used in the sample titration
- W = weight (g) of the sample taken, on the dried basis

Acceptance criteria: NLT 97.0% and not more than 102.0% of carbohydrate, calculated as cellulose

IMPURITIES
Inorganic Impurities
- **CHLORIDE**
  Sample: 5 g
  Analysis: Add 250 mL of water to the *Sample* contained in a 500-mL conical flask and reflux the mixture for 1 h. Filter through Whatman No. 4 filter paper, or equivalent, and reflux the sample with 200 mL of water for 30 min. Filter as before, and combine the filtrates and hot water rinses. Add 1 mL of nitric acid, heat to boiling, and slowly add 5 mL of a 5% solution of silver nitrate. After the precipitate has coagulated, cool and filter through a sintered-glass filtering funnel. Wash with a 1:100 nitric acid solution until free from silver nitrate, rinse with water, dry at 130°, and weigh. Perform a blank determination (see *General Provisions*) to obtain the corrected weight of the sample precipitate, each mg of which is equivalent to 0.247 mg of chloride.
  Acceptance criteria: NMT 0.05%
- **LEAD,** *Lead Limit Test, Flame Atomic Absorption Spectrophotometric Method,* Appendix IIIB
  Sample: 3 g
  Acceptance criteria: NMT 3 mg/kg
- **SULFUR (TOTAL)**
  Sample: 5 g, previously dried
  Analysis: Transfer the *Sample* into a 300-mL conical flask, and add 50 mL of 2:3 perchloric acid: nitric acid (v/v). [**CAUTION**—Handle perchloric acid in an appropriate fume hood.] Heat on a hot plate in a hood, and boil until all organic matter has been destroyed and copious fumes of perchloric acid evolve. If the organic matter chars and cannot be destroyed quickly by further heating for a short time, add 10 to 20 mL of the acid mixture, and continue the treatment until a clear, syrupy residue is obtained. [NOTE—All of the nitric acid must be driven from the flask, because it will otherwise form a double salt with the barium sulfate formed later.] Allow the mixture to cool for a few min, then add 200 mL of hot water, and heat again to boiling. (If the mixture is cloudy, filter, and rinse the filter with a small amount of hot water before boiling.) As soon as the mixture is boiling gently, carefully run in 20 mL of barium chloride TS, boil for a few minutes longer, and allow to stand for at least 12 h on a steam bath. Filter any barium sulfate onto an ashless filter paper, and rinse with five portions of boiling water to remove traces of perchloric acid. Place the paper in a tared platinum dish, dry in an oven at 105°, and ignite at 800° ± 25° for 1 h. Perform a blank determination (see *General Provisions*) to obtain the corrected weight of the sample precipitate, each mg of which is equivalent to 0.137 mg of sulfur.
  Acceptance criteria: NMT 0.01%

SPECIFIC TESTS
- **ASH (TOTAL)**
  Sample: 3 g
  Analysis: Heat the *Sample* at 550° ± 50° until completely charred, then ignite at 800° ± 25° until free from carbon, cool in a desiccator, and weigh.
  Acceptance criteria: NMT 0.3%
- **LOSS ON DRYING,** Appendix IIC: 105° to constant weight
  Acceptance criteria: NMT 7.0%
- **PH,** *pH Determination,* Appendix IIB
  Sample mixture: Mix 10 g of sample in 90 mL of water and allow to stand with occasional stirring for 1 h.
  Analysis: Determine the pH of the supernatant liquid from the *Sample mixture*.
  Acceptance criteria: Between 5.0 and 7.5
- **WATER-SOLUBLE SUBSTANCES**
  Sample: 6 g
  Analysis: Mix the *Sample* with 90 mL of recently boiled and cooled water and allow to stand with occasional stirring for 10 min. Filter through Whatman No. 2 filter paper, or equivalent, discard the first 10 mL of filtrate, and pass the filtrate through the same filter a second time, if necessary, to obtain a clear filtrate. Evaporate a 15-mL portion of the filtrate to dryness in a tared evaporating dish on a steam bath, dry at 105° for 1 h, cool in a desiccator, and weigh.
  Acceptance criteria: NMT 1.5%

Chamomile Oil, English Type
First Published: Prior to FCC 6

CAS: [8015-92-7]
UNII: UB27587839 [chamaemelum nobile flower oil]

DESCRIPTION
Chamomile Oil, English Type occurs as a light blue or light green-blue liquid with a strong, aromatic odor, characteristic of the flowers. The color may change with age to green-yellow or yellow-brown. It is the oil obtained by steam distillation of the dried flowers of the so-called English or Roman Chamomile, *Anthemis nobilis* L. (Fam. Asteraceae). It is soluble in most fixed oils, and it is almost completely soluble in mineral oil. It is soluble, with slight haziness, in propylene glycol, but it is insoluble in glycerin.
Function: Flavoring agent
Packaging and Storage: Store in a cool place protected from light in full, tight containers that are made from steel or aluminum and that are suitably lined.

IDENTIFICATION
- **INFRARED SPECTRA,** *Spectrophotometric Identification Tests,* Appendix IIIC

Acceptance criteria: The spectrum of the sample exhibits relative maxima at the same wavelengths as those of the spectrum below.

SPECIFIC TESTS
- **ACID VALUE (ESSENTIAL OILS AND FLAVORS),** Appendix VI
  Acceptance criteria: NMT 15.0
- **ESTER VALUE,** *Esters,* Appendix VI
  Sample: 1 g
  Acceptance criteria: Between 250 and 310

- **REFRACTIVE INDEX,** Appendix IIB
  [NOTE—Use an Abbé or other refractometer of equal or greater accuracy.]
  Acceptance criteria: Between 1.440 and 1.450 at 20°
- **SOLUBILITY IN ALCOHOL,** Appendix VI
  Acceptance criteria: One mL of sample dissolves in 2 mL of 80% alcohol, sometimes with a slight precipitate.
- **SPECIFIC GRAVITY:** Determine by any reliable method (see *General Provisions*).
  Acceptance criteria: Between 0.892 and 0.910

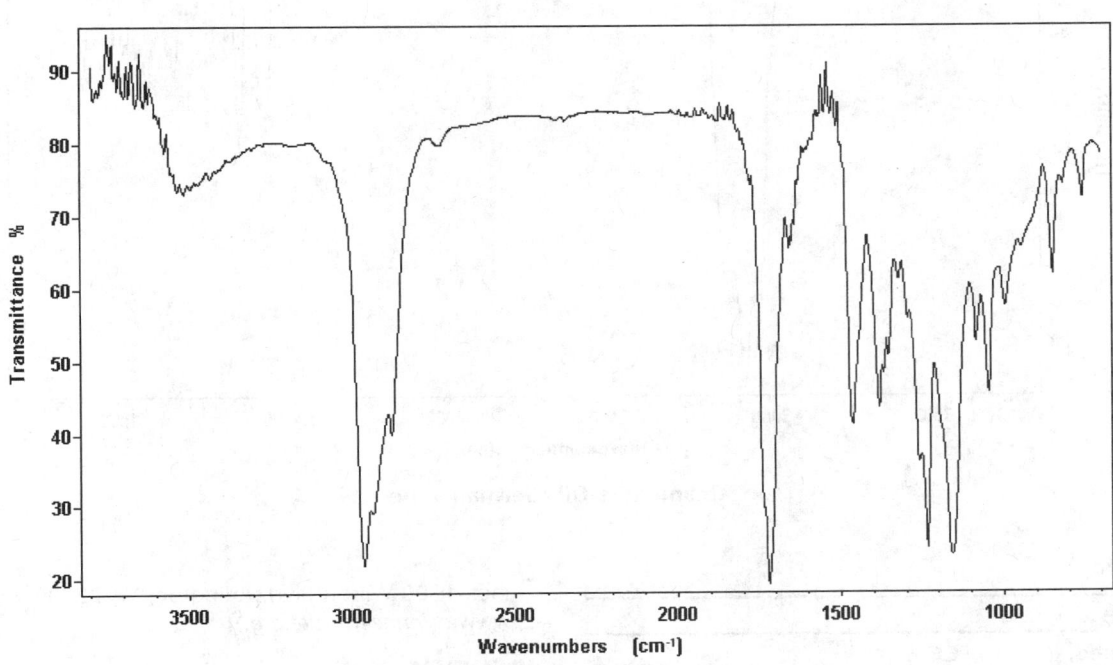

Chamomile Oil, English Type

Chamomile Oil, German Type

First Published: Prior to FCC 6

Chamomile Oil, Hungarian Type
UNII: 60F80Z61A9 [chamomile flower oil]

DESCRIPTION
Chamomile Oil, German Type occurs as a deep blue or blue-green liquid with a strong, characteristic odor and a bitter, aromatic taste. When the oil is exposed to light or air, the blue color changes to green and finally to brown. It is the oil obtained by steam distillation of the flowers and stalks of *Matricaria chamomilla* L. (Fam. Asteraceae). Upon cooling, the oil may become viscous. It is soluble in most fixed oils and in propylene glycol. It is insoluble in glycerin and in mineral oil.
Function: Flavoring agent
Packaging and Storage: Store in a cool place protected from light in full, tight containers that are made from steel or aluminum and that are suitably lined.

IDENTIFICATION
- **INFRARED SPECTRA,** *Spectrophotometric Identification Tests,* Appendix IIIC
  Acceptance criteria: The spectrum of the sample exhibits relative maxima at the same wavelengths as those of the spectrum below.

SPECIFIC TESTS
- **ACID VALUE (ESSENTIAL OILS AND FLAVORS),** Appendix VI
  Acceptance criteria: Between 5 and 50
- **ESTER VALUE,** *Esters,* Appendix VI
  Sample: 5 g
  Acceptance criteria: NMT 40
- **ESTER VALUE AFTER ACETYLATION**
  Sample: 10 mL
  Acetylated sample: Using the *Sample,* prepare 1.5 g of dried, acetylated oil as directed under *Total Alcohols,* Appendix VI.
  Analysis: Using the *Acetylated sample,* proceed as directed in *Esters, Ester Value,* Appendix VI.
  Acceptance criteria: Between 65 and 155

- **SOLUBILITY IN ALCOHOL**, Appendix VI
  Acceptance criteria: The oil does not usually dissolve clearly in 95% alcohol.

- **SPECIFIC GRAVITY:** Determine by any reliable method (see *General Provisions*).
  Acceptance criteria: Between 0.910 and 0.950

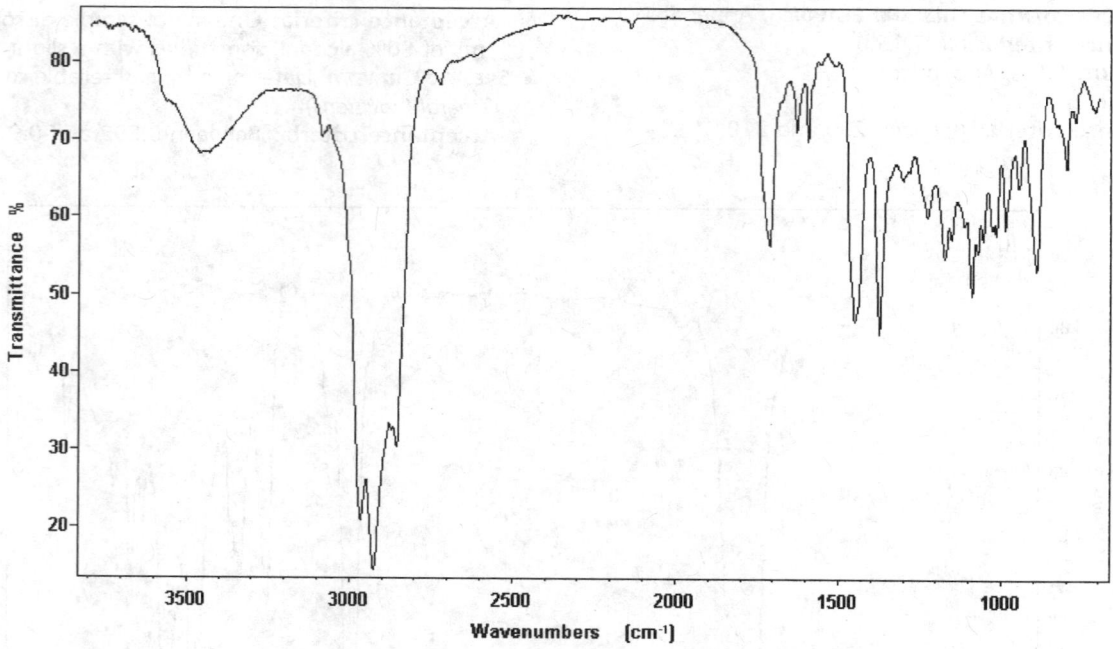

Chamomile Oil, German Type

Chlorine

First Published: Prior to FCC 6

Cl₂
INS: 925
UNII: 4R7X1O2820 [chlorine]
Formula wt 70.91
CAS: [7782-50-5]

DESCRIPTION
Chlorine occurs as a green-yellow gas, normally packaged as a liquid under pressure in containers approved by the U.S. Department of Transportation. At 60° F, it has a vapor pressure of 70.91 psig. Its vapor density is about 2.5 times that of air. About 0.8 lb (0.362 kg) is soluble in 100 lb (45.4 kg) of water at 60° F under atmospheric pressure.

Function: Antimicrobial agent; bleaching agent; oxidizing agent

Packaging and Storage: Store in suitable pressure containers, observing applicable U.S. Department of Transportation regulations pertaining to shipping containers.

[**CAUTION**—Chlorine gas is a respiratory irritant. Large amounts cause coughing, labored breathing, and irritation of the eyes. In extreme cases, the difficulty in breathing may cause death due to suffocation. Liquid Chlorine causes skin and eye burns on contact. (Safety precautions to be observed in handling the material are specified in the *Chlorine Manual*, available from The Chlorine Institute, Inc., 1300 Wilson Blvd, Arlington, VA 22209, www.chlorineinstitute.org.)]

IDENTIFICATION
- **CHLORIDE,** Appendix IIIA
  Sample preparation: Cautiously pass a few mL of sample gas through 10 mL of 1 N sodium hydroxide that has previously been chilled in an ice bath.
  Acceptance criteria: The *Sample preparation* gives positive tests for *Chloride*, and it darkens starch iodide paper.

ASSAY
- **PROCEDURE**
  Analysis: Determine by ASTM Method E 412-93, "*Assay of Liquid Chlorine, Zinc Amalgam Method*."
  Acceptance criteria: NLT 99.5%, by volume

IMPURITIES
Inorganic Impurities
- **LEAD,** *Lead Limit Test,* Appendix IIIB
  Sample stock solution: Dissolve the residue obtained under the test for *Residue* (below) in 2.5 mL of freshly prepared aqua regia, and dilute with water to a volume, in mL, equivalent to the weight, in g, of the initial sample. One mL of the final dilution is equivalent to 1 g of sample.
  Sample solution: Mix a 1.0-mL portion of the *Sample stock solution* with 5 mL of water and 11 mL of 2.7 N hydrochloric acid.

Control: 10 μg Pb (10 mL of *Diluted Standard Lead Solution*)
Acceptance criteria: NMT 10 mg/kg
- **MERCURY,** *Mercury Limit Test, Method I,* Appendix IIIB
  Sample stock solution: Dissolve the residue obtained under the test for *Residue* (below) in 2.5 mL of freshly prepared aqua regia, and dilute with water to a volume, in mL, equivalent to the weight, in g, of the initial sample. One mL of the final dilution is equivalent to 1 g of sample.
  Sample solution: Transfer 2.0 mL of the *Sample stock solution* to a 50-mL beaker and add 10 mL of water, 1 mL of 1:5 sulfuric acid, and 1 mL of a 40 mg/mL potassium permanganate solution. Cover the beaker with a watch glass, boil for a few seconds, and cool.
  Acceptance criteria: NMT 1 mg/kg

SPECIFIC TESTS
- **MOISTURE**
  Analysis: Determine by ASTM Method E 410-92, "*Moisture and Residue in Liquid Chlorine.*"
  [NOTE—Retain the residue obtained for use in tests for *Lead* and *Mercury* (above).]
  Acceptance criteria: NMT 0.015%, by weight
- **RESIDUE**
  Analysis: Determine by ASTM Method E 410-92, "*Moisture and Residue in Liquid Chlorine.*"
  [NOTE—Retain the residue obtained for use in tests for *Lead* and *Mercury* (above).]
  Acceptance criteria: NMT 0.015%, by weight, of nonvolatile matter

Cholic Acid

First Published: Prior to FCC 6
Last Revision: Third Supplement, FCC 7

Cholalic Acid
3,7,12-Trihydroxycholanic Acid

$C_{24}H_{40}O_5$ Formula wt 408.58
INS: 1000   CAS: [81-25-4]
UNII: G1JO7801AE [cholic acid]

DESCRIPTION
Cholic Acid occurs as colorless plates or as a white, crystalline powder. One g dissolves in about 30 mL of alcohol or acetone and in about 7 mL of glacial acetic acid. It is very slightly soluble in water.

Function: Emulsifier
Packaging and Storage: Store in tight containers.

IDENTIFICATION
- **A. INFRARED ABSORPTION,** *Spectrophotometric Identification Tests,* Appendix IIIC
  Reference standard: USP Cholic Acid RS
  Sample and standard preparation: K
  Acceptance criteria: The spectrum of the sample exhibits maxima at the same wavelengths as those in the spectrum of the *Reference standard*.
- **B. PROCEDURE**
  Sample solution: 0.2 mg/mL in 50% acetic acid
  Analysis: To 1 mL of the *Sample solution* add 1 mL of a 1:100 furfural solution. Cool in an ice bath for 5 min, add 15 mL of 1:2 sulfuric acid, mix, and warm in a water bath at 70° for 10 min. Immediately cool in an ice bath, and stir for 2 min.
  Acceptance criteria: A blue color appears.

ASSAY
- **PROCEDURE**
  Sample: 400 mg
  Analysis: Transfer the *Sample* into a 250-mL Erlenmeyer flask, add 20 mL of water and 40 mL of alcohol, cover with a watch glass, heat gently on a steam bath until dissolved, and cool. Add 5 drops of phenolphthalein TS and, using a 10-mL microburet, titrate with 0.1 N sodium hydroxide to the first pink color that persists for 15 s. Perform a blank determination (see *General Provisions*), and make any necessary correction. Each mL of 0.1 N sodium hydroxide is equivalent to 40.86 mg of $C_{24}H_{40}O_5$.
  Acceptance criteria: NLT 98.0% of $C_{24}H_{40}O_5$, calculated on the dried basis

IMPURITIES
Inorganic Impurities
- **LEAD,** *Lead Limit Test, Flame Atomic Absorption Spectrophotometric Method,* Appendix IIIB
  Sample: 10 g
  Acceptance criteria: NMT 4 mg/kg

SPECIFIC TESTS
- **LOSS ON DRYING,** Appendix IIC: 140° under a vacuum of NMT 5 mm Hg, for 4 h
  Acceptance criteria: NMT 0.5%
- **MELTING RANGE OR TEMPERATURE DETERMINATION,** Appendix IIB
  Acceptance criteria: Between 197° and 202°
- **OPTICAL (SPECIFIC) ROTATION,** Appendix IIB
  Sample solution: 20 mg/mL in alcohol
  Acceptance criteria: $[\alpha]_D^{25}$ NLT +37°, calculated on the dried basis
- **RESIDUE ON IGNITION (SULFATED ASH),** Appendix IIC
  Sample: 2 g
  Acceptance criteria: NMT 0.1%

Choline Bitartrate

First Published: Prior to FCC 6
Last Revision: FCC 7

(2-Hydroxyethyl)trimethylammonium-L-(+)-tartrate Salt

$C_9H_{19}NO_7$
INS: 1001(v)
UNII: 6K2W7T9V6Y [choline bitartrate]
Formula wt 253.25
CAS: [87-67-2]

DESCRIPTION
Choline Bitartrate occurs as a white, hygroscopic, crystalline powder. It is freely soluble in water, slightly soluble in alcohol, and insoluble in ether and in chloroform.
Function: Nutrient
Packaging and Storage: Store in tight containers.

IDENTIFICATION
- **A. INFRARED ABSORPTION,** *Spectrophotometric Identification Tests,* Appendix IIIC
  Reference standard: USP Choline Bitartrate RS
  Sample and standard preparation: K
  Acceptance criteria: The spectrum of the sample exhibits maxima at the same wavelengths as those in the spectrum of the *Reference standard*.
- **B. PROCEDURE**
  Sample: 500 mg
  Analysis: Dissolve the *Sample* in 2 mL of iodine TS. A red-brown precipitate forms immediately. Add 5 mL of 1 N sodium hydroxide. The precipitate dissolves, and the solution becomes clear yellow. Heat the solution.
  Acceptance criteria: A pale yellow precipitate forms following the heating step.
- **C. PROCEDURE**
  Sample solution: 10 mg/mL
  Analysis: Add 1 mL of the *Sample solution* and 2 mL of a 20 mg/mL solution of potassium ferrocyanide to 2 mL of cobaltous chloride TS.
  Acceptance criteria: An emerald green color develops immediately.

ASSAY
- **PROCEDURE**
  Sample: 500 mg
  Analysis: Transfer the *Sample* into a 250-mL Erlenmeyer flask. Add 50 mL of glacial acetic acid and warm on a steam bath until dissolution is complete. Cool, add 2 drops of crystal violet TS, and titrate with 0.1 N perchloric acid in glacial acetic acid to a green endpoint. [**CAUTION**—Handle perchloric acid in an appropriate fume hood.] Perform a blank determination (see *General Provisions*), and make any necessary correction. Each mL of 0.1 N perchloric acid is equivalent to 25.36 mg of $C_9H_{19}NO_7$.
  Acceptance criteria: NLT 98.0% of $C_9H_{19}NO_7$, calculated on the anhydrous basis

IMPURITIES
Inorganic Impurities
- **LEAD,** *Lead Limit Test, Flame Atomic Absorption Spectrophotometric Method,* Appendix IIIB
  Sample: 5 g
  Acceptance criteria: NMT 2 mg/kg

Organic Impurities
- **1,4-DIOXANE,** Appendix IIIB
  Acceptance criteria: Passes test

SPECIFIC TESTS
- **OPTICAL (SPECIFIC) ROTATION,** Appendix IIB
  Sample solution: 400 mg/mL
  Acceptance criteria: $[\alpha]_D^{25}$ between 17.5° and 18.5°
- **RESIDUE ON IGNITION (SULFATED ASH),** Appendix IIC
  Sample: 2 g
  Acceptance criteria: NMT 0.1%
- **WATER,** *Water Determination,* Appendix IIB
  Sample solution: 2 g of sample in 50 mL of methanol. [NOTE—Alternatively, the *Water Determination* can be made by drying the sample in a vacuum desiccator over phosphorus pentoxide for 4 h.]
  Acceptance criteria: NMT 0.5%

Choline Chloride

First Published: Prior to FCC 6
Last Revision: FCC 7

(2-Hydroxyethyl)trimethylammonium Chloride

$C_5H_{14}ClNO$
INS: 1001(iii)
UNII: 45I14D8O27 [choline chloride]
Formula wt 139.65
CAS: [67-48-1]

DESCRIPTION
Choline Chloride occurs as colorless or white crystals or as a crystalline powder. It is hygroscopic, and is very soluble in water and in alcohol.
Function: Nutrient
Packaging and Storage: Store in tight containers.

IDENTIFICATION
- **A. CHLORIDE,** Appendix IIIA
  Sample solution: 50 mg/mL
  Acceptance criteria: Passes tests
- **B. INFRARED ABSORPTION,** *Spectrophotometric Identification Tests,* Appendix IIIC
  Reference standard: USP Choline Chloride RS
  Sample and standard preparation: K
  Acceptance criteria: The spectrum of the sample exhibits maxima at the same wavelengths as those in the spectrum of the *Reference standard*.
- **C. PROCEDURE**
  Sample: 500 mg
  Analysis: Dissolve the *Sample* in 2 mL of iodine TS. A red-brown precipitate forms immediately. Add 5 mL of

1 N sodium hydroxide. The precipitate dissolves, and the solution becomes clear yellow. Heat the solution.
Acceptance criteria: A pale yellow precipitate forms following the heating step.
- **D. Procedure**
  Sample solution: 10 mg/mL
  Analysis: Add 1 mL of the *Sample solution* and 2 mL of a 20 mg/mL solution of potassium ferrocyanide to 2 mL of cobaltous chloride TS.
  Acceptance criteria: An emerald green color develops immediately.

ASSAY
- **Procedure**
  Sample: 300 mg
  Analysis: Transfer the *Sample* into a 250-mL Erlenmeyer flask. Add 50 mL of glacial acetic acid and warm on a steam bath until dissolution is complete. Cool, add 10 mL of mercuric acetate and 2 drops of crystal violet TS, and titrate with 0.1 N perchloric acid in glacial acetic acid to a green endpoint. [**Caution**—Handle perchloric acid in an appropriate fume hood.] Perform a blank determination (see *General Provisions*), and make any necessary correction. Each mL of 0.1 N perchloric acid is equivalent to 13.96 mg of $C_5H_{14}ClNO$.
  Acceptance criteria: 98.0%–100.5% of $C_5H_{14}ClNO$, calculated on the anhydrous basis

IMPURITIES
Inorganic Impurities
- **Lead**, *Lead Limit Test, Flame Atomic Absorption Spectrophotometric Method,* Appendix IIIB
  Sample: 5 g
  Acceptance criteria: NMT 2 mg/kg
- **Water**, *Water Determination,* Appendix IIB
  [Note—Alternatively, the *Water Determination* can be made by drying the sample in a vacuum desiccator over phosphorus pentoxide for 4 h.]
  Acceptance criteria: NMT 0.5%

Organic Impurities
- **1,4-Dioxane**, Appendix IIIB
  Acceptance criteria: Passes test

SPECIFIC TESTS
- **Residue on Ignition (Sulfated Ash)**, Appendix IIC
  Sample: 4 g
  Acceptance criteria: NMT 0.05%

Cinnamaldehyde
First Published: Prior to FCC 6
Last Revision: First Supplement, FCC 6

Cinnamal
Cinnamic Aldehyde

C_9H_8O Formula wt 132.16
FEMA: 2286
UNII: SR60A3XG0F [cinnamaldehyde]

DESCRIPTION
Cinnamaldehyde occurs as a yellow, strongly refractive liquid. It may contain a suitable antioxidant.
Odor: Cinnamon, burning aromatic taste
Solubility: Miscible in alcohol, chloroform, ether, fixed and volatile oils; 1 g dissolves in 700 mL of water.
Boiling Point: ~248°
Solubility in Alcohol, Appendix VI: One mL dissolves in 5 mL of 60% alcohol.
Function: Flavoring agent

IDENTIFICATION
- **Infrared Spectra**, *Spectrophotometric Identification Tests,* Appendix IIIC
  Acceptance criteria: The spectrum of the sample exhibits relative maxima at the same wavelengths as those of the spectrum below.

ASSAY
- **Procedure:** Proceed as directed under *M-1b,* Appendix XI.
  Acceptance criteria: NLT 98.0% of C_9H_8O

SPECIFIC TESTS
- **Acid Value, Flavor Chemicals (Other Than Essential Oils),** *M-15,* Appendix XI
  Acceptance criteria: NMT 10.0
- **Refractive Index,** Appendix II: At 20°
  Acceptance criteria: Between 1.619 and 1.623
- **Specific Gravity:** Determine at 25° by any reliable method (see *General Provisions*).
  Acceptance criteria: Between 1.046 and 1.050

OTHER REQUIREMENTS
- **Chlorinated Compounds,** Appendix VI
  Acceptance criteria: Passes test

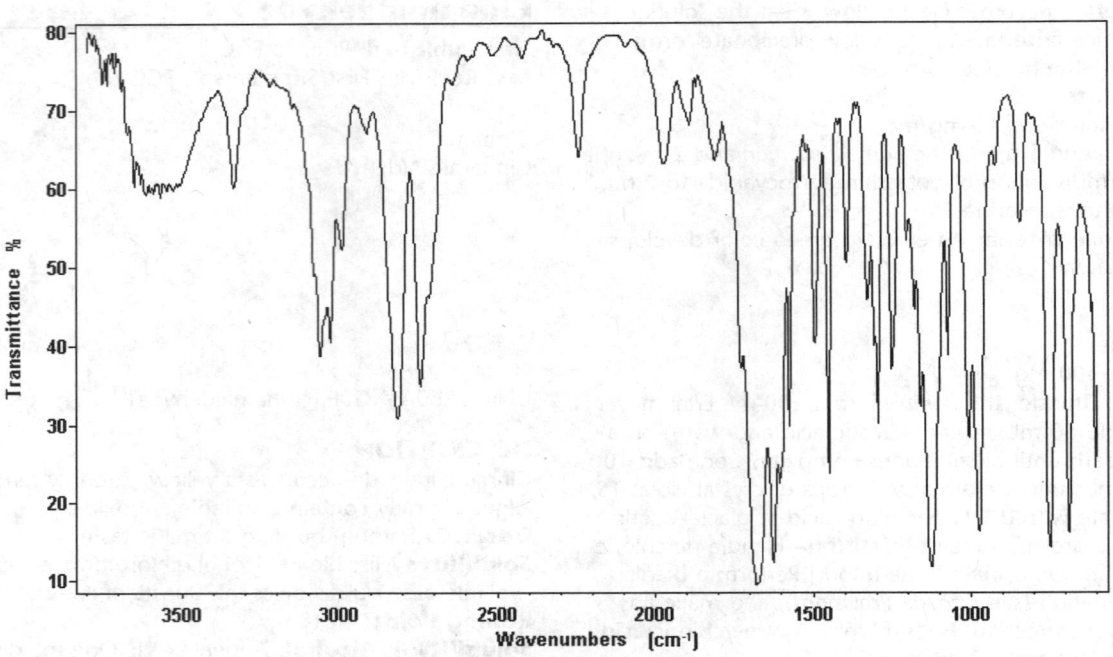

Cinnamaldehyde

Cinnamic Acid

First Published: Prior to FCC 6

3-Phenylpropenoic Acid

C₉H₈O₂ Formula wt 148.16
FEMA: 2288
UNII: U14A832J8D [cinnamic acid]

DESCRIPTION
Cinnamic Acid occurs as white crystalline scales.
Odor: Honey-floral
Solubility: Soluble in acetic acid, acetone, benzene, most fixed oils; 1 g dissolves in 2000 mL water.
Boiling Point: ~300°
Solubility in Alcohol, Appendix VI: One g dissolves in 7 mL of 95% alcohol.

Function: Flavoring agent

IDENTIFICATION
- **INFRARED SPECTRA,** Spectrophotometric Identification Tests, Appendix IIIC
  Acceptance criteria: The spectrum of the sample exhibits relative maxima at the same wavelengths as those of the spectrum below.

ASSAY
- **PROCEDURE:** Proceed as directed under M-3b, Appendix XI.
  Acceptance criteria: NLT 99.0% of C₉H₈O₂ on the dried basis

OTHER REQUIREMENTS
- **MELTING RANGE OR TEMPERATURE DETERMINATION,** Appendix IIB
  Acceptance criteria: NLT 130°
- **RESIDUE ON IGNITION (SULFATED ASH),** Appendix IIC
  Acceptance criteria: NLT 0.05%

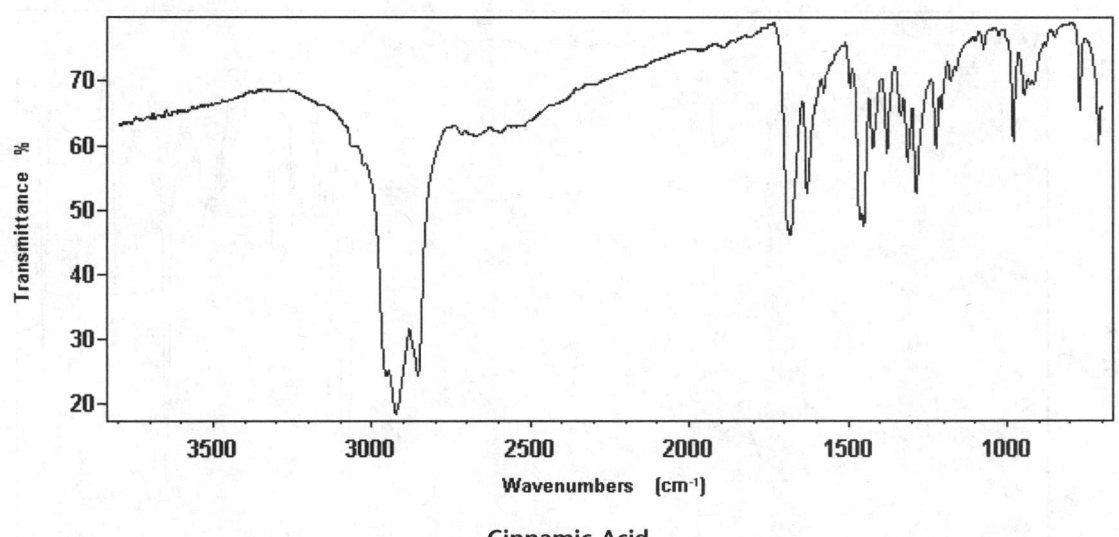

Cinnamic Acid

Cinnamon Bark Oil, Ceylon Type

First Published: Prior to FCC 6

FEMA: 2290

CAS: [8015-91-6]

UNII: XE54U569EC [cinnamon bark oil]

DESCRIPTION

Cinnamon Bark Oil, Ceylon Type occurs as a yellow liquid with an odor of cinnamon and a spicy burning taste. It is the volatile oil obtained by steam distillation from the dried inner bark of the clipped cinnamon shrub *Cinnamomum zeylanicum* Nees (Fam. Lauraceae). It is soluble in most fixed oils and in propylene glycol. It is insoluble in glycerin and in mineral oil.

Function: Flavoring agent

Packaging and Storage: Store in a cool place protected from light in full, tight containers that are made from glass or aluminum or that are lined with tin.

IDENTIFICATION

- **INFRARED SPECTRA,** *Spectrophotometric Identification Tests,* Appendix IIIC

  Acceptance criteria: The spectrum of the sample exhibits relative maxima at the same wavelengths as those of the spectrum below.

ASSAY

- **ALDEHYDES,** Appendix VI

  Sample: 2.5 g

  Analysis: Use 66.10 as the equivalence factor (e) in the calculation.

  Acceptance criteria: NLT 55.0% and NMT 78.0% of aldehydes, calculated as cinnamic aldehyde (C_9H_8O)

SPECIFIC TESTS

- **ANGULAR ROTATION,** *Optical (Specific) Rotation,* Appendix IIB: Use a 100-mm tube.

  Acceptance criteria: Between −2° and 0°

- **REFRACTIVE INDEX,** Appendix IIB

  [NOTE—Use an Abbé or other refractometer of equal or greater accuracy.]

  Acceptance criteria: Between 1.573 and 1.591 at 20°

- **SOLUBILITY IN ALCOHOL,** Appendix VI

  Acceptance criteria: One mL of sample dissolves in 3 mL of 70% alcohol.

- **SPECIFIC GRAVITY:** Determine by any reliable method (see *General Provisions*).

  Acceptance criteria: Between 1.010 and 1.030

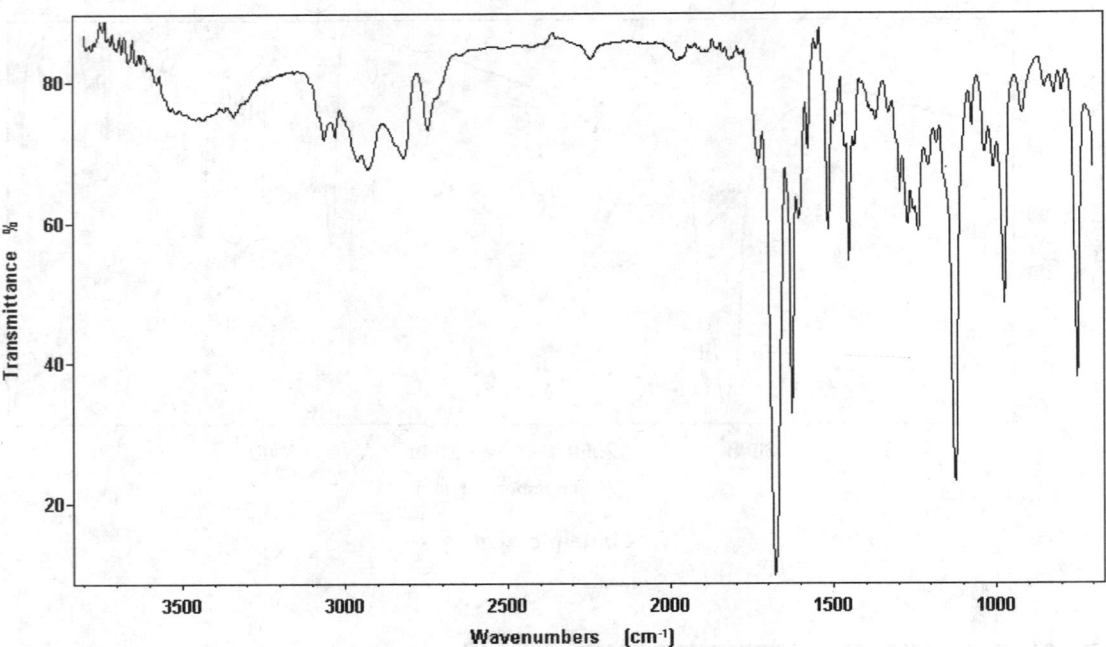

Cinnamon Bark Oil, Ceylon Type

Cinnamon Leaf Oil

First Published: Prior to FCC 6

FEMA: 2292

CAS: [8015-91-6]

UNII: S92U8SQ71V [cinnamon leaf oil]

DESCRIPTION
Cinnamon Leaf Oil occurs as a light to dark brown liquid with a spicy cinnamon–clove odor and taste. It is the volatile oil obtained by steam distillation from the leaves and twigs of the true cinnamon shrub, *Cinnamomum zeylanicum* Nees (Fam. Lauraceae). The commercial oils, according to the geographical origin, are designated as Cinnamon Leaf Oil, Ceylon, or Cinnamon Leaf Oil, Seychelles, and the two types differ in physical and chemical properties. Cinnamon Leaf Oil is soluble in most fixed oils and in propylene glycol. It is soluble, with cloudiness, in mineral oil, but is insoluble in glycerin.

Function: Flavoring agent

Packaging and Storage: Store in a cool place protected from light in full, tight containers that are made from glass or aluminum or that are lined with tin.

IDENTIFICATION
- **INFRARED SPECTRA,** *Spectrophotometric Identification Tests,* Appendix IIIC
  Acceptance criteria: The spectrum of the sample exhibits relative maxima at the same wavelengths as those of the spectrum below.

ASSAY
- **PHENOLS,** Appendix VI
  Sample: Pretreat the oil by shaking a suitable quantity with about 2% powdered tartaric acid, and filter.
  Acceptance criteria
  Ceylon type: NLT 80.0% and NMT 88.0%, by volume, of phenols
  Seychelles type: NLT 87.0% and NMT 96.0%, by volume, of phenols

SPECIFIC TESTS
- **ANGULAR ROTATION,** *Optical (Specific) Rotation,* Appendix IIB: Use a 100-mm tube.
  Acceptance criteria:
  Ceylon type: Between −2° and +1°
  Seychelles type: Between −2° and 0°
- **REFRACTIVE INDEX,** Appendix IIB
  [NOTE—Use an Abbé or other refractometer of equal or greater accuracy.]
  Acceptance criteria
  Ceylon type: Between 1.529 and 1.537
  Seychelles type: Between 1.533 and 1.540 at 20°
- **SOLUBILITY IN ALCOHOL,** Appendix VI
  Acceptance criteria
  Ceylon type: One mL of sample dissolves in 1.5 mL of 70% alcohol. The solution may cloud upon further dilution.
  Seychelles type: One mL of sample dissolves in 1 mL of 70% alcohol. The solution may cloud upon further dilution.
- **SPECIFIC GRAVITY:** Determine by any reliable method (see *General Provisions*).

Acceptance criteria
Ceylon type: Between 1.030 and 1.050
Seychelles type: Between 1.040 and 1.060

OTHER REQUIREMENTS
- LABELING: Indicate whether the oil is the Ceylon or Seychelles type.

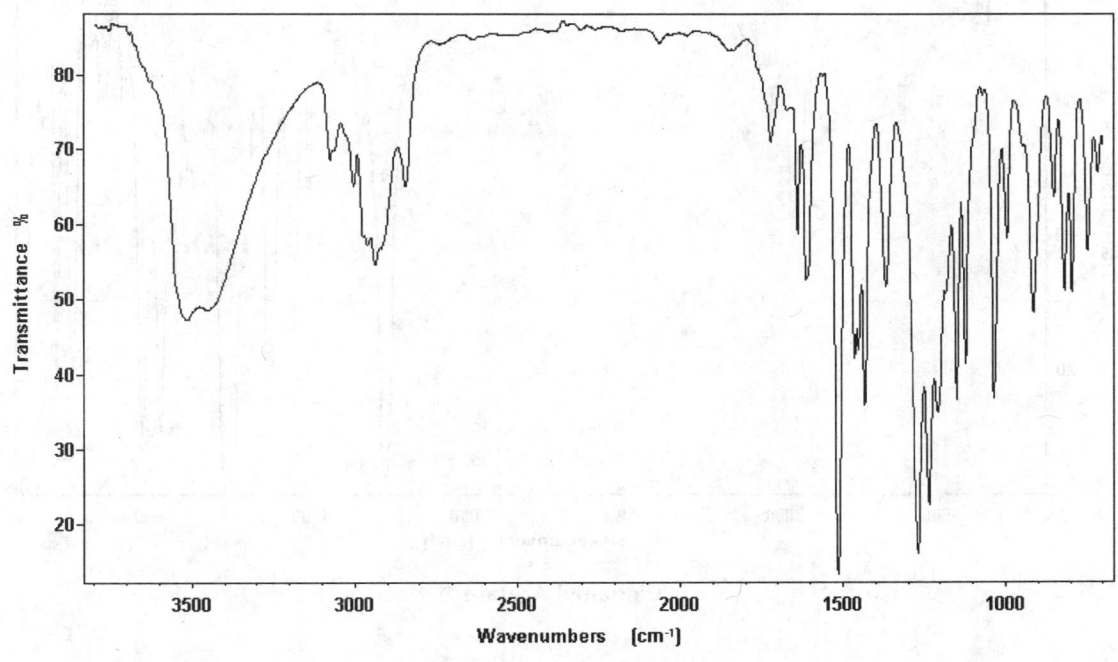

Cinnamon Leaf Oil

Cinnamyl Acetate

First Published: Prior to FCC 6

$C_{11}H_{12}O_2$ Formula wt 176.22
FEMA: 2293
UNII: LFJ36XSV8K [cinnamyl acetate]

DESCRIPTION
Cinnamyl Acetate occurs as a colorless to slightly yellow liquid.
Odor: Sweet, balsamic, floral
Solubility: Miscible in alcohol, chloroform, ether, most fixed oils; insoluble or practically insoluble in glycerin, water
Boiling Point: ~264°
Solubility in Alcohol, Appendix VI: One mL dissolves in 5 mL of 70% alcohol.

Function: Flavoring agent

IDENTIFICATION
- INFRARED SPECTRA, *Spectrophotometric Identification Tests*, Appendix IIIC
  Acceptance criteria: The spectrum of the sample exhibits relative maxima at the same wavelengths as those of the spectrum below.

ASSAY
- PROCEDURE: Proceed as directed under *M-1b*, Appendix XI.
  Acceptance criteria: NLT 98.0% of $C_{11}H_{12}O_2$

SPECIFIC TESTS
- ACID VALUE, FLAVOR CHEMICALS (OTHER THAN ESSENTIAL OILS), *M-15*, Appendix XI
  Acceptance criteria: NMT 1.0
- REFRACTIVE INDEX, Appendix II: At 20°
  Acceptance criteria: Between 1.539 and 1.543
- SPECIFIC GRAVITY: Determine at 25° by any reliable method (see *General Provisions*).
  Acceptance criteria: Between 1.050 and 1.054

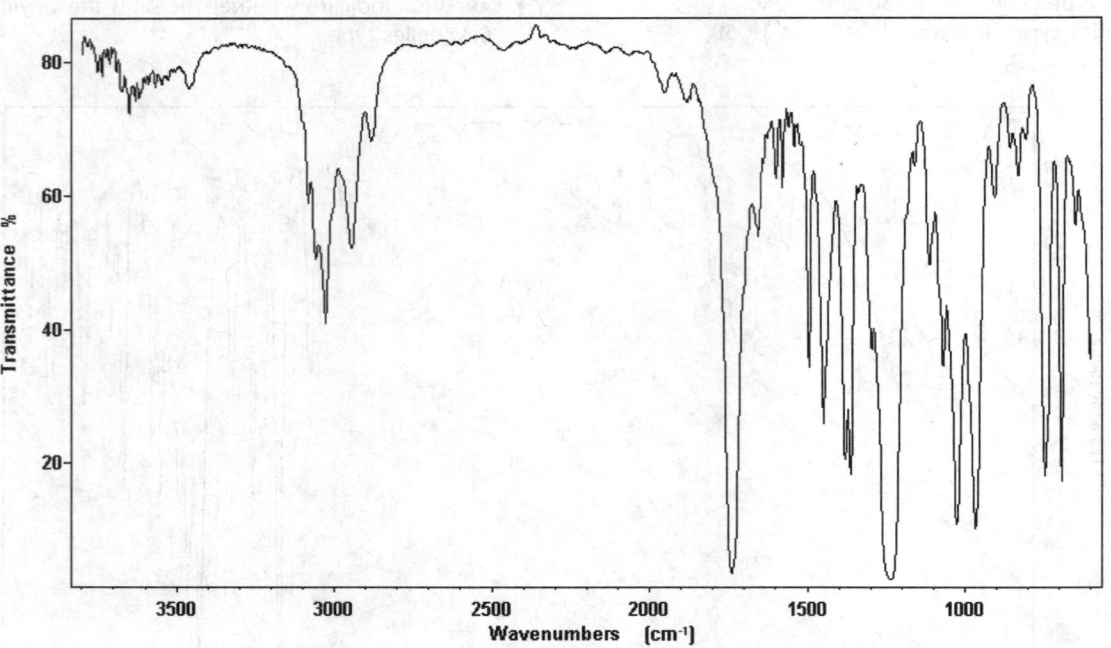

Cinnamyl Acetate

Cinnamyl Alcohol

First Published: Prior to FCC 6

Cinnamic Alcohol

$C_9H_{10}O$ Formula wt 134.18
FEMA: 2294
UNII: SS8YOP444F [cinnamyl alcohol]

DESCRIPTION
Cinnamyl Alcohol occurs as a white to slightly yellow crystalline solid.
Odor: Balsamic
Solubility: Soluble in most fixed oils, propylene glycol; insoluble or practically insoluble in glycerin
Boiling Point: ~258°
Solubility in Alcohol, Appendix VI: One g dissolves in 1 mL of 70% alcohol, and remains in solution on dilution to 10 mL.

Function: Flavoring agent

IDENTIFICATION
- **INFRARED SPECTRA,** Spectrophotometric Identification Tests, Appendix IIIC
  Acceptance criteria: The spectrum of the sample exhibits relative maxima at the same wavelengths as those of the spectrum below.

ASSAY
- **PROCEDURE:** Proceed as directed under M-1b, Appendix XI.
  Acceptance criteria: NLT 98.0% of $C_9H_{10}O$

OTHER REQUIREMENTS
- **ALDEHYDES,** M-1b, Appendix XI
  Acceptance criteria: NMT 1.5%
- **CHLORINATED COMPOUNDS,** Appendix VI
  Acceptance criteria: Passes test
- **SOLIDIFICATION POINT,** Appendix IIB
  Acceptance criteria: NLT 31°

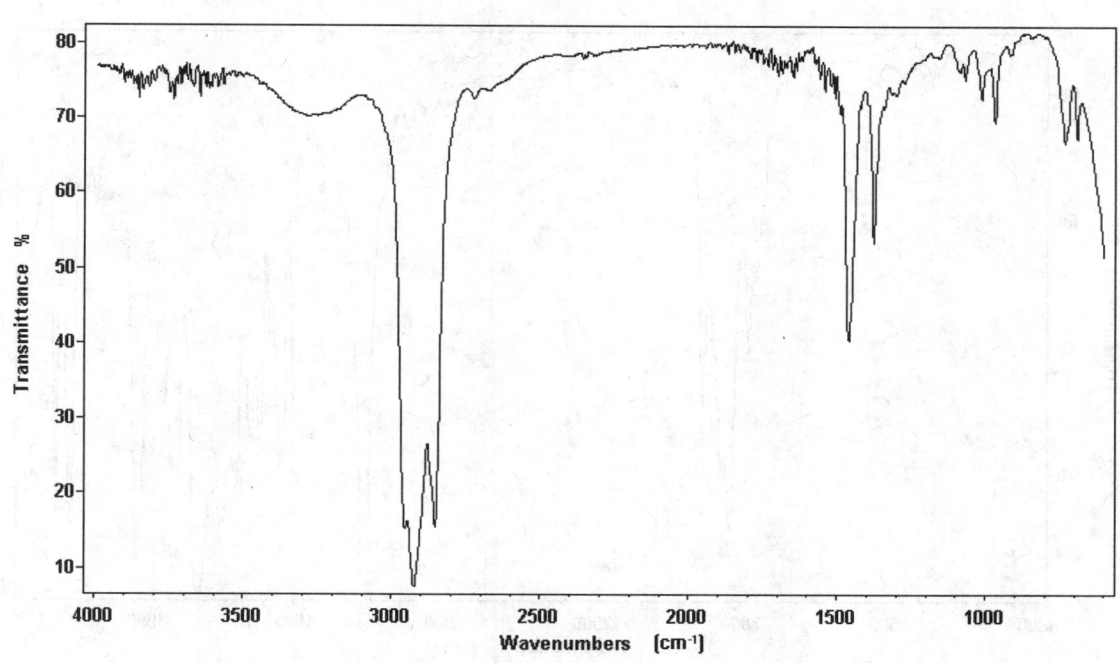

Cinnamyl Alcohol

Cinnamyl Butyrate

First Published: Prior to FCC 6

$C_{13}H_{16}O_2$ Formula wt 204.27
FEMA: 2296
UNII: TKZ9V37P1G [cinnamyl butyrate]

DESCRIPTION
Cinnamyl Butyrate occurs as a colorless to pale yellow liquid.
Odor: Fruity, balsamic
Boiling Point: ~300°
Solubility in Alcohol, Appendix VI: One mL dissolves in 1 mL of 95% alcohol.
Function: Flavoring agent

IDENTIFICATION
- **INFRARED SPECTRA,** *Spectrophotometric Identification Tests,* Appendix IIIC
  Acceptance criteria: The spectrum of the sample exhibits relative maxima at the same wavelengths as those of the spectrum below.

ASSAY
- **PROCEDURE:** Proceed as directed under *M-1b,* Appendix XI.
  Acceptance criteria: NLT 96.0% of $C_{13}H_{16}O_2$

SPECIFIC TESTS
- **ACID VALUE, FLAVOR CHEMICALS (OTHER THAN ESSENTIAL OILS),** *M-15,* Appendix XI
  Acceptance criteria: NMT 1.0
- **REFRACTIVE INDEX,** Appendix II: At 20°
  Acceptance criteria: Between 1.525 and 1.530
- **SPECIFIC GRAVITY:** Determine at 25° by any reliable method (see *General Provisions*).
  Acceptance criteria: Between 1.010 and 1.015

256 / Cinnamyl Butyrate / *Monographs*

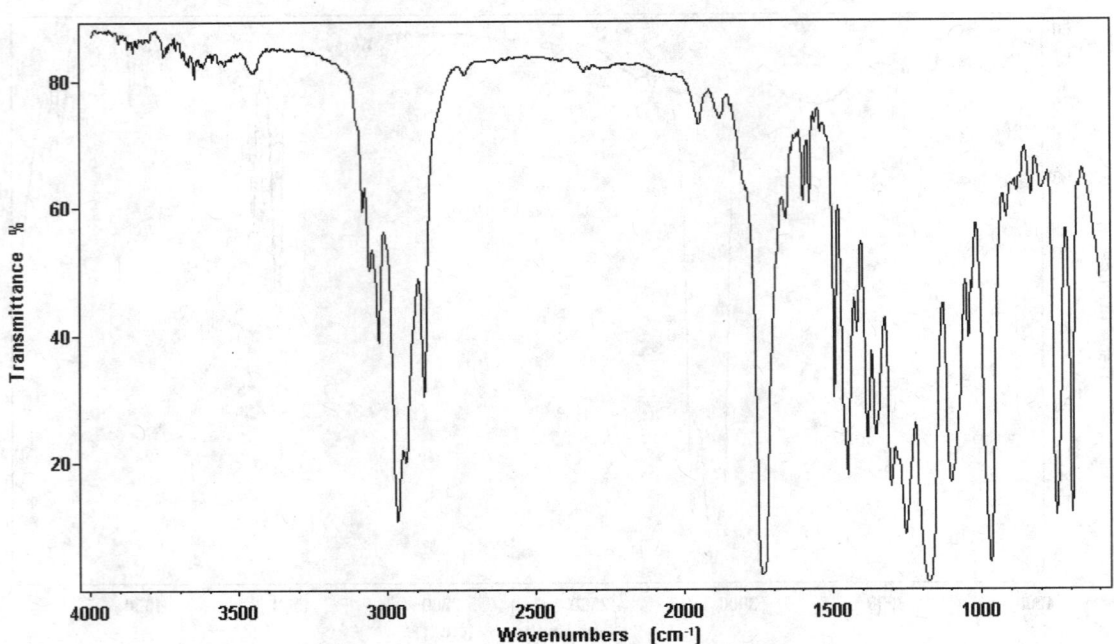

Cinnamyl Butyrate

Cinnamyl Cinnamate

First Published: Prior to FCC 6

$C_{18}H_{16}O_2$ Formula wt 264.32
FEMA: 2298
UNII: F1438569N2 [cinnamyl cinnamate]

DESCRIPTION
Cinnamyl Cinnamate occurs as a mixture of (*Z*) and (*E*) isomers; low-melting solid.
Boiling Point: ~370°
Solubility in Alcohol, Appendix VI: One mL dissolves in 1 mL of 95% alcohol.

Function: Flavoring agent

IDENTIFICATION
- **INFRARED SPECTRA,** *Spectrophotometric Identification Tests,* Appendix IIIC
  Acceptance criteria: The spectrum of the sample exhibits relative maxima at the same wavelengths as those of the spectrum below.

ASSAY
- **PROCEDURE:** Proceed as directed under *M-1b,* Appendix XI.
  Acceptance criteria: NLT 95.0% of $C_{18}H_{16}O_2$

SPECIFIC TESTS
- **ACID VALUE, FLAVOR CHEMICALS (OTHER THAN ESSENTIAL OILS),** *M-15,* Appendix XI
  Acceptance criteria: NMT 2.0

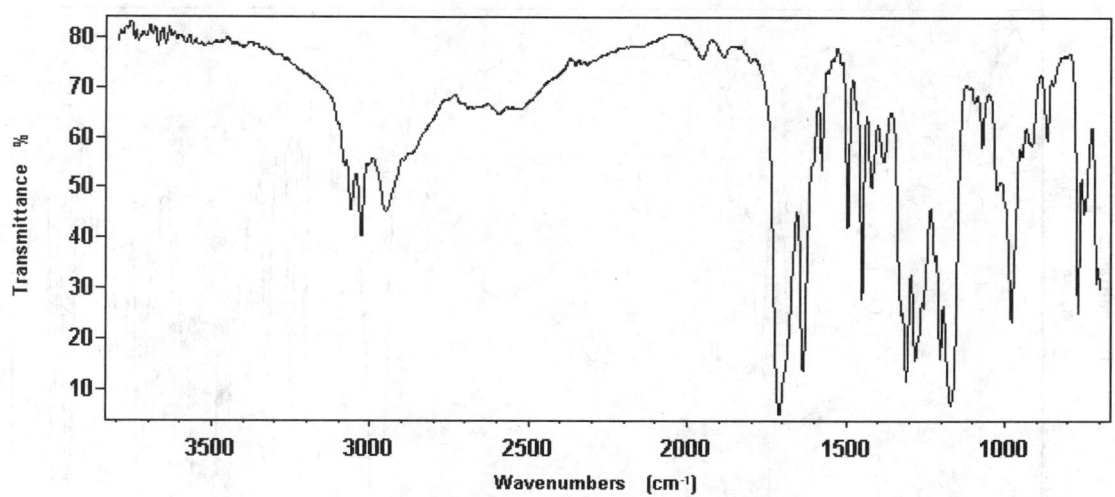

Cinnamyl Cinnamate

Cinnamyl Formate

First Published: Prior to FCC 6

C$_{10}$H$_{10}$O$_2$ Formula wt 162.19
FEMA: 2299
UNII: 896AGS89RD [cinnamyl formate]

DESCRIPTION
Cinnamyl Formate occurs as a colorless to slightly yellow liquid.
Odor: Green, herbaceous, balsamic
Solubility: Miscible in alcohol, chloroform, ether, most fixed oils; insoluble or practically insoluble in water
Boiling Point: ~250°
Solubility in Alcohol, Appendix VI: One mL dissolves in 2 mL of 80% alcohol to give a clear solution.
Function: Flavoring agent

IDENTIFICATION
- **INFRARED SPECTRA,** *Spectrophotometric Identification Tests,* Appendix IIIC
  Acceptance criteria: The spectrum of the sample exhibits relative maxima at the same wavelengths as those of the spectrum below.

ASSAY
- **PROCEDURE:** Proceed as directed under *M-1a,* Appendix XI.
  Acceptance criteria: NLT 92.0% of C$_{10}$H$_{10}$O$_2$

SPECIFIC TESTS
- **ACID VALUE, FLAVOR CHEMICALS (OTHER THAN ESSENTIAL OILS),** *M-15,* Appendix XI
  Acceptance criteria: NMT 3.0
- **REFRACTIVE INDEX,** Appendix II: At 20°
  Acceptance criteria: Between 1.550 and 1.556
- **SPECIFIC GRAVITY:** Determine at 25° by any reliable method (see *General Provisions*).
  Acceptance criteria: Between 1.077 and 1.082

OTHER REQUIREMENTS
- **CINNAMYL ALCOHOL,** *M-1a,* Appendix XI
  Acceptance criteria: NMT 8.0%

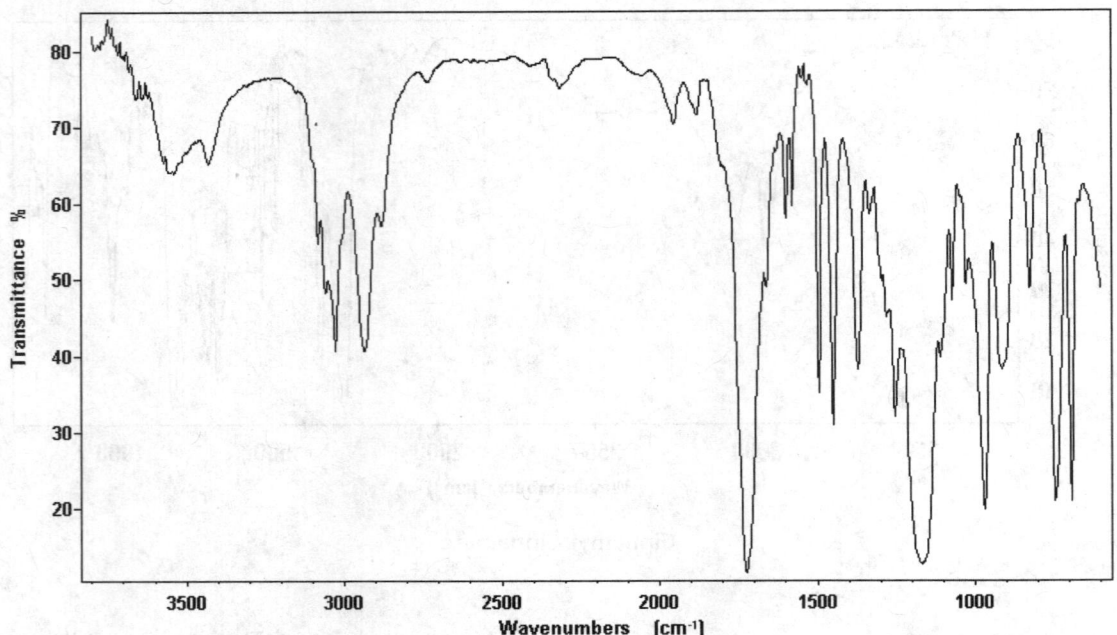

Cinnamyl Formate

Cinnamyl Isobutyrate

First Published: Prior to FCC 6

$C_{13}H_{16}O_2$ Formula wt 204.27
FEMA: 2297
UNII: C286CMK03D [cinnamyl isobutyrate]

DESCRIPTION
Cinnamyl Isobutyrate occurs as a colorless to pale yellow liquid.
Odor: Sweet, balsamic, fruity
Boiling Point: ~254°
Solubility in Alcohol, Appendix VI: One mL dissolves in one mL of 95% alcohol.
Function: Flavoring agent

IDENTIFICATION
- **INFRARED SPECTRA,** *Spectrophotometric Identification Tests,* Appendix IIIC
  Acceptance criteria: The spectrum of the sample exhibits relative maxima at the same wavelengths as those of the spectrum below.

ASSAY
- **PROCEDURE:** Proceed as directed under *M-1b,* Appendix XI.
  Acceptance criteria: NLT 96.0% of $C_{13}H_{16}O_2$

SPECIFIC TESTS
- **ACID VALUE, FLAVOR CHEMICALS (OTHER THAN ESSENTIAL OILS),** *M-15,* Appendix XI
  Acceptance criteria: NMT 3.0
- **REFRACTIVE INDEX,** Appendix II: At 20°
  Acceptance criteria: Between 1.523 and 1.528
- **SPECIFIC GRAVITY:** Determine at 25° by any reliable method (see *General Provisions*).
  Acceptance criteria: Between 1.006 and 1.009

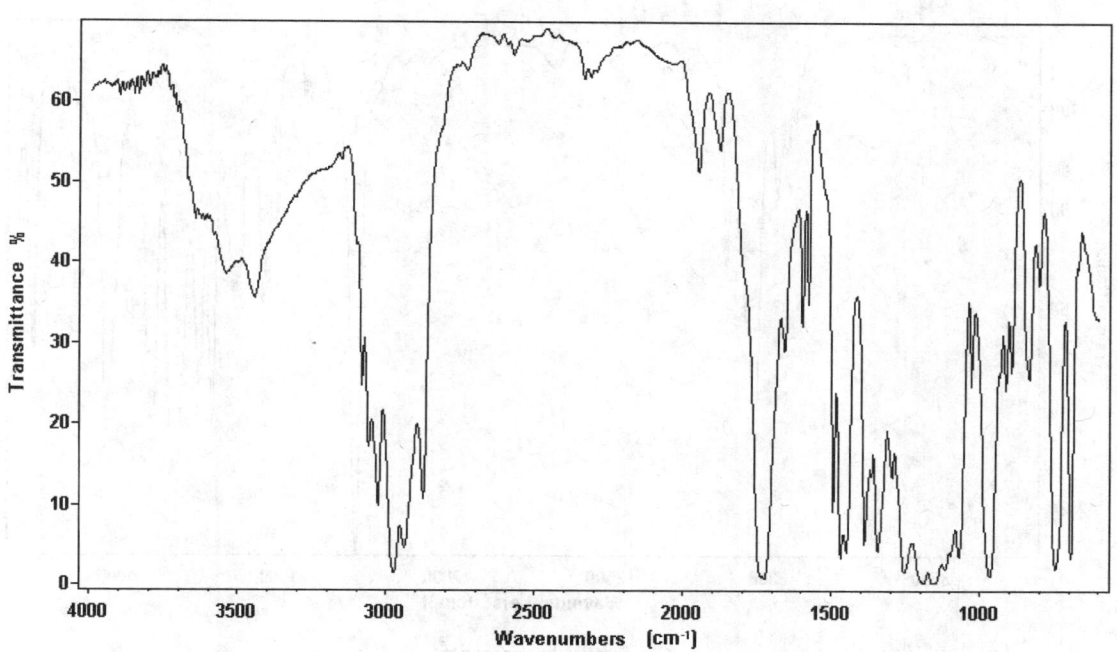

Cinnamyl Isobutyrate

Cinnamyl Isovalerate

First Published: Prior to FCC 6

$C_{14}H_{18}O_2$ Formula wt 218.30
FEMA: 2302
UNII: 5JHK9Y2XRM [cinnamyl isovalerate]

DESCRIPTION
Cinnamyl Isovalerate occurs as a colorless to slightly yellow liquid.
Odor: Spicy, floral, fruity
Solubility: Miscible in alcohol, chloroform, most fixed oils, ether; insoluble or practically insoluble in glycerin, propylene glycol, water
Boiling Point: ~313°
Solubility in Alcohol, Appendix VI: One mL dissolves in 1 mL of 90% alcohol.

Function: Flavoring agent

IDENTIFICATION
- **INFRARED SPECTRA,** *Spectrophotometric Identification Tests,* Appendix IIIC
  Acceptance criteria: The spectrum of the sample exhibits relative maxima at the same wavelengths as those of the spectrum below.

ASSAY
- **PROCEDURE:** Proceed as directed under *M-1b,* Appendix XI.
  Acceptance criteria: NLT 95.0% of $C_{14}H_{18}O_2$ (one major isomer)

SPECIFIC TESTS
- **ACID VALUE, FLAVOR CHEMICALS (OTHER THAN ESSENTIAL OILS),** *M-15,* Appendix XI
  Acceptance criteria: NMT 3.0
- **REFRACTIVE INDEX,** Appendix II: At 20°
  Acceptance criteria: Between 1.518 and 1.524
- **SPECIFIC GRAVITY:** Determine at 25° by any reliable method (see *General Provisions*).
  Acceptance criteria: Between 0.991 and 0.996

260 / Cinnamyl Isovalerate / *Monographs*

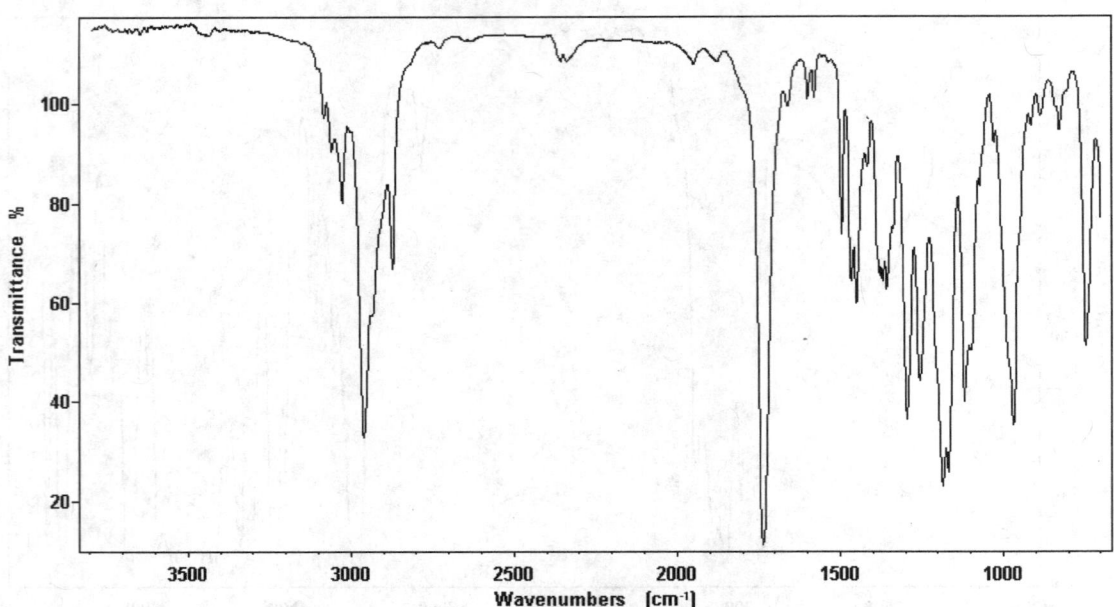

Cinnamyl Isovalerate

Cinnamyl Propionate

First Published: Prior to FCC 6

$C_{12}H_{14}O_2$ Formula wt 190.24
FEMA: 2301
UNII: OI92915815 [cinnamyl propionate]

DESCRIPTION
Cinnamyl Propionate occurs as a colorless to pale yellow liquid.
Odor: Spicy, fruity, balsamic
Solubility: Miscible in alcohol, chloroform, ether, most fixed oils; insoluble or practically insoluble in glycerin, propylene glycol, water
Boiling Point: ~289°
Function: Flavoring agent

IDENTIFICATION
- **INFRARED SPECTRA,** *Spectrophotometric Identification Tests,* Appendix IIIC
  Acceptance criteria: The spectrum of the sample exhibits relative maxima at the same wavelengths as those of the spectrum below.

ASSAY
- **PROCEDURE:** Proceed as directed under *M-1b,* Appendix XI.
  Acceptance criteria: NLT 98.0% of $C_{12}H_{14}O_2$ (one isomer)

SPECIFIC TESTS
- **ACID VALUE, FLAVOR CHEMICALS (OTHER THAN ESSENTIAL OILS),** *M-15,* Appendix XI
  Acceptance criteria: NMT 3.0
- **REFRACTIVE INDEX,** Appendix II: At 20°
  Acceptance criteria: Between 1.532 and 1.537
- **SPECIFIC GRAVITY:** Determine at 25° by any reliable method (see *General Provisions*).
  Acceptance criteria: Between 1.029 and 1.035

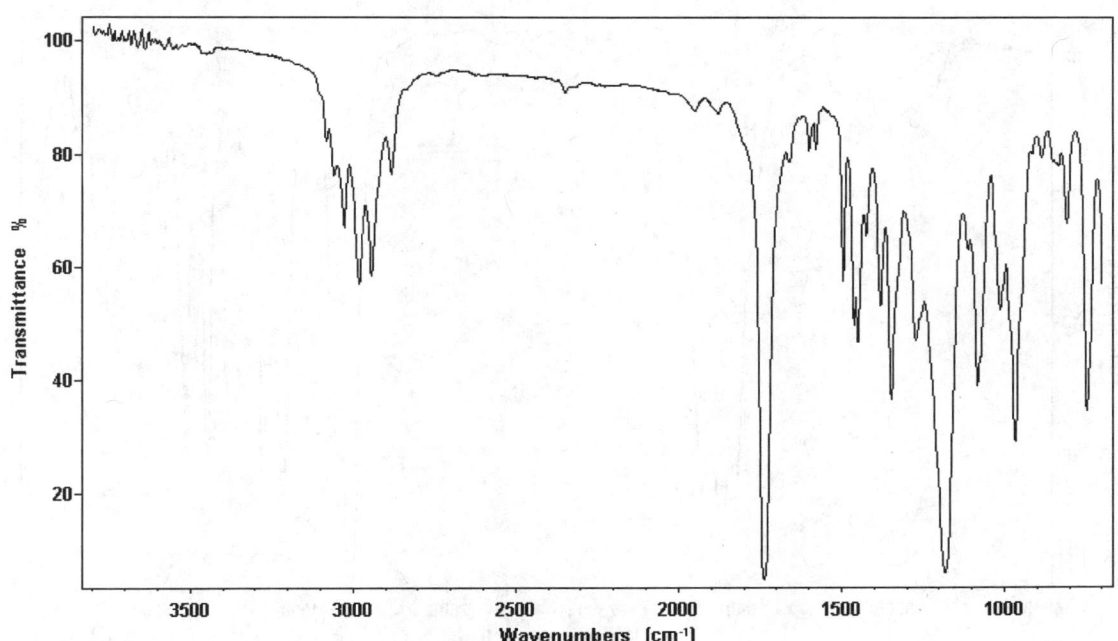

Cinnamyl Propionate

Citral

First Published: Prior to FCC 6
Last Revision: First Supplement, FCC 6

Mixture of Geranial [(*E*)-3,7-dimethyl-2,6-octadien-1-al] and Neral [the (*Z*) isomer]

$C_{10}H_{16}O$ Formula wt 152.24
FEMA: 2303
UNII: T7EU0O9VPP [citral]

DESCRIPTION

Citral occurs as a pale yellow liquid. It may contain a suitable antioxidant.
Odor: Strong, lemon
Solubility: Soluble in most fixed oils, mineral oil, propylene glycol; insoluble or practically insoluble in glycerin
Boiling Point: ~228°
Solubility in Alcohol, Appendix VI: One mL dissolves in 7 mL of 70% alcohol.
Function: Flavoring agent

IDENTIFICATION

- **INFRARED SPECTRA,** *Spectrophotometric Identification Tests,* Appendix IIIC
  Acceptance criteria: The spectrum of the sample exhibits relative maxima at the same wavelengths as those of the spectrum below.

ASSAY

- **PROCEDURE:** Proceed as directed under *M-1b*, Appendix XI.
  Acceptance criteria: NLT 96.0% of $C_{10}H_{16}O$ (sum of neral and geranial)

SPECIFIC TESTS

- **REFRACTIVE INDEX,** Appendix II: At 20°
  Acceptance criteria: Between 1.486 and 1.490
- **SPECIFIC GRAVITY:** Determine at 25° by any reliable method (see *General Provisions*).
  Acceptance criteria: Between 0.885 and 0.891

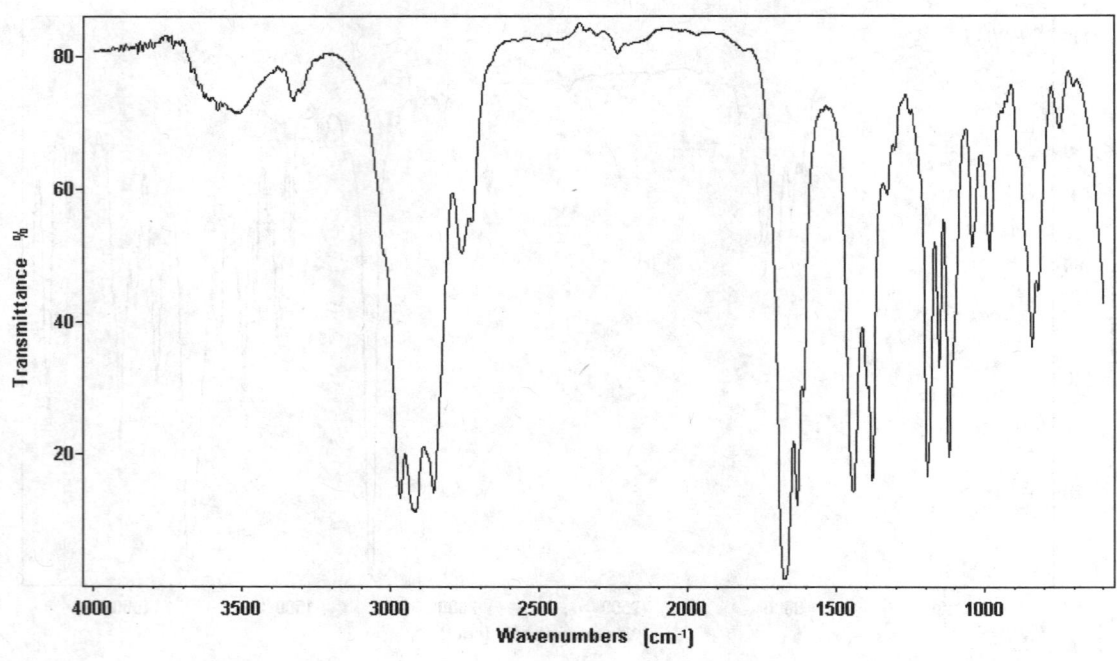

Citral

Citric Acid

First Published: Prior to FCC 6

$C_6H_8O_7$ Formula wt, anhydrous 192.13
$C_6H_8O_7 \cdot H_2O$ Formula wt, monohydrate 210.14
INS: 330   CAS: anhydrous [77-92-9]
                    monohydrate [5949-29-1]
UNII: 2968PHW8QP [citric acid monohydrate]
UNII: XF417D3PSL [anhydrous citric acid]

DESCRIPTION

Citric Acid occurs as colorless, translucent crystals or as a white, granular to fine, crystalline powder. It is anhydrous or contains one molecule of water of hydration. The hydrous form is efflorescent in dry air. It is odorless and has a strongly acid taste. One g is soluble in about 0.5 mL of water, in about 2 mL of alcohol, and in about 30 mL of ether.

Function: Sequestrant; dispersing agent; acidifier; flavoring agent

Packaging and Storage: Store in tight containers.

IDENTIFICATION

- **CITRATE,** Appendix IIIA
  Sample solution: 100 mg/mL
  Acceptance criteria: Passes test

ASSAY

- **PROCEDURE**
  Sample: 3 g
  Analysis: Dissolve the Sample in 40 mL of water, add phenolphthalein TS and titrate with 1 N sodium hydroxide. Each mL of 1 N sodium hydroxide is equivalent to 64.04 mg of $C_6H_8O_7$.
  Acceptance criteria: NLT 99.5% and NMT 100.5% of $C_6H_8O_7$, calculated on the anhydrous basis

IMPURITIES

Inorganic Impurities

- **LEAD,** Lead Limit Test, Atomic Absorption Spectrophotometric Graphite Furnace Method, Method I, Appendix IIIB
  Acceptance criteria: NMT 0.5 mg/kg

Organic Impurities

- **TRIDODECYLAMINE (FOR SOLVENT-EXTRACTED CITRIC ACID ONLY)**
  Buffered indicator solution: Prepare a mixture consisting of 700 mL of 0.1 M citric acid (anhydrous, reagent grade), 200 mL of 0.2 M disodium phosphate, and 50 mL each of 0.2% bromophenol blue and of 0.2% bromocresol green in spectrograde methanol.
  Non-indicator buffer solution: Prepare a mixture consisting of 700 mL of 0.1 M citric acid (anhydrous, reagent grade), 200 mL of 0.2 M disodium phosphate, and 100 mL of spectrograde methanol.
  Standard stock solution: 0.08 mg/mL tridodecylamine in isopropyl alcohol [NOTE—Discard after 3 weeks.]

Standard solution: 4 µg/mL tridodecylamine in isopropyl alcohol: from *Standard stock solution* [NOTE—Prepare this solution fresh on the day of use.]

Sample solution: Either 160 g of anhydrous sample in 320 mL of water, or dissolve 174 g of monohydrate sample in 306 mL of water.

Analysis: Dissolve 160 g of anhydrous, reagent-grade citric acid in 320 mL of water, and divide the solution equally between two 250-mL separatory funnels, S_1 and S_2. Add 5 mL of *Non-indicator buffer solution* to S_1. Add 2.0 mL of *Standard solution* and 5 mL of *Buffered indicator solution* to S_2. Divide the *Sample solution* equally between two additional 250-mL separatory funnels, S_3 and S_4. Add 5 mL of *Non-indicator buffer solution* to S_3 and 5 mL of *Buffered indicator solution* to S_4.

Add 20 mL of a spectrograde chloroform and *n*-heptane (1:1, v/v) to each of the four separatory funnels, shake for 15 min on a mechanical shaker, and allow the phases to separate for 45 min. Drain all except the last few drops of the lower (aqueous) phases, and discard. Add 25 mL of 0.05 N sulfuric acid to the organic phases in each separatory funnel, hand-shake for 30 s, and allow the phases to separate for 30 min. Drain all except the last few drops of the lower (organic) phases through dry Whatman No. 40 (or equivalent) paper and collect the filtrates in separate, small, glass-stoppered containers.

Using a suitable spectrophotometer, determine the absorbance of each solution against chloroform and heptane (1:1, v/v) in a 5-cm cell at 400 nm.

Calculate the *Sample solution* net absorbance (A_U) as the absorbance of S_4 minus the absorbance of S_3. Calculate the *Standard solution* net absorbance (A_S) as the absorbance of S_2 minus the absorbance of S_1.

Acceptance criteria: A_U is NMT A_S (NMT 0.1 mg/kg)

SPECIFIC TESTS
- **OXALATE**
  Sample solution: 100 mg/mL
  Analysis: Neutralize 10 mL of the *Sample solution* with 6 N ammonium hydroxide, add 5 drops of 2.7 N hydrochloric acid, cool, and add 2 mL of calcium chloride TS.
  Acceptance criteria: No turbidity forms.
- **READILY CARBONIZABLE SUBSTANCES**
  Sample: 1.00 ± 0.01 g, finely powdered
  Analysis: Transfer the *Sample* into a 150-mm × 18-mm (od) tube previously rinsed with 10 mL of 95% sulfuric acid at 90° or used exclusively for this test. Add 10 ± 0.1 mL of 95% sulfuric acid, carefully agitate the tube until solution is complete, and immerse the tube in a water bath at 90° ± 1° for 1 h. Occasionally remove the tube from the water bath, and carefully agitate it to ensure that the sample is dissolved and gaseous decomposition products are allowed to escape to the atmosphere. Cool the tube to ambient temperature, carefully shake it to ensure that all gases are removed, and using an adequate spectrophotometer, measure the absorbance and transmission of the solution at 470 nm in a 1-cm cell.
  Acceptance criteria
  Absorbance: NMT 0.52
  Transmission: NLT 30%
- **RESIDUE ON IGNITION (SULFATED ASH)**, Appendix IIC
  Sample: 4 g
  Acceptance criteria: NMT 0.05%
- **WATER**, *Water Determination*, Appendix IIB
  Acceptance criteria
  Anhydrous: NMT 0.5%
  Monohydrate: NMT 8.8%

OTHER REQUIREMENTS
- **LABELING**: Indicate whether it is anhydrous or hydrous.

Citric and Fatty Acid Esters of Glycerol
First Published: Third Supplement, FCC 7

CITREM
Citric Acid Esters of Mono- and Diglycerides
Citroglycerides
INS: 472c

DESCRIPTION
Citric and Fatty Acid Esters of Glycerol occurs as a yellowish to light brown liquid of variable viscosity or as a solid. It consists of mixed esters of citric acid and edible fatty acids with glycerol. It may contain minor amounts of free fatty acids, free glycerol, free citric acid, and mono- and diglycerides, and may be fully or partially neutralized with substances suitable for the purpose (as declared on the label). It is obtained by esterification of glycerol with citric acid and edible fatty acids or by reaction of a mixture of mono- and diglycerides of edible fatty acid with citric acid. Citroglycerides can be differentiated from stearyl citrate by the distinctive amount of stearyl alcohol in the latter. Because the mono- or diglycerides in citroglycerides may include either one or two fatty acids, and because there is a variety of edible fatty acids with chain lengths ranging most commonly from 12 to 18, there is no single molecular or structural formula. It forms a dispersion in hot water; is soluble in oils and fats; insoluble in cold water and in cold ethanol.

Function: Stabilizer; emulsifier; dough conditioner; antioxidant synergist

Packaging and Storage: Store in well-closed containers.

ASSAY
- **TOTAL GLYCERIN**
  Solution A: Mix exactly 99 mL (from a buret) of chloroform and 25 mL of glacial acetic acid in a 1-L volumetric flask.
  Sample solution: Weigh accurately 2 g of sample into a saponification flask, add 50 mL of ethanolic potassium hydroxide solution (0.5 M), and gently boil for 30 min. Quantitatively transfer the content of the saponification flask to the 1-L volumetric flask with *Solution A*, using three 25-mL portions of water. Add about 500 mL of water, and shake vigorously for about 1 min. Dilute with water to volume, mix thoroughly, and set aside for

separation of layers. The aqueous layer result is the *Sample solution*.

Analysis: Pipet 50 mL of acetic periodic acid TS into a series of 400-mL beakers. Prepare two blanks by adding 50 mL of water to each. Pipet 50 mL of the *Sample solution* into one of the beakers containing 50 mL of acetic periodic acid TS, shake gently to mix, cover with a watch glass, and allow to stand 30 min but NMT 90 min. Add 20 mL of 15% ethanolic potassium iodide solution, shake gently to mix, and allow to stand at least 1 min but NMT 5 min. Do not allow to stand in bright or direct sunlight. Add 100 mL of water, and titrate with 0.1 N sodium thiosulfate VS. Use a variable speed electric stirrer to keep the solution thoroughly mixed. Continue the titration until the brown iodine color disappears from the aqueous layer. Add 2 mL of starch TS, and continue the titration until the blue iodine-starch color disappears from both the thin chloroform layer (separated during titration) and the aqueous layer.

Calculate the percentage of total glycerol in the sample taken:

$$\text{Result} = [(B - S) \times N \times K]/W$$

- B = volume of titrant consumed by the blank containing 50 mL of water (mL)
- S = volume of titrant consumed by the *Sample solution* (mL)
- N = exact normality of 0.1 N thiosulfate
- K = molecular weight of glycerin divided by 40, 2.302
- W = weight of the original sample taken (g)

Acceptance criteria: 8%–33%

- **TOTAL FATTY ACID**

  Analysis: Transfer 5 g of sample into a 250-mL round-bottomed flask, add 50 mL of 1 N ethanolic potassium hydroxide, and reflux for 1 h on a water bath. Quantitatively transfer the contents of the saponification flask to a 1000-mL separating funnel, using three 25-mL portions of water, and add 5 drops of methyl orange TS. Cautiously add concentrated hydrochloric acid until the solution color changes clearly to red, and shake well to separate fatty acids. Extract the separated fatty acids with three 100-mL portions of diethyl ether. Combine the extracts, and wash with 50-mL portions of 10% sodium chloride solution until the washed sodium chloride solution becomes neutral. Dry the ether solution with anhydrous sodium sulfate. Then evaporate off ether on a steam bath, leave an additional 10 min on the steam bath, and weigh the residue.

  Acceptance criteria: 37%–81%

- **TOTAL CITRIC ACID**

  [NOTE—In this test, the sample is saponified with an alcoholic potassium hydroxide solution and the fatty acids are removed by extraction. The citric acid present is converted to trimethylsilyl derivatives and analyzed by gas liquid chromatography.]

  Internal standard solution: 1 mg/mL of tartaric acid solution

  Standard stock solution: 3 mg/mL of USP Citric Acid RS solution

  Sample solution: Weigh accurately 1 g of sample into a round-bottomed flask, add 25 mL of 0.5 M ethanolic potassium hydroxide, and reflux for 30 min. Acidify the mixture with hydrochloric acid, and evaporate in a rotary evaporator or by another suitable method. Quantitatively transfer the contents of the flask to a separator, using NMT 50 mL of water, and extract with three 50-mL portions of heptane, discarding the extracts. Transfer the aqueous layer to a 100-mL volumetric flask, neutralize, dilute with water to volume, and mix. Transfer 1 mL of this mixture and 1 mL of the *Internal standard solution* into a 10-mL round-bottom flask, and evaporate to dryness. Add to the flask 1.0 mL of pyridine, 0.2 mL of trimethyl-chlorosilane, 0.4 mL of hexamethyl-disilazane, and 0.1 mL of *N*-methyl-*N*-trimethylsilyl-tri-fluoroacetamide. Cap the flask tightly, and swirl carefully to dissolve completely. Heat the flask in an oven at 60° for 1 h.

  Standard solution: Transfer 1 mL of the *Standard stock solution* and 1 mL of the *Internal standard solution* into a 10-mL round-bottom flask, and evaporate to dryness. Add to the flask 1.0 mL of pyridine, 0.2 mL of trimethyl-chlorosilane, 0.4 mL of hexamethyl-disilazane, and 0.1 mL of *N*-methyl-*N*-trimethylsilyl-tri-fluoroacetamide. Cap the flask tightly, and swirl carefully to dissolve completely. Heat the flask in an oven at 60° for 1 h.

  Chromatographic system, Appendix IIA
  Mode: Gas chromatography
  Detector: Flame ionization
  Column: 1.8-m × 2.0-mm (id) glass column packed with 10% DC-200 on 80- to 100-mesh, chromosorb Q, or equivalent
  Temperature
  Oven: 165°
  Injection block: 240°
  Detector block: 240°
  Carrier gas: Nitrogen
  Flow rate: 24 mL/min
  Injection volume: 5 µL

  Analysis: Separately inject derivatized *Sample solution* and *Standard solution* into the chromatograph. Measure each peak area by a suitable method, and calculate the percentage of citric acid in the sample taken:

  [NOTE—The retention times for citric acid/tartaric acid and tartaric acid are about 2.3 min and 12 min, respectively.]

  $$\text{Result} = R_S \times 100 \times R_O \times 100 \times (W_O/W_S)$$

  - R_S = peak area ratio of citric acid and tartaric acid from the *Sample solution*
  - R_O = peak area ratio of tartaric acid and citric acid from the *Standard solution*
  - W_O = weight of USP Citric Acid RS used in the *Standard solution* (g)
  - W_S = sample weight (g)

  Acceptance criteria: 13%–50%

IMPURITIES

Inorganic Impurities
- **LEAD,** *Lead Limit Test, Flame Atomic Absorption Spectrophotometric Method,* Appendix IIIB
  Sample: 10 g
  Acceptance criteria: NMT 2 mg/kg

SPECIFIC TESTS
- **RESIDUE ON IGNITION (SULFATED ASH),** *Method 1,* Appendix IIC
  Sample: 2 g
  Acceptance criteria: NMT 0.5% for non-neutralized products, NMT 10% for partially or wholly neutralized products
- **FREE GLYCERIN,** *Free Glycerin or Propylene Glycol,* Appendix VII
  Acceptance criteria: NMT 4%

OTHER REQUIREMENTS
- **LABELING:** Indicate substances used to neutralize material.

Citronellal

First Published: Prior to FCC 6
Last Revision: First Supplement, FCC 6

3,7-Dimethyl-6-octen-1-al

$C_{10}H_{18}O$
FEMA: 2307
UNII: QB99VZZ7GZ [citronellal]
Formula wt 154.25

DESCRIPTION
Citronellal occurs as a colorless to slightly yellow liquid. It may contain a suitable antioxidant.

Odor: Intense lemon-citronella-rose
Solubility: Soluble in alcohol, most fixed oils; slightly soluble in propylene glycol; insoluble or practically insoluble in glycerin, water
Boiling Point: ~206°
Solubility in Alcohol, Appendix VI: One mL dissolves in 5 mL of 70% alcohol, and remains clear on dilution.
Function: Flavoring agent

IDENTIFICATION
- **INFRARED SPECTRA,** *Spectrophotometric Identification Tests,* Appendix IIIC
  Acceptance criteria: The spectrum of the sample exhibits relative maxima at the same wavelengths as those of the spectrum below.

ASSAY
- **PROCEDURE:** Proceed as directed under *M-1b,* Appendix XI.
  Acceptance criteria: NLT 85.0% of aldehydes as $C_{10}H_{18}O$ (one isomer)

SPECIFIC TESTS
- **ACID VALUE, FLAVOR CHEMICALS (OTHER THAN ESSENTIAL OILS),** *M-15,* Appendix XI
  Acceptance criteria: NMT 3.0
- **REFRACTIVE INDEX,** Appendix II: At 20°
  Acceptance criteria: Between 1.446 and 1.456
- **SPECIFIC GRAVITY:** Determine at 25° by any reliable method (see *General Provisions*).
  Acceptance criteria: Between 0.850 and 0.860

OTHER REQUIREMENTS
- **ANGULAR ROTATION,** *Optical (Specific) Rotation,* Appendix IIB: Use a 100-mm tube.
  Acceptance criteria: Between −1° and +11°

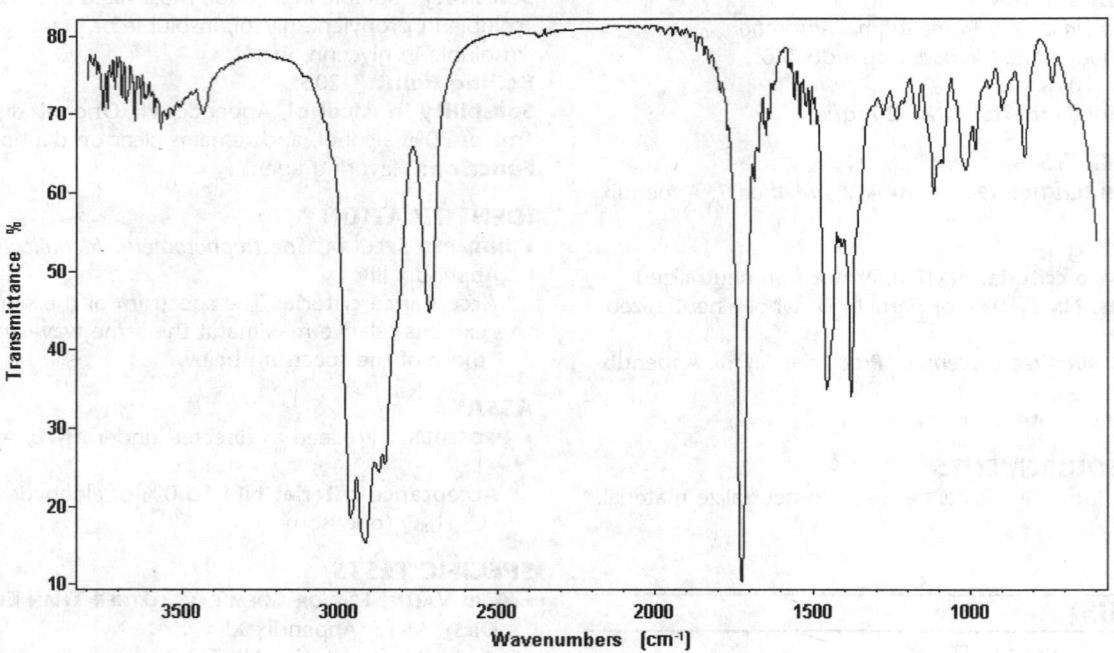

Citronellal

Citronellol

First Published: Prior to FCC 6

3,7-Dimethyl-6-octen-1-ol

$C_{10}H_{20}O$ Formula wt 156.27
FEMA: 2309
UNII: P01OUT964K [β-citronellol, (r)-]

DESCRIPTION
Citronellol occurs as a colorless, oily liquid.
Odor: Rosy
Solubility: Soluble in most fixed oils, propylene glycol; slightly soluble in water; insoluble or practically insoluble in glycerin
Boiling Point: ~225°
Solubility in Alcohol, Appendix VI: One mL dissolves in 2 mL of 70% alcohol and remains in solution on dilution to 10 mL.
Function: Flavoring agent

IDENTIFICATION
- **INFRARED SPECTRA,** Spectrophotometric Identification Tests, Appendix IIIC
  Acceptance criteria: The spectrum of the sample exhibits relative maxima at the same wavelengths as those of the spectrum below.

ASSAY
- **PROCEDURE:** Proceed as directed under Total Alcohols, Appendix VI.
  Sample: 1.2 g
  Analysis: Use 78.13 as the equivalence factor (e).
  Acceptance criteria: NLT 90.0% of total alcohols as $C_{10}H_{20}O$

SPECIFIC TESTS
- **REFRACTIVE INDEX,** Appendix II: At 20°
  Acceptance criteria: Between 1.454 and 1.462
- **SPECIFIC GRAVITY:** Determine at 25° by any reliable method (see General Provisions).
  Acceptance criteria: Between 0.850 and 0.860

OTHER REQUIREMENTS
- **ALDEHYDES,** M-2d, Appendix XI
  Sample: 5 g
  Analysis: Use 66.08 as the equivalence factor (e).
  Acceptance criteria: NMT 1.0% as citronellal
- **ESTERS,** Appendix VI
  Sample: 5 g
  Analysis: Use 99.15 as the equivalence factor (e).
  Acceptance criteria: NMT 1.0% as citronellyl acetate

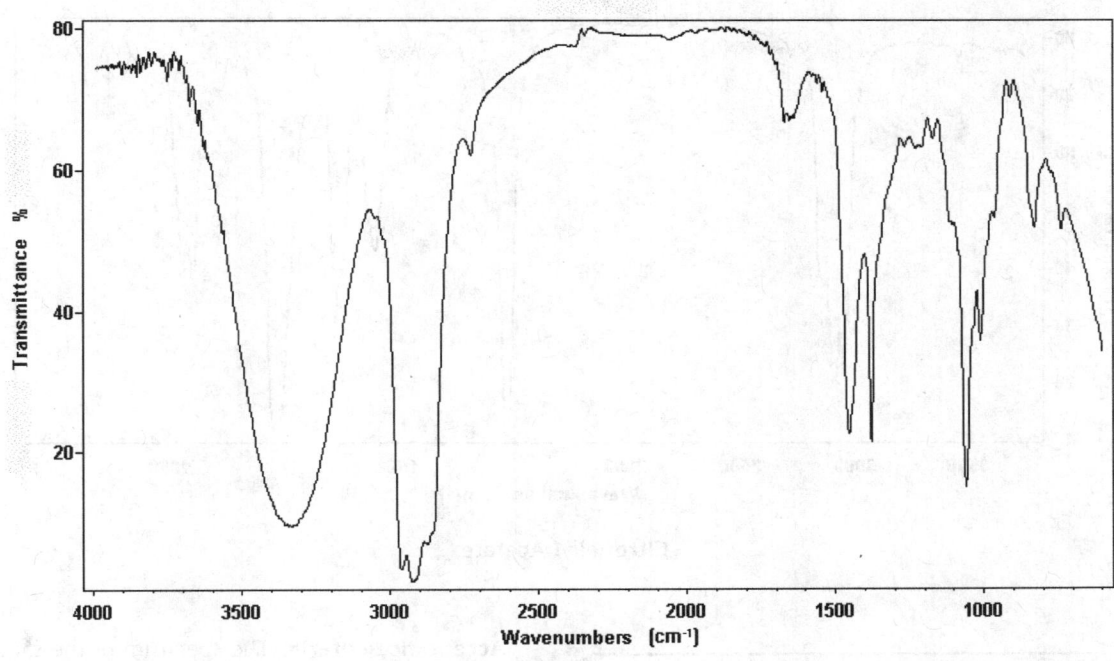

Citronellol

Citronellyl Acetate

First Published: Prior to FCC 6

3,7-Dimethyl-6-octen-1-yl Acetate

$C_{12}H_{22}O_2$ Formula wt 198.31
FEMA: 2311
UNII: IZ420RT3OY [citronellyl acetate]

DESCRIPTION
Citronellyl Acetate occurs as a colorless liquid.
Odor: Fruity
Solubility: Soluble in alcohol, most fixed oils; insoluble or practically insoluble in glycerin, propylene glycol, water
Boiling Point: ~229°
Solubility in Alcohol, Appendix VI: One mL dissolves in 9 mL of 70% alcohol.
Function: Flavoring agent

IDENTIFICATION
- **INFRARED SPECTRA,** *Spectrophotometric Identification Tests,* Appendix IIIC
  Acceptance criteria: The spectrum of the sample exhibits relative maxima at the same wavelengths as those of the spectrum below.

ASSAY
- **PROCEDURE:** Proceed as directed under *Esters,* Appendix VI.
  Sample: 1.4 g
  Analysis: Use 99.15 as the equivalence factor (e).
  Acceptance criteria: NLT 92.0% of total esters as $C_{12}H_{22}O_2$

SPECIFIC TESTS
- **ACID VALUE, FLAVOR CHEMICALS (OTHER THAN ESSENTIAL OILS),** *M-15,* Appendix XI
  Acceptance criteria: NMT 1.0
- **REFRACTIVE INDEX,** Appendix II: At 20°
  Acceptance criteria: Between 1.440 and 1.450
- **SPECIFIC GRAVITY:** Determine at 25° by any reliable method (see *General Provisions*).
  Acceptance criteria: Between 0.883 and 0.893

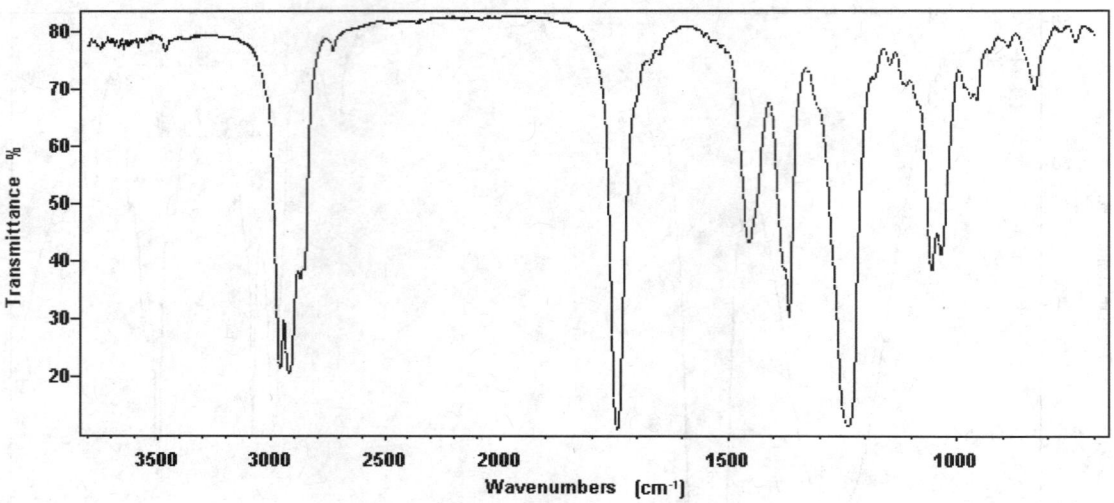

Citronellyl Acetate

Citronellyl Butyrate
First Published: Prior to FCC 6

3,7-Dimethyl-6-octen-1-yl Butyrate

$C_{14}H_{26}O_2$ Formula wt 226.36
FEMA: 2312
UNII: IY68QPD54V [citronellyl butyrate]

DESCRIPTION
Citronellyl Butyrate occurs as a colorless liquid.
Odor: Strong, fruity-rosy
Solubility: Miscible in alcohol, ether, most fixed oils, chloroform; insoluble or practically insoluble in water
Boiling Point: ~245°
Solubility in Alcohol, Appendix VI: One mL dissolves in 6 mL of 80% alcohol to give a clear solution.
Function: Flavoring agent

IDENTIFICATION
- **INFRARED SPECTRA,** *Spectrophotometric Identification Tests,* Appendix IIIC
  Acceptance criteria: The spectrum of the sample exhibits relative maxima at the same wavelengths as those of the spectrum below.

ASSAY
- **PROCEDURE:** Proceed as directed under *Esters,* Appendix VI.
  Sample: 1.5 g
  Analysis: Use 113.2 as the equivalence factor (e).
  Acceptance criteria: NLT 90.0% of total esters as $C_{14}H_{26}O_2$

SPECIFIC TESTS
- **ACID VALUE, FLAVOR CHEMICALS (OTHER THAN ESSENTIAL OILS),** *M-15,* Appendix XI
  Acceptance criteria: NMT 1.0
- **REFRACTIVE INDEX,** Appendix II: At 20°
  Acceptance criteria: Between 1.444 and 1.448
- **SPECIFIC GRAVITY:** Determine at 25° by any reliable method (see *General Provisions*).
  Acceptance criteria: Between 0.873 and 0.883

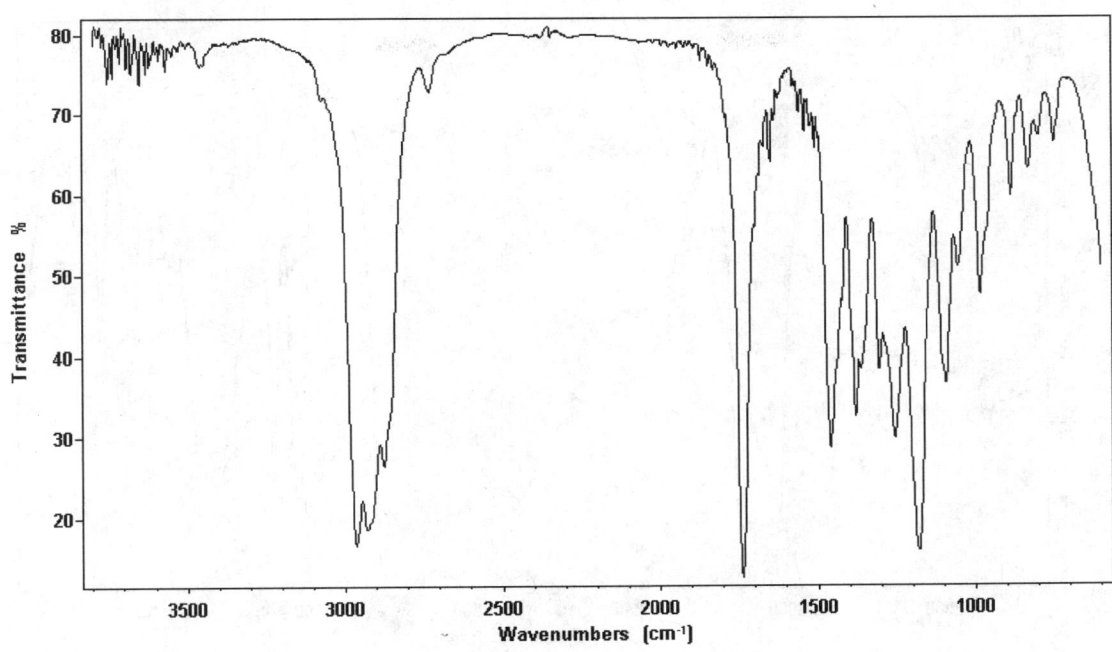

Citronellyl Butyrate

Citronellyl Formate

First Published: Prior to FCC 6

3,7-Dimethyl-6-octen-1-yl Formate

$C_{11}H_{20}O_2$
FEMA: 2314
UNII: 7B1MY2BRDK [citronellyl formate]

Formula wt 184.28

DESCRIPTION
Citronellyl Formate occurs as a colorless liquid.
Odor: Strong, fruity, floral
Solubility: Soluble in alcohol, most fixed oils; slightly soluble in propylene glycol; insoluble or practically insoluble in glycerin, water
Boiling Point: ~235°
Solubility in Alcohol, Appendix VI: One mL dissolves in 3 mL of 80% alcohol, and remains in solution upon dilution to 10 mL.
Function: Flavoring agent

IDENTIFICATION
- **INFRARED SPECTRA,** *Spectrophotometric Identification Tests,* Appendix IIIC
  Acceptance criteria: The spectrum of the sample exhibits relative maxima at the same wavelengths as those of the spectrum below.

ASSAY
- **PROCEDURE:** Proceed as directed under *Esters,* Appendix VI.
  Sample: 1.0 g
  Analysis: Use 92.14 as the equivalence factor (e).
  Acceptance criteria: NLT 86.0% of total esters as $C_{11}H_{20}O_2$

SPECIFIC TESTS
- **ACID VALUE, FLAVOR CHEMICALS (OTHER THAN ESSENTIAL OILS),** *M-15,* Appendix XI
  Acceptance criteria: NMT 3.0
- **REFRACTIVE INDEX,** Appendix II: At 20°
  Acceptance criteria: Between 1.443 and 1.452
- **SPECIFIC GRAVITY:** Determine at 25° by any reliable method (see *General Provisions*).
  Acceptance criteria: Between 0.890 and 0.903

Citronellyl Formate

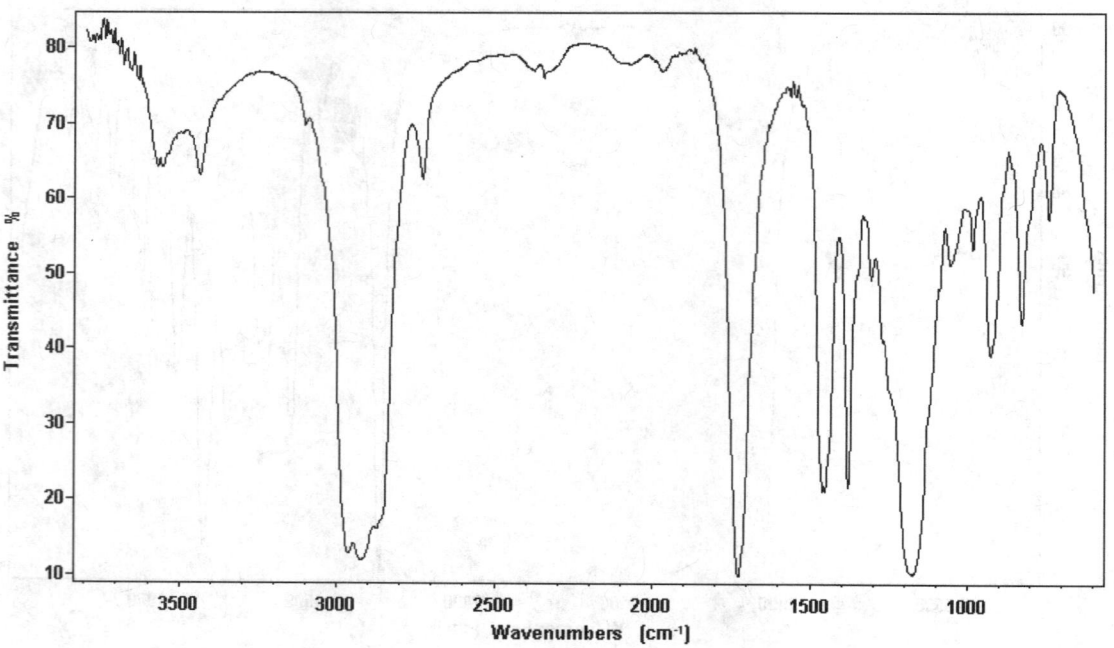

Citronellyl Formate

Citronellyl Isobutyrate

First Published: Prior to FCC 6

3,7-Dimethyl-6-octen-1-yl Isobutyrate

$C_{14}H_{26}O_2$ Formula wt 226.36
FEMA: 2313
UNII: 5RZR3JKW1P [citronellyl isobutyrate]

DESCRIPTION
Citronellyl Isobutyrate occurs as a colorless liquid.
Odor: Fruity-rosy
Solubility: Miscible in alcohol, chloroform, ether, most fixed oils; insoluble or practically insoluble in water
Boiling Point: ~249°
Solubility in Alcohol, Appendix VI: One mL dissolves in 6 mL of 80% alcohol to give a clear solution.
Function: Flavoring agent

IDENTIFICATION
- **INFRARED SPECTRA,** Spectrophotometric Identification Tests, Appendix IIIC
  Acceptance criteria: The spectrum of the sample exhibits relative maxima at the same wavelengths as those of the spectrum below.

ASSAY
- **PROCEDURE:** Proceed as directed under Esters, Appendix VI.
  Sample: 1.5 g
  Analysis: Use 113.2 as the equivalence factor (e).
  Acceptance criteria: NLT 92.0% of total esters as $C_{14}H_{26}O_2$

SPECIFIC TESTS
- **ACID VALUE, FLAVOR CHEMICALS (OTHER THAN ESSENTIAL OILS),** M-15, Appendix XI
  Acceptance criteria: NMT 1.0
- **REFRACTIVE INDEX,** Appendix II: At 20°
  Acceptance criteria: Between 1.440 and 1.448
- **SPECIFIC GRAVITY:** Determine at 25° by any reliable method (see General Provisions).
  Acceptance criteria: Between 0.870 and 0.880

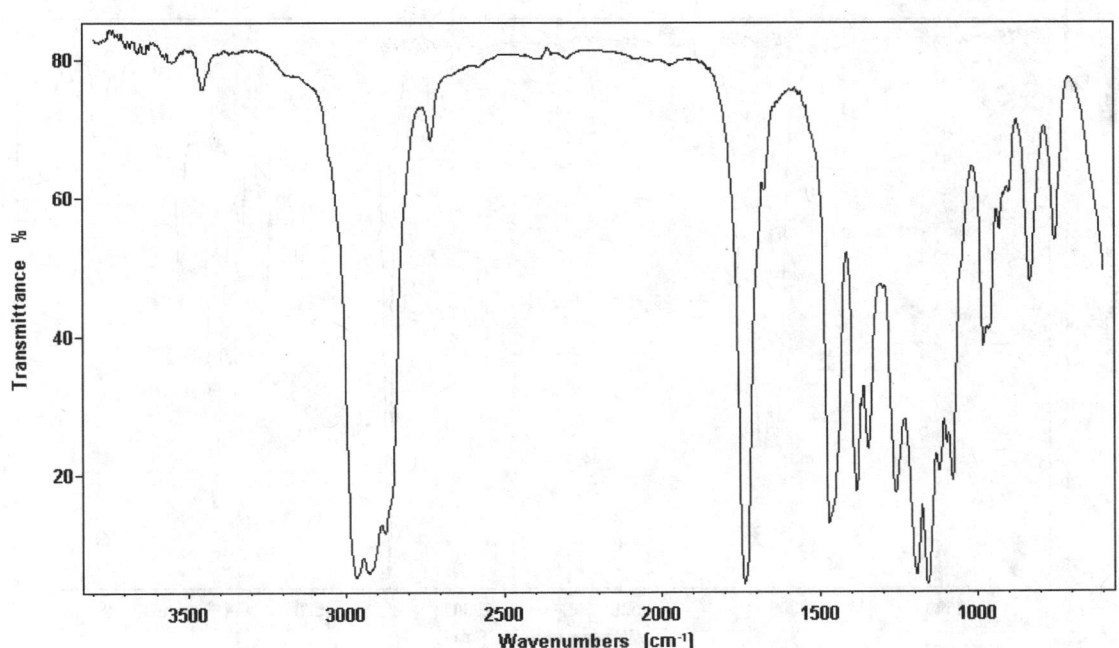

Citronellyl Isobutyrate

Citronellyl Propionate

First Published: Prior to FCC 6

Citronellyl Propanoate
3,7-Dimethyl-6-octen-1-yl Propionate

$C_{13}H_{24}O_2$ Formula wt 212.33
FEMA: 2316
UNII: 87R1092U7J [citronellyl propionate]

DESCRIPTION
Citronellyl Propionate occurs as a colorless liquid.
Odor: Fruity-rosy
Solubility: Miscible in alcohol, most fixed oils; insoluble or practically insoluble in water
Boiling Point: ~242°
Solubility in Alcohol, Appendix VI: One mL dissolves in 4 mL of 80% alcohol to give a clear solution.
Function: Flavoring agent

IDENTIFICATION
- **INFRARED SPECTRA,** Spectrophotometric Identification Tests, Appendix IIIC

  Acceptance criteria: The spectrum of the sample exhibits relative maxima at the same wavelengths as those of the spectrum below.

ASSAY
- **PROCEDURE:** Proceed as directed under Esters, Appendix VI.
  Sample: 1.2 g
  Analysis: Use 95.12 as the equivalence factor (e).
  Acceptance criteria: NLT 90.0% of total esters as $C_{13}H_{24}O_2$

SPECIFIC TESTS
- **ACID VALUE, FLAVOR CHEMICALS (OTHER THAN ESSENTIAL OILS),** M-15, Appendix XI
  Acceptance criteria: NMT 1.0
- **REFRACTIVE INDEX,** Appendix II: At 20°
  Acceptance criteria: Between 1.443 and 1.449
- **SPECIFIC GRAVITY:** Determine at 25° by any reliable method (see General Provisions).
  Acceptance criteria: Between 0.877 and 0.886

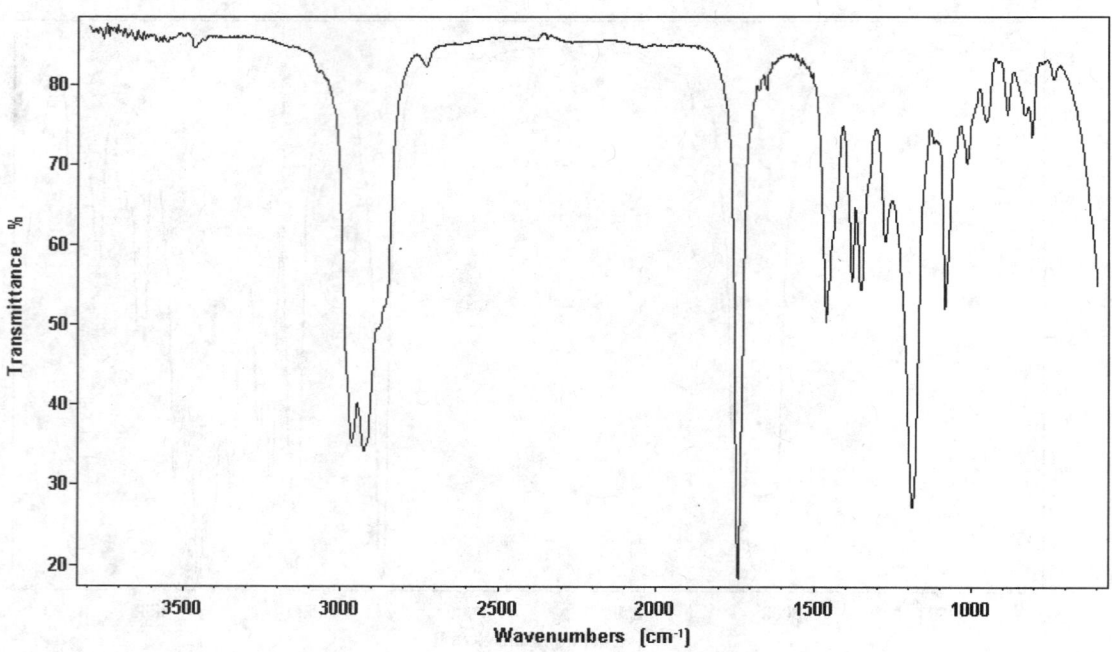

Citronellyl Propionate

Clary Oil

First Published: Prior to FCC 6

Clary Sage Oil

CAS: [8016-63-5]

UNII: 87L0D4U3M0 [clary sage oil]

DESCRIPTION
Clary Oil occurs as a pale yellow to yellow liquid with a herbaceous odor and a winy bouquet. It is the oil obtained by steam distillation from the flowering tops and leaves of the clary sage plant, *Salvia sclarea* L. (Fam. Labiatae). It is soluble in most fixed oils, and in mineral oil up to 3 volumes, but it becomes opalescent on further dilution. It is insoluble in glycerin and in propylene glycol.

Function: Flavoring agent

Packaging and Storage: Store in a cool place protected from light in full, tight containers that are made from steel or aluminum and that are suitably lined.

IDENTIFICATION
- **INFRARED SPECTRA**, *Spectrophotometric Identification Tests*, Appendix IIIC
  Acceptance criteria: The spectrum of the sample exhibits relative maxima at the same wavelengths as those of the spectrum below.

ASSAY
- **ESTERS**, *Ester Determination*, Appendix VI
  Sample: 2 g
  Analysis: Use 98.15 as the equivalence factor (e) in the calculation.
  Acceptance criteria: NLT 48.0% and NMT 75.0% of esters, calculated as linalyl acetate ($C_{12}H_{20}O_2$)

SPECIFIC TESTS
- **ACID VALUE (ESSENTIAL OILS AND FLAVORS)**, Appendix VI
  Acceptance criteria: NMT 2.5
- **ANGULAR ROTATION**, *Optical (Specific) Rotation*, Appendix IIB: Use a 100-mm tube.
  Acceptance criteria: Between −6° and −20°
- **REFRACTIVE INDEX**, Appendix IIB
  [NOTE—Use an Abbé or other refractometer of equal or greater accuracy.]
  Acceptance criteria: Between 1.458 and 1.473 at 20°
- **SOLUBILITY IN ALCOHOL**, Appendix VI
  Acceptance criteria: One mL of sample dissolves in 3 mL of 90% alcohol and becomes opalescent on further dilution.
- **SPECIFIC GRAVITY:** Determine by any reliable method (see *General Provisions*).
  Acceptance criteria: Between 0.886 and 0.929

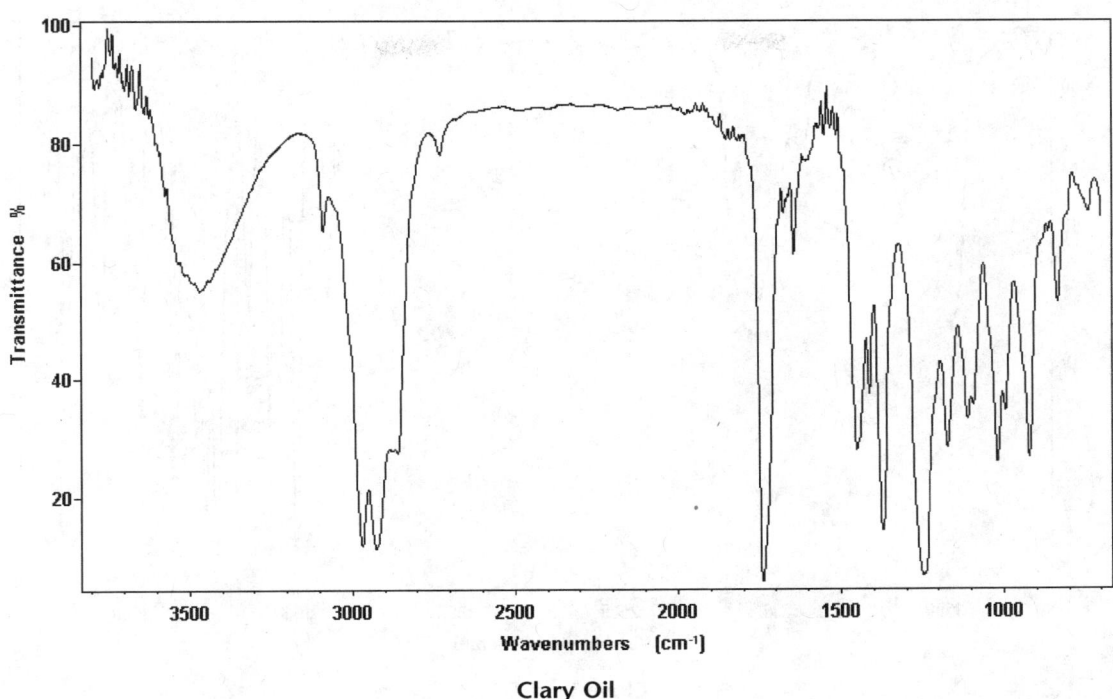

Clary Oil

Clove Leaf Oil

First Published: Prior to FCC 6

CAS: [8015-97-2]

UNII: VCA5491KVF [clove leaf oil]

DESCRIPTION
Clove Leaf Oil occurs as a pale yellow liquid with a sharp, spicy, peppery odor and taste. It is the volatile oil obtained by steam distillation of the leaves of *Eugenia caryophyllata* Thunberg (*Eugenia aromatica* L. Baill.) (Fam. Myrtaceae). It is soluble in propylene glycol and in most fixed oils with slight opalescence, and it is relatively insoluble in glycerin and in mineral oil.

Function: Flavoring agent

Packaging and Storage: Store in a cool place protected from light in full, tight containers that are made from steel or aluminum and that are suitably lined.

IDENTIFICATION
- **INFRARED SPECTRA**, *Spectrophotometric Identification Tests,* Appendix IIIC
  Acceptance criteria: The spectrum of the sample exhibits relative maxima at the same wavelengths as those of the spectrum below.

ASSAY
- **PHENOLS**, Appendix VI
  Sample: Pretreat a suitable quantity of sample by shaking it with 2% powdered tartaric acid for about 2 min, and filtering.
  Analysis: Modify the test by heating the cassia flask in a boiling water bath for 10 min after shaking the pretreated *Sample* with 1 N potassium hydroxide. Remove from the boiling water bath, cool, and proceed as directed.
  Acceptance criteria: NLT 84.0% and NMT 88.0%, by volume, of phenols

SPECIFIC TESTS
- **ANGULAR ROTATION,** *Optical (Specific) Rotation,* Appendix IIB: Use a 100-mm tube.
  Acceptance criteria: Between −2° and 0°
- **REFRACTIVE INDEX,** Appendix IIB
  [NOTE—Use an Abbé or other refractometer of equal or greater accuracy.]
  Acceptance criteria: Between 1.531 and 1.535 at 20°
- **SOLUBILITY IN ALCOHOL,** Appendix VI
  Acceptance criteria: One mL of sample dissolves in 2 mL of 70% alcohol. A slight opalescence may occur when additional solvent is added.
- **SPECIFIC GRAVITY:** Determine by any reliable method (see *General Provisions*).
  Acceptance criteria: Between 1.036 and 1.046

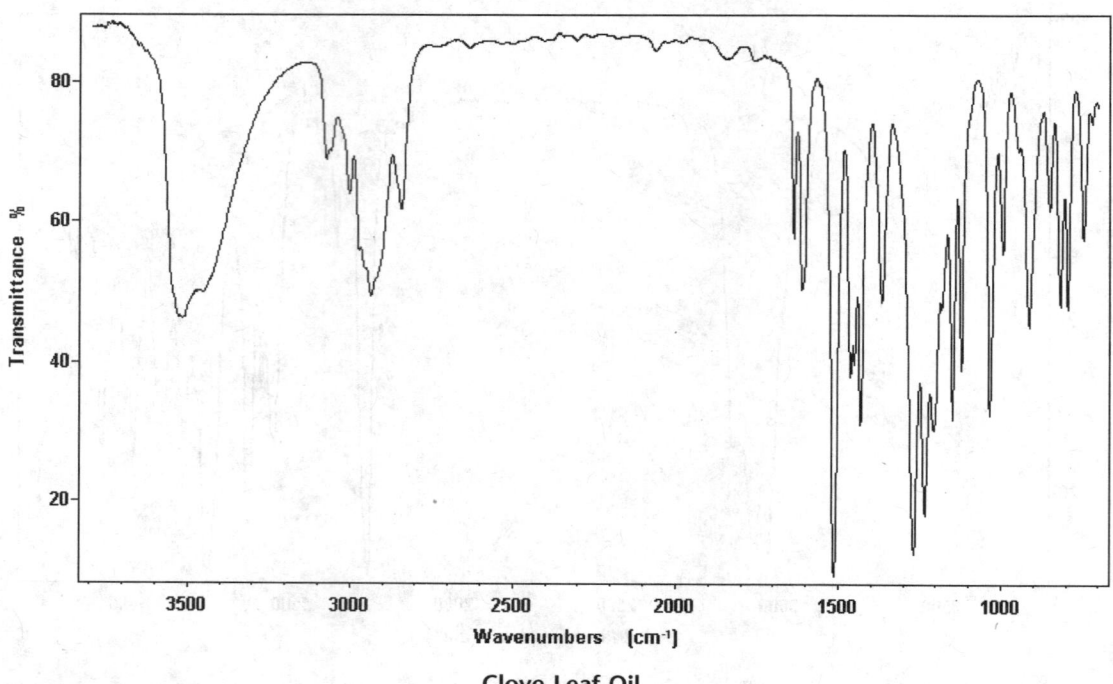

Clove Leaf Oil

Clove Oil

First Published: Prior to FCC 6

Clove Bud Oil

CAS: [8000-34-8]

UNII: 578389D6D0 [clove oil]

DESCRIPTION
Clove Oil occurs as a colorless or pale yellow liquid with a sharp, spicy odor and taste. It is the volatile oil obtained by steam distillation from the dried flower buds of *Eugenia caryophyllata* Thunberg (*Eugenia aromatica* L. Baill.) (Fam. Myrtaceae). It darkens and thickens upon aging or exposure to air.

Function: Flavoring agent

Packaging and Storage: Store in aluminum or tin- or epoxyphenolic-lined, tight, light-resistant containers, and avoid exposure to excessive heat.

IDENTIFICATION
- **INFRARED SPECTRA,** *Spectrophotometric Identification Tests,* Appendix IIIC
  Acceptance criteria: The spectrum of the sample exhibits relative maxima at the same wavelengths as those of the spectrum below.

ASSAY
- **PHENOLS,** Appendix VI
  Acceptance criteria: NLT 85.0%, by volume, of phenols

SPECIFIC TESTS
- **ANGULAR ROTATION,** *Optical (Specific) Rotation,* Appendix IIB: Use a 100-mm tube.
  Acceptance criteria: Between −1.5° and 0°
- **PHENOLS**
  Sample: 1 mL
  Analysis: Shake the *Sample* with 20 mL of hot water. The water shows no more than a scarcely perceptible acid reaction with blue litmus paper. Cool the mixture, pass the water layer through a wetted filter, and treat the clear filtrate with 1 drop of ferric chloride TS.
  Acceptance criteria: The mixture has only a transient gray-green color, but not a blue or violet color.
- **REFRACTIVE INDEX,** Appendix IIB
  [NOTE—Use an Abbé or other refractometer of equal or greater accuracy.]
  Acceptance criteria: Between 1.527 and 1.535 at 20°
- **SOLUBILITY IN ALCOHOL,** Appendix VI
  Acceptance criteria: One mL of sample dissolves in 2 mL of 70% alcohol.
- **SPECIFIC GRAVITY:** Determine by any reliable method (see *General Provisions*).
  Acceptance criteria: Between 1.038 and 1.060

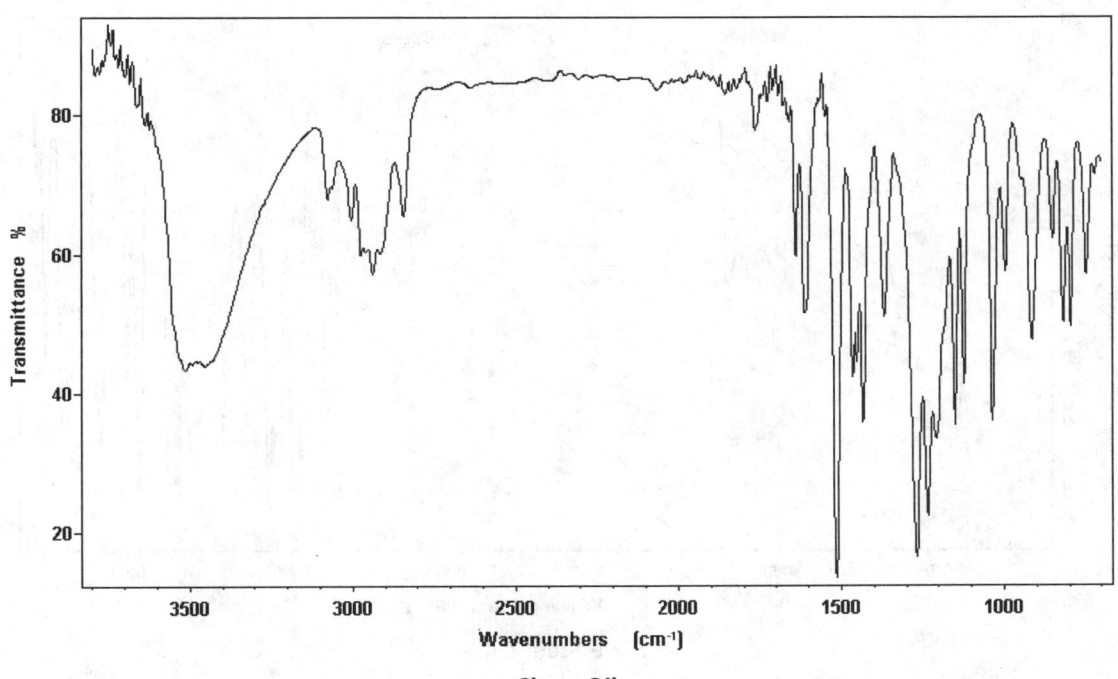
Clove Oil

Clove Stem Oil

First Published: Prior to FCC 6

CAS: [8015-98-3]

UNII: 9368YZM9M4 [clove stem oil]

DESCRIPTION
Clove Stem Oil occurs as a yellow to light brown liquid with a sharp, spicy odor and taste. It is the volatile oil obtained by steam distillation from the dried stems of the buds of *Eugenia caryophyllata* Thunberg (*Eugenia aromatica* L. Baill.) (Fam. Myrtaceae). It is soluble in fixed oils and in propylene glycol, but it is relatively insoluble in glycerin and in mineral oil.
Function: Flavoring agent
Packaging and Storage: Store in a cool place protected from light in full, tight containers that are made from steel or aluminum and that are suitably lined.

IDENTIFICATION
- **INFRARED SPECTRA**, *Spectrophotometric Identification Tests*, Appendix IIIC
  Acceptance criteria: The spectrum of the sample exhibits relative maxima at the same wavelengths as those of the spectrum below.

ASSAY
- **PHENOLS,** Appendix VI
  Sample: Pretreat a suitable quantity of sample by shaking it with 2% powdered tartaric acid for about 2 min and filtering.
  Analysis: Modify the test by heating the cassia flask in a boiling water bath for 10 min after shaking the pretreated *Sample* with 1 N potassium hydroxide. Remove from the boiling water bath, cool, and proceed as directed.
  Acceptance criteria: NLT 89.0% and NMT 95.0%, by volume, of phenols

SPECIFIC TESTS
- **ANGULAR ROTATION,** *Optical (Specific) Rotation,* Appendix IIB: Use a 100-mm tube.
- **REFRACTIVE INDEX,** Appendix IIB
  [NOTE—Use an Abbé or other refractometer of equal or greater accuracy.]
  Acceptance criteria: Between 1.534 and 1.538 at 20°
- **SPECIFIC GRAVITY:** Determine by any reliable method (see *General Provisions*).

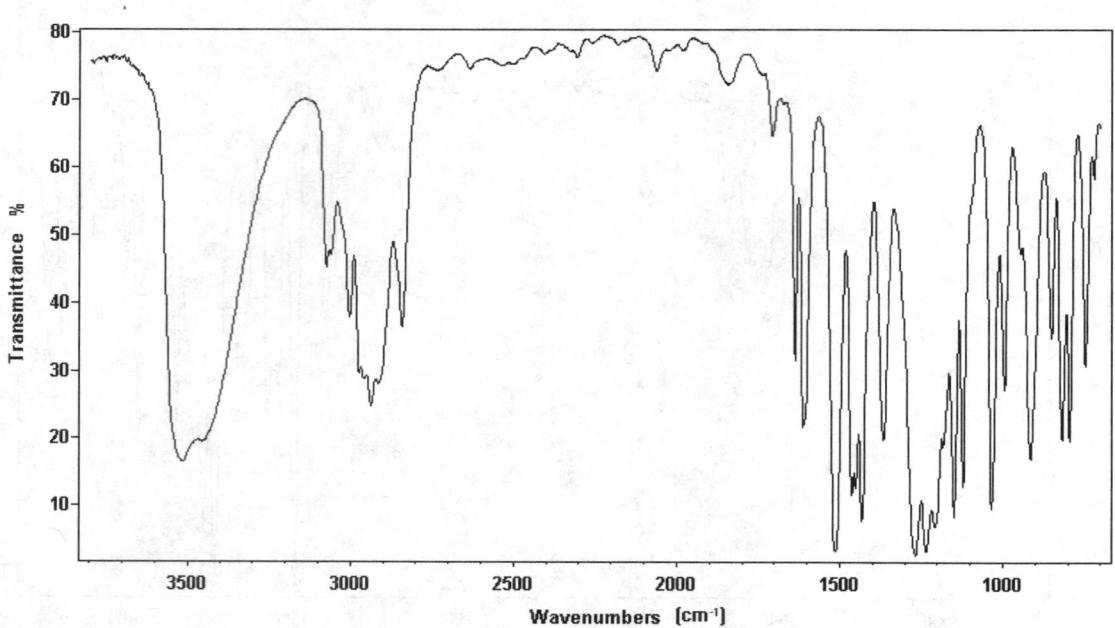

Clove Stem Oil

Cocoa Butter Substitute

First Published: Prior to FCC 6

DESCRIPTION

Cocoa Butter Substitute occurs as a white, waxy solid that is predominantly a mixture of triglycerides derived primarily from palm, safflower, sunflower, or coconut oils. The resulting products may be used directly or with cocoa butter in all proportions for the preparation of coatings. In contrast to many edible oils and hard butters, Cocoa Butter Substitute has an abrupt melting range, changing from a rather firm, plastic solid below 32° to a liquid at about 33.8° to 35.5°.

Function: Coating agent; texturizer
Packaging and Storage: Store in well-closed containers.

IDENTIFICATION

- **FATTY ACID COMPOSITION,** Appendix VII
  Acceptance criteria: Cocoa Butter Substitute exhibits the following composition profile of fatty acids:

Fatty Acid	Weight % (Range)
≤12	0.0
12:0	0.0
14:0	0.0
16:0	21–24
16:1	0.0
18:0	40–44
18:1	31–35

Fatty Acid	Weight % (Range)
18:2	0.5–1.5
≥20	0.3–0.7

IMPURITIES

Inorganic Impurities

- **LEAD,** *Lead Limit Test, Atomic Absorption Spectrophotometric Graphite Furnace Method, Method II,* Appendix IIIB
  Sample: 5 g
  Acceptance criteria: NMT 0.1 mg/kg
- **RESIDUAL CATALYST (AS FLUORIDE),** *Fluoride Limit Test, Method I,* Appendix IIIB
  Sample: Transfer 30 g of sample into a 250-mL distillation flask having a side arm and a trap. Connect the flask with a condenser, and fit it with a thermometer and a capillary tube. Both of these should reach nearly to the bottom of the flask so that they extend into the liquid during the distillation. Add 0.2 g of silver sulfate, three boiling beads, and 25 mL of 1:1 sulfuric acid:water to the flask. Connect a dropping funnel or a steam generator to the capillary tube. Distill until the temperature reaches 135°. Then, through the capillary, add water from the funnel or introduce steam, as necessary, to maintain the temperature as close as possible to 135° until 250 mL of distillate has been collected in a beaker. Cool the distillate. Add 3 mL of 30% hydrogen peroxide to remove any sulfites, let it stand for 5 min, and evaporate the distillate in a dish containing 15 mL of saturated calcium hydroxide suspension. Ash the residue at 600° for 4 h. Use the ashed residue so obtained as the sample in the *Analysis* below.

Analysis: Proceed as directed beginning with "... and 30 mL of water in a 125-mL distillation flask having a side arm and trap..."

Acceptance criteria: The total volume of sodium fluoride TS required for the solutions from both *Distillate A* and *Distillate B* should not exceed 0.75 mL (NMT 0.5 mg/kg).

Organic Impurities

- **HEXANE**

  Standard aliquots: Using a micropipet, transfer and dissolve 34 µL of hexane in 45 g of cold-pressed cottonseed oil that has not been extracted with hexane. As directed under *Standard curve* (below), analyze aliquots of 0.1, 0.25, 0.5, and 5.0 mg; the aliquots correspond to 2, 5, 10, and 100 mg/kg, respectively, of residual hexane in a 25-mg sample.

  Sample preparation: Pack the lower half of 8.5-cm × 9.5-mm (od) borosilicate glass tubing (inlet liner) with glass wool that has been heated at 200° for 16 h to expel volatiles. Transfer 25 mg of sample, accurately weighed, into the glass tubing, and cover it with a small plug of treated glass wool.

  Standard curve: Chromatograph the *Standard aliquots* as directed for the *Sample preparation* under *Analysis* (below), using the same borosilicate glass tubing setup as used for the *Sample preparation*. Measure the peak areas for each of the *Standard aliquots*. Plot a standard curve using the concentration, in mg/kg, of each of the *Standard aliquots* versus its corresponding peak area, and draw the best straight line. To ensure that the relative standard deviation does not exceed 2.0%, chromatograph a sufficient number of replicates of each of the *Standard aliquots*, and record the areas as directed under *Analysis* (below).

  Chromatographic system, Appendix IIA
  - Mode: Gas chromatography
  - Detector: Independent dual flame-ionization
  - Column: 0.6-m × 6.35-mm (od) stainless-steel U-tube, or equivalent, packed with Porapak P, or equivalent
  - Inlet temperature: 70°
  - Detectors temperature: 110°
  - Column temperature: Hold at 70° for 5 min followed by a linear temperature gradient at 5°/min to 180°, and finally hold at 180° or until the column is clean
  - Carrier gas: Helium
  - Carrier gas flow rate: 60 mL/min
  - Fuel gas: Hydrogen
  - Fuel gas flow rate: 52 mL/min (for each flame)
  - Scavenger gas: Air
  - Scavenger gas flow rate: 500 mL/min (for each flame)

  Analysis: Insert the *Sample preparation* into the inlet liner of the gas chromatograph, immediately sealing the base of the inlet and the lower lip of the glass tubing with a silicone O-ring (Applied Science Laboratories, Inc., or equivalent) previously heated at 200° for 2 h to remove volatile impurities. Immediately close the inlet liner with the septum and septum liner. Allow the carrier gas to flow through the *Sample preparation*, chromatograph, and record the chromatograms. Using the peak area of hexane eluting from the *Sample preparation* at the same time as that of the *Standard aliquots*, read directly from the *Standard curve* the concentration, C, of hexane, in mg/kg, of the *Sample preparation*. Calculate the quantity of hexane, in mg/kg, in the sample taken by the formula:

  $$\text{Result} = 25C/W$$

  W = weight of the sample introduced into the gas chromatograph (mg)

  Acceptance criteria: NMT 5 mg/kg

SPECIFIC TESTS

- **COLOR (FATS AND RELATED SUBSTANCES),** Appendix VII

  Acceptance criteria: NMT 2.5 red

- **FREE FATTY ACIDS (AS OLEIC ACID),** Appendix VII

  Sample: Use the diglyceride fraction obtained in the test for *Total Glycerides* (below).

  Analysis: Determine as directed, except add 2 mL of phenolphthalein TS, and titrate with the appropriate normality of sodium hydroxide. Use the following equivalence factor (e) in the formula given in the procedure:

  Free fatty acids as oleic acid, e = 28.2

  Acceptance criteria: NMT 1.0%

- **IODINE VALUE,** Appendix VII

  Acceptance criteria: Between 30 and 33

- **PEROXIDE VALUE,** *Method II,* Appendix VII

  Acceptance criteria: NMT 10 mEq/kg

- **TOTAL GLYCERIDES,** *Total Monoglycerides,* Appendix VII

  Analysis: Proceed as directed, using toluene instead of benzene and saving all three elution fractions to determine the percentages of *Monoglycerides, Diglycerides,* and *Triglycerides*. The diglyceride fraction also contains free fatty acids, the percentage of which is determined under *Free Fatty Acids* (above). Calculate the percentage of Total Glycerides (G), which is the sum of the percentages of *Monoglycerides, Diglycerides,* and *Triglycerides*, by the following formulas:

  $$M = W_M 100/W_U$$

  $$D = (W_D 100/W_U) - F$$

  $$T = W_T 100/W_U$$

  $$G = M + D + T$$

  M = percentage of monoglycerides
  W_M = weight of monoglycerides (g)
  W_U = weight of the sample (g) taken
  D = percentage of diglycerides
  W_D = weight of diglycerides (g)
  F = percentage of free fatty acids (determined above in the test for *Free Fatty Acids*)
  T = percentage of triglycerides
  W_T = weight of triglycerides (g)

  Acceptance criteria

  Total glycerides: NLT 98.0% of total

Monoglycerides: NMT 1.0%
Diglycerides: NMT 7.0%
Triglycerides: NLT 90.0%
- **UNSAPONIFIABLE MATTER,** Appendix VII
  Acceptance criteria: NMT 1.0%

Change to read:

- **WATER,** *Water Determination,* Appendix IIB
  Analysis: Proceed as directed except use 50 mL of a 1:1 solution of chloroform in methanol to dissolve the sample instead of using 35 to 40 mL of •methanol.• (ERR 1-Jan-2012)
  Acceptance criteria: NMT 0.1%

Coconut Oil (Unhydrogenated)

First Published: Prior to FCC 6

CAS: [8001-31-8]
UNII: Q9L0O73W7L [coconut oil]

DESCRIPTION

Coconut Oil (Unhydrogenated) occurs as a viscous, white to light yellow-tan liquid. It is obtained from the kernel of the fruit of the coconut palm *Cocos nucifera* (Fam. Palmae). The crude oil obtained by mechanically pressing dried coconut meat (copra) is refined, bleached, and deodorized to substantially remove free fatty acids, phospholipids, color, odor and flavor components, and other non-oil materials. Compared with many natural fats, Coconut Oil (Unhydrogenated) has an abrupt melting range, changing from a rather firm, plastic solid at about 21° or below or to a liquid at about 27°.

Function: Coating agent; emulsifying agent; texturizer
Packaging and Storage: Store in well-closed containers.

IDENTIFICATION

- **FATTY ACID COMPOSITION,** Appendix VII
  Acceptance criteria: A sample exhibits the following typical composition profile of fatty acids:

Fatty Acid	Weight % (Range)
6:0	0–0.8
8:0	5–9
10:0	4–8
12:0	44–52
14:0	15–21
16:0	8–11
16:1	0–1
18:0	1–4
18:1	5–8
18:2	0–2.5
20:0	0–0.4

IMPURITIES

Inorganic Impurities

- **ARSENIC,** *Arsenic Limit Test,* Appendix IIIB
  Sample solution: Prepare using 2 g of sample
  Analysis: Proceed as directed under *Procedure*, except use 1 µg of As (1.0 mL of *Standard Arsenic Solution*), instead of 3 µg As.
  Acceptance criteria: The absorbance caused by any red color from the *Sample solution* does not exceed that produced by the 1.0 mL of *Standard Arsenic Solution*. (NMT 0.5 mg/kg)
- **LEAD,** *Lead Limit Test, Atomic Absorption Spectrophotometric Graphite Furnace Method, Method II,* Appendix IIIB
  Acceptance criteria: NMT 0.1 mg/kg

SPECIFIC TESTS

- **COLOR (FATS AND RELATED SUBSTANCES),** Appendix VII
  Acceptance criteria: NMT 20 yellow/2.0 red
- **FREE FATTY ACIDS,** Appendix VII
  Analysis: Determine as directed using the following equivalence factor (e) in the formula given in the procedure:
  Free fatty acids as oleic acid, e = 28.2
  Free fatty acids as lauric acid, e = 20.0
  Acceptance criteria:
  Oleic acid: NMT 0.1%
  Lauric acid: NMT 0.07%
- **IODINE VALUE,** Appendix VII
  Acceptance criteria: Between 6 and 11
- **MELTING RANGE (FATS AND RELATED SUBSTANCES),** Appendix VII
  Acceptance criteria: Between 23.5° and 27°
- **PEROXIDE VALUE,** *Method II,* Appendix VII
  Acceptance criteria: NMT 10 mEq/kg
- **UNSAPONIFIABLE MATTER,** Appendix VII
  Acceptance criteria: NMT 1.5%
- **WATER,** *Water Determination,* Appendix IIB
  Analysis: Proceed as directed except use 50 mL of chloroform to dissolve the sample instead of using 35 to 40 mL of methanol.
  Acceptance criteria: NMT 0.1%

Cognac Oil, Green

First Published: Prior to FCC 6

Wine Yeast Oil

CAS: [8016-21-5]
UNII: 930MLC8XGG [grape seed oil]

DESCRIPTION

Cognac Oil, Green occurs as a green to blue-green liquid with the characteristic aroma of cognac. It is the volatile oil obtained by steam distillation from wine lees. It is soluble in most fixed oils and in mineral oil. It is very slightly soluble in propylene glycol, and it is insoluble in glycerin.

Function: Flavoring agent
Packaging and Storage: Store in full, tight containers in a cool place protected from light.

IDENTIFICATION

- **INFRARED SPECTRA,** *Spectrophotometric Identification Tests,* Appendix IIIC

Acceptance criteria: The spectrum of the sample exhibits relative maxima at the same wavelengths as those of the spectrum below.

SPECIFIC TESTS
- **ACID VALUE (ESSENTIAL OILS AND FLAVORS),** Appendix VI
  Acceptance criteria: Between 32 and 70
- **ANGULAR ROTATION,** *Optical (Specific) Rotation,* Appendix IIB: Use a 100-mm tube.
  Acceptance criteria: Between −1° and +2°
- **ESTER VALUE,** *Esters,* Appendix VI
  Sample: 1 g
  Acceptance criteria: Between 200 and 245
- **REFRACTIVE INDEX,** Appendix IIB
  [NOTE—Use an Abbé or other refractometer of equal or greater accuracy.]
  Acceptance criteria: Between 1.427 and 1.430 at 20°
- **SOLUBILITY IN ALCOHOL,** Appendix VI
  Acceptance criteria: One mL of sample dissolves in 2 mL of 80% alcohol.
- **SPECIFIC GRAVITY:** Determine by any reliable method (see *General Provisions*).
  Acceptance criteria: Between 0.864 and 0.870

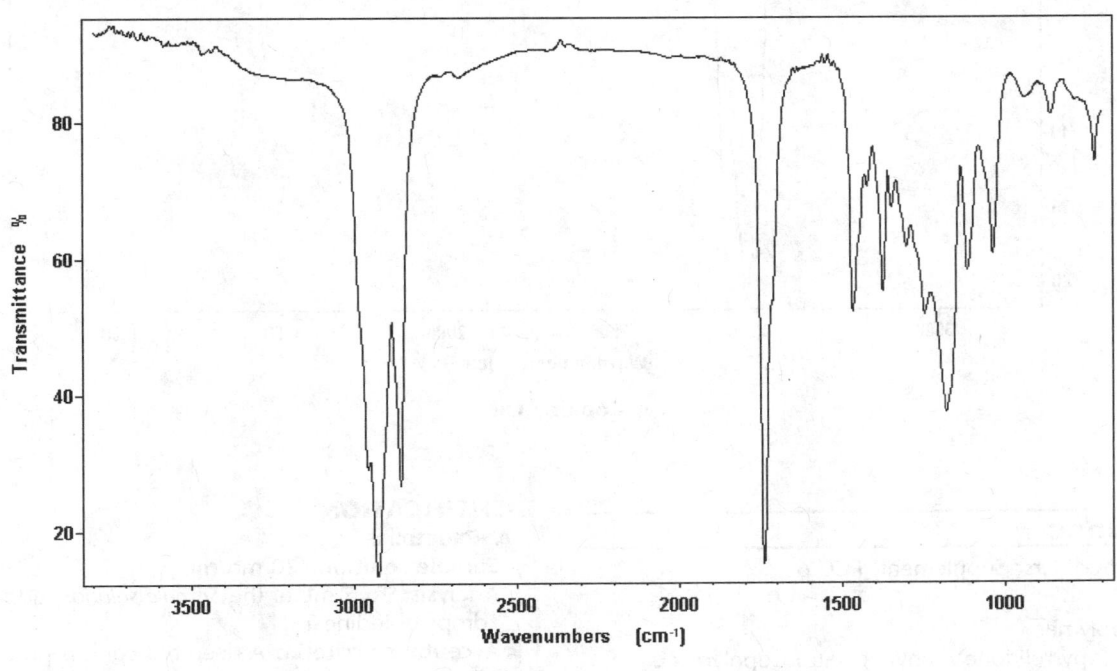

Cognac Oil, Green

Copaiba Oil

First Published: Prior to FCC 6

CAS: [8013-97-6]

UNII: 64VX45Y68N [copaiba oil]

DESCRIPTION
Copaiba Oil occurs as a colorless to slightly yellow liquid with the characteristic odor of copaiba balsam and an aromatic, slightly bitter and pungent taste. It is the volatile oil obtained by steam distillation of copaiba balsam, an exudate from the trunk of various South American species of *Copaifera* L. (Fam. Leguminosae). It is soluble in alcohol, in most fixed oils, and in mineral oil. It is insoluble in glycerin and practically insoluble in propylene glycol.
Function: Flavoring agent
Packaging and Storage: Store in a cool place protected from light in full, tight containers that are made from steel or aluminum and that are suitably lined.

IDENTIFICATION
- **INFRARED SPECTRA,** *Spectrophotometric Identification Tests,* Appendix IIIC
  Acceptance criteria: The spectrum of the sample exhibits relative maxima at the same wavelengths as those of the spectrum below.

SPECIFIC TESTS
- **ANGULAR ROTATION,** *Optical (Specific) Rotation,* Appendix IIB: Use a 100-mm tube.
  Acceptance criteria: Between −7° and −33°
- **GURJUN OIL**
  Analysis: Introduce 5 or 6 drops of sample into 10 mL of glacial acetic acid to which 5 drops of nitric acid has been added.
  Acceptance criteria: No purple color appears within 2 min, indicating the absence of gurjun oil.
- **REFRACTIVE INDEX,** Appendix IIB
  [NOTE—Use an Abbé or other refractometer of equal or greater accuracy.]
  Acceptance criteria: Between 1.493 and 1.500 at 20°

- **SPECIFIC GRAVITY:** Determine by any reliable method (see *General Provisions*).

  Acceptance criteria: Between 0.880 and 0.907

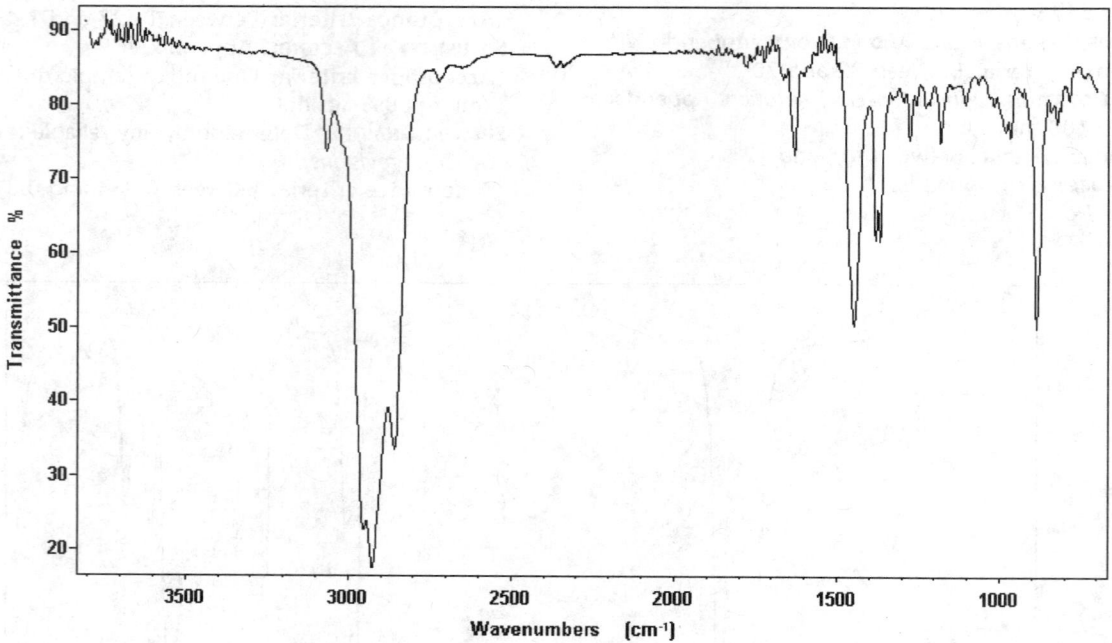

Copaiba Oil

Copovidone

First Published: First Supplement, FCC 6

PVP/VA Copolymer
Poly(1-vinyl-2-pyrrolidone)/(vinyl acetate) Copolymer
1-Vinyl-2-pyrrolidone polymer with vinyl acetate
Acetic acid ethenyl ester polymer with 1-ethenyl-2-pyrrolidone
Copolyvidone

$(C_6H_9NO)_n/(C_4H_6O_2)_m$ CAS: [25086-89-9]
UNII: D9C330MD8B [copovidone]

DESCRIPTION
Copovidone occurs as a white to yellowish-white powder or as flakes. It is a copolymer of 1-vinyl-2-pyrrolidone and vinyl acetate in the mass proportion of 3:2. It is freely soluble in water, in alcohol, and in methylene chloride, but practically insoluble in ether. It is hygroscopic. The pH of a 1:10 aqueous solution is between 3 and 7.

Function: Coating for fresh and fresh-cut fruits and vegetables, film-forming agent, binder, and crystallization inhibitor

Packaging and Storage: Store in tight containers.

IDENTIFICATION
- **A. PROCEDURE**
  Sample solution: 20 mg/mL
  Analysis: To 5 mL of the *Sample solution,* add a few drops of iodine TS.
  Acceptance criteria: A deep red color is produced.
- **B. INFRARED ABSORPTION, INFRARED SPECTRA,** *Spectrophotometric Identification Tests,* Appendix IIIC
  Reference standard: USP Copovidone RS
  Sample and **Standard preparation:** *K*
  Acceptance criteria: The spectrum of the sample exhibits maxima at the same wavelengths as those in the spectrum of the *Reference standard.*

ASSAY
- **NITROGEN DETERMINATION,** *Method II,* Appendix IIIC
  Sample: 100 mg
  Bromocresol green–methyl red solution: Dissolve 0.15 g of bromocresol green and 0.1 g of methyl red in 180 mL of alcohol, and dilute with water to 200 mL.
  Analysis: Modify the procedure as follows: in the wet-digestion step, use 5 g of a 33:1:1 mixture of potassium sulfate–cupric sulfate–titanium dioxide instead of the 10:1 potassium sulfate–cupric sulfate mixture; and omit the use of hydrogen peroxide. Heat until the solution has a clear, yellow-green color and the sides of the flask are free from carbonaceous material. Then heat for an additional 45 min and continue as directed, beginning with "Cautiously add 20 mL of water, cool, then…". Use *Bromocresol green–methyl red solution* instead of methyl red–methylene blue TS. Titrate the distillate with 0.05 N

sulfuric acid until the color of the solution changes from green through pale grayish-blue to pale grayish red-purple. Perform a blank determination, and make any necessary correction. Each mL of 0.05 N sulfuric acid is equivalent to 0.7004 mg of nitrogen.

Acceptance criteria: NLT 7.0% and NMT 8.0%, calculated on the dried basis

- **COPOLYMERIZED VINYL ACETATE**
  Sample: 2 g
  Analysis: Transfer the *Sample* into a 250-mL borosilicate glass flask, add 25 mL of 0.5 N alcoholic potassium hydroxide and a few glass beads, and heat under reflux for 30 min. Add 1 mL of phenolphthalein TS, and titrate the excess 0.5 N alcoholic potassium hydroxide immediately (while still hot) with 0.5 N hydrochloric acid. Perform a blank determination and make any necessary correction. Calculate the percentage of copolymerized vinyl acetate in the sample taken by the formula:

  $$\text{Result} = 0.1 \times (M_{r1}/M_{r2}) \times (M_{r2} \times N_A) \times (V_B - V_U)/W$$

  M_{r1} = molecular weight of vinyl acetate, 86.09
  M_{r2} = molecular weight of potassium hydroxide, 56.11
  N_A = actual normality of the alcoholic potassium hydroxide
  V_B = volume (mL) of 0.5 N hydrochloric acid consumed for the blank determination
  V_U = volume (mL) of 0.5 N hydrochloric acid consumed for the *Sample* determination
  W = weight (g) of *Sample* taken

  Acceptance criteria: NLT 35.3% and NMT 42.0%, calculated on the dried basis

IMPURITIES
Inorganic Impurities
- **LEAD,** *Lead Limit Test, Flame Atomic Absorption Spectrometric Method,* Appendix IIIB
  Sample: 10 g
  Acceptance criteria: NMT 2 mg/kg

Organic Impurities
- **ALDEHYDES**
  Pyrophosphate buffer, 0.05 M: Transfer 8.7 g of potassium pyrophosphate into a 500-mL volumetric flask, and dissolve in 400 mL of water. Adjust, if necessary, to a pH of 9.0 with 1 N potassium hydroxide, dilute to volume, and mix.
  Aldehyde dehydrogenase solution: Transfer a quantity of lyophilized aldehyde dehydrogenase (Sigma A550, or equivalent) equivalent to 70 units into a glass vial, dissolve it in 10.0 mL of water, and mix. [NOTE—This solution is stable for 8 h at 4°.]
  NAD solution: 4.0 mg/mL of nicotinamide adenine dinucleotide in *Pyrophosphate buffer*
  Standard solution: Dissolve 0.140 g of acetaldehyde ammonia trimer trihydrate in 200.0 mL of water, and mix. Pipet 1.0 mL of this solution into a 100-mL volumetric flask, dilute with *Pyrophosphate buffer* to volume, and mix.
  Sample solution: Transfer 1 g of sample into a 100-mL volumetric flask, dissolve it in 50 mL of *Pyrophosphate buffer,* dilute to volume with *Pyrophosphate buffer,* and mix. Stopper the flask loosely, heat at 60° for 1 h, and cool to room temperature.
  Blank: Water
  Analysis: Pipet 0.5 mL each of the *Standard solution,* the *Sample solution,* and *Blank* into separate 1-cm cells. Add 2.5 mL of *Pyrophosphate buffer* and 0.2 mL of *NAD solution* to each cell. Cover the cells to exclude oxygen. Mix them by inversion and allow them to stand for 2 to 3 min at 22° ± 2°. Using a suitable spectrophotometer, measure the absorbances of the solutions at 340 nm. Add 0.05 mL of *Aldehyde dehydrogenase solution* to each cell. Stopper the cells tightly and mix by inversion. Allow them to stand for 5 min at 22 ± 2°. Measure the absorbances of the solutions as before. Calculate the percentage of *Aldehydes* (as acetaldehyde) in the sample taken by the formula:

  $$\text{Result} = 10(C/W)\{[(A_{U2} - A_{U1}) - (A_{B2} - A_{B1})]/[(A_{S2} - A_{S1}) - (A_{B2} - A_{B1})]\}$$

  C = concentration (mg/mL) of acetaldehyde in the *Standard solution* calculated from the weight of the acetaldehyde–ammonia trimer trihydrate with the factor of 0.72
  W = weight (g) of sample taken to prepare the *Sample solution*
  A_{U1} = absorbance of the solution obtained from the *Sample solution,* before the *Aldehyde dehydrogenase solution* was added
  A_{S1} = absorbance of the solution obtained from the *Standard solution* before the *Aldehyde dehydrogenase solution* was added
  A_{B1} = absorbance of the solution obtained from the *Blank,* before the *Aldehyde dehydrogenase solution* was added
  A_{U2} = absorbance of the solution obtained from the *Sample solution,* after the *Aldehyde dehydrogenase solution* was added
  A_{S2} = absorbance of the solution obtained from the *Standard solution* after the *Aldehyde dehydrogenase solution* was added
  A_{B2} = absorbance of the solution obtained from the *Blank,* after the *Aldehyde dehydrogenase solution* was added

  Acceptance criteria: NMT 0.05% (as acetaldehyde)

- **HYDRAZINE,** *Thin-Layer Chromatography,* Appendix IIA
  Salicylaldazine standard solution: 9 μg/mL of salicylaldazine in toluene
  Sample: An amount of sample equivalent to 2.5 g on the dried basis
  Sample solution: Transfer the *Sample* into a 50-mL centrifuge tube, add 25 mL of water, and mix to dissolve. Add 500 μL of a 50 mg/mL solution of salicylaldehyde in methanol, swirl, and heat in a water bath at 60° for 15 min. Allow the solution to cool, add 2.0 mL of toluene, insert a stopper in the tube, shake

the tube vigorously for 2 min, and centrifuge. The clear upper layer is the *Sample solution*.

Adsorbent: 0.25-mm layer of dimethylsilanized chromatographic silica gel mixture with fluorescent indicator

Developing solvent system: Methanol and water (2:1)

Application volume: 10 µL

Detection/Visualization: UV 365 nm

Analysis: Spot the *Sample solution* and the *Salicylaldazine standard solution* onto the plate. Following development, locate the spots on the plate by examination under UV light. Salicylaldazine appears as a fluorescent spot having an R_F value of about 0.3.

Acceptance criteria: The fluorescence of any salicylaldazine spot from the *Sample solution* is not more intense than that produced by the spot obtained from the *Salicylaldazine standard solution* (NMT 1 mg/kg).

- **MONOMERS (1-VINYL-2-PYRROLIDONE, VINYL ACETATE, AND 2-PYRROLIDONE)**

  Solution A: Acetonitrile, methanol, and water (1:1:18)

  Solution B: Acetonitrile, methanol, and water (9:1:10)

  Standard stock solution: 0.5 mg/mL 1-vinyl-2-pyrrolidone, 0.5 mg/mL vinyl acetate, and 3 mg/mL of 2-pyrrolidone in methanol

  Standard solution: 0.25 µg/mL 1-vinyl-2-pyrrolidone, 0.25 µg/mL vinyl acetate, and 1.5 µg/mL of 2-pyrrolidone prepared by diluting the *Standard stock solution* with *Solution A*

  Sample solution: Transfer 250 mg of sample into a 10-mL volumetric flask, add 1 mL of methanol, mix ultrasonically to dissolve, dilute with water to volume, and mix. If necessary, filter this solution to remove undissolved particles.

  Chromatographic system, Appendix IIA
  Mode: High-performance liquid chromatography
  Detectors: UV 205 nm and 235 nm
  Column: 4-mm × 250-mm stainless steel, packed with octadecylsilane silica gel (5 µm particle diameter)[1], with 4-mm × 30-mm guard column with the same packing[2]
  Column temperature: 30°
  Flow rate: About 1.0 mL/min
  Injection volume: About 10 µL
  Mobile phase: See gradient table (below).

Time (min)	Solution A (%)	Solution B (%)
0	100	0
2	100	0
26	80	20
27	0	100
36	0	100
38	100	0

[1]Aquasil C18 (Thermo-Hypersil), or equivalent.
[2]Nucleosil 120-5 C18 (Machery-Nagel), or equivalent.

System suitability
  Sample: *Standard solution*
  Resolution: NLT 2.0 between 2-pyrrolidone, vinyl acetate, and 1-vinyl-2-pyrrolidone peaks
  Relative standard deviation: NMT 2.0% for each analyte for replicate injections

Analysis: Separately inject the *Standard solution* and the *Sample solution* into the chromatograph, record the chromatograms, and measure the responses for the 2-pyrrolidone, vinyl acetate, and 1-vinyl-2-pyrrolidone peak areas. [NOTE—The order of elution is 2-pyrrolidone, vinyl acetate, and 1-vinyl-2-pyrrolidone.] [NOTE—After each injection of the *Sample solution*, wash the polymeric material from the guard column by passing the mobile phase (100% *Solution A*) through the column backwards for about 30 min at the same flow rate.] Calculate the content of the three monomers in the sample taken using the following equations:

$$\text{1-Vinyl-2-pyrrolidone (mg/kg)} = (r_{UA}/r_{SA}) \times (C_{SA}/C_U) \times F_1$$

$$\text{Vinyl acetate (mg/kg)} = (r_{UB}/r_{SB}) \times (C_{SB}/C_U) \times F_1$$

$$\text{2-Pyrrolidone (\%)} = (r_{UC}/r_{SC}) \times (C_{SC}/C_U) \times F_2 \times 100\%$$

r_{UA}, r_{UB}, r_{UC} = peak area responses from the *Sample solution* for 1-vinyl-2-pyrrolidone, vinyl acetate, and 2-pyrrolidone, respectively
r_{SA}, r_{SB}, r_{SC} = peak area responses from the *Standard solution* for 1-vinyl-2-pyrrolidone, vinyl acetate, and 2-pyrrolidone, respectively
C_{SA}, C_{SB}, C_{SC} = concentrations of 1-vinyl-2-pyrrolidone, vinyl acetate, and 2-pyrrolidone, respectively, in the *Standard solution* (µg/mL)
C_U = *Sample solution* concentration (mg/mL)
F_1 = correction factor to convert units from mg/g to mg/kg, 100
F_2 = correction factor to convert units from, 1/1000 µg/mg to µg/µg

Acceptance criteria
  1-Vinyl-2-pyrrolidone: NMT 10 mg/kg
  Vinyl acetate: NMT 10 mg/kg
  2-Pyrrolidone: NMT 0.5%

- **PEROXIDES**

  Sample stock solution: 40 mg/mL

  Titanium trichloride solution: 150 mg/mL titanium trichloride in 10% hydrochloric acid

  Titanium trichloride–sulfuric acid solution: Mix carefully 20 mL of *Titanium trichloride solution* in 13 mL of sulfuric acid. Add sufficient 30% hydrogen peroxide to produce a yellow color. Heat until white fumes are evolved, allow to cool, and dilute with water. Repeat the evaporation and addition of water until a colorless solution is obtained. Dilute with water to 100 mL.

  Sample solution: Transfer 25.0 mL of the *Sample stock solution* to a 50-mL beaker, add 2 mL of *Titanium*

trichloride–sulfuric acid solution, and mix. Allow to stand for 30 min at room temperature.

Blank solution: Transfer 25.0 mL of *Sample stock solution* to a 50-mL beaker, add 2 mL of 13% sulfuric acid, and mix.

Analysis: Measure the absorbances of the *Sample solution* and *Blank solution* in a 1-cm cell at the wavelength of maximum absorbance (about 405 nm), using a suitable spectrophotometer.

Acceptance criteria: The blank-corrected absorbance is NMT 0.35 (corresponding to NMT 0.04%, expressed as hydrogen peroxide).

SPECIFIC TESTS
- **CLARITY AND COLOR**
  Sample solution: 100 mg/mL
  Acceptance criteria: The *Sample solution* is clear or slightly opalescent and colorless to pale yellow or pale red.
- **K-VALUE**
  [NOTE—The molecular weight of the sample is characterized by its viscosity in aqueous solution, relative to that of water, expressed as a *K-Value*.]
  Sample: An amount of sample equivalent to 1.0 g on the dried basis
  Sample solution: Transfer the *Sample* into a 100-mL volumetric flask, dissolve it in about 50 mL of water, dilute with water to volume, mix thoroughly, and allow it to stand for 1 h. Filter the solution. Pipet 15 mL of filtrate into a clean, dry Ubbelholde-type viscometer, and place the viscometer in a water bath maintained at $25° \pm 0.2°$.
  Analysis: After allowing the viscometer and the *Sample solution* to warm in the water bath for 10 min, draw the solution by means of very gentle suction up through the capillary until the meniscus is above the upper etched mark. Release suction, and after the meniscus reaches the upper etched mark, begin timing the flow through the capillary. Record the exact time when the meniscus reaches the lower etched mark, and calculate the flow time to the nearest 0.01 s. Repeat this operation until at least three readings are obtained. The readings must agree within 0.1 s; if not, repeat the determination with additional 15-mL portions of the *Sample solution* after recleaning the viscometer with sulfuric acid–dichromate cleaning solution or with a suitable laboratory cleaning compound that will remove oils, greases, waxes, and other impurities. Calculate the average flow time and then obtain the flow time in a similar manner for 15 mL of water. Calculate the relative viscosity, z, of the *Sample* by dividing the average flow time of the *Sample solution* by that of the water sample, and then calculate the *K-Value* by the formula:

$$\left[\sqrt{300c \log z + (c + 1.5c \log z)^2} + 1.5c \log z - c\right] / (0.15c + 0.003c^2)$$

c = weight (g) of the sample, calculated on the dried basis, in each 100.0 g of solution

z = relative viscosity

Acceptance criteria: NLT 90.0% and NMT 110.0% of the *K-Value* stated on the label

- **LOSS ON DRYING,** Appendix IIC : 105° for 3h
  Acceptance criteria: NMT 5.0%
- **RESIDUE ON IGNITION (SULFATED ASH),** Appendix IIC
  Sample: 2 g
  Analysis: Proceed as directed, but igniting at $600° \pm 50°$ for 30 min.
  Acceptance criteria: NMT 0.1%

OTHER REQUIREMENTS
- **LABELING:** Indicate the nominal *K-Value* of the product.

Copper Gluconate
First Published: Prior to FCC 6

$C_{12}H_{22}CuO_{14}$ Formula wt 453.84
                        CAS: [527-09-3]

UNII: RV823G6G67 [copper gluconate]

DESCRIPTION
Copper Gluconate occurs as a fine, light blue powder. It is very soluble in water, and is very slightly soluble in alcohol.
Function: Nutrient
Packaging and Storage: Store in well-closed containers.

IDENTIFICATION
- **COPPER,** Appendix IIIA
  Sample solution: 50 mg/mL
  Acceptance criteria: Passes tests
- **THIN-LAYER CHROMATOGRAPHY,** Appendix IIA
  Sample solution: 10 mg/mL in water
  Standard solution: 10 mg/mL of USP Potassium Gluconate RS in water
  [NOTE—*Sample solution* and *Standard solution* (above), if necessary, can be heated in a water bath at 60° to aid dissolution.]
  Adsorbent: 0.25-mm layer of chromatographic silica gel
  Application volume: 5 µL
  Developing solvent system: Alcohol, water, ammonium hydroxide, and ethyl acetate (5:3:1:1)
  Spray reagent: 25 mg/mL of ammonium molybdate and 10 mg/mL of ceric sulfate in 2 N sulfuric acid
  Analysis: Following development, dry the plate at 110° for 20 min, and allow to cool. Spray the cooled plate with the *Spray reagent*. After spraying, heat the plate at 110° for about 10 min.
  Acceptance criteria: The principal spot obtained from the *Sample solution* corresponds in color, size, and R_F value to that of the *Standard solution*.

ASSAY
- **PROCEDURE**
  Sample: 1.5 g

Analysis: Dissolve the *Sample* in 100 mL of water in a 250-mL Erlenmeyer flask, add 2 mL of glacial acetic acid and 5 g of potassium iodide, mix well, and titrate with 0.1 N sodium thiosulfate to a light yellow color. Add 2 g of ammonium thiocyanate, mix, then add 3 mL of starch TS and continue titrating to a milk-white endpoint. Each mL of 0.1 N sodium thiosulfate is equivalent to 45.38 mg of $C_{12}H_{22}CuO_{14}$.
Acceptance criteria: NLT 98.0% and NMT 102.0% $C_{12}H_{22}CuO_{14}$

IMPURITIES
Inorganic Impurities
- **LEAD,** *Lead Limit Test,* Appendix IIIB
  Sample solution: 1 g of sample in 25 mL of water
  Control: 5 µg of Pb (5 mL of *Diluted Standard Lead Solution*)
  Acceptance criteria: NMT 5 mg/kg

SPECIFIC TESTS
- **REDUCING SUBSTANCES**
  Sample: 1 g
  Analysis: Dissolve the *Sample* in 10 mL of water in a 250-mL Erlenmeyer flask. Add 25 mL of alkaline cupric citrate TS and cover the flask with a small beaker. Boil gently for exactly 5 min, and cool rapidly to room temperature. Add 25 mL of a 1:10 solution of acetic acid, 10.0 mL of 0.1 N iodine, 10.0 mL of 2.7 N hydrochloric acid, and 3 mL of starch TS and titrate with 0.1 N sodium thiosulfate to the disappearance of the blue color. Calculate the weight, in mg, of reducing substances (as D-glucose) by the formula:

$$Result = (V_1N_1 - V_2N_2) \times F_E$$

  V_1 = volume of the iodine solution (mL)
  N_1 = normality of the iodine solution
  V_2 = volume of the sodium thiosulfate solution (mL)
  N_2 = normality of the sodium thiosulfate solution
  F_E = equivalence factor for D-glucose, 27
  Acceptance criteria: NMT 1.0%

Copper Sulfate

First Published: Prior to FCC 6

Cupric Sulfate

$CuSO_4$ Formula wt, anhydrous 159.6
$CuSO_4 \cdot 5H_2O$ Formula wt, pentahydrate 249.68
INS: 519   CAS: anhydrous [7758-98-7]
                            pentahydrate [7758-99-8]
UNII: KUW2Q3U1VV [cupric sulfate anhydrous]
UNII: LRX7AJ16DT [cupric sulfate]

DESCRIPTION
Copper Sulfate occurs as blue crystals, crystalline granules, or powder. It effloresces slowly in dry air and is freely soluble in water, soluble in glycerin, and slightly soluble in alcohol.
Function: Nutrient
Packaging and Storage: Store in tight containers.

IDENTIFICATION
- **A. COPPER,** Appendix IIIA
  Sample solution: 50 mg/mL
  Acceptance criteria: Passes tests
- **B. SULFATE,** Appendix IIIA
  Sample solution: 50 mg/mL
  Acceptance criteria: Passes tests

ASSAY
- **PROCEDURE**
  Sample: 1 g
  Analysis: Dissolve the *Sample* in 50 mL of water. Add 4 mL of glacial acetic acid and 3 g of potassium iodide, mix well, and titrate with 0.1 N sodium thiosulfate to a light yellow color. Add 2 g of ammonium thiocyanate, mix, and then add 3 mL of starch TS, and continue titrating to a milky white endpoint. Perform a blank titration (see *General Provisions*) and make any necessary correction. Each mL of 0.1 N sodium thiosulfate used is equivalent to 24.97 mg of $CuSO_4 \cdot 5H_2O$.
  Acceptance criteria: NLT 98.0% and NMT 102.0% of $CuSO_4 \cdot 5H_2O$

IMPURITIES
Inorganic Impurities
- **IRON**
  Sample: Residue from *Substances Not Precipitated by Hydrogen Sulfide* (below)
  Control: 0.033 mg iron
  Analysis: Add 2 mL of hydrochloric acid and 0.1 mL of nitric acid to the *Sample*, cover with a watch glass, and digest on a steam bath for 20 min. Remove the watch glass, and evaporate to dryness. Dissolve the residue in 1 mL of hydrochloric acid, and dilute to 60 mL with water. Dilute 5 mL of this solution to 40 mL with water, add 2 mL of hydrochloric acid, and dilute to 50 mL with water. Add 40 mg of ammonium peroxydisulfate crystals and 10 mL of ammonium thiocyanate TS, and mix thoroughly. Repeat the preceding using the *Control* in place of the *Sample*.
  Acceptance criteria: Any red color produced within 1 h by the *Sample* does not exceed that produced by the *Control*. (NMT 0.01%)
- **LEAD,** *Lead Limit Test, APDC Extraction Method,* Appendix IIIB
  Acceptance criteria: NMT 4 mg/kg

SPECIFIC TESTS
- **SUBSTANCES NOT PRECIPITATED BY HYDROGEN SULFIDE**
  Sample: 5 g
  Analysis: Dissolve the *Sample* in 200 mL of 1:100 sulfuric acid, heat to 70°, and pass hydrogen sulfide through the solution until the copper is completely precipitated. Dilute to 250 mL, mix thoroughly, allow the precipitate to settle, and filter. Evaporate 200 mL of the filtrate to dryness in a tared dish, ignite at 800° ±

25° for 15 min, cool, and weigh. [NOTE—Retain the resulting residue for the *Iron* test (above).]
Acceptance criteria: NMT 0.3%

Coriander Oil

First Published: Prior to FCC 6

CAS: [8008-52-4]

UNII: 7626GC95E5 [coriander oil]

DESCRIPTION
Coriander Oil occurs as a colorless or pale yellow liquid with the characteristic odor and taste of coriander. It is the volatile oil obtained by steam distillation from the dried ripe fruit of *Coriandrum sativum* L. (Fam. Umbelliferae).
Function: Flavoring agent
Packaging and Storage: Store in full, tight containers protected from light. Avoid exposure to excessive heat.

IDENTIFICATION
- **INFRARED SPECTRA,** *Spectrophotometric Identification Tests,* Appendix IIIC
  Acceptance criteria: The spectrum of the sample exhibits relative maxima at the same wavelengths as those of the spectrum below.

SPECIFIC TESTS
- **ANGULAR ROTATION,** *Optical (Specific) Rotation,* Appendix IIB: Use a 100-mm tube.
  Acceptance criteria: Between +8° and +15°
- **REFRACTIVE INDEX,** Appendix IIB
  [NOTE—Use an Abbé or other refractometer of equal or greater accuracy.]
  Acceptance criteria: Between 1.462 and 1.472 at 20°
- **SOLUBILITY IN ALCOHOL,** Appendix VI
  Acceptance criteria: One mL of sample dissolves in 3 mL of 70% alcohol.
- **SPECIFIC GRAVITY:** Determine by any reliable method (see *General Provisions*).
  Acceptance criteria: Between 0.863 and 0.875

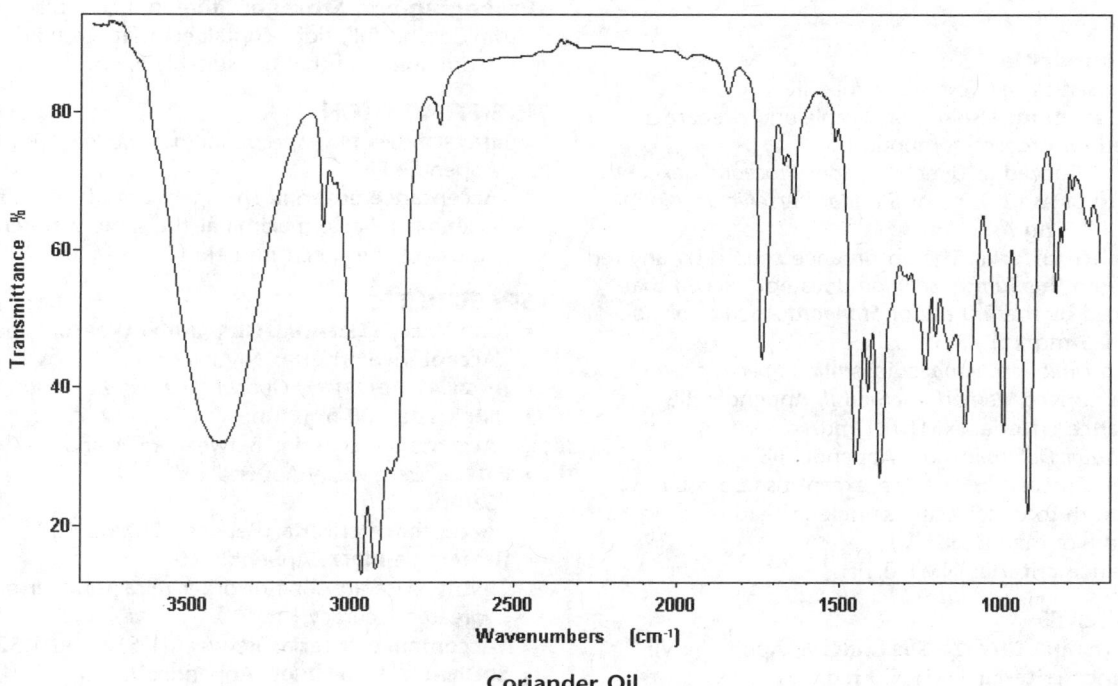

Coriander Oil

Corn Oil (Unhydrogenated)

First Published: Prior to FCC 6

CAS: [8001-30-7]

UNII: 8470G57WFM [corn oil]

DESCRIPTION
Corn Oil (Unhydrogenated) occurs as an amber-colored oil. It is obtained from the corn plant *Zea mays* (Fam. Gramineae), usually by solvent extraction of the corn germ. It is refined, bleached, and deodorized to substantially remove free fatty acids, phospholipids, color, odor and flavor components, and other non-oil materials. It is a liquid at 21° to 27°, but traces of wax, unless they are removed by winterization, may cause the oil to cloud when cooled to low temperature. It is free from visible foreign material (other than wax) at 21° to 27°.
Function: Coating agent; emulsifying agent; texturizer
Packaging and Storage: Store in well-closed containers.

IDENTIFICATION

- **FATTY ACID COMPOSITION,** Appendix VII
  Acceptance criteria: Corn Oil exhibits the following typical composition profile of fatty acids:

Fatty Acid	Weight % (Range)
<14	<0.1
14:0	<1.0
16:0	8.0–19
16:1	<0.5
18:0	0.5–4.0
18:1	19–50
18:2	38–65
18:3	<2.0
20:0	<1.0
20:1	<0.5
22:0	<0.3
22:1	<0.1
24:0	<0.4

IMPURITIES

Inorganic Impurities

- **ARSENIC,** *Arsenic Limit Test,* Appendix IIIB
  Sample solution: Use 4 g of sample and prepare as directed for organic compounds.
  Analysis: Proceed as directed under *Procedure,* except use 2 μg of As (2.0 mL of *Standard Arsenic Solution*) instead of 3 μg As.
  Acceptance criteria: The absorbance caused by any red color from the *Sample solution* does not exceed that produced by the 2.0 mL of *Standard Arsenic Solution.* (NMT 0.5 mg/kg)
- **LEAD,** *Lead Limit Test, Atomic Absorption Spectrophotometric Graphite Furnace Method, Method II,* Appendix IIIB
  Acceptance criteria: NMT 0.1 mg/kg
- **WATER,** *Water Determination,* Appendix IIB
  Analysis: Proceed as directed except use 50 mL of chloroform to dissolve the sample instead of using 35 to 40 mL of methanol.
  Acceptance criteria: NMT 0.1%

SPECIFIC TESTS

- **COLOR (FATS AND RELATED SUBSTANCES),** Appendix VII
  Acceptance criteria: NMT 5.0 red
- **FREE FATTY ACIDS (AS OLEIC ACID),** Appendix VII
  Analysis: Use 28.2 for the equivalence factor (e) in the formula given in the procedure.
  Acceptance criteria: NMT 0.1%
- **IODINE VALUE,** Appendix VII
  Acceptance criteria: Between 120 and 130
- **LINOLENIC ACID,** *Fatty Acid Composition,* Appendix VII
  Acceptance criteria: NMT 2.0%
- **PEROXIDE VALUE,** *Method II,* Appendix VII
  Acceptance criteria: NMT 10 mEq/kg
- **UNSAPONIFIABLE MATTER,** Appendix VII
  Acceptance criteria: NMT 1.5%

Costus Root Oil

First Published: Prior to FCC 6

CAS: [8023-88-9]

UNII: 2WF6750061 [costus root oil]

DESCRIPTION

Costus Root Oil occurs as a light yellow to brown, viscous liquid with a peculiar, persistent odor reminiscent of violet, orris, and vetivert. It is the volatile oil obtained by steam distillation from the dried, triturated roots of the herbaceous perennial plant *Saussurea lappa* Clarke (Fam. Compositae) or by a solvent extraction procedure followed by vacuum distillation of the resinoid extract. It is soluble in most fixed oils and in mineral oil. It is insoluble in glycerin and in propylene glycol.

Function: Flavoring agent

Packaging and Storage: Store in a cool place protected from light in full, tight containers that are made from steel or aluminum and that are suitably lined.

IDENTIFICATION

- **INFRARED SPECTRA,** *Spectrophotometric Identification Tests,* Appendix IIIC
  Acceptance criteria: The spectrum of the sample exhibits relative maxima at the same wavelengths as those of the spectrum below.

SPECIFIC TESTS

- **ACID VALUE (ESSENTIAL OILS AND FLAVORS),** Appendix VI
  Acceptance criteria: NMT 42
- **ANGULAR ROTATION,** *Optical (Specific) Rotation,* Appendix IIB: Use a 100-mm tube.
  Acceptance criteria: Between +10° and +36°
- **ESTERS,** *Ester Value,* Appendix VI
  Sample: 1 g
  Acceptance criteria: Between 90 and 150
- **REFRACTIVE INDEX,** Appendix IIB
  [NOTE—Use an Abbé or other refractometer of equal or greater accuracy.]
  Acceptance criteria: Between 1.512 and 1.523 at 20°
- **SOLUBILITY IN ALCOHOL,** Appendix VI
  Acceptance criteria: One mL of sample dissolves in 0.5 mL of 90% alcohol, but the solution becomes cloudy upon further dilution, and paraffin crystals may occasionally separate.
- **SPECIFIC GRAVITY:** Determine by any reliable method (see *General Provisions*).
  Acceptance criteria: Between 0.995 and 1.039

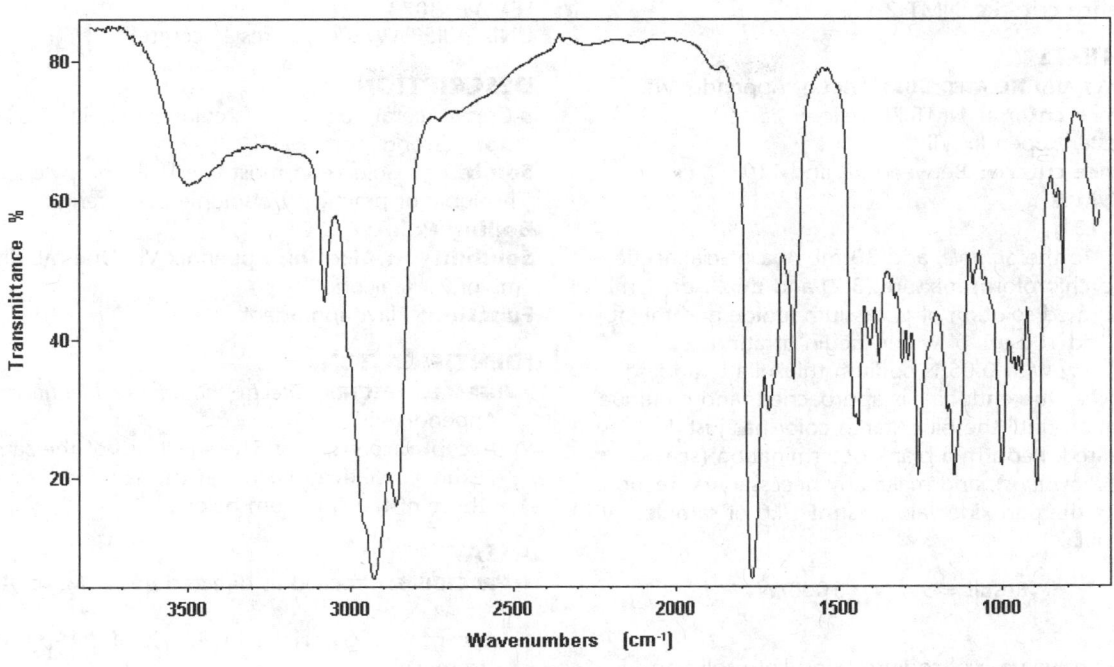

Costus Root Oil

Cottonseed Oil (Unhydrogenated)

First Published: Prior to FCC 6

CAS: [8001-29-4]
UNII: H3E878020N [cottonseed oil]

DESCRIPTION
Cottonseed Oil (Unhydrogenated) occurs as a dark red-brown oil. It is obtained from the seed of the cotton plant *Gossypium hirsutum* (American) or *Gossypium barbadense* (Egyptian) by mechanical expression or solvent extraction. It is refined, bleached, and deodorized to substantially remove free fatty acids, phospholipids, color, odor and flavor components, and miscellaneous other non-oil materials. It is liquid at 21° to 27°, clouds at 21°, and partially solidifies at storage temperatures below 10° to 16°. It is free from visible foreign material at 23° to 27°.

Function: Cooking or salad oil; component of margarine or shortening; tenderizer; carrier; stabilizer; thickener; coating agent; texturizer

Packaging and Storage: Store in well-closed containers.

IDENTIFICATION
- **FATTY ACID COMPOSITION,** Appendix VII
  Acceptance criteria: A sample exhibits the following composition profile of fatty acids:

Fatty Acid	Weight % (Range)
<14	<0.1
14:0	0.5-2.0
16:0	17-29
16:1	<1.5
18:0	1.0-4.0
18:1	13-44
18:2	40-63
18:3	0.1-2.1
20:0	<0.5
20:1	<0.5
22:0	<0.5
22:1	<0.5
24:0	<0.5

IMPURITIES
Inorganic Impurities
- **LEAD,** *Lead Limit Test*, Atomic Absorption Spectrophotometric Graphite Furnace Method, Method II, Appendix IIIB
  Acceptance criteria: NMT 0.1 mg/kg
- **WATER,** *Water Determination*, Appendix IIB
  Analysis: Proceed as directed, except use 50 mL of chloroform to dissolve the sample instead of 35 to 40 mL of methanol.
  Acceptance criteria: NMT 0.1%

Organic Impurities
- **FREE FATTY ACIDS (AS OLEIC ACID),** *Free Fatty Acids*, Appendix VII
  Analysis: Use 28.2 for the equivalence factor (e) in the formula given in the procedure.
  Acceptance criteria: NMT 0.1%

- **Linolenic Acid,** *Fatty Acid Composition,* Appendix VII
  Acceptance criteria: NMT 2.1%

SPECIFIC TESTS
- **Color (Fats and Related Substances),** Appendix VII
  Acceptance criteria: NMT 70 yellow/4.5 red
- **Iodine Value,** Appendix VII
  Acceptance criteria: Between 99 and 119
- **Peroxide Value**
  Sample: 10 g
  Analysis: To the *Sample*, add 30 mL of a glacial acetic acid and chloroform mixture (3:2) and mix. Add 1 mL of a saturated solution of potassium iodide and mix for 1 min. Add 100 mL of water, begin titrating immediately with 0.05 N sodium thiosulfate, adding starch TS as the endpoint is approached, and continue the titration until the blue starch color has just disappeared. Perform a blank determination (see *General Provisions*), and make any necessary correction. Calculate the peroxide value, as mEq/kg of sample, by the formula:

  $$Result = S \times N \times 1000/W$$

  S = net volume of sodium thiosulfate solution required for the sample (mL)
  N = exact normality of the sodium thiosulfate solution
  W = weight of sample taken (g)
  Acceptance criteria: NMT 10 mEq/kg
- **Unsaponifiable Matter,** Appendix VII
  Acceptance criteria: NMT 1.5%

p-Cresyl Acetate

First Published: Prior to FCC 6

p-Methylphenyl Acetate
p-Tolyl Acetate

$C_9H_{10}O_2$ Formula wt 150.18
FEMA: 3073
UNII: 4215PWW20C [p-cresyl acetate]

DESCRIPTION
p-Cresyl Acetate occurs as a colorless liquid.
Odor: Strong, floral
Solubility: Soluble in most fixed oils, propylene glycol; insoluble or practically insoluble in glycerin
Boiling Point: ~212°
Solubility in Alcohol, Appendix VI: One mL dissolves in 2 mL of 70% alcohol.
Function: Flavoring agent

IDENTIFICATION
- **Infrared Spectra,** *Spectrophotometric Identification Tests,* Appendix IIIC
  Acceptance criteria: The spectrum of the sample exhibits relative maxima at the same wavelengths as those of the spectrum below.

ASSAY
- **Procedure:** Proceed as directed under *M-1b,* Appendix XI.
  Acceptance criteria: NLT 98.0% of $C_9H_{10}O_2$ (one isomer)

SPECIFIC TESTS
- **Acid Value, Flavor Chemicals (Other Than Essential Oils),** *M-15,* Appendix XI
  [Note—Use phenol red TS as the indicator.]
  Acceptance criteria: NMT 1.0
- **Refractive Index,** Appendix II: At 20°
  Acceptance criteria: Between 1.499 and 1.502
- **Specific Gravity:** Determine at 25° by any reliable method (see *General Provisions*).
  Acceptance criteria: Between 1.044 and 1.050

OTHER REQUIREMENTS
- **Free Cresol,** *M-17, Cresyl Acetate (Test for Free Cresol),* Appendix XI
  Acceptance criteria: NMT 1.0%

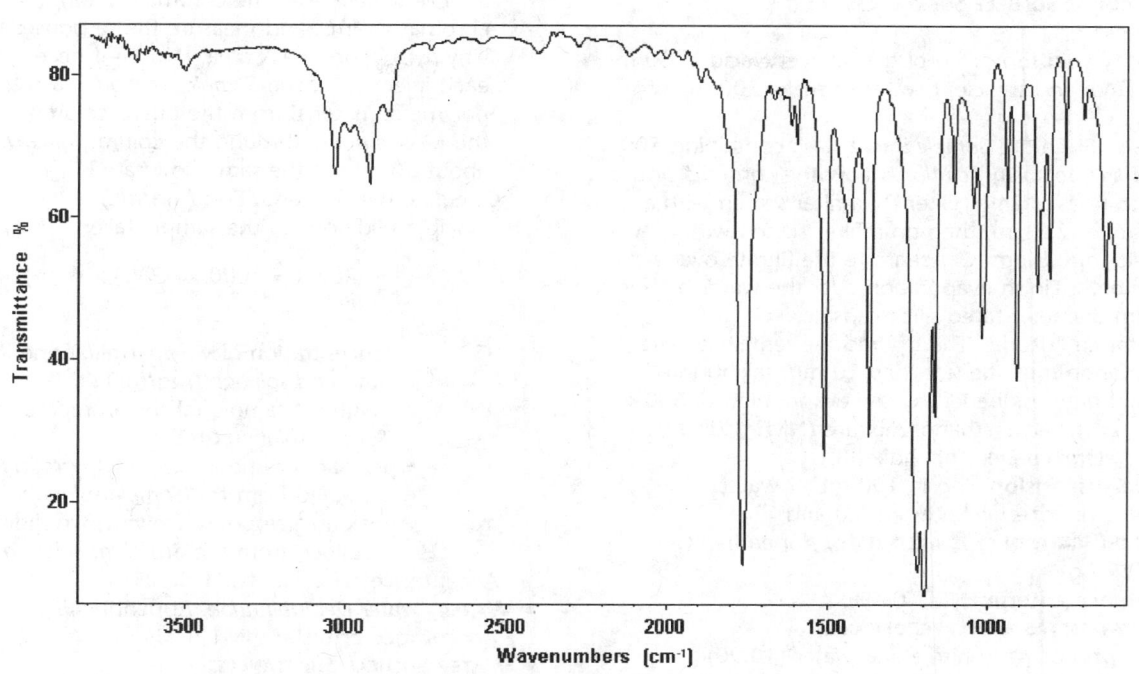

p-Cresyl Acetate

Crospovidone

First Published: Prior to FCC 6
Last Revision: First Supplement, FCC 7

Polyvinylpolypyrrolidone
PVPP
1-Vinyl-2-pyrrolidone Crosslinked Insoluble Polymer

INS: 1202
UNII: 68401960MK [crospovidone]

DESCRIPTION
Crospovidone occurs as a white to off-white, hygroscopic, free-flowing powder. It is a crosslinked homopolymer of purified vinylpyrrolidone, produced catalytically. It is insoluble in water and in other common solvents.
Function: Clarifying agent; stabilizer
Packaging and Storage: Store in tight containers.

IDENTIFICATION
- **A. INFRARED ABSORPTION**, *Spectrophotometric Identification Tests*, Appendix IIIC
  Reference standard: USP Crospovidone RS
  Standard and sample preparation: *K*; previously dried in vacuum at 105° for 1 h
  Acceptance criteria: The spectrum of the sample exhibits maxima at the same wavelengths as those in the spectrum of the *Reference standard*.
- **B. PROCEDURE**
  Sample: 1 g
  Analysis: Add 0.1 mL of iodine TS to a suspension of the *Sample* in 10 mL of water, and shake the mixture for 30 s. [NOTE—The reagent is discolored, a distinction from povidone, which produces a red color.] Add 1 mL of starch TS, and shake the mixture.
  Acceptance criteria: No blue color appears.

ASSAY
- **NITROGEN DETERMINATION,** *Method II,* Appendix IIIC
  Sample: 100 mg
  Analysis: Determine as directed, except in the wet-digestion step, repeat the addition of hydrogen peroxide (usually three to six times) until a clear, light green solution is obtained, then heat for an additional 4 h, and continue as directed, beginning with "Cautiously add 20 mL of water".
  Acceptance criteria: NLT 11.0% and NMT 12.8% of nitrogen (N)

IMPURITIES
Inorganic Impurities
- **LEAD,** *Lead Limit Test, Flame Atomic Absorption Spectrophotometric Method,* Appendix IIIB
  Sample: 10 g
  Acceptance criteria: NMT 2 mg/kg

SPECIFIC TESTS
- **ACID-ALCOHOL SOLUBLE SUBSTANCES**
  Sample: 1 g
  Solubility solution: 15 g of glacial acetic acid in 50 mL of ethanol and sufficient water to make 500 mL of solution
  Analysis: Place the *Sample* into a flask containing 500 mL of the *Solubility solution*. Allow the contents of the flask to rest for 24 h. Filter on a filter screen with a porosity of 2.5 µm, then on a filter screen with a porosity of 0.8 µm. Concentrate the filtrate over a water bath. Finish evaporation over the water bath in a 70-mm diameter tared silica capsule.
  Acceptance criteria: The dry residue remaining after evaporation must be less than 10 mg, taking into account any residue left by the evaporation of 500 mL of the acetic acid–ethanol mixture (NMT 1.0%).
- **pH,** *pH Determination,* Appendix IIB
  Sample suspension: 1 g in 100 mL of water
  Acceptance criteria: Between 5.0 and 11.0
- **RESIDUE ON IGNITION (SULFATED ASH),** Appendix IIC
  Sample: 2 g
  Acceptance criteria: NMT 0.4%
- **UNSATURATION (AS VINYLPYRROLIDONE)**
  Mobile phase: Acetonitrile and water (10:90)
  System suitability solution: Transfer 10 mg of vinylpyrrolidone and 500 mg of vinyl acetate to a 100-mL volumetric flask, and dissolve in and dilute with methanol to volume. Transfer 1.0 mL of this solution to a 100-mL volumetric flask, dilute with *Mobile phase* to volume, and mix.
  Standard solution: Transfer 50 mg of vinylpyrrolidone to a 100-mL volumetric flask, dilute with methanol to volume, and mix. Transfer 1.0 mL of this solution to a 100-mL volumetric flask, dilute with methanol to volume, and mix. Transfer 5.0 mL of this solution to a 100-mL volumetric flask, dilute with *Mobile phase* to volume, and mix.
  Sample solution: Suspend 1.250 g in 50.0 mL of methanol, and shake for 60 min. Leave the bulk to settle, and pass through a 0.2-µm filter.
  Chromatographic system, Appendix IIA
    Mode: High-performance liquid chromatography
    Detector: UV 235 nm
    Column: Stainless steel column about 4-mm × 250-mm, packed with octadecylsilanized silica gel (5 µm in particle diameter), with a guard column about 4-mm × 25-mm with the same packing
    Column temperature: 40°
    Flow rate: Adjust so that the retention time of vinylpyrrolidone is about 10 min.
    Injection volume: About 50 µL
  System suitability
    Samples: *System suitability solution* and *Standard solution*
    Suitability requirement 1: The resolution, *R*, between vinylpyrrolidone and vinyl acetate for the *System suitability solution* is NLT 2.0.
    Suitability requirement 2: The relative standard deviation for replicate injections of the *Standard solution* is NMT 2.0%.
  Analysis: Separately inject the *Standard solution* and the *Sample solution* into the chromatograph, record the chromatograms, and measure the responses for the vinylpyrrolidone peak area. [NOTE—If necessary, after each injection of the *Sample solution*, wash the polymeric material from the guard column by passing the *Mobile phase* through the column backwards for about 30 min at the same flow rate.]
  Calculate the concentration (mg/mL) of vinylpyrrolidinone in the sample taken:

  $$\text{Result} = 1000 \times (C/W) \times (r_U/r_S)$$

  C = concentration of vinylpyrrolidinone in the *Standard solution* (mg/mL)
  W = weight of sample taken to prepare the *Sample solution* (mg)
  r_U = peak area response for vinylpyrrolidinone obtained from the *Sample solution*
  r_S = peak area response for vinylpyrrolidinone obtained from the *Standard solution*
  Acceptance criteria: NMT 0.001%
- **WATER,** *Water Determination,* Appendix IIB
  Acceptance criteria: NMT 6.0%
- **WATER SOLUBLE SUBSTANCES**
  Sample: 10 g
  Analysis: Place the *Sample* into a 200-mL flask containing 100 mL of water. Shake the flask, and allow the contents to rest for 24 h. Pass through a membrane filter having a 0.45-µm porosity, protected against clogging by superimposing a membrane filter having a 3-µm porosity. Evaporate the filtrate over a water bath until dry.
  Acceptance criteria: The residue left by evaporating the filtrate is less than 150 mg (NMT 1.5%).

Cubeb Oil

First Published: Prior to FCC 6

CAS: [8007-87-2]
UNII: HDE20IN4M5 [cubeb oil]

DESCRIPTION
Cubeb Oil occurs as a colorless or light green to blue-green liquid with a spicy odor and a slightly acrid taste. It is the volatile oil obtained by steam distillation from the mature, unripe, sun-dried fruit of the perennial vine *Piper cubeba* L. (Fam. Piperaceae). It is soluble in most fixed oils and in mineral oil, but it is insoluble in glycerin and propylene glycol.
Function: Flavoring agent
Packaging and Storage: Store in a cool place protected from light in full, tight containers that are made from steel or aluminum and that are suitably lined.

IDENTIFICATION
- **INFRARED SPECTRA,** *Spectrophotometric Identification Tests,* Appendix IIIC

Acceptance criteria: The spectrum of the sample exhibits relative maxima at the same wavelengths as those of the spectrum below.

SPECIFIC TESTS

- **ACID VALUE (ESSENTIAL OILS AND FLAVORS),** Appendix VI
  Acceptance criteria: NMT 2.0
- **ANGULAR ROTATION,** Optical (Specific) Rotation, Appendix IIB: Use a 100-mm tube.
  Acceptance criteria: Between −12° and −43°
- **REFRACTIVE INDEX,** Appendix IIB
  [NOTE—Use an Abbé or other refractometer of equal or greater accuracy.]
  Acceptance criteria: Between 1.492 and 1.502 at 20°
- **SAPONIFICATION VALUE,** Appendix VI
  Sample: 5 g
  Acceptance criteria: NMT 8
- **SOLUBILITY IN ALCOHOL,** Appendix VI
  Acceptance criteria: One mL of sample dissolves in 10 mL of 90% alcohol.
- **SPECIFIC GRAVITY:** Determine by any reliable method (see *General Provisions*).
  Acceptance criteria: Between 0.898 and 0.928

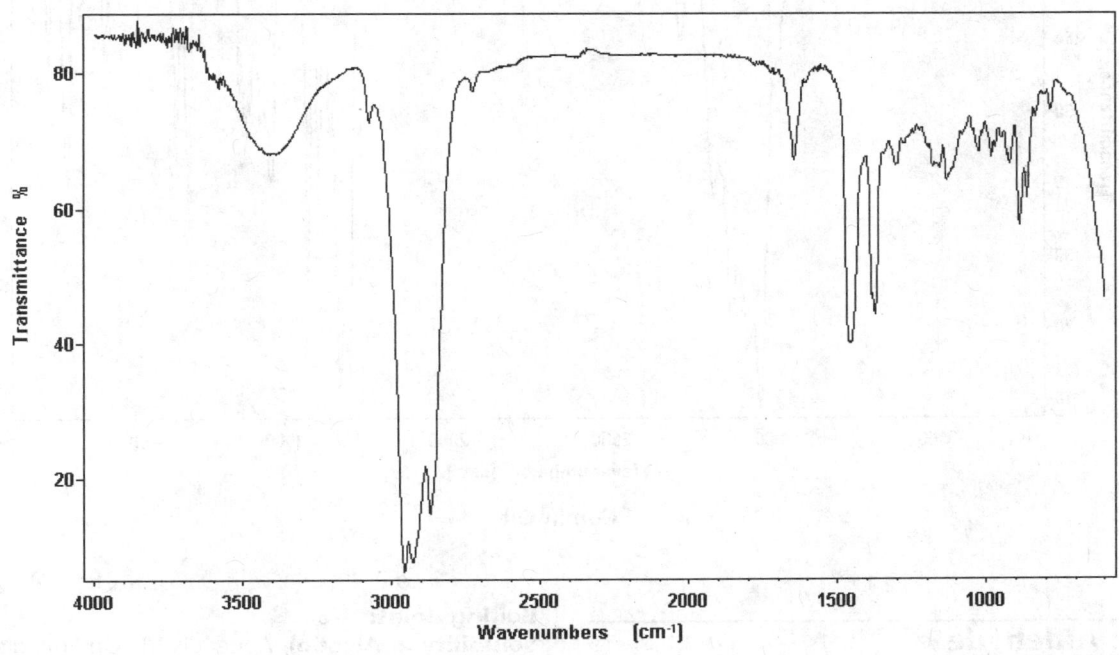

Cubeb Oil

Cumin Oil

First Published: Prior to FCC 6

CAS: [8014-13-9]
UNII: N356X94O43 [cumin oil]

DESCRIPTION

Cumin Oil occurs as a light yellow to brown liquid with a strong and somewhat disagreeable odor. It is the volatile oil obtained by steam distillation from the plant *Cuminum cyminum* L. (Fam. Umbelliferae). It is relatively soluble in most fixed oils and in mineral oil. It is very soluble in glycerin and in propylene glycol.
Function: Flavoring agent
Packaging and Storage: Store in a cool place protected from light in full, tight containers that are made from steel or aluminum and that are suitably lined.

IDENTIFICATION

- **INFRARED SPECTRA,** *Spectrophotometric Identification Tests*, Appendix IIIC
  Acceptance criteria: The spectrum of the sample exhibits relative maxima at the same wavelengths as those of the spectrum below.

ASSAY

- **ALDEHYDES,** Appendix VI
  Sample: 1 g
  Analysis: Proceed as directed, but allow the mixture to stand for 30 min at room temperature before titrating. Use 74.10 as the equivalence factor (e) in the calculation.
  Acceptance criteria: NLT 45.0% and NMT 54.0% of aldehydes, calculated as cuminaldehyde ($C_{10}H_{12}O$)

SPECIFIC TESTS

- **ANGULAR ROTATION,** Optical (Specific) Rotation, Appendix IIB: Use a 100-mm tube.

Acceptance criteria: Between +3° and +8°
- **REFRACTIVE INDEX,** Appendix IIB
  [NOTE—Use an Abbé or other refractometer of equal or greater accuracy.]
  Acceptance criteria: Between 1.500 and 1.506 at 20°
- **SOLUBILITY IN ALCOHOL,** Appendix VI
  Acceptance criteria: One mL of sample dissolves in 8 mL of 80% alcohol. The solution can become hazy on the addition of more alcohol.
- **SPECIFIC GRAVITY:** Determine by any reliable method (see *General Provisions*).
  Acceptance criteria: Between 0.905 and 0.925

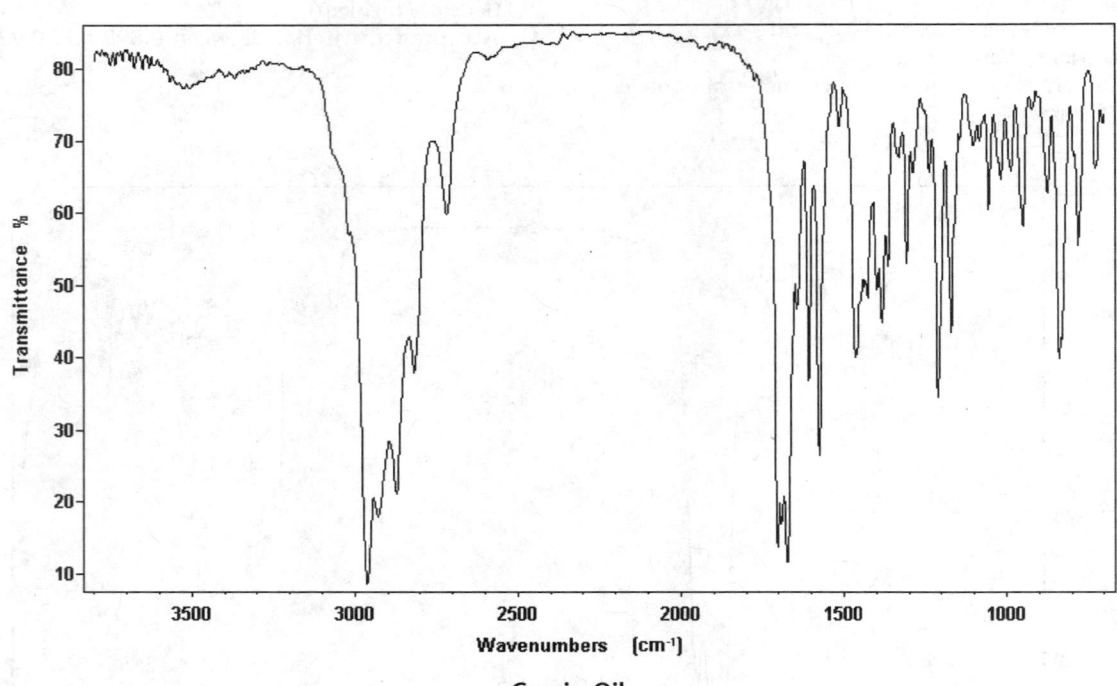

Cumin Oil

Cuminic Aldehyde

First Published: Prior to FCC 6
Last Revision: First Supplement, FCC 6

Cuminal
Cuminaldehyde
p-Cuminic Aldehyde
p-Isopropylbenzaldehyde

$C_{10}H_{12}O$ Formula wt 148.20
FEMA: 2341
UNII: O0893NC35F [cuminaldehyde]

DESCRIPTION
Cuminic Aldehyde occurs as a colorless to pale yellow liquid. It may contain a suitable antioxidant.
Odor: Strong, pungent, cumin oil
Solubility: Soluble in alcohol, ether; insoluble or practically insoluble in water
Boiling Point: ~236°
Solubility in Alcohol, Appendix VI: One mL dissolves in 4 mL of 70% alcohol.
Function: Flavoring agent

IDENTIFICATION
- **INFRARED SPECTRA,** *Spectrophotometric Identification Tests,* Appendix IIIC
  Acceptance criteria: The spectrum of the sample exhibits relative maxima at the same wavelengths as those of the spectrum below.

ASSAY
- **PROCEDURE:** Proceed as directed under *M-2a,* Appendix XI.
  Acceptance criteria: NLT 95.0% of $C_{10}H_{12}O$

SPECIFIC TESTS
- **ACID VALUE, FLAVOR CHEMICALS (OTHER THAN ESSENTIAL OILS),** *M-15,* Appendix XI
  Acceptance criteria: NMT 5.0
- **REFRACTIVE INDEX,** Appendix II: At 20°
  Acceptance criteria: Between 1.528 and 1.534
- **SPECIFIC GRAVITY:** Determine at 25° by any reliable method (see *General Provisions*).
  Acceptance criteria: Between 0.975 and 0.980

OTHER REQUIREMENTS
- **CHLORINATED COMPOUNDS,** Appendix VI
  Acceptance criteria: Passes test

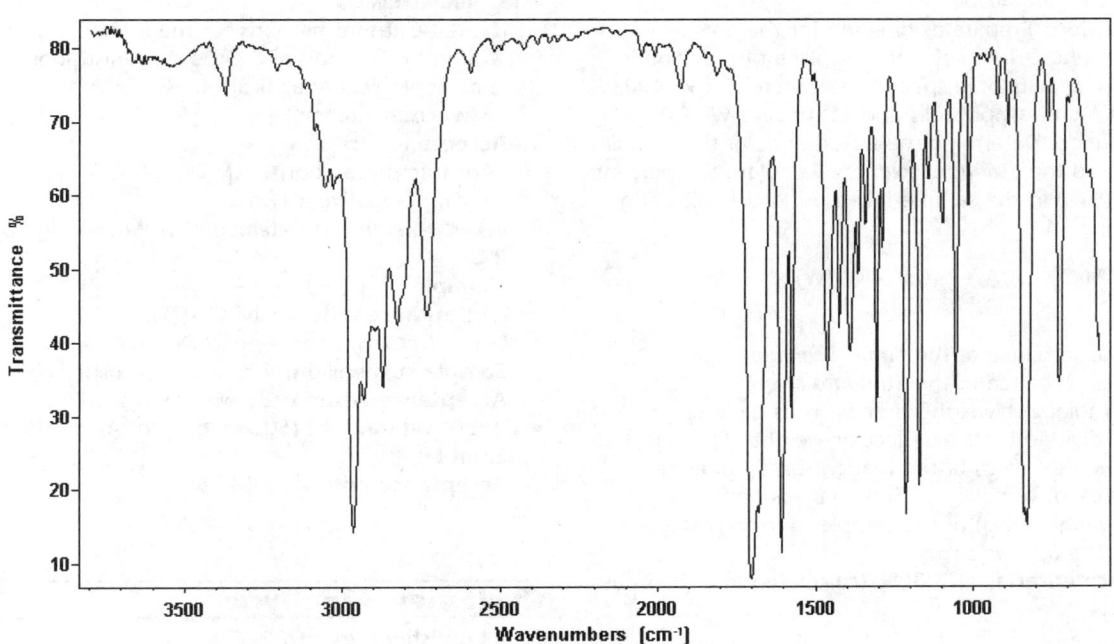

Cuminic Aldehyde

Curdlan
First Published: Prior to FCC 6

Beta-1,3-glucan

$(C_6H_{10}O_5)n$ CAS: [54724-00-4]
UNII: 6930DL209R [curdlan]

DESCRIPTION
Curdlan occurs as a white to nearly white powder. It is a high-molecular-weight polymer of glucose (β-1,3-glucan) produced by pure-culture fermentation of a carbohydrate by a nonpathogenic and nontoxigenic strain of *Agrobacterium biobar* 1 (formerly *Alcaligenes faecalis* var. *myxogenes*) or *Agrobacterium radiobacter*. Curdlan consists of β-(1,3)-linked glucose residues and has the unusual property of forming an elastic gel when its aqueous suspension is heated to a temperature above 54°. It is insoluble in water, but is soluble in alkaline solutions.
Function: Firming agent; gelling agent; stabilizer; thickener
Packaging and Storage: Store in airtight containers.

IDENTIFICATION
- **A. PROCEDURE**
  Sample mixture: 2% aqueous suspension of sample
  Analysis: Add 5 mL of sulfuric acid TS to 10 mL of *Sample mixture*, heat in a boiling water bath for 30 min, and cool. Neutralize the mixture with barium carbonate, and centrifuge it at 900 g for 10 min. Add 1 mL of the supernatant to 5 mL of hot alkaline cupric tartrate TS.
  Acceptance criteria: A copious red precipitate of cuprous oxide forms.
- **B. PROCEDURE**
  Sample mixture: 2% aqueous suspension of sample
  Analysis: Heat the *Sample mixture* in a boiling water bath for 10 min, then cool.
  Acceptance criteria: A firm gel forms.
- **C. PROCEDURE**
  Sample: 0.2 g
  Analysis: Suspend the *Sample* in 5 mL of water, add 1 mL of 3 N sodium hydroxide, and shake.
  Acceptance criteria: The sample dissolves.

ASSAY
- **ANHYDROUS GLUCOSE CONTENT**
  Sample solution: Transfer 100 mg of sample into a 100-mL volumetric flask and dissolve in and dilute to volume with 0.1 N sodium hydroxide. Transfer 5 mL of this solution into a 100-mL volumetric flask, dilute to volume with water, and mix. To 1 mL of this solution, add 1 mL of a 50 mg/mL solution of reagent-grade

phenol and 5 mL of sulfuric acid TS. Shake the flask vigorously, and cool it in ice-cold water.

Standard solution: Prepare as directed for the *Sample solution*, using 100 mg of reagent-grade glucose in place of the sample.

Blank solution: Prepare as directed for the *Sample solution*, using 0.1 mL of water in place of the sample.

Analysis: Use a suitable spectrophotometer set to 490 nm with 1-cm sample cells and set to zero with the *Blank solution*. Determine the absorbance of the *Sample solution* and the *Standard solution*. Calculate the percent curdlan (%C) in the sample taken using the following equation:

$$\%C = (A/A_R) \times (0.9 \times W_R/W) \times 100\%$$

A = absorbance of the *Sample solution*
A_R = absorbance of the *Standard solution*
0.9 = molecular weight of anhydrous glucose divided by the molecular weight of glucose
W_R = weight (mg) of the reagent-grade glucose used to make the *Standard solution*
W = weight (mg) of the sample used to make the *Sample solution*

Acceptance criteria: NLT 80% (calculated as anhydrous glucose)

IMPURITIES
Inorganic Impurities
- **LEAD,** *Lead Limit Test, Atomic Absorption Spectrophotometric Graphite Furnace Method, Method II,* Appendix IIIB
  Acceptance criteria: NMT 0.5 mg/kg

SPECIFIC TESTS
- **GEL STRENGTH**
  2% Sample suspension: Place 200 mg of sample into the tube of a Potter-Elvehjem homogenizer, add 10 mL of water, and homogenize at about 1500 g for 5 min.
  Analysis: Transfer the *2% Sample suspension* into a 16-mm × 150-mm test tube, de-aerate in vacuum for 3 min, and heat in a boiling water bath for 10 min to form a gel. Cool in running water, let it stand for 30 min, and remove the gel from the test tube. Accurately cut the gel at distances of 20 mm and 30 mm from the bottom to obtain a section 10 mm long. Determine the gel strength using a Rheo Meter Model CR-200D (Sun Scientific Co., Ltd., Japan; Load cell: 1000 g; set to a measurement mode 4) or an equivalent instrument capable of uniaxial compression and having a load cell sensitivity of 500 to 1000 g. Use a cylindrical stainless steel plunger with a 0.5-cm diameter. Lower the plunger into the gel at 250 mm/min. The resulting force-time curve is recorded and used for gel strength calculation. Calculate gel strength by the following equation:

$$\text{gel strength (g force/cm}^2\text{)} = f/0.196 \text{ cm}^2$$

f = force on the force-time curve that shows a sharp yielding downward trend associated with rupture of the gel
0.196 = area (cm^2) of the plunger
Acceptance criteria: NLT 600 g/cm^2

- **LOSS ON DRYING,** Appendix IIC: 60° for 5 h in a vacuum
  Acceptance criteria: NMT 10%
- **MICROBIAL LIMITS**
  [NOTE—Current methods for the following tests may be found in the Food and Drug Administration's Bacteriological Analytical Manual online at *www.cfsan.fda.gov.*]
  Acceptance criteria
  Aerobic plate count: NMT 1000 CFU/g
  e. coli: Negative in 1 g
- **NITROGEN,** *Nitrogen Determination, Method II,* Appendix IIIC
  Sample: 1 g
  Acceptance criteria: NMT 0.3%
- **pH,** *pH Determination,* Appendix IIB
  Sample suspension: 1% aqueous suspension
  Acceptance criteria: Between 6.0 and 7.5
- **RESIDUE ON IGNITION (SULFATED ASH),** Appendix IIC
  Sample: 1 g
  Acceptance criteria: NMT 6%

Cyclamen Aldehyde
First Published: Prior to FCC 6
Last Revision: First Supplement, FCC 6

2-Methyl-3-(*p*-isopropylphenyl)propionaldehyde

$C_{13}H_{18}O$ Formula wt 190.29
FEMA: 2743
UNII: 4U37UX0E1E [cyclamen aldehyde]

DESCRIPTION
Cyclamen Aldehyde occurs as a colorless to pale yellow liquid. It may contain a suitable antioxidant.
Odor: Strong, floral
Solubility: Soluble in most fixed oils; insoluble or practically insoluble in glycerin, propylene glycol
Boiling Point: ~270°
Solubility in Alcohol, Appendix VI: One mL dissolves in 3 mL of 80% alcohol.
Function: Flavoring agent

IDENTIFICATION
- **INFRARED SPECTRA,** *Spectrophotometric Identification Tests,* Appendix IIIC
  Acceptance criteria: The spectrum of the sample exhibits relative maxima at the same wavelengths as those of the spectrum below.

ASSAY
- **PROCEDURE:** Proceed as directed under *M-1b,* Appendix XI.

Acceptance criteria
  Sum of two isomers: NLT 90.0% of $C_{13}H_{18}O$
  Major isomer: NLT 85.0% of $C_{13}H_{18}O$

SPECIFIC TESTS
- ACID VALUE, FLAVOR CHEMICALS (OTHER THAN ESSENTIAL OILS), M-15, Appendix XI
  Acceptance criteria: NMT 5.0
- REFRACTIVE INDEX, Appendix II: At 20°
  Acceptance criteria: Between 1.503 and 1.508
- SPECIFIC GRAVITY: Determine at 25° by any reliable method (see General Provisions).
  Acceptance criteria: Between 0.946 and 0.952

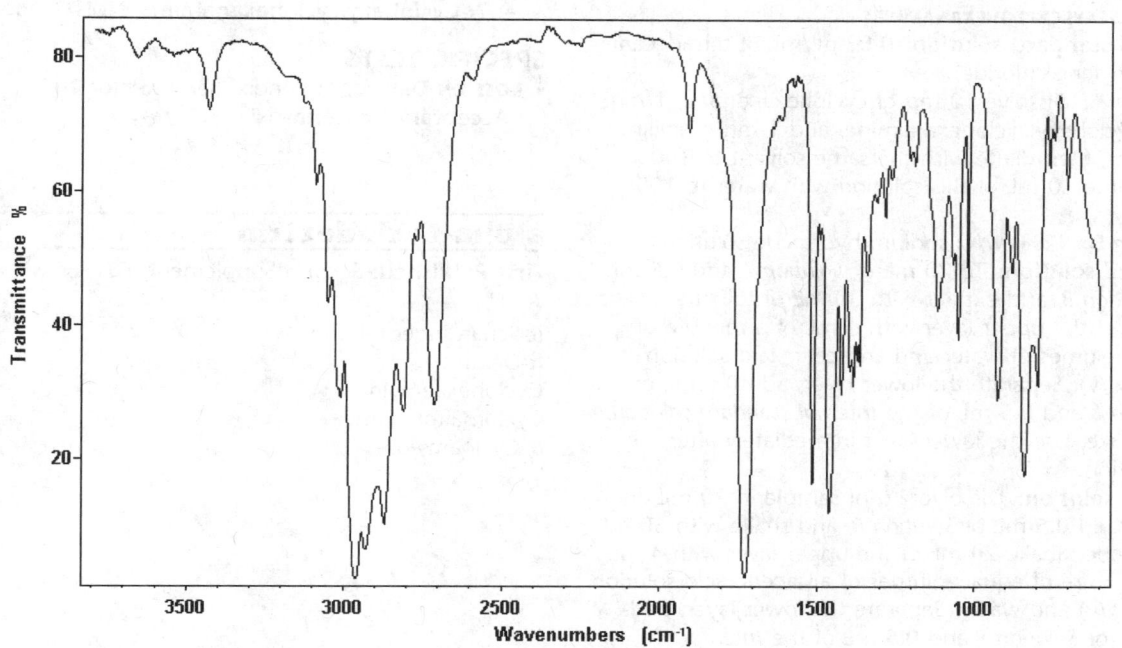

Cyclamen Aldehyde

Add the following:

▲Cyclamic Acid

First Published: FCC 8

Cyclohexanesulfamic Acid
Cyclohexylsulfamic Acid

$C_6H_{13}NO_3S$ Formula wt 179.24
INS: 952   CAS: [100-88-9]
UNII: HN3OFO5036 [cyclamic acid]

DESCRIPTION
Cyclamic Acid occurs as a practically colorless, white crystalline powder. It is soluble in water and in ethanol.
Function: Sweetener
Packaging and Storage: Store in well-closed containers.

IDENTIFICATION
- A. INFRARED ABSORPTION, Spectrophotometric Identification Tests, Appendix III
  Reference standard: USP Cyclamic Acid RS
  Sample and standard preparation: K
  Acceptance criteria: The spectrum of the sample exhibits maxima at the same wavelengths as those in the spectrum of the Reference standard.
- B. PROCEDURE
  Sample solution: 20 mg/mL
  Analysis: Acidify the Sample solution with hydrochloric acid. Add 1 mL of barium chloride TS to the acidified solution, then filter if any turbidity or precipitate forms. When a clear solution is obtained, add 1 mL of 10% sodium nitrite solution.
  Acceptance criteria: A white precipitate forms.

ASSAY
- PROCEDURE
  Phenolphthalein solution: Dissolve 0.2 g of phenolphthalein in 60 mL of 90% ethanol, and dilute with water to 100 mL.
  Sample: 350 mg
  Analysis: Transfer the Sample to a 250-mL flask, and dissolve it in 50 mL of water. Titrate the solution with 0.1 N sodium hydroxide, using Phenolphthalein solution as the indicator. Each mL of 0.1 N sodium hydroxide is equivalent to 17.92 mg of $C_6H_{13}NO_3S$.
  Acceptance criteria: 98.0%–102.0% of $C_6H_{13}NO_3S$, calculated on the dried basis

IMPURITIES

Inorganic Impurities
- **LEAD**, *Lead Limit Test, Flame Atomic Absorption Spectrophotometric Method*, Appendix IIIB
  Sample: 5 g
  Acceptance criteria: NMT 1.0 mg/kg

Organic Impurities
- **CYCLOHEXANAMINE, ANILINE, AND N-CYCLOHEXYLCYCLOHEXANAMINE**
  Internal standard solution: 0.02 µL/mL of tetradecane in methylene chloride
  Solution A: Dissolve 10 mg of cyclohexanamine, 1 mg of N-cyclohexylcyclohexanamine, and 1 mg of aniline in water, then dilute with the same solvent to 1000 mL. Dilute 10 mL of this solution with water to 100 mL.
  Solution B: 42% (w/v) sodium hydroxide solution
  Standard solution: To 20 mL of *Solution A* add 0.5 mL of *Solution B*, and extract with 30 mL of toluene. Shake 20 mL of the upper layer with 4 mL of a mixture of equal volumes of water and an acetic acid solution (12% w/v). Separate the lower layer, add 0.5 mL of *Solution B* and 0.5 mL of the *Internal standard solution*, and shake. Use the lower layer immediately after separation.
  Sample solution: Dissolve 2 g of sample in 20 mL of water, add 0.5 mL of *Solution B*, and shake with 30 mL of toluene. Shake 20 mL of the upper layer with 4 mL of a mixture of equal volumes of an acetic acid solution (12% w/v) and water. Separate the lower layer, add 0.5 mL of *Solution B* and 0.5 mL of the *Internal standard solution*, and shake. Use the lower layer immediately after separation.
  Chromatographic system, Appendix IIA
    Mode: Gas chromatography
    Detector: Flame ionization
    Column: 25-cm × 0.32-mm (i.d.) fused-silica column with poly(dimethyl)(diphenyl)siloxane containing 95% of methyl groups and 5% of phenyl groups[1] as stationary phase (film thickness 0.51 µm)
    Carrier gas: Helium
    Flow rate: 1.8 mL/min
    Temperature
      Injection port: 250°
      Detector: 270°
      Column: See the temperature program in the table below.

Time (min)	Temperature (°)
0–1	85
1–9	85–150
9–13	150

  Injection volume: 1.5 µL. Use a split vent at a flow rate of 20 mL/min.
  Analysis: Separately inject equal volumes of the *Standard solution* and *Sample solution* into the chromatograph, record the chromatograms, and measure the responses. [NOTE—The approximate retention times (relative to cyclohexanamine, which has a retention time of about 2.3 min) for aniline, tetradecane, and N-cyclohexylcyclohexanamine are about 1.4, 4.3, and 4.5 min, respectively.]
  Acceptance criteria
    Cyclohexanamine: NMT 10.0 mg/kg
    Aniline: NMT 1.0 mg/kg
    N-Cyclohexylcyclohexanamine: NMT 1.0 mg/kg

SPECIFIC TESTS
- **LOSS ON DRYING**, Appendix IIC: 105° for 1 h
  Acceptance criteria: NMT 1%▲FCC8

alpha-Cyclodextrin

First Published: Second Supplement, FCC 6

α-Schardinger dextrin
α-Dextrin
Cyclohexaamylose
Cyclomaltohexose
α-Cycloamylose

$(C_6H_{10}O_5)_6$ Formula wt 972.85
INS: 457   CAS: [10016-20-3]
UNII: Z1LH97KTRM [alfadex]

DESCRIPTION
Alpha-Cyclodextrin occurs as a virtually odorless, white or almost white crystalline solid. It is a non-reducing cyclic saccharide consisting of six α-(1→4)-linked D-glucopyranosyl units produced by the action of cyclodextrin glucosyltransferase (CGTase, EC 2.4.1.19) on hydrolyzed starch. Recovery and purification of alpha-cyclodextrin may be carried out using one of the following procedures: precipitation of a complex of alpha-cyclodextrin with 1-decanol, dissolution in water at elevated temperature and re-precipitation, steam-stripping of the complexant, and crystallization of alpha-cyclodextrin from the solution; or chromatography with ion-exchange or gel filtration followed by crystallization of alpha-cyclodextrin from the purified mother liquor; or membrane separation methods such as ultra-filtration and reverse osmosis. It is freely soluble in water and very slightly soluble in ethanol.

Function: Carrier; encapsulating agent; stabilizer
Packaging and storage: Store in tight containers in a dry place.

---
[1] DB-5 available from J&W Scientific, SE-52 available from Restek Corp., or equivalent.

IDENTIFICATION
- **PROCEDURE**
  Acceptance criteria: The retention time of the major peak in the chromatogram of the *Sample solution* is the same as that of the *Standard solution* in the *Assay*.

ASSAY
- **PROCEDURE**
  Mobile phase: Acetonitrile and water (67:33, v/v)
  Standard solution: 10 mg/mL USP alpha-Cyclodextrin RS [NOTE—Ultra-sonication for 10–15 min may be necessary to aid in complete dissolution.]
  Sample solution: 10 mg/mL filtered through a 0.45-µm filter [NOTE—Ultra-sonication for 10–15 min may be necessary to aid in complete dissolution.]
  Chromatographic system, Appendix IIA
  Mode: High-performance liquid chromatography
  Detector: Refractive index
  Column: 25-cm × 4-mm, packed with a monomolecular layer of aminopropylsilane chemically bonded to totally porous silica gel support (10 µm particle diameter)[1]
  Column temperature: 40°
  Flow rate: 2.0 mL/min
  Injection volume: 10 µL
  Analysis: Separately inject equal volumes of the *Standard solution* and *Sample solution* into the chromatograph, and measure the responses for the major peaks on the resulting chromatograms. Calculate the percentage of alpha-cyclodextrin in the portion of the sample taken by the equation:

  $$\text{Result} = (r_U/r_S) \times (C_S/C_U) \times 100\%$$

  r_U = peak response for alpha-cyclodextrin from the *Sample solution*
  r_S = peak response for alpha-cyclodextrin from the *Standard solution*
  C_U = concentration of the sample in the *Sample solution* (mg/mL)
  C_S = concentration of alpha-cyclodextrin in the *Standard solution* (mg/mL)

  Acceptance criteria: NLT 98%, calculated on the anhydrous basis

IMPURITIES
Inorganic Impurities
- **LEAD,** Lead Limit Test, Atomic Absorption Spectrophotometric Graphite Furnace Method, Method I, Appendix IIIB
  Acceptance criteria: NMT 1 mg/kg

Organic Impurities
- **REDUCING SUBSTANCES (AS DEXTROSE)** [NOTE—Dextrose levels are usually lower when determined by the following procedure in the presence of alpha-cyclodextrin, compared to levels determined in its absence. An alpha-cyclodextrin reference standard is therefore utilized in this procedure for the calibration.]
  Reagent solution: Weigh 10.0 g of 3,5-dinitrosalicylic acid in a 1000-mL volumetric flask. Add 80 mL of water, and dissolve the 3,5-dinitrosalicylic acid by heating in a water bath. Prepare a solution of 16.0 g sodium hydroxide in 200 mL of water and a solution of 300 g sodium potassium tartrate in 500 mL of water. Transfer both solutions to the 1000-mL flask. Dilute with water to volume, shake the flask, and let it stand for 24 h. Filter (paper) the reagent solution prior to use if a precipitate appears.
  Standard stock solution: 10 mg/mL dextrose (on the anhydrous basis)
  Standard solutions: 0 to 1.0 mg/mL dextrose prepared as follows: weigh 1.0 g of alpha-cyclodextrin standard[2] into each of eleven 10-mL volumetric flasks (numbered 0 to 10). Add 0, 0.1, 0.2, ..., 1.0 mL of *Standard solution* to flasks nos. 0, 1, ... to 10, respectively. Dilute all flasks with water to volume.
  Sample solutions: 100 mg/mL [NOTE—Ultra-sonication for 10–15 min at 30° may be necessary to aid in complete dissolution.]
  Calibration curve: Assemble a set of eleven 10-mL volumetric flasks. Transfer 1 mL of each of the eleven *Standard solutions* into the flasks, and add 1 mL of *Reagent solution* to each flask. Heat each flask in the boiling water bath for 10 min. Cool rapidly to room temperature, and dilute all flasks with water to volume. For each solution, measure the absorbance against water at 545 nm. Generate a standard curve by plotting absorbance vs. the concentration, in mg/mL, of dextrose in the *Standard solutions*.
  Analysis: Prepare a set of six 10-mL volumetric flasks (labeled a through f), and add 1 mL of *Reagent solution* to each. Transfer 1 mL of the *Sample solution* to flasks "a," "b," and "c". Transfer 1 mL of the *Standard solutions* numbered 0, 3, and 6 to flasks "d," "e," and "f". Thoroughly mix the contents of each flask, and place in a boiling water bath for 10 min. Then, cool the flasks to room temperature, fill to the mark with water, and measure absorbance of the solutions against water at 545 nm. The result is only valid if the absorbances of the solutions in flasks "d," "e," and "f" do not deviate more than 5% from the corresponding absorbances from the *Calibration curve*. Calculate the percentage reducing substance (as dextrose) in the sample taken using the following equation:

  $$\text{Reducing substances} = C_{RS}/C_U \times 100\%$$

  C_{RS} = average of the reducing substance concentrations (as dextrose), in mg/mL, from flasks "a," "b," and "c," calculated using the *Calibration curve*
  C_U = concentration of the sample in the *Sample solution* (mg/mL)

  Acceptance criteria: NMT 0.5% (as dextrose)

- **RESIDUAL COMPLEXANT (1-DECANOL)**
  Tris buffer solution: Dissolve 606 mg of tris (hydroxymethyl) aminomethane and 430 mg of calcium sulfate dihydrate in 500 mL of water. Adjust the pH to 6.5 with phosphoric acid.

---

[1] Nucleosil 100 NH2 (Macherey-Nagel Co, Düren, Germany), or equivalent.

[2] Available from Consortium für Elektrochemische Industrie GmbH (München, Germany), or Wacker Biochem Group (Adrian, MI, USA).

Internal standard solution: Add 50 mg of 1-octanol to 250 mL of tetrahydrofuran.
Standard stock solution: 750 µg/mL 1-decanol in *Internal standard solution*
Standard solution: 7.5 µg/mL 1-decanol in *Internal standard solution*: diluted from *Standard stock solution*
Sample solution: Dissolve 750 mg of sample and 50 mg of glucoamylase[3] (EC 3.2.1.3) in 7 mL of *Tris buffer solution*. Add 100 µL of *Internal standard solution* and 50 µL of cyclodextrin glucosyltransferase preparation (500 U/mL).[4] Close tightly, mix, and incubate in a shaking water bath at 40° for 4 h.
Condition a C18 solid-phase extraction column[5] by washing with methanol (2 × 10 mL) and water (4 × 10 mL). Quantitatively transfer the digested sample solution to the conditioned column, and slowly pass it through the column. Wash the column with water (2 × 10 mL). Gently pass nitrogen through the column to dry it (10 min). Apply 2.5 mL of tetrahydrofuran to the column, let stand for 5 min, and collect the eluate. Use the eluate as the *Sample solution*.
Chromatographic system, Appendix IIA
  Mode: Gas chromatography
  Detector: Flame ionization
  Column: 25-m × 0.32-mm capillary column coated with a 0.5-µm layer of dimethylpolysiloxane gum[6]
  Column temperature: 60° for 1 min, 20°/min to 300°, 300° for 7 min
  Injection port temperature: 265°
  Carrier gas: Helium
  Flow rate: 1 mL/min
  Injection syringe: Heated, gas-tight
  Injection volume: 1 µL
Analysis: Separately inject equal volumes of the *Standard solution* and *Sample solution* into the chromatograph, record the chromatograms, and measure the peak responses. Calculate the concentration (mg/kg) of 1-decanol in the sample taken using the following formula:

$$\text{Result} = (R_U/R_S) \times C_S \times (2.5/S) \times 1000$$

R_U = internal standard ratio (1-decanol peak response/1-octanol response) from the *Sample solution*
R_S = internal standard ratio (1-decanol peak response/1-octanol response) from the *Standard solution*
C_S = concentration of 1-decanol in the *Standard solution* (µg/mL)
2.5 = dilution factor for the *Sample solution* from the mL of tetrahydrofuran applied to the solid-phase extraction column
S = mg of sample taken to prepare the *Sample solution*
1000 = µg/mg to mg/kg conversion factor
Acceptance criteria: NMT 20 mg/kg

---

[3] Gluczyme 8000 (Wacker Chemie, Munich, Germany).
[4] Available from Wacker Chimie (Munich, Germany).
[5] Isolute C18, 10 mL (ICT, Bad Homburg, Germany), or equivalent.
[6] HP-1 (Agilent Technologies), or equivalent.

SPECIFIC TESTS
- **MELTING RANGE OR TEMPERATURE DETERMINATION,** Appendix IIB
  Acceptance criteria: Decomposes above 278°
- **RESIDUE ON IGNITION (SULFATED ASH),** Appendix IIC
  Sample: 1 to 2 g
  Acceptance criteria: NMT 0.1%
- **OPTICAL (SPECIFIC) ROTATION,** Appendix IIB
  Sample solution: 10 mg/mL
  Acceptance criteria: $[\alpha]_D^{25}$ between +145° and +151°
- **WATER,** *Water Determination, Method I,* Appendix IIB
  Acceptance criteria: NMT 11%

---

beta-Cyclodextrin
First Published: Prior to FCC 6

β-Cyclodextrin
BCD

$(C_6H_{10}O_5)_7$ Formula Wt 1135.0
INS: 459   CAS: [7585-39-9]
UNII: JV039JZZ3A [betadex]

DESCRIPTION
Beta-Cyclodextrin occurs as a white, fine, crystalline solid, frequently a fine, crystalline powder. It is a nonreducing cyclic compound consisting of seven alpha-(1,4) linked D-glucopyranosyl units. It is slightly soluble in water.
Function: Encapsulating agent; stabilizer
Packaging and Storage: Store in tight containers in a dry place.

IDENTIFICATION
- **INFRARED ABSORPTION,** *Spectrophotometric Identification Tests,* Appendix IIIC
  Reference standard: USP beta-Cyclodextrin RS
  Sample and Standard preparation: K
  Analysis: The spectrum of the sample exhibits maxima at the same wavelengths as those in the spectrum of the *Reference standard*.
- **CHROMATOGRAPHY,** Appendix IIA
  Analysis: The retention time of the major peak in the chromatogram of *Sample solution* corresponds to that in the chromatogram of *Standard solution*, obtained as directed in the *Assay* (below).

ASSAY
- **PROCEDURE**
  Mobile phase: Acetonitrile and water [65:35], filtered and degassed
  Internal standard solution: 20 mg/mL of glycerol, filtered through a 0.45-µm membrane filter [NOTE—Use fresh or store in a freezer and thaw in hot water.]
  Standard stock solution: 10 mg/mL of USP beta-Cyclodextrin RS [NOTE—Use fresh or store in a freezer and thaw in hot water.]
  Standard solution: Mix 1.0 mL of the *Standard stock solution* with 1.0 mL of *Internal standard solution*.

System suitability solution: 5 mg/mL each of USP alpha-Cyclodextrin RS and USP beta-Cyclodextrin RS, filtered through a 0.45-µm membrane filter
Sample: 1 g
Sample stock solution: Transfer the *Sample* into a 100-mL volumetric flask, dilute to volume with water, and mix. Filter this solution through a 0.45-µm membrane filter.
Sample solution: Mix 1.0 mL of the filtered *Sample stock solution* with 1.0 mL of *Internal standard solution*.
Chromatographic system, Appendix IIA
  Mode: High-performance liquid chromatography
  Detector: Refractive index
  Column: 25-cm × 4.6-mm (id) column packed with 10-µm porous silica gel bonded with aminopropylsilane (Alltech 35643, or equivalent), and a guard column that contains the same packing
  Column temperature: 25° ± 2°
  Detector temperature: 25°
  Flow rate: About 2.0 mL/min
  Injection size: 20 µL
System suitability
  Sample: *System suitability solution*
  Suitability requirement 1: The relative standard deviation for replicate injections is NMT 2.0%.
  Suitability requirement 2: The alpha-cyclodextrin and beta-cyclodextrin peaks exhibit baseline separation. [NOTE—The relative retention times for alpha-cyclodextrin and beta-cyclodextrin are about 0.8 and 1.0, respectively.]
Analysis: Separately inject the *Sample solution* and the *Standard solution* into the chromatograph, record the chromatograms, and measure the responses for the major peaks. Calculate the quantity, in mg, of $(C_6H_{10}O_5)_7$ in the portion of the *Sample* taken by the formula:

$$\text{Result} = C \times (R_U / R_S) \times 100$$

C = concentration (mg/mL) of anhydrous beta-cyclodextrin in the *Standard solution*, corrected for moisture content by a titrimetric water determination
R_U = peak response ratio of the beta-cyclodextrin peak to the internal standard peak obtained from the *Sample solution*
R_S = peak response ratio of the beta-cyclodextrin peak to the internal standard peak obtained from the *Standard solution*

Acceptance criteria: NLT 98.0% and NMT 101.0% of $(C_6H_{10}O_5)_7$ as beta-cyclodextrin, calculated on the anhydrous basis

IMPURITIES
Inorganic Impurities
- **LEAD,** *Lead Limit Test, Flame Absorption Spectrophotometric Method,* Appendix IIIB
  Sample: 10 g
  Acceptance criteria: NMT 1 mg/kg

Organic Impurities
- **REDUCING SUGARS (DEXTROSE EQUIVALENT),** *Reducing Sugars,* Appendix X
  Sample: 60 to 120 mg
  Acceptance criteria: NMT 1.0%, calculated on the anhydrous basis
- **TOLUENE**
  Toluene standard stock solution: 1000 µg/mL (or 1.153 µL/mL) of toluene in methanol
  Toluene standard solutions: 10 µg/mL, 50 µg/mL, 100 µg/mL, 250 µg/mL, and 500 µg/mL of toluene in methanol: from *Toluene standard stock solution*
  Trifluorotoluene standard stock solution: 800 µg/mL (or 0.673 µL/mL) of α,α,α-trifluorotoluene in methanol
  Trifluorotoluene standard solutions: 80 µg/mL, 400 µg/mL, and 800 µg/mL of α,α,α-trifluorotoluene in methanol, from *Trifluorotoluene standard stock solution* [NOTE—These are the surrogate standards.]
  Sample: 500 mg
  Chromatographic system, Appendix IIA
    Mode: Gas chromatography connected to a purge and trap apparatus (below)
    Detector: Photoionization
    Column: 30-m × 0.53-mm (id) fused silica open tubular column, or equivalent, with a 1.5-µm crossbonded 5% diphenyl, 95% dimethyl polysiloxane (Restek RTX-5, or equivalent) stationary phase
    Column temperature: Hold at 40° for 2 min, increase at 20°/min to 180°, hold at 180° for 2 min.
    Flow rate: 20 mL/min
    Carrier gas: Helium (ultra-high-purity)
  Purge and trap apparatus: The purging apparatus uses disposable 15- × 150-mm test tubes. Use ultra-high-purity helium to purge the sample for 15 min at a flow rate of 60 mL/min. Maintain at 100° all lines that the sample vapor passes through in the purge module. The trap consists of a 30.5-cm × 2.7-mm (id) stainless steel tube, with a packing of a porous polymer based on 2,6-diphenyl-*p*-phenylene oxide (Tenax, or equivalent). The length of the packing in the tube is 24 cm. The entire void volume of the trap is at the vented end of the trap column. Maintain the trap at 100°. Recondition the trap for a subsequent run by baking it for 5 min at 190°.
  Calibration: Place an empty purge tube into the purging apparatus. Fill a 5-mL syringe with 0.5 N sodium hydroxide, and inject into this solution an accurately measured 5-µL aliquot of 10 µg/mL of *Toluene standard solution*. Introduce this solution into the purge tube. Start the instrument for the run, automated if desired, by purging for 15 min, then heating the trap at 180° for 3 min. Repeat this sequence for each of the *Toluene standard solutions* and *Trifluorotoluene standard solutions*. Plot standard curves of the standard concentration (C_S), in µg/mL, versus detector response (r_S) for the *Toluene standard solutions* and *Trifluorotoluene standard solutions*.
  Analysis: Place the *Sample* in a purge tube with 0.1 g of salicylic acid. Attach the purge tube to the purging apparatus. Add 5 µL of 400 µg/mL of *Trifluorotoluene*

standard solution to a 5-mL syringe filled with 0.5 N sodium hydroxide. Add the contents of the syringe to the sample/salicylic acid mixture in the purge apparatus, and start the run, automated if desired, by purging for 15 min, then heating the trap at 180° for 3 min. The procedure is valid only when the detector response of the surrogate standard (*Trifluorotoluene standard solution*) in the sample preparation is within ±15% of the value from the standard curve for *Trifluorotoluene standard*. Calculate the concentration, in µg/g (numerically equivalent to mg/kg), of toluene in the *Sample* taken by the formula:

$$\text{Result} = 5C_S / W_S$$

C_S = concentration of toluene (µg/mL) in the sample, calculated from the standard curve for the *Toluene standard solutions*
W_S = weight of *Sample* (g) taken

Acceptance criteria: NMT 1 mg/kg

- **TRICHLOROETHYLENE**
  Standard stock solution: 1 mg/mL of reagent-grade trichloroethylene in methanol
  Standard solutions: Transfer 0.5, 1.0, 2.0, 3.0, and 5.0 mL of the *Standard stock solution* into five 50-mL volumetric flasks and dilute to volume with water. These *Standard solutions* contain 10 ng/µL, 20 ng/µL, 40 ng/µL, 60 ng/µL, and 100 ng/µL of trichloroethylene.
  Sample: 250 mg
  Chromatographic system, Appendix IIA
    Mode: Gas chromatography
    Detector: Flame-ionization
    Column: 30-m × 0.32-mm (id) capillary column coated with a 1-µm film thickness of dimethylpolysiloxane oil (such as DB-1, OV-1, or equivalent)
    Column temperature: Hold at 40° for 3 min, increase at 4°/min to 220°.
    Detector temperature: 280°
    Carrier gas: Helium
    Purge gas: Nitrogen
    Flow rate: 40 mL/min
    Injection size: 20 µL
  Purge and trap apparatus: The apparatus[1] comprises three sections: the sample purge, the trap, and the desorber. The sample purge accepts 5-mL samples with a water column NLT 3 cm deep, and the gaseous headspace between the water column and the trap has a total volume of NMT 15 mL. The purge gas is passed through the water column as finely divided bubbles with a diameter of less than 3 mm at the origin and is introduced NMT 5 mm from the base of the water column. Use a trap not shorter than or narrower than 25 cm × 2.67 mm (id). Pack the trap to contain the indicated minimum lengths of adsorbents in the following order, beginning at the trap inlet: 7.7 cm of 2,6-diphenylene oxide polymer (TENAX GC, or equivalent), 7.7 cm of silica gel, and 7.7 cm of coconut charcoal. The desorber is capable of rapidly heating the trap to 250°, which is the maximum temperature to be used. Condition the assembled trap before use at 225° overnight with an inert gas at a flow rate of not less than 20 mL/min. Before daily use, condition the trap for 15 min at 225°.
  Analysis: Introduce exactly 20 µL of each *Standard solution* on the inner wall of the sample purge. Desorb according to equipment instructions, and record the peak areas. Prepare a calibration curve by plotting the peak area responses versus the weight of trichloroethylene introduced into the purge. Introduce the *Sample* on the fritted sparger of the sample purge. Purge and desorb according to equipment instructions. Record the peak area of trichloroethylene, and read the corresponding weight (*X*) of trichloroethylene from the calibration curve. Calculate the amount of trichloroethylene, in mg/kg, by the formula:

$$\text{Result} = X/W$$

X = weight of trichloroethylene (ng) in the sample, determined from the calibration curve
W = weight of *Sample* (mg) taken

Acceptance criteria: NMT 1 mg/kg

SPECIFIC TESTS

- **OPTICAL (SPECIFIC) ROTATION,** Appendix IIB
  Sample solution: 1 g in 100 mL of water
  Acceptance criteria: $[\alpha]_D^{20}$ between +160° and +164°, calculated on the anhydrous basis
- **RESIDUE ON IGNITION (SULFATED ASH),** Appendix IIC
  Sample: 1 to 2 g
  Acceptance criteria: NMT 0.1%
- **WATER,** *Water Determination,* Appendix IIB
  Acceptance criteria: NMT 14.0%

gamma-Cyclodextrin

First Published: Prior to FCC 6

γ-Cyclodextrin
gamma-CD
Cyclooctaamylose
Cyclomaltooctaose

---

[1] The apparatus used is based on that described in the U.S. Environmental Protection Agency Test Method for Purgeable Halocarbons—Method 601.

Monographs / gamma-Cyclodextrin

$(C_6H_{10}O_5)_8$
Formula wt 1297.14
CAS: [17465-86-0]
UNII: KZJ0BYZ5VA [gamma cyclodextrin]

DESCRIPTION
Gamma-Cyclodextrin occurs as a white or almost white crystalline solid. It is a nonreducing cyclic saccharide consisting of eight α-1,4-linked D-glucopyranosyl units manufactured by the action of cyclomaltodextrin glucanotransferase on hydrolyzed starch followed by purification of the gamma-Cyclodextrin. It is freely soluble in water and is very slightly soluble in ethanol.
Function: Stabilizer; emulsifier; carrier
Packaging and Storage: Store in tight containers in a dry place.

IDENTIFICATION
- **INFRARED SPECTRA,** *Spectrophotometric Identification Tests,* Appendix IIIC
  Sample preparation: Mineral oil mull
  Analysis: The spectrum of the sample exhibits relative maxima at the same wavelengths as those of the spectrum below.

ASSAY
- **PROCEDURE**
  Mobile phase: Deionized water
  Sample solution: 10 mg/mL
  Chromatographic system, Appendix IIA
    Mode: High-performance liquid chromatography
    Detector: Differential refractometer
    Column: 30-cm × 7.8-mm (id); column packed with 25-μm diameter beads of silver bonded to sulfonated divinyl benzene–styrene copolymer (Aminex HPX-42A, Bio-Rad Laboratories, or equivalent)
    Column temperature: 65° ± 10°
    Flow rate: 0.3 to 1.0 mL/min
    Injection size: About 20 μL
  Analysis: Inject the *Sample solution* into the chromatograph, record the chromatogram, and measure the responses for all peaks. Calculate the content of gamma-cyclodextrin in the *Sample* taken by the peak area percentage method using the following equation:

  $$A = (B/C) \times 100$$

  A = percentage of gamma-cyclodextrin in the sample
  B = peak area of gamma-cyclodextrin in the chromatogram
  C = sum of the areas of all peaks recorded in the chromatogram
  Acceptance criteria: NLT 98.0% as $(C_6H_{10}O_5)_8$, calculated on the anhydrous basis

IMPURITIES
Inorganic Impurities
- **LEAD,** *Atomic Absorption Spectrophotometric Graphite Furnace Method, Method I,* Appendix IIIB
  Sample preparation: Reflux 5 g of sample with 30 mL nitric acid for 1 h. Remove the reflux condenser, and attach a condenser to the flask. Continue to heat and collect the distilled nitric acid. Allow the residue to cool, add 20 mL of water, and allow it to cool again. Add 2 mL of orthophosphoric acid, and dilute to 100 mL with water.
  Acceptance criteria: NMT 1 mg/kg

Organic Impurities
- **REDUCING SUGARS (AS GLUCOSE)**
  Sample: 1 g
  Analysis: Transfer the *Sample* into a 250-mL Erlenmeyer flask, dissolve in 10 mL of water, add 25 mL of alkaline cupric citrate TS, and cover the flask with a small beaker. Boil gently for exactly 5 min, and cool rapidly to room temperature. Add 25 mL of 10% acetic acid solution, 10.0 mL of 0.1 N iodine, 10 mL of dilute hydrochloric acid TS, and 3 mL of starch TS, and titrate with 0.1 N sodium thiosulfate to the disappearance of the blue color. Calculate the content of reducing substances, %R, (as D-glucose) by the equation:

  $$\%R = [(V_1N_1 - V_2N_2) \times F_E]/W$$

  V_1 = volume of the iodine solution (mL)
  N_1 = normality of the iodine solution
  V_2 = volume of the sodium thiosulfate solution (mL)
  N_2 = normality of the sodium thiosulfate solution
  F_E = equivalence factor for D-glucose, determined empirically, 2.7
  W = weight of the sample taken (g)
  Acceptance criteria: NMT 0.5%

- **VOLATILE ORGANIC COMPOUNDS**
  Standard solutions: Prepare solutions of 8-cyclohexadecen-1-one in hexane in the range of 1 μg/mL to 60 μg/mL.
  Sample solution: Dissolve 50 g of sample in 700 mL of water in a 1-L round bottom flask and add a magnetic stirrer. Attach the flask to the lower part of a Bleidner apparatus (see *Figure 1,* below), and connect a 100-mL round-bottom flask containing about 70 mL of hexane and a few boiling stones to the other side of the apparatus. Fill the Bleidner apparatus with equal amounts of water and hexane, and place a reflux condenser on the top. Heat both flasks with heating mantels to boiling. Using the magnetic stirrer, stir the contents of the 1-L flask well. Keep the contents of the two flasks boiling for 8 h. After cooling, remove the

100-mL flask, transfer the contents to a 100-mL volumetric flask, and dilute to volume with hexane.

Chromatographic system, Appendix IIA
  Mode: Gas chromatography
  Detector: Flame-ionization
  Column: 30-m × 0.32-mm (id) column with a stationary phase consisting of 0.25-µm, cross-bonded, 95% dimethyl 5% diphenyl polysiloxane (JBW Scientific DB-5.625, or equivalent)
  Temperature
    Injector: 280°
    Detector: 280°
    Column: Hold at 70° for 4 min, increase at 10°/min to 250°.
  Carrier gas: Nitrogen
  Flow rate: 70 mL/min
Analysis: Separately inject the *Standard solutions* and the *Sample solution* into the chromatograph and record the resulting chromatograms. Using the chromatograms from the *Standard solutions*, create a calibration curve of the concentration of 8-cyclohexadecen-1-one versus the response factor. Calculate the area(s) under the peak for each volatile organic compound in the *Sample solution*, and convert it to mg per kg of gamma-cyclodextrin using the calibration curve.
Acceptance criteria: NMT 20 mg/kg

SPECIFIC TESTS
- **IODINE REACTION**
  Sample: 0.2 g
  Analysis: Place the *Sample* in a test tube and add 2 mL of a 0.1 N iodine solution. Heat the mixture in a water bath, and allow to cool at room temperature.
  Acceptance criteria: A clear, brown solution forms.
- **OPTICAL (SPECIFIC) ROTATION,** Appendix IIB
  Sample: 10 mg/mL
  Acceptance criteria: $[\alpha]_D^{25}$ between +174° and +180°
- **RESIDUE ON IGNITION (SULFATED ASH),** Method I (for Solids), Appendix IIC
  Acceptance criteria: NMT 0.1%
- **WATER,** *Water Determination,* Appendix IIB
  Acceptance criteria: NMT 11.0%

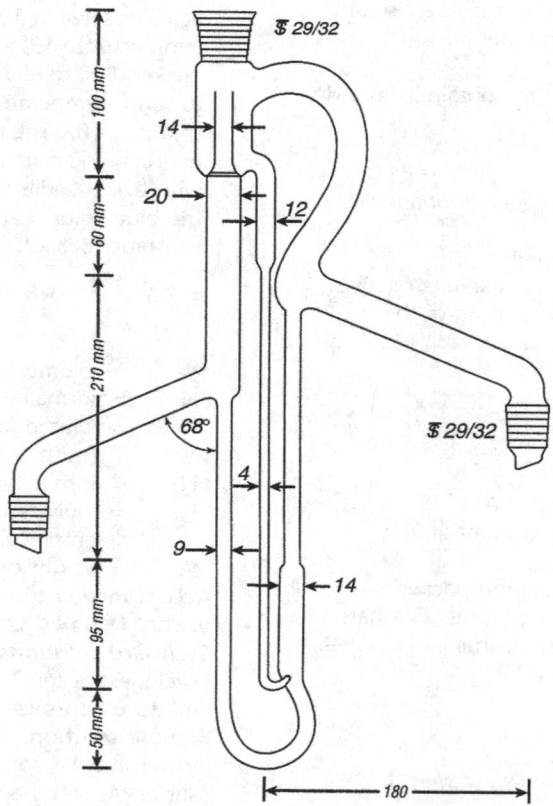

Figure 1. Bleidner Apparatus

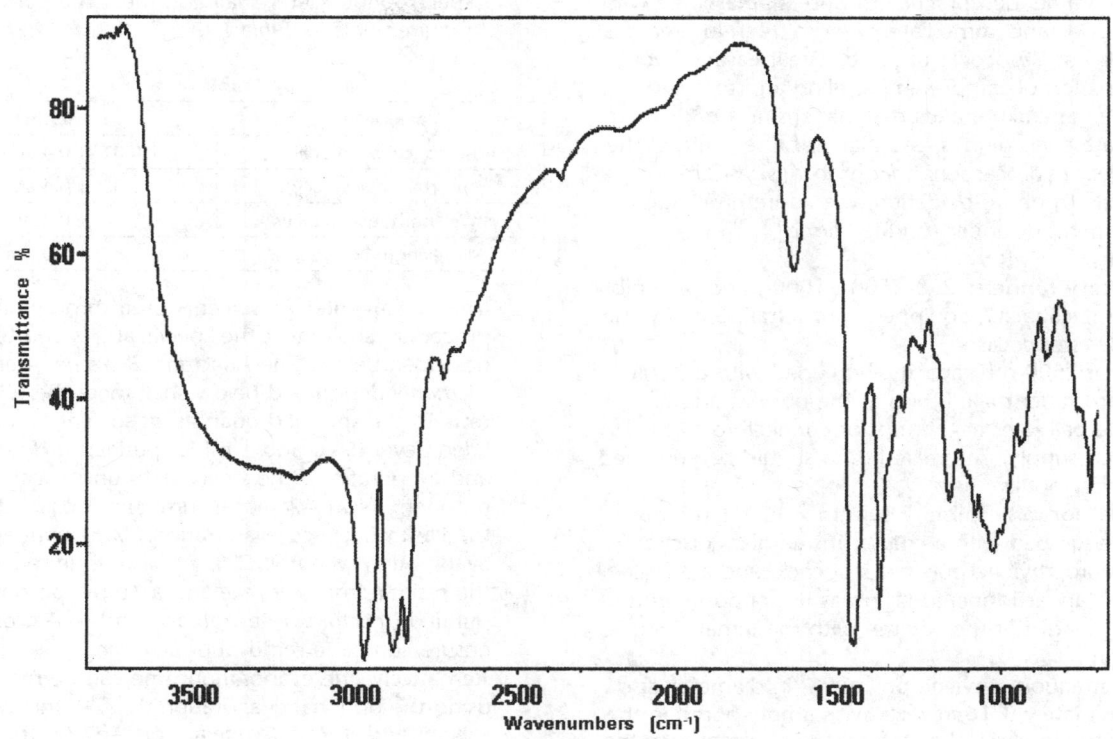

γ-Cyclodextrin (Mineral Oil Mull)

Cyclohexane

First Published: FCC 7

Hexahydrobenzene
Hexamethylene
Hexanaphthene

C₆H₁₂   Formula wt 84.16
                        CAS: [110-82-7]

UNII: 48K5MKG32S [cyclohexane]

DESCRIPTION
Cyclohexane occurs as a clear, colorless, flammable liquid with a faint, characteristic odor that is ether-like. It is produced by reacting benzene with hydrogen. Cyclohexane is insoluble in water and miscible with ethanol and ether.

Function: Extraction solvent

Packaging and Storage: Store in tight containers in a cool place. Store remote from fire. [CAUTION—Cyclohexane is highly flammable.]

IDENTIFICATION
- **SPECIFIC GRAVITY:** Determine by any reliable method (see *General Provisions*).

  Acceptance criteria: Between 0.776 and 0.780 at 20°

ASSAY
- **PROCEDURE**
  Analysis: Proceed as directed under *M-1b*, Appendix XI.
  Acceptance criteria: NLT 99.5% (w/w)

IMPURITIES
Inorganic Impurities
- **LEAD**, *Lead Limit Test, Flame Atomic Absorption Spectrophotometric Method*, Appendix IIIB
  Sample: 5 g
  Analysis: Proceed as directed using the *Diluted Standard Lead Solutions* for the *1 mg/kg Lead Limit*.
  Acceptance criteria: NMT 2 mg/kg
- **SULFUR**, Appendix IIIC
  Acceptance criteria: NMT 10 mg/kg

Organic Impurities
- **BENZENE**, Appendix IIIC
  Analysis: Proceed as directed using the conditions described under *Column No. 6*.
  Acceptance criteria: NMT 0.1%
- **POLYCYCLIC AROMATIC HYDROCARBONS**
  [NOTE—Because of the sensitivity of the test, the possibility of errors arising from contamination is great. It is of the greatest importance, therefore, that all glassware be scrupulously cleaned to remove all organic matter such as oil, grease, detergent residues, etc. Examine all glassware, including stoppers and

stopcocks, under ultraviolet light to detect any residual fluorescent contamination. As a precautionary measure it is a recommended practice to rinse all glassware with purified isooctane immediately before use. No grease is to be used on stopcocks or joints. Great care to avoid contamination of samples in handling and to assure absence of any extraneous material arising from inadequate packaging is essential. Because some of the polynuclear hydrocarbons sought in this test are very susceptible to photo-oxidation, the entire procedure is to be carried out under subdued light.]

Apparatus

Separatory funnels: 250-, 500-, 1000-, and preferably 2000-mL capacity, equipped with tetrafluoroethylene polymer stopcocks

Reservoir: 500-mL capacity, equipped with a 24/40-standard taper male fitting at the bottom and a suitable ball joint at the top for connecting to the nitrogen supply. The male fitting should be equipped with glass hooks.

Chromatographic tube: 180 mm × 15.7 ± 0.1 mm (i.d.), equipped with a coarse, fritted-glass disc, a tetrafluoroethylene polymer stopcock, and a female 24/40-standard tapered fitting at the opposite end. Overall length of the column with the female joint is 235 mm.

Disc: Tetrafluoroethylene polymer 2-in diameter disc approximately 3/16-in thick with a hole bored in the center to closely fit the stem of the chromatographic tube

Heating jacket: Conical, suitable for a 500-mL separatory funnel; used with variable transformer heat control

Suction flask: 250- or 500-mL filter flask

Condenser: 24/40 joints, fitted with a drying tube, length optional

Evaporation flask (optional): 250- or 500-mL capacity all-glass flask equipped with a standard taper stopper having inlet and outlet tubes permitting passage of nitrogen across the surface of the liquid to be evaporated

Vacuum distillation assembly: Use an all glass (for purification of dimethyl sulfoxide) 2-L distillation flask with a heating mantle; a Vigreaux, or equivalent, vacuum-jacketed condenser about 45-cm in length; and a distilling head with a separable cold finger condenser. Use of tetrafluoroethylene polymer sleeves on the glass joints will prevent freezing. Do not use grease on stopcocks or joints.

Nitrogen cylinder: Water-pumped or equivalent purity nitrogen in cylinder equipped with regulator and valve to control flow at 5 psig

Spectrophotometric cells: Use fused quartz cells with an optical path length in the range of 5.000 ± 0.005 cm; also, for checking spectrophotometer performance only, use cells with an optical path length in the range of 1.000 ± 0.005 cm. With distilled water in the cells, determine any absorbance differences.

Spectrophotometer: Use an instrument with a spectral range of 250–400 nm with a spectral slit width of 2 nm or less. Under instrument operating conditions for these absorbance measurements, the spectrophotometer shall also meet the performance requirements in *Table 1*.

Table 1

Parameter	Value
Absorbance repeatability	± 0.01 at 0.4 absorbance
Absorbance accuracy	± 0.05 at 0.4 absorbance
Wavelength repeatability	± 0.2 nm
Wavelength accuracy	± 1.0 nm

Organic solvents: All solvents used throughout this procedure shall meet the specifications and tests described below. The *Isooctane, Benzene, Acetone,* and *Methanol* designated below shall meet the following test: To the specified quantity of solvent in a 250-mL Erlenmeyer flask, add 1 mL of purified *n-Hexadecane* and evaporate on the steam bath under a stream of nitrogen. [NOTE—A loose aluminum foil jacket around the flask will speed evaporation.] Discontinue evaporation when NMT 1 mL of residue remains. To the residue from *Benzene* add a 10-mL portion of purified *Isooctane*, re-evaporate, and repeat once to ensure complete removal of *Benzene*.

Alternatively, the evaporation time can be reduced by using the optional evaporation flask. In this case the solvent and *n-Hexadecane* are placed into the flask on the steam bath, the tube assembly is inserted, and a stream of nitrogen is fed through the inlet tube while the outlet tube is connected to a solvent trap and vacuum line in such a way as to prevent any flow-back of condensate into the flask.

Dissolve the 1 mL of *n-Hexadecane* residue in *Isooctane* and dilute to 25 mL. Determine the absorbance in the 5-cm path length cells compared to *Isooctane* as reference. The absorbance of the solution of the solvent residue (except for *Methanol*) is NMT 0.01 per cm path length between 280 and 400 nm. For *Methanol* this absorbance value is 0.00.

Isooctane (2,2,4-trimethylpentane): Use 180 mL for the test described under *Organic solvents*. Purify, if necessary, by passage through a column of activated silica gel, grade 12, or equivalent, about 90-cm in length and 5- to 8-cm in diameter.

Benzene, reagent grade: Use 150 mL for the test described under *Organic solvents*. Purify, if necessary, by distillation or otherwise.

Acetone, reagent grade: Use 200 mL for the test described under *Organic solvents*. Purify, if necessary, by distillation.

Eluting mixtures

10% Benzene in isooctane: Pipet 50 mL of *Benzene* into a 500-mL glass-stoppered volumetric flask and adjust with *Isooctane* to volume.

20% Benzene in isooctane: Pipet 50 mL of *Benzene* into a 250-mL glass-stoppered volumetric flask and adjust with *Isooctane* to volume.

Acetone–benzene–water mixture: Add 20 mL of water to 390 mL of *Acetone* and 200 mL of *Benzene*.

n-Hexadecane, 99% olefin-free: Dilute 1.0 mL of n-hexadecane with *Isooctane* to 25 mL and determine the absorbance in a 5-cm cell, compared to *Isooctane* as a reference, between 280 and 400 nm. The absorbance per cm path length shall not exceed 0.00 in this range. Purify, if necessary, by percolation through activated silica gel or by distillation.

Methanol, reagent grade: Use 10.0 mL of methanol. Purify, if necessary, by distillation.

Dimethyl sulfoxide: Use a pure grade, clear, water-white product with a melting point of 18°, minimum. Dilute 120 mL with 240 mL of distilled water in a 500-mL separatory funnel, mix, and allow to cool for 5–10 min. Add 40 mL of *Isooctane* to the solution and extract by shaking the funnel vigorously for 2 min. Draw off the lower aqueous layer into a second 500-mL separatory funnel, and repeat the extraction with 40 mL of *Isooctane*. Draw off and discard the aqueous layer. Wash each of the 40-mL isooctane portions three times with 50-mL portions of distilled water. The shaking time for each wash is 1 min. Discard the aqueous layers. Filter the first isooctane portion through *Sodium sulfate, anhydrous* prewashed with *Isooctane* (see *Sodium sulfate* below for preparation of filter), into a 250-mL Erlenmeyer flask, or optionally into the *Evaporation flask*. Wash the first separatory funnel with the second 40-mL isooctane portion, and pass through the sodium sulfate into the flask. Then wash the second and first separatory funnels successively with a 10-mL portion of *Isooctane*, and pass the solvent through the *Sodium sulfate* into the flask. Add 1 mL of *n-Hexadecane* and evaporate the isooctane on the steam bath under nitrogen. Discontinue evaporation when NMT 1 mL of residue remains. To the residue, add a 10-mL portion of *Isooctane* and re-evaporate to 1 mL of *n-Hexadecane*. Again, add 10 mL of *Isooctane* to the residue and evaporate to 1 mL of hexadecane to ensure complete removal of all volatile materials. Dissolve the 1 mL of *n-Hexadecane* in *Isooctane* and dilute to 25 mL. Determine the absorbance in 5-cm path length cells, compared to *Isooctane* as the reference. The absorbance of the solution should not exceed 0.02 per cm path length in the 280–400 nm range. [NOTE—Difficulty in meeting this absorbance specification may be due to organic impurities in the distilled water. Repetition of the test omitting the *Dimethyl sulfoxide* will disclose their presence. If necessary to meet the specification, purify the water by re-distillation, passage through an ion-exchange resin, or otherwise.]

Purify, if necessary, as follows: To 1500 mL of *Dimethyl sulfoxide* in a 2-L glass-stoppered flask, add 6.0 mL of 85% phosphoric acid and 50 g of norit A (decolorizing carbon), or equivalent. Stopper the flask and stir with a magnetic stirrer (tetrafluoroethylene polymer coated bar) for 15 min. Filter the *Dimethyl sulfoxide* through four thicknesses of fluted paper (18.5 cm, Schleicher & Schuell, No. 597, or equivalent). If the initial filtrate contains carbon fines, refilter through the same filter until a clear filtrate is obtained. Protect the sulfoxide from air and moisture during this operation by covering the solvent in the funnel and collection flask with a layer of *Isooctane*. Transfer the filtrate to a 2-L separatory funnel and draw off the dimethyl sulfoxide into the 2-L distillation flask of the *Vacuum distillation assembly* and distill at or below 3 mm Hg. Discard the first 200-mL fraction of the distillate and replace the distillate collection flask with a clean one. Continue the distillation until 1 L of the sulfoxide has been collected. At completion of the distillation, the reagent should be stored in glass-stoppered bottles because it is very hygroscopic and will react with some metal containers in the presence of air.

Magnesium oxide: Use Sea Sorb 43, Food Machinery Company, Westvaco Division, or equivalent. Place 100 g in a large beaker, add 700 mL of distilled water to make a thin slurry, and heat on a steam bath for 30 min with intermittent stirring. Stir well initially to ensure that all of the adsorbent is completely wetted. Using a Buchner funnel and a filter paper (Schleicher & Schuell No. 597, or equivalent) of suitable diameter, filter with suction. Continue suction until water no longer drips from the funnel. Transfer the adsorbent to a glass trough lined with aluminum foil free from rolling oil. Break up the magnesia with a clean spatula and spread out the adsorbent on the foil in a layer 1–2 cm thick. Dry for 24 h at 160 ± 1°. Pulverize the magnesia with a mortar and pestle. Sieve the pulverized adsorbent between 60 and 180 mesh. Use the magnesia retained on the 180-mesh sieve.

Celite 545: Johns-Manville Company, diatomaceous earth, or equivalent

Magnesium oxide–celite 545 mixture: Place the *Magnesium oxide* (60–180 mesh) and *Celite 545* in 2 to 1 proportions, respectively by weight, in a glass-stoppered flask large enough for mixing. Shake vigorously for 10 min, then transfer the mixture to a glass trough lined with aluminum foil free from rolling oil and spread it out in a layer 1–2 cm thick. Reheat the mixture at 160 ± 1° for 2 h, and store in a tightly closed flask

Sodium sulfate, anhydrous, reagent grade: (It is preferable to use a granular form.) For each bottle of *Sodium sulfate, anhydrous, reagent grade* used, establish as follows the necessary prewash to provide such filters required in the method: Place 35 g of *Sodium sulfate, anhydrous* in a 30-mL coarse, fritted-glass funnel or in a 65-mL filter funnel with a glass wool plug; wash with successive 15-mL portions of the indicated solvent until a 15-mL portion of the wash shows 0.00 absorbance per cm path length between 280 and 400 nm when tested as prescribed under *Organic solvents* above. Usually three portions of wash solvent are sufficient.

Sulfoxide–phosphoric acid mixture: Place 300 mL of *Dimethyl sulfoxide* in a 1-L separatory funnel and add 75 mL of 85% phosphoric acid. Mix the contents of the funnel and allow to stand for 10 min. [**CAUTION**—The reaction between the sulfoxide and the acid is exothermic. Release pressure after mixing, then keep the funnel stoppered.] Add 150 mL of *Isooctane* and shake to pre-equilibrate the solvents. Draw off the individual layers and store in glass-stoppered flasks. The layers are *Pre-equilibrated sulfoxide–phosphoric acid mixture* and *Pre-equilibrated isooctane*.

Sample: 25 g

Analysis: Weigh the *Sample* in a beaker and transfer the *Sample* to a 500-mL separatory funnel containing 100 mL of the *Pre-equilibrated sulfoxide–phosphoric acid mixture*. Promptly complete the transfer of the *Sample* to the funnel with portions of the *Pre-equilibrated isooctane*, using a total volume of 50 mL.

When the *Sample* is in solution, shake it vigorously for 2 min. Set up three 250-mL separatory funnels with each containing 30 mL of *Pre-equilibrated isooctane*. After separation of the liquid phases, allow to cool until the main portion of the sample–isooctane solution begins to show a precipitate. Gently swirl the funnel when precipitation first occurs on the inside surface of the funnel to accelerate this process. Carefully draw off the lower layer, filter it slowly through a thin layer of glass wool fitted loosely in a filter funnel into the first 250-mL separatory funnel, and wash in tandem with the 30-mL portions of isooctane contained in the 250-mL separatory funnels. Shaking time for each wash is 1 min. Repeat the extraction operation with two additional portions of the *Sulfoxide–phosphoric acid mixture*, replacing the funnel after each extraction to keep the sample in solution and washing each extractive in tandem through the same three portions of isooctane.

Collect the successive extractives (300 mL total) in a separatory funnel (2-L), containing 480 mL of distilled water, mix, and allow to cool for a few min after the last extractive has been added. Add 80 mL of *Isooctane* to the solution and extract by shaking the funnel vigorously for 2 min. Draw off the lower aqueous layer into a second 2-L separatory funnel, and repeat the extraction with 80 mL of *Isooctane*. Draw off and discard the aqueous layer. Wash each of the 80-mL extractives three times with 100-mL portions of distilled water. Shaking time for each wash is 1 min. Discard the aqueous layers.

Filter the first extractive through *Sodium sulfate, anhydrous* prewashed with *Isooctane* (see *Sodium sulfate* above for preparation of the filter) into a 250-mL Erlenmeyer flask (or, optionally, into the *Evaporation flask*). Wash the first separatory funnel with the second 80-mL isooctane extractive and pass through the sodium sulfate. Then wash the second and first separatory funnels successively with a 20-mL portion of *Isooctane* and pass the solvent through the sodium sulfate into the flask. Add 1 mL of *n-Hexadecane* and evaporate the isooctane on the steam bath under nitrogen. Discontinue evaporation when NMT 1 mL of residue remains. To the residue, add a 10-mL portion of *Isooctane*, re-evaporate to 1 mL of *n-Hexadecane*, and repeat this operation once more.

Transfer the residue with *Isooctane* to a 25-mL volumetric flask and dilute to volume. Determine the absorbance of the solution in the 5-cm path length cells compared to *Isooctane* as reference between 280 and 400 nm. Take care to lose none of the solution in filling the sample cell. Correct the absorbance values for any absorbance derived from the reagents as determined by carrying out the preceding *Analysis* without the *Sample*. If the corrected absorbance does not exceed the limits prescribed under *Acceptance criteria*, the *Sample* meets the ultraviolet absorbance specifications.

If the corrected absorbance per cm path length exceeds the limits prescribed in the *Acceptance criteria*, proceed as follows: Transfer the isooctane solution to a 125-mL flask equipped with a 24/40 joint and evaporate the isooctane on the steam bath under a stream of nitrogen to a volume of 1 mL of hexadecane. Add 10 mL of *Methanol* and 0.3 g of 98% sodium borohydride. Minimize exposure of the borohydride to the atmosphere; a measuring dipper may be used. Immediately fit a water-cooled condenser equipped with a 24/40 joint and with a drying tube into the flask, mix until the borohydride is dissolved, and allow to stand for 30 min at room temperature, with intermittent swirling. At the end of this period, disconnect the flask and evaporate the methanol on the steam bath under nitrogen until the sodium borohydride begins to come out of solution. Add 10 mL of *Isooctane* and evaporate to a volume of 2–3 mL. Again, add 10 mL of *Isooctane* and concentrate to a volume of 5 mL. Swirl the flask repeatedly to assure adequate washing of the sodium borohydride residues.

Fit the *Disc* on the upper part of the stem of the *Chromatographic tube*, then place the tube with the disc on the *Suction flask* and apply the vacuum (135 mm Hg). Weigh out 14 g of the *Magnesium oxide–Celite 545 mixture* and pour the adsorbent mixture into the *Chromatographic tube* in approximately 3-cm layers. After the addition of each layer, level off the top of the adsorbent with a flat glass rod or metal plunger by pressing down firmly until the adsorbent is well-packed. Loosen the topmost few mm of each adsorbent layer with the end of a metal rod before the addition of the next layer. Continue packing in this manner until all of the 14 g of adsorbent is added to the tube. Level off the top of the adsorbent by pressing down firmly with a flat glass rod or metal plunger to make the depth of the adsorbent bed approximately 12.5 cm in depth. Turn off the vacuum and remove the *Suction flask*. Fit the 500-mL *Reservoir* onto the top of the chromatographic column and pre-wet the column by passing 100 mL of *Isooctane* through the column. Adjust the nitrogen pressure so that the rate of descent of the isooctane coming off of the column is between 2 and 3 mL/min. Discontinue pressure just before the last of the isooctane reaches the level of the adsorbent. [**CAUTION**—Do not allow the liquid level to recede below the adsorbent level at any time.]

Remove the *Reservoir* and decant the 5 mL isooctane concentrate solution onto the column, and, with slight pressure, again allow the liquid level to recede to barely above the adsorbent level. Rapidly complete the transfer similarly with two 5-mL portions of isooctane, swirling the flask repeatedly each time to assure adequate washing of the residue. Just before the final

5-mL wash reaches the top of the adsorbent, add 100 mL of *Isooctane* to the *Reservoir* and continue the percolation at the 2–3 mL/min rate. Just before the last of the isooctane reaches the adsorbent level, add 100 mL of *10% Benzene in isooctane* to the *Reservoir* and continue the percolation at the 2–3 mL/min rate. Just before the solvent mixture reaches the adsorbent level, add 25 mL of *20% Benzene in isooctane* to the *Reservoir* and continue the percolation at 2–3 mL/min until all this solvent mixture has been removed from the column. Discard all the elution solvents collected up to this point.

Add 300 mL of the *Acetone–benzene–water mixture* to the *Reservoir* and percolate through the column to elute the polynuclear compounds. Collect the eluate in a clean 1-L separatory funnel. Allow the column to drain until most of the solvent mixture is removed. Wash the eluate three times with 300-mL portions of distilled water, shaking well for each wash. The addition of small amounts of sodium chloride facilitates separation. Discard the aqueous layer after each wash. After the final separation, filter the residual benzene through *Sodium sulfate, anhydrous* prewashed with *Benzene* (see *Sodium sulfate* above for preparation of the filter) into a 250-mL Erlenmeyer flask (or optionally into the *Evaporation flask*). Wash the separatory funnel with two additional 20-mL portions of *Benzene* which are also filtered through the *Sodium sulfate*. Add 1 mL of *n-Hexadecane* and completely remove the benzene by evaporation under nitrogen, using the special procedure to eliminate benzene as previously described under *Organic solvents*. Transfer the residue with *Isooctane* to a 25-mL volumetric flask and adjust the volume. Determine the absorbance of the solution in the 5-cm path length cells compared to *Isooctane* as reference between 250 and 400 nm. Correct for any absorbance derived from the reagents as determined by carrying out the procedure without a wash sample. If either spectrum shows the characteristic benzene peaks in the 250–260 nm region, evaporate the solution to remove benzene by the procedure under *Organic solvents*. Dissolve the residue, transfer with *Isooctane* to a 25-mL volumetric flask, and dilute to volume. Record the absorbance again. If the corrected absorbance does not exceed the limits prescribed in the *Acceptance criteria*, the *Sample* meets the ultraviolet absorbance specifications.

Acceptance criteria: See *Table 2*.

Table 2

Wavelength (nm)	Absorbance
280–289	0.15
290–299	0.12
300–359	0.08
360–400	0.02

SPECIFIC TESTS
- **DISTILLATION RANGE**, Appendix IIB
  Acceptance criteria: Between 80° and 82°

- **NONVOLATILE RESIDUE**
  Sample: 100 mL
  Analysis: Evaporate the *Sample* to dryness in a tared platinum dish on a steam bath, heat at 105° for 30 min or to constant weight, cool in a desiccator, and weigh.
  Acceptance criteria: NMT 1 mg/100 mL

Cyclohexyl Acetate
First Published: Prior to FCC 6

$C_8H_{14}O_2$ Formula wt 142.20
FEMA: 2349
UNII: UL0RS4H1UE [cyclohexyl acetate]

DESCRIPTION
Cyclohexyl Acetate occurs as a colorless to pale yellow liquid.
Odor: Green, fruity
Solubility: Soluble in alcohol
Boiling Point: ~174°
Function: Flavoring agent

ASSAY
- **PROCEDURE:** Proceed as directed under *M-1b*, Appendix XI.
  Acceptance criteria: NLT 98.0% of $C_8H_{14}O_2$

SPECIFIC TESTS
- **ACID VALUE, FLAVOR CHEMICALS (OTHER THAN ESSENTIAL OILS)**, *M-15*, Appendix XI
  Acceptance criteria: NMT 1.0
- **REFRACTIVE INDEX**, Appendix II: At 20°
  Acceptance criteria: Between 1.436 and 1.441
- **SPECIFIC GRAVITY:** Determine at 25° by any reliable method (see *General Provisions*).
  Acceptance criteria: Between 0.966 and 0.970

p-Cymene
First Published: Prior to FCC 6

$C_{10}H_{14}$ Formula wt 134.22
FEMA: 2356
UNII: 1G1C8T1N7Q [p-cymene]

DESCRIPTION
p-Cymene occurs as a colorless to pale yellow liquid.
Odor: Kerosene

308 / *p*-Cymene / *Monographs*

Solubility: Soluble in vegetable oils; insoluble or practically insoluble in water, propylene glycol
Boiling Point: ~177°
Solubility in Alcohol, Appendix VI: One mL dissolves in 1 mL of 95% alcohol.
Function: Flavoring agent

IDENTIFICATION

- **INFRARED SPECTRA,** *Spectrophotometric Identification Tests,* Appendix IIIC
  Acceptance criteria: The spectrum of the sample exhibits relative maxima at the same wavelengths as those of the spectrum below.

ASSAY

- **PROCEDURE:** Proceed as directed under *M-1a*, Appendix XI.
  Acceptance criteria: NLT 97.0% of $C_{10}H_{14}$

SPECIFIC TESTS

- **REFRACTIVE INDEX,** Appendix II: At 20°
  Acceptance criteria: Between 1.489 and 1.491
- **SPECIFIC GRAVITY:** Determine at 25° by any reliable method (see *General Provisions*).
  Acceptance criteria: Between 0.853 and 0.855

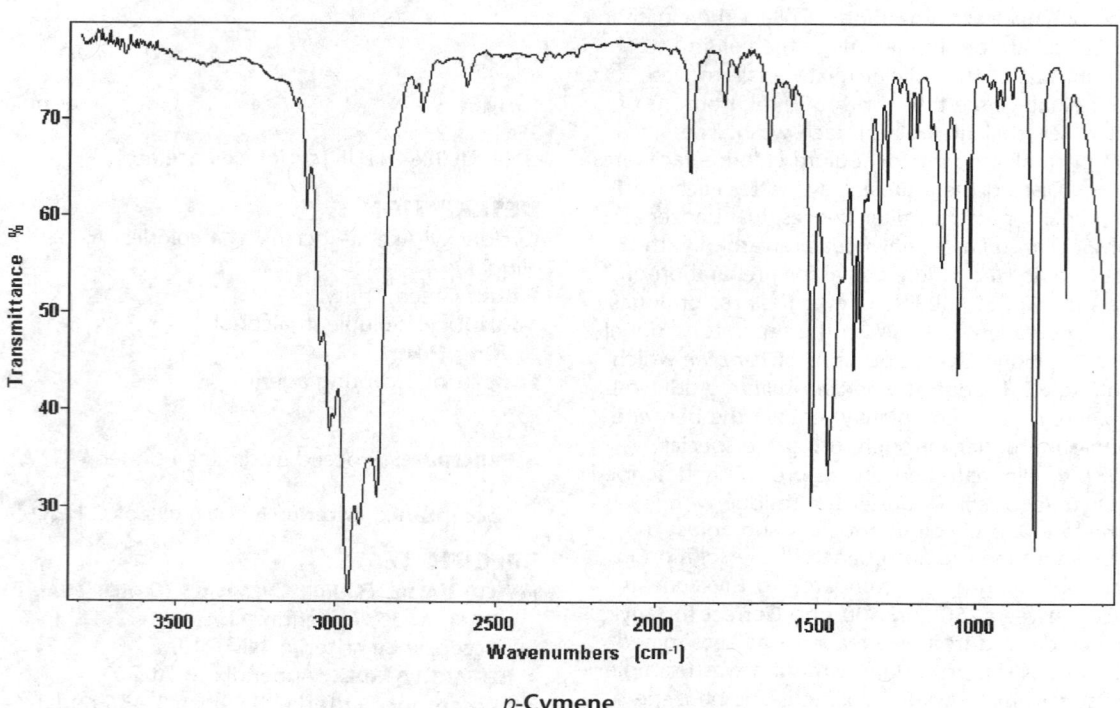

p-Cymene

L-Cysteine Monohydrochloride

First Published: Prior to FCC 6
Last Revision: FCC 6

L-2-Amino-3-mercaptopropanoic Acid Monohydrochloride

$C_3H_7NO_2S \cdot HCl \cdot H_2O$ Formula wt, monohydrate 175.63
$C_3H_7NO_2S \cdot HCl$ Formula wt, anhydrous 157.62
INS: 920   CAS: monohydrate [7048-04-6]
   anhydrous [52-89-1]
UNII: ZT934N0X4W [cysteine hydrochloride]

DESCRIPTION

L-Cysteine Monohydrochloride occurs as a white, crystalline powder. It is freely soluble in water and in alcohol. The anhydrous form melts with decomposition at about 175°.
Function: Nutrient
Packaging and Storage Store in well-closed, light-resistant containers.

IDENTIFICATION

- **INFRARED ABSORPTION,** *Spectrophotometric Identification Tests,* Appendix IIIC.
  Reference standard: USP L-Cysteine Hydrochloride RS
  Sample and Standard preparation: *K*
  Acceptance criteria: The spectrum of the sample exhibits maxima at the same wavelengths as those in the spectrum of the *Reference standard*.

ASSAY

- **PROCEDURE**
  Sample: 300 mg, previously dried

Analysis: Transfer the *Sample* into a 250-mL glass-stoppered flask. Add 20 mL of water, 4 g of potassium iodide, 5 mL of 2.7 N hydrochloric acid, and 25.0 mL of 0.1 N iodine. Stopper the flask, and allow the mixture to stand for 30 min in a dark place. Titrate the excess iodine with 0.1 N sodium thiosulfate. Perform a blank determination (see *General Provisions*), and make any necessary correction. Each mL of 0.1 N iodine is equivalent to 15.76 mg of $C_3H_7NO_2S \cdot HCl$.
Acceptance criteria: NLT 98.0% and NMT 101.5% $C_3H_7NO_2S \cdot HCl$, on the dried basis

IMPURITIES
Inorganic Impurities
- **LEAD,** *Lead Limit Test,* Appendix IIIB
  Sample solution: Prepare as directed for organic compounds.
  Control: 5 µg Pb (5 mL of *Diluted Standard Lead Solution*)
  Acceptance criteria: NMT 5 mg/kg

SPECIFIC TESTS
- **LOSS ON DRYING,** Appendix IIC: room temperature for 24 h in a vacuum desiccator using a suitable desiccant and maintaining a pressure of NMT 5 mm Hg
  Acceptance criteria: NLT 8.0% and NMT 12.0%
- **OPTICAL (SPECIFIC) ROTATION,** Appendix IIB
  Sample: 8 g, undried
  Analysis: Dissolve the *Sample* in sufficient 1 N hydrochloric acid to make 100 mL.
  Acceptance criteria
  $[\alpha]_D^{20}$ between +5.0° and +8.0°, calculated on the dried basis
  $[\alpha]_D^{25}$ between +4.9° and +7.9°, calculated on the dried basis
- **RESIDUE ON IGNITION (SULFATED ASH),** Appendix IIC
  Sample: 1 g
  Acceptance criteria: NMT 0.1%

L-Cystine
First Published: Prior to FCC 6

3,3'-Dithiobis(2-aminopropanoic acid)

$C_6H_{12}N_2O_4S_2$　　　　　　　　Formula wt 240.30

INS: 921　　　　　　　　CAS: [56-89-3]
UNII: 48TCX9A1VT [cystine]

DESCRIPTION
L-Cystine occurs as colorless to white crystals. It is soluble in diluted mineral acids and in alkaline solutions. It is very slightly soluble in water and in alcohol.
Function: Nutrient
Packaging and Storage: Store in well-closed containers.

IDENTIFICATION
- **INFRARED SPECTRA,** *Spectrophotometric Identification Tests,* Appendix IIIC
  Sample preparation: Mineral oil mull
  Acceptance criteria: The spectrum of the sample exhibits relative maxima at the same wavelengths as those of the spectrum below.

ASSAY
- **NITROGEN DETERMINATION,** Appendix IIIC
  Sample: 200 mg
  Analysis: Calculate the percent L-Cystine using the equation:

$$\% \text{ L-Cystine} = N \times 8.58$$

  N = percent nitrogen
  Acceptance criteria: NLT 98.5% and NMT 101.5% $C_6H_{12}N_2O_4S_2$, calculated on the dried basis

IMPURITIES
Inorganic Impurities
- **LEAD,** *Lead Limit Test,* Appendix IIIB
  Sample solution: Prepare as directed for organic compounds.
  Control: 5 µg Pb (5 mL of *Diluted Standard Lead Solution*)
  Acceptance criteria: NMT 5 mg/kg

SPECIFIC TESTS
- **LOSS ON DRYING,** Appendix IIC: 105° for 3 h
  Acceptance criteria: NMT 0.2%
- **OPTICAL (SPECIFIC) ROTATION,** Appendix IIB
  Sample solution: 2 g of previously dried sample in sufficient 1 N hydrochloric acid to make 100 mL
  Acceptance criteria: $[\alpha]_D^{20}$ between −215° and −225°, on the dried basis
- **RESIDUE ON IGNITION (SULFATED ASH),** Appendix IIC
  Sample: 2 g
  Acceptance criteria: NMT 0.1%

L-Cystine (Mineral Oil Mull)

5′-Cytidylic Acid

First Published: First Supplement, FCC 7

Cytidine 5′-monophosphate
Cytidylic acid
CMP
Cytidine 5′-phosphoric acid

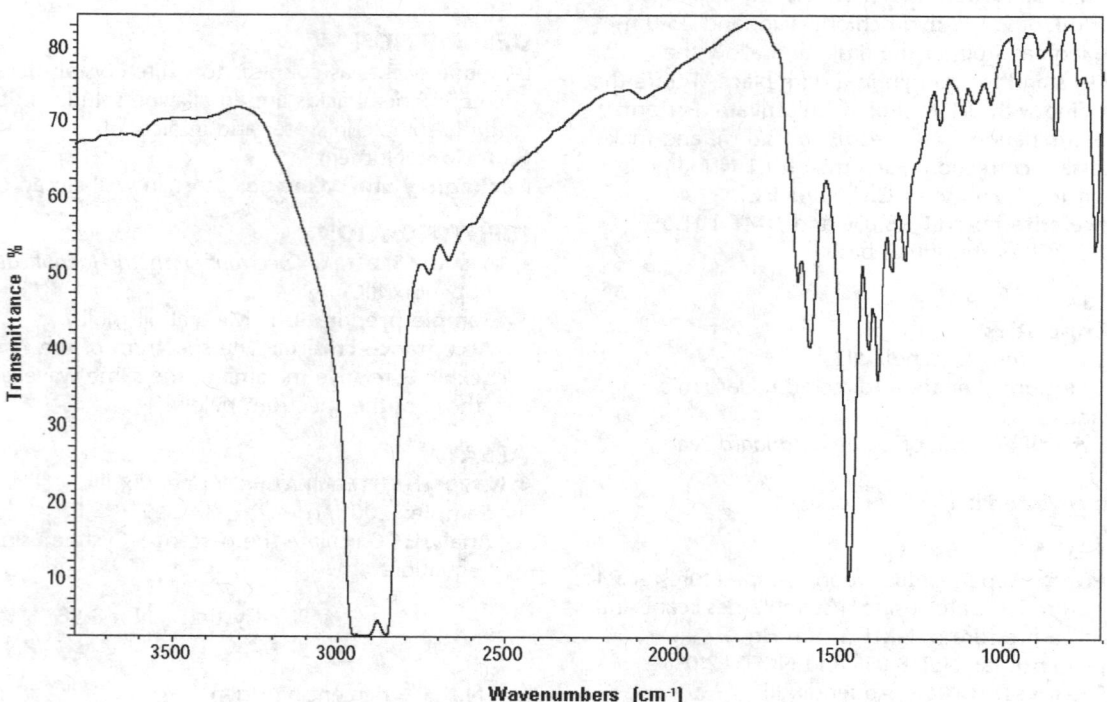

$C_9H_{14}N_3O_8P$ Formula wt 323.20
                       CAS: [63-37-6]

UNII: F469818O25 [5′-cytidylic acid]

DESCRIPTION
5′-Cytidylic Acid occurs as colorless or white crystals, or as a white, crystalline powder. It is very slightly soluble in water, and practically insoluble in alcohol. It is produced by enzymatic cleavage of yeast riboncleic acid (RNA) with a 5′-phosphodiesterase followed by heat treatment, further purification steps, and washing of crystals with ethanol.

Function: Source of 5′-Cytidylic Acid

Packaging and Storage: Store in tight containers protected from light and moisture.

IDENTIFICATION
- **A. INFRARED ABSORPTION**, *Spectrophotometric Identification Tests*, Appendix IIIC
  Reference standard: USP 5′-Cytidylic Acid RS
  Sample and standard preparation: *A*
  Acceptance criteria: The spectrum of the sample exhibits maxima at the same wavelengths as those in the spectrum of the *Reference standard*.
- **B. PROCEDURE**
  Acceptance criteria: The retention time of the major peak (excluding the solvent peak) in the chromatogram of the *Sample solution* corresponds to that of the *Standard solution* in the *Assay*.

ASSAY
- **PROCEDURE**
  Mobile phase: 0.1 M potassium dihydrogen phosphate (KH_2PO_4) in degassed water, adjusted with 0.1 M dipotassium hydrogen phosphate (K_2HPO_4) to a pH of 5.6
  Standard solution: 0.02 mg/mL of USP 5′-Cytidylic Acid RS in *Mobile phase*. [NOTE—Ultrasonication for 15 min at 30° may be necessary to aid in complete dissolution.]
  Sample solution: 0.02 mg/mL in *Mobile phase*. [NOTE—Ultrasonication for 15 min at 30° may be necessary to aid in complete dissolution.]
  Chromatographic system, Appendix IIA
    Mode: High-performance liquid chromatography
    Detector: UV 254 nm

Column: 25-cm × 4.6-mm; packed with 5-μm reversed phase C18 silica gel[1]
Column temperature: Ambient
Flow rate: About 1.0 mL/min
Injection size: 50 μL
System suitability
  Sample: *Standard solution*
  Suitability requirements
    Suitability requirement 1: The relative standard deviation of the 5′-cytidylic acid peak area responses from replicate injections is NMT 2.0%.
    Suitability requirement 2: The resolution, R, between the 5′-cytidylic acid peak and all other peaks is NLT 2.0.
Analysis: Separately inject equal volumes of the *Standard solution* and *Sample solution* into the chromatograph, and measure the responses for the major peaks on the resulting chromatograms. [NOTE—The approximate retention time for 5′-cytidylic acid is 4.6 min.] Calculate the percentage of disodium 5′-cytidylic acid, $C_9H_{14}N_3O_8P$, in the sample taken:

$$\text{Result} = (r_U/r_S) \times (C_S/C_U) \times 100$$

r_U = peak area response of 5′-cytidylic acid in the *Sample solution*
r_S = peak area response of 5′-cytidylic acid in the *Standard solution*
C_S = concentration of 5′-cytidylic acid in the *Standard solution* (mg/mL)
C_U = concentration of sample in the *Sample solution* (mg/mL)

Acceptance criteria: 98.0%–103.0%, calculated on the anhydrous basis

IMPURITIES
Inorganic Impurities
- **ARSENIC**
  [NOTE—When water is specified as a diluent, use deionized ultra-filtered water. When nitric acid is specified, use nitric acid of a grade suitable for trace element analysis with as low a content of arsenic as practical.]
  Diluent: 4% nitric acid in water
  Standard stock solution: 100 μg/mL of arsenic prepared by diluting a commercially available 1000 mg/kg arsenic ICP standard solution
  Standard solutions: 0.05, 0.1, 0.2, 0.5, 1, and 2 μg/mL of arsenic: from *Standard stock solution* diluted with *Diluent*
  Sample: 5 g
  Sample solution: Dissolve the *Sample* in 40 mL of 10% nitric acid in a 100-mL volumetric flask, and dilute with water to volume.
  Spectrophotometric system, *Plasma Spectrochemistry*, Appendix IIC
    Mode: Inductively coupled plasma–optical emission spectroscopy (ICP–OES)
    Setup: Use a suitable ICP–OES configured in a radial optical alignment. [NOTE—This method was developed using a Varian Vista MPX ICP OES unit.] The instrument parameters are as follows: set the ultraviolet detector to scan arsenic at 188.980 nm. Set the sample read time to 20 s. Set the forward power from the RF generator to 1150 watts. Use an argon plasma feed gas flow of 13.5 L/min with the auxiliary gas set to flow at 2.25 L/min. The sample is delivered to the spray chamber by a multi-channel peristaltic pump set to deliver sample at a rate of 20 rpm. Samples are flushed through the system for 20 s prior to analysis. A 40-s read delay is also programmed into the sampling routine to allow for fluid flow equilibration after the high-speed flush, prior to the first analytical read of the sample. Between samples, the pumping system is washed by flushing the *Diluent* for 20 s.
  Analysis: Generate a standard curve using *Diluent* as a *Blank* and the *Standard solutions*. [NOTE—The correlation coefficient for the best-fit line should not be less than 0.999.]
  Similarly, analyze the *Sample solution* on the ICP. Calculate the concentration (mg/kg) of arsenic in the *Sample* taken:

$$\text{Result} = (C/W) \times F$$

  C = concentration of arsenic in the *Sample solution* determined from the standard curve (μg/mL)
  W = weight of *Sample* taken (g)
  F = final volume of the *Sample solution*, 100 mL

  Acceptance criteria: NMT 2 mg/kg

- **CADMIUM**
  [NOTE—When water is specified as a diluent, use deionized ultra-filtered water. When nitric acid is specified, use nitric acid of a grade suitable for trace element analysis with as low a content of cadmium as practical.]
  Diluent: 4% nitric acid in water
  Standard stock solution: 100 μg/mL of cadmium prepared by diluting a commercially available 1000 mg/kg cadmium ICP standard solution
  Standard solutions: 0.005, 0.05, 0.1, 0.2, 0.5, 1, and 2 μg/mL of cadmium: from *Standard stock solution* diluted with *Diluent*
  Sample: 5 g
  Sample solution: Dissolve the *Sample* in 40 mL of 10% nitric acid in a 100-mL volumetric flask, and dilute with water to volume.
  Spectrophotometric system, *Plasma Spectrochemistry*, Appendix IIC
    Mode: Inductively coupled plasma–optical emission spectroscopy (ICP–OES)
    Setup: Same as that described in the test for *Arsenic*, but set to scan for cadmium at 228.802 nm
  Analysis: Generate a standard curve using *Diluent* as a *Blank* and the *Standard solutions*. [NOTE—The correlation coefficient for the best-fit line should not be less than 0.999.]

---
[1] YMC-Pack ODS-AQ (YMC Europe GmbH, Dinslaken, Germany), or equivalent.

Similarly, analyze the *Sample solution* on the ICP. Calculate the concentration (mg/kg) of cadmium in the *Sample* taken:

$$\text{Result} = (C/W) \times F$$

C = concentration of cadmium in the *Sample solution* determined from the standard curve (µg/mL)
W = weight of *Sample* taken (g)
F = final volume of the *Sample solution*, 100 mL

Acceptance criteria: NMT 0.1 mg/kg

- **LEAD**

  [NOTE—When water is specified as a diluent, use deionized ultra-filtered water. When nitric acid is specified, use nitric acid of a grade suitable for trace element analysis with as low a content of lead as practical.]

  Diluent: 4% nitric acid in water
  Standard stock solution: 100 µg/mL of lead prepared by diluting a commercially available 1000 mg/kg lead ICP standard solution
  Standard solutions: 0.05, 0.1, 0.2, 0.5, 1, and 2 µg/mL of lead: from *Standard stock solution* diluted with *Diluent*
  Sample: 5 g
  Sample solution: Dissolve the *Sample* in 40 mL of 10% nitric acid in a 100-mL volumetric flask, and dilute with water to volume.
  Spectrophotometric system, *Plasma Spectrochemistry*, Appendix IIC
  Mode: Inductively coupled plasma–optical emission spectroscopy (ICP–OES)
  Setup: Same as that described in the test for *Arsenic*, but set to scan for lead at 220.353 nm
  Analysis: Generate a standard curve using *Diluent* as a *Blank* and the *Standard solutions*. [NOTE—The correlation coefficient for the best-fit line should not be less than 0.999.]
  Similarly, analyze the *Sample solution* on the ICP. Calculate the concentration (mg/kg) of lead in the *Sample* taken:

  $$\text{Result} = (C/W) \times F$$

  C = concentration of lead in the *Sample solution* determined from the standard curve (µg/mL)
  W = weight of *Sample* taken (g)
  F = final volume of the *Sample solution*, 100 mL

  Acceptance criteria: NMT 1 mg/kg

- **MERCURY**

  [NOTE—When water is specified as a diluent, use deionized ultra-filtered water. When nitric acid is specified, use nitric acid of a grade suitable for trace element analysis with as low a content of mercury as practical.]

  Diluent: 4% nitric acid in water
  Standard stock solution: 100 µg/mL of mercury prepared by diluting a commercially available 1000 mg/kg mercury ICP standard solution
  Standard solutions: 0.025, 0.05, 0.1, 0.2, 0.5, 1, and 2 µg/mL of mercury: from *Standard stock solution* diluted with *Diluent*
  Sample: 5 g
  Sample solution: Dissolve the *Sample* in 40 mL of 10% nitric acid in a 100-mL volumetric flask, and dilute with water to volume.
  Spectrophotometric system, *Plasma Spectrochemistry*, Appendix IIC
  Mode: Inductively coupled plasma–optical emission spectroscopy (ICP–OES)
  Setup: Same as that described in the test for *Arsenic*, but set to scan for mercury at 194.164 nm
  Analysis: Generate a standard curve using *Diluent* as a *Blank* and the *Standard solutions*. [NOTE—The correlation coefficient for the best-fit line should not be less than 0.999.]
  Similarly, analyze the *Sample solution* on the ICP. Calculate the concentration (mg/kg) of mercury in the *Sample* taken:

  $$\text{Result} = (C/W) \times F$$

  C = concentration of mercury in the *Sample solution* determined from the standard curve (µg/mL)
  W = weight of *Sample* taken (g)
  F = final volume of the *Sample solution*, 100 mL

  Acceptance criteria: NMT 0.5 mg/kg

Organic Impurities

- **ETHANOL**

  Standard solution: 20 mg/kg of ethanol in 1 N sodium hydroxide. Add 10 mL of this solution to a 20-mL headspace vial, and cap tightly.
  Sample solution: 100 mg/g in 1 N sodium hydroxide. Add 10 mL of this solution to a 20-mL headspace vial, and cap tightly.
  Chromatographic system, Appendix IIA
  Mode: Gas chromatography equipped with pressure-loop headspace autosampler
  Detector: Flame ionization
  Column: 30-m × 0.53-mm (id) capillary column with a 6% cyanopropylphenyl–94% dimethylpolysiloxane stationary phase and a 3.00-µm film thickness[2]
  Temperature
  Column: 20 min at 40°; increase to 240° at 10°/min; maintain at 240° for 10 min
  Injection port: 140°
  Detector: 250°
  Carrier gas: Nitrogen
  Flow rate: 2.5 mL/min
  Headspace unit: 2.5 mL/min
  Equilibration temperature: 80°
  Equilibration time: 60 min
  Loop temperature: 85°
  Transfer temperature: 90°
  Pressurization time: 0.5 min
  Loop fill time: 0.1 min
  Injection time: 1 min
  Injection size: 1 mL of headspace

---

[2] CP-Select 624 CB (Varian-Chrompack, Palo Alto, CA), or equivalent.

System suitability
  Sample: *Standard solution*
  Suitability requirement: The relative standard deviation of the ethanol peak area responses from replicate injections is NMT 5.0%.
Analysis: Separately inject equal volumes of the *Standard solution* and *Sample solution* into the chromatograph, record the chromatograms, and measure the peak responses. [NOTE—The approximate retention time for ethanol is 11 min.]
Acceptance criteria: The peak area from the *Sample solution* does not exceed that from the *Standard solution* (NMT 200 mg/kg).

- **OTHER RIBONUCLEOTIDES**
  Mobile phase and **Chromatographic system:** Prepare as directed in the *Assay*.
  Standard solution: Mixture of USP Disodium 5'-Uridylate RS, USP 5'-Adenylic Acid RS, USP 5'-Cytidylic Acid RS, USP Disodium Guanylate RS, and USP Disodium Inosinate RS each at 0.02 mg/mL in *Mobile phase*
  Sample solution: 1.0 mg/mL. [NOTE—Ultrasonication for 15 min at 30° may be necessary to aid in complete dissolution.]
  Suitability requirements
    Sample: *Standard solution*
    Suitability requirement 1: The relative standard deviation of the 5'-cytidylic acid peak area responses from replicate injections is NMT 2.0%.
    Suitability requirement 2: The resolution, R, between the 5'-cytidylic acid peak and all other nucleotide peaks is NLT 2.0.
  Analysis: Separately inject equal volumes of the *Standard solution* and *Sample solution* into the chromatograph, and measure the responses for all nucleotide peaks on the resulting chromatograms, except the peak from 5'-cytidylic acid. [NOTE—The approximate retention times are 4.6 min (5'-cytidylic acid), 6.2 min (5'-uridylic acid), 10.3 min (5'-guanylic acid), 11.5 min (5'-inosinic acid), and 27.5 min (5'-adenylic acid).] Separately calculate the percentage of each analyte (disodium 5'-uridylate, 5'-guanylic acid, 5'-inosinic acid, and 5'-adenylic acid) in the sample taken:

$$\text{Result} = (r_U/r_S) \times (C_S/C_U) \times 100$$

  r_U = peak area of the analyte from the *Sample solution*
  r_S = peak area of the analyte from the *Standard solution*
  C_S = concentration of analyte in the *Standard solution* (mg/mL)
  C_U = concentration of analyte in the *Sample solution* (mg/mL)
  Acceptance criteria: The sum of the percentages for all nucleotide impurities is NMT 0.5%, calculated on the anhydrous basis.

SPECIFIC TESTS

- **PH**, *pH Determination*, Appendix IIB
  Sample solution: 5 mg/mL
  Acceptance criteria: 2.7–3.7
- **WATER**, *Water Determination, Method I*, Appendix IIB
  Acceptance criteria: NMT 6.0%
- **BILE-TOLERANT GRAM-NEGATIVE BACTERIA**, Appendix XIIC
  Sample preparation: Proceed as directed using a 10-g sample and incubating at 30°–35° for 18–24 h.
  Acceptance criteria: Negative in 10 g
- **ENTEROBACTER SAKAZAKII** (*Cronobacter spp.*), Appendix XIIC
  Sample preparation: Proceed as directed using a 10-g sample and incubating at 30°–35° for 18–24 h.
  Acceptance criteria: Negative in 10 g
- **SALMONELLA SPP.**, Appendix XIIC
  Sample preparation: Dissolve 25 g of sample at a sample/broth ratio of 1/8, and proceed as directed.
  Acceptance criteria: Negative in 25 g
- **TOTAL AEROBIC MICROBIAL COUNT**, *Method I (Plate Count Method)*, Appendix XIIB
  Acceptance criteria: NMT 1,000 cfu/g
- **TOTAL YEASTS AND MOLDS COUNT**, *Method I (Plate Count Method)*, Appendix XIIB
  Acceptance criteria: NMT 100 cfu/g

Dammar Gum

First Published: Prior to FCC 6

Dammar Resin
Damar Gum
Damar Resin
Dammar

CAS: [9000-16-2]

DESCRIPTION
Crude Dammar Gum occurs as irregular, white to yellow to brown tears, fragments, or powder, sometimes admixed with fragments of bark. Refined grades are white to yellow and are free of fragments of ligneous matter. Dammar Gum is the dried exudate from trees of the *Agathis, Hopea,* or *Shorea* genera. It consists of a complex mixture of acidic and neutral terpenoid compounds together with polysaccharide material. It is insoluble in water and in ethanol and is soluble in toluene and in limonene. A chloroform solution of Dammar Gum is dextrorotatory.

Function: Stabilizer; glazing agent
Packaging and Storage: Store in well-closed containers.

IDENTIFICATION
- **THIN-LAYER CHROMATOGRAPHY,** Appendix IIA
  Sample solution: 100 mg/mL in chloroform
  Adsorbent: 0.2-mm layer of silica (Merck F254, or equivalent)
  Application volume: 20 μL
  Developing solvent system: Diethyl ether:heptane [30:25]
  Analysis: Spray the plate with sulfuric acid, and dry it at 180° for 3 min.
  Acceptance criteria: Two dark spots are observed at R_f of 0.8 and 0.7, and the ratio of the faster-moving spot to the second spot is about 1.1 to 1.

IMPURITIES
Inorganic Impurities
- **LEAD,** *Lead Limit Test,* Appendix IIIB,
  Sample solution: Prepare as directed for organic compounds.
  Control: 5 μg Pb (5 mL of *Diluted Standard Lead Solution*)
  Acceptance criteria: NMT 5 mg/kg

SPECIFIC TESTS
- **ACID NUMBER,** Appendix IX
  Sample: 5 g
  Analysis: Modify the procedure in Appendix IXA by adding 30 mL each of toluene and neutral ethanol to the *Sample* and titrating with 0.5 N alcoholic potassium hydroxide, using phenolphthalein TS as indicator.
  Acceptance criteria: Between 20 and 40
- **ASH (TOTAL),** Appendix IIC
  Acceptance criteria: NMT 0.5%
- **IODINE VALUE,** Appendix VII
  Acceptance criteria: Between 10 and 40
- **LOSS ON DRYING,** Appendix IIC: 105° for 18 h
  Acceptance criteria: NMT 6.0%
- **MELTING RANGE,** *Melting Range or Temperature Determination,* Appendix IIB
  Acceptance criteria: Between 90° and 95°
- **SOFTENING POINT,** *Ring-and-Ball Method,* Appendix IX
  Acceptance criteria: Between 86° and 90°

(*E*),(*E*)-2,4-Decadienal

First Published: Prior to FCC 6
Last Revision: First Supplement, FCC 6

trans,trans-2,4-Decadienal

$C_{10}H_{16}O$ Formula wt 152.24
FEMA: 3135
UNII: 3G88X2RK09 [2,4-decadienal, (2e,4e)-]

DESCRIPTION
(*E*),(*E*)-2,4-Decadienal occurs as a yellow liquid. It may contain a suitable antioxidant.
Odor: Powerful, oily, chicken fat
Solubility: Soluble in alcohol, most fixed oils; insoluble or practically insoluble in water
Boiling Point: ~104° (7 mm Hg)
Solubility in Alcohol, Appendix VI: One mL dissolves in 1 mL of 95% ethanol.
Function: Flavoring agent

IDENTIFICATION
- **INFRARED SPECTRA,** *Spectrophotometric Identification Tests,* Appendix IIIC
  Acceptance criteria: The spectrum of the sample exhibits relative maxima at the same wavelengths as those of the spectrum below.

ASSAY
- **PROCEDURE:** Proceed as directed under *M-1a,* Appendix XI.
  Acceptance criteria: NLT 89.0% of $C_{10}H_{16}O$ (sum of two isomers)

SPECIFIC TESTS
- **REFRACTIVE INDEX,** Appendix II: At 20°
  Acceptance criteria: Between 1.514 and 1.519
- **SPECIFIC GRAVITY:** Determine at 25° by any reliable method (see *General Provisions*).
  Acceptance criteria: Between 0.866 and 0.876

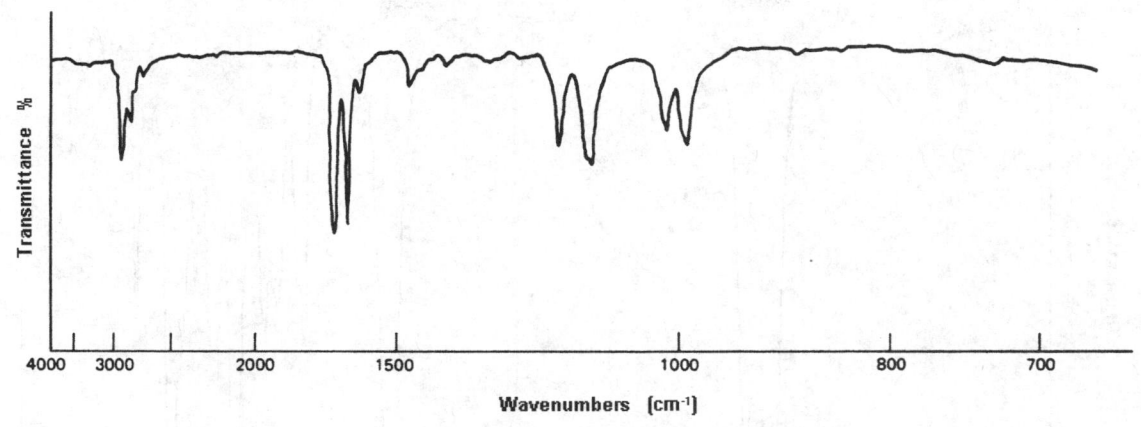

(E),(E)-2,4-Decadienal

δ-Decalactone

First Published: Prior to FCC 6

$C_{10}H_{18}O_2$ Formula wt 170.25
FEMA: 2361
UNII: CNA0S5T234 [δ-decalactone]

DESCRIPTION
δ-Decalactone occurs as a colorless liquid.
Odor: Coconut-fruity, buttery on dilution
Solubility: Very soluble in alcohol, propylene glycol, vegetable oils; insoluble or practically insoluble in water
Boiling Point: ~281°
Solubility in Alcohol, Appendix VI: One mL dissolves in 1 mL of 95% ethanol.
Function: Flavoring agent

IDENTIFICATION
- **INFRARED SPECTRA,** *Spectrophotometric Identification Tests,* Appendix IIIC
  Acceptance criteria: The spectrum of the sample exhibits relative maxima at the same wavelengths as those of the spectrum below.

ASSAY
- **PROCEDURE:** Proceed as directed under *M-1b*, Appendix XI.
  Acceptance criteria: NLT 98.0% of $C_{10}H_{18}O_2$

SPECIFIC TESTS
- **ACID VALUE (FATS AND RELATED SUBSTANCES),** *Method II,* Appendix VII
  Acceptance criteria: NMT 5.0
- **REFRACTIVE INDEX,** Appendix II: At 20°
  Acceptance criteria: Between 1.454 and 1.459
- **SPECIFIC GRAVITY:** Determine at 25° by any reliable method (see *General Provisions*).
  Acceptance criteria: Between 0.964 and 0.971

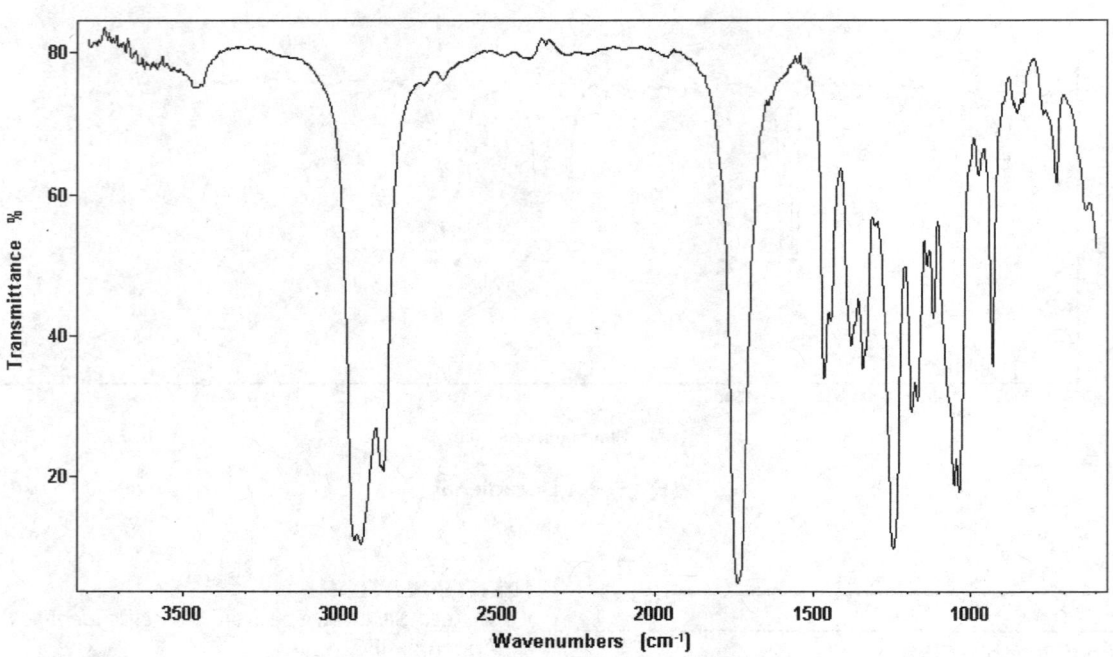

δ-Decalactone

γ-Decalactone

First Published: Prior to FCC 6

4-Hydroxydecanoic Acid Lactone

$C_{10}H_{18}O_2$ Formula wt 170.25
FEMA: 2360
UNII: 7HLS05KP9O [γ-decalactone]

DESCRIPTION
γ-Decalactone occurs as a colorless to pale yellow liquid.
Odor: Fruity, peach
Solubility: Soluble in propylene glycol, vegetable oils; insoluble or practically insoluble in water
Boiling Point: ~281°
Solubility in Alcohol, Appendix VI: One mL dissolves in 1 mL of 95% alcohol.
Function: Flavoring agent

IDENTIFICATION
- **INFRARED SPECTRA,** Spectrophotometric Identification Tests, Appendix IIIC
  Acceptance criteria: The spectrum of the sample exhibits relative maxima at the same wavelengths as those of the spectrum below.

ASSAY
- **PROCEDURE:** Proceed as directed under M-1a, Appendix XI.
  Acceptance criteria: NLT 95.0% of $C_{10}H_{18}O_2$

SPECIFIC TESTS
- **ACID VALUE, FLAVOR CHEMICALS (OTHER THAN ESSENTIAL OILS),** M-15, Appendix XI
  Acceptance criteria: NMT 1.0
- **REFRACTIVE INDEX,** Appendix II: At 20°
  Acceptance criteria: Between 1.447 and 1.451
- **SPECIFIC GRAVITY:** Determine at 25° by any reliable method (see General Provisions).
  Acceptance criteria: Between 0.949 and 0.954

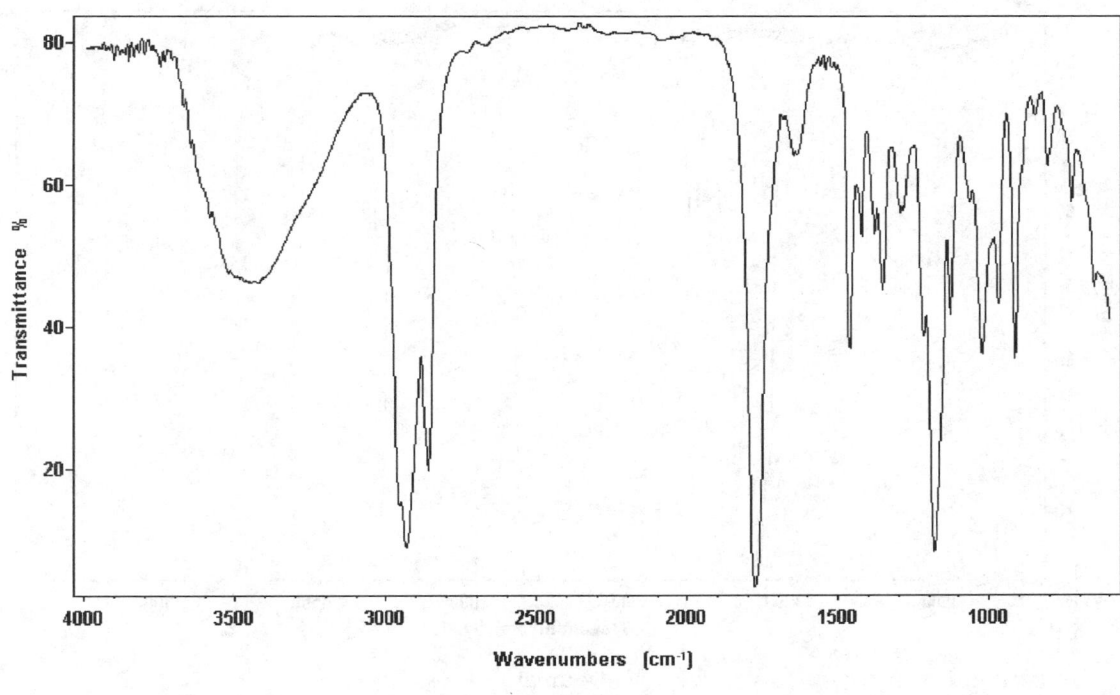

γ-Decalactone

Decanal

First Published: Prior to FCC 6
Last Revision: First Supplement, FCC 6

Aldehyde C-10
Capraldehyde

$C_{10}H_{20}O$ Formula wt 156.27
FEMA: 2362
UNII: 31Z90Q7KQJ [decanal]

DESCRIPTION
Decanal occurs as a colorless to light yellow liquid. It may contain a suitable antioxidant.
Odor: Fatty, floral-orange on dilution
Solubility: Miscible in alcohol, most fixed oils, propylene glycol (may be turbid); insoluble or practically insoluble in glycerin, water
Boiling Point: ~209°

Function: Flavoring agent

IDENTIFICATION
- **INFRARED SPECTRA,** *Spectrophotometric Identification Tests,* Appendix IIIC
  Acceptance criteria: The spectrum of the sample exhibits relative maxima at the same wavelengths as those of the spectrum below.

ASSAY
- **PROCEDURE:** Proceed as directed under *M-1b,* Appendix XI.
  Acceptance criteria: NLT 92.0% of $C_{10}H_{20}O$

SPECIFIC TESTS
- **ACID VALUE, FLAVOR CHEMICALS (OTHER THAN ESSENTIAL OILS),** *M-15,* Appendix XI
  Acceptance criteria: NMT 10.0
- **REFRACTIVE INDEX,** Appendix II: At 20°
  Acceptance criteria: Between 1.426 and 1.430
- **SPECIFIC GRAVITY:** Determine at 25° by any reliable method (see *General Provisions*).
  Acceptance criteria: Between 0.823 and 0.832

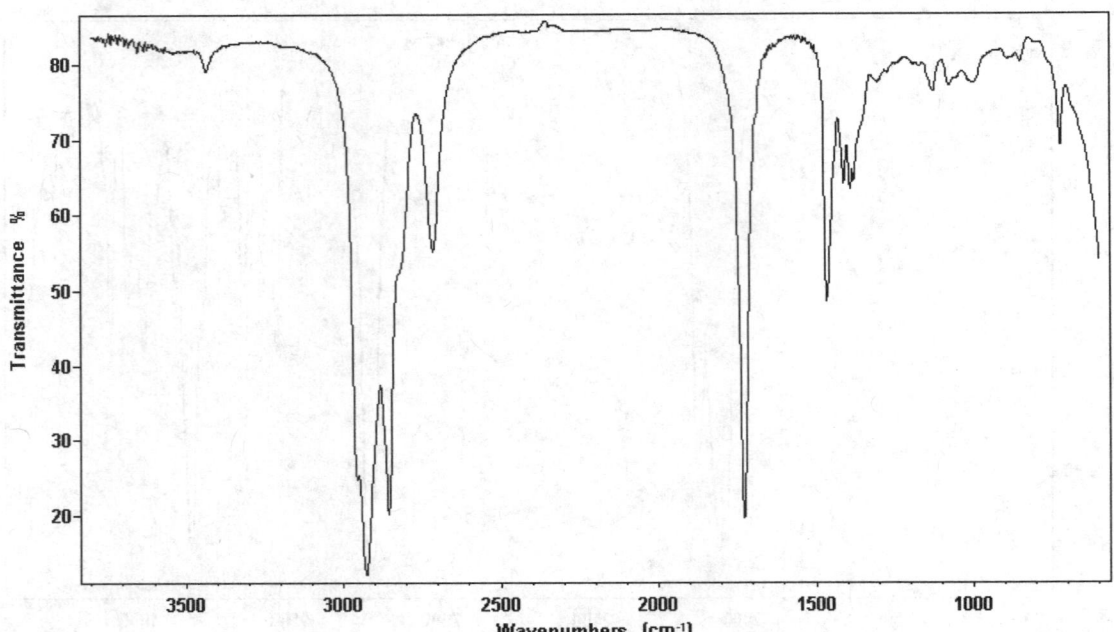

Decanal

Decanoic Acid

First Published: Prior to FCC 6

Capric Acid

C₁₀H₂₀O₂   Formula wt 172.27
FEMA: 2364
                                   CAS: [334-48-5]
UNII: 4G9EDB6V73 [capric acid]

DESCRIPTION
Decanoic Acid occurs as white crystals having a sour, fatty, rancid odor. It is soluble in most organic solvents and practically insoluble in water.
Function: Component in the manufacture of other food-grade additives; defoaming agent; flavoring agent
Packaging and Storage: Store in well-closed containers.

SPECIFIC TESTS
- **ACID VALUE (FATS AND RELATED SUBSTANCES),** *Method I*, Appendix VII
  Acceptance criteria: Between 320 and 329
- **IODINE VALUE,** Appendix VII
  Acceptance criteria: NMT 0.6
- **RESIDUE ON IGNITION (SULFATED ASH),** Appendix IIC
  Sample: 10.0 g
  Acceptance criteria: NMT 0.1%
- **TITER (SOLIDIFICATION POINT),** *Solidification Point*, Appendix IIB
  Acceptance criteria: Between 27° and 32°
- **UNSAPONIFIABLE MATTER,** Appendix VII
  Acceptance criteria: NMT 0.2%
- **WATER,** *Water Determination, Method Ia*, Appendix IIB
  Acceptance criteria: NMT 0.2%

(E)-2-Decenal

First Published: Prior to FCC 6
Last Revision: First Supplement, FCC 6

trans-2-Decenal

C₁₀H₁₈O   Formula wt 154.25
FEMA: 2366
UNII: E93S23U2BU [2-decenal, (2e)-]

DESCRIPTION
(E)-2-Decenal occurs as a slightly yellow liquid. It may contain a suitable antioxidant.
Odor: Orange, wax
Solubility: Soluble in alcohol, most fixed oils; insoluble or practically insoluble in water
Boiling Point: ~229°
Solubility in Alcohol, Appendix VI: One mL dissolves in 1 mL of 95% ethanol.
Function: Flavoring agent

IDENTIFICATION
- **INFRARED SPECTRA,** *Spectrophotometric Identification Tests,* Appendix IIIC
  Acceptance criteria: The spectrum of the sample exhibits relative maxima at the same wavelengths as those of the spectrum below.

ASSAY
- **PROCEDURE:** Proceed as directed under *M-1a,* Appendix XI.
  Acceptance criteria: NLT 92.0% of $C_{10}H_{18}O$ (one isomer)

SPECIFIC TESTS
- **REFRACTIVE INDEX,** Appendix II: At 20°
  Acceptance criteria: Between 1.452 and 1.457
- **SPECIFIC GRAVITY:** Determine at 25° by any reliable method (see *General Provisions*).
  Acceptance criteria: Between 0.836 and 0.846

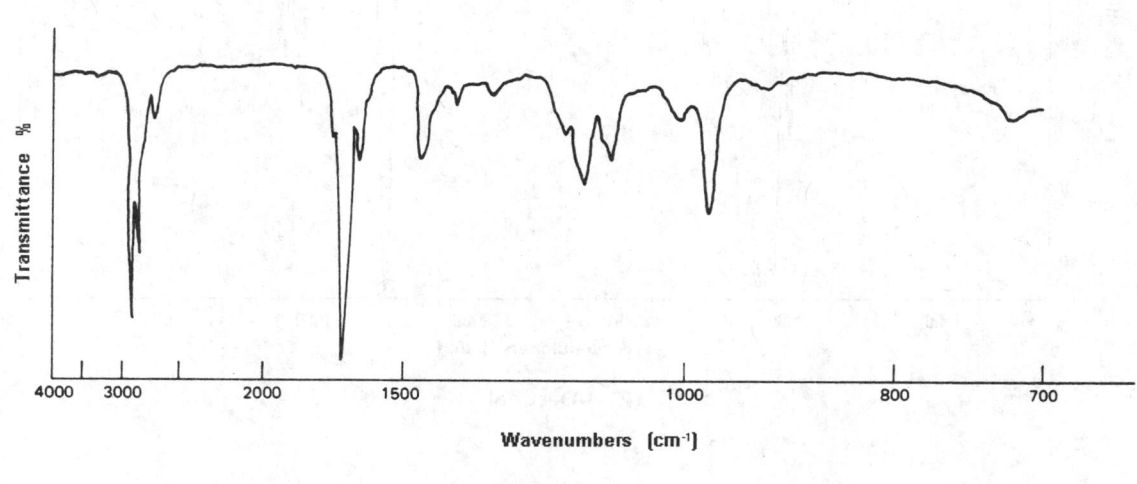

(*E*)-2-Decenal

(Z)-4-Decenal

First Published: Prior to FCC 6
Last Revision: First Supplement, FCC 6

cis-4-Decenal

$C_{10}H_{18}O$　　　　　　　　　　Formula wt 154.25
FEMA: 3264
UNII: 5R675PGU7K [4-decenal, (4z)-]

DESCRIPTION
(*Z*)-4-Decenal occurs as a colorless to slightly yellow liquid. It may contain a suitable antioxidant.
Odor: Orange, fatty
Solubility: Soluble in alcohol, most fixed oils; insoluble or practically insoluble in water
Boiling Point: ~78° to 80° (10 mm Hg)

Solubility in Alcohol, Appendix VI: One mL dissolves in 1 mL of 95% ethanol.
Function: Flavoring agent

IDENTIFICATION
- **INFRARED SPECTRA,** *Spectrophotometric Identification Tests,* Appendix IIIC
  Acceptance criteria: The spectrum of the sample exhibits relative maxima at the same wavelengths as those of the spectrum below.

ASSAY
- **PROCEDURE:** Proceed as directed under *M-1a,* Appendix XI.
  Acceptance criteria: NLT 90.0% of $C_{10}H_{18}O$

SPECIFIC TESTS
- **REFRACTIVE INDEX,** Appendix II: At 20°
  Acceptance criteria: Between 1.442 and 1.447
- **SPECIFIC GRAVITY:** Determine at 25° by any reliable method (see *General Provisions*).
  Acceptance criteria: Between 0.843 and 0.850

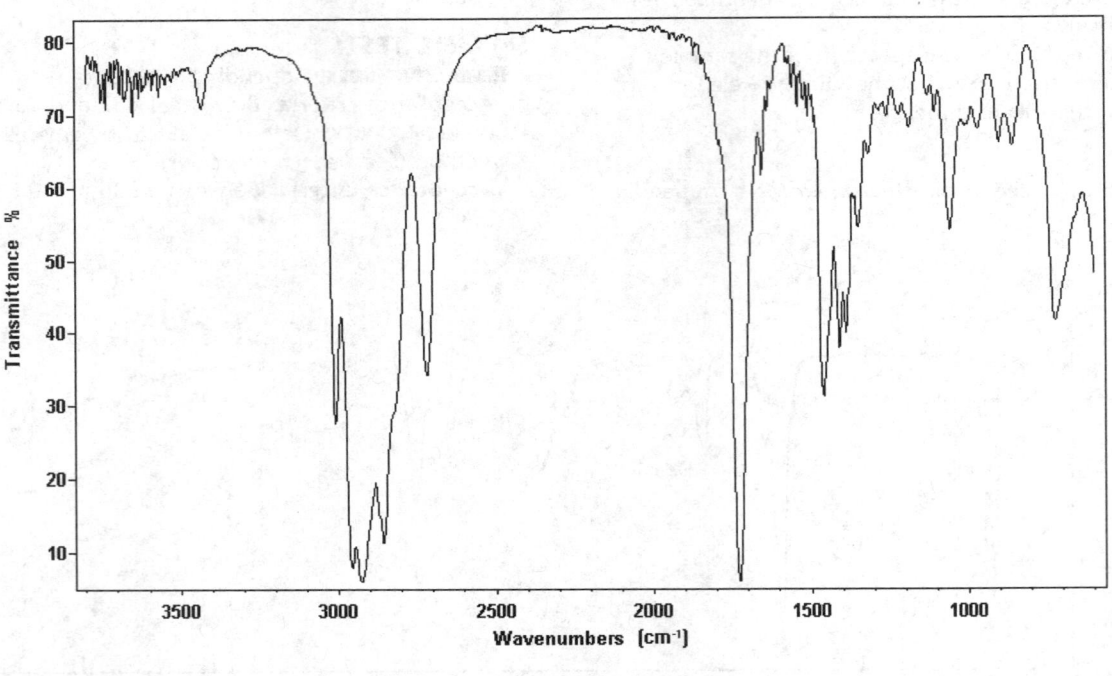

(Z)-4-Decenal

Decyl Alcohol

First Published: Prior to FCC 6

Alcohol C-10
1-Decanol

H₃C~~~~~~~~OH

C₁₀H₂₂O   Formula wt 158.28
FEMA: 2365
UNII: 89V4LX791F [decyl alcohol]

DESCRIPTION
Decyl Alcohol occurs as a colorless liquid.
Odor: Floral, waxy, fruity
Solubility: Soluble in alcohol, ether, mineral oil, propylene glycol, most fixed oils; insoluble or practically insoluble in glycerin, water
Boiling Point: ~233°
Solubility in Alcohol, Appendix VI: One mL dissolves in 3 mL of 60% alcohol.
Function: Flavoring agent

IDENTIFICATION
- **INFRARED SPECTRA,** *Spectrophotometric Identification Tests,* Appendix IIIC

  Acceptance criteria: The spectrum of the sample exhibits relative maxima at the same wavelengths as those of the spectrum below.

ASSAY
- **PROCEDURE:** Proceed as directed under *M-1b,* Appendix XI.
  Acceptance criteria: NLT 98.0% of C₁₀H₂₂O

SPECIFIC TESTS
- **ACID VALUE, FLAVOR CHEMICALS (OTHER THAN ESSENTIAL OILS),** *M-15,* Appendix XI
  Acceptance criteria: NMT 1.0
- **REFRACTIVE INDEX,** Appendix II: At 20°
  Acceptance criteria: Between 1.435 and 1.439
- **SPECIFIC GRAVITY:** Determine at 25° by any reliable method (see *General Provisions*).
  Acceptance criteria: Between 0.826 and 0.831

OTHER REQUIREMENTS
- **SOLIDIFICATION POINT,** Appendix IIB
  Acceptance criteria: NLT 5°

Decyl Alcohol

Dehydroacetic Acid

First Published: Prior to FCC 6

3-Acetyl-6-methyl-1,2-pyran-2,4(3H)-dione
Methylacetopyronone

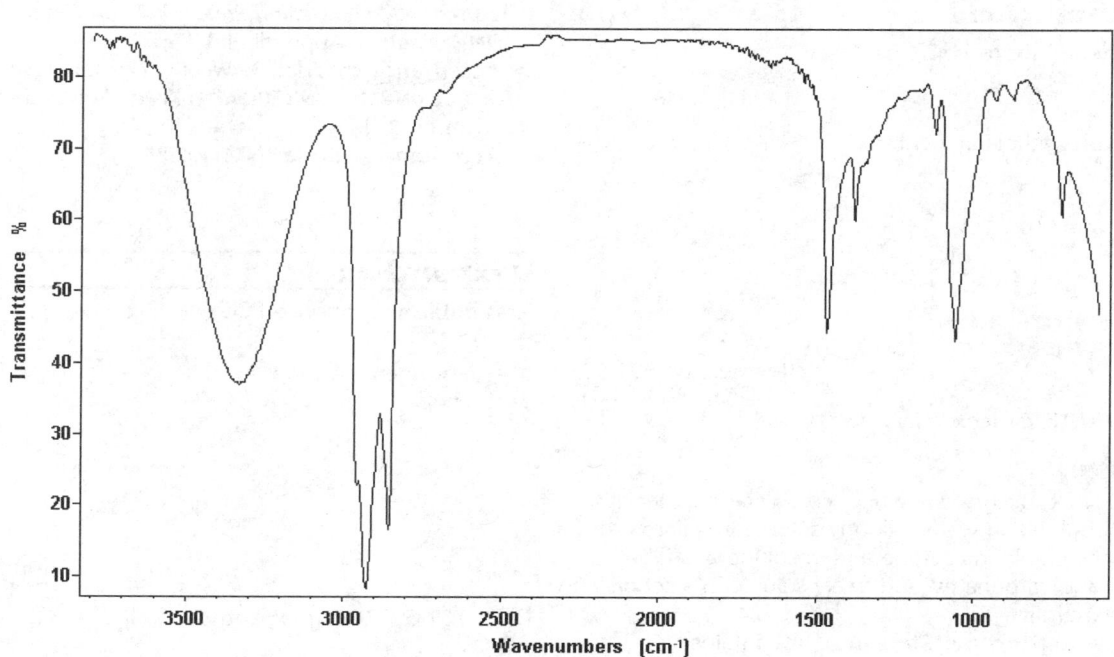

$C_8H_8O_4$
UNII: 2KAG279R6R [dehydroacetic acid]

Formula wt 168.15
CAS: [520-45-6]

DESCRIPTION
Dehydroacetic Acid occurs as a white or nearly white, crystalline powder. It is soluble in aqueous solutions of fixed alkalies, and is very slightly soluble in water. One g of sample dissolves in about 35 mL of alcohol and in 5 mL of acetone.
Function: Antimicrobial agent; preservative
Packaging and Storage: Store in well-closed containers.

IDENTIFICATION
- **INFRARED ABSORPTION,** *Spectrophotometric Identification Tests,* Appendix IIIC
  Reference standard: USP Dehydroacetic Acid RS
  Sample and Standard preparation: *K*
  Acceptance criteria: The spectrum of the sample exhibits maxima at the same wavelengths as those in the spectrum of the *Reference standard.*

ASSAY
- **DEHYDROACETIC ACID**
  Sample: 500 mg
  Analysis: Transfer the *Sample* into a 250-mL Erlenmeyer flask, dissolve it in 75 mL of neutral alcohol, add phenolphthalein TS, and titrate with 0.1 N sodium hydroxide to a pink endpoint that persists for at least 30 s. Each mL of 0.1 N sodium hydroxide is equivalent to 16.82 mg of $C_8H_8O_4$.
  Acceptance criteria: NLT 98.0% and NMT 100.5% of $C_8H_8O_4$, calculated on the dried basis

IMPURITIES
Inorganic Impurities
- **LEAD,** *Lead Limit Test, Atomic Absorption Spectrophotometric Graphite Furnace Method, Method II,* Appendix IIIB
  Acceptance criteria: NMT 0.5 mg/kg

SPECIFIC TESTS
- **LOSS ON DRYING,** Appendix IIC: 80° for 4 h
  Acceptance criteria: NMT 1%
- **MELTING RANGE,** *Melting Range or Temperature Determination,* Appendix IIB
  Acceptance criteria: Between 109° and 111°
- **RESIDUE ON IGNITION (SULFATED ASH),** Appendix IIC
  Sample: 2 g
  Acceptance criteria: NMT 0.1%

Desoxycholic Acid

First Published: Prior to FCC 6

Deoxycholic Acid
3α,12α-Dihydroxycholanic Acid

$C_{24}H_{40}O_4$ Formula wt 392.58
            CAS: [83-44-3]
UNII: 005990WHZZ [deoxycholic acid]

DESCRIPTION
Desoxycholic Acid occurs as a white, crystalline powder. It is practically insoluble in water, slightly soluble in chloroform and in ether, soluble in acetone and in solutions of alkali hydroxides and carbonates, and freely soluble in alcohol.
Function: Emulsifier
Packaging and Storage: Store in tight containers.

IDENTIFICATION
- **Procedure**
  Sample: 10 mg
  Analysis: Add 2 drops of benzaldehyde and 3 drops of 75% sulfuric acid to the *Sample*, heat at 50° for 5 min, and then add 10 mL of glacial acetic acid.
  Acceptance criteria: A green color appears (cholic acid produces a brown color).

ASSAY
- **Procedure**
  Sample: 500 mg
  Analysis: Transfer the *Sample* into a 250-mL Erlenmeyer flask, and add 20 mL of water and 40 mL of alcohol. Cover the flask with a watch glass, heat the mixture gently on a steam bath until the sample is dissolved, and allow the mixture to cool to room temperature. Add a few drops of phenolphthalein TS to the solution, and titrate with 0.1 N sodium hydroxide to a pink endpoint that persists for 15 s. Each mL of 0.1 N sodium hydroxide is equivalent to 39.26 mg of $C_{24}H_{40}O_4$.
  Acceptance criteria: NLT 98.0% and NMT 102.0% of $C_{24}H_{40}O_4$, calculated on the dried basis

IMPURITIES
Inorganic Impurities
- **Lead,** *Lead Limit Test, Flame Atomic Absorption Spectrophotometric Method,* Appendix IIIB
  Sample: 10 g
  Acceptance criteria: NMT 4 mg/kg

SPECIFIC TESTS
- **Loss on Drying,** Appendix IIC: 140° for 4 h under a vacuum of NMT 5 mm Hg
  Acceptance criteria: NMT 1%
- **Melting Range,** *Melting Range or Temperature Determination,* Appendix IIB
  Acceptance criteria: Between 172° and 175°
- **Residue on Ignition (Sulfated Ash),** Appendix IIC
  Sample: 1 g
  Acceptance criteria: NMT 0.2%

Dexpanthenol

First Published: Prior to FCC 6

D(+)-Pantothenyl Alcohol
Panthenol

$C_9H_{19}NO_4$ Formula wt 205.25
             CAS: [81-13-0]
UNII: 1O6C93RI7Z [dexpanthenol]

DESCRIPTION
Dexpanthenol occurs as a clear, viscous, somewhat hygroscopic liquid. It is the dextrorotatory isomer of the alcohol analogue of pantothenic acid. Some crystallization may occur on standing. It is freely soluble in water, in alcohol, in methanol, and in propylene glycol. It is soluble in chloroform and in ether, and is slightly soluble in glycerin. Its solutions are alkaline to litmus.
Function: Nutrient
Packaging and Storage: Store in tight containers.

IDENTIFICATION
- **A. Procedure**
  Sample solution: 100 mg/mL
  Analysis: Add 5 mL of 1 N sodium hydroxide and 1 drop of cupric sulfate TS to 1 mL of the *Sample solution*, and shake vigorously.
  Acceptance criteria: A deep-blue color develops.
- **B. Procedure**
  Sample solution: 10 mg/mL
  Analysis: Add 1 mL of 1 N hydrochloric acid to 1 mL of the *Sample solution*, and heat on a steam bath for about 30 min. Cool, add 100 mg of hydroxylamine hydrochloride, mix, and add 5 mL of 1 N sodium hydroxide. Allow to stand for 5 min, then adjust the pH to within a range of 2.5 to 3.0 with 1 N hydrochloric acid, and add 1 drop of ferric chloride TS.
  Acceptance criteria: A purple-red color develops.
- **C. Infrared Absorption,** *Spectrophotometric Identification Tests,* Appendix IIIC
  Reference standard: USP Dexpanthenol RS
  Sample and **Standard preparation:** E
  Acceptance criteria: The spectrum of the sample exhibits maxima at the same wavelengths as those in the spectrum of the *Reference standard*.

ASSAY
- **PROCEDURE**
  Sample: 400 mg
  Analysis: Transfer the *Sample* into a 300-mL reflux flask fitted with a standard taper glass joint, add 50.0 mL of 0.1 N perchloric acid in glacial acetic acid, and reflux for 5 h. [**CAUTION**—Handle perchloric acid in an appropriate fume hood.] Cool, covering the condenser with foil to prevent contamination by moisture, and rinse the condenser with glacial acetic acid. Add 5 drops of crystal violet TS, and titrate with 0.1 N potassium acid phthalate in glacial acetic acid to a blue-green endpoint. Perform a blank determination (see *General Provisions*) and make any necessary correction. Each mL of 0.1 N perchloric acid is equivalent to 20.53 mg of $C_9H_{19}NO_4$.
  Acceptance criteria: NLT 98.0% and NMT 102.0% of $C_9H_{19}NO_4$, calculated on the anhydrous basis

IMPURITIES
Inorganic Impurities
- **LEAD,** *Lead Limit Test, Flame Atomic Absorption Spectrophotometric Method,* Appendix IIIB
  Sample: 5 g
  Acceptance criteria: NMT 5 mg/kg

Organic Impurities
- **AMINOPROPANOL**
  Sample: 5 g
  Analysis: Transfer the *Sample* into a 50-mL flask, and dissolve in 10 mL of water. Add bromothymol blue TS and titrate with 0.1 N sulfuric acid from a microburet to a yellow endpoint. Each mL of 0.1 N sulfuric acid is equivalent to 7.5 mg of aminopropanol.
  Acceptance criteria: NMT 1%

SPECIFIC TESTS
- **OPTICAL (SPECIFIC) ROTATION,** Appendix IIB
  Sample solution: 50 mg/mL in water (on the anhydrous basis)
  Acceptance criteria: $[\alpha]_D^{25}$ between +29.0° and +31.5°
- **REFRACTIVE INDEX,** Appendix IIB
  [NOTE—Use an Abbé or other refractometer of equal or greater accuracy.]
  Acceptance criteria: Between 1.495 and 1.502 at 20°
- **RESIDUE ON IGNITION (SULFATED ASH),** Appendix IIC
  Sample: 1 g
  Acceptance criteria: NMT 0.1%
- **WATER,** *Water Determination,* Appendix IIB
  Acceptance criteria: NMT 1%

Dextrin

First Published: Prior to FCC 6

INS: 1400   CAS: [9004-53-9]
UNII: 2NX48Z0A9G [icodextrin]

DESCRIPTION
Dextrin occurs as free-flowing white, yellow, or brown powders and consist chiefly of polygonal, rounded, or oblong or truncated granules. Dextrin is partially hydrolyzed starch converted by heat alone, or by heating in the presence of suitable food-grade acids and buffers, from any of several grain- or root-based unmodified native starches (e.g., corn, waxy maize, high-amylose maize, milo, waxy milo, potato, arrowroot, wheat, rice, tapioca, sago, etc.). Dextrin is partially to completely soluble in water.
Function: Thickener; colloidal stabilizer; binder; surface-finishing agent
Packaging and Storage: Store in well-closed containers.

IDENTIFICATION
- **PROCEDURE**
  Sample: 1 g
  Analysis: Suspend the *Sample* in 20 mL of water, and add a few drops of iodine TS.
  Acceptance criteria: A dark blue to red-brown color appears.

IMPURITIES
Inorganic Impurities
- **CHLORIDE**
  Sample solution: Dissolve 1 g of sample in 25 mL of boiling water, cool, dilute to 100 mL with water, and filter.
  Control: 20 µg chloride (Cl) ion
  Analysis: To 1 mL of filtrate from the *Sample solution*, add 24 mL of water, 2 mL of nitric acid, and 1 mL of silver nitrate TS. Repeat the preceding using the *Control* in place of the *Sample solution*.
  Acceptance criteria: Any turbidity produced in the *Sample solution* does not exceed that shown in the *Control*. (NMT 0.2%)
- **LEAD,** Appendix IIIB
  Sample solution: Transfer 4.0 g of sample to an evaporating dish, add 4 mL of sulfuric acid solution (1:4), and evaporate most of the water on a steam bath. Char and dehydrate the sample by heating on a hot plate, while at the same time, heating with an infrared lamp from above, and then heat in a muffle furnace at 500° until the residue is free from carbon. Remove the dish from the furnace, cool, and cautiously wash down the inside of the dish with water. Add 1 mL of 1 N hydrochloric acid, evaporate to dryness on a steam bath, and then add 2 mL of 1 N hydrochloric acid, and heat briefly, while stirring, on a steam bath. Quantitatively transfer the solution into a separatory funnel with the aid of small quantities of water, and neutralize with 1 N ammonium hydroxide.
  Control: 4 µg Pb (4 mL of *Diluted Standard Lead Solution*)
  Acceptance criteria: NMT 1 mg/kg
- **SULFUR DIOXIDE,** *Sulfur Dioxide Determination,* Appendix X
  Acceptance criteria: NMT 0.005%

Organic Impurities
- **REDUCING SUGARS:**
  Sample preparation: Transfer the 10 g of sample into a 200-mL collecting flask, dilute to volume with water, shake for 30 min, and filter through Whatman No. 1 filter paper, or equivalent, collecting the filtrate in a clean, dry flask. Use the collected filtrate as the *Sample preparation*.

Analysis: Pipet 10 mL each of *The Copper Solution (A)* and *The Alkaline Tartrate Solution (B)* (see *Cupric Tartrate TS*, Solutions and Indicators) into a 250-mL Erlenmeyer flask, add 20.0 mL of the *Sample preparation* and 10 mL of water, and mix. Add two small glass beads, cover the mouth of the flask with a small glass funnel or glass bulb, and heat on a hot plate adjusted to bring the solution to a boil in 3 min. Continue boiling for exactly 2 min (total heating time, 5 min), and then quickly cool to room temperature in an ice bath or in a cold running-water bath. Add 10 mL each of 30% potassium iodide solution and 28% sulfuric acid, and titrate immediately with 0.1 N sodium thiosulfate. Near the endpoint, add 1 mL of starch TS, and continue titrating carefully, while agitating the solution continuously, until the blue color is discharged. Record the volume (S), in mL, of 0.1 N sodium thiosulfate required. Conduct two reagent blank determinations in the same manner, substituting water for the sample filtrate, and record the average volume (B), in mL, of the blanks. Obtain the *Titer Difference*, expressed as mL of 0.1 N sodium thiosulfate, using the following equation:

$$\text{Titer Difference} = B - S$$

B = average volume (mL) of sodium thiosulfate used in the blank titration
S = volume (mL) of sodium thiosulfate used in the sample titration

Using the *Titer Difference*, determine the weight, in mg, of reducing sugars, expressed as D-glucose (dextrose), by reference to the table below entitled *Conversion of Titer Difference to Reducing Sugars Content*. Record this value as R.

Calculate the percentage of reducing sugars, as D-glucose, on the dried basis, by the formula:

$$\text{Result} = (R \times 200 \times 100)/(W \times 20 \times 1000)$$

W = weight (g) of the sample taken
R = weight (mg) of reducing sugars determined using the *Titer Difference*

Conversion of Titer Difference to Reducing Sugars Content[a]

Titer Difference (mL)	0.0	0.1	0.2	0.3	0.4	0.5	0.6	0.7	0.8	0.9
Reducing Sugar (as Dextrose) mg										
0.0	0.0	0.3	0.7	1.0	1.3	1.6	1.9	2.2	2.5	2.8
0.1	3.2	3.5	3.8	4.1	4.4	4.7	5.0	5.3	5.6	5.9
2.0	6.4	6.6	6.9	7.2	7.5	7.8	8.1	8.5	8.8	9.1
3.0	9.4	9.8	10.1	10.4	10.7	11.0	11.4	11.7	12.0	12.3
4.0	12.6	13.0	13.3	13.6	14.0	14.3	14.6	15.0	15.3	15.6
5.0	15.9	16.3	16.6	16.9	17.2	17.6	17.9	18.2	18.5	18.9
6.0	19.2	19.5	19.8	20.1	20.5	20.8	21.1	21.4	21.8	22.1
7.0	22.4	22.7	23.0	23.3	23.7	24.0	24.3	24.6	24.9	25.2
8.0	25.6	25.9	26.2	26.6	26.9	27.3	27.6	28.0	28.3	28.6
9.0	28.9	29.3	29.6	30.0	30.3	30.6	31.0	31.3	31.6	31.9
10.0	32.3	32.7	33.0	33.3	33.7	34.0	34.3	34.6	35.0	35.3
11.0	35.7	36.0	36.3	36.7	37.0	37.3	37.6	38.0	38.3	38.7
12.0	39.0	39.3	39.6	40.0	40.3	40.6	41.0	41.3	41.7	42.0
13.0	42.4	42.8	43.1	43.4	43.7	44.1	44.4	44.8	45.2	45.5
14.0	45.8	46.2	46.5	46.9	47.2	47.6	47.9	48.3	48.6	48.9
15.0	49.3	49.6	49.9	50.3	50.7	51.1	51.4	51.7	52.1	52.4
16.0	52.8	53.2	53.5	53.9	54.2	54.5	54.9	55.3	55.6	56.0
17.0	56.3	56.7	57.0	57.3	57.7	58.1	58.4	58.8	59.1	59.5
18.0	59.8	60.1	60.5	60.9	61.2	61.5	61.9	62.3	62.6	63.0
19.0	63.3	63.6	64.0	64.3	64.7	65.0	65.4	65.8	66.1	66.5

[a] Use of this table presumes the ability of the analyst to duplicate exactly the conditions under which the data were developed. The risk of error can be avoided by careful duplicate standardization with known quantities of pure dextrose (five samples, ranging from 10 to 70 mg). A plot of *Titer Difference* versus mg of dextrose is slightly curvilinear, passing through the origin. If use of a standardization curve is adopted, the thiosulfate solution need not be standardized. Some additional increase in accuracy results from use of a 0.065 N sodium thiosulfate solution, which increases the blank titer to about 44 to 45 mL.

Conversion of Titer Difference to Reducing Sugars Content[a] *(continued)*

Titer Difference (mL)	0.0	0.1	0.2	0.3	0.4	0.5	0.6	0.7	0.8	0.9
20.0	66.9	67.2	67.6	68.0	68.4	68.8	69.1	69.5	69.9	70.3
21.0	70.7	71.1	71.5	71.9	72.2	72.6	73.0	73.4	73.7	74.1
22.0	74.5	74.9	75.3	75.7	76.1	76.5	76.9	77.3	77.7	78.1
23.0	78.5	78.9	79.3	79.7	80.1	80.5	80.9	81.3	81.7	82.1
24.0	82.6	83.0	83.4	83.8	84.2	84.6	85.0	85.4	85.8	86.2
25.0	86.6	87.0	87.4	87.8	88.2	88.6	89.0	89.4	89.8	90.2
26.0	90.7	91.1	91.5	91.9	92.3	92.7	93.1	93.5	93.9	94.3
27.0	94.8									

[a] Use of this table presumes the ability of the analyst to duplicate exactly the conditions under which the data were developed. The risk of error can be avoided by careful duplicate standardization with known quantities of pure dextrose (five samples, ranging from 10 to 70 mg). A plot of *Titer Difference* versus mg of dextrose is slightly curvilinear, passing through the origin. If use of a standardization curve is adopted, the thiosulfate solution need not be standardized. Some additional increase in accuracy results from use of a 0.065 N sodium thiosulfate solution, which increases the blank titer to about 44 to 45 mL.

Acceptance criteria: NMT 18.0% (as D-glucose), calculated on the dried basis

SPECIFIC TESTS

- **CRUDE FAT,** Appendix X
  Acceptance criteria: NMT 1.0%
- **LOSS ON DRYING,** Appendix IIC: Under vacuum not exceeding 100 mm Hg, at 120° for 4 h
  Sample: 5.0 g
  Acceptance criteria: NMT 13.0%
- **PROTEIN**
  Sample: 10 g
  Analysis: Transfer the *Sample* into an 800-mL Kjeldahl flask, and add 10 g of anhydrous potassium or sodium sulfate, 300 mg of copper selenite or mercuric oxide, and 60 mL of sulfuric acid. Gently heat the mixture, keeping the flask inclined at about a 45° angle, and, after frothing has ceased, boil briskly until the solution has remained clear for about 1 h. Cool, add 30 mL of water, mix, and cool again. Cautiously pour about 75 mL (or enough to make the mixture strongly alkaline) of 400 mg/mL sodium hydroxide solution down the inside of the flask so that it forms a layer under the acid solution, and then add a few pieces of granular zinc. Immediately connect the flask to a distillation apparatus consisting of a Kjeldahl connecting bulb and a condenser, the delivery tube of which extends well beneath the surface of an accurately measured excess of 0.1 N sulfuric acid contained in a 50-mL flask. Gently rotate the contents of the Kjeldahl flask to mix, and distill until all ammonia has passed into the absorbing acid solution (about 250 mL of distillate). Add 0.25 mL of methyl red-methylene blue TS to the receiving flask, and titrate the excess acid with 0.1 N sodium hydroxide. Perform a blank determination, substituting pure sucrose or dextrose for the sample, and make any necessary correction (see *General Provisions*). Each mL of 0.1 N sulfuric acid consumed is equivalent to 1.401 mg of nitrogen (N).
  Calculate the percent N in the sample, and then calculate the percent protein by multiplying the percent N by 6.25, in the case of starches obtained from corn, or by 5.7, in the case of starches obtained from wheat. Other factors may be applied as necessary for starches obtained from other sources.
  Acceptance criteria: NMT 1.0%
- **RESIDUE ON IGNITION (SULFATED ASH),** Appendix IIC
  Sample: 5 g
  Acceptance criteria: NMT 0.5%

OTHER REQUIREMENTS

- **LABELING:** Indicate the presence of sulfur dioxide if the residual concentration is greater than 10 mg/kg.

Dextrose

First Published: Prior to FCC 6

D-Glucose
Glucose
Corn Sugar

$C_6H_{12}O_6$

Formula wt 180.16
CAS: [50-99-7]

UNII: 5SL0G7R0OK [anhydrous dextrose]
UNII: LX22YL083G [dextrose monohydrate]

DESCRIPTION

Dextrose occurs as white, crystalline granules or as a granular powder. It is purified and crystallized D-glucose. It is anhydrous or contains one molecule of water of crystallization. It is freely soluble in water, very soluble in boiling water, and slightly soluble in alcohol.

Function: Nutritive sweetener; humectant; texturizing agent

Packaging and Storage: Store in tight containers in a dry place.

IDENTIFICATION

- **Procedure**
  Sample: 50 mg/mL
  Analysis: Add a few drops of the *Sample solution* to 5 mL of hot alkaline cupric tartrate TS.
  Acceptance criteria: A copious red precipitate of cuprous oxide forms.

ASSAY

- **Reducing Sugars,** Appendix X
  Acceptance criteria: NLT 99.5% and NMT 100.5% of reducing sugar content (dextrose equivalent), expressed as D-glucose, calculated on the dried basis

IMPURITIES

Inorganic Impurities

- **Arsenic,** *Arsenic Limit Test,* Appendix IIIB
  Sample: 1 g
  Control: 1 µg As (1 mL of *Standard Arsenic Solution*)
  Acceptance criteria: NMT 1 mg/kg
- **Chloride**
  Sample: 2.0 g
  Acceptance criteria: Sample shows no more chloride than corresponds to 0.50 mL of 0.020 N hydrochloric acid. (NMT 0.018%)
  Acceptance criteria: NMT 0.018%
- **Lead,** *Lead Limit Test, Atomic Absorption Spectrophotometric Graphite Furnace Method, Method I,* Appendix IIIB
  Sample: 5 g
  Acceptance criteria: NMT 0.1 mg/kg
- **Sulfur Dioxide,** *Sulfur Dioxide Determination,* Appendix X
  Sample: 75 g
  Acceptance criteria: NMT 0.002%

SPECIFIC TESTS

- **Loss on Drying,** Appendix IIC
  Sample: 10 g of anhydrous sample or 5 g of monohydrate sample
  Analysis: Dry for 2 h at 70° in a vacuum oven not exceeding 50 mm Hg, cool in a desiccator for 30 min, and weigh. Dry for successive 1-h intervals until the weight change is less than 2 mg.
  Acceptance criteria
    Anhydrous: NMT 2.0%
    Monohydrate: NMT 10.0%
- **Optical (Specific) Rotation,** Appendix IIB
  Sample solution: Dissolve 10 g of sample, previously dried, and 0.2 mL of 6 N ammonium hydroxide in sufficient water to make 100 mL.
  Acceptance criteria: $[\alpha]_D^{25}$ between +52.6° and +53.2°, on the dried basis
- **Residue on Ignition (Sulfated Ash),** Appendix IIC
  Sample: 10.0 g
  Acceptance criteria: NMT 0.1%
- **Starch**
  Sample solution: 1 g in 10 mL of water
  Analysis: Add 1 drop of iodine TS to the *Sample solution.*
  Acceptance criteria: A yellow color indicates the absence of soluble starch.

OTHER REQUIREMENTS

- **Labeling:** Indicate the presence of sulfur dioxide if the residual concentration is greater than 10 mg/kg.

DHA from Algal (*Crypthecodinium*) Oil

First Published: First Supplement, FCC 7
Last Revision: FCC 8

Crypthecodinium cohnii Oil
UNII: ZAD9OKH9JC [doconexent]

DESCRIPTION

DHA from Algal (*Crypthecodinium*) Oil occurs as a light yellow to orange colored oil providing a source of docosahexaenoic acid (DHA, $C_{22}H_{32}O_2$) (C22:6 n-3), an omega-3 long-chain polyunsaturated fatty acid. It is obtained from fermentation of the species of microalgae *Crypthecodinium cohnii*, usually by solvent extraction. The oil may be winterized, bleached, and deodorized to substantially remove free fatty acids, phospholipids, odor and flavor components, and other material. Docosahexaenoic acid is the only significant polyunsaturated fatty acid present; DHA content may be standardized with other oils. Suitable antioxidants may be added.

Function: Source of DHA
Packaging and Storage: Store in tight, light-resistant containers. Avoid exposure to excessive heat.

IDENTIFICATION

Change to read:

- **Fatty Acid Composition,** *Fatty Acid Composition (Saturated, cis-Monounsaturated, and cis-Polyunsaturated) in Oils Containing Long Chain Polyunsaturated Fatty Acids,* Appendix VII
  Acceptance criteria: The retention time of the peak of the docosahexaenoic acid methyl ester from the *Sample Preparation* corresponds to that from the *Standard Solution*. The area percentage for the methyl esters of the fatty acids from the *Sample Preparation* meet the requirements for each fatty acid indicated in the table below.

Fatty Acid	Shorthand Notation	Lower Limit (area %)	Upper Limit (area %)
Linoleic acid	18:2 n-6	0	1.0
Dihomo-gamma-linolenic acid	20:3 n-6	0	0.1
Eicosapentanoic acid	20:5 n-3	0	0.1
Docosapentaenoic acid	22:5 n-6	0	0.1
Docosahexaenoic acid	22:6 n-3	▲35.0▲FCC8	47.0

ASSAY
Change to read:
- **DHA**, *Fatty Acid Composition (Saturated, cis-Monounsaturated, and cis-Polyunsaturated) in Oils Containing Long Chain Polyunsaturated Fatty Acids*, Appendix VII

  Acceptance criteria: NLT ▲35.0%▲*FCC8* docosahexaenoic acid (DHA)

IMPURITIES
Inorganic Impurities
- **ARSENIC**

  Apparatus

  Sample digestion: Use a microwave oven (CEM Model MDS-2100, or equivalent) equipped with advanced composite vessels with 100-mL Teflon liners. Use rupture membranes to vent vessels should the pressure exceed 125 psi. The vessels fit into a turntable, and each vessel can be vented into an overflow container. Equip the microwave oven with an exhaust tube to ventilate fumes.

  Sample analysis: Use a suitable graphite furnace atomic absorption spectrophotometer (GFAAS) equipped with an autosampler, pyrolytically coated graphite tubes, solid pyrolytic graphite platforms, and an adequate means of background correction. This method was developed using a Perkin-Elmer Model 5100, HGA-600 furnace, and an AS-60 autosampler with Zeeman effect background correction. An electrodeless discharge lamp serves as the source, argon as the purge gas, and air as the alternate gas. Set up the instrument according to manufacturer's specifications, with consideration of current good GFAAS practices. The instrument parameters are as follows:

  Wavelength: 193.7 nm
  Lamp current: 300 (EDL) modulated
  Pyrolysis: 1000°
  Atomization: 2400°
  Slit: 0.7
  Characteristic mass: 15 pg

  Glassware: Acid wash all glass, Teflon, and plastic vessels by soaking them in a nitric acid bath containing a solution of water and nitric acid (4:1). [**CAUTION**—Wear a full face shield and protective clothing and gloves at all times when working with acid baths.] After acid soaking, rinse acid-washed items in deionized water, dry them, and store them in clean, covered cabinets.

  Calibration standard stock solution: 100 µg/L
  Prepare from a suitable standard, which may be purchased [accuracy certified against National Institute of Standards and Technology (NIST) spectrometric standard solutions].

  Calibration standard solutions: 2.0 µg/L, 5.0 µg/L, 10.0 µg/L, 25.0 µg/L, and 50.0 µg/L in 2% nitric acid from the *Calibration standard stock solution*

  1% Palladium stock solution: Mix 1 g of ultrapure palladium metal with 20 mL of water and 10 mL of nitric acid in a Teflon beaker, and warm the solution on a hot plate to dissolve the palladium. Allow the solution to cool to room temperature, transfer it into a 100-mL volumetric flask, and dilute with deionized water to volume.

  1% Magnesium nitrate stock solution: Mix 1 g of ultrapure magnesium nitrate with 40 mL of water and 1 mL of nitric acid in a Teflon beaker, and warm the solution on a hot plate to dissolve. Allow the solution to cool to room temperature, transfer it into a 100-mL volumetric flask, and dilute with deionized water to volume.

  [NOTE—Because of the difficulty in preparing matrix modifier stock solutions with the required purity, purchasing modifier stock solutions and using them to prepare working modifier solutions is recommended. A palladium (0.3%) and magnesium nitrate (0.2%) solution may be purchased from High Purity Standards, or equivalent.]

  Modifier working solution: Transfer 3 mL of *1% Palladium stock solution* and 2 mL of *1% Magnesium nitrate stock solution* to a 10-mL volumetric flask, and dilute with 2% nitric acid to volume. A volume of 5 µL provides 0.015 mg of palladium and 0.01 mg of magnesium nitrate.

  Sample solution: [**CAUTION**—Wear proper eye protection and protective clothing and gloves during sample preparation. Closely follow the manufacturer's safety instructions for use of the microwave digestion apparatus.]

  Transfer 500 mg of the sample into a Teflon digestion vessel liner. Prepare samples in duplicate. Add 15 mL of nitric acid, and swirl gently. Cover the vessels with lids, leaving the vent fitting off. Predigest overnight under a hood. Place the rupture membrane in the vent fitting, and tighten the lid. Place all vessels on the microwave oven turntable. Connect the vent tubes to the vent trap, and connect the pressure-sensing line to the appropriate vessel. Initiate a two-stage digestion procedure by heating the microwave at 15% power for 15 min followed by 25% power for 45 min. Remove the turntable of vessels from the oven, and allow the vessels to cool to room temperature (a cool water bath may be used to speed the cooling process). Vent the vessels when they reach room temperature. Remove the lids, and slowly add 2 mL of 30% hydrogen peroxide to each. Allow the reactions to subside, and seal the vessels. Return the vessels on the turntable to the microwave oven and heat for an additional 15 min at 30% power. Remove the vessels from the oven, and allow them to cool to room temperature. Transfer the cooled digests into 25-mL volumetric flasks, and dilute with deionized water to volume.

  Analysis: The graphite furnace program is as follows:
  1. Dry at 115° using a 1-s ramp, a 65-s hold, and a 300-mL/min argon flow.
  2. Char the sample at 1000° using a 1-s ramp, a 20-s hold, and a 300-mL/min air flow.
  3. Cool down and purge the air from the furnace for 10 s using a 20° set temperature and a 300-mL/min argon flow.

4. Atomize at 2400° using a 0-s ramp and a 5-s hold with the argon flow stopped.
5. Clean out at 2600° with a 1-s ramp and a 5-s hold.

Use the autosampler to inject 20-μL aliquots of blanks, *Calibration standard solutions*, and *Sample solutions* and 5 μL of *Modifier working solution*. Inject each solution in duplicate, and average the results. Use peak area measurement for all quantitations. After ensuring that the furnace is clean by running a 5% nitric acid blank, check the instrument's sensitivity by running a 20-μL aliquot of the 25-μg *Calibration standard solution*. Compare the results obtained with the expected results for the equipment used, and take the necessary steps to correct any problems.

Calculate the characteristic mass. Record and track the integrated absorbance and characteristic mass for reference and quality assurance.

Inject each *Calibration standard solution* in duplicate. Use the algorithms provided in the instrument software to establish calibration curves. Recheck calibration periodically, and recalibrate if the recheck differs from the original calibration by more than 10%.

Inject the *Sample solution* in duplicate, and record the integrated absorbance. If the instrument response exceeds that of the calibration curve, dilute with 5% nitric acid to bring the sample's response into the working range, and note the dilution factor (DF). All sample analyses should be blank corrected using a sample solution blank.

If a computer-based instrument is used, the data output is reported as μg/L. Calculate the concentration of arsenic, in μg/g (equivalent to mg/kg), in the original sample taken:

$$\text{Result} = (C \times DF \times V)/W$$

C = concentration of arsenic in the sample aliquot injected (μg/L)
DF = dilution factor of the *Sample solution*
V = final volume of the *Sample solution* (L)
W = weight of the sample taken to prepare the *Sample solution* (g)

[NOTE—To monitor recovery and ensure analytical accuracy for proper quality assurance, analyze blanks, spiked blanks, and a spiked oil with each digestion set.]

Acceptance criteria: NMT 0.1 mg/kg

- **LEAD**
  Apparatus
  Sample digestion: Use a microwave oven (CEM Model MDS-2100, or equivalent) equipped with advanced composite vessels with 100-mL Teflon liners. Use rupture membranes to vent vessels should the pressure exceed 125 psi. The vessels fit into a turntable, and each vessel can be vented into an overflow container. Equip the microwave oven with an exhaust tube to ventilate fumes.
  Sample analysis: See *Apparatus* in *Lead Limit Test, Atomic Absorption Spectrophotometric Graphite Furnace Method, Method I,* Appendix IIIB.
  Calibration standard stock solution: 100 μg/L

Prepare from a suitable standard, which may be purchased (accuracy certified against NIST spectrometric standard solutions).

Calibration standard solutions: 2.0 μg/L, 5.0 μg/L, 10.0 μg/L, 25.0 μg/L, and 50.0 μg/L in 2% nitric acid from the *Calibration standard stock solution*

10% Ammonium dihydrogen phosphate stock solution: Mix 10 g of ultrapure ammonium dihydrogen phosphate with 40 mL of water and 1 mL of nitric acid to dissolve the phosphate. Dilute with deionized water to 100 mL.

1% Magnesium nitrate stock solution: Mix 1 g of ultrapure magnesium nitrate with 40 mL of water and 1 mL of nitric acid in a Teflon beaker, and warm on a hot plate to dissolve the solids. Allow the solution to cool to room temperature, transfer it into a 100-mL volumetric flask, and dilute with deionized water to volume.

[NOTE—Because of the difficulty in preparing matrix modifier stock solutions with the required purity, purchasing modifier stock solutions and using them to prepare working solutions is recommended. An ammonium dihydrogen phosphate (4%) and magnesium nitrate (0.2%) solution may be purchased from High Purity Standards, or equivalent.]

Modifier working solution: Transfer 4 mL of *10% Ammonium dihydrogen phosphate stock solution* and 2 mL of *1% Magnesium nitrate stock solution* to a 10-mL volumetric flask, and dilute with 2% nitric acid to volume. A volume of 5 μL provides 0.2 mg of phosphate plus 0.01 mg of magnesium nitrate.

Sample solution: Prepare as directed for the *Sample solution* in the *Arsenic* test (above).

[CAUTION—Wear proper eye protection and protective clothing and gloves during sample preparation. Closely follow the manufacturer's safety instructions for use of the microwave digestion apparatus.]

Analysis: The graphite furnace program is as follows:
1. Dry at 120° using a 1-s ramp, a 55-s hold, and a 300-mL/min argon flow.
2. Char the sample at 850° using a 1-s ramp, a 30-s hold, and a 300-mL/min air flow.
3. Cool down and purge the air from the furnace for 10 s using a 20° set temperature and a 300-mL/min argon flow.
4. Atomize at 2100° using a 0-s ramp and a 5-s hold with the argon flow stopped.
5. Clean out at 2600° with a 1-s ramp and a 5-s hold.

Use the autosampler to inject 20-μL aliquots of blanks, *Calibration standard solutions*, *Sample solutions*, and 5 μL of *Modifier working solution*. Inject each solution in duplicate, and average the results. Use peak-area measurement for all quantitation. After ensuring that the furnace is clean by running a 5% nitric acid blank, check instrument sensitivity by running an aliquot of the 25-μg *Calibration standard solution*. Compare the results obtained with the expected results for the equipment used, and take the necessary steps to correct any problems.

Calculate the characteristic mass, and record and track the integrated absorbance and characteristic mass for reference and quality assurance.

Inject each *Calibration standard solution* in duplicate. Use the algorithms provided in the instrument software to establish calibration curves. Recheck the calibration periodically, and recalibrate if the recheck differs from the original calibration by more than 10%.

Inject the *Sample solution* in duplicate, and record the integrated absorbance. If the instrument response exceeds that of the calibration curve, dilute with 5% nitric acid to bring the sample response into the working range, and note the dilution factor (DF). All sample analyses should be blank corrected using a sample solution blank.

If a computer-based instrument is used, the data output is reported as micrograms per liter. Calculate the concentration, in µg/g (equivalent to mg/kg), of lead in the original sample:

$$\text{Result} = (C \times DF \times V)/W$$

C = concentration of lead in the sample aliquot injected (µg/L)
DF = dilution factor of the *Sample solution*
V = final volume of the *Sample solution* (L)
W = weight of the sample taken to prepare the *Sample solution* (g)

[NOTE—To monitor recovery and ensure analytical accuracy for proper quality assurance, analyze blanks, spiked blanks, and a spiked oil with each digestion set.]

Acceptance criteria: NMT 0.1 mg/kg

- **MERCURY**
  Apparatus
    Sample digestion: Use a microwave oven (CEM Model MDS-2100, or equivalent) equipped with advanced composite vessels with 100-mL Teflon liners. Use rupture membranes to vent vessels should the pressure exceed 125 psi. The vessels fit into a turntable, and each vessel can be vented into an overflow container. Equip the microwave oven with an exhaust tube to ventilate fumes.
    Sample analysis: Use a suitable atomic absorption spectrophotometer equipped with an atomic vapor assembly. This method was developed using a Perkin-Elmer Model 5100 and IL 440 Thermo Jarrell Ash atomic vapor assembly. An electrodeless discharge lamp serves as the source, with an inert gas such as argon or nitrogen as the purge gas. Set up the instrument according to manufacturers specifications. Instrument parameters are as follows:
    Wavelength: 253.6 nm
    Slit: 0.7
    Reagent setting: 5
    Gas flow: 5–6 L/min
    Reaction time: 0.5 min
    Glassware: Acid wash all glass, Teflon, and plastic vessels by soaking them in a nitric acid bath containing a solution of water and nitric acid (4:1).
    [CAUTION—Wear a full face shield and protective clothing and gloves at all times when working with acid baths.] After acid soaking, rinse acid-washed items in deionized water, dry, and store them in clean, covered cabinets.
  Calibration standard stock solution: 200 ng/g of mercury. Prepare from a suitable standard, which may be purchased (accuracy certified against NIST spectrometric standard solutions).
  Calibration standard solutions: 20 ng, 60 ng, 100 ng, 200 ng, and 400 ng of mercury in 1 N hydrochloric acid from the *Calibration standard stock solution*
  Reducing reagent: 5% stannous chloride in 25% hydrochloric acid (trace-metal grade). [NOTE—Prepare daily.]
  Sample solution: Prepare as directed for the *Sample solution* in the *Arsenic* test (above).
    [CAUTION—Wear proper eye protection and protective clothing and gloves during sample preparation. Closely follow the manufacturer's safety instructions for use of the microwave digestion apparatus.]
  Analysis: Optimize the instrument settings for the spectrophotometer as described in the instrument manual. The instrument parameters for cold vapor generation are as follows:
  Wavelength: 253.6 nm
  Slit: 0.70 nm
  Reagent setting: 5
  Gas flow: 5–6 L/min
  Reaction time: 0.5 min
  Use a peak height integration method with a 40-s integration time and a 20-s read delay in an unheated absorption cell. Zero the instrument as follows. Place a Fleaker containing 50 mL of 1 N hydrochloric acid in the sample well of the hydride generator. Press "start" on the vapor generator and "read" on the atomic absorption spectrophotometer. The instrument will automatically flush the sample container with nitrogen, dispense the designated amount of reagent, stir the sample for a designated reaction time, and purge the head volume again with nitrogen, sweeping any vapor into the quartz cell for determination of absorption. The atomic absorption spectrophotometer will automatically zero on this sample when "autozero" is selected from the calibration menu.

  Generate a standard curve of concentration versus absorption by analyzing the five *Calibration standard solutions* prepared as described for daily standards in *Calibration standard solutions*. Analyze each solution in duplicate, generate the calibration curve, and store, using procedures specific for the instrumentation.

  Transfer an appropriate aliquot of the *Sample solution* (usually 2 mL) in a Fleaker containing 50 mL of 1 N hydrochloric acid. Analyze solutions in duplicate using the procedure specified in the instrument manual. Using the calibration algorithm provided in the instrument software, calculate and report the mercury concentration in nanograms of mercury in the aliquot analyzed.

Calculate the level of mercury as μg/g (equivalent to mg/kg) in the original sample:

$$\text{Result} = (A \times DF)/(W \times 1000)$$

A = amount of mercury in the aliquot analyzed (ng)
DF = dilution factor (final volume of *Sample solution*/volume taken for analysis)
W = weight of the sample taken to prepare the *Sample solution* (g)

[NOTE—To monitor recovery and ensure analytical accuracy for proper quality assurance, analyze blanks, spiked blanks, and a spiked oil with each digestion set.]
Acceptance criteria: NMT 0.1 mg/kg

SPECIFIC TESTS
- **ANISIDINE VALUE**, Appendix VII
  Acceptance criteria: NMT 20.0
- **FREE FATTY ACIDS (AS OLEIC ACID)**, Appendix VII
  Analysis: Use 28.2 for the equivalence factor (e) in the formula given in the procedure.
  Acceptance criteria: NMT 0.4%
- **PEROXIDE VALUE**, Appendix VII
  Acceptance criteria: NMT 5.0 mEq/kg
- **TOTAL OXIDATION VALUE**
  Analysis: Calculate by the formula:

  $$\text{Result} = (2 \times PV) + AV$$

  PV = peroxide value, determined above
  AV = anisidine value, determined above
  Acceptance criteria: NMT 26
- **UNSAPONIFIABLE MATTER**, Appendix VII
  Acceptance criteria: NMT 3.5%

OTHER REQUIREMENTS
- **LABELING:** Label to indicate the content of docosahexaenoic acid in mg/g (%). Indicate the name of any added antioxidant and the presence of any other oil(s) used to standardize the docosahexaenoic acid content.

DHA from Algal (*Schizochytrium*) Oil

First Published: First Supplement, FCC 7

Schizochytrium Oil
UNII: ZAD9OKH9JC [doconexent]

DESCRIPTION
DHA from Algal (*Schizochytrium*) Oil occurs as a light yellow to orange colored oil providing a source of docosahexaenoic acid (DHA, $C_{22}H_{32}O_2$) (C22:6 n-3), an omega-3 long-chain polyunsaturated fatty acid. It is obtained from fermentation of the species of microalgae *Schizochytrium* sp., usually by solvent extraction. The oil may be winterized, bleached, and deodorized to substantially remove free fatty acids, phospholipids, odor and flavor components, and other material. Docosahexaenoic acid is the main polyunsaturated fatty acid present; DHA content may be standardized with other oils. Suitable antioxidants may be added.

Function: Source of DHA
Packaging and Storage: Store in tight, light-resistant containers. Avoid exposure to excessive heat.

IDENTIFICATION
- **FATTY ACID COMPOSITION**, Fatty Acid Composition (Saturated, cis-Monounsaturated, and cis-Polyunsaturated) in Oils Containing Long Chain Polyunsaturated Fatty Acids, Appendix VII
  Acceptance criteria: The retention times of the peaks of the docosahexaenoic acid methyl ester and eicosapentanoic acid methyl ester from the *Sample Preparation* correspond to those from the *Standard Solution*. The area percentage for the methyl esters of the fatty acids from the *Sample Preparation* meet the requirements for each fatty acid indicated in the table below.

Fatty Acid	Shorthand Notation	Lower Limit (area %)	Upper Limit (area %)
Dihomo-gamma-linolenic acid	20:3 n-6	1.7	2.8
Arachidonic acid	20:4 n-6	0.6	1.3
Eicosapentanoic acid	20:5 n-3	1.3	3.9
Docosapentaenoic acid	22:5 n-6	10.5	16.5
Docosahexaenoic acid	22:6 n-3	30.0	40.0

ASSAY
- **DHA**, Fatty Acid Composition (Saturated, cis-Monounsaturated, and cis-Polyunsaturated) in Oils Containing Long Chain Polyunsaturated Fatty Acids, Appendix VII
  Acceptance criteria: NLT 30.0% docosahexaenoic acid (DHA)

IMPURITIES
Inorganic Impurities
- **ARSENIC**
  Apparatus
  Sample digestion: Use a microwave oven (CEM Model MDS-2100, or equivalent) equipped with advanced composite vessels with 100-mL Teflon liners. Use rupture membranes to vent vessels should the pressure exceed 125 psi. The vessels fit into a turntable, and each vessel can be vented into an overflow container. Equip the microwave oven with an exhaust tube to ventilate fumes.
  Sample analysis: Use a suitable graphite furnace atomic absorption spectrophotometer (GFAAS) equipped with an autosampler, pyrolytically coated graphite tubes, solid pyrolytic graphite platforms, and an adequate means of background correction. This

method was developed using a Perkin-Elmer Model 5100, HGA-600 furnace, and an AS-60 autosampler with Zeeman effect background correction. An electrodeless discharge lamp serves as the source, argon as the purge gas, and air as the alternate gas. Set up the instrument according to manufacturer's specifications, with consideration of current good GFAAS practices. The instrument parameters are as follows:

Wavelength: 193.7 nm
Lamp current: 300 (EDL) modulated
Pyrolysis: 1000°
Atomization: 2400°
Slit: 0.7
Characteristic mass: 15 pg

Glassware: Acid wash all glass, Teflon, and plastic vessels by soaking them in a nitric acid bath containing a 4:1 solution of water:nitric acid. [**Caution**—Wear a full face shield and protective clothing and gloves at all times when working with acid baths.] After acid soaking, rinse acid-washed items in deionized water, dry them, and store them in clean, covered cabinets.

Calibration standard stock solution: 100 µg/L
Prepare from a suitable standard, which may be purchased [accuracy certified against National Institute of Standards and Technology (NIST) spectrometric standard solutions].

Calibration standard solutions: 2.0, 5.0, 10.0, 25.0, and 50.0 µg/L in 2% nitric acid, from the *Calibration standard stock solution*

1% Palladium stock solution: Mix 1 g of ultrapure palladium metal with 20 mL of water and 10 mL of nitric acid in a Teflon beaker, and warm the solution on a hot plate to dissolve the palladium. Allow the solution to cool to room temperature, transfer it into a 100-mL volumetric flask, and dilute with deionized water to volume.

1% Magnesium nitrate stock solution: Mix 1 g of ultrapure magnesium nitrate with 40 mL of water and 1 mL of nitric acid in a Teflon beaker, and warm the solution on a hot plate to dissolve. Allow the solution to cool to room temperature, transfer it into a 100-mL volumetric flask, and dilute with deionized water to volume.

[Note—Because of the difficulty in preparing matrix modifier stock solutions with the required purity, purchasing modifier stock solutions and using them to prepare working modifier solutions is recommended. A palladium (0.3%) and magnesium nitrate (0.2%) solution may be purchased from High Purity Standards, or equivalent.]

Modifier working solution: Transfer 3 mL of *1% Palladium stock solution* and 2 mL of *1% Magnesium nitrate stock solution* to a 10-mL volumetric flask, and dilute with 2% nitric acid to volume. A volume of 5 µL provides 0.015 mg of palladium and 0.01 mg of magnesium nitrate.

Sample solution: [**Caution**—Wear proper eye protection and protective clothing and gloves during sample preparation. Closely follow the manufacturer's safety instructions for use of the microwave digestion apparatus.]

Transfer 500 mg of sample into a Teflon digestion vessel liner. Prepare samples in duplicate. Add 15 mL of nitric acid, and swirl gently. Cover the vessels with lids, leaving the vent fitting off. Predigest overnight under a hood. Place the rupture membrane in the vent fitting, and tighten the lid. Place all vessels on the microwave oven turntable. Connect the vent tubes to the vent trap, and connect the pressure-sensing line to the appropriate vessel. Initiate a two-stage digestion procedure by heating the microwave at 15% power for 15 min followed by 25% power for 45 min. Remove the turntable of vessels from the oven, and allow the vessels to cool to room temperature (a cool water bath may be used to speed the cooling process). Vent the vessels when they reach room temperature. Remove the lids, and slowly add 2 mL of 30% hydrogen peroxide to each. Allow the reactions to subside, and seal the vessels. Return the vessels on the turntable to the microwave oven, and heat for an additional 15 min at 30% power. Remove the vessels from the oven, and allow them to cool to room temperature. Transfer the cooled digests into 25-mL volumetric flasks, and dilute with deionized water to volume.

Analysis: The graphite furnace program is as follows:
1. Dry at 115° using a 1-s ramp, a 65-s hold, and a 300-mL/min argon flow.
2. Char the sample at 1000° using a 1-s ramp, a 20-s hold, and a 300-mL/min air flow.
3. Cool down and purge the air from the furnace for 10 s using a 20° set temperature and a 300-mL/min argon flow.
4. Atomize at 2400° using a 0-s ramp and a 5-s hold with the argon flow stopped.
5. Clean out at 2600° with a 1-s ramp and a 5-s hold.

Use the autosampler to inject 20-µL aliquots of blanks, *Calibration standard solutions*, and *Sample solutions* and 5 µL of *Modifier working solution*. Inject each solution in duplicate, and average the results. Use peak area measurement for all quantitations. After ensuring that the furnace is clean by running a 5% nitric acid blank, check the instrument's sensitivity by running a 20-µL aliquot of the 25-µg *Calibration standard solution*. Compare the results obtained with the expected results for the equipment used, and take the necessary steps to correct any problems.

Calculate the characteristic mass. Record and track the integrated absorbance and characteristic mass for reference and quality assurance.

Inject each *Calibration standard solution* in duplicate. Use the algorithms provided in the instrument software to establish calibration curves. Recheck calibration periodically, and recalibrate if the recheck differs from the original calibration by more than 10%.

Inject the *Sample solution* in duplicate, and record the integrated absorbance. If the instrument response exceeds that of the calibration curve, dilute with 5% nitric acid to bring the sample's response into the working range, and note the dilution factor (DF). All sample analyses should be blank corrected using a sample solution blank.

If a computer-based instrument is used, the data output is reported as µg/L. Calculate the concentration of arsenic, in µg/g (equivalent to mg/kg), in the original sample taken:

$$\text{Result} = (C \times DF \times V)/W$$

C = concentration of arsenic in the sample aliquot injected (µg/L)
DF = dilution factor of the *Sample solution*
V = final volume of the *Sample solution* (L)
W = weight of the sample taken to prepare the *Sample solution* (g)

[NOTE—To monitor recovery and ensure analytical accuracy for proper quality assurance, analyze blanks, spiked blanks, and a spiked oil with each digestion set.]

Acceptance criteria: NMT 0.1 mg/kg

- **LEAD**
  Apparatus
  Sample digestion: Use a microwave oven (CEM Model MDS-2100, or equivalent) equipped with advanced composite vessels with 100-mL Teflon liners. Use rupture membranes to vent vessels should the pressure exceed 125 psi. The vessels fit into a turntable, and each vessel can be vented into an overflow container. Equip the microwave oven with an exhaust tube to ventilate fumes.
  Sample analysis: See *Apparatus* in *Lead Limit Test, Atomic Absorption Spectrophotometric Graphite Furnace Method, Method I,* Appendix IIIB

  Calibration standard stock solution: 100 µg/L
  Prepare from a suitable standard, which may be purchased [accuracy certified against National Institute of Standards and Technology (NIST) spectrometric standard solutions].

  Calibration standard solutions: 2.0, 5.0, 10.0, 25.0, and 50.0 µg/L in 2% nitric acid, from the *Calibration standard stock solution*

  10% Ammonium dihydrogen phosphate stock solution: Mix 10 g of ultrapure ammonium dihydrogen phosphate with 40 of mL water and 1 mL of nitric acid to dissolve the phosphate. Dilute with deionized water to 100 mL.

  1% Magnesium nitrate stock solution: Mix 1 g of ultrapure magnesium nitrate with 40 mL of water and 1 mL of nitric acid in a Teflon beaker, and warm on a hot plate to dissolve the solids. Allow the solution to cool to room temperature, transfer it into a 100-mL volumetric flask, and dilute with deionized water to volume.

  [NOTE—Because of the difficulty in preparing matrix modifier stock solutions with the required purity, purchasing modifier stock solutions and using them to prepare working solutions is recommended. An ammonium dihydrogen phosphate (4%) and magnesium nitrate (0.2%) solution may be purchased from High Purity Standards, or equivalent.]

  Modifier working solution: Transfer 4 mL of *10% Ammonium dihydrogen phosphate stock solution* and 2 mL of *1% Magnesium nitrate stock solution* to a 10-mL volumetric flask, and dilute with 2% nitric acid to volume. A volume of 5 µL provides 0.2 mg of phosphate plus 0.01 mg of magnesium nitrate.

  Sample solution: Prepare as directed for *Sample solution* in the *Arsenic* test (above).

  [**CAUTION**—Wear proper eye protection and protective clothing and gloves during sample preparation. Closely follow the manufacturer's safety instructions for use of the microwave digestion apparatus.]

  Analysis: The graphite furnace program is as follows:
  1. Dry at 120° using a 1-s ramp, a 55-s hold, and a 300-mL/min argon flow.
  2. Char the sample at 850° using a 1-s ramp, a 30-s hold, and a 300-mL/min air flow.
  3. Cool down and purge the air from the furnace for 10 s using a 20° set temperature and a 300-mL/min argon flow.
  4. Atomize at 2100° using a 0-s ramp and a 5-s hold with the argon flow stopped.
  5. Clean out at 2600° with a 1-s ramp and a 5-s hold.

  Use the autosampler to inject 20-µL aliquots of blanks, *Calibration standard solutions*, *Sample solutions*, and 5 µL of *Modifier working solution*. Inject each solution in duplicate, and average the results. Use peak-area measurement for all quantitation. After ensuring that the furnace is clean by running a 5% nitric acid blank, check instrument sensitivity by running an aliquot of the 25-µg *Calibration standard solution*. Compare the results obtained with the expected results for the equipment used, and take the necessary steps to correct any problems.

  Calculate the characteristic mass, and record and track the integrated absorbance and characteristic mass for reference and quality assurance.

  Inject each *Calibration standard solution* in duplicate. Use the algorithms provided in the instrument software to establish calibration curves. Recheck the calibration periodically, and recalibrate if the recheck differs from the original calibration by more than 10%.

  Inject the *Sample solution* in duplicate, and record the integrated absorbance. If the instrument response exceeds that of the calibration curve, dilute with 5% nitric acid to bring the sample response into the working range, and note the dilution factor (DF). All sample analyses should be blank corrected using a sample solution blank.

  If a computer-based instrument is used, the data output is reported as micrograms per liter. Calculate the concentration, in µg/g (equivalent to mg/kg), of lead in the original sample:

  $$\text{Result} = (C \times DF \times V)/W$$

  C = concentration of lead in the sample aliquot injected (µg/L)
  DF = dilution factor of the *Sample solution*
  V = final volume of the *Sample solution* (L)
  W = weight of the sample taken to prepare the *Sample solution* (g)

[NOTE—To monitor recovery and ensure analytical accuracy for proper quality assurance, analyze blanks, spiked blanks, and a spiked oil with each digestion set.]
Acceptance criteria: NMT 0.1 mg/kg

- **MERCURY**
  Apparatus
  Sample digestion: Use a microwave oven (CEM Model MDS-2100, or equivalent) equipped with advanced composite vessels with 100-mL Teflon liners. Use rupture membranes to vent vessels should the pressure exceed 125 psi. The vessels fit into a turntable, and each vessel can be vented into an overflow container. Equip the microwave oven with an exhaust tube to ventilate fumes.
  Sample analysis: Use a suitable atomic absorption spectrophotometer equipped with an atomic vapor assembly. This method was developed using a Perkin-Elmer Model 5100 and IL 440 Thermo Jarrell Ash atomic vapor assembly. An electrodeless discharge lamp serves as the source, with an inert gas such as argon or nitrogen as the purge gas. Set up the instrument according to manufacturer specifications. Instrument parameters are as follows:
  Wavelength: 253.6 nm
  Slit: 0.7
  Reagent setting: 5
  Gas flow: 5–6 L/min
  Reaction time: 0.5 min
  Glassware: Acid wash all glass, Teflon, and plastic vessels by soaking them in a nitric acid bath containing a 4:1 solution of water:nitric acid.
  [CAUTION—Wear a full face shield and protective clothing and gloves at all times when working with acid baths.] After acid soaking, rinse acid-washed items in deionized water, dry, and store them in clean, covered cabinets.
  Calibration standard stock solution: 200 ng/g of mercury. Prepare from a suitable standard, which may be purchased [accuracy certified against National Institute of Standards and Technology (NIST) spectrometric standard solutions].
  Calibration standard solutions: 20, 60, 100, 200, and 400 ng of mercury in 1 N hydrochloric acid from the *Calibration standard stock solution*
  Reducing reagent: 5% stannous chloride in 25% hydrochloric acid (trace-metal grade) [NOTE—Prepare daily.]
  Sample solution: Prepare as directed for the *Sample solution* in the *Arsenic* test (above).
  [CAUTION—Wear proper eye protection and protective clothing and gloves during sample preparation. Closely follow the manufacturer's safety instructions for use of the microwave digestion apparatus.]
  Analysis: Optimize the instrument settings for the spectrophotometer as described in the instrument manual. The instrument parameters for cold vapor generation are as follows:
  Wavelength: 253.6 nm
  Slit: 0.70 nm
  Reagent setting: 5
  Gas flow: 5–6 L/min
  Reaction time: 0.5 min
  Use a peak height integration method with a 40-s integration time and a 20-s read delay in an unheated absorption cell. Zero the instrument as follows: Place a Fleaker containing 50 mL of 1 N hydrochloric acid in the sample well of the hydride generator. Press "start" on the vapor generator and "read" on the atomic absorption spectrophotometer. The instrument will automatically flush the sample container with nitrogen, dispense the designated amount of reagent, stir the sample for a designated reaction time, and purge the head volume again with nitrogen, sweeping any vapor into the quartz cell for determination of absorption. The atomic absorption spectrophotometer will automatically zero on this sample when "autozero" is selected from the calibration menu.
  Generate a standard curve of concentration versus absorption by analyzing the five *Calibration standard solutions* prepared as described for daily standards under *Calibration standard solutions*. Analyze each solution in duplicate, generate the calibration curve, and store, using procedures specific for the instrumentation.
  Transfer an appropriate aliquot of *Sample solution* (usually 2 mL) in a Fleaker containing 50 mL of 1 N hydrochloric acid. Analyze solutions in duplicate using the procedure specified in the instrument manual. Using the calibration algorithm provided in the instrument software, calculate and report the mercury concentration in nanograms of mercury in the aliquot analyzed.
  Calculate the level of mercury as µg/g (equivalent to mg/kg) in the original sample:

  $$\text{Result} = (A \times DF)/(W \times 1000)$$

  A = amount of mercury in the aliquot analyzed (ng)
  DF = dilution factor (final volume of *Sample solution*/volume taken for analysis)
  W = weight of the sample taken to prepare the *Sample solution* (g)
  [NOTE—To monitor recovery and ensure analytical accuracy for proper quality assurance, analyze blanks, spiked blanks, and a spiked oil with each digestion set.]
  Acceptance criteria: NMT 0.1 mg/kg

SPECIFIC TESTS
- **ANISIDINE VALUE,** Appendix VII
  Acceptance criteria: NMT 20.0
- **FREE FATTY ACIDS (AS OLEIC ACID),** Appendix VII
  Analysis: Use 28.2 for the equivalence factor (e) in the formula given in the procedure.
  Acceptance criteria: NMT 0.4%
- **PEROXIDE VALUE,** Appendix VII
  Acceptance criteria: NMT 5.0 mEq/kg

- **TOTAL OXIDATION VALUE**
  Analysis: Calculate by the formula:

  $$\text{Result} = (2 \times PV) + AV$$

  PV = peroxide value, determined above
  AV = anisidine value, determined above
  Acceptance criteria: NMT 26
- **UNSAPONIFIABLE MATTER,** Appendix VII
  Acceptance criteria: NMT 4.5%

OTHER REQUIREMENTS

- **LABELING:** Label to indicate the content of docosahexaenoic acid in mg/g (%). Indicate the name of any added antioxidant and the presence of any other oil(s) used to standardize the docosahexaenoic acid content.

Add the following:

▲DHA from Algal (*Ulkenia*) Oil

First Published: FCC 8

Ulkenia DHA Oil

DESCRIPTION

DHA from Algal (*Ulkenia*) Oil occurs as a slightly waxy to liquid, light yellow to orange colored oil providing a source of docosahexaenoic acid (DHA, $C_{22}H_{32}O_2$) (C22:6 n-3), an omega-3 long-chain polyunsaturated fatty acid. It is obtained from fermentation of a thraustochytrid microalgae, *Ulkenia* sp., followed by extraction and refining. Extraction can be pure pressing or supported by solvents approved for food processing. Solvents, if used, are subsequently removed by vacuum distillation. The oil may be degummed, deacidified, winterized, bleached, and deodorized to substantially remove free fatty acids, phospholipids, odor and flavor components, and other material. Docosahexaenoic acid is the main polyunsaturated fatty acid present; DHA content may be standardized with other oils. Suitable antioxidants may be added.
Function: Source of DHA
Packaging and Storage: Store in tight, light-resistant containers, under inert gas and below 5°. Avoid exposure to excessive heat.

IDENTIFICATION

- **FATTY ACID COMPOSITION,** *Fatty Acid Composition (Saturated, cis-Monounsaturated, and cis-Polyunsaturated) in Oils Containing Long Chain Polyunsaturated Fatty Acids,* Appendix VII
  Acceptance criteria: The retention time of the peak of the docosahexaenoic acid methyl ester from the *Sample Preparation* corresponds to that from the *Standard Solution*. The percentage of the fatty acids (calculated using the results from the corresponding methyl esters) from the *Sample Preparation*, meets the requirements for each fatty acid as indicated in the table below.

Fatty Acid	Shorthand Notation	Lower Limit (area %)	Upper Limit (area %)
Myristic acid	14:0	1.5	4.5
Stearic acid	18:0	0.5	2.0
Eicosapentaenoic acid	20:5 n-3	0	0.5
Docosapentaenoic acid	22:5 n-6	8.0	14.0
Docosapentaenoic acid	22:5 n-3	0.2	1.5
Docosahexaenoic acid	22:6 n-3	40.0	55.0

ASSAY

- **DHA,** *Fatty Acid Composition (Saturated, cis-Monounsaturated, and cis-Polyunsaturated) in Oils Containing Long Chain Polyunsaturated Fatty Acids,* Appendix VII
  Acceptance criteria: NLT 40.0% docosahexaenoic acid (DHA), as the percentage of total fatty acids (w/w)

IMPURITIES

Inorganic Impurities

- **ARSENIC,** *Elemental Impurities by ICP,* Appendix IIIC
  Acceptance criteria: NMT 0.1 mg/kg
- **CADMIUM,** *Elemental Impurities by ICP,* Appendix IIIC
  Acceptance criteria: NMT 0.1 mg/kg
- **LEAD,** *Elemental Impurities by ICP,* Appendix IIIC
  Acceptance criteria: NMT 0.1 mg/kg
- **MERCURY**
  Apparatus
    Sample digestion: Use a microwave oven[1] equipped with advanced composite vessels with 100-mL Teflon liners. Use rupture membranes to vent vessels should the pressure exceed 125 psi. The vessels fit into a turntable, and each vessel can be vented into an overflow container. Equip the microwave oven with an exhaust tube to ventilate fumes.
    Sample analysis: Use a suitable atomic absorption spectrophotometer equipped with an atomic vapor assembly.[2] An electrodeless discharge lamp serves as the source, with an inert gas such as argon or nitrogen as the purge gas. Set up the instrument according to manufacturer specifications. Instrument parameters are as follows:
    Wavelength: 253.6 nm
    Slit: 0.7
    Reagent setting: 5
    Gas flow: 5–6 L/min
    Reaction time: 0.5 min
    Glassware: Acid wash all glass, Teflon, and plastic vessels by soaking them in a nitric acid bath containing a solution of water and nitric acid (4:1). [**CAUTION**—Wear a full face shield and protective clothing and gloves at all times when working with acid baths.] After acid soaking, rinse acid-washed items in deionized water, dry, and store them in clean, covered cabinets.
    Calibration standard stock solution: 200 ng/g of mercury. Prepare from a suitable standard, which may be purchased [accuracy certified against National

---
[1] CEM Model MDS-2100, or equivalent.
[2] This method was developed using a Perkin-Elmer Model 5100 and IL 440 Thermo Jarrell Ash atomic vapor assembly.

Institute of Standards and Technology (NIST) spectrometric standard solutions].

Calibration standard solutions: 20 ng, 60 ng, 100 ng, 200 ng, and 400 ng of mercury in 1 N hydrochloric acid from the *Calibration standard stock solution*

Reducing reagent: 5% stannous chloride in 25% hydrochloric acid (trace-metal grade). [NOTE—Prepare daily.]

Sample solution

[CAUTION—Wear proper eye protection and protective clothing and gloves during sample preparation. Closely follow the manufacturer's safety instructions for use of the microwave digestion apparatus.]

Transfer 500 mg of sample into a Teflon digestion vessel liner. Prepare samples in duplicate. Add 15 mL of nitric acid, and swirl gently. Cover the vessels with lids, leaving the vent fitting off. Predigest overnight under a hood. Place the rupture membrane in the vent fitting, and tighten the lid. Place all vessels on the microwave oven turntable. Connect the vent tubes to the vent trap, and connect the pressure-sensing line to the appropriate vessel. Initiate a two-stage digestion procedure by heating the microwave at 15% power for 15 min followed by 25% power for 45 min. Remove the turntable of vessels from the oven, and allow the vessels to cool to room temperature (a cool water bath may be used to speed the cooling process). Vent the vessels when they reach room temperature. Remove the lids, and slowly add 2 mL of 30% hydrogen peroxide to each. Allow the reactions to subside, and seal the vessels. Return the vessels on the turntable to the microwave oven, and heat for an additional 15 min at 30% power. Remove the vessels from the oven, and allow them to cool to room temperature. Transfer the cooled digests into 25-mL volumetric flasks, and dilute with deionized water to volume.

Analysis: Optimize the instrument settings for the spectrophotometer as described in the instrument manual. The instrument parameters for cold vapor generation are as follows:

Wavelength: 253.6 nm
Slit: 0.70 nm
Reagent setting: 5
Gas flow: 5–6 L/min
Reaction time: 0.5 min

Use a peak height integration method with a 40-s integration time and a 20-s read delay in an unheated absorption cell. Zero the instrument as follows. Place a Fleaker containing 50 mL of 1 N hydrochloric acid in the sample well of the hydride generator. Press "start" on the vapor generator and "read" on the atomic absorption spectrophotometer. The instrument will automatically flush the sample container with nitrogen, dispense the designated amount of reagent, stir the sample for a designated reaction time, and purge the head volume again with nitrogen, sweeping any vapor into the quartz cell for determination of absorption. The atomic absorption spectrophotometer will automatically zero on this sample when "autozero" is selected from the calibration menu.

Generate a standard curve of concentration vs. absorption by analyzing the five *Calibration standard solutions* prepared as described for daily standards under *Calibration standard solutions*. Analyze each solution in duplicate, generate the calibration curve, and store, using procedures specific for the instrumentation.

Transfer an appropriate aliquot of *Sample solution* (usually 2 mL) to a Fleaker containing 50 mL of 1 N hydrochloric acid. Analyze solutions in duplicate using the procedure specified in the instrument manual. Using the calibration algorithm provided in the instrument software, calculate and report the mercury concentration in ng of mercury in the aliquot analyzed.

Calculate the level of mercury as µg/g (equivalent to mg/kg), in the original sample:

$$\text{Result} = (A \times DF)/(W \times 1000)$$

A = amount of mercury in the aliquot analyzed (ng)
DF = dilution factor (final volume of *Sample solution*/volume taken for analysis)
W = weight of the sample taken to prepare the *Sample solution* (g)

[NOTE—To monitor recovery and ensure analytical accuracy for proper quality assurance, analyze blanks, spiked blanks, and a spiked oil with each digestion set.]

Acceptance criteria: NMT 0.1 mg/kg

SPECIFIC TESTS

- **ACID VALUE (FATS AND RELATED SUBSTANCES),** Appendix VII
  Acceptance criteria: NMT 0.5
- **PEROXIDE VALUE,** Appendix VII
  Acceptance criteria: NMT 5.0 mEq/kg
- **UNSAPONIFIABLE MATTER,** Appendix VII
  Acceptance criteria: NMT 4.5%

OTHER REQUIREMENTS

- **LABELING:** Label to indicate the content of docosahexaenoic acid in mg/g (%). Indicate the name of any added antioxidant and the presence of any other oil(s) used to standardize the docosahexaenoic acid content. ▲FCC8

Diacetyl

First Published: Prior to FCC 6
Last Revision: First Supplement, FCC 6

2,3-Butanedione
Dimethyldiketone
Dimethylglyoxal

Diacetyl

C₄H₆O₂ Formula wt 86.09
FEMA: 2370
UNII: K324J5K4HM [diacetyl]

DESCRIPTION
Diacetyl occurs as a yellow to yellow-green liquid. It may contain a suitable antioxidant.
Odor: Powerful, buttery in very dilute solution
Solubility: Soluble in glycerin, water; miscible in alcohol, most fixed oils, propylene glycol
Boiling Point: ~88°
Function: Flavoring agent

IDENTIFICATION
- **INFRARED SPECTRA**, *Spectrophotometric Identification Tests*, Appendix IIIC
  Acceptance criteria: The spectrum of the sample exhibits relative maxima at the same wavelengths as those of the spectrum below.

ASSAY
- **PROCEDURE:** Proceed as directed under *M-1b*, Appendix XI.
  Acceptance criteria: NLT 95.0% of C₄H₆O₂

SPECIFIC TESTS
- **REFRACTIVE INDEX,** Appendix II: At 20°
  Acceptance criteria: Between 1.393 and 1.397
- **SPECIFIC GRAVITY:** Determine at 25° by any reliable method (see *General Provisions*).
  Acceptance criteria: Between 0.979 and 0.985

OTHER REQUIREMENTS
- **SOLIDIFICATION POINT,** Appendix IIB
  Acceptance criteria: Between −2.0° and −4.0°

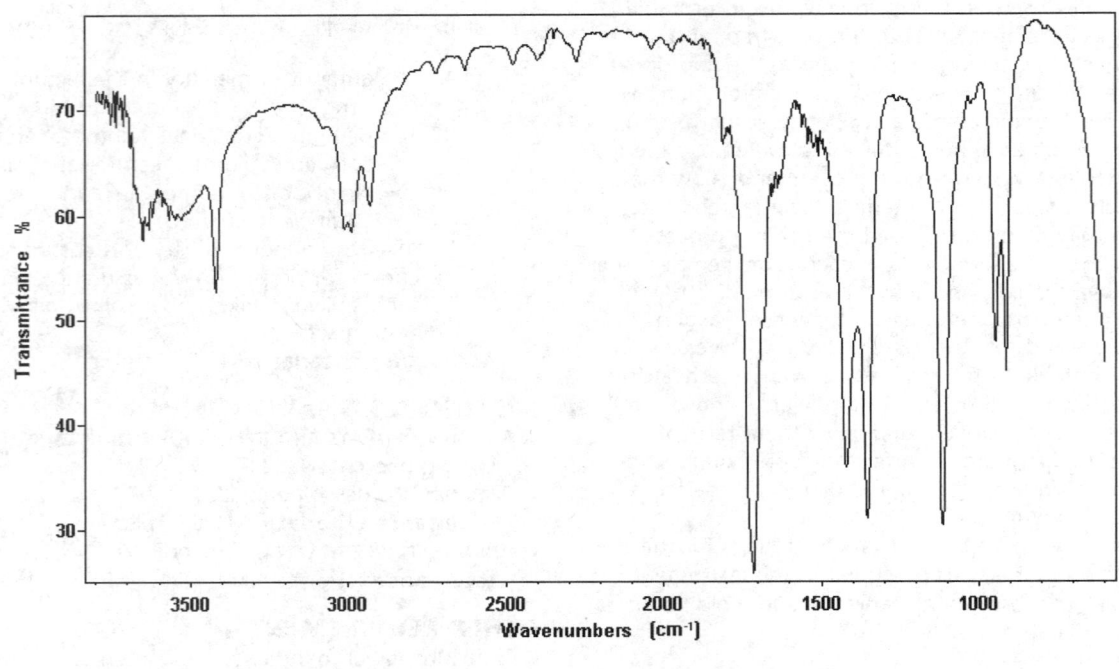

Diacetyl

Diacetyl Tartaric Acid Esters of Mono- and Diglycerides

First Published: Prior to FCC 6
Last Revision: First Supplement, FCC 7

DATEM
INS: 472e CAS: [91052-83-4]
  [100085-39-0]

DESCRIPTION
Diacetyl Tartaric Acid Esters of Mono- and Diglycerides occur over a range in appearance from sticky, viscous liquids through a fatlike consistency to a waxy solid, depending on the iodine value of the oils or fats used in their manufacture. They are the reaction product of partial glycerides of edible oils, fats, or fat-forming fatty acids with diacetyl tartaric anhydride. The diacetyl tartaroyl esters are miscible in all proportions with oils and fats. They are soluble in most common fat solvents, in methanol, in acetone, and in ethyl acetate, but are insoluble in other alcohols, in acetic acid, and in water. They are dispersible in water and resistant to hydrolysis for moderate periods of time. The pH of a 3% dispersion in water is between 2 and 3.

Function: Emulsifier

Packaging and Storage: Store in well-closed containers.

IDENTIFICATION
- **PROCEDURE**
  Sample solution: 500 mg in 10 mL of methanol
  Analysis: Add, dropwise, lead acetate TS to the *Sample solution*.
  Acceptance criteria: A white, flocculent, practically insoluble precipitate forms.

ASSAY
- **TARTARIC ACID**
  Solution A: Transfer 4 g of sample into a 250-mL Erlenmeyer flask, and add 80 mL of 0.5 N potassium hydroxide and 0.5 mL of phenolphthalein TS. Connect an air condenser at least 65 cm long to the flask, and heat the mixture on a hot plate for about 2.5 h. Remove the air condenser and add approximately 10% phosphoric acid to the hot mixture until it is definitely acid to congo red test paper. Reconnect the air condenser, and heat until the fatty acids are liquefied and clear. Cool, and transfer the mixture into a 250-mL separatory funnel with the aid of small portions of water and hexane. Extract the liberated fatty acids with three successive 25-mL portions of hexane, and collect the extracts in a second separatory funnel. Wash the combined hexane extracts with two 25-mL portions of water, and add the washings to the first separatory funnel containing the water layer. Retain the combined hexane extracts for the determination of *Fatty Acids (Total)*. Transfer the contents of the first separatory funnel to a 250-mL beaker, heat on a steam bath to remove traces of hexane, filter through acid-washed, fine-texture filter paper into a 500-mL volumetric flask, and finally dilute with water to volume.
  Solution B: Pipet 25.0 mL of *Solution A* into a 100-mL volumetric flask, and dilute with water to volume (*Solution B*). [NOTE—Retain the rest of *Solution A* for the determination of *Glycerin* (below).]
  Standard stock solution: 1 mg/mL of tartaric acid (reagent-grade)
  Standard solutions: Transfer 3.0-, 4.0-, 5.0-, and 6.0-mL aliquots of the *Standard stock solution* into separate 19-mm × 150-mm matched cuvettes, and add sufficient water to make 10.0 mL. Add 4.0 mL of a freshly prepared 50 mg/mL solution of sodium metavanadate and 1.0 mL of glacial acetic acid to each cuvette. [NOTE—Use these solutions within 10 min after color development.]
  Blank solution: Prepare in the same manner as the *Standard solutions*, using 10.0 mL of water in the cuvette in place of the tartaric acid solutions.
  Sample solution: Prepare in the same manner as the *Standard solutions*, using 10.0 mL of *Solution B* in the cuvette in place of the tartaric acid solutions.
  Analysis: Using a suitable spectrophotometer or photoelectric colorimeter equipped with a 520-nm filter that has been set at zero with the *Blank solution*, determine the absorbance of each of the *Standard solutions* and the *Sample solution*. Prepare a standard curve from the data obtained for the *Standard solutions* by plotting the absorbances on the ordinate against the corresponding quantities, in mg, of tartaric acid in each solution on the abscissa. From the curve, determine the weight, in mg, of tartaric acid in the final dilution (W_T). Calculate the percentage of tartaric acid taken by the formula:

  $$\text{Result} = (W_T/W_S) \times 20$$

  W_T = weight (mg) of tartaric acid in the final dilution
  W_S = weight (mg) of sample taken
  Acceptance criteria: Between 17.0 and 20.0 g of tartaric acid ($C_4H_6O_6$) per 100 g of sample after saponification

IMPURITIES
Inorganic Impurities
- **LEAD,** *Lead Limit Test, Atomic Absorption Spectrophotometric Graphite Furnace Method, Method II,* Appendix IIIB
  Sample: 10 g
  Acceptance criteria: NMT 2 mg/kg

SPECIFIC TESTS
- **ACETIC ACID,** *Volatile Acidity,* Appendix VII
  Sample: 4 g
  Analysis: Use 30.03 as the equivalence factor (e).
  Acceptance criteria: Between 14.0 and 17.0 g of acetic acid (CH_3COOH) per 100 g of sample after hydrolysis
- **ACID VALUE**
  Solvent mixture: Prepare a 20% solution of hexane in methanol (v/v), and add phenol red TS. Neutralize the solution if necessary.
  Analysis: Transfer 1 g of sample into a 125-mL Erlenmeyer flask, and dissolve in 25 mL of *Solvent mixture*. Titrate with 0.1 N methanolic potassium hydroxide to a light red endpoint. Perform a blank determination (see *General Provisions*), using a 25-mL portion of the *Solvent mixture*, and make any necessary correction. Calculate the acid value by the formula:

  $$\text{Result} = 56.1V \times N/W$$

  V = volume (mL) of the methanolic potassium hydroxide used in the titration
  N = normality of the methanolic potassium hydroxide used
  W = weight (g) of the sample taken
  Acceptance criteria: Between 62 and 76
- **FATTY ACIDS (TOTAL)**
  Sample: The combined hexane extracts of fatty acids obtained in the *Assay* for *Tartaric Acid*
  Analysis: Dry the sample by shaking with a few grams of anhydrous sodium sulfate. Filter the solution into a tared, 250-mL beaker, evaporate the hexane on a steam bath, cool, and weigh.
  Acceptance criteria: NLT 56.0 g of total fatty acids per 100 g of sample after hydrolysis
- **GLYCERIN**
  Periodic acid solution: Dissolve 2.7 g of periodic acid (H_5IO_6) in 50 mL of water, add 950 mL of glacial acetic acid, and mix thoroughly. [NOTE—Protect this solution from light.]

Analysis: Transfer 5.0 mL of *Solution A*, prepared in the *Assay* for *Tartaric Acid*, into a 250-mL glass-stoppered Erlenmeyer or iodine flask. Add 15 mL of glacial acetic acid and 25.0 mL of *Periodic acid solution* to the flask, shake the mixture for 1 or 2 min, allow it to stand for 15 min, add 15 mL of a 150 mg/mL potassium iodide solution and 15 mL of water, swirl, and let it stand for 1 min. Titrate the liberated iodine with 0.1 N sodium thiosulfate, using starch TS as the indicator. Perform a residual blank titration (see *General Provisions, Tests and Assays, Blank Tests*), using water in place of sample, and make any necessary correction. The corrected volume is the number of mL of 0.1 N sodium thiosulfate required for the glycerin and the tartaric acid in the sample represented by the 5 mL of *Solution A*. From the percentage determined in the *Assay* for *Tartaric Acid*, calculate the volume of 0.1 N sodium thiosulfate required for the tartaric acid in the titration. The difference between the corrected volume and the calculated volume required for the tartaric acid is the number of mL of 0.1 N sodium thiosulfate consumed because of the glycerin in the sample. One mL of 0.1 N sodium thiosulfate is equivalent to 2.303 mg of glycerin and to 7.505 mg of tartaric acid.

Acceptance criteria: NLT 12.0 g of glycerin ($C_3H_8O_3$) per 100 g of sample after hydrolysis

- **RESIDUE ON IGNITION (SULFATED ASH),** Appendix IIC
  Sample: 10 g
  Acceptance criteria: NMT 0.5%
- **SAPONIFICATION VALUE,** Appendix VII
  Sample: 2 g
  [NOTE—Add 5 to 10 mL of water to samples and blanks before saponification; otherwise, sufficient salts precipitate during saponification to cause serious bumping and spattering.]
  Acceptance criteria: Between 380 and 425

Diacylglycerol Oil

First Published: FCC 6

DAG Oil

CAS: [308082-33-9]
UNII: GN1LK75KSX [diacylglycerol oil]

DESCRIPTION

Diacylglycerol Oil occurs as an opaque white to pale yellow, usually viscous liquid at room temperature, and free from particulate matter. It is manufactured through enzymatic esterification of fatty acids derived from natural, edible plant oils, such as soybean, rapeseed, corn, sunflower, cottonseed, safflower, peanut, palm, coconut, or olive oil, with either monoacylglycerol or glycerol. Its main component is randomized diacylglycerol. Oleic acid, linoleic acid, and linolenic acid are the main constituent fatty acids. It is soluble in ethanol, in isopropanol, in acetone, and in hexane, and insoluble in water.

Function: Component of shortening; coating agent; texturizer

Packaging and Storage: Store in well-closed containers.

IDENTIFICATION

- **FATTY ACID COMPOSITION,** Appendix VII
  Acceptance criteria: A sample exhibits the following composition profile of fatty acids:

Fatty Acid	Weight % (Range)
16:0	≤10
18:0	≤10
18:1	20–65
18:2	15–65
18:3	≤15
20:1	≤0.5

ASSAY

- **PROCEDURE**
  [NOTE—This method is adapted from AOAC Method 965.35.]
  Silica gel preparation: Transfer 10 g of silica gel (Fischer Scientific Co. No. S-679, grade 923, 100- to 200-mesh, or equivalent) into a tared weighing bottle, and cap immediately. Weigh the bottle and its contents to the nearest mg, and subtract the tare weight. Remove the cap and dry the bottle and its contents in an oven for 2 h at 200°. Remove the bottle from the oven, immediately cap it, and let it cool for 30 min at room temperature. Raise the cap briefly to equalize the internal pressure with the atmospheric pressure, weigh, reheat for 5 min at 200°, cool, and reweigh. Repeat the 5-min drying cycle until two consecutive weights agree within 10 mg. Calculate the water content as follows:

$$W_P = L \times 100/S$$

W_P = percentage of water in the original silica gel
L = loss in weight (mg) of the silica gel
S = weight (mg) of the original silica gel

Calculate the amount of water necessary to adjust the final water content of the silica gel to 5% using the following formula:

$$\text{Result} = S \times (5 - W_P)/95$$

S = weight (mg) of the silica gel
W_P = percentage of water in the silica gel

To adjust the water content of the silica gel to 5%, transfer the gel to be adjusted, accurately weighed, into a blender (Patterson-Kelley Twin Shell Blender, or equivalent). Add the calculated amount of water necessary to take the final water content of the silica gel to 5 ± 0.1%, blend the contents for 1 h to ensure complete water distribution, and store the gel in a sealed container. Before use, determine the water content of the adjusted silica gel, as above, and readjust it if necessary.

Column preparation: Use a 250-mL reservoir with Teflon stopcock attached through a standard taper 19/22 drip tip inner joint to a 19- (id) × 290-mm chromatographic tube. The tube has an outer standard taper 19/22 joint at the top and a coarse fritted glass disk and an inner standard taper 19/22 joint at the bottom. The bottom joint connects to an adapter consisting of an outer standard taper 19/22 joint connected to a Teflon stopcock (Lurex Scientific, or equivalent).

[NOTE—Keep the temperature of the work area below the boiling point of ethyl ether (34.6°). Higher temperatures will cause the column packing to separate and permit the solvent to channel.]

[NOTE—Never let the column become dry on top, and maintain a 2-mL/min flow rate throughout elution. If it is necessary to interrupt the elution, do so when a very small volume of eluate is passing through the bottom stopcock. Such interruptions, however, may allow the solvent above the bottom stopcock to cause a pressure buildup, resulting in leakage through the stopcock or cracks in the silica gel packing.]

Assemble the column without the reservoir and without greasing the joints. Transfer 30 g of *Silica gel preparation* into a 150-mL beaker, and add 50 to 60 mL of petroleum ether. Slowly stir the slurry with a glass rod until it is free of air bubbles. Transfer the slurry into the column using a powder funnel. Open the stopcock, and let the liquid level in the column drop to about 2 cm above the level of the silica gel. Transfer any remaining slurry by inverting the beaker over the powder funnel at 45°, and washing it into the column using a wash bottle containing petroleum ether. Use only the minimum amount of petroleum ether necessary to complete the transfer. Rinse the funnel and sides of the column; when the solvent level drops to 2 cm above the silica gel, close the bottom stopcock and remove the powder funnel.

Sample solution: Transfer 0.9 to 1.1 g of prepared sample into a 100-mL beaker. Add 15 mL of chloroform and warm with minimal heat, not to exceed 40°, if necessary for complete dissolution.

[NOTE—If unknown, determine the melting temperature of the sample as directed under *Melting Range or Temperature Determination,* Appendix IIB.]

[NOTE—Use extreme caution to avoid heating samples to more than 50°, as this may cause partial glycerides to rearrange. For samples that melt below 50°, melt by warming at less than 50° for short periods not to exceed 30 min. For samples that melt above 50°, grind 10 g of sample using a mortar and pestle. If needed, chill samples in solid carbon dioxide.]

Analysis: Carefully add the *Sample solution* to the column. Open the stopcock, and adjust the flow to 2 mL/min. Rinse the beaker with 5 mL of chloroform, and add the rinse to the column when the level drops to 2 cm above the silica gel. Attach the reservoir to the column, add 200 mL of benzene, and collect the eluate (triacylglycerol fraction) in a tared 250-mL flask.

[NOTE—After each collection, rinse the tip of the column into the flask with the same solvent used in elution just before changing flasks for the next eluate.]

When all of the benzene has been added from the reservoir and the level in the column drops to 2 cm above the silica gel, add 200 mL of 10% (v/v) diethyl ether in benzene and collect the eluate in a second tared 250-mL flask (diacylglycerol and free fatty acid fraction). When all of the benzene–diethyl ether solvent has been added from the reservoir and the level in the column drops to 2 cm above the silica gel, add 200 mL of diethyl ether and, using a third 250-mL flask, collect the monoacylglycerol fraction.

[NOTE—Adding diethyl ether to a column often creates internal pressure, resulting in an increased flow rate and cracks in the silica gel packing before a fraction is completely eluted. To avoid this event, slightly separate the reservoir from the column for about 30 s, and let the solvent flow into the column at the same rate the eluate is collecting. To ensure quantitative separation of fractions, rinse the tip of the column into the receiver with the same solvent used in elution prior to changing flasks for the next eluate.]

Place the collected fractions in a steam bath, and evaporate the solvents under a stream of nitrogen or dry air. Let the flasks cool at room temperature for at least 15 min, and weigh. Repeat this sequence, heating the flasks for only 5 min, and reweigh until two consecutive weights agree within 2 mg.

Any free fatty acid (FFA) present has eluted with the diacylglycerol fraction. To determine the FFA content, add 25 mL of warm neutral ethanol and 1 drop of phenolphthalein indicator, and titrate with 0.05 M sodium hydroxide.

Calculate the percent FFA, triacylglycerol (T), diacylglycerol (D), and monoacylglycerol (M) using the following equations:

$$\text{FFA (as oleic acid)} = A \times M_O \times 28.2/S$$

A = volume (mL) of sodium hydroxide used in the titration
M_O = molarity of the sodium hydroxide
28.2 = equivalence factor of FFA as oleic acid
S = weight (g) of the sample taken

$$T = T_G \times 100/S$$

T_G = weight (g) of the eluted triacylglycerol fraction after evaporation of the solvents

$$D = D_G \times 100/S - \text{FFA}$$

D_G = weight (g) of the diacylglycerol fraction after evaporation of the solvents

$$M = M_G \times 100/S$$

M_G = weight (g) the monoacylglycerol fraction after evaporation of the solvents

Acceptance criteria
Diacylglycerol: NLT 80%
Triacylglycerol: NMT 18%
Monoacylglycerol: NMT 2%

IMPURITIES
Inorganic Impurities
- **LEAD,** *Lead Limit Test, Atomic Absorption Spectrophotometric Graphite Furnace Method, Method II,* Appendix IIIB
  Acceptance criteria: NMT 0.1 mg/kg
- **WATER,** *Water Determination, Method Ib,* Appendix IIB
  Acceptance criteria: NMT 0.1%

Organic Impurities
- **FREE FATTY ACIDS (AS OLEIC ACID)**
  Analysis: Determine as directed in the *Assay* (above).
  Acceptance criteria: NMT 0.2%
- **FREE GLYCERIN,** *Free Glycerin or Propylene Glycol,* Appendix VII
  Acceptance criteria: NMT 0.5%

SPECIFIC TESTS
- **ACID VALUE (FATS AND RELATED SUBSTANCES),** *Method II,* Appendix VII
  Acceptance criteria: NMT 0.5
- **COLOR (FATS AND RELATED SUBSTANCES),** Appendix VII
  Analysis: Determine as directed using a 133.4-mm cell.
  Acceptance criteria: NMT 5 yellow/0.7 red
- **HYDROXYL VALUE,** *Method II,* Appendix VII
  Acceptance criteria: Between 77 and 85
- **IODINE VALUE,** Appendix VII
  Acceptance criteria: Between 81 and 170
- **PEROXIDE VALUE,** Appendix VII
  Acceptance criteria: NMT 2 mEq/kg
- **RESIDUE ON IGNITION (SULFATED ASH),** Appendix IIC
  Acceptance criteria: NMT 0.1%
- **SAPONIFICATION VALUE,** Appendix VII
  Acceptance criteria: Between 180 and 185
- **UNSAPONIFIABLE MATTER,** Appendix VII
  Acceptance criteria: NMT 1.5%

Diatomaceous Earth

First Published: Prior to FCC 6

Diatomaceous Silica
Diatomite
D.E.

CAS: natural powder and calcined powder [61790-53-2]
flux-calcined powder [68855-54-9]

UNII: 2RF6EJ0M85 [diatomaceous earth]

DESCRIPTION
Diatomaceous Earth occurs as a powder of varying colors consisting of processed siliceous skeletons of diatoms. The *natural powder* (gray to off-white) is air dried and classified by particle size; the *calcined powder* (pink to buff-colored) is air dried, classified, calcined at a high temperature (815° to 982°), and again classified; the *flux-calcined powder* (white) is air dried, classified, calcined in the presence of a suitable flux (generally soda ash or other alkaline salt), and again classified; and the *acid-washed powder* is any of the preceding powders having been further purified by washing in acid and rinsing with water. It is insoluble in water, in acids (except hydrofluoric), and in dilute alkalis.

Function: Filter aid in food processing
Packaging and Storage: Store in well-closed containers.

IDENTIFICATION
- **MICROSCOPY**
  Analysis: Examine the powdered sample with a 100- to 200-power microscope.
  Acceptance criteria: Typical diatom shapes are observed.

IMPURITIES
Inorganic Impurities
- **ARSENIC,** *Arsenic Limit Test,* Appendix IIIB
  Sample solution: Transfer 10.0 g of sample into a 250-mL beaker, add 50 ml of 0.5 N hydrochloric acid, cover with a watch glass, and heat to 70° for 15 min. Cool and decant through a Whatman No. 3 filter paper, or equivalent, into a 100-mL volumetric flask. Wash the slurry with three 10-mL portions of hot water and wash the filter paper with 15 mL of hot water, dilute to volume with water, and mix.
  Analysis: Proceed as directed using a 3.0-mL portion of the *Sample solution*. [NOTE—Retain the remaining *Sample solution* for the test for *Lead* (below).]
  Acceptance criteria: Passes test (NMT 10 mg/kg)
- **LEAD,** *Lead Limit Test,* Appendix IIIB
  Sample: 10.0-mL portion of the *Sample solution* prepared in the test for *Arsenic* (above)
  Control: 10 µg Pb (10 mL of *Diluted Standard Lead Solution*)
  Acceptance criteria: NMT 10 mg/kg

SPECIFIC TESTS
- **LOSS ON DRYING,** Appendix IIC: 105° for 2 h
  Acceptance criteria
    Natural powders: NMT 10.0%
    Acid-washed powders: NMT 10.0%
    Calcined powders: NMT 3.0%
    Flux-calcined powders: NMT 3.0%
- **LOSS ON IGNITION**
  Sample: 1 g
  Analysis: Ignite the *Sample* at 800° to constant weight in a suitable, tared crucible.
  Acceptance criteria
    Natural powders: NMT 7.0%, calculated on the dried basis
    Calcined powders: NMT 0.5%, calculated on the dried basis
    Flux-calcined powders: NMT 0.5%, calculated on the dried basis
- **NONSILICEOUS SUBSTANCES**
  Sample: 200 mg
  Analysis: Transfer the *Sample* into a tared platinum crucible, add 5 mL of hydrofluoric acid and 2 drops of 1:2 sulfuric acid, and evaporate gently to dryness. Cool, add 5 mL of hydrofluoric acid, evaporate again to dryness, and then ignite to constant weight.
  Acceptance criteria: NMT 25.0%, calculated on the dried basis

- **PH,** *pH Determination,* Appendix IIB
  Sample: Boil 10 g of sample with 100 mL of water for 30 min, make up to 100 mL with water, and filter through a fine-porosity sintered-glass funnel. Use the resulting filtrate as the *Sample.*
  Acceptance criteria
  Natural powders: Between 5.0 and 10.0
  Acid-washed powders: Between 5.0 and 10.0
  Calcined powders: Between 5.0 and 10.0
  Flux-calcined powders: Between 8.0 and 11.0

Dibenzyl Ether

First Published: Prior to FCC 6

$C_{14}H_{14}O$ Formula wt 198.26
FEMA: 2371
UNII: 2O6CNO27RJ [dibenzyl ether]

DESCRIPTION
Dibenzyl Ether occurs as a colorless to pale yellow liquid.
Odor: Earthy

Boiling Point: ~298°
Solubility in Alcohol, Appendix VI: One mL dissolves in 1 mL of 95% alcohol.
Function: Flavoring agent

IDENTIFICATION
- **INFRARED SPECTRA,** *Spectrophotometric Identification Tests,* Appendix IIIC
  Acceptance criteria: The spectrum of the sample exhibits relative maxima at the same wavelengths as those of the spectrum below.

ASSAY
- **PROCEDURE:** Proceed as directed under *M-1b,* Appendix XI.
  Acceptance criteria: NLT 98.0% of $C_{14}H_{14}O$

SPECIFIC TESTS
- **REFRACTIVE INDEX,** Appendix II: At 20°
  Acceptance criteria: Between 1.557 and 1.565
- **SPECIFIC GRAVITY:** Determine at 25° by any reliable method (see *General Provisions*).
  Acceptance criteria: Between 1.039 and 1.044

OTHER REQUIREMENTS
- **CHLORINATED COMPOUNDS,** Appendix VI
  Acceptance criteria: Passes test

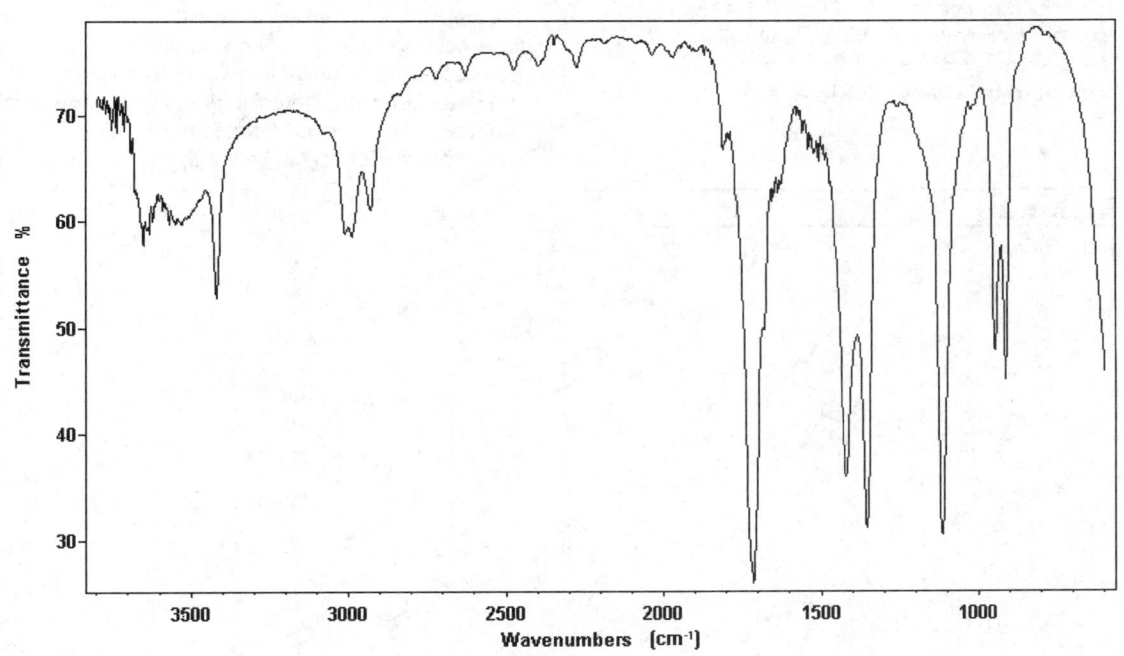

Dibenzyl Ether

1,2-Di[(1'-ethoxy)ethoxy]propane

First Published: Prior to FCC 6

$C_{11}H_{24}O_4$ Formula wt 220.31
FEMA: 3534
UNII: S52T0S2V2J [1,2-di((1'-ethoxy)ethoxy)propane]

DESCRIPTION
1,2-Di[(1'-ethoxy)ethoxy]propane occurs as a colorless to pale yellow liquid.
Odor: Odorless when pure
Function: Flavoring agent

ASSAY
- **PROCEDURE:** Proceed as directed under *M-1b,* Appendix XI.
  Acceptance criteria: NLT 97.0% of $C_{11}H_{24}O_4$

SPECIFIC TESTS
- **ACID VALUE, FLAVOR CHEMICALS (OTHER THAN ESSENTIAL OILS),** *M-15,* Appendix XI
  Acceptance criteria: NMT 0.1
- **REFRACTIVE INDEX,** Appendix II: At 20°
  Acceptance criteria: Between 1.409 and 1.413
- **SPECIFIC GRAVITY:** Determine at 25° by any reliable method (see *General Provisions*).
  Acceptance criteria: Between 0.915 and 0.925

Diethyl Malonate

First Published: Prior to FCC 6

Ethyl Malonate
Malonic Ester

$C_7H_{12}O_4$ Formula wt 160.17
FEMA: 2375
UNII: 53A58PA183 [diethyl malonate]

DESCRIPTION
Diethyl Malonate occurs as a colorless liquid.
Odor: Slight, fruity
Solubility: Soluble in most fixed oils, propylene glycol; slightly soluble in alcohol, water; insoluble or practically insoluble in glycerin, mineral oil
Boiling Point: ~200°
Solubility in Alcohol, Appendix VI: One mL dissolves in 1.5 mL of 60% alcohol.
Function: Flavoring agent

IDENTIFICATION
- **INFRARED SPECTRA,** *Spectrophotometric Identification Tests,* Appendix IIIC
  Acceptance criteria: The spectrum of the sample exhibits relative maxima at the same wavelengths as those of the spectrum below.

ASSAY
- **PROCEDURE:** Proceed as directed under *M-1b,* Appendix XI.
  Acceptance criteria: NLT 98.0% of $C_7H_{12}O_4$

SPECIFIC TESTS
- **ACID VALUE, FLAVOR CHEMICALS (OTHER THAN ESSENTIAL OILS),** *M-15,* Appendix XI
  Acceptance criteria: NMT 1.0
- **REFRACTIVE INDEX,** Appendix II: At 20°
  Acceptance criteria: Between 1.413 and 1.416
- **SPECIFIC GRAVITY:** Determine at 25° by any reliable method (see *General Provisions*).
  Acceptance criteria: Between 1.053 and 1.056

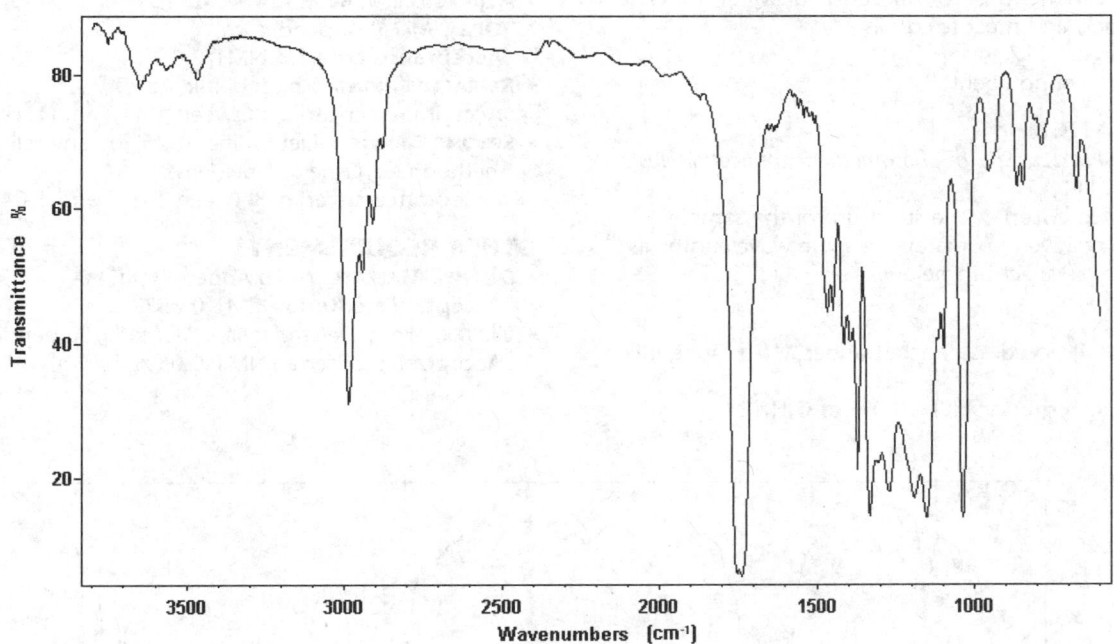

Diethyl Malonate

Diethyl Sebacate

First Published: Prior to FCC 6
Last Revision: First Supplement, FCC 7

Ethyl Sebacate

$C_{14}H_{26}O_4$ Formula wt 258.36
FEMA: 2376
UNII: I41B9FJK6V [diethyl sebacate]

DESCRIPTION
Diethyl Sebacate occurs as a colorless to slightly yellow liquid.
Odor: Faint, winy, fruity
Solubility: Miscible in alcohol, ether, other organic solvents, most fixed oils; insoluble or practically insoluble in water
Boiling Point: ~302°
Function: Flavoring agent

IDENTIFICATION
- **INFRARED ABSORPTION**, *Spectrophotometric Identification Tests,* Appendix IIIC
  Reference standard: USP Diethyl Sebacate RS
  Sample and standard preparation: *F*
  Acceptance criteria: The spectrum of the sample exhibits maxima at the same wavelengths as those in the spectrum of the *Reference standard.*

ASSAY
- **PROCEDURE:** Proceed as directed under *M-1b,* Appendix XI.
  Acceptance criteria: NLT 98.0% of $C_{14}H_{26}O_4$

SPECIFIC TESTS
- **ACID VALUE, FLAVOR CHEMICALS (OTHER THAN ESSENTIAL OILS)**, *M-15,* Appendix XI
  Acceptance criteria: NMT 1.0
- **REFRACTIVE INDEX,** Appendix II: At 20°
  Acceptance criteria: Between 1.435 and 1.438
- **SPECIFIC GRAVITY:** Determine at 25° by any reliable method (see *General Provisions*).
  Acceptance criteria: Between 0.960 and 0.965

Diethyl Succinate

First Published: Prior to FCC 6

Ethyl Succinate

$C_8H_{14}O_4$ Formula wt 174.20
FEMA: 2377
UNII: ELP55C13DR [diethyl succinate]

DESCRIPTION
Diethyl Succinate occurs as a colorless, mobile liquid.

344 / Diethyl Succinate / *Monographs*

Odor: Faint, winy, ethereal
Solubility: One mL dissolves in 50 mL of water; miscible in alcohol, ether, and most fixed oils.
Boiling Point: ~217°
Function: Flavoring agent

IDENTIFICATION
- **INFRARED SPECTRA,** *Spectrophotometric Identification Tests,* Appendix IIIC
  Acceptance criteria: The spectrum of the sample exhibits relative maxima at the same wavelengths as those of the spectrum below.

ASSAY
- **PROCEDURE:** Proceed as directed under *M-1a,* Appendix XI.
  Acceptance criteria: NLT 99.0% of $C_8H_{14}O_4$

SPECIFIC TESTS
- **ACID VALUE, FLAVOR CHEMICALS (OTHER THAN ESSENTIAL OILS),** *M-15,* Appendix XI
  Acceptance criteria: NMT 2.0
- **REFRACTIVE INDEX,** Appendix II: At 20°
  Acceptance criteria: Between 1.419 and 1.423
- **SPECIFIC GRAVITY:** Determine at 25° by any reliable method (see *General Provisions*).
  Acceptance criteria: Between 1.036 and 1.040

OTHER REQUIREMENTS
- **DIETHYL MALEATE,** *M-1b* Appendix XI
  Acceptance criteria: NMT 0.03%
- **WATER,** *Water Determination, Method I,* Appendix IIB
  Acceptance criteria: NMT 0.05%

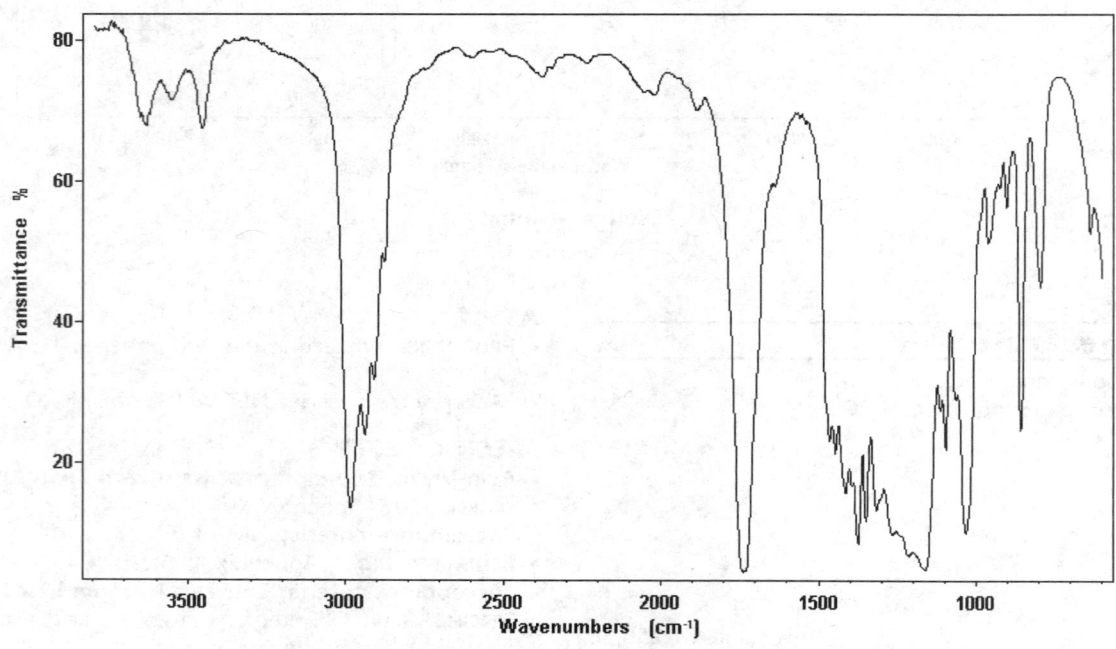

Diethyl Succinate

Dihydrocarveol

First Published: Prior to FCC 6

$C_{10}H_{18}O$ Formula wt 154.25
FEMA: 2379
UNII: 2683FD21WA [dihydrocarveol, (-)-]
UNII: R6OW1F785H [dihydrocarveol, (+)-]
UNII: ZR76810L52 [dihydrocarveol, (+/-)-]

DESCRIPTION
Dihydrocarveol occurs as an almost colorless, oily liquid.
Odor: Spearmint
Solubility: Soluble in alcohol, most fixed oils; insoluble or practically insoluble in water
Boiling Point: ~225°
Solubility in Alcohol, Appendix VI: One mL dissolves in 1 mL of 95% ethanol.
Function: Flavoring agent

ASSAY
- **PROCEDURE:** Proceed as directed under *M-1a,* Appendix XI.
  Acceptance criteria: NLT 96.0% of $C_{10}H_{18}O$ (sum of two isomers)

SPECIFIC TESTS
- **REFRACTIVE INDEX**, Appendix II: At 20°
  Acceptance criteria: Between 1.477 and 1.481
- **SPECIFIC GRAVITY**: Determine at 25° by any reliable method (see *General Provisions*).
  Acceptance criteria: Between 0.921 and 0.926

(+)-Dihydrocarvone

First Published: Prior to FCC 6
Last Revision: Third Supplement, FCC 7

d-Dihydrocarvone
d-2-Methyl-5-(1-methylethenyl)-cyclohexanone

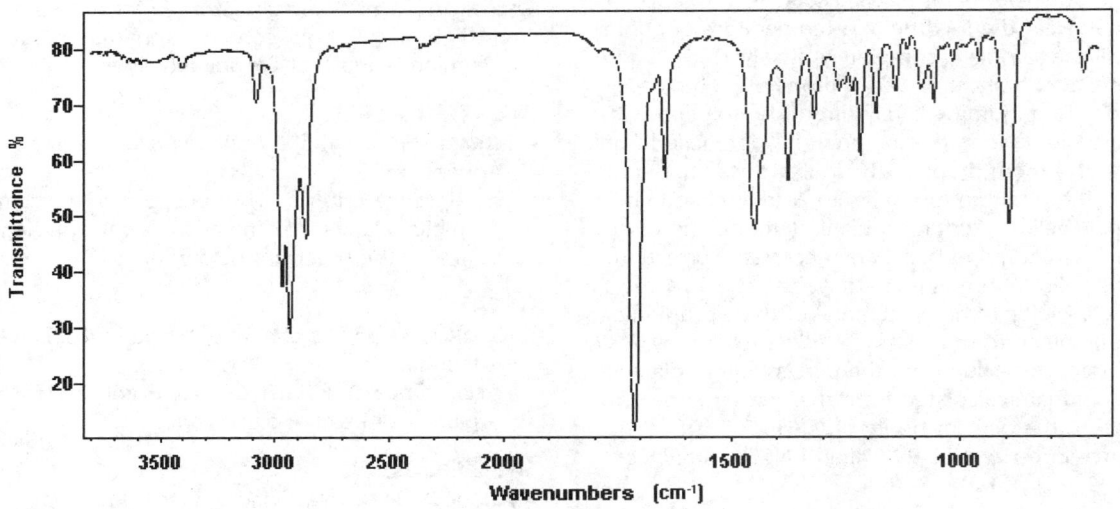

$C_{10}H_{16}O$ Formula wt 154.24
FEMA: 3565
UNII: YQS5CW1O1J [dihydrocarvone, (+)-]

DESCRIPTION
(+)-Dihydrocarvone occurs as an almost colorless liquid.
Odor: Herbaceous, spearmint

Solubility: Soluble in alcohol, most fixed oils; insoluble or practically insoluble in water
Boiling Point: ~222°
SOLUBILITY IN ALCOHOL, Appendix VI: One mL dissolves in 1 mL of 95% alcohol.
Function: Flavoring agent

IDENTIFICATION
- **INFRARED SPECTRA**, *Spectrophotometric Identification Tests*, Appendix IIIC
  Acceptance criteria: The spectrum of the sample exhibits relative maxima at the same wavelengths as those of the spectrum below.

ASSAY
- **PROCEDURE:** Proceed as directed under *M-1a*, Appendix XI.
  Acceptance criteria: NLT 92.0% of $C_{10}H_{16}O$ (sum of two isomers)

SPECIFIC TESTS
- **REFRACTIVE INDEX**, Appendix II: At 20°
  Acceptance criteria: 1.470–1.474
- **SPECIFIC GRAVITY**: Determine at 25° by any reliable method (see *General Provisions*).
  Acceptance criteria: 0.923–0.928

OTHER REQUIREMENTS
- **ANGULAR ROTATION**, *Optical (Specific) Rotation*, Appendix IIB
  Acceptance criteria: Between +14° and +25°

(+)-Dihydrocarvone

Dilauryl Thiodipropionate

First Published: Prior to FCC 6

$C_{30}H_{58}O_4S$ Formula wt 514.85
INS: 389   CAS: [123-28-4]
UNII: V51YH1B080 [dilauryl thiodipropionate]

DESCRIPTION
Dilauryl Thiodipropionate occurs as white, crystalline flakes. It is soluble in most organic solvents, but insoluble in water.
Function: Antioxidant
Packaging and Storage: Store in well-closed containers.

IDENTIFICATION
- **SOLIDIFICATION POINT**
  Acceptance criteria: Dilauryl Thiodiproprionate may be identified by its solidification point as determined under *Solidification Point* (below).

ASSAY
- **PROCEDURE**
  Sample: 700 mg
  Analysis: Transfer the *Sample* into a 250-mL Erlenmeyer flask, and add 100 mL of glacial acetic acid and 50 mL of alcohol. Heat the mixture at a temperature of about 40°, until the sample is completely dissolved, then add 3 mL of hydrochloric acid and 4 drops of *p*-ethoxychrysoidin TS and immediately titrate the solution with 0.1 N bromine. When the endpoint is approached (pink color), add 4 more drops of the indicator solution and continue the titration, dropwise, to a color change from red to pale yellow. Perform a blank determination (see *General Provisions*) and make any necessary correction. Each mL of 0.1 N bromine is equivalent to 25.74 mg of $C_{30}H_{58}O_4S$. Multiply the percentage of thiodipropionic acid, determined in the test for *Acidity* (below), by 2.89, and subtract this value from the percentage of dilauryl thiodipropionate calculated from the titration. The difference is the percent purity of $C_{30}H_{58}O_4S$.
  Acceptance criteria: NLT 99.0% and NMT 100.5% of $C_{30}H_{58}O_4S$

IMPURITIES
Inorganic Impurities
- **LEAD,** *Lead Limit Test,* Appendix IIIB
  Sample solution: Prepare as directed for organic compounds.
  Control: 10 μg Pb (10 mL of *Diluted Standard Lead Solution*)
  Acceptance criteria: NMT 10 mg/kg

SPECIFIC TESTS
- **ACIDITY (AS THIODIPROPIONIC ACID)**
  Sample: 2 g
  Analysis: Transfer the *Sample* into a 250-mL Erlenmeyer flask. Dissolve the *Sample* in 50 mL of a mixture comprising 1 part methyl alcohol and 3 parts and benzene, add 5 drops of phenolphthalein TS, and titrate with 0.1 N alcoholic potassium hydroxide. Each mL of 0.1 N alcoholic potassium hydroxide is equivalent to 8.91 mg of 3,3'-thiodipropionic acid.
  Acceptance criteria: NMT 0.2% of 3,3'-thiodipropionic acid
- **SOLIDIFICATION POINT,** Appendix IIB
  Acceptance criteria: NLT 40°

Dill Seed Oil, European Type

First Published: Prior to FCC 6

UNII: 86T27UW55G [dill seed oil]

DESCRIPTION
Dill Seed Oil, European Type, occurs as a pale yellow to light yellow liquid with a caraway odor and flavor. It is the volatile oil obtained by steam distillation from the crushed, dried fruit or seeds of *Anethum graveolens* L. (Fam. Umbelliferae). It is soluble in most fixed oils and in mineral oil. It is soluble, with slight opalescence, in propylene glycol, but it is practically insoluble in glycerin.
Function: Flavoring agent
Packaging and Storage: Store in a cool place protected from light in full, tight containers that are made from steel or aluminum and that are suitably lined.

IDENTIFICATION
- **INFRARED SPECTRA,** *Spectrophotometric Identification Tests,* Appendix IIIC
  Acceptance criteria: The spectrum of the sample exhibits relative maxima at the same wavelengths as those of the spectrum below.

ASSAY
- **KETONES,** *Aldehydes and Ketones, Neutral Sulfite Method,* Appendix VI
  Acceptance criteria: NLT 42.0% and NMT 60.0%, by volume, of ketones as carvone

SPECIFIC TESTS
- **ANGULAR ROTATION,** *Optical (Specific) Rotation,* Appendix IIB: Use a 100-mm tube.
  Acceptance criteria: Between +70° and +82°
- **REFRACTIVE INDEX,** Appendix IIB
  [NOTE—Use an Abbé or other refractometer of equal or greater accuracy.]
  Acceptance criteria: Between 1.483 and 1.490 at 20°
- **SOLUBILITY IN ALCOHOL,** Appendix VI
  Acceptance criteria: One mL of sample dissolves in 2 mL of 80% alcohol, with slight opalescence that might not disappear on dilution to as much as 10 mL.

- **SPECIFIC GRAVITY:** Determine by any reliable method (see *General Provisions*).
  Acceptance criteria: Between 0.890 and 0.915

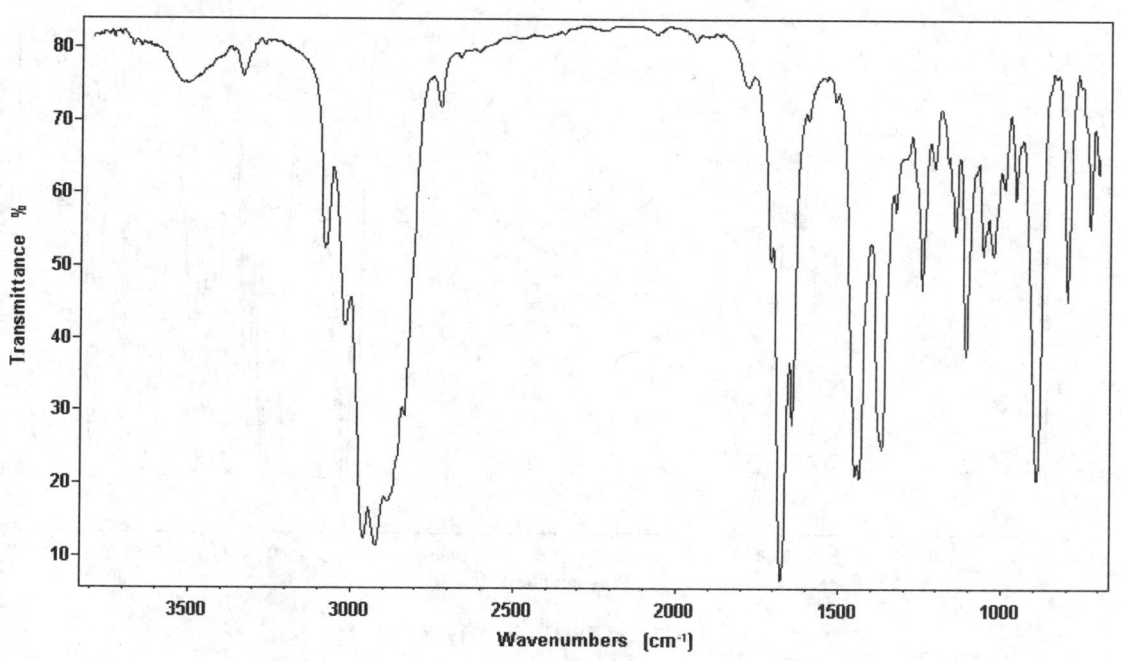

Dill Seed Oil, European Type

Dill Seed Oil, Indian Type
First Published: Prior to FCC 6

Dill Seed Oil, Indian
Dill Oil, Indian Type
UNII: 86T27UW55G [dill seed oil]

DESCRIPTION
Dill Seed Oil, Indian Type, occurs as a light yellow to light brown liquid with a rather harsh, caraway odor and flavor. It is the volatile oil obtained by steam distillation from the crushed mature fruit of Indian Dill, *Anethum sowa* D.C. (Fam. Umbelliferae). It is soluble in most fixed oils and in mineral oil, occasionally with slight opalescence. It is sparingly soluble in propylene glycol and practically insoluble in glycerin.
Function: Flavoring agent
Packaging and Storage: Store in a cool place protected from light in full, tight containers that are made from steel or aluminum and that are suitably lined.

IDENTIFICATION
- **INFRARED SPECTRA,** *Spectrophotometric Identification Tests,* Appendix IIIC

  Acceptance criteria: The spectrum of the sample exhibits relative maxima at the same wavelengths as those of the spectrum below.

ASSAY
- **KETONES,** *Aldehydes and Ketones, Neutral Sulfite Method,* Appendix VI
  Acceptance criteria: NLT 20.0% and NMT 30.0%, by volume, of ketones as carvone

SPECIFIC TESTS
- **ANGULAR ROTATION,** *Optical (Specific) Rotation,* Appendix IIB: Use a 100-mm tube.
  Acceptance criteria: Between +40° and +58°
- **REFRACTIVE INDEX,** Appendix IIB
  [NOTE—Use an Abbé or other refractometer of equal or greater accuracy.]
  Acceptance criteria: Between 1.486 and 1.495 at 20°
- **SOLUBILITY IN ALCOHOL,** Appendix VI
  Acceptance criteria: One mL of sample dissolves in 0.5 mL of 90% alcohol and remains clear on dilution.
- **SPECIFIC GRAVITY:** Determine by any reliable method (see *General Provisions*).
  Acceptance criteria: Between 0.925 and 0.980

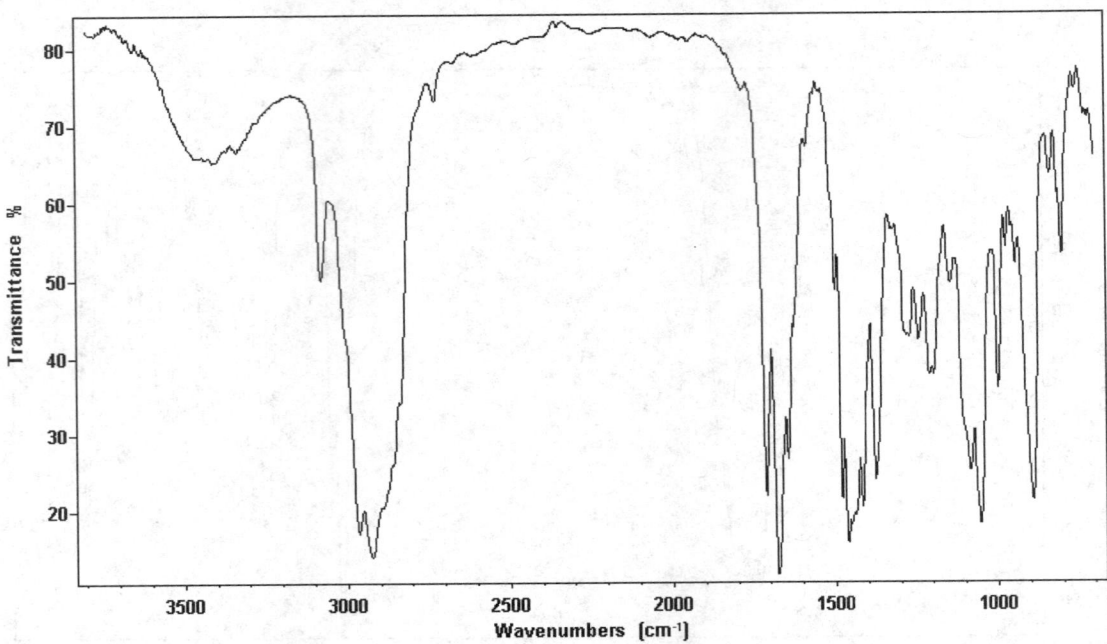

Dill Seed Oil, Indian Type

Dillweed Oil, American Type

First Published: Prior to FCC 6

Dill Oil
Dill Herb Oil, American Type

CAS: [8006-75-5]

UNII: 0MYU0F0FNV [dillweed oil]

DESCRIPTION
Dillweed Oil, American Type occurs as a light yellow to yellow liquid. It is the volatile oil obtained by steam distillation from the freshly cut stalks, leaves, and seeds of the plant *Anethum graveolens* L. (Fam. Umbelliferae). It is soluble in most fixed oils and in mineral oil. It is soluble, usually with opalescence or turbidity, in propylene glycol, but it is practically insoluble in glycerin.
Function: Flavoring agent
Packaging and Storage: Store in a cool place protected from light in full, tight containers that are made from steel or aluminum and that are suitably lined.

IDENTIFICATION
- **INFRARED SPECTRA,** *Spectrophotometric Identification Tests,* Appendix IIIC
    Acceptance criteria: The spectrum of the sample exhibits relative maxima at the same wavelengths as those of the spectrum below.

ASSAY
- **KETONES,** *Aldehydes and Ketones, Neutral Sulfite Method,* Appendix VI

    Acceptance criteria: NLT 28.0% and NMT 45.0%, by volume, of ketones as carvone
    [NOTE—Oil obtained from early season distillation can show a carvone content as low as 25.0% and a correspondingly lower specific gravity, lower refractive index, and higher angular rotation.]

SPECIFIC TESTS
- **ANGULAR ROTATION,** *Optical (Specific) Rotation,* Appendix IIB: Use a 100-mm tube.
    Acceptance criteria: Between +84° and +95° (See NOTE under *Assay*.)
- **REFRACTIVE INDEX,** Appendix IIB
    [NOTE—Use an Abbé or other refractometer of equal or greater accuracy.]
    Acceptance criteria: Between 1.480 and 1.485 at 20° (See NOTE under *Assay*.)
- **SOLUBILITY IN ALCOHOL,** Appendix VI
    Acceptance criteria: One mL of sample dissolves in 1 mL of 90% alcohol, frequently with opalescence that might not disappear on dilution to as much as 10 mL.
- **SPECIFIC GRAVITY:** Determine by any reliable method (see *General Provisions*).
    Acceptance criteria: Between 0.884 and 0.900 (See NOTE under *Assay*.)

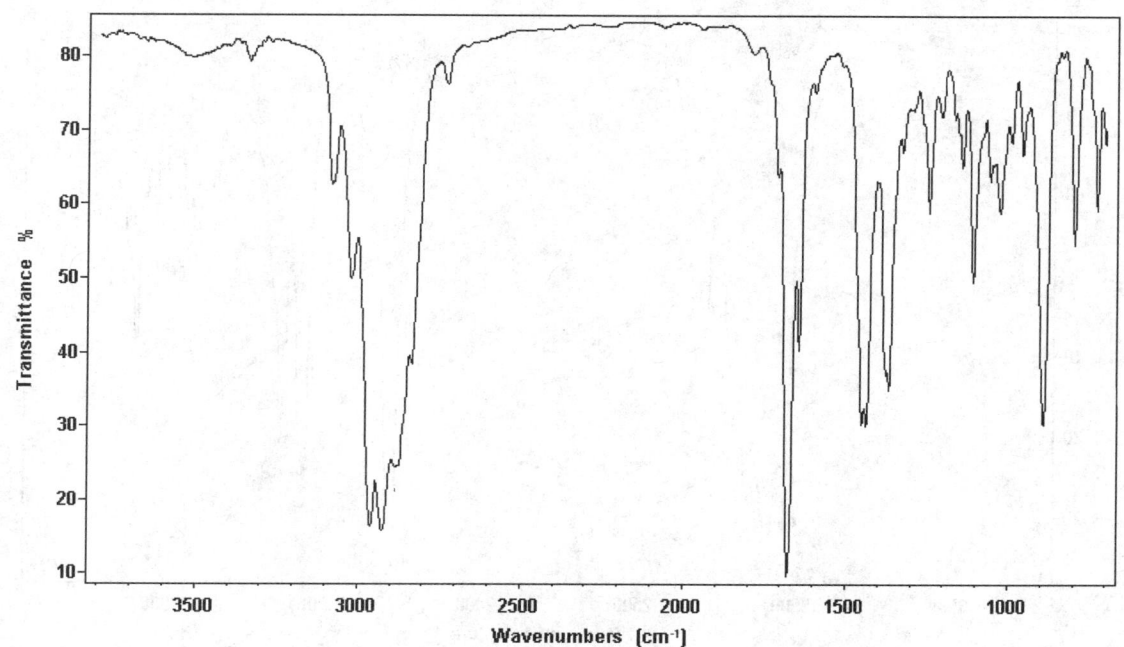

Dillweed Oil, American Type

2,6-Dimethyl-5-heptenal

First Published: Prior to FCC 6
Last Revision: First Supplement, FCC 6

$C_9H_{16}O$ Formula wt 140.23
FEMA: 2389
UNII: Z331YX9EL9 [2,6-dimethyl-5-heptenal]

DESCRIPTION
2,6-Dimethyl-5-heptenal occurs as a pale yellow liquid. It may contain a suitable antioxidant.
Odor: Melon
Solubility: Soluble in vegetable oils; slightly soluble in propylene glycol; insoluble or practically insoluble in water
Boiling Point: ~116° to 124° (100 mm Hg)
Solubility in Alcohol, Appendix VI: One mL dissolves in 1 mL of 95% alcohol.
Function: Flavoring agent

IDENTIFICATION
- **INFRARED SPECTRA**, Spectrophotometric Identification Tests, Appendix IIIC
  Acceptance criteria: The spectrum of the sample exhibits relative maxima at the same wavelengths as those of the spectrum below.

ASSAY
- **PROCEDURE:** Proceed as directed under M-2d, Appendix XI.
  Sample: 1 g
  Analysis: Use 14.01 as the equivalence factor (e).
  Acceptance criteria: NLT 85.0% of $C_9H_{16}O$

SPECIFIC TESTS
- **ACID VALUE, FLAVOR CHEMICALS (OTHER THAN ESSENTIAL OILS),** M-15, Appendix XI
  Acceptance criteria: NMT 5.0
- **REFRACTIVE INDEX,** Appendix II: At 20°
  Acceptance criteria: Between 1.442 and 1.447
- **SPECIFIC GRAVITY:** Determine at 25° by any reliable method (see General Provisions).
  Acceptance criteria: Between 0.848 and 0.854

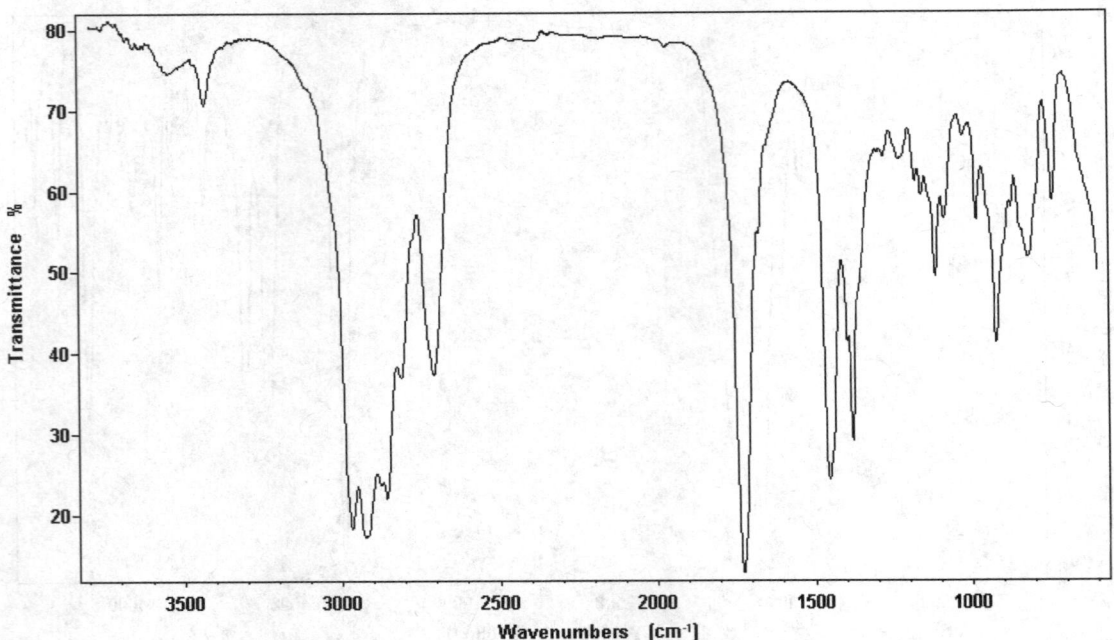

2,6-Dimethyl-5-heptenal

3,4-Dimethyl 1,2-Cyclopentandione

First Published: Prior to FCC 6
Last Revision: First Supplement, FCC 6

$C_7H_{10}O_2$ Formula wt 126.16
FEMA: 3268
UNII: 50AlF51OCl [3,4-dimethyl 1,2-cyclopentandione]

DESCRIPTION
3,4-Dimethyl 1,2-Cyclopentandione occurs as a pale yellow to orange crystal. It may contain a suitable antioxidant.
Odor: Maple
Solubility: Slightly soluble in propylene glycol; insoluble or practically insoluble in vegetable oils, water

Boiling Point: ~142°
Solubility in Alcohol, Appendix VI: One g dissolves in 3 mL of 95% ethanol.
Function: Flavoring agent

IDENTIFICATION
- **INFRARED SPECTRA,** Spectrophotometric Identification Tests, Appendix IIIC
  Acceptance criteria: The spectrum of the sample exhibits relative maxima at the same wavelengths as those of the spectrum below.

ASSAY
- **PROCEDURE:** Proceed as directed under M-1b, Appendix XI.
  Acceptance criteria: NLT 95.0% of $C_7H_{10}O_2$

OTHER REQUIREMENTS
- **MELTING RANGE OR TEMPERATURE DETERMINATION,** Appendix IIB
  Acceptance criteria: Between 64.0° and 72.0°

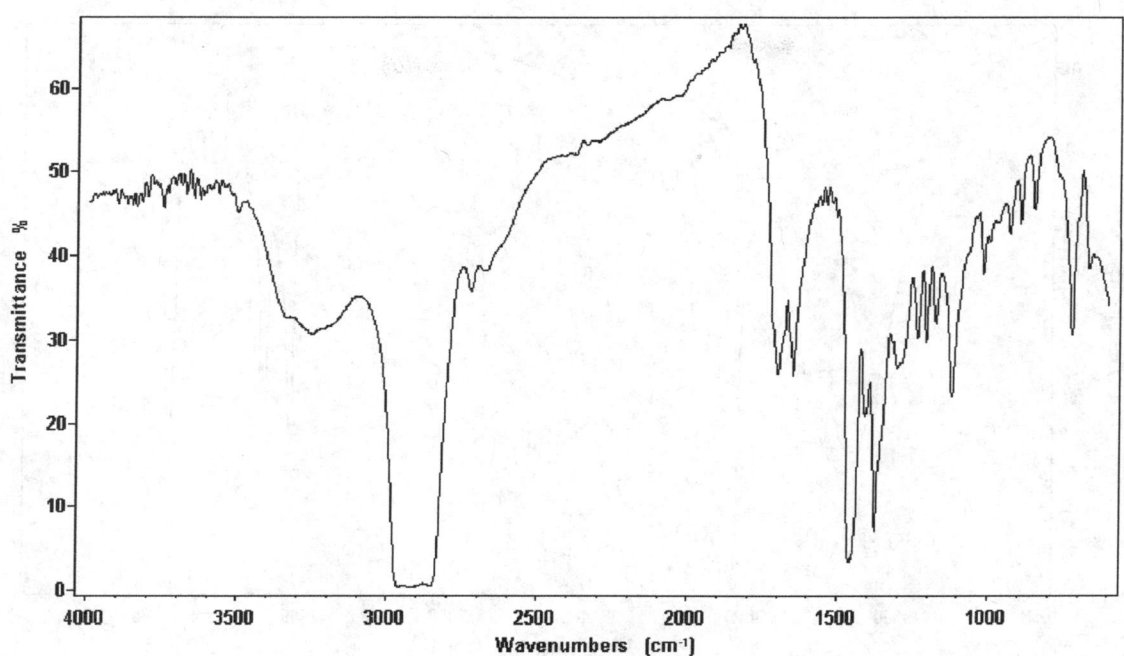

3,4-Dimethyl 1,2-Cyclopentandione

3,7-Dimethyl-1-octanol

First Published: Prior to FCC 6

Dimethyl Octanol
Tetrahydrogeraniol

$C_{10}H_{22}O$ Formula wt 158.28
FEMA: 2391
UNII: DPY9K1927C [3,7-dimethyl-1-octanol]

DESCRIPTION
3,7-Dimethyl-1-octanol occurs as a colorless liquid.
Odor: Sweet, rose
Solubility: Soluble in most fixed oils, propylene glycol; insoluble or practically insoluble in glycerin
Boiling Point: ~213°
Solubility in Alcohol, Appendix VI: One mL dissolves in 3 mL of 70% alcohol.
Function: Flavoring agent

IDENTIFICATION
- **INFRARED SPECTRA,** Spectrophotometric Identification Tests, Appendix IIIC
  Acceptance criteria: The spectrum of the sample exhibits relative maxima at the same wavelengths as those of the spectrum below.

ASSAY
- **PROCEDURE:** Proceed as directed under Total Alcohols, Appendix VI.
  Sample: 1.2 g
  Analysis: Use 79.15 as the equivalence factor (e).
  Acceptance criteria: NLT 90.0% of total alcohols as $C_{10}H_{22}O$

SPECIFIC TESTS
- **ACID VALUE, FLAVOR CHEMICALS (OTHER THAN ESSENTIAL OILS),** M-15, Appendix XI
  Acceptance criteria: NMT 1.0
- **REFRACTIVE INDEX,** Appendix II: At 20°
  Acceptance criteria: Between 1.435 and 1.445
- **SPECIFIC GRAVITY:** Determine at 25° by any reliable method (see General Provisions).
  Acceptance criteria: Between 0.826 and 0.842

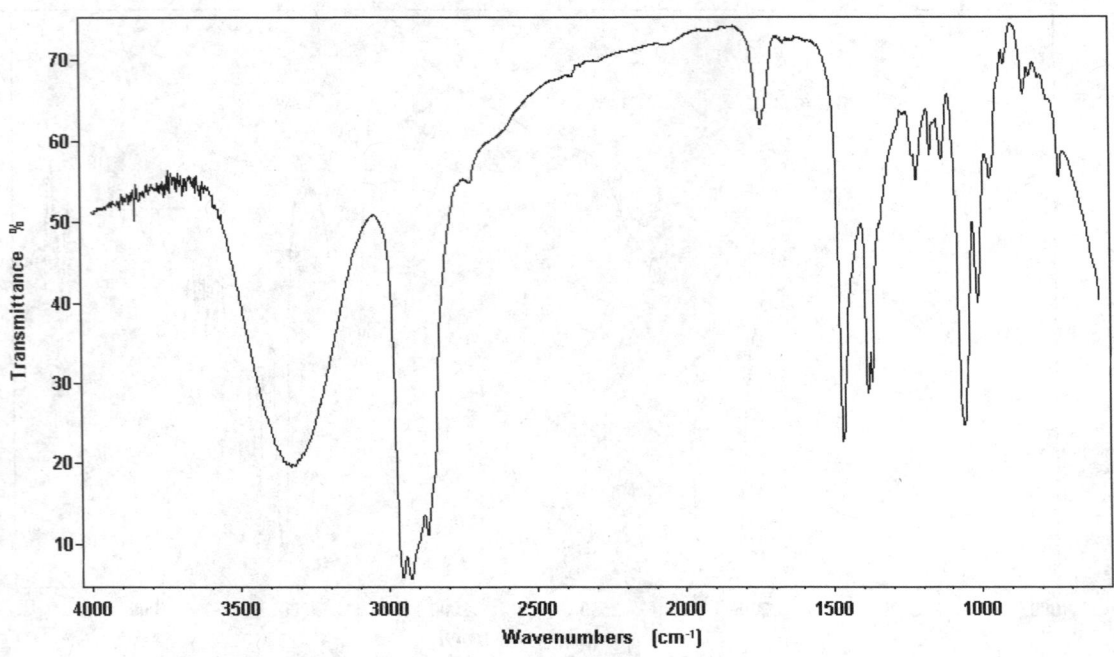

3,7-Dimethyl-1-octanol

Dimethyl Anthranilate

First Published: Prior to FCC 6

Methyl N-Methyl Anthranilate

C₉H₁₁NO₂ Formula wt 165.19
FEMA: 2718
UNII: 5Z37T562P9 [dimethyl anthranilate]

DESCRIPTION
Dimethyl Anthranilate occurs as a pale yellow liquid with pale blue fluorescence.
Odor: Grape
Solubility: Soluble in most fixed oils; slightly soluble in propylene glycol; insoluble or practically insoluble in glycerin, water
Boiling Point: ~256°
Solubility in Alcohol, Appendix VI: One mL dissolves in 3 mL of 80% alcohol, and remains in solution on dilution to 10 mL.
Function: Flavoring agent

ASSAY
- **PROCEDURE:** Proceed as directed under *Esters*, Appendix VI.
  Sample: 1.1 g
  Analysis: Use 82.60 as the equivalence factor (e).

  Acceptance criteria: Between 98.0 and 101.3% of total esters as C₉H₁₁NO₂

SPECIFIC TESTS
- **REFRACTIVE INDEX,** Appendix II: At 20°
  Acceptance criteria: Between 1.577 and 1.583
- **SPECIFIC GRAVITY:** Determine at 25° by any reliable method (see *General Provisions*).
  Acceptance criteria: Between 1.124 and 1.132

OTHER REQUIREMENTS
- **SOLIDIFICATION POINT,** Appendix IIB
  Acceptance criteria: NLT 14°

Dimethyl Benzyl Carbinol

First Published: Prior to FCC 6

α,α-Dimethylphenethyl Alcohol

C₁₀H₁₄O Formula wt 150.22
FEMA: 2393
UNII: N95NCI59MI [dimethyl benzyl carbinol]

DESCRIPTION
Dimethyl Benzyl Carbinol occurs as a white crystalline solid; may exist in supercooled form as a colorless to pale yellow liquid.

Odor: Floral
Solubility: Soluble in mineral oil, most fixed oils, propylene glycol; insoluble or practically insoluble in glycerin
Solubility in Alcohol, Appendix VI: One mL dissolves in 3 mL of 50% alcohol, and remains in solution on dilution to 10 mL.
Function: Flavoring agent

IDENTIFICATION

- **INFRARED SPECTRA,** *Spectrophotometric Identification Tests,* Appendix IIIC
  Acceptance criteria: The spectrum of the sample exhibits relative maxima at the same wavelengths as those of the spectrum below.

ASSAY

- **PROCEDURE:** Proceed as directed under *M-1b,* Appendix XI.
  Acceptance criteria: NLT 97.0% of $C_{10}H_{14}O$

SPECIFIC TESTS

- **ACID VALUE, FLAVOR CHEMICALS (OTHER THAN ESSENTIAL OILS),** *M-15,* Appendix XI
  Acceptance criteria: NMT 1.0
- **REFRACTIVE INDEX,** Appendix II: 20°
  [NOTE—Determine as a supercooled liquid.]
  Acceptance criteria: Between 1.514 and 1.517
- **SPECIFIC GRAVITY:** Determine at 25° by any reliable method (see *General Provisions*).
  Acceptance criteria: Between 0.972 and 0.977

OTHER REQUIREMENTS

- **CHLORINATED COMPOUNDS,** Appendix VI
  Acceptance criteria: Passes test
- **SOLIDIFICATION POINT,** Appendix IIB
  Acceptance criteria: NLT 22°

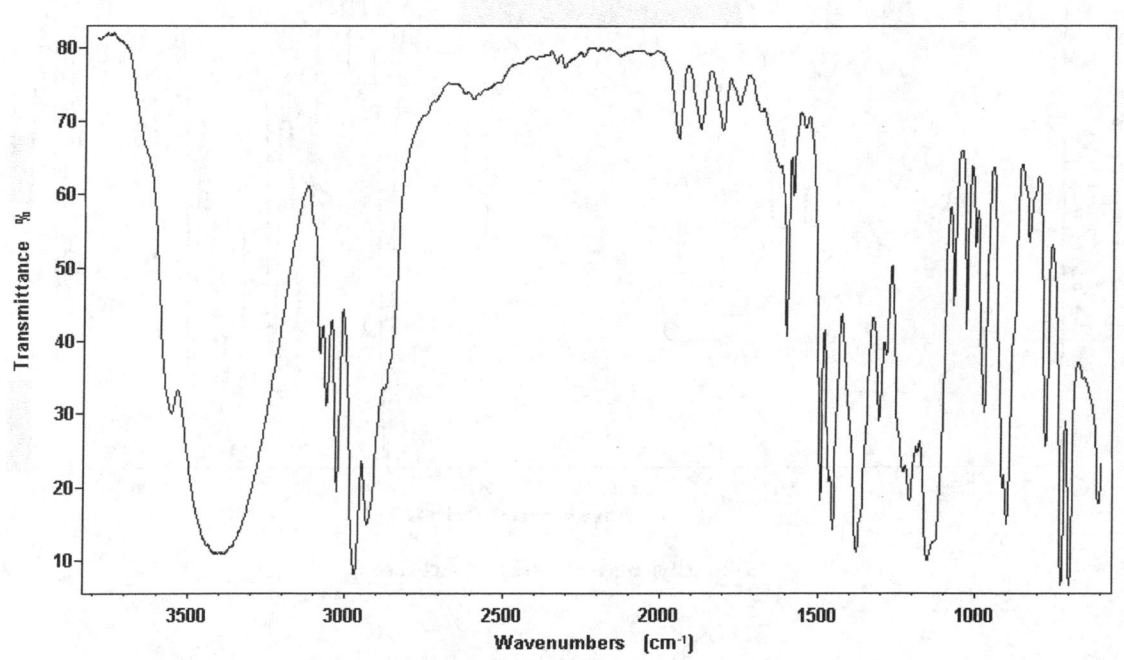

Dimethyl Benzyl Carbinol

Dimethyl Benzyl Carbinyl Acetate

First Published: Prior to FCC 6

α,α-Dimethylphenethyl Acetate

$C_{12}H_{16}O_2$ Formula wt 192.26
FEMA: 2392
UNII: 6Y9488RL8H [dimethyl benzyl carbinyl acetate]

DESCRIPTION

Dimethyl Benzyl Carbinyl Acetate occurs as a colorless liquid; solidifies at room temperature.
Odor: Floral, fruity
Solubility: Soluble in most fixed oils; slightly soluble in propylene glycol; insoluble or practically insoluble in water
Boiling Point: ~250°
Solubility in Alcohol, Appendix VI: One mL dissolves in 4 mL of 70% alcohol.
Function: Flavoring agent

IDENTIFICATION

- **INFRARED SPECTRA,** *Spectrophotometric Identification Tests,* Appendix IIIC

Acceptance criteria: The spectrum of the sample exhibits relative maxima at the same wavelengths as those of the spectrum below.

ASSAY
- **PROCEDURE:** Proceed as directed under *M-1b*, Appendix XI.
  Acceptance criteria: NLT 98.0% of $C_{12}H_{16}O_2$

SPECIFIC TESTS
- **ACID VALUE, FLAVOR CHEMICALS (OTHER THAN ESSENTIAL OILS),** *M-15*, Appendix XI
  Acceptance criteria: NMT 1.0
- **REFRACTIVE INDEX**, Appendix II: At 20°
  Acceptance criteria: Between 1.490 and 1.495
- **SPECIFIC GRAVITY:** Determine at 25° by any reliable method (see *General Provisions*).
  Acceptance criteria: Between 0.995 and 1.002

OTHER REQUIREMENTS
- **CHLORINATED COMPOUNDS,** Appendix VI
  Acceptance criteria: Passes test
- **SOLIDIFICATION POINT,** Appendix IIB
  Acceptance criteria: NLT 28°

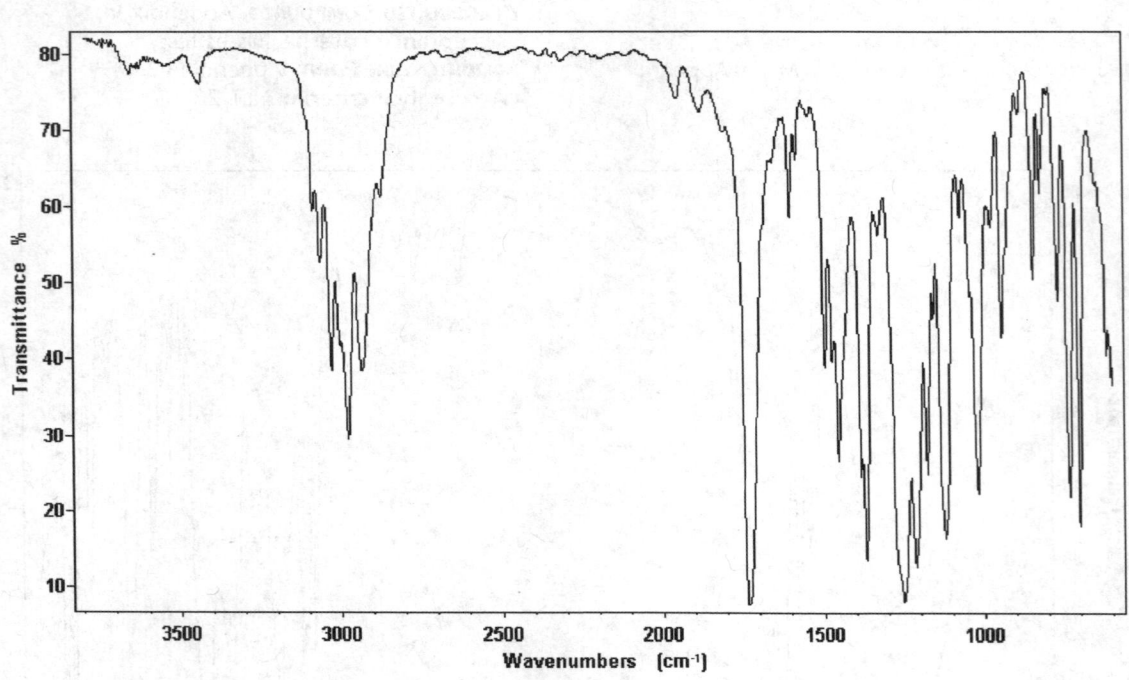

Dimethyl Benzyl Carbinyl Acetate

Dimethyl Benzyl Carbinyl Butyrate
First Published: Prior to FCC 6

α,α-Dimethylphenethyl Butyrate

$C_{14}H_{20}O_2$ Formula wt 220.31
FEMA: 2394
UNII: 3Q0C60547R [dimethyl benzyl carbinyl butyrate]

DESCRIPTION
Dimethyl Benzyl Carbinyl Butyrate occurs as an almost colorless liquid.
Odor: Prune
Solubility: Soluble in alcohol, most fixed oils; insoluble or practically insoluble in propylene glycol, water
Boiling Point: ~237° to 255°
Solubility in Alcohol, Appendix VI: One mL dissolves in 1 mL of 95% ethanol.
Function: Flavoring agent

IDENTIFICATION
- **INFRARED SPECTRA,** *Spectrophotometric Identification Tests,* Appendix IIIC
  Acceptance criteria: The spectrum of the sample exhibits relative maxima at the same wavelengths as those of the spectrum below.

ASSAY
- **PROCEDURE:** Proceed as directed under *M-1b*, Appendix XI.
  Acceptance criteria: NLT 95.0% of $C_{14}H_{20}O_2$

SPECIFIC TESTS
- **REFRACTIVE INDEX,** Appendix II: At 20°
  Acceptance criteria: Between 1.484 and 1.489

- **Specific Gravity:** Determine at 25° by any reliable method (see *General Provisions*).

    Acceptance criteria: Between 0.960 and 0.981

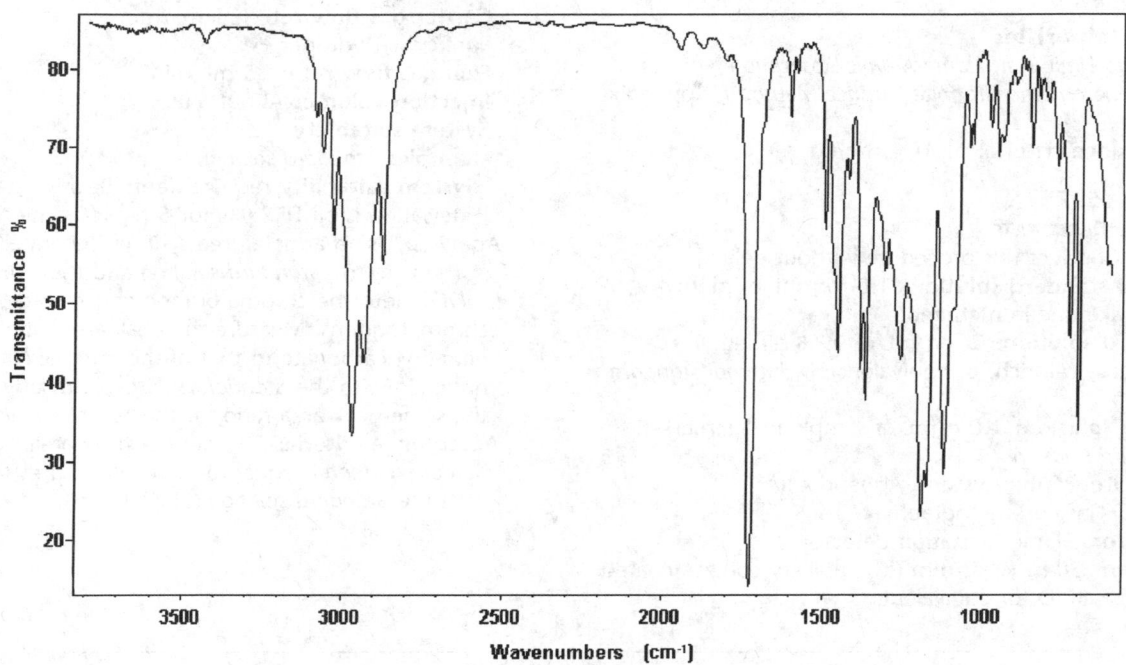

Dimethyl Benzyl Carbinyl Butyrate

Dimethyl Dicarbonate
First Published: Prior to FCC 6

Dicarbonic Acid
Dimethyl Ester
Dimethyl Pyrocarbonate
DMDC

$C_4H_6O_5$　　　　　　　　Formula wt 134.09
INS: 242　　　　　　　　　CAS: [4525-33-1]
UNII: 1AY9229ZMG [dimethyl dicarbonate]

DESCRIPTION
Dimethyl Dicarbonate occurs as a clear, colorless liquid. Its solubility in water is 35 g/L at 20° with decomposition. Its melting point is about 17°, and its flash point is 85°. It reacts quantitatively with water, producing carbon dioxide and methanol.
Function: Preservative; antimicrobial
Packaging and Storage: Store in the original container in a cool (about 20°), dry, and well-ventilated area. Do not repackage because it is particularly susceptible to contamination by water. [**Caution**—Dimethyl Dicarbonate is toxic if inhaled.]

IDENTIFICATION
- **Infrared Spectra**, *Spectrophotometric Identification Tests*, Appendix IIIC
  Acceptance criteria: The spectrum of the sample exhibits relative maxima at the same wavelengths as those of the spectrum below.

ASSAY
- **Procedure**
  1 N Di-*n*-butylamine: 129.3 mg/mL of di-*n*-butylamine in toluene
  Sample: 2 g
  Analysis: Dissolve the *Sample* in 100 mL of acetone contained in a 250-mL beaker. Add 25 mL of *1 N Di-n-butylamine* by pipet. Allow the mixture to stand for 5 min. Titrate with 1 N hydrochloric acid, determining the endpoint potentiometrically. Perform a blank titration (see *General Provisions*) and make any necessary correction. Calculate the percent dimethyl dicarbonate in the sample taken by the formula:

  $$\text{Result} = [100 \times (V_B - V_S) \times F_E]/W$$

  V_B　= volume of hydrochloric acid used for the blank (mL)
  V_S　= volume of hydrochloric acid used for the *Sample* (mL)
  F_E　= milliequivalent weight of dimethyl dicarbonate, 0.134

W = weight of the sample taken (mg)

Acceptance criteria: NLT 99.8% and NMT 101.5% of $C_4H_6O_5$

IMPURITIES
Inorganic Impurities
- **LEAD,** *Lead Limit Test, Flame Atomic Absorption Spectrophotometric Graphite Furnace Method I,* Appendix IIIB

  Acceptance criteria: NMT 1 mg/kg

SPECIFIC TESTS
- **DIMETHYL CARBONATE**

  [NOTE—Conduct this procedure without delay.]

  Internal standard solution: 1.0 mg/mL of methyl isobutylketone in methanol

  Standard solution: 2 mg/mL of 99% dimethyl carbonate (Aldrich, or equivalent), in *Internal standard solution*

  Sample solution: 1.0 g/mL of sample in *Internal standard solution*

  Chromatographic system, Appendix IIA
  Mode: Gas chromatography
  Detector: Flame ionization detector
  Column: 50-m × 0.3-mm (id) capillary column coated with SE 30-D, or equivalent
  Column temperature: Initially at 30° for 5-min hold time, followed by a linear temperature gradient of 40°/min to final temperature of 120° held for 5 min
  Carrier gas: Helium
  Carrier gas flow rate: 11 mL/min
  Fuel gas: Hydrogen
  Fuel gas flow rate: 35 mL/min
  Injection volume: About 5 µL
  System suitability
    Sample: *Standard solution*
    System suitability requirement: Relative standard deviation is NMT 2.0% for 5 replicate injections.
  Analysis: Using a metal-free syringe, separately inject portions of the *Standard solution* and the *Sample solution* into the chromatograph and record the chromatograms. Measure the peak area ratio of dimethyl carbonate to that of the internal standard obtained with the *Standard solution*. Similarly, measure the same peak area ratio for the *Sample solution*.
  Acceptance criteria: The ratio of peak areas for the *Sample solution* is equal to or smaller than that obtained with the *Standard solution* (NMT 0.2%).

Dimethyl Dicarbonate

Dimethyl Succinate
First Published: Prior to FCC 6

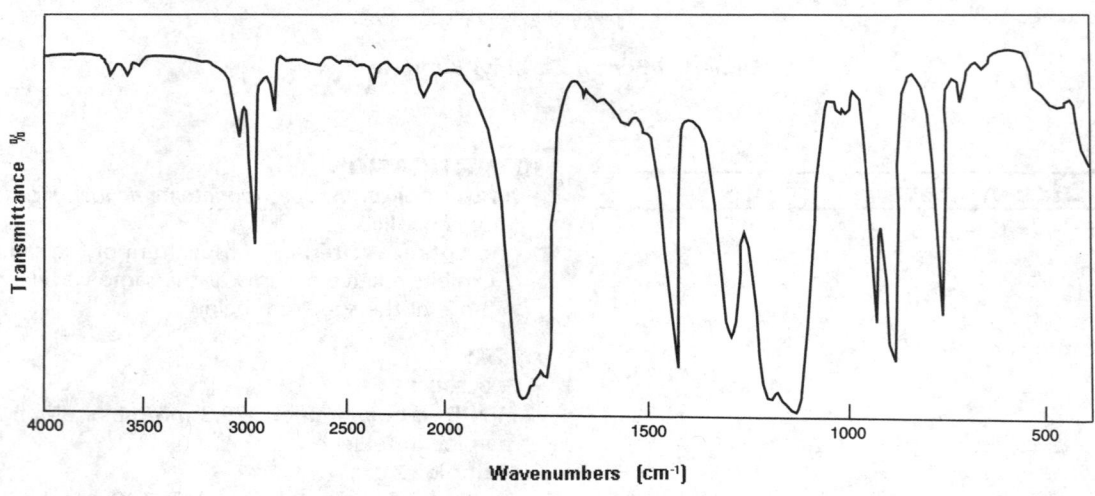

$C_6H_{10}O_4$
FEMA: 2396
UNII: 914I2127JR [dimethyl succinate]

Formula wt 146.14

DESCRIPTION
Dimethyl Succinate occurs as a colorless to pale yellow liquid.
Odor: Mild, fruity
Solubility: Soluble in propylene glycol, vegetable oils; insoluble or practically insoluble in water
Boiling Point: ~196°
Solubility in Alcohol, Appendix VI: One mL dissolves in 1 mL of 95% alcohol.
Function: Flavoring agent

ASSAY
- **PROCEDURE:** Proceed as directed under *M-1b*, Appendix XI.
  Acceptance criteria: NLT 98.0% of $C_6H_{10}O_4$

SPECIFIC TESTS
- **ACID VALUE, FLAVOR CHEMICALS (OTHER THAN ESSENTIAL OILS),** *M-15,* Appendix XI
  Acceptance criteria: NMT 1.0
- **REFRACTIVE INDEX,** Appendix II: At 20°
  Acceptance criteria: Between 1.418 and 1.421
- **SPECIFIC GRAVITY:** Determine at 25° by any reliable method (see *General Provisions*).
  Acceptance criteria: Between 1.114 and 1.118

Dimethyl Sulfide
First Published: Prior to FCC 6

Methyl Sulfide
Thiobismethane

C_2H_6S Formula wt 62.14
FEMA: 2746
UNII: QS3J7O7L3U [methyl sulfide]

DESCRIPTION
Dimethyl Sulfide occurs as a colorless to pale yellow liquid.
Odor: Disagreeable, intense boiled cabbage
Solubility: Soluble in propylene glycol, vegetable oils; insoluble or practically insoluble in water
Boiling Point: ~37°
Solubility in Alcohol, Appendix VI: One mL dissolves in 1 mL of 95% alcohol.
Function: Flavoring agent

IDENTIFICATION
- **INFRARED SPECTRA,** *Spectrophotometric Identification Tests,* Appendix IIIC
  Acceptance criteria: The spectrum of the sample exhibits relative maxima at the same wavelengths as those of the spectrum below.

ASSAY
- **PROCEDURE:** Proceed as directed under *M-1a,* Appendix XI.
  Acceptance criteria: NLT 99.0% of C_2H_6S

SPECIFIC TESTS
- **REFRACTIVE INDEX,** Appendix II: At 20°
  Acceptance criteria: Between 1.431 and 1.441
- **SPECIFIC GRAVITY:** Determine at 25° by any reliable method (see *General Provisions*).
  Acceptance criteria: Between 0.842 and 0.847

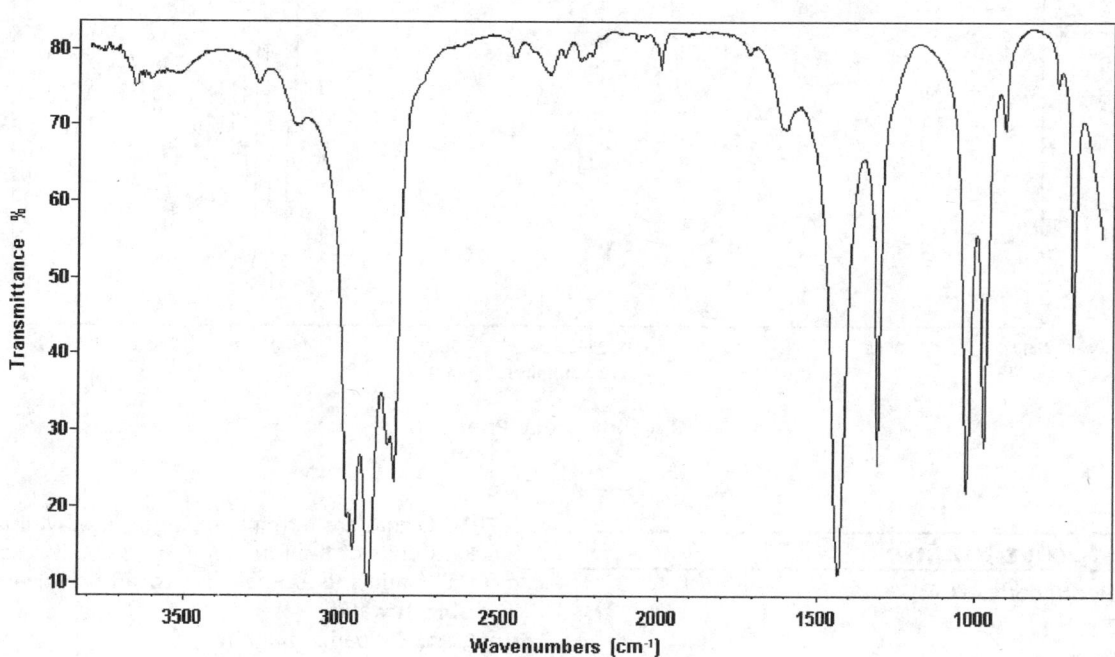

Dimethyl Sulfide

2,6-Dimethoxy Phenol

First Published: Prior to FCC 6

$C_8H_{10}O_3$
FEMA: 3137
UNII: 4UQT464H8K [2,6-dimethoxyphenol]

Formula wt 154.17

DESCRIPTION
2,6-Dimethoxy Phenol occurs as a white to brown crystal.
Odor: Smoky
Solubility: Slightly soluble in propylene glycol, vegetable oils; insoluble or practically insoluble in water
Boiling Point: ~262°
Solubility in Alcohol, Appendix VI: One g dissolves in 2 mL of 95% ethanol.
Function: Flavoring agent

IDENTIFICATION
- **INFRARED SPECTRA,** *Spectrophotometric Identification Tests,* Appendix IIIC
  Acceptance criteria: The spectrum of the sample exhibits relative maxima at the same wavelengths as those of the spectrum below.

ASSAY
- **PROCEDURE:** Proceed as directed under *M-1b,* Appendix XI.
  Acceptance criteria: NLT 98.0% of $C_8H_{10}O_3$

OTHER REQUIREMENTS
- **MELTING RANGE OR TEMPERATURE DETERMINATION,** Appendix IIB
  Acceptance criteria: Between 53.0° and 56.0°

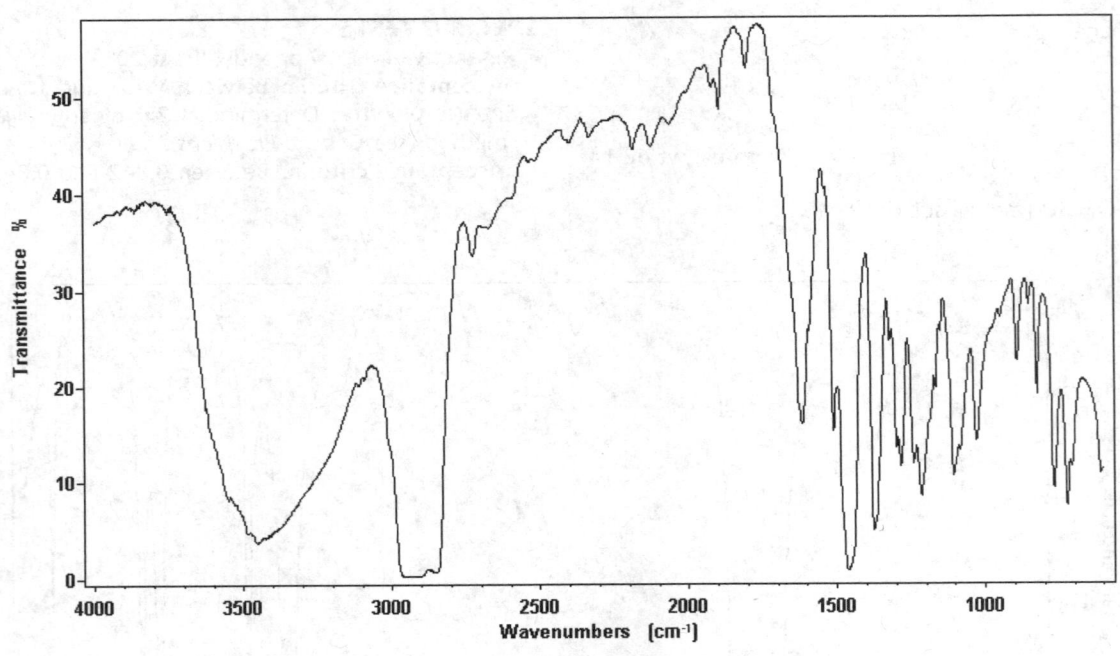

2,6-Dimethoxy Phenol

Dimethylpolysiloxane

First Published: Prior to FCC 6

Dimethyl Silicone
Polydimethylsiloxane

CAS: [9006-65-9]

UNII: 92RU3N3Y1O [dimethicone]

DESCRIPTION
Dimethylpolysiloxane occurs as a clear, colorless, viscous liquid. It is a mixture of fully methylated linear siloxane polymers containing repeating units of the formula $(CH_3)_2SiO$ that are terminated with trimethylsiloxy end-blocking units of the formula $(CH_3)_3SiO-$. It is soluble in most aliphatic and aromatic hydrocarbon solvents, but it is insoluble in water.
Function: Defoaming agent
Packaging and Storage: Store in tightly closed containers.

[NOTE—Dimethylpolysiloxane is frequently used in commerce as such, or as a liquid containing silica (usually 4% to 5%), which must be removed by high-speed centrifugation (about 20,000 rpm) before testing Dimethylpolysiloxane for *Identification, Refractive Index, Specific Gravity,* and *Viscosity.* This monograph does not apply to aqueous emulsions containing emulsifying agents and preservatives in addition to silica.]

IDENTIFICATION
- **INFRARED ABSORPTION,** *Spectrophotometric Identification Tests,* Appendix IIIC
  Reference standard: USP Dimethylpolysiloxane RS
  Sample and standard preparation: *F*
  Acceptance criteria: The spectrum of the sample exhibits maxima at the same wavelengths as those in the spectrum of the *Reference standard*.

IMPURITIES
Inorganic Impurities
- **LEAD,** *Lead Limit Test, Flame Atomic Absorption Spectrophotometric Method,* Appendix IIIB
  Sample: 10.0 g
  Acceptance criteria: NMT 5 mg/kg

SPECIFIC TESTS
- **LOSS ON HEATING**
  Sample: 15 g
  Analysis: Transfer the *Sample* into an open, tared aluminum cup having an internal surface area of about 30 cm^2, weigh the cup and its contents, heat for 4 h at 200° in a circulating air oven, cool, and weigh again.
  Acceptance criteria: NMT 18.0%
- **REFRACTIVE INDEX,** Appendix IIB
  [NOTE—Use an Abbé or other refractometer of equal or greater accuracy.]
  Acceptance criteria: Between 1.4000 and 1.4050
- **SPECIFIC GRAVITY:** Determine by any reliable method (see *General Provisions*).
  Acceptance criteria: Between 0.96 and 0.98
- **VISCOSITY DETERMINATION,** *Viscosity of Dimethylpolysiloxane,* Appendix IIB
  Acceptance criteria: Between 300 and 1500 centistokes

2,3-Dimethylpyrazine
First Published: Prior to FCC 6

$C_6H_8N_2$ Formula wt 108.14
FEMA: 3271

UNII: WHF7883D0V [2,3-dimethylpyrazine]

DESCRIPTION
2,3-Dimethylpyrazine occurs as a colorless to slightly yellow liquid.
Odor: Nutty, cocoa
Solubility: Miscible in organic solvents, water
Boiling Point: ~156°
Solubility in Alcohol, Appendix VI: One mL dissolves in 1 mL of 95% ethanol.
Function: Flavoring agent

IDENTIFICATION
- **INFRARED SPECTRA,** *Spectrophotometric Identification Tests,* Appendix IIIC
  Acceptance criteria: The spectrum of the sample exhibits relative maxima at the same wavelengths as those of the spectrum below.

ASSAY
- **PROCEDURE:** Proceed as directed under *M-1a*, Appendix XI.
  Acceptance criteria: NLT 95.0% of $C_6H_8N_2$

SPECIFIC TESTS
- **REFRACTIVE INDEX,** Appendix II: At 20°
  Acceptance criteria: Between 1.506 and 1.509
- **SPECIFIC GRAVITY:** Determine at 25° by any reliable method (see *General Provisions*).
  Acceptance criteria: Between 1.000 and 1.022

OTHER REQUIREMENTS
- **DISTILLATION RANGE,** Appendix IIB
  Acceptance criteria: Between 152° and 157°
- **SOLIDIFICATION POINT,** Appendix IIB
  Acceptance criteria: 11° to 13°
- **TRI- AND TETRAPYRAZINES**
  Analysis: By GC assay
  Acceptance criteria: NMT 5%
- **WATER,** *Water Determination, Method I,* Appendix IIB
  [NOTE—Use freshly distilled pyridine as solvent.]
  Acceptance criteria: NMT 0.5%

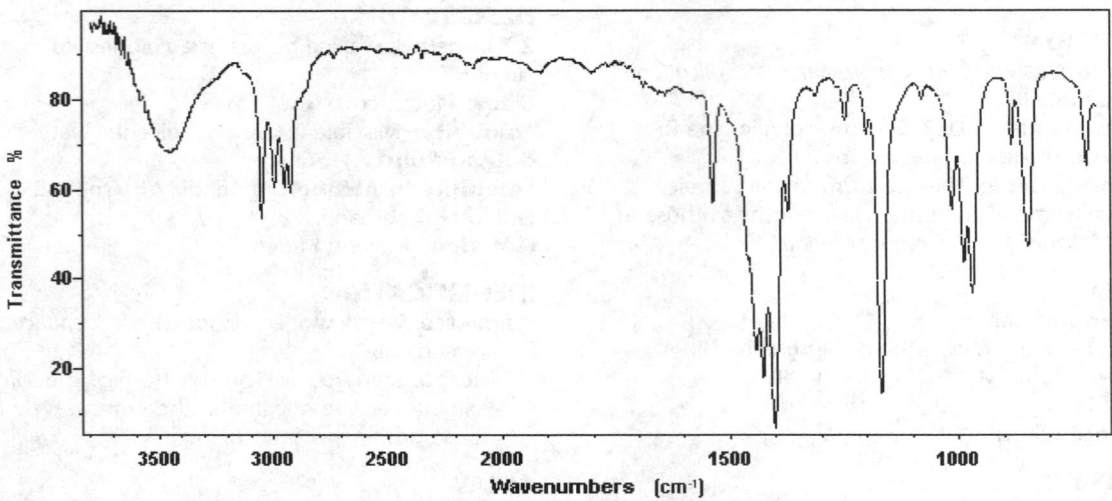

2,3-Dimethylpyrazine

2,5-Dimethylpyrazine

First Published: Prior to FCC 6

$C_6H_8N_2$ Formula wt 108.14
FEMA: 3272
UNII: V99Y0MUY1Q [2,5-dimethylpyrazine]

DESCRIPTION
2,5-Dimethylpyrazine occurs as a colorless to slightly yellow liquid.
Odor: Earthy, potato
Solubility: Miscible in water, organic solvents
Boiling Point: ~155°
Function: Flavoring agent

IDENTIFICATION
- **INFRARED SPECTRA,** *Spectrophotometric Identification Tests,* Appendix IIIC
  Acceptance criteria: The spectrum of the sample exhibits relative maxima at the same wavelengths as those of the spectrum below.

ASSAY
- **PROCEDURE:** Proceed as directed under *M-1a,* Appendix XI.
  Acceptance criteria: NLT 99.0% of $C_6H_8N_2$

SPECIFIC TESTS
- **REFRACTIVE INDEX,** Appendix II: At 20°
  Acceptance criteria: Between 1.497 and 1.501
- **SPECIFIC GRAVITY:** Determine at 25° by any reliable method (see *General Provisions*).
  Acceptance criteria: Between 0.980 and 1.000

OTHER REQUIREMENTS
- **SOLIDIFICATION POINT,** Appendix IIB
  Acceptance criteria: Between 12° and 17°
- **WATER,** *Water Determination, Method I,* Appendix IIB
  [NOTE—Use freshly distilled pyridine as solvent.]
  Acceptance criteria: NMT 0.5%

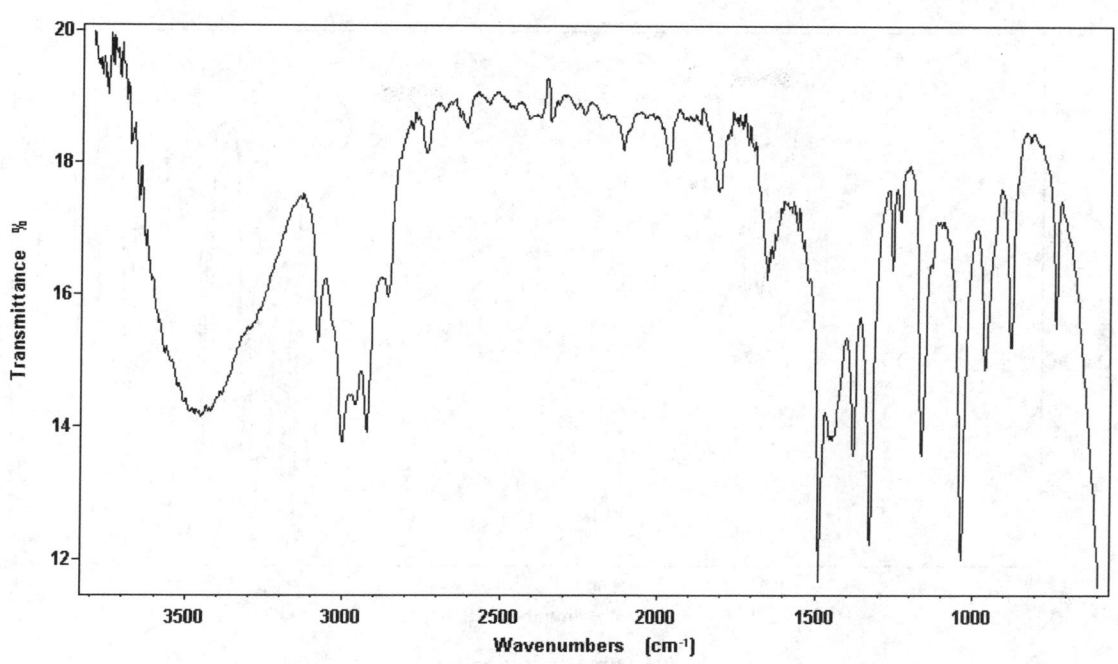

2,5-Dimethylpyrazine

2,6-Dimethylpyrazine

First Published: Prior to FCC 6

$C_6H_8N_2$　　　　　　　　　　　　　　Formula wt 108.14
FEMA: 3273
UNII: N77Q72C9I3 [2,6-dimethylpyrazine]

DESCRIPTION
2,6-Dimethylpyrazine occurs as white to yellow, lumpy crystals.
Odor: Nutty, coffee
Solubility: Soluble in water, organic solvents
Boiling Point: ~155°
Function: Flavoring agent

IDENTIFICATION
- **INFRARED SPECTRA,** Spectrophotometric Identification Tests, Appendix IIIC
  Acceptance criteria: The spectrum of the sample exhibits relative maxima at the same wavelengths as those of the spectrum below.

ASSAY
- **PROCEDURE:** Proceed as directed under M-1a, Appendix XI.
  Acceptance criteria: NLT 98.0% of $C_6H_8N_2$

SPECIFIC TESTS
- **SPECIFIC GRAVITY:** Determine at 50° by any reliable method (see General Provisions).
  Acceptance criteria: 0.965

OTHER REQUIREMENTS
- **MELTING RANGE OR TEMPERATURE DETERMINATION,** Appendix IIB
  Acceptance criteria: Between 35° and 40°
- **RESIDUE ON IGNITION (SULFATED ASH),** Appendix IIC
  Acceptance criteria: NMT 0.1%
- **WATER,** Water Determination Method I, Appendix IIB [NOTE—Use freshly distilled pyridine as solvent.]
  Acceptance criteria: NMT 0.5%

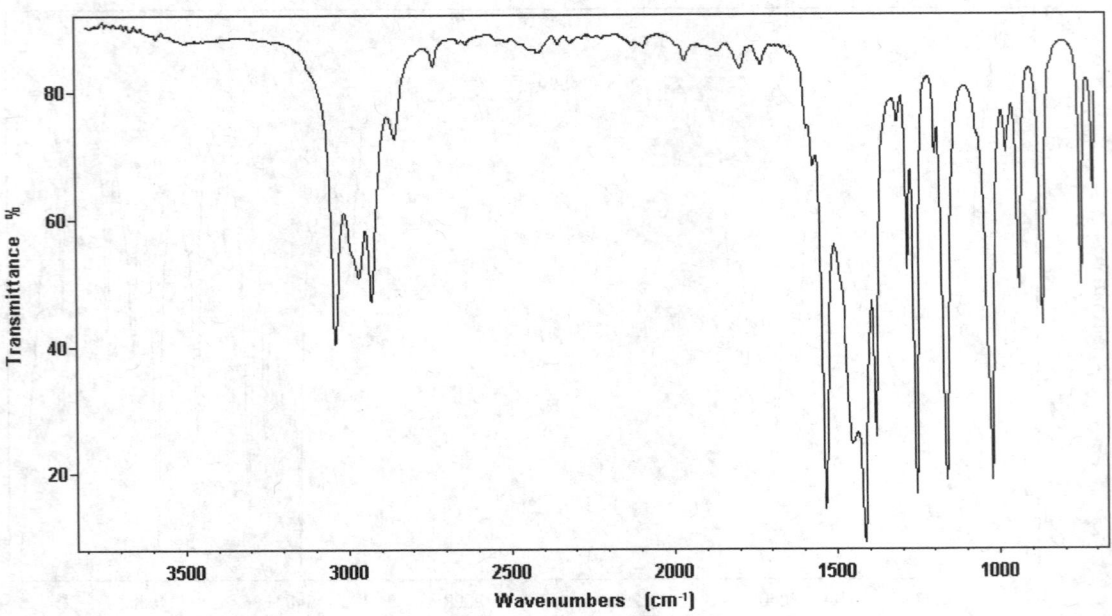

2,6-Dimethylpyrazine

2,5-Dimethylpyrrole

First Published: Prior to FCC 6

C_6H_9N Formula wt 95.14
UNII: MZ3OYF5521 [2,5-dimethylpyrrole]

DESCRIPTION
2,5-Dimethylpyrrole occurs as a colorless to yellow, oily liquid.
Odor: Burnt
Solubility: Very soluble in alcohol, ether; very slightly soluble in water
Boiling Point: ~165°
Function: Flavoring agent

IDENTIFICATION
- **INFRARED SPECTRA,** *Spectrophotometric Identification Tests,* Appendix IIIC
  Acceptance criteria: The spectrum of the sample exhibits relative maxima at the same wavelengths as those of the spectrum below.

ASSAY
- **PROCEDURE:** Proceed as directed under *M-1a,* Appendix XI.
  Acceptance criteria: NLT 98.0% of C_6H_9N

SPECIFIC TESTS
- **REFRACTIVE INDEX,** Appendix II: At 20°
  Acceptance criteria: Between 1.503 and 1.506
- **SPECIFIC GRAVITY:** Determine at 25° by any reliable method (see *General Provisions*).
  Acceptance criteria: Between 0.932 and 0.942

OTHER REQUIREMENTS
- **WATER,** *Method I (Karl Fischer Titrimetric Method),* Appendix IIB
  [NOTE—Use freshly distilled pyridine as solvent.]
  Acceptance criteria: NMT 0.5%

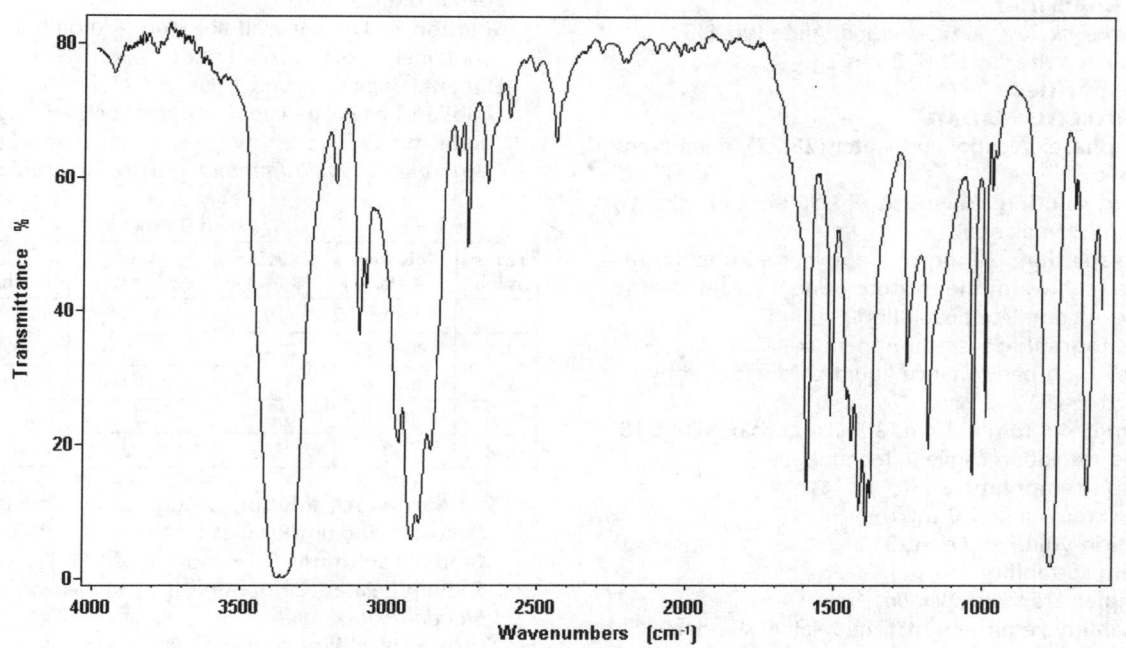

2,5-Dimethylpyrrole

Dioctyl Sodium Sulfosuccinate

First Published: Prior to FCC 6
Last Revision: First Supplement, FCC 6

Docusate Sodium; DSS

$C_{20}H_{37}NaO_7S$ Formula wt 444.56
INS: 480   CAS: [577-11-7]
UNII: F05Q2T2JA0 [docusate sodium]

DESCRIPTION
Dioctyl Sodium Sulfosuccinate occurs as a white, waxlike, plastic solid. One g of sample dissolves slowly in about 70 mL of water. It is freely soluble in alcohol and in glycerin, and it is very soluble in solvent hexane.
Function: Emulsifier; wetting agent
Packaging and Storage: Store in well-closed containers.

IDENTIFICATION
- **INFRARED ABSORPTION,** *Spectrophotometric Identification Tests,* Appendix IIIC
  Reference standard: USP Docusate Sodium RS
  Sample and **Standard preparation:** A
  Acceptance criteria: The spectrum of the sample exhibits maxima at the same wavelengths as those in the spectrum of the *Reference standard.*

ASSAY
- **PROCEDURE**
  Sample solution: Transfer 3.8 g of sample into a 50-mL volumetric flask, dissolve in and dilute with chloroform to volume, and mix.
  Tetra-*n*-butylammonium iodide solution: 2.5 mg/mL tetra-*n*-butylammonium iodide
  Salt solution: 100 mg/mL anhydrous sodium sulfate and 10 mg/mL sodium carbonate, made to 1000 mL
  Analysis: Pipet 10.0 mL of the *Sample solution* into a 250-mL flask, and add 40 mL of chloroform, 50 mL of *Salt solution*, and 10 drops of bromophenol blue TS. Titrate with *Tetra-n-butylammonium iodide solution* to the first appearance of a blue color in the chloroform layer after vigorous shaking. Calculate the percent $C_{20}H_{37}NaO_7S$ by the formula:

  $$\text{Result} = (V \times M_{r1} \times F_1 \times F_2)/(W \times M_{r2})$$

  V = volume of *Tetra-n-butylammonium iodide solution* required (mL)
  M_{r1} = approximate molecular weight of dioctyl sodium sulfosuccinate, 444.6
  F_1 = factor, 10
  F_2 = factor, 1.250
  W = weight of the sample taken to prepare the *Sample solution* (g)
  M_{r2} = molecular weight of tetra-*n*-butylammonium iodide, 369.4

  Acceptance criteria: NLT 98.5% of $C_{20}H_{37}NaO_7S$, on the dried basis

IMPURITIES
Inorganic Impurities
- **LEAD,** *Lead Limit Test, APDC Method,* Appendix IIIB
    Acceptance criteria: NMT 2 mg/kg

Organic Impurities
- **BIS(2-ETHYLHEXYL) MALEATE**
    Mobile phase: Alcohol and water (78:22), filtered and degassed
    Standard solution: 80 µg/mL of USP Bis(2-ethylhexyl) Maleate RS in alcohol
    Sample solution: 20 mg/mL sample in alcohol [NOTE—If necessary, warm the mixture using a steam bath to achieve a complete dissolution.]
    Chromatographic system, Appendix IIA
        Mode: High-performance liquid chromatography
        Detector: UV 210 nm
        Column: 4.6-mm × 3-cm, 3.5-µm Zorbax XDB C18 Rapid resolution (Agilent Technologies)
        Column temperature: 30°
        Flow rate: About 1.0 mL/min
        Injection volume: About 3 µL
    System suitability
        Sample: *Standard solution*
        Suitability requirement: The relative standard deviation for replicate injections is NMT 2.0%.
    Analysis: Separately inject equal volumes of the *Standard solution* and the *Sample solution* into the chromatograph, record the chromatograms, and measure the responses for the bis(2-ethylhexyl) maleate peaks. Calculate the percentage of bis(2-ethylhexyl) maleate in the portion of sample taken by the formula:

    $$\text{Result} = 5C/W(r_U/r_S)$$

    C = concentration of USP Bis(2-ethylhexyl) Maleate RS in the *Standard solution* (µg/mL)
    W = weight of the sample taken to prepare the *Sample solution* (mg)
    r_U = peak response of bis(2-ethylhexyl) maleate obtained from the *Sample solution*
    r_S = peak response of bis(2-ethylhexyl) maleate obtained from the *Standard solution*
    Acceptance criteria: NMT 0.2%

SPECIFIC TESTS
- **CLARITY OF SOLUTION**
    Sample solution: Dissolve 25 g of sample in 94 mL of alcohol.
    Acceptance criteria: The solution does not develop a haze within 24 h.
- **LOSS ON DRYING,** Appendix IIC: 105° for 2 h
    Acceptance criteria: NMT 2.0%
- **RESIDUE ON IGNITION (SULFATED ASH),** Appendix IIC
    Sample: 1 g
    Acceptance criteria: Between 15.5 and 16.2%
- **CHROMATOGRAPHIC PURITY**
    Reference standard: USP Docusate Sodium Related Compound B RS
    Solution A: Dissolve in 1000 mL of water.* Filter and degas prior to use.
    Solution B: Use acetonitrile. Store acetonitrile in a glass container; protect from light.
    Diluent: *Solution A* and *Solution B* (1:1)
    Mobile phase: See *Gradient Table* (below). Make adjustments if necessary (see *System Suitability* in *High-Performance Liquid Chromatography,* Appendix IIA).

Gradient Table

Time (min)	Solution A (%)	Solution B (%)	Flow (mL/min)	Elution
0	80	20	1.25	initial flow
0–3	80→25	20→75	1.25	linear gradient
3–5	25→10	75→90	1.25→1.50	isocratic
5–6	10→80	90→20	1.25	linear gradient
6–8	80	20	1.25	re-equilibration

Standard stock solution: About 0.4 mg/mL of USP Docusate Sodium Related Compound B RS in *Diluent*
Standard solution: 0.16 mg/mL of USP Docusate Sodium Related Compound B RS in *Diluent*: from *Standard stock solution*
System suitability solution: Prepare a solution of USP Docusate Sodium RS in *Diluent* having a concentration of about 4 mg/mL. Transfer 1.0 g of this solution to a 25-mL volumetric flask, add 1.0 g of the *Standard stock solution,* and dilute with *Diluent* to volume.
Sample solution: About 4 mg/mL of Dioctyl Sodium Sulfosuccinate in *Diluent,* made to 25 mL
Chromatographic system, Appendix IIA
    Mode: Liquid chromatography
    Detector: UV 210 nm
    Column: 4.6-mm × 75-mm column that contains 3.5-µm packing, Agilent XDB-C18 Rapid Resolution (Agilent Technologies)
    Column temperature: 45°
    Flow rate: About 1.25 to 1.50 mL/min, see *Gradient Table*
    Injection volume: About 10 µL
System suitability
    Sample 1: *Standard solution*
    Suitability requirement 1: The relative standard deviation for replicate injections is NMT 1.0%.
    Sample 2: *System suitability solution*
    Suitability requirement 2: The resolution between docusate sodium related compound B and dioctyl sodium sulfosuccinate peaks is greater than 2.0.
Analysis: Separately inject equal volumes of the *Standard solution* and the *Sample solution* into the chromatograph, record the chromatograms, and measure the responses of the major peaks. Calculate the percentage of each impurity in the portion of Dioctyl Sodium Sulfosuccinate taken by the formula:

$$\text{Result} = 0.1(C_S/C_T)\,(r_i/r_S)$$

in which C_S is the concentration, in µg/mL, of docusate sodium related compound B in the *Standard solution*; C_T

---
* Waters PIC®B-8 Low UV Reagent (Waters Part Number WAT084283)

is the concentration, in mg/mL, of Dioctyl Sodium Sulfosuccinate in the *Sample solution*; r_i is the peak response for each impurity obtained from the *Sample solution*; and r_S is the dioctyl sodium sulfosuccinate response obtained from the *Standard solution*.

Acceptance criteria: Refer to *Table 1* for the impurity limits.

Table 1

Compound Name	Relative Retention Time (min)	Limit (%)
Salt compound	0.443	0.8
Related compound A[1]	1.687	0.4
Related compound B[1]	2.007	0.6
Related compound C[2]	2.582	1.5
Related compound D[2]	2.679	0.8
Dioctyl sodium sulfosuccinate	~3.48	N/A
Any other individual impurity found	—	0.1
Total, other impurities	—	0.5

[1] One isomer of disodium mono (2-ethylhexyl) sulfosuccinate (CAS# 63782-88-7).

[2] One isomer of butanedioc acid, sulfo-, C-(2-ethylhexyl) C-ethyl ester, sodium salt.

Diphenyl Ether

First Published: Prior to FCC 6

Diphenyl Oxide

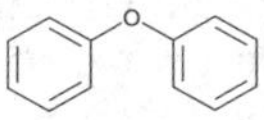

$C_{12}H_{10}O$ Formula wt 170.21

FEMA: 3667
UNII: 3O695R5M1U [diphenyl ether]

DESCRIPTION

Diphenyl Ether occurs as a colorless to white to pale yellow liquid.
Odor: Rose
Solubility: Soluble in vegetable oils; very slightly soluble in water
Boiling Point: ~259°
Solubility in Alcohol, Appendix VI: One g dissolves in 2 mL of 95% ethanol.
Function: Flavoring agent

IDENTIFICATION

- **INFRARED SPECTRA**, *Spectrophotometric Identification Tests*, Appendix IIIC
  Acceptance criteria: The spectrum of the sample exhibits relative maxima at the same wavelengths as those of the spectrum below.

ASSAY

- **PROCEDURE:** Proceed as directed under *M-1b*, Appendix XI.
  Acceptance criteria: NLT 99.0% of $C_{12}H_{10}O$

SPECIFIC TESTS

- **REFRACTIVE INDEX**, Appendix II: At 20°
  Acceptance criteria: Freezes
- **SPECIFIC GRAVITY:** Determine at 25° by any reliable method (see *General Provisions*).
  Acceptance criteria: Between 1.070 and 1.074

OTHER REQUIREMENTS

- **MELTING RANGE OR TEMPERATURE DETERMINATION**, Appendix IIB
  Acceptance criteria: Between 26.0° and 30.0°

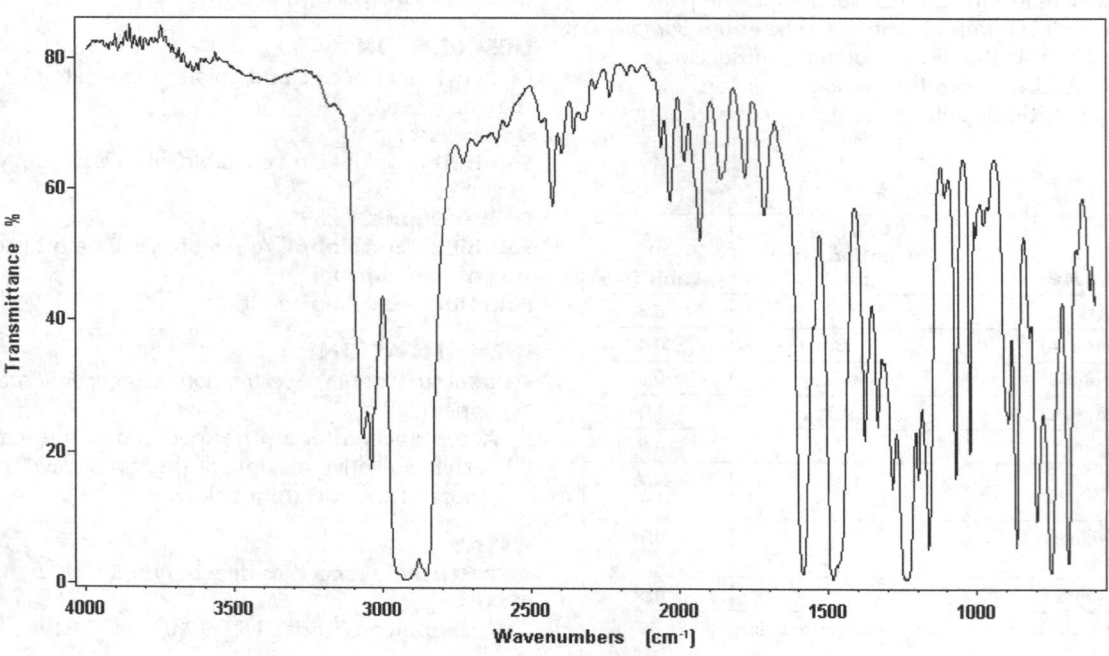

Diphenyl Ether

Disodium EDTA

First Published: Prior to FCC 6

Disodium Ethylenediaminetetraacetate
Disodium (Ethylenedinitrilo)tetraacetate
Disodium Edetate

$C_{10}H_{14}N_2Na_2O_8 \cdot 2H_2O$ Formula wt 372.24
INS: 386   CAS: [6381-92-6]
UNII: 7FLD91C86K [edetate disodium]

DESCRIPTION
Disodium EDTA occurs as a white, crystalline powder. It is soluble in water.
Function: Preservative; sequestrant; stabilizer
Packaging and Storage: Store in well-closed containers.

IDENTIFICATION
- **A. Sodium,** Appendix IIIA
  Sample solution: 50 mg/mL in water
  Acceptance criteria: Responds to the flame test.
- **B. Procedure**
  Sample: 50 mg
  Analysis: Add 2 drops of ammonium thiocyanate TS and 2 drops of ferric chloride TS to 5 mL of water in a test tube. Add the Sample to the deep red solution so obtained, and mix.
  Acceptance criteria: The deep red color disappears.
- **C. Infrared Absorption,** Spectrophotometric Identification Tests, Appendix IIIC
  Reference standard: USP Edetate Disodium RS
  Sample and standard preparation: K
  Analysis: The spectrum of the sample exhibits maxima at the same wavelengths as those in the spectrum of the Reference standard.

ASSAY
- **Procedure**
  Sample: 5 g
  Sample solution: Transfer the Sample into a 250-mL volumetric flask, dissolve in water, dilute to volume, and mix.
  Analysis: Place about 200 mg of chelometric standard calcium carbonate, accurately weighed, in a 400-mL beaker, add 10 mL of water, and swirl to form a slurry. Cover the beaker with a watch glass and introduce 2 mL of 2.7 N hydrochloric acid from a pipet inserted between the lip of the beaker and the edge of the watch glass. Swirl the contents of the beaker to dissolve the calcium carbonate. Wash down the sides of the beaker, the outer surface of the pipet, and the watch glass, and dilute to about 100 mL with water. While stirring, preferably with a magnetic stirrer, add about 30 mL of the Sample solution from a 50-mL buret, then add 15 mL of 1 N sodium hydroxide and 300 mg of hydroxy naphthol blue indicator, and continue the titration with the Sample solution to a blue endpoint.

Calculate the weight, in mg, of $C_{10}H_{14}N_2Na_2O_8 \cdot 2H_2O$ in the *Sample* taken by the formula:

$$\text{Result} = 929.8(W/V)$$

W = weight (mg) of calcium carbonate
V = Volume (mL) of the Sample solution consumed in the titration

Acceptance criteria: NLT 99.0% and NMT 101.0% of $C_{10}H_{14}N_2Na_2O_8 \cdot 2H_2O$

IMPURITIES
Inorganic Impurities
- **CALCIUM**
  Sample solution: 50 mg/mL
  Analysis: Add 2 drops of methyl red TS to the *Sample solution* and neutralize with 6 N ammonium hydroxide. Add 3 N hydrochloric acid dropwise until the solution is just acid, and then add 1 mL of ammonium oxalate TS.
  Acceptance criteria: No precipitate forms.
- **LEAD**, *Lead Limit Test*, Appendix IIIB
  Sample solution: Prepare as directed for organic compounds.
  Control: 10 µg Pb (10 mL of *Diluted Standard Lead Solution*)
  Acceptance criteria: NMT 10 mg/kg

Organic Impurities
- **NITRILOTRIACETIC ACID**
  Mobile phase: Add 10 mL of a 25% solution of tetrabutylammonium hydroxide in methanol to 200 mL of water, and adjust with 1 M phosphoric acid to a pH of 7.5 ± 0.1. Transfer the solution to a 1000-mL volumetric flask, add 90 mL of methanol, dilute with water to volume, mix, filter through a membrane filter (0.5-µm or finer porosity), and de-gas.
  Cupric nitrate solution: 10 mg/mL
  Standard stock solution: Transfer 100 mg of nitrilotriacetic acid to a 10-mL volumetric flask, add 0.5 mL of ammonium hydroxide, and mix. Dilute to volume and mix.
  Standard solution: Transfer 1.0 g of sample to a 100-mL volumetric flask, add 100 µL of *Standard stock solution*, dilute to volume with *Cupric nitrate solution* and mix. If necessary, sonicate to achieve complete dissolution.
  Sample solution: 10 mg/mL in *Cupric nitrate solution*
  Chromatographic system, Appendix IIA
    Mode: High-performance liquid chromatography
    Detector: UV 254 nm
    Column: 4.6-mm × 15-cm column that contains 5- to 10-mm porous microparticles of silica bonded to octylsilane (Zorbax 8, or equivalent)
    Flow rate: About 2 mL/min
    Injection volume: About 50 µL
    System suitability
      Sample: *Standard solution*
      Suitability requirement 1: The resolution factor between nitrilotriacetic acid and disodium EDTA is NLT 4.0.
      Suitability requirement 2: The relative standard deviation for replicate injections is NMT 2.0%.
  Analysis: Separately inject the *Standard solution* and the *Sample solution* into the chromatograph, record the chromatograms, and measure the responses for the major peaks. [NOTE—The retention times for nitrilotriacetic acid and disodium EDTA are about 3.5 min and 9 min, respectively.]
  Acceptance criteria: The response of the nitrilotriacetic acid peak of the *Sample solution* does not exceed the difference between the nitrilotriacetic acid peak responses obtained from the *Standard solution* and the *Sample solution*. (NMT 0.1%)

SPECIFIC TESTS
- **PH**, *pH Determination*, Appendix IIB
  Sample solution: 10 mg/mL
  Acceptance criteria: Between 4.3 and 4.7

Disodium Guanylate
First Published: Prior to FCC 6

Disodium 5'-Guanylate
Disodium Guanosine-5'-monophosphate

$C_{10}H_{12}N_5Na_2O_8P \cdot xH_2O$ Formula wt 407.19
INS: 627   CAS: [5550-12-9]
UNII: B768T44Q8V [disodium 5'-guanylate]

DESCRIPTION
Disodium Guanylate occurs as colorless or white crystals, or as a white, crystalline powder. It contains approximately seven molecules of water of crystallization. It is soluble in water, sparingly soluble in alcohol, and practically insoluble in ether.
Function: Flavor enhancer
Packaging and Storage: Store in well-closed containers.

IDENTIFICATION
- **ULTRAVIOLET ABSORPTION SPECTRUM**
  Sample solution: 20 µg/mL in 0.01 N hydrochloric acid
  Acceptance criteria: The ultraviolet absorption spectrum of the *Sample solution* exhibits an absorbance maximum at 256 ± 2 nm.

ASSAY
- **PROCEDURE**
  Sample solution: 20 µg/mL in 0.01 N hydrochloric acid
  Standard solution: 20 µg/mL of USP Disodium Guanylate RS in 0.01 N hydrochloric acid
  Analysis: Using a suitable spectrophotometer set to the absorbance maximum at about 260 nm with 1-cm cells and 0.01 N hydrochloric acid as the blank, determine the absorbance of the *Sample solution* and of

368 / Disodium Guanylate / Monographs

the *Standard solution*. Calculate the quantity, in mg, of $C_{10}H_{12}N_5Na_2O_8P$ in the sample taken by the formula:

$$\text{Result} = 25C \times A_U / A_S$$

- C = exact concentration (µg/mL) of the *Standard solution*
- A_U = absorbance of the *Sample solution*
- A_S = absorbance of the *Standard solution*

Acceptance criteria: NLT 97.0% and NMT 102.0% of $C_{10}H_{12}N_5Na_2O_8P$, calculated on the dried basis

IMPURITIES
Inorganic Impurities
- **AMMONIUM SALTS**
  Sample: 100 mg
  Analysis: Transfer the *Sample* into a small test tube and add 50 mg of magnesium oxide and 1 mL of water. Moisten a piece of red litmus paper with water, suspend it in the tube, cover the mouth of the tube, and heat in a water bath for 5 min.
  Acceptance criteria: The litmus paper does not change to blue.
- **LEAD**, *Lead Limit Test*, Appendix IIIB
  Sample solution: Prepare as directed for organic compounds.
  Control: 5 µg Pb (5 mL of *Diluted Standard Lead Solution*)
  Acceptance criteria: NMT 5 mg/kg

Organic Impurities
- **AMINO ACIDS**
  Sample solution: 1 mg/mL
  Analysis: Add 1 mL of ninhydrin TS to 5 mL of the *Sample solution* and heat for 3 min.
  Acceptance criteria: No color appears.
- **OTHER NUCLEOTIDES**
  Sample solution: 10 mg/mL
  Chromatographic system, Appendix IIA
    Mode: Descending chromatography (see *Paper Chromatography*, Appendix IIA)
    Stationary phase: Prepare a strip of Whatman No. 2, or equivalent, filter paper about 20 × 40 cm, and draw a line across the narrow dimension about 5 cm from one end.
    Solvent mixture: Saturated ammonium sulfate solution:*tert*-butyl alcohol:0.025 N ammonia (160:3:40)
    Application volume: 10 µL
    Detection/visualization: UV, 254 nm
  Analysis: Using a micropipette, apply the *Sample solution* to the center of the line drawn across the filter paper and dry in air. Fill the trough of an apparatus suitable for descending chromatography with the *Solvent mixture*. Suspend the strip in the chamber, placing the end of the strip in the trough at a distance about 1 cm from the pencil line. Seal the chamber, and allow the chromatogram to develop until the solvent front descends to a distance about 30 cm from the starting line. Remove the strip from the chamber, dry in air, and observe under shortwave (254 nm) ultraviolet light in the dark.
  Acceptance criteria: Only one spot is visible.

SPECIFIC TESTS
- **CLARITY AND COLOR OF SOLUTION**
  Sample solution: 100 mg in 10 mL of water
  Acceptance criteria: The *Sample solution* is colorless and shows no more than a trace of turbidity.
- **LOSS ON DRYING**, Appendix IIC: 120° for 4 h
  Acceptance criteria: NMT 25.0%
- **PH**, *pH Determination*, Appendix IIB
  Sample solution: 50 mg/mL
  Acceptance criteria: Between 7.0 and 8.5

Disodium Inosinate

First Published: Prior to FCC 6

Disodium 5′-Inosinate
Disodium Inosine-5′-monophosphate

$C_{10}H_{11}N_4Na_2O_8P \cdot xH_2O$ Formula wt 392.17
INS: 631   CAS: [4691-65-0]
UNII: T2ZYA7KC05 [disodium 5′-inosinate]

DESCRIPTION
Disodium Inosinate occurs as colorless or white crystals, or as a white, crystalline powder. It contains approximately 7.5 molecules of water of crystallization. It is soluble in water, sparingly soluble in alcohol, and practically insoluble in ether.
Function: Flavor enhancer
Packaging and Storage: Store in well-closed containers.

IDENTIFICATION
- **ULTRAVIOLET ABSORPTION SPECTRUM**
  Sample solution: 20 µg/mL in 0.01 N hydrochloric acid
  Acceptance criteria
    Absorbance maximum: 250 ± 2 nm
    A_{250}/A_{260} **ratio:** Between 1.55 and 1.65
    A_{280}/A_{260} **ratio:** Between 0.20 and 0.30

ASSAY
- **PROCEDURE**
  Sample solution: 20 µg/mL in 0.01 N hydrochloric acid
  Standard solution: 20 µg/mL of USP Disodium Inosinate RS in 0.01 N hydrochloric acid
  Analysis: Using a suitable spectrophotometer set to the absorbance maximum at about 250 nm with 1-cm cells and 0.01 N hydrochloric acid as the blank, determine the absorbance of the *Sample solution* and of the *Standard solution*. Calculate the quantity, in mg, of $C_{10}H_{11}N_4Na_2O_8P$ in the sample taken by the formula:

$$\text{Result} = 25C \times A_U / A_S$$

C = exact concentration (µg/mL) of the *Standard solution*
A_U = absorbance of the *Sample solution*
A_S = absorbance of the *Standard solution*
Acceptance criteria: NLT 97.0% and NMT 102.0% $C_{10}H_{11}N_4Na_2O_8P$, calculated on the anhydrous basis

IMPURITIES
Inorganic Impurities
- **AMMONIUM SALTS**
  Sample: 100 mg
  Analysis: Transfer the *Sample* into a small test tube and add 50 mg of magnesium oxide and 1 mL of water. Moisten a piece of red litmus paper with water, suspend it in the tube, cover the mouth of the tube, and heat in a water bath for 5 min.
  Acceptance criteria: The litmus paper does not change to blue.
- **LEAD,** *Lead Limit Test,* Appendix IIIB
  Sample solution: Prepare as directed for organic compounds.
  Control: 5 µg Pb (5 mL of *Diluted Standard Lead Solution*)
  Acceptance criteria: NMT 5 mg/kg

Organic Impurities
- **AMINO ACIDS**
  Sample solution: 1 mg/mL
  Analysis: Add 1 mL of ninhydrin TS to 5 mL of the *Sample solution*.
  Acceptance criteria: No color appears.
- **OTHER NUCLEOTIDES**
  Sample solution: 10 mg/mL
  Chromatographic system, Appendix IIA
    Mode: Descending chromatography (see *Paper Chromatography,* Appendix IIA)
    Stationary phase: Prepare a strip of Whatman No. 2, or equivalent, filter paper about 20 × 40 cm, and draw a line across the narrow dimension about 5 cm from one end.
    Solvent mixture: Saturated ammonium sulfate solution:*tert*-butyl alcohol:0.025 N ammonia (160:3:40)
    Application volume: 10 µL
    Detection/visualization: UV, 254 nm
  Analysis: Using a micropipette, apply the *Sample solution* to the center of the line drawn across the filter paper and dry in air. Fill the trough of an apparatus suitable for descending chromatography with the *Solvent mixture*. Suspend the strip in the chamber, placing the end of the strip in the trough at a distance about 1 cm from the pencil line. Seal the chamber, and allow the chromatogram to develop until the solvent front descends to a distance about 30 cm from the starting line. Remove the strip from the chamber, dry in air, and observe under shortwave (254 nm) ultraviolet light in the dark.
  Acceptance criteria: Only one spot is visible.

SPECIFIC TESTS
- **CLARITY AND COLOR OF SOLUTION**
  Sample solution: 500 mg in 10 mL of water
  Acceptance criteria: The *Sample solution* is colorless and shows no more than a trace of turbidity.
- **PH,** *pH Determination,* Appendix IIB
  Sample: 50 mg/mL
  Acceptance criteria: Between 7.0 and 8.5
- **WATER,** *Water Determination,* Appendix IIB
  Acceptance criteria: NMT 28.5%

Disodium 5'-Uridylate

First Published: First Supplement, FCC 7

Uridine 5'-monophosphate disodium salt
Disodium uridine 5'-monophosphate
UMP disodium salt

$C_9H_{11}N_2Na_2O_9P \cdot xH_2O$ Formula wt 368.15
                                 CAS: [3387-36-8]
UNII: KD8E20071T [uridine monophosphate disodium]

DESCRIPTION
Disodium 5'-Uridylate occurs as colorless or white crystals. It contains approximately seven molecules of water of crystallization. It is soluble in water, sparingly soluble in alcohol, and practically insoluble in ether. It is produced by enzymatic cleavage of yeast ribonucleic acid (RNA) with a 5'-phosphodiesterase followed by heat treatment, further purification steps, and washing of crystals with ethanol.
Function: Source of Disodium 5'-Uridylate
Packaging and Storage: Store in tight containers, protected from light and moisture.

IDENTIFICATION
- **A. INFRARED ABSORPTION,** *Spectrophotometric Identification Tests,* Appendix IIIC
  Reference standard: USP Disodium 5'-Uridylate RS
  Sample and standard preparation: *A*
  Acceptance criteria: The spectrum of the sample exhibits maxima at the same wavelengths as those in the spectrum of the *Reference standard*.
- **B. PROCEDURE**
  Acceptance criteria: The retention time of the major peak (excluding the solvent peak) in the chromatogram of the *Sample solution* corresponds to that of the *Standard solution* in the *Assay*.

ASSAY
- **PROCEDURE**
  Mobile phase: 0.1 M potassium dihydrogen phosphate (KH_2PO_4) in degassed water, adjusted to pH 5.6 with 0.1 M dipotassium hydrogen phosphate (K_2HPO_4)
  Standard solution: 0.02 mg/mL of USP Disodium 5'-Uridylate RS in *Mobile phase*. [NOTE—Ultrasonication may be necessary to aid in complete dissolution.]

Sample solution: 0.02 mg/mL in *Mobile phase*. [NOTE—Ultrasonication may be necessary to aid in complete dissolution.]
Chromatographic system, Appendix IIA
  Mode: High-performance liquid chromatography
  Detector: UV 254 nm
  Column: 25 cm × 4.6-mm; packed with 5-μm reversed phase C18 silica gel[1]
  Column temperature: Ambient
  Flow rate: About 1.0 mL/min
  Injection size: 50 μL
System suitability
  Sample: *Standard solution*
  Suitability requirements
   Suitability requirement 1: The relative standard deviation of the disodium 5'-uridylate peak area responses from replicate injections is NMT 2.0%.
   Suitability requirement 2: The resolution, R, between the disodium 5'-uridylate peak and all other peaks is NLT 2.0.
Analysis: Separately inject equal volumes of the *Standard solution* and *Sample solution* into the chromatograph, and measure the responses for the major peaks on the resulting chromatograms. [NOTE—The approximate retention time for disodium 5'-uridylate is 6.2 min.] Calculate the percentage of disodium 5'-uridylate, $C_9H_{11}N_2Na_2O_9P$, in the sample taken:

$$\text{Result} = (r_U/r_S) \times (C_S/C_U) \times 100$$

r_U = peak area response for disodium 5'-uridylate in the *Sample solution*
r_S = peak area response for disodium 5'-uridylate in the *Standard solution*
C_S = concentration of disodium 5'-uridylate in the *Standard solution* (mg/mL)
C_U = concentration of sample in the *Sample solution* (mg/mL)

Acceptance criteria: 98.0%–103.0%, calculated on the anhydrous basis

IMPURITIES
Inorganic Impurities
- **ARSENIC**

[NOTE—When water is specified as a diluent, use deionized ultrafiltered water. When nitric acid is specified, use nitric acid of a grade suitable for trace element analysis with as low a content of arsenic as practical.]
Diluent: 4% nitric acid in water
Standard stock solution: 100 μg/mL of arsenic prepared by diluting a commercially available 1000 mg/kg arsenic ICP standard solution
Standard solutions: 0.05, 0.1, 0.2, 0.5, 1, and 2 μg/mL of arsenic: from *Standard stock solution* diluted with *Diluent*
Sample: 5 g
Sample solution: Dissolve the *Sample* in 40 mL of 10% nitric acid in a 100-mL volumetric flask, and dilute with water to volume.

---
[1] YMC-Pack ODS-AQ (YMC Europe GmbH, Dinslaken, Germany), or equivalent.

Spectrophotometric system, *Plasma Spectrochemistry*, Appendix IIC
  Mode: Inductively coupled plasma–optical emission spectroscopy (ICP–OES)
  Setup: Use a suitable ICP–OES configured in a radial optical alignment. [NOTE—This method was developed using a Varian Vista MPX ICP–OES unit.] The instrument parameters are as follows: set the ultraviolet detector to scan arsenic at 188.980 nm. Set the sample read time to 20 s. Set the forward power from the RF generator to 1150 watts. Use an argon plasma feed gas flow of 13.5 L/min with the auxiliary gas set to flow at 2.25 L/min. The sample is delivered to the spray chamber by a multichannel peristaltic pump set to deliver sample at a rate of 20 rpm. Samples are flushed through the system for 20 s prior to analysis. A 40-s read delay is also programmed into the sampling routine to allow for fluid flow equilibration after the high-speed flush, prior to the first analytical read of the sample. Between samples, the pumping system is washed by flushing the *Diluent* for 20 s.
Analysis: Generate a standard curve using *Diluent* as a blank and the *Standard solutions*. [NOTE—The correlation coefficient for the best-fit line should not be less than 0.999.]
Similarly, analyze the *Sample solution* on the ICP. Calculate the concentration (mg/kg) of arsenic in the *Sample* taken:

$$\text{Result} = (C/W) \times F$$

C = concentration of arsenic in the *Sample solution* determined from the standard curve (μg/mL)
W = weight of *Sample* taken (g)
F = *Sample solution* final volume, 100 mL

Acceptance criteria: NMT 2 mg/kg
- **CADMIUM**

[NOTE—When water is specified as a diluent, use deionized ultrafiltered water. When nitric acid is specified, use nitric acid of a grade suitable for trace element analysis with as low a content of cadmium as practical.]
Diluent: 4% nitric acid in water
Standard stock solution: 100 μg/mL of cadmium prepared by diluting a commercially available 1000 mg/kg cadmium ICP standard solution
Standard solutions: 0.005, 0.05, 0.1, 0.2, 0.5, 1, and 2 μg/mL of cadmium: from *Standard stock solution* diluted with *Diluent*
Sample: 5 g
Sample solution: Dissolve the *Sample* in 40 mL of 10% nitric acid in a 100-mL volumetric flask, and dilute with water to volume.
Spectrophotometric system, *Plasma Spectrochemistry*, Appendix IIC
  Mode: ICP–OES
  Setup: Same as that described in the test for *Arsenic*, but set to scan for cadmium at 228.802 nm.
Analysis: Generate a standard curve using *Diluent* as a blank and the *Standard solutions*. [NOTE—The

correlation coefficient for the best-fit line should not be less than 0.999.]

Similarly, analyze the *Sample solution* on the ICP. Calculate the concentration (mg/kg) of cadmium in the *Sample* taken:

$$\text{Result} = (C/W) \times F$$

C = concentration of cadmium in the *Sample solution* determined from the standard curve (μg/mL)
W = weight of *Sample* taken (g)
F = *Sample solution* final volume, 100 mL

Acceptance criteria: NMT 0.1 mg/kg

- **LEAD**

  [NOTE—When water is specified as a diluent, use deionized ultrafiltered water. When nitric acid is specified, use nitric acid of a grade suitable for trace element analysis with as low a content of lead as practical.]

  Diluent: 4% nitric acid in water

  Standard stock solution: 100 μg/mL of lead prepared by diluting a commercially available 1000 mg/kg lead ICP standard solution

  Standard solutions: 0.05, 0.1, 0.2, 0.5, 1, and 2 μg/mL of lead: from *Standard stock solution* diluted with *Diluent*

  Sample: 5 g

  Sample solution: Dissolve the *Sample* in 40 mL of 10% nitric acid in a 100-mL volumetric flask, and dilute with water to volume.

  Spectrophotometric system, *Plasma Spectrochemistry,* Appendix IIC

  Mode: ICP–OES

  Setup: Same as that described in the test for *Arsenic,* but set to scan for lead at 220.353 nm

  Analysis: Generate a standard curve using *Diluent* as a blank and the *Standard solutions.* [NOTE—The correlation coefficient for the best-fit line should not be less than 0.999.]

  Similarly, analyze the *Sample solution* on the ICP. Calculate the concentration (mg/kg) of lead in the *Sample* taken:

  $$\text{Result} = (C/W) \times F$$

  C = concentration of lead in the *Sample solution* determined from the standard curve (μg/mL)
  W = weight of *Sample* taken (g)
  F = *Sample solution* final volume, 100 mL

  Acceptance criteria: NMT 1 mg/kg

- **MERCURY**

  [NOTE—When water is specified as a diluent, use deionized ultrafiltered water. When nitric acid is specified, use nitric acid of a grade suitable for trace element analysis with as low a content of mercury as practical.]

  Diluent: 4% nitric acid in water

  Standard stock solution: 100 μg/mL of mercury prepared by diluting a commercially available 1000 mg/kg mercury ICP standard solution

  Standard solutions: 0.025, 0.05, 0.1, 0.2, 0.5, 1, and 2 μg/mL of mercury: from *Standard stock solution* diluted with *Diluent*

  Sample: 5 g

  Sample solution: Dissolve the *Sample* in 40 mL of 10% nitric acid in a 100-mL volumetric flask, and dilute with water to volume.

  Spectrophotometric system, *Plasma Spectrochemistry,* Appendix IIC

  Mode: ICP–OES

  Setup: Same as that described in the test for *Arsenic,* but set to scan for mercury at 194.164 nm

  Analysis: Generate a standard curve using *Diluent* as a blank and the *Standard solutions.* [NOTE—The correlation coefficient for the best-fit line should not be less than 0.999.]

  Similarly, analyze the *Sample solution* on the ICP. Calculate the concentration (mg/kg) of mercury in the *Sample* taken:

  $$\text{Result} = (C/W) \times F$$

  C = concentration of mercury in the *Sample solution* determined from the standard curve (μg/mL)
  W = weight of *Sample* taken (g)
  F = *Sample solution* final volume, 100 mL

  Acceptance criteria: NMT 0.5 mg/kg

Organic Impurities

- **ETHANOL**

  Standard solution: 100 mg/kg of ethanol in 1 N sodium hydroxide. Add 10 mL of this solution to a 20-mL headspace vial, and cap tightly.

  Sample solution: 100 mg/g in 1 N sodium hydroxide. Add 10 mL of this solution to a 20-mL headspace vial, and cap tightly.

  Chromatographic system, Appendix IIA

  Mode: Gas chromatography equipped with pressure-loop headspace autosampler

  Detector: Flame ionization

  Column: 30-m × 0.53-mm (id) capillary column with a 6% cyanopropylphenyl–94% dimethylpolysiloxane stationary phase and a 3.00-μm film thickness[2]

  Temperature

  Column: 20 min at 40°; increase to 240° at 10°/min; maintain at 240° for 10 min

  Injection port: 140°

  Detector: 250°

  Carrier gas: Nitrogen

  Flow rate: 2.5 mL/min

  Headspace unit: 2.5 mL/min

  Equilibration temperature: 80°

  Equilibration time: 60 min

  Loop temperature: 85°

  Transfer temperature: 90°

  Pressurization time: 0.5 min

  Loop fill time: 0.1 min

  Injection time: 1 min

  Injection size: 1 mL of headspace

  System suitability

---

[2] CP-Select 624 CB (Varian-Chrompack, Palo Alto, CA), or equivalent.

Sample: Standard solution
Suitability requirement: The relative standard deviation of the ethanol peak area responses from replicate injections is NMT 5.0%.
Analysis: Separately inject equal volumes of the Standard solution and Sample solution into the chromatograph, record the chromatograms, and measure the peak responses. [NOTE—The approximate retention time for ethanol is 11 min.]
Acceptance criteria: The peak area from the Sample solution does not exceed that from the Standard solution (NMT 1000 mg/kg).

- **OTHER RIBONUCLEOTIDES**
Mobile phase and Chromatographic system: Prepare as directed in the Assay.
Sample solution: 1.0 mg/mL. [NOTE—Ultrasonication may be necessary to aid in complete dissolution.]
Standard solution: Mixture of USP Disodium 5′-Uridylate RS, USP 5′-Adenylic Acid RS, USP 5′-Cytidylic Acid RS, USP Disodium Guanylate RS, and USP Disodium Inosinate RS, each at 0.02 mg/mL in Mobile phase
Suitability requirements
Sample: Standard solution
Suitability requirement 1: The relative standard deviation of the disodium 5′-uridylate peak area responses from replicate injections is NMT 2.0%.
Suitability requirement 2: The resolution, R, between the disodium 5′-uridylate peak and all other nucleotide peaks is NLT 2.0.
Analysis: Separately inject equal volumes of the Standard solution and Sample solution into the chromatograph, and measure the responses for all nucleotide peaks on the resulting chromatograms, except the peak from disodium 5′-uridylate. [NOTE—The approximate retention times are 4.6 min (5′-cytidylic acid), 6.2 min (5′-uridylic acid), 10.3 min (5′-guanylic acid), 11.5 min (5′-inosinic acid), and 27.5 min (5′-adenylic acid).] Separately calculate the percentage of each analyte (5′-cytidylic acid, 5′-guanylic acid, 5′-inosinic acid, and 5′-adenylic acid) in the sample taken:

Result = $(r_U/r_S) \times (C_S/C_U) \times 100$

r_U = peak area of the analyte from the Sample solution
r_S = peak area of the analyte from the Standard solution
C_S = concentration of analyte in the Standard solution (mg/mL)
C_U = concentration of analyte in the Sample solution (mg/mL)

Acceptance criteria: The sum of the percentages for all nucleotide impurities is NMT 1%, calculated on the anhydrous basis.

SPECIFIC TESTS
- **PH**, pH Determination, Appendix IIB
Sample solution: 50 mg/mL
Acceptance criteria: 7.0–8.5

- **WATER**, Water Determination, Method I, Appendix IIB
Acceptance criteria: NMT 26.0%
- **BILE-TOLERANT GRAM-NEGATIVE BACTERIA**, Appendix XIIC
Sample preparation: Proceed as directed using a 10-g sample and incubating at 30°–35° for 18–24 h.
Acceptance criteria: Negative in 10 g
- **ENTEROBACTER SAKAZAKII** (Cronobacter spp.), Appendix XIIC
Sample preparation: Proceed as directed using a 10-g sample and incubating at 30°–35° for 18–24 h.
Acceptance criteria: Negative in 10 g
- **SALMONELLA SPP.**, Appendix XIIC
Sample preparation: Dissolve 25 g of sample at a sample/broth ratio of 1/8, and proceed as directed.
Acceptance criteria: Negative in 25 g
- **TOTAL AEROBIC MICROBIAL COUNT**, Method I (Plate Count Method), Appendix XIIB
Acceptance criteria: NMT 1,000 cfu/g
- **TOTAL YEASTS AND MOLDS COUNT**, Method I (Plate Count Method), Appendix XIIB
Acceptance criteria: NMT 100 cfu/g

δ-Dodecalactone
First Published: Prior to FCC 6

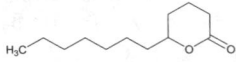

$C_{12}H_{22}O_2$ Formula wt 198.31
FEMA: 2401
UNII: 33DIC582TL [δ-dodecalactone]

DESCRIPTION
δ-Dodecalactone occurs as a colorless to yellow liquid.
Odor: Coconut-fruity, buttery on dilution
Solubility: Very soluble in alcohol, propylene glycol, vegetable oils; insoluble or practically insoluble in water
Boiling Point: ~140° to 141° (1 mm Hg)
Solubility in Alcohol, Appendix VI: One mL dissolves in 1 mL of 95% ethanol.
Function: Flavoring agent

IDENTIFICATION
- **INFRARED SPECTRA**, Spectrophotometric Identification Tests, Appendix IIIC
Acceptance criteria: The spectrum of the sample exhibits relative maxima at the same wavelengths as those of the spectrum below.

ASSAY
- **PROCEDURE:** Proceed as directed under M-1a, Appendix XI.
Acceptance criteria
Sum of two isomers: NLT 98.0% of $C_{12}H_{22}O_2$
δ Isomer: NLT 95.0% of $C_{12}H_{22}O_2$

SPECIFIC TESTS
- **ACID VALUE (FATS AND RELATED SUBSTANCES)**, Method II, Appendix VII

Acceptance criteria: NMT 8.0
- **REFRACTIVE INDEX**, Appendix II: At 20°
  Acceptance criteria: Between 1.458 and 1.461
- **SPECIFIC GRAVITY:** Determine at 25° by any reliable method (see *General Provisions*).
  Acceptance criteria: Between 0.942 and 0.950

OTHER REQUIREMENTS
- **SAPONIFICATION VALUE,** *Esters,* Appendix VI
  Sample: 1 g
  Acceptance criteria: Between 278 and 286

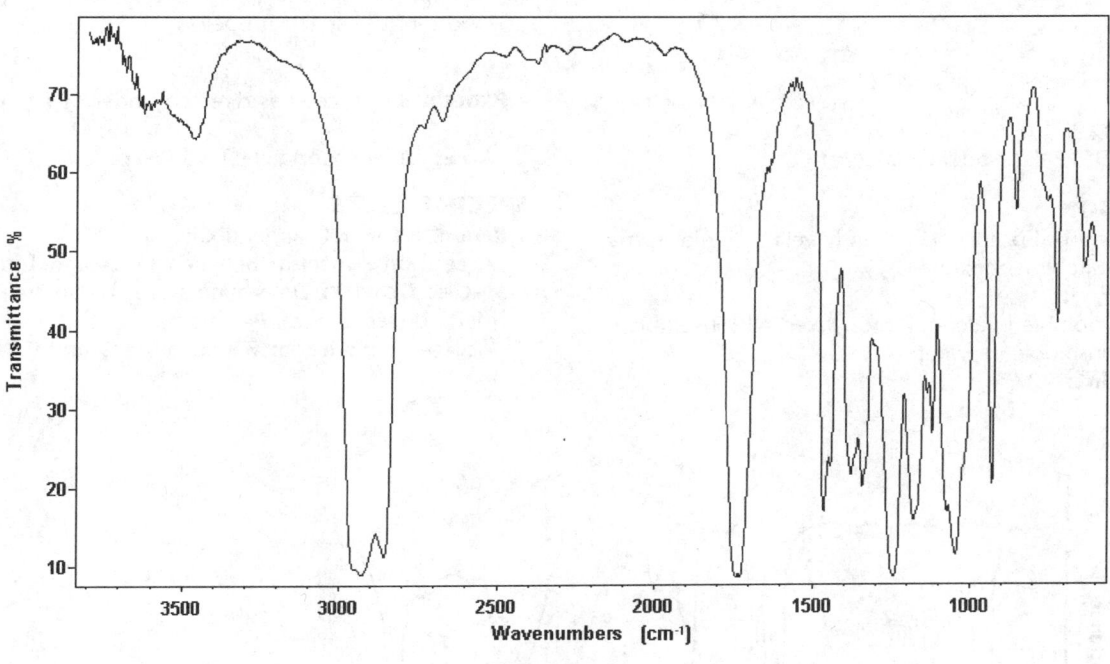

δ-Dodecalactone

γ-Dodecalactone

First Published: Prior to FCC 6

4-Hydroxydodecanoic Acid Lactone

$C_{12}H_{22}O_2$ Formula wt 198.31
FEMA: 2400
UNII: YX9N4581LU [γ-dodecalactone]

DESCRIPTION
γ-Dodecalactone occurs as a colorless to pale yellow liquid.
Odor: Fruity, peach, pear
Solubility: Soluble in propylene glycol, vegetable oils; insoluble or practically insoluble in water
Boiling Point: ~131° (1.5 mm Hg)
Solubility in Alcohol, Appendix VI: One mL dissolves in 1 mL of 95% alcohol.

Function: Flavoring agent

ASSAY
- **PROCEDURE:** Proceed as directed under *M-1a,* Appendix XI.
  Acceptance criteria: NLT 97.0% of $C_{12}H_{22}O_2$

SPECIFIC TESTS
- **ACID VALUE, FLAVOR CHEMICALS (OTHER THAN ESSENTIAL OILS),** *M-15,* Appendix XI
  Acceptance criteria: NMT 1.0
- **REFRACTIVE INDEX**, Appendix II: At 20°
  Acceptance criteria: Between 1.451 and 1.456
- **SPECIFIC GRAVITY:** Determine at 25° by any reliable method (see *General Provisions*).
  Acceptance criteria: Between 0.933 and 0.938

(E)-2-Dodecen-1-al

First Published: Prior to FCC 6
Last Revision: First Supplement, FCC 6

trans-2-Dodecen-1-al

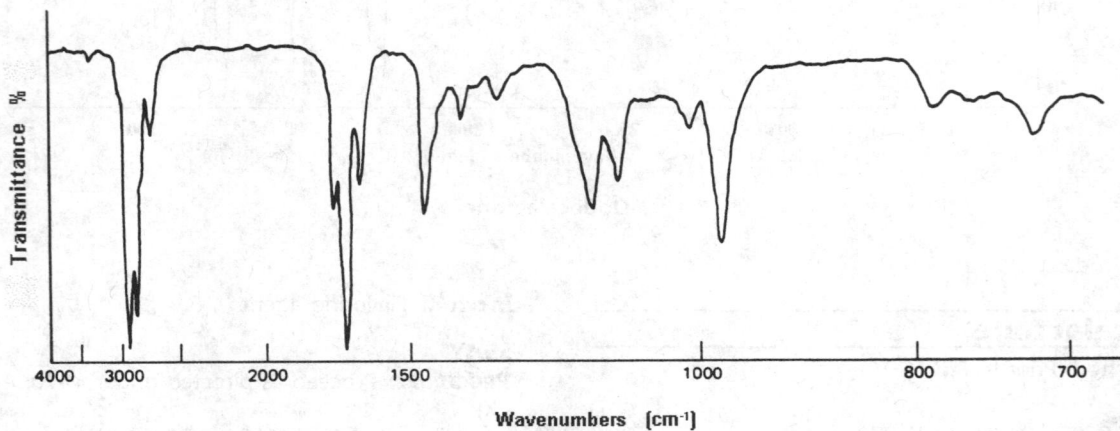

C$_{12}$H$_{22}$O   Formula wt 182.31
FEMA: 2402
UNII: 1D55O81P4E [2-dodecenal, (2e)-]

DESCRIPTION
(E)-2-Dodecen-1-al occurs as a slightly yellow liquid. It may contain a suitable antioxidant.
Odor: Fatty, citrus
Solubility: Soluble in alcohol, most fixed oils; insoluble or practically insoluble in water
Boiling Point: ~272°
Solubility in Alcohol, Appendix VI
Function: Flavoring agent

IDENTIFICATION
- **INFRARED SPECTRA,** Spectrophotometric Identification Tests, Appendix IIIC
  Acceptance criteria: The spectrum of the sample exhibits relative maxima at the same wavelengths as those of the spectrum below.

ASSAY
- **PROCEDURE:** Proceed as directed under M-1a, Appendix XI.
  Acceptance criteria: NLT 93.0% of C$_{12}$H$_{22}$O

SPECIFIC TESTS
- **REFRACTIVE INDEX,** Appendix II: At 20°
  Acceptance criteria: Between 1.454 and 1.460
- **SPECIFIC GRAVITY:** Determine at 25° by any reliable method (see General Provisions).
  Acceptance criteria: Between 0.839 and 0.849

(E)-2-Dodecen-1-al

Enzyme Preparations

First Published: Prior to FCC 6
Last Revision: FCC 6

DESCRIPTION

Enzyme Preparations used in food processing are derived from animal, plant, or microbial sources (see *Classification*, below). They may consist of whole cells, parts of cells, or cell-free extracts of the source used, and they may contain one active component or, more commonly, a mixture of several, as well as food-grade diluents, preservatives, antioxidants, and other substances consistent with good manufacturing practices. The individual preparations usually are named according to the substance to which they are applied, such as *Protease* or *Amylase*. Traditional names such as *Malt*, *Pepsin*, and *Rennet* also are used, however. The color of the preparations—which may be liquid, semiliquid, or dry—may vary from virtually colorless to dark brown. The active components consist of the biologically active proteins, which are sometimes conjugated with metals, carbohydrates, and/or lipids. Known molecular weights of the active components range from approximately 12,000 to several hundred thousand. The activity of enzyme preparations is measured according to the reaction catalyzed by individual enzymes (see below) and is usually expressed in activity units per unit weight of the preparation. In commercial practice (but not for *Food Chemicals Codex* purposes), the activity of the product is sometimes also given as the quantity of the preparation to be added to a given quantity of food to achieve the desired effect. Additional information relating to the nomenclature and the sources from which the active components are derived is provided under *Enzyme Assays*, Appendix V.

Function: Enzyme (see discussion under *Classification*, below)

Packaging and Storage: Store in well-closed containers in a cool, dry place.

IDENTIFICATION
Classification

- **ANIMAL-DERIVED PREPARATIONS**

  Catalase, Bovine Liver: Produced as partially purified liquid or powdered extracts from bovine liver. Major active principle: *catalase*. Typical application: used in the manufacture of certain cheeses.

  Chymotrypsin: Obtained from purified extracts of bovine or porcine pancreatic tissue. Produced as white to tan, amorphous powders soluble in water, but practically insoluble in alcohol, in chloroform, and in ether. Major active principle: *chymotrypsin*. Typical application: used in the hydrolysis of protein.

  Lipase, Animal: Obtained from the edible forestomach tissue of calves, kids, or lambs; and from animal pancreatic tissue. Produced as purified edible tissue preparations or as aqueous extracts dispersible in water, but insoluble in alcohol. Major active principle: *lipase*. Typical applications: used in the manufacture of cheese and in the modification of lipids.

  Lysozyme: Obtained from extracts of purified chicken egg whites. Generally prepared and used in the hydrochloride form as a white powder. Major active principle: *lysozyme*. Typical application: used as an antimicrobial in food processing.

  Pancreatin: Obtained from porcine or bovine (ox) pancreatic tissue. Produced as a white to tan, water-soluble powder. Major active principles: (1) α-amylase; (2) protease; and (3) lipase. Typical applications: used in the preparation of precooked cereals, infant foods, and protein hydrolysates.

  Pepsin: Obtained from the glandular layer of hog stomach. Produced as a white to light tan, water-soluble powder; amber paste; or clear, amber to brown, aqueous liquids. Major active principle: *pepsin*. Typical applications: used in the preparation of fishmeal and other protein hydrolysates and in the clotting of milk in the manufacture of cheese (in combination with rennet).

  Phospholipase A$_2$: Obtained from porcine pancreatic tissue. Produced as a white to tan powder or pale to dark yellow liquid. Major active principle: *phospholipase A$_2$*. Typical application: used in the hydrolysis of lecithins.

  Rennet, Bovine: Aqueous extracts made from the fourth stomach of bovines. Produced as a clear, amber to dark brown liquid or a white to tan powder. Major active principle: *protease* (pepsin). Typical application: used in the manufacture of cheese. Similar preparations may be made from the fourth stomach of sheep or goats.

  Rennet, Calf: Aqueous extracts made from the fourth stomach of calves. Produced as a clear, amber to dark brown liquid or a white to tan powder. Major active principle: *protease* (chymosin). Typical application: used in the manufacture of cheese. Similar preparations may be made from the fourth stomach of lambs or kids.

  Trypsin: Obtained from purified extracts of porcine or bovine pancreas. Produced as white to tan, amorphous powders soluble in water, but practically insoluble in alcohol, in chloroform, and in ether. Major active principle: *trypsin*. Typical applications: used in baking, in the tenderizing of meat, and in the production of protein hydrolysates.

- **PLANT-DERIVED PREPARATIONS**

  Amylase: Obtained from extraction of ungerminated barley. Produced as a clear, amber to dark brown liquid or a white to tan powder. Major active principle: β-amylase. Typical applications: used in the production of alcoholic beverages and sugar syrups.

  Bromelain: The purified proteolytic substance derived from the pineapples *Ananas comosus* and *Ananas bracteatus* L. (Fam. Bromeliaceae). Produced as a white to light tan, amorphous powder soluble in water (the solution is usually colorless to light yellow and somewhat opalescent), but practically insoluble in alcohol, in chloroform, and in ether. Major active principle: *bromelain*. Typical applications: used in the chillproofing of beer, in the tenderizing of meat, in the preparation of precooked cereals, in the production of protein hydrolysates, and in baking.

Ficin: The purified proteolytic substance derived from the latex of *Ficus* sp. (Fam. Moraceae), which includes a variety of tropical fig trees. Produced as a white to off-white powder completely soluble in water. (Liquid fig latex concentrates are light to dark brown.) Major active principle: *ficin*. Typical applications: used in the chillproofing of beer, in the tenderizing of meat, and in the conditioning of dough in baking.

Malt: The product of the controlled germination of barley. Produced as a clear amber to dark brown liquid preparation or as a white to tan powder. Major active principles: (1) α-*amylase* and (2) β-*amylase*. Typical applications: used in baking, in the manufacture of alcoholic beverages and of syrups.

Papain: The purified proteolytic substance derived from the fruit of the papaya *Carica papaya* L. (Fam. Caricaceae). Produced as a white to light tan, amorphous powder or a liquid soluble in water (the solution is usually colorless or light yellow and somewhat opalescent), but practically insoluble in alcohol, in chloroform, and in ether. Major active principles: (1) *papain* and (2) *chymopapain*. Typical applications: used in the chillproofing of beer, in the tenderizing of meat, in the preparation of precooked cereals, and in the production of protein hydrolysates.

- **MICROBIALLY-DERIVED PREPARATIONS**

α-Acetolactatedecarboxylase: (*Bacillus subtilis* containing a *Bacillus brevis* gene) Produced as a brown liquid by controlled fermentation using the modified *Bacillus subtilis*. Soluble in water (the solution is usually a light yellow to brown). Major active principle: *decarboxylase*. Typical application: used in the preparation of beer.

Aminopeptidase, Leucine: (*Aspergillus niger* var., *Aspergillus oryzae* var., and other microbial species) Produced as a light tan to brown powder or as a brown liquid by controlled fermentation using *Aspergillus niger* var., *Aspergillus oryzae* var., or other microbial species. The powder is soluble in water (the solution is usually light yellow to brown). Major active principles: (1) *aminopeptidase*, (2) *protease*, and (3) *carboxypeptidase* activities in varying amounts. Typical applications: used in the preparation of protein hydrolysates and in the development of flavors in processed foods.

Carbohydrase: (*Aspergillus niger* var., including *Aspergillus aculeatus*) Produced as an off-white to tan powder or a tan to dark brown liquid by controlled fermentation using *Aspergillus niger* var. (including *Aspergillus aculeatus*). Soluble in water (the solution is usually light yellow to dark brown), but practically insoluble in alcohol, in chloroform, and in ether. Major active principles: (1) α-*amylase*, (2) *pectinase* (a mixture of enzymes, including *pectin depolymerase, pectin methyl esterase, pectin lyase,* and *pectate lyase*), (3) *cellulase*, (4) *glucoamylase* (amyloglucosidase), (5) *amylo-1,6-glucosidase*, (6) *hemicellulase* (a mixture of enzymes, including *poly(galacturonate) hydrolase, arabinosidase, mannosidase, mannanase,* and *xylanase*), (7) *lactase*, (8) *β-glucanase*, (9) *β-D-glucosidase*, (10) *pentosanase*, and (11) *α-galactosidase*. Typical applications: used in the preparation of starch syrups and dextrose, alcohol, beer, ale, fruit juices, chocolate syrups, bakery products, liquid coffee, wine, dairy products, cereals, and spice and flavor extracts.

Carbohydrase: (*Aspergillus oryzae* var.) Produced as an off-white to tan, amorphous powder or a liquid by controlled fermentation using *Aspergillus oryzae* var. Soluble in water (the solution is usually light yellow to dark brown), but practically insoluble in alcohol, in chloroform, and in ether. Major active principles: (1) α-*amylase*, (2) *glucoamylase* (amyloglucosidase), and (3) *lactase*. Typical applications: used in the preparation of starch syrups, alcohol, beer, ale, bakery products, and dairy products.

Carbohydrase: (*Bacillus acidopullulyticus*) Produced as an off-white to brown, amorphous powder or a liquid by controlled fermentation using *Bacillus acidopullulyticus*. Soluble in water (the solution is usually light yellow to dark brown), but practically insoluble in alcohol, in chloroform, and in ether. Major active principle: *pullulanase*. Typical applications: used in the hydrolysis of amylopectins and other branched polysaccharides.

Carbohydrase: (*Bacillus stearothermophilus*) Produced as an off-white to tan powder or a light yellow to dark brown liquid by controlled fermentation using *Bacillus stearothermophilus*. Soluble in water, but practically insoluble in alcohol, in ether, and in chloroform. Major active principle: α-*amylase*. Typical applications: used in the preparation of starch syrups, alcohol, beer, dextrose, and bakery products.

Carbohydrase: (*Candida pseudotropicalis*) Produced as an off-white to tan, amorphous powder or a liquid by controlled fermentation using *Candida pseudotropicalis*. Soluble in water (the solution is usually light yellow to dark brown) but insoluble in alcohol, in chloroform, and in ether. Major active principle: *lactase*. Typical applications: used in the manufacture of candy and ice cream and in the modification of dairy products.

Carbohydrase: (*Kluyveromyces marxianus* var. *lactis*) Produced as an off-white to tan, amorphous powder or a liquid by controlled fermentation using *Kluyveromyces marxianus* var. *lactis*. Soluble in water (the solution is usually light yellow to dark brown), but insoluble in alcohol, in chloroform, and in ether. Major active principle: *lactase*. Typical applications: used in the manufacture of candy and ice cream and in the modification of dairy products.

Carbohydrase: (*Mortierella vinaceae* var. *raffinoseutilizer*) Produced as an off-white to tan powder or as pellets by controlled fermentation using *Mortierella vinaceae* var. *raffinoseutilizer*. Soluble in water (pellets may be insoluble in water), but practically insoluble in alcohol, in chloroform, and in ether. Major active principle: α-*galactosidase*. Typical application: used in the production of sugar from sugar beets.

Carbohydrase: (*Rhizopus niveus*) Produced as an off-white to brown, amorphous powder or a liquid by controlled fermentation using *Rhizopus niveus*. Soluble in water (the solution is usually light yellow to dark brown), but practically insoluble in alcohol, in chloroform, and in ether. Major active principles: (1) α-

amylase and (2) *glucoamylase*. Typical application: used in the hydrolysis of starch.

Carbohydrase: (*Rhizopus oryzae* var.) Produced as a powder or a liquid by controlled fermentation using *Rhizopus oryzae* var. Soluble in water, but practically insoluble in alcohol, in chloroform, and in ether. Major active principles: (1) α-*amylase*, (2) *pectinase*, and (3) *glucoamylase* (amyloglucosidase). Typical applications: used in the preparation of starch syrups and fruit juices, vegetable purees, and juices and in the manufacture of cheese.

Carbohydrase: (*Saccharomyces* species) Produced as a white to tan, amorphous powder by controlled fermentation using a number of species of *Saccharomyces* traditionally used in the manufacture of food. Soluble in water (the solution is usually light yellow), but practically insoluble in alcohol, in chloroform, and in ether. Major active principles: (1) *invertase* and (2) *lactase*. Typical applications: used in the manufacture of candy and ice cream and in the modification of dairy products.

Carbohydrase: [(*Trichoderma longibrachiatum* var.) (formerly *reesei*)] Produced as an off-white to tan, amorphous powder or as a liquid by controlled fermentation using *Trichoderma longibrachiatum* var. Soluble in water (the solution is usually tan to brown), but practically insoluble in alcohol, in chloroform, and in ether. Major active principles: (1) *cellulase*, (2) β-*glucanase*, (3) β-D-*glucosidase*, (4) *hemicellulase*, and (5) *pentosanase*. Typical applications: used in the preparation of fruit juices, wine, vegetable oils, beer, and baked goods.

Carbohydrase: (*Bacillus subtilis* containing a *Bacillus megaterium* α-*amylase* gene) Produced as an off-white to brown, amorphous powder or liquid by controlled fermentation using the modified *Bacillus subtilis*. Soluble in water (the solution is usually light yellow to dark brown), but practically insoluble in alcohol, in chloroform, and in ether. Major active principle: α-*amylase*. Typical applications: used in the preparation of starch syrups, alcohol, beer, and dextrose.

Carbohydrase: (*Bacillus subtilis* containing a *Bacillus stearothermophilus* α-amylase gene) Produced as an off-white to brown, amorphous powder or a liquid by controlled fermentation using the modified *Bacillus subtilis*. Soluble in water (the solution is usually light yellow to dark brown), but practically insoluble in alcohol, in chloroform, and in ether. Major active principle: maltogenic *amylase*. Typical applications: used in the preparation of starch syrups, dextrose, alcohol, beer, and baked goods.

Carbohydrase and Protease, Mixed: (*Bacillus licheniformis* var.) Produced as an off-white to brown, amorphous powder or as a liquid by controlled fermentation using *Bacillus licheniformis* var. Soluble in water (the solution is usually light yellow to dark brown), but practically insoluble in alcohol, in chloroform, and in ether. Major active principles: (1) α-*amylase* and (2) *protease*. Typical applications: used in the preparation of starch syrups, alcohol, beer, dextrose, fishmeal, and protein hydrolysates.

Carbohydrase and Protease, Mixed: (*Bacillus subtilis* var. including *Bacillus amyloliquefaciens*) Produced as an off-white to tan, amorphous powder or as a liquid by controlled fermentation using *Bacillus subtilis* var. Soluble in water (the solution is usually light yellow to dark brown), but practically insoluble in alcohol, in chloroform, and in ether. Major active principles: (1) α-*amylase*, (2) β-*glucanase*, (3) *protease*, and (4) *pentosanase*. Typical applications: used in the preparation of starch syrups, alcohol, beer, dextrose, bakery products, and fishmeal, in the tenderizing of meat, and in the preparation of protein hydrolysates.

Catalase: (*Aspergillus niger* var.) Produced as an off-white to tan, amorphous powder or as a liquid by controlled fermentation using *Aspergillus niger* var. Soluble in water (the solution is usually tan to brown), but practically insoluble in alcohol, in chloroform, and in ether. Major active principle: *catalase*. Typical applications: used in the manufacture of cheese, egg products, and soft drinks.

Catalase: (*Micrococcus lysodeikticus*) Produced by controlled fermentation using *Micrococcus lysodeikticus*. Soluble in water (the solution is usually light yellow to dark brown), but practically insoluble in alcohol, in chloroform, and in ether. Major active principle: *catalase*. Typical application: used in the manufacture of cheese, egg products, and soft drinks.

Chymosin: (*Aspergillus niger* var. *awamori*, *Escherichia coli K-12*, and *Kluyveromyces marxianus*, each microorganism containing a calf *prochymosin* gene) Produced as a white to tan, amorphous powder or as a light yellow to brown liquid by controlled fermentation using the above-named genetically modified microorganisms. The powder is soluble in water, but practically insoluble in alcohol, in chloroform, and in ether. Major active principle: *chymosin*. Typical application: used in the manufacture of cheese and in the preparation of milk-based desserts.

Glucose Isomerase: (*Actinoplanes missouriensis*, *Bacillus coagulans*, *Streptomyces olivaceus*, *Streptomyces olivochromogenes*, *Microbacterium arborescens*, *Streptomyces rubiginosus* var., or *Streptomyces murinus*) Produced as an off-white to tan, brown, or pink amorphous powder, granules, or liquid by controlled fermentation using any of the above-named organisms. The products may be soluble in water, but practically insoluble in alcohol, in chloroform, and in ether; or if immobilized, may be insoluble in water and partially soluble in alcohol, in chloroform, and in ether. Major active principle: *glucose* (or *xylose*) *isomerase*. Typical applications: used in the manufacture of high-fructose corn syrup and other fructose starch syrups.

Glucose Oxidase: (*Aspergillus niger* var.) Produced as a yellow to brown solution or as a yellow to tan or off-white powder by controlled fermentation using *Aspergillus niger* var. Soluble in water (the solution is usually light yellow to brown), but practically insoluble in alcohol, in chloroform, and in ether. Major active principles: (1) *glucose oxidase* and (2) *catalase*. Typical applications: used in the removal of sugar from liquid eggs and in the deoxygenation of citrus beverages.

Lipase: (*Aspergillus niger* var.) Produced as an off-white to tan, amorphous powder by controlled fermentation using *Aspergillus niger* var. Soluble in water (the solution is usually light yellow), but practically insoluble in alcohol, in chloroform, and in ether. Major active principle: *lipase*. Typical application: used in the hydrolysis of lipids (e.g., fish oil concentrates and cereal-derived lipids).

Lipase: (*Aspergillus oryzae* var.) Produced as an off-white to tan, amorphous powder or a liquid by controlled fermentation using *Aspergillus oryzae* var. Soluble in water (the solution is usually light yellow), but practically insoluble in alcohol, in chloroform, and in ether. Major active principle: *lipase*. Typical applications: used in the hydrolysis of lipids (e.g., fish oil concentrates) and in the manufacture of cheese and cheese flavors.

Lipase: (*Candida rugosa*; formerly *Candida cylindracea*) Produced as an off-white to tan powder by controlled fermentation using *Candida rugosa*. Soluble in water, but practically insoluble in alcohol, in chloroform, and in ether. Major active principle: *lipase*. Typical applications: used in the hydrolysis of lipids, in the manufacture of dairy products and confectionery goods, and in the development of flavor in processed foods.

Lipase: [*Rhizomucor (Mucor) miehei*] Produced as an off-white to tan powder or as a liquid by controlled fermentation using *Rhizomucor miehei*. Soluble in water (the solution is usually light yellow to dark brown), but practically insoluble in alcohol, in chloroform, and in ether. Major active principle: *lipase*. Typical applications: used in the hydrolysis of lipids, in the manufacture of cheese, and in the removal of haze in fruit juices.

Phytase: (*Aspergillus niger* var.) Produced as an off-white to brown powder or as a tan to dark brown liquid by controlled fermentation using *Aspergillus niger* var. Soluble in water, but practically insoluble in alcohol, in chloroform, and in ether. Major active principles: (1) *3-phytase* and (2) *acid phosphatase*. Typical applications: used in the production of soy protein isolate and in the removal of phytic acid from plant materials.

Protease: (*Aspergillus niger* var.) Produced by controlled fermentation using *Aspergillus niger* var. The purified enzyme occurs as an off-white to tan, amorphous powder. Soluble in water (the solution is usually light yellow), but practically insoluble in alcohol, in chloroform, and in ether. Major active principle: *protease*. Typical application: used in the production of protein hydrolysates.

Protease: (*Aspergillus oryzae* var.) Produced by controlled fermentation using *Aspergillus oryzae* var. The purified enzyme occurs as an off-white to tan, amorphous powder. Soluble in water (the solution is usually light yellow), but practically insoluble in alcohol, in chloroform, and in ether. Major active principle: *protease*. Typical applications: used in the chillproofing of beer, in the production of bakery products, in the tenderizing of meat, in the production of protein hydrolysates, and in the development of flavor in processed foods.

Rennet, Microbial: (nonpathogenic strain of *Bacillus cereus*) Produced as a white to tan, amorphous powder or a light yellow to dark brown liquid by controlled fermentation using *Bacillus cereus*. Soluble in water, but practically insoluble in alcohol, in chloroform, and in ether. Major active principle: *protease*. Typical application: used in the manufacture of cheese.

Rennet, Microbial: (*Endothia parasitica*) Produced as an off-white to tan, amorphous powder or as a liquid by controlled fermentation using nonpathogenic strains of *Endothia parasitica*. The powder is soluble in water (the solution is usually tan to dark brown), but practically insoluble in alcohol, in chloroform, and in ether. Major active principle: *protease*. Typical application: used in the manufacture of cheese.

Rennet, Microbial: [*Rhizomucor (Mucor)* sp.] Produced as a white to tan, amorphous powder by controlled fermentation using *Rhizomucor miehei*, or *pusillus* var. Lindt. The powder is soluble in water (the solution is usually light yellow), but practically insoluble in alcohol, in chloroform, and in ether. Major active principle: *protease*. Typical application: used in the manufacture of cheese.

Transglutaminase: (*Streptoverticillium mobaraense* var.) Produced as an off-white to weak yellow-brown, amorphous powder by controlled fermentation using *Streptoverticillium mobaraense* var. Soluble in water but practically insoluble in alcohol, in chloroform, and in ether. Major active principle: *transglutaminase*. Typical applications: used in the processing of meat, poultry, and seafood; production of yogurt, certain cheeses, and frozen desserts; and manufacture of pasta products and noodles, baked goods, meat analogs, ready-to-eat cereals, and other grain-based foods.

- **REACTIONS CATALYZED**

  [NOTE—The reactions catalyzed by any given active component are essentially the same, regardless of the source from which that component is derived.]

  α-Acetolactatedecarboxylase: Decarboxylation of α-cetolactate to acetoin

  Aminopeptidase, Leucine: Hydrolysis of N-terminal amino acid, which is preferably leucine, but may be other amino acids, from proteins and oligopeptides, yielding free amino acids and oligopeptides of lower molecular weight

  α-Amylase: Endohydrolysis of α-1,4-glucan bonds in polysaccharides (starch, glycogen, etc.), yielding dextrins and oligo- and monosaccharides

  β-Amylase: Hydrolysis of α-1,4-glucan bonds in polysaccharides (starch, glycogen, etc.), yielding maltose and betalimit dextrins

  Bromelain: Hydrolysis of polypeptides, amides, and esters (especially at bonds involving basic amino acids, leucine, or glycine), yielding peptides of lower molecular weight

  Catalase: $2H_2O_2 \leftrightarrow O_2 + 2H_2O$

  Cellulase: Hydrolysis of β-1,4-glucan bonds in such polysaccharides as cellulose, yielding β-dextrins

Chymosin (calf and fermentation derived): Cleaves a single bond in kappa casein
Ficin: Hydrolysis of polypeptides, amides, and esters (especially at bonds involving basic amino acids, leucine, or glycine), yielding peptides of lower molecular weight
α-Galactosidase: Hydrolysis of terminal nonreducing α-D-galactose residues in α-D-galactosides
β-Glucanase: Hydrolysis of β-1,3- and β-1,4-linkages in β-D-glucans, yielding oligosaccharides and glucose
Glucoamylase (amyloglucosidase): Hydrolysis of terminal α-1,4- and α-1,6-glucan bonds in polysaccharides (starch, glycogen, etc.), yielding glucose (dextrose)
Glucose Isomerase (xylose isomerase): Isomerization of glucose to fructose, and xylose to xylulose
Glucose Oxidase: β-D-glucose + $O_2 \leftrightarrow$ D-glucono-δ-lactone + H_2O_2
β-D-Glucosidase: Hydrolysis of terminal, nonreducing β-D-glucose residues with the release of β-D-glucose
Hemicellulase: Hydrolysis of β-1,4-glucans, α-L-arabinosides, β-D-mannosides, 1,3-β-D-xylans, and other polysaccharides, yielding polysaccharides of lower molecular weight
Invertase (β-fructofuranosidase): Hydrolysis of sucrose to a mixture of glucose and fructose (invert sugar)
Lactase (β-galactosidase): Hydrolysis of lactose to a mixture of glucose and galactose
Lysozyme: Hydrolysis of cell-wall polysaccharides of various bacterial species leading to the breakdown of the cell wall most often in Gram-positive bacteria
Maltogenic Amylase: Hydrolysis of α-1,4-glucan bonds
Lipase: Hydrolysis of triglycerides of simple fatty acids, yielding mono- and diglycerides, glycerol, and free fatty acids
Pancreatin
  α-Amylase: Hydrolysis of α-1,4-glucan bonds
  Protease: Hydrolysis of proteins and polypepticles
  Lipase: Hydrolysis of triglycerides of simple fatty acids
Pectinase
  Pectate lyase: Hydrolysis of pectate to oligosaccharides
  Pectin depolymerase: Hydrolysis of 1,4 galacturonide bonds
  Pectin lyase: Hydrolysis of oligosaccharides formed by pectate lyase
  Pectinesterase: Demethylation of pectin
Pepsin: Hydrolysis of polypeptides, including those with bonds adjacent to aromatic or dicarboxylic L-amino acid residues, yielding peptides of lower molecular weight
Phospholipase A_2: Hydrolysis of lecithins and phosphatidylcholine, producing fatty acid anions
Phytase
  3-Phytase: myo-Inositol hexakisphosphate + $H_2O \leftrightarrow$ 1,2,4,5,6-pentakisphosphate + ortho-phosphate
  Acid Phosphatase: Orthophosphate monoester + $H_2O \leftrightarrow$ an alcohol + orthophosphate
Protease (generic): Hydrolysis of polypeptides, yielding peptides of lower molecular weight
Pullulanase: Hydrolysis of 1,6-α-D-glycosidic bonds on amylopectin and glycogen and in α-and β-limit dextrins, yielding linear polysaccharides
Rennet (bovine and calf): Hydrolysis of polypeptides; specificity may be similar to pepsin
Transglutaminase: Binding of proteins
Trypsin: Hydrolysis of polypeptides, amides, and esters at bonds involving the carboxyl groups of L-arginine and L-lysine, yielding peptides of lower molecular weight

ASSAY
- **PROCEDURE**
  Analysis: The following procedures, which are included under *Enzyme Assays*, Appendix V, are provided for application as necessary in determining compliance with the declared representations for enzyme activity[1] : α-Acetolactatedecarboxylase Activity, Acid Phosphatase Activity, α-Amylase Activity (Nonbacterial); Bacterial α-Amylase Activity (BAU); Catalase Activity; Cellulase Activity; Chymotrypsin Activity; Diastase Activity (Diastatic Power); α-Galactosidase Activity, β-Glucanase Activity; Glucoamylase Activity (Amyloglucosidase Activity); Glucose Isomerase Activity; Glucose Oxidase Activity; β-D-Glucosidase Activity; Hemicellulase Activity; Invertase Activity; Lactase (Neutral) (β-Galactosidase) Activity; Lactase (Acid) (β-Galactosidase) Activity; Lipase Activity; Lipase/Esterase (Forestomach) Activity; Maltogenic Amylase Activity; Milk-Clotting Activity; Pancreatin Activity; Pepsin Activity; Phospholipase Activity; Phytase Activity; Plant Proteolytic Activity; Proteolytic Activity, Bacterial (PC); Proteolytic Activity, Fungal (HUT); Proteolytic Activity, Fungal (SAP); Pullulanase Activity; and Trypsin Activity.
  Acceptance criteria: NLT 85.0% and NMT 115.0% of the declared units of enzyme activity

IMPURITIES
- **LEAD,** *Lead Limit Test,* Appendix IIIB
  Control: 5 µg Pb (5 mL of *Diluted Standard Lead Solution*)
  Acceptance criteria: NMT 5 mg/kg

SPECIFIC TESTS
- **MICROBIAL LIMITS**
  [NOTE—Current methods for the following tests may be found in the Food and Drug Administration's Bacteriological Analytical Manual online at *www.cfsan.fda.gov/*.]
  Acceptance criteria
  Coliforms: NMT 30 CFU/g
  salmonella: Negative in 25 g

OTHER REQUIREMENTS
Enzyme preparations are produced in accordance with good manufacturing practices. Regardless of the source of derivation, they should cause no increase in the total

---
[1] Because of the varied conditions under which pectinases are employed, and because laboratory hydrolysis of a purified pectin substrate does not correlate with results observed with the natural substrates under use conditions, pectinase suppliers and users should develop their own assay procedures that would relate to the specific application under consideration.

microbial count in the treated food over the level accepted for the respective food.

Animal tissues used to produce enzymes must comply with the applicable U.S. meat inspection requirements and must be handled in accordance with good hygienic practices.

Plant material used to produce enzymes or culture media used to grow microorganisms consist of components that leave no residues harmful to health in the finished food under normal conditions of use.

Preparations derived from microbial sources shall be obtained using a pure culture fermentation of a non-pathogenic and non-toxigenic strain and are produced by methods and under culture conditions that ensure a controlled fermentation, thus preventing the introduction of microorganisms that could be the source of toxic materials and other undesirable substances.

The carriers, diluents, and processing aids used to produce the enzyme preparations shall be substances that are acceptable for general use in foods, including water and substances that are insoluble in foods but removed from the foods after processing.

Although limits have not been established for mycotoxins, appropriate measures should be taken to ensure that the products do not contain such contaminants.

Enzyme-Modified Fats

First Published: Prior to FCC 6

DESCRIPTION
Enzyme-Modified Fats occur as light to medium tan liquids, pastes, or powders with a strong fatty acid odor and flavor. They are produced by enzyme lipolysis of fats obtained from milk, refined beef fat, or steam-rendered chicken fat, using suitable food-grade enzymes. Enzyme-modified milkfat may be prepared from milk, concentrated milk, dry whole milk, cream, concentrated cream(s), dry cream, butter, butter oil, dried butter, or anhydrous milkfat. For enzyme-modified milkfat, optional dairy ingredients such as skim milk, concentrated skim milk, nonfat dry milk, buttermilk, concentrated buttermilk, dried buttermilk, liquid whey, concentrated whey, and dried whey may be used to adjust the concentration of the flavors. Fat emulsions are reacted with suitable food-grade enzymes under controlled conditions to increase the flavor components. Thermoprocessing is then used to destroy the enzyme activity and provide acceptable microbiological quality. Suitable preservatives, emulsifiers, buffers, stabilizers, and antioxidants as well as sodium chloride may be added. The resulting product is concentrated or dried.

Function: Flavoring agent

Packaging and Storage: Store in tight containers in a cool place.

IDENTIFICATION
- **PROCEDURE**
  Acceptance criteria: A sample has a very strong fatty acid odor.

IMPURITIES
Inorganic Impurities
- **LEAD,** *Lead Limit Test, Atomic Absorption Spectrophotometric Graphite Furnace Method, Method II,* Appendix IIIB
  Acceptance criteria: NMT 1 mg/kg

SPECIFIC TESTS
- **ACID VALUE (FATS AND RELATED SUBSTANCES),** *Method II,* Appendix VII
  Sample: 5 g
  Acceptance criteria: NLT 98.0% and NMT 102.0% of the labeled value
- **LOSS ON DRYING,** Appendix IIC: 105° for 48 h
  Acceptance criteria: NMT 4.0% for the dry product
- **MICROBIAL LIMITS**
  [NOTE—Current methods for the following tests may be found by accessing the Food and Drug Administration's Bacteriological Analytical Manual (BAM) online at www.cfsan.fda.gov.]
  Acceptance criteria
  Aerobic plate count: NMT 10,000 CFU/g
  Coliforms: NMT 10 CFU/g
  Salmonella: Negative in 25 g
  Staphylococcal enterotoxins: Negative in 1 g
  Staphylococcus aureus: NMT 100 CFU/g
  Yeasts and molds: NMT 10 CFU/g

OTHER REQUIREMENTS
- **LABELING:** Indicate the *Acid Value*.

Erythorbic Acid

First Published: Prior to FCC 6

D-Araboascorbic Acid

$C_6H_8O_6$ Formula wt 176.13
INS: 315   CAS: 89-65-6
UNII: 3113320II1 [erythorbic acid]

DESCRIPTION
Erythorbic Acid occurs as white or slightly yellow crystals or powder. It gradually darkens when exposed to light. In the dry state, it is reasonably stable in air, but in solution, it rapidly deteriorates in the presence of air. It melts between 164° and 171° with decomposition. One g is soluble in about 2.5 mL of water and in about 20 mL of alcohol. It is slightly soluble in glycerin.

Function: Preservative; antioxidant

Packaging and Storage: Store in tight, light-resistant containers.

IDENTIFICATION
- **A. PROCEDURE**
  Sample solution: 20 mg/mL

Analysis: Add a few drops of sodium nitroferricyanide TS to 2 mL of the *Sample solution*, then add 1 mL of approximately 0.1 N sodium hydroxide.
Acceptance criteria: A transient blue color immediately appears.
- **B. Procedure**
Sample: 15 mg
Analysis: Dissolve the *Sample* in 15 mL of a 50 mg/mL trichloroacetic acid solution, add 200 mg of activated charcoal, and shake the mixture vigorously for 1 min. Filter through a small fluted filter, refiltering if necessary to obtain a clear filtrate. Add 1 drop of pyrrole to 5 mL of the clear filtrate, agitate the mixture until the pyrrole is dissolved, then heat in a water bath at 50°.
Acceptance criteria: A blue color appears.

ASSAY
- **Procedure**
Sample: 400 mg
Analysis: Dissolve the *Sample* in a 100:25 (v/v) mixture of recently boiled and cooled water:2 N sulfuric acid. Titrate the solution immediately with 0.1 N iodine, adding starch TS near the endpoint. Each mL of 0.1 N iodine is equivalent to 8.806 mg of $C_6H_8O_6$.
Acceptance criteria: NLT 99.0% and NMT 100.5% of $C_6H_8O_6$, calculated on the dried basis

IMPURITIES
Inorganic Impurities
- **Lead,** *Lead Limit Test, Flame Atomic Absorption Spectrophotometric Method,* Appendix IIIB
Sample: 10 g
Acceptance criteria: NMT 2 mg/kg

SPECIFIC TESTS
- **Loss on Drying,** Appendix IIC: Dry under reduced pressure over silica gel for 3 h.
Acceptance criteria: NMT 0.4%
- **Optical (Specific) Rotation,** Appendix IIB
Sample solution: 100 mg/mL
Acceptance criteria: $[\alpha]_D^{25}$ between −16.5° and −18.0°
- **Residue on Ignition (Sulfated Ash),** Appendix IIC
Sample: 1.0 g
Acceptance criteria: NMT 0.3%

Erythritol
First Published: Prior to FCC 6
Last Revision: FCC 7

1,2,3,4-Butanetetrol
meso-Erythritol

$C_4H_{10}O_4$ Formula wt 122.12
INS: 968   CAS: [149-32-6]
UNII: RA96B954X6 [erythritol]

DESCRIPTION
Erythritol occurs as white crystals. It is obtained from the fermentation broth of the yeast *Moniliella pollinis* or *Trichosporonoides megachiliensis*. It is stable to heat and is nonhygroscopic. It is soluble in water and is slightly soluble in alcohol. Erythritol melts between 119° and 123°.
Function: Flavor enhancer; humectant; nutritive sweetener; texturizing agent; stabilizer
Packaging and Storage: Store in well-closed containers.

IDENTIFICATION
- **A. Procedure**
Acceptance criteria: The retention time of the major peak in the chromatogram of the *Sample solution* corresponds to that in the chromatogram of the *Standard solution* obtained in the *Assay*.
- **B. Infrared Absorption,** *Spectrophotometric Identification Tests,* Appendix IIIC
Reference standard: USP Erythritol RS
Sample and standard preparation: K
Acceptance criteria: The spectrum of the sample exhibits maxima at the same wavelengths as those in the spectrum of the *Reference standard*.

ASSAY
- **Procedure**
Mobile phase: Twice-distilled water
Standard solution: 5.0 mg/mL USP Erythritol RS on the dried basis, 0.5 mg/mL USP Glycerin RS (glycerol), and 0.5 mg/mL ribitol in *Mobile phase*.
[Note—Save this preparation for the test for *Ribitol and Glycerol*.]
Sample solution: Transfer 4.0 g of sample into a 25-mL volumetric flask, dissolve in and dilute to volume with *Mobile phase* and mix. Pass through a 0.45-μm filter before injecting into the chromatograph.
[Note—Save this preparation for the test for *Ribitol and Glycerol*.]
Chromatographic system, Appendix IIA
Mode: High-performance liquid chromatography with a constant-flow, pulseless pump
Detector: Differential refractive index
Column: Strong cation-exchange resin in the hydrogen form consisting of a macroreticular sulfonated polystyrene divinylbenzene and an 8% cross-linked copolymer, such as MCI-CKO8SH or Shodex KC811 (Mitsubishi Chemical Corp. and Showa Denko, Ltd.), or equivalent
Flow rate: About 0.6 mL/min and maximum pressure system is about 1500 psi
Injection volume: About 10 μL
Analysis: Separately inject the *Standard solution* followed by the *Sample solution* into the chromatograph, and record the peak responses over a period of 60 min. The relative retention times are 1.0 for erythritol, 1.1 for

glycerol, and 0.9 for ribitol. Calculate the percentage of erythritol in the sample using the following formula:

$$\text{Result} = 2.5(C/W)(r_U/r_S)$$

- C = concentration, in mg/mL, of erythritol in the *Standard solution*
- W = weight, in g, of sample taken to prepare the *Sample solution*
- r_U = peak response for erythritol from the *Sample solution*
- r_S = peak response for erythritol from the *Standard solution*.

Acceptance criteria: 99.5%–100.5% of $C_4H_{10}O_4$, calculated on the dried basis

IMPURITIES
Inorganic Impurities
- **LEAD**, *Lead Limit Test, Atomic Absorption Spectrophotometric Graphite Furnace Method, Method I*, Appendix IIIB
  Sample: 5 g
  Acceptance criteria: NMT 1 mg/kg

Organic Impurities
- **RIBITOL AND GLYCEROL**
  Analysis: Determine as directed in the *Assay*. Identify the peak area responses for glycerol and ribitol in the chromatogram of the *Sample solution* by comparison with the chromatogram of the *Standard solution*, and calculate the percentage of glycerol and ribitol by the formula:

  $$\text{Result} = 2.5(C/W)(r_U/r_S)$$

  - C = concentration, in mg/mL, of glycerol or ribitol in the *Standard solution*
  - W = weight, in g, of sample taken to prepare the *Sample solution*
  - r_U = peak response of glycerol or ribitol obtained from the *Sample solution*
  - r_S = peak response of glycerol or ribitol obtained from the *Standard solution*

  Acceptance criteria: The sum of glycerol and ribitol is NMT 0.1%.

SPECIFIC TESTS
- **LOSS ON DRYING**, Appendix IIC: 105° for 4 h
  Acceptance criteria: NMT 0.2%
- **REDUCING SUGARS (AS GLUCOSE)**
  Sample solution: Dissolve 500 mg of sample in 2 mL of water in a 20-mL flask, and mix.
  Control solution: Transfer 2 mL of a glucose solution containing 0.75 mg/mL into a 20-mL flask.
  Analysis: Add 1 mL each of *Fehling's Solution A* and of *Fehling's Solution B* (see *cupric tartrate TS, alkaline*, Solutions and Indicators) to both the *Sample solution* and the *Control solution*, heat to boiling, and cool.
  Acceptance criteria: The resulting *Sample solution* is less turbid than the resulting *Control solution*, which forms a red-brown precipitate (NMT 0.3%).

- **RESIDUE ON IGNITION (SULFATED ASH)**, Appendix IIC
  Sample: 2 g
  Acceptance criteria: NMT 0.1%

Erythrosine[1]
First Published: Prior to FCC 6

CI Food Red 14
CI 45430
Class: Xanthene

$C_{20}H_6O_5I_4Na_2$ Formula wt 879.86
INS: 127
UNII: PN2ZH5LOQY [fd&c red no. 3]   CAS: [16423-68-0]

DESCRIPTION
Erythrosine occurs as a brown powder or granules. It is principally the disodium salt of the monohydrate of 9-(o-carboxyphenyl)-6-hydroxy-2,4,5,7-tetraiodo-3H-xanthen-3-one. It dissolves in water to give a solution red at neutrality, with a yellow-brown precipitate in acid, and with a red precipitate in base. When dissolved in concentrated sulfuric acid, it yields a brown-yellow solution that evolves iodine and a precipitate of the free acid when heated. It is insoluble in ethanol.
Function: Color
Packaging and Storage: Store in well-closed containers.

IDENTIFICATION
- **PROCEDURE**
  Sample solution: 2.8 µg/mL
  Analysis: Adjust the pH of two aliquots of the *Sample solution* to pH 7 and pH 13. Measure the absorbance intensities (A) and wavelength maxima of these solutions with a suitable UV-visible spectrophotometer.
  Acceptance criteria: In neutral and alkaline solutions, A = 0.32 at 527 nm with a shoulder at 490 nm. In acid solution, a yellow-brown precipitate forms.

ASSAY
- **TOTAL COLOR**, *Color Determination, Methods I and III*, Appendix IIIC: Both methods must be used.
  Method I: Spectrophotometric
  Sample: 75 to 100 mg

---

[1] To be used or sold for use to color food that is marketed in the United States, this color additive must be from a batch that has been certified by the U.S. Food and Drug Administration (FDA). If it is not from an FDA-certified batch, it is not a permitted color additive for food use in the United States, even if it is compositionally equivalent. The name FD&C Red No. 3 can be applied only to FDA-certified batches of this color additive. Erythrosine is a common name given to the uncertified colorant. See the monograph entitled *FD&C Red No. 3* for directions for producing an FDA-certified batch.

Analysis: Transfer the *Sample* into a 1-L volumetric flask; dissolve in and dilute to volume with water. Determine as directed at 527 nm using 0.110 L/(mg·cm) for the absorptivity (a) for Erythrosine.

Method III: Gravimetric

Analysis: Determine as directed using 1.074 as the gravimetric conversion factor (F) for Erythrosine.

Acceptance criteria: The average of results obtained from *Methods I and III* is NLT 87.0% total coloring matters.

IMPURITIES
Inorganic Impurities
- **ARSENIC,** *Arsenic Limit Test,* Appendix IIIB
  Sample solution: Prepare as directed for organic compounds.
  Acceptance criteria: NMT 3 mg/kg
- **LEAD,** *Lead Limit Test,* Appendix IIIB
  Sample solution: Prepare as directed for organic compounds.
  Control: 10 µg Pb (10 mL of *Diluted Standard Lead Solution*)
  Acceptance criteria: NMT 10 mg/kg

Organic Impurities
- **UNCOMBINED INTERMEDIATES AND PRODUCTS OF SIDE REACTIONS,** *Color Determination, Method I,* Appendix IIIC
  Sample solution: 20 mg/mL
  Analysis: Calculate the concentrations of 2-(2,4-dihydroxy-3,5-diiodobenzoyl)benzoic acid, iodine, phthalic acid, sodium iodide, and triiodoresorcinol, using the following absorptivities:

  2-(2,4-Dihydroxy-3,5-diiodobenzoyl)benzoic acid: a = 0.047 L/(mg·cm) at 348 nm (alkaline solution)
  Iodine: a = 0.082 L/(mg·cm) at 245 nm (acidic solution)
  Phthalic acid: a = 0.045 L/(mg·cm) at 228 nm (acidic solution)
  Sodium iodide: a = 0.091 L/(mg·cm) at 220 nm (acidic solution).
  Triiodoresorcinol: a = 0.079 L/(mg·cm) at 223 nm (acidic solution)

  Acceptance criteria
  2-(2,4-Dihydroxy-3,5-diiodobenzoyl)benzoic acid: NMT 0.2%
  Sodium iodide: NMT 0.4%
  Triiodoresorcinol: NMT 0.2%
  Unhalogenated intermediates: Total NMT 0.1%

SPECIFIC TESTS
- **COMBINED TESTS**
  Tests
  - **LOSS ON DRYING (VOLATILE MATTER),** *Color Determination,* Appendix IIIC
  - **CHLORIDE,** *Sodium Chloride, Color Determination,* Appendix IIIC
  - **SULFATES (AS SODIUM SALTS),** *Sodium Sulfate, Color Determination,* Appendix IIIC

  Acceptance criteria: NMT 13.0%, in combination
- **ETHER EXTRACTS,** *Color Determination,* Appendix IIIC
  Analysis: Proceed as directed using a solution with a pH of not less than 7.
  Acceptance criteria: NMT 0.2%

- **SUBSIDIARY COLORS,** *Thin-layer Chromatography,* Appendix IIA
  Adsorbent: Silica Gel G
  Developing solvent system: Acetone, chloroform, butylamine, and water (95:25:10:10)
  Sample solution: Transfer 2 g of sample into a 100-mL volumetric flask. Fill the flask about 3/4 full with water, place it in the dark for 1 h, dilute to volume with water, and mix well.
  Application volume: 0.1 mL
  Analysis: Prepare a 20- × 20-cm glass plate coated with a 0.25-mm layer of *Adsorbent*. Spot the *Sample solution* 3 cm from the bottom edge. Allow the plate to dry for about 20 min in the dark, then develop with the *Developing solvent system* in an unlined tank equilibrated for at least 20 min before inserting the plate. Allow the solvent front to reach to within about 3 cm of the top of the plate. Dry the developed plate in the dark. Scrape off each subsidiary color and extract with 3- to 5-mL portions of 50% aqueous ethanol until no color remains on the gel by visual inspection. Dilute each sample to 13 to 15 mL with the 50% ethanol, add a few drops of ammonium hydroxide, and record the final volume. Repeat this procedure for the band of Erythrosine using 10- to 20-mL portions of 50% ethanol, and dilute the eluant to 250 mL in a volumetric flask after adding enough ammonium hydroxide to make the solution slightly alkaline. The approximate band positions (R_F), wavelengths of maximal absorbance (λ), and absorptivities (a) are as follows:

Color	R_F	λ	a
Unknown	0.84	524	0.110
Erythrosine	0.84	526	0.110
2,4,7-isomer	0.76	521	0.140
2,4,5-isomer	0.67	521	0.116
2,4/2,5-isomers	0.45	513	0.145
Unknown	0.45	524	0.110

Record the spectrum of each solution between 400 and 600 nm, and calculate the percent of each subsidiary color by the formula:

$$\text{Result} = (A \times V \times 100)/(a \times W \times b)$$

A = absorbance at the wavelength maximum
V = volume (mL) of the ethanol solution
a = absorptivity (L/(mg·cm)) as given in the table
W = weight (mg) of the sample taken to prepare the *Sample solution*
b = cell pathlength (cm)

Acceptance criteria
Monoiodofluoresceins: NMT 1.0%
Other lower-iodinated fluoresceins: NMT 9.0%

- **WATER-INSOLUBLE MATTER,** *Color Determination,* Appendix IIIC
  Acceptance criteria: NMT 0.2%

Estragole

First Published: Prior to FCC 6

p-Allylanisole
Methyl Chavicol

C₁₀H₁₂O
FEMA: 2411
UNII: 9NIW07V3ET [estragole]

Formula wt 148.20

DESCRIPTION
Estragole occurs as a colorless to light yellow liquid.
Odor: Anise
Solubility: Soluble in alcohol; insoluble or practically insoluble in water
Boiling Point: ~216°

Solubility in Alcohol, Appendix VI: One mL dissolves in 6 mL of 80% alcohol to give a clear solution.
Function: Flavoring agent

IDENTIFICATION
- **INFRARED SPECTRA,** *Spectrophotometric Identification Tests,* Appendix IIIC
  Acceptance criteria: The spectrum of the sample exhibits relative maxima at the same wavelengths as those of the spectrum below.

ASSAY
- **PROCEDURE:** Proceed as directed under *M-1a,* Appendix XI.
  Acceptance criteria: NLT 95.0% of C₁₀H₁₂O

SPECIFIC TESTS
- **REFRACTIVE INDEX,** Appendix II: At 20°
  Acceptance criteria: Between 1.519 and 1.524
- **SPECIFIC GRAVITY:** Determine at 25° by any reliable method (see *General Provisions*).
  Acceptance criteria: Between 0.960 and 0.968

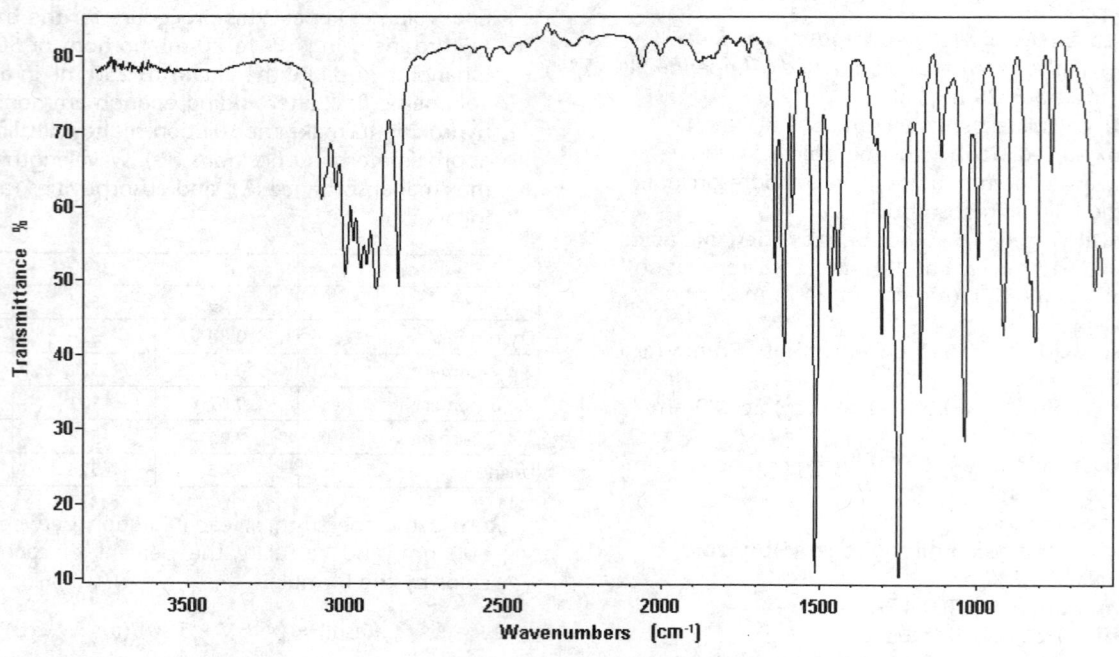

Estragole

Ethone

First Published: Prior to FCC 6

1-(*p*-Methoxyphenyl)-1-penten-3-one

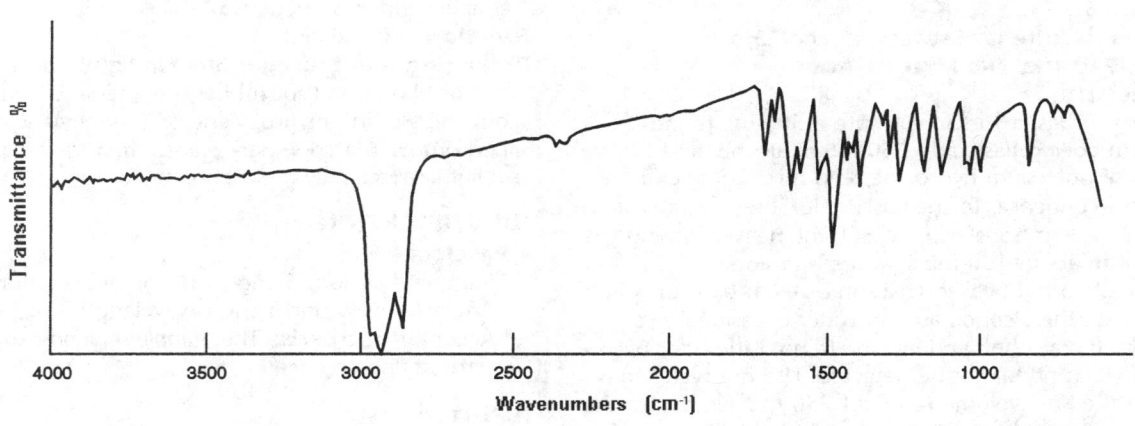

C₁₂H₁₄O₂   Formula wt 190.24
FEMA: 2673
UNII: U0ZZO1ACOR [ethone]

DESCRIPTION
Ethone occurs as a white to pale yellow crystalline solid.
Odor: Nutty, maple
Solubility in Alcohol, Appendix VI: One g dissolves in 7 mL of 95% alcohol.

Function: Flavoring agent

IDENTIFICATION
- **INFRARED SPECTRA,** *Spectrophotometric Identification Tests,* Appendix IIIC
  Sample preparation: Mineral oil mull
  Acceptance criteria: The spectrum of the sample exhibits relative maxima at the same wavelengths as those of the spectrum below.

ASSAY
- **PROCEDURE:** Proceed as directed under *M-1b,* Appendix XI.
  Acceptance criteria: NLT 98.0% of C₁₂H₁₄O₂

OTHER REQUIREMENTS
- **SOLIDIFICATION POINT,** Appendix IIB
  Acceptance criteria: NLT 59.0°

Ethone (Mineral Oil Mull)

Ethoxylated Mono- and Diglycerides

First Published: Prior to FCC 6

Polyoxyethylene (20) Mono- and Diglycerides of Fatty Acids
Polyglycerate (60)
INS: 488

DESCRIPTION
Ethoxylated Mono- and Diglycerides occur as a pale, slightly yellow-colored, oily liquid or semigel. They are a mixture of stearate, palmitate, and lesser amounts of myristate partial esters of glycerin condensed with approximately 20 moles of ethylene oxide per mole of alpha-monoglyceride reaction mixture, having an average molecular weight of 535 (±10%). They are soluble in water, in alcohol, and in xylene. They are partially soluble in mineral oil and in vegetable oils.

Function: Dough conditioner; emulsifier
Packaging and Storage: Store in well-closed containers. [NOTE—If the product is manufactured by direct esterification of glycerin with a mixture of primary stearic, palmitic, and myristic acids, then the intermediate product (before reaction with ethylene oxide) has an acid value of not greater than 0.3 and a water content of not greater than 0.2%.]

IDENTIFICATION
- **A. PROCEDURE**
  Sample solution: 50 mg/mL
  Analysis: Add 5 mL of 1 N sodium hydroxide to 5 mL of the *Sample solution.* Boil the solution for a few min, cool, and acidify with 2.7 N hydrochloric acid.
  Acceptance criteria: The solution is strongly opalescent.
- **B. PROCEDURE**
  Sample solution: 46 : 54 (v/v) mixture of sample:water at 40° or cooler
  Acceptance criteria: A gelatinous mass forms.

386 / Ethoxylated Mono- and Diglycerides / Monographs

IMPURITIES
Inorganic Impurities
- **LEAD**, *Lead Limit Test, Atomic Absorption Spectrophotometric Graphite Furnace, Method II,* Appendix IIIB
  Acceptance criteria: NMT 1 mg/kg
Organic Impurities
- **1,4-DIOXANE**, *1,4-Dioxane Limit Test,* Appendix IIIB
  Acceptance criteria: Passes test

SPECIFIC TESTS
- **ACID VALUE (FATS AND RELATED SUBSTANCES)**, *Method II,* Appendix VII
  Acceptance criteria: NMT 2
- **HYDROXYL VALUE**, *Method II,* Appendix VII
  Acceptance criteria: Between 65 and 80
- **OXYETHYLENE CONTENT (APPARENT)**, *Oxyethylene Determination,* Appendix VII
  Sample: 70 mg
  Acceptance criteria: NLT 60.5% and NMT 65.0%, calculated as ethylene oxide (C_2H_4O), on the anhydrous basis
- **SAPONIFICATION VALUE**, Appendix VII
  Sample: 6 g
  Acceptance criteria: Between 65 and 75
- **STEARIC, PALMITIC, AND MYRISTIC ACIDS**
  Sample: 25 g
  Analysis: Transfer the *Sample* into a 500-mL round-bottom boiling flask, add 250 mL of alcohol and 7.5 g of potassium hydroxide, and mix. Connect a suitable condenser to the flask, reflux the mixture for 1 to 2 h, then transfer to an 800-mL beaker, rinsing the flask with about 100 mL of water and adding the washings to the beaker. Heat on a steam bath to evaporate the alcohol, adding water occasionally to replace the alcohol, and evaporate until the odor of alcohol can no longer be detected. Use hot water to adjust the final volume to about 250 mL. Neutralize the soap solution with 1 : 2 sulfuric acid; add 10% in excess; and while stirring, heat until the fatty acid layer separates. Transfer the fatty acids into a 500- mL separatory funnel, wash with three or four 20-mL portions of hot water, and combine the washings with the original aqueous layer from the saponification. Extract the combined aqueous layer with three 50-mL portions of petroleum ether, add the extracts to the fatty acid layer, evaporate to dryness in a tared dish, cool, and weigh. The product so obtained has an *Acid Value* between 199 and 211 (*Method I,* Appendix VII) and a *Solidification Point* not less than 50° (Appendix IIB).
  Acceptance criteria: Between 31 and 33 g per 100 g of sample
- **WATER**, *Water Determination,* Appendix IIB
  Acceptance criteria: NMT 1.0%

Ethoxyquin
First Published: Prior to FCC 6
Last Revision: First Supplement, FCC 6

6-Ethoxy-1,2-dihydro-2,2,4-trimethylquinoline

$C_{14}H_{19}NO$ Formula wt 217.31
INS: 324 CAS: [91-53-2]
UNII: 9T1410R4OR [ethoxyquin]

DESCRIPTION
Ethoxyquin occurs as a clear yellow to red liquid that may darken with age without affecting its antioxidant activity. It is a mixture consisting predominantly of the monomer ($C_{14}H_{19}NO$). It also contains dimers and other polymers of $C_{14}H_{19}NO$. Its specific gravity is about 1.02, and its refractive index is about 1.57.
Function: Antioxidant
Packaging and Storage: Store in tightly closed carbon steel or black iron (not rubber, neoprene, or nylon) containers or in polypropylene or polyethylene drums or lined drums in a cool, dark place. Prolonged exposure to sunlight causes polymerization.

IDENTIFICATION
- **PROCEDURE**
  Sample solution: 1 mg in 10 mL of acetonitrile
  Analysis: View under short-wavelength UV light.
  Acceptance criteria: The *Sample solution* exhibits a strong fluorescence.

ASSAY
- **PROCEDURE**
  Sample: 200 mg
  Analysis: Transfer the *Sample* into a 150-mL beaker containing 50 mL of glacial acetic acid and immediately titrate with 0.1 N perchloric acid in glacial acetic acid, determining the endpoint potentiometrically. [**CAUTION**—Handle perchloric acid in an appropriate fume hood.] Perform a blank determination (see *General Provisions*) and make any necessary correction. Each mL of 0.1 N perchloric acid is equivalent to 21.73 mg of $C_{14}H_{19}NO$.
  Acceptance criteria: NLT 91.0% $C_{14}H_{19}NO$

IMPURITIES
Inorganic Impurities
- **LEAD**, *Lead Limit Test, Flame Atomic Absorption Spectrophotometric Method,* Appendix IIIB
  Sample: 10 g
  Acceptance criteria: NMT 2 mg/kg
Organic Impurities
- **ETHOXYQUIN-RELATED IMPURITIES:** Low-boiling monomers and high-boiling dimers, trimers, and oligomers of Ethoxyquin

Analysis: Calculate the quantity, in percentage, of related impurities by the formula:

Result = 100 − (%Assay + %*p*-Phenetidine)

Acceptance criteria: NMT 8.0%

- *p*-PHENETIDINE
  Standard solution: [CAUTION—Perform all steps in a fume hood and away from a source of ignition. Wear appropriate protective equipment, including gloves.] Transfer approximately 200 mg of *p*-phenetidine and approximately 200 mg of diphenyl ether, both accurately weighed, into a 4-dram bottle, add 10 mL of toluene and 5 drops of 10% sodium hydroxide, cap, and shake vigorously to dissolve. Prepare in triplicate. [NOTE—Both the *p*-phenetidine and the diphenyl ether must be of known purity. Unless the reagent supplier's reported purity is certified quantitative and traceable, determine the purity of a reagent standard by conducting an area percent profile by injecting 0.1 μL on the same column and at conditions analogous to those described below. The area percent corresponding to the standard in the chromatograph represents its purity.]
  Sample preparation: Transfer 0.1 g of sample into a 4-dram vial. Add between 0.010 and 0.015 g of diphenyl ether, accurately weighed, 10 mL of toluene, and 5 drops of 10% sodium hydroxide solution; cap the vial; and shake well. Allow the vial to stand until the caustic layer settles to the bottom, and filter the neutralized sample through a 0.45-μm polytetrafluoroethylene (PTFE) filter, or equivalent.
  Chromatographic system, Appendix IIA
    Mode: Gas chromatography (HP 6890, or equivalent)
    Detector: Flame-ionization detector (FID)
    Column: 30-m × 0.25-mm (id) GC capillary column (DB-5MS, or equivalent) having a film thickness of 0.25 μm
    Temperatures
      Injector: 250°
      Detector: 280°
      Column: Initially 50° with 1 min hold-time, linear gradient increase of 10°/min to 280°, final hold-time at 280° of 10 min
    Carrier gas: Helium
    Flow rates
      Carrier gas: 2.3 mL/min
      Makeup: 50 mL/min
      Hydrogen (to burner): 45 mL/min
      Air (to burner): 450 mL/min
      Split flow rate: 232 mL/min
      Total flow rate: 237 mL/min
    Injection size: 1.0 μL
    Injector type: Split injector port
  Standardization: Inject the *Standard solution* into the chromatograph. Calculate the *p*-phenetidine factor (F) by the formula:

  Result = $(A_{DE} \times W_{PF} \times P_{PF})/(A_{PF} \times W_{DE} \times P_{DE})$

  A_{DE} = area response for diphenyl ether
  A_{PF} = area response for *p*-phenetidine
  W_{PF} = weight (g) of *p*-phenetidine
  W_{DE} = weight (g) of diphenyl ether
  P_{PF} = purity of *p*-phenetidine
  P_{DE} = purity of diphenyl ether
  Analysis: Inject the *Sample preparation* into the gas chromatograph and calculate the content of *p*-phenetidine, in percentage, by the formula:

  Result = $(A_P \times W_D \times F)/(W_S \times A_D)$

  A_P = area of the *p*-phenetidine peak
  A_D = area of the diphenyl ether peak
  W_D = weight (g) of diphenyl ether in the *Sample preparation*
  W_S = weight (g) of the sample taken
  F = *p*-phenetidine factor (calculated above)
  Acceptance criteria: NMT 3.0%

2-Ethyl Fenchol

First Published: Prior to FCC 6

$C_{12}H_{22}O$ — Formula wt 182.31
FEMA: 3491
UNII: OH8YI97N62 [2-ethyl fenchol]

DESCRIPTION
2-Ethyl Fenchol occurs as a pale yellow liquid.
Odor: Sharp, camphoraceous, earthy
Solubility: Soluble in alcohol, propylene glycol, most fixed oils; insoluble or practically insoluble in water
Boiling Point: ~105° (15 mm Hg)
Function: Flavoring agent

IDENTIFICATION
- INFRARED SPECTRA, *Spectrophotometric Identification Tests,* Appendix IIIC
  Acceptance criteria: The spectrum of the sample exhibits relative maxima at the same wavelengths as those of the spectrum below.

ASSAY
- PROCEDURE: Proceed as directed under *M-1a,* Appendix XI.
  Acceptance criteria: NLT 95.0% of $C_{12}H_{22}O$

SPECIFIC TESTS
- REFRACTIVE INDEX, Appendix II: At 20°
  Acceptance criteria: Between 1.470 and 1.491
- SPECIFIC GRAVITY: Determine at 25° by any reliable method (see *General Provisions*).
  Acceptance criteria: Between 0.946 and 0.967

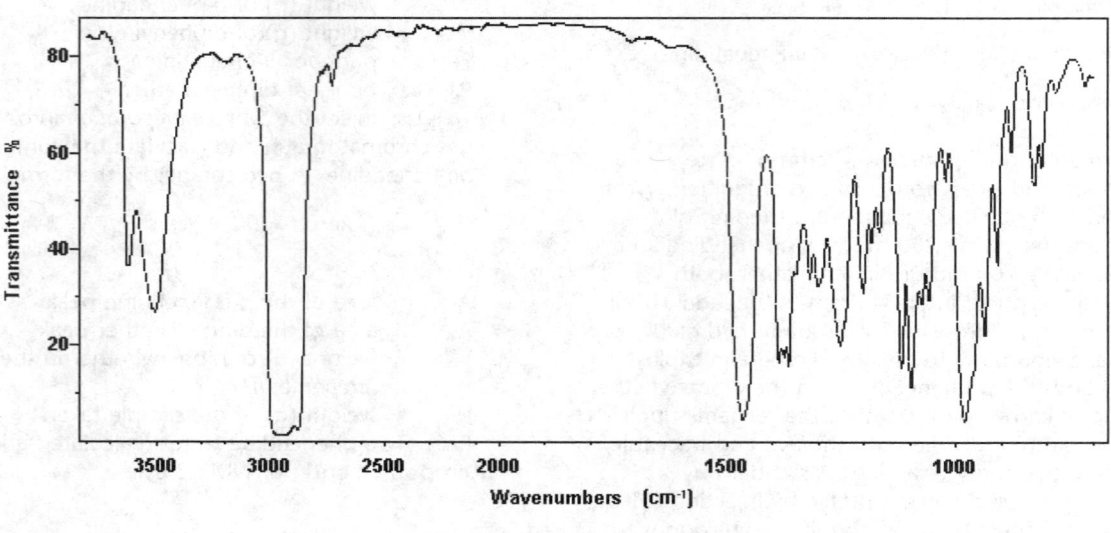

2-Ethyl Fenchol

2-Ethyl Hexanol

First Published: Prior to FCC 6

2-Ethyl-1-hexanol

$C_8H_{18}O$ Formula wt 130.23
FEMA: 3151
UNII: XZV7TAA77P [2-ethylhexanol]

DESCRIPTION
2-Ethyl Hexanol occurs as a colorless to pale yellow liquid.
Odor: Green
Solubility: Soluble in propylene glycol, vegetable oils; insoluble or practically insoluble in water
Boiling Point: ~183°
Solubility in Alcohol, Appendix VI: One mL dissolves in 1 mL of 95% ethanol.
Function: Flavoring agent

ASSAY
- **Procedure:** Proceed as directed under *M-1b*, Appendix XI.
  Acceptance criteria: NLT 97.0% of $C_8H_{18}O$

SPECIFIC TESTS
- **Refractive Index,** Appendix II: At 20°
  Acceptance criteria: Between 1.429 and 1.434
- **Specific Gravity:** Determine at 25° by any reliable method (see *General Provisions*).
  Acceptance criteria: Between 0.830 and 0.834

2-Ethyl-3,5(6)-dimethylpyrazine

First Published: Prior to FCC 6

$C_8H_{12}N_2$ Formula wt 136.20
FEMA: 3149
UNII: 1D80F4PE6E [2-ethyl-3,(5 or 6)-dimethylpyrazine]

DESCRIPTION
2-Ethyl-3,5(6)-dimethylpyrazine occurs as a colorless to slightly yellow liquid.
Odor: Roasted cocoa
Solubility: Soluble in propylene glycol, vegetable oils
Boiling Point: ~180° to 181°
Function: Flavoring agent

IDENTIFICATION
- **Infrared Spectra,** *Spectrophotometric Identification Tests,* Appendix IIIC
  Acceptance criteria: The spectrum of the sample exhibits relative maxima at the same wavelengths as those of the spectrum below.

ASSAY
- **Procedure:** Proceed as directed under *M-1a*, Appendix XI.
  Acceptance criteria: NLT 95.0% of $C_8H_{12}N_2$

SPECIFIC TESTS
- **Refractive Index,** Appendix II: At 20°
  Acceptance criteria: Between 1.500 and 1.503
- **Specific Gravity:** Determine at 25° by any reliable method (see *General Provisions*).

Acceptance criteria: Between 0.950 and 0.970

OTHER REQUIREMENTS
- **WATER,** *Water Determination, Method I,* Appendix IIB
  [NOTE—Use freshly distilled pyridine as solvent.]
  Acceptance criteria: NMT 0.1%

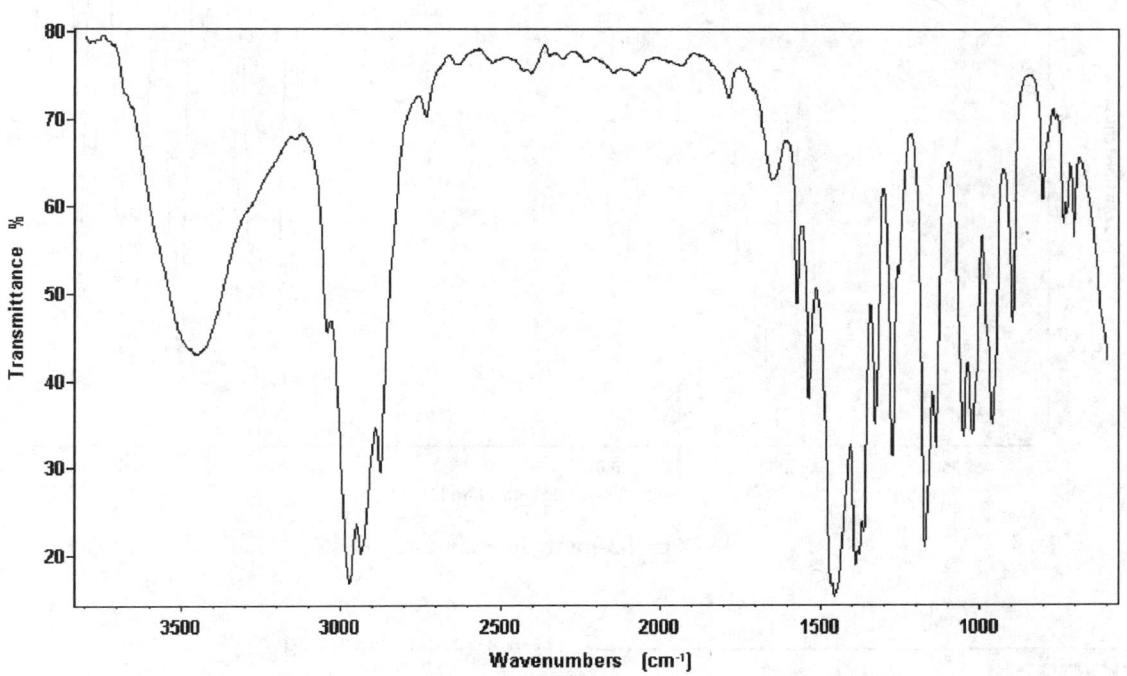

2-Ethyl-3,5(6)-dimethylpyrazine

2-Ethyl-3-methylpyrazine

First Published: Prior to FCC 6

$C_7H_{10}N_2$ Formula wt 122.17
FEMA: 3155
UNII: 9GF35MK66U [2-ethyl-3-methylpyrazine]

DESCRIPTION
2-Ethyl-3-methylpyrazine occurs as a colorless to slightly yellow liquid.
Odor: Strong, raw potato
Solubility: Soluble in propylene glycol, vegetable oils, water
Boiling Point: ~57° (10 mm Hg)
Solubility in Alcohol, Appendix VI: One mL dissolves in 1 mL of 95% ethanol.
Function: Flavoring agent

IDENTIFICATION
- **INFRARED SPECTRA,** *Spectrophotometric Identification Tests,* Appendix IIIC
  Acceptance criteria: The spectrum of the sample exhibits relative maxima at the same wavelengths as those of the spectrum below.

ASSAY
- **PROCEDURE:** Proceed as directed under *M-1a,* Appendix XI.
  Acceptance criteria: NLT 98.0% of $C_7H_{10}N_2$

SPECIFIC TESTS
- **REFRACTIVE INDEX,** Appendix II: (at 20°)
  Acceptance criteria: Between 1.502 and 1.505
- **SPECIFIC GRAVITY:** Determine at 25° by any reliable method (see *General Provisions*).
  Acceptance criteria: Between 0.978 and 0.988

OTHER REQUIREMENTS
- **WATER,** *Water Determination, Method I,* Appendix IIB
  [NOTE—Use freshly distilled pyridine as solvent.]
  Acceptance criteria: NMT 0.1%

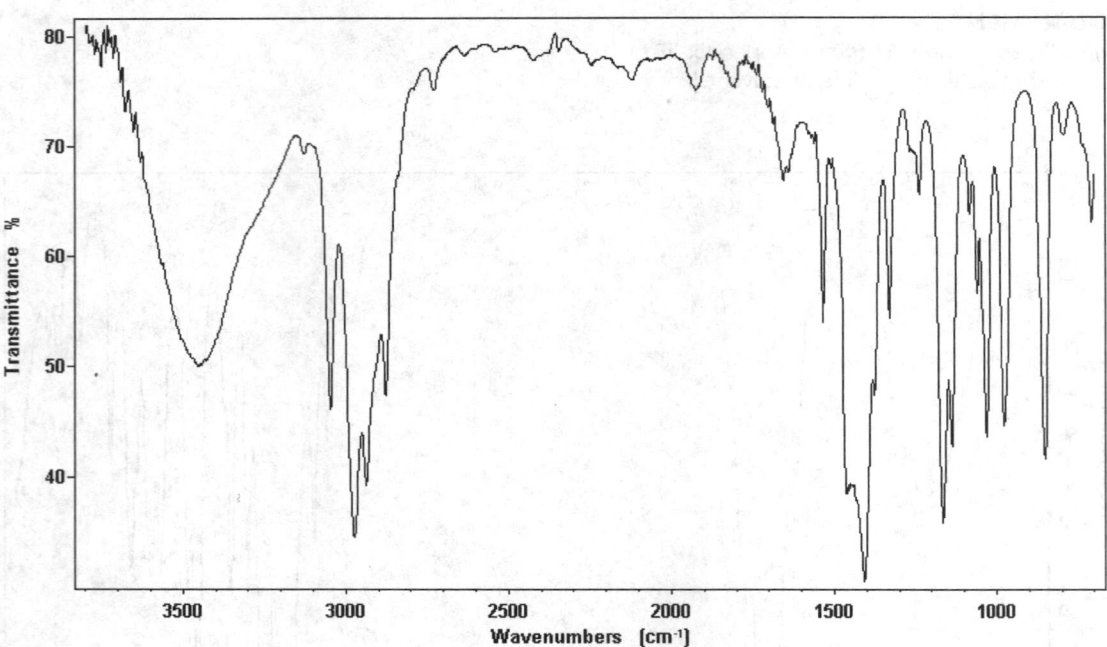

2-Ethyl-3-methylpyrazine

3-Ethyl Pyridine

First Published: Prior to FCC 6

C_7H_9N Formula wt 107.16
FEMA: 3394
UNII: A25I3EZ88V [3-ethylpyridine]

DESCRIPTION
3-Ethyl Pyridine occurs as a colorless to yellow liquid.
Odor: Tobacco
Solubility: Soluble in propylene glycol, vegetable oils; insoluble or practically insoluble in water
Boiling Point: ~166°
Solubility in Alcohol, Appendix VI: One mL dissolves in 1 mL of 95% ethanol.

Function: Flavoring agent

IDENTIFICATION
- **INFRARED SPECTRA,** Spectrophotometric Identification Tests, Appendix IIIC
  Acceptance criteria: The spectrum of the sample exhibits relative maxima at the same wavelengths as those of the spectrum below.

ASSAY
- **PROCEDURE:** Proceed as directed under M-1b, Appendix XI.
  Acceptance criteria: NLT 97.0% of C_7H_9N

SPECIFIC TESTS
- **REFRACTIVE INDEX,** Appendix II: (at 20°)
  Acceptance criteria: Between 1.500 and 1.505
- **SPECIFIC GRAVITY:** Determine at 25° by any reliable method (see General Provisions).
  Acceptance criteria: Between 0.951 and 0.957

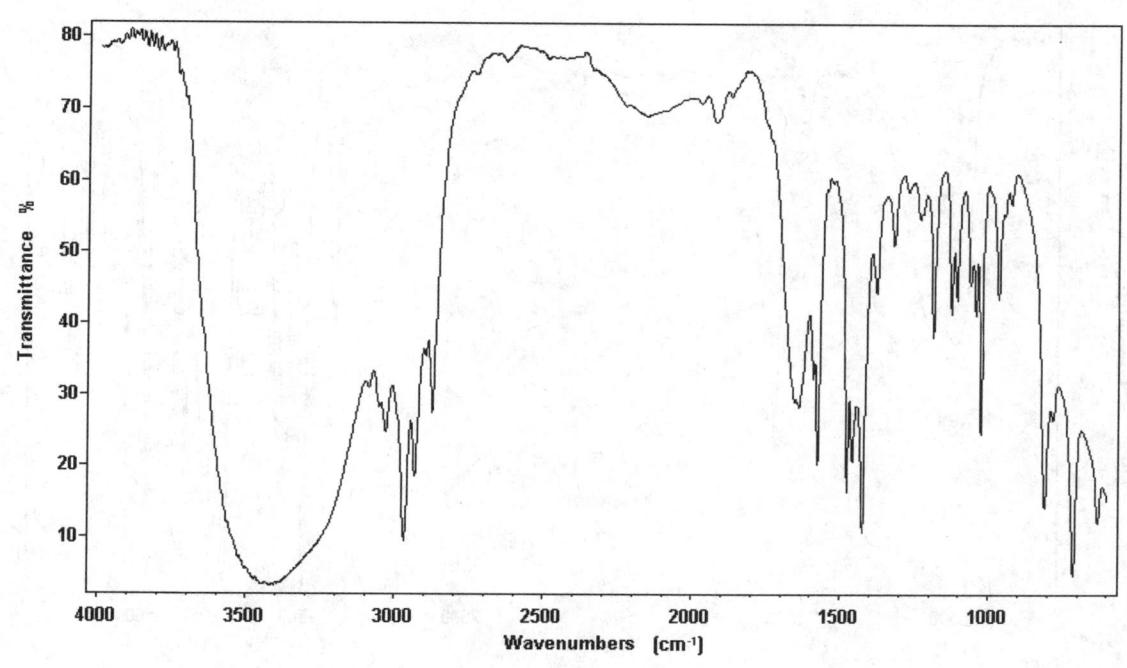

4-Ethyl Guaiacol

First Published: Prior to FCC 6

4-Hydroxy-3-methylethylbenzene

$C_9H_{12}O_2$ Formula wt 152.19
FEMA: 2436
UNII: C9NFD83BJ5 [4-ethylguaiacol]

DESCRIPTION
4-Ethyl Guaiacol occurs as a colorless to pale yellow liquid.
Odor: Warm, spicy, medicinal
Solubility: Soluble in propylene glycol, vegetable oils; insoluble or practically insoluble in water
Boiling Point: ~235°
Solubility in Alcohol, Appendix VI: One mL dissolves in 1 mL of 95% alcohol

Function: Flavoring agent

IDENTIFICATION
- **INFRARED SPECTRA,** *Spectrophotometric Identification Tests,* Appendix IIIC
  Acceptance criteria: The spectrum of the sample exhibits relative maxima at the same wavelengths as those of the spectrum below.

ASSAY
- **PROCEDURE:** Proceed as directed under *M-1a,* Appendix XI.
  Acceptance criteria: NLT 98.0% of $C_9H_{12}O_2$

SPECIFIC TESTS
- **REFRACTIVE INDEX,** Appendix II: At 20°
  Acceptance criteria: Between 1.525 and 1.530
- **SPECIFIC GRAVITY:** Determine at 25° by any reliable method (see *General Provisions*).
  Acceptance criteria: Between 1.061 and 1.064

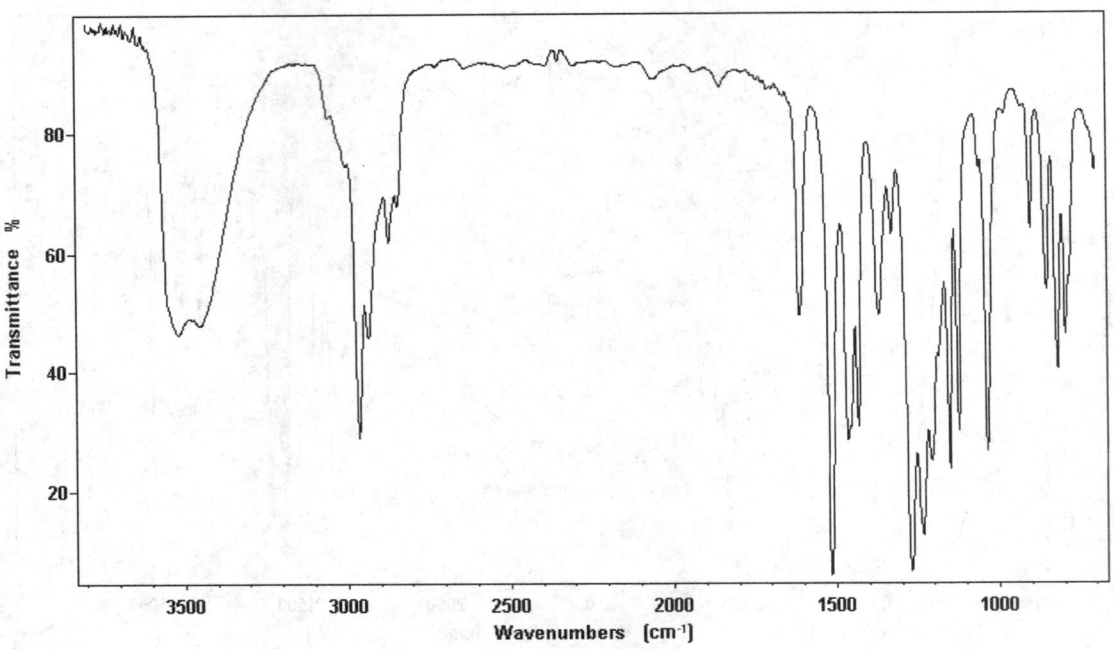

4-Ethyl Guaiacol

5-Ethyl 3-Hydroxy 4-Methyl 2(5H)-Furanone

First Published: Prior to FCC 6

Maple Furanone

$C_7H_{10}O_3$ Formula wt 142.15
FEMA: 3153
UNII: J007136N0N [5-ethyl-3-hydroxy-4-methyl-2(5h)-furanone]

DESCRIPTION
5-Ethyl 3-Hydroxy 4-Methyl 2(5H)-Furanone occurs as a pale yellow to yellow liquid.
Odor: Maple
Solubility: Soluble in propylene glycol, vegetable oils; slightly soluble in water
Boiling Point: ~83° (0.5 mm Hg)
Solubility in Alcohol, Appendix VI: One mL dissolves in 2 mL of 95% ethanol.
Function: Flavoring agent

IDENTIFICATION
- **INFRARED SPECTRA,** Spectrophotometric Identification Tests, Appendix IIIC
  Acceptance criteria: The spectrum of the sample exhibits relative maxima at the same wavelengths as those of the spectrum below.

ASSAY
- **PROCEDURE:** Proceed as directed under *M-1b*, Appendix XI.
  Acceptance criteria: NLT 95% of $C_7H_{10}O_3$

SPECIFIC TESTS
- **REFRACTIVE INDEX,** Appendix II: At 20°
  Acceptance criteria: Between 1.488 and 1.493

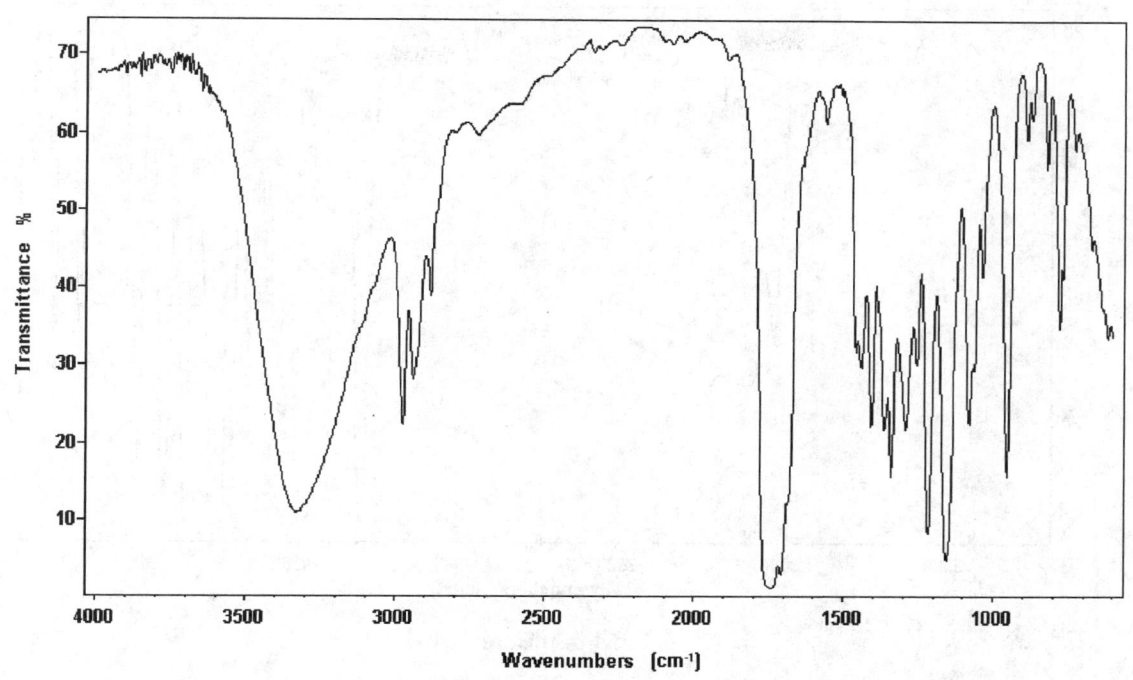

5-Ethyl 3-Hydroxy 4-Methyl 2(5H)-Furanone

Ethyl *p*-Anisate

First Published: Prior to FCC 6

Ethyl *p*-Methoxybenzoate

$C_{10}H_{12}O_3$ Formula wt 180.20
FEMA: 2420
UNII: KJ95H2S7NM [ethyl p-anisate]

DESCRIPTION
Ethyl *p*-Anisate occurs as a colorless to slightly yellow liquid.
Odor: Light, fruity, anise
Solubility: Soluble in alcohol, chloroform, ether; insoluble or practically insoluble in water
Boiling Point: ~270°
Solubility in Alcohol, Appendix VI: One mL dissolves in 7 mL 60% alcohol to give a clear solution

Function: Flavoring agent

IDENTIFICATION
- **INFRARED SPECTRA,** *Spectrophotometric Identification Tests,* Appendix IIIC
  Acceptance criteria: The spectrum of the sample exhibits relative maxima at the same wavelengths as those of the spectrum below.

ASSAY
- **PROCEDURE:** Proceed as directed under *M-1b,* Appendix XI.
  Acceptance criteria: NLT 97.0% of $C_{10}H_{12}O_3$

SPECIFIC TESTS
- **ACID VALUE, FLAVOR CHEMICALS (OTHER THAN ESSENTIAL OILS),** *M-15,* Appendix XI
  Acceptance criteria: NMT 1.0
- **REFRACTIVE INDEX,** Appendix II: At 20°
  Acceptance criteria: Between 1.522 and 1.526
- **SPECIFIC GRAVITY:** Determine at 25° by any reliable method (see *General Provisions*).
  Acceptance criteria: Between 1.101 and 1.104

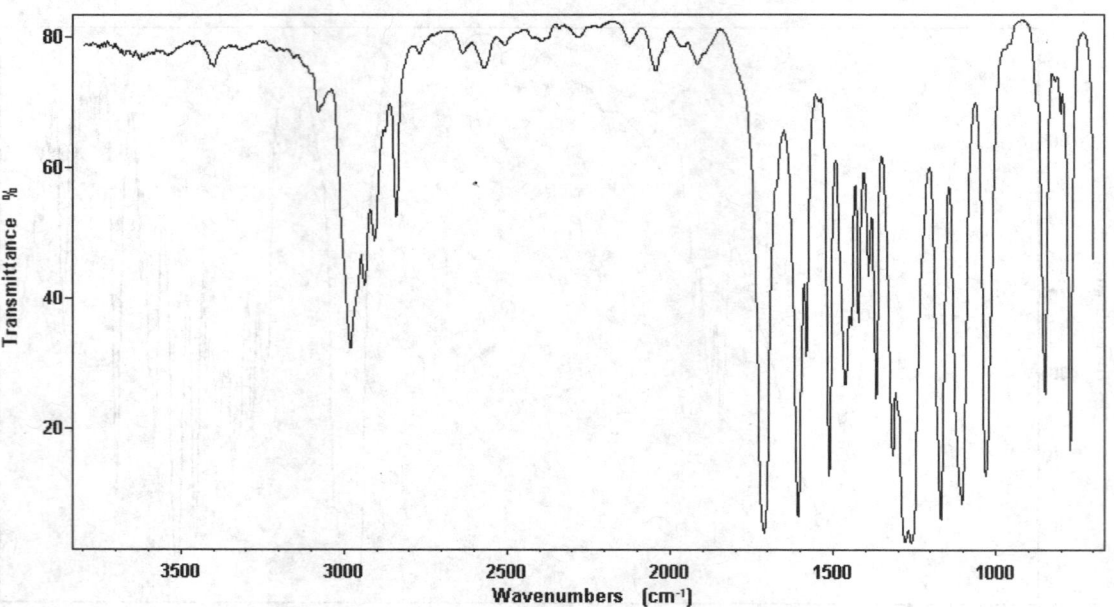

Ethyl p-Anisate

Ethyl 10-Undecenoate

First Published: Prior to FCC 6

C₁₃H₂₄O₂   Formula wt 212.33
FEMA: 2461
UNII: 7P1S77T8BF [ethyl 10-undecenoate]

DESCRIPTION
Ethyl 10-Undecenoate occurs as a colorless to pale yellow liquid.
Odor: Waxy, coconut
Solubility: Soluble in vegetable oils; insoluble or practically insoluble in propylene glycol, water
Boiling Point: ~258° to 259°
Solubility in Alcohol, Appendix VI: One mL dissolves in 1 mL of 95% ethanol.
Function: Flavoring agent

ASSAY
- **Procedure:** Proceed as directed under *M-1b,* Appendix XI.
  Acceptance criteria: NLT 98.0% of C₁₃H₂₄O₂

SPECIFIC TESTS
- **Acid Value, Flavor Chemicals (Other Than Essential Oils),** *M-15,* Appendix XI
  Acceptance criteria: NMT 1.0
- **Refractive Index,** Appendix II: At 20°
  Acceptance criteria: Between 1.436 and 1.440
- **Specific Gravity:** Determine at 25° by any reliable method (see *General Provisions*).
  Acceptance criteria: Between 0.877 and 0.879

Ethyl 2-Methylbutyrate

First Published: Prior to FCC 6

C₇H₁₄O₂   Formula wt 130.19
FEMA: 2443
UNII: L1T4AB29DS [ethyl 2-methylbutyrate]

DESCRIPTION
Ethyl 2-Methylbutyrate occurs as a colorless liquid.
Odor: Strong, green-fruity, apple
Solubility: Soluble in alcohol, propylene glycol; very slightly soluble in water; miscible in most fixed oils
Boiling Point: ~133°
Solubility in Alcohol, Appendix VI: One mL dissolves in 1 mL of 95% ethanol.
Function: Flavoring agent

ASSAY
- **Procedure:** Proceed as directed under *M-1b,* Appendix XI.
  Acceptance criteria: NLT 95.0% of C₇H₁₄O₂ (one isomer)

SPECIFIC TESTS
- **ACID VALUE, FLAVOR CHEMICALS (OTHER THAN ESSENTIAL OILS)**, *M-15*, Appendix XI
  Acceptance criteria: NMT 2.0
- **REFRACTIVE INDEX**, Appendix II: At 20°
  Acceptance criteria: Between 1.393 and 1.400
- **SPECIFIC GRAVITY:** Determine at 25° by any reliable method (see *General Provisions*).
  Acceptance criteria: Between 0.863 and 0.870

Ethyl 2-Methylpentanoate
First Published: Prior to FCC 6

$C_8H_{16}O_2$ Formula wt 144.21
FEMA: 3488
UNII: 405SN8638D [ethyl 2-methylpentanoate]

DESCRIPTION
Ethyl 2-Methylpentanoate occurs as a colorless to pale yellow liquid.
Odor: Fruity

Solubility: Soluble in vegetable oils; insoluble or practically insoluble in propylene glycol, water
Boiling Point: ~153°
Solubility in Alcohol, Appendix VI: One mL dissolves in 1 mL of 95% ethanol.
Function: Flavoring agent

IDENTIFICATION
- **INFRARED SPECTRA**, *Spectrophotometric Identification Tests*, Appendix IIIC
  Acceptance criteria: The spectrum of the sample exhibits relative maxima at the same wavelengths as those of the spectrum below.

ASSAY
- **PROCEDURE:** Proceed as directed under *M-1b*, Appendix XI.
  Acceptance criteria: NLT 98.0% of $C_8H_{16}O_2$

SPECIFIC TESTS
- **ACID VALUE, FLAVOR CHEMICALS (OTHER THAN ESSENTIAL OILS)**, *M-15*, Appendix XI
  Acceptance criteria: NMT 1.0
- **REFRACTIVE INDEX**, Appendix II: At 20°
  Acceptance criteria: Between 1.401 and 1.404
- **SPECIFIC GRAVITY:** Determine at 25° by any reliable method (see *General Provisions*).
  Acceptance criteria: Between 0.859 and 0.865

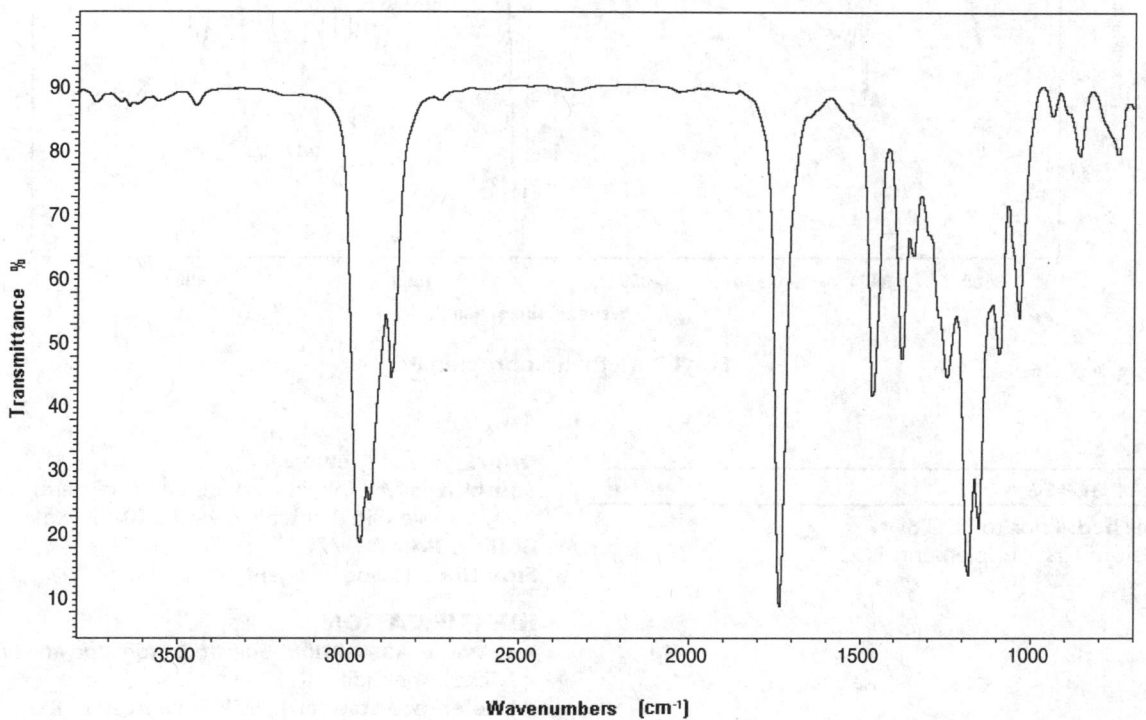

Ethyl 2-Methylpentanoate

Ethyl 3-Methylthiopropionate

First Published: Prior to FCC 6

C₆H₁₂O₂S   Formula wt 148.23
FEMA: 3343
UNII: 1AVT374NII [ethyl 3-methylthiopropionate]

DESCRIPTION
Ethyl 3-Methylthiopropionate occurs as a colorless to pale yellow liquid.
Odor: Onion, fruity, sweet
Solubility: Soluble in propylene glycol, vegetable oils; insoluble or practically insoluble in water
Boiling Point: ~89° to 91° (15 mm Hg)
Solubility in Alcohol, Appendix VI: One mL dissolves in 1 mL of 95% ethanol.

Function: Flavoring agent

IDENTIFICATION
- **INFRARED SPECTRA,** *Spectrophotometric Identification Tests,* Appendix IIIC
  Acceptance criteria: The spectrum of the sample exhibits relative maxima at the same wavelengths as those of the spectrum below.

ASSAY
- **PROCEDURE:** Proceed as directed under *M-1b,* Appendix XI.
  Acceptance criteria: NLT 99.0% of C₆H₁₂O₂S

SPECIFIC TESTS
- **REFRACTIVE INDEX,** Appendix II: At 20°
  Acceptance criteria: Between 1.457 and 1.463
- **SPECIFIC GRAVITY:** Determine at 25° by any reliable method (see *General Provisions*).
  Acceptance criteria: Between 1.030 and 1.035

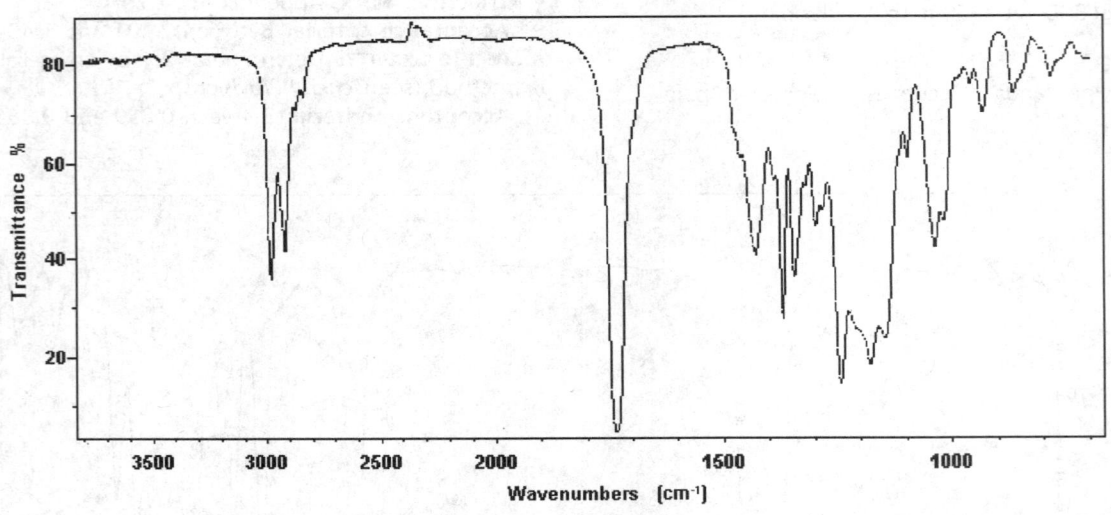

Ethyl 3-Methylthiopropionate

Ethyl Acetate

First Published: Prior to FCC 6
Last Revision: First Supplement, FCC 7

C₄H₈O₂   Formula wt 88.11
FEMA: 2414
UNII: 76845O8NMZ [ethyl acetate]

DESCRIPTION
Ethyl Acetate occurs as a colorless liquid; volatile at low temperatures; flammable.
Odor: Acetous, ethereal
Solubility: Miscible in alcohol, ether, glycerin, most fixed oils, volatile oils; 1 mL dissolves in 10 mL water.
Boiling Point: ~77°
Function: Flavoring agent

IDENTIFICATION
- **INFRARED ABSORPTION,** *Spectrophotometric Identification Tests,* Appendix IIIC
  Reference standard: USP Ethyl Acetate RS
  Sample and standard preparation: F
  Acceptance criteria: The spectrum of the sample exhibits maxima at the same wavelengths as those in the spectrum of the *Reference standard.*

ASSAY
- **PROCEDURE:** Proceed as directed under *M-1b*, Appendix XI.
  Acceptance criteria: NLT 99.0% of $C_4H_8O_2$

SPECIFIC TESTS
- **ACID VALUE, FLAVOR CHEMICALS (OTHER THAN ESSENTIAL OILS),** *M-15,* Appendix XI: Use bromocresol purple TS as the indicator.
  Acceptance criteria: NMT 5.0
- **REFRACTIVE INDEX,** Appendix II: At 20°
  Acceptance criteria: Between 1.370 and 1.375
- **SPECIFIC GRAVITY:** Determine at 25° by any reliable method (see *General Provisions*).
  Acceptance criteria: Between 0.894 and 0.898

OTHER REQUIREMENTS
- **DISTILLATION RANGE,** Appendix IIB
  Acceptance criteria: Between 76° and 77.5°
- **METHYL COMPOUNDS,** *M-10,* Appendix XI
  Acceptance criteria: Passes test
- **READILY CARBONIZABLE SUBSTANCES,** *M-12,* Appendix XI
  Acceptance criteria: Passes test
- **RESIDUE ON EVAPORATION,** *M-16,* Appendix XI: 105°
  Sample: 10 g
  Acceptance criteria: NMT 0.02%

Ethyl Acetoacetate
First Published: Prior to FCC 6

Acetoacetic Ester
Ethyl 3-Oxybutanoate

$C_6H_{10}O_3$ Formula wt 130.14
FEMA: 2415
UNII: IZP61H3TB1 [ethyl acetoacetate]

DESCRIPTION
Ethyl Acetoacetate occurs as a colorless to very light yellow, mobile liquid.
Odor: Fruity
Solubility: Miscible in alcohol, ether, ethyl acetate; 1 mL dissolves in 12 mL water.
Boiling Point: ~181°
Function: Flavoring agent

IDENTIFICATION
- **INFRARED SPECTRA,** *Spectrophotometric Identification Tests,* Appendix IIIC
  Acceptance criteria: The spectrum of the sample exhibits relative maxima at the same wavelengths as those of the spectrum below.

ASSAY
- **PROCEDURE:** Proceed as directed under *M-1b,* Appendix XI.
  Acceptance criteria: NLT 97.5% of $C_6H_{10}O_3$

SPECIFIC TESTS
- **ACID VALUE, FLAVOR CHEMICALS (OTHER THAN ESSENTIAL OILS),** *M-15,* Appendix XI
  [NOTE—Use bromocresol purple TS as the indicator.]
  Acceptance criteria: NMT 5.0
- **REFRACTIVE INDEX,** Appendix II: At 20°
  Acceptance criteria: Between 1.418 and 1.421
- **SPECIFIC GRAVITY:** Determine at 25° by any reliable method (see *General Provisions*).
  Acceptance criteria: Between 1.022 and 1.027

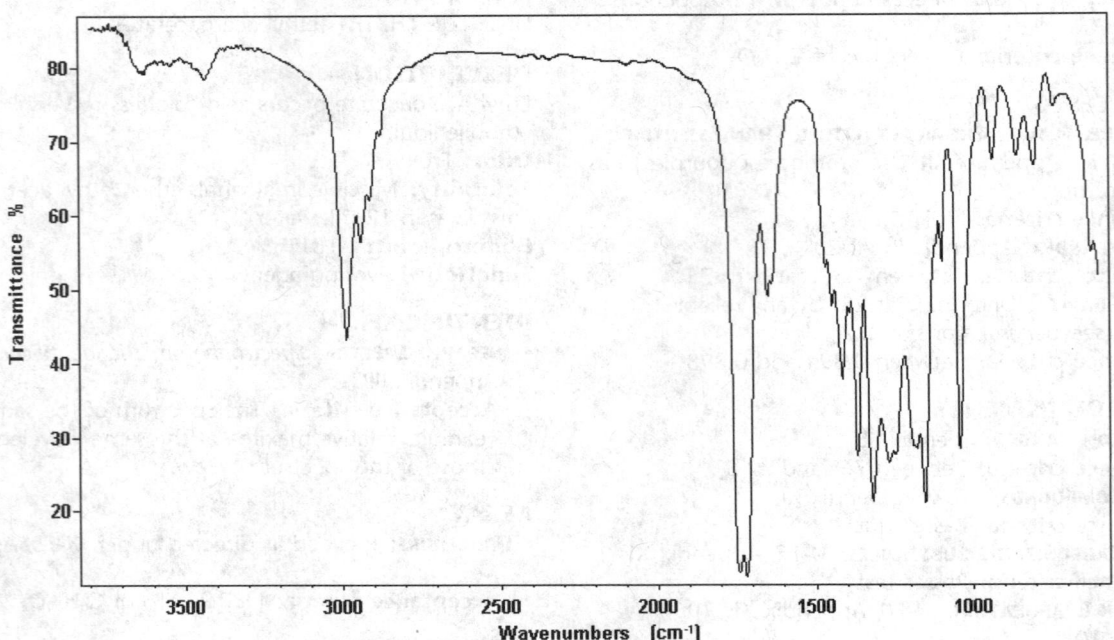

Ethyl Acetoacetate

Ethyl Acrylate

First Published: Prior to FCC 6

C₅H₈O₂   Formula wt 100.12
FEMA: 2418
UNII: 71E6178C9T [ethyl acrylate]

DESCRIPTION
Ethyl Acrylate occurs as a colorless, mobile liquid. It acts as a lachrymator.
Odor: Intense, harsh, fruity
Solubility: Miscible in alcohol, ether; 1 mL dissolves in 50 mL of water.
Boiling Point: ~99°
Function: Flavoring agent

IDENTIFICATION
- **INFRARED SPECTRA,** *Spectrophotometric Identification Tests,* Appendix IIIC
  Acceptance criteria: The spectrum of the sample exhibits relative maxima at the same wavelengths as those of the spectrum below.

ASSAY
- **PROCEDURE:** Proceed as directed under *M-1b*, Appendix XI.
  Acceptance criteria: NLT 99.5% of C₅H₈O₂

SPECIFIC TESTS
- **ACID VALUE, FLAVOR CHEMICALS (OTHER THAN ESSENTIAL OILS),** *M-15,* Appendix XI
  Acceptance criteria: NMT 5.0
- **SPECIFIC GRAVITY:** Determine at 25° by any reliable method (see *General Provisions*).
  Acceptance criteria: Between 0.916 and 0.919

OTHER REQUIREMENTS
- **ANTIOXIDANTS,** *M-6,* Appendix XI
  Acceptance criteria: NMT 0.022%
- **WATER,** *Water Determination, Method I,* Appendix IIB
  Acceptance criteria: NMT 0.05%

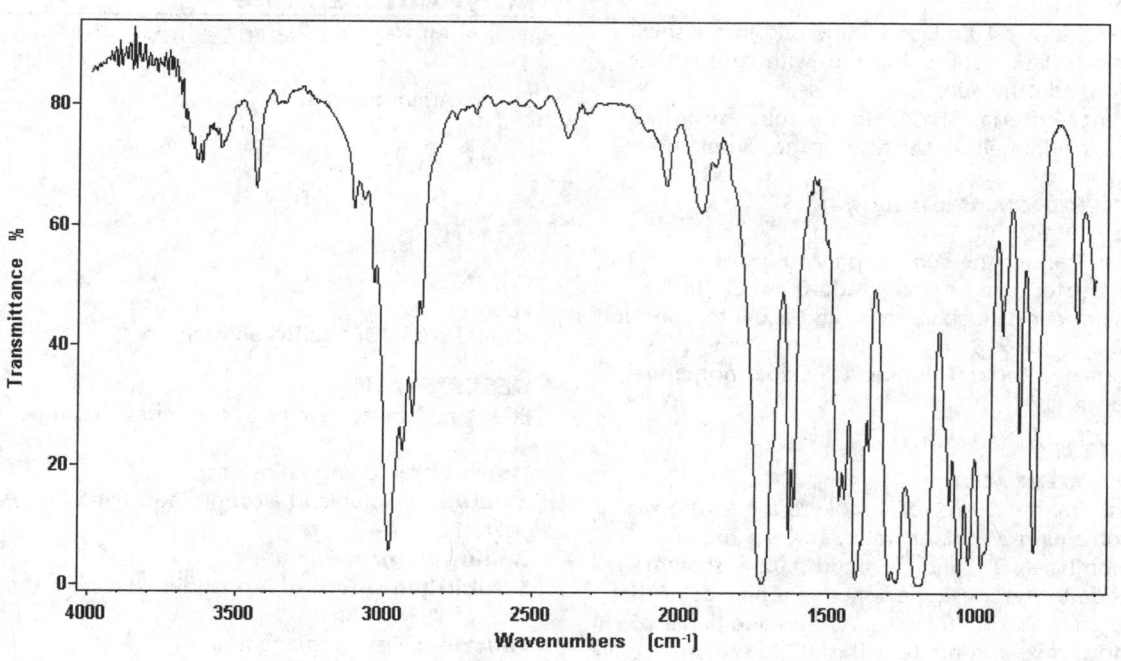

Ethyl Acrylate

Ethyl Alcohol

First Published: Prior to FCC 6

Alcohol
Ethanol

C₂H₆O
UNII: 3K9958V90M [alcohol]

Formula wt 46.07
CAS: [64-17-5]

DESCRIPTION
Ethyl Alcohol occurs as a clear, colorless, mobile liquid. It is miscible with water, with ether, and with chloroform. It boils at about 78° and is flammable. Its refractive index at 20° is about 1.364.
[NOTE—This monograph applies only to undenatured ethyl alcohol.]

Function: Extraction solvent; carrier solvent

Packaging and Storage: Store in tight containers, remote from fire.

ASSAY
- **SPECIFIC GRAVITY:** Determine by any reliable method (see *General Provisions*).
  Acceptance criteria: NMT 0.8096 at 25°/25° (equivalent to 0.8161 at 15.56°/15.56°), and equivalent to NLT 94.9% by volume (92.3% by weight) of C₂H₆O

IMPURITIES
Inorganic Impurities
- **LEAD,** *Lead Limit Test, Atomic Absorption Spectrophotometric Graphite Furnace Method, Method I,* Appendix IIIB
  Sample: 10 g
  Acceptance criteria: NMT 0.5 mg/kg

Organic Impurities
- **FUSEL OIL**
  Sample: 10 mL
  Analysis: Mix the *Sample* with 1 mL of glycerin and 1 mL of water, and allow to evaporate from a piece of clean, odorless, absorbent paper.
  Acceptance criteria: No foreign odor is perceptible when the last traces of alcohol leave the paper.

- **KETONES, ISOPROPYL ALCOHOL**
  Sample: 1 mL
  Analysis: Transfer the *Sample*, 3 mL of water, and 10 mL of mercuric sulfate TS to a test tube; mix; and heat in a boiling water bath.
  Acceptance criteria: No precipitate forms within 3 min.

- **METHANOL**
  Analysis: To 1 drop of sample in a test tube, add 1 drop of 1:20 phosphoric acid and 1 drop of 50 mg/mL potassium permanganate solution, mix, and allow to stand for 1 min. Add, dropwise, 100 mg/mL sodium bisulfite solution until the permanganate color disappears. If a brown color remains, add 1 drop of the phosphoric acid solution. Add 5 mL of freshly prepared chromotropic acid TS to the colorless solution, and heat it in a water bath at 60° for 10 min.
  Acceptance criteria: No violet color appears.

- **SUBSTANCES DARKENED BY SULFURIC ACID**
  Sample: 10 mL
  Analysis: Transfer 10 mL of sulfuric acid into a small Erlenmeyer flask, cool to 10° and, with constant agitation, add the *Sample*, dropwise.
  Acceptance criteria: The mixture is colorless or has no more color than either the acid or the sample before mixing.
- **SUBSTANCES REDUCING PERMANGANATE**
  Sample: 20 mL
  Analysis: Transfer the *Sample*, previously cooled to 15°, to a glass-stoppered cylinder, add 0.1 mL of 0.1 N potassium permanganate, mix, and allow to stand for 5 min.
  Acceptance criteria: The pink color does not entirely disappear.

SPECIFIC TESTS
- **ACIDITY (AS ACETIC ACID)**
  Analysis: Transfer 10 mL of sample to a glass-stoppered flask containing 25 mL of water, add 0.5 mL of phenolphthalein TS, and then add 0.02 N sodium hydroxide to the first appearance of a pink color that persists after shaking for 30 s. Add an additional 25 mL of sample, mix, and titrate with 0.02 N sodium hydroxide until the pink color is restored.
  Acceptance criteria: NMT 0.5 mL of 0.02 N sodium hydroxide is required to restore the pink color. (NMT 0.003%)
- **ALKALINITY (AS NH$_3$)**
  Sample: 25 mL
  Analysis: Add 2 drops of methyl red TS to 25 mL of water, add 0.02 N sulfuric acid until a red color just appears, then add the *Sample*, and mix.
  Acceptance criteria: NMT 0.2 mL of 0.02 N sulfuric acid is required to restore the red color. (NMT 3 mg/kg)
- **NONVOLATILE RESIDUE**
  Sample: 125 mL (about 100 g)
  Analysis: Evaporate the *Sample* to dryness in a tared dish on a steam bath, dry the residue at 105° for 30 min, cool, and weigh.
  Acceptance criteria: NMT 0.003%
- **SOLUBILITY IN WATER**
  Analysis: Transfer 50 mL of sample to a 100-mL glass-stoppered graduated cylinder, dilute to 100 mL with water, and mix. Place the graduated cylinder, in a water bath maintained at 10°, and allow it to stand for 30 min.
  Acceptance criteria: No haze or turbidity develops.

Ethyl Anthranilate

First Published: Prior to FCC 6

Ethyl *o*-Aminobenzoate

$C_9H_{11}NO_2$ Formula wt 165.19
FEMA: 2421
UNII: 38Y050IUE4 [ethyl anthranilate]

DESCRIPTION
Ethyl Anthranilate occurs as a colorless to amber-colored liquid.
Odor: Floral, orange blossom
Solubility: Soluble in alcohol, most fixed oils, propylene glycol
Boiling Point: ~267°
Solubility in Alcohol, Appendix VI: One mL dissolves in 2 mL of 70% alcohol.
Function: Flavoring agent

IDENTIFICATION
- **INFRARED SPECTRA,** *Spectrophotometric Identification Tests,* Appendix IIIC
  Acceptance criteria: The spectrum of the sample exhibits relative maxima at the same wavelengths as those of the spectrum below.

ASSAY
- **PROCEDURE:** Proceed as directed under *Esters,* Appendix VI.
  Sample: 1.5 g
  Analysis: Use 82.6 as the equivalence factor (e).
  Acceptance criteria: NLT 96.0% of total esters as $C_9H_{11}NO_2$

SPECIFIC TESTS
- **ACID VALUE, FLAVOR CHEMICALS (OTHER THAN ESSENTIAL OILS),** *M-15,* Appendix XI
  Acceptance criteria: NMT 1.0
- **REFRACTIVE INDEX,** Appendix II: At 20°
  Acceptance criteria: Between 1.563 and 1.566
- **SPECIFIC GRAVITY:** Determine at 25° by any reliable method (see *General Provisions*).
  Acceptance criteria: Between 1.115 and 1.120

OTHER REQUIREMENTS
- **SOLIDIFICATION POINT,** Appendix IIB
  Acceptance criteria: NLT 13°

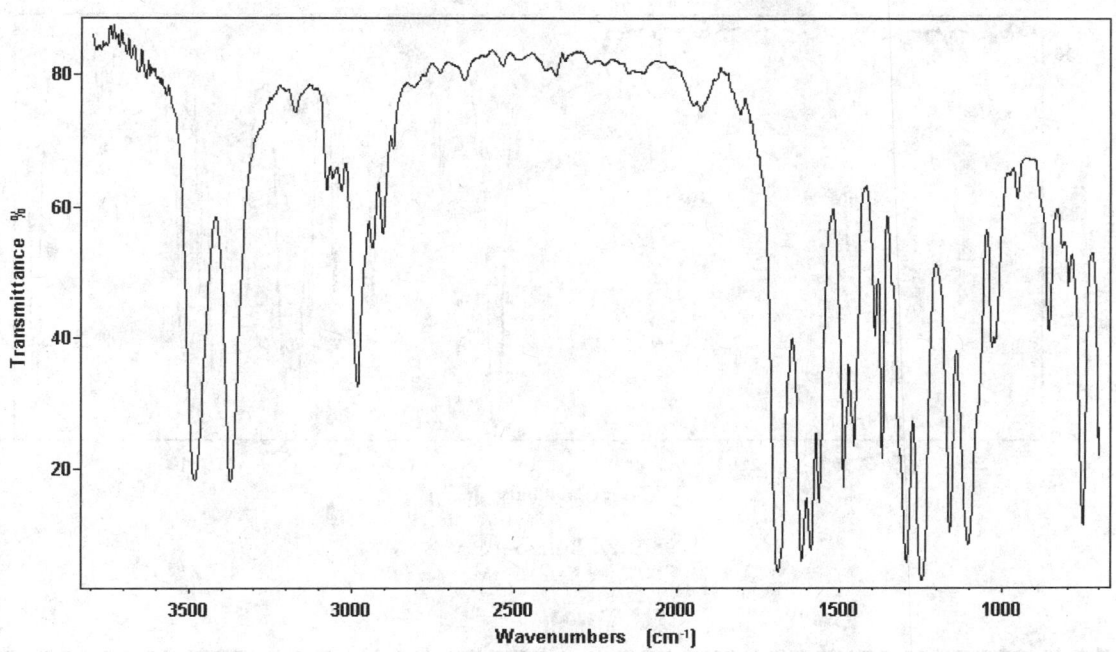

Ethyl Anthranilate

Ethyl Benzoate

First Published: Prior to FCC 6

$C_9H_{10}O_2$ Formula wt 150.18
FEMA: 2422
UNII: J115BRJ15H [ethyl benzoate]

DESCRIPTION
Ethyl Benzoate occurs as a colorless liquid.
Odor: Heavy, floral, fruity
Solubility: Soluble in alcohol, most fixed oils, propylene glycol; insoluble or practically insoluble in glycerin, water
Boiling Point: ~212°
Solubility in Alcohol, Appendix VI: One mL dissolves in 6 mL of 60% alcohol.
Function: Flavoring agent

IDENTIFICATION
- **INFRARED SPECTRA,** *Spectrophotometric Identification Tests,* Appendix IIIC
  Acceptance criteria: The spectrum of the sample exhibits relative maxima at the same wavelengths as those of the spectrum below.

ASSAY
- **PROCEDURE:** Proceed as directed under *M-1b,* Appendix XI.
  Acceptance criteria: NLT 98.0% of $C_9H_{10}O_2$

SPECIFIC TESTS
- **ACID VALUE, FLAVOR CHEMICALS (OTHER THAN ESSENTIAL OILS),** *M-15,* Appendix XI
  Acceptance criteria: NMT 1.0
- **REFRACTIVE INDEX,** Appendix II: At 20°
  Acceptance criteria: Between 1.502 and 1.506
- **SPECIFIC GRAVITY:** Determine at 25° by any reliable method (see *General Provisions*).
  Acceptance criteria: Between 1.043 and 1.046

OTHER REQUIREMENTS
- **CHLORINATED COMPOUNDS,** Appendix VI
  Acceptance criteria: Passes test

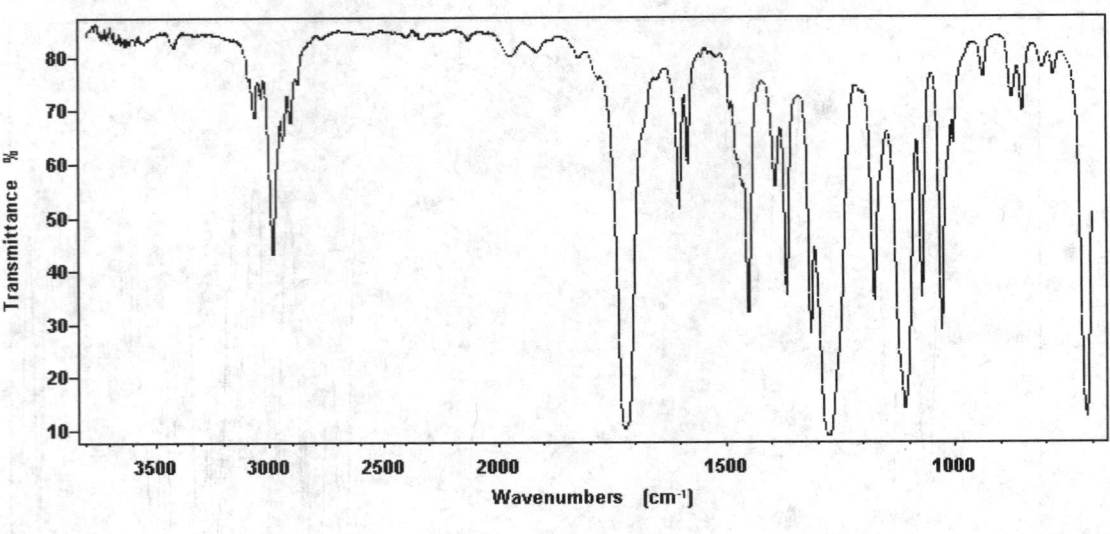

Ethyl Benzoate

Ethyl Benzoyl Acetate
First Published: Prior to FCC 6

C₁₁H₁₂O₃ Formula wt 192.21
FEMA: 2423
UNII: K8CHJ4MKM0 [ethyl benzoyl acetate]

DESCRIPTION
Ethyl Benzoyl Acetate occurs as a colorless to light yellow liquid.
Odor: Whiskey
Boiling Point: ~265°
Function: Flavoring agent

ASSAY
- **PROCEDURE:** Proceed as directed under *M-1b,* Appendix XI.
  Acceptance criteria: NLT 88.0% of C₁₁H₁₂O₃

SPECIFIC TESTS
- **ACID VALUE, FLAVOR CHEMICALS (OTHER THAN ESSENTIAL OILS),** *M-15,* Appendix XI
  Acceptance criteria: NMT 2.0
- **REFRACTIVE INDEX,** Appendix II: At 20°
  Acceptance criteria: Between 1.528 and 1.533
- **SPECIFIC GRAVITY:** Determine at 25° by any reliable method (see *General Provisions*).
  Acceptance criteria: Between 1.107 and 1.120

Ethyl Butyrate
First Published: Prior to FCC 6

C₆H₁₂O₂ Formula wt 116.16
FEMA: 2427
UNII: UFD2LZ005D [ethyl butyrate]

DESCRIPTION
Ethyl Butyrate occurs as a colorless liquid.
Odor: Banana-pineapple
Solubility: Soluble in most fixed oils, propylene glycol; insoluble or practically insoluble in glycerin
Boiling Point: ~121°
Solubility in Alcohol, Appendix VI: One mL dissolves in 3 mL of 60% alcohol.
Function: Flavoring agent

IDENTIFICATION
- **INFRARED SPECTRA,** *Spectrophotometric Identification Tests,* Appendix IIIC
  Acceptance criteria: The spectrum of the sample exhibits relative maxima at the same wavelengths as those of the spectrum below.

ASSAY
- **PROCEDURE:** Proceed as directed under *M-1b,* Appendix XI.
  Acceptance criteria: NLT 98.0% of C₆H₁₂O₂

SPECIFIC TESTS
- **ACID VALUE, FLAVOR CHEMICALS (OTHER THAN ESSENTIAL OILS),** *M-15,* Appendix XI
  Acceptance criteria: NMT 1.0

- **REFRACTIVE INDEX**, Appendix II: At 20°
  Acceptance criteria: Between 1.391 and 1.394
- **SPECIFIC GRAVITY:** Determine at 25° by any reliable method (see General Provisions).
  Acceptance criteria: Between 0.870 and 0.877

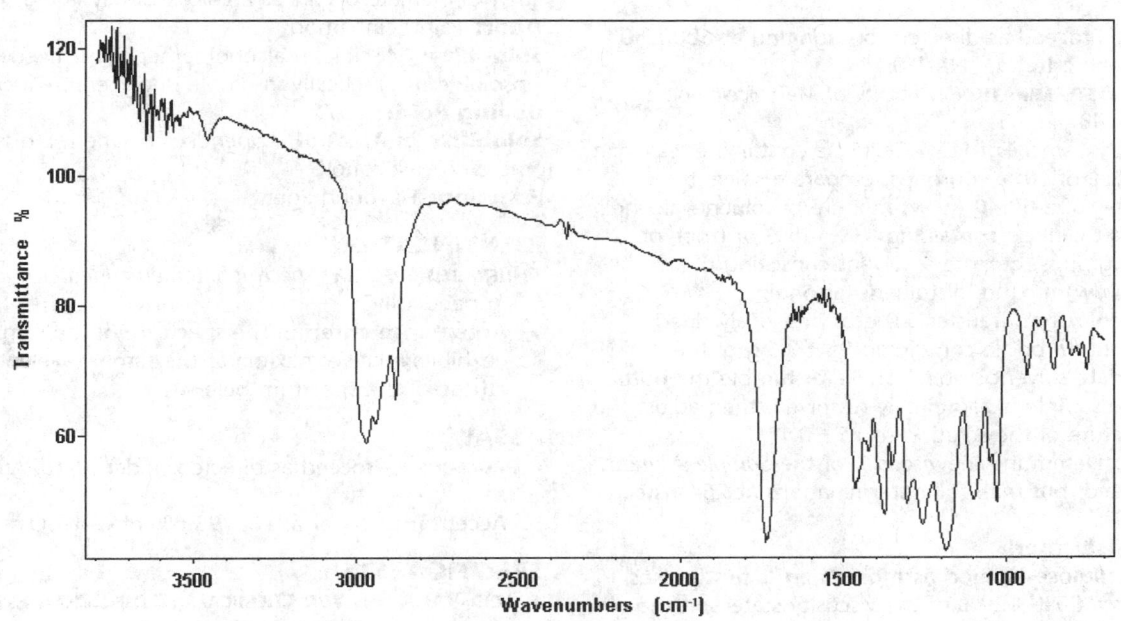

Ethyl Butyrate

Ethyl Cellulose

First Published: Prior to FCC 6
Last Revision: Third Supplement, FCC 7

Modified Cellulose, EC
INS: 462   CAS: [9004-57-3]
UNII: 7Z8S9VYZ4B [ethylcelluloses]

DESCRIPTION
Ethyl Cellulose occurs as a free-flowing, white to light tan powder. It is heat labile, and exposure to high temperatures (240°) causes color degradation and loss of properties. It is practically insoluble in water, in glycerin, and in propylene glycol, but is soluble in varying proportions in certain organic solvents, depending on the ethoxyl content. Ethyl Cellulose containing less than 46%–48% of ethoxyl groups is freely soluble in tetrahydrofuran, in methyl acetate, in chloroform, and in aromatic hydrocarbon–alcohol mixtures. Ethyl Cellulose containing 46%–48% or more of ethoxyl groups is freely soluble in alcohol, in methanol, in toluene, in chloroform, and in ethyl acetate. A 1:20 aqueous suspension is neutral to litmus.

Function: Protective coating; binder; filler
Packaging and Storage: Store in well-closed containers.

IDENTIFICATION
- **PROCEDURE**
  Sample solution: Dissolve 5 g of sample in 95 g of an 80:20 (w/w) mixture of toluene–ethanol.
  Analysis: Pour a few mL of the Sample solution onto a glass plate, and allow the solvent to evaporate.
  Acceptance criteria: The Sample solution is clear, stable, and slightly yellow; and following the Analysis, a thick, tough, clear, flammable film remains.

ASSAY
- **PROCEDURE**
  Sample: Place about 50 mg of sample, previously dried, in a tared gelatin capsule.
  Analysis: Transfer the capsule and its contents into the boiling flask of a methoxyl determination apparatus, and proceed as directed under Methoxyl Determination, Appendix IIIC. Each mL of 0.1 N sodium thiosulfate is equivalent to 751 mg of ethoxyl groups (–OC$_2$H$_5$).
  Acceptance criteria: 44.0%–50.0% of ethoxyl groups (–OC$_2$H$_5$), on the dried basis (equivalent to NMT 2.6 ethoxyl groups per anhydroglucose unit)

IMPURITIES
Inorganic Impurities
- **LEAD**, Lead Limit Test, Appendix IIIB
  Sample solution: Prepare as directed for organic compounds, using a 2-g sample.
  Control: 6 µg of Pb (6 mL of Diluted Standard Lead Solution)
  [NOTE—Alternatively, determine as directed for Flame Atomic Absorption Spectrophotometric Method under Lead Limit Test, Appendix IIIB, using a 10-g sample.]
  Acceptance criteria: NMT 3 mg/kg

SPECIFIC TESTS

- **LOSS ON DRYING,** Appendix IIC: 105° for 2 h
  Acceptance criteria: NMT 3.0%
- **RESIDUE ON IGNITION (SULFATED ASH),** Appendix IIC
  Sample: 1 g
  Analysis: Proceed as directed, but igniting at 600 ± 50°.
  Acceptance criteria: NMT 0.5%
- **VISCOSITY DETERMINATION,** *Viscosity of Methylcellulose,* Appendix IIB
  Solvent systems: For Ethyl Cellulose containing less than 46%–48% of ethoxyl groups, prepare a solvent consisting of a 60:40 (w/w) mixture of toluene–alcohol; for Ethyl Cellulose containing 46%–48% or more of ethoxyl groups, prepare a solvent consisting of an 80:20 (w/w) mixture of toluene–alcohol.
  Sample solution: Transfer 5.0 g of previously dried sample into a bottle containing 95 ± 0.5 g of the appropriate solvent system. Shake or tumble the bottle until the sample is completely dissolved, then adjust the temperature of the solution to 25 ± 0.1°.
  Analysis: Determine the viscosity of the *Sample solution* as directed, but make all determinations at 25° instead of at 20°.
  Acceptance criteria
    Ethyl Cellulose labeled as more than 6 centipoises (mPa·s): 80%–120% of the viscosity stated on the label
    Ethyl Cellulose labeled as 6 centipoises (mPa·s) or less: 75%–140% of the viscosity stated on the label

Ethyl Cinnamate

First Published: Prior to FCC 6

Ethyl 3-Phenylpropenate

$C_{11}H_{12}O_2$ Formula wt 176.22

FEMA: 2430
UNII: C023P3M5JJ [ethyl cinnamate]

DESCRIPTION
Ethyl Cinnamate occurs as a colorless, oily liquid.
Odor: Faint, cinnamon
Solubility: Miscible in alcohol, ether, most fixed oils; insoluble or practically insoluble in glycerin, water
Boiling Point: ~272°
Solubility in Alcohol, Appendix VI: One mL dissolves in 5 mL of 70% alcohol.
Function: Flavoring agent

IDENTIFICATION
- **INFRARED SPECTRA,** *Spectrophotometric Identification Tests,* Appendix IIIC
  Acceptance criteria: The spectrum of the sample exhibits relative maxima at the same wavelengths as those of the spectrum below.

ASSAY
- **PROCEDURE:** Proceed as directed under *M-1b,* Appendix XI.
  Acceptance criteria: NLT 98.0% of $C_{11}H_{12}O_2$

SPECIFIC TESTS
- **ACID VALUE, FLAVOR CHEMICALS (OTHER THAN ESSENTIAL OILS),** *M-15,* Appendix XI
  Acceptance criteria: NMT 1.0
- **REFRACTIVE INDEX,** Appendix II: At 20°
  Acceptance criteria: Between 1.558 and 1.561
- **SPECIFIC GRAVITY:** Determine at 25° by any reliable method (see *General Provisions*).
  Acceptance criteria: Between 1.045 and 1.051

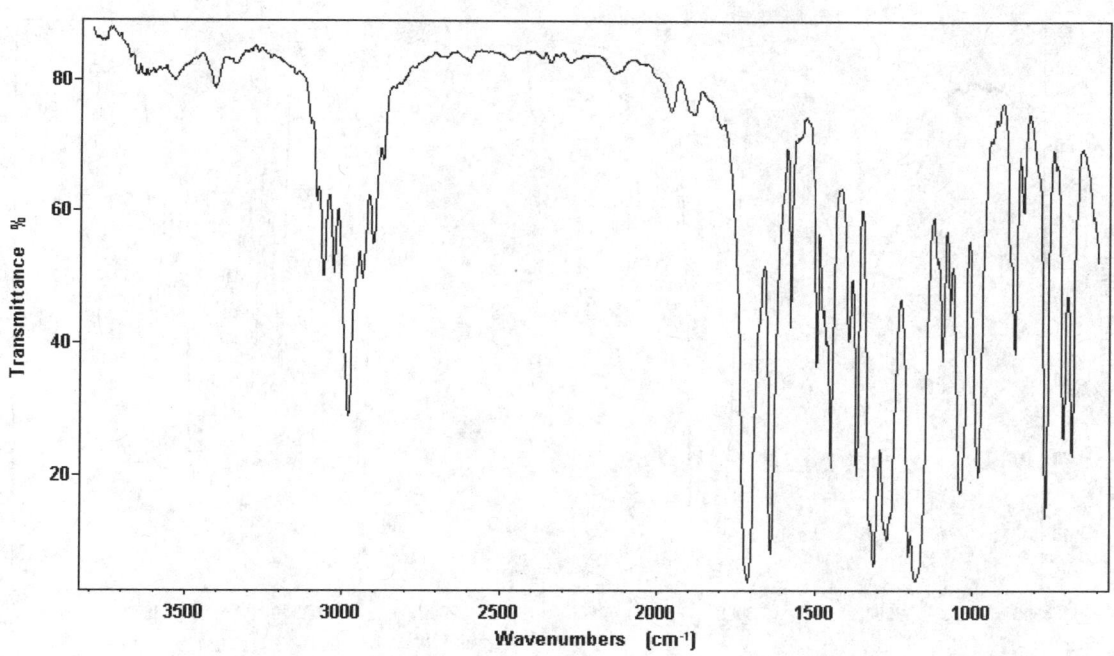

Ethyl Cinnamate

Ethyl Decanoate

First Published: Prior to FCC 6

Ethyl Caprate

$C_{12}H_{24}O_2$
FEMA: 2432
UNII: GY39FB86UO [ethyl decanoate]

Formula wt 200.32

DESCRIPTION
Ethyl Decanoate occurs as a colorless liquid.
Odor: Oily, brandy
Solubility: Soluble in most fixed oils; insoluble or practically insoluble in glycerin, propylene glycol
Boiling Point: ~243°
Solubility in Alcohol, Appendix VI: One mL dissolves in 4 mL of 80% alcohol.
Function: Flavoring agent

IDENTIFICATION
- **INFRARED SPECTRA,** *Spectrophotometric Identification Tests,* Appendix IIIC
  Acceptance criteria: The spectrum of the sample exhibits relative maxima at the same wavelengths as those of the spectrum below.

ASSAY
- **PROCEDURE:** Proceed as directed under *M-1b,* Appendix XI.
  Acceptance criteria: NLT 98.0% of $C_{12}H_{24}O_2$

SPECIFIC TESTS
- **ACID VALUE, FLAVOR CHEMICALS (OTHER THAN ESSENTIAL OILS),** *M-15,* Appendix XI
  Acceptance criteria: NMT 1.0
- **REFRACTIVE INDEX,** Appendix II: At 20°
  Acceptance criteria: Between 1.424 and 1.427
- **SPECIFIC GRAVITY:** Determine at 25° by any reliable method (see *General Provisions*).
  Acceptance criteria: Between 0.862 and 0.867

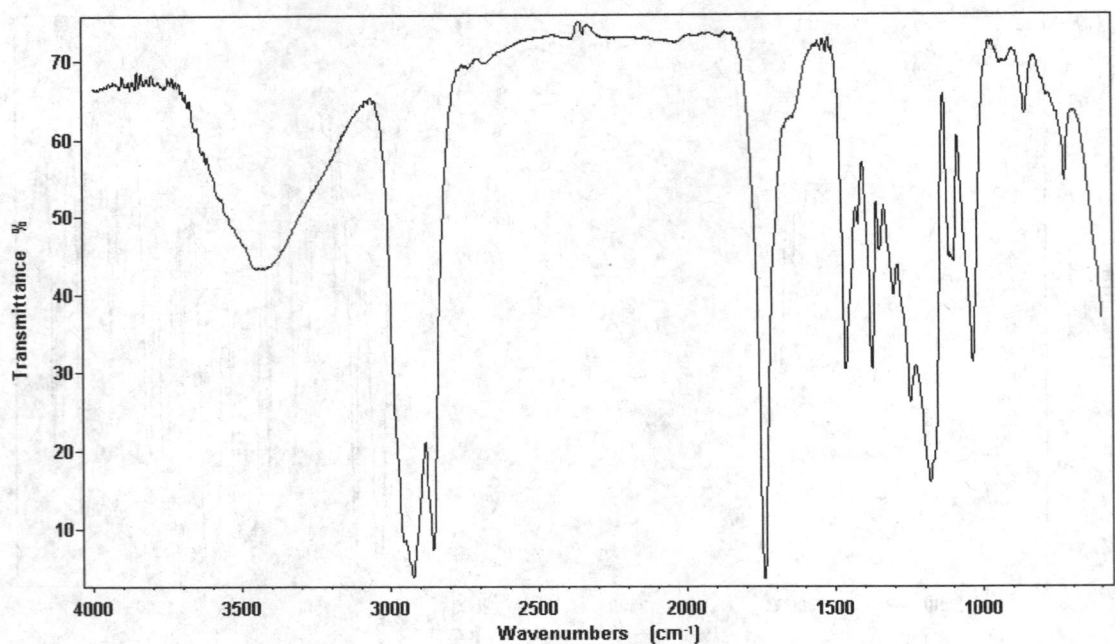

Ethyl Decanoate

Ethyl Formate

First Published: Prior to FCC 6
Last Revision: FCC 7

C$_3$H$_6$O$_2$ Formula wt 74.08
FEMA: 2434
UNII: 0K3E2L5553 [ethyl formate]

DESCRIPTION
Ethyl Formate occurs as a colorless liquid.
Odor: Sharp, rum
Solubility: Soluble in most fixed oils, propylene glycol; slightly soluble in mineral oil; insoluble or practically insoluble in glycerin. Soluble with gradual decomposition in water.
Boiling Point: ~54°
Solubility in Alcohol, Appendix VI: One mL dissolves in 5 mL of 50% alcohol.
Function: Flavoring agent

IDENTIFICATION
- **INFRARED ABSORPTION,** Spectrophotometric Identification Tests, Appendix IIIC
   Reference standard: USP Ethyl Formate RS
   Sample and standard preparation: F
   Acceptance criteria: The spectrum of the sample exhibits maxima at the same wavelengths as those in the spectrum of the Reference standard.

ASSAY
- **PROCEDURE:** Proceed as directed under M-1b, Appendix XI.
   Acceptance criteria: NLT 95.0% of C$_3$H$_6$O$_2$

SPECIFIC TESTS
- **REFRACTIVE INDEX,** Appendix II: At 20°
   Acceptance criteria: Between 1.359 and 1.363
- **SPECIFIC GRAVITY:** Determine at 25° by any reliable method (see General Provisions).
   Acceptance criteria: Between 0.916 and 0.921

OTHER REQUIREMENTS
- **ACIDITY,** M-5, Appendix XI
   Acceptance criteria: NMT 0.2%

Ethyl Heptanoate

First Published: Prior to FCC 6

Ethyl Heptoate

C$_9$H$_{18}$O$_2$ Formula wt 158.24
FEMA: 2437
UNII: 45R404Y5X8 [ethyl oenanthate]

DESCRIPTION
Ethyl Heptanoate occurs as a colorless liquid.
Odor: Winy-brandy
Solubility: Slightly soluble in propylene glycol; miscible in alcohol, chloroform, most fixed oils; insoluble or practically insoluble in glycerin
Boiling Point: ~189° (72% water azeotrope, 98.5°)
Solubility in Alcohol, Appendix VI: One mL dissolves in 3 mL of 70% alcohol.
Function: Flavoring agent

IDENTIFICATION
- **INFRARED SPECTRA,** *Spectrophotometric Identification Tests,* Appendix IIIC
  Acceptance criteria: The spectrum of the sample exhibits relative maxima at the same wavelengths as those of the spectrum below.

ASSAY
- **PROCEDURE:** Proceed as directed under *M-1b,* Appendix XI.
  Acceptance criteria: NLT 98.0% of $C_9H_{18}O_2$

SPECIFIC TESTS
- **ACID VALUE, FLAVOR CHEMICALS (OTHER THAN ESSENTIAL OILS),** *M-15,* Appendix XI
  Acceptance criteria: NMT 1.0
- **REFRACTIVE INDEX,** Appendix II: At 20°
  Acceptance criteria: Between 1.411 and 1.415
- **SPECIFIC GRAVITY:** Determine at 25° by any reliable method (see *General Provisions*).
  Acceptance criteria: Between 0.867 and 0.872

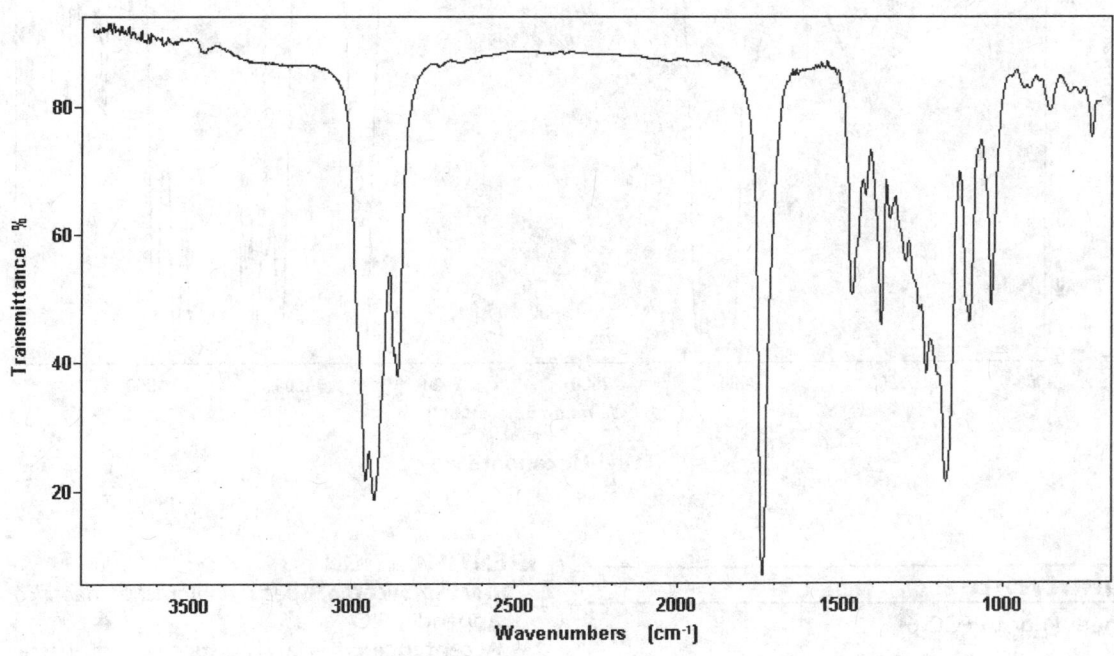

Ethyl Heptanoate

Ethyl Hexanoate
First Published: Prior to FCC 6

Ethyl Caproate
Ethyl Capronate

$C_8H_{16}O_2$ Formula wt 144.21
FEMA: 2439
UNII: FLO6YR1SHT [ethyl caproate]

DESCRIPTION
Ethyl Hexanoate occurs as a colorless liquid.
Odor: Winy
Solubility: Soluble in most fixed oils; slightly soluble in propylene glycol; insoluble or practically insoluble in glycerin
Boiling Point: ~166°
Solubility in Alcohol, Appendix VI: One mL dissolves in 2 mL of 70% alcohol.
Function: Flavoring agent

IDENTIFICATION
- **INFRARED SPECTRA,** *Spectrophotometric Identification Tests,* Appendix IIIC

408 / Ethyl Hexanoate / Monographs

Acceptance criteria: The spectrum of the sample exhibits relative maxima at the same wavelengths as those of the spectrum below.

ASSAY
- **Procedure:** Proceed as directed under *M-1b,* Appendix XI.
  Acceptance criteria: NLT 98.0% of $C_8H_{16}O_2$

SPECIFIC TESTS
- **Acid Value, Flavor Chemicals (Other Than Essential Oils),** *M-15,* Appendix XI
  Acceptance criteria: NMT 1.0
- **Refractive Index,** Appendix II: At 20°
  Acceptance criteria: Between 1.406 and 1.409
- **Specific Gravity:** Determine at 25° by any reliable method (see *General Provisions*).
  Acceptance criteria: Between 0.867 and 0.871

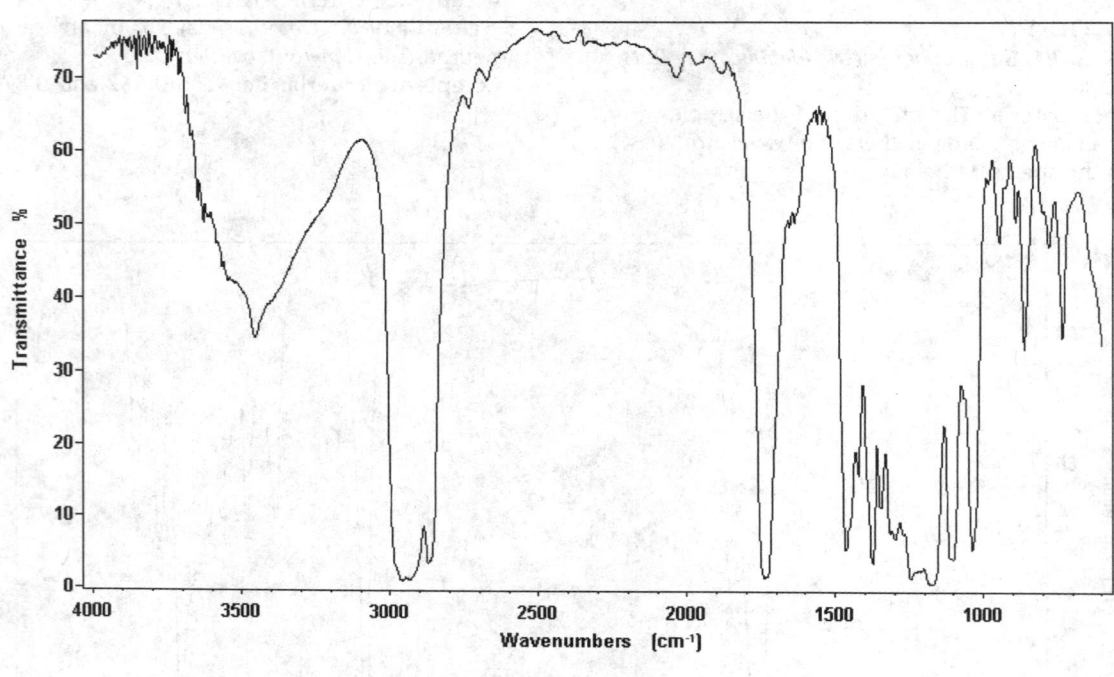

Ethyl Hexanoate

Ethyl Isobutyrate

First Published: Prior to FCC 6

$C_6H_{12}O_2$ Formula wt 116.16
FEMA: 2428
UNII: 9A9661LN4H [ethyl isobutyrate]

DESCRIPTION
Ethyl Isobutyrate occurs as a colorless liquid.
Odor: Fruity
Solubility: Soluble in propylene glycol, vegetable oils; insoluble or practically insoluble in water
Boiling Point: ~112° to 113°
Solubility in Alcohol, Appendix VI: One mL dissolves in 1 mL of 95% alcohol.
Function: Flavoring agent

IDENTIFICATION
- **Infrared Spectra,** *Spectrophotometric Identification Tests,* Appendix IIIC
  Acceptance criteria: The spectrum of the sample exhibits relative maxima at the same wavelengths as those of the spectrum below.

ASSAY
- **Procedure:** Proceed as directed under *M-1b,* Appendix XI.
  Acceptance criteria: NLT 98.0% of $C_6H_{12}O_2$

SPECIFIC TESTS
- **Acid Value, Flavor Chemicals (Other Than Essential Oils),** *M-15,* Appendix XI
  Acceptance criteria: NMT 1.0
- **Refractive Index,** Appendix II: At 20°
  Acceptance criteria: Between 1.385 and 1.391
- **Specific Gravity:** Determine at 25° by any reliable method (see *General Provisions*).
  Acceptance criteria: Between 0.862 and 0.868

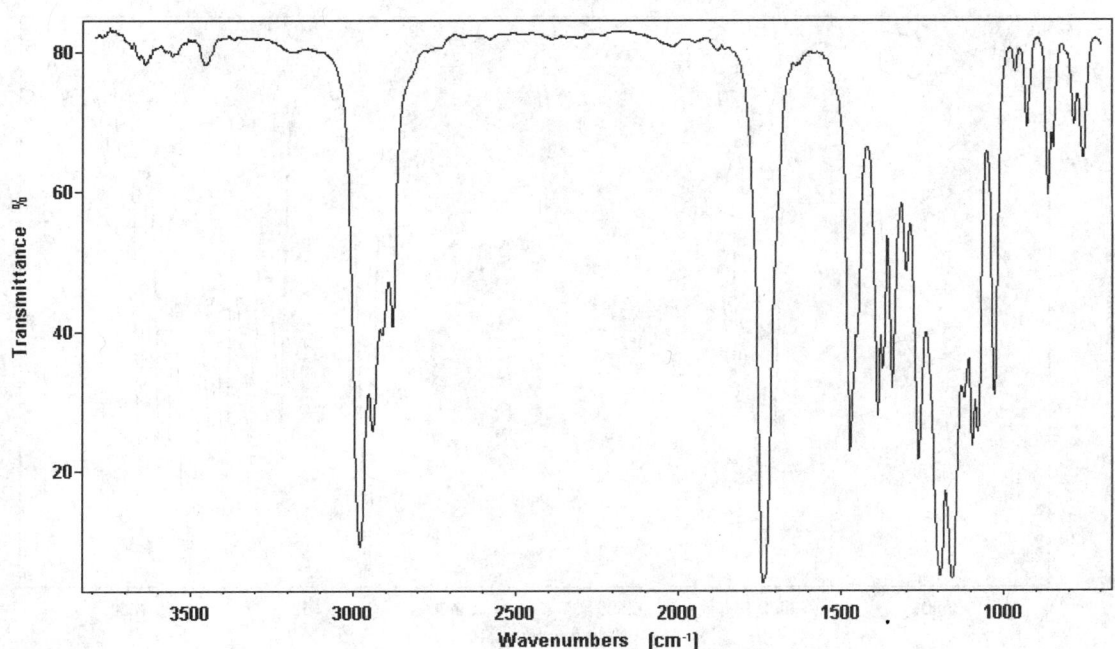

Ethyl Isobutyrate

Ethyl Isovalerate

First Published: Prior to FCC 6

Ethyl 3-Methylbutyrate

C₇H₁₄O₂ Formula wt 130.19
FEMA: 2463
UNII: 9ZZ5597636 [ethyl isovalerate]

DESCRIPTION
Ethyl Isovalerate occurs as a colorless liquid.
Odor: Strong, fruity, vinous, apple on dilution
Solubility: Soluble in propylene glycol; miscible in alcohol, most fixed oils; 1 mL dissolves in 350 mL water
Boiling Point: ~135°
Function: Flavoring agent

IDENTIFICATION
- **INFRARED SPECTRA,** Spectrophotometric Identification Tests, Appendix IIIC

  Acceptance criteria: The spectrum of the sample exhibits relative maxima at the same wavelengths as those of the spectrum below.

ASSAY
- **PROCEDURE:** Proceed as directed under M-1b, Appendix XI.

  Acceptance criteria: NLT 98.0% of C₇H₁₄O₂ (one isomer)

SPECIFIC TESTS
- **ACID VALUE, FLAVOR CHEMICALS (OTHER THAN ESSENTIAL OILS),** M-15, Appendix XI
  Acceptance criteria: NMT 2.0
- **REFRACTIVE INDEX,** Appendix II: At 20°
  Acceptance criteria: Between 1.395 and 1.399
- **SPECIFIC GRAVITY:** Determine at 25° by any reliable method (see General Provisions).
  Acceptance criteria: Between 0.862 and 0.866

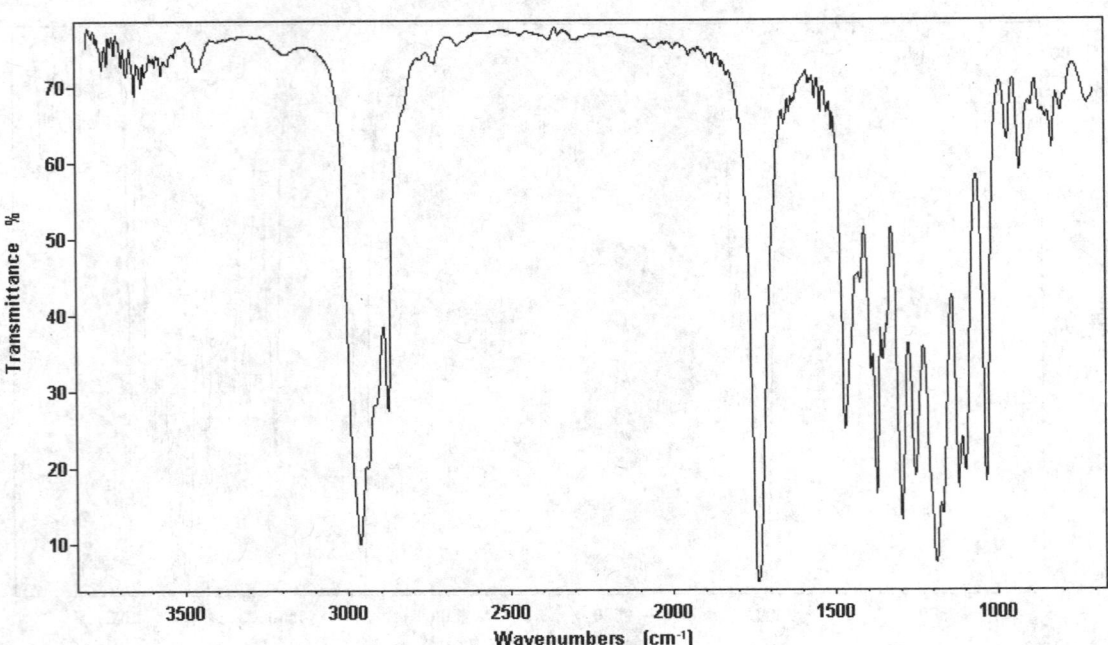

Ethyl Isovalerate

Ethyl Lactate

First Published: Prior to FCC 6

Ethyl 2-Hydroxypropionate

$C_5H_{10}O_3$ Formula wt 118.13
FEMA: 2440
UNII: F3P750VW8I [ethyl lactate]

DESCRIPTION
Ethyl Lactate occurs as a colorless liquid.
Odor: Cheesy
Solubility: Very soluble in alcohol, ether, chloroform, water
Boiling Point: ~154°
Function: Flavoring agent

IDENTIFICATION
- **INFRARED SPECTRA,** *Spectrophotometric Identification Tests,* Appendix IIIC

Acceptance criteria: The spectrum of the sample exhibits relative maxima at the same wavelengths as those of the spectrum below.

ASSAY
- **PROCEDURE:** Proceed as directed under *M-1b,* Appendix XI.
  Acceptance criteria: NLT 98.0% of $C_5H_{10}O_3$

SPECIFIC TESTS
- **ACID VALUE, FLAVOR CHEMICALS (OTHER THAN ESSENTIAL OILS),** *M-15,* Appendix XI
  Acceptance criteria: NMT 1.0
- **REFRACTIVE INDEX,** Appendix II: At 20°
  Acceptance criteria: Between 1.410 and 1.420
- **SPECIFIC GRAVITY:** Determine at 25° by any reliable method (see *General Provisions*).
  Acceptance criteria: Between 1.029 and 1.032

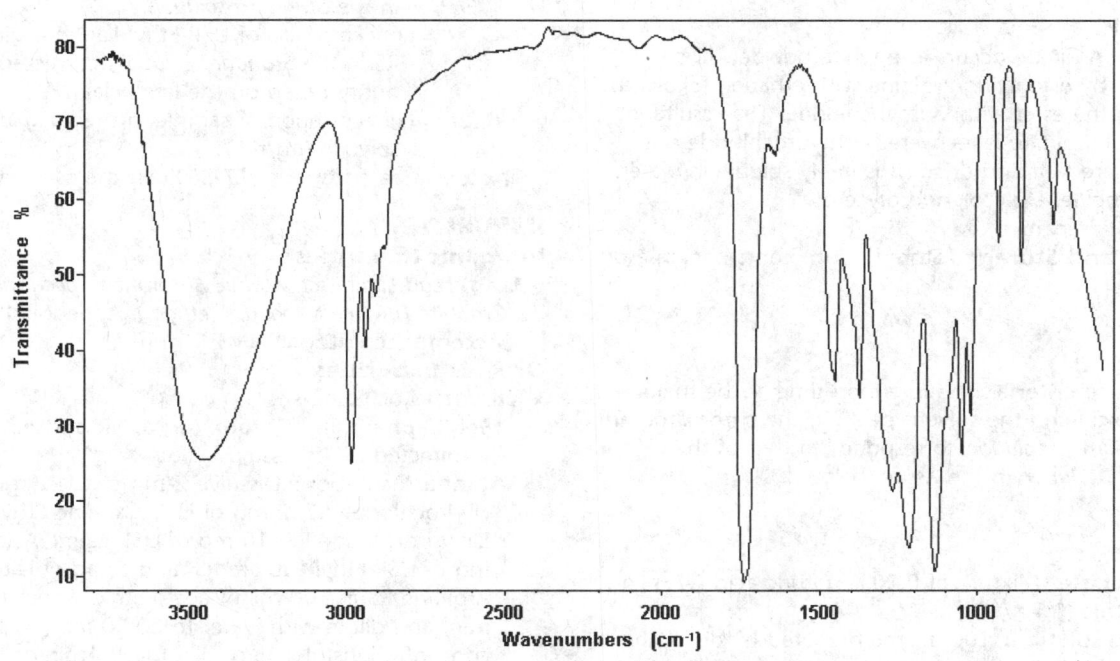
Ethyl Lactate

Ethyl Laurate

First Published: Prior to FCC 6
Last Revision: Second Supplement, FCC 7

Ethyl Dodecanoate

$C_{14}H_{28}O_2$ Formula wt 228.38
FEMA: 2441
UNII: F389D4MD5K [ethyl laurate]

DESCRIPTION
Ethyl Laurate occurs as a colorless, oily liquid.
Odor: Fruity-floral
Solubility: Miscible in alcohol, chloroform, ether; insoluble or practically insoluble in water
Boiling Point: ~269°
Solubility in Alcohol, Appendix VI: One mL dissolves in 9 mL of 80% alcohol to give a clear solution.
Function: Flavoring agent

IDENTIFICATION
- **INFRARED ABSORPTION,** *Spectrophotometric Identification Tests,* Appendix IIIC
  Reference standard: USP Ethyl Laurate RS
  Sample and standard preparation: F
  Acceptance criteria: The spectrum of the sample exhibits maxima at the same wavelengths as those in the spectrum of the *Reference standard*.

ASSAY
- **PROCEDURE:** Proceed as directed under *M-1b,* Appendix XI.
  Acceptance criteria: NLT 98.0% of $C_{14}H_{28}O_2$

SPECIFIC TESTS
- **ACID VALUE, FLAVOR CHEMICALS (OTHER THAN ESSENTIAL OILS),** *M-15,* Appendix XI
  Acceptance criteria: NMT 1.0
- **REFRACTIVE INDEX,** Appendix II: At 20°
  Acceptance criteria: 1.430–1.434
- **SPECIFIC GRAVITY:** Determine at 25° by any reliable method (see *General Provisions*).
  Acceptance criteria: 0.858–0.863

Ethyl Lauroyl Arginate

First Published: Third Supplement, FCC 7

Ethyl-N^α-Lauroyl-L-Arginate · HCl
Ethyl-N^α-Dodecanoyl-L-Arginate · HCl
Lauric Arginate Ethyl Ester
Lauramide Arginine Ethyl Ester
LAE

$C_{20}H_{41}N_4O_3Cl$ Formula wt 421.02

Ethyl Lauroyl Arginate

INS: 243 CAS: [60372-77-2]

DESCRIPTION
Ethyl Lauroyl Arginate occurs as a white powder. It is synthesized by esterifying arginine with ethanol, followed by reacting the ester with lauroyl chloride. The resultant ethyl lauroyl arginate is recovered as hydrochloride salt which is filtered off and dried. It is freely soluble in water, ethanol, propylene glycol, and glycerol.

Function: Preservative

Packaging and Storage: Store in tight containers in a dry place.

IDENTIFICATION
- **PROCEDURE**

  Acceptance criteria: The retention time of the major peak (excluding the solvent peak) in the chromatogram of the *Sample solution* corresponds to that of the *Standard solution* in the *Assay* (below).

ASSAY
- **PROCEDURE**

  Mobile phase: Mixture of 0.20% sulfuric acid (v/v) and acetonitrile (1:1, v/v)

  Standard solution: 100 µg/mL prepared by dissolving 10 mg of USP Ethyl Lauroyl Arginate RS in 50.0 mL of water, sonicating for 3 min, and diluting with acetonitrile to 100.0 mL

  Sample solution: 100 µg/mL prepared by dissolving 10 mg of sample in 50.0 mL of water, sonicating for 3 min, and diluting with acetonitrile to 100.0 mL

  Chromatographic system, Appendix IIA
  Mode: High-performance liquid chromatography
  Detector: UV 209 nm
  Column: 2.1-mm × 150-mm, mixed mode column (reverse phase with embedded acidic ion-pairing groups), 5-µm particle diameter[1]
  Column temperature: 30°
  Flow rate: 0.6 mL/min
  Injection volume: 50 µL
  System suitability
    Sample: *Standard solution*
    Suitability requirement 1: The relative standard deviation for peak area is NMT 0.5% for replicate injections.
    Suitability requirement 2: The peak tailing factor is NMT 2.0%.
  Analysis: Separately inject equal volumes of the *Standard solution* and *Sample solution* into the chromatograph and measure the responses for the major peaks on the resulting chromatograms. [NOTE—The retention time for ethyl lauroyl arginate is approximately 12.8 min.]
  Calculate the percentage of ethyl lauryl arginate in the portion of the sample taken:

  $$\text{Result} = (r_U/r_S) \times (C_S/C_U) \times 100$$

  r_U = peak area response for ethyl lauryl arginate in the *Sample solution*
  r_S = peak area response for ethyl lauryl arginate in the *Standard solution*
  C_S = concentration of USP Ethyl Lauryl Arginate RS in the *Standard solution*, corrected for purity based on the label claim (µg/mL)
  C_U = concentration of sample in the *Sample solution* (µg/mL)

  Acceptance criteria: NLT 85% on the as-is basis

IMPURITIES
Inorganic Impurities
- **LEAD,** *Lead Limit Test, Atomic Absorption Spectrophotometric Graphite Furnace Method, Method I,* Appendix IIIB
  Acceptance criteria: NMT 1 mg/kg

Organic Impurities
- **RELATED COMPOUNDS**

  Mobile phase and **Chromatographic system:** Proceed as directed in the *Assay*.

  Standard solution: Dissolve 2 mg of USP Arginine Hydrochloride RS, 2 mg of USP Arginine Ethyl Ester Dihydrochloride RS, 10 mg of USP Lauric Acid RS, 6 mg of USP Ethyl Laurate RS, and 6 mg of Lauroyl Arginine RS in 100 mL of acetonitrile. Sonicate for 3 min, and dilute with water to 200.0 mL (final concentrations of 10 µg/mL of USP Arginine Hydrochloride RS, 10 µg/mL of Arginine Ethyl Ester Dihydrochloride RS, 50 µg/mL of USP Lauric Acid RS, 30 µg/mL of USP Ethyl Laurate RS, and 30 µg/mL of USP Lauroyl Arginine RS).

  Resolution solution: Dissolve 5 mg of USP Ethyl Lauroyl Arginate RS in 5 mL of the *Standard solution.*

  Sample solution: 1000 µg/mL prepared by dissolving 5 mg of the sample in 2.5 mL of water, sonicating for 3 min, and diluting with acetonitrile to 5.0 mL

  System suitability
    Sample: *Resolution solution*
    Suitability requirement 1: The relative standard deviation for peak area is NMT 2.0% for any of the five measured related compounds, for replicate injections.
    Suitability requirement 2: The resolution is NLT 1.5 between any of the five related compound peaks, and NLT 1.0 between the ethyl laurate and ethyl lauroyl arginate peaks.

  Analysis: Separately inject equal volumes of the *Standard solution* and *Sample solution* into the chromatograph and measure the responses for the major peaks on the resulting chromatograms. [NOTE— The relative retention times for arginine hydrochloride, lauric acid, arginine ethyl ester dihydrochloride, lauroyl arginine, ethyl laurate, and ethyl lauroyl arginate RS are 0.2, 0.3, 0.4, 0.5, 0.8, and 1, respectively.]
  Calculate the percentages of the five related compounds (arginine hydrochloride, lauric acid, arginine ethyl ester dihydrochloride, lauroyl arginine, and ethyl laurate) in the portion of the sample taken:

  $$\text{Result} = (r_U/r_S) \times (C_S/C_U) \times 100$$

  r_U = peak area response for the analyte in the *Sample solution*

---

[1] SIELC Primesep 100 (SIELC Technologies, Prospect Heights, IL), part #100-21.150.0510.

r_S = peak area response for the analyte in the *Standard solution*
C_S = concentration of the corresponding analyte USP RS in the *Standard solution*, corrected for purity based on the label claim if applicable (µg/mL)
C_U = concentration of sample in the *Sample solution* (µg/mL)

Acceptance criteria
Arginine hydrochloride: NMT 1.0% on the as-is basis
Lauric acid: NMT 5.0% on the as-is basis
Arginine ethyl ester dihydrochloride: NMT 1.0% on the as-is basis
Lauroyl arginine: NMT 3.0% on the as-is basis
Ethyl laurate: NMT 3.0% on the as-is basis

SPECIFIC TESTS
- **ASH (TOTAL),** Appendix IIC
  Analysis: Proceed as directed, but igniting at 700° instead of 550°.
  Acceptance criteria: NMT 2%
- **pH,** *pH Determination,* Appendix IIB
  Sample: 10 mg/mL
  Acceptance criteria: 3.0–5.0
- **WATER,** *Water Determination, Method I,* Appendix IIB
  Acceptance criteria: NMT 5%

Ethyl Levulinate
First Published: Prior to FCC 6

$C_7H_{12}O_3$ Formula wt 144.17
FEMA: 2442

UNII: 7BU24CSS2G [ethyl levulinate]

DESCRIPTION
Ethyl Levulinate occurs as a colorless to pale yellow liquid.
Odor: Fruity, apple, green
Solubility: Soluble in propylene glycol, vegetable oils; insoluble or practically insoluble in water
Boiling Point: ~93° to 94° (18 mm Hg)
Solubility in Alcohol, Appendix VI: One mL dissolves in 1 mL of 95% alcohol.
Function: Flavoring agent

IDENTIFICATION
- **INFRARED SPECTRA,** *Spectrophotometric Identification Tests,* Appendix IIIC
  Acceptance criteria: The spectrum of the sample exhibits relative maxima at the same wavelengths as those of the spectrum below.

ASSAY
- **PROCEDURE:** Proceed as directed under *M-1b,* Appendix XI.
  Acceptance criteria: NLT 98.0% of $C_7H_{12}O_3$

SPECIFIC TESTS
- **ACID VALUE, FLAVOR CHEMICALS (OTHER THAN ESSENTIAL OILS),** *M-15,* Appendix XI
  Acceptance criteria: NMT 2.0
- **REFRACTIVE INDEX,** Appendix II: At 20°
  Acceptance criteria: Between 1.420 and 1.425
- **SPECIFIC GRAVITY:** Determine at 25° by any reliable method (see *General Provisions*).
  Acceptance criteria: Between 1.007 and 1.013

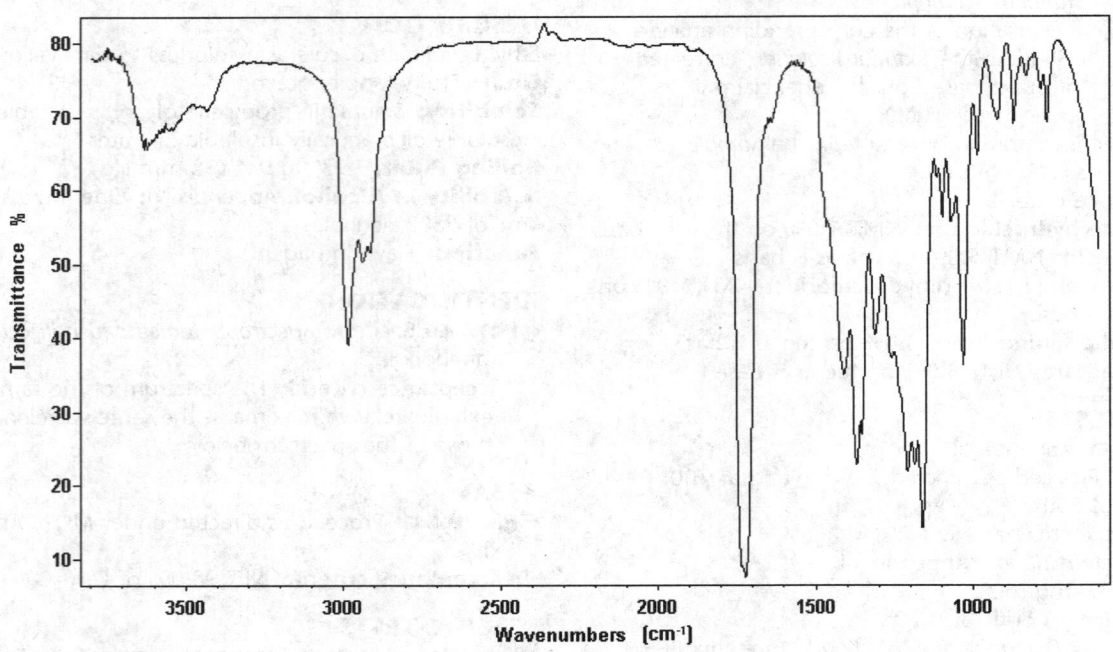

Ethyl Levulinate

Ethyl Maltol

First Published: Prior to FCC 6

2-Ethyl-3-hydroxy-4-pyrone

$C_7H_8O_3$
INS: 637
FEMA: 3487
UNII: L6Q8K29L05 [ethyl maltol]

Formula wt 140.14
CAS: [4940-11-8]

DESCRIPTION
Ethyl Maltol occurs as a white, crystalline powder having a cotton-candy odor and a sweet, fruitlike flavor in dilute solution. One g dissolves in about 55 mL of water, 10 mL of alcohol, 17 mL of propylene glycol, and 5 mL of chloroform. It melts at about 90°.

Function: Flavoring agent; flavor enhancer
Packaging and Storage: Store in tight containers.

IDENTIFICATION
- **INFRARED ABSORPTION,** *Spectrophotometric Identification Tests,* Appendix IIIC
  Reference standard: USP Ethyl Maltol RS
  Sample and standard preparation: *S,* 1:50 in chloroform
  Acceptance criteria: The spectrum of the sample exhibits maxima at the same wavelengths as those in the spectrum of the *Reference standard.*

ASSAY
- **PROCEDURE**
  Standard stock solution: 200 µg/mL USP Ethyl Maltol RS in 0.1 N hydrochloric acid, made to 250 mL
  Standard solution: 10 µg/mL USP Ethyl Maltol RS prepared from *Standard stock solution* and 0.1 N hydrochloric acid
  Sample solution: Dissolve 50 mg of sample in sufficient 0.1 N hydrochloric acid to make 250.0 mL, and mix. Transfer 5.0 mL of this solution into a 100-mL volumetric flask, dilute to volume with 0.1 N hydrochloric acid, and mix.
  Blank: 0.1 N hydrochloric acid
  Analysis: Using a suitable spectrophotometer and a 1-cm cell, determine the absorbance (corrected for the *Blank*) of the *Standard solution,* and of the *Sample solution,* at the wavelength of maximum absorption (about 276 nm). Calculate the quantity (mg) of $C_7H_8O_3$ in the sample taken by the formula:

  Result = $5C(A_u/A_s)$,

  C = concentration (µg/mL) of the USP Ethyl Maltol RS in the Standard solution
  A_u = absorbance of the *Sample solution*
  A_s = absorbance of the *Standard solution*
  Acceptance criteria: NLT 99.0% of $C_7H_8O_3$, calculated on the anhydrous basis

SPECIFIC TESTS

- **RESIDUE ON IGNITION (SULFATED ASH),** Appendix IIC
  Sample: 1 g
  Acceptance criteria: NMT 0.2%
- **WATER,** *Water Determination,* Appendix IIB
  Acceptance criteria: NMT 0.5%

Ethyl Methylphenylglycidate

First Published: Prior to FCC 6

Aldehyde C-16
Strawberry Aldehyde

$C_{12}H_{14}O_3$ Formula wt 206.24
FEMA: 2444
UNII: UD51D5KR4A [ethyl methylphenylglycidate]

DESCRIPTION
Ethyl Methylphenylglycidate occurs as a colorless to pale yellow liquid.
Odor: Strong, fruity, strawberry

Solubility: Soluble in most fixed oils, propylene glycol; insoluble or practically insoluble in glycerin
Boiling Point: ~272° to 275°
Solubility in Alcohol, Appendix VI: One mL dissolves in 3 mL of 70% alcohol.
Function: Flavoring agent

IDENTIFICATION

- **INFRARED SPECTRA,** *Spectrophotometric Identification Tests,* Appendix IIIC
  Acceptance criteria: The spectrum of the sample exhibits relative maxima at the same wavelengths as those of the spectrum below.

ASSAY

- **PROCEDURE:** Proceed as directed under *M-1b,* Appendix XI.
  Acceptance criteria: NLT 98.0% of $C_{12}H_{14}O_3$ (sum of two isomers)

SPECIFIC TESTS

- **ACID VALUE, FLAVOR CHEMICALS (OTHER THAN ESSENTIAL OILS),** *M-15,* Appendix XI
  Acceptance criteria: NMT 2.0
- **REFRACTIVE INDEX,** Appendix II: At 20°
  Acceptance criteria: Between 1.504 and 1.513
- **SPECIFIC GRAVITY:** Determine at 25° by any reliable method (see *General Provisions*).
  Acceptance criteria: Between 1.086 and 1.096

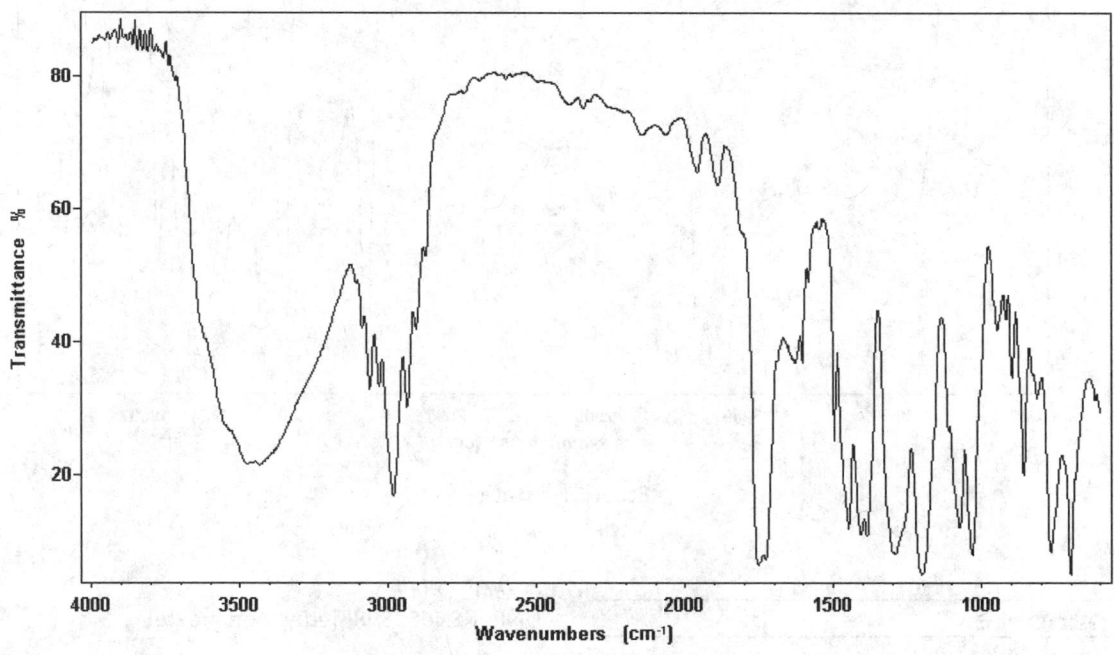

Ethyl Methylphenylglycidate

Ethyl Myristate

First Published: Prior to FCC 6

$C_{16}H_{32}O_2$ Formula wt 256.43
FEMA: 2445
UNII: 6995S49749 [ethyl myristate]

DESCRIPTION
Ethyl Myristate occurs as a colorless to pale yellow liquid.
Odor: Waxy
Solubility: Soluble in vegetable oils; insoluble or practically insoluble in propylene glycol, water
Boiling Point: ~178° to 180° (12 mm Hg)
Solubility in Alcohol, Appendix VI: One mL dissolves in 1 mL of 95% alcohol.
Function: Flavoring agent

IDENTIFICATION
- **INFRARED SPECTRA,** *Spectrophotometric Identification Tests,* Appendix IIIC
   Acceptance criteria: The spectrum of the sample exhibits relative maxima at the same wavelengths as those of the spectrum below.

ASSAY
- **PROCEDURE:** Proceed as directed under *M-1b,* Appendix XI.
   Acceptance criteria: NLT 98.0% of $C_{16}H_{32}O_2$

SPECIFIC TESTS
- **ACID VALUE, FLAVOR CHEMICALS (OTHER THAN ESSENTIAL OILS),** *M-15,* Appendix XI
   Acceptance criteria: NMT 1.0
- **REFRACTIVE INDEX,** Appendix II: At 20°
   Acceptance criteria: Between 1.434 and 1.438
- **SPECIFIC GRAVITY:** Determine at 25° by any reliable method (see *General Provisions*).
   Acceptance criteria: Between 0.857 and 0.862

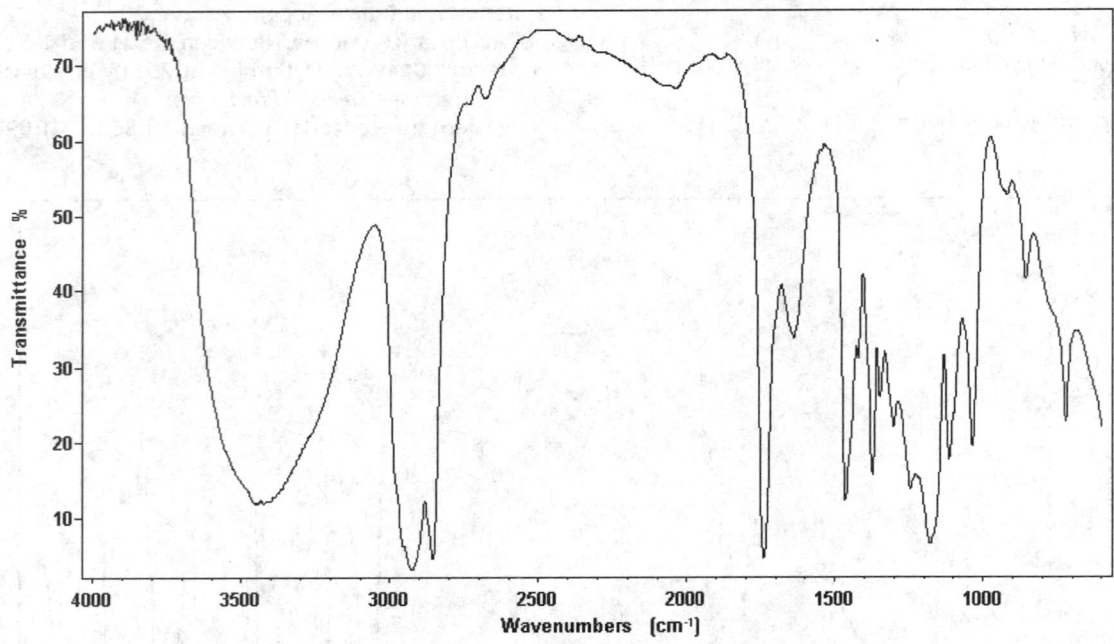

Ethyl Myristate

Ethyl Nonanoate

First Published: Prior to FCC 6

Ethyl Pelargonate

$C_{11}H_{22}O_2$ Formula wt 186.29

FEMA: 2447
UNII: KSH683S98J [ethyl nonanoate]

DESCRIPTION
Ethyl Nonanoate occurs as a colorless liquid.
Odor: Fatty, fruity, cognac
Solubility: Miscible in alcohol, propylene glycol; insoluble or practically insoluble in water
Boiling Point: ~229°
Solubility in Alcohol, Appendix VI: One mL dissolves in 10 mL of 70% alcohol.

Function: Flavoring agent

IDENTIFICATION
- **INFRARED SPECTRA,** *Spectrophotometric Identification Tests,* Appendix IIIC
  Acceptance criteria: The spectrum of the sample exhibits relative maxima at the same wavelengths as those of the spectrum below.

ASSAY
- **PROCEDURE:** Proceed as directed under *M-1b,* Appendix XI.

Acceptance criteria: NLT 98.0% of $C_{11}H_{22}O_2$

SPECIFIC TESTS
- **ACID VALUE, FLAVOR CHEMICALS (OTHER THAN ESSENTIAL OILS),** *M-15,* Appendix XI
  Acceptance criteria: NMT 3.0
- **REFRACTIVE INDEX,** Appendix II: At 20°
  Acceptance criteria: Between 1.420 and 1.424
- **SPECIFIC GRAVITY:** Determine at 25° by any reliable method (see *General Provisions*).
  Acceptance criteria: Between 0.863 and 0.867

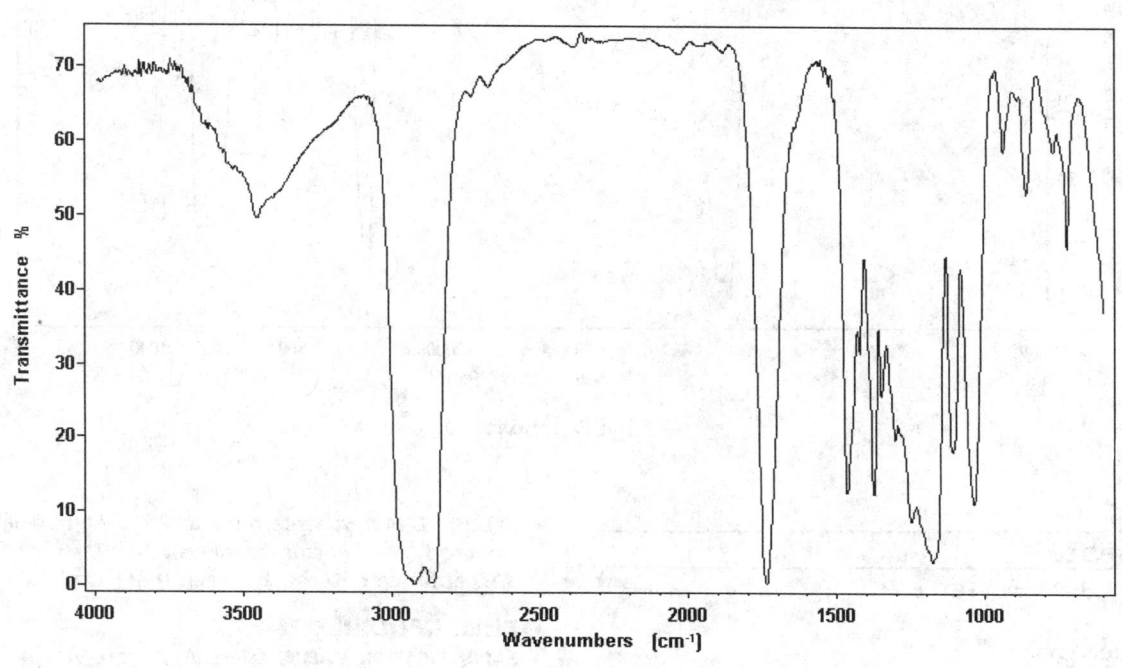

Ethyl Nonanoate

Ethyl Octanoate

First Published: Prior to FCC 6

Ethyl Caprylate
Ethyl Octoate

$C_{10}H_{20}O_2$ Formula wt 172.27
FEMA: 2449
UNII: 81C5MOP582 [ethyl octanoate]

DESCRIPTION
Ethyl Octanoate occurs as a colorless liquid.
Odor: Winy-brandy, fruity-floral
Solubility: Soluble in most fixed oils; slightly soluble in propylene glycol; insoluble or practically insoluble in glycerin, water
Boiling Point: ~209°

Solubility in Alcohol, Appendix VI: One mL dissolves in 4 mL of 70% alcohol.
Function: Flavoring agent

IDENTIFICATION
- **INFRARED SPECTRA,** *Spectrophotometric Identification Tests,* Appendix IIIC
  Acceptance criteria: The spectrum of the sample exhibits relative maxima at the same wavelengths as those of the spectrum below.

ASSAY
- **PROCEDURE:** Proceed as directed under *M-1b,* Appendix XI.
  Acceptance criteria: NLT 98.0% of $C_{10}H_{20}O_2$

SPECIFIC TESTS
- **ACID VALUE, FLAVOR CHEMICALS (OTHER THAN ESSENTIAL OILS),** *M-15,* Appendix XI
  Acceptance criteria: NMT 1.0
- **REFRACTIVE INDEX,** Appendix II: At 20°
  Acceptance criteria: Between 1.416 and 1.420

418 / Ethyl Octanoate / Monographs

- **SPECIFIC GRAVITY:** Determine at 25° by any reliable method (see *General Provisions*).
  Acceptance criteria: Between 0.863 and 0.867

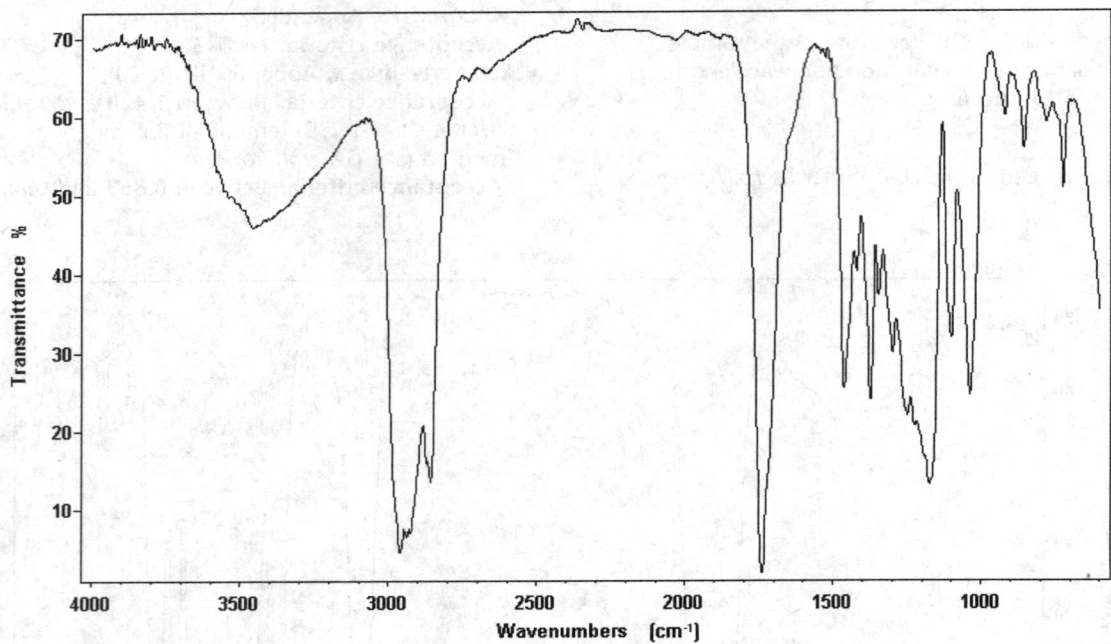

Ethyl Octanoate

Ethyl Oleate

First Published: Prior to FCC 6

Ethyl 9-Octadecenoate

$C_{20}H_{38}O_2$ **Formula wt 310.52**
FEMA: 2450
UNII: Z2Z439864Y [ethyl oleate]

DESCRIPTION
Ethyl Oleate occurs as a colorless to pale yellow liquid.
Odor: Floral
Solubility: Soluble in vegetable oils; insoluble or practically insoluble in propylene glycol, water
Boiling Point: ~205° to 208°
Solubility in Alcohol, Appendix VI: One mL dissolves in 1 mL of 95% ethanol.
Function: Flavoring agent

SPECIFIC TESTS
- **ACID VALUE, FLAVOR CHEMICALS (OTHER THAN ESSENTIAL OILS),** *M-15,* Appendix XI
  Acceptance criteria: NMT 1.0
- **REFRACTIVE INDEX,** Appendix II: At 20°
  Acceptance criteria: Between 1.448 and 1.453
- **SPECIFIC GRAVITY:** Determine at 25° by any reliable method (see *General Provisions*).
  Acceptance criteria: Between 0.868 and 0.873

OTHER REQUIREMENTS
- **SAPONIFICATION VALUE,** *Esters,* Appendix VI
  Acceptance criteria: Between 175 and 190

Ethyl Oxyhydrate (so-called)

First Published: Prior to FCC 6

Rum Ether, So-Called
FEMA: 2996
UNII: LM8ZO3J16V [ethyl oxyhydrate]

DESCRIPTION
Ethyl Oxyhydrate (so-called) occurs as a colorless liquid.
Odor: Sharp rum
Solubility: Miscible in alcohol, glycerin, propylene glycol; insoluble or practically insoluble in vegetable oils, water
Function: Flavoring agent

OTHER REQUIREMENTS
- **ALCOHOL CONTENT,** *M-4,* Appendix XI
  Acceptance criteria: NLT 14.0% by volume, at 15.56°
- **ESTER VALUE,** *Esters,* Appendix VI
  Sample: 1 to 3 g
  Acceptance criteria: NLT 25

Ethyl Phenylacetate

First Published: Prior to FCC 6

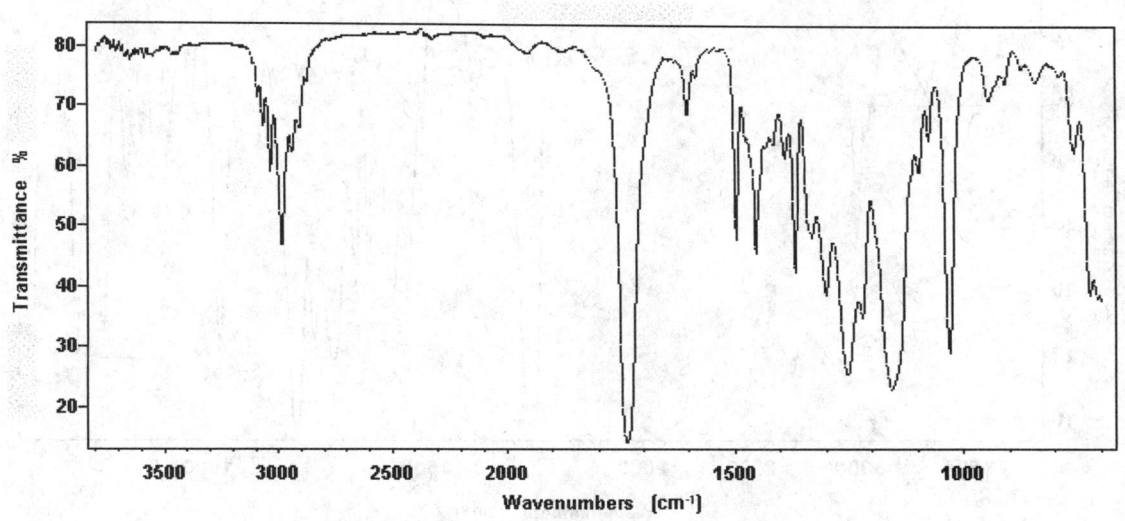

C₁₀H₁₂O₂   Formula wt 164.20
FEMA: 2452
UNII: V6CNZ04D8O [ethyl phenylacetate]

DESCRIPTION
Ethyl Phenylacetate occurs as a colorless or nearly colorless liquid.
Odor: Sweet, honey
Solubility: Soluble in alcohol, most fixed oils; insoluble or practically insoluble in glycerin, propylene glycol, water
Boiling Point: ~228°
Solubility in Alcohol, Appendix VI: One mL dissolves in 3 mL of 70% alcohol.
Function: Flavoring agent

IDENTIFICATION
- **INFRARED SPECTRA,** Spectrophotometric Identification Tests, Appendix IIIC
  Acceptance criteria: The spectrum of the sample exhibits relative maxima at the same wavelengths as those of the spectrum below.

ASSAY
- **PROCEDURE:** Proceed as directed under *M-1b,* Appendix XI.
  Acceptance criteria: NLT 98.0% of C₁₀H₁₂O₂

SPECIFIC TESTS
- **ACID VALUE, FLAVOR CHEMICALS (OTHER THAN ESSENTIAL OILS),** *M-15,* Appendix XI
  Acceptance criteria: NMT 1.0
- **REFRACTIVE INDEX,** Appendix II: At 20°
  Acceptance criteria: Between 1.496 and 1.500
- **SPECIFIC GRAVITY:** Determine at 25° by any reliable method (see *General Provisions*).
  Acceptance criteria: Between 1.027 and 1.032

OTHER REQUIREMENTS
- **CHLORINATED COMPOUNDS,** Appendix VI
  Acceptance criteria: Passes test

Ethyl Phenylacetate

Ethyl Phenylglycidate

First Published: Prior to FCC 6

$C_{11}H_{12}O_3$
FEMA: 2454
UNII: 2VVS520ZWM [ethyl 3-phenylglycidate]

Formula wt 192.21

DESCRIPTION
Ethyl Phenylglycidate occurs as a colorless to slightly yellow liquid.
Odor: Strong, strawberry
Solubility: Soluble in alcohol, chloroform, ether; insoluble or practically insoluble in water
Boiling Point: ~96° (0.5 mm Hg)
Solubility in Alcohol, Appendix VI: One mL dissolves in 6 mL of 70% alcohol, and in 1 mL of 80% alcohol to give a clear solution.

Function: Flavoring agent

IDENTIFICATION
- **INFRARED SPECTRA,** *Spectrophotometric Identification Tests,* Appendix IIIC
  Acceptance criteria: The spectrum of the sample exhibits relative maxima at the same wavelengths as those of the spectrum below.

ASSAY
- **PROCEDURE:** Proceed as directed under *Esters,* Appendix VI
  Sample: 1.4 g
  Analysis: Use 96.11 as the equivalence factor (e).
  Acceptance criteria: NLT 98.0% of $C_{11}H_{12}O_3$

SPECIFIC TESTS
- **REFRACTIVE INDEX,** Appendix II: At 20°
  Acceptance criteria: Between 1.516 and 1.521
- **SPECIFIC GRAVITY:** Determine at 25° by any reliable method (see *General Provisions*).
  Acceptance criteria: Between 1.120 and 1.125

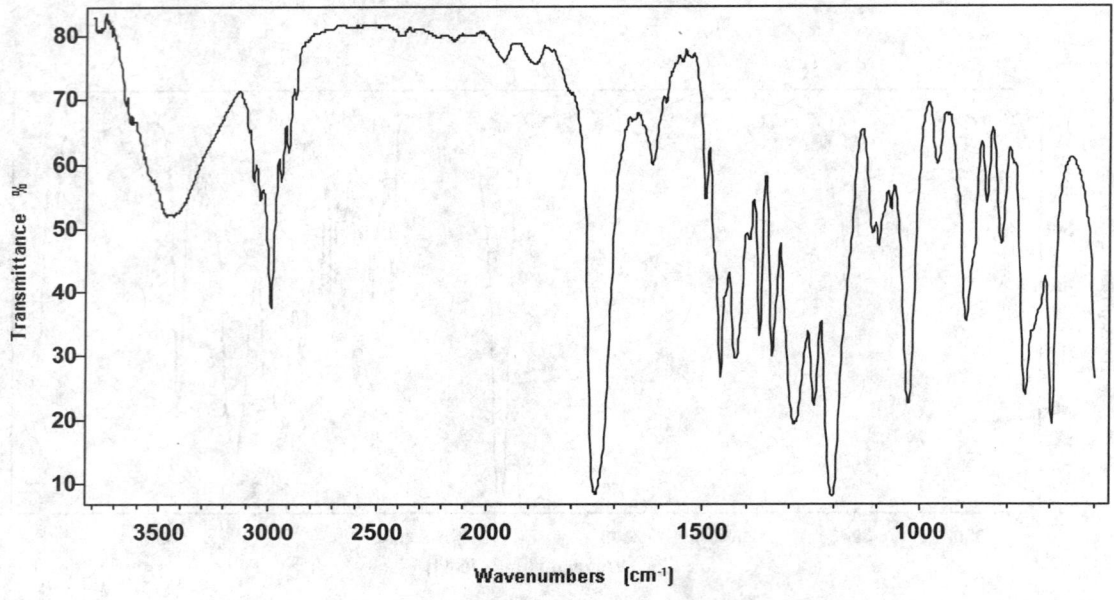

Ethyl Phenylglycidate

Ethyl Propionate

First Published: Prior to FCC 6

$C_5H_{10}O_2$
FEMA: 2456

Formula wt 102.13

UNII: AT9K8FY49U [ethyl propionate]

DESCRIPTION
Ethyl Propionate occurs as a colorless liquid.
Odor: Fruity, rum, ethereal
Solubility: Soluble in most fixed oils; 1 mL dissolves in 42 mL water; miscible in alcohol, propylene glycol
Boiling Point: ~99°
Function: Flavoring agent

IDENTIFICATION
- **INFRARED SPECTRA,** *Spectrophotometric Identification Tests,* Appendix IIIC
  Acceptance criteria: The spectrum of the sample exhibits relative maxima at the same wavelengths as those of the spectrum below.

ASSAY
- **PROCEDURE:** Proceed as directed under *M-1b,* Appendix XI.
  Acceptance criteria: NLT 97.0% of $C_5H_{10}O_2$

SPECIFIC TESTS
- **ACID VALUE, FLAVOR CHEMICALS (OTHER THAN ESSENTIAL OILS),** *M-15,* Appendix XI
  Acceptance criteria: NMT 2.0
- **REFRACTIVE INDEX,** Appendix II: At 20°
  Acceptance criteria: Between 1.383 and 1.385
- **SPECIFIC GRAVITY:** Determine at 25° by any reliable method (see *General Provisions*).
  Acceptance criteria: Between 0.886 and 0.889

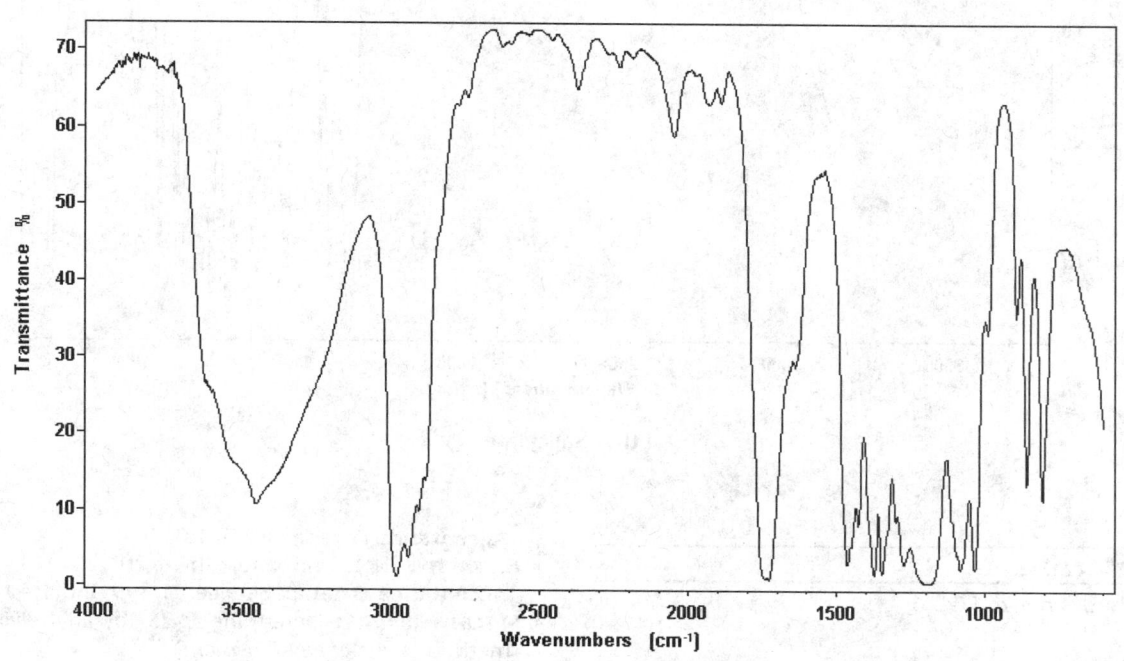

Ethyl Propionate

Ethyl Salicylate

First Published: Prior to FCC 6

$C_9H_{10}O_3$ Formula wt 166.18
FEMA: 2458
UNII: 555U6TZ2MV [ethyl salicylate]

DESCRIPTION
Ethyl Salicylate occurs as a colorless liquid.
Odor: Wintergreen
Solubility: Soluble in alcohol, acetic acid, most fixed oils; slightly soluble in glycerin, water
Boiling Point: ~234°
Solubility in Alcohol, Appendix VI: One mL dissolves in 4 mL of 80% alcohol to give a clear solution.

Function: Flavoring agent

IDENTIFICATION
- **INFRARED SPECTRA,** *Spectrophotometric Identification Tests,* Appendix IIIC
  Acceptance criteria: The spectrum of the sample exhibits relative maxima at the same wavelengths as those of the spectrum below.

ASSAY
- **PROCEDURE:** Proceed as directed under *M-1b,* Appendix XI.
  Acceptance criteria: NLT 99.0% of $C_9H_{10}O_3$

SPECIFIC TESTS
- **ACID VALUE, FLAVOR CHEMICALS (OTHER THAN ESSENTIAL OILS),** *M-15,* Appendix XI: Use phenol red TS as the indicator.
  Acceptance criteria: NMT 1.0
- **REFRACTIVE INDEX,** Appendix II: At 20°
  Acceptance criteria: Between 1.520 and 1.525

422 / Ethyl Salicylate / Monographs

- **SPECIFIC GRAVITY:** Determine at 25° by any reliable method (see *General Provisions*).
  Acceptance criteria: Between 1.126 and 1.130

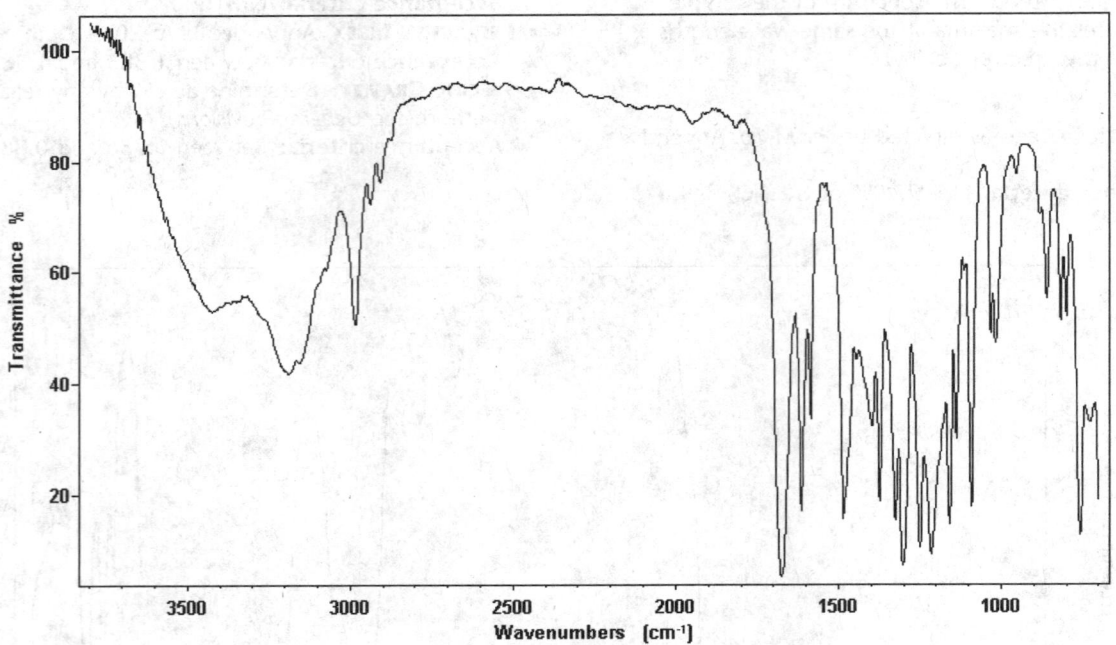

Ethyl Salicylate

Ethyl Valerate

First Published: Prior to FCC 6

Ethyl *n*-Pentanoate

C$_7$H$_{14}$O$_2$ Formula wt 130.19
FEMA: 2462
UNII: 95R258T4P6 [ethyl valerate]

DESCRIPTION
Ethyl Valerate occurs as a colorless to pale yellow liquid.
Odor: Fruity
Solubility: Soluble in vegetable oils; slightly soluble in propylene glycol; insoluble or practically insoluble in water
Boiling Point: ~145°
Solubility in Alcohol, Appendix VI: One mL dissolves in 1 mL of 95% ethanol.
Function: Flavoring agent

ASSAY
- **PROCEDURE:** Proceed as directed under *M-1b*, Appendix XI.
  Acceptance criteria: NLT 98.0% of C$_7$H$_{14}$O$_2$

SPECIFIC TESTS
- **ACID VALUE, FLAVOR CHEMICALS (OTHER THAN ESSENTIAL OILS),** *M-15,* Appendix XI

  Acceptance criteria: NMT 1.0
- **REFRACTIVE INDEX,** Appendix II: At 20°
  Acceptance criteria: Between 1.399 and 1.404
- **SPECIFIC GRAVITY:** Determine at 25° by any reliable method (see *General Provisions*).
  Acceptance criteria: Between 0.870 and 0.875

Ethyl Vanillin

First Published: Prior to FCC 6
Last Revision: FCC 6

3-Ethoxy-4-hydroxybenzaldehyde

C$_9$H$_{10}$O$_3$ Formula wt 166.18
FEMA: 2464
UNII: YC9ST449YJ [ethyl vanillin]

DESCRIPTION
Ethyl Vanillin occurs as a fine white or slightly yellow crystalline powder.
Odor: Strong, vanilla
Solubility: Soluble in alcohol, chloroform, ether, propylene glycol solutions of alkali hydroxides; 1 g dissolves in 100 mL of water at 50°

Solubility in Alcohol, Appendix VI: One g dissolves in 5 mL of 95% ethanol.
Function: Flavoring agent

IDENTIFICATION

- **INFRARED ABSORPTION,** *Spectrophotometric Identification Tests,* Appendix IIIC
  Reference standard: USP Ethyl Vanillin RS
  Sample and standard preparation: *K*
  Acceptance criteria: The spectrum of the sample exhibits maxima at the same wavelengths as those in the spectrum of the *Reference standard*.

ASSAY

- **PROCEDURE:** Proceed as directed under *M-1b,* Appendix XI.
  Acceptance criteria: NLT 98.0% of $C_9H_{10}O_3$

OTHER REQUIREMENTS

- **MELTING RANGE OR TEMPERATURE DETERMINATION,** Appendix IIB
  Sample: Previously dried for 4h over P_2O_5
  Acceptance criteria: 76 to 78°
- **LOSS ON DRYING,** Appendix IIC: 4 h over P_2O_5
  Acceptance criteria: NMT 0.5%
- **RESIDUE ON IGNITION (SULFATED ASH),** Appendix IIC
  Sample: 2 g
  Acceptance criteria: NMT 0.05%

Ethyl-(*E*)-2-butenoate

First Published: Prior to FCC 6

Ethyl-*trans*-2-butenoate
Ethyl Crotonate

$C_6H_{10}O_2$ Formula wt 114.14
FEMA: 3486
UNII: 99YUC7A1X1 [ethyl crotonate]

DESCRIPTION

Ethyl-(*E*)-2-butenoate occurs as a colorless to pale yellow liquid.
Odor: Sweet, ethereal
Solubility: Soluble in propylene glycol, vegetable oils; insoluble or practically insoluble in water
Boiling Point: ~136°
Solubility in Alcohol, Appendix VI: One mL dissolves in 1 mL of 95% alcohol.
Function: Flavoring agent

IDENTIFICATION

- **INFRARED SPECTRA,** *Spectrophotometric Identification Tests,* Appendix IIIC
  Acceptance criteria: The spectrum of the sample exhibits relative maxima at the same wavelengths as those of the spectrum below.

ASSAY

- **PROCEDURE:** Proceed as directed under *M-1b,* Appendix XI.
  Acceptance criteria: NLT 97.0% of $C_6H_{10}O_2$

SPECIFIC TESTS

- **ACID VALUE, FLAVOR CHEMICALS (OTHER THAN ESSENTIAL OILS),** *M-15,* Appendix XI
  Acceptance criteria: NMT 5.0
- **REFRACTIVE INDEX,** Appendix II: At 20°
  Acceptance criteria: Between 1.422 and 1.427
- **SPECIFIC GRAVITY:** Determine at 25° by any reliable method (see *General Provisions*).
  Acceptance criteria: Between 0.913 and 0.920

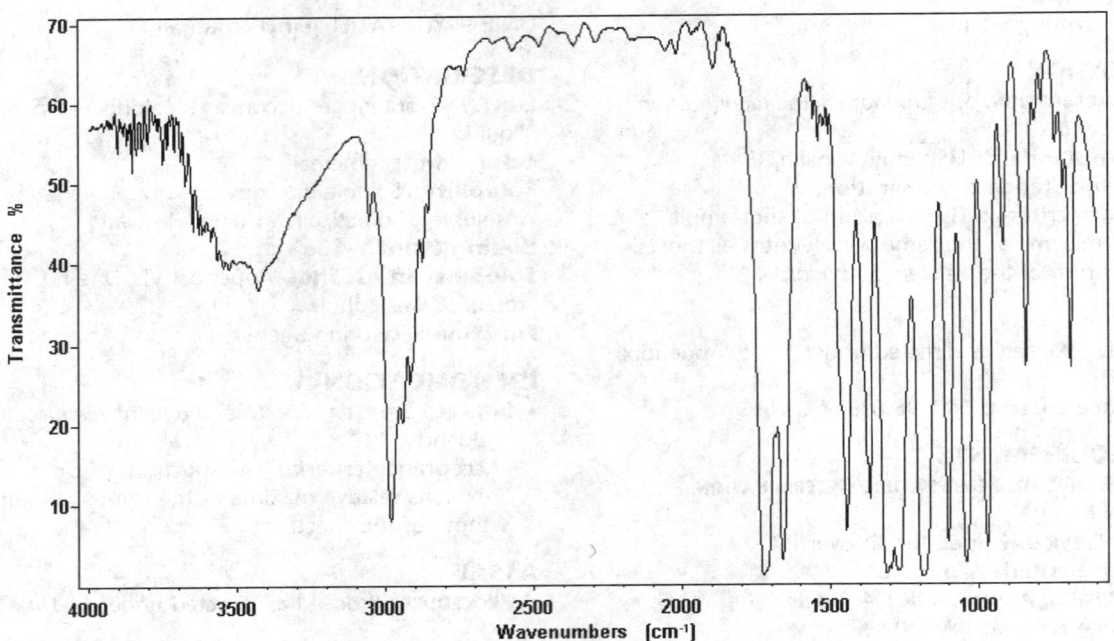

Ethyl-(E)-2-butenoate

Ethylene Brassylate

First Published: Prior to FCC 6

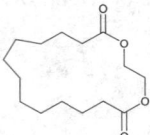

$C_{15}H_{26}O_4$　　　　　　　　　　Formula wt 270.37
FEMA: 3543
UNII: 9A87HC7ROD [ethylene brassylate]

DESCRIPTION
Ethylene Brassylate occurs as a colorless to pale yellow liquid.
Odor: Sweet, musky
Solubility: Soluble in vegetable oils; insoluble or practically insoluble in propylene glycol, water
Boiling Point: ~138° to 142° (1 mm Hg)
Solubility in Alcohol, Appendix VI: One mL dissolves in 1 mL of 95% alcohol.

Function: Flavoring agent

IDENTIFICATION
- **INFRARED SPECTRA,** *Spectrophotometric Identification Tests,* Appendix IIIC
  Acceptance criteria: The spectrum of the sample exhibits relative maxima at the same wavelengths as those of the spectrum below.

ASSAY
- **PROCEDURE:** Proceed as directed under *M-1a,* Appendix XI.
  Acceptance criteria: NLT 95.0% of $C_{15}H_{26}O_4$

SPECIFIC TESTS
- **ACID VALUE, FLAVOR CHEMICALS (OTHER THAN ESSENTIAL OILS),** *M-15,* Appendix XI
  Acceptance criteria: NMT 1.0
- **REFRACTIVE INDEX,** Appendix II: At 20°
  Acceptance criteria: Between 1.468 and 1.473
- **SPECIFIC GRAVITY:** Determine at 25° by any reliable method (see *General Provisions*).
  Acceptance criteria: Between 1.040 and 1.045

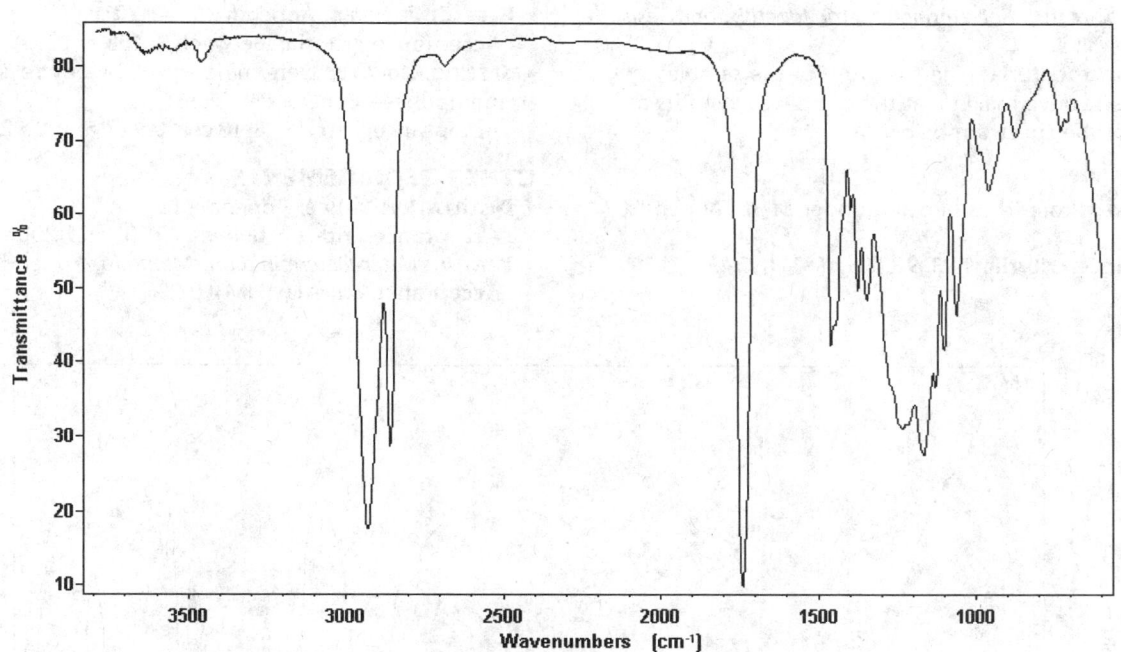

Ethylene Brassylate

2-Ethylbutyraldehyde

First Published: Prior to FCC 6
Last Revision: First Supplement, FCC 6

$C_6H_{12}O$ Formula wt 100.16
FEMA: 2426
UNII: 676JY5569P [2-ethylbutyraldehyde]

DESCRIPTION
2-Ethylbutyraldehyde occurs as a colorless, mobile liquid. It may contain a suitable antioxidant.
Odor: Pungent
Solubility: Miscible in alcohol, ether; 1 mL dissolves in 50 mL water
Boiling Point: ~117°
Function: Flavoring agent

ASSAY
- **PROCEDURE:** Proceed as directed under *M-1b*, Appendix XI.
  Acceptance criteria: NLT 95.0% of $C_6H_{12}O$

SPECIFIC TESTS
- **ACID VALUE, FLAVOR CHEMICALS (OTHER THAN ESSENTIAL OILS),** *M-15*, Appendix XI
  Acceptance criteria: NMT 2.0

- **REFRACTIVE INDEX,** Appendix II: At 20°
  Acceptance criteria: Between 1.398 and 1.404
- **SPECIFIC GRAVITY:** Determine at 25° by any reliable method (see *General Provisions*).
  Acceptance criteria: Between 0.808 and 0.814

OTHER REQUIREMENTS
- **DISTILLATION RANGE,** Appendix IIB
  Acceptance criteria: NLT 95% between 100° and 120°

2-Ethylbutyric Acid

First Published: Prior to FCC 6

$C_6H_{12}O_2$ Formula wt 116.16
FEMA: 2429
UNII: IDY8B990KE [2-ethylbutyric acid]

DESCRIPTION
2-Ethylbutyric Acid occurs as a colorless liquid.
Odor: Mildly rancid
Solubility: Miscible in alcohol, ether; 1 mL dissolves in 65 mL water
Boiling Point: ~99° (18 mm Hg)
Function: Flavoring agent

IDENTIFICATION

- **INFRARED SPECTRA,** *Spectrophotometric Identification Tests,* Appendix IIIC
  Acceptance criteria: The spectrum of the sample exhibits relative maxima at the same wavelengths as those of the spectrum below.

ASSAY

- **PROCEDURE:** Proceed as directed under *M-3b,* Appendix XI.
  Acceptance criteria: NLT 98.0% of $C_6H_{12}O_2$

SPECIFIC TESTS

- **REFRACTIVE INDEX,** Appendix II: At 20°
  Acceptance criteria: Between 1.408 and 1.418
- **SPECIFIC GRAVITY:** Determine at 25° by any reliable method (see *General Provisions*).
  Acceptance criteria: Between 0.917 and 0.922

OTHER REQUIREMENTS

- **DISTILLATION RANGE,** Appendix IIB
  Acceptance criteria: Between 190° and 200°
- **WATER,** *Water Determination, Method I,* Appendix IIB
  Acceptance criteria: NMT 0.2%

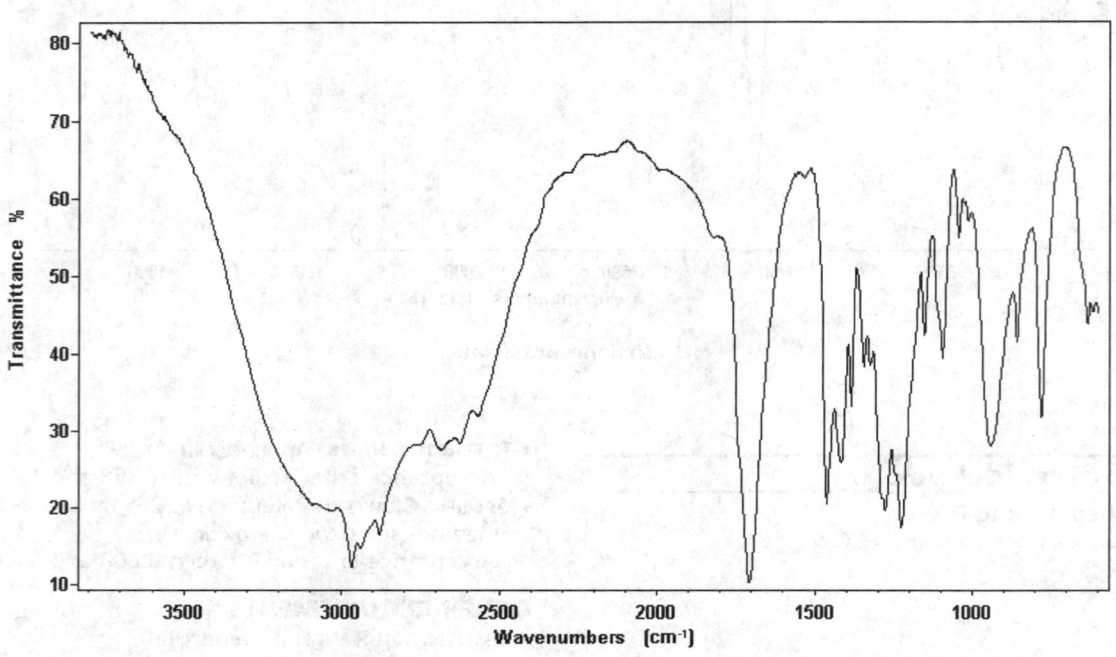

2-Ethylbutyric Acid

Ethylene Dichloride

First Published: Prior to FCC 6

1,2-Dichloroethane

$C_2H_4Cl_2$
UNII: 55163IJI47 [ethylene dichloride]

Formula wt 98.96
CAS: [107-06-2]

DESCRIPTION

Ethylene Dichloride occurs as a clear, colorless, flammable, oily liquid. It is slightly soluble in water, and is soluble in alcohol, in ether, and in acetone. Its refractive index at 20° is about 1.445.

Function: Extraction solvent
Packaging and Storage: Store in tight containers.

IMPURITIES

Inorganic Impurities

- **LEAD** *Lead Limit Test, Atomic Absorption Spectrophotometric Graphite Furnace Method, Method II,* Appendix IIIB
  Sample: 10 g
  Acceptance criteria: NMT 1 mg/kg
- **WATER,** *Water Determination,* Appendix IIB
  Acceptance criteria: NMT 0.03%

SPECIFIC TESTS

- **ACIDITY (AS HCL)**
  Sample: 25 mL
  Analysis: Transfer 25 mL of alcohol to a 100-mL glass-stoppered flask, add 2 drops of phenolphthalein TS, and titrate with 0.01 N sodium hydroxide to the first appearance of a slight pink color. Add the *Sample,* mix, and titrate with 0.01 N sodium hydroxide until the faint pink color is restored.
  Acceptance criteria: NMT 0.85 mL of 0.01 N sodium hydroxide is required to restore the pink color. (NMT 10 mg/kg).

- **DISTILLATION RANGE,** Appendix IIB
  Acceptance criteria: Between 82° and 85°
- **FREE HALOGENS**
  Sample: 10 mL
  Analysis: Mix the Sample with 10 mL of 10% potassium iodide solution and 1 mL of starch TS. Shake the mixture vigorously for 2 min.
  Acceptance criteria: A blue color does not appear in the water layer.
- **NONVOLATILE RESIDUE**
  Sample: 80 mL (~100 g)
  Analysis: Evaporate the Sample to dryness in a tared dish on a steam bath, dry the residue at 105° for 30 min, cool, and weigh. [**CAUTION**—Use an appropriate fume hood.]
  Acceptance criteria: NMT 0.002%
- **SPECIFIC GRAVITY:** Determine by any reliable method (see General Provisions).
  Acceptance criteria: Between 1.245 and 1.255

Eucalyptol

First Published: Prior to FCC 6

1,8-Cineol
1,8 Epoxy-p-menthane
1:8 Oxido-p-menthane

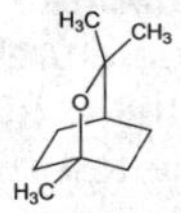

$C_{10}H_{18}O$ Formula wt 154.25

FEMA: 2465
UNII: RV6J6604TK [eucalyptol]

DESCRIPTION
Eucalyptol occurs as a colorless liquid.
Odor: Camphoraceous; pungent, cooling taste
Solubility: Soluble in alcohol, most fixed oils, glycerin, propylene glycol
Boiling Point: ~176°
Solubility in Alcohol, Appendix VI: One mL dissolves in 5 mL of 60% alcohol.
Function: Flavoring agent

IDENTIFICATION
- **INFRARED SPECTRA,** Spectrophotometric Identification Tests, Appendix IIIC
  Acceptance criteria: The spectrum of the sample exhibits relative maxima at the same wavelengths as those of the spectrum below.

ASSAY
- **PROCEDURE:** Proceed as directed under M-1a, Appendix XI.
  Acceptance criteria: NLT 98.5% of $C_{10}H_{18}O$

SPECIFIC TESTS
- **REFRACTIVE INDEX,** Appendix II: At 20°
  Acceptance criteria: Between 1.455 and 1.460
- **SPECIFIC GRAVITY:** Determine at 25° by any reliable method (see General Provisions).
  Acceptance criteria: Between 0.921 and 0.924

OTHER REQUIREMENTS
- **ANGULAR ROTATION,** Optical (Specific) Rotation, Appendix IIB: Use a 100-mm tube.
  Acceptance criteria: Between −0.5° and +0.5°

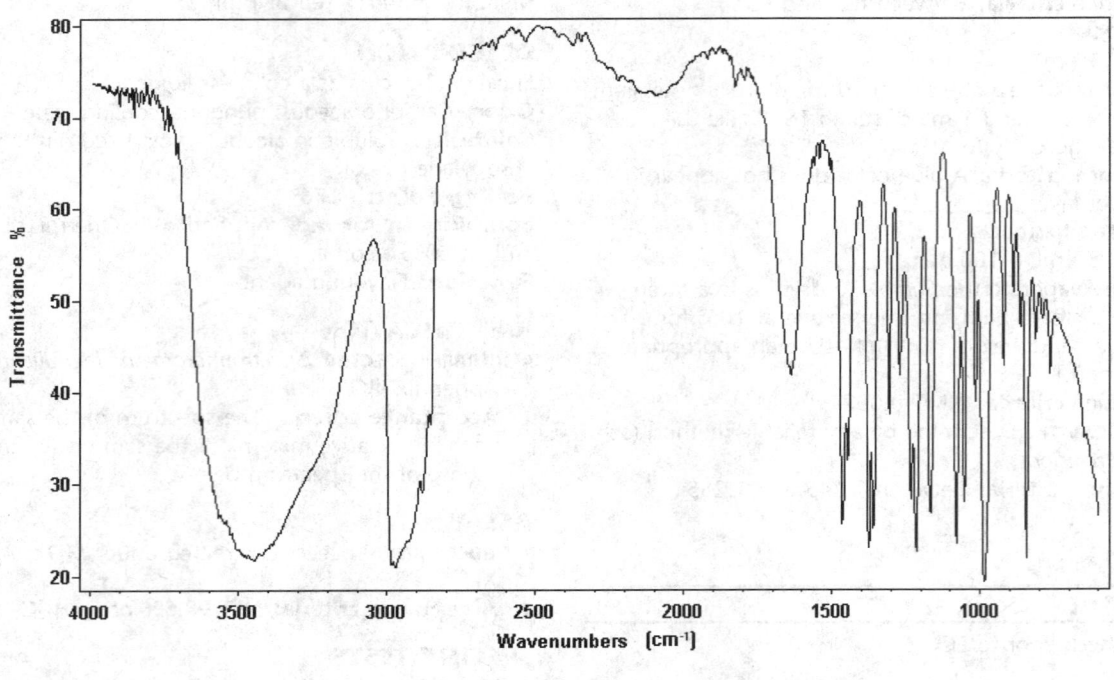

Eucalyptol

Eucalyptus Oil

First Published: Prior to FCC 6

CAS: [8000-48-4]

UNII: 2R04ONI662 [eucalyptus oil]

DESCRIPTION
Eucalyptus Oil occurs as a colorless or pale yellow liquid with a characteristic, aromatic, somewhat camphoraceous odor and a pungent, spicy, cooling taste. It is the volatile oil obtained by steam distillation from the fresh leaves of *Eucalyptus globulus* Labillardiere and other species of *Eucalyptus* L'Heritier (Fam. Myrtaceae).
Function: Flavoring agent
Packaging and Storage: Store in well-filled, tight containers in a cool place protected from light.

IDENTIFICATION
- **INFRARED SPECTRA,** *Spectrophotometric Identification Tests,* Appendix IIIC
  Acceptance criteria: The spectrum of the sample exhibits relative maxima at the same wavelengths as those of the spectrum below.

ASSAY
- **CINEOLE**
  Sample: 3 g, previously dried with anhydrous sodium sulfate
  Analysis: Transfer the *Sample,* into a 25- × 150-mm test tube. Add to the *Sample* 2.100 g of melted o-cresol that is pure and dry, with a solidification point of 30° or higher. [NOTE—Moisture in the o-cresol may cause low results.] Stir the mixture with a thermometer (see *Thermometers,* Appendix I) to induce crystallization, and note the highest temperature reading obtained. Warm the tube gently until the contents are completely melted, then insert the test tube into an apparatus assembled as directed under *Solidification Point,* Appendix IIB. Allow the mixture to cool slowly until crystallization starts, or until the temperature has fallen to the point noted above. Stir the mixture vigorously with the thermometer, rubbing the sides of the test tube with an up and down motion to induce crystallization. Continue the stirring and rubbing until the temperature no longer rises. Record the highest temperature obtained as the solidification point. Repeat the procedure until two results agreeing within 0.1° are obtained. Calculate the percentage of cineole from the *Percentage of Cineole* table, Appendix VI.
  Acceptance criteria: NLT 70.0% of cineole ($C_{10}H_{18}O$)

SPECIFIC TESTS
- **PHELLANDRENE**
  Sample: 2.5 mL
  Analysis: Mix the *Sample* with 5 mL of solvent hexane, add 5 mL of a solution of sodium nitrite (made by dissolving 5 g of sodium nitrite in 8 mL of water), and gradually add 5 mL of glacial acetic acid.
  Acceptance criteria: No crystals form in the mixture within 10 min following the addition of the acetic acid.
- **REFRACTIVE INDEX,** Appendix IIB
  [NOTE—Use an Abbé or other refractometer of equal or greater accuracy.]
  Acceptance criteria: Between 1.458 and 1.470 at 20°

- **SOLUBILITY IN ALCOHOL,** Appendix VI
  Acceptance criteria: One mL of sample dissolves in 5 mL of 70% alcohol.
- **SPECIFIC GRAVITY:** Determine by any reliable method (see *General Provisions*).
  Acceptance criteria: Between 0.905 and 0.925

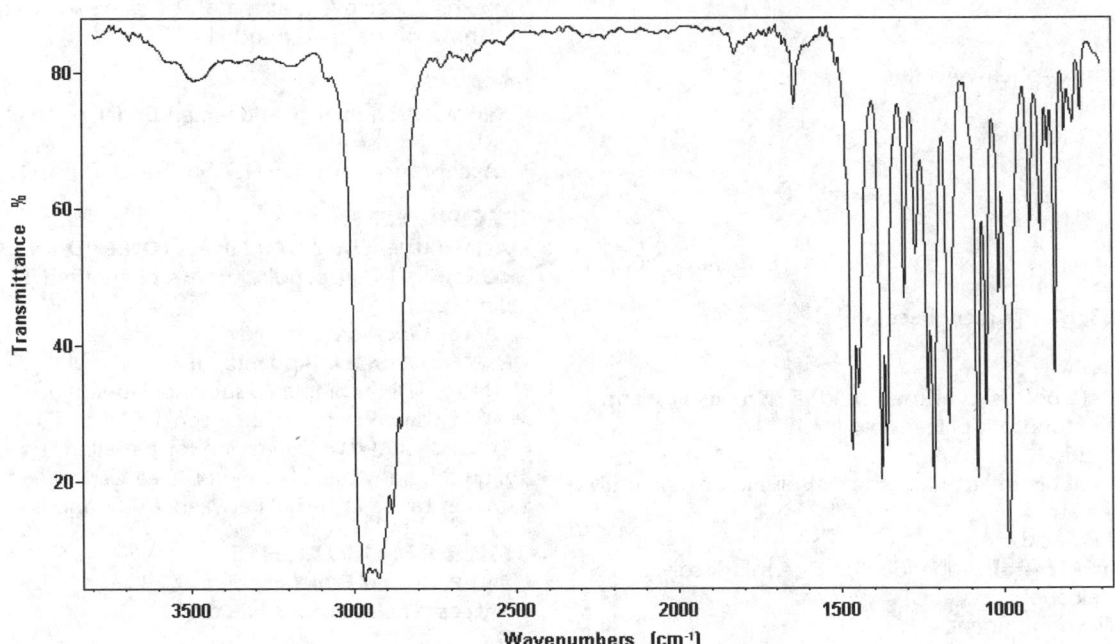

Eucalyptus Oil

Eugenol

First Published: Prior to FCC 6
Last Revision: FCC 6

4-Allylguaiacol
4-Allyl-2-methoxyphenol
Eugenic Acid

$C_{10}H_{12}O_2$ Formula wt 164.20
FEMA: 2467
UNII: 3T8H1794QW [eugenol]

DESCRIPTION
Eugenol occurs as a colorless to pale yellow liquid. It darkens and thickens on air exposure and has a pungent, spicy taste.
Odor: Strong clove
Solubility: Slightly soluble in water; miscible in alcohol, chloroform, ether, most fixed oils
Boiling Point: ~256°
Solubility in Alcohol, Appendix VI: One mL dissolves in 2 mL of 70% alcohol.

Function: Flavoring agent

IDENTIFICATION
Infrared Absorption, *Spectrophotometric Identification Tests,* Appendix IIIC
  Reference standard: USP Eugenol AS
  Sample and standard preparation: *F*
  Acceptance criteria: The spectrum of the sample exhibits maxima at the same wavelengths as those in the spectrum of the *Reference standard.*

ASSAY
- **PROCEDURE:** Proceed as directed under *M-1b,* Appendix XI.
  Acceptance criteria: NLT 98.0% of $C_{10}H_{12}O_2$

SPECIFIC TESTS
- **REFRACTIVE INDEX,** Appendix II: At 20°
  Acceptance criteria: Between 1.540 and 1.542
- **SPECIFIC GRAVITY:** Determine at 25° by any reliable method (see *General Provisions*).
  Acceptance criteria: Between 1.064 and 1.070

OTHER REQUIREMENTS
- **HYDROCARBONS,** *M-7,* Appendix XI
  Acceptance criteria: Passes test

Eugenyl Acetate

First Published: Prior to FCC 6

Aceteugenol
Acetyl Eugenol
4-Allyl-2-methoxy-phenyl Acetate
Eugenol Acetate

$C_{12}H_{14}O_3$
FEMA: 2469
UNII: V9OSB376X8 [eugenol acetate]

Formula wt 206.24

DESCRIPTION
Eugenyl Acetate occurs as a fused solid, and melts at warm room temperature to a pale yellow liquid.
Odor: Mild, clove
Solubility: Soluble in alcohol, ether; insoluble or practically insoluble in water
Boiling Point: ~282°
Solubility in Alcohol, Appendix VI: One mL dissolves in 5 mL of 70% alcohol.
Function: Flavoring agent

IDENTIFICATION
- **INFRARED SPECTRA,** Spectrophotometric Identification Tests, Appendix IIIC
  Acceptance criteria: The spectrum of the sample exhibits relative maxima at the same wavelengths as those of the spectrum below.

ASSAY
- **PROCEDURE:** Proceed as directed under *M-1b*, Appendix XI.
  Acceptance criteria: NLT 98.0% of $C_{12}H_{14}O_3$

SPECIFIC TESTS
- **ACID VALUE, FLAVOR CHEMICALS (OTHER THAN ESSENTIAL OILS),** *M-15,* Appendix XI: Use phenol red TS as the indicator.
  Acceptance criteria: NMT 1.0
- **REFRACTIVE INDEX,** Appendix II
  [NOTE—Determine as a supercooled liquid.]
  Acceptance criteria: Between 1.514 and 1.522
- **SPECIFIC GRAVITY:** Determine for a melted, supercooled liquid by any reliable method (see *General Provisions*).
  Acceptance criteria: Between 1.077 and 1.082

OTHER REQUIREMENTS
- **SOLIDIFICATION POINT,** Appendix IIB
  Acceptance criteria: NLT 25°

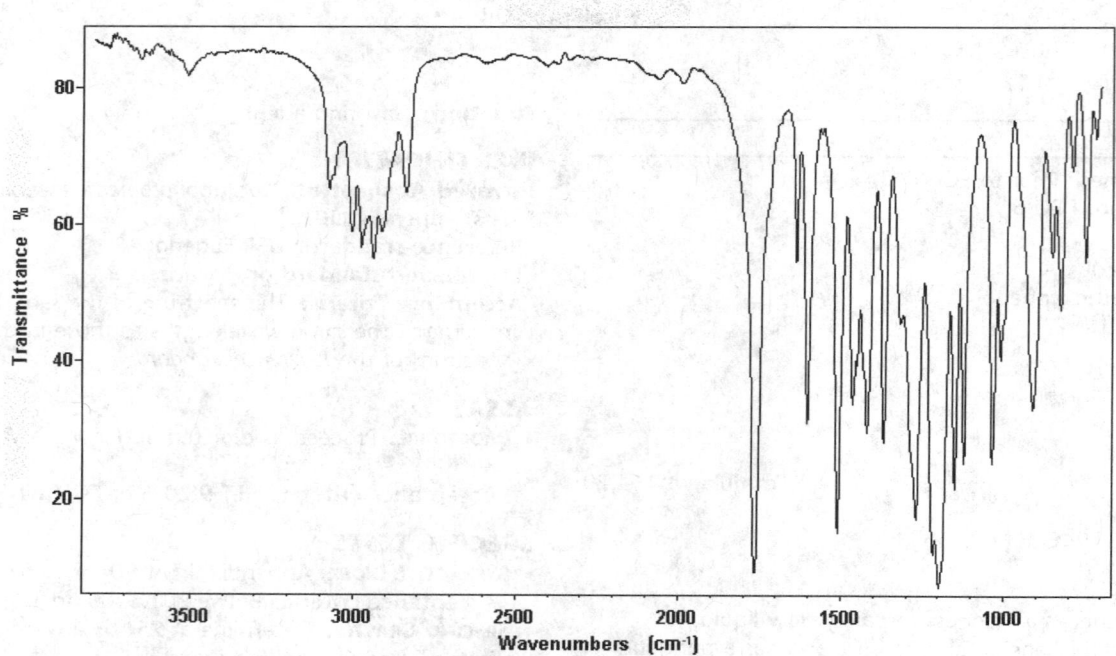

Eugenyl Acetate

Farnesol

First Published: Prior to FCC 6

3,7,11-Trimethyl-2,6,10-dodecatrien-1-ol

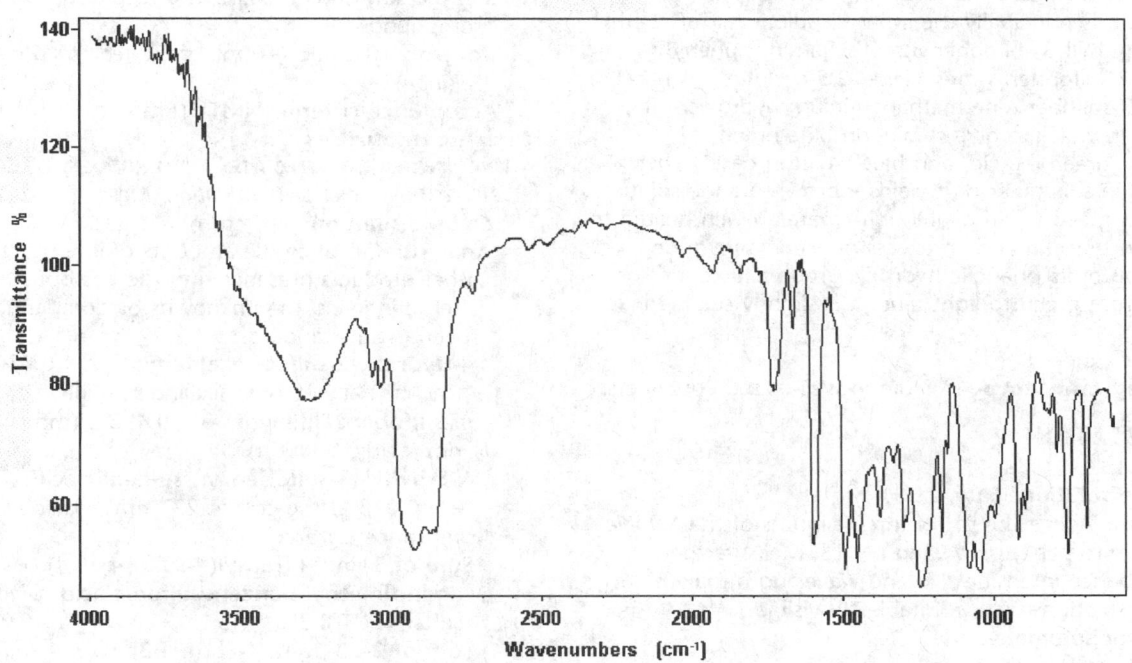

$C_{15}H_{26}O$ Formula wt 222.37
FEMA: 2478
UNII: EB41QIU6JL [farnesol]

DESCRIPTION
Farnesol occurs as a slightly yellow liquid.
Odor: Mild, oily
Solubility: Insoluble or practically insoluble in water
Boiling Point: ~263°
Solubility in Alcohol, Appendix VI: One mL dissolves in 1 mL of 95% ethanol.

Function: Flavoring agent

IDENTIFICATION
- **INFRARED SPECTRA,** *Spectrophotometric Identification Tests,* Appendix IIIC
  Acceptance criteria: The spectrum of the sample exhibits relative maxima at the same wavelengths as those of the spectrum below.

ASSAY
- **PROCEDURE:** Proceed as directed under *M-1a*, Appendix XI.
  Acceptance criteria: NLT 96.0% of $C_{15}H_{26}O$ (sum of four isomers)

SPECIFIC TESTS
- **REFRACTIVE INDEX,** Appendix II: At 20°
  Acceptance criteria: Between 1.487 and 1.492
- **SPECIFIC GRAVITY:** Determine at 25° by any reliable method (see *General Provisions*).
  Acceptance criteria: Between 0.884 and 0.891

Farnesol

Fast Green[1]

First Published: Prior to FCC 6

Fast Green FCF
CI 42053
Class: Triphenylmethane

$C_{37}H_{34}N_2O_{10}S_3Na_2$
INS: 143
UNII: 9J3VQ0Y6BV [fast green]

Formula wt 808.86
CAS: [2353-45-9]

DESCRIPTION
Fast Green occurs as a red to brown-violet powder or granules. It is principally the inner disodium salt of N-ethyl-N-[4-[[4-[ethyl[(3-sulfophenyl)methyl]amino] phenyl](4-hydroxy-2-sulfophenyl)methylene]-2,5-cyclohexadien-1-ylidene]-3-sulfobenzene-methanaminium hydroxide. It dissolves in water to give a solution blue-green at neutrality, green in acid, and blue-violet in base. When dissolved in sulfuric acid, it yields a brown-orange solution that turns green when diluted with water. When heated to 130° with triacetin and an excess of acetic anhydride, acetylation of its phenolic hydroxyl group causes a color change from green to light blue. It is slightly soluble in ethanol.

Function: Color
Packaging and Storage: Store in well-closed containers.

IDENTIFICATION
- **Procedure**
  Sample solution: 5 µg/mL
  Analysis: Adjust the pH of three aliquots of the Sample solution to pH 1, pH 7, and pH 13. Measure the absorbance intensities (A) and wavelength maxima of these solutions with a suitable UV-visible spectrophotometer.
  Acceptance criteria
  pH 1: A = 0.83 at 625 nm and 0.09 at 423 nm
  pH 7: A = 0.80 at 624 nm and 0.08 at 423 nm
  pH 13: A = 0.74 at 610 nm

ASSAY
- **Total Color,** Color Determination, Methods I and II, Appendix IIIC: Both methods must be used.
  Method I (Spectrophotometric)
  Sample: 50 to 75 mg
  Analysis: Transfer the Sample into a 1-L volumetric flask; dissolve in and dilute to volume with water. Determine as directed at 625 nm using 0.156 L/(mg·cm) for the absorptivity (a) for Fast Green.
  Method II (TiCl$_3$ Titration)
  Sample: 0.5 g
  Analysis: Determine as directed using 2.47 as the stoichiometric factor (F_S) for Fast Green.
  Acceptance criteria: The average of results obtained from Methods I and II is NLT 85.0% total coloring matters.

IMPURITIES
Inorganic Impurities
- **Arsenic,** Arsenic Limit Test, Appendix IIIB
  Sample solution: Prepare as directed for organic compounds.
  Acceptance criteria: NMT 3 mg/kg
- **Chromium,** Color Determination, Appendix IIIC
  Acceptance criteria: NMT 0.005%
- **Lead,** Lead Limit Test, Appendix IIIB
  Sample solution: Prepare as directed for organic compounds.
  Control: 10 µg Pb (10 mL of Diluted Standard Lead Solution)
  Acceptance criteria: NMT 10 mg/kg

Organic Impurities
- **Uncombined Intermediates and Products of Side Reactions,** Color Determination, Method I, Appendix IIIC
  Sample solution: 20 mg/mL
  Analysis: Calculate the amounts of intermediates and other products present using the absorptivities below after identifying the unknowns by comparing their spectra with standards:
  4-Hydroxy-2-sulfobenzaldehyde: a = 0.080 L/(mg·cm) at 335 nm (alkaline solution)
  m-Sulfobenzaldehyde: a = 0.495 L/(mg·cm) at 246 nm (acidic solution)
  N-Ethyl-N-(3-sulfobenzyl)-sulfanilic acid: a = 0.078 L/(mg·cm) at 277 nm (alkaline solution)
  Acceptance criteria
  Sum of 3-and 4-[[Ethyl(4-sulfophenyl)amino]methyl]benzenesulfonic acid, Disodium salts: NMT 0.3%
  Sum of 2-, 3-, and 4-Formyl Benzene- sulfonic acids, Sodium salts: NMT 0.5%
  2-Formyl-5-hydroxybenzenesulfonic acid, Sodium salt: NMT 0.5%

SPECIFIC TESTS
- **Combined Tests**
  Tests
  - **Loss on Drying (volatile matter),** Color Determination, Appendix IIIC
  - **Chloride,** Sodium Chloride, Color Determination, Appendix IIIC
  - **Sulfates (as sodium salts),** Sodium Sulfate, Color Determination, Appendix IIIC
  Acceptance criteria: NMT 15.0% in combination
- **Ether Extracts,** Color Determination, Appendix IIIC
  Acceptance criteria: NMT 0.4%

---

[1] To be used or sold for use to color food that is marketed in the United States, this color additive must be from a batch that has been certified by the U.S. Food and Drug Administration (FDA). If it is not from an FDA-certified batch, it is not a permitted color additive for food use in the United States, even if it is compositionally equivalent. The name FD&C Green No. 3 can be applied only to FDA-certified batches of this color additive. Fast Green is a common name given to the uncertified colorant. See the monograph entitled FD&C Green No. 3 for directions for producing an FDA-certified batch.

- **LEUCO BASE,** *Color Determination,* Appendix IIIC
  Sample solution: 130 µg/mL
  Acceptance criteria: NMT 5.0%
- **SUBSIDIARY COLORS,** *Thin-Layer Chromatography,* Appendix IIA
  Adsorbent: Silica Gel G
  Developing solvent system: Acetonitrile, isoamyl alcohol, 2-butanone, water, and ammonium hydroxide [10:10:3:2:1]
  Sample solution: Transfer 1 g of sample into a 100-mL volumetric flask. Fill the flask about 3/4 full with water, place it in the dark for 1 h, dilute to volume with water, and mix well.
  Application volume: 0.1 mL
  Analysis: Prepare a 20- × 20-cm glass plate coated with a 0.25-mm layer of *Adsorbent*. Spot the *Sample solution* 3 cm from the bottom edge. Allow the plate to dry for about 20 min in the dark, then develop with the *Developing solvent system* in an unlined tank equilibrated for at least 20 min before the plate is inserted. Allow the solvent front to reach within about 3 cm of the top of the plate. Dry the developed plate in the dark. When the plate has dried, scrape off all the colored bands above the Fast Green, which remains close to the origin, into a 30-mL beaker. Extract the subsidiary colors with three 6-mL portions of 95% ethanol, or until no color remains on the gel by visual inspection. Record the volume of ethanol used and the spectrum of the solution between 400 and 700 nm. Calculate the percent of subsidiary colors by the formula:

  $$\text{Result} = (A \times V \times 100)/(a \times W \times b)$$

  A = absorbance at the wavelength maximum
  V = volume (mL) of the ethanol extract
  a = absorptivity (0.126 L/(mg·cm))
  W = weight (mg) of the sample taken to prepare the *Sample solution*
  b = cell pathlength (cm)

  Acceptance criteria
  Isomeric inner salt of *N*-ethyl-*N*-[4-[[4-[ethyl[(3-sulfophenyl)methyl] amino]phenyl](4-hydroxy-2-sulfophenyl)-methylene]-2,5-cyclohexadien-1-ylidene]-4-sulfobenzene methanaminium hydroxide, Disodium salt
  and
  N-ethyl-*N*-[4-[[4-[ethyl[(4-sulfophenyl) methyl]amino]phenyl](4-hydroxy-2-sulfophenyl)methylene]-2,5-cyclohexadien-1-ylidene]-4-sulfobenzenemethanaminium hydroxide
  and
  N-ethyl-*N*-[4-[[4-[ethyl[(2-sulfophenyl) methyl] amino] phenyl](4-hydroxy-2-sulfophenyl) methylene]-2,5-cyclohexadien-1-ylidene]-3-sulfobenzenemethanaminium hydroxide:
  NMT 6.0%, combined
- **WATER-INSOLUBLE MATTER,** *Color Determination,* Appendix IIIC
  Acceptance criteria: NMT 0.2%

FD&C Blue No. 1[1]

First Published: Prior to FCC 6

Brilliant Blue FCF[2]
CI 42090[2]
Class: Triphenylmethane

$C_{37}H_{34}N_2O_9S_3Na_2$ Formula wt 792.86
INS: 133   CAS: [3844-45-9]
UNII: H3R47K3TBD [fd&c blue no. 1]

DESCRIPTION

FD&C Blue No. 1 is principally the disodium salt of ethyl[4-[*p*-[ethyl(*m*-sulfobenzyl)amino]-α-(*o*-sulfophenyl) benzylidene]-2,5-cyclohexadien-1-ylidene](*m*-sulfobenzyl)ammonium hydroxide inner salt, with smaller amounts of the isomeric disodium salts of ethyl[4-[*p*-[ethyl(*p*-sulfobenzyl)amino]-α-(*o*-sulfophenyl)benzylidene]-2,5-cyclohexadien-1-ylidene](*p*-sulfobenzyl)ammonium hydroxide inner salt and ethyl[4-[*p*-[ethyl(*o*-sulfobenzyl)amino]-α-(*o*-sulfophenyl)benzylidene]-2,5-cyclohexadien-1-ylidene](*o*-sulfobenzyl)ammonium hydroxide inner salt.

Function: Color
Packaging and Storage: Store in well-closed containers. [NOTE—FDA-certifiable color additives are batch certified by the United States Food and Drug Administration using analytical chemistry methods developed for this purpose by the FDA. The color additive regulations are described in Title 21, Parts 70 to 82, of the United States *Code of Federal Regulations* (21 *CFR* Parts 70 to 82). The batch certification process is described in 21 *CFR* Part 80. Current certification analytical methods are available from the Office of Cosmetics and Colors, Colors Certification Branch (HFS-107), U.S. Food and Drug Administration, 5100 Paint Branch Parkway, College Park, Maryland 20740.]

IDENTIFICATION
- **VISIBLE ABSORPTION SPECTRUM**
  Acceptance criteria: A sample dissolved in 0.04 N aqueous ammonium acetate gives a spectrum exhibiting a wavelength maximum at 630 nm, with an absorptivity of 0.164 L/(mg·cm).

ASSAY
- **TOTAL COLOR**
  Acceptance criteria: NLT 85.0%

---
[1] To be used or sold in the United States, this color additive must be batch certified by the U.S. Food and Drug Administration. The monograph title is the name of the color additive only after batch certification has been completed.

[2] Generic designations; not synonyms for certified batches of color additive

IMPURITIES
Inorganic Impurities
- **ARSENIC (AS AS)**
  Acceptance criteria: NMT 3 mg/kg
- **CHROMIUM (AS CR)**
  Acceptance criteria: NMT 0.005%
- **LEAD (AS PB)**
  Acceptance criteria: NMT 10 mg/kg
- **MANGANESE (AS MN)**
  Acceptance criteria: NMT 0.01%

Organic Impurities
- **UNCOMBINED INTERMEDIATES AND PRODUCTS OF SIDE REACTIONS**
  Acceptance criteria
  o-, m-, and p-Sulfobenzaldehydes: NMT 1.5%, combined
  N-Ethyl-N-(m-sulfobenzyl)sulfanilic acid: NMT 0.3%

SPECIFIC TESTS
- **ETHER EXTRACTS**[3] **(COMBINED)**
  Acceptance criteria: NMT 0.4%
- **LEUCO BASE**
  Acceptance criteria: NMT 5%
- **SUBSIDIARY COLORS**
  Acceptance criteria: NMT 6%
- **VOLATILE MATTER (AT 135°) AND CHLORIDES AND SULFATES (AS SODIUM SALTS)**
  Acceptance criteria: NMT 15.0% in combination
- **WATER-INSOLUBLE MATTER**
  Acceptance criteria: NMT 0.2%

FD&C Blue No. 2[1]

First Published: Prior to FCC 6

Indigotine[2]
Indigo Carmine[2]
CI 73015[2]
Class: Indigoid

Formula wt 466.36
INS: 132   CAS: [860-22-0]
UNII: L06K8R7DQK [fd&c blue no. 2]

DESCRIPTION
FD&C Blue No. 2 is principally the disodium salt of 2-(1,3-dihydro-3-oxo-5-sulfo-2H-indol-2-ylidene)-2,3-dihydro-3-oxo-1H-indole-5-sulfonic acid, with smaller amounts of the disodium salt of 2-(1,3-dihydro-3-oxo-7-sulfo-2H-indol-2-ylidene)-2,3-dihydro-3-oxo-1H-indole-5-sulfonic acid and the sodium salt of 2-(1,3-dihydro-3-oxo-2H-indol-2-ylidene)-2,3-dihydro-3-oxo-1H-indole-5-sulfonic acid.
Function: Color
Packaging and Storage: Store in well-closed containers. [NOTE—FDA-certifiable color additives are batch certified by the United States Food and Drug Administration using analytical chemistry methods developed for this purpose by the FDA. The color additive regulations are described in Title 21, Parts 70 to 82, of the United States Code of Federal Regulations (21 CFR Parts 70 to 82). The batch certification process is described in 21 CFR Part 80. Current certification analytical methods are available from the Office of Cosmetics and Colors, Colors Certification Branch (HFS-107), U.S. Food and Drug Administration, 5100 Paint Branch Parkway, College Park, Maryland 20740.]

IDENTIFICATION
- **VISIBLE ABSORPTION SPECTRUM**
  Acceptance criteria: A sample dissolved in 0.04 N aqueous ammonium acetate gives a spectrum exhibiting a wavelength maximum at 610 nm, with an absorptivity of 0.0478 L/(mg·cm).

ASSAY
- **TOTAL COLOR**
  Acceptance criteria: NLT 85%

IMPURITIES
Inorganic Impurities
- **ARSENIC (AS AS)**
  Acceptance criteria: NMT 3 mg/kg
- **LEAD (AS PB)**
  Acceptance criteria: NMT 10 mg/kg
- **MERCURY (AS HG)**
  Acceptance criteria: NMT 1 mg/kg

Organic Impurities
- **DECOMPOSITION PRODUCTS**
  Acceptance criteria
  Isatin-5-sulfonic acid: NMT 0.4%
  5-Sulfoanthranilic acid: NMT 0.2%

SPECIFIC TESTS
- **ETHER EXTRACTS**[3] **(COMBINED)**
  Acceptance criteria: NMT 0.4%
- **SUBSIDIARY AND ISOMERIC COLORS**
  Acceptance criteria
  2-(1,3-Dihydro-3-oxo-7-sulfo-2H-indol-2-ylidene)-2,3-dihydro-3-oxo-1H-indole-5-sulfonic acid, Disodium salt: NMT 18%
  2-(1,3-Dihydro-3-oxo-2H-indol-2-ylidene)-2,3-dihydro-3-oxo-1H-indole-5-sulfonic acid, Sodium salt: NMT 2%
- **VOLATILE MATTER (AT 135°) AND CHLORIDES AND SULFATES (AS SODIUM SALTS)**
  Acceptance criteria: NMT 15% in combination
- **WATER INSOLUBLE MATTER**
  Acceptance criteria: NMT 0.4%

---
[3] Not required for certification in the United States
[1] To be used or sold in the United States, this color additive must be batch certified by the U.S. Food and Drug Administration. The monograph title is the name of the color additive only after batch certification has been completed.
[2] Generic designations; not synonyms for certified batches of color additive

[3] Not required for certification in the United States

FD&C Green No. 3[1]

First Published: Prior to FCC 6

Fast Green FCF[2]
CI 42053[2]
Class: Triphenylmethane

$C_{37}H_{34}N_2O_{10}S_3Na_2$
INS: 143
UNII: 3P3ONR6O1S [fd&c green no. 3]

Formula wt 808.86
CAS: [2353-45-9]

DESCRIPTION
FD&C Green No. 3 is principally the inner salt disodium salt of N-ethyl-N-[4-[[4-[ethyl[(3-sulfophenyl)methyl]amino]phenyl](4-hydroxy-2-sulfophenyl)methylene]-2,5-cyclohexadien-1-ylidene]-3-sulfobenzenemethanaminium-hydroxide, with smaller amounts of the isomeric inner salt disodium salt of N-ethyl-N-[4-[[4-[ethyl[(3-sulfophenyl)methyl]amino]phenyl](4-hydroxy-2-sulfophenyl)methylene]-2,5-cyclohexadien-1-ylidene]-4-sulfobenzenemethanaminium hydroxide; of N-ethyl-N-[4-[4-[ethyl[(4-sulfophenyl)-methyl]amino]phenyl](4-hydroxy-2-sulfophenyl)methylene]-2,5-cyclohexadien-1-ylidene]-4-sulfobenzenemethanaminium hydroxide; and of N-ethyl-N-[4-[[4-[ethyl[(2-sulfophenyl)methyl]amino] phenyl](4-hydroxy-2-sulfophenyl)methylene]-2,5-cyclohexadien-1-ylidene]-3-sulfobenzene methanaminium hydroxide.

Function: Color

Packaging and Storage: Store in well-closed containers. [NOTE—FDA-certifiable color additives are batch certified by the United States Food and Drug Administration using analytical chemistry methods developed for this purpose by the FDA. The color additive regulations are described in Title 21, Parts 70 to 82, of the United States *Code of Federal Regulations* (21 *CFR* Parts 70 to 82). The batch certification process is described in 21 *CFR* Part 80. Current certification analytical methods are available from the Office of Cosmetics and Colors, Colors Certification Branch (HFS-107), U.S. Food and Drug Administration, 5100 Paint Branch Parkway, College Park, Maryland 20740.]

IDENTIFICATION
- VISIBLE ABSORPTION SPECTRUM
  Acceptance criteria: A sample dissolved in 0.04 N aqueous ammonium acetate gives a spectrum exhibiting a wavelength maximum at 625 nm, with an absorptivity of 0.156 L/(mg·cm).

ASSAY
- TOTAL COLOR
  Acceptance criteria: NLT 85%

IMPURITIES
Inorganic Impurities
- ARSENIC (AS As)
  Acceptance criteria: NMT 3 mg/kg
- CHROMIUM (AS Cr)
  Acceptance criteria: NMT 0.005%
- LEAD (AS Pb)
  Acceptance criteria: NMT 10 mg/kg
- MERCURY (AS Hg)
  Acceptance criteria: NMT 1 mg/kg

Organic Impurities
- UNCOMBINED INTERMEDIATES AND PRODUCTS OF SIDE REACTIONS
  Acceptance criteria
    Sum of 3- and 4-[[Ethyl(4-sulfophenyl)amino]methyl]benzenesulfonic acid, Disodium salts: NMT 0.3%
    Sum of 2-, 3-, and 4-Formylbenzenesulfonic acid, Sodium salts: NMT 0.5%
    2-Formyl-5-hydroxybenzenesulfonic acid, Sodium salt: NMT 0.5%

SPECIFIC TESTS
- ETHER EXTRACTS[3] (COMBINED)
  Acceptance criteria: NMT 0.4%
- LEUCO BASE
  Acceptance criteria: NMT 5%
- SUBSIDIARY COLORS
  Acceptance criteria: NMT 6%
- VOLATILE MATTER (AT 135°) AND CHLORIDES AND SULFATES (AS SODIUM SALTS)
  Acceptance criteria: NMT 15.0% in combination
- WATER-INSOLUBLE MATTER
  Acceptance criteria: NMT 0.2%

FD&C Red No. 3[1]

First Published: Prior to FCC 6

Erythrosine[2]
CI 45430[2]
Class: Xanthene

---

[3] Not required for certification in the United States.

[1] To be used or sold in the United States, this color additive must be batch certified by the U.S. Food and Drug Administration. The monograph title is the name of the color additive only after batch certification has been completed.
[2] Generic designations; not synonyms for certified batches of color additive.

[1] To be used or sold in the United States, this color additive must be batch certified by the U.S. Food and Drug Administration. The monograph title is the name of the color additive only after batch certification has been completed.
[2] Generic designations; not synonyms for certified batches of color additives.

436 / FD&C Red No. 3 / *Monographs*

$C_{20}H_6O_5I_4Na_2$
INS: 127
UNII: PN2ZH5LOQY [fd&c red no. 3]

Formula wt 879.86
CAS: [16423-68-0]

DESCRIPTION
FD&C Red No. 3 is principally the monohydrate of 9-(o-carboxyphenyl)-6-hydroxy-2,4,5,7-tetraiodo-3H-xanthen-3-one, disodium salt, with smaller amounts of lower iodinated fluoresceins.

Function: Color

Packaging and Storage: Store in well-closed containers. [NOTE—FDA-certifiable color additives are batch certified by the United States Food and Drug Administration using analytical chemistry methods developed for this purpose by the FDA. The color additive regulations are described in Title 21, Parts 70 to 82, of the United States *Code of Federal Regulations* (21 *CFR* Parts 70 to 82). The batch certification process is described in 21 *CFR* Part 80. Current certification analytical methods are available from the Office of Cosmetics and Colors, Colors Certification Branch (HFS-107), U.S. Food and Drug Administration, 5100 Paint Branch Parkway, College Park, Maryland 20740.]

IDENTIFICATION
- **VISIBLE ABSORPTION SPECTRUM**
  Acceptance criteria: A sample dissolved in 0.05% aqueous ammonium hydroxide gives a spectrum exhibiting a wavelength maximum at 527 nm, with an absorptivity of 0.110 L/(mg·cm).

ASSAY
- **TOTAL COLOR**
  Acceptance criteria: NLT 87.0%

IMPURITIES
Inorganic Impurities
- **ARSENIC (AS As)**
  Acceptance criteria: NMT 3 mg/kg
- **LEAD (AS Pb)**
  Acceptance criteria: NMT 10 mg/kg

Organic Impurities
- **UNCOMBINED INTERMEDIATES AND PRODUCTS OF SIDE REACTIONS**
  Acceptance criteria
    2-(2,4-Dihydroxy-3,5-diiodobenzoyl) benzoic acid: NMT 0.2%
    Sodium iodide: NMT 0.4%
    Triiodoresorcinol: NMT 0.2%
    Unhalogenated intermediates: NMT 0.1%, total

SPECIFIC TESTS
- **ETHER EXTRACTS**[3]
  Acceptance criteria: NMT 0.2%

---
[3] Not required for certification in the United States.

- **SUBSIDIARY COLORS**
  Acceptance criteria
    Monoiodofluoresceins: NMT 1.0%
    Other lower iodinated fluoresceins: NMT 9.0%
- **VOLATILE MATTER (AT 135°) AND CHLORIDES AND SULFATES (AS SODIUM SALTS)**
  Acceptance criteria: NMT 13% in combination
- **WATER-INSOLUBLE MATTER**
  Acceptance criteria: NMT 0.2%

FD&C Red No. 40[1]

First Published: Prior to FCC 6

Allura Red AC[2]
CI 16035
Class: Monoazo

$C_{18}H_{14}N_2O_8S_2Na_2$
INS: 129
UNII: WZB9127XOA [fd&c red no. 40]

Formula wt 496.43
CAS: [25956-17-6]

DESCRIPTION
FD&C Red No. 40 is principally the disodium salt of 6-hydroxy-5-[(2-methoxy-5-methyl-4-sulfophenyl)azo]-2-naphthalenesulfonic acid.

Function: Color

Packaging and Storage: Store in well-closed containers. [NOTE—FDA-certifiable color additives are batch certified by the United States Food and Drug Administration using analytical chemistry methods developed for this purpose by the FDA. The color additive regulations are described in Title 21, Parts 70 to 82, of the United States *Code of Federal Regulations* (21 *CFR* Parts 70 to 82). The batch certification process is described in 21 *CFR* Part 80. Current certification analytical methods are available from the Office of Cosmetics and Colors, Colors Certification Branch (HFS-107), U.S. Food and Drug Administration, 5100 Paint Branch Parkway, College Park, Maryland 20740.]

IDENTIFICATION
- **VISIBLE ABSORPTION SPECTRUM**
  Acceptance criteria: A sample dissolved in 0.04 N aqueous ammonium acetate gives a spectrum exhibiting a wavelength maximum at 500 nm, with an absorptivity of 0.052 L/(mg·cm).

---
[1] To be used or sold in the United States, this color additive must be batch certified by the U.S. Food and Drug Administration. The monograph title is the name of the color additive only after batch certification has been completed.
[2] Generic designations; not synonyms for certified batches of color additives

ASSAY
- **TOTAL COLOR**
  Acceptance criteria: NLT 85.0%

IMPURITIES
Inorganic Impurities
- **ARSENIC (AS As)**
  Acceptance criteria: NMT 3 mg/kg
- **LEAD (AS Pb)**
  Acceptance criteria: NMT 10 mg/kg

Organic Impurities
- **UNCOMBINED INTERMEDIATES AND PRODUCTS OF SIDE REACTIONS**
  Acceptance criteria
  4-Amino-5-methoxy-o-toluenesulfonic acid: NMT 0.2%
  6,6'-Oxybis(2- naphthalenesulfonic acid), Disodium salt: NMT 1.0%
  6-Hydroxy-2-naphthalenesulfonic acid, Sodium salt: NMT 0.3%

SPECIFIC TESTS
- **SUBSIDIARY COLORS**
  Acceptance criteria
  6-Hydroxy-5-[(2-methoxy-5-methyl-4-sulfophenyl)azo]-8-(2-methoxy-5-methyl-4-sulfophenoxy)-2-naphthalenesulfonic acid, Disodium salt: NMT 1.0%
  Higher sulfonated subsidiary colors (as sodium salts): NMT 1.0%
  Lower sulfonated subsidiary colors (as sodium salts): NMT 1.0%
- **VOLATILE MATTER (AT 135°) AND CHLORIDES AND SULFATES (AS SODIUM SALTS)**
  Acceptance criteria: NMT 14.0%, in combination
- **WATER-INSOLUBLE MATTER**
  Acceptance criteria: NMT 0.2%

FD&C Yellow No. 5[1]

First Published: Prior to FCC 6

Tartrazine[2]
CI 19140[2]
Class: Pyrazolone

$C_{16}H_9N_4O_9S_2Na_3$ Formula wt 534.37
INS: 102   CAS: [1934-21-0]
UNII: I753WB2F1M [fd&c yellow no. 5]

---

[1] To be used or sold in the United States, this color additive must be batch certified by the U.S. Food and Drug Administration. The monograph title is the name of the color additive only after batch certification has been completed.
[2] Generic designations; not synonyms for certified batches of color additives.

DESCRIPTION
FD&C Yellow No. 5 is principally the trisodium salt of 4,5-dihydro-5-oxo-1-(4-sulfophenyl)-4-[4-sulfophenyl-azo]-1H-pyrazole-3-carboxylic acid.
Function: Color
Packaging and Storage: Store in well-closed containers. [NOTE—FDA-certifiable color additives are batch certified by the United States Food and Drug Administration using analytical chemistry methods developed for this purpose by the FDA. The color additive regulations are described in Title 21, Parts 70 to 82, of the United States *Code of Federal Regulations* (21 CFR Parts 70 to 82). The batch certification process is described in 21 CFR Part 80. Current certification analytical methods are available from the Office of Cosmetics and Colors, Colors Certification Branch (HFS-107), U.S. Food and Drug Administration, 5100 Paint Branch Parkway, College Park, Maryland 20740.]

IDENTIFICATION
- **VISIBLE ABSORPTION SPECTRUM**
  Acceptance criteria: A sample dissolved in 0.04 N aqueous ammonium acetate gives a spectrum exhibiting a wavelength maximum at 428 nm, with an absorptivity of 0.053 L/(mg·cm)

ASSAY
- **TOTAL COLOR**
  Acceptance criteria: NLT 87%

IMPURITIES
Inorganic Impurities
- **ARSENIC (AS As)**
  Acceptance criteria: NMT 3 mg/kg
- **LEAD (AS Pb)**
  Acceptance criteria: NMT 10 mg/kg
- **MERCURY (AS Hg)**
  Acceptance criteria: NMT 1 mg/kg

Organic Impurities
- **UNCOMBINED INTERMEDIATES AND PRODUCTS OF SIDE REACTIONS**
  Acceptance criteria
  4,4'-[4,5-Dihydro-5-oxo-4-[(4-sulfophenyl)-hydrazono]-1H-pyrazol-1,3-diyl]bis[benzenesulfonic acid], Trisodium salt: NMT 1%
  4-[(4',5-Disulfo[1,1'-biphenyl]-2-yl)hydrazono]-4,5-dihydro-5-oxo-1-(4-sulfophenyl)-1H-pyrazole-3-carboxylic acid, Tetrasodium salt: NMT 1%
  Ethyl or Methyl 4,5-Dihydro-5-oxo-1-(4-sulfophenyl)-4-[(4-sulfophenyl)hydrazono]-1H-pyrazole-3-carboxylate, Disodium salt: NMT 1%
  Sum of 4,5-Dihydro-5-oxo-1-phenyl-4-[(4-sulfophenyl)azo]-1H-pyrazole-3-carboxylic acid, Disodium Salt and 4,5-Dihydro-5-oxo-4-(phenylazo)-1-(4-sulfophenyl)-1H-pyrazole-3-carboxylic acid, Disodium salt: NMT 0.5%
  4-Aminobenzenesulfonic acid, Sodium salt: NMT 0.2%
  4,5-Dihydro-5-oxo-1-(4-sulfophenyl)-1H-pyrazole-3-carboxylic acid, Disodium salt: NMT 0.2%

Ethyl or Methyl 4,5-dihydro-5-oxo-1-(4-sulfophenyl)-1H-pyrazole-3-carboxylate, Sodium salt: NMT 0.1%
4,4'-(1-Triazene-1,3-diyl)bis [benzenesulfonic acid], Disodium salt: NMT 0.05%
4-Aminoazobenzene: NMT 75 µg/kg
4-Aminobiphenyl: NMT 5 µg/kg
Aniline: NMT 100 µg/kg
Azobenzene: NMT 40 µg/kg
Benzidine: NMT 1 µg/kg
1,3-Diphenyltriazene: NMT 40 µg/kg

SPECIFIC TESTS
- **ETHER EXTRACTS**[3]
  Acceptance criteria: NMT 0.2%
- **VOLATILE MATTER (AT 135°) AND CHLORIDES AND SULFATES (AS SODIUM SALTS)**
  Acceptance criteria: NMT 13% in combination
- **WATER-INSOLUBLE MATTER**
  Acceptance criteria: NMT 0.2%

FD&C Yellow No. 6[1]

First Published: Prior to FCC 6

Sunset Yellow FCF[2]
CI 15985[2]
Class: Monoazo

INS: 110
UNII: H77VEI93A8 [fd&c yellow no. 6]
Formula wt 452.37
CAS: [2783-94-0]

DESCRIPTION
FD&C Yellow No. 6 is principally the disodium salt of 6-hydroxy-5-[(4-sulfophenyl)azo]-2-naphthalene-sulfonic acid. The trisodium salt of 3-hydroxy-4-[(4-sulfophenyl)azo]-2,7-naphthalenedisulfonic acid may be added in small amounts.
Function: Color
Packaging and Storage: Store in well-closed containers.
[NOTE—FDA-certifiable color additives are batch certified by the United States Food and Drug Administration using analytical chemistry methods developed for this purpose by the FDA. The color additive regulations are described in Title 21, Parts 70 to 82, of the United States Code of Federal Regulations (21 CFR Parts 70 to 82). The batch certification process is described in 21 CFR Part 80. Current certification analytical methods are available from the Office of Cosmetics and Colors, Colors Certification Branch (HFS-107), U.S. Food and Drug Administration, 5100 Paint Branch Parkway, College Park, Maryland 20740.]

IDENTIFICATION
- **VISIBLE ABSORPTION SPECTRUM**
  Acceptance criteria: A sample dissolved in 0.04 N aqueous ammonium acetate gives a spectrum exhibiting a wavelength maximum of 484 nm, with an absorptivity of 0.054 L/(mg·cm).

ASSAY
- **TOTAL COLOR**
  Acceptance criteria: NLT 87%

IMPURITIES
Inorganic Impurities
- **ARSENIC (AS As)**
  Acceptance criteria: NMT 3 mg/kg
- **LEAD (AS Pb)**
  Acceptance criteria: NMT 10 mg/kg
- **MERCURY (AS Hg)**
  Acceptance criteria: NMT 1 mg/kg

Organic Impurities
- **UNCOMBINED INTERMEDIATES AND PRODUCTS OF SIDE REACTIONS**
  Acceptance criteria
  4-Aminoazobenzene: NMT 50 µg/kg
  4-Aminobiphenyl: NMT 15 µg/kg
  Aniline: NMT 250 µg/kg
  Azobenzene: NMT 200 µg/kg
  Benzidine: NMT 1 µg/kg
  1,3-Diphenyltriazene: NMT 40 µg/kg
  1-(Phenylazo)-2-naphthalenol: NMT 10 mg/kg
  4-Aminobenzenesulfonic acid, Sodium salt: NMT 0.2%
  6-Hydroxy-2-naphthalenesulfonic acid, Sodium salt: NMT 0.3%
  6,6'-Oxybis[2-naphthalenesulfonic acid], Disodium salt: NMT 1%
  4,4'-(1-Triazene-1,3-diyl)bis[benzenesulfonic acid], Disodium salt: NMT 0.1%
  Sum of 6-Hydroxy-5-(phenylazo)-2-naphthalenesulfonic acid, Sodium salt and 4-[(2-Hydroxy-1-naphthalenyl)azo]benzene-sulfonic acid, Sodium salt: NMT 1%
  Sum of 3-Hydroxy-4-[(4-sulfophenyl)azo]-2,7-naphthalenedisulfonic acid, Trisodium salt and Other higher sulfonated subsidiaries: NMT 5%

SPECIFIC TESTS
- **ETHER EXTRACTS**[3] **(COMBINED)**
  Acceptance criteria: NMT 0.2%
- **VOLATILE MATTER (AT 135°) AND CHLORIDES AND SULFATES (AS SODIUM SALTS)**
  Acceptance criteria: NMT 13.0% in combination
- **WATER-INSOLUBLE MATTER**
  Acceptance criteria: NMT 0.2%

---

[3] Not required for certification in the United States.
[1] To be used or sold in the United States, this color additive must be batch certified by the U.S. Food and Drug Administration. The monograph title is the name of the color additive only after batch certification has been completed.
[2] Generic designations; not synonyms for certified batches of color additives.

[3] Not required for certification in the United States

(+)-Fenchone

First Published: Prior to FCC 6
Last Revision: First Supplement, FCC 7

d-Fenchone

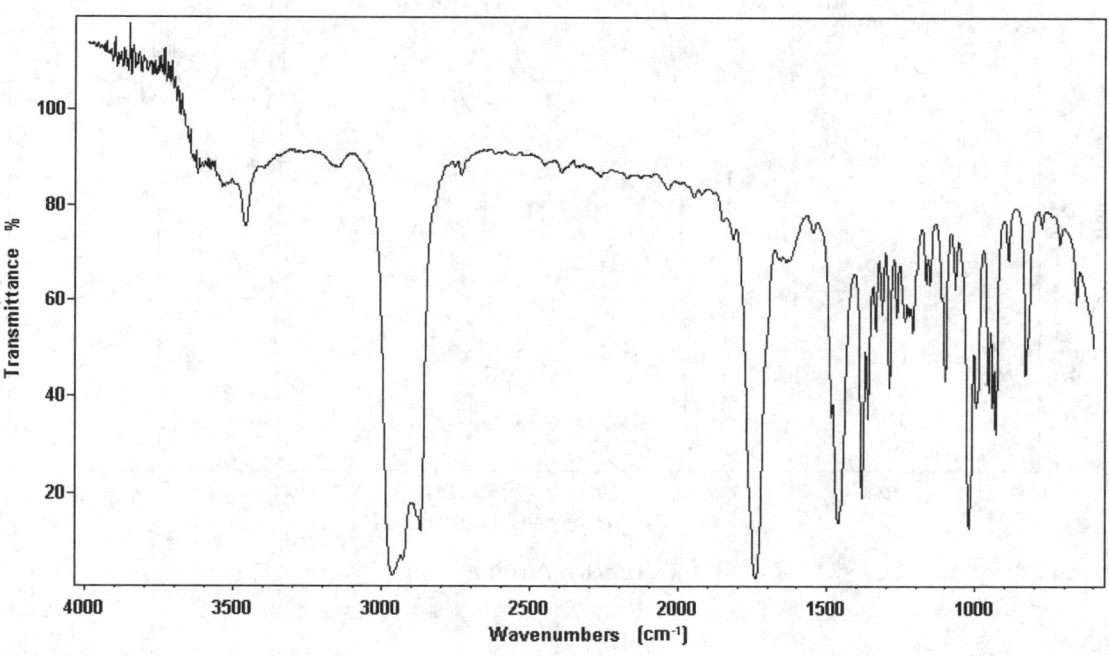

$C_{10}H_{16}O$ Formula wt 152.24
FEMA: 2479
UNII: S436YKU51N [fenchone, (+)-]

DESCRIPTION
(+)-Fenchone occurs as a colorless to pale yellow liquid.
Odor: Camphoraceous
Solubility: Soluble in propylene glycol, vegetable oils; insoluble or practically insoluble in water
Boiling Point: ~192°
Solubility in Alcohol, Appendix VI: One mL dissolves in 1 mL of 95% ethanol.
Function: Flavoring agent

IDENTIFICATION
- **INFRARED SPECTRA**, *Spectrophotometric Identification Tests,* Appendix IIIC
  Acceptance criteria: The spectrum of the sample exhibits relative maxima at the same wavelengths as those of the spectrum below.

ASSAY
- **PROCEDURE:** Proceed as directed under *M-1b*, Appendix XI.
  Acceptance criteria: NLT 97.0% of $C_{10}H_{16}O$

SPECIFIC TESTS
- **REFRACTIVE INDEX,** Appendix II: At 20°
  Acceptance criteria: Between 1.460 and 1.467
- **SPECIFIC GRAVITY:** Determine at 25° by any reliable method (see *General Provisions*).
  Acceptance criteria: Between 0.940 and 0.948

OTHER REQUIREMENTS
- **ANGULAR ROTATION,** *Optical (Specific) Rotation,* Appendix IIB
  Acceptance criteria: Between +46° and −68°

(+)-Fenchone

Fenchyl Alcohol

First Published: Prior to FCC 6

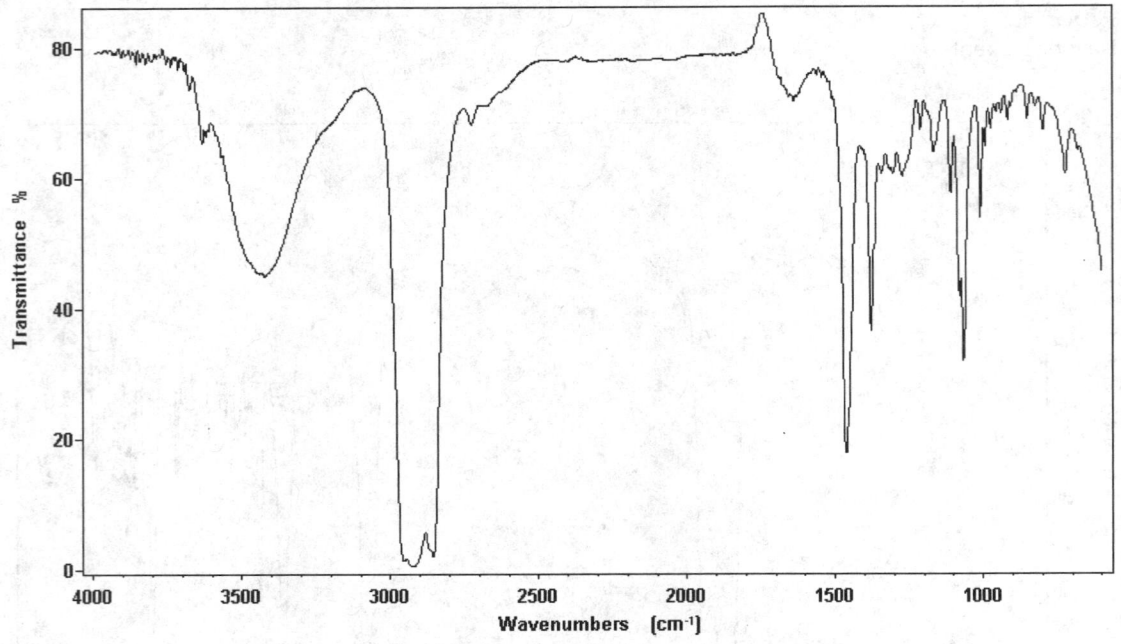

C₁₀H₁₈O
FEMA: 2480
UNII: 410Q2GK1HF [fenchyl alcohol]

Formula wt 154.25

DESCRIPTION
Fenchyl Alcohol occurs as a white to pale yellow crystalline solid.
Odor: Camphoraceous
Solubility: Soluble in vegetable oils; very slightly soluble in water
Boiling Point: ~201°
Solubility in Alcohol, Appendix VI: One g dissolves in 1 mL of 95% ethanol.
Function: Flavoring agent

IDENTIFICATION
- **INFRARED SPECTRA,** *Spectrophotometric Identification Tests,* Appendix IIIC
  Acceptance criteria: The spectrum of the sample exhibits relative maxima at the same wavelengths as those of the spectrum below.

ASSAY
- **PROCEDURE:** Proceed as directed under *M-1b,* Appendix XI.
  Acceptance criteria: NLT 97.0% of C₁₀H₁₈O

OTHER REQUIREMENTS
- **MELTING RANGE OR TEMPERATURE DETERMINATION,** Appendix IIB
  Acceptance criteria: Between 35.0° and 40.0°

Fenchyl Alcohol

Fennel Oil

First Published: Prior to FCC 6

CAS: [8006-84-6]
UNII: 59AAO5F6HT [fennel oil]

DESCRIPTION
Fennel Oil occurs as a colorless or pale yellow liquid with the characteristic odor and taste of fennel. It is the volatile oil obtained by steam distillation from the dried ripe fruit of *Foeniculum vulgare* Miller (Fam. Umbelliferae).

[NOTE—If solid material has separated, carefully warm the sample until it is completely liquefied, and mix it before using.]
Function: Flavoring agent
Packaging and Storage: Store in full, tight containers in a cool place protected from light.

IDENTIFICATION
- **INFRARED SPECTRA,** *Spectrophotometric Identification Tests,* Appendix IIIC

Acceptance criteria: The spectrum of the sample exhibits relative maxima at the same wavelengths as those of the spectrum below.

SPECIFIC TESTS
- **ANGULAR ROTATION,** *Optical (Specific) Rotation,* Appendix IIB: Use a 100-mm tube.
  Acceptance criteria: Between +12° and +24°
- **REFRACTIVE INDEX,** Appendix IIB
  [NOTE—Use an Abbé or other refractometer of equal or greater accuracy.]
  Acceptance criteria: Between 1.532 and 1.543 at 20°
- **SOLIDIFICATION POINT,** Appendix IIB
  Acceptance criteria: NLT 3°
- **SOLUBILITY IN ALCOHOL,** Appendix VI
  Acceptance criteria: One mL of sample dissolves in 1 mL of 90% alcohol.
- **SPECIFIC GRAVITY:** Determine by any reliable method (see *General Provisions*).
  Acceptance criteria: Between 0.953 and 0.973

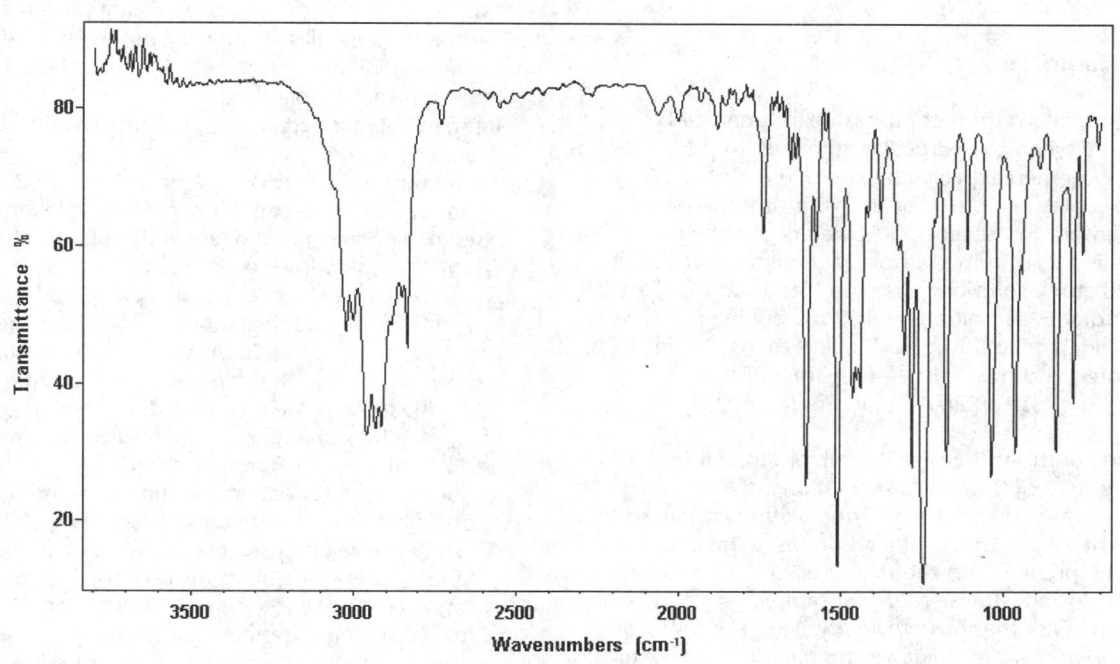

Fennel Oil

Ferric Ammonium Citrate, Brown
First Published: Prior to FCC 6

Iron Ammonium Citrate
INS: 381 CAS: [1185-57-5]
UNII: UVP74NG1C5 [ferric ammonium citrate]

DESCRIPTION
Ferric Ammonium Citrate, Brown, occurs as thin, transparent brown, red-brown, or garnet red scales or granules, or as a brown-yellow powder. It is a complex salt of undetermined structure, composed of iron, ammonia, and citric acid. It is very soluble in water, but is insoluble in alcohol. The pH of a 1:20 aqueous solution is about 5.0 to 8.0. It is deliquescent in air and is affected by light.
Function: Nutrient
Packaging and Storage: Store in tight, light-resistant containers in a cool place.

IDENTIFICATION
- **A. PROCEDURE**
  Sample: 500 mg
  Analysis: Ignite the *Sample.*
  Acceptance criteria: The *Sample* chars and leaves a residue of iron oxide.
- **B. PROCEDURE**
  Sample solution: 100 mg/mL
  Analysis: To 5 mL of the *Sample solution,* add 0.3 mL of potassium permanganate TS and 4 mL of mercuric sulfate TS, and heat the mixture to boiling.
  Acceptance criteria: A white precipitate forms.
- **C. PROCEDURE**
  Sample solution: 500 mg in 5 mL of water
  Analysis: To the *Sample solution,* add 5 mL of 1 N sodium hydroxide.
  Acceptance criteria: A red-brown precipitate forms, and ammonia is evolved when the mixture is heated.

ASSAY
- **IRON CONTENT**
  Sample: 1 g

Analysis: Transfer the *Sample* to a 250-mL glass-stoppered Erlenmeyer flask, and dissolve in 25 mL of water and 5 mL of hydrochloric acid. Add 4 g of potassium iodide, stopper, and allow to stand protected from light for 15 min. Add 100 mL of water, and titrate the liberated iodine with 0.1 N sodium thiosulfate, using starch TS as the indicator. Perform a blank determination (see *General Provisions*) and make any necessary correction. Each mL of 0.1 N sodium thiosulfate is equivalent to 5.585 mg of iron (Fe).

Acceptance criteria: NLT 16.5% and NMT 18.5% of iron (Fe)

IMPURITIES
Inorganic Impurities
- **LEAD**

  [NOTE—The following method has been found to be satisfactory when the particular atomic absorption spectrophotometer specified is used. The method may be modified as necessary for use with other suitable atomic absorption spectrophotometers capable of determining lead in the sample at the limit specified.]

  Standard stock solution: Dissolve 159.8 mg of ACS reagent-grade lead nitrate in 100 mL of water containing 1 mL of nitric acid, dilute to 1000.0 mL with water, and mix. [NOTE—Prepare and store this solution in glass containers that are free from lead salts.]

  Standard solution: Transfer 2.0 mL of *Standard stock solution* into a 500-mL volumetric flask, dilute to volume with water, and mix. This solution contains the equivalent of 0.4 µg/mL of lead. [NOTE—This solution should be prepared on the day of use.]

  Sample solution: Transfer 20 g of sample into a 100-mL volumetric flask that has previously been rinsed with nitric acid and water. Dissolve the sample in a mixture of 50 mL of water and 1 mL of nitric acid, dilute to volume with water, and mix.

  Analysis: Use a Perkin-Elmer 403 atomic absorption spectrophotometer equipped with a deuterium arc background corrector, a digital readout device, and a burner head capable of handling 20% solids content. Blank the instrument with water following the manufacturer's operating instructions. Aspirate a portion of the *Standard solution* and record the absorbance; then aspirate a portion of the *Sample solution* and record the absorbance. Calculate the lead content, in mg/kg, of the sample taken by the formula:

  $$\text{Result} = 100 \times (C/W) \times (A_U/A_S)$$

  C = concentration of lead in the *Standard solution* (µg/mL)
  W = weight of the sample taken (g)
  A_U = absorbance of the *Sample solution*
  A_S = absorbance of the *Standard solution*

  Acceptance criteria: NMT 2 mg/kg

- **MERCURY**

  Standard stock solution: 1 µg/mL of mercury prepared as directed for *Standard Preparation* under *Mercury Limit Test, Method I*, Appendix IIIB

  Standard solutions: Pipet 0.25, 0.50, 1.0 and 3.5 mL of the *Standard stock solution*, respectively, into each of four glass-stoppered bottles of about 300-mL capacity, such as BOD (biological oxygen demand) bottles. Dilute the contents of each bottle to 100 mL with water, and mix. These solutions contain the equivalent of 0.25, 0.50, 1.0 and 3.5 mg/kg of mercury, respectively.

  Sample solution: Transfer 1.000 g of sample into a 200-mL screw-cap centrifuge bottle, and add 5 mL of nitric acid and 5 mL of hydrochloric acid. Close the bottle tightly with a Teflon-lined screw-cap, digest on a steam bath for 1 h, and cool. Quantitatively transfer into a suitable glass-stoppered bottle (see *Standard solutions*), dilute to 100 mL with water, and bubble air through the sample for 2 min.

  Reagent blank: Prepare in the same manner as the *Sample solution*.

  10% Stannous chloride solution: Dissolve 20 g of stannous chloride dihydrate in 40 mL of warm hydrochloric acid and dilute with 160 mL of water. [NOTE—Prepare fresh each week.]

  Analysis: Use a suitable atomic absorption spectrophotometer assembly designed for mercury analysis, such as the Coleman MAS-50 Mercury Analyzer. [NOTE—The *Apparatus* and *Procedure* described under *Mercury Limit Test, Method I*, Appendix IIIB, may be suitably modified for this determination.] Add 5 mL of *10% Stannous chloride solution* to the solution to be tested, and immediately insert the bubbler of the mercury analysis apparatus. Obtain the absorbance reading by following the instrument manufacturer's operating instructions. Correct the sample readings for the *Reagent blank* (see *General Provisions*), and determine the mercury concentration of the *Sample solution* from a standard curve prepared by plotting the readings obtained with the *Standard solutions* against mercury concentration, in mg/kg.

  Acceptance criteria: NMT 1 mg/kg

- **SULFATE**, *Chloride and Sulfate Limit Tests, Sulfate Limit Test*, Appendix IIIB

  Sample: Dissolve 100 mg of sample in 2.7 N hydrochloric acid and dilute to 30 to 40 mL with water.

  Control: 300 µg of sulfate (30 mL of *Standard Sulfate Solution*)

  Analysis: Proceed as directed beginning with the addition of 3 mL of barium chloride TS.

  Acceptance criteria: Any turbidity produced in the solution containing the *Sample* does not exceed that produced in the solution containing the *Control*. (NMT 0.3%)

Organic Impurities
- **FERRIC CITRATE**

  Sample solution: 10 mg/mL

  Analysis: Add potassium ferrocyanide TS to the *Sample solution*.

  Acceptance criteria: No blue precipitate forms.

SPECIFIC TESTS
- **OXALATE**

  Sample: 1 g

  Analysis: Transfer the *Sample* into a 125-mL separatory funnel, dissolve in 10 mL of water, add 2 mL of hydrochloric acid, and extract successively with one 50-mL portion and one 20-mL portion of ether. Transfer the combined ether extracts into a 150-mL beaker, add 10 mL of water, and remove the ether by evaporation on a steam bath. Add 1 drop of glacial acetic acid and 1 mL of a 50 mg/mL calcium acetate solution to the residual aqueous solution.

  Acceptance criteria: No turbidity develops within 5 min.

Ferric Ammonium Citrate, Green

First Published: Prior to FCC 6

Iron Ammonium Citrate
INS: 381 CAS: [1185-57-5]
UNII: UVP74NG1C5 [ferric ammonium citrate]

DESCRIPTION
Ferric Ammonium Citrate, Green, occurs as thin, transparent green scales, as granules, as a powder, or as transparent green crystals. It is a complex salt of undetermined structure, composed of iron, ammonia, and citric acid. It is very soluble in water, but is insoluble in alcohol. Its solutions are acid to litmus. It may deliquesce in air and is affected by light.

Function: Nutrient; anticaking agent for sodium chloride

Packaging and Storage: Store in tight, light-resistant containers in a cool place.

IDENTIFICATION
- **A. PROCEDURE**

  Sample: 500 mg

  Analysis: Ignite the *Sample*.

  Acceptance criteria: The *Sample* chars and leaves a residue of iron oxide.

- **B. PROCEDURE**

  Sample solution: 100 mg/mL

  Analysis: To 5 mL of the *Sample solution*, add 0.3 mL of potassium permanganate TS and 4 mL of mercuric sulfate TS, and heat the mixture to boiling.

  Acceptance criteria: A white precipitate forms.

- **C. PROCEDURE**

  Sample solution: 500 mg in 5 mL of water

  Analysis: To the *Sample solution*, add 5 mL of 1 N sodium hydroxide.

  Acceptance criteria: A red-brown precipitate forms, and ammonia is evolved when the mixture is heated.

ASSAY
- **IRON CONTENT**

  Sample: 1 g

  Analysis: Transfer the *Sample* to a 250-mL glass-stoppered Erlenmeyer flask, and dissolve in 25 mL of water and 5 mL of hydrochloric acid. Add 4 g of potassium iodide, stopper, and allow to stand protected from light for 15 min. Add 100 mL of water, and titrate the liberated iodine with 0.1 N sodium thiosulfate, using starch TS as the indicator. Perform a blank determination (see *General Provisions*) and make any necessary correction. Each mL of 0.1 N sodium thiosulfate is equivalent to 5.585 mg of iron (Fe).

  Acceptance criteria: NLT 14.5% and NMT 16.0% of iron (Fe).

IMPURITIES
Inorganic Impurities
- **LEAD**

  [NOTE—The following method has been found to be satisfactory when the particular atomic absorption spectrophotometer specified is used. The method may be modified as necessary for use with other suitable atomic absorption spectrophotometers capable of determining lead in the sample at the limit specified.]

  Standard stock solution: Dissolve 159.8 mg of ACS reagent-grade lead nitrate in 100 mL of water containing 1 mL of nitric acid, dilute to 1000.0 mL with water, and mix. [NOTE—Prepare and store this solution in glass containers that are free from lead salts.]

  Standard solution: Transfer 2.0 mL of *Standard stock solution* into a 500-mL volumetric flask, dilute to volume with water, and mix. This solution contains the equivalent of 0.4 µg/mL of lead. [NOTE—This solution should be prepared on the day of use.]

  Sample solution: Transfer 20 g of sample into a 100-mL volumetric flask that has previously been rinsed with nitric acid and water. Dissolve the sample in a mixture of 50 mL of water and 1 mL of nitric acid, dilute to volume with water, and mix.

  Analysis: Use a Perkin-Elmer 403 atomic absorption spectrophotometer equipped with a deuterium arc background corrector, a digital readout device, and a burner head capable of handling 20% solids content. Blank the instrument with water following the manufacturer's operating instructions. Aspirate a portion of the *Standard solution* and record the absorbance; then aspirate a portion of the *Sample solution* and record the absorbance. Calculate the lead content, in mg/kg, of the sample taken by the formula:

  $$\text{Result} = 100 \times (C/W) \times (A_U/A_S)$$

  C = concentration of lead in the *Standard solution* (µg/mL)
  W = weight of the sample taken (g)
  A_U = absorbance of the *Sample solution*
  A_S = absorbance of the *Standard solution*

  Acceptance criteria: NMT 2 mg/kg

- **MERCURY**

  Standard stock solution: Prepare a solution containing 1 µg/mL of mercury as directed for *Standard Preparation* under *Mercury Limit Test, Method I*, Appendix IIIB.

  Standard solutions: Pipet 0.25, 0.50, 1.0 and 3.5 mL of the *Standard stock solution*, respectively, into each of

four glass-stoppered bottles of about 300-mL capacity, such as BOD (biological oxygen demand) bottles. Dilute the contents of each bottle to 100 mL with water, and mix. These solutions contain the equivalent of 0.25, 0.50, 1.0 and 3.5 mg/kg of mercury, respectively.

Sample solution: Transfer 1.000 g of sample into a 200-mL screw-cap centrifuge bottle, and add 5 mL of nitric acid and 5 mL of hydrochloric acid. Close the bottle tightly with a Teflon-lined screw-cap, digest on a steam bath for 1 h, and cool. Quantitatively transfer into a suitable glass-stoppered bottle (see *Standard solutions*), dilute to 100 mL with water, and bubble air through the sample for 2 min.

Reagent blank: Prepare in the same manner as the *Sample solution*.

10% Stannous chloride solution: Dissolve 20 g of stannous chloride dihydrate in 40 mL of warm hydrochloric acid and dilute with 160 mL of water. [NOTE—Prepare fresh each week.]

Analysis: Use a suitable atomic absorption spectrophotometer assembly designed for mercury analysis, such as the Coleman MAS-50 Mercury Analyzer. [NOTE—The *Apparatus* and *Procedure* described under *Mercury Limit Test, Method I*, Appendix IIIB, may be suitably modified for this determination.] Add 5 mL of *10% Stannous chloride solution* to the solution to be tested, and immediately insert the bubbler of the mercury analysis apparatus. Obtain the absorbance reading by following the instrument manufacturer's operating instructions. Correct the sample readings for the *Reagent blank* (see *General Provisions*), and determine the mercury concentration of the *Sample solution* from a standard curve prepared by plotting the readings obtained with the *Standard solutions* against mercury concentration, in mg/kg.

Acceptance criteria: NMT 1 mg/kg

- **SULFATE,** *Chloride and Sulfate Limit Tests, Sulfate Limit Test,* Appendix IIIB

  Sample: Dissolve 100 mg of sample in 2.7 N hydrochloric acid and dilute to 30 to 40 mL with water.

  Control: 300 µg of sulfate (30 mL of *Standard Sulfate Solution*

  Analysis: Proceed as directed beginning with the addition of 3 mL of barium chloride TS.

  Acceptance criteria: Any turbidity produced in the solution containing the *Sample* does not exceed that produced in the solution containing the *Control*. (NMT 0.3%)

Organic Impurities
- **FERRIC CITRATE**

  Sample solution: 10 mg/mL

  Analysis: Add potassium ferrocyanide TS to the *Sample solution*.

  Acceptance criteria: No blue precipitate forms.

- **OXALATE**

  Sample: 1 g

  Analysis: Transfer the *Sample* into a 125-mL separatory funnel, dissolve in 10 mL of water, add 2 mL of hydrochloric acid, and extract successively with one 50-mL portion and one 20-mL portion of ether. Transfer the combined ether extracts into a 150-mL beaker, add 10 mL of water, and remove the ether by evaporation on a steam bath. Add 1 drop of glacial acetic acid and 1 mL of a 50 mg/mL calcium acetate solution to the residual aqueous solution.

  Acceptance criteria: No turbidity develops within 5 min.

Ferric Citrate

First Published: Prior to FCC 6

$FeC_6H_5O_7 \cdot xH_2O$ Formula wt, anhydrous 244.95
                               CAS: anhydrous [2338-05-8]
UNII: 63G354M39Z [ferric citrate anhydrous]

DESCRIPTION
Ferric Citrate occurs as brown granules or as thin, transparent, garnet red scales. It is more readily soluble in hot water than in cold, but it is insoluble in alcohol.

Function: Nutrient

Packaging and Storage: Store in well-closed containers.

IDENTIFICATION
- **CITRATE,** Appendix IIIA

  Sample solution: 100 mg/mL

  Acceptance criteria: Passes test

- **IRON (FERRIC SALTS),** Appendix IIIA

  Sample solution: 100 mg/mL

  Acceptance criteria: Passes tests

ASSAY
- **IRON CONTENT**

  Sample: 1 g

  Analysis: Dissolve the *Sample* in a mixture of 5 mL of hydrochloric acid and 25 mL of water contained in a glass-stoppered flask, warming to aid dissolution, if necessary. Cool, add 4 g of potassium iodide, insert the stopper in the flask, and allow the solution to stand for 15 min. Dilute with 100 mL of water, and titrate the liberated iodine with 0.1 N sodium thiosulfate, adding 3 mL of starch TS as the endpoint is approached. Perform a blank determination (see *General Provisions*) and make any necessary correction. Each mL of 0.1 N sodium thiosulfate is equivalent to 5.585 mg of Fe.

  Acceptance criteria: NLT 16.5% and NMT 18.5% of ferric Fe

IMPURITIES
Inorganic Impurities
- **AMMONIA**

  Sample: 500 mg

  Analysis: Heat the *Sample* with 5 mL of 1 N sodium hydroxide.

  Acceptance criteria: The odor of ammonia is not perceptible.

- **CHLORIDE**

  Sample solution: Heat 1 g of sample in a mixture of 25 mL of water and 2 mL of nitric acid until it dissolves. Cool, dilute with water to 100 mL, and mix. [NOTE—

Save the unused portion of this solution for analysis of *Sulfate* (below).]
Analysis: Add 1 mL of silver nitrate TS to 10 mL of the *Sample solution*.
Acceptance criteria: No turbidity immediately develops.
- **LEAD**, *Lead Limit Test, Flame Atomic Absorption Spectrophotometric Method,* Appendix IIIB
  Sample: 1 g
  Acceptance criteria: NMT 2 mg/kg
- **SULFATE**
  Sample solution: Use solution obtained in the test for *Chloride* (above).
  Analysis: Add 1 mL of barium chloride TS to 10 mL of the *Sample solution*.
  Acceptance criteria: No turbidity develops within 15 s.

Organic Impurities
- **ALKALI CITRATE**
  Sample: 500 mg
  Analysis: Ignite the *Sample* until it is thoroughly charred, cool, and add 2 mL of hot water.
  Acceptance criteria: The water is neutral or shows only a slight alkaline reaction to litmus.

Ferric Phosphate

First Published: Prior to FCC 6
Last Revision: First Supplement, FCC 7

Iron Phosphate
Ferric Orthophosphate

FePO$_4 \cdot x$H$_2$O

Formula wt, anhydrous 150.82
CAS: anhydrous [10045-86-0]
dihydrate (strengite) [13824-49-2]
dihydrate (phosphosiderite) [14567-75-0]
trihydrate (koninckite) [14567-93-2]
UNII: N6BAA189V1 [ferric phosphate]

DESCRIPTION
Ferric Phosphate occurs as a crystalline or amorphous material in shades of yellow, white, purple, or pink. It contains from one to four molecules of water of hydration. It is insoluble in water and in glacial acetic acid, but is soluble in hydrochloric and sulfuric acids.
Function: Nutrient
Packaging and Storage: Store in well-closed containers.

IDENTIFICATION
- **PROCEDURE**
  Sample: 1 g
  Analysis: Dissolve the *Sample* in 5 mL of 1:2 hydrochloric acid, and add an excess of 1 N sodium hydroxide. A red-brown precipitate forms. Boil the mixture, filter to remove the iron, and strongly acidify a portion of the filtrate with hydrochloric acid. Cool, mix with an equal volume of magnesia mixture TS, and treat with a slight excess of 6 N ammonium oxide. An abundant white precipitate forms. Wash the precipitate and add a few drops of silver nitrate TS.
  Acceptance criteria: The white precipitate turns green-yellow when treated with the silver nitrate TS.

ASSAY
- **PROCEDURE**
  Sample: 3.5 g
  Analysis: Dissolve the *Sample* in 75 mL of 1:2 hydrochloric acid, heat to boiling, and boil for about 5 min. Cool, transfer into a 100-mL volumetric flask, dilute with the dilute hydrochloric acid to volume, and mix. Add 100 mL of the dilute hydrochloric acid to 25.0 mL of this solution, boil again for 5 min, and add, dropwise and while stirring, stannous chloride TS to the boiling solution until the iron is just reduced as indicated by the disappearance of the yellow color. Add 2 drops in excess (but no more) of the stannous chloride TS, dilute with about 50 mL of water, and cool to room temperature. While stirring vigorously, add 15 mL of a saturated solution of mercuric chloride, and then allow to stand for 5 min. Add 15 mL of a sulfuric acid–phosphoric acid mixture, prepared by slowly adding 75 mL of sulfuric acid to 300 mL of water, cooling, adding 75 mL of phosphoric acid, and then diluting with water to 500 mL. Mix, add 0.5 mL of barium diphenylamine sulfonate TS, and titrate with 0.1 N potassium dichromate to a red-violet endpoint. Each mL of 0.1 N potassium dichromate is equivalent to 5.585 mg of Fe.
  Acceptance criteria: NLT 26.0% and NMT 32.0% of Fe

IMPURITIES
Inorganic Impurities
- **ARSENIC,** *Arsenic Limit Test,* Appendix IIIB
  [NOTE—Assemble the special distillation apparatus as shown in *Figure 13*.]
  Sample solution: Transfer 2 g of sample, 50 mL of hydrochloric acid, and add 5 g of cuprous chloride into the distilling flask (*B*). Reassemble the distillation apparatus and apply gentle suction to flask *F* to produce a continuous stream of bubbles. Heat the solution in flask *B* to boiling and distill until between 30 and 35 mL of distillate has been collected in flask *D*. Quantitatively transfer the distillate to a 100-mL volumetric flask with the aid of water, dilute with water to volume, and mix.
  Standard solution: Prepare this solution in the same manner as the *Sample solution*, but use 6.0 mL of *Standard Arsenic Solution* in place of the sample.
  Blank solution: Prepare this solution in the same manner as the *Sample solution,* but use 6.0 mL of water in place of the sample.
  Analysis: Transfer 50.0 mL of the *Sample solution* into the generator flask, add 2 mL of a 150 mg/mL solution of potassium iodide, and continue as directed in the *Procedure* beginning with "[add] 0.5 mL of *Stannous Chloride Solution*, and mix. ..." Modify the *Procedure* by using 5.0 g of Devarda's metal in place of the 3.0 g of 20-mesh granular zinc, and maintain the temperature of the reaction mixture in the generator flask between 25° and 27°. Treat 50.0 mL each of the *Standard solution* and of the *Blank solution* in the same manner and under the same conditions. Determine the

absorbance at 525 nm produced by each solution as directed under *Procedure*. Calculate the arsenic content (in mg/kg) of the sample taken:

$$\text{Result} = 3 \times (A_U - A_B)/(A_S - A_B)$$

A_U = absorbance produced by the *Sample solution*
A_B = absorbance produced by the *Blank solution*
A_S = absorbance produced by the *Standard solution*

[NOTE—If A_B exceeds 0.300, different samples of reagent-grade cuprous chloride and Devarda's metal should be tested for arsenic content by the procedure described herein, and lots of these reagents should be selected that will give blank readings that do not exceed 0.300.]

Acceptance criteria: NMT 3 mg/kg

- **FLUORIDE**, *Fluoride Limit Test*, Appendix IIIB
  Sample: 1.0 g
  Acceptance criteria: NMT 0.005%

- **LEAD**
  [NOTE—When preparing all aqueous solutions and rinsing glassware before use, employ water that has been passed through a strong-acid, strong-base, mixed-bed ion-exchange resin before use. Select all reagents to have as low a content of lead as practicable, and store all reagent solutions in containers of borosilicate glass. Clean glassware before use by soaking in warm 8 N nitric acid for 30 min and by rinsing with deionized water.]

  Ascorbic acid–sodium iodide solution: 100 mg/mL of ascorbic acid and 192.5 mg/mL of sodium iodide

  Trioctylphosphine oxide solution: 50 mg/mL of trioctylphosphine oxide in 4-methyl-2-pentanone.
  [CAUTION—This solution causes irritation. Avoid contact with eyes, skin, and clothing. Take special precautions in disposing of unused portions of solutions to which this reagent is added.]

  Standard stock solution: Transfer 159.8 mg of reagent-grade lead nitrate to a 1000-mL volumetric flask, dissolve it in 100 mL of water containing 1 mL of nitric acid, and dilute with water to volume. This solution contains 100 µg/mL of lead.

  Standard preparation: Transfer 5.0 mL of *Standard stock solution* into a 100-mL volumetric flask, dilute with water to volume, and mix. Transfer 2.0 mL of this resulting solution into a 50-mL volumetric flask. Add 10 mL of 9 N hydrochloric acid and about 10 mL of water to the volumetric flask. Add 20 mL of *Ascorbic acid–sodium iodide solution* and 5.0 mL of *Trioctylphosphine oxide solution* to the flask. Shake for 30 s and allow the layers to separate. Add water to bring the organic solvent layer into the neck of the flask, shake again, and allow the layers to separate. The organic solvent layer is the *Standard preparation* and contains 2.0 µg/mL of lead.

  Blank preparation: Transfer 10 mL of 9 N hydrochloric acid and about 10 mL of water to a 50-mL volumetric flask. Add 20 mL of *Ascorbic acid–sodium iodide solution* and 5.0 mL of *Trioctylphosphine oxide solution* to the flask. Shake for 30 s and allow the layers to separate. Add water to bring the organic solvent layer into the neck of the flask, shake again, and allow the layers to separate. The organic solvent layer remaining is the *Blank preparation* and contains 0.0 µg/mL of lead.

  Sample preparation: Add 2.5 g of sample, 10 mL of 9 N hydrochloric acid, about 10 mL of water, 20 mL of *Ascorbic acid–sodium iodide solution*, and 5.0 mL of *Trioctylphosphine oxide solution* to a 50-mL volumetric flask, shake for 30 s, and allow the layers to separate. Add water to bring the organic solvent layer into the neck of the flask, shake again, and allow the layers to separate. The organic solvent layer is the *Sample preparation*.

  Analysis: Using a suitable atomic absorption spectrophotometer equipped with a lead hollow-cathode lamp and an air–acetylene flame set at the lead emission line of 283.3 nm, with 4-methyl-2-pentanone used to set the instrument to zero, concomitantly determine the absorbance of the *Blank preparation*, the *Standard preparation*, and the *Sample preparation*. [NOTE—In a suitable analysis, the absorbance of the *Blank preparation* is NMT 20% of the difference between the absorbance of the *Standard preparation* and the absorbance of the *Blank preparation*.]

  Acceptance criteria: The absorbance of the *Sample preparation* does not exceed that of the *Standard preparation* (NMT 4 mg/kg).

- **MERCURY**
  10% Stannous chloride solution: Dissolve 20 g of stannous chloride ($SnCl_2 \cdot 2H_2O$) in 40 mL of warm hydrochloric acid and dilute with 160 mL of water.

  Sample solution: Transfer 5.00 g of sample into a 150-mL beaker, add 25 mL of aqua regia, cover with a watch glass, and allow to stand at room temperature for about 5 min. Heat just to boiling, allow to simmer for about 5 min, and cool. Transfer the solution into a 250-mL volumetric flask, dilute with water to volume, and mix. [NOTE—Disregard any undissolved material that may be present.] Transfer a 50.0-mL aliquot of this solution into a 150-mL beaker, and add 1.0 mL of 1:5 sulfuric acid and 1.0 mL of a filtered solution of 40 mg/mL potassium permanganate. Heat the solution just to boiling, simmer for about 5 min, and cool. Prepare a *Reagent blank* in the same manner.

  Standard stock solution: Dissolve 338.5 mg of mercuric chloride, in 200 mL of water in a 250-mL volumetric flask, add 14 mL of 1:2 sulfuric acid, dilute with water to volume, and mix. Pipet 10.0 mL of this solution into a 1000-mL volumetric flask containing about 800 mL of water and 56 mL of 1:2 sulfuric acid, dilute with water to volume, and mix. Pipet 10.0 mL of the second solution into a second 1000-mL volumetric flask containing 800 mL of water and 56 mL of 50% sulfuric acid, dilute with water to volume, and mix. Each mL of this diluted stock solution contains 0.1 µg of mercury.

  Standard solutions: Pipet 1.25, 2.50, 5.00, 7.50, and 10.00 mL of the *Standard stock solution* (equivalent to 0.125, 0.250, 0.500, 0.750, and 1.00 µg of mercury, respectively) into five separate 150-mL beakers. Add 25 mL of aqua regia to each beaker, cover with watch glasses, heat just to boiling, simmer for about 5 min, and cool to room temperature. Transfer the solutions into separate 250-mL volumetric flasks, dilute with water to volume, and mix. Transfer a 50.0-mL aliquot from each solution into five separate 150-mL beakers, and add 1.0 mL of 1:5 sulfuric acid and 1.0 mL of a filtered solution of 40 mg/mL of potassium permanganate solution to each. Heat the solutions just to boiling, simmer for about 5 min, and cool.

Analysis: Use a Mercury Detection Instrument as described and an Aeration Apparatus as shown in Figure 16 under Mercury Limit Test, Appendix IIIB. For the purposes of the test described in this monograph, the Techtron AA-1000 atomic absorption spectrophotometer, equipped with a 10-cm silica absorption cell (Beckman Part No. 75144, or equivalent) and coupled with a strip chart recorder (Varian Series A-25, or equivalent), is satisfactory. Assemble the Aeration Apparatus as shown in Figure 16 under Mercury Limit Test, Appendix IIIB. Use magnesium perchlorate as the absorbent in the absorption cell (e), fill gas-washing bottle (c) with 60 mL of water, and place stopcock (b) in the bypass position. Connect the assembly to the 10-cm absorption cell (analogous to f in the figure) of the spectrophotometer, and adjust the air or nitrogen flow rate so that, in the following procedure, maximum absorption and reproducibility are obtained without excessive foaming in the test solution. Obtain a baseline reading at 253.7 nm by following the equipment manufacturer's operating instructions. Using the Techtron AA-1000 spectrophotometer, the following conditions are suitable: slit width: 2 Å; lamp current: 3 mA; and scale expansion: × 1. With the strip chart recorder, set the chart speed at 25 in/h and the span at 2 mV. Precondition the apparatus by an appropriate modification of the procedures described below for treatment of the test solutions.

[NOTE—The fritted bubbler in gas-washing bottle (c) should be kept immersed in water between determinations. After each determination, wash the bubbler with a stream of water.]

Treat the Reagent blank, each of the Standard solutions, and the Sample solution as follows: Transfer the solution to be tested into a 125-mL gas-washing bottle (c), using a few drops of 100 mg/mL of hydroxylamine hydrochloride solution to remove any manganese hydroxide from the beaker. Dilute with water to about 55 mL, and add a magnetic stirring bar. Discharge the permanganate color by adding, dropwise, the hydroxylamine hydrochloride solution, swirling after each drop is added. Add 15.0 mL of 10% Stannous chloride solution, and immediately connect gas-washing bottle c to the aeration apparatus. Switch on the magnetic stirrer, turn stopcock b from the bypass to the aerating position, and obtain the absorbance reading. Disconnect bottle c from the aeration apparatus, discard the solution just tested, wash bottle c and the fritted bubbler with water, and repeat the procedure with the remaining solutions. Correct the sample readings for the Reagent blank, and determine the mercury concentration of the Sample solution from a standard curve prepared by plotting the readings obtained with the Standard solutions against mercury concentration, in mg/kg, with suitable adjustments being made for dilution factors.

Acceptance criteria: NMT 3 mg/kg

SPECIFIC TESTS
- **LOSS ON IGNITION**
  Analysis: Ignite a sample at 800° for 1 h.
  Acceptance criteria: NMT 32.5%

Ferric Pyrophosphate

First Published: Prior to FCC 6

Iron Pyrophosphate

$Fe_4(P_2O_7)_3 \cdot xH_2O$ Formula wt, anhydrous 745.22
                                  CAS: [10058-44-3]
UNII: QK8899250F [ferric pyrophosphate]

DESCRIPTION
Ferric Pyrophosphate occurs as a tan or yellow-white powder. It is insoluble in water, but is soluble in mineral acids.

Function: Nutrient
Packaging and Storage: Store in well-closed containers.

IDENTIFICATION
- **PROCEDURE**
  Sample: 500 mg
  Analysis: Dissolve the Sample in 5 mL of 1:2 hydrochloric acid. Add an excess of 1 N sodium hydroxide. A red-brown precipitate forms. Allow the solution to stand for several minutes, and then filter, discarding the first few mL of filtrate. Add 1 drop of bromophenol blue TS to 5 mL of the clear filtrate and titrate with 1 N hydrochloric acid to a green color. Add 10 mL of a 125 mg/mL solution of zinc sulfate, and readjust the pH to 3.8 (green color).
  Acceptance criteria: A white precipitate forms (distinction from orthophosphates).

ASSAY
- **PROCEDURE**
  Sample: 3.5 g
  Analysis: Dissolve the Sample in 75 mL of 1:2 hydrochloric acid, heat to boiling, and boil for about 5 min. Cool, transfer into a 100-mL volumetric flask, dilute to volume with the dilute hydrochloric acid, and mix. Add 100 mL of the dilute hydrochloric acid to 25.0 mL of this solution, boil again for 5 min, and add, dropwise and while stirring, stannous chloride TS to the boiling solution until the iron is just reduced as indicated by the disappearance of the yellow color. Add 2 drops in excess (but no more) of the stannous chloride TS, dilute with about 50 mL of water, and cool to room temperature. While stirring vigorously, add 15 mL of a saturated solution of mercuric chloride, and

then allow to stand for 5 min. Add 15 mL of a sulfuric acid–phosphoric acid mixture, prepared by slowly adding 75 mL of sulfuric acid to 300 mL of water, cooling, adding 75 mL of phosphoric acid, and then diluting to 500 mL with water. Mix, add 0.5 mL of barium diphenylamine sulfonate TS, and titrate with 0.1 N potassium dichromate to a red-violet endpoint. Each mL of 0.1 N potassium dichromate is equivalent to 5.585 mg of Fe.

Acceptance criteria: NLT 24.0% and NMT 26.0% of Fe

IMPURITIES
Inorganic Impurities

- **ARSENIC**, *Arsenic Limit Test,* Appendix IIIB
  [NOTE—Assemble the special distillation apparatus as shown in Fig. 13.]
  Sample solution: Transfer 2 g of sample, 50 mL of hydrochloric acid, and add 5 g of cuprous chloride into the distilling flask (*B*). Reassemble the distillation apparatus and apply gentle suction to flask *F* to produce a continuous stream of bubbles. Heat the solution in flask *B* to boiling and distill until between 30 and 35 mL of distillate has been collected in flask *D*. Quantitatively transfer the distillate to a 100-mL volumetric flask with the aid of water, dilute to volume with water, and mix.
  Standard solution: Prepare this solution in the same manner as the *Sample solution*, but use 6.0 mL of *Standard Arsenic Solution* in place of the sample.
  Blank solution: Prepare this solution in the same manner as the *Sample solution*, but use 6.0 mL of water in place of the sample.
  Analysis: Transfer 50.0 mL of the *Sample solution* into the generator flask, add 2 mL of a 150 mg/mL solution of potassium iodide, and continue as directed in the *Procedure* beginning with "[add] 0.5 mL of *Stannous Chloride Solution*, and mix. ..." Modify the *Procedure* by using 5.0 g of Devarda's metal in place of the 3.0 g of 20-mesh granular zinc, and maintain the temperature of the reaction mixture in the generator flask between 25° and 27°. Treat 50.0 mL each of the *Standard solution* and of the *Blank solution* in the same manner and under the same conditions. Determine the absorbance at 525 nm produced by each solution as directed under *Procedure*. Calculate the arsenic content (in mg/kg) of the sample by the formula:

  $$\text{Result} = 3 \times (A_U - A_B)/(A_S - A_B)$$

  A_U = absorbance produced by the *Sample solution*
  A_B = absorbance produced by the *Blank solution*
  A_S = absorbance produced by the *Standard solution*

  [NOTE—If A_B exceeds 0.300, different samples of reagent-grade cuprous chloride and Devarda's metal should be tested for arsenic content by the procedure described herein, and lots of these reagents should be selected that will give blank readings that do not exceed 0.300.]
  Acceptance criteria: NMT 3 mg/kg

- **LEAD**
  [NOTE—When preparing all aqueous solutions and rinsing glassware before use, employ water that has been passed through a strong-acid, strong-base, mixed-bed ion-exchange resin before use. Select all reagents to have as low a content of lead as practicable, and store all reagent solutions in containers of borosilicate glass. Clean glassware before use by soaking in warm 8 N nitric acid for 30 min and by rinsing with deionized water.]
  Ascorbic acid–sodium iodide solution: 100 mg/mL of ascorbic acid and 192.5 mg/mL of sodium iodide in water
  Trioctylphosphine oxide solution: 50 mg/mL of trioctylphosphine oxide in 4-methyl-2-pentanone
  [CAUTION—This reagent causes irritation. Avoid contact with eyes, skin, and clothing. Take special precautions in disposing of unused portions of solutions to which this reagent is added.]
  Standard stock solution: 100 µg/mL of lead prepared as follows: Transfer 159.8 mg of reagent-grade lead nitrate to a 1000-mL volumetric flask, dissolve it in 100 mL of water containing 1 mL of nitric acid, and dilute to volume with water.
  Standard solution: Transfer 1.0 mL of *Standard stock solution* into a 100-mL volumetric flask, dilute to volume with water, and mix. Transfer 2.0 mL of this resulting solution into a 50-mL volumetric flask. Add 10 mL of 9 N hydrochloric acid and about 10 mL of water to the volumetric flask. Add 20 mL of *Ascorbic acid–sodium iodide solution* and 5.0 mL of *Trioctylphosphine oxide solution* to the flask. Shake for 30 s and allow the layers to separate. Add water to bring the organic solvent layer into the neck of the flask, shake again, and allow the layer to separate. The organic solvent layer is the *Standard solution* and contains 0.4 µg/mL of lead.
  Blank solution: Transfer 10 mL of 9 N hydrochloric acid and about 10 mL of water to a 50-mL volumetric flask. Add 20 mL of *Ascorbic acid–sodium iodide solution* and 5.0 mL of *Trioctylphosphine oxide solution* to the flask. Shake for 30 s and allow the layers to separate. Add water to bring the organic solvent layer into the neck of the flask, shake again, and allow the layer to separate. The organic solvent layer remaining is the *Blank solution* and contains 0.0 µg/mL of lead.
  Sample solution: Add 2.5 g of sample, 10 mL of 9 N hydrochloric acid, about 10 mL of water, 20 mL of *Ascorbic acid–sodium iodide solution*, and 5.0 mL of *Trioctylphosphine oxide solution* to a 50-mL volumetric flask, shake for 30 s, and allow the layers to separate. Add water to bring the organic solvent layer into the neck of the flask, shake again, and allow the layers to separate. The organic solvent layer is the *Sample solution*.
  Analysis: Using a suitable atomic absorption spectrophotometer equipped with a lead hollow-cathode lamp and an air–acetylene flame set at the lead emission line of 283.3 nm, with 4-methyl-2-pentanone used to set the instrument to zero,

concomitantly determine the absorbance of the *Blank solution,* the *Standard solution* and the *Sample solution.*
Acceptance criteria: The absorbance of the *Blank solution* is NMT 20% of the difference between the absorbance of the *Standard solution* and the absorbance of the *Blank solution.* The absorbance of the *Sample solution* does not exceed that of the *Standard solution* (NMT 4 mg/kg).

- **MERCURY**
  10% Stannous chloride solution: Dissolve 20 g of stannous chloride ($SnCl_2 \cdot 2H_2O$) in 40 mL of warm hydrochloric acid and dilute with 160 mL of water.
  Sample solution: Transfer 5.00 g of sample into a 150-mL beaker, add 25 mL of aqua regia, cover with a watch glass, and allow to stand at room temperature for about 5 min. Heat just to boiling, allow to simmer for about 5 min, and cool. Transfer the solution into a 250-mL volumetric flask, dilute to volume with water, and mix. [NOTE—Disregard any undissolved material that may be present.] Transfer a 50.0-mL aliquot of this solution into a 150-mL beaker, and add 1.0 mL of 1:5 sulfuric acid and 1.0 mL of a filtered solution of 40 mg/mL potassium permanganate. Heat the solution just to boiling, simmer for about 5 min, and cool. Prepare a *Reagent blank* in the same manner.
  Standard stock solution: Dissolve 338.5 mg of mercuric chloride, in 200 mL of water in a 250-mL volumetric flask, add 14 mL of 1:2 sulfuric acid, dilute to volume with water, and mix. Pipet 10.0 mL of this solution into a 1000-mL volumetric flask containing about 800 mL of water and 56 mL of 1:2 sulfuric acid, dilute to volume with water, and mix. Pipet 10.0 mL of the second solution into a second 1000-mL volumetric flask containing 800 mL of water and 56 mL of 50% sulfuric acid, dilute to volume with water, and mix. Each mL of this diluted stock solution contains 0.1 µg of mercury.
  Standard solutions: Pipet 1.25, 2.50, 5.00, 7.50, and 10.00 mL of the *Standard stock solution* (equivalent to 0.125, 0.250, 0.500, 0.750, and 1.00 µg of mercury, respectively) into five separate 150-mL beakers. Add 25 mL of aqua regia to each beaker, cover with watch glasses, heat just to boiling, simmer for about 5 min, and cool to room temperature. Transfer the solutions into separate 250-mL volumetric flasks, dilute to volume with water, and mix. Transfer a 50.0-mL aliquot from each solution into five separate 150-mL beakers, and add 1.0 mL of 1:5 sulfuric acid and 1.0 mL of a filtered solution of 40 mg/mL potassium permanganate solution to each. Heat the solutions just to boiling, simmer for about 5 min, and cool.
  Analysis: Use a Mercury Detection Instrument, as described, and an Aeration Apparatus, as shown in Fig. 16 under *Mercury Limit Test,* Appendix IIIB. For the purposes of the test described in this monograph, the Techtron AA-1000 atomic absorption spectrophotometer, equipped with a 10-cm silica absorption cell (Beckman Part No. 75144, or equivalent) and coupled with a strip chart recorder (Varian Series A-25, or equivalent), is satisfactory. Assemble the Aeration Apparatus as shown in Fig. 16 under *Mercury Limit Test,* Appendix IIIB. Use magnesium perchlorate as the absorbent in the absorption cell (*e*). Fill gas washing bottle (*c*) with 60 mL of water, and place stopcock (*b*) in the bypass position. Connect the assembly to the 10-cm absorption cell (analogous to *f* in the figure) of the spectrophotometer, and adjust the air or nitrogen flow rate so that, in the following procedure, maximum absorption and reproducibility are obtained without excessive foaming in the test solution. Obtain a baseline reading at 253.7 nm by following the equipment manufacturer's operating instructions. Using the Techtron AA-1000 spectrophotometer, the following conditions are suitable: slit width: 2 Å; lamp current: 3 mA; and scale expansion: × 1. With the strip chart recorder, set the chart speed at 25 in/h and the span at 2 mV. Precondition the apparatus by an appropriate modification of the procedures described below for treatment of the test solutions. [NOTE—The fritted bubbler in gas washing bottle (*c*) should be kept immersed in water between determinations. After each determination, wash the bubbler with a stream of water.]
  Treat the *Reagent blank,* each of the *Standard solutions,* and the *Sample solution* as follows: Transfer the solution to be tested into a 125-mL gas-washing bottle (*c*), using a few drops of 100 mg/mL hydroxylamine hydrochloride solution to remove any manganese hydroxide from the beaker. Dilute to about 55 mL with water, and add a magnetic stirring bar. Discharge the permanganate color by adding, dropwise, the hydroxylamine hydrochloride solution, swirling after each drop is added. Add 15.0 mL of *10% stannous chloride solution,* and immediately connect gas washing bottle *c* to the aeration apparatus. Switch on the magnetic stirrer, turn stopcock *b* from the bypass to the aerating position, and obtain the absorbance reading. Disconnect bottle *c* from the aeration apparatus, discard the solution just tested, wash bottle *c* and the fritted bubbler with water, and repeat the procedure with the remaining solutions. Correct the sample readings for the *Reagent blank,* and determine the mercury concentration of the *Sample solution* from a standard curve prepared by plotting the readings obtained with the *Standard solutions* against mercury concentration, in mg/kg, with suitable adjustments being made for dilution factors.
  Acceptance criteria: NMT 3 mg/kg

SPECIFIC TESTS
- **LOSS ON IGNITION**
  Analysis: Ignite a sample at 800° for 1 h.
  Acceptance criteria: NMT 20.0%

Ferrous Ammonium Phosphate

First Published: Third Supplement, FCC 7

Ammonium Iron (II) Phosphate
Phosphoric acid, ammonium iron (II) salt

FeNH$_4$PO$_4$ Formula wt 168.85
CAS: [10101-60-7]

DESCRIPTION
Ferrous Ammonium Phosphate occurs as a greyish-green fine powder. It consists primarily of the anhydrous salt with small amounts of the hydrate. The final product is obtained by combining iron powder, phosphoric acid, and ammonia solution in demineralized water. The purification and spray drying processes remove any excess of starting materials (e.g. unreacted iron powder), insoluble salts, and volatiles, such as ammonia. The product is then milled into fine powder with the required particle size. It is insoluble in water, but is soluble in dilute mineral acids.

Function: Nutrient
Packaging and Storage: Store in tightly closed containers. The recommended storage temperature is between 5° and 10°.

IDENTIFICATION
- **AMMONIUM,** Appendix IIIA
   Acceptance criteria: Passes test
- **IRON (FERROUS SALTS),** Appendix IIIA
   Acceptance criteria: Passes test
- **PHOSPHATE,** Appendix IIIA
   Acceptance criteria: Passes test

ASSAY
- **PROCEDURE**
   Analysis: Weigh 300 g of sample into a 250-mL conical flask, add 25 mL of dilute sulfuric acid (16% v/v), and dissolve with heating. Cool, and add 75 mL of water. Add 0.1 mL of ferroin TS (0.1% w/v in water). Titrate immediately with 0.1 N ceric sulfate VS until the color changes from orange to light bluish-green. Each mL of 0.1 N ceric sulfate is equivalent to 5.585 mg of iron (II).
   Acceptance criteria: 22%–30% expressed as iron (II)

IMPURITIES
Inorganic Impurities
- **ARSENIC,** Elemental Impurities by ICP, Appendix IIIC
   Acceptance criteria: NMT 3 mg/kg
- **CADMIUM,** Elemental Impurities by ICP, Method I, Appendix IIIC
   Acceptance criteria: NMT 1 mg/kg
- **FLUORIDE,** Fluoride Limit Test, Method I or Method II, Appendix IIIB
   Acceptance criteria: NMT 0.005%
- **LEAD,** Elemental Impurities by ICP, Method I, Appendix IIIC
   Acceptance criteria: NMT 2 mg/kg
- **MERCURY,** Elemental Impurities by ICP, Appendix IIIC
   Acceptance criteria: NMT 1 mg/kg

SPECIFIC TESTS
- **IRON (III)**
   Procedure: Transfer 1 g of sample into a 250-mL Erlenmeyer flask, add 20 mL of water and 10 mL of hydrochloric acid TS, diluted, heat to dissolve, and cool to room temperature. Add 3 g of potassium iodide, stopper, swirl to mix, and allow to stand in the dark for 15 min. Remove the stopper, add approximately 100 mL of water, and titrate with 0.1 N sodium thiosulfate, adding starch TS near the endpoint. Each mL of 0.1 N sodium thiosulfate is equivalent to 5.585 mg of iron (III).
   Acceptance criteria: NMT 7%
- **WATER DETERMINATION,** Method I (Karl Fischer Titrimetric Method), Appendix IIB
   Acceptance criteria: NMT 3%

Ferrous Citrate

First Published: Prior to FCC 6
Last Revision: FCC 8

FeC$_6$H$_6$O$_7$ Formula wt 245.95
CAS: [23383-11-1]
UNII: 33KM3X4QQW [ferrous citrate]

DESCRIPTION
Ferrous Citrate occurs as a slightly gray-green powder or as white crystals.
Function: Nutrient
Packaging and Storage: Store in well-closed containers.

IDENTIFICATION
- **CITRATE,** Appendix IIIA
   Sample solution: 100 mg/mL
   Acceptance criteria: Passes test
- **IRON (FERROUS SALTS),** Appendix IIIA
   Sample solution: 100 mg/mL
   Acceptance criteria: Passes tests

ASSAY
Change to read:
- **FERROUS IRON CONTENT**
   Sample: 400 mg
   Analysis: Dissolve the Sample in 20 mL of 16:100 sulfuric acid, add 5 mL of 85% phosphoric acid, dilute with approximately 50 mL of water, and immediately titrate with 0.1 N ceric sulfate, using orthophenanthroline TS as the indicator. Perform a blank determination (see General Provisions), and make any necessary correction. Each mL of 0.1 N ceric sulfate is equivalent to 5.585 mg of Fe.
   Acceptance criteria: ▲NLT 20.0%▲FCC8 of ferrous Fe

IMPURITIES
Inorganic Impurities
- **CHLORIDE,** Chloride and Sulfate Limit Tests, Chloride Limit Test, Appendix IIIB
   Sample solution: Heat 100 mg of sample in a mixture of 25 mL of water and 2 mL of nitric acid until it

dissolves. Cool, dilute with water to 100 mL, and mix. Take 10 mL of this solution and dilute to 30–40 mL with water.
  Control: 20 µg chloride (2 mL of *Standard Chloride Solution*)
  Analysis: Proceed as directed in the *Procedure*, beginning with "add 1 mL of silver nitrate TS…"
  Acceptance criteria: Any turbidity produced by the *Sample solution* does not exceed that shown in the *Control*. (NMT 0.2%)
- **FERRIC IRON**
  Sample: 2 g
  Analysis: Dissolve the *Sample* in a mixture of 100 mL of water and 10 mL of hydrochloric acid contained in a 250-mL glass-stoppered flask, add 3 g of potassium iodide, shake well, and allow the mixture to stand in the dark for 5 min. Titrate any liberated iodine with 0.1 N sodium thiosulfate, using starch TS as an indicator. Perform a blank determination (see *General Provisions*), and make any necessary correction. Each mL of 0.1 N sodium thiosulfate is equivalent to 5.585 mg of ferric iron.
  Acceptance criteria: NMT 3.0%
- **LEAD,** *Lead Limit Test, Flame Atomic Absorption Spectrophotometric Method,* Appendix IIIB
  Sample: 1 g
  Acceptance criteria: NMT 2 mg/kg
- **SULFATE,** *Chloride and Sulfate Limit Tests, Chloride Limit Test,* Appendix IIIB
  Sample solution: Dissolve 500 mg of sample in 1 mL of 2.7 N hydrochloric acid, and dilute to 30–40 mL with water.
  Control: 300 µg sulfate (30 mL of *Standard Sulfate Solution*)
  Analysis: Proceed as directed in the *Procedure*, beginning with "add 3 mL of barium chloride TS…"
  Acceptance criteria: Any turbidity produced by the *Sample solution* does not exceed that shown in the *Control*. (NMT 0.06%)

Ferrous Fumarate

First Published: Prior to FCC 6

Iron (II) Fumarate

$C_4H_2FeO_4$ Formula wt 169.90
                              CAS: [141-01-5]
UNII: R5L488RY0Q [ferrous fumarate]

DESCRIPTION
Ferrous Fumarate occurs as a red-orange to red-brown powder. It may contain soft lumps that produce a yellow streak when crushed. It is soluble in water and in alcohol.
Function: Nutrient
Packaging and Storage: Store in well-closed containers.

IDENTIFICATION
- **IRON,** Appendix IIIA
  Sample solution: Use a portion of the filtrate obtained in the test for *Melting Range or Temperature* (below).
  Acceptance criteria: Passes tests
- **MELTING RANGE OR TEMPERATURE DETERMINATION,** Appendix IIB
  Sample preparation: Add 25 mL of 1:2 hydrochloric acid to the 1.5 g of sample, and dilute to 50 mL with water. Heat to complete dissolution; then cool; filter on a fine-porosity, sintered-glass crucible; wash the precipitate with 2:100 hydrochloric acid, [NOTE—Save the filtrate for the *Iron* identification test (above).]; and dry the precipitate at 105°. Add 3 mL of water and 7 mL of 1 N sodium hydroxide to 400 mg of the dried precipitate, and stir until dissolution is complete. Add, dropwise, 2.7 N hydrochloric acid until the solution is just acid to litmus; add 1 g of *p*-nitrobenzyl bromide and 10 mL of alcohol; and reflux the mixture for 2 h. Cool, filter, and wash the precipitate with two small portions of a 2:1 alcohol:water mixture, followed by two small portions of water. Recrystalize the precipitate in hot alcohol and dry at 105°.
  Acceptance criteria: The *Sample preparation*, so obtained, melts at about 152°.

ASSAY
- **PROCEDURE**
  Sample: 500 mg
  Analysis: Transfer the *Sample* into a 500-mL Erlenmeyer flask, add 25 mL of 2:5 hydrochloric acid, and heat to boiling. Add, dropwise, a solution of 5.6 g of stannous chloride in 50 mL of 3:10 hydrochloric acid until the yellow color disappears, and then add 2 drops in excess. Cool the solution in an ice bath to room temperature, add 8 mL of mercuric chloride TS, and allow to stand for 5 min. Add 200 mL of water, 25 mL of 1:2 sulfuric acid, and 4 mL of phosphoric acid; then add orthophenanthroline TS, and titrate with 0.1 N ceric sulfate. Each mL of 0.1 N ceric sulfate is equivalent to 16.99 mg of $C_4H_2FeO_4$.
  Acceptance criteria: NLT 97.0% and NMT 101.0% of $C_4H_2FeO_4$, calculated on the dried basis

IMPURITIES
Inorganic Impurities
- **FERRIC IRON**
  Sample: 2 g
  Analysis: Transfer the *Sample* into a 250-mL glass-stoppered Erlenmeyer flask, add 25 mL of water and 4 mL of hydrochloric acid, and heat on a hot plate until dissolution is complete. Stopper the flask and cool to room temperature. Add 3 g of potassium iodide, stopper, swirl to mix, and allow to stand in the dark for 5 min. Remove the stopper, add 75 mL of water, and titrate with 0.1 N sodium thiosulfate, adding starch TS near the endpoint.
  Acceptance criteria: NMT 7.16 mL of 0.1 N sodium thiosulfate is consumed. (NMT 2.0%)

- **LEAD**

  [NOTE—When preparing all aqueous solutions and rinsing glassware before use, employ water that has been passed through a strong-acid, strong-base, mixed-bed ion-exchange resin before use. Select all reagents to have as low a content of lead as practicable, and store all reagent solutions in containers of borosilicate glass. Clean glassware before use by soaking in warm 8 N nitric acid for 30 min and by rinsing with deionized water.]

  Ascorbic acid–sodium iodide solution: 100 mg/mL of ascorbic acid and 192.5 mg/mL of sodium iodide

  Trioctylphosphine oxide solution: 50 mg/mL of trioctylphosphine oxide in 4-methyl-2-pentanone. [CAUTION—This reagent causes irritation. Avoid contact with eyes, skin, and clothing. Take special precautions in disposing of unused portions of solutions to which this reagent is added.]

  Standard stock solution: Transfer 159.8 mg of reagent-grade lead nitrate to a 1000-mL volumetric flask, dissolve it in 100 mL of water containing 1 mL of nitric acid, and dilute to volume with water. This solution contains 100 µg/mL of lead. [NOTE—Prepare and store this solution in glass containers that are free from lead salts.]

  Standard solution: Transfer 1.0 mL of *Standard stock solution* into a 100-mL volumetric flask, dilute to volume with water, and mix. Transfer 2.0 mL of this resulting solution into a 50-mL volumetric beaker. Add 6 mL of nitric acid and 10 mL of perchloric acid to the beaker and evaporate in a fume hood to dryness. [CAUTION—Handle perchloric acid in an appropriate fume hood.] Cool, dissolve the residue in 10 mL of 9 N hydrochloric acid, and transfer the solution, with the aid of about 10 mL of water into a 50-mL volumetric flask. Add 20 mL of *Ascorbic acid-sodium iodide solution* and 5.0 mL of *Trioctylphosphine oxide solution* to the flask. Shake for 30 s and allow the layers to separate. Add water to bring the organic solvent layer into the neck of the flask, shake again, and allow the layers to separate. The organic solvent layer is the *Standard preparation* and contains 0.4 µg/mL of lead.

  Blank preparation: Transfer 6 mL of nitric acid and 10 mL of perchloric acid to a 50-mL beaker and evaporate in a fume hood to dryness. [CAUTION—Handle perchloric acid in an appropriate fume hood.] Cool, dissolve the residue in 10 mL of 9 N hydrochloric acid and transfer the solution, with the aid of about 10 mL of water to a 50-mL volumetric flask. Add 20 mL of *Ascorbic acid-sodium iodide solution* and 5.0 mL of *Trioctylphosphine oxide solution* to the flask. Shake for 30 s and allow the layers to separate. Add water to bring the organic solvent layer into the neck of the flask, shake again, and allow the layers to separate. The organic solvent layer remaining is the *Blank preparation* and contains 0.0 µg/mL of lead.

  Sample preparation: Transfer 1.0 g of sample to a 50-mL beaker and add 6 mL of nitric acid and 10 mL of perchloric acid. [CAUTION—Handle perchloric acid in an appropriate fume hood.] Cover the beaker with a ribbed watch glass and heat in a fume hood until completely dry. Cool, dissolve the residue in 10 mL of 9 N hydrochloric acid, and transfer the beaker's contents, with the aid of about 10 mL of water, to a 50-mL volumetric flask. Add 20 mL of *Ascorbic acid-sodium iodide solution*, and 5.0 mL of *Trioctylphosphine oxide solution*, shake for 30 s, and allow the layers to separate. Add water to bring the organic solvent layer into the neck of the flask, shake again, and allow the layers to separate. The organic solvent layer is the *Sample preparation*.

  Analysis: Using a suitable atomic absorption spectrophotometer equipped with a lead hollow-cathode lamp and an air–acetylene flame set at the lead emission line of 283.3 nm, with 4-methyl-2-pentanone used to set the instrument to zero, concomitantly determine the absorbance of the *Blank preparation*, the *Standard preparation* and the *Sample preparation*. [NOTE—In a suitable analysis, the absorbance of the *Blank preparation* is NMT 20% of the difference between the absorbance of the *Standard preparation* and the absorbance of the *Blank preparation*.]

  Acceptance criteria: The absorbance of the *Sample preparation* does not exceed that of the *Standard preparation*. (NMT 2 mg/kg)

- **MERCURY,** Mercury Limit Test, Method II, Appendix IIIB

  Acceptance criteria: NMT 3 mg/kg

- **SULFATE**

  Sample: 1 g

  Analysis: Mix the *Sample* with 100 mL of water in a 250-mL beaker and heat on a steam bath, adding hydrochloric acid, dropwise, until dissolution is complete (about 2 mL of the acid will be required). Filter the solution, if necessary, and dilute the clear solution or filtrate to 100 mL with water. Heat to boiling, add 10 mL of barium chloride TS, warm on a steam bath for 2 h, cover, and allow to stand overnight. If crystals of ferrous fumarate form, warm on a steam bath to dissolve them, then filter through paper, wash the residue with hot water, and transfer the paper containing the residue to a tared crucible. Char the paper, without burning, and ignite the crucible and its contents at 600° to constant weight. Each mg of the residue is equivalent to 0.412 mg of sulfate (SO_4).

  Acceptance criteria: NMT 0.2%

SPECIFIC TESTS

- **LOSS ON DRYING,** Appendix IIC: 105° for 16 h

  Acceptance criteria: NMT 1.5%

Ferrous Gluconate

First Published: Prior to FCC 6

Iron (II) Gluconate

$C_{12}H_{22}FeO_{14} \cdot 2H_2O$ Formula wt 482.18
INS: 579 CAS: [299-29-6]
UNII: U1B11I423Z [ferrous gluconate]

DESCRIPTION
Ferrous Gluconate occurs as a fine, yellow-gray or pale green-yellow powder or granules. One g dissolves in about 10 mL of water with slight heating. It is practically insoluble in alcohol. A 1:20 aqueous solution is acid to litmus.
Function: Nutrient; color adjunct
Packaging and Storage: Store in tight containers.

IDENTIFICATION
- **Iron (Ferrous Salts),** Appendix IIIA
  Sample solution: 50 mg/mL
  Acceptance criteria: Passes tests
- **Thin-Layer Chromatography,** Appendix IIA
  Standard solution: 10 mg/mL of USP Potassium Gluconate RS [Note—Heat in a water bath at 60°, if necessary, to dissolve.]
  Sample solution: 10 mg/mL [Note—Heat in a water bath at 60°, if necessary, to dissolve.]
  Adsorbent: 0.25-mm layer of chromatographic silica gel
  Application volume: 5 µL
  Developing solvent system: Alcohol, ethyl acetate, ammonium hydroxide, and water [50:10:10:30]
  Spray reagent: Dissolve 2.5 g of ammonium molybdate in about 50 mL of 2 N sulfuric acid in a 100-mL volumetric flask, add 1.0 g of ceric sulfate, swirl to dissolve, dilute to volume with 2 N sulfuric acid, and mix.
  Analysis: After removing the plate from the developing chamber, allow it to dry at 110° for 20 min, and allow it to cool. Spray the plate with the *Spray reagent*, then heat the plate at 110° for 10 min.
  Acceptance criteria: The principal spot obtained from the *Sample solution* corresponds in color, size, and R_F value to that obtained from the *Standard solution*.

ASSAY
- **Procedure**
  Sample: 1.5 g
  Analysis: Dissolve the *Sample* in a mixture of 75 mL of water and 15 mL of 2 N sulfuric acid in a 300-mL Erlenmeyer flask and add 250 mg of zinc dust. Close the flask with a stopper containing a Bunsen valve, allow to stand at room temperature for 20 min, then filter through a sintered-glass filter crucible containing a thin layer of zinc dust, and wash the crucible and contents with 10 mL of 2 N sulfuric acid, followed by 10 mL of water. Add orthophenanthroline TS, and titrate the filtrate in the suction flask immediately with 0.1 N ceric sulfate. Perform a blank determination (see *General Provisions*) and make any necessary correction. Each mL of 0.1 N ceric sulfate is equivalent to 44.62 mg of $C_{12}H_{22}FeO_{14}$.
  Acceptance criteria: NLT 97.0% and NMT 102.0% of $C_{12}H_{22}FeO_{14}$, calculated on the dried basis

IMPURITIES
Inorganic Impurities
- **Chloride,** *Chloride and Sulfate Limit Tests, Chloride Limit Test,* Appendix IIIB
  Sample solution: 10 mg/mL
  Control: 70 µg of chloride (7 mL of *Standard Chloride Solution*)
  Analysis: Proceed as directed using a 10-mL portion of the *Sample solution*.
  Acceptance criteria: Any turbidity produced by the *Sample solution* does not exceed that shown in the *Control*. (NMT 0.07%)
- **Ferric Iron**
  Sample: 5 g
  Analysis: Dissolve the *Sample* in a mixture of 100 mL of water and 10 mL of hydrochloric acid in a 250-mL glass-stoppered flask, add 3 g of potassium iodide, shake well, and allow to stand in the dark for 5 min. Titrate any liberated iodine with 0.1 N sodium thiosulfate, using starch TS as the indicator. Each mL of 0.1 N sodium thiosulfate is equivalent to 5.585 mg of ferric iron.
  Acceptance criteria: NMT 2.0%
- **Lead**
  [Note—When preparing all aqueous solutions and rinsing glassware before use, employ water that has been passed through a strong-acid, strong-base, mixed-bed ion-exchange resin before use. Select all reagents to have as low a content of lead as practicable, and store all reagent solutions in containers of borosilicate glass. Clean glassware before use by soaking in warm 8 N nitric acid for 30 min and by rinsing with deionized water.]
  Ascorbic acid–sodium iodide solution: 100 mg/mL of ascorbic acid and 192.5 mg/mL of sodium iodide in water
  Trioctylphosphine oxide solution: 50 mg/mL of trioctylphosphine oxide in 4-methyl-2-pentanone [**Caution**—This reagent causes irritation. Avoid contact with eyes, skin, and clothing. Take special precautions in disposing of unused portions of solutions to which this reagent is added.]
  Standard stock solution: 100 µg/mL of lead prepared as follows: Transfer 159.8 mg of reagent-grade lead nitrate to a 1000-mL volumetric flask, dissolve it in 100 mL of water containing 1 mL of nitric acid, and dilute to volume with water.
  Standard solution: Transfer 1.0 mL of *Standard stock solution* into a 100-mL volumetric flask, dilute to volume with water, and mix. Transfer 2.0 mL of this resulting solution into a 50-mL volumetric flask. Add 10 mL of 9 N hydrochloric acid and about 10 mL of water

to the volumetric flask. Add 20 mL of *Ascorbic acid–sodium iodide solution* and 5.0 mL of *Trioctylphosphine oxide solution* to the flask. Shake for 30 s and allow the layers to separate. Add water to bring the organic solvent layer into the neck of the flask, shake again, and allow the layer to separate. The organic solvent layer is the *Standard solution* and contains 0.4 µg/mL of lead.
Blank solution: Transfer 10 mL of 9 N hydrochloric acid and about 10 mL of water to a 50-mL volumetric flask. Add 20 mL of *Ascorbic acid-sodium iodide solution* and 5.0 mL of *Trioctylphosphine oxide solution* to the flask. Shake for 30 s and allow the layers to separate. Add water to bring the organic solvent layer into the neck of the flask, shake again, and allow the layer to separate. The organic solvent layer remaining is the *Blank solution* and contains 0.0 µg/mL of lead.
Sample solution: Add 1.0 g of sample, 10 mL of 9 N hydrochloric acid, about 10 mL of water, 20 mL of *Ascorbic acid-sodium iodide solution*, and 5.0 mL of *Trioctylphosphine oxide solution* to a 50-mL volumetric flask, shake for 30 s, and allow the layers to separate. Add water to bring the organic solvent layer into the neck of the flask, shake again, and allow the layers to separate. The organic solvent layer is the *Sample solution*.
Analysis: Using a suitable atomic absorption spectrophotometer equipped with a lead hollow-cathode lamp and an air–acetylene flame set at the lead emission line of 283.3 nm, with 4-methyl-2-pentanone used to set the instrument to zero, concomitantly determine the absorbance of the *Blank solution*, the *Standard solution*, and the *Sample solution*. [NOTE—In a suitable analysis, the absorbance of the *Blank solution* is NMT 20% of the difference between the absorbance of the *Standard solution* and the absorbance of the *Blank solution*.]
Acceptance criteria: The absorbance of the *Sample solution* does not exceed that of the *Standard solution*. (NMT 2 mg/kg)
- **MERCURY,** *Mercury Limit Test, Method II,* Appendix IIIB
  Acceptance criteria: NMT 3 mg/kg
- **SULFATE,** *Chloride and Sulfate Limit Tests, Chloride Limit Test,* Appendix IIIB
  Sample: 200 mg
  Control: 20 mL of *Standard Sulfate Solution*
  Acceptance criteria: Any turbidity produced by the *Sample* does not exceed that shown in the *Control*. (NMT 0.1%)

Organic Impurities
- **OXALIC ACID**
  Sample: 1 g
  Analysis: Dissolve the *Sample* in 10 mL of water, add 2 mL of hydrochloric acid, transfer to a separatory funnel, and extract successively with 50 and 20 mL of ether. Combine the ether extracts, add 10 mL of water, and evaporate the ether on a steam bath. Add 1 drop of acetic acid (36%) and 1 mL of a 5 mg/mL calcium acetate solution.
  Acceptance criteria: No turbidity forms within 5 min.

- **REDUCING SUGARS**
  Sample: 500 mg
  Analysis: Dissolve the *Sample* in 10 mL of water, warm, and add 1 mL of 6 N ammonium hydroxide to make the solution alkaline. Pass hydrogen sulfide gas into the solution to precipitate the iron, and allow the mixture to stand for 30 min to coagulate the precipitate. Filter, and wash the precipitate with two successive 5-mL portions of water. Acidify the combined filtrate and washings with hydrochloric acid, and add 2 mL of 2.7 N hydrochloric acid in excess. Boil the solution until the vapors no longer darken lead acetate paper, and continue to boil, if necessary, until the solution has been concentrated to about 10 mL. Cool, add 5 mL of sodium carbonate TS and 20 mL of water, filter, and adjust the volume of the filtrate to 100 mL with water. Add 2 mL of alkaline cupric tartrate TS to 5 mL of filtrate, and boil for 1 min.
  Acceptance criteria: No red precipitate forms within 1 min.

SPECIFIC TESTS
- **LOSS ON DRYING,** Appendix IIC: 105° for 16 h
  Acceptance criteria: Between 6.5% and 10.0%

Ferrous Glycinate
First Published: Prior to FCC 6

Diaquo bis(glycinato) iron (II)
Ferrous Bisglycinate

Fe(OH$_2$)$_2$(OOCCH$_2$NH$_2$)$_2$ Formula wt 239.99
                                    CAS: [20150-34-9]
UNII: SFW1D987QV [ferrous bisglycinate]

DESCRIPTION
Ferrous Glycinate occurs as a fine, free-flowing powder. It has an octahedral structure with two water molecules and two chelated glycinate ions coordinated to the central ferrous iron.
Function: Source of dietary iron
Packaging and Storage: Store in tight containers.

IDENTIFICATION
- **IRON (FERROUS SALTS),** Appendix IIIA
  Acceptance criteria: Passes tests

ASSAY
- **PROCEDURE**
  Sample: 1 g
  Analysis: Dissolve the *Sample* in a mixture of 150 mL of water and 10 mL of sulfuric acid in a 300-mL flask. Add 1 drop of orthophenanthroline TS and titrate immediately with 0.1 N ceric sulfate prepared as

indicated under *Volumetric Solutions,* Solutions and Indicators. Perform a blank determination (see *General Provisions*) and make any necessary correction. Each mL of 0.1 N ceric sulfate is equivalent to 24.00 mg of Fe(OH$_2$)$_2$(OOCCH$_2$NH$_2$)$_2$.

Acceptance criteria: NLT 97.0% and NMT 102.0% of Fe(OH$_2$)$_2$(OOCCH$_2$NH$_2$)$_2$, calculated on the dried basis

IMPURITIES
Inorganic Impurities
- **FERRIC IRON**
  Sample: 5 g
  Analysis: Dissolve the *Sample* in a mixture of 100 mL of water and 10 mL of hydrochloric acid in a 250-mL glass-stoppered flask. Add 3 g of potassium iodide, shake well, and allow to stand in the dark for 5 min. Titrate any liberated iodine with 0.1 N sodium thiosulfate, using starch TS as the indicator. Each mL of 0.1 N sodium thiosulfate is equivalent to 5.585 mg of ferric iron.
  Acceptance criteria: NMT 2%
- **LEAD,** *Lead Limit Test, Flame Atomic Absorption Spectrophotometric Method*
  Sample: 10 g
  Acceptance criteria: NMT 1 mg/kg

SPECIFIC TESTS
- **LOSS ON DRYING,** Appendix IIC: 105° for 3 h
  Acceptance criteria: NMT 7%
- **NITROGEN**
  Equipment: Use a LECO CNS 2000, or equivalent, instrument capable of analyzing for carbon, nitrogen, and sulfur simultaneously. The instrument consists of an autosampler, a combustion furnace, and a computer system for determination and calculations required for operation. Before calibrating the instrument, perform appropriate combustion, helium gas line, and ballast leak checks of the system, and correct any detected leaks. Analyze about ten blanks through the system. Check and monitor that the results for carbon, nitrogen, and sulfur are constant. (Inconsistent blank values indicate problems with the instrument that must be corrected.) Use the results of these blank analyses to zero the instrument, then calibrate it by analyzing at least five 0.2-g samples of sulfamethazine, and verify that the results for carbon (51.7%), nitrogen (20.13%), and sulfur (11.52%) are within ±10% of actual values. Use these values to drift-correct the instrument, thus completing calibration. Analyze at least two more samples of sulfamethazine, and verify that the results for carbon, nitrogen, and sulfur are within ±10% of actual values.
  Sample: 0.2 g
  Analysis: Mix the *Sample* in a small amount of comcat (100 g of tungstic anhydride and 15 g of 97% lithium metaphosphate) in a ceramic weigh boat, to facilitate combustion. Analyze the sample through the system.
  Acceptance criteria: Between 10% and 12%
- **TOTAL IRON**
  Sample: 0.500 g [NOTE—Mix the sample thoroughly to achieve homogeneity. Some samples may require additional grinding to attain homogeneity. Do so by placing small amounts of sample into a clean, dry laboratory grinder and grinding until the sample has attained the desired level of homogeneity.]
  Analysis: Place the *Sample* into an appropriate digestion vessel. Add 5 mL of concentrated nitric acid, mix the slurry, and cover the vessel with a watch glass or vapor recovery device. Heat the sample to 95° ± 5° for 30 to 40 min without boiling. If brown fumes evolve after heating for the allotted time, indicating that the nitric acid has incompletely oxidized the sample, add 2 mL of concentrated nitric acid repeatedly, with heating for 15 to 20 min, until no brown fumes evolve. Heat the sample digest until the volume has been reduced to about 3 mL, ensuring that the bottom of the vessel is covered with the sample digest at all times. Remove the vessel from the heating source, and allow its contents to cool thoroughly. Add 2 mL of concentrated hydrochloric acid to the sample digest, and cover with a watch glass. Place the vessel on the heating source, and reflux the sample digest at 95° ± 5° for 15 to 20 min. Before removing the vessel from the heating source, be sure the evolving vapor is clear. Allow the sample digest to cool to room temperature, and dilute it to 50 mL with water. Add 3 g of potassium iodide, shake well, and allow to stand in the dark for 5 min. Titrate any liberated iodine with 0.1 N sodium thiosulfate, using starch TS as the indicator. Each mL of 0.1 N sodium thiosulfate is equivalent to 5.585 mg of iron.
  Acceptance criteria: NLT 20% and NMT 22%

Ferrous Lactate

First Published: Prior to FCC 6

Iron (II) Lactate
Iron (II) 2-Hydroxypropionate

$$Fe^{2+} \left[H_3C\text{-}CH(OH)\text{-}COO^- \right]_2 \cdot xH_2O$$

C$_6$H$_{10}$FeO$_6$·xH$_2$O   Formula wt, anhydrous 233.99
INS: 585   CAS: [5905-52-2]
UNII: 5JU4C2L5A0 [ferrous lactate]

DESCRIPTION
Ferrous Lactate occurs as a green-white powder or as crystals. The *levo* enantiomer occurs as the dihydrate, and the racemic mixture occurs as the trihydrate. It is sparingly soluble in water and practically insoluble in ethanol. A 1:50 aqueous solution has a pH between 5 and 6.
Function: Nutrient
Packaging and Storage: Store in tight containers.

IDENTIFICATION
- **IRON (FERROUS SALTS),** Appendix IIIA
  Sample solution: 20 mg/mL
  Acceptance criteria: Passes tests

- **LACTATE**, Appendix IIIA
  Sample solution: 20 mg/mL
  Acceptance criteria: Passes test

ASSAY
- **PROCEDURE**
  Sample: 800 mg
  Analysis: Dissolve the *Sample* in a mixture of 150 mL of water and 10 mL of sulfuric acid contained in a 300-mL flask. Add 5 mL of phosphoric acid, and cool to room temperature if necessary. Add 1 drop of orthophenanthroline TS and immediately titrate with 0.1 N ceric sulfate. Perform a blank determination (see *General Provisions*) and make any necessary correction. Each mL of 0.1 N ceric sulfate is equivalent to 23.40 mg of $C_6H_{10}FeO_6$.
  Acceptance criteria: NLT 97.0% and NMT 100.5% of $C_6H_{10}FeO_6$, calculated on the anhydrous basis

IMPURITIES
Inorganic Impurities
- **CHLORIDE**, *Chloride and Sulfate Limit Tests, Chloride Limit Test*, Appendix IIIB
  Sample solution: 10 mg/mL [NOTE—Use the same *Sample solution* for the test for *Sulfate*.]
  Control: 100 µg of chloride (10 mL of *Standard Chloride Solution*)
  Acceptance criteria: Any turbidity produced by a 10-mL portion of the *Sample solution* does not exceed that shown in the *Control*. (NMT 0.1%)
- **FERRIC IRON**
  Sample: 5 g
  Analysis: Dissolve the *Sample* in a mixture of 100 mL of water and 10 mL of hydrochloric acid contained in a 250-mL glass-stoppered flask. Add 3 g of potassium iodide, shake the flask well, and allow the mixture to stand in the dark for 5 min. Titrate any liberated iodine with 0.1 N sodium thiosulfate, using starch TS as the indicator. Each mL of 0.1 N sodium thiosulfate is equivalent to 5.585 mg of ferric iron.
  Acceptance criteria: NMT 0.2%
- **LEAD**
  [NOTE—In preparing all aqueous solutions and for rinsing glassware before use, employ water that has been passed through a strong-acid, strong-base, mixed-bed ion-exchange resin before use. Select all reagents to have as low a content of lead as practicable, and store all reagent solutions in containers of borosilicate glass. Clean glassware before use by soaking it in warm 8 N nitric acid for 30 min and then rinsing it with deionized water.]
  Standard stock solution: 1 µg/mL Pb, prepared (weekly) by diluting a single-element 1000 µg/mL lead stock solution with 0.1% nitric acid
  Standard lead solution: 10 ng/mL, prepared (daily) by diluting the *Standard stock solution* with 0.1 N nitric acid
  Modifier stock solution: Weigh an amount of palladium nitrate equivalent to 1 g of palladium, and dilute to 100 mL with 15% nitric acid.
  Modifier solution: Prepare just before use by diluting the *Modifier stock solution* 1:10 with water.
  Blank: 0.1% nitric acid
  Sample solution: Dissolve 2 g of sample in 5 mL of water and 10 mL of 10% nitric acid. Dilute to 100.0 mL with water.
  Solution A: (6:1)(v/v) mixture of *Blank* and the *Modifier Solution*
  Solution B: (2:2:2:1)(v/v/v/v) mixture of *Standard lead solution*, the *Sample solution*, the *Blank*, and the *Modifier solution*
  Solution C: (4:2:1) (v/v/v) mixture of *Standard lead solution*, the *Sample solution*, and the *Modifier solution*
  Solution D: (2:4:1) (v/v/v) mixture of *Sample solution*, the *Blank*, and the *Modifier solution*
  Analysis: Using a suitable graphite furnace atomic absorption spectrophotometer set at 283.3 nm and equipped with an autosampler, follow the time/temperature furnace program in the table below. Separately inject 35 µL aliquots of *Solution A, Solution B, Solution C*, and *Solution D*. Calculate the blank-corrected absorbances of *Solutions B, C*, and *D* by subtracting from each the absorbance measured for *Solution A*. Plot the blank-corrected absorbances of *Solutions B, C*, and *D* (y-axis) versus the quantity of lead, in ng, added to each solution (x-axis). These are equal to 0.1, 0.2, and 0 ng, respectively. Draw the best straight line through the points. Extrapolate the line to the x-axis intercept to obtain the quantity *S* (ng) of lead in 10 µL of the *Sample solution*. Calculate the concentration, in mg/kg, of lead in the sample taken by the formula:

  $$Result = 10S/W$$

  W = weight of the sample taken (g)

  Furnace Program

Temperature (°C)	Time (s)	Gas Flow (Argon) (L/min)
85	5.0	3.0
95	40.0	3.0
120	10.0	3.0
300	30.0	3.0
900	5.0	3.0
900	1.0	3.0
900	2.0	0.0
2100	0.6	0.0
2100	2.0	0.0
2800	3.0	3.0

  Acceptance criteria: NMT 1 mg/kg
- **SULFATE**, *Chloride and Sulfate Limit Tests, Chloride Limit Test*, Appendix IIIB
  Control: 200 µg sulfate (20 mL of *Standard Sulfate Solution*)
  Sample: 20 mL of the *Sample solution* prepared for the test for *Chloride*

Acceptance criteria: Any turbidity produced in the Sample solution does not exceed that shown in the Control. (NMT 0.1%)

SPECIFIC TESTS
- **OPTICAL (SPECIFIC) ROTATION,** Appendix IIB
  Sample: 20 mg/mL in oxygen-free water
  Acceptance criteria
    Dihydrate: $[\alpha]_D^{20}$ between +6.0° and +11.0°, calculated on the anhydrous basis
- **OXALIC ACID**
  Sample: 1 g
  Analysis: Dissolve the Sample in 10 mL of water and 2 mL of hydrochloric acid and transfer the solution to a separatory funnel. Extract the solution with two 35-mL portions of ether. Evaporate the combined ether extracts in a rotary evaporator or on a steam bath. Dissolve any residue in 10 mL of water and add 1 mL of glacial acetic acid and 1 mL of a 1:20 solution of calcium acetate.
  Acceptance criteria: No turbidity develops in 5 min.
- **WATER,** Water Determination, Appendix IIB
  [NOTE—Perform the analysis at 50°.]
  Sample solution: For the Test preparation, dissolve the 100 mg of sample in a freshly prepared mixture of 20 mL of methanol and 20 mL of formamide.
  Acceptance criteria
    Dihydrate: Between 12.0% and 14.0%
    Trihydrate: Between 18.0% and 20.0%

OTHER REQUIREMENTS
- **LABELING:** Indicate the state of hydration of the material.

Ferrous Sulfate

First Published: Prior to FCC 6
Last Revision: First Supplement, FCC 6

$FeSO_4 \cdot 7H_2O$ 　　　　　Formula wt 278.02
　　　　　　　　　　　　CAS: [7782-63-0]
UNII: 39R4TAN1VT [ferrous sulfate]

DESCRIPTION
Ferrous Sulfate occurs as pale, blue-green crystals or granules that are efflorescent in dry air. In moist air, it oxidizes readily to form a brown-yellow, basic ferric sulfate. A 1:10 aqueous solution has a pH of about 3.7. One g dissolves in 1.5 mL of water at 25° and in 0.5 mL of boiling water. It is insoluble in alcohol.
Function: Nutrient
Packaging and Storage: Store in tight containers.

IDENTIFICATION
- **IRON (FERROUS SALTS),** Appendix III
  Acceptance criteria: Passes tests
- **SULFATE,** Appendix IIIA
  Acceptance criteria: Passes tests

ASSAY
- **PROCEDURE**
  Sample: 1 g
  Analysis: Dissolve the Sample in a mixture of 25 mL of 2 N sulfuric acid and 25 mL of recently boiled and cooled water. Titrate with 0.1 N ceric sulfate, using orthophenanthroline TS, as the indicator. Perform a blank determination (see General Provisions), and make any necessary correction. Each mL of 0.1 N ceric sulfate is equivalent to 27.80 mg of $FeSO_4 \cdot 7H_2O$.
  Acceptance criteria: NLT 99.5% and NMT 104.5% $FeSO_4 \cdot 7H_2O$

IMPURITIES
Inorganic Impurities
- **LEAD**
  [NOTE—When preparing all aqueous solutions and rinsing glassware before use, employ water that has been passed through a strong-acid, strong-base, mixed-bed ion-exchange resin before use. Select all reagents to have as low a content of lead as practicable, and store all reagent solutions in containers of borosilicate glass. Clean glassware before use by soaking in warm 8 N nitric acid for 30 min and by rinsing with deionized water.]
  Ascorbic acid–sodium iodide solution: 100 mg/mL of ascorbic acid and 192.5 mg/mL of sodium iodide in water
  Trioctylphosphine oxide solution: 50 mg/mL of trioctylphosphine oxide in 4-methyl-2-pentanone
  [CAUTION—This reagent causes irritation. Avoid contact with eyes, skin, and clothing. Take special precautions in disposing of unused portions of solutions to which this reagent is added.]
  Standard stock solution: 100 µg/mL of lead prepared as follows: Transfer 159.8 mg of reagent-grade lead nitrate to a 1000-mL volumetric flask, dissolve it in 100 mL of water containing 1 mL of nitric acid, and dilute with water to volume.
  Standard solution: Transfer 1.0 mL of Standard stock solution into a 100-mL volumetric flask, dilute with water to volume, and mix. Transfer 2.0 mL of this resulting solution into a 50-mL volumetric flask. Add 10 mL of 9 N hydrochloric acid and about 10 mL of water to the volumetric flask. Add 20 mL of Ascorbic acid–sodium iodide solution and 5.0 mL of Trioctylphosphine oxide solution to the flask. Shake for 30 s and allow the layers to separate. Add water to bring the organic solvent layer into the neck of the flask, shake again, and allow the layers to separate. The organic solvent layer is the Standard solution and contains 0.4 µg/mL of lead.
  Blank solution: Transfer 10 mL of 9 N hydrochloric acid and about 10 mL of water to a 50-mL volumetric flask. Add 20 mL of Ascorbic acid–sodium iodide solution and 5.0 mL of Trioctylphosphine oxide solution to the flask. Shake for 30 s and allow the layers to separate. Add water to bring the organic solvent layer into the neck of the flask, shake again, and allow the layers to separate. The organic solvent layer remaining is the Blank solution and contains 0.0 µg/mL of lead.
  Sample solution: Add 1.0 g of sample, 10 mL of 9 N hydrochloric acid, about 10 mL of water, 20 mL of Ascorbic acid–sodium iodide solution, and 5.0 mL of

Trioctylphosphine oxide solution to a 50-mL volumetric flask, shake for 30 s, and allow the layers to separate. Add water to bring the organic solvent layer into the neck of the flask, shake again, and allow the layers to separate. The organic solvent layer is the *Sample solution*.

Analysis: Using a suitable atomic absorption spectrophotometer equipped with a lead hollow-cathode lamp and an air–acetylene flame set at the lead emission line of 283.3 nm, with 4-methyl-2-pentanone used to set the instrument to zero, concomitantly determine the absorbance of the *Blank solution*, the *Standard solution*, and the *Sample solution*.

Acceptance criteria: The absorbance of the *Blank solution* is NMT 20% of the difference between the absorbance of the *Standard solution* and the absorbance of the *Blank solution*. The absorbance of the *Sample solution* does not exceed that of the *Standard solution*. (NMT 2 mg/kg)

- **MERCURY,** *Mercury Limit Test, Method II,* Appendix IIIB
  Sample solution: Prepare as directed using 3 g of sample.
  Acceptance criteria: NMT 1 mg/kg

Ferrous Sulfate, Dried

First Published: Prior to FCC 6
Last Revision: First Supplement, FCC 6

$FeSO_4 \cdot xH_2O$ Formula wt, anhydrous 151.91
                                     CAS: [7720-78-7]
UNII: RIB00980VW [ferrous sulfate, dried]

DESCRIPTION
Ferrous Sulfate, Dried occurs as a gray-white to buff colored powder consisting primarily of $FeSO_4 \cdot H_2O$, with varying amounts of $FeSO_4 \cdot 4H_2O$. It dissolves slowly in water, but is insoluble in alcohol.
Function: Nutrient
Packaging and Storage: Store in tight containers.

IDENTIFICATION
- **IRON (FERROUS SALTS),** Appendix III
  Acceptance criteria: Passes tests
- **SULFATE,** Appendix IIIA
  Acceptance criteria: Passes tests

ASSAY
- **PROCEDURE**
  Sample: 1 g
  Analysis: Dissolve the *Sample* in a mixture of 25 mL of 2 N sulfuric acid and 25 mL of recently boiled and cooled water. Titrate with 0.1 N ceric sulfate, using orthophenanthroline TS, as the indicator. Perform a blank determination (see *General Provisions*), and make any necessary correction. Each mL of 0.1 N ceric sulfate is equivalent to 15.19 mg of $FeSO_4$.
  Acceptance criteria: NLT 86.0% and NMT 89.0% $FeSO_4$

IMPURITIES
Inorganic Impurities
- **LEAD**
  [NOTE—When preparing all aqueous solutions and rinsing glassware before use, employ water that has been passed through a strong-acid, strong-base, mixed-bed ion-exchange resin before use. Select all reagents to have as low a content of lead as practicable, and store all reagent solutions in containers of borosilicate glass. Clean glassware before use by soaking in warm 8 N nitric acid for 30 min and by rinsing with deionized water.]
  Ascorbic acid–sodium iodide solution: 100 mg/mL of ascorbic acid and 192.5 mg/mL of sodium iodide in water
  Trioctylphosphine oxide solution: 50 mg/mL of trioctylphosphine oxide in 4-methyl-2-pentanone
  [CAUTION—This reagent causes irritation. Avoid contact with eyes, skin, and clothing. Take special precautions in disposing of unused portions of solutions to which this reagent is added.]
  Standard stock solution: 100 µg/mL of lead prepared as follows: Transfer 159.8 mg of reagent-grade lead nitrate to a 1000-mL volumetric flask, dissolve it in 100 mL of water containing 1 mL of nitric acid, and dilute with water to volume.
  Standard solution: Transfer 1.0 mL of *Standard stock solution* into a 100-mL volumetric flask, dilute with water to volume, and mix. Transfer 2.0 mL of this resulting solution into a 50-mL volumetric flask. Add 10 mL of 9 N hydrochloric acid and about 10 mL of water to the volumetric flask. Add 20 mL of *Ascorbic acid–sodium iodide solution* and 5.0 mL of *Trioctylphosphine oxide solution* to the flask. Shake for 30 s and allow the layers to separate. Add water to bring the organic solvent layer into the neck of the flask, shake again, and allow the layer to separate. The organic solvent layer is the *Standard solution* and contains 0.4 µg/mL of lead.
  Blank solution: Transfer 10 mL of 9 N hydrochloric acid and about 10 mL of water to a 50-mL volumetric flask. Add 20 mL of *Ascorbic acid–sodium iodide solution* and 5.0 mL of *Trioctylphosphine oxide solution* to the flask. Shake for 30 s and allow the layers to separate. Add water to bring the organic solvent layer into the neck of the flask, shake again, and allow the layer to separate. The organic solvent layer remaining is the *Blank solution* and contains 0.0 µg/mL of lead.
  Sample solution: Add 1.0 g of sample, 10 mL of 9 N hydrochloric acid, about 10 mL of water, 20 mL of *Ascorbic acid–sodium iodide solution*, and 5.0 mL of *Trioctylphosphine oxide solution* to a 50-mL volumetric flask, shake for 30 s, and allow the layers to separate. Add water to bring the organic solvent layer into the neck of the flask, shake again, and allow the layers to separate. The organic solvent layer is the *Sample solution*.
  Analysis: Using a suitable atomic absorption spectrophotometer equipped with a lead hollow-cathode lamp and an air–acetylene flame set at the lead emission line of 283.3 nm, with 4-methyl-2-

pentanone used to set the instrument to zero, concomitantly determine the absorbance of the *Blank solution*, the *Standard solution*, and the *Sample solution*.
Acceptance criteria: The absorbance of the *Blank solution* is NMT 20% of the difference between the absorbance of the *Standard solution* and the absorbance of the *Blank solution*. The absorbance of the *Sample solution* does not exceed that of the *Standard solution*. (NMT 2 mg/kg)
- **MERCURY,** *Mercury Limit Test, Method II,* Appendix IIIB
  Sample solution: Prepare as directed using 3 g of sample.
  Acceptance criteria: NMT 1 mg/kg

SPECIFIC TESTS
- **INSOLUBLE RESIDUE**
  Sample: 2 g
  Analysis: Dissolve the *Sample* in 20 mL of freshly boiled 1:100 sulfuric acid, heat to boiling, and then digest in a covered beaker on a steam bath for 1 h. Filter through a tared filtering crucible, wash thoroughly, and dry at 105°.
  Acceptance criteria: The weight of the insoluble residue is NMT 1 mg. (NMT 0.05%)

Fir Needle Oil, Canadian Type
First Published: Prior to FCC 6

Balsam Fir Oil
UNII: 2FGT9T2SQC [abies balsamea leaf oil]

DESCRIPTION
Fir Needle Oil, Canadian Type, occurs as a colorless to faintly yellow liquid with a pleasant, balsamic odor. It is the volatile oil obtained by steam distillation from needles and twigs of *Abies balsamea* L., Mill (Fam. Pinaceae). It is soluble in most fixed oils and in mineral oil. It is slightly soluble in propylene glycol, but it is insoluble in glycerin.
Function: Flavoring agent
Packaging and Storage: Store in a cool place protected from light in full, tight containers that are made from steel or aluminum and that are suitably lined.

IDENTIFICATION
- **INFRARED SPECTRA,** *Spectrophotometric Identification Tests,* Appendix IIIC
  Acceptance criteria: The spectrum of the sample exhibits relative maxima at the same wavelengths as those of the spectrum below.

ASSAY
- **ESTERS,** *Ester Determination,* Appendix VI
  Sample: 5 g
  Analysis: Use 98.15 as the equivalence factor (e) in the calculation.
  Acceptance criteria: NLT 8.0% and NMT 16.0% of esters, calculated as bornyl acetate ($C_{12}H_{20}O_2$)

SPECIFIC TESTS
- **ANGULAR ROTATION,** *Optical (Specific) Rotation,* Appendix IIB: Use a 100-mm tube.
  Acceptance criteria: Between −19° and −24°
- **REFRACTIVE INDEX,** Appendix IIB
  [NOTE—Use an Abbé or other refractometer of equal or greater accuracy.]
  Acceptance criteria: Between 1.473 and 1.476 at 20°
- **SOLUBILITY IN ALCOHOL,** Appendix VI
  Acceptance criteria: One mL of sample dissolves in 4 mL of 90% alcohol, occasionally with haziness.
- **SPECIFIC GRAVITY:** Determine by any reliable method (see *General Provisions*).
  Acceptance criteria: Between 0.872 and 0.878

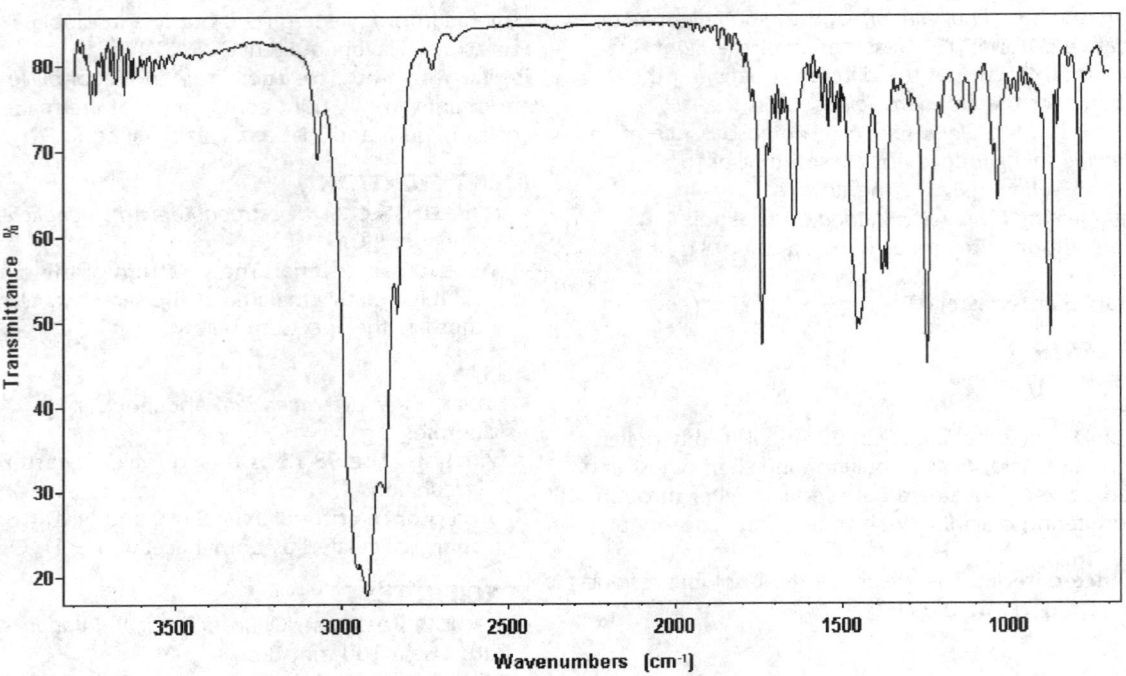

Fir Needle Oil, Canadian Type

Fir Needle Oil, Siberian Type

First Published: Prior to FCC 6

Pine Needle Oil
UNII: XRY0V4VZKZ [abies sibirica leaf oil]

DESCRIPTION
Fir Needle Oil, Siberian Type, occurs as an almost colorless or faintly yellow liquid with a piney, balsamic odor. It is the volatile oil obtained by steam distillation from needles and twigs of *Abies sibirica* Lebed. (Fam. Pinaceae). It is soluble in most fixed oils and in mineral oil. It is insoluble in glycerin and in propylene glycol.
Function: Flavoring agent
Packaging and Storage: Store in a cool place protected from light in full, tight containers that are made from steel or aluminum and that are suitably lined.

IDENTIFICATION
- **INFRARED SPECTRA**, *Spectrophotometric Identification Tests*, Appendix IIIC
  Acceptance criteria: The spectrum of the sample exhibits relative maxima at the same wavelengths as those of the spectrum below.

ASSAY
- **ESTERS**, *Ester Determination*, Appendix VI
  Sample: 2g
  Analysis: Use 98.15 as the equivalence factor (e) in the calculation.
  Acceptance criteria: NLT 32.0% and NMT 44.0% of esters, calculated as bornyl acetate ($C_{12}H_{20}O_2$)

SPECIFIC TESTS
- **ANGULAR ROTATION**, *Optical (Specific) Rotation*, Appendix IIB: Use a 100-mm tube.
  Acceptance criteria: Between −33° and −45°
- **REFRACTIVE INDEX**, Appendix IIB
  [NOTE—Use an Abbé or other refractometer of equal or greater accuracy.]
  Acceptance criteria: Between 1.468 and 1.473 at 20°
- **SOLUBILITY IN ALCOHOL**, Appendix VI
  Acceptance criteria: One mL of sample dissolves in 1 mL of 90% alcohol. Occasionally the solution will become hazy on further dilution.
- **SPECIFIC GRAVITY:** Determine by any reliable method (see *General Provisions*).
  Acceptance criteria: Between 0.898 and 0.912

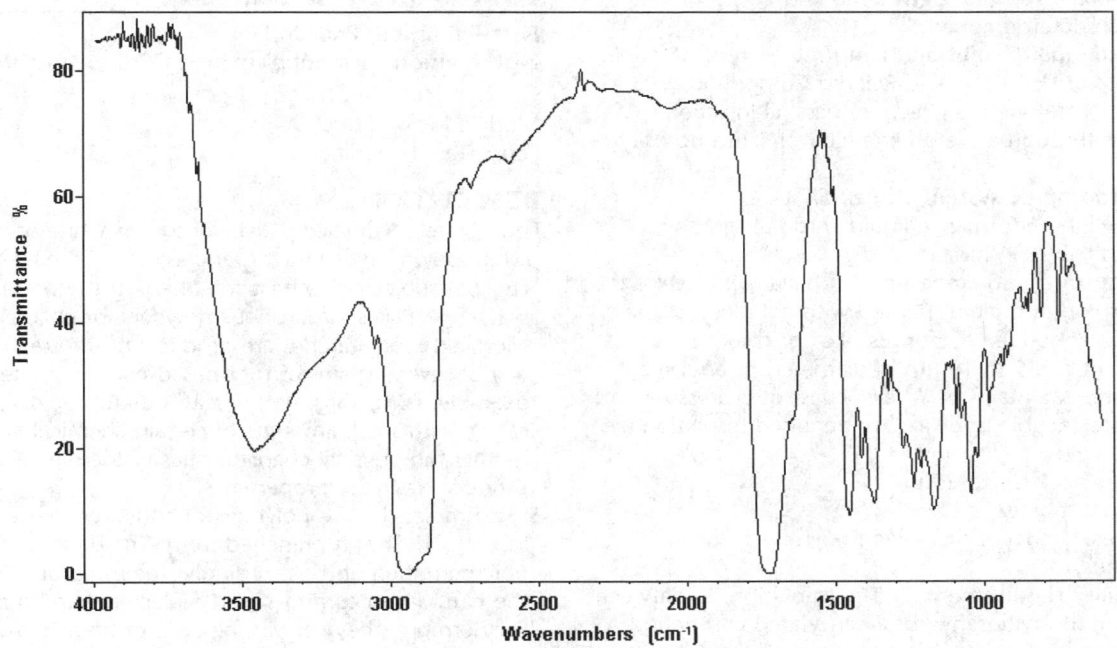

Fir Needle Oil, Siberian Type

Folic Acid

First Published: Prior to FCC 6
Last Revision: FCC 7

N-[4-[[(2-Amino-1,4-dihydro-4-oxo-6-pteridinyl)methyl]amino]benzoyl]-L-glutamic Acid
N-[p-[[(2-Amino-4-hydroxy-6-pteridinyl)methyl]amino]benzoyl]glutamic Acid
Pteroylglutamic Acid

$C_{19}H_{19}N_7O_6$ Formula wt 441.40
                             CAS: [59-30-3]
UNII: 935E97BOY8 [folic acid]

DESCRIPTION
Folic Acid occurs as yellow or yellow-orange crystals or crystalline powder. About 1.6 mg dissolves in 1 mL of water. It is insoluble in acetone, in alcohol, in chloroform, and in ether, but dissolves in solutions of alkali hydroxides and carbonates. The pH of a suspension of 1 g in 10 mL of water is between 4.0 and 4.8.
Function: Nutrient
Packaging and Storage: Store in well-closed, light-resistant containers.

IDENTIFICATION
- **ULTRAVIOLET ABSORPTION**, *Spectrophotometric Identification Tests*, Appendix IIIC
  Standard solution: 10 µg/mL USP Folic Acid RS in 4 mg/mL sodium hydroxide solution
  Sample solution: 10 µg/mL in 4 mg/mL sodium hydroxide solution
  Acceptance criteria
  Maxima/minima: The ultraviolet absorption spectrum of the *Sample solution* exhibits maxima and minima at the same wavelengths as those of the *Standard solution*.
  A_{256}/A_{365} **ratio:** Between 2.80 and 3.00

ASSAY
- **PROCEDURE**
  Mobile phase: Transfer 35.1 g of sodium perchlorate, 1.40 g of monobasic potassium phosphate, 7.0 mL of 1 N potassium hydroxide, and 40 mL of methanol to a 1000-mL volumetric flask. Dilute with water to volume, and mix. Adjust the pH to 7.2 with 1 N potassium hydroxide. [NOTE—The methanol concentration may be varied to meet system suitability and to provide a suitable resolution (R) for the *System suitability solution*.]
  Diluent: 1 g of sodium perchlorate and 2 mL of ammonium hydroxide diluted with water to 100 mL
  Standard solution: Dissolve 30 mg of USP Folic Acid RS, corrected for water content, in *Diluent* adjusting the volume quantitatively, according to the injection size to be used in the *Procedure*, so that between 5 and 20 µg of folic acid is chromatographed.
  Sample solution: Dissolve 30 mg of sample, corrected for water content, in *Diluent* adjusting the volume

quantitatively, according to the injection size to be used in the *Analysis*, so that between 5 and 20 µg of folic acid is chromatographed.

System suitability solution: 1 mg/mL each of USP Folic Acid RS and USP Folic Acid Related Compound A RS in *Diluent*. [NOTE—Before injection, pass all injection solutions through a membrane filter of 1-µm porosity or finer.]

Chromatographic system, Appendix IIA
  Mode: High-performance liquid chromatography
  Detector: UV 254 nm
  Column: 25- to 30-cm × 4-mm (id) stainless-steel column, or equivalent, packed with octadecyl silane chemically bonded to porous silica or ceramic microparticles 5 to 10 µm in diameter, or equivalent
  Flow rate: Maintain the *Mobile phase* at a pressure and flow rate capable of giving the required resolution (see below).
  Injection size: Up to 25 µL
  System suitability
    Samples: *Standard solution* and *System suitability solution*
    Suitability requirement 1: The resolution, R, between calcium formyltetrahydrofolate (related compound A) and folic acid in the chromatogram of the *System suitability solution* is NLT 3.6.
    Suitability requirement 2: The relative standard deviation of the peak responses from the *Standard solution* is NMT 2%.
Analysis: Inject volumes of the *Sample solution* equal to those used for the *Standard solution*. Measure the responses for the major peaks obtained with the *Sample solution* and the *Standard solution*. Calculate the percent of $C_{19}H_{19}N_7O_6$ in the sample taken:

$$\text{Result} = (R_U/R_S) \times (C_S/C_U) \times 100\%$$

R_U = peak response from the *Sample solution*
R_S = peak responses from the *Standard solution*
C_S = concentration of folic acid in the *Standard solution* (mg/mL)
C_U = concentration of folic acid in the *Sample solution* (mg/mL)

Acceptance criteria: 95.0%–102.0% of $C_{19}H_{19}N_7O_6$, calculated on the anhydrous basis

IMPURITIES
Inorganic Impurities
- **LEAD**, *Lead Limit Test, Flame Atomic Absorption Spectrophotometric Method*, Appendix IIIB
  Sample: 10 g
  Acceptance criteria: NMT 2 mg/kg

SPECIFIC TESTS
- **RESIDUE ON IGNITION (SULFATED ASH)**, Appendix IIC
  Sample: 1 g
  Acceptance criteria: NMT 0.3%
- **WATER**, *Water Determination*, Appendix IIB
  Sample: 200 mg
  Acceptance criteria: NMT 8.5%

Food Starch, Modified
First Published: Prior to FCC 6
Last Revision: First Supplement, FCC 6

Modified Food Starch
Food Starch–Modified

DESCRIPTION
Food Starch, Modified usually occurs as white or nearly white powders; as intact granules; and if pregelatinized (that is, subjected to heat treatment in the presence of water), as flakes, amorphous powders, or coarse particles. Modified food starches are products of the treatment of any of several grain- or root-based native starches (for example, corn, sorghum, wheat, potato, tapioca, and sago), with small amounts of certain chemical agents that modify the physical characteristics of the native starches to produce desirable properties.

Starch molecules are polymers of anhydroglucose and occur in both linear and branched form. The degree of polymerization and, accordingly, the molecular weight of the naturally occurring starch molecules vary radically. Furthermore, they vary in the ratio of branched-chain polymers (amylopectin) to linear-chain polymers (amylose), both within a given type of starch and from one type to another. These factors, in addition to any type of chemical modification used, significantly affect the viscosity, texture, and stability of the starch sols.

Starch is chemically modified by mild degradation reactions or by reactions between the hydroxyl groups of the native starch and the reactant selected. One or more of the following processes are used: mild oxidation (bleaching), moderate oxidation, acid and/or enzyme depolymerization, monofunctional esterification, polyfunctional esterification (cross-linking), monofunctional etherification, alkaline gelatinization, and certain combinations of these treatments. These methods of preparation can be used as a basis for classifying the starches thus produced (see *Other Requirements*, below). Generally, however, the products are called Modified Food Starch, or Food Starch—Modified.

Modified food starches are insoluble in alcohol, in ether, and in chloroform. If not pregelatinized, they are practically insoluble in cold water. Upon heating in water, the granules usually begin to swell at temperatures between 45° and 80°, depending on the botanical origin and the degree of modification. They gelatinize completely at higher temperatures. Pregelatinized starches hydrate in cold water.

Function: Thickener; colloidal stabilizer; binder
Packaging and Storage: Store in well-closed containers.

IDENTIFICATION
- **IODINE STAIN**
  Sample suspension: 1 g in 20 mL of water
  Analysis: To the *Sample suspension*, add a few drops of iodine TS.
  Acceptance criteria: A dark blue to red color appears.
- **COPPER REDUCTION**
  Sample: 2.5 g

Analysis: Place the *Sample* in a boiling flask, add 10 mL of 3% hydrochloric acid and 70 mL of water, mix, reflux for about 3 h, and cool. Add 0.5 mL of the resulting solution to 5 mL of hot alkaline cupric tartrate TS.
Acceptance criteria: A copious red precipitate forms.
- **MICROSCOPY**
Analysis: Examine a portion of the sample with a polarizing microscope in polarized light under crossed Nicol prisms.
Acceptance criteria: The typical polarization cross is observed, except in the case of pregelatinized starches.

IMPURITIES
Inorganic Impurities
- **LEAD,** *Lead Limit Test, Flame Atomic Absorption Spectrophotometric Method,* Appendix IIIB
  Sample: 5 g
  Acceptance criteria: NMT 1 mg/kg
- **SULFUR DIOXIDE,** Appendix X
  Acceptance criteria: NMT 0.005%

SPECIFIC TESTS
- **CRUDE FAT,** Appendix X
  Acceptance criteria: NMT 0.15%
- **LOSS ON DRYING,** Appendix IIC: 120° for 4 h, in a vacuum oven not exceeding 100 mm Hg
  Sample: 5 g
  Acceptance criteria
    Cereal starch: NMT 15.0%
    Potato starch: NMT 21.0%
    Sago starch: NMT 18.0%
    Tapioca starch: NMT 18.0%
- **PH,** *pH Determination,* Appendix IIB
  Sample suspension: Mix 20 g of sample with 80 mL of water, and agitate continuously at a moderate rate for 5 min. For pregelatinized starches, suspend 3 g of sample in 97 mL of water. [NOTE—The water used for sample dispersion should require not more than 0.05 mL of 0.1 N acid or alkali per 200 mL of sample to obtain the methyl red or phenolphthalein endpoint, respectively.]
  Acceptance criteria: Between 3.0 and 9.0
- **PROTEIN**
  Sample: 10 g
  Analysis: Transfer the *Sample* into an 800-mL Kjeldahl flask, and add 10 g of anhydrous potassium sulfate or anhydrous sodium sulfate, 300 mg of copper selenite or mercuric oxide, and 60 mL of sulfuric acid. Gently heat the mixture, keeping the flask inclined at about a 45° angle, and after frothing has ceased, boil briskly until the solution remains clear for about 1 h. Cool the solution, add 300 mL of water, mix, and cool again. Cautiously pour about 75 mL (or enough to make the mixture strongly alkaline) of a 2:5 aqueous solution of sodium hydroxide down the inside of the flask so that it forms a layer under the acid solution; then add a few pieces of granular zinc. Immediately connect the flask to a distillation apparatus consisting of a Kjeldahl connecting bulb and a condenser, the delivery tube of which extends well beneath the surface of an accurately measured excess of 0.1 N sulfuric acid contained in a 500-mL flask. Gently rotate the contents of the Kjeldahl flask to mix, and then distill until all ammonia has passed into the absorbing acid solution (about 250 mL of distillate). Titrate the excess acid with 0.1 N sodium hydroxide, using 0.25 mL of methyl red and methylene blue TS as the indicator. Perform a blank determination (see *General Provisions*), substituting pure sucrose or dextrose for the sample, and make any necessary correction. Each mL of 0.1 N sulfuric acid consumed is equivalent to 1.401 mg of nitrogen.
  Calculate the percent of nitrogen in the sample, and then calculate the percent of protein in starches obtained from corn by multiplying the percent of nitrogen by 6.25, or in starches obtained from wheat, by 5.7. Other factors may be applied as necessary for starches obtained from other sources.
  Acceptance criteria: NMT 0.5%; except in modified high-amylose starches, NMT 1%

OTHER REQUIREMENTS
- **LABELING:** Indicate the presence of sulfur dioxide if the residual concentration is greater than 10 mg/kg.

[NOTE—The modified food starches listed below according to method of preparation must meet all of the above requirements under *Identification, Impurities,* and *Specific Tests,* in addition to any requirements for *Residuals Limitation* listed in the tables below. The maximum limits for reagents appearing in the *Treatment* column are for information only and pertain to the requirements of the U.S. Food and Drug Administration (see Title 21 of the U.S. Code of Federal Regulations, Part 172 (21 CFR 172.892: Food Starch, Modified)). For treatments for which a maximum reagent limit is not specified, the amount of reagent used should not exceed that reasonably required to accomplish the intended modification.]

- **TESTS**
  The following *Tests* apply to those entries as specifically cited under *Residuals Limitation* in the tables below:
  - ACETYL GROUPS, Appendix X
  - MANGANESE, Appendix IIIB
  - PHOSPHATE, *Phosphorus,* Appendix IIIB
  - PROPYLENE CHLOROHYDRIN, Appendix X
- **ALKALINE GELATINIZATION (GELATINIZED STARCH)**

Treatment to Produce Gelatinized Starch	Residuals Limitation
Sodium hydroxide, not to exceed 1%	—

- **DEPOLYMERIZATION (THIN-BOILING, OR ACID-MODIFIED STARCH)** This treatment results in partial depolymerization, causing a reduction in viscosity. Any of these treatments may be used in combination with the other treatments that follow.

Treatment to Produce Thin-Boiling Starch	Residuals Limitation
Hydrochloric acid and/or sulfuric acid	—

464 / Food Starch, Modified / *Monographs*

Treatment to Produce Thin-Boiling Starch	Residuals Limitation
Alpha-amylase enzyme	The resulting nonsweet nutritive saccharide polymer has a dextrose equivalent of less than 20

- **ETHERIFICATION AND ESTERIFICATION (STARCH ETHER-ESTERS)**

Treatment to Produce Hydroxypropyl Distarch Phosphate	Residuals Limitation
Phosphorus oxychloride, not to exceed 0.1%; propylene oxide, not to exceed 10%	NMT 3 mg/kg of propylene chlorohydrin

- **ETHERIFICATION WITH OXIDATION (OXIDIZED STARCH ETHERS)**

Treatment to Produce Oxidized Hydroxypropyl Phosphate Starch	Residuals Limitation
Chlorine, as sodium hypochlorite, not to exceed 0.055 lb. (25 g) of chlorine per lb. (454 g) of dry starch; active oxygen obtained from hydrogen peroxide, not to exceed 0.45%; and propylene oxide, not to exceed 25%	NMT 1 mg/kg of propylene chlorohydrin

- **MILD OXIDATION (BLEACHED STARCH):** The starches resulting from mild oxidation are not altered chemically; in all cases, extraneous color bodies are oxidized, solubilized, and removed by washing and filtration. These treatments may be used in combination with the other forms of treatment listed in this section.

Treatment to Produce Bleached Starch	Residuals Limitation
Active oxygen obtained from hydrogen peroxide, and/or peracetic acid, not to exceed 0.45% of active oxygen	—
Ammonium persulfate, not to exceed 0.075%, and sulfur dioxide, not to exceed 0.05%	—
Chlorine, as sodium hypochlorite, not to exceed 0.0082 lb. (3.72 g) of chlorine per lb. (454 g) of dry starch	—
Chlorine, as calcium hypochlorite, not to exceed 0.036% of dry starch	—
Potassium permanganate, not to exceed 0.2%	NMT 0.005% of manganese (as Mn)
Sodium chlorite, not to exceed 0.5%	—

- **MODERATE OXIDATION (OXIDIZED STARCH):** The maximum specified treatment introduces about 1 carboxyl group per 28 anhydroglucose units. The starch is whitened, and its molecular weight and viscosity are reduced.

Treatment to Produce Oxidized Starch	Residuals Limitation
Chlorine, as sodium hypochlorite, not to exceed 0.055 lb. (25 g) of chlorine per lb. (454 g) of dry starch	—

- **MONOFUNCTIONAL AND/OR POLYFUNCTIONAL ESTERIFICATION (STARCH ESTERS):** The starch esters are named individually, depending on the method of preparation.

Treatment to Produce Starch Acetate	Residuals Limitation
Acetic anhydride or vinyl acetate	NMT 2.5% of acetyl groups introduced into finished product

Treatment to Produce Acetylated Distarch Adipate	Residuals Limitation
Adipic anhydride, not to exceed 0.12%, and acetic anhydride	NMT 2.5% of acetyl groups introduced into finished product

Treatment to Produce Starch Phosphate	Residuals Limitation
Monosodium orthophosphate	NMT 0.4% of phosphate (calculated as P)

Treatment to Produce Starch Octenyl Succinate	Residuals Limitation
Octenyl succinic anhydride, not to exceed 3%, followed by treatment with beta-amylase enzyme	—

Treatment to Produce Starch Sodium Octenyl Succinate	Residuals Limitation
Octenyl succinic anhydride, not to exceed 3%	—

Treatment to Produce Starch Aluminium Octenyl Succinate	Residuals Limitation
Octenyl succinic anhydride, not to exceed 2%, and aluminum sulfate, not to exceed 2%	—

Treatment to Produce Distarch Phosphate	Residuals Limitation
Phosphorus oxychloride, not to exceed 0.1%	—
Sodium trimetaphosphate	NMT 0.04% of phosphate (calculated as P)

Treatment to Produce Phosphated Distarch Phosphate	Residuals Limitation
Sodium tripolyphosphate and sodium trimetaphosphate	NMT 0.4% of phosphate (calculated as P)

Treatment to Produce Acetylated Distarch Phosphate	Residuals Limitation
Phosphorus oxychloride, not to exceed 0.1%, followed by either acetic anhydride, not to exceed 8%, or vinyl acetate, not to exceed 7.5%	NMT 2.5% of acetyl groups introduced into finished product

Treatment to Produce Starch Sodium Succinate	Residuals Limitation
Succinic anhydride, not to exceed 4%	—

- **MONOFUNCTIONAL ETHERIFICATION**

Treatment to Produce Hydroxypropyl Starch	Residuals Limitation
Propylene oxide, not to exceed 25%	NMT 1 mg/kg of propylene chlorohydrin

Food Starch, Unmodified

First Published: Prior to FCC 6
Last Revision: First Supplement, FCC 6

DESCRIPTION

Food Starch, Unmodified occurs as white or nearly white powders; as intact granules; and if pregelatinized, as flakes, powders, or coarse particles. Food starches are extracted from any of several grain or root crops, including corn (maize), sorghum, wheat, potato, tapioca, sago, and arrowroot and hybrids of these crops such as waxy maize and high-amylose maize. They are chemically composed of one or a mixture of two glucose polysaccharides (amylose and amylopectin), the composition and relative proportions of which are characteristic of the plant source. Food starches are generally produced by extraction from the plant source using wet-milling processes in which the starch is liberated by grinding aqueous slurries of the raw material. The extracted starch may be subjected to other nonchemical treatments such as purification, extraction, physical treatments, dehydration, heating, and minor pH adjustment during further processing steps. Food starch may be pregelatinized by heat treatment in the presence of water or made cold-water swelling.

Food starches are insoluble in alcohol, in ether, and in chloroform. If they are not treated to be pregelatinized or cold-water swelling, then they are practically insoluble in cold water. Pregelatinized and cold-water swelling starches hydrate in cold water. When heated in water, the granules usually begin to swell at temperatures between 45° and 80°, depending on the botanical origin of the starch. They gelatinize completely at higher temperatures.

Function: Thickener; colloidal stabilizer; binder.
Packaging and Storage: Store in well-closed containers.

IDENTIFICATION
- **A. PROCEDURE**
  Sample: 1 g
  Analysis: Suspend the *Sample* in 20 mL of water, and add a few drops of iodine TS.
  Acceptance criteria: A dark blue to red color appears.
- **B. PROCEDURE**
  Sample: 2.5 g
  Analysis: Place the *Sample* in a boiling flask, add 10 mL of 3% hydrochloric acid and 70 mL of water, mix, reflux for about 3 h, and cool. Add 0.5 mL of the resulting solution to 5 mL of hot alkaline cupric tartrate TS.
  Acceptance criteria: A copious, red precipitate forms.
- **C. MICROSCOPY**
  Analysis: Examine a portion of sample with a polarizing microscope in polarized light under crossed Nicol prisms.
  Acceptance criteria: The typical polarization cross is observed, except in the case of pregelatinized starches.

IMPURITIES
Inorganic Impurities
- **LEAD,** *Lead Limit Test, Atomic Absorption Spectrophotometric Graphite Furnace Method, Method II,* Appendix IIIB
  Acceptance criteria: NMT 1 mg/kg
- **SULFUR DIOXIDE,** *Sulfur Dioxide Determination,* Appendix X
  Sample: 25 g
  Acceptance criteria: NMT 0.005%

SPECIFIC TESTS
- **CRUDE FAT,** Appendix X
  Acceptance criteria: NMT 0.15%
- **LOSS ON DRYING,** Appendix IIC: 120° for 4 h in a vacuum oven not exceeding 100 mm Hg
  Sample: 5 g
  Acceptance criteria
    Cereal starch: NMT 15.0%
    Potato starch: NMT 21.0%
    Sago and Tapioca starch: NMT 18.0%
- **pH OF DISPERSIONS,** *pH Determination,* Appendix IIB
  Sample: 20 g (Use 3 g for pregelatinized starches.)
  Analysis: Mix the *Sample* with 80 mL of water (Use 97 mL for pregelatinized starches), and agitate the suspension continuously at a moderate rate for 5 min. [NOTE—The water used for sample dispersion should

not require more than 0.05 mL of 0.1 N acid or alkali per 200 mL of sample to obtain the methyl red or phenolphthalein endpoint, respectively.]
Acceptance criteria: Between 3.0 and 9.0

- **PROTEIN**
  Sample: 10 g
  Analysis: Transfer the *Sample* into an 800-mL Kjeldahl flask. Add 10 g of anhydrous potassium sulfate or anhydrous sodium sulfate, 300 mg of copper selenite or mercuric oxide, and 60 mL of sulfuric acid. Gently heat the mixture, keeping the Kjeldahl flask inclined at about a 45° angle and, after frothing has ceased, boil briskly until the solution remains clear for about 1 h. Cool, add 300 mL of water, mix, and cool again. Cautiously pour about 75 mL (or enough to make the mixture strongly alkaline) of a 2 : 5 aqueous solution of sodium hydroxide down the inside of the flask so that it forms a layer under the acid solution, and then add a few pieces of granular zinc. Immediately connect the flask to a distillation apparatus consisting of a Kjeldahl connecting bulb and a condenser, the delivery tube of which extends well beneath the surface of an accurately measured excess of 0.1 N sulfuric acid contained in a 500-mL flask. Gently rotate the contents of the Kjeldahl flask to mix, and distill until all ammonia has passed into the absorbing acid solution (about 250 mL of distillate). Titrate the excess acid with 0.1 N sodium hydroxide, using 0.25 mL of methyl red and methylene blue TS as the indicator. Perform a blank determination (see *General Provisions*), substituting pure sucrose or dextrose for the sample and make any necessary correction. Each mL of 0.1 N sulfuric acid consumed is equivalent to 1.401 mg of nitrogen.
  Calculate the percent nitrogen in the sample, and then calculate the percent protein in starches obtained from corn by multiplying the percent of nitrogen by 6.25, or in starches obtained from wheat, by 5.7. Other factors may be applied as necessary for starches obtained from other sources.
  Acceptance criteria: NMT 0.5%; except in high-amylose and other hybrid starches, NMT 1%

OTHER REQUIREMENTS
- **LABELING:** Indicate the presence of sulfur dioxide if the residual concentration is greater than 10 mg/kg (0.001%).

Formic Acid

First Published: Prior to FCC 6

CH_2O_2
INS: 236
FEMA: 2487
Formula wt 46.03
CAS: [64-18-6]
UNII: 0YIW783RG1 [formic acid]

DESCRIPTION
Formic Acid occurs as a clear, colorless, *highly corrosive* liquid with a characteristic, pungent odor. It is miscible with water, with alcohol, with glycerin, and with ether. Its specific gravity is about 1.20.
Function: Flavoring adjunct; preservative
Packaging and Storage: Store in tight containers.

IDENTIFICATION
- **A. PROCEDURE**
  Sample: 5 mL
  Analysis: Add 2 mL of mercuric chloride TS to the *Sample* and warm the mixture.
  Acceptance criteria: A white precipitate of mercurous chloride forms.
- **B. PROCEDURE**
  Sample: 1 mL
  Analysis: Neutralize the *Sample* with sodium hydroxide TS, and then add 2 drops in excess and 1 mL of ferric chloride TS.
  Acceptance criteria: A deep, red-orange color appears that turns to yellow-orange on the addition of mineral acids.
- **C. PROCEDURE**
  Sample: 2 mL
  Analysis: Place the *Sample* in a test tube, add 5 mL of sulfuric acid, and test the gas evolved with a lighted splint.
  Acceptance criteria: A blue flame characteristic of carbon monoxide is produced.

ASSAY
- **FORMIC ACID**
  Sample: 1.5 mL
  Analysis: Tare a small glass-stoppered Erlenmeyer flask containing about 15 mL of water. Transfer the *Sample* into the flask, and weigh. Dilute the solution to 50 mL with water, add phenolphthalein TS, and titrate with 1 N sodium hydroxide. Each mL of 1 N sodium hydroxide is equivalent to 46.03 mg of CH_2O_2.
  Acceptance criteria: NLT 85.0% of CH_2O_2

IMPURITIES
Inorganic Impurities
- **SULFATE**
  Sample: 2.1 mL (2.5 g)
  Control: 100 µg of sulfate
  Analysis: Add about 10 mg of sodium carbonate to the *Sample* and to the *Control* contained in separate beakers. Evaporate to dryness on a steam bath.
  Acceptance criteria: Any turbidity produced by the *Sample* residue does not exceed that shown in the *Control*. (NMT 0.004%)

Organic Impurities
- **ACETIC ACID**
  Sample: 1 mL
  Analysis: Dilute the *Sample* to 100 mL with water. Transfer 50 mL of this solution into a 250-mL boiling flask and add 5 g of yellow mercuric oxide. While continuously stirring, boil the mixture under a reflux condenser for 2 h, cool, filter, and wash the residue with about 25 mL of water. Add phenolphthalein TS to

the combined filtrate and washings, and titrate with 0.02 N sodium hydroxide.

Acceptance criteria: NMT 2.0 mL of 0.02 N sodium hydroxide is required to produce a pink color. (NMT 0.4%)

SPECIFIC TESTS
- **DILUTION TEST**
  Analysis: Dilute 1 volume of sample with 3 volumes of water.
  Acceptance criteria: No turbidity develops within 1 h.

Fructooligosaccharides, Short Chain

First Published: FCC 6

scFOS

DESCRIPTION
Fructooligosaccharides, Short Chain (scFOS), are indigestible carbohydrates synthesized from sucrose and fructose through an enzymatic process or from Inulin by partial enzymatic hydrolysis. These carbohydrates are a mixture of polysaccharides consisting of a sucrose molecule (glucose-fructose disaccharide, GF_1) linked to one (GF_2), two (GF_3), or three (GF_4) additional fructose units added by β2-1 glycosidic linkages to the fructose unit of sucrose for the synthesized scFOS. The scFOS from Inulin consists of oligosaccharides with the same structure but a slightly larger range of polymerization (from GF_2 to GF_9 and from F_3 to F_9). They are very soluble in hot and cold water, and almost insoluble in most organic solvents.

Function: Bulking agent; source of dietary fiber; sweetener; prebiotic

Packaging and Storage: Store tightly closed containers in a cool, dry place.

IDENTIFICATION
- **PROCEDURE**
  Acetate buffer (pH 4.5 ± 0.05): Transfer 22 mL of 0.2 M sodium acetate and 28 mL of 0.2 M acetic acid into a 100-mL volumetric flask, and dilute to volume with water.
  Standard solution: 3.0 mg/mL of GF_2, 4.5 mg/mL of GF_3, 0.50 mg/mL of GF_4 scFOS Reference Standards (Waco Pure Chemical Industries, Ltd., Osaka, Japan, or equivalent) and 0.50 mg/mL each of fructose, glucose, and sucrose in water.
  Sample stock solution: 10 mg/mL using a sample previously dried to constant weight
  Digested sample solution: Transfer 10 mL of *Acetate buffer* and 10 mL of the *Sample stock solution* into a 25-mL volumetric flask. Add 150 units of Fructozyme SP230 enzyme (Novozymes, Denmark), or equivalent. Digest for 30 min at 60°, cool, and dilute to volume with water.
  Mobile phase: Acetonitrile–water (65–70% to 35–30%)
  Chromatographic system, Appendix IIA
    Mode: High-performance liquid chromatography
    Detector: Refractive index [NOTE—Use a detector with a sensitivity of 8×10^{-5}.]
    Column: 25-cm × 4-mm (id) 5-µm LiChrospher 100 NH2 column (Merck Corp.), or equivalent
    Column temperature: 35°
    Flow rate: 1 mL/min
    Run time: 12 min
    Injection volume: 20 µL
    Sample loop: 20 µL
  Analysis: Separately inject the *Digested sample solution* and the *Standard solution* into the chromatograph and record the chromatograms. Determine the percentage of fructose and the percentage of glucose in the *Digested sample solution* using the following formula:

  $$\text{Result} = 100(C_{ST} \times A_{SA})/(A_{ST} \times W)$$

  C_{ST} = concentration of fructose or glucose in the *Standard solution* (mg/100 mL)
  A_{SA} = area of the corresponding sugar peak in the chromatogram of the *Digested sample solution*
  A_{ST} = area of the corresponding sugar peak in the chromatogram of the *Standard solution*
  W = weight of sample (g) contained in each 100 mL of the *Sample stock solution*

  Correct the percent fructose and percent glucose results for the mono- and disaccharide content (obtained in the *Assay* below), and for moisture.
  Acceptance criteria: The sample releases greater than 67% fructose and less than 33% glucose upon enzymatic digestion.

ASSAY
- **PROCEDURE**
  Mobile phase: Acetonitrile–water (65–70% to 35–30%)
  Standard solution: 3.0 mg/mL of GF_2, 4.5 mg/mL of GF_3, 0.50 mg/mL of GF_4 scFOS Reference Standards (Waco Pure Chemical Industries, Ltd., Osaka, Japan, or equivalent) and 0.50 mg/mL each of fructose, glucose, and sucrose in water
  Sample stock solution: 10 mg/mL using a sample previously dried to constant weight
  Chromatographic system, Appendix IIA
    Mode: High-performance liquid chromatography
    Detector: Refractive index [NOTE—Use a detector with a sensitivity of 8×10^{-5}.]
    Column: 25-cm × 4-mm (id) 5-µm LiChrospher 100 NH2 column (Merck Corp.), or equivalent
    Column temperature: 35°

468 / Fructooligosaccharides, Short Chain / Monographs

Flow rate: 1 mL/min
Run time: 12 min
Injection volume: 20 μL
Sample loop: 20 μL
Analysis: Separately inject the *Sample solution* and the *Standard solution* into the chromatograph, and record the area responses for each scFOS. Calculate the percentage of each scFOS, from trimers to nonamers, in the sample taken using the formula:

$$\text{Result} = 100(C_{ST} \times A_{SA})/(A_{ST} \times W)$$

C_{ST} = concentration of the scFOS of interest in the *Standard solution* (mg/100 mL)
A_{SA} = area of the corresponding sugar peak in the chromatogram of the *Sample solution*
A_{ST} = area of the corresponding sugar peak in the chromatogram of the *Standard solution* (for oligomers without a specific standard, use the average area response of the peaks of the standards)
W = weight of sample (g) contained in each 100 mL of the *Sample solution*

Calculate the total percentage of scFOS in the sample by adding the individual percentages of each scFOS, from trimers to nonamers.
Acceptance criteria: NLT 85.0% scFOS (≥ 30.0% trimer, ≥ 45.0% tetramer, and ≥ 5.0% pentamer and larger), with the remainder being glucose, fructose, and sucrose, on the dried basis

IMPURITIES
Inorganic Impurities
- **LEAD,** *Lead Limit Test, Atomic Absorption Spectrophotometric Graphite Furnace Method, Method I,* Appendix IIIB
  Acceptance criteria: NMT 1 mg/kg

SPECIFIC TESTS
- **RESIDUE ON IGNITION (SULFATED ASH),** Appendix IIC
  Analysis: Ignite sample at 525° for 2 h.
  Acceptance criteria: NMT 0.1%
- **TOTAL SOLIDS,** *Water Determination, Karl Fischer Titrimetric Method,* Appendix IIB
  Analysis: Calculate the percent *Total Solids* by the formula:

$$\text{Result} = (W_U - W_W) \times 100/W_U$$

W_U = weight of the sample taken (mg)
W_W = weight of the water determined (mg)
Acceptance criteria: NLT 95.0%

Fructose
First Published: Prior to FCC 6

D-Fructose
Levulose
Fruit Sugar

$C_6H_{12}O_6$ Formula wt 180.16
                  CAS: [57-48-7]
UNII: 6YSS42VSEV [fructose]

DESCRIPTION
Fructose occurs as white, hygroscopic, purified crystals or as a purified crystalline powder. It is a natural constituent of fruit, and is obtained from glucose in corn syrup by the use of glucose isomerase. Its density is about 1.6. It is soluble in methanol and in ethanol, freely soluble in water, and insoluble in ether.
Function: Nutritive sweetener
Packaging and Storage: Store in tight containers protected from humidity.

IDENTIFICATION
- **A. PROCEDURE**
  Sample solution: 100 mg/mL
  Analysis: Add a few drops of a *Sample solution* to 5 mL of hot alkaline cupric tartrate TS.
  Acceptance criteria: A copious red precipitate of cuprous oxide is formed.
- **B. INFRARED ABSORPTION,** *Spectrophotometric Identification Tests,* Appendix IIIC
  Reference standard: USP Fructose RS
  Sample and standard preparation: K
  Acceptance criteria: The spectrum of the sample exhibits maxima at the same wavelengths as those in the spectrum of the *Reference standard*.

ASSAY
- **ANGULAR ROTATION,** *Optical (Specific) Rotation,* Appendix IIB
  Sample: 10 g, previously dried
  Analysis: Transfer the *Sample* into a 100-mL volumetric flask, dissolve in 50 mL of water, add 0.2 mL of 15.2 N ammonium hydroxide, dilute to volume with water, and mix. After 30 min, determine the angular rotation in a 100- or 200-mm tube at 25° with the sodium D line. The observed rotation, in degrees (absolute value), multiplied by 1.124 (or 0.562 for the 200-mm tube), represents the weight, in g, of fructose in the sample taken.
  Acceptance criteria: NLT 98.0% and NMT 102.0% of $C_6H_{12}O_6$, on the dried basis

IMPURITIES
Inorganic Impurities
- **CHLORIDE,** *Chloride and Sulfate Limit Tests, Chloride Limit Test,* Appendix IIIB
  Sample: 2 g
  Control: 0.5 mL of 0.02 N hydrochloric acid
  Acceptance criteria: Any turbidity produced by the *Sample* does not exceed that shown in the *Control*. (NMT 0.018%)
- **LEAD,** *Lead Limit Test, Atomic Absorption Spectrophotometric Graphite Furnace Method, Method I,* Appendix IIIB
  Sample: 5 g

Acceptance criteria: NMT 0.1 mg/kg
- **SULFATE,** *Chloride and Sulfate Limit Tests, Chloride Limit Test,* Appendix IIIB
  Sample: 2 g
  Control: 0.5 mL of 0.02 N sulfuric acid
  Acceptance criteria: Any turbidity produced by the *Sample* does not exceed that shown in the *Control* (NMT 0.025%).

Organic Impurities
- **GLUCOSE**
  0.1 M acetate buffer: Dissolve 13.608 g of sodium acetate trihydrate in sufficient water to make 1000 mL, add 2.7 mL of acetic acid, and adjust the pH to 5.5 with glacial acetic acid or sodium acetate.
  Reagent solution: Dissolve 40 mg of *o*-dianisidine dihydrochloride, 40 mg of horseradish peroxidase (Worthington Biochemical Co., Freehold, NJ, or equivalent), and 0.4 mL of purified glucose oxidase (1000 glucose oxidase units/mL, Miles Laboratories, Inc., or equivalent) in *0.1 M acetate buffer* and dilute to 100 mL with *0.1 M acetate buffer.*
  [NOTE—Commercially available preparations containing the reagents in the proper proportions may also be used.]
  Standard solution: Transfer 300 mg of USP Dextrose RS, previously dried, into a 1000-mL volumetric flask, dissolve in and dilute to volume with water, and mix. Allow to stand for 2 h to allow mutarotation to occur, then transfer 20.0 mL to a 100-mL volumetric flask, dilute to volume with water, and mix. [NOTE—Prepare fresh on the day of use.]
  Sample: 14 g
  Sample solution: Transfer the *Sample* into a 100-mL volumetric flask, dissolve in and dilute to volume with water, and mix. Transfer 20.0 mL of this solution into a second 100-mL volumetric flask, dilute to volume with water, and mix.
  Analysis: Pipet 2 mL each of the *Sample solution, Standard solution,* and water (*Blank*) into separate 150- × 18-mm test tubes. Heat the tubes for 5 min in a water bath maintained at 30°. At zero time and after 30 and 60 s, add 1.0 mL of the *Reagent solution* to the first, second, and third tubes, respectively, mix the contents of the tubes, and allow them to react for exactly 30 min from zero time. Immediately stop the reaction in the first tube by adding 10.0 mL of 25% sulfuric acid. Similarly, add 10.0 mL of 25% sulfuric acid to the remaining tubes after they have reacted for exactly 30 min. Mix the contents of each tube, and cool them to room temperature. Using a suitable spectrophotometer, determine the absorbance values of the mixtures obtained from the *Sample solution* and from the *Standard solution* at 540 nm versus the mixture obtained from the *Blank* in the reference cell. Calculate the percentage of glucose in the sample by the formula:

$$\text{Result} = (50C/W) \times A_U/A_S$$

  C = concentration of the *Standard solution* (mg/mL)
  W = weight of sample (g) taken
  A_U = absorbance of the mixture obtained from the *Sample solution*
  A_S = absorbance of the mixture obtained from the *Standard solution*
  Acceptance criteria: NMT 0.5%
- **HYDROXYMETHYLFURFURAL**
  Sample: 10 mg/mL
  Analysis: Read the absorbance of the *Sample solution* against a water blank at 283 nm in a 1-cm quartz cell in a spectrophotometer. Calculate the percentage of 5-hydroxylmethylfurfural (HMF) by the following equation:

$$\% \text{ HMF} = (0.749 \times A)/C$$

  A = absorbance of the *Sample solution*
  C = concentration of the *Sample solution* (mg/mL) corrected for ash and moisture
  Acceptance criteria: NMT 0.1%, calculated on the dried and ash-free basis

SPECIFIC TESTS
- **LOSS ON DRYING,** Appendix IIC: 70° under vacuum for 4 h
  Acceptance criteria: NMT 0.5%
- **RESIDUE ON IGNITION (SULFATED ASH),** Appendix IIC
  Sample: 2 g
  Acceptance criteria: NMT 0.5%

Fumaric Acid

First Published: Prior to FCC 6

(*E*)-Butenedioic Acid
trans-1,2-Ethylenedicarboxylic Acid

$C_4H_4O_4$ Formula wt 116.07
INS: 297
FEMA: 2488
CAS: [110-17-8]
UNII: 88XHZ13131 [fumaric acid]

DESCRIPTION
Fumaric Acid occurs as white granules or as a crystalline powder. A 1:30 aqueous solution has a pH of 2.0 to 2.5. It is soluble in alcohol, slightly soluble in water and in ether, and very slightly soluble in chloroform.
Function: Acidifier; flavoring agent
Packaging and Storage: Store in well-closed containers.

IDENTIFICATION
- **INFRARED ABSORPTION,** *Spectrophotometric Identification Tests,* Appendix IIIC
  Reference standard: USP Fumaric Acid RS
  Sample and standard preparation: *K*

Acceptance criteria: The spectrum of the sample exhibits maxima at the same wavelengths as those in the spectrum of the *Reference standard*.

ASSAY
- **PROCEDURE**
  Sample: 1 g
  Analysis: Transfer the *Sample* into a 250-mL Erlenmeyer flask, add 50 mL of methanol, and dissolve the sample by warming gently on a steam bath. Cool, add phenolphthalein TS, and titrate with 0.5 N sodium hydroxide to the first appearance of a pink color that persists for at least 30 s. Perform a blank determination (see *General Provisions*), and make any necessary correction. Each mL of 0.5 N sodium hydroxide is equivalent to 29.02 mg of $C_4H_4O_4$.
  Acceptance criteria: NLT 99.5% and NMT 100.5% of $C_4H_4O_4$, calculated on the anhydrous basis

IMPURITIES
Inorganic Impurities
- **LEAD,** *Lead Limit Test, Flame Atomic Absorption Spectrophotometric Method,* Appendix IIIB
  Sample: 5 g
  Acceptance criteria: NMT 2 mg/kg

Organic Impurities
- **MALEIC ACID**
  Mobile phase: 0.005 N sulfuric acid, filtered and degassed
  Standard solution: 1 µg/mL USP Maleic Acid RS in *Mobile phase*
  Sample: 100 mg
  Sample solution: Transfer the *Sample* into a 100-mL volumetric flask, dilute to volume with *Mobile phase*, and mix.
  System suitability solution: 10 µg/mL USP Fumaric Acid RS and 5 µg/mL USP Maleic Acid RS in *Mobile phase*
  Chromatographic system, Appendix IIA
  Mode: High-performance liquid chromatography
  Detector: UV 210 nm
  Column: 22-cm × 4.6-mm column packed with a strong cation exchange resin consisting of sulfonated crosslinked styrene-divinylbenzene copolymer in the hydrogen form (Polypore H from Brownlee Laboratories, Inc., or equivalent)
  Flow rate: About 0.3 mL/min
  Injection volume: About 5 µL
  System suitability
  Sample: *System suitability solution*
  Suitability requirement 1: The resolution, R, between maleic acid and fumaric acid is NLT 2.5.
  Suitability requirement 2: The relative standard deviation for replicate injections is NMT 2.0%.
  Analysis: Separately inject the *Standard solution* and the *Sample solution* into the chromatograph, record the chromatograms, and measure the peak responses. [NOTE—The relative retention times are about 0.5 for maleic acid and 1.0 for fumaric acid.] Calculate the quantity, in mg, of maleic acid in the total weight of the *Sample* taken by the formula:

  $$\text{Result} = 100C\ (R_U/R_S)$$

  C = concentration (mg/mL) of USP Maleic Acid RS in the *Standard solution*
  R_U = responses of the maleic acid peak obtained from the *Sample solution*
  R_S = responses of the maleic acid peak obtained from the *Standard solution*
  Acceptance criteria: NMT 0.1%

SPECIFIC TESTS
- **RESIDUE ON IGNITION (SULFATED ASH),** Appendix IIC
  Sample: 2 g
  Acceptance criteria: NMT 0.1%
- **WATER,** *Water Determination,* Appendix IIB
  Acceptance criteria: NMT 0.5%

Furcelleran

First Published: Prior to FCC 6

Danish Agar

CAS: [9000-21-9]

UNII: 30QS0PF14U [furcelleran]

DESCRIPTION
Furcelleran occurs as a brown or tan to white, coarse to fine powder. It is soluble in water at a temperature of about 80°, forming a viscous, clear or slightly opalescent solution that flows readily. It disperses in water more readily if first moistened with alcohol, glycerin, or a saturated solution of sucrose in water.

Furcelleran is a hydrocolloid obtained from *Furcellaria fastigiata* of the class Rhodophyceae (red seaweeds) by extraction with water or aqueous alkali. It consists mainly of the potassium, sodium, magnesium, calcium, and ammonium sulfate esters of galactose and 3,6-anhydrogalactose copolymers. These hexoses are alternately linked α-1,3 and β-1,4 in the polymer. The relative proportion of cations existing in Furcelleran may be changed during processing to the extent that one may become predominant.

The ester sulfate content of Furcelleran ranges from 8% to 20% (see *Specific Tests*, below). In addition, it contains inorganic salts that originate from the seaweed and the process of recovery from the extract. Furcelleran is recovered by alcohol precipitation, by potassium precipitation, or by freezing. The alcohols used during recovery and purification are restricted to methanol, ethanol, and isopropanol.

Function: Stabilizer; thickener; gelling agent
Packaging and Storage: Store in a well-closed container.

IDENTIFICATION
- **A. PROCEDURE**
  Sample: 4 g

Analysis: Add the *Sample* to 200 mL of water. Heat the mixture in a water bath at 80°, with constant stirring, until dissolved. Replace any water lost by evaporation, and allow the solution to cool to room temperature.
Acceptance criteria: The solution becomes viscous and might form a gel.

- **B. PROCEDURE**
  Sample: The solution or gel obtained from identification test A
  Analysis: Add 200 mg of potassium chloride to 50 mL of the *Sample*, then reheat, mix well, and cool.
  Acceptance criteria: A short-textured (brittle) gel forms.
- **C. PROCEDURE**
  Sample: The solution or gel obtained from identification test A
  Analysis: Add 1 drop of a 1 : 100 solution of methylene blue to 5 mL of the *Sample*.
  Acceptance criteria: A fibrous precipitate forms.
- **D. INFRARED ABSORPTION SPECTRUM**
  Sample solution: 0.2%
  Analysis: Cast films 0.0005 cm thick (when dry) on a suitable non-sticking surface such as Teflon, and obtain the spectrum. (Alternatively, the spectrum may be obtained on potassium bromide pellets if care is taken to avoid moisture.)
  Acceptance criteria: Furcelleran has strong, broad absorption bands in the 1000 to 1100 cm^{-1} region. The absorption maximum is 1065 cm^{-1}. Other characteristic absorption bands and their intensities relative to the absorbance at 1050 cm^{-1} are as follows:

Wavenumber (cm^{-1})	Molecular Assignment	Absorbance Relative to 1050 cm^{-1}
1220–1260	ester sulfate	0.2–0.6
928–933	3,6-anhydrogalactose	0.2–0.3
840–850	galactose-4-sulfate	0.1–0.3

IMPURITIES
Inorganic Impurities
- **ARSENIC,** *Arsenic Limit Test,* Appendix IIIB
  Sample solution: Prepare as directed for organic compounds.
  Acceptance criteria: NMT 3 mg/kg
- **LEAD,** *Lead Limit Test,* Appendix IIIB
  Sample solution: Prepare as directed for organic compounds.
  Control: 5 µg Pb (5 mL of *Diluted Standard Lead Solution*)
  Acceptance criteria: NMT 5 mg/kg

SPECIFIC TESTS
- **ACID INSOLUBLE MATTER**
  Sample: 2 g
  Analysis: Transfer the *Sample* to a 250-mL beaker containing 150 mL of water and 1.5 mL of sulfuric acid. Cover with a watch glass and heat on a steam bath for 6 h; rub down the wall of the beaker frequently with a rubber-tipped stirring rod and replace any water lost by evaporation. Transfer about 500 mg of a suitable filtering aid, accurately weighed, to the beaker, and filter through a tared filtering crucible containing a 2.4-cm glass fiber filter. Wash the residue several times with hot water, dry at 105° for 3 h, cool in a desiccator, and weigh. The difference between the total weight and the sum of the weights of the filter aid, crucible, and glass fiber filter is the weight of the acid-insoluble matter.
  Acceptance criteria: NMT 1.0%
- **ASH (ACID-INSOLUBLE),** Appendix IIC
  Acceptance criteria: NMT 1.0%
- **ASH (TOTAL)**
  Sample: 2 g
  Analysis: Transfer the *Sample* into a previously ignited, tared, silica or platinum crucible. Heat the *Sample* with a suitable infrared heat lamp, increasing the intensity gradually, until the *Sample* is completely charred, and then continue for an additional 30 min. Transfer the crucible and charred matter into a muffle furnace, and ignite at about 550° for 1 h, then cool in a desiccator, and weigh. Repeat the ignition in the muffle furnace until a constant weight is attained. If a carbon-free ash is not obtained after the first ignition, moisten the charred spots with a 1:10 solution of ammonium nitrate, and dry under an infrared heat lamp before reigniting.
  Acceptance criteria: NMT 35.0%
- **LOSS ON DRYING,** Appendix IIC: 105° for 4 h
  Acceptance criteria: NMT 12.0%
- **SOLUBILITY IN WATER**
  Sample: 1 g
  Analysis: Add the *Sample* to 30 mL of cold water, stir well, and heat to a temperature of 80° to completely dissolve the *Sample*.
  Acceptance criteria: NMT 30 mL of water is required to completely dissolve the *Sample* at 80°, and the resulting solution, when maintained at 80°, is uniformly viscous and clear or slightly opalescent.
- **SULFATE**
  Sample: 500 mg, previously dried at 105° for 12 h
  Analysis: Transfer the *Sample* into a 100-mL Kjeldahl flask. Add 10 mL of nitric acid, and heat gently for 30 min, adding more of the acid, if necessary, to prevent evaporation to dryness and to yield a volume of about 3 mL at the end of the heating. Cool the mixture to room temperature, and decompose the excess nitric acid by adding formaldehyde TS, dropwise, heating if necessary, until no brown fumes are evolved. Continue heating until the volume of the reaction mixture is reduced to about 5 mL, and then cool. Transfer the residue quantitatively, with the aid of water, into a 400-mL beaker, dilute it to about 100 mL, and filter, if necessary, to produce a clear solution. Dilute the solution to about 200 mL, and add 1 mL of hydrochloric acid. Heat to boiling and, while constantly stirring, add, dropwise, an excess (about 6 mL) of hot barium chloride TS. Heat the mixture for 1 h on a steam bath, collect the precipitate of barium sulfate on a filter, wash it until it is free from chloride, dry, ignite, and weigh. The weight of the barium sulfate so obtained, multiplied by 0.4116, gives the equivalent of sulfate (SO_4).

Acceptance criteria: Between 8.0% and 20.0%, on the dried basis
- **VISCOSITY OF A 1.5% SOLUTION**
Sample: 7.5 g
Analysis: Transfer the Sample into a tared, 600-mL tall-form (Berzelius) beaker, and disperse with agitation for 10 to 20 min in 450 mL of deionized water. Add sufficient water to bring the final weight to 500 g, and heat in a water bath, with continuous agitation, until a temperature of 80° is reached (20 to 30 min). Add water to adjust for loss by evaporation, cool to 76° to 77°, and place in a constant-temperature bath at 75°. Preheat the bob and guard of a Brookfield LVF or LVT viscometer, or equivalent, to approximately 75° in water, then dry the bob and guard and attach them to the viscometer, which should be equipped with a No. 1 spindle (19-mm diameter, approximately 65 mm long) capable of rotating at 30 rpm. Adjust the height of the bob in the sample solution, start the viscometer rotating at 30 rpm, and after six complete revolutions, take the reading on the 0 to 100 scale. Record the results in centipoises by multiplying the reading by 2. [NOTE—Some samples may be too viscous to be read when a No. 1 spindle is used. Such samples obviously pass the specification, but if a viscosity reading is desired for other reasons, use a No. 2 spindle, take the reading on the 0 to 100 scale, and multiply the reading by 10 to obtain the viscosity in centipoises, or read on the 0 to 500 scale and multiply by 2. If the viscosity is very low, increased precision may be obtained by using the Brookfield UL (ultra low) adapter, in which case the viscometer reading on the 0 to 100 scale should be multiplied by 0.2 to obtain the viscosity in centipoises.]
Acceptance criteria: NLT 5 centipoises at 75°

Furfural

First Published: Prior to FCC 6
Last Revision: First Supplement, FCC 6

2-Furaldehyde
Pyromucic Aldehyde

$C_5H_4O_2$ Formula wt 96.09
FEMA: 2489
UNII: DJ1HGI319P [furfural]

DESCRIPTION
Furfural occurs as a colorless to yellow oily liquid that turns red-brown on long storage. It may contain a suitable antioxidant.
Odor: Sweet, bready
Solubility: Soluble in vegetable oils; slightly soluble in propylene glycol, water
Boiling Point: ~162°
Solubility in Alcohol, Appendix VI: One mL dissolves in 1 mL of 95% ethanol.
Function: Flavoring agent

IDENTIFICATION
- **INFRARED SPECTRA,** Spectrophotometric Identification Tests, Appendix IIIC
Acceptance criteria: The spectrum of the sample exhibits relative maxima at the same wavelengths as those of the spectrum below.

ASSAY
- **PROCEDURE:** Proceed as directed under M-1b, Appendix XI.
Acceptance criteria: NLT 96.0% of $C_5H_4O_2$

SPECIFIC TESTS
- **ACID VALUE, FLAVOR CHEMICALS (OTHER THAN ESSENTIAL OILS),** M-15, Appendix XI
Acceptance criteria: NMT 1.0
- **REFRACTIVE INDEX,** Appendix II: At 20°
Acceptance criteria: Between 1.522 and 1.528
- **SPECIFIC GRAVITY:** Determine at 25° by any reliable method (see General Provisions).
Acceptance criteria: Between 1.154 and 1.158

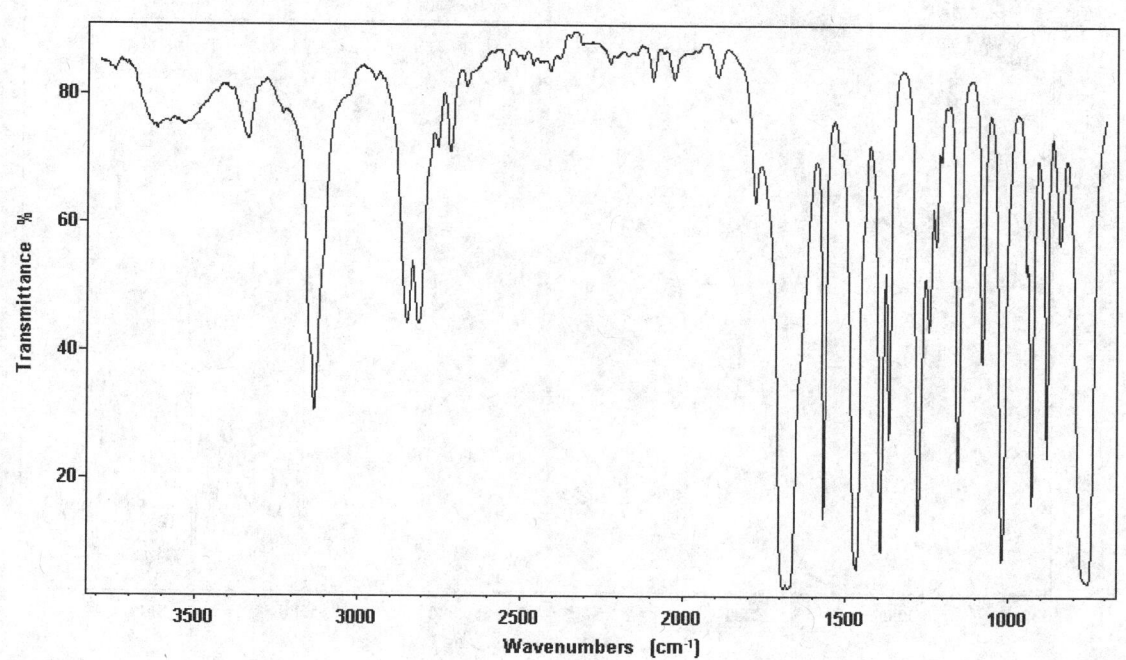

Furfural

Furfuryl Alcohol

First Published: Prior to FCC 6

C₅H₆O₂   Formula wt 98.10
FEMA: 2491
UNII: D582054MUH [furfuryl alcohol]

DESCRIPTION
Furfuryl Alcohol occurs as a pale yellow to brown liquid.
Odor: Caramel
Solubility: Soluble in propylene glycol, vegetable oils, water
Boiling Point: ~169°
Solubility in Alcohol, Appendix VI: One mL dissolves in 1 mL of 95% ethanol.

Function: Flavoring agent

IDENTIFICATION
- **INFRARED SPECTRA,** *Spectrophotometric Identification Tests,* Appendix IIIC
  Acceptance criteria: The spectrum of the sample exhibits relative maxima at the same wavelengths as those of the spectrum below.

ASSAY
- **PROCEDURE:** Proceed as directed under *M-1b,* Appendix XI.
  Acceptance criteria: NLT 95.0% of C₅H₆O₂

SPECIFIC TESTS
- **REFRACTIVE INDEX,** Appendix II: At 20°
  Acceptance criteria: Between 1.481 and 1.490
- **SPECIFIC GRAVITY:** Determine at 25° by any reliable method (see *General Provisions*).
  Acceptance criteria: Between 1.126 and 1.136

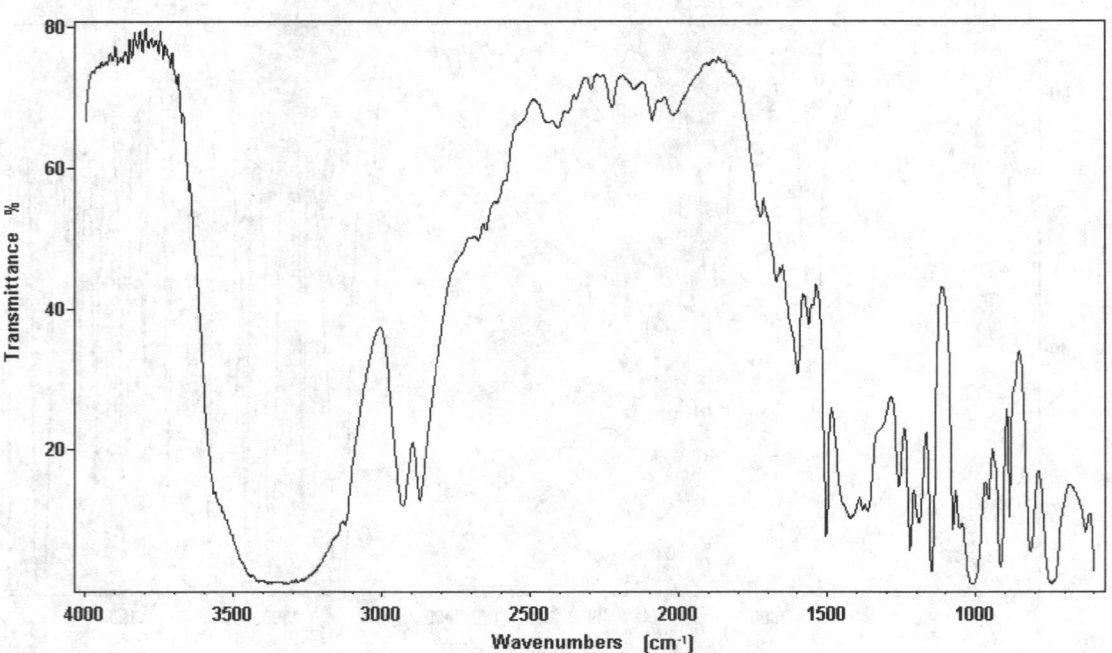

Furfuryl Alcohol

Furfuryl Mercaptan

First Published: Prior to FCC 6

C₅H₆OS   Formula wt 114.16
FEMA: 2493
UNII: 29W096TCPG [furfuryl mercaptan]

DESCRIPTION
Furfuryl Mercaptan occurs as a yellow to brown liquid.
Odor: Coffee
Solubility: Soluble in vegetable oils; slightly soluble in propylene glycol; insoluble or practically insoluble in water
Boiling Point: ~155°
Solubility in Alcohol, Appendix VI: One mL dissolves in 1 mL of 95% ethanol.

Function: Flavoring agent

IDENTIFICATION
- **INFRARED SPECTRA,** *Spectrophotometric Identification Tests,* Appendix IIIC
  Acceptance criteria: The spectrum of the sample exhibits relative maxima at the same wavelengths as those of the spectrum below.

ASSAY
- **PROCEDURE:** Proceed as directed under *M-1b,* Appendix XI.
  Acceptance criteria: NLT 95.0% of C₅H₆OS

SPECIFIC TESTS
- **REFRACTIVE INDEX,** Appendix II: At 20°
  Acceptance criteria: Between 1.529 and 1.534
- **SPECIFIC GRAVITY:** Determine at 25° by any reliable method (see *General Provisions*).
  Acceptance criteria: Between 1.124 and 1.135

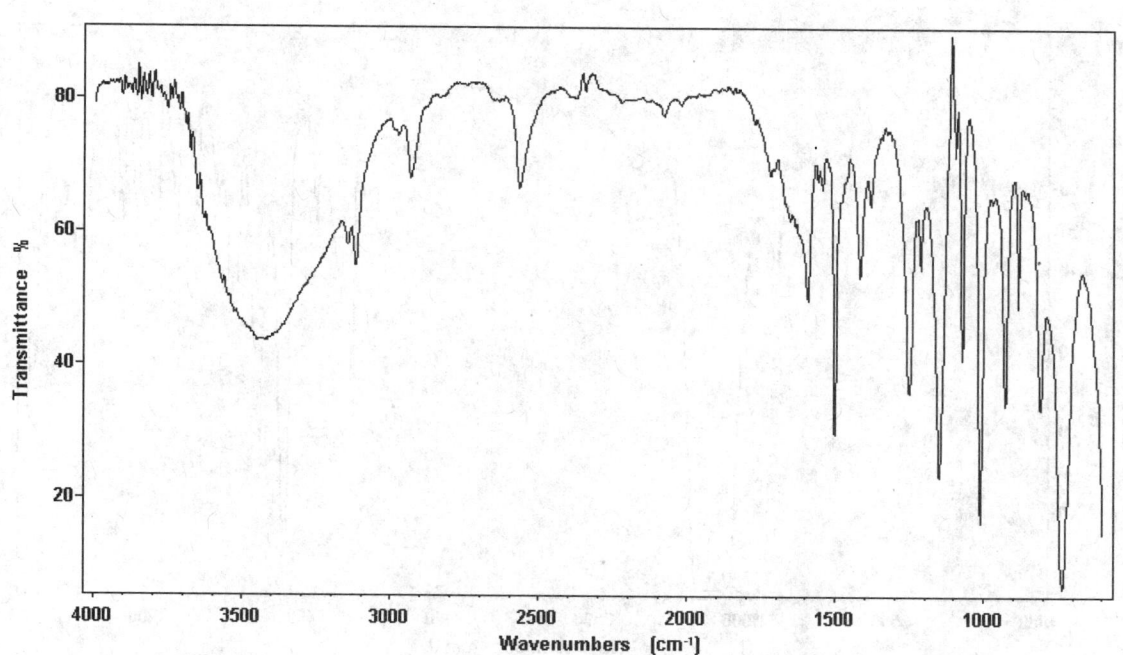

Furfuryl Mercaptan

2-Furyl Methyl Ketone

First Published: Prior to FCC 6

$C_6H_6O_2$ Formula wt 110.11
FEMA: 3163
UNII: Q5ZRP80K02 [2-furyl methyl ketone]

DESCRIPTION
2-Furyl Methyl Ketone occurs as a yellow to brown liquid.
Odor: Coffee
Solubility: Slightly soluble in propylene glycol, vegetable oils; very slightly soluble in water
Boiling Point: ~67° (10 mm Hg)
Solubility in Alcohol, Appendix VI: One mL dissolves in 2 mL of 95% ethanol.

Function: Flavoring agent

IDENTIFICATION
- **INFRARED SPECTRA,** *Spectrophotometric Identification Tests,* Appendix IIIC
  Acceptance criteria: The spectrum of the sample exhibits relative maxima at the same wavelengths as those of the spectrum below.

ASSAY
- **PROCEDURE:** Proceed as directed under *M-1b,* Appendix XI.
  Acceptance criteria: NLT 97.0% of $C_{10}H_6O_2$

SPECIFIC TESTS
- **REFRACTIVE INDEX,** Appendix II: At 20°
  Acceptance criteria: Between 1.505 and 1.510
- **SPECIFIC GRAVITY:** Determine at 25° by any reliable method (see *General Provisions*).
  Acceptance criteria: Between 1.102 and 1.107

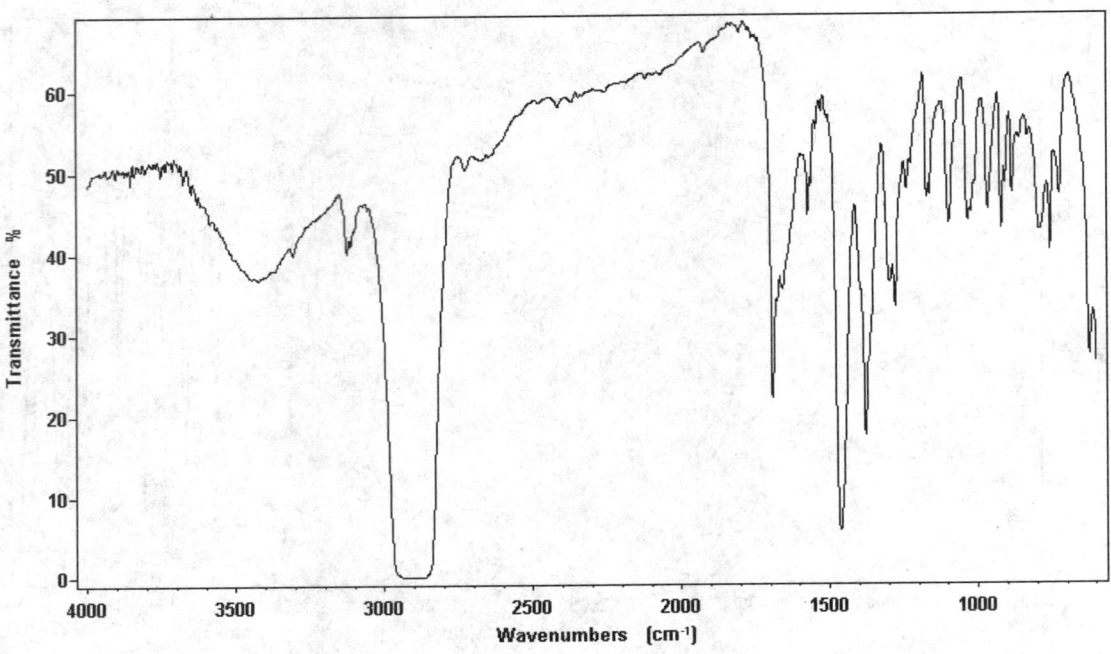

2-Furyl Methyl Ketone

Fusel Oil, Refined

First Published: Prior to FCC 6

FEMA: 2497
UNII: 2NK7O363Q6 [fusel oil]

DESCRIPTION
Fusel Oil, Refined occurs as a colorless to pale yellow liquid.
Odor: Winy, whiskey
Solubility: Soluble in propylene glycol, vegetable oils; insoluble or practically insoluble in water
Boiling Point: ~128° to 130°
Solubility in Alcohol, Appendix VI: One mL dissolves in 1 mL of 95% alcohol.
Function: Flavoring agent

IDENTIFICATION
- **INFRARED SPECTRA,** *Spectrophotometric Identification Tests,* Appendix IIIC
  Acceptance criteria: The spectrum of the sample exhibits relative maxima at the same wavelengths as those of the spectrum below.

ASSAY
- **PROCEDURE:** Proceed as directed under *M-1a,* Appendix XI.
  Acceptance criteria: NLT 95.0% of 2- and 3-methyl butanol

SPECIFIC TESTS
- **REFRACTIVE INDEX,** Appendix II: At 20°
  Acceptance criteria: Between 1.405 and 1.410
- **SPECIFIC GRAVITY:** Determine at 25° by any reliable method (see *General Provisions*).
  Acceptance criteria: Between 0.807 and 0.813

OTHER REQUIREMENTS
- **ANGULAR ROTATION,** *Optical (Specific) Rotation,* Appendix IIB
  Acceptance criteria: Between −0.5° and −2.0°

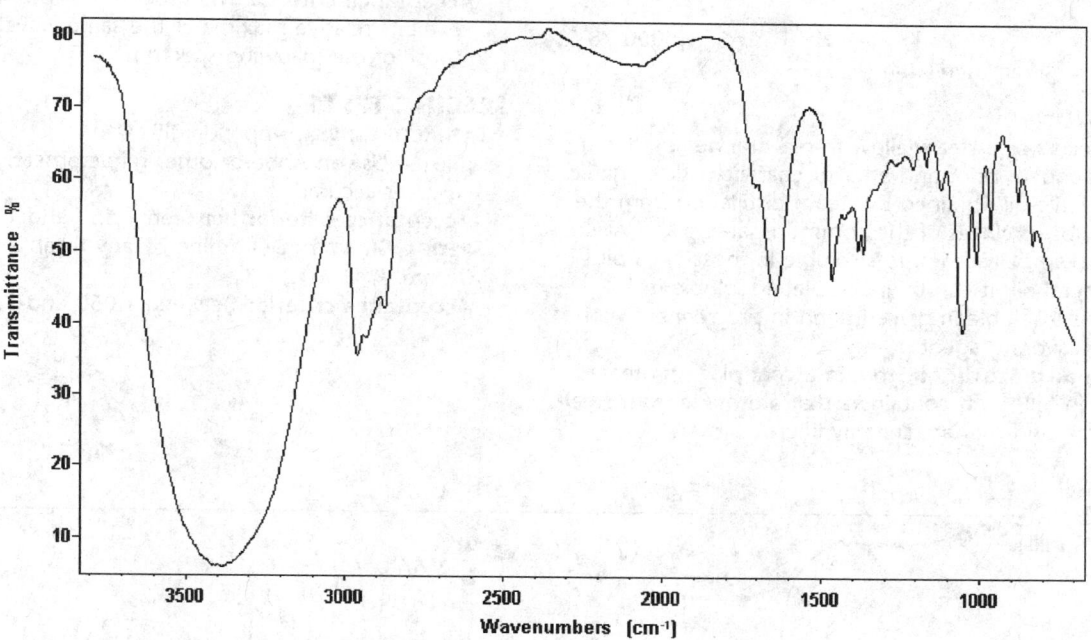

Fusel Oil, Refined

Garlic Oil

First Published: Prior to FCC 6

CAS: [8000-78-0]

UNII: 4WG8U28833 [garlic oil]

DESCRIPTION
Garlic Oil occurs as a clear yellow to red-orange liquid with a strong, pungent odor and a flavor characteristic of garlic. It is the volatile oil obtained by steam distillation from the crushed bulbs or cloves of the common garlic plant, *Allium sativum* L. (Fam. Liliaceae). It is soluble in most fixed oils and in mineral oil. It can be incompletely soluble in alcohol. It is insoluble in glycerin and in propylene glycol.

Function: Flavoring agent

Packaging and Storage: Store in a cool place protected from light in full, tight containers that are made from steel or aluminum and that are suitably lined.

IDENTIFICATION
- **INFRARED SPECTRA,** *Spectrophotometric Identification Tests,* Appendix IIIC
  Acceptance criteria: The spectrum of the sample exhibits relative maxima at the same wavelengths as those of the following spectrum:

SPECIFIC TESTS
- **REFRACTIVE INDEX,** Appendix IIB
  [NOTE—Use an Abbé or other refractometer of equal or greater accuracy.]
  Acceptance criteria: Between 1.550 and 1.580 at 20°
- **SPECIFIC GRAVITY:** Determine by any reliable method (see *General Provisions*).
  Acceptance criteria: Between 1.050 and 1.095

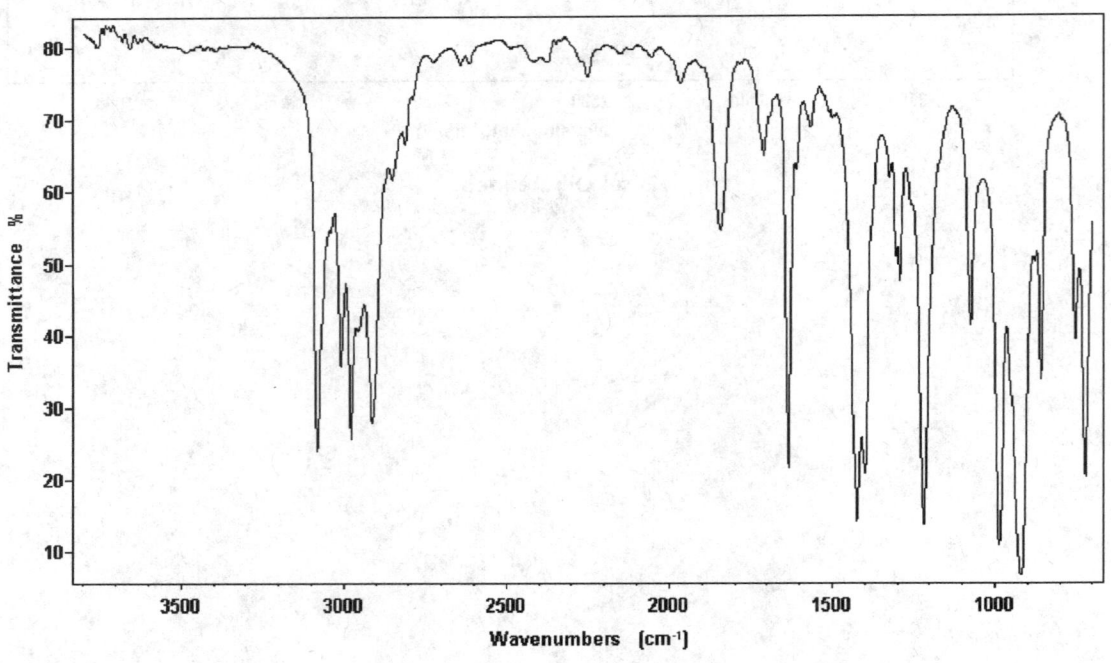

Garlic Oil

Gelatin

First Published: Prior to FCC 6

Food-Grade Gelatin
Edible Gelatin

CAS: [9000-70-8]

UNII: 2G86QN327L [gelatin]

DESCRIPTION
Gelatin is the product obtained from the acid, alkaline, or enzymatic hydrolysis of collagen, the chief protein component of the skin, bones, and connective tissues of animals, including fish and poultry. These animal sources shall not have been exposed to pentachlorophenol.
Type A Gelatin is produced by the acid processing of collagenous raw materials and exhibits an isoelectric point between pH 7 and pH 9. Type B Gelatin is produced by the alkaline or lime processing of collagenous raw materials and exhibits an isoelectric point between pH 4.6 and pH 5.2. Mixtures of Types A and B as well as Gelatins produced by modifications of the above mentioned processes may exhibit isoelectric points outside of the stated ranges.

Gelatin is a vitreous, brittle solid that is faintly yellow. When Gelatin granules are immersed in cold water, they hydrate into discrete, swollen particles. On being warmed, Gelatin disperses into the water, resulting in a stable suspension. Water solutions of Gelatin will form a reversible gel if cooled below the specific gel point of Gelatin. The gel point is dependent on the source of the raw material. Gelatin extracted from the tissues of warm-blooded animals will have a gel point in the range of 30° to 35°. Gelatin extracted from the skin of cold-water ocean fish will have a gel point in the range of 5° to 10°. Gelatin is soluble in aqueous solutions of polyhydric alcohols such as glycerin and propylene glycol. It is insoluble in most organic solvents.

Function: Firming agent; stabilizer and thickener; surface-active agent; surface-finishing agent

Packaging and Storage: Store in tight containers.

IDENTIFICATION
- **A. Procedure**
  Sample: 10 g
  Analysis: Dissolve the *Sample* in 100 mL of hot water contained in a suitable flask, and cool in a refrigerator at 2° for 24 h. Transfer the flask to a water bath heated to 60°.
  Acceptance criteria: A gel forms following the refrigeration step; and within 30 min after transferring to the water bath, when stirred, the gel reverts to the original liquid state.
- **B. Procedure**
  Sample solution: 10 mg/mL
  Analysis: To the *Sample solution*, add trinitrophenol TS or a 1:1.5 solution of potassium dichromate, previously mixed with about one-fourth its volume of 3 N hydrochloric acid.
  Acceptance criteria: A yellow precipitate forms.

IMPURITIES
Inorganic Impurities
- **Chromium**
  Standard stock solution: Dissolve 192.3 mg of chromium trioxide [CrO_3] in 100 mL water and 10 mL nitric acid. Dilute to 1000 mL with water. This solution contains 0.1 mg/mL chromium. Transfer 100.0 mL of this solution into a 1000-mL volumetric flask, dilute to volume with water, and mix. This solution contains 10 µg/mL chromium.
  Standard solutions: 1.0, 3.0, 5.0, and 7.0 µg/mL of chromium: from the *Standard stock solution*
  Sample solution: Transfer 10 g of sample into a 100-mL silica dish. Using a very low flame, heat the dish over a Bunsen burner. [**Caution**—Take care that the sample does not swell over the lip of the dish or catch fire.] Gradually increase the flame until the sample is completely charred, transfer it into a muffle furnace at 550°, and ash overnight. Cool to room temperature, add 10 mL of hydrochloric acid and 10 mL of nitric acid, and heat on a steam bath for 10 min. Cool and transfer into a 25-mL volumetric flask, cautiously dilute to volume with water, and mix.
  Analysis: Using a suitable atomic absorption spectrophotometer equipped with a chromium hollow-cathode lamp and a slightly reducing air-acetylene flame with water as the blank, concomitantly determine the absorbances of the *Standard solutions* and the *Sample solution* at the chromium emission line of 356.9 nm. Plot the absorbances of the *Standard solutions* versus concentration, in µg/mL of chromium, and draw the straight line best fitting the four plotted points. Calculate the concentration of chromium, in mg/kg, in the portion of sample taken, by the formula:

  $$\text{Result} = 25 \times C_S/W$$

  C_S = concentration of chromium in the *Sample solution* determined from the standard curve (µg/mL)
  W = quantity of the sample taken (g)
  Acceptance criteria: NMT 10 mg/kg
- **Lead,** *Lead Limit Test, Atomic Absorption Spectrophotometric Graphite Furnace Method, Method I,* Appendix IIIB
  Acceptance criteria: NMT 1.5 mg/kg
- **Sulfur Dioxide,** *Sulfur Dioxide Determination,* Appendix X
  Sample solution: 200 mg/mL in a 5% alcohol in water mixture
  Analysis: Proceed as directed under *Sample Introduction and Distillation*.
  Acceptance criteria: NMT 0.005%

Organic Impurities
- **Pentachlorophenol**
  Standard stock solution: 4.0 µg/mL pentachlorophenol in pesticide-grade benzene. [Note—Use PCP *Reference Standard*, Standard No. 5260, Pesticide Reference Standards Section, Environmental Protection Agency, Research Triangle Park, NC 27711, or equivalent, available from Aldrich Chemical Co.]
  Standard solutions: 0.0 µg/mL, 0.004 µg/mL, 0.020 µg/mL, 0.040 µg/mL, 0.100 µg/mL, 0.200 µg/mL, and 0.400 µg/mL in hexane: from *Standard stock solution*
  Sample preparation: Transfer 2 g of sample into a 25- × 150-mm screw-cap test tube equipped with a Teflon-lined cap. Add 10 mL of 12 N sulfuric acid, close the tube, tighten the cap, and heat for 1 h in a fume hood in a water bath maintained at 100°, removing the tube periodically and mixing the sample by shaking. Remove the tube from the bath, and allow it to cool to room temperature. Add 10 mL of a 4:1 (v/v) solution of hexane:isopropanol to the tube, and shake vigorously. Centrifuge for 2 min at 1000 × g in a suitable centrifuge (International Equipment Co., or equivalent) with a head equipped to accommodate 25- × 150-mm test tubes. Use a Pasteur pipet to transfer the upper hexane layer to a second 25- × 150-mm test tube. Repeat the extraction and centrifugation two additional times, and combine the hexane extracts in the second test tube. Add 5.0 mL of 1.0 N potassium hydroxide to the combined extracts, tighten the cap, shake the test tube vigorously, and centrifuge for 2 min at 1000 × g as before. Remove the upper layer with a Pasteur pipet, and discard. Add 10 mL of hexane to the test tube, tighten the cap, shake the test tube vigorously, and centrifuge as before. Remove the upper layer with a Pasteur pipet, and discard. Add 5.0 mL of 12 N sulfuric

acid to the test tube, tighten the cap, and mix by carefully swirling the tube. Add 5.0 mL of hexane, tighten the cap, shake the test tube vigorously, centrifuge as before, and transfer the upper layer to a 10-mL volumetric flask. Repeat twice, using 2.0 mL of hexane each time, and transfer the upper layer into the 10-mL volumetric flask. Dilute to volume with hexane.

Blank solution: Prepare as directed under *Sample solution* using 2.0 mL of water instead of sample.

Chromatographic system
 Mode: Gas chromatography
 Detector: ^{63}Ni electron capture detector
 Column: 1.8-m × 4-mm (id) glass column, or equivalent, containing 1% SP-1240DA on 100- to 120-mesh Supelcoport (Supelco Inc.), or equivalent. [NOTE—Place a small plug (2 to 3 mm) of phosphoric acid-washed glass wool in the detector end of the column.]
 Carrier gas: 5% methane in argon
 Temperature
  Column oven: 180°
  Injector port: 250°
  Detector: 350°
 Flow rate: 60 mL/min
 Injection volume: 5 µL
 [NOTE—Use only recently prepared and thoroughly conditioned columns; the appearance of ghost PCP peaks may be noted following the injection of samples containing high levels of PCP; repeated injections of solvent may be necessary until ghost PCP peaks disappear.

 Adjust the electrometer to provide about half of the full-scale deflection when 0.1 ng of PCP is injected.

 Condition the column by purging with carrier gas at ambient temperature for 10 to 15 min; program the column oven to increase from, and hold the temperature at 190° for 8 h while continuing to purge with carrier gas. Inject each *Standard solution* and *Sample preparation* twice to ensure that consistent responses are obtained. Following each injection of the *Standard solutions* or *Sample preparation*, rinse the syringe 10 times with hexane. After each injection of the *Standard solutions* or *Sample preparation*, inject 5 µL of hexane onto the gas chromatograph, or equivalent, and record the chromatogram. If peaks are observed at the retention time for PCP, repeat the hexane injection until such peaks are no longer encountered.]

Analysis: Inject the *Standard solutions* and the *Blank solution* into the gas chromatograph sequentially, and record the chromatograms. Measure the areas under the PCP peaks and the peak heights for each of the *Standard solutions* corrected for the *Blank solution*. [NOTE—The retention time for PCP should be about 10 min.] The maximum acceptable *Blank solution* for satisfactory performance of the method is 0.01 µg/g.

Similarly, inject 5 µL of the *Sample preparation* into the gas chromatograph, and record the chromatogram. Measure the area under the PCP peak and the peak height, corrected for the *Blank solution*. Determine the amount of PCP in the *Sample preparation* by comparing the peak area and height to the peak area and height obtained from injection of known amounts of *Standard solutions*; to ensure valid measurement of PCP in the *Sample preparation*, the size of the PCP peak from the *Sample preparation* and the *Standard solutions* should be within ±10%. The *Sample preparation* may require further dilution.

Calculate the concentration of PCP, in µg/g, in the sample taken by the formula:

$$\text{Result} = 5 \times A_S$$

A_S = amount of PCP in the aliquot of the *Sample preparation* injected (ng)

Acceptance criteria: NMT 0.3 mg/kg

SPECIFIC TESTS
- **ASH (TOTAL),** Appendix IIC
 Sample: 5 g
 Analysis: Before ashing in a muffle furnace at 500° to 550° for 15 to 20 h, add 1.5 to 2.0 g of paraffin to the *Sample*, then heat the crucible on a low-flame hot plate or muffle furnace until the mixture is thoroughly charred.
 Acceptance criteria: NMT 3.0%
- **LOSS ON DRYING,** Appendix IIC: 105° for 16 to 18 h to constant weight
 Sample: 5 g
 Acceptance criteria: NMT 15.0%
- **MICROBIAL LIMITS**
 [NOTE—Current methods for the following tests may be found in the Food and Drug Administration's Bacteriological Analytical Manual online at www.cfsan.fda.gov.]
 Acceptance criteria
  E. coli: Negative in 25 g
  Salmonella: Negative in 25 g
- **PROTEIN,** *Nitrogen Determination,* Appendix IIIC
 Sample: 1 g
 Analysis: Use a 500 mL Kjeldahl flask. Calculate the percent protein with the formula:

$$\text{Result} = N \times F$$

N = percent nitrogen
F = nitrogen-to-protein conversion factor, 5.55

Acceptance criteria: Conforms to the representations of the vendor.

Gellan Gum

First Published: Prior to FCC 6
Last Revision: FCC 8

INS: 418
CAS: [71010-52-1]

DESCRIPTION

Change to read:

Gellan Gum occurs as an off-white powder. It is a high-molecular-weight polysaccharide gum produced by fermentation of a carbohydrate with a pure culture of ▲*Sphingomonas elodea* (previously identified as *Pseudomonas elodea*, but later reclassified),▲FCC8 purified by recovery with isopropyl alcohol, dried, and milled. It is a heteropolysaccharide comprising a tetrasaccharide-repeating unit of one rhamnose, one glucuronic acid, and two glucose units. The glucuronic acid is neutralized to mixed potassium, sodium, calcium, and magnesium salts. It may contain acyl (glyceryl and acetyl) groups as the O-glycosidically linked esters. It is soluble in hot or cold deionized water.

Function: Stabilizer; thickener
Packaging and Storage: Store in well-closed containers.

IDENTIFICATION

- **A. PROCEDURE**
  Sample solution: Prepare a 1% solution by dissolving 1 g of sample in 99 mL of deionized water. Using a motorized stirrer and a propeller-type stirring blade, stir the mixture for about 2 h. [NOTE—Save part of this solution for *Identification* test B.]
  Analysis: Draw a small amount of the *Sample solution* into a wide-bore pipet, and transfer it into a solution of 10% calcium chloride.
  Acceptance criteria: A tough, worm-like gel forms instantly.

- **B. PROCEDURE**
  Sample solution: Use the *Sample solution* from *Identification* test A.
  Analysis: Add 0.5 g of sodium chloride to the *Sample solution*, heat the solution to 80°, stirring constantly, and hold the temperature at 80° for 1 min. Stop heating and stirring the solution, and allow it to cool to room temperature.
  Acceptance criteria: A firm gel forms.

ASSAY

- **ALGINATES ASSAY**, Appendix IIIC
  Sample: 1.2 g, undried
  Acceptance criteria: A sample yields NLT 3.3% and NMT 6.8% of carbon dioxide (CO_2), calculated on the dried basis.

IMPURITIES

Inorganic Impurities

- **LEAD**, *Lead Limit Test*, Appendix IIIB
  Sample solution: Prepare as directed for organic compounds using 2 g of sample.
  Control: 4 µg Pb (4 mL of *Diluted Standard Lead Solution*)
  Acceptance criteria: NMT 2 mg/kg

Organic Impurities

- **ISOPROPYL ALCOHOL**
  IPA standard solution: 1 mg/mL of isopropyl alcohol (chromatography grade) in water
  TBA standard solution: 1 mg/mL of *tert*-butyl alcohol (chromatography grade) in water
  Mixed standard solution: Pipet 4 mL each of the *IPA standard solution* and the *TBA standard solution* into a 125-mL graduated Erlenmeyer flask, dilute to about 100 mL with water, and mix. The solution contains about 40 µg/mL each of isopropyl alcohol and *tert*-butyl alcohol.
  Sample: 5 g
  Sample solution: Disperse 1 mL of a suitable antifoam emulsion, such as Dow-Corning G-10, or equivalent, in 200 mL of water contained in a 1000-mL 24/40 round-bottom distilling flask. Add the *Sample*, and shake for 1 h on a wrist-action mechanical shaker. Connect the flask to a fractionating column, and distill about 100 mL, adjusting the heat so that foam does not enter the column. Add 4.0 mL of *TBA standard solution* to the distillate to obtain the *Sample solution*.
  Chromatographic system, Appendix IIA
    Mode: Gas chromatography
    Detector type: Flame-ionization
    Column: 1.8-m × 3.2-mm (id) stainless steel, or equivalent, packed with 80- to 100-mesh Porapak QS, or equivalent
    Temperature
      Column: 165°
      Injection port: 200°
      Detector: 200°
    Carrier gas: Helium
    Flow rate: 80 mL/min
    Injection volume: About 5 µL
  Analysis: Inject the *Mixed standard solution* and separately inject the *Sample solution*. From the chromatogram of the *Mixed standard solution*, determine the areas of the isopropyl alcohol and *tert*-butyl alcohol peaks and calculate the response factor, F, from the formula:

  $$F = A_{IPA}/A_{TBA}$$

  A_{IPA} = area of the isopropyl alcohol peak
  A_{TBA} = area of the *tert*-butyl alcohol peak
  [NOTE—The retention times of isopropyl alcohol and *tert*-butyl alcohol are about 2 min and 3 min.]
  From the chromatogram of the *Sample solution*, calculate the isopropyl alcohol content, in mg/kg, in the portion of the sample taken by the formula:

  $$\text{Result} = (S_{IPA} \times 4000)/(F \times S_{TBA} \times W)$$

  S_{IPA} = area of the isopropyl alcohol peak in the *Sample preparation* chromatogram
  S_{TBA} = area of the *tert*-butyl alcohol peak in the *Sample preparation* chromatogram
  W = weight of the sample taken (g)

Acceptance criteria: NMT 0.075%

SPECIFIC TESTS
- **Loss on Drying**, Appendix IIC: 105° for 2.5 h
  Acceptance criteria: NMT 15.0%

ADDITIONAL INFORMATION

Add the following:

▲Materials of commerce are often comprised of FCC Gellan Gum standardized with significant amounts of FCC Sucrose or other suitable sugars to create a material suitable for applications requiring specific functionality at low levels of gellan gum, the ratio of which will be determined based on the natural variation of the gellan gum. Such standardized materials should be identified as the standardized form (gellan gum standardized with sugar) to indicate the presence and type of any added FCC-grade or other suitable sugars, and cannot be identified as pure FCC Gellan Gum unless the material meets the monograph requirements.▲FCC8

Geraniol

First Published: Prior to FCC 6

trans-3,7-Dimethyl-2,6-octadien-1-ol
E-3,7-Dimethyl-2,6-octadien-1-ol

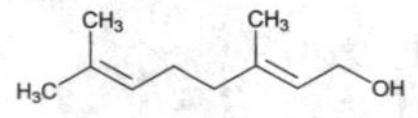

$C_{10}H_{18}O$ Formula wt 154.25
FEMA: 2507
UNII: L837108USY [geraniol]

DESCRIPTION
Geraniol occurs as a colorless liquid.
Odor: Rose

Solubility: Soluble in most fixed oils, propylene glycol; slightly soluble in water; insoluble or practically insoluble in glycerin
Boiling Point: ~230°
Solubility in Alcohol, Appendix VI: One mL dissolves in 3 mL of 70% alcohol, and remains in solution upon dilution to 10 mL.
Function: Flavoring agent

IDENTIFICATION
- **Infrared Spectra,** *Spectrophotometric Identification Tests,* Appendix IIIC
  Acceptance criteria: The spectrum of the sample exhibits relative maxima at the same wavelengths as those of the spectrum below.

ASSAY
- **Procedure:** Proceed as directed under *Total Alcohols,* Appendix VI.
  Sample: 1.2 g
  Analysis: Use 77.13 as the equivalence factor (e).
  Acceptance criteria: NLT 88.0% of total alcohols as $C_{10}H_{18}O$

SPECIFIC TESTS
- **Refractive Index,** Appendix II: At 20°
  Acceptance criteria: Between 1.469 and 1.478
- **Specific Gravity:** Determine at 25° by any reliable method (see *General Provisions*).
  Acceptance criteria: Between 0.870 and 0.885

OTHER REQUIREMENTS
- **Aldehydes,** *M-2d,* Appendix XI
  Sample: 5 g
  Analysis: Use 77.13 as the equivalence factor (e).
  Acceptance criteria: NMT 1.0% as citronellal
- **Esters,** Appendix VI
  Sample: 5 g
  Analysis: Use 98.15 as the equivalence factor (e).
  Acceptance criteria: NMT 1.0% as geranyl acetate

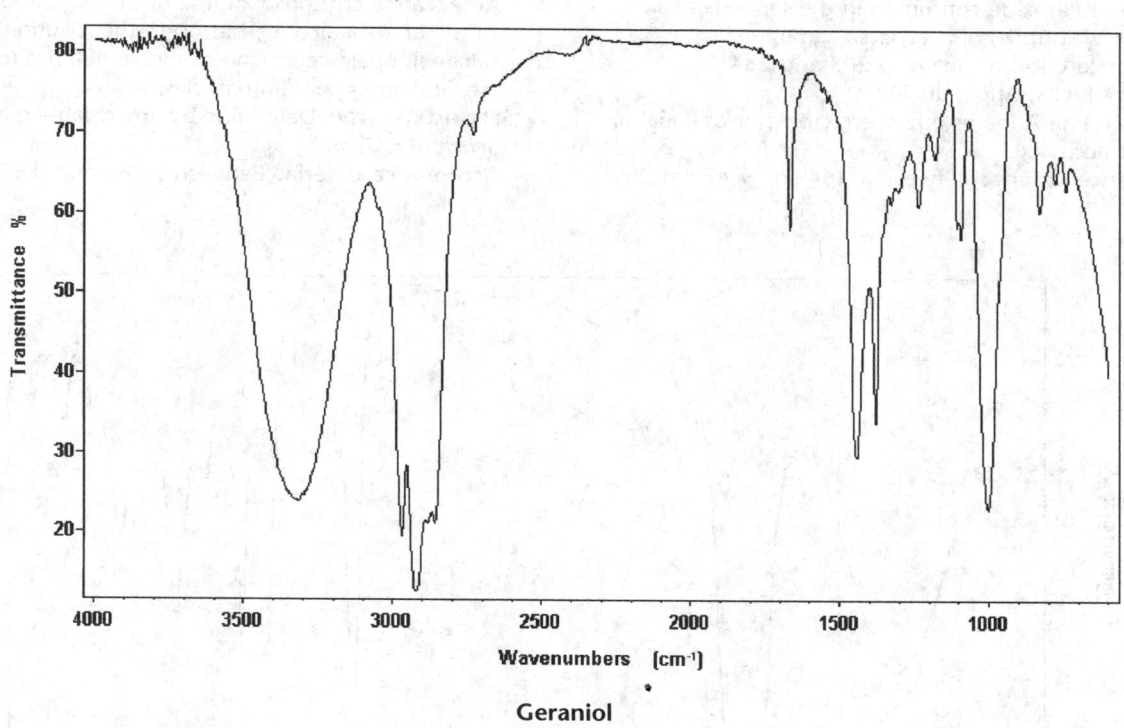

Geraniol

Geranium Oil, Algerian Type

First Published: Prior to FCC 6

Rose Geranium Oil, Algerian Type
　　　　　　　　　　　　　　　　CAS: [8000-46-2]
UNII: 5Q1I94P4WG [geranium oil, algerian type]

DESCRIPTION
Geranium Oil, Algerian Type occurs as a light to deep yellow liquid with a characteristic odor resembling rose and geraniol. It is the oil obtained by steam distillation from the leaves of *Pelargonium graveolens* L'Her (Fam. Geraniaceae). It is soluble in most fixed oils, and it is soluble, usually with opalescence, in mineral oil and in propylene glycol. It is practically insoluble in glycerin.

Function: Flavoring agent

Packaging and Storage: Store in a cool place protected from light in full, tight containers that are made from steel or aluminum and that are suitably lined.

IDENTIFICATION
- **INFRARED SPECTRA,** *Spectrophotometric Identification Tests,* Appendix IIIC
  Acceptance criteria: The spectrum of the sample exhibits relative maxima at the same wavelengths as those of the spectrum below.

ASSAY
- **PROCEDURE**
  Sample: 6 g
  Analysis: Determine as directed in *Esters, Ester Value,* Appendix VI.
  Calculate the percentage of esters (as geranyl tiglate) ($C_{15}H_{24}O_2$) by the formula:

  $$Result = 0.422 \times EV$$

  EV　= ester value
  Acceptance criteria: NLT 13.0% and NMT 29.5% of esters, calculated as geranyl tiglate ($C_{15}H_{24}O_2$)

SPECIFIC TESTS
- **ACID VALUE (ESSENTIAL OILS AND FLAVORS),** Appendix VI
  Sample: 5 g
  Analysis: Modify the procedure by using 15 mL of water, instead of alcohol, as diluent and by agitating the mixture thoroughly during the titration to keep the oil in suspension.
  Acceptance criteria: Between 1.5 and 9.5
- **ANGULAR ROTATION,** *Optical (Specific) Rotation,* Appendix IIB: Use a 100 mm tube.
  Acceptance criteria: Between −7° and −13°
- **ESTER VALUE AFTER ACETYLATION,** *Total Alcohols,* Appendix VI
  Sample: 1.9 g of the acetylated sample
  Analysis: Calculate the ester value after acetylation by the formula:

  $$Result = A \times 28.05/B$$

A = amount (mL) of 0.5 N alcoholic potassium hydroxide consumed in the saponification
B = weight (g) of acetylated sample oil
Acceptance criteria: Between 203 and 234
- **REFRACTIVE INDEX,** Appendix IIB
  [NOTE—Use an Abbé or other refractometer of equal or greater accuracy.]
  Acceptance criteria: Between 1.464 and 1.472 at 20°

- **SOLUBILITY IN ALCOHOL,** Appendix VI
  Acceptance criteria: One mL of the sample dissolves in 3 mL of 70% alcohol, but on further dilution with the alcohol, opalescence can occur, sometimes followed by separation of paraffin particles.
- **SPECIFIC GRAVITY:** Determine by any reliable method (see *General Provisions*).
  Acceptance criteria: Between 0.886 and 0.898

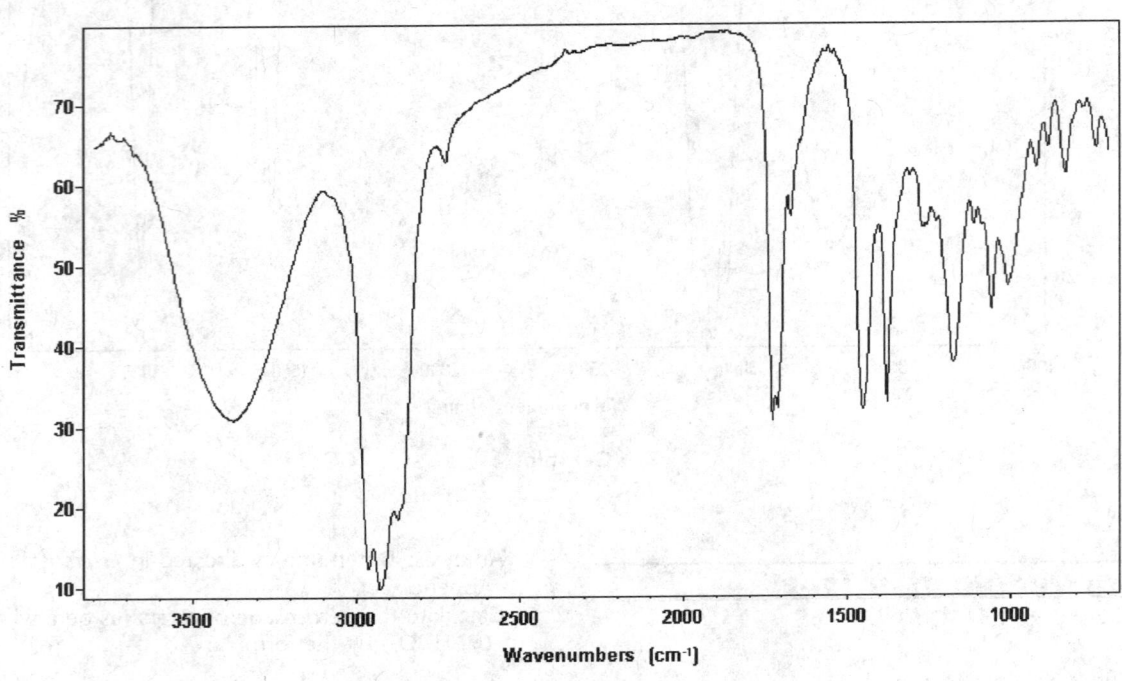

Geranium Oil, Algerian Type

Geranyl Acetate

First Published: Prior to FCC 6

3,7-Dimethyl-2,6-octadien-1-yl Acetate

$C_{12}H_{20}O_2$ Formula wt 196.29
FEMA: 2509
UNII: 3W81YG7P9R [geranyl acetate]

DESCRIPTION
Geranyl Acetate occurs as a colorless liquid.
Odor: Floral
Solubility: Soluble in alcohol, most fixed oils; slightly soluble in propylene glycol; insoluble or practically insoluble in glycerin, water
Boiling Point: ~245°
Solubility in Alcohol, Appendix VI: One mL dissolves in 9 mL of 70% alcohol.

Function: Flavoring agent

IDENTIFICATION
- **INFRARED SPECTRA,** *Spectrophotometric Identification Tests,* Appendix IIIC
  Acceptance criteria: The spectrum of the sample exhibits relative maxima at the same wavelengths as those of the spectrum below.

ASSAY
- **PROCEDURE:** Proceed as directed under *Esters,* Appendix VI.
  Sample: 1.0 g
  Analysis: Use 98.15 as the equivalence factor (e).
  Acceptance criteria: NLT 90.0% of total esters as $C_{12}H_{20}O_2$

SPECIFIC TESTS
- **REFRACTIVE INDEX,** Appendix II: At 20°
  Acceptance criteria: Between 1.458 and 1.464
- **SPECIFIC GRAVITY:** Determine at 25° by any reliable method (see *General Provisions*).
  Acceptance criteria: Between 0.900 and 0.914

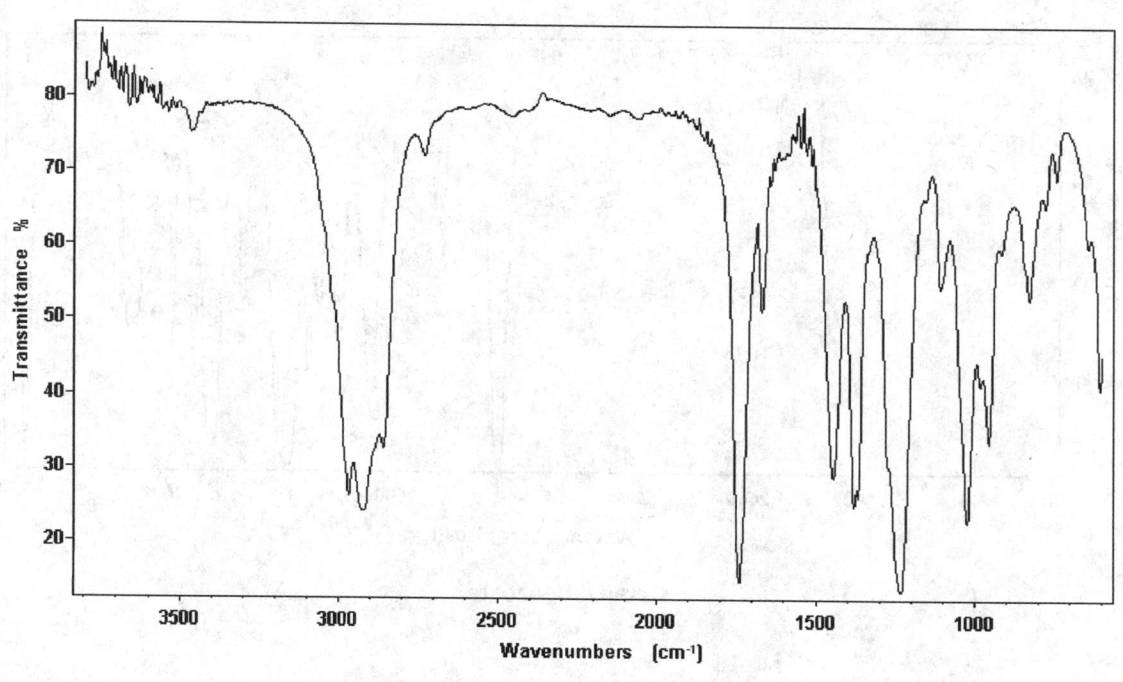

Geranyl Acetate

Geranyl Benzoate
First Published: Prior to FCC 6

3,7-Dimethyl-2,6-octadien-1-yl Benzoate

$C_{17}H_{22}O_2$ Formula wt 258.36
FEMA: 2511
UNII: B4M42WH83V [geranyl benzoate]

DESCRIPTION
Geranyl Benzoate occurs as a slightly yellow liquid.
Odor: Floral, resembling ylang-ylang oil
Solubility: Miscible in alcohol, chloroform; insoluble or practically insoluble in water
Boiling Point: ~305°
Solubility in Alcohol, Appendix VI: One mL dissolves in 4 mL of 90% alcohol to give a clear solution.
Function: Flavoring agent

IDENTIFICATION
- **INFRARED SPECTRA,** Spectrophotometric Identification Tests, Appendix IIIC

Acceptance criteria: The spectrum of the sample exhibits relative maxima at the same wavelengths as those of the spectrum below.

ASSAY
- **PROCEDURE:** Proceed as directed under Esters, Appendix VI.
  Sample: 1.5 g
  Analysis: Use 129.2 as the equivalence factor (e).
  Acceptance criteria: NLT 95.0% of total esters as $C_{17}H_{22}O_2$

SPECIFIC TESTS
- **ACID VALUE, FLAVOR CHEMICALS (OTHER THAN ESSENTIAL OILS),** M-15, Appendix XI
  Acceptance criteria: NMT 1.0
- **REFRACTIVE INDEX,** Appendix II: At 20°
  Acceptance criteria: Between 1.516 and 1.521
- **SPECIFIC GRAVITY:** Determine at 25° by any reliable method (see General Provisions).
  Acceptance criteria: Between 0.983 and 0.989

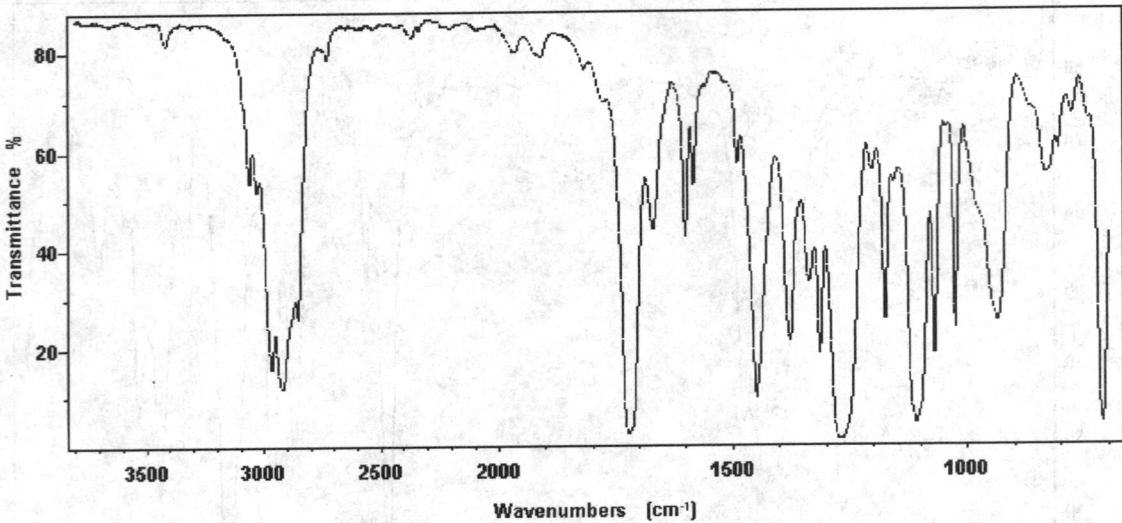

Geranyl Benzoate

Geranyl Butyrate

First Published: Prior to FCC 6

3,7-Dimethyl-2,6-octadien-1-yl Butyrate

$C_{14}H_{24}O_2$ Formula wt 224.34
FEMA: 2512
UNII: 69AVH8L7KL [geranyl butyrate]

DESCRIPTION
Geranyl Butyrate occurs as a colorless to pale yellow liquid.
Odor: Fruity, rose
Solubility: Soluble in alcohol, most fixed oils; insoluble or practically insoluble in glycerin, propylene glycol, water
Boiling Point: ~253°
Solubility in Alcohol, Appendix VI: One mL dissolves in 6 mL of 80% alcohol.
Function: Flavoring agent

IDENTIFICATION
- **INFRARED SPECTRA,** Spectrophotometric Identification Tests, Appendix IIIC

  Acceptance criteria: The spectrum of the sample exhibits relative maxima at the same wavelengths as those of the spectrum below.

ASSAY
- **PROCEDURE:** Proceed as directed under Esters, Appendix VI.
  Sample: 1.0 g
  Analysis: Use 112.2 as the equivalence factor (e).
  Acceptance criteria: NLT 92.0% of total esters as $C_{14}H_{24}O_2$

SPECIFIC TESTS
- **ACID VALUE, FLAVOR CHEMICALS (OTHER THAN ESSENTIAL OILS),** M-15, Appendix XI
  Acceptance criteria: NMT 1.0
- **REFRACTIVE INDEX,** Appendix II: At 20°
  Acceptance criteria: Between 1.455 and 1.462
- **SPECIFIC GRAVITY:** Determine at 25° by any reliable method (see General Provisions).
  Acceptance criteria: Between 0.889 and 0.904

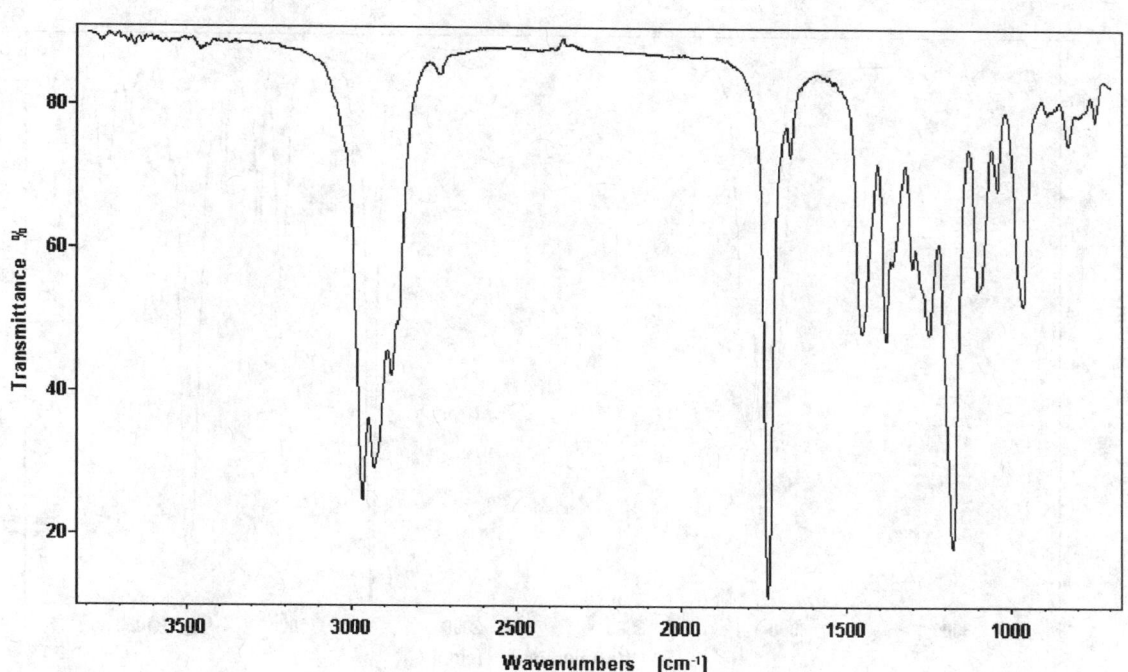

Geranyl Butyrate

Geranyl Formate
First Published: Prior to FCC 6

3,7-Dimethyl-2,6-octadien-1-yl Formate

$C_{11}H_{18}O_2$ Formula wt 182.26
FEMA: 2514
UNII: 72O586X6ZI [geranyl formate]

DESCRIPTION
Geranyl Formate occurs as a colorless to pale yellow liquid.
Odor: Fresh, leafy, rose
Solubility: Soluble in alcohol, most fixed oils; insoluble or practically insoluble in glycerin, propylene glycol, water
Boiling Point: ~216°
Solubility in Alcohol, Appendix VI: One mL dissolves in 3 mL of 80% alcohol.
Function: Flavoring agent

IDENTIFICATION
- **INFRARED SPECTRA,** Spectrophotometric Identification Tests, Appendix IIIC

  Acceptance criteria: The spectrum of the sample exhibits relative maxima at the same wavelengths as those of the spectrum below.

ASSAY
- **PROCEDURE:** Proceed as directed under Esters, Appendix VI.
  Sample: 1.0 g
  Analysis: Use 91.13 as the equivalence factor (e).
  Acceptance criteria: NLT 85.0% of total esters as $C_{11}H_{18}O_2$

SPECIFIC TESTS
- **ACID VALUE (ESSENTIAL OILS AND FLAVORS),** Appendix VI
  Acceptance criteria: NMT 3.0
- **REFRACTIVE INDEX,** Appendix II: At 20°
  Acceptance criteria: Between 1.457 and 1.466
- **SPECIFIC GRAVITY:** Determine at 25° by any reliable method (see General Provisions).
  Acceptance criteria: Between 0.906 and 0.920

488 / Geranyl Formate / *Monographs*

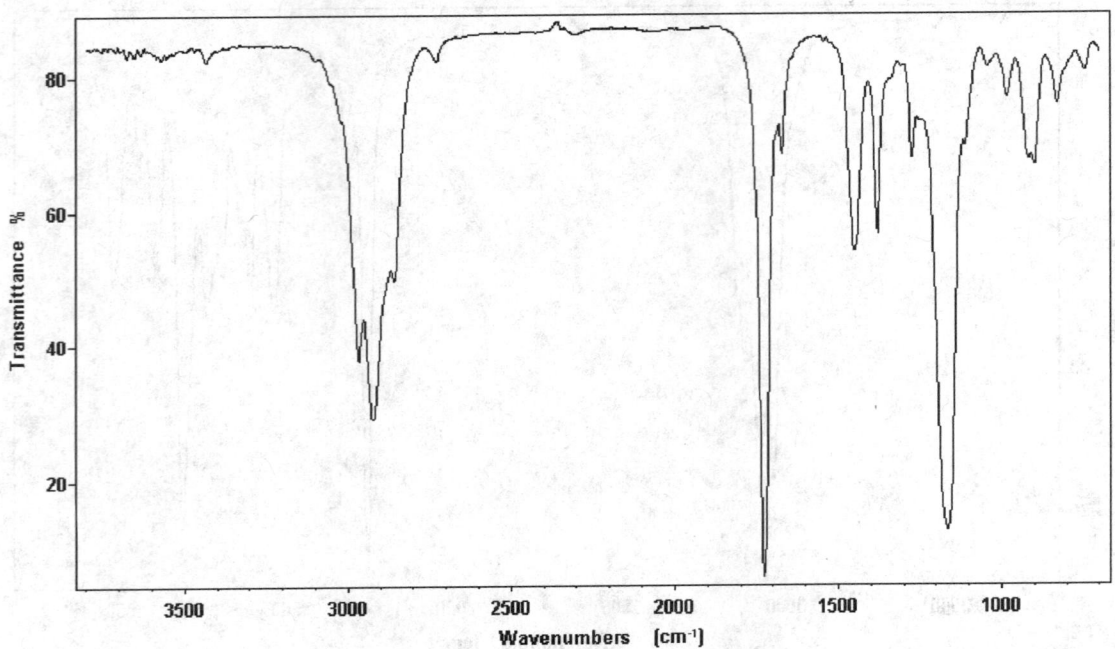

Geranyl Formate

Geranyl Isovalerate
First Published: Prior to FCC 6

$C_{15}H_{26}O_2$ Formula wt 238.37
FEMA: 2518
UNII: OPO8694RK3 [geranyl isovalerate]

DESCRIPTION
Geranyl Isovalerate occurs as a colorless to pale yellow liquid.
Odor: Rose
Solubility: Soluble in propylene glycol, vegetable oils; insoluble or practically insoluble in water
Boiling Point: ~279°
Solubility in Alcohol, Appendix VI: One mL dissolves in 1 mL of 95% ethanol.
Function: Flavoring agent

IDENTIFICATION
- **INFRARED SPECTRA,** *Spectrophotometric Identification Tests,* Appendix IIIC
  Acceptance criteria: The spectrum of the sample exhibits relative maxima at the same wavelengths as those of the spectrum below.

ASSAY
- **PROCEDURE:** Proceed as directed under *M-1b,* Appendix XI
  Acceptance criteria: NLT 95.0% of $C_{15}H_{26}O_2$ (sum of neryl and geranyl isomers)

SPECIFIC TESTS
- **ACID VALUE, FLAVOR CHEMICALS (OTHER THAN ESSENTIAL OILS),** *M-15,* Appendix XI
  Acceptance criteria: NMT 1.0
- **REFRACTIVE INDEX,** Appendix II: At 20°
  Acceptance criteria: Between 1.452 and 1.462
- **SPECIFIC GRAVITY:** Determine at 25° by any reliable method (see *General Provisions*).
  Acceptance criteria: Between 0.881 and 0.894

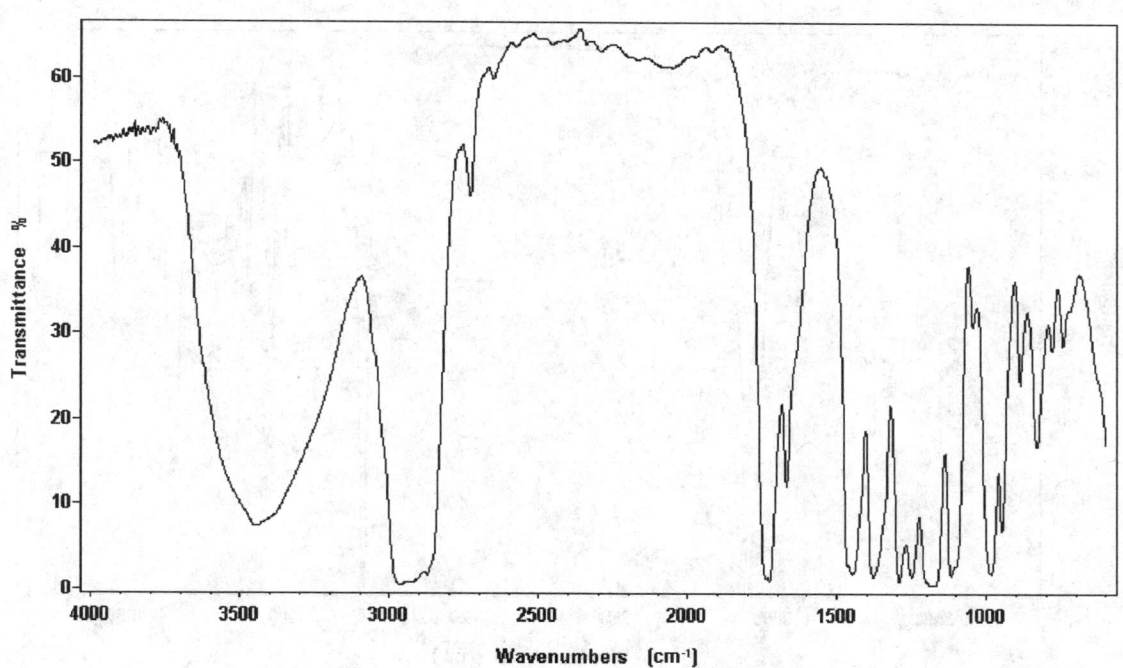

Geranyl Isovalerate

Geranyl Phenylacetate

First Published: Prior to FCC 6

3,7-Dimethyl-2,6-octadien-1-yl Phenylacetate

$C_{18}H_{24}O_2$ Formula wt 272.39
FEMA: 2516
UNII: 62A4GG7D57 [geranyl phenylacetate]

DESCRIPTION
Geranyl Phenylacetate occurs as a yellow liquid.
Odor: Honey-rose
Solubility: Miscible in alcohol, chloroform, ether; insoluble or practically insoluble in water
Boiling Point: ~278°
Solubility in Alcohol, Appendix VI: One mL dissolves in 4 mL of 90% alcohol to give a clear solution.
Function: Flavoring agent

IDENTIFICATION
- **INFRARED SPECTRA,** Spectrophotometric Identification Tests, Appendix IIIC
  Acceptance criteria: The spectrum of the sample exhibits relative maxima at the same wavelengths as those of the spectrum below.

ASSAY
- **PROCEDURE:** Proceed as directed under Esters, Appendix VI.
  Sample: 1.6 g
  Analysis: Use 136.2 as the equivalence factor (e).
  Acceptance criteria: NLT 97.0% of total esters as $C_{18}H_{24}O_2$

SPECIFIC TESTS
- **ACID VALUE, FLAVOR CHEMICALS (OTHER THAN ESSENTIAL OILS),** M-15, Appendix XI
  Acceptance criteria: NMT 2.0
- **REFRACTIVE INDEX,** Appendix II: At 20°
  Acceptance criteria: Between 1.506 and 1.511
- **SPECIFIC GRAVITY:** Determine at 25° by any reliable method (see General Provisions).
  Acceptance criteria: Between 0.971 and 0.978

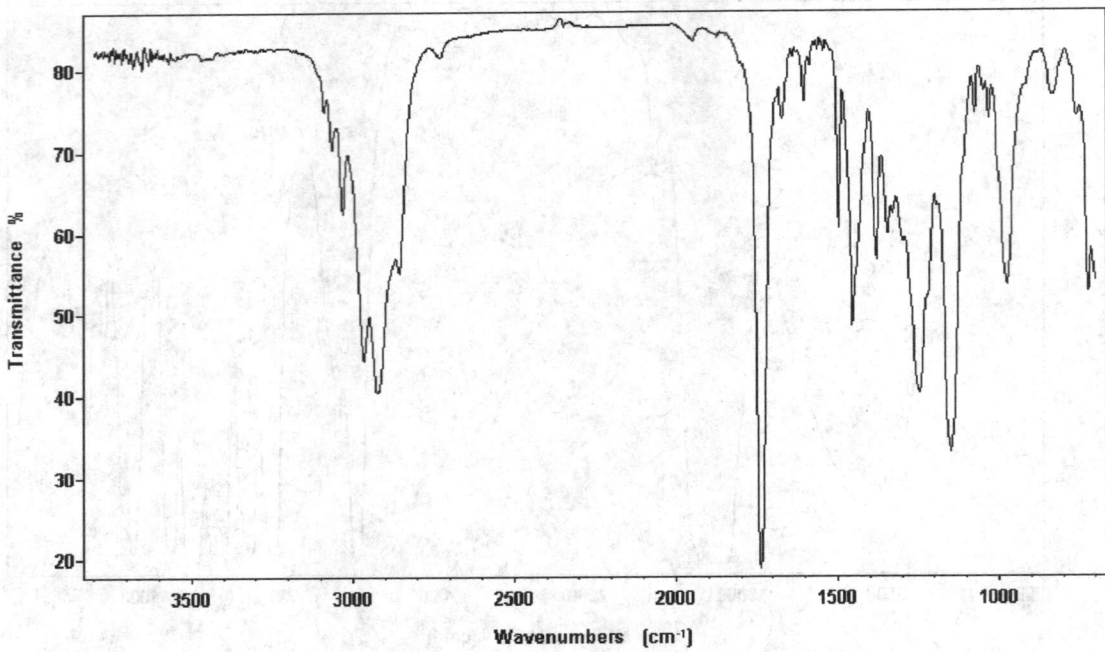

Geranyl Phenylacetate

Geranyl Propionate

First Published: Prior to FCC 6

3,7-Dimethyl-2,6-octadien-1-yl Propionate

$C_{13}H_{22}O_2$ Formula wt 210.32
FEMA: 2517
UNII: U9F1RPB24G [geranyl propionate]

DESCRIPTION
Geranyl Propionate occurs as a colorless liquid.
Odor: Rosy, fruity
Solubility: Soluble in alcohol, most fixed oils; insoluble or practically insoluble in glycerin, propylene glycol, water
Boiling Point: ~253°
Solubility in Alcohol, Appendix VI: One mL dissolves in 4 mL of 80% alcohol.
Function: Flavoring agent

IDENTIFICATION
- **INFRARED SPECTRA,** Spectrophotometric Identification Tests, Appendix IIIC

  Acceptance criteria: The spectrum of the sample exhibits relative maxima at the same wavelengths as those of the spectrum below.

ASSAY
- **PROCEDURE:** Proceed as directed under *Esters*, Appendix VI.
  Sample: 1.6 g
  Analysis: Use 105.2 as the equivalence factor (e).
  Acceptance criteria: NLT 92.0% of total esters as $C_{13}H_{22}O_2$

SPECIFIC TESTS
- **ACID VALUE, FLAVOR CHEMICALS (OTHER THAN ESSENTIAL OILS),** *M-15,* Appendix XI
  Acceptance criteria: NMT 1.0
- **REFRACTIVE INDEX,** Appendix II: At 20°
  Acceptance criteria: Between 1.456 and 1.464
- **SPECIFIC GRAVITY:** Determine at 25° by any reliable method (see *General Provisions*).
  Acceptance criteria: Between 0.896 and 0.913

Geranyl Propionate

Gibberellic Acid

First Published: Prior to FCC 6

2,4α,7-Trihydroxy-1-methyl-8-methylenegibb-3-ene-1,10-dicarboxylic Acid 1,4-α-Lactone

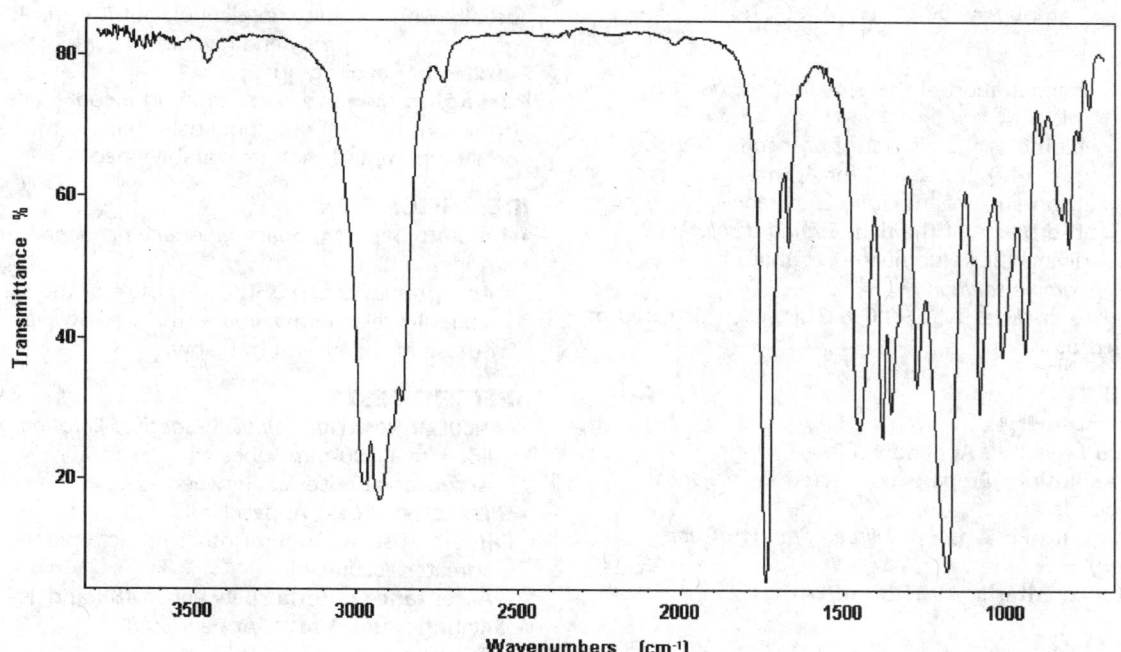

C₁₉H₂₂O₆
Formula wt 346.38
CAS: [77-06-5]

UNII: BU0A7MWB6L [gibberellic acid]

DESCRIPTION
Gibberellic Acid occurs as a white to pale yellow, crystalline powder. It melts at about 234°. It is slightly soluble in water and is soluble in alcohol and in acetone.

Function: Enzyme activator

Packaging and Storage: Store in well-closed containers.

IDENTIFICATION
- **Procedure**

  Analysis: Dissolve a few mg of sample in 2 mL of sulfuric acid.

  Acceptance criteria: A red solution having a green fluorescence forms.

ASSAY
- **Procedure**

  Standard solution: Transfer an accurately weighed quantity of gibberellic acid containing NLT 90% of total gibberellins as gibberellic acid (USP, or equivalent), equivalent to about 25 mg of pure gibberellic acid, in 50 mL methanol, and mix.

  Sample stock solution: 0.80 mg/mL in methanol

  Sample solution: 0.08 mg/mL in methanol: from *Sample stock solution*

  Analysis: Transfer 5.0 mL of the *Sample solution* into a 25- × 200-mm glass-stoppered tube, and transfer 4.0- and 5.0-mL portions of the *Standard solution* into separate, similar tubes. Place the tubes in a boiling water bath, evaporate to dryness, and then dry in an oven at 90° for 10 min. Remove the tubes from the oven, stopper, and allow to cool to room temperature. Dissolve the residue in each tube in 10.0 mL of 8:10 sulfuric acid, heat in a boiling water bath for 10 min, and then cool in a 10° water bath for 5 min. Determine the absorbance of the solutions in 1-cm cells at 535 nm with a suitable spectrophotometer, using dilute sulfuric acid as the blank. [Note—Note the absorbances of the two solutions prepared from the 4.0- and 5.0-mL aliquots of the *Standard solution* and use the nearest one to the solution prepared with the *Sample solution*,

for the calculation below.] Calculate the quantity (mg) of $C_{19}H_{22}O_6$ in the sample taken by the formula:

$$\text{Result} = 500C \times (V/5) \times (A_U/A_S)$$

C = concentration of the *Standard solution* (mg/mL)
V = volume of the aliquot of *Standard solution* used (4.0 or 5.0 mL) for A_S (mL)
A_U = absorbance of the *Sample solution*
A_S = absorbance of the final *Standard solution* giving the value nearest to that of the *Sample solution*

Acceptance criteria: NLT 90.0% $C_{19}H_{22}O_6$, calculated on the dried basis

IMPURITIES
Inorganic Impurities
- **LEAD,** *Lead Limit Test,* Appendix IIIB
  Sample solution: Prepare as directed for organic compounds.
  Control: 5 µg Pb (5 mL of *Diluted Standard Lead Solution*)
  Acceptance criteria: NMT 5 mg/kg

SPECIFIC TESTS
- **LOSS ON DRYING,** Appendix IIC: 100° for 7 h in vacuum
  Acceptance criteria: NMT 3.0%
- **OPTICAL (SPECIFIC) ROTATION,** Appendix IIB
  Sample solution: 100 mg/mL in alcohol. [NOTE—Do not use heat in preparing the solution.]
  Acceptance criteria: $[\alpha]_D^{20}$ between +75.0° and +90.0°, calculated on the dried basis

Ginger Oil

First Published: Prior to FCC 6

CAS: [8007-08-7]

UNII: SAS9Z1SVUK [ginger oil]

DESCRIPTION
Ginger Oil occurs as a light yellow to yellow liquid with the aromatic, characteristic odor of ginger. It is the volatile oil obtained by steam distillation of the dried ground rhizome of *Zingiber officianale*, Roscoe (Fam. Zingiberaceae). It is soluble in most fixed oils and in mineral oil. It is soluble, usually with turbidity, in alcohol, but it is insoluble in glycerin and in propylene glycol.

Function: Flavoring agent

Packaging and Storage: Store in a cool place protected from light in full, tight containers that are made from steel or aluminum and that are suitably lined.

IDENTIFICATION
- **INFRARED SPECTRA,** *Spectrophotometric Identification Tests,* Appendix IIIC
  Acceptance criteria: The spectrum of the sample exhibits relative maxima at the same wavelengths as those of the spectrum below.

SPECIFIC TESTS
- **ANGULAR ROTATION,** *Optical (Specific) Rotation,* Appendix IIB: Use a 100-mm tube.
  Acceptance criteria: Between −28° and −47°
- **REFRACTIVE INDEX,** Appendix IIB
  [NOTE—Use an Abbé or other refractometer of equal or greater accuracy.]
  Acceptance criteria: Between 1.488 and 1.494 at 20°
- **SAPONIFICATION VALUE,** Appendix VI
  Sample: 5 g
  Acceptance criteria: NMT 20
- **SPECIFIC GRAVITY:** Determine by any reliable method (see *General Provisions*).
  Acceptance criteria: Between 0.870 and 0.882

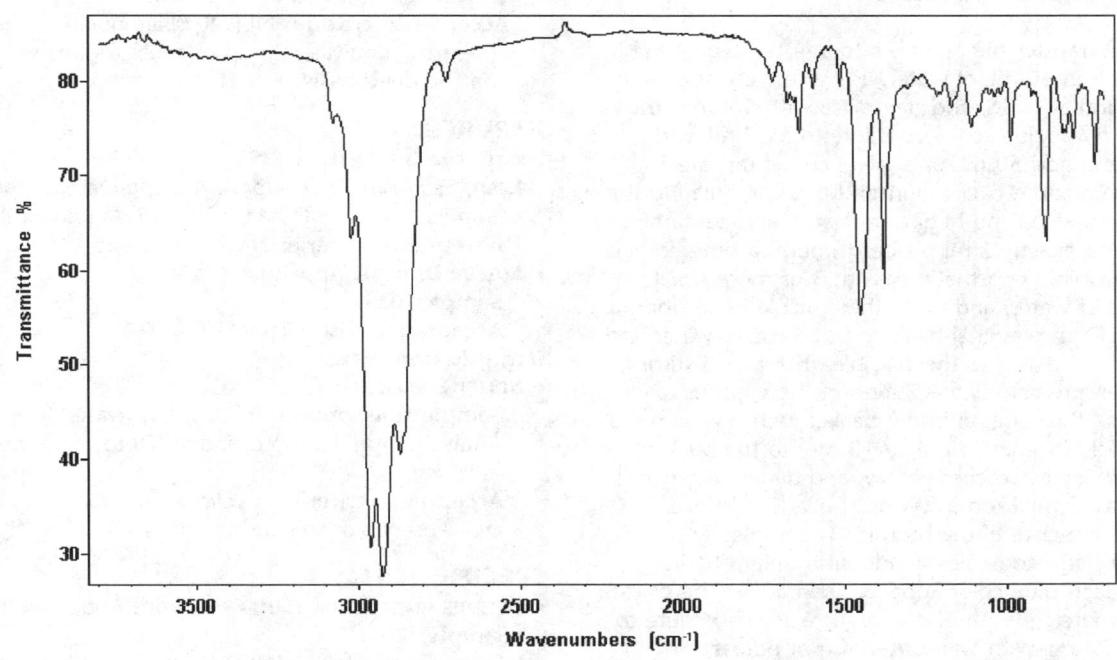

Ginger Oil

Glucono delta-Lactone

First Published: Prior to FCC 6

C₆H₁₀O₆   Formula wt 178.14
INS: 575   CAS: [90-80-2]
UNII: WQ29KQ9POT [gluconolactone]

DESCRIPTION
Glucono delta-Lactone occurs as a fine, white, crystalline powder. It is freely soluble in water and is sparingly soluble in alcohol. It decomposes at about 153°.
Function: Acidifier; leavening agent; sequestrant
Packaging and Storage: Store in well-closed containers.

IDENTIFICATION
- **THIN-LAYER CHROMATOGRAPHY,** Appendix IIA
  Sample solution: 10 mg/mL
  Standard solution: 10 mg/mL USP Potassium Gluconate RS
  [NOTE—The *Sample solution* and the *Standard solution* can be heated at 60° if necessary to aid in dissolution.]
  Adsorbent: 0.25-mm layer of chromatographic silica gel
  Application volume: 5 µL
  Developing solvent system: Ethanol, ethyl acetate, water, and ammonium hydroxide (5:1:3:1)
  Spray reagent: Dissolve 2.5 g of ammonium molybdate in 50 mL of 2 N sulfuric acid in a 100-mL volumetric flask, add 1.0 g of ceric sulfate, swirl to dissolve, dilute to volume with 2 N sulfuric acid, and mix.
  Analysis: Following development, dry the plate at 110° for 20 min, and allow to cool. Spray the cooled plate with the *Spray reagent*. After spraying, heat the plate at 110° for about 10 minutes.
  Acceptance criteria: The principal spot obtained from the *Sample solution* corresponds in color, size, and R_f value to that obtained from the *Standard Solution*.

ASSAY
- **PROCEDURE**
  Sample: 600 mg
  Analysis: Dissolve the *Sample* in 100 mL of water in a 300-mL Erlenmeyer flask, add 50.0 mL of 0.1 N sodium hydroxide, and allow to stand for 15 min. Add phenolphthalein TS and titrate the excess alkali with 0.1 N hydrochloric acid. Perform a blank determination (see *General Provisions*). Each mL of 0.1 N hydrochloric acid is equivalent to 17.81 mg of C₆H₁₀O₆.
  Acceptance criteria: NLT 99.0% and NMT 100.5% C₆H₁₀O₆.

IMPURITIES
Inorganic Impurities
- **LEAD,** Appendix IIIB
  Sample solution: Prepare as directed for organic compounds
  Control: 4 µg Pb (4 mL of *Diluted Standard Lead Solution*)
  Acceptance criteria: NMT 4 mg/kg

Organic Impurities
- **REDUCING SUBSTANCES (AS D-GLUCOSE)**
  Sample: 10.0 g
  Analysis: Transfer the *Sample* into a 400-mL beaker, dissolve it in 40 mL of water, add a few drops of phenolphthalein TS, and neutralize with 500 mg/mL sodium hydroxide solution. Dilute to 50.0 mL with water, and add 50 mL of alkaline cupric tartrate TS. Heat the mixture over a Bunsen burner, regulating the flame so that boiling begins in 4 min, and continue the boiling for exactly 2 min. Filter through a sintered-glass filter crucible, wash the filter with 3 or more small portions of water, and place the crucible in an upright position in the original beaker. Add 5 mL of water and 3 mL of nitric acid to the crucible, mix with a stirring rod to ensure complete solution of the cuprous oxide, and wash the solution into a beaker with several mL of water. Add bromine TS (5 to 10 mL) to the beaker until the color becomes yellow, and dilute with water to about 75 mL. Add a few glass beads, boil over a Bunsen burner until the bromine is completely removed, and cool. Slowly add ammonium hydroxide until a deep blue color appears, then adjust the pH to approximately 4 with glacial acetic acid, and dilute to about 100 mL with water. Add 4 g of potassium iodide, and titrate with 0.1 N sodium thiosulfate, adding starch TS just before the endpoint is reached.
  Acceptance criteria: NMT 16.1 mL of 0.1 N sodium thiosulfate is required in the titration. (NMT 0.5%)

Glucose Syrup

First Published: Prior to FCC 6

Corn Syrup
UNII: 9G5L16BK6N [corn syrup]

DESCRIPTION
Glucose Syrup occurs as a clear, white to light yellow, viscous liquid. It is a clarified, concentrated, aqueous solution of saccharides obtained by the partial hydrolysis of edible starch by food-grade acids and/or enzymes. Depending on the degree of hydrolysis, it contains varying amounts of D-glucose. When obtained from corn starch, it is commonly designated as corn syrup. It is miscible in all proportions with water.
Function: Nutritive sweetener
Packaging and Storage: Store in tightly closed containers in a dry place.

IDENTIFICATION
- **PROCEDURE**
  Sample solution: 50 mg/mL
  Analysis: Add a few drops of the *Sample solution* in 5 mL of hot alkaline cupric tartrate TS
  Acceptance criteria: A red precipitate of cuprous oxide forms.

ASSAY
- **REDUCING SUGARS ASSAY,** Appendix X
  Acceptance criteria: NLT 20.0% reducing sugar content (dextrose equivalent) expressed as D-glucose, calculated on the dried basis

IMPURITIES
Inorganic Impurities
- **LEAD,** *Lead Limit Test, Atomic Absorption Spectrophotometric Graphite Furnace Method, Method I,* Appendix IIIB
  Acceptance criteria: NMT 0.1 mg/kg
- **SULFUR DIOXIDE,** Appendix X
  Sample: 35 g
  Acceptance criteria: NMT 0.004%

Organic Impurities
- **SOLUBLE STARCH**
  Sample solution: 1 g in 10 mL of water
  Analysis: Add 1 drop of iodine TS to the *Sample solution*.
  Acceptance criteria: A yellow color forms, indicating the absence of soluble starch.

SPECIFIC TESTS
- **RESIDUE ON IGNITION (SULFATED ASH),** Appendix IIC
  Sample: 20 g
  Acceptance criteria: NMT 0.5%
- **TOTAL SOLIDS,** *Glucose Syrup (Corn Syrup),* Appendix X
  Analysis: Determine the refractive index of a sample at 20° or 45°. Use the appropriate table to determine *Total Solids*.
  Acceptance criteria: NLT 70.0%

OTHER REQUIREMENTS
- **LABELING:** Indicate the presence of sulfur dioxide if the residual concentration is greater than 10 mg/kg.

Glucose Syrup, Dried

First Published: Prior to FCC 6

Dried Glucose Syrup
Glucose Syrup Solids
UNII: 9G5L16BK6N [corn syrup]

DESCRIPTION
Glucose Syrup, Dried, occurs as a white to light yellow powder or granules. It is a purified, concentrated mixture of nutritive saccharides obtained by the hydrolysis of edible starch and by partially drying the resulting solution (glucose syrup). When obtained from corn starch, it is commonly designated dried corn syrup or corn syrup solids. Depending on the degree of hydrolysis, it contains varying amounts of D-glucose. It is soluble in water.
Function: Nutritive sweetener
Packaging and Storage: Store in tightly closed containers in a dry environment.

IDENTIFICATION
- **PROCEDURE**
  Sample solution: 50 mg/mL

Analysis: Add a few drops of the *Sample solution* in 5 mL of hot alkaline cupric tartrate TS.
Acceptance criteria: A red precipitate of cuprous oxide forms.

ASSAY
- **REDUCING SUGARS ASSAY,** Appendix X
  Acceptance criteria: NLT 20.0% reducing sugar content (dextrose equivalent) expressed as D-glucose, calculated on the dried basis

IMPURITIES
Inorganic Impurities
- **LEAD,** *Lead Limit Test, Atomic Absorption Spectrophotometric Graphite Furnace Method, Method I,* Appendix IIIB
  Acceptance criteria: NMT 0.1 mg/kg
- **SULFUR DIOXIDE,** Appendix X
  Sample: 25 g
  Acceptance criteria: NMT 0.004%

Organic Impurities
- **SOLUBLE STARCH**
  Sample solution: 1 g in 10 mL of water
  Analysis: Add 1 drop of iodine TS to the *Sample solution*.
  Acceptance criteria: A yellow color forms, indicating the absence of soluble starch.

SPECIFIC TESTS
- **RESIDUE ON IGNITION (SULFATED ASH),** Appendix IIC
  Sample: 1 g
  Analysis: Ignite the *Sample* at 525° for 2 h.
  Acceptance criteria: NMT 0.5%
- **TOTAL SOLIDS,** *Water Determination,* Appendix IIB
  Analysis: Determine the water content of a sample as directed. Calculate the percent *Total Solids* by the formula:

  $$\text{Result} = 100(W_U - W_W)/W_U$$

  W_U = weight (mg) of the sample taken
  W_W = weight (mg) of water determined
  Acceptance criteria: NLT 90% when the reducing sugar content is 88% or greater; NLT 93% when the reducing sugar content is between 20.0% and 88.0%

OTHER REQUIREMENTS
- **LABELING:** Indicate the presence of sulfur dioxide if the residual concentration is greater than 10 mg/kg.

L-Glutamic Acid

First Published: Prior to FCC 6
Last Revision: FCC 6

Glutamic Acid
L-2-Aminopentanedioic Acid

$C_5H_9NO_4$　　　　　Formula wt 147.13
INS: 620
UNII: 3KX376GY7L [glutamic acid]　　CAS: [56-86-0]

DESCRIPTION
L-Glutamic Acid occurs as a white, free-flowing, crystalline powder. It is slightly soluble in water, forming acidic solutions. The pH of a saturated solution is about 3.2.
Function: Salt substitute; nutrient
Packaging and Storage: Store in well-closed containers.

IDENTIFICATION
- **INFRARED ABSORPTION,** *Spectrophotometric Identification Tests,* Appendix IIIC
  Reference standard: USP Glutamic Acid RS
  Sample and standard preparation: M
  Acceptance criteria: The spectrum of the sample exhibits maxima at the same wavelengths as those in the spectrum of the *Reference standard*.

ASSAY
- **PROCEDURE**
  Sample: 200 mg
  Analysis: Dissolve the *Sample* in 3 mL of formic acid and 50 mL of glacial acetic acid. Add 2 drops of crystal violet TS, and titrate with 0.1 N perchloric acid to a green endpoint or until the blue color disappears completely. [**CAUTION**—Handle perchloric acid in an appropriate fume hood.] Perform a blank determination (see *General Provisions*), and make any necessary correction. Each mL of 0.1 N perchloric acid is equivalent to 14.71 mg of $C_5H_9NO_4$.
  Acceptance criteria: NLT 98.5% and NMT 101.5% of $C_5H_9NO_4$, calculated on the dried basis

IMPURITIES
Inorganic Impurities
- **LEAD,** *Lead Limit Test,* Appendix IIIB
  Sample solution: Prepare as directed for organic compounds.
  Control: 5 µg Pb (5 mL of *Diluted Standard Lead Solution*)
  Acceptance criteria: NMT 5 mg/kg

SPECIFIC TESTS
- **LOSS ON DRYING,** Appendix IIC: 105° for 3 h
  Acceptance criteria: NMT 0.1%
- **OPTICAL (SPECIFIC) ROTATION,** Appendix IIB
  Sample: 10 g, previously dried
  Analysis: Dissolve the *Sample* in sufficient 2 N hydrochloric acid to make 100 mL.
  Acceptance criteria: $[\alpha]_D^{20}$ between +31.5° and +32.5°, on the dried basis
- **RESIDUE ON IGNITION (SULFATED ASH),** Appendix IIC
  Sample: 1 g
  Acceptance criteria: NMT 0.3%

L-Glutamic Acid Hydrochloride

First Published: Prior to FCC 6

2-Aminopentanedioic Acid Hydrochloride

$C_5H_9NO_4 \cdot HCl$ Formula wt 183.59
                                          CAS: [138-15-8]
UNII: M0C2SP444T [glutamic acid hydrochloride]

DESCRIPTION
L-Glutamic Acid Hydrochloride occurs as a white, crystalline powder. One g dissolves in about 3 mL of water. It is almost insoluble in alcohol and in ether. Its solutions are acid to litmus.
Function: Salt substitute; flavoring agent; nutrient
Packaging and Storage: Store in well-closed, light-resistant containers.

IDENTIFICATION
- **INFRARED SPECTRA,** *Spectrophotometric Identification Tests,* Appendix IIIC
  Acceptance criteria: The spectrum of the sample exhibits relative maxima at the same wavelengths as those of the spectrum below.

ASSAY
- **PROCEDURE**
  Sample: 100 mg, previously dried
  Analysis: Dissolve the *Sample* in 0.5 mL of water, add 15.0 mL of 0.1 N perchloric acid, and heat on a water bath for 30 min. After cooling, add 45 mL of glacial acetic acid, and titrate the excess perchloric acid with 0.1 N sodium acetate, determining the endpoint potentiometrically. [**CAUTION**—Handle perchloric acid in an appropriate fume hood.] Perform a blank determination (see *General Provisions*), and make any necessary correction. Each mL of 0.1 N perchloric acid is equivalent to 18.36 mg of $C_5H_9NO_4 \cdot HCl$.
  Acceptance criteria: NLT 98.5% and NMT 101.5% $C_5H_9NO_4 \cdot HCl$, on the dried basis

IMPURITIES
Inorganic Impurities
- **LEAD,** *Lead Limit Test,* Appendix IIIB,
  Sample solution: Prepare as directed for organic compounds.
  Control: 5 µg Pb (5 mL of *Diluted Standard Lead Solution*)
  Acceptance criteria: NMT 5 mg/kg

SPECIFIC TESTS
- **LOSS ON DRYING,** Appendix IIC: 80° for 4 h
  Acceptance criteria: NMT 0.5%
- **OPTICAL (SPECIFIC) ROTATION,** Appendix IIB
  Sample solution: 10 g of sample in sufficient 2 N hydrochloric acid to make 100 mL
  Acceptance criteria: $[\alpha]_D^{20}$ between +25.2° and +25.8°, calculated on the dried basis
- **RESIDUE ON IGNITION (SULFATED ASH),** Appendix IIC
  Sample: 1g
  Acceptance criteria: NMT 0.25%

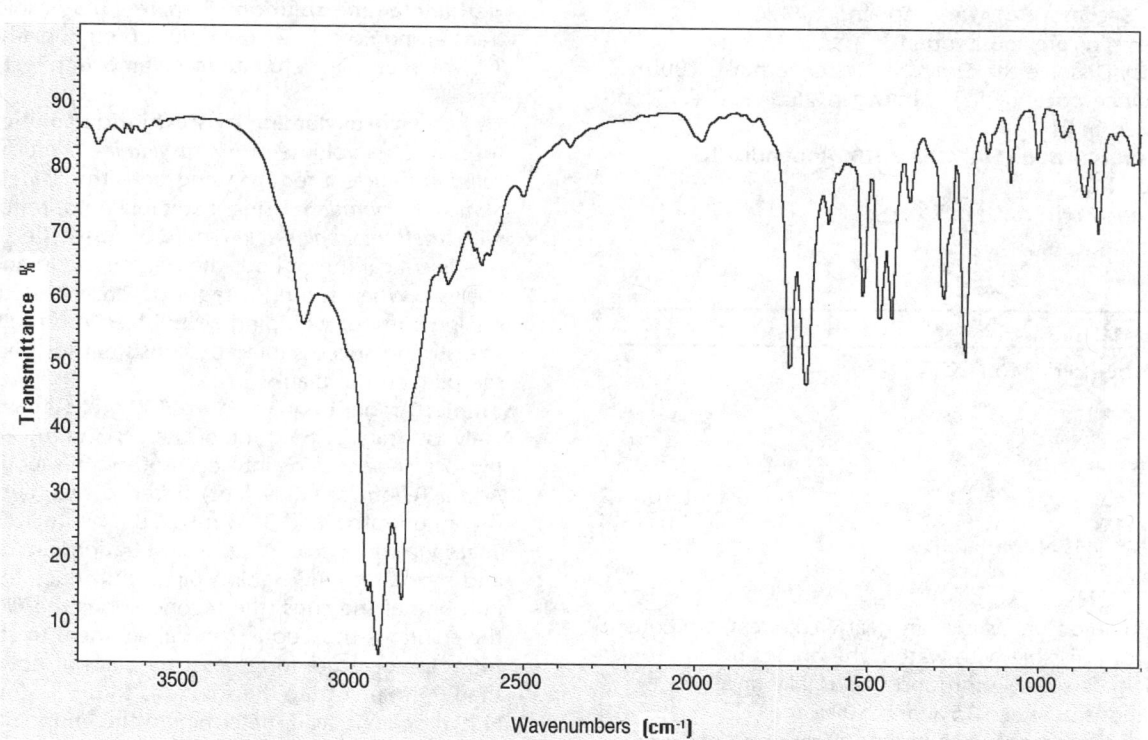

L-Glutamic Acid Hydrochloride

L-Glutamine

First Published: Prior to FCC 6
Last Revision: FCC 6

L-2-Aminoglutaramic Acid

$C_5H_{10}N_2O_3$

Formula wt 146.15
CAS: [56-85-9]

UNII: 0RH81L854J [glutamine]

DESCRIPTION

L-Glutamine occurs as white crystals or a crystalline powder. It is soluble in water and practically insoluble in alcohol and in ether. Its solutions are acid to litmus. It melts with decomposition at about 185°.
Function: Nutrient
Packaging and Storage: Store in well-closed, light-resistant containers.

IDENTIFICATION

- **INFRARED ABSORPTION,** *Spectrophotometric Identification Tests,* Appendix IIIC
  Reference standard: USP Glutamine RS
  Sample and standard preparation: *K*
  Acceptance criteria: The spectrum of the sample exhibits maxima at the same wavelengths as those in the spectrum of the *Reference standard*.

ASSAY

- **PROCEDURE**
  Sample: 150 mg, previously dried
  Analysis: Dissolve the *Sample* in 3 mL of formic acid and 50 mL of glacial acetic acid. Titrate with 0.1 N perchloric acid, determining the endpoint potentiometrically. [**CAUTION**—Handle perchloric acid in an appropriate fume hood.] Perform a blank determination (see *General Provisions*), and make any necessary correction. Each mL of 0.1 N perchloric acid is equivalent to 14.62 mg of $C_5H_{10}N_2O_3$.
  Acceptance criteria: NLT 98.5% and NMT 101.5% $C_5H_{10}N_2O_3$, on the dried basis

IMPURITIES
Inorganic Impurities

- **LEAD,** *Lead Limit Test,* Appendix IIIB
  Sample solution: Prepare as directed for organic compounds.
  Control: 5 μg Pb (5 mL of *Diluted Standard Lead Solution*)
  Acceptance criteria: NMT 5 mg/kg

SPECIFIC TESTS

- **LOSS ON DRYING,** Appendix IIC: 105° for 3 h
  Acceptance criteria: NMT 0.3%

- **OPTICAL (SPECIFIC) ROTATION**, Appendix IIB
  Sample: 4 g, previously dried
  Analysis: Dissolve the *Sample* in water to make 100 mL.
  Acceptance criteria: $[\alpha]_D^{20}$ between +6.3° and +7.3°, on the dried basis
- **RESIDUE ON IGNITION (SULFATED ASH)**, Appendix IIC
  Sample: 1 g
  Acceptance criteria: NMT 0.1%

Glutaraldehyde

First Published: Prior to FCC 6

Glutaral
1,5-Pentanedial

$C_5H_8O_2$ Formula wt 100.12
                              CAS: [111-30-8]

UNII: T3C89M417N [glutaral]

DESCRIPTION
Glutaraldehyde occurs as a clear, nearly colorless, aqueous solution. It is miscible with water. The grades of Glutaraldehyde suitable for food use usually have concentrations between 15% and 50%.
Function: Fixing agent in the immobilization of enzyme preparations; cross-linking agent for microencapsulating flavoring substances; antimicrobial for sugar milling
Packaging and Storage: Store in tight, light-resistant containers protected from heat.

IDENTIFICATION
- **MELTING RANGE OR TEMPERATURE DETERMINATION**, Appendix IIB
  2,4-Dinitrophenylhydrazine reagent: Add 4 mL of sulfuric acid to 0.8 g of 2,4-dinitrophenylhydrazine, then while swirling, add 6 mL of water, dropwise. When dissolution is essentially complete, add 20 mL of alcohol, mix, and filter. The filtrate is the reagent.
  Sample preparation: Add 0.4 mL of sample to 20 mL of *2,4-Dinitrophenylhydrazine reagent*. Mix by swirling, and allow the mixture to stand for 5 min. Collect the precipitate on a filter, and rinse thoroughly with alcohol. Dissolve the precipitate in 20 mL of hot ethylene dichloride, filter, and cool the filtrate in an ice bath until crystallization occurs. Collect the precipitate on a filter. Redissolve the precipitate by refluxing with 30 mL of acetone, filter, and cool the filtrate in an ice bath until crystallization occurs. Collect the precipitate on a filter.
  Acceptance criteria: The 2,4-dinitrophenylhydrazone precipitate so obtained melts between 185° and 195°.

ASSAY
- **PROCEDURE**
  Hydroxylamine hydrochloride solution: Prepare a 0.5 N solution by dissolving 35.0 g of hydroxylamine hydrochloride in water contained in a 1-L volumetric flask, dilute to volume with water, and mix.
  Triethanolamine solution: Prepare a 0.5 N solution by transferring 65 mL (74 g) of 98% triethanolamine into a 1-L volumetric flask, dilute to volume with water, and mix.
  pH 3.60 Hydroxylamine hydrochloride solution: Adjust to pH 3.60 a volume of *Hydroxylamine hydrochloride solution* sufficient for analyzing both the *Blank* and the *Sample preparation*. Using a suitable autotitrator, titrate with *Triethanolamine solution*. [**CAUTION**—The stirring rate is critical throughout the neutralization and analysis. When stirring is required, ensure adequate mixing without whipping air bubbles into the solution. The stirring speed should be consistent for both the sample and the blank.]
  Sample: Amount equivalent to 300 g of Glutaraldehyde
  Analysis: Transfer 65.0 mL of the *pH 3.60 Hydroxylamine hydrochloride solution* into each of two titration cups. Add a Teflon (or equivalent) stirrer to each cup. Using the autotitrator, add 30.8 mL of the neutralized *Triethanolamine solution* to each titration cup, cover, and mix. Using a weighing pipet, introduce the *Sample* into one of the cups (the second cup is the *Blank*). Mix the solutions thoroughly, and allow them to stand at room temperature for at least 60 min but not for more than 90 min. Titrate the solutions to pH 3.60 with 0.5 N hydrochloric acid, determining the endpoint potentiometrically. Calculate the percentage, by weight, of $C_5H_8O_2$ in the *Sample* by the formula:

  $$\text{Result} = [(V_B - V_S) \times N \times F_E \times 100]/W$$

  V_B = volume of 0.5 N hydrochloric acid consumed by the *Blank* solution (mL)
  V_S = volume of 0.5 N hydrochloric acid consumed by the *Sample* solution (mL)
  N = normality of the hydrochloric acid
  F_E = milliequivalent weight of glutaraldehyde, 0.05006 g/mEq
  W = weight of the sample taken (g)
  Acceptance criteria: NLT 100.0% and NMT 105.0% of the labeled amount of $C_5H_8O_2$

IMPURITIES
Inorganic Impurities
- **LEAD**, *Lead Limit Test, Atomic Absorption Spectrophotometric Method*, Appendix IIIB
  Sample: 10 g
  Acceptance criteria: NMT 2 mg/kg

SPECIFIC TESTS
- **pH**, *pH Determination*, Appendix IIB
  Acceptance criteria: Between 3.1 and 4.5

OTHER REQUIREMENTS
- **LABELING:** Indicate the concentration of Glutaraldehyde.

Glycerin

First Published: Prior to FCC 6
Last Revision: Second Supplement, FCC 7

Glycerol

C₃H₈O₃
INS: 422
UNII: PDC6A3C0OX [glycerin]

Formula wt 92.09
CAS: [56-81-5]

DESCRIPTION

Glycerin occurs as a clear, colorless, viscous liquid. It is hygroscopic, and its solutions are neutral. Glycerin is miscible with water and with alcohol. It is insoluble in chloroform, in ether, and in fixed and volatile oils. [NOTE—An informational GC method (not a monograph requirement) for the identification and quantification of diethylene glycol and ethylene glycol in glycerin is available for FCC users interested in testing food-grade materials for these potential adulterants. See *Diethylene Glycol and Ethylene Glycol in Glycerin*, Appendix XIII.]

Function: Humectant; solvent; bodying agent; plasticizer
Packaging and Storage: Store in tight containers.

IDENTIFICATION

- **A. INFRARED ABSORPTION,** *Spectrophotometric Identification Tests,* Appendix IIIC
  Reference standard: USP Glycerin RS
  Sample and standard preparation: F
  Acceptance criteria: The spectrum of the sample exhibits maxima at the same wavelengths as those in the spectrum of the *Reference standard*. [NOTE—A very strong absorption band in the glycerin spectrum at about 10.1 μm can be useful for differentiating glycerin from diethylene glycol and ethylene glycol, which both lack this band.]

- **B. PROCEDURE**
  Standard solution: 2.0 mg/mL of USP Glycerin RS and 0.050 mg/mL of USP Diethylene Glycol RS in methanol
  Sample solution: 50 mg/mL in methanol
  Chromatographic system, Appendix IIA
   Mode: GC
   Detector: Flame-ionization
   Column: 0.53-mm × 30-m fused-silica analytical column coated with 3.0-μm 6% cyanopropylphenyl–94% dimethylpolysiloxane stationary phase[1]
   Temperature
    Injector: 220°
    Detector: 250°
    Column: See the temperature program table below.

Initial Temperature (°)	Temperature Ramp (°/min)	Final Temperature (°)	Hold Time at Final Temperature (min)
100	—	100	4
100	50	120	10
100	50	220	6

   Carrier gas: Helium
   Injection size: 1.0 μL
   Flow rate: 4.5 mL/min
   Injection type: Split flow ratio is about 10:1
   System suitability
    Sample: *Standard solution*
    Suitability requirements
     Resolution: NLT 1.5 between diethylene glycol and glycerin
   Analysis: Separately inject equal volumes of the *Standard solution* and the *Sample solution*. [NOTE—The relative retention times for diethylene glycol and glycerin are about 0.8 and 1.0, respectively.]
   Acceptance criteria: The retention time of the glycerin peak for the *Sample solution* corresponds to that of the glycerin peak for the *Standard solution*.

ASSAY

- **PROCEDURE**
  Sodium periodate solution: Dissolve 60 g of sodium metaperiodate (NaIO₄) in sufficient water containing 120 mL of 0.1 N sulfuric acid to make 1000 mL. Do not heat to dissolve the periodate. If the solution is not clear, pass through a sintered-glass filter. Store the solution in a glass-stoppered, light-resistant container. Test the suitability of this solution as follows: Pipet 10 mL into a 250-mL volumetric flask, dilute to volume, and mix. Dissolve about 550 mg of sample in 50 mL of water, and add 50 mL of the diluted periodate solution by pipet. For a blank, pipet 50 mL of the diluted periodate solution into a flask containing 50 mL of water. Allow the solutions to stand for 30 min, then add 5 mL of hydrochloric acid and 10 mL of potassium iodide TS to each, and rotate to mix. Allow to stand for 5 min, add 100 mL of water, and titrate with 0.1 N sodium thiosulfate, shaking continuously and adding starch TS near the endpoint. The ratio of the volume of 0.1 N sodium thiosulfate required for the sample:periodate mixture to that required for the blank should be between 0.750 and 0.765.
  Sample: 400 mg
  Analysis: Transfer the *Sample* into a 600-mL beaker, dilute with 50 mL of water, add bromothymol blue TS, and acidify with 0.2 N sulfuric acid to a definite green or green-yellow color. Neutralize with 0.05 N sodium hydroxide to a definite blue endpoint free of green color. Prepare a blank containing 50 mL of water, and neutralize in the same manner. Pipet 50 mL of the *Sodium periodate solution* into each beaker, mix by swirling gently, cover with a watch glass, and allow to stand for 30 min at room temperature (not above 35°) in the dark or in subdued light. Add 10 mL of a mixture consisting of equal volumes of ethylene glycol and water to each beaker, and allow to stand for 20

---

[1] DB-624 (J & W Scientific), or equivalent.

min. Dilute each solution to about 300 mL with water, and titrate with 0.1 N sodium hydroxide to a pH of 8.1 ± 0.1 for the *Sample* and 6.5 ± 0.1 for the blank, using a pH meter previously calibrated with pH 4.0 *Acid Phthalate Standard Buffer Solution* (see *Solutions and Indicators*). Each mL of 0.1 N sodium hydroxide, after correction for the blank, is equivalent to 9.210 mg of glycerin ($C_3H_8O_3$).
Acceptance criteria: 99.0%–101.0% of $C_3H_8O_3$ on the as-is basis

IMPURITIES
Inorganic Impurities
- **LEAD,** *Lead Limit Test, Atomic Absorption Spectrophotometric Graphite Furnace Method, Method I,* Appendix IIIB
  Acceptance criteria: NMT 1 mg/kg

Organic Impurities
- **FATTY ACIDS AND ESTERS**
  Sample: 40.0 mL (50 g)
  Analysis: Mix the *Sample* with 50 mL of recently boiled water and 5.0 mL of 0.5 N sodium hydroxide. Boil the mixture for 5 min, cool, add phenolphthalein TS, and titrate the excess alkali with 0.5 N hydrochloric acid.
  Acceptance criteria: More than 4 mL of 0.5 N hydrochloric acid is consumed. (Limit is about 0.1% calculated as butyric acid.)

SPECIFIC TESTS
- **CHLORINATED COMPOUNDS (AS Cl)**
  Sample: 5.0 g
  Analysis: Transfer the *Sample* into a dry, 100-mL round-bottom, ground-joint flask, and add 15 mL of morpholine to it. Connect the flask with a ground joint reflux condenser, and reflux the mixture gently for 3 h. Rinse the condenser with 10 mL of water, receiving the washing into the flask, and cautiously acidify with nitric acid. Transfer the solution to a suitable comparison tube, add 0.5 mL of silver nitrate TS, dilute to 50.0 mL, and mix thoroughly.
  Control: 150 µg of chloride in an equal volume of solution containing the quantities of reagents used in the *Analysis*, but omitting the refluxing
  Acceptance criteria: Any turbidity produced by the *Sample* does not exceed that produced by the *Control*. (NMT 0.003% as Cl)
- **COLOR**
  Sample: 50 mL
  Control: 0.40 mL of ferric chloride CS diluted with water to 50 mL
  Analysis: Transfer the *Sample* and the *Control* to separate 50-mL Nessler tubes of the same diameter and color and view the tubes downward against a white surface.
  Acceptance criteria: The color of the *Sample* is not darker than that of the *Control*.
- **READILY CARBONIZABLE SUBSTANCES,** Appendix IIB
  Sample: 5 mL
  Analysis: Rinse a glass-stoppered 25-mL cylinder with 95% sulfuric acid, and allow it to drain for 10 min. Add the *Sample* and 5 mL of 95% sulfuric acid, gently mix for 1 min at 18°–20°, and allow to stand for 1 h.
  Acceptance criteria: The resulting mixture has no more color than *Matching Fluid H*.
- **RESIDUE ON IGNITION**
  Sample: 50 g
  Analysis: Heat the *Sample* in a tared, open dish, and ignite the vapors, allowing them to burn until the sample has been completely consumed. After cooling, moisten the residue with 0.5 mL of sulfuric acid, and complete the ignition by heating for 15-min periods at 800 ± 25° to constant weight.
  Acceptance criteria: NMT 0.01%
- **SPECIFIC GRAVITY:** Determine by any reliable method (see *General Provisions*).
  Acceptance criteria: NLT 1.259
- **WATER,** *Water Determination, Method I,* Appendix IIB
  Acceptance criteria: NMT 1.0%

Glycerol Ester of Gum Rosin
First Published: Prior to FCC 6
Last Revision: FCC 6

Ester Gum

DESCRIPTION
Glycerol Ester of Gum Rosin occurs as a hard, pale amber-colored resin (color N or paler as determined by ASTM Designation D 509) produced by the esterification of pale gum rosin with food-grade glycerin. When intended for use in chewing gum base, the product is usually purified by steam stripping, but when intended for use in adjusting the density of citrus oils for beverages, it is purified by countercurrent steam distillation. It is soluble in acetone and in toluene, but is insoluble in water.
Function: Masticatory substance in chewing gum base; beverage stabilizer
Packaging and Storage: Store in well-closed containers.

IDENTIFICATION
- **INFRARED SPECTRA,** *Spectrophotometric Identification Tests,* Appendix IIIC
  Sample preparation: Melted sample on a potassium bromide plate
  Acceptance criteria: The spectrum of the sample exhibits relative maxima at the same wavelengths as those of the spectrum below.

IMPURITIES
Inorganic Impurities
- **LEAD,** *Sample Solution for Lead Limit Test,* Appendix IV
  Control: 5 µg Pb (5 mL of *Diluted Standard Lead Solution*)
  Acceptance criteria: NMT 1 mg/kg

SPECIFIC TESTS
- **ACID NUMBER,** Appendix IX
  Acceptance criteria: Between 3 and 9
- **RING-AND-BALL SOFTENING POINT,** *Softening Point, Ring-and-Ball Method,* Appendix IX
  Acceptance criteria: 82° or higher

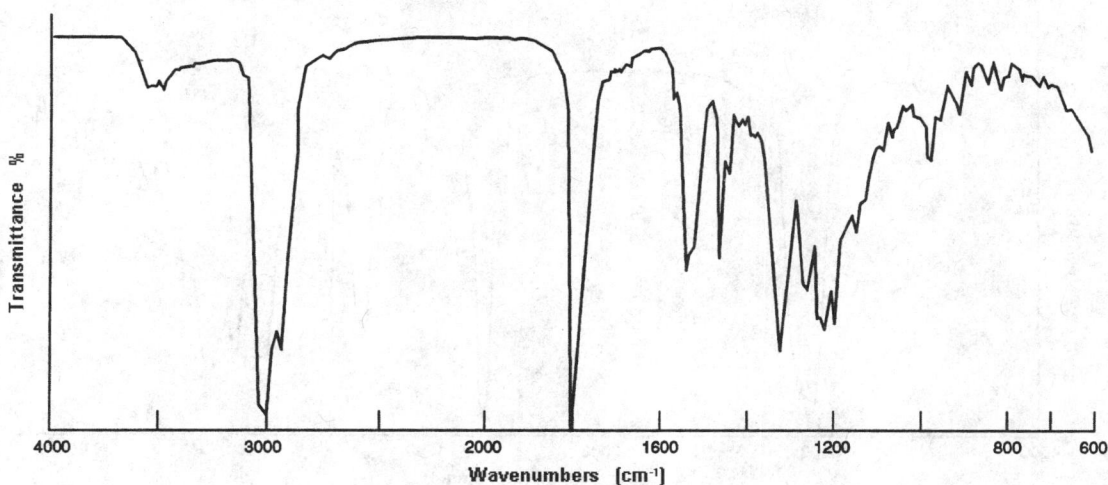

Glycerol Ester of Gum Rosin

Glycerol Ester of Partially Dimerized Rosin

First Published: Prior to FCC 6
Last Revision: FCC 6

DESCRIPTION
Glycerol Ester of Partially Dimerized Rosin occurs as a hard, pale, amber-colored resin (color M or paler as determined by ASTM Designation D 509) produced by the esterification of partially dimerized rosin with food-grade glycerin, and purified by steam stripping. It is soluble in acetone, but is insoluble in water.

Function: Masticatory substance in chewing gum base
Packaging and Storage: Store in well-closed containers.

IDENTIFICATION
- **INFRARED SPECTRA,** Spectrophotometric Identification Tests, Appendix IIIC
  Sample preparation: Melted sample on a potassium bromide plate
  Acceptance criteria: The spectrum of the sample exhibits relative maxima at the same wavelengths as those of the spectrum below.

IMPURITIES
Inorganic Impurities
- **LEAD,** Sample Solution for Lead Limit Test, Appendix IV
  Control: 5 µg Pb (5 mL of Diluted Standard Lead Solution)
  Acceptance criteria: NMT 1 mg/kg

SPECIFIC TESTS
- **ACID NUMBER,** Appendix IX
  Acceptance criteria: Between 3 and 8
- **RING-AND-BALL SOFTENING POINT,** Softening Point, Ring-and-Ball Method, Appendix IX
  Acceptance criteria: 103° or higher

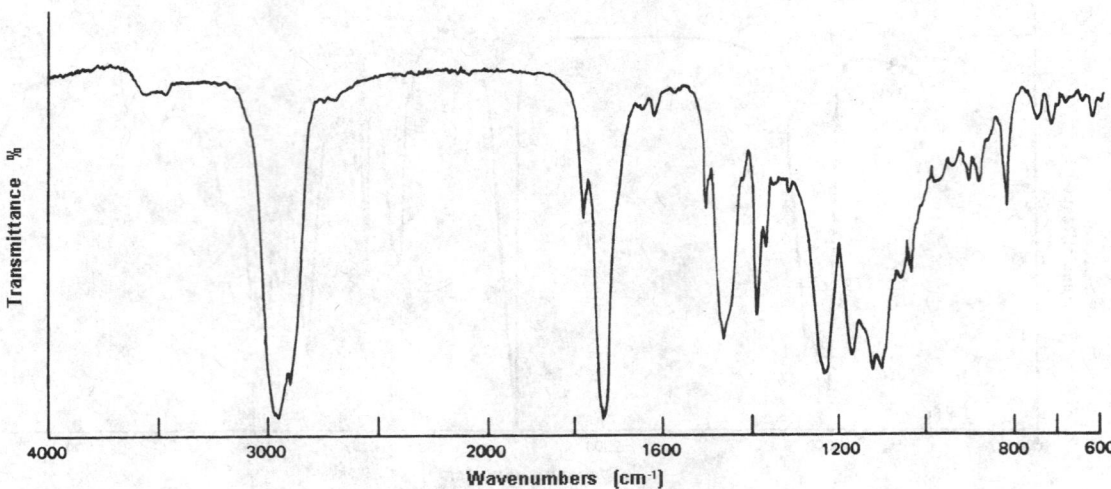

Glycerol Ester of Partially Dimerized Rosin

Glycerol Ester of Partially Hydrogenated Gum Rosin

First Published: Prior to FCC 6
Last Revision: FCC 6

DESCRIPTION
Glycerol Ester of Partially Hydrogenated Gum Rosin occurs as a medium-hard, pale amber-colored resin (color N or paler as determined by ASTM Designation D 509). It is produced by the esterification of partially hydrogenated gum rosin with food-grade glycerin and purified by steam stripping. It is soluble in acetone and in toluene, but is insoluble in water and in alcohol.
Function: Masticatory substance in chewing gum base
Packaging and Storage: Store in well-closed containers.

IDENTIFICATION
- **INFRARED SPECTRA,** Spectrophotometric Identification Tests, Appendix IIIC
  Sample preparation: Melted sample on a potassium bromide plate
  Acceptance criteria: The spectrum of the sample exhibits relative maxima at the same wavelengths as those of the spectrum below.

IMPURITIES
Inorganic Impurities
- **LEAD,** Sample Solution for Lead Limit Test, Appendix IV
  Sample: 5 g
  Control: 5 µg Pb (5 mL of Diluted Standard Lead Solution)
  Acceptance criteria: NMT 1 mg/kg

SPECIFIC TESTS
- **ACID NUMBER,** Appendix IX
  Acceptance criteria: Between 3 and 10
- **DROP SOFTENING POINT,** Softening Point, Drop Method, Appendix IX: Using a bath temperature of 100°
  Acceptance criteria: 79° or higher

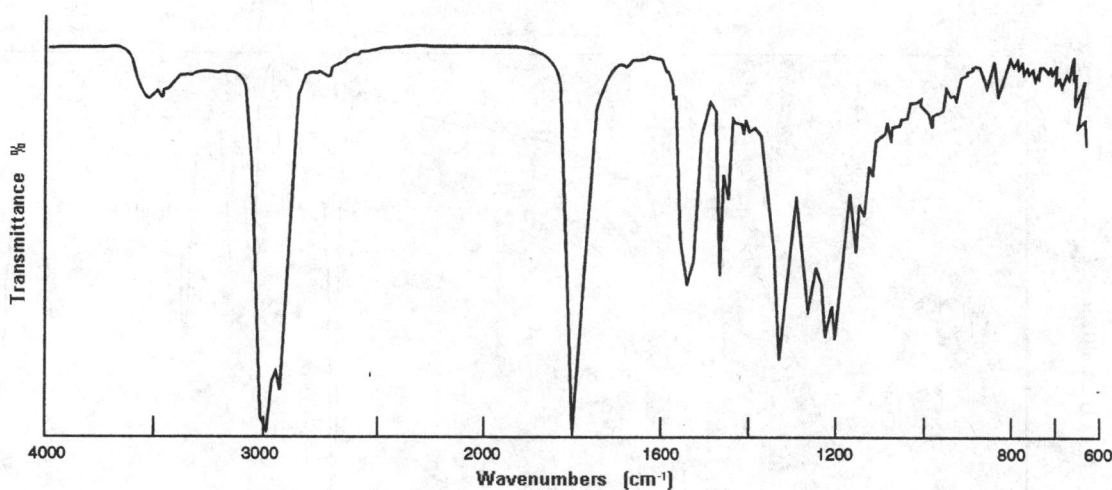

Glycerol Ester of Partially Hydrogenated Gum Rosin

Glycerol Ester of Partially Hydrogenated Wood Rosin

First Published: Prior to FCC 6
Last Revision: FCC 6

DESCRIPTION
Glycerol Ester of Partially Hydrogenated Wood Rosin occurs as a medium-hard, pale amber-colored resin (color N or paler as determined by ASTM Designation D 509). It is produced by the esterification of partially hydrogenated wood rosin with food-grade glycerin and purified by steam stripping. It is soluble in acetone, but is insoluble in water and in alcohol.
Function: Masticatory substance in chewing gum base
Packaging and Storage: Store in well-closed containers.

IDENTIFICATION
- **INFRARED SPECTRA,** *Spectrophotometric Identification Tests,* Appendix IIIC
  Sample preparation: Melted sample on a potassium bromide plate
  Acceptance criteria: The spectrum of the sample exhibits relative maxima at the same wavelengths as those of the spectrum below.

IMPURITIES
Inorganic Impurities
- **LEAD,** *Sample Solution for Lead Limit Test,* Appendix IV
  Control: 5 µg Pb (5 mL of *Diluted Standard Lead Solution*)
  Acceptance criteria: NMT 1 mg/kg

SPECIFIC TESTS
- **ACID NUMBER,** Appendix IX
  Acceptance criteria: Between 3 and 10
- **RING-AND-BALL SOFTENING POINT,** *Softening Point, Ring-and-Ball Method,* Appendix IX: Use a water bath.
  Acceptance criteria: 68° or higher

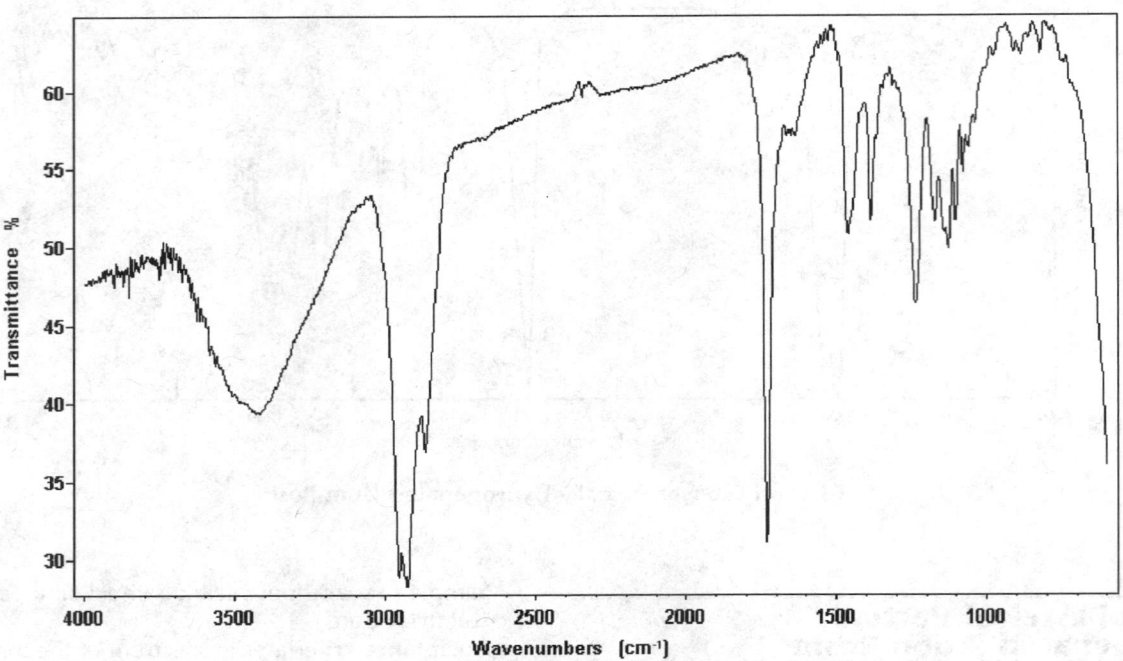

Glycerol Ester of Partially Hydrogenated Wood Rosin

Glycerol Ester of Polymerized Rosin

First Published: Prior to FCC 6
Last Revision: FCC 6

DESCRIPTION
Glycerol Ester of Polymerized Rosin occurs as a hard, pale amber-colored resin (color M or paler as determined by ASTM Designation D 509). It is produced by the esterification of polymerized rosin with food-grade glycerin and purified by steam stripping. It is soluble in acetone, but is insoluble in water and in alcohol.
Function: Masticatory substance in chewing gum base
Packaging and Storage: Store in well-closed containers.

IDENTIFICATION
- **INFRARED SPECTRA,** *Spectrophotometric Identification Tests,* Appendix IIIC
  Sample preparation: Melted sample on a potassium bromide plate
  Acceptance criteria: The spectrum of the sample exhibits relative maxima at the same wavelengths as those of the spectrum below.

IMPURITIES
- **LEAD,** *Sample Solution for Lead Limit Test,* Appendix IV
  Control: 5 µg of Pb (5 mL of *Diluted Standard Lead Solution*)
  Acceptance criteria: NMT 1 mg/kg

SPECIFIC TESTS
- **ACID NUMBER,** Appendix IX
  Acceptance criteria: Between 3 and 12
- **RING-AND-BALL SOFTENING POINT,** *Softening Point, Ring-and-Ball Method,* Appendix IX
  Acceptance criteria: 80° or higher

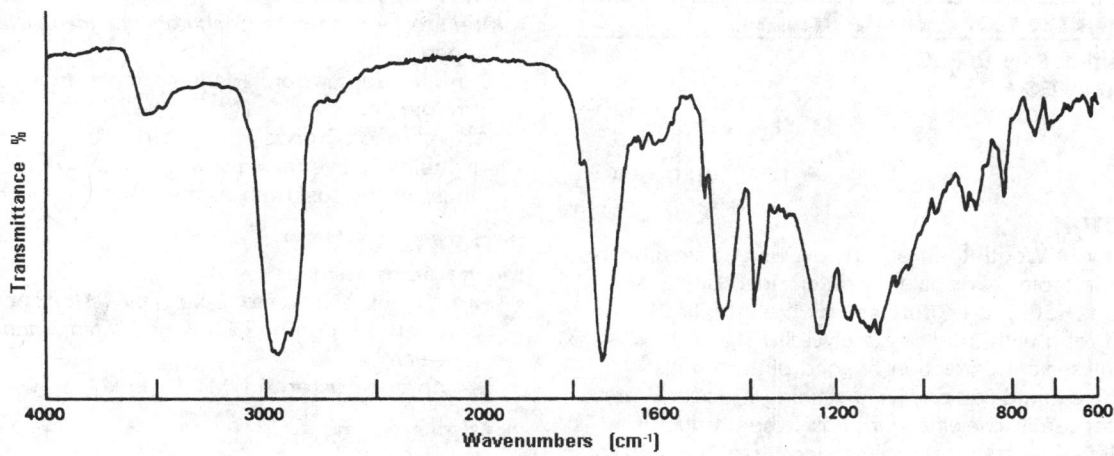

Glycerol Ester of Polymerized Rosin

Glycerol Ester of Tall Oil Rosin

First Published: Prior to FCC 6
Last Revision: FCC 6

DESCRIPTION
Glycerol Ester of Tall Oil Rosin occurs as a pale amber-colored resin (color N or paler as determined by ASTM Designation D 509). It is produced by the esterification of tall oil rosin with food-grade glycerin and purified by steam stripping. It is soluble in acetone, but is insoluble in water.
Function: Masticatory substance in chewing gum base
Packaging and Storage: Store in well-closed containers.

IDENTIFICATION
- **INFRARED SPECTRA**, *Spectrophotometric Identification Tests,* Appendix IIIC
  Sample preparation: Melted sample on a potassium bromide plate
  Acceptance criteria: The spectrum of the sample exhibits relative maxima at the same wavelengths as those of the spectrum below.

IMPURITIES
Inorganic Impurities
- **LEAD,** *Sample Solution for Lead Limit Test,* Appendix IV
  Control: 5 µg Pb (5 mL of *Diluted Standard Lead Solution*)
  Acceptance criteria: NMT 1 mg/kg

SPECIFIC TESTS
- **ACID NUMBER,** Appendix IX
  Acceptance criteria: Between 2 and 12
- **RING-AND-BALL SOFTENING POINT,** *Softening Point, Ring-and-Ball Method,* Appendix IX
  Acceptance criteria: 80° or higher

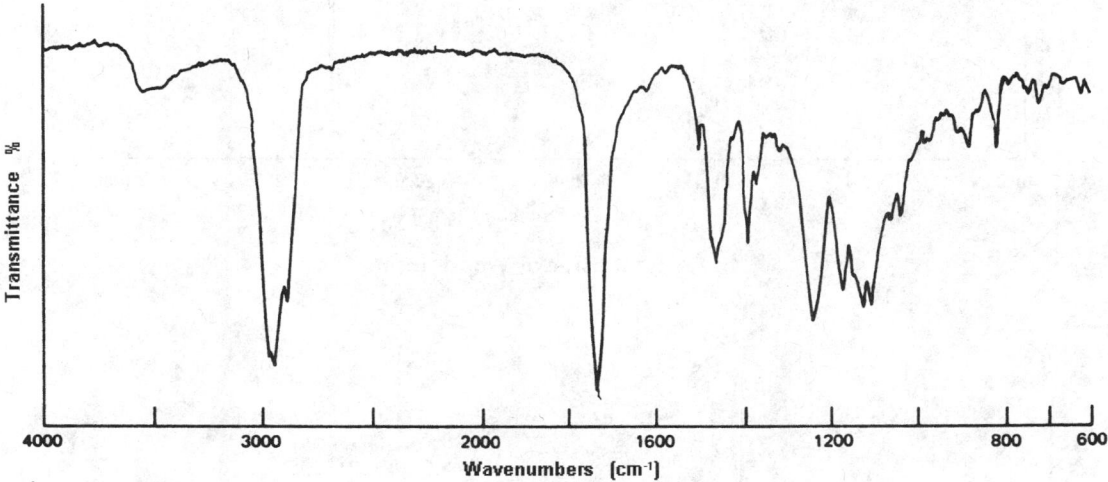

Glycerol Ester of Tall Oil Rosin

Glycerol Ester of Wood Rosin

First Published: Prior to FCC 6
Last Revision: FCC 6

Ester Gum
INS: 445   CAS: [8050-30-4]

DESCRIPTION
Glycerol Ester of Wood Rosin occurs as a hard, pale amber-colored resin (color N or paler as determined by ASTM Designation D 509). It is produced by the esterification of pale wood rosin with food-grade glycerin. The rosin is obtained by solvent extraction of aged pine stumps, followed by a liquid-liquid solvent refining process. When intended for use in chewing gum base, the product is usually purified by steam stripping, but when intended for use in adjusting the density of citrus oils for beverages, it is purified by countercurrent steam distillation. It is soluble in acetone, but it is insoluble in water.

Function: Masticatory substance in chewing gum base; beverage stabilizer

Packaging and Storage: Store in well-closed containers.

IDENTIFICATION
- **INFRARED SPECTRA,** *Spectrophotometric Identification Tests,* Appendix IIIC
  Sample preparation: Melted sample on a potassium bromide plate
  Acceptance criteria: The spectrum of the sample exhibits relative maxima at the same wavelengths as those of the spectrum below.

IMPURITIES
Inorganic Impurities
- **LEAD,** *Sample Solution for Lead Limit Test,* Appendix IV
  Control: 3.3 µg Pb (3.3 mL of *Diluted Standard Lead Solution*)
  Acceptance criteria: NMT 1 mg/kg

SPECIFIC TESTS
- **ACID NUMBER,** Appendix IX
  Acceptance criteria: Between 3 and 9
- **RING-AND-BALL SOFTENING POINT,** *Softening Point, Ring-and-Ball Method,* Appendix IX
  Acceptance criteria: 82° or higher

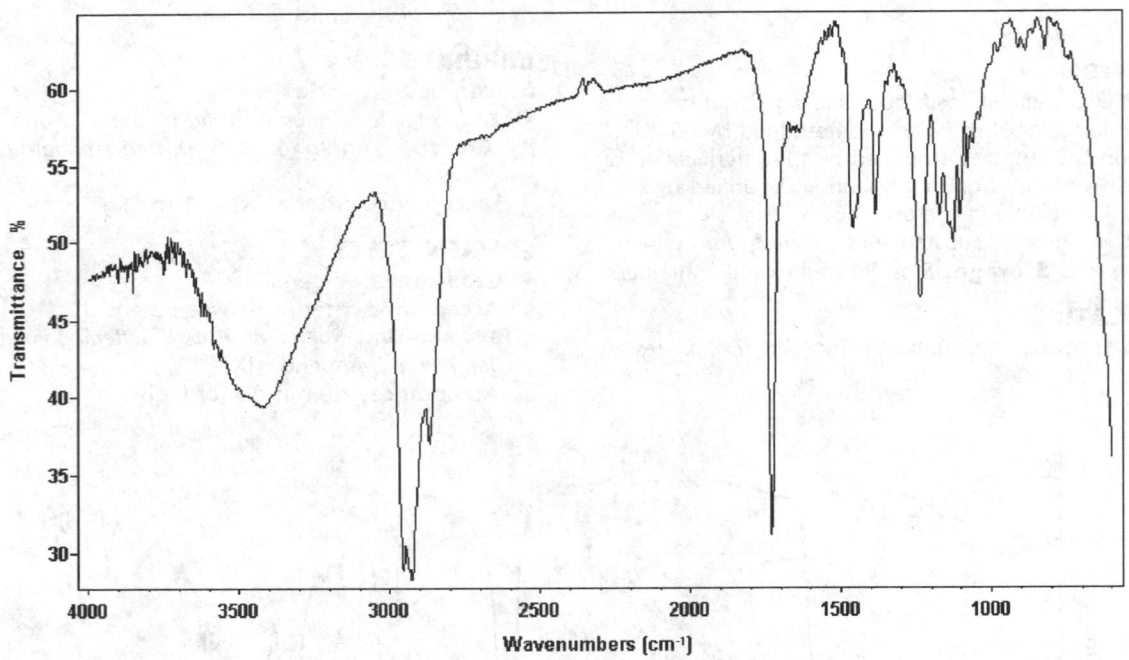

Glycerol Ester of Wood Rosin

Glyceryl Behenate

First Published: Prior to FCC 6

Glyceryl Tribehenate
Glyceryl Tridocosanoate
Tribehenoyl-sn-glycerol
Tridocosanoyl-sn-glycerol

$C_{69}H_{134}O_6$ Formula wt 1059.83
    CAS: [30233-64-8]
UNII: R8WTH25YS2 [glyceryl dibehenate]

DESCRIPTION
Glyceryl Behenate occurs as a fine powder. It is a mixture of fatty acid glycerides, primarily glyceryl esters of behenic acid, that melts at about 70°. It is soluble in chloroform and practically insoluble in water and in alcohol.
Function: Emulsifier; texturizer
Packaging and Storage: Store in tight containers at a temperature not higher than 35°.

IDENTIFICATION
- **THIN-LAYER CHROMATOGRAPHY,** Appendix IIA
  [**CAUTION**—Ether is highly volatile and flammable. Its vapor, when mixed with air and ignited, may explode.]
  Standard solution: 60 mg/mL of USP Glyceryl Behenate RS in chloroform
  Sample solution: 60 mg/mL in chloroform
  Adsorbent: 0.25-mm layer of chromatographic silica gel mixture
  Application volume: 10 µL
  Developing solvent system: Chloroform and acetone (96:4)
  Spray reagent: 0.02% solution of dichlorofluorescein in alcohol
  Analysis: [NOTE—Pretreat the plates by placing them in a chromatographic chamber saturated with ether. Remove the plates from the chamber, allow the ether to evaporate, and immerse them in a 2.5% solution of boric acid in alcohol. After about 1 min, withdraw the plates, and allow them to dry at ambient temperature. Heat to 110° for 30 min to activate the plates, and then keep them in a desiccator.] After developing the plate in the *Developing solvent*, remove the plate from the developing chamber and allow the solvent to evaporate. Spray the chromatogram with the *Spray reagent* and examine the spots under short-wavelength ultraviolet light.
  Acceptance criteria: The R_F values of the spots obtained from the *Sample solution* correspond to those obtained from the *Standard solution*.
- **GAS CHROMATOGRAPHY,** Appendix IIA
  Standard solution: Dissolve 22 mg of USP Glyceryl Behenate RS in 1 mL of toluene in a screw-cap vial with a Teflon-lined septum. Add 0.4 mL of 0.2 N methanolic (*m*-trifluoromethylphenyl) trimethylammonium hydroxide, attach the cap, and mix. Allow the vial to stand at room temperature for at least 30 min.
  Sample solution: Dissolve 22 mg of sample in 1 mL of toluene in a screw-cap vial with a Teflon-lined septum. Add 0.4 mL of 0.2 N methanolic (*m*-trifluoromethylphenyl) trimethylammonium hydroxide, attach the cap, and mix. Allow the vial to stand at room temperature for at least 30 min.
  Chromatographic system
    Mode: Gas chromatography
    Detector: Flame-ionization detector
    Column: 1.8-m × 4-mm (id) column packed with a 10% coating of 50% 3-cyanopropyl-50% phenylmethylsilicone (SP 2300, or equivalent) on a silanized siliceous earth support (Supelcoport, or equivalent)
    Column temperature: About 225°
  Analysis: Separately inject a suitable volume of *Sample solution* and *Standard solution* into the chromatograph and record the resulting chromatograms.
  Acceptance criteria
    Retention time: The retention time of the main peak in the chromatogram of the *Sample solution* corresponds to that of the main peak in the chromatogram of the *Standard solution*.
    Response ratio: The response ratio of the main peak to the sum of all the responses is NLT 0.83.

IMPURITIES
Inorganic Impurities
- **LEAD,** *Lead Limit Test, Atomic Absorption Spectrophotometric Graphite Furnace Method, Method II,* Appendix IIIB
  Acceptance criteria: NMT 1 mg/kg

SPECIFIC TESTS
- **ACID VALUE**
  Sample: 10 g
  Analysis: Suspend the *Sample* in a flask containing 50 mL of a 1:1 mixture of alcohol and ether that has been neutralized to phenolphthalein with 0.1 N sodium hydroxide. Connect the flask with a suitable condenser and, while frequently shaking, warm for about 10 min. Add 1 mL of phenolphthalein TS and titrate with 0.1 N sodium hydroxide until the solution remains faintly pink after shaking for 30 s. Calculate the *Acid Value* by the formula:

  $$\text{Result} = 56.1V \times N/W$$

  V = volume of the 0.1 N sodium hydroxide solution (mL)
  N = normality of the sodium hydroxide solution
  W = weight of the sample taken (g)
  Acceptance criteria: NMT 4
- **FREE GLYCERIN,** *Free Glycerin or Propylene Glycol,* Appendix VII
  Acceptance criteria: NMT 1.0%
- **IODINE VALUE,** Appendix VII
  Acceptance criteria: NMT 3
- **1-MONOGLYCERIDES CONTENT,** *1-Monoglycerides,* Appendix VII
  Sample: 1 g, that has been melted at a temperature not higher than 80°, stirred, and accurately weighed
  Analysis: Proceed as directed. [NOTE—If the sample titration is less than 0.8 volumes of the blank titration, discard and repeat, using a smaller weight of sample.]

508 / Glyceryl Behenate / *Monographs*

Calculate the percentage of 1-monoglycerides, as glyceryl monobehenate, by the formula:

$$\text{Result} = [(V_B \times V_S) \times N \times F]/W$$

- V_B = volume of 0.1 N sodium thiosulfate consumed by the blank (mL)
- V_S = volume of 0.1 N sodium thiosulfate consumed by the sample (mL)
- N = normality of the sodium thiosulfate
- F = 1/20th of the molecular weight of glyceryl monobehenate, 20.73
- W = weight of the sample taken (g)

Acceptance criteria: NLT 12.0% and NMT 18.0%

- **RESIDUE ON IGNITION (SULFATED ASH)**, Appendix IIC
  Sample: 5 g
  Acceptance criteria: NMT 0.1%
- **SAPONIFICATION VALUE**, Appendix VII
  Acceptance criteria: NLT 145 and NMT 165

Glyceryl Monooleate

First Published: Prior to FCC 6
Last Revision: First Supplement, FCC 7

Monoolein

$C_{21}H_{40}O_4$
INS: 471
FEMA: 2526
UNII: 4PC054V79P [glyceryl oleate]

Formula wt 356.54
CAS: [25496-72-4]

DESCRIPTION

Glyceryl Monooleate occurs as a clear liquid at room temperature. It has a mild, fatty taste. It is prepared by esterifying glycerin with food-grade oleic acid in the presence of a suitable catalyst such as aluminum oxide. It also occurs in many animal and vegetable fats such as tallow and cocoa butter. It is soluble in hot alcohol and in chloroform; very slightly soluble in cold alcohol, in ether, and in petroleum ether; and insoluble in water. It melts at around 15°. It may also contain tri- and diesters.

Function: Emulsifier; flavoring agent
Packaging and Storage: Store in tight, light-resistant containers.

IDENTIFICATION

- **FATTY ACID COMPOSITION**, Appendix VII
  Acceptance criteria: A sample exhibits the following composition profile of fatty acids:

Fatty Acid	Weight % (Range)
≤12	0
12:0	0
14:0	<4
16:0	1-5
16:1	<9
18:0	<3.0
18:1	≥82
18:2	3-7
≥20	<1.5

ASSAY

- **PROCEDURE**
  Mobile phase: Tetrahydrofuran
  Standard solution: 20 mg/mL of USP Glyceryl Monooleate 90% RS in *Mobile phase*
  Sample solution: 40 mg/mL in *Mobile phase*
  Chromatographic system, Appendix IIA
  Mode: High-performance liquid chromatography
  Detector: Refractive index
  Column: Two 7.5-mm × 30-cm columns in tandem containing spherical styrene-divinylbenzene copolymer packing (5- to 10-μm particle diameter)[1]. [NOTE—Alternatively, one 7.5-mm × 60-cm column with an equivalent packing can be used provided that system suitability criteria are met.]
  Column temperature: 40°. [NOTE—Column temperature may be lowered to ambient, but working at 40° provides stable separation conditions and ensures better sample solubility.]
  Flow rate: 1 mL/min
  Injection size: 40 μL
  System suitability
    Sample: *Standard solution*
    Suitability requirements
      Suitability requirement 1: The resolution between the diglycerides and monoglycerides peaks is NLT 1.0.
      Suitability requirement 2: The relative standard deviation for the monoglycerides peak area is NMT 2.0%.
  Analysis: Separately inject equal volumes of the *Standard solution* and *Sample solution* into the chromatograph, and measure the responses for the major peaks on the resulting chromatograms.
  [NOTE—The approximate relative retention times for triglycerides, diglycerides, monoglycerides, and glycerin are 0.76, 0.79, 0.85, and 1.0, respectively.]
  Calculate the percentage of monoglycerides in the portion of the sample taken:

$$\text{Result} = (r_U/r_S) \times (C_S/C_U) \times 100$$

- r_U = peak area response for monoglycerides from the *Sample solution*
- r_S = peak area response for monoglycerides from the *Standard solution*
- C_S = concentration of monoglycerides in the *Standard solution* corrected for purity based on the USP RS label claim (mg/mL)

---
[1] PLgel (Phenomenex, Torrance, CA), or equivalent.

C_U = concentration of sample in the *Sample solution* (mg/mL)

Acceptance criteria: NLT 35.0% monoglycerides, calculated on the anhydrous basis

IMPURITIES
Inorganic Impurities
- **LEAD**, *Lead Limit Test, Flame Atomic Absorption Spectrophotometric Method,* Appendix IIIB
  Sample: 10 g
  Acceptance criteria: NMT 1 mg/kg
- **WATER**, *Water Determination,* Appendix IIB
  Sample: 0.5 g
  Analysis: Proceed as directed using 20 mL of a 1:1 methanol and chloroform mixture
  Acceptance criteria: NMT 1.0%

SPECIFIC TESTS
- **ACID VALUE (FATS AND RELATED SUBSTANCES),** Appendix VII
  Acceptance criteria: NMT 6
- **FREE GLYCERIN**
  Glycerin standard solutions: 0.4, 1.0, 2.0, and 4.0 mg/mL of USP Glycerin RS in tetrahydrofuran
  Mobile phase, Sample solution, and **Chromatographic system:** Proceed as directed in the *Assay.*
  System suitabilty solution: Use the *Standard solution* prepared in the *Assay.*
  System suitabilty: Proceed as directed in the *Assay* using the *System suitability solution.*
  Analysis: Separately inject equal volumes of the *Glycerin standard solutions* and *Sample solution* into the chromatograph, and measure the responses for the major peaks on the resulting chromatograms.
  [NOTE—The approximate relative retention times for triglycerides, diglycerides, monoglycerides, and glycerin are 0.76, 0.79, 0.85, and 1.0, respectively.]
  Prepare a standard curve for glycerin by plotting glycerin peak areas (obtained from the chromatograms of the *Glycerin standard solutions*) versus concentrations in mg/mL. Calculate the percentage of glycerin in the portion of the sample taken:

  $$\text{Result} = C_U/C_{SMP} \times 100$$

  C_U = concentration of glycerin in the *Sample solution* determined from the standard curve (mg/mL)
  C_{SMP} = concentration of sample in the *Sample solution* (mg/mL)
  Acceptance criteria: NMT 6.0%
- **HYDROXYL VALUE,** *Method II,* Appendix VII
  Acceptance criteria: Between 300 and 330
- **IODINE VALUE,** Appendix VII
  Acceptance criteria: Between 58 and 80
- **SAPONIFICATION VALUE,** Appendix VII
  Acceptance criteria: Between 160 and 176
- **RESIDUE ON IGNITION (SULFATED ASH),** Appendix IIC
  Sample: 5 g
  Acceptance criteria: NMT 0.1%

Glyceryl Monostearate
First Published: Prior to FCC 6

Monostearin
1,2,3-Propanetriol Octadecanoate

CAS: [31566-31-1]
UNII: 230OU9XXE4 [glyceryl monostearate]

DESCRIPTION
Glyceryl Monostearate occurs as a white, wax-like solid, as flakes, or as beads. It is a mixture of Glyceryl Monostearate and glyceryl monopalmitate. It may contain a suitable antioxidant. It is soluble in hot organic solvents such as acetone, alcohol, and ether and in mineral or fixed oils. It is dispersible in hot water with the aid of soap or suitable surfactants.

Function: Emulsifier
Packaging and Storage: Store in tight, light-resistant containers.

IDENTIFICATION
- **PROCEDURE**
  Analysis: Heat the sample with 3 parts water to between 2° and 5° above its melting point.
  Acceptance criteria: An irreversible gel forms when the sample is held at this temperature.

ASSAY
- **PROCEDURE**
  Propionating reagent: Mix 10 mL of pyridine with 20 mL of propionic anhydride.
  Internal standard solution: 4 mg/mL hexadecyl hexadecanoate in chloroform
  Standard solution: Transfer 50 mg of USP Monoglycerides RS into a 25-mL flask, add 5 mL of *Internal standard solution* by pipet, and mix. When dissolution is complete, immerse the flask in a water bath maintained at a temperature between 45° and 50°, and volatilize the chloroform with the aid of a stream of nitrogen. Add 3.0 mL of *Propionating reagent,* and heat on a hot plate at 75° for 30 min. Evaporate the reagents with the aid of a stream of nitrogen and gentle steam heat. Add 15 mL of chloroform, and swirl to dissolve the residue.
  Sample solution: Transfer 50 mg of sample into a 25-mL conical flask, and add 5 mL of *Internal standard solution* by pipet, and mix. When dissolution is complete, immerse the flask in a water bath maintained at a temperature between 45° and 50°, and volatilize the chloroform with the aid of a stream of nitrogen. Add 3.0 mL of *Propionating reagent,* and heat on a hot plate at 75° for 30 min. Evaporate the reagents with the aid of a stream of nitrogen and gentle steam heat. Add 15 mL of chloroform, and swirl to dissolve the residue.
  Chromatographic system, Appendix IIA
    Mode: Gas chromatography
    Detector: Flame-ionization detector
    Column: 2.4-m × 4-mm (id) borosilicate glass column, or equivalent, packed with 2% liquid phase, 5% phenyl methyl silicone (SE 52 or equivalent) on 80- to

510 / Glyceryl Monostearate / Monographs

100-mesh siliceous earth support (Diatoport S, or equivalent)

Temperature
  Column: Between 270° and 280°, isothermal
  Injection port: About 310°
  Detector block: About 310°
Carrier gas: Helium
Flow rate: About 70 mL/min
System suitability
  Sample: Standard solution (6 to 10 replicate injections)
  Suitability requirements
    Suitability requirement 1: The resolution, R, between the peaks for the derivatized glyceryl hexadecanoate and glyceryl octadecanoate is NLT 2.0.
    Suitability requirement 2: The relative standard deviation of the ratio of the peak area of the derivatized glyceryl octadecanoate to that of the hexadecyl hexadecanoate is NMT 2.0%.
Analysis: Inject a suitable portion of the Standard solution and record the resulting chromatogram. Calculate the response factor, F, by the equation:

$$F = (A_S/A_D)(W_D/W_S)$$

A_S = sum of areas under the derivatized monoglyceride peaks
A_D = area under the hexadecyl hexadecanoate peak
W_D = weight (mg) of hexadecyl hexadecanoate in the Standard solution
W_S = weight (mg) of USP Monoglycerides RS, in the Standard solution

Similarly inject a suitable portion of the Sample solution and record the resulting chromatogram. Calculate the quantity, in mg, of monoglycerides in the amount of sample taken by the formula:

$$Result = (W_D/F)(a_U/a_D)$$

W_D = weight (mg) of hexadecyl hexadecanoate in the Standard solution
F = response factor, determined above
a_U = sum of areas under the derivatized monoglyceride peaks
a_D = area under the hexadecyl hexadecanoate peak

Acceptance criteria: NLT 90.0% monoglycerides of saturated fatty acids

IMPURITIES
Inorganic Impurities
- **LEAD,** Lead Limit Test, Flame Atomic Absorption Spectrophotometric Method, Method II, Appendix IIIB
  Acceptance criteria: NMT 1 mg/kg

SPECIFIC TESTS
- **ACID VALUE (FATS AND RELATED SUBSTANCES),** Appendix VII
  Acceptance criteria: NMT 6

- **FREE GLYCERIN**
  Propionating reagent: 10 mL of pyridine and 20 mL of propionic anhydride
  Internal standard solution: 0.2 mg/mL tributyrin in chloroform
  Standard stock preparation: Transfer 15 mg of glycerin and 50 mg of tributyrin into a 25-mL glass-stoppered conical flask. Add 3.0 mL of Propionating reagent, and heat on a hot plate at 75° for 30 min. Volatilize the reagents with the aid of a stream of nitrogen at room temperature, add about 12 mL of chloroform, and mix.
  Standard preparation: 1 mL of Standard stock preparation diluted to 20 mL with chloroform
  Sample solution: Transfer 50 mg of sample into a 25-mL glass-stoppered conical flask, and add 5 mL of Internal standard solution by pipet, and mix to dissolve. Immerse the flask in a water bath maintained at a temperature between 45° and 50°, and volatilize the chloroform with the aid of a stream of nitrogen. Add 3.0 mL of Propionating reagent, and heat on a hot plate at 75° for 30 min. Evaporate the reagents with the aid of a stream of nitrogen at room temperature. Add 5 mL of chloroform, and mix.
  Chromatographic system, Appendix IIA
    Mode: Gas chromatography
    Detector: Flame-ionization detector
    Column: 2.4-m × 4-mm (id) borosilicate glass column, or equivalent, packed with 2% liquid phase consisting of a high-molecular-weight compound of polyethylene glycol and a diepoxide (Carbowax 20 M, or equivalent) on an 80- to 100-mesh siliceous earth support (Chromosorb W AW DMCS, or equivalent)
    Temperature
      Column: Between 190° and 200°, isothermal
      Injection port: About 300°
      Detector block: About 310°
    Carrier gas: Helium
    Flow rate: About 70 mL/min
    System suitability
      Sample: Standard preparation (6 to 10 replicate injections)
      Suitability requirement 1: The resolution factor, R, between the peaks for the derivatized glycerin and tributyrin is NLT 4.0.
      Suitability requirement 2: The relative standard deviation of the ratio of the peak areas of the derivatized glycerin and tributyrin is NMT 2.0%.
    Analysis: Inject a suitable portion of the Standard preparation and record the resulting chromatogram. Calculate the response factor, F, taken by the formula:

$$F = (A_D/A_S)(W_S/W_D)$$

A_S = area under the tripropionin peak
A_D = area under the tributyrin peak
W_D = weight of tributyrin in the Standard preparation (mg)
W_S = weight of glycerin, in the Standard preparation (mg)

Similarly inject a suitable portion of the *Sample solution* and record the resulting chromatogram. Calculate the percentage of glycerin by the formula:

$$\text{Result} = 100F\,(a_U/a_D)(w_D/w_U)$$

F	= response factor, determined above
a_U	= area under the tripripionin peak
a_D	= area under the tributyrin peak
w_D	= weight of tributyrin in 5 mL of *Internal standard solution* (mg)
w_U	= weight of sample (mg) in the *Sample solution*

Acceptance criteria: NMT 1.2%
- HYDROXYL VALUE, Method II, Appendix VII
  Acceptance criteria: Between 300 and 330
- IODINE VALUE, Appendix VII
  Acceptance criteria: NMT 3
- MELTING RANGE (FATS AND RELATED SUBSTANCES), Appendix VII
  Acceptance criteria: NLT 65°
- SAPONIFICATION VALUE, Appendix VII
  Acceptance criteria: Between 150 and 165
- RESIDUE ON IGNITION (SULFATED ASH), Appendix IIC
  Sample: 5 g
  Acceptance criteria: NMT 0.1%

Glyceryl Palmitostearate

First Published: Prior to FCC 6

UNII: GSY51O183C [glyceryl palmitostearate]

DESCRIPTION
Glyceryl Palmitostearate occurs as a fine powder or waxy solid. It is a mixture of fatty acid glycerides, primarily glyceryl esters of palmitic and stearic acids. The waxy solid melts at about 55°. Glyceryl Palmitostearate is soluble in chloroform, but practically insoluble in water and in alcohol.
Function: Emulsifier
Packaging and Storage: Store in tight containers at a temperature no higher than 25°.

IDENTIFICATION
- PROCEDURE
  Sample solution: Transfer 100 mg of sample into a small, conical flask fitted with a suitable reflux condenser. Add 5.0 mL of a 14% (w/v) solution of boron trifluoride in methanol. [NOTE—Commercial reagent, 14% w/v, may be used (Applied Science, or equivalent).] Swirl to mix, and reflux for 15 min. Cool, transfer the reaction mixture with the aid of 10 mL of chromatographic-grade hexane to a 60-mL separatory funnel, and add 10 mL of water and 10 mL of saturated sodium chloride solution. Shake, allow the mixture to separate, then drain and discard the lower, aqueous layer. Pass the hexane layer through 6 g of anhydrous sodium sulfate into a suitable flask.

Standard solution: Prepare as indicated for the *Sample solution*, using 50 mg each of USP Palmitic Acid RS and USP Stearic Acid RS instead of the sample.
Chromatographic system, Appendix IIA
  Mode: Gas chromatography
  Detector: Flame-ionization detector
  Column: 1.5-m × 3-mm (id) column packed with 15% diethylene glycol succinate polyester on flux-calcined, acid-washed siliceous earth
  Temperature
    Column: 165°
    Inlet port: 210°
    Detector: 210°
  Carrier gas: Helium
  Injection volume: 1 to 2 µL
Analysis: Separately inject the *Sample solution* and *Standard solution* into the chromatograph and record the resulting chromatograms.
Acceptance criteria
  Retention time: The retention times of the main peaks of methyl palmitate and methyl stearate obtained in the *Sample solution* chromatogram correspond to those of the main peaks obtained from the *Standard solution*.
  Response ratio: The ratio of the response of the main peaks to the sum of all the responses is between 0.42 and 0.55 for methyl palmitate, and between 0.43 and 0.55 for methyl stearate.

IMPURITIES
Inorganic Impurities
- LEAD, *Lead Limit Test*, Atomic Absorption Spectrophotometric Graphite Furnace Method, Method II, Appendix IIIB
  Acceptance criteria: NMT 1 mg/kg

SPECIFIC TESTS
- ACID VALUE
  Sample: 10 g
  Analysis: Transfer the *Sample* into a flask, and add 50 mL of a 1:1 ethanol: diethyl ether mixture that has been neutralized to phenolphthalein with 0.1 N sodium hydroxide. Connect the flask to a suitable condenser, and warm it slowly while frequently shaking it. Add 1 ml of phenolphthalein TS and titrate with 0.1 N sodium hydroxide until the solution remains faintly pink after shaking it for 30 s. Calculate the *Acid Value* by the formula:

$$\text{Result} = 56.11V \times (N/W)$$

V	= volume of the 0.1 N sodium hydroxide solution used (mL)
N	= normality of the sodium hydroxide solution
W	= weight of the sample taken (g)

Acceptance criteria: NMT 6
- FREE GLYCERIN, *Free Glycerin or Propylene Glycol*, Appendix VII
  Acceptance criteria: NMT 1%
- IODINE VALUE, Appendix VII
  Acceptance criteria: NMT 3

- **1-MONOGLYCERIDES CONTENT,** *1-Monoglycerides,* Appendix VII
  Sample: 1 g, melted at a temperature not higher than 80° and mixed
  Analysis: Calculate the percentage of 1-monoglycerides as a normalized content of monopalmitin and monostearin by the formula:

  $$\text{Result} = [(V_B - V_S) \times N \times F]/W$$

  V_B = volume of 0.1 N sodium thiosulfate solution consumed by the blank (mL)
  V_S = volume of 0.1 N sodium thiosulfate solution consumed by the sample (mL)
  N = normality of the sodium thiosulfate solution
  F = 1/20th of the formula weight of glyceryl monopalmitostearate, 17.2
  W = weight of the sample taken (g)
  Acceptance criteria: NMT 18.0%
- **RESIDUE ON IGNITION (SULFATED ASH),** Appendix IIC
  Sample: 5 g
  Acceptance criteria: NMT 0.1%
- **SAPONIFICATION VALUE,** Appendix VII
  Acceptance criteria: Between 170 and 200

Glyceryl Tripropanoate

First Published: Prior to FCC 6

Tripropionin

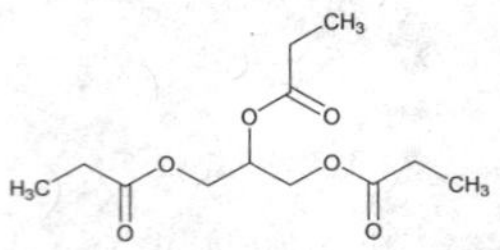

$C_{12}H_{20}O_6$ Formula wt 260.29
FEMA: 3286
UNII: F8L8EVQ6QB [glyceryl tripropanoate]

DESCRIPTION
Glyceryl Tripropanoate occurs as a colorless to pale yellow liquid.
Odor: Odorless with a bitter taste
Boiling Point: ~175° to 176° (20 mm Hg)
Function: Flavoring agent

ASSAY
- **PROCEDURE:** Proceed as directed under *M-1b,* Appendix XI.
  Acceptance criteria: NLT 97.1% of $C_{12}H_{20}O_6$

SPECIFIC TESTS
- **ACID VALUE, FLAVOR CHEMICALS (OTHER THAN ESSENTIAL OILS),** *M-15,* Appendix XI
  Acceptance criteria: NMT 2.0
- **REFRACTIVE INDEX,** Appendix II: At 20°
  Acceptance criteria: Between 1.431 and 1.435

- **SPECIFIC GRAVITY:** Determine at 25° by any reliable method (see *General Provisions*).
  Acceptance criteria: Between 1.078 and 1.082

Glyceryl Tristearate

First Published: Prior to FCC 6

Tristearin
Stearin
Octadecanoic Acid
1,2,3-Propane Tristearoyl Ester

$C_{57}H_{110}O_6$ Formula wt 891.49
                    CAS: [555-43-1]

UNII: P6OCJ2551R [tristearin]

DESCRIPTION
Glyceryl Tristearate occurs as a white, microfine, crystalline powder. It is prepared by reacting glycerin with stearic acid in the presence of a suitable catalyst such as aluminum oxide. It is also found in many animal and vegetable fats such as tallow and cocoa butter. It is soluble in hot alcohol and in chloroform; very slightly soluble in cold alcohol, in ether, and in petroleum ether; but insoluble in water.
Function: Crystallization accelerator; lubricant; surface-finishing agent
Packaging and Storage: Store in tight, light-resistant containers.

IDENTIFICATION
- **FATTY ACID COMPOSITION,** Appendix VII
  Acceptance criteria: A sample exhibits the following composition profile of fatty acids:

Fatty Acid	Weight % (Range)
≤ 12	0.0 - 0.3
12:0	0.0 - 0.5
14:0	0.0 - 1.0
16:0	0.0 - 0.1
16:1	0.0 - 0.1
18:0	> 95
18:1	0.0 - 0.5
18:2	0.0 - 0.5
≥ 20	0.0 - 0.5

IMPURITIES
Inorganic Impurities
- **LEAD,** *Lead Limit Test, Atomic Absorption Spectrophotometric Graphite Furnace Method, Method II,* Appendix IIIB
  Acceptance criteria: NMT 1 mg/kg

SPECIFIC TESTS
- **ACID VALUE (FATS AND RELATED SUBSTANCES),** Appendix VII
  Acceptance criteria: NMT 1.0
- **FREE GLYCERIN,** *Free Glycerin and Propylene Glycol,* Appendix VII
  Acceptance criteria: NMT 0.5%

- **HYDROXYL VALUE**, *Method II*, Appendix VII
  Acceptance criteria: NMT 5.0
- **IODINE VALUE**, Appendix VII
  Acceptance criteria: NMT 1.0
- **MELTING RANGE OR TEMPERATURE DETERMINATION**, *Procedure for Class II*, Appendix IIB
  Acceptance criteria: Between 69° and 73°
- **RESIDUE ON IGNITION (SULFATED ASH)**, Appendix IIC
  Sample: 5 g
  Acceptance criteria: NMT 0.1%
- **SAPONIFICATION VALUE**, Appendix VII
  Acceptance criteria: Between 186 and 192
- **UNSAPONIFIABLE MATTER**, Appendix VII
  Acceptance criteria: NMT 0.5%

Glyceryl-Lacto Esters of Fatty Acids

First Published: Prior to FCC 6

Lactated Mono-Diglycerides
Lactic and Fatty Acid Esters of Glycerol
INS: 472b

DESCRIPTION
Glyceryl-Lacto Esters of Fatty Acids occur as a waxy solid that varies in consistency from soft to hard. They are a mixture of partial lactic and fatty acid esters of glycerin. They are dispersible in hot water and are moderately soluble in hot isopropanol, in xylene, and in cottonseed oil.
Function: Emulsifier; stabilizer
Packaging and Storage: Store in well-closed containers.

IDENTIFICATION
- **PROCEDURE**
  p-Phenylphenol solution: 75 mg of p-phenylphenol dissolved in 5 mL of 1 N sodium hydroxide
  Cupric sulfate solution: 1 g of cupric sulfate pentahydrate dissolved in 25 mL of water
  Sample solution: The solution obtained in the test for *Total Lactic Acid* (below)
  Analysis: Transfer 1 mL of *Sample solution* into a 25-mL glass-stoppered test tube, add 0.1 mL *Cupric sulfate solution* and 6 mL of sulfuric acid, and mix. Stopper loosely, heat in a boiling water bath for 5 min, and then cool in an ice bath for 5 min. Remove from the ice bath, add 0.1 mL of *p-Phenylphenol solution* and mix. Allow to stand at room temperature for 1 min, then heat in a boiling water bath for 1 min.
  Acceptance criteria: A deep, blue-violet color indicates the presence of lactic acid.

IMPURITIES
Inorganic Impurities
- **LEAD**, *Lead Limit Test, Atomic Absorption Spectrophotometric Graphite Furnace Method, Method II*, Appendix IIIB
  Acceptance criteria: NMT 0.5 mg/kg

SPECIFIC TESTS
- **ACID VALUE (FATS AND RELATED SUBSTANCES)**, *Method II*, Appendix VII

  Acceptance criteria: The result conforms to the representations of the vendor.
- **FREE GLYCERIN**, *Free Glycerin or Propylene Glycol*, Appendix VII
  Acceptance criteria: The result conforms to the representations of the vendor.
- **1-MONOGLYCERIDE CONTENT**, *1-Monoglycerides*, Appendix VII
  Acceptance criteria: The result conforms to the representations of the vendor.
- **RESIDUE ON IGNITION (SULFATED ASH)**, Appendix IIC
  Sample: 1 g
  Acceptance criteria: NMT 0.1%
- **TOTAL LACTIC ACID**
  Sample: An amount of melted sample equivalent to between 140 and 170 mg of lactic acid
  Analysis: Transfer the *Sample* into a 250-mL Erlenmeyer flask. Pipet 20 mL of 0.5 N alcoholic potassium hydroxide into the flask, connect an air condenser at least 65 cm long, and reflux for 30 min. In a separate flask, run a blank determination (see *General Provisions*) using the same volume of 0.5 N alcoholic potassium hydroxide. Add 20 mL of water to each flask, then disconnect the condensers, evaporate to a volume of about 20 mL, and cool to about 40°. Add methyl red TS to each flask, and titrate the blank with 0.5 N hydrochloric acid. While swirling the sample flask, add exactly the same volume of 0.5 N hydrochloric acid. Add 50 mL of hexane to each flask. Swirl the sample flask vigorously to dissolve the fatty acids, then quantitatively transfer the contents of each flask into separate 250-mL separatory funnels, and shake for 30 s. Collect the aqueous phases in 300-mL Erlenmeyer flasks, wash the hexane solutions with 50 mL of water, and combine the wash solution with the original aqueous phases in the Erlenmeyer flasks, discarding the hexane solution. Titrate with 0.1 N potassium hydroxide, using phenolphthalein TS as the indicator, to a pink color that persists for at least 30 s. [NOTE—Save the resulting titrated *Sample solution* for use in the *Identification* test (above).]
  Calculate the percent of total lactic acid by the formula:

  $$\text{Result} = [(V_S - V_B) \times N \times F_E]/W$$

  V_S = volume of 0.1 N potassium hydroxide required for the titration of the *Sample* (mL)
  V_B = volume of 0.1 N potassium hydroxide required for the titration of the blank (mL)
  N = exact normality of the potassium hydroxide solution
  F_E = equivalence factor to lactic acid, 9.008
  W = weight of the sample taken (g)
  Acceptance criteria: The result conforms to the representations of the vendor.
- **UNSAPONIFIABLE MATTER**, Appendix VII
  Acceptance criteria: NMT 2.0%
- **WATER**, *Water Determination*, Appendix IIB
  Acceptance criteria: The result conforms to the representations of the vendor.

Glycine

First Published: Prior to FCC 6
Last Revision: FCC 6

Aminoacetic Acid
Glycocoll

$C_2H_5NO_2$
INS: 640
UNII: TE7660XO1C [glycine]
Formula wt 75.07
CAS: [56-40-6]

DESCRIPTION
Glycine occurs as a white, crystalline powder. One g dissolves in about 4 mL of water. It is very slightly soluble in alcohol and in ether. Its solution is acid to litmus.
Function: Nutrient
Packaging and Storage: Store in well-closed containers.

IDENTIFICATION
- **INFRARED ABSORPTION,** *Spectrophotometric Identification Tests,* Appendix IIIC
  Reference standard: USP Glycine RS
  Sample and standard preparation: M
  Acceptance criteria: The spectrum of the sample exhibits maxima at the same wavelengths as those in the spectrum of the *Reference standard.*

ASSAY
- **PROCEDURE**
  Sample: 175 mg, previously dried
  Analysis: Transfer the *Sample* into a 250-mL flask and dissolve in 50 mL of glacial acetic acid. Add 2 drops of crystal violet TS, and titrate with 0.1 N perchloric acid to a blue-green endpoint. [**CAUTION**—Handle perchloric acid in an appropriate fume hood.] Perform a blank determination (see *General Provisions*) and make any necessary correction. Each mL of 0.1 N perchloric acid is equivalent to 7.507 mg of $C_2H_5NO_2$.
  Acceptance criteria: NLT 98.5% and NMT 101.5% of $C_2H_5NO_2$, on the dried basis.

IMPURITIES
Inorganic Impurities
- **LEAD,** *Lead Limit Test,* Appendix IIIB
  Sample solution: Prepare as directed for organic compounds.
  Control: 5 µg Pb (5 mL of *Diluted Standard Lead Solution*)
  Acceptance criteria: NMT 5 mg/kg

SPECIFIC TESTS
- **LOSS ON DRYING,** Appendix IIC: 105° for 3 h
  Acceptance criteria: NMT 0.2%
- **RESIDUE ON IGNITION (SULFATED ASH),** Appendix IIC
  Sample: 2 g
  Acceptance criteria: NMT 0.1%

Grape Skin Extract

First Published: Prior to FCC 6

Enocianina
INS: 163(ii)
UNII: F02KPB2508 [vitis vinifera anthocyanins]
CAS: [11029-12-2]

DESCRIPTION
Grape Skin Extract occurs as a red to purple powder or liquid concentrate. It is prepared by aqueous extraction of grape marc remaining from the pressing of grapes to obtain juice. Extraction is effected with water containing sulfur dioxide. During the steeping process, sulfur dioxide is added, and the sugar content is reduced by fermentation; further concentration removes most of the alcohol. The primary color components are anthocyanins, such as the glucosides of malvidin, peonidin, petunidin, delphinidin, or cyanidin. Other components naturally present are sugars, tartrates, malates, tannins, and minerals. The powder may contain an added carrier, such as maltodextrin, modified starch, or gum. In acid solution, Grape Skin Extract is red; in neutral to alkaline solution, it is unstable and violet to blue.
Function: Color
Packaging and Storage: Store liquid Grape Skin Extract with aseptic packaging or in high-density polyethylene containers at 4° to 14°. Store powdered Grape Skin Extract in fiber drums at room temperature.

IDENTIFICATION
- **PROCEDURE**
  Analysis: Transfer 1 g of sample and 1 g of potassium metabisulfite to a 100-mL volumetric flask. Add about 50 mL of *pH 3.0 Citrate–citric acid buffer* (see *Assay,* below) to dissolve the contents of the flask and dilute to volume with the same buffer, and mix.
  Acceptance criteria: The red color caused by anthocyanins is bleached.

ASSAY
- **PROCEDURE**
  pH 3.0 Citrate–citric acid buffer: Add, dropwise, 0.1 M sodium citrate to 0.1 M citric acid until a pH of 3.0 is reached, as determined by a glass electrode.
  Sample solution: Transfer 0.2 g of sample to a 100-mL volumetric flask, dissolve in and dilute to volume with *pH 3.0 Citrate–citric acid buffer.* Remove any undissolved material by filtration or centrifugation. Adjust the pH to 3.0.
  Analysis: Using a suitable spectrophotometer and a 1-cm cell, measure the absorbance of the *Sample Solution* at the wavelength maximum of about 525 nm. Calculate the color strength, expressed as the absorbance of a 1% solution in a 1-cm cell, using the formula:

  $$\text{Result} = A_{525}/S$$

  A_{525} = absorbance at 525 nm
  S = weight of the sample taken (g)

Acceptance criteria: NLT 90% of the color strength as represented by the vendor

IMPURITIES
Inorganic Impurities
- **ARSENIC,** *Arsenic Limit Test,* Appendix IIIB
  Acceptance criteria: NMT 1 mg/kg
- **LEAD,** *Lead Limit Test,* Appendix IIIB
  Sample solution: Prepare as directed for organic compounds.
  Control: 5 µg Pb (5 mL of *Diluted Standard Lead Solution*)
  Acceptance criteria: NMT 5 mg/kg

Grapefruit Oil, Coldpressed
First Published: Prior to FCC 6

Grapefruit Oil, Expressed
Oil of Shaddock

CAS: [8016-20-4]

UNII: YR377U58W9 [grapefruit oil]

DESCRIPTION
Grapefruit Oil, Coldpressed, occurs as a yellow, sometimes red, liquid that often shows a flocculent separation of waxy material. It is the oil obtained by expression from the fresh peel of the grapefruit *Citrus paradisi* Macfayden (*Citrus decumana* L.) (Fam. Rutaceae). It is soluble in most fixed oils and in mineral oil, often with opalescence or cloudiness. It is slightly soluble in propylene glycol and insoluble in glycerin. It may contain a suitable antioxidant.

Function: Flavoring agent

Packaging and Storage: Store in a cool place protected from light in full, tight containers that are made from steel or aluminum and that are suitably lined.

IDENTIFICATION
- **INFRARED SPECTRA,** *Spectrophotometric Identification Tests,* Appendix IIIC
  Acceptance criteria: The spectrum of the sample exhibits relative maxima at the same wavelengths as those of the spectrum below.

SPECIFIC TESTS
- **ANGULAR ROTATION,** *Optical (Specific) Rotation,* Appendix IIB: Use a 100-mm tube.
  Acceptance criteria: Between +91° and +96°
- **REFRACTIVE INDEX,** Appendix IIB
  [NOTE—Use an Abbé or other refractometer of equal or greater accuracy.]
  Acceptance criteria: Between 1.475 and 1.478 at 20°
- **RESIDUE ON EVAPORATION,** Appendix VI: Heat the sample for 5 h.
  Acceptance criteria: Between 5.0% and 10.0%
- **SPECIFIC GRAVITY:** Determine by any reliable method (see *General Provisions*).
  Acceptance criteria: Between 0.848 and 0.856

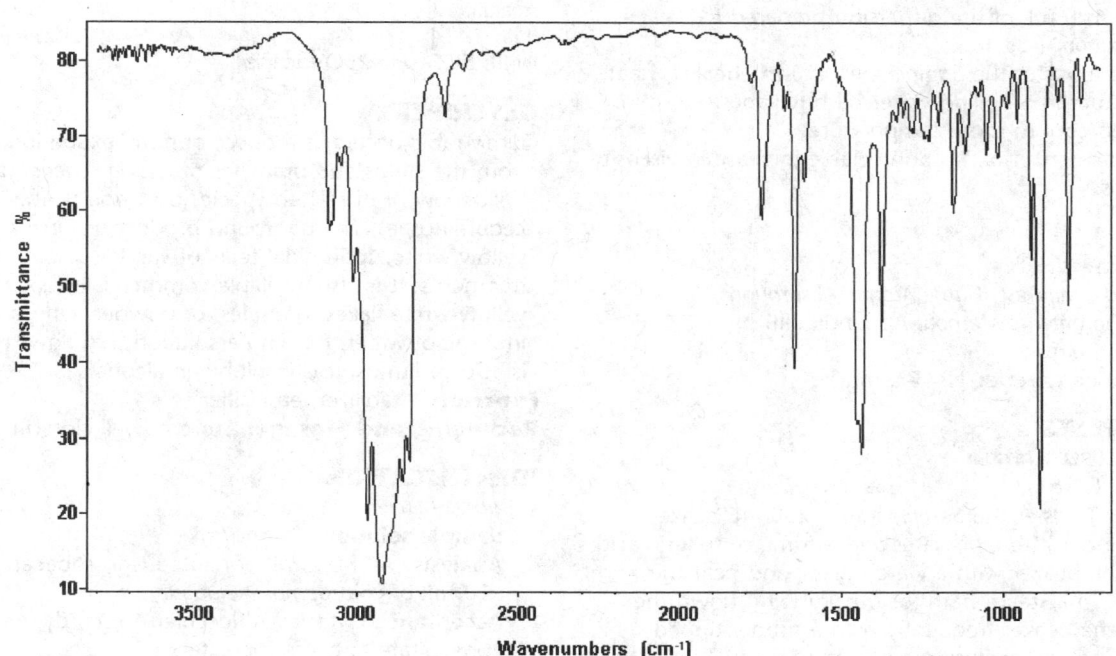

Grapefruit Oil, Coldpressed

Guar Gum

First Published: Prior to FCC 6

INS: 412
UNII: E89I1637KE [guar gum]
CAS: [9000-30-0]

DESCRIPTION
Guar Gum occurs as a white to yellow-white powder. It is a gum obtained from the ground endosperms of *Cyamopsis tetragonolobus* (L.) Taub (Fam. Leguminosae) (synonym *Cyamopsis psoraloides* [Lam.] D.C.). It consists chiefly of a high molecular weight polysaccharide composed of galactose and mannose units and may be described chemically as a galactomannan. It is dispersible in either hot or cold water, forming a sol, having a pH between 5.4 and 7.0, that may be converted to a gel by the addition of small amounts of sodium borate.

Function: Stabilizer; thickener; emulsifier
Packaging and Storage: Store in well-closed containers.

IDENTIFICATION
- **A. Procedure**
  Sample: 2 g
  Analysis: Transfer the *Sample* into a 400-mL beaker, and moisten it thoroughly with about 4 mL of isopropyl alcohol. Add, with vigorous stirring, 200 mL of cold water, and continue to stir until the gum is completely and uniformly dispersed.
  Acceptance criteria: An opalescent, viscous dispersion forms.
- **B. Procedure**
  Sample: 100 mL of the dispersion prepared in *Identification* test A
  Analysis: Transfer the *Sample* into 400-mL beaker, heat the mixture in a boiling water bath for about 10 min, and then cool to room temperature.
  Acceptance criteria: No appreciable increase in viscosity develops.

IMPURITIES
Inorganic Impurities
- **Lead,** *Lead Limit Test, Flame Atomic Absorption Spectrophotometric Method,* Appendix IIIB
  Sample: 10 g
  Acceptance criteria: NMT 2 mg/kg

SPECIFIC TESTS
- **Acid-Insoluble Matter**
  Sample: 1.5 g
  Analysis: Transfer the *Sample* into a 250-mL beaker containing 150-mL of water and 1.5 mL of sulfuric acid. Cover the beaker with a watch glass, and heat the mixture on a steam bath for 6 h, rubbing down the wall of the beaker frequently with a rubber-tipped stirring rod and replacing any water lost by evaporation. At the end of the 6-h heating period, add 500 mg, accurately weighed, of a suitable filter aid, previously dried for 3 h at 105°, and filter through a tared, sintered-glass filter crucible. Wash the residue several times with hot water, dry the crucible and its contents at 105° for 3 h, cool in a desiccator, and weigh. The difference between the weight of the filter aid and that of the residue is the weight of *Acid-Insoluble Matter*.
  Acceptance criteria: NMT 7.0%
- **Ash (Total),** Appendix IIC
  Acceptance criteria: NMT 1.5%
- **Galactomannans**
  Analysis: Determine the difference between 100 and the sum of the percent *Acid-Insoluble Matter*, *Ash (Total)*, *Loss on Drying*, and *Protein*.
  Acceptance criteria: NLT 70.0%
- **Loss on Drying,** Appendix IIC: 105° for 5 h
  Acceptance criteria: NMT 15.0%
- **Protein,** *Nitrogen Determination, Method I,* Appendix IIIC
  Sample: 3.5 g
  Analysis: Transfer the *Sample* into a 500-mL Kjeldahl flask. Multiply the percentage of nitrogen determined by 6.25.
  Acceptance criteria: NMT 10.0%
- **Starch**
  Sample solution: 100 mg/mL
  Analysis: Add a few drops of iodine TS to the *Sample solution*.
  Acceptance criteria: No blue color appears.

Gum Arabic

First Published: Prior to FCC 6
Last Revision: First Supplement, FCC 6

Acacia
INS: 414
UNII: 5C5403N26O [acacia]
CAS: [9000-01-5]

DESCRIPTION
Gum Arabic occurs as a dried, gummy exudation obtained from the stems and branches of *Acacia senegal* (L.) Willdenow or of related species of *Acacia* (Fam. Leguminosae). The unground product occurs as white or yellow-white, spheroidal tears of varying size or in angular fragments. It is also available commercially as white to yellow-white flakes, granules, or powder. One g dissolves in 2 mL of water, forming a solution that flows readily and is acid to litmus. It is insoluble in alcohol.

Function: Stabilizer; emulsifier
Packaging and Storage: Store in well-closed containers.

IDENTIFICATION
- **Procedure**
  Sample solution: 20 mg/mL
  Analysis: Add 0.2 mL of diluted lead subacetate TS to 10 mL of cold *Sample solution*.
  Acceptance criteria: A flocculent or curdy, white precipitate forms immediately.

IMPURITIES
Inorganic Impurities
- **Arsenic,** *Arsenic Limit Test,* Appendix IIIB
  Sample solution: Prepare as directed for organic compounds.

Acceptance criteria: NMT 3 mg/kg
- **Lead,** *Lead Limit Test,* Appendix IIIB
  Sample solution: Prepare as directed for organic compounds.
  Control: 5 µg Pb (5 mL of *Diluted Standard Lead Solution*)
  Acceptance criteria: NMT 5 mg/kg

SPECIFIC TESTS
- **Ash (Acid-Insoluble),** Appendix IIC
  Acceptance criteria: NMT 0.5%
- **Ash (Total),** Appendix IIC
  Analysis: Proceed as directed, but ignite at 675 ± 25°.
  Acceptance criteria: NMT 4.0%
- **Insoluble Matter**
  Sample: 5 g
  Analysis: Dissolve the *Sample* in about 100 mL of water contained in a 250-mL Erlenmeyer flask, add 10 mL of 2.7 N hydrochloric acid, and boil gently for 15 min. Filter the hot solution by suction through a tared filtering crucible, and wash the residue thoroughly with hot water. Dry the residue at 105° for 2 h, and weigh.
  Acceptance criteria: NMT 1.0%
- **Loss on Drying,** Appendix IIC: 105° for 5 h
  [NOTE—Powder unground samples sufficiently to pass through a No. 40 sieve, and mix well before weighing and drying.]
  Acceptance criteria: NMT 15.0%
- **Starch or Dextrin**
  Sample solution: 20 mg/mL
  Analysis: Boil the *Sample solution*, cool, and add a few drops of iodine TS.
  Acceptance criteria: No blue or red color appears.
- **Tannin-Bearing Gums**
  Sample solution: 20 mg/mL
  Analysis: Add about 0.1 mL of ferric chloride TS to 10 mL of *Sample solution*.
  Acceptance criteria: No black coloration or precipitate forms.

Gum Ghatti

First Published: Prior to FCC 6

Indian Gum

UNII: X1N78DL020 [ghatti gum]   CAS: [9000-28-6]

DESCRIPTION
Gum Ghatti occurs as colorless or light to dark tan tears. It is also available as a gray to red-gray powder. It is the dried gummy exudate from the stems of *Anogeissus latifolia* Wall (Fam. Combretaceae). It is a complex, water-soluble, acidic polysaccharide composed of the calcium and magnesium salts of L-arabinose, D-galactose, D-mannose, D-xylose, and D-glucuronic acids in the approximate molar ratio of 10 : 6 : 2 : 1 : 2. It is slightly soluble in water, but it is insoluble in 90% alcohol.
Function: Emulsifier
Packaging and Storage: Store in well-closed containers.

IDENTIFICATION
- **Procedure**
  Sample solution: 10 mg/mL
  Lead acetate solution: [CAUTION—Use gloves and goggles to avoid contact with skin and eyes. Use an effective fume removal device or other respiratory protection.] Activate 50 to 60 g of lead (II) oxide by heating it for 2.5 to 3 h in a furnace at 650° to 670° (cooled product should have a lemon color). Boil 80 g of lead acetate trihydrate and 40 g of the freshly activated lead (II) oxide with 250 g of water in a 500-mL Erlenmeyer flask provided with a reflux condenser for 45 min. Cool, filter off any residue, and dilute with recently boiled water to a density of 1.25 at 20°. Add 4 mL of water to 1 mL of the lead acetate solution, and filter.
  Analysis: Add 0.2 mL of the *Lead acetate solution* to 5 mL of cold *Sample solution*.
  Acceptance criteria: A slight precipitate or clear solution results in which an opaque flocculent precipitate forms on the addition of 1 mL of 3 N ammonia solution.

IMPURITIES
Inorganic Impurities
- **Arsenic,** *Arsenic Limit Test,* Appendix IIIB
  Sample solution: Prepare as directed for organic compounds.
  Acceptance criteria: NMT 3 mg/kg
- **Lead,** *Lead Limit Test,* Appendix IIIB
  Sample solution: Prepare as directed for organic compounds.
  Control: 5 µg Pb (5 mL of *Diluted Standard Lead Solution*)
  Acceptance criteria: NMT 5 mg/kg

SPECIFIC TESTS
- **Ash (Acid-Insoluble),** Appendix IIC
  Acceptance criteria: NMT 1.75%
- **Ash (Total),** Appendix IIC
  Acceptance criteria: NMT 6.0%
- **Insoluble Matter**
  Sample: 5 g
  Analysis: Dissolve the *Sample* in about 100 mL of water contained in a 250-mL Erlenmeyer flask, add 10 mL of 2.7 N hydrochloric acid, and boil gently for 15 min. Filter the hot solution by suction through a tared filtering crucible and wash the residue thoroughly with hot water. Dry the residue at 105° for 2 h, and weigh.
  Acceptance criteria: NMT 1.0%
- **Loss on Drying,** Appendix IIC: Ground sample at 105° for 5 h.
  [NOTE—Powder unground samples to pass through a No. 40 sieve, and mix well before weighing.]
  Acceptance criteria: NMT 14.0%
- **Viscosity Determination,** *Viscosity of Cellulose Gum,* Appendix IIB
  Analysis: Determine at 75° using spindle No. 2 at 60 rpm.
  Acceptance criteria: A 5% solution exhibits a viscosity, within the range stated on the label.

OTHER REQUIREMENTS
- **LABELING:** Indicate the viscosity range (centipoises) of a 5% solution of the gum.

Gum Guaiac
First Published: Prior to FCC 6

Guaiac Resin
INS: 314   CAS: [9000-29-7]
UNII: N0K2Z502R6 [guaiacum officinale resin]

DESCRIPTION
Gum Guaiac occurs as irregular masses enclosing fragments of vegetable tissues; as large, nearly homogeneous masses; and occasionally, as more-or-less rounded or ovoid tears. It is externally brown-black to dusky brown, acquiring a green color on long exposure to air, the fractured surface having a glassy luster, the thin pieces being transparent and varying in color from brown to yellow-orange. The powder is moderate yellow-brown, becoming olive brown on exposure to air. It is the resin of the wood of *Guajacum officinale* L. or *Guajacum sanctum* L. (Fam. Zygophyllaceae). Gum Guaiac dissolves incompletely, but readily, in alcohol, in ether, in chloroform, and in solutions of alkalies. It is slightly soluble in carbon disulfide.
Function: Antioxidant
Packaging and Storage: Store in well-closed containers.

IDENTIFICATION
- **A. PROCEDURE**
  Sample solution: 10 mg/mL in alcohol
  Analysis: Add 1 drop of ferric chloride TS to 5 mL of *Sample solution*.
  Acceptance criteria: A blue color appears that gradually changes to green, finally becoming green-yellow.
- **B. PROCEDURE**
  Sample solution: 10 mg/mL in alcohol
  Analysis: Add 5 mL of water to 5 mL of *Sample solution* and mix. Add 20 mg of lead peroxide and shake the mixture, which becomes blue. Filter the solution.
  Acceptance criteria: After boiling a portion of the filtrate the color disappears, but may be restored by adding lead peroxide and shaking the filtrate. To a second portion of the filtrate, add a few drops of 2.7 N hydrochloric acid. The color immediately disappears.

IMPURITIES
Inorganic Impurities
- **LEAD,** *Lead Limit Test,* Appendix IIIB
  Sample solution: Prepare as directed for organic compounds.
  Control: 4 µg Pb (4 mL of *Diluted Standard Lead Solution*)
  Acceptance criteria: NMT 2 mg/kg

SPECIFIC TESTS
- **ALCOHOL-INSOLUBLE RESIDUE**
  Sample: 2 g, finely powdered
  Analysis: Place the *Sample* in a dry, tared extraction thimble, and extract it with alcohol in a suitable continuous extraction apparatus for 3 h or until completely extracted. Dry the insoluble residue remaining in the thimble for 4 h at 105°, and weigh.
  Acceptance criteria: NMT 15.0%
- **ASH (ACID-INSOLUBLE),** Appendix IIC
  Acceptance criteria: NMT 2.0%
- **ASH (TOTAL),** Appendix IIC
  Acceptance criteria: NMT 5.0%
- **MELTING RANGE OR TEMPERATURE DETERMINATION,** Appendix IIB
  Acceptance criteria: Between 85° and 90°
- **ROSIN**
  Sample solution: 100 mg/mL in petroleum ether
  Analysis: Mix and shake a quantity of *Sample solution*, which should be colorless, with an equal quantity of a freshly prepared, 5 mg/mL aqueous solution of cupric acetate. Prepare a similar solution of cupric acetate in petroleum ether.
  Acceptance criteria: The *Sample solution*/cupric acetate mixture is not more green than the solution of cupric acetate in petroleum ether.

Helium
First Published: Prior to FCC 6

He
INS: 939
UNII: 206GF3GB41 [helium]
Formula wt 4.00
CAS: [7440-59-7]

DESCRIPTION
Helium occurs as a colorless gas that is not combustible and does not support combustion. It is very slightly soluble in water. One L of the gas weighs about 180 mg at 0° and 760 mm Hg.
Function: Processing aid
Packaging and Storage: Store in appropriate gas cylinders.

[NOTE—Reduce the sample gas cylinder pressure with a regulator. Measure the sample gas with a gas volume meter downstream from the detector tube to minimize contamination of or change to the gas samples.]

IDENTIFICATION
- **A. PROCEDURE**
  Analysis: Cautiously insert a burning wood splinter into an inverted test tube filled with sample gas.
  Acceptance criteria: The flame is extinguished.
- **B. PROCEDURE**
  Analysis: Fill a small balloon with sample gas.
  Acceptance criteria: The filled balloon shows buoyancy.

ASSAY
- **PROCEDURE**
  Standard: Air–helium certified standard (A mixture of 1.0% air in industrial-grade helium is available from most suppliers.)
  Chromatographic system, Appendix IIA
    Mode: Gas chromatography
    Detector: Thermal-conductivity detector
    Carrier gas: Helium (industrial grade, 99.99%)
    Column: 6-m × 4-mm (id), or equivalent, packed with porous polymer beads (PoraPak Q, or equivalent) that permit complete separation of nitrogen and oxygen from Helium, although nitrogen and oxygen might not be separated from each other.
    Column temperature: 60°
  Analysis: Select the operating conditions of the gas chromatograph, or equivalent, so that the peak signal from the Standard corresponds to NLT 70% of the full-scale reading. Introduce a gas sample into the gas-sampling valve and record the chromatogram. Compare the sample chromatogram to that produced by the Standard.
  Acceptance criteria: The peak response produced by the sample gas exhibits a retention time corresponding to that produced by the Standard and, when compared with the peak response of that Standard, indicates NMT 1.0% air, by volume (indicating NLT 99.0% of He, by volume).

IMPURITIES
Inorganic Impurities
- **AIR**
  Analysis: Determine as directed under Assay (above).
  Acceptance criteria: NMT 1.0%, by volume
- **CARBON MONOXIDE**
  Sample: 1050 ± 50 mL
  Analysis: Pass the Sample gas through a carbon monoxide detector tube (see Detector Tubes, Solutions and Indicators) at the rate specified for the tube.
  Acceptance criteria: The indicator change corresponds to NMT 10 ppm, by volume.

SPECIFIC TESTS
- **ODOR**
  Analysis: Carefully open the sample gas cylinder valve to produce a moderate flow of sample gas. [CAUTION—Do not direct the gas stream toward the face, but deflect a portion of the stream toward the nose.]
  Acceptance criteria: No appreciable odor is discernible.

(E),(E)-2,4-Heptadienal
First Published: Prior to FCC 6
Last Revision: First Supplement, FCC 6

trans,trans-2,4-Heptadienal

C$_7$H$_{10}$O
FEMA: 3164
UNII: VY79R3SU8X [2,4-heptadienal]
Formula wt 110.16

DESCRIPTION
(E),(E)-2,4-Heptadienal occurs as a slightly yellow liquid. It may contain a suitable antioxidant.
Odor: Fatty, green
Solubility: Soluble in alcohol, most fixed oils; insoluble or practically insoluble in water
Boiling Point: ~100° (35 mm Hg)
Solubility in Alcohol, Appendix VI: One mL dissolves in 1 mL of 95% ethanol.
Function: Flavoring agent

IDENTIFICATION
- **INFRARED SPECTRA,** Spectrophotometric Identification Tests, Appendix IIIC
  Acceptance criteria: The spectrum of the sample exhibits relative maxima at the same wavelengths as those of the spectrum below.

ASSAY
- **PROCEDURE:** Proceed as directed under M-1a, Appendix XI.
  Acceptance criteria: NLT 92.0% of C$_7$H$_{10}$O (sum of isomers)

SPECIFIC TESTS
- **REFRACTIVE INDEX,** Appendix II: At 20°
  Acceptance criteria: Between 1.531 and 1.537
- **SPECIFIC GRAVITY:** Determine at 25° by any reliable method (see *General Provisions*).
  Acceptance criteria: Between 0.878 and 0.888

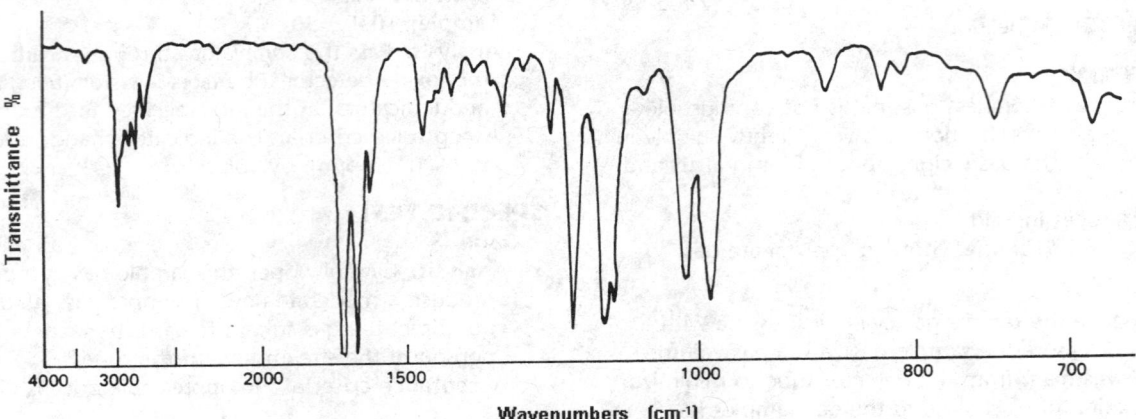

(*E*),(*E*)-2,4-Heptadienal

γ-Heptalactone

First Published: Prior to FCC 6

$C_7H_{12}O_2$
FEMA: 2539
UNII: U4XIN3U7DH [γ-heptalactone]

Formula wt 128.17

DESCRIPTION
γ-Heptalactone occurs as a colorless, slightly oily liquid.
Odor: Coconut, sweet, malty, caramel
Solubility: Soluble in propylene glycol; miscible in alcohol, most fixed oils; insoluble or practically insoluble in water
Boiling Point: ~61° (2 mm Hg)
Function: Flavoring agent

IDENTIFICATION
- **INFRARED SPECTRA,** *Spectrophotometric Identification Tests,* Appendix IIIC
  Acceptance criteria: The spectrum of the sample exhibits relative maxima at the same wavelengths as those of the spectrum below.

ASSAY
- **PROCEDURE:** Proceed as directed under *M-1a,* Appendix XI.
  Acceptance criteria: NLT 98.0% of $C_7H_{12}O_2$

SPECIFIC TESTS
- **REFRACTIVE INDEX,** Appendix II: At 20°
  Acceptance criteria: Between 1.439 and 1.445
- **SPECIFIC GRAVITY:** Determine at 25° by any reliable method (see *General Provisions*).
  Acceptance criteria: Between 0.989 and 0.998

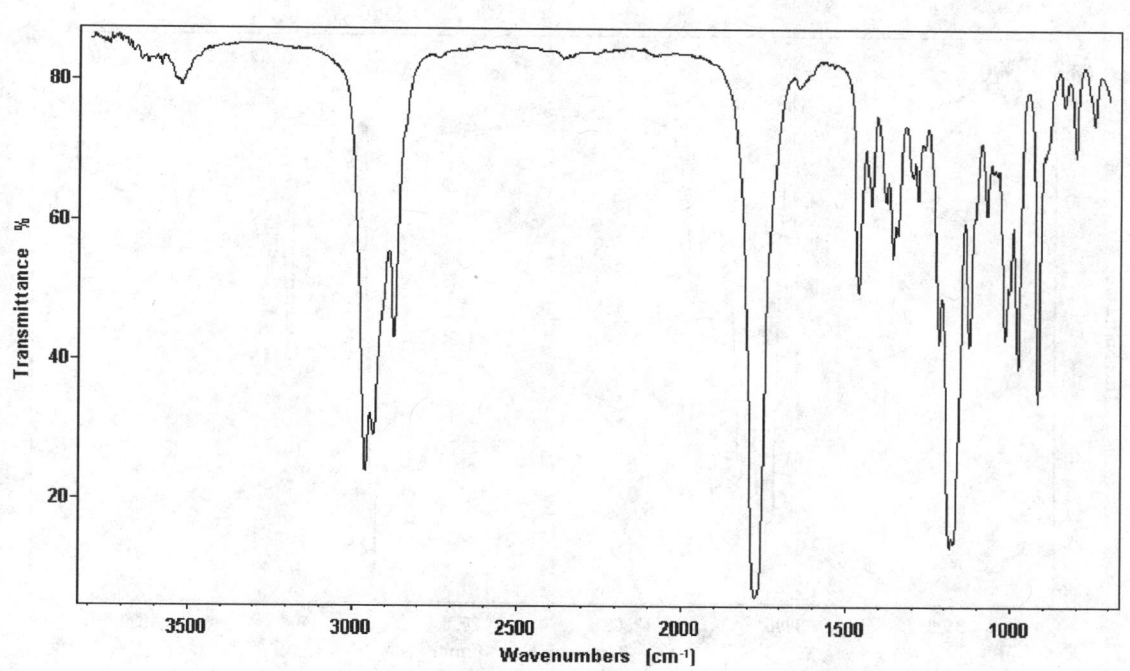

γ-Heptalactone

Heptanal

First Published: Prior to FCC 6
Last Revision: First Supplement, FCC 6

Aldehyde C-7
Heptaldehyde

$C_7H_{14}O$ Formula wt 114.19
FEMA: 2540
UNII: 92N104S3HF [heptanal]

DESCRIPTION
Heptanal occurs as a colorless to slightly yellow liquid. It may contain a suitable antioxidant.
Odor: Penetrating, oily
Solubility: Slightly soluble in water; miscible in alcohol, ether, most fixed oils
Boiling Point: ~153°
Solubility in Alcohol, Appendix VI: One mL dissolves in 2 mL of 70% alcohol to give a clear solution.

Function: Flavoring agent

IDENTIFICATION
- **INFRARED SPECTRA,** *Spectrophotometric Identification Tests,* Appendix IIIC
  Acceptance criteria: The spectrum of the sample exhibits relative maxima at the same wavelengths as those of the spectrum below.

ASSAY
- **PROCEDURE:** Proceed as directed under *M-1b,* Appendix XI.
  Acceptance criteria: NLT 92.0% of $C_7H_{14}O$

SPECIFIC TESTS
- **ACID VALUE, FLAVOR CHEMICALS (OTHER THAN ESSENTIAL OILS),** *M-15,* Appendix XI
  Acceptance criteria: NMT 10.0
- **REFRACTIVE INDEX,** Appendix II: At 20°
  Acceptance criteria: Between 1.412 and 1.420
- **SPECIFIC GRAVITY:** Determine at 25° by any reliable method (see *General Provisions*).
  Acceptance criteria: Between 0.815 and 0.820

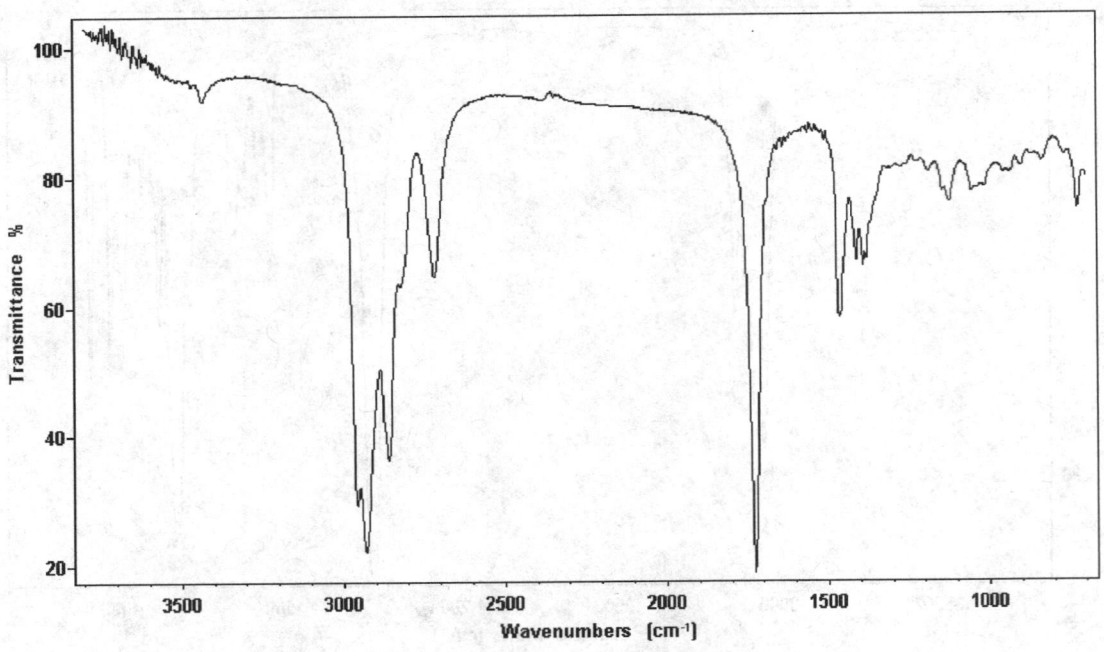

Heptanal

Change to read:

•2,3-Heptanedione• (ERR 1-Jan-2012)

First Published: Prior to FCC 6
Last Revision: First Supplement, FCC 6

Acetyl Valeryl

C₇H₁₂O₂   Formula wt 128.17
FEMA: 2543
UNII: DK55DDE86P [2,3-heptanedione]

DESCRIPTION

Change to read:

•2,3-Heptanedione• (ERR 1-Jan-2012) occurs as a yellow liquid. It may contain a suitable antioxidant.
Odor: Butter, cheese
Solubility: Soluble in propylene glycol, vegetable oils; insoluble or practically insoluble in water

Boiling Point: ~64° (18 mm Hg)
Solubility in Alcohol, Appendix VI: One mL dissolves in 1 mL of 95% ethanol.
Function: Flavoring agent

IDENTIFICATION

Change to read:

- **INFRARED SPECTRA,** *Spectrophotometric Identification Tests,* Appendix IIIC
  Acceptance criteria: The spectrum of the sample exhibits relative maxima at the same wavelengths as those of the spectrum below.

ASSAY

- **PROCEDURE:** Proceed as directed under *M-1b,* Appendix XI.
  Acceptance criteria: NLT 97.0% of C₇H₁₂O₂

SPECIFIC TESTS

- **REFRACTIVE INDEX,** Appendix II: At 20°
  Acceptance criteria: Between 1.411 and 1.418
- **SPECIFIC GRAVITY:** Determine at 25° by any reliable method (see *General Provisions*).
  Acceptance criteria: Between 0.916 and 0.923

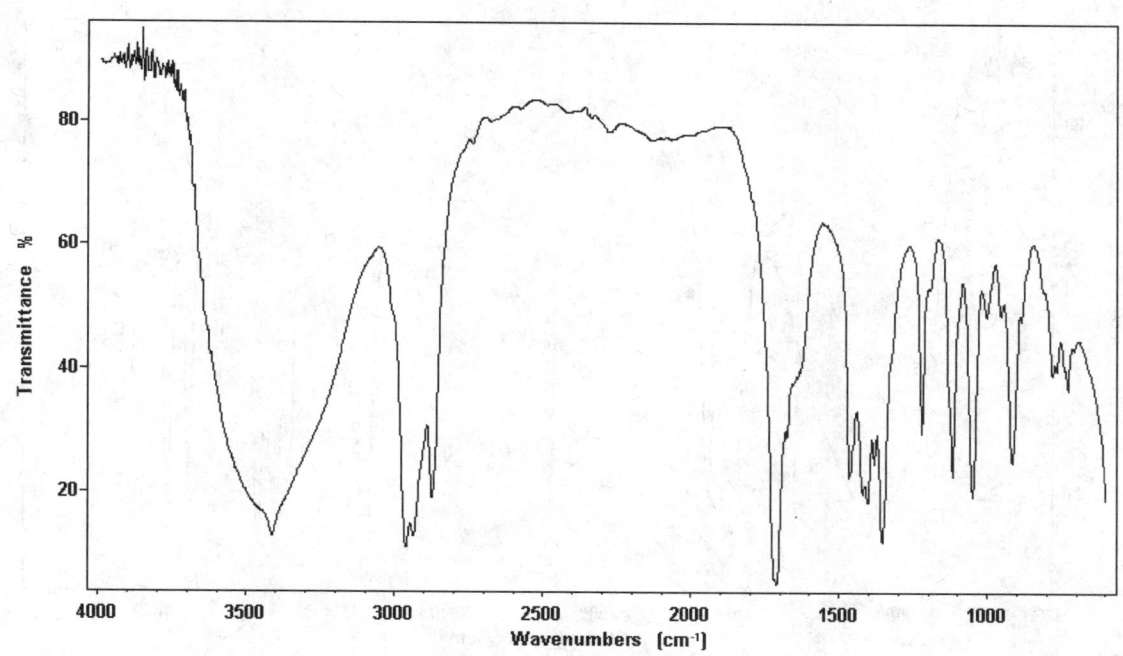

2,3-Heptanedione (ERR 1-Jan-2012)

2-Heptanone

First Published: Prior to FCC 6

Methyl Amyl Ketone

$C_7H_{14}O$ Formula wt 114.19
FEMA: 2544
UNII: 89VVP1B008 [2-heptanone]

DESCRIPTION
2-Heptanone occurs as a colorless, mobile liquid.
Odor: Fruity, spicy
Solubility: Miscible in alcohol, ether; 1 mL dissolves in 250 mL water.
Boiling Point: ~151°
Function: Flavoring agent

IDENTIFICATION
- **INFRARED SPECTRA,** *Spectrophotometric Identification Tests,* Appendix IIIC
  Acceptance criteria: The spectrum of the sample exhibits relative maxima at the same wavelengths as those of the spectrum below.

ASSAY
- **PROCEDURE:** Proceed as directed under *M-1b,* Appendix XI.
  Acceptance criteria: NLT 95.0% of $C_7H_{14}O$

SPECIFIC TESTS
- **ACID VALUE, FLAVOR CHEMICALS (OTHER THAN ESSENTIAL OILS),** *M-15,* Appendix XI
  Acceptance criteria: NMT 2.0
- **REFRACTIVE INDEX,** Appendix II: At 20°
  Acceptance criteria: Between 1.405 and 1.411
- **SPECIFIC GRAVITY:** Determine at 25° by any reliable method (see *General Provisions*).
  Acceptance criteria: Between 0.811 and 0.816

OTHER REQUIREMENTS
- **DISTILLATION RANGE,** Appendix IIB
  Acceptance criteria: Between 147° and 154°
- **RESIDUE ON EVAPORATION,** *M-16,* Appendix XI
  Sample: 100 mL
  Acceptance criteria: NMT 5 mg/100 mL
- **WATER,** *Water Determination, Method I,* Appendix IIB
  [NOTE—Use freshly distilled pyridine as solvent.]
  Acceptance criteria: NMT 0.3%

524 / 2-Heptanone / *Monographs*

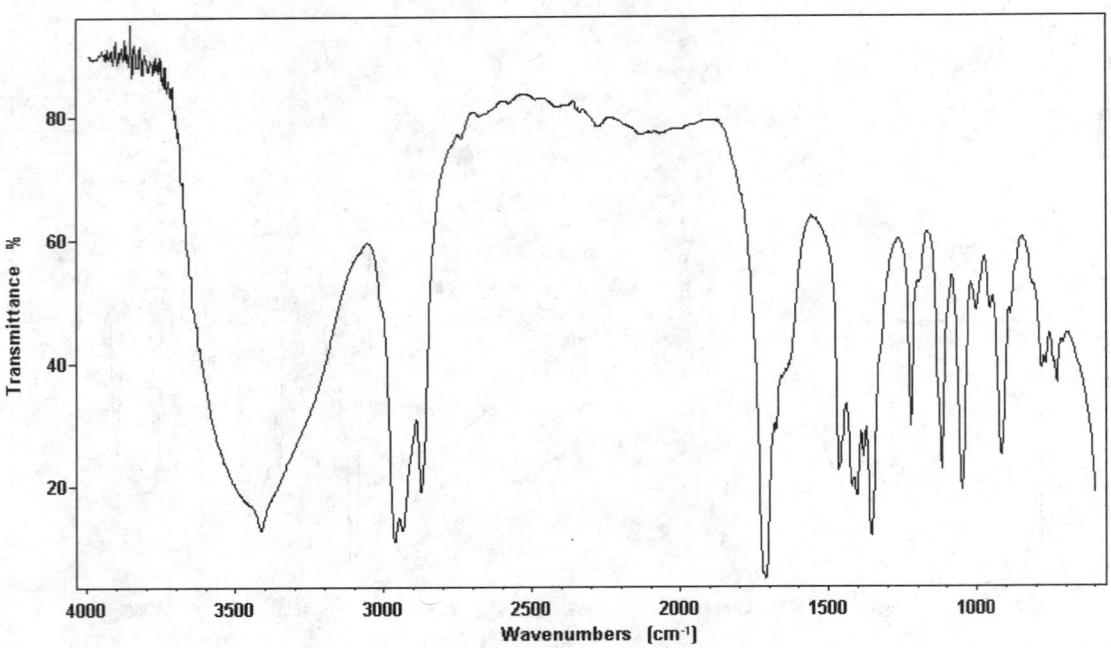

2-Heptanone

3-Heptanone

First Published: Prior to FCC 6

Ethyl Butyl Ketone

$C_7H_{14}O$ Formula wt 114.19
FEMA: 2545
UNII: 10GA6SR3AT [3-heptanone]

DESCRIPTION
3-Heptanone occurs as a colorless, mobile liquid.
Odor: Fruity, green, fatty
Solubility: Miscible in alcohol, ether; 1 mL dissolves in 70 mL water.
Boiling Point: ~149°
Function: Flavoring agent

IDENTIFICATION
- **INFRARED SPECTRA,** *Spectrophotometric Identification Tests,* Appendix IIIC
  Acceptance criteria: The spectrum of the sample exhibits relative maxima at the same wavelengths as those of the spectrum below.

ASSAY
- **PROCEDURE:** Proceed as directed under *M-1b,* Appendix XI.
  Acceptance criteria: NLT 97.0% of $C_7H_{14}O$

SPECIFIC TESTS
- **ACID VALUE, FLAVOR CHEMICALS (OTHER THAN ESSENTIAL OILS),** *M-15,* Appendix XI
  Acceptance criteria: NMT 2.0
- **REFRACTIVE INDEX,** Appendix II: At 20°
  Acceptance criteria: Between 1.404 and 1.411
- **SPECIFIC GRAVITY:** Determine at 25° by any reliable method (see *General Provisions*).
  Acceptance criteria: Between 0.813 and 0.818

OTHER REQUIREMENTS
- **DISTILLATION RANGE,** Appendix IIB
  Acceptance criteria: Between 143° and 151°
- **WATER,** *Water Determination, Method I,* Appendix IIB
  [NOTE—Use freshly distilled pyridine as solvent.]
  Acceptance criteria: NMT 0.3%

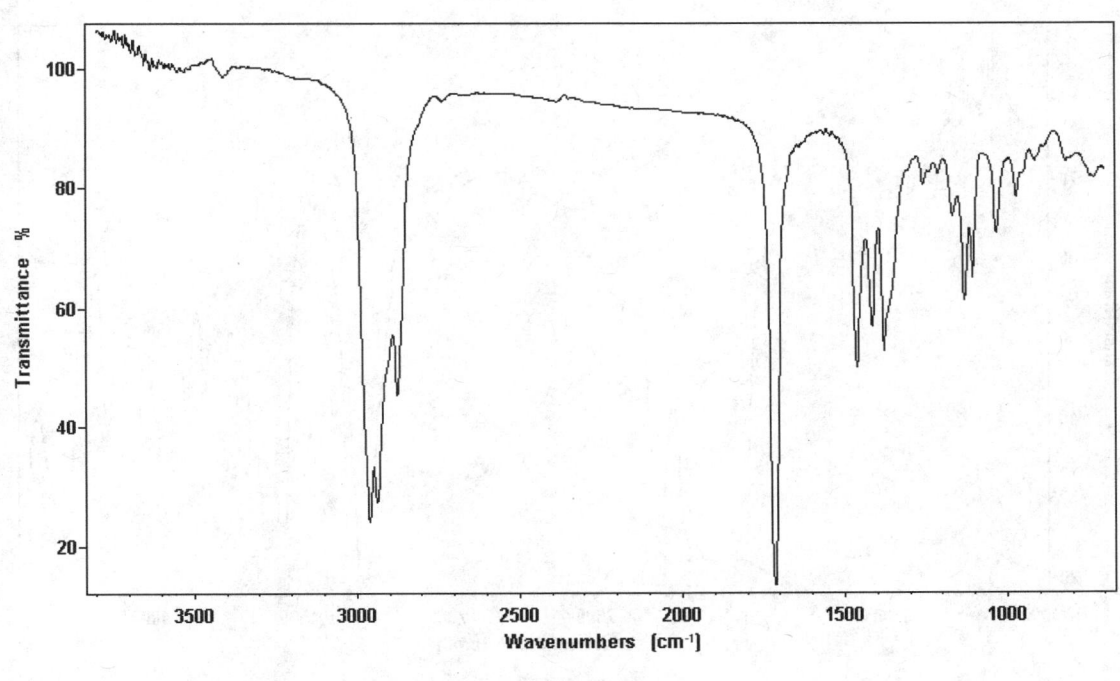

3-Heptanone

(Z)-4-Hepten-1-al

First Published: Prior to FCC 6

cis-4-Hepten-1-al

C₇H₁₂O Formula wt 112.17
FEMA: 3289
UNII: 5BJ99WWP64 [4-heptenal, (4z)-]

DESCRIPTION
(Z)-4-Hepten-1-al occurs as a slightly yellow liquid.
Odor: Fatty, green
Solubility: Soluble in alcohol, most fixed oils; insoluble or practically insoluble in water
Boiling Point: ~60° (25 mm Hg)
Solubility in Alcohol, Appendix VI: One mL dissolves in 1 mL of 95% ethanol.

Function: Flavoring agent

IDENTIFICATION
- **INFRARED SPECTRA,** Spectrophotometric Identification Tests, Appendix IIIC
  Acceptance criteria: The spectrum of the sample exhibits relative maxima at the same wavelengths as those of the spectrum below.

ASSAY
- **PROCEDURE:** Proceed as directed under M-1a, Appendix XI
  Acceptance criteria
  Sum of two isomers: NLT 98.0% of C₇H₁₂O
  (Z)-4-isomer: NLT 93.0% of C₇H₁₂O

SPECIFIC TESTS
- **REFRACTIVE INDEX,** Appendix II: At 20°
  Acceptance criteria: Between 1.432 and 1.436
- **SPECIFIC GRAVITY:** Determine at 25° by any reliable method (see General Provisions).
  Acceptance criteria: Between 0.843 and 0.855

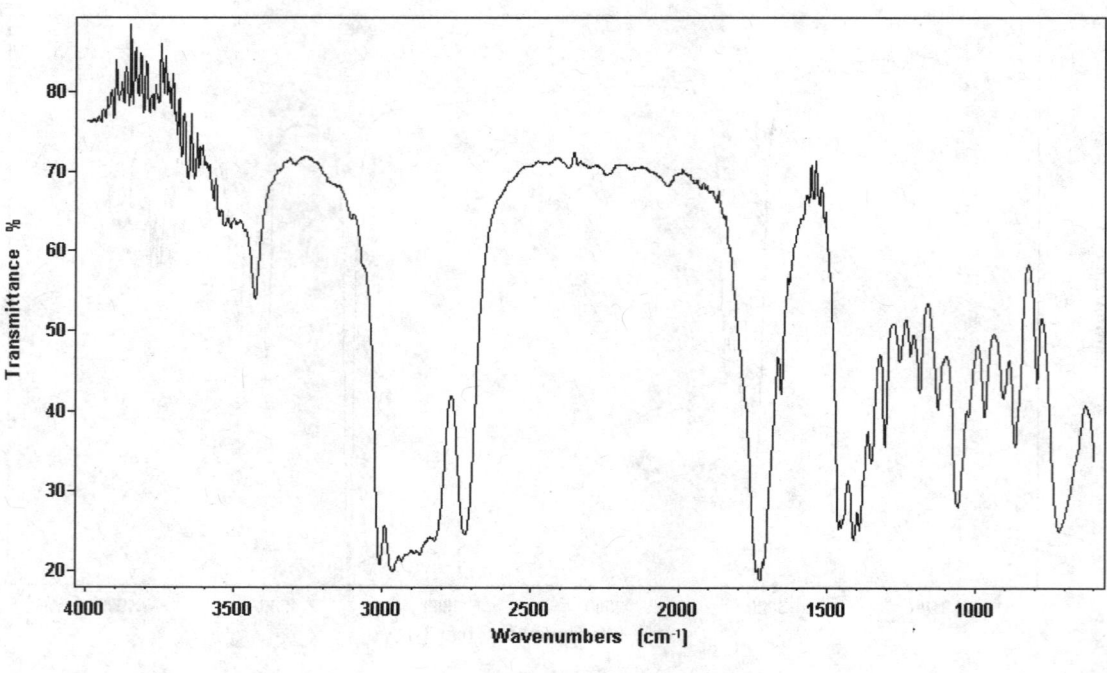

(Z)-4-Hepten-1-al

Heptyl Alcohol

First Published: Prior to FCC 6

Enanthic Alcohol

$C_7H_{16}O$ Formula wt 116.20
FEMA: 2548
UNII: 8JQ5607IO5 [heptyl alcohol]

DESCRIPTION
Heptyl Alcohol occurs as a colorless liquid.
Odor: Fatty, winy
Solubility: Slightly soluble in water; miscible in alcohol, ether, most fixed oils
Boiling Point: ~175°
Solubility in Alcohol, Appendix VI: One mL dissolves in 2 mL of 60% alcohol to give a clear solution.
Function: Flavoring agent

IDENTIFICATION
- **INFRARED SPECTRA,** Spectrophotometric Identification Tests, Appendix IIIC

  Acceptance criteria: The spectrum of the sample exhibits relative maxima at the same wavelengths as those of the spectrum below.

ASSAY
- **PROCEDURE:** Proceed as directed under *M-1b,* Appendix XI.
  Acceptance criteria: NLT 97.0% of $C_7H_{16}O$

SPECIFIC TESTS
- **ACID VALUE, FLAVOR CHEMICALS (OTHER THAN ESSENTIAL OILS),** *M-15,* Appendix XI
  Acceptance criteria: NMT 1.0
- **REFRACTIVE INDEX,** Appendix II: At 20°
  Acceptance criteria: Between 1.423 and 1.427
- **SPECIFIC GRAVITY:** Determine at 25° by any reliable method (see *General Provisions*).
  Acceptance criteria: Between 0.820 and 0.824

OTHER REQUIREMENTS
- **ALDEHYDES,** *M-1b,* Appendix XI
  Acceptance criteria: NMT 1.0% heptanal

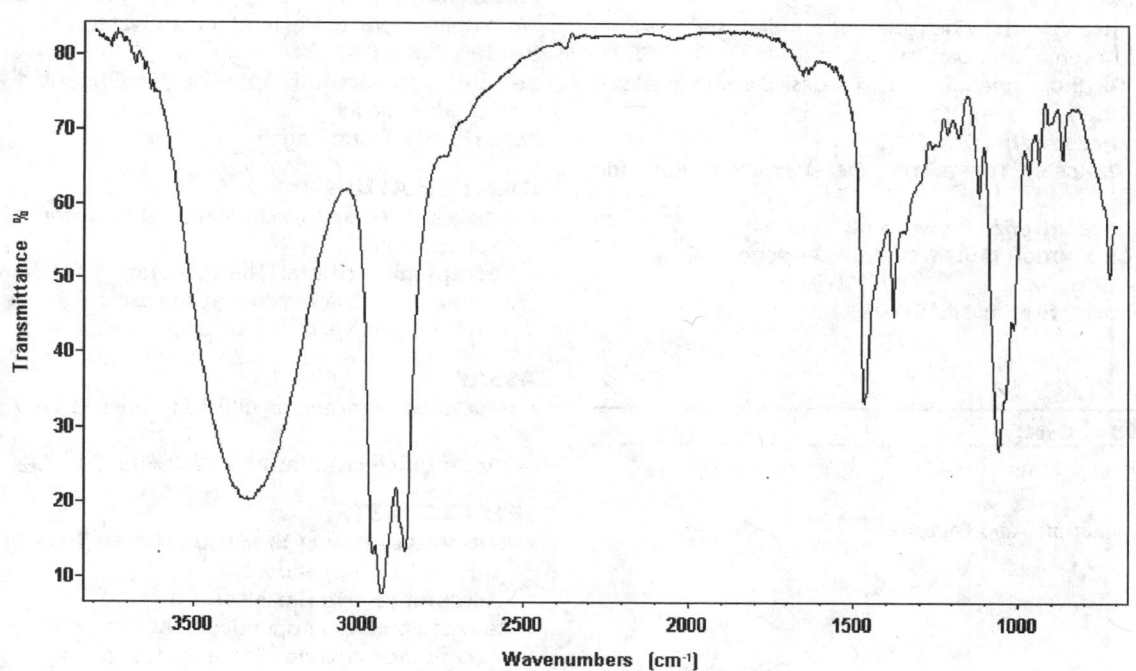

Heptyl Alcohol

Heptylparaben

First Published: Prior to FCC 6

n-Heptyl-p-hydroxybenzoate

$C_{14}H_{20}O_3$　　　　　　　　　　Formula wt 236.31
　　　　　　　　　　　　　　　CAS: [1085-12-7]
UNII: K2CIJ448IX [heptylparaben]

DESCRIPTION
Heptylparaben occurs as small, colorless crystals or as a white, crystalline powder. It is very slightly soluble in water, but is freely soluble in alcohol and in ether.
Function: Preservative; antimicrobial agent
Packaging and Storage: Store in tight containers.

IDENTIFICATION
- **MELTING RANGE OR TEMPERATURE DETERMINATION,** Appendix IIB
  Sample preparation: Dissolve 500 mg of sample in 10 mL of 1 N sodium hydroxide, boil for 30 min, allow the solution to evaporate to a volume of about 5 mL, and cool. Acidify the solution with 2 N sulfuric acid, collect the resulting p-hydroxybenzoic acid crystals on a filter, wash several times with small portions of water, and dry in a desiccator over silica gel.
  Acceptance criteria: The Sample preparation melts between 212° and 217°.

ASSAY
- **PROCEDURE**
  Sample: 3.5 g
  Analysis: Transfer the Sample into a flask, add 40.0 mL of 1 N sodium hydroxide, and rinse the sides of the flask with water. Cover with a watch glass, boil gently for 1 h, and cool. Titrate the excess sodium hydroxide with 1 N sulfuric acid to pH 6.5. Perform a blank determination (see General Provisions) with the same quantities of the same reagents in the same manner, and make any necessary correction. Each mL of 1 N sodium hydroxide is equivalent to 236.3 mg of $C_{14}H_{20}O_3$.
  Acceptance criteria: NLT 99.0% and NMT 100.5% of $C_{14}H_{20}O_3$, calculated on the dried basis

IMPURITIES
Inorganic Impurities
- **LEAD,** Lead Limit Test, Flame Atomic Absorption Spectrophotometric Method, Appendix IIIB
  Sample: 10 g
  Acceptance criteria: NMT 2 mg/kg

SPECIFIC TESTS
- **ACIDITY**
  Sample: 750 mg
  Analysis: Mix the Sample with 15 mL of water, heat at 80° for 1 min, cool, and filter. The filtrate is acid or neutral to litmus. Add 0.2 mL of 0.1 N sodium

hydroxide and 2 drops of methyl red TS to 10 mL of the filtrate.
Acceptance criteria: The resulting solution is yellow, without even a light cast of pink.
- **LOSS ON DRYING,** Appendix IIC: In a desiccator over silica gel for 5 h
  Acceptance criteria: NMT 0.5%
- **MELTING RANGE OR TEMPERATURE DETERMINATION,** Appendix IIB
  Acceptance criteria: Between 48° and 51°
- **RESIDUE ON IGNITION (SULFATED ASH),** Appendix IIC
  Sample: 2 g
  Acceptance criteria: NMT 0.05%

γ-Hexalactone

First Published: Prior to FCC 6

4-Hydroxyhexanoic Acid Lactone

$C_6H_{10}O_2$ Formula wt 114.14
FEMA: 2556
UNII: J16NAT1G41 [γ-hexalactone]

DESCRIPTION
γ-Hexalactone occurs as a colorless to pale yellow liquid.

Odor: Herbaceous, sweet
Solubility: Soluble in propylene glycol, vegetable oils; insoluble or practically insoluble in water
Boiling Point: ~220°
Solubility in Alcohol, Appendix VI: One mL dissolves in 1 mL of 95% alcohol.
Function: Flavoring agent

IDENTIFICATION
- **INFRARED SPECTRA,** *Spectrophotometric Identification Tests,* Appendix IIIC
  Acceptance criteria: The spectrum of the sample exhibits relative maxima at the same wavelengths as those of the spectrum below.

ASSAY
- **PROCEDURE:** Proceed as directed under *M-1a,* Appendix XI.
  Acceptance criteria: NLT 98.0% of $C_6H_{10}O_2$

SPECIFIC TESTS
- **ACID VALUE, FLAVOR CHEMICALS (OTHER THAN ESSENTIAL OILS),** *M-15,* Appendix XI
  Acceptance criteria: NMT 1.0
- **REFRACTIVE INDEX,** Appendix II: At 20°
  Acceptance criteria: Between 1.437 and 1.442
- **SPECIFIC GRAVITY:** Determine at 25° by any reliable method (see *General Provisions*).
  Acceptance criteria: Between 1.020 and 1.025

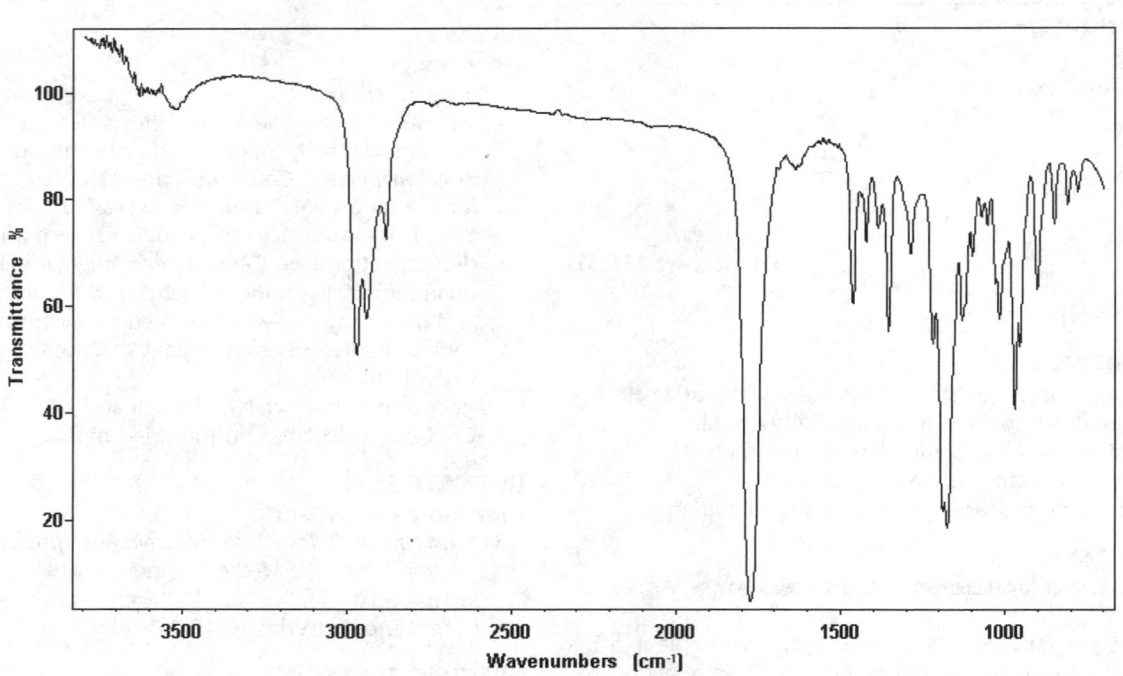

γ-Hexalactone

Hexanal

First Published: Prior to FCC 6
Last Revision: First Supplement, FCC 6

Caproic Aldehyde
Hexaldehyde
Aldehyde C-6

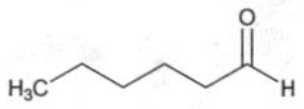

$C_6H_{12}O$ Formula wt 100.16
FEMA: 2557
UNII: 9DC2K31JJQ [hexanal]

DESCRIPTION
Hexanal occurs as an almost colorless liquid. It may contain a suitable antioxidant.
Odor: Fatty-green, grassy
Solubility: Very slightly soluble in water; miscible in alcohol, propylene glycol, most fixed oils
Boiling Point: ~131°
Function: Flavoring agent

ASSAY
- **Procedure:** Proceed as directed under *M-1a*, Appendix XI.
  Acceptance criteria: NLT 97.0% of $C_6H_{12}O$

SPECIFIC TESTS
- **Acid Value, Flavor Chemicals (Other Than Essential Oils),** *M-15,* Appendix XI
  Acceptance criteria: NMT 10.0
- **Refractive Index,** Appendix II: At 20°
  Acceptance criteria: Between 1.402 and 1.407
- **Specific Gravity:** Determine at 25° by any reliable method (see *General Provisions*).
  Acceptance criteria: Between 0.808 and 0.817

Hexanes

First Published: Prior to FCC 6

Mixed Paraffinic Hydrocarbons

C_6H_{14} Formula wt 86.18
CAS: [110-54-3]
UNII: 2DDG612ED8 [hexane]

DESCRIPTION
Hexanes occur as a clear, colorless, flammable liquid. It is composed predominantly of C_6, with some C_5 and C_7, isomeric paraffins. The relative proportion of isomers varies with the producer and the production lot. It is soluble in alcohol, in acetone, and in ether and is insoluble in water.
Function: Extraction solvent
Packaging and Storage: Store in tight containers, protected from fire.

IMPURITIES
Inorganic Impurities
- **Lead,** *Lead Limit Test, Flame Atomic Absorption Spectrophotometric Method,* Appendix IIIB
  Sample: 10 g
  Acceptance criteria: NMT 1 mg/kg

Organic Impurities
- **Benzene,** Appendix IIIC
  Acceptance criteria: NMT 0.05%

SPECIFIC TESTS
- **Color (APHA)**
  Sample: 100 mL
  Control: 2.0 mL of platinum–cobalt stock solution (APHA No. 500) diluted with water to 100 mL (APHA No. 10)
  Analysis: Compare equal volumes of the *Control* with the *Sample* in 100-mL Nessler tubes, viewed vertically over a white background.
  Acceptance criteria: NMT 10
- **Distillation Range,** Appendix IIB
  Acceptance criteria: Between 56° and 71°
- **Nonvolatile Residue**
  Sample: 150 mL (about 100 g)
  Analysis: Evaporate the *Sample* to dryness in a tared dish on a steam bath. Dry the residue at 105° for 30 min, cool, and weigh.
  Acceptance criteria: NMT 10 mg/kg
- **Specific Gravity:** Determine by any reliable method (see *General Provisions*).
  Acceptance criteria: Between 0.655 and 0.675
- **Sulfur,** Appendix IIIC
  Acceptance criteria: NMT 5 mg/kg

Hexanoic Acid

First Published: Prior to FCC 6

Caproic Acid

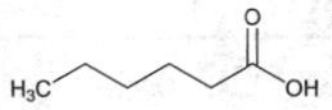

$C_6H_{12}O_2$ Formula wt 116.16
FEMA: 2559
UNII: 1F8SN134MX [caproic acid]

DESCRIPTION
Hexanoic Acid occurs as a colorless to very pale yellow, oily liquid.
Odor: Cheesy, sweat
Solubility: Miscible in alcohol, most fixed oils, ether; 1 mL dissolves in 250 mL water
Boiling Point: ~223°
Function: Flavoring agent

IDENTIFICATION
- **Infrared Spectra,** *Spectrophotometric Identification Tests,* Appendix IIIC

Acceptance criteria: The spectrum of the sample exhibits relative maxima at the same wavelengths as those of the spectrum below.

ASSAY
- **PROCEDURE:** Proceed as directed under *M-3a*, Appendix XI.
  Acceptance criteria: NLT 98.0% of $C_6H_{12}O_2$

SPECIFIC TESTS
- **REFRACTIVE INDEX,** Appendix II: At 20°
  Acceptance criteria: Between 1.415 and 1.418
- **SPECIFIC GRAVITY:** Determine at 25° by any reliable method (see *General Provisions*).
  Acceptance criteria: Between 0.923 and 0.928

OTHER REQUIREMENTS
- **SOLIDIFICATION POINT,** Appendix IIB
  Acceptance criteria: NLT –4.5°

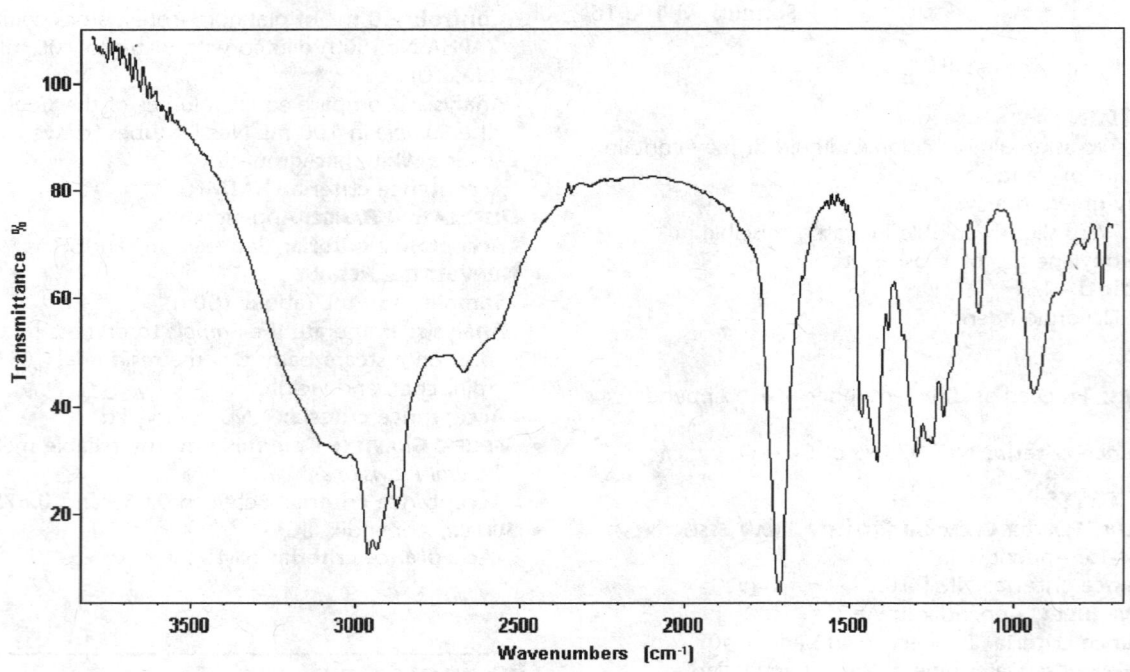

Hexanoic Acid

(E)-2-Hexen-1-al

First Published: Prior to FCC 6
Last Revision: First Supplement, FCC 6

trans-2-Hexen-1-al

$C_6H_{10}O$ Formula wt 98.14
FEMA: 2560
UNII: 69JX3AIR1I [2-hexenal, (2e)-]

DESCRIPTION
(E)-2-Hexen-1-al occurs as a pale yellow liquid. It may contain a suitable antioxidant.
Odor: Strong, fruity-green, vegetable
Solubility: Soluble in alcohol, propylene glycol, most fixed oils; very slightly soluble in water
Boiling Point: ~47° (17 mm Hg)
Solubility in Alcohol, Appendix VI: One mL dissolves in 1 mL of 95% ethanol.
Function: Flavoring agent

ASSAY
- **PROCEDURE:** Proceed as directed under *M-1a*, Appendix XI.
  Acceptance criteria: NLT 92.0% of $C_6H_{10}O$

SPECIFIC TESTS
- **REFRACTIVE INDEX,** Appendix II: At 20°
  Acceptance criteria: Between 1.445 and 1.449
- **SPECIFIC GRAVITY:** Determine at 25° by any reliable method (see *General Provisions*).
  Acceptance criteria: Between 0.841 and 0.850

(E)-2-Hexen-1-ol

First Published: Prior to FCC 6

trans-2-Hexen-1-ol

C₆H₁₂O   Formula wt 100.16
FEMA: 2562
UNII: BVP79C4821 [2-hexen-1-ol, (2e)-]

DESCRIPTION
(*E*)-2-Hexen-1-ol occurs as an almost colorless liquid.
Odor: Strong, fruity-green
Solubility: Soluble in alcohol, propylene glycol, most fixed oils; very slightly soluble in water
Boiling Point: ~158°
Function: Flavoring agent

IDENTIFICATION
- **INFRARED SPECTRA,** *Spectrophotometric Identification Tests,* Appendix IIIC
  Acceptance criteria: The spectrum of the sample exhibits relative maxima at the same wavelengths as those of the spectrum below.

ASSAY
- **PROCEDURE:** Proceed as directed under *M-1a,* Appendix XI.
  Acceptance criteria: NLT 95.0% of C₆H₁₂O

SPECIFIC TESTS
- **REFRACTIVE INDEX,** Appendix II: At 20°
  Acceptance criteria: Between 1.436 and 1.441
- **SPECIFIC GRAVITY:** Determine at 25° by any reliable method (see *General Provisions*).
  Acceptance criteria: Between 0.839 and 0.844

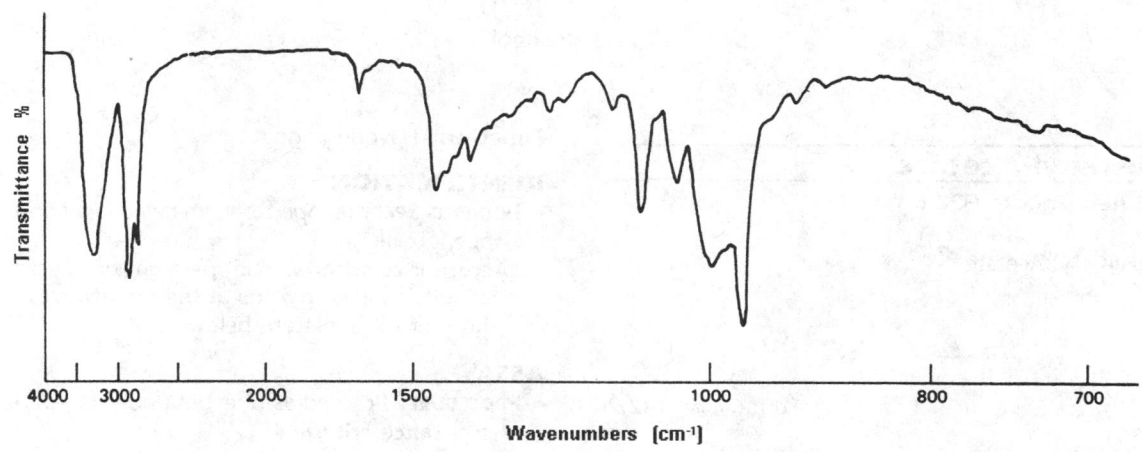

(*E*)-2-Hexen-1-ol

(Z)-3-Hexenol

First Published: Prior to FCC 6

cis-3-Hexen-1-ol

C₆H₁₂O   Formula wt 100.16
FEMA: 2563
UNII: V14F8G75P4 [3-hexen-1-ol, (3z)-]

DESCRIPTION
(*Z*)-3-Hexenol occurs as a colorless liquid.
Odor: Powerful, grassy-green
Solubility: Soluble in alcohol, propylene glycol, most fixed oils; very slightly soluble in water
Boiling Point: ~156°
Function: Flavoring agent

IDENTIFICATION
- **INFRARED SPECTRA,** *Spectrophotometric Identification Tests,* Appendix IIIC
  Acceptance criteria: The spectrum of the sample exhibits relative maxima at the same wavelengths as those of the spectrum below.

ASSAY
- **PROCEDURE:** Proceed as directed under *M-1a,* Appendix XI.
  Acceptance criteria
  Sum of (*Z*) and (*E*) isomers: NLT 98.0% of C₆H₁₂O
  (*Z*) isomer: NLT 92% of C₆H₁₂O

SPECIFIC TESTS
- **REFRACTIVE INDEX,** Appendix II: At 20°
  Acceptance criteria: Between 1.436 and 1.443

- **Specific Gravity:** Determine at 25° by any reliable method (see *General Provisions*).
  Acceptance criteria: Between 0.846 and 0.850

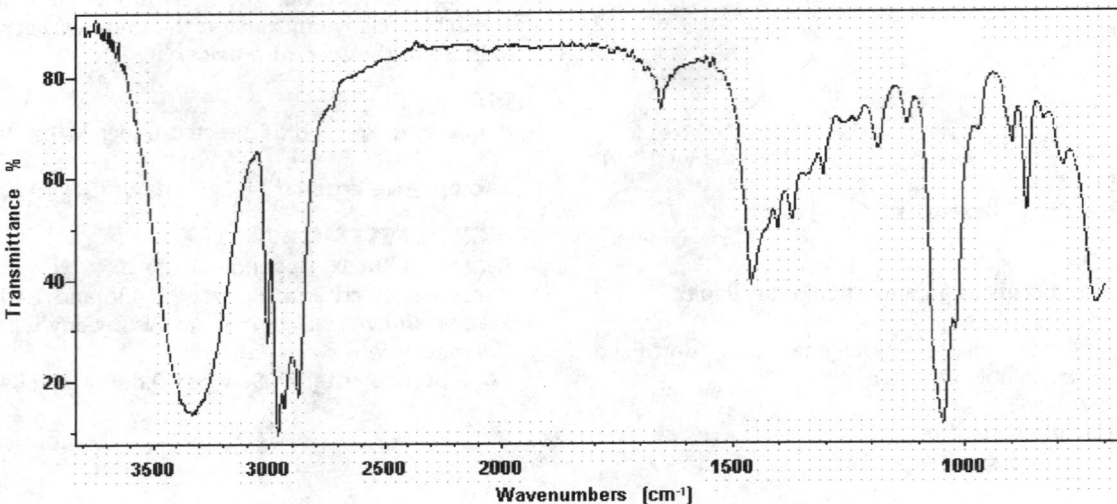

(Z)-3-Hexenol

(E)-2-Hexenyl Acetate

First Published: Prior to FCC 6

trans-2-Hexen-1-yl Acetate

C_8H_14O_2 Formula wt 142.20
FEMA: 2564
UNII: XDV436N45E [2-hexenyl acetate, (2e)-]

DESCRIPTION
(E)-2-Hexenyl Acetate occurs as a colorless to pale yellow liquid.
Odor: Green note
Solubility: Soluble in vegetable oils; slightly soluble in propylene glycol; insoluble or practically insoluble in water
Boiling Point: ~166°
Solubility in Alcohol, Appendix VI: One mL dissolves in 1 mL of 95% alcohol.

Function: Flavoring agent

IDENTIFICATION
- **Infrared Spectra,** *Spectrophotometric Identification Tests,* Appendix IIIC
  Acceptance criteria: The spectrum of the sample exhibits relative maxima at the same wavelengths as those of the spectrum below.

ASSAY
- **Procedure:** Proceed as directed under *M-1a,* Appendix XI
  Acceptance criteria
  Sum of (Z)- and (E)-isomers: NLT 98.0% of C_8H_14O_2
  (E)-isomer: NLT 90% of C_8H_14O_2

SPECIFIC TESTS
- **Refractive Index,** Appendix II: At 20°
  Acceptance criteria: Between 1.425 and 1.430
- **Specific Gravity:** Determine at 25° by any reliable method (see *General Provisions*).
  Acceptance criteria: Between 0.890 and 0.897

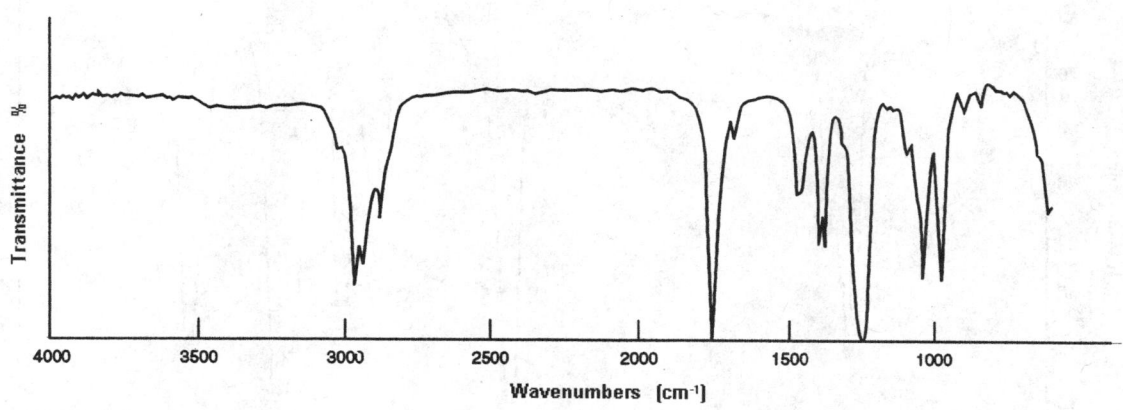

(E)-2-Hexenyl Acetate

(Z)-3-Hexenyl Acetate

First Published: Prior to FCC 6

cis-3-Hexen-1-yl Acetate

C₈H₁₄O₂   Formula wt 142.20
FEMA: 3171
UNII: 6INA6GC5I6 [3-hexenyl acetate, (3z)-]

DESCRIPTION
(Z)-3-Hexenyl Acetate occurs as a colorless to pale yellow liquid.
Odor: Powerful green note
Solubility: Soluble in propylene glycol, vegetable oils; insoluble or practically insoluble in water
Boiling Point: ~198°
Solubility in Alcohol, Appendix VI: One mL dissolves in 1 mL of 95% alcohol.

Function: Flavoring agent

IDENTIFICATION
- **INFRARED SPECTRA,** *Spectrophotometric Identification Tests,* Appendix IIIC
  Acceptance criteria: The spectrum of the sample exhibits relative maxima at the same wavelengths as those of the spectrum below.

ASSAY
- **PROCEDURE:** Proceed as directed under *M-1a,* Appendix XI
  Acceptance criteria
  Sum of (Z)- and (E)-isomers: NLT 98.0% of C₈H₁₄O₂
  (Z)-isomer: NLT 92% of C₈H₁₄O₂

SPECIFIC TESTS
- **ACID VALUE, FLAVOR CHEMICALS (OTHER THAN ESSENTIAL OILS),** *M-15,* Appendix XI
  Acceptance criteria: NMT 1.0
- **REFRACTIVE INDEX,** Appendix II: At 20°
  Acceptance criteria: Between 1.425 and 1.429
- **SPECIFIC GRAVITY:** Determine at 25° by any reliable method (see *General Provisions*).
  Acceptance criteria: Between 0.896 and 0.901

534 / (Z)-3-Hexenyl Acetate / Monographs

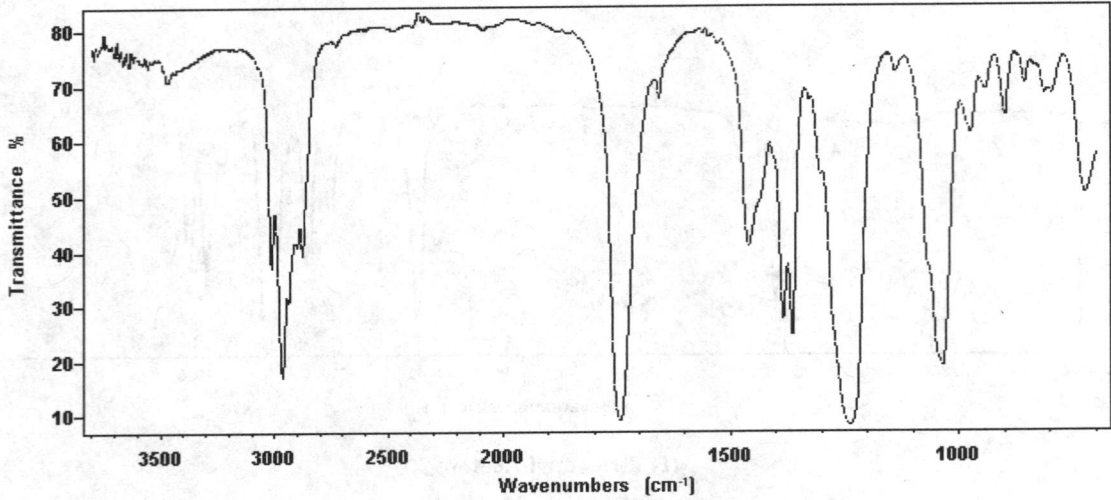

(Z)-3-Hexenyl Acetate

(Z)-3-Hexenyl Butyrate

First Published: Prior to FCC 6

$C_{10}H_{18}O_2$ Formula wt 170.25
FEMA: 3402
UNII: O47B839622 [3-hexenyl butyrate, (3z)-]

DESCRIPTION
(Z)-3-Hexenyl Butyrate occurs as a colorless to pale yellow liquid.
Odor: Green, fruity
Solubility: Soluble in propylene glycol, vegetable oils; insoluble or practically insoluble in water
Boiling Point: ~96° (20 mm Hg)
Solubility in Alcohol, Appendix VI: One mL dissolves in 1 mL of 95% ethanol.

Function: Flavoring agent

IDENTIFICATION
- **INFRARED SPECTRA,** *Spectrophotometric Identification Tests,* Appendix IIIC
  Acceptance criteria: The spectrum of the sample exhibits relative maxima at the same wavelengths as those of the spectrum below.

ASSAY
- **PROCEDURE:** Proceed as directed under *M-1b,* Appendix XI
  Acceptance criteria: NLT 97.0% of $C_{10}H_{18}O_2$ (one isomer)

SPECIFIC TESTS
- **ACID VALUE, FLAVOR CHEMICALS (OTHER THAN ESSENTIAL OILS),** *M-15,* Appendix XI
  Acceptance criteria: NMT 1.0
- **REFRACTIVE INDEX,** Appendix II: At 20°
  Acceptance criteria: Between 1.427 and 1.435
- **SPECIFIC GRAVITY:** Determine at 25° by any reliable method (see *General Provisions*).
  Acceptance criteria: Between 0.880 and 0.887

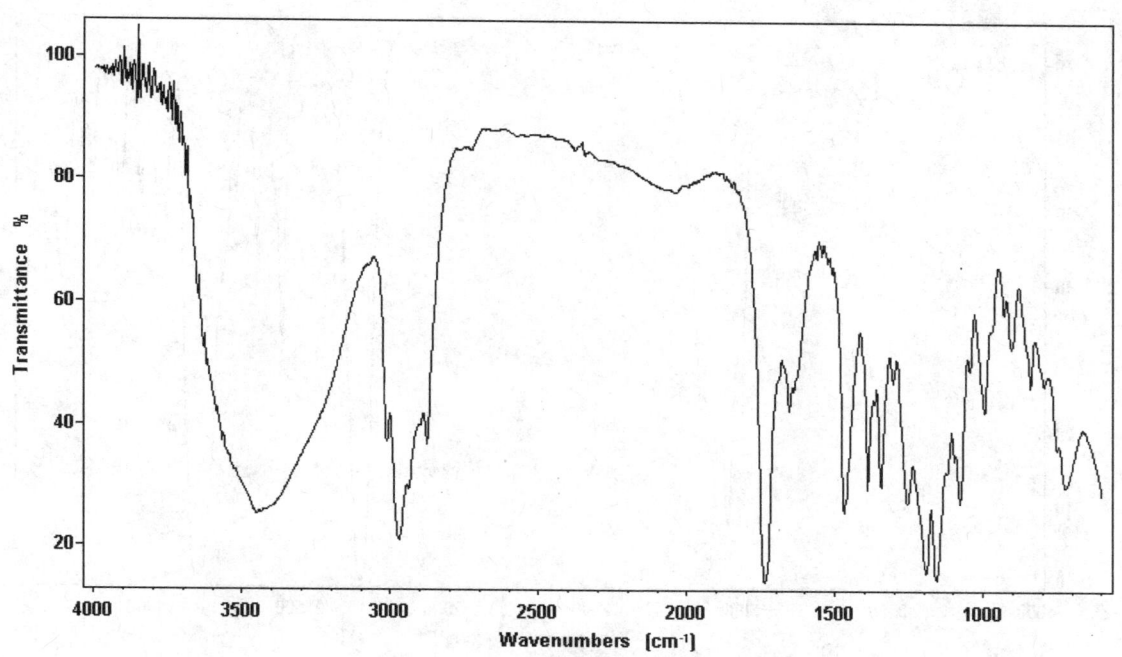

(Z)-3-Hexenyl Butyrate

(Z)-3-Hexenyl Formate

First Published: Prior to FCC 6

$C_7H_{12}O_2$ Formula wt 128.17
FEMA: 3353
UNII: E34OB83TYM [3-hexenyl formate, (3z)-]

DESCRIPTION
(Z)-3-Hexenyl Formate occurs as a colorless to pale yellow liquid.
Odor: Green
Solubility: Soluble in propylene glycol, vegetable oils; insoluble or practically insoluble in water
Boiling Point: ~72° (40 mm Hg)
Solubility in Alcohol, Appendix VI: One mL dissolves in 1 mL of 95% ethanol.
Function: Flavoring agent

IDENTIFICATION
- **INFRARED SPECTRA,** Spectrophotometric Identification Tests, Appendix IIIC
  Acceptance criteria: The spectrum of the sample exhibits relative maxima at the same wavelengths as those of the spectrum below.

ASSAY
- **PROCEDURE:** Proceed as directed under *M-1b,* Appendix XI.
  Acceptance criteria: NLT 95.0% of $C_7H_{12}O_2$

SPECIFIC TESTS
- **ACID VALUE, FLAVOR CHEMICALS (OTHER THAN ESSENTIAL OILS),** *M-15,* Appendix XI
  Analysis: Proceed as directed, but add ice to the solution.
  Acceptance criteria: NMT 5.0
- **REFRACTIVE INDEX,** Appendix II: At 20°
  Acceptance criteria: Between 1.424 and 1.430
- **SPECIFIC GRAVITY:** Determine at 25° by any reliable method (see *General Provisions*).
  Acceptance criteria: Between 0.907 and 0.915

536 / (Z)-3-Hexenyl Formate / *Monographs*

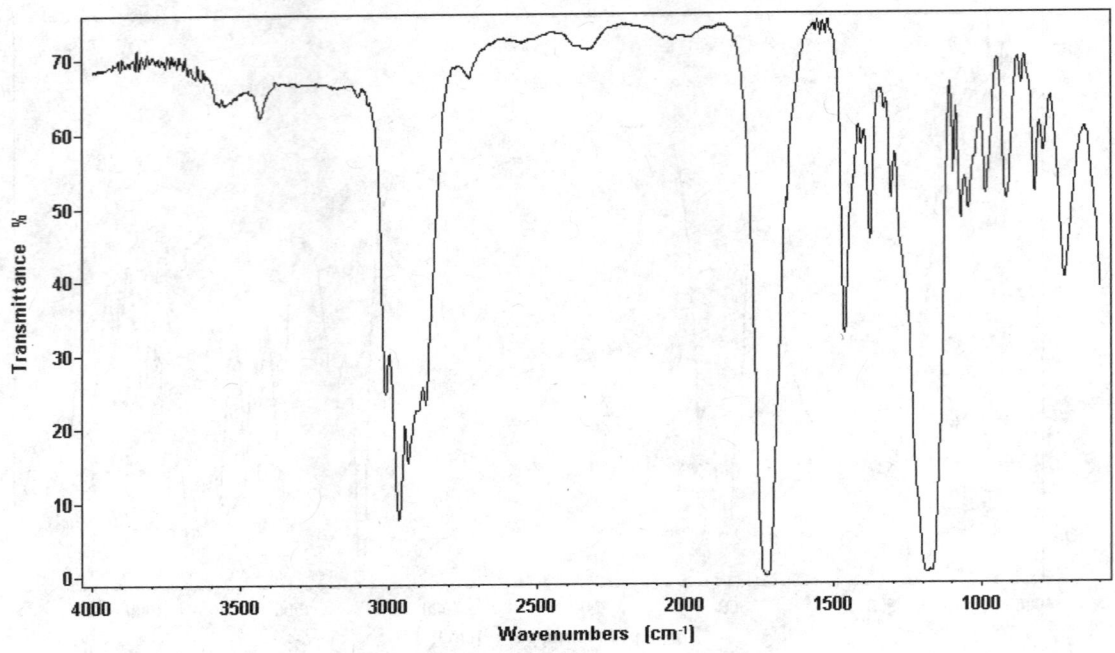

(Z)-3-Hexenyl Formate

(Z)-3-Hexenyl Isovalerate

First Published: Prior to FCC 6

cis-3-Hexen-1-yl Isovalerate

$C_{11}H_{20}O_2$ Formula wt 184.28
FEMA: 3498
UNII: L9KN8775G8 [3-hexenyl 3-methylbutanoate, (3z)-]

DESCRIPTION
(Z)-3-Hexenyl Isovalerate occurs as a colorless liquid.
Odor: Sweet, apple
Solubility: Soluble in alcohol, most fixed oils, propylene glycol; insoluble or practically insoluble in water
Boiling Point: ~199°
Solubility in Alcohol, Appendix VI: One mL dissolves in 1 mL of 95% ethanol.
Function: Flavoring agent

ASSAY
- **Procedure:** Proceed as directed under *M-1a*, Appendix XI.
  Acceptance criteria
  Sum of two isomers: NLT 95.0% of $C_{11}H_{20}O_2$
  (Z)-isomer: NLT 92.0% of $C_{11}H_{20}O_2$

SPECIFIC TESTS
- **Acid Value, Flavor Chemicals (Other Than Essential Oils),** *M-15,* Appendix XI
  Acceptance criteria: NMT 2.0
- **Refractive Index,** Appendix II: At 20°
  Acceptance criteria: Between 1.429 and 1.435
- **Specific Gravity:** Determine at 25° by any reliable method (see *General Provisions*).
  Acceptance criteria: Between 0.872 and 0.877

(Z)-3-Hexenyl 2-Methylbutyrate

First Published: Prior to FCC 6

cis-3-Hexenyl 2-Methylbutyrate

$C_{11}H_{20}O_2$ Formula wt 184.28
FEMA: 3497
UNII: N181NM2UXZ [3-hexenyl 2-methylbutyrate, (3z)-]

DESCRIPTION
(Z)-3-Hexenyl 2-Methylbutyrate occurs as an almost colorless liquid.
Odor: Powerful, fruity, unripe apples
Solubility: Soluble in alcohol, most fixed oils; insoluble or practically insoluble in water
Boiling Point: ~105° (25 mm Hg)

Solubility in Alcohol, Appendix VI: One mL dissolves in 1 mL of 95% ethanol.
Function: Flavoring agent

ASSAY
- **PROCEDURE:** Proceed as directed under *M-1a,* Appendix XI.
  Acceptance criteria
  Sum of two isomers: NLT 95.0% of $C_{11}H_{20}O_2$
  (Z)-isomer: NLT 92.0% of $C_{11}H_{20}O_2$

SPECIFIC TESTS
- **ACID VALUE, FLAVOR CHEMICALS (OTHER THAN ESSENTIAL OILS),** *M-15,* Appendix XI
  Acceptance criteria: NMT 2.0
- **REFRACTIVE INDEX,** Appendix II: At 20°
  Acceptance criteria: Between 1.430 and 1.434
- **SPECIFIC GRAVITY:** Determine at 25° by any reliable method (see *General Provisions*).
  Acceptance criteria: Between 0.876 and 0.880

Hexyl 2-Methylbutyrate
First Published: Prior to FCC 6

$C_{11}H_{22}O_2$ Formula wt 186.29
FEMA: 3499
UNII: UI17LL5Q4P [hexyl 2-methylbutyrate]

DESCRIPTION
Hexyl 2-Methylbutyrate occurs as a colorless liquid.
Odor: Strong, fresh-green, fruity
Solubility: Soluble in alcohol, most fixed oils; insoluble or practically insoluble in water
Boiling Point: ~217° to 219°
Solubility in Alcohol, Appendix VI: One mL dissolves in 1 mL of 95% ethanol.
Function: Flavoring agent

ASSAY
- **PROCEDURE:** Proceed as directed under *M-1a,* Appendix XI.
  Acceptance criteria: NLT 95.0% of $C_{11}H_{22}O_2$ (one isomer)

SPECIFIC TESTS
- **ACID VALUE, FLAVOR CHEMICALS (OTHER THAN ESSENTIAL OILS),** *M-15,* Appendix XI
  Acceptance criteria: NMT 2.0
- **REFRACTIVE INDEX,** Appendix II: At 20°
  Acceptance criteria: Between 1.416 and 1.421
- **SPECIFIC GRAVITY:** Determine at 25° by any reliable method (see *General Provisions*).
  Acceptance criteria: Between 0.854 and 0.859

Hexyl Acetate
First Published: Prior to FCC 6

$C_8H_{16}O_2$ Formula wt 144.21
FEMA: 2565
UNII: 7U7KU3MWT0 [hexyl acetate]

DESCRIPTION
Hexyl Acetate occurs as a colorless liquid.
Odor: Fruity
Solubility: Soluble in vegetable oils; slightly soluble in propylene glycol; insoluble or practically insoluble in water
Boiling Point: ~168° to 170°
Solubility in Alcohol, Appendix VI: One mL dissolves in 1 mL of 95% alcohol.
Function: Flavoring agent

IDENTIFICATION
- **INFRARED SPECTRA,** *Spectrophotometric Identification Tests,* Appendix IIIC
  Acceptance criteria: The spectrum of the sample exhibits relative maxima at the same wavelengths as those of the spectrum below.

ASSAY
- **PROCEDURE:** Proceed as directed under *M-1b,* Appendix XI.
  Acceptance criteria: NLT 98.0% of $C_8H_{16}O_2$

SPECIFIC TESTS
- **ACID VALUE, FLAVOR CHEMICALS (OTHER THAN ESSENTIAL OILS),** *M-15,* Appendix XI
  Acceptance criteria: NMT 1.0
- **REFRACTIVE INDEX,** Appendix II: At 20°
  Acceptance criteria: Between 1.407 and 1.411
- **SPECIFIC GRAVITY:** Determine at 25° by any reliable method (see *General Provisions*).
  Acceptance criteria: Between 0.868 and 0.872

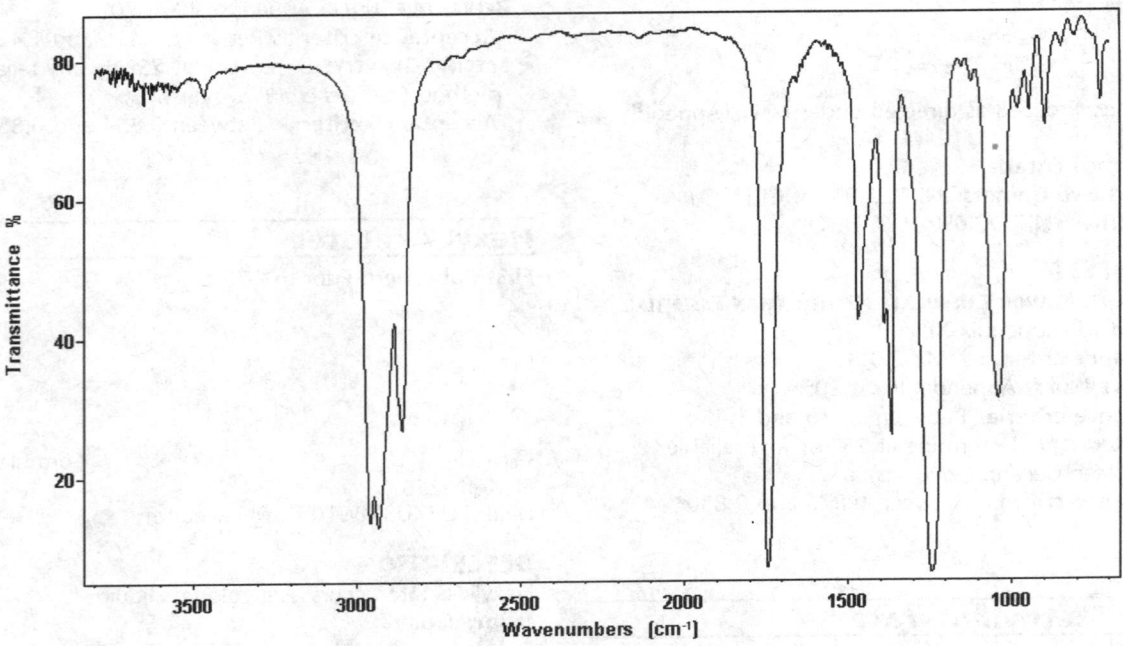

Hexyl Acetate

Hexyl Alcohol

First Published: Prior to FCC 6

1-Hexanol
Alcohol C-6

$C_6H_{14}O$ Formula wt 102.18
FEMA: 2567
UNII: 6CP2QER8GS [1-hexanol]

DESCRIPTION
Hexyl Alcohol occurs as a colorless, mobile liquid.
Odor: Mild, sweet, green
Solubility: Miscible in alcohol, ether; 1 mL dissolves in 175 mL water
Boiling Point: ~157°
Function: Flavoring agent

IDENTIFICATION
- **INFRARED SPECTRA,** Spectrophotometric Identification Tests, Appendix IIIC
  Acceptance criteria: The spectrum of the sample exhibits relative maxima at the same wavelengths as those of the spectrum below.

ASSAY
- **PROCEDURE:** Proceed as directed under M-1b, Appendix XI.
  Acceptance criteria: NLT 97.0% of $C_6H_{14}O$

SPECIFIC TESTS
- **ACID VALUE, FLAVOR CHEMICALS (OTHER THAN ESSENTIAL OILS),** M-15, Appendix XI
  Acceptance criteria: NMT 2.0
- **REFRACTIVE INDEX,** Appendix II: At 20°
  Acceptance criteria: Between 1.415 and 1.420
- **SPECIFIC GRAVITY:** Determine at 25° by any reliable method (see General Provisions).
  Acceptance criteria: Between 0.816 and 0.821

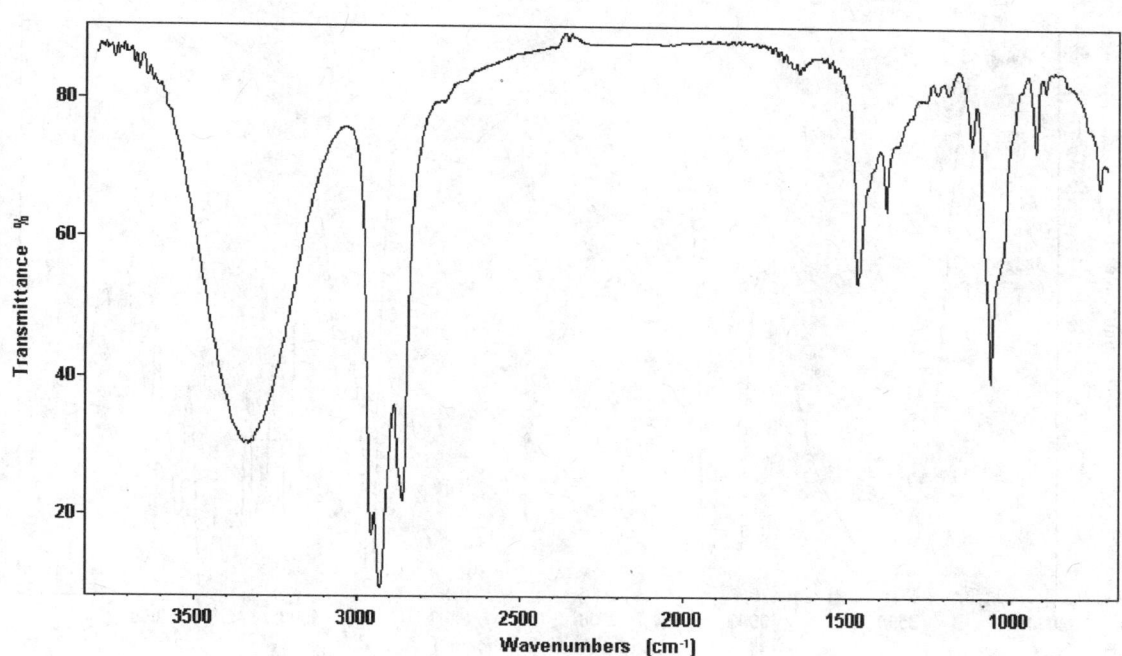

Hexyl Alcohol

Hexyl Butyrate

First Published: Prior to FCC 6

C₁₀H₂₀O₂   Formula wt 172.27
FEMA: 2568
UNII: 74HY6P24G7 [hexyl butyrate]

DESCRIPTION
Hexyl Butyrate occurs as a colorless to pale yellow liquid.
Odor: Fruity
Solubility: Soluble in vegetable oils; slightly soluble in propylene glycol; insoluble or practically insoluble in water
Boiling Point: ~205°
Solubility in Alcohol, Appendix VI: One mL dissolves in 1 mL of 95% ethanol.
Function: Flavoring agent

IDENTIFICATION
- **INFRARED SPECTRA,** *Spectrophotometric Identification Tests,* Appendix IIIC
  Acceptance criteria: The spectrum of the sample exhibits relative maxima at the same wavelengths as those of the spectrum below.

ASSAY
- **PROCEDURE:** Proceed as directed under *M-1b,* Appendix XI.
  Acceptance criteria: NLT 98.0% of C₁₀H₂₀O₂

SPECIFIC TESTS
- **ACID VALUE, FLAVOR CHEMICALS (OTHER THAN ESSENTIAL OILS),** *M-15,* Appendix XI
  Acceptance criteria: NMT 1.0
- **REFRACTIVE INDEX,** Appendix II: At 20°
  Acceptance criteria: Between 1.414 and 1.420
- **SPECIFIC GRAVITY:** Determine at 25° by any reliable method (see *General Provisions*).
  Acceptance criteria: Between 0.860 and 0.866

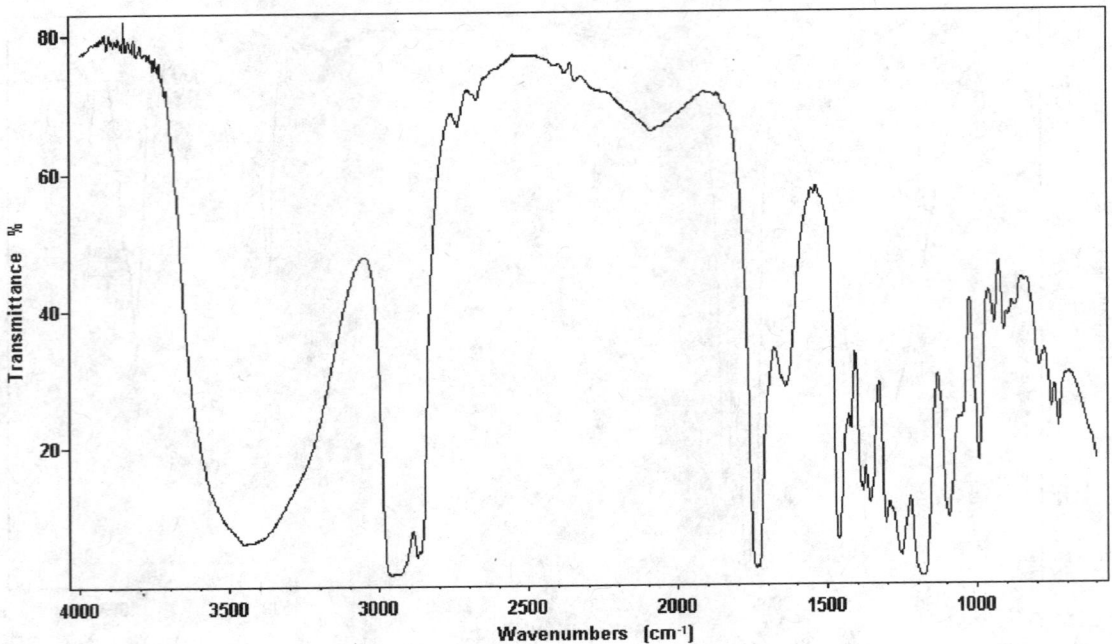

Hexyl Butyrate

Hexyl Hexanoate

First Published: Prior to FCC 6

$C_{12}H_{24}O_2$
FEMA: 2572
UNII: GI6FE1QMW6 [hexyl hexanoate]

Formula wt 200.32

DESCRIPTION
Hexyl Hexanoate occurs as a colorless to pale yellow liquid.
Odor: Fruity
Solubility: Soluble in propylene glycol, vegetable oils; insoluble or practically insoluble in water
Boiling Point: ~245°
Solubility in Alcohol, Appendix VI: One mL dissolves in 1 mL of 95% ethanol.
Function: Flavoring agent

IDENTIFICATION
- **INFRARED SPECTRA,** *Spectrophotometric Identification Tests,* Appendix IIIC
  Acceptance criteria: The spectrum of the sample exhibits relative maxima at the same wavelengths as those of the spectrum below.

ASSAY
- **PROCEDURE:** Proceed as directed under *M-1b,* Appendix XI.
  Acceptance criteria: NLT 98.0% of $C_{12}H_{24}O_2$

SPECIFIC TESTS
- **ACID VALUE, FLAVOR CHEMICALS (OTHER THAN ESSENTIAL OILS),** *M-15,* Appendix XI
  Acceptance criteria: NMT 1.0
- **REFRACTIVE INDEX,** Appendix II: At 20°
  Acceptance criteria: Between 1.421 and 1.427
- **SPECIFIC GRAVITY:** Determine at 25° by any reliable method (see *General Provisions*).
  Acceptance criteria: Between 0.857 and 0.863

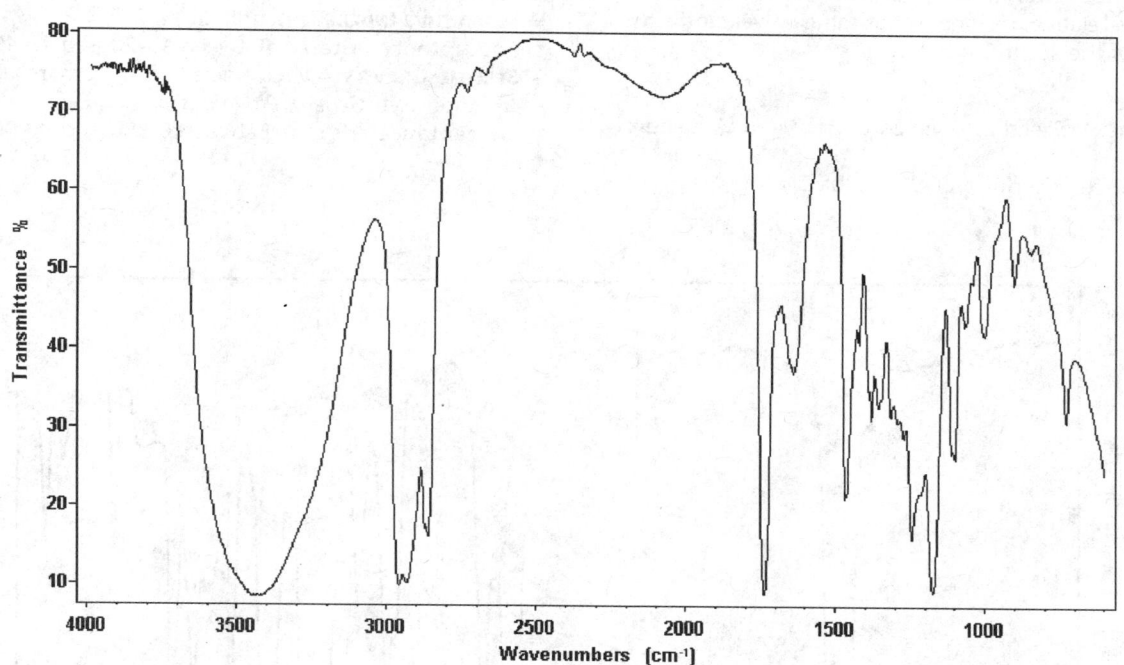

Hexyl Hexanoate

Hexyl Isovalerate

First Published: Prior to FCC 6

$C_{11}H_{22}O_2$ Formula wt 186.29
FEMA: 3500
UNII: 5FJ2M7YCY6 [hexyl isovalerate]

DESCRIPTION
Hexyl Isovalerate occurs as a colorless liquid.
Odor: Pungent, fruity
Solubility: Soluble in alcohol, most fixed oils; insoluble or practically insoluble in water
Boiling Point: ~215°
Solubility in Alcohol, Appendix VI: One mL dissolves in 1 mL of 95% alcohol.
Function: Flavoring agent

ASSAY
- **Procedure:** Proceed as directed under *M-1b,* Appendix XI.
  Acceptance criteria
    Sum of two isomers: NLT 95.0% of $C_{11}H_{22}O_2$
    Isovalerate isomer: NLT 92.0% of $C_{11}H_{22}O_2$

SPECIFIC TESTS
- **Acid Value, Flavor Chemicals (Other Than Essential Oils),** *M-15,* Appendix XI

  Acceptance criteria: NMT 2.0
- **Refractive Index,** Appendix II: At 20°
  Acceptance criteria: Between 1.417 and 1.421
- **Specific Gravity:** Determine at 25° by any reliable method (see *General Provisions*).
  Acceptance criteria: Between 0.853 and 0.857

Hexyl-2-butenoate

First Published: Prior to FCC 6

$C_{10}H_{18}O_2$ Formula wt 170.25
FEMA: 3354
UNII: L8K16M475M [hexyl crotonate]

DESCRIPTION
Hexyl-2-butenoate occurs as a colorless liquid.
Odor: Fruity
Solubility: Soluble in alcohol, most fixed oils; insoluble or practically insoluble in water, propylene glycol
Function: Flavoring agent

IDENTIFICATION
- **Infrared Spectra,** *Spectrophotometric Identification Tests,* Appendix IIIC

542 / Hexyl-2-butenoate / Monographs

Acceptance criteria: The spectrum of the sample exhibits relative maxima at the same wavelengths as those of the spectrum below.

ASSAY
- **Procedure:** Proceed as directed under M-1a, Appendix XI.
  Acceptance criteria: NLT 95.0% of $C_{10}H_{18}O_2$

SPECIFIC TESTS
- **Refractive Index,** Appendix II: At 20°
  Acceptance criteria: Between 1.428 and 1.449
- **Specific Gravity:** Determine at 25° by any reliable method (see General Provisions).
  Acceptance criteria: Between 0.880 and 0.900

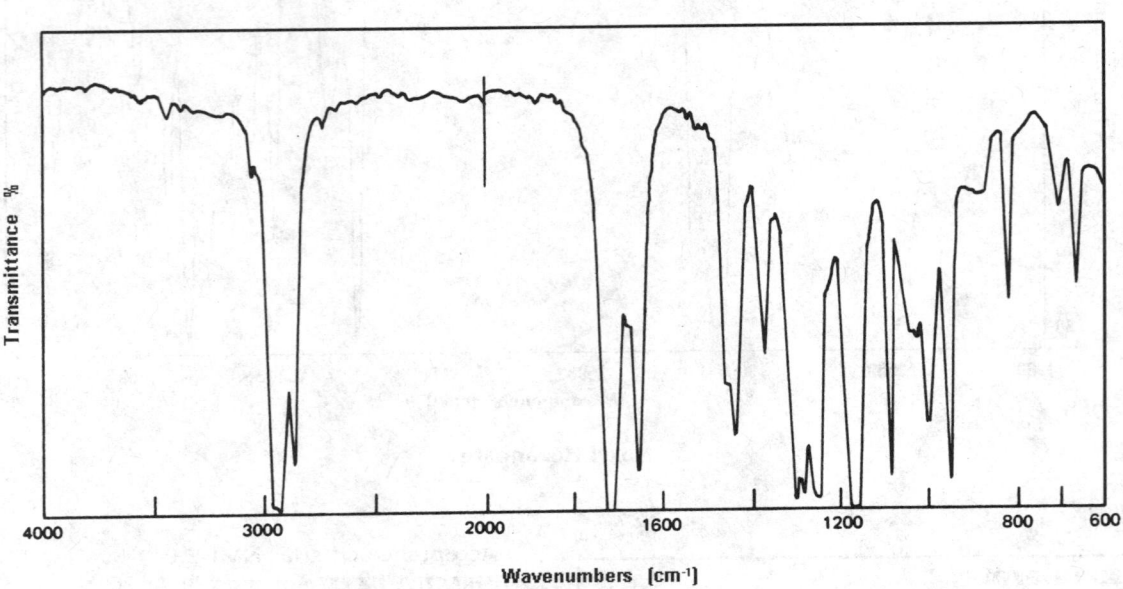

Hexyl-2-butenoate

α-Hexylcinnamaldehyde

First Published: Prior to FCC 6

$C_{15}H_{20}O$ Formula wt 216.32
FEMA: 2569
UNII: 7X6O37OK2I [α-hexylcinnamaldehyde]

DESCRIPTION
α-Hexylcinnamaldehyde occurs as a pale yellow liquid.
Odor: Jasmine
Solubility: Soluble in most fixed oils; insoluble or practically insoluble in glycerin, propylene glycol
Boiling Point: ~174° (15 mm Hg)
Solubility in Alcohol, Appendix VI: One mL dissolves in 1 mL of 90% alcohol.
Function: Flavoring agent

IDENTIFICATION
- **Infrared Spectra,** Spectrophotometric Identification Tests, Appendix IIIC
  Acceptance criteria: The spectrum of the sample exhibits relative maxima at the same wavelengths as those of the spectrum below.

ASSAY
- **Procedure:** Proceed as directed under M-1b, Appendix XI.
  Acceptance criteria: NLT 95.0% of $C_{15}H_{20}O$ (sum of two isomers)

SPECIFIC TESTS
- **Acid Value, Flavor Chemicals (Other Than Essential Oils),** M-15, Appendix XI
  Acceptance criteria: NMT 5.0
- **Refractive Index,** Appendix II: At 20°
  Acceptance criteria: Between 1.548 and 1.552
- **Specific Gravity:** Determine at 25° by any reliable method (see General Provisions).
  Acceptance criteria: Between 0.953 and 0.959

OTHER REQUIREMENTS
- **Chlorinated Compounds,** Appendix VI
  Acceptance criteria: Passes test

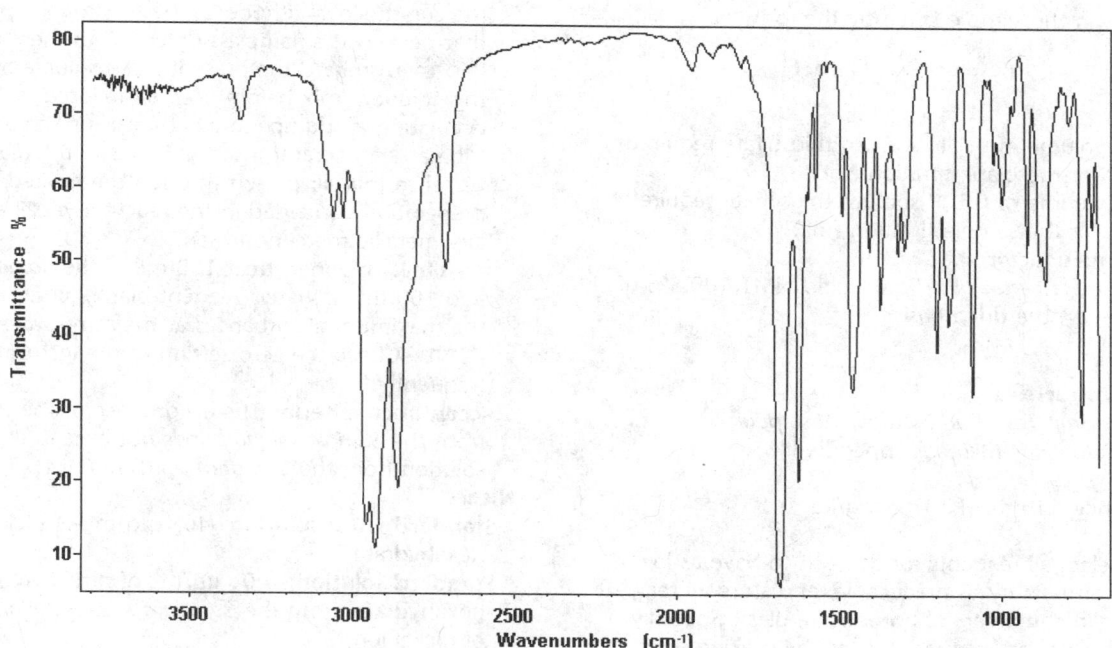
α-Hexylcinnamaldehyde

4-Hexylresorcinol
First Published: Prior to FCC 6

Hexylresorcinol
4-Hexyl-1,3-benzenediol

$C_{12}H_{18}O_2$

UNII: R9QTB5E82N [hexylresorcinol]

Formula wt 194.27
CAS: [136-77-6]

DESCRIPTION
4-Hexylresorcinol occurs as a white powder. It is very slightly soluble in water and freely soluble in ether and in acetone. [CAUTION—4-Hexylresorcinol is irritating to the oral mucosa and respiratory tract and to the skin, and its solution in alcohol has vesicant properties.]
Function: Color stabilizer; enzymatic browning inhibitor
Packaging and Storage: Store in tight, light-resistant containers.

IDENTIFICATION
- **A. PROCEDURE**
  Sample solution: Saturated solution
  Analysis: Add 1 mL of nitric acid to 1 mL of *Sample solution*.
  Acceptance criteria: A light red color appears.
- **B. PROCEDURE**
  Sample solution: Saturated solution
  Analysis: Add 1 mL of bromine TS to 1 mL of *Sample solution*. A yellow flocculent precipitate forms. Add 2 mL of 6 N ammonium hydroxide.
  Acceptance criteria: A yellow precipitate forms after the addition of bromine TS and dissolves following the addition of the ammonium hydroxide, producing a yellow solution.
- **C. INFRARED SPECTRA**, *Spectrophotometric Identification Tests*, Appendix IIIC
  Sample preparation: Potassium bromide dispersion
  Analysis: The spectrum of the sample exhibits relative maxima at the same wavelengths as those of the spectrum below.

ASSAY
- **PROCEDURE**
  Sample: 70 to 100 mg, previously dried over silica gel for 4 h
  Analysis: Dissolve the *Sample* in 10 mL of methanol in a 250-mL iodine flask. Add 30.0 mL of 0.1 N bromine, then quickly add 5 mL of hydrochloric acid, and insert the stopper in the flask immediately. Cool the flask under running water to room temperature, shake vigorously for 5 min, then set aside for 5 min. Add 6 mL of potassium iodide TS around the stopper, cautiously loosen the stopper, again insert the stopper tightly, and swirl gently. Add 1 mL of chloroform. Titrate the liberated iodine with 0.1 N sodium thiosulfate, adding 3 mL of starch TS as the endpoint is approached. Perform a blank determination (see

General Provisions). Calculate the weight (mg) of $C_{12}H_{18}O_2$ in the sample taken by the formula:

$$\text{Result} = (V_B - V_S) \times F_E$$

V_B = volume of 0.1 N sodium thiosulfate required for the blank titration (mL)
V_S = volume of 0.1 N sodium thiosulfate required for the sample titration (mL)
F_E = mEq factor, 4.857

Acceptance criteria: NLT 98.0% and NMT 100.5% of $C_{12}H_{18}O_2$, on the dried basis

IMPURITIES
Inorganic Impurities
- **LEAD**, *Lead Limit Test, Flame Atomic Absorption Spectrophotometric Method,* Appendix IIIB
  Sample: 2 g
  Acceptance criteria: NMT 2 mg/kg
- **MERCURY**
  [NOTE—Select all reagents for this test to have as low a content of mercury as practicable, and store all reagent solutions in containers of borosilicate glass. Specially clean all glassware used in this test by soaking it in warm 8 N nitric acid for 30 min and rinsing with water. Keep flasks for this determination separate from other flasks, and use them only for mercury determinations.]
  Standard stock solution: Transfer 34.0 mg of mercuric chloride to a 250-mL volumetric flask. Add 1 drop of hydrochloric acid, and dissolve in and dilute to volume with water. Transfer 1.0 mL of this solution to a 100-mL volumetric flask, add 1 drop of hydrochloric acid, and dilute with water to volume.
  Standard solution: Transfer 1.0 mL of the *Standard stock solution* to a 500-mL volumetric flask, add 1 drop of hydrochloric acid, and dilute to volume with water.
  Sample solution: Transfer 134 mg of sample to a 250-mL beaker, and cautiously add 10 mL of 11 N nitric acid and 10 mL of 18 N sulfuric acid. Digest with the aid of heat in a well-ventilated hood until brown fumes cease to evolve. Cautiously add an additional 10 mL of 11 N nitric acid, and continue heating until no more fumes evolve. Cool, transfer to a 200-mL volumetric flask, and dilute to volume with water.
  Analysis: Transfer 100 mL of *Standard solution* to a 300-mL mercury analysis reaction vessel, add 2 drops of a 50 mg/mL potassium permanganate solution, and mix. (The solution should be purple; add additional permanganate solution, dropwise, if necessary.) Add 5 mL of 11 N nitric acid, stir, and allow to stand for NLT 15 s. Add 5 mL of 18 N sulfuric acid, stir, and allow to stand for NLT 45 s. Add 5 mL of 15 mg/mL hydroxylamine hydrochloride solution, stir, and allow to stand until the solution turns light yellow or colorless. Add 5 mL of 100 mg/mL stannous chloride solution, immediately insert the aerator connected to an air pump, and determine the maximum absorbance of the treated *Standard solution* at the mercury resonance line of 253.65 nm, with a suitable atomic absorption spectrophotometer equipped with a mercury hollow-cathode lamp and an absorption cell that permits the flameless detection of mercury. [NOTE—Disregard the presence of insoluble matter in this solution; mix before use.] In a closed system with a circulating air pump, connect a calcium chloride drying tube and an aerator inserted in a 300-mL reaction vessel so that air passed through the treated preparation contained in the reaction vessel evaporates any metallic mercury present.
  In a similar manner, treat 100 mL of the *Sample solution* and 100 mL of water (reagent blank), and determine the maximum absorbances at the same wavelength. [NOTE—Check the zero setting of the instrument frequently.]
  Acceptance criteria: The absorbance of the solution from the *Sample solution* does not exceed that of the solution from the *Standard solution*. (NMT 3 mg/kg)
- **NICKEL**
  Standard stock solution: 40.1 μg/mL of nickel chloride hexahydrate
  Standard solution: 4.01 μg/mL of nickel chloride hexahydrate, from the *Standard stock solution* (1 μg/mL of nickel ion)
  Sample: 2 g
  Analysis: Dissolve the *Sample* in sufficient methanol to yield 20 mL. Add 3 mL of bromine TS and 2 mL of 200 mg/mL citric acid solution, and mix. Add 10 mL of 6 N ammonium hydroxide and 1 mL of a 1:100 dimethylglyoxime:ethanol solution. Mix, dilute with water to 50 mL, and allow to stand for 5 min. Repeat the preceding with 4 mL of the *Standard solution*.
  Acceptance criteria: Any color the solution containing the *Sample* produces is not more intense than that of the solution containing the *Standard solution*. (NMT 2 mg/kg)

Organic Impurities
- **RESORCINOL AND OTHER PHENOLS**
  Sample: 1 g
  Analysis: Shake the *Sample* with 50 mL of water for a few minutes, filter, and add 3 drops of ferric chloride TS to the filtrate.
  Acceptance criteria: No red or blue color appears.

SPECIFIC TESTS
- **ACIDITY**
  Sample: 250 mg
  Analysis: Dissolve the *Sample* in 500 mL of water, add a few drops of methyl red TS, and titrate with 0.02 N sodium hydroxide.
  Acceptance criteria: NMT 1.0 mL of 0.02 N sodium hydroxide is required for neutralization. (0.05%)
- **MELTING RANGE OR TEMPERATURE DETERMINATION,** *Procedure for Class I,* Appendix IIB
  Acceptance criteria: Between 62° and 67°
- **RESIDUE ON IGNITION (SULFATED ASH),** Appendix IIC
  Sample: 1 g
  Acceptance criteria: NMT 0.1%

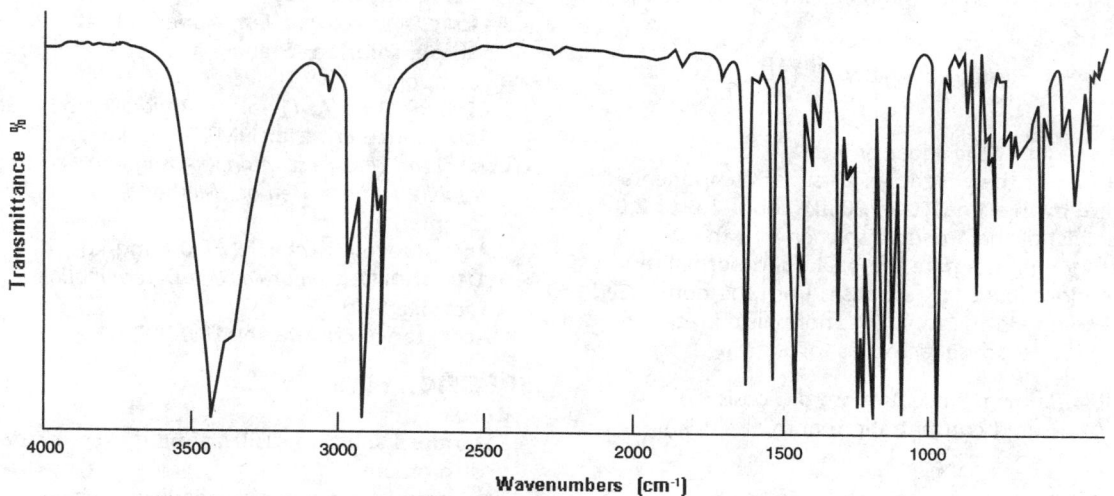

4-Hexylresorcinol

High-Fructose Corn Syrup

First Published: Prior to FCC 6

UNII: XY6UN3QB6S [high fructose corn syrup]

DESCRIPTION
High-Fructose Corn Syrup (HFCS) occurs as a water white to light yellow, somewhat viscous liquid that darkens at high temperatures. It is a saccharide mixture prepared as a clear, aqueous solution from high-dextrose-equivalent corn starch hydrolysate by the partial enzymatic conversion of glucose (dextrose) to fructose, using an insoluble glucose isomerase preparation that complies with 21CFR 184.1372 and that has been obtained from a pure culture fermentation that produces no antibiotics. It is miscible in all proportions with water.

Function: Nutritive sweetener
Packaging and Storage: Store in tight containers.

IDENTIFICATION
- **PROCEDURE**
  Sample solution: 100 mg/mL
  Analysis: Add a few drops of the *Sample solution* to 5 mL of hot alkaline cupric tartrate TS.
  Acceptance criteria: A copious red precipitate of cuprous oxide forms.

ASSAY
- **PROCEDURE**
  Mobile phase: Degassed, purified water passed through a 0.22-μm filter before use. [NOTE—Maintain the water at 85° during operation of the chromatograph.]
  Standard solution: Prepare a solution containing a total of about 10% solids, using sugars of known purity (e.g., USP Fructose RS; USP Dextrose RS or NIST Standard Reference Material; maltose, Aldrich Chemical Company; or equivalent) that approximates, on the dry basis, the composition of the sample to be analyzed. Dissolve each standard sugar, in 20 mL of purified water contained in a 50-mL beaker. Heat on a steam bath until all sugars are dissolved, then cool, and transfer to a 100-mL volumetric flask. Dilute to volume with water and mix. [NOTE—Freeze the solution if it is to be reused.]
  Sample solution: Dilute to approximately 10% solids using the result from the test for *Total Solids* (below).
  Chromatographic system, Appendix IIIC
  [NOTE—Use a suitable high-performance liquid chromatography system such as the one described in *Standard Analytical Methods of the Corn Refiners Association*.]
  Mode: High-performance liquid chromatography
  Detector: Differential refractometer
  Column: 22- to 31-cm stainless steel column, or equivalent with a stationary phase of prepacked macroreticular polystyrene sulfonated divinylbenzene cation-exchange resin (2% to 8% cross-linked, 8- to 25-μm particle size), preferably in the calcium or silver form. Examples of acceptable resins are Bio-Rad Aminex HPX-87C, or equivalent, for separating DP_1-DP_4 saccharides, and Aminex HPX-42C and HPX-42A, or equivalent, for separating DP_1-DP_7 saccharides.
  Column temperature: 85°
  Detector temperature: 45° ± 0.005°
  Injection volume
    Standard solution: 10 to 20 μL
    Sample solution: 10 to 50 μL, appropriate for the specific solids content
  Standardization: If a corn syrup or maltodextrin is used to supply a DP_{4+} fraction, take care to include all saccharides in the standard composition calculation.

Calculate the dry-basis concentration, in percent, of each individual component in the *Standard solution* by the formula:

$$\text{Result} = (W_C/\Sigma W_I) \times 100$$

W_C = weight of the sugar of interest
ΣW_I = sum of the weights of all sugar components

Standardize by injecting 10 to 20 µL (about 1.0 to 2.0 mg of solids) of the *Standard solution* into the chromatograph. Integrate the peaks and normalize. Sum the individual DP_{4+} responses from the normalized printout to obtain the total DP_{4+} normalized response. Calculate the response factors as follows:

$$R_I = \text{(known concentration, dry basis \%)}/\text{(measured concentration, normalized \%)}$$

R_I = response factor for component i

Compute the response factor for each component relative to glucose (R'_I) using the following equation:

$$R'_I = R_I/R_G$$

R_G = response factor for glucose
R_I = response factor for component i
R'_I = response factor relative to glucose for component i

The R'_I for DP_{4+} should be programmed as a default value (if automated equipment is used) and used to compute the concentration of higher saccharides.

Analysis: Inject a volume of the *Sample solution* (sized appropriately for the specific solids content) into the chromatograph and record the resulting chromatogram. Calculate the concentration of each component as follows:

$$C_I = (A_I \times R_I \times 100)/(\Sigma A_N R_N)$$

C_I = concentration of component i
A_I = peak area recorded for component i
R_I = response factor for component i
$\Sigma A_N R_N$ = sum of the product of the areas (A) and response factors (R) for all components detected

Acceptance criteria
42% HFCS: NLT 97.0% total saccharides, expressed as a percent of solids, of which:
  NLT 42.0% consists of fructose
  NLT 92.0% consists of monosaccharides
  NMT 8.0% consists of other saccharides
55% HFCS: NLT 95.0% total saccharides, expressed as a percent of solids, of which:
  NLT 55.0% consists of fructose
  NLT 95.0% consists of monosaccharides
  NMT 5.0% consists of other saccharides

IMPURITIES
Inorganic Impurities
- **ARSENIC,** *Arsenic Limit Test,* Appendix IIIB
  Sample solution: Prepare as directed for organic compounds.
  Control: 1 µg As (1 mL *of Standard Arsenic* Solution)
  Acceptance criteria: NMT 1 mg/kg
- **LEAD,** *Lead Limit Test, Atomic Absorption Spectrophotometric Graphite Furnace Method, Method I,* Appendix IIIB
  Sample: 5 g
  Acceptance criteria: NMT 0.1 mg/kg
- **SULFUR DIOXIDE,** *Sulfur Dioxide Determination,* Appendix X
  Sample: 50 g
  Acceptance criteria: NMT 0.003%

SPECIFIC TESTS
- **COLOR**
  Standard solution: 100 µg/mL reagent-grade potassium dichromate
  Analysis: Use a suitable variable-wavelength spectrophotometer capable of measuring percent transmittance throughout the visible spectrum and designed to permit the use of sample and reference cells with path lengths of 2 to 4 cm. The transmittance of all paired cells should agree within 0.5%.
  Using water in the sample and reference cells of 2-cm pathlength, normalize the percent transmittance scale of the spectrophotometer to 100%. Leave the reference cell in place and replace the water in the sample cell with the *Standard solution*. Determine the wavelength at which the solution exhibits exactly 54.5% transmittance. This wavelength is defined as λ_c, the corrected 450-nm wavelength.
  Remove the 2-cm cells from the spectrophotometer and, with water in the sample and reference cells of 4-cm pathlength, adjust the percent transmittance scale to 100% with the spectrophotometer set at λ_c. Leave the reference cell in place and replace the water in the sample cell with sample. Measure the percent transmittance (T_{450}). Remove the sample cell, set the wavelength at 600 nm, replace the sample with water, and adjust the percent transmittance scale to 100%. Determine the percent transmittance at 600 nm (T_{600}) with the same sample in the sample cell.
  Calculate the *Color* of the *Sample* taken using the formula:

  $$\text{Result} = (\log T_{600} - \log T_{450})/4$$

  T_{600} = percent transmittance at 600 nm
  T_{450} = percent transmittance at λ_c nm
  Acceptance criteria: Within the range specified by the vendor
- **RESIDUE ON IGNITION (SULFATED ASH),** Appendix IIC
  Sample: 10 g
  Acceptance criteria: NMT 0.05%
- **TOTAL SOLIDS,** *High Fructose Corn Syrup Solids,* Appendix X
  Analysis: Determine the refractive index of a sample at 20° or 45° and use the tables in the test referenced to obtain the percent *Total Solids*.

Acceptance criteria
42% HFCS: NLT 70.5%
55% HFCS: NLT 76.5%

OTHER REQUIREMENTS
- **LABELING:** Indicate the color range and presence of sulfur dioxide if the residual concentration is greater than 10 mg/kg.

L-Histidine

First Published: Prior to FCC 6
Last Revision: FCC 6

L-α-Amino-4(or 5)-imidazolepropionic Acid

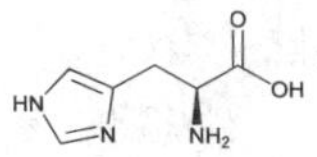

$C_6H_9N_3O_2$　　　　　　　　Formula wt 155.16
　　　　　　　　　　　　　　　CAS: [71-00-1]
UNII: 4QD397987E [histidine]

DESCRIPTION
L-Histidine occurs as white crystals or as a crystalline powder. It is soluble in water, very slightly soluble in alcohol, and insoluble in ether. It melts with decomposition between about 277° and 288°.
Function: Nutrient
Packaging and Storage: Store in well-closed, light-resistant containers.

IDENTIFICATION
- **INFRARED ABSORPTION,** Spectrophotometric Identification Tests, Appendix IIIC
  Reference standard: USP L-Histidine RS
  Sample and standard preparation: K
  Acceptance criteria: The spectrum of the sample exhibits maxima at the same wavelengths as those in the spectrum of the Reference standard.

ASSAY
- **PROCEDURE**
  Sample: 150 mg, previously dried
  Analysis: Dissolve the Sample in 3 mL of formic acid and 50 mL of glacial acetic acid. Titrate with 0.1 N perchloric acid, determining the endpoint potentiometrically. [**CAUTION**—Handle perchloric acid in an appropriate fume hood.] Perform a blank determination (see General Provisions), and make any necessary correction. Each mL of 0.1 N perchloric acid is equivalent to 15.52 mg of $C_6H_9N_3O_2$.
  Acceptance criteria: NLT 98.5% and NMT 101.5% of $C_6H_9N_3O_2$, on the dried basis

IMPURITIES
Inorganic Impurities
- **LEAD,** Lead Limit Test, Appendix IIIB
  Sample solution: Prepare as directed for organic compounds.
  Control: 5 µg Pb (5 mL of Diluted Standard Lead Solution)
  Acceptance criteria: NMT 5 mg/kg

SPECIFIC TESTS
- **LOSS ON DRYING,** Appendix IIC: 105° for 3 h
  Acceptance criteria: NMT 0.2%
- **OPTICAL (SPECIFIC) ROTATION,** Appendix IIB
  Sample: 11g, previously dried
  Analysis: Dissolve the Sample in sufficient 6 N hydrochloric acid to make 100 mL.
  Acceptance criteria
  $[\alpha]_D^{20}$ between +11.5° and +13.5°, on the dried basis; or
  $[\alpha]_D^{25}$ between +12.0° and +14.0°, on the dried basis.
- **RESIDUE ON IGNITION (SULFATED ASH),** Appendix IIC
  Sample: 1 g
  Acceptance criteria: NMT 0.2%

L-Histidine Monohydrochloride

First Published: Prior to FCC 6

L-α-Amino-4(or 5)-imidazolepropionic Acid Monohydrochloride

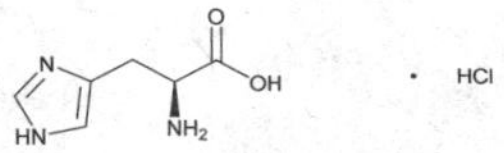

$C_6H_9N_3O_2 \cdot HCl \cdot H_2O$　　　　Formula wt 209.63
　　　　　　　　　　CAS: monohydrate [5934-29-2]
UNII: X573657P6P [histidine monohydrochloride monohydrate]

DESCRIPTION
L-Histidine Monohydrochloride occurs as white crystals or as a crystalline powder. It is soluble in water, and insoluble in alcohol and in ether. It melts with decomposition at about 250° (after drying).
Function: Nutrient
Packaging and Storage: Store in well-closed, light-resistant containers.

IDENTIFICATION
- **INFRARED SPECTRA,** Spectrophotometric Identification Tests, Appendix IIIC
  Acceptance criteria: The spectrum of the sample exhibits relative maxima at the same wavelengths as those of the spectrum below.

ASSAY
- **PROCEDURE**
  Sample: 100 mg, previously dried
  Analysis: Dissolve the Sample in 3 mL of formic acid, add 15.0 mL of 0.1 N perchloric acid, and heat on a water bath for 30 min. [**CAUTION**—Handle perchloric acid in an appropriate fume hood.] After cooling, add 45 mL of glacial acetic acid, and titrate the excess perchloric acid with 0.1 N sodium acetate, determining the endpoint potentiometrically. Perform a blank determination (see General Provisions), and make any

548 / L-Histidine Monohydrochloride / Monographs

necessary correction. Each mL of 0.1N perchloric acid is equivalent to 10.48 mg of $C_6H_9N_3O_2 \cdot HCl \cdot H_2O$.
Acceptance criteria: NLT 98.5% and NMT 101.5% of $C_6H_9N_3O_2 \cdot HCl \cdot H_2O$, on the dried basis

IMPURITIES
Inorganic Impurities
- **LEAD,** *Lead Limit Test,* Appendix IIIB
  Sample solution: Prepare as directed for organic compounds.
  Control: 5 µg Pb (5 mL of *Diluted Standard Lead Solution*)
  Acceptance criteria: NMT 5 mg/kg

SPECIFIC TESTS
- **LOSS ON DRYING,** Appendix IIC: 105° for 3 h
  Acceptance criteria: NMT 0.3%
- **OPTICAL (SPECIFIC) ROTATION,** Appendix IIB
  Sample solution: 11 g of a previously dried sample in sufficient 6 N hydrochloric acid to make 100 mL
  Acceptance criteria: $[\alpha]_D^{20}$ between +8.5° and +10.5°, on the dried basis
- **RESIDUE ON IGNITION (SULFATED ASH),** Appendix IIC
  Sample: 1g
  Acceptance criteria: NMT 0.1%

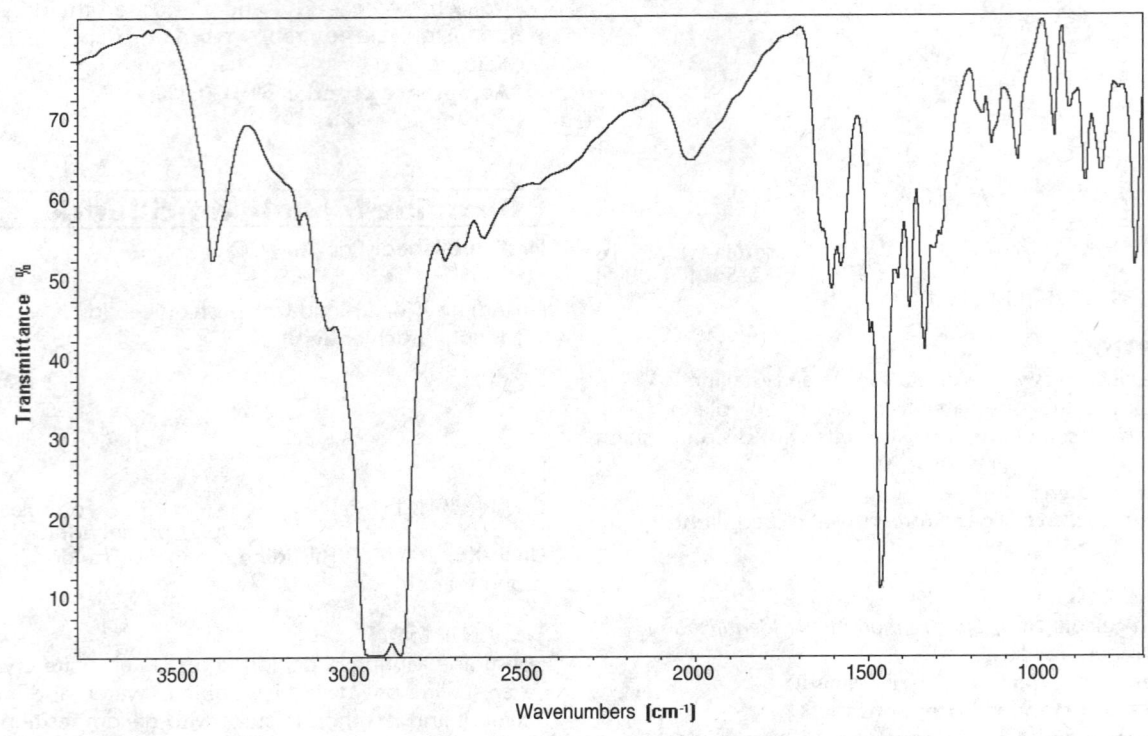

L-Histidine Monohydrochloride

Hops Oil

First Published: Prior to FCC 6

CAS: [8007-04-3]

UNII: 06JI9W529S [hops oil]

DESCRIPTION
Hops Oil occurs as a light yellow to green-yellow liquid with a characteristic, aromatic odor. Age darkens the color, and the oil tends to become viscous. It is the volatile oil obtained by steam distillation of the freshly dried membranous cones of the female plants of *Humulus lupulus* L. or *Humulus americanus* Nutt. (Fam. Moraceae). It is soluble in most fixed oils and, sometimes with opalescence, in mineral oil. It is practically insoluble in glycerin and in propylene glycol.
Function: Flavoring agent

Packaging and Storage: Store in a cool place protected from light in full, tight containers that are made from steel or aluminum and that are suitably lined.

IDENTIFICATION
- **INFRARED SPECTRA,** *Spectrophotometric Identification Tests,* Appendix IIIC
  Acceptance criteria: The spectrum of the sample exhibits relative maxima at the same wavelengths as those of the spectrum below.

SPECIFIC TESTS
- **ACID VALUE (ESSENTIAL OILS AND FLAVORS),** Appendix VI
  Sample: 5 g
  Acceptance criteria: NMT 11.0
- **ANGULAR ROTATION,** *Optical (Specific) Rotation,* Appendix IIB: Use a 100-mm tube.
  Acceptance criteria: Between −2° and +2°5′

- **REFRACTIVE INDEX,** Appendix IIB
  [NOTE—Use an Abbé or other refractometer of equal or greater accuracy.]
  Acceptance criteria: Between 1.470 and 1.494 at 20°
- **SAPONIFICATION VALUE,** *Esters,* Appendix VI
  Sample: 5 g
  Acceptance criteria: Between 14 and 69
- **SOLUBILITY IN ALCOHOL,** Appendix VI
  Acceptance criteria: One mL of sample usually is not soluble in 95% alcohol. Older oils are less soluble than fresh oils.
- **SPECIFIC GRAVITY:** Determine by any reliable method (see *General Provisions*).
  Acceptance criteria: Between 0.825 and 0.926

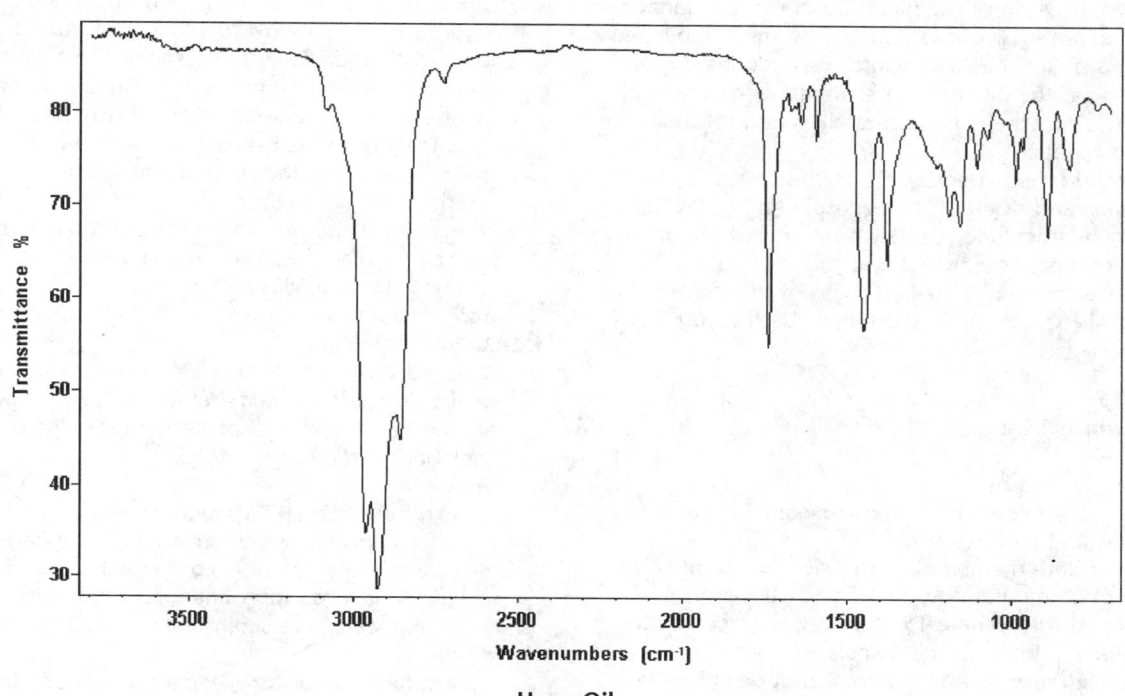

Hops Oil

Hydrochloric Acid

First Published: Prior to FCC 6
Last Revision: Second Supplement, FCC 7

HCl
INS: 507
UNII: QTT17582CB [hydrochloric acid]
Formula wt 36.46
CAS: [7647-01-0]

DESCRIPTION
Hydrochloric Acid occurs as a clear, colorless or slightly yellow, corrosive liquid. It is a water solution of hydrogen chloride of varied concentrations. It is miscible with water and with alcohol. Concentrations of Hydrochloric Acid are expressed in percent by weight or may be expressed in degrees Baumé (°Bé) from which percents of Hydrochloric Acid and specific gravities may readily be derived (see *Hydrochloric Acid Table,* Appendix IIC). The usually available concentrations are 18°, 20°, 22°, and 23°Bé.
Concentrations above 13°Bé (19.6%) fume in moist air, lose hydrogen chloride, and create a corrosive atmosphere. Because of these characteristics, observe suitable precautions during sampling and analysis to prevent losses.

[NOTE—Hydrochloric Acid is produced by various methods that might impart trace amounts of organic compounds as impurities. The manufacturer, vendor, or user is responsible for identifying the specific organic compounds that are present and for meeting the requirements for *Organic Impurities* (below). Methods are likewise provided for their determination. In applying the procedures, use any necessary standards to quantitate the organic compounds present in each specific product.
The variety of organic impurities that might conceivably be found in Hydrochloric Acid is such that it is impossible to provide a comprehensive and accurate list here. Therefore, the manufacturer, vendor, or user is responsible for establishing the suitability of such Hydrochloric Acid for its intended application in foods or food processing in accordance with the provision of *Trace Impurities* (see *General Provisions*).]
Function: Acidifier
Packaging and Storage: Store in tight containers.

IDENTIFICATION
- **CHLORIDE,** Appendix IIIA
  Acceptance criteria: Passes test

ASSAY
- **PROCEDURE**
  Sample preparation: Tare a 125-mL glass-stoppered Erlenmeyer flask containing 35.0 mL of 1 N sodium hydroxide. Without the use of vacuum, partially fill a 10-mL serological pipet from near the bottom of a flask containing the sample, remove any acid adhering to the outside, and discard the first mL flowing from the pipet. Hold the tip of the pipet just above the surface of the sodium hydroxide solution, and transfer between 2.5 and 3 mL of the sample into the flask, leaving at least 1 mL in the pipet. Stopper the flask, gently swirl to mix the contents, and accurately weigh to obtain the sample weight.
  Analysis: Add methyl orange TS to the *Sample preparation* and titrate the excess sodium hydroxide with 1 N hydrochloric acid. Each mL of 1 N sodium hydroxide is equivalent to 36.46 mg of HCl.
  Acceptance criteria: 97.0%–103.0% of the labeled amount of HCl, or within the range specified on the label

IMPURITIES
Inorganic Impurities
- **IRON**
  Sample: 5 g (4.3 mL)
  Control: 25 µg Fe (2.5 mL *Iron Standard Solution*, Solutions and Indicators)
  Analysis: Dilute the *Sample* with water to 40 mL. Add 40 mg of ammonium persulfate and 10 mL of ammonium thiocyanate TS. Repeat the preceding using the *Control* in place of the *Sample*.
  Acceptance criteria: Any red color produced by the *Sample* does not exceed that produced by the *Control*. (NMT 5 mg/kg)
- **LEAD**, *Lead Limit Test, Atomic Absorption Spectrophotometric Graphite Furnace Method, Method I,* Appendix IIIB
  Acceptance criteria: NMT 1 mg/kg
- **MERCURY**, *Mercury Limit Test, Method II,* Appendix IIIB
  Acceptance criteria: NMT 0.10 mg/kg
- **OXIDIZING SUBSTANCES (AS CL$_2$)**
  Sample: 1 mL
  Analysis: Transfer the *Sample* into a 30-mL test tube, dilute to 20 mL with freshly boiled and cooled water, and add 1 mL of potassium iodide TS and 1 mL of starch TS. Stopper the test tube, and mix thoroughly. Prepare a *Control* consisting of 1.0 mL of 0.001 N iodine in an equal volume of water containing the same quantities of the same reagents and 1 mL of ACS reagent-grade hydrochloric acid.
  Acceptance criteria: Any blue color produced by the *Sample* does not exceed that produced by the *Control*. (NMT 0.003%)
- **REDUCING SUBSTANCES (AS SO$_3$)**
  Sample: 1 mL
  Analysis: Transfer 1 mL of ACS reagent-grade hydrochloric acid into a 30-mL test tube, dilute to 20 mL with recently boiled and cooled water, and add 1 mL of potassium iodide TS, 1 mL of starch TS, and 2.0 mL of 0.001 N iodine. Stopper the test tube, and mix thoroughly. Add the *Sample* to the test tube.
  Acceptance criteria: The blue color of the solution does not disappear when the *Sample* is added. (NMT 0.007%)
- **SULFATE**
  Sample solution: 10 mg/mL in water
  Analysis: Transfer 5.0 mL of the *Sample solution* into a 50-mL tall-form Nessler tube, and dilute with water to 20 mL. Add a drop of phenolphthalein TS, neutralize the solution with 6 N ammonium hydroxide, and then add 1 mL of 2.7 N hydrochloric acid. Add 3 mL of barium chloride TS to the resulting clear solution, previously filtered, if necessary, dilute with water to 50 mL, and mix. Prepare a *Control* consisting of 1 mL of ACS reagent-grade hydrochloric acid and 250 µg of sulfate (SO$_4$) and the same quantities of the reagents used for the sample.
  Acceptance criteria: Any turbidity produced by the *Sample solution* does not exceed that shown in the *Control*. (NMT 0.5%)

Organic Impurities
- **ORGANIC COMPOUNDS**
  [NOTE—Use either the *Vapor Partitioning Method* (below) or the *Solvent Extraction Method* (below) for analysis of all listed elements, except for benzene, which requires the *Vapor Partitioning Method*.]
  Tests
  - **VAPOR PARTITIONING METHOD**
    [NOTE—This method is suitable for the determination of extractable organic compounds at 0.05–100 mg/kg but is most appropriate for organic compounds with a vapor pressure greater than 10 mm Hg at 25°.]
    Standard solutions: Prepare a standard solution of each of the organic compounds to be quantitated in hydrochloric acid (known to be free of interfering impurities) at approximate concentrations of 5 mg/kg, or within ±50% of the concentrations in the samples to be analyzed.
    Place a stirring bar in a 1-L volumetric flask equipped with a ground-glass stopper, and tare the combination. Fill the flask with reagent-grade hydrochloric acid so that no air space is present when the flask is stoppered, and determine the weight of the hydrochloric acid.
    Calculate the volume (V), in µL, of each organic component to be added:

    $$V = (C \times W)/(D \times F)$$

    C = desired concentration of the organic compound to be added (mg/kg)
    W = weight of the hydrochloric acid (g)
    D = density of the organic compound to be added (mg/µL)
    F = conversion factor, 1000 (g/kg)

    Add the calculated amount of each component to the hydrochloric acid with a syringe (ensure that the syringe tip is under the solution surface), stopper the flask, and stir the solution for at least 2 h using a magnetic stirrer.

Chromatographic system, Appendix IIA
  Mode: Gas chromatography
  Detector: Flame ionization
  Column: 4-m × 2-mm (id) stainless-steel column, or equivalent, packed with 15%, by weight, methyl trifluoropropyl silicone (DCFS 1265, or QF-1, or OV-210, or SP-2401) stationary phase on 80- to 100-mesh Gas Chrom R, or the equivalent. [NOTE—Condition a newly packed column at 120° and with a 30-mL/min helium flow for at least 2 h (preferably overnight) before it is attached to the detector.]
  Flow rate: 11 mL/min; with fuel gas flows optimized for the gas chromatograph and detector in use
  Temperature
    Column: 105° (isothermal)
    Injection port: 250°
    Detector: 250°
  Suitability requirements
    Suitability requirement 1: The signal-to-noise ratio should be at least 10:1.
    Suitability requirement 2: The relative standard deviation at 5 mg/kg is NMT 15% for five sample analyses.

[NOTE—Change the experimental conditions as necessary for optimal resolution and sensitivity.]

Calibration (non-gaseous standards): Dilute a 10-mL aliquot of *Standard solution* with an equal volume of water. Draw this solution into a 50-mL glass syringe. Then draw 20 mL of air into the syringe, cap with a rubber septum, and place the syringe on a shaker for 5 min. Draw 1 mL of the vapor through the septum, and inject it into the gas chromatograph. Determine a blank for each lot of reagent-grade hydrochloric acid, and calculate a response factor:

$$R = C/(A - B)$$

R = response factor
C = concentration for the standard component of interest (mg/kg)
A = peak area for the standard component of interest
B = peak area for the *Blank*

Calibration (gaseous standards)

[NOTE—Gaseous compounds present special problems in the preparation of standards. Therefore, to determine response factors for gaseous compounds use the following *Method of Multiple Extractions*.]

Dilute a sample of hydrochloric acid known to contain the gaseous compound of interest with an equal volume of water. Draw 20 mL of this solution into a 50-mL glass syringe; then draw 20 mL of air into the syringe, cap with a rubber septum, and place the syringe on a shaker for 5 min. Withdraw 1 mL of the vapor through the septum, and inject it into the chromatograph. Expel the vapor phase from the 50-mL syringe, draw in another 20 mL of air, repeat the extraction, and inject another 1-mL vapor sample into the chromatograph. Carry out the extraction and analysis on the same sample of acid six times. For each impurity, plot the area (A_N) determined for extraction (N) against the difference between A_N and the area determined for extraction (N + 1); that is, plot A_N against ($A_N - A_{N+1}$). The slope of this line is the extraction efficiency (E) for that impurity into the air.

Inject 1 mL of a 0.1% (by volume) standard gas sample of each impurity in air into the chromatograph, and determine the absolute factor (F_A), in g, per peak area:

$$F_A = (M \times 4.0816 \times 10^{-8})/A$$

M = molecular weight of the compound
A = peak area of the compound

The concentration (C), in mg/kg, of the component of interest in the original sample is calculated as:

$$C = (A \times F_A \times 1.6949 \times 10^6)/E$$

A = peak area corresponding to the compound (as above)
F_A = absolute factor (determined above)
E = extraction efficiency (determined above)

The response factor, R, is then calculated as:

$$R = C/A$$

Analysis: Dilute 10-mL of sample with an equal volume of water. Draw this solution into a 50-mL glass syringe. Then draw 20 mL of air into the syringe, cap with a rubber septum, and place the syringe on a shaker for 5 min. Draw 1 mL of the vapor through the septum, and inject it into the gas chromatograph. Approximate elution times, in minutes, for some specific organic compounds are as follows:

   Methane and acetylene: 1.70
   Methyl chloride: 2.21
   Vinyl chloride: 2.29
   1,1,1-Trichlorofluoromethane: 2.62
   Ethyl chloride: 2.90
   Vinylidene chloride: 3.20
   Methylene chloride: 3.64
   Chloroform: 4.49
   1,1-Dichloroethane: 4.53
   Carbon tetrachloride: 4.86
   1,1,1-Trichloroethane: 5.50
   Benzene: 6.00
   Trichloroethylene: 6.22
   Ethylene dichloride: 6.61
   Propylene dichloride: 8.41
   Perchloroethylene: 9.73

[NOTE—Alternative columns may be required to resolve some combinations of components. Methyl chloride and vinyl chloride are resolved by a 3.7-m × 3-mm (id) squalane column, or equivalent, at 45° and a helium flow of 10 mL/min. Chloroform and 1,1-dichloroethane are resolved by a 4-m × 3-mm (id)

DC 550R column, or equivalent, at 110° and a helium flow of 12 mL/min.]

Calculate the concentration, in mg/kg, of each compound by multiplying its corresponding peak area by the appropriate response factor determined in the Calibration protocol:

$$C = R \times A$$

- C = concentration of the compound of interest in the sample taken (mg/kg)
- R = response area for the compound of interest, determined in *Calibration* (above)
- A = peak area for the compound of interest in the chromatogram of the sample

- SOLVENT EXTRACTION METHOD

[NOTE—This method is suitable for the determination of extractable organic compounds at 0.3–100 mg/kg, but is most appropriate for organic compounds with vapor pressures less than 10 mm Hg at 25°.]

Standard solutions: Prepare as described in *Vapor Partitioning Method* (above).

Chromatographic system, Appendix IIA
  Mode: Gas chromatography
  Detector: Flame ionization
  Column: 4-m × 2-mm (id) stainless-steel column, or equivalent, packed with 15%, by weight, methyl trifluoropropyl silicone (DCFS 1265, or QF-1, or OV-210, or SP-2401) stationary phase on 80- to 100-mesh Gas Chrom R, or the equivalent. [NOTE—Condition a newly packed column at 120° and with a 30-mL/min helium flow for at least 2 h (preferably overnight) before it is attached to the detector.]
  Flow rate: 21 mL/min; with fuel gas flows optimized for the gas chromatograph and detector in use
  Temperature
    Column: 120° (isothermal)
    Injection port: 250°
    Detector: 250°
  Suitability requirements
    Suitability requirement 1: The signal-to-noise ratio should be at least 10:1.
    Suitability requirement 2: The relative standard deviation at 5 mg/kg is NMT 15% for five sample analyses.
      [NOTE—Change the experimental conditions as necessary for optimal resolution and sensitivity.]

Calibration: Accurately transfer 90 mL of *Standard solution* and 10 mL of perchloroethylene (free of interfering impurities) into a narrow-mouth, 4-oz bottle. Place the bottle in a mechanical shaker for 30 min. Separate the two phases (perchloroethylene on the bottom) and inject 3 µL of the perchloroethylene extract into the gas chromatograph, or equivalent. Determine a *Blank* for each lot of reagent-grade hydrochloric acid and perchloroethylene by extracting the hydrochloric acid in the same way as for the *Standard solution*. Calculate a response factor:

$$R = C/(A - B)$$

- R = response factor
- C = concentration for the standard component of interest (mg/kg)
- A = peak area for the standard component of interest
- B = peak area for the *Blank*

Analysis: Accurately transfer 90 mL of sample and 10 mL of perchloroethylene (free of interfering impurities) into a narrow-mouth, 4-oz bottle. Place the bottle in a mechanical shaker for 30 min. Separate the two phases (perchloroethylene on the bottom) and inject 3 µL of the perchloroethylene extract into the gas chromatograph, or equivalent. Approximate elution times, in minutes, for some chlorinated organic compounds are as follows:
  Vinylidene chloride: 2.94
  Methylene chloride: 3.27
  Chloroform: 3.83
  Carbon tetrachloride: 4.07
  1,1,1-Trichloroethane: 4.50
  Trichloroethylene: 4.97
  Ethylene dichloride: 5.26
  Propylene dichloride: 6.36
  Perchloroethylene: 6.95
  1,1,1,2-Tetrachloroethane: 10.12
  1,1,2,2-Tetrachloroethane: 13.70
  Pentachloroethane: 16.19

[NOTE—To determine perchloroethylene and higher-boiling impurities, substitute methylene chloride (free of interfering impurities) for perchloroethylene in the extraction step. For higher boiling impurities such as monochlorobenzene and the three dichlorobenzenes, use a 2.74-m × 2.1-mm (id) stainless-steel column packed with 10% carbowax 20M/2% KOH on 80- to 100-mesh chromasorb W (acid washed), set at 150° and with a nitrogen flow of 35 mL/min.]

Calculate the concentration, in mg/kg, of each compound by multiplying its corresponding peak area by the appropriate response factor determined in the *Calibration* protocol:

$$C = R \times (A - B)$$

- C = concentration of the compound of interest in the sample taken (mg/kg)
- R = response area for the compound of interest, determined in *Calibration* (above)
- A = peak area for the compound of interest in the chromatogram of the sample
- B = area obtained from a blank sample

Acceptance criteria
  Total non-fluorine containing organic compounds: NMT 5 mg/kg, including NMT 0.05 mg/kg benzene

Total fluorinated organic compounds: NMT 0.0025%

SPECIFIC TESTS
- **COLOR,** *Readily Carbonizable Substances,* Appendix IIB
  Acceptance criteria: A sample shows no more color than does *Matching Fluid A.*
- **DEGREES BAUMÉ**
  Sample: 200 mL, previously cooled to a temperature below 15°
  Analysis: Transfer the *Sample* into a 250-mL hydrometer cylinder. Insert a suitable Baumé hydrometer graduated at 0.1 °Bé intervals, adjust the temperature to 15.6°, and note the reading at the bottom of the meniscus.
  Acceptance criteria: Within the range shown on the label or claimed by the vendor
- **NONVOLATILE RESIDUE**
  Sample: 1 g
  Analysis: Transfer the *Sample* into a tared glass dish, evaporate to dryness on a steam bath, then dry at 110° for 1 h. Cool in a desiccator and weigh.
  Acceptance criteria: The weight of the residue does not exceed 5 mg. (NMT 0.5%)
- **SPECIFIC GRAVITY**
  Analysis: Determine 15.6° with a hydrometer, or calculate from the degrees Baumé observed in *Degrees Baumé* (above).
  Acceptance criteria: Within the range specified or implied by the vendor

OTHER REQUIREMENTS
- **LABELING:** Indicate the content, by weight, of Hydrochloric Acid (HCl). Alternatively, indicate the range of Hydrochloric Acid content, the range of degrees Baumé, and/or the specific gravity range.

Hydrogen Peroxide

First Published: Prior to FCC 6

H_2O_2
Formula wt 34.01
CAS: [7722-84-1]
UNII: BBX060AN9V [hydrogen peroxide]

DESCRIPTION
Hydrogen Peroxide occurs as a clear, colorless liquid. The grades of Hydrogen Peroxide suitable for food use usually have a concentration between 30% and 50%. It is miscible with water.
[NOTE—Although Hydrogen Peroxide undergoes exothermic decomposition in the presence of dirt and other foreign materials, it is safe and stable under recommended conditions of handling and storage. Information on safe handling and use may be obtained from the supplier.]
Function: Bleaching, oxidizing agent; starch modifier; antimicrobial agent
Packaging and Storage: Store in a cool place in containers with a vent in the stopper.

IDENTIFICATION
- **PROCEDURE**
  Sample: 1 mL
  Analysis: Shake the *Sample* with 10 mL of water containing 1 drop of 2 N sulfuric acid, and add 2 mL of ether. Add one drop of potassium dichromate TS.
  Acceptance criteria: An evanescent blue color is produced in the water layer that, upon agitation and standing, passes into the ether layer.

ASSAY
- **PROCEDURE**
  Sample solution: Dilute an amount of sample equivalent to 300 mg of H_2O_2 to 100 mL with water.
  Analysis: Add 25 mL of 2 N sulfuric acid to 20.0 mL of *Sample solution*, and titrate with 0.1 N potassium permanganate. Each mL of 0.1 N potassium permanganate is equivalent to 1.701 mg of H_2O_2.
  Acceptance criteria: NLT the labeled concentration or within the range stated on the label

IMPURITIES
Inorganic Impurities
- **IRON**
  Sample: 18 mL (20 g)
  Analysis: Evaporate the *Sample* to dryness with 10 mg of sodium chloride on a steam bath. Dissolve the residue in 2 mL of hydrochloric acid and dilute to 50 mL with water. Add 40 mg of ammonium persulfate crystals and 10 mL of ammonium thiocyanate TS, and mix.
  Acceptance criteria: Any red or pink color produced by the *Sample* does not exceed that produced by 1.0 mL of *Iron Standard Solution* (10 μg Fe) in an equal volume of solution containing the quantities of the reagents used in the test. (NMT 0.5 mg/kg)
- **LEAD,** *Lead Limit Test, Flame Atomic Absorption Spectrophotometric Method,* Appendix IIIB
  Analysis: Determine as directed with the following modifications: (1) Prepare only one *Diluted Standard Lead Solution* by transferring 40 mL of *Lead Nitrate Stock Solution* into a 1000-mL volumetric flask and diluting to volume with water to obtain a solution containing 4 μg/mL of lead (Pb) ion; (2) Replace the first paragraph under *Sample Preparation* with the following: Transfer 10 g of sample, into an evaporation dish; (3) Under *Procedure,* determine the absorbances of the *Sample Preparation* and *Diluted Standard Lead Solution* only.
  Acceptance criteria: The absorbance of the *Sample Preparation* is NMT that of the *Diluted Standard Lead Solution.* (NMT 4 mg/kg)
- **PHOSPHATE**
  Sample: 400 mg
  Analysis: Evaporate the *Sample* to dryness on a steam bath. Dissolve the residue in 25 mL of 0.5 N sulfuric acid, add 1 mL of a 50 mg/mL ammonium molybdate tetrahydrate solution and 1 mL of *p*-methylaminophenol sulfate TS, and allow it to stand for 2 h. Prepare a *Control* using 2.0 mL of *Phosphate Standard Solution* (20 μg PO_4) (see *Solutions and*

Indicators) in an equal volume of solution containing the quantities of the reagents used for the *Sample*.
Acceptance criteria: Any blue color produced by the *Sample* does not exceed that produced by the *Control*. (NMT 0.005%)

- **TIN**
  Aluminum chloride solution: 8.93 mg/mL of aluminum chloride (AlCl$_3$·6H$_2$O)
  Gelatin solution: 2 mg/mL of gelatin in boiled water that has been cooled to between 50° and 60°. [NOTE—Prepare on the day of use.]
  Standard stock solution: Dissolve 250.0 mg of lead-free tin foil in 10 to 15 mL of hydrochloric acid, and dilute to 250.0 mL with 1:2 hydrochloric acid.
  Standard solution: Transfer 5.0 mL of *Standard stock solution* into a 100-mL volumetric flask, dilute to volume with water, and mix. Transfer 2.0 mL of this solution (100 µg Sn) into a 250-mL Erlenmeyer flask, and add 15 mL of water, 5 mL of nitric acid, and 2 mL of sulfuric acid. Place a small, stemless funnel in the mouth of the flask, and heat until strong fumes of sulfuric acid evolve. Cool, add 5 mL of water, evaporate again to strong fumes, and cool. Repeat the addition of water and heating to strong fumes, then add 15 mL of water, heat to boiling, and cool. Dilute to about 35 mL with water, add 1 drop of methyl red TS and 2.0 mL of the *Aluminum chloride solution*, and mix. Make the solution just alkaline by adding, dropwise, ammonium hydroxide and stirring gently, then add 0.1 mL in excess. [CAUTION—To avoid dissolving the aluminum hydroxide precipitate, do not add more ammonium hydroxide than 0.1 mL in excess.]
  Centrifuge for about 15 min at 4000 rpm, and then decant the supernatant liquid as completely as possible without disturbing the precipitate. Dissolve the precipitate in 5 mL of 1:2 hydrochloric acid, add 1.0 mL of the *Gelatin solution*, and dilute to 20.0 mL with a saturated solution of aluminum chloride. [NOTE—Prepare on the day of use.]
  Sample solution: Transfer 9 mL (10 g) of sample into a 250-mL Erlenmeyer flask, and add 15 mL of water, 5 mL of nitric acid, and 2 mL of sulfuric acid. Mix, and heat gently on a hot plate to initiate and maintain a vigorous decomposition. When decomposition is complete, place a small, stemless funnel in the mouth of the flask, and continue as directed for the *Standard solution*, beginning with 'and heat until strong fumes of sulfuric acid evolve.'
  Analysis: Rinse a polarographic cell or other vessel with a portion of the *Standard solution*, then add a suitable volume to the cell, immerse it in a constant-temperature bath maintained at 35° ± 0.2°, and deaerate by bubbling oxygen-free nitrogen or hydrogen through the solution for at least 10 min. Insert the dropping mercury electrode of a suitable polarograph, and record the polarogram from −0.2 to −0.7 V at a sensitivity of 0.0003 µA/mm, using a saturated calomel reference electrode. In the same manner, record a polarogram of a portion of the *Sample solution* at the same current sensitivity.
  Acceptance criteria: The height of the wave produced by the *Sample solution* is not greater than that produced by the *Standard solution* at the same half-wave potential. (NMT 10 mg/kg)

SPECIFIC TESTS
- **ACIDITY (AS H$_2$SO$_4$)**
  Sample: 9 mL (10 g)
  Analysis: Dilute the *Sample* in 90 mL of carbon dioxide-free water, add methyl red TS and titrate with 0.02 N sodium hydroxide. Perform a blank determination by repeating the preceding, omitting the addition of the *Sample*.
  Acceptance criteria: The volume of sodium hydroxide solution required for titration of the *Sample* should not be more than 3 mL greater than the volume required for the blank titration. (NMT 0.03%)
- **RESIDUE ON EVAPORATION**
  Sample: 25 g
  Analysis: Evaporate the *Sample* to dryness in a tared porcelain or silica dish on a steam bath, and continue drying to constant weight at 105°.
  Acceptance criteria: The weight of the residue does not exceed 1.5 mg. (NMT 0.006%)

Hydrogenated Starch Hydrolysate

First Published: Prior to FCC 6

Polyglucitol

C$_6$H$_{14}$O$_6$ — Formula wt, Sorbitol 182.17
C$_{12}$H$_{24}$O$_{11}$ — Formula wt, Manitol 344.31
C$_{12}$H$_{24}$O$_{11}$ plus C$_6$H$_{10}$O$_5$ for each additional glucose moiety in the chain — Formula wt, Dextrose Monomer 162.14

CAS: [68425-17-2]

DESCRIPTION
Hydrogenated Starch Hydrolysate occurs as a concentrated, aqueous solution or spray-dried or dried powder. It is a mixture of sorbitol, maltitol, maltitriol, and hydrogenated polysaccharides containing greater than three D-glucopyranosyl units joined by α-1,4-linkages and terminated with a D-glucityl unit. It is soluble in water.
Function: Humectant; texturizing agent; stabilizer; thickener; crystal modification agent
Packaging and Storage: Store in well-closed containers.

ASSAY
- **PROCEDURE**
  Mobile phase: Water (degassed, deionized)

Standard solution: 1 mg/mL USP Sorbitol RS, 1 mg/mL USP Dextrose RS, and 1 mg/mL USP Maltitol RS, 1 mg/mL maltose in *Mobile phase*. (Use Sigma, or equivalent high-purity maltose monohydrate previously dried at 105° to constant weight.)
Sample stock solution: 1 mg/mL
Sample solution: Transfer approximately 10 mL of the *Sample stock solution* into a container and add approximately 0.2 g of an MB-1 mixed-bed resin. Shake this mixture for 30 s, and filter through a 0.45-micron nylon disc filter.
Chromatographic system, Appendix IIA
  Mode: High-performance liquid chromatography
  Detector: Differential refractive index detector
  Column: 20-cm × 10-mm (id) column (Phenomenex "Rezex" 4% silver oligosaccharide, or equivalent)
  Column temperature: 80°
  Flow rate: 0.3 mL/min
  Injection size: About 50 µL
Analysis: Separately inject the *Sample solution* and the *Standard solution* into the chromatograph, record the chromatograms, and measure the responses for the major peaks. The elution order for the *Standard solution* is maltose, maltitol, dextrose, and sorbitol. The differential refractive index detector should show similar response factors.
Calculate the response factors of the *Standard solution* by dividing their concentrations by their peak areas.
Calculate the concentration of each standard component in the sample by multiplying the individual peak areas corresponding to each standard component by the appropriate response factor calculated for its standard, giving the concentration in w/w percent.
Acceptance criteria: A comparison of sorbitol and dextrose peak areas from the *Sample solution* shows that at least 95% of the sum of these peak areas is sorbitol. A similar comparison of maltitol and maltose peak areas shows that at least 95% is maltitol. Neither sorbitol nor maltitol fractions comprise more than 50% of the sample.

IMPURITIES
Inorganic Impurities
- **CHLORIDE,** *Chloride and Sulfate Limit Tests, Chloride Limit Test,* Appendix IIIB
  Sample: 10.0 g
  Control: 50 µg chloride (5 mL of *Chloride Standard Solution*)
  Acceptance criteria: Any turbidity produced by the *Sample* does not exceed that shown in the *Control*. (NMT 50 mg/kg, calculated on the dried basis)
- **LEAD,** *Lead Limit Test, Atomic Absorption Spectrophotometric Graphite Furnace Method, Method I,* Appendix IIIB
  Sample: 5 g
  Acceptance criteria: NMT 1 mg/kg
- **NICKEL,** *Nickel Limit Test,* Appendix IIIB
  Sample: 20 g
  Acceptance criteria: NMT 2 mg/kg

Organic Impurities
- **REDUCING SUGARS**
  Cupric-citric solution: 25 mg/mL of copper sulfate, 50 mg/mL of citric acid, and 144 mg/mL of anhydrous sodium carbonate [**CAUTION**—Add the anhydrous sodium carbonate slowly.]
  Sample: 1.0 g
  Analysis: Dissolve the *Sample* in 6 mL of deionized water. [NOTE—Heat gently, if necessary, to aid in dissolution.] Cool, and add 20-mL of *Cupric-citric solution* and a few glass beads. Heat so that boiling begins after 4 min, and continue boiling for 3 min. Cool rapidly, and add 100 mL of a 2.4% (v/v) solution of glacial acetic acid and 20.0 mL of 0.025 M iodine. While shaking continuously, add 25 mL of a 6:94 (v/v) mixture of hydrochloric acid:deionized water. After the precipitate dissolves, titrate the excess iodine with 0.05 M sodium thiosulfate, using 1 mL of starch solution as the indicator, added towards the end of the titration.
  Acceptance criteria: NLT 12.8 mL of 0.05 M sodium thiosulfate is required for the titration. (NMT 1%, calculated on the dried basis)

SPECIFIC TESTS
- **LOSS ON DRYING,** Appendix IIC
  Sample: 5 g of dry sample or 1 g of liquid sample
  Analysis: Dry the *Sample* at 105° for 4 h. After drying, place the *Sample* in a cool desiccator until it has cooled to room temperature, and weigh.
  Acceptance criteria
    Dry samples: NMT 15%
    Liquid samples: NMT 50%
- **RESIDUE ON IGNITION (SULFATED ASH),** Appendix IIC
  Acceptance criteria: NMT 0.1%

Hydroxycitronellal

First Published: Prior to FCC 6
Last Revision: First Supplement, FCC 6

7-Hydroxy-3,7-dimethyl Octanal

$C_{10}H_{20}O_2$ Formula wt 172.27
FEMA: 2583
UNII: 8SQ0VA4YUR [hydroxycitronellal]

DESCRIPTION
Hydroxycitronellal occurs as a colorless liquid. It may contain a suitable antioxidant.
Odor: Sweet, floral, lily
Solubility: Soluble in most fixed oils, propylene glycol; insoluble or practically insoluble in glycerin
Boiling Point: ~241°
Solubility in Alcohol, Appendix VI: One mL dissolves in 1 mL of 50% alcohol.
Function: Flavoring agent

556 / Hydroxycitronellal / *Monographs*

IDENTIFICATION
- **INFRARED SPECTRA,** *Spectrophotometric Identification Tests,* Appendix IIIC
  Acceptance criteria: The spectrum of the sample exhibits relative maxima at the same wavelengths as those of the spectrum below.

ASSAY
- **PROCEDURE:** Proceed as directed under *M-1b,* Appendix XI.
  Acceptance criteria: NLT 95.0% of $C_{10}H_{20}O_2$

SPECIFIC TESTS
- **ACID VALUE, FLAVOR CHEMICALS (OTHER THAN ESSENTIAL OILS),** *M-15,* Appendix XI
  Acceptance criteria: NMT 5.0
- **REFRACTIVE INDEX,** Appendix II: At 20°
  Acceptance criteria: Between 1.447 and 1.450
- **SPECIFIC GRAVITY:** Determine at 25° by any reliable method (see *General Provisions*).
  Acceptance criteria: Between 0.918 and 0.923

Hydroxycitronellal

Hydroxycitronellal Dimethyl Acetal
First Published: Prior to FCC 6

7-Hydroxy-3,7-dimethyl Octanal Dimethyl Acetal

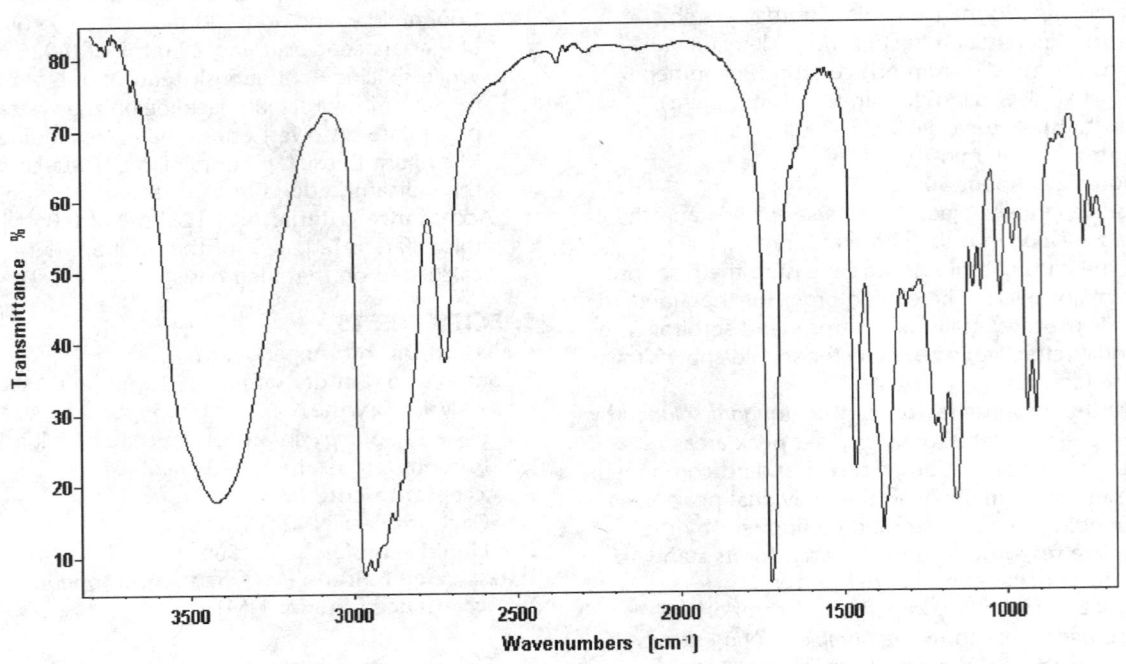

$C_{12}H_{26}O_3$ Formula wt 218.34
FEMA: 2585
UNII: K989V651N4 [hydroxycitronellal dimethyl acetal]

DESCRIPTION
Hydroxycitronellal Dimethyl Acetal occurs as a colorless liquid.
Odor: Floral
Solubility: Soluble in most fixed oils, propylene glycol; insoluble or practically insoluble in glycerin
Boiling Point: ~252°

Solubility in Alcohol, Appendix VI: One mL dissolves in 2 mL of 50% alcohol.
Function: Flavoring agent

IDENTIFICATION
- **INFRARED SPECTRA,** *Spectrophotometric Identification Tests,* Appendix IIIC
  Acceptance criteria: The spectrum of the sample exhibits relative maxima at the same wavelengths as those of the spectrum below.

ASSAY
- **PROCEDURE:** Proceed as directed under *M-1b,* Appendix XI.
  Acceptance criteria: NLT 95.0% of $C_{12}H_{26}O_3$

SPECIFIC TESTS
- **ACID VALUE, FLAVOR CHEMICALS (OTHER THAN ESSENTIAL OILS),** *M-15,* Appendix XI
  Acceptance criteria: NMT 1.0
- **REFRACTIVE INDEX,** Appendix II: At 20°
  Acceptance criteria: Between 1.441 and 1.444

- **SPECIFIC GRAVITY:** Determine at 25° by any reliable method (see *General Provisions*).
  Acceptance criteria: Between 0.925 and 0.930

OTHER REQUIREMENTS
- **FREE HYDROXY CITRONELLAL,** *M-1b,* Appendix XI
  Acceptance criteria: NMT 3.0%

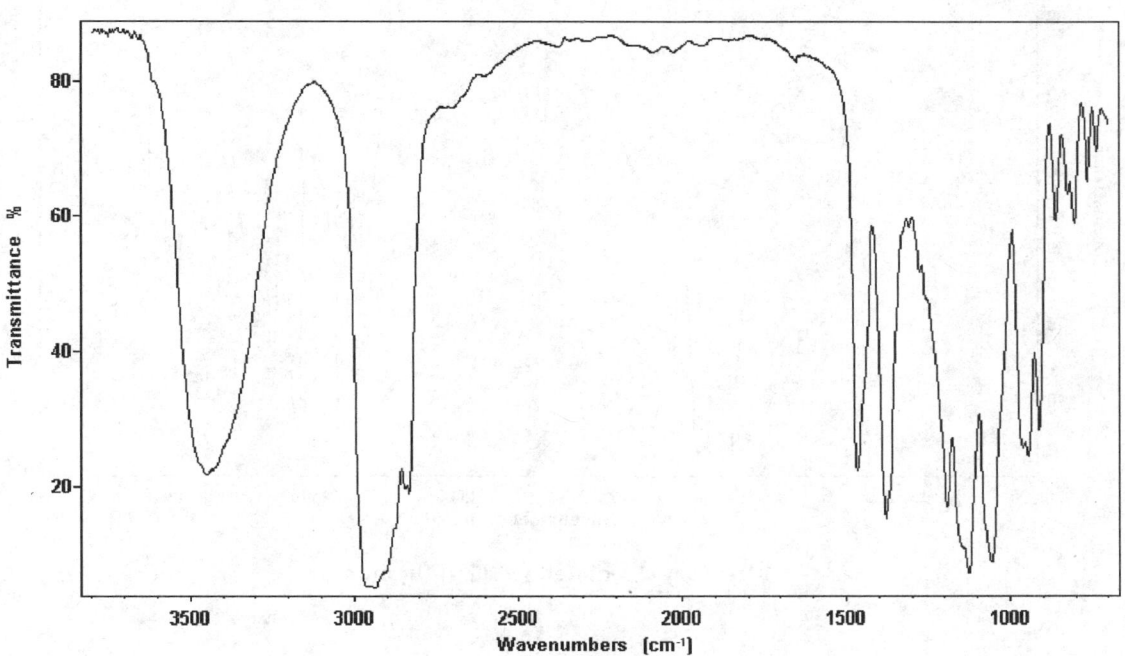

Hydroxycitronellal Dimethyl Acetal

4-Hydroxy-2,5-dimethyl-3(2*H*)-furanone
First Published: Prior to FCC 6
Last Revision: First Supplement, FCC 6

$C_6H_8O_3$ Formula wt 128.13
FEMA: 3174
UNII: 20PI8YZP7A [4-hydroxy-2,5-dimethylfuran-2(3h)-one]

DESCRIPTION
4-Hydroxy-2,5-dimethyl-3(2*H*)-furanone occurs as a white to pale yellow solid. It may contain a suitable antioxidant.
Odor: Fruity, caramel, burnt sugar

Solubility: Soluble in propylene glycol, vegetable oils; insoluble or practically insoluble in water
Solubility in Alcohol, Appendix VI: One g dissolves in 1 mL of 95% alcohol.
Function: Flavoring agent

IDENTIFICATION
- **INFRARED SPECTRA,** *Spectrophotometric Identification Tests,* Appendix IIIC
  Acceptance criteria: The spectrum of the sample exhibits relative maxima at the same wavelengths as those of the spectrum below.

ASSAY
- **PROCEDURE:** Proceed as directed under *M-1a,* Appendix XI.
  Acceptance criteria: NLT 98.0% of $C_6H_8O_3$ in a suitable solvent

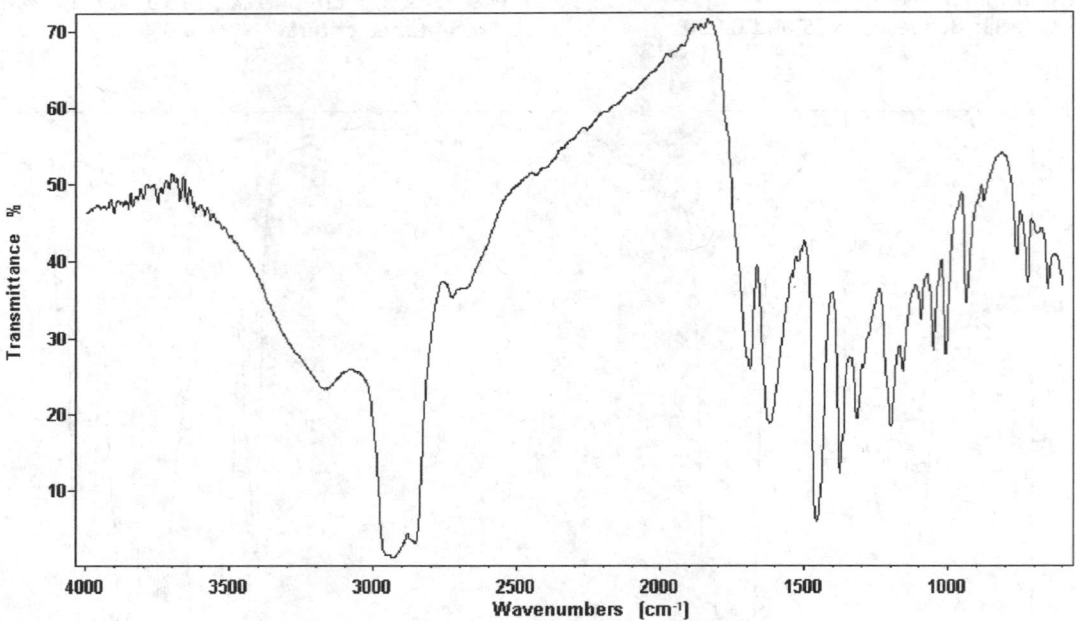

4-Hydroxy-2,5-dimethyl-3(2H)-furanone

6-Hydroxy-3,7-dimethyloctanoic Acid Lactone

First Published: Prior to FCC 6

$C_{10}H_{18}O_2$
FEMA: 3355
UNII: 30YQY8O31P [6-hydroxy-3,7-dimethyloctanoic acid lactone]

Formula wt 170.25

DESCRIPTION
6-Hydroxy-3,7-dimethyloctanoic Acid Lactone occurs as a colorless, low-melting solid.
Odor: Maple syrup or brown sugar
Solubility: Very soluble in water; soluble in alcohol
Function: Flavoring agent

ASSAY
- **Procedure:** Proceed as directed under *M-1a*, Appendix XI.
  Acceptance criteria: NLT 90.0% of $C_{10}H_{18}O_2$

SPECIFIC TESTS
- **Refractive Index,** Appendix II: At 20°
  Acceptance criteria: Between 1.457 and 1.461
- **Specific Gravity:** Determine at 25° by any reliable method (see *General Provisions*).
  Acceptance criteria: Between 0.966 and 0.973

Hydroxylated Lecithin

First Published: Prior to FCC 6

CAS: [8029-76-3]

DESCRIPTION
Hydroxylated Lecithin occurs as a light yellow substance that may vary in consistency from fluid to plastic, depending on the content of free fatty acid and oil and on whether it contains diluents. It is derived from a complex mixture of acetone-insoluble phosphatides from soybean and other plant lecithins, consisting chiefly of phosphatidyl choline, phosphatidyl ethanolamine, and phosphatidyl inositol as well as other minor phospholipids and glycolipids mixed with varying amounts of triglycerides, fatty acids, sterols, and carbohydrates. The mixture is treated with hydrogen peroxide, benzoyl peroxide, lactic acid, and sodium hydroxide or with hydrogen peroxide, acetic acid, and sodium hydroxide to produce a hydroxylated product having an iodine value approximately 10% lower than that of the starting material. It is partially soluble in water but hydrates readily to form emulsions; it is more dispersible and hydrates more readily than crude lecithin.
Function: Emulsifier; clouding agent
Packaging and Storage: Store in well-closed containers.

IMPURITIES
Inorganic Impurities
- **LEAD,** *Lead Limit Test, Flame Atomic Absorption Spectrophotometric Method,* Appendix IIIB
  Sample: 10 g
  Acceptance criteria: NMT 1 mg/kg

SPECIFIC TESTS
- **ACETONE-INSOLUBLE MATTER (AS PHOSPHATIDES)**
  Purified phosphatides preparation: Dissolve 10 g of sample in 20 mL of petroleum ether, add 50 mL of acetone to the solution, chill, and decant. Dry the solids under flowing nitrogen under a hood. Dissolve 5 g of the solids in 10 mL of petroleum ether, and add 25 mL of acetone to the solution. Transfer approximately equal portions of the precipitate to each of two 40-mL centrifuge tubes, using additional portions of acetone to facilitate the transfer. Stir thoroughly, dilute to 40 mL with acetone, stir again, chill for 15 min in an ice bath, stir again, and then centrifuge for 5 min. Decant the acetone, crush the solids with a stirring rod, refill the tube with acetone, stir, chill, centrifuge, and decant as before. The solids after the second centrifugation require no further purification and may be used for preparing the *Phosphatide-acetone solution*.
  Phosphatide-acetone solution: Add a quantity of *Purified phosphatides preparation* to sufficient acetone, previously cooled to about 5°, to form a saturated solution [NOTE—Five g of the *Purified phosphatides preparation* are required to saturate about 16 L of acetone.], and maintain the mixture at this temperature for 2 h, shaking it vigorously at 15-min intervals. Decant the solution through a rapid filter paper, avoiding the transfer of any undissolved solids to the paper and conducting the filtration under refrigerated conditions (not above 5°).
  Sample: 2 g, well-mixed. [NOTE—If the sample is plastic or semisolid, soften a portion by warming it at a temperature not exceeding 60°, and then mix it thoroughly.]
  Analysis: Transfer the *Sample* into a 40-mL centrifuge tube, previously tared with a glass stirring rod, and add 15 mL of *Phosphatide-acetone solution* from a buret. Warm the mixture in a water bath until the *Sample* melts, but avoid evaporation of the acetone. Stir until the *Sample* is completely disintegrated and dispersed, transfer the tube into an ice bath, chill for 5 min, remove from the ice bath, and add about 10 mL of *Phosphatide-acetone solution*, previously chilled for 5 min in an ice bath. Stir the mixture to complete dispersion of the sample, dilute to 40 mL with chilled (5°) *Phosphatide-acetone solution*, stir to complete dispersion of the sample, and return the tube and contents to the ice bath for 15 min. Subsequently stir again while still in the ice bath, remove the stirring rod, and centrifuge the mixture immediately for 5 min. Decant the supernatant liquid from the centrifuge tube; crush the centrifuged solids with the stirring rod; refill the tube to the 40-mL mark with chilled (5°) *Phosphatide-acetone solution*; and repeat the chilling, stirring, centrifugation, and decantation procedure. After the second centrifugation and decantation of the supernatant acetone, again crush the solids with the stirring rod, and place the tube and its contents in a horizontal position at room temperature until the excess acetone has evaporated. Mix the residue again, dry the centrifuge tube and its contents at 105° for 45 min in a forced-draft oven, cool, and weigh. Calculate the percentage of acetone-insoluble substances by the formula:

  $$\text{Result} = (100R/S) - B$$

  R = weight (g) of residue
  S = weight (g) of the sample taken
  B = percentage of hexane-insoluble matter determined as directed under *Hexane-Insoluble Matter* determined below
  Acceptance criteria: NLT 50.0%

- **ACID VALUE**
  Sample solution: 2 g, well-mixed. [NOTE—If the sample is plastic or semisolid, soften a portion by warming it in a water bath at a temperature not exceeding 60°, and then mix it thoroughly.]
  Analysis: Transfer the *Sample* into a 250-mL Erlenmeyer flask and dissolve it in 50 mL of petroleum ether. Add 50 mL of ethanol, previously neutralized to phenolphthalein with 0.1 N sodium hydroxide and mix well. Titrate with 0.1 N sodium hydroxide to a pink endpoint that persists for 5 s, using phenolphthalein TS as an indicator. Calculate the *Acid Value* by the formula:

  $$\text{Result} = 5.6 \times A/W$$

  A = volume (mL) of 0.1 N sodium hydroxide consumed
  W = weight (g) of the sample taken
  Acceptance criteria: NMT 70

- **HEXANE INSOLUBLE MATTER,** Appendix VII
  Acceptance criteria: NMT 0.3%

- **IODINE VALUE,** Appendix VII
  Acceptance criteria: Between 85 and 95

- **PEROXIDE VALUE**
  Sample: 10 g
  Analysis: To the *Sample*, add 30 mL of a 3:2 mixture of glacial acetic acid:chloroform and mix. Add 1 mL of a saturated solution of potassium iodide, mix, and allow to stand for 10 min. Add 100 mL of water and begin titrating with 0.05 N sodium thiosulfate, adding starch TS as the endpoint is approached. Continue the titration until the blue starch color has just disappeared. Perform a blank determination (see *General Provisions*), and make any necessary correction. Calculate the peroxide value, as mEq of peroxide per kg of sample by the formula:

  $$\text{Result} = [S \times N \times 1000]/W$$

  S = net volume (mL) of sodium thiosulfate solution required for the sample

560 / Hydroxylated Lecithin / *Monographs*

N = exact normality of the sodium thiosulfate solution
W = weight of the sample (g) taken
Acceptance criteria: NMT 100
- **WATER,** *Water Determination,* Appendix IIB
  Acceptance criteria: NMT 1.5%

4-(*p*-Hydroxyphenyl)-2-butanone

First Published: Prior to FCC 6
Last Revision: First Supplement, FCC 7

4-(4-Hydroxyphenyl)-2-butanone
Raspberry Ketone

C₁₀H₁₂O₂   Formula wt 164.20
FEMA: 2588
UNII: 7QY1MH15BG [4-(p-hydroxyphenyl)-2-butanone]

DESCRIPTION
4-(*p*-Hydroxyphenyl)-2-butanone occurs as a white solid.
Odor: Raspberry
Solubility: Insoluble or practically insoluble in propylene glycol, vegetable oils, water
Solubility in Alcohol, Appendix VI: One g dissolves in 2 mL of 95% alcohol.
Function: Flavoring agent

IDENTIFICATION
- **INFRARED ABSORPTION,** *Spectrophotometric Identification Tests,* Appendix IIIC
  Reference standard: USP Raspberry Ketone RS
  Sample and standard preparation: *K*
  Acceptance criteria: The spectrum of the sample exhibits maxima at the same wavelengths as those in the spectrum of the *Reference standard.*

ASSAY
- **PROCEDURE:** Proceed as directed under *M-1b,* Appendix XI.
  Acceptance criteria: NLT 98.0% of C₁₀H₁₂O₂

OTHER REQUIREMENTS
- **MELTING RANGE OR TEMPERATURE DETERMINATION,** Appendix IIB
  Acceptance criteria: Between 82° and 84°

Hydroxypropyl Cellulose

First Published: Prior to FCC 6

Modified Cellulose
INS: 463   CAS: [9004-64-2]
UNII: RFW2ET671P [hydroxypropyl cellulose]

DESCRIPTION
Hydroxypropyl Cellulose occurs as a white powder. It is a cellulose ether containing hydroxypropyl substitution. It may contain a suitable anticaking agent. It is soluble in water and in certain organic solvents.
Function: Emulsifier; film coating; protective colloid; stabilizer; suspending agent; thickener
Packaging and Storage: Store in well-closed containers.

IDENTIFICATION
- **A. PROCEDURE**
  Sample solution: 1 mg/mL
  Acceptance criteria: Upon shaking the *Sample solution,* a layer of foam appears (distinction from cellulose gum).
- **B. PROCEDURE**
  Sample solution: 5 mg/mL
  Analysis: Add 5 mL of a 50 mg/mL solution of copper sulfate (or aluminum sulfate) to 5 mL of the *Sample solution.*
  Acceptance criteria: No precipitate forms (distinction from cellulose gum).

ASSAY
- **HYDROXYPROPOXYL GROUPS,** *Hydroxypropyl Determination,* Appendix IIIC
  Sample: 85 mg, previously dried
  Acceptance criteria: NMT 80.5% of hydroxypropoxyl groups (-OCH₂CHOHCH₃), on the dried basis, equivalent to NMT 4.6 hydroxypropyl groups per anhydroglucose unit.

IMPURITIES
Inorganic Impurities
- **LEAD,** *Lead Limit Test,* Appendix IIIB
  Sample solution: Prepare as directed for organic compounds, but with 2 g of sample.
  Control: 6 µg Pb (6 mL of *Diluted Standard Lead Solution*)
  Acceptance criteria: NMT 3 mg/kg

SPECIFIC TESTS
- **LOSS ON DRYING,** Appendix IIC: 105° for 3 h
  Acceptance criteria: NMT 5.0%
- **PH,** *pH Determination,* Appendix IIB
  Sample solution: 10 mg/mL
  Acceptance criteria: Between 5.0 and 8.0
- **RESIDUE ON IGNITION (SULFATED ASH),** Appendix IIC
  Sample: 1 g
  Acceptance criteria: NMT 0.5%
- **VISCOSITY OF A 10% SOLUTION,** *Viscosity of Cellulose Gum,* Appendix IIB
  Sample: Amount equivalent to 40 g of hydroxypropyl cellulose, on the dried basis
  Analysis: Use a tared sample container.
  Acceptance criteria: NLT 145 centipoises

Hydroxypropyl Methylcellulose

First Published: Prior to FCC 6

Propylene Glycol Ether of Methylcellulose
Modified Cellulose
HPMC

INS: 464   CAS: [9004-65-3]

DESCRIPTION

Hydroxypropyl Methylcellulose occurs as a white to off-white, fibrous powder or as granules. It is the propylene glycol ether of methylcellulose in which both the hydroxypropyl and the methyl groups are attached to the anhydroglucose rings of cellulose by ether linkages. Several product types are available that are defined by varying combinations of methoxyl and hydroxypropoxyl content. It is soluble in water and in certain organic solvent systems. Aqueous solutions are surface active, form films upon drying, and undergo a reversible transformation from sol to gel upon heating and cooling, respectively.

Function: Thickening agent; stabilizer; emulsifier
Packaging and Storage: Store in well-closed containers.

IDENTIFICATION

- **A. Procedure**
  Sample: 1 g
  Analysis: Add the *Sample* to 100 mL of water.
  Acceptance criteria: The sample swells and disperses to form a clear to opalescent, mucilaginous solution, depending on the intrinsic viscosity, which is stable in the presence of most electrolytes.
- **B. Procedure**
  Sample: 1 g
  Analysis: Add the *Sample* to 100 mL of boiling water and stir the mixture. [NOTE—Save a portion of this solution for *Identification* test C (below).]
  Acceptance criteria: A slurry forms that, when cooled to 20°, dissolves to form a clear or opalescent, mucilaginous solution.
- **C. Procedure**
  Sample: A few mL of the solution prepared in *Identification* test B (above)
  Analysis: Pour the *Sample* onto a glass plate and allow the water to evaporate.
  Acceptance criteria: A thin, self-sustaining film forms.

ASSAY

- **Procedure**
  [CAUTION—Perform all steps involving hydriodic acid carefully in a well-ventilated hood. Use goggles, acid-resistant gloves, and other appropriate safety equipment. Be extremely careful when handling the hot vials because they are under pressure. In the event of hydriodic acid exposure, wash with copious amounts of water and seek medical attention at once.]
  Internal standard solution: Dilute 2.5 g of toluene to 1000 mL with *o*-xylene.
  Standard solution: Transfer 135 mg of adipic acid into a suitable serum vial, add 4.0 mL of hydriodic acid followed by 4.0 mL of the *Internal standard solution*, and close the vial securely with a septum stopper. Weigh the vial and its contents, add 30 µL of isopropyl iodide with a syringe through the septum, reweigh, and calculate the weight of isopropyl iodide added. Similarly, add 90 µL of methyl iodide, and calculate the weight added. Shake well, and allow the layers to separate.
  Sample solution: Transfer 0.065 g of sample into a 5-mL vial equipped with a pressure-tight septum closure, add an amount of adipic acid equal to the weight of the sample, and pipet 2 mL of the *Internal standard solution* into the vial. Cautiously pipet 2 mL of hydriodic acid into the mixture, immediately secure the closure, and accurately weigh. Shake the vial for 30 s, heat at 150° for 20 min, remove from the heat, shake again, using extreme caution, and heat at 150° for 40 min. Allow the vial to cool for about 45 min, and weigh. If the weight loss is greater than 10 mg, discard the mixture and prepare another *Sample solution*.
  Chromatographic system, Appendix IIA
  Mode: Gas chromatography
  Detector: Thermal conductivity detector
  Column: 1.8-m × 4-mm glass column, or equivalent, packed with 10% methylsilicone oil (UCW 982 or equivalent) on 100- to 120-mesh flux-calcined chromatographic siliceous earth (Chromosorb WHP, or equivalent)
  Temperature
  Column: 100°
  Injector port: 200°
  Detector: 200°
  Carrier gas: Helium
  Flow rate: 20 mL/min
  Injection size: About 2 µL
  Calibration: Inject an aliquot from the upper layer of the *Standard solution* into the chromatograph, and record the chromatogram. [NOTE—The retention times for methyl iodide, isopropyl iodide, toluene, and *o*-xylene are approximately 3, 5, 7, and 13 min, respectively.]
  Calculate the relative response factor, F, of equal weights of toluene and methyl iodide by the formula:

  $$\text{Result} = Q/A$$

  Q = quantity ratio of methyl iodide to toluene in the *Standard solution*
  A = peak area ratio of methyl iodide to toluene obtained from the chromatogram of the *Standard solution*

Calculate the relative response factor, F', of equal weights of toluene and isopropyl iodide by the formula:

$$\text{Result} = Q'/A'$$

Q' = quantity ratio of isopropyl iodide to toluene in the *Standard solution*
A' = peak area ratio of isopropyl iodide to toluene obtained from the chromatogram of the *Standard solution*

Analysis: Inject an aliquot from the upper layer of the *Sample solution* into the chromatograph, and record the chromatogram.

Calculate the percentage of methoxyl groups (–OCH$_3$) in the sample by the formula:

$$\text{Result} = a \times (W/w) \times (M_{r1}/M_{r2}) \times F \times 2$$

a = ratio of the area of the methyl iodide peak to that of the toluene peak in the chromatogram of the *Sample solution*
W = weight of the toluene in the *Internal standard solution* (g)
w = weight of the sample taken (g)
M$_{r1}$ = formula weight of methoxyl group, 31
M$_{r2}$ = formula weight of methyl iodide, 142
F = relative response factor of toluene and methyl iodide determined above

Calculate the percentage of hydroxypropoxyl groups (–OCH$_2$CHOHCH$_3$) in the sample by the formula:

$$\text{Result} = a' \times (W/w) \times (M_{r1}/M_{r2}) \times F' \times 2$$

a' = ratio of the area of the isopropyl iodide peak to that of the toluene peak in the chromatogram of the *Sample solution*
W = weight of toluene in the *Internal standard solution* (g)
w = weight of the sample taken (g)
M$_{r1}$ = formula weight of hydroxypropoxyl iodide, 75
M$_{r2}$ = formula weight of isopropyl iodide, 170
F' = relative response factor of toluene and isopropyl iodide determined above

Acceptance criteria
Methoxyl groups: Between 19.0% and 30.0% of methoxyl groups (and OCH$_3$), within the range claimed by the vendor for any product type
Hydroxypropoxyl groups: Between 3.0% and 12.0% of hydroxypropoxyl groups (and OCH$_2$CHOHCH$_3$), within the range claimed by the vendor for any product type

IMPURITIES
Inorganic Impurities
- **LEAD,** *Lead Limit Test,* Appendix IIIB
  Sample solution: Prepare as directed for organic compounds using a 2 g sample.
  Control: 6 µg Pb (6 mL of *Diluted Standard Lead Solution*)
  Acceptance criteria: NMT 3 mg/kg

SPECIFIC TESTS
- **LOSS ON DRYING,** Appendix IIC: 105° for 2 h
  Sample: 3 g
  Acceptance criteria: NMT 5.0%
- **RESIDUE ON IGNITION (SULFATED ASH),** Appendix IIC
  Sample: 1 g
  Acceptance criteria
  Products with viscosities of 50 cP or above: NMT 1.5%
  Products with viscosities below 50 cP: NMT 3.0%
- **VISCOSITY DETERMINATION,** *Viscosity of Methylcellulose,* Appendix IIB
  Sample solution: Transfer an amount of sample equivalent to 2 g of solids on the dried basis to a wide-mouth 250-mL centrifuge bottle and add 98 g of water, previously heated to between 80° and 90°. Stir with a mechanical stirrer for 10 min, then place the bottle in an ice bath until solution is complete, adjust the weight of the solution with water to 100 g if necessary, and centrifuge it to expel any entrapped air. Adjust the temperature of the *Sample solution* to 20° ± 0.1°.
  Acceptance criteria
  Viscosity types of 100 cP or less: NLT 80.0% and NMT 120.0% of that stated on the label
  Viscosity types of higher than 100 cP: NLT 75.0% and NMT 140.0% of that stated on the label

Indigotine[1]

First Published: Prior to FCC 6

CI Food Blue 1
Indigotine Disulfonate
Indigo Carmine
CI 73015
Class: Indigoid

$C_{16}H_8N_2O_8S_2Na_2$
INS: 132
UNII: L06K8R7DQK [fd&c blue no. 2]
Formula wt 466.36
CAS: [860-22-0]

DESCRIPTION
Indigotine occurs as a blue-brown to red-brown powder or as granules. It is principally the disodium salt of 2-(1,3-dihydro-3-oxo-5-sulfo-2H-indol-2-ylidene)-2,3-dihydro-3-oxo-1H-indole-5-sulfonic acid. It dissolves in water to give a solution that is blue at neutrality, blue-violet in acid, and green to yellow-green in base. When dissolved in concentrated sulfuric acid, it yields a blue-violet solution that turns blue when diluted with water. It is insoluble in ethanol.

Function: Color
Packaging and Storage: Store in well-closed containers.

IDENTIFICATION
- **PROCEDURE**
  Sample solution: 20 μg/mL, freshly prepared
  Analysis: Adjust the pH of three aliquots of the *Sample solution* to pH 1, pH 7, and pH 13. Measure the absorbance intensities (A) and wavelength maxima of these solutions with a suitable UV-visible spectrophotometer.
  Acceptance criteria
  pH 1: A = 0.81 at 610 nm
  pH 7: A = 0.82 at 610 nm
  pH 13: A = 0.2 at 610 nm and A = 0.31 at 442 nm

ASSAY
- **TOTAL COLOR**, Color Determination, Methods I and II, Appendix IIIC: Both methods must be used.
  Method I (Spectrophotometric)
  Sample: 175 to 225 mg
  Analysis: Transfer the *Sample* into a 1-L volumetric flask; dissolve in and dilute to volume with water. Determine as directed at 610 nm using 0.0478 L/(mg·cm) for the absorptivity (a) for Indigotine.
  Method II (TiCl$_3$ Titration)
  Sample: 0.3 g
  Analysis: Determine as directed using 4.29 as the stoichiometric factor (F$_s$) for Indigotine.
  Acceptance criteria: The average of results obtained from *Methods I and II* is NLT 85.0% total coloring matters.

IMPURITIES
Inorganic Impurities
- **ARSENIC**, Arsenic Limit Test, Appendix IIIB
  Sample solution: Prepare as directed for organic compounds.
  Acceptance criteria: NMT 3 mg/kg
- **LEAD**, Lead Limit Test, Appendix IIIB
  Sample solution: Prepare as directed for organic compounds.
  Control: 10 μg Pb (10 mL of *Diluted Standard Lead Solution*)
  Acceptance criteria: NMT 10 mg/kg
- **MERCURY**, Color Determination, Appendix IIIC
  Acceptance criteria: NMT 1 mg/kg

Organic Impurities
- **UNCOMBINED INTERMEDIATES AND PRODUCTS OF SIDE REACTIONS**, Color Determination, Method I, Appendix IIIC
  Analysis: Calculate the concentration of isatin-5-sulfonic acid using an absorptivity of 0.089 L/(mg·cm) at 245 nm.
  Acceptance criteria
  Isatin-5-sulfonic acid: NMT 0.4%
  5-Sulfoanthranilic acid: NMT 0.2%

SPECIFIC TESTS
- **COMBINED TESTS**
  Tests
  - **LOSS ON DRYING (VOLATILE MATTER)**, Color Determination, Appendix IIIC
  - **CHLORIDE**, Sodium Chloride, Color Determination, Appendix IIIC
  - **SULFATES (AS SODIUM SALTS)**, Sodium Sulfate, Color Determination, Appendix IIIC
  Acceptance criteria: NMT 15.0% in combination
- **ETHER EXTRACTS**, Color Determination, Appendix IIIC
  Acceptance criteria: NMT 0.2%
- **SUBSIDIARY AND ISOMERIC COLORS**, Column Chromatography, Appendix IIA
  Mobile phase and stationary phase: Dissolve 20 g of hydroxylamine hydrochloride in 500 mL of water, place the solution into a 2-L separatory funnel, and add 450 mL of butanol, 450 mL of chloroform, 300 mL of water, and 100 mL of hydrochloric acid. Agitate the mixture well, periodically venting the funnel. After settling, separate and store the bottom layer (organic), which is the *Mobile phase*, and the top layer (aqueous), which is the *Stationary phase*.

---

[1] To be used or sold for use to color food that is marketed in the United States, this color additive must be from a batch that has been certified by the U.S. Food and Drug Administration (FDA). If it is not from an FDA-certified batch, it is not a permitted color additive for food use in the United States, even if it is compositionally equivalent. The name FD&C Blue No. 2 can be applied only to FDA-certified batches of this color additive. Indigotine is a common name given to the uncertified colorant. See the monograph entitled *FD&C Blue No. 2* for directions for producing an FDA-certified batch.

Column: Slurry 12 g of Celite (Johns Manville No. 595, or equivalent) with 7 mL of *Stationary phase* and pour the slurry into a glass column (40- × 2.5-cm (id)).
Sample solution: 1 mg/mL in *Stationary phase*. [NOTE—Warm on a steam bath, if necessary, to dissolve the sample.]
Analysis: Mix 5 mL of *Sample solution* with 10 g of Celite and pour the mixture into the column over the slurry, ensuring that the sample is quantitatively transferred to the column. Elute the column with *Mobile phase*. Collect the monosulfonated derivative, the first band eluting, in a 25-mL graduated cylinder, and note the volume. Collect the next band, the isomeric (unsulfonated) derivative, in a similar manner. Mix each aliquot collected with an equal volume of hexane, and transfer to a separatory funnel. Extract this mixture with three 15-mL aliquots of water and combine the extracts. Calculate the percent of the monosulfonated derivative (a = 0.0513 L/(mg·cm) at 615 nm) and the isomeric derivative (a = 0.0478 L/(mg·cm) at 610 nm) by the formula:

$$\text{Result} = (A \times V)/(a \times W \times 10)$$

A = absorbance at the wavelength maximum
V = volume (mL) of extract
a = absorptivity (L/(mg·cm))
W = weight (mg) of the sample taken to prepare the *Sample solution*

Acceptance criteria
2-(1,3-Dihydro-3-oxo-7-sulfo-2*H*-indole-2-ylidene)-2,3-dihydro-3-oxo-1*H*-indole-5-sulfonic acid, Disodium salt: NMT 18.0%
2-(1,3-Dihydro-3-oxo-2*H*-indole-2-ylidene)-2,3-dihydro-3-oxo-1*H*-indole-5-sulfonic acid, Sodium salt: NMT 2.0%

- **WATER-INSOLUBLE MATTER,** *Color Determination,* Appendix IIIC
  Acceptance criteria: NMT 0.4%

Indole
First Published: Prior to FCC 6

C$_8$H$_7$N
FEMA: 2593
UNII: 8724FJW4M5 [indole]

Formula wt 117.15

DESCRIPTION
Indole occurs as a white, lustrous, flaky, crystalline solid.
Odor: Unpleasant odor in high concentration, free of fecal quality; floral on dilution
Solubility: Soluble in alcohol, most fixed oils, propylene glycol; insoluble or practically insoluble in glycerin
Boiling Point: ~253° to 254°
Solubility in Alcohol, Appendix VI: One g dissolves in 3 mL of 70% alcohol.
Function: Flavoring agent

IDENTIFICATION
- **INFRARED SPECTRA,** *Spectrophotometric Identification Tests,* Appendix IIIC
  Sample preparation: Mineral oil mull
  Acceptance criteria: The spectrum of the sample exhibits relative maxima at the same wavelengths as those of the spectrum below.

ASSAY
- **PROCEDURE:** Proceed as directed under *M-1a,* Appendix XI.
  Acceptance criteria: NLT 99.0% of C$_8$H$_7$N

OTHER REQUIREMENTS
- **SOLIDIFICATION POINT,** Appendix IIB: Dry over H$_2$SO$_4$.
  Acceptance criteria: NLT 51°

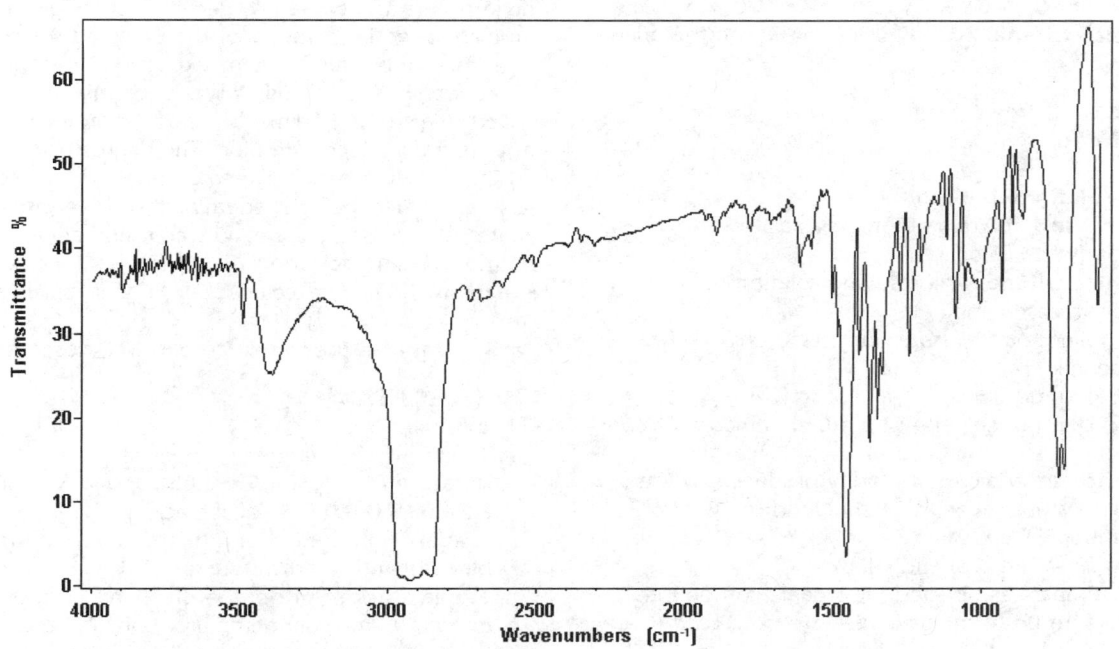

Indole (Mineral Oil Mull)

Inositol

First Published: Prior to FCC 6

1,2,3,5/4,6-Cyclohexanehexol
i-Inositol
meso-Inositol
myo-Inositol

$C_6H_{12}O_6$ Formula wt 180.16
CAS: [87-89-8]

UNII: 4L6452S749 [inositol]

DESCRIPTION
Inositol occurs as fine, white crystals or as a white, crystalline powder. Its solutions are neutral to litmus. It is optically inactive. It is stable in air. One g is soluble in 6 mL of water. It is slightly soluble in alcohol, and is insoluble in ether and in chloroform.

Function: Nutrient
Packaging and Storage: Store in well-closed containers.

IDENTIFICATION
- **A. Procedure**
  Sample solution: 20 mg/mL
  Anlaysis: Add 6 mL of nitric acid to 1 mL of *Sample solution* in a porcelain evaporating dish and evaporate to dryness on a water bath. Dissolve the residue in 1 mL of water, add 0.5 mL of a 100 mg/mL solution of strontium acetate, and again evaporate to dryness on a steam bath.
  Acceptance criteria: A violet color appears.
- **B. Melting Range or Temperature Determination,** Appendix IIB
  Sample: The inositol hexaacetate residue obtained from the *Assay* (below)
  Acceptance criteria: Between 212° and 216°

ASSAY
- **Procedure**
  Sample: 200 mg, previously dried
  Analysis: Transfer the *Sample* to a 250-mL beaker, add 5 mL of a 1:50 mixture of 2 N sulfuric acid:acetic anhydride, and cover the beaker with a watch glass. Heat on a steam bath for 20 min, then chill in an ice bath, and add 100 mL of water. Boil for 20 min, allow to cool, and transfer quantitatively, with the aid of a little water, to a 250-mL separatory funnel. Extract the solution with six successive 30-, 25-, 20-, 15-, 10-, and 10-mL portions of chloroform, using the solvent to rinse the original flask. Collect the chloroform extracts in a second 250-mL separatory funnel, and wash the combined extracts with 10 mL of water. Transfer the chloroform extracts through a funnel containing a pledget of cotton into a 150-mL tared Soxhlet flask. Wash the separatory funnel and funnel with 10 mL of chloroform, and add to the combined extracts. Evaporate to dryness on a steam bath, dry in an oven at 105° for 1 h, cool in a desiccator, and weigh. [NOTE—Save this residue for use in *Identification test B* (above).] The weight of the inositol hexaacetate

obtained, multiplied by 0.4167, represents the equivalent of $C_6H_{12}O_6$.

Acceptance criteria: NLT 97.0% $C_6H_{12}O_6$, on the dried basis

IMPURITIES
Inorganic Impurities
- **CALCIUM**
  Sample solution: 100 mg/mL
  Analysis: Add 1 mL of ammonium oxalate TS to 10 mL of the *Sample solution*.
  Acceptance criteria: The resulting solution remains clear for at least 1 min.
- **CHLORIDE,** *Chloride and Sulfate Limit Tests, Chloride Limit Test,* Appendix IIIB
  Sample: 400 mg
  Control: 20 µg of chloride (2.0 mL of *Standard Chloride Solution*)
  Acceptance criteria: Any turbidity produced by the *Sample* does not exceed that shown in the *Control* (NMT 0.005%).
- **LEAD,** *Lead Limit Test,* Appendix IIIB
  Sample: Prepare as directed for organic compounds.
  Control: 4 µg Pb (4 mL of *Diluted Standard Lead Solution*)
  Acceptance criteria: NMT 4 mg/kg
- **SULFATE,** *Chloride and Sulfate Limit Tests, Chloride Limit Test,* Appendix IIIB
  Sample: 5 g
  Control: 300 µg of sulfate (30 mL of *Standard Sulfate Solution*)
  Acceptance criteria: Any turbidity produced by the *Sample* does not exceed that in the *Control* (NMT 0.006%).

SPECIFIC TESTS
- **LOSS ON DRYING,** Appendix IIC: 105° for 4 h
  Acceptance criteria: NMT 0.5%
- **MELTING RANGE OR TEMPERATURE DETERMINATION,** Appendix IIB
  Acceptance criteria: Between 224° and 227°
- **RESIDUE ON IGNITION (SULFATED ASH),** Appendix IIC
  Sample: 2 g
  Acceptance criteria: NMT 0.1%

Inulin

First Published: FCC 6

CAS: [9005-80-5]

UNII: JOS53KRJ01 [inulin]

DESCRIPTION
Inulin occurs as a white powder. It is an indigestible plant fructan found in members of the *Compositae* family. Commercial production is by extraction from the roots of *Cichorium intybus* Lin. (chicory). It is a mixture composed of polymers of β-2,1-linked fructose residues mostly linked to a terminal glucose residue. The degree of polymerization in the mixture varies between 3 and 60, with the longer-chain polymers being predominant. It is very soluble in hot water, slightly soluble in cold water, and almost insoluble in most organic solvents.

Function: Source of dietary fiber; binder; bulking agent; texturizer

Packaging and Storage: Store in well-closed containers.

IDENTIFICATION
- **PROCEDURE**
  Mobile phase: Water
  Acetate buffer (pH 4.5 ± 0.05): 0.044 M sodium acetate and 0.056 M acetic acid
  Standard solution: 5 mg/mL fructose, 1 mg/mL glucose, and 1 mg/mL sucrose
  Sample stock solution: Transfer 1 to 1.5 g of sample, into a 100-mL volumetric flask. Dissolve the sample in hot (>80°) water and allow the solution to cool before diluting to volume.
  Digested sample solution: Transfer 10 mL of *Acetate buffer* and 10 mL of the *Sample stock solution* into a 25-mL volumetric flask. Add 150 units of Fructozyme SP230 enzyme (Novozymes, Denmark), or equivalent. Digest for 30 min at 60°, cool, and dilute to volume with water.
  Chromatographic system, Appendix IIA
  Mode: High-performance liquid chromatography
  Detector: Refractive index
  Column: Gel filtration column for molecular weight range up to 5000 Da (Shodex KS-802, Showa Denko, K.K., Tokyo, Japan, or equivalent)
  Temperature
  Column: 50°
  Detector: 35°–40°
  Flow rate: 1 mL/min
  Injection volume: 20 µL
  Sample loop: 20 µL
  Analysis: Separately inject the *Digested sample solution* and the *Standard solution* into the chromatograph and record the chromatograms. Determine the percentage of fructose and the percentage of glucose in the *Digested sample solution* using the following formula:

$$\text{Result} = 100(C_{ST} \times A_{SA})/(A_{ST} \times W)$$

C_{ST} = concentration of fructose or glucose in the *Standard solution* (mg/100 mL)
A_{SA} = area of the corresponding sugar peak in the chromatogram of the *Sample solution*
A_{ST} = area of the corresponding sugar peak in the chromatogram of the *Standard solution*
W = weight of sample, in g, contained in each 100 mL of the *Sample stock solution*

Correct the percent fructose and percent glucose results for the mono- and disaccharide content (obtained in the *Assay* below), and for moisture.
Acceptance criteria: The sample releases greater than 90% fructose and less than 10% glucose upon enzymatic digestion.

ASSAY
- **PROCEDURE**
  Mobile phase: Water
  Standard solution: 5 mg/mL fructose, 1 mg/mL glucose, and 1 mg/mL sucrose
  Sample solution: Transfer 1 to 1.5 g of sample, into a 100-mL volumetric flask. Dissolve the sample in hot - (> 80°) water and allow the solution to cool before diluting to volume.
  Chromatographic system, Appendix IIA
    Mode: High-performance liquid chromatography
    Detector: Refractive index
    Column: Gel filtration column for molecular weight range up to 5000 Da (Shodex KS-802, Showa Denko, K.K., Tokyo, Japan, or equivalent)
    Temperature
      Column: 50°
      Detector: 35°–40°
    Flow rate: 1 mL/min
    Injection volume: 20 µL
    Sample loop: 20 µL
  Analysis: Separately inject the *Standard solution* and the *Sample solution* into the chromatograph and record the chromatograms. Determine the percentage of each sugar and of inulin in the *Sample solution* using the following formula:

  $$\text{Result} = 100(C_{ST} \times A_{SA})/(A_{ST} \times W)$$

  C_{ST} = concentration of each sugar in the *Standard solution* (mg/100 mL)
  A_{SA} = area of the corresponding sugar peak in the chromatogram of the *Sample solution*
  A_{ST} = area of the corresponding sugar peak in the chromatogram of the *Standard solution*
  W = weight of the sample taken (g/100 mL)

  Acceptance criteria: NLT 85%, calculated on the dried basis

IMPURITIES
Inorganic Impurities
- **LEAD,** *Lead Limit Test, Atomic Absorption Spectrophotometric Graphite Furnace Method, Method II,* Appendix IIIB
  Acceptance criteria: NMT 1 mg/kg

SPECIFIC TESTS
- **ASH (TOTAL),** Appendix IIC
  Sample: 2.5 g
  Analysis: Ignite at 600°.
  Acceptance criteria: NMT 0.2%
- **LOSS ON DRYING,** Appendix IIC: 103° ± 2°
  Sample: 2.5 g
  Acceptance criteria: NMT 8%

- **MONOSACCHARIDES AND DISACCHARIDES**
  Analysis: Use the results obtained in the *Assay* (above).
  Acceptance criteria: NMT 15% (combined) of monosaccharides (as fructose and glucose) and disaccharides (as sucrose), calculated on the dried basis
- **OPTICAL (SPECIFIC) ROTATION,** Appendix IIB
  Sample solution: 10 mg/mL
  Acceptance criteria: $[\alpha]_D^{20}$ between −15° and −37°

Invert Sugar
First Published: Prior to FCC 6

Invert Sugar Syrup

CAS: [8013-17-0]
UNII: ED959S6ACY [corn invert sugar]

DESCRIPTION
Invert Sugar occurs as a hygroscopic liquid. It is a mixture of glucose and fructose that results from the hydrolysis of sucrose. Invert Sugar is marketed as Invert Sugar Syrup and contains dextrose (glucose), fructose, and sucrose in various amounts as represented by the manufacturer. It is very soluble in water, in glycerin, and in glycols and is very sparingly soluble in acetone and in ethanol.
Function: Nutritive sweetener
Packaging and Storage: Store in tight containers.

IDENTIFICATION
- **A. PROCEDURE**
  Mobile phase: Purified water
  Standard solution: 10 mg/mL of each fructose, glucose, and sucrose
  Sample solution: 100 mg/mL
  Chromatographic system, Appendix IIA
    Mode: High-performance liquid chromatography
    Detector: Differential refractometer
    Column: Packed with a cation exchange resin
    Column temperature: 85°
    Flow rate: 0.7 mL/min
    Injection volume: 7.5 µL
  Analysis: Separately inject aliquots of the *Standard solution* and the *Sample solution* into the chromatograph and record the resulting chromatograms. Compare the elution times for fructose, glucose, and sucrose given in the two chromatograms.
  Acceptance criteria: The chromatogram of the *Sample solution* gives appropriate elution times for fructose, glucose, and sucrose when compared with the *Standard solution*.

ASSAY
- **INVERT SUGAR,** *Total Solids,* Appendix X
  Acceptance criteria: NLT 90.0% and NMT 110.0% of the labeled amount of sucrose and of Invert Sugar

IMPURITIES
Inorganic Impurities
- **LEAD,** *Lead Limit Test, Atomic Absorption Spectrophotometric Graphite Furnace Method, Method I,* Appendix IIIB

Sample: 5 g
Acceptance criteria: NMT 0.1 mg/kg

SPECIFIC TESTS
- **pH**, *pH Determination,* Appendix IIB
  Acceptance criteria: Between 3.0 and 5.5
- **RESIDUE ON IGNITION (SULFATED ASH),** *Method II,* Appendix IIC
  Acceptance criteria: NMT 0.2%
- **TOTAL SOLIDS,** *Invert Sugar,* Appendix X
  Analysis: Determine as directed using the table provided.
  Acceptance criteria: Conforms to the representations of the vendor
- **TOTAL SUGARS**
  Analysis: Calculate the percent total sugars (T_S) by the equation:

  $$T_S = P_I + P_S$$

  P_I = percentage of invert sugar as determined under *Assay*
  P_S = percentage of sucrose as determined under *Assay* (above)
  Acceptance criteria: NLT 99.5% of the *Total Solids* content

OTHER REQUIREMENTS
- **LABELING:** Indicate the percentages of sucrose and Invert Sugar.

α-Ionone

First Published: Prior to FCC 6

4-(2,6,6-Trimethyl-2-cyclohexenyl)-3-butene-2-one

$C_{13}H_{20}O$ Formula wt 192.30

FEMA: 2594
UNII: I9V075M61R [α-ionone]

DESCRIPTION
α-Ionone occurs as a colorless to pale yellow liquid.
Odor: Warm, woody, violet-floral
Solubility: Soluble in alcohol, most fixed oils, propylene glycol; insoluble or practically insoluble in glycerin, water
Boiling Point: ~237°
Solubility in Alcohol, Appendix VI: One mL dissolves in 10 mL of 60% alcohol.
Function: Flavoring agent

IDENTIFICATION
- **INFRARED SPECTRA,** *Spectrophotometric Identification Tests,* Appendix IIIC
  Acceptance criteria: The spectrum of the sample exhibits relative maxima at the same wavelengths as those of the spectrum below.

ASSAY
- **PROCEDURE:** Proceed as directed under *M-1b,* Appendix XI.
  Acceptance criteria
  α-isomer: NLT 85.0% of $C_{13}H_{20}O$
  Sum of α-, β-, γ-, and δ-isomers: NLT 97.0% of $C_{13}H_{20}O$

SPECIFIC TESTS
- **REFRACTIVE INDEX,** Appendix II: At 20°
  Acceptance criteria: Between 1.497 and 1.502
- **SPECIFIC GRAVITY:** Determine at 25° by any reliable method (see *General Provisions*).
  Acceptance criteria: Between 0.927 and 0.933

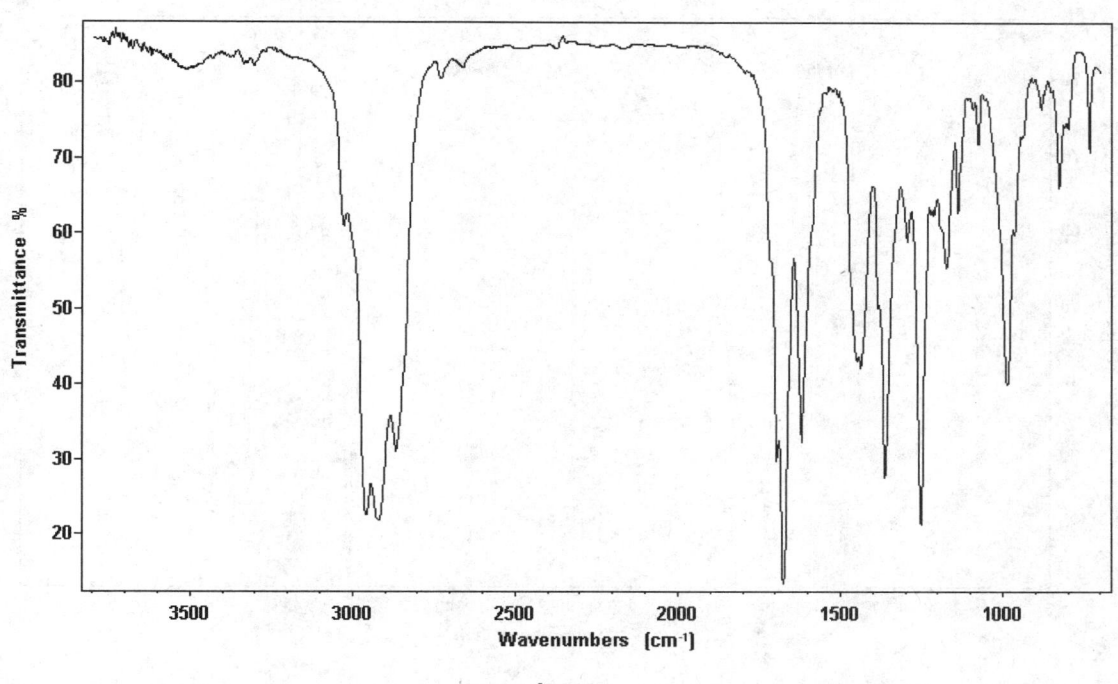

α-Ionone

β-Ionone

First Published: Prior to FCC 6

4-(2,6,6-Trimethyl-1-cyclohexenyl)-3-butene-2-one

$C_{13}H_{20}O$ Formula wt 192.30
FEMA: 2595
UNII: A7NRR1HLH6 [β-ionone]

DESCRIPTION
β-Ionone occurs as a colorless to pale straw-colored liquid.
Odor: Warm, woody, dry
Solubility: Soluble in alcohol, most fixed oils, propylene glycol; insoluble or practically insoluble in glycerin, water
Boiling Point: ~239°
Solubility in Alcohol, Appendix VI: One mL dissolves in 1 mL of 95% ethanol.

Function: Flavoring agent

IDENTIFICATION
- **INFRARED SPECTRA,** *Spectrophotometric Identification Tests,* Appendix IIIC
  Acceptance criteria: The spectrum of the sample exhibits relative maxima at the same wavelengths as those of the spectrum below.

ASSAY
- **PROCEDURE:** Proceed as directed under *M-1b,* Appendix XI.
  Acceptance criteria: NLT 97.0% of $C_{13}H_{20}O$

SPECIFIC TESTS
- **REFRACTIVE INDEX,** Appendix II: At 20°
  Acceptance criteria: Between 1.517 and 1.522
- **SPECIFIC GRAVITY:** Determine at 25° by any reliable method (see *General Provisions*).
  Acceptance criteria: Between 0.940 and 0.947

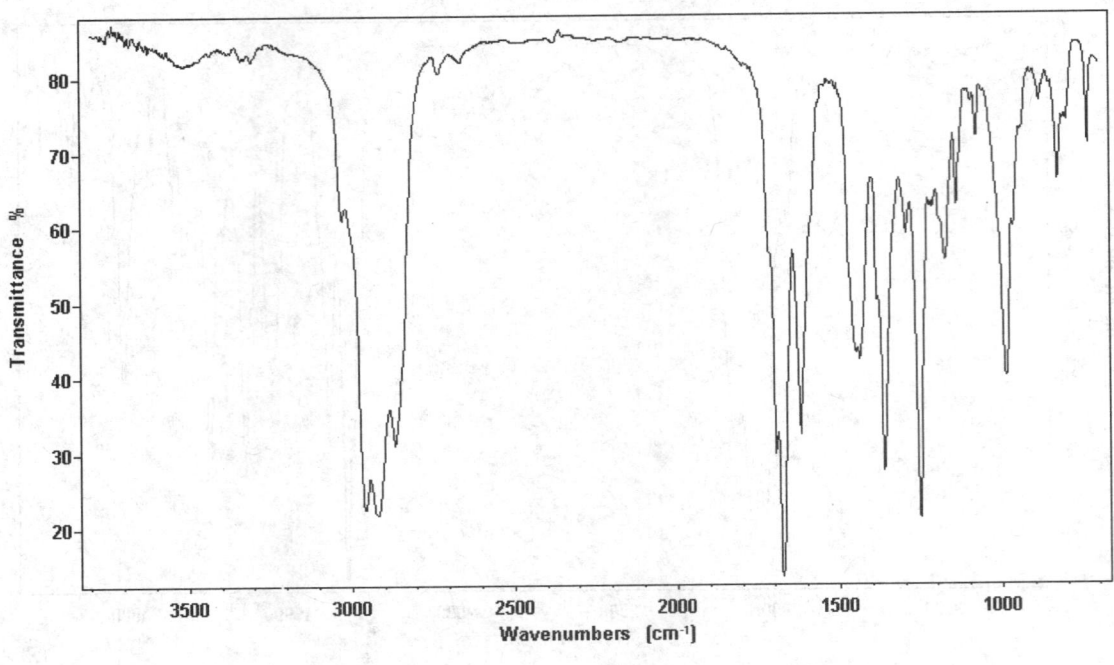

β-Ionone

Iron, Carbonyl

First Published: Prior to FCC 6
Last Revision: First Supplement, FCC 6

Fe Atomic wt 55.85
 CAS: [7439-89-6]
UNII: 6WQ62TAQ6Z [iron pentacarbonyl]

DESCRIPTION
Iron, Carbonyl occurs as a dark gray powder. It is elemental iron produced by the decomposition of iron pentacarbonyl. When viewed under a microscope having a magnifying power of 500 diameters or greater, it appears as spheres built up with concentric shells. It is stable in dry air.
Function: Nutrient
Packaging and Storage: Store in well-closed containers.

IDENTIFICATION
- **FERROUS SALTS,** *Iron,* Appendix IIIA
  Sample solution: Dissolve a sample in a dilute mineral acid. [NOTE—Hydrogen is evolved, and solutions of the corresponding salts are formed.]
  Acceptance criteria: Passes test

ASSAY
- **PROCEDURE**
  Sample: 200 mg
  Analysis: Transfer the *Sample* into a 300-mL Erlenmeyer flask, add 50 mL of 2 N sulfuric acid, and close the flask with a stopper containing a Bunsen valve (made by inserting a glass tube connected to a short piece of rubber tubing with a slit on the side and a glass rod inserted in the other end and arranged so that gases can escape but air cannot enter). Heat on a steam bath to completely dissolve the *Sample*. [NOTE—The solution will be clear.] Remove the flask from the steam bath and allow the solution to cool at room temperature with the stopper in place.
  Add a stir bar and 50 mL of recently boiled and cooled water to the flask. Using an automated titrator[1] equipped with a platinum indicating electrode and a silver–silver chloride reference electrode (or an equivalent combination electrode), titrate the solution with 0.1 N ceric sulfate VS through the inflection point of the titration curve. Perform a blank determination (see *General Provisions*). Each mL of 0.1 N ceric sulfate VS is equivalent to 5.585 mg of Fe.
  Acceptance criteria: NLT 98.0% of Fe

IMPURITIES
Inorganic Impurities
- **ARSENIC,** *Arsenic Limit Test,* Appendix IIIB
  Sample solution: Dissolve 1.0 g of sample in 25 mL of 2 N sulfuric acid, heat on a steam bath until the evolution of hydrogen ceases, cool, and dilute with water to 35 mL.
  Acceptance criteria: NMT 3 mg/kg
- **LEAD**
  [NOTE—When preparing all aqueous solutions and rinsing glassware before use, employ water that has been passed through a strong-acid, strong-base, mixed-bed ion-exchange resin before use. Select all reagents to have as low a content of lead as practicable, and store

---
[1] Metrohm 751 GPD Titrino automatic, PC-based titrator with Titrino Workcell software (Brinkmann, Hauppauge, NY), or equivalent automated titrator.

all reagent solutions in containers of borosilicate glass. Clean glassware before use by soaking in warm 8 N nitric acid for 30 min and by rinsing with deionized water.]

Ascorbic acid–sodium iodide solution: Transfer 20 g of ascorbic acid and 38.5 g of sodium iodide to a 200-mL volumetric flask. Dissolve in and dilute with water to volume, and mix.

Trioctylphosphine oxide solution: Transfer 5.0 g of trioctylphosphine oxide to a 100-mL volumetric flask. Dissolve in and dilute with 4-methyl-2-pentanone to volume, and mix. [**Caution**—This solution causes irritation. Avoid contact with eyes, skin, and clothing. Take special precautions in disposing of unused portions of solutions to which this reagent is added.]

Lead nitrate stock solution: Transfer 159.8 mg of reagent-grade lead nitrate [$Pb(NO_3)_2$] into a 1000-mL volumetric flask. Dissolve it in 100 mL of water containing 1 mL of nitric acid, dilute with water to volume, and mix. (100 µg lead/mL)

Standard solution: Transfer 5.0 mL of *Lead nitrate stock solution* into a 100-mL volumetric flask, dilute with water to volume, and mix. Transfer 2.0 mL of the resulting solution into a 50-mL beaker. Add 8 mL of hydrochloric acid and 2 mL of nitric acid. Place a ribbed watch glass over the beaker, and evaporate to dryness on a steam bath. Add 10 mL of 9 N hydrochloric acid, and transfer the resulting solution, with the aid of about 10 mL of water, to a 50-mL volumetric flask. Add 20 mL of *Ascorbic acid–sodium iodide solution* and 5.0 mL of *Trioctylphosphine oxide solution*; shake the flask for 30 s, and allow the layers to separate. Add water to bring the organic solvent layer into the neck of the flask, shake the flask again, and allow the layers to separate. The organic solvent layer contains 2.0 µg of lead/mL, and is the *Standard solution*.

Blank solution: Into a 50-mL beaker, add 8 mL of hydrochloric acid and 2 mL of nitric acid. Place a ribbed watch glass over the beaker, and evaporate to dryness on a steam bath. Add 10 mL of 9 N hydrochloric acid, and transfer the resulting solution, with the aid of about 10 mL of water, to a 50-mL volumetric flask. Add 20 mL of *Ascorbic acid–sodium iodide solution* and 5.0 mL of *Trioctylphosphine oxide solution*, shake the flask for 30 s, and allow the layers to separate. Add water to bring the organic solvent layer into the neck of the flask, shake the flask again, and allow the layers to separate. The organic solvent layer contains 0.0 µg of lead/mL, and is the *Blank solution*.

Sample solution: Transfer 1.0 g of sample to a 50-mL beaker and cover it with a ribbed watch glass. Slowly add 8 mL of hydrochloric acid and 2 mL of nitric acid, keeping the beaker covered as much as possible. After the initial reaction subsides, evaporate to dryness on a steam bath, cool, and dissolve the residue in 10 mL of 9 N hydrochloric acid, warming if necessary to effect solution. Cool, and transfer the resultant solution, with the aid of about 10 mL of water, into a 50-mL volumetric flask. Add 20 mL of *Ascorbic acid–sodium iodide solution* and 5 mL of *Trioctylphosphine oxide solution*; shake the flask for 30 s and allow the layers to separate. Add water to bring the organic solvent layer into the neck of the flask, shake the flask again, and allow the layers to separate. The organic solvent layer is the *Sample solution*.

Analysis: Concomitantly determine the absorbance of the *Blank solution*, the *Standard solution*, and the *Sample solution* at the lead emission line at 283.3 nm, with a suitable atomic absorption spectrophotometer equipped with a lead hollow-cathode lamp and an air–acetylene flame, using 4-methyl-2-pentanone to set the instrument to zero. In a suitable analysis, the absorbance of the *Blank solution* is not more than 20% of the difference between the absorbance of the *Standard solution* and that of the *Blank solution*.

Acceptance criteria: The absorbance of the *Sample solution* does not exceed that of the *Standard solution*. (NMT 4 mg/kg)

- **Mercury**

Dithizone stock solution: Dissolve 30 mg of dithizone in 1000 mL of chloroform, add 5 mL of alcohol, and mix (0.03 mg/mL). [Note—Store in a refrigerator in a dark bottle; prepare fresh monthly.]

Dithizone extraction solution: On the day of use, dilute 30 mL of *Dithizone stock solution* to 100 mL with chloroform.

Hydroxylamine hydrochloride solution: Dissolve 20 g of hydroxylamine hydrochloride in sufficient water to make about 65 mL. Transfer the solution into a separatory funnel, add a few drops of thymol blue TS, and then add ammonia solution until a yellow color appears. Add 10 mL of 1:25 sodium diethyldithiocarbamate solution, mix, and allow to stand for 5 min. Extract the solution with successive 10- to 15-mL portions of chloroform until a 5-mL test portion of the chloroform extract does not develop a yellow color when shaken with a dilute cupric sulfate solution. Add 2.7 N hydrochloric acid until the extracted solution is pink, adding one or two more drops of thymol blue TS, if necessary, then dilute with water to 100 mL, and mix.

Mercury stock solution: Transfer 33.8 mg of mercuric chloride into a 100-mL volumetric flask, dilute with 1 N hydrochloric acid to volume, and mix (250 µg Hg/mL).

Diluted standard mercury solution: Transfer 4.0 mL of *Mercury stock solution* into a 250-mL volumetric flask, dilute with 1 N hydrochloric acid to volume, and mix (4 µg Hg/mL).

Sodium citrate solution: Dissolve 250 g of sodium citrate dihydrate in 1000 mL of water.

Sample solution: Transfer 2 g of sample into a 250-mL beaker, add 20 mL of 1:2 nitric acid, and digest on a steam bath for about 45 min. Add 5 mL of 1:3 hydrochloric acid, and continue heating on the steam bath until the sample is dissolved. Cool to room temperature and pass, if necessary, through a medium-porosity filter paper. Wash the paper with a few mL of water, add 40 mL of *Sodium citrate solution* and 1 mL of *Hydroxylamine hydrochloride solution* to the filtrate, and adjust the pH to 1.8 with ammonia solution.

Control: Transfer 1.0 mL of *Diluted standard mercury solution* (4 μg Hg) into a 250-mL beaker, add 20 mL of 1:2 nitric acid, and digest on a steam bath for about 45 min. Add 5 mL of 1:3 hydrochloric acid, and continue heating on the steam bath until the sample is dissolved. Cool to room temperature and pass, if necessary, through a medium-porosity filter paper. Wash the paper with a few mL of water, add 40 mL of *Sodium citrate solution* and 1 mL of *Hydroxylamine hydrochloride solution* to the filtrate, and adjust the pH to 1.8 with ammonia solution.

Analysis: [NOTE—Because mercuric dithizonate is light sensitive, this procedure should be performed in subdued light.] Transfer the *Control* and the *Sample solution* into separate 250-mL separatory funnels, and treat both solutions as follows: Extract with 5 mL of *Dithizone extraction solution*, shaking the mixtures vigorously for 1 min. Drain carefully, collecting the chloroform in another separatory funnel. If the chloroform does not show a pronounced green color caused by excess reagent, add another 5 mL of the extraction solution, shake the mixture again, and drain into the separatory funnel. Continue the extraction with 5-mL portions, if necessary, collecting each successive extract in the second funnel, until the final chloroform layer contains dithizone in marked excess. Add 15 mL of 1:3 hydrochloric acid to the combined chloroform extracts, shake the mixture vigorously for 1 min, and discard the chloroform. Extract with 2 mL of chloroform, drain carefully, and discard the chloroform. Add 1 mL of 0.05 M disodium EDTA and 2 mL of 6 N acetic acid to the aqueous layer. Slowly add 5 mL of 6 N ammonia solution and cool the separatory funnel. Transfer the solution into a 150-mL beaker, adjust the pH to 1.8 with 6 N ammonia solution or 1:10 nitric acid, using a pH meter, and return the solution to the funnel. Add 5.0 mL of *Dithizone extraction solution*, and shake the mixture vigorously for 1 min. Allow the layers to separate, insert a plug of cotton into the stem of the funnel, and collect the dithizone extract in a test tube. Determine the absorbance of each solution in 1-cm cells at 490 nm with a suitable spectrophotometer, using chloroform as the blank.

Acceptance criteria: The absorbance of the *Sample solution* does not exceed that of the *Control* (NMT 2 mg/kg).

SPECIFIC TESTS
- **ACID-INSOLUBLE SUBSTANCES**
  Sample: 1 g
  Analysis: Dissolve the *Sample* in 25 mL of 2 N sulfuric acid, and heat on a steam bath until the evolution of hydrogen ceases. Filter through a tared filter crucible, wash the residue with water until free from sulfate, dry at 105° for 1 h, let cool, and weigh.
  Acceptance criteria: NMT 0.2%
- **SIEVE ANALYSIS**, *Sieve Analysis of Granular Metal Powders*, Appendix IIC
  Acceptance criteria: NLT 100% passes through a 200-mesh sieve and NLT 95% passes through a 325-mesh sieve.

Iron, Electrolytic
First Published: Prior to FCC 6

Fe Atomic wt 55.85
CAS: [7439-89-6]
UNII: E1UOL152H7 [iron]

DESCRIPTION
Iron, Electrolytic, occurs as an amorphous, lusterless, gray-black powder. It is elemental iron obtained by electrode deposition. It is stable in dry air.
Function: Nutrient
Packaging and Storage: Store in well-closed containers.

IDENTIFICATION
- **FERROUS SALTS**, *Iron*, Appendix IIIA
  Sample solution: Dissolve a sample in a dilute mineral acid. [NOTE—Hydrogen is evolved, and solutions of the corresponding salts are formed.]
  Acceptance criteria: Passes test

ASSAY
- **PROCEDURE**
  Sample: 200 mg
  Analysis: Transfer the *Sample* into a 300-mL Erlenmeyer flask, add 50 mL of 2 N sulfuric acid, and close the flask with a stopper containing a Bunsen valve (made by inserting a glass tube connected to a short piece of rubber tubing with a slit on the side and a glass rod inserted in the other end and arranged so that gases can escape but air cannot enter). Heat on a steam bath until the iron is dissolved, cool the solution, dilute it with 50 mL of recently boiled and cooled water, add 2 drops of orthophenanthroline TS and titrate with 0.1 N ceric sulfate until the red color changes to a weak blue. Each mL of 0.1 N ceric sulfate is equivalent to 5.585 mg of Fe.
  Acceptance criteria: NLT 97.0% of Fe

IMPURITIES
Inorganic Impurities
- **ARSENIC**, *Arsenic Limit Test*, Appendix IIIB
  Sample solution: Dissolve 1 g of sample in 25 mL of 2 N sulfuric acid, heat on a steam bath until the evolution of hydrogen ceases, cool, and dilute to 35 mL with water.
  Acceptance criteria: NMT 3 mg/kg
- **LEAD**
  [NOTE—When preparing all aqueous solutions and rinsing glassware before use, employ water that has been passed through a strong-acid, strong-base, mixed-bed ion-exchange resin before use. Select all reagents to have as low a content of lead as practicable, and store all reagent solutions in containers of borosilicate glass. Clean glassware before use by soaking in warm 8 N nitric acid for 30 min and by rinsing with deionized water.]
  Ascorbic acid-sodium iodide solution: Transfer 20 g of ascorbic acid and 38.5 g of sodium iodide to a 200-mL volumetric flask. Dissolve in and dilute to volume with water, and mix.

Trioctylphosphine oxide solution: Transfer 5.0 g of trioctylphosphine oxide to a 100-mL volumetric flask. Dissolve in and dilute to volume with 4-methyl-2-pentanone, and mix. [**Caution**—This solution causes irritation. Avoid contact with eyes, skin, and clothing. Take special precautions in disposing of unused portions of solutions to which this reagent is added.]

Lead nitrate stock solution: Transfer 159.8 mg of reagent-grade lead nitrate [$Pb(NO_3)_2$] into a 1000-mL volumetric flask. Dissolve it in 100 ml of water containing 1 mL of nitric acid and dilute to volume with water, and mix (100 µg lead/mL).

Standard solution: Transfer 5.0 mL of *Lead nitrate stock solution* into a 100-mL volumetric flask, dilute to volume with water, and mix. Transfer 2.0 mL of the resulting solution into a 50-mL beaker. Add 8 mL of hydrochloric acid and 2 mL of nitric acid. Place a ribbed watch glass over the beaker, and evaporate to dryness on a steam bath. Add 10 mL of 9 N hydrochloric acid, and transfer the resulting solution, with the aid of about 10 mL of water, to a 50-mL volumetric flask. Add 20 mL of *Ascorbic acid–sodium iodide solution* and 5.0 mL of *Trioctylphosphine oxide solution*, shake the flask for 30 s, and allow the layers to separate. Add water to bring the organic solvent layer into the neck of the flask; shake the flask again and allow the layers to separate. The organic solvent layer contains 2.0 µg of lead/mL, and is the *Standard solution*.

Blank solution: Into a 50-mL beaker, add 8 mL of hydrochloric acid and 2 mL of nitric acid. Place a ribbed watch glass over the beaker, and evaporate to dryness on a steam bath. Add 10 mL of 9 N hydrochloric acid, and transfer the resulting solution, with the aid of about 10 mL of water, to a 50-mL volumetric flask. Add 20 mL of *Ascorbic acid–sodium iodide solution* and 5.0 mL of *Trioctylphosphine oxide solution*; shake the flask for 30 s and allow the layers to separate. Add water to bring the organic solvent layer into the neck of the flask, shake the flask again, and allow the layers to separate. The organic solvent layer contains 0.0 µg of lead/mL, and is the *Blank solution*.

Sample solution: Transfer 1.0 g of sample to a 50-mL beaker and cover it with a ribbed watch glass. Slowly add 8 mL of hydrochloric acid and 2 mL of nitric acid, keeping the beaker covered as much as possible. After the initial reaction subsides, evaporate to dryness on a steam bath, cool, and dissolve the residue in 10 mL of 9 N hydrochloric acid, warming if necessary to effect solution. Cool, and transfer the resultant solution, with the aid of about 10 mL of water, into a 50-mL volumetric flask. Add 20 mL of *Ascorbic acid–sodium iodide solution* and 5 mL of *Trioctylphosphine oxide solution*; shake the flask for 30 s and allow the layers to separate. Add water to bring the organic solvent layer into the neck of the flask, shake the flask again, and allow the layers to separate. The organic solvent layer is the *Sample solution*.

Analysis: Concomitantly determine the absorbance of the *Blank solution*, the *Standard solution*, and the *Sample solution* at the lead emission line at 283.3 nm, with a suitable atomic absorption spectrophotometer equipped with a lead hollow-cathode lamp and an air–acetylene flame, using 4-methyl-2-pentanone to set the instrument to zero. In a suitable analysis, the absorbance of the *Blank solution* is not more than 20% of the difference between the absorbance of the *Standard solution* and that of the *Blank solution*.

Acceptance criteria: The absorbance of the *Sample solution* does not exceed that of the *Standard solution* (NMT 4 mg/kg).

- **Mercury**

    Dithizone stock solution: Dissolve 30 mg of dithizone in 1000 mL of chloroform, add 5 mL of alcohol, and mix (0.03 mg/mL). [NOTE—Store in a refrigerator in a dark bottle; prepare fresh monthly.]

    Dithizone extraction solution: On the day of use, dilute 30 mL of *Dithizone stock solution* to 100 mL with chloroform.

    Hydroxylamine hydrochloride solution: Dissolve 20 g of hydroxylamine hydrochloride in sufficient water to make about 65 mL. Transfer the solution into a separatory funnel, add a few drops of thymol blue TS, and then add ammonia solution until a yellow color appears. Add 10 mL of 1:25 sodium diethyldithiocarbamate solution, mix, and allow to stand for 5 min. Extract the solution with successive 10- to 15-mL portions of chloroform until a 5-mL test portion of the chloroform extract does not develop a yellow color when shaken with a dilute cupric sulfate solution. Add 2.7 N hydrochloric acid until the extracted solution is pink, adding one or two more drops of thymol blue TS, if necessary, then dilute to 100 mL with water, and mix.

    Mercury stock solution: Transfer 33.8 mg of mercuric chloride into a 100-mL volumetric flask, dilute to volume with 1 N hydrochloric acid, and mix (250 µg Hg/mL).

    Diluted standard mercury solution: Transfer 4.0 mL of *Mercury stock solution* into a 250-mL volumetric flask, dilute to volume with 1 N hydrochloric acid, and mix (4 µg Hg/mL).

    Sodium citrate solution: Dissolve 250 g of sodium citrate dihydrate in 1000 mL of water.

    Sample solution: Transfer 2 g of sample into a 250-mL beaker, add 20 mL of 1:2 nitric acid, and digest on a steam bath for about 45 min. Add 5 mL of 1:3 hydrochloric acid and continue heating on the steam bath until the sample is dissolved. Cool to room temperature and filter, if necessary, through a medium-porosity filter paper. Wash the paper with a few mL of water, add 40 mL of *Sodium citrate solution* and 1 mL of *Hydroxylamine hydrochloride solution* to the filtrate, and adjust the pH to 1.8 with ammonia solution.

    Control: Transfer 1.0 mL of *Diluted standard mercury solution* (4 µg Hg) into a 250-mL beaker, add 20 mL of 1:2 nitric acid, and digest on a steam bath for about 45 min. Add 5 mL of 1:3 hydrochloric acid and continue heating on the steam bath until the sample is dissolved. Cool to room temperature and filter, if necessary, through a medium-porosity filter paper. Wash the paper with a few mL of water, add 40 mL of

Sodium citrate solution and 1 mL of Hydroxylamine hydrochloride solution to the filtrate, and adjust the pH to 1.8 with ammonia solution.

Analysis: [NOTE—Because mercuric dithizonate is light sensitive, this procedure should be performed in subdued light.] Transfer the Control and the Sample solution into separate 250-mL separatory funnels, and treat both solutions as follows: Extract with 5 mL of Dithizone extraction solution, shaking the mixtures vigorously for 1 min. Drain carefully, collecting the chloroform in another separatory funnel. If the chloroform does not show a pronounced green color caused by excess reagent, add another 5 mL of the extraction solution, shake the mixture again, and drain into the separatory funnel. Continue the extraction with 5-mL portions, if necessary, collecting each successive extract in the second funnel, until the final chloroform layer contains dithizone in marked excess. Add 15 mL of 1:3 hydrochloric acid to the combined chloroform extracts, shake the mixture vigorously for 1 min, and discard the chloroform. Extract with 2 mL of chloroform, drain carefully, and discard the chloroform. Add 1 mL of 0.05 M disodium EDTA and 2 mL of 6 N acetic acid to the aqueous layer. Slowly add 5 mL of 6 N ammonia solution and cool the separatory funnel. Transfer the solution into a 150-mL beaker, adjust the pH to 1.8 with 6 N ammonia solution or 1:10 nitric acid, using a pH meter, and return the solution to the funnel. Add 5.0 mL of Dithizone extraction solution, and shake the mixture vigorously for 1 min. Allow the layers to separate, insert a plug of cotton into the stem of the funnel, and collect the dithizone extract in a test tube. Determine the absorbance of each solution in 1-cm cells at 490 nm with a suitable spectrophotometer, using chloroform as the blank.

Acceptance criteria: The absorbance of the Sample solution does not exceed that of the Control (NMT 2 mg/kg).

SPECIFIC TESTS
- **ACID-INSOLUBLE SUBSTANCES**
  Sample: 1 g
  Analysis: Dissolve the Sample in 25 mL of 2 N sulfuric acid, and heat on a steam bath until the evolution of hydrogen ceases. Filter through a tared filter crucible, wash the residue with water until free from sulfate, dry at 105° for 1 h, let cool, and weigh.
  Acceptance criteria: NMT 0.2%
- **SIEVE ANALYSIS,** Sieve Analysis of Granular Metal Powders, Appendix IIC
  Acceptance criteria: NLT 100% passes through a 100-mesh sieve; NLT 95% passes through a 325-mesh sieve

Iron, Reduced

First Published: Prior to FCC 6
Last Revision: First Supplement, FCC 6

Fe   Atomic wt 55.85
               CAS: [7439-89-6]

DESCRIPTION
Iron, Reduced occurs as a gray-black powder. It is elemental iron obtained by a chemical process. It is lusterless or has not more than a slight luster. When viewed under a microscope having a magnifying power of 100 diameters, it appears as an amorphous powder, free from particles having a crystalline structure. It is stable in dry air.

Function: Nutrient
Packaging and Storage: Store in well-closed containers.

IDENTIFICATION
- **FERROUS SALTS,** Iron, Appendix IIIA
  Sample solution: Dissolve a sample in a dilute mineral acid. [NOTE—Hydrogen is evolved, and solutions of the corresponding salts are formed.]
  Acceptance criteria: Passes test

ASSAY
- **PROCEDURE**
  Sample: 200 mg
  Analysis: Transfer the Sample into a 300-mL Erlenmeyer flask, add 50 mL of 2 N sulfuric acid, and close the flask with a stopper containing a Bunsen valve (made by inserting a glass tube connected to a short piece of rubber tubing with a slit on the side and a glass rod inserted in the other end and arranged so that gases can escape but air cannot enter). Heat on a steam bath until the iron is dissolved, cool the solution, dilute it with 50 mL of recently boiled and cooled water, add 2 drops of orthophenanthroline TS and titrate with 0.1 N ceric sulfate until the red color changes to a weak blue. Each mL of 0.1 N ceric sulfate is equivalent to 5.585 mg of Fe.
  Acceptance criteria: NLT 97.0% of Fe

IMPURITIES
Inorganic Impurities
- **ARSENIC,** Arsenic Limit Test, Appendix IIIB
  Sample solution: Dissolve 1.0 g of sample in 25 mL of 2 N sulfuric acid, heat on a steam bath until the evolution of hydrogen ceases, cool, and dilute with water to 35 mL.
  Acceptance criteria: NMT 3 mg/kg
- **LEAD**
  [NOTE—When preparing all aqueous solutions and rinsing glassware before use, employ water that has been passed through a strong-acid, strong-base, mixed-bed ion-exchange resin before use. Select all reagents to have as low a content of lead as practicable, and store all reagent solutions in containers of borosilicate glass. Clean glassware before use by soaking in warm 8 N nitric acid for 30 min and by rinsing with deionized water.]
  Ascorbic acid–sodium iodide solution: Transfer 20 g of ascorbic acid and 38.5 g of sodium iodide to a 200-mL volumetric flask. Dissolve in and dilute with water to volume, and mix.
  Trioctylphosphine oxide solution: Transfer 5.0 g of trioctylphosphine oxide to a 100-mL volumetric flask. Dissolve in and dilute with 4-methyl-2-pentanone to volume, and mix. [CAUTION—This solution causes irritation. Avoid contact with eyes, skin, and clothing.

Take special precautions in disposing of unused portions of solutions to which this reagent is added.]

Lead nitrate stock solution: Transfer 159.8 mg of reagent-grade lead nitrate [Pb(NO$_3$)$_2$] into a 1000-mL volumetric flask. Dissolve it in 100 mL of water containing 1 mL of nitric acid, dilute with water to volume, and mix. (100 µg Pb/mL)

Standard solution: Transfer 5.0 mL of *Lead nitrate stock solution* into a 100-mL volumetric flask, dilute with water to volume, and mix. Transfer 2.0 mL of the resulting solution into a 50-mL beaker. Add 8 mL of hydrochloric acid and 2 mL of nitric acid. Place a ribbed watch glass over the beaker, and evaporate to dryness on a steam bath. Add 10 mL of 9 N hydrochloric acid, and transfer the resulting solution, with the aid of about 10 mL of water, to a 50-mL volumetric flask. Add 20 mL of *Ascorbic acid–sodium iodide solution* and 5.0 mL of *Trioctylphosphine oxide solution*, shake the flask for 30 s, and allow the layers to separate. Add water to bring the organic solvent layer into the neck of the flask, shake the flask again, and allow the layers to separate. The organic solvent layer contains 2.0 µg of lead/mL, and is the *Standard solution*.

Blank solution: Into a 50-mL beaker, add 8 mL of hydrochloric acid and 2 mL of nitric acid. Place a ribbed watch glass over the beaker, and evaporate to dryness on a steam bath. Add 10 mL of 9 N hydrochloric acid, and transfer the resulting solution, with the aid of about 10 mL of water, to a 50-mL volumetric flask. Add 20 mL of *Ascorbic acid–sodium iodide solution* and 5.0 mL of *Trioctylphosphine oxide solution*, shake the flask for 30 s, and allow the layers to separate. Add water to bring the organic solvent layer into the neck of the flask, shake the flask again, and allow the layers to separate. The organic solvent layer contains 0.0 µg of lead/mL, and is the *Blank solution*.

Sample solution: Transfer 2.5 g of sample to a 50-mL beaker and cover it with a ribbed watch glass. Slowly add 8 mL of hydrochloric acid and 2 mL of nitric acid, keeping the beaker covered as much as possible. After the initial reaction subsides, evaporate to dryness on a steam bath, cool, and dissolve the residue in 10 mL of 9 N hydrochloric acid, warming if necessary to effect solution. Cool, and transfer the resultant solution, with the aid of about 10 mL of water, into a 50-mL volumetric flask. Add 20 mL of *Ascorbic acid–sodium iodide solution* and 5 mL of *Trioctylphosphine oxide solution*, shake the flask for 30 s, and allow the layers to separate. Add water to bring the organic solvent layer into the neck of the flask, shake the flask again, and allow the layers to separate. The organic solvent layer is the *Sample solution*.

Analysis: Concomitantly determine the absorbance of the *Blank solution*, the *Standard solution*, and the *Sample solution* at the lead emission line at 283.3 nm, with a suitable atomic absorption spectrophotometer equipped with a lead hollow-cathode lamp and an air–acetylene flame, using 4-methyl-2-pentanone to set the instrument to zero. In a suitable analysis, the absorbance of the *Blank solution* is not more than 20% of the difference between the absorbance of the *Standard solution* and that of the *Blank solution*.

Acceptance criteria: The absorbance of the *Sample solution* does not exceed that of the *Standard solution*. (NMT 4 mg/kg)

- **MERCURY**

  Dithizone stock solution: Dissolve 30 mg of dithizone in 1000 mL of chloroform, add 5 mL of alcohol, and mix. (0.03 mg/mL) [NOTE—Store in a refrigerator in a dark bottle; prepare fresh monthly.]

  Dithizone extraction solution: On the day of use, dilute 30 mL of *Dithizone stock solution* to 100 mL with chloroform.

  Hydroxylamine hydrochloride solution: Dissolve 20 g of hydroxylamine hydrochloride in sufficient water to make about 65 mL. Transfer the solution into a separatory funnel, add a few drops of thymol blue TS, and then add ammonia solution until a yellow color appears. Add 10 mL of 1:25 sodium diethyldithiocarbamate solution, mix, and allow to stand for 5 min. Extract the solution with successive 10- to 15-mL portions of chloroform until a 5-mL test portion of the chloroform extract does not develop a yellow color when shaken with a dilute cupric sulfate solution. Add 2.7 N hydrochloric acid until the extracted solution is pink, adding one or two more drops of thymol blue TS, if necessary, then dilute with water to 100 mL, and mix.

  Mercury stock solution: Transfer 33.8 mg of mercuric chloride into a 100-mL volumetric flask, dilute with 1 N hydrochloric acid to volume, and mix. (250 µg Hg/mL)

  Diluted standard mercury solution: Transfer 4.0 mL of *Mercury stock solution* into a 250-mL volumetric flask, and dilute with 1 N hydrochloric acid to volume. (4 µg Hg/mL)

  Sodium citrate solution: Dissolve 250 g of sodium citrate dihydrate in 1000 mL of water.

  Sample solution: Transfer 2 g of sample into a 250-mL beaker, add 20 mL of 1:2 nitric acid, and digest on a steam bath for about 45 min. Add 5 mL of 1:3 hydrochloric acid and continue heating on the steam bath until the sample is dissolved. Cool to room temperature and pass, if necessary, through a medium-porosity filter paper. Wash the paper with a few mL of water, add 20 mL of *Sodium citrate solution* and 1 mL of *Hydroxylamine hydrochloride solution* to the filtrate, and adjust the pH to 1.8 with ammonia solution.

  Control: Transfer 1.0 mL of *Diluted standard mercury solution* (4 µg Hg) into a 250-mL beaker, add 20 mL of 1:2 nitric acid, and digest on a steam bath for about 45 min. Add 5 mL of 1:3 hydrochloric acid and continue heating on the steam bath until the sample is dissolved. Cool to room temperature and pass, if necessary, through a medium-porosity filter paper. Wash the paper with a few mL of water, add 20 mL of *Sodium citrate solution* and 1 mL of *Hydroxylamine hydrochloride solution* to the filtrate, and adjust the pH to 1.8 with ammonia solution.

  Analysis: [NOTE—Because mercuric dithizonate is light sensitive, this procedure should be performed in

subdued light.] Transfer the *Control* and the *Sample solution* into separate 250-mL separatory funnels, and treat both solutions as follows: Extract with 5 mL of *Dithizone extraction solution*, shaking the mixtures vigorously for 1 min. Drain carefully, collecting the chloroform in another separatory funnel. If the chloroform does not show a pronounced green color caused by excess reagent, add another 5 mL of the extraction solution, shake the mixture again, and drain into the separatory funnel. Continue the extraction with 5-mL portions, if necessary, collecting each successive extract in the second funnel, until the final chloroform layer contains dithizone in marked excess. Add 15 mL of 1:3 hydrochloric acid to the combined chloroform extracts, shake the mixture vigorously for 1 min, and discard the chloroform. Extract with 2 mL of chloroform, drain carefully, and discard the chloroform. Add 1 mL of 0.05 M disodium EDTA and 2 mL of 6 N acetic acid to the aqueous layer. Slowly add 5 mL of 6 N ammonia solution and cool the separatory funnel. Transfer the solution into a 150-mL beaker, adjust the pH to 1.8 with 6 N ammonia solution or 1:10 nitric acid, using a pH meter, and return the solution to the funnel. Add 5.0 mL of *Dithizone extraction solution*, and shake the mixture vigorously for 1 min. Allow the layers to separate, insert a plug of cotton into the stem of the funnel, and collect the dithizone extract in a test tube. Determine the absorbance of each solution in 1-cm cells at 490 nm with a suitable spectrophotometer, using chloroform as the blank.
Acceptance criteria: The absorbance of the *Sample solution* does not exceed that of the *Control*. (NMT 2 mg/kg)

SPECIFIC TESTS

- **Acid-Insoluble Substances**
  Sample: 1.0 g
  Analysis: Dissolve the *Sample* in 25 mL of 2 N sulfuric acid, and heat on a steam bath until the evolution of hydrogen ceases. Pass through a tared filter crucible, wash the residue with water until free from sulfate, dry at 105° for 1 h, let cool, and weigh.
  Acceptance criteria: The weight of the residue does not exceed 5.0 mg. (NMT 0.50%)
- **Sieve Analysis**, *Sieve Analysis of Granular Metal Powders*, Appendix IIC
  Acceptance criteria: NLT 100% passes through a 100-mesh sieve and NLT 95% passes through a 325-mesh sieve

Isoamyl Acetate

First Published: Prior to FCC 6

Amyl Acetate
β-Methyl Butyl Acetate

$C_7H_{14}O_2$ Formula wt 130.19
FEMA: 2055
UNII: Z135787824 [isoamyl acetate]

DESCRIPTION

Isoamyl Acetate occurs as a colorless liquid.
Odor: Fruity, pear, banana
Solubility: Slightly soluble in water; miscible in alcohol, ether, ethyl acetate, most fixed oils; insoluble or practically insoluble in glycerin, propylene glycol
Boiling Point: ~145°
Solubility in Alcohol, Appendix VI: One mL dissolves in 3 mL of 60% alcohol to give a clear solution.
Function: Flavoring agent

IDENTIFICATION

- **Infrared Spectra,** *Spectrophotometric Identification Tests*, Appendix IIIC
  Acceptance criteria: The spectrum of the sample exhibits relative maxima at the same wavelengths as those of the spectrum below.

ASSAY

- **Procedure:** Proceed as directed under *M-1b*, Appendix XI.
  Acceptance criteria: NLT 95.0% of $C_7H_{14}O_2$ (sum of 2-methyl butyl, 3-methyl butyl, and *n*-pentyl isomers)

SPECIFIC TESTS

- **Acid Value, Flavor Chemicals (Other Than Essential Oils),** *M-15*, Appendix XI
  Acceptance criteria: NMT 1.0
- **Refractive Index,** Appendix II: At 20°
  Acceptance criteria: Between 1.400 and 1.404
- **Specific Gravity:** Determine at 25° by any reliable method (see *General Provisions*).
  Acceptance criteria: Between 0.868 and 0.878

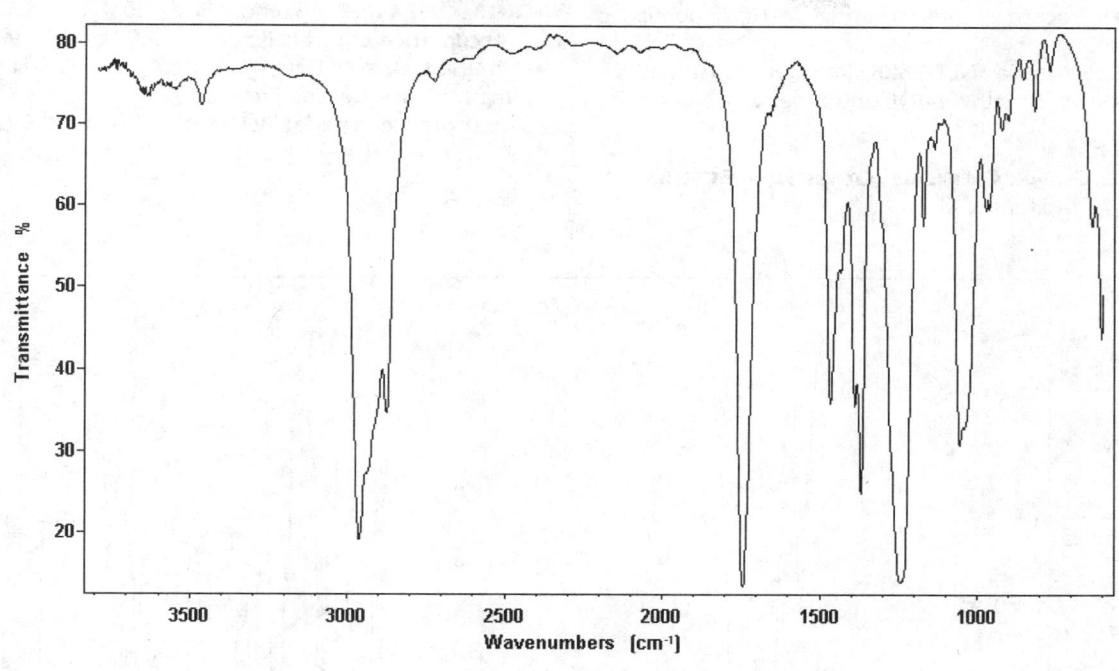

Isoamyl Acetate

Isoamyl Alcohol

First Published: Prior to FCC 6

$C_5H_{12}O$ Formula wt 88.15
FEMA: 2057
UNII: DEM9NIT1J4 [isoamyl alcohol]

DESCRIPTION
Isoamyl Alcohol occurs as a colorless to pale yellow liquid.
Odor: Winy
Solubility: Soluble in propylene glycol, vegetable oils; insoluble or practically insoluble in water
Boiling Point: ~130°
Solubility in Alcohol, Appendix VI: One mL dissolves in 1 mL of 95% ethanol.
Function: Flavoring agent

ASSAY
- **Procedure:** Proceed as directed under *M-1b,* Appendix XI.
  Acceptance criteria: NLT 98.0% of $C_5H_{12}O$ (sum of 2-methyl butyl, 3-methyl butyl, and *n*-pentyl isomers)

SPECIFIC TESTS
- **Refractive Index,** Appendix II: At 20°
  Acceptance criteria: Between 1.405 and 1.410
- **Specific Gravity:** Determine at 25° by any reliable method (see *General Provisions*).
  Acceptance criteria: Between 0.807 and 0.813

Isoamyl Benzoate

First Published: Prior to FCC 6

$C_{12}H_{16}O_2$ Formula wt 196.26
FEMA: 2058
UNII: 0AY72CK43K [isoamyl benzoate]

DESCRIPTION
Isoamyl Benzoate occurs as a colorless to pale yellow liquid.
Odor: Pungent fruit
Boiling Point: ~261° (746 mm Hg)
Solubility in Alcohol, Appendix VI: One mL dissolves in 1 mL of 95% alcohol.
Function: Flavoring agent

IDENTIFICATION
- **Infrared Spectra,** *Spectrophotometric Identification Tests,* Appendix IIIC
  Acceptance criteria: The spectrum of the sample exhibits relative maxima at the same wavelengths as those of the spectrum below.

578 / Isoamyl Benzoate / Monographs

ASSAY
- **PROCEDURE:** Proceed as directed under *M-1a*, Appendix XI.
  Acceptance criteria: NLT 98.0% of $C_{12}H_{16}O_2$ (sum of 2-methyl butyl, 3-methyl butyl, and *n*-pentyl isomers)

SPECIFIC TESTS
- **ACID VALUE, FLAVOR CHEMICALS (OTHER THAN ESSENTIAL OILS),** *M-15*, Appendix XI
  Acceptance criteria: NMT 1.0
- **REFRACTIVE INDEX,** Appendix II: At 20°
  Acceptance criteria: Between 1.492 and 1.496
- **SPECIFIC GRAVITY:** Determine at 25° by any reliable method (see *General Provisions*).
  Acceptance criteria: Between 0.986 and 0.992

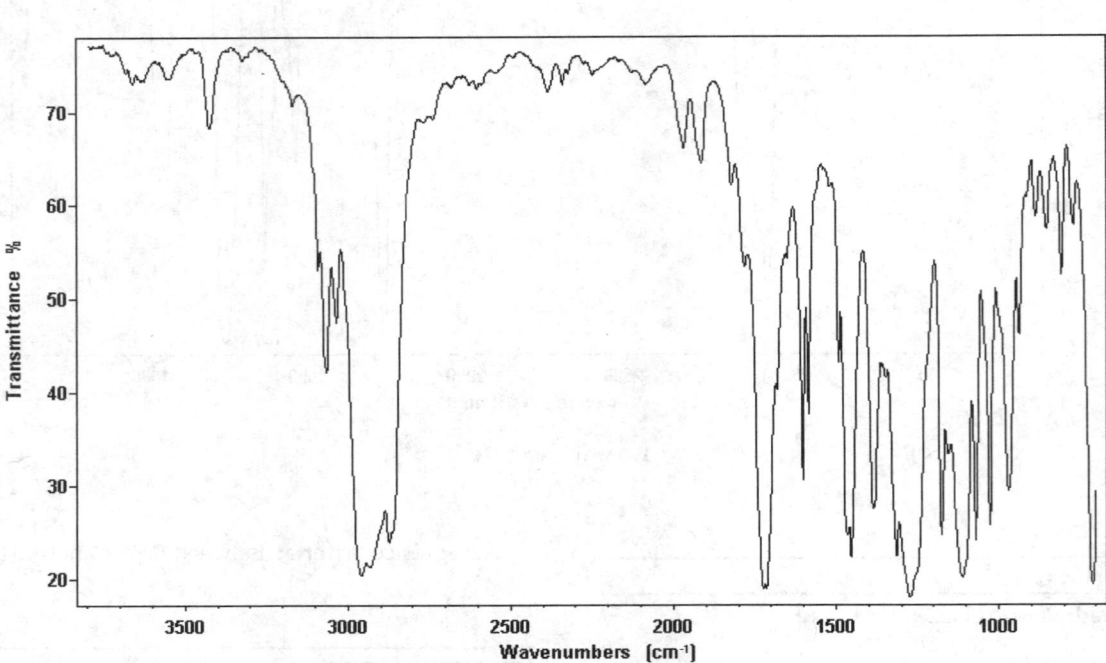

Isoamyl Benzoate

Isoamyl Butyrate

First Published: Prior to FCC 6

Amyl Butyrate

$C_9H_{18}O_2$ Formula wt 158.24
FEMA: 2060
UNII: 505AFM77VU [isoamyl butyrate]

DESCRIPTION
Isoamyl Butyrate occurs as a colorless liquid.
Odor: Fruity
Solubility: Soluble in alcohol, most fixed oils; insoluble or practically insoluble in glycerin, propylene glycol, water
Boiling Point: ~179°
Solubility in Alcohol, Appendix VI: One mL dissolves in 4 mL of 70% alcohol.
Function: Flavoring agent

IDENTIFICATION
- **INFRARED SPECTRA,** *Spectrophotometric Identification Tests*, Appendix IIIC
  Acceptance criteria: The spectrum of the sample exhibits relative maxima at the same wavelengths as those of the spectrum below.

ASSAY
- **PROCEDURE:** Proceed as directed under *M-1b*, Appendix XI.
  Acceptance criteria: NLT 98.0% of $C_9H_{18}O_2$ (sum of 2-methyl butyl, 3-methyl butyl, and *n*-pentyl isomers)

SPECIFIC TESTS
- **ACID VALUE, FLAVOR CHEMICALS (OTHER THAN ESSENTIAL OILS),** *M-15*, Appendix XI
  Acceptance criteria: NMT 1.0
- **REFRACTIVE INDEX,** Appendix II: At 20°
  Acceptance criteria: Between 1.409 and 1.414
- **SPECIFIC GRAVITY:** Determine at 25° by any reliable method (see *General Provisions*).
  Acceptance criteria: Between 0.861 and 0.866

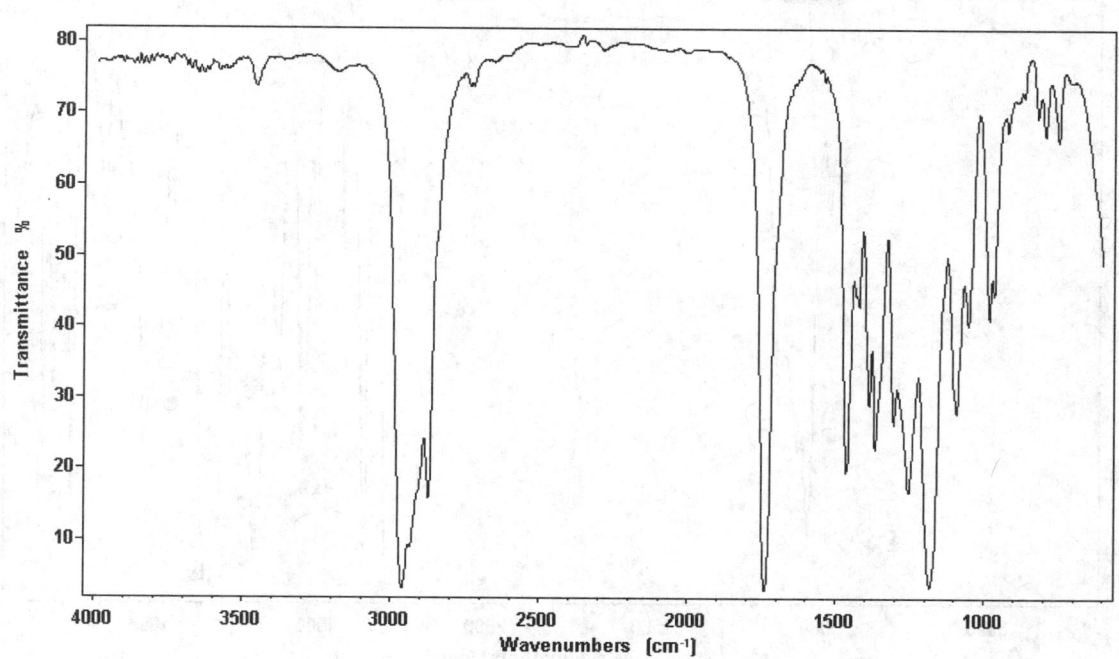

Isoamyl Butyrate

Change to read:

•Isoamyl• (ERR 1-Jan-2012) Cinnamate
First Published: Prior to FCC 6

Change to read:

Isoamyl Cinnamate
Isoamyl 3-Phenyl Propenate
•

• (ERR 1-Jan-2012)

$C_{14}H_{18}O_2$ Formula wt 218.28
FEMA: 2063
UNII: AB60R20S7J [isoamyl cinnamate]

DESCRIPTION

Change to read:

•Isoamyl• (ERR 1-Jan-2012) Cinnamate occurs as a colorless to pale yellow liquid.
Odor: Faint, balsamic, cocoa
Solubility: Soluble in most fixed oils; slightly soluble in propylene glycol; insoluble or practically insoluble in glycerin

Boiling Point: ~310°
Solubility in Alcohol, Appendix VI: One mL dissolves in 7 mL of 80% alcohol, and may be opalescent.
Function: Flavoring agent

IDENTIFICATION

Change to read:

- **INFRARED SPECTRA,** *Spectrophotometric Identification Tests,* Appendix IIIC
  Acceptance criteria: The spectrum of the sample exhibits relative maxima at the same wavelengths as those of the spectrum below.

ASSAY

- **PROCEDURE:** Proceed as directed under *M-1b,* Appendix XI.
  Acceptance criteria: NLT 96.0% of $C_{14}H_{18}O_2$ (sum of n-, 2-methyl butyl, and 3-methyl butyl isomers)

SPECIFIC TESTS

- **ACID VALUE, FLAVOR CHEMICALS (OTHER THAN ESSENTIAL OILS),** *M-15,* Appendix XI
  Acceptance criteria: NMT 1.0
- **REFRACTIVE INDEX,** Appendix II: At 20°
  Acceptance criteria: Between 1.535 and 1.539
- **SPECIFIC GRAVITY:** Determine at 25° by any reliable method (see *General Provisions*).
  Acceptance criteria: Between 0.992 and 0.997

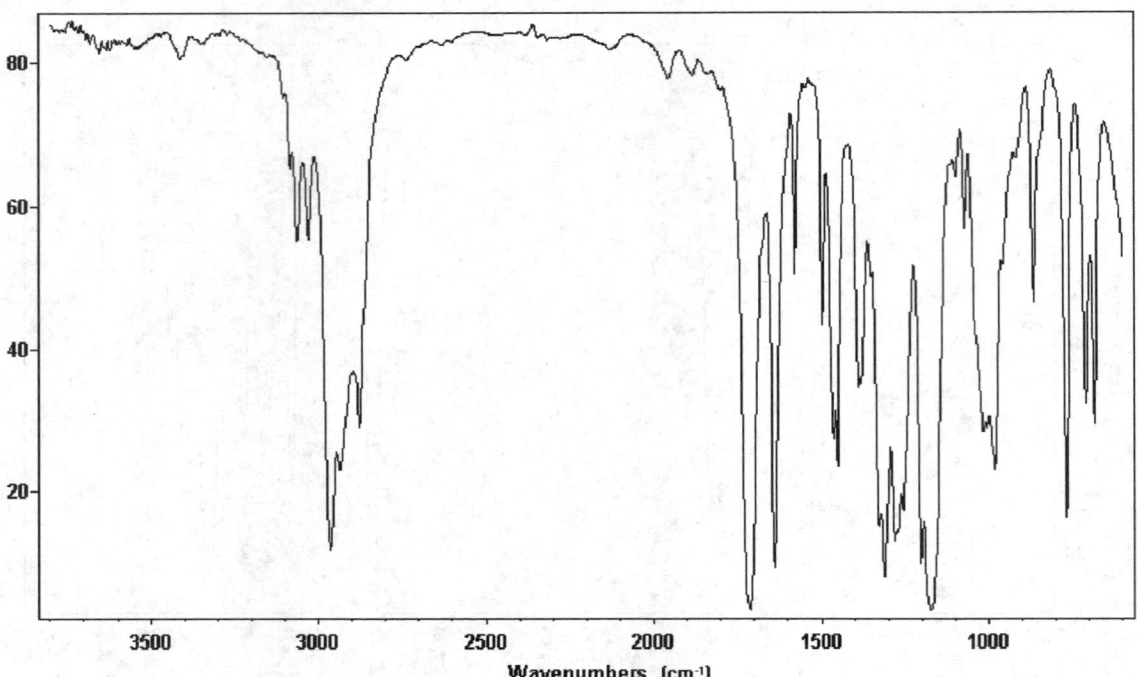

•Isoamyl• (ERR 1-Jan-2012) Cinnamate

Isoamyl Formate

First Published: Prior to FCC 6

Amyl Formate

C₆H₁₂O₂   Formula wt 116.16
FEMA: 2069
UNII: 50L53EN043 [isoamyl formate]

DESCRIPTION
Isoamyl Formate occurs as a colorless liquid.
Odor: Plum
Solubility: Soluble in alcohol, most fixed oils, propylene glycol; slightly soluble in water; insoluble or practically insoluble in glycerin
Boiling Point: ~124°
Solubility in Alcohol, Appendix VI: One mL dissolves in 4 mL of 60% alcohol and remains in solution on dilution to 10 mL.

Function: Flavoring agent

IDENTIFICATION
- **INFRARED SPECTRA,** *Spectrophotometric Identification Tests,* Appendix IIIC
  Acceptance criteria: The spectrum of the sample exhibits relative maxima at the same wavelengths as those of the spectrum below.

ASSAY
- **PROCEDURE:** Proceed as directed under *M-1b,* Appendix XI.
  Acceptance criteria: NLT 92.0% of C₆H₁₂O₂ (sum of 2-methyl butyl, 3-methyl butyl, and *n*-pentyl isomers)

SPECIFIC TESTS
- **ACID VALUE, FLAVOR CHEMICALS (OTHER THAN ESSENTIAL OILS),** *M-15,* Appendix XI
  Acceptance criteria: NMT 3.0
- **REFRACTIVE INDEX,** Appendix II: At 20°
  Acceptance criteria: Between 1.396 and 1.400
- **SPECIFIC GRAVITY:** Determine at 25° by any reliable method (see *General Provisions*).
  Acceptance criteria: Between 0.881 and 0.889

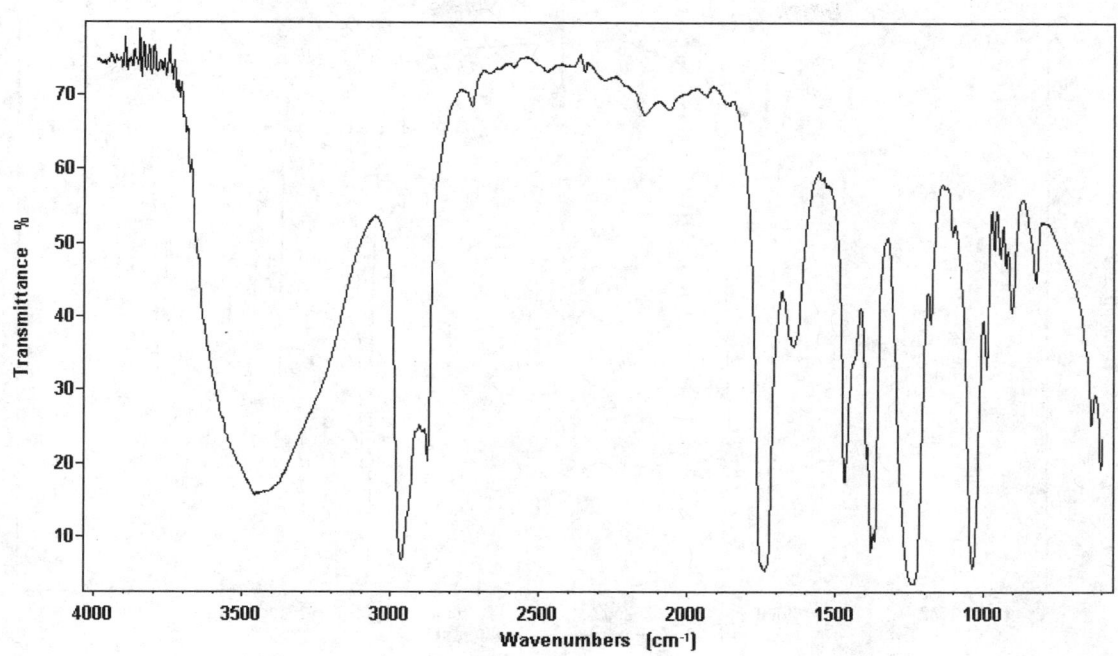

Isoamyl Formate

Isoamyl Hexanoate

First Published: Prior to FCC 6

Amyl Hexanoate
Isoamyl Caproate
Pentyl Hexanoate

$C_{11}H_{22}O_2$ Formula wt 186.29
FEMA: 2075
UNII: 694171CHWH [isoamyl hexanoate]

DESCRIPTION
Isoamyl Hexanoate occurs as a colorless liquid.
Odor: Fruity
Solubility: Soluble in alcohol, most fixed oils; insoluble or practically insoluble in glycerin, propylene glycol, water
Boiling Point: ~222°
Solubility in Alcohol, Appendix VI: One mL dissolves in 3 mL of 80% alcohol to give a clear solution.

Function: Flavoring agent

IDENTIFICATION
- **INFRARED SPECTRA,** *Spectrophotometric Identification Tests,* Appendix IIIC
  Acceptance criteria: The spectrum of the sample exhibits relative maxima at the same wavelengths as those of the spectrum below.

ASSAY
- **PROCEDURE:** Proceed as directed under *M-1b,* Appendix XI.
  Acceptance criteria: NLT 98.0% of $C_{11}H_{22}O_2$ (sum of 2-methyl butyl, 3-methyl butyl, and *n*-pentyl isomers)

SPECIFIC TESTS
- **ACID VALUE, FLAVOR CHEMICALS (OTHER THAN ESSENTIAL OILS),** *M-15,* Appendix XI
  Acceptance criteria: NMT 1.0
- **REFRACTIVE INDEX,** Appendix II: At 20°
  Acceptance criteria: Between 1.418 and 1.422
- **SPECIFIC GRAVITY:** Determine at 25° by any reliable method (see *General Provisions*).
  Acceptance criteria: Between 0.858 and 0.863

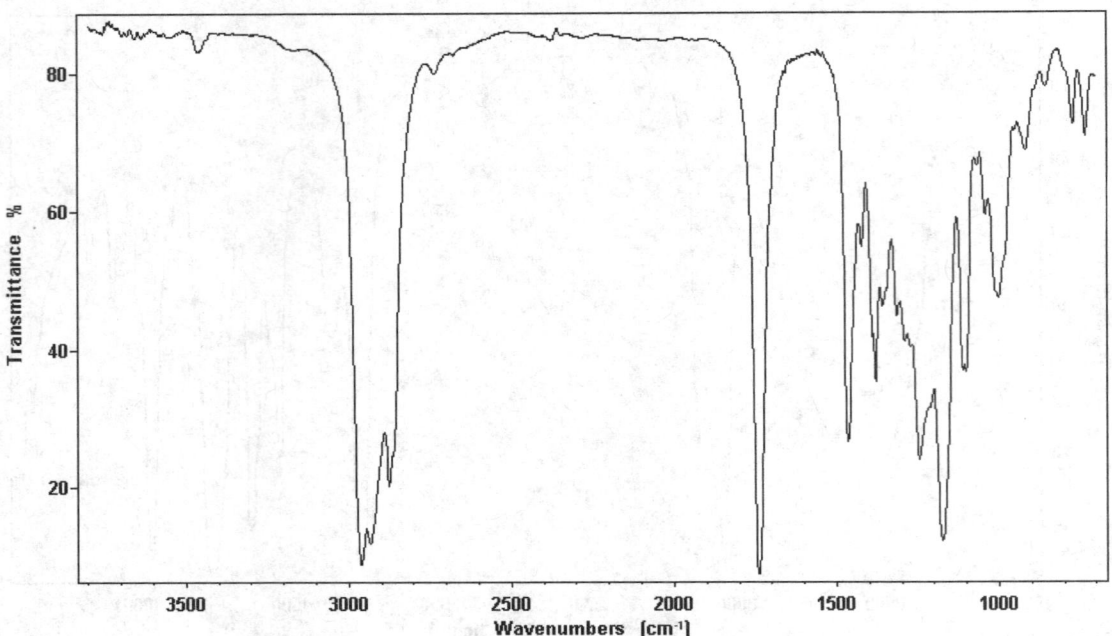

Isoamyl Hexanoate

Isoamyl Isobutyrate
First Published: Prior to FCC 6

C₉H₁₈O₂ Formula wt 158.24
FEMA: 3507
UNII: RF0ZT103EG [isoamyl isobutyrate]

DESCRIPTION
Isoamyl Isobutyrate occurs as a colorless to pale yellow liquid.
Odor: Fruity
Solubility: Soluble in propylene glycol, vegetable oils; insoluble or practically insoluble in water
Boiling Point: ~169°
Solubility in Alcohol, Appendix VI: One mL dissolves in 1 mL of 95% ethanol.

Function: Flavoring agent

IDENTIFICATION
- **INFRARED SPECTRA,** *Spectrophotometric Identification Tests,* Appendix IIIC
  Acceptance criteria: The spectrum of the sample exhibits relative maxima at the same wavelengths as those of the spectrum below.

ASSAY
- **PROCEDURE:** Proceed as directed under *M-1b,* Appendix XI.
  Acceptance criteria: NLT 98.0% of C₉H₁₈O₂

SPECIFIC TESTS
- **ACID VALUE, FLAVOR CHEMICALS (OTHER THAN ESSENTIAL OILS),** *M-15,* Appendix XI
  Acceptance criteria: NMT 1.0
- **REFRACTIVE INDEX,** Appendix II: At 20°
  Acceptance criteria: Between 1.404 and 1.410
- **SPECIFIC GRAVITY:** Determine at 25° by any reliable method (see *General Provisions*).
  Acceptance criteria: Between 0.853 and 0.859

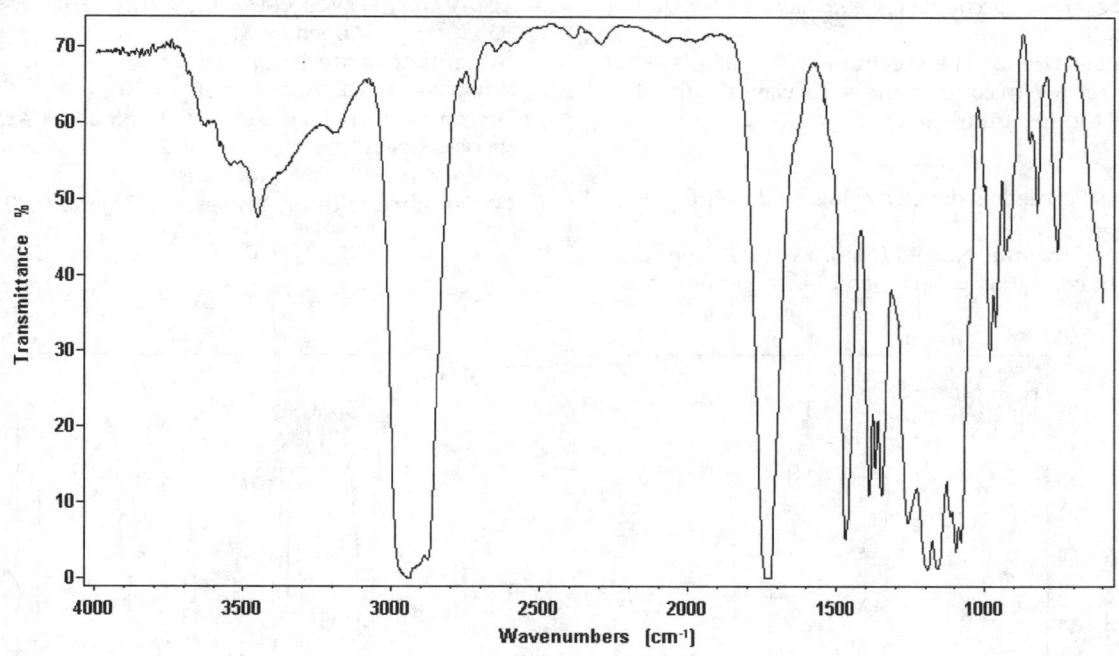

Isoamyl Isobutyrate

Isoamyl Isovalerate

First Published: Prior to FCC 6

Amyl Valerate
Amyl Isovalerate

$C_{10}H_{20}O_2$ Formula wt 172.27
FEMA: 2085
UNII: 16M1VA1FJY [isoamyl isovalerate]

DESCRIPTION
Isoamyl Isovalerate occurs as a colorless liquid.
Odor: Fruity, apple
Solubility: Slightly soluble in propylene glycol; miscible in alcohol, most fixed oils; insoluble or practically insoluble in water
Boiling Point: ~192°
Solubility in Alcohol, Appendix VI: One mL dissolves in 6 mL of 70% alcohol.
Function: Flavoring agent

ASSAY
- **Procedure:** Proceed as directed under *M-1b,* Appendix XI.
  Acceptance criteria: NLT 98.0% of $C_{10}H_{20}O_2$ (sum of 2-methyl butyl, 3-methyl butyl, and *n*-pentyl isomers)

SPECIFIC TESTS
- **Acid Value, Flavor Chemicals (Other Than Essential Oils),** *M-15,* Appendix XI
  Acceptance criteria: NMT 2.0
- **Refractive Index,** Appendix II: At 20°
  Acceptance criteria: Between 1.411 and 1.414
- **Specific Gravity:** Determine at 25° by any reliable method (see *General Provisions*).
  Acceptance criteria: Between 0.851 and 0.857

Isoamyl Phenyl Acetate

First Published: Prior to FCC 6

$C_{13}H_{18}O_2$ Formula wt 206.29
FEMA: 2081
UNII: E5RHQ50DDC [isoamyl phenylacetate]

DESCRIPTION
Isoamyl Phenyl Acetate occurs as a colorless to pale yellow liquid.
Odor: Chocolate, honey
Boiling Point: ~268°
Solubility in Alcohol, Appendix VI: One mL dissolves in 1 mL of 95% alcohol.
Function: Flavoring agent

584 / Isoamyl Phenyl Acetate / Monographs

IDENTIFICATION
- **INFRARED SPECTRA,** *Spectrophotometric Identification Tests,* Appendix IIIC
  Acceptance criteria: The spectrum of the sample exhibits relative maxima at the same wavelengths as those of the spectrum below.

ASSAY
- **PROCEDURE:** Proceed as directed under *M-1b,* Appendix XI.
  Acceptance criteria: NLT 98.0% of $C_{13}H_{18}O_2$ (sum of 2-methyl butyl, 3-methyl butyl, and *n*-pentyl isomers)

SPECIFIC TESTS
- **ACID VALUE, FLAVOR CHEMICALS (OTHER THAN ESSENTIAL OILS),** *M-15,* Appendix XI
  Acceptance criteria: NMT 1.0
- **REFRACTIVE INDEX,** Appendix II: At 20°
  Acceptance criteria: Between 1.485 and 1.490
- **SPECIFIC GRAVITY:** Determine at 25° by any reliable method (see *General Provisions*).
  Acceptance criteria: Between 0.975 and 0.981

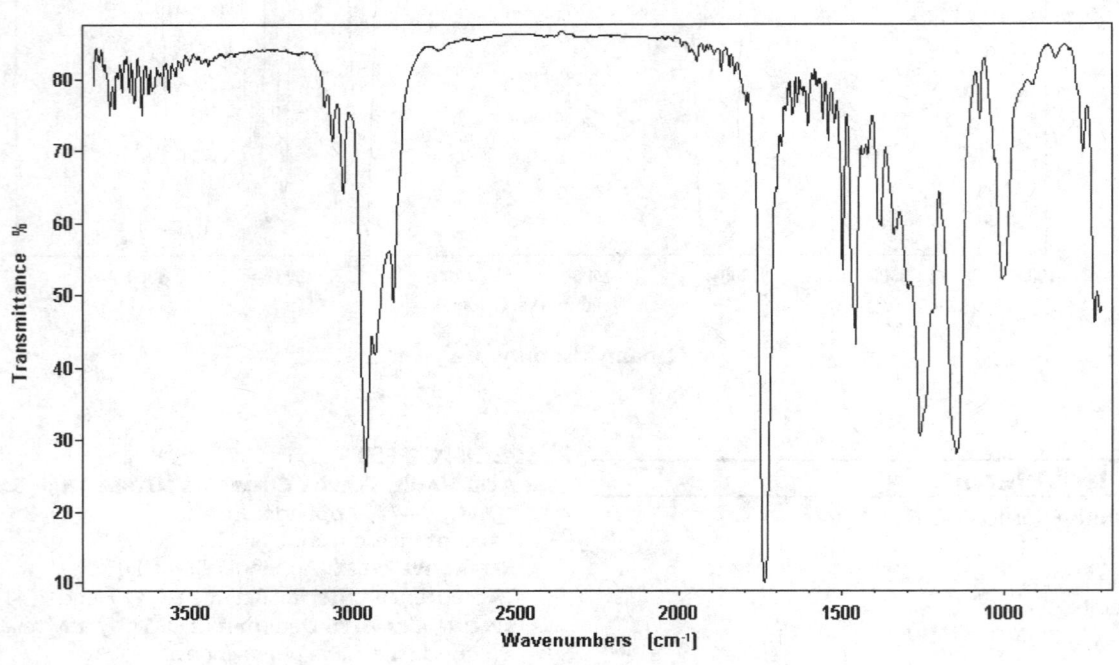

Isoamyl Phenyl Acetate

Isoamyl Salicylate

First Published: Prior to FCC 6

Amyl Salicylate

$C_{12}H_{16}O_3$ Formula wt 208.26
FEMA: 2084
UNII: M25E4ZMR0N [isoamyl salicylate]

DESCRIPTION
Isoamyl Salicylate occurs as a colorless liquid.
Odor: Floral
Solubility: Miscible in alcohol, chloroform, ether, most fixed oils; insoluble or practically insoluble in glycerin, propylene glycol, water
Boiling Point: ~277°
Solubility in Alcohol, Appendix VI: One mL dissolves in 3 mL of 90% alcohol and remains in solution on dilution.
Function: Flavoring agent

IDENTIFICATION
- **INFRARED SPECTRA,** *Spectrophotometric Identification Tests,* Appendix IIIC
  Acceptance criteria: The spectrum of the sample exhibits relative maxima at the same wavelengths as those of the spectrum below.

ASSAY
- **PROCEDURE:** Proceed as directed under *M-1b,* Appendix XI.
  Acceptance criteria: NLT 98.0% of $C_{12}H_{16}O_3$ (sum of 2-methyl butyl, 3-methyl butyl, and *n*-pentyl isomers)

SPECIFIC TESTS
- **ACID VALUE, FLAVOR CHEMICALS (OTHER THAN ESSENTIAL OILS),** *M-15,* Appendix XI: Use phenol red TS as the indicator.
  Acceptance criteria: NMT 1.0
- **REFRACTIVE INDEX,** Appendix II: At 20°
  Acceptance criteria: Between 1.505 and 1.509
- **SPECIFIC GRAVITY:** Determine at 25° by any reliable method (see *General Provisions*).
  Acceptance criteria: Between 1.047 and 1.053

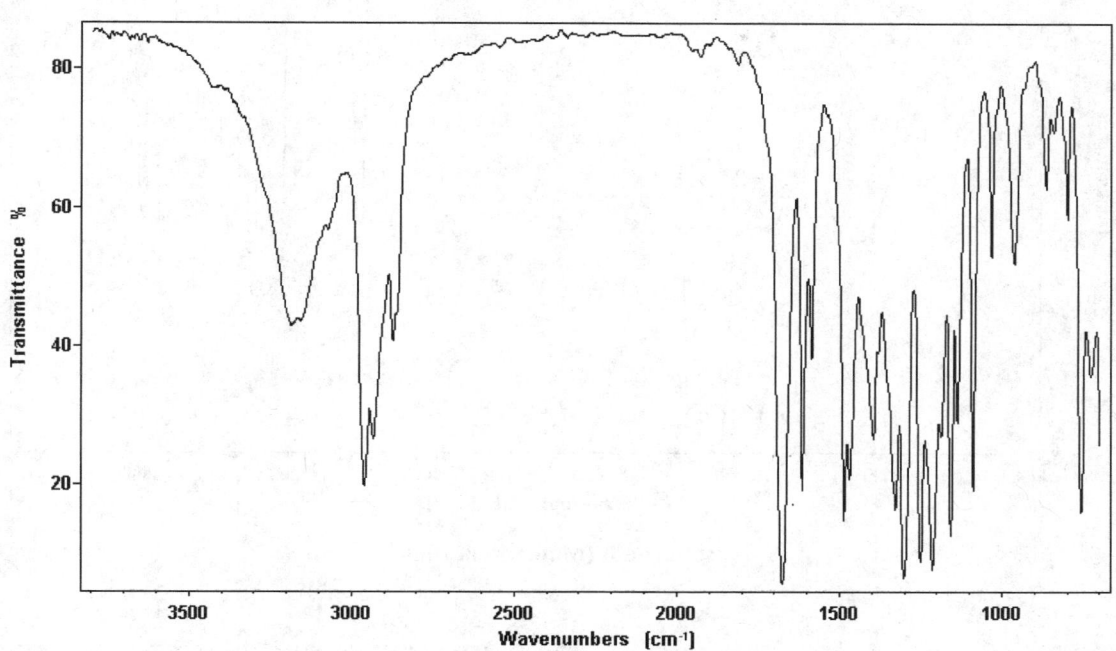

Isoamyl Salicylate

Isoborneol
First Published: Prior to FCC 6

$C_{10}H_{18}O$ Formula wt 154.25
FEMA: 2158
UNII: L88RA8N5EG [isoborneol]

DESCRIPTION
Isoborneol occurs as a white crystalline solid.
Odor: Piney, camphoraceous
Solubility: Slightly soluble in propylene glycol; insoluble or practically insoluble in vegetable oils

Boiling Point: ~214°
Solubility in Alcohol, Appendix VI: One g dissolves in 1 mL of 95% alcohol.
Function: Flavoring agent

IDENTIFICATION
- **INFRARED SPECTRA,** *Spectrophotometric Identification Tests,* Appendix IIIC
  Sample preparation: Mineral oil mull
  Acceptance criteria: The spectrum of the sample exhibits relative maxima at the same wavelengths as those of the spectrum below.

OTHER REQUIREMENTS
- **MELTING RANGE OR TEMPERATURE DETERMINATION,** Appendix IIB
  Acceptance criteria: Between 212° and 214°

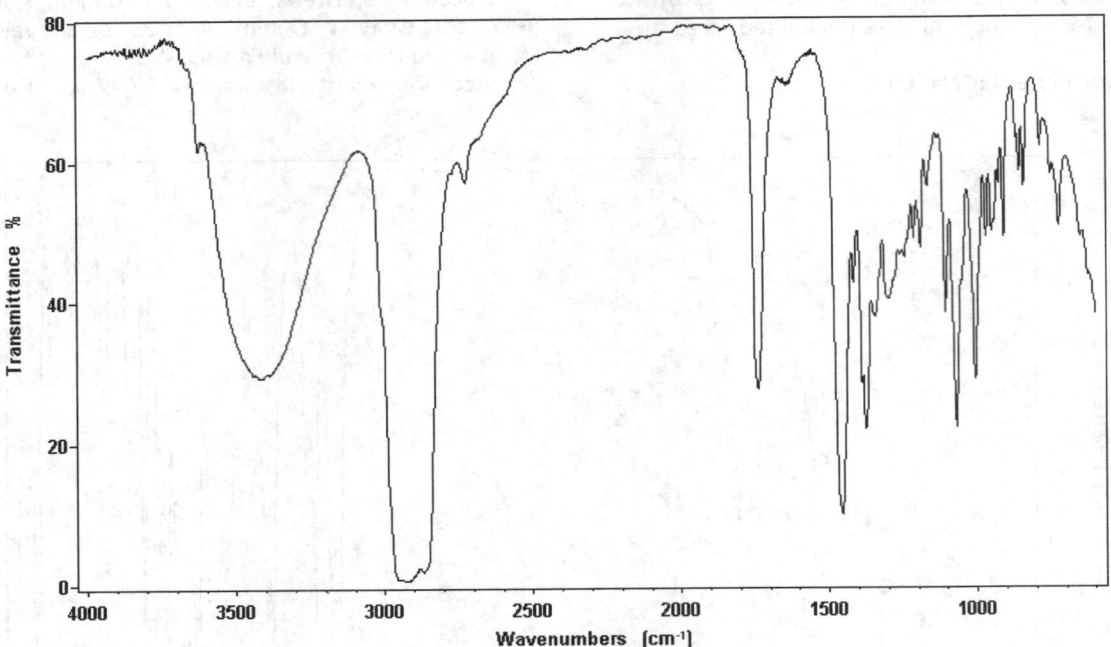

Isoborneol (Mineral Oil Mull)

Isobornyl Acetate

First Published: Prior to FCC 6

$C_{12}H_{20}O_2$ Formula wt 196.29
FEMA: 2160
UNII: 54T6CCU09Z [isobornyl acetate]

DESCRIPTION
Isobornyl Acetate occurs as a colorless liquid when fresh. It yellows upon storage.
Odor: Camphoraceous, piney, balsamic
Solubility: Soluble in alcohol, most fixed oils; slightly soluble in propylene glycol; insoluble or practically insoluble in glycerin, water
Boiling Point: ~227°
Solubility in Alcohol, Appendix VI: One mL dissolves in 3 mL of 70% alcohol.
Function: Flavoring agent

IDENTIFICATION
- **INFRARED SPECTRA,** *Spectrophotometric Identification Tests,* Appendix IIIC

  Acceptance criteria: The spectrum of the sample exhibits relative maxima at the same wavelengths as those of the spectrum below.

ASSAY
- **PROCEDURE:** Proceed as directed under *M-1b,* Appendix XI.
  Acceptance criteria: NLT 97.0% of $C_{12}H_{20}O_2$

SPECIFIC TESTS
- **ACID VALUE, FLAVOR CHEMICALS (OTHER THAN ESSENTIAL OILS),** *M-15,* Appendix XI
  Acceptance criteria: NMT 1.0
- **REFRACTIVE INDEX,** Appendix II: At 20°
  Acceptance criteria: Between 1.462 and 1.465
- **SPECIFIC GRAVITY:** Determine at 25° by any reliable method (see *General Provisions*).
  Acceptance criteria: Between 0.979 and 0.984

OTHER REQUIREMENTS
- **ANGULAR ROTATION,** *Optical (Specific) Rotation,* Appendix IIB: Use a 100-mm tube.
  Acceptance criteria: Between −4° and 0°

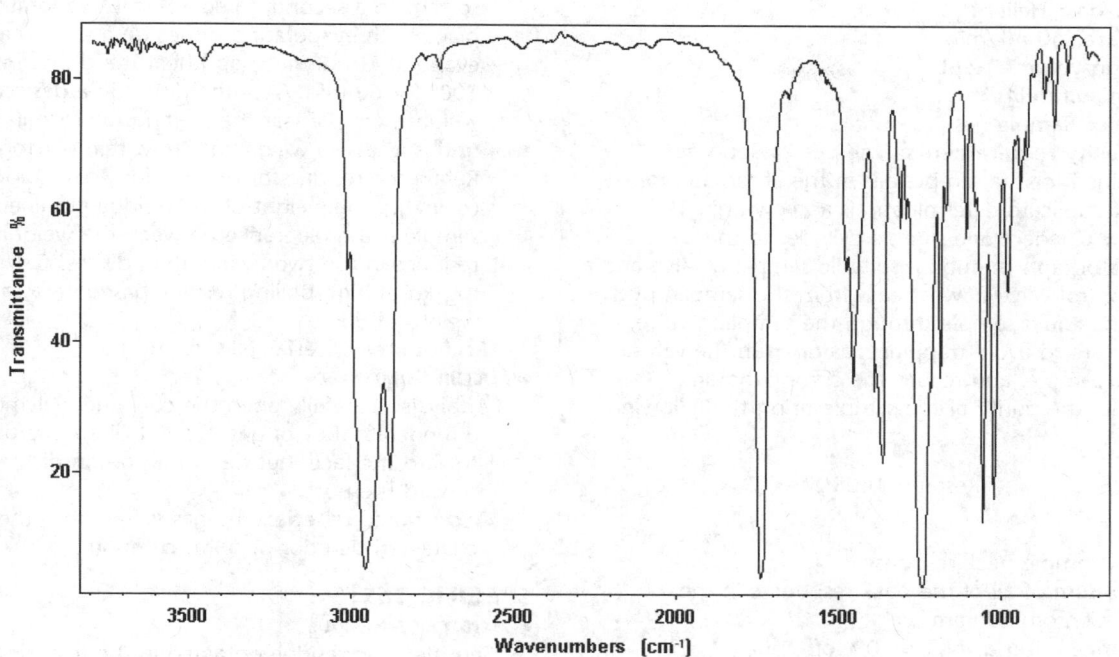

Isobornyl Acetate

Isobutane

First Published: Prior to FCC 6
Last Revision: FCC 6

C_4H_{10}
INS: 943b
UNII: BXR49TP611 [isobutane]
Formula wt 58.12
CAS: [75-28-5]

DESCRIPTION
Isobutane occurs as a colorless, flammable gas. Its boiling temperature is about −11°.
Function: Propellant; aerating agent
Packaging and Storage: Store in tight cylinders protected from excessive heat.
[CAUTION—Isobutane is highly flammable and explosive. Perform sampling and analytical operations in a well-ventilated fume hood.]
[NOTE—For obtaining a test sample of gas, use a stainless steel specimen cylinder equipped with a stainless steel valve and having a capacity of not less than 200 mL and a pressure rating of 240 psi or more. Dry the cylinder with the valve open at 110° for 2 h, and evacuate the hot cylinder to less than 1 mm Hg. Close the valve, and cool and weigh the cylinder. Tightly connect one end of a charging line to the sample cylinder, and loosely connect the other end to the specimen cylinder. Carefully open the sample cylinder, and allow the sample gas to flush out the charging line through the loose connection. Avoid excessive flushing that causes moisture to freeze in the charging line and connections. Tighten the fitting on the specimen cylinder, and open its valve, allowing the sample gas to flow into the evacuated cylinder. Continue until the desired amount of sample gas is obtained, then close the sample cylinder valve, and finally, close the specimen cylinder valve. Weigh the charged specimen cylinder again, and calculate the sample gas weight.]
[CAUTION—Do not overload the specimen cylinder.]

IDENTIFICATION
- **INFRARED ABSORPTION SPECTRUM**
  Acceptance criteria: The spectrum of a sample exhibits absorptions, among others, at approximately 3.4 μm (vs), 6.8 μm (s), 7.2 μm (m), and 10.9 μm (m).
- **VAPOR PRESSURE**
  Analysis: Determine the vapor pressure of the sample gas at 21° by means of a suitable pressure gauge. (See Note above on sampling.)
  Acceptance criteria: 1600 mm Hg (17 psi)

ASSAY
- **PROCEDURE**
  Chromatographic system, Appendix IIA
  Mode: Gas chromatography
  Detector: Thermal conductivity
  Column: 6-m × 3-mm (id) aluminum column, or equivalent, packed with 10 weight percent tetra ethylene glycol dimethyl ether liquid phase, on a support of crushed firebrick (GasChrom R, or equivalent), which has been calcined or burned with a clay binder above 900° and silanized, or equivalent

Column temperature: 33°
Carrier gas: Helium
Flow rate: 50 mL/min
Injection volume: 2 µL
System suitability
  Sample: Sample gas
  Suitability requirements: The peak responses obtained for the sample gas in the chromatograms from duplicate determinations agree within 1%.
Analysis: Connect one sample cylinder to the chromatograph through a suitable sampling valve and a flow control valve downstream from the sampling valve. Flush the liquid sample through the sampling valve, taking care to avoid trapping gas or air in the valve. Inject a sample, and record the chromatogram. Calculate the purity of the sample using the following formula:

$$\text{Result} = 100S/\Sigma s$$

S = sample peak response
Σs = sum of all of the peak responses in the chromatogram

Acceptance criteria: NLT 95.0% of C_4H_{10}

IMPURITIES
Inorganic Impurities
- **WATER,** *Water Determination,* Appendix IIB
  Sample: 100 g (see *Note* above on sampling)
  Analysis: Proceed as directed using the following modifications: (a) Provide the closed-system titrating vessel with an opening, and pass through it a coarse-porosity gas dispersion tube connected to a sampling cylinder. (b) Dilute the reagent with anhydrous methanol to give a water equivalence factor of between 0.2 and 1.0 mg/mL; age this diluted solution for at least 16 h before standardization. (c) Introduce the gas *Sample* into the titration vessel through the gas dispersion tube at a rate of about 100 mL/min; if necessary, heat the sampling cylinder gently to maintain this flow rate.
  Acceptance criteria: NMT 10 mg/kg

Organic Impurities
- **HIGH-BOILING RESIDUE**
  Analysis: Prepare a cooling coil from copper tubing (about 6.1 m × 6 mm (od)) to fit into a suitable vacuum-jacketed flask. Immerse the cooling coil in a mixture of Dry Ice and acetone in a vacuum-jacketed flask, and connect one end of the tubing to the sample cylinder (see *Note* above on sampling). Carefully open the sample cylinder valve, flush the cooling coil with about 50 mL of the liquified sample, and discard this portion of liquid. Continue delivering liquid from the cooling coil, and collect it in a previously chilled 1000-mL sedimentation cone until the cone is filled to the 1000-mL mark (approximately 600 g). Using a warm water bath maintained at about 40° to reduce evaporating time, allow the liquid to evaporate. When all of the liquid has evaporated, rinse the sedimentation cone with two 50-mL portions of pentane, and combine the rinsings in a tared 150-mL evaporating dish. Transfer 100 mL of the pentane solvent to a second, tared 150-mL evaporating dish, place both evaporating dishes on a water bath, evaporate to dryness, and heat the dishes in an oven at 100° for 60 min. Cool the dishes in a desiccator, and weigh them. Repeat the heating for 15-min periods until successive weighings are within 0.1 mg. [NOTE—Retain the residue for the test for *Acidity of Residue* (below).] The weight of the residue obtained from the sample is the difference between the weights of the residues in the two evaporating dishes. Calculate the mg/kg of high-boiling residue based on a sample weight of 600 g.
  Acceptance criteria: NMT 5 mg/kg

- **SULFUR COMPOUND**
  Analysis: Carefully open the container valve to produce a moderate flow of gas. Do not direct the gas stream toward the face, but deflect a portion of the stream toward the nose.
  Acceptance criteria: The gas is free from the characteristic odor of sulfur compounds.

SPECIFIC TESTS
- **ACIDITY OF RESIDUE**
  Sample: The residue obtained in the test for *High-Boiling Residue* (above)
  Analysis: Add 10 mL of water to the *Sample*, mix by swirling for about 30 s, add 2 drops of methyl orange TS, insert the stopper in the tube, and shake the tube vigorously.
  Acceptance criteria: No pink or red color appears in the aqueous layer.

Isobutyl Acetate
First Published: Prior to FCC 6
Last Revision: FCC 7

$C_6H_{12}O_2$ Formula wt 116.16
FEMA: 2175
UNII: 7CR47FO6LF [isobutyl acetate]

DESCRIPTION
Isobutyl Acetate occurs as a colorless liquid.
Odor: Fruity, banana on dilution
Solubility: Soluble in alcohol, most fixed oils, propylene glycol; 1 mL dissolves in 180 mL of water.
Boiling Point: ~116°
Solubility in Alcohol, Appendix VI: One mL dissolves in 1 mL of 95% ethanol.
Function: Flavoring agent

IDENTIFICATION
- **INFRARED ABSORPTION,** *Spectrophotometric Identification Tests,* Appendix IIIC

Reference standard: USP Isobutyl Acetate RS
Sample and standard preparation: F
Acceptance criteria: The spectrum of the sample exhibits maxima at the same wavelengths as those in the spectrum of the Reference standard.

ASSAY
- **PROCEDURE:** Proceed as directed under M-1b, Appendix XI.
  Acceptance criteria: NLT 90.0% of $C_6H_{12}O_2$

SPECIFIC TESTS
- **ACID VALUE, FLAVOR CHEMICALS (OTHER THAN ESSENTIAL OILS)**, M-15, Appendix XI
  Acceptance criteria: NMT 1.0
- **REFRACTIVE INDEX**, Appendix II: At 20°
  Acceptance criteria: Between 1.389 and 1.392
- **SPECIFIC GRAVITY:** Determine at 25° by any reliable method (see General Provisions).
  Acceptance criteria: Between 0.862 and 0.871

Isobutyl Alcohol

First Published: Prior to FCC 6

$C_4H_{10}O$
FEMA: 2179

Formula wt 74.12

UNII: 56F9Z98TEM [isobutyl alcohol]

DESCRIPTION
Isobutyl Alcohol occurs as a colorless, mobile liquid.
Odor: Penetrating, winy
Solubility: Miscible in alcohol, ether; 1 mL dissolves in 140 mL water.
Boiling Point: ~108°
Function: Flavoring agent

IDENTIFICATION
- **INFRARED SPECTRA**, Spectrophotometric Identification Tests, Appendix IIIC
  Acceptance criteria: The spectrum of the sample exhibits relative maxima at the same wavelengths as those of the spectrum below.

ASSAY
- **PROCEDURE:** Proceed as directed under M-1a, Appendix XI.
  Acceptance criteria: NLT 98.0% of $C_4H_{10}O$

SPECIFIC TESTS
- **ACID VALUE, FLAVOR CHEMICALS (OTHER THAN ESSENTIAL OILS)**, M-15, Appendix XI
  Acceptance criteria: NMT 2.0
- **REFRACTIVE INDEX**, Appendix II: At 20°
  Acceptance criteria: Between 1.392 and 1.397
- **SPECIFIC GRAVITY:** Determine at 25° by any reliable method (see General Provisions).
  Acceptance criteria: Between 0.799 and 0.801

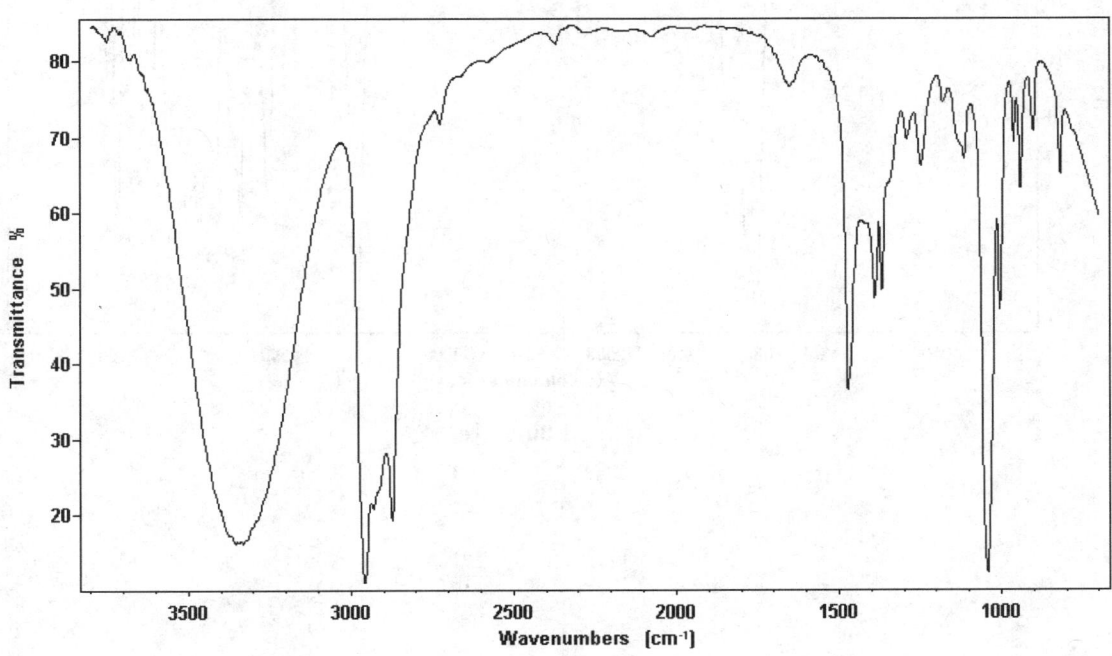

Isobutyl Alcohol

Isobutyl Butyrate

First Published: Prior to FCC 6

2-Methyl Propanyl Butyrate

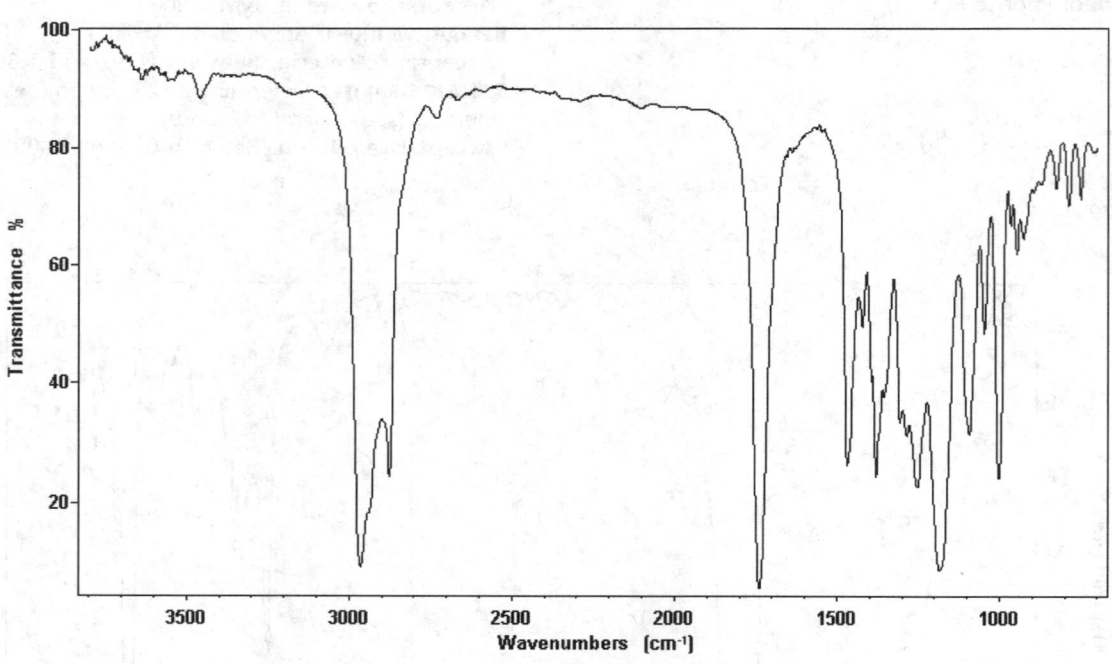

C₈H₁₆O₂
FEMA: 2187
UNII: 827NDQ0P0W [isobutyl butyrate]

Formula wt 144.21

DESCRIPTION
Isobutyl Butyrate occurs as a colorless liquid.
Odor: Sweet, fruity, apple, pineapple
Solubility: Soluble in alcohol, most fixed oils; slightly soluble in water; insoluble or practically insoluble in glycerin
Boiling Point: ~157°
Solubility in Alcohol, Appendix VI: One mL dissolves in 8 mL of 60% alcohol.

Function: Flavoring agent

IDENTIFICATION
- **INFRARED SPECTRA,** *Spectrophotometric Identification Tests,* Appendix IIIC
  Acceptance criteria: The spectrum of the sample exhibits relative maxima at the same wavelengths as those of the spectrum below.

ASSAY
- **PROCEDURE:** Proceed as directed under *M-1b,* Appendix XI.
  Acceptance criteria: NLT 98.0% of C₈H₁₆O₂

SPECIFIC TESTS
- **ACID VALUE, FLAVOR CHEMICALS (OTHER THAN ESSENTIAL OILS),** *M-15,* Appendix XI
  Acceptance criteria: NMT 1.0
- **REFRACTIVE INDEX,** Appendix II: At 20°
  Acceptance criteria: Between 1.402 and 1.405
- **SPECIFIC GRAVITY:** Determine at 25° by any reliable method (see *General Provisions*).
  Acceptance criteria: Between 0.858 and 0.863

Isobutyl Butyrate

Isobutyl Cinnamate

First Published: Prior to FCC 6

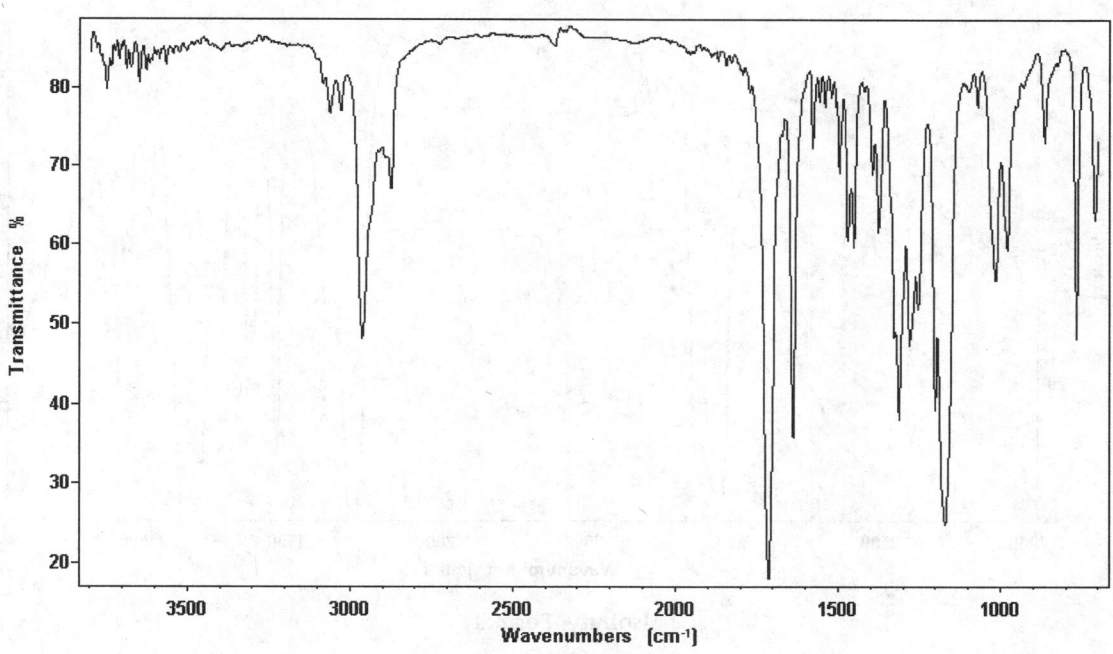

C₁₃H₁₆O₂
FEMA: 2193
UNII: 4NCI0MR7KP [isobutyl cinnamate]

Formula wt 204.27

DESCRIPTION
Isobutyl Cinnamate occurs as a colorless liquid.
Odor: Sweet, fruity, balsamic
Solubility: Miscible in alcohol, chloroform, ether, most fixed oils; insoluble or practically insoluble in water
Boiling Point: ~271°
Solubility in Alcohol, Appendix VI: One mL dissolves in 3 mL of 80% alcohol to give a clear solution.
Function: Flavoring agent

IDENTIFICATION
- **INFRARED SPECTRA,** *Spectrophotometric Identification Tests,* Appendix IIIC
  Acceptance criteria: The spectrum of the sample exhibits relative maxima at the same wavelengths as those of the spectrum below.

ASSAY
- **PROCEDURE:** Proceed as directed under *M-1b,* Appendix XI.
  Acceptance criteria: NLT 98.0% of $C_{13}H_{16}O_2$ (sum of two isomers)

SPECIFIC TESTS
- **ACID VALUE, FLAVOR CHEMICALS (OTHER THAN ESSENTIAL OILS),** *M-15,* Appendix XI
  Acceptance criteria: NMT 1.0
- **REFRACTIVE INDEX,** Appendix II: At 20°
  Acceptance criteria: Between 1.539 and 1.541
- **SPECIFIC GRAVITY:** Determine at 25° by any reliable method (see *General Provisions*).
  Acceptance criteria: Between 1.001 and 1.004

Isobutyl Cinnamate

Isobutyl Formate

First Published: Prior to FCC 6

$C_5H_{10}O_2$ Formula wt 102.13
FEMA: 2197
UNII: 6OCL1KXH0Q [isobutyl formate]

DESCRIPTION
Isobutyl Formate occurs as a colorless to pale yellow liquid.
Odor: Fruity
Solubility: Soluble in propylene glycol, vegetable oils; insoluble or practically insoluble in water
Boiling Point: ~98°
Solubility in Alcohol, Appendix VI: One mL dissolves in 1 mL of 95% ethanol.
Function: Flavoring agent

IDENTIFICATION
- **INFRARED SPECTRA,** *Spectrophotometric Identification Tests,* Appendix IIIC
  Acceptance criteria: The spectrum of the sample exhibits relative maxima at the same wavelengths as those of the spectrum below.

ASSAY
- **PROCEDURE:** Proceed as directed under *M-1b*, Appendix XI.
  Acceptance criteria: NLT 94.0% of $C_5H_{10}O_2$

SPECIFIC TESTS
- **ACID VALUE, FLAVOR CHEMICALS (OTHER THAN ESSENTIAL OILS),** *M-15,* Appendix XI
  [NOTE—Add ice to the solution.]
  Acceptance criteria: NMT 2.0

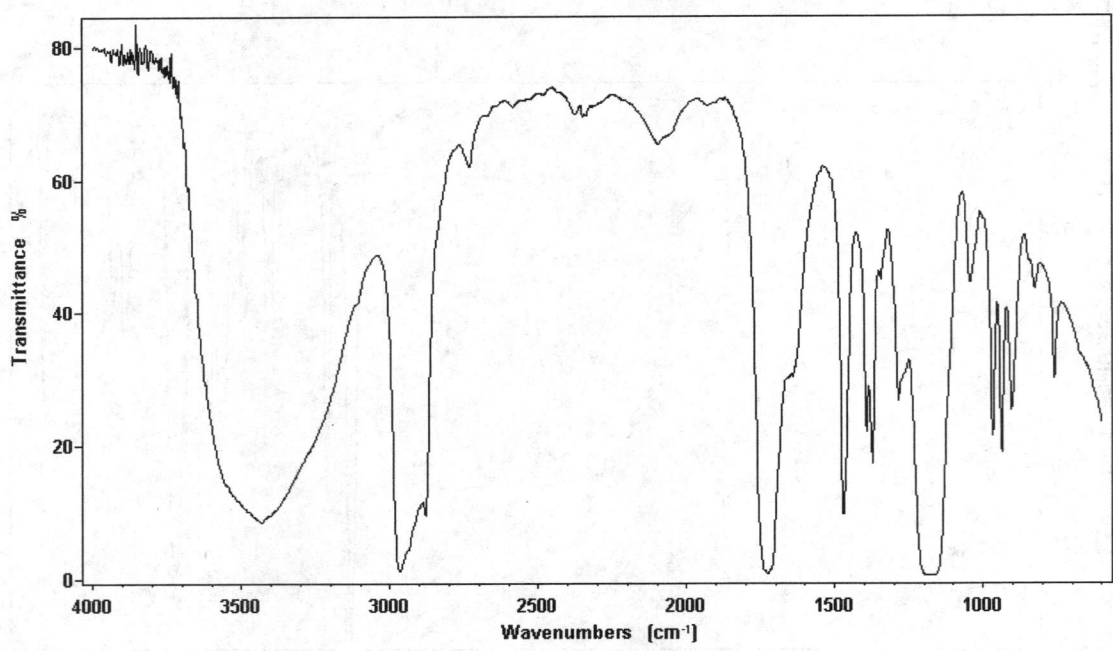

Isobutyl Formate

Isobutyl Hexanoate

First Published: Prior to FCC 6

$C_{10}H_{20}O_2$ Formula wt 172.27
FEMA: 2202
UNII: 2A3X4W9GZ0 [isobutyl hexanoate]

DESCRIPTION
Isobutyl Hexanoate occurs as a colorless to pale yellow liquid.
Odor: Fruity
Solubility: Soluble in propylene glycol, vegetable oils; insoluble or practically insoluble in water
Boiling Point: ~203°
Solubility in Alcohol, Appendix VI: One mL dissolves in 1 mL of 95% ethanol.
Function: Flavoring agent

IDENTIFICATION
- **INFRARED SPECTRA,** *Spectrophotometric Identification Tests,* Appendix IIIC
  Acceptance criteria: The spectrum of the sample exhibits relative maxima at the same wavelengths as those of the spectrum below.

ASSAY
- **PROCEDURE:** Proceed as directed under *M-1b,* Appendix XI.
  Acceptance criteria: NLT 98.0% of $C_{10}H_{20}O_2$

SPECIFIC TESTS
- **ACID VALUE, FLAVOR CHEMICALS (OTHER THAN ESSENTIAL OILS),** *M-15,* Appendix XI
  Acceptance criteria: NMT 1.0
- **REFRACTIVE INDEX,** Appendix II: At 20°
  Acceptance criteria: Between 1.411 and 1.417
- **SPECIFIC GRAVITY:** Determine at 25° by any reliable method (see *General Provisions*).
  Acceptance criteria: Between 0.853 and 0.859

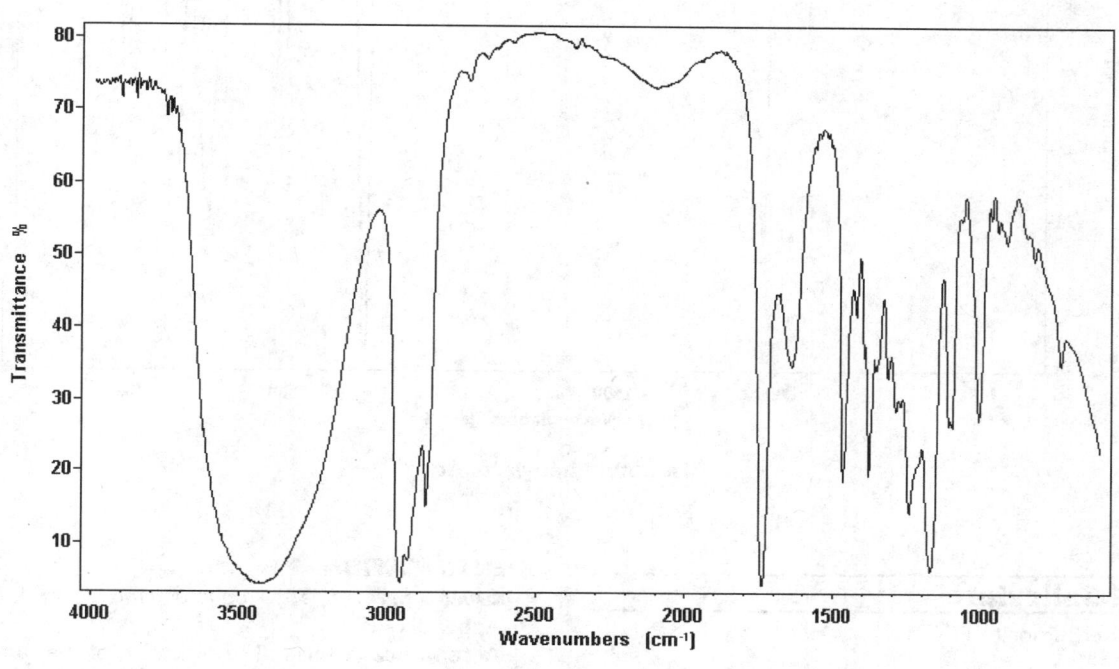

Isobutyl Hexanoate

Isobutyl Phenylacetate
First Published: Prior to FCC 6

$C_{12}H_{16}O_2$ Formula wt 192.26
FEMA: 2210
UNII: 2QK898564G [isobutyl phenylacetate]

DESCRIPTION
Isobutyl Phenylacetate occurs as a colorless liquid.
Odor: Rose, honey
Solubility: Soluble in alcohol, most fixed oils; insoluble or practically insoluble in glycerin, propylene glycol, water
Boiling Point: ~247°

Solubility in Alcohol, Appendix VI: One mL dissolves in 2 mL of 80% alcohol, and remains in solution on dilution to 10 mL.
Function: Flavoring agent

IDENTIFICATION
- **INFRARED SPECTRA,** *Spectrophotometric Identification Tests,* Appendix IIIC
  Acceptance criteria: The spectrum of the sample exhibits relative maxima at the same wavelengths as those of the spectrum below.

ASSAY
- **PROCEDURE:** Proceed as directed under *M-1b,* Appendix XI.
  Acceptance criteria: NLT 98.0% of $C_{12}H_{16}O_2$

SPECIFIC TESTS
- **ACID VALUE, FLAVOR CHEMICALS (OTHER THAN ESSENTIAL OILS),** *M-15,* Appendix XI
  Acceptance criteria: NMT 1.0

- **REFRACTIVE INDEX,** Appendix II: At 20°
  Acceptance criteria: Between 1.486 and 1.488
- **SPECIFIC GRAVITY:** Determine at 25° by any reliable method (see *General Provisions*).
  Acceptance criteria: Between 0.984 and 0.988

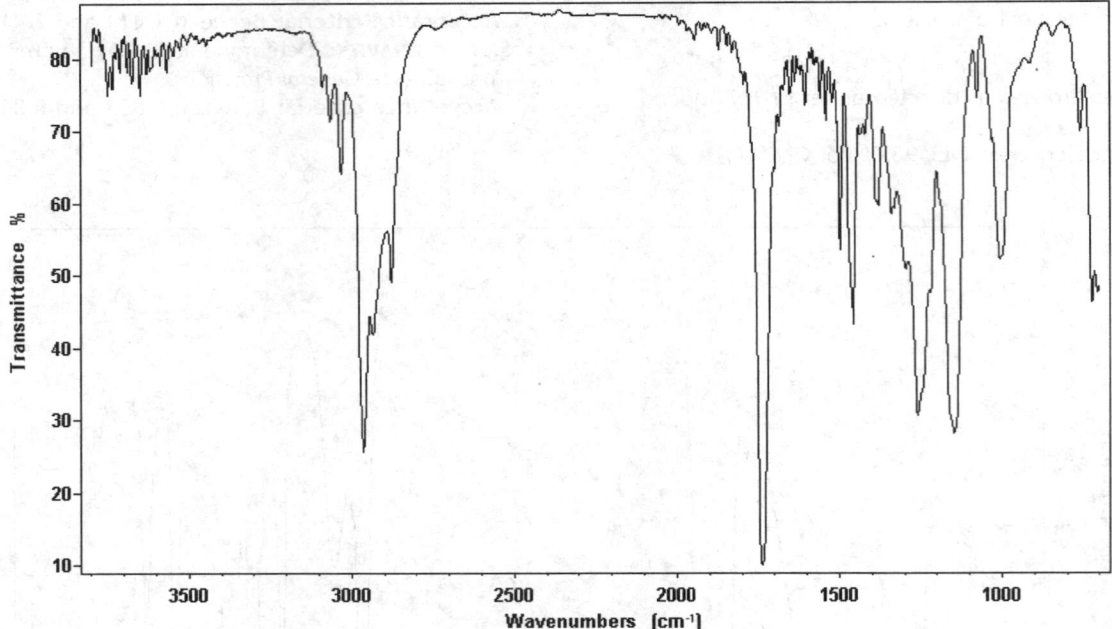

Isobutyl Phenylacetate

Isobutyl Salicylate

First Published: Prior to FCC 6

$C_{11}H_{14}O_3$
FEMA: 2213
UNII: S122C080GX [isobutyl salicylate]

Formula wt 194.23

DESCRIPTION
Isobutyl Salicylate occurs as a colorless liquid.
Odor: Orchid
Solubility: Soluble in most fixed oils; insoluble or practically insoluble in glycerin, propylene glycol
Boiling Point: ~260°
Solubility in Alcohol, Appendix VI: One mL dissolves in 9 mL of 80% alcohol, and remains in solution on dilution to 10 mL.
Function: Flavoring agent

IDENTIFICATION
- **INFRARED SPECTRA,** *Spectrophotometric Identification Tests,* Appendix IIIC
  Acceptance criteria: The spectrum of the sample exhibits relative maxima at the same wavelengths as those of the spectrum below.

ASSAY
- **PROCEDURE:** Proceed as directed under *M-1b,* Appendix XI.
  Acceptance criteria: NLT 98.0% of $C_{11}H_{14}O_3$

SPECIFIC TESTS
- **ACID VALUE, FLAVOR CHEMICALS (OTHER THAN ESSENTIAL OILS),** *M-15,* Appendix XI: Use phenol red TS as the indicator.
  Acceptance criteria: NMT 1.0
- **REFRACTIVE INDEX,** Appendix II: At 20°
  Acceptance criteria: Between 1.507 and 1.510
- **SPECIFIC GRAVITY:** Determine at 25° by any reliable method (see *General Provisions*).
  Acceptance criteria: Between 1.062 and 1.066

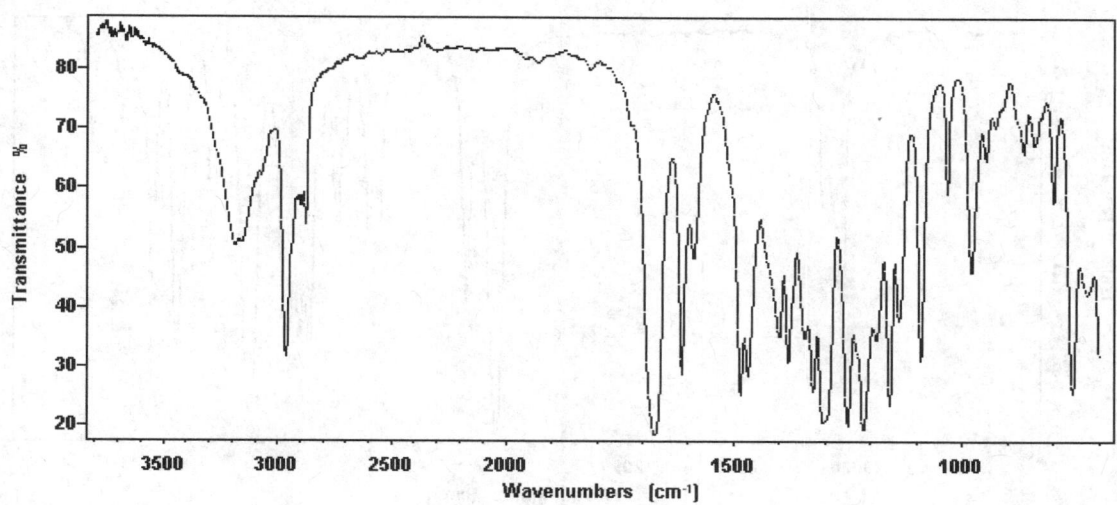

Isobutyl Salicylate

Isobutyl-2-butenoate
First Published: Prior to FCC 6

$C_8H_{14}O_2$ Formula wt 142.20
FEMA: 3432
UNII: 6H6IW50K3Z [isobutyl 2-butenoate]

DESCRIPTION
Isobutyl-2-butenoate occurs as a colorless liquid.
Odor: Powerful, fruity
Solubility: Soluble in alcohol, propylene glycol, most fixed oils; slightly soluble in water
Boiling Point: ~71°
Solubility in Alcohol, Appendix VI: One mL dissolves in 1 mL of 95% ethanol.

Function: Flavoring agent

IDENTIFICATION
- **INFRARED SPECTRA,** *Spectrophotometric Identification Tests,* Appendix IIIC
  Acceptance criteria: The spectrum of the sample exhibits relative maxima at the same wavelengths as those of the spectrum below.

ASSAY
- **PROCEDURE:** Proceed as directed under *M-1a,* Appendix XI.
  Acceptance criteria: NLT 95.0% of $C_8H_{14}O_2$

SPECIFIC TESTS
- **REFRACTIVE INDEX,** Appendix II: At 20°
  Acceptance criteria: Between 1.426 and 1.430
- **SPECIFIC GRAVITY:** Determine at 25° by any reliable method (see *General Provisions*).
  Acceptance criteria: Between 0.880 and 0.900

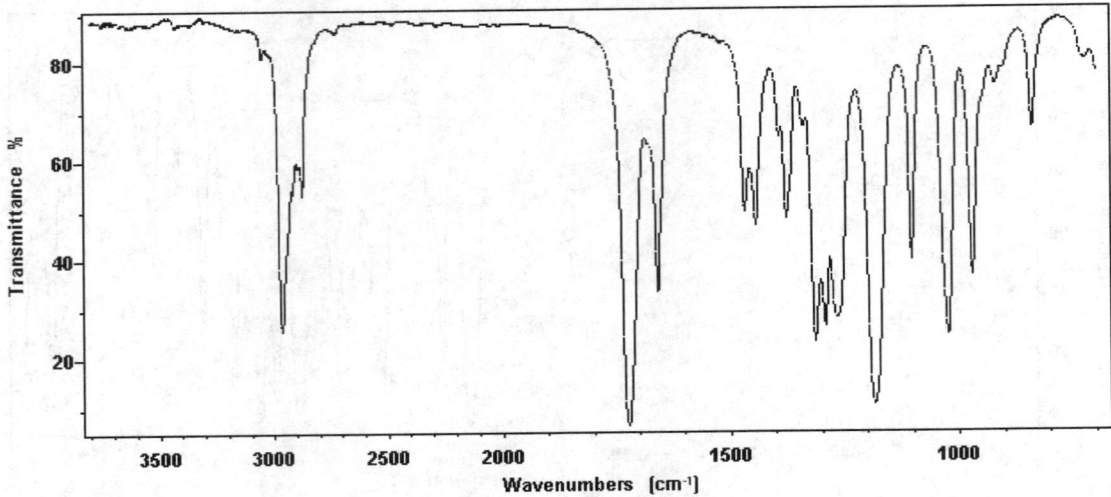

Isobutyl-2-butenoate

Isobutylene-Isoprene Copolymer
First Published: Prior to FCC 6

Butyl Rubber

CAS: [9010-85-9]

DESCRIPTION
Isobutylene–Isoprene Copolymer occurs as a synthetic copolymer containing from 0.5 to 3.0 molar percent of isoprene, the remainder consisting of isobutylene. It is prepared by copolymerization of isobutylene and isoprene in methyl chloride solution, using aluminum chloride as the catalyst. After completion of polymerization, the rubber particles are treated with hot water containing a suitable food-grade deagglomerating agent, such as stearic acid. Finally, the coagulum is dried to remove residual volatiles.
Function: Masticatory substance in chewing gum base
Packaging and Storage: Store in well-closed containers.

IDENTIFICATION
- **INFRARED SPECTRA,** *Spectrophotometric Identification Tests,* Appendix IIIC
  Sample preparation: Dissolve a sample in hot toluene and evaporate on a potassium bromide plate.
  Acceptance criteria: The spectrum of the *Sample preparation* exhibits relative maxima at the same wavelengths as those of the spectrum below.

IMPURITIES
Inorganic Impurities
- **LEAD,** *Sample Solution for Lead Limit Test,* Appendix IV
  Acceptance criteria: NMT 3 mg/kg

SPECIFIC TESTS
- **TOTAL UNSATURATION,** Appendix IV
  Acceptance criteria: NMT 3.0 molar percent, as isoprene

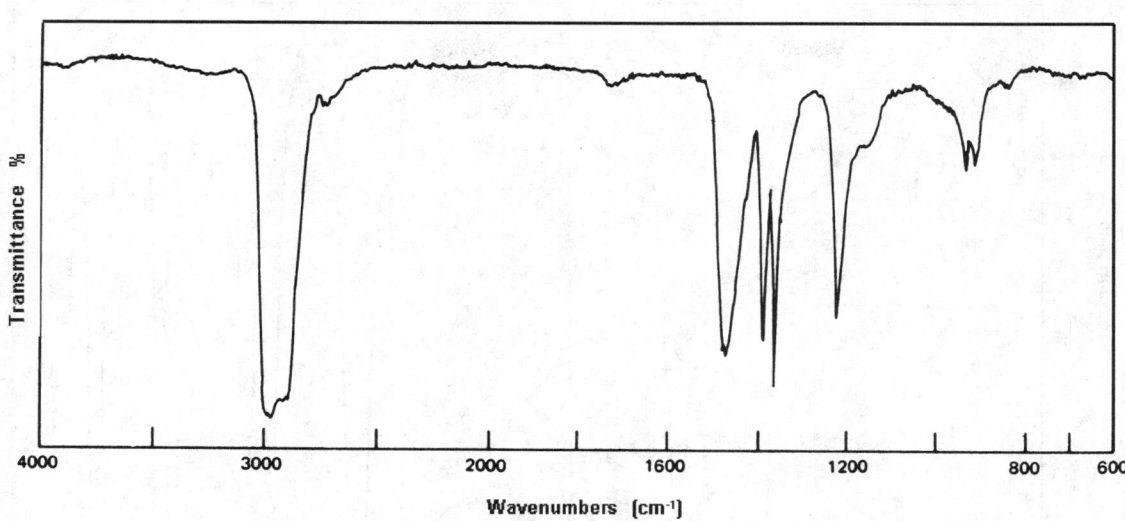

Isobutylene–Isoprene Copolymer

Isobutyraldehyde

First Published: Prior to FCC 6
Last Revision: First Supplement, FCC 6

C_4H_8O Formula wt 72.11
FEMA: 2220
UNII: C42E28168L [isobutyraldehyde]

DESCRIPTION
Isobutyraldehyde occurs as a colorless, mobile liquid. It may contain a suitable antioxidant.
Odor: Sharp, pungent
Solubility: Miscible in alcohol, ether; 1 mL dissolves in 125 mL of water.
Boiling Point: ~64°

Function: Flavoring agent

IDENTIFICATION
- **INFRARED SPECTRA, INFRARED SPECTRA,** *Spectrophotometric Identification Tests,* Appendix IIIC
  Acceptance criteria: The spectrum of the sample exhibits relative maxima at the same wavelengths as those of the spectrum below.

ASSAY
- **PROCEDURE:** Proceed as directed under *M-1b,* Appendix XI.
  Acceptance criteria: NLT 98.0% of C_4H_8O

SPECIFIC TESTS
- **ACID VALUE, FLAVOR CHEMICALS (OTHER THAN ESSENTIAL OILS),** *M-15,* Appendix XI
  [NOTE—Use methyl red TS as the indicator.]
  Acceptance criteria: NMT 5.0
- **SPECIFIC GRAVITY:** Determine at 25° by any reliable method (see *General Provisions*).
  Acceptance criteria: Between 0.783 and 0.788

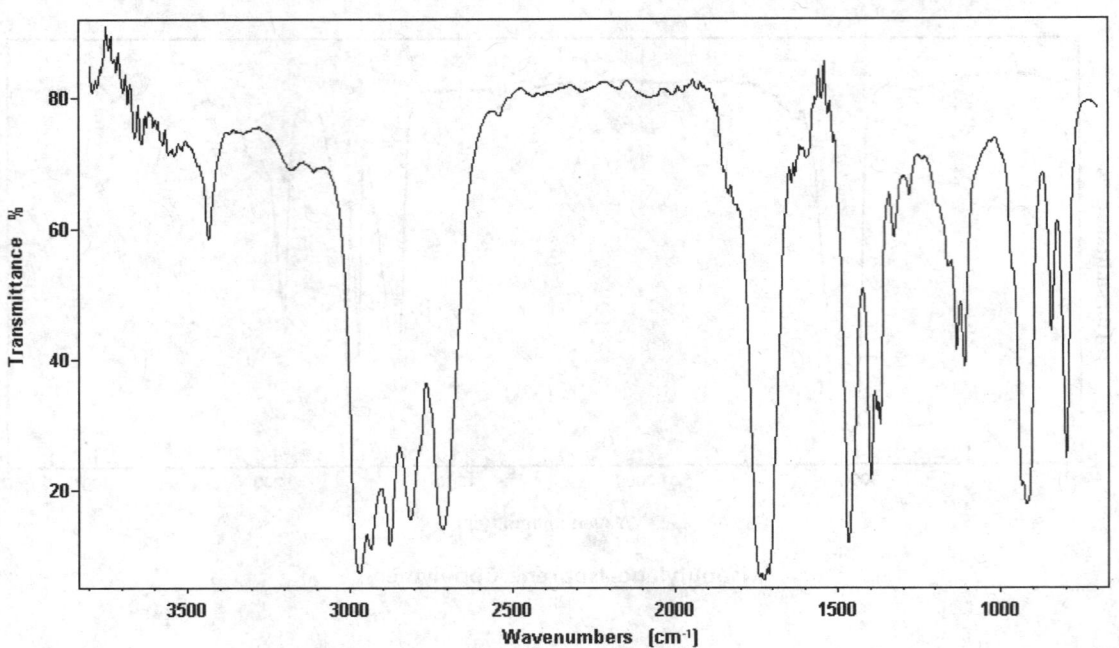

Isobutyraldehyde

Isobutyric Acid

First Published: Prior to FCC 6

2-Methyl Propanoic Acid
Isopropylformic Acid

$C_4H_8O_2$ Formula wt 88.11
FEMA: 2222
UNII: 8LL210O1U0 [isobutyric acid]

DESCRIPTION
Isobutyric Acid occurs as a colorless liquid.
Odor: Strong, penetrating odor of rancid butter
Solubility: Miscible in alcohol, most fixed oils, glycerin, propylene glycol; insoluble or practically insoluble in water
Boiling Point: ~155°
Function: Flavoring agent

IDENTIFICATION
- **INFRARED SPECTRA,** Spectrophotometric Identification Tests, Appendix IIIC

  Acceptance criteria: The spectrum of the sample exhibits relative maxima at the same wavelengths as those of the spectrum below.

ASSAY
- **PROCEDURE:** Proceed as directed under M-3a, Appendix XI.
  Acceptance criteria: Between 99.0 and 101.1% of $C_4H_8O_2$

SPECIFIC TESTS
- **REFRACTIVE INDEX,** Appendix II: At 20°
  Acceptance criteria: Between 1.392 and 1.395
- **SPECIFIC GRAVITY:** Determine at 25° by any reliable method (see General Provisions).
  Acceptance criteria: Between 0.944 and 0.948

OTHER REQUIREMENTS
- **REDUCING SUBSTANCES,** M-14, Appendix XI
  Acceptance criteria: Passes test

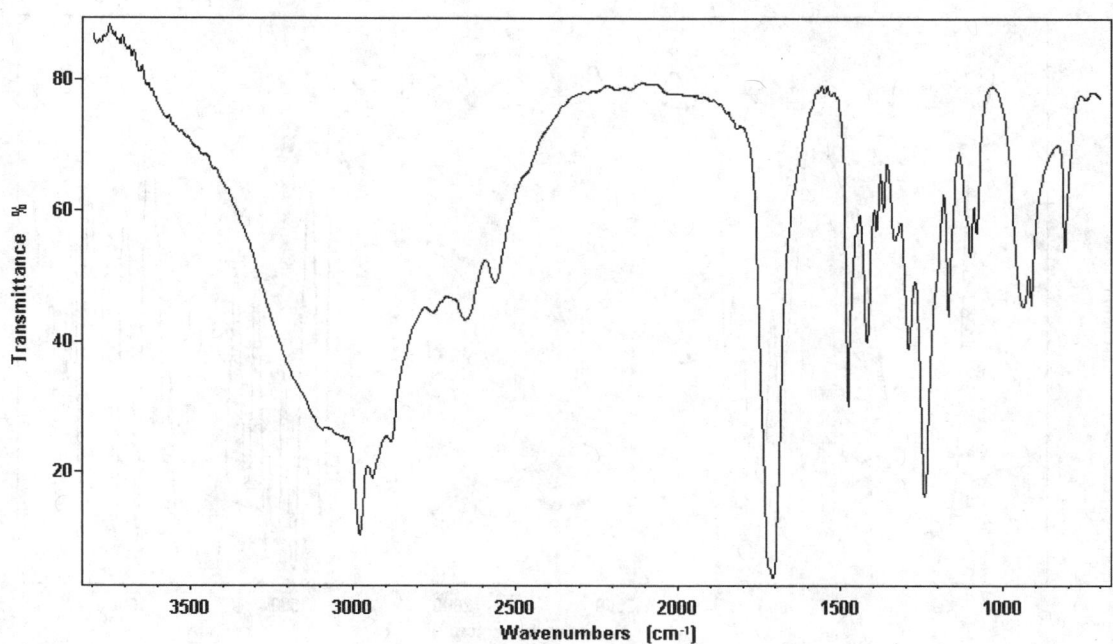

Isobutyric Acid

Isoeugenol

First Published: Prior to FCC 6

2-Methoxy-4-propenylphenol

$C_{10}H_{12}O_2$ Formula wt 164.20
FEMA: 2468
UNII: 5M0MWY797U [isoeugenol]

DESCRIPTION
Isoeugenol occurs as a pale yellow, viscous liquid.
Odor: Floral, carnation
Solubility: Soluble in most fixed oils, ether; insoluble or practically insoluble in glycerin
Boiling Point: ~266°
Solubility in Alcohol, Appendix VI: One mL dissolves in 5 mL of 50% alcohol.
Function: Flavoring agent

IDENTIFICATION
- **INFRARED SPECTRA,** *Spectrophotometric Identification Tests,* Appendix IIIC
  Acceptance criteria: The spectrum of the sample exhibits relative maxima at the same wavelengths as those of the spectrum below.

ASSAY
- **PROCEDURE:** Proceed as directed under *M-1b,* Appendix XI.
  Acceptance criteria: NLT 99.0% of $C_{10}H_{12}O_2$ (sum of two isomers)

SPECIFIC TESTS
- **REFRACTIVE INDEX,** Appendix II: At 20°
  Acceptance criteria: Between 1.572 and 1.577
- **SPECIFIC GRAVITY:** Determine at 25° by any reliable method (see *General Provisions*).
  Acceptance criteria: Between 1.079 and 1.085

OTHER REQUIREMENTS
- **SOLIDIFICATION POINT,** Appendix IIB
  Acceptance criteria: NLT 12°

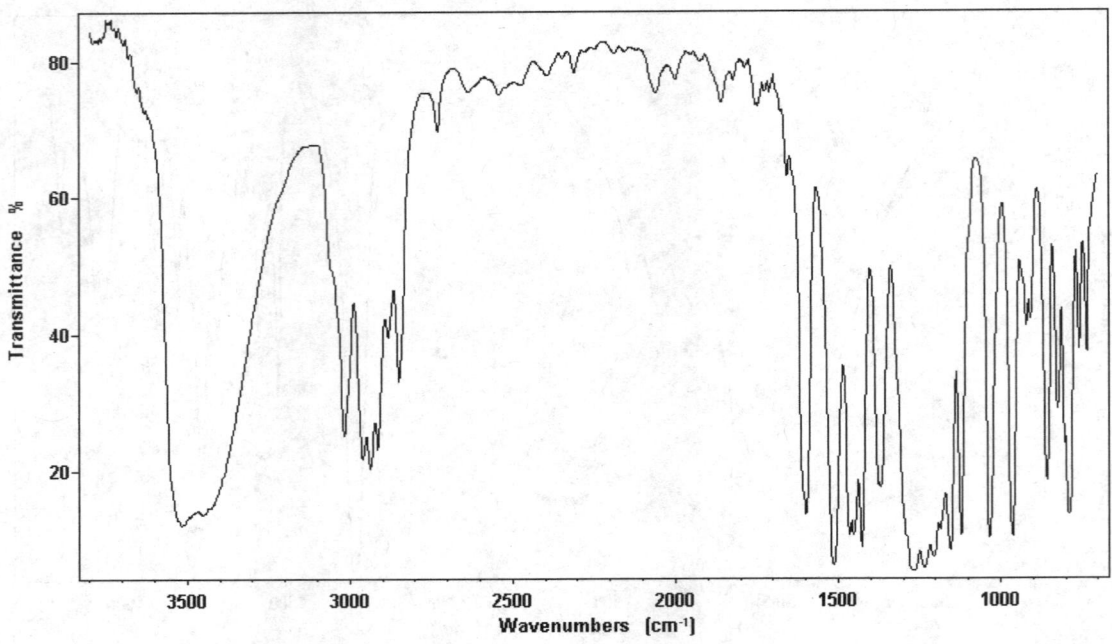

Isoeugenol

Isoeugenyl Acetate

First Published: Prior to FCC 6

2-Methoxy-4-propenyl Phenyl Acetate

$C_{12}H_{14}O_3$ Formula wt 206.24
FEMA: 2470
UNII: 9DF21GI8W6 [isoeugenyl acetate]

DESCRIPTION
Isoeugenyl Acetate occurs as a white crystalline solid.
Odor: Spicy, clove
Solubility: Soluble in alcohol, most fixed oils, chloroform; insoluble or practically insoluble in water
Solubility in Alcohol, Appendix VI: One g dissolves in 27 mL of 95% alcohol to give a clear solution.
Function: Flavoring agent

IDENTIFICATION
- **INFRARED SPECTRA,** *Spectrophotometric Identification Tests,* Appendix IIIC
  Sample preparation: Mineral oil mull
  Acceptance criteria: The spectrum of the sample exhibits relative maxima at the same wavelengths as those of the spectrum below.

ASSAY
- **PROCEDURE:** Proceed as directed under *M-1b,* Appendix XI.
  Acceptance criteria: NLT 98.0% of $C_{12}H_{14}O_3$ (sum of two isomers) and NLT 95.0% of the main isomer

SPECIFIC TESTS
- **ACID VALUE, FLAVOR CHEMICALS (OTHER THAN ESSENTIAL OILS),** *M-15,* Appendix XI
  [NOTE—Use phenol red TS as the indicator.]
  Acceptance criteria: NMT 2.0

OTHER REQUIREMENTS
- **SOLIDIFICATION POINT,** Appendix IIB
  Acceptance criteria: NLT 76°

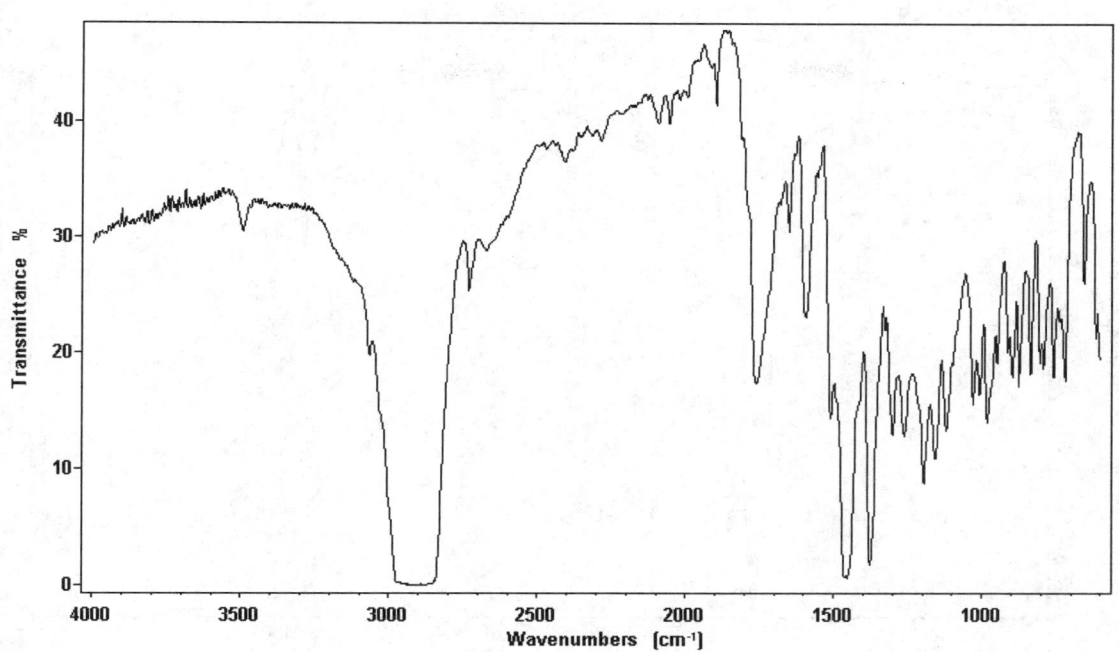

Isoeugenyl Acetate (Mineral Oil Mull)

DL-Isoleucine

First Published: Prior to FCC 6

DL-2-Amino-3-methylvaleric Acid

C₆H₁₃NO₂   Formula wt 131.17
                   CAS: [443-79-8]
UNII: 5HX0BYT4E3 [isoleucine, dl-]

DESCRIPTION
DL-Isoleucine occurs as a white, crystalline powder. It is soluble in water, and practically insoluble in alcohol and in ether. It melts with decomposition at about 292°. The pH of a 1:100 aqueous solution is between 5.5 and 7.0. It is optically inactive.
Function: Nutrient
Packaging and Storage: Store in well-closed containers.

IDENTIFICATION
- **INFRARED SPECTRA,** *Spectrophotometric Identification Tests,* Appendix IIIC
  Sample preparation: Mineral oil mull
  Acceptance criteria: The spectrum of the sample exhibits relative maxima at the same wavelengths as those of the spectrum below.

ASSAY
- **PROCEDURE**
  Sample: 250 mg
  Analysis: Dissolve the *Sample* in 3 mL of formic acid and 50 mL of glacial acetic acid. Add 2 drops of crystal violet TS and titrate with 0.1 N perchloric acid to the first appearance of a pure green color or until the blue color disappears completely. [**CAUTION**—Handle perchloric acid in an appropriate fume hood.] Perform a blank determination (see *General Provisions*) and make any necessary correction. Each mL of 0.1 N perchloric acid is equivalent to 13.12 mg of C₆H₁₃NO₂.
  Acceptance criteria: NLT 98.5% and NMT 101.5% of C₆H₁₃NO₂, calculated on the dried basis

IMPURITIES
Inorganic Impurities
- **LEAD,** *Lead Limit Test,* Appendix IIIB
  Sample solution: Prepare as directed for organic compounds.
  Control: 5 μg Pb (5 mL of *Diluted Standard Lead Solution*)
  Acceptance criteria: NMT 5 mg/kg

SPECIFIC TESTS
- **LOSS ON DRYING,** Appendix IIC: 105° for 3 h
  Acceptance criteria: NMT 0.3%
- **RESIDUE ON IGNITION (SULFATED ASH),** Appendix IIC
  Sample: 1g
  Acceptance criteria: NMT 0.1%

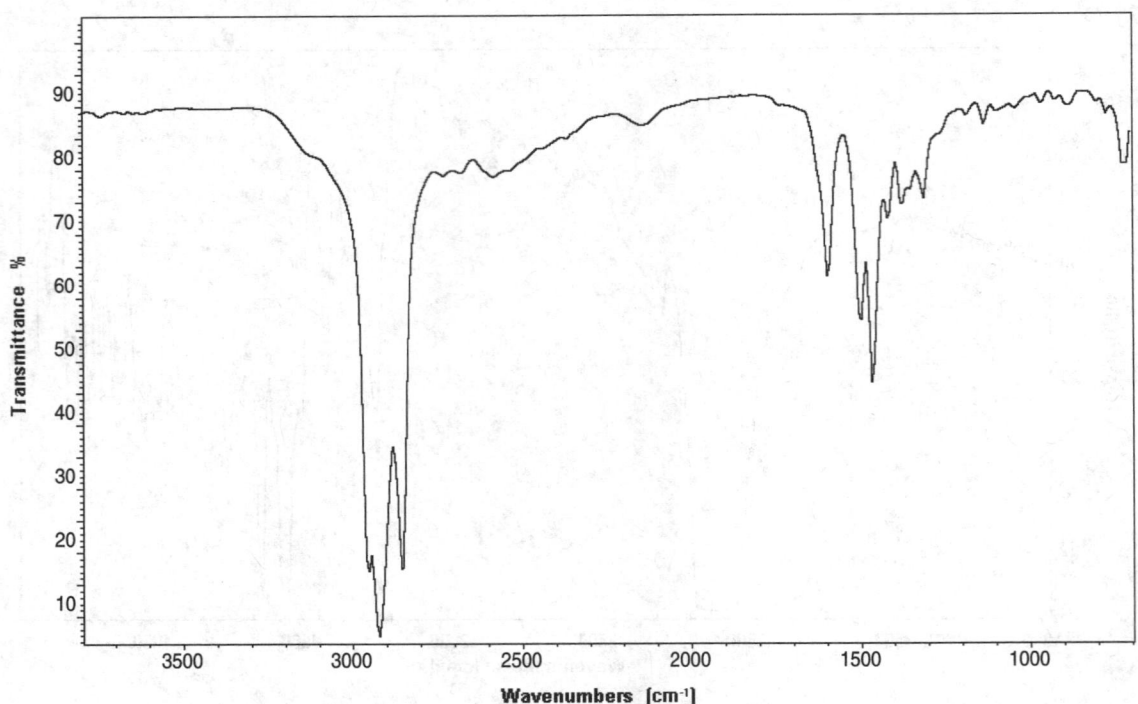

DL-Isoleucine (Mineral Oil Mull)

L-Isoleucine

First Published: Prior to FCC 6
Last Revision: FCC 6

L-2-Amino-3-methylvaleric Acid

C₆H₁₃NO₂
UNII: 04Y7590D77 [isoleucine]

Formula wt 131.17
CAS: [73-32-5]

DESCRIPTION
L-Isoleucine occurs as crystalline leaflets or as a white, crystalline powder. It is soluble in 25 parts of water, slightly soluble in hot alcohol, and soluble in diluted mineral acids and in alkaline solutions. It sublimes at between 168° and 170°, and melts with decomposition at about 284°. The pH of a 1:100 aqueous solution is between 5.5 and 7.0.
Function: Nutrient
Packaging and Storage: Store in well-closed containers.

IDENTIFICATION
- **INFRARED ABSORPTION,** Spectrophotometric Identification Tests, Appendix IIIC
  Reference standard: USP L-Isoleucine RS
  Sample and standard preparation: K
  Acceptance criteria: The spectrum of the sample exhibits maxima at the same wavelengths as those in the spectrum of the Reference standard.

ASSAY
- **PROCEDURE**
  Sample: 250 mg
  Analysis: Dissolve the Sample in 3 mL of formic acid and 50 mL of glacial acetic acid. Add 2 drops of crystal violet TS, and titrate with 0.1 N perchloric acid to the first appearance of a pure green color or until the blue color disappears completely. [**CAUTION**—Handle perchloric acid in an appropriate fume hood.] Perform a blank determination (see General Provisions), and make any necessary correction. Each mL of 0.1 N perchloric acid is equivalent to 13.12 mg of C₆H₁₃NO₂.
  Acceptance criteria: NLT 98.5% and NMT 101.5% of C₆H₁₃NO₂, calculated on the dried basis

IMPURITIES
Inorganic Impurities
- **LEAD,** Lead Limit Test, Appendix IIIB
  Sample solution: Prepare as directed for organic compounds.
  Control: 5 µg Pb (5 mL of Diluted Standard Lead Solution)
  Acceptance criteria: NMT 5 mg/kg

SPECIFIC TESTS
- **LOSS ON DRYING,** Appendix IIC: 105° for 3 h
  Acceptance criteria: NMT 0.3%

- **OPTICAL (SPECIFIC) ROTATION,** Appendix IIB
  Sample: 4 g, previously dried
  Analysis: Dissolve the *Sample* in sufficient 6 N hydrochloric acid to make 100 mL.
  Acceptance criteria
  $[\alpha]_D^{20}$ between +38.6° and +41.5°, on the dried basis; or
  $[\alpha]_D^{25}$ between +38.2° and +41.1°, on the dried basis
- **RESIDUE ON IGNITION (SULFATED ASH),** Appendix IIC
  Sample: 1 g
  Acceptance criteria: NMT 0.2%

Isomalt

First Published: First Supplement, FCC 6

Hydrogenated isomaltulose

6-O-alpha-D-glucopyranosyl-D-sorbitol (1,6-GPS)

1-O-alpha-D-glucopyranosyl-D-mannitol dihydrate (1,1-GPM) · 2 H$_2$O

INS: 953
UNII: S870P55O2W [isomalt]
CAS: [64519-82-0]

DESCRIPTION
Isomalt occurs as an odorless, white, crystalline slightly hygroscopic substance. It is a mixture of hydrogenated mono- and disaccharides whose principal components are the disaccharides 6-O-α-glucopyranosyl-D-sorbitol (1,6-GPS), formula wt, 344.32, and 1-O-α-D-glucopyranosyl-D-mannitol dihydrate (1,1-GPM), formula wt, 380.32. Isomalt is soluble in water; very slightly soluble in ethanol.
Function: Nutritive sweetener, texturizer, formulation aid, surface finishing agent, stabilizer and thickener
Packaging and Storage: Store in well-closed containers.

IDENTIFICATION
- **THIN-LAYER CHROMATOGRAPHY,** Appendix IIA
  Adsorbent: 0.25-mm layer of chromatographic silica gel mixture containing a fluorescent indicator having optimal intensity at 254 nm
  Developing solvent system: Ethyl acetate, pyridine, water, acetic acid, and propionic acid (10:10:2:1:1)
  Standard solution: 5 mg/mL of USP Isomalt RS
  Sample solution: 5 mg/mL
  Application volume: 1 µL
  Analysis: Separately apply each of the *Standard solution* and the *Sample solution* to the chromatographic plate and thoroughly dry the starting points in warm air. Develop over 10 cm using the *Developing solvent system*, dry the plate in a current of hot air, and dip for 3 s in a 1 g/L solution of sodium periodate. Dip the plate for 3 s in a mixture of absolute ethanol, sulfuric acid, acetic acid, and anisaldehyde (90:5:1:1). Dry the plate in a current of hot air until colored spots become visible. The background color may be brightened by exposure to warm steam. Examine in daylight.
  Acceptance criteria: The chromatograms obtained from the *Standard solution* and the *Sample solution* show principal spot(s) similar in position and color.

ASSAY
- **PROCEDURE**
  Mobile phase: Degassed water
  Standard solution: 20 mg/mL USP Isomalt RS
  Sample solution: 20 mg/mL
  Chromatographic system, Appendix IIA
    Mode: High-performance liquid chromatography
    Detector: Refractive index
    Column: 7.8-mm × 30-cm analytical column[1] and a 4.6-mm × 3-cm guard column, both packed with a strong cation-exchange resin consisting of sulfonated cross-linked styrene–divinylbenzene copolymer in the calcium form, about 9 µm in diameter
    Column temperature: 80 ± 1°
    Flow rate: About 0.5 mL/min
    Injection volume: About 20 µL
  System suitability
    Sample: *Standard solution*
    Resolution: NLT 2.0 between 1,1-GPM and 1,6-GPS
    Relative standard deviation: NMT 2.0% determined from the 1,6-GPS and 1,1-GPM peak responses, for replicate injections
  Analysis: Separately inject equal volumes of the *Standard solution* and *Sample solution* into the chromatograph, record the chromatograms, and measure the responses for the 1,6-GPS and 1,1-GPM peaks. [NOTE—The relative retention times for 1,6-GPS and 1,1-GPM are 1.2 and 1.0, respectively.]
  Separately calculate the percentages of 1,6-GPS and 1,1-GPM in the sample taken by the following formula:

  $$\text{Result} = (r_U/r_S) \times (C_S/C_U) \times 100\%$$

  r_U = peak response for 1,6-GPS or 1,1-GPM from the *Sample solution*
  r_S = peak response for 1,6-GPS or 1,1-GPM from the *Standard solution*
  C_S = concentration of 1,6-GPS or 1,1-GPM in the *Standard solution* (mg/mL) [Calculated based on the declared 1,6-GPS or 1,1-GPM content of USP Isomalt RS]
  C_U = concentration of sample in the *Sample solution* (mg/mL)

  Calculate the percentage of total hydrogenated mono- and disaccharides (%THS) in the sample taken using the following equation:

  $$\%THS = A + B$$

---

[1] Aminex Carbohydrate HPX-87C (BioRad), or equivalent.

604 / Isomalt / Monographs

A = sum of the percentages of 1,6-GPS and 1,1-GPM in the sample taken calculated above
B = sum of the percentages of mannitol and sorbitol in the sample, determined separately in the *Mannitol and Sorbitol* test procedure below

Acceptance criteria: NLT 98.0% of total hydrogenated mono- and disaccharides (%THS) and NLT 86% of the mixture of 1,6-GPS and 1,1-GPM, calculated on the anhydrous basis

IMPURITIES
Inorganic Impurities
- **LEAD**, *Lead Limit Test, Atomic Absorption Spectrophotometric Graphite Furnace Method, Method I,* Appendix IIIB
  Acceptance criteria: NMT 1 mg/kg
- **NICKEL**, *Nickel Limit Test, Method II,* Appendix IIIB
  Acceptance criteria: NMT 2 mg/kg

Organic Impurities
- **MANNITOL AND SORBITOL**
  Mobile phase: Degassed water
  Standard solution: 0.1 mg/mL each of USP Sorbitol RS and USP Mannitol RS
  System suitability solution: 20 mg/mL, 0.1 mg/mL, and 0.1 mg/mL of USP Isomalt RS, USP Sorbitol RS, and USP Mannitol RS, respectively
  Sample solution: 20 mg/mL
  Chromatographic system, Appendix IIA
    Mode: High-performance liquid chromatography
    Detector: Refractive index
    Column: 7.8-mm × 30-cm analytical column[1] and a 4.6-mm × 3-cm guard column, both packed with a strong cation-exchange resin consisting of sulfonated cross-linked styrene–divinylbenzene copolymer in the calcium form, about 9 µm in diameter
    Column temperature: 80 ± 1°
    Flow rate: About 0.5 mL/min
    Injection volume: About 20 µL
  System suitability
    Sample: *System suitability solution*
    Resolution: NLT 2.0 between 1,1-GPM and 1,6-GPS
  Analysis: Separately inject equal volumes of the *Standard solution* and *Sample solution* into the chromatograph, record the chromatograms, and measure the responses for the for 1,6-GPS and 1,1-GPM. [NOTE—The typical retention time of 1,1-GPM is about 12.3 min; the relative retention times are about 1.2 for 1,6-GPS, about 1.6 for mannitol, about 2.0 for sorbitol, and 1.0 for 1,1-GPM.]
  Separately calculate the percentages of mannitol and sorbitol in the sample taken by the following formula:

  $$\text{Result} = (r_U/r_S) \times (C_S/C_U) \times 100\%$$

  r_U = peak response for mannitol or sorbitol from the *Sample solution*
  r_S = peak response for mannitol or sorbitol from the *Standard solution*
  C_S = concentration of mannitol or sorbitol in the *Standard solution* (mg/mL)
  C_U = concentration of sample in the *Sample solution* (mg/mL)

  Acceptance criteria: NMT 3% mannitol and NMT 6% sorbitol

- **REDUCING SUGARS**
  Alkaline tartrate solution: Dissolve 34.6 g of potassium sodium tartrate (Rochelle salt) and 10 g of sodium hydroxide in water, dilute to 100 mL, let stand 2 days, and filter through glass wool.
  Sample: 7 g
  Analysis: Dissolve the *Sample* in 35 mL of water in a 400-mL beaker, and mix. Add 25 mL of cupric sulfate TS and 25 mL of *Alkaline tartrate solution*. Cover the beaker with glass and heat the mixture at such a rate that it comes to a boil in approximately 4 min and boils for exactly 2 min. Filter the precipitated cuprous oxide through a tared Gooch crucible previously washed with hot water, ethanol, and ether, and dried at 100° for 30 min. Thoroughly wash the collected cuprous oxide on the filter with hot water, then with 10 mL of ethanol, and finally with 10 mL of ether, and dry at 100° for 30 min. Weigh the filter containing the cuprous oxide.
  Acceptance criteria: The weight of the cuprous oxide does not exceed 50 mg (NMT 0.3% (as glucose)).

SPECIFIC TESTS
- **WATER**, *Water Determination,* Appendix IIB
  Acceptance criteria: NMT 7.0%
- **RESIDUE ON IGNITION (SULFATED ASH),** Appendix IIC
  Sample: 5 g
  Acceptance criteria: NMT 0.05%

Isomaltulose
First Published: FCC 7

Palatinose
6-O-α-D-Glucopyranosyl-D-fructofuranose, Monohydrate

$C_{12}H_{22}O_{11} \cdot H_2O$ Formula wt 360.6
CAS: [13718-94-0]
UNII: 43360LXH8N [isomaltulose monohydrate]

DESCRIPTION
Isomaltulose occurs as a white or colorless, crystalline, sweet substance with a faint, characteristic odor. It is a reducing disaccharide consisting of one glucose and one fructose moiety linked by an α-1,6-glycosidic bond. Isomaltulose is soluble in water.
Function: Nutritive sweetener; formulation and texturizing aid
Packaging and Storage: Store in well-closed containers.

IDENTIFICATION
- **A. PROCEDURE**
  Acceptance criteria: The retention time of the major peak in the chromatogram of the *Sample solution* corresponds to that in the chromatogram of the *Standard solution*, as obtained in the *Assay*.
- **B. THIN-LAYER CHROMATOGRAPHY**, Appendix IIA
  Solution A: 1 g/L of sodium periodate
  Solution B: Absolute ethanol, sulfuric acid, acetic acid, and anisaldehyde (90:5:1:1)
  Standard solution: 5 mg/mL of USP Isomaltulose RS
  Sample solution: 5 mg/mL
  Adsorbent: 0.25-mm layer of chromatographic silica gel mixture containing a fluorescent indicator having optimal intensity at 254 nm
  Developing solvent system: Ethyl acetate, pyridine, acetic acid, propionic acid, and water (10:10:1:1:2)
  Application volume: 1 µL
  Analysis: Separately apply the *Sample solution* and the *Standard solution* to the chromatographic plate and thoroughly dry the starting points in warm air. Develop over 10 cm using the *Developing solvent system*, dry the plate in a current of hot air, and dip for 3 s in *Solution A*. Dry the plate in hot air. Dip the plate for 3 s in *Solution B*. Dry the plate in a current of hot air until colored spots become visible. The background color may be brightened by exposure to warm steam. Examine in daylight.
  Acceptance criteria: The chromatograms obtained from the *Standard solution* and the *Sample solution* show principal spot(s) similar in position and color.

ASSAY
- **PROCEDURE**
  Mobile phase: 70% acetonitrile in water, degassed. [NOTE—The exact concentration can be 60%–75%, depending on the kind and condition of column used.]
  Standard solution: 100 mg/mL of USP Isomaltulose RS
  Sample solution: 100 mg/mL
  System suitability solution: 76 mg/mL of USP Isomaltulose RS; 4 mg/mL each of trehalulose and isomaltose; 5 mg/mL each of USP Fructose RS, USP Sucrose RS, and USP Dextrose RS
  Chromatographic system, Appendix IIA
    Mode: High-performance liquid chromatography
    Detector: Refractive index
    Column: 4.6-mm × 25-cm amino phase analytical column and 4.6-mm × 1-cm amino phase precolumn (ZORBAX-NH$_2$, or equivalent, analytical column and precolumn)
    Column temperature: Ambient
    Flow rate: 1.0–1.8 mL/min
    Injection size: 10 µL
  System suitability
    Sample: *System suitability solution*
    Suitability requirement 1: The resolution between isomaltulose and the previous peak (sucrose) and the following peak (trehalulose) is NLT 1.4.
    Suitability requirement 2: The relative standard deviation of the isomaltulose peak response is NMT 2.0%.
  Analysis: Separately inject the *Standard solution* and the *Sample solution* into the chromatograph, record the chromatograms, and measure the responses for isomaltulose.
  Calculate the percentage of Isomaltulose in the sample taken:

  $$\text{Result} = (r_U/r_S) \times (C_S/C_U) \times 100$$

  r_U = peak response for isomaltulose from the chromatogram of the *Sample solution*
  r_S = peak response for isomaltulose from the chromatogram of the *Standard solution*
  C_S = concentration of isomaltulose in the *Standard solution* (mg/mL)
  C_U = concentration of Isomaltulose in the *Sample solution* (mg/mL)

  Acceptance criteria: NLT 98.0% of isomaltulose, calculated on the anhydrous basis

IMPURITIES
Inorganic Impurities
- **LEAD**, Lead Limit Test, Atomic Absorption Spectrophotometric Graphite Furnace Method, Method I, Appendix IIIB
  Acceptance criteria: NMT 0.1 mg/kg

Organic Impurities
- **OTHER SACCHARIDES**
  Mobile phase: Prepare as directed in the *Assay*.
  Standard solution: 98.5 mg/mL of USP Isomaltulose RS; 0.6 mg/mL each of trehalulose and isomaltose; 0.1 mg/mL each of USP Fructose RS, USP Sucrose RS, and USP Dextrose RS
  Sample solution: 100 mg/mL
  System suitability solution: Prepare as directed in the *Assay*.
  Chromatographic system, Appendix IIA
    Mode: High-performance liquid chromatography
    Detector: Refractive index
    Column: 4.6-mm × 25-cm amino phase analytical column and 4.6-mm × 1-cm amino phase precolumn (ZORBAX-NH$_2$, or equivalent, analytical column and precolumn)
    Column temperature: Ambient
    Flow rate: 1.0–1.8 mL/min
    Injection size: 10 µL
  System suitability
    Sample: *System suitability solution*
    Suitability requirement: The resolution between isomaltulose and the previous peak (sucrose) and the following peak (trehalulose) is NLT 1.4.
  Analysis: Separately inject the *Standard solution* and the *Sample solution* into the chromatograph, record the chromatograms, and measure the responses for the saccharides. [NOTE—The approximate retention time of isomaltulose is 7.7 min; the approximate relative retention times are 0.67 for fructose, 0.74 for dextrose, 0.92 for sucrose, 1.00 for isomaltulose, 1.10 for trehalulose, and 1.2 for isomaltose.]

Calculate the percentage of each saccharide in the sample taken:

$$\text{Result} = (r_U/r_S) \times (C_S/C_U) \times 100$$

- r_U = peak response for the saccharide from the chromatogram of the *Sample solution*
- r_S = peak response for the saccharide from the chromatogram of the *Standard solution*
- C_S = concentration of the saccharide in the *Standard solution* (mg/mL)
- C_U = concentration of the *Sample solution* (mg/mL)

Acceptance criteria: NMT 2% of other saccharides (total), calculated on the anhydrous basis

SPECIFIC TESTS

- **CONDUCTIVITY ASH**
  [NOTE—For preparation of all solutions, twice-distilled or deionized water with a conductivity of less than 2 µS/cm should be used.]
  Sample: 31.3 g, based on the dry substance
  Analysis: Dissolve the *Sample* in carbon dioxide-free water and dilute to 100 mL. Using an appropriate conductivity meter that has been standardized with a potassium chloride conductivity calibration standard, measure the conductivity of the solution while gently stirring with a magnetic stirrer.
  The conductivity ash, in g/100 g of solution, is calculated by the formula:

$$\text{Result} = F \times [C_1 - (0.35 \times C_{WATER})]$$

- F = factor to convert to Conductivity Ash % (0.0006)
- C_1 = measured conductivity of the solution containing the *Sample* at 20° (µS/cm)
- C_{WATER} = specific conductivity of the water at 20° (µS/cm)

Acceptance criteria: NMT 0.01 g/100 g

- **WATER**, *Water Determination, Method 1a,* Appendix IIB
  Acceptance criteria: NMT 6.0%

Isopropyl Acetate

First Published: Prior to FCC 6
Last Revision: FCC 7

$C_5H_{10}O_2$ Formula wt 102.13
FEMA: 2926
UNII: 1Y67AFK870 [isopropyl acetate]

DESCRIPTION
Isopropyl Acetate occurs as a colorless, mobile liquid.
Odor: Ethereal
Solubility: Miscible in alcohol, ether, most fixed oils; 1 g dissolves in 72 mL water.
Boiling Point: ~88°
Function: Flavoring agent

IDENTIFICATION
- **INFRARED ABSORPTION,** *Spectrophotometric Identification Tests,* Appendix IIIC
  Reference standard: USP Isopropyl Acetate RS
  Sample and standard preparation: F
  Acceptance criteria: The spectrum of the sample exhibits maxima at the same wavelengths as those in the spectrum of the *Reference standard*.

ASSAY
- **PROCEDURE:** Proceed as directed under *M-1b,* Appendix XI.
  Acceptance criteria: NLT 99.0% of $C_5H_{10}O_2$

SPECIFIC TESTS
- **ACID VALUE, FLAVOR CHEMICALS (OTHER THAN ESSENTIAL OILS),** *M-15,* Appendix XI
  Acceptance criteria: NMT 2.0
- **SPECIFIC GRAVITY:** Determine at 25° by any reliable method (see *General Provisions*).
  Acceptance criteria: Between 0.866 and 0.869

Isopropyl Alcohol

First Published: Prior to FCC 6
Last Revision: Third Supplement, FCC 7

2-Propanol
Isopropanol

C_3H_8O Formula wt 60.10
                                                      CAS: [67-63-0]
UNII: ND2M416302 [isopropyl alcohol]

DESCRIPTION
Isopropyl Alcohol occurs as a clear, colorless, flammable liquid. It is miscible with water, with ethyl alcohol, with ether, and with many other organic solvents.
Function: Extraction solvent
Packaging and Storage: Store in tight containers, remote from fire.

IDENTIFICATION
- **REFRACTIVE INDEX,** Appendix IIB
  [NOTE—Use an Abbé or other refractometer of equal or greater accuracy.]
  Acceptance criteria: 1.377–1.380 at 20°

ASSAY
- **PROCEDURE**
  System suitability solution: USP 2-Propanol System Suitability RS
  Chromatographic system, Appendix IIA
  Mode: Gas chromatography
  Detector: Flame ionization
  Column: 60-m × 0.25-mm fused silica column with 1.4-μm film thickness of 6% cyanopropylphenyl/94% dimethylpolysiloxane stationary phase[1] with a 4-mm straight liner
  Temperature
   Injector: 150°
   Detector: 200°
   Column: Hold at 35° for 5 min; ramp to 45° at 1°/min; ramp to 100° at 10°/min; hold at 100° for 1 min
  Carrier gas: Helium
  Linear velocity: 35 cm/s
  Injection size: 1 μL
  Split ratio: 50:1
  System suitability
   Sample: System suitability solution
  [NOTE—Approximate relative retention times for ethyl ether, acetone, isopropyl alcohol, diisopropyl ether, 1-propanol, and 2-butanol are 0.7, 0.9, 1.0, 1.4, 1.5, and 2.0, respectively.]
   Suitability requirement 1: The relative standard deviation for the main isopropyl alcohol peak is NMT 2.0% for replicate injections.
   Suitability requirement 2: The resolution for the acetone and isopropyl alcohol peaks is NLT 2.0.
   Suitability requirement 3: The signal-to-noise ratio is NLT 10 for any of the following peaks: ethyl ether, acetone, diisopropyl ether, 1-propanol, and 2-butanol.
  Analysis: Inject the sample into the chromatograph, and record the resulting chromatogram. Determine the percentage of C_3H_8O present in the sample through peak area normalization:

  $$\text{Result} = (R_i/R_T) \times 100$$

  R_i = peak area for isopropyl alcohol
  R_T = sum of all of the peak areas
  Acceptance criteria: NLT 99.7% of C_3H_8O

[1] Restek Rtx®-1301, or equivalent. Available at www.restek.com.

IMPURITIES
Inorganic Impurities
- **LEAD,** Lead Limit Test, Atomic Absorption Spectrophotometric Graphite Furnace Method, Method I, Appendix IIIB
  Acceptance criteria: NMT 1 mg/kg

SPECIFIC TESTS
- **ACIDITY (AS ACETIC ACID)**
  Sample: 50 mL (about 39 g)
  Analysis: Add 2 drops of phenolphthalein TS to 100 mL of water, then add 0.01 N sodium hydroxide to the first pink color that persists for at least 30 s. Add the Sample to this solution, and mix. Continue the addition of 0.01 N sodium hydroxide until the pink color is restored.
  Acceptance criteria: NMT 0.7 mL of sodium hydroxide is required to restore the pink color (NMT 10 mg/kg).
- **DISTILLATION RANGE,** Appendix IIB
  Acceptance criteria: Within a range of 1°, including 82.3°
- **NONVOLATILE RESIDUE**
  Sample: 125 mL (about 100 g)
  Analysis: Evaporate the Sample to dryness in a tared dish on a steam bath, dry the residue at 105° for 30 min, cool, and weigh.
  Acceptance criteria: NMT 10 mg/kg
- **SOLUBILITY IN WATER**
  Sample: 10 mL
  Analysis: Mix the Sample with 40 mL of water.
  Acceptance criteria: After 1 h, the solution is as clear as an equal volume of water.
- **SPECIFIC GRAVITY:** Determine by any reliable method (see General Provisions).
  Acceptance criteria: NMT 0.7840 at 25°/25° (equivalent to 0.7870 at 20°/20°)
- **SUBSTANCES REDUCING PERMANGANATE**
  Sample: 50 mL
  Analysis: Transfer the Sample into a 50-mL glass-stoppered cylinder, add 0.25 mL of 0.1 N potassium permanganate, mix, and allow to stand for 10 min.
  Acceptance criteria: The pink color is not entirely discharged.
- **WATER,** Water Determination, Appendix IIB
  Acceptance criteria: NMT 0.2%

Isopulegol

First Published: Prior to FCC 6

p-Menth-4-en-3-ol

C₁₀H₁₈O Formula wt 154.25
FEMA: 2962
UNII: 3TH92O3BXN [isopulegol]

DESCRIPTION
Isopulegol occurs as a colorless liquid.
Odor: Harsh, camphoraceous, mint, with rose leaf and geranium background
Boiling Point: ~91° (12 mm Hg)
Solubility in Alcohol, Appendix VI: One mL dissolves in 4 mL of 60% alcohol to give a clear solution.
Function: Flavoring agent

IDENTIFICATION
- **INFRARED SPECTRA,** *Spectrophotometric Identification Tests,* Appendix IIIC
   Acceptance criteria: The spectrum of the sample exhibits relative maxima at the same wavelengths as those of the spectrum below.

ASSAY
- **PROCEDURE:** Proceed as directed under *Total Alcohols,* Appendix VI.
   Sample: 1.2 g
   Analysis: Reflux mixture for 2 h instead of the specified 1 h. Use 77.12 as the equivalence factor (e).
   Acceptance criteria: NLT 95.0% of total alcohols as C₁₀H₁₈O

SPECIFIC TESTS
- **ACID VALUE, FLAVOR CHEMICALS (OTHER THAN ESSENTIAL OILS),** *M-15,* Appendix XI
   Acceptance criteria: NMT 1.0
- **REFRACTIVE INDEX,** Appendix II: At 20°
   Acceptance criteria: Between 1.470 and 1.475
- **SPECIFIC GRAVITY:** Determine at 25° by any reliable method (see *General Provisions*).
   Acceptance criteria: Between 0.904 and 0.913

OTHER REQUIREMENTS
- **ANGULAR ROTATION, ALDEHYDES,** *M-2d,* Appendix XI
   Sample: 10 g
   Analysis: Use 77.13 as the equivalence factor (e).
   Acceptance criteria: NMT 1.0% as citronellal
- **ANGULAR ROTATION,** *Optical (Specific) Rotation,* Appendix IIB: Use a 100-mm tube.
   Acceptance criteria: Between 0° and −7°

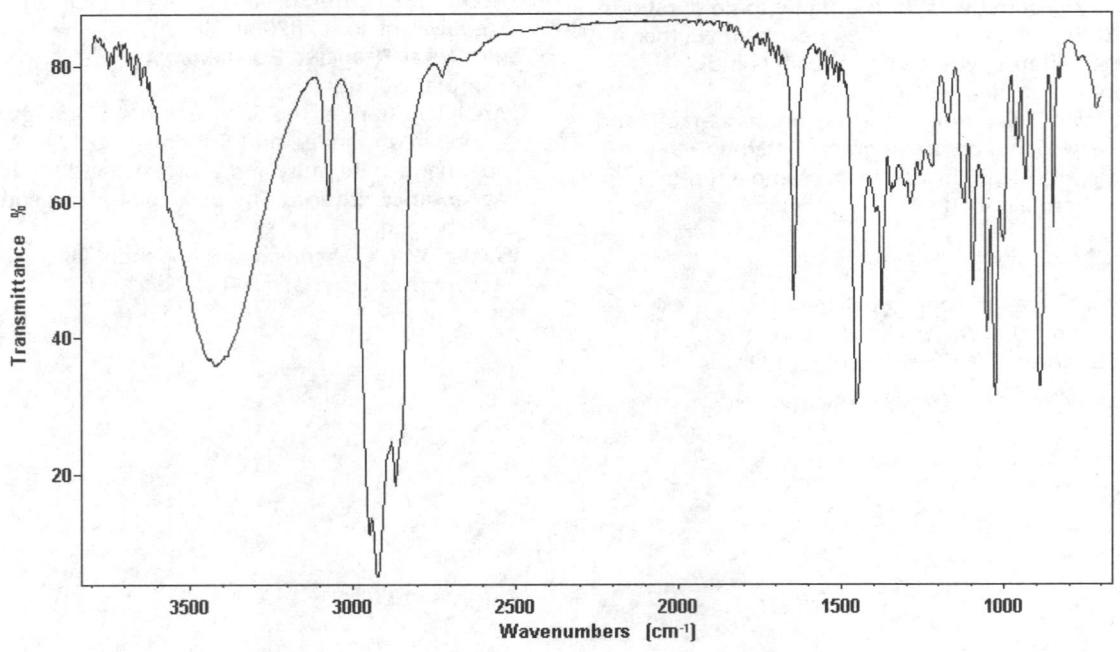

Isopulegol

Isovaleric Acid

First Published: Prior to FCC 6

Isopropylacetic Acid

$C_5H_{10}O_2$　　　　　　　　　　　　Formula wt 102.13
FEMA: 3102
UNII: 1BR7X184L5 [isovaleric acid]

DESCRIPTION
Isovaleric Acid occurs as a colorless to pale yellow liquid.
Odor: Disagreeable, rancid, cheese
Solubility: Soluble in alcohol, chloroform, ether, water
Boiling Point: ~175°
Function: Flavoring agent

IDENTIFICATION
- **INFRARED SPECTRA,** *Spectrophotometric Identification Tests,* Appendix IIIC
  Acceptance criteria: The spectrum of the sample exhibits relative maxima at the same wavelengths as those of the spectrum below.

ASSAY
- **PROCEDURE:** Proceed as directed under *M-3a,* Appendix XI.
  Acceptance criteria: NLT 99.0% of $C_5H_{10}O_2$

SPECIFIC TESTS
- **REFRACTIVE INDEX,** Appendix II: At 20°
  Acceptance criteria: Between 1.401 and 1.405
- **SPECIFIC GRAVITY:** Determine at 25° by any reliable method (see *General Provisions*).
  Acceptance criteria: Between 0.922 and 0.927

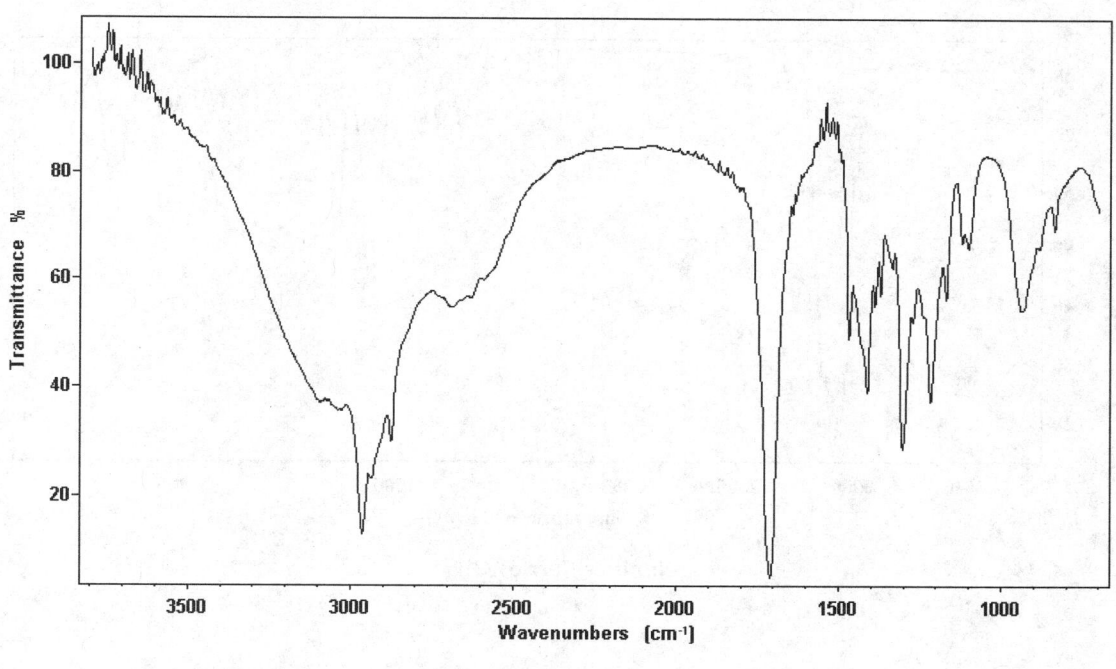

Isovaleric Acid

Juniper Berries Oil

First Published: Prior to FCC 6

CAS: [8012-91-7]

UNII: SZH16H44UY [juniper berry oil]

DESCRIPTION
Juniper Berries Oil occurs as a colorless, faintly green or yellow liquid with a characteristic odor and an aromatic, bitter taste. It is the volatile oil obtained by steam distillation from the dried ripe fruit of the plant *Juniperus communis* L. var. *erecta* Pursh (Fam. Cupressaceae). It is soluble in most fixed oils and in mineral oil. It is insoluble in glycerin and in propylene glycol. The oil tends to polymerize during long storage.

Function: Flavoring agent

Packaging and Storage: Store in a cool place protected from light in full, tight containers that are made from steel or aluminum and that are suitably lined.

IDENTIFICATION
- **INFRARED SPECTRA,** *Spectrophotometric Identification Tests,* Appendix IIIC

  Acceptance criteria: The spectrum of the sample exhibits relative maxima at the same wavelengths as those of the spectrum below.

SPECIFIC TESTS
- **ANGULAR ROTATION,** *Optical (Specific) Rotation,* Appendix IIB: Use a 100-mm tube.

  Acceptance criteria: Between −15° and 0°
- **REFRACTIVE INDEX,** Appendix IIB

  [NOTE—Use an Abbé or other refractometer of equal or greater accuracy.]

  Acceptance criteria: Between 1.474 and 1.484 at 20°
- **SPECIFIC GRAVITY:** Determine by any reliable method (see *General Provisions*).

  Acceptance criteria: Between 0.854 and 0.879

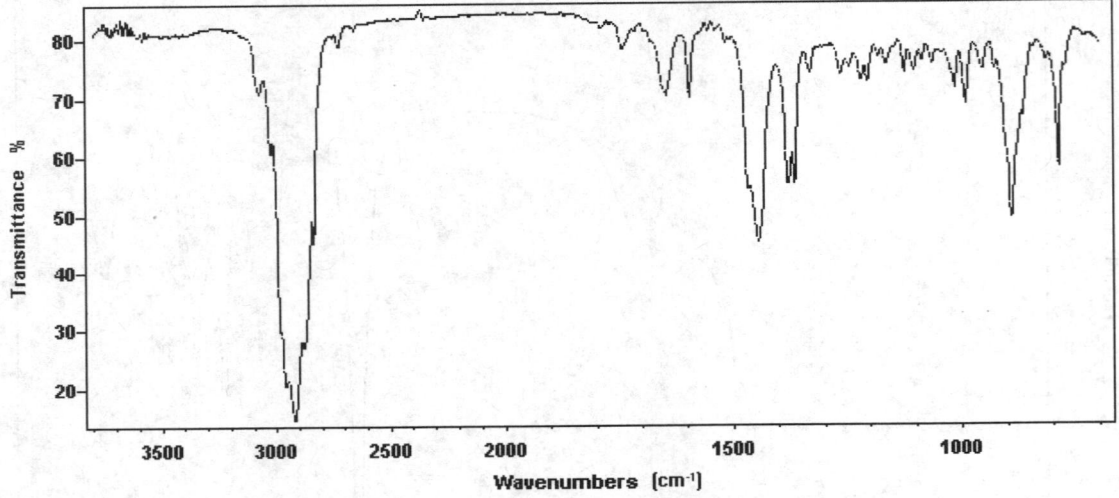

Juniper Berries Oil

Kaolin

First Published: Prior to FCC 6

China Clay

UNII: 24H4NWX5CO [kaolin]   CAS: [1332-58-7]

DESCRIPTION
Kaolin occurs as a fine, white to yellow-white or gray powder that becomes darker when moistened. It is a purified clay consisting mainly of alumina, silica, and water. It is insoluble in water, in alcohol, in dilute acids, and in alkali solutions.
Function: Anticaking agent
Packaging and Storage: Store in well-closed containers.

IDENTIFICATION
- **Procedure**
  Sample: 1 g
  Analysis: Mix the *Sample* with 10 mL of water and 5 mL of sulfuric acid in a porcelain dish and evaporate until the water is removed. Continue heating until dense, white fumes of sulfur trioxide evolve, then cool and cautiously add 20 mL of water. Boil for a few minutes, and filter. A gray residue of silica remains on the filter. Add 6 N ammonium hydroxide to a portion of the filtrate.
  Acceptance criteria: A gelatinous, white precipitate of aluminum hydroxide forms that is insoluble in an excess of 6 N ammonium hydroxide

IMPURITIES
Inorganic Impurities
- **Arsenic,** *Arsenic Limit Test,* Appendix IIIB
  Sample solution: Transfer 10.0 g of sample into a 250-mL flask, and add 50 mL of 0.5 N hydrochloric acid. Attach a reflux condenser to the flask, heat on a steam bath for 30 min, cool, and let the undissolved material settle. Decant the supernatant liquid through Whatman No. 3 filter paper, or equivalent, into a 100-mL volumetric flask, retaining as much as possible of the insoluble material in the beaker. Wash the slurry and beaker with three 10-mL portions of hot water, decanting each washing through the filter into the flask. Finally, wash the filter paper with 15 mL of hot water, cool the filtrate to room temperature, dilute to volume with water, and mix. [NOTE—Save the unused portion of this filtrate for use in the test for *Lead* (below).]
  Analysis: Proceed as directed using 10 mL of the *Sample solution.*
  Acceptance criteria: NMT 3 mg/kg
- **Lead,** *Lead Limit Test,* Appendix IIIB
  Sample: 10 mL of the *Sample solution* prepared in the test for *Arsenic* (above)
  Control: 10 µg Pb (10 mL of *Diluted Standard Lead Solution*)
  Acceptance criteria: NMT 10 mg/kg

SPECIFIC TESTS
- **Acid-Soluble Substances**
  Sample: 1 g
  Analysis: Mix the *Sample* with 20 mL of 2.7 N hydrochloric acid for 15 min and filter. Evaporate 10 mL of the filtrate to dryness in a tared dish, ignite gently, cool, and weigh the residue. Calculate the percent acid-soluble substances by the formula:

  $$\text{Result} = (2R \times 100) / w$$

  R = weight of the residue (g)
  w = weight of the sample (g) taken
  Acceptance criteria: NMT 2.0%
- **Carbonate**
  Sample: 1 g
  Analysis: Mix the *Sample* with 10 mL of water, cool, and keep the mixture cool while adding 5 mL of sulfuric acid.
  Acceptance criteria: No effervescence occurs during the addition of the acid.
- **Loss on Ignition**
  Sample: 2 g
  Analysis: Ignite the *Sample* in a tared crucible at 575° ± 25° to constant weight, cool, and weigh.
  Acceptance criteria: NMT 15.0%
- **Iron**
  Sample: 2 g
  Analysis: Mix the *Sample* with 10 mL of water in a mortar and add 500 mg of sodium salicylate.
  Acceptance criteria: No more than a light red tint appears.
- **Sulfide**
  Sample: 1 g
  Analysis: Add the *Sample* to 25 mL of water in a 250-mL flask, then add 15 mL of 2.7 N hydrochloric acid, and immediately cover the top of the flask with filter paper moistened with lead acetate TS. Heat to boiling, and boil for several minutes.
  Acceptance criteria: The paper does not show any brown coloration.

Karaya Gum

First Published: Prior to FCC 6

Sterculia Gum
INS: 416
UNII: 73W9IQY50Q [karaya gum]   CAS: [9000-36-6]

DESCRIPTION
Karaya Gum occurs in tears of variable size or in broken, irregular pieces having a somewhat crystalline appearance. In this form, it is a pale yellow to pink-brown, translucent substance that is compact and homogeneous with a dull luster. It is sometimes admixed with a few darker fragments and occasional pieces of bark. In the powdered form, it is light to pink-gray. It is a dried, gummy exudation from *Sterculia urens* Roxburgh and other species of Sterculia (Fam. Sterculiaceae), or from *Cochlospermum*

gossypium A. P. De Condolle or other species of *Cochlospermum* Kunth (Fam. Bixaceae). Karaya Gum is insoluble in alcohol, but it swells in water to form a gel.
Function: Stabilizer; thickener; emulsifier
Packaging and Storage: Store in well-closed containers.

IDENTIFICATION
- **A. PROCEDURE**
  Sample: 2 g
  Analysis: Add the *Sample* to 50 mL of water.
  Acceptance criteria: The sample swells to form a stiff, granular, slightly opalescent mucilage.
- **B. PROCEDURE**
  Sample solution: 10 mg/mL in water
  Analysis: Add a few drops of Millon's Reagent to the *Sample solution*.
  Acceptance criteria: A white, curdy precipitate forms.
- **C. PROCEDURE**
  Analysis: Add a sample to 60% alcohol.
  Acceptance criteria: The sample swells.

IMPURITIES
Inorganic Impurities
- **LEAD,** *Lead Limit Test,* Appendix IIIB
  Sample solution: Prepare as directed for organic compounds.
  Control: 2 µg Pb (2 mL of *Diluted Standard Lead Solution*)
  Acceptance criteria: NMT 2 mg/kg

Organic Impurities
- **STARCH**
  Sample solution: 100 mg/mL
  Analysis: Add a few drops of iodine TS to the *Sample solution*.
  Acceptance criteria: No blue color appears.

SPECIFIC TESTS
- **ASH (ACID-INSOLUBLE),** Appendix IIC
  Acceptance criteria: NMT 1.0%
- **INSOLUBLE MATTER**
  Sample: 5 g
  Analysis: Transfer the *Sample* into a 250-mL Erlenmeyer flask, add a 1:1 mixture of 2.7 N hydrochloric acid:water, cover the flask with a watch glass, and boil the solution gently until it loses its viscosity. Filter the solution through a tared filtering crucible, wash the residue with water until the washings are free from acid, dry at 105° for 1 h, and weigh.
  Acceptance criteria: NMT 3.0%
- **LOSS ON DRYING,** Appendix IIC: 105° for 5 h
  Sample: Use an unground sample that has been powdered until it passes through a No. 40 sieve. Mix well before weighing.
  Acceptance criteria: NMT 20.0%

- **VISCOSITY DETERMINATION,** *Viscosity of Cellulose Gum,* Appendix IIB
  Sample preparation: Transfer 4 g of finely powdered sample into the container of a stirring apparatus equipped with blades capable of being adjusted to about 1000 rpm. Add 10 mL of alcohol to the sample, swirl to wet it uniformly, and then add 390 mL of water, avoiding the formation of lumps. Stir the mixture for 7 min, pour the resulting dispersion into a 500-mL bottle, insert a stopper, and allow to stand for about 12 h in a water bath at 25°.
  Analysis: Determine the apparent viscosity at 25° with a model LVF Brookfield, or equivalent, viscometer using suitable spindle, speed, and factor.
  Acceptance criteria: NLT the minimum or within the range claimed by the vendor

Kelp
First Published: Prior to FCC 6

DESCRIPTION
Kelp occurs as a dark green to olive brown, dry substance. It is the dehydrated seaweed obtained from the class Phaeophyceae (brown algae) of the genera *Macrocystis* (including *M. pyrifera* and related species) and *Laminaria* (including *L. digitata, L. cloustoni,* and *L. saccharina*). The seaweed may be chopped to provide coarse particles and/or it may be ground to provide a fine powder.
Function: Nutrient (source of iodine)
Packaging and Storage: Store in well-closed containers.

IMPURITIES
Inorganic Impurities
- **ARSENIC,** *Arsenic Limit Test,* Appendix IIIB
  Distillation-reducing solution: 72 mg/mL of ACS-grade, low-arsenic, ferrous chloride tetrahydrate ($FeCl_2 \cdot 4H_2O$) in 6.6 N hydrochloric acid. [NOTE—Prepare fresh on the day of use.]
  Apparatus: Refer to the figure *Special Apparatus for the Determination of Inorganic Arsenic, Figure 14.* Have all parts available for assembly.
  Control: 6.0 µg As (6.0 mL *Standard Arsenic Solution*). [NOTE—Use this amount rather than the 3.0 mL specified in the *Procedure*.]
  Sample solution: Transfer a 2.00 g sample that has previously been ground to pass through a 60-mesh screen, and transfer to a distillation flask (*A*). Add 50 mL of *Distillation-reducing solution*, connect the flask to the receiver chamber (*B*), complete the assembly of the apparatus, and begin circulating tap water through the condenser (*C*). Half-fill the lower two bulbs of the splash head (*D*) with water.

Maneuver the stopcock to cause the contents of the receiver chamber to drain into the distillation flask, heat the flask until the temperature above the solution reaches 106° to 108°, and continue refluxing at this temperature for 45 min. Close the stopcock, continue heating at 108° to 110°, and collect 30 to 33 mL of distillate in the receiver chamber. Remove the heating source and allow the temperature to drop to about 80°.

Drain the distillate from the receiver chamber into a 250-mL beaker that is contained in an ice-water bath. Close the stopcock, and add a second 50-mL portion of the *Distillation-reducing solution* through the thermometer opening to the distillation flask. Replace the thermometer, increase the temperature to 108° to 110°, and collect a second 30- to 33-mL portion of distillate in the receiver chamber.

Drain the second distillate into the beaker containing the first portion, and continue cooling in the ice-water bath until the combined distillate cools to room temperature. Remove the splash head, and wash its contents into the beaker. Also, wash down the insides of the condenser and receiver chamber with water, collecting the washings in the beaker. Filter the beaker contents through a Whatman No. 40, or equivalent, filter paper, collecting the filtrate in a 300-mL Erlenmeyer flask having a 24/40 standard-taper joint, to be used later as an arsine generator flask. Wash the filter three times with water so that the final volume of filtrate measures 200 mL.

Analysis: Add 2 mL of potassium iodide TS and 0.5 mL of *Stannous Chloride Solution* to the *Sample solution* contained in the Erlenmeyer flask, and proceed as directed in the *Procedure* beginning with "Allow the mixture to stand for 30 min at room temperature…"
Acceptance criteria: NMT 1 mg/kg

- **LEAD,** *Lead Limit Test, Flame Atomic Absorption Spectrophotometric Method,* Appendix IIIB
  Sample: 10 g
  Acceptance criteria: NMT 2 mg/kg

SPECIFIC TESTS

- **ASH (TOTAL),** Appendix IIC
  Acceptance criteria: NMT 45.0%
- **IODINE CONTENT**
  Sample: 2 g
  Analysis: Transfer the *Sample* into a large porcelain crucible and mix thoroughly with 10 g of potassium carbonate. Place the crucible in a muffle furnace, starting with low heat, and then ignite at 500° to 600° for 20 min or until combustion is complete. Dissolve the ash in about 200 mL of boiling water, filter, and wash the filter paper with two 15-mL portions of boiling water, adding the washings to the filtrate. Cool to room temperature, neutralize to methyl red TS with approximately 20 mL of 85% phosphoric acid diluted with 20 mL of water, and then add 5 mL in excess. Cool the reaction mixture on an ice bath, and add bromine TS (about 5 mL) until a permanent yellow color appears. Gently boil the solution to remove all free bromine, adding water if necessary to maintain a volume of 200 mL or more. Boil for an additional 5 min after the bromine color has completely disappeared. Add a few mg of salicylic acid, stir, and cool to about 20°. Add 1 mL of the diluted phosphoric acid solution and 5 mL of potassium iodide TS, and titrate immediately with 0.01 N sodium thiosulfate, using starch TS as the indicator. Each mL of 0.01 N sodium thiosulfate is equivalent to 211.5 µg of iodine (I).
  Acceptance criteria: Between 0.1% and 0.5%
- **LOSS ON DRYING,** Appendix IIC: 105° for 4 h
  Acceptance criteria: NMT 13.0%

Konjac Flour

First Published: Prior to FCC 6

Konjac
Konnyaku
Konjac Gum
Yam Flour

CAS: [37220-17-0]
UNII: F7KU2UY3HE [amorphophallus konjac root]

DESCRIPTION

Konjac Flour occurs as a cream to light tan powder. It is a hydrocolloidal polysaccharide obtained from the tubers of various species of *Amorphophallus*. Konjac Flour is a high-molecular-weight, nonionic glucomannan primarily consisting of mannose and glucose at a respective molar ratio of approximately 1.6:1.0. It is a slightly branched polysaccharide connected by β-1,4 linkages and has an average molecular weight of 200 to 2000 kDa. Acetyl groups along the glucomannan backbone contribute to solubility properties and are located, on average, every 9 to 19 sugar units. Konjac Flour is dispersible in hot or cold water and forms a highly viscous solution with a pH between 4.0 and 7.0. Solubility is increased by heat and mechanical agitation. Addition of mild alkali to the solution results in the formation of a heat-stable gel that resists melting, even under extended heating conditions.

Function: Gelling agent; thickener; film former; stabilizer
Packaging and Storage: Store cool and dry in a closed container away from direct heat and sunlight.

IDENTIFICATION

- **MICROSCOPIC TEST**
  Sample: 0.1 g
  Analysis: Stain the *Sample* with 0.01% methylene blue powder in 50% isopropyl alcohol, and observe microscopically.

Acceptance criteria: The sample should have flattened elliptical particles that are generally 100 to 500 μm in length along the long axis. Unground Konjac Flour is clearly distinguished from other hydrocolloids by the presence of saclike cells that contain glucomannan. The surface of these cells has a reticulated structure. Particles of Konjac Flour are also birefringent under polarized light. These visual characteristics may remain even if the sample is finely ground, but they are less pronounced.

- **GEL TEST**
  Sample mixture: 10 mg/mL
  Analysis: At room temperature, add 5 mL of a 40 mg/mL sodium borate solution to the *Sample mixture* in a test tube, and shake vigorously.
  Acceptance criteria: A gel forms.
  [NOTE—Konjac flour solutions gel in the presence of sodium borate, similar in reaction to that of galactomannans such as guar gum and locust bean gum.]

- **HEAT-STABLE GEL TEST**
  Sample mixture: 20 mg/mL, prepared by heating the mixture in a water bath for 30 min with continuous agitation and then cooling to room temperature
  Analysis: For each 100 mL of *Sample solution* prepared, add 2 mL of 100 mg/mL potassium carbonate solution to the fully hydrated sample at ambient temperature. Heat the mixture in a water bath to 85°, and hold quiescently for 2 h without agitation.
  Acceptance criteria: The sample forms a thermally stable gel under the specified conditions. [NOTE—Related hydrocolloids such as guar gum and locust bean gum do not form thermally stable gels and are negative by this test.]

IMPURITIES
Inorganic Impurities

- **ARSENIC,** *Arsenic Limit Test,* Appendix IIIB
  Sample solution: Prepare as directed for organic compounds.
  Acceptance criteria: NMT 3 mg/kg

- **LEAD,** *Lead Limit Test, Flame Atomic Absorption Spectrophotometric Method,* Appendix IIIB
  Sample: 5 g
  Control: Use the *Diluted Standard Lead Solutions* specified for *1 mg/kg Lead Limit*
  Acceptance criteria: NMT 2 mg/kg

SPECIFIC TESTS

- **ASH (TOTAL),** Appendix IIC
  Acceptance criteria: NMT 5.0%

- **CARBOHYDRATE (TOTAL)**
  Analysis: The remainder, after subtracting from 100% the sum of the percentages of *Ash (Total)*, *Loss on Drying*, and *Protein*, represents the percentage of carbohydrates (glucomannans) in the sample.
  Acceptance criteria: NLT 75.0%

- **LOSS ON DRYING,** Appendix IIC: 105° for 5 h
  Acceptance criteria: NMT 15.0%

- **PROTEIN,** *Nitrogen Determination,* Appendix IIIC
  Sample: 3.5 g
  Analysis: Determine as directed using a 500-mL Kjeldahl flask. Calculate the percent protein using the equation:

  $$\%\text{Protein} = N \times 5.7$$

  N = percent nitrogen
  Acceptance criteria: NMT 8.0%

Labdanum Oil

First Published: Prior to FCC 6

UNII: 67GS9BGA2X [labdanum oil]

CAS: [8016-26-0]

DESCRIPTION
Labdanum Oil occurs as a golden yellow, viscous liquid with a powerful, balsamic odor, which on dilution, is reminiscent of ambergris. It turns dark brown on standing. It is the volatile oil obtained by steam distillation from crude labdanum gum extracted from the perennial shrub *Cistus ladaniferus* L. (Fam. Cistaceae). It is soluble in most fixed oils and in mineral oil, but it is insoluble in glycerin and in propylene glycol.

Function: Flavoring agent

Packaging and Storage: Store in a cool place protected from light in full, tight containers that are made from steel or aluminum and that are suitably lined.

IDENTIFICATION
- **INFRARED SPECTRA**, *Spectrophotometric Identification Tests*, Appendix IIIC

  Acceptance criteria: The spectrum of the sample exhibits relative maxima at the same wavelengths as those of the spectrum below.

SPECIFIC TESTS
- **ACID VALUE (ESSENTIAL OILS AND FLAVORS),** Appendix VI
  Acceptance criteria: Between 18 and 86
- **ANGULAR ROTATION,** *Optical (Specific) Rotation,* Appendix IIB: Use a 100-mm tube.
  Acceptance criteria: Between +0°15′ and +7°
- **ESTER VALUE,** *Esters,* Appendix VI
  Sample: 1 g
  Acceptance criteria: Between 31 and 86
- **REFRACTIVE INDEX,** Appendix IIB
  [NOTE—Use an Abbé or other refractometer of equal or greater accuracy.]
  Acceptance criteria: Between 1.492 and 1.507 at 20°
- **SOLUBILITY IN ALCOHOL,** Appendix VI
  Acceptance criteria: One mL of sample dissolves in 0.5 mL of 90% alcohol, but the solution usually becomes opalescent or turbid on further dilution.
- **SPECIFIC GRAVITY:** Determine by any reliable method (see *General Provisions*).
  Acceptance criteria: Between 0.905 and 0.993

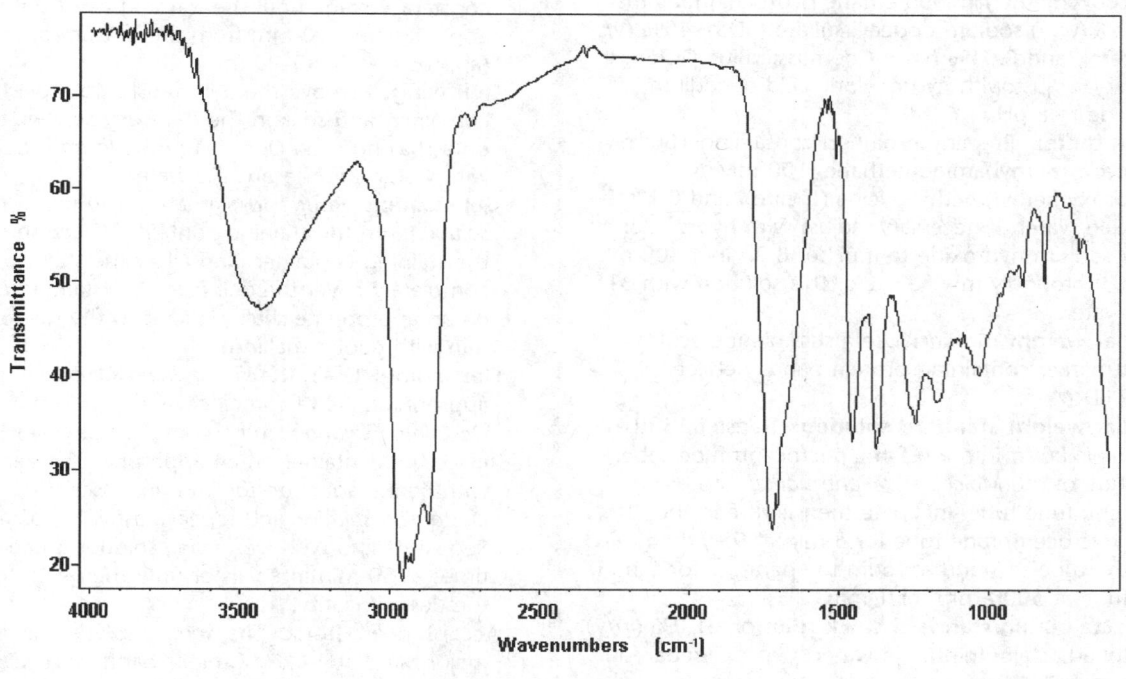

Labdanum Oil

Alpha-Lactalbumin

First Published: First Supplement, FCC 7

$C_{626}H_{958}N_{162}O_{196}S_9$

UNII: G0Y102QI5I [α-lactalbumin]

Formula wt 14,178
CAS: [9051-29-0]

DESCRIPTION
Alpha-Lactalbumin occurs as a homogenous, free-flowing, semi-hygroscopic, light cream-colored powder. It is a lyophilized or spray-dried powder of compact globular metalloprotein that may contain a single bound calcium ion and is capable of binding zinc and other metals. Alpha-Lactalbumin is isolated either from bovine milk or from

whey, both of which should be from edible sources suitable for human use. It may contain suitable stabilizers.
Function: Nutrient; source of tryptophan; source of alpha-lactalbumin
Packaging and Storage: Store in tight containers.

IDENTIFICATION
- **A. Procedure**
  Acceptance criteria: The retention time of the major peak for alpha-lactalbumin in the chromatogram of the *Sample solution* corresponds to that in the chromatogram of the *Standard solution*, as obtained in the *Assay*.
- **B. SDS-Polyacrylamide Gel Electrophoresis**
  Alcoholic solution: Specially denatured alcohol 3A and isopropyl alcohol (95:5)[1]
  Gel fixing solution: *Alcoholic solution*, glacial acetic acid, and water (400:100:500)
  Gel staining solution: 0.25 g/L of Coomassie Blue G-250 in 10% (v/v) acetic acid solution.[2] [Note—Store at room temperature.]
  Destaining solution: 10.0% acetic acid in water (v/v). [Note—This solution may be stored at room temperature for up to 6 months.]
  Sample buffer: Prepare a solution containing 200 mM tris(hydroxymethyl)aminomethane hydrochloride (Tris-HCl), 2% (w/v) sodium dodecyl sulfate (SDS), 40% (v/v) glycerol, and 0.04% (w/v) Coomassie Blue G-250. If necessary, adjust with hydrochloric acid or sodium hydroxide to a pH of 6.8.[3]
  Running buffer: Prepare a solution containing 100 mM tris(hydroxymethyl)aminomethane, 100 mM *N*-tris(hydroxymethyl)methylglycine (tricine), and 0.1% (w/v) SDS in water. If necessary, adjust with hydrochloric acid or sodium hydroxide to a pH of 8.3.[4] In a 400-mL beaker, thoroughly mix 35 mL of this solution with 315 mL of water.
  Molecular weight marker: Use a suitable molecular weight marker containing protein bands between 3.5 and 27 kD.
  Molecular weight standard solution: Transfer 16 µL of the *Sample buffer* into a 0.5-mL microcentrifuge tube. Pipet 4 µL of the *Molecular weight marker* into the microcentrifuge tube. Incubate the mixture in the closed microcentrifuge tube for 5 min at 95°, then allow the tube to stand at room temperature for 5 min. Centrifuge at 5000 rpm for 1 min.
  Alpha-lactalbumin standard stock solution: 1.0% (w/v) USP Alpha-Lactalbumin RS in water. [Note—Prepare in a 2-mL centrifuge tube.]
  Alpha-lactalbumin standard solution: Pipet 21 µL of the *Sample buffer* and 3 µL of the *Alpha-lactalbumin standard stock solution* into a 0.5-mL microcentrifuge tube. Incubate the mixture in the closed microcentrifuge tube for 5 min at 95°, then allow the tube to stand at room temperature for 5 min. Centrifuge at 5000 rpm for 1 min.
  Sample stock solution: 1.0% (w/v) sample in water. [Note—Prepare in a 2-mL centrifuge tube.]
  Sample solution: Pipet 21 µL of the *Sample buffer* and 3 µL of the *Sample stock solution* into a 0.5-mL microcentrifuge tube. Incubate the mixture in the closed microcentrifuge tube for 5 min at 95°, then allow the tube to stand at room temperature for 5 min. Centrifuge at 5000 rpm for 1 min.
  SDS-PAGE gel and apparatus: Following the manufacturer's instructions, assemble and fill a 16.5% Tris-Tricine Ready Gel[5] or equivalent, in the Mini-Protean III Electrophoresis Module[6] or in an equivalent module. Add the *Running buffer* appropriately to the apparatus.
  Gel loading: Load 10 µL of the *Molecular weight standard solution*, 2.5 µL of the *Alpha-lactalbumin standard solution*, and 2.5 µL of the *Sample solution*, respectively, into the 16.5% Tris-Tricine SDS-PAGE gel. [Note—The loaded samples contain approximately 3 µg of protein, based on the sample weight.]
  Running the gel: Set the voltage to 100 V and run at a constant voltage until the tracking dye front is approximately 10 mm from the bottom of the gel (approximately 80–90 min).
  Gel fixing: Remove the gel, transfer to a plastic container, and soak in the *Gel fixing solution* for 30 min on a shaking rack. Decant the *Gel fixing solution*, rinse with water, and decant the water.
  Gel staining: Pour approximately 100 mL of *Gel staining solution* into the staining container. Place the gel into the staining container, and allow the stain to completely cover the gel. Place the staining container on an appropriate shaker and stain the gel for 60–90 min with gentle shaking.
  Destaining: Drain the *Gel staining solution* into an appropriate waste container, and add 100 mL of *Destaining solution* to the container to cover the gel. Place the container on an appropriate shaker and shake with gentle agitation for 30 min. Discard the used *Destaining solution* and repeat destaining as necessary. Repeat rinsing with *Destaining* solution three to four times at 30-min intervals or until the gel is destained to the desired clarity.
  Acceptance criteria: The *Sample solution* gives one major band at 14 kD, a minor band at 16 kD, and has a molecular weight that is similar to that of the *Alpha-lactalbumin standard solution*.

ASSAY
- **Procedure**
  Mobile phase: Prepare a solution containing 0.02 M Tris-HCl, 0.5% SDS, and 0.1 N sodium chloride. Adjust the pH of the solution to 5.95 ± 0.05. Pass the solution

---

[1] A suitable grade of this solution is available, for example, as Reagent Alcohol, catalog number R8382, from www.sigma-aldrich.com.
[2] Suitable gel staining solutions are commercially available, for example, from Bio-Rad. Use Coomassie Brilliant Blue G-250 from Bio-Rad (catalog number 161-0406, www.bio-rad.com), or equivalent.
[3] A suitable sample buffer is commercially available, for example, as Tricine sample buffer from Bio-Rad, catalog number 161-0739, www.bio-rad.com.
[4] A suitable undiluted running buffer is available, for example, as 10x Tris/Tricine/SDS buffer from Bio-Rad, catalog number 161-0744, www.bio-rad.com.
[5] Available from Bio-Rad, catalog number 161-1107 or 161-1179, www.bio-rad.com.
[6] Available from Bio-Rad, catalog number 165-3302, www.bio-rad.com.

through a filter havng a 0.5-μm or finer porosity, and degas.
Standard solution: 1.0 mg/mL of USP Alpha-Lactalbumin RS in *Mobile phase*, calculated on the dried basis. [NOTE—Prepare immediately before use.]
Sample solution: 1.0 mg/mL in *Mobile phase*
System suitability solution: 0.5 mg/mL each of USP Alpha-Lactalbumin RS and beta-lactoglobulin in *Mobile phase*
Chromatographic system, Appendix IIA
  Mode: High-performance liquid chromatography
  Detector: UV 280 nm
  Column: 7.8-mm × 30-cm size exclusion chromatography column containing a hydrophilic bonded silica packing of 5-μm particles (pore size 290Å)[7]
  Flow rate: 0.6 mL/min
  Injection size: 20 μL
System suitability
  [NOTE—Before performing the *System suitability* and *Analysis*, equilibrate the column with *Mobile phase* at 0.6 mL/min for approximately 90 min, or until a stable baseline is achieved.]
  Sample: *System suitability solution*
  [NOTE—The relative retention times are approximately 1.00 for alpha-lactalbumin and 0.91 for beta-lactoglobulin.]
  Suitability requirement 1: The resolution between beta-lactoglobulin and alpha-lactalbumin is NLT 1.65.
  Suitability requirement 2: The tailing factor for the alpha-lactalbumin peak is NMT 1.1.
Analysis: Separately inject the *Standard solution* and the *Sample solution* into the chromatograph, record the chromatograms, and measure the responses for the major peaks.
Calculate the alpha-lactalbumin content of the sample as a percentage of total protein:

$$\text{Result} = (r_U/r_S) \times (C_S/C_U) \times (100/P)$$

r_U = peak response of alpha-lactalbumin obtained from the chromatogram of the *Sample solution*
r_S = peak response of alpha-lactalbumin obtained from the chromatogram of the *Standard solution*
C_S = concentration of Alpha-Lactalbumin in the *Standard solution* (mg/mL)
C_U = concentration of Alpha-Lactalbumin in the *Sample solution* (mg/mL)
P = total protein percentage (labeled)

Acceptance criteria: NLT 90.0% of the labeled total protein content

IMPURITIES
Inorganic Impurities
- **LEAD**, *Lead Limit Test, Atomic Absorption Spectrophotometric Graphite Furnace Method, Method II,* Appendix IIIB
  Acceptance criteria: NMT 0.5 mg/kg, on the dried basis

- **PHOSPHORUS**
  Solution A: Dilute 250 mL of hydrochloric acid with water to 1000 mL.
  Solution B: Dissolve 20 g of ammonium molybdate in 200 mL of water with heat, then allow the solution to cool. Dissolve 1.0 g of ammonium vanadate in 125 mL of water with heat, cool, and add 160 mL of hydrochloric acid. Gradually add, with stirring, the molybdate solution to the vanadate solution, then dilute with water to 1000 mL.
  Standard stock solution 1: 2 mg/mL of phosphorus from monobasic potassium phosphate (KH_2PO_4), previously dried for 2 h at 105°. [NOTE—Store this solution in a refrigerator.]
  Standard stock solution 2: 0.1 mg/mL of phosphorus, from *Standard stock solution 1*. [NOTE—Prepare this solution immediately before use. Store in a refrigerator.]
  Standard solutions: Transfer 5.0, 8.0, 10.0, and 15.0 mL of *Standard stock solution 2* to four separate 100-mL volumetric flasks.
  Sample solution: Transfer 4.0 g of the sample to an ashing dish. Dry the sample on a hot plate or steam bath. Ignite in a muffle furnace at a maximum temperature of 600° until free of carbon. Cool, add 40 mL of *Solution A* and several drops of nitric acid, and bring to a boil on a hot plate. Cool, transfer to a 100-mL volumetric flask, and dilute with water to volume. Pipet 20.0 mL of this solution into a 100-mL volumetric flask.
  Analysis: To each of the flasks containing the *Standard solutions* and the *Sample solution*, add 20.0 mL of *Solution B*, dilute with water to volume, and allow to stand for exactly 10 min for maximum color development. To an empty 100-mL volumetric flask, add 20.0 mL of *Solution B*, dilute with water to volume, and allow to stand for exactly 10 min for maximum color development (this solution will be used as the blank). Concomitantly determine the absorbance of each solution in 1-cm cells with a suitable spectrophotometer at a wavelength of 400 nm, using the blank to zero the instrument. Plot the absorbances of the *Standard solutions* versus concentration, in μg/mL, of phosphorus, and draw the straight line best fitting the plotted points. From the graph so obtained, determine the concentration, C, in μg/mL, of phosphorus in the *Sample solution*.
  Calculate the quantity, in μg/g, of phosphorus in the sample taken:

$$\text{Result} = (F \times C/W) \times 100$$

F = dilution factor, 5
C = concentration of phosphorus in the *Sample solution*, determined from the standard curve (μg/mL)
W = weight of the sample used to prepare the *Sample solution* (g)

Acceptance criteria: NMT 700 μg/g

---
[7] Phenomenex BioSep 3000 SEC, or equivalent, www.phenomenex.com.

Organic Impurities
- **BETA-LACTOGLOBULIN**

  Mobile phase, Sample solution, System suitability solution, Chromatographic system and **System suitability:** Proceed as directed in the *Assay*.

  Standard solution: 1.0 mg/mL of beta-lactoglobulin in *Mobile phase*, calculated on the dried basis. [NOTE—Prepare immediately before use.]

  Analysis: Separately inject the *Standard solution* and the *Sample solution* into the chromatograph, record the chromatograms, and measure the responses for the major peaks.

  Calculate the percentage of beta-lactoglobulin in the portion of the sample taken:

  $$\text{Result} = (r_U/r_S) \times (C_S/C_U) \times (100/P)$$

  r_U = peak response of beta-lactoglobulin obtained from the chromatogram of the *Sample solution*

  r_S = peak response of beta-lactoglobulin obtained from the chromatogram of the *Standard solution*

  C_S = concentration of beta-lactoglobulin in the *Standard solution* (mg/mL)

  C_U = concentration of the *Sample solution* (mg/mL)

  P = percentage of *Total Protein* as determined below

  Acceptance criteria: NMT 6.5%, calculated on total protein basis

- **LACTOSE**

  Solution A: 36.0 mg/mL of potassium ferrocyanide trihydrate ($K_4Fe(CN)_6 \cdot 3H_2O$)

  Solution B: 72.0 mg/mL of zinc sulfate heptahydrate ($ZnSO_4 \cdot 7H_2O$)

  Test reagent 1: 600 mg of lyophilisate consisting of a mixture of citrate buffer (pH 6.6), nicotinamide adenine dinucleotide (NAD) (35 mg), anhydrous magnesium sulfate, and stabilizers (added if necessary). Dissolve lyophilisate in 7.0 mL of water before use.

  Test reagent 2: 1.7 mL of a suspension of β-galactosidase (approximately 100 Units)

  Test reagent 3: 34 mL of a solution consisting of 0.51 M potassium diphosphate buffer (pH 8.6), and stabilizers (added if necessary)

  Test reagent 4: 1.7 mL of a suspension of galactose dehydrogenase (approximately 40 Units). [NOTE—*Test reagents 1–4* are commercially available in a test kit.[8]]

  Sample solution: Transfer 1.0 g of the sample to a 100-mL volumetric flask and add 60 mL of water. Add 5 mL of *Solution A*, mix, then add 5 mL of *Solution B*. Add 10 mL of 0.1 N sodium hydroxide solution and mix vigorously. Dilute with water to volume and pass through a filter paper. Use the clear filtrate. [NOTE—This procedure breaks emulsions, absorbs some colors, and precipitates proteins.]

  Analysis: Label one glass or disposable 1-cm plastic cuvette as "blank" and a second, equivalent, cuvette as "test." To each cuvette, pipet 0.20 mL of *Test reagent 1* and 0.05 mL of *Test reagent 2*. Pipet 0.10 mL of the *Sample solution* into the cuvette that is labeled "test." Mix both cuvettes with stirrers and incubate at 20°–25° for 20 min. Pipet 1.00 mL of *Test reagent 3* into each cuvette. Pipet 2.00 mL of water into the "blank" cuvette and 1.90 mL of water into the cuvette containing the *Sample solution*. Incubate at 20°–25° for 2 min. Determine the absorbances, A_{S1} and A_{B1}, at 340 nm for the *Sample solution* and the blank, respectively. Next, add 0.05 mL of *Test reagent 4* to each cuvette. Incubate at 20°–25° until the reaction has stopped (about 10–15 min). Again determine the absorbances, A_{S2} and A_{B2}, at 340 nm for the *Sample solution* and the blank, respectively. If the reaction has not stopped after 15 min, continue to read the absorbances at 2-min intervals until the absorbance for the *Sample solution* remains constant for two successive measurements.

  Calculate the percentage of lactose in the portion of the sample taken:

  $$\text{Result} = 100 \times V_T \times M_{r1} \times [(A_{S2} - A_{S1}) - (A_{B2} - A_{B1})]/(E \times V_U \times C_U)$$

  V_T = total volume in the cuvette, 3.30 mL

  M_{r1} = molecular weight of lactose monohydrate, 360.32

  E = absorption coefficient of nicotinamide adenine dinucleotide reduced form (NADH) at 340 nm, 6300 L · mol^{-1} · cm^{-1}

  V_U = volume of *Sample solution* in the cuvette, 0.10 mL

  C_U = concentration of the *Sample solution* (mg/L)

  Acceptance criteria: NMT 1.0%

- **LIPID (FAT)**

  Weighing dish preparation: Pre-dry the clean dishes under the same conditions that will be used for final drying after fat extraction. Ensure that all surfaces where weighing dishes will be placed are clean and free of particulates. At the end of the oven drying, place the weighing dishes in a desiccator and cool to room temperature. Immediately before use, weigh the dishes to the nearest 0.1 mg and record the weights. Check the balance zero after weighing each dish. Protect the weighed dishes from contamination with extraneous matter.

  Sample: 0.5 g

  Analysis: Transfer the *Sample* to a Mojonnier-style ether extraction flask that has the capacity to hold a volume of 21–23 mL in the lower bulb plus neck at the bottom of the flask. The flask should have a smooth, round opening at the top that can be sealed when closed with a cork. Add 1.5 mL of ammonium hydroxide to the flask. Add 3 drops of phenolphthalein TS to help sharpen the visual appearance of the interface between the ether and the aqueous layers during extraction. Add 10 mL of alcohol, close the flask with a cork stopper that has been water-soaked, and shake the flask for 15 s.

  For the first extraction, add 25 mL of ether, replace the cork stopper, and shake the flask very vigorously for 1 min, releasing built-up pressure by loosening the

---

[8] Available, for example, from Boehringer-Mannheim (R-Biopharm, Inc., 7950 Old US 27S, Marshall, MI 49068 USA; Tel: 1-877-789-3033 or 1-269-789-3033; Fax: 1-269-789-3070; www.r-biopharm.com).

stopper as necessary. Add 25 mL of petroleum ether, replace the cork stopper, and repeat vigorous shaking for 1 min. Centrifuge the flask at 600 rpm for NLT 30 s to obtain a clean separation of the aqueous (bright pink) and ether phases. Decant the ether solution into a suitable weighing dish prepared as directed in *Weighing dish preparation*. When the ether solution is decanted into the dish, be careful not to pour any suspended solids or aqueous phase into the weighing dish. Ether can be evaporated from the dish at NMT 100° while conducting the second extraction.

For the second extraction, add 5 mL of alcohol to the original flask, close with the cork stopper, and shake vigorously for 15 s. Add 15 mL of ether, replace the cork, and shake vigorously for 1 min. Add 15 mL of petroleum ether, replace the cork stopper, and repeat vigorous shaking for 1 min. Centrifuge the flask at 600 rpm for NLT 30 s to obtain a clean separation of the aqueous (bright pink) and ether phases. If the interface is below the neck of the flask, add water to bring the level about halfway up to the neck. Add water slowly down the inside surface of the flask so that there is minimum disturbance of the interface. Decant the ether solution for the second extraction into the same weighing dish used for the first extraction.

For the third extraction, omit addition of the alcohol and repeat the procedure used for the second extraction. Completely evaporate the solvents in a hood on a hot plate at NMT 100°, avoiding spattering. Dry the extracted fat and the weighing dish to constant weight in a forced air oven at $100 \pm 1°$ for NLT 30 min or in a vacuum oven at 70–75° and NMT 50.8 cm (20 inches) of vacuum for NLT 7 min. Remove the weighing dish from the oven and place in a desiccator to cool to room temperature. Record the weight of the weighing dish containing the fat.

Run a blank determination using water and record the weight of any dry residue collected. The reagent blank should be less than 2.0 mg of residue. [NOTE—A negative number is not acceptable.]

Calculate the weight percent of lipid (fat) in the portion of the sample taken:

$$\text{Result} = 100 \times (W_2 - W_1 - W_3)/W$$

W_2 = weight of the weighing dish containing fat
W_1 = weight of the empty weighing dish
W_3 = weight of the reagent blank residue
W = weight of the *Sample*

Acceptance criteria: NMT 1.0% lipid (fat); the difference between duplicate runs is NMT 0.03% lipid (fat)

SPECIFIC TESTS

- **ASH (TOTAL)**, Appendix IIC
  Sample: 1 g
  Acceptance criteria: NMT 3.5%
- **CALCIUM CONTENT**
  Standard stock solution: Dissolve 1.249 g of calcium carbonate in 270 mL of 3 N hydrochloric acid in a 1000-mL volumetric flask. Dilute with water to volume. Dilute 50 mL of the solution so obtained to 1000 mL. (Contains 25 µg/mL of calcium.)
  Solution A: Weigh 11.7 g (±100 mg) of lanthanum oxide and transfer to a 1000-mL volumetric flask. Add enough water to wet the powder, then slowly add 50 mL of hydrochloric acid. [**CAUTION**—Exothermic reaction.] Let the powder dissolve, then dilute with water to volume. This solution contains 1% (w/v) of lanthanum and is stable for up to 6 months when stored at room temperature.
  Standard solutions: To five identical 25-mL volumetric flasks, add 0, 5, 10, 15, and 20 mL, respectively, of the *Standard stock solution*. Add 2.5 mL of *Solution A* to each flask then dilute with water to volume. The solutions contain 0, 5, 10, 15, and 20 µg/mL of calcium, respectively, and each contains 0.1% (w/v) of lanthanum.
  Sample solution: Transfer 1.0 g of the sample to a 100-mL volumetric flask, add 10 mL of *Solution A*, and dilute with water to volume.
  Blank: Dilute *Solution A* 10-fold.
  Analysis: Concomitantly determine the absorbances of the *Standard solutions* and the *Sample solution* against the *Blank* at the calcium emission line of 422.7 nm with a suitable atomic absorption spectrophotometer equipped with a calcium hollow-cathode lamp and a reduced air–acetylene flame. [NOTE—Optimize flame parameters in accordance with the instrument manufacturer's instructions.] Plot the absorbances of the *Standard solutions* versus the concentration, in µg/mL of calcium, and draw the straight line best fitting the plotted points. From the graph so obtained, determine the concentration, C, in µg/mL, of calcium in the *Sample solution*.
  Calculate the quantity of calcium, in mg, in each g of Alpha-Lactalbumin taken:

  $$\text{Result} = (F \times V \times C)/W$$

  F = factor converting µg to mg, 0.001
  V = final volume of the *Sample solution*, 100 mL
  C = concentration of calcium in the *Sample solution*, determined from the standard curve (µg/mL)
  W = weight of Alpha-Lactalbumin used to prepare the *Sample solution* (g)

  Acceptance criteria: NMT 1 mg/g
- **DENATURATION TEMPERATURE**
  Sample preparation: Prepare a protein dough by mixing 3 g of the sample with 2 g of water. Place the dough into a well-sealed sample container.
  Analysis: Perform two measurements on the *Sample preparation* using a differential scanning calorimeter. Heat to 140° and scan. Cool rapidly to below room temperature, and rescan. Apply a scan rate of 10°/min. Weigh pans before and after scanning to verify that no moisture loss occurs during the scanning process. Measure and record the denaturation temperatures as peak temperatures. The formation of two peaks indicates the presence of both the holo form and the apo form of alpha-lactalbumin.

Acceptance criteria
Apo form: 50°–52°
Holo form: 58°–61°
- **Loss on Drying**, Appendix IIC (vacuum oven at 100° and 660 mm Hg with continuous dry air feed for 5 h)
Sample: 1.0–1.5 g
Acceptance criteria: NMT 6.5%
- **pH**, Appendix IIB
Sample solution: 100 mg/mL
Acceptance criteria: NMT 7.5
- **Total Protein**
Sample: 250 mg
Analysis: Combust the Sample in the presence of pure oxygen (99.9%) in an airtight oven at 950° with a suitable nitrogen analyzer. The components such as carbon dioxide, sulfur dioxide, and moisture are absorbed by various in-line chemical filters. All nitrogenous matter is converted into nitrogen in the presence of catalytic converters. The weight percent of nitrogen is measured by a thermal conductivity detector. Blank the system by analyzing a suitable nitrogen blank material, such as powdered cellulose, and obtaining a zero reading. Calibrate and qualify the system using EDTA. The relative standard deviation for replicate runs is NMT 0.5%.
Calculate the weight percent of total protein in the sample by multiplying the percentage of nitrogen found by 6.23.
Acceptance criteria: NLT 95.0%, calculated on the dried basis

OTHER REQUIREMENTS
- **Labeling:** Label to state protein content, expressed as total protein percentage on the dried basis. Indicate the type of source material, expressed as bovine milk, whey, or both, used to manufacture the final product.

Lactic Acid

First Published: Prior to FCC 6

α-Hydroxypropionic Acid
2-Hydroxypropionic Acid

$C_3H_6O_3$ Formula wt 90.08
INS: 270   CAS: L(+)-Lactic Acid [79-33-4]
                  DL-Lactic Acid [598-82-3]
UNII: 3B8D35Y7S4 [lactic acid, dl-]
UNII: F9S9FFU82N [lactic acid, l-]

DESCRIPTION
Lactic Acid occurs as a colorless or yellow, syrupy liquid consisting of a mixture of lactic acid ($C_3H_6O_3$) and lactic acid lactate ($C_6H_{10}O_5$). It is obtained by the lactic fermentation of sugars or is prepared synthetically. It is usually available in solutions containing the equivalent of from 50% to 90% lactic acid. It is hygroscopic, and when concentrated by boiling, the acid condenses to form lactic acid lactate, 2-(lactoyloxy)propanoic acid, that on dilution and heating, hydrolyzes to Lactic Acid. It is miscible with water and with alcohol.

Function: Acidifier
Packaging and Storage: Store in tight containers.

IDENTIFICATION
- **Lactate**, Appendix IIIA
Acceptance criteria: Passes test

ASSAY
- **Procedure**
Sample: Amount of sample equivalent to 3 g of lactic acid
Analysis: Transfer the Sample into a 250-mL flask, add 50.0 mL of 1 N sodium hydroxide, mix, and boil for 20 min. Add phenolphthalein TS and titrate the excess alkali in the hot solution with 1 N sulfuric acid. Perform a blank determination (see General Provisions), and make any necessary correction. Each mL of 1 N sodium hydroxide is equivalent to 90.08 mg of $C_3H_6O_3$.
Acceptance criteria: NLT 95.0% and NMT 105.0% of the labeled concentration of $C_3H_6O_3$

IMPURITIES
Inorganic Impurities
- **Chloride**, Chloride and Sulfate Limit Tests, Chloride Limit Test, Appendix IIIB
Sample solution: 20 mg/mL
Control: 20 µg chloride (2.0 mL of Standard Chloride Solution)
Acceptance criteria: Any turbidity produced by a 1.0-mL portion of the Sample solution does not exceed that produced by the Control. (NMT 0.1%)
- **Cyanide**
[Caution—Because of the extremely poisonous nature of potassium cyanide, conduct this test in a fume hood, and exercise great care to prevent skin contact and the inhalation of particles or vapors of solutions of the material. Under no conditions pipet solutions by mouth.]
Solution A: Dissolve 200 mg of p-phenylenediamine hydrochloride in 100 mL of water, warming to aid dissolution. Cool, allow the solids to settle, and save the supernatant liquid to make the Solution B.
Solution B: Dissolve 128 mL of pyridine in 365 mL of water, add 10 mL of hydrochloric acid, and mix. To this solution add 30 mL of the supernatant of Solution A and allow to stand for 24 h before using. This solution is stable for about 3 weeks when stored in an amber bottle.
Standard stock solution: 2.5 mg/mL potassium cyanide in 0.1 N sodium hydroxide
Standard solution: 25 µg/mL potassium cyanide in 0.1 N sodium hydroxide made from Standard stock solution. [Note—Each mL of this solution contains 10 µg of cyanide.]
Sample solution: Transfer a quantity of sample equivalent to 20.0 g of lactic acid into a 100-mL volumetric flask, dilute to volume with water, and mix.
Analysis: Pipet a 10-mL aliquot of the Sample solution into a 50-mL beaker. Pipet 1.0 mL of the Standard solution into a second 50-mL beaker, and add 10 mL of water. Place the beakers in an ice bath, and adjust the pH to between 9 and 10 with 20% sodium hydroxide, stirring slowly and adding the reagent slowly to avoid

overheating. Allow the solutions to stand for 3 min, and then slowly add 10% phosphoric acid to reach a pH between 5 and 6, measured with a pH meter. Transfer the solutions into 100-mL separatory funnels each containing 25 mL of cold water, and rinse the beakers and pH meter electrodes with a few mL of cold water, collecting the washings in the respective separatory funnel. To each funnel add 2 mL of bromine TS, stopper, and mix. Add 2 mL of 2% sodium arsenite solution, stopper, and mix. Add 10 mL of *n*-butanol to the clear solutions, stopper, and mix. Finally, add 5 mL of *Solution B*, mix, and allow to stand for 15 min. Remove and discard the aqueous phases, and filter the alcoholic phases into 10-mm spectrophotometry cells. Using a suitable spectrophotometer, determine the absorbances at 480 nm of the solutions from the *Sample solution* and the *Standard solution*.
Acceptance criteria: The absorbance of the solution from the *Sample solution* does not exceed that from the *Standard solution*. (NMT 5 mg/kg)

- **IRON**
  Sample: The ash obtained in the test for *Residue on Ignition* (below)
  Control: 20 µg iron (2.0 mL of *Iron Standard Solution*, Solutions and Indicators)
  Analysis: Add 2 mL of 1:20 hydrochloric acid to the *Sample* and evaporate to dryness on a steam bath. Dissolve the residue in 1 mL of hydrochloric acid, dilute to 40 mL with water, and add about 40 mg of ammonium persulfate crystals and 10 mL of ammonium thiocyanate TS. Repeat the preceding using the *Control*.
  Acceptance criteria: Any red or pink color produced by the *Sample* does not exceed that produced by the *Control*. (NMT 10 mg/kg)

- **LEAD,** *Lead Limit Test, Atomic Absorption Spectrophotometric Graphite Furnace Method, Method I,* Appendix IIIB
  Acceptance criteria: NMT 0.5 mg/kg

- **SULFATE,** *Chloride and Sulfate Limit Tests, Chloride Limit Test,* Appendix IIIB
  Sample solution: 100 mg/mL in water
  Control: 400 µg sulfate (40.0 mL of *Standard Sulfate Solution*)
  Acceptance criteria: Any turbidity produced by a 1.6-mL portion of the *Sample solution* does not exceed that produced by the *Control*. (NMT 0.25%)

Organic Impurities
- **SUGARS**
  Analysis: Add 5 drops of sample to 10 mL of hot alkaline cupric tartrate TS.
  Acceptance criteria: No red precipitate forms.

SPECIFIC TESTS
- **CITRIC, OXALIC, PHOSPHORIC, OR TARTARIC ACID**
  Sample: 1 g
  Analysis: Dilute the *Sample* to 10 mL with water, add 40 mL of calcium hydroxide TS, and boil for 2 min.
  Acceptance criteria: The solution does not become turbid.

- **RESIDUE ON IGNITION (SULFATED ASH),** Appendix IIC
  Sample: 2 g
  [NOTE—Save the resulting ash for the test for *Iron* (above).]
  Acceptance criteria: NMT 0.1%

OTHER REQUIREMENTS
- **LABELING:** Indicate the concentration of Lactic Acid.

Lactitol

First Published: FCC 6

D-Lactitol
Hydrogenated Lactose
β-D-Galactopyranosyl-D-glucitol

$C_{12}H_{24}O_{11}$　　　　　Formula wt, anhydrous 344.31
$C_{12}H_{24}O_{11} \cdot H_2O$　　Formula wt, monohydrate 362.37
INS: 966　　　　　CAS: anhydrous [585-86-4]
　　　　　　　　　　　　monohydrate [81025-04-9]
UNII: L2B0WJF7ZY [lactitol]
UNII: UH2K6W1Y64 [lactitol monohydrate]

DESCRIPTION
Lactitol occurs as a white, crystalline powder. It is a disaccharide containing small amounts of sorbitol and related polyols. It is very soluble in water and slightly soluble in ethanol.
Function: Sweetener; humectant; stabilizer
Packaging and Storage: Store in well-closed containers.

IDENTIFICATION
- **THIN-LAYER CHROMATOGRAPHY,** Appendix IIA
  Sample solution: 2.5 mg/mL (on the dried basis)
  Standard solution: 2.5 mg/mL of USP Lactitol RS (on the dried basis)
  Adsorbent: 0.25-mm layer of chromatographic silica gel
  Application volume: 2 µL
  Developing solvent system: *n*-propyl alcohol:ethyl acetate:water (70:20:10)
  Spray reagent 1: 2 mg/mL sodium metaperiodate
  Spray reagent 2: 1:50 solution of 4,4′-tetra-methyldiaminodiphenylmethane in a 4:1 acetone:glacial acetic acid mixture
  Analysis: Following development, mark the solvent front and allow the solvent to evaporate from the plate. Spray the plate with *Spray reagent 1*, air dry for 15 min, and spray the plate with *Spray reagent 2*.
  Acceptance criteria: The principal spot obtained from the *Sample solution* corresponds in color and R_F value to that obtained from the *Standard solution*.

ASSAY
- **PROCEDURE**
  Mobile phase: Water, degassed
  Standard solution: 10.0 mg/mL USP Lactitol RS
  Sample: 0.7 g
  Sample solution: Transfer the *Sample* into a 50-mL volumetric flask, dilute to volume with water and mix.
  Chromatographic system, Appendix IIA
    Mode: High-performance liquid chromatography

Detector: Refractive index. [NOTE—Maintain the detector at a constant temperature.]
Column: 9-mm × 30-cm column packed with a strong cation-exchange resin, about 9 μm in diameter, consisting of sulfonated cross-linked styrene-divinylbenzene copolymer in the calcium form (Aminex HPX-87c, or equivalent)
Column temperature: 85° ± 0.5°
Flow rate: About 0.5 mL/min
Injection volume: About 20 μL
System suitability
 Sample: Standard solution
 Suitability requirement: Replicate injections have a relative standard deviation of NMT 2.0%.
Analysis: Separately inject the Sample solution and the Standard solution into the chromatograph, record the chromatograms, and measure the responses for the major peaks. The elution pattern includes the higher-molecular-weight hydrogenated polysaccharides, followed by three individual peaks representing maltotriitol, lactitol, and sorbitol. The principal peak is lactitol, which elutes at about twice the retention time of the void volume. The retention time for sorbitol is about 1.7 relative to lactitol. Calculate the quantity, in mg, of D-lactitol in the Sample taken by the formula:

$$Result = 50C(r_U/r_S)$$

C = concentration (mg/mL) of USP Lactitol RS in the Standard solution
r_U = peak response of the other hydrogenated saccharides in the Sample solution
r_S = peak response for lactitol in the Standard solution

Acceptance criteria: NLT 96.0% and NMT 102.0% D-lactitol as $C_{12}H_{24}O_{11}$, calculated on the dried basis

IMPURITIES
Inorganic Impurities
- **LEAD,** Lead Limit Test, Atomic Absorption Spectrophotometric Graphite Furnace Method, Method I, Appendix IIIB
  Acceptance criteria: NMT 1 mg/kg
- **NICKEL,** Nickel Limit Test, Appendix IIIB
  Sample: 20 g
  Acceptance criteria: NMT 1 mg/kg

Organic Impurities
- **OTHER HYDROGENATED SACCHARIDES (POLYOLS)**
  Standard solution: 10.0 mg/mL USP Lactitol RS
  Sample: 0.7 g
  Sample solution: Transfer the Sample into a 50-mL volumetric flask, dilute to volume with water and mix.
  Analysis: Separately inject the Sample solution and the Standard solution into the chromatograph, record the chromatograms, and measure the responses for the major peaks. The elution pattern includes the higher-molecular-weight hydrogenated polysaccharides, followed by three individual peaks representing maltotriitol, lactitol, and sorbitol. The principal peak is lactitol, which elutes at about twice the retention time of the void volume. The retention time for sorbitol is about 1.7 relative to lactitol. Calculate the quantity, in mg, of lactitol and other hydrogenated saccharides in the Sample solution by the following formula:

$$Result = 50C(r_U/r_S)$$

C = concentration (mg/mL) of USP Lactitol RS in the Standard solution
r_U = peak response of the other hydrogenated saccharides in the Sample solution
r_S = peak response for lactitol in the Standard solution

Acceptance criteria: NMT 4.0%
- **REDUCING SUGARS**
  Sample: 21 g
  Analysis: Dissolve the Sample in 35 mL of water contained in a 400-mL beaker and mix. Add 25 mL of cupric sulfate TS and 25 mL of alkaline tartrate TS. Cover the beaker with a watch glass, heat the mixture at such a rate that it comes to a boil in approximately 4 min, and boil for exactly 2 min. Filter the precipitated cuprous oxide through a tared, sintered-glass filter crucible previously washed with hot water, ethanol, and ether, and dry it at 100° for 30 min. Thoroughly wash the collected cuprous oxide on the filter with hot water, then with 10 mL of ethanol, and finally with 10 mL of ether, and dry at 100° for 30 min. Weigh the cuprous oxide residue so obtained.
  Acceptance criteria: The weight of the cuprous oxide residue is NMT 30 mg (NMT 0.3%).

SPECIFIC TESTS
- **PH,** pH Determination, Appendix IIB
  Sample solution: Prepare an aqueous solution of sample.
  Acceptance criteria: Between 4.5 and 7.0
- **RESIDUE ON IGNITION (SULFATED ASH),** Method I, Appendix IIC
  Sample: 2 g
  Acceptance criteria: NMT 0.1%
- **WATER,** Water Determination, Method I: Karl Fischer Titrimetric Method, Appendix IIC
  Acceptance criteria: NMT 5.5%

Lactose
First Published: FCC 6

4-O-β-Galactopyranosyl-D-glucose

$C_{12}H_{22}O_{11}$
$C_{12}H_{22}O_{11} \cdot H_2O$

Formula wt anhydrous 342.30
Formula wt monohydrate 360.32
CAS: anhydrous [63-42-3]
monohydrate [5989-81-1]

UNII: 3SY5LH9PMK [anhydrous lactose]
UNII: EWQ57Q8I5X [lactose monohydrate]

DESCRIPTION

Lactose occurs as a white to creamy white, crystalline powder. It is normally obtained from whey. It may be anhydrous, contain one molecule of water of hydration, or contain a mixture of both forms if it has been prepared by a spray-drying process. It is soluble in water, very slightly soluble in alcohol, and insoluble in chloroform and in ether.

Function: Nutritive sweetener; processing aid; humectant (anhydrous form); texturizer

Packaging and Storage: Store in well-closed containers protected from humidity.

IDENTIFICATION

- **PROCEDURE**
  Analysis: Add 5 mL of 1 N sodium hydroxide to 5 mL of a hot, saturated solution of sample, and gently warm the mixture. The liquid turns yellow and, finally, brown-red. Cool to room temperature, and add a few drops of alkaline cupric tartrate TS.
  Acceptance criteria: A red precipitate of cuprous oxide forms.

ASSAY

- **LACTOSE,** Appendix X
  Sample preparation: Transfer 2 g of sample to a 100-mL volumetric flask. Add 10 mL of *Fructose Internal Standard Solution*, dilute to volume with water, and mix. [NOTE—Perform the analysis within 24 h of making this solution.]
  Acceptance criteria: NLT 98.0% and NMT 100.5% of $C_{12}H_{22}O_{11}$, calculated on the dried basis

IMPURITIES

Inorganic Impurities

- **ARSENIC,** *Arsenic Limit Test,* Appendix IIIB
  Sample solution: 114 mg/mL in water
  Control: 2 µg As (2.0 mL of *Standard Arsenic Solution*)
  Acceptance criteria: NMT 0.5 mg/kg
- **LEAD,** *Lead Limit Test, Atomic Absorption Spectrophotometric Graphite Furnace Method, Method I,* Appendix IIIB
  Sample: 5 g
  Acceptance criteria: NMT 0.5 mg/kg

SPECIFIC TESTS

- **LOSS ON DRYING,** Appendix IIC: 120° for 16 h
  Sample: 2 g
  Acceptance criteria
    Monohydrate and spray-dried mixture: NLT 4.5% and NMT 5.5%
    Anhydrous: NMT 1.0%
- **PH,** *pH Determination,* Appendix IIB
  Sample preparation: Transfer 10 g of sample into a clean, dry 100-mL Erlenmeyer flask and add 90 mL of recently boiled water cooled to 25°. Shake until the particles are evenly suspended and the mixture is free of lumps. Heat the sample to boiling and shake frequently to aid dissolution. Let the suspension stand for 10 min, decant the supernatant into the hydrogen-ion vessel, and quickly cool to 25°.
  Analysis: Proceed as directed using pH 4.01 and 9.18 buffer solutions to standardize the pH meter.
  Acceptance criteria: NLT 4.5 and NMT 7.5
- **RESIDUE ON IGNITION (SULFATED ASH),** *Method I,* Appendix IIC
  Sample: 2 g
  Acceptance criteria: NMT 0.3%

OTHER REQUIREMENTS

- **LABELING:** Indicate whether it is anhydrous or the monohydrate or a mixture of both forms if it has been prepared by a spray-drying process.

Lactylated Fatty Acid Esters of Glycerol and Propylene Glycol

First Published: Prior to FCC 6

Propylene Glycol Lactostearate
INS: 478

DESCRIPTION

Lactylated Fatty Acid Esters of Glycerol and Propylene Glycol occur as a substance that varies in consistency from a soft solid to a hard, waxy solid. They are a mixture of partial lactic and fatty acid esters of propylene glycol and glycerin produced by the lactylation of a product obtained by reacting edible fats or oils with propylene glycol. They are dispersible in hot water, and are moderately soluble in hot isopropanol, in chloroform, and in soybean oil.

Function: Emulsifier; stabilizer; whipping agent; plasticizer
Packaging and Storage: Store in well-closed containers

IDENTIFICATION

- **GAS CHROMATOGRAPHY,** Appendix IIA
  Sample preparation: Place 150 mg of melted sample into a 16- × 125-mm tube equipped with a screw cap having a Teflon liner, and add 4 mL of absolute methanol, 4 drops of a 25% sodium methoxide solution in absolute methanol, and a boiling chip. Cap the tube, reflux for 15 min, and cool to room temperature. Extract as follows: Add 8 drops of a 15% potassium acid sulfate solution, 4 mL of water, and 4 mL of *n*-hexane; cap the tube; shake for 1 min; and centrifuge for 30 to 60 s. Decant and discard the *n*-hexane layer, and repeat the extraction with three additional 4-mL portions of *n*-hexane, discarding each extract. Transfer the aqueous alcoholic phase from the tube into a 50-mL round-bottom, glass-stoppered flask; place the flask in a water bath at 50° to 55°; and evaporate to near dryness (about 0.5 mL of residue) in a rotary film evaporator under full water aspirator vacuum. [**CAUTION**—Do not heat above 55°.] Remove the flask from the evaporator, add 1 mL of a 1:1 solution of 0.5 N hydrochloric acid:methanol, swirl for several minutes, and decant the clear solution into a small flask.

Standard solutions: Prepare solutions containing the following reference substances: propylene glycol, methyl lactate, lactic acid, and glycerin.
Chromatographic system, Appendix IIA
  Mode: Gas chromatography
  Detector: Flame-ionization detector
  Column: 1.8-m × 3-mm (id) column packed with 80- to 100-mesh Porapak Q (ethylvinylbenzene-divinylbenzene polymer porous beads), or equivalent
  Temperature
    Column: 175° to 210° (Increase at 4°/min, and hold at 210° until the glycerin is eluted.)
    Inlet port: 310°
    Detector: 385°
  Flow rate: 50 mL/min
  Carrier gas: Helium
  [NOTE—Use a recorder with a range of 0 to 1 mV and a 1-s full-scale deflection at a chart speed of 6.5 mm/min.]
Analysis: Inject a portion of the *Sample preparation* into the chromatograph. From the chromatogram so obtained, identify the peaks by their relative positions on the chart. Major peaks representing propylene glycol, methylene lactate, lactic acid, and glycerin, in the order listed, may be identified with suitable reference standards, and may also be identified by their relative retention times using a suitable internal standard.
Acceptance criteria: The major peaks from the chromatogram of the *Sample preparation* match appropriate standards.

IMPURITIES
Inorganic Impurities
- **LEAD,** Lead Limit Test, Flame Atomic Absorption Spectrophotometric Method, Appendix IIIB
  Sample: 10 g
  Acceptance criteria: NMT 2 mg/kg

SPECIFIC TESTS
- **ACID VALUE (FATS AND RELATED SUBSTANCES),** Method II, Appendix VII
  Acceptance criteria: NMT 12.0
- **FREE GLYCERIN,** Free Glycerin or Propylene Glycol, Appendix VII
  Acceptance criteria: The result should conform to the representations of the vendor.
- **FREE LACTIC ACID**
  Sample: 15 g
  Analysis: Dissolve the *Sample* in 75 mL of benzene in a beaker and transfer it to a 500-mL glass-stoppered graduated cylinder. Wash the beaker with 125 mL of benzene in divided portions, adding the washings to the graduated cylinder. Add 200 mL of water to the graduated cylinder, and shake vigorously for 1 min. After 125 mL or more of the aqueous phase has separated, pipet 100.0 mL of the aqueous phase into an Erlenmeyer flask, add 1 mL of phenolphthalein TS, and titrate with 0.5 N sodium hydroxide to the first appearance of a slight pink color. Calculate the percentage of free lactic acid in the sample by the formula:

$$\text{Result} = (V \times N \times F_E)/(0.5 \times W)$$

  V = volume of 0.5 N sodium hydroxide required (mL)
  N = exact normality of the sodium hydroxide solution
  F_E = equivalence factor for lactic acid, 45.04
  W = weight of the sample taken (g)
  Acceptance criteria: The result should conform to the representations of the vendor.
- **1-MONOGLYCERIDE CONTENT,** 1-Monoglycerides, Appendix VII
  Acceptance criteria: The result should conform to the representations of the vendor.
- **TOTAL LACTIC ACID**
  Sample: 3 g
  Analysis: Transfer the *Sample* into a 250-mL glass-stoppered flask, pipet 50.0 mL of 0.7 N alcoholic potassium hydroxide into the flask, attach an air condenser, and boil gently on a steam bath for 30 min or until the sample is completely saponified. Remove the flask from the steam bath, immediately remove the air condenser, and allow the solution to cool until it begins to gel. Add 75.0 mL of 0.5 N hydrochloric acid, mix, and transfer the solution into a 500-mL separatory funnel, washing the flask with two 15-mL portions of water and adding them to the solution in the separatory funnel. Cool to 35° or lower, and extract with 100 mL of diethyl ether. Transfer the aqueous layer into a second 500-mL separatory funnel, and wash the ether layer with two 20-mL portions of water, adding the wash water to the original aqueous phase in the second separatory funnel. Retain the ether solution. Extract the aqueous phase with a second 100-mL portion of diethyl ether, and transfer the aqueous phase into a 500-mL Erlenmeyer flask. Combine and wash the ether extracts with five 20-mL portions of water, and add the wash water to the flask. Add 1 mL of phenolphthalein TS to the combined aqueous phases in the Erlenmeyer flask, and titrate with 0.5 N sodium hydroxide to the first appearance of a slight pink color. Perform a blank determination (see *General Provisions*), make any necessary correction, and calculate the percent of total lactic acid in the sample taken by the formula:

$$\text{Result} = [(V_S - V_B) \times N \times F_E]/W$$

  V_S = volume of 0.5 N sodium hydroxide required for titration of the sample (mL)
  V_B = volume of 0.5 N sodium hydroxide required for titration of the blank (mL)
  N = exact normality of the sodium hydroxide solution
  F_E = equivalence factor for lactic acid, 45.04
  W = weight of the sample taken (g)

Acceptance criteria: The result should conform to the representations of the vendor.
- **WATER,** *Water Determination,* Appendix IIB
  Acceptance criteria: The result should conform to the representations of the vendor.
- **WATER-INSOLUBLE COMBINED LACTIC ACID**
  Sample: 3 g
  Analysis: Transfer the *Sample* into a 250-mL separatory funnel with the aid of 100 mL of benzene, and wash with three 30-mL portions of water, discarding the washings. Transfer the benzene layer into a 250-mL glass-stoppered Erlenmeyer flask, wash the separatory funnel with a few mL of benzene, and completely evaporate the combined benzene solution to dryness. Pipet 50.0 mL of 0.7 N alcoholic potassium hydroxide into the flask, attach an air condenser, boil gently on a steam bath for 30 min or until the sample is completely saponified, and remove the flask from the steam bath. Immediately remove the air condenser, and allow the solution to cool until it begins to gel. Add 75.0 mL of 0.5 N hydrochloric acid, mix, and transfer the solution into a 500-mL separatory funnel, washing the flask with two 15-mL portions of water. Cool to 35° or lower, and extract with 100 mL of diethyl ether. Transfer the water layer to a second 500-mL separatory funnel, and wash the diethyl ether with two 20-mL portions of water, adding the wash water to the original aqueous phase in the second separatory funnel. Retain the ether solution. Extract the aqueous phase with a second 100-mL portion of diethyl ether, and transfer the aqueous phase to a 500-mL Erlenmeyer flask. Combine and wash the ether extracts with five 20-mL portions of water, and add the wash water to the flask. Add 1 mL of phenolphthalein TS to the combined aqueous phases in the flask, and titrate with 0.5 N sodium hydroxide to the first appearance of a slight pink color. Perform a blank determination (see *General Provisions*), make any necessary correction, and calculate the percent of water-insoluble combined lactic acid in the sample taken by the formula:

$$\text{Result} = [(V_S - V_B) \times N \times F_E]/W$$

V_S = volume of 0.5 N sodium hydroxide required for titration of the sample (mL)
V_B = volume of 0.5 N sodium hydroxide required for titration of the blank (mL)
N = exact normality of the sodium hydroxide solution
F_E = equivalence factor for lactic acid, 45.04
W = weight of the sample taken (g)

Acceptance criteria: Between 14.0% and 18.0%

Lactylic Esters of Fatty Acids

First Published: Prior to FCC 6

DESCRIPTION
Lactylic Esters of Fatty Acids occur as liquids to hard, waxy solids. They are mixed fatty acid esters of lactic acid and its polymers, with minor quantities of free lactic acid, polylactic acid, and fatty acids. They are dispersible in hot water and are soluble in organic solvents and in vegetable oils.
Function: Emulsifier; surface-active agent
Packaging and Storage: Store in tight, plastic-lined containers in a cool, dry place.

IDENTIFICATION
- **LACTIC ACID**
  Sample: 1 mL of the solution obtained in the test for *Total Lactic Acid* (below)
  Analysis: Transfer the *Sample* into a 25-mL glass-stoppered test tube. Add 0.1 mL of 40 mg/mL cupric sulfate pentahydrate solution and 6 mL of sulfuric acid, and mix. Stopper loosely, heat in a boiling water bath for 5 min, then cool in an ice bath for 5 min, and remove from the bath. Add 0.1 mL of *p*-phenylphenol TS, mix, allow to stand at room temperature for 1 min, and then heat in a boiling water bath for 1 min.
  Acceptance criteria: A deep, blue-violet color appears, indicating the presence of lactic acid.
- **THIN-LAYER CHROMATOGRAPHY,** Appendix IIA
  Sample solution: 100 mg/mL in hexane
  Stearic acid solution: 25 mg/mL in hexane
  Adsorbent: Chromatographic silica gel containing about 13% calcium sulfate
  Developing solvent system: Hexane:acetone:glacial acetic acid: (92:4:4)
  Spray reagent: Saturated solution of chromium trioxide in sulfuric acid
  Analysis: Prepare a 500 mg/mL slurry of *Adsorbent* in water and apply a uniformly thin layer to glass plates of convenient size. Dry in air for 10 min and activate by drying at 100° for 1 h. Spot 2 µL of the *Sample solution* and 1 µL of the *Stearic acid solution* onto the plates, allow them to dry, and place them in a suitable ascending chromatographic chamber containing the *Developing solvent system*. Following development, remove the plate from the chamber, dry thoroughly in air, and spray evenly with *Spray reagent*. Immediately place the sprayed plate on a hot plate in a hood, heat it to about 200°, char until white fumes of sulfur trioxide cease to evolve, and cool to room temperature.
  Acceptance criteria: The spots from the *Sample solution* are located according to the following R_F values:
  Stearic acid: 1.00
  Fatty acid: 1.00
  Acylated monolactic acid: 0.84
  Acylated dilactic acid: 0.76
  Acylated trilactic acid: 0.68
  Tetralactic acid: 0.62

ASSAY

- **ACYLATED MONOLACTIC ACID, ACYLATED POLYLACTIC ACID, AND FREE FATTY ACIDS**

  Boron trifluoride solution: 14% (w/v) solution of boron trifluoride in methanol (A commercial reagent, 14% w/v, may be used; Applied Science, or equivalent.)

  Sample preparation: Transfer 100 mg of sample into a small, conical flask fitted with a suitable reflux condenser. Add 5.0 mL of a *Boron trifluoride solution*. Swirl to mix, and reflux for 15 min. Cool, transfer the reaction mixture with the aid of 10 mL of chromatographic-grade hexane to a 60-mL separatory funnel, and add 10 mL of water and 10 mL of saturated sodium chloride solution. Shake, allow the mixture to separate, then drain and discard the lower, aqueous layer. Pass the hexane layer through 6 g of anhydrous sodium sulfate into a suitable flask. This hexane layer is the *Sample preparation*.

  Chromatographic system, Appendix IIA
  Mode: Gas chromatography
  Detector: Flame-ionization detector
  Column: 1.2-m × 6.3-mm (id) column packed with 20% SE-30 or SE-52, or equivalent grades of silicone rubber gums, on Chromosorb P or W or Diatoport S, or equivalent grades of diatomaceous material
  Temperature
  Column: 150° to 310° (increase at 4°/min)
  Inlet port: 335°
  Detector: 315°
  Carrier gas: Helium
  Flow rate: About 54 mL/min
  [NOTE—Use a recorder that has an attenuation switch, a range of 0 to 1 mV and a 1-s full-scale deflection at a chart speed of 12.7 mm/min.]
  Injection volume: 0.5 to 2.0 μL. [NOTE—Adjust the sample size so that the major peak is not attenuated more than ×8.]
  Analysis: Using a 10-μL capacity Hamilton fixed needle, or equivalent, inject the *Sample preparation* into the chromatograph. From the chromatogram so obtained, identify the peaks by their relative position on the chart. The esters, appearing in the order of increasing number of carbon atoms in the fatty acid and in order of increasing length of the polymer, are eluted as follows:

    myristate
    palmitate
    stearate
    palmitoyl lactylate (2-palmitoyloxypropionate)
    stearoyl lactylate (2-stearoyloxypropionate)
    palmitoyl lactoyl lactylate
    stearoyl lactoyl lactylate
    palmitoyl dilactoyl lactylate
    stearoyl dilactoyl lactylate
    palmitoyl triactoyl lactylate
    stearoyl triactoyl lactylate
    palmitoyl tetralactoyl lactylate

  Other esters may be determined by interpolation of a conventional carbon number-retention plot. Determine the composition of the sample, using the area normalization method, by the equation:

  $$\%_i = 100 \times A_i / \Sigma(A_i + \ldots + A_n)$$

  i = component of interest
  A_i = equalized area for the component of interest

  If free and polylactic acids are present, as determined in *Total Free and Polylactic Acids* (below), the results should be corrected by the following formula:

  $$\text{Result} = \%_i \times [(100 - F)/100]$$

  F = *Total Free and Polylactic Acids* (%), determined below

  Acceptance criteria: The results should conform to the representations of the vendor.

IMPURITIES

Inorganic Impurities

- **LEAD,** *Lead Limit Test, Flame Atomic Absorption Spectrophotometric Method,* Appendix IIB
  Sample: 10 g
  Acceptance criteria: NMT 2 mg/kg

SPECIFIC TESTS

- **ACID VALUE (FATS AND RELATED SUBSTANCES),** *Method II,* Appendix VII
  Acceptance criteria: The result should conform to the representations of the vendor.

- **SAPONIFICATION VALUE,** Appendix VII
  Acceptance criteria: The result should conform to the representations of the vendor.

- **TOTAL FREE AND POLYLACTIC ACIDS**
  Sample: 500 mg, previously melted
  Analysis: Transfer the *Sample* into a 50-mL glass-stoppered separatory funnel with the aid of 15 mL of hexane, and add 10 mL of water. Invert the separatory funnel ten times, and allow it to stand until the layers have separated. Filter the aqueous layer through a plug of glass wool into a 125-mL flask, wash the hexane with two 10-mL portions of water, and combine the aqueous layers. Add 5.0 mL of 0.1 N sodium hydroxide to the flask, then heat the flask on a steam bath for 15 min under a nitrogen atmosphere. Titrate with 0.1 N hydrochloric acid, using phenolphthalein TS as the indicator, to the disappearance of the pink color. Conduct a blank determination (see *General Provisions*), using 30 mL of water and 5.0 mL of 0.1 N sodium hydroxide, and make any necessary correction. Calculate the percent of free and polylactic acids in the sample by the formula:

  $$\text{Result} = [(V_B - V_S) \times F_E]/W$$

  V_B = volume of 0.1 N hydrochloric acid required for the titration of the blank (mL)
  V_S = volume of 0.1 N hydrochloric acid required for the titration of the *Sample* (mL)

F_E = equivalence factor for lactic acid, 9.008
W = weight of the sample taken (g)

Acceptance criteria: The result should conform to the representations of the vendor.

- **TOTAL LACTIC ACID**

  Sample: An amount of melted sample equivalent to between 140 and 170 mg of lactic acid

  Analysis: Transfer the *Sample* into a 250-mL Erlenmeyer flask. Pipet 20 mL of 0.5 N alcoholic potassium hydroxide into the flask, connect an air condenser at least 65 cm long, and reflux for 30 min. In a separate flask, run a blank determination (see *General Provisions*) using the same volume of 0.5 N alcoholic potassium hydroxide. Add 20 mL of water to each flask, then disconnect the condensers, evaporate to a volume of about 20 mL, and cool to about 40°. Add methyl red TS to each flask, and titrate the blank with 0.5 N hydrochloric acid. While swirling the *Sample* flask, add exactly the same volume of 0.5 N hydrochloric acid. Add 50 mL of hexane to each flask. Swirl the *Sample* flask vigorously to dissolve the fatty acids, then quantitatively transfer the contents of each flask into separate 250-mL separatory funnels, and shake for 30 s. Collect the aqueous phases in 300-mL Erlenmeyer flasks, wash the hexane solutions with 50 mL of water, and combine the wash solution with the original aqueous phases in the Erlenmeyer flasks, discarding the hexane solution. Titrate with 0.1 N potassium hydroxide, using phenolphthalein TS as the indicator, to a pink color that persists for at least 30 s. [NOTE—Save the resulting titrated *Sample* solution for use in *Identification* test A (above).] Calculate the percent of total lactic acid by the formula:

  $$\text{Result} = [(V_S - V_B) \times N \times F_E]/W$$

  V_S = volume of 0.1 N potassium hydroxide required for the titration of the *Sample* (mL)
  V_B = volume of 0.1 N potassium hydroxide required for the titration of the blank (mL)
  N = exact normality of the potassium hydroxide solution
  F_E = equivalence factor for lactic acid, 9.008
  W = weight of the sample taken (g)

  Acceptance criteria: The result should conform to the representations of the vendor.

- **WATER**, *Water Determination*, Appendix IIB

  Acceptance criteria: The result should conform to the representations of the vendor.

Lanolin, Anhydrous

First Published: Prior to FCC 6

Wool Fat
INS: 913
UNII: 7EV65EAW6H [lanolin]
CAS: [8006-54-0]

DESCRIPTION

Lanolin, Anhydrous occurs as a purified, yellow-white, semisolid, fat-like substance. It is extracted from the wool of sheep. It is insoluble in water, but mixes with about twice its weight of water without separation. It is soluble in chloroform and in ether.

Function: Masticatory substance in chewing gum base

Packaging and Storage: Store in well-closed containers, preferably at a temperature not exceeding 30°.

IMPURITIES

Inorganic Impurities

- **LEAD,** *Sample Solution for Lead Limit Test*, Appendix IV

  Acceptance criteria: NMT 3 mg/kg

SPECIFIC TESTS

- **ACID VALUE (FATS AND RELATED SUBSTANCES),** *Method I*, Appendix VII

  Acceptance criteria: NMT 1.12

- **IODINE VALUE,** Appendix VII

  Acceptance criteria: Between 18 and 36

- **LOSS ON HEATING**

  Sample: 5 g

  Analysis: Heat the *Sample* on a steam bath, with frequent stirring, to constant weight.

  Acceptance criteria: NMT 0.5%

- **MELTING RANGE OR TEMPERATURE DETERMINATION,** Appendix IIB

  Acceptance criteria: Between 36° and 42°

Lard (Unhydrogenated)

First Published: Prior to FCC 6

UNII: SI6O3IW77Z [lard]

DESCRIPTION

Lard (Unhydrogenated) is an off-white fat obtained by dry or wet (steam) rendering of fresh fatty porcine tissues (cuttings and trimmings) shortly after slaughtering. Rendered Lard may be bleached, or bleached and deodorized. It is soft to semisolid at 27° and melts completely at 42°.

Rendered, Bleached, and Bleached-Deodorized lards are off-white semisolids at 21° to 27°. Bleached, and Bleached-Deodorized lards, which are pale yellow and clear at 54°, differ from Rendered Lard, which is pale yellow, clear to hazy, and may contain extraneous matter.

Function: Coating agent; texturizer

Packaging and Storage: Store in well-closed containers.

IDENTIFICATION

- **FATTY ACID COMPOSITION,** Appendix VII

  Acceptance criteria: A sample exhibits the following composition profile of fatty acids:

Fatty Acid	Weight % (Range)
<14:0	<0.5
14:0	0.5–2.5

Fatty Acid	Weight % (Range)
14:1	0.2
15:0	<0.1
16:0	20–32
16:1	1.7–5
17:0	<1.0
17:1	<0.7
18:0	5.0–24
18:1	35–62
18:2	3.0–16
18:3	<2.0
20:0	<1.0
20:1	<1.0

IMPURITIES
Inorganic Impurities
- **LEAD,** *Lead Limit Test, Atomic Absorption Spectrophotometric Graphite Furnace Method, Method II,* Appendix IIIB
  Sample: 3 g
  Acceptance criteria: NMT 0.1 mg/kg
- **WATER,** *Water Determination,* Appendix IIB
  Analysis: Determine as directed except use 50 mL of chloroform in place of 35 to 40 mL of methanol to dissolve the sample.
  Acceptance criteria
    Rendered lard: NMT 0.5%
    Bleached lard: NMT 0.1%
    Bleached-deodorized lard: NMT 0.1%

SPECIFIC TESTS
- **COLOR (FATS AND RELATED SUBSTANCES),** Appendix VII
  Acceptance criteria
    Rendered lard: NMT 3.0 red
    Bleached lard: NMT 1.5 red
    Bleached-deodorized lard: NMT 1.5 red
- **FREE FATTY ACIDS (AS OLEIC ACID),** *Free Fatty Acids,* Appendix VII
  Analysis: Use the following equivalence factor (e) in the formula given in the procedure:
    Free fatty acids as oleic acid, e = 28.2
  Acceptance criteria
    Rendered lard: NMT 1.0%
    Bleached lard: NMT 1.0%
    Bleached-deodorized lard: NMT 0.1%
- **HEXANE INSOLUBLE MATTER**
  Sample: 100 g, well mixed. [NOTE—If the sample is plastic or semisolid, soften a portion by warming it at a temperature not exceeding 60°, and then mix it thoroughly.]
  Analysis: Transfer the *Sample* into a 1500-mL wide-mouth Erlenmeyer flask, add 1000 mL of solvent hexane, and shake until the *Sample* is dissolved. Filter the resulting solution through a 600-mL Corning "C" porosity, or equivalent, filtering funnel that previously has been dried at 105° for 1 h, cooled in a desiccator, and weighed. Wash the flask with two successive 250-mL portions of solvent hexane, and pass the washings through the filter. Dry the funnel at 105° for 1 h, cool to room temperature in a desiccator, and weigh. From the gain in weight of the funnel, calculate the percentage of the hexane insoluble matter in the sample.
  Acceptance criteria
    Rendered lard: NMT 0.1%
    Bleached lard: NMT 0.05%
    Bleached-deodorized lard: NMT 0.05%
- **IODINE VALUE,** Appendix VII
  Acceptance criteria: Between 46 and 70
- **PEROXIDE VALUE**
  Sample: 10 g
  Analysis: To the *Sample*, add 30 mL of a 3:2 mixture of glacial acetic acid:chloroform and mix. Add 1 mL of a saturated solution of potassium iodide, mix the solution for 1 min, add 100 mL of water and immediately begin titrating with 0.05 N sodium thiosulfate, adding starch TS as the endpoint is approached. Continue the titration until the blue starch color has just disappeared. Perform a blank determination (see *General Provisions*), and make any necessary correction. Calculate the peroxide value, as mEq of peroxide per kg of sample by the formula:

$$\text{Result} = [S \times N \times 1000]/W$$

  S = net volume (mL) of sodium thiosulfate solution required for the sample
  N = exact normality of the sodium thiosulfate solution
  W = weight (g) of the sample taken
  Acceptance criteria: NMT 10 mEq/kg
- **UNSAPONIFIABLE MATTER,** Appendix VII
  Acceptance criteria
    Rendered lard: NMT 1.5%
    Bleached lard: NMT 1.5%
    Bleached-deodorized lard: NMT 1.5%

Laurel Leaf Oil

First Published: Prior to FCC 6

Bay Leaf Oil

CAS: [8006-78-8]

UNII: 5UMH0U3W0V [bay leaf oil]

DESCRIPTION
Laurel Leaf Oil occurs as a light yellow to yellow liquid with an aromatic, spicy odor. It is the oil obtained by steam distillation from the leaves of *Laurus nobilis* L. (Fam. Lauraceae). It is soluble in most fixed oils, and it is soluble with cloudiness in mineral oil and in propylene glycol. It is insoluble in glycerin.
[NOTE—The oil from *Laurus nobilis* L. should not be confused with that of the West Indian bay tree or the California bay laurel.]
Function: Flavoring agent

Packaging and Storage: Store in a cool place protected from light in full, tight containers that are made from steel or aluminum and that are suitably lined.

IDENTIFICATION

- **INFRARED SPECTRA,** *Spectrophotometric Identification Tests,* Appendix IIIC
  Acceptance criteria: The spectrum of the sample exhibits relative maxima at the same wavelengths as those of the spectrum below.

SPECIFIC TESTS

- **ACID VALUE (ESSENTIAL OILS AND FLAVORS),** Appendix VI
  Acceptance criteria: NMT 3.0
- **ANGULAR ROTATION,** *Optical (Specific) Rotation,* Appendix IIB: Use a 100-mm tube.
  Acceptance criteria: Between −10° and −19°
- **REFRACTIVE INDEX,** Appendix IIB
  [NOTE—Use an Abbé or other refractometer of equal or greater accuracy.]
  Acceptance criteria: Between 1.465 and 1.470 at 20°
- **SAPONIFICATION VALUE,** *Esters,* Appendix VI
  Sample: 5 g
  Acceptance criteria: Between 15 and 45
- **SAPONIFICATION VALUE AFTER ACETYLATION,** *Total Alcohols,* Appendix VI
  Sample: 2.5 g of acetylated oil
  Analysis: Calculate the saponification value by the formula:

$$\text{Result} = 28.05 \times A/B$$

  A = amount (mL) of 0.5 N alcoholic potassium hydroxide consumed in the titration
  B = weight (g) of the acetylated oil taken
  Acceptance criteria: Between 36 and 85
- **SOLUBILITY IN ALCOHOL**
  Acceptance criteria: One mL of sample dissolves in 1 mL of 80% alcohol, and it remains in solution upon dilution to 10 mL.
- **SPECIFIC GRAVITY:** Determine by any reliable method (see *General Provisions*).
  Acceptance criteria: Between 0.905 and 0.929

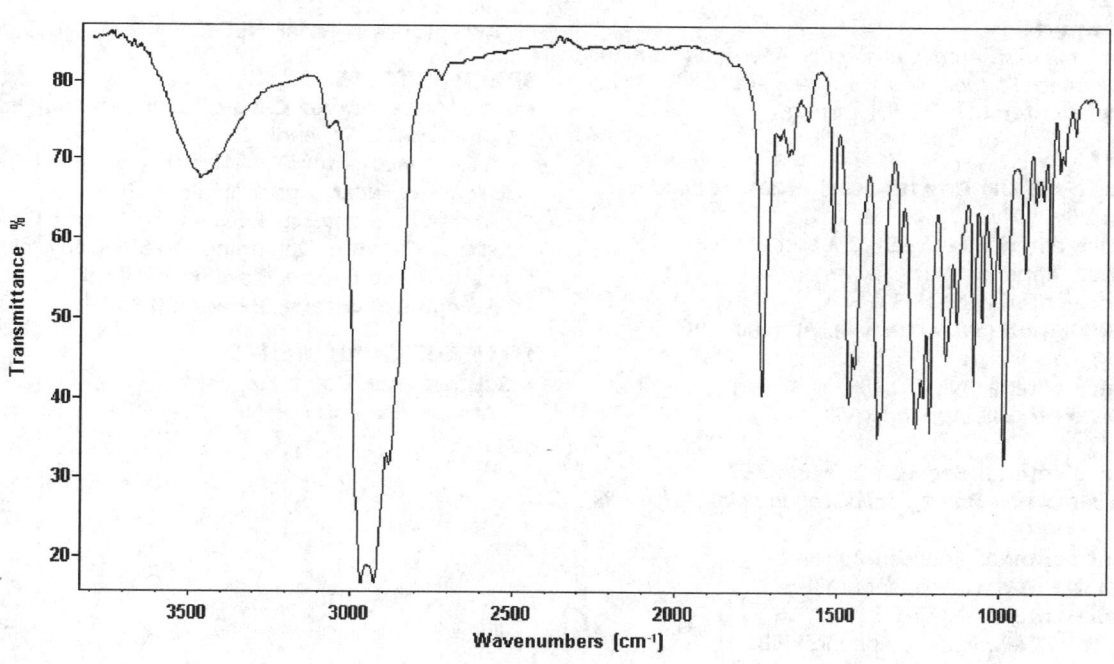

Laurel Leaf Oil

Lauric Acid

First Published: Prior to FCC 6

Dodecanoic Acid

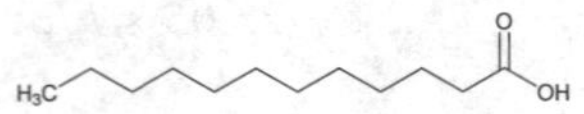

$C_{12}H_{24}O_2$	Formula wt 200.32
	CAS: [143-07-7]

UNII: 1160N9NU9U [lauric acid]

DESCRIPTION
Lauric Acid occurs as a white or faintly yellow, somewhat glossy, crystalline solid or powder. It is obtained from coconut oil and other plant fats. It is practically insoluble in water, but is soluble in alcohol, in chloroform, and in ether.
Function: Component in the manufacture of other food-grade additives; defoaming agent
Packaging and Storage: Store in well-closed containers.

IMPURITIES
Inorganic Impurities
- **LEAD,** *Lead Limit Test, Atomic Absorption Spectrophotometric Graphite Furnace Method, Method II,* Appendix IIIB
  Acceptance criteria: NMT 0.1 mg/kg

SPECIFIC TESTS
- **ACID VALUE (FATS AND RELATED SUBSTANCES),** *Method I,* Appendix VII
  Acceptance criteria: Between 252 and 287
- **IODINE VALUE,** Appendix VII
  Acceptance criteria: NMT 3.0
- **RESIDUE ON IGNITION (SULFATED ASH),** Appendix IIC
  Sample: 10 g
  Acceptance criteria: NMT 0.1%
- **SAPONIFICATION VALUE,** Appendix VII
  Sample: 3 g
  Acceptance criteria: Between 253 and 287
- **TITER (SOLIDIFICATION POINT),** *Solidification Point,* Appendix IIB
  Acceptance criteria: Between 26° and 44°
- **UNSAPONIFIABLE MATTER,** Appendix VII
  Acceptance criteria: NMT 0.3%
- **WATER,** *Water Determination,* Appendix IIB
  Acceptance criteria: NMT 0.2%

Lauryl Alcohol

First Published: Prior to FCC 6

1-Dodecanol
Alcohol C-12

$C_{12}H_{26}O$ Formula wt 186.34
FEMA: 2617
UNII: 178A96NLP2 [lauryl alcohol]

DESCRIPTION
Lauryl Alcohol occurs as a colorless liquid above 21°.
Odor: Fatty
Solubility: Soluble in most fixed oils, propylene glycol; insoluble or practically insoluble in glycerin, water
Boiling Point: ~259°
Solubility in Alcohol, Appendix VI: One mL dissolves in 3 mL of 70% alcohol, and remains in solution on dilution to 10 mL.
Function: Flavoring agent

IDENTIFICATION
- **INFRARED SPECTRA,** *Spectrophotometric Identification Tests,* Appendix IIIC
  Acceptance criteria: The spectrum of the sample exhibits relative maxima at the same wavelengths as those of the spectrum below.

ASSAY
- **PROCEDURE:** Proceed as directed under *M-1b,* Appendix XI.
  Acceptance criteria: NLT 97.0% of $C_{12}H_{26}O$

SPECIFIC TESTS
- **ACID VALUE, FLAVOR CHEMICALS (OTHER THAN ESSENTIAL OILS),** *M-15,* Appendix XI
  Acceptance criteria: NMT 1.0
- **REFRACTIVE INDEX,** Appendix II: At 20°
  Acceptance criteria: Between 1.440 and 1.444
- **SPECIFIC GRAVITY:** Determine at 25° by any reliable method (see *General Provisions*).
  Acceptance criteria: Between 0.830 and 0.836

OTHER REQUIREMENTS
- **SOLIDIFICATION POINT,** Appendix IIB
  Acceptance criteria: NLT 21°

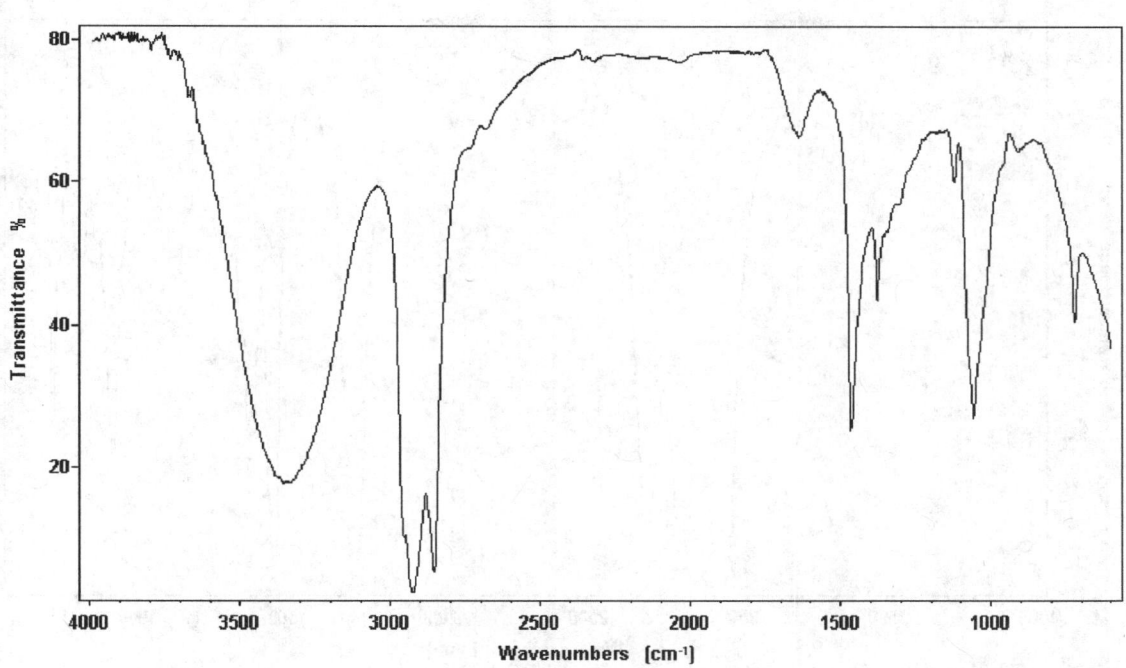

Lauryl Alcohol

Lauryl Aldehyde

First Published: Prior to FCC 6
Last Revision: First Supplement, FCC 6

Aldehyde C-12
Dodecanal

$C_{12}H_{24}O$ Formula wt 184.32
FEMA: 2615
UNII: C42O120SEF [lauryl aldehyde]

DESCRIPTION
Lauryl Aldehyde occurs as a colorless to light yellow liquid (that can solidify at room temperature). It may contain a suitable antioxidant.
Odor: Fatty
Solubility: Soluble in alcohol, most fixed oils, propylene glycol (may be turbid); insoluble or practically insoluble in glycerin, water

Boiling Point: ~249°
Function: Flavoring agent

IDENTIFICATION
- **INFRARED SPECTRA,** Spectrophotometric Identification Tests, Appendix IIIC
  Acceptance criteria: The spectrum of the sample exhibits relative maxima at the same wavelengths as those of the spectrum below.

ASSAY
- **PROCEDURE:** Proceed as directed under M-1b, Appendix XI.
  Acceptance criteria: NLT 92.0% of $C_{12}H_{24}O$

SPECIFIC TESTS
- **ACID VALUE, FLAVOR CHEMICALS (OTHER THAN ESSENTIAL OILS),** M-15, Appendix XI
  Acceptance criteria: NMT 10.0
- **REFRACTIVE INDEX,** Appendix II: At 20°
  Acceptance criteria: Between 1.433 and 1.439
- **SPECIFIC GRAVITY:** Determine at 25° by any reliable method (see General Provisions).
  Acceptance criteria: Between 0.826 and 0.836

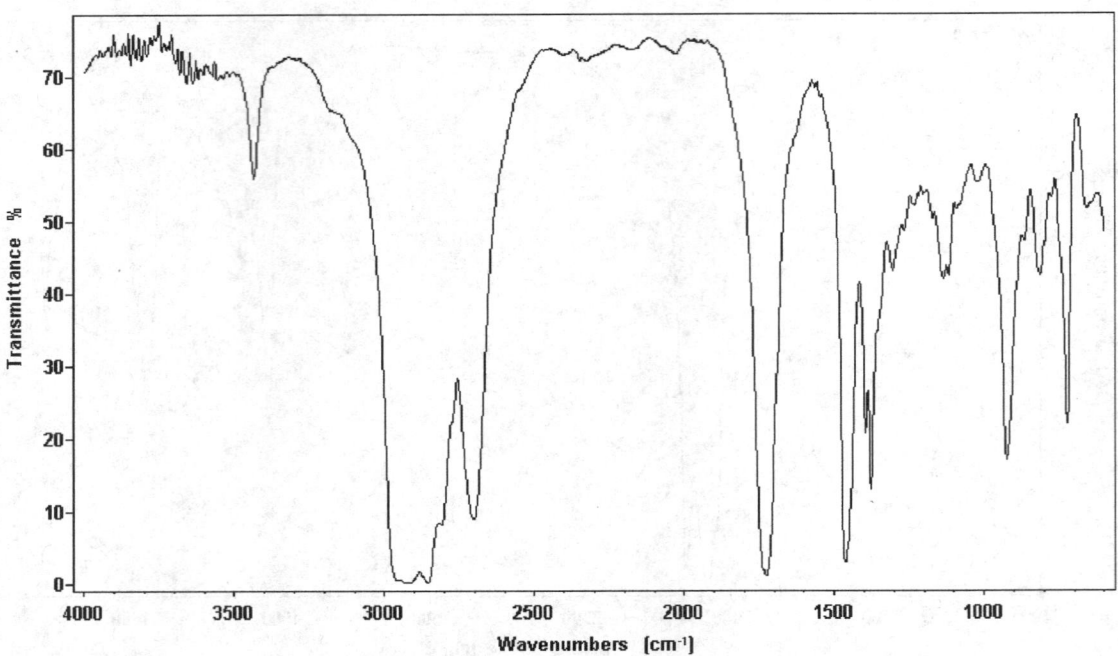

Lauryl Aldehyde

Lavandin Oil, Abrial Type

First Published: Prior to FCC 6

CAS: [8022-15-9]

UNII: 9RES347CKG [lavandin oil]

DESCRIPTION
Lavandin Oil, Abrial Type occurs as a pale yellow to yellow liquid with a slight, camphoraceous odor that is strongly suggestive of lavender. It is obtained by steam distillation of the fresh flowering tops of a hybrid, *Lavandula abrialis* unofficial (Fam. Labiatae), of true lavender, *Lavandula officinalis*, or of spike lavender, *Lavandula latifolia*. It is soluble in most fixed oils and in propylene glycol. It is soluble with opalescence in mineral oil, but it is relatively insoluble in glycerin.

Function: Flavoring agent.

Packaging and Storage: Store in a cool place protected from light in full, tight containers that are made from steel or aluminum and that are suitably lined.

IDENTIFICATION
- **INFRARED SPECTRA**, *Spectrophotometric Identification Tests*, Appendix IIIC
  Acceptance criteria: The spectrum of the sample exhibits relative maxima at the same wavelengths as those of the spectrum below.

ASSAY
- **ESTER DETERMINATION,** *Esters,* Appendix VI
  Sample: 3 g
  Analysis: Use 98.15 as the equivalence factor (e) in the calculation.
  Acceptance criteria: NLT 28.0% and NMT 35.0% of esters, calculated as linalyl acetate ($C_{12}H_{20}O_2$).

SPECIFIC TESTS
- **ANGULAR ROTATION,** *Optical (Specific) Rotation,* Appendix IIB: Use a 100-mm tube.
  Acceptance criteria: Between −2° and −5°
- **REFRACTIVE INDEX,** Appendix IIB
  [NOTE—Use an Abbé or other refractometer of equal or greater accuracy.]
  Acceptance criteria: Between 1.460 and 1.464 at 20°
- **SOLUBILITY IN ALCOHOL**
  Acceptance criteria: One mL of sample dissolves in 2 mL of 70% alcohol. A slight opalescence sometimes develops on further dilution.
- **SPECIFIC GRAVITY:** Determine by any reliable method (see *General Provisions*).
  Acceptance criteria: Between 0.885 and 0.893

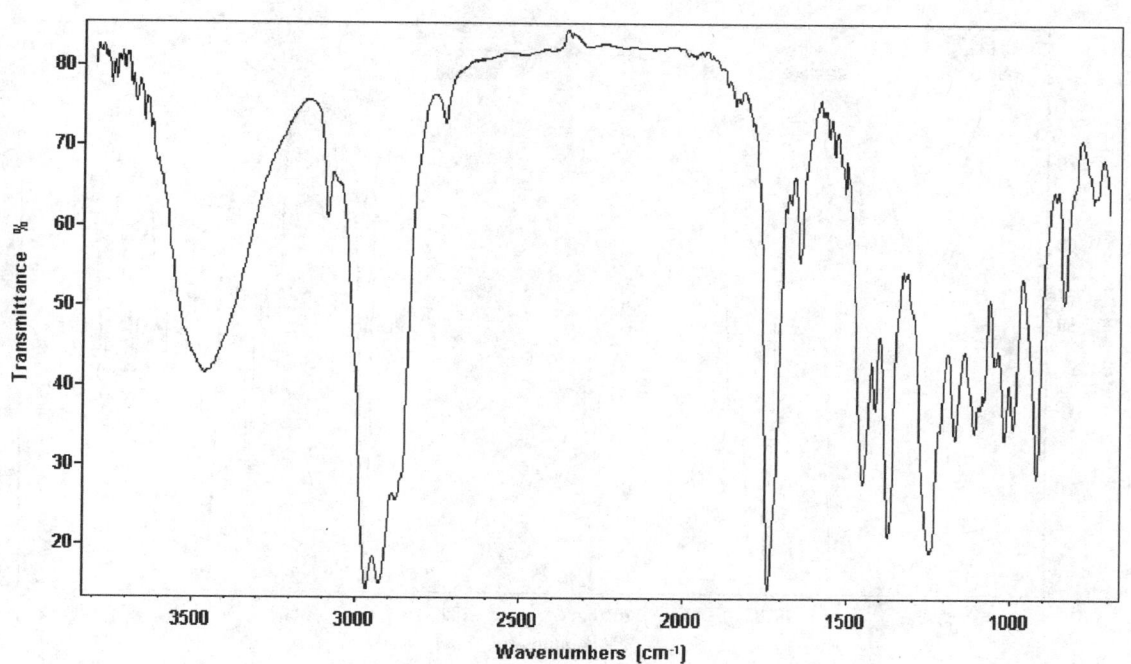

Lavandin Oil, Abrial Type

Lavender Oil

First Published: Prior to FCC 6

FEMA: 2622
CAS: [8000-28-0]
UNII: ZBP1YXW0H8 [lavender oil]

DESCRIPTION
Lavender Oil occurs as a colorless or yellow liquid with the characteristic odor and taste of lavender flowers. It is the volatile oil obtained by steam distillation from the fresh flowering tops of *Lavandula officinalis* Chaix ex Villars (*Lavandula vera* De Candolle) (Fam. Labiatae). It is soluble in alcohol and in most vegetable oils, but is insoluble in propylene glycol.
Function: Flavoring agent
Packaging and Storage: Store in a cool place protected from light in full, tight containers.

IDENTIFICATION
- **INFRARED SPECTRA,** *Spectrophotometric Identification Tests,* Appendix IIIC
  Acceptance criteria: The spectrum of the sample exhibits relative maxima at the same wavelengths as those of the spectrum below.

ASSAY
- **ESTERS,** *Ester Determination,* Appendix VI
  Sample: 5 g
  Analysis: Use 98.15 as the equivalence factor (e) in the calculation.
  Acceptance criteria: NLT 35.0% of esters, calculated as linalyl acetate ($C_{12}H_{20}O_2$).

SPECIFIC TESTS
- **ALCOHOL**
  Sample: 5 mL
  Analysis: Transfer the *Sample* into a narrow, glass-stoppered, 10-mL graduated cylinder and add 5 mL of water; shake the cylinder.
  Acceptance criteria: The volume of the oil does not diminish.
- **ANGULAR ROTATION,** *Optical (Specific) Rotation,* Appendix IIB: Use a 100-mm tube.
  Acceptance criteria: Between −3° and −10°
- **REFRACTIVE INDEX,** Appendix IIB
  [NOTE—Use an Abbé or other refractometer of equal or greater accuracy.]
  Acceptance criteria: Between 1.459 and 1.470 at 20°
- **SOLUBILITY IN ALCOHOL,** Appendix VI
  Acceptance criteria: One mL of sample dissolves in 4 mL of 70% alcohol.
- **SPECIFIC GRAVITY:** Determine by any reliable method (see *General Provisions*).
  Acceptance criteria: Between 0.875 and 0.888

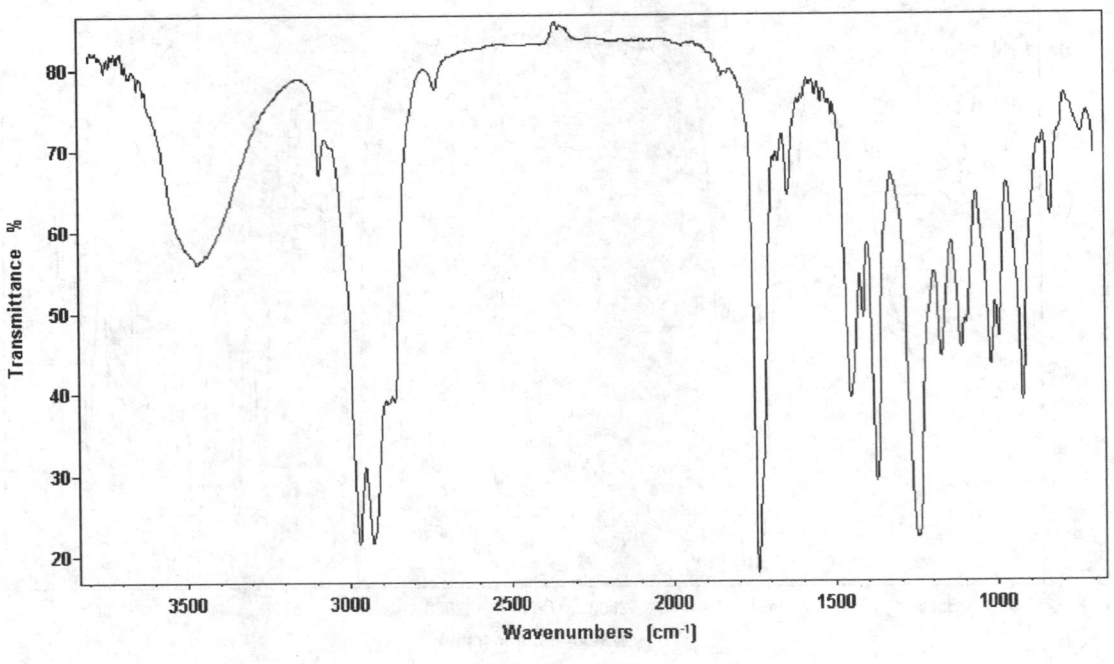

Lavender Oil

Lecithin

First Published: Prior to FCC 6

INS: 322   CAS: [8002-43-5]

DESCRIPTION
Lecithin, both natural and refined grades, occurs as a substance varying in consistency from plastic to fluid depending on free fatty acid and oil content and on the presence or absence of other diluents. Its color varies from light yellow to brown, depending on the source, on crop variations, and on whether it is bleached or unbleached. Lecithin is obtained from soybeans and other plant sources. It is a complex mixture of acetone-insoluble phosphatides that consists chiefly of phosphatidyl choline, phosphatidyl ethanolamine, and phosphatidyl inositol combined with various amounts of other substances such as triglycerides, fatty acids, and carbohydrates. Refined grades of Lecithin may contain any of these components in varying proportions and combinations depending on the type of fractionation used. In its oil-free form, the preponderance of triglycerides and fatty acids is removed and the product contains 90% or more of phosphatides representing all or certain fractions of the total phosphatide complex. Edible diluents, such as cocoa butter and vegetable oils, often replace soybean oil to improve functional and flavor characteristics. Lecithin is only partially soluble in water, but it readily hydrates to form emulsions. The oil-free phosphatides are soluble in fatty acids, but they are practically insoluble in fixed oils. When all phosphatide fractions are present, Lecithin is partially soluble in alcohol and practically insoluble in acetone.

Function: Antioxidant; emulsifier.
Packaging and Storage: Store in well-closed containers.

IMPURITIES
Inorganic Impurities
- **LEAD,** *Lead Limit Test, Flame Atomic Absorption Spectrophotometric Method,* Appendix IIIB
  Sample: 10 g
  Acceptance criteria: NMT 1 mg/kg

SPECIFIC TESTS
- **ACETONE-INSOLUBLE MATTER (AS PHOSPHATIDES)**
  Purified phosphatides preparation: Dissolve 10 g of sample in 20 mL of petroleum ether, add 50 mL of acetone to the solution, chill, and decant. Dry the solids under flowing nitrogen under a hood. Dissolve 5 g of the solids in 10 mL of petroleum ether, and add 25 mL of acetone to the solution. Transfer approximately equal portions of the precipitate to each of two 40-mL centrifuge tubes, using additional portions of acetone to facilitate the transfer. Stir thoroughly, dilute to 40 mL with acetone, stir again, chill for 15 min in an ice bath, stir again, and then centrifuge for 5 min. Decant the acetone, crush the solids with a stirring rod, refill the tube with acetone, stir, chill, centrifuge, and decant as before. The solids after the second centrifugation require no further purification and may be used for preparing the *Phosphatide–acetone solution.*
  Phosphatide–acetone solution: Add a quantity of *Purified phosphatides preparation* to sufficient acetone, previously cooled to about 5°, to form a saturated

solution [NOTE—Five g of the *Purified phosphatides preparation* are required to saturate about 16 L of acetone.], and maintain the mixture at this temperature for 2 h, shaking it vigorously at 15-min intervals. Decant the solution through a rapid filter paper, avoiding the transfer of any undissolved solids to the paper and conducting the filtration under refrigerated conditions (not above 5°).

Sample: 2 g, well-mixed. [NOTE—If the sample is plastic or semisolid, soften a portion by warming it at a temperature not exceeding 60°, and then mix it thoroughly.]

Analysis: Transfer the *Sample* into a 40-mL centrifuge tube, previously tared with a glass stirring rod, and add 15 mL of *Phosphatide–acetone solution* from a buret. Warm the mixture in a water bath until the *Sample* melts, but avoid evaporation of the acetone. Stir until the *Sample* is completely disintegrated and dispersed, transfer the tube into an ice bath, chill for 5 min, remove from the ice bath, and add about 10 mL of *Phosphatide–acetone solution*, previously chilled for 5 min in an ice bath. Stir the mixture to complete dispersion of the sample, dilute to 40 mL with chilled (5°) *Phosphatide–acetone solution*, stir to complete dispersion of the sample, and return the tube and contents to the ice bath for 15 min. Subsequently stir again while still in the ice bath, remove the stirring rod, and centrifuge the mixture immediately for 5 min. Decant the supernatant liquid from the centrifuge tube; crush the centrifuged solids with the stirring rod; refill the tube to the 40-mL mark with chilled (5°) *Phosphatide–acetone solution*; and repeat the chilling, stirring, centrifugation, and decantation procedure. After the second centrifugation and decantation of the supernatant acetone, again crush the solids with the stirring rod, and place the tube and its contents in a horizontal position at room temperature until the excess acetone has evaporated. Mix the residue again, dry the centrifuge tube and its contents at 105° for 45 min in a forced-draft oven, cool, and weigh. Calculate the percentage of acetone-insoluble substances by the formula:

$$\text{Result} = (100R/S) - B$$

- R = weight (g) of residue
- S = weight (g) of the sample taken
- B = percentage *Hexane-Insoluble Matter* determined below

Acceptance criteria: NLT 50.0%

- **ACID VALUE**

  Sample solution: 2 g, well-mixed. [NOTE—If the sample is plastic or semisolid, soften a portion by warming it in a water bath at a temperature not exceeding 60°, and then mix it thoroughly.]

  Analysis: Transfer the *Sample* into a 250-mL Erlenmeyer flask and dissolve it in 50 mL of petroleum ether. Add 50 mL of ethanol, previously neutralized to phenolphthalein with 0.1 N sodium hydroxide and mix well. Titrate with 0.1 N sodium hydroxide to a pink endpoint that persists for 5 s, using phenolphthalein TS as an indicator. Calculate the *Acid Value* by the formula:

  $$\text{Result} = 5.6 \times A / W$$

  - A = volume (mL) of 0.1 N sodium hydroxide consumed
  - W = weight (g) of the sample taken

  Acceptance criteria: NMT 36

- **HEXANE INSOLUBLE MATTER**

  Sample: 10 g, well mixed. [NOTE—If the sample is plastic or semisolid, soften a portion by warming it at a temperature not exceeding 60°, and then mix it thoroughly.]

  Analysis: Transfer the *Sample* into a 250-mL wide-mouth Erlenmeyer flask, add 100 mL of solvent hexane, and shake until the *Sample* is dissolved. Filter the resulting solution through a 30-mL Corning 'C' porosity, or equivalent, filtering funnel that previously has been dried at 105° for 1 h, cooled in a desiccator, and weighed. Wash the flask with two successive 25-mL portions of solvent hexane, and pass the washings through the filter. Dry the funnel at 105° for 1 h, cool to room temperature in a desiccator, and weigh. From the gain in weight of the funnel, calculate the percentage of the hexane insoluble matter in the sample.

  Acceptance criteria: NMT 0.3%

- **PEROXIDE VALUE**

  Sample: 10 g

  Analysis: To the *Sample*, add 30 mL of a 3:2 mixture of glacial acetic acid:chloroform and mix. Add 1 mL of a saturated solution of potassium iodide, mix, and allow to stand for 10 min. Add 100 mL of water and begin titrating with 0.05 N sodium thiosulfate, adding starch TS as the endpoint is approached. Continue the titration until the blue starch color has just disappeared. Perform a blank determination (see *General Provisions*), and make any necessary correction. Calculate the peroxide value, as mEq of peroxide per kg of sample by the formula:

  $$\text{Result} = [S \times N \times 1000]/W$$

  - S = net volume (mL) of sodium thiosulfate solution required for the sample
  - N = exact normality of the sodium thiosulfate solution
  - W = weight of the sample (g) taken

  Acceptance criteria: NMT 100

- **WATER,** *Water Determination,* Appendix IIB

  Acceptance criteria: NMT 1.5%

Lemon Oil, Cold-pressed

First Published: Prior to FCC 6

Lemon Oil, Expressed
FEMA: 2625
CAS: [8008-56-8]
UNII: I9GRO824LL [lemon oil]

DESCRIPTION
Lemon Oil, Cold-pressed occurs as a pale to deep yellow or green-yellow liquid with the characteristic odor and taste of the outer part of fresh lemon peel. It is the volatile oil obtained by expression, without the aid of heat, from the fresh peel of the fruit of *Citrus limon* L. Burmann filius (Fam. Rutaceae) with or without the previous separation of the pulp and the peel. It is miscible with dehydrated alcohol and with glacial acetic acid. It may contain a suitable antioxidant. [NOTE—Do not use if it has a terebinthine odor.]

Function: Flavoring agent

Packaging and Storage: Store in full, tight containers. Avoid exposure to excessive heat.

IDENTIFICATION
- **INFRARED SPECTRA,** *Spectrophotometric Identification Tests,* Appendix IIIC
  Acceptance criteria: The spectrum of the sample exhibits relative maxima at the same wavelengths as those of the spectrum below.

ASSAY
- **ALDEHYDES,** *Aldehydes and Ketones, Hydroxylamine tert-Butyl Alcohol Method,* Appendix VI
  Sample: 5 mL
  Analysis: Before titrating, allow the mixture to stand for 15 min, shaking the flask occasionally. Use 76.12 as the equivalence factor (e) in the calculation.
  Acceptance criteria
  California Type: NLT 2.2% and NMT 3.8% of aldehydes, calculated as citral ($C_{10}H_{16}O$)
  Italian Type: NLT 3.0% and NMT 5.5% of aldehydes, calculated as citral ($C_{10}H_{16}O$)

SPECIFIC TESTS
- **ANGULAR ROTATION,** *Optical (Specific) Rotation,* Appendix IIB: Use a 100-mm tube.
  Acceptance criteria: Between +57° and +65.6°
- **REFRACTIVE INDEX,** Appendix IIB
  [NOTE—Use an Abbé or other refractometer of equal or greater accuracy.]
  Acceptance criteria: Between 1.473 and 1.476 at 20°
- **SOLUBILITY IN ALCOHOL,** Appendix VI
  Acceptance criteria: One mL of sample dissolves in 3 mL of 95% alcohol, sometimes with a slight haze.
- **SPECIFIC GRAVITY:** Determine by any reliable method (see *General Provisions*).
  Acceptance criteria: Between 0.849 and 0.855
- **ULTRAVIOLET ABSORBANCE,** *Ultraviolet Absorbance of Citrus Oils,* Appendix VI
  Sample: 250 mg
  Acceptance criteria: [NOTE—The absorbance maximum occurs at 315 ± 3 nm.]
  California Type: NLT 0.2
  Italian Type: NLT 0.49

OTHER REQUIREMENTS
- **LABELING:** Indicate whether the oil is the California type or the Italian type.

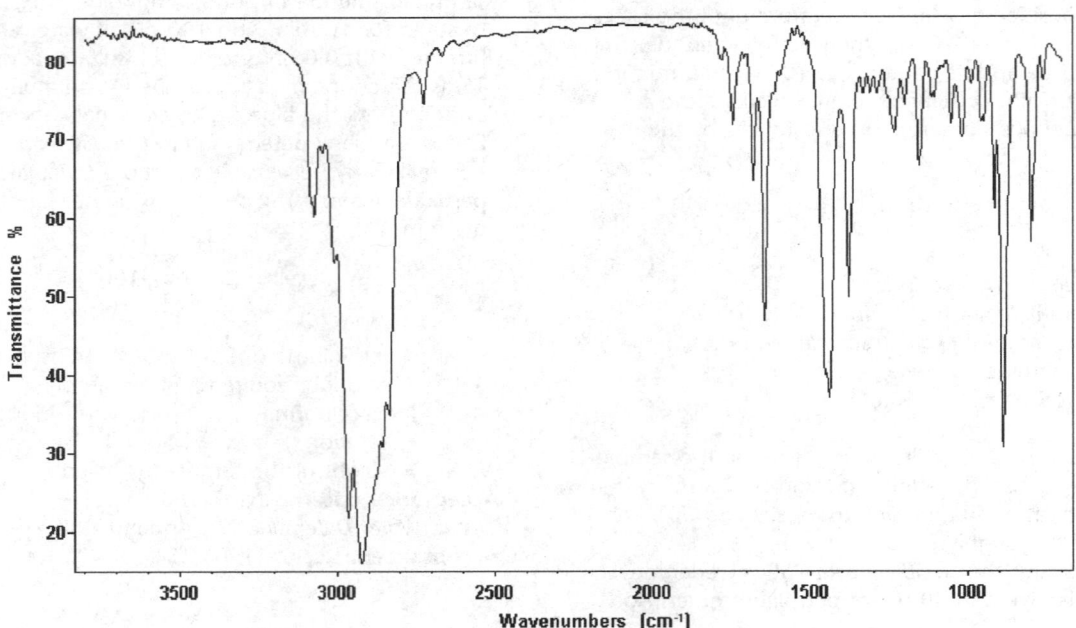

Lemon Oil, Cold-pressed

Lemon Oil, Desert Type, Cold-pressed

First Published: Prior to FCC 6

Lemon Oil Arizona
UNII: I9GRO824LL [lemon oil]

DESCRIPTION
Lemon Oil, Desert Type, Cold-pressed, occurs as a pale to deep yellow or green-yellow liquid with the characteristic odor and taste of the outer part of fresh lemon peel. It is the volatile oil obtained by expression, without the aid of heat, from the fresh peel of the fruit of *Citrus limon* L. Burmann filius (Fam. Rutaceae), with or without the previous separation of the pulp and peel. It is miscible with dehydrated alcohol and with glacial acetic acid. It may contain a suitable antioxidant. [NOTE—Do not use if it has a terebinthine odor.]

Function: Flavoring agent
Packaging and Storage: Store in full, tight containers. Avoid exposure to excessive heat.

IDENTIFICATION
- **INFRARED SPECTRA,** *Spectrophotometric Identification Tests,* Appendix IIIC
  Acceptance criteria: The spectrum of the sample exhibits relative maxima at the same wavelengths as those of the spectrum below.

ASSAY
- **ALDEHYDES,** *Aldehydes and Ketones, Hydroxylamine tert-Butyl Alcohol Method,* Appendix VI
  Sample: 5 mL
  Analysis: Before titrating, allow the mixture to stand for 15 min, shaking the flask occasionally. Use 76.12 as the equivalence factor (e) in the calculation.
  Acceptance criteria: NLT 1.7% of aldehydes, calculated as citral ($C_{10}H_{16}O$)

SPECIFIC TESTS
- **ANGULAR ROTATION,** *Optical (Specific) Rotation,* Appendix IIB: Use a 100-mm tube.
  Acceptance criteria: Between +67° and +78°
- **REFRACTIVE INDEX,** Appendix IIB
  [NOTE—Use an Abbé or other refractometer of equal or greater accuracy.]
  Acceptance criteria: Between 1.473 and 1.476 at 20°
- **SOLUBILITY IN ALCOHOL,** Appendix VI
  Acceptance criteria: One mL of sample dissolves in 3 mL of alcohol, sometimes with a slight haze.
- **SPECIFIC GRAVITY:** Determine by any reliable method (see *General Provisions*).
  Acceptance criteria: Between 0.846 and 0.851
- **ULTRAVIOLET ABSORBANCE,** *Ultraviolet Absorbance of Citrus Oils,* Appendix VI
  Sample: 250 mg
  Acceptance criteria: The absorbance is NLT 0.20.
  [NOTE—The absorbance maximum occurs at 315 ± 3 nm.]

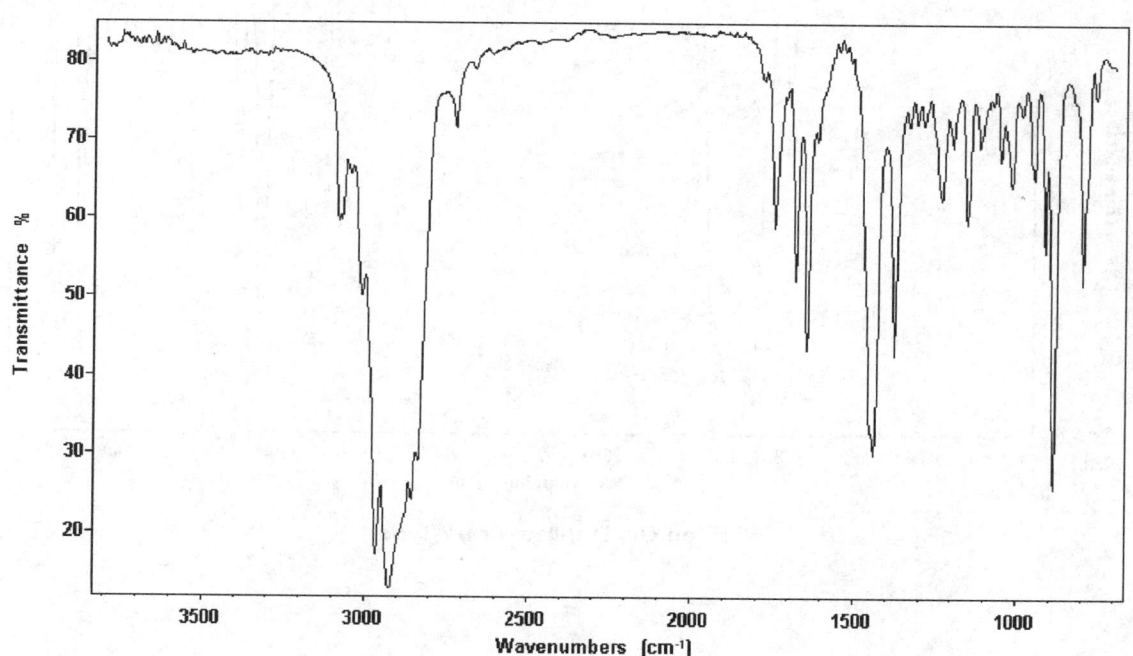

Lemon Oil, Desert Type, Cold-pressed

Lemon Oil, Distilled

First Published: Prior to FCC 6

UNII: ET5GD00TRP [lemon oil, distilled]

DESCRIPTION
Lemon Oil, Distilled, occurs as a colorless to pale yellow liquid with the characteristic odor of fresh lemon peel. It is the volatile oil obtained by distillation from the fresh peel or juice of the fruit of *Citrus limon* L. Burmann filius (Fam. Rutaceae), with or without the previous separation of the juice, pulp, and peel. It is soluble in most fixed oils, in mineral oil, and in alcohol (with haze). It is insoluble in glycerin and in propylene glycol. It may contain a suitable antioxidant.

Function: Flavoring agent

Packaging and Storage: Store in a cool place protected from light in full, tight containers.

IDENTIFICATION
- **INFRARED SPECTRA,** *Spectrophotometric Identification Tests,* Appendix IIIC
  Acceptance criteria: The spectrum of the sample exhibits relative maxima at the same wavelengths as those of the spectrum below.

SPECIFIC TESTS
- **ALDEHYDES,** *Aldehydes and Ketones, Hydroxylamine tert-Butyl Alcohol Method,* Appendix VI
  Sample: 5 mL
  Analysis: Before titrating, allow the mixture to stand for 1 h at room temperature. Use 76.12 as the equivalence factor (e) in the calculation.
  Acceptance criteria: Between 1.0% and 3.5% of aldehydes, calculated as citral ($C_{10}H_{16}O$)
- **ANGULAR ROTATION,** *Optical (Specific) Rotation,* Appendix IIB: Use a 100-mm tube.
  Acceptance criteria: Between +55° and +75°
- **REFRACTIVE INDEX,** Appendix IIB
  [NOTE—Use an Abbé or other refractometer of equal or greater accuracy.]
  Acceptance criteria: Between 1.470 and 1.475 at 20°
- **SPECIFIC GRAVITY:** Determine by any reliable method (see *General Provisions*).
  Acceptance criteria: Between 0.842 and 0.856
- **ULTRAVIOLET ABSORBANCE,** *Ultraviolet Absorbance of Citrus Oils,* Appendix VI
  Sample: 250 mg
  Acceptance criteria: The absorbance is NMT 0.01.
  [NOTE—The absorbance maximum occurs at 315 ± 3 nm.]

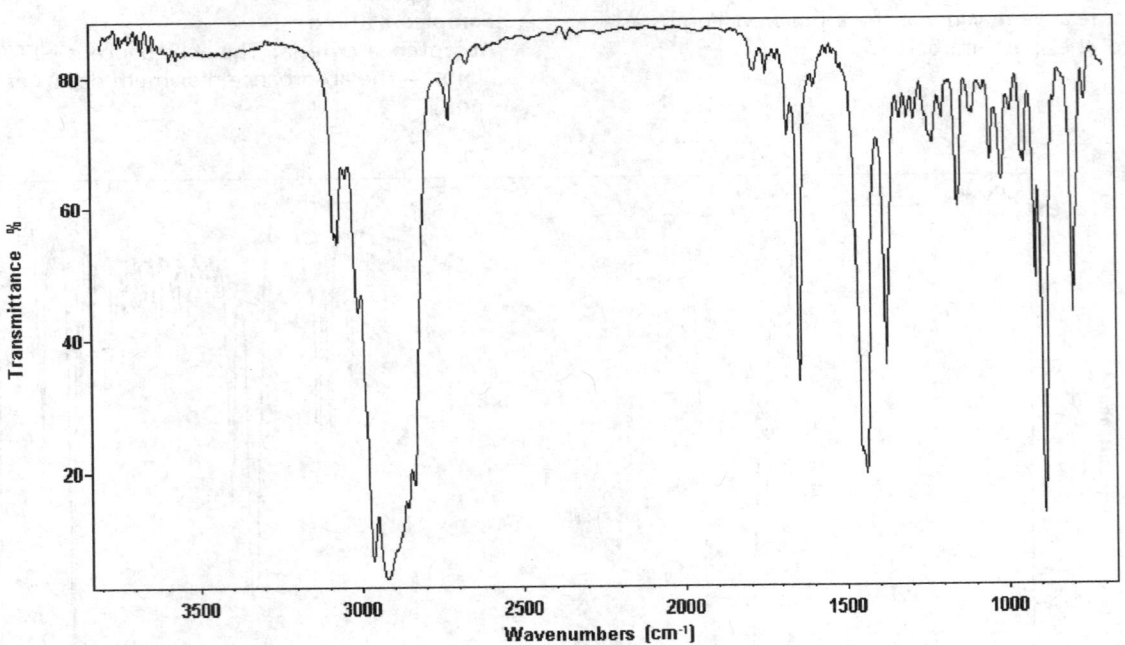

Lemon Oil, Distilled, Brazil Type

Lemongrass Oil

First Published: Prior to FCC 6
Last Revision: FCC 6

FEMA: 2624

CAS: [8007-02-1]
UNII: 5BIA40E9ED [west indian lemongrass oil]

DESCRIPTION
Lemongrass Oil is a volatile oil prepared by steam distillation of freshly cut and partially dried cymbopogon grasses indigenous to tropical and subtropical areas. Two types of Lemongrass Oil are commercially available. The *East Indian* type, also known as Cochin, Native, and British Indian Lemongrass Oil, usually occurs as a dark yellow to light brown-red liquid with a pronounced heavy lemon odor. The *West Indian* type, also known as Madagascar, Guatemala, or other country of origin Lemongrass Oil, occurs as a light yellow to light brown liquid with a lemon odor of a lighter character than the East Indian type oil. Lemongrass oils are soluble in mineral oil, freely soluble in propylene glycol, but practically insoluble in water and in glycerin. The East Indian type dissolves readily in alcohol, but the West Indian type yields cloudy solutions.
Function: Flavoring agent
Packaging and Storage: Store in full, tight containers. Avoid exposure to excessive heat.

IDENTIFICATION
- **INFRARED SPECTRA,** *Spectrophotometric Identification Tests,* Appendix IIIC
  Acceptance criteria: The spectrum of the sample exhibits relative maxima at the same wavelengths as those of the spectrum below.

ASSAY
- **PROCEDURE**
  Sample: 50.0 mL
  Analysis: Mix the *Sample* with 500 mg of tartaric acid, shake for 5 min, and filter. Dry the filtered oil over anhydrous sodium sulfate, and then pipet 10.0 mL of the clear, treated oil into a 150-mL cassia flask. Add 75 mL of a 30% solution of sodium bisulfite, stopper the flask, and shake until a semisolid to solid sodium bisulfite addition product has formed. Allow the mixture to stand at room temperature for 5 min, then loosen the stopper, and immerse the flask in a water bath heated to between 85° and 90°. Maintain the water bath at this temperature, shaking the flask occasionally, until the addition product dissolves, and then continue heating and intermittently shaking for another 30 min. When the liquids have separated completely, add enough 30% sodium bisulfite solution to raise the lower level of the oily layer within the graduated portion of the flask's neck. Calculate the percentage, by volume, of the citral by the formula:

$$\text{Result} = 100 - (V \times 10)$$

  V = amount (mL) of separated oil in the graduated neck of the cassia flask
  Acceptance criteria: NLT 75.0%, by volume, of aldehydes, calculated as citral ($C_{10}H_{16}O$)

SPECIFIC TESTS
- **ANGULAR ROTATION,** *Optical (Specific) Rotation,* Appendix IIB: Use a 100-mm tube.
  Acceptance criteria: Between −10° and 0°
- **REFRACTIVE INDEX,** Appendix IIB
  [NOTE—Use an Abbé or other refractometer of equal or greater accuracy.]
  Acceptance criteria: Between 1.483 and 1.489
- **SOLUBILITY IN ALCOHOL,** Appendix VI
  Acceptance criteria
  East Indian Type: One mL dissolves in 3 mL of 70% alcohol, usually with slight turbidity.
  West Indian Type: Yields a cloudy solution with 70%, 80%, 90%, and 95% alcohol.
- **SPECIFIC GRAVITY:** Determine by any reliable method (see *General Provisions*).
  Acceptance criteria
  East Indian Type: Between 0.890 and 0.904
  West Indian Type: Between 0.869 and 0.894

OTHER REQUIREMENTS
- **LABELING:** Indicate whether the oil is the East Indian or West Indian type.

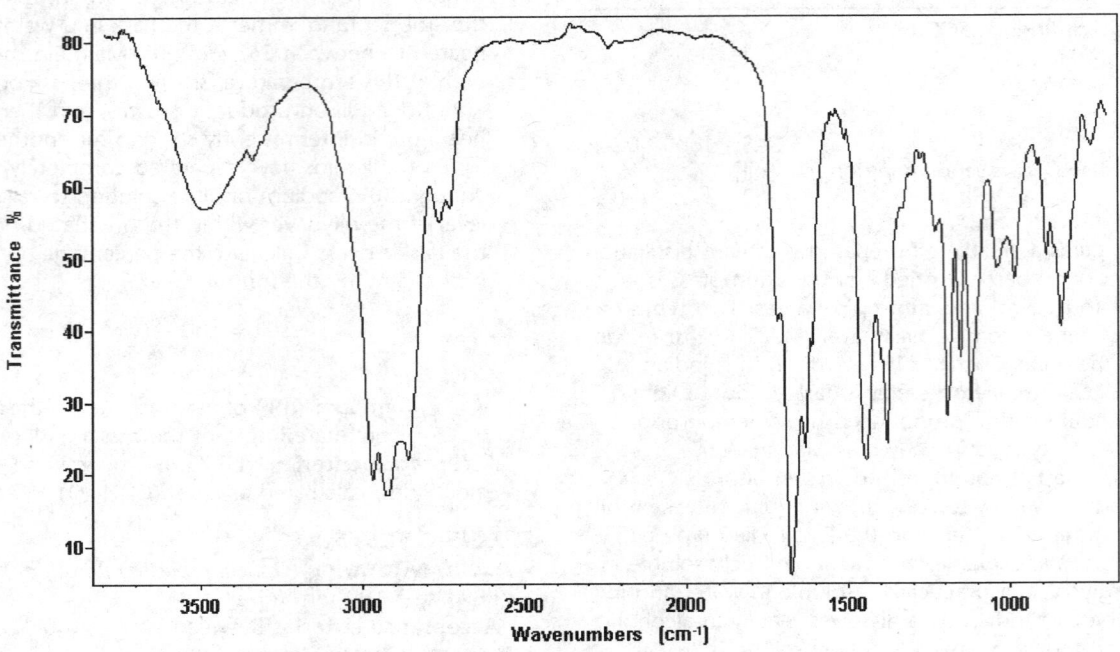

Lemongrass Oil

DL-Leucine

First Published: Prior to FCC 6

DL-2-Amino-4-methylvaleric Acid

$C_6H_{13}NO_2$

Formula wt 131.17
CAS: [328-39-2]

UNII: 1QSS9D5DR6 [leucine, dl-]

DESCRIPTION
DL-Leucine occurs as small, white crystals or as a crystalline powder. It is freely soluble in water, slightly soluble in alcohol, and insoluble in ether. It melts with decomposition at about 290°. The pH of a 1:100 aqueous solution is between 5.5 and 7.0. It is optically inactive.
Function: Nutrient
Packaging and Storage: Store in well-closed containers.

IDENTIFICATION
- **INFRARED SPECTRA,** *Spectrophotometric Identification Tests,* Appendix IIIC
  Sample preparation: Mineral oil mull
  Acceptance criteria: The spectrum of the sample exhibits relative maxima at the same wavelengths as those of the spectrum below.

ASSAY
- **PROCEDURE**
  Sample: 400 mg
  Analysis: Dissolve the *Sample* in 3 mL of formic acid and 50 mL of glacial acetic acid. Add 2 drops of crystal violet TS and titrate with 0.1 N perchloric acid to the first appearance of a pure-green color or until the blue color disappears completely. Perform a blank determination (see *General Provisions*), and make any necessary correction. Each mL of 0.1 N perchloric acid is equivalent to 13.12 mg of $C_6H_{13}NO_2$. [**CAUTION**— Handle perchloric acid in an appropriate fume hood.]
  Acceptance criteria: NLT 98.5% and NMT 101.5% of $C_6H_{13}NO_2$, calculated on the dried basis

IMPURITIES
Inorganic Impurities
- **LEAD,** *Lead Limit Test,* Appendix IIIB
  Sample solution: Prepare as directed for organic compounds.
  Control: 5 µg Pb (5 mL of *Diluted Standard Lead Solution*)
  Acceptance criteria: NMT 5 mg/kg

SPECIFIC TESTS
- **LOSS ON DRYING,** Appendix IIC: 105° for 3 h
  Acceptance criteria: NMT 0.3%
- **RESIDUE ON IGNITION (SULFATED ASH),** Appendix IIC
  Sample: 1 g
  Acceptance criteria: NMT 0.1%

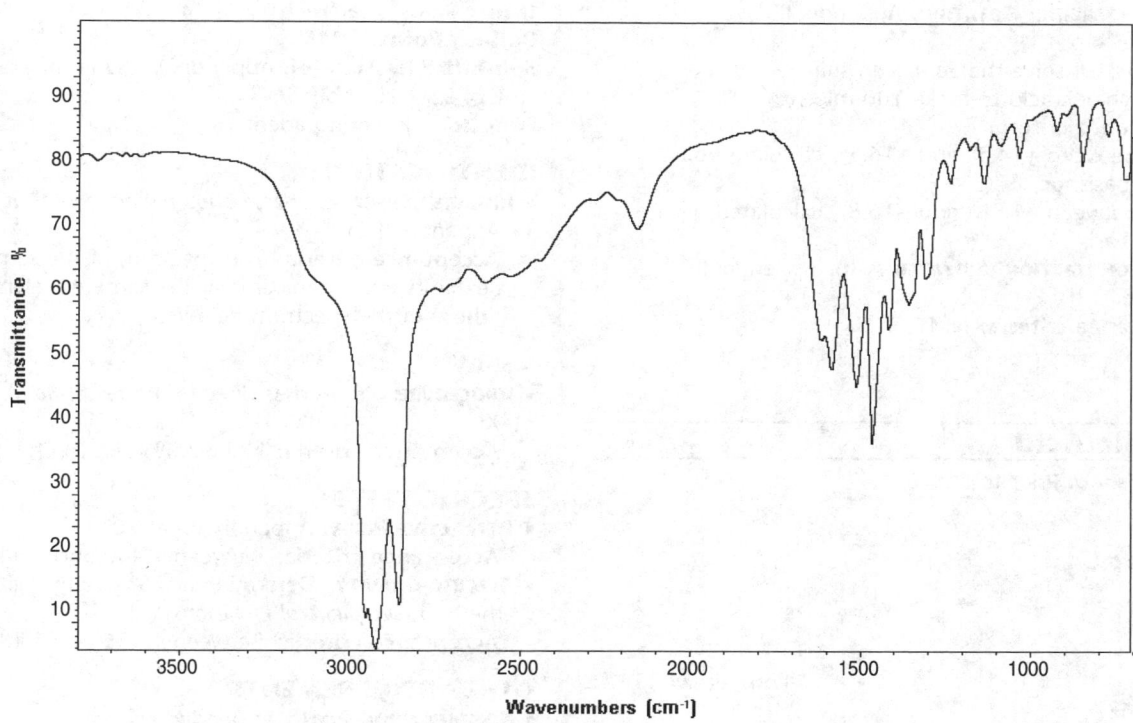

DL-Leucine (Mineral Oil Mull)

L-Leucine

First Published: Prior to FCC 6
Last Revision: FCC 6

L-2-Amino-4-methylvaleric Acid

$C_6H_{13}NO_2$ Formula wt 131.17
INS: 641   CAS: [61-90-5]
UNII: GMW67QNF9C [leucine]

DESCRIPTION
L-Leucine occurs as small, white, lustrous plates, or as a white, crystalline powder. One g dissolves in about 40 mL of water and in about 100 mL of glacial acetic acid. It is sparingly soluble in alcohol, and soluble in dilute hydrochloric acid and in solutions of alkali hydroxides and carbonates.
Function: Nutrient
Packaging and Storage: Store in well-closed containers.

IDENTIFICATION
- **INFRARED ABSORPTION,** *Spectrophotometric Identification Tests,* Appendix IIIC
  Reference standard: USP L-Leucine RS
  Sample and standard preparation: K
  Acceptance criteria: The spectrum of the sample exhibits maxima at the same wavelengths as those in the spectrum of the *Reference standard.*

ASSAY
- **PROCEDURE**
  Sample: 400 mg, previously dried
  Analysis: Transfer the *Sample* into a 250-mL flask. Dissolve the sample in 3 mL of formic acid and about 50 mL of glacial acetic acid. Add 2 drops of crystal violet TS, and titrate with 0.1 N perchloric acid to a blue-green endpoint. [**CAUTION**—Handle perchloric acid in an appropriate fume hood.] Perform a blank determination (see *General Provisions*), and make any necessary correction. Each mL of 0.1 N perchloric acid is equivalent to 13.12 mg of $C_6H_{13}NO_2$.
  Acceptance criteria: NLT 98.5% and NMT 101.5% of $C_6H_{13}NO_2$, on the dried basis

IMPURITIES
Inorganic Impurities
- **LEAD,** *Lead Limit Test,* Appendix IIIB
  Sample solution: Prepare as directed for organic compounds.
  Control: 5 µg Pb (5 mL of *Diluted Standard Lead Solution*)
  Acceptance criteria: NMT 5 mg/kg

SPECIFIC TESTS
- **LOSS ON DRYING,** Appendix IIC: 105° for 3 h
  Acceptance criteria: NMT 0.2%

- **OPTICAL (SPECIFIC) ROTATION,** Appendix IIB
  Sample: 4 g
  Analysis: Dissolve the Sample in sufficient 6 N hydrochloric acid to make 100 mL.
  Acceptance criteria
  $[\alpha]_D^{20}$ between +14.5° and +16.5°, calculated on the dried basis; or
  $[\alpha]_D^{25}$ between +14.8° and +16.8°, calculated on the dried basis
- **RESIDUE ON IGNITION (SULFATED ASH),** Appendix IIC
  Sample: 1 g
  Acceptance criteria: NMT 0.1%

Levulinic Acid

First Published: Prior to FCC 6

$C_5H_8O_3$
FEMA: 2627
UNII: RYX5QG61EI [levulinic acid]

Formula wt 116.12

DESCRIPTION
Levulinic Acid occurs as a yellow to brown liquid; may congeal.

Odor: Smoky, caramel
Boiling Point: ~245°
Solubility in Alcohol, Appendix VI: One mL dissolves in 1 mL of 95% alcohol.
Function: Flavoring agent

IDENTIFICATION
- **INFRARED SPECTRA,** Spectrophotometric Identification Tests, Appendix IIIC
  Acceptance criteria: The spectrum of the sample exhibits relative maxima at the same wavelengths as those of the spectrum below.

ASSAY
- **PROCEDURE:** Proceed as directed under M-3a, Appendix XI.
  Acceptance criteria: NLT 97.0% of $C_5H_8O_3$

SPECIFIC TESTS
- **REFRACTIVE INDEX,** Appendix II: At 20°
  Acceptance criteria: Between 1.440 and 1.445
- **SPECIFIC GRAVITY:** Determine at 25° by any reliable method (see General Provisions).
  Acceptance criteria: Between 1.136 and 1.142

OTHER REQUIREMENTS
- **SOLIDIFICATION POINT,** Appendix IIB
  Acceptance criteria: NLT 27°

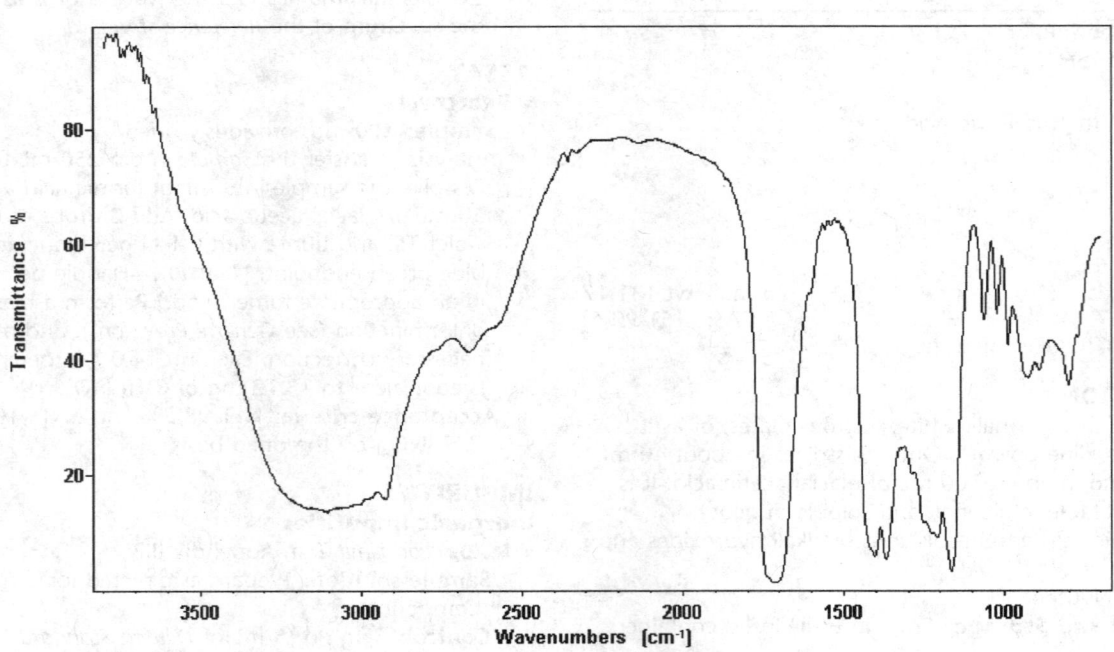

Levulinic Acid

Lime Oil, Cold-pressed

First Published: Prior to FCC 6

Lime Oil, Expressed
FEMA: 2631

UNII: UZH29XGA8G [lime oil]

CAS: [8008-26-2]

DESCRIPTION
Lime Oil, Cold-pressed occurs as a yellow to brown-green to green liquid that often shows a waxy separation and has a fresh lime-peel odor. It is the volatile oil obtained by expression from the fresh peel or crushed whole fruit of *Citrus aurantifolia* Swingle (Mexican type) or *Citrus latifolia* (Tahitian type) (Fam. Rutaceae). It is soluble in most fixed oils and in mineral oil, but is insoluble in glycerin and in propylene glycol. It may contain a suitable antioxidant.

Function: Flavoring agent

Packaging and Storage: Store in full, tight containers. Avoid exposure to excessive heat.

IDENTIFICATION
- **INFRARED SPECTRA,** *Spectrophotometric Identification Tests,* Appendix IIIC
  Acceptance criteria: The spectrum of the sample exhibits relative maxima at the same wavelengths as those of the appropriate spectrum below.

ASSAY
- **ALDEHYDES,** *Aldehydes and Ketones, Hydroxylamine tert-Butyl Alcohol Method,* Appendix VI
  Sample: 5 mL
  Analysis: Before titrating, allow the mixture to stand for 1 h, shaking the flask occasionally. Use 76.12 as the equivalence factor (e) in the calculation.
  Acceptance criteria
    Mexican type: NLT 4.5% and NMT 8.5% of aldehydes, calculated as citral ($C_{10}H_{16}O$)
    Tahitian type: NLT 3.2% and NMT 7.5% of aldehydes, calculated as citral ($C_{10}H_{16}O$)

SPECIFIC TESTS
- **ANGULAR ROTATION,** *Optical (Specific) Rotation,* Appendix IIB: Use a 100-mm tube.
  Acceptance criteria
    Mexican type: Between +35° and +41°
    Tahitian type: Between +38° and +53°
- **REFRACTIVE INDEX,** Appendix IIB
  [NOTE—Use an Abbé or other refractometer of equal or greater accuracy.]
  Acceptance criteria
    Mexican type: Between 1.482 and 1.486
    Tahitian type: Between 1.476 and 1.486
- **RESIDUE ON EVAPORATION,** Appendix VI
  Sample: 3 g
  Analysis: Heat the *Sample* for 6 h
  Acceptance criteria
    Mexican type: Between 10.0% and 14.5%
    Tahitian type: Between 5.0% and 12.0%
- **SPECIFIC GRAVITY:** Determine by any reliable method (see *General Provisions*).
  Acceptance criteria
    Mexican type: Between 0.872 and 0.881
    Tahitian type: Between 0.858 and 0.876
- **ULTRAVIOLET ABSORBANCE,** *Ultraviolet Absorbance of Citrus Oils,* Appendix VI
  Sample: 20 mg
  Acceptance criteria: [NOTE—The absorbance maximum occurs at 315 ± 3 nm.]
    Mexican type: NLT 0.45
    Tahitian type: NLT 0.24

OTHER REQUIREMENTS
- **LABELING:** Indicate whether the oil is the Mexican or Tahitian type.

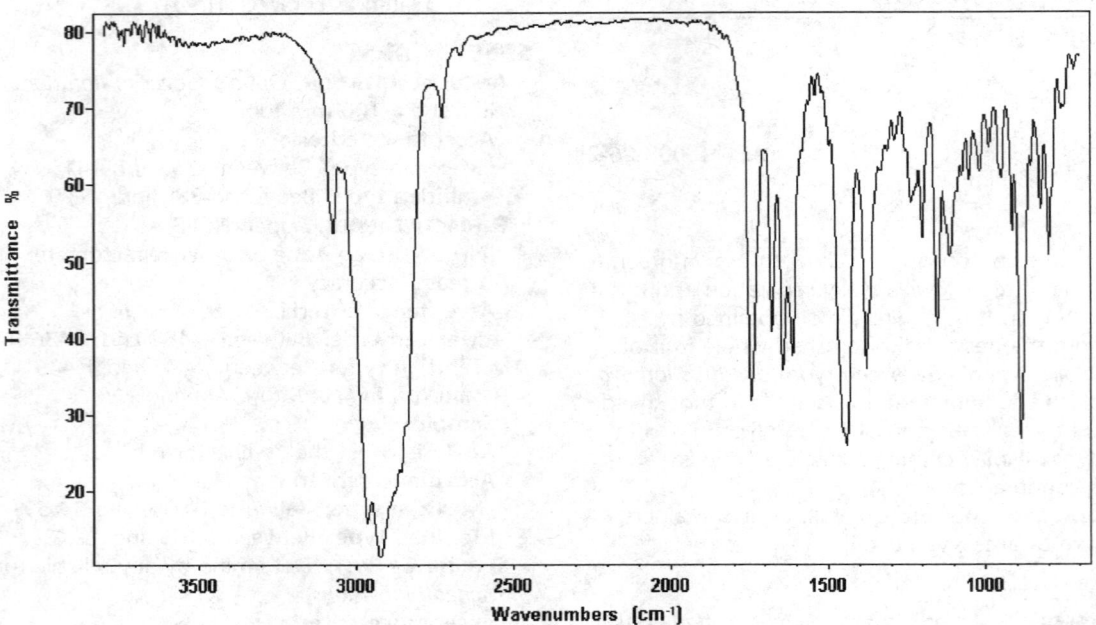

Lime Oil, Cold-pressed, Mexican Type

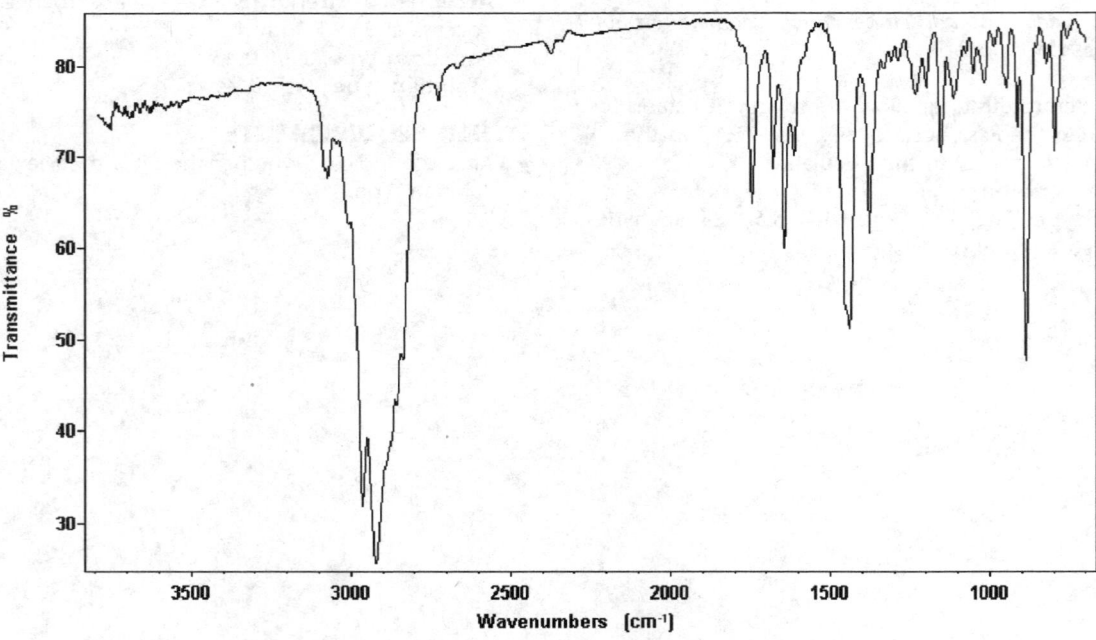

Lime Oil, Cold-pressed, Tahitian Type

Lime Oil, Distilled

First Published: Prior to FCC 6

UNII: 7937R189CB [citrus aurantiifolia fruit oil]

DESCRIPTION
Lime Oil, Distilled, occurs as a colorless to green-yellow liquid with a mild citrus, floral odor. It is the volatile oil obtained by distillation from the juice or the whole crushed fruit of *Citrus aurantifolia* Swingle (Fam. Rutaceae). It is soluble in most fixed oils and in mineral oil, but it is insoluble in glycerin and in propylene glycol. It may contain a suitable antioxidant.
Function: Flavoring agent
Packaging and Storage: Store in a cool place protected from light in full, tight containers that are made from steel or aluminum and that are suitably lined.

IDENTIFICATION
- **INFRARED SPECTRA,** *Spectrophotometric Identification Tests,* Appendix IIIC
  Acceptance criteria: The spectrum of the sample exhibits relative maxima at the same wavelengths as those of the spectrum below.

SPECIFIC TESTS
- **ALDEHYDES,** *Aldehydes and Ketones, Hydroxylamine tert-Butyl Alcohol Method,* Appendix VI
  Sample: 5 g
  Analysis: Before titrating, allow the mixture to stand for 15 min. Use 76.12 as the equivalence factor (e) in the calculation.
  Acceptance criteria: Between 0.5% and 2.5% of aldehydes, calculated as citral ($C_{10}H_{16}O$)
- **ANGULAR ROTATION,** *Optical (Specific) Rotation,* Appendix IIB: Use a 100-mm tube.
  Acceptance criteria: Between +34° and +47°
- **REFRACTIVE INDEX,** Appendix IIB
  [NOTE—Use an Abbé or other refractometer of equal or greater accuracy.]
  Acceptance criteria: Between 1.474 and 1.477 at 20°
- **SOLUBILITY IN ALCOHOL,** Appendix VI
  Acceptance criteria: One mL of sample dissolves in 5 mL of 90% alcohol.
- **SPECIFIC GRAVITY:** Determine by any reliable method (see *General Provisions*).
  Acceptance criteria: Between 0.855 and 0.863

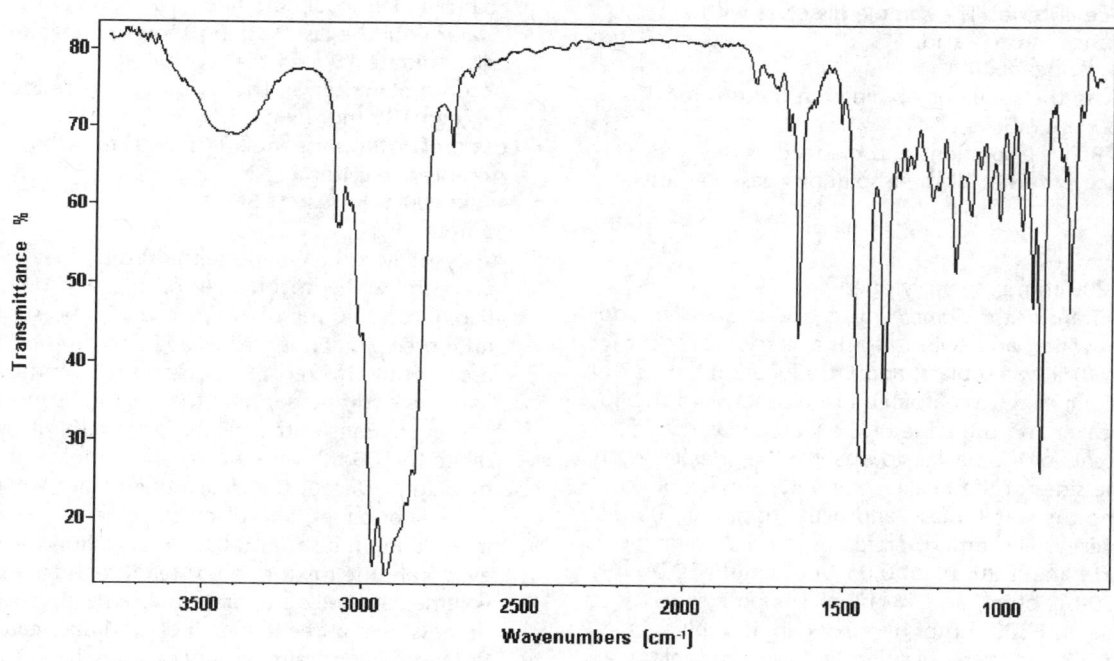

Lime Oil, Distilled

Limestone, Ground

First Published: Prior to FCC 6

UNII: H0G9379FGK [calcium carbonate]

DESCRIPTION

Limestone, Ground is produced as a fine, white to off-white, microcrystalline powder mainly consisting of calcium carbonate. It is obtained by crushing, grinding, and classifying naturally occurring limestone benefited by flotation and/or air classification. It is stable in air. It is practically insoluble in water and in alcohol. The presence of any ammonium salt or carbon dioxide increases its solubility in water, but the presence of any alkali hydroxide reduces its solubility.

Function: Texturizing and release agent and modifier for chewing gum base and chewing gum

Packaging and Storage: Store in well-closed containers.

IDENTIFICATION

- **A. Procedure**
  Analysis: Dissolve the sample separately in 1 N acetic acid, in 2.7 N hydrochloric acid, and in 1.7 N nitric acid. [NOTE—Save the resulting solutions for the *Calcium* identification test (below).]
  Acceptance criteria: The sample dissolves with effervescence in each acid.
- **B. Calcium,** Appendix IIIA
  Sample: Use the solutions obtained in the test for *Identification A* (above).
  Analysis: Boil the solutions and proceed as directed.
  Acceptance criteria: All three solutions pass the tests.

ASSAY

- **Procedure**
  Sample: 200 mg, previously dried
  Analysis: Transfer the *Sample* into a 400-mL beaker, add 10 mL of water, and swirl to form a slurry. Cover the beaker with a watch glass, and introduce 2 mL of 2.7 N hydrochloric acid from a pipet inserted between the lip of the beaker and the edge of the watch glass. Swirl the contents of the beaker to dissolve the *Sample*. Wash down the sides of the beaker, the outer surface of the pipet, and the watch glass, and dilute to about 100 mL with water. While stirring, preferably with a magnetic stirrer, add about 30 mL of 0.05 M disodium EDTA from a 50-mL buret, add 15 mL of 1 N potassium hydroxide and 300 mg of hydroxy naphthol blue indicator. Continue the titration to a blue endpoint. Each mL of 0.05 M disodium EDTA is equivalent to 5.004 mg of $CaCO_3$.
  Acceptance criteria: NLT 94.0% and NMT 100.5% of $CaCO_3$, on the dried basis

IMPURITIES

Inorganic Impurities

- **Arsenic,** *Arsenic Limit Test,* Appendix IIIB
  Sample solution: 1 g in 10 mL of 2.7 N hydrochloric acid
  Acceptance criteria: NMT 3 mg/kg
- **Fluoride,** *Fluoride Limit Test, Method III,* Appendix IIIB
  Acceptance criteria: NMT 0.005%
- **Lead,** *Lead Limit Test,* Appendix IIIB
  Sample solution: Cautiously dissolve 5 g of sample in 25 mL of 1:2 hydrochloric acid, and evaporate to dryness on a steam bath. Dissolve the residue in about 15 mL of water, and dilute to 25 mL.
  Control: 3 µg of Pb (3 mL of *Diluted Standard Lead Solution*)
  Analysis: Proceed as directed using a 5-mL portion of the *Sample solution*.
  Acceptance criteria: NMT 3 mg/kg

SPECIFIC TESTS

- **Acid-Insoluble Substances**
  Sample: 5 g
  Analysis: Suspend the *Sample* in 25 mL of water, agitate while cautiously adding 25 mL of 1:2 hydrochloric acid, and add water to make a volume of about 200 mL. Heat the solution to boiling, cover, digest on a steam bath for 1 h, cool, and filter. Wash the precipitate with water until the last washing shows no chloride with silver nitrate TS, and then ignite it.
  Acceptance criteria: The weight of the residue does not exceed 125 mg. (NMT 2.5%)
- **Loss on Drying,** Appendix IIC: 200° for 4 h
  Acceptance criteria: NMT 2.0%
- **Magnesium and Alkali Salts**
  Sample: 1 g
  Analysis: Mix the *Sample* with 40 mL of water, carefully add 5 mL of hydrochloric acid, mix, and boil for 1 min. Rapidly add 40 mL of oxalic acid TS, and stir vigorously until precipitation is well established. Immediately add 2 drops of methyl red TS, then add 6 N ammonium hydroxide, dropwise, until the mixture is just alkaline, and cool. Transfer the mixture to a 100-mL cylinder, dilute to 100 mL with water, and let it stand for 4 h or overnight. Decant the clear, supernatant liquid through a dry filter paper, and place 50 mL of the clear filtrate in a platinum dish. Add 0.5 mL of sulfuric acid, and evaporate the mixture on a steam bath to a small volume. Carefully evaporate the remaining liquid to dryness over a free flame, and continue heating until the ammonium salts have been completely decomposed and volatilized. Finally, ignite the residue to constant weight.
  Acceptance criteria: The weight of the residue does not exceed 17.5 mg. (NMT 3.5%)

(+)-Limonene

First Published: Prior to FCC 6
Last Revision: FCC 8

d-Limonene
d-p-Mentha-1,8-diene
Cinene

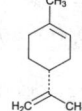

C₁₀H₁₆ Formula wt 136.24
FEMA: 2633
UNII: GFD7C86Q1W [limonene, (+)-]

DESCRIPTION
(+)-Limonene occurs as a colorless liquid. It may contain a suitable antioxidant.
Odor: Mildly citrus, free from camphoraceous and terpene notes
Solubility: Slightly soluble in glycerin; miscible in alcohol, most fixed oils; insoluble or practically insoluble in propylene glycol, water
Boiling Point: ~177°

Function: Flavoring agent

IDENTIFICATION
- **INFRARED SPECTRA**, *Spectrophotometric Identification Tests*, Appendix IIIC
  Acceptance criteria: The spectrum of the sample exhibits relative maxima at the same wavelengths as those of the spectrum below.

ASSAY
- **PROCEDURE:** Proceed as directed under *M-1a*, Appendix XI.
  Acceptance criteria: NLT 93.0% of C₁₀H₁₆

SPECIFIC TESTS
- **REFRACTIVE INDEX**, Appendix II: At 20°
  Acceptance criteria: 1.471–1.474
- **SPECIFIC GRAVITY:** Determine at 25° by any reliable method (see *General Provisions*).
  Acceptance criteria: 0.838–0.843

OTHER REQUIREMENTS

Change to read:

- **ANGULAR ROTATION**, *Optical (Specific) Rotation*, Appendix IIB: Use a 100-mm tube.
  Acceptance criteria: Between +96° and ▲+125°▲FCC8
- **PEROXIDE VALUE**, *M-11*, Appendix XI
  Acceptance criteria: NMT 5.0

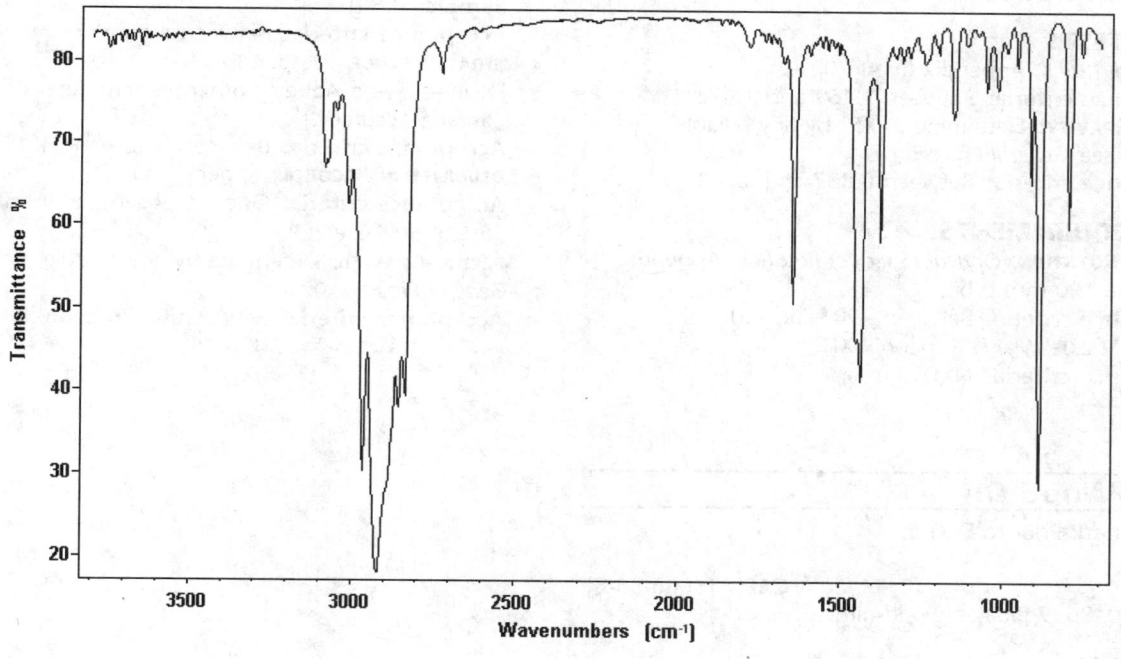

(+)-Limonene

(−)-Limonene

First Published: Prior to FCC 6
Last Revision: First Supplement, FCC 7

l-Limonene
l-*p*-Mentha-1,8-diene

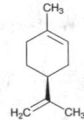

C$_{10}$H$_{16}$ Formula wt 136.24
UNII: 47MAJ1Y2NE [limonene, (-)-]

DESCRIPTION
(−)-Limonene occurs as a colorless liquid. It may contain a suitable antioxidant.
Odor: Refreshing, light, clean
Solubility: Miscible in alcohol, most fixed oils; insoluble or practically insoluble in water
Boiling Point: ~177°
Function: Flavoring agent

ASSAY
- **PROCEDURE:** Proceed as directed under *M-1a*, Appendix XI.
  Acceptance criteria: NLT 95.0% of C$_{10}$H$_{16}$

SPECIFIC TESTS
- **REFRACTIVE INDEX,** Appendix II: At 20°
  Acceptance criteria: Between 1.469 and 1.473
- **SPECIFIC GRAVITY:** Determine at 25° by any reliable method (see *General Provisions*).
  Acceptance criteria: Between 0.837 and 0.841

OTHER REQUIREMENTS
- **ANGULAR ROTATION,** *Optical (Specific) Rotation,* Appendix IIB: Use a 100-mm tube.
  Acceptance criteria: Between −90° and −61°
- **PEROXIDE VALUE,** *M-11,* Appendix XI
  Acceptance criteria: NMT 5.0

Linaloe Wood Oil

First Published: Prior to FCC 6

CAS: [8006-86-8]

UNII: RUV8048639 [linaloe wood oil]

DESCRIPTION
Linaloe Wood Oil occurs as a colorless to yellow liquid with a pleasant, flowery odor. It is the volatile oil obtained by steam distillation from the wood of *Bursera delpechiana* Poiss. (Fam. Burseraceae) and other *Bursera* species. It is soluble in most fixed oils and in propylene glycol. It is soluble in mineral oil, but it becomes opalescent or turbid on dilution. It is insoluble in glycerin.
Function: Flavoring agent
Packaging and Storage: Store in a cool place protected from light in full, tight containers that are made from steel or aluminum and that are suitably lined.

IDENTIFICATION
- **INFRARED SPECTRA,** *Spectrophotometric Identification Tests,* Appendix IIIC
  Acceptance criteria: The spectrum of the sample exhibits relative maxima at the same wavelengths as those of the spectrum below.

ASSAY
- **ALCOHOLS,** *Linalool Determination,* Appendix VI
  Sample: 1.5 g of acetylated oil for the saponification
  Acceptance criteria: NLT 85.0% of alcohols, calculated as linalool (C$_{10}$H$_{18}$O)

SPECIFIC TESTS
- **ACID VALUE (ESSENTIAL OILS AND FLAVORS),** Appendix VI
  Acceptance criteria: NMT 3.0
- **ANGULAR ROTATION,** *Optical (Specific) Rotation,* Appendix IIB: Use a 100-mm tube.
  Acceptance criteria: Between −5° and −13°
- **ESTER VALUE,** *Ester Value,* Appendix VI
  Sample: 2.5 g
  Acceptance criteria: Between 40 and 75
- **REFRACTIVE INDEX,** Appendix IIB
  [NOTE—Use an Abbé or other refractometer of equal or greater accuracy.]
  Acceptance criteria: Between 1.459 and 1.463 at 20°
- **SOLUBILITY IN ALCOHOL,** Appendix VI
  Acceptance criteria: One mL of sample dissolves in 5 mL of 60% alcohol.
- **SPECIFIC GRAVITY:** Determine by any reliable method (see *General Provisions*).
  Acceptance criteria: Between 0.876 and 0.883

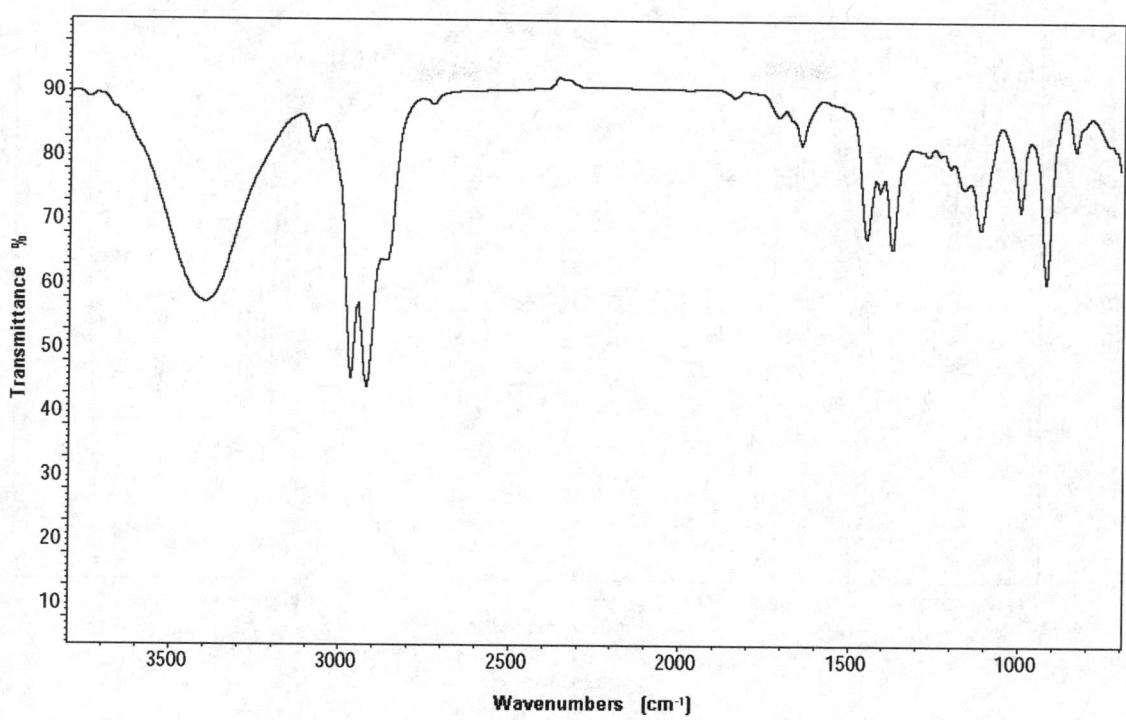

Linaloe Wood Oil

Linalool

First Published: Prior to FCC 6

3,7-Dimethyl-1,6-octadien-3-ol

$C_{10}H_{18}O$ Formula wt 154.25
FEMA: 2635
UNII: D81QY6I88E [linalool, (+/-)-]

DESCRIPTION
Linalool occurs as a colorless liquid.
Odor: Pleasant, floral
Solubility: Soluble in most fixed oils, propylene glycol; insoluble or practically insoluble in glycerin
Boiling Point: ~198°
Solubility in Alcohol, Appendix VI: One mL dissolves in 4 mL of 60% alcohol.
Function: Flavoring agent

IDENTIFICATION
- **INFRARED SPECTRA,** Spectrophotometric Identification Tests, Appendix IIIC

  Acceptance criteria: The spectrum of the sample exhibits relative maxima at the same wavelengths as those of the spectrum below.

ASSAY
- **PROCEDURE:** Proceed as directed under *M-1b*, Appendix XI.
  Acceptance criteria: NLT 92.0% of $C_{10}H_{18}O$

SPECIFIC TESTS
- **REFRACTIVE INDEX,** Appendix II: At 20°
  Acceptance criteria: Between 1.461 and 1.465
- **SPECIFIC GRAVITY:** Determine at 25° by any reliable method (see *General Provisions*).
  Acceptance criteria: Between 0.858 and 0.867

OTHER REQUIREMENTS
- **ESTERS,** Appendix VI
  Sample: 10 g
  Analysis: Use 98.15 as the equivalence factor (e).
  Acceptance criteria: NMT 0.5% as linalylacetate

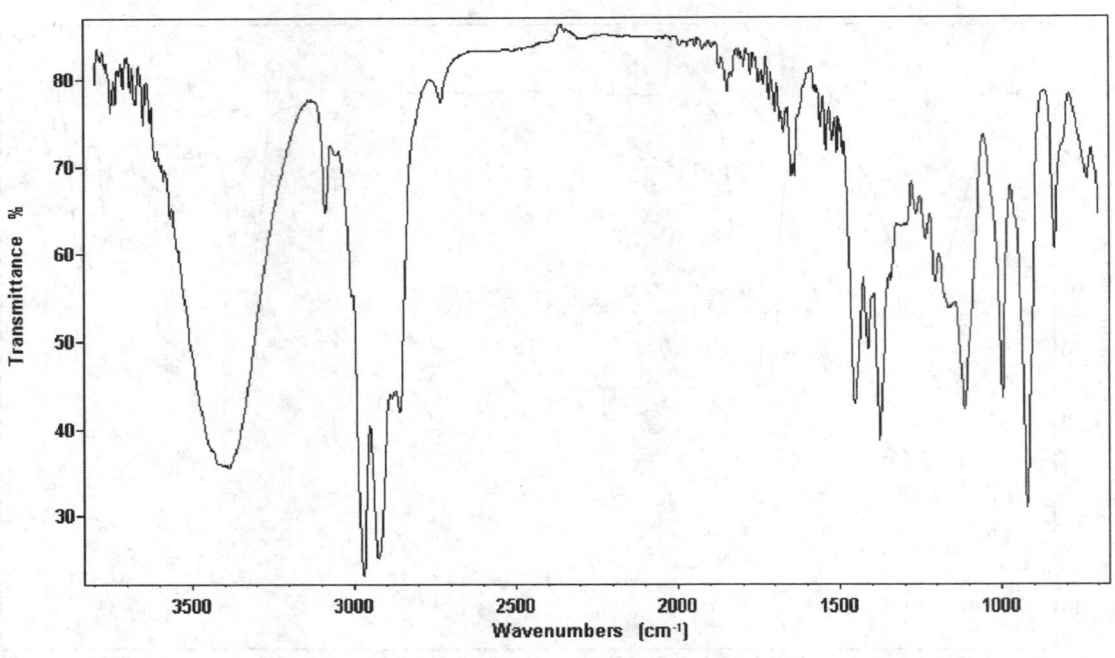

Linalool

Linalool Oxide

First Published: Prior to FCC 6

$C_{10}H_{18}O_2$ Formula wt 170.25
FEMA: 3746
UNII: 4UJJ55KMCS [linalool oxide]

DESCRIPTION
Linalool Oxide occurs as a colorless to pale yellow liquid.
Odor: Floral
Solubility: Soluble in propylene glycol, vegetable oils; insoluble or practically insoluble in water
Boiling Point: ~188°
Solubility in Alcohol, Appendix VI: One mL dissolves in 1 mL of 95% ethanol.

Function: Flavoring agent

IDENTIFICATION
- **INFRARED SPECTRA,** *Spectrophotometric Identification Tests,* Appendix IIIC
  Acceptance criteria: The spectrum of the sample exhibits relative maxima at the same wavelengths as those of the spectrum below.

ASSAY
- **PROCEDURE:** Proceed as directed under *M-1b,* Appendix XI
  Acceptance criteria: NLT 98.0% of $C_{10}H_{18}O_2$ (sum of *cis* and *trans* isomers).

SPECIFIC TESTS
- **REFRACTIVE INDEX,** Appendix II: At 20°
  Acceptance criteria: Between 1.449 and 1.455
- **SPECIFIC GRAVITY:** Determine at 25° by any reliable method (see *General Provisions*).
  Acceptance criteria: Between 0.940 and 0.947

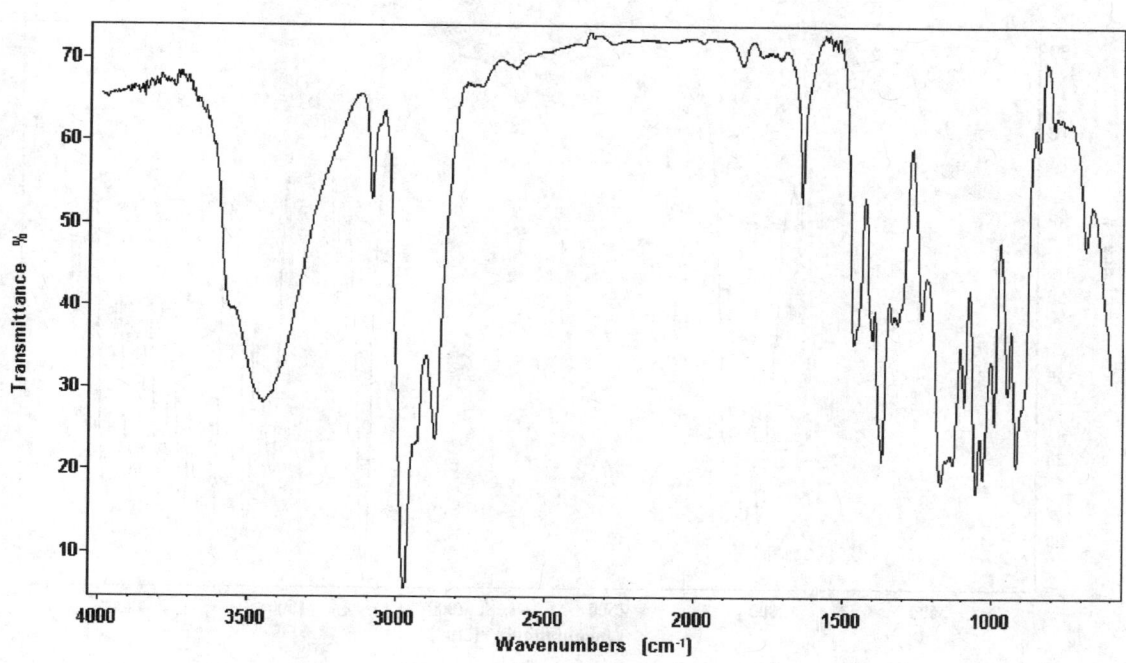

Linalool Oxide

Linalyl Acetate

First Published: Prior to FCC 6

3,7-Dimethyl-1,6-octadien-3-yl Acetate

$C_{12}H_{20}O_2$ Formula wt 196.29
FEMA: 2636
UNII: 5K47SSQ51G [linalyl acetate]

DESCRIPTION
Linalyl Acetate occurs as a colorless liquid.
Odor: Floral, fruity
Solubility: Slightly soluble in propylene glycol; miscible in alcohol, most fixed oils; insoluble or practically insoluble in glycerin, water
Boiling Point: ~220°
Solubility in Alcohol, Appendix VI: One mL dissolves in 5 mL of 70% alcohol.
Function: Flavoring agent

IDENTIFICATION
- **INFRARED SPECTRA,** Spectrophotometric Identification Tests, Appendix IIIC
  Acceptance criteria: The spectrum of the sample exhibits relative maxima at the same wavelengths as those of the spectrum below.

ASSAY
- **PROCEDURE:** Proceed as directed under *M-1b*, Appendix XI.
  Acceptance criteria: NLT 90.0% of total esters as $C_{12}H_{20}O_2$

SPECIFIC TESTS
- **ACID VALUE, FLAVOR CHEMICALS (OTHER THAN ESSENTIAL OILS),** *M-15,* Appendix XI
  Acceptance criteria: NMT 1.0
- **REFRACTIVE INDEX,** Appendix II: At 20°
  Acceptance criteria: Between 1.449 and 1.457
- **SPECIFIC GRAVITY:** Determine at 25° by any reliable method (see *General Provisions*).
  Acceptance criteria: Between 0.895 and 0.914

652 / Linalyl Acetate / *Monographs*

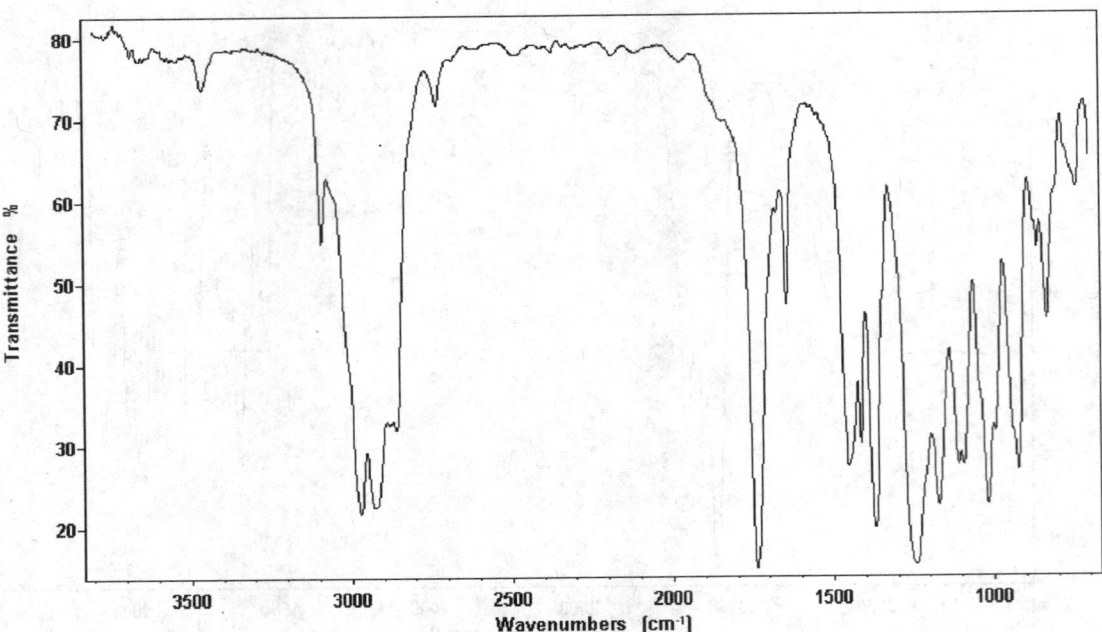

Linalyl Acetate

Linalyl Benzoate

First Published: Prior to FCC 6

3,7-Dimethyl-1,6-octadien-3-yl Benzoate

$C_{17}H_{22}O_2$ Formula wt 258.36
FEMA: 2638
UNII: 2ADP7IT9Y3 [linalyl benzoate]

DESCRIPTION

Linalyl Benzoate occurs as a yellow to brown-yellow liquid.
Odor: Tuberose
Solubility: Soluble in alcohol, chloroform, ether; insoluble or practically insoluble in water
Boiling Point: ~263°
Solubility in Alcohol, Appendix VI: One mL dissolves in 1 mL of 90% alcohol to give a clear solution.

Function: Flavoring agent

IDENTIFICATION

- **INFRARED SPECTRA,** *Spectrophotometric Identification Tests,* Appendix IIIC
  Acceptance criteria: The spectrum of the sample exhibits relative maxima at the same wavelengths as those of the spectrum below.

ASSAY

- **PROCEDURE:** Proceed as directed under *M-1b*, Appendix XI.
  Acceptance criteria: NLT 75.0% of $C_{17}H_{22}O_2$

SPECIFIC TESTS

- **ACID VALUE, FLAVOR CHEMICALS (OTHER THAN ESSENTIAL OILS),** *M-15,* Appendix XI
  Acceptance criteria: NMT 5.0
- **REFRACTIVE INDEX,** Appendix II: At 20°
  Acceptance criteria: Between 1.505 and 1.520
- **SPECIFIC GRAVITY:** Determine at 25° by any reliable method (see *General Provisions*).
  Acceptance criteria: Between 0.980 and 0.999

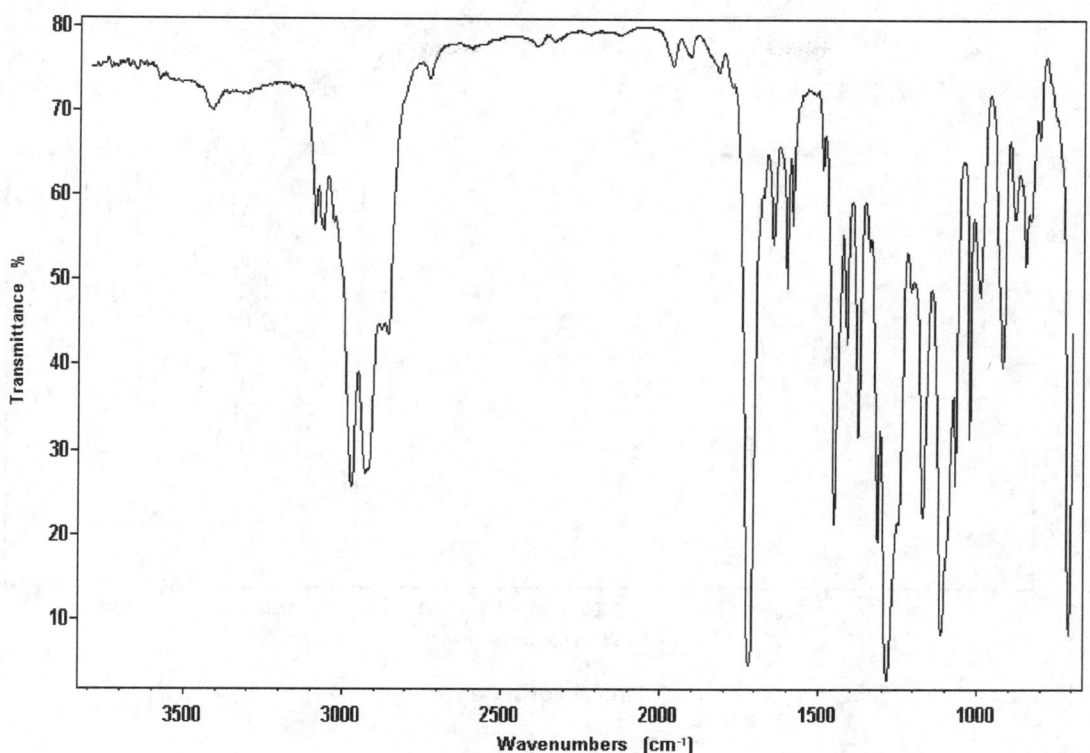

Linalyl Benzoate

Linalyl Formate

First Published: Prior to FCC 6

3,7-Dimethyl-1,6-octadien-3-yl Formate

$C_{11}H_{18}O_2$ Formula wt 182.26
FEMA: 2642
UNII: 3V67WH3R5N [linalyl formate]

DESCRIPTION
Linalyl Formate occurs as a colorless liquid.
Odor: Fresh, citrus, green, herbaceous, bergamot
Solubility: Soluble in alcohol, most fixed oils; slightly soluble in propylene glycol, water; insoluble or practically insoluble in glycerin
Boiling Point: ~202°
Solubility in Alcohol, Appendix VI: One mL dissolves in 6 mL of 70% alcohol.

Function: Flavoring agent

IDENTIFICATION
- **INFRARED SPECTRA,** *Spectrophotometric Identification Tests,* Appendix IIIC
  Acceptance criteria: The spectrum of the sample exhibits relative maxima at the same wavelengths as those of the spectrum below.

ASSAY
- **PROCEDURE:** Proceed as directed under *M-1b,* Appendix XI.
  Acceptance criteria: NLT 90.0% of $C_{11}H_{18}O_2$

SPECIFIC TESTS
- **ACID VALUE, FLAVOR CHEMICALS (OTHER THAN ESSENTIAL OILS),** *M-15,* Appendix XI
  Acceptance criteria: NMT 3.0
- **REFRACTIVE INDEX,** Appendix II: At 20°
  Acceptance criteria: Between 1.453 and 1.458
- **SPECIFIC GRAVITY:** Determine at 25° by any reliable method (see *General Provisions*).
  Acceptance criteria: Between 0.910 and 0.918

654 / Linalyl Formate / *Monographs*

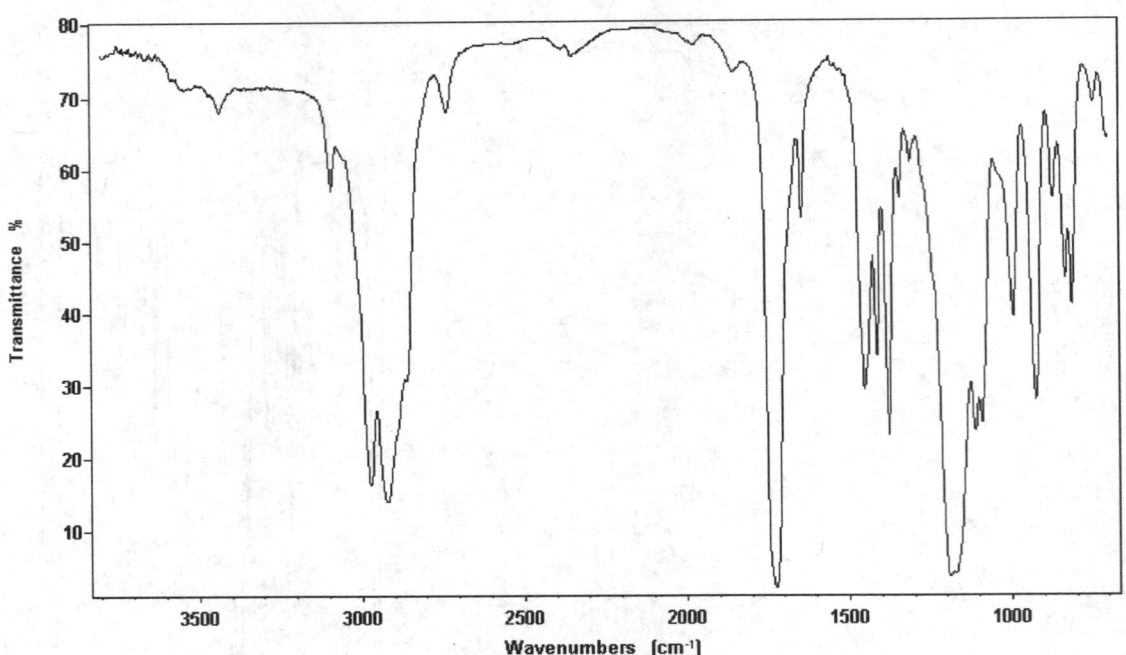

Linalyl Formate

Linalyl Isobutyrate

First Published: Prior to FCC 6

3,7-Dimethyl-6-octadien-3-yl Isobutyrate

$C_{14}H_{24}O_2$ Formula wt 224.34
FEMA: 2640
UNII: 8867Y4G46L [linalyl isobutyrate]

DESCRIPTION
Linalyl Isobutyrate occurs as a colorless to slightly yellow liquid.
Odor: Sweet, fresh, rosy
Solubility: Miscible in alcohol, chloroform, ether; insoluble or practically insoluble in water
Boiling Point: ~230°
Solubility in Alcohol, Appendix VI: One mL dissolves in 3 mL of 80% alcohol to give a clear solution.

Function: Flavoring agent

IDENTIFICATION
- **INFRARED SPECTRA,** *Spectrophotometric Identification Tests,* Appendix IIIC
  Acceptance criteria: The spectrum of the sample exhibits relative maxima at the same wavelengths as those of the spectrum below.

ASSAY
- **PROCEDURE:** Proceed as directed under *M-1b,* Appendix XI.
  Acceptance criteria: NLT 95.0% of $C_{14}H_{24}O_2$

SPECIFIC TESTS
- **ACID VALUE, FLAVOR CHEMICALS (OTHER THAN ESSENTIAL OILS),** *M-15,* Appendix XI
  Acceptance criteria: NMT 1.0
- **REFRACTIVE INDEX,** Appendix II: At 20°
  Acceptance criteria: Between 1.446 and 1.451
- **SPECIFIC GRAVITY:** Determine at 25° by any reliable method (see *General Provisions*).
  Acceptance criteria: Between 0.882 and 0.888

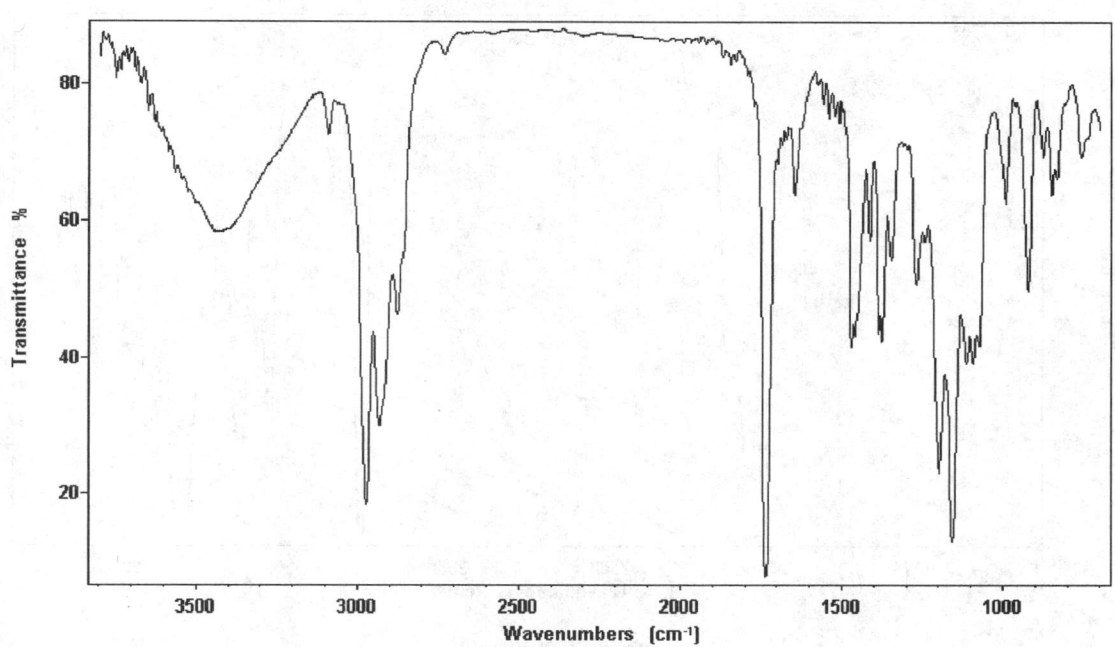

Linalyl Isobutyrate

Linalyl Propionate

First Published: Prior to FCC 6

3,7-Dimethyl-6-octadien-3-yl Propionate

$C_{13}H_{22}O_2$ Formula wt 210.32
FEMA: 2645
UNII: BI845A018T [linalyl propionate]

DESCRIPTION
Linalyl Propionate occurs as a colorless or almost colorless liquid.
Odor: Fresh, floral, sweet, fruity, pear
Solubility: Soluble in alcohol, most fixed oils; slightly soluble in propylene glycol; insoluble or practically insoluble in glycerin
Boiling Point: ~226°
Solubility in Alcohol, Appendix VI: One mL dissolves in 2 mL of 80% alcohol.

Function: Flavoring agent

IDENTIFICATION
- **INFRARED SPECTRA,** *Spectrophotometric Identification Tests,* Appendix IIIC
  Acceptance criteria: The spectrum of the sample exhibits relative maxima at the same wavelengths as those of the spectrum below.

ASSAY
- **PROCEDURE:** Proceed as directed under *M-1b,* Appendix XI.
  Acceptance criteria: NLT 92.0% of $C_{13}H_{22}O_2$

SPECIFIC TESTS
- **ACID VALUE, FLAVOR CHEMICALS (OTHER THAN ESSENTIAL OILS),** *M-15,* Appendix XI
  Acceptance criteria: NMT 1.0
- **REFRACTIVE INDEX,** Appendix II: At 20°
  Acceptance criteria: Between 1.449 and 1.454
- **SPECIFIC GRAVITY:** Determine at 25° by any reliable method (see *General Provisions*).
  Acceptance criteria: Between 0.893 and 0.902

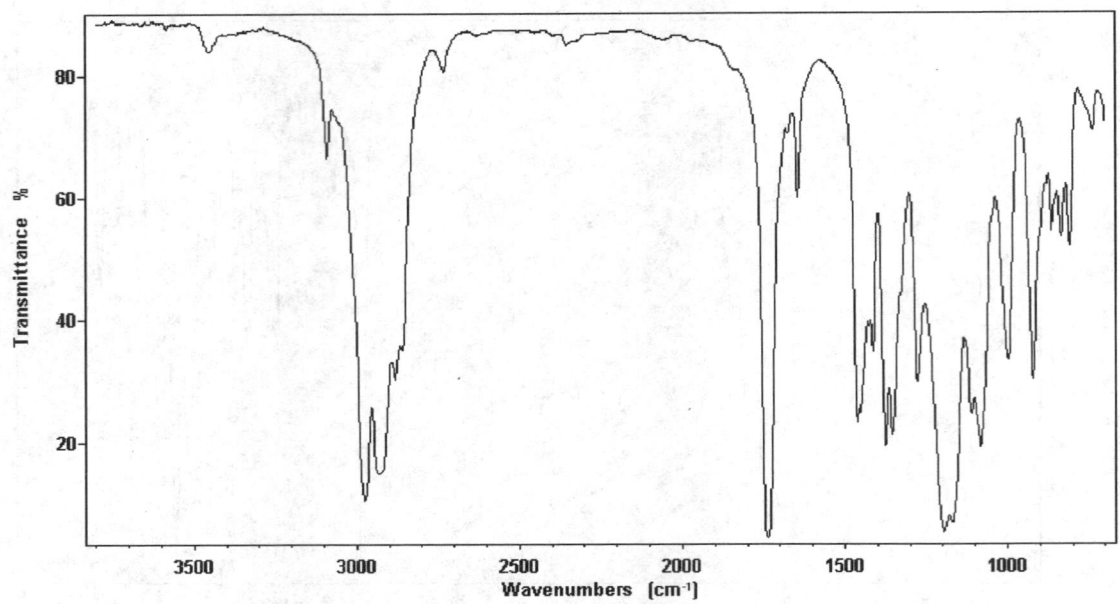

Linalyl Propionate

Linoleic Acid

First Published: Prior to FCC 6

(Z),(Z)-9,12-Octadecadienoic Acid

$C_{18}H_{32}O_2$
Formula wt 280.45
CAS: [60-33-3]

UNII: 9KJL21T0QJ [linoleic acid]

DESCRIPTION
Linoleic Acid occurs as a colorless to pale yellow, oily liquid that is easily oxidized by air. It is an essential fatty acid and the major constituent of many vegetable oils, including cottonseed, soybean, peanut, corn, sunflower seed, safflower, poppy seed, and linseed. Its specific gravity is about 0.901, and its refractive index is about 1.469. It has a boiling point ranging from 225° to 230° and a melting point around −5°. One mL dissolves in 10 mL of petroleum ether. It is freely soluble in ether; soluble in absolute alcohol and in chloroform; and miscible with dimethylformamide, fat solvents, and oils. It is insoluble in water.

Function: Flavoring adjuvant; nutrient
Packaging and Storage: Store in tight containers.

IDENTIFICATION
- **FATTY ACID COMPOSITION,** Appendix VII
  Acceptance criteria: A sample exhibits the following composition profile of fatty acids:

Fatty Acid	Weight % (Range)
14:0	<1.0
16:0	3–5
18:0	<1.0
18:1	<25.0
18:2	>60.0
18:3	<9.0

ASSAY
- **FATTY ACID COMPOSITION,** Appendix VII
  Acceptance criteria: NLT 60.0% of fatty acid C18:2, equivalent to $C_{18}H_{32}O_2$, calculated on the anhydrous basis

IMPURITIES
Inorganic Impurities
- **LEAD,** *Lead Limit Test, Flame Atomic Absorption Spectrophotometric Method,* Appendix IIIB
  Sample: 5 g
  Acceptance criteria: NMT 2 mg/kg
- **WATER,** *Water Determination,* Appendix IIB
  Acceptance criteria: NMT 0.5%

SPECIFIC TESTS
- **ACID VALUE (FATS AND RELATED SUBSTANCES),** Method I, Appendix VII
  Acceptance criteria: Between 196 and 202
- **IODINE VALUE,** Appendix VII
  Acceptance criteria: Between 145 and 160
- **RESIDUE ON IGNITION (SULFATED ASH),** Appendix IIC
  Sample: 10 g
  Acceptance criteria: NMT 0.01%

- **UNSAPONIFIABLE MATTER,** Appendix VII
  Sample: 10 g
  Acceptance criteria: NMT 2.0%

Locust (Carob) Bean Gum

First Published: Prior to FCC 6

Locust Bean Gum
Carob Bean Gum
INS: 410 CAS: [9000-40-2]
UNII: V4716MY704 [locust bean gum]

DESCRIPTION
Locust (Carob) Bean Gum occurs as a white to yellow-white powder. It is obtained from the ground endosperms of *Ceratonia siliqua* (L.) Taub. (Fam. Leguminosae). It consists chiefly of a high-molecular-weight hydrocolloidal polysaccharide, composed of galactose and mannose units combined through glycosidic linkages, which may be described chemically as a galactomannan. It is dispersible in either hot or cold water, forming a sol having a pH between 5.4 and 7.0, which may be converted to a gel by the addition of small amounts of sodium borate.
Function: Stabilizer; thickener
Packaging and Storage: Store in well-closed containers.

IDENTIFICATION
- **A. PROCEDURE**
  Sample: 2 g
  Analysis: Transfer the *Sample* into a 400-mL beaker, moisten it with about 4 mL of isopropyl alcohol, while vigorously stirring add 200 mL of cold water, and continue stirring until the gum is uniformly dispersed. [NOTE—Save the resulting solution for *Identification* test B (below).]
  Acceptance criteria: An opalescent, slightly viscous solution forms.
- **B. PROCEDURE**
  Sample: 100 mL of the solution prepared in *Identification* test A (above)
  Analysis: Transfer the *Sample* into a 400-mL beaker, heat the mixture in a boiling water bath for about 10 min, and then cool to room temperature.
  Acceptance criteria: The viscosity of the solution increases appreciably (distinguishing it from guar gum).

IMPURITIES
Inorganic Impurities
- **ARSENIC,** *Arsenic Limit Test,* Appendix IIIB
  Sample solution: Prepare as directed for organic compounds.
  Acceptance criteria: NMT 3 mg/kg
- **LEAD,** *Lead Limit Test,* Appendix IIIB
  Sample solution: Prepare as directed for organic compounds.
  Control: 5 µg Pb (5 mL of *Diluted Standard Lead Solution*)
  Acceptance criteria: NMT 5 mg/kg

SPECIFIC TESTS
- **ACID-INSOLUBLE MATTER**
  Sample: 1.5 g
  Analysis: Transfer the *Sample* into a 250-mL beaker containing 150 mL of water and 1.5 mL of sulfuric acid. Cover the beaker with a watch glass, and heat the mixture on a steam bath for 6 h, rubbing down the wall of the beaker frequently with a rubber-tipped stirring rod and replacing any water lost by evaporation. Subsequently add 500 mg of a suitable filter aid, previously dried for 3 h at 105° and accurately weighed, and filter through a tared, sintered-glass filter crucible. Wash the residue several times with hot water, dry the crucible and its contents at 105° for 3 h, cool in a desiccator, and weigh. The difference between the weight of the filter aid and that of the residue is the weight of the *Acid-Insoluble Matter*.
  Acceptance criteria: NMT 4.0%
- **ASH (TOTAL),** Appendix IIC
  Acceptance criteria: NMT 1.2%
- **GALACTOMANNANS**
  Analysis: Add the percentages of *Acid-Insoluble Matter, Ash (Total), Loss on Drying,* and *Protein,* and subtract the total from 100%. The difference represents the percentage of galactomannans in the sample.
  Acceptance criteria: NLT 75.0%
- **LOSS ON DRYING,** Appendix IIC: 105° for 5 h
  Acceptance criteria: NMT 14.0%
- **PROTEIN,** *Nitrogen Determination,* Appendix IIIC
  Sample: 3.5 g. [NOTE—Use a 500-mL Kjeldahl flask.]
  Analysis: Calculate the percent protein with the formula:

  $$\text{Result} = F \times N$$

  F = nitrogen-to-protein conversion factor, 6.25
  N = percent nitrogen
  Acceptance criteria: NMT 7.0%
- **STARCH**
  Sample solution: 100 mg/mL
  Analysis: Add a few drops of iodine TS to the *Sample solution*.
  Acceptance criteria: No blue color appears.

Lovage Oil

First Published: Prior to FCC 6

CAS: [8016-31-7]
UNII: 7534M4PQ6U [lovage oil]

DESCRIPTION
Lovage Oil occurs as a yellow-green-brown to deep brown liquid with a strong, characteristic aromatic odor and taste. It is the volatile oil obtained by steam distillation of the fresh root of the plant *Levisticum officinale* L. Koch syn. *Angelica levisticum,* Baillon (Fam. Umbelliferae). It is soluble in most fixed oils and slightly soluble, with opalescence, in mineral oil, but it is relatively insoluble in glycerin and in

propylene glycol. [NOTE—This oil becomes darker and more viscous under the influence of air and light.]
Function: Flavoring agent
Packaging and Storage: Store in a cool place protected from light in full, tight containers that are made from steel or aluminum and that are suitably lined.

IDENTIFICATION
- **INFRARED SPECTRA,** *Spectrophotometric Identification Tests,* Appendix IIIC
  Acceptance criteria: The spectrum of the sample exhibits relative maxima (that may vary in intensity) at the same wavelengths as those of the spectrum below.

SPECIFIC TESTS
- **ACID VALUE (ESSENTIAL OILS AND FLAVORS),** Appendix VI
  Acceptance criteria: Between 2.0 and 16.0
- **ANGULAR ROTATION,** *Optical (Specific) Rotation,* Appendix IIB: Use a 100-mm tube.
  Acceptance criteria: Between −1° and +5°
- **REFRACTIVE INDEX,** Appendix IIB
  [NOTE—Use an Abbé or other refractometer of equal or greater accuracy.]
  Acceptance criteria: Between 1.536 and 1.554 at 20°
- **SAPONIFICATION VALUE,** *Esters,* Appendix VI
  Sample: 1.5 g
  Acceptance criteria: Between 238 and 258
- **SOLUBILITY IN ALCOHOL,** Appendix VI
  Acceptance criteria: One mL of sample dissolves in 4 mL of 95% alcohol, sometimes with slight turbidity. The age of the oil has an adverse effect upon solubility.
- **SPECIFIC GRAVITY:** Determine by any reliable method (see *General Provisions*).
  Acceptance criteria: Between 1.030 and 1.057

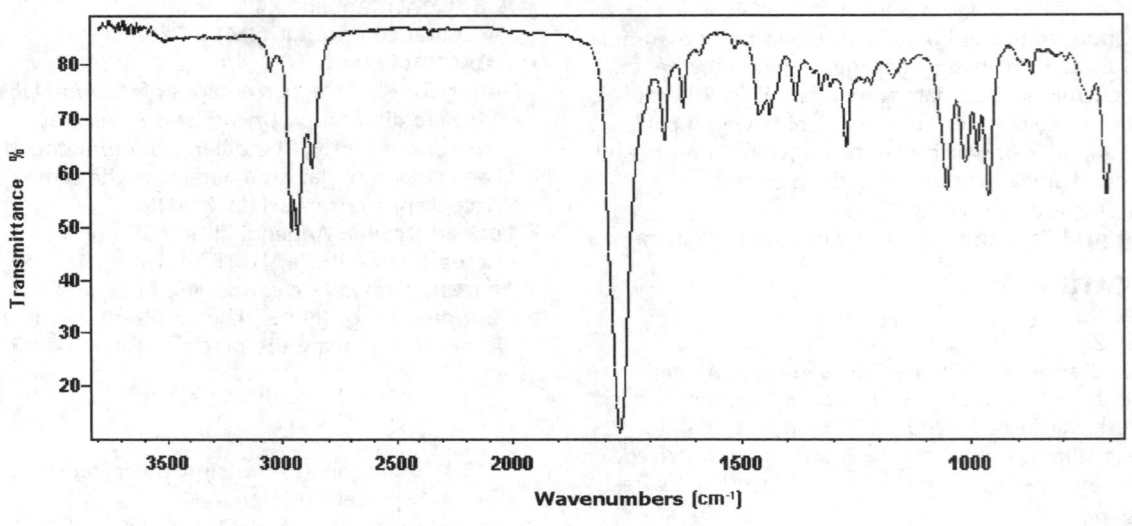

Lovage Oil

Lutein
First Published: FCC 7

Bo-Xan
Vegetable Luteol
Xanthophyll

$C_{40}H_{56}O_2$ Formula wt 568.88
INS: 161b(i) CAS: [127-40-2]
UNII: X72A60C9MT [lutein]

DESCRIPTION
Lutein occurs as a free-flowing, orange-red powder. It is the purified fraction obtained from saponification of the oleoresin of *Tagetes erecta L.* It is insoluble in water.
Function: Source of lutein; color
Packaging and Storage: Store in tight, light-resistant containers in a cool place.

IDENTIFICATION
- **A. UV-VISIBLE ABSORPTION SPECTRUM**
  Sample solution: Prepare as directed in the *Assay for Total Carotenoids.*
  Analysis: Using a suitable UV/Vis spectrophotometer, examine the *Sample solution* in a 1-cm cell over a spectral range of 300 to 700 nm.
  Acceptance criteria: The ratio of A_{446}/A_{474} is between 1.09 and 1.14.
- **B. PROCEDURE**
  Acceptance criteria: The retention time for the major peak in the chromatogram of the *Sample solution*

corresponds to that in the chromatogram of the *Standard solution*, as obtained in the *Assay* for *Lutein*.

ASSAY
- **LUTEIN**
  [NOTE—Use low-actinic glassware.]
  Mobile phase: Hexane and ethyl acetate (75:25), filtered and degassed. Make adjustments if necessary.
  Standard solution: 150 µg/mL of USP Lutein RS in *Mobile phase*
  Sample solution: Evaporate 1 mL of *Sample stock solution* (prepared as directed in the *Assay* for *Total Carotenoids*) under a stream of nitrogen to dryness. Add 1 mL of *Mobile phase* and sonicate to dissolve.
  Chromatographic system, Appendix IIA
    Mode: High-performance liquid chromatography
    Detector: 446 nm
    Column: 4.6-mm × 25-cm column that contains 5- to 10-µm porous silica packing[1]
    Flow rate: 1.5 mL/min
    Injection size: 10 µL
    System suitability
      Sample: *Standard solution*
    [NOTE—The approximate relative retention times are 1.0 for lutein and 1.05 for zeaxanthin.]
      Suitability requirement 1: The resolution between lutein and zeaxanthin is NLT 1.0.
      Suitability requirement 2: The tailing factor is NMT 2.
      Suitability requirement 3: The relative standard deviation for replicate injections is NMT 2.0%.
  Analysis: Inject the *Sample solution* into the chromatograph, record the chromatogram, and measure the peak area responses. [NOTE—The peak area of lutein is NLT 85.0% of the total detected area of peaks in the chromatogram.]
  Calculate the percentage of Lutein in the sample taken by the formula:

  $$\text{Result} = T \times (R_I/R_S)$$

  T = percentage of *Total Carotenoids* determined below
  R_I = peak response of lutein
  R_S = sum of the responses of all of the peaks
  Acceptance criteria: NLT 74.0%

- **TOTAL CAROTENOIDS**
  [NOTE—Use low-actinic glassware.]
  Solution A: Hexanes, acetone, toluene, and dehydrated alcohol (10:7:7:6)
  Sample stock solution: 0.30 mg/mL of sample in *Solution A*
  Sample solution: 3.0 µg/mL of sample in dehydrated alcohol: from *Sample stock solution*
  Blank: Dehydrated alcohol
  Analysis: Determine the absorbance of the *Sample solution* against that of the *Blank* at the wavelength of maximum absorbance at about 446 nm, with a suitable spectrophotometer.
  Calculate the percentage of total carotenoids as lutein ($C_{40}H_{56}O_2$) by the formula:

  $$\text{Result} = A/(C \times F)$$

  A = absorbance of the *Sample solution*
  C = concentration of the *Sample solution* (g/mL)
  F = absorptivity of lutein in alcohol (2550 mL · g^{-1} · cm^{-1})
  Acceptance criteria: NLT 80.0%

IMPURITIES
Inorganic Impurities
- **LEAD,** *Lead Limit Test, Flame Atomic Absorption Spectrophotometric Method,* Appendix IIIB
  Sample: 10 g
  Acceptance criteria: NMT 1 mg/kg

Organic Impurities
- **ZEAXANTHIN AND OTHER RELATED COMPOUNDS**
  [NOTE—Use low-actinic glassware.]
  Mobile phase: Hexane and ethyl acetate (75:25), filtered and degassed. Make adjustments if necessary.
  Standard solution: 150 µg/mL of USP Lutein RS in *Mobile phase*
  Sample solution: Evaporate 1 mL of *Sample stock solution* (prepared as directed in the *Assay* for *Total Carotenoids*) under a stream of nitrogen to dryness. Add 1 mL of *Mobile phase* and sonicate to dissolve.
  Chromatographic system, Appendix IIA
    Mode: High-performance liquid chromatography
    Detector: 446 nm
    Column: 4.6-mm × 25-cm column that contains 5- to 10-µm porous silica packing[1]
    Flow rate: 1.5 mL/min
    Injection size: 10 µL
    System suitability
      Sample: *Standard solution*
      [NOTE—The approximate relative retention times are 1.0 for lutein and 1.05 for zeaxanthin.]
      Suitability requirement 1: The resolution between lutein and zeaxanthin is NLT 1.0.
      Suitability requirement 2: The tailing factor is NMT 2.
      Suitability requirement 3: The relative standard deviation for replicate injections is NMT 2.0%.
  Analysis: Inject the *Sample solution* into the chromatograph, record the chromatogram, and measure the peak area responses.
  Calculate the percentage of zeaxanthin in the sample taken by the formula:

  $$\text{Result} = T \times (R_I/R_S)$$

  T = percentage of *Total Carotenoids* determined above
  R_I = peak response of zeaxanthin
  R_S = sum of the responses of all of the peaks

---
[1] Agilent Zorbax Rx-SIL, or equivalent.

Calculate the percentage of other related compounds in the sample taken by the formula:

$$Result = 100 \times (R_O/R_S)$$

R_O = individual peak response of any other peak in the chromatogram, excluding zeaxanthin and lutein
R_S = sum of the responses of all of the peaks

Acceptance criteria
Zeaxanthin: NMT 9.0%
Other related compounds: NMT 1.0% of any other single related compound

SPECIFIC TESTS
- **WATER**, *Water Determination*, Appendix IIB
  Acceptance criteria: NMT 1.0%
- **RESIDUE ON IGNITION (SULFATED ASH)**, Appendix IIC
  Analysis: Proceed as directed, but igniting at 600 ± 50°.
  Acceptance criteria: NMT 1.0%

Lycopene from *Blakeslea trispora*

First Published: Second Supplement, FCC 7

All-*trans*-lycopene

$C_{40}H_{56}$ Formula wt 536.85
INS: 160d(iii)   CAS: [502-65-8]
UNII: SB0N2N0WV6 [lycopene]

DESCRIPTION
Lycopene from *Blakeslea trispora* occurs as a red crystalline powder. It is a fermentation product that accumulates inside the biomass of the fungus and is extracted and purified using suitable solvents. It is predominantly all-*trans*-lycopene, but also contains minor quantities of other carotenoids. Commercial preparations containing Lycopene from *Blakeslea trispora* are available as suspensions in edible oils or as water-dispersible powders and are stabilized using suitable food-grade antioxidants. Lycopene from *Blakeslea trispora* is freely soluble in chloroform and insoluble in water.
Function: Source of lycopene; color
Packaging and Storage: Preserve in tight, light-resistant containers under inert gas, and store in a cool place.

IDENTIFICATION
- **A. PRESENCE OF CAROTENOIDS**
  Sample solution: Solution in acetone
  Analysis: To the *Sample solution*, successively add a 5% solution of sodium nitrite and 1 N sulfuric acid.
  Acceptance criteria: The color of the *Sample solution* disappears.
- **B. PROCEDURE**
  Acceptance criteria: The retention time of the major peak in the chromatogram of the *Sample solution* corresponds to that of the major peak in the chromatogram of *Standard solution A*, as determined in the *Assay* for *Lycopene*.
- **C. UV-VIS ABSORPTION SPECTRUM**
  Sample solution: Solution in hexane
  Acceptance criteria: The absorption spectrum of the *Sample solution* exhibits an absorption maximum at about 470 nm.

ASSAY
- **LYCOPENE**
  Mobile phase: Methanol and acetonitrile (60:40)
  Standard solution A: Transfer an amount of USP Lycopene RS equivalent to 5 mg of lycopene to a 250-mL volumetric flask, add about 60 units of bacterial alkaline protease preparation or another suitable enzyme, and about 25 mg of butylated hydroxytoluene. Add 2.50 mL of dilute ammonium hydroxide (2 in 100) in water, mix, place in an ultrasonic bath at 50° for 10 min, rotate the flask occasionally to avoid having the material stick to the glass surface, and continue until the material is dispersed with no lumps. Add 5 mL of tetrahydrofuran, 40 mL of dehydrated alcohol, mix, and place in the ultrasonic bath for about 1 min. Cool to room temperature, and dilute with *tert*-butyl methyl ether to volume. Shake vigorously, allow the precipitate to settle, and filter the supernatant for use as *Standard solution A*.
  Standard solution B: [NOTE—Preparation of *Standard solution B* is required to determine the exact concentration of *Standard solution A*.] Dilute 1 mL of *Standard solution A* with hexane to 10 mL.
  To determine the purity of the USP Lycopene RS used to prepare *Standard solution A*, P_S, measure the absorbance of *Standard solution B* in a 1-cm optical cell at the wavelength of maximum absorption of approximately 470 nm, using hexane as a blank. Calculate P_S by:

$$P_S = A_{MAX}/(F \times C_{SSB})$$

A_{MAX} = absorbance of *Standard solution B* at the wavelength of maximum absorbance
F = absorptivity of pure lycopene in hexane, 345
C_{SSB} = concentration of USP Lycopene RS in *Standard solution B* (mg/mL)

[NOTE—P_S, the purity of the USP Lycopene RS, equals 1.0 for a 100% pure standard and is less than 1.0 for a standard with purity below 100%.]
  Standard solution C: Dilute 25 mL of *Standard solution A* with acetone to 100 mL.
  Sample stock solution: Transfer an amount of sample equivalent to 25 mg of lycopene to a 100-mL volumetric flask, and dissolve in 10 mL of methylene chloride. Dilute with hexane to volume.
  Sample solution: Dilute 1 mL of the *Sample stock solution* with acetone to 50 mL.
  Chromatographic system, Appendix IIA
  Mode: Liquid chromatography
  Detector: UV-Vis 470 nm

Column: 4.6-mm × 25-cm; packing of octadecylsilane chemically bonded to 5-μm porous (300 Å pore size) silica micro-particles[1]
Temperature
  Column: 30°
  Injector: 10°
Flow rate: 1 mL/min
Injection size: 10 μL
Analysis: Inject *Standard solution C* into the chromatograph and record the chromatogram. [NOTE—The retention time of all-*trans*-lycopene is approximately 11.5–12.5 min. The relative retention time of 13-*cis*-lycopene with respect to all-*trans*-lycopene is 1.25. The relative retention times for other carotenoids with respect to all-*trans*-lycopene are 1.2 for β-carotene and 1.1 for γ-carotene.]
Record the total peak area of all-*trans*-lycopene and *cis*-lycopene isomers and calculate the response factor, RF, in AU mL/mg, for lycopene:

$$RF = r_{ST}/(C_S \times P_S)$$

r_{ST} = total lycopene peak area for all-*trans*-lycopene and *cis*-lycopene, as determined from the chromatogram of the *Standard solution*
C_S = concentration of *Standard solution C* (mg/mL)
P_S = purity of the USP Lycopene RS, as determined above

Inject the *Sample solution* into the chromatograph and record the chromatogram, measuring the peak areas for all-*trans*-lycopene (r_1); total lycopene (all-*trans*-lycopene + *cis*-lycopene, r_2); other carotenoids (r_3); and all carotenoids (all-*trans*-lycopene + *cis*-lycopene + other carotenoids, r_4).
Calculate the percentages of total lycopene and all-*trans*-lycopene in the sample taken:

$$\text{Total lycopene} = r_2/(C_U \times RF) \times 100$$

$$\text{All-}trans\text{-lycopene} = (r_1/r_2) \times 100$$

C_U = concentration of the *Sample solution* (mg/mL)

Acceptance criteria
  Total lycopene: NLT 95%
  All-*trans*-lycopene: NLT 90%

IMPURITIES
Inorganic Impurities
- **LEAD**, *Elemental Impurities by ICP, Method I,* Appendix IIIC
  Acceptance criteria: NMT 1 mg/kg

Organic Impurities
- **RESIDUAL SOLVENTS**
  [NOTE—Perform this test to determine the amount of residual isopropanol and isobutyl acetate in the sample.]
  Internal standard: 3-methyl-2-pentanone

Internal standard solution: Add 50.0 mL of methanol to a 50-mL headspace vial and seal. Weigh and inject 15 μL of the *Internal standard* through the septum. Re-weigh the vial to within 0.01 mg.
Blank: Use a portion of the sample with very low solvent content.
Blank solution: Weigh 0.20 g of the *Blank* to a 50-mL headspace vial. Add 5.0 mL of methanol and 1.0 mL of *Internal standard solution*. Heat at 60° for 10 min and shake vigorously for 10 s.
Standard stock solution: Add 50.0 mL of methanol to a 50-mL headspace vial and seal. Weigh the vial and inject 50 μL of the component of interest through the septum. Re-weigh the vial and mix the solution well.
Standard solution: Weigh 0.20 g of the *Blank* into a 50-mL headspace vial, and add 4.9 mL of methanol and 1.0 mL of *Internal standard solution*. Introduce 0.1 mL of the *Standard stock solution* to the vial, mix well, and heat at 60° for 10 min. Shake vigorously for 10 s.
Sample solution: Weigh 0.20 g of the sample into a 50-mL headspace vial. Add 5.0 mL of methanol and 1.0 mL of the *Internal standard solution*. Heat at 60° for 10 min and shake vigorously for 10 s.
Chromatographic system, Appendix IIA
  Mode: Headspace gas chromatography
  Detector: Flame ionization
  Column: 0.8-m × 0.53-mm (i.d.) megabore fused silica column coated with a 1-μm film of polyethylene glycol (average molecular weight about 15,000) coupled with a second 30-m × 0.53-mm (i.d.) fused silica column coated with a 5-μm film of dimethylpolysiloxane gum
  Carrier gas: Helium
  Flow rate: 5 mL/min (209 kPa)
  Temperature
    Injector: 140°
    Detector: 300°
    Oven: Hold at 35° for 5 min; ramp to 90° at 5°/min; hold at 90° for 6 min
    Syringe: 70°
    Transfer: 80°
  Headspace sampler
    Sample heating temperature: 60°
    Sample heating period: 10 min
  Injection size: 1000 μL
  Injection mode: Split
  [NOTE—The approximate retention time for isopropanol is 5.23 min. The approximate retention time for isobutyl acetate is not available for this system and should be determined experimentally.]
Analysis: Place the *Sample solution*, *Blank solution*, and *Standard solution* into the sample tray of the headspace gas chromatograph. Record the resulting chromatograms and determine the calibration factor, C, for each component of interest:

$$C = W_S/[W_{ISS} \times (r_S - r_{SB}) \times F_1]$$

C = calibration factor
W_S = amount of the component of interest in the *Standard stock solution* (mg)

---
[1] Vydac 281TP54, or equivalent, available from Grace Davison Discovery Sciences at www.discoverysciences.com.

W_{ISS} = amount of Internal standard in the 1.0-mL aliquot of Internal standard solution used to prepare the Standard solution (mg)

r_S = relative peak area of the component of interest in the chromatogram of the Standard solution

r_{SB} = relative peak area of the component of interest in the chromatogram of the Blank solution

F_1 = dilution factor for the Stock standard solution, 10

Calculate the amount of each component of interest in the sample taken, in mg/headspace vial:

$$Result = (r_U \times W_{ISU} \times C)/F_2$$

r_U = relative peak area of the component of interest in the chromatogram of the Sample solution

W_{ISU} = amount of Internal standard in the 1.0-mL aliquot of Internal standard solution used to prepare the Sample solution (mg)

F_2 = factor, 50

From the calculations, determine the percentage of each component of interest in the sample taken.

Acceptance criteria
Isobutyl acetate: NMT 1.0%
Isopropanol: NMT 0.1%

SPECIFIC TESTS

- **CONTENT OF OTHER CAROTENOIDS**
  Mobile phase, Sample stock solution, Sample solution, and Chromatographic system: Prepare as directed in the Assay for Lycopene.
  Analysis: Proceed as directed in the Assay for Lycopene. Calculate the percentage of other carotenoids in the sample taken:

  $$Other\ carotenoids = (r_3/r_4) \times 100$$

  Acceptance criteria: NMT 5%

- **LOSS ON DRYING**, Appendix IIC: 40°, 4 h at 20 mm Hg
  Acceptance criteria: NMT 0.5%

Lycopene Extract from Tomato

First Published: Second Supplement, FCC 7

All-*trans*-lycopene
Lycopene (Tomato)
Lycopene, Tomato Extract
Tomato Oleoresin Extract

$C_{40}H_{56}$ Formula wt 536.85
INS: 160d(ii)   CAS: [502-65-8]
UNII: SB0N2N0WV6 [lycopene]

DESCRIPTION

Lycopene Extract from Tomato occurs as a dark-red viscous liquid. It is obtained through ethyl acetate extraction of the pulp of ripe red tomatoes (*Lycopersicon esculentum* L.) followed by removal of the solvent. The ingredient contains only the fat-soluble solids extracted from the fruit. Lycopene is the major coloring component in tomato extract; minor amounts of other carotenoid pigments may also be present. Lycopene Extract from Tomato also contains oils, fats, waxes, and flavor components naturally occurring in tomatoes. It is freely soluble in ethyl acetate and *n*-hexane; partially soluble in ethanol and acetone; and insoluble in water. Tocopherols may be added as antioxidants. While not a requirement for this monograph, users interested in analyzing this ingredient for potential pesticide residues may use the informational method found under *Pesticide Residues* in Appendix XIII.

Function: Antioxidant; source of lycopene; color
Packaging and Storage: Preserve in tight, light-resistant containers, and store in a cool place.

IDENTIFICATION

- **PRESENCE OF LYCOPENE, PHYTOFLUENE, AND PHYTOENE**
  Butylated hydroxytoluene solution, Diluent, Standard solution C, Sample stock solution, and Sample solution: Proceed as directed in the Assay for Lycopene.
  Chromatographic system: Proceed as directed in the test for Content of Other Carotenoids and Tocopherols in Specific Tests.
  Acceptance criteria: The retention times for the lycopene, phytofluene, and phytoene peaks of the Sample solution correspond to those of Standard solution C, as obtained in the test for Content of Other Carotenoids and Tocopherols (under System suitability).

- **RATIO OF ALL-*E*-LYCOPENE AND 5*Z*-LYCOPENE**
  Butylated hydroxytoluene solution: Proceed as directed in the Assay for Lycopene.
  Mobile phase: 0.05% diisopropylethylamine in *n*-hexane; sonicate for 3–4 min
  Sample stock solution: Proceed as directed in the Assay for Lycopene.
  Sample solution: Dilute 5 mL of the Sample stock solution with *n*-hexane to 100 mL.
  Chromatographic system, Appendix IIA
    Mode: Liquid chromatography
    Detector: UV-Vis 472 nm
    Column: Two 4.0-mm × 25-cm columns; 5-µm packing of porous silica particles (300 Å pore size); connected in series
    Temperature: 22°
    Flow rate: 0.5 mL/min
    Injection size: 10 µL
  Analysis: Inject the Sample solution into the chromatograph, record the chromatogram, and measure the peak responses of the two major peaks. [NOTE—The approximate relative retention times for all-*E*-lycopene and 5*Z*-lycopene are 1.00 and 1.04–1.10, respectively. The approximate retention time for the all-*E*-lycopene peak is 30–45 min.]

Calculate the ratio of the peak areas:

$$\text{Result} = r_{U1}/r_{U2}$$

r_{U1} = peak response of 5Z-lycopene
r_{U2} = peak response of all-E-lycopene

Acceptance criteria: The peak area ratio is NMT 0.10.

ASSAY
- **LYCOPENE**

  Butylated hydroxytoluene solution: 5 mg/mL in methylene chloride

  Mobile phase: Prepare a solution containing acetonitrile, methanol, methylene chloride, and n-hexane (850:100:25:25). Add 0.05% of diisopropylethylamine and sonicate for 3–4 min.

  Diluent: Prepare a solution containing acetonitrile, methylene chloride, methanol, n-hexane, and butylated hydroxytoluene (600:150:150:100:0.5). Add 0.05% of diisopropylethylamine and sonicate for 3–4 min.

  Standard solution A: Transfer an amount of USP Lycopene RS equivalent to 5 mg of lycopene into a 100-mL volumetric flask, add 60 units of bacterial alkaline protease preparation or another suitable enzyme, and 25 mg of butylated hydroxytoluene. Add 2.5 mL of dilute ammonium hydroxide (2 in 100) in water, and place in an ultrasonic bath at 50° for 10 min, rotating the flask occasionally to avoid having material stick to the glass surface. Continue ultrasonication until the material is dispersed with no lumps. Add 5 mL of tetrahydrofuran, and shake until no colored precipitate remains. Add an additional 2-mL portion of tetrahydrofuran, 40 mL of *Diluent*, and shake until the mixture is homogeneous. Dilute with *Diluent* to volume, shake vigorously, and allow to stand, if necessary, until the solid has settled.

  Standard solution B: [NOTE—Preparation of *Standard solution B* is required to determine the exact concentration of *Standard solution A*.] Transfer 2.0 mL of *Standard solution A* to a 100-mL volumetric flask, add 10 mL of alcohol and 10 mL of *Butylated hydroxytoluene solution*, and dilute with n-hexane to volume. Prepare in triplicate.

  Determine the absorbance of *Standard solution B* at the wavelength of maximum absorbance at 472 nm using a mixture of alcohol, *Butylated hydroxytoluene solution*, and n-hexane (10:10:80) as the blank. Calculate the concentration of lycopene, in μg/mL, in *Standard solution A*:

  $$\text{Result} = (A_{MAX}/F) \times 50{,}000$$

  A_{MAX} = absorbance of *Standard solution B*
  F = absorptivity of pure lycopene in n-hexane at 472 nm, 345

  Standard solution C: Transfer an amount of USP Tomato Extract Containing Lycopene RS equivalent to 6 mg of lycopene to a 100-mL volumetric flask, and dissolve in 1 mL of *Butylated hydroxytoluene solution* and 9 mL of methylene chloride, using a sonicator. Dilute with *Diluent* to volume (0.06 mg/mL of lycopene).

  Sample stock solution: Warm several grams of the extract to 50° in a water bath. Mix well with a glass rod or spatula, then weigh 1–1.2 g into a 100-mL volumetric flask. Add 10 mL of *Butylated hydroxytoluene solution* and 30 mL of methylene chloride to the flask and sonicate for 1 min in order to dissolve the sample completely. Cool to room temperature, and dilute with methylene chloride to volume.

  Sample solution: Transfer 5.0 mL of *Sample stock solution* to a 50-mL volumetric flask, and dilute with *Diluent* to volume.

  Chromatographic system, Appendix IIA
    Mode: Liquid chromatography
    Detector: UV-Vis 472 nm
    Column: 4.6-mm × 25-cm; with octylsilane chemically bonded to 5-μm porous silica particles
    Temperature: 39 ± 1°
    Flow rate: 0.7 mL/min
    Injection size: 10 μL

  System suitability
    Sample: *Standard solution A*
    Suitability requirement: The relative standard deviation is NMT 1.5% for the lycopene peak area for replicate injections.

  Analysis
  [NOTE—Both *Standard solution A* and *Standard solution C* will be necessary for use in *Content of Other Carotenoids and Tocopherols*, but analysts may choose which solution to use in the *Assay* for *Lycopene*.] Separately inject *Standard solution A* or *Standard solution C* into the chromatograph, record the chromatograms, and measure the responses of the major lycopene peak in each chromatogram. [NOTE—The approximate retention time for lycopene is 6 min.]

  Calculate the percentage of lycopene in the sample taken:

  $$\text{Result} = (C_S/C_U) \times (r_U/r_S) \times 100$$

  C_S = concentration of lycopene in *Standard solution A* or *Standard solution C* (μg/mL)
  C_U = concentration of the *Sample solution* (μg/mL)
  r_U = peak response for lycopene obtained from the chromatogram for the *Sample solution*
  r_S = peak response for lycopene obtained from the chromatogram of *Standard solution A* or *Standard solution B*

  Acceptance criteria: 5.0%–15.0%

IMPURITIES
Inorganic Impurities
- **ARSENIC**, Elemental Impurities by ICP, Method I, Appendix IIIC
  Acceptance criteria: NMT 3 mg/kg
- **LEAD**, Elemental Impurities by ICP, Method I, Appendix IIIC
  Acceptance criteria: NMT 1 mg/kg

Organic Impurities
- **RESIDUAL SOLVENTS**
  Standard stock solution: 10.00 mg/g of ethyl acetate in diethylphthalate. [NOTE—Use an ultrasonic bath to dissolve. This solution is stable for 2 months at room temperature.]

Standard solution 1: Dilute 500 mg of *Solution A* to 50.00 g with diethylphthalate (100 µg/g). [NOTE—Use an ultrasonic bath to dissolve. This solution is stable for 2 months at room temperature.]

Standard solution 2: Dilute 500 mg of *Standard solution 1* to 10.00 g (±0.1 mg) with diethylphthalate in a pre-weighed and tared 20-mm headspace vial (5 µg/g). Insert a 12–15 mm magnetic stirrer and seal the vial.

Standard solution 3: Dilute 1000 mg of *Standard solution 1* to 10.00 g (±0.1 mg) with diethylphthalate in a pre-weighed and tared 20-mm headspace vial (10 µg/g). Insert a 12–15 mm magnetic stirrer and seal the vial.

Standard solution 4: Dilute 1750 mg of *Standard solution 1* to 10.00 g (±0.1 mg) with diethylphthalate in a pre-weighed and tared 20-mm headspace vial (17.5 µg/g). Insert a 12–15 mm magnetic stirrer and seal the vial.

Standard solution 5: Dilute 2500 mg of *Standard solution 1* to 10.00 g (±0.1 mg) with diethylphthalate in a pre-weighed and tared 20-mm headspace vial (25 µg/g). Insert a 12–15 mm magnetic stirrer and seal the vial.

Sample solution: Heat a portion of sample material to 40°–50° in a water bath while stirring mechanically. Remove a 30-g portion of the sample material and warm to 50° in a water bath. Mix well with a glass rod or spatula and weigh 5000 mg into a pre-weighed and tared 20-mm headspace vial. Bring the weight of the sample to 10.00 g (total weight; ±0.1 mg) with diethylphthalate. Insert a 12–15 mm magnetic stirrer and seal the vial. Mix the sample using the stirrer.

Chromatographic system, Appendix IIA
  Mode: Headspace gas chromatography
  Detector: Flame ionization
  Column: 30-m × 0.53-mm (i.d.) megabore fused silica column coated with a 3-µm film of 5% diphenyl/95% dimethyl polysiloxane
  Carrier gas: Nitrogen
  Temperature
    Injector: 180°
    Detector: 230°
    Oven: Hold at 73° for 5 min; ramp to 160° at 25°/min; hold at 160° for 1 min. [NOTE—The run time is about 9.5 min.]
  Flow rate: 4 mL/min
  Injection size: 1000 µL
  Injection mode: Splitless 1:6

Analysis: Place *Standard solutions 2, 3, 4,* and *5*, and the *Sample solution* in a water bath held at 70° for exactly 2 h, stirring each solution for 1 min every 30 min. Separately inject each of the *Standard solutions* into the head-space gas chromatograph, record the peak area, and calculate the mean ratio of the standard concentration to peak area based on concentrations and peak areas of *Standard solutions 2, 3, 4,* and *5*.

Inject the *Sample solution* into the chromatograph, record the peak area, and calculate the concentration of ethyl acetate, in mg/kg:

$$\text{Result} = A_U \times F \times (W_{TU}/W_U)$$

A_U = peak area obtained from the chromatogram of the *Sample solution*
F = mean ratio of the concentration of *Standard solutions 2, 3, 4,* and *5* to the peak areas obtained on the solutions
W_{TU} = total weight of the *Sample solution* prepared (g)
W_U = amount of the sample used to prepare the *Sample solution* (g)

Acceptance criteria: NMT 50 mg/kg

SPECIFIC TESTS

- **CONTENT OF OTHER CAROTENOIDS AND TOCOPHEROLS**
  Butylated hydroxytoluene solution, Diluent, Standard solution A, Standard solution B, Standard solution C, Sample stock solution, and **Sample solution:** Prepare as directed in the *Assay* for *Lycopene*.
  Mobile phase: Prepare a solution containing acetonitrile, methanol, methylene chloride, and *n*-hexane (475:475:25:25). Add 0.05% of diisopropylethylamine and sonicate for 3–4 min.
  Chromatographic system, Appendix IIA
    Mode: Liquid chromatography
    Detector: UV-Vis 472 nm (lycopene); 450 nm (beta-carotene); 350 nm (phytofluene); 288 nm (phytoene and tocopherol)
    Column: 4.6-mm × 25-cm; with octadecylsilane chemically bonded to 5-µm porous silica particles
    Temperature: 39 ± 1°
    Flow rate: 0.6 mL/min
    Injection size: 10 µL
    System suitability
      Sample: *Standard solution C*
      [NOTE—The chromatogram obtained from *Standard solution C* should be similar to the reference chromatogram provided with the USP Tomato Extract Containing Lycopene RS. Approximate relative retention times are 0.6 for the peaks of the tocopherol isomers, 1.0 for the peak of all-*E*-lycopene, 1.5–1.7 for the peaks of beta carotene isomers, 1.6–1.8 for the peaks of the phytofluene isomers, and 1.8–2.2 for the phytoene peak.]
      Suitability requirement: The relative standard deviation is NMT 2% for the peak responses for the lycopene isomers for replicate injections.
  Analysis: Separately inject *Standard solution A* and the *Sample solution* into the chromatograph and record the chromatograms. Identify the locations of the peaks for the lycopene isomers, beta carotene isomers, phytofluene isomers, and phytoene by comparison with the reference chromatogram provided with the corresponding lot of USP Tomato Extract Containing Lycopene RS. Measure the sum of the peak responses of the lycopene isomers at 472 in *Standard solution A*. Determine the concentration of *Standard solution A* as directed in the *Assay* for *Lycopene*. [NOTE—The lycopene

isomers may be resolved in more than one peak in this chromatographic system.]

In the chromatogram of the *Sample solution*, measure the sum of the peak responses of the beta carotene isomers at 450 nm, the sum of the peak responses of the phytofluene isomers at 350 nm, the response of phytoene at 288 nm, and the sum of the peak responses of all tocopherols at 288 nm.

Calculate the percentage of beta carotene in the portion of the sample taken:

$$\text{Result} = (C_S/C_U) \times (r_{U1}/r_S) \times (F_1/F_2) \times 100$$

C_S = concentration of *Standard solution A* (μg/mL)
C_U = concentration of the *Sample solution* (μg/mL)
r_{U1} = sum of the peak responses for the beta carotene isomers at 450 nm obtained from the chromatogram of the *Sample solution*
r_S = sum of the peak responses for the lycopene isomers at 473 nm obtained from the chromatogram of *Standard solution A*
F_1 = absorptivity for pure lycopene, 345
F_2 = absorptivity for pure beta carotene, 259.2

Calculate the percentage of phytofluene in the portion of the sample taken:

$$\text{Result} = (C_S/C_U) \times (r_{U2}/r_S) \times (F_1/F_3) \times 100$$

C_S = concentration of *Standard solution A* (μg/mL)
C_U = concentration of the *Sample solution* (μg/mL)
r_{U2} = sum of the peak responses for the phytofluene isomers at 350 nm obtained from the chromatogram of the *Sample solution*
r_S = sum of the peak responses for the lycopene isomers at 472 nm obtained from the chromatogram of *Standard solution A*
F_1 = absorptivity for pure lycopene, 345
F_3 = absorptivity for pure phytofluene, 135

Calculate the percentage of phytoene in the portion of the sample taken:

$$\text{Result} = (C_S/C_U) \times (r_{U3}/r_S) \times (F_1/F_4) \times 100$$

C_S = concentration of *Standard solution A* (μg/mL)
C_U = concentration of the *Sample solution* (μg/mL)
r_{U3} = peak area for phytoene at 288 nm obtained from the chromatogram of the *Sample solution*
r_S = sum of the peak responses for the lycopene isomers at 472 nm obtained from the chromatogram of *Standard solution A*
F_1 = absorptivity for pure lycopene, 345
F_4 = absorptivity for pure phytoene, 125

Calculate the percentage of tocopherols in the portion of the sample taken:

$$\text{Result} = (C_S/C_U) \times (r_{U4}/r_S) \times (F_1/F_5) \times 100$$

C_S = concentration of *Standard solution A* (μg/mL)
C_U = concentration of the *Sample solution* (μg/mL)
r_{U4} = sum of the peak responses for all the tocopherol peaks at 288 nm obtained from the chromatogram of the *Sample solution*
r_S = sum of the peak responses for the lycopene isomers at 472 nm obtained from the chromatogram of *Standard solution A*
F_1 = absorptivity for pure lycopene, 345
F_5 = average absorptivity for tocopherols, 8.5

Acceptance criteria
Phytofluene and phytoene (combined): NLT 0.8%, on the anhydrous basis
Beta carotene: NLT 0.2%, on the anhydrous basis
Tocopherols: NLT 1.0%, on the anhydrous basis

- **RESIDUE ON IGNITION (SULFATED ASH)**, Appendix IIC
Sample: 1–2 g
Acceptance criteria: NMT 1.0%

Lycopene, Synthetic

First Published: FCC 6

$C_{40}H_{56}$ Formula wt 536.88
CAS: All-*E*(*trans*) lycopene [502-65-8]
5*Z*(*cis*) lycopene [101468-86-4]
UNII: 32A47J0H1R [lycopene, synthetic]

DESCRIPTION
Lycopene, Synthetic occurs as dark red to dark violet crystals or crystalline powder. It is an open-chain, unsaturated C_{40} carotenoid made up of eight isoprene units, and consists of a mixture of geometric isomers. It is insoluble in water and in acids and alkalis, and nearly insoluble in methanol and in ethanol, but it is soluble in chloroform and in tetrahydrofuran. It is sparingly soluble in ether, in hexane, and in vegetable oils.

Function: Source of lycopene
Packaging and Storage: Store under inert gas in tight, light-resistant containers in a cool place.

IDENTIFICATION

- **A. UV-VISIBLE ABSORPTION SPECTRUM**

    Standard stock solution: Transfer 25 mg of lycopene Reference Standard (Chromadex, Inc., Santa Ana, CA; Sigma, St. Louis, MO, or equivalent) into a 100-mL volumetric flask, add about 25 mg of butylated hydroxytoluene and about 60 mL of methylene chloride, and sonicate to dissolve. Dilute to volume with methylene chloride.

    Standard solution: Transfer 2.0 mL of the *Standard stock solution* into a 200-mL volumetric flask and dilute to volume with cyclohexane.

    Sample stock solution: Transfer 25 mg of sample into a 100-mL volumetric flask, add about 25 mg of butylated hydroxytoluene and about 60 mL of methylene chloride, and sonicate to dissolve. Dilute to volume with methylene chloride.

    Sample solution: Transfer 2.0 mL of the *Sample stock solution* into a 200-mL volumetric flask and dilute to volume with cyclohexane.

    Analysis: Using a suitable UV/VIS spectrophotometer, examine the *Sample solution* and the *Standard solution* in 1-cm cells over a spectral range of 300 to 700 nm. Record and compare the spectra from each solution.

    Acceptance criteria: The ratio of A_{476}/A_{508} is between 1.10 and 1.14.

- **B. PROCEDURE**

    Acceptance criteria: The retention time of the major peak in the chromatogram of the *Sample solution* corresponds to that in the chromatogram of the *Standard solution* as obtained in the test for *Content of all-E-Lycopene, 5Z-Lycopene, and Related Compounds* (below).

ASSAY

- **PROCEDURE**

    Sample stock solution: Transfer 25 mg of sample into a 100-mL volumetric flask, add about 25 mg of butylated hydroxytoluene and about 60 mL of methylene chloride, and sonicate to dissolve. Dilute to volume with methylene chloride.

    Sample solution: Transfer 2.0 mL of the *Sample stock solution* into a 200-mL volumetric flask and dilute to volume with cyclohexane.

    Analysis: Determine the absorbance of the *Sample solution* at the wavelength of maximum absorbance at about 476 nm using cyclohexane as the blank. Calculate the percent lycopene in the portion of the sample taken by the formula:

    $$\text{Result} = 1000A/331W$$

    A = absorbance of the *Sample solution*
    W = weight of the sample (g) taken to make the *Sample stock solution*
    331 = absorptivity of pure lycopene in cyclohexane

    Acceptance criteria: NLT 96.0% and NMT 101.0% of lycopene ($C_{40}H_{56}$), calculated on the dried basis

IMPURITIES

Inorganic Impurities

- **LEAD,** *Lead Limit Test, Atomic Absorption Spectrophotometric Graphite Furnace Method, Method II,* Appendix IIIB

    Acceptance criteria: NMT 1 mg/kg

Organic Impurities

- **ORGANIC VOLATILE IMPURITIES**

    Standard solution: 1.0 µg/mL of 1,4-dioxane, 12.0 µg/mL of ethanol, 6.0 µg/mL of methanol, and 1.0 µg/mL of *n*-propyl alcohol in dimethylformamide. Pipet 5 mL of this solution into a vial that contains 1 g of anhydrous sodium sulfate and that is fitted with a septum and a crimp cap, seal, and heat at 80° for 1 h.

    Sample solution: Transfer 100 mg of sample into a vial, add 5.0 mL of dimethylformamide and 1 g of anhydrous sodium sulfate, and seal with a septum and crimp cap. Heat the sealed vial at 80° for 1 h.

    Chromatographic system, Appendix IIA
    Mode: Gas chromatography
    Detector: Flame ionization detector
    Column: 30-m × 0.53-mm (id) column coated with 3.0-µm 6% cyanopropylphenyl-94% dimethylpolysiloxane (DB-624, J&W, or equivalent), and a 5-m × 0.53-mm (id) silica guard column deactivated with phenylmethylsiloxane

    Temperature
    Column: Hold at 40° for 20 min, then increase rapidly to 240° and hold for 20 min
    Injection port: 140°
    Detector: 260°
    Carrier gas: Helium
    Linear velocity: About 35 cm/s
    Injection volume: About 1 µL

    System suitability
    Sample: *Standard solution*
    Suitability requirement 1: All of the components in the *Standard solution* are resolved in the chromatogram.
    Suitability requirement 2: The resolution, R, between any two components is NLT 3.
    Suitability requirement 3: The relative standard deviation of the individual peak responses from replicate injections is NMT 15%.

Analysis: Separately inject the *Standard solution* and *Sample solution* into the chromatograph, record the chromatograms, and measure the peak responses. Based on the retention time, identify any peaks present in the chromatogram of the *Sample solution*. Use mass spectrometry to establish the presence and identity of any peaks in the chromatogram from any of the organic volatile impurities listed below or from some other volatile impurity eluting with a comparable retention time by mass spectrometric relative abundance methods or by using a second validated column containing a different stationary phase.

Acceptance criteria
 1,4-Dioxane: NMT 50 mg/kg
 Ethanol: NMT 600 mg/kg
 Methanol: NMT 300 mg/kg
 Propyl alcohol: NMT 50 mg/kg

SPECIFIC TESTS

- **CONTENT OF ALL *E*-LYCOPENE, 5*Z*-LYCOPENE, AND RELATED COMPOUNDS**
 Mobile phase: *tert*-butyl methyl ether:methanol:tetrahydrofuran [784:665:74] (v/v/v), filtered and degassed. [NOTE—Adjust as necessary. See *System suitability* below.]
 Standard solution: 20 μg/mL of lycopene using lycopene reference standard (Chromadex, Inc., Santa Ana, CA; Sigma, St. Louis, MO, or equivalent) in *Mobile phase*
 Sample: 15 mg
 Sample stock solution: Transfer the *Sample* into a 25-mL volumetric flask, dissolve in and dilute to volume with tetrahydrofuran containing 50 mg of butylated hydroxytoluene per L.
 Sample solution: Pipet 2 mL of the *Sample stock solution* into a 50-mL volumetric flask, add 8 mL of tetrahydrofuran, and dilute to volume with *tert*-butyl methyl ether.
 Chromatographic system, *Appendix IIA*
  Mode: High-performance liquid chromatography
  Detector: 472 nm
  Column: 25-cm × 4.6-mm (id) column containing 5-μm C30, polymerically bonded, non-end-capped packing, preceding in series by a guard column containing 3-μm C30 packing
  Flow rate: 1.0 mL/min
  Injection volume: About 10 μL
 System suitability
  Sample: *Standard solution*
  Suitability requirement 1: The resolution, *R*, between all-*E*-lycopene and 5*Z*-lycopene is NLT 1.0.
  Suitability requirement 2: The tailing factor is NLT 0.8 and NMT 2.0.
  Suitability requirement 3: The relative standard deviation for replicate injections for the all-*E*-lycopene is NMT 2.0%.

 [NOTE—New columns may require up to 30 injections before the system suitability requirements are met.]
 Analysis: Inject the *Sample solution* into the chromatograph, record the chromatogram, and measure the peak area responses. [NOTE—Relative retention times are about 1.07 for 5*Z*-lycopene and 1.0 for all-*E*-lycopene.] Calculate the percentage of related compounds in the portion of the *Sample* taken by the formula:

$$\text{Result} = T(r_S/r_T)$$

 T = percent total lycopene isomers obtained in the *Assay* (above)
 r_S = sum of the responses of all peaks, excluding the peak for all-*E*-lycopene and the peak for 5*Z*-lycopene
 r_T = total detected area

 Calculate the percent 5*Z*-lycopene isomer in the portion of the sample taken by the formula:

$$\text{Result} = T(r_{5Z}/r_T)$$

 T = percent total lycopene isomers obtained in the *Assay* (above)
 r_{5Z} = peak response for 5*Z*-lycopene isomer
 r_T = total detected area

 Calculate the percent all-*E*-lycopene taken by the formula:

$$\text{Result} = T(r_E/r_T)$$

 T = percent total lycopene isomers obtained in the *Assay* (above)
 r_E = peak response for all-*E*-lycopene isomer
 r_T = total detected area

 Acceptance criteria
  5*Z*-lycopene: NMT 23.0%
  all-*E*-lycopene: NLT 70%
  Other related compounds: NMT 9.0%

- **LOSS ON DRYING,** *Appendix IIC*: 40° over phosphorus pentoxide, under vacuum for 4 h
 Acceptance criteria: NMT 0.2%

- **RESIDUE ON IGNITION (SULFATED ASH),** *Appendix IIC*
 Analysis: 2 g
 Acceptance criteria: NMT 0.2%

OTHER REQUIREMENTS

- **LABELING:** Label as Lycopene, Synthetic.

L-Lysine Monohydrochloride

First Published: Prior to FCC 6
Last Revision: FCC 6

L-2,6-Diaminohexanoic Acid Hydrochloride

$C_6H_{14}N_2O_2 \cdot HCl$ Formula wt 182.65
                             CAS: [657-27-2]
UNII: JNJ23Q2COM [lysine hydrochloride]

DESCRIPTION
L-Lysine Monohydrochloride occurs as a white or nearly white, free-flowing, crystalline powder. It is freely soluble in water and almost insoluble in alcohol and in ether. It melts at about 260° with decomposition.
Function: Nutrient
Packaging and Storage: Store in well-closed containers.

IDENTIFICATION
- **INFRARED ABSORPTION,** *Spectrophotometric Identification Tests,* Appendix IIIC
  Reference standard: USP L-Lysine Hydrochloride RS
  Sample and standard preparation: *K*
  Acceptance criteria: The spectrum of the sample exhibits maxima at the same wavelengths as those in the spectrum of the *Reference standard*.

ASSAY
- **PROCEDURE**
  Sample: 100 mg, previously dried
  Analysis: Dissolve the *Sample* in 2 mL of formic acid, add exactly 15.0 mL of 0.1 N perchloric acid, and heat on a water bath for 30 min. [**CAUTION**—Handle perchloric acid in an appropriate fume hood.] After cooling, add 45 mL of glacial acetic acid, and titrate the excess perchloric acid with 0.1 N sodium acetate, determining the endpoint potentiometrically. Perform a blank determination (see *General Provisions*), and make any necessary correction. Each mL of 0.1 N perchloric acid is equivalent to 9.133 mg of $C_6H_{14}N_2O_2 \cdot HCl$.
  Acceptance criteria: NLT 98.5% and NMT 101.5% of $C_6H_{14}N_2O_2 \cdot HCl$, on the dried basis

IMPURITIES
Inorganic Impurities
- **LEAD,** *Lead Limit Test,* Appendix IIIB
  Sample solution: Prepare as directed for organic compounds.
  Control: 5 µg Pb (5 mL of *Diluted Standard Lead Solution*)
  Acceptance criteria: NMT 5 mg/kg

SPECIFIC TESTS
- **LOSS ON DRYING,** Appendix IIC: 105° for 3 h
  Acceptance criteria: NMT 1.0%
- **OPTICAL (SPECIFIC) ROTATION,** Appendix IIB
  Sample: 8 g, previously dried
  Analysis: Dissolve the *Sample* in sufficient 6 N hydrochloric acid to make 100 mL.
  Acceptance criteria
  $[\alpha]_D^{20}$ between +20.3° and +21.5°, on the dried basis; or
  $[\alpha]_D^{25}$ between +20.4° and +21.4°, on the dried basis
- **RESIDUE ON IGNITION (SULFATED ASH),** Appendix IIC
  Sample: 2 g
  Acceptance criteria: NMT 0.2%

Mace Oil

First Published: Prior to FCC 6

UNII: 9KKX6I0U7Z [mace oil] CAS: [8007-12-3]

DESCRIPTION
Mace Oil occurs as a colorless to pale yellow liquid with the characteristic odor and taste of nutmeg. It is the volatile oil obtained by steam distillation from the ground, dried arillode of the ripe seed of *Myristica fragrans* Houtt. (Fam. Myristicaceae). Two types of oil, the East Indian and the West Indian, are commercially available. It is soluble in most fixed oils and in mineral oil, but it is insoluble in glycerin and in propylene glycol.

Function: Flavoring agent

Packaging and Storage: Store in a cool place protected from light in full, tight containers that are made from steel or aluminum and that are suitably lined.

IDENTIFICATION
- **INFRARED SPECTRA,** *Spectrophotometric Identification Tests,* Appendix IIIC

  Acceptance criteria: The spectrum of the sample exhibits relative maxima at the same wavelengths as those of the spectrum below.

SPECIFIC TESTS
- **ANGULAR ROTATION,** *Optical (Specific) Rotation,* Appendix IIB: Use a 100-mm tube.

  Acceptance criteria
  East Indian type: Between +2° and +30°
  West Indian type: Between +20° and +45°
- **REFRACTIVE INDEX,** Appendix IIB

  [NOTE—Use an Abbé or other refractometer of equal or greater accuracy.]

  Acceptance criteria
  East Indian type: Between 1.474 and 1.488 at 20°
  West Indian type: Between 1.469 and 1.480 at 20°
- **SOLUBILITY IN ALCOHOL,** Appendix VI

  Acceptance criteria: One mL of sample dissolves in 4 mL of 90% alcohol.
- **SPECIFIC GRAVITY:** Determine by any reliable method (see *General Provisions*).

  Acceptance criteria
  East Indian type: Between 0.880 and 0.930
  West Indian type: Between 0.854 and 0.880

OTHER REQUIREMENTS
- **LABELING:** Indicate whether the oil is the East Indian or West Indian type.

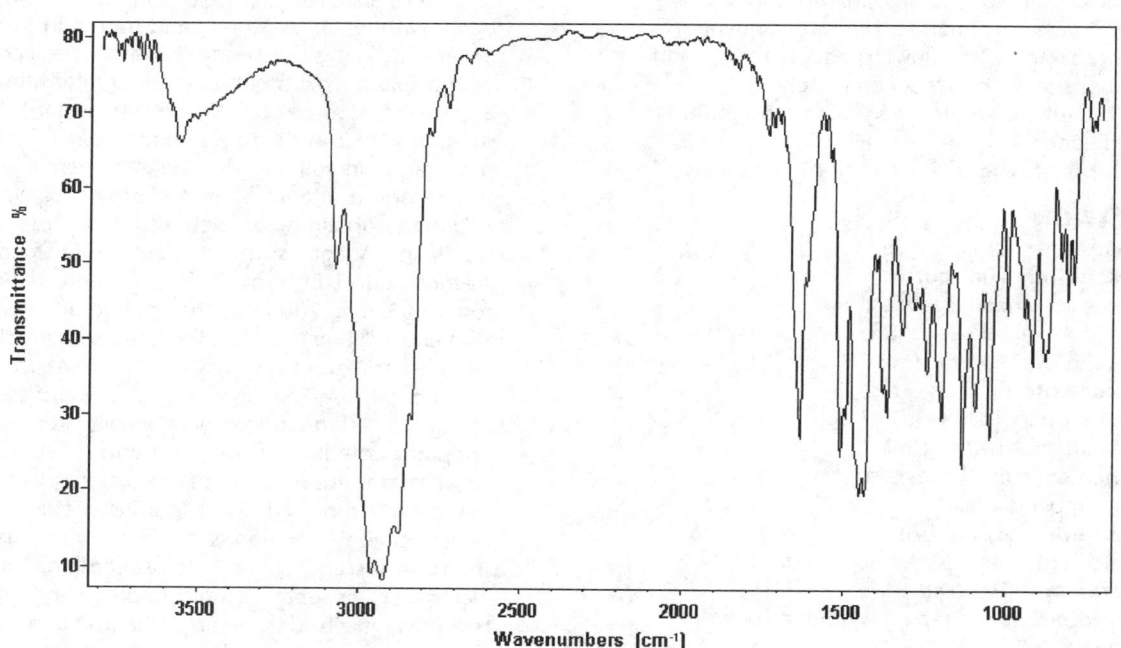

Mace Oil

Magnesium Ammonium Potassium Chloride, Hydrate

First Published: Second Supplement, FCC 7

Ammonium Magnesium Potassium Chloride, Hydrate
Magnesal
Magnesium Ammonium Potassium Carnallite
Magnesium Ammonium Potassium Chloride, Triple Salt

$Mg_4K(NH_4)_3Cl_{12} \cdot 24H_2O$ Formula wt 1048.23
CAS: [1044829-32-4]

DESCRIPTION
Magnesium Ammonium Potassium Chloride, Hydrate occurs as a white co-crystalline triple salt (solid) containing 24 waters of hydration for each unit of the magnesium/potassium/ammonium chloride complex. The method of manufacture involves dissolving stoichiometric amounts of the individual magnesium, potassium, and ammonium chloride salts in water, boiling the solution and removing the vapor formed, then cooling the mixture, crystallizing, filtering or centrifuging, drying and sieving the product. Magnesium Ammonium Potassium Chloride, Hydrate is freely soluble in water and remains dry in air at relative humidity below 70%, but may become deliquescent at higher humidity. It may contain suitable food-grade anticaking or free-flowing agents, such as silicon dioxide (SiO_2) or calcium silicate (Ca_2SiO_4). Magnesium Ammonium Potassium Chloride, Hydrate containing water insoluble anticaking or free-flowing agents may produce cloudy solutions and dissolve incompletely.

Function: Salt substitute; flavoring agent and intensifier; dough conditioner

Packaging and Storage: Store in tight containers.

IDENTIFICATION
- **Ammonium**, Appendix IIIA
    Sample solution: 100 mg/mL
    Acceptance criteria: Passes test
- **Chloride**, Appendix IIIA
    Sample solution: 100 mg/mL
    Acceptance criteria: Passes test
- **Magnesium**, Appendix IIIA
    Sample solution: 100 mg/mL
    Acceptance criteria: Passes test
- **Potassium**, Appendix IIIA
    Sample solution: 100 mg/mL
    Acceptance criteria: Passes tests
- **X-Ray Diffraction Pattern**
    Sample preparation: Prepare a random powder specimen of the sample.
    Analysis: Record the x-ray diffraction pattern of the Sample preparation using a copper source, and calculate the d values.
    Acceptance criteria: The Sample preparation exhibits intense reflections at the following d values: 6.59Å, 3.79Å, 2.96Å, 2.34Å, and 2.10Å.

ASSAY
[Note—In the following procedures, it may be necessary to filter solutions of the sample to avoid interference from insoluble or suspended added anticaking or free-flowing agents.]

- **Ammonium**
    Sample: 700 mg–2.2 g, previously dried at 60° for 2 h
    Analysis: Proceed as directed under Nitrogen Determination, Appendix IIIC. From the mg of nitrogen determined, N, calculate the percentage of ammonium in the Sample:

    $$Result = N/(F \times W) \times 100$$

    F = factor representing the percentage of nitrogen in ammonium, by weight, 0.776
    W = weight of the Sample taken (mg)
    Acceptance criteria: 4.9%–5.4%

- **Chloride**[1]
    [Note—Use distilled or deionized water that is halogen-free when tested as follows: Add 1 mL of 0.1 M silver nitrate and 5 mL of HNO_3 (20% v/v, diluted with water) to 100 mL of the water. No more than slight turbidity is produced.]
    Solution A: 2% nitric acid in water (v/v)
    Sodium chloride standard solution: 5.000 mg/mL NaCl (0.0856 M); prepared from sodium chloride primary standard that has been previously dried at 110° for 2 h
    Silver nitrate standard solution: 14.451 mg/mL $AgNO_3$ (0.0856 M). Standardize as follows: pipet 25 mL of Sodium chloride standard solution into a 250-mL beaker, dilute with water to 50 mL, and then add 50 mL of Solution A. Using the Electrode system specified below with a suitable pH meter and a magnetic stirrer (stir at a constant, vigorous rate without splashing), titrate the solution with Silver nitrate standard solution, recording the change in voltage with the incremental addition of titrant. Add a total of 50 mL of Silver nitrate standard solution to obtain a complete titration curve. Plot the results in mV against mL of Silver nitrate standard solution added. Determine the inflection point of the resulting curve, and from the volume of Silver nitrate standard solution used to titrate the sodium chloride, calculate the exact molarity of the Silver nitrate standard solution. [Note—The Silver nitrate standard solution should be restandardized occasionally. Recheck the endpoint potential occasionally, and redetermine it if any changes are made in the Electrode system, or if the pH meter is replaced. Store in a Pyrex container out of direct sunlight. Solution is stable in room light.]
    Electrode system: Use a Ag billet combination electrode[2], or separate indicating Ag[3] and glass reference[4] electrodes. Before initial use and before use each day, if necessary, clean the Ag billet electrode tip with scouring powder or other suitable material, and rinse thoroughly with water. Clean other electrodes as recommended by the manufacturer(s), and reclean as

---
[1] Based on AOAC Official Method 971.27, Sodium Chloride in Canned Vegetables, Method III (Potentiometric Method).
[2] Beckman No. 39261, or equivalent.
[3] Beckman No. 39261, Orion No. 94-17-BN, Fisher No. 13-639-122, or equivalent.
[4] Beckman No. 39419, Orion No. 90-02-00, Fisher No. 9-313-216, or equivalent.

frequently as necessary to prevent drifting of the endpoint reading. Store and care for all electrodes as directed by the manufacturer(s).

Sample solution: Transfer 5.00 g of sample, previously dried at 60° for 2 h, to a 100-mL volumetric flask, and dilute with water to volume.

Analysis: Transfer 5 mL of the *Sample solution* to a 250-mL beaker, dilute with water to 50 mL, and then add 50 mL of *Solution A*. Using the *Electrode system* specified above with a suitable pH meter and a magnetic stirrer (stir at a constant, vigorous rate without splashing), titrate the solution with *Silver nitrate standard solution*, recording the change in voltage with the incremental addition of titrant. Add a total of 50 mL of *Silver nitrate standard solution* to obtain a complete titration curve. Plot the results in mV against mL of *Silver nitrate standard solution* added. Determine the inflection point of the resulting curve, and from the volume of *Silver nitrate standard solution* used to titrate the sodium chloride, calculate the percentage of chloride in the *Sample*:

$$\text{Result} = [V_T \times M_T \times M_{r1}]/[F \times V_S \times C_U] \times 100$$

- V_T = volume of *Silver nitrate standard solution* used to titrate the sample to the inflection point (mL)
- M_T = exact molarity of the *Silver nitrate standard solution* used in the titration (mol/L)
- M_{r1} = atomic weight of chlorine, 35.453 g/mol
- F = conversion from mL to L, 1000 mL/L
- C_U = concentration of the *Sample solution* (g/mL)
- V_S = volume of *Sample solution* titrated, 5 mL

Acceptance criteria: 38.6%–42.2%

- **MAGNESIUM**

[NOTE—Thoroughly clean all glassware by soaking overnight in 20% nitric acid (v/v). Triple-rinse all glassware with distilled and deionized water. All water used for cleaning glassware and for preparation of solutions should have a resistance of NLT 18 megaohms.]

Solution A: 0.1% (w/v) lanthanum chloride; prepare by dissolving 1.33 g of lanthanum chloride heptahydrate in water and diluting with water to 500 mL [NOTE—This solution is stable for up to 6 months when stored at room temperature.]

Standard stock solution: 1000 µg/mL magnesium; commercially prepared, certified atomic absorption standard

Standard solutions: Using serial dilutions of *Standard stock solution* in *Solution A*, prepare three standard solutions containing 0.05 µg/mL, 0.1 µg/mL, and 0.2 µg/mL of magnesium.

Sample solution: 10 mg/mL, using a sample previously dried at 60° for 2 h

Blank: *Solution A*

Analysis: Using a suitable atomic absorption spectrophotometer equipped with a lead hollow-cathode lamp set at the magnesium emission line of 285.21 nm and an air–acetylene flame, and optimized according to the instrument manufacturer's instructions, concomitantly determine the absorbance of the *Blank*, the three *Standard solutions*, and the *Sample solution*. If the absorbance of the *Sample solution* is above the absorbance of the most concentrated *Standard solution*, further dilute the *Sample solution* with *Solution A* until its absorbance falls within the range of the *Standard solutions*. Correct the readings from the *Standard solutions* and the final dilution of the *Sample solution* for the *Blank* reading. Plot the absorbance readings of the *Standard solutions* against the magnesium concentration, in µg/mL, and determine the magnesium concentration of the *Sample solution* from the curve so obtained.

Calculate the percentage of magnesium in the sample:

$$\text{Result} = (C/C_U) \times F \times 100$$

- C = concentration of magnesium in the solution of the sample, determined from the standard curve (µg/mL)
- C_U = concentration of sample in the final solution used for the determination (mg/mL)
- F = factor converting µg to mg, 0.001

Acceptance criteria: 8.8%–9.6%

- **POTASSIUM**

[NOTE—Thoroughly clean all glassware by soaking overnight in 20% nitric acid (v/v). Triple-rinse all glassware with distilled and deionized water. All water used for cleaning glassware and for preparation of solutions should have a resistance of NLT 18 megaohms.]

Solution A: 0.5% (w/v) cesium; prepare by dissolving 1.58 g of cesium chloride in water and diluting with water to 250 mL [NOTE—Prepare fresh every 6 months.]

Standard stock solution: 1000 µg/mL potassium; commercially prepared, certified atomic absorption standard

Standard solutions: Using serial dilutions of *Standard stock solution* in *Solution A*, prepare three standard solutions containing 0.1 µg/mL, 0.5 µg/mL, and 1.0 µg/mL of potassium.

Sample solution: 10 mg/mL, using a sample previously dried at 60° for 2 h

Blank: *Solution A*

Analysis: Using a suitable atomic absorption spectrophotometer equipped with a lead hollow-cathode lamp set at the potassium emission line of 766.7 nm and an air–acetylene flame, and optimized according to the instrument manufacturer's instructions, concomitantly determine the absorbance of the *Blank*, the three *Standard solutions*, and the *Sample solution*. If the absorbance of the *Sample solution* is above the absorbance of the most concentrated *Standard solution*, further dilute the *Sample solution* with *Solution A* until its absorbance falls within the range of the *Standard solutions*. Correct the readings from the *Standard solutions* and the final dilution of the *Sample solution* for the *Blank* reading. Plot the absorbance readings of the *Standard solutions* against the potassium concentration, in µg/mL, and determine the potassium concentration of the *Sample solution* from the curve so obtained.

Calculate the percentage of potassium in the sample:

$$\text{Result} = (C/C_U) \times F \times 100$$

- C = concentration of potassium in the *Sample solution*, determined from the standard curve (µg/mL)
- C_U = concentration of sample in the final solution used for the determination (mg/mL)
- F = factor converting µg to mg, 0.001

Acceptance criteria: 3.5%–3.9%

IMPURITIES
- **Cadmium**, *Elemental Impurities by ICP*, Appendix IIIC
  Acceptance criteria: NMT 0.3 mg/kg
- **Lead**, *Elemental Impurities by ICP*, Appendix IIIC
  Acceptance criteria: NMT 2 mg/kg
- **Mercury**, *Elemental Impurities by ICP*, Appendix IIIC
  Acceptance criteria: NMT 0.5 mg/kg

Magnesium Carbonate

First Published: Prior to FCC 6

MgCO₃   Formula wt, anhydrous 84.31
4MgCO₃·Mg(OH)₂·5H₂O   Formula wt, basic 485.65
MgCO₃·H₂O   Formula wt, monohydrate 102.33
INS: 504(i)   CAS: anhydrous [546-93-0]
    basic [39409-82-0]
    monohydrate [23389-33-5]
UNII: 0E53J927NA [magnesium carbonate]

DESCRIPTION
Magnesium Carbonate occurs as light, white, friable masses, or as a bulky, white powder. It is a basic hydrated magnesium carbonate or a normal hydrated magnesium carbonate. It is stable in air. It is practically insoluble in water, to which, however, it imparts a slightly alkaline reaction. It is insoluble in alcohol, but dissolves, with effervescence, in dilute acids.
Function: pH control; drying agent; color-retention agent; anticaking agent; carrier
Packaging and Storage: Store in well-closed containers

IDENTIFICATION
- **Magnesium**, Appendix IIIA
  Sample solution: Dissolve sample in 2.7 N hydrochloric acid (solution will dissolve with effervescence)
  Acceptance criteria: Passes tests

ASSAY
- **Procedure**
  Sample: 1 g
  Analysis: Dissolve the *Sample* in 30.0 mL of 1 N sulfuric acid, add methyl orange TS, and titrate the excess acid with 1 N sodium hydroxide. From the volume of 1 N sulfuric acid consumed, deduct the volume of 1 N sulfuric acid corresponding to the content of calcium oxide in the weight of the sample taken for the assay. The difference is the volume of 1 N sulfuric acid equivalent to the magnesium oxide present. Each mL of 1 N sulfuric acid is equivalent to 20.16 mg of MgO and to 28.04 mg of CaO.
  Acceptance criteria: NLT 40.0% and NMT 43.5% of MgO

IMPURITIES
Inorganic Impurities
- **Calcium Oxide**
  Sample: 1 g
  Analysis: Dissolve the *Sample* in a mixture of 3 mL of sulfuric acid and 22 mL of water. Add 50 mL of alcohol, and allow the mixture to stand overnight. If crystals of magnesium sulfate separate, warm the mixture to about 50° to dissolve them. Filter through a suitable tared porous bottom porcelain crucible, previously washed with 2 N sulfuric acid, water, and alcohol. Wash the crystals on the porous disk several times with a 2:1 (v/v) mixture of alcohol:2 N sulfuric acid. Ignite the crucible and contents at 450° ± 25° to constant weight. [Note—Avoid exposing the crucible to sudden temperature changes.] The weight of calcium sulfate so obtained, multiplied by 0.4119, gives the equivalent of calcium oxide in the sample taken for the test.
  Acceptance criteria: NMT 0.6%
- **Lead**, *Lead Limit Test, APDC Extraction Method*, Appendix IIIB
  Acceptance criteria: NMT 2 mg/kg

SPECIFIC TESTS
- **Acid-Insoluble Substances**
  Sample: 5 g
  Analysis: Mix the *Sample* with 75 mL of water; while agitating, add hydrochloric acid in small portions until no more of the sample dissolves. Boil for 5 min. If an insoluble residue remains, filter through a suitable tared porous bottom porcelain crucible, wash well with water until the last washing is free from chloride, ignite at 800° ± 25° for 45 min, cool, and weigh. [Note—Avoid exposing the crucible to sudden temperature changes.]
  Acceptance criteria: NMT 0.05%
- **Soluble Salts**
  Sample: 2.0 g
  Analysis: Mix the *Sample* with 100 mL of a 1:1 (v/v) mixture of n-propyl alcohol:water. Heat the mixture to the boiling point with constant stirring, cool to room temperature, add water to make 100 mL, and filter. Evaporate 50 mL of the filtrate on a steam bath to dryness, and dry in an oven at 105° for 1 h.
  Acceptance criteria: The weight of the residue does not exceed 10 mg (NMT 1%).

Magnesium Chloride

First Published: Prior to FCC 6

MgCl₂·6H₂O   Formula wt 203.30
INS: 511   CAS: [7791-18-6]
UNII: 02F3473H9O [magnesium chloride]

DESCRIPTION
Magnesium Chloride occurs as colorless flakes or crystals. It contains six molecules of water of hydration. It is hygroscopic, very soluble in water, and freely soluble in alcohol.

Function: Color-retention agent; firming agent
Packaging and Storage: Store in tight containers.

IDENTIFICATION
- **MAGNESIUM,** Appendix IIIA
  - Sample solution: 100 mg/mL
  - Acceptance criteria: Passes tests
- **CHLORIDE,** Appendix IIIA
  - Sample solution: 100 mg/mL
  - Acceptance criteria: Passes test

ASSAY
- **PROCEDURE**
  - Sample: 450 mg
  - Analysis: Dissolve the Sample in 25 mL of water, add 5 mL ammonia–ammonium chloride buffer TS and 0.1 mL of eriochrome black TS and titrate with 0.05 M disodium EDTA until the solution turns blue. Each mL of 0.05 M disodium EDTA titrant is equivalent to 10.16 mg of $MgCl_2 \cdot 6H_2O$.
  - Acceptance criteria: NLT 99.0% and NMT 105.0% of $MgCl_2 \cdot 6H_2O$

IMPURITIES
Inorganic Impurities
- **AMMONIUM ION**
  - Sample solution: Dissolve 1 g of sample in 90 mL of water and slowly add 10 mL of a freshly boiled and cooled 100 mg/mL sodium hydroxide solution. Allow the mixture to settle, then decant 20 mL of the supernatant liquid into a color comparison tube and dilute to 50 mL with water.
  - Control solution: 10 µg of ammonium ion in 48 mL of water and 2 mL of a freshly boiled and cooled 100 mg/mL sodium hydroxide solution; transfer the solution to a color comparison tube
  - Analysis: Add 2 mL of Nessler's reagent to both color comparison tubes.
  - Acceptance criteria: Any color produced by the Sample solution does not exceed that produced by the Control solution. (NMT 0.005%)
- **LEAD,** Lead Limit Test, Appendix IIIB
  - Sample solution: 1 g in 10 mL of water
  - Control: 4 µg Pb (4 mL of Diluted Standard Lead Solution)
  - Acceptance criteria: NMT 4 mg/kg
- **SULFATE,** Chloride and Sulfate Limit Tests, Chloride Limit Test, Appendix IIIB
  - Sample: 1 g
  - Control: 300 µg sulfate (30 mL of Standard Sulfate Solution)
  - Acceptance criteria: Any turbidity produced by the Sample does not exceed that shown in the Control. (NMT 0.03%)

Magnesium Gluconate
First Published: Prior to FCC 6

$C_{12}H_{22}MgO_{14}$ Formula wt, anhydrous 414.60
$C_{12}H_{22}MgO_{14} \cdot 2H_2O$ Formula wt, dihydrate 450.63
INS: 580   CAS: anhydrous [3632-91-5]
           dihydrate [59625-89-7]
UNII: T42NAD2KHC [magnesium gluconate]

DESCRIPTION
Magnesium Gluconate occurs as a white to off-white powder or granulate. It is anhydrous, the dihydrate, or a mixture of both. It is very soluble in water and is sparingly soluble in alcohol. It is insoluble in ether.

Function: Nutrient
Packaging and Storage: Store in well-closed containers.

IDENTIFICATION
- **A. MAGNESIUM,** Appendix IIIA
  - Sample solution: 50 mg/mL
  - Acceptance criteria: Passes test
- **B. THIN-LAYER CHROMATOGRAPHY,** Appendix IIA
  - Sample solution: 10 mg/mL. [NOTE—Heat in a water bath at 60° if necessary to dissolve the sample.]
  - Standard solution: 10 mg/mL of USP Potassium Gluconate RS. [NOTE—Heat in a water bath at 60°, if necessary, to dissolve the sample.]
  - Adsorbent: 0.25-mm layer of chromatographic silica gel
  - Developing solvent system: Alcohol, water, ethyl acetate, and ammonium hydroxide (50:30:10:10)
  - Spray reagent: Dissolve 2.5 g of ammonium molybdate in 50 mL of 2 N sulfuric acid in a 100-mL volumetric flask. Add 1.0 g of ceric sulfate, swirl to dissolve, dilute to volume with 2 N sulfuric acid, and mix.
  - Application volume: 5 µL
  - Analysis: After removing the plate from the developing chamber, allow it to dry at 110° for 20 min, and allow it to cool. Spray the plate with the Spray reagent and heat the plate at 110° for 10 min.
  - Acceptance criteria: The principal spot obtained from the Sample solution corresponds in color, size, and R_F value to that obtained from the Standard solution.

ASSAY
- **PROCEDURE**
  - Sample: 800 mg
  - Analysis: Dissolve the Sample in 20 mL of water, add 5 mL of ammonia–ammonium chloride buffer TS and 0.1 mL of eriochrome black TS. Titrate with 0.05 M disodium EDTA to a blue endpoint. Each mL of 0.05 M disodium EDTA is equivalent to 20.73 mg of $C_{12}H_{22}MgO_{14}$.
  - Acceptance criteria: NLT 98.0% and NMT 102.0% of $C_{12}H_{22}MgO_{14}$, calculated on the anhydrous basis

674 / Magnesium Gluconate / Monographs

IMPURITIES
Inorganic Impurities
- **CHLORIDE**, *Chloride and Sulfate Limit Tests*, *Chloride Limit Test*, Appendix IIIB
  Sample solution: 1 g in 100 mL of water
  Control: 50 µg of chloride (5 mL of *Standard Chloride Solution*)
  Analysis: Proceed as directed using 10 mL of the *Sample solution*.
  Acceptance criteria: Any turbidity produced by the *Sample* does not exceed that shown in the *Control* (NMT 0.05%).
- **LEAD**, *Lead Limit Test, Flame Atomic Absorption Spectrophotometric Method*, Appendix IIIB
  Sample: 10 g
  Acceptance criteria: NMT 2 mg/kg
- **SULFATE**, *Chloride and Sulfate Limit Tests*, *Sulfate Limit Test*, Appendix IIIB
  Sample: 200 mg
  Control: 100 µg of sulfate (10 mL of *Standard Sulfate Solution*)
  Acceptance criteria: Any turbidity produced by the *Sample* does not exceed that in the *Control* (NMT 0.05%).

SPECIFIC TESTS
- **REDUCING SUBSTANCES:**
  Sample: 1 g
  Analysis: Transfer the *Sample* into a 250-mL Erlenmeyer flask, dissolve it in 10 mL of water, add 25 mL of alkaline cupric citrate TS, and cover the flask with a small beaker. Boil gently for exactly 5 min and cool rapidly to room temperature. Add 25 mL of a 1:10 acetic acid solution, 10.0 mL of 0.1 N iodine, 10 mL of 2.7 N hydrochloric acid, and 3 mL of starch TS. Titrate with 0.1 N sodium thiosulfate, to the disappearance of the blue color. Calculate the weight (mg) of reducing substances (as D-glucose) by the formula:

  $$\text{Result} = 27(V_1 N_1 - V_2 N_2)$$

  27 = an empirically determined equivalence factor for D-glucose
  V_1 = volume of the iodine solution
  N_1 = normality of the iodine solution
  V_2 = volume (mL) of the sodium thiosulfate solution
  N_2 = normality of the sodium thiosulfate solution
  Acceptance criteria: NMT 1.0%
- **WATER**, *Water Determination, Method Ib (Residual Titration)*, Appendix IIB
  Analysis: Allow 30 min for the sample to dissolve, perform a blank determination (see *General Provisions*) and make any necessary corrections.
  Acceptance criteria: Between 3.0% and 12.0%

Magnesium Hydroxide
First Published: Prior to FCC 6

Mg(OH)$_2$ Formula wt 58.32
INS: 528 CAS: [1309-42-8]
UNII: NBZ3QY004S [magnesium hydroxide]

DESCRIPTION
Magnesium Hydroxide occurs as a white, bulky powder. It is soluble in dilute acids but practically insoluble in water and in alcohol.
Function: pH control; drying agent; color-retention agent
Packaging and Storage: Store in tight containers.

IDENTIFICATION
- **MAGNESIUM**, Appendix IIIA
  Sample solution: 50 mg/mL in 2.7 N hydrochloric acid
  Acceptance criteria: Passes tests

ASSAY
- **PROCEDURE**
  Sample: 400 mg, previously dried at 105° for 2 h
  Analysis: Transfer the *Sample* into an Erlenmeyer flask. Add 25.0 mL of 1 N sulfuric acid and, after solution is complete, add methyl red TS. Titrate the excess acid with 1 N sodium hydroxide. From the volume of 1 N sulfuric acid consumed, deduct the volume of 1 N sulfuric acid corresponding to the content of calcium oxide in the sample taken for the assay. The difference is the volume of 1 N sulfuric acid equivalent to the Mg(OH)$_2$ in the sample taken. Each mL of 1 N sulfuric acid is equivalent to 29.16 mg of Mg(OH)$_2$ and to 28.04 mg of CaO.
  Acceptance criteria: NLT 95.0% and NMT 100.5% Mg(OH)$_2$, on the dried basis

IMPURITIES
Inorganic Impurities
- **LEAD**, *Lead Limit Test, APDC Extraction Method*, Appendix IIIB
  Acceptance criteria: NMT 2 mg/kg
- **CALCIUM OXIDE**
  Sample: 500 mg
  Analysis: Dissolve the *Sample* in 3 mL of sulfuric acid and 22 mL of water. Add 50 mL of alcohol, and allow the mixture to stand overnight. If crystals of magnesium sulfate separate, warm the mixture to about 50° to dissolve them. Filter through a suitable tared porous-bottom porcelain crucible, previously washed with 2 N sulfuric acid, water, and alcohol. Wash the crystals on the porous disk several times with a 2:1 (v/v) mixture of alcohol:2 N sulfuric acid. Ignite the crucible and contents at 450° ± 25° to constant weight. [NOTE—Avoid exposing the crucible to sudden temperature changes.] The weight of the calcium sulfate thus obtained, multiplied by 0.4119, gives the equivalent of calcium oxide in the sample taken for the test.
  Acceptance criteria: NMT 1%

SPECIFIC TESTS
- **ALKALIES (FREE) AND SOLUBLE SALTS**
  Sample solution: Boil 2 g of sample with 100 mL of water for 5 min in a covered beaker, then filter while hot.
  Analysis: Titrate 50 mL of the cooled *Sample solution* with 0.1 N sulfuric acid, using methyl red TS as the indicator. Not more than 2 mL of the acid is consumed. Evaporate 25 mL of the filtrate to dryness and dry at 105° for 3 h.
  Acceptance criteria: NMT 10 mg of residue remains
- **LOSS ON DRYING,** Appendix IIC: 105° for 2 h
  Acceptance criteria: NMT 2%
- **LOSS ON IGNITION**
  Sample: 500 mg
  Analysis: Transfer the *Sample* to a tared platinum crucible, and ignite, increasing the heat gradually, to constant weight at 800° ± 25°.
  Acceptance criteria: Between 30.0% and 33.0%

Magnesium Lactate

First Published: FCC 7

Lactic Acid Magnesium Salt
Magnesium bis(2-hydroxypropanoate)

$Mg(C_3H_5O_3)_2$ Formula wt anhydrous 202.45
$Mg(C_3H_5O_3)_2 \cdot H_2O$ Formula wt dihydrate 238.47
INS: 329   CAS: [18917-93-6]
UNII: MT6QI8324A [magnesium lactate]

DESCRIPTION
Magnesium Lactate occurs as a white or almost white, crystalline or granular powder and may be enantiomerically pure or mixed enantiomers. It is slightly soluble in water, soluble in boiling water, and practically insoluble in ethanol.
Function: Buffer; dough conditioner; nutrient
Packaging and Storage: Store in tight containers.

IDENTIFICATION
- **LACTATE,** Appendix IIIA
  Acceptance criteria: Passes the test
- **MAGNESIUM,** Appendix IIIA
  Acceptance criteria: Passes the tests

ASSAY
- **PROCEDURE**
  Sample: 200 mg
  Analysis: Dissolve the *Sample* in 25 mL of water, add 10 mL of ammonia–ammonium chloride buffer TS, and 0.1 mL of eriochrome black TS and titrate with 0.05 M disodium EDTA until the solution turns blue. Each mL of 0.05 M disodium EDTA titrant is equivalent to 10.12 mg of $Mg(C_3H_5O_3)_2$.
  Acceptance criteria: 98.0%–102.0% of $Mg(C_3H_5O_3)_2$, calculated on the dried basis

IMPURITIES
Inorganic Impurities
- **CHLORIDE,** *Chloride and Sulfate Limit Tests, Chloride Limit Test,* Appendix IIIB
  Sample: 1.0 g
  Control: 100 µg of chloride (10 mL of *Standard Chloride Solution*)
  Acceptance criteria: Any turbidity produced by the *Sample* does not exceed that shown in the *Control* (NMT 100 ppm).
- **IRON**
  Sample solution: Dissolve 1 g in 40 mL of water.
  Control: 40 µg of iron (4 mL of *Iron Standard solution;* see *Standard Solutions for the Preparation of Controls and Standards,* Solutions and Indicators)
  Analysis: To the *Sample solution,* add 2 mL of hydrochloric acid and dilute with water to 50 mL. Add 40 mg of ammonium persulfate crystals and 3 mL of ammonium thiocyanate TS. Repeat the preceding with the *Control.*
  Acceptance criteria: Any color produced by the *Sample solution* does not exceed that produced by the *Control* (NMT 40 ppm).
- **LEAD,** *Lead Limit Test, Flame Atomic Absorption Spectrophotometric Method,* Appendix IIIB
  Sample: 10 g
  Acceptance criteria: NMT 2 mg/kg
- **SULFATE,** *Chloride and Sulfate Limit Tests, Sulfate Limit Test,* Appendix IIIB
  Sample: 1.0 g
  Control: 50 µg of sulfate (5 mL of *Standard Sulfate Solution*)
  Acceptance criteria: Any turbidity produced by the *Sample* does not exceed that shown in the *Control* (NMT 50 ppm).

SPECIFIC TESTS
- **APPEARANCE**
  Solution A: 10 mg/mL of hydrazine sulfate in water. [NOTE—Allow to stand 4–6 h before use.]
  Solution B: Dissolve 2.5 g of hexamethylenetetramine in 25.0 mL of water in a 100-mL ground-glass stoppered flask.
  Opalescent stock suspension: To the flask containing *Solution B,* add 25.0 mL of *Solution A.* Mix the solutions and allow to stand for 24 h before use. [NOTE—The suspension is stable for 2 months, provided that it is stored in a glass container free from surface defects. The suspension must not adhere to the glass and must be well-mixed before use.]
  Opalescence reference solution: Mix 10.0 mL of *Opalescent stock suspension* and 90.0 mL of water. Shake before use.
  Yellow solution: 45.0 mg/mL of iron trichloride hexahydrate in water
  Red solution: 59.5 mg/mL of cobalt (II) chloride hexahydrate in water
  Blue solution: 62.4 mg/mL of copper (II) sulfate pentahydrate in water

Color reference stock solution: Combine 2.4 mL of *Yellow solution*, 1.0 mL of *Red solution*, 0.4 mL of *Blue solution*, and 6.2 mL of 10 mg/mL hydrochloric acid.
Color reference solution: Combine 5.0 mL of *Color reference stock solution* and 95.0 mL of 10 mg/mL hydrochloric acid.
Sample solution: Dissolve 5.0 g (with heating) in carbon dioxide-free water and, after cooling, dilute to 100 mL.
Analysis: Using colorless, transparent, neutral glass test tubes with a flat base and an internal diameter of 15–25 mm, compare the *Sample solution* to the *Opalescence reference solution* by examining a 40-mm depth of solution of each in diffused daylight 5 min after preparation of the *Opalescence reference solution*. View the tubes vertically and against a black background. Next, compare the *Sample solution* to the *Color reference solution* using test tubes as described above and examining a 40-mm depth of each solution vertically against a white background.
Acceptance criteria: The *Sample solution* is not more opalescent than the *Opalescence reference solution* and not more intensely colored than the *Color reference solution*. When compared directly against a white background, the sample material, prior to dilution in water, should be white.
- **Loss on Drying**, Appendix IIC: 120° for 24 h
  Sample: 2 g
  Acceptance criteria
    Anhydrous: NMT 1.0%
    Dihydrate: 14.0%–17.0%
- **pH**, *pH Determination*, Appendix IIB
  Sample solution: 50 mg/mL (Heat to dissolve, if necessary.)
  Acceptance criteria: 6.5–8.5

Magnesium Oxide

First Published: Prior to FCC 6

MgO
INS: 530
UNII: 3A3U0GI71G [magnesium oxide]
Formula wt 40.30
CAS: [1309-48-4]

DESCRIPTION
Magnesium Oxide occurs as a very bulky, white powder known as Light Magnesium Oxide or as a relatively dense, white powder known as Heavy Magnesium Oxide. Five grams of Light Magnesium Oxide occupies a volume of approximately 40 to 50 mL, while 5 g of Heavy Magnesium Oxide occupies a volume of approximately 10 to 20 mL. It is soluble in dilute acids, practically insoluble in water, and insoluble in alcohol.
Function: pH control; neutralizer; anticaking agent; free-flowing agent; firming agent
Packaging and Storage: Store in tight containers.

IDENTIFICATION
- **Magnesium**, Appendix IIIA
  Sample solution: Dissolve a sample in 2.7 N hydrochloric acid.
  Acceptance criteria: Passes tests

ASSAY
- **Procedure**
  Sample: 500 mg
  Analysis: Ignite the *Sample* to constant weight at 800° ± 25° in a tared platinum crucible, accurately weigh the residue, dissolve it in 30.0 mL of 1 N sulfuric acid, boil gently to remove any carbon dioxide, cool, and add methyl orange TS. Titrate the excess acid with 1 N sodium hydroxide. From the volume of 1 N sulfuric acid consumed deduct the volume of 1 N sulfuric acid corresponding to the content of calcium oxide in the sample taken for the assay. The difference is the volume of 1 N sulfuric acid equivalent to the MgO in the sample taken. Each mL of 1 N sulfuric acid is equivalent to 20.15 mg of MgO and to 28.04 mg of CaO.
  Acceptance criteria: NLT 96.0% and NMT 100.5% of MgO after ignition

IMPURITIES
Inorganic Impurities
- **Arsenic**, *Arsenic Limit Test*, Appendix IIIB
  Sample solution: 1 g in 10 mL of 2.7 N hydrochloric acid
  Acceptance criteria: NMT 3 mg/kg
- **Calcium Oxide**
  Sample: 400 mg
  Analysis: Dissolve the *Sample* in 3 mL of sulfuric acid and 22 mL of water. Add 50 mL of alcohol, and allow the mixture to stand overnight. If crystals of magnesium sulfate separate, warm the mixture to about 50° to dissolve them. Filter through a suitable tared porous-bottom porcelain crucible, previously washed with 2 N sulfuric acid, water, and alcohol. Wash the crystals on the porous disk several times with a 2:1 (v/v) mixture of alcohol:2 N sulfuric acid. Ignite the crucible and contents at 450° ± 25° to constant weight. [Note—Avoid exposing the crucible to sudden temperature changes.] The weight of the calcium sulfate thus obtained, multiplied by 0.4119, gives the equivalent of calcium oxide in the sample taken for the test.
  Acceptance criteria: NMT 1.5%
- **Lead**, *Lead Limit Test*, Appendix IIIB
  Sample solution: 1 g in 20 mL of 2.7 N hydrochloric acid
  Control: 4 µg Pb (4 mL of *Dilute Standard Lead Solution*)
  Acceptance criteria: NMT 4 mg/kg

SPECIFIC TESTS
- **Acid-Insoluble Substances**
  Sample: 2.0 g
  Analysis: Mix the *Sample* in 75 mL of water and, while agitating, add hydrochloric acid in small portions until no more of the sample dissolves. Boil for 5 min. If an insoluble residue remains, filter it through a suitable tared porous bottom porcelain crucible, wash well with

water until the last washing is free from chloride, ignite at 800° ± 25° for 45 min, cool, and weigh. [NOTE— Avoid exposing the crucible to sudden temperature changes.]
Acceptance criteria: NMT 0.1%
- **ALKALIES (FREE) AND SOLUBLE SALTS**
Sample: 2 g
Analysis: Boil the Sample with 100 mL of water for 5 min in a covered beaker, then filter while hot. Add methyl red TS and titrate 50 mL of the cooled filtrate with 0.1 N sulfuric acid. NMT 2 mL of the acid is consumed. Evaporate 25 mL of the filtrate to dryness, and dry at 105° for 1 h.
Acceptance criteria: NMT 10 mg of residue remains
- **LOSS ON IGNITION**
Sample: 500 mg
Analysis: Transfer the Sample to a tared, covered, platinum crucible, and ignite at 800° ± 25° for 15 min. Cool and weigh.
Acceptance criteria: NMT 10.0%

OTHER REQUIREMENTS
- **LABELING:** Indicate whether it is Light Magnesium Oxide or Heavy Magnesium Oxide.

Magnesium Phosphate, Dibasic, Mixed Hydrates

First Published: Prior to FCC 6

$MgHPO_4 \cdot xH_2O$

DESCRIPTION
Magnesium Phosphate, Dibasic, Mixed Hydrates occurs as a white, crystalline powder that is a partially dehydrated form of a mixture of magnesium phosphate, dibasic—in the trihydrate, dihydrate, and anhydrous forms—and of magnesium pyrophosphate. It is slightly soluble in water and insoluble in alcohol, but is soluble in dilute acids.
Function: Nutrient; leavening agent; pH control agent
Packaging and Storage: Store in well-closed containers.

IDENTIFICATION
- **A. PROCEDURE**
Sample: 200 mg
Analysis: Dissolve the Sample in 10 mL of 1.7 N nitric acid and add, dropwise, ammonium molybdate TS.
Acceptance criteria: A green-yellow precipitate of ammonium phosphomolybdate forms that is soluble in 6 N ammonium hydroxide.
- **B. MAGNESIUM,** Appendix IIIA
Sample solution: Dissolve a 100-mg sample in 0.5 mL of 1 N acetic acid and 20 mL of water. Add 1 mL of ferric chloride TS, let the solution stand for 5 min, and filter.
Acceptance criteria: Filtrate passes test.

ASSAY
- **PROCEDURE**
Sample: 500 mg of the residue obtained in the test for Loss on Ignition (below)
Analysis: Dissolve the Sample by heating in a mixture of 50 mL of water and 2 mL of hydrochloric acid. Cool, dilute to 100.0 mL with water, and mix. Transfer 50.0 mL of this solution into a 400-mL beaker, add 100 mL of water, and heat to 55° to 60°. Add 15 mL of 0.1 M disodium EDTA from a buret and, while stirring with a magnetic stirring bar, adjust with 1 N sodium hydroxide to pH 10. Add 10 mL of ammonia–ammonium chloride buffer TS, and 12 drops of eriochrome black TS. Titrate with 0.1 M disodium EDTA, determining the endpoint until the wine-red color changes to pure blue. Calculate the weight, in mg, of $Mg_2P_2O_7$ in the residue taken by the formula:

$$Result = 2 \times 11.13 \times V$$

V = volume of 0.1 M disodium EDTA required in the titration of the 50.0-mL aliquot (mL)
Acceptance criteria: NLT 96.0% $Mg_2P_2O_7$, on the ignited basis.

IMPURITIES
Inorganic Impurities
- **ARSENIC,** Arsenic Limit Test, Appendix IIIB
Sample solution: 1 g in 5 mL of 2.7 N hydrochloric acid
Acceptance criteria: NMT 3 mg/kg
- **FLUORIDE,** Fluoride Limit Test, Appendix IIIB
Analysis: Determine as directed in Method III, except in the Procedure use 10 mL of 1 N hydrochloric acid instead of 20 mL to dissolve the sample.
Alternatively, use the following procedure, based on Method I:
Sample: 5.0 g
Analysis: Prepare a 200-mL distilling flask connected with a condenser and carrying a thermometer and a dropping funnel equipped with a stopcock. Transfer the Sample into the distilling flask, dissolve the sample in 25 mL of 1:4 sulfuric acid, add six glass beads, and connect the apparatus for distillation, using a 600-mL beaker to collect the distillate. Add 40 mL of the dilute sulfuric acid to the flask through the dropping funnel, then fill the funnel with water, heat the solution to boiling, and continue heating until the temperature reaches 165°. Adjust the stopcock of the dropping funnel so that the temperature is maintained at 165° ± 5°, and continue the distillation until about 300 mL has been collected. Rinse the condenser and condenser arm with water, collecting the rinsings in the beaker. Add 1 N sodium hydroxide to the distillate to make it alkaline to litmus paper, and then add 5 mL in excess. Add 5 mL of 30% hydrogen peroxide and six glass beads to the beaker, boil until a volume of about 30 mL is reached, and cool. Transfer the condensed distillate, including the glass beads, into a 125-mL distilling flask connected with a condenser and carrying a thermometer and a capillary tube, both of which

must extend into the liquid. Add 30 mL of perchloric acid. [CAUTION—Handle perchloric acid in an appropriate fume hood.] Continue as directed under *Method I* beginning with "Connect a small dropping funnel or a steam generator to the capillary tube…"
Acceptance criteria: NMT 25 mg/kg
- **LEAD**, *Lead Limit Test, APDC Extraction Method,* Appendix IIIB
  Sample: 10 g
  Acceptance criteria: NMT 2 mg/kg

SPECIFIC TESTS
- **LOSS ON IGNITION**
  Sample: 1 g
  Analysis: Ignite the *Sample* at 800° ± 25°, preferably in a muffle furnace, to constant weight. [NOTE—Save the residue for the *Assay* (above).]
  Acceptance criteria: Between 15.0% and 28.9%

OTHER REQUIREMENTS
- **LABELING:** When used as a magnesium supplement, state the amount, in mg/g, of magnesium.

Magnesium Phosphate, Dibasic, Trihydrate

First Published: Prior to FCC 6
Last Revision: FCC 7

Dimagnesium Phosphate

MgHPO$_4$·3H$_2$O Formula wt 174.33
INS: 343(ii) CAS: [7782-75-4]
UNII: HF539G9L3Q [magnesium phosphate, dibasic trihydrate]

DESCRIPTION
Magnesium Phosphate, Dibasic, Trihydrate, occurs as a white, dibasic, crystalline powder. It contains three molecules of water of hydration. It is slightly soluble in water and insoluble in alcohol, but is soluble in dilute acids.
Function: Nutrient; leavening agent; pH control agent
Packaging and Storage: Store in well-closed containers.

IDENTIFICATION
- **A. PROCEDURE**
  Sample: 200 mg
  Analysis: Dissolve the *Sample* in 10 mL of 1.7 N nitric acid and add, dropwise, ammonium molybdate TS.
  Acceptance criteria: A green-yellow precipitate of ammonium phosphomolybdate forms that is soluble in 6 N ammonium hydroxide.
- **B. MAGNESIUM**, Appendix IIIA
  Sample solution: Dissolve a 100-mg sample in 0.5 mL of 1 N acetic acid and 20 mL of water. Add 1 mL of ferric chloride TS, let the solution stand for 5 min, and filter.
  Acceptance criteria: Filtrate passes test.

ASSAY
- **PROCEDURE**
  Sample: 500 mg of the residue obtained in the test for *Loss on Ignition*
  Analysis: Dissolve the *Sample* by heating in a mixture of 50 mL of water and 2 mL of hydrochloric acid. Cool, dilute to 100.0 mL with water, and mix. Transfer 50.0 mL of this solution into a 400-mL beaker, add 100 mL of water, and heat to 55° to 60°. Add 15 mL of 0.1 M disodium EDTA from a buret and, while stirring with a magnetic stirring bar, adjust with 1 N sodium hydroxide to pH 10. Add 10 mL of ammonia–ammonium chloride buffer TS, and 12 drops of eriochrome black TS. Titrate with 0.1 M disodium EDTA, determining the endpoint until the wine-red color changes to pure blue. Calculate the weight, in mg, of Mg$_2$P$_2$O$_7$ in the residue taken by the formula:

$$\text{Result} = 2 \times 11.13 \times V$$

V = volume (mL) of 0.1 M disodium EDTA required in the titration of the 50.0-mL aliquot
Acceptance criteria: NLT 96.0% Mg$_2$P$_2$O$_7$, on the ignited basis

IMPURITIES
Inorganic Impurities
- **ARSENIC**, *Arsenic Limit Test,* Appendix IIIB
  Sample solution: 1 g in 5 mL of 2.7 N hydrochloric acid
  Acceptance criteria: NMT 3 mg/kg
- **FLUORIDE**, *Fluoride Limit Test,* Appendix IIIB
  Analysis: Determine as directed in *Method III,* except in the *Procedure* use 10 mL of 1 N hydrochloric acid instead of 20 mL to dissolve the sample.
  Alternatively, use the following procedure, based on *Method I.*
  Sample: 5.0 g
  Analysis: Prepare a 200-mL distilling flask connected with a condenser and carrying a thermometer and a dropping funnel equipped with a stopcock. Transfer the *Sample* into the distilling flask, dissolve the sample in 25 mL of 1:4 sulfuric acid, add six glass beads, and connect the apparatus for distillation, using a 600-mL beaker to collect the distillate. Add 40 mL of the dilute sulfuric acid to the flask through the dropping funnel, then fill the funnel with water, heat the solution to boiling, and continue heating until the temperature reaches 165°. Adjust the stopcock of the dropping funnel so that the temperature is maintained at 165 ± 5°, and continue the distillation until about 300 mL has been collected. Rinse the condenser and condenser arm with water, collecting the rinsings in the beaker. Add 1 N sodium hydroxide to the distillate to make it alkaline to litmus paper, and then add 5 mL in excess. Add 5 mL of 30% hydrogen peroxide and six glass beads to the beaker, boil until a volume of about 30 mL is reached, and cool. Transfer the condensed distillate, including the glass beads, into a 125-mL distilling flask connected with a condenser and carrying

a thermometer and a capillary tube, both of which must extend into the liquid. Add 30 mL of perchloric acid. [CAUTION—Handle perchloric acid in an appropriate fume hood.] Continue as directed under *Method I* beginning with "Connect a small dropping funnel or a steam generator to the capillary tube..."
  Acceptance criteria: NMT 25 mg/kg
- **LEAD**, *Lead Limit Test, APDC Extraction Method*, Appendix IIIB
  Sample: 10 g
  Acceptance criteria: NMT 2 mg/kg

SPECIFIC TESTS
- **LOSS ON IGNITION**
  Sample: 1 g
  Analysis: Ignite the *Sample* at 800 ± 25°, preferably in a muffle furnace, to constant weight. [NOTE—Save the residue for the *Assay*.]
  Acceptance criteria: Between 29.0% and 36.5%

OTHER REQUIREMENTS
- **LABELING:** When used as a magnesium supplement, state the amount, in mg/g, of magnesium.

Magnesium Phosphate, Monobasic

First Published: Second Supplement, FCC 7

Acid Magnesium Phosphate
Magnesium Biphosphate
Magnesium Dihydrogen Phosphate
Monomagnesium Dihydrogen Phosphate
Monomagnesium Orthophosphate
Monomagnesium Phosphate

$Mg(H_2PO_4)_2 \cdot xH_2O$
Formula wt, anhydrous 218.28
Formula wt, dihydrate 254.31
Formula wt, tetrahydrate 290.34
INS: 343(i)
CAS: anhydrous [13092-66-5]
dihydrate [15609-87-7]
UNII: H3992158BT [magnesium phosphate, monobasic, dihydrate]
UNII: XG6J0SHI70 [magnesium phosphate, monobasic, tetrahydrate]

DESCRIPTION
Magnesium Phosphate, Monobasic, occurs as a white, odorless, crystalline powder. It may contain two or four molecules of water of hydration. It is produced by partially neutralizing phosphoric acid with magnesium oxide and drying the resulting material. It is slightly soluble in water.
Function: Nutrient; pH control agent
Packaging and Storage: Store in well-closed containers.

IDENTIFICATION
- **MAGNESIUM**, Appendix IIIA
  Sample solution: Dissolve a 100-mg sample in 0.5 mL of 1 N acetic acid and 20 mL of water. Add 1 mL of ferric chloride TS, let the solution stand for 5 min, and filter. Use the filtrate to carry out the *Magnesium* identification test procedure in Appendix IIIA.
  Acceptance criteria: Filtrate passes tests
- **PHOSPHATE**, Appendix IIIA
  Sample: 200 mg
  Analysis: Dissolve the *Sample* in 10 mL of 1.7 N nitric acid and add, dropwise, ammonium molybdate TS.
  Acceptance criteria: A green-yellow precipitate of ammonium phosphomolybdate forms that is soluble in 6 N ammonium hydroxide.

ASSAY
- **PROCEDURE**
  Sample: 200 mg of the residue obtained from the *Loss on Ignition* test
  Analysis: Transfer the *Sample* into a 250-mL beaker, dissolve in 2 mL of hydrochloric acid (16%), and add 100 mL of water. Heat the solution to 50° to 60° and add 10 mL of 0.1 M disodium EDTA from a buret. Add a magnetic stirring bar and, while stirring, adjust with 1 N sodium hydroxide to a pH of 10. Add 10 mL of ammonia–ammonium chloride buffer TS, 12 drops of eriochrome black TS, and continue the titration with 0.1 M disodium EDTA until the red color changes to green. [NOTE—The solution must be clear when the endpoint is reached.] Each mL of 0.1 M disodium EDTA consumed is equivalent to 9.14 mg of $Mg_2P_2O_7$.
  Acceptance criteria: 96%–102% of $Mg_2P_2O_7$ on the ignited basis

IMPURITIES
Inorganic Impurities
- **ARSENIC**, *Arsenic Limit Test*, Appendix IIIB
  Sample solution: 1 g in 10 mL of 2.7 N hydrochloric acid
  Acceptance criteria: NMT 3 mg/kg
- **FLUORIDE**, *Fluoride Limit Test, Method III*, Appendix IIIB
  Analysis: Determine as directed, except in the *Procedure* use 10 mL of 1 N hydrochloric acid instead of 20 mL to dissolve the sample.
  Acceptance criteria: NMT 25 mg/kg
- **LEAD**, *Lead Limit Test, APDC Extraction Method*, Appendix IIIB
  Acceptance criteria: NMT 4 mg/kg

SPECIFIC TESTS
- **LOSS ON DRYING**, Appendix IIC: 105° for 4 h
  Acceptance criteria
    Anhydrous: NMT 1.5%
- **LOSS ON IGNITION**
  Sample: 2 g
  Analysis: Ignite the *Sample* in a platinum, quartz, or porcelain dish at about 800° for 30 min, preferably in a muffle furnace. [NOTE—Save the residue for the *Assay*.]
  Acceptance criteria
    Anhydrous: NMT 18.5%
    Dihydrate: NMT 33%
    Tetrahydrate: NMT 43%

Magnesium Phosphate, Tribasic

First Published: Prior to FCC 6
Last Revision: Second Supplement, FCC 6

Trimagnesium Phosphate

$Mg_3(PO_4)_2 \cdot xH_2O$ Formula wt, anhydrous 262.86
INS: 343(iii)   CAS: [7757-87-1]
UNII: XMK14ETW2D [magnesium phosphate anhydrous]

DESCRIPTION
Magnesium Phosphate, Tribasic, occurs as a white, crystalline powder. It may contain four, five, or eight molecules of water of hydration. It is readily soluble in dilute mineral acids, but is almost insoluble in water.
Function: Nutrient
Packaging and Storage: Store in well-closed containers.

IDENTIFICATION
- **A. Procedure**
  Sample: 200 mg
  Analysis: Dissolve the *Sample* in 10 mL of 1.7 N nitric acid and add, dropwise, ammonium molybdate TS.
  Acceptance criteria: A green-yellow precipitate of ammonium phosphomolybdate forms that is soluble in 6 N ammonium hydroxide.
- **B. Magnesium,** Appendix IIIA
  Sample solution: Dissolve 100 mg sample in 0.7 mL of 1 N acetic acid and 20 mL of water. Add 1 mL of ferric chloride TS, let the solution stand for 5 min, and filter.
  Acceptance criteria: Filtrate passes test.

ASSAY
- **Procedure**
  Sample: 1.2 g, previously heated at 425° to constant weight and cooled
  Analysis: Transfer the *Sample* into a glass funnel positioned in the neck of a 200-mL flat-bottom boiling flask. Wash down the flask with a small amount of water and exactly 4 mL of concentrated hydrochloric acid. With the funnel still in place, pour 100 mL of water into the flask and place the flask. Remove the funnel and place the flask on a hotplate. Bring the solution to a boil, and while gently and frequently swirling the flask, let the solution boil for 5 min. [**Caution**—Use proper precautions when handling concentrated acids. When the flask is not swirled sufficiently, the solution may erupt unexpectedly from the neck of the flask. Wear protective clothing and goggles to avoid possible serious injury. Use flask tongs to hold the neck of the flask while swirling the contents.] Immediately after the boiling time has elapsed, carefully cool the flask in an ice bath to room temperature. Transfer the solution into a 200-mL volumetric flask, dilute to volume with water, mix, and pipet a 50-mL portion of the resulting solution into a 250-mL beaker. Add 50 mL of water, insert a 1-in stirring bar, and place the flask on a hotplate equipped with temperature and stirring controls. Insert pH and temperature probes, and heat with stirring until the temperature reaches 50°. Add 25.0 mL of 0.1 M disodium ethylenediaminetetraacetate (EDTA) solution from a buret. Adjust the pH to 10.0 using 1 N sodium hydroxide TS. Add 10 mL of ammonia–ammonium chloride buffer TS and 12 drops of eriochrome black TS. Adjust the heat to maintain the temperature at 55° to 60°. Continue the titration with disodium EDTA, to a blue to blue-green endpoint. Each mL of 0.1 M disodium EDTA consumed by the aliquot taken is equivalent to 8.76 mg of $Mg_3(PO_4)_2$.
  Acceptance criteria: NLT 98.0% and NMT 101.5% of $Mg_3(PO_4)_2$, on the ignited basis

IMPURITIES
Inorganic Impurities
- **Arsenic,** *Arsenic Limit Test,* Appendix IIIB
  Sample solution: 1 g in 10 mL of 2.7 N hydrochloric acid
  Acceptance criteria: NMT 3 mg/kg
- **Fluoride,** *Fluoride Limit Test, Method III,* Appendix IIIB
  Analysis: Determine as directed in *Method III*, except in the *Procedure* use 10 mL of 1 N hydrochloric acid instead of 20 mL to dissolve the sample.
  Acceptance criteria: NMT 25 mg/kg
- **Lead,** *Lead Limit Test, APDC Extraction Method,* Appendix IIIB
  Acceptance criteria: NMT 2 mg/kg

SPECIFIC TESTS
- **Loss on Heating**
  Sample: 2 g
  Analysis: Heat the *Sample* at 425° to constant weight.
  Acceptance criteria
    Tetrahydrate: Between 15.0% and 23.0%
    Pentahydrate: Between 20.0% and 27.0%
    Octahydrate: Between 30.0% and 37.0%

Magnesium Silicate

First Published: Prior to FCC 6

Synthetic Magnesium Silicate
INS: 553(i)   CAS: [1343-88-0]
UNII: 9B9691B2N9 [magnesium silicate]

DESCRIPTION
Magnesium Silicate occurs as a very fine, white powder free from grittiness. It is a synthetic, usually amorphous form of magnesium silicate in which the molar ratio of magnesium oxide (MgO) to silicon dioxide (SiO_2) is approximately 2:5. It is insoluble in water and in alcohol, but is readily decomposed by mineral acids. The pH of a 1:10 slurry is between 7.0 and 10.8.
Function: Anticaking agent; filter aid
Packaging and Storage: Store in well-closed containers.

IDENTIFICATION
- **A. Magnesium,** Appendix IIIA
  Sample solution: Mix 500 mg of sample with 10 mL of 2.7 N hydrochloric acid, filter, and neutralize the filtrate to litmus paper with 6 N ammonium hydroxide.

Acceptance criteria: The neutralized filtrate from the *Sample solution* passes the test.
- **B. Procedure**
  Analysis: Prepare a bead by fusing a few crystals of sodium ammonium phosphate on a platinum loop in the flame of a Bunsen burner. Place the hot, transparent bead in contact with a sample, and again fuse.
  Acceptance criteria: Silica floats about in the bead, producing, upon cooling, an opaque bead with a weblike structure.

ASSAY
- **Magnesium Oxide**
  Sample: 1.5 g
  Analysis: Transfer the *Sample* into a 250-mL conical flask. Add 50.0 mL of 1 N sulfuric acid, and digest on a steam bath for 1 h. Cool to room temperature and add methyl orange TS. Titrate the excess acid with 1 N sodium hydroxide. Each mL of 1 N sulfuric acid is equivalent to 20.15 mg of MgO.
  Acceptance criteria: NLT 15.0% MgO, calculated on the ignited basis
- **Silicon Dioxide**
  Sample: 700 mg
  Analysis: Transfer the *Sample* into a 150-mL beaker. Add 20 mL of 1 N sulfuric acid and heat on a steam bath for 1 h and 30 min. Decant the supernatant liquid through an ashless filter paper and wash the residue, by decantation, three times with hot water. Add 25 mL of water to the residue and digest on a steam bath for 15 min. Finally, transfer the residue to the filter paper, and wash thoroughly with hot water. Transfer the filter paper and its contents to a platinum crucible. Heat to dryness, incinerate, then ignite strongly for 30 min, cool, and weigh. Moisten the residue with water, and add 6 mL of hydrofluoric acid and 3 drops of sulfuric acid. Evaporate to dryness, ignite for 5 min, cool, and weigh. The loss in weight represents the weight of SiO_2.
  Acceptance criteria: NLT 67.0% SiO_2, calculated on the ignited basis

IMPURITIES
Inorganic Impurities
- **Fluoride**
  0.2 N EDTA/0.2 N TRIS solution: Transfer 18.6 g of disodium ethylenediaminetetraacetate (EDTA) and 6.05 g of tris (hydroxymethyl) aminomethane (TRIS), into a single 250-mL beaker. Add 200 mL of hot, deionized water, and stir until dissolved. Adjust the pH to 7.5 to 7.6 by adding 5 N sodium hydroxide. Cool the solution, and adjust the pH to 8.0 with 5 N sodium hydroxide. Transfer the solution into a 250-mL volumetric flask and dilute to volume with deionized water. Mix well and store in a plastic container.
  Standard stock solution: Dissolve 2.210 g of sodium fluoride in 50 mL of deionized water. Transfer the solution into a 1-L volumetric flask and dilute to volume. To further dilute, pipet 10 mL of this solution into a 100-mL volumetric flask and dilute to volume. The resulting solution is 100 mg/kg fluoride. [Note—Store this solution and all fluoride solutions in plastic containers.]
  [Note—The *Standard solutions* and *Sample preparation* (below) must be prepared on the day of use, and not in advance.]
  Standard solutions: Pipet 10 mL and 1 mL of *Standard stock solution* into separate 100-mL volumetric flasks and dilute each to volume with deionized water. The resulting *Standard solutions* are 10 and 1 mg/kg fluoride respectively.
  Sample preparation: Transfer 5 g of sample into a 150-mL Teflon beaker. Add 40 mL of deionized water and 20 mL of 1 N hydrochloric acid. Heat to near boiling for 1 min while stirring continuously. Cool in an ice bath, transfer into a 100-mL volumetric flask, and dilute to volume with deionized water. The sample does not dissolve completely.
  Calibration curve: Pipet 20 mL of the two *Standard solutions* into separate 100-mL plastic beakers. Add 10 mL of *0.2 N EDTA/0.2 N TRIS solution* to each beaker. Measure the potential, in mV, of each solution with a suitable fluoride-selective, ion-indicating electrode and a calomel reference electrode connected to a pH meter capable of measuring potentials with a reproducibility of ±0.2 mV (Orion model 96-09 combination fluoride electrode, or equivalent). Generate a standard curve by plotting the logarithms of the fluoride ion concentrations, in mg/kg, of the *Standard solutions* versus the potential, in mV, or calibrate an Orion Expandable Ion Analyzer EA-940 (or an equivalent instrument) for a direct concentration reading.
  Analysis: Pipet a 20-mL aliquot of *Sample preparation* into a 100-mL plastic beaker, add 10 mL of *0.2 N EDTA/0.2 N TRIS solution*, and measure the solution potential as described for the *Calibration curve* (above). From the measured potential of the *Sample preparation*, calculate the concentration, in mg/kg, of fluoride ion using the *Calibration curve*.
  Acceptance criteria: NMT 10 mg/kg
- **Lead,** *Lead Limit Test,* Appendix IIIB
  Sample solution: Transfer 10.0 g of sample into a 250-mL flask, and add 50 mL of 0.5 N hydrochloric acid. Attach a reflux condenser to the flask, heat on a steam bath for 30 min, cool, and let the undissolved material settle. Decant the supernatant liquid through Whatman No. 3, or equivalent, filter paper, into a 100-mL volumetric flask, retaining as much as possible of the insoluble material in the original flask. Wash the slurry and flask with three 10-mL portions of hot water, decanting each washing through the filter into the volumetric flask. Finally, wash the filter paper with 15 mL of hot water, cool the filtrate to room temperature, dilute to volume with water, and mix. Proceed with the test using 10 mL of this *Sample solution*.
  Control: 5 µg Pb (5 mL of *Diluted Standard Lead Solution*)
  Acceptance criteria: NMT 5 mg/kg

SPECIFIC TESTS

- **FREE ALKALI (AS NaOH)**
  Analysis: To 20 mL of *Sample solution* filtrate prepared for the test for *Soluble salts* (below) (representing 1 g of magnesium silicate), add 2 drops of phenolphthalein TS.
  Acceptance criteria: If a pink color develops, NMT 2.5 mL of 0.1 N hydrochloric acid is required to discharge it. (NMT 1%)

- **LOSS ON DRYING,** Appendix IIC: 105° for 2 h
  [NOTE—Retain the sample for determination of *Loss on Ignition*.]
  Acceptance criteria: NMT the percentage stated or within the range claimed by the vendor

- **LOSS ON IGNITION**
  Sample: Sample retained from the test for *Loss on Drying*.
  Analysis: Ignite the *Sample* at 900° to 1000° for 20 min and calculate the percent weight loss.
  Acceptance criteria: NMT the percentage stated or within the range claimed by the vendor

- **SOLUBLE SALTS**
  Sample solution: Boil 10 g of sample with 150 mL of water for 15 min. Cool to room temperature, and add water to restore the original volume. Allow the mixture to stand for 15 min, and filter until clear. Reserve 20 mL of the filtrate for the test for *Free Alkali* (above).
  Analysis: Add 25 mL of water to 75 mL of the *Sample solution* filtrate. Evaporate 50 mL of this solution, representing 2.5 g of magnesium silicate, in a tared platinum dish on a steam bath to dryness, and ignite gently to constant weight.
  Acceptance criteria: The weight of the residue does not exceed 75 mg. (NMT 3.0%)

- **SOLIDIFICATION POINT,** Appendix IIB
  Sample preparation: Mix 25 g of sample with 200 mL of hot water, then add 60 mL of 2 N sulfuric acid and, while stirring frequently, heat the mixture until the fatty acids separate cleanly as a transparent layer. Wash the fatty acids with boiling water until they are free from sulfate, collect them in a small beaker, and warm them on a steam bath until the water has separated and the fatty acids are clear. Allow the acids to cool, pour off the water layer, then melt the acids, filter into a dry beaker, and dry at 105° for 20 min.
  Acceptance criteria: The solidification point of the fatty acids so obtained is not below 54°.

ASSAY

- **PROCEDURE**
  Sample: 1 g
  Analysis: Boil the *Sample* with 50 mL of 0.1 N hydrochloric acid for about 30 min, or until the separated fatty acid layer is clear, adding water if necessary to maintain the original volume. Cool, filter, and wash the filter and the container thoroughly with water until the last washing is not acid to litmus. Neutralize the filtrate to litmus with 1 N sodium hydroxide. While stirring, preferably with a magnetic stirrer, add about 30 mL of 0.05 M disodium EDTA from a 50-mL buret, then add 5 mL of ammonia–ammonium chloride buffer TS and 0.15 mL of eriochrome black TS. Continue the titration with 0.05 M disodium EDTA, to a blue endpoint. Each mL of 0.05 M disodium EDTA is equivalent to 2.015 mg of MgO.
  Acceptance criteria: NLT 6.8% and NMT 8.3% of MgO

IMPURITIES

Inorganic Impurities

- **LEAD,** *Lead Limit Test*, Appendix IIIB
  Sample solution: Ignite, in a muffle furnace at 475° to 500° for 15 to 20 min, 500 mg of sample contained in a silica crucible. Cool, add 3 drops of nitric acid, evaporate over a low flame to dryness, and re-ignite at 475° to 500° for 30 min. Dissolve the residue in 1 mL of a mixture of 1:1 (v/v) nitric acid:water, and wash into a separatory funnel with several successive portions of water.
  Control: Add 0.25 mL of the *Standard Lead Solution* containing 10 μg/mL of lead (Pb) ion, 4 mL of *Ammonia–Cyanide Solution*, and 2 drops of *Hydroxylamine Hydrochloride Solution* to 20 mL of 1:100 nitric acid, and shake for 30 s with 10 mL of *Standard Dithizone Solution*. Filter through an acid-washed filter paper into a Nessler tube.
  Analysis: Add 3 mL of *Ammonium Citrate Solution* and 0.5 mL of *Hydroxylamine Hydrochloride Solution* to the *Sample solution*, and make the combined solutions alkaline to phenol red TS with ammonium hydroxide. Add 10 mL of *Potassium Cyanide Solution*. Immediately extract the solution with successive 5-mL portions of *Dithizone Extraction Solution*, draining off each extract into another separatory funnel, until the last portion of *Dithizone Extraction Solution* retains its green color. Shake the combined extracts for 30 s with 20 mL of 1:100 nitric acid, and discard the chloroform layer. Add

Magnesium Stearate

First Published: Prior to FCC 6

CAS: [557-04-0]
UNII: 70097M6I30 [magnesium stearate]

DESCRIPTION

Magnesium Stearate occurs as a fine, white, bulky powder that is unctuous and free from grittiness. It is a compound of magnesium with a mixture of solid organic acids obtained from edible sources and consists chiefly of variable proportions of Magnesium Stearate and magnesium palmitate. It is insoluble in water, in alcohol, and in ether.
Function: Anticaking agent; binder; emulsifier
Packaging and Storage: Store in well-closed containers.

IDENTIFICATION

- **MAGNESIUM,** Appendix IIIA
  Sample preparation: Heat 1 g of sample with a mixture of 25 mL of water and 5 mL of hydrochloric acid. Liberated fatty acids float as an oily layer on the surface of the liquid.
  Acceptance criteria: The water layer passes the tests.

exactly 4 mL of *Ammonia–Cyanide Solution* and 2 drops of *Hydroxylamine Hydrochloride Solution* to the acid solution. Add 10 mL of *Standard Dithizone Solution*, and shake the mixture for 30 s. Filter the chloroform layer through an acid-washed filter paper into a Nessler tube, and compare the color with that of the *Control*.
Acceptance criteria: The color of the *Sample solution* does not exceed that in the *Control* (NMT 5 mg/kg).

SPECIFIC TESTS
- **Loss on Drying,** Appendix IIC: 105° to constant weight, weighing at 2-h increments
  Acceptance criteria: NMT 4.0%

Magnesium Sulfate

First Published: Prior to FCC 6

Epsom Salt

$MgSO_4 \cdot xH_2O$

INS: 518

Formula wt, monohydrate 138.38
Formula wt, heptahydrate 246.47
CAS: monohydrate [14168-73-1]
heptahydrate [10034-99-8]
dried [15244-36-7]

UNII: E2L2TK027P [magnesium sulfate monohydrate]
UNII: SK47B8698T [magnesium sulfate heptahydrate]

DESCRIPTION
Magnesium Sulfate occurs as a colorless crystal or a granular crystalline powder. It is produced with one or seven molecules of water of hydration or in a dried form containing the equivalent of about 2.3 waters of hydration. It is readily soluble in water, slowly soluble in glycerin, and sparingly soluble in alcohol.
Function: Nutrient
Packaging and Storage: Store in well-closed containers.

IDENTIFICATION
- **Magnesium,** Appendix IIIA
  Sample solution: 50 mg/mL
  Acceptance criteria: Passes tests
- **Sulfate,** Appendix IIIA
  Sample solution: 50 mg/mL
  Acceptance criteria: Passes tests

ASSAY
- **Procedure**
  Sample: 500 mg of the residue obtained in the test for *Loss on Ignition*
  Analysis: Dissolve the *Sample* in a 1:50 mixture of hydrochloric acid:water, dilute with water to 100.0 mL, and mix. Transfer 50.0 mL of this solution into a 250-mL Erlenmeyer flask. Add 10 mL of ammonia–ammonium chloride buffer TS and 12 drops of eriochrome black TS. Titrate with 0.1 M disodium EDTA, until the wine red color changes to pure blue. Each mL of 0.1 M disodium EDTA is equivalent to 12.04 mg of $MgSO_4$.
  Acceptance criteria: NLT 99.5% $MgSO_4$, on the ignited basis

IMPURITIES
Inorganic Impurities
- **Lead,** *Lead Limit Test, APDC Extraction Method,* Appendix IIIB
  Acceptance criteria: NMT 4 mg/kg
- **Selenium,** *Selenium Limit Test, Method II,* Appendix IIIB
  Sample: 200 mg
  Acceptance criteria: NMT 0.003%

SPECIFIC TESTS
- **Loss on Ignition**
  Sample: 1 g
  Analysis: Transfer the *Sample* to a crucible, heat at 105° for 2 h, then ignite in a muffle furnace at 450° ± 25°, to constant weight.
  [NOTE—Reserve the residue after ignition for use in the *Assay* (above).]
  Acceptance criteria
  Monohydrate: Between 13.0% and 16.0%
  Heptahydrate: Between 40.0% and 52.0%
  Dried: Between 22.0% and 28.0%

OTHER REQUIREMENTS
- **Labeling:** Indicate whether it is the monohydrate, the heptahydrate, or the dried form.

Malic Acid

First Published: Prior to FCC 6

DL-Malic Acid
Hydroxysuccinic Acid
2-Hydroxybutanedioic Acid

$C_4H_6O_5$
INS: 296
UNII: 817L1N4CKP [malic acid]

Formula wt 134.09
CAS: [617-48-1]

DESCRIPTION
Malic Acid occurs as a white or nearly white, crystalline powder or granules having a strongly acid taste. One g dissolves in 0.8 mL of water and in 1.4 mL of alcohol. Its solutions are optically inactive. It melts at about 130°.
Function: Acidifier; flavoring agent
Packaging and Storage: Store in well-closed containers.

IDENTIFICATION
- **Infrared Absorption,** *Spectrophotometric Identification Tests,* Appendix IIIC
  Reference standard: USP Malic Acid RS
  Sample and Standard preparation: K
  Acceptance criteria: The spectrum of the sample exhibits maxima at the same wavelengths as those in the spectrum of the *Reference standard*.

ASSAY
- **PROCEDURE**
  Sample: 2 g
  Analysis: Dissolve the *Sample* in 40 mL of recently boiled and cooled water. Titrate with 1 N sodium hydroxide, using phenolphthalein TS as the indicator, to the first appearance of a faint pink color that persists for at least 30 s. Each mL of 1 N sodium hydroxide is equivalent to 67.04 mg of $C_4H_6O_5$.
  Acceptance criteria: NLT 99.0% and NMT 100.5% of $C_4H_6O_5$

IMPURITIES
Inorganic Impurities
- **LEAD,** *Lead Limit Test, Flame Atomic Absorption Spectrophotometric Method,* Appendix IIIB
  Sample: 5 g
  Acceptance criteria: NMT 2 mg/kg

Organic Impurities
- **FUMARIC AND MALEIC ACIDS**
  [NOTE—For all reference standards, do not dry before use and keep the containers tightly closed and protected from light. Determine the water content of the USP Fumaric Acid RS titrimetrically before use and make the necessary correction in preparing the *Standard solution*.]
  Mobile phase: 0.01 N sulfuric acid, filtered and degassed
  System suitability solution: 1 mg/mL of sample, 10 μg/mL of USP Fumaric Acid RS, and 4 μg/mL USP Maleic Acid RS in *Mobile phase*
  Standard solution: 5 μg/mL of USP Fumaric Acid RS and 2 μg/mL of USP Maleic Acid RS in *Mobile phase*
  Sample: 100 mg
  Sample solution: Transfer the *Sample* into a 100-mL volumetric flask, dilute to volume with *Mobile phase*, and mix.
  Chromatographic system, Appendix IIA
    Mode: High-performance liquid chromatography
    Detector: UV 210 nm
    Column: 30-cm × 6.5-mm (id) column packed with a strong cation exchange resin consisting of sulfonated crosslinked styrene-divinylbenzene copolymer in the hydrogen form (Polypore H from Brownlee Laboratories, Inc., or equivalent)
    Column temperature: 37° ± 1°
    Flow rate: About 0.6 mL/min
    Injection volume: About 20 μL
  System suitability
    Sample: *System suitability solution*
    Suitability requirement 1: From the *System suitability solution*, the resolution, R, between maleic acid and sample peaks is NLT 2.5.
    Suitability requirement 2: From the *System suitability solution*, the resolution, R, between fumaric acid and sample peaks is NLT 7.0.
    Suitability requirement 3: From the *System suitability solution*, the maleic acid peak relative standard deviation for replicate injections is NMT 2.0%.
  Analysis: Separately inject the *Standard solution* and the *Sample solution* into the chromatograph, record the chromatograms, and measure the peak responses. [NOTE—The relative retention times are approximately 0.6 for maleic acid, 1.0 for malic acid, and 1.5 for fumaric acid.] Calculate the quantity, in mg, of maleic acid and fumaric acid in the portion of the *Sample* taken by the formula:

  $$\text{Result} = 100C \times (r_U/r_S)$$

  C = concentration (mg/mL) of the corresponding *Reference standard* in the *Standard solution*
  r_U = response of the corresponding peak from the chromatogram of the *Sample solution*
  r_S = response of the corresponding peak from the chromatogram of the *Standard solution*
  Acceptance criteria
    Fumaric acid: NMT 1.0%
    Maleic acid: NMT 0.05%

SPECIFIC TESTS
- **OPTICAL (SPECIFIC) ROTATION,** Appendix IIB
  Sample solution: 85 mg/mL at 25°
  Acceptance criteria: $[\alpha]_D^{25}$ between −0.10° and +0.10°
- **RESIDUE ON IGNITION (SULFATED ASH),** Appendix IIC
  Sample: 2 g
  Acceptance criteria: NMT 0.1%
- **WATER-INSOLUBLE MATTER**
  Sample: 25 g
  Analysis: Dissolve the *Sample* in 100 mL of water and filter through a tared, sintered-glass filter crucible of suitable porosity. Wash the filter with hot water, dry at 100° to constant weight, cool, and weigh.
  Acceptance criteria: NMT 0.1%

Malt Syrup
First Published: Prior to FCC 6

Malt Extract

CAS: [8002-48-0]

DESCRIPTION
Malt is the product of barley (*Hordeum vulgare* L.) (Fam. Gramineae) germinated under controlled conditions. Malt Syrup and Malt Extract are interchangeable terms for a concentrate of the water extract of germinated barley grain with or without added food-grade preservatives. Malt Syrup is usually a yellow to brown, sweet, and viscous liquid containing varying amounts of amylolytic enzymes and plant constituents.

Function: Color; enzyme; flavoring agent; humectant; nutritive sweetener; stabilizer; thickener; and texturizer
Packaging and Storage: Store in tight containers.

IDENTIFICATION
- **PROCEDURE**
  Sample solution: 1:10 aqueous solution
  Analysis: Add a few drops of *Sample solution* to 5 mL of hot alkaline cupric tartrate TS.

Acceptance criteria: A red precipitate of cuprous oxide forms.

ASSAY

- **PROCEDURE**
  Sample solution: 10 mg/mL
  Analysis: Pipet 10.0 mL each of *Fehling's Solutions A* and *B* (see *Alkaline Cupric Tartrate TS* Solutions and Indicators) into a 250-mL flask. Add 20.0 mL (choose the size of the aliquot so that the sample titration will be about half that of the blank titration) of the *Sample solution*, add water to make a total volume of 50 mL, and mix the contents of the flask by swirling gently. Add two small glass beads and close the mouth of the flask with a small funnel or glass bulb. Heat the solution, preferably on a hot plate, at such a rate that the solution is brought to boiling within 3 min, and then continue boiling for exactly 2 min (total heating time, 5 min). Cool quickly to room temperature in an ice bath or with cold running water and then rinse down the funnel or bulb and the walls of the flask with a few mL of water. Add 10 mL each of 30% potassium iodide solution and 28% sulfuric acid, and titrate rapidly with 0.1 N sodium thiosulfate until the iodine color almost disappears. Add 1 mL of starch TS and titrate dropwise with continuous agitation, until the blue color disappears. Record the volume (S), in mL, of 0.1 N sodium thiosulfate required for the *Sample solution*. Conduct two blank determinations (see *General Provisions*), substituting 20.0 mL (or the same volume as the aliquot of the *Sample solution* taken) of water for the *Sample solution*, and record the average volume (B), in mL, of 0.1 N sodium thiosulfate required for the blanks. Obtain the titer difference (T_S), expressed as mL of 0.1 N sodium thiosulfate, for the sample by the equation:

$$T_S = B - S$$

T_S = titer difference, expressed as mL of 0.1 N sodium thiosulfate, for the sample
B = average volume (mL) of 0.1 N sodium thiosulfate required for the blanks
S = volume (mL) of 0.1 N sodium thiosulfate required for the *Sample solution*

By reference to the following table, determine the weight, in mg, of reducing sugars (as maltose) equivalent to the volume T_S and record the value thus obtained as W_S. Calculate the percent of total reducing sugars (as maltose) in the sample taken by the formula:

$$\text{Result} = W_S \times (1/F) \times (1/C_U) \times 100$$

W_S = weight of reducing sugars (as maltose) calculated above (mg)
F = volume of the *Sample solution* used as the aliquot in the *Assay* (20.0 mL unless otherwise adjusted)
C_U = concentration of sample in the *Sample solution* (mg/mL)

Acceptance criteria: NLT 40.0% and NMT 65.0% of reducing sugars content, expressed as maltose.

Conversion of Titer Differences to Reducing Sugars Content											
Titer Diff. (mL)	0.0	0.1	0.2	0.3	0.4	0.5	0.6	0.7	0.8	0.9
	Reducing Sugars Content (as mg of Maltose)										
5.0	27.0	27.6	28.1	28.7	29.2	29.8	30.3	30.9	31.4	32.0
6.0	32.5	33.1	33.6	34.2	34.7	35.3	35.8	36.3	36.9	37.5
7.0	38.0	38.6	39.1	39.7	40.2	40.8	41.3	41.9	42.4	43.0
8.0	43.5	44.1	44.6	45.2	45.7	46.3	46.8	47.4	47.9	48.5
9.0	49.0	49.6	50.2	50.8	51.4	52.0	52.6	53.2	53.8	54.4
10.0	55.0	55.6	56.1	56.7	57.2	57.8	58.3	58.9	59.4	60.0
11.0	60.5	61.1	61.6	62.2	62.7	63.3	63.8	64.4	64.9	65.5
12.0	66.0	66.6	67.2	67.8	68.4	69.0	69.6	70.2	70.8	71.4
13.0	72.0	72.6	73.2	73.8	74.4	75.0	75.6	76.2	76.8	77.4
14.0	78.0	78.6	79.1	79.7	80.2	80.8	81.3	81.9	82.4	83.0
15.0	83.5	84.1	84.6	85.2	85.7	86.3	86.8	87.4	87.9	88.5
16.0	89.0	89.6	90.2	90.8	91.4	92.0	92.6	93.2	93.8	94.4
17.0	95.0	95.6	96.2	96.8	97.4	98.0	98.6	99.2	99.8	100.4
18.0	101.0	101.6	102.2	102.8	103.4	104.0	104.6	105.2	105.8	106.4
19.0	107.0	107.6	108.1	108.7	109.2	109.8	110.3	110.9	111.4	112.0
20.0	112.5	113.1	113.7	114.3	114.9	115.5	116.1	116.7	117.3	117.9

IMPURITIES
Inorganic Impurities
- **LEAD,** *Lead Limit Test, Atomic Absorption Spectrophotometric Graphite Furnace Method, Method I,* Appendix IIIB
  Acceptance criteria: NMT 0.5 mg/kg

Organic Impurities
- **N-NITROSODIMETHYLAMINE** (Based on AOAC method 982.12)

  [CAUTION—*N*-Nitrosamines are potent carcinogens. Take adequate precaution to avoid exposure. Carry out all steps in a well-ventilated fume hood, and wear protective gloves while handling nitrosamine standards. Because these compounds are highly photolabile, carry out all procedures under subdued light. Do not pipet solutions by mouth, and do not use the same pipet for other reagents. Destroy all nitrosamine solutions by boiling with hydrochloric acid, potassium iodide, and sulfamic acid before disposal.]

  [NOTE—Thoroughly clean all glassware before use. After normal cleaning and washing, wash with chromic acid. If contamination still exists, rinse all glassware with dichloromethane before use. Let the charred residue in the distillation flask soak with diluted alkali, and then wash in a normal manner.]

  Distillation apparatus: Set up the apparatus using a 1000-mL distillation flask, a heating mantle, an adapter, and a 200-mm Graham condenser (Kontes, or equivalent) so that the connecting adapter slopes downward toward the vertical Graham condenser. Loosely wrap glass wool around the distillation flask and connecting adapter. Set up a 100-mL graduate under the condenser to collect the distillate. The temperature of the cooling water for the condenser should be ≤20°. Assemble a 250-mL Kuderna-Danish evaporative concentrator that has a 24/40 column connection and a 19/22 lower joint (Kontes, or equivalent) with a 4-mL Kuderna-Danish concentrator tube (Kontes, or equivalent) that has a 19/22 joint and 0.1-mL subdivisions from 0 to 2.0 mL at the bottom.

  NDMA standard stock solution: 1 mg/mL of *N*-nitrosodimethylamine (NDMA) (Sigma or equivalent) in dichloromethane

  NDMA standard solutions: 500, 200, 100, 40, 20, 10, and 5 ng/mL of *N*-nitrosodimethylamine in dichloromethane: from *NDMA standard stock solution*. [NOTE—Store these solutions at 20°, and warm to room temperature before use. After 30 days, dispose of the *NDMA standard solutions*.]

  NDPA standard solution: 250 µg/mL of *N*-nitrosodi-*N*-propylamine (NDPA) in anhydrous ethanol

  Sample solution: Transfer 50 g of sample into a 1000-mL distillation flask, and add 1.0 mL of 10% sulfamic acid, 1.0 mL of *NDPA standard solution*, 1.0 mL of 1 N hydrochloric acid, and 15 mL of water. Mix the contents by gently swirling, and let the flask stand in the dark for 10 min. Add 10.0 mL of 3 N potassium hydroxide and two small boiling chips, mix, and connect the flask to the distillation apparatus.

  During the initial 10 min of distillation, adjust the heating mantle so the mixture boils smoothly without too much frothing or bumping. Watch constantly for excessive foaming, and if necessary, turn off the heat for 1 to 2 min. After 10 min, increase the temperature, and continue distillation (watch for foaming) until approximately 55 mL of distillate is collected in a graduated cylinder. Do not boil the distilling flask to complete dryness; this may give erroneous results. Total distillation time should be ≤1 h. If any portion of the sample foams over during distillation, discontinue the distillation, and start over with a fresh sample.

  Add 2.0 mL of 10 N potassium hydroxide to the distillate and transfer the mixture into a 250-mL separatory funnel. Use the same graduated cylinder for all subsequent measuring of dichloromethane. Rinse the condenser with 50 mL of dichloromethane, and collect the rinsing directly into the separatory funnel containing the distillate and potassium hydroxide. Extract the distillate with dichloromethane by shaking the funnel vigorously for 2 min. Drain off the lower dichloromethane layer into a second separatory funnel. Extract the aqueous layer with two additional 50-mL portions of dichloromethane and combine all dichloromethane extracts in the second separatory funnel. Discard the aqueous layer.

  Place 40 g of anhydrous sodium sulfate into a coarse, sintered-glass Büchner funnel, wash with about 20 mL of dichloromethane, and discard the washing. Dry the combined dichloromethane extract by passing it through the sodium sulfate bed in the Büchner funnel and collect the extract directly in the Kuderna-Danish evaporative concentrator. Wash the sodium sulfate bed with an additional 20 mL of dichloromethane and collect the washing in the Kuderna-Danish evaporative concentrator.

  Add a 1- to 2-mm boiling chip to the contents of the Kuderna-Danish evaporative concentrator, attach a three-section Snyder column with three chambers and a 24/40 joint (Kontes or equivalent), and concentrate the extract by heating the flask in a 50° to 60° water bath. Initially maintain the outside water level close to the level of dichloromethane inside the flask, and continue heating until the amount of concentrated extract is about 4 mL (about 40 min). (If excessive boiling occurs during concentration, control it either by raising the flask slightly out of the water bath or by decreasing the bath temperature.) Finally, raise the flask above the water and let condensed dichloromethane in the Snyder column drain into the flask. Add about 1 mL of dichloromethane to the top of the Snyder column and let it drain into the flask. Disconnect the concentrator tube from the flask.

  Add another boiling chip to the contents and attach a micro-Snyder column with three chambers and a 19/22 joint (Kontes or equivalent) to the concentrator tube. Concentrate the extract to about 0.8 mL by heating the concentrator tube in a 50° to 60° water bath. Lift out or immerse the tube in water to control the boiling rate, but do not lift the tube completely out of the water bath because this will stop the action of the boiling chip. Avoid overheating and excessive accumulation of dichloromethane in the column chambers. Stop concentration when the dichloromethane level reaches 0.8 mL; do not concentrate to less than 0.8 mL. Carry out this final concentrating step slowly, taking at least 30 min. Raise the tube, and with the bottom still touching the water, let the liquid drain, and note the volume to see if it is around 0.8 mL. If it is greater than 0.8 mL, continue the concentration as above. Finally, rinse the micro-Snyder column with a few drops of dichloromethane, let the rinsing drain to the tube, disconnect the column, and dilute the extract to 1.0 or 1.1 mL, but not greater than 1.1 mL. (Do not use a nitrogen stream for concentrating the extract at any stage.) Stopper the tube, mix in a vortex mixer, and store at 4° in the dark until analysis. The resulting extract is the *Sample solution*.

To ensure the absence of contamination, carry the reagent blank taken through all of the steps mentioned above, except use 50 mL of 4% alcohol in water instead of 50 g of sample.

Chromatographic system, Appendix IIA
   Mode: Gas chromatography
   Detector: Thermal energy analyzer (Thermo Electron Corporation, or equivalent)
   Column: 1.8-m × 3mm (od) stainless steel column, or equivalent, packed with 20% Carbowax 20M, or equivalent, and 2% sodium hydroxide on 80- to 100-mesh, acid-washed Chromosorb P, or equivalent.
   Column temperature: 170°
   Injection port temperature: 220°
   Carrier gas: Argon
   Flow rate: 25 to 30 mL/min
      [NOTE—Operate with a −110° to −130° slush bath. Adjust instrument parameters such as vacuum chamber pressure, oxygen flow, and calibration knob to obtain the proper sensitivity.]

Analysis: Set attenuation (usually 4) of the chromatograph's detector so that an injection of 30 pg of NDMA gives a definite peak with acceptable background. Using this attenuation, analyze 5- to 6-µL aliquots, in duplicate, of *NDMA standard solutions* of 5, 10, 20, and 40 ng/mL. (Note the volume injected.)

Next, choose a higher attenuation setting that gives an on-scale peak for 6 µL of *NDMA standard solution* at 500 ng/mL. Using this setting, analyze 6-µL aliquots, in duplicate, of *NDMA standard solutions* of 500, 200, 100, and 40 ng/mL.

Accurately measure the peak heights (±0.1 cm), and determine the average peak heights of two injections at each concentration. If the aliquots injected were not exactly 6 µL, make appropriate corrections and convert all peak heights equivalent to 5-µL injections. Draw two standard curves, one for each attenuation setting, of peak heights versus picogram injection.

As above, inject a 6-µL aliquot of *Sample solution*, in duplicate, using the lowest attenuation setting sensitive to 30 pg of NDMA. [NOTE—Let the *Sample solution* warm to room temperature and note its volume before analyzing it.] Measure and determine the average peak height. Compare the sample response with the standard curve that produces the closest peak height at the same attenuation. Choose the *NDMA standard solution* that gives the closest peak height, inject 6-µL aliquots, in duplicate, and determine the average peak height.

For a *Sample solution* giving an off-scale peak at an attenuation of 32, dilute the *Sample solution* extracts to 5.0 mL with dichloromethane contained in a volumetric flask, and reanalyze. Analyze the sample extract and corresponding standard under the same attenuation setting, and all within 60 min.

If the extract gives a negative result for NDMA, or if the peak is too small to measure, inject 10-µL aliquots, in duplicate, using a 25-µL syringe. Similarly, inject duplicate 10-µL aliquots of the 5 ng/mL *NDMA standard solution* for quantitation. To achieve a 0.1 to 1 µg/kg detection limit, analyze 10-µL aliquots of *Sample solution* under an attenuation setting that gives a detectable peak corresponding to 30 pg of NDMA. [NOTE—If using a 25-µL syringe, which usually has a thick needle, watch for septum damage, and check for leaks. Use a new septum daily.] Calculate the concentration of uncorrected NDMA in the sample, in micrograms per kilogram, using the following formula:

$$\text{Result} = (H_1 P V_2)/(H_2 G V_1)$$

H_1 = average NDMA peak height (cm) from the *Sample solution*
P = weight (pg) of NDMA producing the H_2 peak height
V_2 = final volume (mL) of the *Sample solution*
H_2 = average peak height (cm) of the corresponding *NDMA standard solution*
G = weight (g) of the sample taken for analysis
V_1 = volume (µL) of *Sample solution* injected

Correction for percent recovery of NDPA: Accurately measure the peak height of the NDPA peak on each sample chromatogram, and calculate the average peak height of two injections. Make appropriate corrections if the final volume of sample is not exactly 1.0 mL or the injection volume is not exactly 6.0 µL. Then inject, in duplicate, within 60 min, 6-µL of the *NDPA standard solution* under the same attenuation setting. Calculate the average peak height and correct the value if exactly 6.0 µL is not injected. Calculate the percent recovery of NDPA for each sample. If recovery of NDPA is less than 80%, repeat the analysis from the beginning. Finally, correct the results as follows:

Corrected NDMA (mg/kg) in the sample = (uncorrected µg/kg/% recovery of NDPA) × 0.1.

Acceptance criteria: NMT 0.005 mg/kg

SPECIFIC TESTS
- **PH,** *pH Determination,* Appendix IIB
   Sample solution: 1:10 aqueous solution
   Acceptance criteria: Between 4.5 and 5.5
- **PROTEIN,** *Nitrogen Determination,* Appendix IIIC
   Sample: 0.25 g

688 / Malt Syrup / Monographs

Analysis: Calculate the percent protein by the formula:

$$Result = 6.25 \times N$$

6.25 = nitrogen to protein conversion factor
N = percent nitrogen
Acceptance criteria: NMT 7.0%
- **SULFUR DIOXIDE,** Appendix X
  Sample: 100 g
  Acceptance criteria: NMT 10 mg/kg
- **TOTAL SOLIDS,** *Water Determination,* Appendix IIB
  Analysis: Use an accurately weighed portion of sample. Calculate the percent of total solids by the formula:

$$Result = 100[(W_U - W_W)/W_U]$$

W_U = weight (mg) of the sample taken
W_W = weight (mg) of water determined
Acceptance criteria: Between 77.0% and 83.0%.

Maltitol

First Published: Prior to FCC 6
Last Revision: First Supplement, FCC 7

D-Maltitol
Hydrogenated Maltose
α-D-Glucopyranosyl-1,4-D-glucitol

$C_{12}H_{24}O_{11}$ Formula wt 344.31
INS: 965   CAS: [585-88-6]
UNII: D65DG142WK [maltitol]

DESCRIPTION
Maltitol occurs as a white, crystalline powder containing small amounts of sorbitol and related polyhydric alcohols. It is very soluble in water and slightly soluble in ethanol.
Function: Sweetener; humectant; stabilizer
Packaging and Storage: Store in well-closed containers.

IDENTIFICATION
- **THIN-LAYER CHROMATOGRAPHY,** Appendix IIA
  Adsorbent: 0.25-mm layer of chromatographic silica gel
  Standard solution: 2.5 mg/mL of USP Maltitol RS
  Sample solution: 2.5 mg/mL, on the anhydrous basis
  Application volume: 2 μL
  Developing solvent system: *n*-propyl alcohol, ethyl acetate, and water (70:20:10)
  Spray reagent A: 2 mg/mL of sodium metaperiodate
  Spray reagent B: 20 mg/mL of 4,4′-tetramethyl-diaminodiphenylmethane in 4:1 acetone–glacial acetic acid

Analysis: Following development, spray the plate with *Spray reagent A,* air-dry for 15 min, and spray with *Spray reagent B.*
Acceptance criteria: The principal spot obtained from the *Sample solution* corresponds in R_F value and color to that obtained from the *Standard solution.*

ASSAY
- **PROCEDURE**
  Mobile phase: Degassed water
  Standard solution: 10.0 mg/mL of USP Maltitol RS
  Sample solution: Transfer 0.7 g of the sample into a 50-mL volumetric flask, dilute with water to volume, and mix.
  Chromatographic system, Appendix IIA
    Mode: High-performance liquid chromatography
    Detector: Refractive index
    Column: 9-mm × 30-cm column packed with a strong cation-exchange resin, about 9 μm in diameter, or equivalent, consisting of sulfonated cross-linked styrene–divinylbenzene copolymer in the calcium form (Aminex HPX-87c, or equivalent)
    Column temperature: 85° ± 0.5°
    Flow rate: About 0.5 mL/min
    Injection volume: About 20 μL
  System suitability
    Sample: *Standard solution*
    Suitability requirement: The relative standard deviation for replicate injections is NMT 2.0%.
  Analysis: Separately inject the *Standard solution* and the *Sample solution* into the chromatograph, record the chromatograms, and measure the responses for the major peaks. [NOTE—The elution pattern includes the higher-molecular-weight hydrogenated polysaccharides, followed by three individual peaks representing maltotriitol, maltitol, and sorbitol. The principal peak is maltitol, which elutes at about twice the retention time of the void volume, and the retention time for sorbitol is about 1.7 relative to maltitol.]
  Calculate the quantity, in mg, of maltitol in the portion of the sample taken:

$$Result = (r_U/r_S) \times C \times 50$$

r_U = peak response of maltitol obtained from the *Sample solution*
r_S = peak response of maltitol obtained from the *Standard solution*
C = concentration of maltitol in the *Standard solution* (mg/mL)
Acceptance criteria: NLT 92.0% and NMT 100.5% of maltitol as $C_{12}H_{24}O_{11}$, calculated on the dried basis

IMPURITIES
Inorganic Impurities
- **LEAD,** *Lead Limit Test, Atomic Absorption Spectrophotometric Graphite Furnace Method, Method I,* Appendix IIIB
  Acceptance criteria: NMT 1 mg/kg
- **NICKEL,** *Nickel Limit Test,* Appendix IIIB
  Sample: 20.0 g
  Acceptance criteria: NMT 1 mg/kg

SPECIFIC TESTS

- **OTHER HYDROGENATED SACCHARIDES**
  Analysis: Proceed as directed under *Assay*, but use the following calculation:
  Calculate the quantity, in mg, of maltitol and other hydrogenated saccharides in the *Sample solution*:

  $$\text{Result} = (r_U/r_S) \times C \times 50$$

  r_U = peak response of hydrogenated saccharide obtained from the *Sample solution*
  r_S = peak response of maltitol obtained from the *Standard solution*
  C = concentration of maltitol in the *Standard solution* (mg/mL)

  Add the percentages of higher-molecular-weight hydrogenated polysaccharides, maltotriitol, and sorbitol to obtain the total.
  Acceptance criteria: NMT 7.0%

- **REDUCING SUGARS (AS GLUCOSE)**
  0.05 N Iodine VS: Dilute 0.1 N iodine VS with water (1:1).
  0.05 N Sodium thiosulfate VS: Dilute 0.1 N sodium thiosulfate VS with water (1:1).
  Sample: 3.3 g
  Analysis: Dissolve the *Sample* in 3 mL of water with the aid of gentle heat. Cool, and add 20.0 mL of alkaline cupric citrate TS and a few glass beads. Heat so that boiling begins after 4 min, and maintain the boiling for 3 min. Cool rapidly, and add 40 mL of diluted acetic acid TS, 60 mL of water, and 20.0 mL of *0.05 N Iodine VS*. With continuous shaking, add 25 mL of a mixture of 6 mL of hydrochloric acid and 94 mL of water. When the precipitate has dissolved, titrate the excess iodine with *0.05 N Sodium thiosulfate VS*. Use 2 mL of starch TS, added toward the end of the titration, as an indicator.
  Acceptance criteria: NLT 12.8 mL of *0.05 N Sodium thiosulfate VS* is required. (NMT 0.3% reducing sugars, as glucose)

- **RESIDUE ON IGNITION (SULFATED ASH),** Method I (for solids), Appendix IIC
  Sample: 2 g
  Acceptance criteria: NMT 0.1%

- **LOSS ON DRYING,** Appendix IIC
  Sample: 1.5 g
  Analysis: 80° for 3 hr in a vacuum of NMT 10 mm Hg
  Acceptance criteria: NMT 1.5%

Maltitol Syrup

First Published: Prior to FCC 6
Last Revision: First Supplement, FCC 6

Hydrogenated Glucose Syrup
INS: 965

DESCRIPTION

Maltitol Syrup occurs as a clear, colorless, syrupy liquid. It is a water solution of a hydrogenated, partially hydrolyzed starch containing maltitol, sorbitol, and hydrogenated oligo- and polysaccharides. It is miscible with water and with glycerin, and slightly miscible with alcohol.
Function: Humectant; texturizing agent; stabilizer; sweetener
Packaging and Storage: Store in well-closed containers.

IDENTIFICATION

- **A. PROCEDURE**
  Sample: 18.7 mg/mL
  Analysis: Transfer 3 mL of the *Sample solution* into a 15-cm test tube, add 3 mL of a freshly prepared 1:10 catechol solution, and mix. Add 6 mL of sulfuric acid, mix again, then gently heat the tube in a flame for about 30 s.
  Acceptance criteria: A deep pink or wine red color appears.

- **B. PROCEDURE**
  Acceptance criteria: The retention time of the major peak in the chromatogram of the *Sample solution* corresponds to that in the chromatogram of the *Standard solution* as obtained from the *Assay* (below).

ASSAY

- **PROCEDURE**
  Mobile phase: Degassed water
  Standard solution: 10.0 mg/g USP Maltitol RS and 1.6 mg/g USP Sorbitol RS
  Sample solution: 20 mg/g
  Chromatographic system, Appendix IIA
    Mode: High-performance liquid chromatography
    Detector: Refractive index detector
    Column: 10-cm × 7.8-mm column containing packing L34 (Bio-Rad Laboratories), or equivalent
    Temperature
      Column: 60° ± 2°
      Detector: About 35° (Maintain at constant temperature.)
    Flow rate: About 0.5 mL/min
    Injection volume: About 10 μL
  System suitability
    Sample: *Standard solution*
    Suitability requirement 1: The relative standard deviation for replicate injections is NMT 2.0%.
    Suitability requirement 2: The tailing factor for maltitol and sorbitol is NMT 1.2.
  Analysis: Separately inject the *Sample solution* and the *Standard solution* into the chromatograph, record the chromatograms, and measure the responses for the major peaks. [NOTE—The elution pattern includes the higher-molecular-weight hydrogenated polysaccharides, followed by three individual peaks representing maltotriitol, maltitol, and sorbitol. The relative retention times are about 0.38 for maltotriitol, 0.48 for maltitol, and 1.0 for sorbitol.]

690 / Maltitol Syrup / Monographs

Separately calculate the percentages, on the anhydrous basis, of maltitol and sorbitol in the portion of sample taken by the formula:

$$\text{Result} = [(C_S/C_U) \times (r_U/r_S) \times 10{,}000]/(100 - w)$$

C_S = concentration (mg/g) of the appropriate USP RS in the *Standard solution*
C_U = concentration (mg/g) of sample in the *Sample solution*
r_U = peak response of the corresponding analyte obtained from the chromatogram of the *Sample solution*
r_S = peak response of the corresponding analyte obtained from the chromatogram of the *Standard solution*
w = percent water as determined in the test for *Water* (below)

Acceptance criteria
D-Maltitol: NLT 50.0%, by weight, calculated on the anhydrous basis
D-Sorbitol: NMT 8.0%, calculated on the anhydrous basis

IMPURITIES
Inorganic Impurities
- **LEAD,** *Lead Limit Test, Atomic Absorption Spectrophotometric Graphite Furnace Method, Method I,* Appendix IIIB
  Acceptance criteria: NMT 1 mg/kg, calculated on the anhydrous basis
- **NICKEL,** *Nickel Limit Test,* Appendix IIIB
  Acceptance criteria: NMT 1 mg/kg, calculated on the anhydrous basis

Organic Impurities
- **REDUCING SUGARS**
  0.05 N iodine: Dilute 0.1 N iodine VS 1:1(v/v) with water.
  0.05 N sodium thiosulfate: Dilute 0.1 N sodium thiosulfate VS 1:1 (v/v) with water.
  Sample: Amount equivalent to 3.3 g on the anhydrous basis
  Analysis: Add 3 mL of water, 20.0 mL of alkaline cupric citrate TS and a few glass beads to the *Sample*. Heat so that boiling begins after 4 min, and maintain the boiling for 3 min. Cool rapidly and add 40 mL of diluted acetic acid TS, 60 mL of water, and 20.0 mL of 0.05 N iodine. With continuous shaking, add 25 mL of a mixture of 6 mL of hydrochloric acid and 94 mL of water. When the precipitate has dissolved, titrate the excess iodine with 0.05 N sodium thiosulfate. Use 2 mL of starch TS, added toward the end of the titration, as an indicator.
  Acceptance criteria: NLT 12.8 mL of 0.05 N sodium thiosulfate is required for the titration. (NMT 0.3%, on the anhydrous basis, as glucose)

SPECIFIC TESTS
- **PH,** *pH Determination,* Appendix IIB
  Sample solution: 140 mg/g in carbon dioxide-free water
  Acceptance criteria: Between 5.0 and 7.5
- **RESIDUE ON IGNITION (SULFATED ASH),** *Method II (for Liquids),* Appendix IIC
  Sample: 2 g
  Acceptance criteria: NMT 0.1%, calculated on the anhydrous basis
- **WATER,** *Water Determination,* Appendix IIB
  Acceptance criteria: NMT 31.5%

Maltodextrin
First Published: Prior to FCC 6

UNII: 7CVR7L4A2D [maltodextrin]

DESCRIPTION
Maltodextrin occurs as a white, slightly hygroscopic powder, as granules of similar description, or as a clear to hazy solution in water. It is a purified, concentrated, nutritive mixture of saccharide polymers obtained by the partial hydrolysis of edible starch. Powders or granules are freely soluble or readily dispersible in water.
Function: Anticaking and free-flowing agent; bulking agent; stabilizer and thickener; surface-finishing agent
Packaging and Storage: Keep dry, and store at ambient temperatures.

IDENTIFICATION
- **PROCEDURE**
  Sample solution: 100 mg/mL
  Analysis: Add a few drops of *Sample solution* to 5 mL of hot alkaline cupric tartrate TS.
  Acceptance criteria: A red precipitate of cuprous oxide forms.

ASSAY
- **REDUCING SUGARS ASSAY,** Appendix X
  Acceptance criteria: Less than 20.0% reducing sugar content (dextrose equivalent) expressed as D-glucose

IMPURITIES
Inorganic Impurities
- **LEAD,** *Lead Limit Test, Atomic Absorption Spectrophotometric Graphite Furnace Methods, Method I,* Appendix IIIB
  Sample: 5 g
  Acceptance criteria: NMT 0.5 mg/kg
- **SULFUR DIOXIDE,** *Sulfur Dioxide Determination,* Appendix X
  Acceptance criteria: NMT 0.0025%

Organic Impurities
- **PROTEIN (TOTAL),** *Nitrogen Determination,* Appendix IIIC
  Analysis: Determine the percent nitrogen as directed. Calculate the percent protein using the equation:

$$\% \text{ Protein} = N \times 6.25$$

N = percent nitrogen
6.25 = nitrogen to protein conversion factor
Acceptance criteria
Maltodextrins produced from high-amylose starches: NMT 1.0%
All other types of maltodextrins: NMT 0.5%

SPECIFIC TESTS
- **RESIDUE ON IGNITION (SULFATED ASH)**, Appendix IIC
  Sample: 1 g
  Acceptance criteria: NMT 0.5%
- **TOTAL SOLIDS**, Appendix X
  Powders and granules
  Sample solution: 60 g of sample made to 100 g with water. [NOTE—Heat the solution slightly, if necessary, to complete dissolution.]
  Analysis: Determine the refractive index of the *Sample solution* at 20° or 45°, and refer to the tables under *Total Solids, Maltodextrin*, Appendix X to determine the *Total Solids* for the *Sample solution*. Calculate the *Total Solids* of the sample taken by the formula:

  $$\text{Result} = (TS \times W_T/W_S)$$

  TS = percent *Total Solids* in the *Sample solution*, determined in the *Analysis*
  W_T = total weight (g) of the prepared *Sample solution*
  W_S = weight of the sample (g) taken to prepare the *Sample solution*

  Liquids
  Analysis: Determine the refractive index of a sample at 20° or 45°, and refer to the tables in *Total Solids, Maltodextrin*, Appendix X.
  Acceptance criteria
  Powders and granules: NLT 90.0%
  Liquids: NLT 50.0%

OTHER REQUIREMENTS
- **LABELING:** Indicate the presence of sulfur dioxide if the residual concentration is greater than 10 mg/kg.

Maltol

First Published: Prior to FCC 6

3-Hydroxy-2-methyl-4-pyrone

$C_6H_6O_3$ Formula wt 126.11
INS: 636 CAS: [118-71-8]
UNII: 3A9RD92BS4 [maltol]

DESCRIPTION
Maltol occurs as a white, crystalline powder with a characteristic caramel-butterscotch odor, and is suggestive of a fruity-strawberry aroma in dilute solution. One g dissolves in about 82 mL of water, in 21 mL of alcohol, in 80 mL of glycerin, and in 28 mL of propylene glycol.
Function: Flavoring agent
Packaging and Storage: Store in tight containers.

IDENTIFICATION
- **UV-VISIBLE ABSORPTION SPECTRUM**
  Sample solution: 10 µg/mL in 0.1 N hydrochloric acid
  Acceptance criteria: The *Sample solution* exhibits an absorbance maximum at 274 ± 2 nm.

ASSAY
- **PROCEDURE**
  Standard solution: 10 µg/mL USP Maltol RS in 0.1 N hydrochloric acid
  Sample solution: 10 µg/mL in 0.1 N hydrochloric acid
  Analysis: Using 0.1 N hydrochloric acid as the blank, determine the absorbance of each solution in a 1-cm quartz cell at the wavelength of maximum absorption at about 274 nm, using a suitable spectrophotometer. Calculate the quantity, in mg, of $C_6H_6O_3$ in the sample taken by the formula:

  $$\text{Result} = (R_U/R_S) \times (C_S/C_U) \times 100$$

  R_U = absorbance of the *Sample solution*
  R_S = absorbance of the *Standard solution*
  C_S = concentration of the *Standard solution* (µg/mL)
  C_U = concentration of the *Sample solution* (µg/mL)

  Acceptance criteria: NLT 99.0% of $C_6H_6O_3$, calculated on the anhydrous basis

IMPURITIES
Inorganic Impurities
- **WATER**, *Water Determination*, Appendix IIB
  Acceptance criteria: NMT 0.5%

SPECIFIC TESTS
- **MELTING RANGE OR TEMPERATURE DETERMINATION**, *Procedure for Class Ia*, Appendix IIB
  Acceptance criteria: Between 160° and 164°
- **RESIDUE ON IGNITION (SULFATED ASH)**, Appendix IIC
  Sample: 1 g
  Acceptance criteria: NMT 0.2%

Maltol Isobutyrate

First Published: Prior to FCC 6

$C_{10}H_{12}O_4$ Formula wt 196.20
FEMA: 3462
UNII: 6LE3UBK142 [maltyl isobutyrate]

DESCRIPTION
Maltol Isobutyrate occurs as a colorless to yellow liquid.
Odor: Strawberry
Solubility: Soluble in propylene glycol, vegetable oils; insoluble or practically insoluble in water
Boiling Point: ~176° (7 mm Hg)

Solubility in Alcohol, Appendix VI: One mL dissolves in 1 mL of 95% ethanol.
Function: Flavoring agent

IDENTIFICATION
- **INFRARED SPECTRA,** *Spectrophotometric Identification Tests,* Appendix IIIC
  Acceptance criteria: The spectrum of the sample exhibits relative maxima at the same wavelengths as those of the spectrum below.

ASSAY
- **PROCEDURE:** Proceed as directed under *M-1b,* Appendix XI.

Acceptance criteria: NLT 96.0% of $C_{10}H_{12}O_4$

SPECIFIC TESTS
- **ACID VALUE, FLAVOR CHEMICALS (OTHER THAN ESSENTIAL OILS),** *M-15,* Appendix XI
  Acceptance criteria: NMT 10.0
- **REFRACTIVE INDEX,** Appendix II: At 20°
  Acceptance criteria: Between 1.493 and 1.501
- **SPECIFIC GRAVITY:** Determine at 25° by any reliable method (see *General Provisions*).
  Acceptance criteria: Between 1.140 and 1.153

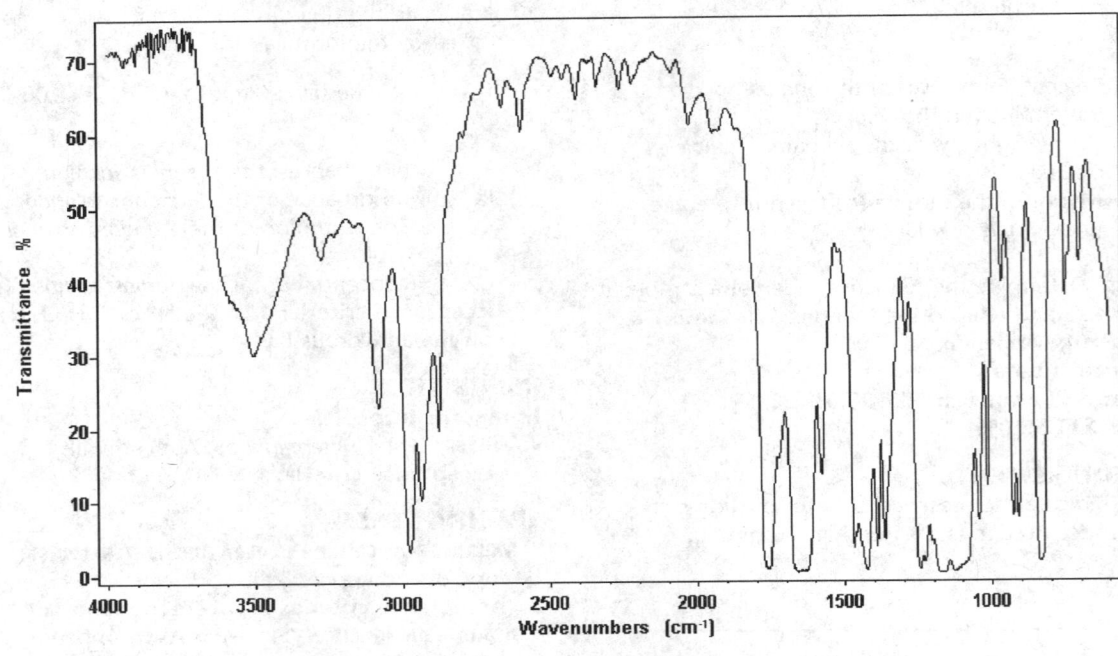

Maltol Isobutyrate

Mandarin Oil, Cold-pressed
First Published: Prior to FCC 6

Mandarin Oil, Expressed
FEMA: 2657
CAS: [8008-31-9]
UNII: NJO720F72R [mandarin oil]

DESCRIPTION
Mandarin Oil, Cold-pressed occurs as a clear, dark orange to red-yellow or brown-orange liquid with a pleasant, orange odor. It often shows a blue fluorescence in diffused light. Oils produced from unripe fruit often show a green color. It is the oil obtained by expression of the peels of the ripe fruit of the mandarin orange, *Citrus reticulata* Blanco var. *Mandarin* (Fam. Rutaceae). It is soluble in most fixed oils and in mineral oil, slightly soluble in propylene glycol, but insoluble in glycerin. It may contain a suitable antioxidant.

Function: Flavoring agent
Packaging and Storage: Store in a cool place protected from light in full, tight containers that are made from steel or aluminum and that are suitably lined.

IDENTIFICATION
- **INFRARED SPECTRA,** *Spectrophotometric Identification Tests,* Appendix IIIC
  Acceptance criteria: The spectrum of the sample exhibits relative maxima at the same wavelengths as those of the spectrum below.

ASSAY
- **ALDEHYDES,** *Aldehydes and Ketones, Hydroxylamine tert-Butyl Alcohol Method,* Appendix VI
  Sample: 10 g
  Analysis: Before titrating, allow the mixture to stand for 30 min at room temperature. Use 156.26 as the equivalence factor (e) in the calculation.

Acceptance criteria: NLT 0.4% and NMT 1.8% of aldehydes, calculated as decyl aldehyde ($C_{10}H_{20}O$)

SPECIFIC TESTS
- **ANGULAR ROTATION,** Optical (Specific) Rotation, Appendix IIB: Use a 100-mm tube.
  Acceptance criteria: Between +63° and +78°
- **REFRACTIVE INDEX,** Appendix IIB
  [NOTE—Use an Abbé or other refractometer of equal or greater accuracy.]
  Acceptance criteria: Between 1.473 and 1.477 at 20°
- **RESIDUE ON EVAPORATION,** Appendix VI
  Sample: 5 g
  Analysis: Heat the Sample for 5 h.
  Acceptance criteria: Between 2.0% and 5.0%
- **SPECIFIC GRAVITY:** Determine by any reliable method (see General Provisions).
  Acceptance criteria: Between 0.846 and 0.852

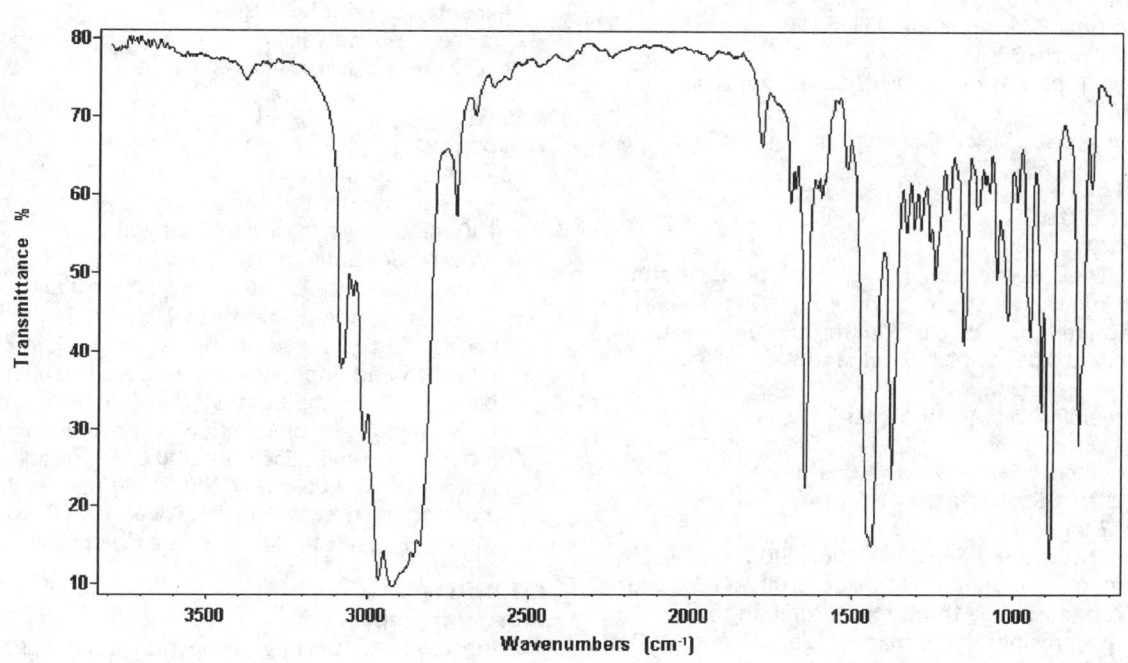

Mandarin Oil, Cold-pressed

Manganese Chloride
First Published: Prior to FCC 6

$MnCl_2$ Formula wt, anhydrous 125.84
$MnCl_2 \cdot 4H_2O$ Formula wt, tetrahydrate 197.91
CAS: anhydrous [7773-01-5]
tetrahydrate [13446-34-9]
UNII: QQE170PANO [manganese chloride]

DESCRIPTION
Manganese Chloride occurs as large, irregular, pink, translucent crystals. It is freely soluble in water at room temperature and very soluble in hot water.
Function: Nutrient
Packaging and Storage: Store in well-closed containers.

IDENTIFICATION
- **MANGANESE,** Appendix IIIA
  Sample solution: 50 mg/mL
  Acceptance criteria: Passes test
- **CHLORIDE,** Appendix IIIA
  Sample solution: 50 mg/mL
  Acceptance criteria: Passes test

ASSAY
- **PROCEDURE**
  Sample solution: 16 mg/mL, made to 250 mL.
  Analysis: Transfer 25.0 mL of the Sample solution into a 400-mL beaker, add 10 mL of a 1:10 solution of hydroxylamine hydrochloride, 25 mL of 0.05 M disodium EDTA measured from a buret, 25 mL of ammonia–ammonium chloride buffer TS, and 5 drops of eriochrome black TS. Heat the solution to between 55° and 65° and titrate from the buret to a blue endpoint. Each mL of 0.05 M disodium EDTA is equivalent to 9.896 mg of $MnCl_2 \cdot 4H_2O$.
  Acceptance criteria: NLT 98.0% and NMT 102.0% of $MnCl_2 \cdot 4H_2O$

IMPURITIES
Inorganic Impurities
- **IRON**
  Sample solution: 2.0 g in 20 mL of water

Control solution: (10 μg Fe): 1.0 mL of *Iron Standard Solution* (see *Standard Solutions for the Preparation of Controls and Standards,* Solutions and Indicators)
Analysis: To the *Sample solution,* add 1 mL of hydrochloric acid and dilute to 50 mL with water. Add about 40 mg of ammonium persulfate crystals and 3 mL of ammonium thiocyanate TS. Repeat the preceding with the *Control solution.*
Acceptance criteria: Any red or pink color produced by the *Sample solution* does not exceed that produced by the *Control solution* (NMT 5 mg/kg).
- **LEAD,** *Lead Limit Test,* Appendix IIIB
  Sample: 1 g in 10 mL of water
  Control: 4 μg Pb (4 mL *of Diluted Standard Lead Solution*)
  Acceptance criteria: NMT 4 mg/kg

SPECIFIC TESTS
- **INSOLUBLE MATTER**
  Sample: 20 g
  Analysis: Dissolve the *Sample* in 200 mL of water and allow to stand on a steam bath for 1 h. Filter through a tared, sintered-glass crucible, wash thoroughly with hot water, dry at 105° for 1 h, cool, and weigh.
  Acceptance criteria: NMT 0.005%
- **pH,** *pH Determination,* Appendix IIB
  Sample solution: 50 mg/mL
  Acceptance criteria: Between 4.0 and 6.0
- **SUBSTANCES NOT PRECIPITATED BY SULFIDE**
  Sample: 2.0 g
  Analysis: Dissolve the *Sample* in about 90 mL of water, add 4 mL of ammonium hydroxide, heat to 80°, and pass hydrogen sulfide through the solution to completely precipitate the manganese. Dilute to 100 mL, mix, and allow the precipitate to settle. Decant the supernatant liquid through a filter, and evaporate 50 mL of the filtrate to dryness in a tared dish. Add 0.5 mL of sulfuric acid, ignite to constant weight, cool, and weigh.
  Acceptance criteria: NMT 0.2% after ignition
- **SULFATE**
  Sample: 10.0 g
  Analysis: Dissolve the *Sample* in 100 mL of water, add 1 mL of 2.7 N hydrochloric acid, mix, and filter. Heat to boiling, then add 10 mL of barium chloride TS, and allow to stand overnight. Filter out any precipitate in a tared crucible, wash, ignite gently, cool, and weigh.
  Acceptance criteria: The weight of the ignited precipitate should not be more than 1.2 mg greater than the weight obtained in a complete blank test (NMT 0.005%).

Manganese Citrate

First Published: Prior to FCC 6

$Mn_3(C_6H_5O_7)_2 \cdot 10H_2O$ Formula wt, decahydrate 723.177
$Mn_3(C_6H_5O_7)_2$ Formula wt, anhydrous 543.02
    CAS: [10024-66-5]

UNII: 4Z2OA6A13N [manganese citrate]

DESCRIPTION
Manganese Citrate occurs as a light pink or pink-white, fine, granular solid. It is very slightly soluble in water.
Function: Nutrient
Packaging and Storage: Store in well-closed containers.

IDENTIFICATION
- **MANGANESE,** Appendix IIIA
  Sample solution: 1 g in 20 mL of 1 N hydrochloric acid
  Acceptance criteria: Passes test
- **CITRATES,** Appendix IIIA
  Acceptance criteria: Passes test

ASSAY
- **PROCEDURE**
  Sample: 350 mg
  Analysis: Transfer the *Sample* into a 250-mL beaker. Add 100 mL of water and 1 mL of hydrochloric acid. While stirring constantly, heat to approximately 75° to 80° on a hot plate. Add 25 mL of 0.05 M disodium EDTA, and if necessary, adjust the pH to 10.0 ± 0.2 with 1 N NaOH. Add 10 mL of ammonia–ammonium chloride buffer TS and approximately 8 drops of eriochrome black TS. Continue titrating with 0.05 M disodium EDTA until a true blue endpoint is reached and holds for at least 3 min. Each mL of 0.05 M disodium EDTA is equivalent to 9.05 mg of $Mn_3(C_6H_5O_7)_2$.
  Acceptance criteria: NLT 96.5% and NMT 104.8% of $Mn_3(C_6H_5O_7)_2$, calculated on the dried basis

IMPURITIES
Inorganic Impurities
- **ARSENIC,** *Arsenic Limit Test,* Appendix IIIB
  Sample: 1 g in 35 mL of water
  Acceptance criteria: NMT 3 mg/kg
- **LEAD,** *Lead Limit Test, APDC Extraction Method,* Appendix IIIB
  Acceptance criteria: NMT 2 mg/kg

SPECIFIC TESTS
- **LOSS ON DRYING,** Appendix IIC: 135° for 16 h under vacuum
  Acceptance criteria: Between 23.0% and 26.0%
- **SULFATES**
  Sample: 10.0 g
  Analysis: Dissolve the *Sample* in 200 mL of water and sufficient hydrochloric acid to make the solution acid to methyl red. Heat to boiling, add 10 mL of barium chloride TS, and allow to digest on a steam bath for 2 h. Filter the precipitate through a 1-μm tared filtering crucible, wash, ignite gently, cool, and weigh.
  Acceptance criteria: The weight of the ignited precipitate multiplied by 0.4113 is NMT 0.02% of the original sample weight.

Manganese Gluconate

First Published: Prior to FCC 6

$C_{12}H_{22}MnO_{14} \cdot 2H_2O$ — Formula wt, dihydrate 481.27
$C_{12}H_{22}MnO_{14}$ — Formula wt, anhydrous 445.24
CAS: [6485-39-8]
UNII: 0O43J7044T [manganese gluconate dihydrate]
UNII: 7G09WJ8QIR [manganese gluconate anhydrous]

DESCRIPTION
Manganese Gluconate occurs as a slightly pink powder. The anhydrous form is obtained by spray-drying and the dihydrate is obtained by crystallization. It is very soluble in hot water and is very slightly soluble in alcohol.
Function: Nutrient
Packaging and Storage: Store in well-closed containers.

IDENTIFICATION
- **MANGANESE,** Appendix IIIA
  Sample solution: 50 mg/mL
  Acceptance criteria: Passes tests
- **THIN-LAYER CHROMATOGRAPHY,** Appendix IIA
  Standard solution: 10 mg/mL of USP Potassium Gluconate RS. [NOTE—Heat in a water bath at 60° if necessary to dissolve sample.]
  Sample solution: 10 mg/mL. [NOTE—Heat in a water bath at 60° if necessary to dissolve sample.]
  Adsorbent: 0.25-mm layer of chromatographic silica gel
  Application volume: 5 µL
  Developing solvent system: Alcohol, ethyl acetate, ammonium hydroxide, water (50:10:10:30)
  Spray reagent: Dissolve 2.5 g of ammonium molybdate in about 50 mL of 2 N sulfuric acid in a 100-mL volumetric flask, add 1.0 g of ceric sulfate, swirl to dissolve, dilute to volume with 2 N sulfuric acid, and mix.
  Analysis: After removing the plate from the developing chamber, allow it to dry at 110° for 20 min, and allow it to cool. Spray the plate with the *Spray reagent*, then heat the plate at 110° for 10 min.
  Acceptance criteria: The principal spot obtained from the *Sample solution* corresponds in color, size, and R_F value to that obtained from the *Standard solution*.

ASSAY
- **PROCEDURE**
  Sample: 700 mg
  Analysis: Dissolve the *Sample* in 50 mL of water, add 1 g of ascorbic acid, 10 mL of ammonia–ammonium chloride buffer TS, and 5 drops of eriochrome black TS. Titrate with 0.05 M disodium EDTA to a deep blue color. Each mL of 0.05 M disodium EDTA is equivalent to 22.26 mg of $C_{12}H_{22}MnO_{14}$.
  Acceptance criteria: NLT 98.0% and NMT 102.0% of $C_{12}H_{22}MnO_{14}$, calculated on the anhydrous basis.

IMPURITIES
Inorganic Impurities
- **ARSENIC,** *Arsenic Limit Test,* Appendix IIIB
  Sample solution: 1 g in 35 mL of hot water
  Acceptance criteria: NMT 3 mg/kg
- **LEAD,** *Lead Limit Test, APDC Extraction Method,* Appendix IIIB
  Acceptance criteria: NMT 2 mg/kg

SPECIFIC TESTS
- **REDUCING SUBSTANCES**
  Sample: 1 g
  Analysis: Transfer the *Sample* into a 250-mL Erlenmeyer flask, dissolve in 10 mL of water, add 25 mL of alkaline cupric citrate TS, and cover the flask with a small beaker. Boil gently for exactly 5 min, and cool rapidly to room temperature. Add 25 mL of 1:10 acetic acid solution, 10 mL of 0.1 N iodine, 10 mL of 2.7 N hydrochloric acid, and 3 mL of starch TS. Titrate with 0.1 N sodium thiosulfate to the disappearance of the blue color. Calculate the weight, in mg, of reducing substances (as D-glucose) by the formula:

$$\text{Result} = (V_1 N_1 - V_2 N_2) \times 27$$

V_1 = volume of the iodine solution (mL)
N_1 = normality of the iodine solution
V_2 = volume of the sodium thiosulfate solution (mL)
N_2 = normality of the sodium thiosulfate solution
27 = empirically determined equivalence factor for D-glucose

  Acceptance criteria: NMT 1.0%
- **WATER,** *Water Determination,* Appendix IIB
  Analysis: Stir the mixture containing the *Sample solution,* maintained at 50°, for 30 min before titrating with the reagent.
  Acceptance criteria
    Anhydrous: Between 3.0% and 9.0%
    Dihydrate: Between 6.0% and 9.0%

OTHER REQUIREMENTS
- **LABELING:** Indicate whether it has been obtained through spray drying or from crystallization.

Manganese Glycerophosphate

First Published: Prior to FCC 6

$C_3H_7MnO_6P \cdot xH_2O$ — Formula wt, anhydrous 225.00
CAS: [1320-46-3]
UNII: LR135I04CJ [manganese glycerophosphate]

DESCRIPTION
Manganese Glycerophosphate occurs as a white or pink-white powder. One gram dissolves in about 5 mL of 1:4 citric acid solution. It is slightly soluble in water, and is insoluble in alcohol.
Function: Nutrient
Packaging and Storage: Store in well-closed containers.

IDENTIFICATION
- **MANGANESE**, Appendix IIIA
  Sample solution: 50 mg/mL in 2.7 N hydrochloric acid
  Acceptance criteria: Passes tests

ASSAY
- **PROCEDURE**
  Sample: 1 g, previously dried at 110° to constant weight
  Analysis: Dissolve the *Sample* in 1.5 mL of nitric acid and 5 mL of warm water. Dilute to 125 mL with water, add 2.0 g of dibasic ammonium phosphate and a few drops of methyl red TS, and heat to boiling. While the solution is boiling, slowly add ammonium hydroxide, dropwise and with constant stirring, until the solution is alkaline, and then add 2.0 mL in excess. Let the solution stand for 2 h at room temperature. Filter through a tared, porous-bottom porcelain filter crucible, and wash the precipitate with 1:100 ammonia. Dry at 105°, and ignite to constant weight at 800° ± 25. [NOTE—Avoid exposing the crucible to sudden temperature changes.] Each g of manganese pyrophosphate so obtained is equivalent to 1.585 g of $C_3H_7MnO_6P$.
  Acceptance criteria: NLT 98.0% and NMT 100.5% of $C_3H_7MnO_6P$, on the dried basis

IMPURITIES
Inorganic Impurities
- **LEAD**, *Lead Limit Test*, Appendix IIIB
  Sample solution: Mix 1 g of sample with 3 mL of 1:2 nitric acid and 10 mL of water, and boil until brown fumes evolve. Add 10 mL of water, boil for 2 min, cool, and dilute to 100 mL with water. Use 25 mL of this solution for the *Analysis*.
  Control: 4 µg Pb (4 mL of *Diluted Standard Lead Solution*)
  Analysis: Proceed as described under *Procedure*, but with the following modifications: 100 mL of *Ammonium Citrate Solution* instead of 6 mL, 1 mL of *Potassium Cyanide Solution* instead of 2 mL, and 0.5 mL of *Hydroxylamine Hydrochloride Solution* instead of 2 mL.
  Acceptance criteria: NMT 4 mg/kg

SPECIFIC TESTS
- **LOSS ON DRYING**, Appendix IIC: 110° to constant weight
  Acceptance criteria: NMT 12.0%

Manganese Hypophosphite
First Published: Prior to FCC 6

$Mn(H_2PO_2)_2 \cdot xH_2O$ Formula wt, anhydrous 184.92
                                      CAS: [10043-84-2]
UNII: 4O05955R9G [manganese hypophosphite]

DESCRIPTION
Manganese Hypophosphite occurs as a pink, granular or crystalline powder that is stable in air. One g dissolves in about 6.5 mL of water at 25° or in about 6 mL of boiling water. It is soluble in alcohol.
Function: Nutrient
Packaging and Storage: Store in well-closed containers. [CAUTION—Mix Manganese Hypophosphite with nitrates, chlorates, or other oxidizing agents very carefully because an explosion may occur if it is triturated or heated.]

IDENTIFICATION
- **MANGANESE**, Appendix IIIA
  Sample solution: 50 mg/mL
  Acceptance criteria: Passes test
- **HYPOPHOSPHITE**, Appendix IIIA
  Sample solution: 50 mg/mL
  Acceptance criteria: Passes tests

ASSAY
- **PROCEDURE**
  Sample solution: 1.20 mg/mL, made to 100 mL (using a previously dried sample)
  Analysis: Transfer 50.0 mL of the *Sample solution* to a 250-mL glass-stoppered iodine flask, add 50.0 mL of 0.1 N bromine and 20 mL of 2 N sulfuric acid and stopper the flask. Place a few mL of a saturated solution of potassium iodide in the lip around the stopper, shake the flask well, and allow it to stand for 3 h. Place the flask in an ice bath for 5 min, then carefully remove the stopper and allow the potassium iodide solution to be drawn into the flask. Add 2 g of potassium iodide dissolved in 10 mL of recently boiled water, shake the flask, and titrate the liberated iodine with 0.1 N sodium thiosulfate, using starch TS as the indicator. Each mL of 0.1 N bromine is equivalent to 2.311 mg of $Mn(H_2PO_2)_2$.
  Acceptance criteria: NLT 97.0% and NMT 100.5% of $Mn(H_2PO_2)_2$, on the dried basis

IMPURITIES
Inorganic Impurities
- **LEAD**, *Lead Limit Test*, Appendix IIIB
  Sample solution: Dissolve 625 mg of sample in 10 mL of water, add 2 mL of 1:2 nitric acid, and boil until brown fumes evolve. Add 10 mL of water, boil for 2 min, then cool and dilute with water to about 25 mL.
  Control: 2.5 µg Pb (2.5 mL of *Diluted Standard Lead Solution*)
  Analysis: Proceed as directed under *Procedure*, but using the following modifications: 25 mL of *Ammonium Citrate Solution* instead of 6 mL, 1 mL of *Potassium Cyanide Solution* instead of 2 mL, and 0.5 mL of *Hydroxylamine Hydrochloride Solution* instead of 2 mL.
  Acceptance criteria: NMT 4 mg/kg

SPECIFIC TESTS
- **LOSS ON DRYING**, Appendix IIC: 105° for 1 h
  Acceptance criteria: NMT 9.0%

Manganese Sulfate

First Published: Prior to FCC 6
Last Revision: First Supplement, FCC 6

MnSO$_4$·H$_2$O Formula wt 169.02
 CAS: [7785-87-7]
UNII: W00LYS4T26 [manganese sulfate]

DESCRIPTION
Manganese Sulfate occurs as a pale pink, granular powder. It is freely soluble in water, but is insoluble in alcohol.
Function: Nutrient
Packaging and Storage: Store in well-closed containers.

IDENTIFICATION
- **A. MANGANESE,** Appendix IIIA
  Sample solution: 100 mg/mL
  Acceptance criteria: Passes test
- **B. SULFATE,** Appendix IIIA
  Sample solution: 100 mg/mL
  Acceptance criteria: Passes tests

ASSAY
- **PROCEDURE**
  Sample solution: 16 mg/mL
  Analysis: Transfer a 25.0-mL portion of the *Sample solution* into a 400-mL beaker, and add 10 mL of 100 mg/mL hydroxylamine hydrochloride solution, 25 mL of 0.05 M disodium EDTA measured from a buret, 25 mL of ammonia–ammonium chloride buffer TS, and 5 drops of eriochrome black TS. Heat the solution to between 55° and 65° and titrate with 0.05 M disodium EDTA from the buret to a blue endpoint. Each mL of 0.05 M disodium EDTA is equivalent to 8.450 mg of MnSO$_4$·H$_2$O.
  Acceptance criteria: NLT 98.0% and NMT 102.0% of MnSO$_4$·H$_2$O

IMPURITIES
Inorganic Impurities
- **ARSENIC,** *Arsenic Limit Test,* Appendix IIIB
  Sample solution: 1 g in 35 mL of water
  Acceptance criteria: NMT 3 mg/kg
- **LEAD,** *Lead Limit Test, APDC Extraction Method,* Appendix IIIB
  Acceptance criteria: NMT 4 mg/kg
- **SELENIUM,** *Selenium Limit Test, Method II,* Appendix IIIB
  Sample: 200 mg
  Acceptance criteria: NMT 0.003%

SPECIFIC TESTS
- **LOSS ON HEATING**
  Sample: 1 g
  Analysis: Heat the *Sample*, in a crucible tared in a stoppered weighing bottle, to constant weight at 400° to 500°. Cool in a desiccator, transfer to the stoppered weighing bottle, and weigh.
  Acceptance criteria: Between 10.0% and 13.0%

Mannitol

First Published: Prior to FCC 6
Last Revision: First Supplement, FCC 6

D-Mannitol
Mannite
1,2,3,4,5,6-Hexanehexol

C$_6$H$_{14}$O$_6$ Formula wt 182.17
INS: 421 CAS: [69-65-8]
UNII: 3OWL53L36A [mannitol]

DESCRIPTION
Mannitol occurs as a white, crystalline powder or as free-flowing granules consisting of D-mannitol and a small quantity of sorbitol. It is soluble in water and in pyridine, very slightly soluble in alcohol, and practically insoluble in chloroform and ether.
Function: Nutritive sweetener; texturizing agent
Packaging and Storage: Store in well-closed containers.

IDENTIFICATION
- **A. PROCEDURE**
  Sample solution: 13.3 mg/mL
  Analysis: Transfer 3 mL of the *Sample solution* into a 15-cm test tube, add 3 mL of a freshly prepared 100 mg/mL catechol solution, and mix. Add 6 mL of sulfuric acid, mix again, then gently heat the tube in a flame for about 30 s.
  Acceptance criteria: A deep pink or wine red color appears.
- **B. PROCEDURE**
  Acceptance criteria: The retention time of the major peak in the chromatogram of the *Sample solution* corresponds to that in the chromatogram of the *Standard solution* as obtained from the *Assay* (below).

ASSAY
- **PROCEDURE**
  Mobile phase: Degassed water
  System suitability solution: 4.8 mg/g each of sorbitol and USP Mannitol RS
  Standard solution: 4.8 mg/g USP Mannitol RS
  Sample solution: 5 mg/g in water
  Chromatographic system, Appendix IIA
   Mode: High-performance liquid chromatography
   Detector: Refractive index
   Column: 10-cm × 7.8-mm column containing packing L34 (Bio-Rad Laboratories), or equivalent
   Column temperature: 50° ± 2°, isothermal
   Detector temperature: 35°
   Flow rate: About 0.7 mL/min
   Injection volume: About 10 µL
  System suitability
   Sample: *System suitability solution* and *Standard solution*

Suitability requirement 1: The resolution, R, between sorbitol and mannitol from the *System suitability solution* is NLT 2.0.
Suitability requirement 2: The relative standard deviation for replicate injections is NMT 2.0% for the *Standard solution*.
Analysis: Separately inject the *Sample solution* and the *Standard solution* into the chromatograph, record the chromatograms, and measure the responses for the major peaks. [NOTE—The relative retention times are about 0.6 for mannitol and 1.0 for sorbitol.]
Calculate the percentage of $C_6H_{14}O_6$ in the sample taken by the formula:

$$\text{Result} = [(C_S/C_U) \times (r_U/r_S) \times 10{,}000]/(100 - w)$$

C_S = concentration (mg/g) of the *Standard solution*
C_U = concentration (mg/g) of the *Sample solution*
r_U = peak responses obtained from the chromatogram of the *Sample solution*
r_S = peak responses obtained from the chromatogram of the *Standard solution*
w = percent loss on drying determined below for the sample

Acceptance criteria: NLT 96.0% and NMT 101.5% of $C_6H_{14}O_6$, calculated on the dried basis

IMPURITIES
Inorganic Impurities
- **LEAD,** *Lead Limit Test, Atomic Absorption Spectrophotometric Graphite Furnace Method, Method I,* Appendix IIIB
  Acceptance criteria: NMT 1 mg/kg
- **NICKEL,** *Nickel Limit Test,* Appendix IIIB
  Acceptance criteria: NMT 1 mg/kg

SPECIFIC TESTS
- **LOSS ON DRYING,** Appendix IIC: 105° for 4 h
  Acceptance criteria: NMT 0.3%
- **PH,** *pH Determination* Appendix IIB
  Sample: 10% (w/w) solution in carbon dioxide-free water
  Acceptance criteria: Between 4.0 and 7.5
- **REDUCING SUGARS**
  0.05 N Iodine VS: Dilute 0.1 N iodine VS with water (1:1).
  0.05 N Sodium thiosulfate VS: Dilute 0.1 N sodium thiosulfate VS with water (1:1).
  Sample: 3.3 g
  Analysis: Dissolve the *Sample* in 25 mL of water with the aid of gentle heat. Cool the solution and add 20 mL alkaline cupric citrate TS and a few glass beads. Heat the solution so that boiling begins after 4 min, and maintain the boiling for 3 min. Cool rapidly and add 40 mL of diluted acetic acid TS, 60 mL of water, and 20.0 mL of *0.05 N Iodine VS*. While continuously shaking the solution, add 25 mL of a mixture of 6 mL of hydrochloric acid and 94 mL of water. When the precipitate has dissolved, titrate the excess iodine with *0.05 N Sodium thiosulfate VS*. Use 2 mL of starch TS, added toward the end of the titration, as an indicator.
  Acceptance criteria: NLT 12.8 mL of *0.05 N Sodium thiosulfate VS* is required for the titration. (NMT 0.3% of reducing sugars, as glucose)
- **RESIDUE ON IGNITION (SULFATED ASH),** Appendix IIC
  Sample: 1.5 g
  Acceptance criteria: NMT 0.1%

Maritime Pine Extract

First Published: Second Supplement, FCC 7

Pinus pinaster Extract
UNII: 50JZ5Z98QY [maritime pine]

DESCRIPTION
Maritime Pine Extract occurs as a fine, brown powder. It is extracted and purified from pulverized Maritime Pine (*Pinus pinaster*) using suitable solvents. While not a requirement for this monograph, users interested in analyzing this ingredient for potential pesticide residues may use the informational method found in *Pesticide Residues* under Appendix XIII.
Function: Source of procyanidins and other phenolic compounds
Packaging and Storage: Store in a tight, light-resistant container protected from excessive heat.

IDENTIFICATION
- **A. PROCEDURE**
  Sample solution: Dissolve 50 mg of sample in 6 mL of a mixture of butanol and hydrochloric acid (95:5).
  Analysis: Heat the *Sample solution* in a boiling water bath for 2 min.
  Acceptance criteria: The *Sample solution* so treated turns dark red.
- **B. PROCEDURE**
  Solution A: Methanol
  Solution B: 0.1% phosphoric acid in water (w/v)
  Mobile phase: See gradient table below.

Time (min)	Solution A (%)	Solution B (%)
0	8	92
40	34	66
45	2	98
50	2	98
52	8	92
57	8	92

Standard solution: 2 mg/mL of USP Maritime Pine Extract RS in *Solution A*. Pass through a membrane filter having a 0.45-μm or finer porosity.
Sample solution: Add 20 mg of sample to 10 mL of *Solution A* and sonicate for 10 min to dissolve. Pass through a membrane filter having a 0.45-μm or finer porosity, discarding the first 4 mL of filtrate.
Chromatographic system, Appendix IIA
Mode: High-performance liquid chromatography
Detector: UV 280 nm

Column: 4.6-mm × 15-cm; contains base-deactivated octylsilane bonded to porous silica particles of less than 5 μm[1]
Temperature: 40°
Flow rate: 1 mL/min
Injection size: 10 μL
System suitability
[NOTE—The chromatogram obtained is similar to the Reference Chromatogram provided with the USP Maritime Pine Extract RS.]
   Sample: Standard solution
   Suitability requirement 1: The resolution between taxifolin and ferulic acid is NLT 3.0.
   Suitability requirement 2: The tailing factor for taxifolin is NMT 2.0.
Analysis: Separately inject the Sample solution and the Standard solution into the chromatograph, record the chromatograms, and identify the peaks for catechin, caffeic acid, taxifolin, and ferulic acid by comparing the chromatogram of the Standard solution with the Reference Chromatogram provided with the USP Maritime Pine Extract RS.
Acceptance criteria: The chromatogram of the Sample solution exhibits peaks for catechin, caffeic acid, taxifolin, and ferulic acid at the retention times corresponding to those in the chromatogram of the Standard solution.

- **C. THIN-LAYER CHROMATOGRAPHY**, Appendix IIA
   Sample solution: 25 mg/mL in methanol
   Standard solution A: 25 mg/mL of USP Maritime Pine Extract RS in methanol
   Standard solution B: 1 mg/mL each of USP Ferulic Acid RS[2] and USP Protocatechuic Acid RS[3] in methanol
   Adsorbent: 0.25-mm layer of chromatographic silica gel mixture
   Application volume: 5 μL
   Developing solvent system: Methylene chloride, methanol, glacial acetic acid, and water (80:15:2:2)
   Spray reagent: 5% ferric chloride in methanol
   Analysis: Develop the chromatogram in the Developing solvent system until the solvent front has moved about three-fourths of the length of the plate. Remove the plate from the chamber, dry at 110°, and examine under short-wavelength and long-wavelength UV light. The chromatograms of Standard solution A and Standard solution B exhibit bands in the middle third and upper third that correspond to protocatechuic acid and ferulic acid, respectively. Spray the plate with the Spray reagent, and heat at 115° for 15 min. The bands due to ferulic acid and protocatechuic acid turn grayish green. Grayish-green bands become visible in the chromatogram of Standard solution A above and below protocatechuic acid, indicating the presence of caffeic acid and catechin, respectively.
   Acceptance criteria: The chromatogram of the Sample solution exhibits bands due to catechin, protocatechuic acid, caffeic acid, and ferulic acid that correspond in color and R_F values to those in the chromatograms of Standard solution A and Standard solution B.

- **D. THIN-LAYER CHROMATOGRAPHY**, Appendix IIA
   Sample solution: Use the Sample solution prepared as directed in Identification test C.
   Standard solution: Use Standard solution A prepared as directed in Identification test C.
   Adsorbent: 0.25-mm layer of chromatographic silica gel mixture
   Application volume: 5 μL
   Developing solvent system: Ethyl acetate, formic acid, and water (50:5:3)
   Spray reagent: Phosphoric acid and alcohol (1:1), containing 1% of vanillin
   Analysis: Develop the chromatogram in the Developing solvent system until the solvent front has moved about three-fourths of the length of the plate. Remove the plate and dry it with the aid of a current of air. Spray the plate with the Spray reagent and heat at 115° for 15 min. Three red bands appear in the middle third of the chromatogram of the Standard solution corresponding to two dimeric procyanidins and catechin. The chromatogram of the Standard solution also exhibits a blue band between the upper band due to upper dimeric procyanidins and the band due to catechin.
   Acceptance criteria: The chromatogram of the Sample solution contains bands that correspond to those found in the chromatogram of the Standard solution.

ASSAY
- **PROCYANIDINS**
   Solution A: Butanol and hydrochloric acid (95:5). [NOTE—Prepare this solution on the day of use.]
   Solution B: Dissolve 2 g of ferric ammonium sulfate in a mixture of 100 mL of water and 17.5 mL of hydrochloric acid. [NOTE—This solution can be used within 15 days of preparation.]
   Standard solution: 95 μg/mL of procyanidins from USP Maritime Pine Extract RS in methanol
   Sample solution: 0.125 mg/mL in methanol
   Analysis: Transfer 1.0 mL each of the Standard solution, Sample solution, and methanol to three 10-mL vials. To each vial add 6.0 mL of Solution A and 0.25 mL of Solution B. Seal the vials with crimp caps. Mix, and heat the vials in a boiling water bath for 40 min. Quickly cool to room temperature in an ice bath. Transfer each solution, with the aid of Solution A, to three separate 10-mL volumetric flasks, and dilute with Solution A to volume.

   Using a suitable spectrophotometer, determine the absorbance of the three solutions at 551 nm, using the methanol-containing solution as a blank. Calculate the percentage of total procyanidins in the portion of the sample taken:

$$\text{Result} = (A_U/A_S) \times (C_S/C_U) \times 100$$

A_U = absorbance of the solution from the Sample solution
A_S = absorbance of the solution from the Standard solution

---
[1] Zorbax SB-C8, or equivalent.
[2] USP Ferulic Acid RS is trans-4-hydroxy-3-methoxycinnamic acid.
[3] USP Protocatechuic Acid RS is 3,4-dihydroxybenzoic acid.

C_S = concentration of the *Standard solution* (µg/mL)
C_U = concentration of the *Sample solution* (µg/mL)

Acceptance criteria: 65%–75%, calculated on the dried basis

IMPURITIES
Inorganic Impurities
- **ARSENIC**, *Elemental Impurities by ICP*, Appendix IIIC
  Acceptance criteria: NMT 1.5 mg/kg
- **CADMIUM**, *Elemental Impurities by ICP*, Appendix IIIC
  Acceptance criteria: NMT 0.5 mg/kg
- **LEAD**, *Elemental Impurities by ICP*, Appendix IIIC
  Acceptance criteria: NMT 1.0 mg/kg
- **MERCURY**, *Elemental Impurities by ICP*, Appendix IIIC
  Acceptance criteria: NMT 1.5 mg/kg

SPECIFIC TESTS
- **ASH (TOTAL)**, Appendix IIC
  Analysis: Proceed as directed, heating the material to 675 ± 25°.
  Acceptance criteria: NMT 0.7%
- **LOSS ON DRYING**, Appendix IIC: 110° for 3 h
  Sample: 1.0 g
  Acceptance criteria: NMT 8.0%
- **WATER-INSOLUBLE SUBSTANCES**
  Sample solution: Add 0.5 g of sample to 50 mL of water at 20° and stir for 15 min.
  Analysis: Pass the *Sample solution* through a fine sintered-glass filter, previously weighed. Dry the filter at 110° for 3 h, cool to room temperature, and weigh the filter. Calculate the amount of water-insoluble substances in the sample taken.
  Acceptance criteria: NMT 10%

Marjoram Oil, Spanish Type

First Published: Prior to FCC 6

CAS: [8015-01-8]
UNII: 9NP0832457 [thymus mastichina flowering top oil]

DESCRIPTION
Marjoram Oil, Spanish Type occurs as a slightly yellow liquid with a camphoraceous note. It is a volatile oil obtained by steam distillation from the flowering plant *Thymus mastichina* L. (Fam. Labiatae). It is soluble in most fixed oils, but it is insoluble in glycerin, in propylene glycol, and in mineral oil.

Function: Flavoring agent
Packaging and Storage: Store in a cool place protected from light in full, tight containers that are made from steel or aluminum and that are suitably lined.

IDENTIFICATION
- **INFRARED SPECTRA**, *Spectrophotometric Identification Tests*, Appendix IIIC
  Acceptance criteria: The spectrum of the sample exhibits relative maxima at the same wavelengths as those of the spectrum below.

ASSAY
- **CINEOLE**
  Sample: 3 g previously dried over anhydrous sodium sulfate
  Analysis: Proceed as directed under *Solidification Point*, Appendix IIB. Transfer the *Sample* into a test tube, and add 2.1 g of melted *o*-cresol. The *o*-cresol must be pure and dry and have a solidification point not below 30°. Insert the thermometer, stir, and warm the tube gently until the mixture is completely melted. Continue as directed in the method. Repeat the procedure until two successive readings agree within 0.10°. Compute the percentage of cineole from the table found under *Percentage of Cineole*, Appendix VI.
  Acceptance criteria: NLT 49.0% and NMT 65.0% of cineole

SPECIFIC TESTS
- **ACID VALUE (ESSENTIAL OILS AND FLAVORS)**, Appendix VI
  Acceptance criteria: NMT 2.0
- **ANGULAR ROTATION**, *Optical (Specific) Rotation*, Appendix IIB: Use a 100-mm tube.
  Acceptance criteria: Between −5° and +10°
- **REFRACTIVE INDEX**, Appendix IIB
  [NOTE—Use an Abbé or other refractometer of equal or greater accuracy.]
  Acceptance criteria: Between 1.463 and 1.468 at 20°
- **SAPONIFICATION VALUE**, *Esters*, Appendix VI
  Sample: 10 g
  Acceptance criteria: Between 5 and 20
- **SOLUBILITY IN ALCOHOL**, Appendix VI
  Acceptance criteria: One mL of sample dissolves in 1 mL of 80% alcohol, and remains in solution upon further addition of alcohol to a total volume of 10 mL.
- **SPECIFIC GRAVITY:** Determine by any reliable method (see *General Provisions*).
  Acceptance criteria: Between 0.904 and 0.920

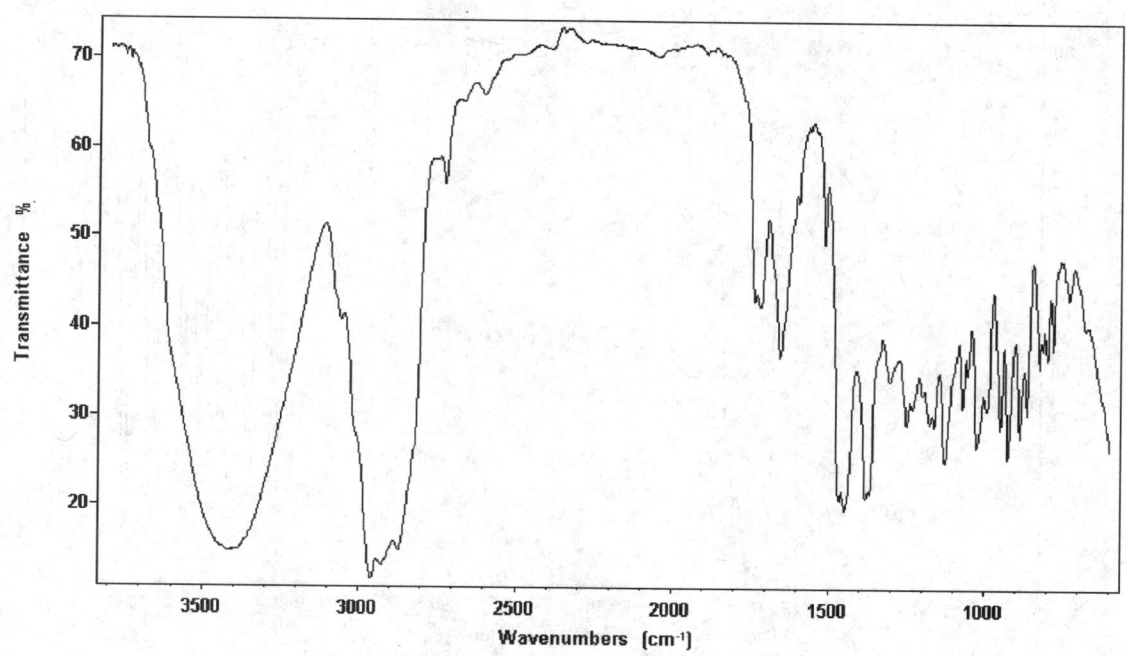

Marjoram Oil, Spanish Type

Marjoram Oil, Sweet

First Published: Prior to FCC 6

UNII: ICH7BE016E [sweet marjoram oil]

DESCRIPTION
Marjoram Oil, Sweet occurs as a yellow or green-yellow oil with a spicy or cardamom note. It is the volatile oil obtained by steam distillation of the dried herb of the marjoram shrub *Marjoram hortensis* L. (Fam. Labiatae). It is soluble in most fixed oils and in mineral oil (with turbidity). It is only partly soluble in propylene glycol, and it is insoluble in glycerin.

Function: Flavoring agent

Packaging and Storage: Store in a cool place protected from light in full, tight containers.

IDENTIFICATION
- **INFRARED SPECTRA,** *Spectrophotometric Identification Tests,* Appendix IIIC
  Acceptance criteria: The spectrum of the sample exhibits relative maxima at the same wavelengths as those of the spectrum below.

SPECIFIC TESTS
- **ACID VALUE (ESSENTIAL OILS AND FLAVORS),** Appendix VI
  Acceptance criteria: NMT 2.5
- **ANGULAR ROTATION,** *Optical (Specific) Rotation,* Appendix IIB: Use a 100-mm tube.
  Acceptance criteria: Between +14° and +24°
- **REFRACTIVE INDEX,** Appendix IIB
  [NOTE—Use an Abbé or other refractometer of equal or greater accuracy.]
  Acceptance criteria: Between 1.470 and 1.475 at 20°
- **SAPONIFICATION VALUE,** *Esters,* Appendix VI
  Sample: 5 g
  Acceptance criteria: Between 23 and 40
- **SAPONIFICATION VALUE AFTER ACETYLATION,** *Total Alcohols,* Appendix VI
  Sample: 2.5 g of acetylated oil
  Analysis: Calculate the saponification value by the formula:

  $$Result = 28.05 \times A/B$$

  A = amount (mL) of 0.5 N alcoholic potassium hydroxide consumed in the titration
  B = weight (g) of the acetylated oil taken
  Acceptance criteria: Between 68 and 86
- **SOLUBILITY IN ALCOHOL,** Appendix VI
  Acceptance criteria: One mL of sample dissolves in 2 mL of 80% alcohol.
- **SPECIFIC GRAVITY:** Determine by any reliable method (see *General Provisions*).
  Acceptance criteria: Between 0.890 and 0.906

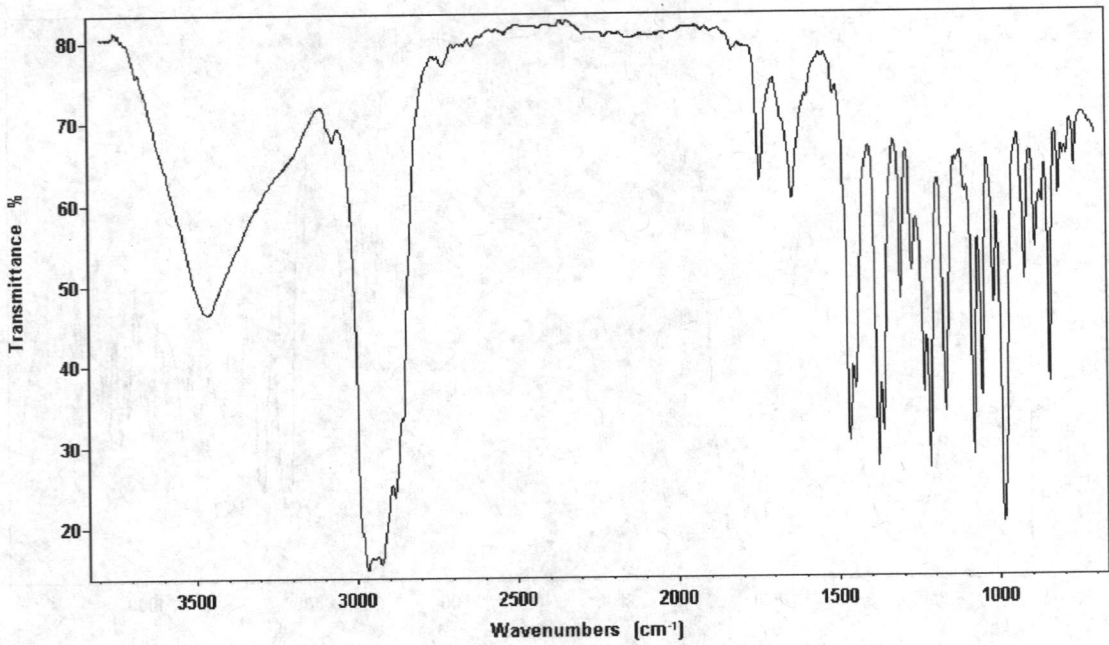

Marjoram Oil, Sweet

Masticatory Substances, Natural

First Published: Prior to FCC 6

Coagulated or Concentrated Latices of Vegetable Origin

DESCRIPTION

Masticatory Substances, Natural, of vegetable origin occur as a coagulated material that vary in color from white to brown, depending on their moisture content and heat treatment during purification. They consist of the gums from the trees of Sapotaceae, Apocynaceae, Moraceae, and Euphorbiaceae as listed below. The gums are purified by extensive treatment either alone or in combination with other gums or food-grade materials. They are heat-treated and then clarified by centrifugation or by any appropriate means of filtration.

Family and Products	Genus and Species
Sapotaceae	
Chicle	*Manilkara zapotilla* Gilly and *Manilkara chicle* Gilly
Chiquibul	*Manilkara zapotilla* Gilly
Crown gum	*Manilkara zapotilla* Gilly and *Manilkara chicle* Gilly
Gutta hang kang	*Palaquium leiocarpum* Boerl. and *Palaquium oblongifolium* Burck
Gutta Katiau	*Palaquium ganua moteleyana* Clarke (also known as *Sideroxylon glabrescens*)
Massaranduba balata (and the solvent-free resin extract of Massaranduba balata)	*Manilkara huberi* (Ducke) Chevalier
Massaranduba chocolate	*Manilkara solimoesensis* Gilly
Nispero	*Manilkara zapotilla* Gilly and *Manilkara chicle* Gilly
Rosidinha (rosadinha)	*Micropholis* (also known as *Sideroxylon*) spp.
Venezuelan chicle	*Manilkara williamsii* Standley and related spp.
Apocynaceae	
Jelutong	*Dyera costulata* Hook. F. and *Dyera lowii* Hook. F.
Leche caspi (sorva)	*Couma macrocarpa* Barb. Rodr.
Pendare	*Couma macrocarpa* Barb. Rodr. and *Couma utilis* (Mart.) Muell. Arg.
Perillo	*Couma macrocarpa* Barb. Rodr. and *Couma utilis* (Mart.) Muell. Arg.

Family and Products	Genus and Species
Moraceae	
Leche de vaca	*Brosimum utile* (H.B.K.) Pittier and *Poulsenia* ssp.; also *Lacmellea standleyi* (Woodson), Monachino (Apocynaceae)
Niger Gutta	*Ficus platyphylla* Del.
Tunu (tuno)	*Castilla fallax* Cook
Euphorbiaceae	
Chilte	*Cnidoscolus* (also known as *Jatropha*) *elasticus* Lundell and *Cnidoscolus tepiquensis* (Cost. and Gall.) McVaugh
Natural rubber (latex solids)	*Hevea brasiliensis*

Function: Masticatory substance in chewing gum base
Packaging and Storage: Store in well-closed containers.

IMPURITIES
Inorganic Impurities
- **Arsenic,** *Arsenic Limit Test,* Appendix IIIB
  Analysis: Prepare a sample solution as directed under *Sample Solution for Arsenic Limit Test,* Appendix IV.
  Acceptance criteria: NMT 3 mg/kg
- **Lead,** *Sample Solution for Lead Limit Test,* Appendix IV
  Acceptance criteria: NMT 3 mg/kg

SPECIFIC TESTS
- **Procedure**
  The following specifications, where applicable, should conform to the representations of the vendor (*Cleanliness, Color, Texture, Odor,* and *Loss on Drying*).

Menhaden Oil, Hydrogenated

First Published: Prior to FCC 6

HMO
FHMO
PHMO

CAS: [8016-14-6]
UNII: 736VD7888J [hydrogenated menhaden oil]

DESCRIPTION
Menhaden Oil, Hydrogenated occurs as an opaque, white solid or semisolid. It belongs to a family of products obtained from menhaden fish, *Brevoortia* sp. (Fam. Clupeidae). It is available as a partially hydrogenated and as a fully hydrogenated product. It is rich in long-chain fatty acids.
Function: Coating agent; crystal stabilizer; used as a blend with other fats and oils
Packaging and Storage: Store in well-closed containers.

IDENTIFICATION
- **Fatty Acid Composition,** Appendix VII
  [NOTE—Menhaden oil can be differentiated from animal fats and vegetable oils by the distinctive significant amount of long-chain C20 and C22 fatty acids.]
  Acceptance criteria: A sample exhibits the following composition profile of fatty acids:

Partially Hydrogenated Menhaden Oil:

Fatty Acid	Weight % Range
<12	Tr[1]
12:0	Tr
14:0	8 – 12
16:0	20 – 30
16:1	5 – 15
18:0	5 – 18
18:1	Tr – 13
18:2	Tr – 4
18:3	Tr
20:0	Tr – 15
20:1	Tr – 10
20:p[2]	Tr – 10
22:0	8 – 12
22:1	Tr – 6
22:p	Tr – 10

[1] Tr indicates trace.
[2] p indicates dienes and higher unsaturation.

Fully Hydrogenated Menhaden Oil:

Fatty Acid	Weight % Range
<12	Tr
12:0	Tr
14:0	8 – 12
16:0	30 – 35
16:1	Tr – 2
18:0	18 – 21
18:1	Tr – 2
18:2	Tr – 1
20:0	14 – 18
20:1	Tr – 2
20:p	Tr
22:0	10 – 12
22:1	Tr – 3
22:p	Tr

IMPURITIES
Inorganic Impurities
[NOTE—The atomic absorption spectrophotometric graphite furnace methods for arsenic, lead, mercury, and nickel in this monograph were developed at the National Marine Fisheries Service (NMFS) Southeast Fisheries Science

Center, Charleston Laboratory, for the determination of these trace element contaminants in materials derived from fish oil. This method is intended for the quantitation of arsenic, lead, mercury, and nickel in marine oils at levels as low as 0.10 µg/g for arsenic and for lead and as low as 0.50 µg/g for mercury and for nickel.]

- **ARSENIC**

  Apparatus

  Sample digestion: Use a microwave oven (CEM Model MDS-2100, or equivalent) equipped with advanced composite vessels with 100-mL Teflon liners. Use rupture membranes to vent vessels should the pressure exceed 125 psi. The vessels fit into a turntable, and each vessel can be vented into an overflow container. Equip the microwave oven with an exhaust tube to ventilate fumes.

  Sample analysis: Use a suitable graphite furnace atomic absorption spectrophotometer (GFAAS) equipped with an autosampler, pyrolytically coated graphite tubes, solid pyrolytic graphite platforms, and an adequate means of background correction. This method was developed using a Perkin-Elmer Model 5100, HGA-600 furnace, and an AS-60 autosampler with Zeeman effect background correction. An electrodeless discharge lamp serves as the source, argon as the purge gas, and air as the alternate gas. Set up the instrument according to manufacturer's specifications, with consideration of current good GFAAS practices. The instrument parameters are as follows:

  Wavelength: 193.7 nm
  Lamp current: 300 (EDL) modulated
  Pyrolysis: 1000°
  Atomization: 2400°
  Slit: 0.7
  Characteristic mass: 15 pg

  Glassware: Acid wash all glass, Teflon, and plastic vessels by soaking them in a nitric acid bath containing a 4:1 solution of water:nitric acid. [CAUTION—Wear a full face shield and protective clothing and gloves at all times when working with acid baths.] After acid soaking, rinse acid-washed items in deionized water, dry them, and store them in clean, covered cabinets.

  Calibration standard stock solution: 100 µg/L Prepare from a suitable standard, which may be purchased [accuracy certified against National Institute of Standards and Technology (NIST) spectrometric standard solutions].

  Calibration standard solutions: 2.0, 5.0, 10.0, 25.0, and 50.0 µg/L in 2% nitric acid; from the *Calibration standard stock solution*

  1% Palladium stock solution: Mix 1 g of ultrapure palladium metal, with 20 mL water and 10 mL nitric acid in a Teflon beaker, and warm the solution on a hot plate to dissolve the palladium. Allow the solution to cool to room temperature, transfer it into a 100-mL volumetric flask, and dilute to volume with deionized water.

  1% Magnesium nitrate stock solution: Mix 1 g of ultrapure magnesium nitrate, with 40 mL water and 1 mL nitric acid in a Teflon beaker, and warm the solution on a hot plate to dissolve. Allow the solution to cool to room temperature, transfer it into a 100-mL volumetric flask, and dilute to volume with deionized water.

  [NOTE—Because of the difficulty in preparing matrix modifier stock solutions with the required purity, purchasing modifier stock solutions and using them to prepare working modifier solutions is recommended. A palladium (0.3%) and magnesium nitrate (0.2%) solution may be purchased from High Purity Standards, or equivalent.]

  Modifier working solution: Transfer 3 mL of *1% Palladium stock solution* and 2 mL *1% Magnesium nitrate stock solution* to a 10-mL volumetric flask and dilute to volume with 2% nitric acid. A volume of 5 µL provides 0.015 mg of palladium and 0.01 mg of magnesium nitrate.

  Sample solution: [CAUTION—Wear proper eye protection and protective clothing and gloves during sample preparation. Closely follow the manufacturer's safety instructions for use of the microwave digestion apparatus.]

  Transfer 500 mg of sample into a Teflon digestion vessel liner. Prepare samples in duplicate. Add 15 mL of nitric acid, and swirl gently. Cover the vessels with lids, leaving the vent fitting off. Predigest overnight under a hood. Place the rupture membrane in the vent fitting, and tighten the lid. Place all vessels on the microwave oven turntable. Connect the vent tubes to the vent trap, and connect the pressure-sensing line to the appropriate vessel. Initiate a two-stage digestion procedure by heating the microwave at 15% power for 15 min followed by 25% power for 45 min. Remove the turntable of vessels from the oven, and allow the vessels to cool to room temperature (a cool water bath may be used to speed the cooling process). Vent the vessels when they reach room temperature. Remove the lids, and slowly add 2 mL of 30% hydrogen peroxide to each. Allow the reactions to subside, and seal the vessels. Return the vessels on the turntable to the microwave oven and heat for an additional 15 min at 30% power. Remove the vessels from the oven, and allow them to cool to room temperature. Transfer the cooled digests into 25-mL volumetric flasks, and dilute to volume with deionized water.

  Analysis: The graphite furnace program is as follows:
  1. Dry at 115° using a 1-s ramp, a 65-s hold, and a 300-mL/min argon flow.
  2. Char the sample at 1000° using a 1-s ramp, a 20-s hold, and a 300-mL/min air flow.
  3. Cool down and purge the air from the furnace for 10 s using a 20° set temperature and a 300-mL/min argon flow.
  4. Atomize at 2400° using a 0-s ramp and a 5-s hold with the argon flow stopped.
  5. Clean out at 2600° with a 1-s ramp and a 5-s hold.

  Use the autosampler to inject 20-µL aliquots of blanks, *Calibration standard solutions*, and *Sample solutions* and 5 µL of *Modifier working solution*. Inject each solution in duplicate, and average the results. Use peak area measurement for all quantitations. After ensuring that the furnace is clean by running a 5% nitric acid blank, check the instrument's sensitivity by running a 20-μL aliquot of the 25-μg *Calibration standard solution*. Compare the results obtained with the expected results for the equipment used, and take the necessary steps to correct any problems.

Calculate the characteristic mass. Record and track the integrated absorbance and characteristic mass for reference and quality assurance.

Inject each *Calibration standard solution* in duplicate. Use the algorithms provided in the instrument software to establish calibration curves. Recheck calibration periodically, and recalibrate if the recheck differs from the original calibration by more than 10%.

Inject the *Sample solution* in duplicate, and record the integrated absorbance. If the instrument response exceeds that of the calibration curve, dilute with 5% nitric acid to bring the sample's response into the working range, and note the dilution factor (DF). All sample analyses should be blank corrected using a sample solution blank.

If a computer-based instrument is used, the data output is reported as μg/L. Calculate the concentration of arsenic, in μg/g (equivalent to mg/kg), in the original sample taken by the formula:

$$Result = (C \times DF \times V)/W$$

C = concentration (μg/L) of arsenic in the sample aliquot injected
DF = dilution factor of the *Sample solution*
V = final volume (L) of the *Sample solution*
W = weight of the sample (g) taken to prepare the *Sample solution*

[NOTE—To monitor recovery and ensure analytical accuracy for proper quality assurance, analyze blanks, spiked blanks, and a spiked oil with each digestion set.]

Acceptance criteria: NMT 0.1 mg/kg

- **LEAD**

  Apparatus
  Sample digestion: Use a microwave oven (CEM Model MDS-2100, or equivalent) equipped with advanced composite vessels with 100-mL Teflon liners. Use rupture membranes to vent vessels should the pressure exceed 125 psi. The vessels fit into a turntable, and each vessel can be vented into an overflow container. Equip the microwave oven with an exhaust tube to ventilate fumes.

  Sample analysis: See *Apparatus* in *Lead Limit Test, Atomic Absorption Spectrophotometric Graphite Furnace Method, Method I,* Appendix IIIB

  Calibration standard stock solution: 100 μg/L Prepare from a suitable standard, which may be purchased [accuracy certified against National Institute of Standards and Technology (NIST) spectrometric standard solutions].

  Calibration standard solutions: 2.0, 5.0, 10.0, 25.0, and 50.0 μg/L in 2% nitric acid; from the *Calibration standard stock solution*

10% Ammonium dihydrogen phosphate stock solution: Mix 10 g of ultrapure ammonium dihydrogen phosphate, with 40 mL water and 1 mL nitric acid to dissolve the phosphate. Dilute to 100 mL with deionized water.

1% Magnesium nitrate stock solution: Mix 1 g of ultrapure magnesium nitrate, with 40 mL water and 1 mL nitric acid in a Teflon beaker, and warm on a hot plate to dissolve the solids. Allow the solution to cool to room temperature, transfer it into a 100-mL volumetric flask, and dilute to volume with deionized water.

[NOTE—Because of the difficulty in preparing matrix modifier stock solutions with the required purity, purchasing modifier stock solutions and using them to prepare working solutions is recommended. An ammonium dihydrogen phosphate (4%) and magnesium nitrate (0.2%) solution may be purchased from High Purity Standards, or equivalent.]

Modifier working solution: Transfer 4 mL of *10% Ammonium dihydrogen phosphate stock solution* and 2 mL of *1% Magnesium nitrate stock solution* to a 10-mL volumetric flask and dilute to volume with 2% nitric acid. A volume of 5 μL provides 0.2 mg of phosphate plus 0.01 mg of magnesium nitrate.

Sample solution: Prepare as directed for *Sample solution* in the *Arsenic* test (above).

[CAUTION—Wear proper eye protection and protective clothing and gloves during sample preparation. Closely follow the manufacturer's safety instructions for use of the microwave digestion apparatus.]

Analysis: The graphite furnace program is as follows:
1. Dry at 120° using a 1-s ramp, a 55-s hold, and a 300-mL/min argon flow.
2. Char the sample at 850° using a 1-s ramp, a 30-s hold, and a 300-mL/min air flow.
3. Cool down and purge the air from the furnace for 10 s using a 20° set temperature and a 300-mL/min argon flow.
4. Atomize at 2100° using a 0-s ramp and a 5-s hold with the argon flow stopped.
5. Clean out at 2600° with a 1-s ramp and a 5-s hold.

Use the autosampler to inject 20-μL aliquots of blanks, *Calibration standard solutions*, *Sample solutions*, and 5 μL of *Modifier working solution*. Inject each solution in duplicate, and average the results. Use peak-area measurement for all quantitation. After ensuring that the furnace is clean by running a 5% nitric acid blank, check instrument sensitivity by running an aliquot of the 25-μg *calibration standard*. Compare the results obtained with the expected results for the equipment used, and take the necessary steps to correct any problems.

Calculate the characteristic mass, and record and track the integrated absorbance and characteristic mass for reference and quality assurance.

Inject each *Calibration standard solution* in duplicate. Use the algorithms provided in the instrument software to establish calibration curves. Recheck the calibration periodically and recalibrate if recheck differs from the original calibration by more than 10%.

Inject the *Sample solution* in duplicate, and record the integrated absorbance. If the instrument response exceeds that of the calibration curve, dilute with 5% nitric acid to bring the sample response into the working range, and note the dilution factor (*DF*). All sample analyses should be blank corrected using a sample solution blank.

If a computer-based instrument is used, the data output is reported as micrograms per liter. Calculate the concentration, in µg/g (equivalent to mg/kg), of lead in the original sample by the following formula:

$$\text{Result} = (C \times DF \times V)/W$$

- C = concentration (µg/L) of lead in the sample aliquot injected
- DF = dilution factor of the *Sample solution*
- V = final volume (L) of the *Sample solution*
- W = weight of the sample (g) taken to prepare the *Sample solution*

[NOTE—To monitor recovery and ensure analytical accuracy for proper quality assurance, analyze blanks, spiked blanks, and a spiked oil with each digestion set.]

Acceptance criteria: NMT 0.1 mg/kg

- **MERCURY**

  Apparatus

  Sample digestion: Use a microwave oven (CEM Model MDS-2100, or equivalent) equipped with advanced composite vessels with 100-mL Teflon liners. Use rupture membranes to vent vessels should the pressure exceed 125 psi. The vessels fit into a turntable, and each vessel can be vented into an overflow container. Equip the microwave oven with an exhaust tube to ventilate fumes.

  Sample analysis: Use a suitable atomic absorption spectrophotometer equipped with an atomic vapor assembly. This method was developed using a Perkin-Elmer Model 5100 and IL 440 Thermo Jarrell Ash atomic vapor assembly. An electrodeless discharge lamp serves as the source, with an inert gas such as argon or nitrogen as the purge gas. Set up the instrument according to manufacturer specifications. Instrument parameters are as follows:

  Wavelength: 253.6 nm
  Slit: 0.7
  Reagent setting: 5
  Gas flow: 5 to 6 L/min
  Reaction time: 0.5 min

  Glassware: Acid wash all glass, Teflon, and plastic vessels by soaking them in a nitric acid bath containing a 4:1 solution of water:nitric acid. [CAUTION—Wear a full face shield and protective clothing and gloves at all times when working with acid baths.] After acid soaking, rinse acid-washed items in deionized water, dry, and store them in clean, covered cabinets.

  Calibration standard stock solution: 200 ng/g of mercury. Prepare from a suitable standard, which may be purchased [accuracy certified against National Institute of Standards and Technology (NIST) spectrometric standard solutions].

  Calibration standard solutions: 20, 60, 100, 200, and 400 ng of mercury in 1N hydrochloric acid from the *Calibration standard stock solution*

  Reducing reagent: 5% Stannous chloride in 25% hydrochloric acid (trace-metal grade). [NOTE—Prepare daily.]

  Sample solution: Prepare as directed for *Sample solution* in the Arsenic test (above).

  [CAUTION—Wear proper eye protection and protective clothing and gloves during sample preparation. Closely follow the manufacturer's safety instructions for use of the microwave digestion apparatus.]

  Analysis: Optimize the instrument settings for the spectrophotometer as described in the instrument manual. The instrument parameters for cold vapor generation are as follows:

  Wavelength: 253.6 nm
  Slit: 0.70 nm
  Reagent setting: 5
  Gas flow: 5 to 6 L/min
  Reaction time: 0.5 min

  Use a peak height integration method with a 40-s integration time and a 20-s read delay in an unheated absorption cell. Zero the instrument as follows: Place a Fleaker containing 50 mL of 1 N hydrochloric acid in the sample well of the hydride generator. Press "start" on the vapor generator and "read" on the atomic absorption spectrophotometer. The instrument will automatically flush the sample container with nitrogen, dispense the designated amount of reagent, stir the sample for a designated reaction time, and purge the head volume again with nitrogen, sweeping any vapor into the quartz cell for determination of absorption. The atomic absorption spectrophotometer will automatically zero on this sample when "autozero" is selected from the calibration menu.

  Generate a standard curve of concentration versus absorption by analyzing the five *Calibration standard solutions* prepared as described for daily standards under *Calibration standard solutions*. Analyze each solution in duplicate, generate the calibration curve, and store, using procedures specific for the instrumentation.

  Transfer an appropriate aliquot of *Sample solution* (usually 2 mL) in a Fleaker containing 50 mL of 1 N hydrochloric acid. Analyze solutions in duplicate using the procedure specified in the instrument manual. Using the calibration algorithm provided in the instrument software, calculate and report the mercury concentration in nanograms of mercury in the aliquot analyzed.

  Calculate the level of mercury as µg/g (equivalent to mg/kg), in the original sample by the formula:

  $$\text{Result} = (A \times DF)/(W \times 1000)$$

A = amount of mercury (ng) in the aliquot analyzed
DF = dilution factor (final volume of *Sample solution*/volume taken for analysis)
W = weight of the sample (g) taken to prepare the *Sample solution*

[NOTE—To monitor recovery and ensure analytical accuracy for proper quality assurance, analyze blanks, spiked blanks, and a spiked oil with each digestion set.]

Acceptance criteria: NMT 0.5 mg/kg

- **NICKEL**

  Apparatus

  Sample digestion: Use a microwave oven (CEM Model MDS-2100, or equivalent) equipped with advanced composite vessels with 100-mL Teflon liners. Use rupture membranes to vent vessels should the pressure exceed 125 psi. The vessels fit into a turntable, and each vessel can be vented into an overflow container. Equip the microwave oven with an exhaust tube to ventilate fumes.

  Sample analysis: Use a suitable graphite furnace atomic absorption spectrophotometer equipped with an autosampler, pyrolytically coated graphite tubes, solid pyrolytic graphite platforms, and an adequate means of background correction. This method was developed using a Perkin-Elmer Model 5100, HGA-600, furnace and an AS-60 autosampler with Zeeman effect background correction. A single-element, hollow-cathode lamp serves as the source, argon as the purge gas, and air as the alternate gas. Set up the instruments according to manufacturer specifications, with consideration of current good GFAAS practices. Instrument parameters are as follows:

  Wavelength: 232.0 nm
  Slit: 0.2
  Lamp current: 25 ma
  Pyrolysis: 1400°
  Characteristic mass: 13 pg
  Atomization: 2500°

  Glassware: Acid wash all glass, Teflon, and plastic vessels by soaking them in a nitric acid bath containing a 4:1 solution of water:nitric acid. [**CAUTION**—Wear a full face shield and protective clothing and gloves at all times when working with acid baths.] After acid soaking, rinse acid-washed items in deionized water, dry, and store them in clean, covered cabinets.

  Calibration standard stock solution: 100 µg/L Prepare from a suitable standard, which may be purchased [accuracy certified against National Institute of Standards and Technology (NIST) spectrometric standard solutions].

  Calibration standard solutions: 2.0, 5.0, 10.0, 25.0, and 50.0 µg/L in 2% nitric acid; from the *Calibration standard stock solution*

  Sample solution: Prepare as directed for *Sample solution* in the *Arsenic* test (above).

  [**CAUTION**—Wear proper eye protection and protective clothing and gloves during sample preparation. Closely follow the manufacturer's safety instructions for use of the microwave digestion apparatus.]

  Analysis: The graphite furnace program is as follows:
  1. Dry at 120° using a 1-s ramp, a 50-s hold, and a 300-mL/min argon flow.
  2. Char the sample at 1400° using a 1-s ramp, a 20-s hold, and a 300-mL/min air flow.
  3. Cool down, and purge the air from the furnace for 15 s using a 20° set temperature and a 300-mL/min argon flow.
  4. Atomize at 2500° using a 0-s ramp and a 5-s hold with the argon flow stopped.
  5. Clean out at 2600° with a 1-s ramp and a 5-s hold.

  Use the autosampler to inject 20-µL aliquots of blanks, calibration standards, and sample solutions. Inject each solution in duplicate, and average the results. Use the peak area measurement for all quantitations. After ensuring that the furnace is clean by running a 5% nitric acid blank, check instrument sensitivity by running a 20-µL aliquot of the 25-µg *calibration standard solution*. Compare the results obtained with the expected results for the equipment used, and take the necessary steps to correct any problems. Calculate the characteristic mass. Record and track the integrated absorbance and characteristic mass for reference and quality assurance.

  Inject each of the *Calibration standard solutions* in duplicate. Use the algorithm provided in the instrument software to establish calibration curves. Recheck the calibration periodically, and recalibrate if the recheck differs from the original calibration by more than 10%.

  Inject the *Sample solution* in duplicate, and record the integrated absorbance. If the instrument response exceeds that of the calibration curve, dilute with 5% nitric acid to bring the sample response into the working range, and note the dilution factor (*DF*). All sample analyses should be blank corrected using the sample solution blank.

  If a computer-based instrument is used, the data output is reported as micrograms per liter. Calculate the concentration of nickel, in µg/g (equivalent to mg/kg) in the original sample taken by the formula:

  $$\text{Result} = C \times DF \times V/W$$

  C = concentration (µg/L) of nickel in the sample aliquot injected
  DF = dilution factor of the *Sample solution*
  V = volume (L) of the final *Sample solution*
  W = weight of the sample (g) taken to prepare the *Sample solution*

  [NOTE—To monitor recovery and ensure analytical accuracy for proper quality assurance, analyze blanks, spiked blanks, and a spiked oil with each digestion set.]

  Acceptance criteria: NMT 0.5 mg/kg

Organic Impurities
- **FREE FATTY ACIDS (AS OLEIC ACID),** Appendix VII
  Analysis: Determine as directed. Use the following equivalence factor (e) in the formula:

  Free fatty acids as oleic acid, e = 28.2

  Acceptance criteria: NMT 0.1%

SPECIFIC TESTS
- **IODINE NUMBER,** *Iodine Determination,* Appendix VII
  Acceptance criteria
    Partially hydrogenated: Between 11 and 119
    Fully hydrogenated: NMT 10
- **PEROXIDE VALUE,** Appendix VII
  Acceptance criteria: NMT 5 mEq/kg
- **SAPONIFICATION VALUE,** Appendix VII
  Acceptance criteria: Between 180 and 200
- **UNSAPONIFIABLE MATTER,** Appendix VII
  Acceptance criteria: NMT 1.5%

OTHER REQUIREMENTS
- **LABELING:** Label to indicate whether it is *Fully Hydrogenated Menhaden Oil* or *Partially Hydrogenated Menhaden Oil.*

Menhaden Oil, Refined

First Published: Prior to FCC 6

CAS: [8002-50-4]
UNII: 1D8HWC57D0 [menhaden oil]

DESCRIPTION
Menhaden Oil, Refined, is prepared from fish of the genus, *Brevoortia,* commonly known as menhaden, by cooking, pressing, and refining. Winterization may separate the oil and produce a solid fraction.
Function: A source of long-chain (greater than C18) ω-3 polyunsaturated fatty acids. It is used as a blend with other fats and oils.
Packaging and Storage: Store in well-closed containers.

IDENTIFICATION
- **FATTY ACID COMPOSITION,** Appendix VII
  [NOTE—Menhaden oil can be differentiated from animal fats and vegetable oils by the distinctive significant amount of long-chain C20 and C22 fatty acids.]
  Acceptance criteria: A sample exhibits the following composition profile of fatty acids:
  Partially Hydrogenated Menhaden Oil:

Fatty Acid	Weight % Range
<12	Tr[1]
12:0	Tr
14:0	7–11
16:0	12–31
16:1	7–13
16:p[2]	4–5
18:0	2–5
18:1	9–11
18:p	6–9
20:0	Tr
20:1	1–2
20:4	1.5–2.5
20:5	11–14
22:0	Tr
22:1	Tr
22:5	1–3
22:6	7–11

[1] Tr indicates trace.
[2] p indicates dienes and higher unsaturation.

IMPURITIES
[NOTE—The atomic absorption spectrophotometric graphite furnace methods for arsenic, lead, mercury, and nickel in this monograph were developed at the National Marine Fisheries Service (NMFS) Southeast Fisheries Science Center, Charleston Laboratory, for the determination of these trace element contaminants in materials derived from fish oil. This method is intended for the quantitation of arsenic, lead, mercury, and nickel in marine oils at levels as low as 0.10 μg/g for arsenic and for lead and as low as 0.50 μg/g for mercury and for nickel.]

Inorganic Impurities
- **ARSENIC**
  Apparatus
  Sample digestion: Use a microwave oven (CEM Model MDS-2100, or equivalent) equipped with advanced composite vessels with 100-mL Teflon liners. Use rupture membranes to vent vessels should the pressure exceed 125 psi. The vessels fit into a turntable, and each vessel can be vented into an overflow container. Equip the microwave oven with an exhaust tube to ventilate fumes.
  Sample analysis: Use a suitable graphite furnace atomic absorption spectrophotometer (GFAAS) equipped with an autosampler, pyrolytically coated graphite tubes, solid pyrolytic graphite platforms, and an adequate means of background correction. This method was developed using a Perkin-Elmer Model 5100, HGA-600 furnace, and an AS-60 autosampler with Zeeman effect background correction. An electrodeless discharge lamp serves as the source, argon as the purge gas, and air as the alternate gas. Set up the instrument according to manufacturers' specifications, with consideration of current good GFAAS practices. The instrument parameters are as follows:
  Wavelength: 193.7 nm
  Lamp current: 300 (EDL) modulated
  Pyrolysis: 1000°
  Atomization: 2400°

Slit: 0.7
Characteristic mass: 15 pg

Glassware: Acid wash all glass, Teflon, and plastic vessels by soaking them in a nitric acid bath containing a 4:1 solution of water:nitric acid. [**CAUTION**—Wear a full face shield and protective clothing and gloves at all times when working with acid baths.] After acid soaking, rinse acid-washed items in deionized water, dry them, and store them in clean, covered cabinets.

Calibration standard stock solution: 100 µg/L of arsenic; Prepare from a suitable standard, which may be purchased [accuracy certified against National Institute of Standards and Technology (NIST) spectrometric standard solutions].

Calibration standard solutions: 2.0, 5.0, 10.0, 25.0, and 50.0 µg/L in 2% nitric acid; from the *Calibration standard stock solution*

1% Palladium stock solution: Mix 1 g of ultrapure palladium metal, with 20 mL water and 10 mL nitric acid in a Teflon beaker, and warm the solution on a hot plate to dissolve the palladium. Allow the solution to cool to room temperature, transfer it into a 100-mL volumetric flask, and dilute to volume with deionized water.

1% Magnesium nitrate stock solution: Mix 1 g of ultrapure magnesium nitrate, with 40 mL water and 1 mL nitric acid in a Teflon beaker, and warm the solution on a hot plate to dissolve. Allow the solution to cool to room temperature, transfer it into a 100-mL volumetric flask, and dilute to volume with deionized water.

[NOTE—Because of the difficulty in preparing matrix modifier stock solutions with the required purity, purchasing modifier stock solutions and using them to prepare working modifier solutions is recommended. A palladium (0.3%) and magnesium nitrate (0.2%) solution may be purchased from High Purity Standards, or equivalent.]

Modifier working solution: Transfer 3 mL of *1% Palladium stock solution* and 2 mL *1% Magnesium nitrate stock solution* to a 10-mL volumetric flask and dilute to volume with 2% nitric acid. A volume of 5 µL provides 0.015 mg of palladium and 0.01 mg of magnesium nitrate.

Sample solution: [**CAUTION**—Wear proper eye protection and protective clothing and gloves during sample preparation. Closely follow the manufacturer's safety instructions for use of the microwave digestion apparatus.]

Transfer 500 mg of sample into a Teflon digestion vessel liner. Prepare samples in duplicate. Add 15 mL of nitric acid, and swirl gently. Cover the vessels with lids, leaving the vent fitting off. Predigest overnight under a hood. Place the rupture membrane in the vent fitting, and tighten the lid. Place all vessels on the microwave oven turntable. Connect the vent tubes to the vent trap, and connect the pressure-sensing line to the appropriate vessel. Initiate a two-stage digestion procedure by heating the microwave at 15% power for 15 min followed by 25% power for 45 min. Remove the turntable of vessels from the oven, and allow the vessels to cool to room temperature (a cool water bath may be used to speed the cooling process). Vent the vessels when they reach room temperature. Remove the lids, and slowly add 2 mL of 30% hydrogen peroxide to each. Allow the reactions to subside, and seal the vessels. Return the vessels on the turntable to the microwave oven and heat for an additional 15 min at 30% power. Remove the vessels from the oven, and allow them to cool to room temperature. Transfer the cooled digests into 25-mL volumetric flasks, and dilute to volume with deionized water.

Analysis: The graphite furnace program is as follows:
1. Dry at 115° using a 1-s ramp, a 65-s hold, and a 300-mL/min argon flow.
2. Char the sample at 1000° using a 1-s ramp, a 20-s hold, and a 300-mL/min air flow.
3. Cool down and purge the air from the furnace for 10 s using a 20° set temperature and a 300-mL/min argon flow.
4. Atomize at 2400° using a 0-s ramp and a 5-s hold with the argon flow stopped.
5. Clean out at 2600° with a 1-s ramp and a 5-s hold.

Use the autosampler to inject 20-µL aliquots of blanks, *Calibration standard solutions*, and *Sample solutions* and 5 µL of *Modifier working solution*. Inject each solution in duplicate, and average the results. Use peak area measurement for all quantitations. After ensuring that the furnace is clean by running a 5% nitric acid blank, check the instrument's sensitivity by running a 20-µL aliquot of the 25-µg *Calibration standard solution*. Compare the results obtained with the expected results for the equipment used, and take the necessary steps to correct any problems.

Calculate the characteristic mass. Record and track the integrated absorbance and characteristic mass for reference and quality assurance.

Inject each *Calibration standard solution* in duplicate. Use the algorithms provided in the instrument software to establish calibration curves. Recheck calibration periodically, and recalibrate if the recheck differs from the original calibration by more than 10%.

Inject the *Sample solution* in duplicate, and record the integrated absorbance. If the instrument response exceeds that of the calibration curve, dilute with 5% nitric acid to bring the sample's response into the working range, and note the dilution factor (DF). All sample analyses should be blank corrected using a sample solution blank.

If a computer-based instrument is used, the data output is reported as µg/L. Calculate the concentration of arsenic, in µg/g (equivalent to mg/kg), in the original sample taken by the formula:

$$\text{Result} = (C \times DF \times V)/W$$

C = concentration (µg/L) of arsenic in the sample aliquot injected
DF = dilution factor of the *Sample solution*
V = final volume (L) of the *Sample solution*

W = weight (g) of the sample taken to prepare the *Sample solution*

[NOTE—To monitor recovery and ensure analytical accuracy for proper quality assurance, analyze blanks, spiked blanks, and a spiked oil with each digestion set.]

Acceptance criteria: NMT 0.1 mg/kg

- **LEAD**

  Apparatus

  Sample digestion: Use a microwave oven (CEM Model MDS-2100, or equivalent) equipped with advanced composite vessels with 100-mL Teflon liners. Use rupture membranes to vent vessels should the pressure exceed 125 psi. The vessels fit into a turntable, and each vessel can be vented into an overflow container. Equip the microwave oven with an exhaust tube to ventilate fumes.

  Sample analysis: See *Apparatus* in *Lead Limit Test, Atomic Absorption Spectrophotometric Graphite Furnace Method, Method I,* Appendix IIIB

  Calibration standard stock solution: 100 µg/L of lead; Prepare from a suitable standard, which may be purchased [accuracy certified against National Institute of Standards and Technology (NIST) spectrometric standard solutions].

  Calibration standard solutions: 2.0, 5.0, 10.0, 25.0, and 50.0 µg/L in 2% nitric acid; from the *Calibration standard stock solution*

  10% Ammonium dihydrogen phosphate stock solution: Mix 10 g of ultrapure ammonium dihydrogen phosphate, with 40 mL water and 1 mL nitric acid to dissolve the phosphate. Dilute to 100 mL with deionized water.

  1% Magnesium nitrate stock solution: Mix 1 g of ultrapure magnesium nitrate, with 40 mL water and 1 mL nitric acid in a Teflon beaker, and warm on a hot plate to dissolve the solids. Allow the solution to cool to room temperature, transfer it into a 100-mL volumetric flask, and dilute to volume with deionized water.

  [NOTE—Because of the difficulty in preparing matrix modifier stock solutions with the required purity, purchasing modifier stock solutions and using them to prepare working solutions is recommended. An ammonium dihydrogen phosphate (4%) and magnesium nitrate (0.2%) solution may be purchased from High Purity Standards, or equivalent.]

  Modifier working solution: Transfer 4 mL of *10% Ammonium dihydrogen phosphate stock solution* and 2 mL of *1% Magnesium nitrate stock solution* to a 10-mL volumetric flask and dilute to volume with 2% nitric acid. A volume of 5 µL provides 0.2 mg of phosphate plus 0.01 mg of magnesium nitrate.

  Sample solution: Prepare as directed for *Sample solution* in the *Arsenic* test (above).

  [CAUTION—Wear proper eye protection and protective clothing and gloves during sample preparation. Closely follow the manufacturer's safety instructions for use of the microwave digestion apparatus.]

  Analysis: The graphite furnace program is as follows:

  1. Dry at 120° using a 1-s ramp, a 55-s hold, and a 300-mL/min argon flow.
  2. Char the sample at 850° using a 1-s ramp, a 30-s hold, and a 300-mL/min air flow.
  3. Cool down and purge the air from the furnace for 10 s using a 20° set temperature and a 300-mL/min argon flow.
  4. Atomize at 2100° using a 0-s ramp and a 5-s hold with the argon flow stopped.
  5. Clean out at 2600° with a 1-s ramp and a 5-s hold.

  Use the autosampler to inject 20-µL aliquots of blanks, *Calibration standard solutions, Sample solutions,* and 5 µL of *Modifier working solution*. Inject each solution in duplicate, and average the results. Use peak-area measurement for all quantitation. After ensuring that the furnace is clean by running a 5% nitric acid blank, check instrument sensitivity by running an aliquot of the 25 µg calibration standard. Compare the results obtained with the expected results for the equipment used, and take the necessary steps to correct any problems.

  Calculate the characteristic mass, and record and track the integrated absorbance and characteristic mass for reference and quality assurance.

  Inject each *Calibration standard solution* in duplicate. Use the algorithms provided in the instrument software to establish calibration curves. Recheck the calibration periodically and recalibrate if recheck differs from the original calibration by more than 10%.

  Inject the *Sample solution* in duplicate, and record the integrated absorbance. If the instrument response exceeds that of the calibration curve, dilute with 5% nitric acid to bring the sample response into the working range, and note the dilution factor (DF). All sample analyses should be blank corrected using a sample solution blank.

  If a computer-based instrument is used, the data output is reported as micrograms per liter. Calculate the concentration, in µg/g (equivalent to mg/kg), of lead in the original sample by the following formula:

  $$\text{Result} = (C \times DF \times V)/W$$

  C = concentration (µg/L) of lead in the sample aliquot injected
  DF = dilution factor of the *Sample solution*
  V = final volume (L) of the *Sample solution*
  W = weight (g) of the sample taken to prepare the *Sample solution*

  [NOTE—To monitor recovery and ensure analytical accuracy for proper quality assurance, analyze blanks, spiked blanks, and a spiked oil with each digestion set.]

  Acceptance criteria: NMT 0.1 mg/kg

- **MERCURY**

  Apparatus

  Sample digestion: Use a microwave oven (CEM Model MDS-2100, or equivalent) equipped with advanced composite vessels with 100-mL Teflon liners. Use rupture membranes to vent vessels should the pressure exceed 125 psi. The vessels fit into a turntable, and each vessel can be vented into an overflow container. Equip the microwave oven with an exhaust tube to ventilate fumes.

Sample analysis: Use a suitable atomic absorption spectrophotometer equipped with an atomic vapor assembly. This method was developed using a Perkin-Elmer Model 5100 and IL 440 Thermo Jarrell Ash atomic vapor assembly. An electrodeless discharge lamp serves as the source, with an inert gas such as argon or nitrogen as the purge gas. Set up the instrument according to manufacturer specifications. Instrument parameters are as follows:
  Wavelength: 253.6 nm
  Slit: 0.7
  Reagent setting: 5
  Gas flow: 5 to 6 L/min
  Reaction time: 0.5 min

Glassware: Acid wash all glass, Teflon, and plastic vessels by soaking them in a nitric acid bath containing a 4:1 solution of water:nitric acid. [CAUTION—Wear a full face shield and protective clothing and gloves at all times when working with acid baths.] After acid soaking, rinse acid-washed items in deionized water, dry, and store them in clean, covered cabinets.

Calibration standard stock solution: 200 ng/g of mercury; Prepare from a suitable standard, which may be purchased [accuracy certified against National Institute of Standards and Technology (NIST) spectrometric standard solutions].

Calibration standard solutions: 20, 60, 100, 200, and 400 ng of mercury in 1N hydrochloric acid; from the *Calibration standard stock solution*

Reducing reagent: 5% stannous chloride in 25% hydrochloric acid (trace-metal grade). [NOTE—Prepare daily.]

Sample solution: Prepare as directed for *Sample solution* in the *Arsenic* test (above).
  [CAUTION—Wear proper eye protection and protective clothing and gloves during sample preparation. Closely follow the manufacturer's safety instructions for use of the microwave digestion apparatus.]

Analysis: Optimize the instrument settings for the spectrophotometer as described in the instrument manual. The instrument parameters for cold vapor generation are as follows:
Wavelength: 253.6 nm
Slit: 0.70 nm
Reagent setting: 5
Gas flow: 5 to 6 L/min
Reaction time: 0.5 min

Use a peak height integration method with a 40-s integration time and a 20-s read delay in an unheated absorption cell. Zero the instrument as follows: Place a Fleaker containing 50 mL of 1 N hydrochloric acid in the sample well of the hydride generator. Press "start" on the vapor generator and "read" on the atomic absorption spectrophotometer. The instrument will automatically flush the sample container with nitrogen, dispense the designated amount of reagent, stir the sample for a designated reaction time, and purge the head volume again with nitrogen, sweeping any vapor into the quartz cell for determination of absorption. The atomic absorption spectrophotometer will automatically zero on this sample when "autozero" is selected from the calibration menu.

Generate a standard curve of concentration versus absorption by analyzing the five *Calibration standard solutions* prepared as described for daily standards under *Calibration standard solutions*. Analyze each solution in duplicate, generate the calibration curve, and store, using procedures specific for the instrumentation.

Transfer an appropriate aliquot of *Sample solution* (usually 2 mL) in a Fleaker containing 50 mL of 1 N hydrochloric acid. Analyze solutions in duplicate using the procedure specified in the instrument manual. Using the calibration algorithm provided in the instrument software, calculate and report the mercury concentration in nanograms of mercury in the aliquot analyzed.

Calculate the level of mercury as µg/g (equivalent to mg/kg), in the original sample by the formula:

$$\text{Result} = (A \times DF)/(W \times 1000)$$

A = amount of mercury (ng) in the aliquot analyzed
DF = dilution factor (final volume of *Sample solution*/volume taken for analysis)
W = weight of the sample (g) taken to prepare the *Sample solution*

[NOTE—To monitor recovery and ensure analytical accuracy for proper quality assurance, analyze blanks, spiked blanks, and a spiked oil with each digestion set.]

Acceptance criteria: NMT 0.5 mg/kg

Organic Impurities
- **FREE FATTY ACIDS (AS OLEIC ACID),** Appendix VII
  Analysis: Determine as directed. Use the following equivalence factor (e) in the formula:

  Free fatty acids as oleic acid, e = 28.2.

  Acceptance criteria: NMT 0.1%

SPECIFIC TESTS
- **IODINE NUMBER,** *Iodine Determination,* Appendix VII
  Acceptance criteria: NLT 120
- **PEROXIDE VALUE,** Appendix VII
  Acceptance criteria: NMT 5 mEq/kg
- **SAPONIFICATION VALUE,** Appendix VII
  Acceptance criteria: Between 180 and 200
- **UNSAPONIFIABLE MATTER,** Appendix VII
  Acceptance criteria: NMT 1.5%

Mentha Arvensis Oil, Partially Dementholized

First Published: Prior to FCC 6

Cornmint Oil, Partially Dementholized

CAS: [68917-18-0]

DESCRIPTION
Mentha Arvensis Oil, Partially Dementholized occurs as a colorless to yellow liquid with a characteristic minty odor. It is the portion of oil remaining after the partial removal of menthol, by freezing operations only, from the oil of *Mentha arvensis* var. *piperascens* Holmes (forma piperascens Malinvaud) (Fam. Lamiaceae). It is soluble in most fixed oils, in mineral oil, and in propylene glycol. It is insoluble in glycerin.

Function: Flavoring agent

Packaging and Storage: Store in a cool place protected from light in full, tight containers.

IDENTIFICATION
- **INFRARED SPECTRA,** *Spectrophotometric Identification Tests,* Appendix IIIC

  Acceptance criteria: The spectrum of the sample exhibits relative maxima (that may vary in intensity) at the same wavelengths as those of the spectrum below.

ASSAY
- **TOTAL ALCOHOLS,** Appendix VI

  Sample: 1.5 g of the acetylated oil

  Analysis: Calculate the percentage of alcohol, as menthol, in the sample by the formula:

  $$\text{Result} = A \times 7.813(1 - 0.0021E)/(B - 0.021A)$$

  A = amount (mL) of 0.5 N alcoholic potassium hydroxide consumed in the saponification

  E = percentage of esters, as menthyl acetate determined as directed under *Total Esters* (below)

  B = weight (g) of the acetylated oil taken

  Acceptance criteria: NLT 40.0% and NMT 60.0% of total alcohols, calculated as menthol ($C_{10}H_{20}O$)

SPECIFIC TESTS
- **ANGULAR ROTATION,** *Optical (Specific) Rotation,* Appendix IIB: Use a 100-mm tube.

  Acceptance criteria: Between −30° and −10°

- **REFRACTIVE INDEX,** Appendix IIB

  [NOTE—Use an Abbé or other refractometer of equal or greater accuracy.]

  Acceptance criteria: Between 1.458 and 1.465 at 20°

- **SOLUBILITY IN ALCOHOL,** Appendix VI

  Acceptance criteria: One mL of sample dissolves in 2.5 to 4 mL of 80% alcohol, and can become hazy on further dilution.

- **SPECIFIC GRAVITY:** Determine by any reliable method (see *General Provisions*).

  Acceptance criteria: Between 0.888 and 0.908

- **TOTAL ESTERS,** *Esters, Ester Determination,* Appendix VI

  Sample: 10 g

  Analysis: Use 99.15 as the equivalence factor (e) in the calculation.

  Acceptance criteria: Between 5.0% and 20.0%, calculated as menthyl acetate ($C_{12}H_{22}O_2$)

- **TOTAL KETONES,** *Aldehydes and Ketones Hydroxylamine Method,* Appendix VI

  Sample: 1 g

  Analysis: Use 77.12 as the equivalence factor (e) in the calculation.

  Acceptance criteria: Between 30.0% and 50.0%, calculated as menthone ($C_{10}H_{18}O$)

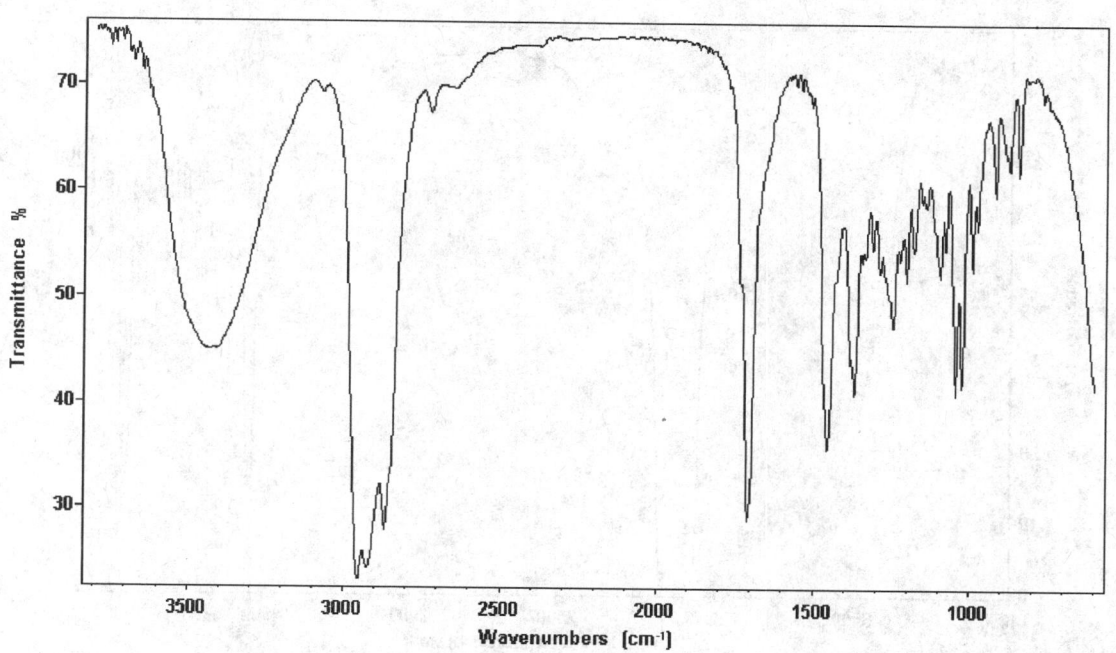

Mentha Arvensis Oil, Partially Dementholized

Menthol

First Published: Prior to FCC 6

3-*p*-Menthanol [NOTE—L-Menthol is natural or synthetic; DL-Menthol is synthetic.]

C₁₀H₂₀O
FEMA: 2665
UNII: BZ1R15MTK7 [levomenthol]
UNII: YS08XHA860 [racementhol]

Formula wt 156.27

DESCRIPTION

Menthol occurs as colorless, hexagonal crystals, usually like needles, as fused masses, or as a crystalline powder.
Odor: Peppermint
Solubility: Very soluble in alcohol, volatile oils; slightly soluble in water
Boiling Point: ~212°
Solubility in Alcohol, Appendix VI: One mL dissolves in 1 mL of 95% ethanol.
Function: Flavoring agent

IDENTIFICATION

- **INFRARED SPECTRA,** *Spectrophotometric Identification Tests,* Appendix IIIC
  Acceptance criteria: The spectrum of the sample exhibits relative maxima at the same wavelengths as those of the spectrum below.

OTHER REQUIREMENTS

- **MELTING RANGE OR TEMPERATURE DETERMINATION,** Appendix IIB: L-menthol
  Acceptance criteria: 41° to 44°
- **RESIDUE ON EVAPORATION,** *M-16,* Appendix XI
  Acceptance criteria: NMT 0.05%
- **READILY OXIDIZABLE SUBSTANCE,** *M-13,* Appendix XI (DL-menthol)
  Acceptance criteria: Passes test
- **SPECIFIC ROTATION,** Appendix IIB
  Acceptance criteria
  L-Menthol: Between −45° and −51°
  DL-Menthol: Between −2° and +2°

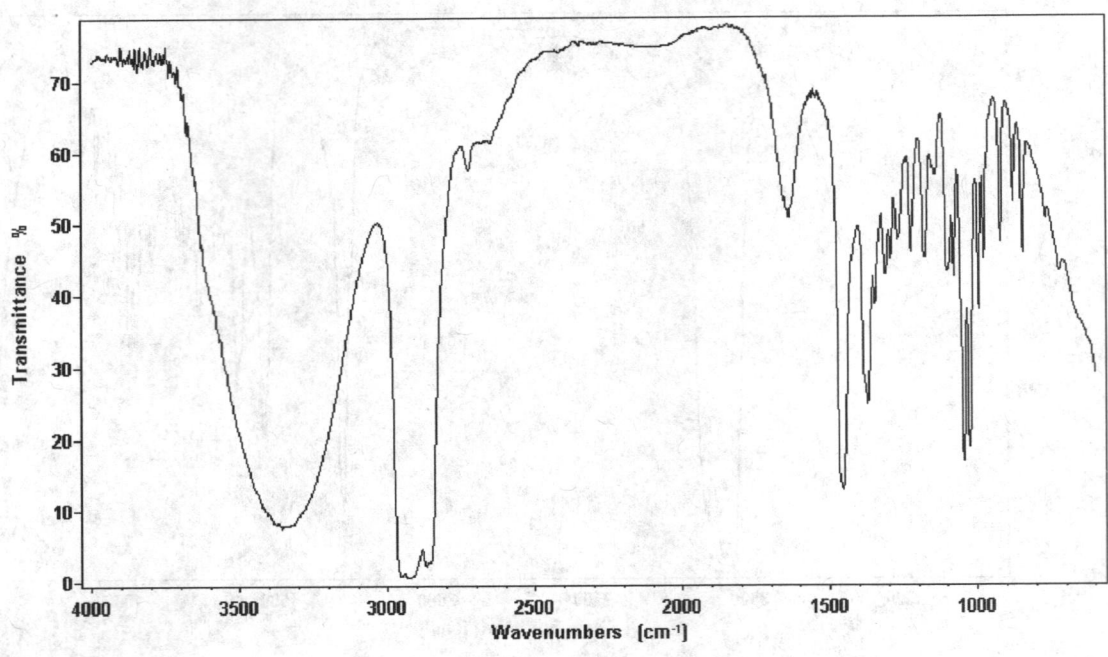

Menthol

(–)-Menthone

First Published: Prior to FCC 6
Last Revision: First Supplement, FCC 7

l-p-Menthan-3-one
l-Menthone

$C_{10}H_{18}O$ Formula wt 154.25
FEMA: 2667
UNII: 5F709W4OG4 [menthone, (-)-]

DESCRIPTION
(–)-Menthone occurs as an almost colorless liquid.
Odor: Mint
Solubility: Soluble in alcohol, most fixed oils; very slightly soluble in water
Boiling Point: ~207°
Solubility in Alcohol, Appendix VI: One mL dissolves in 1 mL of 95% ethanol.
Function: Flavoring agent

ASSAY
- **PROCEDURE:** Proceed as directed under *M-1b*, Appendix XI.
  Acceptance criteria: NLT 96.0% of $C_{10}H_{18}O$ (sum of two isomers)

SPECIFIC TESTS
- **ACID VALUE, FLAVOR CHEMICALS (OTHER THAN ESSENTIAL OILS),** *M-15,* Appendix XI
  Acceptance criteria: NMT 1.0
- **REFRACTIVE INDEX,** Appendix II: At 20°
  Acceptance criteria: Between 1.448 and 1.453
- **SPECIFIC GRAVITY:** Determine at 25° by any reliable method (see *General Provisions*).
  Acceptance criteria: Between 0.888 and 0.895

OTHER REQUIREMENTS
- **ANGULAR ROTATION,** *Optical (Specific) Rotation,* Appendix IIB: Use a 100-mm tube.
  Acceptance criteria: Between 0° and –25°

Menthyl Acetate, Racemic

First Published: Prior to FCC 6
Last Revision: First Supplement, FCC 7

dl-p-Menthan-3-yl Acetate
dl-Menthyl Acetate

$C_{12}H_{22}O_2$ Formula wt 198.31
FEMA: 2668
UNII: LF3LEI45OH [menthyl acetate, (+/-)-]

DESCRIPTION

Menthyl Acetate, Racemic occurs as a colorless liquid.
Odor: Mild, minty
Solubility: Soluble in alcohol, most fixed oils, propylene glycol; slightly soluble in glycerin, water
Boiling Point: ~228° to 229°
SOLUBILITY IN ALCOHOL, Appendix VI: One mL dissolves in 1 mL of 95% ethanol.
Function: Flavoring agent

ASSAY

- **PROCEDURE:** Proceed as directed under *M-1b*, Appendix XI.
  Acceptance criteria: NLT 97.0% of $C_{12}H_{22}O_2$ (sum of two isomers)

SPECIFIC TESTS

- **ACID VALUE, FLAVOR CHEMICALS (OTHER THAN ESSENTIAL OILS)**, *M-15*, Appendix XI
  Acceptance criteria: NMT 2.0
- **REFRACTIVE INDEX**, Appendix II: At 20°
  Acceptance criteria: Between 1.443 and 1.450
- **SPECIFIC GRAVITY:** Determine at 25° by any reliable method (see *General Provisions*).
  Acceptance criteria: Between 0.921 and 0.926

(−)-Menthyl Acetate

First Published: Prior to FCC 6
Last Revision: Third Supplement, FCC 7

l-p-Menthan-3-yl Acetate
l-Menthyl Acetate

$C_{12}H_{22}O_2$ Formula wt 198.31
FEMA: 2668
UNII: W8C5F4H1OA [menthyl acetate]

DESCRIPTION

(−)-Menthyl Acetate occurs as a colorless liquid.
Odor: Mild, minty
Solubility: Soluble in alcohol, propylene glycol, most fixed oils; slightly soluble in water
Boiling Point: ~229° to 230°
Function: Flavoring agent

ASSAY

- **PROCEDURE:** Proceed as directed under *M-1b*, Appendix XI.
  Acceptance criteria: NLT 98.0% of $C_{12}H_{22}O_2$

SPECIFIC TESTS

- **ACID VALUE, FLAVOR CHEMICALS (OTHER THAN ESSENTIAL OILS)**, *M-15*, Appendix XI
  Acceptance criteria: NMT 2.0
- **REFRACTIVE INDEX**, Appendix II: At 20°
  Acceptance criteria: 1.443–1.447
- **SPECIFIC GRAVITY:** Determine at 25° by any reliable method (see *General Provisions*).
  Acceptance criteria: 0.921–0.926

OTHER REQUIREMENTS

- **ANGULAR ROTATION**, *Optical (Specific) Rotation*, Appendix IIB: Use a 100-mm tube.
  Acceptance criteria: Between −75° and −69°

2-Mercaptopropionic Acid

First Published: Prior to FCC 6

$C_3H_6O_2S$ Formula wt 106.16
FEMA: 3180
UNII: 318OLS586D [ethyl 2-mercaptopropionate]

DESCRIPTION

2-Mercaptopropionic Acid occurs as a colorless to pale yellow liquid.
Odor: Roasted, meaty
Solubility: Miscible in water, alcohol, ether, acetone
Boiling Point: ~117°
Solubility in Alcohol, Appendix VI: One mL dissolves in 1 mL of 95% alcohol.
Function: Flavoring agent

IDENTIFICATION

- **INFRARED SPECTRA**, *Spectrophotometric Identification Tests*, Appendix IIIC
  Acceptance criteria: The spectrum of the sample exhibits relative maxima at the same wavelengths as those of the spectrum below.

ASSAY

- **PROCEDURE:** Proceed as directed under *M-3a*, Appendix XI.
  Acceptance criteria: NLT 98.0% of $C_3H_6O_2S$

SPECIFIC TESTS

- **REFRACTIVE INDEX**, Appendix II: At 20°
  Acceptance criteria: Between 1.479 and 1.484
- **SPECIFIC GRAVITY:** Determine at 25° by any reliable method (see *General Provisions*).
  Acceptance criteria: Between 1.192 and 1.200

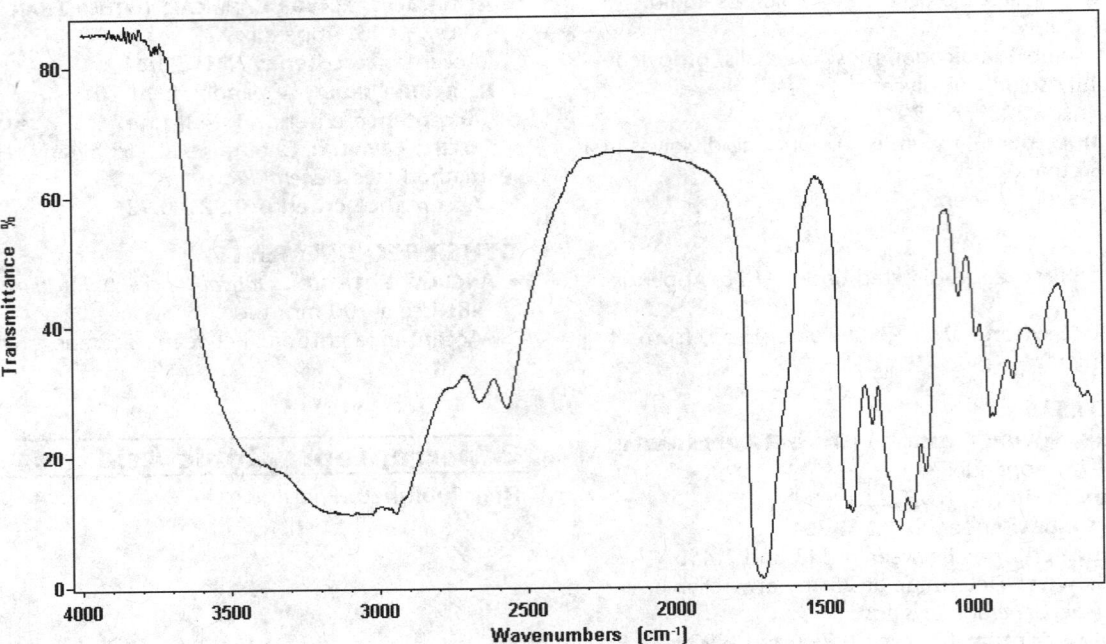

2-Mercaptopropionic Acid

DL-Methionine

First Published: Prior to FCC 6

DL-2-Amino-4-(methylthio)butyric Acid

C₅H₁₁NO₂S
UNII: 73JWT2K6T3 [racemethionine]

Formula wt 149.21
CAS: [59-51-8]

DESCRIPTION
DL-Methionine occurs as white crystalline platelets or a powder. One g dissolves in about 30 mL of water. It is soluble in dilute acids and in solutions of alkali hydroxides. It is very slightly soluble in alcohol, and practically insoluble in ether. It is optically inactive. The pH of a 1:100 aqueous solution is between 5.6 and 6.1.

Function: Nutrient

Packaging and Storage: Store in well-closed, light-resistant containers.

IDENTIFICATION
- **INFRARED SPECTRA,** *Spectrophotometric Identification Tests,* Appendix IIIC
  Sample preparation: Mineral oil mull
  Acceptance criteria: The spectrum of the sample exhibits relative maxima at the same wavelengths as those of the spectrum below.

ASSAY
- **PROCEDURE**
  Sample: 140 mg, previously dried
  Analysis: Dissolve the *Sample* in 3 mL of formic acid and 50 mL of glacial acetic acid. Titrate with 0.1 N perchloric acid, determining the end point potentiometrically. [**CAUTION**—Handle perchloric acid in an appropriate fume hood.] Perform a blank determination (see *General Provisions*) and make any necessary correction. Each mL of 0.1 N perchloric acid is equivalent to 14.92 mg of C₅H₁₁NO₂S.
  Acceptance criteria: NLT 98.5% and NMT 101.5% of C₅H₁₁NO₂S, on the dried basis

IMPURITIES
Inorganic Impurities
- **LEAD,** *Lead Limit Test,* Appendix IIIB
  Sample solution: Prepare as directed for organic compounds.
  Control: 5 µg Pb (5 mL of *Diluted Standard Lead Solution*)
  Acceptance criteria: NMT 5 mg/kg

SPECIFIC TESTS
- **LOSS ON DRYING,** Appendix IIC: 105° for 3 h
  Acceptance criteria: NMT 0.5%
- **RESIDUE ON IGNITION (SULFATED ASH),** Appendix IIC
  Sample: 1 g
  Acceptance criteria: NMT 0.1%

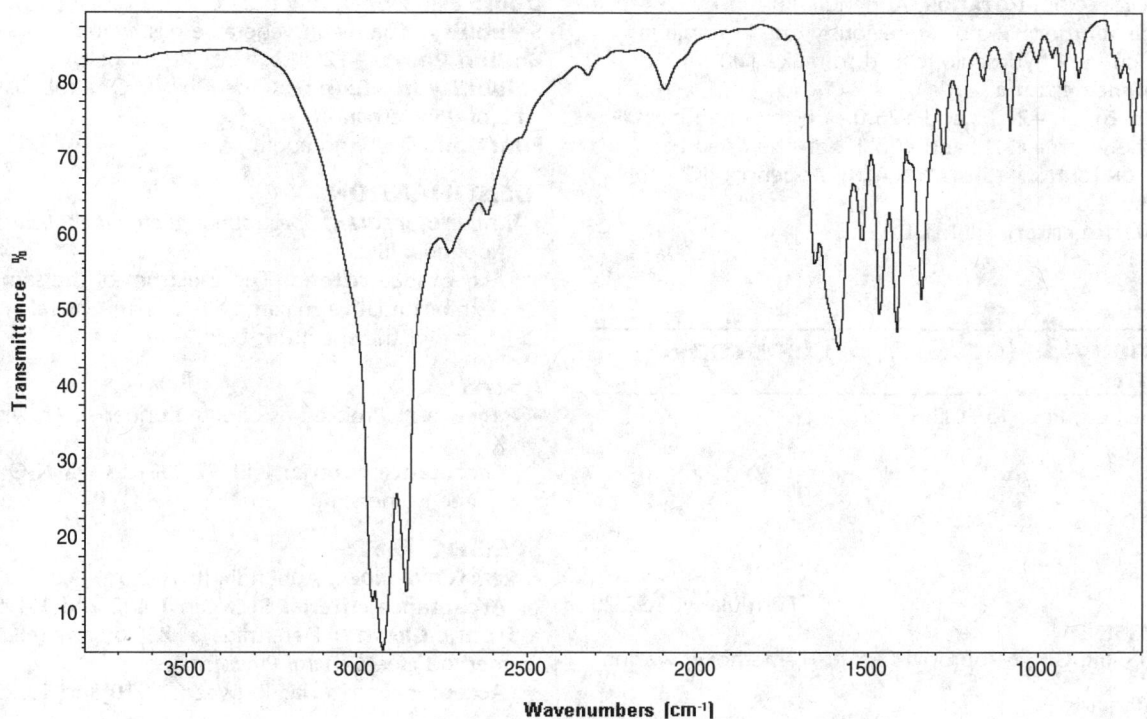

DL-Methionine (Mineral Oil Mull)

L-Methionine

First Published: Prior to FCC 6
Last Revision: FCC 7

L-2-Amino-4-(methylthio)butyric Acid

$C_5H_{11}NO_2S$ Formula wt 149.21
CAS: [63-68-3]
UNII: AE28F7PNPL [methionine]

DESCRIPTION
L-Methionine occurs as colorless or white, lustrous plates, or as a white, crystalline powder. It is soluble in water, in alkali solutions, and in dilute mineral acids; slightly soluble in alcohol; and practically insoluble in ether.
Function: Nutrient
Packaging and Storage: Store in well-closed, light-resistant containers.

IDENTIFICATION
- **INFRARED ABSORPTION**, *Spectrophotometric Identification Tests,* Appendix IIIC
  Reference standard: USP L-Methionine RS
  Sample and standard preparation: M
  Acceptance criteria: The spectrum of the sample exhibits maxima at the same wavelengths as those in the spectrum of the *Reference standard*.

ASSAY
- **PROCEDURE**
  Sample: 140 mg, previously dried
  Analysis: Dissolve the *Sample* in 3 mL of formic acid and 50 mL of glacial acetic acid. Titrate with 0.1 N perchloric acid, determining the end point potentiometrically. [**CAUTION**—Handle perchloric acid in an appropriate fume hood.] Perform a blank determination (see *General Provisions*) and make any necessary correction. Each mL of 0.1 N perchloric acid is equivalent to 14.92 mg of $C_5H_{11}NO_2S$.
  Acceptance criteria: 98.5%–101.5% of $C_5H_{11}NO_2S$, on the dried basis

IMPURITIES
Inorganic Impurities
- **LEAD**, *Lead Limit Test,* Appendix IIIB
  Sample solution: Prepare as directed for organic compounds.
  Control: 5 μg Pb (5 mL of *Diluted Standard Lead Solution*)
  Acceptance criteria: NMT 5 mg/kg

SPECIFIC TESTS
- **LOSS ON DRYING**, Appendix IIC: 105° for 3 h
  Acceptance criteria: NMT 0.5%

718 / L-Methionine / Monographs

- **OPTICAL (SPECIFIC) ROTATION**, Appendix IIB
  Sample solution: 2 g of a previously dried sample in sufficient 6 N hydrochloric acid to make 100 mL
  Acceptance criteria
  $[\alpha]_D^{20}$ between +21.0° and +25.0°, on the dried basis
  $[\alpha]_D^{25}$ between +21.1° and +25.1°, on the dried basis
- **RESIDUE ON IGNITION (SULFATED ASH)**, Appendix IIC
  Sample: 1 g
  Acceptance criteria: NMT 0.1%

2-Methoxy 3- (or 5- or 6-) Isopropyl Pyrazine

First Published: Prior to FCC 6

$C_8H_{12}N_2O$ Formula wt 152.20
FEMA: 3358
UNII: C90S36R5GY [2-isopropyl-(3,5 or 6)-methoxypyrazine]

DESCRIPTION
2-Methoxy 3- (or 5- or 6-) Isopropyl Pyrazine occurs as a colorless to pale yellow liquid.

Odor: Bell pepper, raw potato
Solubility: Soluble in vegetable oils, water
Boiling Point: ~120° to 125° (20 mm Hg)
Solubility in Alcohol, Appendix VI: One mL dissolves in 1 mL of 95% ethanol.
Function: Flavoring agent

IDENTIFICATION
- **INFRARED SPECTRA,** Spectrophotometric Identification Tests, Appendix IIIC
  Acceptance criteria: The spectrum of the sample exhibits relative maxima at the same wavelengths as those of the spectrum below.

ASSAY
- **PROCEDURE:** Proceed as directed under *M-1b,* Appendix XI.
  Acceptance criteria: NLT 97.0% of $C_8H_{12}N_2O$ (sum of three isomers)

SPECIFIC TESTS
- **REFRACTIVE INDEX,** Appendix II: At 20°
  Acceptance criteria: Between 1.492 and 1.499
- **SPECIFIC GRAVITY:** Determine at 25° by any reliable method (see *General Provisions*).
  Acceptance criteria: Between 1.010 and 1.022

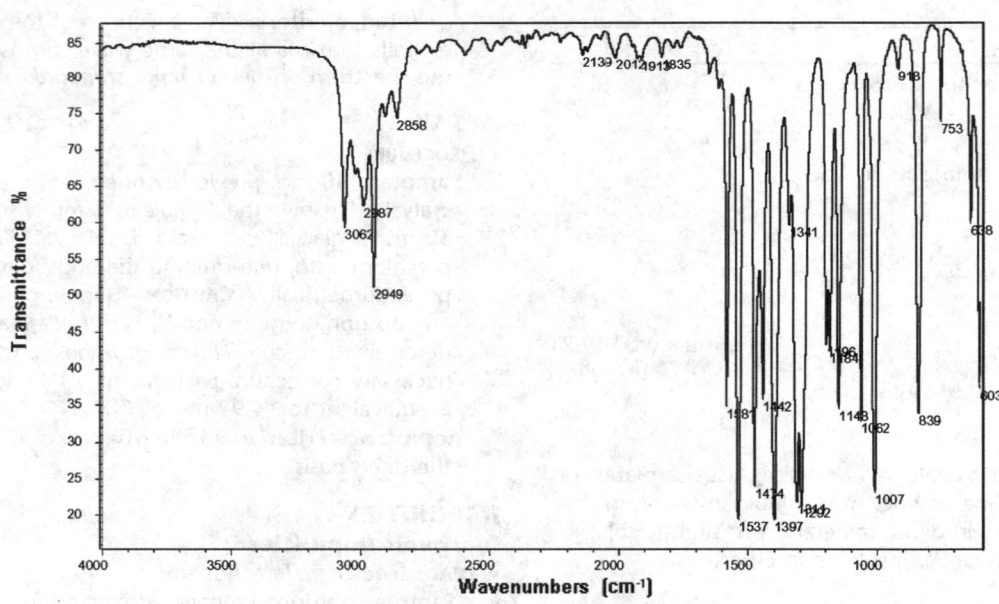

2-Methoxy 3- (or 5- or 6-) Isopropyl Pyrazine

2-Methoxy-3(5)-methylpyrazine

First Published: Prior to FCC 6

$C_6H_8N_2O$ Formula wt 124.14
FEMA: 3183
UNII: 457UQ35J2T [2-methoxy-(3,5 or 6)-methylpyrazine]

DESCRIPTION
2-Methoxy-3(5)-methylpyrazine occurs as a colorless liquid.
Odor: Roasted, hazelnut
Solubility: Soluble in organic solvents, water
Solubility in Alcohol, Appendix VI: One mL dissolves in 1 mL of 95% ethanol.
Function: Flavoring agent

IDENTIFICATION
- **INFRARED SPECTRA,** Spectrophotometric Identification Tests, Appendix IIIC
  Acceptance criteria: The spectrum of the sample exhibits relative maxima at the same wavelengths as those of the spectrum below.

ASSAY
- **PROCEDURE:** Proceed as directed under *M-1b*, Appendix XI.
  Acceptance criteria: NLT 99.0% of $C_6H_8N_2O$ (sum of two isomers)

SPECIFIC TESTS
- **REFRACTIVE INDEX,** Appendix II: At 20°
  Acceptance criteria: Between 1.506 and 1.510
- **SPECIFIC GRAVITY:** Determine at 25° by any reliable method (see *General Provisions*).
  Acceptance criteria: Between 1.070 and 1.090

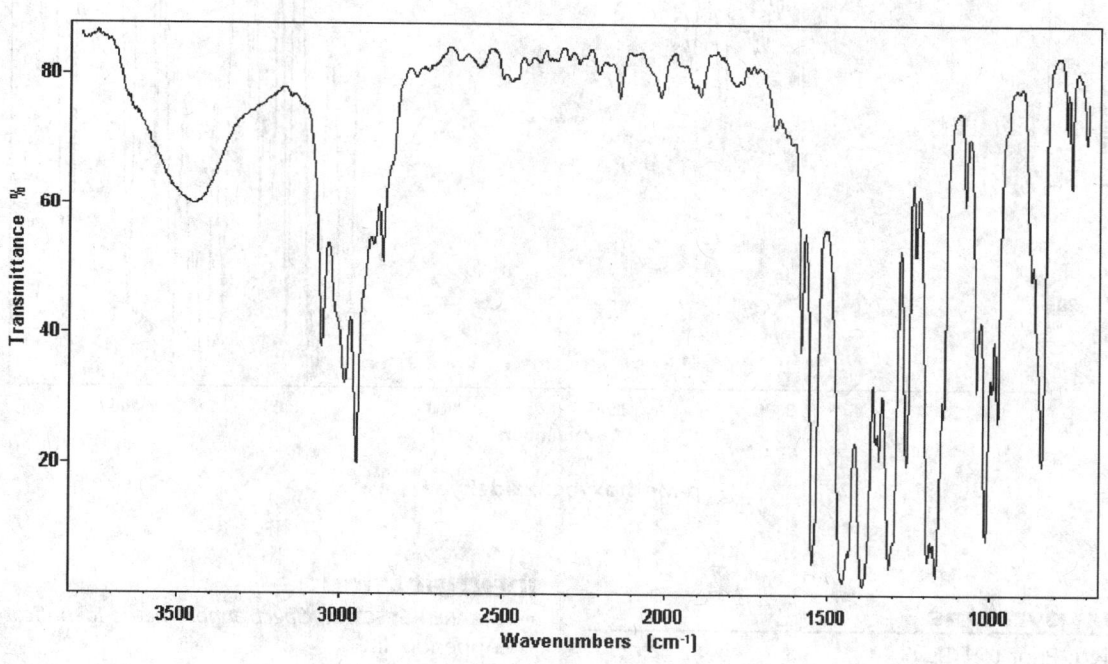

2-Methoxy-3(5)-methylpyrazine

p-Methoxybenzaldehyde

First Published: Prior to FCC 6

Anisic Aldehyde
p-Anisaldehyde

$C_8H_8O_2$ Formula wt 136.15

FEMA: 2670
UNII: 9PA5V6656V [p-anisaldehyde]

DESCRIPTION
p-Methoxybenzaldehyde occurs as a colorless to slightly yellow liquid.
Odor: Hawthorn
Solubility: Soluble in propylene glycol; miscible in alcohol, ether, most fixed oils; insoluble or practically insoluble in alcohol, water
Boiling Point: ~248°
Solubility in Alcohol, Appendix VI: One mL dissolves in 3 mL of 60% alcohol to give a clear solution.

720 / *p*-Methoxybenzaldehyde / Monographs

Function: Flavoring agent

IDENTIFICATION
- **INFRARED SPECTRA,** *Spectrophotometric Identification Tests,* Appendix IIIC
  Acceptance criteria: The spectrum of the sample exhibits relative maxima at the same wavelengths as those of the spectrum below.

ASSAY
- **PROCEDURE:** Proceed as directed under *M-1b,* Appendix XI.
  Acceptance criteria: NLT 97.5% of $C_8H_8O_2$

SPECIFIC TESTS
- **ACID VALUE, FLAVOR CHEMICALS (OTHER THAN ESSENTIAL OILS),** *M-15,* Appendix XI
  Acceptance criteria: NMT 6.0
- **REFRACTIVE INDEX,** Appendix II: At 20°
  Acceptance criteria: Between 1.571 and 1.574
- **SPECIFIC GRAVITY:** Determine at 25° by any reliable method (see *General Provisions*).
  Acceptance criteria: Between 1.119 and 1.123

OTHER REQUIREMENTS
- **CHLORINATED COMPOUNDS,** Appendix VI
  Acceptance criteria: Passes test

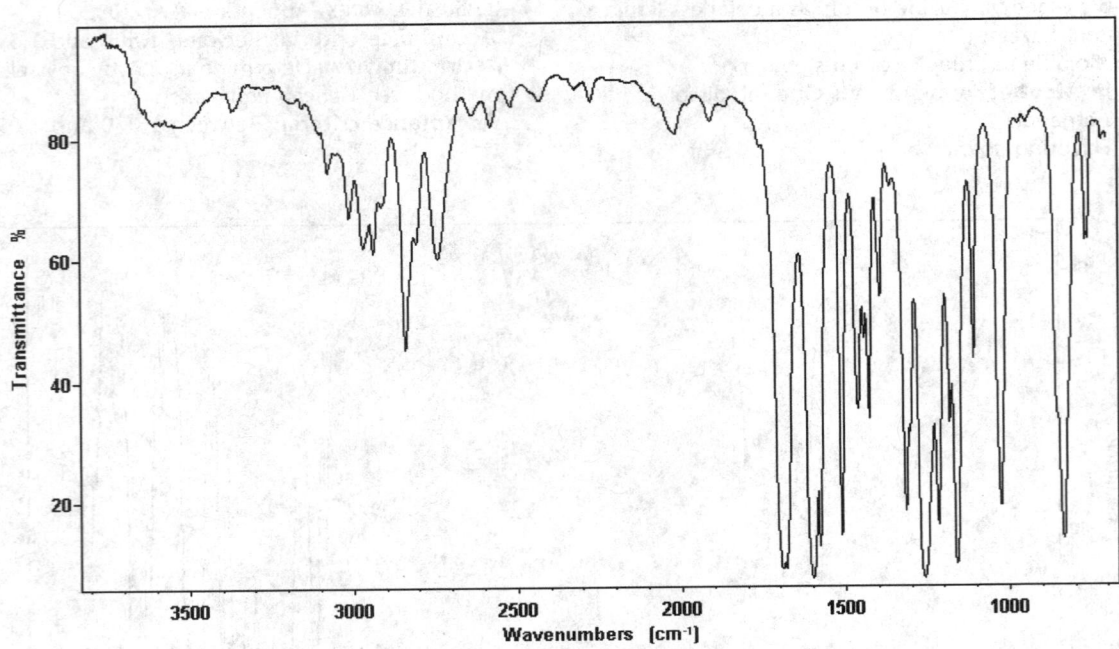

p-Methoxybenzaldehyde

2-Methoxypyrazine
First Published: Prior to FCC 6

$C_5H_6N_2O$ Formula wt 110.12
FEMA: 3302
UNII: RYD35T7F4T [2-methoxypyrazine]

DESCRIPTION
2-Methoxypyrazine occurs as a colorless to yellow liquid.
Odor: Nutty, cocoa
Solubility: Soluble in alcohol; insoluble or practically insoluble in water
Boiling Point: ~61° (29 mm Hg)
Function: Flavoring agent

IDENTIFICATION
- **INFRARED SPECTRA,** *Spectrophotometric Identification Tests,* Appendix IIIC
  Acceptance criteria: The spectrum of the sample exhibits relative maxima at the same wavelengths as those of the spectrum below.

ASSAY
- **PROCEDURE:** Proceed as directed under *M-1b,* Appendix XI.
  Acceptance criteria: NLT 99.0% of $C_5H_6N_2O$

SPECIFIC TESTS
- **REFRACTIVE INDEX,** Appendix II: At 20°
  Acceptance criteria: Between 1.508 and 1.511
- **SPECIFIC GRAVITY:** Determine at 20° by any reliable method (see *General Provisions*).
  Acceptance criteria: Between 1.110 and 1.140

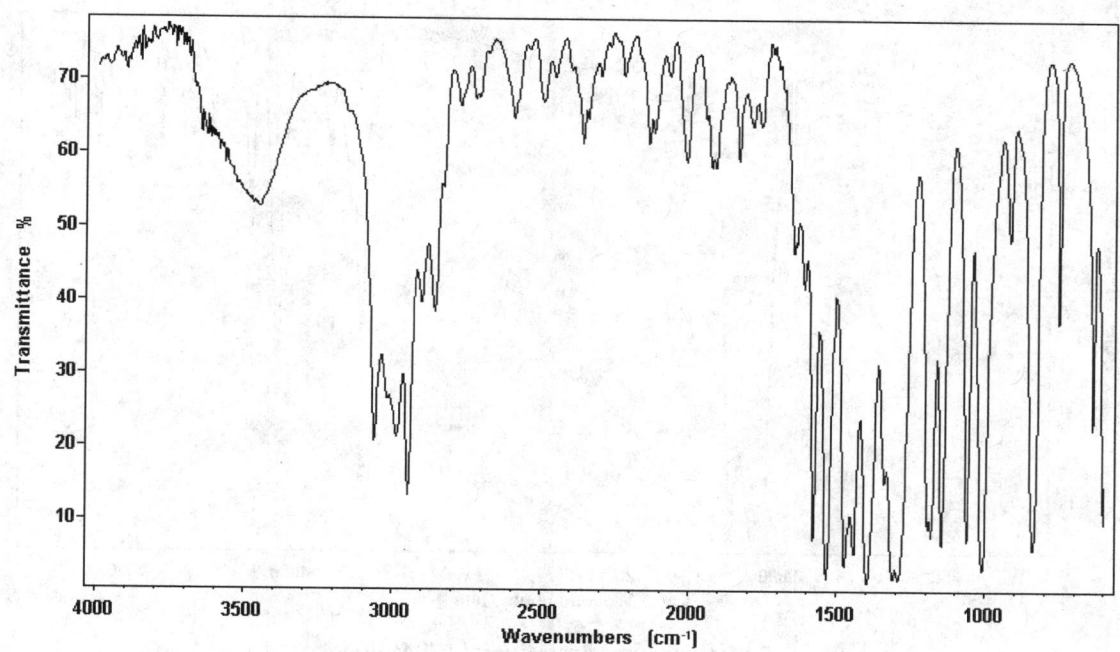

2-Methoxypyrazine

6-Methylcoumarin

First Published: Prior to FCC 6

$C_{10}H_8O_2$ Formula wt 160.17
FEMA: 2699
UNII: EHP8W0L01A [6-methylcoumarin]

DESCRIPTION
6-Methylcoumarin occurs as a white crystalline solid.
Odor: Coconut
Solubility: Insoluble or practically insoluble in propylene glycol, vegetable oils, water
Boiling Point: ~303° (725 mm Hg)
Solubility in Alcohol, Appendix VI: One g dissolves in 20 mL of 95% alcohol.

Function: Flavoring agent

IDENTIFICATION
- **INFRARED SPECTRA,** *Spectrophotometric Identification Tests,* Appendix IIIC
  Sample preparation: Mineral oil mull
  Acceptance criteria: The spectrum of the sample exhibits relative maxima at the same wavelengths as those of the spectrum below.

ASSAY
- **PROCEDURE:** Proceed as directed under *M-1a,* Appendix XI.
  Acceptance criteria: NLT 99.0% of $C_{10}H_8O_2$

OTHER REQUIREMENTS
- **MELTING RANGE OR TEMPERATURE DETERMINATION,** Appendix IIB
  Acceptance criteria: Between 73° and 76°

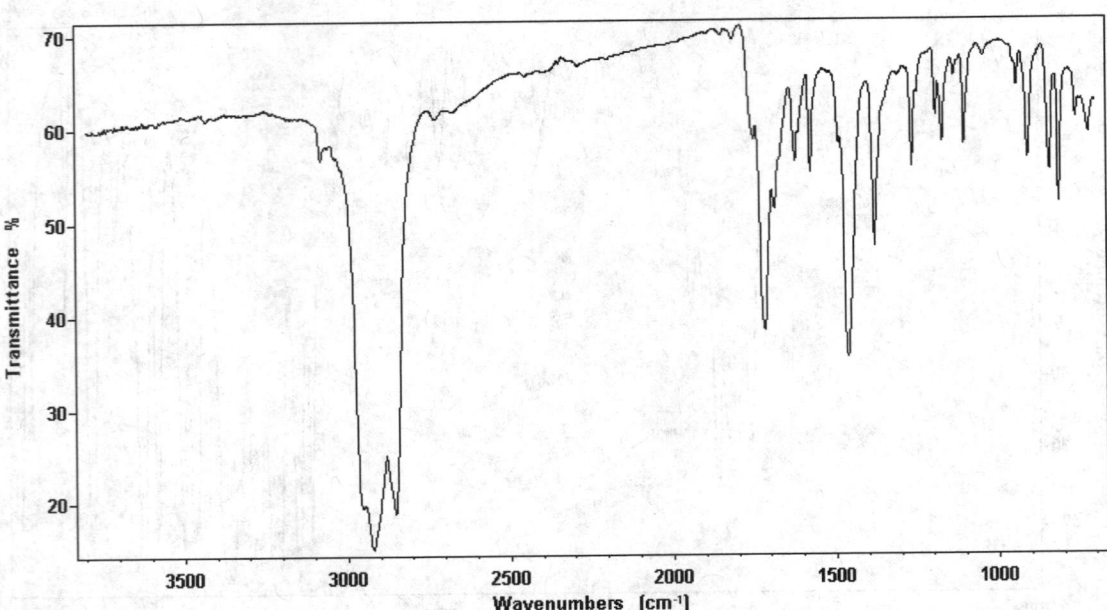

6-Methylcoumarin (Mineral Oil Mull)

4-Methylpentanoic Acid

First Published: Prior to FCC 6

$C_6H_{12}O_2$
FEMA: 3463
UNII: 4G4U8JA28T [isocaproic acid]

Formula wt 116.16

DESCRIPTION
4-Methylpentanoic Acid occurs as a colorless to pale yellow liquid.
Odor: Sour, penetrating
Boiling Point: ~199° to 201°
Solubility in Alcohol, Appendix VI: One mL dissolves in 1 mL of 95% alcohol.

Function: Flavoring agent

IDENTIFICATION
- **INFRARED SPECTRA,** *Spectrophotometric Identification Tests,* Appendix IIIC
  Acceptance criteria: The spectrum of the sample exhibits relative maxima at the same wavelengths as those of the spectrum below.

ASSAY
- **PROCEDURE:** Proceed as directed under *M-3a,* Appendix XI.
  Acceptance criteria: NLT 98.0% of $C_6H_{12}O_2$

SPECIFIC TESTS
- **REFRACTIVE INDEX,** Appendix II: At 20°
  Acceptance criteria: Between 1.412 and 1.417
- **SPECIFIC GRAVITY:** Determine at 25° by any reliable method (see *General Provisions*).
  Acceptance criteria: Between 0.919 and 0.926

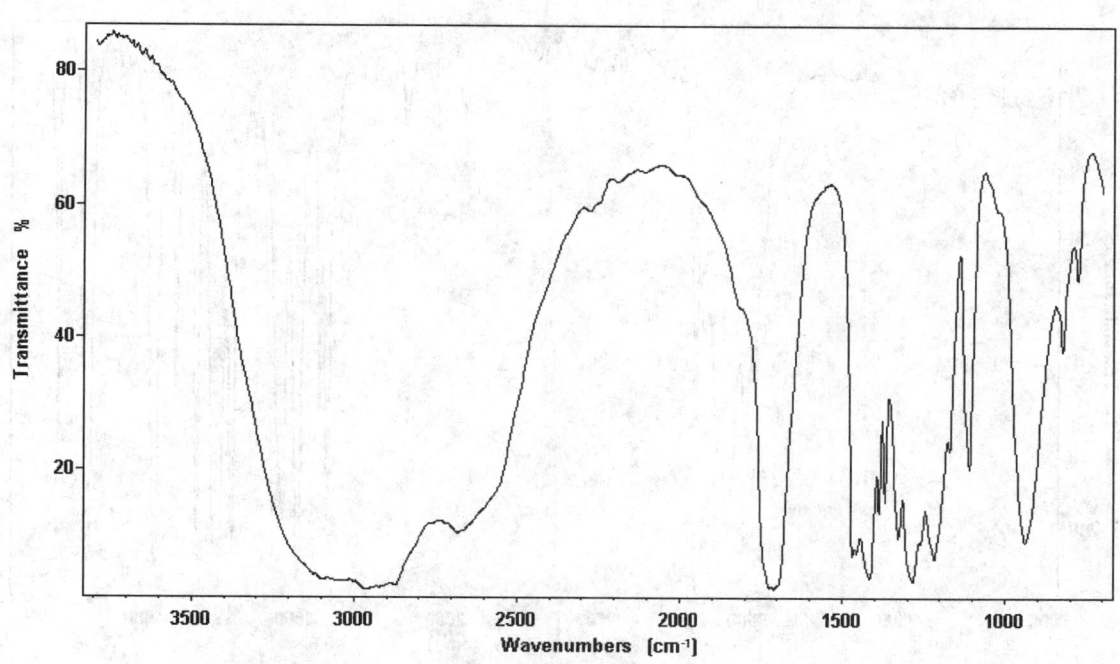

4-Methylpentanoic Acid

p-Methyl Anisole

First Published: Prior to FCC 6

p-Cresyl Methyl Ether
Methyl p-Cresol

$C_8H_{10}O$ Formula wt 122.17
FEMA: 2681
UNII: 10FAI0OR9W [p-methyl anisole]

DESCRIPTION
p-Methyl Anisole occurs as a colorless liquid.
Odor: Ylang-ylang
Solubility: Soluble in most fixed oils; insoluble or practically insoluble in glycerin, propylene glycol
Boiling Point: ~174°
Solubility in Alcohol, Appendix VI: One mL dissolves in 3 mL of 80% alcohol, and remains in solution on dilution.
Function: Flavoring agent

IDENTIFICATION
- **INFRARED SPECTRA,** Spectrophotometric Identification Tests, Appendix IIIC
  Acceptance criteria: The spectrum of the sample exhibits relative maxima at the same wavelengths as those of the spectrum below.

ASSAY
- **PROCEDURE:** Proceed as directed under M-1a, Appendix XI.
  Acceptance criteria: NLT 98.5% of $C_8H_{10}O$

SPECIFIC TESTS
- **REFRACTIVE INDEX,** Appendix II: At 20°
  Acceptance criteria: Between 1.510 and 1.513
- **SPECIFIC GRAVITY:** Determine at 25° by any reliable method (see General Provisions).
  Acceptance criteria: Between 0.966 and 0.970

OTHER REQUIREMENTS
- **CRESOL,** M-1b, Appendix XI
  Acceptance criteria: NMT 0.5%

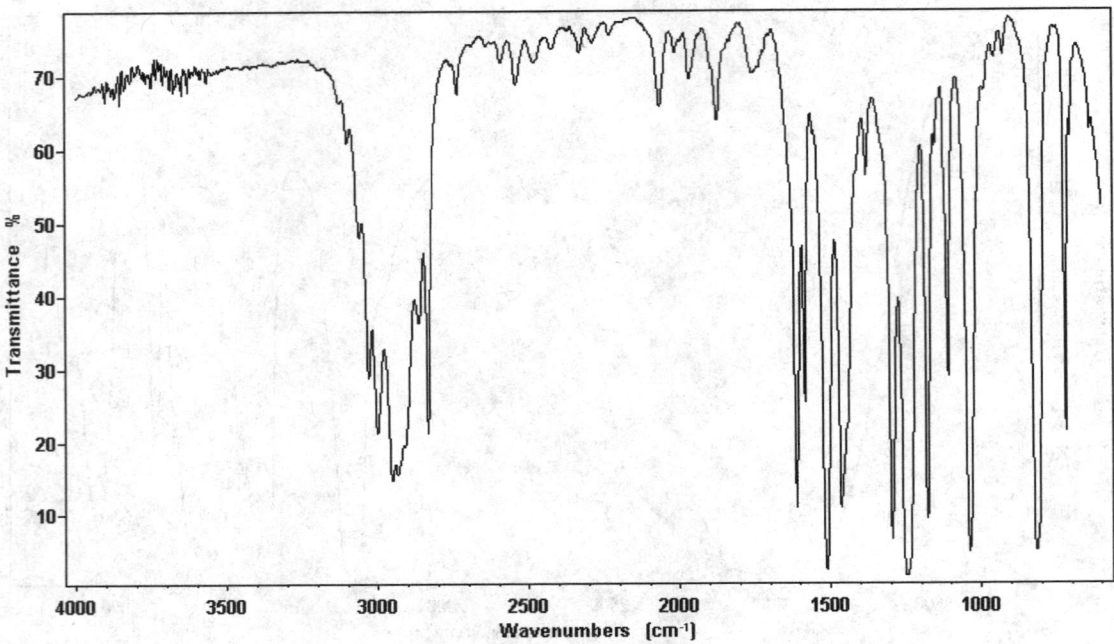

p-Methyl Anisole

2-Methyl Butanal

First Published: Prior to FCC 6
Last Revision: First Supplement, FCC 6

C₅H₁₀O Formula wt 86.13
FEMA: 2691
UNII: 47H597M1YY [2-methylbutyraldehyde]

DESCRIPTION
2-Methyl Butanal occurs as a colorless to pale yellow liquid. It may contain a suitable antioxidant.
Odor: Chocolate
Solubility: Soluble in propylene glycol, vegetable oils; insoluble or practically insoluble in water
Boiling Point: ~93°
Solubility in Alcohol, Appendix VI: One mL dissolves in 1 mL of 95% ethanol.
Function: Flavoring agent

ASSAY
- **PROCEDURE:** Proceed as directed under *M-1b,* Appendix XI.
  Acceptance criteria: NLT 97.0% of C₅H₁₀O

SPECIFIC TESTS
- **ACID VALUE, FLAVOR CHEMICALS (OTHER THAN ESSENTIAL OILS),** *M-15,* Appendix XI

  Acceptance criteria: NMT 10.0
- **REFRACTIVE INDEX,** Appendix II: At 20°
  Acceptance criteria: Between 1.388 and 1.393
- **SPECIFIC GRAVITY:** Determine at 25° by any reliable method (see *General Provisions*).
  Acceptance criteria: Between 0.799 and 0.804

2-Methyl Propyl 3-Methyl Butyrate

First Published: Prior to FCC 6

Isobutyl Isovalerate

C₉H₁₈O₂ Formula wt 158.24
FEMA: 3369
UNII: 6VCJ0UB168 [isobutyl isovalerate]

DESCRIPTION
2-Methyl Propyl 3-Methyl Butyrate occurs as a colorless to pale yellow liquid.
Odor: Fruity
Solubility: Miscible in alcohol
Boiling Point: ~170°
Function: Flavoring agent

ASSAY
- **PROCEDURE:** Proceed as directed under *M-1b*, Appendix XI.
  Acceptance criteria: NLT 98.0% of $C_9H_{18}O_2$

SPECIFIC TESTS
- **ACID VALUE, FLAVOR CHEMICALS (OTHER THAN ESSENTIAL OILS),** *M-15,* Appendix XI
  Acceptance criteria: NMT 1.0
- **REFRACTIVE INDEX,** Appendix II: At 20°
  Acceptance criteria: Between 1.404 and 1.408
- **SPECIFIC GRAVITY:** Determine at 25° by any reliable method (see *General Provisions*).
  Acceptance criteria: Between 0.850 and 0.854

2-Methyl-2-pentenoic Acid
First Published: Prior to FCC 6

$C_6H_{10}O_2$ Formula wt 114.14
FEMA: 3195
UNII: 44I99E898B [2-methyl-2-pentenoic acid]

DESCRIPTION
2-Methyl-2-pentenoic Acid occurs as a colorless to pale yellow liquid (high-purity material may solidify at room temperature, with a melting point range of 24°–26°).
Boiling Point: ~123° (30 mm Hg)
Solubility in Alcohol, Appendix VI: One mL dissolves in 1 mL of 95% alcohol.
Function: Flavoring agent

IDENTIFICATION
- **INFRARED SPECTRA,** *Spectrophotometric Identification Tests,* Appendix IIIC
  Acceptance criteria: The spectrum of the sample exhibits relative maxima at the same wavelengths as those of the spectrum below.

ASSAY
- **PROCEDURE:** Proceed as directed under *M-3a,* Appendix XI.
  Acceptance criteria: NLT 98.0% of $C_6H_{10}O_2$

SPECIFIC TESTS
- **REFRACTIVE INDEX,** Appendix II: At 20°
  Acceptance criteria: Between 1.455 and 1.465
- **SPECIFIC GRAVITY:** Determine at 25° by any reliable method (see *General Provisions*).
  Acceptance criteria: Between 0.978 and 0.985

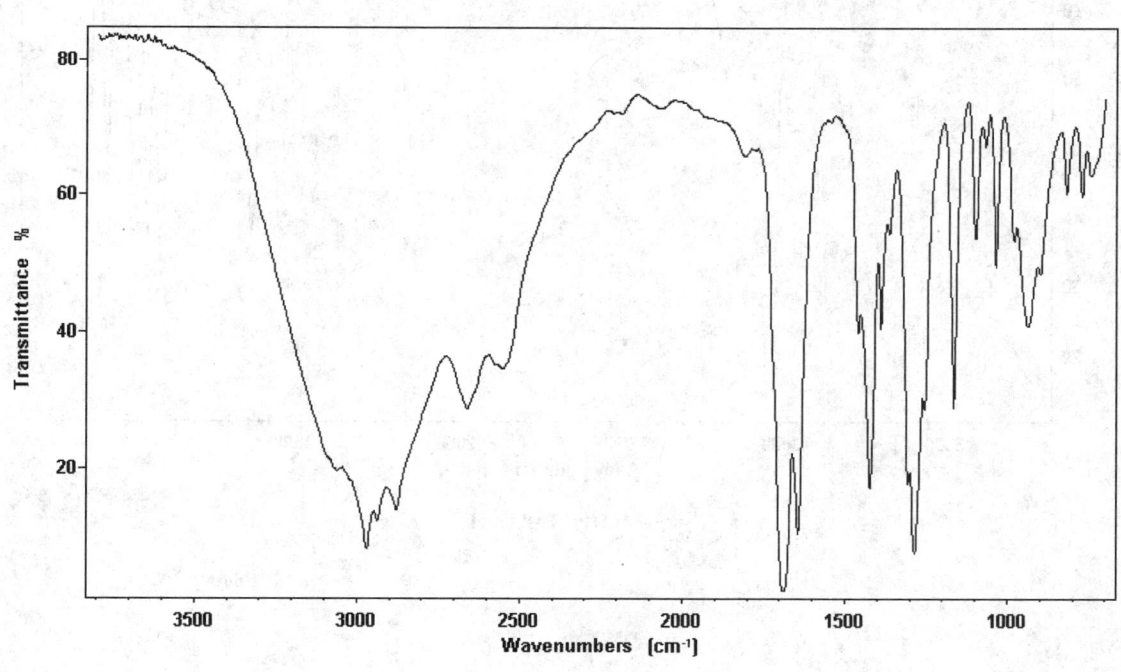

2-Methyl-2-pentenoic Acid

3-Methyl Butanal

First Published: Prior to FCC 6
Last Revision: First Supplement, FCC 6

Isovaleraldehyde

$C_5H_{10}O$ Formula wt 86.13
FEMA: 2692
UNII: 69931RWI96 [isovaleraldehyde]

DESCRIPTION
3-Methyl Butanal occurs as a colorless to pale yellow liquid. It may contain a suitable antioxidant.
Odor: Chocolate
Solubility: Soluble in propylene glycol, vegetable oils; insoluble or practically insoluble in water
Boiling Point: ~93°
Solubility in Alcohol, Appendix VI: One mL dissolves in 1 mL of 95% ethanol.
Function: Flavoring agent

IDENTIFICATION
- **INFRARED SPECTRA,** Spectrophotometric Identification Tests, Appendix IIIC
  Acceptance criteria: The spectrum of the sample exhibits relative maxima at the same wavelengths as those of the spectrum below.

ASSAY
- **PROCEDURE:** Proceed as directed under M-1b, Appendix XI.
  Acceptance criteria: NLT 97.0% of $C_5H_{10}O$

SPECIFIC TESTS
- **ACID VALUE, FLAVOR CHEMICALS (OTHER THAN ESSENTIAL OILS),** M-15, Appendix XI
  Acceptance criteria: NMT 10.0
- **REFRACTIVE INDEX,** Appendix II: At 20°
  Acceptance criteria: Between 1.388 and 1.391
- **SPECIFIC GRAVITY:** Determine at 25° by any reliable method (see General Provisions).
  Acceptance criteria: Between 0.795 and 0.802

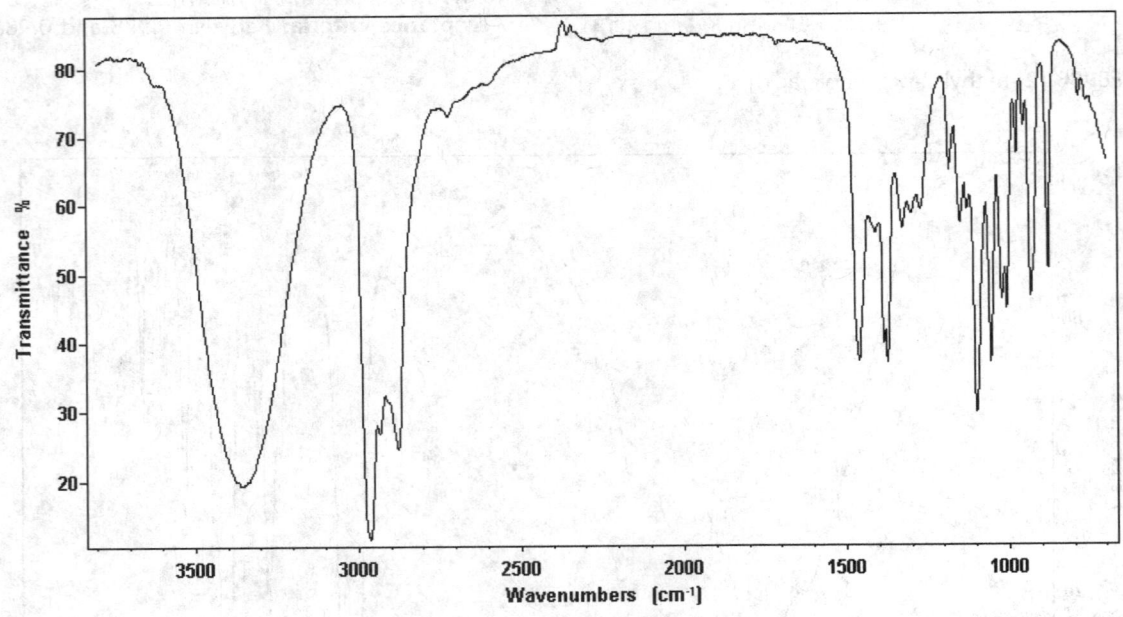

3-Methyl Butanal

4-Methyl Acetophenone
First Published: Prior to FCC 6

Methyl *p*-Tolyl Ketone

C₉H₁₀O Formula wt 134.18
FEMA: 2677
UNII: AX66V0KX3Y [4′-methylacetophenone]

DESCRIPTION
4-Methyl Acetophenone occurs as a colorless or nearly colorless liquid.
Odor: Fruity-floral, resembling acetophenone
Solubility: Soluble in most fixed oils, propylene glycol; insoluble or practically insoluble in glycerin
Boiling Point: ~226°
Solubility in Alcohol, Appendix VI: One mL dissolves in 10 mL of 50% alcohol.

Function: Flavoring agent

IDENTIFICATION
- **INFRARED SPECTRA,** *Spectrophotometric Identification Tests,* Appendix IIIC
  Acceptance criteria: The spectrum of the sample exhibits relative maxima at the same wavelengths as those of the spectrum below.

ASSAY
- **PROCEDURE:** Proceed as directed under *M-1b,* Appendix XI.
  Acceptance criteria: NLT 95.0% of C₉H₁₀O

SPECIFIC TESTS
- **REFRACTIVE INDEX,** Appendix II: At 20°
  Acceptance criteria: Between 1.530 and 1.535
- **SPECIFIC GRAVITY:** Determine at 25° by any reliable method (see *General Provisions*).
  Acceptance criteria: Between 0.996 and 1.004

OTHER REQUIREMENTS
- **CHLORINATED COMPOUNDS,** Appendix VI
  Acceptance criteria: Passes test

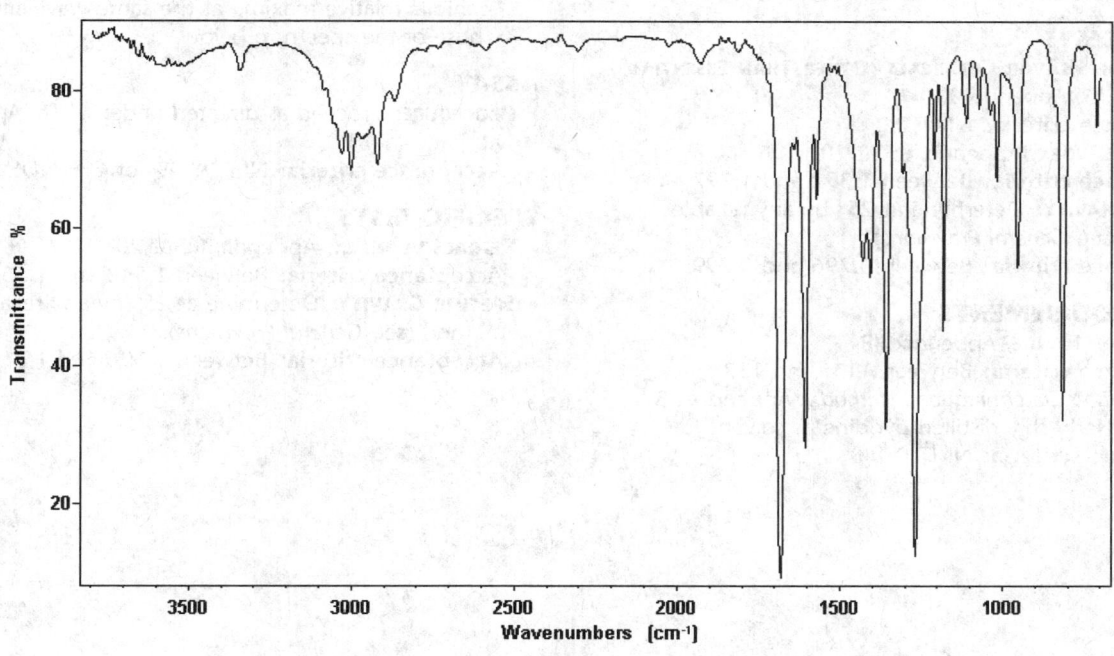

4-Methyl Acetophenone

4-Methyl-2-pentanone

First Published: Prior to FCC 6

Methyl Isobutyl Ketone

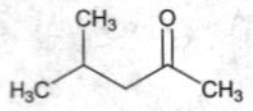

$C_6H_{12}O_2$ — Formula wt 100.16
FEMA: 2731
UNII: U5T7B88CNP [methyl isobutyl ketone]

DESCRIPTION
4-Methyl-2-pentanone occurs as a colorless, mobile liquid.
Odor: Fruity, ethereal
Solubility: Miscible in alcohol, ether; 1 mL dissolves in 50 mL water
Boiling Point: ~117°
Function: Flavoring agent

ASSAY
- **PROCEDURE:** Proceed as directed under *M-2d*, Appendix XI.
  Acceptance criteria: NLT 99.0% of $C_6H_{12}O$

SPECIFIC TESTS
- **ACID VALUE, FLAVOR CHEMICALS (OTHER THAN ESSENTIAL OILS),** *M-15,* Appendix XI
  Acceptance criteria: NMT 2.0
- **REFRACTIVE INDEX,** Appendix II: At 20°
  Acceptance criteria: Between 1.392 and 1.397
- **SPECIFIC GRAVITY:** Determine at 25° by any reliable method (see *General Provisions*).
  Acceptance criteria: Between 0.796 and 0.799

OTHER REQUIREMENTS
- **DISTILLATION RANGE,** Appendix IIB
  Acceptance criteria: Between 114° and 117°
- **WATER,** *Water Determination, Method I,* Appendix IIB
  [NOTE—Use freshly distilled pyridine as solvent.]
  Acceptance criteria: NMT 0.1%

4-Methyl-5-thiazole Ethanol

First Published: Prior to FCC 6

Sulfurol

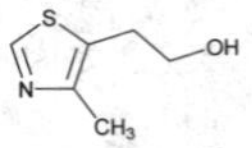

C_9H_9NOS — Formula wt 143.20
FEMA: 3204
UNII: 3XYV4I47I8 [4-methyl-5-thiazoleethanol]

DESCRIPTION
4-Methyl-5-thiazole Ethanol occurs as a colorless to pale yellow liquid; may darken upon aging.
Odor: Meaty
Boiling Point: ~135° (7 mm Hg)
Function: Flavoring agent

IDENTIFICATION
- **INFRARED SPECTRA,** *Spectrophotometric Identification Tests,* Appendix IIIC
  Acceptance criteria: The spectrum of the sample exhibits relative maxima at the same wavelengths as those of the spectrum below.

ASSAY
- **PROCEDURE:** Proceed as directed under *M-1b*, Appendix XI.
  Acceptance criteria: NLT 98.0% of C_9H_9NOS

SPECIFIC TESTS
- **REFRACTIVE INDEX,** Appendix II: At 20°
  Acceptance criteria: Between 1.548 and 1.552
- **SPECIFIC GRAVITY:** Determine at 25° by any reliable method (see *General Provisions*).
  Acceptance criteria: Between 1.196 and 1.210

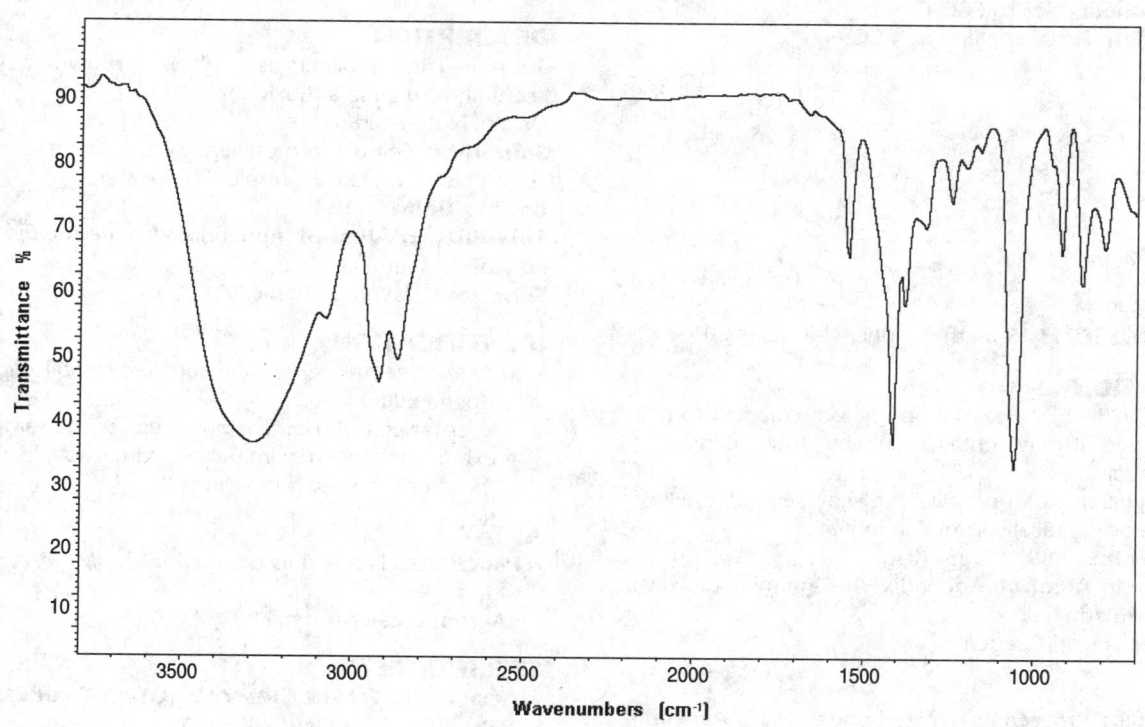

4-Methyl-5-thiazole Ethanol

5H-5-Methyl-6,7-dihydrocyclopenta[b]pyrazine

First Published: Prior to FCC 6

C$_8$H$_{10}$N$_2$ Formula wt 134.18
FEMA: 3306
UNII: L5IDR3PHAV [5-methyl-6,7-dihydro-5h-cyclopentylpyrazine]

DESCRIPTION
5H-5-Methyl-6,7-dihydrocyclopenta[b]pyrazine occurs as a yellow to brown liquid.
Odor: Peanut
Solubility: Soluble in propylene glycol, vegetable oils; slightly soluble in water

Boiling Point: ~200°
Solubility in Alcohol, Appendix VI: One mL dissolves in 1 mL of 95% ethanol.
Function: Flavoring agent

ASSAY
- **PROCEDURE:** Proceed as directed under *M-1b,* Appendix XI.
  Acceptance criteria: NLT 98.0% of C$_8$H$_{10}$N$_2$

SPECIFIC TESTS
- **REFRACTIVE INDEX,** Appendix II: At 20°
  Acceptance criteria: Between 1.525 and 1.535
- **SPECIFIC GRAVITY:** Determine at 25° by any reliable method (see *General Provisions*).
  Acceptance criteria: Between 1.048 and 1.059

5-Methyl 2-Phenyl 2-Hexenal

First Published: Prior to FCC 6
Last Revision: First Supplement, FCC 6

$C_{13}H_{16}O$ Formula wt 188.27
FEMA: 3199
UNII: 57UW55EC13 [5-methyl-2-phenyl-2-hexenal]

DESCRIPTION
5-Methyl 2-Phenyl 2-Hexenal occurs as a colorless to pale yellow liquid. It may contain a suitable antioxidant.
Odor: Cocoa
Solubility: Soluble in propylene glycol, vegetable oils; insoluble or practically insoluble in water
Boiling Point: ~89° (26 mm Hg)
Solubility in Alcohol, Appendix VI: One mL dissolves in 1 mL of 95% ethanol.
Function: Flavoring agent

ASSAY
- **PROCEDURE:** Proceed as directed under *M-1b,* Appendix XI.
  Acceptance criteria: NLT 92.0% of $C_{13}H_{16}O$ (sum of (*E*)- and (*Z*)-isomers)

SPECIFIC TESTS
- **ACID VALUE, FLAVOR CHEMICALS (OTHER THAN ESSENTIAL OILS),** *M-15,* Appendix XI
  Acceptance criteria: NMT 4.0
- **REFRACTIVE INDEX,** Appendix II: At 20°
  Acceptance criteria: Between 1.529 and 1.536
- **SPECIFIC GRAVITY:** Determine at 25° by any reliable method (see *General Provisions*).
  Acceptance criteria: Between 0.963 and 0.979

5-Methyl Furfural

First Published: Prior to FCC 6
Last Revision: First Supplement, FCC 6

$C_6H_6O_2$ Formula wt 110.11
FEMA: 2702
UNII: 4482BZC72D [5-methyl-2-furaldehyde]

DESCRIPTION
5-Methyl Furfural occurs as a yellow to brown liquid. It may contain a suitable antioxidant.
Odor: Nutty, caramel
Solubility: Soluble in propylene glycol, vegetable oils; insoluble or practically insoluble in water
Boiling Point: ~187°
Solubility in Alcohol, Appendix VI: One mL dissolves in 1 mL of 95% ethanol.
Function: Flavoring agent

IDENTIFICATION
- **INFRARED SPECTRA,** *Spectrophotometric Identification Tests,* Appendix IIIC
  Acceptance criteria: The spectrum of the sample exhibits relative maxima at the same wavelengths as those of the spectrum below.

ASSAY
- **PROCEDURE:** Proceed as directed under *M-1b,* Appendix XI.
  Acceptance criteria: NLT 97.0% of $C_6H_6O_2$

SPECIFIC TESTS
- **ACID VALUE, FLAVOR CHEMICALS (OTHER THAN ESSENTIAL OILS),** *M-15,* Appendix XI
  Acceptance criteria: NMT 5.0
- **REFRACTIVE INDEX,** Appendix II: At 20°
  Acceptance criteria: Between 1.525 and 1.535
- **SPECIFIC GRAVITY:** Determine at 25° by any reliable method (see *General Provisions*).
  Acceptance criteria: Between 1.095 and 1.110

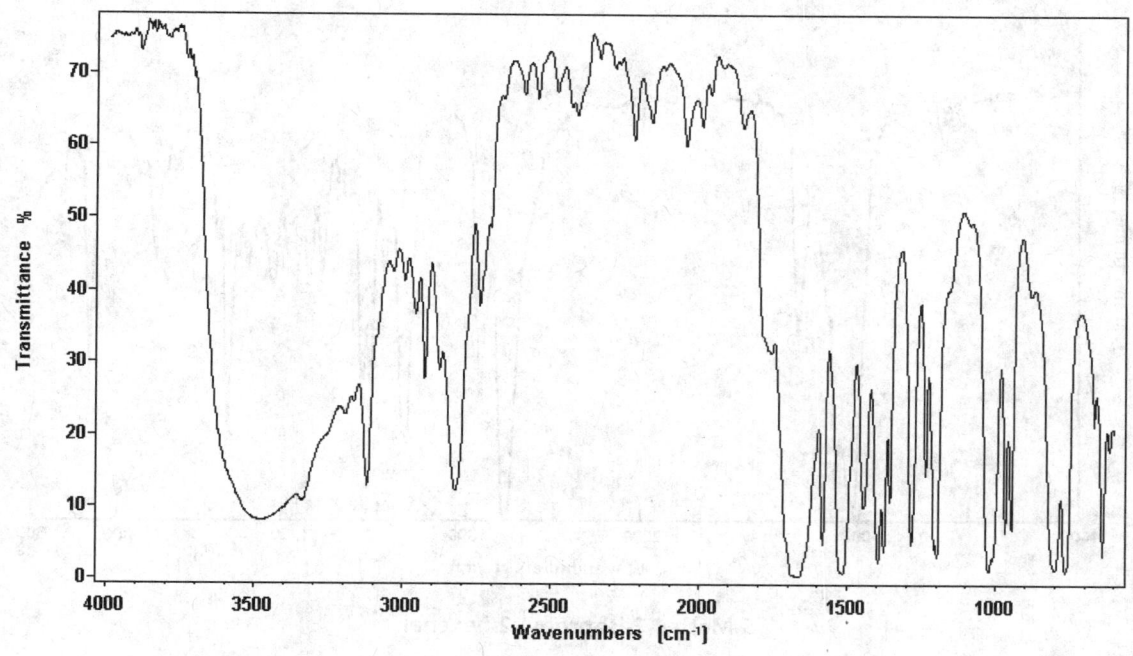

5-Methyl Furfural

5-Methyl-2-isopropyl-2-hexenal

First Published: Prior to FCC 6
Last Revision: First Supplement, FCC 6

Isodihydrolavandulal

$C_{10}H_{18}O$ Formula wt 154.25
FEMA: 3406
UNII: 7F8Q5STQ11 [5-methyl-2-isopropyl-2-hexenal]

DESCRIPTION
5-Methyl-2-isopropyl-2-hexenal occurs as a slightly yellow liquid. It may contain a suitable antioxidant.
Odor: Herbaceous, woody, fruity, chocolate
Solubility: Soluble in alcohol, most fixed oils; insoluble or practically insoluble in water, propylene glycol
Boiling Point: ~73° (10 mm Hg)
Function: Flavoring agent

IDENTIFICATION
- **INFRARED SPECTRA,** *Spectrophotometric Identification Tests,* Appendix IIIC
  Acceptance criteria: The spectrum of the sample exhibits relative maxima at the same wavelengths as those of the spectrum below.

ASSAY
- **PROCEDURE:** Proceed as directed under *M-1a,* Appendix XI.
  Acceptance criteria: NLT 90.0% of $C_{10}H_{18}O$ (sum of isomers)

SPECIFIC TESTS
- **REFRACTIVE INDEX,** Appendix II: At 20°
  Acceptance criteria: Between 1.448 and 1.454
- **SPECIFIC GRAVITY:** Determine at 25° by any reliable method (see *General Provisions*).
  Acceptance criteria: Between 0.842 and 0.850

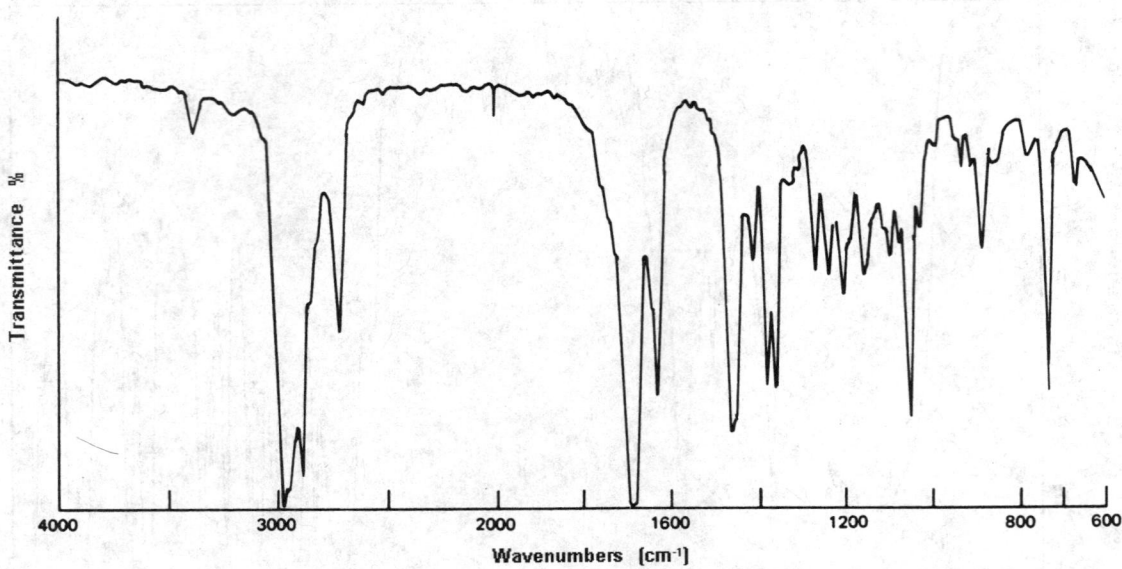

5-Methyl-2-isopropyl-2-hexenal

6-Methyl-5-hepten-2-one

First Published: Prior to FCC 6

Methyl Heptenone

$C_8H_{14}O$
FEMA: 2707
UNII: 448353S93V [methyl heptenone]

Formula wt 126.20

DESCRIPTION
6-Methyl-5-hepten-2-one occurs as a slightly yellow liquid.
Odor: Sharp, citrus-lemongrass
Solubility: Miscible in alcohol, most fixed oils, ether; insoluble or practically insoluble in water
Boiling Point: ~73° (18 mm Hg)
Solubility in Alcohol, Appendix VI: One mL dissolves in 2 mL of 70% alcohol to give a clear solution.

Function: Flavoring agent

IDENTIFICATION
- **INFRARED SPECTRA,** Spectrophotometric Identification Tests, Appendix IIIC
  Acceptance criteria: The spectrum of the sample exhibits relative maxima at the same wavelengths as those of the spectrum below.

ASSAY
- **PROCEDURE:** Proceed as directed under M-1b, Appendix XI.
  Acceptance criteria: NLT 98.0% of $C_8H_{14}O$

SPECIFIC TESTS
- **REFRACTIVE INDEX,** Appendix II: At 20°
  Acceptance criteria: Between 1.438 and 1.442
- **SPECIFIC GRAVITY:** Determine at 25° by any reliable method (see General Provisions).
  Acceptance criteria: Between 0.846 and 0.851

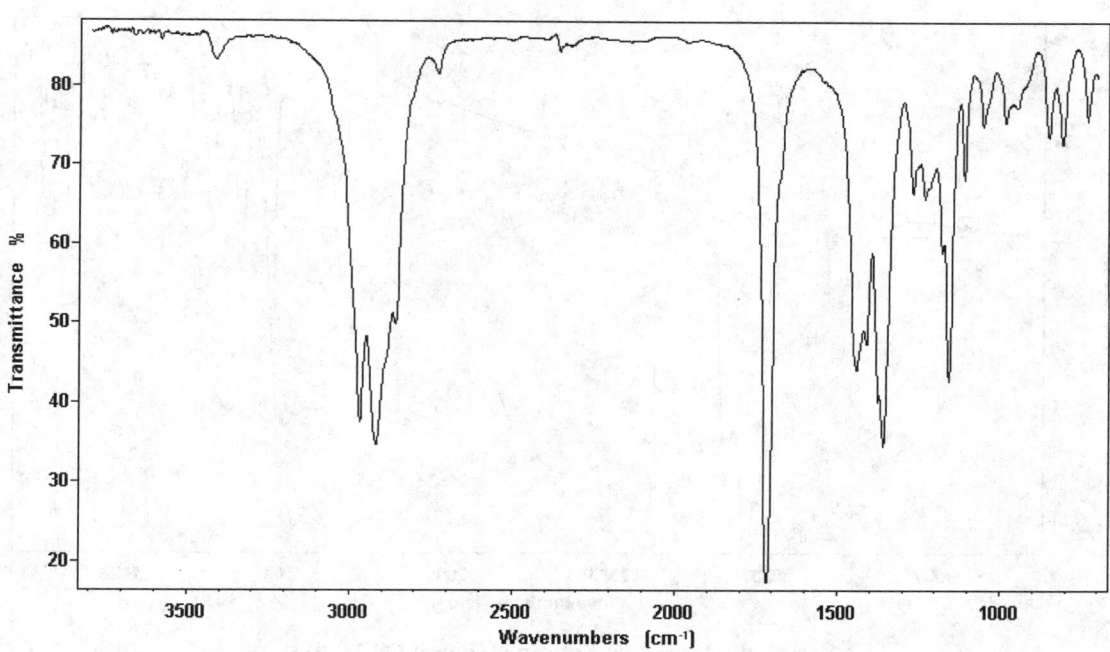

6-Methyl-5-hepten-2-one

Methyl β-Naphthyl Ketone

First Published: Prior to FCC 6

2-Acetonaphthone

C₁₂H₁₀O Formula wt 170.21
FEMA: 2723
UNII: 21D49LOP2T [2-acetonaphthone]

DESCRIPTION
Methyl β-Naphthyl Ketone occurs as a white or nearly white crystalline solid.
Odor: Orange blossom
Solubility: Soluble in most fixed oils; slightly soluble in propylene glycol; insoluble or practically insoluble in glycerin
Boiling Point: ~300°
Solubility in Alcohol, Appendix VI: One g dissolves in 5 mL of 95% alcohol.
Function: Flavoring agent

IDENTIFICATION
- **INFRARED SPECTRA,** Spectrophotometric Identification Tests, Appendix IIIC
  Sample preparation: Mineral oil mull
  Acceptance criteria: The spectrum of the sample exhibits relative maxima at the same wavelengths as those of the spectrum below.

ASSAY
- **PROCEDURE:** Proceed as directed under *M-1b,* Appendix XI.
  Acceptance criteria: NLT 99.0% of C₁₂H₁₀O

OTHER REQUIREMENTS
- **SOLIDIFICATION POINT,** Appendix IIB
  Acceptance criteria: NLT 53°

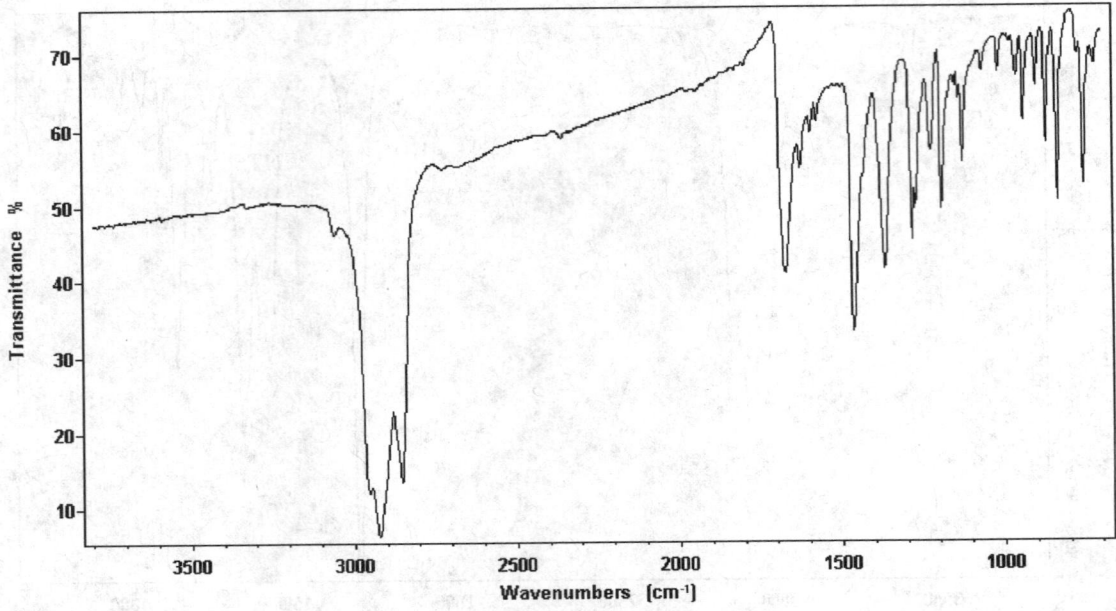

Methyl β-Naphthyl Ketone (Mineral Oil Mull)

Methyl 2-Methylbutyrate

First Published: Prior to FCC 6

Methyl 2-Methylbutanoate

$C_6H_{12}O_2$ Formula wt 116.16
FEMA: 2719
UNII: OLG4D4939V [methyl 2-methylbutyrate]

DESCRIPTION
Methyl 2-Methylbutyrate occurs as an almost colorless liquid.
Odor: Sweet, fruity, apple
Solubility: Soluble in alcohol, most fixed oils; insoluble or practically insoluble in water
Boiling Point: ~115°
Function: Flavoring agent

ASSAY
- **PROCEDURE:** Proceed as directed under *M-1b*, Appendix XI.
  Acceptance criteria: NLT 92.0% of $C_6H_{12}O_2$

SPECIFIC TESTS
- **ACID VALUE, FLAVOR CHEMICALS (OTHER THAN ESSENTIAL OILS),** *M-15,* Appendix XI
  Acceptance criteria: NMT 2.0
- **REFRACTIVE INDEX,** Appendix II: At 20°
  Acceptance criteria: Between 1.393 and 1.397
- **SPECIFIC GRAVITY:** Determine at 25° by any reliable method (see *General Provisions*).
  Acceptance criteria: Between 0.879 and 0.883

Methyl 2-Octynoate

First Published: Prior to FCC 6

Methyl Heptine Carbonate

$C_9H_{14}O_2$ Formula wt 154.21
FEMA: 2729
UNII: 0TTP6YT2T3 [methyl heptine carbonate]

DESCRIPTION
Methyl 2-Octynoate occurs as a colorless to slightly yellow liquid.
Odor: Powerful, unpleasant, violet when diluted
Solubility: Soluble in most fixed oils; slightly soluble in propylene glycol; insoluble or practically insoluble in glycerin
Boiling Point: ~217°
Solubility in Alcohol, Appendix VI: One mL dissolves in 5 mL of 70% alcohol.
Function: Flavoring agent

IDENTIFICATION
- **INFRARED SPECTRA,** *Spectrophotometric Identification Tests,* Appendix IIIC

Acceptance criteria: The spectrum of the sample exhibits relative maxima at the same wavelengths as those of the spectrum below.

ASSAY
- **PROCEDURE:** Proceed as directed under *M-1b,* Appendix XI.
  Acceptance criteria: NLT 96.0% of $C_9H_{14}O_2$

SPECIFIC TESTS
- **ACID VALUE, FLAVOR CHEMICALS (OTHER THAN ESSENTIAL OILS),** *M-15,* Appendix XI
  Acceptance criteria: NMT 1.0
- **REFRACTIVE INDEX,** Appendix II: At 20°
  Acceptance criteria: Between 1.446 and 1.449
- **SPECIFIC GRAVITY:** Determine at 25° by any reliable method (see *General Provisions*).
  Acceptance criteria: Between 0.919 and 0.924

OTHER REQUIREMENTS
- **CHLORINATED COMPOUNDS,** Appendix VI
  Acceptance criteria: Passes test

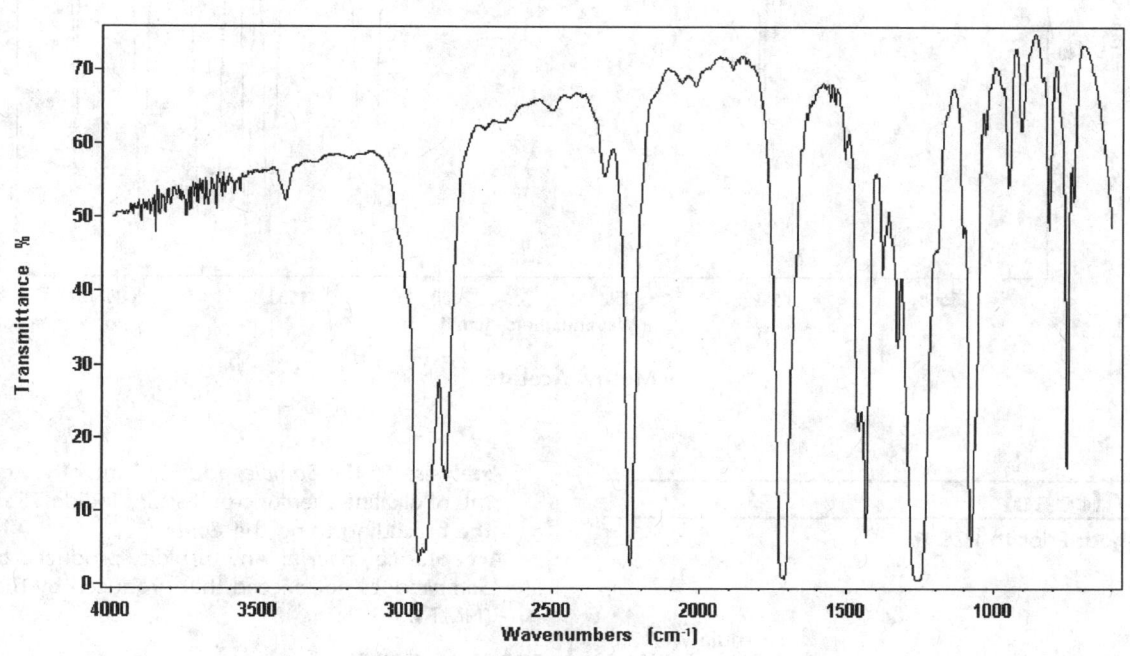

Methyl 2-Octynoate

Methyl Acetate

First Published: Prior to FCC 6

$C_3H_6O_2$ Formula wt 74.08
FEMA: 2676
UNII: W684QT396F [methyl acetate]

DESCRIPTION
Methyl Acetate occurs as a colorless liquid.
Odor: Ethereal, fruity
Boiling Point: ~57.5°
Solubility in Alcohol, Appendix VI: One mL dissolves in 1 mL of 95% alcohol.
Function: Flavoring agent

IDENTIFICATION
- **INFRARED SPECTRA,** *Spectrophotometric Identification Tests,* Appendix IIIC
  Acceptance criteria: The spectrum of the sample exhibits relative maxima at the same wavelengths as those of the spectrum below.

ASSAY
- **PROCEDURE:** Proceed as directed under *M-1b,* Appendix XI.
  Acceptance criteria: NLT 98.0% of $C_3H_6O_2$

SPECIFIC TESTS
- **ACID VALUE, FLAVOR CHEMICALS (OTHER THAN ESSENTIAL OILS),** *M-15,* Appendix XI
  Acceptance criteria: NMT 1.0
- **REFRACTIVE INDEX,** Appendix II: At 20°
  Acceptance criteria: Between 1.358 and 1.363
- **SPECIFIC GRAVITY:** Determine at 25° by any reliable method (see *General Provisions*).
  Acceptance criteria: Between 0.927 and 0.932

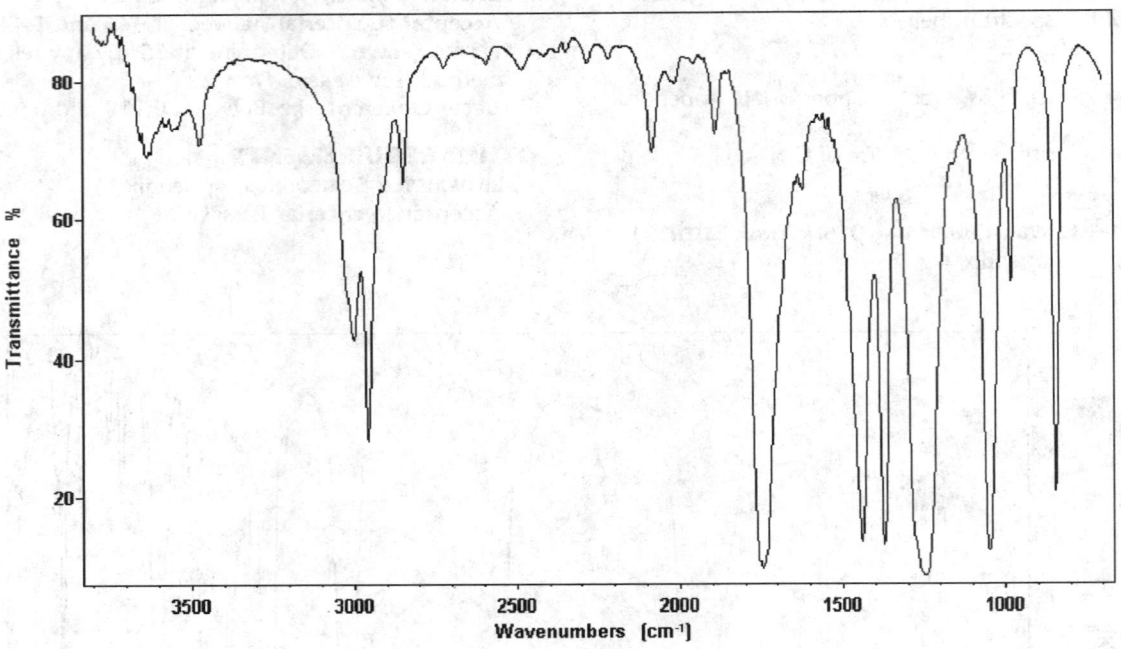

Methyl Acetate

Methyl Alcohol

First Published: Prior to FCC 6

Methanol

CH₃OH   Formula wt 32.04
CAS: [67-56-1]

UNII: Y4S76JWI15 [methyl alcohol]

DESCRIPTION
Methyl Alcohol occurs as a clear, colorless, flammable liquid. It is miscible with water, with ethyl alcohol, and with ether. Its refractive index at 20° is about 1.329.
Function: Extraction solvent
Packaging and Storage: Store in tight containers remote from heat, sparks, and open flames.

ASSAY
- **SPECIFIC GRAVITY:** Determine by any reliable method (see *General Provisions*).
  Acceptance criteria: NMT 0.7893 at 25°/25° (equivalent to 0.7928 at 20°/20°), corresponding to NLT 99.85% of CH₃OH, by weight

IMPURITIES
Inorganic Impurities
- **LEAD,** *Lead Limit Test, Atomic Absorption Spectrophotometric Graphite Furnace Method, Method I,* Appendix IIIB
  Acceptance criteria: NMT 1 mg/kg

Organic Impurities
- **ACETONE AND ALDEHYDES**
  Sample: 1.25 mL
  Control: 30 µg acetone
  Analysis: To the *Sample*, add 3.75 mL of water and 5.0 mL of alkaline mercuric-potassium iodide TS. Repeat the preceding using the *Control*.
  Acceptance criteria: Any turbidity produced by the *Sample* does not exceed that produced by the *Control*. (NMT 0.003%)

SPECIFIC TESTS
- **ACIDITY (AS FORMIC ACID)**
  Sample: 19 mL (about 15 g)
  Analysis: Add 0.5 mL phenolphthalein TS to a mixture of 10 mL of alcohol and 25 mL of water, and titrate with 0.02 N sodium hydroxide to the first pink color that persists for at least 30 s. Add the *Sample*, mix, and titrate with 0.02 N sodium hydroxide until the pink color is restored.
  Acceptance criteria: NMT 0.25 mL of 0.02 N sodium hydroxide is required to restore the pink color (NMT 0.0015%).
- **ALKALINITY (AS NH₃)**
  Sample: 29 mL
  Analysis: Add 1 drop of methyl red TS to 25 mL of water, add 0.02 N sulfuric acid until a red color just appears, then add the *Sample*, and mix and titrate with 0.02 N sulfuric acid until the red color is restored.
  Acceptance criteria: NMT 0.2 mL of 0.02 N sulfuric acid is required to restore the red color (NMT 3 mg/kg)
- **DISTILLATION RANGE,** Appendix IIB
  Acceptance criteria: Within a range of 1°, including 64.6° ± 0.1°
- **NONVOLATILE RESIDUE**
  Sample: 125 mL (about 100 g)

Analysis: Evaporate the *Sample* to dryness in a tared dish on a steam bath, dry the residue at 105° for 30 min, cool, and weigh.
Acceptance criteria: NMT 10 mg/kg
- **READILY CARBONIZABLE SUBSTANCES,** Appendix IIB
  Sample solution: 25 mL of sample in 25 mL of 95% sulfuric acid. [NOTE—The sulfuric acid should be cooled to 10°.]
  Control solution: 3.5 mL of platinum-cobalt CS diluted to 50 mL
  Acceptance criteria: The *Sample solution* has no more color than the *Control solution*. (Equivalent to NMT 35 APHA color units)
- **SOLUBILITY IN WATER**
  Analysis: Mix 15 mL of sample and 45 mL of water.
  Acceptance criteria: After 1 h, the resulting solution is as clear as an equal volume of water.
- **SUBSTANCES REDUCING PERMANGANATE**
  Sample: 20 mL, previously cooled to 15°
  Analysis: Transfer the *Sample*, to a glass-stoppered cylinder, add 0.1 mL of 0.1 N potassium permanganate, mix, and allow to stand for 5 min.
  Acceptance criteria: The pink color is not entirely discharged.
- **WATER,** *Water Determination,* Appendix IIB
  Acceptance criteria: NMT 0.1%

Methyl Anthranilate

First Published: Prior to FCC 6

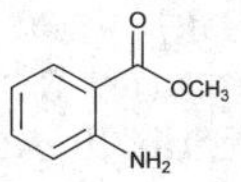

$C_8H_9NO_2$
FEMA: 2682

Formula wt 151.16

UNII: 98II0C1E5W [methyl anthranilate]

DESCRIPTION
Methyl Anthranilate occurs as a colorless to pale yellow liquid with blue fluorescence.
Odor: Grape
Solubility: Soluble in most fixed oils, propylene glycol; insoluble or practically insoluble in glycerin
Boiling Point: ~256°
Solubility in Alcohol, Appendix VI: One mL dissolves in 5 mL of 60% alcohol, and remains in solution upon dilution to 10 mL.
Function: Flavoring agent

IDENTIFICATION
- **INFRARED SPECTRA,** *Spectrophotometric Identification Tests,* Appendix IIIC
  Acceptance criteria: The spectrum of the sample exhibits relative maxima at the same wavelengths as those of the spectrum below.

ASSAY
- **PROCEDURE:** Proceed as directed under *Esters,* Appendix VI.
  Sample: 1.0 g
  Analysis: Use 75.59 as the equivalence factor (*e*).
  Acceptance criteria: NLT 98.0% of total esters as $C_8H_9NO_2$

SPECIFIC TESTS
- **REFRACTIVE INDEX,** Appendix II [NOTE—Determine as a supercooled liquid.]
  Acceptance criteria: Between 1.581 and 1.585
- **SPECIFIC GRAVITY:** Determine at 25° by any reliable method (see *General Provisions*).
  Acceptance criteria: Between 1.161 and 1.169

OTHER REQUIREMENTS
- **SOLIDIFICATION POINT,** Appendix IIB
  Acceptance criteria: NLT 23.8°

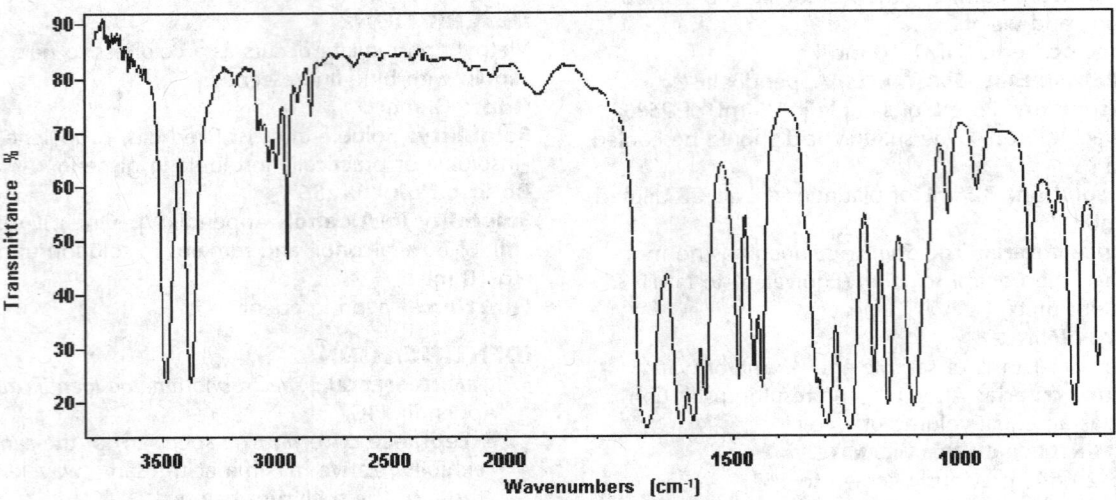

Methyl Anthranilate

Methyl Benzoate

First Published: Prior to FCC 6

C₈H₈O₂   Formula wt 136.15
FEMA: 2683
UNII: 6618K1VJ9T [methyl benzoate]

DESCRIPTION
Methyl Benzoate occurs as a colorless liquid.
Odor: Deep, pungent, floral
Solubility: Soluble in alcohol, most fixed oils, propylene glycol; insoluble or practically insoluble in glycerin
Boiling Point: ~198°
Solubility in Alcohol, Appendix VI: One mL dissolves in 4 mL of 60% alcohol.
Function: Flavoring agent

IDENTIFICATION
- **INFRARED SPECTRA,** *Spectrophotometric Identification Tests,* Appendix IIIC
  Acceptance criteria: The spectrum of the sample exhibits relative maxima at the same wavelengths as those of the spectrum below.

ASSAY
- **PROCEDURE:** Proceed as directed under *M-1b,* Appendix XI.
  Acceptance criteria: NLT 98.0% of C₈H₈O₂

SPECIFIC TESTS
- **ACID VALUE, FLAVOR CHEMICALS (OTHER THAN ESSENTIAL OILS),** *M-15,* Appendix XI
  Acceptance criteria: NMT 1.0
- **REFRACTIVE INDEX,** Appendix II: At 20°
  Acceptance criteria: Between 1.514 and 1.518
- **SPECIFIC GRAVITY:** Determine at 25° by any reliable method (see *General Provisions*).
  Acceptance criteria: Between 1.082 and 1.088

OTHER REQUIREMENTS
- **CHLORINATED COMPOUNDS,** Appendix VI
  Acceptance criteria: Passes test

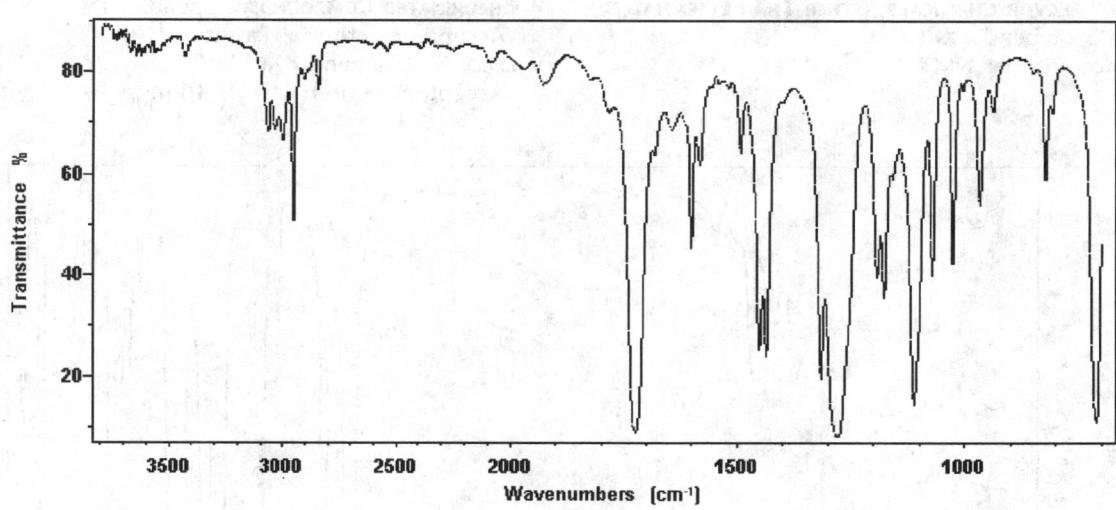

Methyl Benzoate

Methyl Butyrate

First Published: Prior to FCC 6

C₅H₁₀O₂ Formula wt 102.13
FEMA: 2693
UNII: CGX598508O [methyl butyrate]

DESCRIPTION
Methyl Butyrate occurs as a colorless liquid.
Odor: Fruity
Boiling Point: ~102°
Solubility in Alcohol, Appendix VI: One mL dissolves in 1 mL of 95% ethanol.
Function: Flavoring agent

ASSAY
- **PROCEDURE:** Proceed as directed under *M-1b*, Appendix XI.
  Acceptance criteria: NLT 98.0% of C₅H₁₀O₂

SPECIFIC TESTS
- **ACID VALUE, FLAVOR CHEMICALS (OTHER THAN ESSENTIAL OILS),** *M-15,* Appendix XI
  Acceptance criteria: NMT 1.0
- **REFRACTIVE INDEX,** Appendix II: At 20°
  Acceptance criteria: Between 1.386 and 1.390
- **SPECIFIC GRAVITY:** Determine at 25° by any reliable method (see *General Provisions*).
  Acceptance criteria: Between 0.892 and 0.897

Methyl Cinnamate

First Published: Prior to FCC 6

C₁₀H₁₀O₂ Formula wt 162.19
FEMA: 2698
UNII: 533CV2ZCQL [methyl cinnamate]

DESCRIPTION
Methyl Cinnamate occurs as a white to slightly yellow crystalline mass.
Odor: Fruity, balsamic
Solubility: Soluble in alcohol, most fixed oils, glycerin, propylene glycol; insoluble or practically insoluble in water
Boiling Point: ~260°
Solubility in Alcohol, Appendix VI: One g dissolves in 4 mL of 80% alcohol.
Function: Flavoring agent

IDENTIFICATION
- **INFRARED SPECTRA,** *Spectrophotometric Identification Tests,* Appendix IIIC
  Acceptance criteria: The spectrum of the sample exhibits relative maxima at the same wavelengths as those of the spectrum below.

ASSAY
- **PROCEDURE:** Proceed as directed under *M-1b*, Appendix XI.
  Acceptance criteria: NLT 98.0% of C₁₀H₁₀O₂

740 / Methyl Cinnamate / Monographs

SPECIFIC TESTS
- **ACID VALUE, FLAVOR CHEMICALS (OTHER THAN ESSENTIAL OILS),** *M-15,* Appendix XI
  Acceptance criteria: NMT 2.0

OTHER REQUIREMENTS
- **CHLORINATED COMPOUNDS,** Appendix VI
  Acceptance criteria: Passes test
- **LEAD,** *M-9,* Appendix XI
  Acceptance criteria: NMT 10 mg/kg

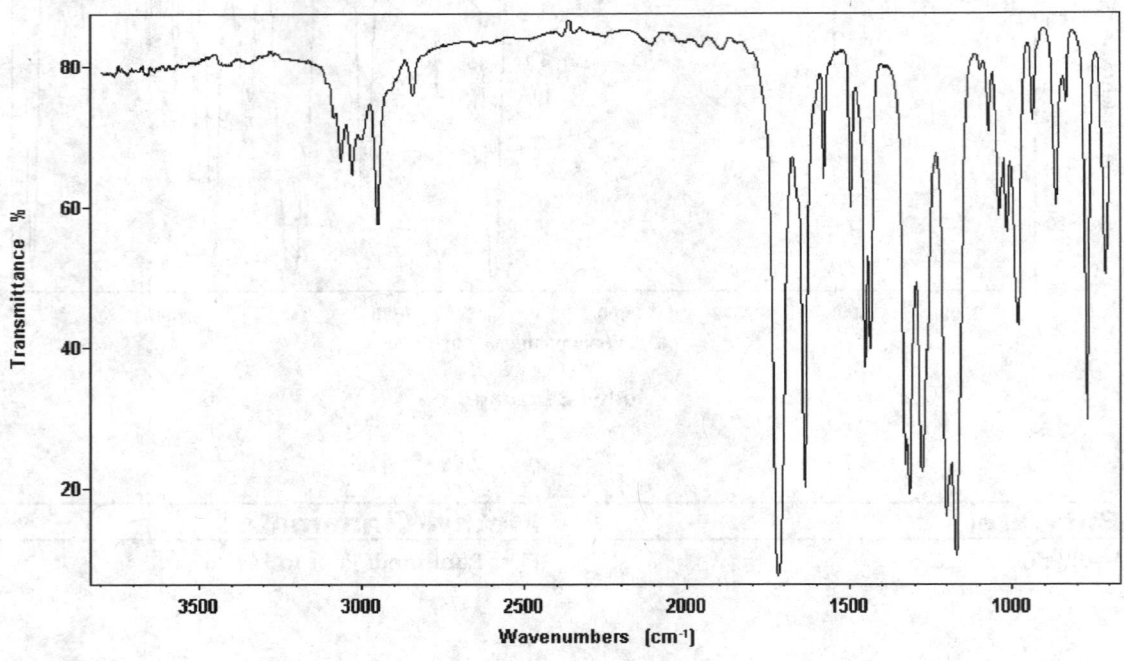

Methyl Cinnamate

Methyl Cyclopentenolone

First Published: Prior to FCC 6

3-Methylcyclopentane-1,2-dione

$C_6H_8O_2$
FEMA: 2700
UNII: 627E92X64B [methylcyclopentenolone]

Formula wt 112.13

DESCRIPTION
Methyl Cyclopentenolone occurs as a white, crystalline powder.
Odor: Nutty, maple-licorice aroma in dilute solution

Solubility: Soluble in alcohol, propylene glycol; slightly soluble in most fixed oils; 1 g dissolves in 72 mL water
Solubility in Alcohol, Appendix VI: One g dissolves in 5 mL of 90% alcohol.
Function: Flavoring agent

IDENTIFICATION
- **INFRARED SPECTRA,** *Spectrophotometric Identification Tests,* Appendix IIIC
  Acceptance criteria: The spectrum of the sample exhibits relative maxima at the same wavelengths as those of the spectrum below.

OTHER REQUIREMENTS
- **MELTING RANGE OR TEMPERATURE DETERMINATION,** Appendix IIB
  Acceptance criteria: Between 104° and 108°

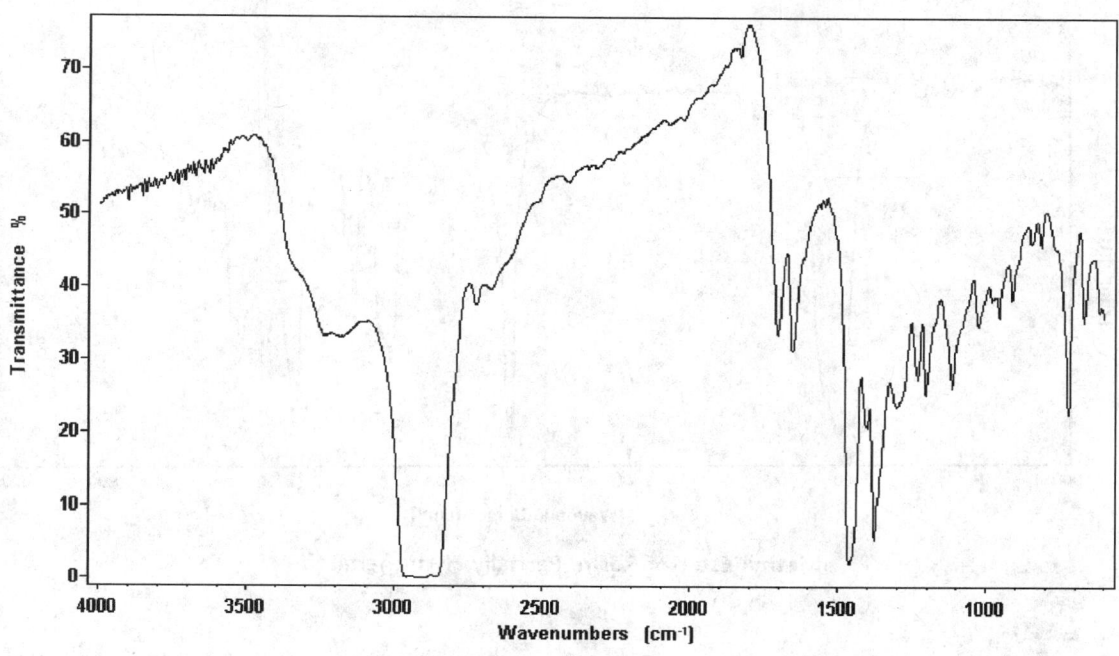

Methyl Cyclopentenolone

Methyl Ester of Rosin, Partially Hydrogenated

First Published: Prior to FCC 6

DESCRIPTION
Methyl Ester of Rosin, Partially Hydrogenated, occurs as a light amber-colored liquid resin. It is soluble in acetone but insoluble in water.
Function: Masticatory substance in chewing gum base
Packaging and Storage: Store in well-closed containers.

IDENTIFICATION
- **INFRARED SPECTRA,** *Spectrophotometric Identification Tests,* Appendix IIIC
  Sample preparation: Neat dispersion of sample on a potassium bromide plate
  Acceptance criteria: The spectrum of the sample exhibits relative maxima at the same wavelengths as those of the spectrum below.

IMPURITIES
Inorganic Impurities
- **LEAD,** *Sample Solution for Lead Limit Test,* Appendix IV
  Control: 5 µg Pb (5 mL of *Diluted Standard Lead Solution*)
  Acceptance criteria: NMT 1 mg/kg

SPECIFIC TESTS
- **ACID NUMBER,** Appendix IX
  Acceptance criteria: Between 4 and 8
- **REFRACTIVE INDEX,** Appendix IIB
  [NOTE—Use an Abbé or other refractometer of equal or greater accuracy.]
  Acceptance criteria: Between 1.517 and 1.520 at 20°
- **VISCOSITY (ROSINS AND RELATED SUBSTANCES),** Appendix IX
  Acceptance criteria: Between 23 and 76 poises

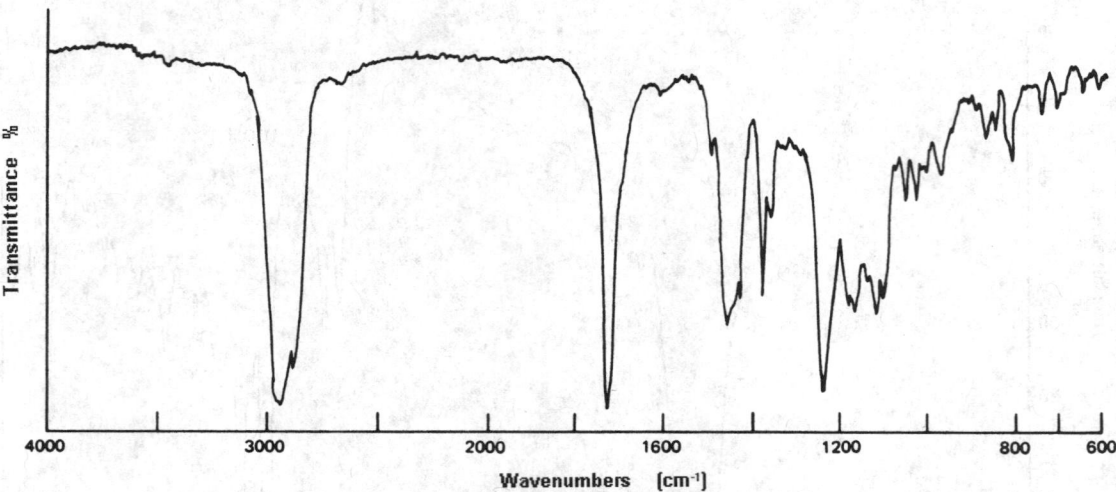

Methyl Ester of Rosin, Partially Hydrogenated

Methyl Ethyl Cellulose

First Published: Prior to FCC 6

Modified Cellulose
INS: 465 CAS: [9004-69-7]

DESCRIPTION
Methyl Ethyl Cellulose occurs as a white or pale cream, fibrous solid or powder. It is the methyl ether of ethyl cellulose in which both the methyl and the ethyl groups are attached to the anhydroglucose units by ether linkages. It disperses in cold water to form aqueous sols that undergo a reversible transformation to gel upon heating and cooling, respectively.
Function: Emulsifier; stabilizer; foaming agent
Packaging and Storage: Store in well-closed containers.

IDENTIFICATION
- **A. PROCEDURE**
  Sample: 1 g
  Analysis: Add the *Sample* to 100 mL of water. [NOTE—Save this solution for use in *Identification* tests *B* and *C*.]
  Acceptance criteria: The sample disperses to form an opalescent, fibrous solution.
- **B. PROCEDURE**
  Sample: A few mL of the solution prepared in *Identification* test *A* (above)
  Analysis: Heat the *Sample* to about 60°.
  Acceptance criteria: The solution becomes cloudy, and a gelatinous precipitate forms that redissolves upon cooling.
- **C. PROCEDURE**
  Sample: The remaining solution from *Identification* test *A* (above)
  Analysis: Whip the *Sample* with a kitchen-type mixer (as if whipping egg whites).
  Acceptance criteria: A stable air/liquid foam is produced.

ASSAY
- **ASSAY FOR ETHOXYL GROUPS,** *Hydroxypropoxyl Determination,* Appendix IIIC
  Analysis: Each mL of 0.02 N sodium hydroxide is equivalent to 0.9 mg of ethoxyl groups ($-OC_2H_5$)
  Acceptance criteria: NLT 14.5% and NMT 19.0% of ethoxyl groups ($-OC_2H_5$).
- **ASSAY FOR METHOXYL GROUPS,** *Methoxyl Determination,* Appendix IIIC
  Sample: 50 mg, previously dried, placed in a tared gelatin capsule
  Analysis: Determine as directed, but calculate the total alkoxyl content as ethoxyl groups ($-OC_2H_5$). Each mL of 0.1 N sodium thiosulfate is equivalent to 0.7510 mg of ethoxyl groups ($-OC_2H_5$). Calculate the methoxyl groups ($-OCH_3$) by the formula:

$$Result = (A - B) \times 31/45$$

  A = total alkoxyl content, calculated as $-OC_2H_5$
  B = $-OC_2H_5$ determined in the *Assay* for Ethoxyl Groups (above)
  31 = molecular weight of $-OCH_3$
  45 = molecular weight of $-OC_2H_5$
  Acceptance criteria: NLT 3.5% and NMT 6.5% of methoxyl groups ($-OCH_3$).

IMPURITIES
Inorganic Impurities
- **LEAD,** *Lead Limit Test,* Appendix IIIB
  Sample: Prepare as directed for organic compounds using 2 g of sample.
  Control: 6 µg Pb (6 mL of *Diluted Standard Lead Solution*)

Acceptance criteria: NMT 3 mg/kg

SPECIFIC TESTS
- **LOSS ON DRYING**, Appendix IIC: 105° for 4 h
  Sample: 3 g
  Acceptance criteria
   Fibrous form: NMT 15.0%
   Powdered form: NMT 10.0%
- **RESIDUE ON IGNITION (SULFATED ASH)**, Appendix IIC
  Sample: 1 g
  Acceptance criteria: NMT 0.6%
- **VISCOSITY DETERMINATION**, *Viscosity of Methylcellulose*, Appendix IIB
  Sample solution: Transfer an amount of sample equivalent to 5.0 g on the dried basis into a 250-mL beaker. Adjust the rotor of a variable-speed stirrer about 1 in above the sample, add 195 mL of recently boiled and cooled water, and stir at a speed that will avoid undue aeration. Continue stirring for about 1.5 h, then either set aside for 3 h to overnight, or centrifuge to expel any entrapped air. Adjust the temperature to 20° ± 0.1°.
  Analysis: Determine as directed using a *Viscometer for High Viscosity*.
  Acceptance criteria: NLT 80% and NMT 120% of that stated on the label or otherwise represented by the vendor. [NOTE—The usual range of viscosity types is between 20 and 60 cP.]

Methyl Eugenol

First Published: Prior to FCC 6

Eugenyl Methyl Ether
1,2-Dimethoxy-4-allylbenzene

$C_{11}H_{14}O_2$ Formula wt 178.23
FEMA: 2475
UNII: 29T9VA6R7M [methyl eugenol]

DESCRIPTION
Methyl Eugenol occurs as a colorless to pale yellow liquid.
Odor: Delicate, clove-carnation
Solubility: Soluble in most fixed oils; insoluble or practically insoluble in glycerin, propylene glycol
Boiling Point: ~249°
Solubility in Alcohol, Appendix VI: One mL dissolves in 2 mL of 70% alcohol, and remains in solution on dilution to 10 mL.
Function: Flavoring agent

IDENTIFICATION
- **INFRARED SPECTRA**, *Spectrophotometric Identification Tests*, Appendix IIIC
  Acceptance criteria: The spectrum of the sample exhibits relative maxima at the same wavelengths as those of the spectrum below.

ASSAY
- **PROCEDURE:** Proceed as directed under *M-1b*, Appendix XI.
  Acceptance criteria: NLT 98.0% of $C_{11}H_{14}O_2$ (one major isomer)

SPECIFIC TESTS
- **REFRACTIVE INDEX**, Appendix II: At 20°
  Acceptance criteria: Between 1.532 and 1.536
- **SPECIFIC GRAVITY:** Determine at 25° by any reliable method (see *General Provisions*).
  Acceptance criteria: Between 1.032 and 1.036

OTHER REQUIREMENTS
- **EUGENOL,** *M-1b*, Appendix XI
  Acceptance criteria: NMT 1.0%

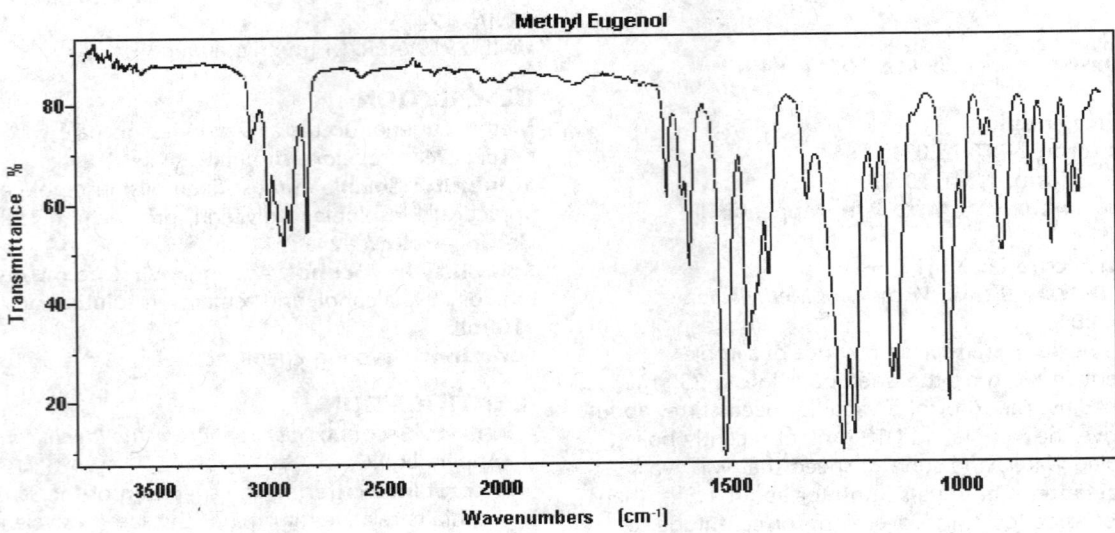

Methyl Eugenol

Methyl Furoate

First Published: Prior to FCC 6

C₆H₆O₃ Formula wt 126.11
FEMA: 2703
UNII: O9A8D29YDE [methyl 2-furoate]

DESCRIPTION
Methyl Furoate occurs as a pale yellow to brown liquid.
Odor: Fruity
Solubility: Soluble in propylene glycol, vegetable oils; insoluble or practically insoluble in water
Boiling Point: ~181°
Solubility in Alcohol, Appendix VI: One mL dissolves in 1 mL of 95% ethanol.
Function: Flavoring agent

IDENTIFICATION
- **INFRARED SPECTRA,** Spectrophotometric Identification Tests, Appendix IIIC
  Acceptance criteria: The spectrum of the sample exhibits relative maxima at the same wavelengths as those of the spectrum below.

ASSAY
- **PROCEDURE:** Proceed as directed under M-1b, Appendix XI.
  Acceptance criteria: NLT 98.0% of C₆H₆O₃

SPECIFIC TESTS
- **ACID VALUE, FLAVOR CHEMICALS (OTHER THAN ESSENTIAL OILS),** M-15, Appendix XI
  Acceptance criteria: NMT 5.0
- **REFRACTIVE INDEX,** Appendix II: At 20°
  Acceptance criteria: Between 1.483 and 1.500
- **SPECIFIC GRAVITY:** Determine at 25° by any reliable method (see General Provisions).
  Acceptance criteria: Between 1.174 and 1.180

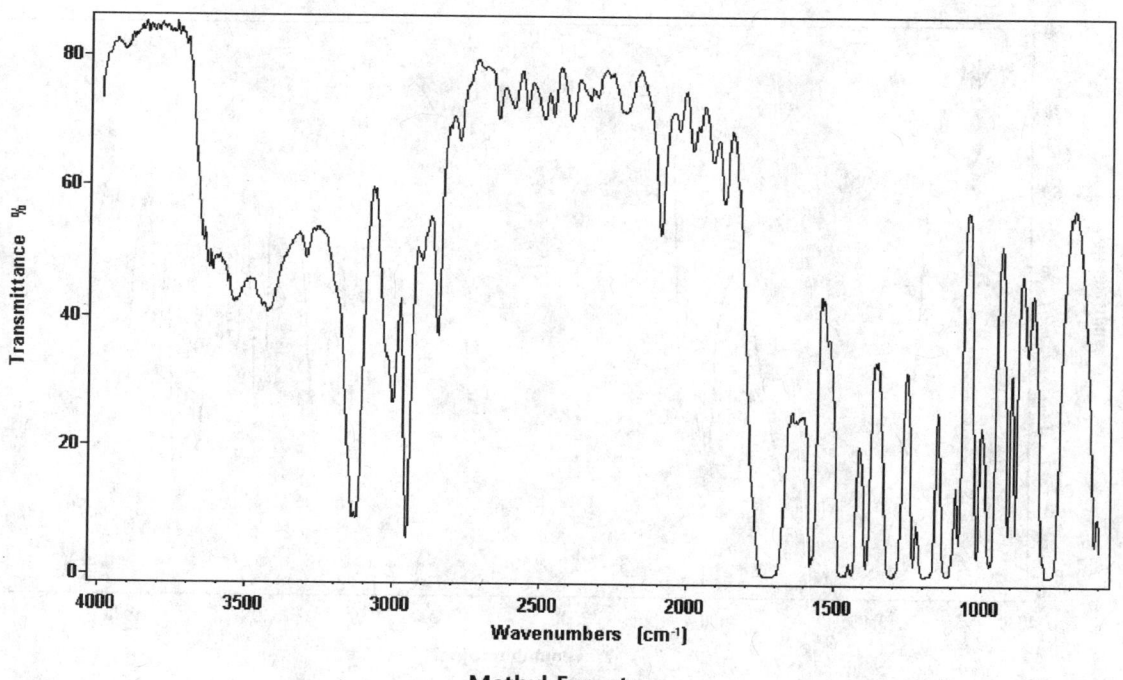

Methyl Furoate

Methyl Hexanoate

First Published: Prior to FCC 6

C₇H₁₄O₂ Formula wt 130.19
FEMA: 2708
UNII: 246364VPJS [methyl caproate]

DESCRIPTION
Methyl Hexanoate occurs as a colorless to pale yellow liquid.
Odor: Fruity
Solubility: Soluble in propylene glycol, vegetable oils; insoluble or practically insoluble in water
Boiling Point: ~151°
Solubility in Alcohol, Appendix VI: One mL dissolves in 1 mL of 95% ethanol.
Function: Flavoring agent

IDENTIFICATION
- **INFRARED SPECTRA,** Spectrophotometric Identification Tests, Appendix IIIC
  Acceptance criteria: The spectrum of the sample exhibits relative maxima at the same wavelengths as those of the spectrum below.

ASSAY
- **PROCEDURE:** Proceed as directed under M-1b, Appendix XI.
  Acceptance criteria: NLT 98.0% of C₇H₁₄O₂

SPECIFIC TESTS
- **ACID VALUE, FLAVOR CHEMICALS (OTHER THAN ESSENTIAL OILS),** M-15, Appendix XI
  Acceptance criteria: NMT 2.0
- **REFRACTIVE INDEX,** Appendix II: At 20°
  Acceptance criteria: Between 1.402 and 1.408
- **SPECIFIC GRAVITY:** Determine at 25° by any reliable method (see General Provisions).
  Acceptance criteria: Between 0.880 and 0.886

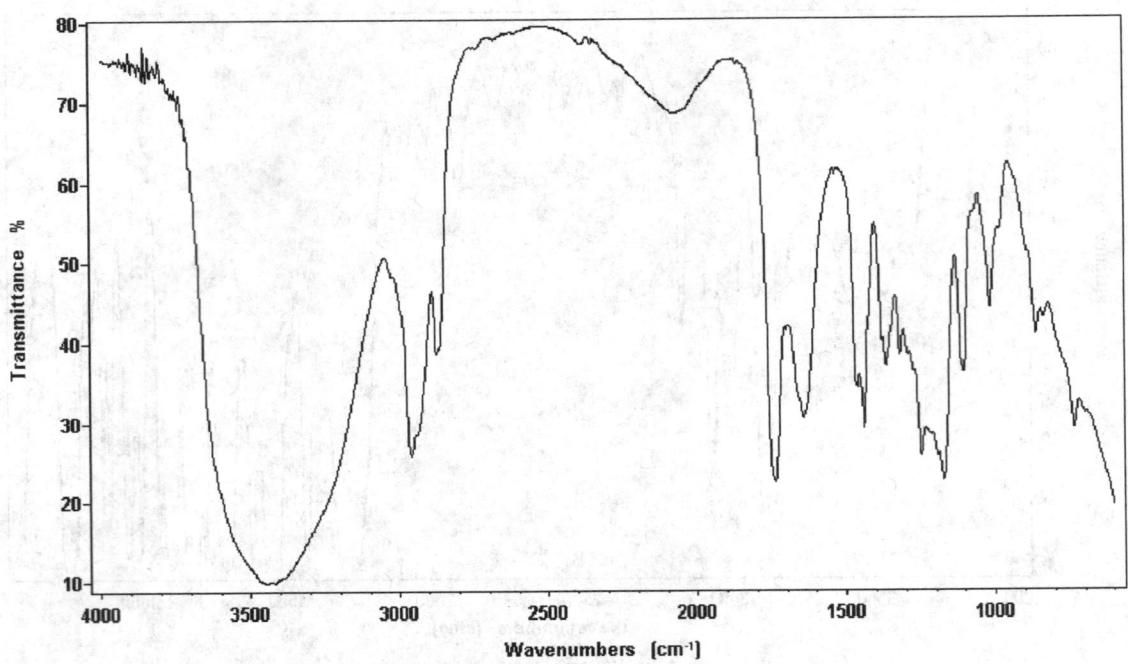

Methyl Hexanoate

Methyl Hexyl Ketone

First Published: Prior to FCC 6

2-Octanone

$C_8H_{16}O$ Formula wt 128.21
FEMA: 2802
UNII: J2G84H29AF [2-octanone]

DESCRIPTION
Methyl Hexyl Ketone occurs as a colorless to pale yellow liquid.
Odor: Apple
Solubility: Soluble in propylene glycol, vegetable oils; insoluble or practically insoluble in water
Boiling Point: ~175°
Solubility in Alcohol, Appendix VI: One mL dissolves in 1 mL of 95% alcohol.

Function: Flavoring agent

IDENTIFICATION
- **INFRARED SPECTRA,** Spectrophotometric Identification Tests, Appendix IIIC
  Acceptance criteria: The spectrum of the sample exhibits relative maxima at the same wavelengths as those of the spectrum below.

ASSAY
- **PROCEDURE:** Proceed as directed under M-1a, Appendix XI.
  Acceptance criteria: NLT 95.0% of $C_8H_{16}O$

SPECIFIC TESTS
- **ACID VALUE, FLAVOR CHEMICALS (OTHER THAN ESSENTIAL OILS),** M-15, Appendix XI
  Acceptance criteria: NMT 1.0
- **REFRACTIVE INDEX,** Appendix II: At 20°
  Acceptance criteria: Between 1.414 and 1.418
- **SPECIFIC GRAVITY:** Determine at 25° by any reliable method (see General Provisions).
  Acceptance criteria: Between 0.813 and 0.818

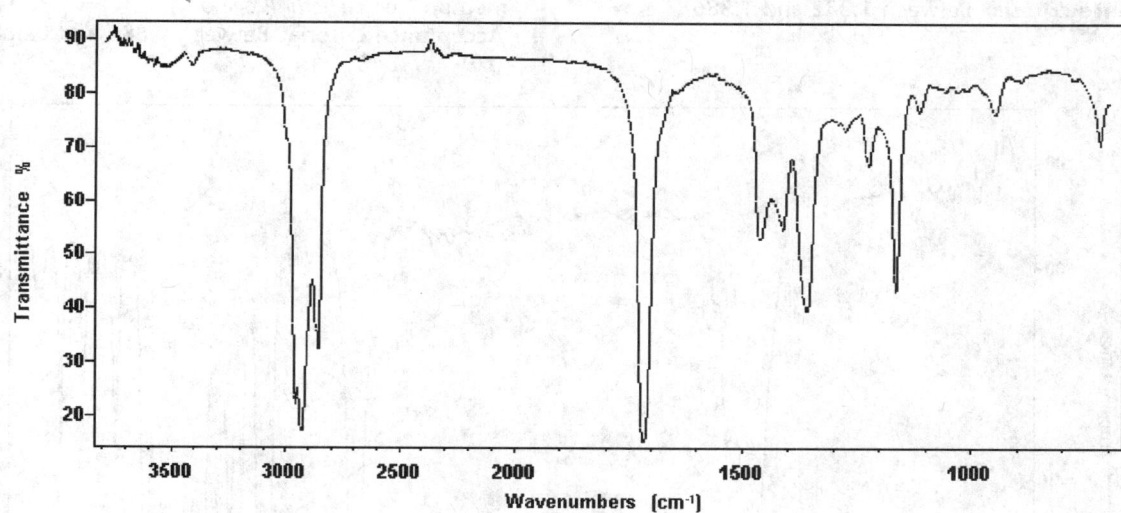

Methyl Hexyl Ketone

Methyl Ionones

First Published: Prior to FCC 6

Mixture of α-, β-, γ- or α-iso, and δ-isomers

$C_{14}H_{22}O$ Formula wt 206.3
UNII: EL78BGX1LO [methyl ionones]

DESCRIPTION
Methyl Ionones occur as clear to pale yellow to yellow liquids.
Odor: Woody, orris
Boiling Point: ~232° to 270°
Solubility in Alcohol, Appendix VI: One mL dissolves in 1 mL of 95% ethanol.
Function: Flavoring agent

ASSAY
- **Procedure:** Proceed as directed under *M-1b*, Appendix XI.
  Acceptance criteria: NLT 88.0% of $C_{14}H_{22}O$ (sum of four isomers)

SPECIFIC TESTS
- **Acid Value, Flavor Chemicals (Other Than Essential Oils),** *M-15*, Appendix XI
  Acceptance criteria: NMT 5.0
- **Refractive Index,** Appendix II: At 20°
  Acceptance criteria: Between 1.497 and 1.507
- **Specific Gravity:** Determine at 25° by any reliable method (see *General Provisions*).
  Acceptance criteria: Between 0.925 and 0.934

Methyl Isobutyrate

First Published: Prior to FCC 6

$C_5H_{10}O_2$ Formula wt 102.13
FEMA: 2694
UNII: EM286QL922 [methyl isobutyrate]

DESCRIPTION
Methyl Isobutyrate occurs as a colorless liquid.
Odor: Fruity
Boiling Point: ~90°
Solubility in Alcohol, Appendix VI: One mL dissolves in 1 mL of 95% alcohol.
Function: Flavoring agent

IDENTIFICATION
- **Infrared Spectra,** *Spectrophotometric Identification Tests,* Appendix IIIC
  Acceptance criteria: The spectrum of the sample exhibits relative maxima at the same wavelengths as those of the spectrum below.

ASSAY
- **Procedure:** Proceed as directed under *M-1b*, Appendix XI.
  Acceptance criteria: NLT 97.0% of $C_5H_{10}O_2$

SPECIFIC TESTS
- **Acid Value, Flavor Chemicals (Other Than Essential Oils),** *M-15*, Appendix XI
  Acceptance criteria: NMT 1.0

748 / Methyl Isobutyrate / Monographs

- **REFRACTIVE INDEX,** Appendix II: At 20°
  Acceptance criteria: Between 1.382 and 1.386
- **SPECIFIC GRAVITY:** Determine at 25° by any reliable method (see *General Provisions*).
  Acceptance criteria: Between 0.884 and 0.888

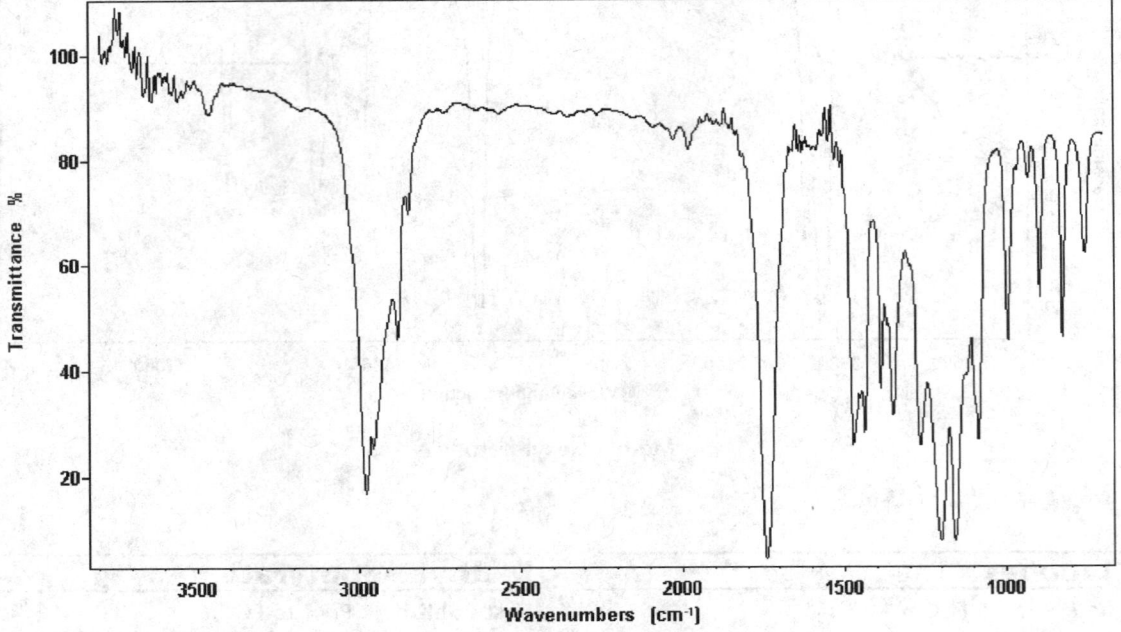

Methyl Isobutyrate

Methyl Isoeugenol

First Published: Prior to FCC 6

4-Allyl-1,2-dimethoxy Benzene
Isoeugenyl Methyl Ether
4-Propenyl Veratrole

$C_{11}H_{14}O_2$ Formula wt 178.23
FEMA: 2476
UNII: 46RN7Q97DE [methyl isoeugenol]

DESCRIPTION
Methyl Isoeugenol occurs as a colorless to pale yellow liquid.
Odor: Delicate, clove-carnation
Solubility: Soluble in most fixed oils; insoluble or practically insoluble in glycerin, propylene glycol
Boiling Point: ~270°
Solubility in Alcohol, Appendix VI: One mL dissolves in 2 mL of 70% alcohol, and remains in solution upon dilution to 10 mL.

Function: Flavoring agent

IDENTIFICATION
- **INFRARED SPECTRA,** *Spectrophotometric Identification Tests,* Appendix IIIC
  Acceptance criteria: The spectrum of the sample exhibits relative maxima at the same wavelengths as those of the spectrum below.

ASSAY
- **PROCEDURE:** Proceed as directed under *M-1a,* Appendix XI.
  Acceptance criteria: NLT 85.0% of $C_{11}H_{14}O_2$ (one isomer)

SPECIFIC TESTS
- **REFRACTIVE INDEX,** Appendix II: At 20°
  Acceptance criteria: Between 1.566 and 1.569
- **SPECIFIC GRAVITY:** Determine at 25° by any reliable method (see *General Provisions*).
  Acceptance criteria: Between 1.047 and 1.053

OTHER REQUIREMENTS
- **ISOEUGENOL,** *M-1b,* Appendix XI
  Acceptance criteria: NMT 1.0%

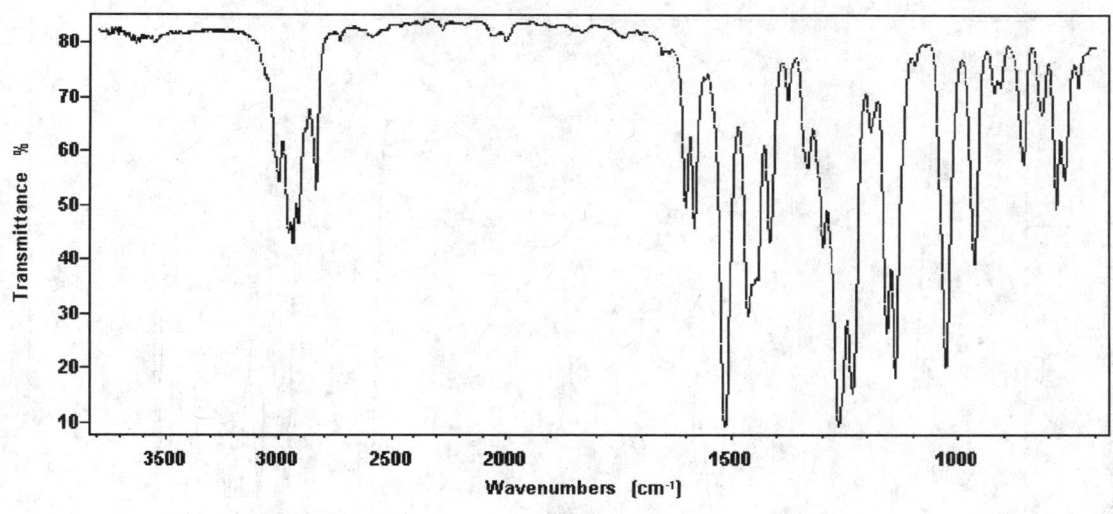
Methyl Isoeugenol

Methyl Isovalerate
First Published: Prior to FCC 6

C₆H₁₂O₂ Formula wt 116.16
FEMA: 2753
UNII: QPS4788198 [methyl isovalerate]

DESCRIPTION
Methyl Isovalerate occurs as a colorless to pale yellow liquid.
Odor: Apple
Solubility: Soluble in propylene glycol, vegetable oils; insoluble or practically insoluble in water
Boiling Point: ~114°
Solubility in Alcohol, Appendix VI: One mL dissolves in 1 mL of 95% ethanol.
Function: Flavoring agent

IDENTIFICATION
- **INFRARED SPECTRA,** Spectrophotometric Identification Tests, Appendix IIIC
  Acceptance criteria: The spectrum of the sample exhibits relative maxima at the same wavelengths as those of the spectrum below.

ASSAY
- **PROCEDURE:** Proceed as directed under *M-1b*, Appendix XI.
  Acceptance criteria: NLT 95.0% of C₁₀H₁₂O₂

SPECIFIC TESTS
- **ACID VALUE, FLAVOR CHEMICALS (OTHER THAN ESSENTIAL OILS),** *M-15,* Appendix XI
  Acceptance criteria: NMT 1.0
- **REFRACTIVE INDEX,** Appendix II: At 20°
  Acceptance criteria: Between 1.390 and 1.396
- **SPECIFIC GRAVITY:** Determine at 25° by any reliable method (see *General Provisions*).
  Acceptance criteria: Between 0.878 and 0.884

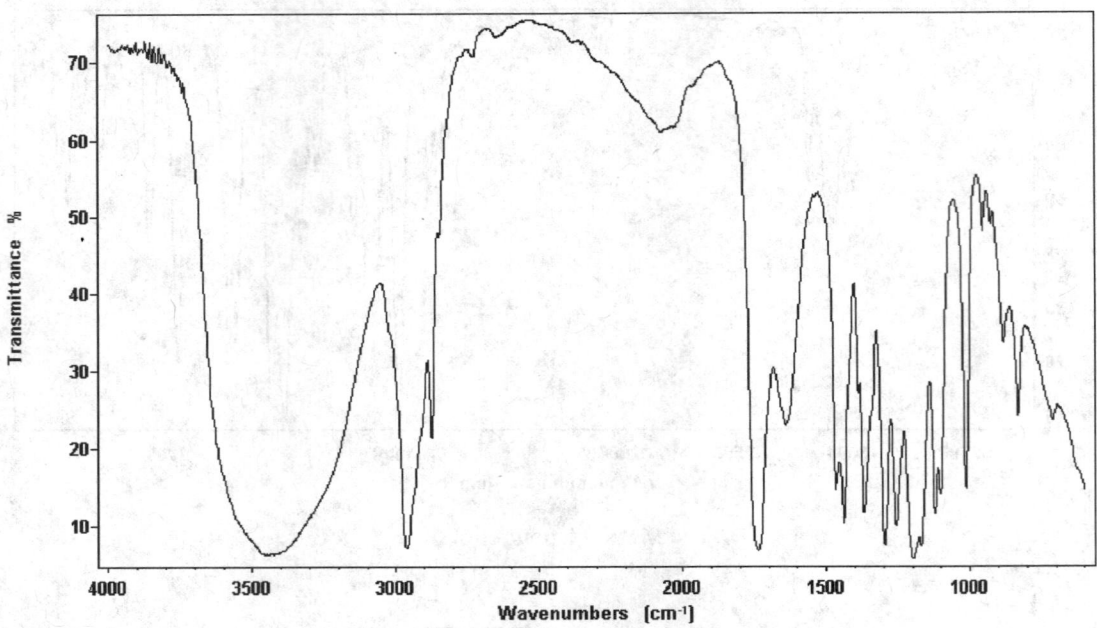

Methyl Isovalerate

Methyl Phenylacetate

First Published: Prior to FCC 6

C₉H₁₀O₂   Formula wt 150.18
FEMA: 2733
UNII: D4PDC41X96 [methyl phenylacetate]

DESCRIPTION
Methyl Phenylacetate occurs as a colorless or nearly colorless liquid.
Odor: Honey, jasmine
Solubility: Soluble in alcohol, most fixed oils; insoluble or practically insoluble in glycerin, propylene glycol, water
Boiling Point: ~215°
Solubility in Alcohol, Appendix VI: One mL dissolves in 6 mL of 60% alcohol.
Function: Flavoring agent

IDENTIFICATION
- **INFRARED SPECTRA,** Spectrophotometric Identification Tests, Appendix IIIC
  Acceptance criteria: The spectrum of the sample exhibits relative maxima at the same wavelengths as those of the spectrum below.

ASSAY
- **PROCEDURE:** Proceed as directed under *M-1b*, Appendix XI.
  Acceptance criteria: NLT 98.0% of C₉H₁₀O₂

SPECIFIC TESTS
- **ACID VALUE, FLAVOR CHEMICALS (OTHER THAN ESSENTIAL OILS),** *M-15,* Appendix XI
  Acceptance criteria: NMT 1.0
- **REFRACTIVE INDEX,** Appendix II: At 20°
  Acceptance criteria: Between 1.503 and 1.509
- **SPECIFIC GRAVITY:** Determine at 25° by any reliable method (see *General Provisions*).
  Acceptance criteria: Between 1.061 and 1.067

OTHER REQUIREMENTS
- **CHLORINATED COMPOUNDS,** Appendix VI
  Acceptance criteria: Passes test

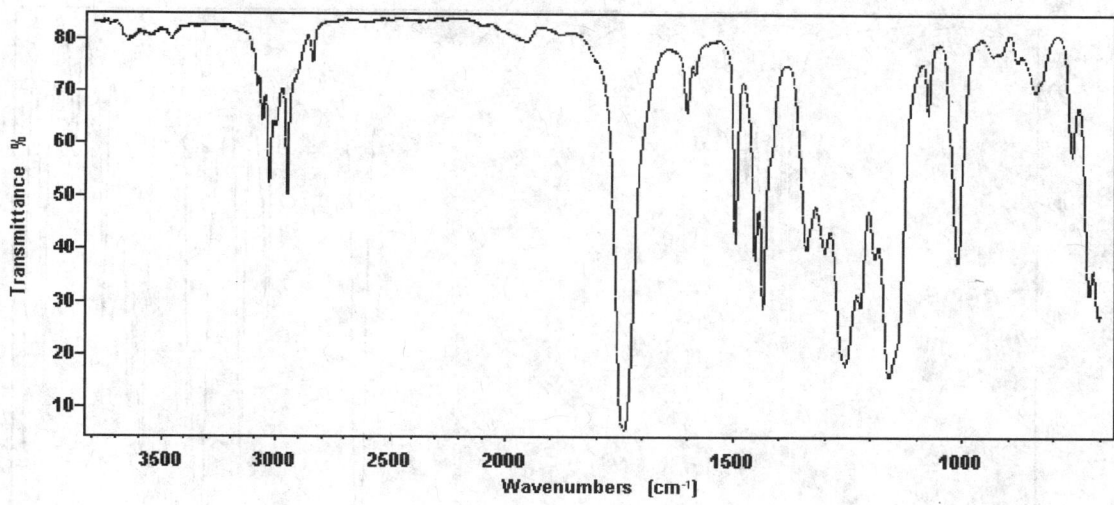

Methyl Phenylacetate

Methyl Phenylcarbinyl Acetate

First Published: Prior to FCC 6

α-Phenyl Ethyl Acetate

$C_{10}H_{12}O_2$ Formula wt 164.20
FEMA: 2684
UNII: FYS3E9NBA3 [α-methylbenzyl acetate]

DESCRIPTION
Methyl Phenylcarbinyl Acetate occurs as a colorless liquid.
Odor: Gardenia
Solubility: Soluble in most fixed oils, glycerin; insoluble or practically insoluble in water
Boiling Point: ~214°
Solubility in Alcohol, Appendix VI: One mL dissolves in 7 mL of 60% alcohol.
Function: Flavoring agent

IDENTIFICATION
- **INFRARED SPECTRA,** Spectrophotometric Identification Tests, Appendix IIIC
  Acceptance criteria: The spectrum of the sample exhibits relative maxima at the same wavelengths as those of the spectrum below.

ASSAY
- **PROCEDURE:** Proceed as directed under *M-1b*, Appendix XI.
  Acceptance criteria: NLT 97.0% of $C_{10}H_{12}O_2$

SPECIFIC TESTS
- **ACID VALUE, FLAVOR CHEMICALS (OTHER THAN ESSENTIAL OILS),** *M-15,* Appendix XI
  Acceptance criteria: NMT 2.0
- **REFRACTIVE INDEX,** Appendix II: At 20°
  Acceptance criteria: Between 1.493 and 1.497
- **SPECIFIC GRAVITY:** Determine at 25° by any reliable method (see *General Provisions*).
  Acceptance criteria: Between 1.023 and 1.026

OTHER REQUIREMENTS
- **CHLORINATED COMPOUNDS,** Appendix VI
  Acceptance criteria: Passes test

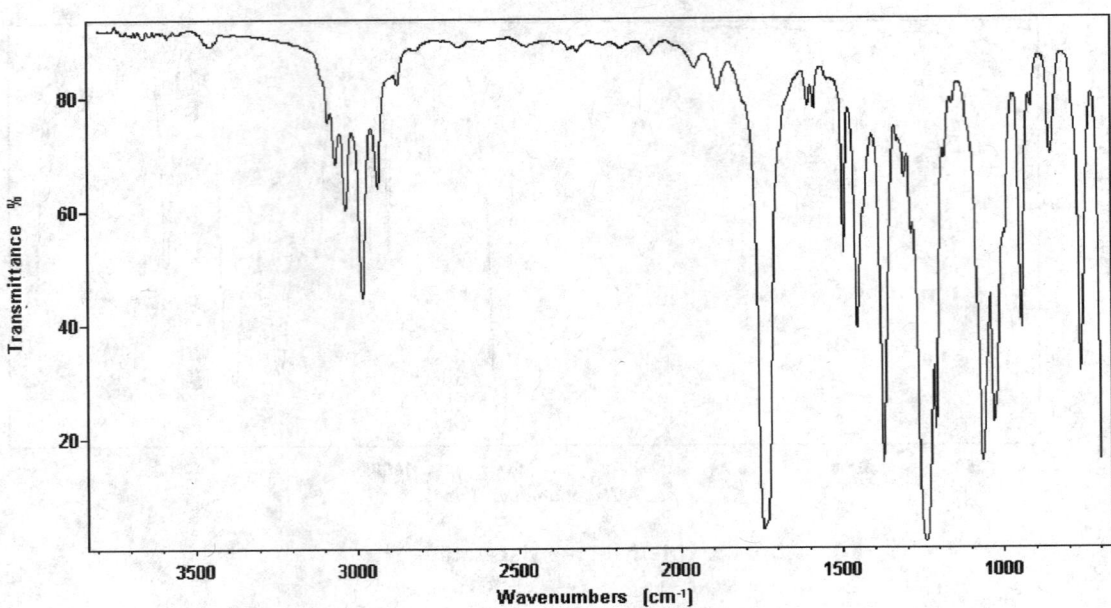

Methyl Phenylcarbinyl Acetate

Methyl Salicylate

First Published: Prior to FCC 6
Last Revision: Third Supplement, FCC 7

$C_8H_8O_3$ Formula wt 152.15
FEMA: 2745
UNII: LAV5U5022Y [methyl salicylate]

DESCRIPTION
Methyl Salicylate occurs as a colorless to yellow liquid.
Odor: Wintergreen
Solubility: Soluble in alcohol, glacial acetic acid; slightly soluble in water
Boiling Point: ~222° (decomp)
Solubility in Alcohol, Appendix VI: One mL dissolves in 7 mL of 70% alcohol, and may be slightly cloudy.
Function: Flavoring agent

IDENTIFICATION
- **INFRARED SPECTRA,** *Spectrophotometric Identification Tests,* Appendix IIIC
  Reference standard: USP Methyl Salicylate RS
  Sample and standard preparation: *F*
  Acceptance criteria: The spectrum of the sample exhibits maxima at the same wavelengths as those in the spectrum of the *Reference standard.*

ASSAY
- **PROCEDURE:** Proceed as directed under *M-1b,* Appendix XI.
  Acceptance criteria: NLT 98.0% of $C_8H_8O_3$

SPECIFIC TESTS
- **ACID VALUE, FLAVOR CHEMICALS (OTHER THAN ESSENTIAL OILS),** *M-15,* Appendix XI
  [NOTE—Use phenol red TS as the indicator.]
  Acceptance criteria: NMT 1.0
- **REFRACTIVE INDEX,** Appendix II: At 20°
  Acceptance criteria: 1.535–1.538
- **SPECIFIC GRAVITY:** Determine at 25° by any reliable method (see *General Provisions*).
  Acceptance criteria: 1.180–1.185

Methyl Thiobutyrate

First Published: Prior to FCC 6

$C_5H_{10}OS$ Formula wt 118.20
FEMA: 3310
UNII: 2P1E432MYZ [methyl thiobutyrate]

DESCRIPTION
Methyl Thiobutyrate occurs as a colorless to pale yellow liquid.
Odor: Pungent

Solubility: Soluble in propylene glycol, vegetable oils; insoluble or practically insoluble in water
Boiling Point: ~143°
Solubility in Alcohol, Appendix VI: One mL dissolves in 1 mL of 95% ethanol.
Function: Flavoring agent

IDENTIFICATION
- **INFRARED SPECTRA,** *Spectrophotometric Identification Tests,* Appendix IIIC
  Acceptance criteria: The spectrum of the sample exhibits relative maxima at the same wavelengths as those of the spectrum below.

ASSAY
- **PROCEDURE:** Proceed as directed under *M-1b,* Appendix XI.
  Acceptance criteria: NLT 97.0% of $C_5H_{10}OS$

SPECIFIC TESTS
- **ACID VALUE, FLAVOR CHEMICALS (OTHER THAN ESSENTIAL OILS),** *M-15,* Appendix XI
  Acceptance criteria: NMT 3.0
- **REFRACTIVE INDEX,** Appendix II: At 20°
  Acceptance criteria: Between 1.461 and 1.467
- **SPECIFIC GRAVITY:** Determine at 25° by any reliable method (see *General Provisions*).
  Acceptance criteria: Between 0.964 and 0.970

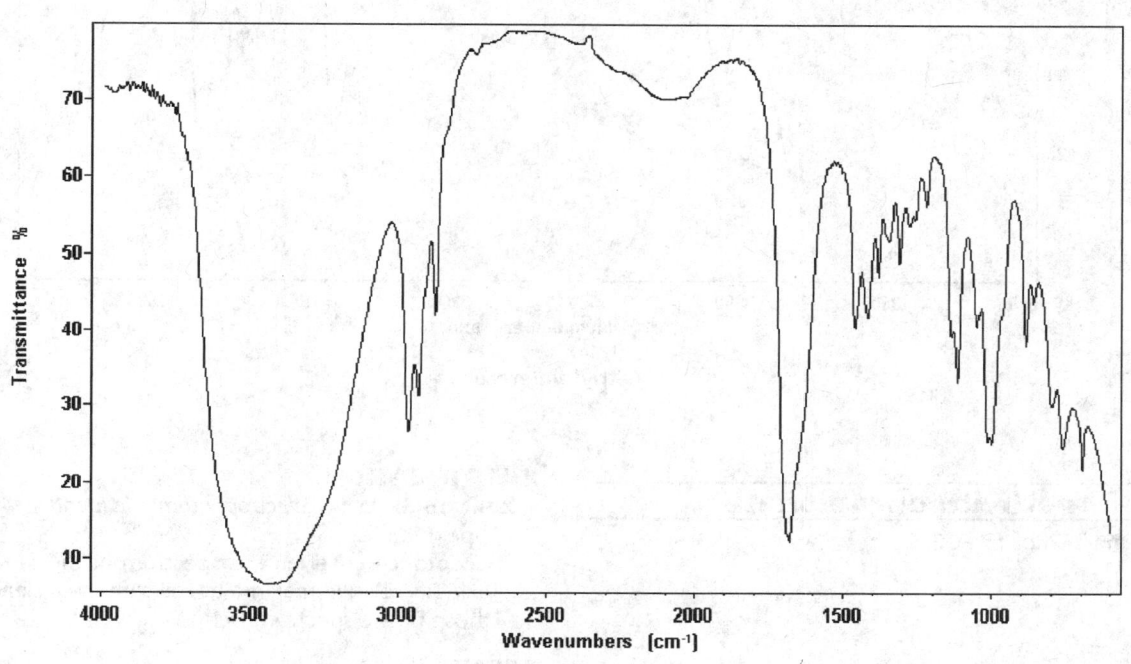

Methyl Thiobutyrate

Methyl Valerate

First Published: Prior to FCC 6

$C_6H_{12}O_2$ Formula wt 116.16
FEMA: 2752
UNII: ZW21JJJ9VN [methyl valerate]

DESCRIPTION
Methyl Valerate occurs as a colorless to pale yellow liquid.
Odor: Fruity
Solubility: Soluble in propylene glycol, vegetable oils; insoluble or practically insoluble in water
Boiling Point: ~128°
Solubility in Alcohol, Appendix VI: One mL dissolves in 1 mL of 95% ethanol.
Function: Flavoring agent

IDENTIFICATION
- **INFRARED SPECTRA,** *Spectrophotometric Identification Tests,* Appendix IIIC
  Acceptance criteria: The spectrum of the sample exhibits relative maxima at the same wavelengths as those of the spectrum below.

ASSAY
- **PROCEDURE:** Proceed as directed under *M-1b,* Appendix XI.
  Acceptance criteria: NLT 98.0% of $C_6H_{12}O_2$

SPECIFIC TESTS
- **ACID VALUE, FLAVOR CHEMICALS (OTHER THAN ESSENTIAL OILS),** *M-15,* Appendix XI

Acceptance criteria: NMT 1.0
- **REFRACTIVE INDEX,** Appendix II: At 20°
  Acceptance criteria: Between 1.395 and 1.401
- **SPECIFIC GRAVITY:** Determine at 25° by any reliable method (see *General Provisions*).
  Acceptance criteria: Between 0.885 and 0.891

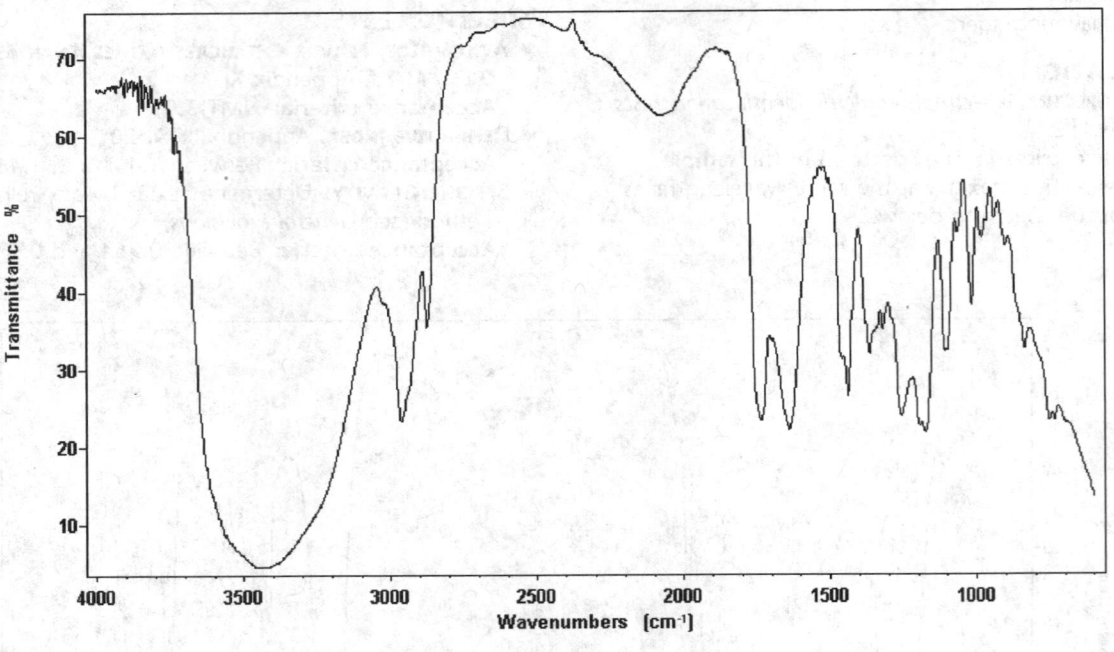

Methyl Valerate

Methyl-3-methylthiopropionate

First Published: Prior to FCC 6

$C_5H_{10}O_2S$ Formula wt 134.19
FEMA: 2720
UNII: 28913SS9T9 [methyl 3-methylthiopropionate]

DESCRIPTION
Methyl-3-methylthiopropionate occurs as a colorless to pale yellow liquid.
Odor: Onion
Solubility: Soluble in propylene glycol, vegetable oils; insoluble or practically insoluble in water
Boiling Point: ~74° to 75° (18 mm Hg)
Solubility in Alcohol, Appendix VI: One mL dissolves in 1 mL of 95% ethanol.
Function: Flavoring agent

IDENTIFICATION
- **INFRARED SPECTRA,** *Spectrophotometric Identification Tests,* Appendix IIIC
  Acceptance criteria: The spectrum of the sample exhibits relative maxima at the same wavelengths as those of the spectrum below.

ASSAY
- **PROCEDURE:** Proceed as directed under *M-1a,* Appendix XI.
  Acceptance criteria: NLT 97.0% of $C_5H_{10}O_2S$

SPECIFIC TESTS
- **ACID VALUE, FLAVOR CHEMICALS (OTHER THAN ESSENTIAL OILS),** *M-15,* Appendix XI
  Acceptance criteria: NMT 1.0
- **REFRACTIVE INDEX,** Appendix II: At 20°
  Acceptance criteria: Between 1.462 and 1.468
- **SPECIFIC GRAVITY:** Determine at 25° by any reliable method (see *General Provisions*).
  Acceptance criteria: Between 1.069 and 1.078

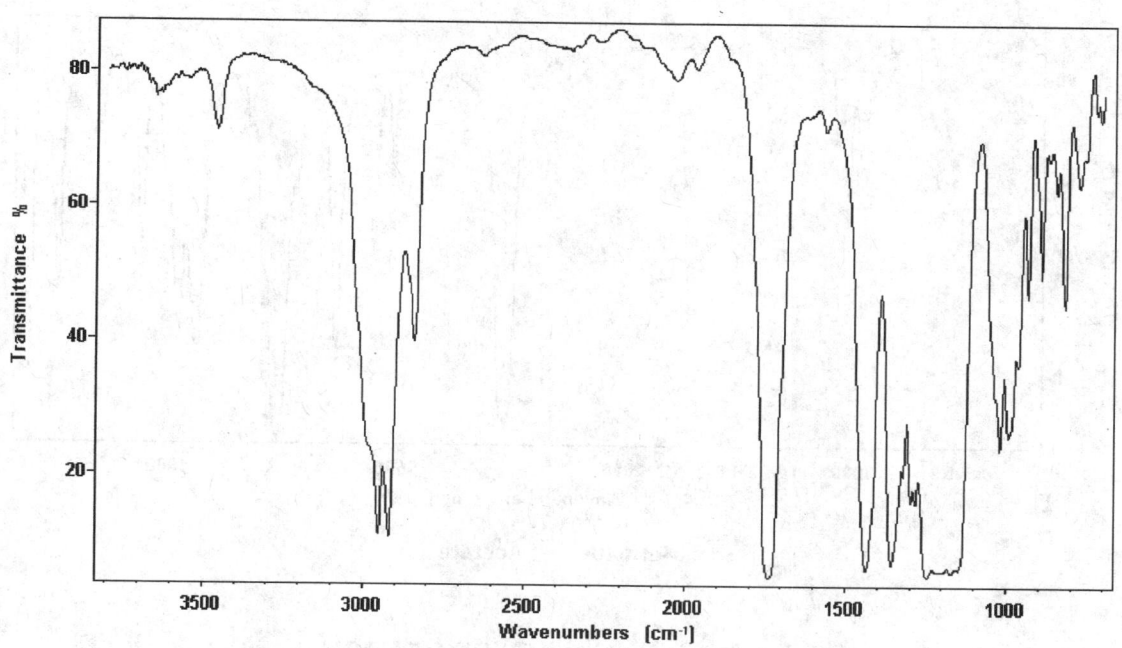

Methyl-3-methylthiopropionate

Methylbenzyl Acetate

First Published: Prior to FCC 6

o-Tolyl Acetate

C₁₀H₁₂O₂ Formula wt 164.20
FEMA: 3072
UNII: 606K99GR0L [o-cresol acetate]

DESCRIPTION
Methylbenzyl Acetate occurs as a colorless liquid.
Odor: Sweet, nutty
Solubility: Soluble in most fixed oils; slightly soluble in propylene glycol; insoluble or practically insoluble in glycerin
Solubility in Alcohol, Appendix VI: One mL dissolves in 2 mL of 70% alcohol, and remains clear on dilution.
Function: Flavoring agent

IDENTIFICATION
- **INFRARED SPECTRA,** *Spectrophotometric Identification Tests,* Appendix IIIC
  Acceptance criteria: The spectrum of the sample exhibits relative maxima at the same wavelengths as those of the spectrum below.

ASSAY
- **PROCEDURE:** Proceed as directed under *M-1b*, Appendix XI.
  Acceptance criteria: NLT 98.0% of C₁₀H₁₂O₂

SPECIFIC TESTS
- **ACID VALUE, FLAVOR CHEMICALS (OTHER THAN ESSENTIAL OILS),** *M-15,* Appendix XI
  Acceptance criteria: NMT 1.0
- **REFRACTIVE INDEX,** Appendix II: At 20°
  Acceptance criteria: Between 1.501 and 1.504
- **SPECIFIC GRAVITY:** Determine at 25° by any reliable method (see *General Provisions*).
  Acceptance criteria: Between 1.030 and 1.035

OTHER REQUIREMENTS
- **CHLORINATED COMPOUNDS,** Appendix VI
  Acceptance criteria: Passes test

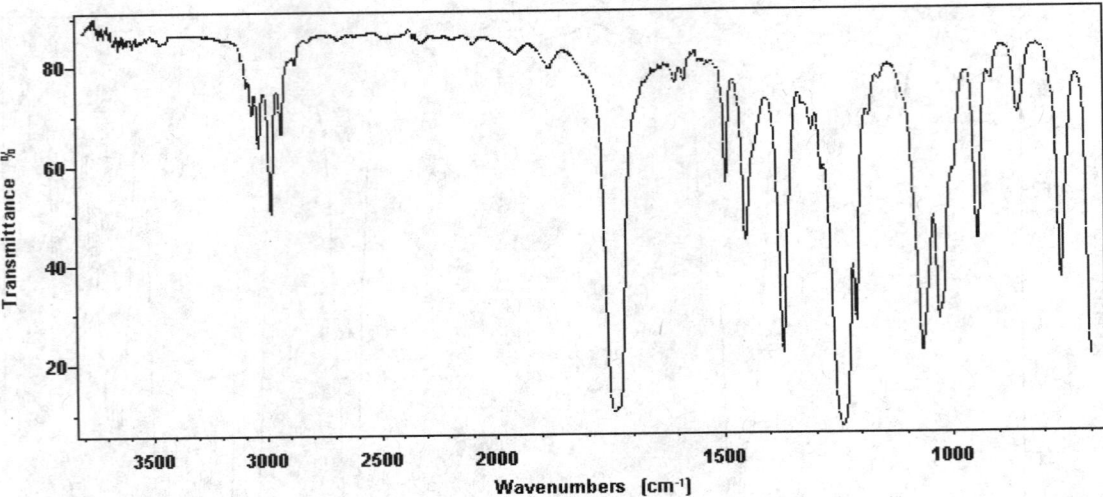

Methylbenzyl Acetate

α-Methylbenzyl Alcohol

First Published: Prior to FCC 6

Methyl Phenylcarbinol
α-Phenethyl Alcohol

$C_8H_{10}O$ Formula wt 122.17
FEMA: 2685
UNII: E6O895DQ52 [1-phenylethanol, (+/-)-]

DESCRIPTION
α-Methylbenzyl alcohol occurs as a colorless liquid above room temperature.
Odor: Mild, hyacinth
Solubility: Very soluble in glycerin; soluble in most fixed oils, propylene glycol
Boiling Point: ~204°
Solubility in Alcohol, Appendix VI: One mL dissolves in 3 mL of 50% alcohol.
Function: Flavoring agent

IDENTIFICATION
- **INFRARED SPECTRA,** Spectrophotometric Identification Tests, Appendix IIIC
  Acceptance criteria: The spectrum of the sample exhibits relative maxima at the same wavelengths as those of the spectrum below.

ASSAY
- **PROCEDURE:** Proceed as directed under M-1b, Appendix XI.
  Acceptance criteria: NLT 99.0% of $C_8H_{10}O$

SPECIFIC TESTS
- **REFRACTIVE INDEX,** Appendix II: At 20°
  Acceptance criteria: Between 1.525 and 1.529
- **SPECIFIC GRAVITY:** Determine at 25° by any reliable method (see General Provisions).
  Acceptance criteria: Between 1.009 and 1.014

OTHER REQUIREMENTS
- **KETONES,** M-2d, Appendix XI
  Sample: 10.0 g
  Analysis: Use 60.07 as the equivalence factor (e).
  Acceptance criteria: NMT 1.0% as acetophenone
- **SOLIDIFICATION POINT,** Appendix IIB
  Acceptance criteria: NLT 19°

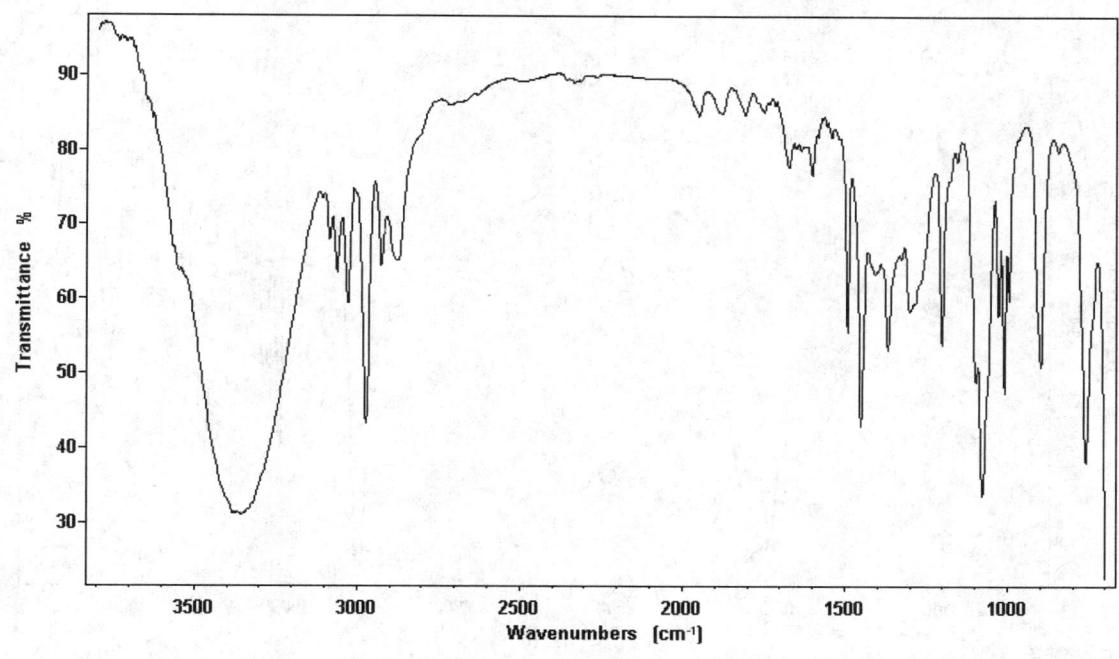

α-Methylbenzyl Alcohol

2-Methylbutyric Acid

First Published: Prior to FCC 6

$C_5H_{10}O_2$ Formula wt 102.13
FEMA: 2695
UNII: PX7ZNN5GXK [2-methylbutyric acid]

DESCRIPTION
2-Methylbutyric Acid occurs as a colorless to pale yellow liquid.
Odor: Fruity
Solubility: Soluble in propylene glycol, vegetable oils; insoluble or practically insoluble in water
Boiling Point: ~176°
Solubility in Alcohol, Appendix VI: One mL dissolves in 1 mL of 95% alcohol.

Function: Flavoring agent

IDENTIFICATION
- **INFRARED SPECTRA,** *Spectrophotometric Identification Tests,* Appendix IIIC
  Acceptance criteria: The spectrum of the sample exhibits relative maxima at the same wavelengths as those of the spectrum below.

ASSAY
- **PROCEDURE:** Proceed as directed under *M-3a,* Appendix XI.
  Acceptance criteria: NLT 98.0% of $C_5H_{10}O_2$

SPECIFIC TESTS
- **REFRACTIVE INDEX,** Appendix II: At 20°
  Acceptance criteria: Between 1.404 and 1.408
- **SPECIFIC GRAVITY:** Determine at 25° by any reliable method (see *General Provisions*).
  Acceptance criteria: Between 0.932 and 0.936

758 / 2-Methylbutyric Acid / *Monographs*

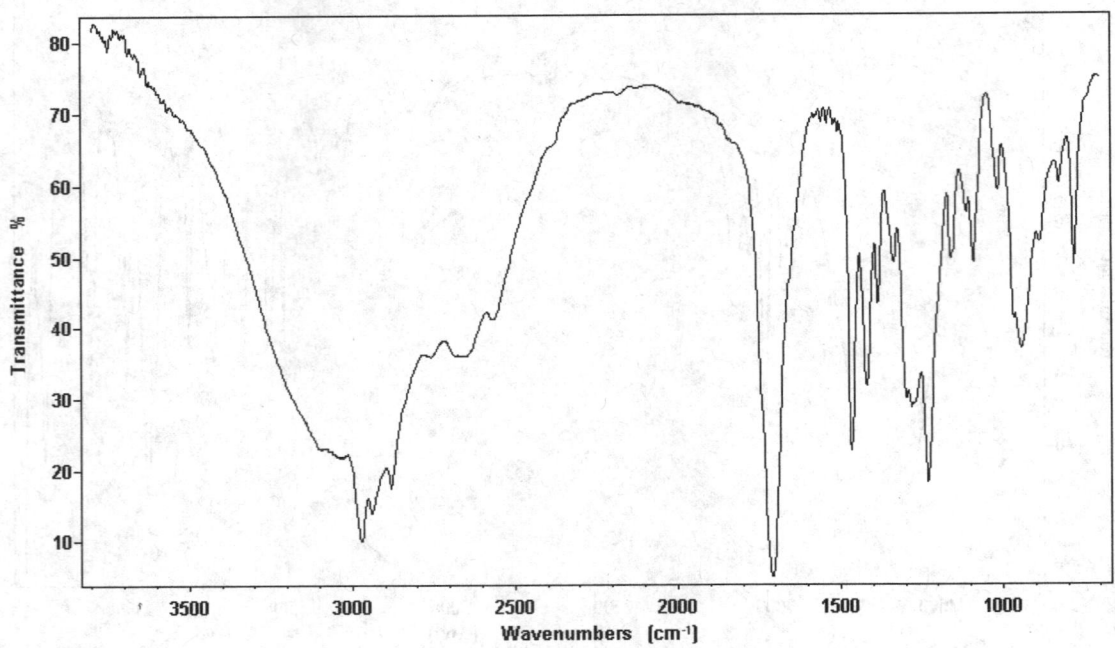

2-Methylbutyric Acid

2-Methylbutyl Acetate

First Published: Prior to FCC 6

C₇H₁₄O₂   Formula wt 130.18
FEMA: 3644
UNII: IY8732E0YC [2-methylbutyl acetate]

DESCRIPTION
2-Methylbutyl Acetate occurs as a colorless to pale yellow liquid.
Odor: Banana
Boiling Point: ~138°
Function: Flavoring agent

ASSAY
- **PROCEDURE:** Proceed as directed under *M-1b*, Appendix XI.
  Acceptance criteria: NLT 97.0% of C₇H₁₄O₂

SPECIFIC TESTS
- **ACID VALUE, FLAVOR CHEMICALS (OTHER THAN ESSENTIAL OILS),** *M-15,* Appendix XI
  Acceptance criteria: NMT 1.0
- **REFRACTIVE INDEX,** Appendix II: At 20°
  Acceptance criteria: Between 1.399 and 1.404
- **SPECIFIC GRAVITY:** Determine at 25° by any reliable method (see *General Provisions*).
  Acceptance criteria: Between 0.872 and 0.877

2-Methylbutyl Isovalerate

First Published: Prior to FCC 6

2-Methylbutyl-3-methylbutanoate

C₁₀H₂₀O₂   Formula wt 172.27
FEMA: 3506
UNII: 7G5TZ5034W [2-methylbutyl isovalerate]

DESCRIPTION
2-Methylbutyl Isovalerate occurs as a colorless liquid.
Odor: Herbaceous, fruity
Solubility: Soluble in alcohol, most fixed oils; insoluble or practically insoluble in water
Boiling Point: ~191° to 195°
Function: Flavoring agent

ASSAY
- **PROCEDURE:** Proceed as directed under *M-1a,* Appendix XI.
  Acceptance criteria: NLT 98.0% of C₁₀H₂₀O₂

SPECIFIC TESTS
- **ACID VALUE, FLAVOR CHEMICALS (OTHER THAN ESSENTIAL OILS),** *M-15,* Appendix XI

Acceptance criteria: NMT 2.0
- **REFRACTIVE INDEX**, Appendix II: At 20°
  Acceptance criteria: Between 1.413 and 1.416
- **SPECIFIC GRAVITY:** Determine at 25° by any reliable method (see *General Provisions*).
  Acceptance criteria: Between 0.852 and 0.857

Methylcellulose

First Published: Prior to FCC 6

Modified Cellulose
MC

INS: 461   CAS: [9004-67-5]

DESCRIPTION

Methylcellulose occurs as a white, fibrous powder or granules. It is the methyl ether of cellulose. It is soluble in water and in a limited number of organic solvent systems. Aqueous solutions of Methylcellulose are surface active, form films upon drying, and undergo a reversible transformation from sol to gel upon heating and cooling, respectively.

Function: Thickener; stabilizer; emulsifier; bodying agent; bulking agent; binder; film former

Packaging and Storage: Store in well-closed containers.

IDENTIFICATION

- **A. PROCEDURE**
  Sample: 1 g
  Analysis: Add the *Sample* to 100 mL of water. [NOTE—Save this solution for use in *Identification* tests B and C.]
  Acceptance criteria: The sample swells and disperses to form a clear to opalescent, mucilaginous solution, depending upon the intrinsic viscosity, which is stable in the presence of most electrolytes and alcohol in concentrations up to 40%.
- **B. PROCEDURE**
  Sample: A few mL of the solution prepared in *Identification* test A (above)
  Analysis: Heat the *Sample*.
  Acceptance criteria: The solution becomes cloudy, and a flaky precipitate forms that redissolves as the solution cools.
- **C. PROCEDURE**
  Sample: A few mL of the solution prepared in *Identification* test A (above)
  Analysis: Pour the *Sample* onto a glass plate, and allow the water to evaporate.
  Acceptance criteria: A thin, self-sustaining film results.

ASSAY

- **PROCEDURE**
  [CAUTION—Perform all steps involving hydriodic acid carefully in a well-ventilated hood. Use goggles, acid-resistant gloves, and other appropriate safety equipment. Be extremely careful when handling the hot vials because they are under pressure. In the event of hydriodic acid exposure, wash with copious amounts of water and seek medical attention at once.]
  Internal standard solution: 25 mg/mL toluene in *o*-xylene
  Standard solution: Transfer 135 mg of adipic acid into a suitable serum vial, add 4.0 mL of hydriodic acid followed by 4.0 mL of the *Internal standard solution*, and close the vial securely with a septum stopper. Weigh the vial and its contents, add 90 µL of methyl iodide with a syringe through the septum, reweigh, and calculate the weight of methyl iodide added. Shake well, and allow the layers to separate.
  Sample solution: Transfer 65 mg of sample into a 5-mL vial equipped with a pressure-tight septum closure, add an amount of adipic acid equal to the weight of the sample, and pipet 2 mL of the *Internal standard solution* into the vial. Cautiously pipet 2 mL of hydriodic acid into the mixture, immediately secure the closure, and accurately weigh. Shake the vial for 30 s, heat at 150° for 20 min, remove from the heat, shake again, using extreme caution, and heat at 150° for 40 min. Allow the vial to cool for about 45 min, and weigh. If the weight loss is greater than 10 mg, discard the mixture and prepare another *Sample solution*.
  Chromatographic system, Appendix IIA
    Mode: Gas chromatography
    Detector: Thermal conductivity detector
    Column: 1.8-m × 4-mm (id) glass column, or equivalent, packed with 10% methylsilicone oil (UCW 982 or equivalent) on 100- to 120-mesh flux-calcined chromatographic siliceous earth (Chromosorb WHP, or equivalent)
    Temperature
      Column: 100°
      Injector port: 200°
      Detector: 200°
    Carrier gas: Helium
    Flow rate: 20 mL/min
    Injection size: About 2 µL
  Calibration: Inject an aliquot from the upper layer of the *Standard solution* into the chromatograph, and record the chromatogram. [NOTE—The retention times for methyl iodide, toluene, and *o*-xylene are approximately 3, 7, and 13 min, respectively.]
  Calculate the relative response factor, F, of equal weights of toluene and methyl iodide by the formula:

  $$\text{Result} = Q/A$$

  Q = quantity ratio of methyl iodide to toluene in the *Standard solution*

A = peak area ratio of methyl iodide to toluene obtained from the chromatogram of the *Standard solution*

Analysis: Inject an aliquot from the upper layer of the *Sample solution* into the chromatograph, and record the chromatogram.

Calculate the percentage of methoxyl groups (–OCH$_3$) in the sample by the formula:

$$\text{Result} = a \times (W/w) \times (M_{r1}/M_{r2}) \times F \times 2$$

a = ratio of the area of the methyl iodide peak to that of the toluene peak in the chromatogram of the *Sample solution*
W = weight of toluene in the *Internal standard solution* (g)
w = weight of the sample taken (g)
M_{r1} = molecular weight of methoxyl group, 31
M_{r2} = molecular weight of methyl iodide, 142
F = relative response factor of toluene and methyl iodide (determined above)

Acceptance criteria: NLT 27.5% and NMT 31.5% of methoxyl groups (–OCH$_3$), calculated on the dried basis

IMPURITIES
Inorganic Impurities
- **LEAD,** *Lead Limit Test,* Appendix IIIB
  Sample solution: Prepare as directed for organic compounds using 2 g of sample.
  Control: 6 μg Pb (6 mL of *Diluted Standard Lead Solution*)
  Acceptance criteria: NMT 3 mg/kg

SPECIFIC TESTS
- **LOSS ON DRYING,** Appendix IIC: 105° for 2 h
  Sample: 3 g
  Acceptance criteria: NMT 5.0%
- **RESIDUE ON IGNITION (SULFATED ASH),** Appendix IIC
  Sample: 1 g
  Acceptance criteria: NMT 1.5%
- **VISCOSITY DETERMINATION,** *Viscosity of Methylcellulose,* Appendix IIB
  Sample solution: Transfer an amount of sample equivalent to 2 g of solids on the dried basis to a wide-mouth 250-mL centrifuge bottle and add 98 g of water, previously heated to between 80° and 90°. Stir with a mechanical stirrer for 10 min, then place the bottle in an ice bath until dissolution is complete, adjust the weight of the solution with water to 100 g if necessary, and centrifuge it to expel any entrapped air. Adjust the temperature of the *Sample solution* to 20° ± 0.1°.
  Acceptance criteria
  Viscosity types of 100 cP or less: NLT 80% and NMT 120% of that stated on the label
  Viscosity types of higher than 100 cP: NLT 75% and NMT 140% of that stated on the label

α-Methylcinnamaldehyde
First Published: Prior to FCC 6
Last Revision: First Supplement, FCC 6

C$_{10}$H$_{10}$O   Formula wt 146.19
FEMA: 2697
UNII: 1C647N9853 [α-methylcinnamaldehyde]

DESCRIPTION
α-Methylcinnamaldehyde occurs as a yellow liquid. It may contain a suitable antioxidant.
Odor: Cinnamon
Solubility: Soluble in most fixed oils, propylene glycol; insoluble or practically insoluble in glycerin
Boiling Point: ~148° (27 mm Hg)
Solubility in Alcohol, Appendix VI: One mL dissolves in 3 mL of 70% alcohol, and remains clear on dilution.
Function: Flavoring agent

IDENTIFICATION
- **INFRARED SPECTRA,** *Spectrophotometric Identification Tests,* Appendix IIIC
  Acceptance criteria: The spectrum of the sample exhibits relative maxima at the same wavelengths as those of the spectrum below.

ASSAY
- **PROCEDURE:** Proceed as directed under *M-1b,* Appendix XI
  Acceptance criteria: NLT 97.0% of C$_{10}$H$_{10}$O (one major isomer)

SPECIFIC TESTS
- **ACID VALUE, FLAVOR CHEMICALS (OTHER THAN ESSENTIAL OILS),** *M-15,* Appendix XI
  Acceptance criteria: NMT 5.0
- **REFRACTIVE INDEX,** Appendix II: At 20°
  Acceptance criteria: Between 1.602 and 1.607
- **SPECIFIC GRAVITY:** Determine at 25° by any reliable method (see *General Provisions*).
  Acceptance criteria: Between 1.035 and 1.039

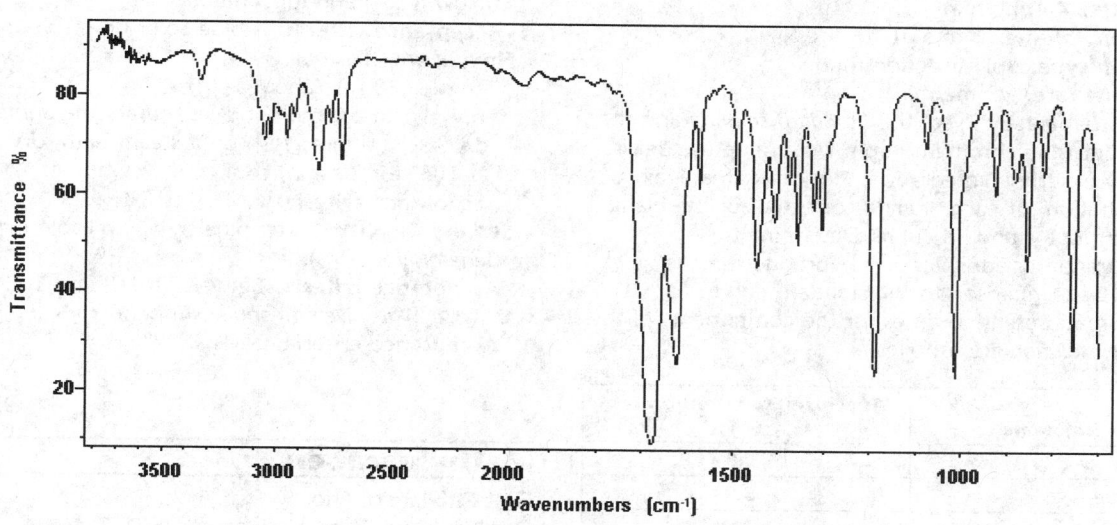

α-Methylcinnamaldehyde

Methylene Chloride

First Published: Prior to FCC 6

Dichloromethane
Methylene Dichloride

CH₂Cl₂
Formula wt 84.93
CAS: [75-09-2]

UNII: 588X2YUY0A [methylene chloride]

DESCRIPTION
Methylene Chloride occurs as a clear, colorless, nonflammable liquid. It is soluble in about 50 parts of water, and is miscible with alcohol, with acetone, with chloroform, and with ether. Its refractive index at 20° is about 1.424.

Function: Extraction solvent
Packaging and Storage: Store in tight containers.

ASSAY
- **PROCEDURE**

  Standard solution: Prepare a standard solution containing appropriate concentrations of methyl chloride, chloroform, methylene chloride, vinyl chloride, ethyl chloride, vinylidene chloride, 2-methyl-2-butene, trans-1,2-dichloroethylene, cyclohexane, and propylene oxide in high-purity dichloromethane (DCM) by adding each reagent to DCM in a glass bottle fitted with a silicone rubber septum. Inject the listed analytes into the bottle by accurately weighing a syringe containing the analyte, injecting the analyte through the septum, and reweighing the syringe to determine the amount of analyte added. Add sufficient amounts of each analyte to obtain these approximate concentrations:

Analyte	Concentration (% w/w)
methyl chloride	0.014
vinyl chloride	0.007
ethyl chloride	0.0084
propylene oxide	2.4
vinylidene chloride	0.0098
trans-1,2-dichloroethylene	0.017
chloroform	0.012
cyclohexane	0.047
2-methyl-2-butene	0.009

  Dilute the standard stepwise with high-purity DCM to create a series of standards in the range of approximately 10 to 300 mg/kg, except for propylene oxide, which should be in the range of 0.06 to 2.4 (w/w%).

  [NOTE—Assay the DCM used to prepare the Standard solution without the analytes to determine the possible presence of the analytes, and make any necessary corrections.]

  Chromatographic system, Appendix IIA
  Mode: Gas chromatography
  Detector: Flame ionization
  Column 1: 30-m × 0.32-mm (id) fused-silica capillary column, or equivalent, coated with 1.8-μm film of (6% cyanopropylphenyl) methylpolysiloxane liquid phase, or equivalent
  Column 2: 25-m × 0.53-mm (id) fused-silica capillary column coated with a 2.0-μm film of 5% phenyl/95% methylsilicone liquid phase, or equivalent
  [NOTE—Connect the two columns in series with Column 2 being behind Column 1.]
  Temperature
  Column oven: 40° (isothermal)
  Injector: 150°
  Detector: 250°

Carrier gas: Helium
Flow rate: 4.4 mL/min
Injection volume: 1 to 5 µL
Injection type: Split injection mode
Split flow rate: 98 mL/min
Analysis: Separately inject the *Standard solution* and the sample into the chromatograph. Determine the peak areas by electronic integration. Plot peak area against concentration for each analyte corrected for the blank to construct a standard curve. Determine the concentration of additives and byproducts in the sample by comparison to the standard curve. Approximate retention times for the components of the *Standard solution* are as follows:

Chemical name	Approximate retention time (RT)
methyl chloride	2.8
vinyl chloride	3.0
ethyl chloride	3.5
propylene oxide	4.1
2-methyl-2-butene	4.5
vinylidene chloride	4.6
dichloromethane	5.3
trans-1,2-dichloroethylene	5.9
chloroform	8.7
cyclohexane	10.5
carbon tetrachloride	12.0

Acceptance criteria: The sum of the concentrations of the impurities and stabilizers is less than 1.0%. (NLT 99.0% CH_2Cl_2)

IMPURITIES
Inorganic Impurities
- **LEAD,** *Lead Limit Test, Atomic Absorption Spectrophotometric Graphite Furnace Method, Method I,* Appendix IIIB
  Acceptance criteria: NMT 1 mg/kg

SPECIFIC TESTS
- **ACIDITY (AS HCL)**
  Sample: 100 mL
  Analysis: Transfer the *Sample* into a separatory funnel, add 100 mL of neutralized water, and shake vigorously for 2 min. Allow the layers to separate, transfer the aqueous phase into an Erlenmeyer flask, add 4 drops of bromothymol blue TS, and titrate with 0.01 N sodium hydroxide.
  Acceptance criteria: Not more than 3.6 mL 0.01 N sodium hydroxide is required for the titration of the *Sample*. (NMT 10 mg/kg)
- **DISTILLATION RANGE,** Appendix IIB
  Acceptance criteria: Between 39.0° and 41.0°
- **FREE HALOGENS**
  Sample: 10 mL
  Analysis: Transfer the *Sample* to a separatory funnel, add 25 mL of water, and shake vigorously for 1 min. Allow the layers to separate, and then remove and discard the lower sample layer. Add 1 mL of potassium iodide TS

and a few drops of starch TS to the aqueous phase, and allow it to stand for 5 min.
Acceptance criteria: A blue color does not appear.
- **NONVOLATILE RESIDUE**
  Sample: 38 mL (about 50 g)
  Analysis: In a fume hood, evaporate the *Sample* to dryness in a tared dish on a steam bath, dry the residue at 105° for 30 min, cool, and weigh.
  Acceptance criteria: NMT 0.015%
- **SPECIFIC GRAVITY:** Determine by any reliable method (see *General Provisions*).
  Acceptance criteria: Between 1.318 and 1.323
- **WATER,** *Water Determination,* Appendix IIB
  Acceptance criteria: NMT 0.02%

Methylparaben

First Published: Prior to FCC 6
Last Revision: Third Supplement, FCC 7

Methyl *p*-Hydroxybenzoate

$C_8H_8O_3$ Formula wt 152.15
INS: 218   CAS: [99-76-3]
UNII: A2I8C7HI9T [methylparaben]

DESCRIPTION
Methylparaben occurs as small, colorless crystals or as a white, crystalline powder. One g dissolves in about 400 mL of water at 25°, in about 50 mL of water at 80°, in about 2.5 mL of alcohol, in about 7 mL of ether, and in about 4 mL of propylene glycol. It is slightly soluble in glycerin and in fixed oils.
Function: Preservative; antimicrobial agent
Packaging and Storage: Store in well-closed containers.

IDENTIFICATION
- **INFRARED ABSORPTION,** *Spectrophotometric Identification Tests,* Appendix IIIC
  Reference standard: USP Methylparaben RS
  Sample and standard preparation: M
  Acceptance criteria: The spectrum of the sample exhibits maxima at the same wavelengths as those in the spectrum of the *Reference standard*.
- **MELTING RANGE OR TEMPERATURE DETERMINATION,** Appendix IIB
  Sample preparation: Dissolve 500 mg of sample in 10 mL of 1 N sodium hydroxide, boil for 30 min, allow the solution to evaporate to a volume of about 5 mL, and cool. Acidify the solution with 2 N sulfuric acid, collect the resulting *p*-hydroxybenzoic acid crystals on a filter, wash several times with small portions of water, and dry in a desiccator over silica gel.
  Acceptance criteria: The *Sample preparation* so obtained melts between 212° and 217°.

ASSAY
- **PROCEDURE**
  Mobile phase: Methanol and a 6.8-g/L solution of potassium dihydrogen phosphate (65:35 v/v)
  Sample solution: Dissolve 50.0 mg in 2.5 mL of methanol, and dilute with *Mobile phase* to 50 mL. Dilute 10.0 mL of this solution with *Mobile phase* to 100 mL.
  Standard solution: Dissolve 50.0 mg of USP Methylparaben RS in 2.5 mL of methanol, and dilute with *Mobile phase* to 50 mL. Dilute 10.0 mL of this solution with *Mobile phase* to 100 mL.
  Chromatographic system, Appendix IIA
  Mode: High-performance liquid chromatography
  Detector: UV 272 nm
  Column: 4.6-mm × 15-cm column packed with octadecyl silane chemically bonded to porous silica or ceramic microparticles 5 μm in diameter
  Flow rate: 1.3 mL/min
  [NOTE—The run time is about 5 times the retention time of methylparaben.]
  Injection size: 10 μL
  System suitability
  Sample: *Standard solution*
  Suitability requirement: The relative standard deviation for 6 injections is NMT 0.85%.
  Analysis: Separately inject the *Sample solution* and the *Standard solution* into the chromatograph. Record the chromatograms and calculate the percentage of methylparaben in the sample taken:

  $$\text{Result} = (r_U/r_S) \times (C_S/C_U) \times 100$$

  r_U = peak area of methylparaben from the chromatogram of the *Sample solution*
  r_S = peak area of methylparaben from the chromatogram of the *Standard solution*
  C_S = concentration of USP Methylparaben RS in the *Standard solution*, corrected for purity (mg/mL)
  C_U = concentration of the *Sample solution* (mg/mL)

  Acceptance criteria: 99.0%–100.5%, calculated on the dried basis

IMPURITIES
Inorganic Impurities
- **LEAD,** *Lead Limit Test, Flame Atomic Absorption Spectrophotometric Method,* Appendix IIIB
  Sample: 10 g
  Acceptance criteria: NMT 2 mg/kg

SPECIFIC TESTS
- **ACIDITY**
  Sample: 750 mg
  Analysis: Mix the *Sample* with 15 mL of water, heat at 80° for 1 min, cool, and filter. The filtrate is acid or neutral to litmus. Add 0.2 mL of 0.1 N sodium hydroxide and 2 drops of methyl red TS to 10 mL of the filtrate.
  Acceptance criteria: The solution is yellow, without even a light cast of pink.
- **LOSS ON DRYING,** Appendix IIC: Over silica gel for 5 h
  Acceptance criteria: NMT 0.5%
- **MELTING RANGE OR TEMPERATURE DETERMINATION,** Appendix IIB
  Acceptance criteria: 125°–128°
- **RESIDUE ON IGNITION (SULFATED ASH),** Appendix IIC
  Sample: 4 g
  Acceptance criteria: NMT 0.05%

2-Methylpentanoic Acid
First Published: Prior to FCC 6

$C_6H_{12}O_2$ Formula wt 116.16
FEMA: 2754
UNII: 26A19CG6J9 [2-methylpentanoic acid]

DESCRIPTION
2-Methylpentanoic Acid occurs as a colorless to pale yellow liquid.
Odor: Caramel, pungent
Boiling Point: ~196° to 197°
Solubility in Alcohol, Appendix VI: One mL dissolves in 1 mL of 95% alcohol.
Function: Flavoring agent

IDENTIFICATION
- **INFRARED SPECTRA,** *Spectrophotometric Identification Tests,* Appendix IIIC
  Acceptance criteria: The spectrum of the sample exhibits relative maxima at the same wavelengths as those of the spectrum below.

ASSAY
- **PROCEDURE:** Proceed as directed under *M-3a,* Appendix XI.
  Acceptance criteria: NLT 98.0% of $C_6H_{12}O_2$

SPECIFIC TESTS
- **REFRACTIVE INDEX,** Appendix II: At 20°
  Acceptance criteria: Between 1.411 and 1.416
- **SPECIFIC GRAVITY:** Determine at 25° by any reliable method (see *General Provisions*).
  Acceptance criteria: Between 0.916 and 0.923

764 / 2-Methylpentanoic Acid / *Monographs*

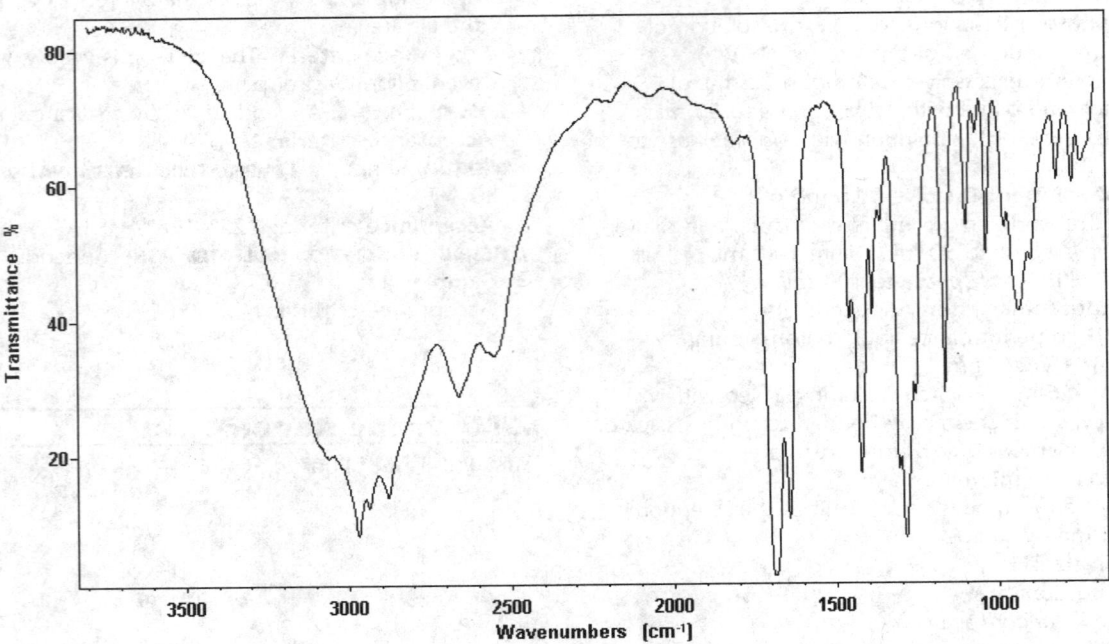

2-Methylpentanoic Acid

2-Methylpyrazine

First Published: Prior to FCC 6

C$_5$H$_6$N$_2$ Formula wt 94.12
FEMA: 3309
UNII: RVC6500U9C [2-methylpyrazine]

DESCRIPTION
2-Methylpyrazine occurs as a colorless to slightly yellow liquid.
Odor: Nutty, cocoa
Solubility: Miscible in water, alcohol, acetone, most fixed oils
Boiling Point: ~137°
Function: Flavoring agent

IDENTIFICATION
- **INFRARED SPECTRA,** *Spectrophotometric Identification Tests,* Appendix IIIC
  Acceptance criteria: The spectrum of the sample exhibits relative maxima at the same wavelengths as those of the spectrum below.

ASSAY
- **PROCEDURE:** Proceed as directed under *M-1a,* Appendix XI.
  Acceptance criteria: NLT 99.0% of C$_5$H$_6$N$_2$

SPECIFIC TESTS
- **REFRACTIVE INDEX,** Appendix II: At 20°
  Acceptance criteria: Between 1.504 and 1.506
- **SPECIFIC GRAVITY:** Determine at 25° by any reliable method (see *General Provisions*).
  Acceptance criteria: Between 1.010 and 1.030

OTHER REQUIREMENTS
- **WATER,** *Water Determination, Method I,* Appendix IIB
  [NOTE—Use freshly distilled pyridine as solvent.]
  Acceptance criteria: NMT 0.5%

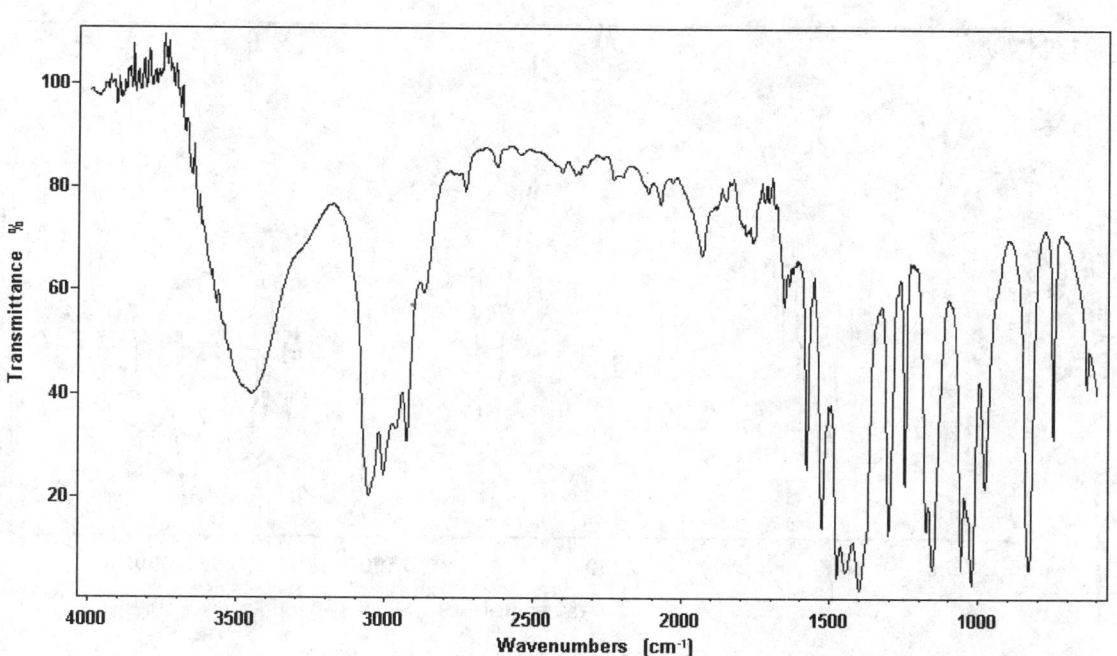

2-Methylpyrazine

3-Methylthiopropionaldehyde

First Published: Prior to FCC 6
Last Revision: First Supplement, FCC 6

Methional

C_4H_8OS Formula wt 104.17
FEMA: 2747
UNII: 0AAO8V0F1R [3-methylthiopropionaldehyde]

DESCRIPTION
3-Methylthiopropionaldehyde occurs as a colorless to pale yellow liquid. It may contain a suitable antioxidant.
Odor: Meaty potato
Boiling Point: ~165° to 166°
Solubility in Alcohol, Appendix VI: One mL dissolves in 1 mL of 95% alcohol.

Function: Flavoring agent

IDENTIFICATION
- **INFRARED SPECTRA,** Spectrophotometric Identification Tests, Appendix IIIC
  Acceptance criteria: The spectrum of the sample exhibits relative maxima at the same wavelengths as those of the spectrum below.

ASSAY
- **PROCEDURE:** Proceed as directed under M-1a, Appendix XI.
  Acceptance criteria: NLT 98.0% of C_4H_8OS

SPECIFIC TESTS
- **REFRACTIVE INDEX,** Appendix II: At 20°
  Acceptance criteria: Between 1.484 and 1.493
- **SPECIFIC GRAVITY:** Determine at 25° by any reliable method (see General Provisions).
  Acceptance criteria: Between 1.038 and 1.048

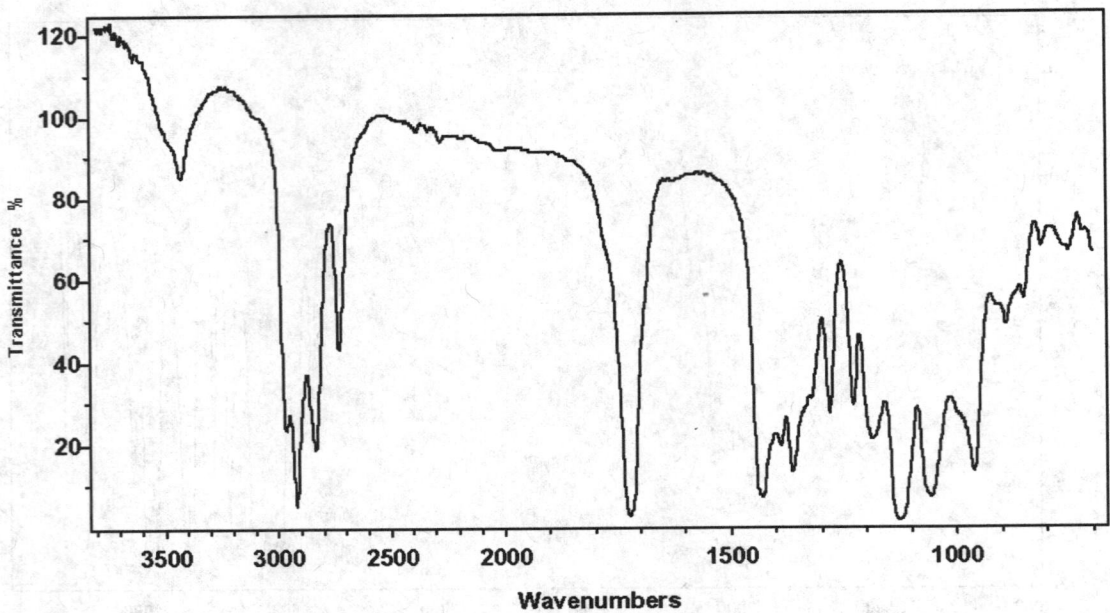

3-Methylthiopropionaldehyde

2-Methylundecanal

First Published: Prior to FCC 6
Last Revision: First Supplement, FCC 6

Aldehyde C-12 MNA
Methyl *n*-Nonyl Acetaldehyde

$C_{12}H_{24}O$ Formula wt 184.32
FEMA: 2749
UNII: S94QNS2VY5 [2-methylundecanal]

DESCRIPTION
2-Methylundecanal occurs as a colorless to slightly yellow liquid. It may contain a suitable antioxidant.
Odor: Fatty
Solubility: Soluble in most fixed oils, alcohol, propylene glycol (may be turbid); insoluble or practically insoluble in glycerin

Boiling Point: ~171°
Function: Flavoring agent

IDENTIFICATION
- **INFRARED SPECTRA,** *Spectrophotometric Identification Tests,* Appendix IIIC
  Acceptance criteria: The spectrum of the sample exhibits relative maxima at the same wavelengths as those of the spectrum below.

ASSAY
- **PROCEDURE:** Proceed as directed under *M-1b*, Appendix XI.
  Acceptance criteria: NLT 94.0% of $C_{12}H_{24}O$

SPECIFIC TESTS
- **ACID VALUE, FLAVOR CHEMICALS (OTHER THAN ESSENTIAL OILS),** *M-15,* Appendix XI
  Acceptance criteria: NMT 10.0
- **REFRACTIVE INDEX,** Appendix II: At 20°
  Acceptance criteria: Between 1.431 and 1.436
- **SPECIFIC GRAVITY:** Determine at 25° by any reliable method (see *General Provisions*).
  Acceptance criteria: Between 0.822 and 0.830

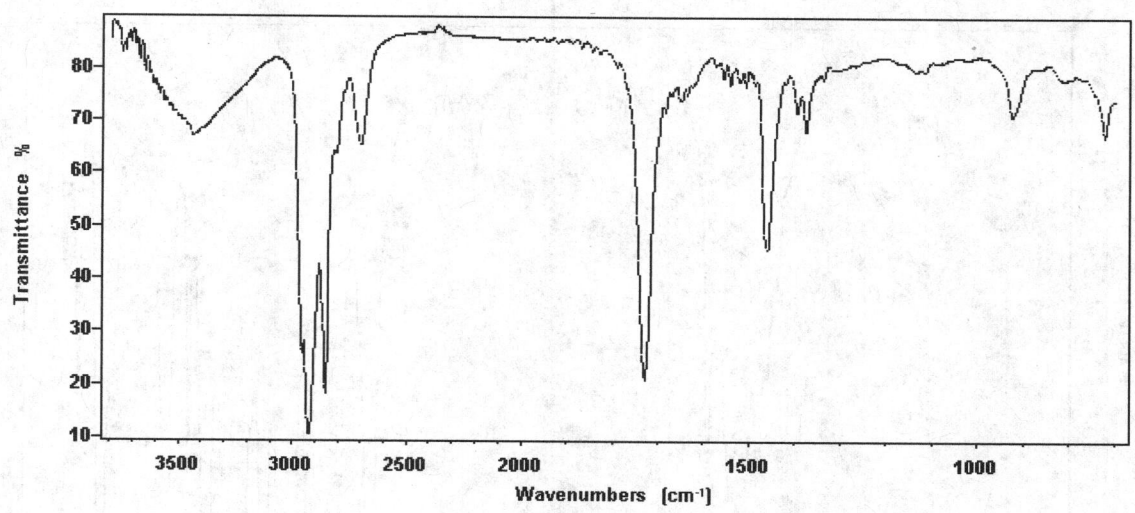

2-Methylundecanal

4-*p*-Methoxyphenyl-2-butanone

First Published: Prior to FCC 6

Anisyl Acetone

$C_{11}H_{14}O_2$ Formula wt 178.23
FEMA: 2672
UNII: GVG47S4S5V [anisylacetone]

DESCRIPTION
4-*p*-Methoxyphenyl-2-butanone occurs as a colorless to pale yellow liquid.
Odor: Sweet, floral, fruity
Boiling Point: ~277°
Solubility in Alcohol, Appendix VI: One mL dissolves in 1 mL of 95% alcohol.

Function: Flavoring agent

IDENTIFICATION
- **INFRARED SPECTRA,** *Spectrophotometric Identification Tests,* Appendix IIIC
  Acceptance criteria: The spectrum of the sample exhibits relative maxima at the same wavelengths as those of the spectrum below.

ASSAY
- **PROCEDURE:** Proceed as directed under *M-1a,* Appendix XI.
  Acceptance criteria: NLT 98.0% of $C_{11}H_{14}O_2$

SPECIFIC TESTS
- **REFRACTIVE INDEX,** Appendix II: At 20°
  Acceptance criteria: Between 1.517 and 1.521
- **SPECIFIC GRAVITY:** Determine at 25° by any reliable method (see *General Provisions*).
  Acceptance criteria: Between 1.042 and 1.048

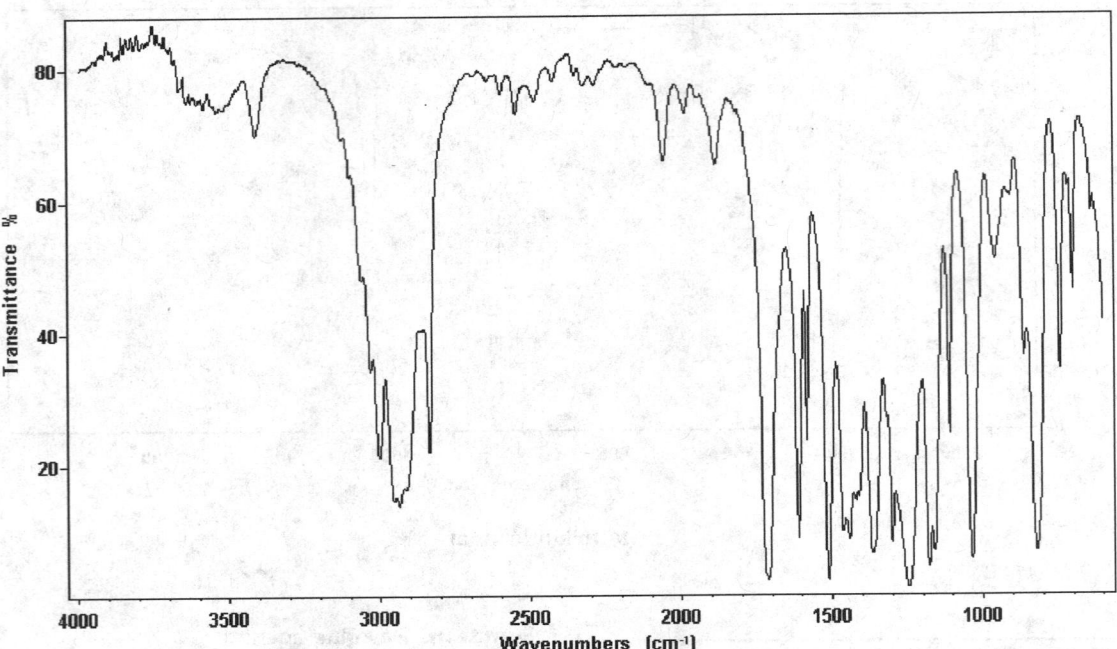

4-*p*-Methoxyphenyl-2-butanone

Mineral Oil, High Viscosity

First Published: Second Supplement, FCC 7

Liquid Petrolatum
Liquid Paraffin

CAS: [8012-95-1]

INS: 905a
UNII: N6K5787QVP [light mineral oil]

DESCRIPTION
Mineral Oil, High Viscosity occurs as a colorless, transparent, oily liquid, free or nearly free from fluorescence. It is a mixture of refined liquid hydrocarbons, essentially paraffinic and naphthenic in nature, obtained from petroleum by solvent extraction and/or crystallization with subsequent purification by acid treatment and/or hydrogen treatment. It has an initial boiling point above 350°. Its average molecular weight is NLT 500. It is insoluble in water and sparingly soluble in alcohol, soluble in volatile oils, and miscible with most fixed oils, but not with castor oil. It may contain any antioxidant permitted in food in an amount not greater than that required to produce its intended effect.

Function: Lubricant; release agent; protective coating
Packaging and Storage: Store in tight containers.

IDENTIFICATION
- **CARBON NUMBER AT 5% DISTILLATION POINT**[1]
  [NOTE—"Carbon Number" is the number of carbon atoms in a molecule.]
  System suitability solution: 1% each of hexadecane and octadecane in *n*-octane
  Calibration solution: Prepare a mixture of hydrocarbons of known boiling points covering the range of the sample. At least one compound must have a boiling point lower than the initial boiling point of the sample.
  Chromatographic system, Appendix IIA
  [NOTE—Use a suitable gas chromatograph. Typical conditions that may be used in the system are identified below.]
  Mode: Gas chromatography
  Detector: Flame ionization
  Packed column: 5% SE-30 or equivalent
  Carrier gas: Helium
  Column temperature: 10°–350°, at a rate of 6.5°/min
  Detector temperature: 370°
  Injection block temperature: 370°
  System suitability
    Suitability requirement 1: The peak height for the dodecane peak is NLT 10% of full scale under the conditions used for the *Calibration solution*.
    Suitability requirement 2: The baseline drift, when the chromatographic system is operated at the

---
[1] As determined by ASTM D2887 Standard Test Method for Boiling Range Distribution of Petroleum Fractions by Gas Chromatography. The original ASTM method is available in its entirety from ASTM International, 100 Barr Harbor Drive, West Conshohocken, PA 19428. Phone: 610-832-9555; email: service@astm.org; website: www.astm.org.

required sensitivity level to meet *Suitability requirement 1*, is NMT 1% of full scale per hour for the *Calibration solution*.

Suitability requirement 3: Retention times have a repeatability of NMT 6 s for each component of the *Calibration solution*.

Suitability requirement 4: The resolution, R, determined for the *System suitability solution* is between 3 and 8 when calculated by:

$$R = 2d/(W_1 + W_2)$$

d = distance between the peak maxima of hexadecane and octadecane (mm)
W_1 = hexadecane peak width at baseline (mm)
W_2 = octadecane peak width at baseline (mm)

Calibration curve: Cool the column to the selected starting temperature (the retention time for the initial boiling point must be NLT 1 min) and inject the *Calibration solution*. For each component, record the retention time of the peak maximum and the peak areas. Plot the retention time of each peak versus the corresponding normal boiling point of that component, in C°, to obtain a calibration curve.

Analysis: Using the conditions for the *Calibration curve*, inject a sample. Record the area of each time segment at fixed time intervals NMT 1% of the retention time equivalent to a boiling point of 538° obtained from the *Calibration curve*.

Sum the area segments to obtain the cumulative area at each time interval during the run. At the point of the chromatogram where the baseline at the end first becomes steady, observe the cumulative area counts. Move back along the record until a cumulative area equal to 99.5% of the total at the steady point appears. Mark this point as the final boiling point. Observe the area counts at the start of the run until the point is reached where the cumulative area count is equal to 0.5% of the total area. Mark this point as the initial boiling point of the sample. Divide the cumulative area at each interval between the initial and final boiling points by the total cumulative area and multiply by 100. This will give the cumulative percent of the sample recovered at each time interval. Tabulate the cumulative percent recovered at each interval and the retention time at the end of the interval. Using linear interpolation, if necessary, determine the retention time associated with 5% and read the corresponding boiling temperature from the *Calibration curve*.

Acceptance criteria: The carbon number is NLT 28 at 5% distillation. The boiling point at 5% distillation is higher than 422°.

IMPURITIES
Inorganic Impurities
- **LEAD**, *Lead Limit Test, Atomic Absorption Spectrophotometric Graphite Furnace Method, Method II*, Appendix IIIB
  Acceptance criteria: NMT 1 mg/kg

SPECIFIC TESTS
- **READILY CARBONIZABLE SUBSTANCES**
  Chromic acid cleaning mixture: Dissolve 200 g of sodium dichromate in 100 mL of water to which 1500 mL of sulfuric acid has been added, slowly with stirring.
  Sample: 5 mL
  Control solution: Mix 3 mL of ferric chloride CS, 1.5 mL of cobaltous chloride CS, and 0.5 mL of cupric sulfate CS in a glass-stoppered test tube that previously has been rinsed with *Chromic acid cleaning mixture*, then rinsed with water, and dried. Overlay this mixture with 5 mL of mineral oil.
  Analysis: Place the *Sample* in a glass-stoppered test tube that previously has been rinsed with *Chromic acid cleaning mixture*, then rinsed with water, and dried. Add 5 mL of 94.5% to 94.9% sulfuric acid; while simultaneously starting a stopwatch, place the tube in a boiling water bath. After the test tube has been in the bath for 30 s, use a 3-s time span to remove it, and while holding the stopper in place, give three vigorous vertical shakes over an amplitude of about 5 in, then return it to the bath. Repeat every 30 s until exactly 10 min has passed, then remove the test tube.
  Acceptance criteria: The *Sample* remains unchanged in color, and the acid does not become darker than the standard color of the *Control solution*.

- **SPECIFIC GRAVITY** Determine by any reliable method (see *General Provisions*).
  Acceptance criteria: NLT that stated, or within the range claimed by the vendor

- **ULTRAVIOLET ABSORBANCE (POLYNUCLEAR HYDROCARBONS)**
  Hexane: Use a pure grade of hexane (predominantly *n*-hexane and methylcyclopentane) having an ultraviolet absorbance not exceeding 0.10 down to 220 nm and not exceeding 0.02 down to 260 nm. The purity should be such that the *Solvent control* as defined below, has an absorbance curve, compared to water, showing no extraneous impurity peaks and no absorbance exceeding that of dimethyl sulfoxide, compared to water, at any wavelength in the range 260–400 nm. If necessary to obtain the prescribed purities, the hexane may be passed through activated silica gel.
  Dimethyl sulfoxide: Use a pure grade of dimethyl sulfoxide (99.9%, melting point: 18°) that has a clear, water-white appearance; has an absorbance curve, compared with water, not exceeding 1.0 at 264 nm; and shows no extraneous impurity peaks in the wavelength range up to 400 nm. Store in glass-stoppered bottles.
  Apparatus: Use 125-mL glass-stoppered separatory funnels equipped with tetrafluoroethylene polymer stopcocks or other suitable stopcocks that will not contaminate the solvents.
  Sample preparation: Transfer 25 mL of the sample and 25 mL of *Hexane* to a separatory funnel and mix. Add 5.0 mL of *Dimethyl sulfoxide*, shake the mixture vigorously for at least 1 min, and allow it to stand until the lower layer is clear. Completely transfer the lower layer to a second separatory funnel, add 2 mL of *Hexane*, and shake the mixture vigorously. Allow it to

stand until the lower layer is clear, and then draw off the lower layer, designated as the *Sample preparation*.

Solvent control: In a separatory funnel, vigorously shake 5.0 mL of *Dimethyl sulfoxide* with 25 mL of *Hexane* for at least 1 min, allow it to stand until the lower layer is clear, and draw off this layer, designated as *Solvent control*.

Standard solution: Use a standard reference solution of naphthalene (National Institute of Standards and Technology, Standard Material No. 577 or a solution of equivalent purity) containing a concentration of 7.0 mg/mL in purified isooctane.

Analysis: Determine the absorbance of the *Sample preparation* and the *Solvent control* in a 1-cm cell in the range 260–400 nm.

Determine the absorbance of the *Standard solution* at 275 nm measured against isooctane of the same spectral purity in 1-cm cells. (The absorbance will be approximately 0.30.)

[NOTE—Make suitable corrections of the absorbance when testing samples containing added antioxidants.]

Acceptance criteria: The absorbance of the *Sample preparation* does not exceed that of the *Solvent control* at any wavelength in the specified range by more than one-third of the absorbance of the *Standard solution*.

- **VISCOSITY:** Determine by any reliable method (see *Viscosity Determination*, Appendix IIB).

  Acceptance criteria: NLT 11 centistokes at 100°

Mineral Oil, Medium and Low Viscosity

First Published: Prior to FCC 6
Last Revision: Second Supplement, FCC 7

Liquid Petrolatum
Liquid Paraffin
White Mineral Oil

CAS: [8042-47-5]

UNII: T5L8T28FGP [mineral oil]

DESCRIPTION

Mineral Oil, Medium and Low Viscosity occurs as a colorless, transparent, oily liquid, free or nearly free from fluorescence. It is a mixture of refined liquid hydrocarbons, essentially paraffinic and naphthenic in nature, obtained from petroleum by solvent extraction and/or crystallization with subsequent purification by acid treatment and/or hydrogen treatment. It has an initial boiling point above 200°. Its average molecular weight is between 300 and 500. It is insoluble in water and in alcohol, is soluble in volatile oils, and is miscible with most fixed oils, but not with castor oil. It may contain any antioxidant permitted in food in an amount not greater than that required to produce its intended effect.

Function: Defoaming agent; release agent; glazing agent; sealing agent

Packaging and Storage: Store in tight containers.

IDENTIFICATION

- **CARBON NUMBER AT 5% DISTILLATION POINT**[1]

  [NOTE—"Carbon Number" is number of carbon atoms in a molecule.]

  System suitability solution: 1% each of hexadecane and octadecane in *n*-octane

  Calibration solution: Prepare a mixture of hydrocarbons of known boiling points covering the range of the sample. At least one compound must have a boiling point lower than the initial boiling point of the sample.

  Chromatographic system, Appendix IIA

  [NOTE—Use a suitable gas chromatograph. Typical conditions that may be used in the system are identified below.]

  Mode: Gas chromatography
  Detector: Flame ionization
  Packed column: 5% SE-30 or equivalent
  Carrier gas: Helium
  Temperature
    Column: 10°–350°, at a rate of 6.5°/min
    Detector: 370°
    Injection block: 370°
  System suitability
  Suitability requirement 1: The peak height for the dodecane peak is NLT 10% of full scale under the conditions used for the *Calibration solution*.
  Suitability requirement 2: The baseline drift, when the *Chromatographic system* is operated at the required sensitivity level to meet *Suitability requirement 1*, is NMT 1% of full scale per hour for the *Calibration solution*.
  Suitability requirement 3: Retention times have a repeatability of NMT 6 s for each component of the *Calibration solution*.
  Suitability requirement 4: The resolution, R, determined for the *System suitability solution* is between 3 and 8 when calculated by:

  $$R = 2d/(W_1 + W_2)$$

  d = distance between the peak maxima of hexadecane and octadecane (mm)
  W_1 = hexadecane peak width at baseline (mm)
  W_2 = octadecane peak width at baseline (mm)

  Calibration curve: Cool the column to the selected starting temperature (the retention time for the initial boiling point must be NLT 1 min) and inject the *Calibration solution*. Record for each component the retention time of each peak maximum and the peak areas. Plot the retention time of each peak versus the corresponding normal boiling point of that component, in °C, to obtain a calibration curve.

  Analysis: Using the conditions for the *Calibration curve*, inject a sample. Record the area of each time segment at fixed time intervals NMT 1% of the retention time equivalent to a boiling point of 538° obtained from the *Calibration curve*.

---

[1] As determined by ASTM D2887 Standard Test Method for Boiling Range Distribution of Petroleum Fractions by Gas Chromatography. The original ASTM method is available in its entirety from ASTM International, 100 Barr Harbor Drive, West Conshohocken, PA 19428. Phone: 610-832-9555; email: service@astm.org; website: www.astm.org.

Sum the area segments to obtain the cumulative area at each time interval during the run. At the point of the chromatogram where the baseline at the end first becomes steady, observe the cumulative area counts. Move back along the record until a cumulative area equal to 99.5% of the total at the steady point appears. Mark this point as the final boiling point. Observe the area counts at the start of the run until the point is reached where the cumulative area count is equal to 0.5% of the total area. Mark this point as the initial boiling point of the sample. Divide the cumulative area at each interval between the initial and final boiling points by the total cumulative area and multiply by 100. This will give the cumulative percent of the sample recovered at each time interval. Tabulate the cumulative percent recovered at each interval and the retention time at the end of the interval. Using linear interpolation, if necessary, determine the retention time associated with 5% and read the corresponding boiling temperature from the *Calibration curve*.

Acceptance criteria: Carbon number is between 17 and 25 at 5% distillation. The boiling point at the 5% distillation is between 287° and 422°.

IMPURITIES
Inorganic Impurities
- **LEAD,** *Lead Limit Test, Atomic Absorption Spectrophotometric Graphite Furnace Method, Method II,* Appendix IIIB
  Acceptance criteria: NMT 1 mg/kg

SPECIFIC TESTS
- **READILY CARBONIZABLE SUBSTANCES**
  Chromic acid cleaning mixture: Dissolve 200 g of sodium dichromate in 100 mL of water to which 1500 mL of sulfuric acid has been added, slowly with stirring.
  Sample: 5 mL
  Control solution: Mix 3 mL of ferric chloride CS, 1.5 mL of cobaltous chloride CS, and 0.5 mL of cupric sulfate CS in a glass-stoppered test tube that previously has been rinsed with *Chromic acid cleaning mixture*, then rinsed with water, and dried. Overlay this mixture with 5 mL of mineral oil.
  Analysis: Place the *Sample* in a glass-stoppered test tube that previously has been rinsed with *Chromic acid cleaning mixture*, then rinsed with water, and dried. Add 5 mL of 94.5%–94.9% sulfuric acid; while simultaneously starting a stopwatch, place the tube in a boiling water bath. After the test tube has been in the bath for 30 seconds, use a 3-second time span to remove it, and while holding the stopper in place, give three vigorous vertical shakes over an amplitude of about 5 in, then return it to the bath. Repeat every 30 seconds until exactly 10 min has passed, then remove the test tube.
  Acceptance criteria: The *Sample* remains unchanged in color, and the acid does not become darker than the standard color of the *Control solution*.
- **SPECIFIC GRAVITY:** Determine by any reliable method (see *General Provisions*).
  Acceptance criteria: NLT that stated, or within the range claimed by the vendor

- **ULTRAVIOLET ABSORBANCE (POLYNUCLEAR HYDROCARBONS)**
  Hexane: Use a pure grade of hexane (predominantly *n*-hexane and methylcyclopentane) having an ultraviolet absorbance not exceeding 0.10 down to 220 nm and not exceeding 0.02 down to 260 nm. The purity should be such that the *Solvent control* as defined below, has an absorbance curve, compared to water, showing no extraneous impurity peaks and no absorbance exceeding that of dimethyl sulfoxide, compared to water, at any wavelength in the range 260 to 420 nm, inclusive. If necessary to obtain the prescribed purities, the hexane may be passed through activated silica gel.
  Dimethyl sulfoxide: Use a pure grade of dimethyl sulfoxide (99.9%, melting point: 18°) that has a clear, water-white appearance; has an absorbance curve, compared with water, not exceeding 1.0 at 264 nm; and shows no extraneous impurity peaks in the wavelength range up to 420 nm. Store in glass-stoppered bottles.
  Apparatus: Use 125-mL glass-stoppered separatory funnels equipped with tetrafluoroethylene polymer stopcocks or other suitable stopcocks that will not contaminate the solvents.
  Sample preparation: Transfer 25 mL of sample and 25 mL of *Hexane* to a separatory funnel and mix. Add 5.0 mL of *Dimethyl sulfoxide*, shake the mixture vigorously for at least 1 min, and allow it to stand until the lower layer is clear. Completely transfer the lower layer to a second separatory funnel, add 2 mL of *Hexane*, and shake the mixture vigorously. Allow it to stand until the lower layer is clear, and then draw off the lower layer, designated as the *Sample preparation*.
  Solvent control: In a separatory funnel, vigorously shake 5.0 mL of *Dimethyl sulfoxide* with 25 mL of *Hexane* for at least 1 min, allow it to stand until the lower layer is clear, and draw off this layer, designated as *Solvent control*.
  Standard solution: Use a standard reference solution of naphthalene (National Institute for Standards and Technology Standard Material No. 577, or a solution of equivalent purity) containing a concentration of 7.0 mg/1000 mL in purified isooctane.
  Analysis: Determine the absorbance of the *Sample preparation* and the *Solvent control* in a 1-cm cell in the range 260 to 420 nm, inclusive.
  Determine the absorbance of the *Standard solution* at 275 nm measured against isooctane of the same spectral purity in 1-cm cells. (The absorbance will be approximately 0.30.)
  [NOTE—Make suitable corrections of the absorbance when testing samples containing added antioxidants.]
  Acceptance criteria: The absorbance of the *Sample preparation* does not exceed that of the *Solvent control* at any wavelength in the specified range by more than one-third of the absorbance of the *Standard solution*.
- **VISCOSITY:** Determine by any reliable method (see *Viscosity Determincation,* Appendix IIB).
  Acceptance criteria: Between 3 and 11 centistokes at 100°

Monk Fruit Extract

First Published: Third Supplement, FCC 7

Luo Han Fruit Concentrate
Luo Han Guo Concentrate
Luo Han Guo Extract
Monk Fruit Concentrate
Siraitia grosvenorii Extract

$C_{60}H_{102}O_{29}$ (Mogroside V) Formula wt, Mogroside V 1286
CAS: Mogroside V [88901-36-4]

DESCRIPTION

Monk Fruit Extract occurs as an off-white to light yellow powder. It is an extract of the fruit luo han guo (*Siraitia grosvenorii* Swingle, also known as monk fruit) that has been concentrated to optimize the concentration of mogroside V. It is obtained through water extraction of the mechanically crushed or shredded pulp of the fruit. Precipitate is removed by decanting, and the supernatant is cooled and passed through a food-grade copolymer resin which binds the target compounds. The resin is flushed with cold ethanol to release the extracted compounds, and the effluent is heated under vacuum to remove the ethanol, then spray dried. Monk Fruit Extract is composed primarily of cucurbitane glycosides, known as mogrosides, with mogroside V being the principal sweetening component. Other components are mogroside II, mogroside III, mogroside IV, mogroside VI, flavonoids, melanoidins, and protein fragments. Monk Fruit Extract is freely soluble in water. While not a requirement for this monograph, users interested in analyzing this ingredient for potential pesticide residues may use the informational method found under *Pesticide Residues* in Appendix XIII.

Function: Non-nutritive sweetener

Packaging and Storage: Store in tight, light-resistant containers. Avoid exposure to excessive heat.

IDENTIFICATION

- **THIN-LAYER CHROMATOGRAPHY,** Appendix IIA

    Standard solution A: 7.5 mg/mL of USP Mogroside V RS in methanol. Sonicate to aid dissolution.

    Standard solution B: Prepare a solution by dissolving 50 mg of USP Monk Fruit Extract RS in 20 mL of water. Extract the aqueous solution twice, using 10 mL of *n*-butanol each time, and combine the *n*-butanol extracts. Evaporate the combined *n*-butanol extract at room temperature, and dissolve the residue in 2 mL of methanol.

    Sample solution: Prepare a solution by dissolving 50 mg of the sample in 20 mL of water. Extract the aqueous solution twice, using 10 mL of *n*-butanol each time, and combine the *n*-butanol extracts. Evaporate the combined *n*-butanol extract at room temperature, and dissolve the residue in 2 mL of methanol.

    Adsorbent: 0.25-mm layer of chromatographic silica gel, prepared with a gypsum (calcium sulfate hemihydrate) binder

    Developing solvent system: *n*-Butanol, acetic acid, and water (4:1:1)

    Spray reagent: 10% sulfuric acid solution

    Application volume: 2 µL

    Analysis: After developing the plate in the *Developing solvent system*, remove the plate from the developing chamber, and allow the solvent to evaporate. Spray the plate with the *Spray reagent*, and heat at 105° to allow color development.

    Acceptance criteria: The principal spot obtained from the *Sample solution* corresponds in color and R_F value to that obtained from *Standard solution A*. The chromatogram obtained from the *Sample solution* corresponds to that obtained from *Standard solution B* in the placement and color of the spots.

ASSAY

- **MOGROSIDE V CONTENT**

    Mobile phase: Acetonitrile and water (22:78)

    Standard solution: 0.10 mg/mL of USP Mogroside V RS in *Mobile phase*

    Sample solution: Dissolve 30 mg of the sample in *Mobile phase* in a 50-mL volumetric flask. Sonicate the solution for 40 min, cool to room temperature, and dilute with *Mobile phase* to volume. Filter the solution through a 0.45-µm membrane.

    Chromatographic system, Appendix IIA

    Mode: High-performance liquid chromatography

    Detector: UV 203 nm

    Column: 4.6-mm × 250-mm column that contains 5-µm porous silica microparticles chemically bonded to octadecylsilane[1]

    Column temperature: 25°

    Flow rate: 1.0 mL/min

    Injection size: 20 µL

    Analysis: Separately inject the *Standard solution* and the *Sample solution* into the chromatograph, record the chromatograms, and measure the areas for the major peaks in the respective chromatograms. [NOTE—The approximate retention time for mogroside V is 15.7 min.] Using the peak area obtained from the

---

[1] ZORBAX SB-C18 (Agilent Technologies); Symmetry Shield RP 18 (Waters Corporation); or equivalent. Use a compatible guard column (C18, 5-µm, 4.6-mm × 7.5-mm).

chromatogram of the *Standard solution*, determine the percentage of mogroside V in the *Sample solution*:

$$\text{Result} = (r_U/r_S) \times (C_S/C_U) \times 100$$

r_U = peak area response for mogroside V obtained from the chromatogram of the *Sample solution*
r_S = peak area response for mogroside V obtained from the chromatogram of the *Standard solution*
C_S = concentration of mogroside V in the *Standard solution* (mg/mL)
C_U = concentration of the *Sample solution* (mg/mL)

Acceptance criteria: NLT 30.0%

IMPURITIES
Inorganic Impurities
- **ARSENIC**, *Elemental Impurities by ICP*, Appendix IIIC
  Acceptance criteria: NMT 0.5 mg/kg
- **CADMIUM**, *Elemental Impurities by ICP*, Appendix IIIC
  Acceptance criteria: NMT 1.0 mg/kg
- **LEAD**, *Elemental Impurities by ICP*, Appendix IIIC
  Acceptance criteria: NMT 1.0 mg/kg

SPECIFIC TESTS
- **ASH (TOTAL)**, Appendix IIC
  Sample: 2 g
  Analysis: Proceed as directed, holding the furnace at 600° for 2 h.
  Acceptance criteria: NMT 5.0%
- **LOSS ON DRYING**, Appendix IIC
  Acceptance criteria: NMT 6.0%

Mono- and Diglycerides

First Published: Prior to FCC 6

DESCRIPTION
Mono- and Diglycerides occur as a substance that varies in consistency from yellow liquids through white- to pale yellow-colored plastics to hard, ivory-colored solids. They consist of mixtures of glycerol mono- and diesters, with minor amounts of triesters, and of edible fats or oils or edible fat-forming fatty acids. They are insoluble in water, but are soluble in alcohol, in ethyl acetate, and in chloroform and other chlorinated hydrocarbons.
Function: Emulsifier; stabilizer
Packaging and Storage: Store in well-closed containers.

IMPURITIES
Inorganic Impurities
- **ARSENIC**, *Arsenic Limit Test*, Appendix IIIB
  Sample solution: Prepare as directed for organic compounds.
  Acceptance criteria: NMT 3 mg/kg
- **LEAD**, *Lead Limit Test, Flame Atomic Absorption Spectrophotometric Method*, Appendix IIIB
  Sample: 10 g
  Acceptance criteria: NMT 2 mg/kg

SPECIFIC TESTS
- **ACID VALUE (FATS AND RELATED SUBSTANCES)**, *Method II*, Appendix VII
  Acceptance criteria: NMT 6
- **FREE GLYCERIN**, *Free Glycerin or Propylene Glycol*, Appendix VII
  Acceptance criteria: NMT 7.0%
- **HYDROXYL VALUE**, *Method II*, Appendix VII
  Acceptance criteria: Results should conform to the representations of the vendor.
- **IODINE VALUE**, Appendix VII
  Acceptance criteria: Results should conform to the representations of the vendor.
- **1-MONOGLYCERIDE CONTENT**, *1-Monoglycerides*, Appendix VII
  Acceptance criteria: Results should conform to the representations of the vendor.
- **RESIDUE ON IGNITION (SULFATED ASH)**, Appendix IIC
  Sample: 5 g
  Acceptance criteria: NMT 0.5%
- **SAPONIFICATION VALUE**, Appendix VII
  Sample: 4 g
  Acceptance criteria: Results should conform to the representations of the vendor.
- **TOTAL MONOGLYCERIDES**, Appendix VII
  Acceptance criteria: Results should conform to the representations of the vendor.

Monoammonium L-Glutamate

First Published: Prior to FCC 6

Monoammonium Glutamate Monohydrate
Ammonium Glutamate

$C_5H_{12}N_2O_4 \cdot H_2O$ Formula wt 182.18
INS: 624   CAS: [7558-63-6]
UNII: 245K560GAW [ammonium glutamate]

DESCRIPTION
Monoammonium L-Glutamate occurs as a white, free-flowing, crystalline powder. It is freely soluble in water, but practically insoluble in common organic solvents. The pH of a 1:20 aqueous solution is between 6.0 and 7.0.
Function: Flavor enhancer; salt substitute
Packaging and Storage: Store in tight containers.

774 / Monoammonium L-Glutamate / Monographs

IDENTIFICATION
- **INFRARED SPECTRA,** *Spectrophotometric Identification Tests,* Appendix IIIC
  Sample preparation: Mineral oil mull
  Acceptance criteria: The spectrum of the sample exhibits relative maxima at the same wavelengths as those of the spectrum below.

ASSAY
- **PROCEDURE**
  Sample: 250 mg
  Analysis: Dissolve the *Sample* in 100 mL of glacial acetic acid. [NOTE—A few drops of water may be added first to speed dissolution.] Titrate with 0.1 N perchloric acid in glacial acetic acid, determining the endpoint potentiometrically. [CAUTION—Handle perchloric acid in an appropriate fume hood.] Perform a blank determination (see *General Provisions*) and make any necessary correction. Each mL of 0.1 N perchloric acid is equivalent to 9.109 mg of $C_5H_{12}N_2O_4 \cdot H_2O$.
  Acceptance criteria: NLT 98.5% and NMT 101.5% of $C_5H_{12}N_2O_4 \cdot H_2O$, calculated on the dried basis

IMPURITIES
Inorganic Impurities
- **LEAD,** *Lead Limit Test,* Appendix IIIB
  Sample solution: Prepare as directed for organic compounds.
  Control: 5 µg Pb (5 mL of *Diluted Standard Lead Solution*)
  Acceptance criteria: NMT 5 mg/kg

SPECIFIC TESTS
- **LOSS ON DRYING,** Appendix IIC: 50° for 4 h
  Acceptance criteria: NMT 0.5%
- **OPTICAL (SPECIFIC) ROTATION,** Appendix IIB
  Sample solution: 100 mg/mL in 2 N hydrochloric acid
  Acceptance criteria: $[\alpha]_D^{20}$ NLT +25.4° and NMT +26.40°, calculated on the dried basis
- **RESIDUE ON IGNITION (SULFATED ASH),** Appendix IIC
  Sample: 1 g
  Acceptance criteria: NMT 0.1%

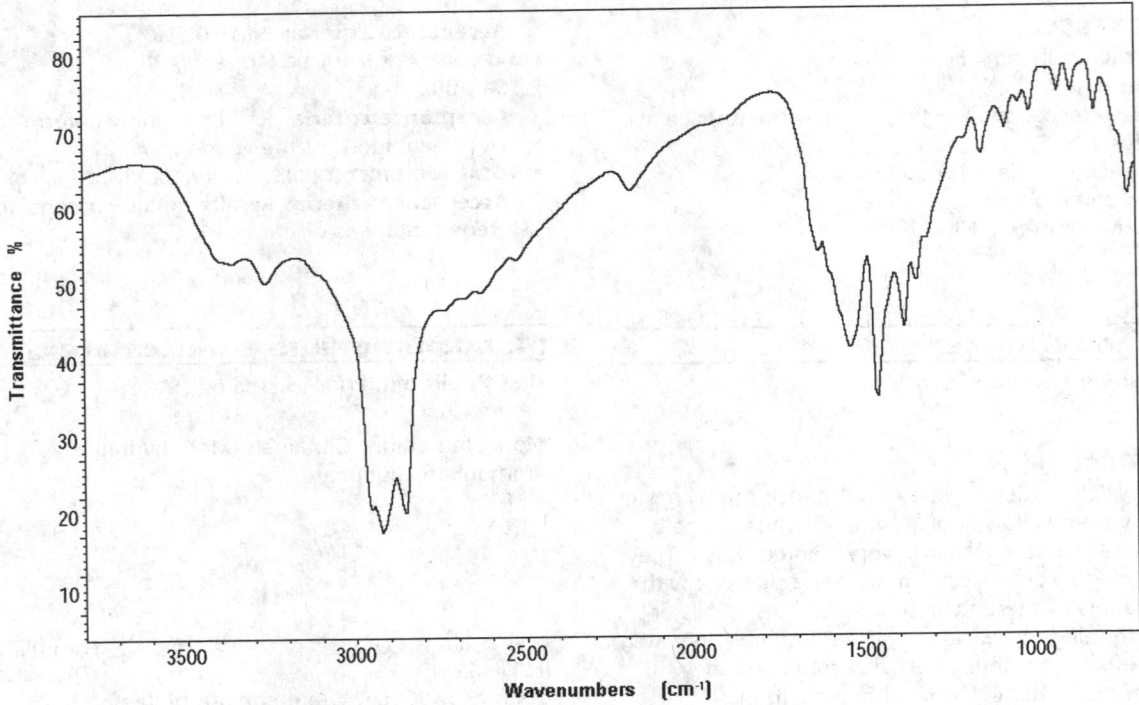

Monoammonium L-Glutamate (Mineral Oil Mull)

Monoammonium Glycyrrhizinate

First Published: Prior to FCC 6

Ammonium Glycyrrhizinate, Pentahydrate
Ammonium Glycyrrhizinate

$C_{42}H_{65}NO_{16} \cdot 5H_2O$ Formula wt anhydrous 839.98
INS: 958
UNII: 3VRD35U26C [ammonium glycyrrhizate]

DESCRIPTION
Monoammonium Glycyrrhizinate occurs as a white powder with an intensely sweet taste. It is obtained by extraction from ammoniated glycyrrhizin. It is soluble in ammonia water and is insoluble in glacial acetic acid.
Function: Flavoring agent
Packaging and Storage: Store in a cool, dry place in a tight container.

IDENTIFICATION
- **AMMONIUM,** Appendix IIIA
  Acceptance criteria: Passes test

ASSAY
- **PROCEDURE**
  [NOTE—This procedure is based on AOAC method 982.19.]
  Mobile phase: Acetonitrile, acetic acid and water (38:1:61), degassed. [NOTE—The water used should be glass-distilled and filtered through a 0.45-μm filter (Millipore, or equivalent).]
  Standard solution: Dissolve 10 mg (on the dried basis) of monoammonium glycyrrhizinate standard for analytical use (available from Sigma) in 20 mL of a 1:1 solution of acetonitrile:water, and filter through a 0.45-μm Millipore filter, or equivalent. [NOTE—Prepare fresh daily.]
  Sample solution: Dissolve 10 mg of sample in 20 mL of a 1:1 solution of acetonitrile:water, and filter through a 0.45-μm Millipore filter, or equivalent.
  Chromatographic system, Appendix IIA
    Mode: High-performance liquid chromatography
    Detector: UV-254 nm (0.2 to 0.1 AUFS range)
    Column: 30-cm × 4-mm (id), 10 μm particle size C18 reverse-phase column (μBondapak C18, Waters Corp., or equivalent)
    Temperature: Room temperature
    Flow rate: 2.0 mL/min. [NOTE—Maintain the Mobile phase at a pressure and flow rate capable of giving the required elution time (see System Suitability in High-Performance Liquid Chromatography).]
    Injection volume: About 10 μL
  System suitability
    Sample: Standard solution
    Suitability requirement: The relative standard deviation for duplicate injections is NMT 2.0%.
  Analysis: Separately inject, in duplicate, volumes of the Standard solution and the Sample solution into the chromatograph and determine the mean peak area for each solution. [NOTE—The approximate retention time for monoammonium glycyrrhizinate is 6 min.]
  Calculate the percent monoammonium glycyrrhizinate, equivalent to $C_{42}H_{65}NO_{16}$, in the sample taken by the formula:

  $$\text{Result} = 100 \times (20 C_S / W_U) \times (A_U / A_S)$$

  C_S = concentration (mg/mL) of the Standard solution
  W_U = weight of sample (mg) taken to prepare the Sample solution
  A_U = peak area of the Sample solution
  A_S = peak area of the Standard solution
  Acceptance criteria: NLT 85.0% and NMT 102.0% of $C_{42}H_{65}NO_{16}$, calculated on the dried basis

SPECIFIC TESTS
- **ASH (TOTAL),** Appendix IIC
  Acceptance criteria: NMT 0.5%
- **LOSS ON DRYING,** Appendix IIC: 78° for 4 h at 1-mm Hg
  Sample: 1 g
  Acceptance criteria: NMT 6.0%
- **OPTICAL (SPECIFIC) ROTATION,** Appendix IIB
  Sample solution: 15 mg/mL in 40% ethanol. [NOTE—Prepare using undried sample.]
  Acceptance criteria: $[\alpha]_D^{20}$ between +45° and +53°, on the as-is basis

Monoglyceride Citrate

First Published: Prior to FCC 6

CAS: [36291-32-4]

DESCRIPTION
Monoglyceride Citrate occurs as a viscous, amber liquid. It is a mixture of glyceryl monooleate and its citric acid monoester, manufactured by the reaction of glyceryl monooleate with citric acid under controlled conditions. It is dispersible in most common fat solvents and in alcohol, and it is insoluble in water.
Function: Solubilizer for antioxidants
Packaging and Storage: Store in well-closed containers.

IMPURITIES
Inorganic Impurities
- **LEAD,** Lead Limit Test, Flame Atomic Absorption Spectrophotometric Method, Appendix IIIB
  Sample: 10 g

Acceptance criteria: NMT 2 mg/kg

SPECIFIC TESTS

- **ACID VALUE (FATS AND RELATED SUBSTANCES)**, *Method II*, Appendix VII
  Acceptance criteria: Between 70 and 100
- **RESIDUE ON IGNITION (SULFATED ASH)**, Appendix IIC
  Sample: 1 g
  Acceptance criteria: NMT 0.3%
- **SAPONIFICATION VALUE**, Appendix VII
  Acceptance criteria: Between 260 and 265
- **TOTAL CITRIC ACID**
  Standard solution: Transfer 35 mg of sodium citrate dihydrate into a 100-mL volumetric flask, dissolve in and dilute to volume with water and mix. Calculate the concentration (μg/mL) of citric acid in the *Standard solution* by the formula:

  $$Result = 1000 \times F \times W/100$$

  F = factor converting sodium citrate dihydrate to citric acid, 0.6533
  W = weight of the sodium citrate dihydrate taken to prepare the *Standard solution* (mg)

  Sample preparation: Transfer 150 mg into a saponification flask, add 50 mL of 4% alcoholic potassium hydroxide solution, and reflux for 1 h. Acidify the reaction mixture with hydrochloric acid to a pH of 2.8 to 3.2, transfer into a 400-mL beaker, and evaporate to dryness on a steam bath. Quantitatively transfer the contents of the beaker into a separatory funnel, using NMT 50 mL of water to rinse the beaker, and then extract with three 50-mL portions of petroleum ether (b.p. 30° to 60°), discarding the extracts. Transfer the water layer to a 100-mL volumetric flask, dilute to volume with water, and mix. This dilution of the water layer is the *Sample preparation*.
  Analysis: Pipet 2.0 mL each the *Standard solution* and of the *Sample preparation* into separate, 40-mL graduated centrifuge tubes, and add 2 mL of 1:2 sulfuric acid and 11 mL of water to each tube. Boil for 3 min, cool, and add 5 mL of bromine TS to each tube. Dilute to 20 mL, allow to stand for 10 min, and centrifuge. Transfer 4.0 mL of each solution into separate 19- × 110-mm test tubes, add 1 mL of water, 0.5 mL of 1:2 sulfuric acid, and 0.3 mL of 1 M potassium bromide, and shake. Add 0.3 mL of 1.5 N potassium permanganate, shake, and allow to stand for 2 min. Add 1 mL of a saturated solution of ferrous sulfate, shake, allow to stand for 2 min, and then dilute to 10 mL with water. Add 10.0 mL of *n*-hexane (previously washed with sulfuric acid, followed by a water wash, and then dried over anhydrous sodium sulfate), shake vigorously for 2 min, and then centrifuge at a low speed for 1 min. Transfer 5.0 mL of the hexane extract into a 20- × 145-mm tube containing 10.0 mL of 40 mg/mL sodium sulfide nonahydrate solution, and briefly shake vigorously (3 oscillations only). Centrifuge the mixture at low speed for 1 min. Immediately determine the absorbance of each aqueous layer in a 1-cm cell at 450 nm with a suitable spectrophotometer, using a reagent blank in the reference cell.
  Calculate the quantity, in mg, of citric acid in the sample taken by the formula:

  $$Result = (A_U/A_S) \times 0.1C$$

  A_U = absorbance of the final solution from the *Sample solution*
  A_S = absorbance of the final solution from the *Standard solution*
  C = concentration of citric acid in the *Standard solution* (μg/mL)

  Acceptance criteria: Between 14.0% and 17.0%
- **WATER**, *Water Determination*, Appendix IIB
  Acceptance criteria: NMT 0.2%

Monopotassium L-Glutamate

First Published: Prior to FCC 6

Monopotassium Glutamate Monohydrate
Potassium Glutamate
MPG

$C_5H_8KNO_4 \cdot H_2O$ Formula wt 203.24
INS: 622 CAS: [19473-49-5]
UNII: B5ZC7FHO6O [monopotassium glutamate]

DESCRIPTION

Monopotassium L-Glutamate occurs as a white, free-flowing, crystalline powder. It is hygroscopic, is freely soluble in water, and is slightly soluble in alcohol. The pH of a 1:50 aqueous solution is between 6.7 and 7.3.
Function: Flavor enhancer; salt substitute
Packaging and Storage: Store in tight containers.

IDENTIFICATION

- **INFRARED SPECTRA**, *Spectrophotometric Identification Tests*, Appendix IIIC
  Sample preparation: Mineral oil mull
  Acceptance criteria: The spectrum of the sample exhibits relative maxima at the same wavelengths as those of the spectrum below.

ASSAY

- **PROCEDURE**
  Sample: 250 mg
  Analysis: Dissolve the *Sample* in 100 mL of glacial acetic acid. [NOTE—A few drops of water may be added first to speed dissolution.] Titrate with 0.1 N perchloric acid in glacial acetic acid, determining the endpoint potentiometrically. [CAUTION—Handle perchloric acid in an appropriate fume hood.] Perform a blank determination (see *General Provisions*) and make any

necessary correction. Each mL of 0.1 N perchloric acid is equivalent to 10.16 mg of $C_5H_8KNO_4 \cdot H_2O$.
Acceptance criteria: NLT 98.5% and NMT 101.5% of $C_5H_8KNO_4 \cdot H_2O$, calculated on the dried basis

IMPURITIES
Inorganic Impurities
- **LEAD,** *Lead Limit Test,* Appendix IIIB
  Sample solution: Prepare as directed for organic compounds.
  Control: 5 µg Pb (5 mL of *Diluted Standard Lead Solution*)

Acceptance criteria: NMT 5 mg/kg

SPECIFIC TESTS
- **LOSS ON DRYING,** Appendix IIC: 80° for 5 h in vacuum
  Acceptance criteria: NMT 0.2%
- **OPTICAL (SPECIFIC) ROTATION,** Appendix IIB
  Sample solution: 100 mg/mL in 2 N hydrochloric acid
  Acceptance criteria: $[\alpha]_D^{20}$ NLT +22.5° and NMT +24.0°, calculated on the dried basis

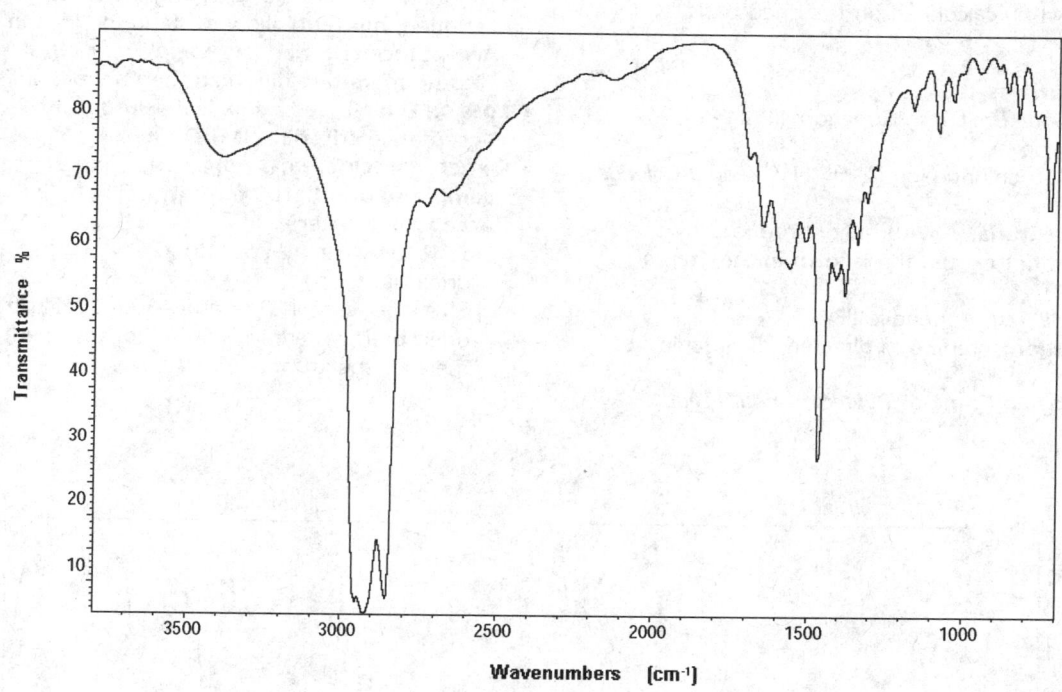

Monopotassium L-Glutamate (Mineral Oil Mull)

Monosodium L-Glutamate

First Published: Prior to FCC 6

Monosodium Glutamate Monohydrate
Monosodium Glutamate
Sodium Glutamate
MSG

$C_5H_8NNaO_4 \cdot H_2O$
INS: 621
UNII: W81N5U6R6U [monosodium glutamate]
Formula wt 187.13
CAS: monohydrate [6106-04-3]

DESCRIPTION
Monosodium L-Glutamate occurs as white, free-flowing crystals or crystalline powder. It is freely soluble in water, and is sparingly soluble in alcohol. The pH of a 1:20 aqueous solution is between 6.7 and 7.2.
Function: Flavor enhancer
Packaging and Storage: Store in tight containers.

IDENTIFICATION
- **INFRARED SPECTRA,** *Spectrophotometric Identification Tests,* Appendix IIIC
  Sample preparation: Mineral oil mull
  Acceptance criteria: The spectrum of the sample exhibits relative maxima at the same wavelengths as those of the spectrum below.

ASSAY

- **PROCEDURE**

  Sample: 250 mg

  Analysis: Dissolve the *Sample* in 100 mL of glacial acetic acid. [NOTE—A few drops of water may be added first to speed dissolution.] Titrate with 0.1 N perchloric acid in glacial acetic acid, determining the endpoint potentiometrically. [CAUTION—Handle perchloric acid in an appropriate fume hood.] Perform a blank determination (see *General provisions*) and make any necessary correction. Each mL of 0.1 N perchloric acid is equivalent to 9.356 mg of $C_5H_8NNaO_4 \cdot H_2O$.

  Acceptance criteria: NLT 98.5% and NMT 101.5% of $C_5H_8NNaO_4 \cdot H_2O$, calculated on the dried basis

IMPURITIES

Inorganic Impurities

- **CHLORIDE,** *Chloride Limit Test,* Appendix IIIB

  Sample: 10 mg

  Control: 20 μg chloride ion (2 mL of *Standard Chloride Solution*)

  Acceptance criteria: Any turbidity produced by the *Sample* does not exceed that shown in the *Control* (NMT 0.2%).

- **LEAD,** *Lead Limit Test,* Appendix IIIB

  Sample solution: Prepare as directed for organic compounds.

  Control: 5 μg Pb (5 mL of *Diluted Standard Lead Solution*)

  [NOTE—Alternatively, determine as directed under *Lead Limit Test, Atomic Absorption Spectrophotometric Graphite Furnace Method, Method I,* Appendix IIIB using a 10-g sample.]

  Acceptance criteria: NMT 5 mg/kg

SPECIFIC TESTS

- **CLARITY AND COLOR OF SOLUTION**

  Sample solution: 100 mg/mL

  Control solution: Dilute 0.2 mL of *Standard Chloride Solution* (see *Chloride and Sulfate Limit Tests, Chloride Limit Test,* Appendix IIIB) with water to 20 mL; add 1 mL of 1:3 nitric acid, 0.2 mL of a 20 mg/mL dextrin solution, and 1 mL of a 20 mg/mL silver nitrate solution; mix, and allow to stand for 15 min.

  Acceptance criteria: The *Sample solution* is colorless and has no more turbidity than the *Control solution*.

- **LOSS ON DRYING,** Appendix IIC: 100° for 5 h

  Acceptance criteria: NMT 0.5%

- **OPTICAL (SPECIFIC) ROTATION,** Appendix IIB

  Sample solution: 100 mg/mL in 2 N hydrochloric acid

  Acceptance criteria:

  $[\alpha]_D^{20}$: between +24.5° and +25.5°, calculated on the dried basis; or

  $[\alpha]_M^{25}$: between +29.4° and +30.4°, calculated on the dried basis, where M = 546.1 for the line from the mercury spectrum

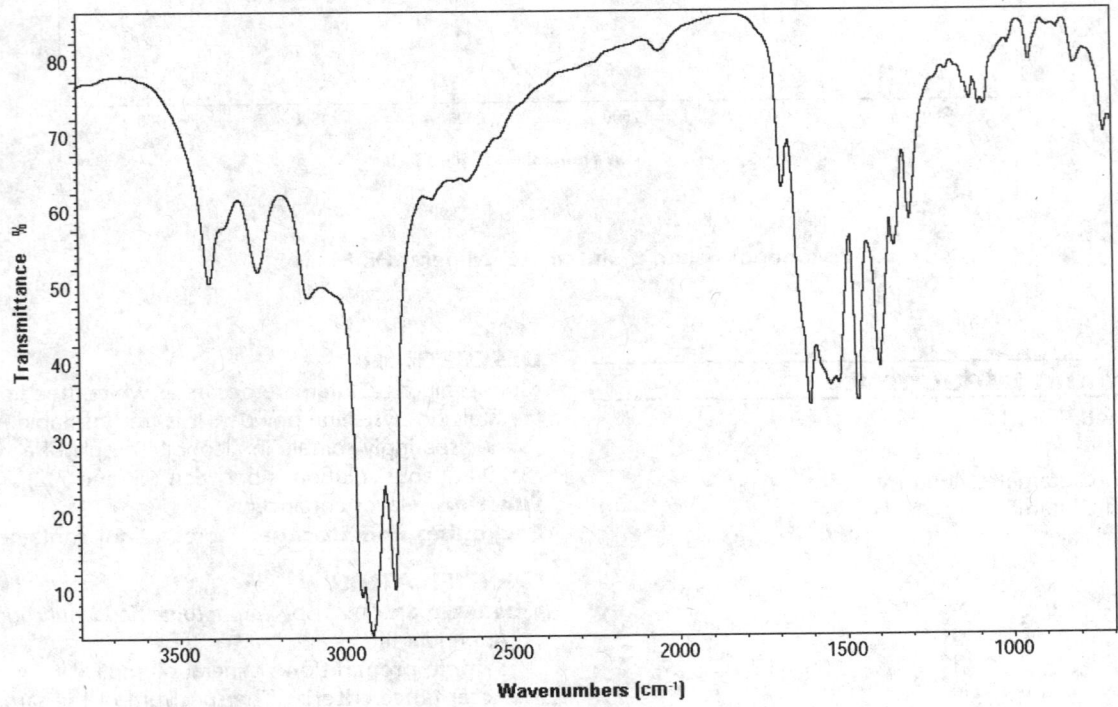

Monosodium L-Glutamate (Mineral Oil Mull)

Morpholine

First Published: Prior to FCC 6

Tetrahydro-2H-1,4-oxazine
Diethylene Oximide
Diethylene Imidoxide

C₄H₉NO
UNII: 8B2ZCK305O [morpholine]

Formula wt 87.12
CAS: [110-91-8]

DESCRIPTION
Morpholine occurs as a clear, colorless, mobile, hygroscopic liquid. It is miscible with water with the evolution of some heat. It is also miscible with acetone, with ether, with castor oil, with methanol, with alcohol, and with many oils such as linseed and pine.

Function: Boiler water additive; component of coatings for fruits and vegetables

Packaging and Storage: Store in tight containers.

IDENTIFICATION
- **INFRARED SPECTRA,** *Spectrophotometric Identification Tests,* Appendix IIIC

  Sample preparation: Neat dispersion of sample between two sodium chloride plates

  Acceptance criteria: The spectrum of the sample exhibits relative maxima at the same wavelengths as those of the spectrum below.

ASSAY
- **PROCEDURE**

  Solution A: 0.1% bromocresol green in methanol

  Solution B: 0.1% sodium salt of methyl red in water

  Mixed indicator solution: *Solution A:Solution B* (5:1) (v/v)

  Sample: 1.4 to 1.6 g

  Analysis: Transfer 50 mL of water into a 250-mL flask. Add 0.4 mL of *Mixed indicator solution*, and neutralize, adding 0.1 N hydrochloric acid dropwise just to the disappearance of the green color. Transfer the *Sample* into the flask and swirl to complete dissolution. Titrate with 0.5 N hydrochloric acid to the disappearance of the green color. Each mL of 0.5 N hydrochloric acid is equivalent to 43.56 mg of C₄H₉NO.

  Acceptance criteria: NLT 99.0%

IMPURITIES
Inorganic Impurities
- **LEAD,** *Lead Limit Test, Atomic Absorption Spectrophotometric Graphite Furnace Method, Method I,* Appendix IIIB

  Acceptance criteria: NMT 1 mg/kg

SPECIFIC TESTS
- **DISTILLATION RANGE,** Appendix IIB

  Acceptance criteria: Between 126.0° and 130.0°
- **REFRACTIVE INDEX,** Appendix IIB

  [NOTE—Use an Abbé or other refractometer of equal or greater accuracy.]

  Acceptance criteria: Between 1.454 and 1.455 at 20°
- **SPECIFIC GRAVITY:** Determine by any reliable method (see *General Provisions*).

  Acceptance criteria: Between 0.997 and 1.000

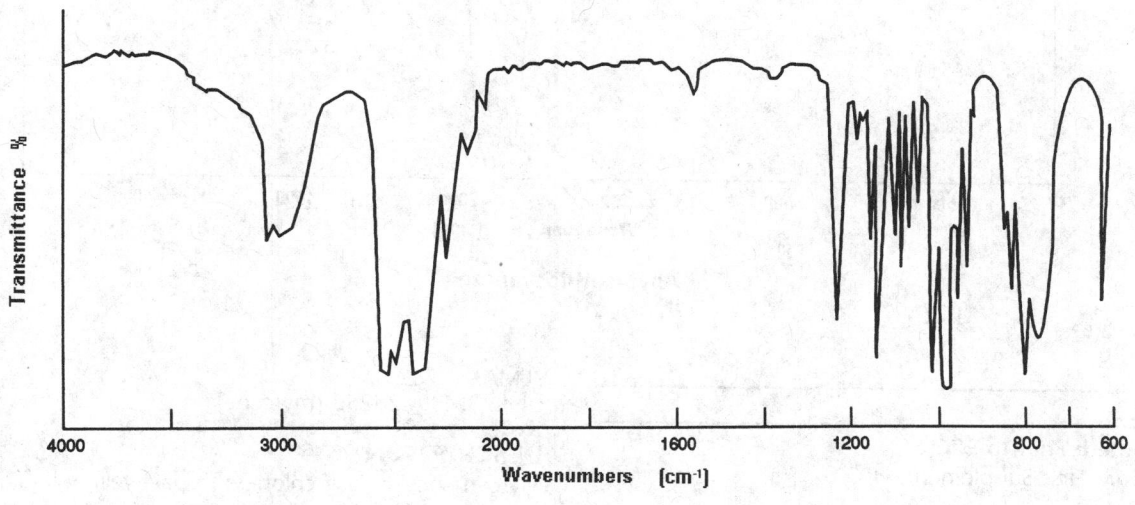

Morpholine

Mustard Oil

First Published: Prior to FCC 6

UNII: TYY1MA9BSY [mustard oil]

DESCRIPTION

Mustard Oil occurs as a clear, pale yellow liquid with a sharp, pungent taste. It is the volatile oil obtained by the steam and water distillation of the comminuted press cakes of the seeds from *Brassica nigra* (Linnaeus) W.D.J. Koch or *Brassica juncea* (Linnaeus) Czernjajev (Fam. Cruciferae). The essential oil forms upon maceration of the comminuted seeds in warm water, which releases sinigrin, a β-glucopyranoside, that is subsequently enzymatically hydrolyzed to allyl isothiocyanate. [**Caution**—Mustard Oil is a lacrimator.]

Function: Flavoring agent

Packaging and Storage: Store in a cool, dry place protected from light in tight containers.

IDENTIFICATION

- **Infrared Spectra**, *Spectrophotometric Identification Tests*, Appendix IIIC

  Acceptance criteria: The spectrum of the sample exhibits relative maxima at the same wavelengths as those of the spectrum for Allyl Isothiocyanate below.

ASSAY

- **Allyl Isothiocyanate**, *M-1a*, Appendix XI

  Acceptance criteria: NLT 93.0%, as C_3H_5NCS (allyl isothiocyanate).

SPECIFIC TESTS

- **Refractive Index**, Appendix IIB

  [Note—Use an Abbé or other refractometer of equal or greater accuracy.]

  Acceptance criteria: Between 1.524 and 1.534 at 20°

- **Specific Gravity:** Determine by any reliable method (see *General Provisions*).

  Acceptance criteria: Between 1.008 and 1.019

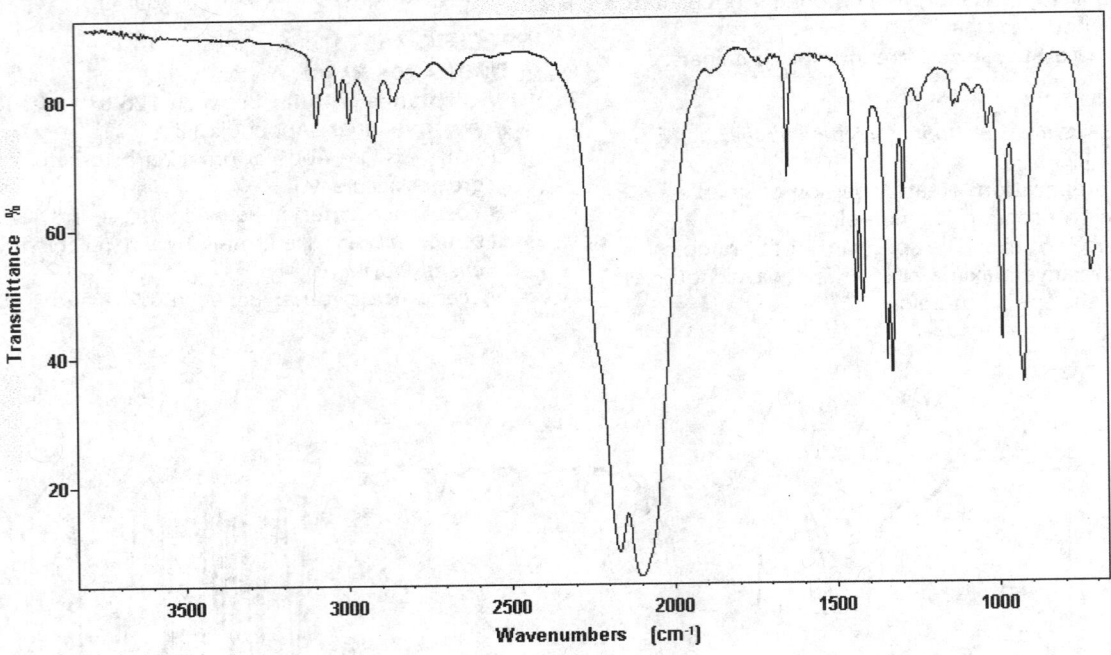

Allyl Isothiocyanate

Myrcene

First Published: Prior to FCC 6
Last Revision: First Supplement, FCC 6

7-Methyl-3-methylene-1,6-octadiene

$C_{10}H_{16}$ Formula wt 136.24

FEMA: 2762
UNII: 3M39CZS25B [myrcene]

DESCRIPTION

Myrcene occurs as a colorless to pale yellow liquid. It may contain a suitable antioxidant.

Odor: Sweet, balsamic
Solubility: Soluble in alcohol, most fixed oils; insoluble or practically insoluble in water
Boiling Point: ~167°
Function: Flavoring agent

ASSAY
- **Procedure:** Proceed as directed under *M-1a,* Appendix XI.
  Acceptance criteria: NLT 90.0% of $C_{10}H_{16}$

SPECIFIC TESTS
- **Refractive Index,** Appendix II: At 20°
  Acceptance criteria: Between 1.466 and 1.471
- **Specific Gravity:** Determine at 25° by any reliable method (see *General Provisions*).
  Acceptance criteria: Between 0.789 and 0.793

OTHER REQUIREMENTS
- **Peroxide Value,** *M-11,* Appendix XI
  Acceptance criteria: NMT 50.0

Myristaldehyde
First Published: Prior to FCC 6

Tetradecanal

$C_{14}H_{28}O$ Formula wt 212.38
FEMA: 2763
UNII: 44AJ2LT15N [tetradecanal]

DESCRIPTION
Myristaldehyde occurs as a colorless to pale yellow liquid.
Odor: Fatty, orris
Solubility: Insoluble or practically insoluble in ethanol, propylene glycol, vegetable oils, water
Boiling Point: ~260°
Function: Flavoring agent

ASSAY
- **Procedure:** Proceed as directed under *M-2a,* Appendix XI.
  Acceptance criteria: NLT 85.0% of $C_{14}H_{28}O$

SPECIFIC TESTS
- **Acid Value, Flavor Chemicals (Other Than Essential Oils),** *M-15,* Appendix XI
  Acceptance criteria: NMT 5.0
- **Refractive Index,** Appendix II: At 20°
  Acceptance criteria: Between 1.438 and 1.445
- **Specific Gravity:** Determine at 25° by any reliable method (see *General Provisions*).
  Acceptance criteria: Between 0.825 and 0.830

Myristic Acid
First Published: Prior to FCC 6

Tetradecanoic Acid

$C_{14}H_{28}O_2$ Formula wt 228.37
                 CAS: [544-63-8]
UNII: 0I3V7S25AW [myristic acid]

DESCRIPTION
Myristic Acid occurs as a hard, white or faintly yellow, somewhat glossy, crystalline solid or as a white or yellow-white powder. It is obtained from coconut oil and other fats. Myristic Acid is practically insoluble in water, but it is soluble in alcohol, in chloroform, and in ether.
Function: Component in the manufacture of other food-grade additives; defoaming agent
Packaging and Storage: Store in well-closed containers.

IMPURITIES
Inorganic Impurities
- **Lead,** *Lead Limit Test, Flame Atomic Absorption Spectrophotometric Method,* Appendix IIIB
  Sample: 5 g
  Acceptance criteria: NMT 2 mg/kg

SPECIFIC TESTS
- **Acid Value (Fats and Related Substances),** Method I, Appendix VII
  Acceptance criteria: Between 242 and 249
- **Iodine Value,** Appendix VII
  Acceptance criteria: NMT 1.0
- **Residue on Ignition (Sulfated Ash),** Appendix IIC
  Sample: 2 g
  Acceptance criteria: NMT 0.1%
- **Saponification Value,** Appendix VII
  Sample: 3 g
  Acceptance criteria: Between 242 and 251
- **Solidification Point,** Appendix IIB
  Acceptance criteria: Between 48° and 55.5°
- **Unsaponifiable Matter,** Appendix VII
  Acceptance criteria: NMT 1%
- **Water,** *Water Determination,* Appendix IIB
  Acceptance criteria: NMT 0.2%

Myristyl Alcohol

First Published: Prior to FCC 6

1-Tetradecanol
Tetradecyl Alcohol

$C_{14}H_{30}O$ Formula wt 214.38
UNII: V42034O9PU [myristyl alcohol]

DESCRIPTION
Myristyl alcohol occurs as colorless to white, waxy, solid flakes.
Odor: Waxy
Solubility: Soluble in ether; slightly soluble in alcohol; insoluble or practically insoluble in water
Boiling Point: ~289°
Function: Flavoring agent

ASSAY
- **Procedure:** Proceed as directed under *M-1b*, Appendix XI.
  Acceptance criteria: NLT 98.0% of $C_{14}H_{30}O$

SPECIFIC TESTS
- **Acid Value, Flavor Chemicals (Other Than Essential Oils)**, *M-15*, Appendix XI
  Acceptance criteria: NMT 1.0

OTHER REQUIREMENTS
- **Melting Range or Temperature Determination**, Appendix IIB
  Acceptance criteria: Between 38° and 41°
- **Iodine Value**, Appendix VII
  Acceptance criteria: NMT 3.0
- **Saponification Value**, *Esters*, Appendix VI
  Acceptance criteria: NMT 1.0

Myrrh Oil

First Published: Prior to FCC 6

FEMA: 2766

CAS: [9000-45-7]

UNII: H74221J5J4 [myrrh oil]

DESCRIPTION
Myrrh Oil occurs as a light brown or green liquid having the characteristic odor of the gum. It is the volatile oil obtained by steam distillation from myrrh gum obtained from several species of *Commiphora* (Fam. Burseraceae). It is soluble in most fixed oils, but is only slightly soluble in mineral oil. It is insoluble in glycerin and in propylene glycol. It becomes darker in color and more viscous under the influence of air and light.
Function: Flavoring agent
Packaging and Storage: Store in a cool place protected from light in full, tight containers that are made from steel or aluminum and that are suitably lined.

IDENTIFICATION
- **Infrared Spectra**, *Spectrophotometric Identification Tests*, Appendix IIIC
  Acceptance criteria: The spectrum of the sample exhibits relative maxima at the same wavelengths as those of the spectrum below.

SPECIFIC TESTS
- **Acid Value (Essential Oils and Flavors)**, Appendix VI
  Acceptance criteria: Between 2 and 13
- **Angular Rotation**, *Optical (Specific) Rotation*, Appendix IIB: Use a 100-mm tube.
  Acceptance criteria: Between −60° and −98°
- **Refractive Index**, Appendix IIB
  [Note—Use an Abbé or other refractometer of equal or greater accuracy.]
  Acceptance criteria: Between 1.519 and 1.528 at 20°
- **Saponification Value**, Appendix VII
  Sample: 5 g
  Acceptance criteria: Between 9 and 35
- **Solubility in Alcohol**, Appendix VI
  Acceptance criteria: One mL of sample dissolves in 10 mL of 90% alcohol, occasionally with opalescence or turbidity.
- **Specific Gravity:** Determine by any reliable method (see *General Provisions*).
  Acceptance criteria: Between 0.985 and 1.014

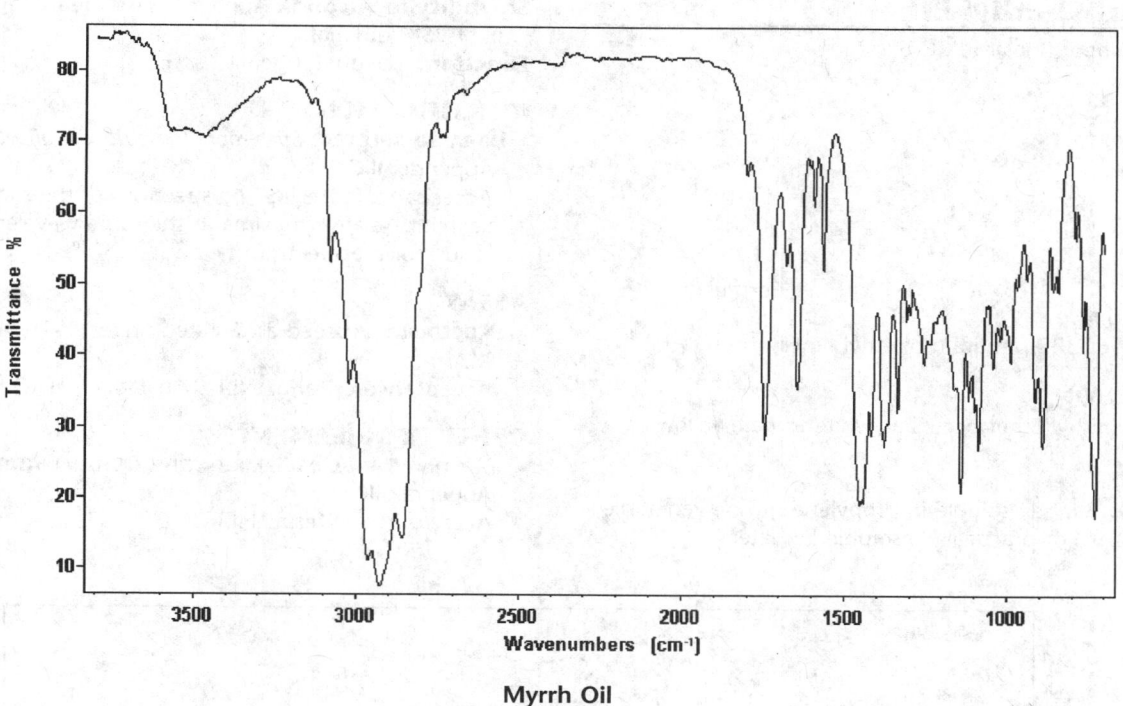
Myrrh Oil

β-Naphthyl Ethyl Ether

First Published: Prior to FCC 6

Nerolin II
Nerolin Bromelia

$C_{12}H_{12}O$ — Formula wt 172.23
FEMA: 2768
UNII: ZF3IS6G3R7 [β-naphthol ethyl ether]

DESCRIPTION
β-Naphthyl Ethyl Ether occurs as white to pale yellow crystals.

Odor: Floral

Solubility: Slightly soluble in propylene glycol, vegetable oils; insoluble or practically insoluble in water

Boiling Point: ~282°

Solubility in Alcohol, Appendix VI: One mL dissolves in 5 mL of 95% ethanol.

Function: Flavoring agent

IDENTIFICATION
- **INFRARED SPECTRA,** *Spectrophotometric Identification Tests,* Appendix IIIC

  Acceptance criteria: The spectrum of the sample exhibits relative maxima at the same wavelengths as those of the spectrum below.

ASSAY
- **PROCEDURE:** Proceed as directed under *M-1b,* Appendix XI.

  Acceptance criteria: NLT 97.0% of $C_{12}H_{12}O$

OTHER REQUIREMENTS
- **MELTING RANGE OR TEMPERATURE DETERMINATION,** Appendix IIB

  Acceptance criteria: NLT 30.0°

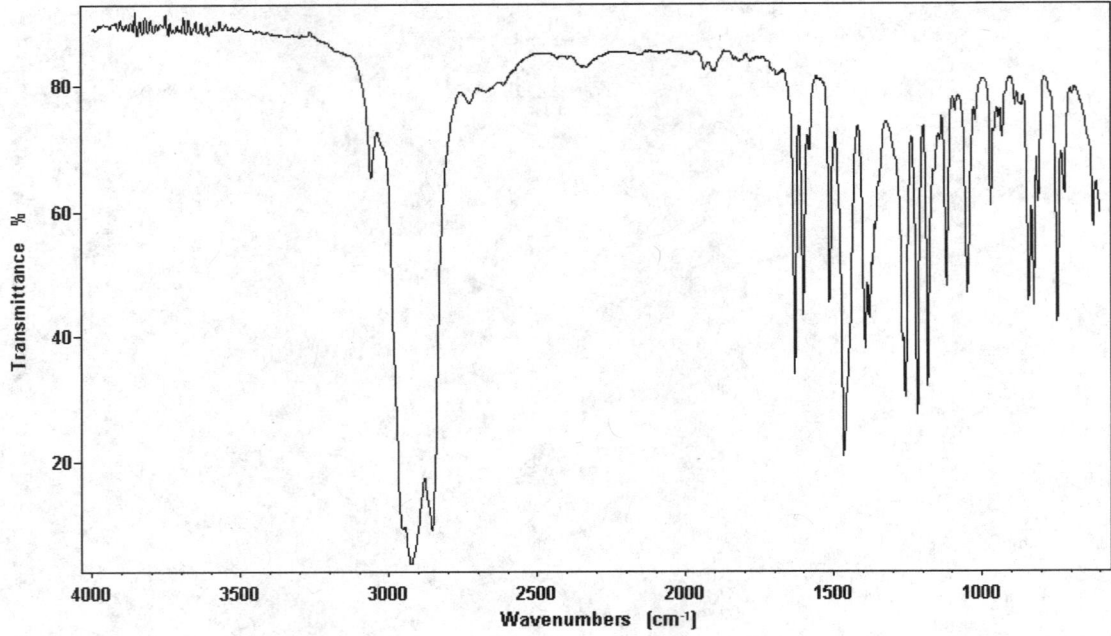

β-Naphthyl Ethyl Ether

Natamycin

First Published: Prior to FCC 6

Pimaricin

$C_{33}H_{47}NO_{13}$　　　　　　　Formula wt 665.73
INS: 235　　　　　　　　　　　CAS: [7681-93-8]
UNII: 8O0C852CPO [natamycin]

DESCRIPTION
Natamycin occurs as an off-white to cream colored powder that may contain up to 3 moles of water. It melts with decomposition at about 280°. It is practically insoluble in water, slightly soluble in methanol, and soluble in glacial acetic acid and in dimethylformamide.
Function: Antimycotic
Packaging and Storage: Store in tight, light-resistant containers in a cool place.

IDENTIFICATION
- **ULTRAVIOLET ABSORPTION,** *Spectrophotometric Identification Tests,* Appendix IIIC
  Standard stock solution: Transfer 50 mg of USP Natamycin RS into a 200-mL volumetric flask, add 5.0 mL of water and moisten the sample. Add 100 mL of glacial acetic acid in methanol (1:1000) and shake by mechanical means in the dark until dissolved. Dilute to volume with the 1:1000 acetic acid-methanol solution.
  Standard solution: Transfer 2.0 mL of *Standard stock solution* into a 100-mL volumetric flask, dilute to volume with the 1:1000 acetic acid-methanol solution, and mix.
  Sample stock solution: Transfer 50 mg of sample into a 200-mL volumetric flask, add 5.0 mL of water and moisten the sample. Add 100 mL of glacial acetic acid in methanol (1:1000) and shake by mechanical means in the dark until dissolved. Dilute to volume with the 1:1000 acetic acid-methanol solution.
  Sample solution: Transfer 2.0 mL of *Sample stock solution* into a 100-mL volumetric flask, dilute to volume with the 1:1000 acetic acid-methanol solution, and mix.
  Acceptance criteria: The spectrum of the *Sample solution* exhibits maxima and minima at the same wavelengths as those in the spectrum of the *Standard solution.*

ASSAY
- **PROCEDURE**
  [NOTE—Throughout this *Assay,* protect all solutions containing natamycin from direct light.]
  Mobile phase: Dissolve 3.0 g of ammonium acetate and 1.0 g of ammonium chloride in 760 mL of water, and mix. Add 5.0 mL of tetrahydrofuran and 240 mL of acetonitrile, mix, and filter through a 0.5-µm or finer porosity filter. If necessary, make adjustments to meet the system suitability requirements.
  System suitability solution: Dissolve 20 mg of sample in 99:1 (v/v) methanol:0.1 N hydrochloric acid mixture, and allow to stand for 2 h. [NOTE—Use this solution within 1 h.]
  Standard solution: Transfer 20 mg of USP Natamycin RS into a 100-mL volumetric flask. Add 5.0 mL of tetrahydrofuran, and sonicate for 10 min. Add 60 mL of methanol, and swirl to dissolve. Add 25 mL of water, and mix. Allow to cool to room temperature. Dilute to volume with water, mix, and filter through a membrane filter of 5-µm or finer porosity.
  Sample solution: Transfer 20 mg of sample into a 100-mL volumetric flask. Add 5.0 mL of tetrahydrofuran, and sonicate for 10 min. Add 60 mL of methanol, and swirl to dissolve. Add 25 mL of water, and mix. Allow to cool to room temperature. Dilute to volume with water, mix, and filter through a membrane filter of 5-µm or finer porosity.
  Chromatographic system, Appendix IIA
    Mode: High-performance liquid chromatography
    Detector: UV 303 nm
    Column: 25-cm × 4.6-mm (id) column packed with octadecylsilanized silica (Supelcosil LC 18, or equivalent)
    Flow rate: About 3 mL/min
    Injection volume: About 20 µL
  System suitability
    Sample: *Standard solution* and *System suitability solution*
    Suitability requirement 1: The column efficiency is NLT 3000 theoretical plates for the *Standard solution.*
    Suitability requirement 2: The tailing factor is between 0.8 and 1.3 for the *Standard solution.*
    Suitability requirement 3: The relative standard deviation for three replicate injections of the *Standard solution* is NMT 1.0%.
    Suitability requirement 4: The resolution between the sample and its methyl ester from the chromatogram of the *System suitability solution* is NLT 2.5.
  Analysis: Separately inject the *Standard solution* and the *Sample solution* into the chromatograph, and record the peak areas of the major peaks. [NOTE—The relative retention times are about 0.7 for natamycin and 1.0 for its methyl ester.]
  Calculate the percentage of natamycin in the portion of sample taken by the formula:

  $$\text{Result} = 0.1(W_S P_S / W_U)(r_U / r_S)$$

  W_S = weight of USP Natamycin RS taken to prepare the *Standard solution* (mg)
  P_S = stated content of USP Natamycin RS (µg/mg)
  W_U = weight of sample taken to prepare the *Sample solution* (mg)
  r_U = peak area response obtained from the chromatogram of the *Sample solution*

r_S = peak area response obtained from the chromatogram of the *Standard solution*

Acceptance criteria: NLT 97.0% and NMT 102.0% $C_{33}H_{47}NO_{13}$, calculated on the anhydrous basis

IMPURITIES
Organic Impurities
- **LEAD**, *Lead Limit Test, Flame Atomic Absorption Spectrophotometric Method*, Appendix IIIB
  Sample: 10 g
  Acceptance criteria: NMT 2 mg/kg

SPECIFIC TESTS
- **OPTICAL (SPECIFIC) ROTATION**, Appendix IIB
  Sample solution: 10 mg/mL in glacial acetic acid
  Acceptance criteria: $[\alpha]_D^{20}$ between +276° and +280°
- **PH**, *pH Determination*, Appendix IIB
  Sample suspension: 10 mg/mL
  Acceptance criteria: Between 5.0 and 7.5
- **WATER**, *Water Determination*, Appendix IIB
  Acceptance criteria: Between 6.0% and 9.0%

Add the following:

▲Neohesperidine Dihydrochalcone
First Published: FCC 8

1-[4-[[2-O-(6-Deoxy-α-L-mannopyranosyl)-β-D-glucopyranosyl]oxy]-2,6-dihydroxyphenyl]-3-(3-hydroxy-4-methoxyphenyl)propan-1-one
Hesperetin dihydrochalcone-4′-β-neohesperidoside
NHDC
Neohesperidin-Dihydrochalcone
Neohesperidine DC

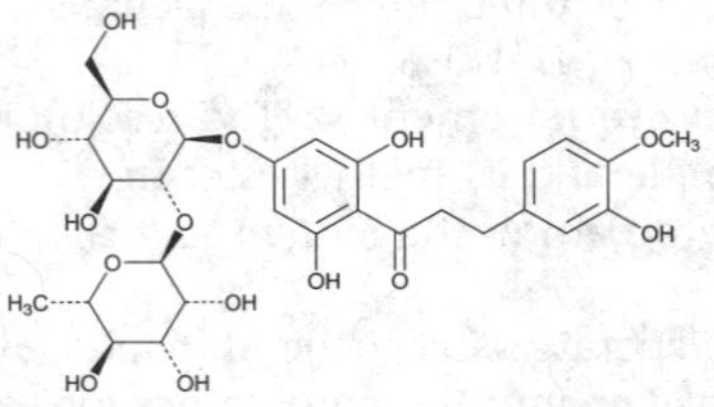

$C_{28}H_{36}O_{15}$ Formula wt 612.6
INS: 959   CAS: [20702-77-6]
FEMA: 3811
UNII: 3X476D83QV [neohesperidine dihydrochalcone]

DESCRIPTION
Neohesperidine Dihydrochalcone occurs as a white to off-white or yellowish-white powder. It is a flavonoid dihydrochalcone, and is practically insoluble in water and in methylene chloride, soluble in methanol, and freely soluble in dimethyl sulfoxide.
Function: Sweetener; flavor enhancer
Packaging and Storage: Store in well-closed containers protected from light.

IDENTIFICATION
- **A. INFRARED ABSORPTION**, *Spectrophotometric Identification Tests*, Appendix III
  Reference standard: USP Neohesperidine Dihydrochalcone RS
  Sample and standard preparation: K
  Acceptance criteria: The spectrum of the sample exhibits maxima at the same wavelengths as those in the spectrum of the *Reference standard*.
- **B. PROCEDURE**
  Acceptance criteria: The retention time for the principal peak in the chromatogram of the *Sample solution* corresponds to that in the chromatogram of the *Standard solution*, as obtained in the *Assay*.

ASSAY
- **PROCEDURE**
  Solution A: 0.5% (v/v) glacial acetic acid in water
  Mobile phase: Acetonitrile and *Solution A* (20:80)
  Sample solution: 1.0 mg/mL in dimethyl sulfoxide
  System suitability solution: Suspend 100 mg of Neohesperidine Dihydrochalcone in 10.0 mL of a 100-g/L solution of concentrated sulfuric acid in water. Heat the suspension for 5 min on a boiling water bath. Immediately dilute 1.0 mL of the resulting solution with dimethyl sulfoxide to 50.0 mL. [NOTE—Related compounds F[1] and G[2] are prepared in situ in this solution.]
  Standard solution: 1.0 mg/mL of USP Neohesperidine Dihydrochalcone RS in dimethyl sulfoxide
  Chromatographic system, Appendix IIA
  Mode: High-performance liquid chromatography
  Detector: UV 282 nm
  Column: 15-cm × 3.9-mm column packed with octadecylsilane chemically bonded to spherical silica particles, 3–10 μm in diameter, with a carbon loading of 7%
  Flow rate: 1.0 mL/min
  Injection size: 10 μL
  System suitability
    Samples: *System suitability solution* and *Standard solution*
    Suitability requirement 1: The resolution, R, between the peaks for neohesperidine dihydrochalcone (the first peak) and related compound F (the second peak) is NLT 2.5 for the *System suitability solution*.
    Suitability requirement 2: The relative standard deviation is NMT 2.0% for the peak response of the main peak in the chromatogram of the *Standard solution*.
  Analysis: Separately inject the *Standard solution* and the *Sample solution* into the chromatograph, record the chromatograms, and measure the peak responses for neohesperidine dihydrochalcone in each chromatogram.
  [NOTE—The approximate relative retention times are 0.4 for related compound B, 0.7 for related compound D,

---

[1] Related compound F is: 1-[4-(β-D-glucopyranosyloxy)-2,6-dihydroxyphenyl]-3-(3-hydroxy-4-methoxyphenyl)propan-1-one (hesperetin-dihydrochalcone dihydrochalcone 7′-glucoside).
[2] Related compound G is: 3-(3-hydroxy-4-methoxyphenyl)-1-(2,4,6-trihydroxyphenyl)propan-1-one (hesperetin-dihydrochalcone).

1.0 for neohesperidine dihydrochalcone, 1.2 for related compound F, and 3.7 for related compound G. The run time for the experiment should be 5 times the retention time of neohesperidine dihydrochalcone. The chromatogram obtained from the Standard solution should be similar to the chromatogram provided with USP Neohesperidine Dihydrochalcone RS.]

Calculate the percentage of Neohesperidine Dihydrochalcone in the sample taken:

$$\text{Result} = (r_U/r_S) \times (C_S/C_U) \times 100$$

r_U = peak response for neohesperidine dihydrochalcone from the chromatogram of the Sample solution

r_S = peak response for neohesperidine dihydrochalcone from the chromatogram of the Standard solution

C_S = concentration of Neohesperidine Dihydrochalcone in the Standard solution (mg/mL)

C_U = concentration of the Sample solution (mg/mL)

Acceptance criteria: NLT 96.0% of $C_{28}H_{36}O_{15}$, calculated on the dried basis

IMPURITIES

Inorganic Impurities
- **ARSENIC**, Elemental Impurities by ICP, Method I, Appendix IIIC
  Acceptance criteria: NMT 3 mg/kg, calculated on the dried basis
- **LEAD**, Elemental Impurities by ICP, Method I, Appendix IIIC
  Acceptance criteria: NMT 2 mg/kg, calculated on the dried basis

Organic Impurities
- **RELATED COMPOUNDS**
  Solution A and **Mobile phase:** Prepare as directed in the Assay.
  Sample solution: 2.0 mg/mL in dimethyl sulfoxide
  Standard solution A: Use the Standard solution, as prepared in the Assay.
  Standard solution B: Dilute 1.0 mL of Standard solution A with dimethyl sulfoxide to 100.0 mL. (Contains 10 μg/mL of USP Neohesperidine Dihydrochalcone RS.)
  Standard solution C: Use the System suitability solution, as prepared in the Assay.
  Chromatographic system, Appendix IIA
    Mode: High-performance liquid chromatography
    Detector: UV 282 nm
    Column: 15-cm × 3.9-mm column packed with octadecylsilane chemically bonded to spherical silica particles, 3–10 μm in diameter, with a carbon loading of 7%
    Flow rate: 1.0 mL/min
    Injection size: 10 μL
  System suitability
    Sample: Standard solution C
    Suitability requirement: The resolution, R, between the peaks for neohesperidine dihydrochalcone (the first peak) and related compound F (the second peak) is NLT 2.5.
  Analysis: Separately inject each of the Standard solutions and the Sample solution into the chromatograph, record the chromatograms, and measure the peak areas for neohesperidine dihydrochalcone in each chromatogram. Compare the peak areas obtained for each related compound to the relevant standard, as described in the Acceptance criteria, disregarding all peaks with a peak area of less than 0.05 times the area of the principal peak in the chromatogram obtained from Standard solution B. [NOTE—The approximate relative retention times are 0.4 for related compound B, 0.7 for related compound D, 1.0 for neohesperidine dihydrochalcone, 1.2 for related compound F, and 3.7 for related compound G. The run time for the experiment should be 5 times the retention time of neohesperidine dihydrochalcone. The chromatogram obtained from Standard solution A should be similar to the chromatogram provided with USP Neohesperidine Dihydrochalcone RS.]
  Acceptance criteria
    Related compound B[3]**:** The peak area for related compound B is NMT the area of the principal peak in the chromatogram obtained from Standard solution B (NMT 2%).
    Related compound D[4] **:** The peak area for related compound D is NMT twice the area of the principal peak in the chromatogram obtained from Standard solution B (NMT 2%).
    Any other single related compound: The peak area for any other single related compound is NMT 0.5 times the area of the principal peak in the chromatogram obtained from Standard solution B (NMT 0.5%).
    Total of all related compounds (apart from related compound B): The total of the peak areas for all related compounds, apart from related compound B, is NMT 2.5 times the area of the principal peak in the chromatogram obtained from Standard solution B (NMT 2.5%).

SPECIFIC TESTS
- **LOSS ON DRYING,** Appendix IIC: 105° for 3 h
  Acceptance criteria: NMT 11%
- **RESIDUE ON IGNITION (SULFATED ASH)**, Appendix IIC
  Sample: 1.0 g
  Acceptance criteria: NMT 0.2%, calculated on the dried basis▲FCC8

---

[3] Related compound B is: 7-[[2-O-(6-deoxy-α-L-mannopyranosyl)β-D-glucopyranosyl]oxy]-5-hydroxy-2-(3-hydroxy-4-methoxyphenyl)-4H-1-benzopyran-4-one (neodiosmin).

[4] Related compound D is: 1-[4-[[2-O-(6-deoxy-α-L-mannopyranosyl)-β-D-glucopyranosyl]oxy]-2,6-dihydroxyphenyl]-3-(4-hydroxyphenyl)propan-1-one (naringin-dihydrochalcone).

Neotame

First Published: FCC 6
Last Revision: FCC 7

N-[*N*-(3,3-Dimethylbutyl)-L-α-aspartyl]-L-phenylalanine 1-Methyl Ester

$C_{20}H_{30}N_2O_5$

INS: 961
UNII: VJ597D52EX [neotame]

Formula wt 378.47
CAS: [165450-17-9]

DESCRIPTION

Neotame occurs as a white to off-white powder. It is sparingly soluble in water and is very soluble in alcohol and in ethyl acetate. The pH of a 0.5% solution is between 5.0 and 7.0.

Function: Non-nutritive sweetener; flavor enhancer
Packaging and Storage: Store in well-closed containers in a cool, dry place.

IDENTIFICATION

- **INFRARED ABSORPTION**, *Spectrophotometric Identification Tests*, Appendix IIIC
  Reference standard: USP Neotame RS
  Sample and standard preparation: *K*
  Acceptance criteria: The spectrum of the sample exhibits maxima at the same wavelengths as those in the spectrum of the *Reference standard*.

ASSAY

- **PROCEDURE**
  Mobile phase: Dissolve 3.0 g of sodium 1-heptanesulfonate in 740 mL of water in a suitable 1000-mL vessel, and add 3.8 mL of triethylamine. Adjust the resulting solution with phosphoric acid to a pH of 3.5, and dilute with water to 750 mL. Add 250 mL of acetonitrile, adjust with phosphoric acid to an apparent pH of 3.7, filter, and degas.
  Standard solution: 1.0 mg/mL of USP Neotame RS in *Mobile phase*
  Sample solution: 1.0 mg/mL in *Mobile phase*. [NOTE—This solution is stable for up to 32 h when stored at a temperature of 0°–10°.]
  Chromatographic system, Appendix IIA
    Mode: High-performance liquid chromatography
    Detector: UV 210 nm
    Column: 4.6-mm × 10-cm; packed with octadecyl silanized silica (5-μm Partisil ODS-3, Whatman Co., or equivalent)
    Column temperature: 45°
    Flow rate: 1.5 mL/min
    Injection size: 25 μL
  System suitability
    Sample: *Standard solution*
    Suitability requirement 1: The tailing factor is NMT 2.0.
    Suitability requirement 2: The relative standard deviation is NMT 2.0%.
  Analysis: Separately inject the *Standard solution* and the *Sample solution* into the chromatograph, record the chromatograms, and measure the neotame peak responses. Calculate the percentage of neotame in the sample:

  $$\text{Result} = (r_U/r_S) \times (C_S/C_U) \times 100$$

  r_U = peak response of the *Sample solution*
  r_S = peak response of the *Standard solution*
  C_S = concentration of the *Standard solution* (mg/mL)
  C_U = concentration of the *Sample solution* (mg/mL)

  Acceptance criteria: 97.0%–102.0% of $C_{20}H_{30}N_2O_5$, calculated on the anhydrous basis

IMPURITIES

Inorganic Impurities

- **LEAD**
  [NOTE—Prepare all lead solutions in 0.2% sub-boiling distilled nitric acid.]
  Standard stock solution: 10 μg/mL of lead prepared weekly from a single-element lead stock solution at 1000 μg/mL
  Standard solutions: 0.03 μg/mL and 0.015 μg/mL of lead, from the *Standard stock solution*
  Sample solution: Transfer 0.16 g of sample into a 10-mL volumetric flask. Dissolve in and dilute to volume with 0.2% sub-boiling distilled nitric acid.
  Reagent blank: 0.2% sub-boiling distilled nitric acid
  Apparatus: Use a suitable graphite furnace atomic absorption spectrophotometer equipped with an autosampler, pyrolytically coated graphite tubes, a solid pyrolytic graphite platform, and an adequate means of background correction. (Zeeman effect, Smith-Hieftje, or deuterium arc background correction, or equivalent, are acceptable.) Use a hollow-cathode lamp as the source, argon as the purge gas, and breathing-quality air as the alternate gas. Set up the instrument according to the manufacturer's instructions. To avoid contamination, use autosampler cups acid cleaned with a mixture of 5% sub-boiling, distilled nitric acid and 5% sub-boiling, distilled hydrochloric acid in water (18 megaohm) and thoroughly rinsed with water. Use micropipets with disposable, lead-free tips for dilutions. Use acid-cleaned volumetric glassware to prepare standards and samples. Store standards and samples in acid-cleaned polyethylene containers. Optimize the instrument program following the manufacturer's recommendations for lead, using a char temperature of 500° and an atomization temperature of 2000°.
  Analysis: Separately inject equal volumes (about 15 μL) of the *Standard solutions*, the *Reagent blank*, and the *Sample solution* into the spectrophotometer in triplicate, and measure the area responses with the lead lamp set at wavelengths of 217.0 or 283.3 nm.

Set the peak area for the 0.015 µg/mL standard equal to 0.015 µg/mL and the 0.030 µg/mL equal to 0.030 µg/mL. Correct the area responses of the *Sample solution* and *Standard solutions* for the *Reagent blank* area response. Generate the appropriate lead calibration algorithm and determine the lead concentration, in µg/mL, in the *Sample solution*. Calculate the concentration of lead, in mg/kg, in the portion of sample taken:

$$\text{Result} = (C_X)(10)/(W_X)$$

C_X = blank-corrected lead concentration in the *Sample solution* (µg/mL)
W_X = weight of the sample taken to prepare the *Sample solution* (g)

Acceptance criteria: NMT 1 mg/kg

Organic Impurities

- **N-[N-(3,3-DIMETHYLBUTYL)-L-α–ASPARTYL]-L-PHENYLALANINE**

  Mobile phase: Proceed as directed in the *Assay*.
  Standard solution: 0.03 mg/mL of USP Neotame Related Compound A RS[1] in *Mobile phase*
  Detector sensitivity solution: Transfer 2 mL of the *Standard solution* to a 50-mL volumetric flask, and dilute with *Mobile phase* to volume.
  Sample solution: 2 mg/mL in *Mobile phase*. [NOTE—This solution is stable for up to 32 h when stored at a temperature of 0°–10°.]
  Chromatographic system, Appendix IIA
    Mode: High-performance liquid chromatography
    Detector: UV 210 nm
    Column: 100- × 4.6-mm; packed with octadecyl silanized silica (5-µm Partisil ODS-3, Whatman Co., or equivalent)
    Column temperature: 45°
    Flow rate: 1.5 mL/min
    Injection volume: 25 µL
    System suitability
      Samples: *System suitability solution* and *Standard solution*
      Suitability requirement 1: The signal-to-noise ratio for the *System suitability solution* is NLT 10.
      Suitability requirement 2: The relative standard deviation for the *Standard solution* is NMT 5.0%.
  Analysis: Separately inject the *Standard solution* and the *Sample solution* into the chromatograph, record the chromatograms, and measure the responses for the neotame and neotame related compound A peaks. Calculate the percentage of neotame related compound A in the portion of sample taken:

  $$\text{Result} = (r_U/r_S) \times (C_S/C_U) \times 100$$

  r_U = peak response for neotame related compound A in the chromatogram of the *Sample solution*
  r_S = peak response for neotame related compound A in the chromatogram of the *Standard solution*
  C_S = concentration of USP Neotame Related Compound A RS in the *Standard solution* (mg/mL)
  C_U = concentration of Neotame in the *Sample solution* (mg/mL)

  Acceptance criteria: NMT 1.5%

- **OTHER RELATED SUBSTANCES**

  Mobile phase, Standard solution, Detector sensitivity solution, Sample solution, and **Chromatographic system:** Proceed as directed in the test for N-[N-(3,3-Dimethylbutyl)-L-α-aspartyl]-L-phenylalanine.
  Neotame standard solution: Proceed as directed for the *Standard solution* in the *Assay*.
  Analysis: Separately inject the *Neotame standard solution* and the *Sample solution* into the chromatograph, record the chromatograms, and measure the responses for the all of the major peaks. Calculate the percentage of other related substances in the sample taken:

  $$\text{Result} = (r_T/r_S) \times (C_S/C_U) \times 100$$

  r_T = sum of the responses of all impurity peaks (except that of related compound A and the solvent peak, if observed) in the chromatogram of the *Sample solution*
  r_S = peak response for neotame in the chromatogram of the *Neotame standard solution*
  C_S = concentration of USP Neotame RS in the *Neotame standard solution* (mg/mL)
  C_U = concentration of Neotame in the *Sample solution* (mg/mL)

  Acceptance criteria: NMT 2.0%

SPECIFIC TESTS

- **OPTICAL (SPECIFIC) ROTATION**

  Standard solution: Transfer 6.50 ± 0.05 g of USP Sucrose RS, previously dried for 2–3 h in an oven at 105° and stored in a desiccator, into each of three 25-mL volumetric flasks. Dissolve in and dilute with water to volume.
  Sample solution: Transfer 250.0 ± 2.0 mg of sample into each of three 50-mL volumetric flasks, and record the weight of each flask to the nearest 0.1 mg. Dissolve in and dilute with water to volume, and mix well. Alternate vortex mixing and sonication to expedite dissolution.

---

[1] USP Neotame Related Compound A RS is N-[N-(3,3-dimethylbutyl)-L-α-aspartyl]-L-phenylalanine.

Analysis: Use a polarimeter having a precision of at least 0.001° and equipped with a sodium lamp. Adjust the absorbance setting to 589 nm. Equilibrate the three *Sample solution* flasks and a water blank for 20 min in a water bath set at 20°, and monitor the temperature with a thermometer. Similarly equilibrate the three *Standard solution* flasks and a water blank, but use a water bath set at 25°. The temperature readings of the *Sample solutions* and *Standard solutions* should be ±2° of the designated temperature. Rinse a quartz cell with water and then with *Standard solution*. Fill the cell with *Standard solution*, and eliminate any bubbles in the light pathway. Place the cell in the polarimeter, and record the optical rotation to three decimal places. [NOTE—If the average reading of three measurements of the *Standard solution* less the water blank is not 65.9° or greater, and the relative standard deviation is not 2.00% or less, check the calibration of the polarimeter, and repeat the *Standard solution* preparation and reading.]

Rinse the quartz cell with *Sample solution*, fill it with *Sample solution*, place it in the polarimeter, and record the optical rotation, in triplicate, as before. Repeat the procedure using water as the *Blank*.

Calculate the *Optical (Specific) Rotation* [α] of the sample with the formula:

$$\text{Result} = 100A/LC$$

A = average reading of the *Sample solution* minus the reading of the *Blank*
C = concentration (g/100 mL) of the sample
L = length (dm) of the quartz cell

Acceptance criteria: $[\alpha]_D^{20}$ between −40.0° and −43.4°, calculated on the dried basis

- **RESIDUE ON IGNITION (SULFATED ASH)**, Method I, Appendix IIC
  Analysis: 1 g
  Acceptance criteria: NMT 0.2%
- **WATER**, *Water Determination, Karl Fischer Titrimetric Method, Method Ic (Coulometric Titration)*, Appendix IIC
  Acceptance criteria: NMT 5.0%

Nerol

First Published: Prior to FCC 6

cis-3,7-Dimethyl-2,6-octadien-1-ol

$C_{10}H_{18}O$ Formula wt 154.25
FEMA: 2770
UNII: 38G5P53250 [nerol]

DESCRIPTION
Nerol occurs as a colorless liquid.
Odor: Fresh, sweet, rose
Solubility: Miscible in alcohol, chloroform, ether; insoluble or practically insoluble in water
Boiling Point: ~227°
Solubility in Alcohol, Appendix VI: One mL dissolves in 9 mL of 50% alcohol to give a clear solution.
Function: Flavoring agent

IDENTIFICATION
- **INFRARED SPECTRA,** *Spectrophotometric Identification Tests,* Appendix IIIC
  Acceptance criteria: The spectrum of the sample exhibits relative maxima at the same wavelengths as those of the spectrum below.

ASSAY
- **PROCEDURE:** Proceed as directed under *Total Alcohols,* Appendix VI.
  Sample: 1.2 g
  Analysis: Use 77.13 as the equivalence factor (e).
  Acceptance criteria: NLT 95.0% of total alcohols as $C_{10}H_{18}O$

SPECIFIC TESTS
- **REFRACTIVE INDEX,** Appendix II: At 20°
  Acceptance criteria: Between 1.467 and 1.478
- **SPECIFIC GRAVITY:** Determine at 25° by any reliable method (see *General Provisions*).
  Acceptance criteria: Between 0.875 and 0.880

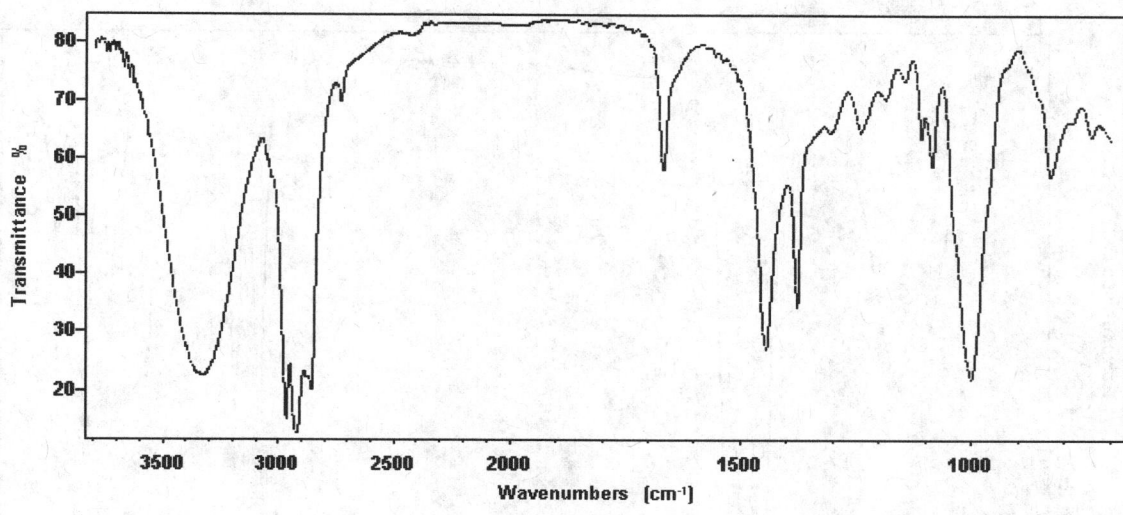

Nerol

Nerolidol

First Published: Prior to FCC 6

3,7,11-Trimethyl-1,6,10-dodecatrien-3-ol

$C_{15}H_{26}O$ Formula wt 222.37
FEMA: 2772
UNII: QR6IP857S6 [nerolidol]

DESCRIPTION
Nerolidol occurs as a colorless to straw-colored liquid.
Odor: Faint, floral, rose, apple
Solubility: Soluble in most fixed oils, propylene glycol; insoluble or practically insoluble in glycerin
Boiling Point: ~276°
Solubility in Alcohol, Appendix VI: One mL dissolves in 4 mL of 70% alcohol.
Function: Flavoring agent

IDENTIFICATION
- **INFRARED SPECTRA,** *Spectrophotometric Identification Tests,* Appendix IIIC

  Acceptance criteria: The spectrum of the sample exhibits relative maxima at the same wavelengths as those of the spectrum below.

ASSAY
- **PROCEDURE:** Proceed as directed under *M-1b*, Appendix XI.
  Acceptance criteria: NLT 97.0% of $C_{15}H_{26}O$ (sum of two isomers)

SPECIFIC TESTS
- **REFRACTIVE INDEX,** Appendix II: At 20°
  Acceptance criteria: Between 1.478 and 1.483
- **SPECIFIC GRAVITY:** Determine at 25° by any reliable method (see *General Provisions*).
  Acceptance criteria: Between 0.870 and 0.880

OTHER REQUIREMENTS
- **ANGULAR ROTATION** *Optical (Specific) Rotation,* Appendix IIB: Use a 100-mm tube.
  Acceptance criteria
    Natural: Between +11° and +14°
- **ESTERS,** Appendix VI
  Sample: 10 g
  Analysis: Use 132.7 as the equivalence factor (e).
  Acceptance criteria: NMT 0.5% as nerolidyl acetate

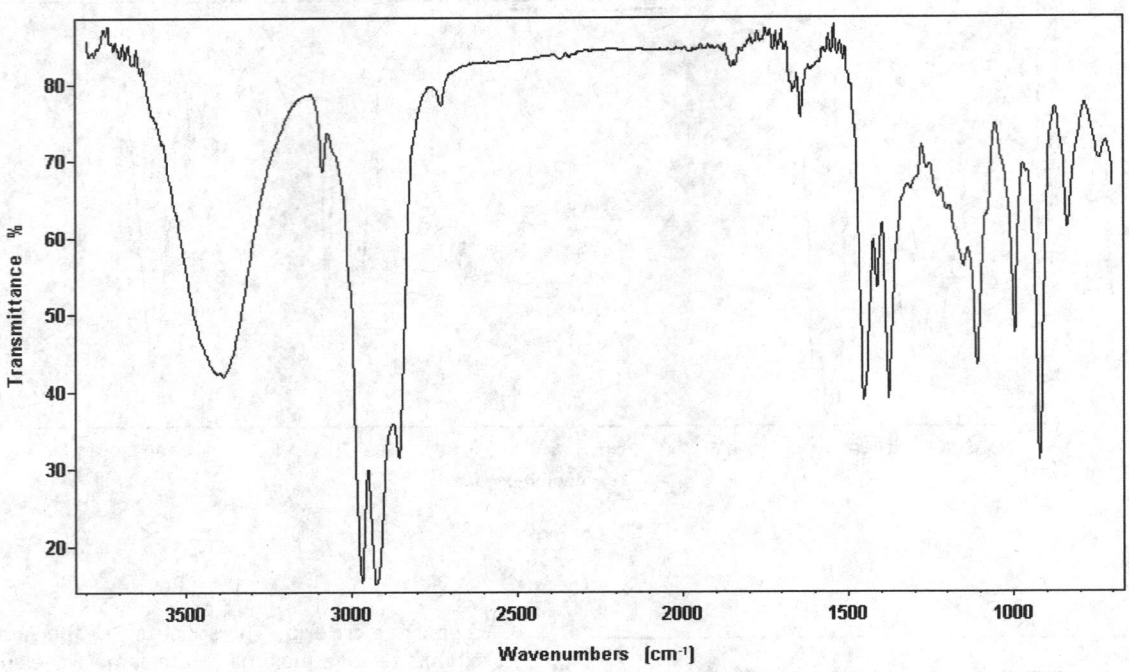

Nerolidol

Neryl Acetate

First Published: Prior to FCC 6

cis-3,7-Dimethyl-2,6-octadien-1-yl Acetate

$C_{12}H_{20}O_2$ Formula wt 196.29
FEMA: 2773
UNII: OF82IJU18H [neryl acetate]

DESCRIPTION
Neryl Acetate occurs as a colorless to pale yellow liquid.
Odor: Sweet, floral
Solubility: Soluble in vegetable oils; slightly soluble in propylene glycol; insoluble or practically insoluble in water
Boiling Point: ~134° (25 mm Hg)
Solubility in Alcohol, Appendix VI: One mL dissolves in 1 mL of 95% alcohol.
Function: Flavoring agent

IDENTIFICATION
- **INFRARED SPECTRA,** Spectrophotometric Identification Tests, Appendix IIIC
  Acceptance criteria: The spectrum of the sample exhibits relative maxima at the same wavelengths as those of the spectrum below.

ASSAY
- **PROCEDURE:** Proceed as directed under M-1a and M-1b, Appendix XI.
  Acceptance criteria: NLT 96.0% of $C_{12}H_{20}O_2$ (predominantly (Z)-isomer)

SPECIFIC TESTS
- **ACID VALUE, FLAVOR CHEMICALS (OTHER THAN ESSENTIAL OILS),** M-15, Appendix XI
  Acceptance criteria: NMT 1.0
- **REFRACTIVE INDEX,** Appendix II: At 20°
  Acceptance criteria: Between 1.458 and 1.464
- **SPECIFIC GRAVITY:** Determine at 25° by any reliable method (see General Provisions).
  Acceptance criteria: Between 0.905 and 0.914

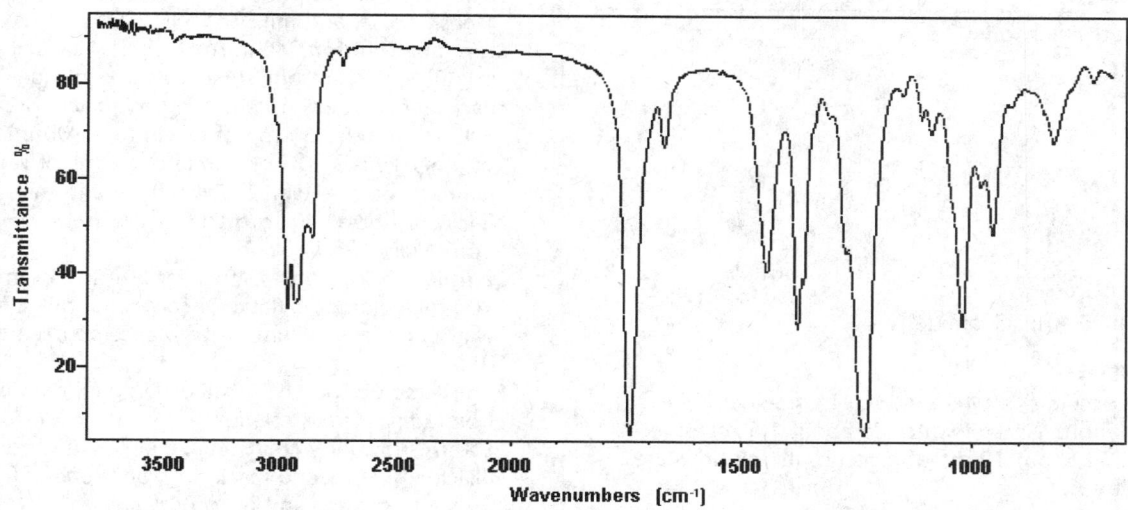

Neryl Acetate

Niacin

First Published: Prior to FCC 6

Nicotinic Acid
3-Pyridinecarboxylic Acid

$C_6H_5NO_2$ Formula wt 123.11
                                CAS: [59-67-6]
UNII: 2679MF687A [niacin]

DESCRIPTION
Niacin occurs as white or light yellow crystals or as a crystalline powder. One gram of sample dissolves in 60 mL of water. It is freely soluble in boiling water and in boiling alcohol and also in solutions of alkali hydroxides and carbonates. It is almost insoluble in ether.
Function: Nutrient
Packaging and Storage: Store in well-closed containers.

IDENTIFICATION
- **A. INFRARED ABSORPTION,** *Spectrophotometric Identification Tests,* Appendix IIIC
  Reference standard: USP Niacin RS
  Sample and **Standard preparation:** *M* (Use a sample that has been previously dried at 105° for 1 h.)
  Acceptance criteria: The spectrum of the sample exhibits maxima at the same wavelengths as those in the spectrum of the *Reference Standard.*

- **B. PROCEDURE**
  Sample: 50 mg
  Analysis: Dissolve the *Sample* in 20 mL of water, neutralize to litmus paper with 0.1 N sodium hydroxide, and add 3mL of cupric sulfate TS.
  Acceptance criteria: A blue precipitate gradually forms.

- **C. PROCEDURE**
  Sample solution: 20 µg /mL
  Analysis: Determine the absorbance, A, of the *Sample solution* in a 1-cm cell at 237 nm and 262 nm, using water as the blank.
  Acceptance criteria: A_{237}/A_{262} is between 0.35 and 0.39.

ASSAY
- **PROCEDURE**
  Sample: 300 mg
  Analysis: Dissolve the *Sample* in 50 mL of water, add phenolphthalein TS, and titrate with 0.1 N sodium hydroxide. Perform a blank determination (see *General Provisions*). Each mL of 0.1 N sodium hydroxide is equivalent to 12.31 mg of $C_6H_5NO_2$.
  Acceptance criteria: NLT 99.5% and NMT 101.0% of $C_6H_5NO_2$, calculated on the dried basis

SPECIFIC TESTS
- **LOSS ON DRYING,** Appendix IIC: 105° for 1 h
  Acceptance criteria: NMT 1.0%
- **MELTING RANGE,** *Melting Range or Temperature Determination,* Appendix IIB
  Acceptance criteria: Between 234° and 238°
- **RESIDUE ON IGNITION (SULFATED ASH),** Appendix IIC
  Sample: 1 g
  Acceptance criteria: NMT 0.1%

Niacinamide

First Published: Prior to FCC 6

Nicotinamide

$C_6H_6N_2O$
UNII: 25X5118RD4 [niacinamide]

Formula wt 122.13
CAS: [98-92-0]

DESCRIPTION
Niacinamide occurs as a white, crystalline powder. One g dissolves in about 1 mL of water, in about 1.5 mL of alcohol, and in about 10 mL of glycerin. Its solutions are neutral to litmus.
Function: Nutrient
Packaging and Storage: Store in tight containers.

IDENTIFICATION
- **UV ABSORBANCE**
  Sample solution: 20 μg/mL
  Analysis: Determine the absorbance of the *Sample solution* in a 1-cm cell at 245 nm and at 262 nm with a suitable spectrophotometer, using water as the blank.
  Acceptance criteria: The ratio A_{245}/A_{262} is 0.65 ± 0.02.
- **INFRARED ABSORPTION**, *Spectrophotometric Identification Tests*, Appendix IIIC
  Reference standard: USP Niacinamide RS
  Standard and Sample preparation: K
  Acceptance criteria: The spectrum of the sample exhibits maxima at the same wavelengths as those in the spectrum of the *Reference standard*.

ASSAY
- **PROCEDURE**
  [NOTE—Use either *Method 1* or *Method 2* to assay a sample.]
  Method 1
  Sample: 300 mg
  Analysis: Dissolve the *Sample* in 20 mL of glacial acetic acid, warming slightly if necessary to complete dissolution. Add 100 mL of toluene and 2 drops of crystal violet TS, and titrate with 0.1 N perchloric acid. [CAUTION—Handle perchloric acid in an appropriate fume hood.] Perform a blank determination (see *General provisions*) and make any necessary correction. Each mL of 0.1 N perchloric acid is equivalent to 12.21 mg of $C_6H_6N_2O$.
  Acceptance criteria: NLT 98.5% and NMT 101.0% $C_6H_6N_2O$, calculated on the dried basis
  Method 2
  [NOTE—For standard and sample solutions, use low-actinic glassware, and prepare fresh solutions daily.]
  Mobile phase: 0.005 M sodium 1-heptanesulfonate and methanol (70:30), filtered and degassed
  Standard stock solution: 0.50 mg/mL USP Niacinamide RS prepared as follows: Transfer 50 mg of USP Niacinamide RS to a 100-mL volumetric flask. Dissolve in about 3 mL of water, dilute to volume with *Mobile phase*, and mix.
  Standard solution: 40 μg/mL of USP Niacinamide RS in *Mobile phase*; from *Standard stock solution*
  Niacin stock solution: 0.50 mg/mL niacin prepared as follows: Transfer 50 mg of niacin to a 100-mL volumetric flask. Dissolve in about 3 mL of water, dilute to volume with *Mobile phase*, and mix.
  Niacin solution: 40 μg/mL of niacin in *Mobile phase*; from *Niacin stock solution*
  Sample stock solution: Transfer 50 mg of sample to a 100-mL volumetric flask. Dissolve in about 3 mL of water, dilute to volume with *Mobile phase*, and mix. (0.50 mg/mL)
  Sample solution: 40 μg/mL of sample in *Mobile phase*; from *Sample stock solution*
  System suitability solution: 20 μg/mL each of USP Niacinamide RS and niacin in *Mobile phase*; from *Standard solution* and *Niacin solution*
  Chromatographic system, Appendix IIA
    Mode: High-performance liquid chromatography
    Detector: UV 254-nm
    Column: 30-cm × 3.9-mm column packed with octadecylsilanized silica (μBondapak C18, or equivalent)
    Flow rate: About 2 mL/min
    Injection volume: About 20 μL
  System suitability
    Sample: *System suitability solution*
    Suitability requirement 1: The resolution, R, between niacin and niacinamide is NLT 3.0.
    Suitability requirement 2: The relative standard deviation for replicate injections is NMT 2.0%.
  Analysis: Separately inject the *Standard solution* and the *Sample solution* into the chromatograph, record the chromatograms, and measure the responses for the major peaks.
  Calculate the quantity, in mg, of $C_6H_6N_2O$ in the portion of sample taken by the formula:

  $$Result = 1250C(r_U/r_S)$$

  C = concentration of niacinamide in the *Standard solution* (mg/mL)
  r_U = peak response for the *Sample solution*
  r_S = peak response for the *Standard solution*
  Acceptance criteria: NLT 98.5% and NMT 101.0% of $C_6H_6N_2O$, calculated on the dried basis

IMPURITIES
Inorganic Impurities
- **LEAD**, *Lead Limit Test, Flame Atomic Absorption Spectrophotometric Method*, Appendix IIIB
  Sample: 10 g
  Acceptance criteria: NMT 2 mg/kg

SPECIFIC TESTS
- **LOSS ON DRYING**, Appendix IIC: Over silica gel for 4 h
  Acceptance criteria: NMT 0.5%

- **MELTING RANGE OR TEMPERATURE DETERMINATION,** Appendix IIB
  Acceptance criteria: Between 128° and 131°
- **READILY CARBONIZABLE SUBSTANCES,** Appendix IIB
  Sample solution: 200 mg in 5 mL of 95% sulfuric acid
  Acceptance criteria: The resulting solution has no more color than *Matching Fluid A*.
- **RESIDUE ON IGNITION (SULFATED ASH),** Appendix IIC
  Sample: 1 g
  Acceptance criteria: NMT 0.1%

Niacinamide Ascorbate

First Published: Prior to FCC 6

Nicotinamide Ascorbate

CAS: [1987-71-9]
UNII: JTL8B7TVW7 [niacinamide ascorbate]

DESCRIPTION
Niacinamide Ascorbate occurs as a yellow colored powder that may gradually darken upon exposure to air. It is a complex of ascorbic acid ($C_6H_8O_6$) and niacinamide ($C_6H_6N_2O$). One g is soluble in 3.5 mL of water and in about 20 mL of alcohol. It is very slightly soluble in chloroform and in ether and is sparingly soluble in glycerin.
Function: Nutrient
Packaging and Storage: Store in tight, light-resistant containers.

IDENTIFICATION
- **A. PROCEDURE**
  Sample solution: 20 mg/mL
  Acceptance criteria: The *Sample solution* slowly reduces alkaline cupric tartrate TS at 25°, but more readily upon heating.
- **B. INFRARED ABSORPTION,** *Spectrophotometric Identification Tests,* Appendix IIIC
  Reference standard: 1 part USP Niacinamide RS and 3 parts USP Ascorbic Acid RS, thoroughly mixed
  Standard and sample preparation: *K*
  Acceptance criteria: The spectrum of the sample exhibits maxima at the same wavelengths as those in the spectrum of the *Reference Standard*.

ASSAY
- **ASCORBIC ACID**
  Sample: 400 mg
  Analysis: Dissolve the *Sample* in a mixture of 100 mL of water, recently boiled and cooled, and 25 mL of 2 N sulfuric acid. Titrate the solution immediately with 0.1 N iodine, adding starch TS near the endpoint. Each mL of 0.1 N iodine is equivalent to 8.806 mg of ascorbic acid, $C_6H_8O_6$.
  Acceptance criteria: NLT 73.5%, calculated on the anhydrous basis
- **NIACINAMIDE**
  Sample: 300 mg
  Analysis: Dissolve the *Sample* in 20 mL of glacial acetic acid, warming slightly if necessary to complete dissolution. Add 100 mL of toluene and 2 drops of crystal violet TS, and titrate with 0.1 N perchloric acid. [CAUTION—Handle perchloric acid in an appropriate fume hood.] Perform a blank determination (see *General Provisions*) and make any necessary correction. Each mL of 0.1 N perchloric acid is equivalent to 12.21 mg of niacinamide, $C_6H_6N_2O$.
  Acceptance criteria: NLT 24.5%, calculated on the anhydrous basis
- **TOTAL OF ASCORBIC ACID AND NIACINAMIDE**
  Calculation: Add the results obtained above for *Ascorbic Acid* and *Niacinamide*.
  Acceptance criteria: NLT 99.0%

IMPURITIES
Inorganic Impurities
- **LEAD,** *Lead Limit Test, Flame Atomic Absorption Spectrophotometric Method,* Appendix IIIB
  Sample: 10 g
  Acceptance criteria: NMT 2 mg/kg

SPECIFIC TESTS
- **LOSS ON DRYING,** Appendix IIC: 75° to constant weight
  Acceptance criteria: NMT 0.5%
- **MELTING RANGE OR TEMPERATURE DETERMINATION,** *Procedure for Class Ia,* Appendix IIB
  Acceptance criteria: Between 141° and 145°
- **RESIDUE ON IGNITION (SULFATED ASH),** Appendix IIC
  Sample: 2 g
  Acceptance criteria: NMT 0.1%

Nickel

First Published: Prior to FCC 6
Last Revision: Second Supplement, FCC 6

Nickel Catalysts

Ni

Atomic wt 58.69
CAS: [7440-02-0]

UNII: 7OV03QG267 [nickel]

DESCRIPTION
Nickel metal occurs as a lustrous, white, hard, ferromagnetic, metallic solid. Nickel is commonly used as a catalyst for hydrogenation reactions for food chemicals. Depending on the use, Nickel catalysts fall into two general categories: *Sponge Nickel Catalyst* and *Supported Nickel Catalyst*.
Sponge Nickel Catalyst is typically used in the manufacture of amines and polyols. It is prepared by chemically treating a Nickel–aluminum amalgam with sodium hydroxide to remove the majority of aluminum, thus leaving a highly porous (skeletal) Nickel solid. The resulting *Sponge Nickel Catalyst* is extremely pyrophoric in air and must be stored under an inert liquid.
Supported Nickel Catalyst is typically used in the manufacture of edible oils. It is prepared from a Nickel salt deposited onto an inert carrier consisting of various types of

acceptable silicas, aluminas, or combinations thereof. The Nickel salt–carrier complex is not catalytically active and is converted to *Supported Nickel Catalyst* in a stream of hydrogen at elevated temperatures. After activation, *Supported Nickel Catalyst* also is pyrophoric and must be protected from air, typically by suspending it in a food-grade stearine. It usually is supplied as droplets or flakes.

Function: Catalyst for hydrogenation reactions

Packaging and Storage
  Sponge nickel catalyst: Store under liquids such as water, alcohol, or methylcyclohexane in a cool, dry place.
  Supported nickel catalyst: Store in tight containers in a cool, dry place.

IDENTIFICATION
- **Procedure**
  Sample preparation
    Sponge nickel catalyst: Dissolve a 100-mg sample in about 2 mL of hydrochloric acid, and dilute to about 20 mL with water.
    Supported nickel catalyst: Ash as described under *Assay* (below). Use 5 mL of the ashed sample solution for the *Analysis*.
  Analysis: Place 5 mL of the *Sample preparation* into a test tube, add a few drops of bromine water, and make it slightly alkaline with ammonium hydroxide. Add 2 to 3 mL of a 1% solution of dimethylglyoxime in alcohol.
  Acceptance criteria: An intense red color or precipitate forms.

ASSAY
[Note—Perform the appropriate assay below based on the type of nickel sample being analyzed.]
[Caution—Because of the danger of combustion, wear goggles and other appropriate protective gear.]

- **Sponge Nickel Catalyst**
  Sample solution: Place 5 g of wet sample into a 20-mL beaker, add 10 mL of ethanol, and decant the supernatant fluid. Repeat the sequence of adding ethanol and decanting the fluid five times. Weigh a clean, 30-mL round-bottom flask and record that weight as W_F. Transfer the catalyst sample into the tared flask, and dry for 5 h under vacuum, warming on a 60° water bath. Using nitrogen, return the flask to atmospheric pressure, and cool it to room temperature. Weigh the flask with the dried catalyst sample, and record that weight as W_C. [Caution—Sponge nickel is pyrophoric when dried. Handle with extreme care.]
  Calculate the weight of the dried catalyst, W_S (g), by the formula:

  $$\text{Result} = W_C - W_F$$

  W_C = weight of the flask with the dried catalyst (g)
  W_F = weight of the empty flask (g)

  Place 30 mL of water into a 500-mL beaker, and add the dried catalyst. Wash the flask with 50 mL of 1:1 hydrochloric acid, and add the wash to the beaker. Heat the beaker gently to dissolve the catalyst, then cool to room temperature. Filter the solution through Whatman number 5, or equivalent, filter paper into a 250-mL volumetric flask and dilute with water to volume. The resulting diluted filtrate is the *Sample solution*.

  Analysis: Place 5 mL of the *Sample solution* into a 200-mL beaker. Add 2 g of tartaric acid and 100 mL of water, heat to about 80°, and add 30 mL of 1% dimethylglyoxime in ethanol. Add ammonium hydroxide until the solution is slightly basic and place the mixture on a steam bath for 20 min. Filter the precipitated material into a tared, fritted-glass, medium-porosity filter crucible, and wash with hot water until the filtrate is free of chloride. Dry the precipitate at 120° for 2 h, and then dry to constant weight, and weigh.
  Calculate the percent nickel by the following formula:

  $$\text{Result} = 50 \times (W_P \times N_P)/W_S$$

  W_P = weight of the precipitate (g)
  N_P = percent nickel in the precipitate, 20.32
  W_S = weight of the dried sample, obtained above (g)

  Acceptance criteria: NLT 83.0% of Ni, calculated on the dried basis

- **Supported Nickel Catalyst**
  Sample solution: Fill a 100-mL porcelain crucible half-full of ashless filter paper pulp. Place 2 g of the finished catalyst, in droplet or flake form and accurately weighed, on top of the paper pulp. Transfer the crucible to a muffle furnace set at room temperature, and slowly raise the temperature to 650° so that the stearine melts into the paper, and the organic mass burns and chars slowly. Continue heating at 650° for 2 h or until the carbon is burned off. Cool, add 20 mL of hydrochloric acid, quantitatively transfer the solution or suspension into a 400-mL beaker, and carefully evaporate to dryness on a steam bath. Cool, add 20 mL of hydrochloric acid, warm to aid dissolution (catalysts containing silica will not dissolve completely), transfer into a 500-mL volumetric flask, dilute with water to volume, and mix. Allow any solids to settle, pipet a clear, 50-mL aliquot into a 400-mL beaker, and dilute with water to 250 mL. [Note—If there is suspended matter in the volumetric flask, filter a portion through a dry, medium-speed filter paper into a dry receiver, and pipet from the receiver.]

  Analysis: Proceed as directed above under the *Assay* for *Sponge Nickel Catalyst* beginning with "Add 2 g of tartaric acid…"
  Calculate the percent nickel by the following formula:

  $$\text{Result} = 10 \times (W_P \times N_P)/W_S$$

  W_P = weight of the precipitate (g)
  N_P = percent of nickel in the precipitate, 20.32
  W_S = weight of the sample taken to prepare the *Sample solution* (g)

  Acceptance criteria: NLT 10.0% and NMT 30.0% of Ni, calculated on the as-is basis

Nisin A Preparation

First Published: Prior to FCC 6
Last Revision: First Supplement, FCC 7

(contains 34 amino acids and has an approximate empirical formula $C_{143}H_{230}O_{37}N_{42}S_7$)

	Formula wt ~3348
INS: 234	CAS: Nisin A [1414-45-5]
UNII: EN8XKG133D [nisin a]	

DESCRIPTION
Nisin A Preparation occurs as a white, free-flowing powder. It is a mixture of closely related polypeptides produced by strains of the *Lactococcus lactis* subsp. *lactis* in an appropriate growth medium. Nisin A in the fermentation broth can be recovered by various methods, such as injecting sterile, compressed air (froth concentration), acidification, salting out, and spray-drying. The product comprises Nisin A and sodium chloride that is adjusted to an activity level of not less than 900 IU/mg by the addition of sodium chloride.
Function: Antimicrobial agent
Packaging and Storage: Store in well-closed containers at temperatures not exceeding 22°.

ASSAY
- **PROCEDURE**
  Assay organism: *Lactococcus lactis* subsp. *cremoris* (ATCC 14365[1], NCDO 495[2]) is subcultured daily in sterile separated milk by transferring one loopful to a McCartney bottle of litmus milk and incubating at 30°.
  Inoculated milk: Inoculate a suitable quantity of sterile skim milk with 2% of a 24-h culture of the *Assay organism*, and place it in a water bath at 30° for 90 min. [NOTE—Use immediately after preparation.]
  Standard stock solution: Dissolve 1 g of standard nisin A in 1 L of 0.02 N hydrochloric acid (1000 units/mL). [NOTE—Nisin A Preparation containing 2.5% nisin A, minimum potency of 10^6 IU/g, obtainable from Sigma, St. Louis, MO or Fluka Buchs, Switzerland, may be used for the *Standard stock solution*. A similar preparation is available from Danisco, Copenhagen, Denmark.]
  Standard solution: Dilute a portion of the *Standard stock solution* in 0.02 N hydrochloric acid to 50 units/mL. [NOTE—Prepare immediately before use.]
  Sample solution: Weigh an amount of sample sufficient to ensure that corresponding tubes of the sample and standard series match (i.e. within close limits, the nisin A content in the sample and standard is the same). Dilute in 0.02 N hydrochloric acid to 50 units/mL of nisin A.
  Resazurin solution: 0.0125% solution of resazurin in water. [NOTE—Prepare immediately before use.]
  Analysis: Separately pipet graded volumes (0.60, 0.55, 0.50, 0.45, 0.41, 0.38, 0.34, 0.31, 0.28, and 0.26 mL) of the *Standard solution* and the *Sample solution* into two rows of 10 dry 6-in × 5/8-in bacteriological test tubes. Add 4.6 mL of *Inoculated milk* to each tube by means of an automatic pipetting device. The addition of *Inoculated milk* should be made in turn across each row of tubes containing the same nominal concentration, not along each row of 10 tubes. Place the tubes in a water bath at 30° for 15 min, then cool in an ice water bath while adding 1 mL of *Resazurin solution* to each using an automatic pipetting device and in the same order used for the addition of the *Inoculated milk*. Thoroughly mix the contents of the tubes by shaking. Continue incubation at 30° in a water bath for a further 3–5 min.
  Examine the tubes under fluorescent light in a black matte-finish cabinet. The tube containing the highest concentration of the *Sample solution* which shows the first clear difference in color (i.e., has changed from blue to mauve) is compared with tubes containing the *Standard solution* to find the nearest in color. Make further matches of tubes containing the next two lower concentrations of the *Sample solution* and the *Standard solution*. Interpolation of matches may be made at half dilution steps. Calculate the concentration of nisin A in the *Sample solution* using the known amounts of nisin A in the *Standard solution*. Obtain three readings of the solution and average them. Calculate the activity in terms of IU/g of preparation.
  Acceptance criteria: NLT 900 IU of nisin A/mg of sample

IMPURITIES
Inorganic Impurities
- **LEAD**, *Lead Limit Test, Flame Atomic Absorption Spectrophotometric Method,* Appendix IIIB
  Sample: 10 g
  Acceptance criteria: NMT 2 mg/kg

SPECIFIC TESTS
- **DIFFERENTIATION OF NISIN A FROM OTHER ANTIMICROBIAL SUBSTANCES, STABILITY TO ACID, NON-STABILITY TO ALKALI**
  Sample stock preparation: Dissolve 1 g of sample in 1 L of 0.02 N hydrochloric acid to give a solution containing 1000 units/mL.
  Sample preparation: Dilute the *Sample stock preparation* further with 0.02 N hydrochloric acid to a concentration of 50 units/mL. [NOTE—Prepare immediately before use.]
  Analysis 1: Boil the *Sample preparation* for 5 min. Determine the nisin A concentration of the boiled *Sample preparation* as directed in the *Assay*. [NOTE—Save the unused portion of the boiled *Sample preparation* for use in *Analysis 2*.]
  Analysis 2: Adjust the pH of the solution obtained in *Analysis 1* to 11.0 by adding 5 N sodium hydroxide. Heat the solution at 65° for 30 min, and then cool. Adjust the pH to 2.0 by adding hydrochloric acid dropwise. Determine the nisin A concentration of the resulting solution as directed in the *Assay*.
  Acceptance criteria
    Analysis 1: The calculated nisin A concentration of the boiled sample is 100 ± 5% of the *Assay* value

---
[1] ATCC is the American Type Culture Collection, 10801 University Boulevard, Manassas, VA 20110.
[2] NCDO is the National Collection of Dairy Organisms. Contact NCDO c/o NCIMB, 23 St. Marchar Drive, Aberdeen, Scotland AB24 3RY.

(indicating no significant loss of activity due to heat treatment).
Analysis 2: Complete loss of the antimicrobial activity is observed following the treatment described.

- **DIFFERENTIATION OF NISIN A FROM OTHER ANTIMICROBIAL SUBSTANCES, TOLERANCE OF *Lactococcus lactis* TO HIGH CONCENTRATIONS OF NISIN A**
  Assay medium: Prepare one or more flasks containing 100 mL of litmus milk, and sterilize at 121° for 15 min.
  Assay organism: Prepare cultures of *Lactococcus lactis* (ATCC 11454, NCIMB 8586) in sterile skim milk by incubating for 18 h at 30°.
  Sample: 0.1 g
  Analysis: Suspend the *Sample* in the *Assay medium* and allow to stand at room temperature for 2 h. Add 0.1 mL of the *Assay organism*, and incubate at 30° for 24 h.
  Acceptance criteria: The *Assay organism* (*L. lactis*) grows in this concentration of the *Sample* (about 1000 IU/mL), but it will not grow in similar concentrations of other antimicrobial substances. [NOTE—This test will not differentiate nisin A from subtilin.]

- **LOSS ON DRYING**, Appendix IIC: 105° for 2 h, dry to constant weight
  Sample: 2 g
  Acceptance criteria: NMT 3.0%

- **MICROBIAL LIMITS** [NOTE—Current methods for the following tests may be found by accessing the Food and Drug Administration's Bacteriological Analytical Manual (BAM) online at www.cfsan.fda.gov.]
  Acceptance criteria
  Aerobic plate count: NMT 10 cfu/g
   E. coli: Negative in 25 g
   Salmonella: Negative in 25 g

- **SODIUM CHLORIDE CONTENT**
  Sample: 200 mg
  Analysis: Dissolve the *Sample* in 50 mL of water in a glass-stoppered flask. While agitating, add 3 mL of nitric acid, 5 mL of nitrobenzene, 50.0 mL of standardized 0.1 N silver nitrate, and 2 mL of ferric ammonium sulfate TS. Shake well, and titrate the excess silver nitrate with 0.1 N ammonium thiocyanate. The titration endpoint is indicated by the appearance of a red color. Perform a blank determination (see *General Provisions*), and subtract the volume required for the blank titration from the volume required for the *Sample* titration; the difference in these volumes is the amount of ammonium thiocyanate consumed by the *Sample*, V. Each mL of reacted 0.1 N silver nitrate is equivalent to 5.844 mg of NaCl. Calculate the percentage (w/w) of sodium chloride in the *Sample*:

  $$\text{Result} = F \times [(50 \times A) - (V \times B)]/W \times 100$$

  F = formula weight of sodium chloride, 58.44
  A = concentration of the silver nitrate solution (mol/L)
  V = volume of the ammonium thiocyanate consumed by the *Sample* (mL)
  B = concentration of the ammonium thiocyanate solution (mol/L)
  W = weight of the *Sample* (mg)
  Acceptance criteria: NLT 50.0%

Nitrogen

First Published: Prior to FCC 6

N_2 Formula wt 28.01
INS: 941   CAS: [7727-37-9]
UNII: N762921K75 [nitrogen]

DESCRIPTION
Nitrogen occurs as a colorless gas that is not combustible and does not support combustion. It may be condensed to a colorless liquid boiling at −195.8° or to a white solid melting at −209.8°. One L of the gas weighs about 1.25 g at 0° and 760 mm Hg. One volume of the gas dissolves in about 62 volumes of water and in about 8 volumes of alcohol at 20° and 760 mm Hg.
Function: *Gas*: air and oxygen displacer; propellant and aerating agent; packaging gas; *Liquid*: direct-contact freezing agent
Packaging and Storage: Store in tight cylinders.

[NOTE—Reduce the sample gas cylinder pressure with a regulator. Measure the sample gas with a gas volume meter downstream from the detector tubes to minimize contamination of or change to the gas samples. The detector tubes called for in certain tests are described under *Detector Tubes*, Solutions and Indicators.]

IDENTIFICATION
- **FLAME TEST**
  Analysis: Cautiously insert a burning wood splinter into a test tube filled with sample gas.
  Acceptance criteria: The flame is extinguished.

ASSAY
- **PROCEDURE**
  Standard: Oxygen–helium certified standard (A mixture of 1.0% oxygen in industrial-grade helium is available from most suppliers.)
  Chromatographic system, Appendix IIA
  Mode: Gas chromatography
  Detector: Thermal conductivity
  Column: 3-m × 4-mm (id), packed with a molecular sieve, or equivalent. [NOTE—The packing is prepared from a synthetic alkali–metal aluminosilicate capable of absorbing molecules with diameters of up to 0.5 nm, which permits complete separation of oxygen from nitrogen.]
  Carrier gas: Helium (99.99%)
  Analysis: Introduce the *Standard* into the gas-sampling valve. Select the operating conditions of the chromatograph so that the oxygen peak signal of the *Standard* corresponds to not less than 70% of the full-scale reading. Inject the same volume of the sample gas and record the chromatogram.
  Acceptance criteria: The peak response produced by the sample gas exhibits a retention time corresponding to that produced by the *Standard*, and the peak response is equivalent to NMT 1.0% of oxygen, by volume, when compared with the peak response of the *Standard* (indicating NLT 99.0% of N_2, by volume).

IMPURITIES
Inorganic Impurities
- **CARBON DIOXIDE**
  Sample: 1050 ± 50 mL
  Analysis: Pass the *Sample* through a carbon dioxide detector tube at the rate specified for the tube. Note the indicator change.
  Acceptance criteria: NMT 0.03%, by volume
- **CARBON MONOXIDE**
  Sample: 1050 ± 50 mL
  Analysis: Pass the *Sample* through a carbon monoxide detector tube at the rate specified for the tube. Note the indicator change.
  Acceptance criteria: NMT 10 ppm, by volume
- **OXYGEN**
  Analysis: Determine as directed under *Assay* (above).
  Acceptance criteria: NMT 1.0%, by volume
- **WATER**
  Sample: 24,000 mL
  Analysis: Pass the *Sample* through a suitable water-absorption tube not less than 100 mm long, which previously has been flushed with about 500 mL of sample gas and weighed. Regulate the flow so that about 60 min will be required for passage of the gas. Then weigh the absorption tube and calculate its weight gain.
  Acceptance criteria: NMT 1.0 mg

Nitrogen-Enriched Air

First Published: Prior to FCC 6

N_2 Formula wt 28.01

DESCRIPTION
Nitrogen-Enriched Air occurs as a colorless gas. It is produced from air *in situ* by physical separation methods. It contains not less than 90% and not more than 99% nitrogen, by volume. The remaining components are noble gases and, primarily, oxygen.
Function: Air and oxygen displacer
Packaging and Storage: Store in metal cylinders or in a low-pressure collecting tank.

[NOTE—Reduce the sample gas cylinder pressure with a regulator. Measure the sample gas with a gas volume meter downstream from the detector tubes to minimize contamination of or change to the gas samples. The detector tubes called for in certain tests are described under *Detector Tubes,* Solutions and Indicators.]

IDENTIFICATION
- **FLAME TEST**
  Analysis: Cautiously insert a burning wood splinter into a test tube filled with sample gas.
  Acceptance criteria: The flame is extinguished.

ASSAY
- **PROCEDURE**
  Standard: Oxygen–helium certified standard (A mixture of 5.0% oxygen in industrial-grade helium is available from most suppliers.)
  Chromatographic system, Appendix IIA
  Mode: Gas chromatography
  Detector: Thermal conductivity
  Column: 3-m × 4-mm (id), packed with a molecular sieve, or equivalent. [NOTE—The packing is prepared from a synthetic alkali–metal aluminosilicate capable of absorbing molecules with diameters of up to 0.5 nm, which permits complete separation of oxygen from nitrogen.]
  Carrier gas: Helium (99.99%)
  Analysis: Introduce the *Standard* into the gas-sampling valve. Select the operating conditions of the chromatograph so that the oxygen peak signal of the *Standard* corresponds to approximately 45% of the full-scale reading. Introduce the same volume of the sample gas and record the chromatogram.
  Acceptance criteria: The peak response produced by the sample gas exhibits a retention time corresponding to that produced by the *Standard* and the peak response is equivalent to NLT 1.0% and NMT 10.0% of oxygen, by volume, when compared with the peak response of the *Standard* (indicating NLT 90.0% and NMT 99.0% of N_2, by volume).

IMPURITIES
Inorganic Impurities
- **CARBON DIOXIDE**
  Sample: 1050 ± 50 mL
  Analysis: Pass the *Sample* through a carbon dioxide detector tube at the rate specified for the tube. Note the indicator change.
  Acceptance criteria: NMT 0.03%, by volume
- **CARBON MONOXIDE**
  Sample: 1050 ± 50 mL
  Analysis: Pass the *Sample* through a carbon monoxide detector tube at the rate specified for the tube. Note the indicator change.
  Acceptance criteria: NMT 10 ppm, by volume
- **NITRIC OXIDE AND NITROGEN DIOXIDE**
  Sample: 550 ± 50 mL
  Analysis: Pass the *Sample* through a nitric oxide–nitrogen dioxide detector tube at the rate specified for the tube. Note the indicator change.
  Acceptance criteria: NMT 2.5 ppm, by volume
- **OXYGEN**
  Analysis: Determine as directed under *Assay* (above).
  Acceptance criteria: NLT 1.0% and NMT 10.0%, by volume
- **SULFUR DIOXIDE**
  Sample: 1050 ± 50 mL

800 / Nitrogen-Enriched Air / *Monographs*

Analysis: Pass the *Sample* through a sulfur dioxide detector tube at the rate specified for the tube. Note the indicator change.
Acceptance criteria: NMT 5 ppm, by volume

- **WATER**
  Sample: 24,000 mL
  Analysis: Pass the *Sample* through a suitable water-absorption tube NLT 100 mm long, which previously has been flushed with about 500 mL of sample gas and weighed. Regulate the flow so that about 60 min will be required for passage of the gas. Then weigh the absorption tube and calculate its weight gain.
  Acceptance criteria: NMT 1.0 mg

OTHER REQUIREMENTS

- **LABELING:** Where the gas is piped from cylinders or directly from the collecting tank to the point of use, label each outlet "Nitrogen-Enriched Air".

Nitrous Oxide

First Published: Prior to FCC 6

Nitrogen Oxide

N_2O
INS: 942
UNII: K50XQU1029 [nitrous oxide]

Formula wt 44.01
CAS: [10024-97-2]

DESCRIPTION

Nitrous Oxide occurs as a colorless gas. One L at 0° and 760 mm Hg weighs about 1.97 g. One volume dissolves in about 1.4 volumes of water at 20° and 760 mm Hg. It is freely soluble in alcohol and soluble in ether and in oils.
Function: Propellant; aerating agent; packaging gas
Packaging and Storage: Preserve in cylinders.

[NOTE—The following tests are designed to reflect the quality of Nitrous Oxide in both its vapor and its liquid phases, which are present in previously unopened cylinders. Reduce the sample gas cylinder pressure with a regulator. Withdraw the samples for the tests with the least possible release of sample gas consistent with proper purging of the sample apparatus. Measure the gases with a gas volume meter downstream from the detector tubes to minimize contamination of or change to the samples. The detector tubes called for in certain tests are described under *Detector Tubes*, Solutions and Indicators.]

IDENTIFICATION

- **A. PROCEDURE**
  Analysis: With the cylinder temperatures the same and maintained between 15° and 25°, concomitantly read the pressure of the cylinder of sample gas and of a cylinder of 99.9% Nitrous Oxide certified standard. [NOTE—Do not use the Nitrous Oxide certified standard if its cylinder has been depleted to less than half of its full capacity.]
  Acceptance criteria: The pressure of the sample gas cylinder is within 50 psi of that of the Nitrous Oxide certified standard cylinder.

- **B. PROCEDURE**
  Analysis: Pass 100 ± 5 mL of sample gas released from the vapor phase of the contents of the sample gas cylinder through a carbon dioxide detector tube at the rate specified for the tube.
  Acceptance criteria: No color change occurs (distinction from carbon dioxide).

[NOTE—The tests below should be performed in the following sequence: *Carbon Monoxide, Nitric Oxide, Nitrogen Dioxide, Halogens (AS CL), Carbon Dioxide, Ammonia, Water, Odor, Air,* and *Assay*.]

ASSAY

- **PROCEDURE**
  Standard: Air–helium certified standard (A mixture of 1.0% air in industrial-grade helium is available from most suppliers.)
  Chromatographic system, Appendix IIA
    Mode: Gas chromatography
    Detector: Thermal conductivity
    Column: 6-m × 4-mm (id), packed with porous polymer beads, or equivalent, that permit complete separation of nitrogen and oxygen from nitrous oxide, although the nitrogen and oxygen may not be separated from each other
    Carrier gas: Helium (99.99%)
  Analysis: Introduce the *Standard* into the gas-sampling valve. Select the operating conditions of the chromatograph so that the air (nitrogen/oxygen) peak signal of the *Standard* corresponds to approximately 70% of the full-scale reading. The sample gas is obtained by first arranging the sample gas cylinder so that when its valve is opened, a portion of the liquid phase of the contents is released through a piece of tubing of sufficient length to allow all of the liquid to vaporize during passage through it. Then, the vaporized sample is introduced into the chromatograph by means of a gas-sampling valve.
  Acceptance criteria: The peak response produced by the sample gas exhibits a retention time corresponding to that produced by the *Standard*, and the peak response is equivalent to not more than 1.0% of air, by volume, when compared with the peak response of the *Standard* (indicating NLT 99.0% of N_2O, by volume).

IMPURITIES
Inorganic Impurities

- **AIR**
  Analysis: Determine as directed under *Assay*.
  Acceptance criteria: NMT 1.0%, by volume

- **AMMONIA**
  Sample: 1050 ± 50 mL
  Analysis: Pass the *Sample*, released from the vapor phase of the contents of the sample gas cylinder, through an ammonia detector tube at the rate specified for the tube. Note the indicator change.
  Acceptance criteria: NMT 0.0025%, by volume

- **CARBON DIOXIDE**
  Sample: 1050 ± 50 mL
  Analysis: Pass the *Sample*, released from the vapor phase of the contents of the sample gas cylinder,

through a carbon dioxide detector tube at the rate specified for the tube. Note the indicator change.
Acceptance criteria: NMT 0.03%, by volume
- **CARBON MONOXIDE**
Sample: 1050 ± 50 mL
Analysis: Pass the *Sample*, released from the vapor phase of the contents of the sample gas cylinder, through a carbon monoxide detector tube at the rate specified for the tube. Note the indicator change.
Acceptance criteria: NMT 10 ppm, by volume
- **HALOGENS (AS CL)**
Sample: 1050 ± 50 mL
Analysis: Pass the *Sample*, released from the vapor phase of the contents of the sample gas cylinder, through a chlorine detector tube at the rate specified for the tube. Note the indicator change.
Acceptance criteria: NMT 1 ppm, by volume
- **NITROGEN DIOXIDE**
Sample: 550 ± 50 mL
Analysis: Arrange a sample gas cylinder so that when its valve is opened, a portion of the liquid phase of the contents is released through a piece of tubing of sufficient length to allow all of the liquid to vaporize during passage through it and to prevent frost from reaching the inlet of the detector tube. Release a flow of liquid into the tubing to provide sufficient vaporized *Sample* plus any excess necessary to ensure adequate flushing of air from the system. Pass the *Sample* through a nitric oxide–nitrogen dioxide detector tube at the rate specified for the tube. Note the indicator change.
Acceptance criteria: NMT 1 ppm, by volume
- **NITRIC OXIDE**
Sample: 550 ± 50 mL
Analysis: Pass the *Sample*, released from the vapor phase of the contents of the sample gas cylinder, through a nitric oxide–nitrogen dioxide detector tube at the rate specified for the tube. Note the indicator change.
Acceptance criteria: NMT 1 ppm, by volume
- **WATER**
Sample: 50 ± 5 L
Analysis: Flush the sample gas regulator with 5 or more L of the sample gas. Pass the *Sample*, released from the vapor phase of the contents of the sample gas cylinder, through a water-vapor detector tube connected to the regulator with a minimal length of metal or polyethylene tubing. Measure the gas passing through the detector tube with a gas flowmeter set at a flow rate of 2 L/min. Record the corrected indicator change.
Acceptance criteria: NMT 150 mg/m³

SPECIFIC TESTS
- **ODOR**
Analysis: Carefully open the sample gas cylinder valve to produce a moderate flow of gas. Do not direct the gas stream toward the face, but deflect a portion of the stream toward the nose.
Acceptance criteria: No appreciable odor is discernible.

(*E*),(*E*)-2,4-Nonadienal
First Published: Prior to FCC 6
Last Revision: First Supplement, FCC 6

trans,trans-2,4-Nonadienal

$C_9H_{14}O$ Formula wt 138.21
FEMA: 3212
UNII: Y411G77SH7 [2,4-nonadienal, (2e,4e)-]

DESCRIPTION
(*E*),(*E*)-2,4-Nonadienal occurs as a slightly yellow liquid. It may contain a suitable antioxidant.
Odor: Strong, fatty, floral
Solubility: Soluble in alcohol, most fixed oils; insoluble or practically insoluble in water
Boiling Point: ~97° (10 mm Hg)
Solubility in Alcohol, Appendix VI: One mL dissolves in 1 mL of 95% ethanol.
Function: Flavoring agent

IDENTIFICATION
- **INFRARED SPECTRA,** *Spectrophotometric Identification Tests,* Appendix IIIC
Acceptance criteria: The spectrum of the sample exhibits relative maxima at the same wavelengths as those of the spectrum below.

ASSAY
- **PROCEDURE:** Proceed as directed under *M-1a*, Appendix XI.
Acceptance criteria: NLT 89.0% of $C_9H_{14}O$ (one major isomer)

SPECIFIC TESTS
- **REFRACTIVE INDEX,** Appendix II: At 20°
Acceptance criteria: Between 1.517 and 1.523
- **SPECIFIC GRAVITY:** Determine at 25° by any reliable method (see *General Provisions*).
Acceptance criteria: Between 0.865 and 0.880

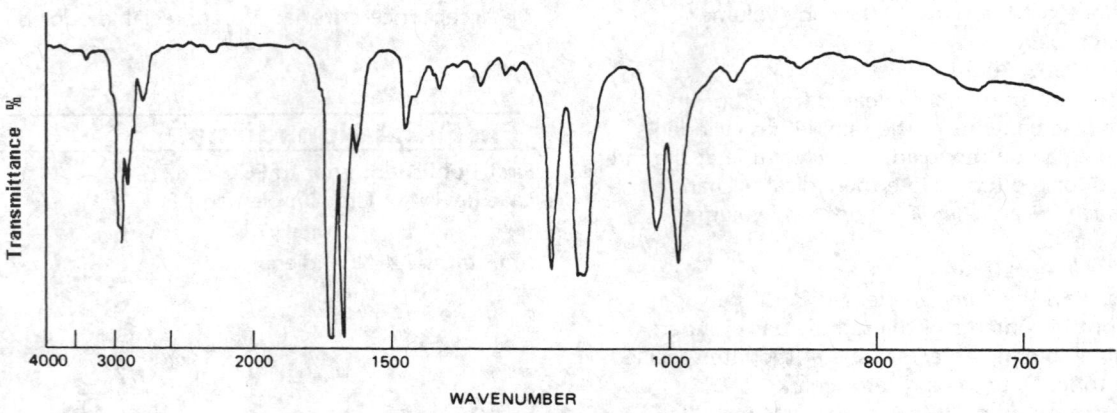

(E),(E)-2,4-Nonadienal

(E),(Z)-2,6-Nonadienal

First Published: Prior to FCC 6
Last Revision: First Supplement, FCC 6

trans,cis-2,6-Nonadienal

C$_9$H$_{14}$O Formula wt 138.21
FEMA: 3377
UNII: 93E895X03C [2,6-nonadienal, (2e,6z)-]

DESCRIPTION
(E),(Z)-2,6-Nonadienal occurs as a slightly yellow liquid. It may contain a suitable antioxidant.
Odor: Powerful, violet, cucumber
Solubility: Soluble in alcohol, most fixed oils; insoluble or practically insoluble in water
Boiling Point: ~94° (18 mm Hg)
Solubility in Alcohol, Appendix VI: One mL dissolves in 1 mL of 95% ethanol.

Function: Flavoring agent

IDENTIFICATION
- **INFRARED SPECTRA,** Spectrophotometric Identification Tests, Appendix IIIC
  Acceptance criteria: The spectrum of the sample exhibits relative maxima at the same wavelengths as those of the spectrum below.

ASSAY
- **PROCEDURE:** Proceed as directed under M-1a, Appendix XI
  Acceptance criteria
  Sum of two isomers: NLT 96.0% of C$_9$H$_{14}$O
  Major isomer: NLT 90% of C$_9$H$_{14}$O

SPECIFIC TESTS
- **REFRACTIVE INDEX,** Appendix II: At 20°
  Acceptance criteria: Between 1.470 and 1.475
- **SPECIFIC GRAVITY:** Determine at 25° by any reliable method (see General Provisions).
  Acceptance criteria: Between 0.850 and 0.870

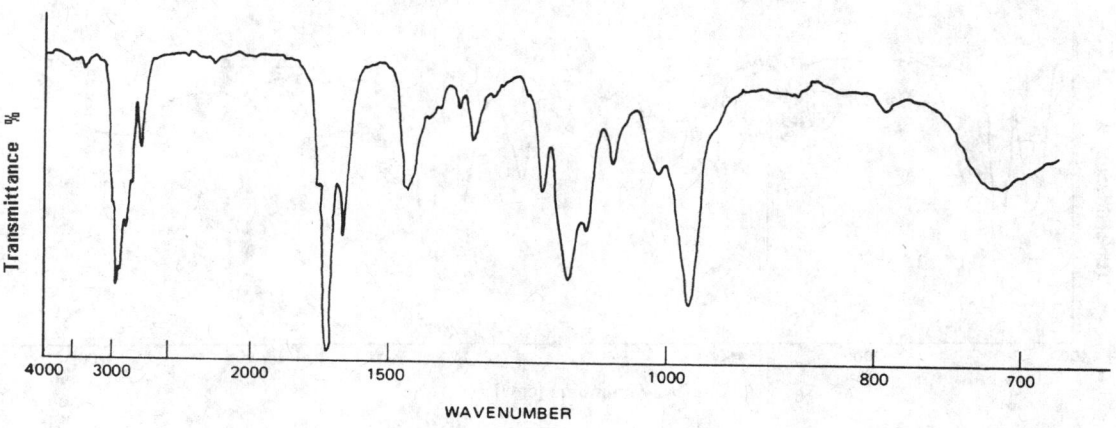

(E),(Z)-2,6-Nonadienal

(E),(Z)-2,6-Nonadienol

First Published: Prior to FCC 6

trans,cis-2,6-Nonadienol

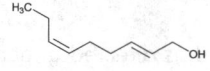

C₉H₁₆O   Formula wt 140.22
FEMA: 2780
UNII: 5DX8YYV2FV [2,6-nonadien-1-ol, (2e,6z)-]

DESCRIPTION
(E),(Z)-2,6-Nonadienol occurs as a white to yellow liquid.
Odor: Powerful, green, vegetable
Solubility: Insoluble or practically insoluble in water
Boiling Point: ~196°
Solubility in Alcohol, Appendix VI: One mL dissolves in 1 mL of 95% ethanol.

Function: Flavoring agent

IDENTIFICATION
- **INFRARED SPECTRA,** *Spectrophotometric Identification Tests,* Appendix IIIC
  Acceptance criteria: The spectrum of the sample exhibits relative maxima at the same wavelengths as those of the spectrum below.

ASSAY
- **PROCEDURE:** Proceed as directed under *M-1a,* Appendix XI.
  Acceptance criteria: NLT 92.0% of C₉H₁₆O (one major isomer)

SPECIFIC TESTS
- **REFRACTIVE INDEX,** Appendix II: At 20°
  Acceptance criteria: Between 1.464 and 1.471
- **SPECIFIC GRAVITY:** Determine at 25° by any reliable method (see *General Provisions*).
  Acceptance criteria: Between 0.860 and 0.880

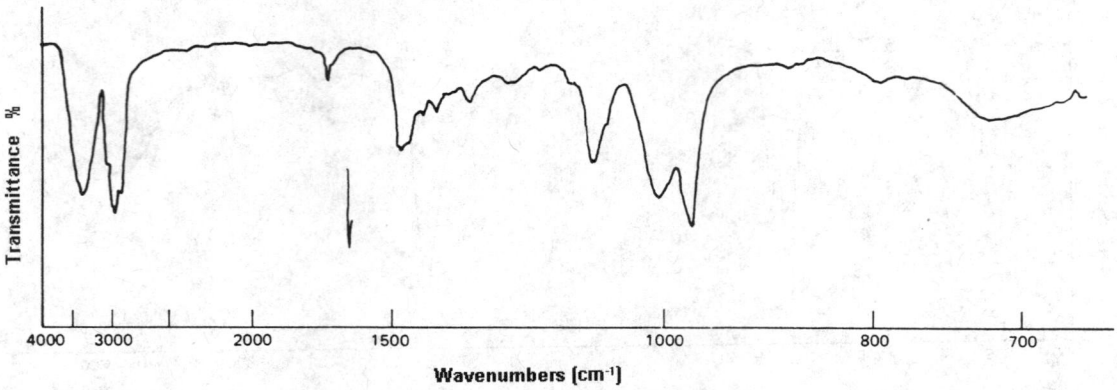

(E),(Z)-2,6-Nonadienol

δ-Nonalactone

First Published: Prior to FCC 6

5-Hydroxynonanoic Acid, Lactone

$C_9H_{16}O_2$　　　　　　　　　　　　Formula wt 156.22
FEMA: 3356
UNII: DMB99B4WCF [δ-nonalactone]

DESCRIPTION
δ-Nonalactone occurs as a colorless to pale yellow liquid.
Odor: Coconut
Solubility: Soluble in propylene glycol, vegetable oils; insoluble or practically insoluble in water
Boiling Point: ~250°
Solubility in Alcohol, Appendix VI: One mL dissolves in 1 mL of 95% alcohol.

Function: Flavoring agent

IDENTIFICATION
- **INFRARED SPECTRA,** *Spectrophotometric Identification Tests,* Appendix IIIC
  Acceptance criteria: The spectrum of the sample exhibits relative maxima at the same wavelengths as those of the spectrum below.

ASSAY
- **PROCEDURE:** Proceed as directed under *M-1a,* Appendix XI.
  Acceptance criteria: NLT 98.0% of $C_9H_{16}O_2$

SPECIFIC TESTS
- **REFRACTIVE INDEX,** Appendix II: At 20°
  Acceptance criteria: Between 1.454 and 1.459
- **SPECIFIC GRAVITY:** Determine at 25° by any reliable method (see *General Provisions*).
  Acceptance criteria: Between 0.980 and 0.986

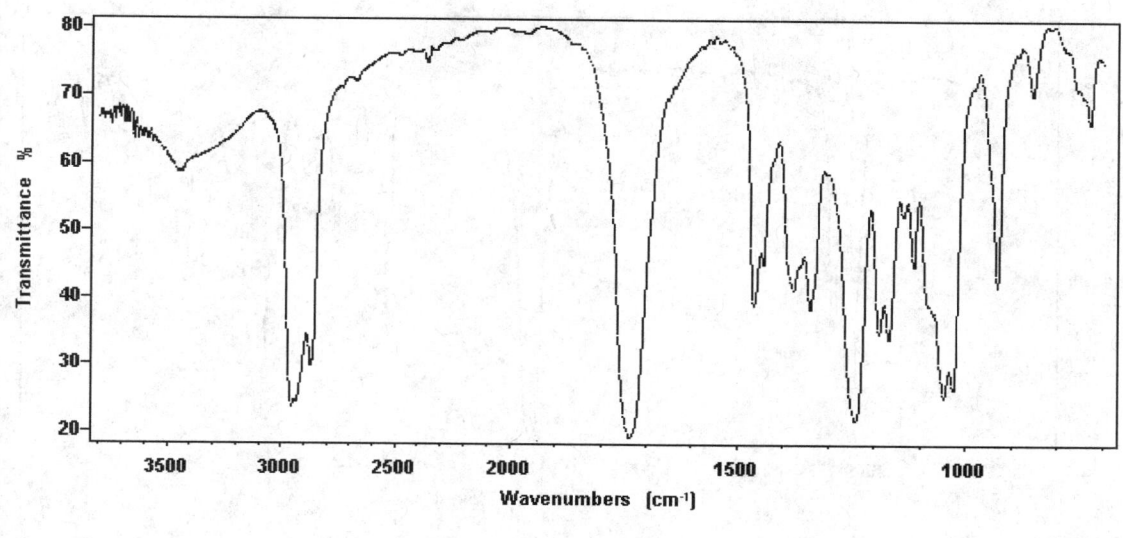
δ-Nonalactone

γ-Nonalactone

First Published: Prior to FCC 6

Aldehyde C-18, So-Called

$C_9H_{16}O_2$
FEMA: 2781
UNII: I1XGH66S8P [γ-nonalactone]

Formula wt 156.22

DESCRIPTION
γ-Nonalactone occurs as a colorless to slightly yellow liquid.
Odor: Coconut
Solubility: Soluble in alcohol, most fixed oils, propylene glycol; insoluble or practically insoluble in water
Boiling Point: ~121° to 122° (6 mm Hg)
Solubility in Alcohol, Appendix VI: One mL dissolves in 5 mL of 60% alcohol.
Function: Flavoring agent

IDENTIFICATION
- **INFRARED SPECTRA,** *Spectrophotometric Identification Tests,* Appendix IIIC
  Acceptance criteria: The spectrum of the sample exhibits relative maxima at the same wavelengths as those of the spectrum below.

ASSAY
- **PROCEDURE:** Proceed as directed under *M-1b,* Appendix XI.
  Acceptance criteria: NLT 98.0% of $C_9H_{16}O_2$

SPECIFIC TESTS
- **ACID VALUE, FLAVOR CHEMICALS (OTHER THAN ESSENTIAL OILS),** *M-15,* Appendix XI
  Acceptance criteria: NMT 2.0
- **REFRACTIVE INDEX,** Appendix II: At 20°
  Acceptance criteria: Between 1.446 and 1.450
- **SPECIFIC GRAVITY:** Determine at 25° by any reliable method (see *General Provisions*).
  Acceptance criteria: Between 0.958 and 0.966

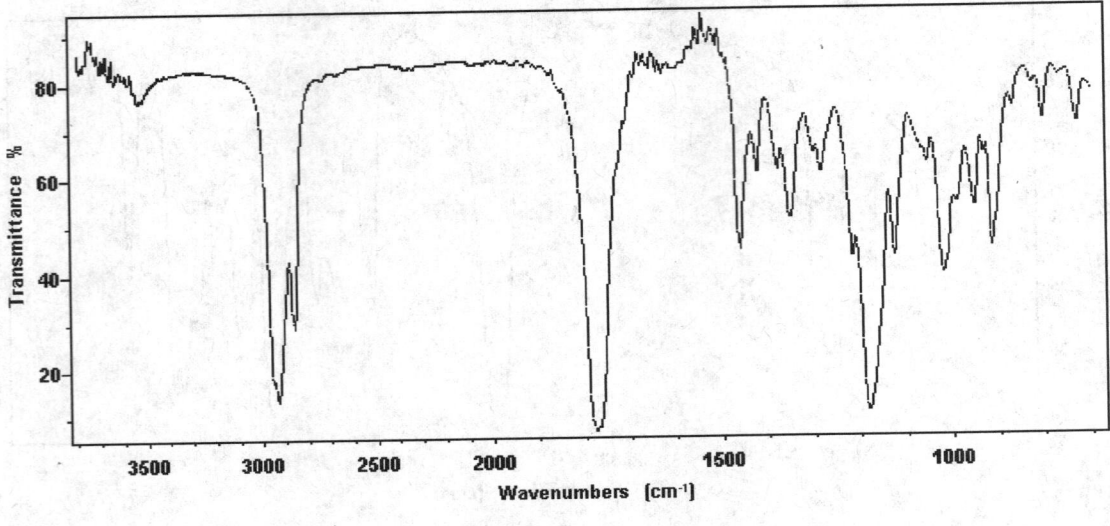

γ-Nonalactone

Nonanal

First Published: Prior to FCC 6
Last Revision: First Supplement, FCC 6

Aldehyde C-9
Pelargonic Aldehyde

$C_9H_{18}O$ Formula wt 142.24
FEMA: 2782
UNII: 2L2WBY9K6T [nonanal]

DESCRIPTION
Nonanal occurs as a colorless to light yellow liquid. It may contain a suitable antioxidant.
Odor: Fatty; citrus–rose on dilution
Solubility: Soluble in alcohol, most fixed oils, propylene glycol; insoluble or practically insoluble in glycerin
Boiling Point: ~93° (23 mm Hg)

Function: Flavoring agent

IDENTIFICATION
- **INFRARED SPECTRA,** *Spectrophotometric Identification Tests,* Appendix IIIC
  Acceptance criteria: The spectrum of the sample exhibits relative maxima at the same wavelengths as those of the spectrum below.

ASSAY
- **PROCEDURE:** Proceed as directed under *M-1b,* Appendix XI.
  Acceptance criteria: NLT 92.0% of $C_9H_{18}O$

SPECIFIC TESTS
- **ACID VALUE, FLAVOR CHEMICALS (OTHER THAN ESSENTIAL OILS),** *M-15,* Appendix XI
  Acceptance criteria: NMT 10.0
- **REFRACTIVE INDEX,** Appendix II: At 20°
  Acceptance criteria: Between 1.422 and 1.429
- **SPECIFIC GRAVITY:** Determine at 25° by any reliable method (see *General Provisions*).
  Acceptance criteria: Between 0.820 and 0.830

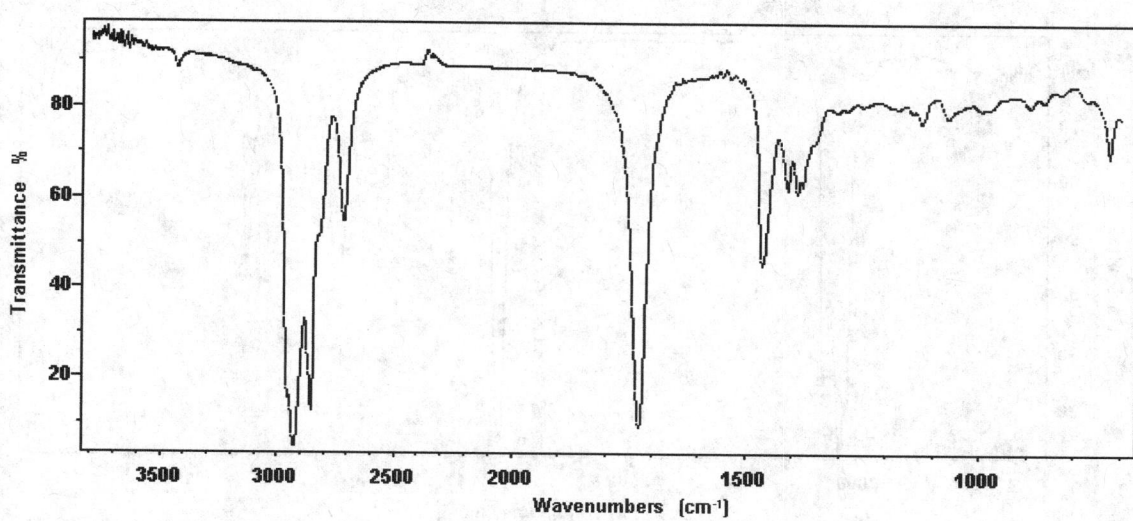
Nonanal

2-Nonanone

First Published: Prior to FCC 6

Methyl Heptyl Ketone

C$_9$H$_{18}$O Formula wt 142.24
FEMA: 2785
UNII: ZE5K73YN2Z [2-nonanone]

DESCRIPTION
2-Nonanone occurs as a colorless to pale yellow liquid.
Odor: Fruity, floral, fatty, herbaceous
Solubility: Soluble in propylene glycol, vegetable oils; insoluble or practically insoluble in water
Boiling Point: ~195°
Solubility in Alcohol, Appendix VI: One mL dissolves in 1 mL of 95% alcohol.

Function: Flavoring agent

IDENTIFICATION
- **INFRARED SPECTRA,** *Spectrophotometric Identification Tests,* Appendix IIIC
  Acceptance criteria: The spectrum of the sample exhibits relative maxima at the same wavelengths as those of the spectrum below.

ASSAY
- **PROCEDURE:** Proceed as directed under *M-1a,* Appendix XI.
  Acceptance criteria: NLT 97.0% of C$_9$H$_{18}$O

SPECIFIC TESTS
- **REFRACTIVE INDEX,** Appendix II: At 20°
  Acceptance criteria: Between 1.418 and 1.423
- **SPECIFIC GRAVITY:** Determine at 25° by any reliable method (see *General Provisions*).
  Acceptance criteria: Between 0.817 and 0.823

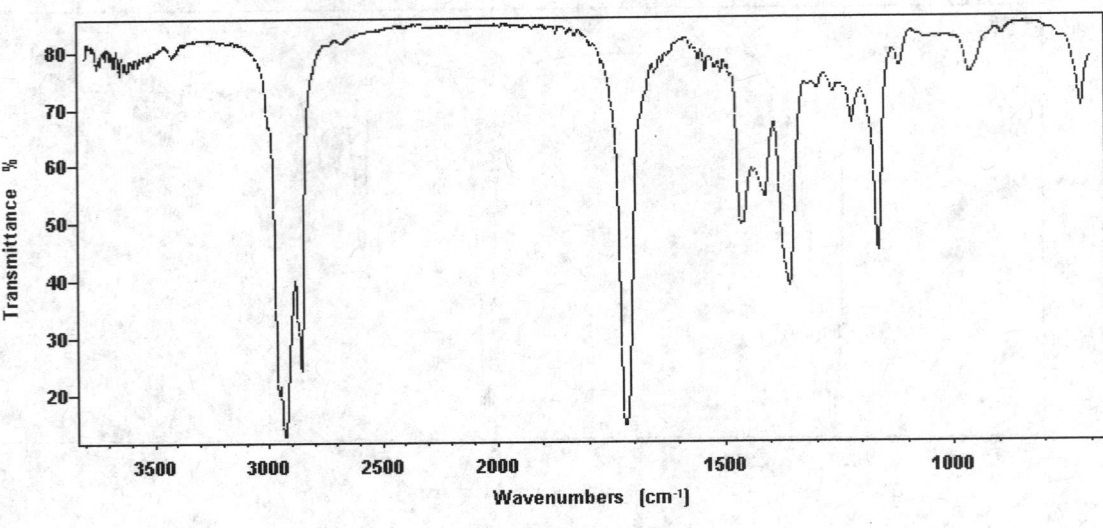
2-Nonanone

Nonanoic Acid

First Published: Prior to FCC 6

$C_9H_{18}O_2$ Formula wt 158.24
FEMA: 2784
UNII: 97SEH7577T [pelargonic acid]

DESCRIPTION
Nonanoic Acid occurs as a colorless to pale yellow liquid.
Odor: Fatty
Solubility: Soluble in propylene glycol, vegetable oils; insoluble or practically insoluble in water
Boiling Point: ~254°
Solubility in Alcohol, Appendix VI: One mL dissolves in 1 mL of ethanol.
Function: Flavoring agent

ASSAY
- **Procedure:** Proceed as directed under *M-3a*, Appendix XI.
  Acceptance criteria: NLT 98.0% of $C_9H_{18}O_2$

SPECIFIC TESTS
- **Refractive Index,** Appendix II: At 20°
  Acceptance criteria: Between 1.431 and 1.435
- **Specific Gravity:** Determine at 25° by any reliable method (see *General Provisions*).
  Acceptance criteria: Between 0.901 and 0.906

(E)-2-Nonen-1-ol

First Published: Prior to FCC 6

trans-2-Nonenol

$C_9H_{18}O$ Formula wt 142.24
FEMA: 3379
UNII: 164F9RI0BJ [2-nonen-1-ol, (2e)-]

DESCRIPTION
(E)-2-Nonen-1-ol occurs as a white liquid.
Odor: Fatty, violet
Solubility: Insoluble or practically insoluble in water
Boiling Point: ~105° (12 mm Hg)
Solubility in Alcohol, Appendix VI: One mL dissolves in 1 mL of 95% ethanol.
Function: Flavoring agent

IDENTIFICATION
- **Infrared Spectra,** *Spectrophotometric Identification Tests,* Appendix IIIC.
  Acceptance criteria: The spectrum of the sample exhibits relative maxima at the same wavelengths as those of the spectrum below.

ASSAY
- **Procedure:** Proceed as directed under *M-1a*, Appendix XI.
  Acceptance criteria: NLT 96.0% of $C_9H_{18}O$ (one major isomer)

SPECIFIC TESTS
- **REFRACTIVE INDEX,** Appendix II: At 20°
  Acceptance criteria: Between 1.444 and 1.452
- **SPECIFIC GRAVITY:** Determine at 25° by any reliable method (see *General Provisions*).
  Acceptance criteria: Between 0.830 and 0.850

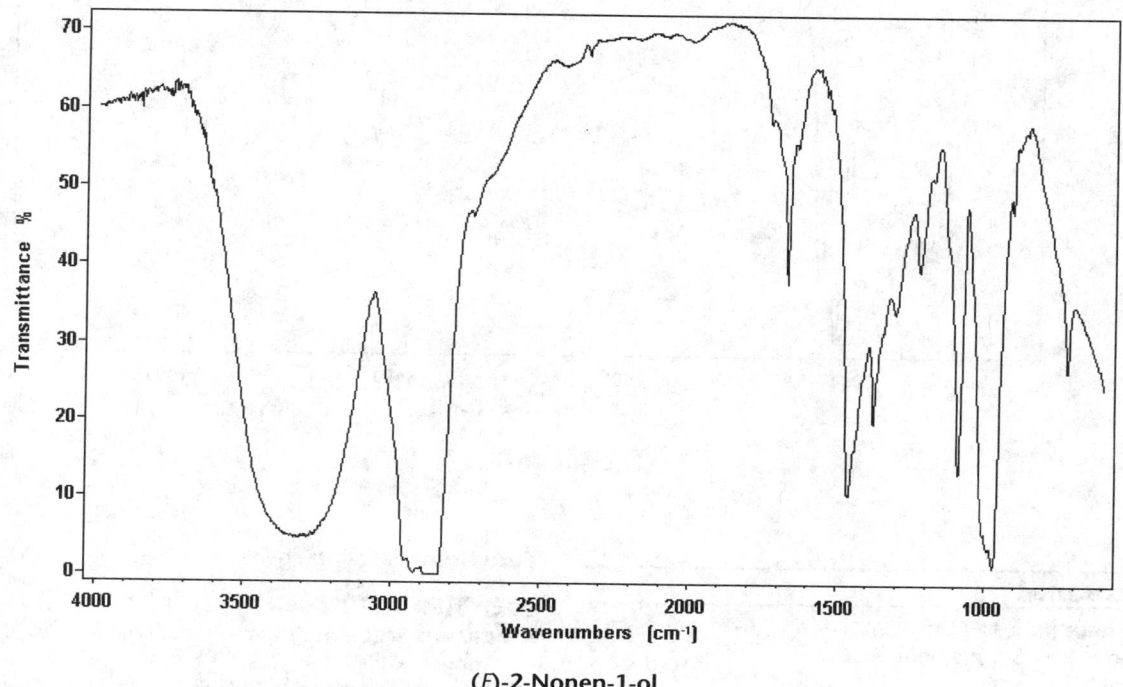

(*E*)-2-Nonen-1-ol

(*Z*)-6-Nonen-1-ol

First Published: Prior to FCC 6

cis-6-Nonen-1-ol

C₉H₁₈O Formula wt 142.24
FEMA: 3465
UNII: 05401NS64Z [6-nonen-1-ol, (6z)-]

DESCRIPTION
(*Z*)-6-Nonen-1-ol occurs as a white to slightly yellow liquid.
Odor: Powerful, melon
Solubility: Insoluble or practically insoluble in water
Boiling Point: ~115° (20 mm Hg)
Solubility in Alcohol, Appendix VI: One mL dissolves in 1 mL of 95% ethanol.

Function: Flavoring agent

IDENTIFICATION
- **INFRARED SPECTRA,** *Spectrophotometric Identification Tests,* Appendix IIIC
  Acceptance criteria: The spectrum of the sample exhibits relative maxima at the same wavelengths as those of the spectrum below.

ASSAY
- **PROCEDURE:** Proceed as directed under *M-1a,* Appendix XI.
  Acceptance criteria: NLT 95.0% of C₉H₁₈O (one major isomer)

SPECIFIC TESTS
- **REFRACTIVE INDEX,** Appendix II: At 20°
  Acceptance criteria: Between 1.446 and 1.452
- **SPECIFIC GRAVITY:** Determine at 25° by any reliable method (see *General Provisions*).
  Acceptance criteria: Between 0.850 and 0.870

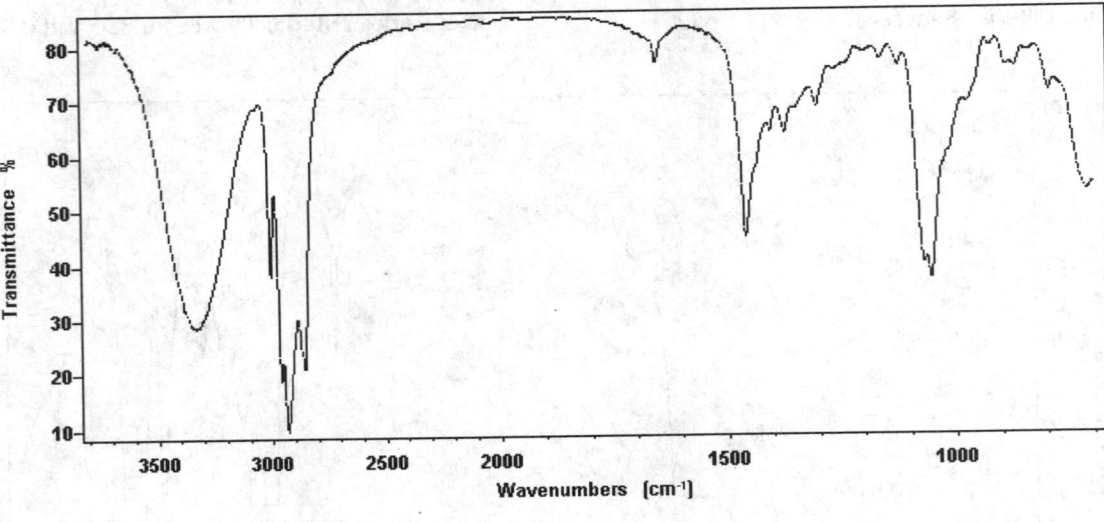

(Z)-6-Nonen-1-ol

(E)-2-Nonenal

First Published: Prior to FCC 6
Last Revision: First Supplement, FCC 6

trans-2-Nonenal

C₉H₁₆O   Formula wt 140.22
FEMA: 3213
UNII: 8VEO649985 [2-nonenal, (2e)-]

DESCRIPTION
(E)-2-Nonenal occurs as a white to slightly yellow liquid. It may contain a suitable antioxidant.
Odor: Fatty, violet
Solubility: Soluble in alcohol, most fixed oils; insoluble or practically insoluble in water
Boiling Point: ~88° (12 mm Hg)
Solubility in Alcohol, Appendix VI: One mL dissolves in 1 mL of 95% ethanol.

Function: Flavoring agent

IDENTIFICATION
- **INFRARED SPECTRA,** *Spectrophotometric Identification Tests,* Appendix IIIC
  Acceptance criteria: The spectrum of the sample exhibits relative maxima at the same wavelengths as those of the spectrum below.

ASSAY
- **PROCEDURE:** Proceed as directed under *M-1a,* Appendix XI.
  Acceptance criteria: NLT 92.0% of C₉H₁₆O (one major isomer)

SPECIFIC TESTS
- **REFRACTIVE INDEX,** Appendix II: At 20°
  Acceptance criteria: Between 1.450 and 1.460
- **SPECIFIC GRAVITY:** Determine at 25° by any reliable method (see *General Provisions*).
  Acceptance criteria: Between 0.840 and 0.850

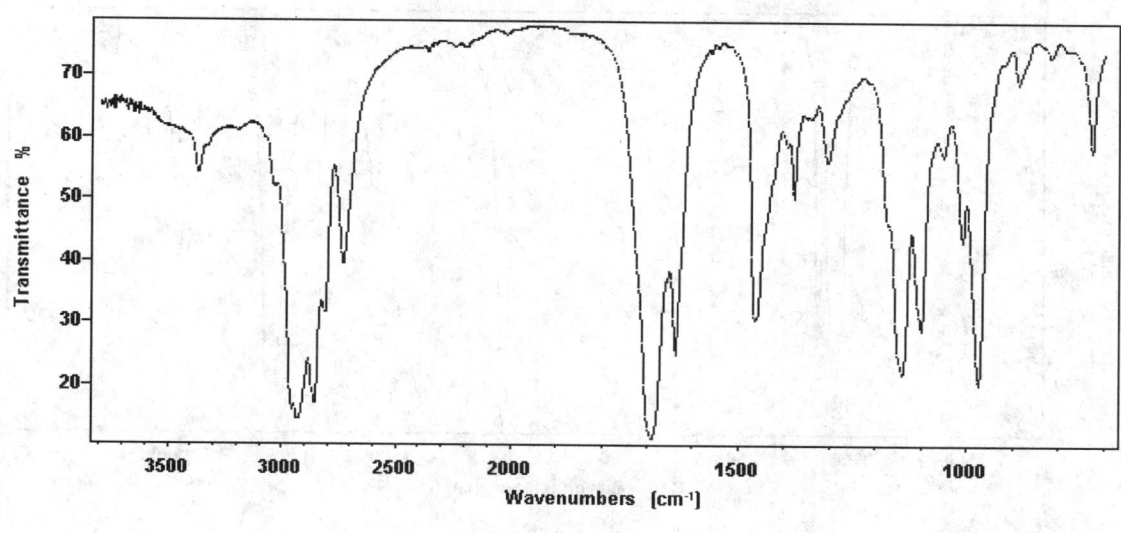

(E)-2-Nonenal

Nonyl Acetate
First Published: Prior to FCC 6

$C_{11}H_{22}O_2$　　　　　　　　　　Formula wt 186.29
FEMA: 2788
UNII: M2SE618B1L [nonyl acetate]

DESCRIPTION
Nonyl Acetate occurs as a colorless liquid.
Odor: Floral, fruity
Solubility: Soluble in alcohol, ether; insoluble or practically insoluble in water
Boiling Point: ~212°
Solubility in Alcohol, Appendix VI: One mL dissolves in 6 mL of 70% alcohol to give a clear solution.
Function: Flavoring agent

IDENTIFICATION
- **INFRARED SPECTRA,** *Spectrophotometric Identification Tests,* Appendix IIIC
  Acceptance criteria: The spectrum of the sample exhibits relative maxima at the same wavelengths as those of the spectrum below.

ASSAY
- **PROCEDURE:** Proceed as directed under *M-1b,* Appendix XI.
  Acceptance criteria: NLT 97.0% of $C_{11}H_{22}O_2$

SPECIFIC TESTS
- **ACID VALUE, FLAVOR CHEMICALS (OTHER THAN ESSENTIAL OILS),** *M-15,* Appendix XI
  Acceptance criteria: NMT 1.0
- **REFRACTIVE INDEX,** Appendix II: At 20°
  Acceptance criteria: Between 1.422 and 1.426
- **SPECIFIC GRAVITY:** Determine at 25° by any reliable method (see *General Provisions*).
  Acceptance criteria: Between 0.864 and 0.868

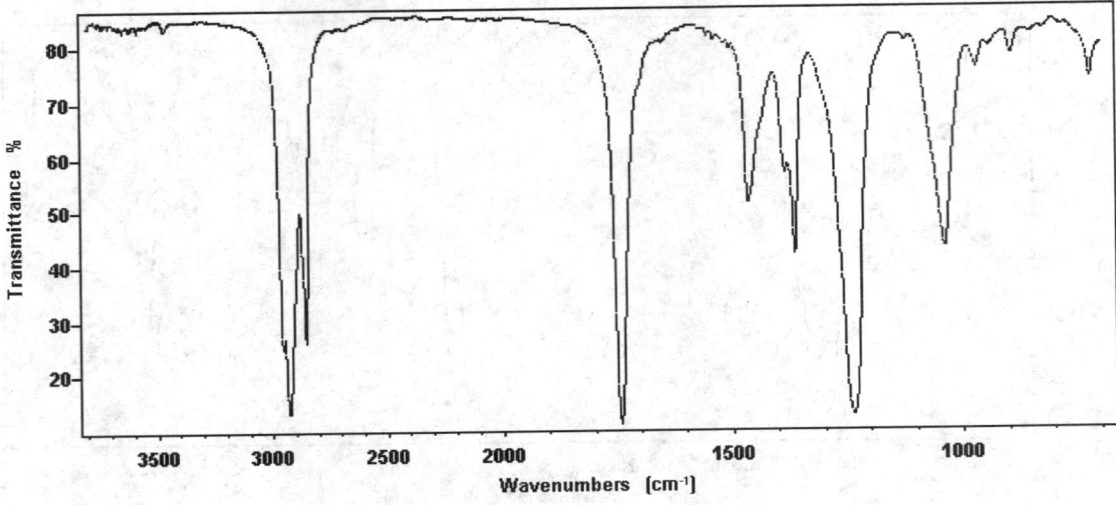

Nonyl Acetate

Nonyl Alcohol

First Published: Prior to FCC 6

1-Nonanol
Alcohol C-9

$C_9H_{20}O$ Formula wt 144.26
FEMA: 2789
UNII: NGK73Q6XMC [nonyl alcohol]

DESCRIPTION
Nonyl Alcohol occurs as a colorless liquid.
Odor: Rose-citrus
Solubility: Miscible in alcohol, chloroform, ether; insoluble or practically insoluble in water
Boiling Point: ~213°
Solubility in Alcohol, Appendix VI: One mL dissolves in 3 mL of 60% alcohol to give a clear solution.
Function: Flavoring agent

IDENTIFICATION
- **INFRARED SPECTRA,** Spectrophotometric Identification Tests, Appendix IIIC
  Acceptance criteria: The spectrum of the sample exhibits relative maxima at the same wavelengths as those of the spectrum below.

ASSAY
- **PROCEDURE:** Proceed as directed under M-1b, Appendix XI.
  Acceptance criteria: NLT 97.0% of $C_9H_{20}O$

SPECIFIC TESTS
- **ACID VALUE, FLAVOR CHEMICALS (OTHER THAN ESSENTIAL OILS),** M-15, Appendix XI
  Acceptance criteria: NMT 1.0
- **REFRACTIVE INDEX,** Appendix II: At 20°
  Acceptance criteria: Between 1.431 and 1.435
- **SPECIFIC GRAVITY:** Determine at 25° by any reliable method (see General Provisions).
  Acceptance criteria: Between 0.824 and 0.830

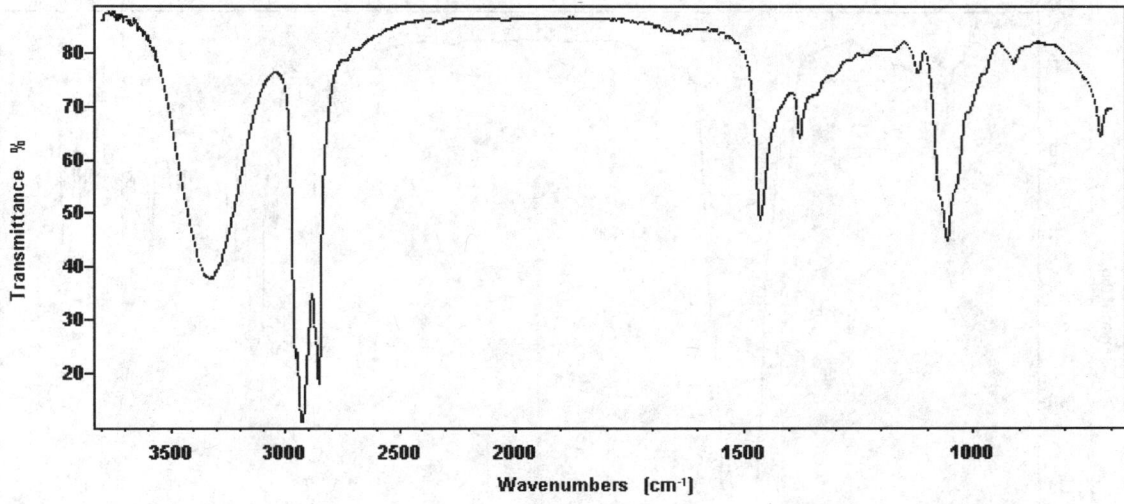

Nonyl Alcohol

Nutmeg Oil

First Published: Prior to FCC 6

Myristica Oil

CAS: [8008-45-5]

UNII: Z1CLM48948 [nutmeg oil]

DESCRIPTION

Nutmeg Oil occurs as a colorless or pale yellow liquid with the characteristic odor and taste of nutmeg. It is the volatile oil obtained by steam distillation from the dried kernels of the ripe seed of *Myristica fragrans* Houttuyn (Fam. Myristicaceae). Two types of oil, the East Indian and the West Indian, are commercially available. It is soluble in alcohol.

Function: Flavoring agent

Packaging and Storage: Store in a cool place protected from light in full, tight containers that are made from steel or aluminum and that are suitably lined.

IDENTIFICATION

- **INFRARED SPECTRA,** *Spectrophotometric Identification Tests,* Appendix IIIC
  Acceptance criteria: The spectrum of the sample exhibits relative maxima at the same wavelengths as those of the spectrum below.

SPECIFIC TESTS

- **ANGULAR ROTATION,** *Optical (Specific) Rotation,* Appendix IIB: Use a 100-mm tube.
  Acceptance criteria
  East Indian type: Between +8° and +30°
  West Indian type: Between +25° and +45°

- **REFRACTIVE INDEX,** Appendix IIB
  [NOTE—Use an Abbé or other refractometer of equal or greater accuracy.]
  Acceptance criteria
  East Indian type: Between 1.474 and 1.488 at 20°
  West Indian type: Between 1.469 and 1.476 at 20°

- **RESIDUE ON EVAPORATION,** Appendix VI
  Sample: 3 mL
  Analysis: Proceed as directed in Appendix VI, but heat the evaporating dish containing the *Sample* on the steam bath for 5 h, and then heat at 105° for 1 h.
  Acceptance criteria
  East Indian type: NMT 60 mg per 3 mL
  West Indian type: NMT 50 mg per 3 mL

- **SOLUBILITY IN ALCOHOL,** Appendix VI
  Acceptance criteria
  East Indian type: One mL of sample dissolves in 3 mL of 90% alcohol.
  West Indian type: One mL of sample dissolves in 4 mL of 90% alcohol.

- **SPECIFIC GRAVITY:** Determine by any reliable method (see *General Provisions*).
  Acceptance criteria
  East Indian type: Between 0.880 and 0.910
  West Indian type: Between 0.854 and 0.880

OTHER REQUIREMENTS

- **LABELING:** Indicate whether the oil is the East Indian or West Indian type.

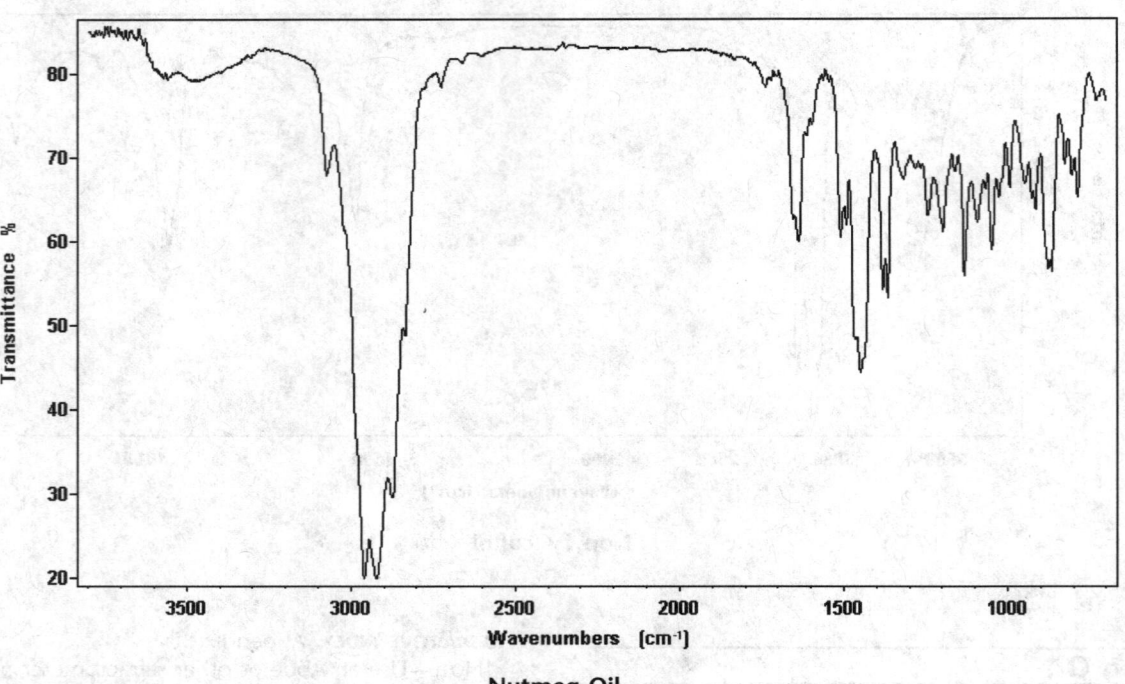

Nutmeg Oil

δ-Octalactone

First Published: Prior to FCC 6

5-Hydroxyoctanoic Acid Lactone

C₈H₁₄O₂   Formula wt 142.20
FEMA: 3214
UNII: 8AA944C37V [δ-octalactone]

DESCRIPTION
δ-Octalactone occurs as a colorless to pale yellow liquid.
Odor: Coconut
Solubility: Soluble in propylene glycol, vegetable oils; insoluble or practically insoluble in water
Boiling Point: ~234°
Solubility in Alcohol, Appendix VI: One mL dissolves in 1 mL of 95% ethanol.

Function: Flavoring agent

IDENTIFICATION
- **INFRARED SPECTRA,** *Spectrophotometric Identification Tests,* Appendix IIIC
  Acceptance criteria: The spectrum of the sample exhibits relative maxima at the same wavelengths as those of the spectrum below.

ASSAY
- **PROCEDURE:** Proceed as directed under *M-1a,* Appendix XI.
  Acceptance criteria: NLT 98.0% of C₈H₁₄O₂

SPECIFIC TESTS
- **REFRACTIVE INDEX,** Appendix II: At 20°
  Acceptance criteria: Between 1.452 and 1.458
- **SPECIFIC GRAVITY:** Determine at 25° by any reliable method (see *General Provisions*).
  Acceptance criteria: Between 0.995 and 1.000

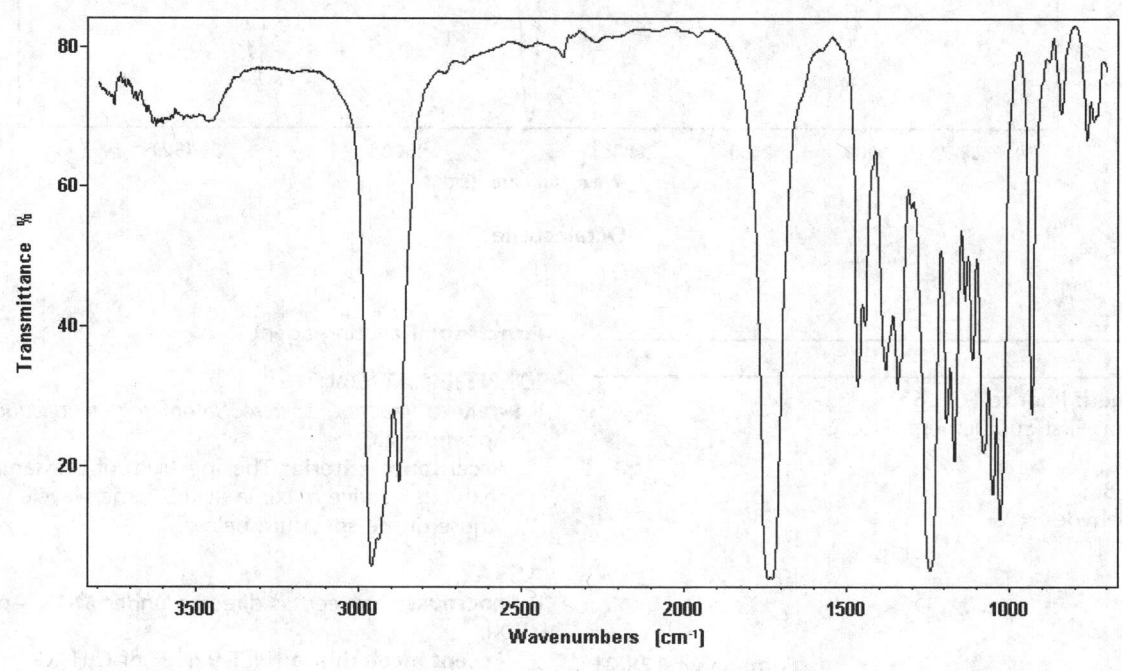

δ-Octalactone

γ-Octalactone

First Published: Prior to FCC 6

C₈H₁₄O₂   Formula wt 142.20
FEMA: 2796

UNII: UHD6M52X0K [γ-octalactone]

DESCRIPTION
γ-Octalactone occurs as a colorless to slightly yellow liquid.
Odor: Sweet, coconut, fruity
Solubility: Soluble in alcohol; slightly soluble in water
Boiling Point: ~234°
Function: Flavoring agent

γ-Octalactone

IDENTIFICATION
- **INFRARED SPECTRA,** *Spectrophotometric Identification Tests,* Appendix IIIC
  Acceptance criteria: The spectrum of the sample exhibits relative maxima at the same wavelengths as those of the spectrum below.

ASSAY
- **PROCEDURE:** Proceed as directed under *M-1a,* Appendix XI.
  Acceptance criteria: NLT 95.0% of $C_8H_{14}O_2$

SPECIFIC TESTS
- **ACID VALUE, FLAVOR CHEMICALS (OTHER THAN ESSENTIAL OILS),** *M-15,* Appendix XI
  Acceptance criteria: NMT 8.0
- **REFRACTIVE INDEX,** Appendix II: At 20°
  Acceptance criteria: Between 1.443 and 1.447
- **SPECIFIC GRAVITY:** Determine at 25° by any reliable method (see *General Provisions*).
  Acceptance criteria: Between 0.970 and 0.980

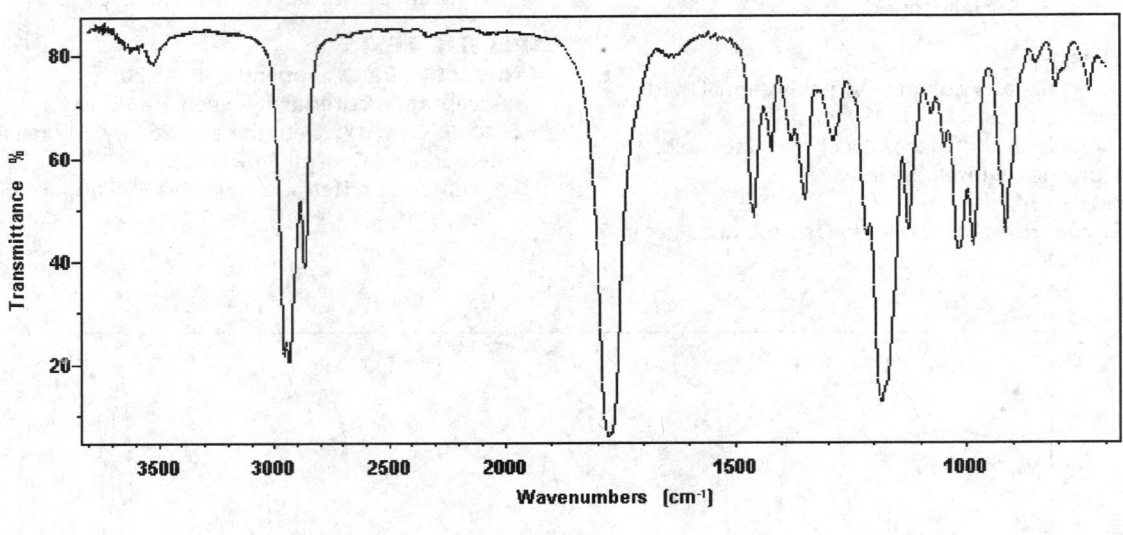

γ-Octalactone

Octanal

First Published: Prior to FCC 6
Last Revision: First Supplement, FCC 6

Aldehyde C-8
Caprylic Aldehyde

$C_8H_{16}O$　　　　　　　　　　　　　Formula wt 128.21
FEMA: 2797
UNII: XGE9999H19 [caprylaldehyde]

DESCRIPTION
Octanal occurs as a colorless to light yellow liquid. It may contain a suitable antioxidant.
Odor: Fatty-orange
Solubility: Soluble in alcohol, most fixed oils, propylene glycol; insoluble or practically insoluble in glycerin
Boiling Point: ~171°

Function: Flavoring agent

IDENTIFICATION
- **INFRARED SPECTRA,** *Spectrophotometric Identification Tests,* Appendix IIIC
  Acceptance criteria: The spectrum of the sample exhibits relative maxima at the same wavelengths as those of the spectrum below.

ASSAY
- **PROCEDURE:** Proceed as directed under *M-1b,* Appendix XI.
  Acceptance criteria: NLT 92.0% of $C_8H_{16}O$

SPECIFIC TESTS
- **ACID VALUE, FLAVOR CHEMICALS (OTHER THAN ESSENTIAL OILS),** *M-15,* Appendix XI
  Acceptance criteria: NMT 10.0
- **REFRACTIVE INDEX,** Appendix II: At 20°
  Acceptance criteria: Between 1.417 and 1.425
- **SPECIFIC GRAVITY:** Determine at 25° by any reliable method (see *General Provisions*).
  Acceptance criteria: Between 0.810 and 0.830

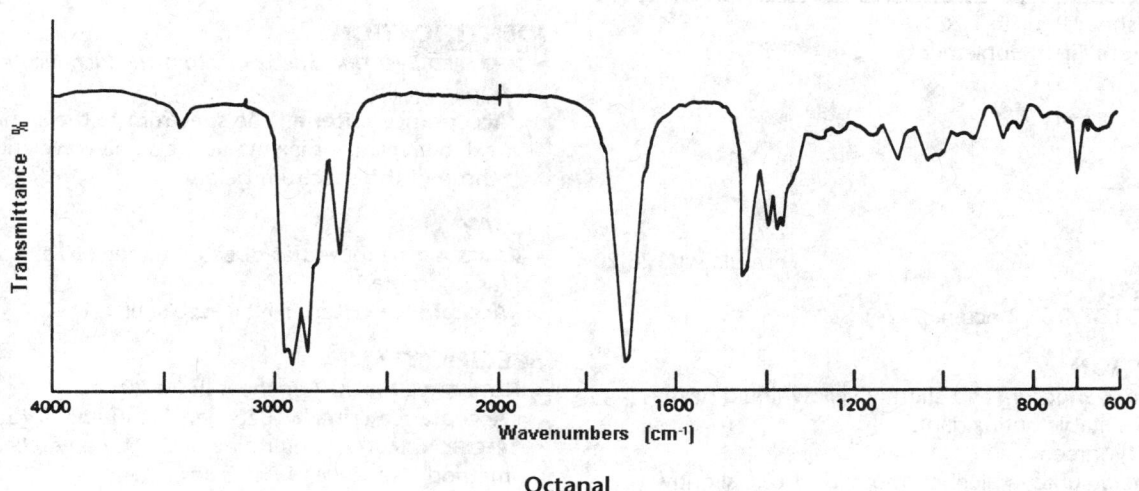

Octanal

Octanoic Acid

First Published: Prior to FCC 6

Caprylic Acid

C$_8$H$_{16}$O$_2$ Formula wt 144.21
FEMA: 2799
                              CAS: [124-07-2]
UNII: OBL58JN025 [octanoic acid]

DESCRIPTION
Octanoic Acid occurs as a colorless, oily liquid. It is slightly soluble in water and soluble in most organic solvents. Its specific gravity is about 0.910.
Function: Component in the manufacture of other food-grade additives; defoaming agent; flavoring agent
Packaging and Storage: Store in tight containers.

IMPURITIES
Inorganic Impurities
- **WATER,** *Water Determination,* Appendix IIB
  Acceptance criteria: NMT 0.4%

SPECIFIC TESTS
- **ACID VALUE (FATS AND RELATED SUBSTANCES),** *Method I,* Appendix VII
  Acceptance criteria: Between 366 and 396
- **IODINE VALUE,** Appendix VII
  Acceptance criteria: NMT 2.0
- **RESIDUE ON IGNITION (SULFATED ASH),** Appendix IIC
  Sample: 10 g
  Acceptance criteria: NMT 0.1%
- **TITER (SOLIDIFICATION POINT),** *Solidification Point,* Appendix IIB
  Acceptance criteria: Between 8° and 17°

- **UNSAPONIFIABLE MATTER,** Appendix VII
  Acceptance criteria: NMT 0.2%

3-Octanol

First Published: Prior to FCC 6

C$_8$H$_{18}$O   Formula wt 130.23
FEMA: 3581
UNII: 73DZ0U3U1E [3-octanol]

DESCRIPTION
3-Octanol occurs as a colorless liquid.
Odor: Strong, oily-nutty, herbaceous
Solubility: Soluble in alcohol, most fixed oils; insoluble or practically insoluble in water
Boiling Point: ~174°
Solubility in Alcohol, Appendix VI: One mL dissolves in 1 mL of 95% ethanol.
Function: Flavoring agent

ASSAY
- **PROCEDURE:** Proceed as directed under *M-1a,* Appendix XI.
  Acceptance criteria: NLT 97.0% of C$_8$H$_{18}$O

SPECIFIC TESTS
- **REFRACTIVE INDEX,** Appendix II: At 20°
  Acceptance criteria: Between 1.425 and 1.429
- **SPECIFIC GRAVITY:** Determine at 25° by any reliable method (see *General Provisions*).
  Acceptance criteria: Between 0.817 and 0.824

(E)-2-Octen-1-al

First Published: Prior to FCC 6
Last Revision: First Supplement, FCC 6

trans-2-Octen-1-al

C₈H₁₄O   Formula wt 126.20
FEMA: 3215
UNII: 55N91D7775 [2-octenal, (2e)-]

DESCRIPTION

(*E*)-2-Octen-1-al occurs as a slightly yellow liquid. It may contain a suitable antioxidant.
Odor: Fatty, green
Solubility: Soluble in alcohol, most fixed oils; slightly soluble in water
Boiling Point: ~84° (19 mm Hg)
Function: Flavoring agent

IDENTIFICATION

- **INFRARED SPECTRA,** *Spectrophotometric Identification Tests,* Appendix IIIC
  Acceptance criteria: The spectrum of the sample exhibits relative maxima at the same wavelengths as those of the spectrum below.

ASSAY

- **PROCEDURE:** Proceed as directed under *M-1a*, Appendix XI (as (*E*)-isomer).
  Acceptance criteria: NLT 92.0% of C₈H₁₄O

SPECIFIC TESTS

- **REFRACTIVE INDEX,** Appendix II: At 20°
  Acceptance criteria: Between 1.450 and 1.455
- **SPECIFIC GRAVITY:** Determine at 25° by any reliable method (see *General Provisions*).
  Acceptance criteria: Between 0.830 and 0.850

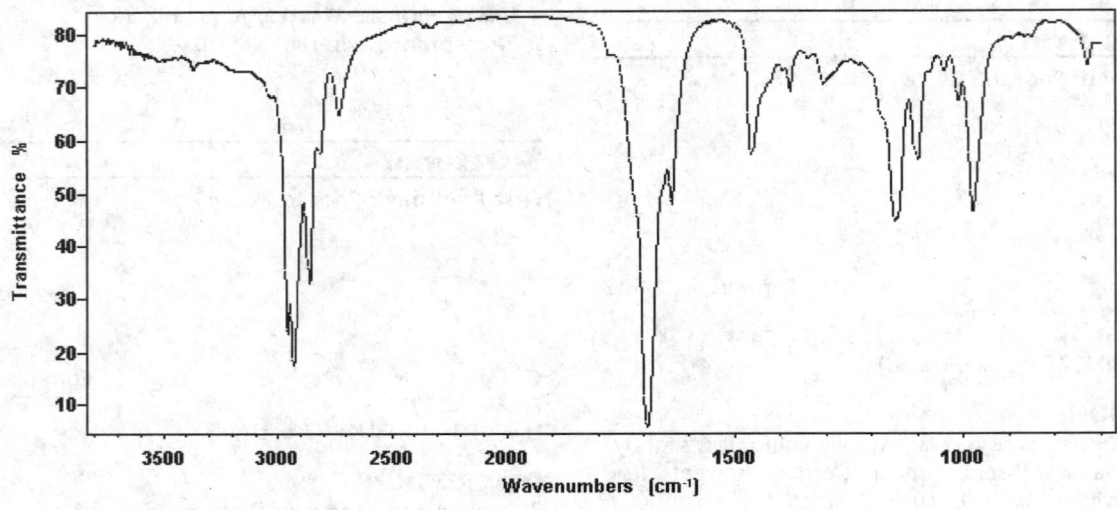

(*E*)-2-Octen-1-al

(Z)-3-Octen-1-ol

First Published: Prior to FCC 6
Last Revision: Second Supplement, FCC 7

cis-3-Octen-1-ol

C₈H₁₆O   Formula wt 128.21
FEMA: 3467
UNII: 34A1X2Y8M9 [3-octen-1-ol, (3z)-]

DESCRIPTION

(*Z*)-3-Octen-1-ol occurs as a colorless to slightly yellow liquid.
Odor: Musty, mushroom
Solubility: Insoluble or practically insoluble in water
Boiling Point: ~174°
Solubility in Alcohol, Appendix VI: One mL dissolves in 1 mL of 95% ethanol.
Function: Flavoring agent

IDENTIFICATION

- **INFRARED SPECTRA,** *Spectrophotometric Identification Tests,* Appendix IIIC
  Acceptance criteria: The spectrum of the sample exhibits relative maxima at the same wavelengths as those of the spectrum below.

ASSAY
- **PROCEDURE:** Proceed as directed under *M-1a*, Appendix XI (as (*Z*)-isomer).
  Acceptance criteria: NLT 95.0% of $C_8H_{16}O$

SPECIFIC TESTS
- **REFRACTIVE INDEX,** Appendix II: At 20°
  Acceptance criteria: 1.444–1.450
- **SPECIFIC GRAVITY:** Determine at 25° by any reliable method (see *General Provisions*).
  Acceptance criteria: 0.844–0.848

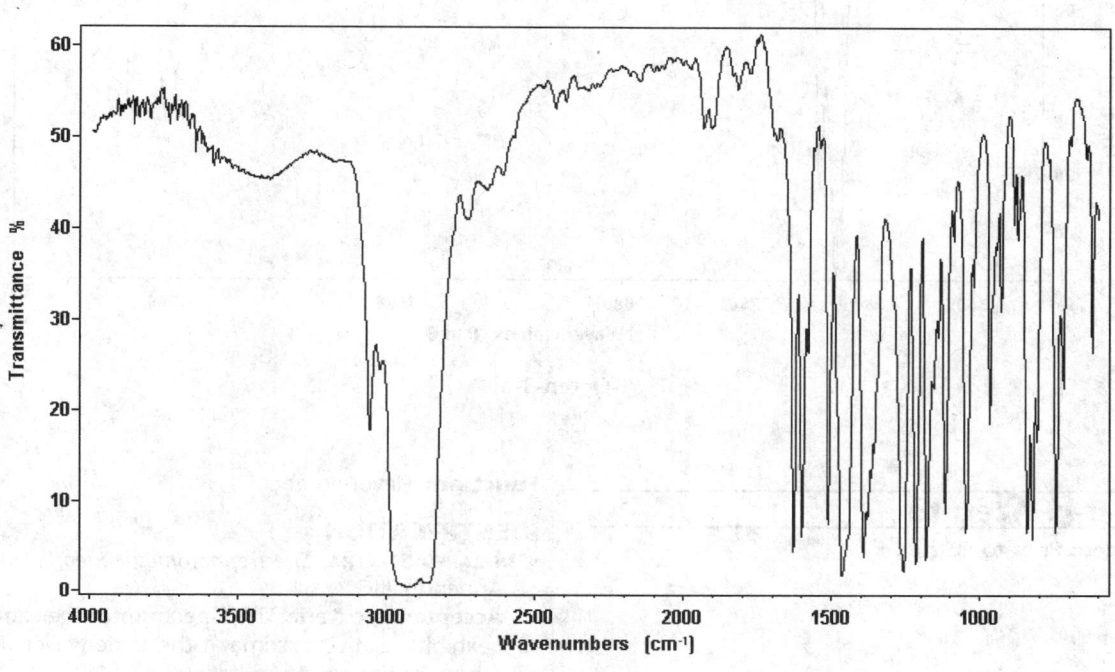

(*Z*)-3-Octen-1-ol

1-Octen-3-ol

First Published: Prior to FCC 6

Amyl Vinyl Carbinol

$C_8H_{16}O$ Formula wt 128.21
FEMA: 2805
UNII: WXB511GE38 [1-octen-3-ol]

DESCRIPTION
1-Octen-3-ol occurs as a colorless to pale yellow liquid.
Odor: Mushroom, herbaceous
Solubility: Soluble in propylene glycol, vegetable oils; insoluble or practically insoluble in water
Boiling Point: ~175°
Solubility in Alcohol, Appendix VI: One mL dissolves in 1 mL of 95% alcohol.

Function: Flavoring agent

IDENTIFICATION
- **INFRARED SPECTRA,** *Spectrophotometric Identification Tests,* Appendix IIIC
  Acceptance criteria: The spectrum of the sample exhibits relative maxima at the same wavelengths as those of the spectrum below.

ASSAY
- **PROCEDURE:** Proceed as directed under *M-1a*, Appendix XI.
  Acceptance criteria: NLT 97.0% of $C_8H_{16}O$

SPECIFIC TESTS
- **REFRACTIVE INDEX,** Appendix II: At 20°
  Acceptance criteria: Between 1.434 and 1.442
- **SPECIFIC GRAVITY:** Determine at 25° by any reliable method (see *General Provisions*).
  Acceptance criteria: Between 0.831 and 0.839

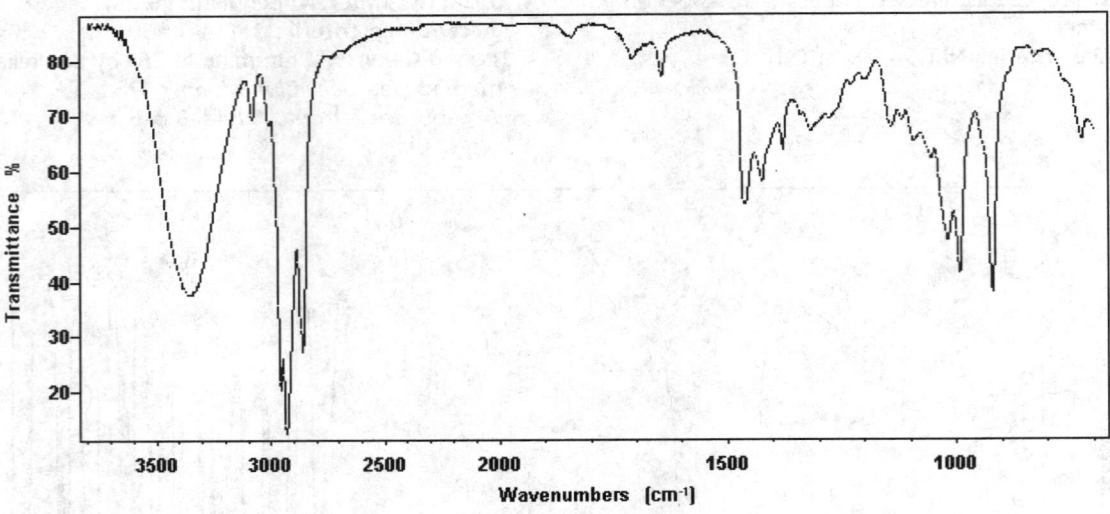

1-Octen-3-ol

1-Octen-3-yl Acetate

First Published: Prior to FCC 6

$C_{10}H_{18}O_2$ Formula wt 170.25
FEMA: 3582
UNII: 2PZ32LCA02 [1-octen-3-yl acetate]

DESCRIPTION
1-Octen-3-yl Acetate occurs as an almost colorless liquid.
Odor: Metallic, mushroom
Solubility: Soluble in alcohol, most fixed oils; insoluble or practically insoluble in water, propylene glycol
Boiling Point: ~80° (15 mm Hg)
Solubility in Alcohol, Appendix VI: One mL dissolves in 1 mL of 95% ethanol.

Function: Flavoring agent

IDENTIFICATION
- **INFRARED SPECTRA,** *Spectrophotometric Identification Tests,* Appendix IIIC
  Acceptance criteria: The spectrum of the sample exhibits relative maxima at the same wavelengths as those of the spectrum below.

ASSAY
- **PROCEDURE:** Proceed as directed under *M-1b,* Appendix XI.
  Acceptance criteria: NLT 95.0% of $C_{10}H_{18}O_2$

SPECIFIC TESTS
- **REFRACTIVE INDEX,** Appendix II: At 20°
  Acceptance criteria: Between 1.418 and 1.428
- **SPECIFIC GRAVITY:** Determine at 25° by any reliable method (see *General Provisions*).
  Acceptance criteria: Between 0.865 and 0.886

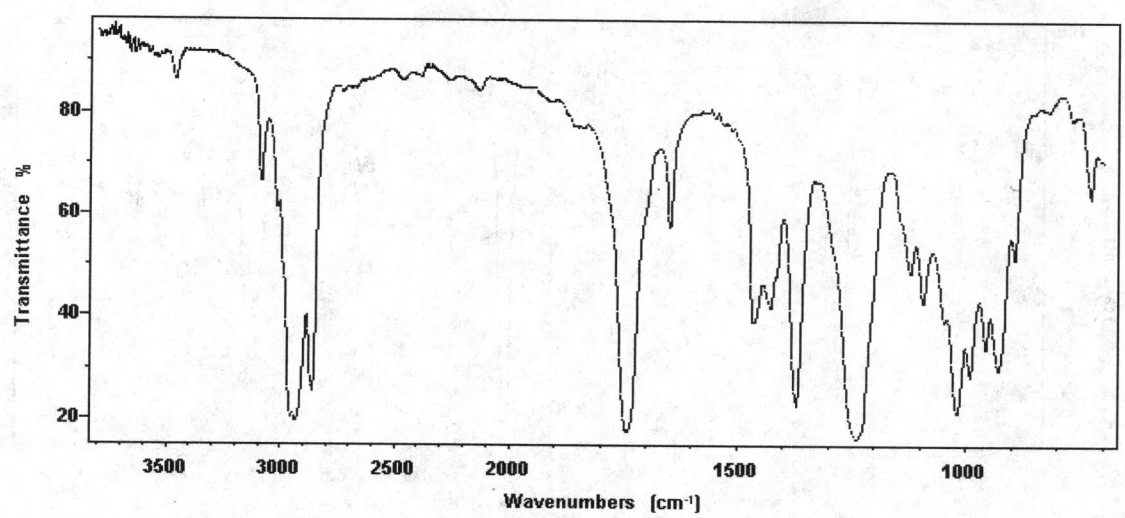

1-Octen-3-yl Acetate

1-Octen-3-yl Butyrate

First Published: Prior to FCC 6

$C_{12}H_{22}O_2$ Formula wt 198.31
FEMA: 3612
UNII: H8J989X4KJ [1-octen-3-yl butyrate]

DESCRIPTION
1-Octen-3-yl Butyrate occurs as an almost colorless liquid.
Odor: Metallic, mushroom
Solubility: Soluble in alcohol, most fixed oils; slightly soluble in propylene glycol; insoluble or practically insoluble in water
Boiling Point: ~225° to 229°
Solubility in Alcohol, Appendix VI: One mL dissolves in 1 mL of 95% ethanol.

Function: Flavoring agent

IDENTIFICATION
- **INFRARED SPECTRA,** Spectrophotometric Identification Tests, Appendix IIIC
  Acceptance criteria: The spectrum of the sample exhibits relative maxima at the same wavelengths as those of the spectrum below.

ASSAY
- **PROCEDURE:** Proceed as directed under M-1b, Appendix XI.
  Acceptance criteria: NLT 95.0% of $C_{12}H_{22}O_2$

SPECIFIC TESTS
- **REFRACTIVE INDEX,** Appendix II: At 20°
  Acceptance criteria: Between 1.423 and 1.433
- **SPECIFIC GRAVITY:** Determine at 25° by any reliable method (see General Provisions).
  Acceptance criteria: Between 0.859 and 0.880

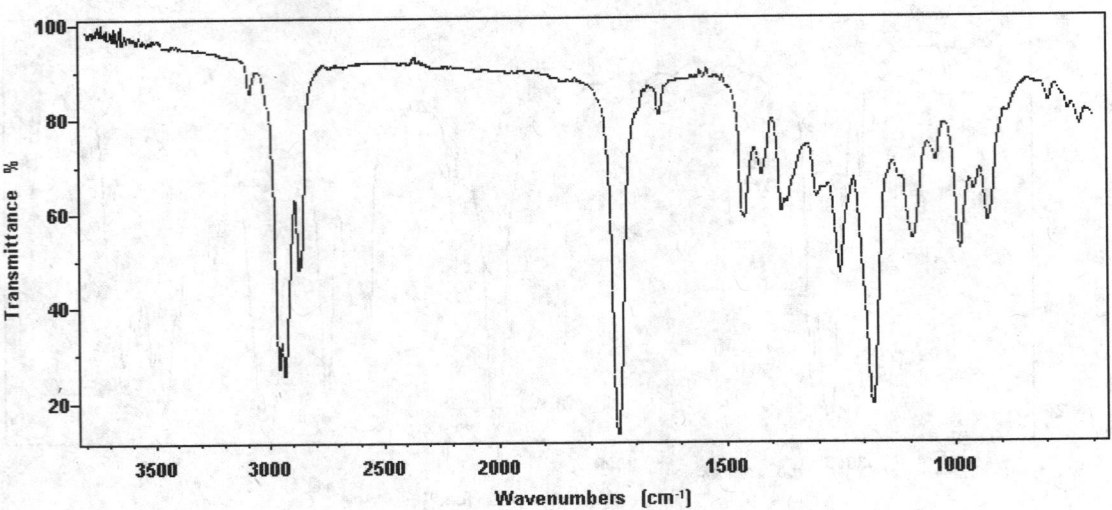

1-Octen-3-yl Butyrate

3-Octyl Acetate

First Published: Prior to FCC 6

$C_{10}H_{20}O_2$ Formula wt 172.27
FEMA: 3583
UNII: 8M41FR2J6W [3-octyl acetate]

DESCRIPTION
3-Octyl Acetate occurs as a colorless liquid.
Odor: Rosy-minty
Solubility: Soluble in alcohol, propylene glycol, most fixed oils; slightly soluble in water
Boiling Point: ~187°
Function: Flavoring agent

ASSAY
- **PROCEDURE:** Proceed as directed under *M-1b*, Appendix XI.
  Acceptance criteria: NLT 98.0% of $C_{10}H_{20}O_2$

SPECIFIC TESTS
- **ACID VALUE, FLAVOR CHEMICALS (OTHER THAN ESSENTIAL OILS),** *M-15,* Appendix XI
  Acceptance criteria: NMT 2.0
- **REFRACTIVE INDEX,** Appendix II: At 20°
  Acceptance criteria: Between 1.414 and 1.419
- **SPECIFIC GRAVITY:** Determine at 25° by any reliable method (see *General Provisions*).
  Acceptance criteria: Between 0.856 and 0.860

Octyl Acetate

First Published: Prior to FCC 6

$C_{10}H_{20}O_2$ Formula wt 172.27
FEMA: 2806
UNII: X0FN2J413S [octyl acetate]

DESCRIPTION
Octyl Acetate occurs as a colorless liquid.
Odor: Fruity, orange, jasmine
Solubility: Miscible in alcohol, most fixed oils, organic solvents; insoluble or practically insoluble in water
Boiling Point: ~208°
Solubility in Alcohol, Appendix VI: One mL dissolves in 4 mL of 70% alcohol to give a clear solution.
Function: Flavoring agent

IDENTIFICATION
- **INFRARED SPECTRA,** *Spectrophotometric Identification Tests,* Appendix IIIC
  Acceptance criteria: The spectrum of the sample exhibits relative maxima at the same wavelengths as those of the spectrum below.

ASSAY
- **PROCEDURE:** Proceed as directed under *M-1b,* Appendix XI.
  Acceptance criteria: NLT 98.0% of $C_{10}H_{20}O_2$

SPECIFIC TESTS
- **ACID VALUE, FLAVOR CHEMICALS (OTHER THAN ESSENTIAL OILS),** *M-15,* Appendix XI
  Acceptance criteria: NMT 1.0

- **REFRACTIVE INDEX,** Appendix II: At 20°
  Acceptance criteria: Between 1.418 and 1.421
- **SPECIFIC GRAVITY:** Determine at 25° by any reliable method (see *General Provisions*).
  Acceptance criteria: Between 0.865 and 0.868

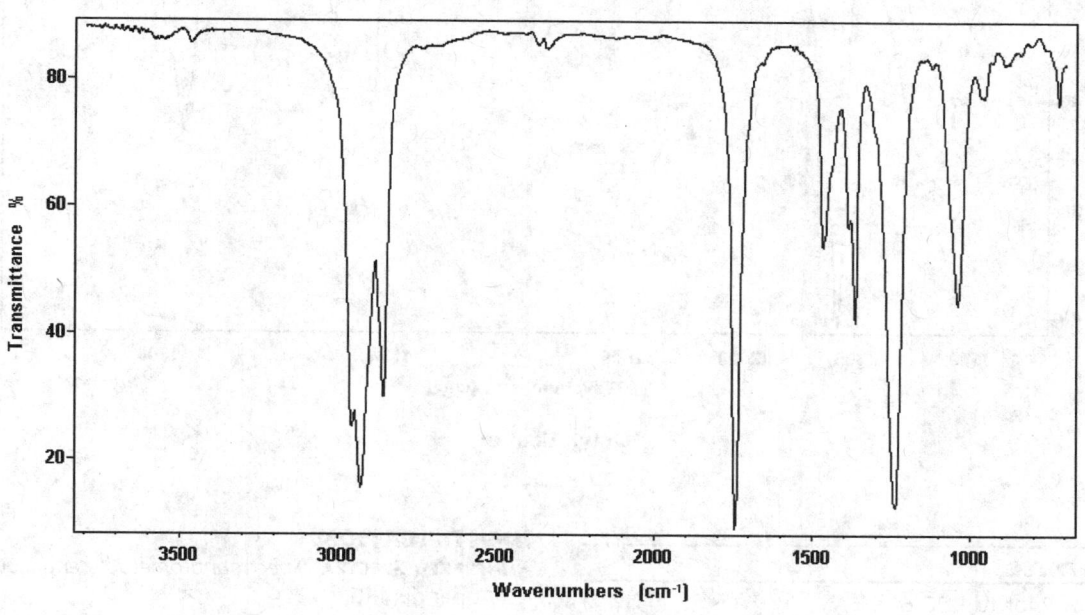

Octyl Acetate

Octyl Alcohol

First Published: Prior to FCC 6

Alcohol C-8
1-Octanol
Capryl Alcohol

$C_8H_{14}O$ Formula wt 130.23
FEMA: 2800
UNII: NV1779205D [caprylic alcohol]

DESCRIPTION
Octyl Alcohol occurs as a colorless liquid.
Odor: Sharp fatty-citrus
Solubility: Soluble in most fixed oils, propylene glycol; insoluble or practically insoluble in glycerin
Boiling Point: ~195°
Solubility in Alcohol, Appendix VI: One mL dissolves in 5 mL of 50% alcohol.

Function: Flavoring agent

IDENTIFICATION
- **INFRARED SPECTRA,** *Spectrophotometric Identification Tests,* Appendix IIIC
  Acceptance criteria: The spectrum of the sample exhibits relative maxima at the same wavelengths as those of the spectrum below.

ASSAY
- **PROCEDURE:** Proceed as directed under *M-1b*, Appendix XI.
  Acceptance criteria: NLT 98.0% of $C_8H_{18}O$

SPECIFIC TESTS
- **ACID VALUE, FLAVOR CHEMICALS (OTHER THAN ESSENTIAL OILS),** *M-15*, Appendix XI
  Acceptance criteria: NMT 1.0
- **REFRACTIVE INDEX,** Appendix II: At 20°
  Acceptance criteria: Between 1.428 and 1.431
- **SPECIFIC GRAVITY:** Determine at 25° by any reliable method (see *General Provisions*).
  Acceptance criteria: Between 0.822 and 0.830

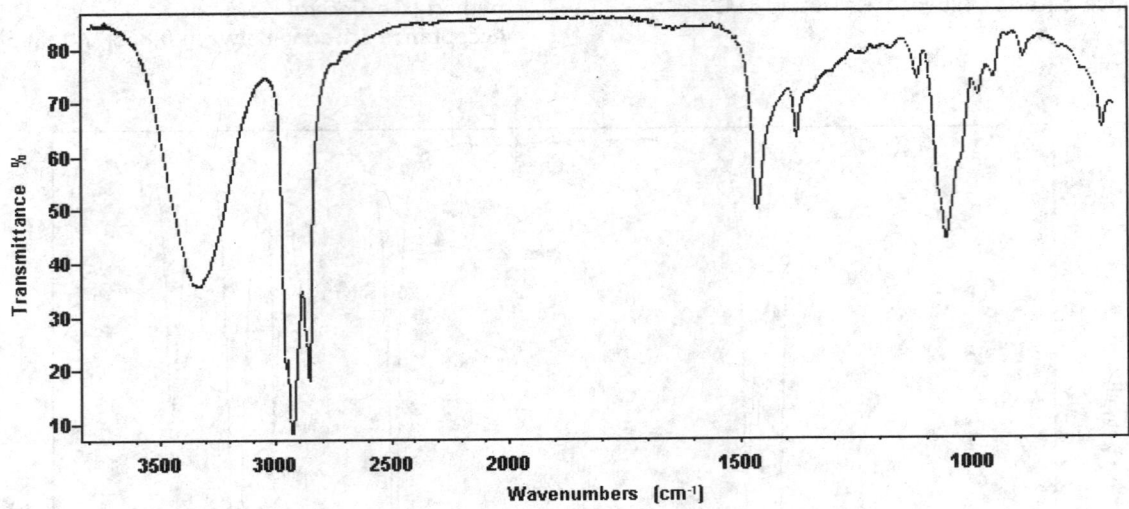

Octyl Alcohol

Octyl Formate

First Published: Prior to FCC 6

C₉H₁₈O₂
FEMA: 2809
UNII: 2XZ47CUU7G [octyl formate]

Formula wt 158.24

DESCRIPTION
Octyl Formate occurs as a colorless liquid.
Odor: Fruity
Solubility: Soluble in most fixed oils, mineral oil, propylene glycol; insoluble or practically insoluble in glycerin
Boiling Point: ~200°
Solubility in Alcohol, Appendix VI: One mL dissolves in 5 mL of 70% alcohol, and remains in solution on dilution to 10 mL.
Function: Flavoring agent

IDENTIFICATION
- **INFRARED SPECTRA,** *Spectrophotometric Identification Tests,* Appendix IIIC
  Acceptance criteria: The spectrum of the sample exhibits relative maxima at the same wavelengths as those of the spectrum below.

ASSAY
- **PROCEDURE:** Proceed as directed under *M-1b,* Appendix XI.
  Acceptance criteria: NLT 96.0% of C₉H₁₈O₂

SPECIFIC TESTS
- **ACID VALUE, FLAVOR CHEMICALS (OTHER THAN ESSENTIAL OILS),** *M-15,* Appendix XI
  Acceptance criteria: NMT 1.0
- **REFRACTIVE INDEX,** Appendix II: At 20°
  Acceptance criteria: Between 1.418 and 1.420
- **SPECIFIC GRAVITY:** Determine at 25° by any reliable method (see *General Provisions*).
  Acceptance criteria: Between 0.869 and 0.874

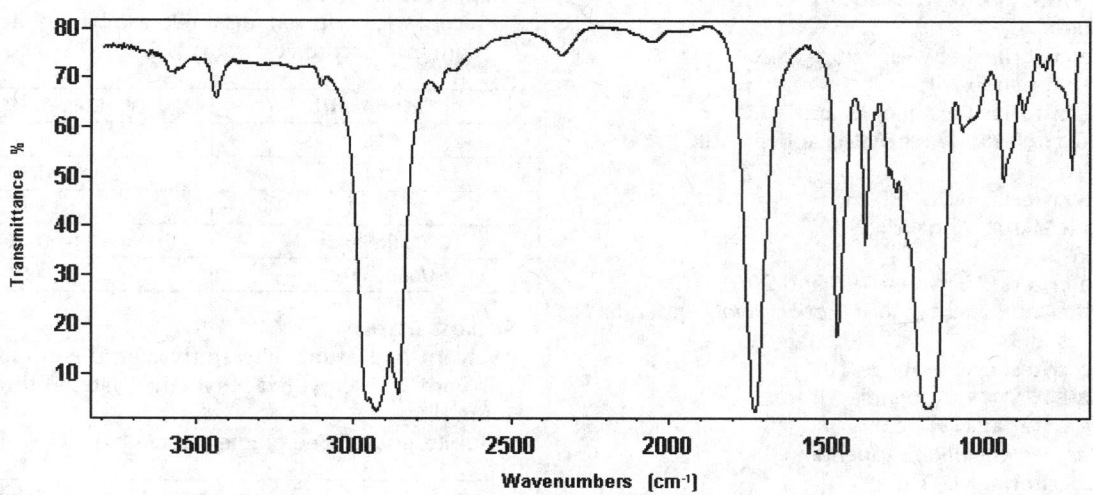

Octyl Formate

Octyl Isobutyrate

First Published: Prior to FCC 6

Octyl 2-Methylpropanoate

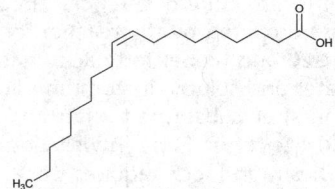

$C_{12}H_{24}O_2$ Formula wt 200.32
FEMA: 2808
UNII: T5819VWJ3T [octyl isobutyrate]

DESCRIPTION
Octyl Isobutyrate occurs as a colorless to pale yellow liquid.
Odor: Refreshing, herbaceous
Boiling Point: ~245°
Solubility in Alcohol, Appendix VI: One mL dissolves in 1 mL of 95% alcohol.
Function: Flavoring agent

ASSAY
- **Procedure:** Proceed as directed under *M-1a,* Appendix XI.
  Acceptance criteria: NLT 98.0% of $C_{12}H_{24}O_2$

SPECIFIC TESTS
- **Acid Value, Flavor Chemicals (Other Than Essential Oils),** *M-15,* Appendix XI
  Acceptance criteria: NMT 1.0
- **Refractive Index,** Appendix II: At 20°
  Acceptance criteria: Between 1.420 and 1.425
- **Specific Gravity:** Determine at 25° by any reliable method (see *General Provisions*).
  Acceptance criteria: Between 0.853 and 0.858

Oleic Acid

First Published: Prior to FCC 6

(Z)-9-Octadecenoic Acid

$C_{18}H_{34}O_2$ Formula wt 282.47
                                 CAS: [112-80-1]

UNII: 2UMI9U37CP [oleic acid]

DESCRIPTION
Oleic Acid occurs as a colorless to pale yellow, oily liquid when freshly prepared, but upon exposure to air it gradually absorbs oxygen and darkens. It is an unsaturated acid obtained from fats. When strongly heated in air, it decomposes and produces acrid vapors. Its specific gravity is about 0.895. It is practically insoluble in water, but is miscible with alcohol, with ether, and with fixed and volatile oils.
Function: Component in the manufacture of other food-grade additives; defoaming agent; lubricant; binder
Packaging and Storage: Store in tight containers.

IMPURITIES
Inorganic Impurities
- **Lead,** *Lead Limit Test, Atomic Absorption Spectrophotometric Graphite Furnace Method, Method II,* Appendix IIIB
  Acceptance criteria: NMT 0.1 mg/kg

SPECIFIC TESTS

- **ACID VALUE (FATS AND RELATED SUBSTANCES)**, *Method I*, Appendix VII
  Acceptance criteria: Between 196 and 204
- **IODINE VALUE**, Appendix VII
  Acceptance criteria: Between 83 and 103
- **RESIDUE ON IGNITION (SULFATED ASH)**, Appendix IIC
  Sample: 10 g
  Acceptance criteria: NMT 0.01%
- **SAPONIFICATION VALUE**, Appendix VII
  Sample: 3 g
  Acceptance criteria: Between 196 and 206
- **TITER (SOLIDIFICATION POINT)**, *Solidification Point*, Appendix IIB
  Acceptance criteria: Not above 10°
- **UNSAPONIFIABLE MATTER**, Appendix VII
  Acceptance criteria: NMT 2.0%
- **WATER**, *Water Determination*, Appendix IIB
  Acceptance criteria: NMT 0.4%

Olestra

First Published: Prior to FCC 6

UNII: 6742Y30KGK [olestra]

DESCRIPTION

Olestra occurs as a solid, soft gel, or liquid at room temperature depending on the fatty acids used in manufacture. It is a mixture of the octa-, hepta-, and hexa-esters of sucrose prepared by the reaction of sucrose with edible C12 to C20 and higher fatty acid methyl esters. It is insoluble in water and soluble in common lipid solvents.

Function: Calorie-free substitute for fats and oils
Packaging and Storage: Store in well-closed containers.
[NOTE—Use of Olestra in foods requires the addition of specific amounts of vitamins A, D, E, and K to these foods.]

IDENTIFICATION

- **FATTY ACID COMPOSITION**, Appendix VII
  [NOTE—Determine as directed using the following *Sample preparation* and *Chromatographic system*.]
  Sample preparation: Prepare as directed using 55 mg of sample per 10 mL.
  Chromatographic system, Appendix IIA
    Mode: Gas chromatography. [NOTE—Use a system suitable for headspace analysis with a capillary injection port and an integrator.]
    Detector: Flame ionization detector
    Column: 60-m × 0.25-mm (id) column, coated with a 0.20-μm layer of 2-cyanopropylpolysiloxane (Supelco SP-2340, or equivalent)
    Temperature
      Column: Set at 150°, heat at 1.3°/min to 225°, hold at 225° for 10 min
      Injection port: 210°
      Detector: 230°
    Linear velocity: 25 cm/s
    Injection volume: 0.1–1.0 μL
    Split ratio: 1:100
  Acceptance criteria: A sample exhibits the following composition profile of fatty acids:

Fatty Acid	Weight % (Range)
C12	NMT 1
C14	NMT 1
C16–18	NLT 78
C20 and longer	NMT 20
Unsaturated	25–83

- **SUCROSE ESTERS**
  Solvent A: Hexane, filtered through 0.2-μm filter
  Solvent B: Methyl-*tert*-butyl ether, filtered through 0.2-μm filter
  Mobile phase: See gradient table below.

Time (min)	Solvent A %	Solvent B %
0	95.2	4.8
5	84	16
8	75	25
10	50	50
12	0	100

  Standard solution: 10 mg/mL of olestra sample with known amounts of various esters (from Sigma Chemical, Nu-Chek-Prep, or equivalent), in *Solvent A*, filtered through a 0.5-μm filter
  Sample solution: 10 mg/mL in *Solvent A*, filtered through a 0.5-μm filter
  Chromatographic system, Appendix IIA
    Mode: High-performance liquid chromatography [NOTE—Use a system suitable for programmed gradient mobile phase delivery with an electronic integrator.]
    Detector: Evaporative light-scattering detector (Applied Chromatography Systems 750/14, or equivalent)
    Column: 80- × 4-mm (id), 5-μm silica Zorbax Reliance, or equivalent, normal phase column
    Column oven temperature: 37°
    Flow rate: 2 mL/min
    Injection volume: 20 μL
  System suitability
    Sample: *Standard solution*
    Suitability requirement: The results are within two standard deviations of the known values.
  Analysis: Inject the *Sample solution* into the chromatograph and record the resulting chromatogram. Identify the peaks for the octa-, hepta-, hexa-, and penta-esters in the chromatogram by comparison with the *Standard solution* chromatogram. Calculate the percentage of each ester, i, by the equation:

$$\% \text{ ester}_i = OA_i / \Sigma_{i=1}^{n} OA_i \times 100$$

OA_i = peak area of each individual ester in the chromatogram of the *Sample solution* that has a retention time corresponding to that of the same esters in the chromatogram of the *Standard solution*

Acceptance criteria: A sample exhibits the following typical distribution of sucrose esters (weight %) constrained by a minimum octa-ester content, a maximum lower ester content, and the hepta-ester as the remainder:

Octa-: NLT 70%
Hexa-: NMT 1%
Penta-: NMT 0.5%

ASSAY

- **PROCEDURE**

  Mobile phase: Tetrahydrofuran, filtered through a 0.2-μm filter

  Standard solution: 30 mg/mL of an olestra sample with a known amount of olestra monomer (from Sigma Chemical, Nu-Chek-Prep, or equivalent), in *Mobile phase*, filtered through a 0.5-μm filter

  Sample solution: 30 mg/mL in *Mobile phase*, filtered through a 0.5-μm filter

  Chromatographic system, Appendix IIA
    Mode: High-performance liquid chromatography
    Detector: Refractive index detector
    Column: 60-cm × 7.5-mm (id) column packed with 5-μm, 500Å porosity PL-Gel, or equivalent
    Temperature
      Column: 40°
      Detector: 40°
    Flow rate: 1 mL/min
    Injection volume: 20 μL
    Pressure: 500 to 1500 psi
    System suitability
      Sample: *Standard solution*
      Suitability requirement: The results are within two standard deviations of the known values.
  Analysis: Inject the *Sample solution* into the chromatograph and record the resulting chromatogram. Identify the peak for the olestra monomer in the *Standard solution* chromatogram. Calculate the percentage of olestra monomer, m, in the *Sample solution* by the formula:

  $$\text{Result} = 100(r_M/r_T)$$

  r_M = peak area of the olestra monomer in the chromatogram of the *Sample solution*
  r_T = sum of all peaks in the chromatogram of the *Sample solution* eluting in about 17.5 min

Acceptance criteria: NLT 97% of the combined octa-, hepta-, and hexa-esters of sucrose

IMPURITIES

Inorganic Impurities

- **LEAD,** *Lead Limit Test, Atomic Absorption Spectrophotometric Graphite Furnace Method, Method II,* Appendix IIIB
  Sample: 3 g
  Acceptance criteria: NMT 0.1 mg/kg

Organic Impurities

- **FREE FATTY ACIDS,** Appendix VII
  Analysis: Determine as directed using the following equivalence factor (e):
  Free fatty acids as oleic acid, e = 28.2
  Acceptance criteria: NMT 0.5%

- **METHANOL**
  Alkaline alumina: Mix 500 g of 60- to 200-mesh neutral alumina (Brockman Activity 1) with 166.5 g of a 40% potassium hydroxide solution contained in a 1-qt wide-mouth polypropylene jar by shaking vigorously until the alumina becomes uniform. Allow the mixture to equilibrate for 16 h before using.
  Internal standard solution: 1 mg/mL of butyl stearate (from Sigma Chemical, or equivalent) in hexane
  Standard solution: 40 mg/mL of methyl oleate (from Nu-Chek-Prep, or equivalent) in hexane
  Sample preparations: Prepare four 50-mL serum bottles. Pipet 2.0 mL of *Internal standard solution* into each bottle. Pipet 5.0, 10.0, and 20.0 μL of the *Standard solution*, equivalent to about 21.6, 43.2, and 86.3 μg of methanol, into three of the bottles, and evaporate the solvent at room temperature under nitrogen. Transfer 300 mg of sample into each of the four serum bottles. Heat the mixtures for about 5 min at 90°, and immediately add 5 g of the *Alkaline alumina*. Mix, cap each serum bottle with a Teflon-backed rubber septum, and hold at 70.0° for 3 h.
  Chromatographic system, Appendix IIA
    Mode: Gas chromatography. [NOTE—Use a system suitable for headspace analysis.]
    Detector: Flame ionization detector
    Column: 1.8-m × 2-mm (id) column packed with 100- to 120-mesh styrene-divinyl copolymer (Chromosorb 101, or equivalent)
    Temperature
      Column: Hold at 100° for 2 min then heat at 10°/min to 195°
      Injection port: 225°
      Detector: 225°
    Injection volume: 3 mL
  Analysis: Using a 5-mL gas-tight syringe, withdraw 3.0 mL of the headspace from the serum bottles for the *Standard solution* and the four *Sample preparations*, inject into the chromatograph, and record the resulting chromatograms. Measure the peak areas for methanol and butanol. [NOTE—Methanol and butanol elute at about 3 and 10 min, respectively.]
  Prepare a standard addition plot of the ratio of peak area responses of methanol to that of the *Internal standard solution* versus the amount, in μg, of methanol in each of the four *Sample preparations*.

828 / Olestra / Monographs

Calculate the quantity, in mg/kg, of methanol in the sample taken by the formula:

$$\text{Result} = 3.3 \times A$$

A = amount of methanol (μg) determined from the standard addition plot

Acceptance criteria: NMT 300 mg/kg

SPECIFIC TESTS

- **PEROXIDE VALUE,** Appendix VII
  Sample: 10 g
  Analysis: To the *Sample*, add 30 mL of a 3:2 mixture of glacial acetic acid:chloroform and mix. Add 1 mL of a saturated solution of potassium iodide and mix for 1 min. Immediately add 100 mL of water and begin titrating with 0.05 N sodium thiosulfate, adding starch TS as the endpoint is approached. Continue the titration until the blue starch color has just disappeared. Perform a blank determination (see *General Provisions*), and make any necessary correction.
  Calculate the peroxide value, as mEq of peroxide per kg of sample, by the formula:

  $$\text{Result} = [S \times N \times 1000]/W$$

  S = net volume (mL) of sodium thiosulfate solution required for the sample
  N = exact normality of the sodium thiosulfate solution
  W = weight of the sample (g) taken
  Acceptance criteria: NMT 10 mEq/kg

- **RESIDUE ON IGNITION (SULFATED ASH),** Appendix IIC
  Sample: 5 g
  Acceptance criteria: NMT 0.5%

- **THIXOTROPHY (STIFFNESS)**
  Sample preparation: Prepare samples in quadruplicate. Transfer 8.0 g of sample into a 57-mm aluminum pan. Heat the sample to above 113° until completely liquid, then temper it by cooling to 29° with agitation. The controlled cooling rate should follow the profile shown within 8° at each time noted:

Time (min)	Temperature
0	113
30	70
60	49
90	40
120	35
150	33
180	29

  Hold the sample at 21° for 7 days.
  Apparatus: Use a suitable cone and plate rheometer [Contraves Rheomat 115A (cone CP-6), Physica Rheolab MC 100 (cone MK23), or equivalent] maintained at 37.8° and capable of measuring the non-Newtonian flow curve hysteresis for ascending and descending shear rates programmed from 0 to 800 s^{-1}. Hold the rheometer at 0 s^{-1} for 120 s, raise it to 800 s^{-1} in 7.5 min, hold for 1 s, then decrease to 0 s^{-1} in 7.5 min to measure the thixotropic area. Check the accuracy of the rheometer with viscosity standards (Cannon ASTM Certified Viscosity Standards, S-2000 and N-350, or equivalent). The measured viscosity must be within 0.20% of the stated viscosity at 37.8°, or the rheometer's cone factor must be recalculated.
  Analysis: Place a sufficient amount of the *Sample preparation* on the rheometer plate to fill the gap between the plate and cone. Measure the thixotropic area. The relative standard deviation of the mean area for the four replicate samples must be within 15% or the *Sample preparation* must be repeated.
  Acceptance criteria: NLT 50 kPa/s

- **WATER,** *Water Determination,* Appendix IIB
  Analysis: Determine as directed, however, in place of 35 to 40 mL of methanol, use 30 mL of chloroform followed by 10 mL of methanol to dissolve the sample.
  Acceptance criteria: NMT 0.1%

Olibanum Oil

First Published: Prior to FCC 6

Oil of Frankincense

CAS: [8016-36-2]

UNII: 67ZYA5T02K [frankincense oil]

DESCRIPTION

Olibanum Oil occurs as a pale yellow liquid with a balsamic odor with a faint lemon note. It is the volatile oil distilled from a gum obtained from the tree *Boswellia carterii* Birdw. and other *Boswellia* species (Fam. Burseraceae). It is soluble in most fixed oils and, with a slight haze, in mineral oil. It is insoluble in glycerin and in propylene glycol.

Function: Flavoring agent

Packaging and Storage: Store in a cool place protected from light in full, tight containers that are made from steel or aluminum and that are suitably lined.

IDENTIFICATION

- **INFRARED SPECTRA,** *Spectrophotometric Identification Tests,* Appendix IIIC
  Acceptance criteria: The spectrum of the sample exhibits relative maxima at the same wavelengths as those of the spectrum below.

SPECIFIC TESTS

- **ACID VALUE (ESSENTIAL OILS AND FLAVORS),** Appendix VI
  Acceptance criteria: NMT 4.0
- **ANGULAR ROTATION,** *Optical (Specific) Rotation,* Appendix IIB: Use a 100-mm tube.
  Acceptance criteria: Between −15° and +35°
- **ESTER VALUE,** *Esters,* Appendix VI
  Sample: 5 g
  Acceptance criteria: Between 4 and 40

- **REFRACTIVE INDEX,** Appendix IIB
  [NOTE—Use an Abbé or other refractometer of equal or greater accuracy.]
  Acceptance criteria: Between 1.465 and 1.482 at 20°

- **SOLUBILITY IN ALCOHOL,** Appendix VI
  Acceptance criteria: One mL of sample dissolves in 6 mL of 90% alcohol, occasionally with opalescence.
- **SPECIFIC GRAVITY:** Determine by any reliable method (see *General Provisions*).
  Acceptance criteria: Between 0.862 and 0.889

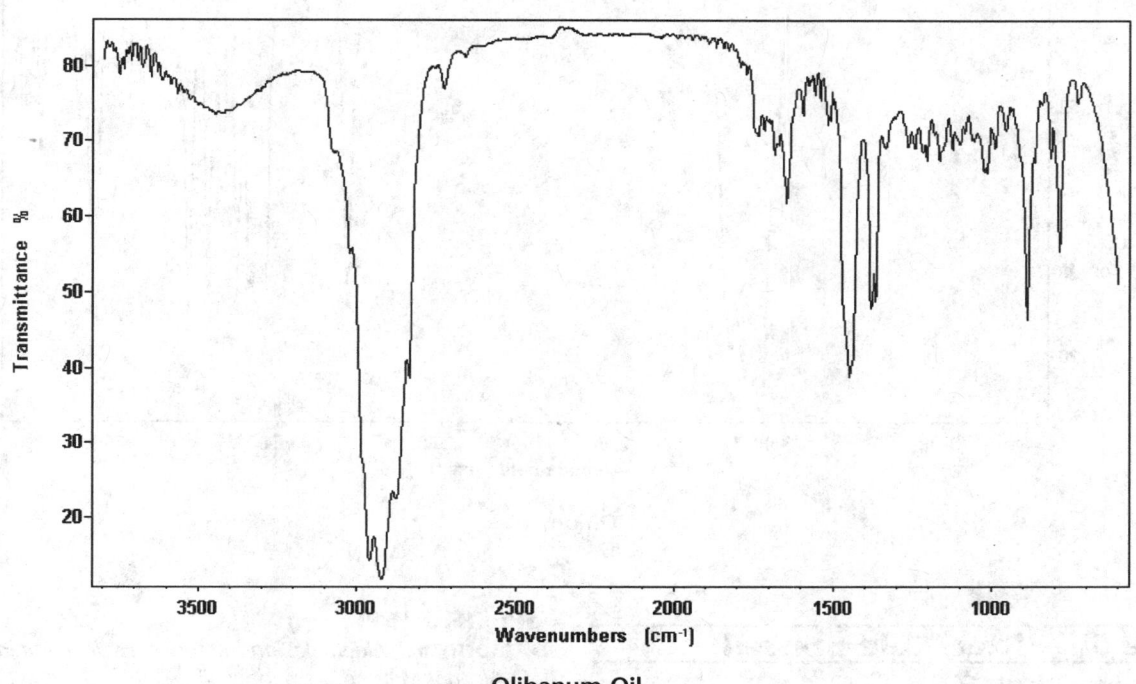

Olibanum Oil

Onion Oil
First Published: Prior to FCC 6

CAS: [8002-72-0]
UNII: 4P3VLD98FL [onion oil]

DESCRIPTION
Onion Oil occurs as a clear, amber yellow to amber orange liquid with a strong, pungent odor and taste characteristic of onion. It is the volatile oil obtained by steam distillation of the bulbs of *Allium cepa* L. (Fam. Liliaceae). It is soluble in most fixed oils, in mineral oil, and in alcohol. It is insoluble in glycerin and in propylene glycol.
Function: Flavoring agent
Packaging and Storage: Store in a cool place protected from light in full, tight containers that are made from steel or aluminum and that are suitably lined.

IDENTIFICATION
- **INFRARED SPECTRA,** *Spectrophotometric Identification Tests,* Appendix IIIC
  Acceptance criteria: The spectrum of the sample exhibits relative maxima at the same wavelengths as those of the spectrum below.

SPECIFIC TESTS
- **REFRACTIVE INDEX,** Appendix IIB
  [NOTE—Use an Abbé or other refractometer of equal or greater accuracy.]
  Acceptance criteria: Between 1.549 and 1.570 at 20°
- **SPECIFIC GRAVITY:** Determine by any reliable method (see *General Provisions*).
  Acceptance criteria: Between 1.050 and 1.135

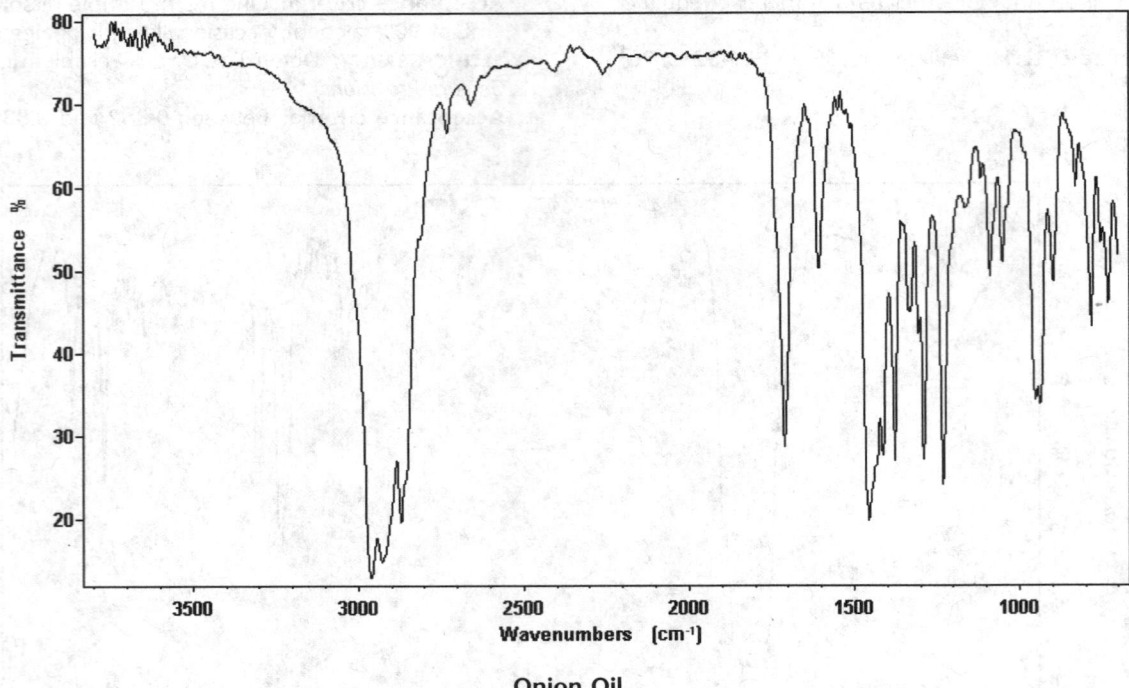

Onion Oil

Orange Oil, Bitter, Cold-pressed

First Published: Prior to FCC 6

UNII: 9TLV70SV6I [bitter orange oil]

DESCRIPTION
Orange Oil, Bitter, Cold-pressed, occurs as a pale yellow or yellow-brown liquid with the characteristic aromatic odor of the Seville orange and an aromatic, somewhat bitter taste. It is the volatile oil obtained by expression, without the use of heat, from the fresh peel of the fruit of *Citrus aurantium* L. (Fam. Rutaceae). It is miscible with absolute alcohol and with an equal volume of glacial acetic acid. It is soluble in fixed oils and in mineral oil. It is slightly soluble in propylene glycol, but it is relatively insoluble in glycerin. It is affected by light, and its alcohol solutions are neutral to litmus. It may contain a suitable antioxidant.

Function: Flavoring agent

Packaging and Storage: Store in a cool place protected from light in full, tight containers that are made from steel or aluminum and that are suitably lined.

IDENTIFICATION
- **INFRARED SPECTRA,** *Spectrophotometric Identification Tests,* Appendix IIIC
  Acceptance criteria: The spectrum of the sample exhibits relative maxima at the same wavelengths as those of the spectrum below.

SPECIFIC TESTS
- **ALDEHYDES,** *Aldehydes and Ketones, Hydroxylamine tert-Butyl Alcohol Method,* Appendix VI
  Sample: 10 g
  Analysis: Before titrating, allow the mixture to stand for 30 min at room temperature. Use 78.14 as the equivalence factor (e) in the calculation.
  Acceptance criteria: NLT 0.5% and NMT 1.0% of aldehydes, calculated as decyl aldehyde ($C_{10}H_{20}O$)
- **ANGULAR ROTATION,** *Optical (Specific) Rotation,* Appendix IIB: Use a 100-mm tube.
  Acceptance criteria: Between +88° and +98°
- **REFRACTIVE INDEX,** Appendix IIB
  [NOTE—Use an Abbé or other refractometer of equal or greater accuracy.]
  Acceptance criteria: Between 1.472 and 1.476 at 20°
- **RESIDUE ON EVAPORATION,** Appendix VI
  Sample: 5 g
  Analysis: Heat for 4.5 h
  Acceptance criteria: Between 2.0% and 5.0%
- **SPECIFIC GRAVITY:** Determine by any reliable method (see *General Provisions*).
  Acceptance criteria: Between 0.845 and 0.851

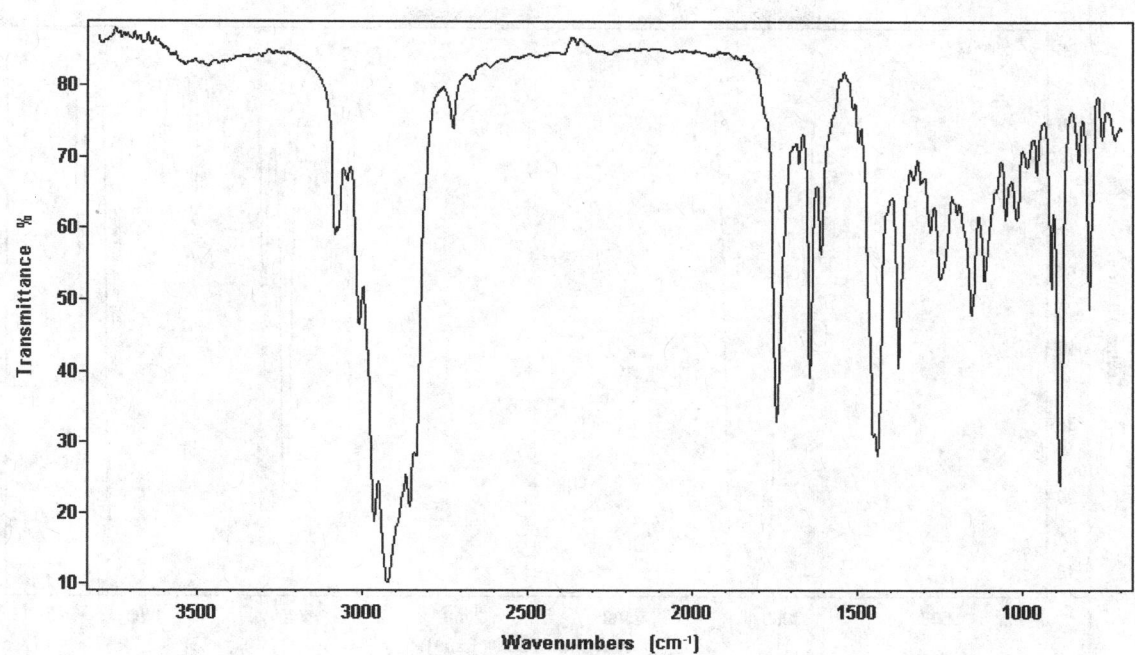

Orange Oil, Bitter, Cold-pressed

Orange Oil, Cold-pressed

First Published: Prior to FCC 6

Sweet Orange Oil

CAS: [8028-48-6]

UNII: AKN3KSD11B [orange oil]

DESCRIPTION
Orange Oil, Cold-pressed occurs as an intensely yellow, orange, or deep orange liquid with the characteristic odor and taste of the outer part of fresh, sweet orange peel. It is the volatile oil obtained by expression, without the use of heat, from the fresh peel of the ripe fruit of *Citrus sinensis* L. Osbeck (Fam. Rutaceae). It is miscible with dehydrated alcohol and with carbon disulfide. It is soluble in glacial acetic acid. It may contain a suitable antioxidant. [NOTE—Do not use Orange Oil, Cold-pressed that has a terebinthine odor.]

Function: Flavoring agent

Packaging and Storage: Store in a cool place protected from light in full, tight containers that are made from steel or aluminum and that are suitably lined.

IDENTIFICATION
- **INFRARED SPECTRA**, *Spectrophotometric Identification Tests,* Appendix IIIC
  Acceptance criteria: The spectrum of the sample exhibits relative maxima at the same wavelengths as those of the spectrum below.

ASSAY
- **ALDEHYDES**, *Aldehydes and Ketones, Hydroxylamine tert-Butyl Alcohol Method,* Appendix VI
  Sample: 10 g
  Analysis: Before titrating, allow the mixture to stand for 15 min, shaking the flask occasionally. Use 78.14 as the equivalence factor (e) in the calculation.
  Acceptance criteria: NLT 1.2% and NMT 2.5% of aldehydes, calculated as decyl aldehyde ($C_{10}H_{20}O$)

SPECIFIC TESTS
- **ANGULAR ROTATION**, *Optical (Specific) Rotation,* Appendix IIB: Use a 100-mm tube.
  Acceptance criteria: Between +94° and +99°
- **REFRACTIVE INDEX**, Appendix IIB
  [NOTE—Use an Abbé or other refractometer of equal or greater accuracy.]
  Acceptance criteria: Between 1.472 and 1.474 at 20°
- **SPECIFIC GRAVITY:** Determine by any reliable method (see *General Provisions*).
  Acceptance criteria: Between 0.842 and 0.846
- **ULTRAVIOLET ABSORBANCE**, *Ultraviolet Absorbance of Citrus Oils,* Appendix VI
  Sample: 250 mg
  Acceptance criteria: [NOTE—The absorbance maximum occurs at 330 ± 3 nm.]
  California type: NLT 0.130
  Florida type: NLT 0.240

OTHER REQUIREMENTS
- **LABELING:** Indicate whether the oil is the California or Florida type.

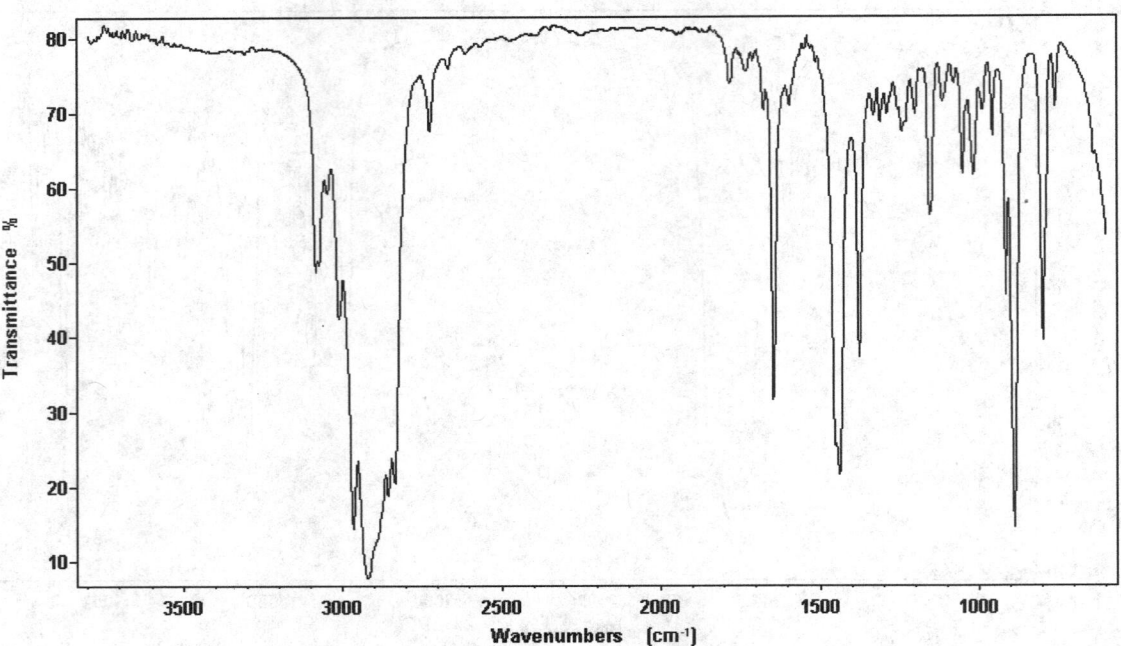

Orange Oil, Cold-pressed

Orange Oil, Distilled

First Published: Prior to FCC 6

UNII: H4QNH2ZN7A [orange oil, expressed]

DESCRIPTION
Orange Oil, Distilled occurs as a colorless to pale yellow liquid with a mild citrus floral odor. It is the volatile oil obtained by distillation from the fresh peel or juice of the fruit of *Citrus sinensis* L. Osbeck (Fam. Rutaceae), with or without the previous separation of the juice, pulp, or peel. It is soluble in most fixed oils, in mineral oil, and in alcohol (with haze). It is insoluble in glycerin and in propylene glycol. It may contain a suitable antioxidant.
Function: Flavoring agent
Packaging and Storage: Store in a cool place protected from light in full, tight containers.

IDENTIFICATION
- **INFRARED SPECTRA,** *Spectrophotometric Identification Tests,* Appendix IIIC
  Acceptance criteria: The spectrum of the sample exhibits relative maxima at the same wavelengths as those of the spectrum below.

SPECIFIC TESTS
- **ALDEHYDES,** *Aldehydes and Ketones, Hydroxylamine tert-Butyl Alcohol Method,* Appendix VI
  Sample: 5 mL
  Analysis: Before titrating, allow the mixture to stand for 1 h at room temperature. Use 78.14 as the equivalence factor (e) in the calculation.
  Acceptance criteria: NLT 1.0% and NMT 2.5% of aldehydes, calculated as decyl aldehyde ($C_{10}H_{20}O$)
- **ANGULAR ROTATION,** *Optical (Specific) Rotation,* Appendix IIB: Use a 100-mm tube.
  Acceptance criteria: Between +94° and +99°
- **REFRACTIVE INDEX,** Appendix IIB
  [NOTE—Use an Abbé or other refractometer of equal or greater accuracy.]
  Acceptance criteria: Between 1.471 and 1.474 at 20°
- **SPECIFIC GRAVITY:** Determine by any reliable method (see *General Provisions*).
  Acceptance criteria: Between 0.840 and 0.844
- **ULTRAVIOLET ABSORBANCE,** *Ultraviolet Absorbance of Citrus Oils,* Appendix VI
  Sample: 250 mg
  Acceptance criteria: The difference in absorbance is NMT 0.01. [NOTE—The absorbance maximum occurs at 330 ± 3 nm.]

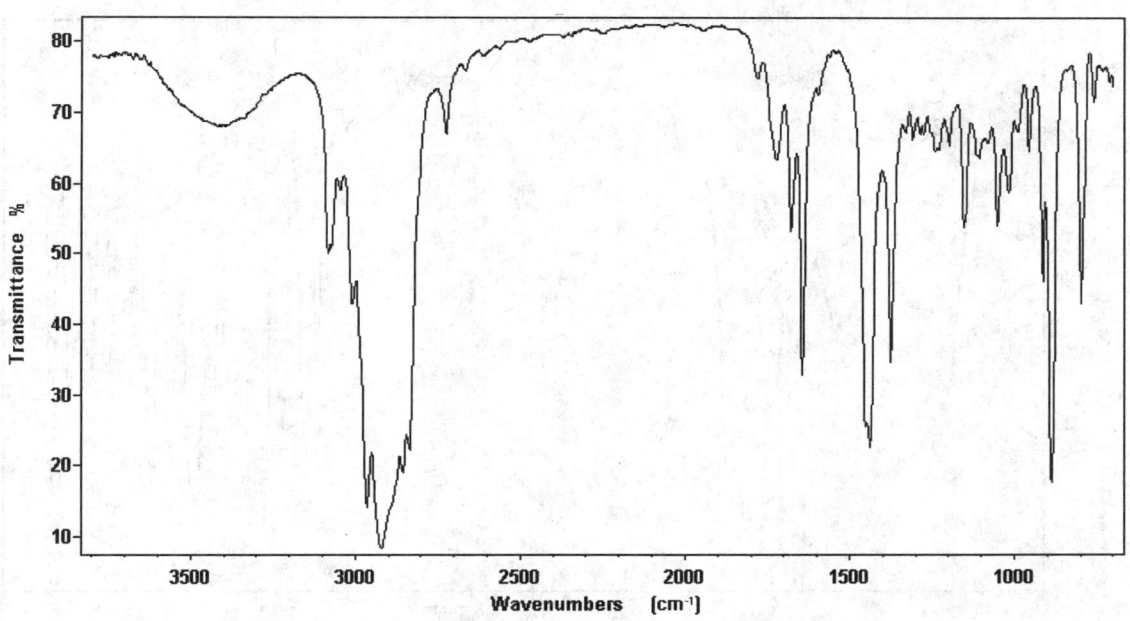

Orange Oil, Distilled

Origanum Oil, Spanish Type
First Published: Prior to FCC 6

UNII: 39736Z7Q8W [origanum oil] CAS: [8007-11-2]

DESCRIPTION
Origanum Oil, Spanish Type, occurs as a yellow-red to a dark, brown-red liquid with a pungent, spicy odor suggestive of thyme oil. It is the volatile oil obtained by steam distillation from the flowering herb *Thymus capitatus* Hoffm. et Link and various species of *Origanum* (Fam. Labiatae). It is soluble in most fixed oils and in propylene glycol. It is soluble, with turbidity, in mineral oil, but it is insoluble in glycerin.
Function: Flavoring agent
Packaging and Storage: Store in a cool place protected from light in full, tight containers that are made from steel or aluminum and that are suitably lined.

IDENTIFICATION
- **INFRARED SPECTRA,** *Spectrophotometric Identification Tests,* Appendix IIIC
  Acceptance criteria: The spectrum of the sample exhibits relative maxima at the same wavelengths as those of the spectrum below.

ASSAY
- **PHENOLS,** Appendix VI
  Sample: Pretreat by shaking a suitable quantity with 2% powdered tartaric acid and filtering.
  Acceptance criteria: NLT 60.0% and NMT 75.0%, by volume, of phenols

SPECIFIC TESTS
- **ANGULAR ROTATION,** *Optical (Specific) Rotation,* Appendix IIB: Use a 100-mm tube. [NOTE—Occasionally the oil is too dark to read in a 100-mm tube.]
  Acceptance criteria: Between −2° and +3°
- **REFRACTIVE INDEX,** Appendix IIB
  [NOTE—Use an Abbé or other refractometer of equal or greater accuracy.]
  Acceptance criteria: Between 1.506 and 1.512 at 20°
- **SOLUBILITY IN ALCOHOL,** Appendix VI
  Acceptance criteria: One mL of sample is soluble in 2 mL of 70% alcohol. The solution may become cloudy on dilution.
- **SPECIFIC GRAVITY:** Determine by any reliable method (see *General Provisions*).
  Acceptance criteria: Between 0.935 and 0.960

834 / Origanum Oil, Spanish Type / *Monographs*

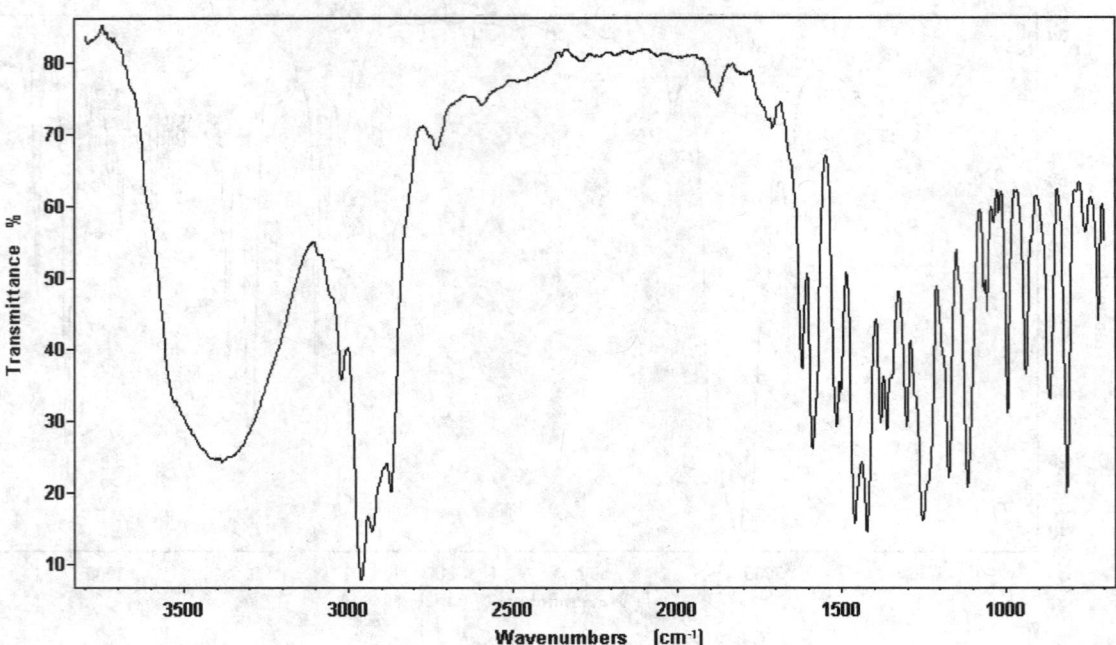

Origanum Oil, Spanish Type

Orris Root Oil

First Published: Prior to FCC 6

UNII: C60YYT168M [orris root oil]

DESCRIPTION
Orris Root Oil occurs as a light yellow to brown-yellow mass at room temperature and melts to form a yellow to yellow-brown liquid. It is the volatile oil obtained by steam distillation from the peeled, dried, and aged rhizomes of *Iris pallida* Lam. (Fam. Iridaceae). It is soluble in most fixed oils, in mineral oil, and in propylene glycol. It is insoluble in glycerin.

Function: Flavoring agent

Packaging and Storage: Store in a cool place protected from light in full, tight containers that are made from steel or aluminum and that are suitably lined.

IDENTIFICATION
- **INFRARED SPECTRA,** *Spectrophotometric Identification Tests,* Appendix IIIC

  Acceptance criteria: The spectrum of the sample exhibits relative maxima at the same wavelengths as those of the spectrum below.

ASSAY
- **KETONES,** *Aldehydes,* Appendix VI

  Sample: 1 g

  Analysis: Before titrating, allow the mixture to stand for 1 h at room temperature. Use 103.2 as the equivalence factor (e) in the calculation.

  Acceptance criteria: NLT 9.0% and NMT 20.0% of ketones, calculated as irone ($C_{14}H_{22}O$)

SPECIFIC TESTS
- **ACID VALUE (ESSENTIAL OILS AND FLAVORS),** Appendix VI

  Sample: 1 g

  Acceptance criteria: Between 175 and 235
- **ESTERS,** *Ester Value,* Appendix VI

  Sample: 1 g

  Acceptance criteria: Between 4 and 35
- **MELTING RANGE,** *Melting Range or Temperature Determination, Procedure for Class II,* Appendix IIB

  Acceptance criteria: Between 38° and 50°

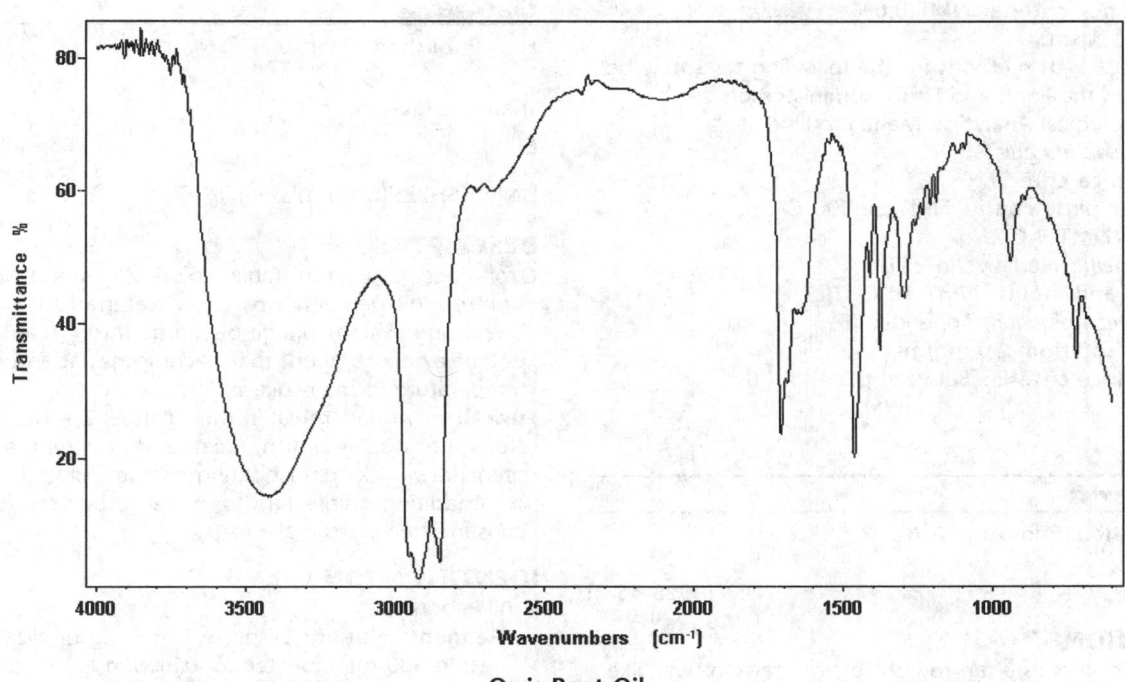

Orris Root Oil

Ox Bile Extract

First Published: Prior to FCC 6

Sodium Choleate
Purified Oxgall

$C_{24}H_{39}NaO_5$ Formula wt 430.56 (as sodium choleate)
UNII: ET3651ZLOU [bos taurus bile]

DESCRIPTION
Ox Bile Extract occurs as a yellow-green powder. It contains ox bile acids, chiefly glycocholic and taurocholic, as sodium salts, equivalent to not less than 45.0% cholic acid, $C_{24}H_{40}O_5$. It is the purified portion of the bile of an ox, obtained by evaporating the alcohol extract of concentrated bile. It is soluble in water and in alcohol.
Function: Surfactant
Packaging and Storage: Store in tight containers.

IDENTIFICATION
- **A. Sodium,** Appendix IIIA
  Acceptance criteria: Passes tests
- **B. Procedure**
  Sample solution: 100 mg/mL in alcohol
  Analysis: Add 0.5 mL of iodine TS to the *Sample solution*.
  Acceptance criteria: A blue color develops.

ASSAY
- **Procedure**
  Standard solution: 0.5 mg/mL USP Cholic Acid RS in 60% acetic acid. [Note—When stored in a refrigerator, this solution may be used over several months.]
  Sample solution: Dissolve 50 mg of sample in 100 mL of 60% acetic acid and mix. After preparing, filter the solution and discard the first 10 mL of the filtrate.
  Analysis: Transfer 1.0 mL each of the *Standard solution* and the *Sample solution* into separate containers. Add 1.0 mL of a freshly prepared 1:100 furfural solution to each container. Cool the containers in an ice bath for 5 min. Add 13 mL of a dilute sulfuric acid solution, prepared by cautiously mixing 50 mL of sulfuric acid with 65 mL of water. Thoroughly mix the contents in each container, and place them for 10 min in a water bath maintained at 70°. Immediately place the containers in an ice bath for 2 min. Determine the absorbance of each solution in a 1-cm cell at the wavelength of maximum absorbance at about 650 nm. Calculate the quantity (mg) of cholic acid in the sample taken by the formula:

$$\text{Result} = 100C\,(A_U/A_S)$$

C = concentration (mg/mL) of USP Cholic Acid RS in the *Standard solution*
A_U = absorbance at 650 nm of the *Sample solution*
A_S = absorbance at 650 nm of the *Standard solution*

Acceptance criteria: NLT 45.0% of cholic acid ($C_{24}H_{40}O_5$)

SPECIFIC TESTS
- **Ash (Total),** Appendix IIC
  Acceptance criteria: NMT 10.0%

- **Loss on Drying,** Appendix IIC: 105° for 16 h
  Acceptance criteria: NMT 6.0%
- **Microbial Limits**
  [NOTE—Current methods for the following tests may be found in the Food and Drug Administration's Bacteriological Analytical Manual online at www.cfsan.fda.gov.]
  Acceptance criteria
    Aerobic plate count: NMT 20,000 CFU/g
    E. coli: NMT 3 CFU/g
    Salmonella: Negative in 25 g
    Yeasts and molds: NMT 10 CFU/g
- **pH,** *pH Determination,* Appendix IIB
  Sample solution: 50 mg/mL
  Acceptance criteria: Between 6.3 and 7.0

Oxystearin

First Published: Prior to FCC 6

INS: 387   CAS: [8028-45-3]

DESCRIPTION
Oxystearin occurs as a tan to light brown, fatty or wax-like substance. It is a mixture of the glycerides of partially oxidized stearic and other fatty acids. It is soluble in ether, in hexane, and in chloroform.
Function: Crystallization inhibitor in salad and cooking oils; sequestrant; defoaming agent
Packaging and Storage: Store in well-closed containers.

IMPURITIES
Inorganic Impurities
- **Lead,** *Lead Limit Test, Flame Atomic Absorption Spectrophotometric Method,* Appendix IIIB
  Sample: 10 g
  Acceptance criteria: NMT 2 mg/kg

SPECIFIC TESTS
- **Acid Value (Fats and Related Substances),** Method II, Appendix VII
  Acceptance criteria: NMT 15
- **Hydroxyl Value,** Method II, Appendix VII
  Sample: 5 g
  Acceptance criteria: Between 30 and 45
- **Iodine Value,** Appendix VII
  Acceptance criteria: NMT 15
- **Refractive Index,** Appendix IIB
  Analysis: Determine at 48° with an Abbé or butyro refractometer, using a melted sample filtered through filter paper.
  Acceptance criteria: Between 59 and 61 at 48° on the butyro scale (equivalent to 1.465 to 1.467 on the Abbé scale)
- **Saponification Value,** Appendix VII
  Sample: 3 g
  Acceptance criteria: Between 225 and 240
- **Unsaponifiable Matter,** Appendix VII
  Acceptance criteria: NMT 0.8%

Ozone

First Published: Prior to FCC 6

Triatomic Oxygen

O_3 Formula wt 48.00
          CAS: [10028-15-6]
UNII: 66H7ZZK23N [ozone]

DESCRIPTION
Ozone occurs as an unstable, colorless gas. It is produced *in situ* from oxygen either by ultraviolet irradiation of air or by passing a high-voltage discharge through air. It is a potent oxidizing agent that decomposes at ambient temperature to molecular oxygen.
Function: Antimicrobial in the treatment, processing, and storage or display of fish, meat, and poultry and in preparing, packing, or holding raw agricultural commodities; disinfectant for water to be used for direct consumption or to make ice.

IDENTIFICATION
- **A. Procedure**
  Reagent solution: Disperse 124.5 mg of alizarin violet 3R in 500 mL of water contained in a 1-L volumetric flask. Mechanically stir overnight. Add 20 mg of sodium hexametaphosphate, 48.5 g of ammonium chloride, and 6.2 mL of ammonium hydroxide (equivalent to 1.6 g of NH_3). Dilute to volume with water, and stir overnight. [NOTE—A 10-fold aqueous dilution of this solution in a 1-cm cell has an absorbance of 0.155 at 548 nm. The pH of dilutions with sample waters is between 8.1 and 8.5.]
  Sample: Ozonated water
  Blank: Ozone-free water
  Analysis: Introduce 20 mL of the *Reagent solution* into each of two 200-mL volumetric flasks. Fill one flask with the *Blank.* Fill the other with the *Sample* by directly introducing it, with the aid of a long-stemmed funnel or pipet, below the surface of the *Reagent solution* to prevent ozone loss by degassing. Immediately mix and measure the absorbance of both solutions at 548 nm, using 1- to 5-cm cells.
  Acceptance criteria: Ozone is present if the solution of the *Sample* has a lower absorbance than the *Blank* solution.

ASSAY
- **Procedure**
  Indigo stock solution: Dissolve 0.770 g of potassium indigotrisulfonate in 500 mL of water and 1 mL of phosphoric acid in a 1-L volumetric flask, dilute to volume with water, and mix. [NOTE—A 1:100 dilution of this reagent has an absorbance of 0.20 ± 0.010 cm^{-1} at 600 nm.]
  Indigo reagent I: Just before use, transfer 20 mL of *Indigo stock solution*, 10 g of monobasic sodium phosphate, and 7 mL of phosphoric acid in water, into a 1-L volumetric flask, dilute to volume with water, and mix.

Indigo reagent II: Prepare as directed for *Indigo reagent I*, using 100 mL of *Indigo stock solution* instead of 20 mL.
Malonic acid reagent: 50 mg/mL
Sample: Ozonated water
Blank: Ozone-free water
Analysis
  Ozone concentrations of 0.01 to 0.1 mg/L: Add 10.0 mL of *Indigo reagent I* to each of two 100-mL flasks. If chlorine is present in the *Sample* or *Blank*, add 1 mL of *Malonic acid reagent* to both flasks. Fill one flask with the *Blank*. Fill the other with the *Sample* (nominally 90 mL) by directly introducing it, with the aid of a long-stemmed funnel or pipet, below the surface of the dye solution to prevent ozone loss by degassing.
  Immediately mix and measure the absorbance of each solution at 600 nm, preferably in 10-cm cells. Calculate the concentration (mg/L) of ozone in the *Sample* by the formula:

$$\text{Result} = 100 \times D/(0.42 \times b \times V)$$

D = difference in absorbance between the solution of the *Sample* and the *Blank* solution
b = cell path length (cm)
V = volume (mL) of *Sample*

Ozone concentrations of 0.05 to 0.5 mg/L: Proceed as above, using *Indigo reagent II*.
Acceptance criteria: Between 0.01 and 0.5 mg/L of O_3

Palm Kernel Oil (Unhydrogenated)

First Published: Prior to FCC 6

CAS: [8023-79-8]

UNII: B0S90M0233 [palm kernel oil]

DESCRIPTION
Palm Kernel Oil (Unhydrogenated) is a fat obtained from the kernel of the fruit of the oil palm *Elaeis guineensis* Jacq. (Fam. Arecaceae) by mechanical expression or solvent extraction. It is refined, bleached, and deodorized to substantially remove free fatty acids, phospholipids, color, odor and flavor components, and miscellaneous other non-oil materials. Like coconut oil, it has a more abrupt melting range than other fats and oils.

Function: Coating agent; texturizer

Packaging and Storage: Store in well-closed containers.

IDENTIFICATION
- **FATTY ACID COMPOSITION,** Appendix VII

    Acceptance criteria: Palm Kernel Oil (Unhydrogenated) exhibits the following composition profile of fatty acids:

Fatty Acid	Weight % (Range)
6:0	0–1.5
8:0	3–5
10:0	2.5–6
12:0	40–52
14:0	14–18
16:0	7–10
16:1	0–1
18:0	1–3
18:1	11–19
18:2	0.5–4
20:0	tr.–1

IMPURITIES
Inorganic Impurities
- **LEAD,** *Lead Limit Test, Atomic Absorption Spectrophotometric Graphite Furnace Method II,* Appendix IIIB

    Acceptance criteria: NMT 0.1 mg/kg

SPECIFIC TESTS
- **COLOR (FATS AND RELATED SUBSTANCES),** Appendix VII

    Acceptance criteria: NMT 20 yellow/2.0 red
- **FREE FATTY ACIDS,** Appendix VII

    Analysis: Use the following equivalence factors (e) in the formula given in the procedure:

    Free fatty acids as oleic acid, e = 28.2

    Free fatty acids as lauric acid, e = 20.0

    Acceptance criteria
    Oleic Acid: NMT 0.1%
    Lauric Acid: NMT 0.07%

- **IODINE VALUE,** Appendix VII

    Acceptance criteria: Between 13 and 23
- **MELTING RANGE (FATS AND RELATED SUBSTANCES),** Appendix VII

    Acceptance criteria: Between 27° and 29°
- **PEROXIDE VALUE,** Appendix VII

    Acceptance criteria: NMT 10 mEq/kg
- **UNSAPONIFIABLE MATTER,** Appendix VII

    Acceptance criteria: NMT 1.5%
- **WATER,** *Water Determination,* Appendix IIB: Use 50 mL of chloroform to dissolve the sample, rather than 35 and 40 mL of methanol.

    Acceptance criteria: NMT 0.1%

Palm Oil (Unhydrogenated)

First Published: Prior to FCC 6

CAS: [8002-75-3]

UNII: 5QUO05548Z [palm oil]

DESCRIPTION
Palm Oil (Unhydrogenated) is a deep orange-red fat obtained from the pulp of the fruit of the oil palm *Elaeis guineensis* Jacq. (Fam. Aracaceae) usually by boiling, centrifugation, and mechanical expression. It is refined, bleached, and deodorized to substantially remove free fatty acids, phospholipids, color, odor and flavor components, and miscellaneous other non-oil materials. It is a semisolid at 21° to 27°.

Function: Coating agent; emulsifying agent; texturizer

Packaging and Storage: Store in well-closed containers.

IDENTIFICATION
- **FATTY ACID COMPOSITION,** Appendix VII

    Acceptance criteria: Palm Oil (Unhydrogenated) exhibits the following composition profile of fatty acids:

Fatty Acid	Weight % (Range)
14:0	0.5–5.9
16:0	32–47
18:0	2–8
18:1	34–44
18:2	7–12

IMPURITIES
Inorganic Impurities
- **LEAD,** *Lead Limit Test, Atomic Absorption Spectrophotometric Graphite Furnace Method II,* Appendix IIIB

    Acceptance criteria: NMT 0.1 mg/kg

SPECIFIC TESTS
- **COLOR (FATS AND RELATED SUBSTANCES),** Appendix VII

    Acceptance criteria: Not more than 35 yellow/5.0 red
- **FREE FATTY ACIDS,** Appendix VII

    Analysis: Use the following equivalence factors (e) in the formula given in the procedure:

    Free fatty acids as oleic acid, e = 28.2

Free fatty acids as lauric acid, e = 25.6
Acceptance criteria
  Oleic Acid: NMT 0.1%
  Palmitic Acid: NMT 0.09%
- **IODINE VALUE,** Appendix VII
  Acceptance criteria: Between 50 and 55
- **PEROXIDE VALUE,** Appendix VII
  Acceptance criteria: NMT 10 mEq/kg
- **STABILITY,** Appendix VII
  Acceptance criteria: NLT 50 h
- **UNSAPONIFIABLE MATTER,** Appendix VII
  Acceptance criteria: NMT 1.5%
- **WATER,** *Water Determination,* Appendix IIB: Use 50 mL of chloroform to dissolve the sample, rather than 35–40 mL of methanol.
  Acceptance criteria: NMT 0.1%

Palmarosa Oil

First Published: Prior to FCC 6

Geranium Oil, East Indian Type
Geranium Oil, Turkish Type
FEMA: 2831

CAS: [8014-19-5]

UNII: 0J3G3O53ST [palmarosa oil]

DESCRIPTION
Palmarosa Oil occurs as light yellow to yellow oil that is often hazy and brown with a rosy, floral, geranium odor. It is the volatile oil obtained by steam distillation from the partially dried grass *Cymbopogon martini* Stapf. var. *motia* (Fam. Gramineae). It is soluble in most fixed oils and in propylene glycol. It is soluble, usually with opalescence or turbidity, in mineral oil. It is practically insoluble in glycerin.
Function: Flavoring agent

Packaging and Storage: Store in a cool place protected from light in full, tight containers that are made from steel or aluminum and that are suitably lined.

IDENTIFICATION
- **INFRARED SPECTRA,** *Spectrophotometric Identification Tests,* Appendix IIIC
  Acceptance criteria: The spectrum of the sample exhibits relative maxima at the same wavelengths as those of the spectrum below.

ASSAY
- **TOTAL ALCOHOLS,** Appendix VI
  Sample: 1 g of the acetylated oil
  Analysis: Use 77.13 as the equivalence factor (e) in the calculation.
  Acceptance criteria: NLT 88.0% of total alcohols
- **ESTERS,** *Ester Determination,* Appendix VI
  Sample: 5 g
  Analysis: Use 98.15 as the equivalence factor (e) in the calculation.
  Acceptance criteria: NLT 4.0% and NMT 18.0% of esters calculated as geranyl acetate ($C_{12}H_{20}O_2$)

SPECIFIC TESTS
- **ANGULAR ROTATION,** *Optical (Specific) Rotation* Appendix IIB: Use a 100-mm tube.
  Acceptance criteria: Between −2° and +3°
- **REFRACTIVE INDEX,** Appendix IIB
  [NOTE—Use an Abbé or other refractometer of equal or greater accuracy.]
  Acceptance criteria: Between 1.470 and 1.476 at 20°
- **SOLUBILITY IN ALCOHOL,** Appendix VI
  Acceptance criteria: One mL of the sample dissolves in 2 mL of 70% alcohol.
- **SPECIFIC GRAVITY:** Determine by any reliable method (see *General Provisions*).
  Acceptance criteria: Between 0.879 and 0.892

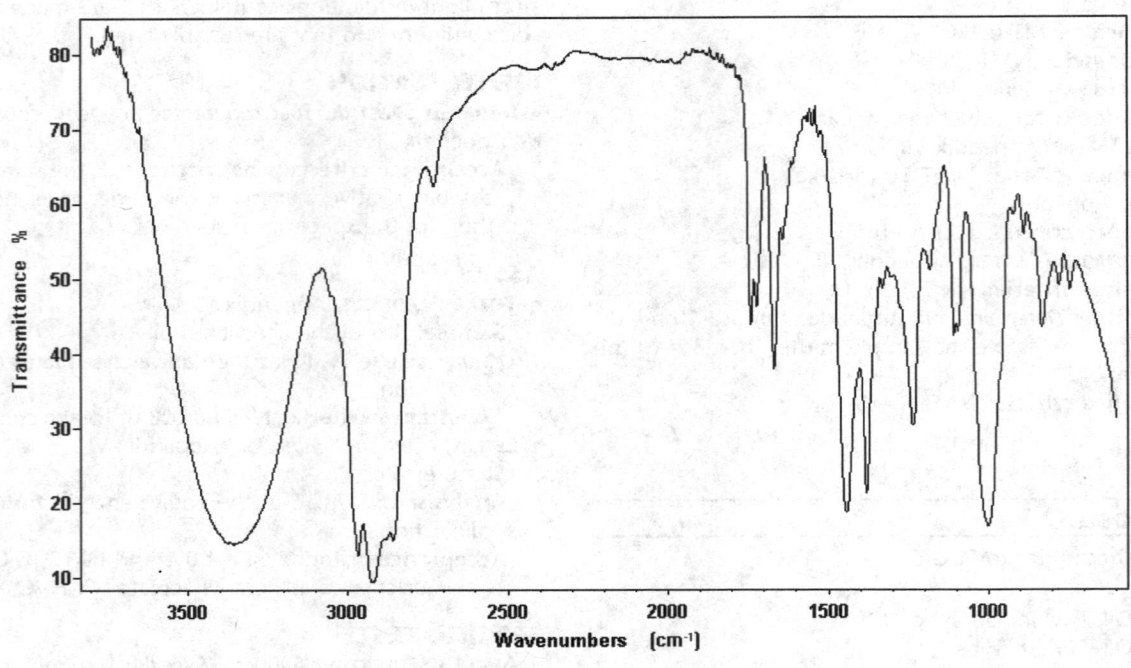

Palmarosa Oil

Palmitic Acid

First Published: Prior to FCC 6

Hexadecanoic Acid

$C_{16}H_{32}O_2$ Formula wt 256.43
　　　　　　　　CAS: [57-10-3]

UNII: 2V16EO95H1 [palmitic acid]

DESCRIPTION
Palmitic Acid occurs as a hard, white or faintly yellow, somewhat glossy crystalline solid, or as a white or pale yellow powder. It is a mixture of solid organic acids obtained from fats consisting chiefly of Palmitic Acid ($C_{16}H_{32}O_2$) with varying amounts of stearic acid ($C_{16}H_{36}O_2$). Palmitic Acid is practically insoluble in water. It is soluble in alcohol, in ether, and in chloroform.
Function: Component in the manufacture of other food-grade additives; defoaming agent
Packaging and Storage: Store in well-closed containers.

IMPURITIES
Inorganic Impurities
- **Lead,** *Lead Limit Test, Atomic Absorption Spectrophotometric Graphite Furnace Method, Method II,* Appendix IIIB
  Acceptance criteria: NMT 0.1 mg/kg

SPECIFIC TESTS
- **Acid Value (Fats and Related Substances),** *Method I,* Appendix VII
  Acceptance criteria: Between 204 and 220
- **Iodine Value,** Appendix VII
  Acceptance criteria: NMT 2.0
- **Residue on Ignition (Sulfated Ash),** Appendix IIC
  Sample: 2 g
  Acceptance criteria: NMT 0.1%
- **Saponification Value,** Appendix VII
  Sample: 3 g
  Acceptance criteria: Between 205 and 221
- **Solidification Point (Titer),** Appendix IIB
  Acceptance criteria: Between 53.3° and 62°
- **Unsaponifiable Matter,** Appendix VII
  Acceptance criteria: NMT 1.5%
- **Water,** *Water Determination,* Appendix IIB
  Acceptance criteria: NMT 0.2%

DL-Panthenol

First Published: Prior to FCC 6

DL-Pantothenyl Alcohol
Racemic Pantothenyl Alcohol

$C_9H_{19}NO_4$ Formula wt 205.25
　　　　　　　　CAS: [16485-10-2]

UNII: WV9CM0O67Z [panthenol]

DESCRIPTION
DL-Panthenol occurs as a white to creamy white, crystalline powder. It is a racemic mixture of the dextrorotatory

(active) and levorotatory (inactive) isomers of panthenol, the alcohol analogue of pantothenic acid. It is freely soluble in water, in alcohol, and in propylene glycol. It is soluble in chloroform and in ether, and is slightly soluble in glycerin. Its solutions are neutral or alkaline to litmus. [NOTE—The physiological activity of DL-Panthenol is one-half that of dexpanthenol (D-Panthenol).]
Function: Nutrient
Packaging and Storage: Store in tight containers.

IDENTIFICATION
- **A. PROCEDURE**
  Sample solution: 100 mg/mL
  Analysis: Add 5 mL of 1 N sodium hydroxide and 1 drop of cupric sulfate TS to 1 mL of the *Sample solution*, and shake vigorously.
  Acceptance criteria: A deep-blue color develops.
- **B. PROCEDURE**
  Sample solution: 10 mg/mL
  Analysis: Add 1 mL of 1 N hydrochloric acid to 1 mL of the *Sample solution*, and heat on a steam bath for about 30 min. Cool, add 100 mg of hydroxylamine hydrochloride, mix, and add 5 mL of 1 N sodium hydroxide. Allow to stand for 5 min, then adjust the pH to within a range of 2.5 to 3.0 with 1 N hydrochloric acid, and add 1 drop of ferric chloride TS.
  Acceptance criteria: A purple-red color develops.
- **C. INFRARED ABSORPTION,** *Spectrophotometric Identification Tests,* Appendix IIIC
  Reference standard: USP Dexpanthenol RS
  Sample and **Standard preparation:** E
  Analysis: The spectrum of the sample exhibits maxima at the same wavelengths as those in the spectrum of the *Reference standard*.

ASSAY
- **PROCEDURE**
  Sample: 400 mg
  Analysis: Transfer the *Sample* into a 300-mL reflux flask fitted with a standard taper glass joint, add 50.0 mL of 0.1 N perchloric acid in glacial acetic acid, and reflux for 5 h. [**CAUTION**—Handle perchloric acid in an appropriate fume hood.] Cool, covering the condenser with foil to prevent contamination by moisture, and rinse the condenser with glacial acetic acid. Add 5 drops of crystal violet TS, and titrate with 0.1 N potassium acid phthalate in glacial acetic acid to a blue-green endpoint. Perform a blank determination (see *General Provisions*) and make any necessary correction. Each mL of 0.1 N perchloric acid is equivalent to 20.53 mg of $C_9H_{19}NO_4$.
  Acceptance criteria: NLT 99.0% and NMT 102.0% of $C_9H_{19}NO_4$ (DL-Panthenol), calculated on the dried basis

IMPURITIES
Inorganic Impurities
- **LEAD,** *Lead Limit Test, Flame Atomic Absorption Spectrophotometric Method,* Appendix IIIB
  Sample: 5 g
  Acceptance criteria: NMT 2 mg/kg

Organic Impurities
- **AMINOPROPANOL**
  Sample: 10 g
  Analysis: Transfer the *Sample* into a 50-mL flask, and dissolve in 25 mL of water. Add bromothymol blue TS and titrate with 0.1 N sulfuric acid from a microburet to a yellow endpoint. Each mL of 0.1 N sulfuric acid is equivalent to 0.75 mg (750 µg) of aminopropanol.
  Acceptance criteria: NMT 0.1%

SPECIFIC TESTS
- **LOSS ON DRYING,** Appendix IIC: 56° for 4 h in vacuum over phosphorus pentoxide
  Acceptance criteria: NMT 0.5%
- **MELTING RANGE OR TEMPERATURE DETERMINATION,** Appendix IIB
  Sample: 1 g
  Acceptance criteria: Between 64.5° and 68.5°
- **RESIDUE ON IGNITION (SULFATED ASH),** Appendix IIC
  Sample: 1 g
  Acceptance criteria: NMT 0.1%

Paraffin, Synthetic
First Published: Prior to FCC 6

Fischer-Tropsch Paraffin

CAS: [8002-74-2]

DESCRIPTION
Paraffin, Synthetic occurs as a white wax that is very hard at room temperature. It is synthesized by the Fischer-Tropsch process from carbon monoxide and hydrogen, which are catalytically converted to a mixture of paraffin hydrocarbons; the lower-molecular-weight fractions are removed by distillation, and the residue is hydrogenated and further treated by percolation through activated charcoal. It is soluble in hot hydrocarbon solvents.
Function: Masticatory substance in chewing gum base
Packaging and Storage: Store in well-closed containers.

IDENTIFICATION
- **INFRARED SPECTRA,** *Spectrophotometric Identification Tests,* Appendix IIIC
  Sample preparation: Mineral oil mull
  Acceptance criteria: The spectrum of the sample exhibits relative maxima at the same wavelengths as those of the spectrum below.

IMPURITIES
Inorganic Impurities
- **LEAD,** *Sample Solution for Lead Limit Test,* Appendix IV
  Control: 10 µg Pb (10 mL of *Diluted Standard Lead Solution*)
  Acceptance criteria: NMT 3 mg/kg

Organic Impurities
- **OIL CONTENT,** *Oil Content of Synthetic Paraffin,* Appendix IIC
  Acceptance criteria: NMT 0.50%

SPECIFIC TESTS

- **ABSORPTIVITY**

  Sample solution: 1 mg/mL in decahydronaphthalene that has been previously heated to 88°

  Analysis: Use an accurately calibrated spectrophotometer capable of measuring absorbance with a repeatability of ±0.1% or better from an average of 0.4 absorbance level at 290 nm, having a spectral bandwidth of 2 nm or less, capable of making wavelength measurements repeatable within ±0.2 nm, and having cell holders with temperature control.

  Determine the absorbance of the Sample solution in a 10-cm cell at 290 nm, maintaining the temperature of the sample cell and the reference cell at 88°. Use decahydronaphthalene at 88° in a matched cell as the blank (see *General Provisions*). Cell lengths should be known to within ±0.5% or better of the nominal pathlength.

  Calculate the absorptivity of the Sample solution by the formula:

  $$Result = A/bc$$

  A = absorbance of the *Sample solution*, corrected for the solvent blank
  b = exact pathlength (cm) of the sample cell
  c = exact concentration (g/L) of the *Sample solution*

  Acceptance criteria: Less than 0.01 at 290 nm in decahydronaphthalene at 88°

- **CONGEALING POINT**

  [NOTE—The congealing point is the temperature at which the molten sample, when allowed to cool under the prescribed conditions, ceases to flow.]

  Analysis: Place a representative sample in a casserole or other suitable dish, and heat slowly in a water bath to a temperature approximately 15°F above the expected congealing point. Use an ASTM Congealing Point Thermometer with a temperature range of 68° to 213°F and that conforms to the requirements for an ASTM 54 F thermometer (see *Thermometers*, Appendix I). Using a cork, as needed, fit the thermometer into a jacket consisting of a 1-oz glass vial that has a 25-mm diameter and is 55 mm long, and adjust the thermometer so that the bottom of the bulb is 10 to 15 mm from the bottom of the vial.

  Heat the thermometer jacket assembly to approximately the same temperature as the prepared sample. When both the sample and the assembly have reached the required temperature, remove the assembly from the bath, then immediately remove the thermometer from its jacket, and immerse the thermometer bulb into the molten sample until the bulb is completely covered, taking care not to cover any part of the thermometer stem with the sample.

  As rapidly as possible, remove the thermometer and any adhering sample from the sample dish and place the thermometer in the jacket, holding both the thermometer and its jacket in a horizontal position during this operation. Rotate the thermometer horizontally at the rate of approximately one revolution every 2 s, pausing momentarily at the completion of each revolution to inspect the drop of sample on the thermometer bulb. When the drop rotates with the bulb, record the thermometer reading as the congealing point, reported to the nearest 0.5°F. Repeat the determination. If the variation is greater than 1°F, make a third determination, and record the average of the three determinations as the congealing point.

  Acceptance criteria: Between 200° and 210°F (93.3° and 98.9°C)

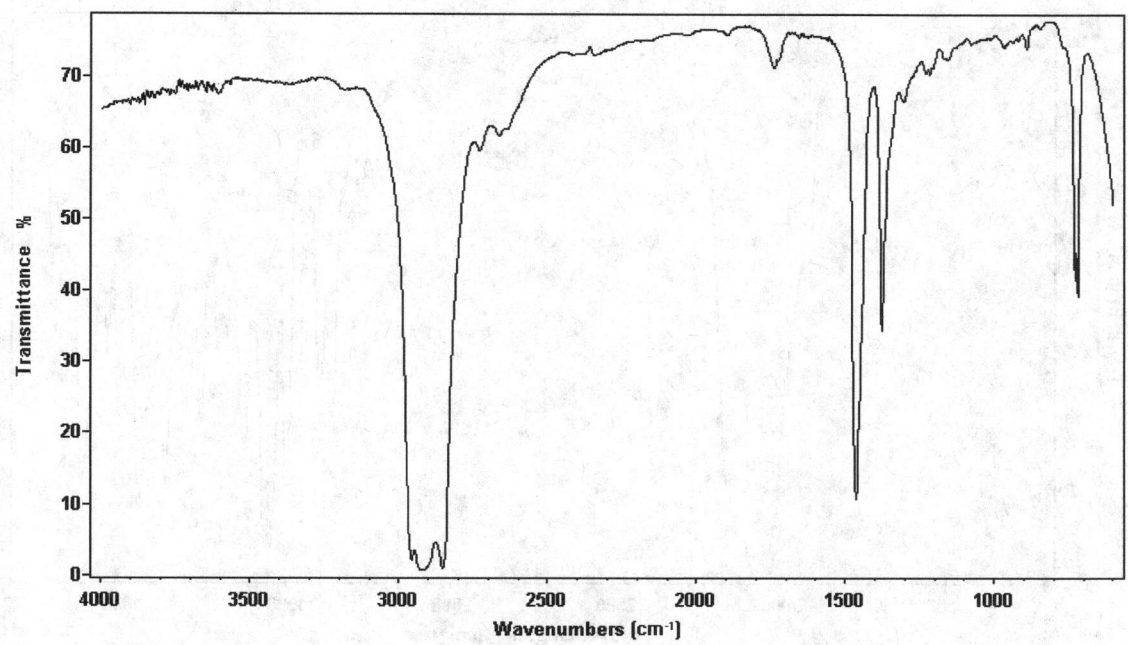

Paraffin Synthetic (Mineral Oil Mull)

Parsley Herb Oil

First Published: Prior to FCC 6

UNII: IXK9N7RJ7J [parsley oil] CAS: [8000-68-8]

DESCRIPTION
Parsley Herb Oil occurs as a yellow to light brown liquid with the odor of parsley herb. It is the oil obtained by steam distillation of the above-ground parts of the plant *Petroselinum crispum* (Fam. Umbelliferae), including the immature seed. It is soluble in most fixed oils, in mineral oil, and in alcohol (with opalescence). It is slightly soluble in propylene glycol, but it is insoluble in glycerin.
Function: Flavoring agent
Packaging and Storage: Store in a cool place protected from light in full, tight containers.

IDENTIFICATION
- **INFRARED SPECTRA,** *Spectrophotometric Identification Tests,* Appendix IIIC
  Acceptance criteria: The spectrum of the sample exhibits relative maxima at the same wavelengths as those of the spectrum below.

SPECIFIC TESTS
- **ACID VALUE (ESSENTIAL OILS AND FLAVORS),** Appendix VI
  Acceptance criteria: NMT 2.0
- **ANGULAR ROTATION,** *Optical (Specific) Rotation* Appendix IIB: Use a 100-mm tube.
  Acceptance criteria: Between +1° and −9°
- **REFRACTIVE INDEX,** Appendix IIB
  [NOTE—Use an Abbé or other refractometer of equal or greater accuracy.]
  Acceptance criteria: Between 1.503 and 1.530 at 20°
- **SPECIFIC GRAVITY:** Determine by any reliable method (see *General Provisions*).
  Acceptance criteria: Between 0.908 and 0.940

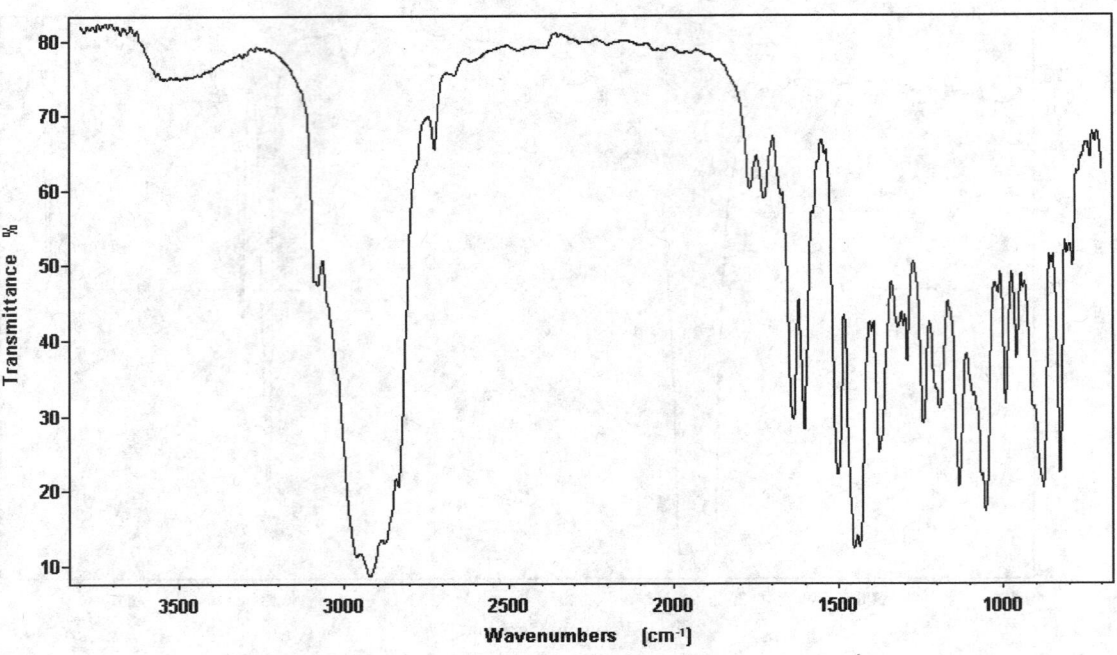

Parsley Herb Oil

Parsley Seed Oil

First Published: Prior to FCC 6

CAS: [8000-68-8]

UNII: XB8Q500O0Z [parsley seed oil]

DESCRIPTION
Parsley Seed Oil occurs as a yellow to light brown liquid with a green, herbal odor. It is the oil obtained by steam distillation of the ripe seed of *Petroselinum crispum* (Fam. Umbelliferae). It is soluble in most fixed oils and in mineral oil. It is slightly soluble in propylene glycol, but it is insoluble in glycerin.

Function: Flavoring agent

Packaging and Storage: Store in a cool place protected from light in full containers that are made from steel or aluminum and that are suitably lined.

IDENTIFICATION
- **INFRARED SPECTRA,** *Spectrophotometric Identification Tests,* Appendix IIIC

  Acceptance criteria: The spectrum of the sample exhibits relative maxima at the same wavelengths as those of the spectrum below.

SPECIFIC TESTS
- **ACID VALUE (ESSENTIAL OILS AND FLAVORS),** Appendix VI

  Acceptance criteria: NMT 4.0
- **ANGULAR ROTATION,** *Optical (Specific) Rotation,* Appendix IIB: Use a 100-mm tube

  Acceptance criteria: Between −4° and −10°
- **REFRACTIVE INDEX,** Appendix IIB

  [NOTE—Use an Abbé or other refractometer of equal or greater accuracy.]

  Acceptance criteria: Between 1.513 and 1.522 at 20°
- **SAPONIFICATION VALUE,** *Esters,* Appendix VI

  Sample: 5 g

  Acceptance criteria: Between 2 and 10
- **SOLUBILITY IN ALCOHOL,** Appendix VI

  Acceptance criteria: One mL of the sample dissolves in 6 mL of 80% alcohol, occasionally with slight haziness.
- **SPECIFIC GRAVITY:** Determine by any reliable method (see *General Provisions*)

  Acceptance criteria: Between 1.040 and 1.080

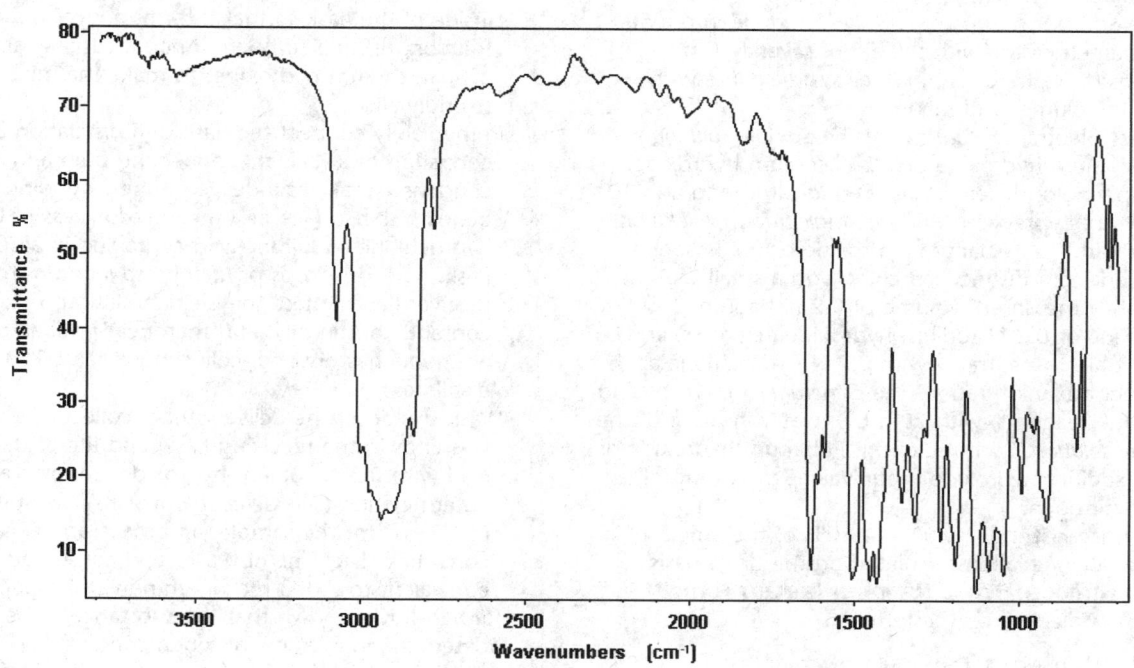

Parsley Seed Oil

Partially Hydrolyzed Proteins

First Published: Prior to FCC 6
Last Revision: Second Supplement, FCC 7

Enzyme-Hydrolyzed (Source) Protein
Partially Hydrolyzed (Source) Protein
(Source) Peptone
Enzyme-Modified (Source) Protein
Partial Enzymatic Digest of (Source) Protein
Partial Acid Digest of (Source) Protein
INS: 429

DESCRIPTION
Partially Hydrolyzed Proteins occur as liquid, paste, powder, or granules. They are composed of peptides and polypeptides resulting from the partial or incomplete hydrolysis of peptide bonds present in edible proteinaceous materials catalyzed by heat, food-grade proteolytic enzymes, and/or suitable food-grade acids. Their degree of hydrolysis typically ranges from 3% to 85% on the basis of peptide bond cleavage. During processing, the proteinaceous raw material may be treated with safe and suitable alkaline materials. The edible proteinaceous materials used as raw materials are derived from casein and other milk products such as whey protein; from animal tissue, including gelatin, defatted animal tissue, and egg albumen; from yeast; and from soy protein products, wheat protein products, or other suitable and safe plant sources.

[CAUTION—Depending on the protein source and the degree of hydrolysis, partially hydrolyzed proteins may present an allergenic risk to sensitized individuals.]
Function: Binder; dough conditioner; emulsifier and emulsifier salt; flavoring agent; flavor enhancer; nutrient; fermentation aid; surface-active agent; texturizer
Packaging and Storage: Store in tight containers.

[NOTE—All analyses should be calculated on the dried basis, based on a sample previously dried as follows: evaporate liquid and paste samples to dryness in a suitable tared container on a steam bath, then, as for the powdered and granular forms, dry to constant weight at 105°.]

ASSAY
- **TOTAL NITROGEN,** *Nitrogen Determination,* Appendix IIIC
  Acceptance criteria: NLT 7.0%, calculated on the dried basis

IMPURITIES
Inorganic Impurities
- **LEAD,** *Lead Limit Test, Flame Atomic Absorption Spectrophotometric Method,* Appendix IIIB
  Sample: 10 g
  Acceptance criteria: NMT 2 mg/kg, calculated on the dried basis

SPECIFIC TESTS
- **α-AMINO NITROGEN**
  Phenolphthalein-formol solution: 50 mL of 40% formaldehyde containing 1 mL of 0.05% phenolphthalein in 50% alcohol neutralized exactly to a

pH of 7 with 0.2 N barium hydroxide or 0.2 N sodium hydroxide

Sample solution: Transfer 7–25 g of sample into a 500-mL volumetric flask with the aid of several 50-mL portions of warm, ammonia-free water, dilute with water to volume, and mix.

Analysis: Neutralize 20.0 mL of the *Sample solution* with 0.2 N barium hydroxide or 0.2 N sodium hydroxide, using phenolphthalein TS as the indicator, and add 10 mL of freshly prepared *Phenolphthalein-formol solution*. Titrate with 0.2 N barium hydroxide or 0.2 N sodium hydroxide to a distinct red color, add a small, but accurately measured, volume of 0.2 N barium hydroxide or 0.2 N sodium hydroxide in excess, and back titrate to neutrality with 0.2 N hydrochloric acid. Conduct a blank titration (see *General Provisions*), using the same reagents, with 20 mL of water in place of the *Sample solution*. Each mL of 0.2 N barium hydroxide or 0.2 N sodium hydroxide is equivalent to 2.8 mg of α-amino nitrogen.

Acceptance criteria: 90.0%–110.0% of the amount claimed on the label, calculated on the dried basis

- **α-AMINO NITROGEN/TOTAL NITROGEN PERCENT RATIO**
  Analysis: Calculate by the formula:

  $$Result = 100[(AN - P)/(TN - P)]$$

  AN = percent α-*Amino Nitrogen*, determined in the previous test
  P = percent *Ammonia Nitrogen*, determined in the following test
  TN = percent *Total Nitrogen*, determined in the *Assay*

  Acceptance criteria: 2.0%–62.0%, when calculated on an ammonia nitrogen-free and dried basis

- **AMMONIA NITROGEN**
  [**CAUTION**—Provide adequate ventilation.]
  [NOTE—Use nitrogen-free reagents, where available, or reagents very low in nitrogen content.]
  Methyl red indicator: 1 g of methyl red in 200 mL of alcohol
  Sample: 0.700 g–2.2 g
  Analysis: Transfer the *Sample* into a 500- to 800-mL Kjeldahl digestion flask of hard, moderately thick, well-annealed glass. [NOTE—If desired, wrap the sample, if solid or semisolid, in nitrogen-free filter paper to facilitate the transfer.] Add about 200 mL of water, and mix. Add a few granules of zinc to prevent bumping, tilt the flask, and cautiously pour sodium hydroxide pellets, or a 2:5 sodium hydroxide solution, down the inside of the flask so that it forms a layer under the solution, using a sufficient amount (usually about 25 g of solid sodium hydroxide) to make the mixture strongly alkaline.

  Immediately connect the flask to a distillation apparatus consisting of a Kjeldahl connecting bulb and a condenser that has a delivery tube extending well beneath the surface of a measured excess of 0.5 N hydrochloric or sulfuric acid contained in a 500-mL flask. Add 5–7 drops of *Methyl red indicator* to the receiver flask. Rotate the Kjeldahl flask to mix its contents thoroughly, and then heat until all of the ammonia has distilled, collecting at least 150 mL of distillate.

  Wash the tip of the delivery tube, collecting the washings in the receiving flask, and titrate the excess acid with 0.5 N sodium hydroxide. Perform a blank determination (see *General Provisions*), substituting 2 g of sucrose for the sample, and make any necessary correction. Each mL of 0.5 N acid consumed is equivalent to 7.003 mg of ammonia nitrogen (A). [NOTE—If it is known that the substance to be determined has a low nitrogen content, 0.1 N acid and alkali may be used, in which case each mL of 0.1 N acid consumed is equivalent to 1.401 mg of nitrogen.] Calculate the percentage of ammonia nitrogen:

  $$Result = 100(A/S)$$

  A = weight of ammonia nitrogen (mg)
  S = weight of the *Sample* taken (mg)

  Acceptance criteria: NMT 1.5%, calculated on the dried basis

- **ASH (TOTAL),** Appendix IIC
  Sample: 1 g
  Acceptance criteria: NMT 40.0%, calculated on the dried basis

- **GLUTAMIC ACID**, Appendix IIIC
  Acceptance criteria: NMT 20.0% as glutamic acid ($C_5H_9NO_4$), and NMT 35.0% of the total protein, calculated on the dried basis

OTHER REQUIREMENTS

- **LABELING:** Indicate the source of protein, including type.

Patent Blue V[1]

First Published: Second Supplement, FCC 7

Patent Blue 5
CI Food Blue 5
CI No. 42051
Class: Triarylmethane
Calcium or sodium salt of 2-[(4-diethylaminophenyl)(4-diethylimino-2,5-cyclohexandien-1-ylidene)methyl]-4-hydroxy-1,5-benzene disulfonate
Calcium or sodium salt of [4-[*alpha*-(4-diethyl-aminophenyl)-5-hydroxy-2,4-disulfonatophenylmethylidene]-2,5-cyclohexadien-1-ylidene] diethylammonium hydroxide inner salt

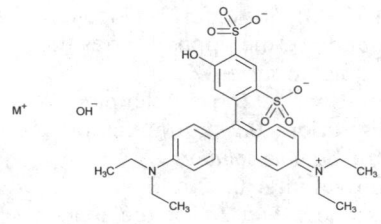

M^+ = 1/2 Ca^{2+}, or Na^+

Calcium salt: $C_{27}H_{31}N_2O_7S_2{}^1/_2Ca$ Formula wt, calcium salt 579.72
Sodium salt: $C_{27}H_{31}N_2O_7S_2Na$ Formula wt, sodium salt 582.67
INS: 131   CAS: [3536-49-0]
UNII: 8QE473DV1Z [patent blue v]

DESCRIPTION
Patent Blue V occurs as a blue powder or granules. It is principally the calcium or sodium salt of 2-[4-[*alpha*-(4-diethyl-aminophenyl)-5-hydroxy-2,4-disulfonatophenylmethylidene]-2,5-cyclohexadien-1-ylidene] diethylammonium hydroxide inner salt, and subsidiary coloring matters. Water, sodium chloride, sodium sulfate, calcium chloride, and calcium sulfate can be present as the principal uncolored components. It is soluble in water and slightly soluble in ethanol.
Function: Color
Packaging and Storage: Store in well-closed containers.

IDENTIFICATION
- **VISIBLE ABSORPTION SPECTRUM**
  Sample solution: Dissolve a sample in water and adjust the pH to 5.
  Analysis: Measure the absorption spectrum of the *Sample solution* using a suitable UV-visible spectrophotometer.
  Acceptance criteria: The *Sample solution* exhibits a wavelength maximum at 638 nm.

ASSAY
- **TOTAL COLOR**, *Color Determination*, Methods I and II, Appendix IIIC [NOTE—Both methods must be used.]

Method I (Spectrophotometric)
  Sample solution: 10 mg/mL adjusted to pH 5
  Analysis: Determine as directed at 638 nm using 0.2 L/(mg·cm) for the absorptivity (*a*) for Patent Blue V.
Method II ($TiCl_3$ Titration)
  Sample: 1.3–1.4 g
  Analysis: Determine as directed, except under *Procedure* use 15 g of *Sodium Bitartrate* instead of 21 to 22 g and use 150 mL of water instead of 275 mL. For the calculation, use 3.336 and 3.433 as the stoichiometric factor (F_S) for the calcium and sodium salts of Patent Blue V, respectively.
Acceptance criteria: The average of results obtained from *Method I* and *Method II* is NLT 85.0% total coloring matters.

IMPURITIES
Inorganic Impurities
- **CHROMIUM**, *Color Determination*, Appendix IIIC
  Acceptance criteria: NMT 0.005%
- **LEAD**, *Lead Limit Test*, Appendix IIIB
  Sample solution: Prepare as directed for organic compounds.
  Control: 2 µg Pb (2 mL of *Diluted Standard Lead Solution*)
  Acceptance criteria: NMT 2 mg/kg

Organic Impurities
- **UNCOMBINED INTERMEDIATES AND PRODUCTS OF SIDE REACTIONS**
  Solution A: 10% (w/v) aqueous acetate buffer pH 4.6 prepared using 1 M sodium hydroxide, 1 M acetic acid, and water (5:10:35)
  Solution B: Acetonitrile
  Mobile phase: See the gradient table below.

Time (min)	Solution A (%)	Solution B (%)	Flow Rate (mL/min)
0	85	15	1
12	85	15	1
25	20	80	2
28	20	80	2
40	85	15	1

  Sample solution: 5 mg/mL in 0.02 M ammonium acetate
  Standard solution: Solution containing 3-hydroxybenzaldehyde, 3-hydroxybenzoic acid, 3-hydroxy-4-sulfonatobenzoic acid, and *N,N*-diethylaminobenzenesulfonic acid in 0.2 M ammonium acetate
  Chromatographic system, Appendix IIA
    Mode: High-performance liquid chromatography
    Detector: UV 254 nm
    Column: 25-cm × 4-mm C18 column (7-µm)[2]
    Temperature: Ambient
    Flow rate: See the gradient table above.
    Injection volume: 20 µL
  Analysis: Separately inject equal volumes of the *Standard solution* and *Sample solution* into the

---
[1] Patent Blue V is approved for use in some countries, but banned in other countries such as the United States and Australia.

[2] LiChrosorb RP 18 (Merck), or equivalent.

chromatograph, and measure the responses for the major peaks on the resulting chromatograms. Calculate the percentages of all four impurities (3-hydroxybenzaldehyde, 3-hydroxybenzoic acid, 3-hydroxy-4-sulfonatobenzoic acid, and N,N-diethylaminobenzenesulfonic acid) in the sample taken:

$$\text{Result} = (r_U/r_S) \times (C_S/C_U) \times 100$$

r_U = peak area response for the analyte in the *Sample solution*
r_S = peak area response for the analyte in the *Standard solution*
C_S = concentration of analyte in the *Standard solution* (mg/mL)
C_U = concentration of sample in the *Sample solution* (mg/mL)

Acceptance criteria
3-hydroxybenzaldehyde, 3-hydroxybenzoic acid, 3-hydroxy-4-sulfonatobenzoic acid, and N,N-diethylaminobenzenesulfonic acid: NMT 0.5%, combined

SPECIFIC TESTS
- **COMBINED TESTS**
  Tests
  - LOSS ON DRYING (VOLATILE MATTER), *Color Determination*, Appendix IIIC
  - CHLORIDE, *Sodium Chloride, Color Determination*, Appendix IIIC
  - SULFATES (AS SODIUM SALTS), *Sodium Sulfate, Color Determination*, Appendix IIIC

  Acceptance criteria: NMT 15.0%, combined as the sum of all three tests

- **ETHER EXTRACTS**, *Color Determination*, Appendix IIIC
  Acceptance criteria: NMT 0.2%

- **LEUCO BASE**, *Color Determination*, Appendix IIIC
  Sample solution: 110 µg/mL
  Analysis: Proceed as directed using an absorptivity constant, a, of 0.200 L/(mg·cm) at 638 nm for Patent Blue V. For the ratio of the molecular weight of colorant and leuco base, r, use 0.95960 (582.15/606.66) and 0.96401 (579.14/600.76) for the sodium and calcium salts, respectively.
  Acceptance criteria: NMT 4%

- **SUBSIDIARY COLORING MATTERS**
  [NOTE—In this method, subsidiary coloring matters are separated from the main coloring matter of Patent Blue V by ascending paper chromatography (see *Paper Chromatography*, Appendix IIA), and extracted separately from the chromatographic paper. The absorbance of each extract is measured at the wavelength of maximum absorption for Patent Blue V (638 nm) by visible spectrophotometry. Because it is impractical to identify each subsidiary coloring matter using this procedure, and because the subsidiary coloring matters are usually minor components of food colors, the method assumes that the maximum absorbance of each subsidiary coloring matter is the same as that of the total coloring matters. The subsidiary coloring matters content is calculated by adding together the absorbances of the extracts in conjunction with the total coloring matters content of the sample.]

  Chromatographic apparatus: The chromatography tank (*Figures 1* and *2*) is comprised of a glass tank (A) and cover (B); frame to support chromatography paper (C); solvent tray (D); secondary frame (E) for supporting "drapes" of the filter paper; and 20-cm × 20-cm chromatography grade paper[3]. Mark out the chromatography paper as shown in *Figure 3*.

  Chromatographic solvent: Prepare a mixture of n-butanol, water, ethanol, and ammonia (s.g. 0.880) (600:264:135:6). Shake for 2 min, allow the layers to separate, and use the upper layer as the chromatographic solvent.

  Sample solution: 10 mg/mL sample
  Standard solution: 0.2 mg/mL sample prepared by diluting the *Sample solution*
  Application volume: 0.10 mL
  Analysis: No less than 2 h before analysis, arrange the filter-paper drapes in the glass tank and pour sufficient *Chromatographic solvent* over the drapes and into the bottom of the tank to cover the bottom of the tank to a depth of 1 cm. Place the solvent tray in position and fit the cover to the tank. Using a microsyringe capable of delivering 0.1 mL with a tolerance of ±0.002 mL, apply to separate chromatograph sheets 0.1 mL aliquots of *Sample solution* and *Standard solution*, as uniformly as possible within the confines of the 18-cm × 7-mm rectangle, holding the nozzle of the microsyringe steadily in contact with the paper. Allow the papers to dry at room temperature for 1–2 h or at 50° in a drying cabinet for 5 min followed by 15 min at room temperature. Mount the dried sheets, together with two plain sheets to act as blanks on the supporting frame. [NOTE—If required, several dried sheets may be developed simultaneously.]

  Pour sufficient *Chromatography solvent* into the solvent tray to bring the surface of the solvent about 1 cm below the base line of the chromatography sheets. The volume necessary will depend on the dimensions of the apparatus and should be predetermined. Put the supporting frame into position and replace the cover. Allow the solvent front to ascend approximately 17 cm above baseline, then remove the supporting frame and transfer it to a drying cabinet at 50°–60° for 10–15 min. Remove the sheets from the frame.

---
[3] Whatman No 1, or equivalent.

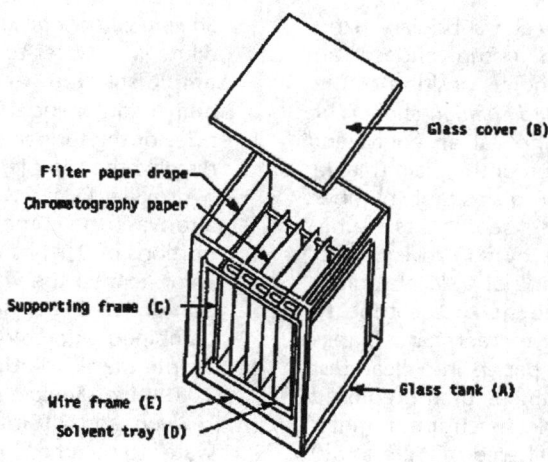

Figure 1. Assembly of the Chromatographic Apparatus

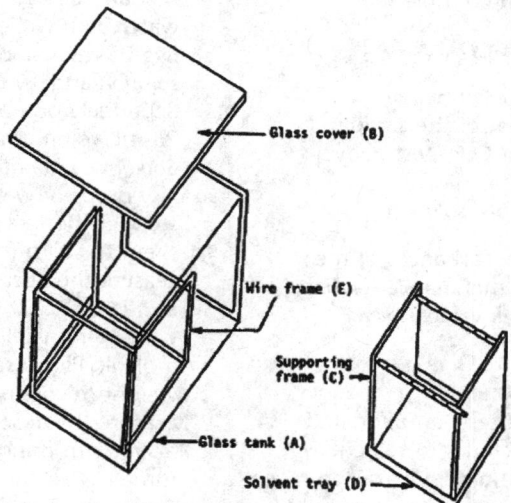

Figure 2. Components of the Chromatographic Apparatus

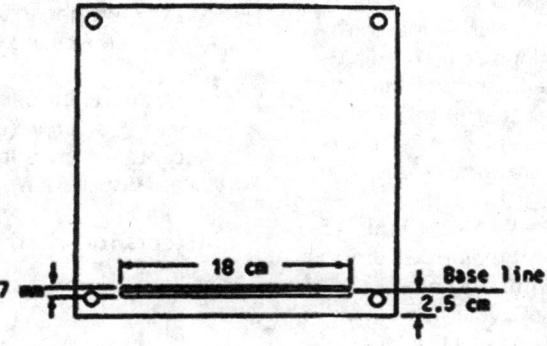

Figure 3. Method for Marking the Chromatographic Paper

For the *Sample solution* sheets, cut each subsidiary band from each chromatogram sheet as a strip, and cut an equivalent strip from the corresponding position of the plain (blank) sheet. For the *Standard solution* sheet, cut the entire band from the sheet, and cut an equivalent strip from the corresponding position of the plain (blank) sheet. Place each strip, subdivided into a suitable number of approximately equal portions, in a separate test tube. Add 5.0 mL of water:acetone (1:1 by vol) to each test tube, swirl for 2–3 min, add 15.0 mL of 0.05 N sodium hydrogen carbonate solution, and shake the tube to ensure mixing. Filter the colored extracts and blanks through 9-cm coarse porosity filter papers into clean test tubes and determine the absorbances of the colored extracts at 638 nm using a suitable spectrophotometer with 40-mm closed cells against a filtered mixture of 5.0 mL of water:acetone (1:1 by vol) and 15.0 mL of the 0.05 N sodium hydrogen carbonate solution. Measure the absorbances of the extracts of the blank strips at 638 nm and correct the absorbances of the colored extracts with the blank values. Calculate the percent subsidiary coloring matter in the portion of the sample taken:

$$\text{Result} = 0.2 \times D \times [(A_a + A_b + A_c \ldots A_n)/A_s]$$

0.2 = dilution factor for the *Standard solution*
D = total coloring matter content of the sample, determined from the *Total Color* test above and expressed as percent
A_s = absorbance from the *Standard solution*

$A_a + A_b + A_c \ldots A_n$ = sum of the absorbances of the subsidiary coloring matters from the *Sample solution*, corrected for the blank values

Acceptance criteria: NMT 2%

- **UNSULFONATED PRIMARY AROMATIC AMINES**
[NOTE—Under the conditions of this test, unsulfonated primary aromatic amines are extracted into toluene from an alkaline solution of the sample, re-extracted into acid, and then determined spectrophotometrically after diazotization and coupling.]
R salt solution: 0.05 N 2-naphthol-3,6-disulfonic acid, disodium salt
Sodium carbonate solution: 2 N
Standard stock solution: Weigh 0.100 g of redistilled aniline into a small beaker and transfer to a 100-mL volumetric flask, rinsing the beaker several times with water. Add 30 mL of 3 N hydrochloric acid and dilute to the mark with water at room temperature. Dilute 10.0 mL of this solution with water to 100 mL, and mix well; 1 mL of this solution is equivalent to 0.0001 g of aniline. [NOTE—Prepare this *Standard stock solution* fresh.]
Standard solutions: Separately dilute 5-mL, 10-mL, 15-mL, 20-mL, and 25-mL aliquots of the *Standard stock solution* with 1 N hydrochloric acid to 100 mL.
Standard blank solution: In a 25-mL volumetric flask mix 10.0 mL of 1 N hydrochloric acid, 10.0 mL of *Sodium carbonate solution*, 2.0 mL of *R salt solution*, and dilute with water to volume.
Sample solution: Add 2.0 g of sample into a separatory funnel containing 100 mL of water, rinse down the sides of the funnel with 50 mL of water, swirling to dissolve the sample, and add 5 mL of 1 N sodium hydroxide. Extract with two 50-mL portions of toluene and wash the combined toluene extracts with 10-mL portions of 0.1 N sodium hydroxide to remove traces of color. Extract the washed toluene with three 10-mL portions of 3 N hydrochloric acid, and dilute the combined extract with water to 100 mL.
Sample blank solution: In a 25-mL volumetric flask mix 10.0 mL of *Sample solution*, 10 mL of *Sodium carbonate solution*, and 2.0 mL of *R salt solution*, and dilute with water to volume.
Analysis: Into separate clean dry test tubes, pipet 10.0-mL aliquots of *Sample solution* and each of the *Standard solutions*, cool for 10 min by immersion in a beaker of ice water, and add 1 mL of 50% potassium bromide solution and 0.05 mL of 0.5 N sodium nitrite solution. Mix and allow the tubes to stand for 10 min in the ice water bath while the aniline is diazotized. Into each of five 25-mL volumetric flasks, measure 1 mL of *R salt solution* and 10 mL the *Sodium carbonate solution*. Separately pour each diazotized aniline solution into a 25-mL volumetric flask containing *R salt solution* and *Sodium carbonate solution*; rinse each test tube with a few drops of water. Dilute to the mark with water, stopper the flasks, mix the contents well, and allow them to stand for 15 min in the dark.
Measure the absorbance of each of the coupled *Standard solutions* at 510 nm using a suitable spectrophotometer with 40-mm cells against the *Standard blank solution* as a blank. Plot a standard curve relating absorbance to weight (g) of aniline in each of the *Standard solutions*. Measure the absorbance of the coupled *Sample solution* at 510 nm using a suitable spectrophotometer with 40-mm cells against the *Sample blank solution* as a blank. From the standard curve, determine the weight (g) of aniline in each 100 mL of the *Sample solution*. Calculate the percent unsulfonated primary aromatic amine (as aniline) in the portion of the sample taken:

$$\text{Result} = W_A/W \times 100$$

W_A = weight of aniline in the *Sample solution* calculated from the standard curve (g/100 mL)
W = weight of sample used to prepare the *Sample solution* (g)

Acceptance criteria: NMT 0.01%, calculated as aniline
- **WATER-INSOLUBLE MATTER**, *Color Determination*, Appendix IIIC
Acceptance criteria: NMT 0.5%

Peanut Oil (Unhydrogenated)
First Published: Prior to FCC 6

UNII: 5TL50QU0W4 [peanut oil]
CAS: [8002-03-7]

DESCRIPTION
Peanut Oil (Unhydrogenated) is a pale yellow oil obtained from the kernel of the peanut plant *Arachis hypogaea* L. (Fam. Fabaceae) by mechanical expression or solvent extraction. It is refined, bleached, and deodorized to substantially remove free fatty acids, phospholipids, color, odor and flavor components, and miscellaneous other non-oil materials. It is a liquid at 21° to 27°, but solidifies to a gel-like consistency at 2° to 4°. It is free from visible foreign matter at 21° to 27°, but sometimes clouds at temperatures above 21°.
Function: Coating agent; texturizer
Packaging and Storage: Store in well-closed containers.

IDENTIFICATION
- **FATTY ACID COMPOSITION,** Appendix VII
  Acceptance criteria: Peanut Oil exhibits the following typical composition profile of fatty acids:

Fatty Acid	Weight % (Range)
<14	<0.1
14:0	<0.2
16:0	6–15
16:1	<1.0
18:0	1.3–6.5
18:1	36–72
18:2	13–45
18:3	<2.0
20:0	<1.0–2.5
20:1	0.5–2.1
22:0	1.5–4.8
22:1	<0.1
24:0	1.0–2.5

IMPURITIES
Inorganic Impurities
- **LEAD,** *Lead Limit Test, Atomic Absorption Spectrophotometric Graphite Furnace Method, Method II,* Appendix IIIB
  Acceptance criteria: NMT 0.1 mg/kg

SPECIFIC TESTS
- **COLOR (FATS AND RELATED SUBSTANCES),** Appendix VII
  Acceptance criteria: NMT 5.0 red
- **FREE FATTY ACIDS (as oleic acid),** *Free Fatty Acids,* Appendix VII
  Analysis: Use the following equivalence factor (e) in the formula given in the procedure under *Free Fatty Acids*, e = 28.2.
  Acceptance criteria: NMT 0.1%
- **IODINE VALUE,** Appendix VII
  Acceptance criteria: Between 84 and 100
- **LINOLENIC ACID,** *Fatty Acid Composition,* Appendix VII
  Acceptance criteria: NMT 2.0%
- **PEROXIDE VALUE,** Appendix VII
  Acceptance criteria: NMT 10 mEq/kg
- **UNSAPONIFIABLE MATTER,** Appendix VII
  Acceptance criteria: NMT 1.5%
- **WATER,** *Water Determination, Method I,* Appendix IIB
  Analysis: Use 50 mL of chloroform to dissolve the sample, rather than 35-40 mL of methanol.
  Acceptance criteria: NMT 0.1%

Pectins
First Published: Prior to FCC 6

INS: 440
UNII: 89NA02M4RX [pectin]
CAS: [9000-69-5]

DESCRIPTION
Pectins occur as white, yellow, light gray, or light brown powders. They consist mainly of the partial methyl esters of polygalacturonic acid and their sodium, potassium, calcium, and ammonium salts. They are obtained by extraction in an aqueous medium of appropriate edible plant material, usually citrus fruits or apples. No organic precipitants shall be used other than methanol, ethanol, and isopropanol. In some types of Pectins, a portion of the methyl esters may have been converted to primary amides by treatment with ammonia under alkaline conditions. Pectins dissolve in water, forming an opalescent, colloidal dispersion. They are practically insoluble in ethanol. The commercial product is normally diluted with sugars for standardization purposes. In addition to sugars, Pectins may be mixed with suitable food-grade salts required for pH control and desirable setting characteristics.
Function: Gelling agent; thickener; stabilizer
Packaging and Storage: Store in well-closed containers.

[NOTE—The following tests and procedures apply to the Pectins as supplied, whether standardized or not, except for specifications covering amide substitution and the weight percent of total galacturonic acid in the Pectin component, in which cases the test procedures include provisions for removing the sugars and soluble salts before analysis of the Pectin component.]

IDENTIFICATION
- **PROCEDURE**
  Sample stock solution: Add 0.05 g of sample into a 100-mL volumetric flask, moisten with pure isopropanol. Add 50 mL of water, and mix with a magnetic stirrer. Using 0.5 M sodium hydroxide, adjust the pH to 12, stop the stirrer, and leave the solution undisturbed and at room temperature for 15 min. Reduce the pH to 7.0 with 0.5 M hydrochloric acid. Dilute to 100.0 mL with water.
  Tris buffer solution: Dissolve 6.055 g of Tris (hydroxymethyl) aminomethane and 0.147g of calcium chloride dihydrate in 1L water. Adjust the pH to 7.0 with 1 M hydrochloric acid.

Enzyme solution: 10 mg/mL of pectate lyase in *Tris buffer solution* [NOTE—Solutions to which this solution is added should be analyzed immediately (see *Analysis*.)]
Sample blank: In a quartz cuvette, mix thoroughly 0.5 mL *Tris buffer solution*, 1.0 mL *Sample solution*, and 1.0 mL water.
Enzyme Blank: In a quartz cuvette, mix thoroughly 0.5 mL *Tris buffer solution*, 1.5 mL water, and 0.5 mL *Enzyme solution*.
Sample solution: In a quartz cuvette, mix thoroughly 0.5 mL *Tris buffer solution*, 1.0 mL *Sample stock solution*, 0.5 mL water, and 0.5 mL *Enzyme solution*.
Analysis: Using a suitable UV spectrophotometer, measure the absorbance of the solutions at 235 nm immediately following addition of the *Enzyme solution* (time 0) and at 10 min after. Using the absorbance values measured for each solution at the specified times, calculate the corrected absorbance, A_t, at $t = 0$ min and $t = 10$ min with the following equation:

$$A_t = A_S - (A_{EB} + A_{SB})$$

A_S = absorbance of the *Sample solution* at time t
A_{EB} = absorbance of the *Enzyme blank* at time t
A_{SB} = absorbance of the *Sample blank* at time t

Calculate the amount of unsaturated product (U) produced as follows:

$$U = (A_{t=10} - A_{t=0})/(4600 \times I)$$

I = thickness (cm) of the cuvette
Report the value of U as $U \times 10^5$
Acceptance criteria: U is greater than 0.5, whereas other gums show essentially no change

IMPURITIES
Inorganic Impurities
- **LEAD**
  [NOTE—Use deionized water throughout this procedure.]
  Standard stock solution: 1000 µg/mL Pb [NOTE—Use a commercially available certified solution.]
  Standard solution: 2 µg/mL Pb, prepared immediately before use by pipetting 0.10 mL of *Standard stock solution* into a 50-mL volumetric flask containing 30 mL of water, 4 mL of 20% (v/v) hydrochloric acid, and 4 mL of 0.1 M EDTA. Dilute to volume with water, and mix.
  Control solution: 0.4 µg/mL Pb, prepared by pipetting 5.0 mL of the *Standard solution* into a 25-mL volumetric flask containing 10 mL of water, 2 mL of 20% (v/v) hydrochloric acid, and 2 mL of 0.1 M EDTA. Dilute to volume with water, and mix.
  Blank solution: Add 30 mL of water, 4 mL of 20% (v/v) hydrochloric acid, and 4 mL of 0.1 M EDTA into a 50-mL volumetric flask. Dilute to volume with water, and mix.
  Sample: 2.0 g
  Sample solution: Transfer the *Sample* into a clean, 100-mL glass beaker, add 25 mL of 70% (v/v) nitric acid, cover with a watch glass, and heat at low to moderate heat on a hot plate in a fume hood for 2 h. Remove the watch glass and continue to heat until the sample is dry with no visible fumes. Add 0.5 mL of 70% (v/v) nitric acid and heat to dryness. Cool to room temperature and add 2 mL of 20% (v/v) hydrochloric acid and 2 mL of 0.1 M EDTA. Quantitatively transfer the solution to a 25-mL volumetric flask, dilute to volume with water, and mix.
  Analysis: Set up an inductively coupled plasma emission spectrometer according to manufacturer's instructions. Using the lead emission line of 220.35 nm, calibrate the instrument with the *Blank solution* and the *Standard solution*. Then analyze the *Sample solution* and the *Control solution*.
  Acceptance criteria: The concentration in the *Sample solution* is not more than that in the *Control solution*. (NMT 5 mg/kg)
- **SULFUR DIOXIDE**, *Sulfur Dioxide Determination*, Appendix X
  Analysis: Proceed as directed, but use the following modification for the *Sample Introduction and Distillation*. Transfer 20 g of sample into the round-bottom flask, C, and add 20 mL of ethanol to moisten the sample. Add 400 mL of water, swirling vigorously to disperse the sample. Reassemble the apparatus, making sure that the tapered joints are clean and greased with stopcock grease, and continue as directed beginning with, "the nitrogen flow through the 3% Hydrogen Peroxide Solution...," in the first paragraph.
  Acceptance criteria: NMT 0.005%

Organic Impurities
- **METHANOL, ETHANOL, AND ISOPROPANOL**
  Internal standard solution: 0.05 mg/mL of n-propanol
  Sample solution: 100 mg of sample dissolved in 10 mL of water [NOTE—Use sodium chloride as a dispersing agent, if necessary.]
  Standard alcohol solution: Using a micropipet, transfer 50 mg each of methanol (63.21 µL); ethanol (63.35 µL); and isopropanol (63.65 µL) into a 1000-mL volumetric flask, dilute to volume, and mix.
  Sodium nitrite solution: 250 mg/mL sodium nitrite
  Chromatographic system, Appendix IIA
  Mode: Gas chromatography
  Detector: Flame ionization
  Column: 90-cm × 4-mm (id) glass column, or equivalent, with the first 15 cm packed with Chromopack (or equivalent) and the remainder packed with 120- to 150-mesh Porapak R (or equivalent)
  Column temperature: Isothermal at 150°
  Injection port temperature: 250°
  Carrier gas: Nitrogen
  Flow rate: 80 mL/min
  Analysis: Weigh 200 mg of urea, and place it in a 25-mL amber-glass vial.[1] Purge the urea with nitrogen for 5 min, add 1 mL of saturated oxalic acid solution, close the vial with a rubber stopper, and swirl. Add 1 mL of *Sample solution* and 1 mL of *Internal standard solution*; simultaneously start a stopwatch (t = 0). Swirl the vial and recap it with an open screw cap fitted with a silicone rubber septum. Swirl the vial until t = 30 s. At

---
[1] Reacti-Flasks, or equivalent

t = 45 s, inject 0.5 mL of *Sodium nitrite solution* through the septum. Swirl until t = 70 s, and at t = 150 s, use a pressure lock syringe[2] to withdraw 1.0 mL of the headspace through the septum. Inject the headspace sample into the injection port of the gas chromatograph. Repeat this procedure, but use 1 mL of the *Standard alcohol solution* instead of the *Sample solution*. Calculate the total amount (mg) of methanol, ethanol, and isopropanol (*T*) present in 1 mL of the *Sample solution* by the equation:

$$T = [V_{MS} \times (R_{MU}/R_{MS}) \times d_M] + [V_{ES} \times (R_{EU}/R_{ES}) \times d_E] + [V_{IS} \times (R_{IU}/R_{IS}) \times d_I]$$

V_{MS} = volume of methanol in the *Standard alcohol solution* (mL)
R_{MU} = ratio of the peak area of methanol in the *Sample solution* to that of *n*-propanol in the *Internal standard solution*
R_{MS} = ratio of the peak area of methanol in the *Standard alcohol solution* to that of *n*-propanol in the *Internal Standard solution*
d_M = density of methanol, 0.791 g/mL
V_{ES} = volume of ethanol in the *Standard alcohol solution* (mL)
R_{EU} = ratio of the peak area of ethanol in the *Sample solution* to that of *n*-propanol in the *Internal standard solution*
R_{ES} = ratio of the peak area of ethanol in the *Standard alcohol solution* to that of *n*-propanol in the *Internal Standard solution*
d_E = density of ethanol, 0.7893 g/mL
V_{IS} = volume of isopropanol in the *Standard alcohol solution* (mL)
R_{IU} = ratio of the peak area of isopropanol in the *Sample solution* to that of *n*-propanol in the *Internal standard solution*
R_{IS} = ratio of the peak area of isopropanol in the *Standard alcohol solution* to that of *n*-propanol in the *Internal Standard solution*
d_I = density of isopropanol, 0.7855 g/mL

Calculate the total percent methanol, ethanol, and isopropanol present in the sample by the following formula:

$$Result = (1000T)/W$$

W = weight of the sample taken to prepare the *Sample solution* (mg)

Acceptance criteria: NMT 1.0% total

- **SODIUM METHYL SULFATE**

  Mobile phase: Prepare a 0.04 M potassium hydrogen phthalate solution by transferring 16.4 g of potassium hydrogen phthalate into a 2-L volumetric flask, diluting to volume with water, and mixing. Then, filter the solution through a 0.45-μm pore-size filter.

  Standard solution: 0.1 mg/mL of anhydrous sodium methyl sulfate in *Mobile phase*

  Sample solution: Suspend 1 g of the sample in 10.0 mL of 50% (v/v) ethanol solution. Stir for 30 min using a Teflon-coated stirring bar. Allow the suspension to precipitate and filter. Evaporate a 1.0-mL aliquot to dryness under reduced pressure (10 mm Hg) and heat at 60°. Redissolve the residue in 1.0 mL of the *Mobile phase*.

  Chromatographic system, Appendix IIA
  Mode: Liquid chromatography
  Detector: Refractive index
  Column: 25-cm × 4.6-mm (id) column packed with Nucleosil 10SB (or equivalent)
  Column temperature: 40°
  Flow rate: 1 mL/min
  Injection volume: 20 μL

  System suitability
  Sample: *Standard solution*
  Suitability requirement: The relative standard deviation for three replicate injections is NMT 4.0% for the response factor of the sodium methyl sulfate peak obtained using the formula:

  $$Result = (A_S/C_S)$$

  A_S = peak area response of the *Standard solution*
  C_S = concentration (mg/mL) of sodium methyl sulfate in the *Standard solution*

  Analysis: Separately inject the *Standard solution* and *Sample solution* into the chromatograph and record the peak areas. Calculate the percent of methyl sulfate in the sample by the formula:

  $$Result = (C_S A_U)/(A_S W)$$

  C_S = concentration (mg/mL) of sodium methyl sulfate in the *Standard solution*
  A_U = peak area response obtained from the *Sample solution*
  A_S = peak area response obtained from the *Standard solution*
  W = weight of the sample taken to prepare the *Sample solution* (g)

  Acceptance criteria: NMT 0.1%

SPECIFIC TESTS

- **ASH (ACID-INSOLUBLE),** Appendix IIC
  Acceptance criteria NMT 1.0%

- **DEGREE OF AMIDE SUBSTITUTION AND TOTAL GALACTURONIC ACID IN THE PECTIN COMPONENT**

  Clark's solution: Mix 100 g of magnesium sulfate heptahydrate with 0.3 mL of sulfuric acid and sufficient water to make 180 mL of solution.

  Sample: 5 g

  Sample solution: Transfer the *Sample* to a suitable beaker, add a mixture of 5 mL of 2.7 N hydrochloric acid and 100 mL of 60% ethanol, and stir for 10 min.

  Analysis:
  Step 1: Transfer the *Sample solution* to a fritted-glass filter tube (30- to 60-mL capacity) and wash the filtrate with six 15-mL portions of the same

---

[2] Precision Sampling Corporation, or equivalent

hydrochloric acid-60% ethanol mixture, followed by 60% ethanol, until the filtrate is free of chlorides. Finally, wash with 20 mL of ethanol, dry for 2.5 h in an oven at 105°, cool, and weigh. Transfer exactly one-tenth of the total net weight of the now ash-free, dried sample (representing 0.5 g of the original, unwashed sample) to a 250-mL conical flask and moisten the sample with 2 mL of ethanol. Add 100 mL of recently boiled and cooled water, stopper the flask, and swirl occasionally until a complete solution is formed. Add 5 drops of phenolphthalein TS, titrate with 0.1 N sodium hydroxide, and record the results as the initial titer (V_1).

Step 2: Add exactly 20 mL of 0.5 N sodium hydroxide to the flask, stopper, shake the flask vigorously, and let it stand for 15 min. Add exactly 20 mL of 0.5 N hydrochloric acid, and shake the flask until the pink color disappears. Titrate with 0.1 N sodium hydroxide to a faint pink color that persists after vigorous shaking; record this value as the saponification titer (V_2).

Step 3: Quantitatively transfer the contents of the conical flask into a 500-mL distillation flask fitted with a Kjeldahl trap and a water-cooled condenser, the delivery tube of which extends well beneath the surface of a mixture of 150 mL of carbon dioxide-free water and 20.0 mL of 0.1 N hydrochloric acid in a receiving flask. Add 20 mL of a 1:10 sodium hydroxide solution to the distillation flask, seal the connections, and begin heating carefully to avoid excessive foaming. Continue heating until 80 to 120 mL of distillate has been collected. Add a few drops of methyl red TS to the receiving flask, titrate the excess acid with 0.1 N sodium hydroxide, and record the volume required (mL) as S. Perform a blank determination (see *General Provisions*) on 20.0 mL of 0.1 N hydrochloric acid and record the volume of 0.1 N sodium hydroxide required (mL) as B. Record the amide titer (B − S) as V_3.

Step 4: Transfer exactly one-tenth of the total net weight of the dried sample (representing 0.5 g of the original, unwashed sample) prepared in *Step 1* to a 50-mL beaker and wet with about 2 mL of ethanol. Dissolve the sample in 25 mL of 0.125 M sodium hydroxide. Agitate the solution for 1 h at room temperature. Quantitatively transfer the saponified solution to a 50-mL volumetric flask and dilute to volume with water. Transfer 25.0 mL of this solution to the round-bottom flask of the distillation apparatus and add 20 mL of *Clark's solution*. Start the distillation by heating the round-bottom flask. Collect the first 15 mL of distillate separately in a graduated cylinder. Then start the steam supply and continue distillation until 150 mL of distillate has been collected in a 200-mL beaker. Quantitatively combine the distillates, titrate with 0.05 M sodium hydroxide to pH 8.5 and record the volume of titrant required (mL) as S. Perform a blank determination (see *General Provisions*) using 20 mL of water. Record the required volume of 0.05 M sodium hydroxide (mL) as B. Record acetate ester titer (S − B) as V_4.

Calculations: Calculate the degree of amidation (as the percent of total carboxyl groups) by the formula:

$$\text{Result} = 100[V_3/(V_1 + V_2 + V_3 - V_4)]$$

Calculate the weight of galacturonic acid (mg) by the formula:

$$\text{Result} = 19.41(V_1 + V_2 + V_3 - V_4)$$

The amount (mg) of galacturonic acid obtained in this way is the content of one-tenth of the weight of the washed and dried sample. To calculate the percent galacturonic acid on a moisture- and ash-free basis, multiply the number of mg obtained by 1000/x, in which x is the weight, (mg), of the washed and dried sample. If the sample is known to be of the non-amidated type, only V_1 and V_2 need to be determined; V_3 may be regarded as zero in the formula for calculating mg of galacturonic acid.

Acceptance criteria
Degree of amide substitution in the pectin component: NMT 25% of total carboxylic groups
Total galacturonic acid in the pectin component: NLT 65.0%, calculated on the ash-free, dried basis

- **Loss on Drying,** Appendix IIC: 105° for 2 h
  Acceptance criteria: NMT 12.0%
- **Total Insoluble Substances**
  [NOTE—Use deionized water free from dust on insoluble particles throughout this procedure.]
  Sample: 1 g
  Analysis: Dry 70-mm glass fiber filter paper[3] for 1 h in an oven equipped with a fan and set to 105°. Transfer the paper to a desiccator containing silica gel, allow it to cool, and weigh.
  Transfer the *Sample* into a 250-mL beaker, add 5 mL of isopropanol to the beaker and, while stirring, add 100 mL of a previously mixed and filtered solution of 0.03 M sodium hydroxide containing 0.1% (w/w) tetrasodium ethylenediamine tetraacetic acid (EDTA). Stir the mixture for 30 min at room temperature, then heat to boiling. [**Caution**—Some Pectins foam when heated.] Filter the hot solution through the previously dried filter paper under a vacuum. Rinse the beaker and filter five times with 100 mL of warm (approximately 50°) water. Dry the filter paper in the oven at 105° for 1 h. Transfer it to the desiccator and allow it to cool. Weigh the paper. Calculate the percentage of insoluble material using the formula:

$$\text{Result} = [(M_2 - M_1)/S] \times 100$$

S = sample weight (g)
M_1 = weight of the filter paper before filtration step (g)
M_2 = weight of the filter paper after filtration and drying steps (g)

Acceptance criteria: NMT 3.0%

---

[3] GF/B (Whatman 1821 070, or equivalent)

OTHER REQUIREMENTS
- **LABELING:** Indicate the presence of sulfur dioxide if the residual concentration is greater than 10 mg/kg.

Pennyroyal Oil
First Published: Prior to FCC 6

FEMA: 2839

CAS: [8013-99-8]

UNII: AK85U7Y3MV [pennyroyal oil]

DESCRIPTION
Pennyroyal Oil occurs as a light yellow to yellow, aromatic liquid with a minty odor. It is the volatile oil obtained by steam distillation from the fresh or partly dried plant *Mentha pulegium* L. (Fam. Labiatae). It is soluble in most fixed oils and in propylene glycol. It is soluble, with slight cloudiness, in mineral oil, but it is practically insoluble in glycerin.

Function: Flavoring agent

Packaging and Storage: Store in a cool place protected from light in full, tight containers that are made from steel or aluminum and that are suitably lined.

IDENTIFICATION
- **INFRARED SPECTRA,** *Spectrophotometric Identification Tests,* Appendix IIIC

  Acceptance criteria: The spectrum of the sample exhibits relative maxima at the same wavelengths as those of the spectrum below.

ASSAY
- **KETONES,** *Aldehydes and Ketones, Neutral Sulfite Method,* Appendix VI

  Acceptance criteria: NLT 88.0% and NMT 96.0% by volume, of ketones

SPECIFIC TESTS
- **ANGULAR ROTATION,** *Optical (Specific) Rotation,* Appendix IIB: Use a 100-mm tube.

  Acceptance criteria: Between +18° and +25°
- **REFRACTIVE INDEX,** Appendix IIB

  [NOTE—Use an Abbé or other refractometer of equal or greater accuracy.]

  Acceptance criteria: Between 1.483 and 1.488 at 20°
- **SOLUBILITY IN ALCOHOL,** Appendix VI

  Acceptance criteria: One mL of the sample dissolves in 2 mL of 70% alcohol.
- **SPECIFIC GRAVITY:** Determine by any reliable method (see *General Provisions*)

  Acceptance criteria: Between 0.928 and 0.940

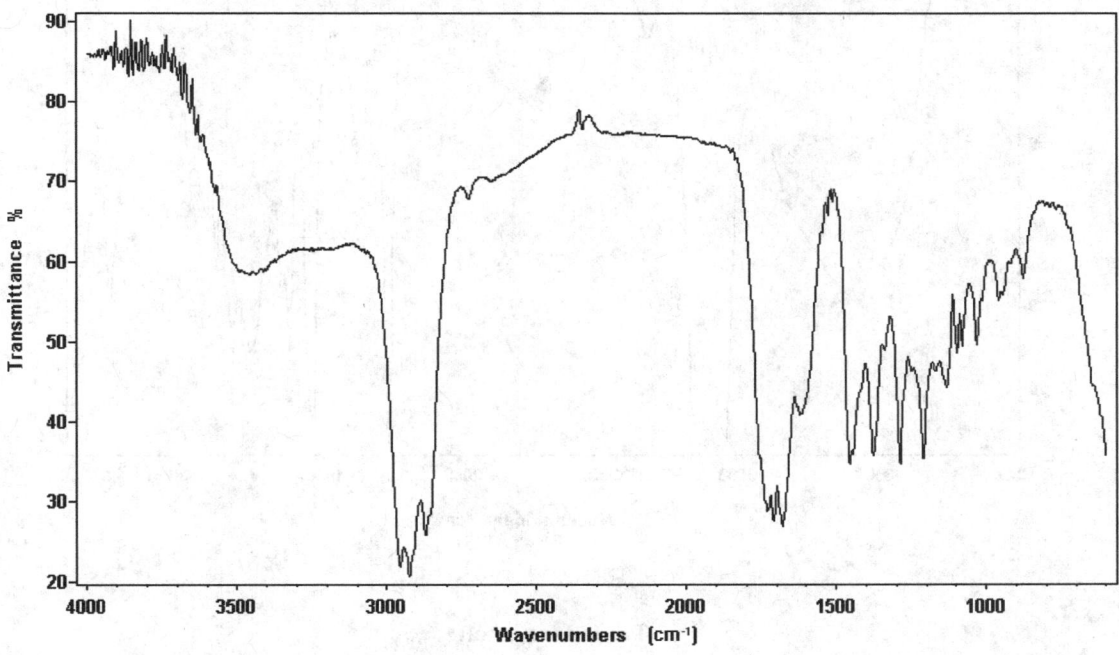

Pennyroyal Oil

ω-Pentadecalactone

First Published: Prior to FCC 6

Cyclopentadecanolide
Exaltolide
Thibetolide

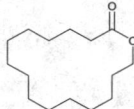

$C_{15}H_{28}O_2$
FEMA: 2840
UNII: OK17S3S98K [pentadecalactone]

Formula wt 240.38

DESCRIPTION
ω-Pentadecalactone occurs as a white to tan or blue-gray crystalline solid.
Odor: Musky
Solubility: Soluble in vegetable oils; insoluble or practically insoluble in propylene glycol
Boiling Point: ~137° (2 mm Hg)
Solubility in Alcohol, Appendix VI: One g dissolves in 1 mL of 95% alcohol.
Function: Flavoring agent

IDENTIFICATION
- **INFRARED SPECTRA,** *Spectrophotometric Identification Tests,* Appendix IIIC
  Acceptance criteria: The spectrum of the sample exhibits relative maxima at the same wavelengths as those of the spectrum below.

ASSAY
- **PROCEDURE:** Proceed as directed under *M-1b,* Appendix XI.
  Acceptance criteria: NLT 99.0% of $C_{15}H_{28}O_2$

OTHER REQUIREMENTS
- **SOLIDIFICATION POINT,** Appendix IIB
  Acceptance criteria: NLT 35°

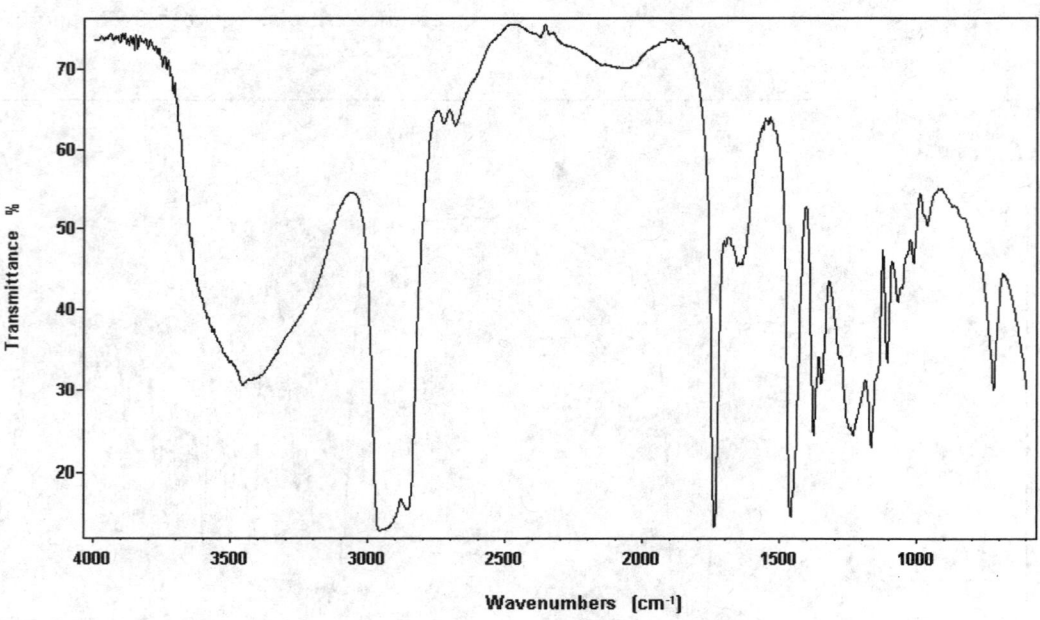

ω-Pentadecalactone

Pentaerythritol Ester of Partially Hydrogenated Wood Rosin

First Published: Prior to FCC 6
Last Revision: FCC 6

DESCRIPTION
Pentaerythritol Ester of Partially Hydrogenated Wood Rosin occurs as a hard, amber-colored resin (color K or paler as determined by ASTM Designation D 509). It is soluble in acetone, but insoluble in water.
Function: Masticatory substance in chewing gum base
Packaging and Storage: Store in well-closed containers.

IDENTIFICATION
- **INFRARED SPECTRA,** *Spectrophotometric Identification Tests,* Appendix IIIC

Sample preparation: Melted sample on a potassium bromide plate
Acceptance criteria: The spectrum of the sample exhibits relative maxima at the same wavelengths as those of the spectrum below.

IMPURITIES
Inorganic Impurities
- **LEAD,** *Sample Solution for Lead Limit Test,* Appendix IV
  Acceptance criteria: NMT 1 mg/kg

SPECIFIC TESTS
- **ACID NUMBER,** Appendix IX
  Acceptance criteria: Between 7 and 18
- **RING-AND-BALL SOFTENING POINT,** *Softening Point, Ring-and-Ball Method,* Appendix IX
  Acceptance criteria: 94° or higher

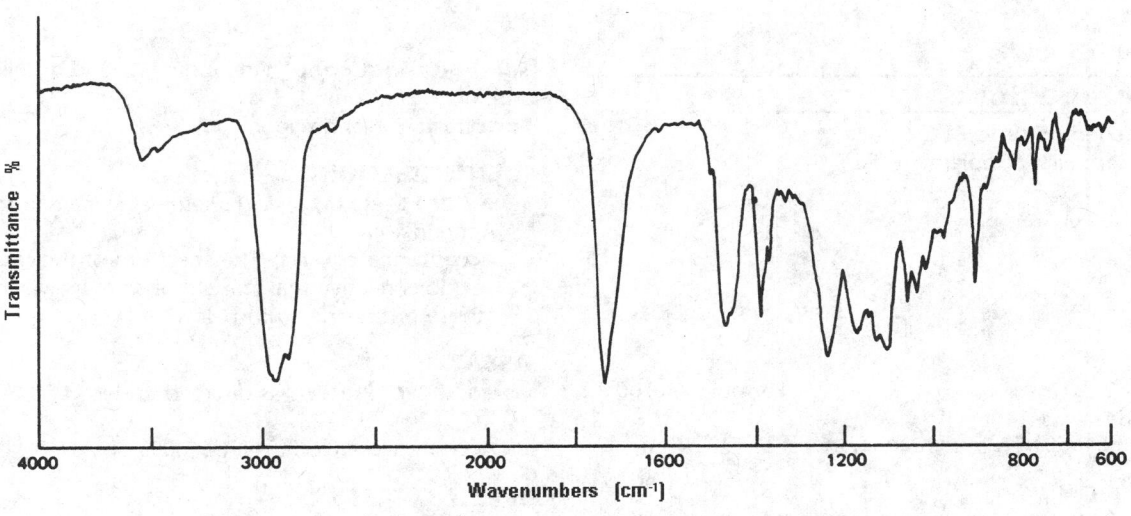

Pentaerythritol Ester of Partially Hydrogenated Wood Rosin

Pentaerythritol Ester of Wood Rosin

First Published: Prior to FCC 6
Last Revision: FCC 6

DESCRIPTION
Pentaerythritol Ester of Wood Rosin occurs as a hard, pale amber-colored resin (color M or paler, as determined by ASTM Designation D 509). It is soluble in acetone, but is insoluble in water and in alcohol.
Function: Masticatory substance in chewing gum base
Packaging and Storage: Store in well-closed containers.

IDENTIFICATION
- **INFRARED SPECTRA,** *Spectrophotometric Identification Tests,* Appendix IIIC

Sample preparation: Melted sample on a potassium bromide plate
Acceptance criteria: The spectrum of the sample exhibits relative maxima at the same wavelengths as those of the spectrum below.

IMPURITIES
Inorganic Impurities
- **LEAD,** *Sample Solution for Lead Limit Test,* Appendix IV
  Acceptance criteria: NMT 1 mg/kg

SPECIFIC TESTS
- **ACID NUMBER,** Appendix IX
  Acceptance criteria: Between 6 and 16
- **RING-AND-BALL SOFTENING POINT,** *Softening Point, Ring-and-Ball Method,* Appendix IX
  Acceptance criteria: 100° or higher

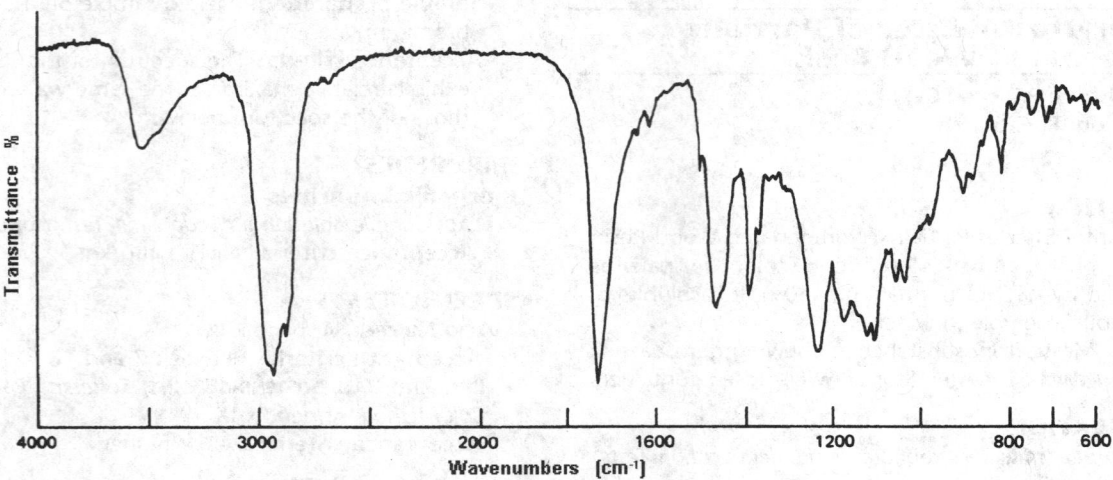

Pentaerythritol Ester of Wood Rosin

2,3-Pentanedione

First Published: Prior to FCC 6
Last Revision: First Supplement, FCC 6

Acetyl Propionyl

$C_5H_8O_2$ Formula wt 100.12
FEMA: 2841
UNII: K4WBE45SCM [2,3-pentanedione]

DESCRIPTION
2,3-Pentanedione occurs as a yellow to yellow-green liquid. It may contain a suitable antioxidant.
Odor: Penetrating, buttery on dilution
Solubility: Miscible in alcohol, propylene glycol, most fixed oils; insoluble or practically insoluble in glycerin, water
Boiling Point: ~108°

Solubility in Alcohol, Appendix VI: One mL dissolves in 3 mL of 50% alcohol.
Function: Flavoring agent

IDENTIFICATION
- **INFRARED SPECTRA,** *Spectrophotometric Identification Tests,* Appendix IIIC
  Acceptance criteria: The spectrum of the sample exhibits relative maxima at the same wavelengths as those of the spectrum below.

ASSAY
- **PROCEDURE:** Proceed as directed under *M-1b,* Appendix XI.
  Acceptance criteria: NLT 93.0% of $C_5H_8O_2$

SPECIFIC TESTS
- **REFRACTIVE INDEX,** Appendix II: At 20°
  Acceptance criteria: Between 1.402 and 1.406
- **SPECIFIC GRAVITY:** Determine at 25° by any reliable method (see *General Provisions*).
  Acceptance criteria: Between 0.952 and 0.962

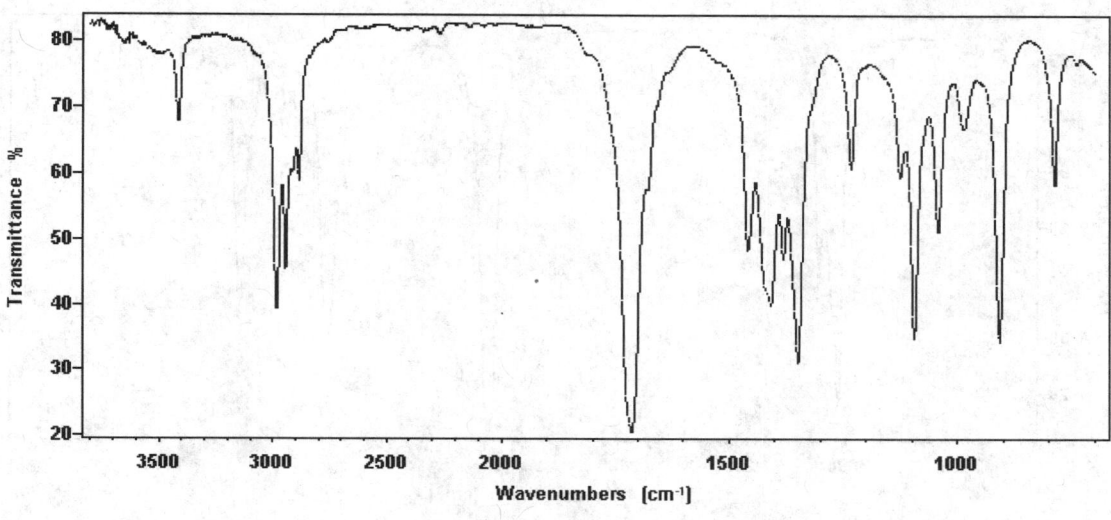

2,3-Pentanedione

2-Pentanone

First Published: Prior to FCC 6

Methyl Propyl Ketone

C₅H₁₀O Formula wt 86.13
FEMA: 2842
UNII: I97392I10V [methyl propyl ketone]

DESCRIPTION

2-Pentanone occurs as a colorless, mobile liquid.
Odor: Fruity, ethereal
Solubility: Miscible in alcohol, ether; 1 mL dissolves in 25 mL water
Boiling Point: ~102°
Function: Flavoring agent

IDENTIFICATION

- **INFRARED SPECTRA**, *Spectrophotometric Identification Tests*, Appendix IIIC

  Acceptance criteria: The spectrum of the sample exhibits relative maxima at the same wavelengths as those of the spectrum below.

ASSAY

- **PROCEDURE:** Proceed as directed under *M-1b*, Appendix XI.
  Acceptance criteria: NLT 95.0% of C₅H₁₀O

SPECIFIC TESTS

- **ACID VALUE, FLAVOR CHEMICALS (OTHER THAN ESSENTIAL OILS)**, *M-15*, Appendix XI
  Acceptance criteria: NMT 2.0
- **REFRACTIVE INDEX**, Appendix II: At 20°
  Acceptance criteria: Between 1.387 and 1.392
- **SPECIFIC GRAVITY:** Determine at 25° by any reliable method (see *General Provisions*).
  Acceptance criteria: Between 0.801 and 0.806

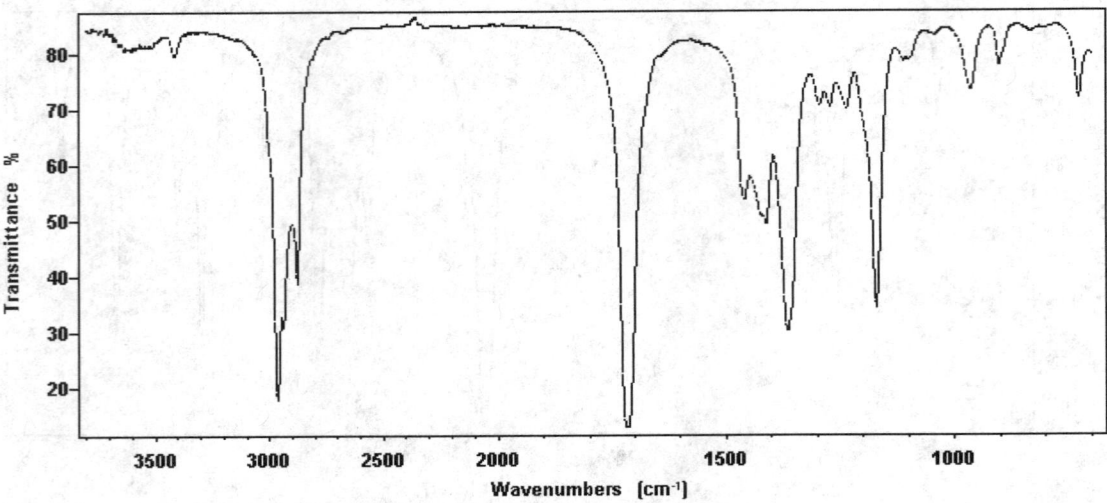

2-Pentanone

Peppermint Oil

First Published: Prior to FCC 6

FEMA: 2848

CAS: [8006-90-4]

UNII: AV092KU4JH [peppermint oil]

DESCRIPTION

Peppermint Oil occurs as a colorless or pale yellow liquid with a strong, penetrating odor of peppermint and a pungent taste that is followed by a sensation of coldness when air is drawn into the mouth. It is the essential oil obtained by steam distillation from the fresh overground parts of the flowering plant of *Mentha piperita* L. (Fam. Labiatae); it may be rectified by distillation, but is neither partially nor wholly dementholized. It is soluble in alcohol and in most vegetable oils, but it is insoluble in propylene glycol.

Function: Flavoring agent

Packaging and Storage: Store in a cool place protected from light in full, tight containers.

IDENTIFICATION

- **A. INFRARED SPECTRA,** *Spectrophotometric Identification Tests,* Appendix IIIC

  Acceptance criteria: The spectrum of the sample exhibits relative maxima at the same wavelengths as those of the spectrum below.

- **B. PROCEDURE**

  Analysis: Mix 3 drops of sample with 5 mL of a 1:300 solution of nitric acid: glacial acetic acid in a dry test tube, and place the tube in a beaker of boiling water.

  Acceptance criteria: A blue color appears within 5 min which, on continued heating, deepens and shows a copper-colored fluorescence, and then fades, leaving a golden yellow solution.

ASSAY

- **TOTAL ESTERS,** *Esters, Ester Determination,* Appendix VI,

  Sample: 10 g

  Analysis: Use 99.16 as the Equivalence factor (e) in the calculation.

  Acceptance criteria: NLT 5.0%, calculated as menthyl acetate ($C_{12}H_{22}O_2$)

- **TOTAL MENTHOL,** *Total Alcohols,* Appendix VI

  Sample: 2.5 g of acetylated sample

  Analysis: Calculate the percentage of total menthol by the formula:

  $$\text{Result} = 7.814A(1 - 0.0021E)/(B - 0.021A)$$

  A = difference between the mL of 0.5 N hydrochloric acid required in the titration and the mL of 0.5 N hydrochloric acid required in the residual blank titration

  E = percentage of *Total Esters*

  B = weight (g) of the acetylated sample

  Acceptance criteria: NLT 50.0% of menthol ($C_{10}H_{20}O$)

SPECIFIC TESTS

- **ANGULAR ROTATION,** *Optical (Specific) Rotation,* Appendix IIB: Use a 100-mm tube.

  Acceptance criteria: Between −18° and −32°

- **DIMETHYL SULFIDE**

  Sample: 25 mL

  Analysis: Distill 1 mL of the *Sample,* and carefully superimpose the distillate on 5 mL of mercuric chloride TS in a test tube.

  Acceptance criteria

  Rectified Oil: A white film does not form at the zone of contact within 1 min.

  Natural Oil: A white film forms at the zone of contact within 1 min.

- **REFRACTIVE INDEX,** Appendix IIB
  [NOTE—Use an Abbé or other refractometer of equal or greater accuracy.]
  Acceptance criteria: Between 1.459 and 1.465 at 20°
- **SOLUBILITY IN ALCOHOL,** Appendix VI
  Acceptance criteria: One mL of the sample dissolves in 3 mL of 70% alcohol.
- **SPECIFIC GRAVITY:** Determine by any reliable method (see *General Provisions*).
  Acceptance criteria: Between 0.896 and 0.908

OTHER REQUIREMENTS
- **LABELING:** Indicate whether it is natural or rectified.

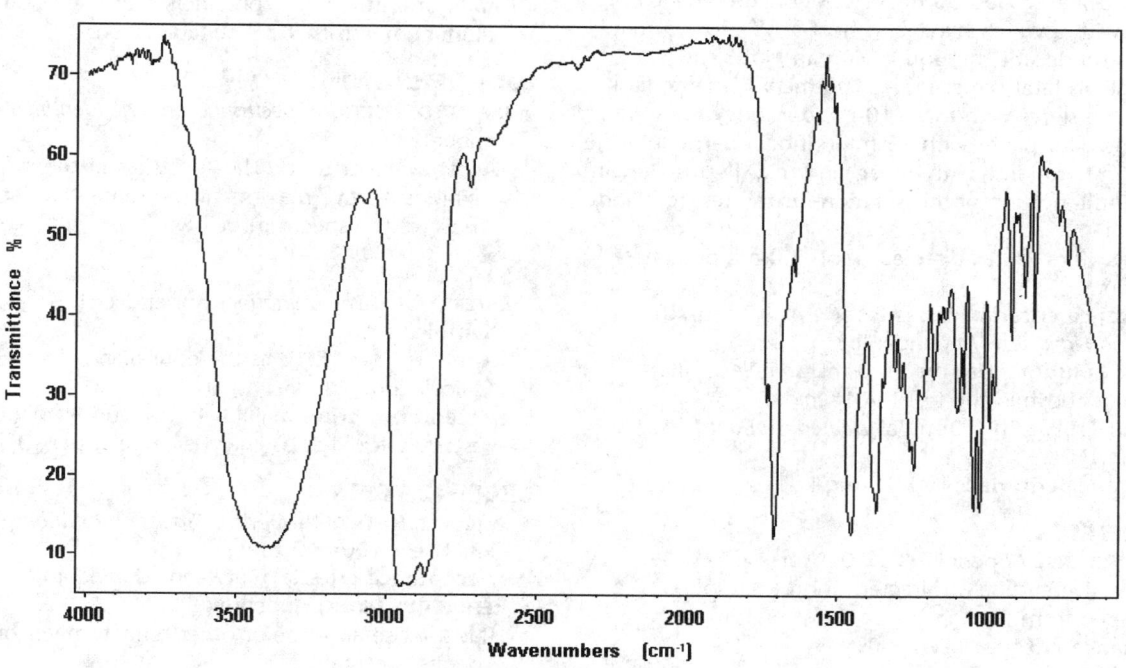

Peppermint Oil

Perlite

First Published: Prior to FCC 6

Expanded Perlite

DESCRIPTION
In its natural state, Perlite occurs as a dense, gray to brown, glassy volcanic rock consisting essentially of fused sodium potassium aluminum silicate plus 3% to 5% water. When fractured and heated at high temperature (900° to 1100°) under proper conditions, it pops like popcorn, caused by the presence of occluded water, expanding to 20 or more times its original volume. The expanded material is crushed to yield a white, nonhygroscopic powder having a bulk density of 32 to 400 kg/m^3 (2 to 25 lb/ft^3) and a particle size ranging from less than one to several hundred micrometers. It is in this latter expanded and powdered state that Perlite is used as a filter aid in food processing. Acceptable food-grade free-flowing agents such as sodium carbonate and sodium silicate may be added. The powder is slightly soluble in water and sparingly soluble in dilute acids and alkalis.
Function: Filter aid in food processing
Packaging and Storage: Store in well-closed containers.

IDENTIFICATION
- **ALUMINUM,** Appendix IIIA
  Sample solution: Mix the 1 g of sample with 25 mL of 2.7 N hydrochloric acid contained in a beaker. Cover the beaker with a watch glass, heat on a steam bath for 15 min, and cool. Filter, and neutralize the filtrate to litmus paper with 6 N ammonium hydroxide. Use the filtrate as the *Sample solution*. [NOTE—Retain any remaining *Sample solution* for the tests for *Potassium* and *Sodium*, below.]
  Acceptance criteria: Passes tests
- **POTASSIUM,** Appendix IIIA
  Sample solution: Use the retained *Sample solution* from the test for *Aluminum*, above.
  Acceptance criteria: Passes tests
- **SODIUM,** Appendix IIIA
  Sample solution: Use the retained *Sample solution* from the test for *Aluminum*, above.
  Acceptance criteria: Passes tests
- **SILICA TEST**
  Analysis: Prepare a bead by fusing a few crystals of sodium ammonium phosphate on a platinum loop in the flame of a burner. Place the hot, transparent bead in contact with a sample, and fuse.

Acceptance criteria: Silica floats about in the bead, producing, upon cooling, an opaque bead with a web-like structure.

IMPURITIES
Inorganic Impurities
- **ARSENIC**, *Arsenic Limit Test,* Appendix IIIB
  Sample solution: Transfer the 10.0 g of sample into a 250-mL beaker, add 50 mL of 0.5 N hydrochloric acid, cover with a watch glass, and heat at 70° for 15 min. Cool, and decant through Whatman No. 3, or equivalent, filter paper into a 100-mL volumetric flask. Wash the slurry with three 10 mL portions of hot water and the filter paper with 15 mL of hot water; dilute the solution to volume with water, and mix. [NOTE—Retain a 10.0-mL portion of this solution for the test for *Lead,* below.]
  Analysis: Proceed as directed using 3.0 mL of *Sample solution.*
  Acceptance criteria: Passes test (NMT 10 mg/kg)
- **LEAD**, *Lead Limit Test,* Appendix IIIB
  Sample solution: Use the 10.0 mL *Sample solution* retained above in the test for *Arsenic.*
  Control: 10 µg Pb (10 mL of *Diluted Standard Lead Solution*)
  Acceptance criteria: NMT 10 mg/kg

SPECIFIC TESTS
- **LOSS ON DRYING,** Appendix IIC: 105° for 2 h
  Analysis: Determine as directed using a sample of the powdered form.
  Acceptance criteria: NMT 3.0%
- **LOSS ON IGNITION**
  Sample: 250 mg of glassy form sample, crushed
  Analysis: Ignite the *Sample* at 1000° to constant weight.
  Acceptance criteria: NMT 7.0%
- **PH,** *pH Determination,* Appendix IIB
  Sample solution: Boil 10 g of sample with 100 mL of water for 30 min, dilute to 100 mL with water, and filter through a fine-pore, sintered-glass funnel.
  Analysis: Proceed as directed using the filtrate from the *Sample solution.*
  Acceptance criteria: Between 5 and 11

Petitgrain Oil, Paraguay Type
First Published: Prior to FCC 6

CAS: [8014-17-3]
UNII: 59JDQ5VT0T [citrus aurantium fruit oil]

DESCRIPTION
Petitgrain Oil, Paraguay Type, occurs as a yellow to brown-yellow liquid with a somewhat harsh, bittersweet, floral odor. It is the volatile oil obtained by steam distillation from the leaves and small twigs of the bitter orange tree, *Citrus aurantium* L. subspecies amara (Fam. Rutaceae). It is soluble in most fixed oils and is soluble, with opalescence or turbidity, in mineral oil and in propylene glycol. It is relatively insoluble in glycerin.
Function: Flavoring agent
Packaging and Storage: Store in a cool place protected from light in full, tight containers that are made from steel or aluminum and that are suitably lined.

IDENTIFICATION
- **INFRARED SPECTRA,** *Spectrophotometric Identification Tests,* Appendix IIIC
  Acceptance criteria: The spectrum of the sample exhibits relative maxima at the same wavelengths as those of the spectrum below.

ASSAY
- **ESTERS,** *Ester Determination,* Appendix VI
  Sample: 2 g
  Analysis: Use 98.15 as the equivalence factor (e) in the calculation.
  Acceptance criteria: NLT 45.0% and NMT 60.0% of esters, calculated as linalyl acetate ($C_{12}H_{20}O_2$)

SPECIFIC TESTS
- **ANGULAR ROTATION,** *Optical (Specific) Rotation,* Appendix IIB: Use a 100-mm tube.
  Acceptance criteria: Between −4° and +1°
- **REFRACTIVE INDEX,** Appendix IIB
  [NOTE—Use an Abbé or other refractometer of equal or greater accuracy.]
  Acceptance criteria: Between 1.455 and 1.462 at 20°
- **SOLUBILITY IN ALCOHOL,** Appendix VI
  Acceptance criteria: One mL of the sample dissolves in 4 mL of 70% alcohol. The solution usually develops opalescence or turbidity upon further dilution.
- **SPECIFIC GRAVITY:** Determine by any reliable method (see *General Provisions*).
  Acceptance criteria: Between 0.878 and 0.889

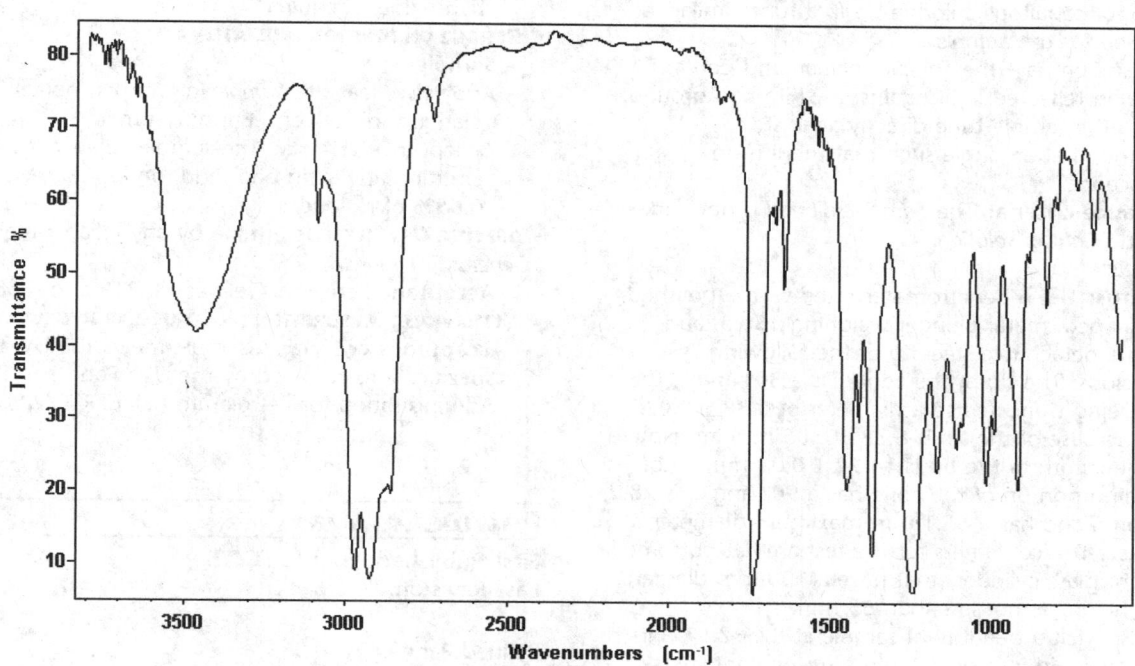

Petitgrain Oil, Paraguay Type

Petrolatum

First Published: Prior to FCC 6
Last Revision: FCC 6

White Petrolatum
Yellow Petrolatum
Petroleum Jelly
INS: 905b

CAS: [8009-03-8]
[92045-77-7]
[100684-33-1]

UNII: 4T6H12BN9U [petrolatum]

DESCRIPTION
Petrolatum occurs as an unctuous mass varying in color from white to yellow or light amber. It is transparent in thin layers, and has not more than a slight fluorescence, even after being melted. It is a purified mixture of semisolid saturated hydrocarbons, mainly paraffinic in nature, obtained from petroleum. In general, it has a viscosity of not less than 3 centistokes at 100°. At 5% initial distillation, 95% of material has a carbon number equal to or greater than 18. It has a minimum average molecular weight of 350. It is partially soluble in ether, insoluble in water, and is almost insoluble in cold or hot alcohol and in cold absolute alcohol. It is partially soluble in solvent hexane, and in most fixed and volatile oils, and is freely soluble in chloroform and in turpentine oil. It may contain any antioxidant permitted by the U.S. Food and Drug Administration in an amount not greater than that required to produce its intended effect.

Function: Defoaming agent; lubricant; protective coating; release agent
Packaging and Storage: Store in tight containers.

IMPURITIES
Inorganic Impurities
- **LEAD,** *Sample Solution for Lead Limit Test,* Appendix IV
  Control: 5 µg Pb (5 mL of *Diluted Standard Lead Solution*)
  Acceptance criteria: NMT 1 mg/kg

SPECIFIC TESTS
- **ACIDITY OR ALKALINITY**
  Sample: 35 g
  Analysis: Transfer *Sample* into a 250-mL separatory flask, add 100 mL of boiling water, and shake vigorously for 5 min. After the sample and water have separated, draw off the water into a casserole, wash the sample in the separator with two 50-mL portions of boiling water, and add the washings to the casserole. Add 1 drop of phenolphthalein TS to the accumulated 200 mL of water, and boil. If the addition of phenolphthalein produces no pink color, add 0.1 mL of methyl orange TS.
  Acceptance criteria: No pink color is produced after the addition of phenolphthalein, and no red or pink color appears after the addition of the methyl orange.
- **COLOR**
  Sample solution: Melt about 10 g of sample on a steam bath, and pour about 5 mL of the liquid into a 150- × 50-mm, clear-glass, bacteriological test tube, keeping the sample liquid.

Control solution: Mix 3.8 mL of ferric chloride CS and 1.2 mL of cobaltous chloride CS in a tube similar to that used for the *Sample*.
Analysis: Compare the *Sample solution* and *Control solution* in reflected light against a white background, holding the sample tube directly against the background at an angle such that there is no fluorescence.
Acceptance criteria: The *Sample solution* is not darker than the *Control solution*.

- **CONSISTENCY**
  Apparatus: Use a penetrometer fitted with a polished, cone-shaped, metal plunger weighing 150 g, and having a detachable steel tip of the following dimensions: The tip of the cone has a 30° angle, the point being truncated to a diameter of 0.38 ± 0.025-mm; the base of the tip is 8.38 ± 0.05 mm in diameter; and the length of the tip is 14.94 ± 0.05 mm long. The remaining portion of the cone has a 90° angle, is 28.2 mm long, and has a 65.1-mm maximum diameter at the base. The containers for the test are flat-bottomed metal or glass cylinders that have a 100-mm diameter and a height of not less than 65 mm.
  Analysis: Melt a quantity of sample at 82 ± 2.5°, and pour the liquid into one or more of the containers, filling each to within 6 mm of the rim. Cool at 25 ± 2.5° for at least 16 h, protecting from drafts. Two hours before the test, place the containers in a water bath at 25 ± 0.5°. If the room temperature is below 23.5° or above 26.5°, adjust the temperature of the cone to 25 ± 0.5° by placing it in the water bath as well.
  Without disturbing the surface of the sample, place a container on the penetrometer table, and lower the plunger until the tip of the cone just touches the top surface of the sample at a spot 25 to 38 mm from the edge of the container. Adjust the zero setting, and quickly release the plunger, then hold it free for 5 s. Secure the plunger, and read the total penetration, to the nearest 0.1 mm, from the scale. Make three or more trials, each so spaced that there is no overlapping of the areas of penetration. If the penetration exceeds 20 mm, use a separate container of the sample for each trial. Calculate the average of the three or more readings, and conduct further trials to a total of ten if the individual results differ from the average by more than ±3%.
  Acceptance criteria: The final average of the trials is NLT 10.0 mm and NMT 30.0 mm, indicating a consistency value between 100 and 300.

- **MELTING RANGE OR TEMPERATURE DETERMINATION,** *Procedure for Class III,* Appendix IIB
  Acceptance criteria: Between 38° and 60°

- **ORGANIC ACIDS**
  Sample: 20 g
  Analysis: Add *Sample* to 50 mL of alcohol, previously neutralized to phenolphthalein TS with sodium hydroxide, and 50 mL of water. Agitate thoroughly, and heat to boiling. Add 1 mL of phenolphthalein TS, and while vigorously agitating the solution, titrate rapidly to the appearance of a sharp-pink endpoint, noting the change in the alcohol-water layer.
  Acceptance criteria: NMT 0.4 mL of 0.1 N sodium hydroxide is required.

- **RESIDUE ON IGNITION (SULFATED ASH)**
  Sample: 4 g
  Analysis: Heat the *Sample* in an open porcelain or platinum dish over a Bunsen burner.
  Acceptance criteria: The sample volatilizes without emitting any acrid odor and, on ignition, yields NMT 0.05% of residue.

- **SPECIFIC GRAVITY:** Determine by any reliable method (see *General Provisions*).
  Acceptance criteria: Between 0.815 and 0.880 at 60°

- **ULTRAVIOLET ABSORPTION (POLYNUCLEAR HYDROCARBONS)**
  Acceptance criteria: A sample meets the UV absorbance specifications required by the U.S. Food and Drug Administration for Petrolatum (21 CFR 172.880).

Petroleum Wax

First Published: Prior to FCC 6
Last Revision: FCC 6

Refined Paraffin Wax
Refined Microcrystalline Wax
INS: 905c   CAS: [8002-74-2]
    Hydrotreated Paraffin Wax CAS: [64742-51-4]
    Hydrotreated Microcrystalline Wax CAS: [64742-60-5]
        Microcrystalline Wax CAS: [63231-60-7]
UNII: I9O0E3H2ZE [paraffin]

DESCRIPTION
Petroleum Wax occurs as a translucent wax that ranges in color from amber to almost white. It is a refined mixture of solid hydrocarbons, paraffinic in nature, obtained from petroleum. It may be prepared as "refined paraffin wax" or as "refined microcrystalline wax." The refined paraffin wax is usually obtained from a lower-molecular-weight fraction of petroleum and has lower viscosities when molten than the refined microcrystalline wax. The refined microcrystalline wax is usually higher in molecular weight, in flash point, and in melting point than the refined paraffin wax. These waxes are graded and sold according to color and to melting point, which ranges from about 48° to 102°. They exhibit low solubility in organic solvents, but they are most soluble in aromatic hydrocarbons and least soluble in ketones, in esters, and in alcohols.
Function: Masticatory substance in chewing gum base; protective coating; defoaming agent; microcapsules for spices and flavoring agents
Packaging and Storage: Store in well-closed containers that are properly vented for liquid materials.

IDENTIFICATION
- **INFRARED SPECTRA,** *Spectrophotometric Identification Tests,* Appendix IIIC
  Sample preparation: Melted sample on a potassium bromide plate
  Acceptance criteria: The spectrum of the sample exhibits relative maxima at the same wavelengths as those of the appropriate spectrum below.

IMPURITIES
Inorganic Impurities
- **LEAD,** *Sample Solution for Lead Limit Test,* Appendix IV
  Control: 5 µg Pb (5 mL of *Diluted Standard Lead Solution*)
  Acceptance criteria: NMT 1 mg/kg

SPECIFIC TESTS
- **COLOR:** Determine by any suitable method, such as ASTM D 1500.
  Acceptance criteria: Where applicable, conforms to the representations of the vendor.
- **MELTING POINT:** Determine by any suitable method, such as ASTM D 127.
  Acceptance criteria: Where applicable, conforms to the representations of the vendor.
- **ODOR:** Determine by any suitable method, such as ASTM D 1833.
  Acceptance criteria: Where applicable, conforms to the representations of the vendor.
- **ULTRAVIOLET ABSORBANCE (POLYNUCLEAR HYDROCARBONS)**
  Analysis: Determine as directed in the U.S. Food and Drug Administration regulation for Petroleum Wax (21 *CFR* 172.886).
  Acceptance criteria
  280–289 nm: NMT 0.15
  290–299 nm: NMT 0.12
  300–359 nm: NMT 0.08
  360–400 nm: NMT 0.02

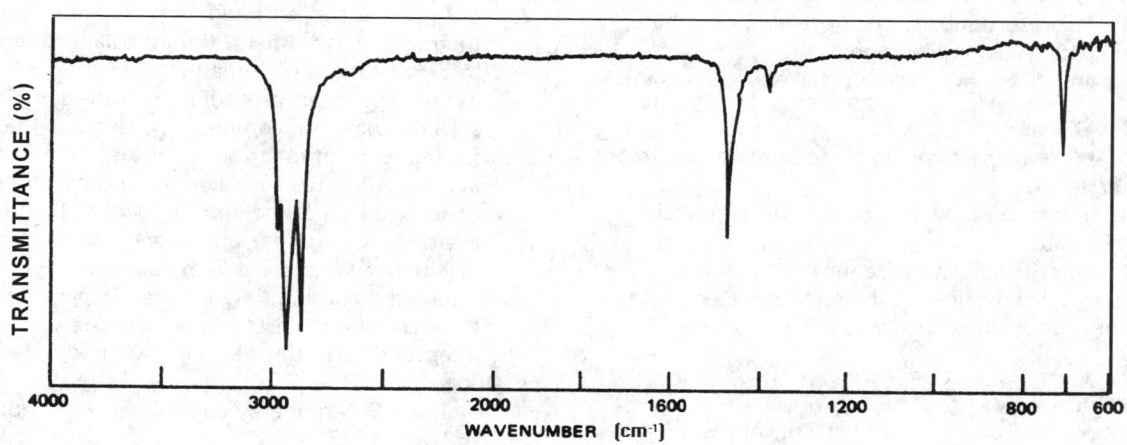

Petroleum Wax (Refined)

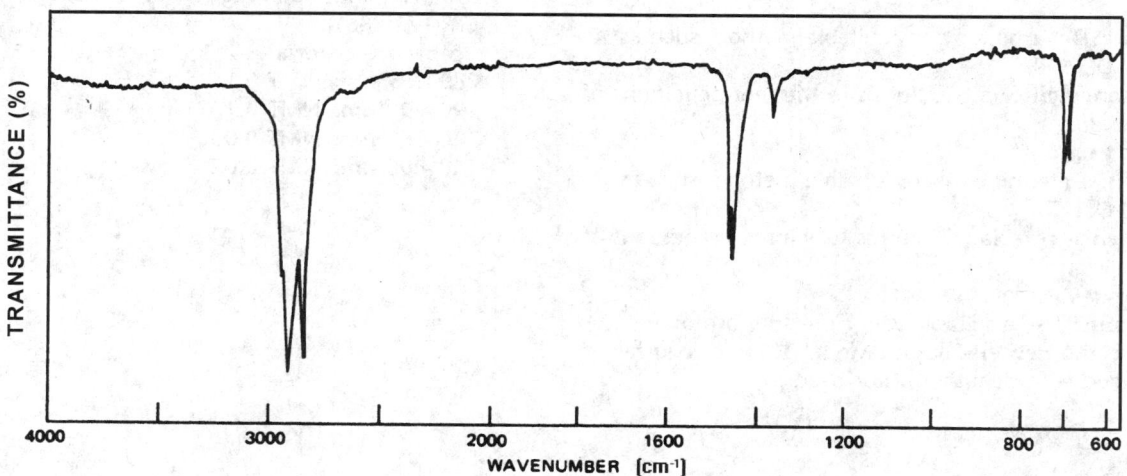

Petroleum Wax (Microcrystalline)

Petroleum Wax, Synthetic

First Published: Prior to FCC 6

Synthetic Wax (Ethylene Polymer or Ethylene Copolymer with Alpha-Olefins)

DESCRIPTION
Petroleum Wax, Synthetic, occurs as an off-white to white wax. It is a refined mixture of solid hydrocarbons, paraffinic in nature, prepared by the catalytic polymerization of ethylene or copolymer of ethylene with linear (C_3–C_{12}) alpha-olefins. Synthetic Petroleum Wax ranges in melting point from about 77° to 116° (170° to 240°F). It is most soluble in aromatic hydrocarbons and least soluble in ketones, in esters, and in alcohols.

Function: Masticatory substance in chewing gum base; protective coating; defoaming agent

Packaging and Storage: Store in well-closed containers.

IDENTIFICATION
- **INFRARED SPECTRA**, *Spectrophotometric Identification Tests*, Appendix IIIC

  Sample preparation: Melted sample on a potassium bromide plate

  Acceptance criteria: The spectrum of the sample exhibits relative maxima at the same wavelengths as those of the spectrum below.

IMPURITIES
Inorganic Impurities
- **LEAD**, *Sample Solution for Lead Limit Test*, Appendix IV

  Control: 5 µg Pb (5 mL of *Diluted Standard Lead Solution*)

  Acceptance criteria: NMT 1 mg/kg

SPECIFIC TESTS
- **COLOR**

  Analysis: Determine by any suitable method, such as ASTM D 1500.

  Acceptance criteria: Conforms to the representations of the vendor.

- **MELTING POINT**

  Analysis: Determine by any suitable method, such as ASTM D 127.

  Acceptance criteria: Conforms to the representations of the vendor.

- **MOLECULAR WEIGHT (AVERAGE)**

  Apparatus: Use a suitable vapor pressure osmometer, such as the Hewlett-Packard Model 302A, or equivalent, equipped with dual thermistor beads.

  Calibration standards: Dissolve benzil ($C_6H_5COCOC_6H_5$) in *o*-dichlorobenzene to produce solutions containing 3, 7, 10, and 15 mg of benzil, respectively, per gram of solution, and heat to 100° on a steam bath.

  Sample solutions: Dissolve sample in *o*-dichlorobenzene to produce solutions containing 10, 20, 35, and 50 mg of sample, respectively, per gram of solution, and heat to 100° on a steam bath. (Other suitable concentrations that give ΔR readings between 5 and 25 may be used in the *Analysis* below.)

  Analysis: Following the manufacturer's instructions, balance the osmometer to zero with *o*-dichlorobenzene on both thermistor beads, and establish the calibration constant, K_S, at 100°, using the four *Calibration standards*. When the temperature within the osmometer has re-equilibrated to 100°, place an aliquot of the most concentrated *Sample solution* on the sample thermistor bead. After 4.0 min, balance the instrument to zero with the potentiometer, and record the ΔR value. Repeat this procedure with the same *Sample solution* two or three times, and average the ΔR values for that concentration. In a similar manner, obtain the average ΔR values for each of the other three concentrations of the *Sample solution*. Plot the four average ΔR values for the *Sample solutions* as a function of ΔR/concentration, and extrapolate the line to zero to obtain the constant, K_U, for the sample. Divide K_S by K_U to obtain the molecular weight of the sample tested.

  Acceptance criteria: Between 500 and 1200

- **ODOR**

  Analysis: Determine by any suitable method, such as ASTM D 1833.

  Acceptance criteria: Conforms to the representations of the vendor.

- **ULTRAVIOLET ABSORBANCE (POLYNUCLEAR HYDROCARBONS)**

  Analysis: Determine as directed in the U.S. Food and Drug Administration regulation for Petroleum Wax (21 *CFR* 172.886).

  Acceptance criteria
  280–289 nm: NMT 0.15
  290–299 nm: NMT 0.12
  300–359 nm: NMT 0.08
  360–400 nm: NMT 0.02

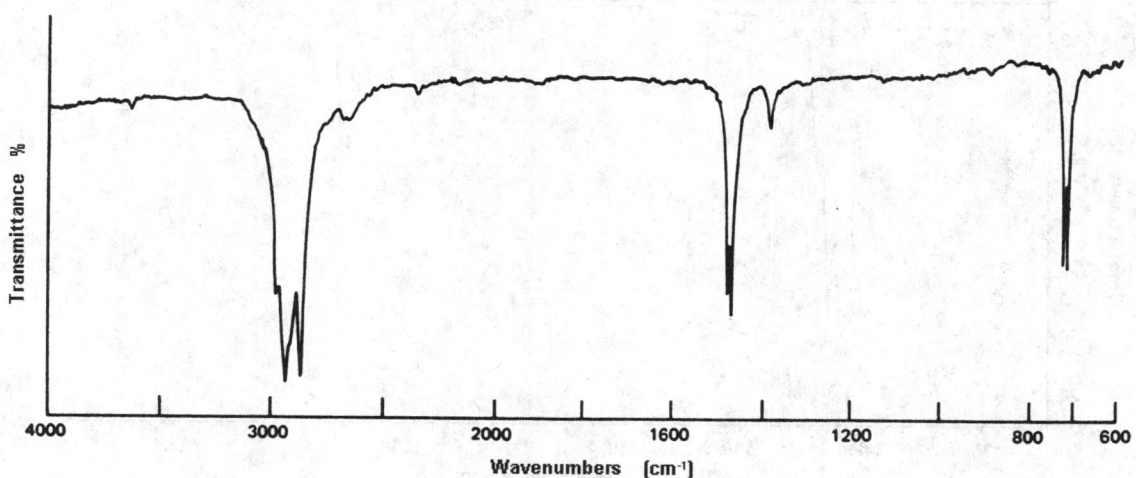

Petroleum Wax, Synthetic

α-Phellandrene

First Published: Prior to FCC 6
Last Revision: First Supplement, FCC 6

p-Mentha-1,5-diene

$C_{10}H_{16}$ Formula wt 136.24
FEMA: 2856
UNII: 49JV13XE39 [α-phellandrene, (+/−)-]

DESCRIPTION
α-Phellandrene occurs as a colorless to slightly yellow liquid. It may contain a suitable antioxidant.
Odor: Herbaceous; minty background
Solubility: Soluble in alcohol; insoluble or practically insoluble in water
Solubility in Alcohol, Appendix VI: One mL dissolves in 1 mL of 95% alcohol to give a clear solution.
Function: Flavoring agent

IDENTIFICATION
- **INFRARED SPECTRA,** Spectrophotometric Identification Tests, Appendix IIIC
  Acceptance criteria: The spectrum of the sample exhibits relative maxima at the same wavelengths as those of the spectrum below.

SPECIFIC TESTS
- **REFRACTIVE INDEX,** Appendix II: At 20°
  Acceptance criteria: Between 1.471 and 1.477
- **SPECIFIC GRAVITY:** Determine at 25° by any reliable method (see General Provisions).
  Acceptance criteria: Between 0.835 and 0.865

OTHER REQUIREMENTS
- **ANGULAR ROTATION,** Optical (Specific) Rotation, Appendix IIB: Use a 100-mm tube.
  Acceptance criteria: Between −80° and −120°

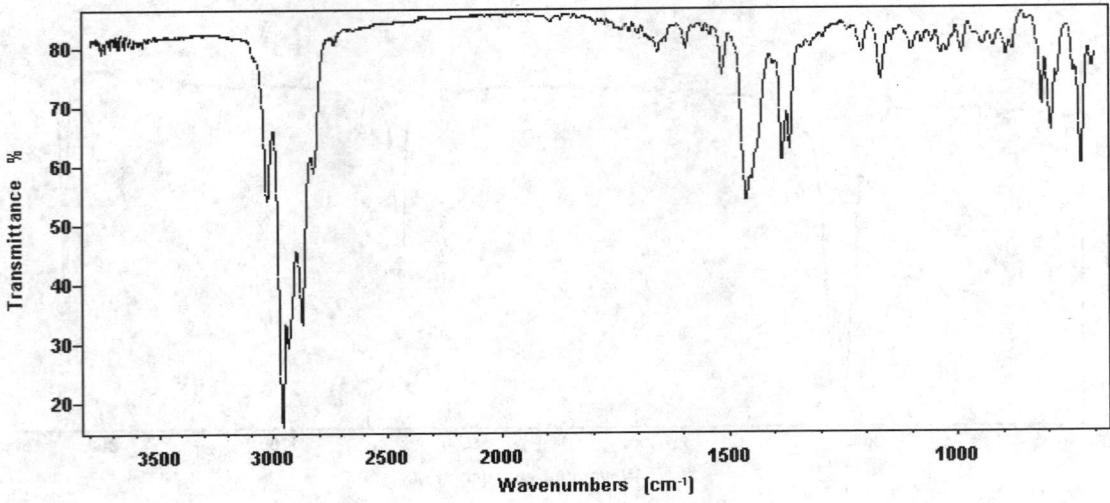

α-Phellandrene

Phenethyl Acetate

First Published: Prior to FCC 6

2-Phenethyl Acetate

$C_{10}H_{12}O_2$ Formula wt 164.20
FEMA: 2857
UNII: 67733846OW [phenethyl acetate]

DESCRIPTION
Phenethyl Acetate occurs as a colorless liquid.
Odor: Sweet, rosy, honey
Solubility: Soluble in alcohol, most fixed oils, propylene glycol; insoluble or practically insoluble in glycerin, water
Boiling Point: ~232°
Solubility in Alcohol, Appendix VI: One mL dissolves in 2 mL of 70% alcohol, and remains in solution on dilution to 10 mL.

Function: Flavoring agent

IDENTIFICATION
- **INFRARED SPECTRA,** *Spectrophotometric Identification Tests,* Appendix IIIC
  Acceptance criteria: The spectrum of the sample exhibits relative maxima at the same wavelengths as those of the spectrum below.

ASSAY
- **PROCEDURE:** Proceed as directed under *M-1b,* Appendix XI.
  Acceptance criteria: NLT 98.0% of $C_{10}H_{12}O_2$

SPECIFIC TESTS
- **ACID VALUE, FLAVOR CHEMICALS (OTHER THAN ESSENTIAL OILS),** *M-15,* Appendix XI
  Acceptance criteria: NMT 1.0
- **REFRACTIVE INDEX,** Appendix II: At 20°
  Acceptance criteria: Between 1.497 and 1.501
- **SPECIFIC GRAVITY:** Determine at 25° by any reliable method (see *General Provisions*).
  Acceptance criteria: Between 1.030 and 1.034

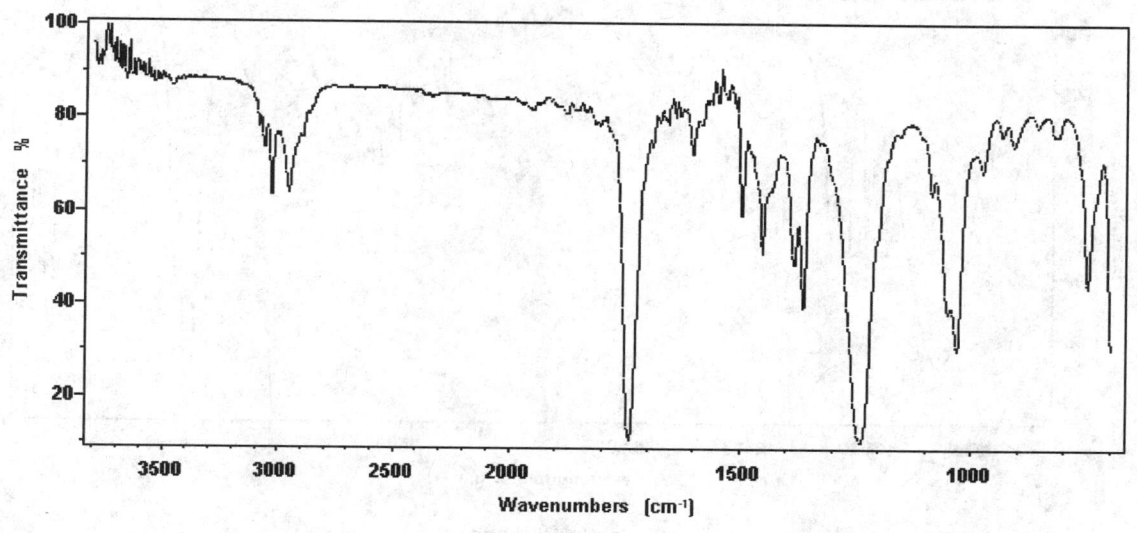

Phenethyl Acetate

Phenethyl Alcohol

First Published: Prior to FCC 6

2-Phenylethyl Alcohol

$C_8H_{10}O$ Formula wt 122.17
FEMA: 2858
UNII: ML9LGA7468 [phenylethyl alcohol]

DESCRIPTION
Phenethyl Alcohol occurs as a colorless liquid.
Odor: Rose
Solubility: Soluble in most fixed oils, water, propylene glycol
Boiling Point: ~219°
Solubility in Alcohol, Appendix VI: One mL dissolves in 2 mL of 50% alcohol, and remains in solution on dilution to 10 mL.
Function: Flavoring agent

IDENTIFICATION
- **INFRARED SPECTRA,** *Spectrophotometric Identification Tests,* Appendix IIIC
  Acceptance criteria: The spectrum of the sample exhibits relative maxima at the same wavelengths as those of the spectrum below.

ASSAY
- **PROCEDURE:** Proceed as directed under *M-1a,* Appendix XI (one isomer).
  Acceptance criteria: NLT 99.0% of $C_8H_{10}O$

SPECIFIC TESTS
- **REFRACTIVE INDEX,** Appendix II: At 20°
  Acceptance criteria: Between 1.531 and 1.534
- **SPECIFIC GRAVITY:** Determine at 25° by any reliable method (see *General Provisions*).
  Acceptance criteria: Between 1.017 and 1.020

OTHER REQUIREMENTS
- **CHLORINATED COMPOUNDS,** Appendix VI
  Acceptance criteria: Passes test

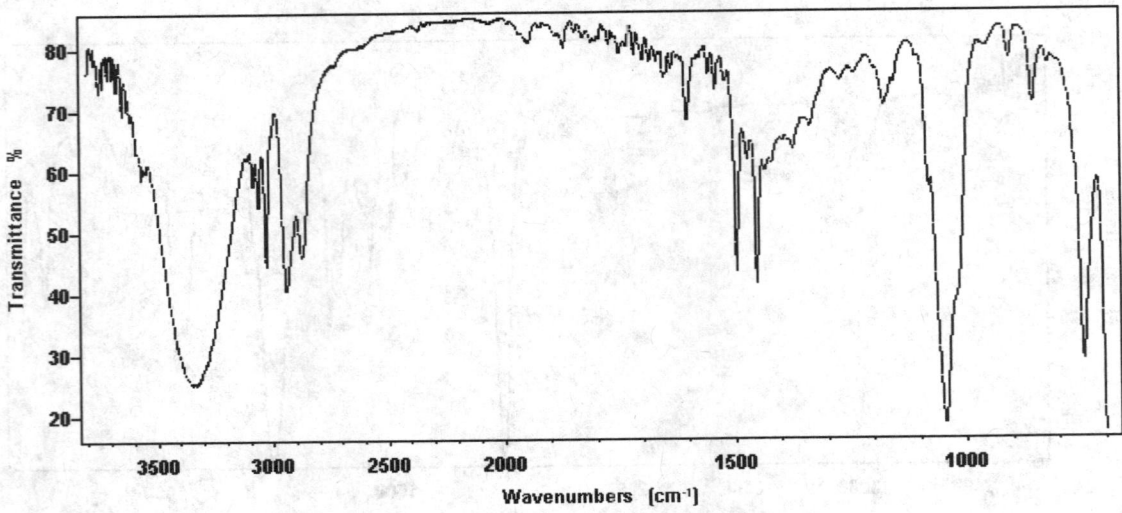

Phenethyl Alcohol

Phenethyl Isobutyrate

First Published: Prior to FCC 6

C₁₂H₁₆O₂   Formula wt 192.26
FEMA: 2862
UNII: QRZ4RE7DCL [2-phenylethyl isobutyrate]

DESCRIPTION
Phenethyl Isobutyrate occurs as a colorless to slightly yellow liquid.
Odor: Fruity, rosy
Solubility: Soluble in alcohol, most fixed oils; insoluble or practically insoluble in water
Boiling Point: ~230°
Solubility in Alcohol, Appendix VI: One mL dissolves in 3 mL of 80% alcohol to give a clear solution.

Function: Flavoring agent

IDENTIFICATION
- **INFRARED SPECTRA,** *Spectrophotometric Identification Tests,* Appendix IIIC
  Acceptance criteria: The spectrum of the sample exhibits relative maxima at the same wavelengths as those of the spectrum below.

ASSAY
- **PROCEDURE:** Proceed as directed under *M-1b,* Appendix XI.
  Acceptance criteria: NLT 98.0% of C₁₂H₁₆O₂

SPECIFIC TESTS
- **ACID VALUE, FLAVOR CHEMICALS (OTHER THAN ESSENTIAL OILS),** *M-15,* Appendix XI
  Acceptance criteria: NMT 1.0
- **REFRACTIVE INDEX,** Appendix II: At 20°
  Acceptance criteria: Between 1.486 and 1.490
- **SPECIFIC GRAVITY:** Determine at 25° by any reliable method (see *General Provisions*).
  Acceptance criteria: Between 0.987 and 0.990

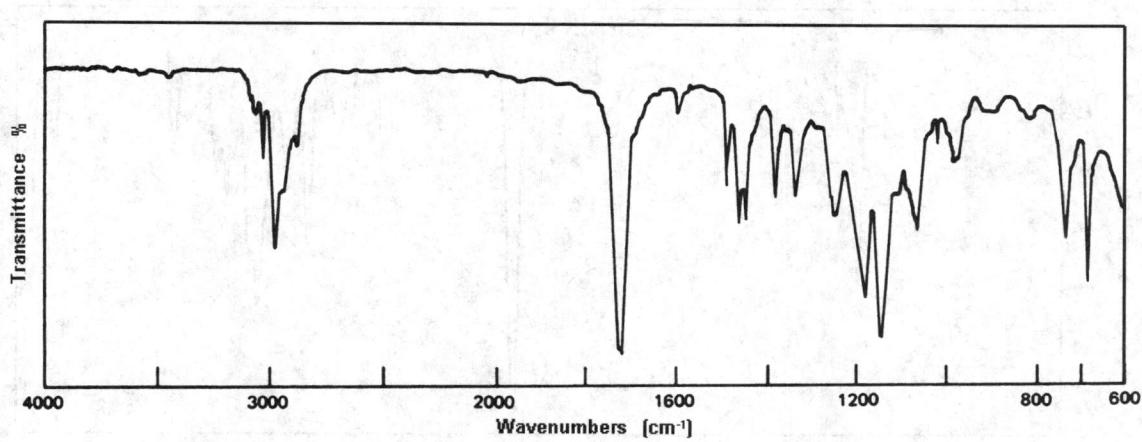
Phenethyl Isobutyrate

Phenethyl Isovalerate

First Published: Prior to FCC 6

$C_{13}H_{18}O_2$ Formula wt 206.28
FEMA: 2871
UNII: K86JE60K0L [phenethyl isovalerate]

DESCRIPTION
Phenethyl Isovalerate occurs as a colorless to slightly yellow liquid.
Odor: Fruity, rosy
Solubility: Soluble in alcohol, most fixed oils; insoluble or practically insoluble in water
Boiling Point: ~263°
Solubility in Alcohol, Appendix VI: One mL dissolves in 3 mL of 80% alcohol to give a clear solution.
Function: Flavoring agent

IDENTIFICATION
- **INFRARED SPECTRA,** *Spectrophotometric Identification Tests,* Appendix IIIC
  Acceptance criteria: The spectrum of the sample exhibits relative maxima at the same wavelengths as those of the spectrum below.

ASSAY
- **PROCEDURE:** Proceed as directed under *M-1b,* Appendix XI (one major isomer).
  Acceptance criteria: NLT 98.0% of $C_{13}H_{18}O_2$

SPECIFIC TESTS
- **ACID VALUE, FLAVOR CHEMICALS (OTHER THAN ESSENTIAL OILS),** *M-15,* Appendix XI
  Acceptance criteria: NMT 1.0
- **REFRACTIVE INDEX,** Appendix II: At 20°
  Acceptance criteria: Between 1.484 and 1.486
- **SPECIFIC GRAVITY:** Determine at 25° by any reliable method (see *General Provisions*).
  Acceptance criteria: Between 0.973 and 0.976

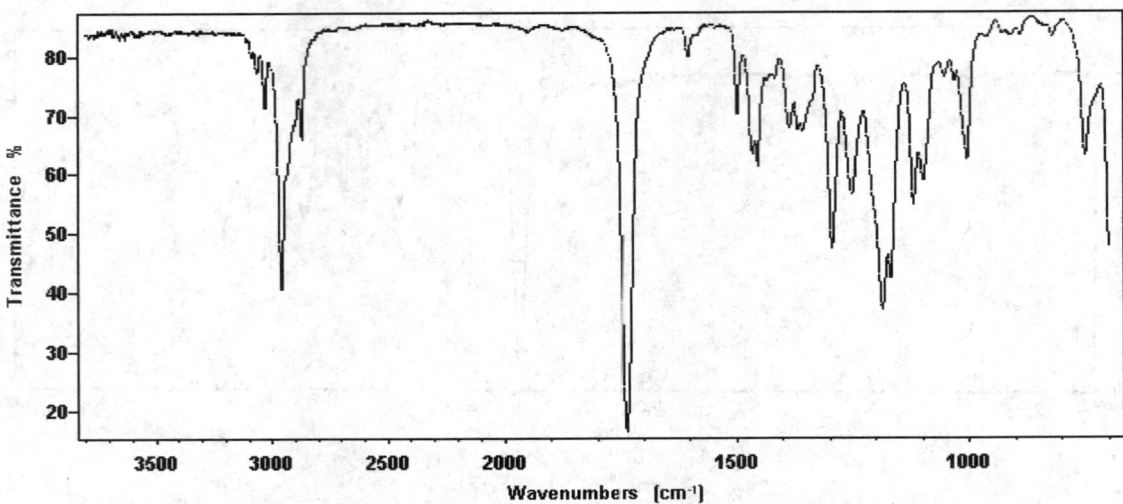

Phenethyl Isovalerate

Phenethyl Phenylacetate

First Published: Prior to FCC 6
Last Revision: Second Supplement, FCC 7

$C_{16}H_{16}O_2$ Formula wt 240.30
FEMA: 2866
UNII: 5J5OJ7GH15 [phenethyl phenylacetate]

DESCRIPTION
Phenethyl Phenylacetate occurs as a colorless to slightly yellow liquid above 26°.
Odor: Rosy, hyacinth
Solubility: Soluble in alcohol; insoluble or practically insoluble in water
Boiling Point: ~325°
Solubility in Alcohol, Appendix VI: One mL dissolves in 4 mL of 90% alcohol to give a clear solution.
Function: Flavoring agent

IDENTIFICATION
- **INFRARED SPECTRA,** Spectrophotometric Identification Tests, Appendix IIIC
  Acceptance criteria: The spectrum of the sample exhibits relative maxima at the same wavelengths as those of the spectrum below.

ASSAY
- **PROCEDURE:** Proceed as directed under *M-1b,* Appendix XI.
  Acceptance criteria: NLT 98.0% of $C_{16}H_{16}O_2$

SPECIFIC TESTS
- **ACID VALUE, FLAVOR CHEMICALS (OTHER THAN ESSENTIAL OILS),** *M-15,* Appendix XI
  Acceptance criteria: NMT 1.0
- **REFRACTIVE INDEX,** Appendix II: At 20°
  [NOTE—It may solidify.]
  Acceptance criteria: 1.548–1.552
- **SPECIFIC GRAVITY:** Determine at 25° by any reliable method (see *General Provisions*).
  Acceptance criteria: 1.075–1.082

OTHER REQUIREMENTS
- **SOLIDIFICATION POINT,** Appendix IIB
  Acceptance criteria: NLT 26°

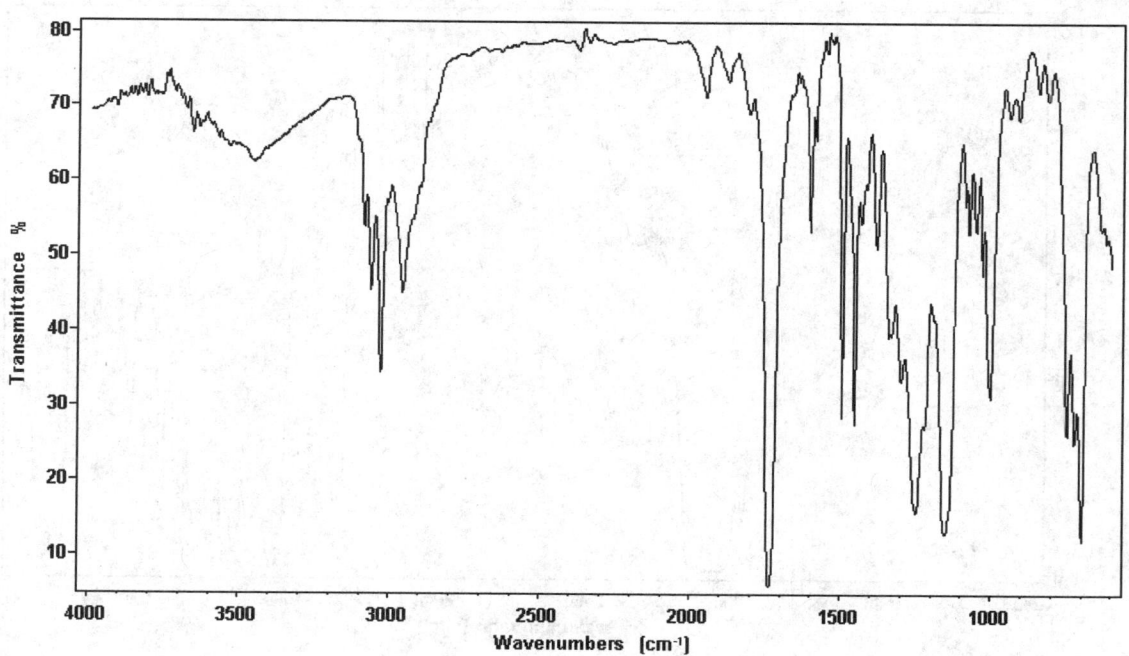

Phenethyl Phenylacetate

Phenethyl Salicylate

First Published: Prior to FCC 6

C$_{15}$H$_{14}$O$_3$ Formula wt 242.27
FEMA: 2868
UNII: 6LDP0U8UB0 [phenethyl salicylate]

DESCRIPTION
Phenethyl Salicylate occurs as a white crystalline solid.
Odor: Balsamic
Solubility: Soluble in alcohol; insoluble or practically insoluble in water
Boiling Point: ~370°
Solubility in Alcohol, Appendix VI: One g dissolves in 20 mL of 95% alcohol to give a clear solution.
Function: Flavoring agent

IDENTIFICATION
- **INFRARED SPECTRA,** *Spectrophotometric Identification Tests,* Appendix IIIC
  Acceptance criteria: The spectrum of the sample exhibits relative maxima at the same wavelengths as those of the spectrum below.

ASSAY
- **PROCEDURE:** Proceed as directed under *M-1b*, Appendix XI.
  Acceptance criteria: NLT 98.0% of C$_{15}$H$_{14}$O$_3$

SPECIFIC TESTS
- **ACID VALUE, FLAVOR CHEMICALS (OTHER THAN ESSENTIAL OILS),** *M-15*, Appendix XI
  [NOTE—Use phenol red TS as the indicator.]
  Acceptance criteria: NMT 1.0

OTHER REQUIREMENTS
- **SOLIDIFICATION POINT,** Appendix IIB
  Acceptance criteria: NLT 41°

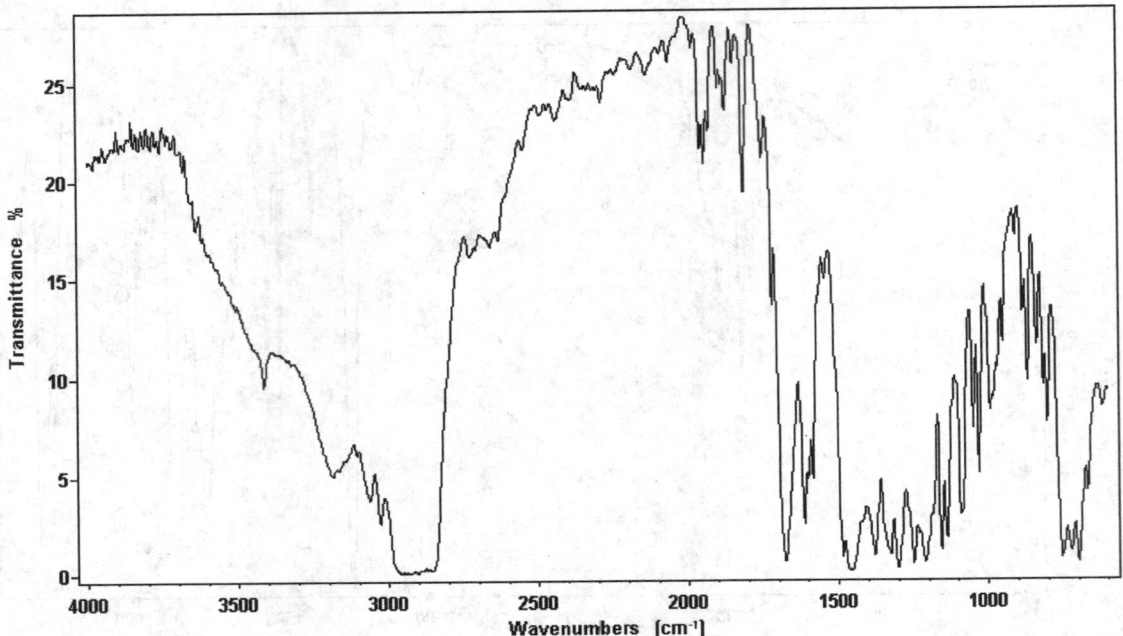

Phenethyl Salicylate

2-Phenethyl 2-Methylbutyrate

First Published: Prior to FCC 6

C₁₃H₁₈O₂　　Formula wt 206.28
FEMA: 3632
UNII: 4D2I5SJ45Q [phenethyl 2-methylbutyrate]

DESCRIPTION
2-Phenethyl 2-Methylbutyrate occurs as a colorless liquid.
Odor: Floral-fruity
Solubility: Soluble in alcohol, most fixed oils; insoluble or practically insoluble in water
Function: Flavoring agent

ASSAY
- **PROCEDURE:** Proceed as directed under *M-1b*, Appendix XI.
  Acceptance criteria: NLT 95.0% of C₁₃H₁₈O₂

SPECIFIC TESTS
- **ACID VALUE, FLAVOR CHEMICALS (OTHER THAN ESSENTIAL OILS),** *M-15*, Appendix XI
  Acceptance criteria: NMT 2.0
- **REFRACTIVE INDEX,** Appendix II: At 20°
  Acceptance criteria: Between 1.484 and 1.488
- **SPECIFIC GRAVITY:** Determine at 25° by any reliable method (see *General Provisions*).

Acceptance criteria: Between 0.973 and 0.977

Phenoxyethyl Isobutyrate

First Published: Prior to FCC 6

C₁₂H₁₆O₃　　Formula wt 208.26
FEMA: 2873
UNII: 43ENB1627Z [2-phenoxyethyl isobutyrate]

DESCRIPTION
Phenoxyethyl Isobutyrate occurs as a colorless liquid.
Odor: Honey, rose
Solubility: Miscible in alcohol, chloroform, ether; insoluble or practically insoluble in water
Boiling Point: ~125° to 127° (4 mm Hg)
Solubility in Alcohol, Appendix VI: One mL dissolves in 1 mL of 95% alcohol to give a clear solution.
Function: Flavoring agent

IDENTIFICATION
- **INFRARED SPECTRA,** *Spectrophotometric Identification Tests,* Appendix IIIC
  Acceptance criteria: The spectrum of the sample exhibits relative maxima at the same wavelengths as those of the spectrum below.

ASSAY
- **PROCEDURE:** Proceed as directed under *M-1b*, Appendix XI.
  Acceptance criteria: NLT 97.0% of $C_{12}H_{16}O_3$

SPECIFIC TESTS
- **ACID VALUE, FLAVOR CHEMICALS (OTHER THAN ESSENTIAL OILS),** *M-15*, Appendix XI
  Acceptance criteria: NMT 1.0
- **REFRACTIVE INDEX,** Appendix II: At 20°
  Acceptance criteria: Between 1.492 and 1.495
- **SPECIFIC GRAVITY:** Determine at 25° by any reliable method (see *General Provisions*).
  Acceptance criteria: Between 1.044 and 1.048

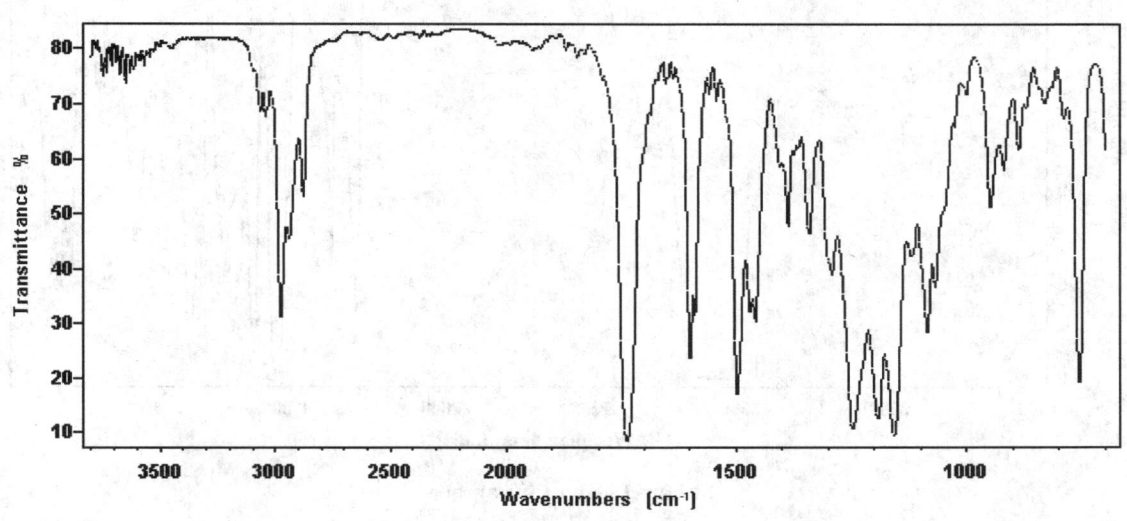

Phenoxyethyl Isobutyrate

Phenyl Ethyl Cinnamate
First Published: Prior to FCC 6

$C_{17}H_{16}O_2$ Formula wt 252.31
FEMA: 2863
UNII: EY056ZZ9MG [phenethyl cinnamate]

DESCRIPTION
Phenyl Ethyl Cinnamate occurs as a white to pale yellow crystalline solid.
Odor: Floral
Solubility: Soluble in propylene glycol, vegetable oils; insoluble or practically insoluble in water
Solubility in Alcohol, Appendix VI: One mL dissolves in 1 mL of 95% ethanol.
Function: Flavoring agent

IDENTIFICATION
- **INFRARED SPECTRA,** *Spectrophotometric Identification Tests,* Appendix IIIC
  Acceptance criteria: The spectrum of the sample exhibits relative maxima at the same wavelengths as those of the spectrum below.

ASSAY
- **PROCEDURE:** Proceed as directed under *M-1b*, Appendix XI.
  Acceptance criteria: NLT 99.0% of $C_{17}H_{16}O_2$

SPECIFIC TESTS
- **ACID VALUE, FLAVOR CHEMICALS (OTHER THAN ESSENTIAL OILS),** *M-15,* Appendix XI
  Acceptance criteria: NMT 1.0

OTHER REQUIREMENTS
- **MELTING RANGE OR TEMPERATURE DETERMINATION,** Appendix IIB
  Acceptance criteria: NLT 54.0°

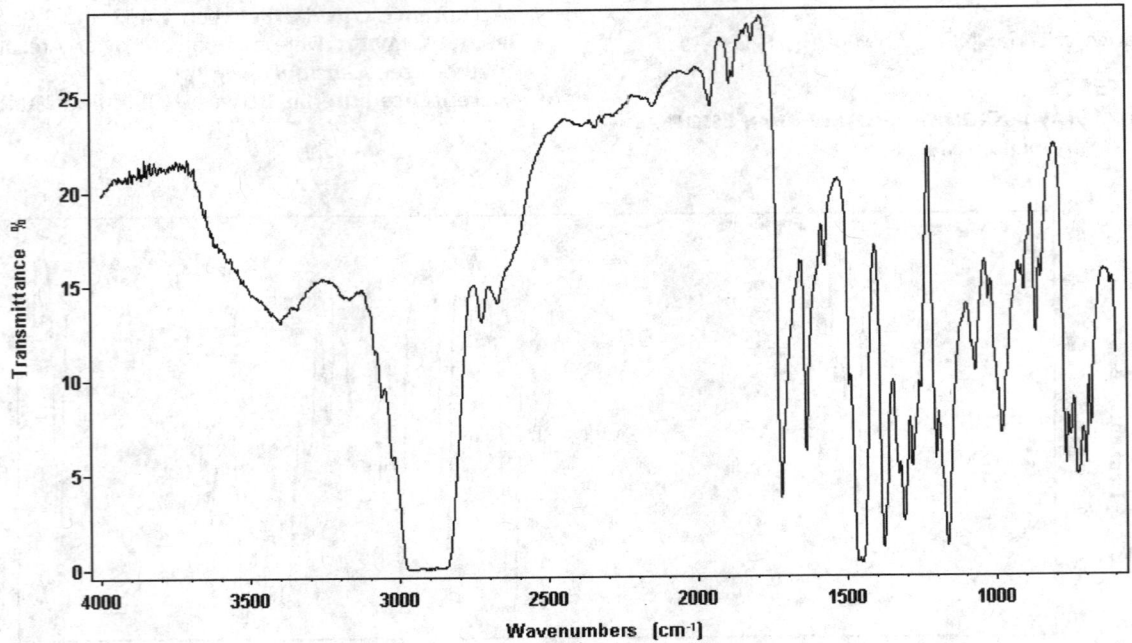

Phenyl Ethyl Cinnamate

Phenyl Ethyl Propionate

First Published: Prior to FCC 6

$C_{11}H_{14}O_2$
FEMA: 2867
UNII: 9VFI60EUHW [phenethyl propionate]

Formula wt 178.23

DESCRIPTION
Phenyl Ethyl Propionate occurs as a colorless to pale yellow liquid.
Odor: Rose
Solubility: Soluble in propylene glycol, vegetable oils; insoluble or practically insoluble in water
Boiling Point: ~245°
Solubility in Alcohol, Appendix VI: One mL dissolves in 1 mL of 95% ethanol.
Function: Flavoring agent

IDENTIFICATION
- **INFRARED SPECTRA,** *Spectrophotometric Identification Tests,* Appendix IIIC
  Acceptance criteria: The spectrum of the sample exhibits relative maxima at the same wavelengths as those of the spectrum below.

ASSAY
- **PROCEDURE:** Proceed as directed under *M-1b,* Appendix XI.
  Acceptance criteria: NLT 98.0% of $C_{11}H_{14}O_2$

SPECIFIC TESTS
- **ACID VALUE, FLAVOR CHEMICALS (OTHER THAN ESSENTIAL OILS),** *M-15,* Appendix XI
  Acceptance criteria: NMT 1.0
- **REFRACTIVE INDEX,** Appendix II: At 20°
  Acceptance criteria: Between 1.491 and 1.497
- **SPECIFIC GRAVITY:** Determine at 25° by any reliable method (see *General Provisions*).
  Acceptance criteria: Between 1.009 and 1.015.

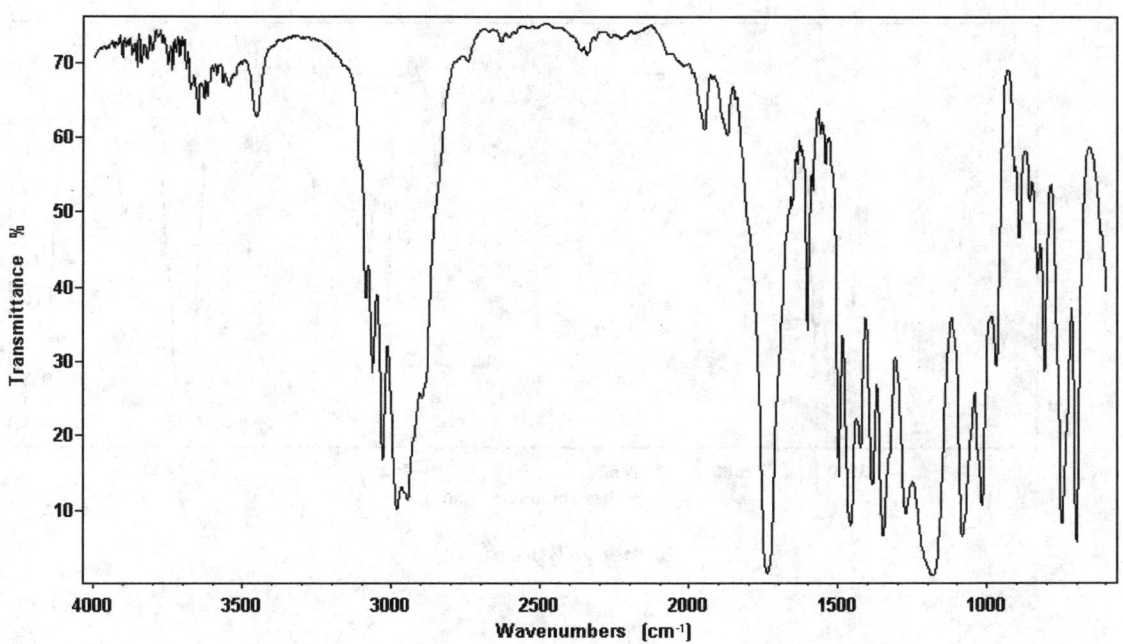

Phenyl Ethyl Propionate

3-Phenyl-1-propanol

First Published: Prior to FCC 6

Phenylpropyl Alcohol
Hydrocinnamyl Alcohol

$C_9H_{12}O$ Formula wt 136.19
FEMA: 2885
UNII: U04IC2765C [3-phenyl-1-propanol]

DESCRIPTION
3-Phenyl-1-propanol occurs as a colorless, slightly viscous liquid.
Odor: Sweet, hyacinth-mignonette
Solubility: Soluble in most fixed oils, propylene glycol; insoluble or practically insoluble in glycerin
Boiling Point: ~236°
Solubility in Alcohol, Appendix VI: One mL dissolves in 1 mL of 70% alcohol.

Function: Flavoring agent

IDENTIFICATION
- **INFRARED SPECTRA,** Spectrophotometric Identification Tests, Appendix IIIC
  Acceptance criteria: The spectrum of the sample exhibits relative maxima at the same wavelengths as those of the spectrum below.

ASSAY
- **PROCEDURE:** Proceed as directed under M-1b, Appendix XI.
  Acceptance criteria: NLT 98.0% of $C_9H_{12}O$

SPECIFIC TESTS
- **REFRACTIVE INDEX,** Appendix II: At 20°
  Acceptance criteria: Between 1.524 and 1.528
- **SPECIFIC GRAVITY:** Determine at 25° by any reliable method (see General Provisions).
  Acceptance criteria: Between 0.998 and 1.002

OTHER REQUIREMENTS
- **FREE 3-PHENYL PROPIONALDEHYDE,** M-1b, Appendix XI
  Acceptance criteria: NMT 0.5%

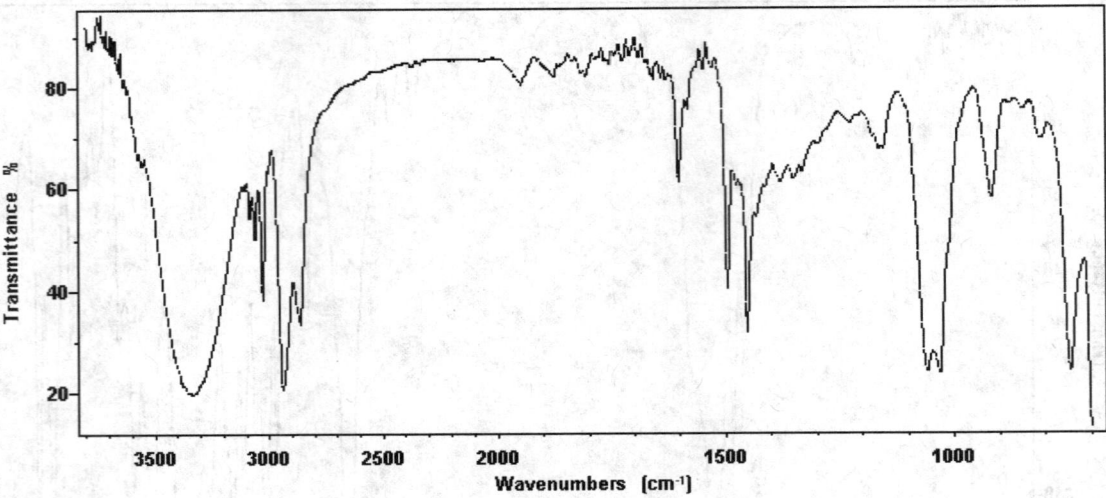

3-Phenyl-1-propanol

Phenylacetaldehyde Dimethyl Acetal
First Published: Prior to FCC 6

$C_{10}H_{14}O_2$ Formula wt 166.22
FEMA: 2876
UNII: P8C94L4MUR [phenyl acetaldehyde dimethyl acetal]

DESCRIPTION
Phenylacetaldehyde Dimethyl Acetal occurs as a colorless liquid.
Odor: Green, spicy, floral
Solubility: Soluble in most fixed oils, propylene glycol; insoluble or practically insoluble in glycerin
Boiling Point: ~219°
Solubility in Alcohol, Appendix VI: One mL dissolves in 2 mL of 70% alcohol, and remains in solution on dilution to 10 mL.
Function: Flavoring agent

IDENTIFICATION
- **INFRARED SPECTRA,** Spectrophotometric Identification Tests, Appendix IIIC
  Acceptance criteria: The spectrum of the sample exhibits relative maxima at the same wavelengths as those of the spectrum below.

ASSAY
- **PROCEDURE:** Proceed as directed under *M-1b,* Appendix XI.
  Acceptance criteria: NLT 95.0% of $C_{10}H_{14}O_2$

SPECIFIC TESTS
- **ACID VALUE, FLAVOR CHEMICALS (OTHER THAN ESSENTIAL OILS),** *M-15,* Appendix XI
  Acceptance criteria: NMT 1.0
- **REFRACTIVE INDEX,** Appendix II: At 20°
  Acceptance criteria: Between 1.493 and 1.496
- **SPECIFIC GRAVITY:** Determine at 25° by any reliable method (see *General Provisions*).
  Acceptance criteria: Between 1.000 and 1.006

OTHER REQUIREMENTS
- **CHLORINATED COMPOUNDS,** Appendix VI
  Acceptance criteria: Passes test
- **FREE PHENYL ACETALDEHYDE,** *M-1b* Appendix XI
  Acceptance criteria: NMT 1.0%

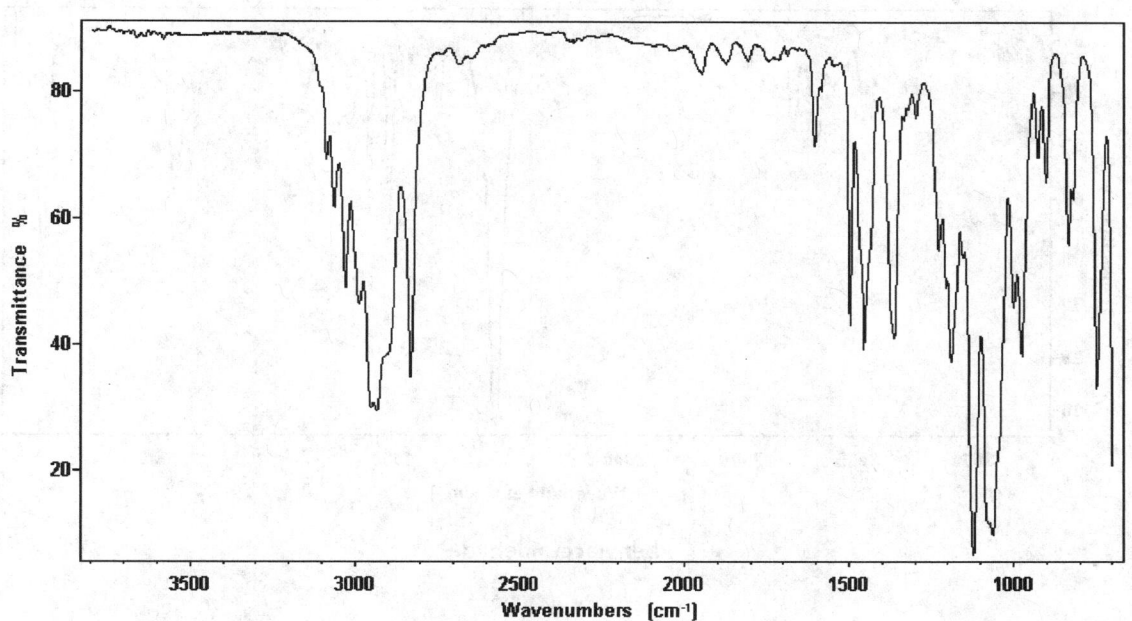

Phenylacetaldehyde Dimethyl Acetal

Phenylacetaldehyde

First Published: Prior to FCC 6
Last Revision: First Supplement, FCC 6

α-Toluic Aldehyde

C_8H_8O Formula wt 120.15
FEMA: 2874
UNII: U8J5PLW9MR [phenylacetaldehyde]

DESCRIPTION
Phenylacetaldehyde occurs as a colorless to slightly yellow, oily liquid; becomes more viscous on aging. It may contain a suitable antioxidant.
Odor: Harsh; hyacinth on dilution
Solubility: Soluble in most fixed oils, propylene glycol; insoluble or practically insoluble in glycerin
Boiling Point: ~195°
Solubility in Alcohol, Appendix VI: One mL dissolves in 2 mL of 80% alcohol.

Function: Flavoring agent

IDENTIFICATION
- **INFRARED SPECTRA,** *Spectrophotometric Identification Tests,* Appendix IIIC
  Acceptance criteria: The spectrum of the sample exhibits relative maxima at the same wavelengths as those of the spectrum below.

ASSAY
- **PROCEDURE:** Proceed as directed under *M-1b,* Appendix XI.
  Acceptance criteria: NLT 90.0% of C_8H_8O

SPECIFIC TESTS
- **ACID VALUE, FLAVOR CHEMICALS (OTHER THAN ESSENTIAL OILS),** *M-15,* Appendix XI
  Acceptance criteria: NMT 5.0
- **REFRACTIVE INDEX,** Appendix II: At 20°
  Acceptance criteria: Between 1.525 and 1.545
- **SPECIFIC GRAVITY:** Determine at 25° by any reliable method (see *General Provisions*).
  Acceptance criteria: Between 1.025 and 1.045

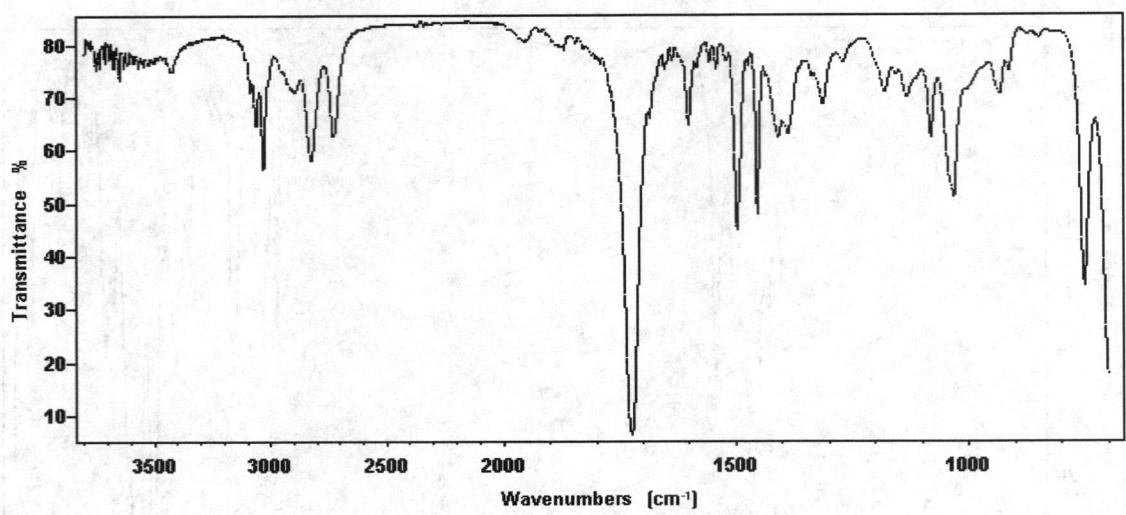

Phenylacetaldehyde

Phenylacetic Acid

First Published: Prior to FCC 6

α-Toluic Acid

C₈H₈O₂ Formula wt 136.15
FEMA: 2878
UNII: ER5I1W795A [phenylacetic acid]

DESCRIPTION
Phenylacetic Acid occurs as a glistening white crystalline solid.
Odor: Persistent, disagreeable, suggestive of geranium leaf and rose when diluted
Solubility: Soluble in most fixed oils, glycerin; slightly soluble in water
Boiling Point: ~265°

Function: Flavoring agent

IDENTIFICATION
- **INFRARED SPECTRA,** *Spectrophotometric Identification Tests,* Appendix IIIC
  Acceptance criteria: The spectrum of the sample exhibits relative maxima at the same wavelengths as those of the spectrum below.

ASSAY
- **PROCEDURE:** Proceed as directed under *M-3b,* Appendix XI.
  Sample: Previously dried over sulfuric acid for 3 h
  Acceptance criteria: NLT 99.0% of C₈H₈O₂, on the dried basis

OTHER REQUIREMENTS
- **MELTING RANGE OR TEMPERATURE DETERMINATION,** *Procedure for Class Ia,* Appendix IIB
  Acceptance criteria: Between 76° and 78°
- **LEAD,** *M-9,* Appendix XI
  Acceptance criteria: NMT 10 mg/kg

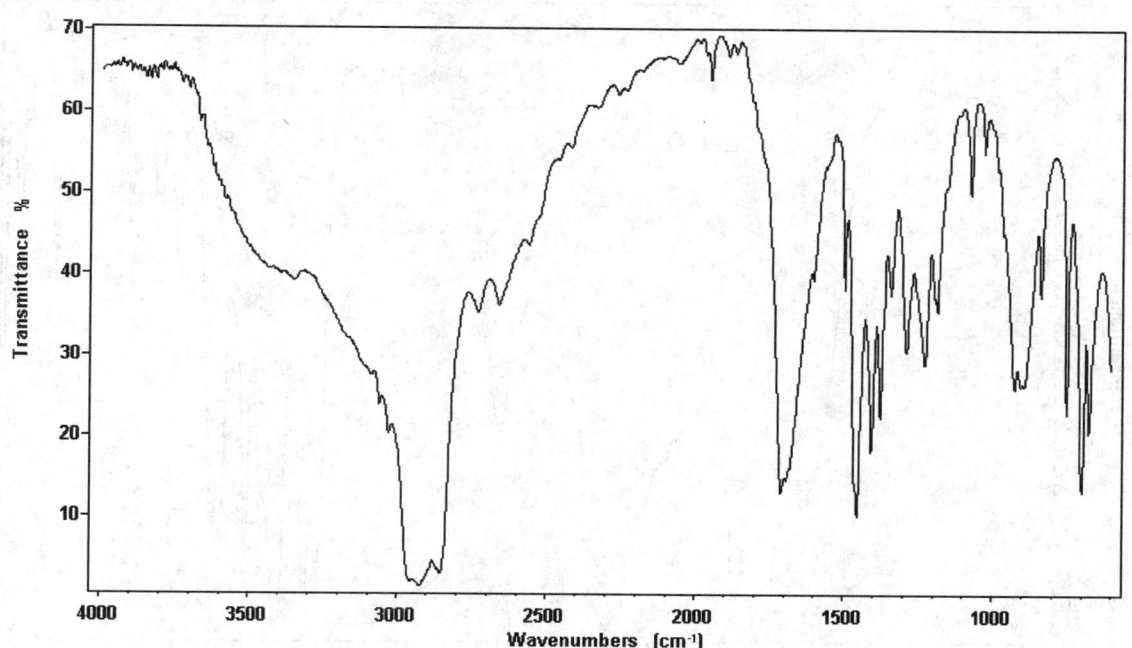

Phenylacetic Acid

DL-Phenylalanine

First Published: Prior to FCC 6

DL-α-Amino-β-phenylpropionic Acid

$C_9H_{11}NO_2$
UNII: 8P946UF12S [phenylalanine, dl-]
Formula wt 165.19
CAS: [150-30-1]

DESCRIPTION
DL-Phenylalanine occurs as white crystalline platelets. It is soluble in water, in dilute mineral acids, and in solutions of alkali hydroxides. It is very slightly soluble in alcohol. It is optically inactive.
Function: Nutrient
Packaging and Storage: Store in well-closed containers.

IDENTIFICATION
- **INFRARED SPECTRA,** *Spectrophotometric Identification Tests,* Appendix IIIC
  Sample preparation: Mineral oil mull
  Acceptance criteria: The spectrum of the sample exhibits relative maxima at the same wavelengths as those of the spectrum below.

ASSAY
- **PROCEDURE**
  Sample: 500 mg, previously dried
  Analysis: Transfer the *Sample* into a 250-mL flask. Dissolve the *Sample* in 75 mL of glacial acetic acid, add 2 drops of crystal violet TS, and titrate with 0.1 N perchloric acid, to a blue-green endpoint. [**CAUTION**—Handle perchloric acid in an appropriate fume hood.] Perform a blank determination (see *General Provisions*), and make any necessary correction. Each mL of 0.1 N perchloric acid is equivalent to 16.52 mg of $C_9H_{11}NO_2$.
  Acceptance criteria: NLT 98.5% and NMT 101.5% of $C_9H_{11}NO_2$, on the dried basis

IMPURITIES
- **LEAD,** *Lead Limit Test,* Appendix IIIB
  Sample solution: Prepare as directed for organic compounds.
  Control: 5 µg Pb (5 mL *Diluted Standard Lead Solution*)
  Acceptance criteria: NMT 5 mg/kg

SPECIFIC TESTS
- **LOSS ON DRYING,** Appendix IIC: 105° for 3 h
  Acceptance criteria: NMT 0.2%
- **RESIDUE ON IGNITION (SULFATED ASH),** Appendix IIC
  Sample: 1 g
  Acceptance criteria: NMT 0.3%

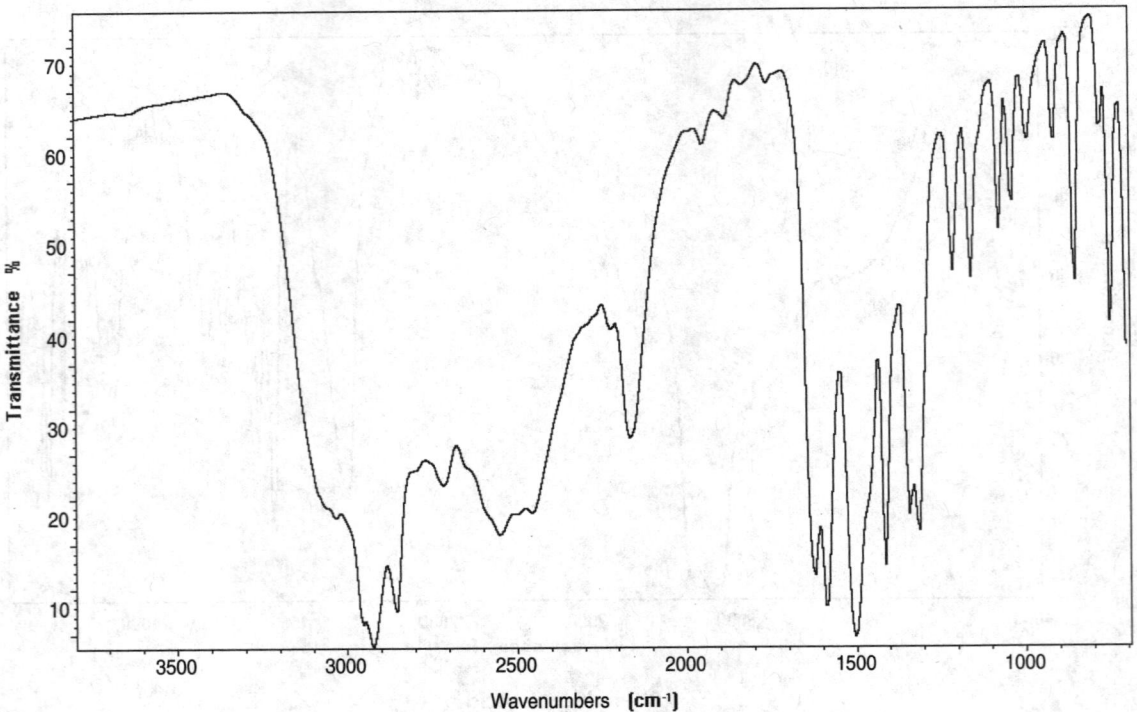

DL-Phenylalanine (Mineral Oil Mull)

L-Phenylalanine

First Published: Prior to FCC 6
Last Revision: FCC 7

L-α-Amino-β-phenylpropionic Acid

$C_9H_{11}NO_2$ Formula wt 165.19
 CAS: [63-91-2]
UNII: 47E5O17Y3R [phenylalanine]

DESCRIPTION
L-Phenylalanine occurs as colorless or white, plate-like crystals or as a white crystalline powder. One g is soluble in about 35 mL of water. It is slightly soluble in alcohol, in dilute mineral acids, and in alkali hydroxide solutions. It melts with decomposition at about 283°. The pH of a 1:100 aqueous solution is between 5.4 and 6.0.
Function: Nutrient
Packaging and Storage: Store in well-closed, light-resistant containers.

IDENTIFICATION
- **INFRARED ABSORPTION**, *Spectrophotometric Identification Tests*, Appendix IIIC
  Reference standard: USP L-Phenylalanine RS
  Sample and standard preparation: *M*
  Acceptance criteria: The spectrum of the sample exhibits maxima at the same wavelengths as those in the spectrum of the *Reference standard*.

ASSAY
- **PROCEDURE**
  Sample: 300 mg
  Analysis: Dissolve the *Sample* in 3 mL of formic acid and 50 mL of glacial acetic acid, add 2 drops of crystal violet TS, and titrate with 0.1 N perchloric acid to a blue-green endpoint. [**CAUTION**—Handle perchloric acid in an appropriate fume hood.] Perform a blank determination (see *General Provisions*), and make any necessary correction. Each mL of 0.1 N perchloric acid is equivalent to 16.52 mg of $C_9H_{11}NO_2$.
  Acceptance criteria: 98.5%–101.5% of $C_9H_{11}NO_2$, calculated on the dried basis

IMPURITIES
Inorganic Impurities
- **LEAD**, *Lead Limit Test*, Appendix IIIB
  Sample solution: Prepare as directed for organic compounds.
  Control: 5 μg Pb (5 mL of *Diluted Standard Lead Solution*)
  Acceptance criteria: NMT 5 mg/kg

SPECIFIC TESTS
- **LOSS ON DRYING**, Appendix IIC: 105° for 3 h
  Acceptance criteria: NMT 0.2%
- **OPTICAL (SPECIFIC) ROTATION**, Appendix IIB
  Sample: 2 g, previously dried

Analysis: Dissolve the *Sample* in sufficient water to make 100 mL.
Acceptance criteria
$[\alpha]_D^{20}$ between $-33.2°$ and $-35.2°$, calculated on the dried basis; or
$[\alpha]_D^{25}$ between $-32.7°$ and $-34.7°$, calculated on the dried basis
- **RESIDUE ON IGNITION (SULFATED ASH)**, Appendix IIC
  Sample: 1 g
  Acceptance criteria: NMT 0.1%

Phenylethyl Anthranilate

First Published: Prior to FCC 6

$C_{15}H_{15}NO_2$ Formula wt 241.29
FEMA: 2859
UNII: 8HBK71OD81 [phenethyl anthranilate]

DESCRIPTION
Phenylethyl Anthranilate occurs as a colorless to pale yellow crystalline mass.

Odor: Neroli, grape undertone
Solubility: Soluble in alcohol
Boiling Point: ~324°
Function: Flavoring agent

IDENTIFICATION
- **INFRARED SPECTRA**, *Spectrophotometric Identification Tests*, Appendix IIIC
  Acceptance criteria: The spectrum of the sample exhibits relative maxima at the same wavelengths as those of the spectrum below.

ASSAY
- **PROCEDURE:** Proceed as directed under *M-1b*, Appendix XI.
  Acceptance criteria: NLT 98.0% of $C_{15}H_{15}NO_2$

SPECIFIC TESTS
- **ACID VALUE, FLAVOR CHEMICALS (OTHER THAN ESSENTIAL OILS)**, *M-15*, Appendix XI
  Acceptance criteria: NMT 1.0

OTHER REQUIREMENTS
- **SOLIDIFICATION POINT**, Appendix IIB
  Acceptance criteria: NLT 40°

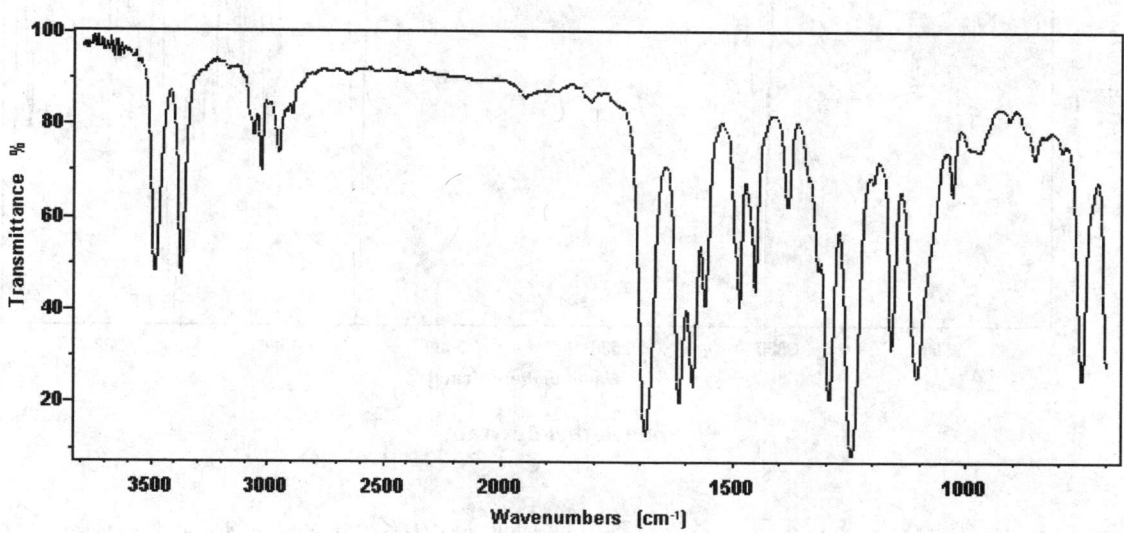

Phenylethyl Anthranilate

Phenylethyl Butyrate

First Published: Prior to FCC 6

$C_{12}H_{16}O_2$
FEMA: 2861
UNII: 02E08ZN98R [phenethyl butyrate]

Formula wt 192.26

DESCRIPTION
Phenylethyl Butyrate occurs as a colorless to pale yellow liquid.
Odor: Green, hay
Boiling Point: ~238°
Solubility in Alcohol, Appendix VI: One mL dissolves in 1 mL of 95% alcohol.
Function: Flavoring agent

IDENTIFICATION
- **INFRARED SPECTRA,** *Spectrophotometric Identification Tests,* Appendix IIIC
  Acceptance criteria: The spectrum of the sample exhibits relative maxima at the same wavelengths as those of the spectrum below.

ASSAY
- **PROCEDURE:** Proceed as directed under *M-1b,* Appendix XI.
  Acceptance criteria: NLT 98.0% of $C_{12}H_{16}O_2$

SPECIFIC TESTS
- **ACID VALUE, FLAVOR CHEMICALS (OTHER THAN ESSENTIAL OILS),** *M-15,* Appendix XI
  Acceptance criteria: NMT 1.0
- **REFRACTIVE INDEX,** Appendix II: At 20°
  Acceptance criteria: Between 1.487 and 1.492
- **SPECIFIC GRAVITY:** Determine at 25° by any reliable method (see *General Provisions*).
  Acceptance criteria: Between 0.991 and 0.995.

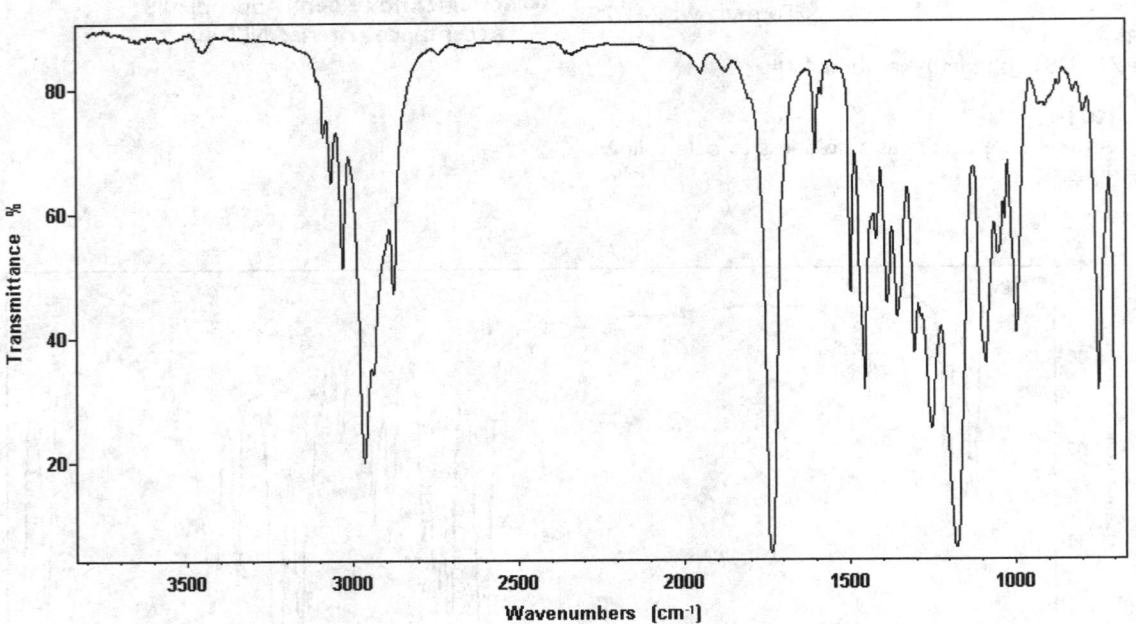

Phenylethyl Butyrate

3-Phenylpropyl Acetate

First Published: Prior to FCC 6

$C_{11}H_{14}O_2$
FEMA: 2890

Formula wt 178.23

UNII: AKW166708I [3-phenylpropyl acetate]

DESCRIPTION
3-Phenylpropyl Acetate occurs as a colorless liquid.
Odor: Spicy, floral
Solubility: Soluble in alcohol; insoluble or practically insoluble in water
Boiling Point: ~244°
Solubility in Alcohol, Appendix VI: One mL dissolves in 3 mL of 70% alcohol to give a clear solution.
Function: Flavoring agent

IDENTIFICATION

- **INFRARED SPECTRA**, *Spectrophotometric Identification Tests,* Appendix IIIC
  Acceptance criteria: The spectrum of the sample exhibits relative maxima at the same wavelengths as those of the spectrum below.

ASSAY

- **PROCEDURE:** Proceed as directed under *M-1b,* Appendix XI.
  Acceptance criteria: NLT 98.0% of $C_{11}H_{14}O_2$

SPECIFIC TESTS

- **ACID VALUE, FLAVOR CHEMICALS (OTHER THAN ESSENTIAL OILS),** *M-15,* Appendix XI
  Acceptance criteria: NMT 1.0
- **REFRACTIVE INDEX,** Appendix II: At 20°
  Acceptance criteria: Between 1.494 and 1.497
- **SPECIFIC GRAVITY:** Determine at 25° by any reliable method (see *General Provisions*).
  Acceptance criteria: Between 1.012 and 1.015

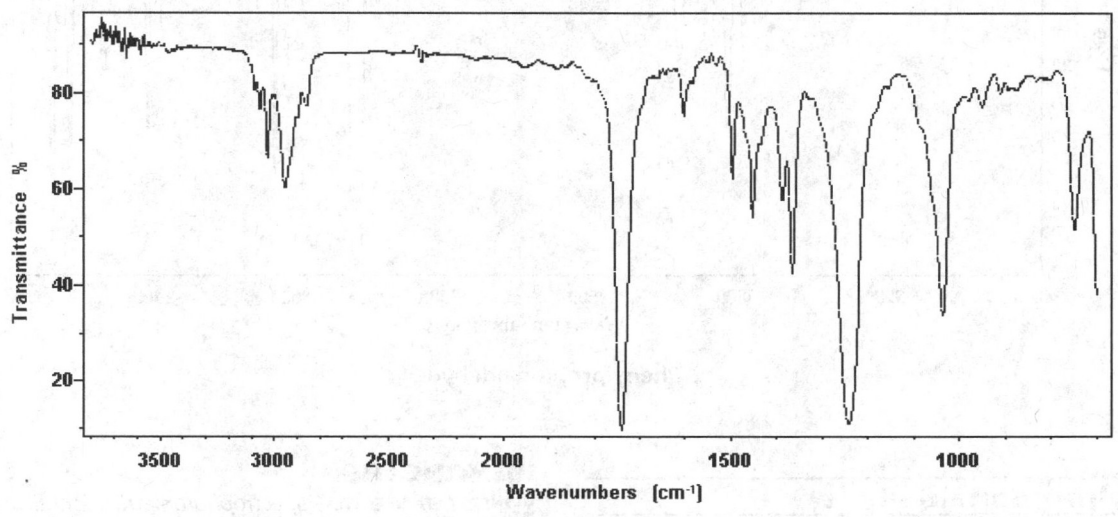

3-Phenylpropyl Acetate

2-Phenylpropionaldehyde

First Published: Prior to FCC 6
Last Revision: First Supplement, FCC 6

Hydratropic Aldehyde
α-Methyl Phenylacetaldehyde

$C_9H_{10}O$ Formula wt 134.18
FEMA: 2886
UNII: 8JKX55PKZQ [2-phenylpropanal]

DESCRIPTION

2-Phenylpropionaldehyde occurs as a water-white to pale yellow liquid. It may contain a suitable antioxidant.
Odor: Floral
Solubility: Soluble in most fixed oils; slightly soluble in propylene glycol; insoluble or practically insoluble in glycerin

Boiling Point: ~222°
Function: Flavoring agent

IDENTIFICATION

- **INFRARED SPECTRA**, *Spectrophotometric Identification Tests,* Appendix IIIC
  Acceptance criteria: The spectrum of the sample exhibits relative maxima at the same wavelengths as those of the spectrum below.

ASSAY

- **PROCEDURE:** Proceed as directed under *M-1b,* Appendix XI.
  Acceptance criteria: NLT 95.0% of $C_9H_{10}O$

SPECIFIC TESTS

- **ACID VALUE, FLAVOR CHEMICALS (OTHER THAN ESSENTIAL OILS),** *M-15,* Appendix XI
  Acceptance criteria: NMT 5.0
- **REFRACTIVE INDEX,** Appendix II: At 20°
  Acceptance criteria: Between 1.515 and 1.520
- **SPECIFIC GRAVITY:** Determine at 25° by any reliable method (see *General Provisions*).
  Acceptance criteria: Between 0.998 and 1.006

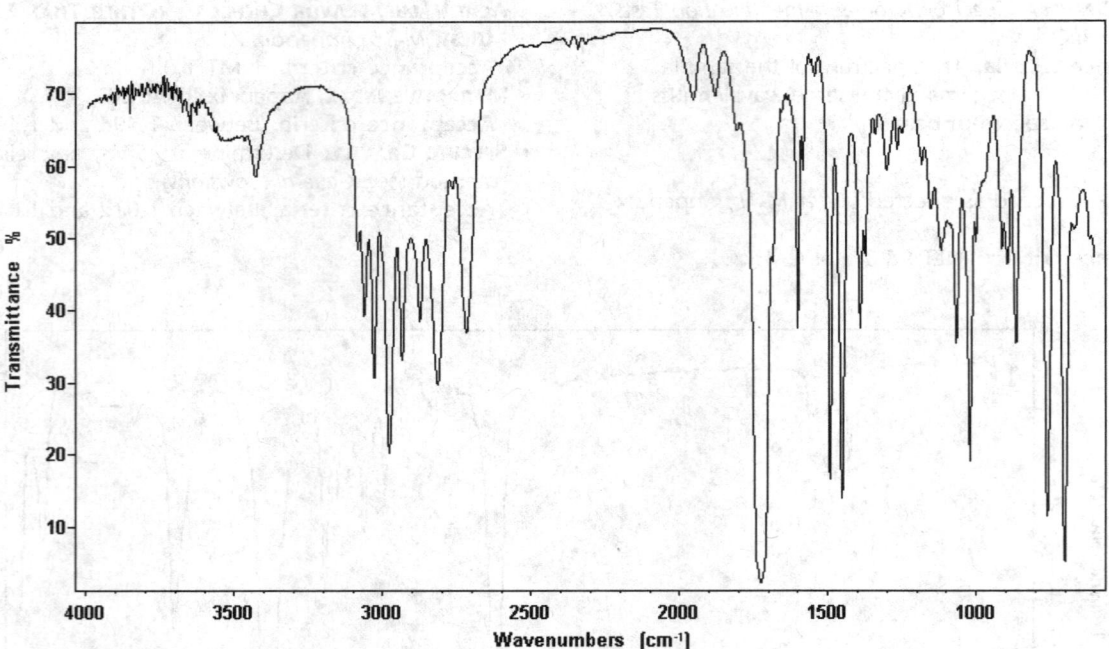

2-Phenylpropionaldehyde

3-Phenylpropionaldehyde

First Published: Prior to FCC 6
Last Revision: First Supplement, FCC 6

Hydrocinnamaldehyde
Phenylpropyl Aldehyde

$C_9H_{10}O$ Formula wt 134.18
FEMA: 2887
UNII: LP1E86N30T [3-phenylpropionaldehyde]

DESCRIPTION
3-Phenylpropionaldehyde occurs as a colorless to slightly yellow liquid. It may contain a suitable antioxidant.
Odor: Strong, pungent, floral, hyacinth
Solubility: Miscible in alcohol, ether; insoluble or practically insoluble in water
Boiling Point: ~97° to 98° (12 mm Hg)
Solubility in Alcohol, Appendix VI: One mL dissolves in 7 mL of 60% alcohol, and remains clear on dilution.
Function: Flavoring agent

IDENTIFICATION
- **INFRARED SPECTRA,** Spectrophotometric Identification Tests, Appendix IIIC
  Acceptance criteria: The spectrum of the sample exhibits relative maxima at the same wavelengths as those of the spectrum below.

ASSAY
- **PROCEDURE:** Proceed as directed under M-1b, Appendix XI.
  Acceptance criteria: NLT 90.0% of aldehydes

SPECIFIC TESTS
- **ACID VALUE, FLAVOR CHEMICALS (OTHER THAN ESSENTIAL OILS),** M-15, Appendix XI
  Acceptance criteria: NMT 10.0.
- **REFRACTIVE INDEX,** Appendix II: At 20°
  Acceptance criteria: Between 1.520 and 1.532
- **SPECIFIC GRAVITY:** Determine at 25° by any reliable method (see General Provisions).
  Acceptance criteria: Between 1.010 and 1.020

OTHER REQUIREMENTS
- **CHLORINATED COMPOUNDS,** Appendix VI
  Acceptance criteria: Passes test

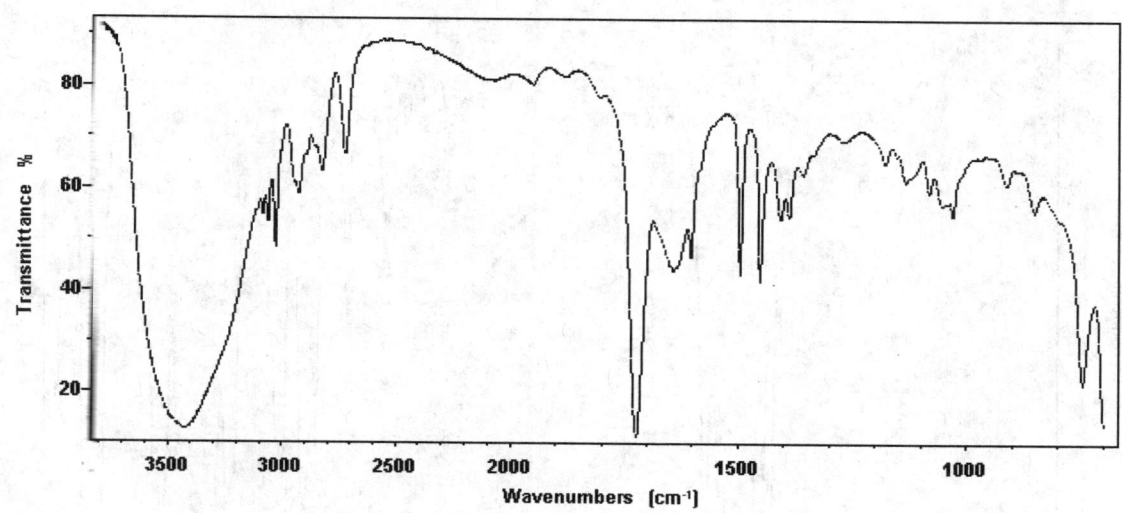

3-Phenylpropionaldehyde

2-Phenylpropionaldehyde Dimethyl Acetal

First Published: Prior to FCC 6

Hydratropic Aldehyde Dimethyl Acetal

$C_{11}H_{16}O_2$
FEMA: 2888
UNII: H41WGL6C 2 [2-phenylpropionaldehyde dimethyl acetal]

Formula wt 180.25

DESCRIPTION
2-Phenylpropionaldehyde Dimethyl Acetal occurs as a colorless to slightly yellow liquid.
Odor: Mushroom
Solubility: Soluble in alcohol, ether; insoluble or practically insoluble in water
Boiling Point: ~241°
Solubility in Alcohol, Appendix VI: One mL dissolves in 7 mL of 60% alcohol, and in 3 mL of 70% alcohol to give clear solutions.

Function: Flavoring agent

IDENTIFICATION
- **INFRARED SPECTRA,** Spectrophotometric Identification Tests, Appendix IIIC
  Acceptance criteria: The spectrum of the sample exhibits relative maxima at the same wavelengths as those of the spectrum below.

ASSAY
- **PROCEDURE:** Proceed as directed under M-1b, Appendix XI.
  Acceptance criteria: NLT 95.0% of $C_{11}H_{16}O_2$

SPECIFIC TESTS
- **REFRACTIVE INDEX,** Appendix II: At 20°
  Acceptance criteria: Between 1.492 and 1.497
- **SPECIFIC GRAVITY:** Determine at 25° by any reliable method (see General Provisions).
  Acceptance criteria: Between 0.989 and 0.994

OTHER REQUIREMENTS
- **FREE 2-PHENYLPROPIONALDEHYDE,** M-1b, Appendix XI
  Acceptance criteria: NMT 3.0%

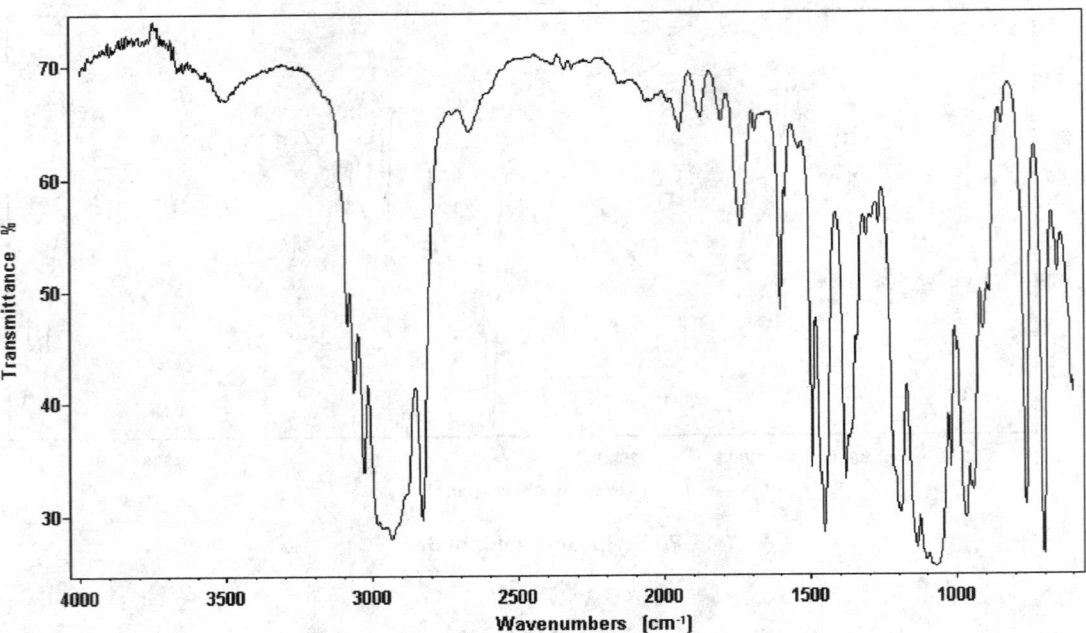

2-Phenylpropionaldehyde Dimethyl Acetal

Phosphoric Acid

First Published: Prior to FCC 6
Last Revision: Second Supplement, FCC 7

Orthophosphoric Acid

H_3PO_4 Formula wt 98.00
INS: 338 CAS: [7664-38-2]
UNII: E4GA8884NN [phosphoric acid]

DESCRIPTION
Phosphoric Acid occurs as a colorless, aqueous solution, usually available in concentrations ranging from 75.0% to 85.0%. It is miscible with water and with alcohol.
Function: Acidifier; sequestrant
Packaging and Storage: Store in tight containers.

IDENTIFICATION
- **PHOSPHATE**, Appendix IIIA
  Sample solution: 100 mg/mL
  Acceptance criteria: Passes tests

ASSAY
- **PROCEDURE**
  Sample: 1.5 g
  Analysis: Transfer the *Sample* into a 250-mL beaker, and dilute with water to 120 mL. Place the electrodes of a suitable pH meter into the solution, and titrate with 1 N sodium hydroxide to the inflection point occurring between pH 8.9 and 9.2. Each mL of 1 N sodium hydroxide is equivalent to 49.00 mg of H_3PO_4.
  Acceptance criteria: NLT the minimum or within the range of percentage claimed by the vendor

IMPURITIES
Inorganic Impurities
- **ARSENIC**, *Arsenic Limit Test*, Appendix IIIB
  [NOTE—Alternatively, use the Inductively Coupled Plasma Emission Method under *Cadmium* to determine the arsenic content.]
  Sample solution: 1 g dissolved in 35 mL of water
  Acceptance criteria: NMT 3 mg/kg
- **CADMIUM**, *Cadmium Limit Test*, Appendix IIIB
  [NOTE—Alternately, use the Inductively Coupled Plasma Emission Method below to determine the cadmium content.]
  Apparatus: Inductively Coupled Plasma Emission Spectrophotometer set to 226.502 nm for cadmium (188.979 nm for arsenic; 220.353 nm for lead) and to 371.029 for yttrium (internal standard) with an axial view mode. [NOTE—This method was developed using a Perkin-Elmer Model 3300 DV equipped with a sapphire injector, low-flow GemCone nebulizer, cyclonic spray chamber, and yttrium internal standard.] Use acid-rinsed plastic volumetric flasks and other labware.
  Standard stock solution: Use commercially available certified stock standard solutions of 10, 100, or 1000 μg/mL of cadmium (and/or of arsenic, lead) in 2% to 5% nitric acid. Use higher purity nitric acid for standards and samples. Where possible, match the sample matrix by adding a material of known high purity to the standards.
  Internal standard solution: 10 μg/mL of yttrium in 2% nitric acid, from a certified stock solution
  Standard solutions: 0.250, 0.050, and 0 μg/mL of cadmium (and/or of arsenic, lead) containing 5% nitric

acid; 0.100 µg/mL of yttrium; and 5% high-purity sample matrix matching reagent (if available): prepared from *Standard stock solution* and *Internal standard solution*. [NOTE—Prepare monthly.]

Sample solution: Dissolve 2.5 g of sample in water, and add 2.5 mL of nitric acid and 500 µL of 10-µg/mL yttrium. Dilute to 50 mL.

Analysis: Set up the instrumental method to measure the intensities of the 0-, 0.050-, and 0.250- µg/mL *Standard solutions*, correcting the cadmium (and/or arsenic, lead) intensities based on the intensity of the yttrium *Internal standard solution*. The calibration curve for cadmium (and/or arsenic, lead) should be linear. Examine the spectra of the cadmium (and/or arsenic, lead) and yttrium, and make any necessary adjustments to the exact peak locations and baselines to ensure proper measurement of the respective peak intensities. Analyze the *Sample solution*, and calculate the concentration, in µg/mL, of the cadmium (and/or arsenic, lead) in the *Sample solution*, again correcting based on the intensity of the yttrium internal standard. Calculate the quantity, in mg/kg, of cadmium in the sample by multiplying this value by 20.

[NOTE—Some sample types may naturally contain significant levels of yttrium. In these cases, choose a suitable alternative internal standard, or run the test without an internal standard. Use of the internal standard is not required, but it is helpful when there are variations in the viscosity among sample types. Samples may be prepared in higher or lower concentrations as needed. Standard concentrations may be adjusted as needed. Alternative procedures should be validated before use.]

Acceptance criteria: NMT 3 mg/kg

- **FLUORIDE**

  Fluoride standard solution: 100 µg/mL of fluoride ion; prepare by dissolving 22.2 mg of sodium fluoride, previously dried at 200° for 4 h, in sufficient water to make 100.0 mL.

  Electrode calibration: Determine the electrode slope, S, according to the manufacturer's instructions or according to the method described under *Fluoride Limit Test, Method IV*, Appendix IIIB.

  Sample preparation: Weigh 5 g of sample into a 100-mL volumetric flask, add 30 mL of water, and place the uncapped flask on a hot plate capable of maintaining a temperature of 80°–90° for 10 min without boiling. (Alternatively, suspend the uncapped flask in a boiling water bath for 10 min.) Allow the contents to cool to room temperature, and dilute with water to volume.

  Analysis: Transfer the *Sample preparation* to a 150-mL plastic beaker with a magnetic stir bar. Place in the solution the fluoride ion and reference electrodes (or a combination fluoride electrode) of a suitable ion-selective apparatus with a magnetic stirrer. Begin stirring slowly, and allow the instrument to equilibrate. Obtain the initial mV reading, E1, from the instrument. Add 1 mL of the *Fluoride standard solution* to the beaker, allow the electrode to equilibrate with continued stirring, and take the final mV reading, E2. [NOTE—The ion-selective electrode responds more slowly than does a pH electrode, and a stable reading may not be obtained for 2–3 min. The mV displayed should be stable for 30 s before taking readings.] Calculate the amount of fluoride, in mg/kg, in the sample:

  $$\text{Result} = 20/[10^{(E2-E1)/S} - 1]$$

  Acceptance criteria: NMT 10 mg/kg

- **LEAD,** *Lead Limit Test, APDC Extraction Method,* Appendix IIIB

  [NOTE—Alternatively, use the Inductively Coupled Plasma Emission Method under *Cadmium* to determine the lead content.]

  Acceptance criteria: NMT 3 mg/kg

OTHER REQUIREMENTS

- **LABELING:** Indicate the percent or the percent range of phosphoric acid (H_3PO_4).

Pimenta Oil

First Published: Prior to FCC 6

Pimenta Berries Oil
Pimento Oil
Allspice Oil
UNII: 032LND7FYA [allspice oil]

DESCRIPTION

Pimenta Oil occurs as a colorless, yellow, or orange liquid that becomes darker with age. It has the characteristic odor and taste of allspice. It is the volatile oil distilled from the fruit of *Pimenta officinalis*, Lindley (Fam. Myrtaceae). It is soluble in alcohol, in propylene glycol, and in most vegetable oils.

Function: Flavoring agent

Packaging and Storage: Store in a cool place protected from light in full, tight containers that are made from steel or aluminum and that are suitably lined.

IDENTIFICATION

- **INFRARED SPECTRA,** *Spectrophotometric Identification Tests*, Appendix IIIC

  Acceptance criteria: The spectrum of the sample exhibits relative maxima at the same wavelengths as those of the spectrum below.

ASSAY

- **PHENOLS,** Appendix VI

  Analysis: Modify the procedure by heating the cassia flask and its contents on a steam bath for 10 min, after shaking the flask for 5 min. Then cool and let stand overnight, or until the liquids are clear. Continue as directed with the addition of 1 N potassium hydroxide.

  Acceptance criteria: NLT 65.0%, by volume, of phenols

SPECIFIC TESTS

- **ANGULAR ROTATION,** *Optical (Specific) Rotation* Appendix IIB: Use a 100-mm tube.

  Acceptance criteria: Between −4° and 0°

890 / Pimenta Oil / Monographs

- **REFRACTIVE INDEX,** Appendix IIB
  [NOTE—Use an Abbé or other refractometer of equal or greater accuracy.]
  Acceptance criteria: Between 1.527 and 1.540 at 20°
- **SOLUBILITY IN ALCOHOL,** Appendix VI
  Acceptance criteria: One mL of the sample dissolves in 2 mL of 70% alcohol.
- **SPECIFIC GRAVITY:** Determine by any reliable method (see *General Provisions*).
  Acceptance criteria: Between 1.018 and 1.048

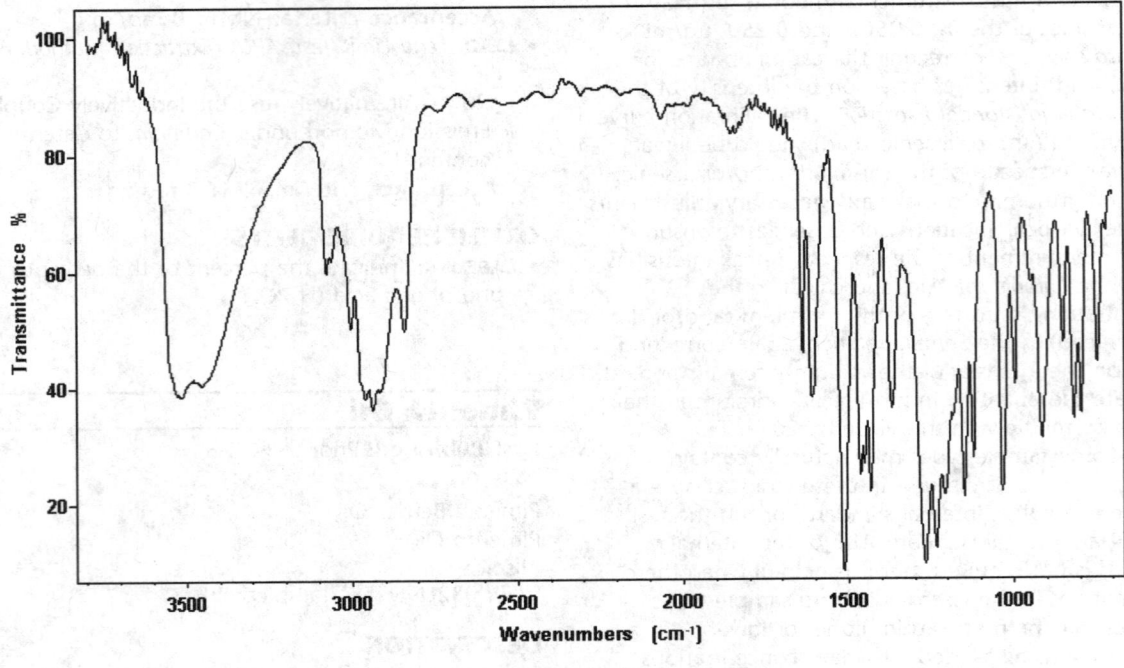

Pimenta Oil

Pimenta Leaf Oil

First Published: Prior to FCC 6

Pimento Leaf Oil
FEMA: 2901
UNII: 60T6W3867P [pimenta leaf oil]
CAS: [8016-45-3]

DESCRIPTION
Pimenta Leaf Oil occurs as a pale yellow to light brown-yellow liquid when freshly distilled, becoming darker with age. In contact with iron, it acquires a blue shade, turning to dark brown on extended contact. It has a spicy odor. It is the volatile oil obtained by steam distillation from the leaves of the evergreen shrub *Pimenta officinalis* Lindl. (Fam. Myrtaceae). It is soluble in propylene glycol, and it is soluble, with slight opalescence, in most fixed oils. It is relatively insoluble in glycerin and in mineral oil.
Function: Flavoring agent
Packaging and Storage: Store in a cool place protected from light in full, tight containers that are made from steel or aluminum and that are suitably lined.

IDENTIFICATION
- **INFRARED SPECTRA,** *Spectrophotometric Identification Tests,* Appendix IIIC
  Acceptance criteria: The spectrum of the sample exhibits relative maxima at the same wavelengths as those of the spectrum below.

ASSAY
- **PHENOLS,** Appendix VI
  Analysis: Use a suitable quantity of sample shaken with about 2% of powdered tartaric acid for about 2 min and filtered. Modify the test by heating the cassia flask on a boiling water bath for 10 min and cooling, after shaking the mixture of sample and 1 N potassium hydroxide for the specified 5 min.
  Acceptance criteria: NLT 80.0% and NMT 91.0%, by volume, of phenols

SPECIFIC TESTS
- **ANGULAR ROTATION,** *Optical (Specific) Rotation* Appendix IIB: Use a 100-mm tube.
  Acceptance criteria: Between −2° and +0.5°
- **REFRACTIVE INDEX,** Appendix IIB
  [NOTE—Use an Abbé or other refractometer of equal or greater accuracy.]
  Acceptance criteria: Between 1.531 and 1.536 at 20°
- **SOLUBILITY IN ALCOHOL,** Appendix VI
  Acceptance criteria: One mL of the sample dissolves in 2 mL of 70% alcohol; a slight opalescence may occur when additional solvent is added.

- **SPECIFIC GRAVITY:** Determine by any reliable method (see *General Provisions*).
  Acceptance criteria: Between 1.037 and 1.050

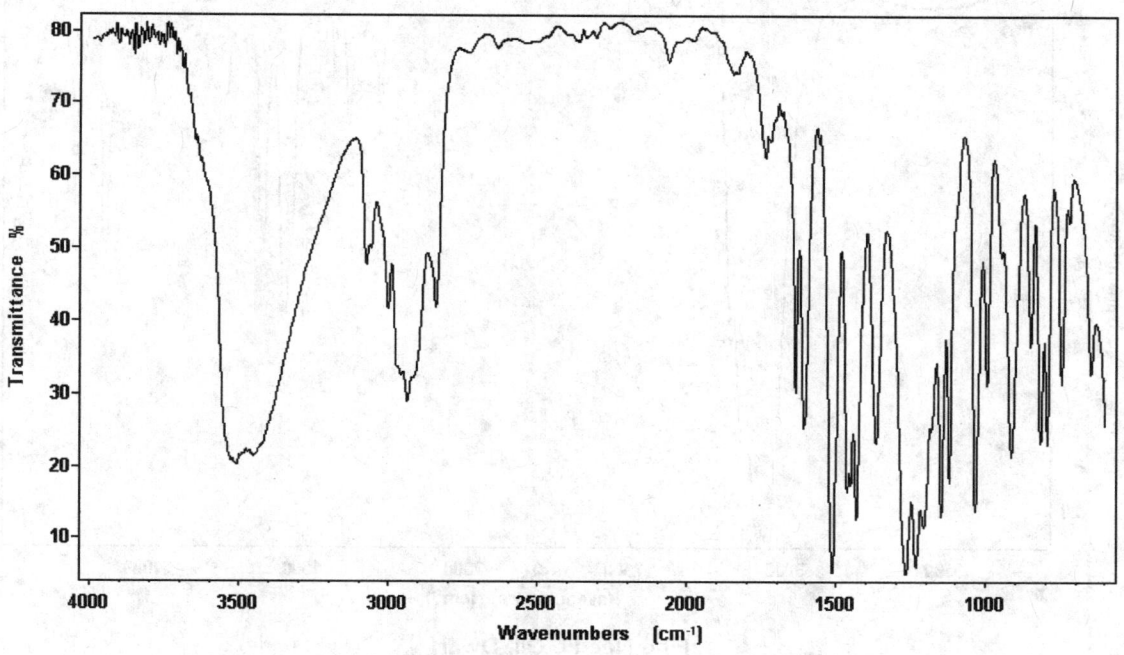

Pimenta Leaf Oil

Pine Needle Oil, Dwarf

First Published: Prior to FCC 6

Pine Needle Oil
FEMA: 2904
CAS: [8000-26-8]
UNII: 6KF1RLN1CI [pine needle oil (pinus mugo)]

DESCRIPTION
Pine Needle Oil, Dwarf occurs as a colorless or yellow liquid with a pleasant, aromatic odor and a bitter, pungent taste. It is the volatile oil obtained by steam distillation of fresh leaves of *Pinus mugo* Turra var. *pumilio* (Haenke) Zenari (Fam. Pinaceae). It is soluble in most vegetable oils, but insoluble in alcohol and in propylene glycol.
Function: Flavoring agent
Packaging and Storage: Store in a cool place protected from light in full, tight containers that are made from steel or aluminum and that are suitably lined.

IDENTIFICATION
- **INFRARED SPECTRA,** *Spectrophotometric Identification Tests,* Appendix IIIC
  Acceptance criteria: The spectrum of the sample exhibits relative maxima at the same wavelengths as those of the spectrum below.

ASSAY
- **ESTERS,** *Ester Determination,* Appendix VI
  Sample: 10 g
  Analysis: Use 98.15 as the equivalence factor (e) in the calculation.
  Acceptance criteria: NLT 3.0% and NMT 10.0% of esters, calculated as bornyl acetate ($C_{12}H_{20}O_2$)

SPECIFIC TESTS
- **ANGULAR ROTATION,** *Optical (Specific) Rotation,* Appendix IIB: Use a 100-mm tube.
  Acceptance criteria: Between −5° and −15°
- **DISTILLATION RANGE,** Appendix IIB
  Acceptance criteria: NMT 10% distills below 165°.
- **REFRACTIVE INDEX,** Appendix IIB
  [NOTE—Use an Abbé or other refractometer of equal or greater accuracy.]
  Acceptance criteria: Between 1.475 and 1.480 at 20°
- **SOLUBILITY IN ALCOHOL,** Appendix VI
  Acceptance criteria: One mL of the sample dissolves in 10 mL of 90% alcohol, often with turbidity.
- **SPECIFIC GRAVITY:** Determine by any reliable method (see *General Provisions*).
  Acceptance criteria: Between 0.853 and 0.871

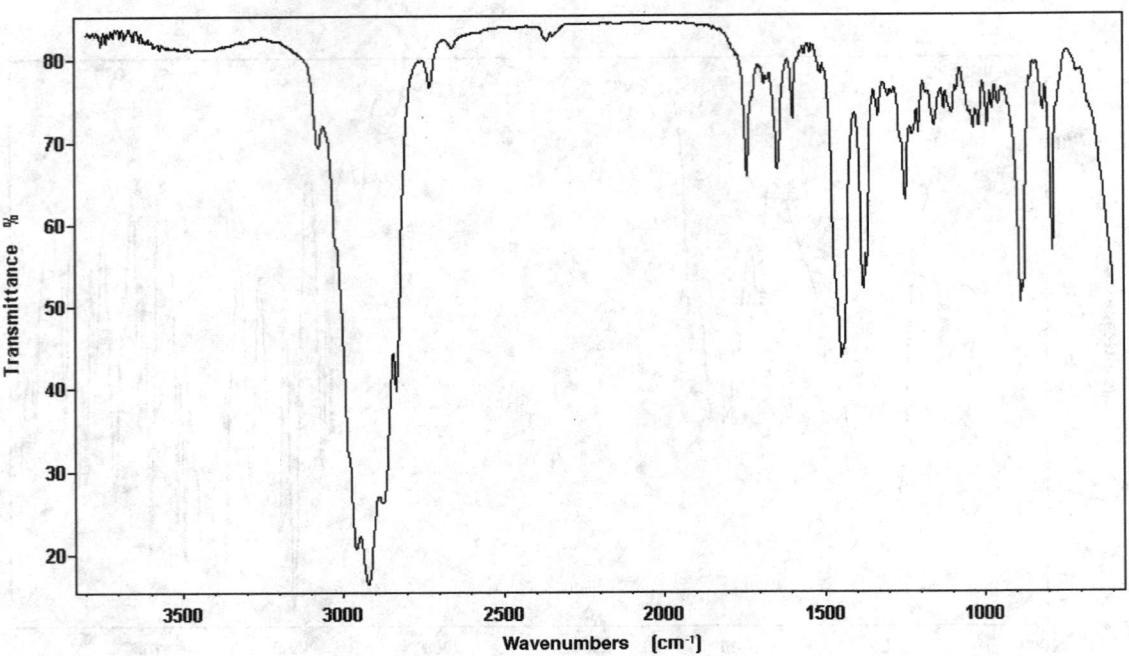

Pine Needle Oil, Dwarf

Pine Needle Oil, Scotch Type

First Published: Prior to FCC 6

FEMA: 2906

CAS: [8023-99-2]

UNII: 5EXL5H740Y [pine needle oil (pinus sylvestris)]

DESCRIPTION
Pine Needle Oil, Scotch Type, occurs as a colorless or yellow liquid with an aromatic, turpentine odor. It is the volatile oil obtained by steam distillation from the needles of *Pinus sylvestris* L. (Fam. Pinaceae). It is soluble in most fixed oils; soluble, with faint opalescence, in mineral oil; and slightly soluble in propylene glycol. It is practically insoluble in glycerin.

Function: Flavoring agent

Packaging and Storage: Store in a cool place protected from light in full, tight containers that are made from steel or aluminum and that are suitably lined.

IDENTIFICATION
- **INFRARED SPECTRA,** *Spectrophotometric Identification Tests,* Appendix IIIC

  Acceptance criteria: The spectrum of the sample exhibits relative maxima at the same wavelengths as those of the spectrum below.

ASSAY
- **PROCEDURE**

  Sample: 10 g

  Analysis: Determine as directed under *Esters, Ester Determination,* Appendix VI. Use 98.15 as the equivalence factor (e) in the calculation.

  Acceptance criteria: NLT 1.5% and NMT 5.0% of esters, calculated as bornyl acetate ($C_{12}H_{20}O_2$)

SPECIFIC TESTS
- **ANGULAR ROTATION,** *Optical (Specific) Rotation* Appendix IIB: Use a 100-mm tube

  Acceptance criteria: Between −4° and +10°

- **REFRACTIVE INDEX,** Appendix IIB

  [NOTE—Use an Abbé or other refractometer of equal or greater accuracy.]

  Acceptance criteria: Between 1.473 and 1.479 at 20°

- **SOLUBILITY IN ALCOHOL,** Appendix VI

  Acceptance criteria: One mL of the sample dissolves in 6 mL of 90% alcohol, occasionally with slight opalescence.

- **SPECIFIC GRAVITY:** Determine by any reliable method (see *General Notices*).

  Acceptance criteria: Between 0.857 and 0.885

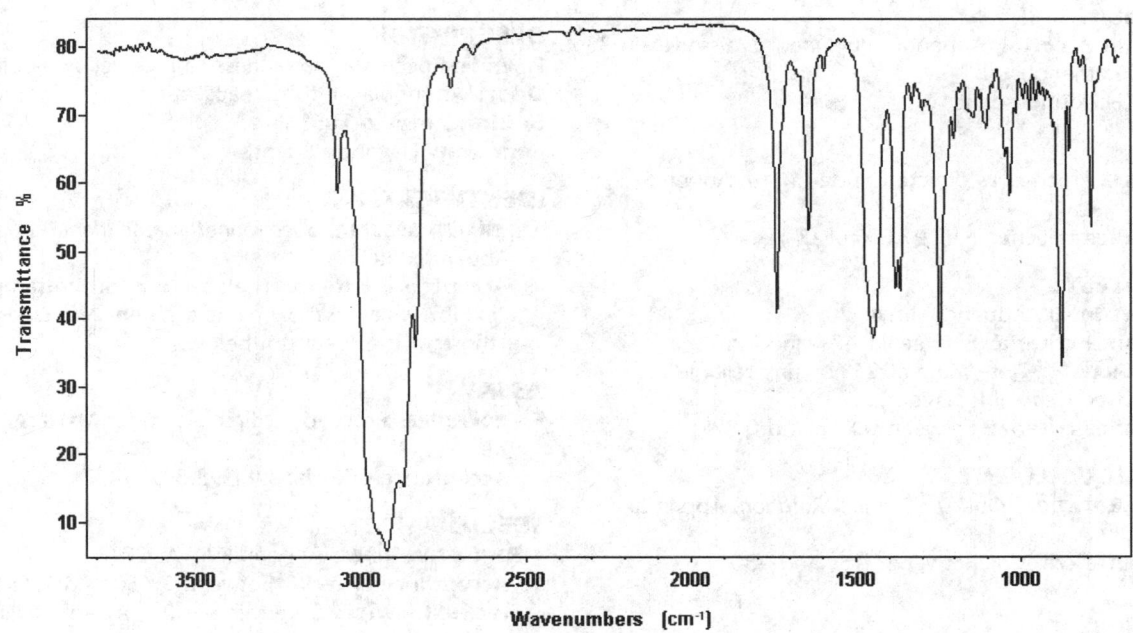

Pine Needle Oil, Scotch Type

α-Pinene

First Published: Prior to FCC 6
Last Revision: First Supplement, FCC 6

2,6,6-Trimethylbicyclo(3.1.1)hept-2-ene
2-Pinene
1-α-Pinene

$C_{10}H_{16}$ Formula wt 136.24
FEMA: 2902
UNII: JPF3YI7O34 [α-pinene]

DESCRIPTION
α-Pinene occurs as a colorless liquid. It may contain a suitable antioxidant.
Odor: Fresh, piney
Solubility: Soluble in alcohol, most fixed oils; insoluble or practically insoluble in water
Boiling Point: ~155°
Solubility in Alcohol, Appendix VI: One mL dissolves in 3 mL of 95% ethanol.
Function: Flavoring agent

ASSAY
- **Procedure:** Proceed as directed under *M-1a,* Appendix XI.
  Acceptance criteria: NLT 97.0% of $C_{10}H_{16}$

SPECIFIC TESTS
- **Refractive Index,** Appendix II: At 20°
  Acceptance criteria: Between 1.464 and 1.468
- **Specific Gravity:** Determine at 25° by any reliable method (see *General Provisions*).
  Acceptance criteria: Between 0.855 and 0.860

OTHER REQUIREMENTS
- **Angular Rotation,** *Optical (Specific) Rotation,* Appendix IIB
  Acceptance criteria: Between −20° and −50°

β-Pinene

First Published: Prior to FCC 6
Last Revision: First Supplement, FCC 6

6,6-Dimethyl-2-methylenebicyclo[3.1.1]heptane

$C_{10}H_{16}$ Formula wt 136.24
FEMA: 2903
UNII: 4MS8VHZ1HJ [β-pinene]

DESCRIPTION
β-Pinene occurs as a colorless liquid. It may contain a suitable antioxidant.
Odor: Resinous-piney

Solubility: Soluble in most fixed oils; insoluble or practically insoluble in water, propylene glycol
Boiling Point: ~165°
Solubility in Alcohol, Appendix VI: One mL dissolves in 3 mL of 95% ethanol.
Function: Flavoring agent

ASSAY
- **Procedure:** Proceed as directed under *M-1a*, Appendix XI.
  Acceptance criteria: NLT 97.0% of $C_{10}H_{16}$

SPECIFIC TESTS
- **Refractive Index,** Appendix II: At 20°
  Acceptance criteria: Between 1.477 and 1.481
- **Specific Gravity:** Determine at 25° by any reliable method (see *General Provisions*).
  Acceptance criteria: Between 0.867 and 0.871

OTHER REQUIREMENTS
- **Angular Rotation,** *Optical (Specific) Rotation,* Appendix IIB
  Acceptance criteria: Between −15° and −30°

Piperidine

First Published: Prior to FCC 6

Hexahydropyridine

$C_5H_{11}N$ Formula wt 85.15

FEMA: 2908
UNII: 67I85E138Y [piperidine]

DESCRIPTION
Piperidine occurs as a colorless to pale yellow liquid.
Odor: Ammoniacal, fishy, nauseating
Boiling Point: ~106°
Function: Flavoring agent

IDENTIFICATION
- **Infrared Spectra,** *Spectrophotometric Identification Tests,* Appendix IIIC
  Acceptance criteria: The spectrum of the sample exhibits relative maxima at the same wavelengths as those of the spectrum below.

ASSAY
- **Procedure:** Proceed as directed under *M-1a*, Appendix XI.
  Acceptance criteria: NLT 98.0% of $C_5H_{11}N$

SPECIFIC TESTS
- **Refractive Index,** Appendix II: At 20°
  Acceptance criteria: Between 1.450 and 1.454
- **Specific Gravity:** Determine at 25° by any reliable method (see *General Provisions*).
  Acceptance criteria: Between 0.858 and 0.862

Piperidine

Piperonal

First Published: Prior to FCC 6

3,4-(Methylenedioxy)-benzaldehyde
Heliotropine
Piperonyl Aldehyde

$C_8H_6O_3$ Formula wt 150.13
FEMA: 2911
UNII: KE109YAK00 [piperonal]

DESCRIPTION
Piperonal occurs as a white crystalline substance.
Odor: Floral, heliotrope, free from safrole by-odor
Solubility: Very soluble in alcohol; soluble in most fixed oils, propylene glycol; insoluble or practically insoluble in glycerin, water
Boiling Point: ~264°
Solubility in Alcohol, Appendix VI: One g dissolves in 4 mL of 70% alcohol.
Function: Flavoring agent

IDENTIFICATION
- **INFRARED SPECTRA,** Spectrophotometric Identification Tests, Appendix IIIC
  Acceptance criteria: The spectrum of the sample exhibits relative maxima at the same wavelengths as those of the spectrum below.

ASSAY
- **PROCEDURE:** Proceed as directed under M-1b, Appendix XI.
  Acceptance criteria: NLT 99.0% of $C_8H_6O_3$

OTHER REQUIREMENTS
- **LEAD,** M-9, Appendix XI
  Acceptance criteria: NMT 10 mg/kg
- **SOLIDIFICATION POINT,** Appendix IIB
  Acceptance criteria: NLT 35°

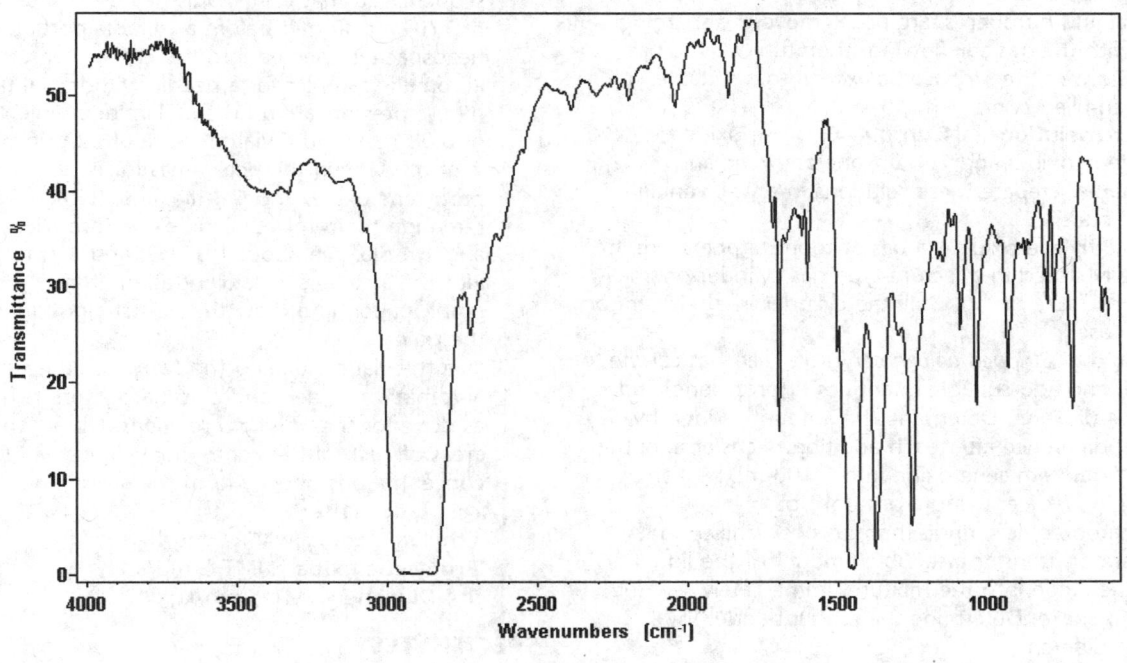

Piperonal

Poloxamer 331

First Published: Prior to FCC 6

α-Hydro-*omega*-hydroxy-poly(oxyethylene)-poly(oxypropylene)(51-57 moles)poly(oxyethylene) Block Copolymer

Formula wt (avg.) 3800
UNII: IS93EQR73R [poloxamer 331]

DESCRIPTION
Poloxamer 331 occurs as a practically colorless liquid. It is a block copolymer condensate of ethylene oxide and propylene oxide with an average formula weight of 3800, a specific gravity of about 1.02, and a refractive index of about 1.452. It is very slightly soluble in water at 25°, but is freely soluble at 0°; it is freely soluble in alcohol, but is insoluble in propylene glycol and in ethylene glycol.
Function: Solubilizing and stabilizing agent in flavor concentrates

Packaging and Storage: Store in tight containers.

IMPURITIES
Inorganic Impurities
- **LEAD**, *Lead Limit Test, Flame Atomic Absorption Spectrophotometric Method,* Appendix IIIB
  Sample: 10 g
  Acceptance criteria: NMT 2 mg/kg

Organic Impurities
- **ETHYLENE OXIDE, PROPYLENE OXIDE, AND 1,4-DIOXANE**
  Stripped poloxamer: Place between 100 and 300 g of sample into a suitable four-neck, round-bottom flask, equipped with a stirrer, a thermometer, a gas dispersion tube, a dry ice trap, a vacuum outlet, and a heating mantle. At room temperature, evacuate the flask carefully to a pressure of less than 1 mm Hg, applying the vacuum slowly while observing for excessive foaming caused by entrapped gases. After any foaming has subsided, sparge with nitrogen, allowing the pressure to rise to 10 mm Hg. Heat the flask to 130° while increasing the pressure to about 60 mm Hg. Continue stripping for 4 h, then cool to room temperature. Shut off the vacuum pump, and bring the flask back to atmospheric pressure while maintaining nitrogen sparging. Remove the sparging tube with the gas still flowing, then turn off the gas flow. Transfer the *Stripped poloxamer* to a suitable, nitrogen-filled container.
  Standard solutions: [**CAUTION**—Ethylene oxide, propylene oxide, and 1,4-dioxane are toxic and flammable. Prepare these solutions in a well-ventilated fume hood.]
  [NOTE—Ethylene oxide is a gas at room temperature. It is usually stored in a lecture-type gas cylinder or small metal pressure bomb. Chill the cylinder in a refrigerator before use.]
  Place 50 g of *Stripped poloxamer* into a vial that can be sealed, and add suitable quantities of propylene oxide and 1,4-dioxane. Determine the amounts added by weight difference after each addition. Transfer about 5 mL of liquid ethylene oxide into a 100-mL beaker chilled in wet ice. Using a gas-tight gas chromatographic syringe that has been chilled in a refrigerator, transfer a suitable amount of the liquid ethylene oxide into the mixture. Immediately seal the vial and shake. Determine the amount added by weight difference.
  By appropriate dilution with *Stripped poloxamer*, prepare four solutions, covering the range from 1 to 20 mg/kg for the three components added to the matrix (e.g., 5, 10, 15, and 20 mg/kg). Transfer 1 ± 0.01 g of each of these solutions to separate 22-mL pressure headspace vials, seal each with a silicone septum, star spring, and pressure-relief safety aluminum sealing cap, and crimp the cap closed with a cap-sealing tool.
  Sample solution: Transfer 1 ± 0.01 g of sample to a 22-mL pressure headspace vial, and seal, cap, and crimp as directed for the *Standard solutions*.
  Chromatographic system, Appendix IIA
  Mode: Gas chromatography [NOTE—Use a system equipped with a balanced pressure automatic headspace sampler.]
  Detector: Flame-ionization detector
  Column: 50-m × 0.32-mm fused silica capillary column bonded with a 5-µm film of 5% phenyl-95% methylsiloxane, or equivalent
  Temperature
    Column: Increase from 70° to 250° at 10°/min
    Transfer line: 140°
    Detector: 250°
  Flow rate: About 0.8 mL/min
  Carrier gas: Helium
  System suitability:
    Sample: *Standard solutions*
    Suitability requirement 1: The resolution, R, between ethylene oxide and propylene oxide is NLT 2.0.
    Suitability requirement 2: On the three calibration plots obtained in the *Analysis*, no point digresses from its line by more than 10%.
  Analysis: Place the vials containing the *Standard solutions* in the automated sampler, and start the sequence so that each vial is heated at a temperature of 110° for 30 min before a suitable portion of its headspace is injected into the chromatograph. Set the automatic sampler for a needle withdrawal time of 0.3 min, a pressurization time of 1 min, an injection time of 0.08 min, and a vial pressure of 22 psig with the vial vent off. Obtain the peak areas for ethylene oxide, propylene oxide, and 1,4-dioxane. [NOTE—Relative retention times for ethylene oxide, propylene oxide, and 1,4-dioxane about 1.0, 1.3, and 3.1, respectively.] Plot the area versus concentration, in mg/kg, on linear graph paper, and draw the best straight line through the points.
  Place the vial containing the *Sample solution* in the automatic sampler, and chromatograph its headspace as done for the *Standard solutions*. Obtain the peak areas of each of the components, and read the concentrations directly from the calibration plots.
  Acceptance criteria
    Ethylene oxide: NMT 5 mg/kg
    Propylene oxide: NMT 5 mg/kg
    1,4-Dioxane: NMT 5 mg/kg

SPECIFIC TESTS
- **CLOUD POINT**
  Sample solution: 100 mg/mL, prepared at a temperature below the expected cloud point
  Analysis: Transfer 100 mL of the *Sample solution* into a 50- × 120-mm test tube. Immerse the tube in a water bath, previously cooled to at least 10° below the expected cloud point, so that the water level is a few mL above that of the test solution. Place a suitable thermometer (see *Thermometers*, Appendix I) in the test solution, and position it so that the immersion line will be at the surface of the liquid. Stir the solution slowly with a mechanical stirrer (about 200 rpm), and heat gradually so that the test solution is heated at a rate of about 1°/min. Do not allow the temperature of the

water bath to rise more than 10° above that of the test solution at any time. Continue heating in this manner, and record the temperature (cloud point) at which the test solution becomes cloudy.
Acceptance criteria: Between 9° and 12°

- **HYDROXYL VALUE**
  Distilled pyridine: Distill pyridine over phthalic anhydride (60 g of phthalic anhydride for each 1000 mL of pyridine), discarding the first 25 mL and the last 50 mL of distillate from each 1000 mL distilled.
  Phenolphthalein indicator: 1% phenolphthalein in undistilled pyridine
  Phthalation reagent: Prepare a 144 mg/mL solution of phthalic anhydride in *Distilled pyridine* and store in a brown bottle. Allow to stand at least 2 h before use. Determine the suitability of *Phthalation reagent* as follows: Mix 10.0 mL of *Phthalation reagent* with 25 mL of undistilled pyridine and 50 mL of water, allow to stand for 15 min, then add a few drops of *Phenolphthalein indicator*, and titrate with 0.5 N sodium hydroxide. Multiply the volume, in mL, of the alkali solution required by its exact normality; if the result is not within the range 18.8 to 20.0, adjust the concentration of *Phthalation reagent* accordingly.
  Sample solution: Transfer 15 g of sample into a 250-mL hydroxyl flask, and add 25.0 mL of *Phthalation reagent*, using a pipet previously rinsed with *Phthalation reagent* and touching the tip of the pipet against the protrusion of the flask approximately 15 s after the pipet has drained. Add a few glass beads to the flask, swirl to dissolve the sample, and reflux for 1 h. Cool the flask to room temperature, and wash the condenser with two 10-mL portions of undistilled pyridine. Disconnect the condenser, add 10 mL of water to the flask, stopper, swirl, and allow to stand for 10 min. Add 50.0 mL of approximately 0.66 N sodium hydroxide to the flask, then add 0.5 mL of *Phenolphthalein indicator*.
  Blank solution: Prepare as directed under *Sample solution* (above), omitting the addition of sample to the hydroxyl flask.
  Analysis: Titrate the *Sample solution* and the *Blank solution* with 0.5 N sodium hydroxide to the first pink color that persists for at least 15 s.
  Calculate the uncorrected hydroxyl value, h, by the formula:

  $$\text{Result} = (B - S) \times (N \times 56.1/W)$$

  B = volume (mL) of 0.5 N sodium hydroxide required for the blank titration
  S = volume (mL) of 0.5 N sodium hydroxide required for the sample titration
  N = exact normality of the sodium hydroxide solution
  W = weight of the sample (g) taken to prepare the *Sample solution*

  If the sample contains significant acidity or alkalinity, correct the results as follows: Dissolve 15 g of sample in 40 mL of undistilled pyridine, and add 60 mL of water and 0.5 mL of *Phenolphthalein indicator*. If the solution is colorless, titrate with 0.1 N sodium hydroxide to a light pink endpoint, recording the volume required, in mL, as v. If the solution is pink, titrate with 0.1 N hydrochloric acid to the disappearance of the pink color, recording the volume required, in mL, as v'. Calculate the acidity correction factor, A, or the alkalinity correction factor, A', by the appropriate following equation:

  $$A = v \times N \times 56.1/W$$

  or

  $$A' = v' \times N' \times 56.1/W$$

  N = exact normality of the sodium hydroxide solution
  N' = exact normality of the hydrochloric acid solution
  W = weight of the sample (g) taken to prepare the *Sample solution*

  Finally, calculate the corrected hydroxyl value, H, by whichever formula, below, is appropriate:

  $$\text{Result} = h + A \quad \text{or} \quad h - A'$$

  h = the uncorrected hydroxyl value calculated above
  A = acidity correction factor calculate above
  A' = alkalinity correction factor calculate above
  Acceptance criteria: Between 27.2 and 32.1

- **MOLECULAR WEIGHT**
  Analysis: Calculate by the formula:

  $$\text{Result} = 56{,}100 \times (2/H)$$

  H = *Hydroxyl Value* obtained above
  Acceptance criteria: Between 3500 and 4125

- **PH**, *pH Determination*, Appendix IIB
  Sample solution: 25 mg/mL
  Acceptance criteria: Between 6.0 and 7.4

Poloxamer 407

First Published: Prior to FCC 6

α-Hydro-*omega*-hydroxy-poly(oxyethylene)-poly(oxypropylene)(63-71 moles)poly(oxyethylene) Block Copolymer

Formula wt (avg.) 12,500
UNII: TUF2IVW3M2 [poloxamer 407]

DESCRIPTION
Poloxamer 407 occurs as a white solid. It is a block copolymer condensate of ethylene oxide and propylene oxide with a melting range of about 52° to 56°. It is freely soluble in alcohol and in water, but is insoluble in propylene glycol and in ethylene glycol.
Function: Solubilizing and stabilizing agent in flavor concentrates

Packaging and Storage: Store in tight containers.

IMPURITIES
Inorganic Impurities
- **LEAD**, *Lead Limit Test, Flame Atomic Absorption Spectrophotometric Method,* Appendix IIIB
  Sample: 10 g
  Acceptance criteria: NMT 2 mg/kg

Organic Impurities
- **ETHYLENE OXIDE, PROPYLENE OXIDE, AND 1,4-DIOXANE**
  Stripped poloxamer: Place between 100 and 300 g of sample into a suitable four-neck, round-bottom flask, equipped with a stirrer, a thermometer, a gas dispersion tube, a dry ice trap, a vacuum outlet, and a heating mantle. At room temperature, evacuate the flask carefully to a pressure of less than 1 mm Hg, applying the vacuum slowly while observing for excessive foaming caused by entrapped gases. After any foaming has subsided, sparge with nitrogen, allowing the pressure to rise to 10 mm Hg. Heat the flask to 130° while increasing the pressure to about 60 mm Hg. Continue stripping for 4 h, then cool to room temperature. Shut off the vacuum pump, and bring the flask back to atmospheric pressure while maintaining nitrogen sparging. Remove the sparging tube with the gas still flowing, then turn off the gas flow. Transfer the *Stripped poloxamer* to a suitable, nitrogen-filled container.
  Standard solutions: [CAUTION—Ethylene oxide, propylene oxide, and 1,4-dioxane are toxic and flammable. Prepare these solutions in a well-ventilated fume hood.]
  [NOTE—Ethylene oxide is a gas at room temperature. It is usually stored in a lecture-type gas cylinder or small metal pressure bomb. Chill the cylinder in a refrigerator before use.]
  Place 50 g of *Stripped poloxamer* into a vial that can be sealed, and add suitable quantities of propylene oxide and 1,4-dioxane. Determine the amounts added by weight difference after each addition. Transfer about 5 mL of liquid ethylene oxide into a 100-mL beaker chilled in wet ice. Using a gas-tight gas chromatographic syringe that has been chilled in a refrigerator, transfer a suitable amount of the liquid ethylene oxide into the mixture. Immediately seal the vial, and shake. Determine the amount added by weight difference.
  By appropriate dilution with *Stripped poloxamer,* prepare four solutions, covering the range from 1 to 20 mg/kg for the three components added to the matrix (e.g., 5, 10, 15, and 20 mg/kg). Transfer 1 ± 0.01 g of each of these solutions to separate 22-mL pressure headspace vials, seal each with a silicone septum, star spring, and pressure-relief safety aluminum sealing cap, and crimp the cap closed with a cap-sealing tool.
  Sample solution: Transfer 1 ± 0.01 g of sample to a 22-mL pressure headspace vial, and seal, cap, and crimp as directed for the *Standard solutions.*
  Chromatographic system, Appendix IIA
  Mode: Gas chromatography [NOTE—Use a system equipped with a balanced pressure automatic headspace sampler.]
  Detector: Flame-ionization detector
  Column: 50-m × 0.32-mm fused silica capillary column bonded with a 5-µm film of 5% phenyl-95% methylsiloxane, or equivalent
  Temperature:
    Column: Increase from 70° to 250° at 10°/min
    Transfer line: 140°
    Detector: 250°
  Flow rate: About 0.8 mL/min
  Carrier gas: Helium
  System suitability
    Sample: *Standard solutions*
    Suitability requirement 1: The resolution, R, between ethylene oxide and propylene oxide is NLT 2.0.
    Suitability requirement 2: On the three calibration plots obtained in the *Analysis,* no point digresses from its line by more than 10%.
  Analysis: Place the vials containing the *Standard solutions* in the automated sampler, and start the sequence so that each vial is heated at a temperature of 110° for 30 min before a suitable portion of its headspace is injected into the chromatograph. Set the automatic sampler for a needle withdrawal time of 0.3 min, a pressurization time of 1 min, an injection time of 0.08 min, and a vial pressure of 22 psig with the vial vent off. Obtain the peak areas for ethylene oxide, propylene oxide, and 1,4-dioxane. [NOTE—Relative retention times for ethylene oxide, propylene oxide, and 1,4-dioxane about 1.0, 1.3, and 3.1, respectively.] Plot the area versus concentration, in mg/kg, on linear graph paper, and draw the best straight line through the points.
  Place the vial containing the *Sample solution* in the automatic sampler, and chromatograph its headspace as done for the *Standard solutions.* Obtain the peak areas of each of the components, and read the concentrations directly from the calibration plots.
  Acceptance criteria
    Ethylene oxide: NMT 5 mg/kg
    Propylene oxide: NMT 5 mg/kg
    1,4-Dioxane: NMT 5 mg/kg

SPECIFIC TESTS
- **CLOUD POINT**
  Sample solution: 100 mg/mL
  Analysis: Transfer 50 mL of *Sample solution* to a test tube. Place the tube in a boiling water bath and heat to 100°.
  Acceptance criteria: The solution does not become cloudy, indicating the cloud point is above 100°.
- **HYDROXYL VALUE**
  Distilled pyridine: Distill pyridine over phthalic anhydride (60 g of phthalic anhydride for each 1000 mL of pyridine), discarding the first 25 mL and the last 50 mL of distillate from each 1000 mL distilled.
  Phenolphthalein indicator: 1% phenolphthalein in undistilled pyridine

Phthalation reagent: Prepare 144 mg/mL solution of phthalic anhydride in *Distilled pyridine*, and store in a brown bottle. Allow to stand at least 2 h before use. Determine the suitability of *Phthalation reagent* as follows: Mix 10.0 mL of *Phthalation reagent* with 25 mL of undistilled pyridine and 50 mL of water, allow to stand for 15 min, then add a few drops of *Phenolphthalein indicator*, and titrate with 0.5 N sodium hydroxide. Multiply the volume, in mL, of the alkali solution required by its exact normality; if the result is not within the range 18.8 to 20.0, adjust the concentration of *Phthalation reagent* accordingly.

Sample solution: Transfer 45 g of sample into a 250-mL hydroxyl flask, and add 25.0 mL of *Phthalation reagent*, using a pipet previously rinsed with *Phthalation reagent* and touching the tip of the pipet against the protrusion of the flask approximately 15 s after the pipet has drained. Add 25.0 mL of *Distilled pyridine* and a few glass beads to the flask, swirl to dissolve the sample, and reflux for 1 h. Cool the flask to room temperature, and wash the condenser with two 10-mL portions of undistilled pyridine. Disconnect the condenser, add 10 mL of water to the flask, stopper, swirl, and allow to stand for 10 min. Add 50.0 mL of approximately 0.66 N sodium hydroxide to the flask, then add 0.5 mL of *Phenolphthalein indicator*.

Blank solution: Prepare as directed under *Sample preparation* (above), omitting the addition of sample to the hydroxyl flask.

Analysis: Titrate the *Sample solution* and the *Blank solution* with 0.5 N sodium hydroxide to the first pink color that persists for at least 15 s.

Calculate the uncorrected hydroxyl value, h, by the formula:

$$\text{Result} = (B - S) \times (N \times 56.1/W)$$

- B = volume (mL) of 0.5 N sodium hydroxide required for the blank titration
- S = volume (mL) of 0.5 N sodium hydroxide required for the sample titration
- N = exact normality of the sodium hydroxide solution
- W = weight (g) of the sample taken to prepare the *Sample solution*

If the sample contains significant acidity or alkalinity, correct the results as follows: Dissolve 15 g of sample in 40 mL of undistilled pyridine, and add 60 mL of water and 0.5 mL of *Phenolphthalein indicator*. If the solution is colorless, titrate with 0.1 N sodium hydroxide to a light pink endpoint, recording the volume required, in mL, as v. If the solution is pink, titrate with 0.1 N hydrochloric acid to the disappearance of the pink color, recording the volume required, in mL, as v'. Calculate the acidity correction factor, A, or the alkalinity correction factor, A', by the appropriate following equation:

$$A = v \times N \times 56.1/W$$

or

$$A' = v' \times N' \times 56.1/W$$

- N = exact normality of the sodium hydroxide solution
- N' = exact normality of the hydrochloric acid solution
- W = weight (g) of the sample taken to prepare the *Sample solution*

Finally, calculate the corrected hydroxyl value, H, by whichever formula, below, is appropriate:

$$\text{Result} = h + A \quad \text{or} \quad h - A'$$

- h = the uncorrected hydroxyl value calculated above
- A = acidity correction factor calculate above
- A' = alkalinity correction factor calculate above

Acceptance criteria: Between 8.5 and 11.5

- **MOLECULAR WEIGHT**
  Analysis: Calculate by the formula:

  $$\text{Result} = 56,100 \times (2/H)$$

  - H = *Hydroxyl Value* obtained above

  Acceptance criteria: Between 9,760 and 13,200

- **PH,** *pH Determination,* Appendix IIB
  Sample solution: 25 mg/mL
  Acceptance criteria: Between 6.0 and 7.4

Polydextrose

First Published: Prior to FCC 6
Last Revision: FCC 6

INS: 1200 CAS: [68424-04-4]
UNII: VH2XOU12IE [polydextrose]

DESCRIPTION

Polydextrose occurs as an off-white to light tan solid. It is a randomly bonded polymer prepared by the condensation of a melt that consists of approximately 90% D-glucose, 10% sorbitol, and 1% citric acid or 0.1% phosphoric acid on a weight basis. The 1,6-glycosidic linkage predominates in the polymer, but other possible bonds are present. The product contains small quantities of free glucose, sorbitol, and D-anhydroglucoses (levoglucosan), with traces of citric acid or phosphoric acid. It may be partially reduced by transition metal catalytic hydrogenation in an aqueous solution. It may be neutralized with any food-grade base and decolorized and deionized for further purification. It is very soluble in water.

Function: Bulking agent; humectant; texturizer
Packaging and Storage: Store in tight, light-proof containers.

IDENTIFICATION

- **A. PROCEDURE**
  Sample solution: 100 mg/mL
  Analysis: Add 4 drops of 5% aqueous phenol solution to 1 drop *Sample solution*, then rapidly add 15 drops of sulfuric acid.
  Acceptance criteria: A deep yellow to orange color appears.

- **B. PROCEDURE**
  Sample solution: 100 mg/mL
  Analysis: While vigorously swirling (vortex mixer), add 1.0 mL of acetone to 1.0 mL of *Sample solution*. [NOTE—Retain this solution for *Identification* test C (below).]
  Acceptance criteria: The solution remains clear.

- **C. PROCEDURE**
  Analysis: While vigorously swirling, add 2.0 mL of acetone to the retained solution from *Identification* test B.
  Acceptance criteria: A heavy, milky turbidity develops immediately.

- **D. PROCEDURE**
  Sample solution: 20 mg/mL
  Sample: Add 4 mL of alkaline cupric citrate TS to 1 mL of *Sample solution*. Boil vigorously for 2 to 4 min. Remove from heat, and allow the precipitate (if any) to settle.
  Acceptance criteria: The supernatant is blue or blue-green.

ASSAY

- **PROCEDURE**
  Standard stock solution: 0.2 mg/mL α-D-glucose
  Standard solutions: 50, 40, 20, 10, and 5 µg/mL α-D-glucose: made from *Standard stock solution*
  Sample stock solution: 1.0 mg/mL
  Sample solution: 40 µg/mL: made from *Sample stock solution*
  Phenol solution: Add 20 mL of water to 80 g of phenol.
  Analysis: On a daily basis, pipet 2.0 mL of each *Standard solution* and the *Sample solution* into separate, acetone-free, 15-mL screw-cap vials. Add 0.12 mL of the *Phenol solution*, and mix gently. Uncap each vial and rapidly add 5.0 mL of sulfuric acid. Immediately recap each vial, and shake vigorously. [**CAUTION**—Wear rubber gloves and a safety shield while adding sulfuric acid.]
  Let the vials stand at room temperature for 45 min, then determine the absorbance of each sample at 490 nm in a suitable spectrophotometer, using a *Phenol solution*–sulfuric acid reagent blank in the reference cell. Repeat the procedure three times and obtain the mean absorbance value. For the standard curve, plot mean absorbance values versus concentrations, in µg/mL, obtained from triplicate *Standard solutions*. Calculate the percent polymer by the formula:

  $$\text{Result} = 1.05[100(A - Y)/(S \times C) - P_G - 1.11 P_L]$$

  1.05 = an experimentally derived correction factor to account for the polymer (which also contains a small amount of sorbitol) not giving the exact amount of color given by an equivalent amount of glucose monomers
  A = sample absorbance
  Y = the y-intercept of the standard curve
  S = slope (approximately 0.02) of absorbance versus glucose concentration, in g/mL, obtained from the standard curve
  C = concentration (g/mL) of the *Sample stock solution*, adjusted for ash and moisture
  P_G = percentage of glucose determined under the test for *Monomers* (below)
  P_L = percentage of levoglucosan determined under the test for *Monomers* (below)
  1.11 = conversion factor from levoglucosan, which gives an equivalent amount of color to an equivalent weight of glucose

  Acceptance criteria: NLT 90.0% polymer, calculated on the anhydrous, ash-free basis

IMPURITIES

Inorganic Impurities

- **LEAD**
  [NOTE—For this test, use reagent-grade chemicals with as low a lead content as is practicable, as well as high-purity water and gases. Before use in this analysis, rinse all glassware and plasticware twice with 10% nitric acid and twice with 10% hydrochloric acid, and then rinse them thoroughly with high-purity water, preferably obtained from a mixed-bed, strong-acid, strong-base, ion-exchange cartridge capable of producing water with an electrical resistivity of 12 to 15 megohms.]
  Apparatus: Use a suitable spectrophotometer (Perkin-Elmer Model 6000, or equivalent), a graphite furnace containing a L'vov platform (Perkin-Elmer Model HGA-500, or equivalent), and an autosampler (Perkin-Elmer Model AS-40, or equivalent). Use a lead hollow-cathode lamp (lamp current of 10 mA), a slit width of 0.7 mm (set low), the wavelength set at 283.3 nm, and a deuterium arc lamp for background correction.
  Lead nitrate solution: 100 µg of lead (Pb) ion/mL prepared as follows: Dissolve 159.8 mg of lead nitrate in 100 mL of water containing 1 mL of nitric acid. Dilute with water to 1000.0 mL, and mix. Prepare and store this solution in glass containers that are free from lead salts.
  Standard stock solution: 10 µg of lead (Pb) ion/mL: from *Lead nitrate solution* [NOTE—Prepare on the day of use.]
  [NOTE—As an alternative to preparing the *Lead nitrate solution* and *Standard stock solution* NIST Standard Reference Material containing 10 mg of lead/kg, or equivalent may be used.]
  Standard solutions: 0.02, 0.05, 0.1, and 0.2 µg of lead (Pb) ion/mL: from *Standard stock solution*
  Matrix modifier solution: 10 mg/mL of dibasic ammonium phosphate

Sample solution: Transfer 1 g of sample into a 10-mL volumetric flask, add 5 mL of water, and mix. Dilute to volume, and mix.

Spiked sample solution: Prepare a solution as directed under *Sample solution*, but add 100 µL of the *Standard stock solution*, dilute to volume, and mix. This solution contains 0.1 µg of lead/mL.

Analysis: With the use of an autosampler, atomize 10-µL aliquots of the four *Standard solutions*, using the following sequence of conditions:

(1) Dry at 130° with a 20-s ramp period, a 40-s hold time, and a 300-mL/min argon flow rate;

(2) Char at 800° with a 20-s ramp period, a 40-s hold time, and a 300-mL/min argon flow rate;

(3) Atomize at 2400° for 6 s with a 50-mL/min argon flow rate;

(4) Clean at 2600° with a 1-s ramp period, a 5-s hold time, and a 300-mL/min argon flow rate; and

(5) Recharge at 20° with a 2-s ramp period, a 20-s hold time, and a 300-mL/min argon flow rate.

Atomize 10 µL of the *Matrix modifier solution* in combination with either 10 mL of the *Sample solution* or 10 µL of the *Spiked sample solution* under identical conditions used for the *Standard solutions*.

Plot a standard curve using the concentration, in µg/mL, of each *Standard solution* versus its maximum absorbance value compensated for background correction, and draw the best straight line. From the standard curve, determine the concentrations, C_S and C_A, in µg/mL, of the *Sample solution* and the *Spiked sample solution*, respectively. Calculate the quantity, in mg/kg, of lead in the sample taken by the formula:

$$\text{Result} = 10C_S/W$$

W = weight (g) of sample taken

Calculate the recovery by the formula:

$$\text{Result} = 100[(C_A - C_S)/0.1]$$

0.1 = amount of lead (µg/mL) added to the *Spiked sample solution*

Acceptance criteria: NMT 0.5 mg/kg

- **NICKEL**, *Nickel Limit Test*, *Method II*, Appendix IIIB: For Hydrogenated Polydextrose
  Acceptance criteria: NMT 2 mg/kg

Organic Impurities

- **5-HYDROXYMETHYLFURFURAL AND RELATED COMPOUNDS**
  Sample solution: 10 mg/mL
  Analysis: Read the absorbance of the *Sample solution* against a water blank at 283 nm in a 1-cm quartz cell in a spectrophotometer. Calculate the percent 5-hydroxymethylfurfural and related compounds by the formula:

$$\text{Result} = (0.749 \times A)/C$$

0.749 = a composite proportionality constant that includes the extinction coefficient and other molecular weight, unit, and volume conversions

A = absorbance of the *Sample solution*

C = Concentration (mg/mL) of *Sample solution*, corrected for ash and moisture

Acceptance criteria: NMT 0.1%, calculated on the anhydrous, ash-free basis

- **MONOMERS**
  Octadecane solution: 0.5 mg/mL *n*-octadecane in pyridine
  Standard solution: Transfer 50 mg of α-D-glucose[1], 40 mg of anhydrous D-sorbitol, and 35 mg of D-anhydroglucoses, all accurately weighed, into a 100-mL volumetric flask; dissolve in and dilute to volume with pyridine.
  Silylated standard solution: Transfer 1.0 mL of *Standard solution* to a screw-cap vial, and add 1.0 mL of *Octadecane solution* and 0.5 mL of *N*-trimethylsilylimidazole. Cap the vial, and immerse it in an ultrasonic bath at 70° for 60 min.
  Sample solution: Transfer 20 mg of sample into a screw-cap vial, and add 1.0 mL of *Octadecane solution*, 1 mL of pyridine, and 0.5 mL of *N*-trimethylsilylimidazole. Cap the vial, and immerse it in an ultrasonic bath at 70° for 60 min.
  Chromatographic system, Appendix IIA
    Mode: Gas chromatography
    Detector: Flame-ionization detector
    Column: 250-cm × 2-mm (id) glass column, or equivalent, packed with 3% OV-1 stationary phase on 100- to 120-mesh Gas Chrom Q, or equivalent
    Temperature
      Column: 175°
      Injection port: 210°
      Detector: 230°
  Injection volume: About 3 µL
  Analysis: Initially, inject the *Silylated standard solution* into the gas chromatograph. Repeat twice, then inject duplicate portions of the *Sample solution*. [NOTE—Relative retention times (min) are: D-anhydroglucoses (levoglucosan), pyranose form (3.7); furanose form (not present in standard) (4.3); *n*-octadecane (5.1); α-D-glucose (8.7); D-sorbitol (11.3); β-D-glucose (13.3).] Calculate the percentage of each monomer by the formula:

$$\text{Result} = (R \times W_S)/(R_S \times W)$$

R = ratio of the area of the monomer peak to the area of the octadecane peak in the sample injection

W_S = weight (mg) of the respective monomer in the *Silylated standard solution*

R_S = mean ratio of the area of the monomer peak to the area of the octadecane peak in the standard injections

---
[1] Available from NIST

W = weight (mg) of sample taken, adjusted for residue on ignition and moisture

Acceptance criteria
D-Anhydroglucoses: NMT 4.0%, calculated on the anhydrous, ash-free basis
Glucose and Sorbitol: NMT 6.0%, calculated on the anhydrous, ash-free basis

SPECIFIC TESTS

- **MOLECULAR WEIGHT LIMIT**
  Mobile phase: Dissolve 35.0 g of sodium nitrate and 1.0 g of sodium azide in 100 mL of HPLC-grade water. Filter through a 0.45-μm filter into a 4-L flask. Dilute to volume with HPLC-grade water. Degas by applying an aspirator vacuum for 30 min. The resulting eluent is 0.1 N sodium nitrate containing 0.025% sodium azide.
  Standard solution: Transfer 20 mg each of dextrose[2]; stachyose[2]; and 5800, 23,700, and 100,000 molecular weight (MW) pullulan standards[2] into a 10-mL volumetric flask. Dissolve in and dilute to volume with *Mobile phase*. Filter through a 0.45-μm syringe filter.
  Sample solution: 5 mg/mL in *Mobile phase*, and filtered through a 0.45-μm filter
  Chromatographic system, Appendix IIA
    Mode: High-performance liquid chromatography
    Detector: Differential refractometer
    Column: Waters Ultrahydrogel 250 A size-exclusion column, or equivalent
    Column temperature: 45°
    Detector cell temperature: 35° ± 0.1°
    Flow rate: 0.8 mL/min, reproducible to 0.5%
    Injection volume: 50 μL
    Setup: Use either a loop injector or suitable autosampler, a column heating block or oven and a computing integrator, or a computer data handling system with molecular weight determination capabilities. Set the differential refractometer at a sensitivity of 4×10^{-6} refractive index units full scale, and set the plotter of the integrator to 64 mV full scale. Noise attributable to the detector and electronics should be less than 0.1% full scale.
    Column equilibration: After installing a new column in the HPLC, pump *Eluent* through it overnight at 0.3 mL/min. Before calibration or analysis, increase the flow slowly to 0.8 mL/min over a 1-min period, then pump at 0.8 mL/min for at least 1 h before the first injection. Check the flow gravimetrically, and adjust it if necessary. Reduce the flow to 0.1 mL/min when the system is not in use.
    Data system setup: Set the integrator or computerized data-handling system as its respective manual instructs for normal gel permeation chromatographic determinations. Set the integration time to 15 min.
    Column standardization: After equilibrating the HPLC system at a flow rate of 0.8 mL/min for at least 1 h, inject 50 μL of the *Standard solution* five times, allowing 15 min between injections. Record the retention times of the various components in the *Standard solution*. Retention times for each component should agree within ±2 s. Insert the average retention time along with the molecular weight of each component into the calibration table of the molecular weight distribution software.
    System suitability: Check the regression results for a cubic fit of the calibration points. They should have an R^2 value of 0.9999+. Dextrose and stachyose should be baseline resolved from one another and from the 5800 MW pullulan standard. Elevated valleys are usually observed between the 5800, the 23,700, and the 100,000 MW pullulan standards.
    Analysis: Inject 50 μL of the *Sample solution*, following the same conditions and procedure as described under *Column standardization*. Using the Molecular Weight Distribution software of the data-reduction system, generate a molecular weight distribution curve of the sample.
  Acceptance criteria: There is no measurable peak above a molecular weight of 22,000.

- **PH,** *pH Determination,* Appendix IIB
  Sample solution: 100 mg/mL
  Acceptance criteria
    Untreated Polydextrose: Between 2.5 and 7.0
    Neutralized or Decolorized Polydextrose: Between 5.0 and 6.0

- **RESIDUE ON IGNITION (SULFATED ASH),** *Method I,* Appendix IIC
  Acceptance criteria:
    Untreated Polydextrose: NMT 0.3%;
    Neutralized or Decolorized Polydextrose: NMT 2.0%

- **WATER,** *Water Determination,* Appendix IIB
  Analysis: Determine as directed, but using pyridine instead of methanol in the titration vessel.
  Acceptance criteria: NMT 4.0%

Polydextrose Solution

First Published: Prior to FCC 6
Last Revision: FCC 6

UNII: VH2XOU12IE [polydextrose]

DESCRIPTION
Polydextrose Solution occurs as a clear, straw-colored liquid. It is a 70% to 80% water solution of polydextrose.
Function: Bulking agent; humectant; texturizer
Packaging and Storage: Store in tight, light-resistant containers.

IDENTIFICATION

- **A. PROCEDURE**
  Sample solution: 100 mg/mL
  Analysis: Add 4 drops of 5% aqueous phenol solution to 1 drop *Sample solution*, then rapidly add 15 drops of sulfuric acid.
  Acceptance criteria: A deep yellow to orange color appears.

- **B. PROCEDURE**
  Sample solution: 100 mg/mL

---

[2] Available from Polymer Laboratories, Inc., Technical Center, Amherst Fields Research Park, 160 Old Farm Road, Amherst, MA 01002.

Analysis: While vigorously swirling (vortex mixer), add 1.0 mL of acetone to 1.0 mL of *Sample solution*. [NOTE—Retain this solution for *Identification* test C (below).]
Acceptance criteria: The solution remains clear.
- **C. PROCEDURE**
  Analysis: While vigorously swirling, add 2.0 mL of acetone to the retained solution from *Identification* test B.
  Acceptance criteria: A heavy, milky turbidity develops immediately.
- **D. PROCEDURE**
  Sample solution: 20 mg/mL
  Sample: Add 4 mL of alkaline cupric citrate TS to 1 mL of *Sample solution*. Boil vigorously for 2 to 4 min. Remove from heat, and allow the precipitate (if any) to settle.
  Acceptance criteria: The supernatant is blue or blue-green.

ASSAY
- **PROCEDURE**
  Standard stock solution: 0.2 mg/mL α-D-glucose
  Standard solutions: 50, 40, 20, 10, and 5 µg/mL α-D-glucose made from *Standard Stock Solution*
  Sample stock solution: 1.44 mg/mL
  Sample solution: 57.6 µg/mL, made from *Sample stock solution*
  Phenol solution: Add 20 mL of water to 80 g of phenol.
  Analysis: On a daily basis, pipet 2.0 mL of each *Standard solution* and the *Sample solution* into separate, acetone-free, 15-mL screw-cap vials. Add 0.12 mL of the *Phenol Solution*, and mix gently. Uncap each vial and rapidly add 5.0 mL of sulfuric acid. Immediately recap each vial, and shake vigorously. [CAUTION—Wear rubber gloves and a safety shield while adding sulfuric acid.]

Let the vials stand at room temperature for 45 min, then determine the absorbance of each sample at 490 nm in a suitable spectrophotometer, using a *Phenol Solution*-sulfuric acid reagent blank in the reference cell. Repeat the procedure three times and obtain the mean absorbance value. For the standard curve, plot mean absorbance values versus concentrations, in µg/mL, obtained from triplicate *Standard Solutions*. Calculate the percent polymer by the formula:

$$\text{Result} = 1.05[100(A - Y)/(S \times C) - P_G - 1.11 P_L]$$

1.05	= an experimentally derived correction factor to account for the polymer (which also contains a small amount of sorbitol) not giving the exact amount of color given by an equivalent amount of glucose monomers
A	= sample absorbance
Y	= the y-intercept of the standard curve
S	= slope (approximately 0.02) of absorbance versus glucose concentration, in g/mL, obtained from the standard curve
C	= concentration (g/mL) of the *Sample stock solution*, adjusted for ash and moisture
P_G	= percentage of glucose determined under the test for *Monomers* (below)
P_L	= percentage of levoglucosan determined under the test for *Monomers* (below)
1.11	= conversion factor from levoglucosan, which gives an equivalent amount of color to an equivalent weight of glucose

Acceptance criteria: NLT 90.0% polymer, calculated on the anhydrous, ash-free basis

IMPURITIES
Inorganic Impurities
- **LEAD**
  [NOTE—For this test, use reagent-grade chemicals with as low a lead content as is practicable, as well as high-purity water and gases. Before use in this analysis, rinse all glassware and plasticware twice with 10% nitric acid and twice with 10% hydrochloric acid, and then rinse them thoroughly with high-purity water, preferably obtained from a mixed-bed, strong-acid, strong-base, ion-exchange cartridge capable of producing water with an electrical resistivity of 12 to 15 megohms.]
  Apparatus: Use a suitable spectrophotometer (Perkin-Elmer Model 6000, or equivalent), a graphite furnace containing a L'vov platform (Perkin-Elmer Model HGA-500, or equivalent), and an autosampler (Perkin-Elmer Model AS-40, or equivalent). Use a lead hollow-cathode lamp (lamp current of 10 mA), a slit width of 0.7 mm (set low), the wavelength set at 283.3 nm, and a deuterium arc lamp for background correction.
  Lead nitrate solution: 100 µg of lead (Pb) ion/mL prepared as follows: Dissolve 159.8 mg of lead nitrate in 100 mL of water containing 1 mL of nitric acid. Dilute with water to 1000.0 mL, and mix. Prepare and store this solution in glass containers that are free from lead salts.
  Standard stock solution: 10 µg of lead (Pb) ion/mL, from *Lead nitrate solution* [NOTE—Prepare on the day of use.]
  [NOTE—As an alternative to preparing the *Lead nitrate solution* and *Standard stock solution*, NIST Standard Reference Material containing 10 mg of lead/kg, or equivalent, may be used.]
  Standard solutions: 0.02, 0.05, 0.1, and 0.2 µg of lead (Pb) ion/mL, from *Standard stock solution*
  Matrix modifier solution: 10 mg/mL of dibasic ammonium phosphate
  Sample solution: Transfer an amount of sample equivalent to 1 g of Polydextrose into a 10-mL volumetric flask, add 5 mL of water, and mix. Dilute to volume, and mix.
  Spiked sample solution: Prepare a solution as directed under *Sample solution*, but add 100 µL of the *Standard stock solution*, dilute to volume, and mix. This solution contains 0.1 µg of lead/mL.
  Analysis: With the use of an autosampler, atomize 10-µL aliquots of the four *Standard solutions*, using the following sequence of conditions:

(1) Dry at 130° with a 20-s ramp period, a 40-s hold time, and a 300-mL/min argon flow rate;

(2) Char at 800° with a 20-s ramp period, a 40-s hold time, and a 300-mL/min argon flow rate;

(3) Atomize at 2400° for 6 s with a 50-mL/min argon flow rate;

(4) Clean at 2600° with a 1-s ramp period, a 5-s hold time, and a 300-mL/min argon flow rate; and

(5) Recharge at 20° with a 2-s ramp period, a 20-s hold time, and a 300-mL/min argon flow rate.

Atomize 10 µL of the *Matrix modifier solution* in combination with either 10 mL of the *Sample solution* or 10 µL of the *Spiked sample solution* under identical conditions used for the *Standard solutions*.

Plot a standard curve using the concentration, in µg/mL, of each *Standard Solution* versus its maximum absorbance value compensated for background correction, and draw the best straight line. From the standard curve, determine the concentrations, C_S and C_A, in µg/mL, of the *Sample solution* and the *Spiked sample solution*, respectively. Calculate the quantity, in mg/kg, of lead in the sample taken by the formula:

$$\text{Result} = 10 C_S / W$$

W = weight (g) of sample taken

Calculate the recovery by the formula:

$$\text{Result} = 100[(C_A - C_S)/0.1]$$

0.1 = amount of lead (µg/mL) added to the *Spiked sample solution*

Acceptance criteria: NMT 0.5 mg/kg

- **NICKEL,** Nickel Limit Test, Method II, Appendix IIIB
  Acceptance criteria: NMT 2 mg/kg

Organic Impurities

- **5-HYDROXYMETHYLFURFURAL**
  Sample solution: 14 mg/mL
  Analysis: Read the absorbance of the *Sample solution* against a water blank at 283 nm in a 1-cm quartz cell in a spectrophotometer. Calculate the percent 5-hydroxymethylfurfural and related compounds by the formula:

$$\text{Result} = (0.749 \times A)/C$$

0.749 = a composite proportionality constant that includes the extinction coefficient and other molecular weight, unit, and volume conversions

A = absorbance of the *Sample solution*

C = concentration (mg/mL) of *Sample solution*, corrected for ash and moisture

Acceptance criteria: NMT 0.1%, calculated on the anhydrous, ash-free basis

- **MONOMERS**
  Octadecane solution: 0.5 mg/mL *n*-octadecane in pyridine

Standard solution: Transfer 50 mg of α-D-glucose[2], 40 mg of anhydrous D-sorbitol, and 35 mg of D-anhydroglucoses, all accurately weighed, into a 100-mL volumetric flask; dissolve in and dilute to volume with pyridine.

Silylated standard solution: Transfer 1.0 mL of *Standard solution* to a screw-cap vial, and add 1.0 mL of *Octadecane solution* and 0.5 mL of *N*-trimethylsilylimidazole. Cap the vial, and immerse it in an ultrasonic bath at 70° for 60 min.

Sample solution: Transfer 30 mg of sample into a screw-cap vial, and add about 2 mL of pyridine. While flushing the vial with a stream of dry air or nitrogen, heat at 80° to 90° until the solution volume is reduced to 0.2 to 0.5 mL. Add a second portion of pyridine, and repeat the evaporation procedure.

Chromatographic system, Appendix IIA
Mode: Gas chromatography
Detector: Flame-ionization detector
Column: 250-cm × 2-mm (id) glass column, or equivalent, packed with 3% OV-1 stationary phase on 100- to 120-mesh Gas Chrom Q, or equivalent
Temperature
  Column: 175°
  Injection port: 210°
  Detector: 230°
Injection volume: About 3 µL
Analysis: Initially, inject the *Silylated standard solution* into the gas chromatograph. Repeat twice, then inject duplicate portions of the *Sample solution*. [NOTE—Relative retention times (min) are: D-anhydroglucoses (levoglucosan), pyranose form (3.7); furanose form (not present in standard) (4.3); *n*-octadecane (5.1); α-D-glucose (8.7); D-sorbitol (11.3); β-D-glucose (13.3)] Calculate the percentage of each monomer by the formula:

$$\text{Result} = (R \times W_S)/(R_S \times W)$$

R = ratio of the area of the monomer peak to the area of the octadecane peak in the sample injection

W_S = weight (mg) of the respective monomer in the *Silylated standard solution*

R_S = mean ratio of the area of the monomer peak to the area of the octadecane peak in the standard injections

W = weight (mg) of sample taken, adjusted for residue on ignition and moisture

Acceptance criteria:
  1,6-Anhydro-D-glucose: NMT 4.0%, calculated on the anhydrous, ash-free basis
  Glucose and Sorbitol: NMT 6.0%, calculated on the anhydrous, ash-free basis

SPECIFIC TESTS

- **MOLECULAR WEIGHT LIMIT**
  Mobile phase: Dissolve 35.0 g of sodium nitrate and 1.0 g of sodium azide in 100 mL of HPLC-grade water. Filter through a 0.45-µm filter into a 4-L flask. Dilute to volume with HPLC-grade water. Degas by applying an

aspirator vacuum for 30 min. The resulting eluent is 0.1 N sodium nitrate containing 0.025% sodium azide.

Standard solution: Transfer 20 mg each of dextrose[1]; stachyose[2]; and 5800, 23,700, and 100,000 molecular weight (MW) pullulan standards[2] into a 10-mL volumetric flask. Dissolve in and dilute to volume with *Mobile phase*. Filter through a 0.45-μm syringe filter.

Sample solution: 72 mg/mL in *Mobile phase*, and filtered through a 0.45-μm filter

Chromatographic system, Appendix IIA
 Mode: High-performance liquid chromatography
 Detector: Differential refractometer
 Column: Waters Ultrahydrogel 250 A size-exclusion column, or equivalent
 Column temperature: 45°
 Detector cell temperature: 35° ± 0.1°
 Flow rate: 0.8 mL/min, reproducible to 0.5%
 Injection volume: 50 μL
 Setup: Use either a loop injector or suitable autosampler, a column heating block or oven and a computing integrator, or a computer data handling system with molecular weight determination capabilities. Set the differential refractometer at a sensitivity of 4×10^{-6} refractive index units full scale, and set the plotter of the integrator to 64 mV full scale. Noise attributable to the detector and electronics should be less than 0.1% full scale.
 Column equilibration: After installing a new column in the HPLC, pump *Eluent* through it overnight at 0.3 mL/min. Before calibration or analysis, increase the flow slowly to 0.8 mL/min over a 1-min period, then pump at 0.8 mL/min for at least 1 h before the first injection. Check the flow gravimetrically, and adjust it if necessary. Reduce the flow to 0.1 mL/min when the system is not in use.
 Data system setup: Set the integrator or computerized data-handling system as its respective manual instructs for normal gel permeation chromatographic determinations. Set the integration time to 15 min.
 Column standardization: After equilibrating the HPLC system at a flow rate of 0.8 mL/min for at least 1 h, inject 50 μL of the *Standard solution* five times, allowing 15 min between injections. Record the retention times of the various components in the Standard Solution. Retention times for each component should agree within ±2 s. Insert the average retention time along with the molecular weight of each component into the calibration table of the molecular weight distribution software.
 System suitability: Check the regression results for a cubic fit of the calibration points. They should have an R^2 value of 0.9999+. Dextrose and stachyose should be baseline resolved from one another and from the 5800 MW pullulan standard. Elevated valleys are usually observed between the 5800, the 23,700, and the 100,000 MW pullulan standards.
 Analysis: Inject 50 μL of the *Sample solution*, following the same conditions and procedure as described under *Column standardization*. Using the Molecular Weight Distribution software of the data-reduction system, generate a molecular weight distribution curve of the sample.
 Acceptance criteria: There is no measurable peak above a molecular weight of 22,000.
- **pH,** *pH Determination,* Appendix IIB
 Sample solution: 0.14 g/mL
 Acceptance criteria: Between 3.5 and 6.5
- **RESIDUE ON IGNITION (SULFATED ASH),** *Method II,* Appendix IIC
 Acceptance criteria: NMT 2.0%
- **WATER**
 Sample: 1 to 2 mL
 Analysis: Transfer the *Sample* into a dropper vial, and weigh the dropper, vial, and sample combined. Add 50 mL of pyridine to a clean, dry reaction jar previously flushed with dry air for 1 min. Titrate the pyridine with Karl Fischer reagent (see *Reagent* in *Method Ia* under *Water Determination,* Appendix IIB) to the endpoint to consume any water present. Transfer one drop of sample (50 to 100 mg) from the weighed sample vial to the reaction jar. Reweigh the dropper, vial, and remaining sample. Stir the pyridine-sample mixture for 5 to 10 min. Titrate with Karl Fischer reagent to the endpoint. For each determination, calculate the percentage of water (W) in the sample by the equation:

$$W = (V \times F \times 100)/S$$

V = volume (mL) of Karl Fischer reagent consumed in the second titration
F = karl Fischer reagent standardization factor (mg/mL)
S = sample weight (mg) equal to the difference between the initial and final weighings of the dropper, vial, and sample combination

Calculate the water content of the sample as the average of two determinations
 Acceptance criteria: Between 27.5% and 32.5%

Polyethylene

First Published: Prior to FCC 6

$(C_2H_4)x$ CAS: [9002-88-4]

DESCRIPTION

Polyethylene occurs as a white, translucent, partially crystalline and partially amorphous resin. It is produced by the direct polymerization of ethylene at high temperatures and high pressure. Various grades and types, differing from one another in molecular weight, molecular weight distribution, degree of chain branching, and extent of crystallization, are available. It is insoluble in water.

Function: Masticatory substance in chewing gum base
Packaging and Storage: Store in well-closed containers.

---

[1] Available from Polymer Laboratories, Inc., Technical Center, Amherst Fields Research Park, 160 Old Farm Road, Amherst, MA 01002.
[2] Available from NIST.

IDENTIFICATION

- **INFRARED SPECTRA,** *Spectrophotometric Identification Tests,* Appendix IIIC
  Sample preparation: Dissolve the sample in hot toluene and evaporate on a potassium bromide plate.
  Acceptance criteria: The spectrum of the sample exhibits relative maxima at the same wavelengths as those of the spectrum below.

IMPURITIES
Inorganic Impurities
- **LEAD,** *Sample Solution for Lead Limit Test,* Appendix IV
  Acceptance criteria: NMT 3 mg/kg

SPECIFIC TESTS

- **MOLECULAR WEIGHT,** Appendix IV
  Acceptance criteria: Between 2000 and 21,000
- **VOLATILES**
  Sample: 4 g
  Analysis: Determine as directed under *Loss on Drying,* Appendix IIC, drying the *Sample* for 45 min at 105°.
  [**CAUTION**—To reduce explosion hazard, pass carbon dioxide or nitrogen into the lower part of the drying oven at a rate of about 100 mL/min.]
  Acceptance criteria: NMT 0.5%

Polyethylene

Polyethylene Glycols

First Published: Prior to FCC 6

PEG

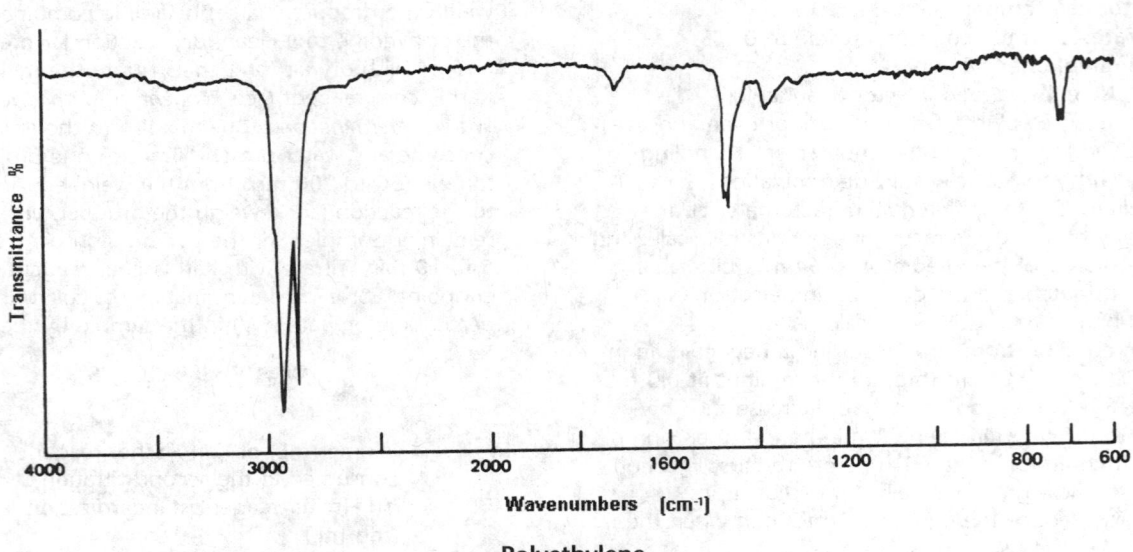

INS: 1521   CAS: [25322-68-3]
UNII: 3WJQ0SDW1A [polyethylene glycols]

DESCRIPTION

Polyethylene Glycols are addition polymers of ethylene oxide and water, ranging in molecular weight from about 200 to about 9500. Commercially available Polyethylene Glycols are usually designated by a number that roughly corresponds to the nominal molecular weight. Polyethylene Glycols having a nominal molecular weight of 600 or below occur as clear to slightly hazy, colorless or practically colorless, viscous, slightly hygroscopic liquids that are miscible with water. Polyethylene Glycols having a nominal molecular weight of 1000 or above are freely soluble in water and occur as creamy white, waxy solids or as flakes resembling paraffin. The Polyethylene Glycols are soluble in many organic solvents, including aliphatic ketones and alcohols, chloroform, glycol ethers, esters, and aromatic hydrocarbons; they are insoluble in ether and in most aliphatic hydrocarbons. As their molecular weight increases, water solubility, vapor pressure, hygroscopicity, and solubility in organic solvents decrease, while solidification point, specific gravity, flash point, and viscosity increase. They may contain a suitable antioxidant.

Function: Dispersing, coating, binding, plasticizing agent; lubricant; flavoring adjuvant
Packaging and Storage: Store in tight containers.

IMPURITIES
Inorganic Impurities
- **LEAD,** *Lead Limit Test, Atomic Absorption Spectrophotometric Graphite Furnace Method, Method I,* Appendix IIIB
  Acceptance criteria: NMT 1 mg/kg

Organic Impurities
- **ETHYLENE OXIDE AND 1,4-DIOXANE**
  Stripped polyethylene glycol 400: Place 3000 g of polyethylene glycol 400 into a 5000-mL, 4-neck, round-bottom flask equipped with a stirrer, a thermometer, a gas dispersion tube, a dry ice trap, a

vacuum outlet, and a heating mantle. At room temperature, evacuate the flask carefully to a pressure of less than 1 mm Hg, applying the vacuum slowly while observing for excessive foaming due to entrapped gases.

After any foaming has subsided, sparge with nitrogen, allowing the pressure to rise to 10 mm Hg. Heat the flask to 60° while increasing the pressure to about 60 mm Hg. Continue stripping for 4 h, then cool to room temperature. Shut off the vacuum pump, and bring the flask pressure back to atmospheric while maintaining nitrogen sparging. Remove the sparging tube with the gas still flowing, then turn off the gas flow.

Transfer the *Stripped polyethylene glycol 400* to a suitable nitrogen-filled container.

Standard solutions: [CAUTION—Ethylene oxide and 1, 4-dioxane are toxic and flammable. Prepare these solutions in a well-ventilated fume hood.]

Add a suitable quantity of 1,4-dioxane to a known weight of organic-free water in a vial that can be sealed. Determine the amount added by weight difference.

Transfer 5 mL of the liquid ethylene oxide to a 100-mL beaker chilled in wet ice. [NOTE—Ethylene oxide is a gas at room temperature. It is usually stored in a lecture-type gas cylinder or small metal pressure bomb. Chill the cylinder in a refrigerator before use.] Using a gas-tight gas chromatographic syringe that has been chilled in a refrigerator, transfer a suitable amount of the liquid ethylene oxide into the mixture. Immediately seal the vial, and shake. Determine the amount added by weight difference.

By appropriate dilution with *Stripped ethylene glycol 400*, prepare four solutions, covering the range from 1 to 20 mg/kg for the two components added to the matrix (e.g., 5, 10, 15, and 20 mg/kg). Transfer 10 mL of each of these solutions to separate 22-mL pressure headspace vials, seal each with a silicone septum, star spring, and pressure-relief safety aluminum sealing cap, and crimp the cap closed with a cap-sealing tool. Shake for 2 min.

Sample solution: Transfer 10 ± 0.01 g of sample to a 22-mL pressure headspace vial, and seal, cap, and crimp as directed for the *Standard solutions*.

Chromatographic system, Appendix IIA
  Mode: Gas chromatography [NOTE—Use a system equipped with a balanced pressure automatic headspace sampler.]
  Detector: Flame-ionization detector
  Column: 50-m × 0.32-mm fused silica capillary column bonded with a 5-μm film of 5% phenyl–95% methylsiloxane, or equivalent
  Temperature
    Column: Program from 70° to 250° at 10°/min.
    Transfer line: 140°
    Detector: 250°
  Flow rate: About 0.8 mL/min
  Carrier gas: Helium
System suitability
  Sample: *Standard solutions*

  Suitability requirement: On the two standard curves obtained below under *Analysis*, no point digresses from the best fit line by more than 10%.

Analysis: Place the vials containing the *Standard solutions* in the automated sampler, and start the sequence so that each vial is heated at a temperature of 50° for 30 min before a suitable portion of its headspace is injected into the chromatograph. Set the automatic sampler for a needle withdrawal time of 0.3 min, a pressurization time of 1 min, an injection time of 0.08 min, and a vial pressure of 22 psig with the vial vent off. Obtain the peak areas for ethylene oxide and 1,4-dioxane. [NOTE—Relative retention times for ethylene oxide and 1,4-dioxane are about 1.0 and 3.1, respectively.] Generate standard curves by plotting the peak area responses versus concentration, in mg/kg.

Place the vial containing the *Sample solution* in the automatic sampler, and chromatograph its headspace as done for the *Standard solutions*. Obtain the peak areas for ethylene oxide and 1,4-dioxane, and read their concentrations directly from the corresponding standard curve.

Acceptance criteria
  Ethylene oxide: NMT 10 mg/kg
  1,4-Dioxane: NMT 10 mg/kg

- **ETHYLENE GLYCOL AND DIETHYLENE GLYCOL**
  - METHOD FOR POLYETHYLENE GLYCOLS HAVING NOMINAL MOLECULAR WEIGHT BELOW 450:

  Ethylene glycol standard solution: 0.2 to 1 mg/mL each of ethylene glycol [NOTE—Purify standards by distillation before use if necessary.]

  Diethylene glycol standard solution: 0.2 to 1 mg/mL each of diethylene glycol [NOTE—Purify standards by distillation before use if necessary.]

  Sample solution: Transfer 4 g of sample into a 10-mL volumetric flask, dilute to volume with water, and mix.

  Chromatographic system, Appendix IIA
    Mode: Gas chromatography
    Detector: Hydrogen flame ionization detector (Varian Aerograph 600D, or equivalent)
    Column: 1.5-m × 3-mm (id) stainless-steel column, or equivalent, packed with sorbitol 12%, by weight, on 60- to 80-mesh non-acid-washed diatomaceous earth[1]
    Column temperature: 165°
    Inlet temperature: 260°
    Carrier gas: Nitrogen (or other suitable inert gas)
    Flow rate: 70 mL/min
    Burner gas: Hydrogen and air, optimized to give maximum sensitivity
    Recorder: 0.5 to +1.05 mV, full span, (1-s full-response time)
    Injection volume: 2 μL

  Analysis: Inject the *Ethylene glycol standard solution*, the *Diethylene glycol standard solution* and the *Sample solution* into the chromatograph and record the resulting chromatogram for each solution. [NOTE—Under the stated conditions, the elution time is approximately 2.0 min for ethylene glycol and 6.5 for

---
[1] Chromosorb W, or equivalent

diethylene glycol.] Measure the peak heights, and record the values as follows:

Calculate the percentage of ethylene glycol in the sample by the formula:

$$\text{Result} = (E \times B)/(A \times C)$$

A = height of the ethylene glycol peak in the chromatogram of *Ethylene glycol standard solution* (mm)
B = concentration of ethylene glycol in the *Ethylene glycol standard solution* (mg/mL)
E = height of the ethylene glycol peak in the chromatogram of the *Sample solution* (mm)
C = concentration of the *Sample solution* (mg/mL)

Calculate the percentage of diethylene glycol in the sample by the formula:

$$\text{Result} = (F \times D)/(G \times C)$$

G = height of the diethylene glycol peak in the chromatogram of *Diethylene glycol standard solution* (mm)
D = concentration of ethylene glycol in *Diethylene glycol standard solution* (mg/mL)
F = height of the diethylene glycol peak in the chromatogram of the *Sample solution* (mm)
C = concentration of the *Sample solution* (mg/mL)

Acceptance criteria: NMT 0.25% of total ethylene and diethylene glycols, combined

- **METHOD FOR POLYETHYLENE GLYCOLS HAVING NOMINAL MOLECULAR WEIGHT OF 450 OR HIGHER:**
  Standard solution: 2.5 mg/mL of diethylene glycol in a 1:1 mixture of freshly distilled acetonitrile and water
  Sample solution: Dissolve 50.0 g of sample in 75 mL of diphenyl ether in a 250-mL distillation flask. Warm the mixture, if necessary, just enough to melt the crystals. Slowly distill at a pressure of 1 to 2 mm Hg into a receiver graduated to 100 mL in 1-mL subdivisions, until 25 mL of distillate has been collected.
  Add 20.0 mL of water to the distillate, shake vigorously, and allow the layers to separate. Cool in an ice bath to solidify the diphenyl ether and facilitate its removal. Filter the water layer, wash the diphenyl ether with 5.0 mL of ice-cold water, pass the washings through the filter, and collect the filtrate and washings in a 25-mL volumetric flask. Warm to room temperature, dilute to volume with water, if necessary, and mix. Mix this solution with 25.0 mL of freshly distilled acetonitrile in a 125-mL glass-stoppered flask to obtain the *Sample solution*.
  Analysis: Transfer 10.0 mL each of the *Sample solution* and of the *Standard solution* into separate 50-mL flasks, each containing 15 mL of ceric ammonium nitrate TS, and mix. Within 2 to 5 min, using a suitable spectrophotometer, determine the absorbance of each solution in a 1-cm cell at the wavelength of maximum absorbance occurring between 400 and 600 nm, using a blank consisting of 15 mL of ceric ammonium nitrate TS and 10 mL of a 1:1 mixture of acetonitrile and water.
  Acceptance criteria: The absorbance of the solution from the *Sample solution* does not exceed that from the *Standard solution*. (NMT 0.25% total of ethylene and diethylene glycols)

SPECIFIC TESTS
- **COMPLETENESS AND COLOR OF SOLUTION**
  Sample solution: 5 g in 50 mL of water
  Acceptance criteria: The *Sample solution* is colorless; it is clear for liquid grades and not more than slightly hazy for solid grades.
- **NOMINAL MOLECULAR WEIGHT**
  Phthalic anhydride solution: Place 49.0 g of phthalic anhydride in an amber bottle, and dissolve it in 300 mL of pyridine that has been freshly distilled over phthalic anhydride. Shake the bottle vigorously until solution is effected, and allow to stand overnight before using.
  Sample solution:
    Liquid polyethylene glycols: Carefully introduce 25.0 mL of the *Phthalic anhydride solution* into a clean, dry, heat-resistant pressure bottle. Add an amount of sample equivalent to its expected average molecular weight divided by 160 to the bottle. (e.g., A sample of about 1.3 g would be taken for polyethylene glycol 200, or about 3.8 g for polyethylene glycol 600.) Stopper the bottle, and wrap it securely in a fabric bag.
    Solid polyethylene glycols: Carefully introduce 25.0 mL of the *Phthalic anhydride solution* into a clean, dry, heat-resistant pressure bottle. Add an amount of sample, previously melted, equivalent to its expected molecular weight divided by 160 to the bottle; because of limited solubility, however, do not use more than 25 g of any sample. Add 25 mL of pyridine, freshly distilled over phthalic anhydride, swirl to complete dissolution, stopper the bottle, and wrap it securely in a fabric bag.
  Analysis: Immerse the capped bottle containing the *Sample solution* in a water bath, maintained between 96° and 100°, to the same depth as that of the mixture in the bottle. Heat the bottle in the water bath for 30 to 60 min, using 60 min for polyethylene glycols having molecular weights of 3000 or higher, then remove the bottle from the bath, and allow it to cool to room temperature. Uncap the bottle carefully to release any pressure. Remove the bottle from the fabric bag, add 5 drops of a 1:100 solution of phenolphthalein: pyridine, and titrate with 0.5 N sodium hydroxide to the first pink color that persists for 15 s, recording the volume, in mL, of 0.5 N sodium hydroxide required as S.
  Perform a blank determination (see *General Provisions*) on 25.0 mL of the *Phthalic anhydride solution* plus any additional pyridine added to the sample bottle, and record the volume, in mL, of 0.5 N sodium hydroxide required as B.

Calculate the nominal molecular weight of the sample by the formula:

$$\text{Result} = 2000W/(B - S)N$$

W = weight of the sample taken to prepare the *Sample solution* (g)
N = exact normality of the sodium hydroxide solution
B = volume of 0.5 N sodium hydroxide required for titration of the blank (mL)
S = volume of 0.5 N sodium hydroxide required for titration of the *Sample solution* (mL)

Acceptance criteria
Polyethylene glycols having nominal molecular weights below 1000: NLT 95.0% and NMT 105.0% of the labeled value
Polyethylene glycols having nominal molecular weights between 1000 and 7000: NLT 90.0% and NMT 110.0% of the labeled value
Polyethylene glycols having nominal molecular weights above 7000: NLT 87.5% and NMT 112.5% of the labeled value

- **pH**
  Sample solution: 5 g of sample in 100 mL of carbon dioxide-free water
  Analysis: Add 0.3 mL of saturated potassium chloride solution to the *Sample solution* and determine the pH potentiometrically.
  Acceptance criteria: Between 4.5 and 7.5
- **Residue on Ignition (Sulfated Ash),** *Method I*, Appendix II
  Sample: 25 g
  Acceptance criteria: NMT 0.2%
- **Viscosity,** *Viscosity of Dimethylpolysiloxane*, Appendix IIIB
  Analysis: Determine as directed maintaining the constant-temperature bath at 100° ± 0.3° and using a capillary viscometer having a flow time of at least 200 s for the sample being tested.
  Acceptance criteria: The viscosity is within the limits specified in the table below. (For polyethylene glycols not listed in the table, calculate the limits by interpolation.)

Nominal Average Mol Wt	Viscosity Range (centistokes)	Nominal Average Mol Wt	Viscosity Range (centistokes)
200	3.9 and 4.8	2400	49–65
300	5.4–6.4	2500	51–70
400	6.8–8.0	2600	54–74
500	8.3–9.6	2700	57–78
600	9.9–11.3	2800	60–83
700	11.5–13.0	2900	64–88
800	12.5–14.5	3000	67–93
900	15.0–17.0	3250	73–105
1000	16.0–19.0	3350	76–110
1100	18.0–22.0	3500	87–123
1200	20.0–24.5	3750	99–140
1300	22.0–27.5	4000	110–158
1400	24–30	4250	123–177
1450	25–32	4500	140–200
1500	26–33	4750	155–228
1600	28–36	5000	170–250
1700	31–39	5500	206–315
1800	33–42	6000	250–390
1900	35–45	6500	295–480
2000	38–49	7000	350–590
2100	40–53	7500	405–735
2200	43–56	8000	470–900
2300	46–60		

OTHER REQUIREMENTS
- **Labeling:** Indicate the nominal average molecular weight.

Polyglycerol Esters of Fatty Acids

First Published: Prior to FCC 6

INS: 475

DESCRIPTION
Polyglycerol Esters of Fatty Acids are mixed partial esters formed by reacting polymerized glycerols with edible fats, oils, or fatty acids. Minor amounts of mono-, di-, and triglycerides; free glycerol and polyglycerols; free fatty acids; and sodium salts of fatty acids may be present. The polyglycerols vary in degree of polymerization, which is specified by a number (such as tri-, penta-, deca-, etc.) that is related to the average number of glycerol residues per polyglycerol molecule. A specified polyglycerol consists of a distribution of molecular species characteristic of its nominal degree of polymerization. By varying the proportions as well as the nature of the fats or fatty acids to be reacted with the polyglycerols, a large and diverse class of products may be obtained. They include light yellow to amber, oily to very viscous liquids; light tan to medium brown, plastic or soft solids; and light tan to brown, hard, waxy solids. The esters range from very hydrophilic to very lipophilic, but as a class tend to be dispersible in water and soluble in organic solvents and oils.

Function: Emulsifier
Packaging and Storage: Store in well-closed containers.

IMPURITIES
Inorganic Impurities
- **Lead,** *Lead Limit Test, Flame Atomic Absorption Spectrophotometric Method*, Appendix IIIB
  Sample: 10 g
  Acceptance criteria: NMT 2 mg/kg

SPECIFIC TESTS
- **Acid Value (Fats and Related Substances),** *Method II*, Appendix VII

Acceptance criteria: Conforms to the representations of the vendor.

- **HYDROXYL VALUE**
  Sample: An amount equivalent, in g, to 561 divided by the expected hydroxyl value ±10%
  Solution A: Pyridine and acetic anhydride [9 : 1] (v/v)
  Analysis: Transfer the *Sample* into a 300-mL Erlenmeyer flask. Add 25.0 mL of *Solution A* into the sample flask, and pipet 25.0 mL of *Solution A* into a separate 300-mL Erlenmeyer flask to serve as the blank. Add boiling stones to each flask, and fit the flasks with air condensers, lubricating the joints only with a few drops of pyridine. Reflux the sample solution gently by heating on a hot plate, confining the vapors in the lower portion of the condenser, and continue refluxing for 45 min. Do not heat the blank. Cool the sample flask to room temperature, and rinse the condenser, the condenser tip, and the sides of the flask with 25 mL of pyridine. Add about 50 mL of 0.55 N sodium hydroxide to each flask, mix by swirling for about 45 s, then add 1 mL of phenolphthalein TS and 75 mL of isopropanol, and continue the titration with stirring to the first pink color that persists for at least 30 s.
  Calculate the hydroxyl value by the formula

  $$\text{Result} = AV + [(56.1)(B - S)(N/W)]$$

  AV = *Acid Value*, determined as directed above
  B = volume of 0.55 N sodium hydroxide required for the blank titration (mL)
  S = volume of 0.55 N sodium hydroxide required for titration of the *Sample* (mL)
  N = exact normality of the sodium hydroxide solution
  W = weight of the sample taken (g)
  Acceptance criteria: Conforms to the representations of the vendor.

- **IODINE VALUE**, Appendix VII
  Acceptance criteria: Conforms to the representations of the vendor.

- **RESIDUE ON IGNITION (SULFATED ASH)**, Appendix IIC
  Acceptance criteria: Conforms to the representations of the vendor.

- **SAPONIFICATION VALUE**, Appendix VII
  Sample: An amount equivalent to 700 divided by the expected saponification value
  Acceptance criteria: Conforms to the representations of the vendor.

- **SODIUM SALTS OF FATTY ACIDS**
  Sample: 5 g
  Analysis: Dissolve the *Sample* in 75 mL of glacial acetic acid, add 2 drops of crystal violet TS, and titrate with 0.1 N perchloric acid in glacial acetic acid to an emerald green endpoint. [**CAUTION**—Handle perchloric acid in an appropriate fume hood.] Perform a blank determination (see *General Provisions*), and make any necessary correction.

Calculate the number of mg of potassium hydroxide equivalent to the sodium salts per g of sample by the formula:

$$\text{Result} = 56.1 \times (VN/W)$$

N = exact normality of the perchloric acid
W = weight of the sample taken (g)
V = volume of perchloric acid consumed by the *Sample* minus any volume consumed by the blank (mL)

Acceptance criteria: Conforms to the representations of the vendor.

Polyglycerol Polyricinoleic Acid

First Published: Prior to FCC 6
Last Revision: FCC 6

Glycerol Esters of Condensed Castor Oil Fatty Acids
Polyglycerol Esters of Interesterified Ricinoleic Acid
Polyglycerol Polyricinoleate

$n = 2 - 6$
R = H or polyricinoleic acid ester

INS: 476

DESCRIPTION
Polyglycerol Polyricinoleic Acid occurs as a clear, light brown, viscous liquid. It is prepared by esterification of polyglycerol with condensed castor oil fatty acids. The castor oil fatty acids are mainly composed of 80% to 90% ricinoleic acid. It is soluble in ether, in hydrocarbons, and in halogenated hydrocarbons. It is insoluble in water and in alcohol.

Function: Emulsifier
Packaging and Storage: Store in well-closed containers.

IDENTIFICATION
[**CAUTION**—Conduct these tests in a fume hood.]

- **A. FATTY ACIDS**
  Sample: 1 g
  Analysis: Reflux *Sample* with 15 mL of 0.5 N ethanolic potassium hydroxide for 1 h. Add 15 mL of water, and acidify with dilute hydrochloric acid TS (about 6 mL).
  Acceptance criteria: Oily drops or a white to yellow-white solid is produced that is soluble in 5 mL of hexane.

- **B. RICINOLEIC ACID**
  Analysis: Remove the hexane layer obtained in *Identification* test *A*, extract again with 5 mL of hexane, and remove the hexane layer.
  Acceptance criteria: The fatty acids thus extracted have a hydroxyl value corresponding to that of castor oil fatty acids (about 150 to 170).

ASSAY
- **PROCEDURE**

  Sample solution: Reflux 0.5 g of sample with 20 mL of ethanolic 1 N potassium hydroxide solution for 2 h. Reduce the volume of ethanol by evaporation at 45 to 50° in a stream of nitrogen. Add 10 mL of water, and acidify with concentrated hydrochloric acid. Extract the fatty acids from the aqueous phase with successive 20-mL volumes of hexane. Wash the hexane extracts with 20 mL of water, and combine the wash with the aqueous phase. With the aid of a pH meter, adjust the aqueous polyol solution to pH 7.0 with aqueous potassium hydroxide solution. Evaporate to 2 to 3 mL under reduced pressure, and extract three times with 30 mL of boiling ethanol. Filter off any residue, and evaporate the ethanol under reduced pressure to yield a viscous liquid mixture of polyols. Transfer 0.1 g of the mixture into a 10-mL capped vial containing 0.5 mL of warm pyridine previously dried over potassium hydroxide, and dissolve. Add 0.2 mL of hexamethyldisilazane, shake, add 2 mL of trimethylchlorosilate, and shake again. Place the vial on a warm plate at about 80° for 3 to 5 min. Check that white fumes are evolving, indicating an excess of reagent.

  Chromatographic system, Appendix IIA
  Mode: Gas chromatography
  Detector: Flame ionization detector
  Column: 1.5-m × 4-mm (id); 3% OV-1 on 100- to 120-mesh diatomite CQ or 100- to 120-mesh Gas Chrom Q, or equivalent
  Oven temperature: Increase from 90 to 330° at 4 to 6°/min.
  Injection block temperature: 275°
  Detector block temperature: 350°
  Carrier gas: Nitrogen
  Flow rate: 86 mL/min
  Injection volume: 2.0 µL
  Analysis: Inject 2.0 µL of the *Sample solution* into the chromatograph. The resultant chromatogram displays the following sequence of peaks:

Identity	Description	Elution Sequence of Peaks (and Typical Attenuation Settings)
1	Solvent	Overloaded
2	Glycerol	Single peak (2 × 10³)
3	Cyclic diglycerols	Single peak (2 × 10³)
4	Diglycerols	Single peak (32 × 10³)
5	Cyclic triglycerols	Single peak (2 × 10³)
6	Triglycerols	Single peak (16 × 10³)
7	Cyclic tetraglycerols	Single peak (2 × 10³)
8	Tetraglycerols	Multiple peaks (8 × 10³)
9	Pentaglycerols	Single peak (4 × 10³)
10	Hexaglycerols	Single peak (2 × 10³)
11	Heptaglycerols	Single peak (2 × 10³)
12	Octaglycerols	Single peak (1 × 10³)
13	Nonaglycerols	Barely discernible in the tail of peak 12

Measure each peak area, and correct for attenuation changes to obtain the corrected area (S_N) of each peak. Calculate the percentage of the total di-, tri-, and tetraglycerols using the following formula:

$$\text{Result} = [(\Sigma S_3 \text{ to } S_8)/(\Sigma S_3 \text{ to } S_{13})]100$$

Calculate the percentage of polyols equal to or greater than heptaglycerol using the following formula:

$$\text{Result} = [(\Sigma S_{11} \text{ to } S_{13})/(\Sigma S_3 \text{ to } S_{13})]100$$

Acceptance criteria
  NLT 75% of di-, tri-, and tetraglycerols, and NMT 10% of polyglycerols equal to or higher than heptaglycerol

IMPURITIES
Inorganic Impurities
- **LEAD,** *Lead Limit Test, Atomic Absorption Spectrophotometric Graphite Furnace Method, Method II,* Appendix IIIB
  Acceptance criteria: NMT 1 mg/kg

SPECIFIC TESTS
- **ACID VALUE (FATS AND RELATED SUBSTANCES),** *Method II,* Appendix VII
  Acceptance criteria: NMT 6
- **HYDROXYL VALUE,** *Method II,* Appendix VII
  Acceptance criteria: Between 80 and 100
- **IODINE VALUE,** Appendix VII
  Acceptance criteria: Between 72 and 103
- **REFRACTIVE INDEX,** Appendix IIB: At 65°
  [NOTE—Use an Abbé or other refractometer of equal or greater accuracy.]
  Acceptance criteria: Between 1.463 and 1.467
- **SAPONIFICATION VALUE,** Appendix VII
  Sample: 4 g
  Acceptance criteria: Between 170 and 210

Polyisobutylene

First Published: Prior to FCC 6

CAS: [9003-27-4]

DESCRIPTION
Polyisobutylene is a synthetic polymer. Low-molecular-weight grades are soft and gummy; high-molecular-weight grades are tough and elastic. All grades are light in color, are soluble in diisobutylene and in benzene, but are insoluble in water.

Function: Masticatory substance in chewing gum base
Packaging and Storage: Store low-molecular-weight grades in boxes or drums with a release liner or coating;

912 / Polyisobutylene / *Monographs*

store high-molecular-weight grades wrapped in polyethylene film.

IDENTIFICATION
- **INFRARED SPECTRA,** *Spectrophotometric Identification Tests,* Appendix IIIC
  Sample preparation: Dissolve the sample in hot toluene and evaporate on a potassium bromide plate.
  Acceptance criteria: The spectrum of the sample exhibits relative maxima at the same wavelengths as those of the spectrum below.

IMPURITIES
Inorganic Impurities
- **LEAD,** *Sample Solution for Lead Limit Test,* Appendix IV
  Control: 3 µg Pb (3 mL of *Diluted Standard Lead Solution*)
  Acceptance criteria: NMT 3 mg/kg

SPECIFIC TESTS
- **MOLECULAR WEIGHT,** *Polyisobutylene (Flory Method),* Appendix IV
  Acceptance criteria: NLT 37,000
- **VOLATILES**
  Sample: 5 g
  Analysis: Determine as directed under *Loss on Drying,* Appendix IIC, drying the *Sample* for 2 h at 105°.
  [**CAUTION**—To reduce explosion hazard, pass carbon dioxide or nitrogen into the lower part of the drying oven at a rate of about 100 mL/min.]
  Acceptance criteria: NMT 0.3%

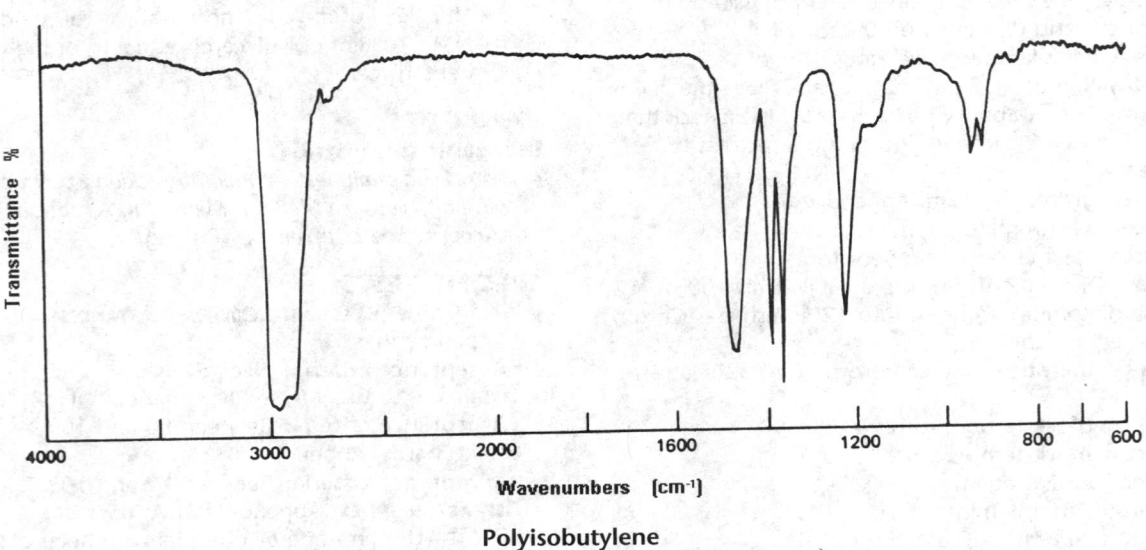

Polyisobutylene

Polypropylene Glycol

First Published: Prior to FCC 6

CAS: [25322-69-4]

DESCRIPTION
Polypropylene Glycol occurs as a clear, colorless or practically colorless, viscous liquid. It is an addition polymer of propylene glycol and water represented by the formula HO(C$_3$H$_6$O)$_n$-C$_3$H$_6$OH, in which n represents the average number of oxypropylene groups. It is soluble in water and in such organic solvents as aliphatic ketones and alcohols, but it is insoluble in ether and in most aliphatic hydrocarbons.
Function: Defoaming agent
Packaging and Storage: Store in tight containers.

IMPURITIES
Inorganic Impurities
- **LEAD,** *Lead Limit Test, Atomic Absorption Spectrophotometric Graphite Furnace Method, Method I,* Appendix IIIB
  Acceptance criteria: NMT 1 mg/kg

Organic Impurities
- **PROPYLENE OXIDE**
  Magnesium chloride stock solution: Add 100 mL of 10 N hydrochloric acid to 950 g of magnesium chloride (MgCl$_2$·6H$_2$O), dissolve in and dilute to 1000 mL with water, and mix.
  Magnesium chloride solution: Carefully add 400 mL of anhydrous methanol to 100 mL of *Magnesium chloride stock solution,* and allow the mixture to come to room temperature before using.
  Indicator: 1 mg/mL of bromocresol green in anhydrous methanol
  Analysis: Place 150 mL of anhydrous methanol into each of two 500-mL glass-stoppered, conical flasks, the second of which is used as the reagent blank. Pressure-

pipet 25.0 mL of the *Magnesium chloride solution* into each flask, allowing the same drainage time for each transfer, and mix thoroughly. Add 50 g of sample to the first flask and dissolve it by swirling. Add about 1 mL of the *Indicator* to each flask, and titrate the contents of the sample flask with 0.1 N alcoholic potassium hydroxide to a brilliant blue endpoint, recording the volume required, in mL, as S. Titrate the reagent blank flask in the same manner and record the volume required, in mL, as B.

To correct for the alkalinity in the sample, place 150 mL of anhydrous methanol into a 500-mL conical flask, add 50 g of sample, and swirl to complete dissolution. Add 1 mL of *Indicator* and titrate with 0.1 N hydrochloric acid to a yellow endpoint, recording the volume required, in mL, as C.

Calculate the percent of propylene oxide in the sample taken by the formula:

$$\text{Result} = 5.81 \times \{[(B - S)N_1]/W_1\} - (CN_2/W_2)$$

N_1 = exact normality of the potassium hydroxide
W_1 = weight of the sample (g) taken for the reaction
N_2 = Exact normality of the hydrochloric acid
W_2 = weight of the sample (g) taken for the alkalinity correction

Acceptance criteria: NMT 0.02%

SPECIFIC TESTS

- **NOMINAL MOLECULAR WEIGHT**

    Phthalic anhydride solution: 163 mg/mL of phthalic anhydride in pyridine that has been freshly distilled over phthalic anhydride, made to 300 mL [NOTE—Prepare in an amber bottle. Shake the bottle vigorously to complete dissolution. Allow the solution to stand overnight before using.]

    Sample solution: Carefully introduce 25.0 mL of the *Phthalic anhydride solution* into a clean, dry, heat-resistant pressure bottle. Add an amount of sample, equivalent to its expected nominal molecular weight divided by 160, into the bottle, cap the bottle tightly, and encase it in a fabric bag.

    Analysis: Immerse the capped bottle containing the *Sample solution* in a water bath, maintained between 96° and 100°, to the same depth as that of the mixture in the bottle. Heat the bottle in the water bath for 30 min, then remove the bottle from the bath, and allow it to cool to room temperature. Uncap the bottle carefully to release any pressure. Remove the bottle from the fabric bag, add 5 drops of a 1:100 solution of phenolphthalein:pyridine, and titrate with 0.5 N sodium hydroxide to the first pink color that persists for 15 s, recording the volume, in mL, of 0.5 N sodium hydroxide required as S.

    Perform a blank determination (see *General provisions*) on 25.0 mL of the *Phthalic anhydride solution* plus any additional pyridine added to the sample bottle. Make any necessary correction, and record the volume, in mL, of 0.5 N sodium hydroxide required as B.

    Calculate the nominal molecular weight of the sample by the formula:

    $$\text{Result} = 2000W/N(B - S)$$

    W = weight of the sample (g) taken to prepare the *Sample solution*
    N = exact normality of the sodium hydroxide solution
    B = volume (mL) of 0.5 N sodium hydroxide required for titration of the blank
    S = volume (mL) of 0.5 N sodium hydroxide required for titration of the *Sample solution*

    Acceptance criteria: NLT 90.0% and NMT 110.0% of the labeled value

- **pH**

    Sample: 10 mL

    Analysis: Using a pH meter, neutralize 100 mL of methanol with either 0.1 N hydrochloric acid or 0.1 N sodium hydroxide. Add the *Sample* and dissolve. Record the pH of the resulting solution.

    Acceptance criteria: Between 6.0 and 9.0

- **RESIDUE ON IGNITION (SULFATED ASH),** Appendix IIC

    Sample: 25 g

    Acceptance criteria: NMT 0.01%

- **VISCOSITY DETERMINATION,** *Viscosity of Dimethylpolysiloxane,* Appendix IIB

    Analysis: Determine as directed, maintaining the constant-temperature bath at 37.8° ± 0.2° and using a capillary viscometer having a flow time of at least 200 s for the sample being tested.

    Acceptance criteria:

    Sample with nominal molecular weight of 1000: The viscosity of the sample is between 85 and 97 centistokes.

    Sample with nominal molecular weight of 2000: The viscosity of the sample is between 150 and 175 centistokes.

Polysorbate 20

First Published: Prior to FCC 6

Polyoxyethylene (20) Sorbitan Monolaurate
Sorbitan Monododecanoate
Poly(oxy-1,2-ethanediyl) Derivative

INS: 432
UNII: 7T1F30V5YH [polysorbate 20]
CAS: [9005-64-5]

DESCRIPTION

Polysorbate 20 occurs as a yellow- to amber-colored liquid. It is a mixture of laurate partial esters of sorbitol and sorbitol anhydrides condensed with approximately 20 moles of ethylene oxide (C_2H_4O) for each mole of sorbitol and its mono- and dianhydrides. It is soluble in water, in alcohol, in ethyl acetate, in methanol, and in dioxane, but it is insoluble in mineral oil and in mineral spirits.

Function: Emulsifier; stabilizer

Packaging and Storage: Store in tight containers.

IDENTIFICATION

- **PROCEDURE**
  Sample solution: 1:20
  Analysis: Add 5 mL of 1 N sodium hydroxide to 5 mL of *Sample solution*, boil for a few minutes, cool, and acidify with 2.7 N hydrochloric acid.
  Acceptance criteria: The solution is strongly opalescent.

ASSAY

- **OXYETHYLENE CONTENT,** *Oxyethylene Determination*, Appendix VII
  Sample: 65 mg
  Acceptance criteria: NLT 70.0% and NMT 74.0% of oxyethylene groups (—C_2H_4O—), equivalent to between 97.3% and 103.0% of polysorbate 20, calculated on the anhydrous basis

IMPURITIES

Inorganic Impurities

- **LEAD,** *Lead Limit Test, Flame Atomic Absorption Spectrophotometric Method*, Appendix IIIB
  Sample: 10 g
  Acceptance criteria: NMT 2 mg/kg

Organic Impurities

- **1,4-DIOXANE**
  Stripped polysorbate: Prepare an appropriate quantity of 1,4-dioxane-free sample by stripping a sample of polysorbate at 10 mm Hg, with nitrogen sparge at 130° for 4 h or until, when tested as directed under *Analysis*, no 1,4-dioxane is detected.
  Standard solution: 10 µg/mL 1,4 dioxane, prepared by appropriate quantitative dilutions of HPLC-grade (99.8%) 1,4-dioxane with *Stripped polysorbate* and water
  Sample: 5 g
  Chromatographic system, Appendix IIA
    Mode: Gas chromatography
    [NOTE—Use a system equipped with a headspace sampler, backflush valve, and 1 mL gas sample loop.]
    Detector: Flame ionization detector
    Column: 1-m × 3.2-mm (id) nickel precolumn and a 6-m × 3.2-mm (id) nickel analytical column, or equivalent, containing 60- to 80-mesh TENAX TA support, or equivalent
    Temperature
      Column: 190°
      Detector: 250°
      Injector: 250°
    Flow rate: About 30 mL/min
    Injection volume: 1 mL, using the gas sample loop
    Carrier gas: Helium
    [NOTE—Program the backflush valve to initiate backflushing after 1,4-dioxane elutes into the analytical column.]
  Analysis: Transfer 5.0 g of the *Standard solution* into a 22-mL pressure headspace vial; seal with a silicone septum, star spring, and pressure-relief safety aluminum sealing cap; and crimp the cap closed with a cap sealing tool. Repeat with the *Sample*. Place the vial containing the *Standard solution* in the automated sampler and start the operating sequence so that each vial is heated at 90° for a minimum of 30 min. Using appropriate headspace sampler settings, inject the *Standard solution*, and measure the peak area for 1,4-dioxane. Similarly, place the vial containing the *Sample* in the automatic sampler, obtain the chromatogram, and measure the peak area for 1,4-dioxane.
  Acceptance criteria: The peak area due to the *Sample* is not greater than that of the *Standard solution*. (NMT 10 mg/kg)

SPECIFIC TESTS

- **ACID VALUE (FATS AND RELATED SUBSTANCES),** Method II, Appendix VII
  Acceptance criteria: NMT 2
- **HYDROXYL VALUE,** Method II, Appendix VII
  Acceptance criteria: Between 96 and 108
- **LAURIC ACID**
  Sample: 25 g
  Analysis: Transfer the *Sample* into a 500-mL round-bottom boiling flask, add 250 mL of alcohol and 7.5 g of potassium hydroxide, and mix. Connect a suitable condenser to the flask, reflux the mixture for 1 to 2 h, then transfer to an 800-mL beaker, rinsing the flask with about 100 mL of water and adding it to the beaker. Heat the beaker on a steam bath to evaporate the alcohol, adding water occasionally to replace the alcohol, and evaporate until the odor of alcohol can no longer be detected. Use hot water to adjust the final volume to about 250 mL. Neutralize the soap solution with 1:2 sulfuric acid, add 10% in excess, and heat, while stirring, until the fatty acid layer separates. Transfer the fatty acids into a 500-mL separatory funnel, wash with three or four 20-mL portions of hot water, and combine the washings with the original aqueous layer from the saponification. Extract the combined aqueous layer with three 50-mL portions of petroleum ether, add the extracts to the fatty acid layer, evaporate to dryness in a tared dish, cool, and weigh. Determine the weight of the lauric acid and its acid value as directed in *Acid Value (Fats and Related Substances), Method I*, Appendix VII.
  Acceptance criteria
    Lauric acid recovered: Between 15 and 17 g/100 g of *Sample*
    Acid value: Between 250 and 275
- **RESIDUE ON IGNITION (SULFATED ASH),** Appendix IIC
  Sample: 5 g
  Acceptance criteria: NMT 0.25%
- **SAPONIFICATION VALUE,** Appendix VII
  Sample: 8 g

Acceptance criteria: Between 40 and 50
- **WATER**, *Water Determination*, Appendix IIB
Acceptance criteria: NMT 3.0%

Polysorbate 40

First Published: FCC 7

Polyoxyethylene (20) Sorbitan Monopalmitate
Sorbitan, Monohexadecanoate, Poly(oxy-1,2-ethanediyl) Derivative

INS: 434
UNII: STI11B5A2X [polysorbate 40]
CAS: [9005-66-7]

DESCRIPTION
Polysorbate 40 occurs as a lemon-to-orange colored oily liquid or semi-gel at 25°, with a faint, characteristic odor. It is a mixture of the partial esters of sorbitol and its mono- and dianhydrides (which have an acid value below 7.5 and a water content below 0.2%) with edible commercial palmitic acid condensed with approximately 20 moles of ethylene oxide per mole of sorbitol and its anhydrides. Polysorbate 40 is soluble in water, ethanol, methanol, ethyl acetate, and acetone; and is insoluble in mineral oil.
Function: Emulsifier; stabilizer
Packaging and Storage: Store in tight containers.

IDENTIFICATION
- **A. PROCEDURE**
Sample solution: 1:20
Analysis: Add 5 mL of 1 N sodium hydroxide to 5 mL of *Sample solution*, boil for a few minutes, cool, and acidify with 2.7 N hydrochloric acid.
Acceptance criteria: The solution is strongly opalescent.
- **B. PROCEDURE**
Analysis: Prepare a mixture of sample and water (60:40, v/v) at 25° or cooler.
Acceptance criteria: A gelatinous mass is produced.
- **C. PROCEDURE**
Sample solution: 1:20
Analysis: To 2 mL of *Sample solution*, add 0.5 mL of bromine TS, dropwise.
Acceptance criteria: The bromine is not decolorized.

ASSAY
- **OXYETHYLENE CONTENT**, *Oxyethylene Determination*, Appendix VII
Sample: 65 mg
Acceptance criteria: 66.0%–70.5% of oxyethylene groups (–C$_2$H$_4$O–), equivalent to 97.0%–103.0% of polysorbate 40, calculated on the anhydrous basis

IMPURITIES
Inorganic Impurities
- **LEAD**, *Lead Limit Test, Flame Atomic Absorption Spectrophotometric Method*, Appendix IIIB
Sample: 10 g
Acceptance criteria: NMT 2 mg/kg

SPECIFIC TESTS
- **ACID VALUE (FATS AND RELATED SUBSTANCES)**, *Method II*, Appendix VII
Acceptance criteria: NMT 2
- **HYDROXYL VALUE**, *Method II*, Appendix VII
Acceptance criteria: 90–107
- **RESIDUE ON IGNITION (SULFATED ASH)**, Appendix IIC
Sample: 5 g
Acceptance criteria: NMT 0.25%
- **SAPONIFICATION VALUE**, Appendix VII
Acceptance criteria: 41–52
- **WATER**, *Water Determination*, Appendix IIB
Acceptance criteria: NMT 3.0%

Polysorbate 60

First Published: Prior to FCC 6

Polyoxyethylene (20) Sorbitan Monostearate
Sorbitan Monooctadecanoate
Poly(oxy-1,2-ethanediyl) Derivative

INS: 435
UNII: CAL22UVI4M [polysorbate 60]
CAS: [9005-67-8]

DESCRIPTION
Polysorbate 60 occurs as a yellow to orange colored, oily liquid or semigel. It is a mixture of stearate and palmitate partial esters of sorbitol and sorbitol anhydrides condensed with approximately 20 moles of ethylene oxide (C$_2$H$_4$O) for each mole of sorbitol and its mono- and dianhydrides. It is soluble in water, in aniline, in ethyl acetate, and in toluene; but, it is insoluble in mineral oil and in vegetable oils.
Function: Emulsifier; stabilizer
Packaging and Storage: Store in tight containers.

IDENTIFICATION

- **A. Procedure**
  Sample solution: 1:20
  Analysis: Add 5 mL of 1 N sodium hydroxide to 5 mL of *Sample solution*, boil for a few minutes, cool, and acidify with 2.7 N hydrochloric acid.
  Acceptance criteria: The solution is strongly opalescent.
- **B. Procedure**
  Analysis: Prepare a mixture of sample and water 60:40 (v/v) at 25° or cooler.
  Acceptance criteria: A gelatinous mass is produced.

ASSAY

- **Oxyethylene Content,** *Oxyethylene Determination,* Appendix VII
  Sample: 65 mg
  Acceptance criteria: NLT 65.0% and NMT 69.5% of oxyethylene groups (—C_2H_4O—), equivalent to between 97.0% and 103.0% of polysorbate 60, calculated on the anhydrous basis

IMPURITIES

Inorganic Impurities

- **Lead,** *Lead Limit Test, Flame Atomic Absorption Spectrophotometric Method,* Appendix IIIB
  Sample: 10 g
  Acceptance criteria: NMT 2 mg/kg

Organic Impurities

- **1,4-Dioxane**
  Stripped polysorbate: Prepare an appropriate quantity of 1,4-dioxane-free sample by stripping a sample of polysorbate at 10 mm Hg, with nitrogen sparge at 130° for 4 h or until, when tested as directed under *Analysis*, no 1,4-dioxane is detected.
  Standard solution: 10 µg/mL 1,4 dioxane, prepared by appropriate quantitative dilutions of HPLC-grade (99.8%) 1,4-dioxane with *Stripped polysorbate* and water
  Sample: 5 g
  Chromatographic system, Appendix IIA
    Mode: Gas chromatography
    [Note—Use a system equipped with a headspace sampler, backflush valve, and 1 mL gas sample loop.]
    Detector: Flame ionization detector
    Column: 1-m × 3.2-mm (id) nickel precolumn and a 6-m × 3.2-mm (id) nickel analytical column, or equivalent, containing 60- to 80-mesh TENAX TA support, or equivalent
    Temperature
      Column: 190°
      Detector: 250°
      Injector: 250°
    Flow rate: About 30 mL/min
    Injection volume: 1 mL, using the gas sample loop
    Carrier gas: Helium
    [Note—Program the backflush valve to initiate backflushing after 1,4-dioxane elutes into the analytical column.]
  Analysis: Transfer 5.0 g of the *Standard solution* into a 22-mL pressure headspace vial; seal with a silicone septum, star spring, and pressure-relief safety aluminum sealing cap; and crimp the cap closed with a cap sealing tool. Repeat with the *Sample*. Place the vial containing the *Standard solution* in the automated sampler and start the operating sequence so that each vial is heated at 90° for a minimum of 30 min. Using appropriate headspace sampler settings, inject the *Standard solution*, and measure the peak area for 1,4-dioxane. Similarly, place the vial containing the *Sample* in the automatic sampler, obtain the chromatogram, and measure the peak area for 1,4-dioxane.
  Acceptance criteria: The peak area due to the *Sample* is not greater than that of the *Standard solution*. (NMT 10 mg/kg)

SPECIFIC TESTS

- **Acid Value (Fats and Related Substances),** *Method II,* Appendix VII
  Acceptance criteria: NMT 2
- **Hydroxyl Value,** *Method II,* Appendix VII
  Acceptance criteria: Between 81 and 96
- **Residue on Ignition (Sulfated Ash),** Appendix IIC
  Sample: 5 g
  Acceptance criteria: NMT 0.25%
- **Saponification Value,** Appendix VII
  Sample: 8 g
  Acceptance criteria: Between 45 and 55
- **Stearic and Palmitic Acids**
  Sample: 25 g
  Analysis: Transfer the *Sample* into a 500-mL round-bottom boiling flask, add 250 mL of alcohol and 7.5 g of potassium hydroxide, and mix. Connect a suitable condenser to the flask, reflux the mixture for 1 to 2 h, then transfer to an 800-mL beaker, rinsing the flask with about 100 mL of water and adding it to the beaker. Heat the beaker on a steam bath to evaporate the alcohol, adding water occasionally to replace the alcohol; continue the evaporation until the odor of alcohol can no longer be detected. Use hot water to adjust the final volume to about 250 mL. Neutralize the soap solution with 1:2 sulfuric acid, add 10% in excess, and heat, while stirring, until the fatty acid layer separates. Transfer the fatty acids into a 500-mL separatory funnel, wash with three or four 20-mL portions of hot water, and combine the washings with the original aqueous layer from the saponification. Extract the combined aqueous layer with three 50-mL portions of petroleum ether, add the extracts to the fatty acid layer, evaporate to dryness in a tared dish, cool, and weigh. Determine the weight of the acids; the acid value of the product as directed in *Acid Value (Fats and Related Substances), Method I,* Appendix VII; and the solidification point as directed in *Solidification Point,* Appendix IIB.
  Acceptance criteria
    Product recovered: Between 21.5 and 26.0 g/100 g of *Sample*
    Acid value: Between 200 and 212
    Solidification point: NLT 52°
- **Water,** *Water Determination,* Appendix IIB
  Acceptance criteria: NMT 3.0%

Polysorbate 65

First Published: Prior to FCC 6

Polyoxyethylene (20) Sorbitan Tristearate
CAS: [9005-71-4]
UNII: 14BGY2Y3MJ [polysorbate 65]

DESCRIPTION
Polysorbate 65 occurs as a tan, waxy solid. It is a mixture of stearate and palmitate partial esters of sorbitol and its anhydrides condensed with approximately 20 moles of ethylene oxide (C_2H_4O) for each mole of sorbitol and its mono- and dianhydrides. It is soluble in mineral oil and in vegetable oils, in mineral spirits, in acetone, in ether, in dioxane, in alcohol, and in methanol, and it is dispersible in water.
Function: Emulsifier; stabilizer
Packaging and Storage: Store in tight containers.

IDENTIFICATION
- **PROCEDURE**
  Sample solution: 1:20
  Analysis: Add 5 mL of 1 N sodium hydroxide to 5 mL of the *Sample solution*, boil for a few minutes, cool, and acidify with 2.7 N hydrochloric acid.
  Acceptance criteria: The solution is strongly opalescent.

ASSAY
- **OXYETHYLENE CONTENT,** *Oxyethylene Determination,* Appendix VII
  Sample: 90 mg
  Acceptance criteria: NLT 46.0% and NMT 50.0% of oxyethylene groups (—C_2H_4O—), equivalent to between 96.0% and 104.0% of polysorbate 65, calculated on the anhydrous basis

IMPURITIES
Inorganic Impurities
- **LEAD,** *Lead Limit Test, Flame Atomic Absorption Spectrophotometric Method,* Appendix IIIB
  Sample: 10 g
  Acceptance criteria: NMT 2 mg/kg

Organic Impurities
- **1,4-DIOXANE**
  Stripped polysorbate: Prepare an appropriate quantity of 1,4-dioxane free sample by stripping a sample of polysorbate at 10 mm Hg, with nitrogen sparge at 130° for 4 h or until, when tested as directed under *Analysis*, no 1,4-dioxane is detected.
  Standard solution: 10 µg/mL 1,4-dioxane, prepared by appropriate quantitative dilutions of HPLC-grade (99.8%) 1,4-dioxane with *Stripped polysorbate* and water
  Sample: 5 g
  Chromatographic system, Appendix IIA
    Mode: Gas chromatography
    [NOTE—Use a system equipped with a headspace sampler, backflush valve, and 1 mL gas sample loop.]
    Detector: Flame ionization detector
    Column: 1-m × 3.2-mm (id) nickel precolumn and a 6-m × 3.2-mm (id) nickel analytical column, or equivalent, containing 60- to 80-mesh TENAX TA support, or equivalent
    Column temperature: 190°
    Detector temperature: 250°
    Injector temperature: 250°
    Flow rate: About 30 mL/min
    Injection volume: 1 mL, using the gas sample loop
    Carrier gas: Helium
    [NOTE—Program the backflush valve to initiate backflushing after 1,4-dioxane elutes into the analytical column.]
  Analysis: Transfer 5.0 g of the *Standard solution* into a 22-mL pressure headspace vial; seal with a silicone septum, star spring, and pressure-relief safety aluminum sealing cap; and crimp the cap closed with a cap sealing tool. Repeat with the *Sample*. Place the vial containing the *Standard solution* in the automated sampler and start the operating sequence so that each vial is heated at 90° for a minimum of 30 min. Using appropriate headspace sampler settings, inject the *Standard solution*, and measure the peak area for 1,4-dioxane. Similarly, place the vial containing the *Sample* in the automatic sampler, obtain the chromatogram, and measure the peak area for 1,4-dioxane.
  Acceptance criteria: The peak area due to the *Sample* is not greater than that of the *Standard solution* (NMT 10 mg/kg).

SPECIFIC TESTS
- **ACID VALUE (FATS AND RELATED SUBSTANCES),** Method II, Appendix VII
  Acceptance criteria: NMT 2
- **HYDROXYL VALUE,** Method II, Appendix VII
  Acceptance criteria: Between 44 and 60
- **RESIDUE ON IGNITION (SULFATED ASH),** Appendix IIC
  Sample: 5 g
  Acceptance criteria: NMT 0.25%
- **SAPONIFICATION VALUE,** Appendix VII
  Sample: 6 g
  Acceptance criteria: Between 88 and 98
- **STEARIC AND PALMITIC ACIDS**
  Sample: 25 g
  Analysis: Transfer the *Sample* into a 500-mL round-bottom boiling flask, add 250 mL of alcohol and 7.5 g of potassium hydroxide, and mix. Connect a suitable condenser to the flask, reflux the mixture for 1 to 2 h, then transfer to an 800-mL beaker, rinsing the flask with about 100 mL of water and adding it to the beaker. Heat the beaker on a steam bath to evaporate the alcohol, adding water occasionally to replace the alcohol; continue the evaporation until the odor of alcohol can no longer be detected. Use hot water to adjust the final volume to about 250 mL. Neutralize the soap solution with 1:2 sulfuric acid, add 10% in excess, and heat, while stirring, until the fatty acid layer separates. Transfer the fatty acids into a 500-mL separatory funnel, wash with three or four 20-mL portions of hot water, and combine the washings with the original aqueous layer from the saponification.

Extract the combined aqueous layer with three 50-mL portions of petroleum ether, add the extracts to the fatty acid layer, evaporate to dryness in a tared dish, cool, and weigh. Determine the weight of the acids; the acid value of the product as directed in *Acid Value (Fats and Related Substances), Method I,* Appendix VII; and the solidification point as directed in *Solidification Point,* Appendix IIB.
Acceptance criteria
Product recovered: Between 42 and 44 g/100 g of *Sample*
Acid value: Between 200 and 212
Solidification point: NLT 52°
- **WATER,** *Water Determination,* Appendix IIB
Acceptance criteria: NMT 3.0%

Polysorbate 80
First Published: Prior to FCC 6

Polyoxyethylene (20) Sorbitan Monooleate
Sorbitan Mono-9-octadecenoate
Poly(oxy-1,2-ethanediyl) Derivative

INS: 433 CAS: [9005-65-6]
UNII: 6OZP39ZG8H [polysorbate 80]

DESCRIPTION
Polysorbate 80 occurs as a yellow to orange colored, oily liquid. It is a mixture of oleate partial esters of sorbitol and sorbitol anhydrides condensed with approximately 20 moles of ethylene oxide (C_2H_4O) for each mole of sorbitol and its mono- and dianhydrides. It is very soluble in water, producing a nearly colorless solution, and it is soluble in alcohol, in fixed oils, in ethyl acetate, and in toluene. It is insoluble in mineral oil.
Function: Emulsifier; stabilizer
Packaging and Storage: Store in tight containers.

IDENTIFICATION
- **A. PROCEDURE**
Sample solution: 1:20
Analysis: Add 5 mL of 1 N sodium hydroxide to 5 mL of *Sample solution*, boil for a few minutes, cool, and acidify with 2.7 N hydrochloric acid.
Acceptance criteria: The solution is strongly opalescent.

- **B. PROCEDURE**
Sample solution: 1:20
Analysis: Add bromine TS, dropwise, to the *Sample solution*.
Acceptance criteria: The bromine is decolorized.
- **C. PROCEDURE**
Analysis: Prepare a mixture of sample and water 60:40 (v/v) at 25° or cooler.
Acceptance criteria: A gelatinous mass is produced.

ASSAY
- **OXYETHYLENE CONTENT,** *Oxyethylene Determination,* Appendix VII
Sample: 65 mg
Acceptance criteria: NLT 65.0% and NMT 69.5% of oxyethylene groups ($—C_2H_4O—$), equivalent to between 96.5% and 103.5% of polysorbate 80, calculated on the anhydrous basis

IMPURITIES
Inorganic Impurities
- **LEAD,** *Lead Limit Test, Flame Atomic Absorption Spectrophotometric Method,* Appendix IIIB
Sample: 10 g
Acceptance criteria: NMT 2 mg/kg

Organic Impurities
- **1,4-DIOXANE**
Stripped polysorbate: Prepare an appropriate quantity of 1,4-dioxane-free sample by stripping a sample of polysorbate at 10 mm Hg, with nitrogen sparge at 130° for 4 h or until, when tested as directed under *Analysis*, no 1,4-dioxane is detected.
Standard solution: 10 µg/mL 1,4 dioxane, prepared by appropriate quantitative dilutions of HPLC-grade (99.8%) 1,4-dioxane with *Stripped polysorbate* and water
Sample: 5 g
Chromatographic system, Appendix IIA
Mode: Gas chromatography
[NOTE—Use a system equipped with a headspace sampler, backflush valve, and 1 mL gas sample loop.]
Detector: Flame ionization detector
Column: 1-m × 3.2-mm (id) nickel precolumn and a 6-m × 3.2-mm (id) nickel analytical column, or equivalent, containing 60- to 80-mesh TENAX TA support, or equivalent
Column temperature: 190°
Detector temperature: 250°
Injector temperature: 250°
Flow rate: About 30 mL/min
Injection volume: 1 mL using the gas sample loop
Carrier gas: Helium
[NOTE—Program the backflush valve to initiate backflushing after 1,4-dioxane elutes into the analytical column.]
Analysis: Transfer 5.0 g of the *Standard solution* into a 22-mL pressure headspace vial; seal with a silicone septum, star spring, and pressure-relief safety aluminum sealing cap; and crimp the cap closed with a cap sealing tool. Repeat with the *Sample*. Place the vial containing the *Standard solution* in the automated

sampler and start the operating sequence so that each vial is heated at 90° for a minimum of 30 min. Using appropriate headspace sampler settings, inject the *Standard solution*, and measure the peak area for 1,4-dioxane. Similarly, place the vial containing the *Sample* in the automatic sampler, obtain the chromatogram, and measure the peak area for 1,4-dioxane.

Acceptance criteria: The peak area due to the *Sample* is not greater than that of the *Standard solution* (NMT 10 mg/kg).

SPECIFIC TESTS

- **ACID VALUE (FATS AND RELATED SUBSTANCES)**, *Method II*, Appendix VII
  Acceptance criteria: NMT 2
- **HYDROXYL VALUE**, *Method II*, Appendix VII
  Acceptance criteria: Between 65 and 80
- **OLEIC ACID**
  Sample: 25 g
  Analysis: Transfer the *Sample* into a 500-mL round-bottom boiling flask, add 250 mL of alcohol and 7.5 g of potassium hydroxide, and mix. Connect a suitable condenser to the flask, reflux the mixture for 1 to 2 h, then transfer to an 800-mL beaker, rinsing the flask with about 100 mL of water and adding it to the beaker. Heat the beaker on a steam bath to evaporate the alcohol, adding water occasionally to replace the alcohol; Continue the evaporation until the odor of alcohol can no longer be detected. Use hot water to adjust the final volume to about 250 mL. Neutralize the soap solution with 1:2 sulfuric acid, add 10% in excess, and heat, while stirring, until the fatty acid layer separates. Transfer the fatty acids into a 500-mL separatory funnel, wash with three or four 20-mL portions of hot water, and combine the washings with the original aqueous layer from the saponification. Extract the combined aqueous layer with three 50-mL portions of petroleum ether, add the extracts to the fatty acid layer, evaporate to dryness in a tared dish, cool, and weigh. Determine the weight of the oleic acid, its acid value as directed in *Acid Value (Fats and Related Substances), Method I*, Appendix VII, and its iodine value as directed in *Iodine Value*, Appendix VII.
  Acceptance criteria
    Oleic acid recovered: Between 22 and 24 g/100 g of *Sample*
    Acid value: Between 193 and 206
    Iodine value: Between 80 and 92
- **RESIDUE ON IGNITION (SULFATED ASH)**, Appendix IIC
  Sample: 5 g
  Acceptance criteria: NMT 0.25%
- **SAPONIFICATION VALUE**, Appendix VII
  Sample: 8 g
  Acceptance criteria: Between 45 and 55
- **WATER**, *Water Determination*, Appendix IIB
  Acceptance criteria: NMT 3.0%

Polyvinyl Acetate

First Published: Prior to FCC 6
Last Revision: Second Supplement, FCC 6

Poly(vinyl acetate)

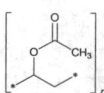

(C$_4$H$_6$O$_2$)$_n$ CAS: 9003-20-7

DESCRIPTION
Polyvinyl Acetate occurs as a clear, water white to pale yellow, solid resin. It is prepared by the polymerization of vinyl acetate. After completion of polymerization, the resin is freed of traces of residual catalyst (usually a peroxide), monomer, and/or solvent by vacuum drying, steam sparging, washing, or any combination of these treatments. The resin is soluble in acetone, but it is insoluble in water.

Function: Masticatory substance in chewing gum base
Packaging and Storage: Store in well-closed containers.

IDENTIFICATION
- **INFRARED ABSORPTION**, *Spectrophotometric Identification Tests*, Appendix IIIC
  Reference standard: USP Polyvinyl Acetate RS
  Sample and standard preparation: F (Melt the sample onto a potassium bromide plate.)
  Acceptance criteria: The spectrum of the sample exhibits maxima at the same wavelengths as those in the spectrum of the *Reference standard*.

IMPURITIES
Inorganic Impurities
- **LEAD**, *Sample Solution for Lead Limit Test*, Appendix IV
  Control: 10 µg Pb (10 mL of *Diluted Standard Lead Solution*)
  Acceptance criteria: NMT 3 mg/kg

Organic Impurities
- **FREE ACETIC ACID**
  Sample: 10 g
  Analysis: Transfer the *Sample* into a 250-mL glass-stoppered Erlenmeyer flask, dissolve it in 75 mL of ethylene dichloride, add 60 mL of specially denatured ethanol formula 2B, and mix. Add phenolphthalein TS and titrate with 0.02 N of methanolic potassium hydroxide to a faint pink endpoint. Perform a blank determination (see *General Provisions*), and make any necessary correction. Each mL of 0.02 N methanolic potassium hydroxide is equivalent to 1.201 mg of C$_2$H$_4$O$_2$.
  Acceptance criteria: NMT 0.05%
- **FREE VINYL ACETATE**
  Sample solution: 333.3 mg/g sample in *N,N*-dimethylacetamide
  Standard solutions: Prepare at least four standard solutions of vinyl acetate in *N,N*-dimethylacetamide with concentrations between 0.25 and 5.0 mg/kg,

each with diethylether as an internal standard at 5.0 mg/kg.

Chromatographic system, Appendix IIA
 Mode: Gas chromatography equipped with a balanced-pressure headspace autosampler
 Detector: Flame ionization
 Column: 30-m × 0.54-mm (id) porous layer open tubular capillary column with divinylbenzene polymer stationary phase[1]
 Column temperature: 6 min at 50°; increase to 110° at 12°/min; maintain at 110° for 9 min
 Injection port temperature: 200°
 Detector temperature: 200°
 Sampler parameters
  Transferline temperature: 110°
  Needle temperature: 110°
  Thermostating temperature: 70°
  Thermostating time: 50 min
  Pressure rising time: 1 min
  Injection time: 0.2 min
  Remaining time: 0.2 min
  Cycle time: 29 min
 Carrier gas: Helium
 Flow rate: 10 mL/min
 System suitability
  Sample: 5.0 mg/kg Standard solution
  Suitability requirement 1: The relative standard deviation of the vinyl acetate peak area responses from replicate injections is NMT 5%.
  Suitability requirement 2: The resolution, R, between the vinyl acetate peak and all other peaks is NLT 1.0. [NOTE—N,N-dimethylacetamide may contain impurities whose peaks may interfere in the vinyl acetate range.]
Analysis: Separately inject equal volumes of the Standard solutions and Sample solution into the chromatograph, record the chromatograms, and measure the peak responses. [NOTE—The approximate retention time for vinylacetate is 14.6 min.]
Prepare a standard curve for vinyl acetate by plotting on the y-axis the ratios of vinyl acetate peak area to internal standard peak area and on the x-axis the concentration of vinyl acetate (mg/kg). [NOTE—The coefficient of determination for the standard curve should be NLT 0.99.]
Using the standard curve, determine the concentration (C_U), in mg/kg, of vinyl acetate in the Sample solution using the ratio of vinyl acetate peak area to internal standard peak area from the Sample solution chromatogram. Determine the concentration (mg/kg) of vinyl acetate in the portion of the sample taken by the following formula:

$$\text{Result} = C_U/C_{SMP} \times F$$

C_U = concentration of vinyl acetate in the Sample solution determined from the standard curve (mg/kg)
C_{SMP} = concentration of sample in the Sample solution (mg/g)

F = correction factor taking into account units conversion from g/kg to mg/kg, 1000
Acceptance criteria: NMT 5 mg/kg

SPECIFIC TESTS
- **LOSS ON DRYING,** Appendix IIC: 100° for 2 h in vacuum
 Sample: 1.5 g
 Acceptance criteria: NMT 1.0%
- **MOLECULAR WEIGHT,** Appendix IV
 Acceptance criteria: NLT 2000

Polyvinyl Alcohol
First Published: FCC 6

Poly(vinyl alcohol)
Vinyl alcohol polymer
PVOH

INS: 1203   CAS: [9002-89-5]
UNII: 532B59J990 [polyvinyl alcohol]

DESCRIPTION
Polyvinyl Alcohol occurs as an odorless translucent, white or cream-colored granular powder. It is soluble in water and sparingly soluble in ethanol.
Function: Coating; binder; sealing agent; and surface-finishing agent

IDENTIFICATION
- **COLOR REACTION A**
 Sample solution: Dissolve 0.01 g of sample in 100 mL of water with warming and let the solution cool to room temperature.
 Analysis: To 5 mL of the Sample solution, add one drop of iodine TS and a few drops of boric acid solution (1 in 25).
 Acceptance criteria: A blue color is produced.
- **COLOR REACTION B**
 Sample solution: Dissolve 0.5 g of sample in 10 mL of water with warming and let the solution cool to room temperature.
 Analysis: Add 1 drop of iodine TS to 5 mL of the Sample solution and allow to stand. [NOTE—Save the remaining Sample solution for Precipitation Reaction below.]
 Acceptance criteria: A dark red to blue color is produced.
- **PRECIPITATION REACTION**
 Analysis: Add 10 mL of ethanol to the remaining 5 mL of solution prepared for Color Reaction B.
 Acceptance criteria: A white, turbid, or flocculent precipitate is formed.
- **INFRARED ABSORPTION,** Spectrophotometric Identification Tests, Appendix IIIC.
 Reference standard: USP Polyvinyl Alcohol RS
 Sample and **standard preparation:** K

---
[1] Supel-Q PLOT (Sigma-Aldrich Co., St. Louis, MO), or equivalent.

Acceptance criteria: The spectrum of the sample exhibits maxima at the same wavelengths as those in the spectrum of the *Reference standard*.

IMPURITIES
Inorganic Impurities
- **LEAD,** *Lead Limit Test, Atomic Absorption Spectrophotometric Graphite Furnace Method, Method I,* Appendix IIIB
  Acceptance criteria: NMT 2.0 mg/kg

Organic Impurities
- **LIMIT OF METHANOL (METHYL ALCOHOL) AND METHYL ACETATE**
  Standard solution: Prepare an aqueous solution having known concentrations of 1.2% (v/v) each for USP Methyl Alcohol RS and USP Methyl Acetate RS and transfer 2 mL of the solution into a 100-mL screw-cap bottle. Add 30 µL of USP Acetone RS and 98 mL of water (this solution contains 0.24 µL/mL each of USP Methyl Alcohol RS and USP Methyl Acetate RS). Close the bottle tightly with the screw cap and heat in a boiling water-bath, stirring continuously. Once the solution becomes clear, remove the bottle from the water bath and allow it to cool to room temperature.
  Sample solution: Transfer a quantity of sample, equivalent to 2.0 g on the dried basis into a 100-mL screw-cap bottle and add a magnetic stirring bar. Add 98 mL of water and 30 µL of USP Acetone RS. Close the bottle tightly with the screw cap and heat in a boiling water-bath, stirring continuously. Once the solution becomes clear, remove the bottle from the water bath and allow it to cool to room temperature.
  Chromatographic system, Appendix IIA
  Mode: Gas chromatography
  Detector: Flame ionization
  Column: 3.2 mm i.d. × 3 m glass, packed with a highly cross-linked copolymer of ethylvinylbenzene and divinylbenzene, such as Sunpak A (Shinawa Chemical Industries, LTD), or equivalent
  Column temperature: 160°
  Injection port temperature: 160°
  Detector temperature: 160°
  Carrier gas: Nitrogen
  Flow rate: About 30 mL/min
  Injection volume: About 0.4 µL
  System suitability
    Sample: *Standard solution*
    Suitability requirement: The relative standard deviation for replicate injections is NMT 2.0%.
  Analysis: Separately inject equal volumes of the *Standard solution* and the *Sample solution* into the chromatograph, record the chromatograms, and measure the areas for the major peaks. Calculate the percentages of methanol (methyl alcohol) or methyl acetate in the sample taken by the formula:

  $$\text{Result} = 10G(C/W)(R_U/R_S)$$

  G = specific gravity of methanol (methyl alcohol) (0.79) or methyl acetate (0.93)
  C = concentration (µL/mL) of methanol (methyl alcohol) or methyl acetate in the *Standard solution*
  W = weight (g) of the sample taken to prepare the *Sample solution*
  R_U = peak response ratios of the methanol (methyl alcohol) peak relative to the acetone peak obtained from the *Sample solution*
  R_S = peak response ratios of the methyl acetate peak relative to the acetone peak obtained from the *Standard solution*
  Acceptance criteria
    Methanol (methyl alcohol): NMT 1.0%
    Methyl acetate: NMT 1.0%

SPECIFIC TESTS
- **ACID VALUE**
  Sample solution: Add 200 mL of water and a stir bar into a 500-mL round-bottom flask, attach a reflux condenser, and begin heating in a boiling water bath. Add 10.0 g of the sample and continue heating for 30 minutes while stirring continuously. Remove the flask from the water-bath and continue stirring until the solution reaches room temperature. Quantitatively transfer this solution to a 250-mL volumetric flask and dilute with water to volume.
  Analysis: Take 50 mL of the *Sample solution*, add 1 mL of phenolphthalein TS, and titrate with 0.05 M potassium hydroxide until the pink color persists for 15 s; record the titre in mL (V). Calculate the *Acid Value*, A, according to the formula:

  $$A = 5.0 (56.1 \times V \times M)/W$$

  5.0 = dilution factor
  56.1 = the formula weight of KOH
  M = molarity of the KOH solution
  W = weight (g) of sample taken
  Acceptance criteria: NMT 3.0

- **ESTER VALUE**
  Sample solution: Weigh 1.0 g of sample into a 250-mL round-bottom flask, add 25.0 mL 0.5 M alcoholic potassium hydroxide, 25.0 mL of water and a few glass beads. Attach a condenser and allow the contents to reflux for 30 min in a boiling water-bath.
  Analysis: Let flask cool to room temperature, remove the condenser, add 1 mL of phenolphthalein TS, and titrate immediately with 0.5 M hydrochloric acid; record the titre in mL (V_1). Carry out a blank test under the same conditions. Titrate with 0.5 M hydrochloric acid and record the titre in mL (V_2). Calculate the saponification value, S, according to the formula:

  $$S = 56.1 (V_2 - V_1) \times M/W$$

  56.1 = formula weight of KOH
  M = molarity of the hydrochloric acid solution
  W = weight (g) of sample taken

Calculate the *Ester Value*, E, according to the formula:

$$E = S - A$$

S = saponification value (calculated above)
A = acid value
Acceptance criteria: Between 125 and 153 mg KOH/g

- **DEGREE OF HYDROLYSIS**
  Analysis: Convert the saponification value obtained during the determination of the *Ester Value* to the "dried basis" (S_{db}):

  $$S_{db} = (S \times 100)/(100 - LOD)$$

  LOD = *Loss on Drying* (determined below)
  The degree of hydrolysis is:

  $$\text{Result} = 100 - [7.84\, S_{db}/(100 - 0.075\, S_{db})]$$

  Acceptance criteria: Between 86.5 and 89.0%

- **LOSS ON DRYING**, Appendix IIC: 105° for 3 h
  Acceptance criteria: NMT 5.0%

- **pH**, *pH Determination*, Appendix IIB
  Sample solution: 1:25
  Acceptance criteria: 5.0–6.5

- **PARTICLE SIZE**
  Sample: 100 g
  Analysis: Sieve the sample for 30 min through a 100-mesh sieve and weigh the material passing through.
  Acceptance criteria: NLT 99.0% material passes through

- **RESIDUE ON IGNITION (SULFATED ASH)**, Appendix IIC
  Sample: 1 g
  Acceptance criteria: NMT 1.0%

- **VISCOSITY**
  Calibration of capillary-type viscometers: An oil of known viscosity is used to determine the viscometer constant (k).
  Ostwald-type viscometer: Fill the tube with the exact amount of oil (adjusted to 20.0 ± 0.1°) as specified by the manufacturer. Use either pressure or suction to adjust the meniscus of the column of liquid in the capillary tube to the level of the top graduation line. Allow the liquid to flow into the reservoir against atmospheric pressure by opening both the filling and capillary tubes. If either of the tubes is not opened, false values may be obtained. Record the time (s), for the liquid to flow from the upper mark to the lower mark in the capillary tube (efflux time).
  Ubbelohde-type viscometer: Place a quantity of the oil (adjusted to 20.0 ± 0.1°) in the filling tube, and transfer to the capillary tube by gentle suction. Keep the air vent tube closed in order to prevent bubble formation in the liquid. Adjust the meniscus of the column of liquid in the capillary tube to the level of the top graduation line. Allow the liquid to flow into the reservoir against atmospheric pressure by opening both the filling and capillary tubes. If either of the tubes is not opened, false values may be obtained. Record the efflux time(s).

Calculation of viscosity constant: For capillary-type viscometers the constant is given by:

$$k = v/dt$$

v = known viscosity (mPa·s) of the oil used for viscometer calibration
d = density (g/mL) of the liquid tested at 20°/20°
t = efflux time (s)

Sample solution: Weigh a quantity of undried sample equivalent to 6.00 g on the dried basis. Into a tared 250-mL flask containing a magnetic stir bar and approximately 140 mL of water, quickly (seconds) transfer the sample, while simultaneously stirring slowly and continuously. Once the sample appears thoroughly saturated, slowly increase the stirring rate to minimize the entrainment of air in the mixture. Heat the mixture to 90°, and maintain it at this temperature for approximately 5 min; discontinue heating and continue stirring for 1 h. Add water in small amounts to attain a total mixture weight of 150 g, and resume stirring until the mixture appears homogenous and cool to about 15° by mixing.

Analysis: Determine viscosity of the *Sample solution* at 20° using an appropriate viscometer (follow the manufacturer's instructions). [NOTE—The temperature at which the viscosity measurement is made must be strictly controlled.] For measurements using *capillary-type viscometers*, the viscosity is given by the formula:

$$v = kdt$$

t = the efflux time for the *Sample solution*
d = the *Sample solution* density at 20°
Acceptance criteria: 4.8–5.8 mPa·s (4% solution at 20°)

- **WATER-INSOLUBLE SUBSTANCES**
  Sample: 10 g
  Analysis: Add 100 mL of hot water to the *Sample* and stir for one hour as sample temperature decreases. Then filter through a tared 100-mesh screen. Wash the insoluble residue with hot water, dry at 105° for 2 h, cool and weigh.
  Acceptance criteria: NMT 0.1%

Add the following:

▲Ponceau 4R[1]

First Published: FCC 8

CI Food Red 7
Cochineal Red A
New Coccine
CI No. 16255
Class: Mono-Azo

---

[1] Ponceau 4R is approved for use in some countries but banned in others, such as the United States.

Trisodium-2-hydroxy-1-(4-sulfonato-1-naphthylazo)-6,8-naphthalenedisulfonate

$C_{20}H_{11}N_2Na_3O_{10}S_3 \cdot 1.5H_2O$ Formula wt 631.51
INS: 124 CAS: [2611-82-7]
UNII: Z525CBK9PG [ponceau 4r]

DESCRIPTION
Ponceau 4R occurs as reddish powder or granules. It is principally the trisodium salt of 2-hydroxy-1-(4-sulfonato-1-naphthylazo)-6,8-naphthalenedisulfonate and subsidiary coloring matters, with sodium chloride and/or sodium sulfate as the principal uncolored components. It is soluble in water and sparingly soluble in ethanol.
Function: Color
Packaging and Storage: Store in well-closed containers.

IDENTIFICATION
- **VISIBLE ABSORPTION SPECTRUM**
  Sample solution: Dissolve a sample in water and dilute appropriately.
  Analysis: Measure the absorption spectrum of the *Sample solution* using a suitable UV-visible spectrophotometer.
  Acceptance criteria: The *Sample solution* exhibits a wavelength maximum at 505 nm.

ASSAY
- **TOTAL COLOR**, *Colors, Methods I and II*, Appendix IIIC: Both methods must be used.
  Method I: (Spectrophotometric)
  Sample solution: 10 mg/mL
  Analysis: Determine as directed at 505 nm, using 0.043 L/(mg · cm) for the absorptivity (*a*) for Ponceau 4R.
  Method II: (TiCl$_3$ Titration)
  Sample: 0.7–0.8 g
  Analysis: Determine as directed, except under *Procedure*, use 15 g of *Sodium Bitartrate* instead of 21–22 g, and use 150 mL of water instead of 275 mL. For the calculation, use 6.337 as the stoichiometric factor (F_S) for the disodium salt of Ponceau 4R.
  Acceptance criteria: The average of results obtained from *Method I* and *Method II* is NLT 85% total coloring matters.

IMPURITIES
Inorganic Impurities
- **LEAD**, *Lead Limit Test,* Appendix IIIB
  Sample solution: Prepare as directed for organic compounds.
  Control: 2 µg of Pb (2 mL of the *Diluted Standard Lead Solution*)
  Acceptance criteria: NMT 2 mg/kg

Organic Impurities
- **UNCOMBINED INTERMEDIATES AND PRODUCTS OF SIDE REACTIONS**
  Solution A: 0.2 N ammonium acetate
  Solution B: Methanol
  Mobile phase: See *Table 1*.

Table 1

Time (min)	Solution A (%)	Solution B (%)	Comments
0	98	2	Analysis
49	0	100	Wash
55	0	100	Return to initial gradient and column equilibration
60	100	0	

  Standard solution: 25 µg/mL of 4-amino-1-naphthalenesulfonic acid, 25 µg/mL of 7-hydroxy-1,3-naphthalenedisulfonic acid, 25 µg/mL of 3-hydroxy-2,7-naphthalenesulfonic acid, 25 µg/mL of 6-hydroxy-2-naphthalenesulfonic acid, and 25 µg/mL of 7-hydroxy-1,3,6-naphthalenetrisulfonic acid in 0.02 M ammonium acetate
  Sample solution: 5 mg/mL in 0.02 M ammonium acetate
  Chromatographic system, Appendix IIA
    Mode: High-performance liquid chromatography
    Detector: UV-Vis
    Column
      Guard column: 4.6-mm × 15-mm; 5-µm C18 column
      Analytical column: 4.6-mm × 25-cm; 5-µm C18 column
    Column temperature: Ambient
    Flow rate: 1.0 mL/min
    Injection volume: 20 µL
  Analysis: Separately inject equal volumes of the *Standard solution* and *Sample solution* into the chromatograph, and measure the responses for the major peaks on the resulting chromatograms. Calculate the percentage of all impurities (4-amino-1-naphthalenesulfonic acid, 7-hydroxy-1,3-naphthalenedisulfonic acid, 3-hydroxy-2,7-naphthalenesulfonic acid, 6-hydroxy-2-naphthalenesulfonic acid, and 7-hydroxy-1,3,6-naphthalenetrisulfonic acid) in the portion of the sample taken:

$$\text{Result} = (r_U/r_S) \times (C_S/C_U) \times F \times 100$$

  r_U = peak area for analyte in the *Sample solution*
  r_S = peak area for analyte in the *Standard solution*
  C_S = concentration of analyte in the *Standard solution* (µg/mL)
  C_U = concentration of sample in the *Sample solution* (mg/mL)
  F = mg-to-µg conversion factor, 1000
  Acceptance criteria: NMT 0.5% for all five impurities combined

SPECIFIC TESTS
- **COMBINED TESTS**
  Tests
    - LOSS ON DRYING (VOLATILE MATTER), *Colors,* Appendix IIIC
    - CHLORIDE, *Sodium Chloride, Colors,* Appendix IIIC
    - SULFATES (AS SODIUM SALTS), *Sodium Sulfate, Colors,* Appendix IIIC

  Acceptance criteria: NMT 20%, combined as the sum of all three tests

- **ETHER EXTRACTS**, *Colors,* Appendix IIIC
  Acceptance criteria: NMT 0.2%

- **SUBSIDIARY COLORING MATTERS**
  [NOTE—In this method, subsidiary coloring matters are separated from the main coloring matter of Ponceau 4R by ascending paper chromatography (see *Paper Chromatography,* Appendix IIA) and extracted separately from the chromatographic paper. The absorbance of each extract is measured at the wavelength of maximum absorption for Ponceau 4R (505 nm) by visible spectrophotometry. Because it is impractical to identify each subsidiary coloring matter using this procedure, and because the subsidiary coloring matters are usually minor components of food colors, the method assumes that the maximum absorbance of each subsidiary coloring matter is the same as that of the total coloring matters. The subsidiary coloring matters content is calculated by adding together the absorbances of the extracts in conjunction with the total coloring matters content of the sample.]

  Chromatographic apparatus: The chromatography tank (*Figures 1* and *2*) is composed of a glass tank (A) and cover (B); frame to support chromatography paper (C); solvent tray (D); wire secondary frame (E) for supporting "drapes" of the filter paper; and 20-cm × 20-cm chromatography grade paper.[2] Mark out the chromatography paper as shown in *Figure 3*.

  Chromatographic solvent: Prepare a mixture of 2-butanone, acetone, and water (7:3:3). Shake for 2 min, allow the layers to separate, and use the upper layer.

  Sample solution: 10 mg/mL sample

  Standard solution: 0.1 mg/mL sample prepared by diluting the *Sample solution*

  Application volume: 0.10 mL

  Analysis: No less than 2 h before analysis, arrange the filter-paper drapes in the glass tank, and pour sufficient *Chromatographic solvent* over the drapes and into the bottom of the tank to cover the bottom of the tank to a depth of 1 cm. Place the solvent tray in position, and fit the cover to the tank. Using a microsyringe capable of delivering 0.1 mL with a tolerance of ±0.002 mL, apply to separate chromatography sheets 0.1 mL aliquots of *Sample solution* and *Standard solution,* as uniformly as possible within the confines of the 7-mm × 18-cm rectangle, holding the nozzle of the microsyringe steadily in contact with the paper. Allow the papers to dry at room temperature for 1–2 h or at 50° in a drying cabinet for 5 min followed by 15 min at room temperature. Mount the dried sheets, together with two plain sheets to act as a blank on the supporting frame. [NOTE—If required, several dried sheets may be developed simultaneously.]

  Pour sufficient *Chromatographic solvent* into the solvent tray to bring the surface of the solvent about 1 cm below the base line of the chromatography sheets. The volume necessary will depend on the dimensions of the apparatus and should be predetermined. Put the supporting frame into position and replace the cover. Allow the solvent front to ascend approximately 17 cm above base line, then allow for 1 hr of further development. Remove the supporting frame and transfer it to a drying cabinet at 50–60° for 10–15 min. Remove the sheets from the frame.

  For the *Sample solution* sheets, cut each subsidiary band from each chromatogram sheet as a strip, and cut an equivalent strip from the corresponding position of the plain (blank) sheet. For the *Standard solution* sheet, cut the entire band from the sheet, and cut an equivalent strip from the corresponding position of the plain (blank) sheet. Place each strip, subdivided into a suitable number of approximately equal portions, in a separate test tube. Add 5.0 mL of a mixture of water and acetone (1:1 by volume) to each test tube, swirl for 2–3 min, add 15.0 mL of 0.05 N sodium hydrogen carbonate solution, and shake the tube to ensure mixing.

  Filter the colored extracts and blanks through 9-cm coarse porosity filter papers into clean test tubes and determine the absorbances of the colored extracts at 505 nm using a suitable spectrophotometer with 40-mm closed cells against a filtered mixture of 5.0 mL of water and acetone (1:1 by vol) and 15.0 mL of the 0.05 N sodium hydrogen carbonate solution. Measure the absorbances of the extracts of the blank strips at 505 nm and correct the absorbances of the colored extracts with the blank values.

  Calculate the percentage of subsidiary coloring matter in the portion of the sample taken:

  $$\text{Result} = 0.01 \times D \times [(A_a + A_b + A_c \ldots A_n)/A_s] \times 100$$

  0.01 = dilution factor for the *Standard solution*
  D = total coloring matter content of the sample, determined from the *Total Color* test above and expressed as a decimal
  A_s = the absorbance from the *Standard solution*

  $A_a + A_b + A_c \ldots A_n$ = the sum of the absorbances of the subsidiary coloring matters from the *Sample solution,* corrected for the blank values

  Acceptance criteria: NMT 1%

---
[2] Whatman No 1, or equivalent

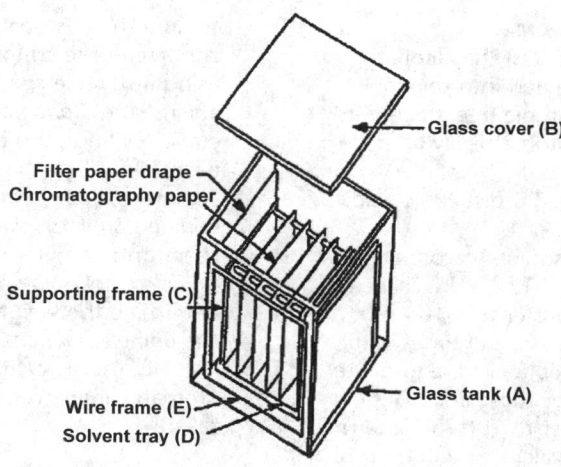

Figure 1. Assembly of the Chromatographic Apparatus

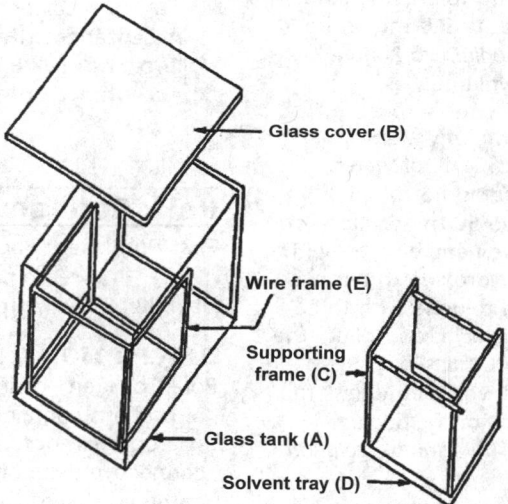

Figure 2. Components of the Chromatographic Apparatus

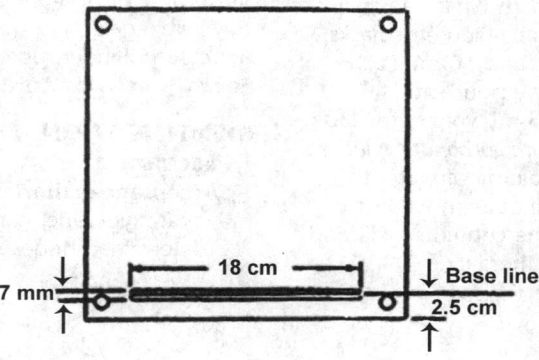

Figure 3. Method for Marking the Chromatographic Paper

- **UNSULFONATED PRIMARY AROMATIC AMINES**
  [NOTE—Under the conditions of this test, unsulfonated primary aromatic amines are extracted into toluene from an alkaline solution of the sample, reextracted into acid, then determined spectrophotometrically after diazotization and coupling.]
  R salt solution: 0.05 N 2-naphthol-3,6-disulfonic acid, disodium salt
  Sodium carbonate solution: 2 N sodium carbonate
  Standard stock solution: Weigh 0.100 g of redistilled aniline into a small beaker and transfer to a 100-mL volumetric flask, rinsing the beaker several times with water. Add 30 mL of 3 N hydrochloric acid, and dilute with water at room temperature to the mark. Dilute 10.0 mL of this solution with water to 100 mL, and mix well; 1 mL of this solution is equivalent to 0.0001 g of aniline. [NOTE—Prepare the Standard stock solution fresh.]
  Standard solutions: Separately dilute 5-, 10-, 15-, 20-, and 25-mL aliquots of the Standard stock solution to 100 mL with 1 N hydrochloric acid.
  Standard blank solution: In a 25-mL volumetric flask mix 10.0 mL of 1 N hydrochloric acid, 2.0 mL of the R salt solution, and 10.0 mL of the Sodium carbonate solution, and dilute with water to volume.
  Sample solution: Add 2.0 g of the sample to a separatory funnel containing 100 mL of water; rinse down the sides of the funnel with 50 mL of water, swirling to dissolve the sample; and add 5 mL of 1 N sodium hydroxide. Extract with two 50-mL portions of toluene, and wash the combined toluene extracts with 10-mL portions of 0.1 N sodium hydroxide to remove traces of color. Extract the washed toluene with three 10-mL portions of 3 N hydrochloric acid, and dilute the combined extract with water to 100 mL.
  Sample blank solution: In a 25-mL volumetric flask mix 2.0 mL of the R salt solution, 10 mL of the Sodium carbonate solution, and 10.0 mL of the Sample solution, and dilute with water to volume.
  Analysis: Pipet 10-mL aliquots of each of the Standard solutions and the Sample solution into separate clean, dry test tubes. Cool the tubes for 10 min by immersion in a beaker of ice water, and add 1 mL of 50% potassium bromide solution and 0.05 mL of 0.5 N sodium nitrite solution. Mix and allow the tubes to stand for 10 min in the ice water bath while the aniline is diazotized. Into each of five 25-mL volumetric flasks, measure 1 mL of the R salt solution and 10 mL of the Sodium carbonate solution. Separately pour each diazotized aniline solution into a 25-mL volumetric flask containing R salt solution and Sodium carbonate solution; rinse each test tube with a small volume of water to allow for a quantitative transfer. Dilute with water to the mark, stopper the flasks, mix the contents well, and allow them to stand for 15 min in the dark.
  Measure the absorbance of each of the solutions containing the coupled Standard solutions at 510 nm, using a suitable spectrophotometer with 40-mm cells against the Standard blank solution. Plot a standard curve relating absorbance to weight (g) of aniline in each 100 mL of the Standard solutions.
  Measure the absorbance of the solutions containing the coupled Sample solution at 510 nm, using a suitable spectrophotometer with 40-mm cells against the Sample blank solution. From the standard curve, determine the weight (g) of aniline in each 100 mL of the Sample solution.
  Calculate the percentage of unsulfonated primary aromatic amine (as aniline) in the portion of the sample taken:

  $$\text{Result} = W_A/W \times 100$$

  W_A = weight of aniline in the Sample solution calculated from the standard curve (g/100 mL)
  W = weight of sample used to prepare the Sample solution (g)
  Acceptance criteria: NMT 0.01%, calculated as aniline
- **WATER-INSOLUBLE MATTER**, Colors, Appendix IIIC
  Acceptance criteria: NMT 0.2%▲FCC8

Pork Collagen

First Published: Prior to FCC 6

UNII: I8442U2G7J [pork collagen]

DESCRIPTION
Pork Collagen occurs as a light tan powder. It is a mixture of proteins containing 40% to 50% collagen, a scleroprotein occurring in animal tendons, ligaments, and connective tissue. It is derived from porcine fatty trimmings gathered during the production of fresh pork meat. During processing, the trimmings are ground, heated, and stabilized, followed by centrifugal separation to reduce the fat. The partially defatted tissue is then dried and further reduced in fat content, resulting in a high-protein material that may be milled or ground into powder or granular form. It is dispersible in water, and forms thermally reversible gels.
Function: Binder; purge reduction
Packaging and Storage: Store in tight containers.

IDENTIFICATION
- **PROCEDURE**
  Acceptance criteria: A sample contains NLT 5.52% hydroxyproline, corresponding to 40.0% collagen, as determined under Assay (below).

ASSAY
- **HYDROXYPROLINE CONTENT**
  [NOTE—This method is based on AOAC Method 990.26.]
  Buffer solution: Transfer 30 g of citric acid monohydrate, 15 g of sodium hydroxide, and 90 g of sodium acetate trihydrate into a 1-L volumetric flask containing 500 mL of water. Add 290 mL of 1-propanol. Adjust the pH to 6.0 with acid or base, and dilute to volume with water.
  Oxidant solution: 14.1 mg/mL of chloramine-T in *Buffer solution*. [NOTE—The solution is stable for 1 week when stored in dark bottles at 4°.]
  Color reagent: 286 mg/mL of 4-dimethylaminobenzaldehyde in 60% (w/w) perchloric acid. [CAUTION—Handle perchloric acid in an appropriate fume hood.] [NOTE—Prepare solution daily.]
  Standard stock solution: 600 µg/mL of *trans*-4-hydroxyproline (Sigma, or equivalent) [NOTE—The solution is stable for up to 2 months at 4°.]
  Standard solutions: 0.6, 1.2, 1.8, and 2.4 µg/mL of *trans*-4-hydroxyproline: from *Standard stock solution*. [NOTE—Prepare these solutions on the day of use.]
  Sample stock solution: Transfer 4.0 g of sample into an Erlenmeyer flask. Add 30 mL of 7 N sulfuric acid, cover with a watch glass, and place the flasks in a drying oven at 105° for 16 h. [CAUTION—Use an oven resistant to corrosion by acids such as those used in analyses involving perchloric acid. Use caution in handling the hot hydrolysate.] Transfer the hot hydrolysate quantitatively into a 500-mL volumetric flask with the aid of water. Dilute to volume with water, and mix. Filter some of the solution into a 100-mL Erlenmeyer flask. The resulting filtrate is the *Sample stock solution*. [NOTE—The filtrate is stable for up to 2 weeks at 4°.]
  Sample solution: Dilute an appropriate volume of *Sample stock solution* with water to 100 mL so that the concentration of hydroxyproline will be 0.5 - 2.4 µg per 2 mL. [NOTE—Typically a dilution of 5 mL of *Sample stock solution* to 100 mL is suitable.]
  Analysis: Transfer 2.0 mL of the *Sample solution* into a test tube and 2.0 mL of water into a second test tube as a blank. Add 1.0 mL of *Oxidant solution* to each tube, shake, and let stand for about 30 min. Add 2.0 mL of *Color reagent* to each tube, mix thoroughly, cap the tubes with foil or screw caps, and place them in a water bath at 60° ± 0.5° for exactly 15 min. Cool the tubes in running water for 3 min, and dry the outside of the tubes. Measure the absorbance of the solution against the blank in 10-mm glass cells, using an appropriate spectrophotometer, at 558 nm.
  Repeat the preceding using each of the *Standard solutions*. Draw a standard curve by plotting the absorbance values of the *Standard solutions* on the Y-axis and the hydroxyproline concentration, in µg per 2 mL, on the X-axis.
  Calculate the percent hydroxyproline content in the sample by the formula:

  $$\text{Result} = (X \times 2.5)/(W \times V)$$

  X = hydroxyproline content of the *Sample solution* (µg per 2 mL) obtained from the standard curve
  W = weight of the sample (mg) taken to prepare the *Sample stock solution*
  V = volume of *Sample stock solution* used (mL) to prepare the *Sample solution*

  Calculate the percent collagen in the sample by multiplying the percent hydroxyproline by 7.25.
  Acceptance criteria: NLT 40.0% collagen

IMPURITIES
Inorganic Impurities
- **LEAD,** *Lead Limit Test, Atomic Absorption Spectrophotometric Graphite Furnace Method, Method II,* Appendix IIIB
  Sample: 10 g
  Acceptance criteria: NMT 1 mg/kg

SPECIFIC TESTS
- **ASH (TOTAL),** Appendix IIIC
  Acceptance criteria: NMT 3.0%
- **FAT**
  Sample: 1 g
  Analysis: Transfer the *Sample* into a fat-extraction flask, add 10 mL of water, and shake until homogeneous. [NOTE—Warm the solution, if necessary, to obtain a homogeneous mixture.] Add approximately 1 mL of ammonium hydroxide to the mixture, and heat in a water bath for 15 min at 60° to 70°, shaking occasionally. Add 10 mL of alcohol, and mix well. Add 25 mL of peroxide-free ether, stopper, and shake vigorously for 1 min, allow to cool if necessary, add 25 mL of petroleum ether, and shake vigorously. Allow the layers to separate and clarify, or centrifuge to expedite the process. Decant the organic layer into a suitable flask or dish, and repeat the extraction twice with 15 mL each of peroxide-free ether and petroleum ether for each extraction. Evaporate the combined ether extractions on a steam bath, and dry the residue to a constant weight at 102°, or 70° to 75° at less than 50 mm Hg.
  Calculate the percent of fat in the sample taken by the formula:

  $$\text{Result} = (R \times 100)/S$$

  R = weight of the residue (mg)
  S = weight of the sample taken (mg)
  Acceptance criteria: NMT 14.0%
- **LOSS ON DRYING,** Appendix IIC
  Acceptance criteria: NMT 5.0%
- **MICROBIAL LIMITS**
  [NOTE—The current method for the following test may be found by accessing the Food and Drug Administration's Bacteriological Analytical Manual (BAM) online at www.cfsan.fda.gov.]
  Acceptance criteria
  Salmonella: Negative in 25 g

- **PROTEIN,** *Nitrogen Determination,* Appendix IIIC
  Analysis: Calculate the percent protein with the formula

  Result = 6.25 × N

  N = percent nitrogen
  6.25 = nitrogen to protein conversion factor
  Acceptance criteria: NLT 85.0% (including collagen)

Potassium Acid Tartrate

First Published: Prior to FCC 6

Potassium Bitartrate
Cream of Tartar

$C_4H_5KO_6$ Formula wt 188.18
INS: 336   CAS: [868-14-4]
UNII: NPT6P8P3UU [potassium bitartrate]

DESCRIPTION
Potassium Acid Tartrate occurs as colorless or slightly opaque crystals, or as a white, crystalline powder. It is a salt of L(+)-tartaric acid. One g dissolves in 165 mL of water at 25°, in 16 mL of boiling water, and in 8820 mL of alcohol. A saturated solution is acid to litmus.
Function: Acidifier; buffer
Packaging and Storage: Store in tight containers.

IDENTIFICATION
- **A. PROCEDURE**
  Analysis: Heat the sample until it chars (it will emit a flammable vapor having an odor resembling that of burning sugar). Further heat at a higher temperature and with free access to air until the heat consumes the carbon of the black residue. Expose the remaining white, fused mass of potassium carbonate to a nonluminous flame.
  Acceptance criteria: A red-purple color is emitted.
- **B. PROCEDURE**
  Sample solution: A saturated solution of the sample in water
  Analysis: Mix the *Sample solution* with sodium cobaltinitrite TS.
  Acceptance criteria: A yellow-orange precipitate forms.
- **C. PROCEDURE**
  Sample solution: A saturated solution of the sample in water
  Analysis: Neutralize the *Sample solution* with 1 N sodium hydroxide in a test tube, add silver nitrate TS, then just sufficient 6 N ammonium hydroxide to dissolve the white precipitate. Boil the solution.
  Acceptance criteria: A mirror forms on the inner surface of the test tube from the silver deposited there.

ASSAY
- **PROCEDURE**
  Sample: 6 g, previously dried at 105° for 3 h
  Analysis: Dissolve the *Sample* in 100 mL of boiling water, and titrate with 1 N sodium hydroxide, determining the endpoint using phenolphthalein TS as an indicator. Each mL of 1 N sodium hydroxide is equivalent to 188.2 mg of $C_4H_5KO_6$.
  Acceptance criteria: NLT 99.0% and NMT 101.0% of $C_4H_5KO_6$, on the dried basis

IMPURITIES
Inorganic Impurities
- **LEAD,** *Lead Limit Test, Flame Atomic Absorption Spectrophotometric Method,* Appendix IIIB
  Sample: 5 g
  Acceptance criteria: NMT 2 mg/kg

SPECIFIC TESTS
- **AMMONIA**
  Sample solution: 100 mg/mL in 1 N sodium hydroxide
  Analysis: Heat a 5-mL portion of the *Sample solution*.
  Acceptance criteria: No odor of ammonia is detected.
- **INSOLUBLE MATTER**
  Analysis: Agitate 500 mg of sample with 3 mL of 6 N ammonium hydroxide.
  Acceptance criteria: No undissolved residue remains.

Potassium Alginate

First Published: Prior to FCC 6

Algin

$(C_6H_7O_6K)_n$ Equiv wt, calculated, 214.22
                                 Equiv wt, actual (avg.) 238.00
INS: 402   CAS: [9005-36-1]
UNII: 44ZPJ5W2J1 [potassium alginate]

DESCRIPTION
Potassium Alginate occurs as a white to yellow, fibrous or granular powder. It is the potassium salt of alginic acid (see the monograph for *Alginic Acid*). It dissolves in water to form a viscous, colloidal solution. It is insoluble in alcohol and in hydroalcoholic solutions in which the alcohol content is greater than 30% by weight. It is insoluble in chloroform, in ether, and in acids having a pH lower than about 3.
Function: Stabilizer; thickener; gelling agent
Packaging and Storage: Store in well-closed containers.

IDENTIFICATION
- **A. PROCEDURE**
  Sample solution: 10 mg/mL
  Analysis: To 5 mL of *Sample solution*, add 1 mL of calcium chloride TS.
  Acceptance criteria: A voluminous, gelatinous precipitate forms.
- **B. PROCEDURE**
  Sample solution: 10 mg/mL

Analysis: To 10 mL of *Sample solution*, add 1 mL of 2 N sulfuric acid.
Acceptance criteria: A heavy, gelatinous precipitate forms.
- **C. PROCEDURE**
  Sample: 5 mg
  Analysis: To the *Sample* add 5 mL of water, 1 mL of freshly prepared 1:100 naphtholresorcinol:ethanol solution, and 5 mL of hydrochloric acid. Heat the mixture to boiling, boil gently for about 3 min, and then cool to about 15°. Transfer the contents of the test tube into a 30-mL separatory funnel with the aid of 5 mL of water, and extract with 15 mL of isopropyl ether. Perform a blank determination (see *General Provisions*) and make any necessary correction.
  Acceptance criteria: The isopropyl ether extract from the sample exhibits a deeper purple hue than that from the blank.

ASSAY
- **ALGINATES ASSAY,** Appendix IIIC
  Analysis: Each mL of 0.25 N sodium hydroxide consumed in the assay is equivalent to 28.75 mg of potassium alginate (equiv wt 238.00).
  Acceptance criteria: A sample yields NLT 16.5% and NMT 19.5% of carbon dioxide (CO_2), corresponding to between 89.2% and 105.5% of potassium alginate (equiv wt 238.00), calculated on the dried basis.

IMPURITIES
Inorganic Impurities
- **ARSENIC,** Appendix IIIB: Using a *Sample solution* prepared as directed for organic compounds
  Acceptance criteria: NMT 3 mg/kg
- **LEAD,** *Lead Limit Test,* Appendix IIIB
  Sample solution: Prepare as directed for organic compounds.
  Control: 5 μg of Pb (5 mL of *Diluted Standard Lead Solution*)
  Acceptance criteria: NMT 5 mg/kg

SPECIFIC TESTS
- **LOSS ON DRYING,** Appendix IIC: 105° for 4 h
  Acceptance criteria: NMT 15.0%

Potassium Benzoate
First Published: Prior to FCC 6

$C_7H_5KO_2$ Formula wt 160.22
INS: 212   CAS: [582-25-2]
UNII: 763YQN2K7K [potassium benzoate]

DESCRIPTION
Potassium Benzoate occurs as white granules, crystalline powder, or flakes. One g dissolves in 2 mL of water, in 75 mL of alcohol, and in 50 mL of 90% alcohol.
Function: Preservative; antimicrobial agent
Packaging and Storage: Store in well-closed containers.

IDENTIFICATION
- **BENZOATE,** Appendix IIIA
  Sample solution: 200 mg/mL
  Acceptance criteria: Passes tests
- **POTASSIUM,** Appendix IIIA
  Sample solution: 200 mg/mL
  Acceptance criteria: The *Sample solution* responds to the flame test.

ASSAY
- **PROCEDURE**
  Sample: 600 mg
  Analysis: Transfer the *Sample* into a 250-mL beaker, add 100 mL of glacial acetic acid, and stir until the sample is completely dissolved. Add crystal violet TS and titrate with 0.1 N perchloric acid in glacial acetic acid.
  [**CAUTION**—Handle perchloric acid in an appropriate fume hood.] Each mL of 0.1 N perchloric acid is equivalent to 16.02 mg of $C_7H_5KO_2$.
  Acceptance criteria: NLT 99.0% and 100.5% of $C_7H_5KO_2$, calculated on the anhydrous basis

IMPURITIES
Inorganic Impurities
- **LEAD,** *Lead Limit Test, Flame Atomic Absorption Spectrophotometric Method,* Appendix IIIB
  Sample: 10 g
  Acceptance criteria: NMT 2 mg/kg

SPECIFIC TESTS
- **ALKALINITY:** As KOH
  Sample solution: 2 g of sample in 20 mL of hot water
  Analysis: To the *Sample solution*, add 2 drops of phenolphthalein TS. If a pink color appears, add 0.1 N sulfuric acid to discharge it.
  Acceptance criteria: NMT 0.2 mL of 0.1 N sulfuric acid is required to discharge pink color (NMT 0.06%).
- **WATER,** *Water Determination,* Appendix IIB
  Acceptance criteria: NMT 1.5%

Potassium Bicarbonate
First Published: Prior to FCC 6

$KHCO_3$ Formula wt 100.12
INS: 501(ii)   CAS: [298-14-6]
UNII: HM5Z15LEBN [potassium bicarbonate]

DESCRIPTION
Potassium Bicarbonate occurs as colorless, transparent, monoclinic prisms or as a white, granular powder. It is stable in air. Its solutions are neutral or alkaline to phenolphthalein TS. One g dissolves in 2.8 mL of water. It is almost insoluble in alcohol.

Function: pH control; leavening agent
Packaging and Storage: Store in well-closed containers.

IDENTIFICATION
- **BICARBONATE,** Appendix IIIA
  Sample solution: 100 mg/mL
  Acceptance criteria: Passes tests
- **POTASSIUM,** Appendix IIIA
  Sample solution: 100 mg/mL
  Acceptance criteria: Passes tests

ASSAY
- **PROCEDURE**
  Sample: 4 g
  Analysis: Dissolve the *Sample* in 100 mL of water. Add 2 drops of methyl red TS and, while constantly stirring, slowly titrate with 1 N hydrochloric acid until the solution becomes faintly pink. Heat the solution to boiling, cool, and continue the titration until the pink color no longer fades after boiling. Each mL of 1 N hydrochloric acid is equivalent to 100.1 mg of $KHCO_3$.
  Acceptance criteria: NLT 99.0% and NMT 101.5% of $KHCO_3$, calculated on the dried basis

IMPURITIES
Inorganic Impurities
- **CARBONATE**
  Sample: 1 g
  Analysis: Dissolve the *Sample*, without agitation, in 20 mL of water at a temperature not above 5°. Then add 2 mL of 0.1 N hydrochloric acid and 2 drops of phenolphthalein TS.
  Acceptance criteria: The solution does not immediately turn more than a faint pink color.
- **LEAD,** *Lead Limit Test, APDC Extraction Method,* Appendix IIIB
  Acceptance criteria: NMT 2 mg/kg

SPECIFIC TESTS
- **LOSS ON DRYING,** Appendix IIC: Dry over silica gel for 4 h.
  Acceptance criteria: NMT 0.25%

Potassium Bromate
First Published: Prior to FCC 6

$KBrO_3$ Formula wt 167.00
INS: 924a CAS: [7758-01-2]
UNII: 04MB35W6ZA [potassium bromate]

DESCRIPTION
Potassium Bromate occurs as white crystals or as a granular powder. It is soluble in water and slightly soluble in alcohol. The pH of a 1:20 aqueous solution is between 5 and 9.
Function: Maturing agent; oxidizing agent
Packaging and Storage: Store in well-closed containers.

IDENTIFICATION
- **A. POTASSIUM**
  Sample solution: 50 mg/mL
  Acceptance criteria: A small quantity of the *Sample solution* imparts a violet color to a non-luminous flame.
- **B. PROCEDURE**
  Sample solution: 50 mg/mL
  Analysis: Add sulfurous acid, dropwise, to the *Sample solution.*
  Acceptance criteria: A yellow color appears that disappears upon the addition of an excess of sulfurous acid.

ASSAY
- **PROCEDURE**
  Sample: 100 mg, previously dried to constant weight over a suitable desiccant
  Analysis: Dissolve the *Sample* in 50 mL of water, contained in a 250-mL glass-stoppered Erlenmeyer flask. Add 3 g of potassium iodide, followed by 3 mL of hydrochloric acid. Allow the mixture to stand for 5 min and add 100 mL of cold water. Titrate the liberated iodine with 0.1 N sodium thiosulfate, adding starch TS as the end point is approached. Perform a blank determination (see *General Provisions*), and make any necessary correction. Each mL of 0.1 N sodium thiosulfate consumed is equivalent to 2.783 mg of $KBrO_3$.
  Acceptance criteria: NLT 99.0% and NMT 101.0% of $KBrO_3$, on the dried basis

IMPURITIES
Inorganic Impurities
- **CHLORIDE,** *Chloride and Sulfate Limit Tests, Chloride Limit Test,* Appendix IIIB
  Sample: 100 mg
  Control: 50 µg chloride (5 mL of *Standard Chloride Solution*)
  Acceptance criteria: Any turbidity produced by the *Sample* does not exceed that shown in the *Control.* (NMT 0.05%)
- **LEAD,** *Lead Limit Test, Flame Atomic Absorption Spectrophotometric Method,* Appendix IIIB
  Sample: 10 g
  Acceptance criteria: NMT 4 mg/kg
- **SULFATE,** *Chloride and Sulfate Limit Tests, Sulfate Limit Test,* Appendix IIIB
  Sample: 100 mg
  Control: 10 µg sulfate (1 mL of *Standard Sulfate Solution*)
  Acceptance criteria: Any turbidity produced by the *Sample* does not exceed that in the *Control.* (NMT 0.01%)

SPECIFIC TESTS
- **LOSS ON DRYING,** Appendix IIC: Dry a sample over a suitable desiccant to constant weight.
  Acceptance criteria: NMT 0.1%

Potassium Carbonate

First Published: Prior to FCC 6

K_2CO_3 Formula wt, anhydrous 138.21
$K_2CO_3 \cdot 1\frac{1}{2}H_2O$ Formula wt, hydrated 165.23
INS: 501(i) CAS: [584-08-7]
UNII: BQN1B9B9HA [potassium carbonate]

DESCRIPTION
Potassium Carbonate is anhydrous or contains 1.5 molecules of water of crystallization. The anhydrous form occurs as a white, granular powder and the hydrated form as small, white, translucent crystals or granules. It is very deliquescent, and its solutions are alkaline. One g dissolves in 1 mL of water at 25° and in about 0.7 mL of boiling water. It is insoluble in alcohol.
Function: pH control
Packaging and Storage: Store in tight containers.

IDENTIFICATION
- **CARBONATE,** Appendix IIIA
  Sample solution: 100 mg/mL
  Acceptance criteria: Passes tests
- **POTASSIUM,** Appendix IIIA
  Sample solution: 100 mg/mL
  Acceptance criteria: Passes tests

ASSAY
- **PROCEDURE**
  Sample: 1 g previously dried
  Analysis: Transfer the *Sample* to a beaker and dissolve it in 50 mL of water. Add 2 drops of methyl red TS and, while constantly stirring, slowly titrate with 1 N hydrochloric acid until the solution becomes faintly pink. Heat the solution to boiling, cool, and continue the titration until the faint pink color no longer fades after boiling. Each mL of 1 N hydrochloric acid is equivalent to 69.11 mg of K_2CO_3.
  Acceptance criteria: NLT 99.0% and NMT 100.5% of K_2CO_3, on the dried basis

IMPURITIES
Inorganic Impurities
- **LEAD,** *Lead Limit Test, APDC Extraction Method,* Appendix IIIB
  [NOTE—Alternatively, determine as directed under *Lead Limit Test, Atomic Absorption Spectrophotometric Graphite Furnace Method I,* Appendix IIIB.]
  Acceptance criteria: NMT 2 mg/kg

SPECIFIC TESTS
- **INSOLUBLE SUBSTANCES**
  Sample: 1 g
  Analysis: Dissolve the *Sample* in 20 mL of water.
  Acceptance criteria: No residue remains.
- **LOSS ON DRYING,** Appendix IIC: 180° for 4 h
  Sample: 3 g
  Acceptance criteria:
    Anhydrous: NMT 1%
    Hydrated: Between 10.0% and 16.5%

Potassium Carbonate Solution

First Published: Prior to FCC 6

INS: 501(i)
UNII: HM5Z15LEBN [potassium bicarbonate]

DESCRIPTION
Potassium Carbonate Solution occurs as a clear or slightly turbid, colorless, alkaline solution that absorbs carbon dioxide when exposed to air, forming potassium bicarbonate. It is available as solutions with concentrations of about 50.0% (w/w).
Function: pH control
Packaging and Storage: Store in tight containers.

IDENTIFICATION
- **CARBONATE,** Appendix IIIA
  Acceptance criteria: Passes tests
- **POTASSIUM,** Appendix IIIA
  Acceptance criteria: Passes tests

ASSAY
- **PROCEDURE**
  Sample: Based on the labeled percentage of K_2CO_3, weigh a volume of the sample solution equivalent to 1 g of potassium carbonate.
  Analysis: Add the *Sample* to 50.0 mL of 1 N sulfuric acid. Add 2 drops of methyl orange TS and titrate the excess acid with 1 N sodium hydroxide. Each mL of 1 N sulfuric acid is equivalent to 69.11 mg of K_2CO_3.
  Acceptance criteria: NLT 97.0% and NMT 103.0%, by weight, of the labeled amount of K_2CO_3

IMPURITIES
Inorganic Impurities
- **LEAD,** *Lead Limit Test, APDC Extraction Method,* Appendix IIIB
  Sample: Use the equivalent of 1 g of potassium carbonate (K_2CO_3), calculated on the basis of the *Assay*.
  Acceptance criteria: NMT 2 mg/kg, calculated on the basis of potassium carbonate (K_2CO_3) determined in the *Assay*.

Potassium Chloride

First Published: Prior to FCC 6

KCl
Formula wt 74.55
INS: 508 CAS: [7447-40-7]
UNII: 660YQ98I10 [potassium chloride]

DESCRIPTION
Potassium Chloride occurs as colorless, elongated, prismatic, or cubical crystals, or as a white, granular powder. It is stable in air. Its solutions are neutral to litmus. It may contain up to 1.0% (total) of suitable food-grade anticaking, free-flowing, or conditioning agents such as

calcium stearate or silicon dioxide, either singly or in combination. One g dissolves in 2.8 mL of water at 25°, and in about 2 mL of boiling water. Potassium Chloride containing anticaking, free-flowing, or conditioning agents may produce cloudy solutions or dissolve incompletely. It is insoluble in alcohol.

Function: Nutrient; gelling agent; salt substitute; yeast food

Packaging and Storage: Store in well-closed containers.

IDENTIFICATION
- **CHLORIDE,** Appendix IIIA
  Sample solution: 50 mg/mL
  Acceptance criteria: Passes test
- **POTASSIUM,** Appendix IIIA
  Sample solution: 50 mg/mL
  Acceptance criteria: Passes tests

ASSAY
- **PROCEDURE**
  Sample: 250 mg, previously dried
  Analysis: Dissolve the *Sample* in 150 mL of water. Add 1 mL of nitric acid, and immediately titrate with 0.1 N silver nitrate, determining the endpoint potentiometrically, using silver-calomel electrodes and a salt bridge containing 4% agar in a saturated potassium nitrate solution. Perform a blank determination (see *General Provisions*), and make any necessary correction. Each mL of 0.1 N silver nitrate is equivalent to 7.455 mg of KCl.
  Acceptance criteria
  Potassium Chloride not containing added substance(s): NLT 99.0% of KCl, on the dried basis
  Potassium Chloride containing added substance(s): NLT 98.0% of KCl, on the dried basis

IMPURITIES
Inorganic Impurities
- **IODIDE AND/OR BROMIDE**
  Sample: 2 g
  Analysis: Dissolve the *Sample* in 6 mL of water, add 1 mL of chloroform, and then add, dropwise and with constant agitation, 5 mL of a mixture of equal parts of chlorine TS and water.
  Acceptance criteria: The chloroform is free from even a transient violet or permanent orange color.
- **HEAVY METALS (AS PB)**
  [NOTE—This test is designed to limit the content of common metallic impurities colored by sulfide ion (Ag, As, Bi, Cd, Cu, Hg, Pb, Sb, Sn) by comparing the color with a standard containing lead (Pb) ion under the specified test conditions. It demonstrates that the test substance is not grossly contaminated by such heavy metals, and within the precision of the test, that it does not exceed the *Heavy Metals* limit given as determined by concomitant visual comparison with a control solution. In the specified pH range, the optimum concentration of lead (Pb) ion for matching purposes by this method is 20 µg in 50 mL of solution.
  The most common limitation of the *Heavy Metals* test is that the color the sulfide ion produces in the *Sample solution* depends on the metals present and may not match the color in the dilution of the *Standard lead solution* used for matching purposes. Lead sulfide is brown, as are Ag, Bi, Cu, Hg, and Sn sulfides. While it is possible that ions not mentioned here may also yield nonmatching colors, among the nine common metallic impurities listed above, the sulfides with different colors are those of As and Cd, which are yellow, and that of Sb, which is orange. If a yellow or orange color is observed, the following action is indicated: Because this monograph does not include an arsenic requirement, As should be determined. Any As found should not exceed 3 mg/kg. If these criteria are met, Cd may be a contributor to the yellow color, so the Cd content should be determined. If an orange color is observed, the Sb content should be determined. These additional tests are in accord with the section on *Trace Impurities* in the *General Provisions* of this book, as follows: "if other possible impurities may be present, additional tests may be required, and should be applied, as necessary, by the manufacturer, vendor, or user to demonstrate that the substance is suitable for its intended application."
  Determine the amount of heavy metals by *Method I* or *Method II* as the following criteria specify: Use *Method I* for samples that yield clear, colorless solutions before adding sulfide ion. Use *Method II* for samples that do not yield clear, colorless solutions under the test conditions specified for *Method I*. Use *Method III*, a wet digestion method, only in those cases where neither *Method I* nor *Method II* can be used.]

  Lead nitrate stock solution: Dissolve 159.8 mg of Reagent-Grade ACS Lead Nitrate [Pb(NO$_3$)$_2$] in 100 mL of water containing 1 mL of nitric acid, dilute to 1000.0 mL and mix. [NOTE—Prepare and store this solution in glass containers that are free from lead salts.]
  Standard lead solution: Dilute 10.0 mL of *Lead nitrate stock solution* to 100.0 mL with water.
  [NOTE—Prepare on the day of use.] Each mL is equivalent to 10 µg of lead (Pb) ion.
  [NOTE—In the following tests, failure to accurately adjust the pH of the solution within the specified limits may result in a significant loss of test sensitivity.]

- **METHOD I**
  Sample solution: 4 g in 25 mL of water
  Solution A: Pipet 2.0 mL of *Standard lead solution* (20 µg of Pb) into a 50-mL color-comparison tube, and add water to make 25 mL. Adjust the pH to between 3.0 and 4.0 (using short-range pH indicator paper) by adding 1 N acetic acid or 6 N ammonia, dilute to 40 mL with water, and mix.
  Solution B: Transfer 25 mL of the *Sample solution* into a 50-mL color-comparison tube that matches the one used for *Solution A*, adjust the pH to between 3.0 and 4.0 (using short-range pH indicator paper) by adding 1 N acetic acid or 6 N ammonia, dilute to 40 mL with water, and mix.
  Solution C: Transfer 25 mL of the *Sample solution* into a third color-comparison tube that matches those used for *Solutions A* and *B*, and add 2.0 mL of *Standard lead*

solution. Adjust the pH to between 3.0 and 4.0 (using short-range pH indicator paper) by adding 1 N acetic acid or 6 N ammonia, dilute to 40 mL with water, and mix.

Analysis: Add 10 mL of freshly prepared hydrogen sulfide TS to each tube, mix, allow to stand for 5 min, and view downward over a white surface.

Acceptance criteria: The color of *Solution B* is not darker than that of *Solution A*, and the intensity of the color of *Solution C* is equal to or greater than that of *Solution A*. (NMT 5 mg/kg) [NOTE—If the color of *Solution C* is lighter than that of *Solution A*, the sample is interfering with the test procedure and *Method II* must be used.]

- **METHOD II**

  Solution A: Prepare as directed in *Method I*.

  Solution B: Place a quantity of sample into a suitable crucible, add sufficient sulfuric acid to wet the sample, and carefully ignite at a low temperature until thoroughly charred, covering the crucible loosely with a suitable lid during the ignition. After the sample is thoroughly carbonized, add 2 mL of nitric acid and 5 drops of sulfuric acid, cautiously heat until white fumes no longer evolve, then ignite, preferably in a muffle furnace, at 500° to 600° until all of the carbon is burned off. Cool, add 4 mL of 1:2 hydrochloric acid, cover, and digest on a steam bath for 10 to 15 min. Uncover, and slowly evaporate on a steam bath to dryness. Moisten the residue with 1 drop of hydrochloric acid, add 10 mL of hot water, and digest for 2 min. Add 6 N ammonia dropwise until the solution is just alkaline to litmus paper, dilute to 25 mL with water, and adjust the pH to between 3.0 and 4.0 (using short-range pH indicator paper) by adding 1 N acetic acid. Filter if necessary, rinse the crucible and the filter with 10 mL of water, transfer the solution and rinsings into a 50-mL color-comparison tube, dilute to 40 mL with water, and mix.

  Analysis: Add 10 mL of freshly prepared hydrogen sulfide TS to each tube, mix, allow to stand for 5 min, and view downward over a white surface.

  Acceptance criteria: The color of *Solution B* is not darker than that of *Solution A*. (NMT 5 mg/kg)

- **METHOD III**

  Sample: 4 mg

  Solution A: Transfer an 8:10 (v/v) mixture of sulfuric acid and nitric acid into a 100-mL Kjeldahl flask, clamp the flask at an angle of 45°, and then add, in small increments, an additional volume of nitric acid equal to that added in the preparation of *Solution B* (below). Heat the solution to dense, white fumes, cool, and cautiously add 10 mL of water. Add a volume of 30% hydrogen peroxide equal to that added in the preparation of *Solution B* (below) then boil gently to dense, white fumes, and cool. Cautiously add 5 mL of water, mix, and boil gently to dense, white fumes. Continue boiling until the volume is reduced to about 2 or 3 mL, then cool, and dilute cautiously with a few mL of water. Pipet 2.0 mL of *Standard lead solution* into this solution, and mix. Transfer the solution into a 50-mL color-comparison tube, rinse the flask with water, add the rinsings to the tube until the volume is 25 mL, and mix. Adjust the pH to between 3.0 and 4.0 (using short-range pH indicator paper), initially with ammonium hydroxide and then with 6 N ammonia as the desired range is neared, dilute to 40 mL with water, and mix.

  Solution B: Transfer the *Sample* into a 100-mL Kjeldahl flask (or into a 300-mL flask if the reaction foams excessively), clamp the flask at an angle of 45°, and add a sufficient amount of an 8:10 (v/v) mixture of sulfuric acid:nitric acid to moisten the sample thoroughly. Warm gently until the reaction begins, allow the reaction to subside, and then add additional portions of the acid mixture, heating after each addition, until all of the 18 mL of acid mixture has been added. Increase the heat, and boil gently until the reaction mixture darkens. Remove the flask from the heat, add 2 mL of nitric acid, and heat to boiling again. Continue the intermittent heating and addition of 2-mL portions of nitric acid until no further darkening occurs, then heat strongly to dense, white fumes, and cool. Cautiously add 5 mL of water, mix, boil gently to dense, white fumes, and continue heating until the volume is reduced to about 2 or 3 mL. Cool, cautiously add 5 mL of water, and examine. If the solution is yellow, cautiously add 1 mL of 30% hydrogen peroxide, and again evaporate to dense, white fumes and to a volume of about 2 or 3 mL. Cool, dilute cautiously with a few mL of water, and mix. Transfer into a 50-mL color-comparison tube, rinse the flask with water, add the rinsings to the tube until the volume is 25 mL, and mix. Adjust the pH to between 3.0 and 4.0 (using short-range pH indicator paper), initially with ammonium hydroxide and then with 6 N ammonia as the desired range is neared, dilute to 40 mL with water, and mix.

  Analysis: Add 10 mL of freshly prepared hydrogen sulfide TS to each tube, mix, allow to stand for 5 min, and view downward over a white surface.

  Acceptance criteria: The color of *Solution B* is not darker than that of *Solution A*. (NMT 5 mg/kg)

SPECIFIC TESTS

- **ACIDITY OR ALKALINITY**

  Sample solution: 5 g of sample in 50 mL of recently boiled and cooled water

  Analysis 1: Add 3 drops of phenolphthalein TS to the *Sample solution*.

  Analysis 2: Add 0.3 mL of 0.02 N sodium hydroxide to the solution from *Analysis 1*.

  Acceptance criteria: No pink color appears after the addition of phenolphthalein TS in *Analysis 1*; and a pink color appears after addition of sodium hydroxide in *Analysis 2*.

  [NOTE—A sample containing no added substance(s) passes this test.]

- **LOSS ON DRYING,** Appendix IIC: 105° for 2 h

  Acceptance criteria: NMT 1.0%.

- **SODIUM**

  Sample without added substances

  Sample solution: 50 mg/mL

Analysis: Test the *Sample solution* on a platinum wire in a nonluminous flame.
Acceptance criteria: The *Sample solution* does not impart a pronounced yellow color to a nonluminous flame.

Sample with added substances
Standard stock solution: 1000 µg/mL of sodium, prepared by diluting 1.2711 g of reagent-grade sodium chloride to 500 mL with water
Standard solutions: From the *Standard stock solution*, prepare separate dilutions to cover the range 0 to 10 µg/mL of sodium at intervals of 2 µg/mL using 500-mL volumetric flasks and adding 0.5 g of reagent-grade potassium chloride to each volumetric flask before diluting to volume.
Sample stock solution: 10 mg/mL
Sample solution: 1 mg/mL; from the *Sample stock solution*
Standard curve: Atomize portions of the *Standard solutions* as described under *Analysis* (below) until readings for the series are reproducible, adjusting the instrument so that the solution containing 10 µg/mL gives a full-scale reading. Prepare a standard curve by plotting the absorbance against the concentration.
Analysis: Determine the absorbances of the *Standard solutions* and the *Sample solution* at the sodium emission line of 589.6 nm with a flame atomic absorption spectrophotometer equipped with a sodium hollow-cathode lamp and an air–acetylene flame, using water as the blank. Determine the concentration, C, in µg/mL, of sodium from the standard curve, and calculate the percent sodium in the sample taken by the formula:

$$Result = C/10$$

Acceptance criteria: NMT 0.5%

OTHER REQUIREMENTS
- **LABELING:** Indicate the name and quantity of any added substance(s) if the material contains such substances.

Potassium Citrate

First Published: Prior to FCC 6

Tripotassium Citrate

$C_6H_5K_3O_7 \cdot H_2O$ Formula wt 324.41
INS: 332(ii)   CAS: [6100-05-6]
UNII: EE90ONI6FF [potassium citrate]

DESCRIPTION
Potassium Citrate occurs as transparent crystals or as a white, granular powder. It is deliquescent when exposed to moist air. One g dissolves in about 0.5 mL of water. It is almost insoluble in alcohol.
Function: Buffer; sequestrant; stabilizer
Packaging and Storage: Store in tight containers.

IDENTIFICATION
- **CITRATE,** Appendix IIIA
  Sample solution: 50 mg/mL
  Acceptance criteria: Passes test
- **POTASSIUM,** Appendix IIIA
  Sample solution: 50 mg/mL
  Acceptance criteria: Passes tests

ASSAY
- **PROCEDURE**
  Sample: 250 mg, previously dried
  Analysis: Dissolve the *Sample* in 40 mL of glacial acetic acid warming slightly to aid in dissolution. Cool the solution to room temperature, add 2 drops of crystal violet TS and titrate with 0.1 N perchloric acid. Perform a blank determination (see *General Provisions*) and make any necessary correction. Each mL of 0.1 N perchloric acid is equivalent to 10.213 mg of $C_6H_5K_3O_7$.
  [**CAUTION**—Handle perchloric acid in an appropriate fume hood.]
  Acceptance criteria: NLT 99.0% and NMT 100.5% of $C_6H_5K_3O_7$, on the dried basis

IMPURITIES
Inorganic Impurities
- **LEAD,** *Lead Limit Test*, *Flame Atomic Absorption Spectrophotometric Method*, Appendix IIIB
  Sample: 10 g
  Acceptance criteria: NMT 2 mg/kg

SPECIFIC TESTS
- **LOSS ON DRYING,** Appendix IIC: 180° to constant weight
  Acceptance criteria: Between 3.0% and 6.0%
- **ALKALINITY**
  Sample solution: 50 mg/mL
  Analysis: Confirm that the *Sample solution* is alkaline to litmus paper. Then add 0.2 mL of 0.1 N sulfuric acid to 10 mL of the *Sample solution* and follow with 1 drop of phenolphthalein TS.
  Acceptance criteria: No pink color appears.

Potassium Gibberellate

First Published: Prior to FCC 6

$C_{19}H_{21}KO_6$ Formula wt 384.47
    CAS: [125-67-7]
UNII: H52L7VZB7S [potassium gibberellate]

DESCRIPTION

Potassium Gibberellate occurs as a white to slightly off-white, crystalline powder. It is soluble in water, in alcohol, and in acetone. The pH of a 1:20 aqueous solution is about 6. It is deliquescent.

Function: Enzyme activator

Packaging and Storage: Store in tight containers protected from light.

IDENTIFICATION

- **A. Procedure**
  Analysis: Dissolve a few mg of sample in 2 mL of sulfuric acid.
  Acceptance criteria: A red solution having a green fluorescence forms.
- **B. Potassium,** Appendix IIIA
  Sample solution: 100 mg/mL
  Acceptance criteria: Passes tests

ASSAY

- **Gibberellic Acid**
  Sample solution: Transfer 65 mg of the sample to a 50-mL volumetric flask, dilute to volume with methanol, and mix. Transfer 10.0 mL of this solution into a 100-mL volumetric flask, dilute to volume with methanol, and mix.
  Standard solution: Transfer an amount of USP Gibberellic Acid RS, equivalent to about 25 mg of pure gibberellic acid (corrected for phase purity and volatiles content), to a 50-mL volumetric flask, dilute to volume with methanol, and mix. Transfer 10.0 mL of this solution into a second 50-mL volumetric flask, dilute to volume with methanol, and mix.
  Analysis: Transfer 5.0 mL of the *Sample solution* to a 25- × 200-mm glass-stoppered tube, and transfer 4.0-mL and 5.0-mL portions of the *Standard solution* into separate, similar tubes. Place the tubes in a boiling water bath, evaporate to dryness, and then dry in an oven at 90° for 10 min. Remove the tubes from the oven, stopper, and allow to cool to room temperature. Dissolve the residue in each tube in 10.0 mL of 8:10 sulfuric acid, heat in a boiling water bath for 10 min, and then cool in a 10° water bath for 5 min. Using a suitable spectrophotometer set at wavelength 535 nm with a 1-cm cell and dilute sulfuric acid as the blank, record the absorbance of the solutions. Note the absorbance of the two solutions prepared from the 4.0-mL and 5.0-mL aliquots of the *Standard solution*, and record the absorbance of the final solution giving the value nearest to that of the *Sample solution*. Calculate the quantity, in mg, of $C_{19}H_{21}KO_6$ in the sample taken by the formula:

  $$\text{Result} = (A_U/A_S) \times [C \times (M_{r2}/M_{r1})] \times (V/F) \times 500$$

  A_U = absorbance of the *Sample solution*
  A_S = absorbance of the *Standard solution* that has the absorbance value nearest to the absorbance of the *Sample solution* (A_U)
  C = concentration of the *Standard solution* (mg/mL)
  M_{r2} = molecular weight of potassium gibberellate, 384.47
  M_{r1} = molecular weight of gibberellic acid, 346.38
  V = volume of the aliquot of the *Standard solution* used to obtain A_S (either 4.0 or 5.0 mL)
  F = factor, 5

  Acceptance criteria: NLT 80.0% and NMT 87.0% of $C_{19}H_{21}KO_6$, equivalent to between 72.1% and 78.4% of $C_{19}H_{22}O_6$ (gibberellic acid)

IMPURITIES

Inorganic Impurities

- **Lead,** *Lead Limit Test,* Appendix IIIB
  Sample solution: Use a *Sample solution* prepared as directed for organic compounds.
  Control: 5 μg Pb (5 mL of *Diluted Standard Lead Solution*)
  Acceptance criteria: NMT 5 mg/kg

SPECIFIC TESTS

- **Loss on Drying,** Appendix IIC 100° in vacuum for 4 h
  Acceptance criteria: Between 5.0% and 13.0%
- **Optical (Specific) Rotation,** Appendix IIB
  Sample solution: 50 mg/mL
  Acceptance criteria: $[\alpha]_D^{20}$ between +43.0° and +60.0°
- **Residue on Ignition (Sulfated Ash),** Appendix IIC
  Sample: 1 g
  Acceptance criteria: Between 19.0% and 23.0%

Potassium Gluconate

First Published: Prior to FCC 6

D-Gluconic Acid, Monopotassium Salt
Monopotassium D-Gluconate

$C_6H_{11}KO_7$ — Formula wt anhydrous 234.25
$C_6H_{11}KO_7 \cdot H_2O$ — Formula wt monohydrate 252.26
INS: 577
CAS: anhydrous [299-27-4]
monohydrate [35398-15-3]
UNII: 12H3K5QKN9 [potassium gluconate]

DESCRIPTION

Potassium Gluconate occurs as a white or yellow-white, crystalline powder or granules. It is anhydrous or the monohydrate. It is freely soluble in water and in glycerin, slightly soluble in alcohol, and insoluble in ether.

Function: Nutrient; sequestrant

Packaging and Storage: Store in well-closed containers.

IDENTIFICATION

- **A. Potassium,** Appendix IIIA
  Acceptance criteria: Passes the flame test

- **B. Thin-Layer Chromatography,** Appendix IIA
  Sample solution: 10 mg/mL [Note—Heat in a water bath at 60° if necessary to dissolve the sample.]
  Standard solution: 10 mg/mL of USP Potassium Gluconate RS [Note—Heat in a water bath at 60° if necessary to dissolve the sample.]
  Adsorbent: 0.25-mm layer of chromatographic silica gel
  Developing solvent system: Alcohol, water, ethyl acetate, and ammonium hydroxide (50:30:10:10)
  Spray reagent: Dissolve 2.5 g of ammonium molybdate in 50 mL of 2 N sulfuric acid in a 100-mL volumetric flask, add 1.0 g of ceric sulfate, swirl to dissolve, dilute to volume with 2 N sulfuric acid, and mix.
  Application volume: 5 µL
  Analysis: After removing the plate from the developing chamber, allow it to dry at 110° for 20 min, and allow it to cool. Spray the plate with the *Spray reagent*, then heat the plate at 110° for 10 min.
  Acceptance criteria: The principal spot obtained from the *Sample solution* corresponds in color, size, and R_F value to that obtained from the *Standard solution*.
- **C. Infrared Absorption,** *Spectrophotometric Identification Tests*, Appendix IIIC
  Reference standard: USP Potassium Gluconate RS
  Sample and standard preparation: *M* (Use a previously dried sample.)
  Acceptance criteria: The spectrum of the *Sample* in the range of 2 to 12 µm exhibits maxima at the same wavelengths as those in the spectrum of the Reference standard.

ASSAY
- **Procedure**
  Sample: 175 mg
  Analysis: Transfer the *Sample* into a 200-mL clean, dry Erlenmeyer flask, add 75 mL of glacial acetic acid, and dissolve the *Sample* by heating the flask on a hot plate. Cool, add quinaldine red TS, and titrate with 0.1 N perchloric acid in glacial acetic acid to a colorless endpoint, using a 10-mL microburet. Each mL of 0.1 N perchloric acid is equivalent to 23.42 mg of $C_6H_{11}KO_7$. [**Caution**—Handle perchloric acid in an appropriate fume hood.]
  Acceptance criteria: NLT 98.0% of $C_6H_{11}KO_7$, calculated on the dried basis

IMPURITIES
Inorganic Impurities
- **Lead,** *Lead Limit Test, Flame Atomic Absorption Spectrophotometric Method*, Appendix IIIB
  Sample: 10 g
  Acceptance criteria: NMT 2 mg/kg

SPECIFIC TESTS
- **Loss on Drying,** Appendix IIC: 105° for 4 h under vacuum
  Acceptance criteria:
  Anhydrous: NMT 3.0%
  Monohydrate: Between 6.0% and 7.5%
- **Reducing Substances**
  Sample: 1 g
  Analysis: Transfer the *Sample* to a 250-mL Erlenmeyer flask, dissolve it in 10 mL of water, add 25 mL of alkaline cupric citrate TS, and cover the flask with a small beaker. Boil gently for exactly 5 min and cool rapidly to room temperature. Add 25 mL of a 1:10 solution of acetic acid, 10.0 mL of 0.1 N iodine, 10 mL of 2.7 N hydrochloric acid, and 3 mL of starch TS. Titrate with 0.1 N sodium thiosulfate to the disappearance of the blue color. Calculate the weight (mg) of reducing substances (as D-glucose) by the formula:

  $$\text{Result} = 27(V_1N_1 - V_2N_2)$$

  27 = an empirically determined equivalence factor for D-glucose
  V_1 = volume of the iodine solution
  N_1 = normality of the iodine solution
  V_2 = volume (mL) of the sodium thiosulfate solution
  N_2 = normality of the sodium thiosulfate solution
  Acceptance criteria: NMT 1.0%

OTHER REQUIREMENTS
- **Labeling:** Indicate whether the product is anhydrous or monohydrate.

Potassium Glycerophosphate
First Published: Prior to FCC 6

$C_3H_7K_2O_6P \cdot 3H_2O$ Formula wt 302.30
  CAS: [1319-70-6]
UNII: 13659SD1OI [potassium glycerophosphate trihydrate]

DESCRIPTION
Potassium Glycerophosphate occurs as a pale yellow, syrupy liquid containing three molecules of water of hydration, or as a colorless to pale yellow, syrupy solution having a concentration of 50% to 75%. It is very soluble in water, and its solutions are alkaline to litmus.
Function: Nutrient
Packaging and Storage: Store in tight containers.

IDENTIFICATION
- **Potassium,** Appendix IIIA
  Sample solution: 100 mg/mL
  Acceptance criteria: Passes tests

ASSAY
- **Procedure**
  Sample: An amount equivalent to 4 g of $C_3H_7K_2O_6P$
  Analysis: Dissolve the *Sample* in 30 mL of water. Add methyl orange and titrate with 0.5 N hydrochloric acid. Each mL of 0.5 N hydrochloric acid is equivalent to 124.13 mg of $C_3H_7K_2O_6P$.
  Acceptance criteria
  Trihydrate: NLT 80.0% of $C_3H_7K_2O_6P$

Potassium glycerophosphate solutions: NLT 95.0% and NMT 105.0% of the labeled concentration of $C_3H_7K_2O_6P$

IMPURITIES
Inorganic Impurities
- **LEAD,** *Lead Limit Test,* Appendix IIIB
  Sample solution: Prepare as directed for organic compounds.
  Control: 4 μg Pb (4 mL of *Diluted Standard Lead Solution*)
  Acceptance criteria: NMT 4 mg/kg

Potassium Hydroxide Solution

First Published: Prior to FCC 6

INS: 525
UNII: WZH3C48M4T [potassium hydroxide]

DESCRIPTION
Potassium Hydroxide Solution occurs as a clear or slightly turbid, colorless or slightly colored, strongly caustic, hygroscopic solution. It absorbs carbon dioxide when exposed to the air, forming potassium carbonate. It is available as solutions of varying nominal concentrations.
Function: pH control
Packaging and Storage: Store in tight containers.

IDENTIFICATION
- **POTASSIUM,** Appendix IIIA
  Acceptance criteria: Passes tests

ASSAY
- **TOTAL ALKALI (AS KOH)**
  Sample solution: Amount equivalent to 1.5 g of potassium hydroxide (based on the stated or labeled percentage of KOH), diluted to 40 mL with recently boiled and cooled water.
  Analysis: Cool the *Sample solution* to 15°, and titrate with 1 N sulfuric acid using phenolphthalein TS as the indicator. When the pink color disappears, record the volume of acid required, then add methyl orange TS as the indicator, and continue the titration until a persistent pink color appears. Record the total volume of acid required for the titration. Each mL of the combined amount of 1 N sulfuric acid used is equivalent to 56.11 mg of total alkali, calculated as KOH.
  Acceptance criteria: NLT 97.0% and NMT 103.0% by weight, of the labeled amount of KOH, calculated as total alkali

IMPURITIES
Inorganic Impurities
- **LEAD,** *Lead Limit Test,* Appendix IIIB
  Sample solution: Dilute the equivalent of 1 g of potassium hydroxide, calculated on the basis of the *Assay,* with a mixture of 5 mL of water and 11 mL of 2.7 N hydrochloric acid.
  Control: 2 μg Pb (2 mL of *Diluted Standard Lead Solution*)
  Acceptance criteria: NMT 2 mg/kg, calculated on the basis of potassium hydroxide determined in the *Assay* (above)
- **MERCURY,** *Mercury Limit Test, Method I,* Appendix IIIB
  [NOTE—Substitute the following for the *Sample Preparation* given under *Method I.*]
  Sample solution: Transfer an amount of sample equivalent to 2.0 g of potassium hydroxide, calculated on the basis of the *Assay,* into a 50-mL beaker, add 10 mL of water and 2 drops of phenolphthalein TS. While constantly stirring, slowly neutralize with 1:2 hydrochloric acid. Add 1 mL of 1:5 sulfuric acid and 1 mL of a 1:25 solution of potassium permanganate. Cover the beaker with a watch glass, boil for a few seconds and cool.
  Acceptance criteria: NMT 0.1 mg/kg, calculated on the basis of potassium hydroxide determined in the *Assay* (above)

SPECIFIC TESTS
- **CARBONATE (AS K_2CO_3)**
  Analysis: Each mL of 1 N sulfuric acid required between the phenolphthalein and methyl orange endpoints in the *Assay* is equivalent to 138.2 mg of carbonate.
  Acceptance criteria: NMT 3.5%, calculated on the basis of the potassium hydroxide (KOH) determined in the *Assay* (above)

OTHER REQUIREMENTS
- **LABELING:** Indicate the percent of potassium hydroxide.

Potassium Hydroxide

First Published: Prior to FCC 6

Caustic Potash

KOH   Formula wt 56.11
INS: 525   CAS: [1310-58-3]
UNII: WZH3C48M4T [potassium hydroxide]

DESCRIPTION
Potassium Hydroxide occurs as white or nearly white pellets, flakes, sticks, fused masses, or other forms. Upon exposure to air, it readily absorbs carbon dioxide and moisture, and it deliquesces. One g dissolves in 1 mL of water, in about 3 mL of alcohol, and in about 2.5 mL of glycerin. It is very soluble in boiling alcohol.
Function: pH control
Packaging and Storage: Store in tight containers.

IDENTIFICATION
- **POTASSIUM,** Appendix IIIA
  Sample solution: 40 mg/mL
  Acceptance criteria: Passes tests

ASSAY
- **TOTAL ALKALI**
  Sample: 1.5 g

Analysis: Dissolve the *Sample* in 40 mL of recently boiled and cooled water, cool to 15°, and titrate with 1 N sulfuric acid using phenolphthalein TS as the indicator. When the pink color disappears, record the volume of acid required, then add methyl orange TS as the indicator, and continue the titration until a persistent pink color appears. Record the total volume of acid required for the titration. Each mL of the combined amount of 1 N sulfuric acid used is equivalent to 56.11 mg of total alkali, calculated as KOH.
Acceptance criteria: NLT 85.0% and NMT 100.5% of total alkali, calculated as KOH

IMPURITIES
Inorganic Impurities
- **CARBONATE (AS K_2CO_3)**
   Analysis: Each mL of 1 N sulfuric acid required between the phenolphthalein and methyl orange endpoints in the *Assay* (above) is equivalent to 138.2 mg of carbonate.
   Acceptance criteria: NMT 3.5%
- **LEAD,** Lead Limit Test, Appendix IIIB
   Sample solution: Dissolve 1 g of sample in a mixture of 5 mL of water and 11 mL of 2.7 N hydrochloric acid, and cool.
   Control: 2 µg Pb (2 mL of *Diluted Standard Lead Solution*)
   Acceptance criteria: NMT 2 mg/kg
- **MERCURY,** Mercury Limit Test, Method I, Appendix IIIB
   [NOTE—Substitute the following for the *Standard Preparation* and *Sample preparation* given under *Method I*.]
   Standard solution: Prepare the stock solution and the dilutions as directed under *Method I* to obtain a final solution of 1 µg mercury/mL. Transfer 0.5 mL of this solution into a 50 mL beaker and add 20 mL of water, 1 mL of 1:5 sulfuric acid, and 1 mL of a 1:25 solution of potassium permanganate. Cover the beaker with a watch glass, boil for a few seconds and cool.
   Sample solution: Transfer 10.0 g of sample into a 100-mL beaker, dissolve in 15 mL of water, add 2 drops of phenolphthalein TS and, while constantly stirring, slowly neutralize with 1:2 hydrochloric acid. Add 1 mL of 1:5 sulfuric acid and 1 mL of a 1:25 solution of potassium permanganate. Cover the beaker with a watch glass, boil for a few seconds and cool.
   Acceptance criteria: NMT 0.1 mg/kg

SPECIFIC TESTS
- **INSOLUBLE SUBSTANCES**
   Sample solution: 50 mg/mL
   Acceptance criteria: The *Sample solution* is complete, clear, and colorless.

Potassium Iodate
First Published: Prior to FCC 6

KIO_3 Formula wt 214.00
INS: 917 CAS: [7758-05-6]
UNII: I139E44NHL [potassium iodate]

DESCRIPTION
Potassium Iodate occurs as a white, crystalline powder. One g dissolves in about 15 mL of water. It is insoluble in alcohol. The pH of a 1:20 aqueous solution is between 5 and 8.
Function: Maturing agent; oxidizing agent; dough conditioner
Packaging and Storage: Store in well-closed containers.

IDENTIFICATION
- **PROCEDURE**
   Sample solution: 100 mg/mL
   Analysis: Add 1 drop of starch TS and a few drops of 20% hypophosphorous acid to 1 mL of the *Sample solution*.
   Acceptance criteria: A transient blue color appears.

ASSAY
- **PROCEDURE**
   Sample solution: 12 mg/mL (sample previously dried at 105° for 3 h)
   Analysis: Transfer 10.0 mL of the *Sample solution* into a 250-mL glass-stoppered flask, add 40 mL of water, 3 g of potassium iodide, and 10 mL of 3:10 hydrochloric acid, and stopper the flask. Allow to stand for 5 min, add 100 mL of cold water, and titrate the liberated iodine with 0.1 N sodium thiosulfate. Add starch TS near the endpoint. Perform a blank determination (see *General Provisions*), and make any necessary correction. Each mL of 0.1 N sodium thiosulfate is equivalent to 3.567 mg of KIO_3.
   Acceptance criteria: NLT 99.0% and NMT 101.0% of KIO_3, on the dried basis

IMPURITIES
Inorganic Impurities
- **CHLORATE**
   Sample solution: 2 g
   Analysis: Add 2 mL of sulfuric acid to the *Sample solution* contained in a beaker.
   Acceptance criteria: The sample remains white, and no odor or gas evolves (limit about 0.01%).
- **IODIDE**
   Sample solution: 1 g of sample in 10 mL of water
   Analysis: Add 1 mL of 2 N sulfuric acid and 1 drop of starch TS to the *Sample solution*.
   Acceptance criteria: No blue color appears (limit about 0.002%).
- **LEAD,** Lead Limit Test, Flame Atomic Absorption Spectrophotometric Method, Appendix IIIB
   Sample: 10 g
   Acceptance criteria: NMT 4 mg/kg

SPECIFIC TESTS
- **Loss on Drying**, Appendix IIC: 105° for 3 h
  Acceptance criteria: NMT 0.5%

Potassium Iodide
First Published: Prior to FCC 6

KI Formula wt 166.00
CAS: [7681-11-0]
UNII: 1C4QK22F9J [potassium iodide]

DESCRIPTION
Potassium Iodide occurs as hexahedral crystals, either transparent and colorless or somewhat opaque and white, or as a white, granular powder. It is stable in dry air but slightly hygroscopic in moist air. One g is soluble in 0.7 mL of water at 25°, in 0.5 mL of boiling water, in 2 mL of glycerin, and in 22 mL of alcohol.
Function: Nutrient
Packaging and Storage: Store in well-closed containers

IDENTIFICATION
- **Potassium**, Appendix IIIA
  Sample solution: 100 mg/mL
  Acceptance criteria: Passes tests
- **Iodide**, Appendix IIIA
  Sample solution: 100 mg/mL
  Acceptance criteria: Passes tests
- **pH**
  Sample solution: 50 mg/mL
  Acceptance criteria: The pH of the Sample solution is between 6 and 10.

ASSAY
- **Procedure**
  Sample solution: 500 mg, previously dried at 105° for 4 h
  Analysis: Dissolve the Sample in about 10 mL of water, add 35 mL of hydrochloric acid and 5 mL of chloroform. Titrate with 0.05 M potassium iodate until the purple color of iodine disappears from the chloroform. Add the last portions of the 0.05 M potassium iodate solution dropwise, agitating vigorously and continuously. After the chloroform is decolorized, allow the mixture to stand for 5 min. If the chloroform develops a purple color, titrate further with the 0.05 M potassium iodate solution. Each mL of 0.05 M potassium iodate used is equivalent to 16.60 mg of KI.
  Acceptance criteria: NLT 99.0% and NMT 101.5% KI, on the dried basis

IMPURITIES
Inorganic Impurities
- **Iodate**
  Sample: 1.1 g
  Control: Contains, in each 10 mL, 100 mg of potassium iodide, 1 mL of standard iodate solution (prepared by diluting 1 mL of a 1:2500 solution of potassium iodate to 100 mL with water), 1 mL of starch TS, and 0.25 mL of 1 N sulfuric acid
  Analysis: Dissolve the Sample in sufficient ammonia- and carbon dioxide-free water to make 10 mL of solution. Transfer this solution to a color-comparison tube. Add 1 mL of starch TS and 0.25 mL of 1 N sulfuric acid, mix, and compare the color with that of the Control.
  Acceptance criteria: Any color in the solution prepared from the Sample does not exceed that in the Control. (NMT 4 mg/kg).
- **Lead,** Lead Limit Test, Flame Atomic Absorption Spectrophotometric Method, Appendix IIIB
  Sample: 10 g
  Acceptance criteria: NMT 4 mg/kg
- **Nitrate, Nitrite, and Ammonia**
  Sample: 1 g
  Analysis: Dissolve the Sample in 5 mL of water in a 40-mL test tube, add 5 mL of 1 N sodium hydroxide and about 200 mg of aluminum wire. Insert a cotton plug in the upper portion of the tube, and place a piece of moistened red litmus paper over the mouth of the tube. Heat in a steam bath for about 15 min.
  Acceptance criteria: No blue coloration of the paper is discernible.
- **Thiosulfate and Barium**
  Sample: 500 mg
  Analysis: Dissolve the Sample in 10 mL of ammonia- and carbon dioxide-free water and add 2 drops of diluted sulfuric acid.
  Acceptance criteria: No turbidity develops within 1 min.

SPECIFIC TESTS
- **Loss on Drying**, Appendix IIC: 105° for 4 h
  Acceptance criteria: NMT 1%

Potassium Lactate Solution
First Published: Prior to FCC 6

2-Hydroxypropanoic Acid, Monopotassium Salt

$C_3H_5KO_3$ Formula wt 128.17
INS: 326 CAS: [996-31-6]
UNII: 276897E67U [potassium lactate, dl-]

DESCRIPTION
Potassium Lactate Solution occurs as a clear, colorless, or practically colorless, viscous liquid that is odorless or has a slight, not unpleasant, odor. It is miscible with water. It is available in solutions with concentrations ranging from about 50% to 70% by weight.
Function: Emulsifier; flavor enhancer; flavoring agent or adjuvant; humectant; pH control agent
Packaging and Storage: Store in tight containers.

IDENTIFICATION
- **LACTATE,** Appendix IIIA
  Acceptance criteria: Passes test
- **POTASSIUM,** Appendix IIIA
  Acceptance criteria: Passes test

ASSAY
- **PROCEDURE**
  Sample: Amount equivalent to 500 mg of potassium lactate
  Analysis: Transfer the *Sample* into a suitable flask, add 60 mL of 1:5 acetic anhydride:glacial acetic acid, mix, and allow to stand for 20 min. Titrate with 0.1 N perchloric acid in glacial acetic acid, determining the endpoint potentiometrically.
  [**CAUTION**—Handle perchloric acid in an appropriate fume hood.] Perform a blank determination (see *General Provisions*), and make any necessary correction. Each mL of 0.1 N perchloric acid is equivalent to 12.82 mg of $C_3H_5KO_3$.
  Acceptance criteria: NLT 50.0%, by weight, and NLT 98.0% and NMT 102.0%, by weight, of the labeled amount of $C_3H_5KO_3$

IMPURITIES
Inorganic Impurities
- **CHLORIDE,** *Chloride and Sulfate Limit Tests, Chloride Limit Test,* Appendix IIIB
  Sample: Amount containing the equivalent of 40 mg of potassium lactate
  Control: 20 µg chloride (2 mL of *Standard Chloride Solution*)
  Acceptance criteria: Any turbidity produced does by the *Sample* not exceed that shown in the *Control* (NMT 0.05%).

- **CYANIDE**
  [**CAUTION**—Because of the extremely poisonous nature of potassium cyanide, conduct this test in a fume hood, and exercise great care to prevent skin contact and the inhalation of particles or vapors of solutions of the material. Under no conditions pipet solutions by mouth.]
  Solution A: Dissolve 200 mg of *p*-phenylenediamine hydrochloride in 100 mL of water, warming to aid dissolution. Cool, allow the solids to settle, and save the supernatant liquid to make the *Solution B*.
  Solution B: Dissolve 128 mL of pyridine in 365 mL of water, add 10 mL of hydrochloric acid, and mix. To this solution add 30 mL of the supernatant of *Solution A* and allow to stand for 24 h before using. This solution is stable for about 3 weeks when stored in an amber bottle.
  Standard stock solution: 2.5 mg/mL potassium cyanide in 0.1 N sodium hydroxide made to 100 mL
  Standard solution: 25 µg/mL potassium cyanide in 0.1 N sodium hydroxide made from *Standard stock solution* [NOTE—Each mL of this solution contains 10 µg of cyanide.]
  Sample solution: Transfer a quantity of sample equivalent to 20.0 g of potassium lactate into a 100-mL volumetric flask, dilute to volume with water, and mix.
  Analysis: Pipet a 10-mL aliquot of the *Sample solution* into a 50-mL beaker. Pipet 0.1 mL of the *Standard solution* into a second 50-mL beaker, and add 10 mL of water. Place the beakers in an ice bath, and adjust the pH to between 9 and 10 with 20% sodium hydroxide, stirring slowly and adding the reagent slowly to avoid overheating. Allow the solutions to stand for 3 min, and then slowly add 10% phosphoric acid to reach a pH between 5 and 6, measured with a pH meter. Transfer the solutions into 100-mL separatory funnels each containing 25 mL of cold water, and rinse the beakers and pH meter electrodes with a few mL of cold water, collecting the washings in the respective separatory funnel. To each funnel add 2 mL of bromine TS, stopper, and mix. Add 2 mL of 2% sodium arsenite solution, stopper, and mix. Add 10 mL of *n*-butanol to the clear solutions, stopper, and mix. Finally, add 5 mL of *Solution B*, mix, and allow to stand for 15 min. Remove and discard the aqueous phases, and filter the alcoholic phases into 1-cm spectrophotometry cells. Using a suitable spectrophotometer, determine the absorbances at 480 nm of the solutions from the *Sample solution*, and the *Standard solution*.
  Acceptance criteria: The absorbance of the solution from the *Sample solution* does not exceed that from the *Standard solution*. (NMT 0.5 mg/kg)

- **LEAD,** *Lead Limit Test, Flame Atomic Absorption Spectrophotometric Method,* Appendix IIIB
  Sample: 5 g
  Acceptance criteria: NMT 2 mg/kg

- **SODIUM**
  Potassium chloride solution: 100 mg/mL, made to 1000 mL
  Standard stock solution: Transfer 127.1 mg of sodium chloride, previously dried at 105° for 2 h, into a 500-mL volumetric flask, dilute to volume with water, and mix. Transfer 10.0 mL of this solution to a 100-mL volumetric flask, dilute to volume with water, and mix to obtain a solution containing 10 µg of sodium per mL.
  Standard solutions: Pipet 1, 2, 5, and 10 mL aliquots of the *Standard stock solution* into separate 100 mL volumetric flasks. Add 1.0 mL of *Potassium chloride solution* followed by 1.0 mL of nitric acid to each flask; dilute to volume with water; and mix to obtain *Standard solutions* containing 0.1, 0.2, 0.5, and 1.0 µg/mL of sodium, respectively.
  Sample solution: Transfer a quantity of sample equivalent to 4 g of potassium lactate into a 50-mL flask, dilute to volume with water, and mix. Pipet 1 mL of this solution into a 100-mL volumetric flask, add 1.0 mL of *Potassium chloride solution* followed by 1.0 mL of nitric acid, dilute to volume with water, and mix.
  Blank solution: Transfer 1.0 mL of *Potassium chloride solution* into a 100-mL volumetric flask, add 1.0 mL of nitric acid, dilute to volume with water, and mix.
  Analysis: Use a suitable atomic absorption spectrophotometer equipped with a sodium hollow-cathode lamp and an oxidizing air–acetylene flame. After using the *Blank solution* to zero the instrument,

concomitantly determine the absorbances of the *Standard solutions* and the *Sample solution* at the sodium emission line of 589 nm. Plot the absorbances of the *Standard solutions* versus concentration, in µg/mL, of sodium, and draw the straight line that best fits the plotted points. From the graph so obtained, determine the concentration, C, in µg/mL, of sodium in the *Sample solution*. Calculate the percentage of sodium in the portion of potassium lactate taken by the formula:

$$\text{Result} = CD/10{,}000W$$

C = concentration (µg/mL) of sodium in the *Sample solution*
D = dilution factor for the *Sample solution*
W = quantity (g) of potassium lactate taken to prepare the *Sample solution*

Acceptance criteria: NMT 0.1%

- **Sulfate,** *Chloride and Sulfate Limit Tests, Chloride Limit Test,* Appendix IIIB
  Sample: Amount containing the equivalent of 4.0 g of potassium lactate
  Control: 200 µg of sulfate (20 mL of *Standard Sulfate Solution*)
  Acceptance criteria: Any turbidity produced does not exceed that shown in the control (NMT 0.005%).

Organic Impurities
- **Methanol and Methyl Esters**
  Solution A: Dissolve 3 g of potassium permanganate in a mixture of 15 mL of phosphoric acid and 70 mL of water. Dilute to 100 mL with water.
  Solution B: Cautiously add 50 mL of sulfuric acid to 50 mL of water, mix, cool, add 5 g of oxalic acid, and mix to dissolve.
  Standard solution: Transfer 10.0 mg of methanol to a 100-mL volumetric flask, dilute to volume with a 1:10 mixture of ethanol:water, and mix.
  Sample solution: Transfer 40.0 g of sample into a glass-stoppered, round-bottom flask, add 10 mL of water, and cautiously add 30 mL of 5 N potassium hydroxide. Connect a condenser to the flask, and steam-distill, collecting the distillate in a suitable 100-mL graduated vessel containing 10 mL of ethanol. Continue the distillation until the volume in the receiver reaches approximately 95 mL, and dilute the distillate to 100.0 mL with water.
  Analysis: Transfer 10.0 mL each of the *Standard solution* and the *Sample solution* to 25-mL volumetric flasks. Add 5.0 mL of *Solution A* to each, and mix. After 15 min, add 2.0 mL of *Solution B* to each, stir with a glass rod until the solutions are colorless, add 5.0 mL of fuchsin-sulfurous acid TS, dilute to volume with water, and mix. After 2 h, using a suitable spectrophotometer, concomitantly determine the absorbances of both solutions in 1-cm cells at the wavelength of maximum absorbance (about 575 nm); use water as the blank.
  Acceptance criteria: The absorbance of the solution from the *Sample solution* does not exceed that from the *Standard solution*. (NMT 0.025%)

- **Sugars**
  Analysis: Add 5 drops of sample to 10 mL of hot alkaline cupric tartrate TS.
  Acceptance criteria: No red precipitate forms.

SPECIFIC TESTS
- **Citrate, Oxalate, Phosphate, or Tartrate**
  Sample: 5 mL
  Analysis: Dilute the *Sample* to 50 mL with recently boiled and cooled water. Take 4 mL of this solution and, if necessary, adjust the pH to between 7.3 and 7.7 with addition of 6 N ammonia solution or 3 N hydrochloric acid. Add 1 mL of calcium chloride TS, and heat in a boiling water bath for 5 min.
  Acceptance criteria: The solution remains clear.
- **pH,** *pH Determination,* Appendix IIB
  Acceptance criteria: Between 5.0 and 9.0

OTHER REQUIREMENTS
- **Labeling:** Indicate its content, by weight, of Potassium Lactate ($C_3H_5KO_3$).

Potassium Metabisulfite

First Published: Prior to FCC 6
Last Revision: Second Supplement, FCC 6

Potassium Pyrosulfite

$K_2S_2O_5$ Formula wt 222.31
INS: 224   CAS: [16731-55-8]
UNII: 65OE787Q7W [potassium metabisulfite]

DESCRIPTION
Potassium Metabisulfite occurs as white or colorless, free-flowing crystals, as a crystalline powder, or as granules. It gradually oxidizes in air to the sulfate. It is soluble in water, but it is insoluble in alcohol. Its solutions are acid to litmus.
Function: Preservative; antioxidant; bleaching agent
Packaging and Storage: Store in well-filled, tight containers, and avoid exposure to excessive heat.

IDENTIFICATION
- **Potassium,** Appendix IIIA
  Sample solution: 100 mg/mL
  Acceptance criteria: Passes tests
- **Sulfite,** Appendix IIIA
  Sample solution: 100 mg/mL
  Acceptance criteria: Passes test

ASSAY
- **Procedure**
  Sample: 250 mg
  Analysis: Add the *Sample* to 50 mL of 0.1 N iodine contained in a glass-stoppered flask. Allow to stand for 5 min, add 1 mL of hydrochloric acid, and back-titrate the excess iodine with 0.1 N sodium thiosulfate, using starch TS as the indicator. The mL of iodine consumed are equivalent to 50 minus the mL of 0.1 N sodium thiosulfate used. Each mL of 0.1 N iodine consumed is equivalent to 5.558 mg of $K_2S_2O_5$.

Acceptance criteria: NLT 90.0% of K$_2$S$_2$O$_5$

IMPURITIES
Inorganic Impurities
- **Iron**
  Sample: 1 g
  Control: 10 µg Fe (1.0 mL of *Iron Standard Solution*, *Standard Solutions for the Preparation of Controls and Standards*, Solutions and Indicators)
  Analysis: Add 2 mL of hydrochloric acid to the *Sample*, and evaporate to dryness on a steam bath. Dissolve the residue in 2 mL of hydrochloric acid and 20 mL of water, add a few drops of bromine TS, and boil the solution to remove the bromine. Cool, dilute with water to 25 mL, then add 50 mg of ammonium persulfate and 5 mL of ammonium thiocyanate TS. Repeat the preceding using the *Control*.
  Acceptance criteria: Any red or pink color produced by the *Sample* does not exceed that produced by the *Control*. (NMT 10 mg/kg)
- **Lead**, *Lead Limit Test, Flame Atomic Absorption Spectrophotometric Method*, Appendix IIIB
  Sample: 10 g
  Acceptance criteria: NMT 2 mg/kg
- **Selenium**, *Selenium Limit Test, Method I*, Appendix IIIB
  Sample: 600 mg of sample and 600 mg of magnesium oxide for the combustion step under *Sample Preparation*
  Acceptance criteria: The absorbance of the extract from the *Sample Preparation* is NMT one-half the absorbance of the extract from the *Standard Preparation*. (NMT 5 mg/kg)

Potassium Nitrate

First Published: Prior to FCC 6
Last Revision: Third Supplement, FCC 7

KNO$_3$ Formula wt 101.10
INS: 252   CAS: [7757-79-1]
UNII: RU45X2JN0Z [potassium nitrate]

DESCRIPTION
Potassium Nitrate occurs as colorless, transparent prisms, as white granules, or as a white, crystalline powder. It is slightly hygroscopic in moist air. One g dissolves in 3 mL of water at 25°, in 0.5 mL of boiling water, and in about 620 mL of alcohol. Its solutions are neutral to litmus.
Function: Antimicrobial agent; preservative
Packaging and Storage: Store in tight containers.

IDENTIFICATION
- **Nitrate**, Appendix IIIA
  Sample solution: 100 mg/mL
  Acceptance criteria: Passes tests
- **Potassium**, Appendix IIIA
  Sample solution: 100 mg/mL
  Acceptance criteria: Passes tests

ASSAY
- **Procedure**
  Sample: 0.4 g, previously dried at 105° for 4 h
  Analysis: Weigh the *Sample* into a 250-mL iodine flask. Add 10 mL of hydrochloric acid to dissolve the *Sample*, then evaporate to dryness on a steam bath. Dissolve the residue in 10 mL of hydrochloric acid, and again evaporate to dryness. After evaporating to dryness the second time, heat the flask on a hot plate at a medium to high setting for 1 h. Allow the flask to cool to room temperature, then dissolve the residue in 25 mL of water. Add, separately, to the flask 50.0 mL of 0.1 N silver nitrate, 3 mL of nitric acid, and 10 mL of nitrobenzene, then stopper the flask and shake it vigorously. [**Caution**—Nitrobenzene is highly flammable and is a poison that can cause cyanosis. Handle with caution, and avoid inhaling or contact with skin.] Sonicate the contents of the flask for 5 min. Remove the flask from the sonicator, and add 3 mL of ferric ammonium sulfate TS as the indicator. Titrate the excess silver nitrate in the solution with 0.1 N ammonium thiocyanate to the first appearance of a reddish-brown color. Calculate the percentage of potassium nitrate in the sample taken:

  $$\text{Result} = [(V \times N) - (V_T \times N_T)] \times (F/W)$$

  V = volume of 0.1 N silver nitrate added to the flask (50 mL)
  N = exact normality of the 0.1 N silver nitrate used (mol/L)
  V_T = volume of 0.1 N ammonium thiocyanate used to titrate the solution (mL)
  N_T = exact normality of the 0.1 N ammonium thiocyanate used (mol/L)
  F = factor representing the amount of potassium nitrate, in mg, equivalent to 1 mL of 0.1 N silver nitrate (10.11)
  W = quantity of the *Sample* (g)

  Acceptance criteria: 99.0%–100.5% of KNO$_3$ on the dried basis

IMPURITIES
Inorganic Impurities
- **Chlorate**
  Sample: 100 mg
  Analysis: Sprinkle the dried *Sample* on 1 mL of sulfuric acid.
  Acceptance criteria: The mixture does not turn yellow.
- **Lead**, *Lead Limit Test*, Appendix IIIB
  Sample solution: 100 mg/mL made to 10 mL
  Control: 4 µg of Pb (4 mL of *Diluted Standard Lead Solution*)
  Acceptance criteria: NMT 4 mg/kg

SPECIFIC TESTS
- **Loss on Drying**, Appendix IIC: 105° for 4 h
  Acceptance criteria: NMT 1%

Potassium Nitrite

First Published: Prior to FCC 6

KNO$_2$
INS: 249
UNII: 794654G42L [potassium nitrite]
Formula wt 85.10
CAS: [7758-09-0]

DESCRIPTION
Potassium Nitrite occurs as small, white or yellow, deliquescent granules or cylindrical sticks. It is very soluble in water, but is sparingly soluble in alcohol.
Function: Color fixative in meat and meat products; antimicrobial agent
Packaging and Storage: Store in tight containers.

IDENTIFICATION
- **ALKALINITY**
  Sample solution: 100 mg/mL
  Analysis: Expose sample to litmus.
  Acceptance criteria: Sample is alkaline.
- **NITRITE**, Appendix IIIA
  Sample solution: 100 mg/mL
  Acceptance criteria: Passes tests
- **POTASSIUM**, Appendix IIIA
  Sample solution: 100 mg/mL
  Acceptance criteria: Passes tests

ASSAY
- **PROCEDURE**
  Sample solution: 12 mg/mL, made to 100 mL
  Analysis: Pipet 10 mL of the *Sample solution* into a mixture of 50.0 mL of 0.1 N potassium permanganate, 100 mL of water, and 5 mL of sulfuric acid, keeping the tip of the pipet well below the surface of the liquid. Warm the solution to 40°, allow it to stand for 5 min, and add 25.0 mL of 0.1 N oxalic acid. Heat the mixture to about 80°, and titrate with 0.1 N potassium permanganate. Each mL of 0.1 N potassium permanganate is equivalent to 4.255 mg of KNO$_2$.
  Acceptance criteria: NLT 90.0% and NMT 100.5% of KNO$_2$

IMPURITIES
Inorganic Impurities
- **LEAD**, *Lead Limit Test,* Appendix IIIB
  Sample solution: 1 g of sample in 10 mL of water
  Control: 4 μg Pb (4 mL of *Diluted Standard Lead Solution*)
  Acceptance criteria: NMT 4 mg/kg

Potassium Phosphate, Dibasic

First Published: Prior to FCC 6
Last Revision: First Supplement, FCC 7

Dipotassium Monophosphate
Dipotassium Phosphate

K$_2$HPO$_4$
INS: 340(ii)
Formula wt 174.18
CAS: [7758-11-4]
UNII: CI71S98N1Z [potassium phosphate, dibasic]

DESCRIPTION
Potassium Phosphate, Dibasic, occurs as a colorless or white, granular salt that is deliquescent when exposed to moist air. One g is soluble in about 3 mL of water. It is insoluble in alcohol. The pH of a 1% solution is about 9.
Function: Buffer; sequestrant; yeast food
Packaging and Storage: Store in tight containers.

IDENTIFICATION
- **PHOSPHATE**, Appendix IIIA
  Sample solution: 50 mg/mL
  Acceptance criteria: Passes tests
- **POTASSIUM**, Appendix IIIA
  Sample solution: 50 mg/mL
  Acceptance criteria: Passes tests

ASSAY
- **PROCEDURE**
  Sample: 6.5 g, previously dried
  Analysis: Transfer the *Sample* into a 250-mL beaker. Add 50.0 mL of 1 N hydrochloric acid and 50.0 mL of water, and stir until the sample is completely dissolved. Place the electrodes of a suitable pH meter in the solution and, stirring constantly, slowly titrate the excess acid with 1 N sodium hydroxide to the inflection point occurring at about pH 4. Record the buret reading, and calculate the volume (A), if any, of 1 N hydrochloric acid consumed by the sample:

$$A = 50 - x$$

  x = volume of 1 N sodium hydroxide used in the titration (mL)

  Continue the titration with 1 N sodium hydroxide until the inflection point occurring at about pH 8.8 is reached, record the buret reading, and calculate the volume (B) of 1 N sodium hydroxide required in the titration between the two inflection points (pH 4 to pH 8.8). When A is equal to or less than B, each mL of the volume A of 1 N hydrochloric acid is equivalent to 174.2 mg of K$_2$HPO$_4$. When A is greater than B, each mL of the volume 2B − A of 1 N sodium hydroxide is equivalent to 174.2 mg of K$_2$HPO$_4$.
  Acceptance criteria: NLT 98.0% of K$_2$HPO$_4$, on the dried basis

IMPURITIES
Inorganic Impurities
- **ARSENIC**, *Arsenic Limit Test,* Appendix IIIB
  Sample solution: 1 g in 10 mL
  Acceptance criteria: NMT 3 mg/kg
- **FLUORIDE**, *Fluoride Limit Test, Method IV,* Appendix IIIB
  Sample: 2 g
  Acceptance criteria: NMT 10 mg/kg
- **LEAD**, *Lead Limit Test, APDC Extraction Method,* Appendix IIIB
  Acceptance criteria: NMT 2 mg/kg

SPECIFIC TESTS
- **INSOLUBLE SUBSTANCES**
  Sample: 10 g

944 / Potassium Phosphate, Dibasic / *Monographs*

Analysis: Dissolve the *Sample* in 100 mL of hot water and filter through a tared filtering crucible. Wash the insoluble residue with hot water, dry it at 105° for 2 h, cool, and weigh.
Acceptance criteria: NMT 0.2%
- **Loss on Drying,** Appendix IIC: 105° for 4 h
Acceptance criteria: NMT 2.0%

Potassium Phosphate, Monobasic

First Published: Prior to FCC 6
Last Revision: First Supplement, FCC 7

Potassium Biphosphate
Potassium Dihydrogen Phosphate
Monopotassium Phosphate

KH_2PO_4 Formula wt 136.09
INS: 340(i)   CAS: [7778-77-0]
UNII: 4J9FJ0HL51 [potassium phosphate, monobasic]

DESCRIPTION
Potassium Phosphate, Monobasic, occurs as colorless crystals or as a white, granular or crystalline powder. It is stable in air. It is freely soluble in water, but is insoluble in alcohol. The pH of a 1:100 aqueous solution is between 4.2 and 4.7.
Function: Buffer; sequestrant; yeast food
Packaging and Storage: Store in tight containers.

IDENTIFICATION
- **Phosphate,** Appendix IIIA
  Sample solution: 50 mg/mL
  Acceptance criteria: Passes tests
- **Potassium,** Appendix IIIA
  Sample solution: 50 mg/mL
  Acceptance criteria: Passes tests

ASSAY
- **Procedure**
  Sample: 5 g, previously dried
  Analysis: Transfer the *Sample* into a 250-mL beaker. Add 5.0 mL of 1 N hydrochloric acid and 100 mL of water, and stir until the sample is completely dissolved. Place the electrodes of a suitable pH meter in the solution, and, stirring constantly, slowly titrate the excess acid with 1 N sodium hydroxide to the inflection point occurring at about pH 4. Record the buret reading, and calculate the volume (A), if any, of 1 N hydrochloric acid consumed by the sample:

$$A = 5 - x$$

x   = volume of 1 N sodium hydroxide used in the titration (mL)

Continue the titration with 1 N sodium hydroxide until the inflection point occurring at about pH 8.8 is reached, record the buret reading, and calculate the volume (B) of 1 N sodium hydroxide required in the titration between the two inflection points (pH 4 to pH 8.8). Each mL of the volume (B − A) of 1 N sodium hydroxide is equivalent to 136.1 mg of KH_2PO_4.
Acceptance criteria: NLT 98.0% of KH_2PO_4, on the dried basis

IMPURITIES
Inorganic Impurities
- **Arsenic,** *Arsenic Limit Test,* Appendix IIIB
  Sample solution: 1 g in 10 mL
  Acceptance criteria: NMT 3 mg/kg
- **Fluoride,** *Fluoride Limit Test, Method IV,* Appendix IIIB
  Sample: 2 g
  Acceptance criteria: NMT 10 mg/kg
- **Lead,** *Lead Limit Test, APDC Extraction Method,* Appendix IIIB
  Acceptance criteria: NMT 2 mg/kg

SPECIFIC TESTS
- **Insoluble Substances**
  Sample: 10 g
  Analysis: Dissolve the *Sample* in 100 mL of hot water, and filter through a tared filtering crucible. Wash the insoluble residue with hot water, dry it at 105° for 2 h, cool, and weigh.
  Acceptance criteria: NMT 0.2%
- **Loss on Drying,** Appendix IIC: 105° for 4 h
  Acceptance criteria: NMT 1.0%

Potassium Phosphate, Tribasic

First Published: Prior to FCC 6
Last Revision: First Supplement, FCC 7

Tripotassium Phosphate

K_3PO_4 Formula wt 212.27
INS: 340(iii)   CAS: [7778-53-2]
UNII: 16D59922JU [potassium phosphate, tribasic]

DESCRIPTION
Potassium Phosphate, Tribasic occurs as white, hygroscopic crystals or granules. It is anhydrous or may contain one molecule of water of hydration. It is freely soluble in water, but is insoluble in alcohol. The pH of a 1:100 aqueous solution is about 11.5.
Function: Emulsifier
Packaging and Storage: Store in tight containers.

IDENTIFICATION
- **Phosphate,** Appendix IIIA
  Sample solution: 50 mg/mL
  Acceptance criteria: Passes test
- **Potassium,** Appendix IIIA
  Sample solution: 50 mg/mL
  Acceptance criteria: Passes test

ASSAY
- **Procedure**
  Sample: Quantity equivalent to 8 g of anhydrous K_3PO_4
  Analysis: Dissolve the *Sample* in 40 mL of water in a 400-mL beaker, and add 100.0 mL of 1 N hydrochloric

acid. Pass a stream of fine bubbles of carbon dioxide-free air through the solution for 30 min to expel carbon dioxide, covering the beaker loosely to prevent any loss by spraying. Wash the cover and sides of the beaker with a few mL of water, and place the electrodes of a suitable pH meter in the solution. Protect the solution from absorbing carbon dioxide. Titrate the solution with 1 N sodium hydroxide until the inflection point occurs at about pH 4, and then calculate the volume (A) of 1 N hydrochloric acid consumed:

$$A = 100 - x$$

x = volume of 1 N sodium hydroxide used in the titration (mL)

Continue the titration with 1 N sodium hydroxide until the inflection point occurs at about pH 8.8. Calculate the volume (B) of 1 N sodium hydroxide consumed in this titration. When A is equal to or greater than 2B, each mL of the volume B of 1 N sodium hydroxide is equivalent to 212.3 mg of K_3PO_4. When A is less than 2B, each mL of the volume A − B of 1 N sodium hydroxide is equivalent to 212.3 mg of K_3PO_4.

Acceptance criteria: NLT 97.0% of K_3PO_4, calculated on the ignited basis

IMPURITIES
Inorganic Impurities
- **ARSENIC**, *Arsenic Limit Test*, Appendix IIIB
  Sample solution: 1 g in 10 mL of water
  Acceptance criteria: NMT 3 mg/kg
- **FLUORIDE**, *Fluoride Limit Test, Method IV*, Appendix IIIB
  Sample: 2 g
  Acceptance criteria: NMT 10 mg/kg
- **LEAD**, *Lead Limit Test, APDC Extraction Method*, Appendix IIIB
  Sample: 10 g
  Acceptance criteria: NMT 2 mg/kg

SPECIFIC TESTS
- **INSOLUBLE SUBSTANCES**
  Sample: 10 g
  Analysis: Dissolve the *Sample* in 100 mL of hot water, and filter through a tared filtering crucible. Wash the insoluble residue with hot water, dry at 105° for 2 h, cool, and weigh.
  Acceptance criteria: NMT 0.2%
- **LOSS ON IGNITION**
  Analysis: Ignite a sample at 800° for 30 min using a platinum, quartz, or porcelain dish instead of the weighing bottle.
  Acceptance criteria
  Anhydrous: NMT 5.0%
  Monohydrate: Between 8% and 20.0%

Potassium Polymetaphosphate
First Published: Prior to FCC 6

Potassium Metaphosphate
Potassium Polyphosphates
Potassium Kurrol's Salt

$(KPO_3)_n$
INS: 452(ii) CAS: [7790-53-6]
UNII: 01DMT14Z63 [potassium metaphosphate]

DESCRIPTION
Potassium Polymetaphosphate occurs as a white powder. It is a straight-chain polyphosphate having a high degree of polymerization. It is insoluble in water, but is soluble in dilute solutions of sodium salts.
Function: Emulsifier; moisture-retaining agent
Packaging and Storage: Store in well-closed containers.

IDENTIFICATION
- **A. PROCEDURE**
  Sample: 1 g, finely powdered
  Analysis: While stirring vigorously, add the *Sample* slowly to 100 mL of a 20 mg/mL sodium chloride solution.
  Acceptance criteria: A gelatinous mass forms.
- **B. PHOSPHATE**, Appendix IIIA
  Sample solution: Mix 500 mg of sample with 10 mL of nitric acid and 50 mL of water, boil for about 30 min, and cool.
  Acceptance criteria: Passes tests
- **C. POTASSIUM**, Appendix IIIA
  Sample solution: Mix 500 mg of sample with 10 mL of nitric acid and 50 mL of water, boil for about 30 min, and cool.
  Acceptance criteria: Passes tests

ASSAY
- **PROCEDURE**
  Sample: 1 g
  Analysis: Transfer the *Sample* into a 400-mL beaker, add 100 mL of water and 25 mL of nitric acid, cover the beaker with a watch glass, and boil the solution for 10 min on a hot plate. Rinse any condensate on the watch glass into the beaker, cool the solution to room temperature, transfer it quantitatively to a 500-mL volumetric flask, dilute to volume with water, and mix thoroughly. Pipet 20.0 mL of this solution into a 500-mL Erlenmeyer flask, add 100 mL of water, and heat just to boiling. While stirring, add 50 mL of quimociac TS, then cover with a watch glass, and boil for 1 min in a well-ventilated hood. Cool to room temperature, swirling occasionally while cooling, then filter through a tared, sintered-glass crucible of medium porosity, and wash with five 25-mL portions of water. Dry at about 225° for 30 min, cool, and weigh. Each mg of precipitate thus obtained is equivalent to 32.074 μg of P_2O_5.
  Acceptance criteria: NLT 59.0% and NMT 61.0% of P_2O_5

IMPURITIES
Inorganic Impurities
- **ARSENIC**, *Arsenic Limit Test,* Appendix IIIB
  Sample solution: 1 g of sample in 15 mL of 2.7 N hydrochloric acid
  Acceptance criteria: NMT 3 mg/kg
- **FLUORIDE**
  Sample: 5 g
  Sample distillate: Place the *Sample*, 25 mL of water, 50 mL of sulfuric acid, 5 drops of a 1:2 silver nitrate solution, and a few glass beads in a 250-mL distilling flask connected to a condenser and carrying a thermometer and a capillary tube, both of which must extend into the liquid. Connect a small dropping funnel, filled with water, or a steam generator to the capillary tube. Support the flask on a fireproof mat with a hole that exposes about one-third of the flask to the flame. Distill the mixture into a 250-mL volumetric flask until the temperature reaches 135°. Add water from the funnel or introduce steam through the capillary tube to maintain the temperature between 135° and 140°. Continue the distillation until 225 to 240 mL has been collected, then dilute to 250 mL with water, and mix.
  Analysis: Place a 50-mL aliquot of the *Sample distillate* in a 100-mL Nessler tube. In another, similar Nessler tube, place 50 mL of water as a control. Add 0.1 mL of a filtered solution of 1:1000 sodium alizarinsulfonate and 1 mL of a freshly prepared 1:4000 hydroxylamine hydrochloride solution to each tube, and mix well. While stirring, add, dropwise, 0.05 N sodium hydroxide to the tube containing the *Sample distillate* until its color just matches that of the control, which is faintly pink. Then add exactly 1.0 mL of 0.1 N hydrochloric acid to each tube, and mix well. Use a buret, graduated in 0.05-mL units, to add slowly enough of a 1:4000 thorium nitrate solution to the tube containing the *Sample distillate* so that after mixing, the color of the liquid just changes to a faint pink. Note the volume of the solution added, and mix exactly the same volume to the control. Use a buret to add sodium fluoride TS (10 μg/mL fluoride) to the control until the color of the solution in the control tube matches that of the solution in the tube containing the *Sample distillate*. Mix well, and allow all air bubbles to escape before making the final color comparison. Check the endpoint by adding 1 or 2 drops of sodium fluoride TS to the control. A distinct color change should take place. Note the volume of sodium fluoride TS added to the control solution.
  Acceptance criteria: The volume of sodium fluoride TS added to the control solution does not exceed 1.0 mL (NMT 10 mg/kg).
- **LEAD**, *Lead Limit Test*, Lead Limit Test, APDC Extraction Method, Appendix IIIB
  Acceptance criteria: NMT 2 mg/kg

SPECIFIC TESTS
- **VISCOSITY**
  Sample: 300 mg
  Tetrasodium pyrophosphate solution: 3.5 g of tetrasodium pyrophosphate in 1000 mL of water
  Analysis: Using a magnetic stirrer, dissolve the *Sample* in 200 mL of *Tetrasodium pyrophosphate solution*. When dissolution is complete, or after 30 min (whichever occurs first), transfer 10 mL of the solution into an Ostwald-Fenske viscometer, and determine the time, T, in seconds, required for the liquid to flow from the upper to the lower mark in the capillary tube. Calculate the viscosity, in centipoises (cP), by the formula:

  $$\text{Result} = Tv/dt$$

  T = time, in seconds, required for the *Sample solution* to flow from the upper to lower mark of the capillary tube
  t = time, in seconds, required for a glycerin-water mixture of known viscosity, and specific gravity to flow from the upper to the lower mark of the capillary tube during calibration of the viscometer under similar conditions
  v = viscosity of the glycerin-water mixture used during calibration in centipoises (cP)
  d = Specific gravity of the glycerin-water mixture used during calibration
  Acceptance criteria: Between 6.5 and 15 centipoises

Potassium Pyrophosphate

First Published: Prior to FCC 6

Tetrapotassium Pyrophosphate

$K_4P_2O_7$ Formula wt 330.34
INS: 450v   CAS: [7320-34-5]
UNII: B9W4019H5G [potassium pyrophosphate]

DESCRIPTION
Potassium Pyrophosphate occurs as colorless or white crystals or as a white, crystalline or granular powder. It is hygroscopic. It is very soluble in water, but is insoluble in alcohol. The pH of a 1:100 aqueous solution is about 10.5.
Function: Emulsifier; texturizer
Packaging and Storage: Store in tight containers.

IDENTIFICATION
- **A. POTASSIUM,** Appendix IIIA
  Sample solution: 50 mg/mL
  Acceptance criteria: Passes tests
- **B. PROCEDURE**
  Sample solution: 100 mg in 100 mL of 1.7 N nitric acid
  Analysis 1: Add 0.5 mL of the *Sample solution* to 30 mL of quimociac TS and note any precipitate formed.
  Analysis 2: Heat the remaining *Sample solution* for 10 min at 95°, add 0.5 mL of it to 30 mL of quimociac TS, and note any precipitate formed.
  Acceptance criteria: A yellow precipitate does not form for *Analysis 1*, but forms immediately for *Analysis 2*.

ASSAY
- **PROCEDURE**
  Zinc sulfate solution: 125 g of $ZnSO_4 \cdot 7H_2O$ dissolved in water, diluted to 1000 mL, filtered, and adjusted to pH 3.8 with hydrochloric acid
  Sample: 600 mg
  Analysis: Dissolve the *Sample* in 100 mL of water contained in a 400-mL beaker and, using a pH meter, adjust the pH of the solution to exactly 3.8 with hydrochloric acid. Add 50 mL of *Zinc sulfate solution* and allow the mixture to stand for 2 min. Titrate the liberated acid with 0.1 N sodium hydroxide until a pH of 3.8 is again reached. After each addition of sodium hydroxide near the endpoint, allow time for any precipitated zinc hydroxide to redissolve. Each mL of 0.1 N sodium hydroxide is equivalent to 16.52 mg of $K_4P_2O_7$.
  Acceptance criteria: NLT 95.0% of $K_4P_2O_7$, calculated on the ignited basis

IMPURITIES
Inorganic Impurities
- **ARSENIC,** *Arsenic Limit Test,* Appendix IIIB
  Sample solution: 1 g in 35 mL
  Acceptance criteria: NMT 3 mg/kg
- **FLUORIDE,** *Fluoride Limit Test, Method IV,* Appendix IIIB
  Sample: 2 g
  Acceptance criteria: NMT 10 mg/kg
- **LEAD,** *Lead Limit Test, APDC Extraction Method,* Appendix IIIB
  Acceptance criteria: NMT 2 mg/kg

SPECIFIC TESTS
- **INSOLUBLE SUBSTANCES**
  Sample: 10 g
  Analysis: Dissolve the *Sample* in 100 mL of hot water and filter through a tared filtering crucible. Wash the insoluble residue with hot water, dry it at 105° for 2 h, cool, and weigh.
  Acceptance criteria: NMT 0.1%
- **LOSS ON IGNITION**
  Analysis: Ignite a sample at 800° for 30 min.
  Acceptance criteria: NMT 0.5%

Potassium Sorbate

First Published: Prior to FCC 6

2,4-Hexadienoic Acid, Potassium Salt

$C_6H_7KO_2$ Formula weight 150.22
INS: 202 CAS: [590-00-1]
UNII: 1VPU26JZZ4 [potassium sorbate]

DESCRIPTION
Potassium Sorbate occurs as white to off-white crystals, crystalline powder, or pellets. It decomposes at about 270°.

Function: Antimicrobial agent; preservative
Packaging and Storage: Store in tight containers.

IDENTIFICATION
- **A. POTASSIUM,** Appendix IIIA
  Sample solution: 100 mg/mL
  Acceptance criteria: The *Sample solution* responds to the flame test.
- **B. PROCEDURE**
  Sample solution: 100 mg/mL
  Analysis: Add a few drops of bromine TS to 2 mL of the *Sample solution*.
  Acceptance criteria: The color disappears.

ASSAY
- **PROCEDURE**
  Sample: 250 mg
  Analysis: Dissolve the *Sample* in 40 mL of glacial acetic acid contained in a 250-mL glass-stoppered Erlenmeyer flask, warming if necessary to aid in dissolution. Cool to room temperature, add 2 drops of crystal violet TS, and titrate with 0.1 N perchloric acid in glacial acetic acid to a blue-green endpoint that persists for at least 30 s. [**CAUTION**—Handle perchloric acid in an appropriate fume hood.] Perform a blank determination (see *General Provisions*) and make any necessary correction. Each mL of 0.1 N perchloric acid is equivalent to 15.02 mg of $C_6H_7KO_2$.
  Acceptance criteria: NLT 98.0% and NMT 101.0% of $C_6H_7KO_2$, calculated on the dried basis

IMPURITIES
Inorganic Impurities
- **LEAD,** *Lead Limit Test, Flame Atomic Absorption Spectrophotometric Method,* Appendix IIIB
  Sample: 10 g
  Acceptance criteria: NMT 2 mg/kg

SPECIFIC TESTS
- **ACIDITY (AS SORBIC ACID)**
  Sample: 1.1 g
  Analysis: Dissolve the *Sample* in 20 mL of water and add 3 drops of phenolphthalein TS. If the solution is colorless, titrate with 0.1 N sodium hydroxide to a pink color that persists for 15 s.
  Acceptance criteria: NMT 1.1 mL of 0.1 N sodium hydroxide is required to achieve a persistent pink color (about 1%).
- **ALKALINITY (AS K_2CO_3)**
  Sample: 1.1 g
  Analysis: Dissolve the *Sample* in 20 mL of water and add 3 drops of phenolphthalein TS. If the solution is pink, titrate with 0.1 N hydrochloric acid.
  Acceptance criteria: NMT 0.8 mL of 0.1 N hydrochloric acid is required to discharge the pink color (about 1%).
- **LOSS ON DRYING,** Appendix IIC: 105° for 3 h
  Acceptance criteria: NMT 1.0%

Potassium Sulfate

First Published: Prior to FCC 6
Last Revision: Second Supplement, FCC 6

K$_2$SO$_4$ Formula wt 174.26
INS: 515 CAS: [7778-80-5]
UNII: 1K573LC5TV [potassium sulfate]

DESCRIPTION
Potassium Sulfate occurs as colorless or white crystals or as a crystalline powder. One g dissolves in about 8.5 mL of water. It is insoluble in alcohol. The pH of a 1:20 aqueous solution is about 5.5 to 8.5.
Function: pH control
Packaging and Storage: Store in well-closed containers.

IDENTIFICATION
- **POTASSIUM,** Appendix IIIA
  Sample solution: 100 mg/mL
  Acceptance criteria: Passes tests

ASSAY
- **PROCEDURE**
  Sample: 500 mg
  Analysis: Dissolve the Sample in 200 mL of water, add 1 mL of hydrochloric acid, and heat to boiling. Gradually add, in small portions and while stirring constantly, an excess of hot barium chloride TS (about 8 or 9 mL), and heat the mixture on a steam bath for 1 h. Collect the precipitate on a retentive, ashless filter paper, wash until free from chloride, and place the filter in a suitable tared crucible. Carefully burn away the paper, and ignite at 800° ± 25° to constant weight. The weight of the barium sulfate so obtained, multiplied by 0.7466, indicates its equivalent of K$_2$SO$_4$.
  Acceptance criteria: NLT 99.0% and NMT 100.5% of K$_2$SO$_4$

IMPURITIES
Inorganic Impurities
- **LEAD,** Lead Limit Test, APDC Extraction Method, Appendix IIIB
  Acceptance criteria: NMT 2 mg/kg
- **SELENIUM,** Selenium Limit Test, Method II, Appendix IIIB
  Sample: 1.2 g
  Acceptance criteria: The absorbance of the extract from the Sample Preparation is NMT the absorbance of the extract from the Standard Preparation. (NMT 5 mg/kg)

Potassium Sulfite

First Published: Prior to FCC 6
Last Revision: Second Supplement, FCC 6

K$_2$SO$_3$ Formula wt 158.26
INS: 225 CAS: [10117-38-1]
UNII: 015KZC652E [potassium sulfite]

DESCRIPTION
Potassium Sulfite occurs as a white granular powder. It undergoes oxidation in air. One g dissolves in about 3.5 mL of water. It is slightly soluble in alcohol.
Function: Preservative; antioxidant
Packaging and Storage: Store in tight containers.

IDENTIFICATION
- **POTASSIUM,** Appendix IIIA
  Sample solution: 50 mg/mL
  Acceptance criteria: Passes tests
- **SULFITE,** Appendix IIIA
  Sample solution: 50 mg/mL
  Acceptance criteria: Passes test

ASSAY
- **PROCEDURE**
  Sample: 750 mg
  Analysis: Dissolve the Sample in a mixture of 100 mL of 0.1 N iodine and 5 mL of 2.7 N hydrochloric acid, and titrate the excess iodine with 0.1 N sodium thiosulfate, using starch TS as the indicator. Each mL of 0.1 N iodine is equivalent to 7.912 mg of K$_2$SO$_3$.
  Acceptance criteria: NLT 90.0% and NMT 100.5% of K$_2$SO$_3$

IMPURITIES
Inorganic Impurities
- **LEAD,** Lead Limit Test APDC Extraction Method, Appendix IIIB
  Acceptance criteria: NMT 2 mg/kg
- **SELENIUM,** Selenium Limit Test, Method I, Appendix IIIB
  Sample: 1.2 g and 600 mg of magnesium oxide for the combustion step described under Sample Preparation
  Acceptance criteria: The absorbance of the extract from the Sample Preparation is NMT the absorbance of the extract from the Standard Preparation. (NMT 5 mg/kg)

SPECIFIC TESTS
- **ALKALINITY (AS K$_2$CO$_3$)**
  Sample: 1 g
  Analysis: Dissolve the Sample in 20 mL of water. Add 25 mL of 3% hydrogen peroxide, previously neutralized to methyl red TS, mix thoroughly, and cool to room temperature. Titrate with 0.02 N hydrochloric acid. Perform a blank determination (see General Provisions) using 25 mL of the neutralized hydrogen peroxide solution, and make any necessary correction. Each mL of 0.02 N hydrochloric acid is equivalent to 1.38 mg of K$_2$CO$_3$.
  Acceptance criteria: Between 0.25% and 0.45%

Potassium Tripolyphosphate

First Published: Prior to FCC 6

Pentapotassium Triphosphate
Potassium Triphosphate

K$_5$P$_3$O$_{10}$ Formula wt 448.41

INS: 451(ii)   CAS: [13845-36-8]
UNII: NCS08RO8PB [pentapotassium triphosphate]

DESCRIPTION
Potassium Tripolyphosphate occurs as white granules or as a white powder. It is hygroscopic and is very soluble in water. The pH of a 1:100 aqueous solution is between 9.2 and 10.1.
Function: Texturizer
Packaging and Storage: Store in tight containers.

IDENTIFICATION
- **A. Potassium,** Appendix IIIA
  Sample solution: 50 mg/mL
  Acceptance criteria: Passes tests
- **B. Procedure**
  Sample solution: 10 mg/mL
  Analysis: Add a few drops of silver nitrate TS to the *Sample solution*.
  Acceptance criteria: A white precipitate forms that is soluble in 1.7 N nitric acid.

ASSAY
- **Procedure**
  Potassium acetate buffer (pH 5.0): Dissolve 78.5 g of potassium acetate in 1000 mL of water and adjust the pH of the solution to 5.0 with glacial acetic acid. Add a few mg of mercuric iodide to inhibit mold growth.
  0.3 M Potassium chloride solution: Dissolve 22.35 g of potassium chloride in water, add 5 mL of *Potassium acetate buffer*, dilute to 1000 mL with water, and mix. Add a few mg of mercuric iodide to inhibit mold growth.
  0.6 M Potassium chloride solution: Dissolve 44.7 g of potassium chloride in water, add 5 mL of *Potassium acetate buffer*, dilute to 1000 mL with water, and mix. Add a few mg of mercuric iodide to inhibit mold growth.
  1 M Potassium chloride solution: Dissolve 74.5 g of potassium chloride in water, add 5 mL of *Potassium acetate buffer*, dilute to 1000 mL with water, and mix. Add a few mg of mercuric iodide to inhibit mold growth.
  Chromatographic column: Use a standard chromatographic column, 20- to 40-cm long with a 20- to 28-mm id, or equivalent, that has a sealed-in, coarse-porosity, fritted disk. If a stopcock is not provided, attach a stopcock having a 3- to 4-mm diameter bore to the outlet of the column with a short length of flexible vinyl tubing.
  Chromatographic column preparation: Close the column stopcock, fill the space between the fritted disk and the stopcock with water, and connect a vacuum line to the stopcock. Prepare a 1:1 water slurry of Dowex 1 × 8, chloride form, 100- to 200- or 200- to 400-mesh, or a comparable grade of styrene–divinylbenzene ion exchange resin, and decant off any very fine particles and any foam. Repeat two or three times or until no more finely suspended material or foaming is observed. Fill the column with the slurry, and open the stopcock to allow the vacuum to pack the resin bed until the water level is slightly above the top of the resin, then immediately close the stopcock. Do not allow the liquid level to fall below the resin level at any time. Repeat this procedure until the packed resin column is 15 cm above the fritted disk. Place one circle of tightly fitting glass-fiber filter paper on top of the resin bed, then place a perforated polyethylene disk on top of the paper. Alternatively, place a loosely packed plug of glass wool on top of the bed. Close the top of the column with a rubber stopper in which a 7.6-cm length of capillary tubing (1.5-mm id, 7-mm od), or equivalent, has been inserted through the center, so that about 12 mm of the tubing extends through the bottom of the stopper. Connect the top of the capillary tubing to the stem of a 500-mL separatory funnel with flexible vinyl tubing, and clamp the separatory funnel to a ring stand above the column. Wash the column by adding 100 mL of water to the separatory funnel with all stopcocks closed. First open the separatory funnel stopcock, then open the column stopcock. The rate of flow should be about 5 mL/min. When the separatory funnel is empty, close the column stopcock, then close the separatory funnel stopcock.
  Sample preparation: Transfer 500 mg of sample into a 250-mL volumetric flask, dissolve in and dilute to volume with water, and mix. Transfer 10.0 mL of this solution into the separatory funnel, open both stopcocks, and allow the solution to drain into the column, rinsing the separator with 20 mL of water. Discard the eluate. Add 370 mL of *0.3 M Potassium chloride solution* to the separatory funnel, and allow this solution to pass through the column, discarding the eluate. Add 250 mL of *0.6 M Potassium chloride solution* to the column, allow the solution to pass through the column, and receive the eluate in a 400-mL beaker. [Note—To ensure a clean column for the next run, pass 100 mL of *1 M Potassium chloride solution* through the column, and then follow with 100 mL of water. Discard all washings.]
  Analysis: Add 15 mL of nitric acid to the beaker containing the column eluate, mix, and boil for 15 to 20 min. Add methyl orange TS, and neutralize the solution with ammonium hydroxide. Add 1 g of ammonium nitrate crystals, stir to dissolve, and cool. While stirring, add 15 mL of ammonium molybdate TS, and stir vigorously for 3 min, or allow the mixture to stand with occasional stirring for 10 to 15 min. Filter the contents of the beaker by means of suction through a 6- to 7-mm paper-pulp filter pad supported in a 25-mm porcelain disk. The filter pad should be covered with a suspension of infusorial earth. After the contents of the beaker have been transferred to the filter, wash the beaker with five 10-mL portions of a 10 mg/mL solution of sodium or potassium nitrate, passing the washings through the filter, then wash the filter with five 5-mL portions of the 10 mg/mL sodium or potassium nitrate wash solution. Return the filter pad and the precipitate to the beaker, wash the funnel thoroughly with water into the beaker, and dilute to about 150 mL. Add 0.1 N sodium hydroxide from a buret until the yellow precipitate is dissolved, then add 5 to 8 mL in excess. Add phenolphthalein TS, and

950 / Potassium Tripolyphosphate / Monographs

titrate the excess alkali with 0.1 N nitric acid. Finally, titrate with 0.1 N sodium hydroxide to the first appearance of a pink color. The difference between the total volume of 0.1 N sodium hydroxide added and the volume of nitric acid required represents the volume, V, in mL, of 0.1 N sodium hydroxide consumed by the phosphomolybdate complex. Calculate the quantity, in mg, of $K_5P_3O_{10}$ in the sample taken by the formula:

$$\text{Result} = 0.650 \times 25V$$

V = volume (mL) of 0.1 N sodium hydroxide consumed by the phosphomolybdate complex

Acceptance criteria: NLT 85.0% of $K_5P_3O_{10}$

IMPURITIES
Inorganic Impurities
- **ARSENIC**, *Arsenic Limit Test*, Appendix IIIB
  Sample solution: 1 g in 35 mL of water
  Acceptance criteria: NMT 3 mg/kg
- **FLUORIDE**, *Fluoride Limit Test, Method IV*, Appendix IIIB
  Sample: 2 g
  Acceptance criteria: NMT 10 mg/kg
- **LEAD**, *Lead Limit Test, APDC Extraction Method*, Appendix IIIB
  Acceptance criteria: NMT 2 mg/kg

SPECIFIC TESTS
- **INSOLUBLE SUBSTANCES**
  Sample: 10 g
  Analysis: Dissolve the *Sample* in 100 mL of hot water and filter the solution through a tared filtering crucible. Wash the insoluble residue with hot water, dry at 105° for 2 h, cool, and weigh.
  Acceptance criteria: NMT 2.0%
- **LOSS ON DRYING**, Appendix IIC: 105° for 1 h
  Acceptance criteria: NMT 0.7%

Povidone

First Published: Prior to FCC 6
Last Revision: First Supplement, FCC 6

PVP
Polyvinylpyrrolidone
Poly[1-(2-oxo-1-pyrrolidinyl)ethylene]

$(C_6H_9NO)_x$ Lower mol wt range product ~40,000
Higher mol wt range product ~360,000
INS: 1201 CAS: [9003-39-8]
UNII: FZ989GH94E [povidone]

DESCRIPTION
Povidone occurs as a white to tan powder. It is a polymer of purified 1-vinyl-2-pyrrolidone produced catalytically. It is soluble in water, in alcohol, and in chloroform, and is insoluble in ether. The pH of a 1 : 20 aqueous solution is between 3 and 7.

Function: Clarifying agent; separation/filtration aid; stabilizer; bodying agent; tableting aid; dispersant; coating on fresh fruit

Packaging and Storage: Store in tight containers.

IDENTIFICATION
- **A. PROCEDURE**
  Sample solution: 20 mg/mL
  Analysis: Add 20 mL of 1 N hydrochloric acid and 5 mL of potassium dichromate TS to 10 mL of *Sample solution*.
  Acceptance criteria: An orange-yellow precipitate forms.
- **B. PROCEDURE**
  Sample solution: 20 mg/mL
  Sample: Add 5 mL of *Sample solution* to 75 mg of cobalt nitrate and 300 mg of ammonium thiocyanate dissolved in 2 mL of water, mix, and make the resulting solution acid with 2.7 N hydrochloric acid.
  Acceptance criteria: A pale blue precipitate forms.
- **C. PROCEDURE**
  Sample solution: 5 mg/mL
  Sample: Add a few drops of iodine TS to 5 mL of *Sample solution*.
  Acceptance criteria: A deep red color appears.

ASSAY
- **NITROGEN**, *Nitrogen Determination, Method II*, Appendix IIIC
  Sample: 100 mg
  Analysis: In the wet-digestion step, omit the use of hydrogen peroxide, and use 5 g of a 33:1:1 mixture of potassium sulfate–cupric sulfate–titanium dioxide instead of the 10:1 potassium sulfate–cupric sulfate mixture. Heat until a clear, light green solution appears, heat for an additional 45 min, and continue as directed, beginning with "Cautiously add 20 mL of water, cool, then…", except use 70 mL of water instead of 20.
  Acceptance criteria: NLT 11.5% and NMT 12.8% as nitrogen (N), calculated on the anhydrous basis

IMPURITIES
Inorganic Impurities
- **LEAD**, *Lead Limit Test, Flame Atomic Absorption Spectrophotometric Method*, Appendix IIIB
  Sample: 10 g
  Acceptance criteria: NMT 2 mg/kg

Organic Impurities
- **ALDEHYDES (AS ACETALDEHYDE)**
  Phosphate buffer: Transfer 50.0 g of potassium pyrophosphate into a 500-mL volumetric flask, and dissolve in 400 mL of water. Adjust, if necessary, to a pH of 9.0 with 1 N hydrochloric acid, dilute to volume, and mix.
  Aldehyde dehydrogenase solution: Transfer a quantity of lyophilized aldehyde dehydrogenase (Sigma A550, or equivalent) equivalent to 70 units into a glass vial, dissolve it in 10.0 mL of water, and mix. [NOTE—This solution is stable for 8 h at 4°.]

NAD solution: 4.0 mg/mL of nicotinamide adenine dinucleotide in *Phosphate buffer*
Standard stock solution: 1 mg/mL of acetaldehyde in water. [NOTE—Store at 4° for about 20 h.]
Standard solution: 0.01 mg/mL of acetaldehyde in water: from *Standard stock solution*
Sample solution: Transfer 2 g of sample into a 100-mL volumetric flask, dissolve it in 50 mL of *Phosphate buffer*, dilute with *Phosphate buffer* to volume, and mix. Stopper the flask loosely, heat at 60° for 1 h, and cool to room temperature.
Analysis: Pipet 0.5 mL each of the *Standard solution*, the *Sample solution*, and water (the reagent blank) into separate 1-cm cells. Determine the absorbances of the solutions at 340 nm, using water as the reference. Add 2.5 mL of *Phosphate buffer* and 0.2 mL of *NAD solution* to each cell. Cover the cells to exclude oxygen. Mix by inversion, and allow them to stand for 2 to 3 min at $22 \pm 2°$. Determine the absorbances of the solutions as before. Calculate the percentage of aldehydes, as acetaldehyde, in the sample by the formula:

$$10(C/W)\{[(A_{U2} - A_{U1}) - (A_{B2} - A_{B1})]/[(A_{S2} - A_{S1}) - (A_{B2} - A_{B1})]\}$$

C = concentration (mg/mL) of acetaldehyde in the *Standard solution*
W = weight (g) of sample taken to prepare the *Sample solution*
A_{U1} = absorbance of the solution obtained from the *Sample solution*, before the *Phosphate buffer* and *NAD solution* were added
A_{S1} = absorbance of the solution obtained from the *Standard solution*, before the *Phosphate buffer* and *NAD solution* were added
A_{B1} = absorbance of the solution obtained from the water reagent blank, before the *Phosphate buffer* and *NAD solution* were added
A_{U2} = absorbance of the solution obtained from the *Sample solution*, after the *Phosphate buffer* and *NAD solution* were added
A_{S2} = absorbance of the solution obtained from the *Standard solution*, after the *Phosphate buffer* and *NAD solution* were added
A_{B2} = absorbance of the solution obtained from the water reagent blank, after the *Phosphate buffer* and *NAD solution* were added

Acceptance criteria: NMT 0.05%

- **HYDRAZINE,** *Thin-Layer Chromatography*, Appendix II
Salicylaldazine standard solution: Dissolve 300 mg of hydrazine sulfate in 5 mL of water, add 1 mL of glacial acetic acid and 2 mL of a freshly prepared 20% (v/v) solution of salicylaldehyde in isopropyl alcohol, mix, and allow the solution to stand until a yellow precipitate forms. Extract the mixture with two 15-mL portions of methylene chloride. Combine the methylene chloride extracts, and dry over anhydrous sodium sulfate. Decant the methylene chloride solution, and evaporate it to dryness. Recrystallize the residue of salicylaldazine from a 60:40 mixture of warm toluene and methanol by cooling. Filter, and dry the crystals in a vacuum. The crystals have a melting range of 213° to 219°, but the range between the beginning and end of melting is not to exceed 10°. Prepare a salicylaldazine solution in toluene containing 9.38 μg/mL.
Sample solution: Transfer 2.5 g of sample into a 50-mL centrifuge tube, add 25 mL of water, and mix to dissolve. Add 500 μL of a 1:20 solution of salicylaldehyde–methanol, swirl, and heat in a water bath at 60° for 15 min. Allow the solution to cool, add 2.0 mL of toluene, insert a stopper in the tube, shake vigorously for 2 min, and centrifuge.
Adsorbent: 0.25-mm layer of dimethylsilanized chromatographic silica gel mixture
Developing solvent system: Methanol and water (2:1)
Application volume: 10 μL
Detection/Visualization: UV 365 nm
Analysis: Spot the clear upper toluene layer from the *Sample solution* and the *Salicylaldazine standard solution* onto the plate. Following development, locate the spots on the plate by examination under UV light. Salicylaldazine appears as a fluorescent spot having an R_F value of about 0.3.
Acceptance criteria: The fluorescence of any salicylaldazine spot from the *Sample solution* is not more intense than that produced by the spot obtained from the *Salicylaldazine standard solution*. (NMT 1 mg/kg)

- **UNSATURATION (AS VINYLPYRROLIDONE)**
Mobile phase: Acetonitrile and water (10 : 90)
System suitability solution: Transfer 10 mg of vinylpyrrolidone and 500 mg of vinyl acetate to a 100-mL volumetric flask, and dissolve in and dilute with methanol to volume. Transfer 1.0 mL of this solution to a 100-mL volumetric flask, dilute with *Mobile phase* to volume, and mix.
Standard solution: Transfer 50 mg of vinylpyrrolidone to a 100-mL volumetric flask, dilute with methanol to volume, and mix. Transfer 1.0 mL of this solution to a 100-mL volumetric flask, dilute with methanol to volume, and mix. Transfer 5.0 mL of this solution to a 100-mL volumetric flask, dilute with *Mobile phase* to volume, and mix.
Sample solution: Transfer 250 mg of sample into a 10-mL volumetric flask, dilute with *Mobile phase* to volume, and mix.
Chromatographic system, Appendix IIA
Mode: High-performance liquid chromatography
Detector: UV 235 nm
Column: Stainless steel column about 4-mm × 250-mm, packed with octadecylsilanized silica gel (5 μm in particle diameter), with a guard column about 4-mm × 25-mm with the same packing
Column temperature: 40°
Flow rate: Adjust so that the retention time of vinylpyrrolidone is about 10 min.
Injection volume: About 50 μL

952 / Povidone / Monographs

System suitability
 Sample: *System suitability solution* and *Standard solution*
 Suitability requirement 1: The resolution, R, between vinylpyrrolidone and vinyl acetate for the *System suitability solution* is NLT 2.0.
 Suitability requirement 2: The relative standard deviation for replicate injections of the *Standard solution* is NMT 2.0%.
Analysis: Separately inject the *Standard solution* and the *Sample solution* into the chromatograph, record the chromatograms, and measure the responses for the vinylpyrrolidone peak area. [NOTE—If necessary, after each injection of the *Sample solution*, wash the polymeric material from the guard column by passing the *Mobile phase* through the column backwards for about 30 min at the same flow rate.]
Calculate the concentration (mg/mL) of vinylpyrrolidinone in the sample by the formula:

Result = $1000(C/W)(r_U/r_S)$

C = concentration (mg/mL) of vinylpyrrolidinone in the *Standard solution*
W = weight (mg) of sample taken to prepare the *Sample solution*
r_U = peak area response for vinylpyrrolidinone obtained from the *Sample solution*
r_S = peak area response for vinylpyrrolidinone obtained from the *Standard solution*
Acceptance criteria: NMT 0.001%

SPECIFIC TESTS
- **K-VALUE**
 [NOTE—The molecular weight of the sample is characterized by its viscosity in aqueous solution, relative to that of water, expressed as a *K-Value*.]
 Sample: An amount of sample equivalent to 1 g on the anhydrous basis
 Sample solution: Transfer the *Sample* into a 100-mL volumetric flask, dissolve it in about 50 mL of water, dilute with water to volume, mix thoroughly, and allow it to stand for 1 h. Filter the solution. Pipet 15 mL of filtrate into a clean, dry Ubbelohde-type viscometer, and place the viscometer in a water bath maintained at 25 ± 0.2°.
 Analysis: After allowing the viscometer and the *Sample solution* to warm in the water bath for 10 min, draw the solution by means of very gentle suction up through the capillary until the meniscus is above the upper etched mark. Release suction, and after the meniscus reaches the upper etched mark, begin timing the flow through the capillary. Record the exact time when the meniscus reaches the lower etched mark, and calculate the flow time to the nearest 0.01 s. Repeat this operation until at least three readings are obtained. The readings must agree within 0.1 s; if not, repeat the determination with additional 15-mL portions of *Sample solution* after recleaning the viscometer with sulfuric acid–dichromate cleaning solution or with a suitable laboratory cleaning compound that will remove oils, greases, waxes, and other impurities. Calculate the average flow time, and then obtain the flow time in a similar manner for 15 mL of water. Calculate the relative viscosity, z, of the sample by dividing the average flow time of the *Sample solution* by that of the water sample, and then calculate the *K-Value* by the formula:

$$\left[\sqrt{300c\log z + (c + 1.5c\log z)^2} + 1.5c\log z - c\right] / (0.15c + 0.003c^2)$$

c = weight (g) of the sample, on the anhydrous basis, in each 100.0 g of solution
z = relative viscosity
Acceptance criteria
 Lower-molecular-weight-range product: Between 27 and 32
 Higher-molecular-weight-range product: Between 81 and 97
- **RESIDUE ON IGNITION (SULFATED ASH),** Appendix IIC
 Sample: 2 g
 Acceptance criteria: NMT 0.1%
- **WATER,** *Water Determination,* Appendix IIB
 Acceptance criteria: NMT 5.0%

OTHER REQUIREMENTS
- **LABELING:** Indicate the *K-value* or the *K-value* range.

L-Proline

First Published: Prior to FCC 6
Last Revision: FCC 7

L-2-Pyrrolidinecarboxylic Acid

$C_5H_9NO_2$ Formula wt 115.13
         CAS: [147-85-3]
UNII: 9DLQ4CIU6V [proline]

DESCRIPTION
L-Proline occurs as white crystals or a crystalline powder. It is very soluble in water and in alcohol, but insoluble in ether.
Function: Nutrient
Packaging and Storage: Store in well-closed, light-resistant containers.

IDENTIFICATION
- **INFRARED ABSORPTION,** *Spectrophotometric Identification Tests,* Appendix IIIC
 Reference standard: USP L-Proline RS
 Sample and standard preparation: M
 Acceptance criteria: The spectrum of the sample exhibits maxima at the same wavelengths as those in the spectrum of the *Reference standard*.

ASSAY
- **PROCEDURE**
  Sample: 220 mg, previously dried
  Analysis: Dissolve the *Sample* in 3 mL of formic acid and 50 mL of glacial acetic acid. Add 2 drops of crystal violet TS and titrate with 0.1 N perchloric acid to a blue-green endpoint. Perform a blank determination (see *General Provisions*), and make any necessary correction. Each mL of 0.1 N perchloric acid is equivalent to 11.51 mg of $C_5H_9NO_2$. [**CAUTION**—Handle perchloric acid in an appropriate fume hood.]
  Acceptance criteria: 98.5%–101.5% of $C_5H_9NO_2$, on the dried basis

IMPURITIES
Inorganic Impurities
- **LEAD**, *Lead Limit Test*, Appendix IIIB
  Sample solution: Prepare as directed for organic compounds.
  Control: 5 μg Pb (5 mL of *Diluted Standard Lead Solution*)
  Acceptance criteria: NMT 5 mg/kg

SPECIFIC TESTS
- **LOSS ON DRYING**, Appendix IIC: 105° for 3 h
  Acceptance criteria: NMT 0.3%
- **OPTICAL (SPECIFIC) ROTATION**, Appendix IIB
  Sample: 4 g of a previously dried sample
  Analysis: Dissolve the *Sample* in sufficient water to make 100 mL.
  Acceptance criteria: $[\alpha]_D^{20}$ between –84.0° and –86.3°, on the dried basis
- **RESIDUE ON IGNITION (SULFATED ASH)**, Appendix IIC
  Sample: 1 g
  Acceptance criteria: NMT 0.1%

Propane
First Published: Prior to FCC 6

$H_3C\diagup\diagdown CH_3$

C_3H_8 Formula wt 44.10
     CAS: [74-98-6]
UNII: T75W9911L6 [propane]

DESCRIPTION
Propane occurs as a colorless, flammable gas (boiling temperature is about –42°). One hundred volumes of water dissolves 6.5 volumes at 17.8° and 753 mm Hg; 100 volumes of anhydrous alcohol dissolves 790 volumes at 16.6° and 754 mm Hg; 100 volumes of ether dissolves 926 volumes at 16.6° and 757 mm Hg; 100 volumes of chloroform dissolves 1299 volumes at 21.6° and 757 mm Hg. Vapor pressure at 21° is about 10,290 mm Hg (108 psi).
Function: Propellant; aerating agent
Packaging and Storage: Store in tight cylinders protected from excessive heat. [**CAUTION**—Propane is highly flammable and explosive. Observe precautions and perform sampling and analytical operations in a well-ventilated fume hood.]

[NOTE—For obtaining a test sample of gas, use a stainless steel specimen cylinder equipped with a stainless steel valve and having a capacity of not less than 200 mL and a pressure rating of 240 psi or more. Dry the cylinder at 110° for 2 h with the valve open, and evacuate the hot cylinder to less than 1 mm Hg. Close the valve, and cool and weigh the cylinder. Tightly connect one end of a charging line to the sample cylinder and loosely connect the other end to the specimen cylinder. Carefully open the sample cylinder and allow the sample gas to flush out the charging line through the loose connection. Avoid excessive flushing that causes moisture to freeze in the charging line and connections. Tighten the fitting on the specimen cylinder and open its valve, allowing the sample gas to flow into the evacuated cylinder. Continue until the desired amount of sample gas is obtained, close the sample cylinder valve, and then close the specimen cylinder valve. [**CAUTION**— Do not overload the specimen cylinder.] Weigh the charged specimen cylinder again and calculate the sample gas weight.]

IDENTIFICATION
- **INFRARED ABSORPTION SPECTRUM**
  Acceptance criteria: The spectrum of a sample exhibits maxima, among others, at approximately 3.4 μm (vs), 6.8 μm (s), and 7.2 μm (m).
- **VAPOR PRESSURE**
  Analysis: Determine the vapor pressure of the sample gas at 21° by means of a suitable pressure gauge.
  Acceptance criteria: Between 820 and 875 kPa absolute (119 and 127 psia, respectively)

ASSAY
- **PROCEDURE**
  Chromatographic system, Appendix IIA
  Mode: Gas chromatography
  Detector: Thermal conductivity detector
  Column: 6-m × 3-mm (id) aluminum column, or equivalent, packed with 10 weight percent tetraethylene glycol dimethyl ether liquid phase, or equivalent, on a support of crushed firebrick (Gas Chrom R) that has been calcined or burned with a clay binder above 900° and silanized, or equivalent
  Column temperature: 33°
  Flow rate: 50 mL/min
  Carrier gas: Helium
  Injection volume: 2 μL
  System suitability
  Sample: Propane
  Suitability requirement: The propane peak responses from duplicate determinations agree within 1%.
  Analysis: Connect one sample cylinder to the chromatograph through a suitable sampling valve and a flow-control valve downstream from the sampling valve. Flush the liquid specimen through the sampling valve, taking care to avoid trapping sample gas or air in the valve. Inject the sample gas and record the

chromatogram. Calculate the percent purity by the following formula:

$$\text{Result} = 100S/\Sigma s$$

S = propane peak response
Σs = sum of all of the peak responses in the chromatogram

Acceptance criteria: NLT 98.0% of *Propane* (C_3H_8)

IMPURITIES
Inorganic Impurities
- **WATER,** *Water Determination, Method I (Karl Fischer Titrimetric Method), Appendix IIB*
  Sample: 100 g (see *Note* above on sampling)
  Analysis: Proceed as directed using the following modifications: (a) Provide the closed-system titrating vessel with an opening through which passes a coarse-porosity gas dispersion tube connected to the sampling cylinder. (b) Dilute the reagent with anhydrous methanol to give a water equivalence factor of between 0.2 and 1.0 mg/mL; age this diluted solution for not less than 16 h before standardization. (c) Introduce the *Sample*, contained in the specimen cylinder, into the titration vessel through the gas dispersion tube at a rate of about 100 mL/min; if necessary, heat the specimen cylinder gently to maintain this flow rate.
  Acceptance criteria: NMT 10 mg/kg

Organic Impurities
- **HIGH BOILING RESIDUE**
  Analysis: Prepare a cooling coil from copper tubing (about 6.1 m × about 6 mm (od)) to fit into a suitable vacuum-jacketed flask. Immerse the cooling coil in a mixture of Dry Ice and acetone in a vacuum-jacketed flask and connect one end of the tubing to a sample cylinder (see *Note* above on sampling). Carefully open the sample cylinder valve, flush the cooling coil with about 50 mL of the liquefied sample, and discard this portion of liquid. Continue delivering liquid from the cooling coil, and collect it in a previously chilled 1000-mL sedimentation cone until the cone is filled to the 1000-mL mark (approximately 600 g). Using a warm water bath maintained at about 40° to reduce evaporating time, allow the liquid to evaporate. When all of the liquid has evaporated, rinse the sedimentation cone with two 50-mL portions of pentane, and combine the rinsings in a tared 150-mL evaporating dish. Transfer 100 mL of the pentane solvent to a second tared 150-mL evaporating dish, place both evaporating dishes on a water bath, evaporate to dryness, and heat the dishes in an oven at 100° for 60 min. Cool the dishes in a desiccator and weigh them. Repeat the heating for 15-min periods until successive weighings are within 0.1 mg. [NOTE—Retain the residue for the test for *Acidity of Residue* (below).] The weight of the residue obtained from the specimen is the difference between the weights of the residues in the two evaporating dishes. Calculate the mg/kg of high-boiling residue based on a sample weight of 600 g.
  Acceptance criteria: NMT 5 mg/kg

- **SULFUR COMPOUNDS**
  Analysis: Carefully open the sample cylinder valve to produce a moderate flow of gas. Do not direct the gas stream toward the face, but deflect a portion of the stream toward the nose.
  Acceptance criteria: The gas is free from the characteristic odor of sulfur compounds.

SPECIFIC TESTS
- **ACIDITY OF RESIDUE**
  Sample: The residue obtained under *High-Boiling Residue* (above)
  Analysis: Add 10 mL of water to the *Sample*, mix by swirling for about 30 s, add 2 drops of methyl orange TS, insert the stopper in the tube, and shake the tube vigorously.
  Acceptance criteria: No pink or red color appears in the aqueous layer.

1,3-Propanediol

First Published: Third Supplement, FCC 7

1,3-Dihydroxypropane
Propane, 1-3-diol
Trimethylene Glycol

$C_3H_8O_2$ Formula wt 76.09
                CAS: [504-63-2]

DESCRIPTION
1,3-Propanediol is a clear, colorless, hygroscopic liquid with a mild, sweet odor. It is produced from corn-derived glucose in a multi-step fermentation process using a non-pathogenic strain of *Escherichia coli* K-12 as a biocatalyst. Principle steps include fermentation, separation, and distillation. It is soluble in water, alcohols, and acetone, and miscible with many polar solvents. 1,3-Propanediol produced from a biobased carbon source (modern carbon source such as plant-derived glucose) can be distinguished from 1,3-propanediol produced from fossil carbon sources (such as fossil fuel) using carbon isotope analysis.
[NOTE—An informational (not a monograph requirement) carbon isotope analysis method is available to determine the biobased content of 1,3-propanediol, see *Biobased Content of 1,3-Propanediol, Markers for Authenticity Testing*, Appendix XIV.]
Function: Solvent; wetting agent; humectant
Packaging and storage: Store in tight containers.

IDENTIFICATION
- **A. INFRARED ABSORPTION,** *Spectrophotometric Identification Tests*, Appendix IIIC
  Reference standard: USP 1,3-Propanediol RS
  Sample and standard preparation: F
  Acceptance criteria: The spectrum of the sample exhibits maxima at the same wavelengths as those in the spectrum of the *Reference standard*.

- **B. Procedure**
  Acceptance criteria: The retention time of the major peak in the chromatogram of the *Sample solution* corresponds to the 1,3-propanediol peak in the chromatogram of the *System suitability solution*.

ASSAY
- **Procedure**
  System suitability solution: Mix quantities of USP Propylene Glycol RS and USP 1,3-Propanediol RS to obtain about a 5% propylene glycol/95% propanediol solution.
  Sample solution: Neat
  Chromatographic system, Appendix IIA
    Mode: Gas chromatography
    Detector: Flame ionization
    Column: 0.25-mm × 30-m; bonded with a 0.25-μm layer of polyethylene glycol compound[1]
    Carrier gas: Helium
    Temperature
      Inlet: 250°
      Detector: 250°
      Column: See the temperature program table below.

Temperature(°)	Rate(°/min)	Hold Time(min)
50→200	15	—
200→250	40	17

  Split ratio: 18:1
  Flow rate: About 1.0 mL/min
  Injection size: 0.2 μL
  System suitability
    Sample: *System suitability solution*
    Suitability requirement: The resolution between 1,3-propanediol and propylene glycol is NLT 1.5.
  Analysis: Inject the *Sample solution* into the chromatograph, record the chromatogram, and measure all peak areas. Calculate the percentage of 1,3-propanediol in the portion of the sample taken:

  $$Result = (A/B) \times 100$$

  A = response of 1,3-propanediol
  B = sum of the responses of all the peaks
  Acceptance criteria: NLT 99.9%

IMPURITIES
Inorganic Impurities
- **Cobalt,** *Elemental Impurities by ICP,* Appendix IIIC
  Acceptance criteria: NMT 1.0 mg/kg
- **Lead,** *Elemental Impurities by ICP,* Appendix IIIC
  Acceptance criteria: NMT 1.0 mg/kg
- **Nickel,** *Elemental Impurities by ICP,* Appendix IIIC
  Acceptance criteria: NMT 1.0 mg/kg

SPECIFIC TESTS
- **Specific Gravity:** Determine by any reliable method (see *General Provisions*).
  Acceptance criteria: 1.040–1.065
- **Water,** *Water Determination, Method I,* Appendix IIB
  Acceptance criteria: NMT 0.1%

OTHER REQUIREMENTS
- **Labeling:** 1,3-Propanediol may be labeled as "biobased", indicating that it was produced using a plant derived carbon source. The biobased content of 1,3-propanediol can be determined using carbon isotope analysis, see *Biobased Content of 1,3-Propanediol, Markers for Authenticity Testing,* Appendix XIV.

Propenylguaethol

First Published: Prior to FCC 6

1-Ethoxy-2-hydroxy-4-propenylbenzene

$C_{11}H_{14}O_2$ Formula wt 178.23
FEMA: 2922
UNII: JP95W81L3F [propenyl guaethol]

DESCRIPTION
Propenylguaethol occurs as a white crystalline powder.
Odor: Vanilla
Solubility: Soluble in vegetable oils; insoluble or practically insoluble in water; 1 g dissolves in 20 mL of 95% alcohol
Solubility in Alcohol, Appendix VI: One g dissolves in 15 mL of 95% ethanol.
Function: Flavoring agent

IDENTIFICATION
- **Infrared Spectra,** *Spectrophotometric Identification Tests,* Appendix IIIC
  Acceptance criteria: The spectrum of the sample exhibits relative maxima at the same wavelengths as those of the spectrum below.

ASSAY
- **Procedure:** Proceed as directed under *M-1a,* Appendix XI.
  Acceptance criteria: NLT 99.0% of $C_{11}H_{14}O_2$

OTHER REQUIREMENTS
- **Melting Range or Temperature Determination,** Appendix IIB
  Acceptance criteria: Between 85° and 88°
- **Residue on Ignition (Sulfated Ash),** Appendix IIC
  Sample: 2 g
  Acceptance criteria: NMT 0.1%

---
[1] ZB Wax (Phenomenex, Torrance, CA), or equivalent.

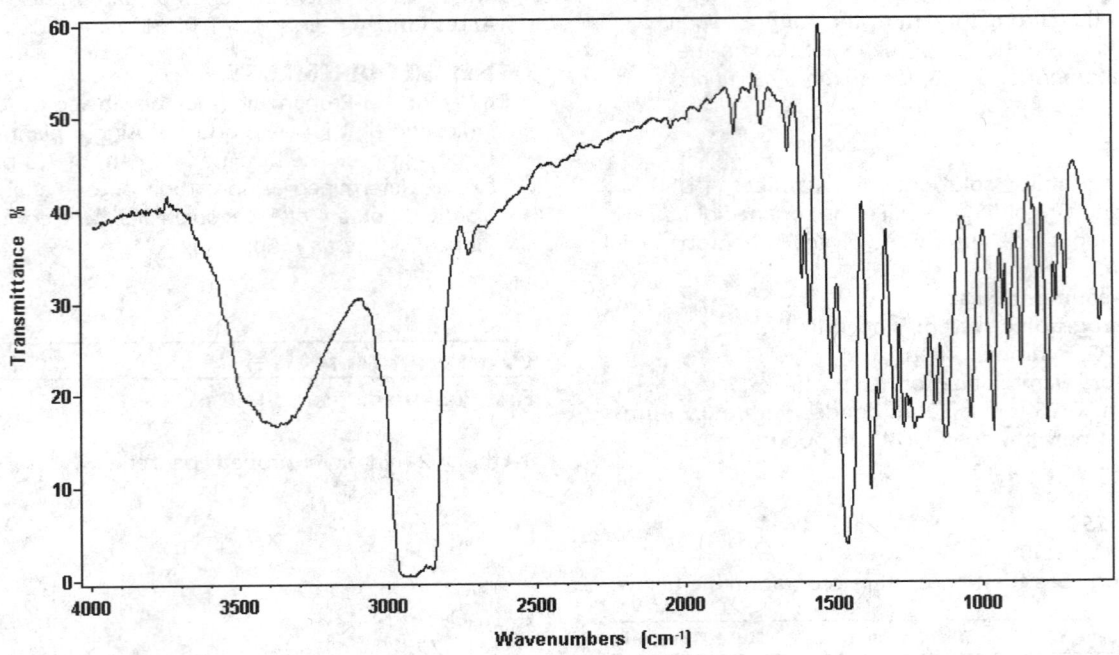

Propenylguaethol

Propionaldehyde

First Published: Prior to FCC 6
Last Revision: First Supplement, FCC 6

C₃H₆O   Formula wt 58.08
FEMA: 2923
UNII: AMJ2B4M67V [propionaldehyde]

DESCRIPTION
Propionaldehyde occurs as a colorless, mobile liquid. It may contain a suitable antioxidant.
Odor: Sharp, pungent
Solubility: Miscible in alcohol, ether, water
Boiling Point: ~49°
Function: Flavoring agent

IDENTIFICATION
- **INFRARED SPECTRA**, *Spectrophotometric Identification Tests,* Appendix IIIC
  Acceptance criteria: The spectrum of the sample exhibits relative maxima at the same wavelengths as those of the spectrum below.

ASSAY
- **PROCEDURE:** Proceed as directed under *M-2c,* Appendix XI.
  Acceptance criteria: NLT 97.0% of C₃H₆O

SPECIFIC TESTS
- **ACID VALUE, FLAVOR CHEMICALS (OTHER THAN ESSENTIAL OILS),** *M-15,* Appendix XI
  Acceptance criteria: NMT 5.0
- **SPECIFIC GRAVITY:** Determine at 25° by any reliable method (see *General Provisions*).
  Acceptance criteria: Between 0.800 and 0.805

OTHER REQUIREMENTS
- **DISTILLATION RANGE,** Appendix IIB
  Acceptance criteria: 46° to 50° (first 97%)
- **WATER,** *Water Determination, Method I,* Appendix IIB
  [NOTE—Use freshly distilled pyridine as solvent.]
  Acceptance criteria: NMT 2.5%

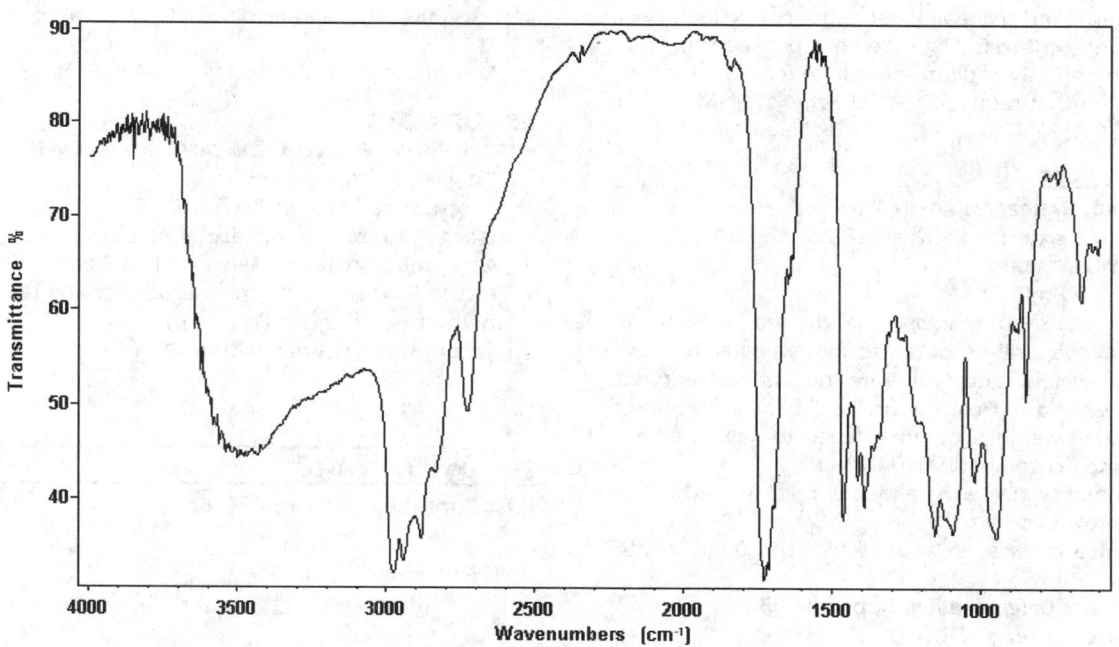
Propionaldehyde

Propionic Acid

First Published: Prior to FCC 6

C₃H₆O₂
INS: 280
UNII: JHU490RVYR [propionic acid]
Formula wt 74.08
CAS: [79-09-4]

DESCRIPTION
Propionic Acid occurs as an oily liquid. It is miscible with water, with alcohol, and with various other organic solvents.

Function: Preservative; mold inhibitor
Packaging and Storage: Store in well-closed containers.

ASSAY
- **PROCEDURE**
  Sample: 1.5 g
  Analysis: Mix the *Sample* with 100 mL of recently boiled and cooled water contained in a 250-mL Erlenmeyer flask, add phenolphthalein TS, and titrate with 0.5 N sodium hydroxide to the first appearance of a faint-pink endpoint that persists for at least 30 s. Each mL of 0.5 N sodium hydroxide is equivalent to 37.04 mg of C₃H₆O₂.
  Acceptance criteria: NLT 99.5% and NMT 100.5% C₃H₆O₂, calculated on the anhydrous basis

IMPURITIES
Inorganic Impurities
- **LEAD,** *Lead Limit Test, Flame Atomic Absorption Spectrophotometric Method,* Appendix IIIB
  Sample: 10 g
  Acceptance criteria: NMT 2 mg/kg

Organic Impurities
- **ALDEHYDES (AS PROPIONALDEHYDE)**
  Sample: 10 mL
  Analysis: Transfer the *Sample* into 250-mL glass-stoppered Erlenmeyer flask containing 50 mL of water and 10.0 mL of a 12.5 mg/mL aqueous solution of sodium bisulfite. Stopper the flask, and shake vigorously. Allow the mixture to stand for 30 min, then titrate with 0.1 N iodine to the same brown-yellow endpoint obtained with a blank treated with the same quantities of the same reagents (see *General Provisions*).
  Acceptance criteria: The difference between the volume of 0.1 N iodine required for the blank and that required for the *Sample* is NMT 1.75 mL (about 0.05%).

- **READILY OXIDIZABLE SUBSTANCES (AS FORMIC ACID)**
  Sample: 10 mL
  Analysis: Dissolve 15 g of sodium hydroxide in 50 mL of water, cool, add 6 mL of bromine, stirring to aid dissolution, and dilute to 2000 mL with water. Transfer 25.0 mL of this solution into a 250-mL glass-stoppered Erlenmeyer flask containing 100 mL of water, and add 10 mL of a 200 mg/mL sodium acetate solution and the *Sample*. Allow to stand for 15 min, add 5 mL of a 250 mg/mL potassium iodide solution and 10 mL of hydrochloric acid, and titrate with 0.1 N sodium thiosulfate just to the disappearance of the brown

958 / Propionic Acid / *Monographs*

color. Perform a blank determination (see *General Provisions*), and make any necessary correction.
Acceptance criteria: The difference between the volume of 0.1 N sodium thiosulfate required for the blank and that required for the *Sample* is NMT 2.2 mL (about 0.05%).

SPECIFIC TESTS
- **DISTILLATION RANGE,** Appendix IIB
  Acceptance criteria: Between 138.5° and 142.5°
- **NONVOLATILE RESIDUE**
  Sample: 100 mL
  Analysis: Transfer the *Sample* into a tared, 125-mL platinum evaporating dish, previously heated at 105° to constant weight, and evaporate the *Sample* to dryness on a steam bath. Heat the dish at 105° for 30 min or to constant weight, cool in a desiccator, and weigh.
  Acceptance criteria: NMT 0.01%
- **SPECIFIC GRAVITY:** Determine by any reliable method (see *General provisions*).
  Acceptance criteria: Between 0.993 and 0.997 at 20°/20°
- **WATER,** *Water Determination,* Appendix IIB
  Acceptance criteria: NMT 0.15%

Propyl Acetate

First Published: Prior to FCC 6
Last Revision: FCC 7

n-Propyl Acetate

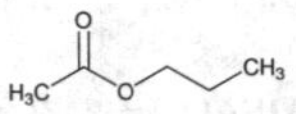

$C_5H_{10}O_2$ Formula wt 102.13
FEMA: 2925
UNII: 4AWM8C91G6 [propyl acetate]

DESCRIPTION
Propyl Acetate occurs as a colorless liquid.
Odor: Ethereal
Boiling Point: ~102°
Solubility in Alcohol, Appendix VI: One mL dissolves in 1 mL of 95% alcohol.
Function: Flavoring agent

IDENTIFICATION
- **INFRARED ABSORPTION,** *Spectrophotometric Identification Tests,* Appendix IIIC
  Reference standard: USP Propyl Acetate RS
  Sample and standard preparation: F
  Acceptance criteria: The spectrum of the sample exhibits maxima at the same wavelengths as those in the spectrum of the *Reference standard*.

ASSAY
- **PROCEDURE:** Proceed as directed under *M-1b,* Appendix XI.
  Acceptance criteria: NLT 97.0% of $C_5H_{10}O_2$

SPECIFIC TESTS
- **ACID VALUE, FLAVOR CHEMICALS (OTHER THAN ESSENTIAL OILS),** *M-15,* Appendix XI
  Acceptance criteria: NMT 1.0
- **REFRACTIVE INDEX,** Appendix II: At 20°
  Acceptance criteria: Between 1.382 and 1.387
- **SPECIFIC GRAVITY:** Determine at 25° by any reliable method (see *General Provisions*).
  Acceptance criteria: 0.880–0.886

Propyl Alcohol

First Published: Prior to FCC 6

n-Propanol

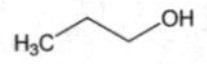

C_3H_8O Formula wt 60.09
FEMA: 2928
UNII: 96F264O9SV [propyl alcohol]

DESCRIPTION
Propyl Alcohol occurs as a colorless liquid.
Odor: Ethereal
Solubility: Soluble in propylene glycol, vegetable oils; miscible in water
Boiling Point: ~97°
Solubility in Alcohol, Appendix VI: One mL dissolves in 1 mL of 95% alcohol.
Function: Flavoring agent

IDENTIFICATION
- **INFRARED SPECTRA,** *Spectrophotometric Identification Tests,* Appendix IIIC
  Acceptance criteria: The spectrum of the sample exhibits relative maxima at the same wavelengths as those of the spectrum below.

ASSAY
- **PROCEDURE:** Proceed as directed under *M-1b,* Appendix XI.
  Acceptance criteria: NLT 99.0% of C_3H_8O

SPECIFIC TESTS
- **REFRACTIVE INDEX,** Appendix II: At 20°
  Acceptance criteria: Between 1.383 and 1.388
- **SPECIFIC GRAVITY:** Determine at 25° by any reliable method (see *General Provisions*).
  Acceptance criteria: Between 0.800 and 0.805

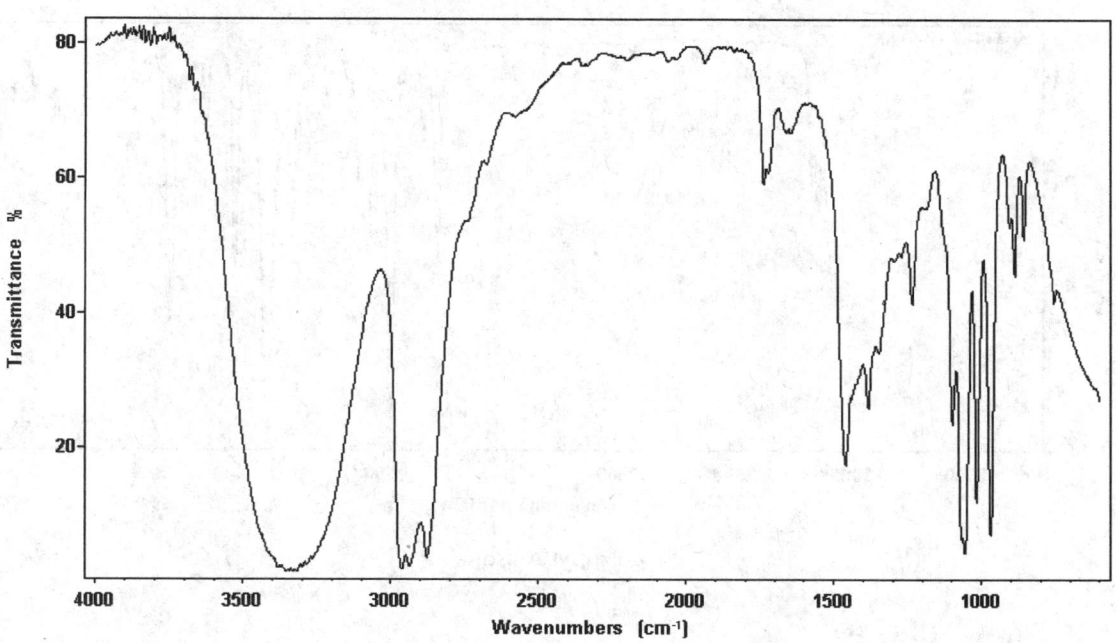

Propyl Alcohol

p-Propyl Anisole

First Published: Prior to FCC 6

Dihydroanethole

$C_{10}H_{14}O$ Formula wt 150.22
FEMA: 2930
UNII: 932XJ1O77X [4-propylanisole]

DESCRIPTION
p-Propyl Anisole occurs as a colorless to pale yellow liquid.
Odor: Anise, with sassafras background
Solubility: Soluble in most fixed oils; insoluble or practically insoluble in glycerin, propylene glycol
Boiling Point: ~215°
Solubility in Alcohol, Appendix VI: One mL dissolves in 5 mL of 80% alcohol and remains in solution on dilution.

Function: Flavoring agent

IDENTIFICATION
- **INFRARED SPECTRA,** Spectrophotometric Identification Tests, Appendix IIIC
  Acceptance criteria: The spectrum of the sample exhibits relative maxima at the same wavelengths as those of the spectrum below.

ASSAY
- **PROCEDURE:** Proceed as directed under M-1a, Appendix XI.
  Acceptance criteria: NLT 99.0% of $C_{10}H_{14}O$

SPECIFIC TESTS
- **REFRACTIVE INDEX,** Appendix II: At 20°
  Acceptance criteria: Between 1.502 and 1.506
- **SPECIFIC GRAVITY:** Determine at 25° by any reliable method (see General Provisions).
  Acceptance criteria: Between 0.940 and 0.943

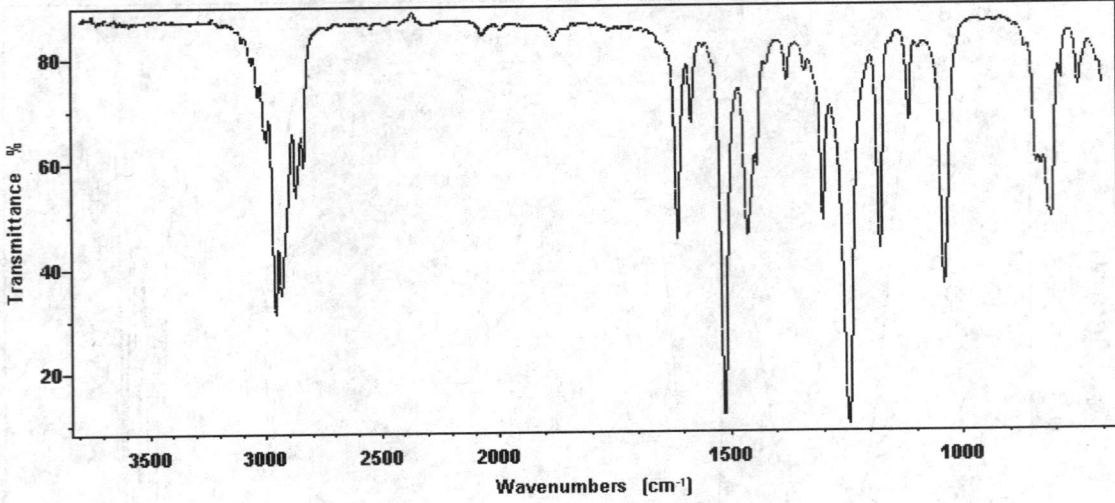

p-Propyl Anisole

Propyl Formate

First Published: Prior to FCC 6

C₄H₈O₂   Formula wt 88.11
FEMA: 2943
UNII: WO1ARV6GTW [propyl formate]

DESCRIPTION
Propyl Formate occurs as a colorless to pale yellow liquid.
Odor: Ethereal
Solubility: Soluble in propylene glycol, vegetable oils; insoluble or practically insoluble in water
Boiling Point: ~80°
Solubility in Alcohol, Appendix VI: One mL dissolves in 1 mL of 95% ethanol.
Function: Flavoring agent

IDENTIFICATION
- **INFRARED SPECTRA,** Spectrophotometric Identification Tests, Appendix IIIC

  Acceptance criteria: The spectrum of the sample exhibits relative maxima at the same wavelengths as those of the spectrum below.

ASSAY
- **PROCEDURE:** Proceed as directed under *M-1b*, Appendix XI.
  Acceptance criteria: NLT 95.0% of C₄H₈O₂

SPECIFIC TESTS
- **ACID VALUE, FLAVOR CHEMICALS (OTHER THAN ESSENTIAL OILS),** *M-15,* Appendix XI
  Analysis: Modify the procedure by adding ice to the solution.
  Acceptance criteria: NMT 5.0
- **REFRACTIVE INDEX,** Appendix II: At 20°
  Acceptance criteria: Between 1.374 and 1.380
- **SPECIFIC GRAVITY:** Determine at 25° by any reliable method (see *General Provisions*).
  Acceptance criteria: Between 0.898 and 0.904

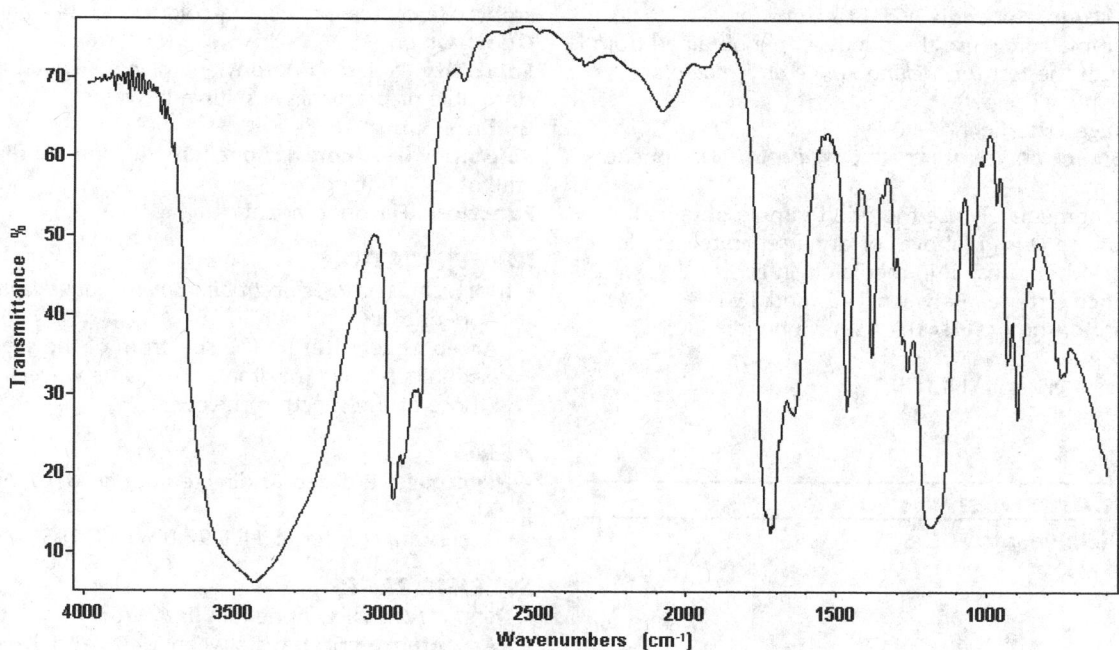

Propyl Formate

Propyl Gallate

First Published: Prior to FCC 6

Gallic Acid Propyl Ester

$C_{10}H_{12}O_5$ Formula wt 212.20
INS: 310 CAS: [121-79-9]
UNII: 8D4SNN7V92 [propyl gallate]

DESCRIPTION
Propyl Gallate occurs as a fine, white to nearly white powder. It is slightly soluble in water and freely soluble in alcohol and in ether.
Function: Antioxidant
Packaging and Storage: Store in well-closed containers.

IDENTIFICATION
- **MELTING RANGE OR TEMPERATURE DETERMINATION,** Appendix IIB
  Sample preparation: Place 5 g of sample and several boiling chips into a 500-mL round-bottom flask, connect a water-cooled condenser to the flask, and introduce a steady stream of nitrogen into the flask, maintaining the flow of nitrogen at all times during the remainder of the procedure. Pour 100 mL of 1 N sodium hydroxide through the top of the condenser, heat the solution to boiling, boil for 30 min, and cool. Place the round-bottom flask in an ice bath, and slowly, with occasional swirling, add dilute sulfuric acid (10%) until a pH of 2 to 3 is obtained (using pH paper). Filter the precipitate through a sintered-glass crucible, wash with a minimum amount of water, and dry at 110° for 2 h.
  Acceptance criteria: The gallic acid so obtained melts at about 240° with decomposition.

ASSAY
- **PROCEDURE**
  Sample: 200 mg, previously dried
  Analysis: Transfer the *Sample* into a 400-mL beaker, dissolve it in 150 mL of water, and heat to boiling. With constant and vigorous stirring, add 50 mL of bismuth nitrate TS, continue stirring and heating until precipitation is complete, and cool. Filter the yellow precipitate in a tared, sintered-glass crucible, wash it with cold 1:300 nitric acid, and dry at 110° to constant weight. The weight of the precipitate so obtained, multiplied by 0.4866, represents its equivalent of $C_{10}H_{12}O_5$.
  Acceptance criteria: NLT 98.0% and NMT 102.0% of $C_{10}H_{12}O_5$, on the dried basis

IMPURITIES
Inorganic Impurities
- **LEAD,** *Lead Limit Test, Flame Atomic Absorption Spectrophotometric Method,* Appendix IIIB
  Sample: 3 g
  Acceptance criteria: NMT 1 mg/kg

SPECIFIC TESTS

- **Loss on Drying,** Appendix IIC: 110° for 4 h
  [NOTE—Immediately use the dried sample obtained from this test in the test for *Melting Range or Temperature Determination* (below).]
  Acceptance criteria: NMT 0.5%
- **Melting Range or Temperature Determination,** Appendix IIB
  Sample: Immediately use the dried sample obtained from *Loss on Drying* (above) or dry a separate sample at 110° for 4 h and use it immediately in this test.
  Acceptance criteria: Between 146° and 150°
- **Residue on Ignition (Sulfated Ash),** Appendix IIC
  Sample: 2 g
  Acceptance criteria: NMT 0.1%

Propyl Mercaptan

First Published: Prior to FCC 6

C_3H_8S Formula wt 76.16
FEMA: 3521
UNII: 4AB0N08V2H [propyl mercaptan]

DESCRIPTION

Propyl Mercaptan occurs as a colorless to pale yellow liquid.
Odor: Onion
Solubility: Soluble in propylene glycol, vegetable oils; insoluble or practically insoluble in water
Boiling Point: ~67°
Solubility in Alcohol, Appendix VI: One mL dissolves in 1 mL of 95% ethanol.
Function: Flavoring agent

IDENTIFICATION

- **Infrared Spectra,** *Spectrophotometric Identification Tests,* Appendix IIIC
  Acceptance criteria: The spectrum of the sample exhibits relative maxima at the same wavelengths as those of the spectrum below.

ASSAY

- **Procedure:** Proceed as directed under *M-1b,* Appendix XI.
  Acceptance criteria: NLT 97.0% of C_3H_8S

SPECIFIC TESTS

- **Refractive Index,** Appendix II: At 20°
  Acceptance criteria: Between 1.436 and 1.442
- **Specific Gravity:** Determine at 25° by any reliable method (see *General Provisions*).
  Acceptance criteria: Between 0.838 and 0.844

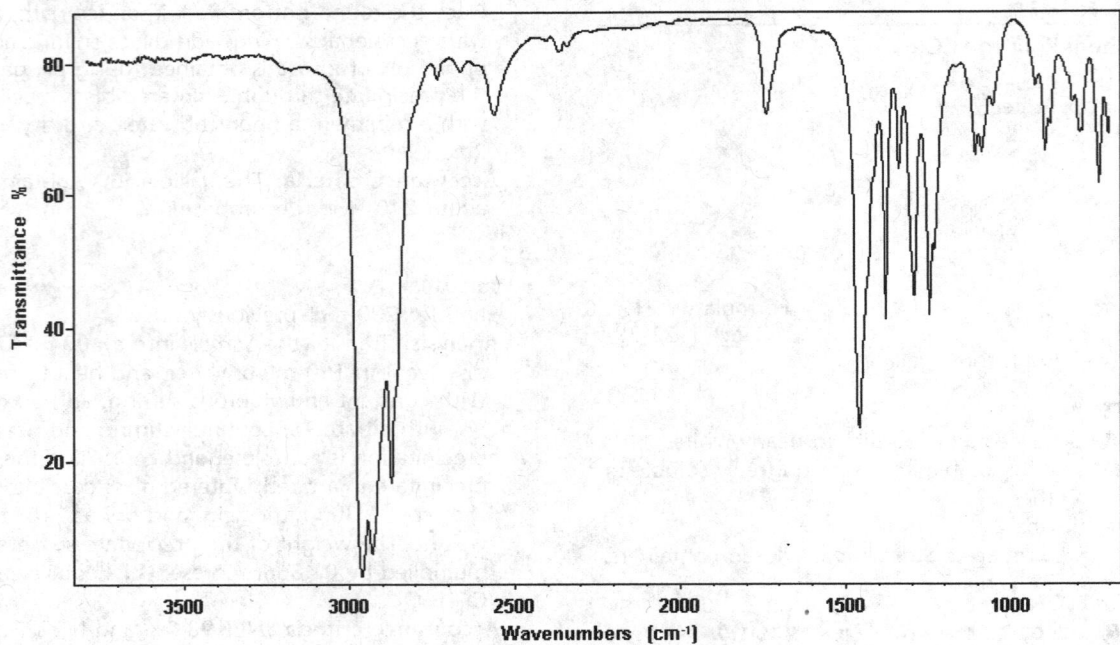

Propyl Mercaptan

Propyl Propionate

First Published: Prior to FCC 6

n-Propyl Propionate

C₆H₁₂O₂
FEMA: 2958
UNII: G09TRV00GK [propyl propionate]

Formula wt 116.16

DESCRIPTION
Propyl Propionate occurs as a colorless to pale yellow liquid.
Odor: Fruity
Boiling Point: ~123°
Solubility in Alcohol, Appendix VI: One mL dissolves in 1 mL of 95% alcohol.
Function: Flavoring agent

IDENTIFICATION
- **INFRARED SPECTRA,** *Spectrophotometric Identification Tests,* Appendix IIIC
  Acceptance criteria: The spectrum of the sample exhibits relative maxima at the same wavelengths as those of the spectrum below.

ASSAY
- **PROCEDURE:** Proceed as directed under *M-1b,* Appendix XI.
  Acceptance criteria: NLT 98.0% of C₆H₁₂O₂

SPECIFIC TESTS
- **ACID VALUE, FLAVOR CHEMICALS (OTHER THAN ESSENTIAL OILS),** *M-15,* Appendix XI
  Acceptance criteria: NMT 1.0
- **REFRACTIVE INDEX,** Appendix II: At 20°
  Acceptance criteria: Between 1.391 and 1.396
- **SPECIFIC GRAVITY:** Determine at 25° by any reliable method (see *General Provisions*).
  Acceptance criteria: Between 0.873 and 0.879

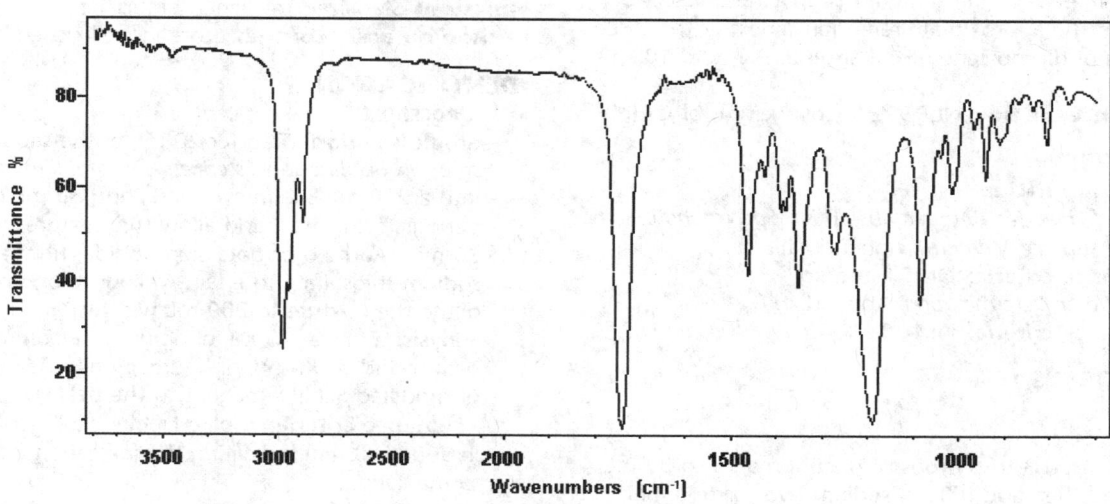

Propyl Propionate

Propylene Glycol

First Published: Prior to FCC 6

1,2-Propanediol
1,2-Dihydroxypropane
Methyl Glycol

C₃H₈O₂
INS: 1520
UNII: 6DC9Q167V3 [propylene glycol]

Formula wt 76.10
CAS: [57-55-6]

DESCRIPTION
Propylene Glycol occurs as a clear, colorless, viscous liquid. It absorbs moisture when exposed to moist air. It is miscible with water, with acetone, and with chloroform in all proportions. It is soluble in ether and will dissolve many essential oils, but is immiscible with fixed oils.
Function: Solvent; wetting agent; humectant
Packaging and Storage: Store in tight containers.

IDENTIFICATION
- **INFRARED ABSORPTION,** *Spectrophotometric Identification Tests,* Appendix IIIC
  Reference standard: USP Propylene Glycol RS
  Sample and Standard preparation: F
  Acceptance criteria: The spectrum of the sample exhibits maxima at the same wavelengths as those in the spectrum of the *Reference standard.*

ASSAY
- **PROCEDURE**
  Chromatographic system, Appendix IIA
  Mode: Gas chromatography
  Detector: Thermal conductivity detector
  Column: 1-m × 8-mm (id) stainless steel tubing (Perkin Elmer Instruments, or equivalent) packed with 4% Carbowax compound 20 M on 40- to 60- mesh Chromosorb T, or equivalent materials)
  Temperature
    Column: 120° to 200° (at 5°/min)
    Injection port: 240°
    Detector block: 250°
  Carrier gas: Helium
  Flow rate: 75 mL/min
  Injection volume: 10 µL
  Analysis: Inject the sample into the chromatograph. Measure the area under all peaks by any convenient means, calculate the normalized area percentage of propylene glycol, and report as weight percentage. [NOTE—Under the conditions described, the approximate retention time for propylene glycol is 5.7 min and the approximate retention times for the three isomers of dipropylene glycol are 8.2, 9.0, and 10.2 min.]
  Acceptance criteria: NLT 99.5%, by weight, of $C_3H_8O_2$

IMPURITIES
Inorganic Impurities
- **LEAD,** Lead Limit Test, Atomic Absorption Spectrophotometric Graphite Furnace Method I, Appendix IIIB
  Acceptance criteria: NMT 1 mg/kg
- **WATER,** Water Determination, Appendix IIB
  Acceptance criteria: NMT 0.2%

SPECIFIC TESTS
- **ACIDITY**
  Sample: 50 g
  Analysis: Add 3 to 6 drops of phenol red TS to 50 mL of water, then add 0.01 N sodium hydroxide until the solution remains red for 30 s. Add the Sample to this solution and titrate with 0.01 N sodium hydroxide until the original red color returns and remains for 15 s.
  Acceptance criteria: NMT 1.67 mL of 0.01 N sodium hydroxide is required to return the solution to its original red color.
- **DISTILLATION RANGE,** Appendix IIB
  Acceptance criteria: Between 185° and 189°
- **RESIDUE ON IGNITION (SULFATED ASH),** Appendix IIC
  Sample: 50 g
  Analysis: Heat the Sample in a tared, 100-mL shallow dish until it ignites, and allow it to burn without further application of heat in a place free from drafts. Cool, moisten the residue with 5 mL of sulfuric acid, and ignite at about 800° for 15 min.
  Acceptance criteria: NMT 0.007%
- **SPECIFIC GRAVITY:** Determine by any reliable method (see General Provisions).
  Acceptance criteria: Between 1.035 and 1.037

Propylene Glycol Alginate
First Published: Prior to FCC 6

Hydroxypropyl Alginate
Algin Derivative

$(C_9H_{14}O_7)_n$ (esterified)   Equiv wt, calculated 234.21
INS: 405   CAS: [9005-37-2]
UNII: 26CD3J2R0C [propylene glycol alginate]

DESCRIPTION
Propylene Glycol Alginate occurs as a white to yellow, fibrous or granular powder. It is the propylene glycol ester of alginic acid (See the monograph for Alginic Acid.). It varies in composition according to its degree of esterification and the percentages of free and neutralized carboxyl groups in the molecule. It dissolves in water, in solutions of dilute organic acids, and depending upon the degree of esterification, in hydroalcoholic mixtures containing up to 60% by weight of alcohol to form stable, viscous, colloidal solutions at pH 3.
Function: Stabilizer; thickener; emulsifier
Packaging and Storage: Store in well-closed containers.

IDENTIFICATION
- **A. PROCEDURE**
  Sample solution: Transfer 20 mL of the saponified solution obtained in Esterified Carboxyl Groups (below) into a 250-mL Erlenmeyer flask, add 50 mL of 0.1 M periodic acid, swirl, and allow the mixture to stand for 30 min. Add 2 g of potassium iodide, titrate with 0.1 N sodium thiosulfate to a faint yellow color, and then dilute the mixture to 200 mL with water.
  Analysis: Transfer 10 mL of Sample solution to a small beaker and add 5 mL of hydrochloric acid and 10 mL of modified Schiff's reagent to the beaker.
  Acceptance criteria: A blue to blue-violet color appears in about 20 min indicating the formation of formaldehyde.
- **B. PROCEDURE**
  Analysis: Transfer a 10-mL aliquot of the Sample solution prepared for Identification test A (above) to a small beaker and add 1 mL of a saturated solution of piperazine hydrate and 0.5 mL of sodium nitroferricyanide TS to the beaker.
  Acceptance criteria: A green color appears indicating the formation of acetaldehyde.

ASSAY
- **ALGINATES ASSAY,** Appendix IIIC
  Acceptance criteria: A sample yields NLT 16.0% and NMT 20.0% of carbon dioxide (CO_2), calculated on the dried basis.

IMPURITIES
Inorganic Impurities
- **ARSENIC,** Arsenic Limit Test, Appendix IIIB
  Procedure: Prepare as directed for organic compounds.
  Acceptance criteria: NMT 3 mg/kg
- **LEAD,** Lead Limit Test, Appendix IIIB
  Procedure: Prepare as directed for organic compounds.

Control: 5 µg Pb (5 mL of *Diluted Standard Lead Solution*)
Acceptance criteria: NMT 5 mg/kg

SPECIFIC TESTS
- **ESTERIFIED CARBOXYL GROUPS**
  Sample: Use the solution obtained in the test for *Free Carboxyl Groups* (below).
  Analysis: Quantitatively transfer the *Sample* into a 1-L Erlenmeyer flask, add a few drops of phenolphthalein TS and 50.0 mL of 0.1 N sodium hydroxide. Stopper the flask, swirl the solution, and then allow it to stand for 30 min at room temperature. Titrate the excess sodium hydroxide to a faint pink endpoint with 0.1 N hydrochloric acid. Transfer the solution to a 600-mL beaker, and complete the titration to a pH of 7.0, determining the endpoint potentiometrically. Calculate the percentage of esterified carboxyl groups by the formula:

  $$\text{Result} = (V \times F)/(CD_S \times W)$$

  V = volume of 0.1 N sodium hydroxide consumed (mL)
  F = factor, 44
  CD_S = percentage of carbon dioxide in the sample as determined by the *Assay*
  W = weight of the sample (calculated on the dried basis) for the test for *Free Carboxyl Groups*

  Acceptance criteria: NLT 40.0% calculated on the dried basis

- **FREE CARBOXYL GROUPS**
  Sample: 1 g
  Analysis: Transfer the *Sample* into a 600-mL beaker and dissolve it in 200 mL of water, stirring mechanically for a minimum of 30 min. Titrate the solution with 0.1 N sodium hydroxide to pH 7.0, determining the endpoint potentiometrically. [NOTE—Retain this resulting solution for the test for *Esterified Carboxyl Groups* (above).] Calculate the percentage of free carboxyl groups by the formula:

  $$\text{Result} = (V \times F)/(CD_S \times W)$$

  V = volume of 0.1 N sodium hydroxide consumed (mL)
  F = factor, 44
  CD_S = percentage of carbon dioxide in the sample as determined by the *Assay*
  W = weight of the sample taken, calculated on the dried basis (g)

  Acceptance criteria: NMT 35.0%, calculated on the dried basis

- **LOSS ON DRYING**, Appendix IIC: 105° for 4 h
  Acceptance criteria: NMT 20.0%

- **NEUTRALIZED CARBOXYL GROUPS**
  Analysis: Calculate the percentage of *Neutralized Carboxyl Groups* by subtracting the sum of the percentage of *Free Carboxyl Groups* and the percentage of *Esterified Carboxyl Groups* from 100%.
  Acceptance criteria: NMT 45.0%

Propylene Glycol Mono- and Diesters

First Published: Prior to FCC 6

Propylene Glycol Mono- and Diesters of Fatty Acids
Propylene Glycol Monostearate (or other appropriate ester)
INS: 477
UNII: F76354LMGR [propylene glycol monopalmitostearate]

DESCRIPTION
Propylene Glycol Mono- and Diesters occur as a clear liquid or as white to yellow-white beads, flakes, or other solid material. It is a mixture of Propylene Glycol Mono- and Diesters of fats and/or fatty acids. It is insoluble in water, but it is soluble in alcohol, in ethyl acetate, and in chloroform and other chlorinated hydrocarbons.
Function: Emulsifier; stabilizer
Packaging and Storage: Store in well-closed containers.

IMPURITIES
Inorganic Impurities
- **LEAD**, *Lead Limit Test, Flame Atomic Absorption Spectrophotometric Method*, Appendix IIIB
  Sample: 10 g
  Acceptance criteria: NMT 2 mg/kg

SPECIFIC TESTS
- **ACID VALUE (FATS AND RELATED SUBSTANCES)**, Method II, Appendix VII
  Acceptance criteria: NMT 4
- **FREE PROPYLENE GLYCOL**, *Free Glycerin or Propylene Glycol*, Appendix VII
  Acceptance criteria: NMT 1.5%
- **HYDROXYL VALUE**, Method II, Appendix VII
  Sample: 2 g
  Acceptance criteria: The result should conform to the representations of the vendor.
- **IODINE VALUE**, Appendix VII
  Acceptance criteria: The result should conform to the representations of the vendor.
- **RESIDUE ON IGNITION (SULFATED ASH)**, Appendix IIC
  Sample: 5 g
  Acceptance criteria: NMT 0.5%
- **SAPONIFICATION VALUE**, Appendix VII
  Sample: 4 g
  Acceptance criteria: The result should conform to the representations of the vendor.
- **SOAP (AS POTASSIUM STEARATE)**, *Soap*, Appendix VII
  Sample: 5 g
  Analysis: Use 31.0 as the equivalence factor (e) in the calculation.
  Acceptance criteria: NMT 7.0%
- **TOTAL MONOESTER CONTENT**
  Sample preparation: Transfer 25 g of sample into a 500-mL round-bottom boiling flask, add 250 mL of alcohol and 7.5 g of potassium hydroxide, and mix.

Connect a suitable condenser to the flask, reflux the mixture for 1 to 2 h, then transfer to an 800-mL beaker, rinsing the flask with about 100 mL of water and adding it to the beaker. Heat on a steam bath to evaporate the alcohol, adding water occasionally to replace the alcohol, and evaporate until the odor of alcohol can no longer be detected. Adjust the final volume to about 250 mL with hot water. Neutralize the soap solution with 1:2 sulfuric acid, add 10% in excess, and heat, while stirring, until the fatty acid layer separates. Use the separated fatty acids as the *Sample preparation*.

Analysis: Determine the acid value (AV) of the *Sample preparation* as directed under *Acid Value (Fats and Related Substances), Method I*, Appendix VII. Calculate the average molecular weight (MW) of the monoester by the equation:

$$MW = (56{,}109/AV) + 76.10 - 18.02$$

Calculate the hydroxyl equivalent of free propylene glycol (F) by the equation:

$$F = 561.1G/38.05$$

G = percentage of free propylene glycol (determined above in the test for *Free Propylene Glycol*)

Finally, calculate the percentage of total monoester in the original sample by the formula:

$$Result = [(H - F) \times MW]/561$$

H = hydroxyl value (determined above in the test for *Hydroxyl Value*)

Acceptance criteria: NLT the minimum percentage claimed by the vendor

Propylene Oxide

First Published: First Supplement, FCC 7

Epoxypropane
Methyl Ethylene Oxide
Methyl Oxirane
Propene Oxide
1,2-Propylene Oxide

C$_3$H$_6$O
Formula wt 58.08
CAS: [75-56-9]

UNII: Y4Y7NYD4BK [propylene oxide]

DESCRIPTION

Propylene Oxide occurs as a colorless volatile liquid with an ether-like odor. It is usually produced by peroxide-based epoxidation of propylene or dehydrochlorination of propylene chlorohydrin. Propylene Oxide is freely soluble in water and miscible in ethanol and ether.

Function: Reactive chemical intermediate used in the manufacture of food ingredients (polyols, propylene glycol, modified food starch, etc.); preservative; antimicrobial agent

Packaging and Storage: Store in tight containers in a cool place, remote from fire. [**Caution**—Propylene Oxide is highly volatile and flammable and is classified as a suspect human carcinogen. Keep away from sources of ignition. The material should be handled with appropriate ventilation and personal protective equipment.]

IDENTIFICATION

- **A. Infrared Absorption**, *Spectrophotometric Identification Tests*, Appendix IIIC
  Reference standard: USP Propylene Oxide RS
  Sample and standard preparation: *F*
  Acceptance criteria: The spectrum of the sample exhibits maxima at the same wavelengths as those in the spectrum of the *Reference standard*.

- **B. Procedure**
  Acceptance criteria: The major peak in the chromatogram of the sample is at the same retention time as the major peak in the chromatogram of the *Standard*, as determined from the *Assay* below.

- **C. Specific Gravity:** Determine by any reliable method (see *General Provisions*).
  Acceptance criteria: 0.829–0.831 at 20°/20°

ASSAY

- **Procedure**
  Standard: USP Propylene Oxide RS
  Chromatographic system, Appendix IIA
  Mode: Gas chromatography
  Detector: Flame ionization
  Column: 60-m × 0.32-mm (i.d.) fused silica capillary column with a 1.5-μm trifluoropropylmethylpolysiloxane stationary phase[1]
  Temperature
  Injector: 65°
  Detector: 175°
  Column: See table below.

Time (min)	Temperature (°)
0	33
7.5	33
19.7	94
22	94
24.8	150
28	150

Carrier gas: Hydrogen
Detector gas flows
  Hydrogen carrier: 28 mL/min
  Make-up (helium): 30 mL/min
  Air: 400 mL/min
Head pressure: 8.3 psi

---

[1] Restek Chromatography Products RTX-200, or equivalent. Available at www.restek.com.

Linear velocity: 40 cm/s
Flow rate: 1.97 mL/min
Injection size: 1 µL
Split ratio: 25:1
Septum purge: 2.0 mL/min
Analysis: Separately inject a sample of Propylene Oxide and the *Standard* into the chromatograph and record the chromatograms.

Identify the impurities present and calculate their concentrations using pre-determined response factors. [NOTE—Potential organic impurities include acetone, methanol, methyl formate, and propionaldehyde.] Calculate the percentage of propylene oxide in the sample as the difference between 100.0 and the sum of all impurities detected from the chromatogram of the sample.

Acceptance criteria: The percentage of propylene oxide in the sample is NLT 99.90%.

IMPURITIES
Inorganic Impurities
- **TOTAL CHLORIDES**[2]

  Apparatus

  Combustion furnace: Electric furnace capable of maintaining a temperature of 800°

  Combustion tube: Quartz; constructed such that the sample, vaporized in the inlet section, is swept into the oxidation zone by an inert gas (argon, helium, nitrogen, or carbon dioxide of high purity grade) where it mixes with oxygen and is burned. The inlet end of the tube contains a septum and has side arms for the introduction of oxygen and the inert gas. The center section of the tube should be of sufficient volume to allow complete oxidation of the sample.

  Titration cell: The cell should contain a sensor-reference pair of electrodes (to detect changes in silver-ion concentration), a generator anode-cathode pair of electrodes (to maintain constant silver-ion concentration), and an inlet for the gaseous sample from the pyrolysis tube. The sensor, reference, and anode electrodes should be silver electrodes and the cathode electrode should be a platinum wire. The reference electrode should reside in a saturated silver acetate half-cell and the electrolyte should contain 70% acetic acid in water.

  Microcoulometer: Use a microcoulometer having variable gain and bias control, capable of measuring the potential of the sensing-reference electrode pair and of comparing this potential with a bias potential, and of applying the amplified difference to the working-auxiliary electrode pair so as to generate a titrant. The output of the microcoulometer signal should be proportional to the generating current. Use an apparatus with a digital meter and circuitry to convert the output signal directly to mass (in ng or µg) of chloride.

Sampling syringe: A µL sampling syringe capable of delivering 5- to 50-µL samples into the pyrolysis tube should be used. The recommended needle length is 3- or 6-in in order to reach the inlet zone.

Pump: A constant-rate syringe pump or manual dispensing adapter may be used to regulate flow of the sample into the combustion tube. Flow rate should not exceed 0.5 µL/s.

Operating conditions
[NOTE—Set up the analyzer as directed by the manufacturer. Typical operating conditions are given below.]

Reactant gas flow (O$_2$)	160 mL/min
Carrier gas flow (argon, helium, nitrogen, or carbon dioxide)	40 mL/min
Furnace temperature:	
Inlet zone	700°
Center/outlet zones	800°
Coulometer:	
Bias voltage	240–265 mV
Gain	~1200

Sample: Propylene Oxide

Standard solution: Dissolve 3.174 mg/mL of chlorobenzene in 2,2,4-trimethyl pentane and dilute with the same solvent to 500 mL (1000 mg/L of chloride). Dilute 1.0 mL of this solution with the same solvent to 100 mL (10 mg/L of chloride).

Blank: 2,2,4-trimethyl pentane

Injection size: 40 µL

Analysis: Separately inject the *Standard solution*, *Sample*, and *Blank* into the pyrolysis tube at a rate of NMT 0.5 µL/s. Use the readouts obtained from the microcoulometer to calculate the chloride content, in µg/g, in the sample taken:

$$\text{Result} = [R_U/(V_U \times D_U \times RF)] - [R_B/(V_B \times D_B \times RF)]$$

R_U = microcoulometer readout obtained from the *Sample* (ng)
V_U = injection size for the *Sample* (µL)
D_U = density of the *Sample* (g/mL)
RF = recovery factor; calculate as directed below
R_B = microcoulometer readout obtained from the *Blank* (ng)
V_B = injection size for the *Blank* (µL)
D_B = density of the *Blank* (g/mL)

Recovery Factor, $RF = [R_S/(V_S \times D_S \times C_S)] - [R_B/(V_B \times D_B)]$

R_S = microcoulometer readout obtained from the *Standard solution* (ng)
V_S = injection size for the *Standard solution* (µL)
D_S = density of the *Standard solution* (g/mL)
C_S = concentration of chloride in the *Standard solution* (mg/kg)
R_B = microcoulometer readout obtained from the *Blank*
V_B = injection size for the *Blank* (µL)
D_B = density of the *Blank* (g/mL)

---
[2] Adapted from ASTM D4929-07 Standard Test Methods for Determination of Organic Chloride Content in Crude Oil, Method B. The original ASTM method is available in its entirety from ASTM International, 100 Barr Harbor Drive, West Conshocken, PA 19428. Phone: 610-832-9585, Fax: 610-832-9555, Email: service@astm.org, Website: www.astm.org.

Acceptance criteria: NMT 10 µg/g

Organic Impurities
- **ACIDITY (AS ACETIC ACID)**
  Solution A: Dissolve 0.2 g of phenolphthalein in 60 mL of 90% ethanol. Dilute with water to 100 mL.
  Sample: 50 mL (measure in a chilled graduated cylinder)
  Analysis: Transfer the Sample to a chilled 250-mL Erlenmeyer flask, add 1 mL of Solution A, and titrate with 0.01 N sodium hydroxide to a faint pink endpoint which persists for NLT 15 s.
  Calculate the percentage of acetic acid present:

  $$\text{Result} = V_T \times 0.060 \times (1/V_{PO}) \times (1/S) \times 100$$

  V_T = volume of 0.01 N sodium hydroxide required for the titration (mL)
  V_{PO} = volume of the propylene oxide Sample taken (mL)
  S = specific gravity of the Sample
  Acceptance criteria: NMT 0.002%

SPECIFIC TESTS
- **NONVOLATILE RESIDUE**
  [NOTE—Perform analysis in a fume hood to avoid exposure to propylene oxide vapors.]
  Sample: 100 mL
  Analysis: Evaporate the Sample to dryness in a tared platinum dish (previously heated at 105° to constant weight) on a steam bath, heat at 105° for 30 min or to constant weight, cool in a desiccator, and weigh.
  Acceptance criteria: NMT 0.002 g/100 mL
- **WATER**, Water Determination, Appendix IIB
  Acceptance criteria: NMT 0.01%

Propylparaben

First Published: Prior to FCC 6
Last Revision: Third Supplement, FCC 7

Propyl *p*-Hydroxybenzoate

$C_{10}H_{12}O_3$ Formula wt 180.20
INS: 216   CAS: [94-13-3]
UNII: Z8IX2SC1OH [propylparaben]

DESCRIPTION
Propylparaben occurs as small, colorless crystals or as a white powder. One g dissolves in about 2500 mL of water at 25°, in about 400 mL of boiling water, in about 1.5 mL of alcohol, and in about 3 mL of ether.
Function: Preservative; antimicrobial agent
Packaging and Storage: Store in well-closed containers.

IDENTIFICATION
- **INFRARED ABSORPTION**, Spectrophotometric Identification Tests, Appendix IIIC
  Reference standard: USP Propylparaben RS
  Sample and standard preparation: M
  Acceptance criteria: The spectrum of the sample exhibits maxima at the same wavelengths as those in the spectrum of the Reference standard.
- **MELTING RANGE OR TEMPERATURE DETERMINATION**, Appendix IIB
  Sample preparation: Dissolve 500 mg of sample in 10 mL of 1 N sodium hydroxide, boil for 30 min, allow the solution to evaporate to a volume of about 5 mL, and cool. Acidify the solution with 2 N sulfuric acid, collect the resulting, liberated *p*-hydroxybenzoic acid crystals on a filter, wash several times with small portions of water, and dry in a desiccator over silica gel.
  Acceptance criteria: The *p*-hydroxybenzoic acid thus obtained melts between 212° and 217°.

ASSAY
- **PROCEDURE**
  Mobile phase: Methanol and a 6.8-g/L solution of potassium dihydrogen phosphate (65:35 v/v)
  Standard solution: Dissolve 50.0 mg of USP Propylparaben RS in 2.5 mL of methanol, and dilute with Mobile phase to 50 mL. Dilute 10.0 mL of this solution with Mobile phase to 100 mL.
  Sample solution: Dissolve 50.0 mg in 2.5 mL of methanol, and dilute with Mobile phase to 50 mL. Dilute 10.0 mL of this solution with Mobile phase to 100 mL.
  Chromatographic system, Appendix IIA
    Mode: High-performance liquid chromatography
    Detector: UV 272 nm
    Column: 4.6-mm × 15-cm column packed with octadecyl silane chemically bonded to porous silica or ceramic microparticles 5-µm in diameter
    Flow rate: 1.3 mL/min
    [NOTE—The run time is about 2.5 times the retention time of propylparaben.]
    Injection size: 10 µL
  System suitability
    Sample: Standard solution
    Suitability requirement: The relative standard deviation for 6 injections is NMT 0.85%.
  Analysis: Separately inject the Sample solution and the Standard solution into the chromatograph. Record the chromatograms and calculate the percentage of propylparaben in the sample taken:

  $$\text{Result} = (r_U/r_S) \times (C_S/C_U) \times 100$$

  r_U = peak area of propylparaben from the chromatogram of the Sample solution
  r_S = peak area of propylparaben from the chromatogram of the Standard solution
  C_S = concentration of USP Propylparaben RS in the Standard solution, corrected for purity (mg/mL)
  C_U = concentration of the Sample solution (mg/mL)
  Acceptance criteria: 99.0%–100.5%, calculated on the dried basis

IMPURITIES
Inorganic Impurities
- **LEAD,** *Lead Limit Test, Flame Atomic Absorption Spectrophotometric Method,* Appendix IIIB
  Sample: 10 g
  Acceptance criteria: NMT 2 mg/kg

SPECIFIC TESTS
- **ACIDITY**
  Sample: 750 mg
  Analysis: Mix the *Sample* with 15 mL of water, heat at 80° for 1 min, cool, and filter. The filtrate is acid or neutral to litmus. Add 0.2 mL of 0.1 N sodium hydroxide and 2 drops of methyl red TS to 10 mL of the filtrate.
  Acceptance criteria: The resulting solution is yellow, without even a light cast of pink.
- **LOSS ON DRYING,** Appendix IIC: Over silica gel for 5 h
  Acceptance criteria: NMT 0.5%
- **MELTING RANGE OR TEMPERATURE DETERMINATION,** Appendix IIB
  Acceptance criteria: Between 95° and 98°
- **RESIDUE ON IGNITION (SULFATED ASH),** Appendix IIC
  Sample: 4 g
  Acceptance criteria: NMT 0.05%

Pullulan

First Published: First Supplement, FCC 6
Last Revision: FCC 7

Poly[6-α-D-glucopyranosyl-(1→4)-α-D-glucopyranosyl-(1→4)-α-D-glucopyranosyl-(1→]

$(C_{18}H_{30}O_{15})_n$

INS: 1204
UNII: 8ZQ0AYU1TT [pullulan]
CAS: [9057-02-07]

DESCRIPTION
Pullulan occurs as a white to off-white odorless powder. It is a neutral simple polysaccharide produced by the fermentation of hydrolyzed starch using *Aureobasidium pullulans*. After completion of the fermentation, the fungal cells are removed by microfiltration, the filtrate is heat-sterilized, and pigments and other impurities are removed by adsorption and ion exchange chromatography. It is a linear glucan consisting predominately of α-(1→6)-linked maltotriose subunits. It may also contain some maltotetraose subunits. It is freely soluble in water, and practically insoluble in dehydrated alcohol.
Function: Glazing agent; film-forming agent; thickener
Packaging and Storage: Store in well-closed containers.

IDENTIFICATION
- **A. PROCEDURE**
  Analysis: In small increments, dissolve 10 g of sample in 100 mL of water with stirring.
  Acceptance criteria: A viscous solution is produced.
  [NOTE—Retain this solution for *Identification* test B.]
- **B. DEPOLYMERIZATION WITH PULLULANASE**
  Sample: 10 mL of the viscous solution obtained in *Identification* test A
  Pullulanase solution: Prepare a solution of pullulanase containing 10 units/mL as directed in *Enzyme Assays, Pullulanase Activity,* Appendix V.
  Analysis: Mix the *Sample* with 0.1 mL of *Pullulanase solution*, and allow the mixture to incubate at 25° for about 20 min.
  Acceptance criteria: A significant loss of viscosity is observed.
- **C. PROCEDURE**
  Sample solution: 20 mg/mL
  Analysis: To 10 mL of *Sample solution*, add 2 mL of polyethylene glycol 600.
  Acceptance criteria: A white precipitate immediately forms.

ASSAY
- **PROCEDURE**
  Analysis: Calculate the percentage of glucan in the sample:

  $$\text{Result} = 100 - [L + (R/F_1) + (N \times F_2) + C]$$

  L = percent *Loss on Drying*
  R = percent *Residue on Ignition (Sulfated Ash)*
  N = percent *Nitrogen Content*
  C = Percent *Mono-, Di-, and Oligosaccharides*
  F_1 = sulfate correction factor, 1.3
  F_2 = nitrogen-to-protein conversion factor, 6.25
  Acceptance criteria: More than 90%

IMPURITIES
Inorganic Impurities
- **LEAD,** *Lead Limit Test, Atomic Absorption Spectrophotometric Graphite Furnace Method, Method I,* Appendix IIIB
  Acceptance criteria: Less than 0.1 mg/kg

SPECIFIC TESTS
- **LOSS ON DRYING,** Appendix IIC: 90° for 6 h in vacuum
  Acceptance criteria: Less than 6.0%
- **MONO-, DI-, AND OLIGOSACCHARIDES**
  Sample stock solution: 8 mg/mL of sample using a previously dried sample
  Sample solution: To 1.0 mL of the *Sample stock solution* add 0.1 mL of saturated potassium chloride solution, and shake vigorously with 3 mL of methyl alcohol. Centrifuge, and use the supernatant.
  Reference solution: 160-µg/mL sample, from *Sample stock solution*
  Blank: Use water
  Analysis: Transfer 0.2 mL each of the *Reference solution*, the *Sample solution*, and the *Blank* to a test tube containing 5 mL of a 1 in 500 solution of anthrone in

75% (v/v) sulfuric acid, with the test tube placed in ice water. Mix each tube immediately, and then heat the test tube at 90° for 10 min. Remove the tube, and allow it to cool in cold running water. Perform the test with the solutions so obtained using a suitable UV/visible spectrophotometer, and using water as a blank. Determine the absorbances A_U, A_B, and A_S at 620 nm, for the *Sample solution*, the *Blank*, and the *Reference solution*, respectively. Determine the percentage of monosaccharide, disaccharide, and oligosaccharides in the portion of dried sample taken:

$$\text{Result} = (A_U - A_B)/(A_S - A_B) \times (D_1/D_2) \times 100$$

A_U = absorbance of the *Sample solution*
A_B = absorbance of the *Blank*
A_S = absorbance of the *Reference solution*
D_1 = dilution factor for the *Sample solution*, 4.1
D_2 = dilution factor for the *Reference solution*, 50

Acceptance criteria: Less than 10.0%, on the dried basis

- **NITROGEN CONTENT**, *Nitrogen Determination*, Appendix IIIC
  Sample: 3 g, previously dried
  Analysis: Determine as directed using 12 mL of sulfuric acid for the decomposition and 40 mL of the sodium hydroxide (400 mg/mL) solution.
  Acceptance criteria: Less than 0.05%
- **PH**, *pH Determination*, Appendix IIB
  Sample solution: 1.0 g in 10 mL of freshly boiled and cooled water
  Acceptance criteria: 5.0–7.0
- **RESIDUE ON IGNITION (SULFATED ASH)**, Appendix IIC
  Sample: 2.0 g
  Analysis: Proceed as directed, but igniting at 450°–550° for 3 h.
  Acceptance criteria: Less than 1.5%
- **VISCOSITY DETERMINATION**, Appendix IIB
  Sample: 10.0 g, previously dried
  Sample solution: Dissolve the *Sample* in water to make 100 g of solution.
  Analysis: Use an Ubbelohde viscometer and perform the test at 30.0 ± 0.1°.
  Acceptance criteria: 100–180 mm^2s^{-1}

Pyridoxine Hydrochloride

First Published: Prior to FCC 6

5-Hydroxy-6-methyl-3,4-pyridinedimethanol Hydrochloride
Pyridoxol Hydrochloride
Vitamin B6 Hydrochloride
Vitamin B6

$C_8H_{11}NO_3 \cdot HCl$ Formula wt 205.64
CAS: [58-56-0]
UNII: 68Y4CF58BV [pyridoxine hydrochloride]

DESCRIPTION
Pyridoxine Hydrochloride occurs as colorless or white crystals or as a white, crystalline powder. It is stable in air, but is slowly affected by sunlight. Its solutions are acid to litmus, having a pH of about 3. One g dissolves in 5 mL of water and in about 100 mL of alcohol. It is insoluble in ether. It melts at about 206° with some decomposition.
Function: Nutrient
Packaging and Storage: Store in tight, light-resistant containers, and avoid exposure to sunlight.

IDENTIFICATION
- **A. PROCEDURE**
  Sample solution: 100 μg/mL
  Analysis: Place 1 mL of the *Sample solution* into each of two test tubes marked *A* and *B*, and add 2 mL of a 1:5 sodium acetate solution to each tube. Add 1 mL of water to tube *A*, and add 1 mL of a 40 mg/mL boric acid solution to tube *B*, and mix. Cool both tubes to about 20°, and rapidly add 1 mL of a 5 mg/mL solution of 2,6-dichloroquinonechlorimide in alcohol to each tube.
  Acceptance criteria: A blue color appears in tube *A*, which fades rapidly and becomes red in a few minutes, but no blue color appears in tube *B*.
- **B. PROCEDURE**
  Sample solution: 5 mg/mL
  Analysis: Add 0.5 mL of phosphotungstic acid TS to 2 mL the *Sample solution*.
  Acceptance criteria: A white precipitate forms.
- **C. CHLORIDE**, Appendix IIIA
  Acceptance criteria: Passes test

ASSAY
- **PROCEDURE**
  Sample: 400 mg
  Analysis: Dissolve the *Sample* in a mixture of 10 mL of glacial acetic acid and 10 mL of mercuric acetate TS, warming slightly to aid in dissolution. Cool to room temperature, add 2 drops of crystal violet TS, and titrate with 0.1 N perchloric acid. [**CAUTION**—Handle perchloric acid in an appropriate fume hood.] Perform a blank determination (see *General Provisions*) and make any necessary correction. Each mL of 0.1 N perchloric acid is equivalent to 20.56 mg of $C_8H_{11}NO_3 \cdot HCl$.
  Acceptance criteria: NLT 98.0% and NMT 100.5% of $C_8H_{11}NO_3 \cdot HCl$, calculated on the dried basis

IMPURITIES
Inorganic Impurities
- **LEAD**, *Lead Limit Test, Flame Atomic Absorption Spectrophotometric Method*, Appendix IIIB
  Sample: 5 g
  Acceptance criteria: NMT 2 mg/kg

SPECIFIC TESTS
- **CHLORIDE CONTENT**
  Sample: 500 mg

Analysis: Dissolve the *Sample* in 50 mL of methanol in a glass-stoppered flask. Add 5 mL of glacial acetic acid and 2 to 3 drops of eosin Y TS and titrate with 0.1 N silver nitrate. Each mL of 0.1 N silver nitrate is equivalent to 3.545 mg of chloride.
  Acceptance criteria: NLT 16.9% and NMT 17.6% of chloride, calculated on the dried basis
- **Loss on Drying,** Appendix IIC: in vacuum over silica gel for 4 h
  Acceptance criteria: NMT 0.5%
- **Residue on Ignition (Sulfated Ash),** Appendix IIC
  Sample: 2 g
  Acceptance criteria: NMT 0.1%

Pyrrole

First Published: Prior to FCC 6

C_4H_5N Formula wt 67.09
FEMA: 3386
UNII: 86S1ZD6L2C [pyrrole]

DESCRIPTION
Pyrrole occurs as a colorless to yellow liquid. It darkens on aging.

Odor: Nutty, sweet, warm, ethereal
Solubility: Soluble in alcohol, most fixed oils; slightly soluble in water
Boiling Point: ~130° (decomp)
Function: Flavoring agent

IDENTIFICATION
- **Infrared Spectra,** *Spectrophotometric Identification Tests,* Appendix IIIC
  Acceptance criteria: The spectrum of the sample exhibits relative maxima at the same wavelengths as those of the spectrum below.

ASSAY
- **Procedure:** Proceed as directed under *M-1a,* Appendix XI.
  Acceptance criteria: NLT 98.0% of C_4H_5N

SPECIFIC TESTS
- **Refractive Index,** Appendix II: At 20°
  Acceptance criteria: Between 1.507 and 1.510
- **Specific Gravity:** Determine at 20° by any reliable method (see *General Provisions*).
  Acceptance criteria: Between 0.950 and 0.980

OTHER REQUIREMENTS
- **Distillation Range,** Appendix IIB
  Acceptance criteria: Between 125° and 130°
- **Water,** *Water Determination, Method I,* Appendix IIB [Note—Use freshly distilled pyridine as solvent.]
  Acceptance criteria: NMT 0.5%

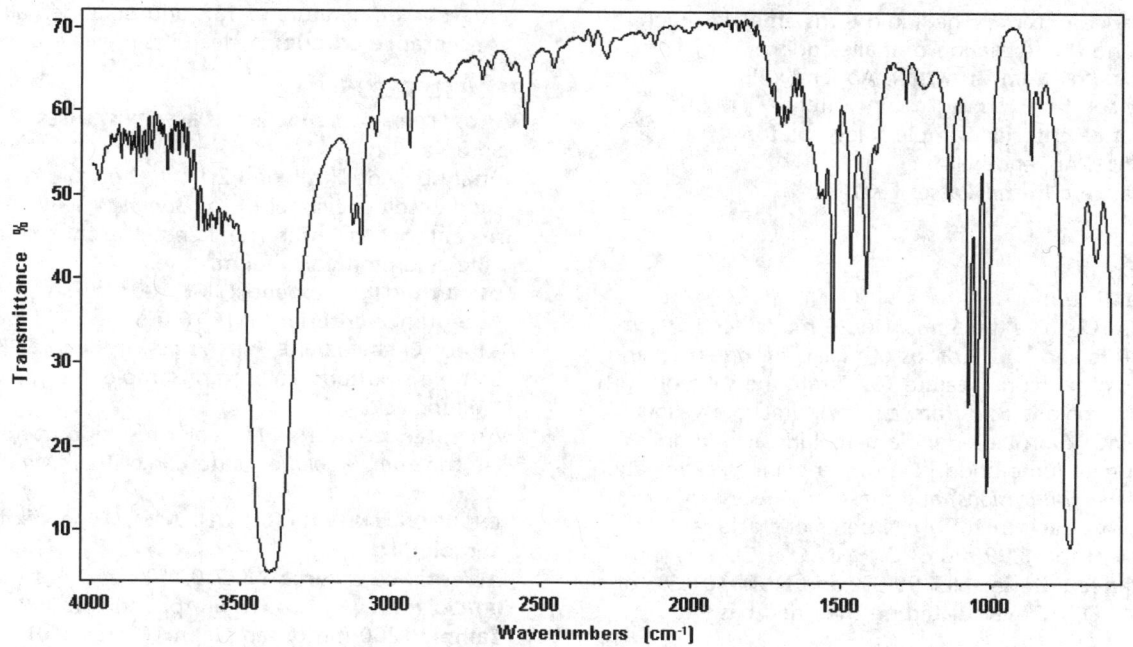

Pyrrole

Quinine Hydrochloride

First Published: Prior to FCC 6

C$_{20}$H$_{24}$N$_2$O$_2$·HCl·2H$_2$O

Formula wt 396.91
CAS: [130-89-2]

UNII: 711S8Y0T33 [quinine hydrochloride]

DESCRIPTION
Quinine Hydrochloride occurs as odorless, white, silky, glistening needle-like crystals with a very bitter taste. It effloresces when exposed to warm air. Its solutions are neutral or alkaline to litmus. One g dissolves in 16 mL of water, in 1 mL of alcohol, in about 7 mL of glycerin, and in about 1 mL of chloroform. It is very slightly soluble in ether.

Function: Flavoring agent
Packaging and Storage: Store in tight, light-resistant containers.

IDENTIFICATION
- **A. PROCEDURE**
  Sample solution: 1 mg/mL
  Analysis: Add 1 or 2 drops of bromine TS followed by 1 mL of 6 N ammonium hydroxide to 5 mL of the *Sample solution*.
  Acceptance criteria: The liquid turns emerald green indicating the formation of thalleioquin.
- **B. OPTICAL (SPECIFIC) ROTATION,** Appendix IIB
  Sample solution: 10 mg/mL in water
  Acceptance criteria: Sample is levorotatory.
- **C. CHLORIDE,** Appendix IIIA
  Acceptance criteria: Passes test

ASSAY
- **PROCEDURE**
  Sample: 150 mg
  Analysis: Dissolve the *Sample* in 20 mL of acetic anhydride and add 2 drops of malachite green TS and 5.5 mL of mercuric acetate TS. Titrate the solution with 0.1 N perchloric acid from a microburet to a yellow endpoint. [**CAUTION**—Handle perchloric acid in an appropriate fume hood.] Perform a blank determination (see *General Provisions*) and make any necessary correction. Each mL of 0.1 N perchloric acid is equivalent to 17.99 mg of C$_{20}$H$_{24}$N$_2$O$_2$·HCl.
  Acceptance criteria: NLT 99.0% and NMT 101.5% of C$_{20}$H$_{24}$N$_2$O$_2$·HCl, calculated on the dried basis

IMPURITIES
Inorganic Impurities
- **SULFATE,** *Chloride and Sulfate Limit Tests, Chloride Limit Test,* Appendix IIIB
  Sample: 500 mg
  Control: 250 μg of sulfate (25 mL of *Standard Sulfate Solution*)
  Acceptance criteria: Any turbidity produced by the *Sample* does not exceed that shown in the *Control*. (NMT 0.05%)

Organic Impurities
- **OTHER CINCHONA ALKALOIDS**
  Sample: 2.5 g
  Analysis: Dissolve the *Sample* in 60 mL of water contained in a separatory funnel, add 10 mL of 6 N ammonium hydroxide, extract the mixture successively with 30 mL and 20 mL of chloroform, and evaporate the combined chloroform extracts to dryness on a steam bath. Dissolve 1.5 g of the residue in 25 mL of alcohol; dilute the solution with 50 mL of hot water; add 1 N sulfuric acid (about 5 mL) until the solution is acid, using 2 drops of methyl red TS as the indicator; and neutralize the excess acid with 1 N sodium hydroxide. Evaporate the solution to dryness on a steam bath, powder the residue, and agitate it in a test tube with 20 mL of water at 65° for 30 min. Cool the mixture to 15°; macerate it at this temperature for 2 h, shaking it occasionally; and filter it through an 8- to 10-cm filter paper. Transfer 5 mL of the filtrate, at a temperature of 15°, into a test tube, and mix and shake it gently with 6 mL of 6 N ammonium hydroxide (which must contain between 10% and 10.2% of NH$_3$, have a temperature of 15°, and be added all at once).
  Acceptance criteria: A clear liquid evolves.

SPECIFIC TESTS
- **CHLOROFORM–ALCOHOL INSOLUBLE SUBSTANCES**
  Sample: 1 g
  Analysis: Add 7 mL of a 2:1 (v/v) mixture of chloroform and absolute alcohol to the *Sample*.
  Acceptance criteria: The *Sample* dissolves completely in the chloroform-alcohol mixture.
- **LOSS ON DRYING,** Appendix IIC: 120° for 3 h
  Acceptance criteria: NMT 10.0%
- **READILY CARBONIZABLE SUBSTANCES,** Appendix IIB
  Sample solution: 100 mg of sample in 2 mL of 95% sulfuric acid
  Acceptance criteria: The color resulting from treatment of the *Sample solution* is no darker than *Matching Fluid M*.
- **RESIDUE ON IGNITION (SULFATED ASH),** Appendix IIC
  Sample: 1g
  Acceptance criteria: NMT 0.15%
- **OPTICAL (SPECIFIC) ROTATION,** Appendix IIB
  Sample: 200 mg of sample in 10 mL of 0.1 N hydrochloric acid
  Acceptance criteria: $[\alpha]_D^{25}$: between −247° and −252°

Quinine Sulfate

First Published: Prior to FCC 6

$(C_{20}H_{24}N_2O_2)_2 \cdot H_2SO_4 \cdot 2H_2O$ Formula wt 782.96
CAS: anhydrous [804-63-7]
UNII: KF7Z0E0Q2B [quinine sulfate]

DESCRIPTION
Quinine Sulfate occurs as odorless, fine, white, needle-like crystals, usually lusterless, with a persistent, very bitter taste. It makes a light and readily compressible mass. It darkens on exposure to light. Its saturated solution is neutral or alkaline to litmus. One g dissolves in about 500 mL of water and in about 120 mL of alcohol at 25°, in about 35 mL of water at 100°, and in about 10 mL of alcohol at 80°. It is slightly soluble in chloroform and in ether, but is freely soluble in a 2:1 (v/v) mixture of chloroform:absolute alcohol.
Function: Flavoring agent
Packaging and Storage: Store in well-closed, light-resistant containers.

IDENTIFICATION
- **A. PROCEDURE**
  Sample solution: 1 mg/mL
  Analysis: Add 1 or 2 drops of bromine TS followed by 1 mL of 6 N ammonium hydroxide to 5 mL of the *Sample solution*.
  Acceptance criteria: The liquid turns emerald green, indicating the formation of thalleioquin.
- **B. OPTICAL (SPECIFIC) ROTATION,** Appendix IIB
  Sample solution: Saturated solution acidified with 2 N sulfuric acid
  Acceptance criteria: The *Sample solution* has a vivid blue fluorescence and is levorotatory.
- **C. SULFATE,** Appendix IIIA
  Sample solution: 20 mg/mL in water, made with the aid of few drops of hydrochloric acid
  Acceptance criteria: Passes tests

ASSAY
- **PROCEDURE**
  Sample: 200 mg
  Analysis: Dissolve the *Sample* in 20 mL of acetic anhydride and add 2 drops of malachite green TS. Titrate the solution with 0.1 N perchloric acid from a microburet to a yellow endpoint. [**CAUTION**—Handle perchloric acid in an appropriate fume hood.] Perform a blank determination (see *General Provisions*) and make any necessary correction. Each mL of 0.1 N perchloric acid is equivalent to 24.9 mg of $(C_{20}H_{24}N_2O_2)_2 \cdot H_2SO_4$.
  Acceptance criteria: NLT 99.0% and NMT 101.0% of $(C_{20}H_{24}N_2O_2)_2 \cdot H_2SO_4$, calculated on the dried basis

IMPURITIES
Organic Impurities
- **OTHER CINCHONA ALKALOIDS**
  Sample: 1.8 g, previously dried at 50° for 2 h
  Analysis: Agitate the *Sample* with 20 mL of water at 65° for 30 min. Cool the mixture to 15°; macerate it at this temperature for 2 h, shaking it occasionally; and filter. Transfer 5 mL of the filtrate, at a temperature of 15°, into a test tube, and mix it gently, without shaking, with 6 mL of 6 N ammonium hydroxide (which must contain between 10% and 10.2% of NH_3, have a temperature of 15°, and be added all at once).
  Acceptance criteria: A clear liquid evolves.

SPECIFIC TESTS
- **CHLOROFORM–ALCOHOL INSOLUBLE SUBSTANCES**
  Sample: 2 g
  Analysis: Mix the *Sample* with 15 mL of a 2:1 (v/v) mixture of chloroform:absolute alcohol and warm at 50° for 10 min. Filter through a tared, sintered-glass filter, using gentle suction, and wash the filter with five 10-mL portions of the chloroform-alcohol mixture. Dry at 105° for 1 h, cool, and weigh.
  Acceptance criteria: NMT 0.1%
- **LOSS ON DRYING,** Appendix IIC: 120° for 3 h
  Acceptance criteria: NMT 5.0%
- **OPTICAL (SPECIFIC) ROTATION,** Appendix IIB
  Sample solution: 200 mg of sample in 10 mL of 0.1 N hydrochloric acid
  Acceptance criteria: $[\alpha]_D^{25}$ between −240° and −244°
- **READILY CARBONIZABLE SUBSTANCES,** Appendix IIB
  Sample solution: 200 mg of sample dissolved in 5 mL of 95% sulfuric acid
  Acceptance criteria: The color resulting from treatment of the *Sample solution* is no darker than *Matching Fluid M*.
- **RESIDUE ON IGNITION,** Appendix IIC
  Sample: 2 g
  Acceptance criteria: NMT 0.05%

Rapeseed Oil, Fully Hydrogenated

First Published: Prior to FCC 6

Fully Hydrogenated Rapeseed Oil
INS: 441　　　　　　　　　　CAS: [84681-71-0]
UNII: K168T6Y0YU [fully hydrogenated rapeseed oil]

DESCRIPTION

Rapeseed Oil, Fully Hydrogenated, occurs as a white, waxy solid. It is a mixture of triglycerides. The saturated fatty acids are found in the same proportions that result from the full hydrogenation of fatty acids occurring in natural high-erucic acid rapeseed oil. The rapeseed oil is obtained from *Brassica juncea*, *Brassica napus*, and *Brassica rapa* (Fam. Cruciferae). It is made by hydrogenating high-erucic acid rapeseed oil in the presence of a nickel catalyst at temperatures not exceeding 245°.

Function: Cooking or salad oil; component of margarine or shortening; coating agent; emulsifying agent; stabilizer; thickener; texturizer

Packaging and Storage: Store in tightly closed containers.

IDENTIFICATION

- **FATTY ACID COMPOSITION,** Appendix VII
  Acceptance criteria: A sample exhibits the following composition profile of fatty acids:

Fatty Acid	Weight % (Range)
14.0	<1.0
16:0	3–5
18:0	38–42
18:1	1.0
18:2	<1.0
20:0	8–10
20:1	<1.0
22:0	42–50
22:1	<1.0
24:0	1.0–2.0

IMPURITIES

Inorganic Impurities

- **LEAD,** *Lead Limit Test, Atomic Absorption Spectrophotometric Graphite Furnace Method, Method II,* Appendix IIIB
  Acceptance criteria: NMT 0.1 mg/kg
- **WATER,** *Water Determination,* Appendix IIB
  Analysis: Proceed as directed, except use 50 mL of a 1:1 solution of chloroform:methanol to dissolve the sample in place of 35 to 40 mL of methanol.
  Acceptance criteria: NMT 0.05%

Organic Impurities

- **ERUCIC ACID,** *Fatty Acid Composition,* Appendix VII
  Acceptance criteria: NMT 1.0%

SPECIFIC TESTS

- **ACID VALUE (FATS AND RELATED SUBSTANCES)** *Method II,* Appendix VII
  Acceptance criteria: NMT 6
- **COLOR (FATS AND RELATED SUBSTANCES),** Appendix VII: Use a 13.34-cm cell.
  Acceptance criteria: NMT 1.5 red/15 yellow
- **FREE FATTY ACIDS (AS OLEIC ACID),** *Free Fatty Acids,* Appendix VII
  Analysis: Use 28.2 for the equivalence factor (e) in the formula given in the procedure.
  Acceptance criteria: NMT 2.0%
- **IODINE VALUE,** Appendix VII
  Acceptance criteria: NMT 4
- **1-MONOGLYCERIDE CONTENT,** *1-Monoglycerides,* Appendix VII
  Acceptance criteria: Conforms to the representation of the vendor.
- **PEROXIDE VALUE,** *Method II,* Appendix VII
  Acceptance criteria: NMT 2.0 mEq/kg
- **RESIDUE ON IGNITION (SULFATED ASH),** *Method I,* Appendix IIC
  Sample: 5 g
  Acceptance criteria: NMT 0.5%
- **UNSAPONIFIABLE MATTER,** Appendix VII
  Acceptance criteria: NMT 1.5%

OTHER REQUIREMENTS

- **LABELING:** Rapeseed Oil products that have been fully hydrogenated should be labeled as Fully Hydrogenated Rapeseed Oil. Label to indicate the *1-Monoglyceride Content* as well.

Rapeseed Oil, Superglycerinated

First Published: Prior to FCC 6

Superglycerinated Fully Hydrogenated Rapeseed Oil

DESCRIPTION

Rapeseed Oil, Superglycerinated, occurs as a white solid. It is a mixture of mono-, di-, and triglycerides, with triglycerides as a minor component. The saturated fatty acids are found in the same proportions that result from the full hydrogenation of fatty acids occurring in natural high-erucic acid rapeseed oil. The rapeseed oil is typically obtained by *n*-hexane extraction from *Brassica juncea*, *Brassica napus*, and *Brassica rapa* (Fam. Cruciferae). It is made by adding excess glycerin to fully hydrogenated rapeseed oil and heating to about 165° in the presence of a sodium hydroxide catalyst under partial vacuum and steam sparging agitation.

Function: Cooking or salad oil; component of margarine or shortening; coating agent; emulsifying agent; texturizer

Packaging and Storage: Store in tightly closed containers.

IDENTIFICATION

- **FATTY ACID COMPOSITION,** Appendix VII
  Acceptance criteria: A sample exhibits the following composition profile of fatty acids:

Fatty Acid	Weight % (Range)
14:0	<1.0
16:0	3–5
18:0	38–42
18:1	1.0
18:2	<1.0
20:0	8–10
20:1	<1.0
22:0	42–50
22:1	<1.0
24:0	1.0–2.0

IMPURITIES
Inorganic Impurities
- **LEAD,** *Lead Limit Test, Atomic Absorption Spectrophotometric Graphite Furnace Method, Method II,* Appendix IIIB
  Acceptance criteria: NMT 0.1 mg/kg
- **WATER,** *Water Determination,* Appendix IIB
  Analysis: Proceed as directed, except use 50 mL of a 1:1 solution of chloroform:methanol to dissolve the sample in place of 35 to 40 mL of methanol.
  Acceptance criteria: NMT 0.05%

Organic Impurities
- **ERUCIC ACID,** *Fatty Acid Composition,* Appendix VII
  Acceptance criteria: NMT 1.0%
- **FREE GLYCERIN,** *Free Glycerin or Propylene Glycol,* Appendix VII
  Acceptance criteria: NMT 1%

SPECIFIC TESTS
- **ACID VALUE (FATS AND RELATED SUBSTANCES)** *Method II,* Appendix VII
  Acceptance criteria: NMT 6
- **COLOR (FATS AND RELATED SUBSTANCES),** Appendix VII: Use a 13.34-cm cell.
  Acceptance criteria: NMT 1.5 red/15 yellow
- **FREE FATTY ACIDS (AS OLEIC ACID),** *Free Fatty Acids,* Appendix VII
  Analysis: Use 28.2 for the equivalence factor (e) in the formula given in the procedure.
  Acceptance criteria: NMT 2.0%
- **HYDROXYL VALUE,** *Method II,* Appendix VII
  Acceptance criteria: Conforms to the representation of the vendor.
- **IODINE VALUE,** Appendix VII
  Acceptance criteria: NMT 4
- **1-MONOGLYCERIDE CONTENT,** *1-Monoglycerides,* Appendix VII
  Acceptance criteria: Conforms to the representation of the vendor.
- **PEROXIDE VALUE,** *Method II,* Appendix VII
  Acceptance criteria: NMT 2.0 mEq/kg
- **RESIDUE ON IGNITION (SULFATED ASH),** *Method I,* Appendix IIC
  Sample: 5 g
  Acceptance criteria: NMT 0.5%
- **UNSAPONIFIABLE MATTER,** Appendix VII
  Acceptance criteria: NMT 1.5%

OTHER REQUIREMENTS
- **LABELING:** Rapeseed Oil products that have added glycerin (glycerol) and that are fully hydrogenated should be labeled as Fully Hydrogenated and Superglycerinated Rapeseed Oil. The *1-Monoglyceride Content* and *Hydroxyl Value* should be indicated as well.

Rebaudioside A

First Published: Second Supplement, FCC 6
Last Revision: First Supplement, FCC 7

Reb A
Rebiana
Kaur-16-en-18-oic acid, 13-[(O-β-D-glucopyranosyl-(1→2)-O-[β-D-glucopyranosyl-(1→3)]-β-D-glucopyranosyl)oxy]-, β-D-glucopyranosyl ester, (4α)
13-[(2-O-β-D-glucopyranosyl-3-O-β-D-glucopyranosyl-β-D-glucopyranosyl)oxy] kaur-16-en-18-oic acid β-D-glucopyranosyl ester

$C_{44}H_{70}O_{23}$

Formula wt 967.01
CAS: [58543-16-1]

UNII: B3FUD0528F [rebaudioside a]

DESCRIPTION
Rebaudioside A is a white to off-white, hygroscopic fine crystal, granule, or powder having a sweet taste. It is freely soluble in ethanol:water 50/50 (v/v), sparingly soluble in water and sparingly soluble in ethanol. It is obtained from the leaves of the *Stevia rebaudiana* (Bertoni) plant in a multi-step separation and purification process. Principle steps include extraction of steviol glycosides from the leaves using an aqueous or aqueous alcoholic (ethanol or methanol) solvent, and purification of rebaudioside A from the resulting mixture of steviol glycosides by resin absorption followed by recrystallization from an aqueous or aqueous alcoholic (ethanol or methanol) solvent. It is composed predominantly of rebaudioside A, a glycoside of the *ent*-kaurenoid diterpenoid aglycone known as steviol.
Function: Nonnutritive sweetener; sugar substitute
Packaging and Storage: Keep dry, and store in tight containers at ambient temperature.

IDENTIFICATION
- **A. INFRARED ABSORPTION,** *Spectrophotometric Identification Tests,* Appendix IIIC
  Reference standard: USP Rebaudioside A RS
  Sample and standard preparation: A

Acceptance criteria: The spectrum of the sample exhibits maxima at the same wavelengths as those in the spectrum of the *Reference standard.*
- **B. PROCEDURE**
Acceptance criteria: The retention time of the major peak (excluding the solvent peak) in the chromatogram of the *Sample solution* is the same as that of the 4750 mg/L *Rebaudioside A standard solution* in the *Assay.*

ASSAY
- **PROCEDURE**
[NOTE—Rebaudioside A is hygroscopic, and accurate quantitative analysis requires moisture equilibration before analysis. Equilibrate sample and rebaudioside A standard specimens in the lab NLT 24 h before weighing. Intermittent stirring will ensure uniform moisture absorption. The *Water* content used in the calculation should be determined at the time of weighing and after equilibration.]
Acetate buffer: Dissolve 0.125 g of ammonium acetate in 900 mL of water, adjust to a pH of 4.3 with glacial acetic acid solution, and dilute to 1 L. [NOTE—It may be necessary to adjust the ratio of ammonium acetate to acetic acid. Changing the pH adjusts the retention time of rebaudioside A and related glycosides. Decreasing the pH of the buffer will decrease the retention time of rebaudioside A.]
Mobile phase: 13% (v/v) *Acetate buffer* in acetonitrile
Diluent: 25% (v/v) *Acetate buffer* in acetonitrile. [NOTE—Allow *Diluent* to come to room temperature before use.]
Rebaudioside A standard solutions: 250, 1000, 2500, and 5000 mg/L of USP Rebaudioside A RS in *Diluent*
Stevioside standard stock solution: 250 mg/L of USP Stevioside RS in *Diluent*
Stevioside standard solutions: 0.5, 5.0, 25, and 250 mg/L of USP Stevioside RS in *Diluent*: from *Stevioside standard stock solution*
Sample solution: 5000 mg/L in *Diluent*
Chromatographic system, Appendix IIA
 Mode: High-performance liquid chromatography
 Detector: UV 210 nm
 Column: 15-cm × 4.6-mm, packed with a propyl-amino silane phase bonded to silica gel (5-μm particle diameter)[1]
 Column temperature: 30°
 Flow rate: 1.5 mL/min
 Injection size: 15 μL
 System suitability
  Samples: 5000 mg/L *Rebaudioside A standard solution* and 0.5 mg/L *Stevioside standard solution*
  Suitability requirements
   Detector response: Peak-to-noise ratio (peak height/baseline noise) is NLT 3 for the stevioside peak from the 0.5 mg/L *Stevioside standard solution*, where peak height is expressed in mAU, and baseline noise is the maximum deflection of the baseline (mAU) in a blank at the retention time of stevioside over the same baseline peak width in min.

---
[1] Cosmosil Sugar-D (Nacalai Tesque), or equivalent.

Relative standard deviation: NMT 2.0% for rebaudioside A peak area and retention time from the 5000 mg/L *Rebaudioside A standard solution*
Retention time: The retention time for the rebaudioside A peak from the 5000 mg/L *Rebaudioside A standard solution* is less than 15.0 min.
Tailing factor: NMT 2.0 for the rebaudioside A peak from the 5000 mg/L *Rebaudioside A standard solution*
Analysis: Separately inject equal volumes of the *Rebaudioside A standard solutions, Stevioside standard solutions,* and *Sample solution* into the chromatograph, and measure the responses for the major peaks on the resulting chromatograms. [NOTE—The approximate retention times for rebaudioside A and its related steviol glycosides are listed in *Chromatographic Profile Table 1*. If the retention time for rebaudioside A is below 11 min, adjust the ratio of ammonium acetate to acetic acid.]

Chromatographic Profile Table 1

Compound	Approx. Retention Time (min)	Molecular Weight (g/mol)
Rubusoside	2.6	642.73
Dulcoside A	4.3	788.87
Stevioside	6.6	804.88
Rebaudioside C	8.5	951.01
Rebaudioside F	9.6	936.99
Rebaudioside A	14	967.01
Steviolbioside	29	642.73
Rebaudioside D	41	1129.15
Rebaudioside B	66	804.88

Prepare a standard curve for rebaudioside A by plotting rebaudioside A peak areas versus concentrations in mg/L, corrected for purity, based on the USP Reference Standard label claim. [NOTE—Peak responses for all other steviol glycosides besides rebaudioside A are used in the *Related Steviol Glycosides* impurities test procedure.] From the standard curve, calculate the concentration (C_U) of rebaudioside A in the *Sample solution* in mg/L. Calculate the percentage of rebaudioside A in the portion of the sample taken:

$$\text{Result} = C_U/C_{SMP} \times 100$$

C_U = concentration of rebaudioside A in the *Sample solution* determined from the standard curve (mg/L)
C_{SMP} = concentration of the sample in the *Sample solution* (mg/L)

Acceptance criteria: NLT 95.0%, calculated on the anhydrous and solvent-free basis

IMPURITIES
Inorganic Impurities
- **ARSENIC,** *Arsenic Limit Test,* Appendix IIIB
[NOTE—Alternatively, the arsenic content may be determined by the following method.]

[NOTE—When water is specified as a diluent, use deionized ultra-filtered water. When nitric acid is specified, use nitric acid of a grade suitable for trace element analysis with as low a content of arsenic as practical.]

Dilute nitric acid: Dilute 2.0 mL of nitric acid with water to 100 mL.

Yttrium internal standard solution: Use a commercially available 1000 µg/kg yttrium ICP standard solution.
 [NOTE—The internal standard should be 20 µg/kg in all blanks, standards, and samples.]

Standard stock solution: Dilute a 1000 mg/kg commercially available arsenic ICP standard solution to 1000 µg/kg with *Dilute nitric acid*, transfer 10.0 mL of this solution to a 100-mL volumetric flask, add 2.0 mL of *Dilute nitric acid*, and dilute with water to volume (100 µg/kg). [NOTE—Prepare this solution fresh every 2 weeks.]

Standard solution: 10 µg/kg arsenic prepared as follows: transfer 5.0 mL of the *Standard stock solution* to a 50-mL volumetric flask, add 3.0 mL of *Dilute nitric acid*, add 1.0 mL of *Yttrium internal standard solution*, and dilute with water to volume (10 µg/kg). [NOTE—Prepare this solution fresh weekly.]

Standard blank solution: Transfer 1.0 mL of the *Yttrium internal standard solution* to a 50-mL volumetric flask, add 3.0 mL of *Dilute nitric acid*, and dilute with water to volume.

Sample solution
 [CAUTION—Wear proper eye protection, protective clothing, and gloves during sample preparation. Closely follow the manufacturer's safety instructions for use of the microwave digestion apparatus.] Transfer 500 mg of sample into a Teflon digestion vessel liner. Prepare samples in duplicate. Add 10 mL of nitric acid, and swirl gently. Cover the vessels with lids, leaving the vent fitting off. Predigest for at least 1 h under a hood. Place the rupture membrane in the vent fitting, and tighten the lid. Place all vessels on the turntable of a microwave oven with a magnetron frequency of about 2455 MHz and a selectable output power of 0 to 950 watts in 1% increments, equipped with advanced composite vessels with 100-mL polytef liners[2]. Connect the vent tubes to the vent trap, and connect the pressure-sensing line to the appropriate vessel. Initiate a two-stage digestion procedure by heating the microwave at 15% power for 10 min, followed by 25% power for 10 min. Remove the turntable of vessels from the oven, and allow the vessels to cool to room temperature (a cool water bath may be used to speed the cooling process). Vent the vessels when they reach room temperature. Transfer the cooled digests into 50-mL volumetric flasks, add 1.0 mL of the *Yttrium internal standard solution*, and dilute with deionized water to volume.

Spectrophotometric system, *Plasma Spectrochemistry,* Appendix IIC

Mode: Inductively coupled plasma-mass spectrometer (ICP-MS)

ICP-MS: Use a system equipped with a quadrupole mass spectrometer and an ion detector maintained under vacuum; the system may include a suppression system to mitigate interference from the $^{40}Ar^{35}Cl^+$ ion. If not, correction for this interference must be determined by a suitable method, such as that recommended by the instrument manufacturer. The isotope ratio of $^{40}Ar^{35}Cl^+/^{40}Ar^{37}Cl^+$ in the *Standard blank solution* may be used to correct this interference.

Analysis: [NOTE—Instrument performance must be verified to conform to the manufacturer's specifications for resolution and sensitivity. Before analyzing samples, the instrument must pass a suitable performance check.] Aspirate the *Standard blank solution*, *Standard solution*, and *Sample solution*, at least in duplicate. The *Standard blank solution* should not yield a significant intensity for arsenic. Calculate the internal standard ratios for the *Sample solution* and *Standard solution* as ratio of the arsenic to the yttrium intensities. Calculate the concentration (mg/kg) of arsenic in the sample taken:

$$\text{Result} = (R_U/R_S) \times C_S \times (50/S)$$

R_U = internal standard ratio (arsenic response/yttrium response) from the *Sample solution*
R_S = internal standard ratio (arsenic response/yttrium response) from the *Standard solution*
C_S = concentration of arsenic in the *Standard solution* (µg/kg)
50 = sample dilution factor
S = weight of sample used to prepare the *Sample solution* (mg)

Acceptance criteria: NMT 1 mg/kg, calculated on the anhydrous basis

- **LEAD**, Lead Limit Test, Atomic Absorption Spectrophotometric Graphite Furnace Method, Method I, Appendix IIIB
 [NOTE—Alternatively, the lead content may be determined by the following method.]
 [NOTE—When water is specified as a diluent, use deionized ultra-filtered water. When nitric acid is specified, use nitric acid of a grade suitable for trace element analysis with as low a content of lead as practical.]

Dilute nitric acid: Dilute 2.0 mL of nitric acid with water to 100 mL.

Thallium internal standard solution: Commercially available 1000 µg/kg thallium ICP standard solution.
 [NOTE—The internal standard should be 20 µg/kg in all blanks, standards, and samples.]

Standard stock solution: Dilute a 1000 mg/kg commercially available lead ICP standard solution to 1000 µg/kg with *Dilute nitric acid*, transfer 10.0 mL of this solution to a 100-mL volumetric flask, add 2.0 mL of *Dilute nitric acid*, and dilute with water to volume (100 µg/kg). [NOTE—Prepare this solution fresh every 2 weeks.]

---
[2] MDS 2100 (CEM Corporation, Matthews, NC, USA) or equivalent.

Standard solution: 10 µg/kg of lead prepared as follows: transfer 5.0 mL of the *Standard stock solution* to a 50-mL volumetric flask, add 3.0 mL of *Dilute nitric acid*, add 1.0 mL of *Thallium internal standard solution*, and dilute with water to volume (10 µg/kg). [NOTE—Prepare this solution fresh weekly.]

Standard blank solution: Transfer 1.0 mL of the *Thallium internal standard solution* to a 50-mL volumetric flask, add 3.0 mL of *Dilute nitric acid*, and dilute with water to volume.

Sample solution

[CAUTION—Wear proper eye protection, protective clothing, and gloves during sample preparation. Closely follow the manufacturer's safety instructions for use of the microwave digestion apparatus.] Transfer 500 mg of sample into a Teflon digestion vessel liner. Prepare samples in duplicate. Add 10 mL of nitric acid, and swirl gently. Cover the vessels with lids, leaving the vent fitting off. Predigest for at least 1 h under a hood. Place the rupture membrane in the vent fitting, and tighten the lid. Place all vessels on the turntable of a microwave oven with a magnetron frequency of about 2455 MHz and a selectable output power of 0 to 950 watts in 1% increments, equipped with advanced composite vessels with 100-mL polytef liners[2]. Connect the vent tubes to the vent trap, and connect the pressure-sensing line to the appropriate vessel. Initiate a two-stage digestion procedure by heating the microwave at 15% power for 10 min, followed by 25% power for 10 min. Remove the turntable of vessels from the oven, and allow the vessels to cool to room temperature (a cool water bath may be used to speed the cooling process). Vent the vessels when they reach room temperature. Transfer the cooled digests into 50-mL volumetric flasks, add 1.0 mL of the *Thallium internal standard solution*, and dilute with deionized water to volume.

Spectrophotometric system, *Plasma Spectrochemistry*, Appendix IIC

Mode: Inductively coupled plasma-mass spectrometer (ICP-MS)

ICP-MS: Use a system equipped with a quadrupole mass spectrometer and an ion detector maintained under vacuum: the instrument should read all isotopes for lead (206, 207, and 208 amu) and the thallium internal standard (205 amu), and should report the total lead content using the most naturally abundant isotope at 208 amu.

Analysis: [NOTE—Instrument performance must be verified to conform to the manufacturer's specifications for resolution and sensitivity. Before analyzing samples, the instrument must pass a suitable performance check.] Aspirate the *Standard blank solution, Standard solution,* and *Sample solution,* at least in duplicate. The *Standard blank solution* should not yield a significant intensity for lead. Calculate the internal standard ratios for the *Sample solution* and *Standard solution* as ratio of the lead to the thallium intensities. Calculate the concentration (mg/kg) of lead in the sample taken:

$$\text{Result} = (R_U/R_S) \times C_S \times (50/S)$$

R_U = internal standard ratio (lead response/thallium response) from the *Sample solution*

R_S = internal standard ratio (lead response/thallium response) from the *Standard solution*

C_S = concentration of lead in the *Standard solution* (µg/kg)

50 = sample dilution factor

S = weight of sample used to prepare the *Sample solution* (mg)

Acceptance criteria: NMT 1 mg/kg, calculated on the anhydrous basis

Organic Impurities

- **ETHANOL AND METHANOL**

Internal standard solution: 10 µg/mL of 1-butanol

Standard stock solution: 12.5 mg/mL of ethanol and 12.5 mg/mL of methanol. [NOTE—Use water free of organics. Prepare fresh daily.]

Standard solutions: By serial dilution of the *Standard stock solution*, prepare solutions with ethanol and methanol concentrations of 1250, 625, 125, 62.5, 12.5, and 1.25 µg/mL. Separately add 4.0 mL each of these ethanol–methanol solutions and 1.0 mL of *Internal standard solution* to headspace vials, and cap tightly.

Sample: 100 mg

Sample solution: Transfer the *Sample* into a headspace vial, add 4.0 mL of water, add 1 mL of *Internal standard solution*, and cap tightly.

Blank: Transfer 4.0 mL of water into a headspace vial, and cap tightly.

Chromatographic system, Appendix IIA

Mode: Gas chromatography equipped with a headspace analyzer

Detector: Flame ionization

Column: 30-m × 0.32-mm (id) high polarity capillary column with a crosslinked and bonded poly(ethylene glycol) stationary phase and a 1-µm film thickness[3]

Column temperature: 3 min at 35°; increase to 180° at 10°/min; maintain at 180° for 1 min

Injection port temperature: 250°

Detector temperature: 250°

Carrier gas: Helium

Flow rate: 35 cm/s linear velocity

Incubation: 80° for 20 min

Injection syringe: Heated, gas-tight, 85°

Injection size: 1 mL of headspace

System suitability

Sample: *Standard solution*

Suitability requirement 1: The resolution, *R*, between any two components is NLT 3.

Suitability requirement 2: The relative standard deviation of the individual peak responses from replicate injections is NMT 15%.

---

[3] DB-WAXetr (Agilent Technologies), or equivalent.

Analysis: Separately inject equal volumes of the *Standard solutions* and *Sample solution* into the chromatograph, record the chromatograms, and measure the peak responses. [NOTE—The approximate retention times for ethanol and methanol are 8.1 and 7.4 min, respectively.]

Prepare standard curves for ethanol and methanol by plotting on the y-axis the ratios of analyte peak area to internal standard peak area and on the x-axis the concentration of analyte (μg/mL). [NOTE—The coefficent of determination for each standard curve should be NLT 0.995.]

Determine the concentration (C_U), in μg/mL, of each analyte in the *Sample solution* using the appropriate standard curve and the ratio of each analyte peak area to the internal standard peak area from the *Sample solution* chromatogram. Determine the percentage of each analyte (ethanol and methanol) in the portion of the *Sample* taken:

$$\text{Result} = C_U \times 4/S \times 0.1$$

C_U = concentration of analyte in the *Sample solution* determined from the standard curve (μg/mL)
4 = total volume of water used dissolve the *Sample* for the *Sample solution* (mL)
S = *Sample* weight (mg)
0.1 = correction factor, taking into account unit conversion from μg/mg to μg/μg and conversion to percentage

Acceptance criteria
Ethanol: NMT 0.50%
Methanol: NMT 0.020%

- **RELATED STEVIOL GLYCOSIDES**
 Acetate buffer, Mobile phase, Diluent, Rebaudioside A standard solutions, Stevioside standard stock solution, Stevioside standard solutions, Sample solution, Chromatographic system, and *System suitability:* Prepare as directed in the *Assay*.
 Analysis: Proceed as directed in the *Assay,* but with the following modifications for the standard curve and calculations.
 Using the peak area responses from the *Stevioside standard solutions,* prepare a standard curve for stevioside by plotting stevioside peak areas versus concentrations, in mg/L, corrected for purity, based on the USP Reference Standard label claim. From this standard curve, determine the concentration (mg/L) of stevioside in the *Sample solution*. Calculate the percentage of stevioside in the sample taken:

$$\text{Result} = C_U/C_{SMP} \times 100$$

C_U = concentration of stevioside in the *Sample solution* determined from the standard curve (mg/L)
C_{SMP} = concentration of the sample in the *Sample solution* (mg/L)

For the seven other steviol glycoside impurities (rubusoside, dulcoside A, rebaudioside C, rebaudioside F, rebaudioside D, steviolbioside, and rebaudioside B) use the stevioside standard curve prepared above to calculate the mg/L stevioside equivalents for each. Separately calculate the percentage of each analyte (rubusoside, dulcoside A, rebaudioside C, rebaudioside F, rebaudioside D, steviolbioside, and rebaudioside B) in the sample taken, which takes into account the differences in molecular weights between the analytes and stevioside:

$$\text{Result} = (C_U \times M_{r1}/M_{r2})/C_{SMP} \times 100$$

C_U = concentration of stevioside equivalents in the *Sample solution* determined from the standard curve (mg/L)
M_{r1} = molecular weight of the analyte (see *Chromatographic Profile Table 1* in the *Assay*)
M_{r2} = molecular weight of stevioside, 804.88
C_{SMP} = concentration of the sample in the *Sample solution* (mg/L)

Acceptance criteria: The sum of the percentages for all eight steviol glycoside impurities is NMT 5%, calculated on the anhydrous and solvent-free basis.

SPECIFIC TESTS

- **pH**, *pH Determination,* Appendix IIB
 Sample: 10 mg/mL
 Acceptance criteria: Between 4.5 and 7.0
- **RESIDUE ON IGNITION (SULFATED ASH)**, Appendix IIC
 Sample: 1 g
 Acceptance criteria: NMT 1%, calculated on the anhydrous basis
- **WATER**, *Water Determination, Method I,* Appendix IIB
 Acceptance criteria: NMT 6%

Rhodinol

First Published: Prior to FCC 6

FEMA: 2980
UNII: 1V437W60X9 [rhodinol]

DESCRIPTION

[NOTE—See Citronellol, Geraniol, and Nerol]
Rhodinol occurs as a colorless liquid.
Odor: Pronounced rose
Solubility: Soluble in most fixed oils, propylene glycol; insoluble or practically insoluble in glycerin
Boiling Point: ~68°–70° (1.8 mm Hg)
Solubility in Alcohol, Appendix VI: One mL dissolves in 1.2 mL of 70% alcohol.
Function: Flavoring agent

IDENTIFICATION

- **INFRARED SPECTRA**, *Spectrophotometric Identification Tests,* Appendix IIIC
 Acceptance criteria: The spectrum of the sample exhibits relative maxima at the same wavelengths as those of the spectrum below.

ASSAY

- **PROCEDURE:** Proceed as directed under *Total Alcohols*, Appendix VI.
  Sample: 1.2 g
  Analysis: Use 78.14 as the equivalence factor (e).
  Acceptance criteria: NLT 82.0% of total alcohols as $C_{10}H_{20}O$

SPECIFIC TESTS

- **REFRACTIVE INDEX,** Appendix II: At 20°
  Acceptance criteria: Between 1.463 and 1.473
- **SPECIFIC GRAVITY:** Determine at 25° by any reliable method (see *General Provisions*).
  Acceptance criteria: Between 0.860 and 0.880

OTHER REQUIREMENTS

- **ANGULAR ROTATION,** *Optical (Specific) Rotation,* Appendix IIB: Use a 100-mm tube.
  Acceptance criteria: Between −4° and −9°
- **ESTERS,** Appendix VI
  Sample: 5 g
  Analysis: Use 99.15 as the equivalence factor (e).
  Acceptance criteria: NMT 1.0% as citronellyl acetate

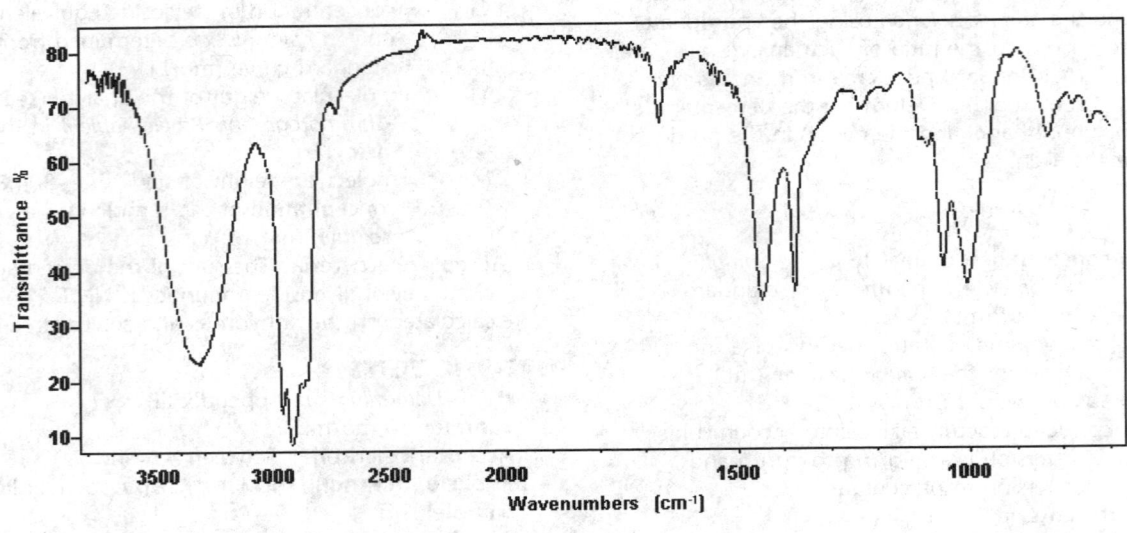

Rhodinol

Rhodinyl Acetate

First Published: Prior to FCC 6

FEMA: 2981
UNII: 90XIH89W4M [rhodinyl acetate]

DESCRIPTION

[NOTE—See Citronellyl Acetate and Geranyl Acetate]
Rhodinyl Acetate occurs as colorless to slightly yellow liquid.
Odor: Light, fresh, rose
Solubility: Soluble in alcohol, most fixed oils; insoluble or practically insoluble in glycerin, propylene glycol, water
Boiling Point: ~237°
Solubility in Alcohol, Appendix VI: One mL dissolves in 2 mL of 80% alcohol, and remains in solution on dilution to 10 mL.
Function: Flavoring agent

IDENTIFICATION

- **INFRARED SPECTRA,** *Spectrophotometric Identification Tests,* Appendix IIIC
  Acceptance criteria: The spectrum of the sample exhibits relative maxima at the same wavelengths as those of the spectrum below.

ASSAY

- **PROCEDURE:** Proceed as directed under *Esters,* Appendix VI.
  Sample: 1.3 g
  Analysis: Use 99.15 as the equivalence factor (e).
  Acceptance criteria: NLT 87.0% of total esters as $C_{12}H_{22}O_2$

SPECIFIC TESTS

- **ACID VALUE, FLAVOR CHEMICALS (OTHER THAN ESSENTIAL OILS),** *M-15,* Appendix XI
  Acceptance criteria: NMT 1.0
- **REFRACTIVE INDEX,** Appendix II: At 20°
  Acceptance criteria: Between 1.450 and 1.458
- **SPECIFIC GRAVITY:** Determine at 25° by any reliable method (see *General Provisions*).
  Acceptance criteria: Between 0.895 and 0.908

OTHER REQUIREMENTS

- **ANGULAR ROTATION,** *Optical (Specific) Rotation,* Appendix IIB: Use a 100-mm tube.
  Acceptance criteria: Between −2° and −6°

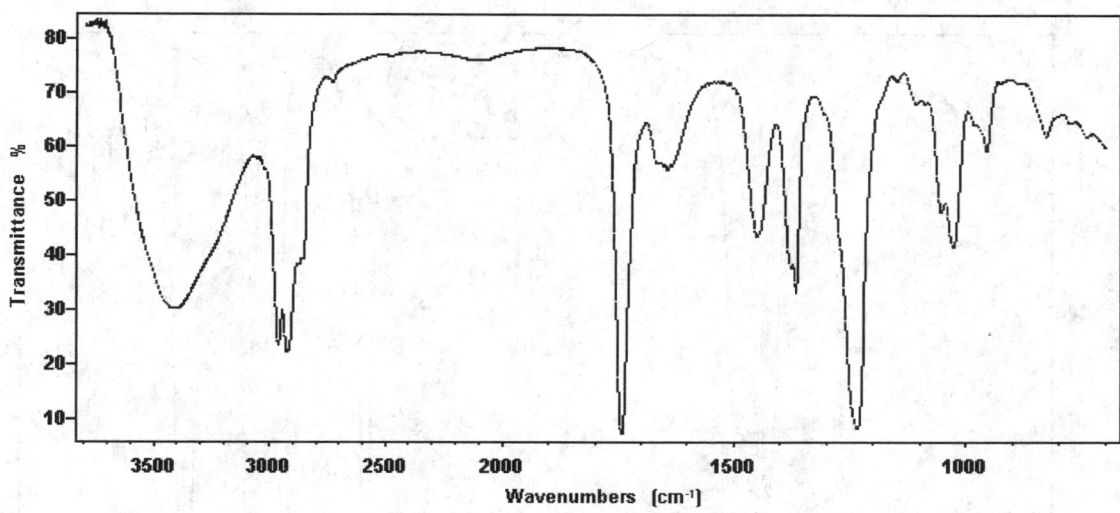

Rhodinyl Acetate

Rhodinyl Formate

First Published: Prior to FCC 6

FEMA: 2984
UNII: 9BZN2JVQ2E [rhodinyl formate]

DESCRIPTION
[NOTE—See Citronellyl Formate.]
Rhodinyl Formate occurs as a colorless to slightly yellow liquid.
Odor: Leafy, rose
Solubility: Soluble in alcohol, most fixed oils; insoluble or practically insoluble in glycerin, propylene glycol, water
Boiling Point: ~220°
Solubility in Alcohol, Appendix VI: One mL dissolves in 2 mL of 80% alcohol to give a clear solution.
Function: Flavoring agent

IDENTIFICATION
- **INFRARED SPECTRA,** Spectrophotometric Identification Tests, Appendix IIIC
  Acceptance criteria: The spectrum of the sample exhibits relative maxima at the same wavelengths as those of the spectrum below.

ASSAY
- **PROCEDURE:** Proceed as directed under Esters, Appendix VI.
  Sample: 1.3 g
  Analysis: Use 92.14 as the equivalence factor (e).
  Acceptance criteria: NLT 85.0% of total esters as $C_{11}H_{20}O_2$

SPECIFIC TESTS
- **ACID VALUE, FLAVOR CHEMICALS (OTHER THAN ESSENTIAL OILS),** M-15, Appendix XI
  Acceptance criteria: NMT 2.0
- **REFRACTIVE INDEX,** Appendix II: At 20°
  Acceptance criteria: Between 1.453 and 1.458
- **SPECIFIC GRAVITY:** Determine at 25° by any reliable method (see General Provisions).
  Acceptance criteria: Between 0.901 and 0.908

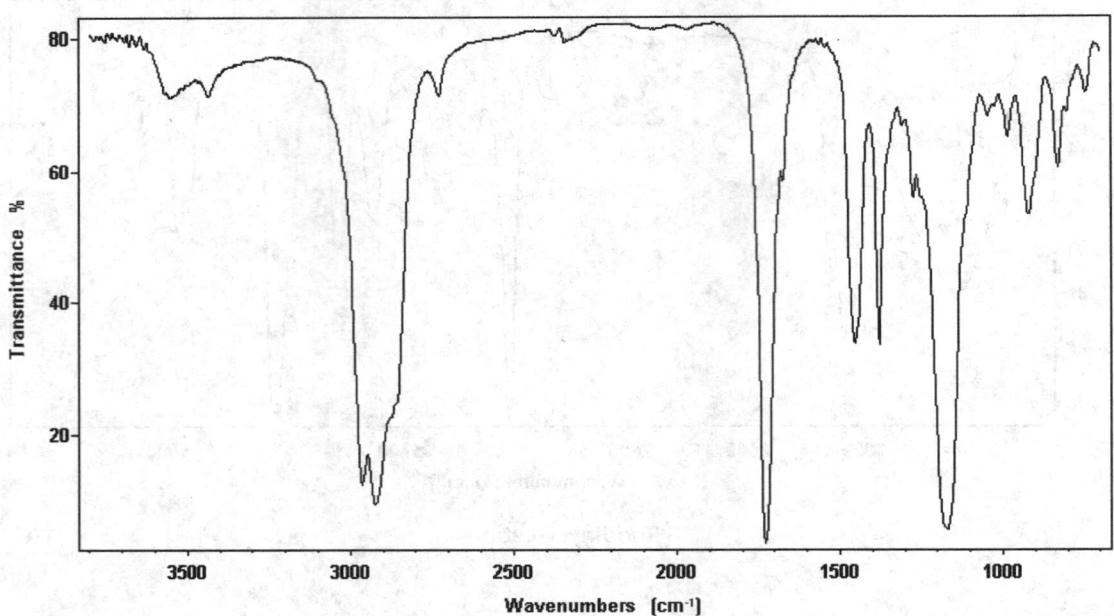

Rhodinyl Formate

Riboflavin

First Published: Prior to FCC 6

Vitamin B₂

$C_{17}H_{20}N_4O_6$ Formula wt 376.37
INS: 101(i) CAS: CAS [83-88-5]
UNII: TLM2976OFR [riboflavin]

DESCRIPTION
Riboflavin occurs as a yellow to orange-yellow, crystalline powder. When dry, it is not affected by diffused light, but when in solution, light induces deterioration. It melts at about 280° with decomposition, and its saturated solution is neutral to litmus. One g dissolves in 3000 to about 20,000 mL of water, the variations being due to differences in the internal crystalline structure. It is less soluble in alcohol than in water. It is insoluble in ether and in chloroform, but it is very soluble in dilute solutions of alkalies.

Function: Nutrient

Packaging and Storage: Store in tight, light-resistant containers.

IDENTIFICATION
- **PROCEDURE**
  Sample solution: 1 mg in 100 mL of water
  Acceptance criteria: The *Sample solution* is pale green-yellow by transmitted light and has an intense yellow-green fluorescence that disappears on the addition of mineral acids or alkalies.

ASSAY
- **PROCEDURE**
  [NOTE—Conduct this assay so that the solutions are protected from direct sunlight at all stages.]
  Sample solution: Transfer 50 mg of sample into a 1000-mL volumetric flask containing about 50 mL of water. Add 5 mL of 6 N acetic acid and sufficient water to make about 800 mL. Heat on a steam bath, protected from light, with frequent agitation until dissolved. Cool to about 25°, add water to volume, and mix. Dilute this solution with water, quantitatively and stepwise, to bring it within the operating sensitivity of the fluorometer used.
  Standard solution: In the same manner, prepare a standard solution to contain, in each mL, a quantity of USP Riboflavin RS equivalent to that of the *Sample solution*.
  Analysis: Using a fluorometer at about 530 nm, using an excitation wavelength of about 440 nm, measure the intensity of the *Standard solution's* fluorescence. Directly after the reading, add about 10 mg of sodium hydrosulfite to the *Standard solution*, stirring with a glass rod until dissolved, and immediately measure the fluorescence again. The difference between the two readings represents the intensity of the fluorescence

caused by the USP Riboflavin RS. Similarly, measure the intensity of the fluorescence of the *Sample solution*, both before and after the addition of sodium hydrosulfite. Calculate the quantity of $C_{17}H_{20}N_4O_6$ in the *Sample solution* by the formula:

Result = $C(I_U/I_S)$

C = concentration of USP Riboflavin RS (mg/mL) in the final solution of the *Standard solution*
I_U = corrected fluorescence values observed for the *Sample solution*
I_S = corrected fluorescence values observed for the *Standard solution*

Acceptance criteria: NLT 98.0% and NMT 102.0% of $C_{17}H_{20}N_4O_6$, calculated on the dried basis

IMPURITIES
Organic Impurities
- **LUMIFLAVIN**
  Alcohol-free chloroform: Shake 20 mL of chloroform gently, but thoroughly, with 20 mL of water for 3 min, draw off the chloroform layer, and wash twice more with 20-mL portions of water. Finally, filter the chloroform through a dry filter paper, shake it well for 5 min with 5 g of powdered anhydrous sodium sulfate, allow the mixture to stand for 2 h, and decant or filter the clear chloroform.
  Sample preparation: Shake 25 mg of sample with 10 mL of *Alcohol-free chloroform*, for 5 min and filter.
  Analysis: Determine the absorbance of the *Sample preparation* with a suitable spectrophotometer set at 440 nm using a 1-cm cell and *Alcohol-free chloroform* as the blank.
  Acceptance criteria: The absorbance of the *Sample preparation* is NMT 0.025.

SPECIFIC TESTS
- **LOSS ON DRYING,** Appendix IIC: 105° for 2 h
  Acceptance criteria: NMT 1.5%
- **OPTICAL (SPECIFIC) ROTATION,** Appendix IIB
  Sample solution: 5 mg/mL in hydrochloric acid
  Acceptance criteria: $[\alpha]_D^{25}$ between + 56.5° and +59.5°, calculated on the dried basis
- **RESIDUE ON IGNITION (SULFATED ASH),** Appendix IIC
  Sample: 1 g
  Acceptance criteria: NMT 0.3%

Riboflavin 5'-Phosphate Sodium

First Published: Prior to FCC 6

Flavin Mononucleotide, Sodium Salt
Riboflavin 5'-Phosphate Ester Monosodium Salt
Riboflavin 5'-Phosphate Ester Monosodium Salt, Dihydrate

$C_{17}H_{20}N_4NaO_9P \cdot 2H_2O$ Formula wt 514.36
INS: 101(ii)   CAS: [130-40-5]
UNII: 20RD1DZH99 [riboflavin 5'-phosphate sodium]

DESCRIPTION
Riboflavin 5'-Phosphate Sodium occurs as a fine, orange-yellow, crystalline powder. One g dissolves in about 30 mL of water. When dry, it is not affected by diffused light, but when in solution, light induces deterioration rapidly. It is hygroscopic.
Function: Nutrient
Packaging and Storage: Store in tight, light-resistant containers.

IDENTIFICATION
- **PROCEDURE**
  Sample solution: 15 mg/mL
  Acceptance criteria: The *Sample solution* is pale green-yellow by transmitted light and has an intense yellow-green fluorescence that disappears on the addition of mineral acids or alkalies.

ASSAY
- **PROCEDURE**
  [NOTE—Use low-actinic glassware, and conduct this assay so that all solutions are protected from direct sunlight at all stages.]
  Standard stock solution: Transfer 35 mg of USP Riboflavin RS into a 250-mL Erlenmeyer flask, add 20 mL of pyridine and 75 mL of water and aid dissolution by frequent shaking. Transfer the solution into a 1000-mL volumetric flask, dilute to volume with water, and mix.
  Standard solution: Transfer 10.0 mL of the *Standard stock solution* into a 1000-mL volumetric flask, add sufficient 0.1 N sulfuric acid (about 4 mL) so that the final pH of the solution is between 5.9 and 6.1, dilute to volume with water, and mix.
  Sample stock solution: Transfer 50 mg of sample into a 250-mL Erlenmeyer flask, add 20 mL of pyridine and 75 mL of water and aid dissolution by frequent shaking. Transfer the solution into a 1000-mL volumetric flask, dilute to volume with water, and mix.
  Sample solution: Transfer 10.0 mL of the *Sample stock solution* into a 1000-mL volumetric flask, add sufficient 0.1 N sulfuric acid (about 4 mL) so that the final pH of the solution is between 5.9 and 6.1, dilute to volume with water, and mix.
  Analysis: Using a suitable fluorometer, determine the intensity of the fluorescence of the *Standard solution* and the *Sample solution* at about 530 nm, using an excitation wavelength of about 440 nm. Calculate the

quantity, in mg, of $C_{17}H_{20}N_4O_6$ in the sample taken, by the formula:

$$Result = 100C \times I_U/I_S$$

C = concentration (µg/mL) of the *Standard solution*, corrected for loss on drying
I_U = fluorescence value observed for the *Sample solution*
I_S = fluorescence value observed for the *Standard solution*

Acceptance criteria: NLT the equivalent of 73.0% and NMT the equivalent of 79.0% of riboflavin ($C_{17}H_{20}N_4O_6$), calculated on the dried basis

IMPURITIES

Inorganic Impurities

- **LEAD**, *Lead Limit Test, Flame Atomic Absorption Spectrophotometric Method*, Appendix IIIB
  Sample: 10 g
  Acceptance criteria: NMT 2 mg/kg

- **FREE PHOSPHATE**
  Ammonium molybdate solution: 70 mg/mL of ammonium molybdate tetrahydrate
  Acid molybdate solution: Dilute 25 mL of *Ammonium molybdate solution* to 200 mL with water, and slowly add 25 mL of 7.5 N sulfuric acid.
  Ferrous sulfate solution: 100 mg/mL ferrous sulfate in water containing 2 mL of 7.5 N sulfuric acid per 100 mL of final solution
  Standard stock solution: 220.0 µg/mL monobasic potassium phosphate in water
  Standard solution: 44.0 µg/mL monobasic potassium phosphate in water: from *Standard stock solution*
  Sample solution: 3.0 mg/mL in water
  Blank: Mix 10.0 mL of water, 10.0 mL of *Acid molybdate solution*, and 5.0 mL of *Ferrous sulfate solution*.
  Analysis: Transfer 10.0 mL each of the *Standard solution* and the *Sample solution* into separate 50-mL Erlenmeyer flasks, add 10.0 mL of *Acid molybdate solution* and 5.0 mL of *Ferrous sulfate solution* to each flask, and mix. Determine the absorbance of each resulting solution and the *Blank* in a 1-cm cell at 700 nm using a suitable visible spectrophotometer.
  Acceptance criteria: The absorbance of the solution prepared from the *Sample solution* is NMT that of the solution prepared from the *Standard solution*. (NMT 1.0%, calculated as PO_4)

Organic Impurities

- **FREE RIBOFLAVIN AND RIBOFLAVIN DIPHOSPHATE**
  [NOTE—Conduct this test so that all solutions are protected from actinic light at all stages, preferably by using low-actinic glassware.]

  Mobile phase: 0.054 M monobasic potassium phosphate and methanol (85:15)(v/v), filtered and degassed. [NOTE—Make adjustments if necessary.]
  System suitability solution: Dissolve USP Phosphated Riboflavin RS in water to obtain a solution containing 2 mg/mL. Add an equal volume of *Mobile phase* and mix. Dilute 8 mL of this solution to 50 mL with *Mobile phase* and mix.
  Standard stock solution: Dissolve 60 mg of USP Riboflavin RS in 1 mL of hydrochloric acid in a 250-mL volumetric flask. Dilute to volume with water and mix.
  Standard solution: Pipet a 4-mL aliquot of the *Standard stock solution* into a 100-mL volumetric flask, dilute to volume with *Mobile phase*, and mix.
  Sample stock solution: Dissolve about 100.0 mg of sample in 50 mL of water in a 100-mL volumetric flask, dilute to volume with *Mobile phase*, and mix.
  Sample solution: Pipet 8 mL of *Sample stock solution* into a 50-mL volumetric flask, dilute to volume with *Mobile phase*, and mix.
  Chromatographic system, Appendix IIA
    Mode: High-performance liquid chromatography
    Detector: Fluorometric detector set at 440-nm excitation wavelength and provided with a 470-nm emission filter or set at about 530 nm for a fluorescence detector that uses a monochromator for emission wavelength selection
    Column: 30-cm × 3.9-mm (id) column packed with µBondapak C18, or equivalent
    Flow rate: About 2.0 mL/min
    Injection volume: About 100 µL
  System suitability
    Sample: *System suitability solution*
    Suitability requirement 1: The resolution, R, between riboflavin 4'- monophosphate and riboflavin 5'-monophosphate is NLT 1.0.
    Suitability requirement 2: The relative standard deviation of the response for riboflavin 5'-monophosphate in replicate injections is NMT 1.5%.
    [NOTE—The retention time for riboflavin 5'-monophosphate is about 20 to 25 min. The approximate relative retention times for the components are as listed in the list that follows.]

Riboflavin 3'4'-diphosphate:	0.23
Riboflavin 3'5'-diphosphate:	0.39
Riboflavin 4'5'-diphosphate:	0.58
Riboflavin 3'-monophosphate:	0.70
Riboflavin 4'-monophosphate:	0.87
Riboflavin 5'-monophosphate:	1.00
Riboflavin	1.63

Analysis: Separately inject equal volumes of the *Standard solution,* the *Sample solution,* and the *System suitability solution* into the chromatograph. Measure the peak responses obtained from the *Standard solution* and the *Sample solution,* identifying the peaks to be measured in the chromatogram of the *Sample solution* by comparing retention times with those of the peaks in the chromatogram of the *System suitability solution.* Calculate the percentage of free riboflavin by the formula:

$$\text{Result} = 625C(r_F/r_S)$$

Calculate the percentage of riboflavin in the form of riboflavin diphosphates by the formula:

$$\text{Result} = 625C(r_D/r_S)$$

C = concentration (mg/mL) of USP Riboflavin RS in the *Standard solution*
r_F = riboflavin peak response, if any, in the chromatogram of the *Sample solution*
r_D = sum of the responses for any of the three riboflavin diphosphate peaks obtained from the *Sample solution*
r_S = riboflavin peak response in the chromatogram of the *Standard solution*

Acceptance criteria
Free riboflavin: NMT 6.0%, calculated on dried basis
Riboflavin diphosphates: NMT 6.0% as riboflavin ($C_{17}H_{20}N_4O_6$), calculated on dried basis

SPECIFIC TESTS
- **LOSS ON DRYING,** Appendix IIC: 100° in a vacuum over phosphorus pentoxide for 5 h
  Acceptance criteria: NMT 7.5%
- **OPTICAL (SPECIFIC) ROTATION,** Appendix IIB
  Sample solution: 15 mg/mL in 20% hydrochloric acid
  Analysis: Proceed as directed using a 1-dm tube and analyzing the *Sample solution* within 15 min of preparing it.
  Acceptance criteria: $[\alpha]_D^{25}$ between +37.0° and +42.0°, calculated on the dried basis
- **PH,** *pH Determination,* Appendix IIB
  Sample solution: 10 mg/mL
  Acceptance criteria: Between 5.0 and 6.5

- **RESIDUE ON IGNITION (SULFATED ASH),** Appendix IIC
  Sample: 1 g
  Acceptance criteria: NMT 25.0%

Rice Bran Wax

First Published: Prior to FCC 6

INS: 908   CAS: [8016-60-2]

DESCRIPTION
Rice Bran Wax occurs as a hard, slightly crystalline substance that ranges in color from tan to light brown. It is a refined wax obtained from rice bran. It is soluble in chloroform, but is insoluble in water.
Function: Masticatory substance in chewing gum base; coating agent
Packaging and Storage: Store in well-closed containers.

IDENTIFICATION
- **INFRARED SPECTRA,** *Spectrophotometric Identification Tests,* Appendix IIIC
  Sample and standard preparation: Melted on a potassium bromide plate
  Acceptance criteria: The spectrum of the sample exhibits relative maxima at the same wavelengths as those of the spectrum below.

IMPURITIES
Inorganic Impurities
- **LEAD,** *Sample Solution for Lead Limit Test,* Appendix IV
  Acceptance criteria: NMT 3 mg/kg

SPECIFIC TESTS
- **FREE FATTY ACIDS,** Appendix VII
  Acceptance criteria: NMT 10.0%
- **IODINE VALUE,** Appendix VII
  Acceptance criteria: NMT 20
- **MELTING RANGE OR TEMPERATURE DETERMINATION,** *Procedure for Class II,* Appendix IIB
  Acceptance criteria: Between 75° and 80°
- **SAPONIFICATION VALUE,** Appendix VII
  Acceptance criteria: Between 75 and 120

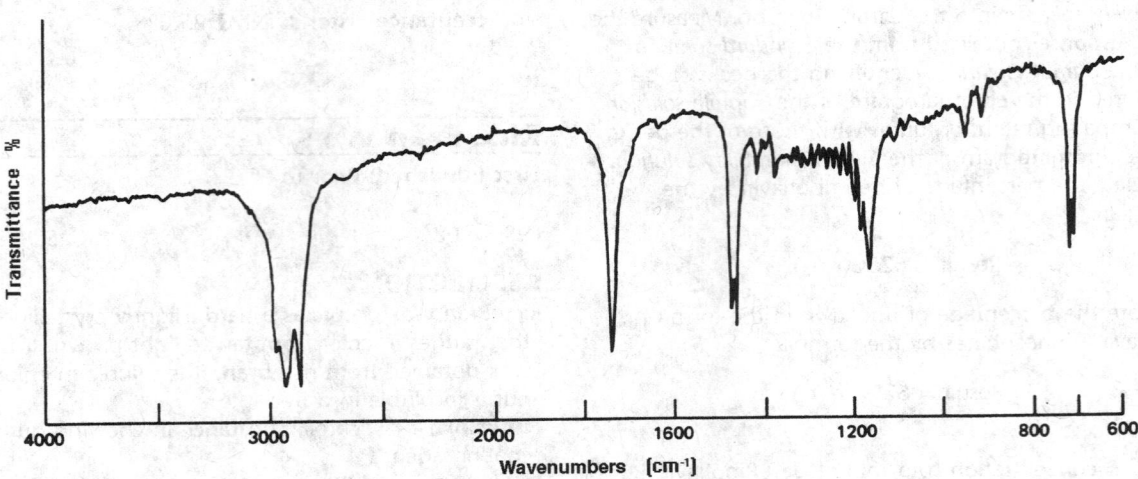

Rice Bran Wax

Rose Oil

First Published: Prior to FCC 6

FEMA: 2989

CAS: [8007-01-0]

UNII: WUB68Y35M7 [rose oil, unspecified]

DESCRIPTION
Rose Oil occurs as a colorless or yellow liquid with the characteristic odor and taste of rose. It is the volatile oil obtained by steam distillation from the fresh flowers of *Rosa gallica* L., *Rosa damascena* Miller, *Rosa alba* L., *Rosa centifolia* L., and varieties of these species (Fam. Rosaceae). At 25°, it is a viscous liquid. Upon gradual cooling it changes to a translucent, crystalline mass, which may be liquefied by warming.
Function: Flavoring agent
Packaging and Storage: Store in a cool place protected from light in full, tight containers.

IDENTIFICATION
- **INFRARED SPECTRA,** *Spectrophotometric Identification Tests,* Appendix IIIC
  Acceptance criteria: The spectrum of the sample exhibits relative maxima at the same wavelengths as those of the spectrum below.

SPECIFIC TESTS
- **ANGULAR ROTATION,** *Optical (Specific) Rotation,* Appendix IIB: Use a 100-mm tube.
  Acceptance criteria: Between −1° and −4°
- **REFRACTIVE INDEX,** Appendix IIB
  [NOTE—Use an Abbé or other refractometer of equal or greater accuracy.]
  Acceptance criteria: Between 1.457 and 1.463 at 30°
- **SOLUBILITY**
  A. One mL of sample is miscible with 1 mL of chloroform without turbidity.
  B. Add 20 mL of 90% alcohol to the mixture from *A*.
  Acceptance criteria: The resulting liquid is neutral or acid to moistened litmus paper and, on standing at 20°, deposits crystals within 5 min.
- **SPECIFIC GRAVITY:** Determine by any reliable method (see *General Provisions*).
  Acceptance criteria: Between 0.848 and 0.863 at 30°/15°

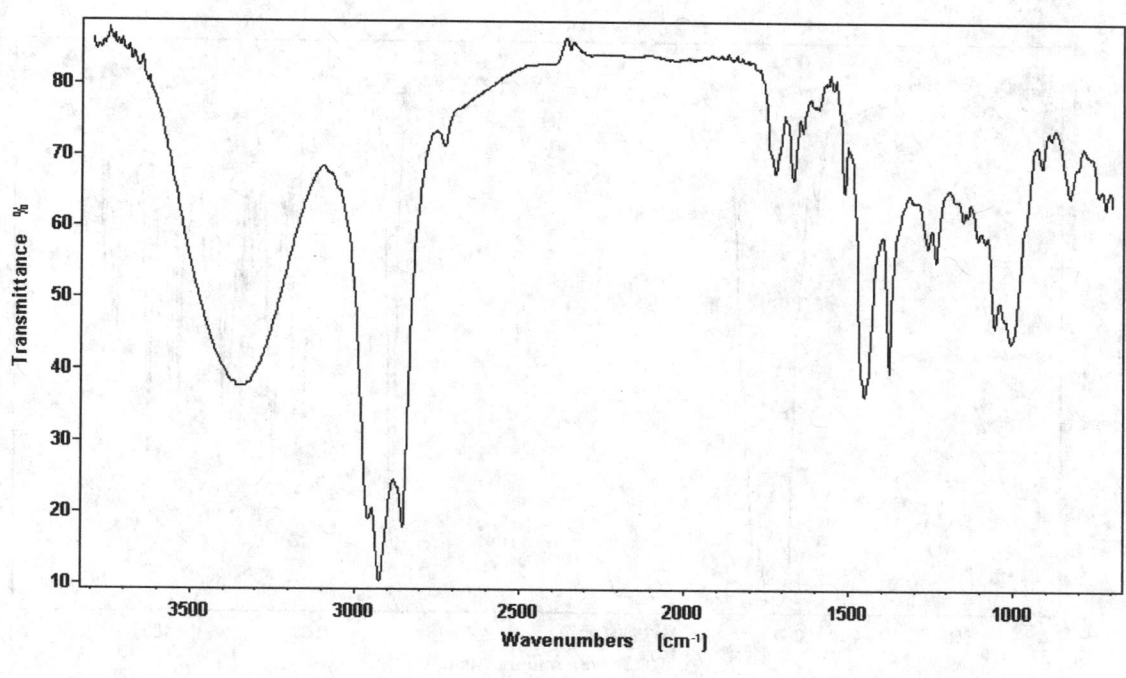

Rose Oil

Rosemary Oil

First Published: Prior to FCC 6

FEMA: 2992

CAS: [8000-25-7]

UNII: 8LGU7VM393 [rosemary oil]

DESCRIPTION
Rosemary Oil occurs as a colorless or pale yellow liquid with the characteristic odor of rosemary and a warm, camphoraceous taste. It is the volatile oil obtained by steam distillation from the fresh flowering tops of *Rosemarinus officinalis* L. (Fam. Labiatae). It is soluble in most vegetable oils, but insoluble in alcohol and in propylene glycol.
Function: Flavoring agent
Packaging and Storage: Store in full, tight containers. Avoid exposure to excessive heat.

IDENTIFICATION
- **INFRARED SPECTRA,** *Spectrophotometric Identification Tests,* Appendix IIIC
  Acceptance criteria: The spectrum of the sample exhibits relative maxima at the same wavelengths as those of the spectrum below.

ASSAY
- **ESTERS,** *Ester Determination,* Appendix VI
  Sample: 10 mL
  Analysis: Use 98.15 as the equivalence factor (e).
  Acceptance criteria: NLT 1.5%, calculated as bornyl acetate ($C_{12}H_{20}O_2$)

- **TOTAL BORNEOL,** *Total Alcohols,* Appendix VI
  Sample: 5 mL of dried, acetylated sample
  Analysis: Calculate the percentage of total borneol by the formula:

  $$\text{Result} = 7.712A(1 - 0.0021E)/(B - 0.021A)$$

  A = difference between the number of mL of 0.5 N hydrochloric acid required for the *Sample* and the number of mL of 0.5 N hydrochloric acid required for the residual blank titration
  E = percentage of esters calculated as bornyl acetate ($C_{12}H_{20}O_2$)
  B = weight of the acetylated *Sample* taken (g)
  Acceptance criteria: NLT 8.0% of borneol ($C_{10}H_{18}O$)

SPECIFIC TESTS
- **ANGULAR ROTATION,** *Optical (Specific) Rotation,* Appendix IIB: Use a 100-mm tube.
  Acceptance criteria: Between −5° and +10°
- **REFRACTIVE INDEX,** Appendix IIB
  [NOTE—Use an Abbé or other refractometer of equal or greater accuracy.]
  Acceptance criteria: Between 1.464 and 1.476 at 20°
- **SOLUBILITY IN ALCOHOL,** Appendix VI
  Acceptance criteria: One mL of the sample dissolves in 1 mL of 90% alcohol. Upon further dilution, the solution may become turbid.
- **SPECIFIC GRAVITY:** Determine by any reliable method (see *General Provisions*).
  Acceptance criteria: Between 0.894 and 0.912

988 / Rosemary Oil / Monographs

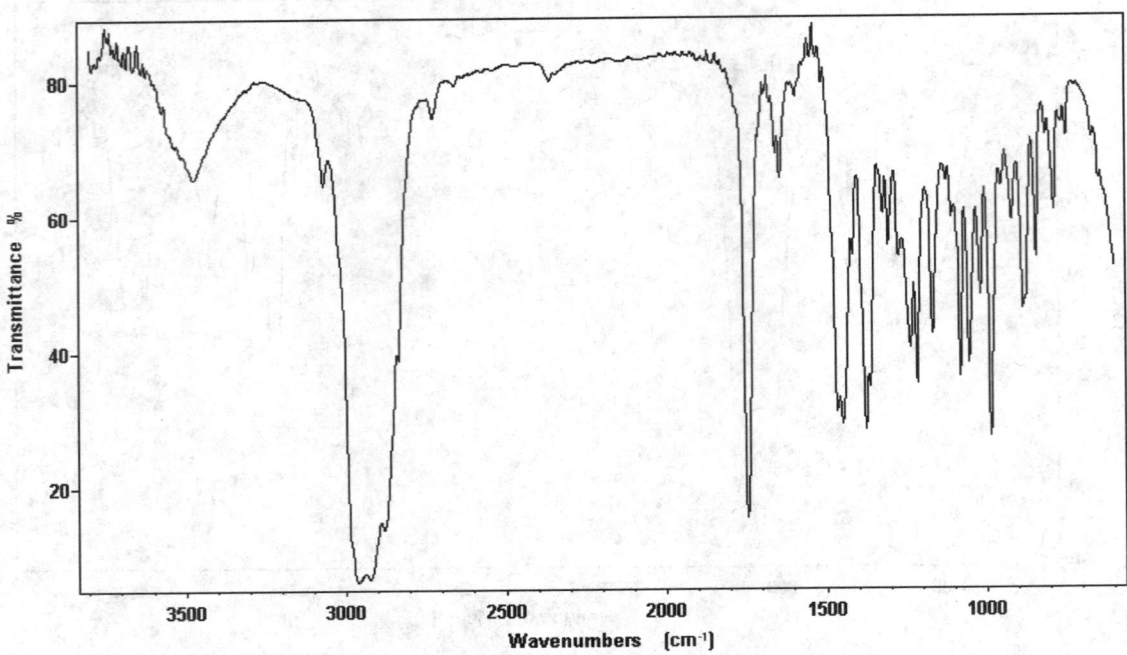

Rosemary Oil

Rue Oil

First Published: Prior to FCC 6

FEMA: 2995

CAS: [8014-29-7]

UNII: VDI0O08XRA [ruta graveolens flowering top oil]

DESCRIPTION
Rue Oil occurs as a yellow to yellow-amber liquid with a characteristic fatty odor. It is the volatile oil obtained by steam distillation from the fresh blossoming plants *Ruta graveolens* L., *Ruta montana* L., or *Ruta bracteosa* L. (Fam. Rutaceae). It is soluble in most fixed oils and in mineral oil, but it is relatively insoluble in glycerin and in propylene glycol.
Function: Flavoring agent
Packaging and Storage: Store in a cool place protected from light in full, tight containers that are made from steel or aluminum and that are suitably lined.

IDENTIFICATION
- **INFRARED SPECTRA**, *Spectrophotometric Identification Tests*, Appendix IIIC
  Acceptance criteria: The spectrum of the sample exhibits relative maxima at the same wavelengths as those of the spectrum below.

ASSAY
- **KETONES**, *Aldehydes and Ketones, Hydroxylamine Method*, Appendix VI
  Sample: 1 g
  Analysis: Use 85.10 as the equivalence factor (e) in the calculation.
  Acceptance criteria: NLT 90.0% of ketones, calculated as methyl nonyl ketone ($C_{11}H_{22}O$)

SPECIFIC TESTS
- **ANGULAR ROTATION**, *Optical (Specific) Rotation*, Appendix IIB: Use a 100-mm tube.
  Acceptance criteria: Between −1° and +3°
- **REFRACTIVE INDEX**, Appendix IIB
  [NOTE—Use an Abbé or other refractometer of equal or greater accuracy.]
  Acceptance criteria: Between 1.430 and 1.440 at 20°
- **SOLIDIFICATION POINT**, Appendix IIB
  Acceptance criteria: Between 7.5° and 10.5°
- **SOLUBILITY IN ALCOHOL**, Appendix VI
  Acceptance criteria: One mL of the sample dissolves in 4 mL of 70% alcohol, occasionally with opalescence or precipitation of solids.
- **SPECIFIC GRAVITY:** Determine by any reliable method (see *General Provisions*).
  Acceptance criteria: Between 0.826 and 0.838

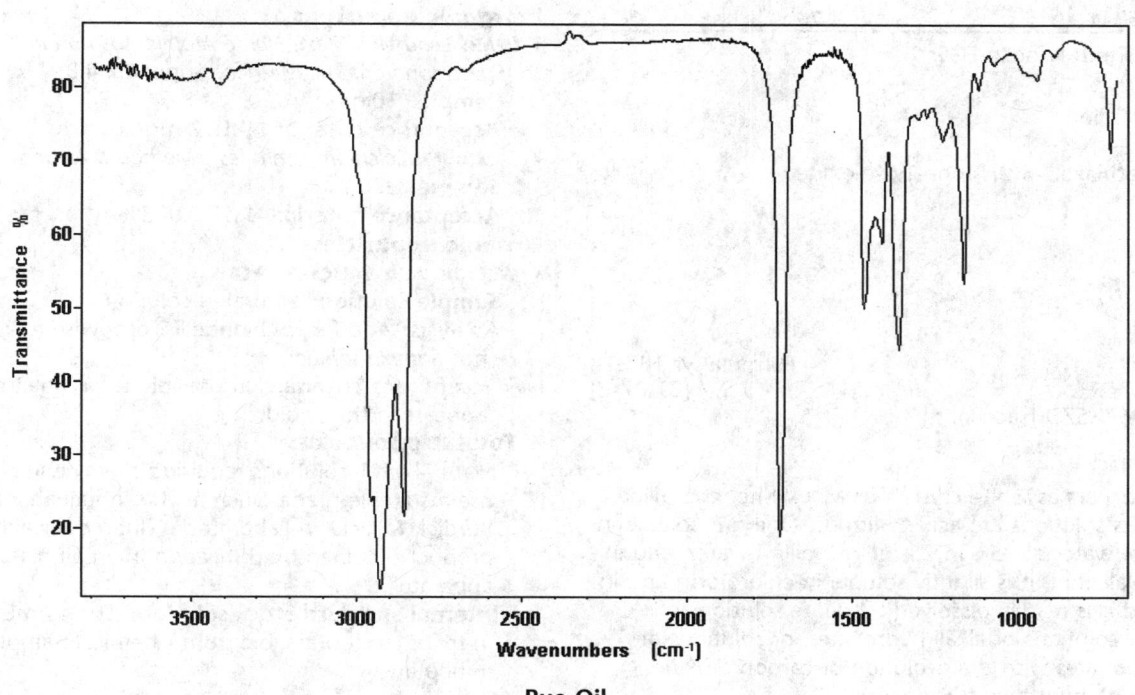

Rue Oil

Saccharin

First Published: Prior to FCC 6

o-Benzosulfimide
Gluside
1,2-Benzisothiazole-3(2H)-one-1,1-dioxide

$C_7H_5NO_3S$ Formula wt 183.18
INS: 954 CAS: [81-07-2]
UNII: FST467XS7D [saccharin]

DESCRIPTION
Saccharin occurs as white crystals or as a white, crystalline powder. Its solutions are acid to litmus. One g is soluble in 290 mL of water at 25°, in 25 mL of boiling water, and in 30 mL of alcohol. It is slightly soluble in chloroform and in ether, and it is readily dissolved by dilute solutions of ammonia, solutions of alkali hydroxides, or solutions of alkali carbonates with the evolution of carbon dioxide.
Function: Nonnutritive sweetener
Packaging and Storage: Store in well-closed containers.

IDENTIFICATION
- **A. Procedure**
    Sample: 100 mg
    Analysis: Dissolve the Sample in 5 mL of a 50 mg/mL solution of sodium hydroxide, evaporate to dryness, and gently fuse the residue over a small flame until ammonia no longer evolves. After the residue has cooled, dissolve it in 20 mL of water, neutralize the solution with 2.7 N hydrochloric acid, and filter. Add 1 drop of ferric chloride TS to the filtrate.
    Acceptance criteria: A violet color appears.
- **B. Procedure**
    Sample: 20 mg
    Analysis: Mix the Sample with 40 mg of resorcinol, cautiously add 10 drops of sulfuric acid, and heat the mixture in a liquid bath at 200° for 3 min. After cooling, add 10 mL of water and an excess of 1 N sodium hydroxide.
    Acceptance criteria: A fluorescent green liquid is produced.

ASSAY
- **Procedure**
    Sample: 500 mg, previously dried
    Analysis: Dissolve the Sample in 75 mL of hot water, cool quickly, add phenolphthalein TS, and titrate with 0.1 N sodium hydroxide. Perform a blank determination (see General Provisions), and make any necessary correction. Each mL of 0.1 N sodium hydroxide is equivalent to 18.32 mg of $C_7H_5NO_3S$.
    Acceptance criteria: NLT 98.0% and NMT 101.0% of $C_7H_5NO_3S$, on the dried basis

IMPURITIES
Inorganic Impurities
- **Lead,** Lead Limit Test, Flame Atomic Absorption Spectrophotometric Method, Appendix IIIB
    Sample: 10 g
    Acceptance criteria: NMT 2 mg/kg
- **Selenium,** Selenium Limit Test, Method I, Appendix IIIB
    Sample: 200 mg
    Acceptance criteria: NMT 0.003%

Organic Impurities
- **Benzoic and Salicylic Acids**
    Sample solution: Saturated solution
    Analysis: Add ferric chloride TS dropwise to 10 mL of hot Sample solution.
    Acceptance criteria: No precipitate or violet color appears in the liquid.
- **Toluenesulfonamides**
    [NOTE—For all solutions requiring methylene chloride, use a suitable grade (such as that obtainable from Burdick & Jackson Laboratories, Inc.) equivalent to the product obtained by distillation in an all-glass apparatus.]
    Internal standard stock solution: 10 mg/mL 95% n-tricosane (obtainable from Chemical Samples Co.) in n-heptane
    Standard stock solution: 2 mg/mL each of reagent-grade o-toluenesulfonamide and p-toluenesulfonamide in methylene chloride
    Standard solutions: Pipet 0.1, 0.25, 1.0, 2.5, and 5.0 mL, respectively, of the Standard stock solution into five 10-mL volumetric flasks. Pipet 0.25 mL of the Internal standard stock solution into each flask, dilute each to volume with methylene chloride, and mix. These solutions contain, respectively, 20, 50, 200, 500, and 1000 µg/mL of each toluenesulfonamide, in addition to 250 µg of n-tricosane.
    Sample solution: Dissolve 2.00 g of sample in 8.0 mL of sodium carbonate TS, and mix the solution thoroughly with 10.0 g of chromatographic siliceous earth (Celite 545, Johns-Manville, or equivalent). Transfer the mixture into a 250-mm × 25-mm chromatographic tube, or equivalent, having a fritted-glass disk and a Teflon stopcock at the bottom and a reservoir at the top. Pack the contents of the tube by tapping the column on a padded surface, and then by tamping firmly from the top. Place 100 mL of methylene chloride in the reservoir, and adjust the stopcock so that 50 mL of eluate is collected in 20 to 30 min. Add 25 µL of Internal standard stock solution to the eluate, mix, and then concentrate the solution to a volume of 1.0 mL in a suitable concentrator tube fitted with a modified Snyder column, using a Kontes tube heater maintained at 90°.
    Chromatographic system, Appendix IIA
        Mode: Gas chromatography
        Detector: Flame-ionization detector
        Column: 3-m × 2-mm (id) glass column, or equivalent, packed with 3% phenyl methyl silicone (OV-17, Applied Science Laboratories, Inc., or equivalent) on 100- to 120-mesh, silanized and calcined diatomaceous silica (Gas-Chrom Q, Applied

Science, or equivalent). [CAUTION—The glass column should extend into the injector for on-column injection and into the detector base to avoid contact with metal.]
Temperature
 Oven: 180°
 Injection port: 225°
 Detector: 250°
Carrier gas: Helium
Flow rate: 30 mL/min
Injection volume: 2.5 µL
Analysis: Set the instrument attenuation so that 2.5 µL of the *Standard solution* that contains 200 µg/mL of each toluenesulfonamide gives a response of 40% to 80% of full-scale deflection. [NOTE—The retention times for *o*-toluenesulfonamide, *p*-toluenesulfonamide, and *n*-tricosane are about 5, 6, and 15 min, respectively.]
Separately inject each of the five *Standard solutions* and the *Sample solution* into the chromatograph, record the chromatograms, and, for each solution, determine the areas of the *o*-toluenesulfonamide, *p*-toluenesulfonamide, and *n*-tricosane peaks. From the values thus obtained from the *Standard solutions*, prepare standard curves by plotting the concentration of each toluenesulfonamide (µg/mL) versus the ratio of the respective toluenesulfonamide peak area to that of *n*-tricosane.
From the standard curve, determine the concentration (µg/mL) of each toluenesulfonamide in the *Sample solution*. Divide each value by 2 to convert the result to mg/kg of the toluenesulfonamide in the 2 g sample taken for analysis.
[NOTE—If the toluenesulfonamide content of the sample is greater than about 500 mg/kg, the impurity may crystallize out of the methylene chloride concentrate (see *Sample solution*). Although this level of impurity exceeds that permitted by the specification, the analysis may be completed by diluting the concentrate with methylene chloride containing 250 µg/mL of *n*-tricosane, and by applying appropriate dilution factors in the calculation. Care must be taken to redissolve completely any crystalline toluenesulfonamide to give a homogeneous solution.]
Acceptance criteria: NMT 0.0025%

SPECIFIC TESTS
- **LOSS ON DRYING,** Appendix IIC: 105° for 2 h
  Acceptance criteria: NMT 1%
- **MELTING RANGE OR TEMPERATURE DETERMINATION,** *Procedure for Class Ia,* Appendix IIB
  Acceptance criteria: Between 226° and 230°
- **READILY CARBONIZABLE SUBSTANCES,** Appendix IIB
  Sample: 200 mg
  Analysis: Dissolve the *Sample* in 5 mL of 95% sulfuric acid and keep it at 48° to 50° for 10 min. Proceed as directed.
  Acceptance criteria: The color of the resulting solution is no darker than that of *Matching Fluid A*.
- **RESIDUE ON IGNITION (SULFATED ASH),** Appendix IIC
  Sample: 1 g
  Acceptance criteria: NMT 0.2%

Safflower Oil (Unhydrogenated)
First Published: Prior to FCC 6

CAS: [8001-23-8]
UNII: 65UEH262IS [safflower oil]

DESCRIPTION
Safflower Oil, Unhydrogenated, occurs as a light yellow oil. It is obtained from the plant *Carthamus tinctorius* (Fam. Asteraceae) by mechanical expression or solvent extraction. It is refined, bleached, and deodorized to substantially remove free fatty acids, phospholipids, color, odor and flavor components, and miscellaneous other non-oil materials. It is a liquid at 21° to 27°, but traces of wax may cause the oil to cloud unless removed by winterization. Safflower Oil has the highest linoleic acid [(Z),(Z)-9,12-octadecadienoic acid] content (typically about 78% of total fatty acids) of any known oil. It is free from visible foreign matter at 21° to 27°
Function: Coating agent; texturizer
Packaging and Storage: Store in well-closed containers.

IDENTIFICATION
- **FATTY ACID COMPOSITION,** Appendix VII
  Acceptance criteria: Safflower Oil exhibits the following composition profile of fatty acids:

Fatty Acid	Weight % (Range)
<14	<0.1
14:0	<1.0
16:0	2–10
16:1	<0.5
18:0	1–10
18:1	7–16
18:2	72–81
18:3	<1.5
20:0	<0.5
20:1	<0.5

IMPURITIES
Inorganic Impurities
- **LEAD,** *Lead Limit Test, Atomic Absorption Spectrophotometric Graphite Furnace Method II,* Appendix IIIB
  Acceptance criteria: NMT 0.1 mg/kg

SPECIFIC TESTS
- **COLD TEST,** Appendix VII
  Acceptance criteria: Passes test
- **COLOR (FATS AND RELATED SUBSTANCES),** Appendix VII
  Acceptance criteria: NMT 1.0 red
- **FREE FATTY ACIDS (AS OLEIC ACID),** *Free Fatty Acids,* Appendix VII
  Analysis: Use the following equivalence factor (e) in the formula given in the procedure under *Free Fatty Acids,* e = 28.2.
  Acceptance criteria: NMT 0.1%

- **Iodine Value,** Appendix VII
  Acceptance criteria: Between 135 and 150
- **Linoleic Acid,** *Fatty Acid Composition,* Appendix VII
  Acceptance criteria: NLT 72% of total fatty acids
- **Linolenic Acid,** *Fatty Acid Composition,* Appendix VII
  Acceptance criteria: NMT 1.5%
- **Peroxide Value,** Appendix VII
  Acceptance criteria: NMT 10 mEq/kg
- **Unsaponifiable Matter,** Appendix VII
  Acceptance criteria: NMT 1.5%
- **Water,** *Water Determination, Method Ia,* Appendix IIB
  Analysis: Use 50 mL of chloroform to dissolve the sample, instead of 35 to 40 mL of methanol, in the *Procedure.*
  Acceptance criteria: NMT 0.1%

Sage Oil, Dalmatian Type

First Published: Prior to FCC 6

FEMA: 3001   CAS: [8022-56-8]

UNII: U27K0H1H2O [sage oil]

DESCRIPTION
Sage Oil, Dalmatian Type, occurs as a yellow or green-yellow liquid with a warm, camphoraceous and thujone odor and flavor. It is the oil obtained by steam distillation from the partially dried leaves of the plant *Salvia officinalis* L. (Fam. Labiatae). It is soluble in most fixed oils and in mineral oil. Frequently the solutions in mineral oil are opalescent. It is slightly soluble in propylene glycol, but it is practically insoluble in glycerin.
Function: Flavoring agent
Packaging and Storage: Store in a cool place protected from light in full, tight containers that are made from steel or aluminum and that are suitably lined.

IDENTIFICATION
- **Infrared Spectra,** *Spectrophotometric Identification Tests,* Appendix IIIC
  Acceptance criteria: The spectrum of the sample exhibits relative maxima at the same wavelengths as those of the spectrum below.

ASSAY
- **Procedure**
  Sample: 1 g
  Analysis: Determine as directed under *Aldehydes and Ketones, Hydroxylamine Method,* Appendix VI. Use 76.12 as the equivalence factor (e) in the calculation.
  Acceptance criteria: NLT 50.0% of ketones, calculated as thujone ($C_{10}H_{16}O$)

SPECIFIC TESTS
- **Angular Rotation,** *Optical (Specific) Rotation,* Appendix IIB: Use a 100-mm tube.
  Acceptance criteria: Between +2° and +29°
- **Ester Value After Acetylation,** *Total Alcohols,* Appendix VI
  Sample: 2.5 g of acetylated oil
  Analysis: Calculate the *Ester value after acetylation* using the formula

  $$\text{Result} = A \times F/B$$

  F = saponification factor (28.05)
  A = volume of 0.5 N alcoholic potassium hydroxide consumed in the saponification of the acetylated oil (mL)
  B = weight of the acetylated oil sample taken (g)

  Acceptance criteria: Between 25 and 60
- **Refractive Index,** Appendix IIB
  [Note—Use an Abbé or other refractometer of equal or greater accuracy.]
  Acceptance criteria: Between 1.457 and 1.469 at 20°
- **Saponification Value,** *Esters,* Appendix VI
  Sample: 5 g
  Acceptance criteria: Between 5 and 20
- **Solubility in Alcohol,** Appendix VI
  Acceptance criteria: One mL of the sample dissolves in 1 mL of 80% alcohol.
- **Specific Gravity:** Determine by any reliable method (see *General Provisions*).
  Acceptance criteria: Between 0.903 and 0.925

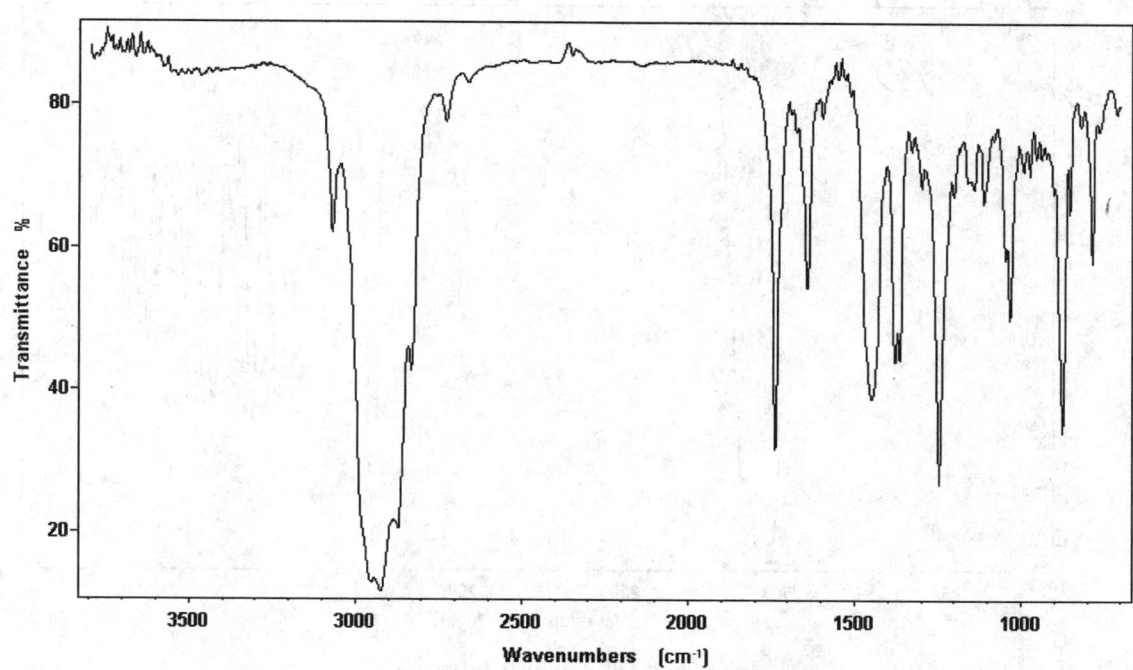

Sage Oil, Dalmatian Type

Sage Oil, Spanish Type
First Published: Prior to FCC 6

FEMA: 3003
CAS: [8016-65-7]
UNII: K69SG4X28I [salvia lavandulifolia leaf oil]

DESCRIPTION
Sage Oil, Spanish-Type, occurs as a colorless to slightly yellow oil with a camphoraceous odor that has a cineole top note. It is the volatile oil obtained by distillation from the plants of *Salvia lavandulaefolia* Vahl. or *Salvia hispanorium* Lag. (Fam. Labiatae). It is soluble in most fixed oils and in glycerin. It is soluble, usually with opalescence, in mineral oil and in propylene glycol.
Function: Flavoring agent
Packaging and Storage: Store in a cool place protected from light in full, tight containers that are made from steel or aluminum and that are suitably lined.

IDENTIFICATION
- **INFRARED SPECTRA,** *Spectrophotometric Identification Tests,* Appendix IIIC
  Acceptance criteria: The spectrum of the sample exhibits relative maxima at the same wavelengths as those of the spectrum below.

SPECIFIC TESTS
- **ANGULAR ROTATION,** *Optical (Specific) Rotation,* Appendix IIB : Use a 100-mm tube.
  Acceptance criteria: Between −3° and +24°
- **REFRACTIVE INDEX,** Appendix IIB
  [NOTE—Use an Abbé or other refractometer of equal or greater accuracy.]
  Acceptance criteria: Between 1.468 and 1.473 at 20°
- **SAPONIFICATION VALUE** *Esters,* Appendix VI
  Sample: 5 g
  Acceptance criteria: Between 14 and 57
- **SAPONIFICATION VALUE AFTER ACETYLATION**
  Sample: 10 mL
  Acetylated sample: Using the *Sample,* prepare 2.5 g of dried, acetylated oil as directed under *Total Alcohols,* Appendix VI.
  Analysis: Using the *Acetylated sample,* proceed as directed in *Saponification Value, Esters,* Appendix VI. Use the weight (g), of the *Acetylated sample* for W in the calculation formula.
  Acceptance criteria: Between 56 and 98
- **SOLUBILITY IN ALCOHOL,** Appendix VI
  Acceptance criteria: One mL of the sample dissolves in 2 mL of 80% alcohol. The solution might become opalescent on dilution.
- **SPECIFIC GRAVITY:** Determine by any reliable method (see *General Provisions*).
  Acceptance criteria: Between 0.909 and 0.932

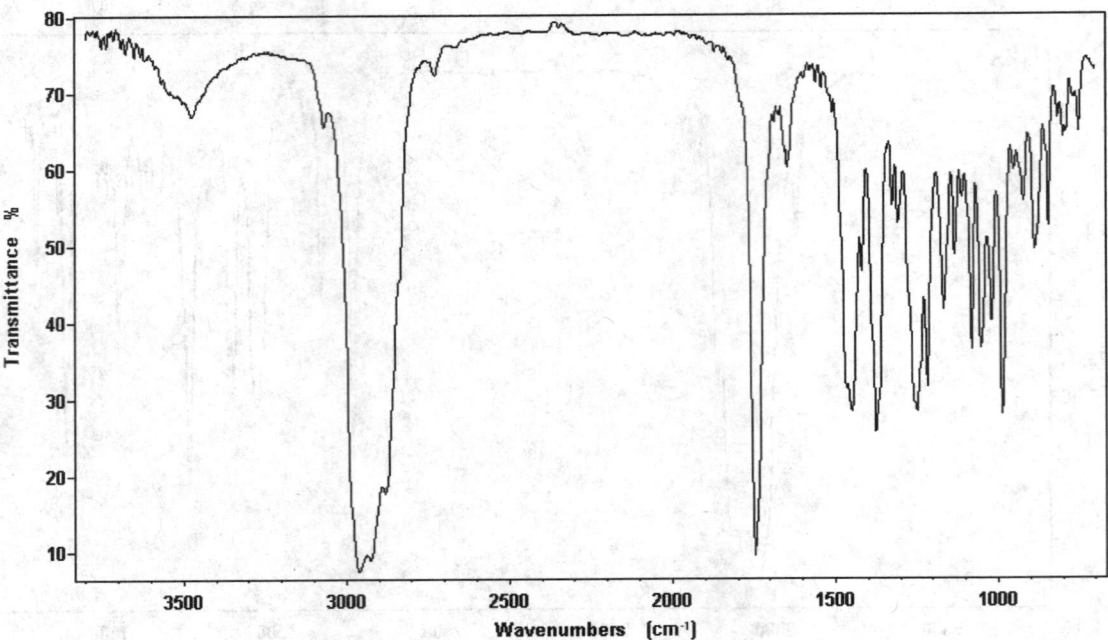

Sage Oil, Spanish Type

Salatrim

First Published: Prior to FCC 6

Short- and Long-Chain Acyl Triglyceride Molecules

$x + y + z = 12 - 42$

CAS: [177403-56-4]

UNII: 99YC50WUBY [salatrim]

DESCRIPTION
Salatrim ranges from a slightly viscous, clear amber liquid to a light-colored, waxy solid. Salatrim is the abbreviated name for short- and long-chain acyl triglyceride molecules. It is prepared by interesterification of triacetin, tripropionin, tributyrin, or of their mixtures, with hydrogenated canola, soybean, sunflower, or cottonseed oil. The process removes triglycerides with three short-chain fatty acids. Salatrim triglycerides typically contain 30 to 42 mol-% short-chain fatty acids (SCFA) and 58 to 70 mol-% long-chain fatty acids (LCFA); stearic acid is the predominant LCFA. It is free of particulate matter. It is soluble in hexane, in cyclohexane, in acetone, in ether, in tetrahydrofuran, and in liquid triglyceride oils, but is insoluble in water. It melts at 16° to 71° depending on triglyceride composition.

Function: Reduced-energy fat replacement for conventional fats and oils

Packaging and Storage: Store in well-closed containers.

IDENTIFICATION
- **INFRARED SPECTRA,** *Spectrophotometric Identification Tests,* Appendix IIIC
  Sample preparation: Contained in a sodium chloride cell or between two sodium chloride plates
  Acceptance criteria: The spectrum of the sample exhibits relative maxima at the same wavelengths as those of the spectrum below.

ASSAY
[NOTE—The following procedures were excerpted with permission from *J. Agric. Food Chem.* 1994, 42:453–460. Copyright 1994 American Chemical Society.]
- **MONOGLYCERIDE AND TRIGLYCERIDE CONTENT**
  [NOTE—This method permits the quantitation of monoglycerides (MG) with one long-chain fatty acid (LCFA) and triglycerides (TG) with the same acyl carbon number (ACN) in salatrim by high-temperature capillary gas chromatography. The ACN is the sum of the number of carbons of each carboxylic acid side chain of each TG. For example, the ACN for tristearin is 54 (i.e., 3×18), and the ACNs for both dipropionylstearoylglycerol and diacetylarachidoylglycerol are 24, that is, $[(2 \times 3) + 18]$ and $[(2 \times 2) + 20]$, respectively. MG and TG are identified by comparison with standards. The weight percent of each MG and TG in salatrim is determined from the peak areas and calibration curves constructed using data from analyses of standard solutions.]
  MG stock standards (2 standards): Obtain monopentadecanoin (mono-C15) and monostearin

(mono-C18) with a minimum purity of 99% (available from Nu Check Prep., Inc., Elysian, MN).

TG stock standards (13 standards): Obtain tricaproin (tri-C6), triheptanoin (tri-C7), tricaprylin (tri-C8), trinonanoin (tri-C9), tricaprin (tri-C10), triundecanoin (tri-C11), trilaurin (tri-C12), tritridecanoin (tri-C13), trimyristin (tri-C14), tripentadecanoin (tri-C15), tripalmitin (tri-C16), triheptadecanoin (tri-C17), and tristearin (tri-C18) with a minimum purity of 99% (available from Nu Check Prep., Inc., Elysian, MN).

Internal standard solution: 0.100 mg/mL of tri-C11 in spectroscopic-grade undecane and toluene (95:5) (v/v)

MG standard solutions: 500 mg/L, 250 mg/L, 125 mg/L, 62.5 mg/L, 31 mg/L, 15.6 mg/L, and 7.8 mg/L of each *MG stock standard* in *Internal standard solution*

TG standard solutions: 1600 mg/L, 800 mg/L, 400 mg/L, 200 mg/L, 100 mg/L, 50 mg/L, 32 mg/L, 25 mg/L, 20 mg/L, 18 mg/L, 16 mg/L, 14 mg/L, 12 mg/L, 10 mg/L, 9 mg/L, 8 mg/L, 7 mg/L, 6 mg/L, 5 mg/L, 4 mg/L, 3 mg/L, and 2 mg/L of each *TG stock standard* in *Internal standard solution*

Sample solution: 2 mg/mL in *Internal standard solution*

Chromatographic system, Appendix IIA

Mode: Gas chromatography. [NOTE—Use a Hewlett-Packard 5890 Series II GC, or equivalent.]

Detector: Flame ionization detector

Injector: Pressure-programmable, on-column

Autosampler: HP 7673, or equivalent

Integrator: HP Series II, or equivalent

Column system: Chromapack SIM-DIST CB fused-silica GC column (Chromapack, Inc. Raritan, NJ), or equivalent, with a 5-m × 0.32-mm (id) and a 0.1-μm film thickness, or equivalent. Use a deactivated fused-silica precolumn (0.5-m × 0.53-mm id) coupled to the analytical column via a butt connector (Quadrex Corp., New Haven, CT), or equivalent.

Oven temperature: Set to ramp 140° to 350° at 10°/min (total run time of 21.0 min). [NOTE—Set the track mode to "on" (injector temperature follows the oven temperature conditions).]

Detector temperature: 375°

Injection mode: On-column injection

Carrier gas: Hydrogen

Gas flow: Constant

Gas pressure: 5.5 psi (140°)

Injection volume: 0.5 μL

Analysis for MG content: Separately inject each of the *MG standard solutions* into the chromatograph and record the resulting chromatograms. From each chromatogram, establish the response factors (RF_i) for each *MG standard solution* (i) using the following equation:

$$RF_i = (C_{IS}/C_i) \times (A_i/A_{IS})$$

C_{IS} = concentration of the *Internal standard solution* (mg/L)

C_i = concentration of the *MG Standard solution* of interest (mg/L)

A_i = peak area of the MG of interest

A_{IS} = peak area of the *Internal standard solution*

For each *MG standard solution*, construct a standard curve by plotting the peak area ratios of (A_i/A_{IS}) (x-axis) versus the RF_i (y-axis) for each solution.

Inject the *Sample solution* into the chromatograph and record the resulting chromatogram. From the chromatograms, obtain the peak area of each MG (A_i) and of the *Internal standard solution* (A_{IS}). Calculate the peak area ratio (A_i/A_{IS}), and determine the response factor for each MG (RF_i) from the calibration curve prepared above. Determine the concentration, in mg/mL, of each MG (C_i) in the sample by the equation:

$$C_i = (C_{IS}/RF_i) \times (A_i/A_{IS})$$

C_{IS} = concentration of the *Internal standard solution* (mg/L)

Determine the weight percent [$(W\%)_i$] of each MG in the sample by the equation:

$$(W\%)_i = (C_i/C_T) \times 100$$

C_T = concentration of the *Sample solution* (mg/L)

Determine the total weight percent of MG in the sample by the formula:

$$\text{Result} = \Sigma_i \, (W\%)_i$$

Analysis for TG content: To determine the RF for *TG standards*, inject each of the *TG standard solutions* into the chromatograph and record the resulting chromatograms.

Determine the RF for each *TG standard solution* (j) by the formula:

$$RF_{nj} = (C_{IS}/C_{nj}) \times (A_{nj}/A_{IS})$$

C_{IS} = concentration of the *Internal standard solution* (mg/L)

C_{nj} = concentration of the *TG standard solution* of interest (mg/L)

A_{IS} = peak area of the *Internal standard solution*

A_{nj} = peak area of the TG of interest, with an acetyl carbon number equaling n (n is between 18 and 54; see the table below for the acetyl carbon numbers of the *TG standard solutions*).

TG standard	n
tri-C6	18
tri-C7	21
tri-C8	24
tri-C9	27
tri-C10	30
tri-C11	33
tri-C12	36
tri-C13	39
tri-C14	42

TG standard	n
tri-C15	45
tri-C16	48
tri-C17	51
tri-C18	54

The relative peak area of each *TG standard solution*, with ACN = n and concentration C_{nj}, to that of the *Internal standard solution* is given by the equation:

$$RA_{nj} = A_{nj}/A_{IS}$$

[NOTE—The notations "j + 1," "j," and "j − 1" denote consecutive concentration values in the series of *TG standard solutions*. For example, for a *TG standard solution* with ACN = n and concentrations of 100, 200, and 400 mg/L, the relative peak areas RA_{nj+1} and RA_{nj-1} correspond to data for standards with concentrations of 400 mg/L and 100 mg/L, respectively.]

Calculate the RF and relative peak areas for each TG with ACN = n + 1 and with ACN = n + 2 from the measured RF and RA values for *TG standard solutions* with ACN = n and n + 3 at the same concentration, C_{nj}, according to the following equations:

$$RF_{n+1j} = RF_{nj} + (RF_{n+3j} - RF_{nj}) \times 1/3$$

$$RA_{n+1j} = RA_{nj} + (RA_{n+3j} - RA_{nj}) \times 1/3$$

$$RF_{n+2j} = RF_{nj} + (RF_{n+3j} - RF_{nj}) \times 2/3$$

$$RA_{n+2j} = RA_{nj} + (RA_{n+3j} - RA_{nj}) \times 2/3$$

For the *Sample solution*, calculate the RF for the TG with a relative peak area RA_{nj} by the equation:

$$RF_{nj} = RF_{nj-1} + (RF_{nj+1} - RF_{nj-1}) \times [(RA_{nj} - RA_{nj-1})/(RA_{nj+1} - RA_{nj-1})]$$

RF_{nj-1} and RF_{nj+1} = response factors
RA_{nj-1} and RA_{nj+1} = relative peak areas of the TG standard solutions with the same ACN value
RA_{nj+1} and RA_{nj-1} must meet the following condition:

$$Result = RA_{nj-1} \leq RA_{nj} < RA_{nj+1}$$

RA_{nj} = ratio of the peak area of the TG in salatrim with ACN = n (A_{nj}), to the peak area for the *Internal standard solution* (A_{IS})

To determine the weight percent of salatrim TG components, the concentration (mg/L) of TG in the sample with ACN = n is given by the equation:

$$C_{nj} = (C_{IS}/RF_{nj}) \times (A_{nj}/A_{IS})$$

C_{IS} = concentration of the *Internal standard solution* (mg/L)

Determine the weight percent of TG with ACN = n in the sample by the equation:

$$(W\%)_n = (C_{nj}/C_T) \times 100$$

C_T = concentration of the *Sample solution* (mg/L)

Determine the total weight percent of TG in the sample with the formula:

$$Result = \Sigma_n (W\%)_n$$

Acceptance criteria: NLT 87% triglycerides

- **SHORT-CHAIN FATTY ACIDS (SCFA)/LONG-CHAIN FATTY ACIDS (LCFA) MOLE RATIO**

0.5 N sodium butoxide: 96.2 mg/mL of sodium butoxide solution in 50% 1-butanol

Butyl ester stock standards: Butyl butyrate (98%); *n*-butyl acetate (99%); butyl propionate; butyl palmitate; butyl stearate (93%)

Standard solutions: [NOTE—Melt the butyl stearate standard before sampling. More than one standard reference solution may be necessary if impurities co-elute with standard peaks.] Transfer 50 mg of each *Butyl ester stock standard* into a single 100-mL volumetric flask. Dilute to volume with HPLC-grade hexane (95%), and mix.

Sample solution: Transfer 50 mg of sample, previously melted, into a 100- mL volumetric flask. Dilute to volume with hexane, and mix.

Blank: Hexane

Chromatographic system, Appendix IIA
  Mode: Gas chromatography. [NOTE—Use a Hewlett-Packard 5890 Series II GC, or equivalent.]
  Detector: Flame ionization detector
  Autosampler: HP 7673, or equivalent
  Integrator: HP 3365 Series II, or equivalent
  Column system: Retention gap, deactivated fused silica, 1- × 0.32-mm (id) with capillary column connectors. DB 5-HT, 15-m × 0.32-mm (id) fused silica capillary column (J&W Scientific, Inc., 91 Blue Ravine Road, Folsom, CA 95630-4714, catalog number 123-5711, or equivalent)
  Temperature
    Column oven: Hold at 40° for 6 min and increase to 280° at 15°/min increments over 5 min.
    Injector: Use track mode at 3° above *Oven temperature*.
    Detector: 380°
  Carrier gas: Helium
  Gas flow: 2.0 psi, constant flow
  Injection volume: 0.5 µL. [NOTE—Use a 5-µL syringe for 0.32-mm (id) columns.]

[NOTE—Use crimp caps and vials (HP 5181-3375, or equivalent) for an on-line autosampler.]

Analysis: For each sample to be analyzed (*Blank, Standard solutions,* and *Sample solution*), pipet 5.0 mL of solution into a clean 8-mL clear glass vial. Add 0.5 mL of *0.5 N Sodium butoxide*, seal, and shake vigorously. The solution will turn yellow. For the *Blank* and the *Sample solution* only, allow the solution to stand for 2 min. Neutralize the mixture by adding 1.0 mL of 0.5 N hydrochloric acid. Seal the vial, and shake well until the solution is clear. Check the pH with pH paper. The solution should be acidic. If it is not, the column will degrade.

[NOTE—1-Butanol and water may be substituted for *0.5 N Sodium butoxide* and 0.5 N hydrochloric acid, respectively, for the *Standard solution*.]

Allow the butyl ester sample phases to separate (centrifugation may be used to hasten the separation). Transfer approximately 1 mL of the hexane layer into an autosampler vial. Run the gas chromatography program and record the resulting chromatograms.

Determine the response factors (RF_i) for each of the *Standard solutions* with the equation:

$$RF_i = 100\% \times A_i/[W_i \times P_i]$$

A_i = average peak area counts for the ith butyl ester in the *Standard solution*
W_i = weight of the ith standard in the *Standard solution* (mg)
P_i = purity of the ith standard (%)

Determine the weights of butyl esters in the sample with the equation:

$$W_i = A_i/RF_i$$

W_i = weight of the ith ester in the sample (mg)
A_i = peak area counts for the ith ester in the *Sample solution*
RF_i = response factor for the ith butyl ester standard (average area counts/mg)

Determine the weights of fatty acids in the sample with the equation:

$$(W_i)_{fatty\ acid} = (W_i)_{butyl\ ester} \times (MW_i)_{fatty\ acid}/(MW_i)_{butyl\ ester}$$

$(W_i)_{fatty\ acid}$ and $(W_i)_{butyl\ ester}$ = Weights of the ith fatty acid and its butyl ester in the sample (mg)
$(MW_i)_{fatty\ acid}$ and $(MW_i)_{butyl\ ester}$ = Molecular weights of the ith fatty acid and its butyl ester

Calculate the short/long (S/L) mole ratio with the following equations:

$$(mmoles_i)_{fatty\ acid} = (W_i)_{fatty\ acid}/[1000 \times (MW_i)_{fatty\ acid}]$$

$$S/L\ mole\ ratio = \Sigma_i\ (mmoles_i)_{SCFA}/\Sigma_i\ (mmoles_i)_{LCFA}$$

$(W_i)_{fatty\ acid}$ = Weight (mg)
$(MW_i)_{fatty\ acid}$ = Molecular weight (mg/mmol)
$\Sigma_i\ (mmoles_i)_{SCFA}$ = Sum of the millimoles of short-chain fatty acids (C2–C4)
$\Sigma_i\ (mmoles_i)_{LCFA}$ = Sum of the millimoles of long-chain fatty acids (C14–C18)

Acceptance criteria
Triglycerides with an SCFA/LCFA mole ratio in the range of 0.5-2.0: NLT 90%

- **TOTAL SATURATED LCFAs**
  Analysis: Calculate the weight percent of saturated LCFAs with the formula below using the *SCFA/LCFA mole ratio* assay method above.

  $$Result = 100 \times [(W_i)_{stearic\ acid} + (W_i)_{palmitic\ acid}]/W_S$$

  W_S = weight of the sample taken (μg)
  Acceptance criteria: NMT 70%, by weight, saturated long-chain fatty acids

IMPURITIES
Inorganic Impurities
- **LEAD,** *Lead Limit Test, Atomic Absorption Spectrophotometric Graphite Furnace Method, Method II,* Appendix IIIB
  Acceptance criteria: NMT 0.1 mg/kg

Organic Impurities
- **FREE FATTY ACIDS (AS OLEIC ACID),** Appendix VII
  Analysis: Determine as directed. Use the following equivalence factor (e) in the formula given in the procedure: *Free Fatty Acids* as oleic acid, e = 28.2.
  Acceptance criteria: NMT 0.5%
- **MONOGLYCERIDES**
  Analysis: Determine as directed in the *Assay* (above) using the *Analysis for MG content*.
  Acceptance criteria: NMT 2%

SPECIFIC TESTS
- **PEROXIDE VALUE**
  Acetic acid–chloroform solution: Acetic acid and chloroform mixture (3:2) (v/v)
  Saturated potassium iodide solution: Dissolve excess potassium iodide in freshly boiled water. Excess solid must remain. Store this solution in the dark. [NOTE—Test the solution daily by adding 0.5 mL to 30 mL of the *Acetic acid–chloroform solution*, then add 2 drops of starch TS. If the solution turns blue, requiring more than 1 drop of 0.1 N sodium thiosulfate to discharge the color, prepare a fresh solution.]
  Sample: 5 g
  Analysis: Transfer the *Sample* into a 250-mL Erlenmeyer flask. Add 30 mL of the *Acetic acid–chloroform solution*, and swirl to dissolve. Add 0.5 mL of the *Saturated potassium iodide solution*, allow the mixture to stand, shaking it occasionally, for 1 min, and add 30 mL of water. Slowly titrate with 0.01 N sodium thiosulfate, shaking the flask vigorously until the yellow color is almost gone. Add about 0.5 mL of starch TS, and continue the titration, shaking the flask vigorously to release all the iodine from the chloroform layer until the blue color disappears. Perform a blank determination (see *General Provisions*), and make any necessary correction.
  Determine the peroxide value (PV, mEq of peroxide per kg of sample) using the following equation:

  $$PV = (S \times N \times 1000)/W$$

S = volume of 0.01 N sodium thiosulfate used in the titration (mL)
N = normality of the sodium thiosulfate solution
W = weight of the sample taken (g)

Acceptance criteria: NMT 2.0

- **RESIDUE ON IGNITION (SULFATED ASH)**, *Method I*, Appendix IIC
  Sample: 2 g
  Acceptance criteria: NMT 0.1%

- **UNSAPONIFIABLE MATTER**
  Calcium chloride–diatomaceous earth mixture: Using a mortar and pestle, grind 1 part anhydrous calcium chloride with 1 part water, and add 3 parts diatomaceous earth, nonacid washed (Celite 545, or equivalent). Grind to a uniform consistency. [NOTE—This mixture may be stored in a covered amber jar for up to 1 month.]
  Potassium hydroxide–diatomaceous earth mixture: Using a mortar and pestle, grind 2 parts potassium hydroxide pellets with 1 part water. [CAUTION—This action generates considerable heat; wear eye protection and gloves.] Add 4 parts diatomaceous earth. Grind the mixture to a uniform consistency. [NOTE—For multiple analyses, prepare in lots of 75 g or more. Store it in a covered amber jar for up to 10 days.]
  Sample: 5 g
  Analysis: Place 10 g of *Potassium hydroxide–diatomaceous earth mixture* in a 400-mL mortar. Transfer the *Sample* into the mortar. Grind the mixture until the sample is uniformly distributed. [CAUTION—This action generates considerable heat; wear eye protection and gloves.] Add another 10 g of *Potassium hydroxide–diatomaceous earth mixture*, and grind to a uniform consistency. Transfer the mixture to a jar. Transfer any residual sample by using the pestle to sweep 5 g of diatomaceous earth along the sides of the mortar and into the jar. Cap the jar securely, and shake until the mixture is uniform. Heat for 20 to 30 min in an oven at 130°.
  Transfer the cooled mixture into the mortar, and regrind it for approximately 30 s to a uniform granular consistency. Loosely fit a plug of glass wool into the tip of a glass chromatography column (30-mm id, 30-cm long overall, with a drip tip 5-cm × 8-mm od, or equivalent). Pack the column with 5 g of *Calcium chloride–diatomaceous earth mixture*, and transfer the contents of the mortar to the column. Pack to a total height of 50 to 60 mm. Place a 150-mL tared flask under the column. Qualitatively transfer the residue of *Sample* from the mortar to the column with about 25 mL of dichloromethane. Once this solution has percolated into the column bed, add sufficient dichloromethane so that the column bed is wet and a few drops of eluate have been collected in the flask. Charge the column with 150 mL of dichloromethane, and collect the entire volume in the flask (approximately 25 min).
  While gently heating, remove the solvent under a stream of nitrogen while the eluate is collected. Take the contents of the flask to constant weight under vacuum. Determine the weight of the residue (W_R). To check for completeness of extraction, add 20 mL of dichloromethane to the column, and collect the eluate in a second tared flask. Evaporate the contents of the second flask to dryness, and examine it for residue. Determine the weight of the residue (W_R^1), if present. If residue is present, repeat the procedure with an additional 20 mL of dichloromethane.
  Use the total residue weight and the weight of the original sample to calculate the percent of unsaponifiable matter using the following equation:

  $$\text{\%unsaponifiable matter} = [(W_R + W_R^1 + \ldots)/W_S] \times 100$$

  W_S = weight of the sample taken (g)
  W_R = weight of the residue after column chromatography (g)
  W_R^1 = weight, if any, of residue left after extraction (g)

  Acceptance criteria: NMT 1.0%

- **WATER**, *Water Determination*, Appendix IIB
  Acceptance criteria: NMT 0.3%

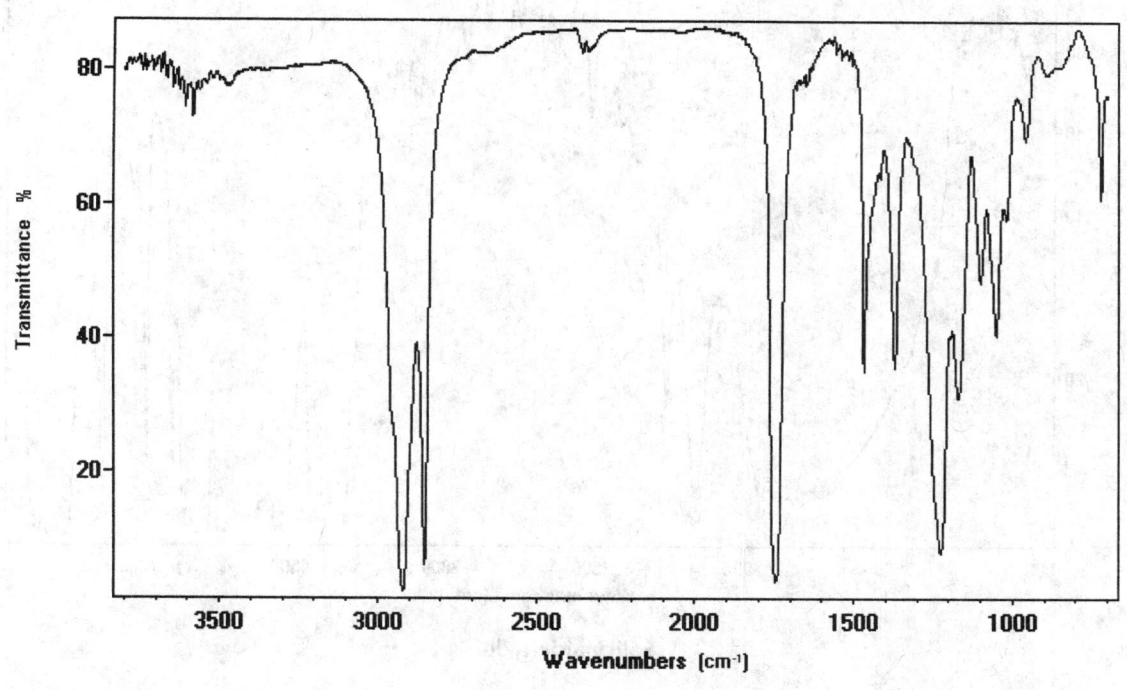
Salatrim

Salicylaldehyde

First Published: Prior to FCC 6
Last Revision: First Supplement, FCC 6

C₇H₆O₂   Formula wt 122.12
FEMA: 3004
UNII: 17K64GZH20 [salicylaldehyde]

DESCRIPTION
Salicylaldehyde occurs as a colorless to yellow liquid. It may contain a suitable antioxidant.
Odor: Phenolic
Solubility: Soluble in propylene glycol, vegetable oils; insoluble or practically insoluble in water
Boiling Point: ~197°
Solubility in Alcohol, Appendix VI: One mL dissolves in 1 mL of 95% ethanol.

Function: Flavoring agent

IDENTIFICATION
- **INFRARED SPECTRA,** *Spectrophotometric Identification Tests,* Appendix IIIC
  Acceptance criteria: The spectrum of the sample exhibits relative maxima at the same wavelengths as those of the spectrum below.

ASSAY
- **PROCEDURE:** Proceed as directed under *M-1b,* Appendix XI.
  Acceptance criteria: NLT 97.0% of C₇H₆O₂

SPECIFIC TESTS
- **ACID VALUE, FLAVOR CHEMICALS (OTHER THAN ESSENTIAL OILS),** *M-15,* Appendix XI
  [NOTE—Use phenol red TS as the indicator.]
  Acceptance criteria: NMT 10.0
- **REFRACTIVE INDEX,** Appendix II: At 20°
  Acceptance criteria: Between 1.570 and 1.576
- **SPECIFIC GRAVITY:** Determine at 25° by any reliable method (see *General Provisions*).
  Acceptance criteria: Between 1.159 and 1.170

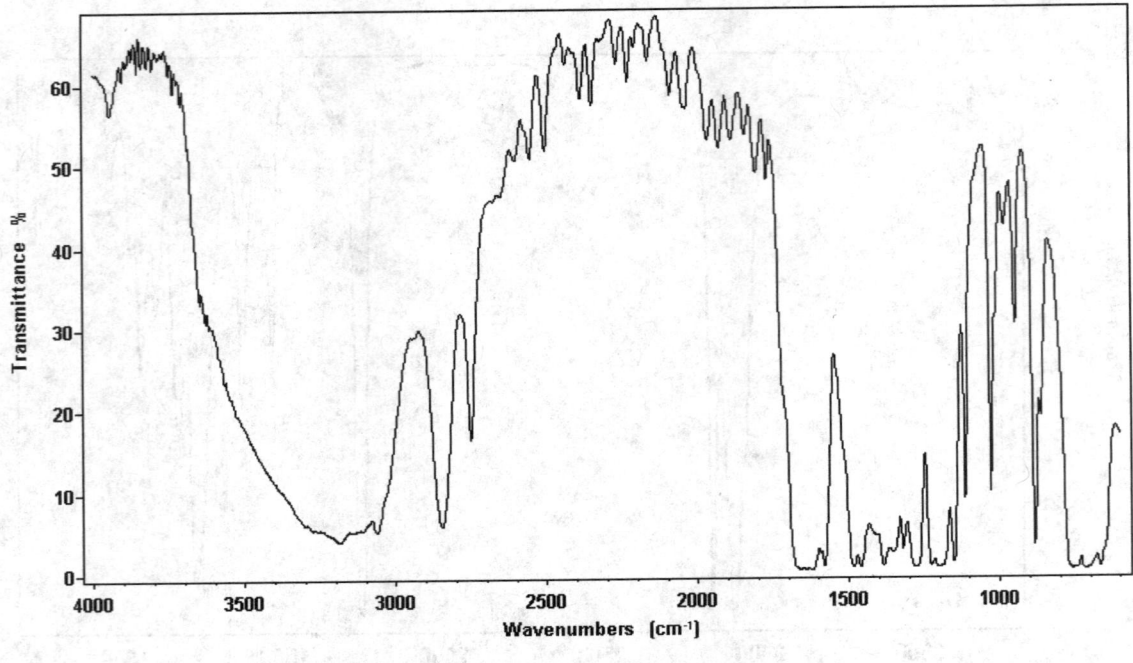

Salicylaldehyde

Sandalwood Oil, East Indian Type

First Published: Prior to FCC 6

CAS: [84787-70-2]
UNII: X7X01WMQ5F [sandalwood oil]

DESCRIPTION
Sandalwood Oil, East Indian Type, occurs as a pale yellow to yellow, somewhat viscous, oily liquid with a strong, persistent, characteristic odor. It is the volatile oil obtained by steam distillation from the dried, ground roots and wood of *Santalum album* L. (Fam. Santalaceae). It is soluble in most fixed oils, in propylene glycol, and in mineral oil, sometimes with haziness. It is insoluble in glycerin.

Function: Flavoring agent

Packaging and Storage: Store in a cool place protected from light in full, tight containers that are made from steel or aluminum and that are suitably lined.

IDENTIFICATION
- **INFRARED SPECTRA,** *Spectrophotometric Identification Tests,* Appendix IIIC
  Acceptance criteria: The spectrum of the sample exhibits relative maxima at the same wavelengths as those of the spectrum below.

ASSAY
- **TOTAL ALCOHOLS,** Appendix VI
  Sample: 1.2 g of the acetylated alcohol, prepared as described in *Total Alcohols*
  Analysis: Use 110.2 as the equivalence factor (e) in the calculation.
  Acceptance criteria: NLT 90.0% of alcohol, calculated as santalol, $C_{15}H_{24}O$

SPECIFIC TESTS
- **ANGULAR ROTATION,** *Optical (Specific) Rotation,* Appendix IIB: Use a 100-mm tube.
  Acceptance criteria: Between −15° and −20°
- **REFRACTIVE INDEX,** Appendix IIB
  [NOTE—Use an Abbé or other refractometer of equal or greater accuracy.]
  Acceptance criteria: Between 1.500 and 1.510 at 20°
- **SOLUBILITY IN ALCOHOL,** Appendix VI
  Acceptance criteria: One mL of the sample dissolves in 5 mL of 70% alcohol and remains in solution on dilution to 10 mL.
  Acceptance criteria: Passes test
- **SPECIFIC GRAVITY:** Determine by any reliable method (see *General Provisions*).
  Acceptance criteria: Between 0.965 and 0.980

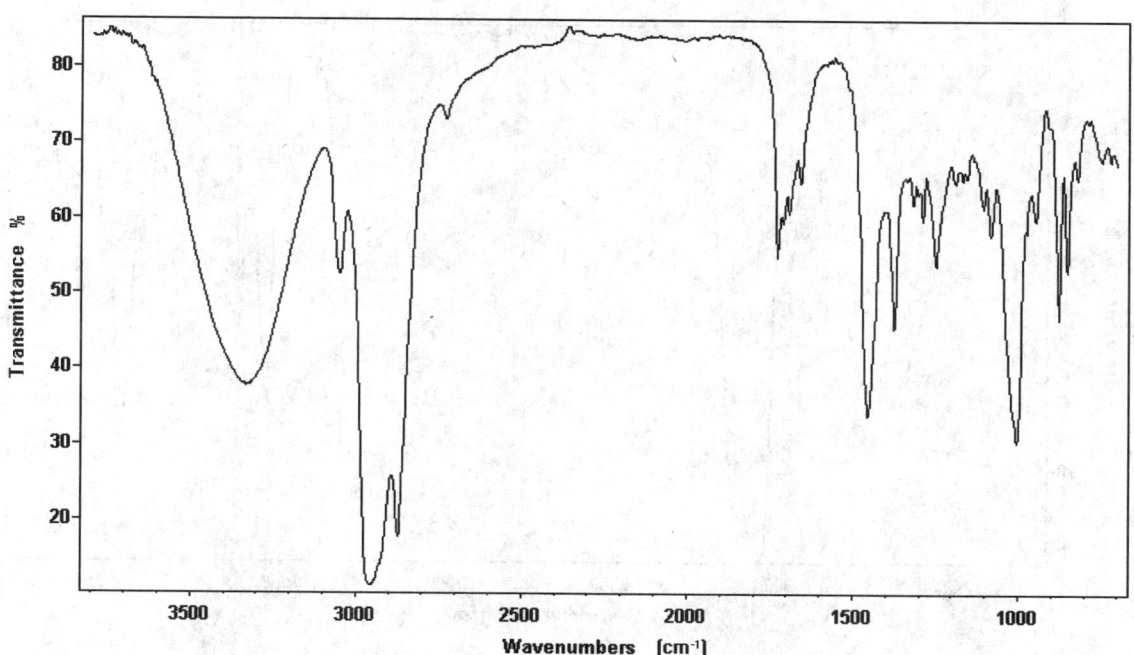
Sandalwood Oil, East Indian Type

Santalol

First Published: Prior to FCC 6

$C_{15}H_{24}O$
FEMA: 3006
UNII: 1DGG9VW8SA [santalol]

Formula wt 220.35

DESCRIPTION
Santalol occurs as a colorless to slightly yellow, viscous liquid. It is a mixture of α- and β-isomers of santalol obtained from sandalwood oils.
Odor: Sandalwood
Solubility: Very soluble in alcohol, most fixed oils, propylene glycol; insoluble or practically insoluble in glycerin, water
Boiling Point: ~302°
Solubility in Alcohol, Appendix VI: One mL dissolves in 4 mL of 70% alcohol to give a clear solution.
Function: Flavoring agent

IDENTIFICATION
- **INFRARED SPECTRA,** *Spectrophotometric Identification Tests,* Appendix IIIC
  Acceptance criteria: The spectrum of the sample exhibits relative maxima at the same wavelengths as those of the spectrum below.

ASSAY
- **PROCEDURE:** Proceed as directed under *Total Alcohols,* Appendix VI.
  Sample: 1.6 g
  Analysis: Use 110.18 as the equivalence factor (e).
  Acceptance criteria: NLT 95.0% of total alcohols as $C_{15}H_{24}O$

SPECIFIC TESTS
- **REFRACTIVE INDEX,** Appendix II: At 20°
  Acceptance criteria: Between 1.505 and 1.509
- **SPECIFIC GRAVITY:** Determine at 25° by any reliable method (see *General Provisions*).
  Acceptance criteria: Between 0.965 and 0.975

OTHER REQUIREMENTS
- **ANGULAR ROTATION,** *Optical (Specific) Rotation,* Appendix IIB: Use a 100-mm tube.
  Acceptance criteria: Between −11° and −19°

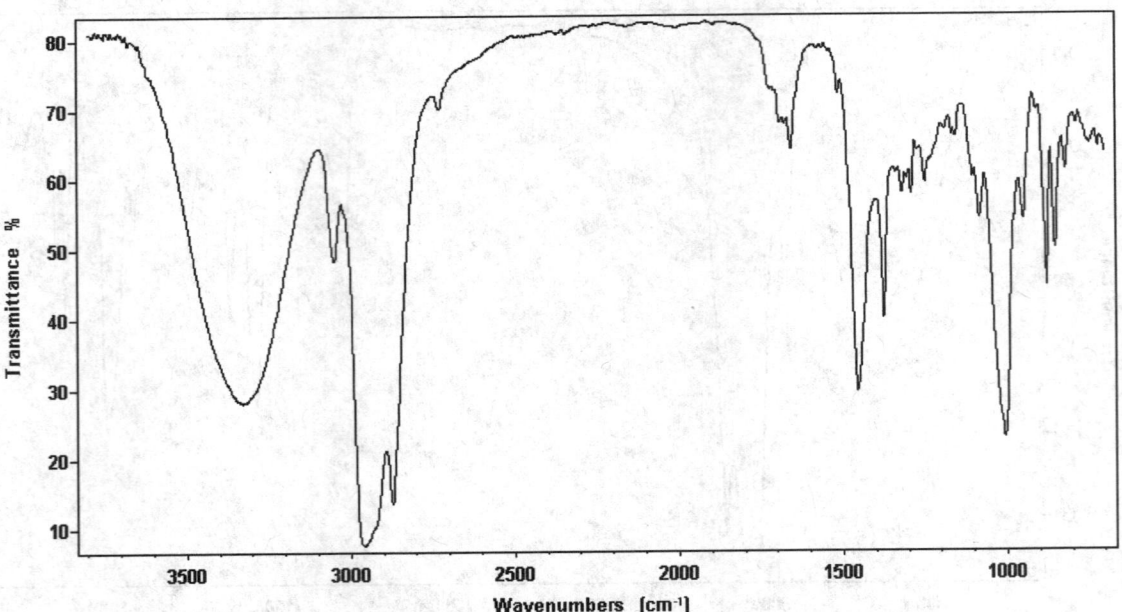
Santalol

Santalyl Acetate

First Published: Prior to FCC 6

FEMA: 3007
UNII: NI0P5374LY [santalyl acetate]

DESCRIPTION
Santalyl Acetate occurs as a colorless to slightly yellow liquid. It is a mixture of α- and β-isomers obtained by the acetylation of santalol.
Odor: Sandalwood
Solubility: Soluble in alcohol; insoluble or practically insoluble in water
Boiling Point: ~315°
Solubility in Alcohol, Appendix VI: One mL dissolves in 9 mL of 80% alcohol to give a clear solution.
Function: Flavoring agent

IDENTIFICATION
- **INFRARED SPECTRA,** *Spectrophotometric Identification Tests,* Appendix IIIC
  Acceptance criteria: The spectrum of the sample exhibits relative maxima at the same wavelengths as those of the spectrum below.

ASSAY
- **PROCEDURE:** Proceed as directed under *Esters,* Appendix VI.
  Sample: 1.6 g
  Analysis: Use 131.2 as the equivalence factor (e).
  Acceptance criteria: NLT 95.0% of total esters as $C_{17}H_{26}O_2$

SPECIFIC TESTS
- **ACID VALUE, FLAVOR CHEMICALS (OTHER THAN ESSENTIAL OILS),** *M-15,* Appendix XI
  Acceptance criteria: NMT 1.0
- **REFRACTIVE INDEX,** Appendix II: At 20°
  Acceptance criteria: Between 1.488 and 1.491
- **SPECIFIC GRAVITY:** Determine at 25° by any reliable method (see *General Provisions*).
  Acceptance criteria: Between 0.980 and 0.986

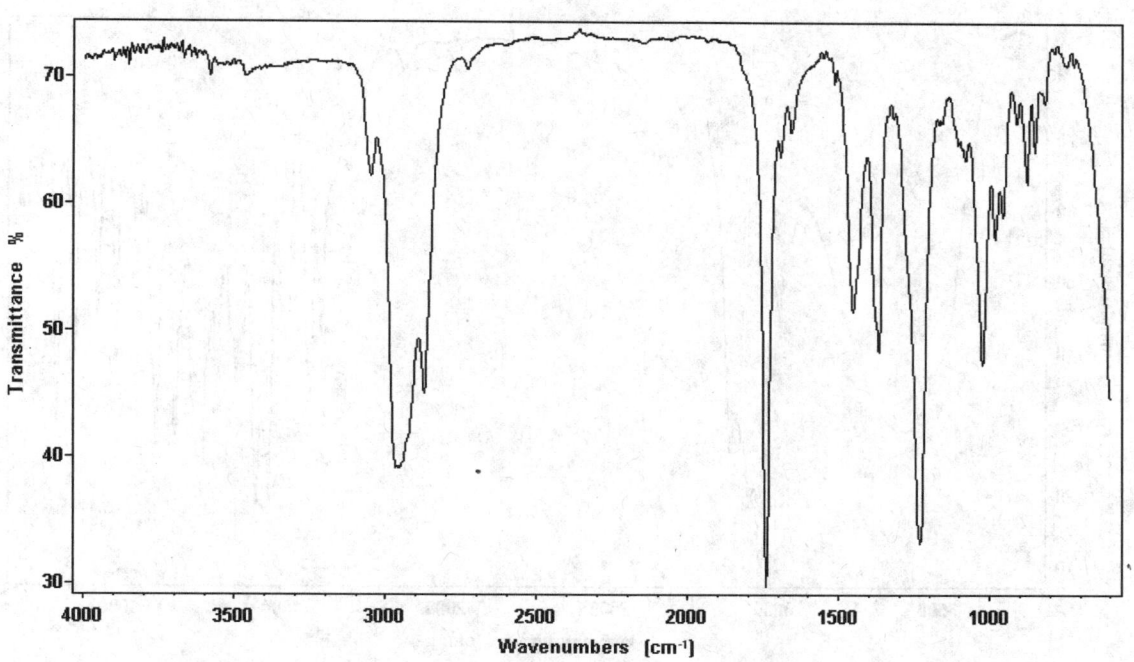

Santalyl Acetate

Savory Oil (Summer Variety)

First Published: Prior to FCC 6

Summer Savory Oil

CAS: [8016-68-0]

UNII: 2T136O9R3W [summer savory oil]

DESCRIPTION
Savory Oil (Summer Variety) occurs as a light yellow to dark brown liquid with a spicy, aromatic note suggestive of thyme or origanum. It is the volatile oil obtained by steam distillation from the whole dried plant *Satureia hortensis* L. (Fam. Labiatae). It is soluble in most fixed oils and in mineral oil, but it is practically insoluble in glycerin and in propylene glycol.
Function: Flavoring agent
Packaging and Storage: Store in a cool place protected from light in full, tight containers that are made from steel or aluminum and that are suitably lined.

IDENTIFICATION
- **INFRARED SPECTRA,** *Spectrophotometric Identification Tests,* Appendix IIIC
  Acceptance criteria: The spectrum of the sample exhibits relative maxima at the same wavelengths as those of the spectrum below.

ASSAY
- **PHENOLS,** Appendix VI
  Acceptance criteria: NLT 20.0% and NMT 57.0% of phenols as carvacrol ($C_{10}H_{14}O$)

SPECIFIC TESTS
- **ANGULAR ROTATION,** *Optical (Specific) Rotation,* Appendix IIB: Use a 100-mm tube.
  Acceptance criteria: Between −5° and +4°
- **REFRACTIVE INDEX,** Appendix IIB
  [NOTE—Use an Abbé or other refractometer of equal or greater accuracy.]
  Acceptance criteria: Between 1.486 and 1.505 at 20°
- **SAPONIFICATION VALUE,** *Esters,* Appendix VI
  Sample: 5 g
  Acceptance criteria: NMT 6
- **SOLUBILITY IN ALCOHOL,** Appendix VI
  Acceptance criteria: One mL of sample usually dissolves in 2 mL of 80% alcohol. Some oils may be slightly hazy in 10 mL of 90% alcohol.
- **SPECIFIC GRAVITY:** Determine by any reliable method *(see General Notices).*
  Acceptance criteria: Between 0.875 and 0.954

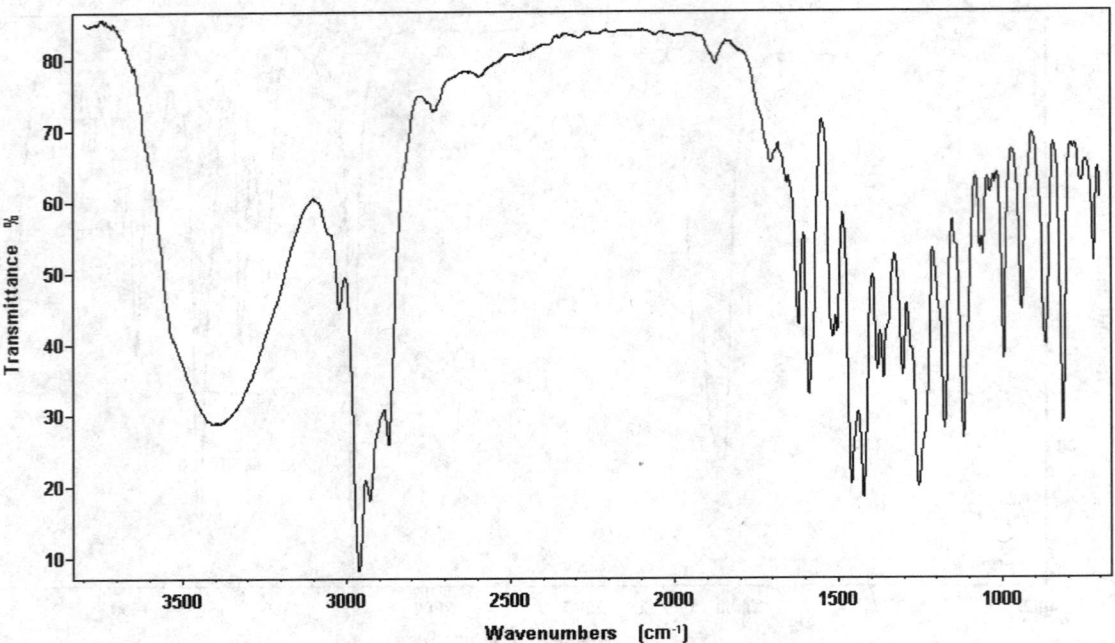

Savory Oil (Summer Variety)

Seaweed-Derived Calcium

First Published: FCC 6

DESCRIPTION
Seaweed-Derived Calcium occurs as an inert, non-hygroscopic, white powder composed of approximately 85.0% calcium carbonate and 11.5% magnesium carbonate. It is obtained from mineralized seaweed (*Lithothamnion* sp.) found on the seabed in mineral-rich waters. It is soluble in weak acids, but almost insoluble in water.

Function: Source of dietary calcium

Packaging and Storage: Store in containers lined with polyethylene in a cool, dry, indoor area.

IDENTIFICATION
- **CALCIUM**, Appendix IIIA
  Acceptance criteria: Passes tests
- **MAGNESIUM**, Appendix IIIA
  Acceptance criteria: Passes tests

ASSAY
- **CALCIUM CONTENT**

  Lanthanum chloride solution: 58.5 mg/mL of lanthanum oxide prepared as follows: mix 117 ± 0.1 g of lanthanum oxide with about 500 mL of water contained in a 2-L volumetric flask; slowly add 200 mL of concentrated hydrochloric acid; dilute to volume with water, and mix well. This solution is stable for 6 months.

  Calcium stock solution: 1 mg/mL of calcium, from standard calcium solution (NIST, or equivalent) or standard calcium nitrate solution (Sigma-Aldrich, or equivalent). This solution is stable for 3 months.

  Magnesium stock solution: 1 mg/mL of magnesium, from standard magnesium solution (NIST, or equivalent) or standard magnesium nitrate solution (Sigma-Aldrich, or equivalent)

  Mixed standard stock solution: 100 µg/mL of calcium and 10 µg/mL of magnesium, from *Calcium stock solution* and *Magnesium stock solution*, made to 100 mL. This solution is stable for 3 months.

  Mixed standard solutions: Place 50.0 mL of *Lanthanum chloride solution* into each of three 1000-mL volumetric flasks. Dilute the contents in the first flask to volume with water. Add 25 mL of *Mixed standard stock solution* to the second flask and dilute to volume with water. Add 50 mL of *Mixed standard stock solution* to the third flask and dilute to volume with water. These flasks contain calcium/magnesium at levels of 0/0 µg/mL, 2.50/0.25 µg/mL and 5.0/0.5 µg/mL, respectively. All three *Mixed standard solutions* contain 0.25% lanthanum. These solutions are stable for 1 month.

  [NOTE—Acid-wash all glassware before use by soaking in a 10% nitric acid solution for a minimum of 1 h or boiling for 5 min, followed by at least three rinses with water. Rinse well with water before each use.]

  Sample solution: To prepare an acid extract of the sample, ash 1.0 g of sample, carefully heat the residue with 10 mL of 1:1 aqueous solution of hydrochloric acid, place the solution into a 1-L volumetric flask, and dilute it to volume with water. Transfer 1 mL of the solution into a 100-mL volumetric flask, add 5 mL of *Lanthanum chloride solution* to give a final concentration of 0.25% lanthanum, and dilute to volume with water. The calcium and magnesium concentration of the resulting solution should be approximately 3.0 µg/mL and 0.3 µg/mL, respectively, and be within range of the spectrometer calibration.

Blank solution: Prepare a *Blank solution* as directed in the *Sample solution* preparation containing all reagents and following all the steps from ashing to dilution with water.

Apparatus: Use an atomic absorption spectrometer equipped with an air–acetylene flame. It must be capable of determining absorbance response to three decimal places and must show a linear relationship between the concentration of the standards used and their absorbance. Set up the spectrometer according to the manufacturer's instructions and using the conditions in the *Analysis* (below).

Analysis: Set up the spectrometer using the following parameters for calcium:

Background correction: No
Band pass: 0.7
Number of decimals used for reading concentration: 3
Lamp current: 25
Standard concentration: 5.00 µg/mL
Minimum acceptable absorbance: 0.250

Adjust the burner head alignment and turn the lamp current to its maximum. Record the lamp energy. Turn on the flame, and aspirate water. Allow the lamp to warm up for 20 to 30 min (10 min for the flame) before reading samples. Set the spectrometer to read absorbance, and use water to zero the instrument.

[NOTE—Aspirate water after each sample or standard to avoid carry over. Aspirate water to clean the nebulizer and burner head at the end of each run.]

Run the the *Mixed standard solutions*, and record their absorbance. [NOTE—If the *Mixed standard solutions* do not have a wavelength of 422.7, recheck the instrument settings and rerun the solutions.]

Set the instrument to read concentration. Aspirate the 0/0 µg/mL *Mixed standard solution*, and zero the instrument. Aspirate the other two *Mixed standard solutions* in turn, and use them to calibrate the instrument when a steady reading is obtained. Aspirate the middle range *Mixed standard solution*, and record the instrument reading. Use this standard as a drift standard throughout the run.

Aspirate the *Blank solution*, and record the reading. If this reading deviates from that of the 0/0 µg/mL *Mixed standard solution* by more than 0.05 µg/mL of calcium, repeat preparation of the *Sample solution*. Once the readings are within range, aspirate the *Sample solution* and record the concentration when a steady reading is obtained.

At regular intervals during a run (minimally every six samples) and at the end of each run, monitor the drift standard to ensure that no drift has occurred in the calibration. These should not vary by more than 5% of the value read using the 2.5/0.25 µg/mL *Mixed standard solution* (2.37 to 2.63 µg/mL of calcium). If the drift standard is outside these limits, check the instrument settings, and recalibrate the spectrometer from the beginning of this section, starting with "Turn on the flame, and aspirate water."

Calculate the amount of calcium, in percent, in the sample taken by the formula:

$$\text{Result} = 10\,[(S - B) \times D]/W$$

10 = factor combining sample dilution times the conversion to percent divided by the conversion from µg to g
S = *Sample solution* reading from the spectrometer (µg/mL)
B = *Blank solution* reading from the spectrometer (µg/mL)
D = any additional dilution factor of the sample, if used
W = weight of the sample taken before ashing (g)

Acceptance criteria: NLT 29%

- **MAGNESIUM CONTENT**

[NOTE—Proceed as directed in *Calcium Content* (above), but use the following *Analysis*.]

Analysis: Set up the spectrometer using the following parameters:

Background correction: Yes
Band pass: 0.7
Number of decimals used for reading concentration: 3
Lamp current: 25
Standard concentration: 0.500 µg/mL
Minimum acceptable absorbance: 0.225

The absorbance of the *Mixed standard solutions* should agree with the value 285.2. Aspirate the *Blank solution*. If the reading deviates from the 0/0 µg/mL *Mixed standard solution* by more than 0.005 µg/mL of magnesium, repeat preparation of the *Sample solution*. While monitoring the drift standard, the value for magnesium at 7.7 is based on 0.237 to 0.263 µg/mL of magnesium.

Calculate the amount of magnesium, in percent, in the sample taken by the formula:

$$\text{Result} = 10\,[(S - B) \times D]/W$$

10 = factor combining sample dilution times the conversion to percent divided by the conversion from µg to g
S = *Sample solution* reading from the spectrometer (µg/mL)
B = *Blank solution* reading from the spectrometer (µg/mL)
D = any additional dilution factor of the sample, if used
W = weight of the sample taken before ashing (g)

Acceptance criteria: NMT 3.5%

- **SUM OF CALCIUM CARBONATE AND MAGNESIUM CARBONATE**
  Analysis: Calculate the *Sum of Calcium Carbonate and Magnesium Carbonate*, in percent, using the formula:

  Result = (Ca × 100.09/40.08) + (Mg × 84.31/24.31)

  Ca = *Calcium Content* (above) in percent
  Mg = *Magnesium Content* (above) in percent
  Acceptance criteria: NLT 85.0%, as the sum of calcium carbonate and magnesium carbonate, on the dried basis

IMPURITIES
Inorganic Impurities
- **ARSENIC**, *Arsenic Limit Test*, Appendix IIIB
  Sample solution: 1 g in 10 mL of 2.7 N hydrochloric acid
  Acceptance criteria: NMT 1 mg/kg
- **LEAD**, *Lead Limit Test, Atomic Absorption Spectrophotometric Graphite Furnace Method, Method II*, Appendix IIIB
  Acceptance criteria: NMT 1 mg/kg

SPECIFIC TESTS
- **ASH (ACID-INSOLUBLE)**, Appendix IIC
  Acceptance criteria: NMT 1.5%
- **ASH (TOTAL)**, Appendix IIC
  Acceptance criteria: NLT 90%
- **LOSS ON DRYING**, Appendix IIC: 200° for 4 h
  Acceptance criteria: NMT 5%
- **RESIDUE ON IGNITION (SULFATED ASH)**, Appendix IIC
  Analysis: 4 g
  Acceptance criteria: NLT 96.5%

L-Selenomethionine
First Published: Second Supplement, FCC 7

(S)-2-Amino-4-(methylselenyl)butyric Acid
Butanoic Acid, 2-amino-4-(methylseleno)-, (S)-

$C_5H_{11}NO_2Se$ Formula wt 196.11
CAS: [1464-42-2]
UNII: 964MRK2PEL [selenomethionine]

DESCRIPTION
L-Selenomethionine occurs as a white to off-white crystalline powder. It is soluble in hot water and has a melting point of about 260° (with decomposition).
Function: Nutrient; source of selenium
Packaging and Storage: Store in a tight container in a cool place.

IDENTIFICATION
- **A. INFRARED ABSORPTION**, *Spectrophotometric Identification Tests*, Appendix IIIC
  Reference standard: USP Selenomethionine RS
  Sample and standard preparation: K
  Acceptance criteria: The spectrum of the sample exhibits maxima at the same wavelengths as those in the spectrum of the *Reference standard*.
- **B. PROCEDURE**
  Acceptance criteria: The retention times for the major peaks in the chromatogram of the *Sample solution* correspond to those in the chromatogram of the *Standard solution*, as determined in the *Assay*.
- **C. PROCEDURE**
  Acceptance criteria: The R_F value of the principal spot obtained from the chromatogram of the *Sample solution* corresponds to that obtained from the chromatogram of the *Standard solution*, as determined in the test for *Chromatographic Purity*.

ASSAY
- **PROCEDURE**
  Mobile phase: Dissolve 6.8 g of monobasic potassium phosphate in 1 L of water. Filter and degas, then adjust with phosphoric acid to a pH of 2.75 ± 0.25. [NOTE—Make adjustments if necessary.]
  System suitability solution: Prepare a solution containing 0.8 mg/mL of USP L-Methionine RS and 0.16 mg/mL of USP Selenomethionine RS in *Mobile phase*.
  Standard solution: 0.16 mg/mL of USP Selenomethionine RS in *Mobile phase*
  Sample solution: 0.16 mg/mL in *Mobile phase*. Dilute sample with sonication prior to bringing to volume. Filter the volumetric solution through a 0.45-μm membrane.
  Chromatographic system, Appendix IIA
    Mode: High-performance liquid chromatography
    Detector: UV 220 nm
    Column: 4.6-mm × 25-cm column packed with octadecylsilane chemically bonded to porous silica or ceramic particles 1.5- to 10-μm in diameter (with polar end-capping)
    Flow rate: 1.0 mL/min
    Injection volume: 20 μL
  System suitability
    Sample: *System suitability solution*
    Suitability requirement 1: The resolution between methionine and selenomethionine is NLT 3.0.
    Suitability requirement 2: The tailing factor is NMT 2.
    Suitability requirement 3: The relative standard deviation is NMT 2.0%.
  Analysis: Separately inject the *Standard solution* and the *Sample solution* into the chromatograph, record the chromatograms, and measure the responses for the major peaks. [NOTE—The approximate relative retention times for methionine and selenomethionine are 0.8 and 1.0, respectively.]
  Calculate the percentage of $C_5H_{11}NO_2Se$ in the portion of the sample taken:

  $$\text{Result} = (r_U/r_S) \times (C_S/C_U) \times 100$$

  r_U = peak response obtained from the chromatogram of the *Sample solution*

r_S = peak response obtained from the chromatogram of the *Standard solution*
C_S = concentration of the *Standard solution* (mg/mL)
C_U = concentration of the *Sample solution* (mg/mL)

Acceptance criteria: 97.0%–103.0%

IMPURITIES
Inorganic Impurities
- **LEAD**, *Elemental Impurities by ICP,* Appendix IIIC
  Acceptance criteria: NMT 1 mg/kg
- **SODIUM**
  Solution A: Potassium chloride and water (1 in 5)
  Standard stock solution: 10 µg/mL of sodium in water from sodium chloride previously dried at 105° for 2 h
  Standard solutions: Transfer 2.0 mL, 5.0 mL, and 10.0 mL of the *Standard stock solution*, respectively, to three separate 100-mL volumetric flasks. To each flask add 2.0 mL of *Solution A* and 1.0 mL of hydrochloric acid, and dilute with water to volume. The resulting solutions contain 0.2 µg/mL, 0.5 µg/mL, and 1.0 µg/mL of sodium, respectively.
  Sample stock solution: 10 mg/mL in water
  Sample solution: Transfer 10.0 mL of the *Sample stock solution* to a 100-mL volumetric flask, add 2.0 mL of *Solution A* and 1.0 mL of hydrochloric acid, and dilute with water to volume.
  Analysis: Using a suitable atomic absorption spectrophotometer equipped with a sodium hollow-cathode lamp and an oxidizing air–acetylene flame, determine the absorbances of the *Standard solutions* and the *Sample solution* at the sodium emission line of 589 nm, using water as the blank. Plot the absorbances of the *Standard solutions* versus their concentrations, in µg/mL, of sodium, and draw the straight line best fitting the plotted points. From the standard curve so obtained, determine the concentration of sodium, in µg/mL, in the *Sample solution*.
  Calculate the percentage of sodium in the portion of the sample taken:

  $$\text{Result} = S/C_U \times 100$$

  S = concentration of sodium in the *Sample solution*, as determined from the standard curve (µg/mL)
  C_U = concentration of L-Selenomethionine in the *Sample solution* (µg/mL)

  Acceptance criteria: NMT 0.1%

Organic Impurities
- **CHROMATOGRAPHIC PURITY**, *Thin-Layer Chromatography,* Appendix IIA
  Standard solution: Dissolve 50 mg of USP Selenomethionine RS in 2 mL of water, warming if necessary, then dilute with methanol to 10.0 mL (5 mg/mL).
  Dilute standard solution: Dilute 1 mL of the *Standard solution* with methanol to 100 mL (50 µg/mL).
  Sample solution: Dissolve 50 mg of the sample in 2 mL of water, warming if necessary, then dilute with methanol to 10.0 mL.
  Adsorbent: 0.25-mm layer of chromatographic silica gel
  Application volume: 10 µL
  Developing solvent system: Butanol, glacial acetic acid, and water (80:20:20)
  Spray reagent: 200 mg of ninhydrin in 100 mL of alcohol
  Analysis: Separately apply portions of the *Standard solution*, *Dilute standard solution*, and *Sample solution* to a suitable thin-layer chromatographic plate. Following development, remove the plate from the chromatographic chamber, mark the solvent front, and allow the solvent to evaporate. Spray the plate with *Spray reagent*, and dry it at 110° for 10 min.
  Acceptance criteria: The R_F value of the principal spot obtained from the chromatogram of the *Sample solution* corresponds to that obtained from the chromatogram of the *Standard solution*, and no spot, other than the principal spot, in the chromatogram of the *Sample solution* is larger or more intense than the principal spot obtained from the *Dilute standard solution* (NMT 1.0%).

SPECIFIC TESTS
- **OPTICAL (SPECIFIC) ROTATION**, Appendix IIB
  Sample solution: 10 mg/mL in hydrochloric acid
  Acceptance criteria: $[\alpha]_D^{20}$ between +17.0° and +19.5°
- **SELENIUM**
  [**CAUTION**—Selenium is toxic; handle with care.]
  Standard stock solution: 1000 µg/mL of selenium prepared as follows: Dissolve 100 mg of metallic selenium in a minimum volume of nitric acid, evaporate to dryness, add 0.2 mL of water, and evaporate to dryness once more. Repeat the addition of water and evaporation to dryness three times. Dissolve the residue obtained in 3 N hydrochloric acid, transfer to a 100-mL volumetric flask, and dilute with 3 N hydrochloric acid to volume.
  Standard solutions: Transfer 2.0 mL, 5.0 mL, and 10.0 mL of the *Standard stock solution*, respectively, to three separate 100-mL volumetric flasks. Dilute the contents of each flask with water to volume. The resulting solutions contain 20 µg/mL, 50 µg/mL, and 100 µg/mL of selenium, respectively.
  Sample solution: 125 µg/mL in water
  Analysis: Using a suitable atomic absorption spectrophotometer equipped with a selenium hollow-cathode lamp and an air–acetylene flame, determine the absorbances of the *Standard solutions* and the *Sample solution* at the selenium emission line of 196 nm, using water as the blank. Plot the absorbances of the *Standard solutions* versus their concentrations, in µg/mL, of selenium, and draw the straight line best fitting the plotted points. From the standard curve so obtained, determine the concentration of selenium, in µg/mL, in the *Sample solution*.

Calculate the percentage of selenium in the portion of the sample taken:

$$Result = S/C_U \times 100$$

- S = concentration of selenium in the *Sample solution*, as determined from the standard curve (μg/mL)
- C_U = concentration of L-Selenomethionine in the *Sample solution* (μg/mL)

Acceptance criteria: 39.0%–41.0%

DL-Serine

First Published: Prior to FCC 6

DL-2-Amino-3-hydroxypropanoic Acid

$C_3H_7NO_3$
UNII: 00PAR1C66F [serine, dl-]

Formula wt 105.09
CAS: [302-84-1]

DESCRIPTION
DL-Serine occurs as white crystals or as a crystalline powder. It is soluble in water, but insoluble in alcohol and in ether. It melts with decomposition at about 246° using a closed capillary tube and a bath preheated to 225°. It is optically inactive.

Function: Nutrient
Packaging and Storage: Store in well-closed containers.

IDENTIFICATION
- **INFRARED SPECTRA,** *Spectrophotometric Identification Tests,* Appendix IIIC
  Sample preparation: Mineral oil mull
  Acceptance criteria: The spectrum of the sample exhibits relative maxima at the same wavelengths as those of the spectrum below.

ASSAY
- **PROCEDURE**
  Sample: 200 mg
  Analysis: Dissolve the *Sample* in 3 mL of formic acid and 50 mL of glacial acetic acid. Titrate with 0.1 N perchloric acid in glacial acetic acid, determining the endpoint potentiometrically. Perform a blank determination (see *General Provisions*), and make any necessary correction. Each mL of 0.1 N perchloric acid is equivalent to 10.51 mg of $C_3H_7NO_3$.
  [**CAUTION**—Handle perchloric acid in an appropriate fume hood.]
  Acceptance criteria: NLT 98.5% and NMT 101.5% of $C_3H_7NO_3$, calculated on the dried basis

IMPURITIES
Inorganic Impurities
- **LEAD,** *Lead Limit Test,* Appendix IIIB
  Sample solution: Prepare as directed for organic compounds.
  Control: 5 μg Pb (5 mL of *Diluted Standard Lead Solution*)
  Acceptance criteria: NMT 5 mg/kg

SPECIFIC TESTS
- **LOSS ON DRYING,** Appendix IIC: 105° for 3 h
  Acceptance criteria: NMT 0.3%
- **RESIDUE ON IGNITION (SULFATED ASH),** Appendix IIC
  Sample: 1 g
  Acceptance criteria: NMT 0.1%

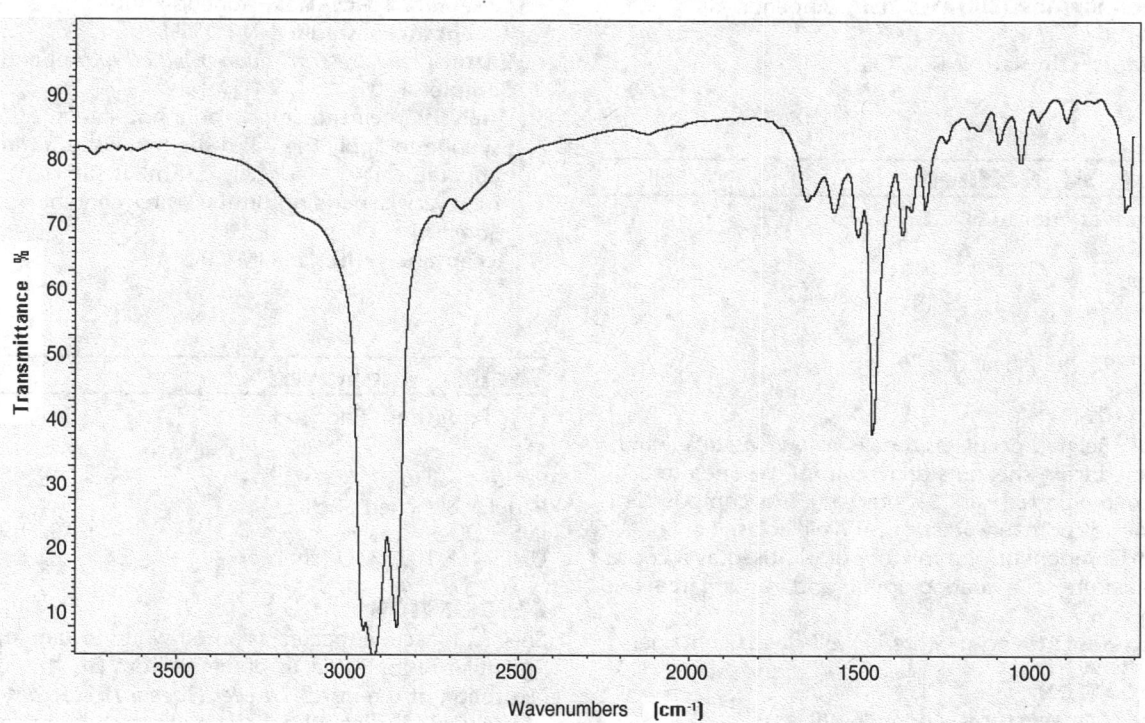

DL-Serine (Mineral Oil Mull)

L-Serine

First Published: Prior to FCC 6
Last Revision: FCC 7

L-2-Amino-3-hydroxypropanoic Acid

$C_3H_7NO_3$　　　　　　　　　Formula wt 105.09
　　　　　　　　　　　　　　　CAS: [56-45-1]
UNII: 452VLY9402 [serine]

DESCRIPTION
L-Serine occurs as a white crystalline powder. It is soluble in water, but is insoluble in alcohol and in ether. It melts with decomposition at about 228°.
Function: Nutrient
Packaging and Storage: Store in well-closed containers.

IDENTIFICATION
- **INFRARED ABSORPTION**, *Spectrophotometric Identification Tests,* Appendix IIIC
  Reference standard: USP L-Serine RS
  Sample and standard preparation: *M*
  Acceptance criteria: The spectrum of the sample exhibits maxima at the same wavelengths as those in the spectrum of the *Reference standard.*

ASSAY
- **PROCEDURE**
  Sample: 200 mg
  Analysis: Dissolve the *Sample* in 3 mL of formic acid and 50 mL of glacial acetic acid. Titrate with 0.1 N perchloric acid in glacial acetic acid, determining the endpoint potentiometrically. Perform a blank determination (see *General Provisions*), and make any necessary correction. Each mL of 0.1 N perchloric acid is equivalent to 10.51 mg of $C_3H_7NO_3$. [**CAUTION—** Handle perchloric acid in an appropriate fume hood.]
  Acceptance criteria: 98.5%–101.5% of $C_3H_7NO_3$, calculated on the dried basis

IMPURITIES
Inorganic Impurities
- **LEAD**, *Lead Limit Test,* Appendix IIIB
  Sample solution: Prepare as directed for organic compounds.
  Control: 5 µg Pb (5 mL of *Diluted Standard Lead Solution*)

SPECIFIC TESTS
- **LOSS ON DRYING**, Appendix IIC: 105° for 3 h
  Acceptance criteria: NMT 0.3%
- **OPTICAL (SPECIFIC) ROTATION**, Appendix IIB
  Sample: 10 g, previously dried
  Analysis: Dissolve the *Sample* in sufficient 2 N hydrochloric acid to make 100 mL.
  Acceptance criteria
  $[\alpha]_D^{20}$ between +13.6° and +16.0°, on the dried basis; or
  $[\alpha]_D^{25}$ between +13° and +15.6°, on the dried basis

Sheanut Oil, Refined

First Published: Prior to FCC 6

Shea Butter
Karite
Galam
UNII: O88E196QRF [sheanut oil]

DESCRIPTION
Sheanut Oil, Refined occurs as a pale yellow, viscous liquid. It is obtained from sheanuts derived from the Shea tree *Butyrospermum parkii* (Fam. Sapotaceae). It is composed of triglycerides of primarily stearic and oleic acids.
Function: Component of a mixture of oils used as a cocoa butter substitute; as a coating agent; and in margarine and shortening
Packaging and Storage: Store in well-closed containers.

IDENTIFICATION
- **FATTY ACID COMPOSITION,** Appendix VII
  Acceptance criteria: Refined Sheanut Oil exhibits the following typical composition profile of fatty acids:

Fatty Acid	Weight % (Range)
16:0	3.8–4.1
18:0	41.2–56.8
18:1	34.0–46.9
18:2	3.7–6.5
20:0	1.0–2.0

IMPURITIES
Inorganic Impurities
- **LEAD,** *Lead Limit Test, Atomic Absorption Spectrophotometric Graphite Furnace Method II,* Appendix IIIB
  Acceptance criteria: NMT 0.1 mg/kg

SPECIFIC TESTS
- **COLOR (FATS AND RELATED SUBSTANCES),** Appendix VII
  Acceptance criteria: NMT 4 red/40 yellow
- **FREE FATTY ACIDS (AS OLEIC ACID),** *Free Fatty Acids,* Appendix VII
  Analysis: Use the following equivalence factor (e) in the formula given in the procedure under *Free Fatty Acids,* e = 28.2.
  Acceptance criteria: NMT 0.1%
- **IODINE VALUE,** Appendix VII
  Acceptance criteria: Between 28 and 43
- **PEROXIDE VALUE,** Appendix VII
  Acceptance criteria: NMT 10 mEq/kg
- **SAPONIFICATION VALUE,** Appendix VII
  Sample: 4 g
  Acceptance criteria: Between 185 and 195
- **UNSAPONIFIABLE MATTER,** Appendix VII
  Acceptance criteria: NMT 1.5%
- **WATER,** *Water Determination, Method Ia,* Appendix IIB
  Sample: 100 g
  Analysis: Melt the *Sample* on a hotplate at 60°. Use a syringe to apply the oil to the Karl Fisher titrimetric apparatus. [NOTE—Usually 1.0 mL is sufficient, but this may vary depending on the water content of the *Sample.*]
  Acceptance criteria: NMT 0.5%

Shellac, Bleached

First Published: Prior to FCC 6

White Shellac
Regular Bleached Shellac
INS: 904   CAS: [9000-59-3]
UNII: 46N107B71O [shellac]

DESCRIPTION
Shellac, Bleached, occurs as an off-white to tan, amorphous, granular resin. Shellac is obtained from lac, the resinous secretion of the insect *Laccifer (Tachardia) lacca* Kerr (Fam. Coccidae). Shellac, Bleached, is obtained by dissolving the lac in aqueous sodium carbonate, followed by bleaching with sodium hypochlorite, precipitation of the bleached lac with a dilute sulfuric acid solution, and drying. It is freely (though very slowly) soluble in alcohol, insoluble in water, and slightly soluble in acetone and in ether. Shellac, Bleached, is usually dissolved in a suitable solvent for application to food products.
Function: Coating agent; surface-finishing agent; glaze
Packaging and Storage: Store in well-closed containers in a cool place protected from heat.

IDENTIFICATION
- **PROCEDURE**
  Sample: 50 mg
  Analysis: Prepare a solution of 1 g of ammonium molybdate in 3 mL of sulfuric acid and add a few drops of this solution to the *Sample*.
  Acceptance criteria: A green color appears and changes to lilac when the solution is neutralized with 6 N ammonium hydroxide.

IMPURITIES
Inorganic Impurities
- **LEAD,** *Lead Limit Test, Flame Atomic Absorption Spectrophotometric Method,* Appendix IIIB
  Sample: 10 g
  Acceptance criteria: NMT 2 mg/kg

SPECIFIC TESTS
- **ACID VALUE**
  Sample: 2 g, finely ground
  Analysis: Dissolve the *Sample* in 50 mL of alcohol previously neutralized to phenolphthalein with sodium hydroxide. Add additional phenolphthalein TS, if

necessary, and titrate with 0.1 N sodium hydroxide to a pink endpoint. Calculate the acid value by the formula:

$$Result = V \times N/W \times 56.1$$

V = volume (mL) of 0.1 N sodium hydroxide
N = normality of the sodium hydroxide solution
W = weight (g) of sample taken, calculated on the dried basis

Acceptance criteria: Between 73 and 89

- **LOSS ON DRYING**, Appendix IIC: 41° ± 2° to constant weight
  Acceptance criteria: NMT 6.0%
- **ROSIN**
  Sample: 2 g
  Analysis: Dissolve the *Sample* in 10 mL of dehydrated alcohol and add 50 mL of hexane slowly, with shaking. Transfer the solution to a separatory funnel, wash with two 50-mL portions of water, and discard the washings. Filter the hexane layer, evaporate it to dryness, and add 2 mL of 1:2 (v/v) liquefied phenol in methylene chloride to the residue. Stir and transfer a portion of the mixture to a cavity of a color-reaction plate. Fill an adjacent cavity with 1:4 (v/v) bromine in methylene chloride, and cover both cavities with an inverted watch glass.
  Acceptance criteria: No purple or deep indigo blue color appears in or above the liquid containing the sample residue.
- **WAX**
  Sample: 10 g, finely ground
  Analysis: Transfer the *Sample* and 2.5 g of sodium carbonate into a 200-mL tall-form beaker. Add 150 mL of hot water, immerse the beaker in a boiling water bath, and stir until the *Sample* is dissolved. Cover the beaker with a watch glass, heat it for 3 h without agitation, and cool it in a cold water bath. When the wax has floated to the surface, filter the mixture through medium-speed, quantitative, ashless filter paper, thus transferring the wax to the paper. Wash the filter with water. Pour 5 to 10 mL of alcohol onto the filter to accelerate drying. Wrap the paper loosely in a larger piece of filter paper, bind with a piece of fine wire, and dry with the aid of gentle heat. Extract with chloroform in a suitable continuous-extraction apparatus for 2 h, using a previously dried and accurately weighed flask to receive the extracted wax and solvent. Evaporate the solvent, dry the wax at 105° to constant weight, and calculate the percentage of wax in the sample taken.
  Acceptance criteria: NMT 5.5%

Shellac, Bleached, Wax-Free

First Published: Prior to FCC 6

Refined Bleached Shellac
INS: 904
UNII: 46N107B71O [shellac]
CAS: [9000-59-3]

DESCRIPTION

Shellac, Bleached, Wax-Free, occurs as an amorphous, light yellow, granular resin. It is obtained from lac, the resinous secretion of the insect *Laccifer (Tachardia) lacca* Kerr (Fam. Coccidae). Shellac, Bleached, Wax-Free, is obtained by the same process as that described in the monograph for *Bleached Shellac*, except that, in addition, wax is removed by filtration. Its solubility is the same as that of *Bleached Shellac*. Shellac, Bleached, Wax-Free, is usually dissolved in a suitable solvent for application to food products.

Function: Coating agent; surface-finishing agent; glaze
Packaging and Storage: Store in well-closed containers in a cool place protected from heat.

IDENTIFICATION

- **PROCEDURE**
  Sample: 50 mg
  Analysis: Prepare a solution of 1 g of ammonium molybdate in 3 mL of sulfuric acid and add a few drops of this solution to the *Sample*.
  Acceptance criteria: A green color appears and changes to lilac when the solution is neutralized with 6 N ammonium hydroxide.

IMPURITIES

Inorganic Impurities

- **LEAD**, *Lead Limit Test, Flame Atomic Absorption Spectrophotometric Method,* Appendix IIIB
  Sample: 10 g
  Acceptance criteria: NMT 2 mg/kg

SPECIFIC TESTS

- **ACID VALUE**
  Sample: 2 g, finely ground
  Analysis: Dissolve the *Sample* in 50 mL of alcohol previously neutralized to phenolphthalein with sodium hydroxide. Add additional phenolphthalein TS, if necessary, and titrate with 0.1 N sodium hydroxide to a pink endpoint. Calculate the acid value by the formula:

$$Result = V \times N/W \times 56.1$$

V = volume (mL) of 0.1 N sodium hydroxide
N = normality of the sodium hydroxide solution
W = weight (g) of sample taken, calculated on the dried basis

Acceptance criteria: Between 75 and 91

- **LOSS ON DRYING**, Appendix IIC: 41° ± 2° to constant weight
  Acceptance criteria: NMT 6.0%
- **ROSIN**
  Sample: 2 g
  Analysis: Dissolve the *Sample* in 10 mL of dehydrated alcohol and add 50 mL of hexane slowly, with shaking. Transfer the solution to a separatory funnel, wash with two 50-mL portions of water, and discard the washings. Filter the hexane layer, evaporate it to dryness, and add 2 mL of 1:2 (v/v) liquefied phenol in methylene chloride to the residue. Stir and transfer a portion of the mixture to a cavity of a color-reaction plate. Fill an adjacent cavity with 1:4 (v/v) bromine in methylene

chloride, and cover both cavities with an inverted watch glass.
Acceptance criteria: No purple or deep indigo blue color appears in or above the liquid containing the sample residue.

- **WAX**
  Sample: 10 g, finely ground
  Analysis: Transfer the *Sample* and 2.5 g of sodium carbonate into a 200-mL tall-form beaker. Add 150 mL of hot water, immerse the beaker in a boiling water bath, and stir until the *Sample* is dissolved. Cover the beaker with a watch glass, heat for 3 h without agitation, and cool in a cold water bath. When the wax has floated to the surface, filter the mixture through medium-speed, quantitative, ashless filter paper, thus transferring the wax to the paper. Wash the filter with water. Pour 5 to 10 mL of alcohol onto the filter to accelerate drying. Wrap the paper loosely in a larger piece of filter paper, bind with a piece of fine wire, and dry with the aid of gentle heat. Extract with chloroform in a suitable continuous extraction apparatus for 2 h, using a previously dried and accurately weighed flask to receive the extracted wax and solvent. Evaporate the solvent, dry the wax at 105° to constant weight, and calculate the percentage of wax in the sample taken.
  Acceptance criteria: NMT 0.2%

Silicon Dioxide

First Published: Prior to FCC 6

Synthetic Amorphous Silica

SiO_2 Formula wt 60.08
INS: 551   CAS: [7631-86-9]
UNII: ETJ7Z6XBU4 [silicon dioxide]

DESCRIPTION
Silicon Dioxide occurs as an amorphous substance that shows a noncrystalline pattern when examined by X-ray diffraction. It is produced synthetically, either by a vapor-phase hydrolysis process, yielding *fumed silica*, or by a wet process, yielding *precipitated silica*, *silica gel*, *colloidal silica*, or *hydrous silica*. *Fumed silica* is produced in an essentially anhydrous state, whereas the wet-process products are obtained as hydrates or contain surface-adsorbed water. *Fumed silica* occurs as a white, fluffy, non-gritty powder of extremely fine particle size and is hygroscopic. The wet-process silicas occur as white, fluffy powders or as white, microcellular beads or granules and are hygroscopic or absorb moisture from the air in varying amounts. All of these forms of Silicon Dioxide are insoluble in water and in organic solvents, but they are soluble in hydrofluoric acid and in hot, concentrated solutions of alkalies.
Function: Anticaking agent; defoaming agent; carrier; conditioning agent; chillproofing agent in malt beverages; filter aid
Packaging and Storage: Store in well-closed containers.

IDENTIFICATION
- **A. PROCEDURE**
  Sample: 5 mg
  Analysis: Place *Sample* into a platinum crucible, mix with 200 mg of anhydrous potassium carbonate, and ignite over a burner at a red heat for about 10 min. Cool, dissolve the melt in 2 mL of freshly distilled water, warming if necessary, and slowly add 2 mL of ammonium molybdate TS.
  Acceptance criteria: A deep yellow color appears.

Change to read:

- **B. PROCEDURE**
  Sample: Solution remaining from *Identification* test *A*
  Analysis: Place 1 drop of *Sample* from *Identification* test *A* on a filter paper, and evaporate the solvent. Add 1 drop of a saturated solution of •o-tolidine• (ERR 1-Jan-2012) in glacial acetic acid, and place the paper over ammonium hydroxide.
  Acceptance criteria: A green-blue spot develops.

ASSAY
- **PROCEDURE**
  Sample: 1 g, previously dried
  Analysis: Transfer *Sample* into a tared platinum crucible, ignite as directed in the test for *Loss on Ignition* (below), cool in a desiccator, and weigh to obtain the ignited sample weight (W). Moisten the residue with 3 or 4 drops of alcohol, add 2 drops of sulfuric acid, and then add enough hydrofluoric acid to cover the wetted sample. [**CAUTION**—Handle hydrofluoric acid in an appropriate fume hood.] Evaporate to dryness on a hot plate, using medium heat (95° to 105°), then add 5 mL of hydrofluoric acid, swirl the dish carefully to wash down the sides, and again evaporate to dryness. Ignite the dried residue over a Meker burner to a red heat, cool in a desiccator, and weigh to obtain the residual weight (w). The difference between the ignited sample weight and the residual weight (W − w) represents the weight, in g, of SiO_2 in the ignited sample.
  Acceptance criteria
  Fumed Silica: NLT 99.0% of SiO_2 on the ignited basis
  Precipitated Silica, Silica Gel, and **Hydrous Silica:** NLT 94.0% of SiO_2 on the ignited basis

IMPURITIES
Inorganic Impurities
- **LEAD**
  Standard stock solution: 100 μg/mL Pb prepared as follows: Dissolve 159.8 mg of lead nitrate, $Pb(NO_3)_2$, in 100 mL of water containing 1 mL of nitric acid, dilute to 1000.0 mL with water, and mix. [NOTE—Prepare and store this solution in glass containers that are free from lead salts.]
  Standard solution: 0.25 μg/mL Pb: from *Standard stock solution*. [NOTE—Prepare on the day of use.]
  Sample solution: Transfer 5.0 g of sample into a 250-mL beaker, add 50 mL of 0.5 N hydrochloric acid, cover with a watch glass, and slowly heat to boiling. Boil gently for 15 min, cool, and let the undissolved material settle. Decant the supernatant liquid through a Whatman No. 3, or equivalent, filter paper into a 100-

mL volumetric flask, retaining as much as possible of the insoluble material in the beaker. Wash the slurry and beaker with three 10-mL portions of hot water, decanting each washing through the filter into the flask. Finally, wash the filter paper with 15 mL of hot water, cool the filtrate to room temperature, dilute with water to volume, and mix.
  Analysis: Set a suitable atomic absorption spectrophotometer to a wavelength of 217 nm and adjust the instrument to zero absorbance against water. Measure the absorbance of the *Standard solution* and of the *Sample solution*.
  Acceptance criteria: The absorbance obtained from the *Sample solution* is not greater than that obtained from the *Standard solution*. (NMT 5 mg/kg)

SPECIFIC TESTS
- **Loss on Drying,** Appendix IIC: 105° for 2 h
  Acceptance criteria
    Fumed Silica: NMT 2.5%
    Precipitated Silica and **Silica Gel:** NMT 7.0%
    Hydrous Silica: NMT 70.0%
    Colloidal Silica: NMT 85.0%
- **Loss on Ignition**
  Sample: 1 g, previously dried
  Analysis: Transfer the *Sample* into a suitable tared crucible, place in a cold muffle furnace and raise the temperature to 900° to 1000° during a 1-h period. Ignite at this temperature for 1 h, cool in a desiccator, and weigh.
  Acceptance criteria
    Fumed Silica: NMT 2.0% on the dried basis
    Precipitated Silica, Silica Gel, and **Hydrous Silica:** NMT 8.5% on the dried basis
- **Soluble Ionizable Salts (as Na₂SO₄)**
  Sample: 5 g, previously dried
  Control solution: 1 mg/mL anhydrous sodium sulfate, made to 250 mL
  Analysis: Stir *Sample* with 150 mL of water for at least 5 min in a high-speed mixer. Filter with the aid of suction, and wash the mixer and filter with 100 mL of water in divided portions, adding the washings to the filtrate. Dilute the filtrate to 250 mL with water. Determine the conductances of the diluted filtrate and of the *Control solution* with a suitable conductance bridge assembly.
  Acceptance criteria
    Precipitated Silica, Silica Gel, and **Hydrous Silica:** The conductance produced by the *Sample* is not greater than that produced by the *Control solution*. (equivalent to NMT 5.0%)

Sodium Acetate
First Published: Prior to FCC 6

$C_2H_3NaO_2$ Formula wt anhydrous 82.03
$C_2H_3NaO_2 \cdot 3H_2O$ Formula wt trihydrate 136.08
INS: 262(i)   CAS: anhydrous [127-09-3]
                              trihydrate [6131-90-4]
UNII: 4550K0SC9B [sodium acetate]

DESCRIPTION
Sodium Acetate occurs as colorless, transparent crystals or as a granular, crystalline or white powder. The anhydrous form is hygroscopic; the trihydrate effloresces in warm, dry air. One g of the anhydrous form dissolves in about 2 mL of water; 1 g of the trihydrate dissolves in about 0.8 mL of water and in about 19 mL of alcohol.
Function: Buffer
Packaging and Storage: Store in tight containers.

IDENTIFICATION
- **Acetate,** *Identification Tests,* Appendix IIIA
  Sample solution: 50 mg/mL
  Acceptance criteria: Passes test
- **Sodium,** *Identification Tests,* Appendix IIIA
  Sample solution: 50 mg/mL
  Acceptance criteria: Passes test

ASSAY
- **Procedure**
  Sample: 400 mg of the dried sample obtained in the test for *Loss on Drying*
  Analysis: Dissolve the *Sample* in 40 mL of glacial acetic acid, add 2 drops of crystal violet TS, and titrate with 0.1 N perchloric acid in glacial acetic acid. Perform a blank determination (see *General Provisions*), and make any necessary correction. Each mL of 0.1 N perchloric acid is equivalent to 8.203 mg of $C_2H_3NaO_2$.
  [**Caution**—Handle perchloric acid in an appropriate fume hood.]
  Acceptance criteria: NLT 99.0% and NMT 101.0% of $C_2H_3NaO_2$, on the dried basis

IMPURITIES
Inorganic Impurities
- **Lead,** *Lead Limit Test, Flame Atomic Absorption Spectrophotometric Method,* Appendix IIIB
  Sample: 10 g
  Acceptance criteria: NMT 2 mg/kg

SPECIFIC TESTS
- **Loss on Drying,** Appendix IIC: 80° overnight, followed by drying it at 120° to constant weight
  Acceptance criteria
    Anhydrous: NMT 1.0%
    Trihydrate: Between 36.0% and 41.0%
- **Alkalinity**
  Sample: 2 g
  Analysis: Dissolve the *Sample* in about 20 mL of water and add 3 drops of phenolphthalein TS.
  Acceptance criteria: Not more than 0.4 mL or 0.1 mL of 0.1 N sulfuric acid for the anhydrous and trihydrate,

respectively, is required to discharge any pink color that appears (Anhydrous: NMT 0.2%; Trihydrate: NMT 0.05%).
- **POTASSIUM COMPOUNDS**
  Sample solution: 5 mL of a clear, saturated solution
  Analysis: Mix a few drops of sodium bitartrate TS with the *Sample solution*.
  Acceptance criteria: No turbidity develops within 5 min.

Sodium Acid Pyrophosphate

First Published: Prior to FCC 6

Disodium Pyrophosphate
Disodium Dihydrogen Pyrophosphate
Disodium Dihydrogen Diphosphate
Acid Sodium Pyrophosphate

$Na_2H_2P_2O_7$ Formula wt 221.94
INS: 450(i)   CAS: [7758-16-9]
UNII: H5WVD9LZUD [sodium acid pyrophosphate]

DESCRIPTION
Sodium Acid Pyrophosphate occurs as a white, crystalline powder or granules. It is soluble in water. The pH of a 1:100 aqueous solution is about 4. It may contain a suitable aluminum and/or calcium salt to control the rate of reaction in leavening systems.
Function: Buffer; emulsifier; leavening agent; sequestrant
Packaging and Storage: Store in tight containers.

IDENTIFICATION
- **A. SODIUM,** Appendix IIIA
  Sample solution: 50 mg/mL
  Acceptance criteria: Passes tests
- **B. PROCEDURE**
  Sample solution: Dissolve 100 mg of sample in 100 mL of 1.7 N nitric acid.
  Solution A: Add 0.5 mL of the *Sample solution* to 30 mL of quimociac TS.
  Solution B: Heat the remaining portion of the *Sample solution* for 10 min at 95°, and add 0.5 mL of it to 30 mL of quimociac TS.
  Acceptance criteria: A yellow precipitate forms immediately in *Solution B*, but does not form in *Solution A*.

ASSAY
- **PROCEDURE**
  Sample: 500 mg
  Solution A: 125 g of $ZnSO_4 \cdot 7H_2O$ dissolved in water, diluted to 1000 mL, filtered, and adjusted to pH 3.8 with hydrochloric acid
  Sodium hydroxide solution: 0.1 N, standardized as directed in *Sodium Hydroxide, Volumetric Solutions,* Solutions and Indicators
  Analysis: Dissolve the *Sample* in 100 mL of water contained in a 400-mL beaker. Using a pH meter, adjust the pH of the solution to 3.8 with hydrochloric acid, then add 50 mL of *Solution A*, and allow the mixture to stand for 2 min. Titrate the liberated acid with *Sodium hydroxide solution* until a pH of 3.8 is again reached. After each addition of 0.1 N sodium hydroxide near the endpoint, allow time for any precipitated zinc hydroxide to redissolve. Each mL of 0.1 N sodium hydroxide is equivalent to 11.10 mg of $Na_2H_2P_2O_7$.
  Acceptance criteria: NLT 93.0% and NMT 100.5% of $Na_2H_2P_2O_7$

IMPURITIES
Inorganic Impurities
- **ARSENIC,** *Arsenic Limit Test,* Appendix IIIB
  Sample solution: 1 g in 10 mL of water
  Acceptance criteria: NMT 3 mg/kg
- **FLUORIDE,** *Fluoride Limit Test, Method IV,* Appendix IIIB
  Sample: 2 g
  Acceptance criteria: NMT 0.005%
- **LEAD,** *Lead Limit Test, APDC Extraction Method,* Appendix IIIB
  Acceptance criteria: NMT 2 mg/kg

SPECIFIC TESTS
- **INSOLUBLE SUBSTANCES**
  Sample: 10 g
  Analysis: Dissolve the *Sample* in 100 mL of hot water and filter the solution through a tared filtering crucible. Wash the insoluble residue with hot water, dry at 105° for 2 h, cool, and weigh.
  Acceptance criteria: NMT 1%

Sodium Alginate

First Published: Prior to FCC 6

Algin

$(C_6H_7O_6Na)_n$ Equiv wt, calculated 198.11
    Equiv wt, actual (avg.) 222.00
INS: 401   CAS: [9005-38-3]
UNII: C269C4G2ZQ [sodium alginate]

DESCRIPTION
Sodium Alginate occurs as a white to yellow-brown, fibrous or granular powder. It is the sodium salt of alginic acid (see the monograph for *Alginic Acid*). It dissolves in water to form a viscous, colloidal solution. It is insoluble in alcohol and in hydroalcoholic solutions in which the alcohol content is greater than about 30% by weight. It is insoluble in chloroform, in ether, and in acids having a pH lower than about 3.
Function: Stabilizer; thickener; emulsifier; gelling agent
Packaging and Storage: Store in well-closed containers.

IDENTIFICATION
- **A. PROCEDURE**
  Sample solution: 10 mg/mL
  Analysis: To 5 mL of the *Sample solution*, add 1 mL of calcium chloride TS.
  Acceptance criteria: A voluminous, gelatinous precipitate forms.

- **B. Procedure**
  Sample solution: 10 mg/mL
  Analysis: To 10 mL of the *Sample solution*, add 1 mL of 2 N sulfuric acid.
  Acceptance criteria: A heavy, gelatinous precipitate forms.
- **C. Procedure**
  Sample: About 5 mg
  Analysis: Place the *Sample* in a test tube, add 5 mL of water, 1 mL of a freshly prepared 1:100 naphtholresorcinol in ethanol solution, and 5 mL of hydrochloric acid. Heat the mixture to boiling, boil gently for about 3 min, and then cool to about 15°. Transfer the contents of the test tube to a 30-mL separatory funnel with the aid of 5 mL of water, and extract with 15 mL of isopropyl ether. Perform a blank determination (see *General Provisions*), and make any necessary correction.
  Acceptance criteria: The isopropyl ether extract from the sample exhibits a deeper purple hue than that from the blank.

ASSAY
- **Alginates Assay,** Appendix IIIC
  Analysis: Each mL of 0.25 N sodium hydroxide consumed is equivalent to 27.75 mg of sodium alginate (equiv. wt. 222.00), calculated on the dried basis.
  Acceptance criteria: NLT 18.0% and NMT 21.0% of carbon dioxide, corresponding to between 90.8% and 106.0% of sodium alginate (equiv wt 222.00)

IMPURITIES
Inorganic Impurities
- **Arsenic,** *Arsenic Limit Test,* Appendix IIIB
  Sample solution: Prepare as directed for organic compounds.
  Acceptance criteria: NMT 3 mg/kg
- **Lead,** *Lead Limit Test,* Appendix IIIB
  Sample solution: Prepare as directed for organic compounds.
  Control: 5 µg of Pb (5 mL of *Diluted Standard Lead Solution*)
  Acceptance criteria: NMT 5 mg/kg

SPECIFIC TESTS
- **Loss on Drying,** Appendix IIC: 105° for 4 h
  Acceptance criteria: NMT 15.0%

Sodium Aluminosilicate
First Published: Prior to FCC 6

Sodium Silicoaluminate
INS: 554 CAS: [1344-00-9]
UNII: 058TS43PSM [sodium aluminium silicate]

DESCRIPTION
Sodium Aluminosilicate occurs as a fine, white, amorphous powder, or as beads. It is a series of hydrated sodium aluminum silicates having $Na_2O:Al_2O_3:SiO_2$ molar ratios of approximately 1:1:13, respectively. It is insoluble in water and in alcohol and other organic solvents, but at 80° to 100°, it is partially soluble in strong acids and solutions of alkali hydroxides.
Function: Anticaking agent
Packaging and Storage: Store in well-closed containers.

IDENTIFICATION
- **A. Procedure**
  Sample: 500 mg
  Analysis: Mix the *Sample* with 2.5 g of anhydrous potassium carbonate, and heat the mixture in a platinum or nickel crucible until it melts completely. Cool, add 5 mL of water, and allow to stand for 3 min. Heat the bottom of the crucible gently, detach the melt, and transfer it into a beaker with the aid of about 50 mL of water. Gradually add hydrochloric acid until no effervescence is observed, add 10 mL more of the acid, and evaporate to dryness on a steam bath. Cool, add 20 mL of water, boil, and filter through ash-free filter paper. An insoluble residue of silica remains. [Note—Retain the filtrate for *Identification* test B and *Identification* test C (below).] Transfer the gelatinous residue to a platinum dish, and cautiously add 5 mL of hydrofluoric acid. [Caution—Handle hydrofluoric acid in an appropriate fume hood.] The precipitate dissolves. (If it does not dissolve, repeat the treatment with hydrofluoric acid.) Heat the solution and introduce a glass stirring rod with a drop of water on the tip into the resulting vapors.
  Acceptance criteria: The drop of water becomes turbid.
- **B. Aluminum,** Appendix IIIA
  Sample: A portion of the filtrate obtained in *Identification* test A.
  Acceptance criteria: Passes tests
- **C. Sodium,** Appendix IIIA
  Sample: A portion of the filtrate obtained in *Identification* test A.
  Acceptance criteria: Passes tests

ASSAY
- **Silicon Dioxide**
  Sample: 500 mg, previously dried
  Analysis: Transfer the *Sample* into a 250-mL beaker, wash the sides of the beaker with a few mL of water, and add 30 mL of sulfuric acid and 15 mL of hydrochloric acid. Heat the solution on a hot plate in a hood until dense, white fumes evolve. Cool, add an additional 15 mL of hydrochloric acid and heat again to dense, white fumes. Cool, add 70 mL of water, and filter through Whatman No. 40, or equivalent, filter paper. Wash the filter paper and precipitate thoroughly with hot water to remove the sulfuric acid residue. Transfer the filter paper and precipitate into a tared platinum crucible, char, and ignite at 900° to constant weight. Moisten the residue with a few drops of water, add 15 mL of hydrofluoric acid and 8 drops of sulfuric acid, and heat on a hot plate in a hood until white fumes of sulfur trioxide evolve. Cool; add 5 mL of water, 10 mL of hydrofluoric acid, and 3 drops of sulfuric acid; and evaporate to dryness on the hot plate. Heat cautiously over an open flame until sulfur trioxide fumes cease to evolve, and ignite at 900° to constant

weight. The weight loss after the addition of hydrofluoric acid represents the weight of SiO₂ in the *Sample*.

Acceptance criteria: NLT 66.0% and NMT 76.0% SiO₂, on the dried basis

- **ALUMINUM OXIDE**

  Sample stock solution: Transfer 500 mg of sample, previously dried, into a tared platinum dish and moisten with 8 to 10 drops of water. Add 25 mL of 70% perchloric acid and 10 mL of hydrofluoric acid, and heat on a hot plate until dense, white fumes of perchloric acid evolve. [**CAUTION**—Handle perchloric acid in an appropriate fume hood.] Cool, add an additional 10 mL of hydrofluoric acid, and heat again to dense, white fumes. Cool, dissolve in sufficient water, quantitatively transfer it with the aid of additional water into a 250-mL volumetric flask, and dilute to volume with water. [NOTE—Retain the unused portion of this solution for the test for *Sodium oxide* (below).]

  Sample solution: 10.0 mL of *Sample stock solution* diluted to 100 mL with water

  Standard solutions: Prepare 5 µg/mL, 10 µg/mL, 20 µg/mL, and 50 µg/mL aqueous solutions of aluminum, in the form of the chloride.

  Analysis: Set a suitable atomic absorption spectrophotometer to a wavelength of 309.3 nm and adjust the instrument to zero absorbance against water. Read the absorbance of the *Standard solutions* and plot the standard curve as absorbance versus concentration of aluminum.

  Aspirate the *Sample solution* into the spectrophotometer, read the absorbance in the same manner, and by reference to the standard curve, determine the concentration (C) of aluminum, in µg/mL, in the *Sample stock solution*. Calculate the quantity, in mg, of Al₂O₃ in the sample taken by the formula:

  $$\text{Result} = (250C \times 10 \times 1.8895)/1000$$

  C = concentration of aluminum (µg/mL) in the *Sample stock solution*, calculated from the standard curve

  Acceptance criteria: NLT 9.0% and NMT 13.0% of Al₂O₃, on the dried basis

- **SODIUM OXIDE**

  Sample solution: A portion of the *Sample stock solution* from the test for *Aluminum oxide* (above)

  Standard solutions: Prepare 50 µg/mL, 100 µg/mL, and 150 µg/mL, 200 µg/mL aqueous solutions of sodium, in the form of the chloride.

  Correction for sodium sulfate content: Transfer 1 g of sample, previously dried, into a tared platinum dish and moisten with 8 to 10 drops of water. Add 25 mL of 70% perchloric acid and 10 mL of hydrofluoric acid, and heat on a hot plate in a hood until dense, white fumes of perchloric acid evolve. Add 10 mL of hydrofluoric acid, and heat again to dense, white fumes. [**CAUTION**—Handle perchloric acid in an appropriate fume hood.] Quantitatively transfer the solution into a 400-mL beaker, add 200 mL of water, and heat to boiling. Gradually add, in small portions and while stirring constantly, an excess of hot barium chloride TS (about 10 mL), and heat the mixture on a steam bath for 1 h. Collect the precipitate on a filter, wash until free from chloride, dry, ignite, and weigh the resulting barium sulfate so obtained. Calculate the correction factor (F) by the formula:

  $$\text{Result} = 0.437(C' \times w/W)$$

  C' = weight (mg) of barium sulfate obtained multiplied by 0.6086 (to convert to Na₂SO₄ equivalents)
  w = weight (mg) of the sample taken for the *Sodium Oxide* determination
  W = weight of the sample taken for the *Correction for sodium sulfate content* determination (mg)

  Analysis: Set a suitable flame photometer to a wavelength of 589 nm and adjust the instrument to zero transmittance against water. Adjust the instrument to 100.0% transmittance with the *Standard solution* containing 200 µg/mL of sodium, in the form of the chloride. Read the percent transmittance of the remaining three *Standard solutions* and plot the standard curve as percent transmittance versus concentration of sodium.

  Aspirate the *Sample solution* into the photometer, read the percent transmittance in the same manner, and by reference to the standard curve, determine the concentration (C) of sodium, in µg/mL, in the *Sample solution*. Calculate the quantity, in mg, of Na₂O in the sample taken by the formula:

  $$\text{Result} = (250C \times 1.348/1000) - F$$

  C = concentration of sodium (µg/mL) in the *Sample solution*, calculated from the standard curve
  F = quantity of sodium oxide equivalent to any sodium sulfate present in the sample (calculated in *Correction for sodium sulfate content* above)

  Acceptance criteria: NLT 4.0% and NMT 7.0% of Na₂O, on the dried basis

IMPURITIES
Inorganic Impurities

- **LEAD**

  Standard stock solution: 100 µg/mL of Pb prepared as follows: Dissolve 159.8 mg of ACS reagent-grade lead nitrate [Pb(NO₃)₂] in 100 mL of water containing 1 mL of nitric acid, dilute to 1000.0 with water, and mix. [NOTE—Prepare and store this solution in glass containers that are free from lead salts.]

  Standard solution: 0.50 µg/mL Pb: from *Standard stock solution*. [NOTE—Prepare this solution on the day of use.]

  Sample solution: Transfer 10.0 g of sample into a 250-mL beaker, add 50 mL of 0.5 N hydrochloric acid, cover with a watch glass, and heat slowly to boiling.

Boil gently for 15 min, cool, and let the undissolved material settle. Decant the supernatant liquid through Whatman No. 4, or equivalent, filter paper into a 100-mL volumetric flask, retaining as much as possible of the insoluble material in the beaker. Wash the slurry and beaker with three 10-mL portions of hot water, decanting each washing through the filter into the flask. Finally, wash the filter paper with 15 mL of hot water, cool the filtrate to room temperature, dilute to volume with water, and mix.
Analysis: Set a suitable atomic absorption spectrophotometer to a wavelength of 217 nm. Adjust the instrument to zero absorbance against water. Read the absorbance of the *Standard solution*. Aspirate the *Sample solution* into the spectrophotometer and measure the absorbance in the same manner.
Acceptance criteria: The absorbance obtained from the *Sample solution* is NMT that obtained from the *Standard solution*. (NMT 5 mg/kg)

SPECIFIC TESTS
- **Loss on Drying,** Appendix IIC: 105° for 2 h
  Acceptance criteria: NMT 8.0%
- **Loss on Ignition**
  Sample: 5 g, previously dried
  Analysis: Transfer the *Sample* into a suitable tared crucible and ignite at 900° to constant weight.
  Acceptance criteria: Between 8.0% and 13.0%, on the dried basis
- **pH,** *pH Determination,* Appendix IIB
  Sample mixture: 200 mg/mL in carbon dioxide-free water
  Acceptance criteria: Between 6.5 and 10.5

Sodium Aluminum Phosphate, Acidic

First Published: Prior to FCC 6
Last Revision: FCC 6

SALP

$Na_3Al_2H_{15}(PO_4)_8$	Formula wt, anhydrous 897.82
$NaAl_3H_{14}(PO_4)_8 \cdot 2H_2O$	Formula wt, dihydrate 913.85
$NaAl_3H_{14}(PO_4)_8 \cdot 4H_2O$	Formula wt, tetrahydrate 949.88
INS: 541(i)	CAS: anhydrous [10279-59-1]
	dihydrate [15136-87-5]
	tetrahydrate [10305-76-7]

DESCRIPTION
Sodium Aluminum Phosphate, Acidic occurs as a white powder. It is anhydrous or contains two or four molecules of water of hydration. It is insoluble in water, but is soluble in hydrochloric acid.
Function: Leavening agent
Packaging and Storage: Store in tightly closed containers.

IDENTIFICATION
- **Aluminum,** Appendix IIIA
  Sample solution: 100 mg/mL in 1:2 hydrochloric acid
  Acceptance criteria: Passes tests
- **Phosphate,** Appendix IIIA
  Sample solution: 100 mg/mL in 1:2 hydrochloric acid
  Acceptance criteria: Passes tests
- **Sodium,** Appendix IIIA
  Sample solution: 100 mg/mL in 1:2 hydrochloric acid
  Acceptance criteria: Responds to the flame test for sodium compounds.

ASSAY
- **Procedure**
  Sample: 800 mg
  Analysis: Transfer the *Sample* into a 400-mL beaker, add 100 mL of water and 25 mL of nitric acid, cover with a watch glass, and boil for 10 min on a hot plate. Rinse any condensate from the watch glass into the beaker, cool the solution to room temperature, transfer it quantitatively to a 500-mL volumetric flask, dilute to volume with water, and mix thoroughly. Pipet 20.0 mL of this solution into a 500-mL Erlenmeyer flask, add 100 mL of water, and heat just to boiling. While stirring, add 50 mL of quimociac TS, cover with a watch glass, and boil for 1 min in a well-ventilated hood. Cool to room temperature, swirling occasionally while cooling; filter through a tared, sintered-glass filter crucible of medium porosity, and wash with five 25-mL portions of water. Dry at about 225° for 30 min, cool, and weigh. Each mg of precipitate thus obtained is equivalent to 53.66 µg of $NaAl_3H_{14}(PO_4)_8 \cdot 4H_2O$ or 50.72 µg of $Na_3Al_2H_{15}(PO_4)_8$.
  Acceptance criteria
    Anhydrous: NLT 95.0%
    Tetrahydrate: NLT 95.0%

IMPURITIES
Inorganic Impurities
- **Arsenic,** *Arsenic Limit Test,* Appendix IIIB
  Sample solution: 1 g of sample in 10 mL of 1:2 hydrochloric acid
  Acceptance criteria: NMT 3 mg/kg
- **Fluoride,** *Fluoride Limit Test, Method II,* Appendix IIIB
  Sample: 2 g
  Acceptance criteria: NMT 0.0025%
- **Lead,** *Lead Limit Test, APDC Extraction Method,* Appendix IIIB
  Acceptance criteria: NMT 2 mg/kg

SPECIFIC TESTS
- **Loss on Ignition:** 750° to 800° for 2 h
  Acceptance criteria
    Anhydrous: Between 15.0% and 16.0%
    Tetrahydrate: Between 19.5% and 21.0%

Sodium Aluminum Phosphate, Basic

First Published: Prior to FCC 6

KASAL
INS: 541(ii)   CAS: [7785-88-8]

DESCRIPTION
Sodium Aluminum Phosphate, Basic, occurs as a white powder consisting of an autogenous mixture of an alkaline sodium aluminum phosphate [approximately $Na_8Al_2(OH)_2(PO_4)_4$] with about 30% dibasic sodium phosphate. It is soluble in hydrochloric acid; the sodium phosphate moiety is soluble in water, whereas the sodium aluminum phosphate moiety is only sparingly soluble in water.

Function: Emulsifier
Packaging and Storage: Store in tightly closed containers.

IDENTIFICATION
- **ALUMINUM,** Appendix IIIA
  Sample solution: 100 mg/mL in 1:2 hydrochloric acid
  Acceptance criteria: Passes tests
- **PHOSPHATE,** Appendix IIIA
  Sample solution: 100 mg/mL in 1:2 hydrochloric acid
  Acceptance criteria: Passes tests
- **SODIUM,** Appendix IIIA
  Sample: 100 mg/mL in 1:2 hydrochloric acid
  Acceptance criteria: Responds to flame test for sodium compounds.

ASSAY
- **PROCEDURE**
  Sample: 2.5 g
  Analysis: Transfer the Sample into a 400-mL beaker. Add 15 mL of hydrochloric acid and one glass bead, cover with a watch glass, and boil gently for about 5 min. Rinse any condensate on the watch glass into the beaker, cool the solution to room temperature, transfer it quantitatively to a 250-mL volumetric flask, dilute to volume with water, and mix thoroughly. Transfer 10.0 mL of this solution to a 250-mL beaker, add phenolphthalein TS, and neutralize with 6 N ammonium hydroxide. Add 1:2 hydrochloric acid until the precipitate just dissolves, then dilute to 100 mL with water and heat to 70° to 80°. Add 10 mL of 8-hydroxyquinoline TS and sufficient ammonium acetate TS until a yellow precipitate forms, then add 30 mL in excess. Digest at 70° for 30 min, filter through a previously dried and weighed sintered glass filter crucible, and wash thoroughly with hot water. Dry at 105° for 2 h, cool, and weigh. Each mg of the precipitate corresponds to 0.111 mg of Al_2O_3.
  Acceptance criteria: NLT 9.5% and NMT 12.5% of Al_2O_3, calculated on the ignited basis

IMPURITIES
Inorganic Impurities
- **ARSENIC,** Arsenic Limit Test, Appendix IIIB
  Sample solution: 1 g in 10 mL of 1:2 hydrochloric acid
  Acceptance criteria: NMT 3 mg/kg
- **FLUORIDE,** Fluoride Limit Test, Appendix IIIB
  Sample: 2 g
  Acceptance criteria: NMT 0.0025%
- **LEAD,** Lead Limit Test, APDC Extraction Method, Appendix IIIB
  Acceptance criteria: NMT 2 mg/kg

SPECIFIC TESTS
- **LOSS ON IGNITION**
  Analysis: Ignite at 750° to 800° for 2 h.
  Acceptance criteria: NMT 9.0%

Sodium Ascorbate

First Published: Prior to FCC 6

Vitamin C Sodium
Sodium L-Ascorbate

$C_6H_7NaO_6$ Formula wt 198.11
INS: 301   CAS: [134-03-2]
UNII: S033EH8359 [sodium ascorbate]

DESCRIPTION
Sodium Ascorbate occurs as a white to yellow crystalline powder that does not darken on exposure to light. One g is soluble in 2 mL of water. The pH of a 1:10 aqueous solution is about 7.5.

Function: Antioxidant; meat curing aid; nutrient
Packaging and Storage: Store in tight, light-resistant containers.

IDENTIFICATION
- **A. PROCEDURE**
  Sample solution: 20 mg/mL
  Acceptance criteria: The Sample solution slowly reduces alkaline cupric tartrate TS at 25°, and does so more readily upon heating.
- **B. PROCEDURE**
  Sample solution: 20 mg/mL
  Analysis: Acidify 2 mL of the Sample solution with 0.5 mL of 0.1 N hydrochloric acid, add 4 drops of methylene blue TS, and warm to 40°.
  Acceptance criteria: A deep blue color forms, then disappears almost completely within 3 min.
- **C. PROCEDURE**
  Sample: 15 mg
  Analysis: Dissolve the Sample in 15 mL of a 1:20 trichloroacetic acid:water solution, add about 200 mg of activated charcoal, shake vigorously for 1 min, and filter through a small fluted filter, returning the filtrate, if necessary, until clear. Add 1 drop of pyrrole to 5 mL of the filtrate, agitate gently until dissolved, and then heat in a water bath at 50°.
  Acceptance criteria: A blue color appears.

- D. SODIUM, Appendix IIIA
  Acceptance criteria: Passes test

ASSAY
- PROCEDURE
  Sample: 400 mg previously dried over phosphorus pentoxide for 24 h
  Analysis: Dissolve the Sample in a mixture of 100 mL of water, recently boiled and cooled, and 25 mL of 2 N sulfuric acid, and titrate with 0.1 N iodine, adding starch TS near the endpoint. Each mL of 0.1 N iodine is equivalent to 9.905 mg of $C_6H_7NaO_6$.
  Acceptance criteria: NLT 99.0% and NMT 101.0% of $C_6H_7NaO_6$, on the dried basis

IMPURITIES
Inorganic Impurities
- LEAD, Lead Limit Test, Flame Atomic Absorption Spectrophotometric Method, Appendix IIIB
  Sample: 10 g
  Acceptance criteria: NMT 2 mg/kg

SPECIFIC TESTS
- LOSS ON DRYING, Appendix IIC: 60° for 4 h in vacuum over phosphorus pentoxide
  Acceptance criteria: NMT 0.25%
- OPTICAL (SPECIFIC) ROTATION, Appendix IIB
  Sample solution: 100 mg/mL
  Acceptance criteria: $[\alpha]_D^{25}$ between +103° and +108°

Sodium Benzoate

First Published: Prior to FCC 6

$C_7H_5NaO_2$ Formula wt 144.11
INS: 211   CAS: [532-32-1]
UNII: OJ245FE5EU [sodium benzoate]

DESCRIPTION
Sodium Benzoate occurs as white granules, a crystalline powder, or flakes. One g dissolves in 2 mL of water, in 75 mL of alcohol, and in 50 mL of 90% alcohol.
Function: Preservative; antimicrobial agent
Packaging and Storage: Store in well-closed containers.

IDENTIFICATION
- BENZOATE, Appendix IIIA
  Acceptance criteria: Passes test
- SODIUM, Appendix IIIA
  Acceptance criteria: Passes test

ASSAY
- PROCEDURE
  Sample: 600 mg
  Analysis: Transfer the Sample to a 250 mL beaker, add 100 mL of glacial acetic acid, and stir until the sample is completely dissolved. Titrate with 0.1 N perchloric acid in glacial acetic acid, using crystal violet TS as the indicator. Each mL of 0.1 N perchloric acid is equivalent to 14.41 mg of $C_7H_5NaO_2$. [CAUTION—Handle perchloric acid in an appropriate fume hood.]
  Acceptance criteria: NLT 99.0% and NMT 100.5% of $C_7H_5NaO_2$, calculated on the anhydrous basis

IMPURITIES
Inorganic Impurities
- LEAD, Lead Limit Test, Flame Atomic Absorption Spectrophotometric Method, Appendix IIIB
  Sample: 10 g
  Acceptance criteria: NMT 2 mg/kg

SPECIFIC TESTS
- ALKALINITY (as NaOH)
  Sample: 2 g
  Analysis: Dissolve the Sample in 20 mL of hot water and add 2 drops of phenolphthalein TS.
  Acceptance criteria: Not more than 0.2 mL of 0.1 N sulfuric acid is required to discharge any pink color that forms. (NMT 0.04%)
- WATER, Water Determination, Appendix IIB
  Acceptance criteria: NMT 1.5%

Sodium Bicarbonate

First Published: Prior to FCC 6

Sodium Hydrogen Carbonate
Baking Soda

$NaHCO_3$ Formula wt 84.01
INS: 500(ii)   CAS: [144-55-8]
UNII: 8MDF5V39QO [sodium bicarbonate]

DESCRIPTION
Sodium Bicarbonate occurs as a white, crystalline powder. It is stable in dry air, but it slowly decomposes in moist air. One g dissolves in 10 mL of water. It is insoluble in alcohol. Its solutions, when freshly prepared with cold water without shaking, are alkaline to litmus. The alkalinity increases as the solutions stand, are agitated, or are heated.
Function: pH control agent; leavening agent
Packaging and Storage: Store in well-closed containers.

IDENTIFICATION
- BICARBONATE, Identification Tests, Appendix IIIA
  Sample solution: 100 mg/mL
  Acceptance criteria: Passes test
- SODIUM, Identification Tests, Appendix IIIA
  Sample solution: 100 mg/mL
  Acceptance criteria: Passes test

ASSAY
- PROCEDURE
  Sample: 3 g previously dried over silica gel for 4 h
  Analysis: Dissolve the Sample in 100 mL of water. Add 2 drops of methyl red TS, and titrate with 1 N

hydrochloric acid. Add the acid slowly, with constant stirring, until the solution becomes faintly pink. Heat the solution to boiling, cool, and continue the titration until the faint pink color no longer fades after boiling. Each mL of 1 N hydrochloric acid is equivalent to 84.01 mg of NaHCO$_3$.

Acceptance criteria: NLT 99.0% and NMT 100.5%, on the dried basis

IMPURITIES
Inorganic Impurities
- **LEAD,** *Lead Limit Test, APDC Extraction Method,* Appendix IIIB
  Acceptance criteria: NMT 2 mg/kg

SPECIFIC TESTS
- **LOSS ON DRYING,** Appendix IIC: Room temperature, 4 h over silica gel
  Acceptance criteria: NMT 0.25%
- **AMMONIA**
  Analysis: Heat 1 g of sample in a test tube.
  Acceptance criteria: No odor of ammonia is detected.
- **INSOLUBLE SUBSTANCES**
  Acceptance criteria: One g of sample dissolves in 20 mL of water to give a clear solution.

Sodium Bisulfate

First Published: Prior to FCC 6
Last Revision: Second Supplement, FCC 6

Sodium Acid Sulfate
Nitre Cake

NaHSO$_4$ Formula wt 120.06
      CAS: [7681-38-1]

UNII: BU8V88OWIQ [sodium bisulfate]

DESCRIPTION
Sodium Bisulfate occurs as white crystals or granules. It is soluble in water, and its solutions are strongly acid. It is decomposed by alcohol into sodium sulfate and free sulfuric acid.
Function: Acidifier
Packaging and Storage: Store in tight containers.

IDENTIFICATION
- **SODIUM,** Appendix IIIA
  Acceptance criteria: Passes tests
- **SULFATE,** Appendix IIIA
  Acceptance criteria: Passes test

ASSAY
- **PROCEDURE**
  Sample: 5 g
  Analysis: Dissolve the *Sample* in about 125 mL of water, add phenolphthalein TS, and titrate with 1 N sodium hydroxide. Each mL of 1 N sodium hydroxide is equivalent to 49.04 mg of H$_2$SO$_4$, or to 120.06 mg of NaHSO$_4$.

Acceptance criteria: NLT 35.0% and NMT 39.0% of available H$_2$SO$_4$, equivalent to NLT 85.4% and NMT 95.2% of NaHSO$_4$

IMPURITIES
Inorganic Impurities
- **LEAD,** *Lead Limit Test, APDC Extraction Method,* Appendix IIIB
  Acceptance criteria: NMT 2 mg/kg
- **SELENIUM,** *Selenium Limit Test, Method II,* Appendix IIIB
  Sample: 1.2 g
  Acceptance criteria: The absorbance of the extract from the *Sample Preparation* is NMT the absorbance of the extract from the *Standard Preparation*. (NMT 5 mg/kg)

SPECIFIC TESTS
- **LOSS ON DRYING,** Appendix IIC: Dry sample in a desiccator over phosphorus pentoxide for 24 h.
  Acceptance criteria: NMT 0.8%
- **WATER-INSOLUBLE SUBSTANCES**
  Sample: 50 g
  Analysis: Dissolve the *Sample* in 300 mL of hot water contained in a 600-mL beaker. Allow the insoluble matter to settle. Filter by decanting through a tared, sintered-glass filter crucible, washing the insoluble matter into the crucible with additional hot water. Dry the residue at 100° to 110° for 1 h, cool in a desiccator, and weigh.
  Acceptance criteria: NMT 0.05%

Sodium Bisulfite

First Published: Prior to FCC 6
Last Revision: Second Supplement, FCC 6

Sodium Acid Sulfite
Sodium Hydrogen Sulfite

NaHSO$_3$ Formula wt 104.06
INS: 222   CAS: [7631-90-5]
UNII: TZX5469Z6I [sodium bisulfite]

DESCRIPTION
Sodium Bisulfite occurs as white or yellow-white crystals or as a granular powder. It consists of sodium bisulfite (NaHSO$_3$) and sodium metabisulfite (Na$_2$S$_2$O$_5$) in varying proportions and, for all practical purposes, possesses properties of the true bisulfite. It is unstable in air. One g dissolves in 4 mL of water. It is slightly soluble in alcohol.
Function: Preservative
Packaging and Storage: Store in well-filled, tight containers, and avoid exposure to excessive heat.

IDENTIFICATION
- **SODIUM,** Appendix IIIA
  Sample solution: 100 mg/mL in water
  Acceptance criteria: Passes tests
- **SULFITE,** Appendix IIIA
  Sample solution: 100 mg/mL in water
  Acceptance criteria: Passes test

ASSAY
- **PROCEDURE**
  Sample: 200 mg
  Analysis: Add the *Sample* to 50.0 mL of 0.1 N iodine contained in a glass-stoppered flask and stopper the flask. Allow the mixture to stand for 5 min, add 1 mL of hydrochloric acid, and titrate the excess iodine with 0.1 N sodium thiosulfate, adding starch TS as the indicator. Each mL of 0.1 N iodine is equivalent to 3.203 mg of SO_2.
  Acceptance criteria: NLT 58.5% and NMT 67.4% of SO_2

IMPURITIES
Inorganic Impurities
- **IRON**
  Sample: 500 mg
  Control: 25 µg Fe (2.5 mL of *Iron Standard Solution*, Solutions and Indicators)
  Analysis: Add 2 mL of hydrochloric acid to the *Sample*, and evaporate to dryness on a steam bath. Dissolve the residue in 2 mL of hydrochloric acid and 20 mL of water, add a few drops of bromine TS, and boil the solution to remove the bromine. Cool, dilute with water to 25 mL, then add 50 mg of ammonium persulfate and 5 mL of ammonium thiocyanate TS. Repeat the above *Analysis* using the *Control* in place of the *Sample*.
  Acceptance criteria: Any red or pink color produced by the *Sample* does not exceed that produced by the *Control*. (NMT 0.005%)
- **LEAD,** *Lead Limit Test, APDC Extraction Method,* Appendix IIIB
  Acceptance criteria: NMT 2 mg/kg
- **SELENIUM,** *Selenium Limit Test, Method I,* Appendix IIIB
  Sample: 1.2 g
  Acceptance criteria: The absorbance of the extract from the *Sample Preparation* is NMT the absorbance of the extract from the *Standard Preparation*. (NMT 5 mg/kg)

Sodium Carbonate
First Published: Prior to FCC 6

Soda Ash

Na_2CO_3	Formula wt, anhydrous 105.99
$Na_2CO_3 \cdot H_2O$	Formula wt, monohydrate 124.00
$Na_2CO_3 \cdot 10H_2O$	Formula wt, decahydrate 286.14
INS: 500(i)	CAS: anhydrous [497-19-8]
	monohydrate [5968-11-6]
	decahydrate [6132-02-1]

UNII: 45P3261C7T [sodium carbonate]

DESCRIPTION
Sodium Carbonate occurs as colorless crystals or as a white, granular or crystalline powder. It is anhydrous or may contain 1 or 10 molecules of water of hydration. It is freely soluble in water and insoluble in ethanol. Its solutions are alkaline to litmus. The anhydrous salt is hygroscopic, and the two hydrates are efflorescent. The decahydrate melts at about 32°.
Function: pH control
Packaging and Storage: Store the anhydrous salt and the decahydrate in tight containers; store the monohydrate in well-closed containers.

IDENTIFICATION
- **CARBONATE,** Appendix IIIA
  Acceptance criteria: Passes test
- **SODIUM,** Appendix IIIA
  Acceptance criteria: Passes test

ASSAY
- **PROCEDURE**
  Sample: 2 g, previously dried (see *Loss on Drying* below)
  Analysis: Dissolve the *Sample* in 50 mL of water. Add 2 drops of methyl red TS, and titrate with 1 N hydrochloric acid, adding the acid slowly, while constantly stirring, until the solution becomes faintly pink. Heat the solution to boiling, cool, and continue the titration until the faint pink color no longer fades after boiling. Each mL of 1 N hydrochloric acid is equivalent to 53.00 mg of Na_2CO_3.
  Acceptance criteria: NLT 99.5% and NMT 100.5% of Na_2CO_3, on the dried basis

IMPURITIES
Inorganic Impurities
- **LEAD,** *Lead Limit Test, APDC Extraction Method,* Appendix IIIB
  Acceptance criteria: NMT 4 mg/kg

SPECIFIC TESTS
- **LOSS ON DRYING,** Appendix IIC
  Sample
    Anhydrous or monohydrate: 3 g
    Decahydrate: 8 g
  Analysis
    Anhydrous or monohydrate: Dry the *Sample* at 275° to 300° to constant weight.
    Decahydrate: Heat the *Sample* first at 70°, then gradually raise the temperature, and dry at 275° to 300° to constant weight.
  Acceptance criteria
    Anhydrous: NMT 1%
    Monohydrate: Between 12.0% and 15.0%
    Decahydrate: Between 55.0% and 65.0%

Sodium Carboxymethyl Cellulose, Enzymatically Hydrolyzed
First Published: First Supplement, FCC 6

Enzymatically Hydrolyzed Carboxymethyl Cellulose, Sodium
CMC-ENZ
Cellulose Gum, Enzymatically Hydrolyzed

INS: 469

DESCRIPTION
Sodium Carboxymethyl Cellulose (CMC), Enzymatically Hydrolyzed occurs as a white or slightly yellowish or grayish granular or fibrous powder. It is the odorless and slightly hygroscopic product of the sodium salt of a carboxymethyl ether of cellulose, which has been partially hydrolyzed by enzymatic treatment with food-grade cellulase [*Trichoderma longibrachiatum* (formerly *reesei*)]. The total content of mono- and disaccharides is typically about 7.5%. It is soluble in water and insoluble in ether.
Function: Thickener, stabilizer
Packaging and Storage: Store in well-closed containers.

IDENTIFICATION
- **A. Procedure**
  Sample solution: 1 mg/mL
  Analysis: Shake the *Sample solution*.
  Acceptance criteria: No layer of foam appears (distinction from other cellulose ethers).
- **B. Procedure**
  Sample solution: 5 mg/mL
  Analysis: Add 5 mL of a 50 mg/mL solution of copper sulfate (or aluminum sulfate) to 5 mL of the *Sample solution*.
  Acceptance criteria: A precipitate forms (distinction from other cellulose ethers).
- **C. Procedure**
  Sample solution: 10 mg/mL
  1-Naphthol solution: 1 g of 1-naphthol in 25 mL of methanol
  Analysis: Dilute 1 mL of the *Sample solution* with 1 mL of water in a small test tube. Add 5 drops of 1-naphthol solution to the test tube, tilt the tube, and carefully add 2 mL of sulfuric acid down the side of the tube so that it forms a lower layer.
  Acceptance criteria: A red-purple color develops at the liquid–liquid interface.
- **D. Viscosity**
  Sample solution: 60 g of sample in 40 mL of water, with continuous stirring; refrigerate the solution at 4° for several hours before testing.
  Analysis: Using a Bohlin viscometer or equivalent instrument, measure the viscosity of the *Sample solution* at 25° using a shear rate of 147 sec^{-1}.
  Acceptance criteria: NLT 2500 mPa (corresponds to an average molecular weight of 5000 Da). [NOTE—This test distinguishes enzymatically hydrolyzed CMC from non-hydrolyzed CMC.]

ASSAY
- **Percent Sodium Chloride**
  Sample solution: Transfer 5 g of sample into a 250-mL beaker, add 50 mL of water and 5 mL of 30% hydrogen peroxide, and heat on a steam bath for 20 min, stirring occasionally to ensure complete dissolution.
  Analysis: Cool the *Sample solution*, add 100 mL of water and 10 mL of nitric acid, and titrate with 0.05 N silver nitrate to a potentiometric endpoint, using a silver/calomel (AgCl) electrode set, and stirring constantly. Calculate the percent sodium chloride in the sample by the formula:

  $$\text{Result} = (584.4 \times V \times N)/(100 - b)W$$

  584.4 = calculation factor including the equivalence factor for sodium chloride, percentage factor, and conversion of sample weight from g to mg
  V = volume of the silver nitrate (mL)
  N = normality of the silver nitrate
  b = percent *Loss on Drying*, determined separately (below)
  W = weight of the sample (g) taken

- **Percent Sodium Glycolate**
  Standard stock solution: 1 mg/mL of glycolic acid (using glycolic acid previously dried in a desiccator at room temperature overnight). [NOTE—Use this solution within 30 days.]
  Standard solutions: Transfer 1.0, 2.0, 3.0, and 4.0 mL, respectively, of the *Standard solution* into separate 100-mL volumetric flasks, add sufficient water to each flask to make 5 mL, then add 5 mL of glacial acetic acid, and dilute with acetone to volume.
  Sample solution: Transfer 500 mg of sample into a 100-mL beaker, moisten thoroughly with 5 mL of glacial acetic acid followed by 5 mL of water, and stir with a glass rod until dissolution is complete (usually about 15 min). While stirring, slowly add 50 mL of acetone, then add 1 g of sodium chloride, and stir for several minutes to ensure complete precipitation of the cellulose gum. Filter through a soft, open-textured paper, previously wetted with a small amount of acetone, and collect the filtrate in a 100-mL volumetric flask. Use an additional 30 mL of acetone to facilitate transfer of the solids and to wash the filter cake, then dilute with acetone to volume, and mix.
  Blank solution: 5% each of glacial acetic acid and water in acetone
  Analysis: Transfer 2.0 mL of the *Sample solution*, 2.0 mL of each of the *Standard solutions*, and 2.0 mL of the *Blank solution* into separate 25-mL volumetric flasks. Place the uncovered flasks in a boiling water bath for exactly 20 min to remove the acetone, remove from the bath, and cool. Add to each flask 5.0 mL of 2,7-dihydroxynaphthalene TS, mix thoroughly, add an additional 15 mL, and again mix thoroughly. Cover the mouth of each flask with a small piece of aluminum foil. Place the flasks upright in a boiling water bath for 20 min, then remove from the bath, cool, dilute with sulfuric acid to volume, and mix. Using a suitable spectrophotometer, determine the absorbance of the solutions prepared from the *Sample solution* and from the *Standard solutions* at 540 nm against the solution prepared from the *Blank solution*. Prepare a standard

curve using the absorbance obtained from each of the *Standard solutions.* From the standard curve and the absorbance of the *Sample solution,* determine the weight (w), in mg, of glycolic acid in the sample taken, and calculate the percent sodium glycolate in the sample by the formula:

Result = (12.9 × w)/(100 − b)W

- 12.9 = calculation factor including conversion of glycolic acid to sodium glycolate, percentage factor, and conversion of sample weight from g to mg
- b = percent *Loss on Drying,* determined separately (below)
- W = weight of the sample (g) taken
- w = weight of glycolic acid in the *Sample,* as determined from the standard curve

• **PERCENT ENZYMATICALLY HYDROLYZED SODIUM CARBOXYMETHYL CELLULOSE**
Calculation: Calculate the *Percent Enzymatically Hydrolyzed Sodium Carboxymethyl Cellulose* by subtracting from 100 the *Percent Sodium Chloride* and *Percent Sodium Glycolate* determined above.
Acceptance criteria: NLT 99.5% (including mono- and di-saccharides), calculated on the dried basis

IMPURITIES
Inorganic Impurities
• **LEAD,** *Lead Limit Test, Flame Atomic Absorption Spectrophotometric Method,* Appendix IIIB
Sample: 3 g
Acceptance criteria: NMT 3 mg/kg

SPECIFIC TESTS
• **DEGREE OF SUBSTITUTION**
Electrode system: Use a standard glass electrode and a calomel electrode modified as follows: Discard the aqueous potassium chloride solution contained in the electrode, rinse and fill with the supernatant obtained by shaking thoroughly 2 g each of potassium chloride and silver chloride (or silver oxide) with 100 mL of methanol, then add a few crystals of potassium chloride and silver chloride (or silver oxide) to the electrode.
Sample: 200 mg, previously dried
Analysis: Add 75 mL of glacial acetic acid to the *Sample* contained in a 250-mL glass stoppered Erlenmeyer flask, connect the flask with a water-cooled condenser, and reflux gently on a hot plate for 2 h. Cool, transfer the solution to a 250-mL beaker with the aid of 50 mL of glacial acetic acid, and titrate with 0.1 N perchloric acid in dioxane while stirring with a magnetic stirrer. [**CAUTION**—Handle perchloric acid in an appropriate fume hood.] Determine the endpoint potentiometrically with a pH meter equipped with the *Electrode system* described. Record the mL of 0.1 N perchloric acid versus mV (0- to 700-mV range), and continue the titration to a few mL beyond the endpoint. Plot the titration curve and read the volume (A), in mL, of 0.1 N perchloric acid at the inflection point. Calculate the degree of substitution by the formula:

Result = (162 × V × N)/[W − (80 × V × N)]

- 162 = molecular weight of one anhydroglucose unit
- V = volume of perchloric acid used in the titration (mL)
- N = normality of the perchloric acid titrant solution
- W = weight of the sample taken (mg)
- 80 = molecular weight of one sodium carboxymethyl group

Acceptance criteria: NLT 0.2 and NMT 1.50 carboxymethyl groups (−CH$_2$COOH) per anhydroglucose unit, on the dried basis
• **LOSS ON DRYING,** Appendix IIC: 105° to constant weight
Acceptance criteria: NMT 12%
• **pH,** *pH Determination,* Appendix IIB
Sample solution: 10 mg/mL
Acceptance criteria: Between 6.0 and 8.5
• **RESIDUAL ENZYME ACTIVITY**
Sample solution: 200 mg/mL
CMC solution: 50 mg/mL of sodium carboxymethyl cellulose. (Use a CMC that gives a viscosity of 25–50 mPa for a 2% solution.)
Analysis: To 20 g of the *CMC solution,* add 2 g of the *Sample solution.* Using a Bohlin viscometer or equivalent, follow the viscosity of the mixture for 10 min at 25°, using a shear rate of 147 sec^{-1}. Perform a blank determination using 2 g of water in place of the *Sample solution.*
Acceptance criteria: The change in viscosity in the *CMC solution* to which the *Sample solution* is added is not greater than that of the blank determination.

Sodium Chloride

First Published: Prior to FCC 6
Last Revision: Third Supplement, FCC 7

Salt

NaCl   Formula wt 58.44
CAS: [7647-14-5]

UNII: 451W47IQ8X [sodium chloride]

DESCRIPTION
Sodium Chloride occurs as a transparent to opaque, white crystalline solid of variable particle size. Salt is a generic term applied to commercially produced Sodium Chloride. It is available in various crystalline forms, referred to as dendritic salt, evaporated salt, rock salt (may be white to off-white), solar salt, or simply salt. It may contain up to 2% (total) of suitable food-grade anticaking, free-flowing, or conditioning agents, either singly or in combination. It may contain not more than 14 mg/kg of calcium, potassium, sodium ferrocyanide alone or in combination, expressed as anhydrous sodium ferrocyanide,

or not more than 25 mg/kg of green ferric ammonium citrate as a crystal-modifying and anticaking agent. Food-grade dendritic salt can contain NMT 29 mg/kg of calcium, potassium, or sodium ferrocyanide, expressed as anhydrous sodium ferrocyanide. If labeled as iodized, it contains not less than 0.006% and not more than 0.010% of potassium iodide. Sodium Chloride remains dry in air at a relative humidity below 75%, but becomes deliquescent at higher humidity. One g is soluble in 2.8 mL of water at 25°, in 2.7 mL of boiling water, and in about 10 mL of glycerin. Sodium Chloride containing water-insoluble anticaking, free-flowing, and conditioning agents may produce cloudy solutions or may dissolve incompletely. A 1:20 aqueous solution usually has a pH between 5.5 and 8.5 (the pH may be higher if alkaline conditioning agents have been added).

Function: Nutrient; preservative; flavoring agent and intensifier; curing agent; dough conditioner

Packaging and Storage: Store in well-closed containers.

IDENTIFICATION
- **SODIUM,** Appendix IIIA
  Acceptance criteria: Passes tests
- **CHLORIDE,** Appendix IIIA
  Acceptance criteria: Passes test

[NOTE—In the following procedures under *Assay*, *Impurities*, and *Specific Tests*, it may be necessary to filter the sample solutions to avoid interference from insoluble or suspended anticaking, free-flowing, or conditioning agents.]

ASSAY
- **PROCEDURE**
  Sample: 250 mg, previously dried at 625° for 2 h
  Analysis: Dissolve the *Sample* in 50 mL of water in a glass-stoppered flask. Add, while agitating, 3 mL of nitric acid, 5 mL of nitrobenzene, 50.0 mL of 0.1 N silver nitrate, and 2 mL of ferric ammonium sulfate TS. Shake well, and titrate the excess silver nitrate with 0.1 N ammonium thiocyanate. Each mL of 0.1 N silver nitrate is equivalent to 5.844 mg of NaCl.
  Acceptance criteria
  Evaporated salt with up to 2% of suitable free-flowing or conditioning agents and anticaking agents such as calcium, potassium, or sodium ferrocyanide: NLT 97.5% and NMT 100.5% of NaCl, on the dried basis
  Evaporated salt with only anticaking agents such as calcium, potassium, or sodium ferrocyanide: 99.0%–100.5%, on the dried basis
  Rock or solar salt: 97.5%–100.5% of NaCl, on the dried basis, the remainder consisting chiefly of minor amounts of naturally occurring components such as alkaline and/or alkaline earth sulfates and chlorides

IMPURITIES
Inorganic Impurities
- **ARSENIC,** *Arsenic Limit Test,* Appendix IIIB
  Sample solution: 3 g in 25 mL of water
  Acceptance criteria: NMT 1 mg/kg
- **CALCIUM AND MAGNESIUM**
  Standard EDTA solution: 4.0 mg/mL of disodium EDTA ($C_{10}H_{14}N_2Na_2O_8 \cdot 2H_2O$)
  Magnesium sulfate solution: 2.6 mg/mL of magnesium sulfate ($MgSO_4 \cdot 7H_2O$)
  Buffer solution A: Transfer 67.5 mg of ammonium chloride into a 1000-mL volumetric flask and dissolve in 570 mL of ammonium hydroxide. Use 2 mL of this solution as directed under *Titer determination* (below).
  Buffer solution B: Pipet 50.0 mL of *Magnesium sulfate solution* into the *Buffer solution A* flask; add exactly the volume, T, in mL, of *Standard EDTA solution,* determined as directed under *Titer determination* (below); then dilute with water to volume, and mix.
  Titer determination (T): Pipet 50 mL of *Magnesium sulfate solution* into a 400-mL beaker; and add 200 mL of water, 2 mL of *Buffer solution A*, 1.0 mL of 1:20 potassium cyanide solution, and 5 drops of eriochrome black TS or another suitable indicator. While stirring with a magnetic stirrer, titrate with the *Standard EDTA solution* to a true blue endpoint. Record the volume, T, in mL, of *Standard EDTA solution* equivalent to 50.0 mL of *Magnesium sulfate solution.*
  Standardization of EDTA solution: Transfer 1 g of primary standard calcium carbonate ($CaCO_3$) into a 1000-mL volumetric flask, dissolve in 800 mL of water containing 5 mL of hydrochloric acid, dilute with water to volume, and mix. Pipet 25.0 mL of this solution into a 400-mL beaker, and add 200 mL of water, 2 mL of *Buffer solution B*, 1.0 mL of 1:20 potassium cyanide solution, and 20 drops of eriochrome black TS or another suitable indicator. While stirring with a magnetic stirrer, titrate with the *Standard EDTA solution* to a true blue endpoint.
  Calculate the factor, F, giving the number of mg of calcium (Ca) equivalent to 1.0 mL of *Standard EDTA solution*:

  $$\text{Result} = 10.011 \times w/v$$

  w = exact weight of the primary standard calcium carbonate taken (g)
  v = volume of *Standard EDTA solution* required in the titration (mL)

  Sample solution
  Rock and solar salts: Transfer 50.0 g of sample into a 500-mL volumetric flask, dissolve in 400 mL of water containing 2 mL of hydrochloric acid, dilute to volume, and mix. Filter a 50-mL aliquot, pipet 10.0 mL of the filtrate into a 400-mL beaker, and add 190 mL of water.
  Evaporated salt: Transfer 10.0 g of sample into a 400-mL beaker and dissolve in 100 mL of water. If free-flowing agents are present, filter and rinse

quantitatively. Dilute the solution or filtrate with water to 200 mL.

Analysis: Add 5.0 mL of *Buffer solution B*, 1 mL of a 1:20 potassium cyanide solution, and 5 drops of eriochrome black TS or another suitable indicator to the *Sample solution*. Begin stirring with a magnetic stirrer, and titrate with *Standard EDTA solution* to a true blue endpoint, recording the volume, in mL, required as V. Calculate the mg/kg of total calcium and magnesium (both expressed as Ca) in the sample:

$$\text{Result} = V \times F \times 1000/W$$

- V = volume of *Standard EDTA solution* required for the titration (mL)
- F = standardization factor determined above
- W = weight of sample in the final solution titrated (g)

Acceptance criteria
Salt other than evaporated salt with only anticaking agents such as calcium, potassium, or sodium ferrocyanide: NMT 0.9%
Evaporated salt with only anticaking agents such as calcium, potassium, or sodium ferrocyanide: NMT 0.35%

- **HEAVY METALS (AS PB)**
  [NOTE—This test is designed to limit the content of common metallic impurities colored by sulfide ion (Ag, As, Bi, Cd, Cu, Hg, Pb, Sb, Sn) by comparing the color with a standard containing lead (Pb) ion under the specified test conditions. It demonstrates that the test substance is not grossly contaminated by such heavy metals, and within the precision of the test, that it does not exceed the *Heavy Metals* limit given as determined by concomitant visual comparison with a control solution. In the specified pH range, the optimum concentration of lead (Pb) ion for matching purposes by this method is 20 µg in 50 mL of solution.

  The most common limitation of the *Heavy Metals* test is that the color the sulfide ion produces in the *Sample solution* depends on the metals present and may not match the color in the dilution of the *Standard lead solution* used for matching purposes. Lead sulfide is brown, as are Ag, Bi, Cu, Hg, and Sn sulfides. While it is possible that ions not mentioned here may also yield nonmatching colors, among the nine common metallic impurities listed above, the sulfides with different colors are those of As and Cd, which are yellow, and that of Sb, which is orange. If a yellow or orange color is observed, the following action is indicated: Because this monograph includes an arsenic requirement, any As found should not exceed 1 mg/kg. If these criteria are met, Cd may be a contributor to the yellow color, so the Cd content should be determined. If an orange color is observed, the Sb content should be determined. These additional tests are in accord with the section on *Trace Impurities* in the *General Provisions* of this book, as follows: "if other possible impurities may be present, additional tests may be required, and should be applied, as necessary, by the manufacturer, vendor, or user to demonstrate that the substance is suitable for its intended application."

  Determine the amount of heavy metals by *Method I* or *Method II* as the following criteria specify: Use *Method I* for samples that yield clear, colorless solutions before adding sulfide ion. Use *Method II* for samples that do not yield clear, colorless solutions under the test conditions specified for *Method I*. Use *Method III*, a wet digestion method, only in those cases where neither *Method I* nor *Method II* can be used.]

  Lead nitrate stock solution: Dissolve 159.8 mg of reagent-grade ACS lead nitrate [Pb(NO$_3$)$_2$] in 100 mL of water containing 1 mL of nitric acid, dilute to 1000.0 mL and mix. [NOTE—Prepare and store this solution in glass containers that are free from lead salts.]

  Standard lead solution: Dilute 10.0 mL of *Lead nitrate stock solution* to 100.0 mL with water. [NOTE—Prepare on the day of use.] Each mL is equivalent to 10 µg of lead (Pb) ion.

  [NOTE—In the following tests, failure to accurately adjust the pH of the solution within the specified limits may result in a significant loss of test sensitivity.]

- **METHOD I**
  Sample solution: 10 g in 35 mL of water
  Solution A: Pipet 2.0 mL of *Standard lead solution* (20 µg of Pb) into a 50-mL color-comparison tube, and add water to make 25 mL. Adjust the pH to between 3.0 and 4.0 (using short-range pH indicator paper) by adding 1 N acetic acid or 6 N ammonia, dilute with water to 40 mL, and mix.
  Solution B: Transfer 25 mL of the *Sample solution* into a 50-mL color-comparison tube that matches the one used for *Solution A*, adjust the pH to between 3.0 and 4.0 (using short-range pH indicator paper) by adding 1 N acetic acid or 6 N ammonia, dilute with water to 40 mL, and mix.
  Solution C: Transfer 25 mL of the *Sample solution* into a third color-comparison tube that matches those used for *Solutions A* and *B*, and add 2.0 mL of *Standard lead solution*. Adjust the pH to between 3.0 and 4.0 (using short-range pH indicator paper) by adding 1 N acetic acid or 6 N ammonia, dilute with water to 40 mL, and mix.
  Analysis: Add 10 mL of freshly prepared hydrogen sulfide TS to each tube, mix, allow to stand for 5 min, and view downward over a white surface.
  Acceptance criteria: The color of *Solution B* is not darker than that of *Solution A*, and the intensity of the color of *Solution C* is equal to or greater than that of *Solution A* (NMT 2 mg/kg). [NOTE—If the color of *Solution C* is lighter than that of *Solution A*, the sample is interfering with the test procedure, and *Method II* must be used.]

- **METHOD II**
  Solution A: Prepare as directed in *Method I*.
  Solution B: Place a quantity of sample into a suitable crucible, add sufficient sulfuric acid to wet the sample, and carefully ignite at a low temperature until thoroughly charred, covering the crucible loosely with

a suitable lid during the ignition. After the sample is thoroughly carbonized, add 2 mL of nitric acid and 5 drops of sulfuric acid, cautiously heat until white fumes no longer evolve, then ignite, preferably in a muffle furnace, at 500°–600° until all of the carbon is burned off. Cool, add 4 mL of 1:2 hydrochloric acid, cover, and digest on a steam bath for 10–15 min. Uncover, and slowly evaporate on a steam bath to dryness. Moisten the residue with 1 drop of hydrochloric acid, add 10 mL of hot water, and digest for 2 min. Add 6 N ammonia dropwise until the solution is just alkaline to litmus paper, dilute with water to 25 mL, and adjust the pH to between 3.0 and 4.0 (using short-range pH indicator paper) by adding 1 N acetic acid. Filter if necessary, rinse the crucible and the filter with 10 mL of water, transfer the solution and rinsings into a 50-mL color-comparison tube, dilute with water to 40 mL, and mix.

Analysis: Add 10 mL of freshly prepared hydrogen sulfide TS to each tube, mix, allow to stand for 5 min, and view downward over a white surface.

Acceptance criteria: The color of *Solution B* is not darker than that of *Solution A* (NMT 2 mg/kg).

- **METHOD III**
  Sample: 4 mg
  Solution A: Transfer an 8:10 (v/v) mixture of sulfuric acid and nitric acid into a 100-mL Kjeldahl flask, clamp the flask at an angle of 45°, and then add, in small increments, an additional volume of nitric acid equal to that added in the preparation of *Solution B* (below). Heat the solution to dense, white fumes, cool, and cautiously add 10 mL of water. Add a volume of 30% hydrogen peroxide equal to that added in the preparation of *Solution B* (below), then boil gently to dense, white fumes, and cool. Cautiously add 5 mL of water, mix, and boil gently to dense, white fumes. Continue boiling until the volume is reduced to about 2 or 3 mL, then cool, and dilute cautiously with a few mL of water. Pipet 2.0 mL of *Standard lead solution* into this solution, and mix. Transfer the solution into a 50-mL color-comparison tube, rinse the flask with water, add the rinsings to the tube until the volume is 25 mL, and mix. Adjust the pH to between 3.0 and 4.0 (using short-range pH indicator paper), initially with ammonium hydroxide and then with 6 N ammonia as the desired range is neared, dilute with water to 40 mL, and mix.
  Solution B: Transfer the *Sample* into a 100-mL Kjeldahl flask (or into a 300-mL flask if the reaction foams excessively), clamp the flask at an angle of 45°, and add a sufficient amount of an 8:10 (v/v) mixture of sulfuric acid:nitric acid to moisten the sample thoroughly. Warm gently until the reaction begins, allow the reaction to subside, and then add additional portions of the acid mixture, heating after each addition, until all of the 18 mL of acid mixture has been added. Increase the heat, and boil gently until the reaction mixture darkens. Remove the flask from the heat, add 2 mL of nitric acid, and heat to boiling again. Continue the intermittent heating and addition of 2-mL portions of nitric acid until no further darkening occurs, then heat strongly to dense, white fumes, and cool. Cautiously add 5 mL of water, mix, boil gently to dense, white fumes, and continue heating until the volume is reduced to about 2 or 3 mL. Cool, cautiously add 5 mL of water, and examine. If the solution is yellow, cautiously add 1 mL of 30% hydrogen peroxide, and again evaporate to dense, white fumes and to a volume of about 2 or 3 mL. Cool, dilute cautiously with a few mL of water, and mix. Transfer into a 50-mL color-comparison tube, rinse the flask with water, add the rinsings to the tube until the volume is 25 mL, and mix. Adjust the pH to between 3.0 and 4.0 (using short-range pH indicator paper), initially with ammonium hydroxide and then with 6 N ammonia as the desired range is neared, dilute with water to 40 mL, and mix.
  Analysis: Add 10 mL of freshly prepared hydrogen sulfide TS to each tube, mix, allow to stand for 5 min, and view downward over a white surface.
  Acceptance criteria: The color of *Solution B* is not darker than that of *Solution A* (NMT 2 mg/kg).

SPECIFIC TESTS

- **LOSS ON DRYING,** Appendix IIC: 110° for 2 h
  Acceptance criteria: NMT 0.5%
- **IODINE**
  [NOTE—This specification applies only to iodized salt.]
  Sample: 20 g
  Analysis: Dissolve *Sample* in about 300 mL of water in a 600-mL beaker. Add a few drops of methyl orange TS, neutralize the solution with 85% phosphoric acid, and then add 1 mL excess of the acid. Add 25 mL of bromine TS and a few glass beads, boil until the solution is clear, then boil for an additional 5 min. Add about 50 mg of salicylic acid crystals, 1 mL of phosphoric acid, and 10 mL of a 1:20 potassium iodide solution, and titrate to a pale yellow color with 0.01 N sodium thiosulfate. Add 1 mL of starch TS, and continue the titration to the disappearance of the blue color. Each mL of 0.01 N sodium thiosulfate is equivalent to 0.2767 mg of potassium iodide (KI).
  Acceptance criteria: 0.006%–0.010% of potassium iodide
- **IRON**
  [NOTE—This specification applies only to products to which green ferric ammonium citrate has been added.]
  Sample solution: Dissolve 625.0 mg of sample in 10 mL of 2.7 N hydrochloric acid, and dilute with water to 50 mL. Add 40 mg of ammonium persulfate crystals and 10 mL of ammonium thiocyanate TS.
  Control solution: Dissolve 10 mL of *Iron Standard Solution* (10 µg of Fe) (see *Standard Solutions for the Preparation of Controls and Standards*, Solutions and Indicators) in 2 mL of 2.7 N hydrochloric acid, and dilute with water to 50 mL.
  Analysis: To the *Sample solution*, add 40 mg of ammonium persulfate crystals and 10 mL of ammonium thiocyanate TS. Repeat the preceding, using the *Control solution* in place of the *Sample solution*.

Acceptance criteria: Any red or pink color produced by the *Sample solution* does not exceed that produced the *Control solution* (NMT 0.0016% of iron [Fe]).

- **FERROCYANIDES**
  [NOTE—This specification applies only to products to which calcium, potassium, or sodium ferrocyanide have been added.]
  Sample: 9.62 g
  Control solution: 135 µg/mL of sodium ferrocyanide [$Na_4Fe(CN)_6$] prepared as follows: dissolve 107.5 mg of decahydrate ferrocyanide [$Na_4Fe(CN)_6 \cdot 10\ H_2O$] in 500 mL of water.
  [NOTE—If dendritic salt is analyzed, dissolve 230 mg of decahydrate ferrocyanide in 500 mL of water to obtain a solution with 290 µL/mL of sodium ferrocyanide [$Na_4Fe(CN)_6$].]
  [NOTE—Although decahydrate ferrocyanide is stable, it usually loses hydration water over time. To avoid this, a prior drying step (105°, overnight) should be incorporated to obtain anhydrous sodium ferrocyanide. Once dried, use 62.5 mg in the *Control solution* instead of the decahydrate ferrocyanide.]
  Analysis: Dissolve the *Sample* in 80 mL of water in a 150-mL glass-stoppered cylinder or flask. Transfer 1.0 mL of *Control solution* into a separate 150-mL container similar to that used for the *Sample*. Add 2 mL of ferrous sulfate TS and 1 mL of 2 N sulfuric acid to each container, dilute with water to 100 mL, and mix. Transfer 50-mL portions of the resulting solutions into matched color-comparison tubes.
  Acceptance criteria: The solution resulting from treatment of the *Sample* shows no more blue color that the solution resulting from treatment of the *Standard solution* (NMT 0.0014% of ferrocyanides, expressed as anhydrous sodium ferrocyanide [$Na_4Fe(CN)_6$]; for dendritic salt, NMT 0.0029% of ferrocyanides, expressed as anhydrous sodium ferrocyanide [$Na_4Fe(CN)_6$]).

OTHER REQUIREMENTS
- **LABELING:** Indicate whether the article is iodized.

Sodium Citrate

First Published: Prior to FCC 6

Trisodium Citrate

$C_6H_5Na_3O_7$ Formula wt, anhydrous 258.07
$C_6H_5Na_3O_7 \cdot 2H_2O$ Formula wt, dihydrate 294.10
INS: 331(iii)   CAS: anhydrous [68-04-2]
                             dihydrate [6132-04-3]

UNII: B22547B95K [trisodium citrate dihydrate]
UNII: RS7A450LGA [anhydrous trisodium citrate]

DESCRIPTION
Sodium Citrate occurs as colorless crystals or as a white, crystalline powder. It is anhydrous or contains two molecules of water of crystallization. One g of the dihydrate dissolves in 1.5 mL of water at 25° and in 0.6 mL of boiling water. It is insoluble in alcohol.
Function: Buffer; sequestrant; emulsion stabilizer; nutrient for cultured buttermilk
Packaging and Storage: Store in tight containers.

IDENTIFICATION
- **CITRATE,** Appendix IIIA
  Sample solution: 50 mg/mL
  Acceptance criteria: Passes test
- **SODIUM,** Appendix IIIA
  Sample solution: 50 mg/mL
  Acceptance criteria: Passes test

ASSAY
- **PROCEDURE**
  Sample: 350 mg
  Analysis: Transfer the *Sample* into a 250-mL beaker. Add 100 mL of glacial acetic acid, stir until completely dissolved, and titrate with 0.1 N perchloric acid, using crystal violet TS as the indicator. Each mL of 0.1 N perchloric acid is equivalent to 8.602 mg of $C_6H_5Na_3O_7$. [CAUTION—Handle perchloric acid in an appropriate fume hood.]
  Acceptance criteria: NLT 99.0% and NMT 100.5% of $C_6H_5Na_3O_7$, calculated on the anhydrous basis

IMPURITIES
Inorganic Impurities
- **LEAD,** *Lead Limit Test, Flame Atomic Absorption Spectrophotometric Method,* Appendix IIIB
  Sample: 5 g
  Acceptance criteria: NMT 2 mg/kg

SPECIFIC TESTS
- **ALKALINITY**
  Sample solution: 1 g in 20 mL of water
  Analysis: Confirm that the *Sample solution* is alkaline to litmus paper. Then, add 0.2 mL of 0.1 N sulfuric acid to the *Sample solution* and follow with one drop of phenolphthalein TS.
  Acceptance criteria: No pink color appears after addition of the phenolphthalein TS.
- **WATER,** *Water Determination,* Appendix IIB
  Acceptance criteria
    Anhydrous: NMT 1%
    Dihydrate: Between 10.0% and 13.0%

Sodium Cyclamate

First Published: Third Supplement, FCC 7

Sodium Cyclohexanesulfamate
Sodium Cyclohexylsulfamate

C₆H₁₂NNaO₃S
INS: 952(iv)
Formula wt 201.22
CAS: [139-05-9]

DESCRIPTION
Sodium Cyclamate occurs as colorless to white crystals or crystalline powder. It is soluble in water and practically insoluble in ethanol.
Function: Sweetener
Packaging and Storage: Store in tight containers in a cool, dry place.

IDENTIFICATION
- **SODIUM,** Appendix IIIA
   Acceptance criteria: Passes test
- **INFRARED ABSORPTION,** Spectrophotometric Identification Tests, Appendix IIIC
   Reference standard: USP Sodium Cyclamate RS
   Sample and standard preparation: K
   Acceptance criteria: The spectrum of the sample exhibits maxima at the same wavelengths as those in the spectrum of the Reference standard.

ASSAY
- **PROCEDURE**
   Sample: 0.4 g
   Analysis: Dissolve the Sample in a mixture of 50 mL of water and 5 mL of hydrochloric acid TS, diluted. Titrate the solution with 0.1 M sodium nitrite. Add the last mL of titrant dropwise until a blue color is produced immediately when a glass rod dipped into the titrated solution is streaked on a piece of starch iodide test paper. Alternatively, the endpoint may be determined potentiometrically. When the titration is complete, the endpoint is reproducible after the mixture has been allowed to stand for 1 min. Each mL of 0.1 M sodium nitrite is equivalent to 20.12 mg of C₆H₁₂NNaO₃S.
   Acceptance criteria: 99.0%–101.0%, calculated on the dried basis

IMPURITIES
Inorganic Impurities
- **LEAD,** Lead Limit Test, Flame Atomic Absorption Spectrophotometric Method, Appendix IIIB
   Sample: 5 g
   Acceptance criteria: NMT 1.0 mg/kg

Organic Impurities
- **CYCLOHEXANAMINE, ANILINE, AND N-CYCLOHEXYLCYCLOHEXANAMINE**
   Internal standard solution: Dissolve 0.02 µL/mL of tetradecane in methylene chloride.
   Solution A: Dissolve 10 mg of cyclohexanamine, 1 mg of N-cyclohexylcyclohexanamine, and 1 mg of aniline in water, then dilute with water to 1000 mL. Dilute 10 mL of this solution with water to 100 mL.
   Solution B: 42% w/v sodium hydroxide solution
   Standard solution: To 20 mL of Solution A, add 0.5 mL of Solution B, and extract with 30 mL of toluene. Shake 20 mL of the upper layer with 4 mL of a mixture of equal volumes of water and an acetic acid solution (12% w/v). Separate the lower layer, add 0.5 mL of Solution B and 0.5 mL of the Internal standard solution, and shake. Use the lower layer immediately after separation.
   Sample solution: Dissolve 2 g of sample in 20 mL of water, add 0.5 mL of Solution B, and shake with 30 mL of toluene. Shake 20 mL of the upper layer with 4 mL of a mixture of equal volumes of an acetic acid solution (12% w/v) and water. Separate the lower layer, add 0.5 mL of Solution B and 0.5 mL of the Internal standard solution, and shake. Use the lower layer immediately after separation.
   Chromatographic system, Appendix IIA
      Mode: Gas chromatography
      Detector: Flame ionization
      Column: 25-m × 0.32-mm (i.d.) fused-silica column with poly(dimethyl)(diphenyl)siloxane containing 95% of methyl groups and 5% of phenyl groups (DB-5, SE52) as stationary phase (film thickness 0.51 µm)
      Temperature
         Injection port: 250°
         Detector: 270°
      Column: See the temperature program table below.

Time (min)	Temperature (°)
0–1	85
1–9	85–150
9–13	150

   Carrier gas: Helium
   Flow rate: 1.8 mL/min
   Injection volume: 1.5 µL. Use a split vent at a flow rate of 20 mL/min.
   Analysis: Separately inject equal volumes of the Standard solution and Sample solution into the chromatograph, record the chromatograms, and measure the responses. [NOTE—The approximate retention times (relative to cyclohexanamine, which has a retention time of about 2.3 min) for aniline, tetradecane, and N-cyclohexylcyclohexanamine are about 1.4, 4.3, and 4.5, respectively.]
   Acceptance criteria
      Cyclohexanamine: NMT 10.0 mg/kg
      Aniline: NMT 1.0 mg/kg
      N-Cyclohexylcyclohexanamine: NMT 1.0 mg/kg

SPECIFIC TESTS
- **LOSS ON DRYING,** Appendix IIC: 105° for 4 h
   Acceptance criteria: NMT 1.0%

Sodium Dehydroacetate

First Published: Prior to FCC 6

Sodium 3-(1-Hydroxyethylidene)-6-methyl-1,2-pyran-2, 4(3H)-dione

$C_8H_7NaO_4 \cdot H_2O$ Formula wt 208.15
INS: 266 CAS: [4418-26-2]
UNII: 8W46YN971G [sodium dehydroacetate]

DESCRIPTION
Sodium Dehydroacetate occurs as a white or nearly white powder. One g dissolves in about 3 mL of water, in 2 mL of propylene glycol, and in 7 mL of glycerin.
Function: Preservative
Packaging and Storage: Store in well-closed containers.

IDENTIFICATION
- **MELTING RANGE OR TEMPERATURE DETERMINATION,** Appendix IIB
  Sample solution: About 1.5 g of sample in 10 mL of water
  Analysis: To the *Sample solution*, add 5 mL of 2.7 N hydrochloric acid, collect the crystals with suction, wash with 10 mL of water, and dry between 75° and 80° for 4 h.
  Acceptance criteria: The crystals melt between 109° and 111°.

ASSAY
- **PROCEDURE**
  Sample: 500 mg
  Analysis: Transfer the *Sample* to a 125 mL conical flask and add 25 mL of glacial acetic acid containing 1 drop of a 1:100 *p*-naphtholbenzene in glacial acetic acid solution that has been previously neutralized to a blue color. After the *Sample* has dissolved, titrate with 0.1 N perchloric acid to the original blue color. Each mL of 0.1 N perchloric acid is equivalent to 19.01 mg of $C_8H_7NaO_4$. [**CAUTION**—Handle perchloric acid in an appropriate fume hood.]
  Acceptance criteria: NLT 98.0% and NMT 100.5% of $C_8H_7NaO_4$, calculated on the anhydrous basis

IMPURITIES
Inorganic Impurities
- **LEAD,** *Lead Limit Test, Flame Atomic Absorption Spectrophotometric Method,* Appendix IIIB
  Sample: 10 g
  Acceptance criteria: NMT 2 mg/kg

SPECIFIC TESTS
- **WATER,** *Water Determination,* Appendix IIB
  Acceptance criteria: Between 8.5% and 10.0%

Sodium Diacetate

First Published: Prior to FCC 6

Sodium Hydrogen Diacetate

$C_4H_7NaO_4 \cdot xH_2O$ Formula wt, anhydrous 142.09
INS: 262 CAS: [126-96-5]
UNII: 26WJH3CS0B [sodium diacetate]

DESCRIPTION
Sodium Diacetate occurs as a white, hygroscopic, crystalline solid. It is a molecular compound of sodium acetate and acetic acid. One g is soluble in about 1 mL of water. The pH of a 1:10 aqueous solution is between 4.5 and 5.0.
Function: Sequestrant; preservative; antimicrobial agent; mold inhibitor
Packaging and Storage: Store in tight containers.

IDENTIFICATION
- **ACETATE,** Appendix IIIA
  Sample solution: 100 mg/mL
  Acceptance criteria: Passes tests
- **SODIUM,** Appendix IIIA
  Sample solution: 100 mg/mL
  Acceptance criteria: Passes tests

ASSAY
- **FREE ACETIC ACID**
  Sample: 4 g
  Analysis: Dissolve the *Sample* in 50 mL of water, add phenolphthalein TS, and titrate with 1 N sodium hydroxide. Each mL of 1 N sodium hydroxide is equivalent to 60.05 mg of acetic acid.
  Acceptance criteria: NLT 39.0% and NMT 41.0%, calculated on the anhydrous basis
- **SODIUM ACETATE**
  Sample: 500 mg
  Analysis: Dissolve the *Sample* in 50 mL of glacial acetic acid and titrate with 0.1 N perchloric acid, determining the endpoint potentiometrically. Each mL of 0.1 N perchloric acid is equivalent to 8.203 mg of sodium acetate. [**CAUTION**—Handle perchloric acid in an appropriate fume hood.]
  Acceptance criteria: NLT 58.0% and NMT 60.0%, calculated on the anhydrous basis

IMPURITIES
Inorganic Impurities
- **LEAD,** *Lead Limit Test, Flame Atomic Absorption Spectrophotometric Method,* Appendix IIIB
  Sample: 10 g
  Acceptance criteria: NMT 2 mg/kg

SPECIFIC TESTS
- **READILY OXIDIZABLE SUBSTANCES** (as formic acid)
  Sample: 1 g
  Analysis: Dissolve the *Sample* in about 50 mL of water, add 10 mL of 2 N sulfuric acid, and heat the solution to

between 80° and 90°. Titrate the hot solution with 0.1 N potassium permanganate to a faint pink color that persists for at least 15 s. Each mL of 0.1 N potassium permanganate is equivalent to 2.301 mg of formic acid.
Acceptance criteria: NMT 0.2%
- **WATER,** *Water Determination,* Appendix IIB
Acceptance criteria: NMT 2.0%

Sodium Erythorbate

First Published: Prior to FCC 6

$C_6H_7NaO_6 \cdot H_2O$
Formula wt 216.12
CAS: [6381-77-7]

UNII: BZ468R6XRD [sodium erythorbate]

DESCRIPTION
Sodium Erythorbate occurs as a white, crystalline powder or as granules. In the dry state it is reasonably stable in air, but in solution it deteriorates in the presence of air, trace metals, heat, and light. One g dissolves in about 7 mL of water. The pH of a 1:20 aqueous solution is between 5.5 and 8.0.
Function: Preservative; antioxidant
Packaging and Storage: Store in tight, light-resistant containers.

IDENTIFICATION
- **A. PROCEDURE**
  Sample solution: 20 mg/mL
  Acceptance criteria: The *Sample solution* slowly reduces alkaline cupric tartrate TS at 25°, but does so more readily upon heating.
- **B. PROCEDURE**
  Sample solution: 20 mg/mL
  Analysis: To 2 mL of *Sample solution*, acidified with 0.5 mL of 0.1 N hydrochloric acid, add a few drops of sodium nitroferricyanide TS, followed by 1 mL of 0.1 N sodium hydroxide.
  Acceptance criteria: A transient blue color immediately appears.
- **C. SODIUM,** Appendix IIIA
  Acceptance criteria: Passes test

ASSAY
- **PROCEDURE**
  Sample: 400 mg
  Analysis: Dissolve the *Sample* in a mixture of water (recently boiled and cooled) and 25 mL of 2 N sulfuric acid. Immediately titrate with 0.1 N iodine, adding starch TS as the indicator near the endpoint. Each mL of 0.1 N iodine is equivalent to 10.81 mg of $C_6H_7NaO_6 \cdot H_2O$.
  Acceptance criteria: NLT 98.0% and NMT 100.5% of $C_6H_7NaO_6 \cdot H_2O$

IMPURITIES
Inorganic Impurities
- **LEAD,** *Lead Limit Test,* Appendix IIIB
  Sample solution: Prepare as directed for organic compounds, but use 2 g of sample.
  Control: 10 µg Pb (10 mL of *Diluted Standard Lead Solution*)
  Acceptance criteria: NMT 5 mg/kg

SPECIFIC TESTS
- **LOSS ON DRYING,** Appendix IIC : Room temperature in a vacuum over silica gel for 24 h
  Acceptance criteria: NMT 0.25%
- **OPTICAL (SPECIFIC) ROTATION,** Appendix IIB
  Sample solution: 100 mg/mL
  Acceptance criteria: $[\alpha]_D^{25}$ between +95.5° and +98.0°
- **OXALATE**
  Sample: 1 g
  Analysis: To a solution of the *Sample* in 10 mL of water, add 2 drops of glacial acetic acid and 5 mL of a 1:10 solution of calcium acetate.
  Acceptance criteria: The solution remains clear.

Sodium Ferric Pyrophosphate

First Published: Prior to FCC 6

Sodium Iron Pyrophosphate

$Na_8Fe_4(P_2O_7)_5 \cdot xH_2O$
Formula wt, anhydrous 1277.02
CAS: [1332-96-3]

DESCRIPTION
Sodium Ferric Pyrophosphate occurs as a white to tan powder. It is insoluble in water, but is soluble in hydrochloric acid.
Function: Nutrient
Packaging and Storage: Store in well-closed containers.

IDENTIFICATION
- **PROCEDURE**
  Sample: 500 mg
  Analysis: Dissolve the *Sample* in 5 mL of 1:2 hydrochloric acid and add an excess of 1 N sodium hydroxide. A red-brown precipitate forms. Age the solution for several minutes, and then filter, discarding the first few milliliters. Add 1 drop of bromophenol blue TS to 5 mL of the clear filtrate, and titrate with 1 N hydrochloric acid to a green color. Add 10 mL of a 1:8 zinc sulfate solution, and readjust the pH to 3.8 (green color).
  Acceptance criteria: A white precipitate forms (distinction from orthophosphates).

ASSAY
- **PROCEDURE**
  Sample: 3.5 g
  Analysis: Dissolve the *Sample* in 75 mL of 1:2 hydrochloric acid, heat to boiling, and boil for about 5 min. Cool, transfer into a 100-mL volumetric flask, dilute to volume with the 1:2 hydrochloric acid, and

mix. Add 100 mL of the 1:2 hydrochloric acid to 25.0 mL of this solution and boil again for 5 min. Add, dropwise, while stirring, stannous chloride TS to the boiling solution, until the iron is just reduced as indicated by the disappearance of the yellow color. Add 2 drops in excess (but no more) of the stannous chloride TS, dilute with about 50 mL of water, and cool to room temperature. While stirring vigorously, add 15 mL of a saturated solution of mercuric chloride and then allow to stand for 5 min. Add 15 mL of a sulfuric acid–phosphoric acid mixture (prepared by slowly adding 75 mL of sulfuric acid to 300 mL of water, cooling, adding 75 mL of phosphoric acid, and then diluting to 500 mL with water). Mix, add 0.5 mL of barium diphenylamine sulfonate TS, and titrate with 0.1 N potassium dichromate to a red-violet endpoint. Each mL of 0.1 N potassium dichromate is equivalent to 5.585 mg of Fe.

Acceptance criteria: NLT 14.5% and NMT 16.0% of Fe

IMPURITIES
Inorganic Impurities
- **ARSENIC,** *Arsenic Limit Test,* Appendix IIIB
  Sample solution: 1 g in 15 mL of 2.7 N hydrochloric acid
  Acceptance criteria: NMT 3 mg/kg
- **FLUORIDE,** *Fluoride Limit Test,* Appendix IIIB
  Sample: 1 g
  Acceptance criteria: NMT 0.005%
- **LEAD**
  [NOTE—In preparing all aqueous solutions and in rinsing glassware before use, use water that has been passed through a strong-acid, strong-base, mixed-bed ion-exchange resin before use. Select all reagents to have as low a lead content as practicable, and store all reagent solutions in containers of borosilicate glass. Clean glassware before use by soaking in warm 8 N nitric acid for 30 min and by rinsing with deionized water.]
  Ascorbic acid-sodium iodide solution: 100 mg/mL of ascorbic acid and 192.5 mg/mL of sodium iodide in water
  Trioctylphosphine oxide solution: 50 mg/mL of trioctylphosphine oxide in 4-methyl-2-pentanone.
  [CAUTION—This reagent causes irritation. Avoid contact with eyes, skin, and clothing. Take special precautions in disposing of unused portions of solutions to which this reagent is added.]
  Standard stock solution: 100 µg/mL Pb, prepared by transferring 159.8 mg of reagent-grade lead nitrate to a 1000-mL volumetric flask, dissolving it in 100 mL of water containing 1 mL of nitric acid, and diluting to volume with water.
  Standard solution: 2.0 µg/mL Pb, prepared by first transferring 5.0 mL of the *Standard stock solution* to a 100 mL volumetric flask, diluting to volume with water, and mixing. Then, transfer 2.0 mL of this resulting solution to a 50-mL volumetric flask, add 10 mL of 9 N hydrochloric acid, and about 10 mL of water. Add 20 mL of *Ascorbic acid-sodium iodide solution* and 5.0 mL of *Trioctylphosphine oxide solution*. Shake the flask for 30 s and allow the layers to separate. Add water to bring the organic layer into the neck of the flask, shake the flask again, and allow the layers to separate. The organic solvent layer is the *Standard solution*.
  Blank solution: Introduce 10 mL of 9 N hydrochloric acid, and about 10 mL of water into a 50-mL volumetric flask. Add 20 mL of *Ascorbic acid-sodium iodide solution* and 5.0 mL of *Trioctylphosphine oxide solution*. Shake the flask for 30 s and allow the layers to separate. Add water to bring the organic layer into the neck of the flask, shake the flask again, and allow the layers to separate. The organic solvent layer, which is the *Blank solution*, contains 0.0 µg/mL of lead.
  Sample solution: Add 2.5 g of sample, 10 mL of 9 N hydrochloric acid, about 10 mL of water, 20 mL of *Ascorbic acid-sodium iodide solution,* and 5.0 mL of *Trioctylphosphine oxide solution* to a 50-mL volumetric flask. Shake the flask for 30 s and allow the layers to separate. Add water to bring the organic solvent layer into the neck of the flask, shake it again, and allow the layers to separate. The organic solvent layer is the *Sample solution*.
  Analysis: Using a suitable atomic absorption spectrophotometer equipped with a lead hollow-cathode lamp and an air-acetylene flame, set at the lead emission line of 283.3 nm, with 4-methyl-2-pentanone used to set the instrument to zero. Concomitantly determine the absorbance of the *Blank solution*, the *Standard solution* and the *Sample solution*.
  Acceptance criteria: The absorbance of the *Blank solution* is not greater than 20% of the difference between the absorbance of the *Standard solution* and the absorbance of the *Blank solution*. The absorbance of the *Sample solution* does not exceed that of the *Standard solution*. (NMT 4 mg/kg)
- **MERCURY**
  Standard stock solution: 0.1 µg/mL of mercury prepared as follows: Dissolve 338.5 mg of mercuric chloride in about 200 mL of water in a 250-mL volumetric flask, add 14 mL of 1:2 sulfuric acid, dilute to volume with water, and mix. Pipet 10.0 mL of this solution into a 1000-mL volumetric flask containing 800 mL of water and 56 mL of 1:2 sulfuric acid, dilute to volume with water, and mix. Pipet 10.0 mL of the resulting solution into a 1000-mL volumetric flask containing 800 mL of water and 56 mL of 1:2 sulfuric acid, dilute to volume with water, and mix.
  Standard solutions: Pipet 1.25, 2.50, 5.00, 7.50, and 10.00 mL of the *Standard stock solution* (equivalent to 0.125, 0.250, 0.500, 0.750, and 1.00 µg of mercury, respectively) into five separate 150-mL beakers. Add 25 mL of aqua regia to each beaker, cover with watch glasses, heat just to boiling, simmer for about 5 min, and cool to room temperature. Transfer the solutions into separate 250-mL volumetric flasks, dilute to volume with water, and mix. Transfer a 50.0-mL aliquot from each solution into five separate 150-mL beakers, and add 1.0 mL of 1:5 sulfuric acid and 1.0 mL of a 1:25 filtered potassium permanganate solution to each. Heat the solutions just to boiling, simmer for about 5 min, and cool.

Sample solution: Transfer 5.00 g of sample into a 150-mL beaker, add 25 mL of aqua regia, cover with a watch glass, and allow to stand at room temperature for about 5 min. Heat just to boiling, allow to simmer for about 5 min, and cool. Transfer the solution into a 250-mL volumetric flask, dilute to volume with water, and mix. [NOTE—Disregard any undissolved material that may be present.] Transfer a 50.0-mL aliquot of this solution into a 150-mL beaker, and add 1.0 mL of 1:5 sulfuric acid and 1.0 mL of a filtered 1:25 potassium permanganate solution. Heat the solution just to boiling, simmer for about 5 min, and cool.

Blank: Introduce 25 mL of aqua regia into a 250-mL volumetric flask, dilute to volume with water, and mix. Transfer a 50-mL aliquot of this solution into a 150-mL beaker, and add 1.0 mL of 1:5 sulfuric acid and 1.0 mL of a filtered 1:25 potassium permanganate solution. Heat the solution just to boiling, simmer for about 5 min, and cool.

Apparatus: Use a Mercury Detection Instrument as described and an Aeration Apparatus as shown in Fig. 16 under *Mercury Limit Test,* Appendix IIIB. For the purposes of the analysis described in this monograph, the Techtron AA-1000 atomic absorption spectrophotometer, equipped with a 10-cm silica absorption cell (Beckman Part No. 75144, or equivalent) and coupled with a strip chart recorder (Varian Series A-25, or equivalent), is satisfactory.

Analysis: Assemble the Aeration Apparatus as shown in Fig. 16 under *Mercury Limit Test,* Appendix IIIB. Use magnesium perchlorate as the absorbent in the absorption cell (*e*), fill gas-washing bottle (*c*) with 60 mL of water, and place stopcock (*b*) in the bypass position. Connect the assembly to the 10-cm absorption cell (analogous to (*f*) in the figure) of the spectrophotometer, and adjust the air or nitrogen flow rate so that, in the following procedure, maximum absorption and reproducibility are obtained without excessive foaming in the test solution. Obtain a baseline reading at 253.7 nm by following the equipment manufacturer's operating instructions. [NOTE—Using the Techtron AA-1000 spectrophotometer, the following conditions are suitable: slit width: 2 Å; lamp current: 3 mA; and scale expansion: × 1. With the strip chart recorder, set the chart speed at 25 in./h and the span at 2 mV.] Precondition the apparatus by an appropriate modification of the procedures described below for treatment of the test solutions. [NOTE—Keep the fritted bubbler in gas-washing bottle (*c*) immersed in water between determinations. After each determination, wash the bubbler with a stream of water.] Treat the *Blank*, each of the *Standard solutions,* and the *Sample Solution* as follows: Transfer the solution to be tested into a 125-mL gas-washing bottle (*c*), using a few drops of 1:10 hydroxylamine hydrochloride solution to remove any manganese hydroxide from the beaker. Dilute to about 55 mL with water, and add a magnetic stirring bar. Discharge the permanganate color by adding, dropwise, the 1:10 hydroxylamine hydrochloride solution, swirling after each drop is added. Add 15.0 mL of 10% stannous chloride solution (prepared by dissolving 20 g of stannous chloride ($SnCl_2 \cdot 2H_2O$) in 40 mL of warm hydrochloric acid and diluting with 160 mL of water) and immediately connect gas-washing bottle (*c*) to the aeration apparatus. Switch on the magnetic stirrer, turn stopcock (*b*) from the bypass to the aerating position, and obtain the absorbance reading. Disconnect bottle (*c*) from the aeration apparatus, discard the solution just tested, wash bottle (*c*) and the fritted bubbler with water, and repeat the procedure with the remaining solutions. Correct the readings for the *Sample solution* and the *Standard solutions* with the reading for the *Blank,* and determine the mercury concentration of the *Sample solution* from a standard curve prepared by plotting the blank-corrected readings obtained with the *Standard solutions* against mercury concentration, in mg/kg, suitable adjustments being made for dilution factors.

Acceptance criteria: NMT 3 mg/kg

SPECIFIC TESTS

- **LOSS ON IGNITION**
  Analysis: Ignite a sample to 800° for 1 h.
  Acceptance criteria: NMT 8.0%

Sodium Ferrocyanide

First Published: Prior to FCC 6

Yellow Prussiate of Soda

$Na_4Fe(CN)_6 \cdot 10H_2O$ Formula wt 484.07
INS: 535   CAS: [13601-19-9]
UNII: 5HT6X21AID [sodium ferrocyanide]

DESCRIPTION

Sodium Ferrocyanide occurs as yellow crystals or as a crystalline powder. It is soluble in water, but it is practically insoluble in most organic solvents.
Function: Anticaking agent for sodium chloride
Packaging and Storage: Store in tight containers.

IDENTIFICATION

- **PROCEDURE**
  Sample solution: 10 mg/mL
  Analysis: To 10 mL of the *Sample solution,* add 1 mL of ferric chloride TS.
  Acceptance criteria: A dark blue precipitate forms.

ASSAY

- **PROCEDURE**
  Sample: 3 g
  Analysis: Transfer the *Sample* into a 400-mL beaker, dissolve it in 225 mL of water, and cautiously add about 25 mL of 95% sulfuric acid. Add, with stirring, 1 drop of orthophenanthroline TS, and titrate with 0.1 N ceric sulfate until the color changes sharply from orange to pure yellow. Each mL of 0.1 N ceric sulfate is equivalent to 96.81 mg of $Na_4Fe(CN)_6 \cdot 10H_2O$.
  Acceptance criteria: NLT 99.0% of $Na_4Fe(CN)_6 \cdot 10H_2O$

IMPURITIES
Inorganic Impurities
- **CHLORIDE,** *Chloride Limit Test,* Appendix IIIB
  Sample solution: 1 mg/mL
  Control: 20 µg chloride (2 mL of *Standard Chloride Solution*)
  Acceptance criteria: Any turbidity produced by the *Sample* does not exceed that produced by the *Control*. (NMT 0.05%)
  Acceptance criteria: Any turbidity produced by a 10-mL portion of *Sample solution* does not exceed that produced by the *Control*. (NMT 0.2%)
- **CYANIDE**
  Sample solution: 1%
  Analysis: Dissolve 10 mg of copper sulfate in a mixture of 8 mL of water and 2 mL of 6 N ammonium hydroxide. Wet a strip of filter paper with this solution, and place the wet paper in a stream of hydrogen sulfide.
  Acceptance criteria: No white circle appears when 1 drop of the *Sample solution* is placed on the brown reagent paper.
- **FERRICYANIDE**
  Sample solution: 1 mg/mL
  Analysis: Place 1 drop of the *Sample solution* on a spot plate and add 1 drop of a 1% solution of lead nitrate, followed by a few drops of a solution prepared by saturating cold 2 N acetic acid with benzidine.
  Acceptance criteria: No blue precipitate or blue color appears.
- **SULFATE,** *Chloride and Sulfate Limit Tests, Chloride Limit Test,* Appendix IIIB
  Sample: 500 mg
  Control: 350 µg sulfate (35 mL of *Standard Sulfate Solution*)
  Acceptance criteria: Any turbidity produced by the *Sample* does not exceed that produced by the *Control*. (NMT 0.07%)

SPECIFIC TESTS
- **FREE MOISTURE**
  Sample: 20 g
  Analysis: Heat the *Sample* at 105° for 6 h, cool in a desiccator, and weigh. Grind the dried sample rapidly, heat 3 g of the powder to constant weight at 105°, and calculate the total water content (W). Calculate the percent free moisture in the sample by the formula:

  $$Result = W - 0.3721A$$

  A = percentage of $Na_4Fe(CN)_6 \cdot 10H_2O$ found in the *Assay*

  Acceptance criteria: NMT 1%
- **INSOLUBLE MATTER**
  Sample: 50 g
  Analysis: Dissolve the *Sample* in 300 mL of hot water, and filter off the insoluble matter into a tared, sintered-glass filter crucible. Wash the residue thoroughly with hot water, dry the crucible in an oven at 105° for 1 h, cool in a desiccator, and weigh.
  Acceptance criteria: NMT 0.03%

Sodium Fumarate
First Published: Second Supplement, FCC 6

Monosodium Fumarate
Fumaric Acid, Sodium Salt

$C_4H_3NaO_4$ — Formula wt 138.06
INS: 365 — CAS: [7704-73-6]
UNII: F119499241 [sodium fumarate]

DESCRIPTION
Sodium Fumarate occurs as an odorless, white crystalline powder. It is soluble in water.
Function: Buffering agent; acidulant; flavoring enhancer
Packaging and Storage: Store in well-closed containers.

IDENTIFICATION
- **A. PROCEDURE**
  Sample: 50 mg
  Analysis: Place the *Sample* in a test tube, add 2 to 3 mg of resorcinol and 1 mL of sulfuric acid, shake, heat at 130° for 5 min, and cool. Dilute with water to 5 mL, and add sodium hydroxide solution (2 in 5) dropwise to render the solution alkaline. Cool, and dilute with water to 10 mL.
  Acceptance criteria: A greenish-blue fluorescence is observed under an ultraviolet lamp.
- **B. PROCEDURE**
  Sample: 0.5 g
  Analysis: Add 10 mL of water to the *Sample*, and dissolve by boiling. Add 2 or 3 drops of bromine TS to the hot solution.
  Acceptance criteria: The color of the bromine TS disappears.
- **C. PH,** *pH Determination,* Appendix II
  Sample solution: 1 in 30
  Analysis: Determine using the potentiometric method.
  Acceptance criteria: Between 3 and 4
- **D. SODIUM,** Appendix IIIA
  Acceptance criteria: Passes the flame test

ASSAY
- **PROCEDURE**
  Phenolphthalein solution: Dissolve 0.2 g of phenolphthalein in 60 mL of 90% ethanol, and dilute with water to 100 mL. [NOTE—Save the unused portion of this solution for use in the *Sulfate* test.]
  Sample: 300 mg, previously dried
  Analysis: Dissolve the *Sample* in 30 mL of water. Titrate with 0.1 N sodium hydroxide, using 2 drops of *Phenolphthalein solution* as the indicator. Each mL of 0.1 N sodium hydroxide is equivalent to 13.81 mg of $C_4H_3NaO_4$.
  Acceptance criteria: NLT 98.0% and NMT 102.0% of $C_4H_3NaO_4$, on the dried basis

IMPURITIES
Inorganic Impurities
- **LEAD,** *Lead Limit Test, Flame Atomic Absorption Spectrophotometric Method,* Appendix IIIB
  Sample: 5 g
  Acceptance criteria: NMT 2 mg/kg
- **SULFATE**
  Sample: 1 g
  Analysis: To the *Sample,* add 30 mL of water, shake, and add 1 drop of *Phenolphthalein solution* prepared under the *Assay.* Add ammonia TS dropwise until a slight pink color is produced, then add 1 mL of diluted hydrochloric acid TS, and dilute with water to 50 mL. Transfer the resulting solution to a Nessler tube. Transfer 0.2 mL of 0.01 N sulfuric acid to a second Nessler tube to serve as the standard, add 1 mL of diluted hydrochloric acid TS to the second Nessler tube, and dilute with water to 50 mL.
  If the solution containing the *Sample* is not clear, filter both solutions under the same conditions. Add 2 mL of barium chloride TS to each solution, mix thoroughly, and allow to stand for 10 min. Compare the turbidity of the two solutions by observing the Nessler tubes from the sides and the tops against a black background.
  Acceptance criteria: The turbidity of the solution containing the *Sample* does not exceed that of the standard. (NMT 0.01%)

Organic Impurities
- **MALEIC ACID**
  Mobile phase: 0.01 N sulfuric acid, filtered and degassed
  Standard solution: 2 µg/mL USP Maleic Acid RS in *Mobile phase.* [NOTE—Do not dry the USP Maleic Acid RS prior to use, and keep containers tightly closed and protected from light.]
  Sample solution: 1 mg/mL in *Mobile phase*
  System suitability solution: 4 µg/mL USP Maleic Acid RS and 1 mg/mL Sodium Fumarate in *Mobile phase*
  Chromatographic system, Appendix IIA
    Mode: High-performance liquid chromatography
    Detector: UV 210 nm
    Column: 30-cm × 6.5-mm column, or equivalent, packed with a strong cation exchange resin consisting of sulfonated crosslinked styrene-divinylbenzene copolymer in the hydrogen form (Polypore H from Brownlee Laboratories, Inc., or equivalent)
    Column temperature: 37 ± 1°
    Flow rate: 0.6 mL/min
    Injection volume: 20 µL
  System suitability
    Sample: *System suitability solution*
    Suitability requirement 1: The resolution, R, between maleic acid and sodium fumarate is NLT 2.5.
    Suitability requirement 2: The relative standard deviation for sodium fumarate from replicate injections is NMT 2.0%.
  Analysis: Separately inject the *Standard solution* and the *Sample solution* into the chromatograph, record the chromatograms, and measure the peak responses. Calculate the percentage of maleic acid in the sample taken by the formula:

$$\text{Result} = (C_S/C_U) \times (R_U/R_S) \times 100$$

  C_S = concentration of USP Maleic Acid RS in the *Standard solution* (mg/mL)
  C_U = concentration of the *Sample solution* (mg/mL)
  R_U = peak response for maleic acid from the *Sample solution*
  R_S = peak response for maleic acid from the *Standard solution*
  Acceptance criteria: NMT 0.05%

SPECIFIC TESTS
- **LOSS ON DRYING,** Appendix IIC: 120° for 4 h
  Acceptance criteria: NMT 0.5%

Sodium Gluconate
First Published: Prior to FCC 6

Sodium D-Gluconate

$C_6H_{11}NaO_7$ Formula wt 218.14
INS: 576   CAS: [527-07-1]
UNII: R6Q3791S76 [sodium gluconate]

DESCRIPTION
Sodium Gluconate occurs as a white to tan, granular to fine, crystalline powder. It is very soluble in water, and is sparingly soluble in alcohol. It is insoluble in ether.
Function: Nutrient; sequestrant
Packaging and Storage: Store in well-closed containers.

IDENTIFICATION
- **SODIUM,** Appendix IIIA
  Sample solution: 50 mg/mL
  Acceptance criteria: Passes tests
- **THIN-LAYER CHROMATOGRAPHY,** Appendix IIA
  Sample solution: 10 mg/mL
  Standard solution: 10 mg/mL USP Potassium Gluconate RS
  [NOTE—*Sample solution* and *Standard solution* (above), if necessary, can be heated in a water bath at 60° to aid dissolution.]
  Adsorbent: 0.25-mm layer of chromatographic silica gel
  Application volume: 5 µL
  Developing solvent system: Alcohol, water, ammonium hydroxide, and ethyl acetate [5:3:1:1]
  Spray reagent: 25 mg/mL of ammonium molybdate and 10 mg/mL of ceric sulfate in 2 N sulfuric acid
  Analysis: Following development, dry the plate at 110° for 20 min, and allow to cool. Spray the cooled plate

with the *Spray reagent*, and heat the plate at 110° for about 10 minutes.

Acceptance criteria: The principal spot obtained from the *Sample solution* corresponds in color, size, and R_F value to that obtained from the *Standard solution*.

ASSAY
- **PROCEDURE**
  Sample: 150 mg
  Analysis: Transfer the *Sample* into a clean, dry 200-mL Erlenmeyer flask, add 75 mL of glacial acetic acid, and dissolve by heating on a hot plate.
  Cool, add quinaldine red TS, and using a 10-mL microburet, titrate with 0.1 N perchloric acid in glacial acetic acid to a colorless endpoint. Each mL of 0.1 N perchloric acid is equivalent to 21.81 mg of $C_6H_{11}NaO_7$.
  [**CAUTION**—Handle perchloric acid in an appropriate fume hood.]
  Acceptance criteria: NLT 98.0% and NMT 102.0% of $C_6H_{11}NaO_7$

IMPURITIES
Inorganic Impurities
- **LEAD,** *Lead Limit Test, Flame Atomic Absorption Spectrophotometric Method,* Appendix IIIB
  Sample: 10 g
  Acceptance criteria: NMT 2 mg/kg

SPECIFIC TESTS
- **REDUCING SUBSTANCES**
  Sample: 1 g
  Analysis: Transfer the *Sample* into a 250-mL Erlenmeyer flask, dissolve it in 10 mL of water, and 25 mL of alkaline cupric citrate TS, and cover the flask with a small beaker. Boil gently for exactly 5 min, and cool rapidly to room temperature. Add 25 mL of a 1:10 solution of acetic acid, 10.0 mL of 0.1 N iodine, 10 mL of 2.7 N hydrochloric acid, and 3 mL of starch TS. Titrate with 0.1 N sodium thiosulfate to the disappearance of the blue color. Calculate the weight, in mg, of reducing substances (as D-glucose) by the formula:

$$\text{Result} = 27(V_1N_1 - V_2N_2)$$

  27 = empirically determined equivalence factor for D-glucose (27)
  V_1 = volume of the iodine solution (mL)
  V_2 = volume of the sodium thiosulfate solution (mL)
  N_1 = normality of the iodine solution
  N_2 = normality of the sodium thiosulfate solution
  Acceptance criteria: NMT 0.5%, calculated as D-glucose

Sodium Hydroxide Solutions

First Published: Prior to FCC 6

Caustic Soda Solutions
Lye Solutions
UNII: 55X04QC32I [sodium hydroxide]

DESCRIPTION
Sodium Hydroxide Solutions occur as clear or slightly turbid, colorless or slightly colored liquids. They are usually available in nominal concentrations of 50% and 73% (w/w) of NaOH. These solutions are strongly caustic and hygroscopic. When exposed to air, they absorb carbon dioxide, forming sodium carbonate.
Function: pH control agent
Packaging and Storage: Store in tight containers.
[**CAUTION**—*Sodium Hydroxide Solutions* are a corrosive irritant to skin, eyes, and mucous membranes.]

IDENTIFICATION
- **SODIUM,** Appendix IIIA
  Acceptance criteria: Passes tests

ASSAY
- **TOTAL ALKALINITY**
  Sample: Amount equivalent to 1.5 g of sodium hydroxide (based on the stated or label percentage)
  Analysis: Dilute the *Sample* to 40 mL with recently boiled and cooled water and cool to 15°. Add phenolphthalein TS, and titrate with 1 N sulfuric acid. When the pink color disappears, record the volume of acid required, add methyl orange TS, and continue the titration until a persistent pink color appears. Record the total volume of acid required for the titration. Each mL of 1 N sulfuric acid is equivalent to 40.00 mg of total alkali, calculated as NaOH.
  Acceptance criteria: NLT 97.0% and NMT 103.0%, by weight, of the labeled amount of NaOH, calculated as total alkalinity

IMPURITIES
Inorganic Impurities
- **ARSENIC,** *Arsenic Limit Test,* Appendix IIIB
  Sample solution: Weigh an amount equivalent to 1 g of sodium hydroxide, calculated on the basis of the *Assay,* and dilute to 10 mL with water. Cautiously neutralize to litmus paper with sulfuric acid and cool.
  Acceptance criteria: NMT 3 mg/kg, calculated on the basis of NaOH determined in the *Assay*
- **CARBONATE (AS NA_2CO_3)**
  Analysis: Each mL of 1 N sulfuric acid required between the phenolphthalein and methyl orange endpoints in the *Assay* is equivalent to 106.0 mg of disodium carbonate.
  Acceptance criteria: NMT 3.0%, calculated on the basis of NaOH determined in the *Assay*
- **LEAD,** *Lead Limit Test,* Appendix IIIB
  Sample solution: Weigh an amount equivalent to 1 g of sodium hydroxide, calculated on the basis of the *Assay,* and dilute with a mixture of 5 mL of water and 11 mL of 2.7 N hydrochloric acid.

Control: 2 µg Pb (2 mL of *Diluted Standard Lead Solution*)
Acceptance criteria: NMT 2 mg/kg, calculated on the basis of NaOH determined in the *Assay*
- **MERCURY,** *Mercury Limit Test, Method I,* Appendix IIIB:
[NOTE—Substitute the following for the *Standard Preparation* and *Sample Preparation* given under *Method I.*]
Standard solution: Prepare a solution containing 1 µg of mercury per mL as directed in *Mercury Limit Test, Standard Preparation, Method I,* Appendix IIIB. Transfer 0.5 mL of the solution to a 50-mL beaker and add 20 mL of water, 1 mL of 1:5 sulfuric acid, and 1 mL of a 40 mg/mL solution of potassium permanganate. Cover the beaker with a watch glass, boil for a few seconds and cool.
Sample solution: Transfer 10.0 g of sample into a 100-mL beaker, dissolve in 15 mL of water, add 2 drops of phenolphthalein TS and, while constantly stirring, slowly neutralize with 1:2 hydrochloric acid. Add 1 mL of 1:5 sulfuric acid and 1 mL of a 40 mg/mL solution of potassium permanganate. Cover the beaker with a watch glass, boil for a few seconds and cool.
Acceptance criteria: NMT 0.1 mg/kg, calculated on the basis of NaOH determined in the *Assay*

OTHER REQUIREMENTS
- **LABELING:** Indicate the percent of Sodium Hydroxide (NaOH).

Sodium Hydroxide
First Published: Prior to FCC 6

Caustic Soda
Lye

NaOH	Formula wt 40.00
INS: 524	CAS: [1310-73-2]
UNII: 55X04QC32I [sodium hydroxide]	

DESCRIPTION
Sodium Hydroxide occurs as white or nearly white pellets, flakes, sticks, fused masses, or other forms. Upon exposure to air it readily absorbs carbon dioxide and moisture. One g dissolves in 1 mL of water. It is freely soluble in alcohol.
Function: pH control agent
Packaging and Storage: Store in tight containers.

IDENTIFICATION
- **SODIUM,** Appendix IIIA
Sample solution: 40 mg/mL
Acceptance criteria: Passes test

ASSAY
- **PROCEDURE**
Sample: 1.5 g
Analysis: Dissolve the *Sample* in 40 mL of recently boiled and cooled water. Cool to 15°. Add phenolphthalein TS, and titrate with 1 N sulfuric acid. When the pink color disappears, record the volume of acid required, add methyl orange TS, and continue the titration until a persistent pink color appears. Record the total volume of acid required for the titration. Each mL of 1 N sulfuric acid is equivalent to 40.00 mg of total alkali, calculated as NaOH.
Acceptance criteria: NLT 95.0% and NMT 100.5% of total alkali, calculated as NaOH

IMPURITIES
Inorganic Impurities
- **ARSENIC,** *Arsenic Limit Test,* Appendix IIIB
Sample solution: Dissolve 1 g of sample in 10 mL of water, cautiously neutralize to litmus paper with sulfuric acid, and cool.
Acceptance criteria: NMT 3 mg/kg
- **CARBONATE** (as Na_2CO_3)
Analysis: Each mL of 1 N sulfuric acid required between the phenolphthalein and methyl orange endpoints in the *Assay* is equivalent to 106.0 mg of disodium carbonate.
Acceptance criteria: NMT 3.0%
- **LEAD,** *Lead Limit Test,* Appendix IIIB
Sample solution: Dissolve 1 g of sample in a mixture of 5 mL of water and 11 mL of 2.7 N hydrochloric acid, and cool.
Control: 2 µg Pb (2 mL of *Diluted Standard Lead Solution*)
Acceptance criteria: NMT 2 mg/kg
- **MERCURY,** *Mercury Limit Test, Method I,* Appendix IIIB
[NOTE—Substitute the following for the *Standard Preparation* and *Sample Preparation* given under *Method I.*]
Standard solution: Prepare a solution containing 1 µg of mercury per mL as directed in *Mercury Limit Test, Standard Preparation, Method I,* Appendix IIIB. Transfer 0.5 mL of the solution to a 50-mL beaker and add 20 mL of water, 1 mL of 1:5 sulfuric acid, and 1 mL of a 40 mg/mL solution of potassium permanganate. Cover the beaker with a watch glass, boil for a few seconds and cool.
Sample solution: Transfer 10.0 g of sample into a 100-mL beaker, dissolve in 15 mL of water, add 2 drops of phenolphthalein TS and, while constantly stirring, slowly neutralize with 1:2 hydrochloric acid. Add 1 mL of 1:5 sulfuric acid and 1 mL of a 40 mg/mL solution of potassium permanganate. Cover the beaker with a watch glass, boil for a few seconds and cool.
Acceptance criteria: NMT 0.1 mg/kg

SPECIFIC TESTS
- **INSOLUBLE SUBSTANCES AND ORGANIC MATTER**
Sample solution: 50 mg/mL
Acceptance criteria: The *Sample solution* is complete, clear, and colorless to slightly colored.

Sodium Hypophosphite

First Published: Prior to FCC 6

NaH$_2$PO$_2$·H$_2$O
Formula wt 105.99
CAS: [7681-53-0]
UNII: 8TU1537O43 [sodium hypophosphite]

DESCRIPTION
Sodium Hypophosphite occurs as a white, crystalline powder; as white granules; or as colorless, pearly crystalline plates. It is very deliquescent. One mL of water dissolves about 1 g at 25° and about 6 g at 100°. It is slightly soluble in alcohol.

Function: Preservative; antioxidant

Packaging and Storage: Store in tight containers.
[CAUTION—Take care in mixing Sodium Hypophosphite with nitrates, chlorates, or other oxidizing agents because an explosion may occur if the mixtures are triturated or heated.]

IDENTIFICATION
- **HYPOPHOSPHITES,** Appendix IIIA
  Sample solution: 50 mg/mL
  Acceptance criteria: Passes test
- **SODIUM,** Appendix IIIA
  Sample solution: 50 mg/mL
  Acceptance criteria: Passes test

ASSAY
- **PROCEDURE**
  Sample: 100 mg
  Analysis: Dissolve the *Sample* in 20 mL of water; add 40.0 mL of 0.1 N ceric sulfate prepared as directed in *Solutions and Indicators* v (or use a commercially available solution); mix well and add 2 mL of silver sulfate solution (5 g of Ag$_2$SO$_4$ dissolved in 95 mL of concentrated sulfuric acid). Cover, heat nearly to boiling, and continue heating for 30 min. Cool to room temperature, and titrate with 0.1 N ferrous ammonium sulfate to a pale yellow color. Add 2 drops of orthophenanthroline TS, and continue the titration to a salmon-colored endpoint, recording the volume required, in mL, as *S*. Perform a residual blank titration (see *General Provisions*) and record the volume required as *B*. Each mL of the volume $B - S$ is equivalent to 2.650 mg of NaH$_2$PO$_2$·H$_2$O.
  Acceptance criteria: NLT 97.0% and NMT 103.0% of NaH$_2$PO$_2$·H$_2$O

IMPURITIES
Inorganic Impurities
- **ARSENIC,** *Arsenic Limit Test,* Appendix IIIB
  Sample solution: 1 g in 35 mL of water
  Acceptance criteria: NMT 3 mg/kg
- **FLUORIDE,** *Fluoride Limit Test,* Appendix IIIB
  Acceptance criteria: NMT 10 mg/kg
- **LEAD,** *Lead Limit Test, APDC Extraction Method,* Appendix IIIB
  Acceptance criteria: NMT 4 mg/kg

SPECIFIC TESTS
- **INSOLUBLE SUBSTANCES**
  Sample: 10 g
  Analysis: Dissolve *Sample* in 100 mL of hot water and filter through a tared filtering crucible. Wash the residue with hot water, dry at 105° for 2 h, cool, and weigh.
  Acceptance criteria: NMT 0.1%

Sodium Iron EDTA

First Published: FCC 7
Last Revision: Second Supplement, FCC 7

Sodium Iron (III) Ethylenediaminetetraacetate, Trihydrate
Ferric Sodium EDTA Trihydrate
Ferric Sodium Edetate
Sodium Feredetate

C$_{10}$H$_{12}$FeN$_2$NaO$_8$·3H$_2$O
Formula wt 421.09
CAS: anhydrous [15708-41-5]
trihydrate [18154-32-0]
UNII: 403J23EMFA [sodium feredetate]

DESCRIPTION
Sodium Iron EDTA occurs as an odorless, light-yellow to yellow-brown powder that is highly stable and unaffected by storage. It contains three molecules of water of hydration. It is freely soluble in water.

Function: Nutrient

Packaging and Storage: Store in well-closed containers.

IDENTIFICATION
- **INFRARED ABSORPTION,** *Spectrophotometric Identification Tests,* Appendix IIIC
  Reference standard: USP Sodium Iron EDTA RS
  Standard and sample preparation: *K*
  Acceptance criteria: The spectrum of the sample exhibits maxima at the same wavelengths as those in the spectrum of the *Reference standard.*

ASSAY
- **EDTA**
  0.1 M Calcium chloride solution: Transfer 14.7 g of calcium chloride dihydrate to a 1-L volumetric flask, and dissolve in and dilute with water to volume. Standardize the solution using the following procedure.
  Weigh 0.4–0.5 g of ethylenediamine–tetraacetic acid (EDTA acid) into each of three 250-mL conical flasks. Add 100 mL of *Triethanolamine solution* to each flask, and adjust to a pH of 12.6 ± 0.1 with 33% (w/v) sodium hydroxide solution. Add 10 mL of *Calmagite indicator solution* to each flask, adjust the transmission to 70%, and titrate with *0.1 M Calcium chloride solution* to the first significant color change using a photometer

operated at a wavelength of 520 nm. [NOTE—The correct endpoint is found at the crossing of the intersection lines. It can also be determined from the first significant deviation of the first derivative dU/mV from zero.]
Calculate the exact molarity of the *0.1 M Calcium chloride solution*:

$$\text{Result} = (W_{EDTA} \times 1000)/(V \times F)$$

W_{EDTA} = quantity of EDTA acid taken (g)
1000 = conversion factor (mL/L)
V = volume of titrant used (mL)
F = molecular weight of EDTA acid, 292.24

Calmagite indicator solution: Dissolve 100 mg of calmagite, 3-hydroxy-4-(2-hydroxy-5-methylphenylazo)-1-naphthalenesulfonic acid in 1 L of water.
Triethanolamine solution: Dilute 100 mL of triethanolamine with water to 1 L.
Sample: 0.65 g
Analysis: Transfer the *Sample* to a 250-mL beaker. Add 100 mL of *Triethanolamine solution* and dissolve. Adjust to a pH of 12.6 ± 0.1 with 33% (w/v) sodium hydroxide solution. [NOTE—The resulting solution should be clear and colorless.] Add 10 mL of *Calmagite indicator solution*, adjust the transmission to 70%, and titrate with *0.1 M Calcium chloride solution* to the first significant color change using a photometer operated at a wavelength of 520 nm. [NOTE—The correct endpoint is found at the crossing of the intersection lines. It can also be determined from the first significant deviation of the first derivative dU/mV from zero.]
Perform a blank determination (see *General Provisions*).
Calculate the percentage of EDTA acid:

$$\text{Result} = [(V_S - V_B) \times M \times F]/(1000 \times W_S) \times 100$$

V_S = volume of *0.1 M Calcium chloride solution* used for the *Sample* titration (mL)
V_B = volume of *0.1 M Calcium chloride solution* used for the blank titration (mL)
M = exact molarity of the *0.1 M Calcium chloride solution*
F = molecular weight of EDTA acid, 292.24
1000 = conversion factor (mL/L)
W_S = quantity of *Sample* taken (g)

Acceptance criteria: 67.5%–71.5%

- **IRON**
Solution A: 1 M sodium hydrogen carbonate (NaHCO$_3$)
Sample: 0.65 g
Analysis: Dissolve the *Sample* in 100 mL of water in an iodine flask. Add 10 mL of *Solution A* and carefully add 20 mL of concentrated hydrochloric acid. Add 15 g of potassium iodide, close the flask immediately, and mix. Allow to stand in the dark for 10 min at 25 ± 5°. Titrate the liberated iodine with 0.1 N sodium thiosulfate, using starch TS as the indicator. Avoid vigorous mixing during the titration. Perform a blank determination (see *General Provisions*). Calculate the percentage of iron in the Sodium Iron EDTA:

$$\text{Result} = [(T_S - T_B) \times N \times F \times 100]/W_S$$

T_S = volume of titrant used for the *Sample* titration (mL)
T_B = volume of titrant used for the blank titration (mL)
N = exact normality of the sodium thiosulfate used in the titration
F = atomic weight of iron × 10^{-3}, 0.05585
W_S = quantity of *Sample* taken (g)

Acceptance criteria: 13.0%–13.5%

IMPURITIES
Inorganic Impurities
- **ARSENIC**, *Arsenic Limit Test*, Appendix IIIB
Sample solution: Prepare as directed for organic compounds, using a 3.0-g sample.
Acceptance criteria: NMT 1 mg/kg

- **CHLORIDE**
Polyvinyl alcohol solution: Dissolve, with heating, 2 g of polyvinyl alcohol (suitable for argentometric titrations) in 1 L of water.
Sample: 5.0 g
Analysis: Transfer the *Sample* to a 250-mL beaker. Add 80 mL of water, dissolve, and add 80 mL of methanol. Using a volumetric pipet, add 5.00 mL of 0.01 M hydrochloric acid and 5 mL of *Polyvinyl alcohol solution*. Titrate with 0.01 M silver nitrate solution, using a combined silver/reference electrode. Perform a blank determination (see *General Provisions*).
Calculate the concentration of chloride, in mg/kg:

$$\text{Result} = [(V_S - V_B) \times M \times F \times 1000]/W_S$$

V_S = volume of titrant used for the *Sample* titration (mL)
V_B = volume of titrant used for the blank titration (mL)
M = exact molarity of the silver nitrate solution used in the titration
F = atomic weight of chloride, 35.45
W_S = quantity of *Sample* taken (g)

Acceptance criteria: NMT 600 mg/kg

- **LEAD**, *Lead Limit Test, Atomic Absorption Spectrophotometric Graphite Furnace Method, Method I*, Appendix IIIB
Acceptance criteria: NMT 1 mg/kg

- **SULFATE (AS BARIUM SULFATE)**
Barium chloride solution: 0.5 M; prepare by diluting 30.5 g of barium chloride dihydrate with water to 250 mL.
Zinc chloride solution: 1 M zinc chloride; prepare by dissolving 13.6 g of zinc chloride in water containing 1 mL of 2 M hydrochloric acid and diluting to 100 mL.
Standard sulfate solution: 2.113 mg/mL sodium sulfate (1.430 mg/mL sulfate)
Solution A: Dilute 5 mL of the *Barium chloride solution* with 55 mL of water and 20 mL of 96% ethanol. Add 0.5 mL of the *Standard sulfate solution*, and mix. [NOTE—Prepare immediately before use.]

Indicator solution: 0.25% *p*-nitrophenol in water
Sample: 1.8 g
Control: Transfer 25 mL of water to a colorless, clear glass test tube with a 50-mL mark. Add 1.8 mL of 5 M sodium hydroxide and 100 µL of the *Indicator solution* to the tube. Neutralize with 2 M hydrochloric acid until the yellow solutions turn colorless. Add 2.0 mL of *Zinc chloride solution*, and adjust to a pH of 2.0 with the addition of either 2 M hydrochloric acid or 2 M sodium hydroxide. Using a positive displacement (piston) pipet, transfer 300 µL of the *Standard sulfate solution* to the test tube. Dilute the contents of the tube to 50 mL, and add 5.0 mL of *Solution A*. Mix the contents of the tube, and visually compare the turbidity of the solution to the solution prepared in the *Analysis*.
Analysis: Transfer the *Sample* to a 50-mL test tube identical to that used in the *Control*, and dissolve in 30 mL of water. Carefully add 4.5 mL of 5 M sodium hydroxide, and stir with a stir bar for 15 min. Remove the stir bar, and dilute the solution with water to the 50-mL mark on the tube. Filter the solution,[1] and transfer 20 mL of the filtrate to another identical test tube. Add 100 µL of the *Indicator solution* to the tube containing the 20 mL of filtrate, and neutralize the filtrate with 2 M hydrochloric acid until the yellow solution turns colorless. Add 2.0 mL of *Zinc chloride solution* to the tube, and adjust to a pH of 2.0 with the addition of 2 M hydrochloric acid. Dilute the contents of the tube to 50 mL, and add 5.0 mL of *Solution A*. Mix the contents of the tube, and visually compare the turbidity of the solution to the solution prepared in the *Control*. Alternatively, a turbidimeter may be used.
Acceptance criteria: The turbidity of the solution prepared in the *Analysis* is NMT the turbidity of the solution prepared in the *Control* (NMT 0.06%).

Organic Impurities
- **NITRILOTRIACETIC ACID**
  [NOTE—Carry out the test protected from light.]
  Mobile phase: Dissolve 50.0 mg of ferric sulfate pentahydrate in 50 mL of 0.5 M sulfuric acid, and add 750 mL of water. Adjust to a pH of 1.5 with 0.5 M sulfuric acid or 1 M sodium hydroxide, and add 20 mL of ethylene glycol. Dilute with water to 1 L.
  Solvent mixture: Dissolve 10.0 g of ferric sulfate pentahydrate in 20 mL of 0.5 M sulfuric acid, and add 780 mL of water. Adjust to a pH of 2.0 with 1 M sodium hydroxide. Dilute with water to 1 L.
  Standard stock solution: 0.40 mg/mL of USP Nitrilotriacetic Acid RS in *Solvent mixture*
  Standard solution: Transfer 1.0 mL of *Standard stock solution* and 0.1 mL of *Sample solution* to a 100-mL volumetric flask. Dilute with *Solvent mixture* to volume.
  Sample solution: 4.0 mg/mL in *Solvent mixture*.
  [NOTE—Sonicate, if necessary, to achieve complete dissolution.]
  Chromatographic system, Appendix IIA
    Mode: High-performance liquid chromatography
    Detector: UV 273 nm
    Column: 4.6-mm × 10-cm column that contains spherical graphitized carbon for chromatography (5 µm) with a specific surface area of 120 m^2/g and a pore size of 25 nm (Hypercarb, or equivalent)
    Flow rate: 1 mL/min
    Injection size: 20 µL
  System suitability
    Sample: *Standard solution* (three replicate injections)
    Suitability requirement 1: The resolution factor between nitrilotriacetic acid and sodium iron EDTA is NLT 4.0.
    Suitability requirement 2: The relative standard deviation for nitrilotriacetic acid is NMT 2.0%.
  Analysis: Separately inject the *Standard solution* and the *Sample solution* into the chromatograph, record the chromatograms, and measure the responses for the major peaks. [NOTE—The retention times for nitrilotriacetic acid and sodium iron EDTA are about 5 and 10 min, respectively.]
  Acceptance criteria: The response of the nitrilotriacetic acid peak of the *Sample solution* does not exceed the response of the nitrilotriacetic acid peak obtained from the *Standard solution* (NMT 0.1% nitrilotriacetic acid).

SPECIFIC TESTS
- **FREE IRON**
  Electrode system: Combined platinum/reference electrode[2]; condition in a 0.1 M solution of iron (II) sulfate before use.
  Buffer solution: 84 mg/mL of monochloroacetic acid and 76 mg/mL of sodium acetate trihydrate (pH 3)
  Starch solution: Add, while stirring, 2 g of a suitable soluble starch to 150 mL of boiling water. Continue boiling until the solution is clear, then dilute with water to 1 L.
  Iodine solution: 0.05 M I$_2$; prepare from a commercially available concentrated iodine solution.
  EDTA standard solution: 0.1 M EDTA–Na$_2$H$_2$; prepare from a commercially available concentrated EDTA disodium salt solution.
  Iron (III) chloride standard solution: Dissolve 27.0 g of iron (III) chloride hexahydrate in water containing 1 mL of hydrochloric acid, then dilute with water to 1 L.
  Sample: 5 g
  Analysis: Transfer the *Sample* to a 250-mL beaker and dissolve in 100 mL of water. Adjust to a pH of 3 with 4 M hydrochloric acid. To the beaker, add 10 mL of the *Buffer solution* and 3 mL of the *Starch solution*. Add a quantity of the *Iodine solution* to the beaker until the solution turns blue, then add an excess 2-mL portion of the *Iodine solution*. Titrate with standardized 0.1 M sodium thiosulfate solution, using the *Electrode system* described. Stop the titration just beyond the equivalence point. Add 5.00 mL of the *EDTA standard solution* to the beaker, then titrate a second time with the *Iron (III) chloride standard solution* to beyond the equivalence point. Perform a blank determination (see *General Provisions*).

---

[1] Use Schleicher & Schuell filter paper 595 1/2 No. 311.647, or equivalent, folded.

[2] Metrohm 6.0415.100, or equivalent.

1040 / Sodium Iron EDTA / *Monographs*

Calculate the percentage of free iron in the sample taken:

$$\text{Result} = (V_0 - V) \times C \times 55.85 \times F \times (1/M_S) \times 100$$

V_0 = volume of *Iron (III) chloride standard solution* used for the *Sample* titration (mL)

V = volume of *Iron (III) chloride standard solution* used for the blank titration (mL)

C = exact concentration of the *Iron (III) chloride standard solution* (mol/L)

F = factor converting mL to L (0.001)

M_S = quantity of the *Sample* used (g)

Acceptance criteria: NMT 0.05%

- **LOSS ON DRYING**
  Sample: 1.0 g
  Analysis: Mix the *Sample* immediately before analysis. Transfer the *Sample* to a suitable halogen dryer/moisture analyzer[3], and dry at 170° for 30 min.
  Acceptance criteria: 12.5%–13.5%
- **PH**, *pH Determination*, Appendix IIB
  Sample: 10 mg/mL
  Acceptance criteria: 4.5–5.5
- **UV ABSORBANCE**
  Buffer solution: 7.94 mg/mL of potassium dihydrogen phosphate and 1.49 mg/mL of disodium hydrogen phosphate, dihydrate
  Sample solution: Transfer 1.0 g of the sample to a 100-mL volumetric flask, and dilute with water to volume. Transfer 1.00 mL of this solution to a 1-L volumetric flask. Add 20 mL of *Buffer solution* to the flask, and dilute with water to volume.
  Analysis: Using a suitable spectrophotometer, measure the absorbance of the *Sample solution* at 260 nm in a 1-cm cell, using water as the blank.
  Acceptance criteria: The absorbance of the *Sample solution* is NMT 0.240.
- **WATER-INSOLUBLE MATTER**, Appendix IIC
  Acceptance criteria: NMT 0.1%

Sodium Lactate Solution

First Published: Prior to FCC 6

2-Hydroxypropanoic Acid, Monosodium Salt

$C_3H_5NaO_3$ Formula wt, anhydrous 112.06
INS: 325 CAS: [72-17-3]
UNII: TU7HW0W0QT [sodium lactate]

DESCRIPTION

Sodium Lactate Solution occurs as a clear, colorless or practically colorless, slightly viscous liquid that is odorless or has a slight, not unpleasant odor. It is miscible with water. It is normally available in solutions with concentrations ranging from 60% to about 80%, by weight.

Function: Emulsifier; flavor enhancer; flavoring agent or adjuvant; humectant; pH control agent

Packaging and Storage: Store in tight containers.

IDENTIFICATION

- **LACTATE**, Appendix IIIA
  Acceptance criteria: Passes test
- **SODIUM**, Appendix IIIA
  Acceptance criteria: Passes tests

ASSAY

- **PROCEDURE**
  Sample: Amount equivalent to 300 mg of sodium lactate
  Analysis: Transfer *Sample* to a suitable flask. Add 60 mL of 1 : 5 acetic anhydride:glacial acetic acid, mix, and allow to stand for 20 min. Titrate with 0.1 N perchloric acid in glacial acetic acid, determining the endpoint potentiometrically. Perform a blank determination (see *General Provisions*), and make any necessary correction. Each mL of 0.1 N perchloric acid is equivalent to 11.21 mg of $C_3H_5NaO_3$. [CAUTION—Handle perchloric acid in an appropriate fume hood.]
  Acceptance criteria: NLT 50.0%, by weight; and NLT 98.0% and NMT 102.0%, by weight, of the labeled amount of $C_3H_5NaO_3$

IMPURITIES

Inorganic Impurities

- **CHLORIDE**, *Chloride Limit Test*, Appendix IIIB
  Sample: Amount containing the equivalent of 40 mg of sodium lactate
  Control: 20 µg chloride (2 mL of *Standard Chloride Solution*)
  Acceptance criteria: Any turbidity produced by the *Sample* does not exceed that produced by the *Control*. (NMT 0.05%)

- **CYANIDE**
  [CAUTION—Because of the extremely poisonous nature of potassium cyanide, conduct this test in a fume hood, and exercise great care to prevent skin contact and the inhalation of particles or vapors of solutions of the material. Under no conditions pipet solutions by mouth.]
  Solution A: Dissolve 200 mg of *p*-phenylenediamine hydrochloride in 100 mL of water, warming to aid dissolution. Cool, allow the solids to settle, and save the supernatant liquid to make the *Solution B*.
  Solution B: Dissolve 128 mL of pyridine in 365 mL of water, add 10 mL of hydrochloric acid, and mix. To this solution add 30 mL of the supernatant of *Solution A* and allow to stand for 24 h before using. [NOTE—This solution is stable for about 3 weeks when stored in an amber bottle.]
  Standard stock solution: 2.5 mg/mL potassium cyanide in 0.1 N sodium hydroxide made to 100 mL
  Standard solution: 25 µg/mL potassium cyanide in 0.1 N sodium hydroxide made from *Standard stock solution*. [NOTE—Each mL of this solution contains 10 µg of cyanide.]

---
[3] Mettler Toledo HG53, HG63, or equivalent.

Sample solution: Transfer a quantity of sample equivalent to 20.0 g of sodium lactate into a 100-mL volumetric flask, dilute to volume with water, and mix.

Analysis: Pipet a 10-mL aliquot of the *Sample solution* into a 50-mL beaker. Pipet 0.1 mL of the *Standard solution* into a second 50-mL beaker, and add 10 mL of water. Place the beakers in an ice bath, and adjust the pH to between 9 and 10 with 20% sodium hydroxide, stirring slowly and adding the reagent slowly to avoid overheating. Allow the solutions to stand for 3 min, and then slowly add 10% phosphoric acid to reach a pH between 5 and 6, measured with a pH meter. Transfer the solutions into 100-mL separatory funnels each containing 25 mL of cold water, and rinse the beakers and pH meter electrodes with a few mL of cold water, collecting the washings in the respective separatory funnel. To each funnel add 2 mL of bromine TS, stopper, and mix. Add 2 mL of 2% sodium arsenite solution, stopper, and mix. Add 10 mL of *n*-butanol to the clear solutions, stopper, and mix. Finally, add 5 mL of *Solution B*, mix, and allow to stand for 15 min. Remove and discard the aqueous phases, and filter the alcoholic phases into 1-cm spectrophotometry cells. Using a suitable spectrophotometer, determine the absorbances at 480 nm of the solutions from the *Sample solution* and the *Standard solution*.

Acceptance criteria: The absorbance of the solution from the *Sample solution* does not exceed that from the *Standard solution* (NMT 0.5 mg/kg).

- **LEAD,** *Lead Limit Test, Flame Atomic Absorption Spectrophotometric Method,* Appendix IIIB
  Sample: 5 g
  Acceptance criteria: NMT 2 mg/kg
- **SULFATE,** *Chloride and Sulfate Limit Tests, Chloride Limit Test,* Appendix IIIB
  Sample: Amount containing the equivalent of 40 mg of sodium lactate
  Control: 200 µg sulfate (20 mL of *Standard Sulfate Solution*)
  Acceptance criteria: Any turbidity produced by the *Sample* does not exceed that produced by the *Control* (NMT 0.005%).

Organic Impurities
- **METHANOL AND METHYL ESTERS**
  Solution A: Dissolve 3 g of potassium permanganate in a mixture of 15 mL of phosphoric acid and 70 mL of water. Dilute to 100 mL with water.
  Solution B: Cautiously add 50 mL of sulfuric acid to 50 mL of water, mix, cool, add 5 g of oxalic acid, and mix to dissolve.
  Standard solution: 100 µg/mL methanol in a 1 : 10 mixture of ethanol:water, made to 100 mL
  Sample solution: Transfer 40.0 g of sample into a glass-stoppered, round-bottom flask, add 10 mL of water, and cautiously add 30 mL of 5 N potassium hydroxide. Connect a condenser to the flask, and steam-distill, collecting the distillate in a suitable 100-mL graduated vessel containing 10 mL of ethanol. Continue the distillation until the volume in the receiver reaches approximately 95 mL, and dilute the distillate to 100.0 mL with water.
  Analysis: Transfer 10.0 mL each of the *Standard solution* and the *Sample solution* to separate 25-mL volumetric flasks. Add 5.0 mL of *Solution A* to each, and mix. After 15 min, add 2.0 mL of *Solution B* to each, stir with a glass rod until the solutions are colorless, add 5.0 mL of fuchsin-sulfurous acid TS, dilute to volume with water, and mix. After 2 h, using a suitable spectrophotometer, concomitantly determine the absorbances of both solutions in 1-cm cells at the wavelength of maximum absorbance (about 575 nm); use water as the blank.
  Acceptance criteria: The absorbance of the solution from the *Sample solution* does not exceed that from the *Standard solution* (NMT 0.025%).
- **SUGARS**
  Sample: 5 drops
  Analysis: Add the *Sample* to 10 mL of hot alkaline cupric tartrate TS.
  Acceptance criteria: No red precipitate forms.

SPECIFIC TESTS
- **CITRATE, OXALATE, PHOSPHATE, OR TARTRATE**
  Sample: 5 mL
  Analysis: Dilute the *Sample* to 50 mL with recently boiled and cooled water. Take 4 mL of this solution and, if necessary, adjust the pH to between 7.3 and 7.7 with addition of 6 N ammonium hydroxide or 3 N hydrochloric acid. Add 1 mL of calcium chloride TS, and heat in a boiling water bath for 5 min.
  Acceptance criteria: The solution remains clear.
- **PH,** *pH Determination,* Appendix IIB
  Acceptance criteria: Between 5.0 and 9.0

OTHER REQUIREMENTS
- **LABELING:** Indicate the content of the solution, by weight, of sodium lactate ($C_3H_5NaO_3$).

Sodium Lauryl Sulfate
First Published: Prior to FCC 6

Sodium Dodecyl Sulfate
INS: 487   CAS: [151-21-3]
UNII: 368GB5141J [sodium lauryl sulfate]

DESCRIPTION
Sodium Lauryl Sulfate occurs as small, white or light yellow crystals. It is a mixture of sodium alkylsulfates consisting chiefly of Sodium Lauryl Sulfate [$CH_3(CH_2)_{10}CH_2OSO_3Na$]. One g dissolves in 10 mL of water, forming an opalescent solution.

Function: Surface-active agent

1042 / Sodium Lauryl Sulfate / Monographs

Packaging and Storage: Store in well-closed containers.

IDENTIFICATION
- **SODIUM,** Appendix IIIA
  Sample solution: 100 mg/mL
  Acceptance criteria: Passes tests
- **SULFATE,** Appendix IIIA
  Sample solution: 100 mg/mL, acidified with hydrochloric acid and boiled gently for 20 min
  Acceptance criteria: Passes tests

ASSAY
- **TOTAL ALCOHOLS**
  Sample: 5 g
  Analysis: Transfer the *Sample* to an 800-mL Kjeldahl flask, add 150 mL of water, 50 mL of hydrochloric acid, and a few boiling chips. Attach a reflux condenser to the flask, heat carefully to avoid excessive frothing, and then boil for about 4 h. Cool the flask, and rinse the condenser with ether, collecting the ether in the flask. Transfer the contents to a 500-mL separatory funnel, rinsing the flask twice with ether and adding the washings to the separatory funnel. Extract the solution with two 75-mL portions of ether, evaporate the combined ether extracts in a tared beaker on a steam bath, dry the residue at 105° for 30 min, cool, and weigh. The residue represents the total alcohols.
  Acceptance criteria: NLT 59.0% of total alcohols

IMPURITIES
Inorganic Impurities
- **LEAD,** *Lead Limit Test, Flame Atomic Absorption Spectrophotometric Method,* Appendix IIIB
  Sample: 10 g
  Acceptance criteria: NMT 2 mg/kg

SPECIFIC TESTS
- **ALKALINITY (AS NaOH)**
  Sample: 1 g
  Analysis: Dissolve the *Sample* in 100 mL of water, add phenol red TS, and titrate with 0.1 N hydrochloric acid.
  Acceptance criteria: NMT 0.5 mL is required for neutralization (about 0.25%).
- **COMBINED SODIUM CHLORIDE AND SODIUM SULFATE**
  Sodium Chloride:
  Sample: 5 g
  Analysis: Dissolve the *Sample* in 50 mL of water. Neutralize the solution with 1:20 nitric acid, using litmus paper as the indicator. Add 2 mL of potassium chromate TS; and titrate with 0.1 N silver nitrate. Each mL of 0.1 N silver nitrate is equivalent to 5.844 mg of sodium chloride (NaCl).
  Sodium Sulfate
  Sample: 1 g
  Analysis: Transfer the *Sample* to a 400-mL beaker, add 10 mL of water, heat the mixture, and stir until completely dissolved. Add 100 mL of alcohol to the hot solution, cover, and digest at a temperature just below the boiling point for 2 h. Filter while hot through a sintered-glass filter crucible, and wash the precipitate with 100 mL of hot alcohol. Dissolve the precipitate in the crucible by washing it with about 150 mL of water, collecting the washings in a beaker. Acidify the beaker's contents with 10 mL of hydrochloric acid, heat to boiling, add 25 mL of barium chloride TS, and allow to stand overnight. Collect the precipitate of barium sulfate on a suitable tared, porous-bottom porcelain filter crucible, wash until free from chloride, dry, and ignite to constant weight at 800° ± 25°. The weight of barium sulfate so obtained, multiplied by 0.6086, represents the weight of sodium sulfate (Na_2SO_4). [NOTE—Avoid exposing the crucible to sudden temperature changes.]
  Calculation: Combine the results from *Sodium Chloride* and *Sodium Sulfate* to obtain *Combined Sodium Chloride and Sodium Sulfate.*
  Acceptance criteria: NMT 8.0%
- **UNSULFATED ALCOHOLS**
  Sample: 10 g
  Analysis: Dissolve the *Sample* in 100 mL of water and add 100 mL of alcohol. Transfer the solution to a separatory funnel, and extract with three 50-mL portions of solvent hexane. If an emulsion forms, add sodium chloride to promote separation of the two layers. Wash the combined solvent hexane extracts with three 50-mL portions of water, and dry with anhydrous sodium sulfate. Filter the solvent hexane extract into a tared beaker, evaporate on a steam bath until the odor of solvent hexane no longer is perceptible, dry the residue at 105° for 30 min, cool, and weigh. The residue represents the unsulfated alcohols.
  Acceptance criteria: NMT 4.0%

Sodium Lignosulfonate

First Published: Prior to FCC 6
Last Revision: First Supplement, FCC 6

CAS: [8061-51-6]
UNII: XY2KOA860T [polignate sodium]

DESCRIPTION
Sodium Lignosulfonate occurs as a brown, amorphous polymer. It is obtained from the spent sulfite and sulfate pulping liquor of wood or from the sulfate (Kraft) pulping process. It may contain up to 30% reducing sugars. It is soluble in water, but not in any of the common organic solvents. The pH of a 1:100 aqueous solution is approximately between 3 and 11.
Function: Binder; dispersant; boiler water additive
Packaging and Storage: Store in well-closed containers.

IDENTIFICATION
- **A. SODIUM,** Appendix IIIA
  Sample solution: 0.15 mg/mL
  Acceptance criteria: Passes test

- **B. Procedure**
  Sample: 100 mg
  Analysis: Dissolve the *Sample* in 50 mL of water. Add 1 mL each of 10% acetic acid and 10% sodium nitrite solutions. Mix the solution by swirling, and allow it to stand for 15 min at room temperature.
  Acceptance criteria: A brown color appears.
- **C. Ultraviolet Absorption**
  Sample solution: 0.1 mg/mL at pH 5
  Acceptance criteria: The spectrum of the *Sample solution* exhibits a peak between 275 and 280 nm.

ASSAY
- **Sulfonate Sulfur**
  Sample: 1.0 g
  Analysis: Dissolve the *Sample* in 400 mL of water in a beaker. Direct a gentle stream of nitrogen gas over the liquid's surface. Add 10 mL of nitric acid and swirl the solution thoroughly until the reaction subsides. Add 10 mL of 70% perchloric acid, and swirl thoroughly again. [**Caution**—Handle perchloric acid in an appropriate fume hood.] Place the uncovered beaker on a hot plate, and heat the contents vigorously until the center of the bottom of the beaker becomes clear. Remove the beaker, and cool to room temperature. Add 5 mL of hydrochloric acid, and heat again until white fumes evolve. After cooling, dilute the solution with water to approximately 100 mL, adjust to pH 6 ± 0.2 with 10% sodium hydroxide, and heat the solution to boiling. Add 15 mL of 10% barium chloride solution, and leave the solution overnight in a fresh beaker in a steam bath at 90° to 95°. Pass the solution through ashless filter paper (Whatman No. 42, or equivalent), and wash the precipitate with 200 mL of warm water. Transfer the paper and precipitate into a tared crucible. Heat the crucible slowly on a Bunsen burner to expel moisture. Place the crucible and contents in a muffle furnace at 850° for 1 h. Let the crucible cool in a desiccator, and then weigh the residue to the nearest 0.0001 g. Calculate the percent sulfonate sulfur by the formula:

  $$\text{Result} = (R/S) \times 13.7$$

  R = weight of the residue (g)
  S = weight of the *Sample* taken (g)
  Acceptance criteria: NLT 5.0% sulfonate sulfur

IMPURITIES
Inorganic Impurities
- **Lead,** *Lead Limit Test, Atomic Absorption Spectrophotometric Graphite Furnace Method I,* Appendix IIIB
  Acceptance criteria: NMT 1 mg/kg

SPECIFIC TESTS
- **Loss on Drying,** Appendix IIC: 105° for 24 h
  Acceptance criteria: NMT 10.0%
- **Reducing Sugars**
  Copper reagent solution: [Note—This solution must be prepared several days in advance of use.] Dissolve 28 g of anhydrous dibasic sodium phosphate and 40 g of potassium sodium tartrate tetrahydrate in 700 mL of water. Add 100 mL of 1 N sodium hydroxide and 8 g of copper sulfate pentahydrate. Add 180 g of anhydrous sodium sulfate. Then, add 0.7134 g of potassium iodate and dilute to 1 L. Allow to stand for several days, then filter the clear top part of the solution through a medium-porosity, sintered-glass funnel.
  Lead subacetate solution: Dissolve 80 g of lead subacetate in 220 mL of water. Stir overnight, and pass through Whatman No. 42 filter paper, or equivalent. Dilute the supernatant solution to a specific gravity of 1.254 with freshly boiled water.
  Dextrose standard solution: 280 µg/mL of dried dextrose, made to 500 mL
  Dibasic sodium phosphate solution: 190 mg/mL of dibasic sodium phosphate heptahydrate, made to 100 mL
  Sample solution: Dissolve 1 g of sample in 150 mL of water, and adjust the pH to between 6.9 and 7.2 with sodium hydroxide solution or acetic acid. Add *Lead subacetate solution* in increments until no further precipitation is observed. Bring the volume to 250.0 mL with water, and mix well. Centrifuge the mixture, pipet 10 mL of the supernatant into a 50-mL volumetric flask, and dilute with water to about 35 mL. Add 2 mL or more of *Dibasic sodium phosphate solution* until no further precipitation forms. Dilute with water to 50 mL, and mix. Centrifuge at 2100 × gravity for 10 min. The supernatant is the *Sample solution*.
  Analysis: Pipet 5 mL of the *Sample solution* into a test tube containing exactly 5 mL of *Copper reagent solution* and mix. Loosely plug the tube and place it in a boiling water bath for 40 min ± 10 s. At the end of the heating period, cool the tube immediately in cold water. Add 2 mL of 2.5% potassium iodide solution and 1.5 mL of 2 N sulfuric acid. Mix well and titrate with 0.005 N sodium thiosulfate, using starch as the indicator. Record the volume of 0.005 N sodium thiosulfate consumed as V_S. Run a corresponding blank titration, V_B, using 5 mL of water and 5 mL of *Copper reagent solution*. Repeat the entire procedure using 5 mL of *Dextrose standard solution* and 5 mL of *Copper reagent solution*, and noting the volume of 0.005 N sodium thiosulfate consumed as V_D. Run a corresponding blank titration, V_B, using 5 mL of water and 5 mL of *Copper reagent solution*. Calculate the percent reducing sugars by the formula:

  $$\text{Result} = 35(V_B - V_S)/(V_B - V_D)$$

  $V_B - V_S$ = Quantity of 0.005 N sodium thiosulfate (mL) consumed by the 5-mL aliquot of *Sample solution*
  $V_B - V_D$ = Quantity of 0.005 N sodium thiosulfate (mL) consumed by 5 mL of *Dextrose standard solution*
  Acceptance criteria: NMT 30.0%
- **Residue on Ignition (Sulfated Ash),** Appendix IIC
  Sample: 1 g
  Acceptance criteria: NMT 20.0%
- **Sodium**
  Standard solution: 2 µg/mL prepared by diluting a certified 1000-ppm Sodium Standard Solution (Mallinckrodt or equivalent) quantitatively and stepwise

with deionized water. Store the *Standard solution* in polyethylene bottles because of its instability in glass.

Sample solution: Transfer 1.00 ± 0.05 g of a previously dried sample into a silica or porcelain dish. Ash in a muffle furnace at 246° to 260° for 2 to 4 h. Allow the ash to cool, and dissolve it in 5 mL of 20% hydrochloric acid, warming the solution, if necessary, to completely dissolve the residue. Pass the solution through acid-washed filter paper into a 500-mL volumetric flask. Wash the filter paper with hot water, dilute with water to volume, and mix. Prepare a 1:100 aqueous dilution of this solution to obtain the final *Sample solution*.

Analysis: Using a suitably calibrated atomic absorption spectrophotometer, determine the absorbance of the *Standard solution* and *Sample solution* at 589.0 nm.

Acceptance criteria: The absorbance of the *Sample solution* is not greater than that of the *Standard solution*. (NMT 10.0%)

- **VISCOSITY OF A 50% SOLUTION**
  Sample: An amount of sample equivalent to 200 g calculated on the dried basis
  Analysis: Dissolve the *Sample* in 200 mL of water contained in a 500-mL beaker. Equilibrate the solution at 25° and measure its relative viscosity with a Brookfield viscometer (Model RVT, or equivalent), using a number 2 spindle at 20 rpm.
  Acceptance criteria: NMT 3000 centipoises

Sodium Magnesium Aluminosilicate

First Published: Prior to FCC 6

CAS: [12040-43-6]

DESCRIPTION
Sodium Magnesium Aluminosilicate occurs as synthetic, amorphous, food-grade coprecipitates that are fine, white powders or beads. It comprises a series of hydrated sodium magnesium aluminosilicates having $Na_2O:MgO:Al_2O_3:SiO_2$ molar ratios of approximately 2:1:2:24, respectively. It has a specific gravity of about 2. It is insoluble in water, in alcohol, and in other organic solvents, but it is partially soluble in strongly acidic and alkaline solutions.

Function: Anticaking agent
Packaging and Storage: Store in well-closed containers.

IDENTIFICATION
- **A. PROCEDURE**
  Sample: 500 mg
  Analysis: Mix the *Sample* with 2.5 g of anhydrous potassium carbonate, and heat the mixture in a platinum or nickel crucible until it melts completely. Cool, add 5 mL of water, and allow to stand for 3 min. Heat the bottom of the crucible gently, detach the melt, and transfer it into a beaker with the aid of about 50 mL of water. Gradually add hydrochloric acid until no effervescence is observed, add 10 mL more of the acid, and evaporate to dryness on a steam bath. Cool, add 20 mL of water, boil, and filter through ash-free filter paper. An insoluble residue of silica remains.
  [NOTE—Retain the filtrate for *Identification* test *B*, *Identification* test *C* and *Identification* test *D* (below).] Transfer the gelatinous residue to a platinum dish, and cautiously add 5 mL of hydrofluoric acid. [**CAUTION**—Handle hydrofluoric acid in an appropriate fume hood.] The precipitate dissolves. (If it does not dissolve, repeat the treatment with hydrofluoric acid.) Heat the solution and introduce a glass stirring rod with a drop of water on the tip into the resulting vapors.
  Acceptance criteria: The drop of water becomes turbid.
- **B. ALUMINUM,** Appendix IIIA
  Sample: A portion of the filtrate obtained in *Identification* test *A*.
  Acceptance criteria: Passes tests
- **C. MAGNESIUM,** Appendix IIIA
  Sample: A portion of the filtrate obtained in *Identification* test *A*.
  Acceptance criteria: Passes tests
- **D. SODIUM,** Appendix IIIA
  Sample: A portion of the filtrate obtained in *Identification* test *A*.
  Acceptance criteria: Passes tests

ASSAY
- **SILICON DIOXIDE**
  Sample: 500 mg, previously dried
  Analysis: Transfer the *Sample* into a 250-mL beaker, wash the sides of the beaker with a few mL of water, and add 30 mL of sulfuric acid and 15 mL of hydrochloric acid. Heat the solution on a hot plate in a hood until dense, white fumes evolve. Cool, add an additional 15 mL of hydrochloric acid and heat again to dense, white fumes. Cool, add 70 mL of water, and filter through Whatman No. 40, or equivalent, filter paper. Wash the filter paper and precipitate thoroughly with hot water to remove the sulfuric acid residue. Transfer the filter paper and precipitate into a tared platinum crucible, char, and ignite at 900° to constant weight. Moisten the residue with a few drops of water, add 15 mL of hydrofluoric acid and 8 drops of sulfuric acid, and heat on a hot plate in a hood until white fumes of sulfur trioxide evolve. Cool; add 5 mL of water, 10 mL of hydrofluoric acid, and 3 drops of sulfuric acid; and evaporate to dryness on the hot plate. Heat cautiously over an open flame until sulfur trioxide fumes cease to evolve, and ignite at 900° to constant weight. The weight loss after the addition of hydrofluoric acid represents the weight of SiO_2 in the *Sample*.
  Acceptance criteria: NLT 65.0% and NMT 75.0% SiO_2, on the dried basis
- **ALUMINUM OXIDE**
  Sample stock solution: Transfer 500 mg of sample, previously dried, into a tared platinum dish and moisten with 8 to 10 drops of water. Add 25 mL of 70% perchloric acid and 10 mL of hydrofluoric acid, and heat on a hot plate until dense, white fumes of perchloric acid evolve. [**CAUTION**—Handle perchloric acid in an appropriate fume hood.] Cool, add an additional 10 mL of hydrofluoric acid, and heat again to dense, white fumes. Cool, dissolve in sufficient water,

quantitatively transfer it with the aid of additional water into a 250-mL volumetric flask, and dilute to volume with water. [NOTE—Retain the unused portion of this solution for the tests for *Magnesium Oxide* and *Sodium Oxide* analysis (below).]

Sample solution: 10.0 mL of *Sample stock solution* diluted to 100 mL with water

Standard solutions: Prepare 5 µg/mL, 10 µg/mL, 20 µg/mL, and 50 µg/mL aqueous solutions of aluminum, in the form of the chloride.

Analysis: Set a suitable atomic absorption spectrophotometer to a wavelength of 309.3 nm and adjust the instrument to zero absorbance against water. Read the absorbance of the *Standard solutions* and plot the standard curve as absorbance versus concentration of aluminum.

Aspirate the *Sample solution* into the spectrophotometer, read the absorbance in the same manner, and by reference to the standard curve, determine the concentration (C) of aluminum, in µg/mL, in the *Sample stock solution*. Calculate the quantity, in mg, of Al_2O_3 in the sample taken by the formula:

$$Result = (250C \times 10 \times 1.8895)/1000$$

C = concentration of aluminum (µg/mL) in the *Sample stock solution*, calculated from the standard curve

Acceptance criteria: NLT 9.0% and NMT 13.0% of Al_2O_3, on the dried basis

- **MAGNESIUM OXIDE**

  Sample solution: A portion of the *Sample stock solution* from the test for *Aluminum oxide* (above)

  Standard solutions: Prepare 5 µg/mL, 10 µg/mL, and 25 µg/mL, 50 µg/mL aqueous solutions of magnesium, in the form of the chloride.

  Analysis: Set a suitable atomic absorption spectrophotometer to a wavelength of 285.2 nm and adjust the instrument to zero absorbance against water. Read the absorbance of the *Standard solutions* and plot the standard curve as absorbance versus concentration of magnesium.

  Aspirate the *Sample solution* into the spectrophotometer, read the absorbance in the same manner, and by reference to the standard curve, determine the concentration (C) of magnesium, in µg/mL, in the *Sample solution*. Calculate the quantity, in mg, of MgO in the sample taken by the formula:

  $$Result = 250C \times 1.6579/1000$$

  C = concentration of magnesium (µg/mL) in the *Sample solution*, calculated from the standard curve

  Acceptance criteria: NLT 1.0% and NMT 3.0%, on the dried basis

- **SODIUM OXIDE**

  Sample solution: A portion of the *Sample stock solution* from the test for *Aluminum oxide* (above)

  Standard solutions: Prepare 50 µg/mL, 100 µg/mL, and 150 µg/mL, 200 µg/mL aqueous solutions of sodium, in the form of the chloride.

  Correction for sodium sulfate content: Transfer 1 g of sample, previously dried, into a tared platinum dish and moisten with 8 to 10 drops of water. Add 25 mL of 70% perchloric acid and 10 mL of hydrofluoric acid, and heat on a hot plate in a hood until dense, white fumes of perchloric acid evolve. Add 10 mL of hydrofluoric acid, and heat again to dense, white fumes. [**CAUTION**—Handle perchloric acid in an appropriate fume hood.] Quantitatively transfer the solution into a 400-mL beaker, add 200 mL of water, and heat to boiling. Gradually add, in small portions and while stirring constantly, an excess of hot barium chloride TS (about 10 mL), and heat the mixture on a steam bath for 1 h. Collect the precipitate on a filter, wash until free from chloride, dry, ignite, and weigh the resulting barium sulfate so obtained. Calculate the correction factor (F) by the formula:

  $$Result = 0.437 \times (C' \times w/W)$$

  C' = weight (mg) of barium sulfate obtained multiplied by 0.6086 (to convert to Na_2SO_4 equivalents)
  w = weight (mg) of the sample taken for the *Sodium Oxide* determination
  W = weight of the sample taken for the *Correction for sodium sulfate content* determination (mg)

  Analysis: Set a suitable flame photometer to a wavelength of 589 nm and adjust the instrument to zero transmittance against water. Adjust the instrument to 100.0% transmittance with the *Standard solution* containing 200 µg/mL of sodium, in the form of the chloride. Read the percent transmittance of the remaining three *Standard solutions* and plot the standard curve as percent transmittance versus concentration of sodium.

  Aspirate the *Sample solution* into the photometer, read the percent transmittance in the same manner, and by reference to the standard curve, determine the concentration (C) of sodium, in µg/mL, in the *Sample solution*. Calculate the quantity, in mg, of Na_2O in the sample taken by the formula:

  $$Result = (250C \times 1.348/1000) - F$$

  C = concentration of sodium (µg/mL) in the *Sample solution*, calculated from the standard curve
  F = quantity of sodium oxide equivalent to any sodium sulfate present in the sample (calculated in *Correction for sodium sulfate content* above)

  Acceptance criteria: NLT 3.0% and NMT 9.0% of Na_2O, on the dried basis

IMPURITIES
Inorganic Impurities
- **LEAD**

  Standard stock solution: 100 µg/mL of Pb prepared as follows: Dissolve 159.8 mg of ACS reagent-grade lead nitrate [Pb(NO$_3$)$_2$] in 100 mL of water containing 1 mL of nitric acid, dilute to 1000.0 with water, and mix. [NOTE—Prepare and store this solution in glass containers that are free from lead salts.]

  Standard solution: 0.50 µg/mL Pb: from *Standard stock solution*. [NOTE—Prepare this solution on the day of use.]

  Sample solution: Transfer 10.0 g of sample into a 250-mL beaker, add 50 mL of 0.5 N hydrochloric acid, cover with a watch glass, and heat slowly to boiling. Boil gently for 15 min, cool, and let the undissolved material settle. Decant the supernatant liquid through Whatman No. 4, or equivalent, filter paper into a 100-mL volumetric flask, retaining as much as possible of the insoluble material in the beaker. Wash the slurry and beaker with three 10-mL portions of hot water, decanting each washing through the filter into the flask. Finally, wash the filter paper with 15 mL of hot water, cool the filtrate to room temperature, dilute to volume with water, and mix.

  Analysis: Set a suitable atomic absorption spectrophotometer to a wavelength of 217 nm. Adjust the instrument to zero absorbance against water. Read the absorbance of the *Standard solution*. Aspirate the *Sample solution* into the spectrophotometer and measure the absorbance in the same manner.

  Acceptance criteria: The absorbance obtained from the *Sample solution* is NMT that obtained from the *Standard solution*. (NMT 5 mg/kg)

SPECIFIC TESTS
- **LOSS ON DRYING,** Appendix IIC: 105° for 2 h

  Acceptance criteria: NMT 8.0%

- **LOSS ON IGNITION**

  Sample: 5 g, previously dried

  Analysis: Transfer the *Sample* into a suitable tared crucible and ignite at 900° to constant weight.

  Acceptance criteria: Between 8.0% and 11.0%, on the dried basis

- **PH,** *pH Determination,* Appendix IIB

  Sample mixture: 200 mg/mL in carbon dioxide-free water

  Acceptance criteria: Between 6.5 and 11.0

- **SOLUBLE SALT (AS NA$_2$SO$_4$)**

  Analysis: Calculate the percent sodium sulfate from the weight of barium sulfate obtained in the *Correction for sodium sulfate content* in the *Sodium Oxide* test by the formula:

  $$\text{Result} = N \times 60.86 / W$$

  N = weight of barium sulfate (mg)
  W = weight of the sample taken for the *Correction for sodium sulfate content* determination (mg)

  Acceptance criteria: NMT 7.5%

Sodium Metabisulfite

First Published: Prior to FCC 6
Last Revision: Second Supplement, FCC 6

Sodium Pyrosulfite

Na$_2$S$_2$O$_5$ Formula wt 190.11
INS: 223 CAS: [7681-57-4]
UNII: 4VON5FNS3C [sodium metabisulfite]

DESCRIPTION
Sodium Metabisulfite occurs as colorless crystals or as a white to yellow, crystalline powder. It is freely soluble in water and slightly soluble in alcohol. Its solutions are acid to litmus.

Function: Preservative; antioxidant

Packaging and Storage: Store in well-filled, tight containers, and avoid exposure to excessive heat.

IDENTIFICATION
- **SODIUM,** Appendix IIIA

  Sample solution: 100 mg/mL

  Acceptance criteria: Passes test

- **SULFITE,** Appendix IIIA

  Sample solution: 100 mg/mL

  Acceptance criteria: Passes test

ASSAY
- **PROCEDURE**

  Sample: 200 mg

  Analysis: Add the *Sample* to 50 mL of 0.1 N iodine contained in a glass-stoppered flask. Allow the solution to stand for 5 min, add 1 mL of hydrochloric acid, and titrate the excess iodine with 0.1 N sodium thiosulfate, adding starch TS as the indicator. Each mL of 0.1 N iodine is equivalent to 4.752 mg of Na$_2$S$_2$O$_5$.

  Acceptance criteria: NLT 90.0% and NMT 100.5% of Na$_2$S$_2$O$_5$

IMPURITIES
Inorganic Impurities
- **IRON**

  Sample: 500 mg

  Control: 1.0 mL (10 µg Fe) *Iron Standard Solution* (see *Standard Solutions for the Preparation of Controls and Standards,* Solutions and Indicators)

  Analysis: Add 2 mL of hydrochloric acid to the *Sample* and evaporate to dryness on a steam bath. Dissolve the residue in 2 mL of hydrochloric acid and 20 mL of water, add a few drops of bromine TS, and boil the solution to remove the bromine. Cool, dilute with water to 25 mL, then add 50 mg of ammonium persulfate and 5 mL of ammonium thiocyanate TS. Repeat the preceding using the *Control* in place of the *Sample*.

  Acceptance criteria: Any red or pink color produced by the *Sample* does not exceed that produced by the *Control*. (NMT 10 mg/kg)

- **LEAD,** *Lead Limit Test, APDC Extraction Method,* Appendix IIIB

  Acceptance criteria: NMT 2 mg/kg

- **SELENIUM,** *Selenium Limit Test, Method I,* Appendix IIIB
  Sample: 1.2 g (with 600 mg of magnesium oxide)
  Acceptance criteria: The absorbance of the extract from the *Sample Preparation* is NMT the absorbance of the extract from the *Standard Preparation*. (NMT 5 mg/kg)

Sodium Metaphosphate, Insoluble

First Published: Prior to FCC 6
Last Revision: First Supplement, FCC 6

Insoluble Sodium Polyphosphate
IMP
Maddrell's Salt

CAS: [50813-16-6]
UNII: P1BM4ZH95L [sodium polymetaphosphate]

DESCRIPTION
Sodium Metaphosphate, Insoluble, occurs as a white, crystalline powder. It is a high-molecular-weight sodium polyphosphate composed of two long metaphosphate chains (NaPO$_3$) that spiral in opposite directions about a common axis. The Na$_2$O:P$_2$O$_5$ ratio is about 1 : 1. It is practically insoluble in water but dissolves in mineral acids and in solutions of potassium and ammonium (but not sodium) chlorides. The pH of a 1 : 3 slurry in water is about 6.5.
Function: Emulsifier; sequestrant; texturizer
Packaging and Storage: Store in tight containers.

IDENTIFICATION
- **A. PROCEDURE**
  Sample: 1 g
  Analysis: Finely powder the *Sample* and add it slowly to 100 mL of a 50 mg/mL solution of potassium chloride in water while stirring vigorously.
  Acceptance criteria: A gelatinous mass forms.
- **B. PHOSPHATES,** Appendix IIIA
  Sample solution: Mix 500 mg of sample with 10 mL of nitric acid and 50 mL of water, boil for about 30 min and cool. [NOTE—Retain remaining solution for *Identification* test C (below).]
  Acceptance criteria: Passes tests
- **C. SODIUM,** Appendix IIIA
  Sample solution: Solution prepared for *Identification* test B (above)
  Acceptance criteria: Passes tests

ASSAY
- **PROCEDURE**
  Sample: 800 mg
  Analysis: Transfer the *Sample* to a 400-mL beaker, add 100 mL of water and 25 mL of nitric acid, cover with a watch glass, and boil for 10 min on a hot plate. Rinse any condensate from the watch glass into the beaker, cool the solution to room temperature, transfer it quantitatively to a 500-mL volumetric flask, dilute with water to volume, and mix thoroughly. Pipet 20.0 mL of this solution into a 500-mL Erlenmeyer flask, add 100 mL of water, and heat just to boiling. While stirring, add 50 mL of quimociac TS, then cover with a watch glass, and boil for 1 min in a well-ventilated hood. Cool to room temperature, swirling occasionally while cooling, then filter through a tared, sintered-glass filter crucible of medium porosity, and wash with five 25-mL portions of water. Dry at about 225° for 30 min, cool, and weigh. Each mg of precipitate thus obtained is equivalent to 32.074 µg of P$_2$O$_5$.
  Acceptance criteria: NLT 68.7% and NMT 70.0% of P$_2$O$_5$

IMPURITIES
Inorganic Impurities
- **ARSENIC,** *Arsenic Limit Test,* Appendix IIIB
  Sample solution: 1 g in 15 mL of 2.7 N hydrochloric acid
  Acceptance criteria: NMT 3 mg/kg
- **FLUORIDE,** *Fluoride Limit Test, Method III,* Appendix IIIB
  Acceptance criteria: NMT 0.005%
- **LEAD,** *Lead Limit Test, APDC Extraction Method,* Appendix IIIB
  Acceptance criteria: NMT 4 mg/kg

Sodium Metasilicate

First Published: Prior to FCC 6

Na$_2$O·SiO$_2$·xH$_2$O
INS: 550

Formula wt, anhydrous 122.06
CAS: [6834-92-0]

DESCRIPTION
Sodium Metasilicate occurs as a white, free-flowing, granular material. It is a hydrous (pentahydrate) or anhydrous silicate having a 1 : 1 molar ratio of SiO$_2$ to Na$_2$O. At 30°, the anhydrous Sodium Metasilicate is readily soluble in water (270 g/L) as is its pentahydrate (610 g/L). The pH values of 1% solutions of anhydrous Sodium Metasilicate and its pentahydrate are about 12.6 and 12.4, respectively.
Function: Saponifying agent; boiler water additive
Packaging and Storage: Store in tight containers.
[CAUTION—Sodium Metasilicate and its solutions are caustic materials and can cause eye and skin burns. Use proper protective equipment and avoid contact with the eyes, skin, and clothing. Do not inhale vapors from Sodium Metasilicate solutions.]

IDENTIFICATION
- **SILICATE**
  Sample solution: 20 mg/mL, made to 10 mL
  Ammonium molybdate solution: 50 mg/mL, made to 10 mL, to which 3 mL of sulfuric acid is subsequently added
  Analysis: Place a drop of *Sample solution* on a spot plate. Add 1 drop of 4 M sodium hydroxide and 1 drop of *Ammonium molybdate solution*. [NOTE—Retain the final solution for the test for *Sodium* (below).]
  Acceptance criteria: A deep yellow color develops.

- **SODIUM**
  Sample solution: The final solution prepared in the test for *Silicate* (above)
  Analysis: Dip a clean nichrome wire into the *Sample solution* and place the wire in the flame of a Bunsen burner.
  Acceptance criteria: A bright yellow-colored flame is produced.

ASSAY
- **SILICON DIOXIDE**
  Sample: 1 g
  Analysis: In a beaker, acidify the *Sample* with 5 mL of hydrochloric acid and evaporate to dryness on a steam bath. Repeat the treatment with an additional 5 mL of hydrochloric acid, and mix the residue with a 1 : 20 (v/v) solution of hydrochloric acid. Digest the residue on the steam bath to dissolve the soluble salts, filter the contents of the beaker through an ashless filter paper, and quantitatively transfer the residue to the paper. Wash the paper and residue thoroughly with hot water, transfer the paper to a platinum crucible, dry the paper for 1 h at 105°, and carefully char it at low heat. Gradually increase the heat to burn away the paper and finally ignite the crucible and its contents to constant weight at 1000°. Cool the crucible in a desiccator, and weigh. Moisten the ignited residue with a few drops of water, and cautiously add 15 mL of hydrofluoric acid and 5 drops of 1 : 3 sulfuric acid. Heat the crucible on a hot plate in a fume hood until all of the acid is driven off. Then ignite the residue to constant weight at a temperature of 1000°. Cool the crucible in a desiccator, and weigh. The loss in weight is equivalent to the weight of SiO_2 in the sample taken.
  Acceptance criteria: NLT 90.0% and NMT 110.0% of the percentage claimed on the label

- **SODIUM OXIDE**
  Sample: 500 mg
  Analysis: Disperse the *Sample* in 150 mL of water and heat to ensure its dissolution. Add 2 to 3 drops of phenolphthalein TS and 100.0 mL of 0.1 N sulfuric acid. Titrate with 0.1 N sodium hydroxide until a permanent pink color first appears. Subtract the volume of 0.1 N sodium hydroxide from the volume of 0.1 N sulfuric acid. Each mL of 0.1 N sulfuric acid is equivalent to 3.099 mg of sodium oxide.
  Acceptance criteria: NLT 90.0% and NMT 110.0% of the percentage claimed on the label

IMPURITIES
Inorganic Impurities
- **LEAD**
  Standard stock solution: Dissolve 159.8 mg of ACS reagent-grade lead nitrate in 100 mL of water containing 1 mL of nitric acid; dilute to 1000.0 mL with water and mix. Each mL of this solution contains 100 µg of lead. [NOTE—Prepare and store this solution in glass containers that are free from lead salts.]
  Standard solution: 0.50 µg/mL of lead prepared from the *Standard stock solution*. [NOTE—Prepare this solution on the day of use.]
  Sample: 10 g
  Sample solution: Transfer the *Sample* to a 250-mL beaker, add 50 mL of 0.5 N hydrochloric acid, cover with a watch glass, and heat slowly to boiling. Boil gently for 15 min, cool, and let the undissolved material settle. Decant the supernatant liquid through Whatman No. 4, or equivalent, filter paper into a 100-mL volumetric flask, retaining as much as possible of the insoluble material in the beaker. Wash the slurry and beaker with three 10-mL portions of hot water, decanting each washing through the filter into the flask. Finally, wash the filter paper with 15 mL of hot water, cool the filtrate to room temperature, dilute to volume with water, and mix.
  Analysis: Set a suitable atomic absorption spectrophotometer to a wavelength of 217 nm and adjust the instrument to zero absorbance against water. Measure the absorbance of the *Standard solution* and of the *Sample solution*.
  Acceptance criteria: The absorbance of the *Sample solution* does not exceed that of the *Standard solution*. (NMT 5 mg/kg)

SPECIFIC TESTS
- **LOSS ON IGNITION**
  Analysis: Ignite an accurately weighed sample in a suitable tared crucible at 1000° for 20 min.
  Acceptance criteria
  Anhydrous: NMT 0.5%
  Pentahydrate: Between 40.5% and 42.7%

OTHER REQUIREMENTS
- **LABELING:** Indicate the percent, each, of SiO_2 and Na_2O, and whether the material is anhydrous or the pentahydrate.

Sodium Methylate

First Published: Prior to FCC 6

Sodium Methoxide

CH_3ONa Formula wt 54.02
                                   CAS: [124-41-4]

UNII: IG663U5EMC [sodium methoxide]

DESCRIPTION
Sodium Methylate occurs as a white, amorphous, hygroscopic, free-flowing powder. It is soluble in fats, in esters, and in alcohols. It decomposes without melting above 127°.
Function: Catalyst for the trans-esterification of fats
Packaging and Storage: Store in airtight containers, and take all necessary precautions to prevent combustion during handling.
[CAUTION—Sodium Methylate and its solutions are caustic and flammable. Avoid contact with the eyes, skin, and clothing, and do not inhale vapors from Sodium Methylate solutions.]

IDENTIFICATION
- **REACTIVITY**
  Analysis: Expose a sample to oxygen, carbon dioxide, and water.
  Acceptance criteria: The sample reacts with decomposition in each case.
- **SODIUM,** Appendix IIIA.
  Sample: The solution resulting from the test for *Reactivity* with water (above)
  Acceptance criteria: Passes test

ASSAY
- **ALKALINITY** (as CH_3ONa): [NOTE—Conduct the test with minimal exposure of the sample to air, preferably in a hood with nitrogen atmosphere.]
  Sample: 12 to 15 g
  Analysis: Select two tared weighing bottles of the approximate dimensions 30 mm × 80 mm. Fill each almost to volume with *Sample*, securely fit the covers, and weigh. Remove the top from one of the bottles and immediately place it into a 500-mL Erlenmeyer flask containing 200 mL of ice-cold, carbon dioxide-free water, sliding the weighing bottle gently down the side of the flask to prevent splashing. Immediately stopper the flask with a rubber stopper, and swirl until the *Sample* dissolves. Wash this solution into a 250-mL volumetric flask, and dilute nearly to volume with carbon dioxide-free water. Allow the solution to reach room temperature, then dilute to volume with water, and mix. Transfer 50.0 mL of this solution into a 500-mL glass-stoppered Erlenmeyer flask, add 150 mL of carbon dioxide-free water and 5 mL of barium chloride TS. Stopper the flask, mix, and allow to stand for 5 min. Add 3 drops of phenolphthalein TS and titrate with 1 N hydrochloric acid to the disappearance of the pink color. [NOTE—Retain the titrated solution for the test for *Sodium Carbonate*, below.] Calculate the percentage of alkalinity as CH_3ONa (% A) by the formula:

  $$Result = (V_1 \times N \times 5.403)/(W \times 0.2)$$

  V_1 = volume (mL) of hydrochloric acid used
  N = normality of the hydrochloric acid
  W = weight (g) of the sample taken
  Acceptance criteria: NLT 97.0% of CH_3ONa

IMPURITIES
Inorganic Impurities
- **ARSENIC,** *Arsenic Limit Test,* Appendix IIIB
  Sample solution: Cautiously dissolve 1 g of the sample in 10 mL of water, neutralize to litmus paper with 2 N sulfuric acid, and dilute to 35 mL with water.
  Acceptance criteria: NMT 3 mg/kg
- **LEAD,** *Lead Limit Test,* Appendix IIIB
  Sample solution: Cautiously dissolve 1 g of the sample in 10 mL of water, add 10 mL of diluted hydrochloric acid, and heat to boiling. Cool and dilute to 25 mL with water.
  Control: 5 µg Pb (5 mL of *Diluted Standard Lead Solution*)
  Acceptance criteria: NMT 5 mg/kg
- **MERCURY,** *Mercury Limit Test, Method I,* Appendix IIIB: [NOTE—For the *Sample preparation* in the Appendix, use the following *Sample solution*.]
  Sample solution: Cautiously dissolve 2 g of sample in 10 mL of water in a small beaker. Add 2 drops of phenolphthalein TS and slowly neutralize, with constant stirring, using 1 : 5 sulfuric acid. Add 1 mL of the 1 : 5 sulfuric acid solution and 1 mL of a 1 : 25 solution of potassium permanganate, and mix.
  Acceptance criteria: NMT 1 mg/kg
- **SODIUM CARBONATE:** [NOTE—Conduct the test with minimal exposure of the sample to air, preferably in a hood with nitrogen atmosphere.]
  Sample solution: The titrated solution retained from the test for *Alkalinity* (above)
  Analysis: Add 2 drops of methyl orange TS to the *Sample solution*, and continue the titration with 1 N hydrochloric acid to a permanent pink color. Calculate the percentage of Na_2CO_3 by the formula:

  $$Result = (V_2 \times N \times 5.30)/(W \times 0.2)$$

  V_2 = volume (mL) of 1 N hydrochloric acid used in this titration
  N = normality of the hydrochloric acid
  W = weight (g) of the sample taken
  Acceptance criteria: NMT 0.4%
- **SODIUM HYDROXIDE:** [NOTE—Conduct the test with minimal exposure of the sample to air, preferably in a hood with nitrogen atmosphere.]
  Analysis: Adapt the *Water Determination, Method I (Karl Fischer Titrimetric Method),* Appendix IIB
  Acceptance criteria: NMT 1.7%

Add the following:

▲Sodium Molybdate Dihydrate
First Published: FCC 8

Molybdic Acid Disodium Salt, Dihydrate
Disodium Molybdate Dihydrate
Sodium Molybdate (VI)

$Na_2MoO_4 \cdot 2H_2O$ Formula wt 241.9
CAS: [10102-40-6]
UNII: 8F2SXI1704 [sodium molybdate dihydrate]

DESCRIPTION
Sodium Molybdate Dihydrate occurs as a white or almost white powder, or colorless crystals. It is freely soluble in water.
Function: Nutrient

1050 / Sodium Molybdate Dihydrate / Monographs

Packaging and Storage: Store in a tightly sealed container in a cool, dry place, away from direct light and moisture.

IDENTIFICATION

- **SODIUM**, Appendix IIIA
  Sample solution: 75 mg/mL
  Acceptance criteria: A dense white precipitate is formed.
- **MOLYBDENUM**
  Sample: 0.2 g
  Analysis: Dissolve the *Sample* in 5 mL of a mixture of equal volumes of nitric acid and water, and add 0.1 g of ammonium chloride. Add 0.3 mL of a 9% w/v solution of dibasic sodium phosphate, and heat slowly at 50°–60°. A yellow precipitate is formed.
  Acceptance criteria: Passes test
- **INFRARED ABSORPTION**, *Spectrophotometric Identification Tests*, Appendix IIIC
  Reference standard: USP Sodium Molybdate Dihydrate RS
  Sample and standard preparation: M
  Acceptance criteria: The spectrum of the sample exhibits maxima at the same wavelengths as those in the spectrum of the *Reference standard*.

ASSAY

- **PROCEDURE**
  Sample: 0.100 g
  Analysis: Dissolve the dry *Sample* in 30 mL of water, add 0.5 g of hexamethylenetetramine and 0.1 mL of a 250 g/L solution of nitric acid. Heat until the mixture reaches 60°, and titrate with 0.05 M lead nitrate using 4-(2-pyridylazo) resorcinol monosodium salt as indicator. Each mL of 0.05 M lead nitrate is equivalent to 10.30 mg of Na_2MoO_4.
  Acceptance criteria: 99.0%–101.0% on the dried basis

IMPURITIES

Inorganic Impurities

- **AMMONIUM**
  Ammonium standard solution: Transfer 0.741 g of ammonium chloride to a 1000-mL volumetric flask, and dilute with water to volume. Transfer 10 mL of this solution to a 1000-mL volumetric flask, and dilute again with water to volume. Transfer 400 mL of this solution to a 1000-mL volumetric flask, and dilute further with water to volume. Each mL contains 1 ppm of NH_4^+. [NOTE—Prepare this solution immediately before use.]
  Silver manganese paper: Immerse strips of slow filter paper into a solution containing 8.5 g/L of manganese sulfate and 8.5 g/L of silver nitrate. Maintain strips in the solution for a few minutes, remove, and allow to dry over diphosphorus pentoxide protected from acid and alkaline vapors.
  Sample: 0.1 g
  Analysis: Transfer the *Sample* to a 25-mL container fitted with a cap, dissolve in 1 mL of water, and add 0.30 g of magnesium oxide. Place a 5-mm square of *Silver manganese paper* wetted with a few drops of water under the polyethylene cap, and close immediately. Swirl, avoiding projections of liquid, and allow to stand at 40° for 30 min. The silver manganese paper shows a grey color that should not be more intense than that of a standard prepared using 1 mL of *Ammonium standard solution*, 1 mL of water, and 0.30 g of magnesium oxide.
  Acceptance criteria: NMT 10 mg/kg
- **CHLORIDE**, *Chloride and Sulfate Limit Tests, Chloride Limit Test*, Appendix IIIB
  Sample: 400 mg
  Control: 20 µg of chloride (2 mL of *Standard Chloride Solution*). [NOTE—Prepare this solution immediately before use.]
  Acceptance criteria: Any turbidity produced by the *Sample* does not exceed that produced by the *Control* (NMT 50 mg/kg).
- **PHOSPHATES**
  Phosphate standard solution: Transfer 0.286 g of monobasic potassium phosphate to a 1000-mL volumetric flask, and dilute with water to volume. Each mL of this solution contains 200 ppm of PO_4^{-3}. [NOTE—Prepare this solution immediately before use.]
  Sample: 2 g
  Analysis: Mix the *Sample* with 13 mL of water, and heat. Then dissolve 8.0 g of ammonium nitrate in the still hot solution. Add this solution to 27 mL of a mixture of equal volumes of nitric acid and water. Prepare the standard solution at the same time and in the same manner by dissolving 1.0 g of ammonium nitrate in 12 mL of water and adding 1 mL of the *Phosphate standard solution*. Any yellow color or opalescence in the sample solution should not be more intense within 3 h than the prepared standard solution.
  Acceptance criteria: NMT 200 mg/kg of PO_4^{-3}
- **ARSENIC**, *Elemental Impurities by ICP, Method I*, Appendix IIIC
  Acceptance criteria: NMT 1 mg/kg
- **CADMIUM**, *Elemental Impurities by ICP, Method I*, Appendix IIIC
  Acceptance criteria: NMT 5 mg/kg
- **LEAD**, *Elemental Impurities by ICP, Method I*, Appendix IIIC
  Acceptance criteria: NMT 1 mg/kg
- **MERCURY**, *Elemental Impurities by ICP, Method I*, Appendix IIIC
  Acceptance criteria: NMT 1 mg/kg

SPECIFIC TESTS

- **LOSS ON DRYING**, Appendix IIC: 140° for 3h
  Acceptance criteria: 14.0%–16.0% ▲FCC8

Sodium Nitrate

First Published: Prior to FCC 6

$NaNO_3$ Formula wt 85.00
INS: 251 CAS: [7631-99-4]
UNII: 8M4L3H2ZVZ [sodium nitrate]

DESCRIPTION

Sodium Nitrate occurs as colorless crystals or white crystalline granules or powder. It is moderately deliquescent in moist air. It is freely soluble in water, and is sparingly soluble in alcohol.

Function: Antimicrobial agent; preservative
Packaging and Storage: Store in tight containers.

IDENTIFICATION

- **NITRATE,** Appendix IIIA
  Sample solution: 200 mg/mL
  Acceptance criteria: Passes tests
- **SODIUM,** Appendix IIIA
  Sample solution: 200 mg/mL
  Acceptance criteria: Passes tests
- **PH**
  Sample solution: 200 mg/mL
  Acceptance criteria: Neutral to litmus

ASSAY

- **PROCEDURE**
  Sample: 350 mg, previously dried at 105° for 4 h
  Analysis: Dissolve the *Sample* in 10 mL of hydrochloric acid in a small beaker or porcelain dish and evaporate to dryness on a steam bath. Dissolve the residue in 10 mL of hydrochloric acid, and again evaporate to dryness, continuing the heating until the residue, when dissolved in water, is neutral to litmus. Transfer the residue, with the aid of 25 mL of water, into a glass-stoppered flask and add exactly 50 mL of 0.1 N silver nitrate. Then, add 3 mL of nitric acid and 3 mL of nitrobenzene and shake the flask vigorously. Add ferric ammonium sulfate TS and titrate the excess silver nitrate with 0.1 N ammonium thiocyanate. Each mL of 0.1 N silver nitrate is equivalent to 8.50 mg of $NaNO_3$.
  Acceptance criteria: NLT 99.0% and NMT 100.5% $NaNO_3$, on the dried basis

IMPURITIES

Inorganic Impurities
- **LEAD,** *Lead Limit Test,* Appendix IIIB
  Sample solution: 100 mg/mL, made to 10 mL
  Control: 4 μg Pb (4 mL of *Diluted Standard Lead Solution*)
  Acceptance criteria: NMT 4 mg/kg

SPECIFIC TESTS

- **TOTAL CHLORINE**
  Sample: 1 g
  Analysis: Dissolve the *Sample* in 100 mL of water and add enough 6% sulfurous acid to give the solution a distinct odor of sulfur dioxide. Boil the solution gently until the odor of the sulfur dioxide is no longer evident and adjust the volume to 100 mL with water. Add 1.0 mL of 0.1 N silver nitrate followed by 3 mL of nitric acid and 3 mL of nitrobenzene, and shake vigorously. Add ferric ammonium sulfate TS, and titrate the excess silver nitrate with 0.1 N ammonium thiocyanate.
  Acceptance criteria: NMT 0.6 mL of the 0.1 N silver nitrate is consumed (Approximately 0.2%).

Sodium Nitrite

First Published: FCC 6

$NaNO_2$ Formula wt 69.00
INS: 250
UNII: M0KG633D4F [sodium nitrite]   CAS: [7632-00-0]

DESCRIPTION

Sodium Nitrite occurs as a white to slightly yellow, granular powder, or as white or nearly white, opaque, fused masses or sticks. It is hygroscopic in air. Its solutions are alkaline to litmus. One g dissolves in 1.5 mL of water, but it is sparingly soluble in alcohol.

Function: Color fixative in meat and meat products; antimicrobial agent; preservative
Packaging and Storage: Store in tight containers.

IDENTIFICATION

- **NITRITE,** Appendix IIIA
  Sample solution: Prepare an aqueous solution.
  Acceptance criteria: Passes test
- **SODIUM,** Appendix IIIA
  Sample solution: Prepare an aqueous solution.
  Acceptance criteria: Passes test

ASSAY

- **SODIUM NITRITE**
  Sample: 3 g, previously dried
  Analysis: Dissolve the *Sample* in water to make 100 mL. Pipet 10 mL of this solution into a mixture of 100.0 mL of 0.1 N potassium permanganate, 50 mL of water, and 5 mL of sulfuric acid, keeping the tip of the pipet well below the surface of the liquid. Warm the solution to 40°, allow it to stand for 5 min, and add 25.0 mL of 0.1 N oxalic acid. Heat the mixture to about 80° and titrate with 0.1 N potassium permanganate. Each mL of 0.1 N potassium permanganate is equivalent to 3.450 mg of $NaNO_2$.
  Acceptance criteria: NLT 97.0% and NMT 100.5% $NaNO_2$, on the dried basis

IMPURITIES

Inorganic Impurities
- **LEAD,** *Lead Limit Test,* Appendix IIIB
  Sample solution: 100 mg/mL, made to 10 mL
  Control: 4 μg Pb (4 mL of *Diluted Standard Lead Solution*)
  Acceptance criteria: NMT 4 mg/kg

SPECIFIC TESTS

- **LOSS ON DRYING,** Appendix IIC: Dry over silica gel for 4 h.
  Acceptance criteria: NMT 0.25%

Sodium Phosphate, Dibasic

First Published: Prior to FCC 6
Last Revision: FCC 8

Disodium Monohydrogen Phosphate
Disodium Phosphate

Na_2HPO_4 Formula wt, anhydrous 141.96
$Na_2HPO_4 \cdot 2H_2O$ Formula wt, dihydrate 177.99
INS: 339(ii) CAS: anhydrous [7558-79-4]
  dihydrate [10028-24-7]
UNII: 22ADO53M6F [sodium phosphate, dibasic, anhydrous]
UNII: 9425516E2T [sodium phosphate, dibasic, dihydrate]
UNII: GR686LBA74 [sodium phosphate, dibasic, unspecified]

DESCRIPTION
Sodium Phosphate, Dibasic occurs as a white, crystalline powder or as granules. It may be anhydrous or contain two molecules of water of hydration. The anhydrous form is hygroscopic. Both forms are freely soluble in water and insoluble in alcohol.
Function: Emulsifier; texturizer; buffer; nutrient
Packaging and Storage: Store in tightly closed containers.

IDENTIFICATION
- **PHOSPHATE**, Appendix IIIA
  Sample solution: 50 mg/mL
  Acceptance criteria: Passes test
- **SODIUM**, Appendix IIIA
  Sample solution: 50 mg/mL
  Acceptance criteria: Passes test

ASSAY
- **PROCEDURE**
  Sample: 6.5 g, previously dried at 105° for 4 h
  Analysis: Transfer the *Sample* into a 250-mL beaker. Add 50.0 mL of 1 N hydrochloric acid and 50.0 mL of water, and stir until the sample is completely dissolved. Place the electrodes of a suitable pH meter in the solution, and titrate the excess acid with 1 N sodium hydroxide to the inflection point occurring at about pH 4. Record the buret reading, and calculate the volume (A) of 1 N hydrochloric acid consumed by the sample:

  $$A = 50 - x$$

  x = volume of 1 N sodium hydroxide used in the titration (mL)

  Continue the titration with 1 N sodium hydroxide until the inflection point occurring at about pH 8.8 is reached, record the buret reading, and calculate the volume (B) of 1 N sodium hydroxide required in the titration between the two inflection points (pH 4 to pH 8.8). When A is equal to or less than B, each mL of the volume A of 1 N hydrochloric acid is equivalent to 142.0 mg of Na_2HPO_4. When A is greater than B, each mL of the volume 2B − A of 1 N sodium hydroxide is equivalent to 142.0 mg of Na_2HPO_4.
  Acceptance criteria: NLT 98.0% of Na_2HPO_4, on the dried basis

IMPURITIES
Inorganic Impurities
- **ARSENIC**, *Arsenic Limit Test*, Appendix IIIB
  Sample solution: 1 g in 35 mL of water
  Acceptance criteria: NMT 3 mg/kg
- **FLUORIDE**, *Fluoride Limit Test, Method IV*, Appendix IIIB
  Sample: 2 g
  Acceptance criteria: NMT 0.005%
- **LEAD**, *Lead Limit Test, APDC Extraction Method*, Appendix IIIB
  Acceptance criteria: NMT 4 mg/kg

SPECIFIC TESTS
Add the following:
- ▲**PYROPHOSPHATE**
  Mobile phase: 20 mM to 70 mM KOH linear gradient, electrochemically generated, from 0 to 20 min
  Standard stock solution: In a 100-mL volumetric flask, dissolve 0.256 g of tetra sodium pyrophosphate decahydrate (> 99% $Na_4P_2O_7 \cdot 10H_2O$) in water and dilute to volume. The resulting solution contains 1000 µg/mL of pyrophosphate anion ($P_2O_7^{4-}$).
  Standard solutions: 0.5 µg/mL, 2.0 µg/mL, and 10 µg/mL of pyrophosphate anion in water, from the *Standard stock solution*
  System suitability solutions: Add commercial orthophosphate ion chromatographic standard (1000 µg/mL) to the 10 µg/mL *Standard solution* for a final solution of 10 µg/mL orthophosphate (PO_4^{3-}).
  Sample solution: 100 µg/mL sample in water
  Chromatographic system, Appendix IIA
    Mode: High-performance liquid chromatography, ion chromatography[1]
    Detector: Electrolytic conductivity detector with eluent suppression
    Column: 2-mm × 25-cm, anion-exchange analytical column[2], and 2-mm × 50-mm anion–exchange guard column[3]
    Flow rate: About 0.25 mL/min
    Injection size: 10 µL
  System suitability
    Samples: *System suitability solutions* and 0.5 µg/mL *Standard solution*
    Suitability requirements
      Suitability requirement 1: Resolution of NLT 5 between 10 µg/mL orthophosphate (PO_4^{3-}) and pyrophosphate ($P_2O_7^{4-}$) anions (from the *System suitability solutions*)
      Suitability requirement 2: Signal-to-noise ratio is NLT 10 for an injection of 0.5 µg/mL pyrophosphate *Standard solution*, where peak height is expressed in µs, and baseline noise is the maximum deflection of the baseline (µs) in a blank at the retention time of pyrophosphate over the same baseline peak width in min.

---
[1] Ion exchange chromatograph ICS-2000, ICS-3000 Dionex Corporation (Sunnyvale, CA), or equivalent.
[2] IonPac AS11 (Dionex Corporation, Sunnyvale, CA), or equivalent.
[3] IonPac AG11 (Dionex Corporation, Sunnyvale, CA), or equivalent.

[NOTE—Conditions may be adjusted for other analytical conditions or brands of equipment.]

Analysis: Establish an eluent flow through the columns until a stable baseline is obtained. Separately inject equal volumes of the *Standard solutions* and *Sample solution* into the chromatograph, and measure the responses for the major peaks on the resulting chromatograms. Prepare a calibration curve by plotting the peak areas versus concentrations of the *Standard solutions* in µg/mL pyrophosphate ion. From the calibration curve, determine the concentration (C_U) of pyrophosphate in the *Sample solution* in µg/mL. Calculate the percentage of pyrophosphate in the sample:

$$\text{Result} = C_U/C_{smp} \times 100$$

C_U = concentration of pyrophosphate in the *Sample solution* determined from the standard curve (µg/mL)
C_{smp} = concentration of the sample in the *Sample solution* (µg/mL)

To determine % tetra sodium pyrophosphate ($Na_4P_2O_7$) multiply the Result by 1.53.

Acceptance criteria: NMT 2% pyrophosphate calculated as $Na_4P_2O_7$ ▲FCC8

- **LOSS ON DRYING**, Appendix IIC: 120° for 4 h
  Acceptance criteria
   Anhydrous: NMT 5.0%
   Dihydrate: 18.0%–22.0%
- **INSOLUBLE SUBSTANCES**
  Sample: 10 g
  Analysis: Dissolve the *Sample* in 100 mL of hot water, and pass through a tared filtering crucible (not glass). Wash the insoluble residue with hot water, dry at 105° for 2 h, cool, and weigh.
  Acceptance criteria: NMT 0.2%

Sodium Phosphate, Monobasic

First Published: Prior to FCC 6
Last Revision: First Supplement, FCC 7

Monosodium Phosphate
Sodium Biphosphate
Monosodium Dihydrogen Phosphate

NaH_2PO_4 Formula wt, anhydrous 119.98
$NaH_2PO_4 \cdot H_2O$ Formula wt, monohydrate 137.99
INS: 339(i) CAS: anhydrous [7558-80-7]
  monohydrate [10049-21-5]
UNII: 3980JIH2SW [sodium phosphate, monobasic, unspecified]
UNII: 593YOG76RN [sodium phosphate, monobasic, monohydrate]
UNII: KH7I04HPUU [sodium phosphate, monobasic, anhydrous]

DESCRIPTION

Sodium Phosphate, Monobasic is anhydrous or contains one or two molecules of water of hydration and is slightly hygroscopic. The anhydrous form occurs as a white, crystalline powder or granules. The hydrated forms occur as white or transparent crystals or granules. All forms are freely soluble in water, but are insoluble in alcohol. The pH of a 1:100 solution is between 4.1 and 4.7.

Function: Buffer; emulsifier; nutrient
Packaging and Storage: Store in tightly closed containers.

IDENTIFICATION

- **PHOSPHATE**, Appendix IIIA
  Sample solution: 50 mg/mL
  Acceptance criteria: Passes tests
- **SODIUM**, Appendix IIIA
  Sample solution: 50 mg/mL
  Acceptance criteria: Passes tests

ASSAY

- **PROCEDURE**
  Sample: 5 g, previously dried at 105° for 4 h
  Analysis: Transfer the *Sample* into a 250-mL beaker and add 100 mL of water and 5.0 mL of 1 N hydrochloric acid. Stir until the *Sample* is completely dissolved. Place the electrodes of a suitable pH meter in the solution and slowly titrate the excess acid, stirring constantly, with 1 N sodium hydroxide to the inflection point occurring at about pH 4. Record the buret reading and calculate the volume (A), if any, of 1 N hydrochloric acid consumed by the sample using the equation:

$$A = 5 - x$$

  x = volume of 1 N sodium hydroxide used in the titration (mL)

  Continue the titration with 1 N sodium hydroxide to the inflection point occurring at about pH 8.8. Record the buret reading and calculate the volume (B) of 1 N sodium hydroxide required in the titration between the two inflection points (pH 4 and pH 8.8). Each mL of the volume B − A of 1 N sodium hydroxide is equivalent to 120.0 mg of NaH_2PO_4.
  Acceptance criteria: NLT 98.0% and NMT 103.0% NaH_2PO_4, on the dried basis

IMPURITIES
Inorganic Impurities

- **ARSENIC**, *Arsenic Limit Test*, Appendix IIIB
  Sample solution: 1 g in 35 mL of water
  Acceptance criteria: NMT 3 mg/kg
- **FLUORIDE**, *Fluoride Limit Test, Method IV*, Appendix IIIB
  Sample: 2 g
  Acceptance criteria: NMT 0.005%
- **LEAD**, *Lead Limit Test, APDC Extraction Method*, Appendix IIIB
  Acceptance criteria: NMT 4 mg/kg

SPECIFIC TESTS
- **INSOLUBLE SUBSTANCES**
  Sample solution: 10 g
  Analysis: Dissolve the *Sample* in 100 mL of hot water, and pass the solution through a tared filtering crucible (not glass). Wash the insoluble residue with hot water, dry at 105° for 2 h, cool, and weigh.
  Acceptance criteria: NMT 0.2%
- **LOSS ON DRYING,** Appendix IIC: 60° for 1 h, then 105° for 4 h
  Acceptance criteria
  Anhydrous: NMT 2.0%
  Monohydrate: Between 10.0% and 15.0%
  Dihydrate: Between 20.0% and 25.0%

Sodium Phosphate, Tribasic

First Published: Prior to FCC 6

Trisodium Phosphate

Na$_3$PO$_4$ Formula wt, anhydrous 163.94
Na$_3$PO$_4$·12H$_2$O   Formula wt, dodecahydrate 380.12
INS: 339(iii)   CAS: anhydrous [7601-54-9]
     dodecahydrate [10101-89-0]
UNII: B70850QPHR [sodium phosphate, tribasic, dodecahydrate]
UNII: SX01TZO3QZ [sodium phosphate, tribasic, anhydrous]

DESCRIPTION
Sodium Phosphate, Tribasic, occurs as white crystals or granules or as a crystalline material. It may be anhydrous or contain 1 to 12 molecules of water of hydration. The formula for a crystalline material is approximately 4(Na$_3$PO$_4$·12H$_2$O)NaOH. It is freely soluble in water, but is insoluble in alcohol. The pH of a 1:100 aqueous solution is between 11.5 and 12.5.
Function: Antimicrobial; buffer; emulsifier; nutrient
Packaging and Storage: Store in well-closed containers.

IDENTIFICATION
- **PHOSPHATE,** Appendix IIIA
  Sample solution: 50 mg/mL
  Acceptance criteria: Passes tests
- **SODIUM,** Appendix IIIA
  Sample solution: 50 mg/mL
  Acceptance criteria: Passes tests

ASSAY
- **PROCEDURE**
  Sample: Amount equivalent to between 5.5 and 6 g of anhydrous Na$_3$PO$_4$
  Analysis: Transfer the *Sample* to a 400-mL beaker, dissolve in 40 mL of water, and add 100.0 mL of 1N hydrochloric acid. While stirring the solution with a magnetic stirrer, pass a stream of fine bubbles of nitrogen using flexible latex tubing ending in a plastic pipet tip at a rate of about five bubbles per second through the solution for 15 min to expel carbon dioxide. Simultaneously, cover the beaker loosely to prevent any loss by spraying. Wash the cover and sides of the beaker and wash the plastic tip inside and out with a few mL of water. Place the electrodes of a standard pH meter in the solution. Titrate the solution with 1 N sodium hydroxide to the inflection point occurring at about pH 4. Calculate the volume (A) of 1N hydrochloric acid consumed using the equation:

$$A = 100 - x$$

x   = volume (mL) of 1 N sodium hydroxide used in the titration

Protect the solution from absorbing carbon dioxide from the air and continue the titration with 1 N sodium hydroxide to the inflection point occurring at about pH 8.8. Calculate the volume (B) of 1 N sodium hydroxide consumed in the titration between the two inflection points (pH 4 to pH 8.8). When A is equal to or greater than 2B, each mL of the volume B of 1 N sodium hydroxide is equivalent to 163.9 mg of Na$_3$PO$_4$. When A is less than 2B, each mL of the volume (A − B) of 1 N sodium hydroxide is equivalent to 163.9 mg of Na$_3$PO$_4$.
Acceptance criteria
Anhydrous and monohydrate: NLT 97.0% Na$_3$PO$_4$, calculated on the ignited basis
Dodecahydrate: NLT 90.0% Na$_3$PO$_4$, calculated on the ignited basis

IMPURITIES
Inorganic Impurities
- **ARSENIC,** *Arsenic Limit Test,* Appendix IIIB
  Sample solution: 1 g in 35 mL of water
  Acceptance criteria: NMT 3 mg/kg
- **FLUORIDE,** *Fluoride Limit Test, Method IV,* Appendix IIIB
  Sample: 2 g
  Acceptance criteria: NMT 0.005%
- **LEAD,** *Lead Limit Test, APDC Extraction Method,* Appendix IIIB
  Acceptance criteria: NMT 4 mg/kg

SPECIFIC TESTS
- **INSOLUBLE SUBSTANCES**
  Sample: 10 g
  Analysis: Dissolve the *Sample* in 100 mL of hot water and filter the solution through a tared filtering crucible (not glass). Wash the insoluble residue with hot water, dry at 105° for 2 h, cool, and weigh.
  Acceptance criteria: NMT 0.2%
- **LOSS ON IGNITION**
  Analysis: Dry the sample at 110° for 5 h, then ignite at about 800° for 30 min.
  Acceptance criteria
  Anhydrous: NMT 2.0%
  Monohydrate: Between 8.0% and 11.0%
  Dodecahydrate: Between 45.0% and 57.0%

Sodium Polyphosphates, Glassy

First Published: Prior to FCC 6
Last Revision: First Supplement, FCC 6

Sodium Hexametaphosphate
Sodium Tetrapolyphosphate
Graham's Salt

INS: 452(i)   CAS: [68915-31-1]
[10361-03-2]
UNII: P1BM4ZH95L [sodium polymetaphosphate]

DESCRIPTION
Sodium Polyphosphates, Glassy, occur as colorless or white, transparent platelets, granules, or powders. They belong to a class consisting of several amorphous, water-soluble polyphosphates composed of linear chains of metaphosphate units $(NaPO_3)x$ for which $x \geq 2$, terminated by Na_2PO_4–groups. They are usually identified by their Na_2O/P_2O_5 ratio or their P_2O_5 content. The Na_2O/P_2O_5 ratios vary from about 1.5 for sodium tetrapolyphosphate, for which x = approximately 2 through about 1.1 for Graham's salt, commonly called sodium hexametaphosphate, for which x = 10 to 18; to about 1.0 for the higher molecular weight sodium polyphosphates, for which x = 20 to 100 or more. Glassy Sodium Polyphosphates are very soluble in water. The pH of their solutions varies from about 3.0 to 9.0.
Function: Emulsifier; sequestrant; texturizer
Packaging and Storage: Store in tightly closed containers.

IDENTIFICATION
- **A. Sodium,** Appendix IIIA
  Sample solution: 50 mg/mL
  Acceptance criteria: Passes tests
- **B. Procedure**
  Sample: 100 mg
  Analysis: Dissolve the *Sample* in 5 mL of hot 1.7 N nitric acid, warm on a steam bath for 10 min, and cool. Neutralize to litmus paper with 1 N sodium hydroxide, and add silver nitrate TS.
  Acceptance criteria: A yellow precipitate forms that is soluble in 1.7 N nitric acid.

ASSAY
- **Procedure**
  Sample: 800 mg
  Sample solution: Transfer the *Sample* into a 400-mL beaker, add 100 mL of water and 25 mL of nitric acid, cover with a watch glass, and boil for 10 min on a hot plate. Rinse any condensate from the watch glass into the beaker, cool the solution to room temperature, transfer it quantitatively into a 500-mL volumetric flask, dilute with water to volume, and mix thoroughly.
  Analysis: Pipet 20.0 mL of *Sample solution* into a 500-mL Erlenmeyer flask, add 100 mL of water, and heat just to boiling. While stirring, add 50 mL of quimociac TS, cover with a watch glass, and boil for 1 min in a well-ventilated hood. Cool to room temperature, swirling occasionally while cooling, then pass through a tared, sintered-glass filter crucible of medium porosity, and wash with five 25-mL portions of water. Dry at about 225° for 30 min, cool, and weigh. Each mg of precipitate thus obtained is equivalent to 32.074 µg of P_2O_5.
  Acceptance criteria: Between 60.0% and 71.0% of P_2O_5

IMPURITIES
Inorganic Impurities
- **Arsenic,** *Arsenic Limit Test,* Appendix IIIB
  Sample solution: 1 g of sample in 35 mL of water
  Acceptance criteria: NMT 3 mg/kg
- **Fluoride,** *Fluoride Limit Test, Method III,* Appendix IIIB
  Sample: 2 g
  Acceptance criteria: NMT 0.005%
- **Lead,** *Lead Limit Test, APDC Extraction Method,* Appendix IIIB
  Acceptance criteria: NMT 4 mg/kg

SPECIFIC TESTS
- **Insoluble Substances**
  Sample: 10 g
  Analysis: Dissolve *Sample* in 100 mL of hot water, and pass through a tared filtering crucible. Wash the insoluble residue with hot water, dry at 105° for 2 h, cool, and weigh.
  Acceptance criteria: NMT 0.1%

Sodium Potassium Tartrate

First Published: Prior to FCC 6

Potassium Sodium Tartrate
Rochelle Salt
Seignette Salt

$C_4H_4KNaO_6 \cdot 4H_2O$ Formula wt 282.22
INS: 337   CAS: [304-59-6]
UNII: QH257BPV3J [potassium sodium tartrate]

DESCRIPTION
Sodium Potassium Tartrate occurs as colorless crystals or as a white, crystalline powder. As it effloresces slightly in warm, dry air, the crystals are often coated with a white powder. It is a salt of L(+)-tartaric acid. One g dissolves in 1 mL of water. It is practically insoluble in alcohol.
Function: Buffer; sequestrant
Packaging and Storage: Store in tight containers.

IDENTIFICATION
- **A. Procedure**
  Acceptance criteria: Upon ignition, a sample emits the odor of burning sugar and leaves a residue that is alkaline to litmus and that effervesces with acids.
- **B. Procedure**
  Sample solution: 50 mg/mL
  Analysis: To 10 mL of the *Sample solution*, add 10 mL of acetic acid.
  Acceptance criteria: A white, crystalline precipitate forms within 15 min.
- **C. Tartrate,** Appendix IIIA
  Sample solution: 100 mg/mL
  Acceptance criteria: Passes test

ASSAY
- **Procedure**
  Sample: 0.5 g
  Analysis: Mix the *Sample* with 50 mL of glacial acetic acid, 30 mL of 96% formic acid, and 45 mL of acetic anhydride. Heat and stir until dissolution is complete and titrate with 0.1 N perchloric acid in glacial acetic acid to a green endpoint with crystal violet indicator. [**Caution**—Handle perchloric acid in an appropriate fume hood.] Perform a blank determination (see *General Provisions*), and make any necessary correction. Each mL of 0.1 N perchloric acid is equivalent to 14.11 mg of $C_4H_4KNaO_6 \cdot 4H_2O$.
  Acceptance criteria: NLT 99.0% and NMT 102.0% of $C_4H_4KNaO_6 \cdot 4H_2O$, calculated on the anhydrous basis

IMPURITIES
Inorganic Impurities
- **Lead,** *Lead Limit Test, Flame Atomic Absorption Spectrophotometric Method,* Appendix IIIB
  Sample: 10 g
  Acceptance criteria: NMT 2 mg/kg

SPECIFIC TESTS
- **Alkalinity**
  Sample solution: 50 mg/mL
  Analysis: To 10 mL of the *Sample solution*, add 0.2 mL of 0.1 N sulfuric acid, and 1 drop of phenolphthalein TS.
  Acceptance criteria: The *Sample solution* is alkaline to litmus and produces no pink color following the addition of the phenolphthalein TS.
- **Water,** *Water Determination,* Appendix IIB: Use 35 mL of methanol in the *Procedure*.
  Sample: 200 mg
  Acceptance criteria: Between 21.0% and 26.0%

Sodium Potassium Tripolyphosphate
First Published: Prior to FCC 6

Trisodium Dipotassium Tripolyphosphate

$Na_3K_2P_3O_{10}$ Formula wt 400.08
CAS: [24315-83-1]

DESCRIPTION
Sodium Potassium Tripolyphosphate occurs as white, slightly hygroscopic granules or as a powder. It is anhydrous. It is freely soluble in water. The pH of a 1:100 aqueous solution is about 10.
Function: Texturizer; sequestrant
Packaging and Storage: Store in tight containers.

IDENTIFICATION
- **Sodium,** Appendix IIIA
  Sample solution: 50 mg/mL
  Acceptance criteria: Passes tests
- **Potassium,** Appendix IIIA
  Sample solution: 50 mg/mL
  Acceptance criteria: Passes tests
- **Phosphate,** Appendix IIIA
  Sample solution: 50 mg/mL
  Acceptance criteria: Passes tests

ASSAY
- **Procedure**
  Potassium acetate buffer (pH 5.0): Dissolve 78.5 g of potassium acetate in 1000 mL of water, and adjust the pH of the solution to 5.0 with glacial acetic acid. Add a few mg of mercuric iodide to inhibit mold growth.
  0.3 M potassium chloride solution: Dissolve 22.35 g of potassium chloride in water, add 5 mL of *Potassium acetate buffer*, dilute to 1000 mL with water, and mix. Add a few mg of mercuric iodide to inhibit mold growth.
  0.6 M potassium chloride solution: Dissolve 44.7 g of potassium chloride in water, add 5 mL of *Potassium acetate buffer*, dilute to 1000 mL with water, and mix. Add a few mg of mercuric iodide to inhibit mold growth.
  1 M potassium chloride solution: Dissolve 74.5 g of potassium chloride in water, add 5 mL of *Potassium acetate buffer*, dilute to 1000 mL with water, and mix. Add a few mg of mercuric iodide to inhibit mold growth.
  Chromatographic column: Use a standard chromatographic column, 20- to 40-cm long with a 20- to 28-mm id, or equivalent, that has a sealed-in, coarse-porosity, fritted disk. If a stopcock is not provided, attach a stopcock having a 3- to 4-mm diameter bore to the outlet of the column with a short length of flexible vinyl tubing.
  Chromatographic column preparation: Close the column stopcock, fill the space between the fritted disk and the stopcock with water, and connect a vacuum line to the stopcock. Prepare a 1:1 water slurry of Dowex 1 × 8, chloride form, 100- to 200- or 200- to 400-mesh, or a comparable grade of styrene-divinylbenzene ion exchange resin, and decant off any very fine particles and any foam. Repeat two or three times or until no more finely suspended material or foaming is observed. Fill the column with the slurry, and open the stopcock to allow the vacuum to pack the resin bed until the water level is slightly above the top of the resin, then immediately close the stopcock. Do not allow the liquid level to fall below the resin level

at any time. Repeat this procedure until the packed resin column is 15 cm above the fritted disk. Place one circle of tightly fitting glass-fiber filter paper on top of the resin bed, then place a perforated polyethylene disk on top of the paper. Alternatively, place a loosely packed plug of glass wool on top of the bed. Close the top of the column with a rubber stopper in which a 7.6-cm length of capillary tubing (1.5-mm id, 7-mm od), or equivalent, has been inserted through the center, so that about 12 mm of the tubing extends through the bottom of the stopper. Connect the top of the capillary tubing to the stem of a 500-mL separatory funnel with flexible vinyl tubing, and clamp the separatory funnel to a ring stand above the column. Wash the column by adding 100 mL of water to the separatory funnel with all stopcocks closed. First open the separatory funnel stopcock, then open the column stopcock. The rate of flow should be about 5 mL/ min. When the separatory funnel is empty, close the column stopcock, then close the separatory funnel stopcock.

Sample preparation: Transfer 500 mg of sample into a 250-mL volumetric flask, dissolve in and dilute to volume with water, and mix. Transfer 10.0 mL of this solution into the separatory funnel connected to the chromatographic column described above under *Chromatographic column preparation*. Open both stopcocks, and allow the solution to drain into the column, rinsing the separator with 20 mL of water. Discard the eluate. Add 370 mL of *0.3 M Potassium chloride solution* to the separatory funnel, and allow this solution to pass through the column, discarding the eluate. Add 250 mL of *0.6 M Potassium chloride solution* to the column, allow the solution to pass through the column, and receive the eluate in a 400-mL beaker. Use this retained eluate as the *Sample preparation*. [NOTE— To ensure a clean column for the next run, pass 100 mL of *1 M Potassium chloride solution* through the column, and then follow with 100 mL of water. Discard all washings.]

Analysis: Add 15 mL of nitric acid to the beaker containing the *Sample preparation*, mix, and boil for 15 to 20 min. Add methyl orange TS, and neutralize the solution with ammonium hydroxide. Add 1 g of ammonium nitrate crystals, stir to dissolve, and cool. While stirring, add 15 mL of ammonium molybdate TS, and stir vigorously for 3 min, or allow the mixture to stand with occasional stirring for 10 to 15 min. Filter the contents of the beaker by means of suction through a 6- to 7-mm paper-pulp filter pad supported in a 25-mm porcelain disk. The filter pad should be covered with a suspension of infusorial earth. After the contents of the beaker have been transferred to the filter, wash the beaker with five 10-mL portions of a 10 mg/mL solution of sodium or potassium nitrate, passing the washings through the filter, then wash the filter with five 5-mL portions of the 10 mg/mL sodium or potassium nitrate wash solution. Return the filter pad and the precipitate to the beaker, wash the funnel thoroughly with water into the beaker, and dilute to about 150 mL. Add 0.1 N sodium hydroxide from a buret until the yellow precipitate is dissolved, then add 5 to 8 mL in excess. Add phenolphthalein TS, and titrate the excess alkali with 0.1 N nitric acid. Finally, titrate with 0.1 N sodium hydroxide to the first appearance of a pink color. The difference between the total volume of 0.1 N sodium hydroxide added and the volume of nitric acid required represents the volume, V, in mL, of 0.1 N sodium hydroxide consumed by the phosphomolybdate complex. Calculate the quantity, in mg, of $Na_3K_2P_3O_{10}$ in the sample taken by the formula:

$$Result = 0.533 \times 25V$$

V = volume (mL) of 0.1 N sodium hydroxide consumed by the phosphomolybdate complex

Acceptance criteria: NLT 85.0% and NMT 100.5% of $Na_3K_2P_3O_{10}$

IMPURITIES
Inorganic Impurities
- **ARSENIC,** *Arsenic Limit Test,* Appendix IIIB
  Sample solution: 1 g of sample in 35 mL of water
  Acceptance criteria: NMT 3 mg/kg
- **FLUORIDE,** *Fluoride Limit Test, Method IV,* Appendix IIIB
  Sample: 2 g
  Acceptance criteria: NMT 0.005%
- **LEAD,** *Lead Limit Test, APDC Extraction Method,* Appendix IIIB
  Acceptance criteria: NMT 2 mg/kg

SPECIFIC TESTS
- **INSOLUBLE SUBSTANCES**
  Sample: 10 g
  Analysis: Dissolve the *Sample* in 100 mL of hot water and filter the solution through a tared filtering crucible. Wash the insoluble residue with hot water, dry at 105° for 2 h, cool, and weigh.
  Acceptance criteria: NMT 0.1%

Sodium Propionate
First Published: Prior to FCC 6

Sodium Propanoate

$C_3H_5NaO_2$ Formula wt 96.06
INS: 281 CAS: [137-40-6]
UNII: DK6Y9P42IN [sodium propionate]

DESCRIPTION
Sodium Propionate occurs as white or colorless, transparent crystals or as a granular, crystalline powder. It is hygroscopic in moist air. One gram is soluble in about 1 mL of water at 25°, in about 0.65 mL of boiling water, and in about 24 mL of alcohol. The pH of a 1:10 aqueous solution is between 8.0 and 10.5.
Function: Preservative; mold inhibitor

1058 / Sodium Propionate / Monographs

Packaging and Storage: Store in tight containers.

IDENTIFICATION
- **A. SODIUM,** Appendix IIIA
  Sample solution: 50 mg/mL
  Acceptance criteria: Passes test
- **B. PROCEDURE**
  Acceptance criteria: Upon ignition, a sample yields an alkaline residue that effervesces with acids.
- **C. PROCEDURE**
  Analysis: Warm a small sample with sulfuric acid.
  Acceptance criteria: Propionic acid, recognized by its odor, evolves.

ASSAY
- **PROCEDURE**
  Sample: 250 mg, previously dried at 105° for 1 h
  Analysis: Dissolve the *Sample* in 40 mL of glacial acetic acid, warming if necessary to aid dissolution. Cool to room temperature, add 2 drops of crystal violet TS, and titrate with 0.1 N perchloric acid. [**CAUTION**—Handle perchloric acid in an appropriate fume hood.] Perform a blank determination (see *General Provisions*), and make any necessary correction. Each mL of 0.1 N perchloric acid is equivalent to 9.606 mg of $C_3H_5NaO_2$.
  Acceptance criteria: NLT 99.0% and NMT 100.5% of $C_3H_5NaO_2$, on the dried basis

IMPURITIES
Inorganic Impurities
- **IRON**
  Sample: 300 mg
  Sample solution: Dissolve the *Sample* in 40 mL of water, and add 2 mL of hydrochloric acid, about 40 mg ammonium persulfate, and 10 mL of ammonium thiocyanate TS.
  Control solution: Combine 0.9 mL of *Iron Standard Solution* (9 μg Fe, see *Standard Solutions for the Preparation of Controls and Standards*, Solutions and Indicators), with the same quantities of reagents used in the preparation of the *Sample solution*.
  Acceptance criteria: Any red or pink color produced by the *Sample solution* does not exceed that of the *Control solution* (NMT 0.003%).
- **LEAD,** *Lead Limit Test, Flame Atomic Absorption Spectrophotometric Method,* Appendix IIIB
  Sample: 10 g
  Acceptance criteria: NMT 2 mg/kg

SPECIFIC TESTS
- **ALKALINITY (AS NA_2CO_3)**
  Sample: 4 g of sample in 20 mL of water
  Analysis: Add 3 drops of phenolphthalein TS.
  Acceptance criteria: If a pink color appears, NMT 0.6 mL of 0.1 N sulfuric acid is required to discharge it (about 0.15%).
- **WATER,** *Water Determination,* Appendix IIB
  Acceptance criteria: NMT 1%

Sodium Pyrophosphate

First Published: Prior to FCC 6
Last Revision: First Supplement, FCC 6

Tetrasodium Diphosphate
Tetrasodium Pyrophosphate

$Na_4P_2O_7$ Formula wt, anhydrous 265.90
$Na_4P_2O_7 \cdot 10H_2O$ Formula wt, decahydrate 446.06
INS: 450(iii)   CAS: anhydrous [7722-88-5]
    decahydrate [13472-36-1]
UNII: O352864B8Z [sodium pyrophosphate]

DESCRIPTION
Sodium Pyrophosphate occurs as colorless or white crystals or as a white, crystalline or granular powder. It is anhydrous or contains 10 molecules of water of hydration. The decahydrate effloresces slightly in dry air. It is soluble in water, but is insoluble in alcohol. The pH of a 1:100 aqueous solution is about 10.

Function: Emulsifier; buffer; nutrient; sequestrant; texturizer

Packaging and Storage: Store in tight containers.

IDENTIFICATION
- **A. SODIUM,** Appendix IIIA
  Sample solution: 50 mg/mL
  Acceptance criteria: Passes tests
- **B. PROCEDURE**
  Sample solution: Dissolve 100 mg of sample in 100 mL of 1.7 N nitric acid.
  Analysis 1: Add 0.5 mL of the *Sample solution* to 30 mL of quimociac TS.
  Analysis 2: Heat the remaining portion of *Sample solution* (~99.5 mL) for 10 min at 95°, then add 0.5 mL of the solution to 30 mL of quimociac TS.
  Acceptance criteria: A yellow precipitate does not form in *Analysis 1*, but does form immediately in *Analysis 2*.

ASSAY
- **PROCEDURE**
  Sample: Amount equivalent to 500 mg of anhydrous $Na_4P_2O_7$
  Analysis: Dissolve the *Sample* in 100 mL of water contained in a 400-mL beaker. Using a pH meter, adjust the pH of the solution to 3.8 with hydrochloric acid, then add 50 mL of a 1:8 solution of zinc sulfate (125 g of $ZnSO_4 \cdot 7H_2O$ dissolved in water, diluted to 1000 mL, filtered, and adjusted to pH 3.8), and allow the mixture to stand for 2 min. Titrate the liberated acid with 0.1 N sodium hydroxide until a pH of 3.8 is again reached. After each addition of sodium hydroxide near the endpoint, allow time for any precipitated zinc hydroxide to redissolve. Each mL of 0.1 N sodium hydroxide is equivalent to 13.30 mg of $Na_4P_2O_7$.
  Acceptance criteria: NLT 95.0% and NMT 100.5% of $Na_4P_2O_7$, calculated on the ignited basis

IMPURITIES
Inorganic Impurities
- **ARSENIC,** *Arsenic Limit Test,* Appendix IIIB
  Sample solution: 1 g of sample in 35 mL of water
  Acceptance criteria: NMT 3 mg/kg
- **FLUORIDE**
  [NOTE—Prepare and store all solutions in plastic containers.]
  Buffer solution: Dissolve 73.5 g sodium citrate in water, made to 250 mL.
  Standard stock solution: 1.1052 mg/mL USP Sodium Fluoride RS
  Standard solution: Transfer 20.0 mL of the *Standard stock solution* to a 100-mL volumetric flask containing 50 mL of *Buffer solution,* dilute with water to volume, and mix (100 µg/mL fluoride ion).
  Sample solution: Transfer 2.0 g of sample to a beaker containing a plastic-coated stirring bar, add 20 mL of water and 2.0 mL of hydrochloric acid, and stir until the sample is dissolved. Add 50.0 mL of *Buffer solution* and sufficient water to make 100 mL.
  Electrode system: Use a fluoride-specific, ion-indicating electrode and a silver–silver chloride reference electrode connected to a pH meter capable of measuring potentials with a minimum reproducibility of ±0.2 mV.
  Standard response line: Transfer 50.0 mL of *Buffer solution* and 2.0 mL of hydrochloric acid into a beaker and add water to make 100 mL. Add a plastic-coated stirring bar, insert the electrodes into the solution, stir for 15 min, and read the potential (mV). Continue stirring, and at 5-min intervals, add 100 µL, 100 µL, 300 µL, and 500 µL of *Standard solution,* reading the potential 5 min after each addition. Plot the logarithms of the cumulative fluoride ion concentrations (0.1, 0.2, 0.5, and 1.0 µg/mL) versus potential, in mV.
  Analysis: Rinse and dry the electrodes, insert them into the *Sample solution,* stir for 5 min, and read the potential (mV). From the measured potential and the *Standard response line,* determine the concentration, C (µg/mL), of fluoride ion in the *Sample solution.* Calculate the percentage of fluoride in the sample taken by the formula:

  Result = C × 0.005

  Acceptance criteria: NMT 0.005%
- **LEAD,** *Lead Limit Test, APDC Extraction Method,* Appendix IIIB
  Acceptance criteria: NMT 4 mg/kg

SPECIFIC TESTS
- **INSOLUBLE SUBSTANCES**
  Sample: 10 g
  Analysis: Dissolve the *Sample* in 100 mL of hot water, and pass the solution through a tared filtering crucible. Wash the insoluble residue with hot water, dry at 105° for 2 h, cool, and weigh.
  Acceptance criteria: NMT 0.2%
- **LOSS ON IGNITION**
  Analysis: Dry a sample at 110° for 4 h, and then ignite it at about 800° for 30 min.
  Acceptance criteria
  Anhydrous: NMT 0.5%
  Decahydrate: Between 38.0% and 42.0%

Sodium Saccharin
First Published: Prior to FCC 6

1,2-Benzisothiazole-3(2H)-one 1,1-Dioxide Sodium Salt
Sodium *o*-Benzosulfimide
Soluble Saccharin

$C_7H_4NNaO_3S \cdot 2H_2O$ Formula wt 241.19
INS: 954 CAS: [128-44-9]
UNII: I4807BK602 [saccharin sodium anhydrous]

DESCRIPTION
Sodium Saccharin occurs as white crystals or as a white, crystalline powder. In powdered form, it effloresces to the extent that it usually contains only about one-third the amount of water indicated in its molecular formula. One g is soluble in 1.5 mL of water and in about 50 mL of alcohol.
Function: Non-nutritive sweetener
Packaging and Storage: Store in well-closed containers.

IDENTIFICATION
- **A. PROCEDURE**
  Sample: 100 mg
  Analysis: Dissolve the *Sample* in 5 mL of a 50 mg/mL solution of sodium hydroxide, evaporate to dryness, and gently fuse the residue over a small flame until ammonia no longer evolves. After the residue has cooled, dissolve it in 20 mL of water, neutralize the solution with 2.7 N hydrochloric acid, and filter. Add 1 drop of ferric chloride TS to the filtrate.
  Acceptance criteria: A violet color appears.
- **B. PROCEDURE**
  Sample: 20 mg
  Analysis: Mix the *Sample* with 40 mg of resorcinol, cautiously add 10 drops of sulfuric acid, and heat the mixture in a liquid bath at 200° for 3 min. After cooling, add 10 mL of water and an excess of 1 N sodium hydroxide.
  Acceptance criteria: A fluorescent green liquid is produced.
- **C. SODIUM,** Appendix IIIA
  Sample: Residue obtained by igniting a 2-g sample
  Acceptance criteria: Passes tests
- **D. MELTING RANGE OR TEMPERATURE DETERMINATION,** Appendix IIB
  Sample solution: 100 mg/mL
  Analysis: Add 1 mL of hydrochloric acid to 10 mL of the *Sample solution.* A crystalline precipitate of saccharin

forms. Wash the precipitate well with cold water, and dry it at 105° for 2 h.

Acceptance criteria: The saccharin thus obtained melts between 226° and 230°.

ASSAY
- **PROCEDURE**
  Sample: 500 mg
  Analysis: With the aid of 10 mL of water, quantitatively transfer the *Sample* into a separatory funnel. Add 2 mL of 2.7 N hydrochloric acid, and extract the precipitated saccharin, first with 30 mL, then with five 20-mL, portions of solvent comprising 9:1 (v/v) chloroform:alcohol. Filter each extract through a small filter paper moistened with the solvent mixture, and evaporate the combined filtrates to dryness on a steam bath with the aid of a current of air. Dissolve the residue in 40 mL of alcohol and 40 mL of water, mix, add 3 drops of phenolphthalein TS, and titrate with 0.1 N sodium hydroxide. Perform a blank determination (see *General Provisions*) with a 40:40 alcohol:water (w/w) mixture, and make any necessary correction. Each mL of 0.1 N sodium hydroxide is equivalent to 20.52 mg of $C_7H_4NNaO_3S$.
  Acceptance criteria: NLT 98.0% and NMT 101.0% of $C_7H_4NNaO_3S$, calculated on the anhydrous basis

IMPURITIES
Inorganic Impurities
- **LEAD,** *Lead Limit Test, Flame Atomic Absorption Spectrophotometric Method,* Appendix IIIB
  Sample: 10 g
  Acceptance criteria: NMT 2 mg/kg
- **SELENIUM,** *Selenium Limit Test, Method I,* Appendix IIIB
  Sample: 200 mg
  Acceptance criteria: NMT 0.003%

Organic Impurities
- **BENZOATE AND SALICYLATE**
  Sample solution: 50 mg/mL
  Analysis: Add 3 drops of ferric chloride TS to 10 mL of *Sample solution,* previously acidified with 5 drops of glacial acetic acid.
  Acceptance criteria: No precipitate or violet color appears.
- **TOLUENESULFONAMIDES**
  [NOTE—For all solutions requiring methylene chloride, use a suitable grade (such as that obtainable from Burdick & Jackson Laboratories, Inc.) equivalent to the product obtained by distillation in an all-glass apparatus.]
  Internal standard stock solution: 10 mg/mL 95% *n*-tricosane (obtainable from Chemical Samples Co.) in *n*-heptane, made to 10 mL
  Standard stock solution: 2 mg/mL each of reagent-grade *o*-toluenesulfonamide and *p*-toluenesulfonamide in methylene chloride, made to 10 mL
  Standard solutions: Pipet 0.1, 0.25, 1.0, 2.5, and 5.0 mL, respectively, of the *Standard stock solution* into five 10-mL volumetric flasks. Pipet 0.25 mL of the *Internal standard stock solution* into each flask, dilute each to volume with methylene chloride, and mix. These solutions contain, respectively, 20, 50, 200, 500, and 1000 µg/mL of each toluenesulfonamide, in addition to 250 µg of *n*-tricosane.
  Sample solution: Dissolve 2.00 g of sample in 8.0 mL of 5% sodium bicarbonate solution, and mix the solution thoroughly with 10.0 g of chromatographic siliceous earth (Celite 545, Johns-Manville, or equivalent). Transfer the mixture into a 250–mm × 25–mm chromatographic tube, or equivalent, having a fritted-glass disk and a Teflon stopcock at the bottom and a reservoir at the top. Pack the contents of the tube by tapping the column on a padded surface, and then by tamping firmly from the top. Place 100 mL of methylene chloride in the reservoir, and adjust the stopcock so that 50 mL of eluate is collected in 20 to 30 min. Add 25 µL of *Internal standard stock solution* to the eluate, mix, and then concentrate the solution to a volume of 1.0 mL in a suitable concentrator tube fitted with a modified Snyder column, using a Kontes tube heater maintained at 90°.
  Chromatographic system, Appendix IIA
    Mode: Gas chromatography
    Detector: Flame-ionization detector
    Column: 3-m × 2-mm (id) glass column, or equivalent, packed with 3% phenyl methyl silicone (OV-17, Applied Science Laboratories, Inc., or equivalent) on 100- to 120-mesh, silanized and calcined diatomaceous silica (Gas-Chrom Q, Applied Science, or equivalent). [CAUTION—The glass column should extend into the injector for on-column injection and into the detector base to avoid contact with metal.]
    Temperature
      Oven temperature: 180°
      Injection port temperature: 225°
      Detector temperature: 250°
    Carrier gas: Helium
    Flow rate: 30 mL/min
    Injection volume: 2.5 µL
  Analysis: Set the instrument attenuation so that 2.5 µL of the *Standard solution* that contains 200 µg/mL of each toluenesulfonamide gives a response of 40% to 80% of full-scale deflection. [NOTE—The retention times for *o*-toluenesulfonamide, *p*-toluenesulfonamide, and *n*-tricosane are about 5, 6, and 15 min, respectively.] Separately inject each of the five *Standard solutions* and the *Sample solution* into the chromatograph, record the chromatograms, and, for each solution, determine the areas of the *o*-toluenesulfonamide, *p*-toluenesulfo-namide, and *n*-tricosane peaks. From the values thus obtained from the *Standard solutions*, prepare standard curves by plotting the concentration of each toluenesulfonamide (µg/mL) versus the ratio of the respective toluenesulfonamide peak area to that of *n*-tricosane. From the standard curve, determine the concentration (µg/mL) of each toluenesulfonamide in the *Sample solution*. Divide each value by 2 to convert the result to mg/kg of the toluenesulfonamide in the 2 g sample taken for analysis.
  [NOTE—If the toluenesulfonamide content of the sample is greater than about 500 mg/kg, the impurity may crystallize out of the methylene chloride concentrate

(see *Sample solution*). Although this level of impurity exceeds that permitted by the specification, the analysis may be completed by diluting the concentrate with methylene chloride containing 250 μg/mL of *n*-tricosane and by applying appropriate dilution factors in the calculation. Care must be taken to redissolve completely any crystalline toluenesulfonamide to give a homogeneous solution.]
Acceptance criteria: NMT 0.0025%

SPECIFIC TESTS
- **ALKALINITY**
  Sample solution: 100 mg/mL
  Acceptance criteria: The *Sample solution* is neutral or alkaline to litmus, but produces no red color with phenolphthalein TS.
- **READILY CARBONIZABLE SUBSTANCES,** Appendix IIB
  Sample: 200 mg
  Analysis: Dissolve the *Sample* in 5 mL of 95% sulfuric acid and hold the solution at 48° to 50° for 10 min.
  Acceptance criteria: The color of the resulting solution is no darker than that of *Matching Fluid A*.
- **WATER,** *Water Determination*, Appendix IIB
  Acceptance criteria: NMT 15.0%

Sodium Sesquicarbonate
First Published: Prior to FCC 6

Sodium Monohydrogendicarbonate
Magadi Soda

$Na_2CO_3 \cdot NaHCO_3 \cdot 2H_2O$ Formula wt 226.03
INS: 500(iii)   CAS: [533-96-0]
UNII: Y1X815621J [sodium sesquicarbonate]

DESCRIPTION
Sodium Sesquicarbonate occurs as white crystals or flakes or as a crystalline powder. It is soluble in water and its solutions are alkaline to litmus.
Function: pH control agent; neutralizer in dairy products; buffer
Packaging and Storage: Store in well-closed containers.

IDENTIFICATION
- **CARBONATE,** Appendix IIIA
  Sample solution: 100 mg/mL
  Acceptance criteria: Passes tests
- **SODIUM,** Appendix IIIA
  Sample solution: 100 mg/mL
  Acceptance criteria: Passes tests

ASSAY
- **SODIUM BICARBONATE**
  Sample: 3 g
  Analysis: Dissolve the *Sample* in 150 mL of carbon dioxide-free water in a 600-mL beaker containing 50.0 mL of 0.5 N sodium hydroxide. While stirring, add 200 mL of 0.48 M barium chloride that has been adjusted to pH 8.0 with the aid of a pH meter. Using a pH meter that has been standardized to pH 9.0, titrate the solution with 0.5 N hydrochloric acid until a pH of 8.8 remains for 1 min, and record the volume, S (mL), of 0.5 N hydrochloric acid required. Perform a blank determination (see *General Provisions*) using 2.1 g of primary standard sodium carbonate, and record the volume, B (mL), of 0.5 N hydrochloric acid required. Each mL of the volume (B − S) of 0.5 N hydrochloric acid is equivalent to 42.00 mg of sodium bicarbonate ($NaHCO_3$).
  Acceptance criteria: NLT 35.0% and NMT 38.6% of $NaHCO_3$
- **SODIUM CARBONATE**
  Sample: 4.2 g
  Analysis: Dissolve the *Sample* in 100 mL of water contained in a 250-mL beaker. Add methyl orange TS and titrate with 1 N sulfuric acid, stirring vigorously near the endpoint to expel carbon dioxide. Each mL of 1 N sulfuric acid is equivalent to 30.99 mg of sodium oxide. Calculate the percentage of sodium oxide (% Na_2O) in the sample taken. Then, calculate the percentage of sodium carbonate in the sample by the formula:

$$Result = [\%SO - (\%SB \times F_1)] \times F_2$$

%SO = percentage of sodium oxide
%SB = percentage of sodium bicarbonate determined in the *Assay* for *Sodium Bicarbonate*
F_1 = factor converting sodium bicarbonate to sodium oxide, 0.3689
F_2 = factor converting sodium oxide to sodium carbonate, 1.7099

Acceptance criteria: NLT 46.4% and NMT 50.0% of Na_2CO_3

IMPURITIES
Inorganic Impurities
- **IRON**
  Sample: 500 mg
  Sample solution: Dissolve the *Sample* in 10 mL of 2.7 N hydrochloric acid and dilute to 50 mL with water. Add about 40 mg of ammonium persulfate crystals and 10 mL of ammonium thiocyanate TS.
  Control: 10 μg Fe (1.0 mL of *Iron Standard Solution*) (see *Standard Solutions for the Preparation of Controls and Standards*, Solutions and Indicators)
  Control solution: Prepare a volume of solution equal to that of the *Sample solution* using the *Control* in place of the *Sample*, 2 mL of hydrochloric acid, and the same quantities of ammonium persulfate and ammonium thiocyanate TS used for the *Sample solution*.
  Acceptance criteria: Any red or pink color in the *Sample solution* does not exceed that produced in the *Control solution* (NMT 0.002%).
- **LEAD,** *Lead Limit Test, APDC Extraction Method*, Appendix IIIB
  Acceptance criteria: NMT 2 mg/kg
- **SODIUM CHLORIDE**
  Sample: 10 g

Analysis: Dissolve the *Sample* in 50 mL of water in a 250-mL beaker. Add sufficient nitric acid to make the solution slightly acid, then add 1 mL of ferric ammonium sulfate TS and 1.00 mL of 0.05 N ammonium thiocyanate, and titrate with 0.05 N silver nitrate, stirring constantly until the red color completely disappears. Finally, back titrate with 0.05 N ammonium thiocyanate until a faint red color appears. Subtract the total volume of 0.05 N ammonium thiocyanate added from the volume of 0.05 N silver nitrate required. Each mL of 0.05 N silver nitrate is equivalent to 2.922 mg of sodium chloride (NaCl). Calculate the percentage of sodium chloride in the sample taken.
Acceptance criteria: NMT 0.5%

SPECIFIC TESTS
- **WATER**
  Analysis: Sum the percentages of *Sodium Bicarbonate*, *Sodium Carbonate*, and *Sodium Chloride* and subtract the sum from 100.
  Acceptance criteria: Between 13.8% and 16.7%

Sodium Stearoyl Lactylate
First Published: Prior to FCC 6

INS: 481(i)   CAS: [25383-99-7]
UNII: IN99IT31LN [sodium stearoyl lactylate]

DESCRIPTION
Sodium Stearoyl Lactylate occurs as a cream-colored powder or brittle solid. It is a mixture of sodium salts of stearoyl lactylic acids and minor proportions of other sodium salts of related acids, manufactured by the reaction of stearic acid and lactic acid, neutralized to the sodium salts. It is slightly hygroscopic. It is soluble in ethanol and in hot oil or fat, and is dispersible in warm water.
Function: Emulsifier; dough conditioner; stabilizer; whipping agent
Packaging and Storage: Store in tight containers in a cool, dry place.

IDENTIFICATION
- **SODIUM,** Appendix IIIA
  Sample: 1 g
  Analysis: Heat the *Sample* with a mixture of 25 mL of water and 5 mL of hydrochloric acid to liberate the fatty acids floating as an oily layer on the surface of the liquid. Test the water layer for *Sodium*.
  Acceptance criteria: Passes tests
- **MELTING RANGE OR TEMPERATURE DETERMINATION,** Appendix IIB
  Sample: 25 g
  Analysis: Mix the *Sample* with 50 g of a 15% alcoholic potassium hydroxide solution in an Erlenmeyer flask and reflux for 1 h or until saponification is complete. Cool, add 150 mL of water, and mix. After complete solution of the soap, add 60 mL of 2 N sulfuric acid and, while stirring frequently, heat the mixture until the fatty acids separate cleanly as a transparent layer. Wash the fatty acids with boiling water until free from sulfate, collect them in a small beaker, and warm the beaker on a steam bath until the water has separated and the fatty acids are clear. Allow the acids to cool, pour off the water layer, then melt the acids, filter into a dry beaker, and dry at 105° for 20 min.
  Acceptance criteria: The fatty acids so obtained do not melt below 54°.

IMPURITIES
Inorganic Impurities
- **LEAD,** *Lead Limit Test, Flame Atomic Absorption Spectrophotometric Method,* Appendix IIIB
  Sample: 10 g
  Acceptance criteria: NMT 2 mg/kg

SPECIFIC TESTS
- **ACID VALUE**
  Sample: 1 g
  Analysis: Transfer the *Sample* to a 125-mL Erlenmeyer flask, add 25 mL of alcohol, previously neutralized to phenolphthalein TS, and heat on a hot plate until the *Sample* is dissolved. Cool, add 5 drops of phenolphthalein TS, and titrate rapidly with 0.1 N sodium hydroxide to the first pink color that persists for at least 30 s. Calculate the acid value by the formula:

  $$\text{Result} = F \times V \times N/W$$

  F = factor, 56.1
  V = volume of the sodium hydroxide solution used (mL)
  N = normality of the sodium hydroxide solution
  W = weight of the sample taken (g)
  [NOTE—Retain the neutralized solution for the determination of *Ester Value*.]
  Acceptance criteria: Between 60 and 80
- **ESTER VALUE**
  Sample: Neutralized solution retained from determination of *Acid Value*
  Analysis: Add 10.0 mL of alcoholic potassium hydroxide solution (prepared by dissolving 11.2 g of potassium hydroxide in 250 mL of alcohol and diluting with 25 mL of water) to the *Sample*. Add 5 drops of phenolphthalein TS, connect a suitable condenser, and reflux for 2 h. Cool the solution, add 5 additional drops of phenolphthalein TS, and titrate the excess alkali with 0.1 N sulfuric acid. Perform a blank determination (see *General Provisions*) using 10.0 mL of the alcoholic potassium hydroxide solution, and make any necessary correction. Calculate the ester value by the formula:

  $$\text{Result} = [F \times (V_B - V_S) \times N]/W$$

F = factor, 56.1
V_B = volume of 0.1 N sulfuric acid required for the blank (mL)
V_S = volume of 0.1 N sulfuric acid required for the sample (mL)
N = normality of the sulfuric acid
W = weight of the sample taken (g)

Acceptance criteria: Between 120 and 190

- **SODIUM CONTENT**

[NOTE—Do not use ordinary glassware in this test because of possible contamination by sodium; instead, use suitable plastic (e.g., polyethylene) vessels where necessary.]

Stock lanthanum solution: Transfer 5.86 g of lanthanum oxide (La_2O_3) into a 100-mL volumetric flask, wet with a few mL of water, slowly add 25 mL of hydrochloric acid, and swirl until the material is completely dissolved. Dilute to volume with water, and mix.

Stock sodium solution: 1 mg/mL (1000 mg/kg Na). [NOTE—Obtain this solution commercially or prepare as follows. Transfer 1.271 g of sodium chloride (previously dried at 105° for 2 h) into a 500-mL volumetric flask, dilute to volume with water, and mix.]

Standard solutions: Transfer 10.0 mL of the *Stock lanthanum solution* into each of three 100-mL volumetric flasks. Using a microliter syringe, transfer 0.20 mL of the *Stock sodium solution* to the first flask, 0.40 mL to the second flask, and 0.50 mL to the third flask. Dilute the contents of each flask to volume with water and mix. The flasks contain 2.0, 4.0, and 5.0 µg/mL of sodium, respectively. [NOTE—Prepare these solutions fresh daily.]

Sample solution: Transfer 250 mg of sample to a 30-mL beaker, dissolve with heating in 10 mL of alcohol, and quantitatively transfer the solution into a 25-mL volumetric flask. Wash the beaker with two 5-mL portions of alcohol, adding the washings to the flask. Dilute to volume with alcohol and mix. Transfer 2.5 mL of the *Stock lanthanum solution* to a second 25-mL volumetric flask. Using a microliter syringe, transfer 0.25 mL of the alcoholic solution of the sample into the second flask, dilute to volume with water, and mix.

Analysis: Set a suitable atomic absorption spectrophotometer to a wavelength of 589 nm. Measure the absorbances of the *Standard solutions* and the *Sample solution*. Plot the absorbances of the *Standard solutions* versus the concentration of sodium, in µg/mL. From the curve, determine the concentration, C (µg/mL), of sodium in the *Sample solution*. Calculate the quantity (mg), of sodium in the sample taken by the formula:

$$Result = 2.5C$$

Acceptance criteria: Between 3.5% and 5.0%

- **TOTAL LACTIC ACID**

Standard stock solution: 106.7 µg/mL lithium lactate made to 100.0 mL

Standard solutions: Transfer 1.0, 2.0, 4.0, 6.0, and 8.0 mL of the *Standard stock solution* into separate 100-mL volumetric flasks; dilute each flask to volume with water, and mix. Transfer 1.0 mL of each solution into separate test tubes. These standards represent 1, 2, 4, 6, and 8 µg/mL lactic acid, respectively.

Sample solution: Transfer 200 mg of sample into a 125-mL Erlenmeyer flask, add 10 mL of 0.5 N alcoholic potassium hydroxide and 10 mL of water. Attach an air condenser and reflux gently for 45 min. Wash the sides of the flask and the condenser with about 40 mL of water and heat on a steam bath until no odor of alcohol remains. Add 6 mL of 1:2 sulfuric acid, heat until the fatty acids are melted, then cool to about 60° and add 25 mL of petroleum ether. Swirl the mixture gently and quantitatively transfer to a separatory funnel. Collect the water layer in a 100-mL volumetric flask and wash the petroleum ether layer with two 20-mL portions of water, adding the washings to the volumetric flask. Dilute to volume with water, and mix. Transfer 1.0 mL of this solution into a second 100-mL volumetric flask, dilute to volume with water, and mix.

Analysis: Transfer 1.0 mL of the *Sample solution* into a test tube and 1.0 mL of water into another test tube to serve as a blank. Treat the contents of these two test tubes and the five test tubes containing the *Standard solutions* as follows: To each tube add 1 drop of cupric sulfate TS, swirl gently, and rapidly add 9.0 mL of sulfuric acid from a buret. Loosely stopper the tubes and heat in a water bath at 90° for exactly 5 min. Immediately cool them below 20° in an ice bath for 5 min, add 3 drops of *p*-phenylphenol TS to each, shake the tubes immediately, and heat in a water bath at 30° for 30 min, shaking each tube twice during this time to disperse the reagent. Heat the tubes in a water bath at 90° for exactly 90 s, and then cool them immediately to room temperature in an ice-water bath. Using a suitable spectrophotometer set to a wavelength of 570 nm, determine the absorbance of the solution in each tube in a 1-cm cell. Construct a standard curve by plotting the absorbance obtained for each of the *Standard solutions* versus micrograms of lactic acid. Obtain the weight (µg) of lactic acid in the *Sample solution* from the standard curve.

Acceptance criteria: Between 23.0% and 34.0%

Sodium Stearyl Fumarate

First Published: Prior to FCC 6
Last Revision: FCC 7

$C_{22}H_{39}NaO_4$ Formula wt 390.54
INS: 1169   CAS: [4070-80-8]
UNII: 7CV7WJK4UI [sodium stearyl fumarate]

Sodium Stearyl Fumarate

DESCRIPTION
Sodium Stearyl Fumarate occurs as a fine, white powder. It is slightly soluble in methanol, but is practically insoluble in water.

Function: Dough conditioner

Packaging and Storage: Store in well-closed containers.

IDENTIFICATION
- **INFRARED ABSORPTION**, *Spectrophotometric Identification Tests,* Appendix IIIC

    Reference standard: USP Sodium Stearyl Fumarate RS

    Sample and standard preparation: *K* (1:300 dispersion)

    Acceptance criteria: The spectrum of the sample exhibits maxima at the same wavelengths as those in the spectrum of the *Reference standard*.

ASSAY
- **PROCEDURE**

    Sample: 250 mg

    Analysis: Transfer the *Sample* into a 50-mL Erlenmeyer flask, mix with 1 mL of chloroform, and add 20 mL of glacial acetic acid to dissolve the sample. Add quinaldine red TS and titrate with 0.1 N perchloric acid in glacial acetic acid. [**CAUTION**—Handle perchloric acid in an appropriate fume hood.] Each mL of 0.1 N perchloric acid is equivalent to 39.05 mg of $C_{22}H_{39}NaO_4$.

    Acceptance criteria: 99.0%–101.5% of $C_{22}H_{39}NaO_4$, calculated on the anhydrous basis

IMPURITIES
Inorganic Impurities
- **LEAD**, *Lead Limit Test, Flame Atomic Absorption Spectrophotometric Method,* Appendix IIIB

    Sample: 10 g

    Acceptance criteria: NMT 2 mg/kg

Organic Impurities
- **SODIUM STEARYL MALEATE AND STEARYL ALCOHOL**

    Diluent: 10% acetic acid in chloroform

    Standard solution A: 0.10 mg/mL of USP Sodium Stearyl Maleate RS in *Diluent*

    Standard solution B: 0.20 mg/mL of USP Stearyl Alcohol RS in *Diluent*

    Standard mixture: Mix one part of *Standard solution A* with one part of *Standard solution B*, and shake well. [NOTE—This mixture represents 0.25% of sodium stearyl maleate and 0.5% of stearyl alcohol, based upon the weight (200 mg) of the sample taken.]

    Sample solution: 20 mg/mL in *Diluent*. [NOTE—If necessary, heat the mixture carefully in a glass-stoppered volumetric flask to dissolve the sample, and then cool before diluting with the solvent mixture to volume.]

    Thin-layer chromatography, Appendix IIA

    Adsorbent plates: Prepare a slurry of 24 g of chromatographic silica gel G in 75 mL of water and apply a uniformly thin layer to 23-cm square, or other convenient size, glass plates. Dry in the air at room temperature for 2 h.

    Developing solvent system: Toluene, hexane, and glacial acetic acid (5:5:1, v/v/v), previously equilibrated

    Spray reagent: 0.5% of potassium permanganate and 0.3% of sodium carbonate in water

    Application volume: 10 μL

    Analysis: Apply the *Standard mixture* and the *Sample solution* to the bottom of the chromatographic plate. Place the plate in a suitable chromatographic chamber containing *Developing solvent system*, and develop by ascending chromatography for 30 min to effect one pass. Remove the plate from the tank, dry in the air for 10 min, and then heat in an oven at 90° for 2 min. After cooling to room temperature, replace the plate in the chamber for a second pass of 30 min. After the second pass, remove the plate from the chamber and dry in the air for 15–20 min. Spray evenly with *Spray reagent*. [NOTE—Maleate and fumarate appear as yellow spots against a pink background.] Spray with sulfuric acid and heat in an oven at 150° to detect the stearyl alcohol. Visually compare any spots from the *Sample solution* against the R_F of the spots from the *Standard mixture*.

    Acceptance criteria: The spots from the *Sample solution* do not appear to be stronger than the respective spots from the *Standard mixture* (NMT 0.25% sodium stearyl maleate and NMT 0.5% stearyl alcohol).

SPECIFIC TESTS
- **SAPONIFICATION VALUE**

    Ethanolic potassium hydroxide solution: 5.5 mg/mL of potassium hydroxide in absolute ethanol. [NOTE—If necessary for complete dissolution, heat the solution prior to bringing it to volume. Prepare fresh daily and filter if necessary to remove carbonate.]

    Sample: 450 mg

    Analysis: Transfer the *Sample* into a 300-mL Erlenmeyer flask, and add 50.0 mL of *Ethanolic potassium hydroxide solution*, rinsing down the inside of the flask during the addition. Reflux the mixture gently on a steam bath for at least 2 h, occasionally swirling gently but avoiding splashing the mixture up into the condenser. Rinse the condenser with 10 mL of 70% alcohol, followed by three 10-mL portions of water, collecting the rinsings in the flask. Cool, rinse the sides of the flask with two 10-mL portions of 70% alcohol, add phenolphthalein TS, and titrate with 0.1 N hydrochloric acid to the disappearance of any pink color. Perform a blank determination (see *General Provisions*) using the same amount of *Ethanolic potassium hydroxide*, and make any necessary correction. Calculate the *Saponification Value* by the formula:

    $$\text{Result} = 56.1(B - S) \times N/W$$

    B = volume of 0.1 N hydrochloric acid required for the blank (mL)
    S = volume of 0.1 N hydrochloric acid required for the sample (mL)
    N = exact normality of the hydrochloric acid
    W = weight of the sample taken (g)

    Acceptance criteria: Between 142.2 and 146.0, calculated on the anhydrous basis

- **WATER**, *Water Determination*, Appendix IIB
  Acceptance criteria: NMT 5.0%

Sodium Sulfate

First Published: FCC 6

Na₂SO₄ — Formula wt, anhydrous 142.04
Na₂SO₄·10H₂O — Formula wt, decahydrate 322.19
INS: 514
CAS: anhydrous [7757-82-6]
decahydrate [7727-73-3]
UNII: 0YPR65R21J [sodium sulfate]

DESCRIPTION
Sodium Sulfate occurs as colorless crystals or as a fine, white, crystalline powder. It is anhydrous or contains 10 molecules of water of crystallization. The decahydrate is efflorescent. It is freely soluble in water and practically insoluble in alcohol. A 1:20 aqueous solution is neutral or slightly alkaline to litmus paper.
Function: Agent in caramel production
Packaging and Storage: Store in well-closed containers.

IDENTIFICATION
- **SULFATE**, Appendix IIIA
  Sample solution: 50 mg/mL
  Acceptance criteria: Passes test
- **SODIUM**, Appendix IIIA
  Sample solution: 50 mg/mL
  Acceptance criteria: Passes test

ASSAY
- **PROCEDURE**
  Sample: 500 mg, previously dried at 105° for 4 h
  Analysis: Dissolve the *Sample* in 200 mL of water, add 1 mL of hydrochloric acid, and heat to boiling. Gradually add, in small portions and while constantly stirring, an excess of hot barium chloride TS (about 10 mL), and heat the mixture on a steam bath for 1 h. Collect the precipitate on a retentive, ashless filter paper, wash until free from chloride, and place the filter into a suitable tared crucible. Carefully burn away the paper, and ignite at 800° ± 25° to constant weight. The weight of the barium sulfate so obtained, multiplied by 0.6086, indicates its equivalent of Na₂SO₄.
  Acceptance criteria: NLT 99.0% and NMT 100.5% of Na₂SO₄, on the dried basis

IMPURITIES
Inorganic Impurities
- **LEAD**, *Lead Limit Test, Lead Limit Test, APDC Extraction Method*, Appendix IIIB
  Acceptance criteria: NMT 2 mg/kg
- **SELENIUM**, *Selenium Limit Test, Method II*, Appendix IIIB
  Sample: 200 mg
  Acceptance criteria: NMT 0.003%

SPECIFIC TESTS
- **LOSS ON DRYING**, Appendix IIC: 105° for 4 h
  Acceptance criteria
    Anhydrous: NMT 1%
    Decahydrate: Between 51.0% and 57.0%

OTHER REQUIREMENTS
- **LABELING:** Indicate whether it is anhydrous or the decahydrate.

Sodium Sulfite

First Published: Prior to FCC 6

Na₂SO₃ — Formula wt 126.04
INS: 221
CAS: [7757-83-7]
UNII: VTK01UQK3G [sodium sulfite]

DESCRIPTION
Sodium Sulfite occurs as a white or tan to slightly pink powder. It undergoes oxidation in air. Its solutions are alkaline to litmus and to phenolphthalein. One g dissolves in about 4 mL of water. It is sparingly soluble in alcohol.
Function: Preservative; antioxidant; bleaching agent
Packaging and Storage: Store in tight containers.

IDENTIFICATION
- **SODIUM**, Appendix IIIA
  Sample solution: 50 mg/mL
  Acceptance criteria: Passes test
- **SULFITE**, Appendix IIIA
  Sample solution: 50 mg/mL
  Acceptance criteria: Passes test

ASSAY
- **PROCEDURE**
  Sample: 250 mg
  Analysis: Add the *Sample* to 50 mL of 0.1 N iodine contained in a glass-stoppered flask and stopper the flask. Allow the flask to stand for 5 min, add 1 mL of hydrochloric acid, and titrate the excess iodine with 0.1 N sodium thiosulfate, adding starch TS as the indicator. Each mL of 0.1 N iodine is equivalent to 6.302 mg of Na₂SO₃.
  Acceptance criteria: NLT 95.0% Na₂SO₃

IMPURITIES
Inorganic Impurities
- **LEAD**, *Lead Limit Test, APDC Extraction Method*, Appendix IIIB
  Acceptance criteria: NMT 2 mg/kg
- **SELENIUM**, *Selenium Limit Test, Method I*, Appendix IIIB
  Sample: 200 g (with 100 mg of magnesium oxide)
  Acceptance criteria: NMT 0.003%

Sodium Tartrate

First Published: Prior to FCC 6

Disodium Tartrate
Disodium L-Tartrate

$C_4H_4Na_2O_6 \cdot 2H_2O$ Formula wt 230.08
INS: 335   CAS: [868-18-8]
UNII: QTO9JB4MDD [sodium tartrate]

DESCRIPTION
Sodium Tartrate occurs as transparent, colorless crystals. It is the disodium salt of L(+)-tartaric acid. One g dissolves in 3 mL of water. It is insoluble in alcohol. The pH of a 1:20 aqueous solution is between 7 and 9. Upon ignition, it emits the odor of burning sugar and leaves a residue that is alkaline to litmus and that effervesces with acids.
Function: Sequestrant
Packaging and Storage: Store in tight containers.

IDENTIFICATION
- **SODIUM,** Appendix IIIA
  Acceptance criteria: Passes test
- **TARTRATE,** Appendix IIIA
  Acceptance criteria: Passes test

ASSAY
- **PROCEDURE**
  Sample: 250 mg, previously dried at 150° for 3 h
  Analysis: Transfer the Sample to a 250-mL beaker. Add 150 mL of glacial acetic acid, heat to near boiling, stir (preferably with a magnetic stirrer) until the sample is dissolved, and cool to room temperature. Titrate with 0.1 N perchloric acid in glacial acetic acid, determining the endpoint potentiometrically. Each mL of 0.1 N perchloric acid is equivalent to 9.703 mg of $C_4H_4Na_2O_6$.
  [**CAUTION**—Handle perchloric acid in an appropriate fume hood.]
  Acceptance criteria: NLT 99.0% and NMT 100.5% of $C_4H_4Na_2O_6$, on the dried basis

IMPURITIES
Inorganic Impurities
- **LEAD,** Lead Limit Test, Flame Atomic Absorption Spectrophotometric Method, Appendix IIIB
  Sample: 10 g
  Acceptance criteria: NMT 2 mg/kg

Organic Impurities
- **OXALATE**
  Sample: 1 g
  Analysis: Dissolve the Sample in 10 mL of water, and add 5 drops of 1 N acetic acid and 2 mL of calcium chloride TS
  Acceptance criteria: No turbidity develops within 1 h. (NMT about 0.1%)

SPECIFIC TESTS
- **LOSS ON DRYING,** Appendix IIC: 150° for 3 h
  Acceptance criteria: Between 14.0% and 17.0%

Sodium Thiosulfate

First Published: Prior to FCC 6

Sodium Hyposulfite

$Na_2S_2O_3 \cdot 5H_2O$ Formula wt 248.19
INS: 539   CAS: [10102-17-7]
UNII: HX1032V43M [sodium thiosulfate]

DESCRIPTION
Sodium Thiosulfate occurs as large, colorless crystals or as a coarse, crystalline powder. It is deliquescent in moist air and effloresces in dry air at temperatures above 33°. Its solutions are neutral or faintly alkaline to litmus. One g dissolves in 0.5 mL of water. It is insoluble in alcohol.
Function: Sequestrant; antioxidant
Packaging and Storage: Store in tight containers.

IDENTIFICATION
- **A. PROCEDURE**
  Sample solution: 100 mg/mL
  Analysis: Add a few drops of iodine TS to the Sample solution.
  Acceptance criteria: The color disappears.
- **B. THIOSULFATE,** Appendix IIIA
  Sample solution: 50 mg/mL
  Acceptance criteria: Passes tests
- **C. SODIUM,** Appendix IIIA
  Sample solution: 50 mg/mL
  Acceptance criteria: Passes tests

ASSAY
- **PROCEDURE**
  Sample: 500 mg of dried sample (see Water determination)
  Analysis: Dissolve it in 30 mL of water, and titrate with 0.1 N iodine, using starch TS as the indicator. Each mL of 0.1 N iodine is equivalent to 15.81 mg of $Na_2S_2O_3$.
  Acceptance criteria: NLT 99.0% and NMT 100.5% of $Na_2S_2O_3$, on the anhydrous basis

IMPURITIES
Inorganic Impurities
- **LEAD,** Lead Limit Test, APDC Extraction Method, Appendix IIIB
  Acceptance criteria: NMT 2 mg/kg
- **SELENIUM,** Selenium Limit Test, Method I, Appendix IIIB
  Sample: 200 mg
  Acceptance criteria: NMT 0.003%

SPECIFIC TESTS
- **WATER**
  Sample: 1 g
  Analysis: Dry the Sample in a vacuum at 40° to 45° for 16 h, cool, and weigh.
  Acceptance criteria: Between 32.0% and 37.0%

Sodium Trimetaphosphate

First Published: Prior to FCC 6

(NaPO$_3$)$_3$ Formula wt 305.89
   CAS: [7785-84-4]
UNII: 3IH6169RL0 [sodium trimetaphosphate]

DESCRIPTION
Sodium Trimetaphosphate occurs as white crystals or as a white, crystalline powder. It is a cyclic polyphosphate composed of three metaphosphate units. It is freely soluble in water. The pH of a 1:100 aqueous solution is about 6.0.
Function: Starch-modifying agent
Packaging and Storage: Store in tight containers.

IDENTIFICATION
- **A. SODIUM,** Appendix IIIA
  Sample solution: 1:20
  Acceptance criteria: Passes test
- **B. SAMPLE:** 100 mg
  Analysis: Dissolve the *Sample* in 5 mL of hot 1.7 N nitric acid. Warm on a steam bath for 10 min, and cool. Neutralize to litmus paper with 1 N sodium hydroxide, and add silver nitrate TS.
  Acceptance criteria: A yellow precipitate forms that is soluble in 1.7 N nitric acid.

ASSAY
- **PROCEDURE**
  Sample: 800 mg
  Analysis: Transfer the *Sample* into a 400-mL beaker, add 100 mL of water and 25 mL of nitric acid, cover with a watch glass, and boil for 10 min on a hot plate. Rinse any condensate from the watch glass into the beaker, cool the solution to room temperature, transfer it quantitatively to a 500-mL volumetric flask, dilute to volume with water, and mix thoroughly. Pipet 20.0 mL of this solution into a 500-mL Erlenmeyer flask, add 100 mL of water, and heat just to boiling. While stirring, add 50 mL of quimociac TS, then cover with a watch glass, and boil for 1 min in a well-ventilated hood. Cool to room temperature, swirling occasionally while cooling, then filter through a tared, sintered-glass filter crucible of medium porosity, and wash the precipitate with five 25-mL portions of water. Dry the precipitate at about 225° for 30 min, cool, and weigh. Each mg of precipitate is equivalent to 32.074 μg of P$_2$O$_5$.
  Acceptance criteria: Between 68.0% and 70.0% of P$_2$O$_5$

IMPURITIES
Inorganic Impurities
- **ARSENIC,** *Arsenic Limit Test,* Appendix IIIB
  Sample solution: 1 g in 35 mL of water
  Acceptance criteria: NMT 3 mg/kg
- **FLUORIDE,** *Fluoride Limit Test, Method IV,* Appendix IIIB
  Sample: 2 g
  Acceptance criteria: NMT 0.005%
- **LEAD,** *Lead Limit Test, APDC Extraction Method,* Appendix IIIB
  Acceptance criteria: NMT 4 mg/kg

SPECIFIC TESTS
- **INSOLUBLE SUBSTANCES**
  Sample: 10 g
  Analysis: Dissolve the *Sample* in 100 mL of hot water and filter the solution through a tared filtering crucible. Wash the insoluble residue with hot water, dry at 105° for 2 h, cool, and weigh.
  Acceptance criteria: NMT 0.1%

Sodium Tripolyphosphate

First Published: Prior to FCC 6

Pentasodium Triphosphate
Triphosphate
Sodium Triphosphate

Na$_5$P$_3$O$_{10}$ Formula wt, anhydrous 367.86
Na$_5$P$_3$O$_{10}$·6H$_2$O   Formula wt, hexahydrate 475.96
INS: 451(i)   CAS: anhydrous [7758-29-4]
   hexahydrate [15091-98-2]
UNII: 5HK03SA80J [sodium tripolyphosphate, unspecified]
UNII: 9SW4PFD2FZ [sodium tripolyphosphate, anhydrous]
UNII: T7Y93S4UXX [sodium tripolyphosphate, hexahydrate]

DESCRIPTION
Sodium Tripolyphosphate occurs as white, slightly hygroscopic granules, or as a powder. It is anhydrous or contains six molecules of water of hydration. It is freely soluble in water, but insoluble in alcohol. The pH of a 1:100 aqueous solution is about 9.5.
Function: Emulsifier; sequestrant
Packaging and Storage: Store in tight containers.

IDENTIFICATION
- **A. SODIUM,** Appendix IIIA
  Sample solution: 50 mg/mL
  Acceptance criteria: Passes tests
- **B. PROCEDURE**
  Sample solution: 10 mg/mL
  Analysis: Add a few drops of silver nitrate TS to 1 mL of the *Sample solution*.
  Acceptance criteria: A white precipitate forms that is soluble in 1.7 N nitric acid.

ASSAY
- **PROCEDURE**
  Potassium acetate buffer (pH 5.0): Dissolve 78.5 g of potassium acetate in 1000 mL of water, and adjust the pH of the solution to 5.0 with glacial acetic acid. Add a few mg of mercuric iodide to inhibit mold growth.
  0.3 M Potassium chloride solution: Dissolve 22.35 g of potassium chloride in water, add 5 mL of *Potassium acetate buffer*, dilute to 1000 mL with water, and mix. Add a few mg of mercuric iodide to inhibit mold growth.
  0.6 M Potassium chloride solution: Dissolve 44.7 g of potassium chloride in water, add 5 mL of *Potassium acetate buffer*, dilute to 1000 mL with water, and mix. Add a few mg of mercuric iodide to inhibit mold growth.

1 M Potassium chloride solution: Dissolve 74.5 g of potassium chloride in water, add 5 mL of *Potassium acetate buffer*, dilute to 1000 mL with water, and mix. Add a few mg of mercuric iodide to inhibit mold growth.

Chromatographic column: Use a standard chromatographic column, 20- to 40-cm long with a 20- to 28-mm id, or equivalent, that has a sealed-in, coarse-porosity, fritted disk. If a stopcock is not provided, attach a stopcock having a 3- to 4-mm diameter bore to the outlet of the column with a short length of flexible vinyl tubing.

Chromatographic column preparation: Close the column stopcock, fill the space between the fritted disk and the stopcock with water, and connect a vacuum line to the stopcock. Prepare a 1:1 water slurry of Dowex 1 × 8, chloride form, 100- to 200- or 200- to 400-mesh, or a comparable grade of styrene-divinylbenzene ion exchange resin, and decant off any very fine particles and any foam. Repeat two or three times or until no more finely suspended material or foaming is observed. Fill the column with the slurry, and open the stopcock to allow the vacuum to pack the resin bed until the water level is slightly above the top of the resin, then immediately close the stopcock. Do not allow the liquid level to fall below the resin level at any time. Repeat this procedure until the packed resin column is 15 cm above the fritted disk. Place one circle of tightly fitting glass-fiber filter paper on top of the resin bed, then place a perforated polyethylene disk on top of the paper. Alternatively, place a loosely packed plug of glass wool on top of the bed. Close the top of the column with a rubber stopper in which a 7.6-cm length of capillary tubing (1.5-mm id, 7-mm od), or equivalent, has been inserted through the center, so that about 12 mm of the tubing extends through the bottom of the stopper. Connect the top of the capillary tubing to the stem of a 500-mL separatory funnel with flexible vinyl tubing, and clamp the separatory funnel to a ring stand above the column. Wash the column by adding 100 mL of water to the separatory funnel with all stopcocks closed. First open the separatory funnel stopcock, then open the column stopcock. The rate of flow should be about 5 mL/min. When the separatory funnel is empty, close the column stopcock, then close the separatory funnel stopcock.

Sample preparation: Transfer 500 mg of sample into a 250-mL volumetric flask, dissolve in and dilute to volume with water, and mix. Transfer 10.0 mL of this solution into the separatory funnel connected to the chromatographic column described above under *Chromotographic column preparation*. Open both stopcocks, and allow the solution to drain into the column, rinsing the separator with 20 mL of water. Discard the eluate. Add 370 mL of *0.3 M Potassium chloride solution* to the separatory funnel, and allow this solution to pass through the column, discarding the eluate. Add 250 mL of *0.6 M Potassium chloride solution* to the column, allow the solution to pass through the column, and receive the eluate in a 400-mL beaker. Use this retained eluate as the *Sample preparation*. [NOTE—To ensure a clean column for the next run, pass 100 mL of *1 M Potassium chloride solution* through the column, and then follow with 100 mL of water. Discard all washings.]

Analysis: Add 15 mL of nitric acid to the beaker containing the *Sample preparation*, mix, and boil for 15 to 20 min. Add methyl orange TS, and neutralize the solution with ammonium hydroxide. Add 1 g of ammonium nitrate crystals, stir to dissolve, and cool. While stirring, add 15 mL of ammonium molybdate TS, and stir vigorously for 3 min, or allow the mixture to stand with occasional stirring for 10 to 15 min. Filter the contents of the beaker by means of suction through a 6- to 7-mm paper-pulp filter pad supported in a 25-mm porcelain disk. The filter pad should be covered with a suspension of infusorial earth. After the contents of the beaker have been transferred to the filter, wash the beaker with five 10-mL portions of a 10 mg/mL solution of sodium or potassium nitrate, passing the washings through the filter, then wash the filter with five 5-mL portions of the 10 mg/mL sodium or potassium nitrate wash solution. Return the filter pad and the precipitate to the beaker, wash the funnel thoroughly with water into the beaker, and dilute to about 150 mL. Add 0.1 N sodium hydroxide from a buret until the yellow precipitate is dissolved, then add 5 to 8 mL in excess. Add phenolphthalein TS, and titrate the excess alkali with 0.1 N nitric acid. Finally, titrate with 0.1 N sodium hydroxide to the first appearance of a pink color. The difference between the total volume of 0.1 N sodium hydroxide added and the volume of nitric acid required represents the volume, V, in mL, of 0.1 N sodium hydroxide consumed by the phosphomolybdate complex. Calculate the quantity, in mg, of $Na_5P_3O_{10}$ in the sample taken by the formula:

$$Result = 0.533 \times 25V$$

V = volume (mL) of 0.1 N sodium hydroxide consumed by the phosphomolybdate complex

Acceptance criteria
  Anhydrous: NLT 85.0% of $Na_5P_3O_{10}$
  Hexahydrate: NLT 65.0% of $Na_5P_3O_{10}$

IMPURITIES
Inorganic Impurities
- **ARSENIC,** *Arsenic Limit Test,* Appendix IIIB
  Sample solution: 1 g of sample in 35 mL of water
  Acceptance criteria: NMT 3 mg/kg
- **FLUORIDE,** *Fluoride Limit Test, Method IV,* Appendix IIIB
  Sample: 2 g
  Acceptance criteria: NMT 0.005%
- **LEAD,** *Lead Limit Test, APDC Extraction Method,* Appendix IIIB
  Acceptance criteria: NMT 2 mg/kg

SPECIFIC TESTS
- **INSOLUBLE SUBSTANCES**
  Sample: 10 g

Analysis: Dissolve the *Sample* in 100 mL of hot water and filter the solution through a tared filtering crucible. Wash the insoluble residue with hot water, dry at 105° for 2 h, cool, and weigh.
Acceptance criteria: NMT 0.1%

Solin Oil

First Published: Prior to FCC 6

Low Linolenic Acid Flaxseed Oil (Unhydrogenated)
Low Linolenic Acid Linseed Oil
UNII: 84XB4DV00W [linseed oil]

DESCRIPTION
Solin Oil occurs as a light yellow oil. It is obtained from the seed of certain varieties of the flaxseed plant *Linum usitatissimum* L. (Fam. Linaceae) by mechanical expression and/or solvent extraction, differing from linseed oil in having a linolenic acid (C18:3) content of less than 5%. The oil is refined, bleached, and deodorized to remove free fatty acids, phospholipids, color, odor and flavor components, and miscellaneous non-oil materials. It is liquid at 21° to 27° and free from visible foreign material, but traces of wax may cause the oil to cloud at refrigeration temperatures (2° to 5°) unless removed by winterization.
Function: Coating agent; texturizer
Packaging and Storage: Store in tightly closed containers blanketed with an inert gas.

IDENTIFICATION
- **Fatty Acid Composition,** Appendix VII
  Acceptance criteria: Solin Oil exhibits the following composition profile of fatty acids:

Fatty Acid	Weight % (Range)
<14:0	<0.1
14:0	<0.5
16:0	2–9
16:1	<0.5
18:0	2–5
18:1	8–60
18:2	40–80
18:3	<5.0
20:0	<0.3
20:1	<0.3
22:0	<0.3
22:1	<0.2
24:0	<0.2

IMPURITIES
Inorganic Impurities
- **Lead,** *Lead Limit Test, Atomic Absorption Spectrophotometric Graphite Furnace, Method II,* Appendix IIIB
  Acceptance criteria: NMT 0.1 mg/kg

- **Water,** *Water Determination, Method I,* Appendix IIB: Use 50 mL of chloroform to dissolve the sample, instead of 35 to 40 mL of methanol, in the *Procedure*.
  Acceptance criteria: NMT 0.1%

SPECIFIC TESTS
- **Cold Test,** Appendix VII
  Acceptance criteria: Passes test
- **Color (Fats and Related Substances),** Appendix VII
  Acceptance criteria: NMT 5.0 red
- **Free Fatty Acids (as Oleic Acid),** *Free Fatty Acids,* Appendix VII
  Analysis: Use the following equivalence factor (e) in the formula given in the procedure under *Free Fatty Acids*: e = 28.2.
  Acceptance criteria: NMT 0.1%
- **Iodine Value,** Appendix VII
  Acceptance criteria: Between 100 and 160
- **Linolenic Acid,** *Fatty Acid Composition,* Appendix VII
  Acceptance criteria: NMT 5.0%
- **Peroxide Value,** *Method II,* Appendix VII
  Acceptance criteria: NMT 10 mEq/kg
- **Unsaponifiable Matter,** Appendix VII
  Acceptance criteria: NMT 1.5%

Sorbic Acid

First Published: Prior to FCC 6

2,4-Hexadienoic Acid

$C_6H_8O_2$ Formula wt 112.13
INS: 200   CAS: [110-44-1]
UNII: X045WJ989B [sorbic acid]

DESCRIPTION
Sorbic Acid occurs as colorless needles or as a white to off-white, free-flowing powder. It is slightly soluble in water. One g dissolves in about 10 mL of ethanol and in about 20 mL of ether.
Function: Preservative; mold inhibitor
Packaging and Storage: Store in tight containers protected from light, preferably at a temperature not exceeding 38°.

IDENTIFICATION
- **A. Procedure**
  Sample solution: 100 mg/mL in alcohol
  Analysis: To 2 mL of the *Sample solution*, add a few drops of Bromine TS.
  Acceptance criteria: The color disappears.
- **B. UV-Visible Absorption Spectrum**
  Sample solution: 2.5 μg/mL in isopropanol
  Acceptance criteria: The *Sample solution* exhibits an absorbance maximum at 254 ± 2 nm.

ASSAY
- **PROCEDURE**
  Sample: 250 mg
  Analysis: Dissolve the *Sample* in 50 mL of anhydrous methanol that has been neutralized with 0.1 N sodium hydroxide. Add phenolphthalein TS and titrate with 0.1 N sodium hydroxide to the first pink color that persists for at least 30 s. Each mL of 0.1 N sodium hydroxide is equivalent to 11.21 mg of $C_6H_8O_2$.
  Acceptance criteria: NLT 99.0% and NMT 101.0% of $C_6H_8O_2$, calculated on the anhydrous basis

IMPURITIES
Inorganic Impurities
- **LEAD**, *Lead Limit Test, Flame Atomic Absorption Spectrophotometric Method*, Appendix IIIB
  Sample: 5 g
  Acceptance criteria: NMT 2 mg/kg
- **WATER**, *Water Determination*, Appendix IIB
  Acceptance criteria: NMT 0.5%

SPECIFIC TESTS
- **MELTING RANGE OR TEMPERATURE DETERMINATION**, *Procedure for Class Ia*, Appendix IIB
  Analysis: Proceed as directed, except increase the heat at a rate of 1°/min until melting is complete.
  Acceptance criteria: Between 132° and 135°
- **RESIDUE ON IGNITION (SULFATED ASH)**, Appendix IIC
  Sample: 2 g
  Acceptance criteria: NMT 0.2%

Sorbitan Monolaurate
First Published: FCC 7

INS: 493 CAS: [1338-39-2]
UNII: 6W9PS8B71J [sorbitan monolaurate]

DESCRIPTION
Sorbitan Monolaurate occurs as an amber-colored, oily, viscous liquid; light cream to tan beads or flakes; or a hard, waxy solid with a slight odor. It is a mixture of the partial esters of sorbitol and its mono- and dianhydrides with edible lauric acid. It contains lauric acid esterified with polyols derived from sorbitol. It is dispersible in hot and cold water.
Function: Emulsifier; stabilizer
Packaging and Storage: Store in well-closed containers.

IDENTIFICATION
- **ACID VALUE (FATS AND RELATED SUBSTANCES)**, Method I, Appendix VII
  Sample: 1 g of the fatty acid residue obtained in the *Assay*
  Acceptance criteria: 260–280
- **IODINE VALUE**, Appendix VII
  Sample: Use the fatty acid residue obtained in the *Assay*.
  Acceptance criteria: NMT 5
- **THIN-LAYER CHROMATOGRAPHY**, Appendix IIA
  Sample solution: 500 mg of the polyols obtained in the *Assay*, diluted with water to volume in a 2-mL volumetric flask
  Standard solution: 25 mg/mL of USP Sorbitol RS, 25 mg/mL of USP 1,4-Sorbitan RS, and 25 mg/mL of USP Isosorbide RS in water
  Adsorbent: 0.25-mm layer of chromatographic silica gel
  Application volume: 2 µL
  Developing solvent system: Acetone and glacial acetic acid (100:2)
  Spray reagent: Sulfuric acid and water (1:2)
  Analysis: Following development remove the plate from the chamber, dry thoroughly in air, and spray evenly with *Spray reagent*. [**CAUTION**—Do not overspray.] Immediately place the chromatographic plate on a hot plate maintained at 200° in a hood. Char until white fumes of sulfur trioxide cease, then cool the chromatographic plate to room temperature. [NOTE— The approximate R_F values for sorbitol, 1,4-sorbitan, and isosorbide are 0.07, 0.40, and 0.77, respectively.]
  Acceptance criteria: The spots from the *Sample solution* are located at the same R_F values as those of the polyols from the *Standard solution*.

ASSAY
- **PROCEDURE**
  Sample: 10 g
  Analysis: Transfer the *Sample* to a 500-mL conical flask, cautiously add 100 mL of alcohol and 3.5 g of potassium hydroxide, and mix. Connect a suitable condenser to the flask, reflux the mixture on a hot plate for 2 h, add 100 mL of water, and heat on a steam bath to evaporate the alcohol. Continue the evaporation until the odor of alcohol can no longer be detected, and transfer the saponification mixture, with the aid of 100 mL of hot water, to a 500-mL separatory funnel. Using extreme caution, neutralize to litmus with a mixture of equal volumes of sulfuric acid and water, noting the volume used, and add a 10% excess of the dilute acid. Allow the solution to cool. If salt appears, add sufficient water to produce a clear solution. Cautiously add 100 mL of solvent hexane, shake thoroughly, and withdraw the lower layer into a 500-mL separatory funnel. Similarly extract with two more 100-mL portions of solvent hexane. Extract the combined hexane layers with 50-mL portions of water until neutral to litmus paper, and combine the extracts with the original aqueous phase. [NOTE—This is the polyol solution and will be analyzed separately.] Evaporate the solvent hexane in a tared beaker on a steam bath nearly to dryness, dry in vacuum at 60° for 1 h, cool in a desiccator, and weigh the fatty acids. [NOTE—Save the fatty acid residue so obtained for use in the *Acid Value* and *Iodine Value* tests under *Identification*.]
  Neutralize the polyol solution with a 1:10 potassium hydroxide solution to pH 7 using a suitable pH meter. Evaporate on a steam bath to a moist residue, extract the polyols from the salts with three 150-mL portions of dehydrated alcohol, boiling the salt residue for 3 min

and crushing it, as necessary, with the flattened end of a stirring rod during each extraction, filtering each extract (while hot) through a medium-porosity sintered-glass funnel, provided with a sheet of retentive filter paper on which a layer of purified siliceous earth has been superimposed, and receiving the filtrates in a 1-L suction flask. Transfer the clear alcoholic polyols solution to a tared beaker, evaporate the alcohol on a steam bath, dry in a vacuum at 60° for 1 h, cool in a desiccator, and weigh the polyols. [NOTE—Save the polyols so obtained for use in the *Thin-Layer Chromatography* test under *Identification*.]

Acceptance criteria
Fatty acids: 55.0%–63.0%
Polyols (as sorbitol, 1,4-sorbitan, and isosorbide): 39.0%–45.0%

IMPURITIES
Inorganic Impurities
- **LEAD**, *Lead Limit Test, Flame Atomic Absorption Spectrophotometric Method*, Appendix IIIB
  Sample: 10 g
  Acceptance criteria: NMT 2 mg/kg

SPECIFIC TESTS
- **ACID VALUE (FATS AND RELATED SUBSTANCES)**, *Method II*, Appendix VII
  Acceptance criteria: NMT 8
- **HYDROXYL VALUE**, *Method II*, Appendix VII
  Acceptance criteria: 330–360
- **RESIDUE ON IGNITION (SULFATED ASH)**, Appendix IIC
  Sample: 1–2 g
  Analysis: Proceed as directed, but ignite at 600 ± 50°.
  Acceptance criteria: NMT 0.5%
- **SAPONIFICATION VALUE**, Appendix VII
  Sample: 4 g
  Acceptance criteria: 153–170
- **WATER**, *Water Determination*, Appendix IIB
  Acceptance criteria: NMT 1.5%

Sorbitan Monooleate

First Published: Second Supplement, FCC 6

INS: 494   CAS: [1338-43-8]
UNII: 06XEA2VD56 [sorbitan monooleate]

DESCRIPTION
Sorbitan Monooleate occurs as an amber-colored, oily, viscous liquid; light cream to tan beads or flakes; or a hard, waxy solid with a slight odor. It is a mixture of the partial esters of sorbitol and its mono- and dianhydrides with edible oleic acid. The constituent in greatest abundance is 1,4-sorbitan monooleate, with lesser abundance of isosorbide monooleate, sorbitan dioleate, and sorbitan trioleate. It is soluble at temperatures above its melting point in ethanol, ether, ethyl acetate, aniline, toluene, dioxane, petroleum ether, and carbon tetrachloride. It is insoluble in cold water, but dispersible in warm water.

Function: Emulsifier; stabilizer

Packaging and Storage: Store in well-closed containers.

IDENTIFICATION
- **IODINE VALUE**, Appendix VII
  Sample: The residue of oleic acid, obtained from the saponification of Sorbitan Monooleate in the *Assay*
  Acceptance criteria: Between 80 and 100
- **THIN-LAYER CHROMATOGRAPHY**, Appendix IIA
  Sample solution: 500 mg of the polyols obtained in the *Assay* (below), diluted with water to volume in a 2-mL volumetric flask
  Standard solution: 25 mg/mL USP Sorbitol RS, 25 mg/mL USP 1,4-Sorbitan RS, and 25 mg/mL USP Isosorbide RS in water
  Adsorbent: 0.25-mm layer of chromatographic silica gel
  Application volume: 2 µL
  Developing solvent system: Acetone and glacial acetic acid (100:2)
  Spray reagent: 1:2 sulfuric acid in water
  Analysis: Following development, remove the plate from the chamber, dry thoroughly in air, and spray evenly with the *Spray reagent*. [**CAUTION**—Do not overspray.] Immediately place the chromatographic plate on a hot plate maintained at 200° in a hood. Char until white fumes of sulfur trioxide cease, then cool the chromatographic plate to room temperature. [NOTE—The approximate R_F values for sorbitol, 1,4-sorbitan, and isosorbide are 0.07, 0.40, and 0.77, respectively.]
  Acceptance criteria: The spots from the *Sample solution* are located at the same R_F values as those of the polyols from the *Standard solution*.

ASSAY
- **PROCEDURE**
  Sample: 25 g
  Analysis: Transfer the *Sample* into a 500-mL round-bottom flask. Add 250 mL of alcohol and 7.5 g of potassium hydroxide, and mix. Connect a suitable condenser to the flask, reflux the mixture for 1 to 2 h, then transfer it to an 800-mL beaker, rinsing the flask with about 100 mL of water, and adding it to the beaker. Heat on a steam bath to evaporate the alcohol, adding water occasionally to replace the alcohol, and evaporate until the odor of alcohol can no longer be detected. Adjust the final volume to about 250 mL with hot water. Neutralize the soap solution with 1:2 sulfuric acid, add 10% in excess, and heat, while stirring, until the fatty acid layer separates. Transfer the fatty acids to a 500-mL separatory funnel, wash with three or four 20-mL portions of hot water to remove polyols, and combine the washings with the original aqueous polyol layer from the saponification. Extract the combined aqueous layer with three 20-mL portions of petroleum ether, add the extracts to the fatty acid layer, evaporate to dryness in a tared dish, cool, and weigh. [NOTE—Save the fatty acid residue so obtained for use in the *Iodine Value* test under *Identification*.]

  Neutralize the polyol solution with a 1:10 potassium hydroxide solution to pH 7 using a suitable pH meter. Evaporate this solution to a moist residue, and separate the polyols from the salts by several extractions with hot alcohol. Evaporate the alcohol extracts to dryness in

1072 / Sorbitan Monooleate / Monographs

a tared dish on a steam bath, cool, and weigh. Avoid excessive drying and heating. [NOTE—Save the polyols so obtained for use in the Thin-Layer Chromatography test under Identification.]
Acceptance criteria
Fatty acids: NLT 73% and NMT 77%
Polyols (as sorbitol, 1,4-sorbitan and isosorbide): NLT 26.6% and NMT 30.4%

IMPURITIES
Inorganic Impurities
- **LEAD**, Lead Limit Test, Flame Atomic Absorption Spectrophotometric Method, Appendix IIIB
  Sample: 10 g
  Acceptance criteria: NMT 2 mg/kg

SPECIFIC TESTS
- **ACID VALUE (FATS AND RELATED SUBSTANCES)**, Method II, Appendix VII
  Acceptance criteria: NMT 8
- **HYDROXYL VALUE**, Method II, Appendix VII
  Acceptance criteria: Between 193 and 210
- **RESIDUE ON IGNITION (SULFATED ASH)**, Appendix IIC
  Sample: 1 to 2 g
  Acceptance criteria: NMT 0.5%
- **SAPONIFICATION VALUE**, Appendix VII
  Sample: 4 g
  Acceptance criteria: Between 145 and 160
- **WATER**, Water Determination, Appendix IIB
  Acceptance criteria: NMT 2%

Sorbitan Monopalmitate
First Published: FCC 7

INS: 495   CAS: [26266-57-9]
UNII: 77K6Z421KU [sorbitan monopalmitate]

DESCRIPTION
Sorbitan Monopalmitate occurs as light cream to tan beads or flakes, or a hard, waxy solid with a characteristic odor. It is a mixture of the partial esters of sorbitol and its mono- and dianhydrides with edible palmitic acid. It contains palmitic acid esterified with polyols derived from sorbitol. It is soluble at temperatures above its melting point in ethanol, methanol, ether, ethyl acetate, aniline, toluene, dioxane, petroleum ether, and carbon tetrachloride. It is insoluble in cold water, but dispersible in warm water.
Function: Emulsifier; stabilizer
Packaging and Storage: Store in well-closed containers.

IDENTIFICATION
- **ACID VALUE (FATS AND RELATED SUBSTANCES)**, Method I, Appendix VII
  Sample: 1 g of the fatty acid residue obtained in the Assay
  Acceptance criteria: 210–225
- **IODINE VALUE**, Appendix VII
  Sample: Use the fatty acid residue obtained in the Assay.
  Acceptance criteria: NMT 4

- **THIN-LAYER CHROMATOGRAPHY**, Appendix IIA
  Sample solution: 500 mg of the polyols obtained in the Assay, diluted with water to volume in a 2-mL volumetric flask
  Standard solution: 25 mg/mL of USP Sorbitol RS, 25 mg/mL of USP 1,4-Sorbitan RS, and 25 mg/mL of USP Isosorbide RS in water
  Adsorbent: 0.25-mm layer of chromatographic silica gel
  Application volume: 2 µL
  Developing solvent system: Acetone and glacial acetic acid (100:2)
  Spray reagent: Sulfuric acid and water (1:2)
  Analysis: Following development, remove the plate from the chamber, dry thoroughly in air, and spray evenly with the Spray reagent. [CAUTION—Do not overspray.] Immediately place the chromatographic plate on a hot plate maintained at 200° in a hood. Char until white fumes of sulfur trioxide cease, then cool the chromatographic plate to room temperature. [NOTE—The approximate R_F values for sorbitol, 1,4-sorbitan, and isosorbide are 0.07, 0.40, and 0.77, respectively.]
  Acceptance criteria: The spots from the Sample solution are located at the same R_F values as those of the polyols from the Standard solution.

ASSAY
- **PROCEDURE**
  Sample: 10 g
  Analysis: Transfer the Sample to a 500-mL conical flask, cautiously add 100 mL of alcohol and 3.5 g of potassium hydroxide, and mix. Connect a suitable condenser to the flask, reflux the mixture on a hot plate for 2 h, add 100 mL of water, and heat on a steam bath to evaporate the alcohol. Continue the evaporation until the odor of alcohol can no longer be detected, and transfer the saponification mixture, with the aid of 100 mL of hot water, to a 500-mL separatory funnel. Using extreme caution, neutralize to litmus with a mixture of equal volumes of sulfuric acid and water, noting the volume used, and add a 10% excess of the dilute acid. Allow the solution to cool. If salt appears, add sufficient water to produce a clear solution. Cautiously add 100 mL of solvent hexane, shake thoroughly, and withdraw the lower layer into a 500-mL separatory funnel. Similarly extract with two more 100-mL portions of solvent hexane. Extract the combined hexane layers with 50-mL portions of water until neutral to litmus paper, and combine the extracts with the original aqueous phase. [NOTE—This is the polyol solution and will be analyzed separately.] Evaporate the solvent hexane in a tared beaker on a steam bath nearly to dryness, dry in vacuum at 60° for 1 h, cool in a desiccator, and weigh the fatty acids. [NOTE—Save the fatty acid residue so obtained for use in the Acid Value and Iodine Value tests under Identification.]
  Neutralize the polyol solution with a 1:10 potassium hydroxide solution to pH 7 using a suitable pH meter. Evaporate on a steam bath to a moist residue, extract the polyols from the salts with three 150-mL portions of dehydrated alcohol, boiling the salt residue for 3 min

and crushing it, as necessary, with the flattened end of a stirring rod during each extraction, filtering each extract (while hot) through a medium-porosity sintered-glass funnel, provided with a sheet of retentive filter paper on which a layer of purified siliceous earth has been superimposed, and receiving the filtrates in a 1-L suction flask. Transfer the clear alcoholic polyols solution to a tared beaker, evaporate the alcohol on a steam bath, dry in a vacuum at 60° for 1 h, cool in a desiccator, and weigh the polyols. [NOTE—Save the polyols so obtained for use in the *Thin-Layer Chromatography* test under *Identification*.]
  Acceptance critera
  Fatty acids: 63.0%–71.0%
  Polyols (as sorbitol, 1,4-sorbitan, and isosorbide): 32.0%–38.0%

IMPURITIES
Inorganic Impurities
- **LEAD**, *Lead Limit Test, Flame Atomic Absorption Spectrophotometric Method*, Appendix IIIB
  Sample: 10 g
  Acceptance criteria: NMT 2 mg/kg

SPECIFIC TESTS
- **ACID VALUE (FATS AND RELATED SUBSTANCES)**, *Method II*, Appendix VII
  Acceptance criteria: NMT 8
- **HYDROXYL VALUE**, *Method II*, Appendix VII
  Acceptance criteria: 275–305
- **RESIDUE ON IGNITION (SULFATED ASH)**, Appendix IIC
  Sample: 1–2 g
  Analysis: Proceed as directed, but ignite at 600 ± 50°.
  Acceptance criteria: NMT 0.5%
- **SAPONIFICATION VALUE**, Appendix VII
  Sample: 4 g
  Acceptance criteria: 140–150
- **WATER**, *Water Determination*, Appendix IIB
  Acceptance criteria: NMT 1.5%

Sorbitan Monostearate

First Published: Prior to FCC 6

INS: 491   CAS: [1338-41-6]
UNII: NVZ4I0H58X [sorbitan monostearate]

DESCRIPTION
Sorbitan Monostearate occurs as an off-white to tan colored, hard, waxy solid. It is a mixture of partial stearic and palmitic acid esters of sorbitol and its mono- and dianhydrides. It is manufactured by reacting edible commercial stearic acid (usually containing associated fatty acids, chiefly palmitic) with sorbitol. It is soluble at temperatures above its melting point in toluene, dioxane, ether, ethanol, methanol, and aniline. It is insoluble in cold water, and in mineral spirits and acetone, but is dispersible in warm water and soluble, with haze, above 50° in mineral oil and in ethyl acetate.
Function: Emulsifier; stabilizer; defoaming agent

Packaging and Storage: Store in well-closed containers.

IDENTIFICATION
- **ACID VALUE (FATS AND RELATED SUBSTANCES)**, *Method I*, Appendix VII
  Sample: The fatty acid residue obtained in the *Assay* (below)
  Acceptance criteria: Between 200 and 215
- **IODINE VALUE**, Appendix VII
  Sample: The fatty acid residue obtained in the *Assay* (below)
  Acceptance criteria: NMT 4
- **THIN-LAYER CHROMATOGRAPHY**, Appendix IIA
  Sample solution: 500 mg of the polyols obtained in the *Assay* (below), diluted to volume with water in a 2-mL volumetric flask
  Standard mixture: 25 mg/mL sorbitol, 25 mg/mL USP 1,4-Sorbitan RS, and 25 mg/mL USP Isosorbide RS in water
  Adsorbent: 0.25-mm layer of chromatographic silica gel
  Application volume: 2 µL
  Developing solvent system: Acetone and glacial acetic acid [100:2]
  Spray reagent: 1:2 sulfuric acid in water
  Analysis: Following development, remove the plate from the chamber, dry thoroughly in air, and spray evenly with the *Spray reagent*. [CAUTION—Do not overspray.] Immediately place the chromatographic plate on a hot plate maintained at 200° in a hood. Char until white fumes of sulfur trioxide cease, then cool the chromatographic plate to room temperature. [NOTE—The approximate R_f values for sorbitol, 1,4-sorbitan, and isosorbide are 0.07, 0.40, and 0.77, respectively.]
  Acceptance criteria: The spots from the *Sample solution* are located at the same R_f values as those of the polyols from the *Standard mixture*.

ASSAY
- **PROCEDURE**
  Sample: 25 g
  Analysis: Transfer the *Sample* into a 500-mL round-bottom flask. Add 250 mL of alcohol and 7.5 g of potassium hydroxide, and mix. Connect a suitable condenser to the flask, reflux the mixture for 1 to 2 h, then transfer it to an 800-mL beaker, rinsing the flask with about 100 mL of water and adding it to the beaker. Heat on a steam bath to evaporate the alcohol, adding water occasionally to replace the alcohol, and evaporate until the odor of alcohol can no longer be detected. Adjust the final volume to about 250 mL with hot water. Neutralize the soap solution with 1:2 sulfuric acid, add 10% in excess, and heat, while stirring, until the fatty acid layer separates. Transfer the fatty acids to a 500-mL separatory funnel, wash with three or four 20-mL portions of hot water to remove polyols, and combine the washings with the original aqueous polyol layer from the saponification. Extract the combined aqueous layer with three 20-mL portions of petroleum ether, add the extracts to the fatty acid layer, evaporate to dryness in a tared dish, cool, and weigh. [NOTE—Save the fatty acid residue so obtained for use in the

Identification tests for Acid Value and Iodine Value (above).]

Neutralize the polyol solution with a 1:10 potassium hydroxide solution to pH 7 using a suitable pH meter. Evaporate this solution to a moist residue, and separate the polyols from the salts by several extractions with hot alcohol. Evaporate the alcohol extracts to dryness in a tared dish on a steam bath, cool, and weigh. Avoid excessive drying and heating. [NOTE—Save the polyols so obtained for use in the Thin-Layer Chromatography Identification test (above).]

Acceptance criteria
Fatty acids: NLT 68% and NMT 76%, calculated on the anhydrous basis
Polyols (as sorbitol and its mono- and dianhydrides): NLT 27.0% and NMT 34.0%, calculated on the anhydrous basis

IMPURITIES
Inorganic Impurities
- **LEAD,** Lead Limit Test, Flame Atomic Absorption Spectrophotometric Method, Appendix IIIB
  Sample: 10 g
  Acceptance criteria: NMT 2 mg/kg

SPECIFIC TESTS
- **ACID VALUE (FATS AND RELATED SUBSTANCES),** Method II, Appendix VII
  Acceptance criteria: Between 5 and 10
- **HYDROXYL VALUE,** Method II, Appendix VII
  Acceptance criteria: Between 235 and 260
- **SAPONIFICATION VALUE,** Appendix VII
  Sample: 4 g
  Acceptance criteria: Between 147 and 157
- **WATER,** Water Determination, Appendix IIB
  Acceptance criteria: NMT 1.5%

Sorbitan Tristearate
First Published: FCC 7

INS: 492   CAS: [26658-19-5]
UNII: 6LUM696811 [sorbitan tristearate]

DESCRIPTION
Sorbitan Tristearate occurs as light cream to tan beads or flakes or a hard, waxy solid. It is a mixture of the partial esters of sorbitol and its mono- and dianhydrides with edible stearic acid. It contains stearic acid esterified with polyols derived from sorbitol. Sorbitan Tristearate is slightly soluble in toluene, ether, carbon tetrachloride, and ethyl acetate and is dispersible in petroleum ether, mineral oil, vegetable oils, acetone, and dioxane. It is insoluble in water, methanol, and ethanol.
Function: Emulsifier
Packaging and Storage: Store in well-closed containers.

IDENTIFICATION
- **CONGEALING RANGE**
  Sample: 5 g
  Analysis: Melt the Sample in a test tube 25-mm in diameter and 100-mm in length (the thickness of the glass being 1-mm) by heating gently to 15°–20° above the expected congealing range. Using a perforated stopper, fasten the tube in a wide-mouthed bottle of clear glass, about 70-mm in diameter and 150-mm in height. Suspend an appropriate thermometer (see Thermometers, Appendix I) in the melted Sample so that it will serve as a stirrer. Cool the sample slowly until the temperature remains unchanged for 30 s. Discontinue stirring and allow the thermometer to hang with the bulb in the center of the Sample. Observe the rise in temperature. The highest point to which the temperature rises is the congealing temperature.
  Acceptance criteria: Between 47° and 50°
- **THIN-LAYER CHROMATOGRAPHY,** Appendix IIA
  Sample solution: 500 mg of the polyols obtained in the Assay, diluted with water to volume in a 2-mL volumetric flask
  Standard solution: 25 mg/mL of USP Sorbitol RS, 25 mg/mL of USP 1,4-Sorbitan RS, and 25 mg/mL of USP Isosorbide RS in water
  Adsorbent: 0.25-mm layer of chromatographic silica gel
  Application volume: 2 µL
  Developing solvent system: Acetone and glacial acetic acid (100:2)
  Spray reagent: Sulfuric acid and water (1:2)
  Analysis: Following development remove the plate from the chamber, dry thoroughly in air, and spray evenly with the Spray reagent. [**CAUTION**—Do not overspray.] Immediately place the chromatographic plate on a hot plate maintained at 200° in a hood. Char until white fumes of sulfur trioxide cease, then cool the chromatographic plate to room temperature. [NOTE— The approximate R_F values for sorbitol, 1,4-sorbitan, and isosorbide are 0.07, 0.40, and 0.77, respectively.]
  Acceptance criteria: The spots from the Sample solution are located at the same R_F values as those of the polyols from the Standard solution.

ASSAY
- **PROCEDURE**
  Sample: 25 g
  Analysis: Transfer the Sample to a 500-mL round-bottom flask. Add 250 mL of alcohol and 7.5 g of potassium hydroxide. Connect a suitable condenser to the flask, reflux the mixture for 1–2 h, then transfer it to an 800-mL beaker, rinsing the flask with 100 mL of water and adding it to the beaker. Heat on a steam bath to evaporate the alcohol, adding water occasionally to replace the alcohol, and evaporate until the odor of alcohol can no longer be detected. Adjust the final volume to 250 mL with hot water. Neutralize the soap solution with 1:2 sulfuric acid, add 10% in excess, and heat, while stirring, until the fatty acid layer separates. Transfer the fatty acids to a 500-mL separatory funnel, wash with three or four 20-mL portions of hot water to remove polyols, and combine the washings with the original aqueous polyol layer from the saponification. Extract the combined aqueous layer with three 20-mL portions of petroleum ether, add the extracts to the

fatty acid layer, evaporate to dryness in a tared dish, cool, and weigh.

Neutralize the polyol solution with a 1:10 potassium hydroxide solution to a pH of 7 using a suitable pH meter. Evaporate this solution to a moist residue, and separate the polyols from the salts by several extractions with hot alcohol. Evaporate the alcohol extracts to dryness in a tared dish on a steam bath, cool, and weigh. Avoid excessive drying and heating. [NOTE—Save the polyols so obtained for use in the *Thin-Layer Chromatography* test under *Identification*.]

Acceptance criteria
Fatty acids: 85%–92%
Polyols (as sorbitol, 1,4-sorbitan, and isosorbide): 13.3%–20.0%

IMPURITIES
Inorganic Impurities
- **LEAD**, *Lead Limit Test, Flame Atomic Absorption Spectrophotometric Method*, Appendix IIIB
  Sample: 10 g
  Acceptance criteria: NMT 2 mg/kg

SPECIFIC TESTS
- **ACID VALUE (FATS AND RELATED SUBSTANCES)**, *Method II*, Appendix VII
  Acceptance criteria: NMT 15
- **HYDROXYL VALUE**, *Method II*, Appendix VII
  Acceptance criteria: 66–80
- **RESIDUE ON IGNITION (SULFATED ASH)**, Appendix IIC
  Sample: 1–2 g
  Acceptance criteria: NMT 0.5%
- **SAPONIFICATION VALUE**, Appendix VII
  Sample: 4 g
  Acceptance criteria: 176–188
- **WATER**, *Water Determination*, Appendix IIB
  Acceptance criteria: NMT 1.5%

Sorbitol

First Published: Prior to FCC 6
Last Revision: First Supplement, FCC 6

D-Sorbitol
D-Glucitol
D-Sorbite
1,2,3,4,5,6-Hexanehexol

$C_6H_{14}O_6$
INS: 420
UNII: 506T60A25R [sorbitol]

Formula wt 182.17
CAS: [50-70-4]

DESCRIPTION
Sorbitol occurs as a white powder, as granules, or as crystalline masses. It is very soluble in water; slightly soluble in ethanol, in methanol, and in acetic acid; and insoluble in ether. It is hygroscopic.

Function: Humectant; texturizing agent; nutritive sweetener
Packaging and Storage: Store in tight containers.

IDENTIFICATION
- **A. PROCEDURE**
  Sample solution: 13.33 mg/mL
  Analysis: Transfer 3 mL of the *Sample solution* into a 15-cm test tube, add 3 mL of a freshly prepared 1:10 catechol solution, and mix. Add 6 mL of sulfuric acid, mix again, then gently heat the tube in a flame for about 30 s.
  Acceptance criteria: A deep pink or wine red color appears.
- **B. PROCEDURE**
  Acceptance criteria: The retention time of the major peak in the chromatogram of the *Sample solution* corresponds to that in the chromatogram of the *Standard solution* obtained in the *Assay* (below).

ASSAY
- **PROCEDURE**
  Mobile phase: Degassed water
  Standard solution: 4.8 mg/g USP Sorbitol RS
  System suitability solution: 4.8 mg/g each of USP Mannitol RS and USP Sorbitol RS
  Sample solution: 5 mg/g
  Chromatographic system, Appendix IIA
    Mode: High-performance liquid chromatography
    Detector: Refractive index
    Column: 10 cm × 7.8-mm; containing packing L34 (Bio-Rad Laboratories), or equivalent
    Column temperature: 50° ± 2°
    Detector temperature: 35°
    Flow rate: About 0.7 mL/min
    Injection size: About 10 µL
  System suitability
    Samples: *System suitability solution* and *Standard solution*
    Suitability requirement 1: Resolution, *R*, between the sorbitol and mannitol in the *System suitability solution* is NLT 2.0.
    Suitability requirement 2: Relative standard deviation for three replicate injections of the *Standard solution* is NMT 2.0%.
  Analysis: Separately inject volumes of the *Standard solution* and *Sample solution* into the chromatograph and measure the responses for the major peaks on the resulting chromatograms. [NOTE—Approximate relative retention times for mannitol and sorbitol are 0.6 and 1.0, respectively.] Calculate the percentage of $C_6H_{14}O_6$ (on the anhydrous basis) in the sample taken by the formula:

$$\text{Result} = [(C_S/C_U) \times (r_U/r_S) \times 10{,}000]/(100 - w)$$

C_S = concentration of USP Sorbitol RS in the *Standard solution* (mg/g)

C_U = concentration of sample in the *Sample solution* (mg/g)
r_U = peak response obtained with the *Sample solution*
r_S = peak response obtained with the *Standard solution*
w = percent water as determined under *Water* (below)

Acceptance criteria: NLT 91.0% and NMT 100.5% of D-Sorbitol ($C_6H_{14}O_6$), calculated on the anhydrous basis

IMPURITIES
Inorganic Impurities
- **LEAD**, *Lead Limit Test, Atomic Absorption Spectrophotometric Graphite Furnace Method, Method I*, Appendix IIIB
  Sample: 10 g
  Acceptance criteria: NMT 1 mg/kg
- **NICKEL**, *Nickel Limit Test*, Appendix IIIB
  Acceptance criteria: NMT 1 mg/kg

Organic Impurities
- **REDUCING SUGARS**
  0.05 N Iodine VS: Dilute 0.1 N iodine VS with water (1:1).
  0.05 N Sodium thiosulfate VS: Dilute 0.1 N sodium thiosulfate VS with water (1:1).
  Sample: 3.3 g
  Analysis: Dissolve the *Sample* in 3 mL of water with the aid of gentle heat. Cool and add 20.0 mL of alkaline cupric citrate TS and a few glass beads. Heat so that boiling begins after 4 min, and maintain the boiling for 3 min. Cool rapidly, and add 40 mL of diluted acetic acid TS, 60 mL of water, and 20.0 mL of *0.05 N Iodine VS*. With continuous shaking, add 25 mL of a mixture of 6 mL of hydrochloric acid and 94 mL of water. When the precipitate has dissolved, titrate the excess iodine with *0.05 N Sodium thiosulfate VS*. Use 2 mL of starch TS, added toward the end of the titration, as an indicator.
  Acceptance criteria: NLT 12.8 mL of *0.05 N Sodium thiosulfate VS* is required (NMT 0.3% reducing sugars, as glucose).

SPECIFIC TESTS
- **PH**, *pH Determination*, Appendix IIB
  Sample: 10% w/w solution of sample in carbon dioxide-free water
  Acceptance criteria: Between 3.5 and 7.0
- **RESIDUE ON IGNITION (SULFATED ASH)**, *Method I (for Solids)*, Appendix IIC
  Sample: 2 g
  Acceptance criteria: NMT 0.1%
- **WATER**, *Water Determination*, Appendix IIB
  Acceptance criteria: NMT 1.5%

Sorbitol Solution
First Published: Prior to FCC 6
Last Revision: First Supplement, FCC 6

INS: 420
UNII: 506T60A25R [sorbitol]

DESCRIPTION
Sorbitol Solution occurs as a clear, colorless, syrupy liquid. It is a water solution of sorbitol ($C_6H_{14}O_6$) containing a small amount of mannitol and other isomeric polyhydric alcohols. It is miscible with water, with ethanol, with glycerin, and with propylene glycol. It sometimes separates into crystalline masses.

Function: Humectant; texturizing agent; nutritive sweetener
Packaging and Storage: Store in well closed containers.

IDENTIFICATION
- **A. PROCEDURE**
  Sample solution: 1.4 g of sample in 75 mL of water
  Analysis: Transfer 3 mL of the *Sample solution* into a 15-cm test tube, add 3 mL of a freshly prepared 1:10 catechol solution, and mix. Add 6 mL of sulfuric acid, mix again, then gently heat the tube in a flame for about 30 s.
  Acceptance criteria: A deep pink or wine red color appears.
- **B. PROCEDURE**
  Acceptance criteria: The retention time of the major peak in the chromatogram of the *Sample solution* corresponds to that in the chromatogram of the *Standard solution* obtained in the *Assay* (below).

ASSAY
- **PROCEDURE**
  Mobile phase: Degassed water
  Standard solution: 4.8 mg/g USP Sorbitol RS
  System suitability solution: 4.8 mg/g each of USP Mannitol RS and USP Sorbitol RS
  Sample solution: 6 mg/g
  Chromatographic system, Appendix IIA
    Mode: High-performance liquid chromatography
    Detector: Refractive index
    Column: 10 cm × 7.8-mm, containing packing L34 (Bio-Rad Laboratories), or equivalent
    Column temperature: 50° ± 2°
    Detector temperature: 35°
    Flow rate: About 0.7 mL/min
    Injection size: About 10 µL
  System suitability
    Samples: *System suitability solution* and *Standard solution*
    Suitability requirement 1: Resolution, R, between the sorbitol and mannitol in the *System suitability solution* is NLT 2.0
    Suitability requirement 2: Relative standard deviation for three replicate injections of the *Standard solution* is NMT 2.0%

Analysis: Separately inject volumes of the *Standard solution* and *Sample solution* into the chromatograph and measure the responses for the major peaks on the resulting chromatograms. [NOTE—Approximate relative retention times for mannitol and sorbitol are 0.6 and 1.0, respectively.] Calculate the percentage of $C_6H_{14}O_6$ in the portion of the sample taken by the formula:

$$\text{Result} = 100(C_S/C_U)(r_U/r_S)$$

C_S = concentration of USP Sorbitol RS in the *Standard solution* (mg/g)
C_U = concentration of sample in the *Sample solution* (mg/g)
r_U = peak response obtained with the *Sample solution*
r_S = peak response obtained with the *Standard solution*

Acceptance criteria: NLT 64.0% sorbitol ($C_6H_{14}O_6$)

IMPURITIES
Inorganic Impurities
- **LEAD**, *Lead Limit Test, Atomic Absorption Spectrophotometric Graphite Furnace Method, Method I,* Appendix IIIB
  Sample: 10 g
  Acceptance criteria: NMT 1 mg/kg, calculated on the anhydrous basis
- **NICKEL**, *Nickel Limit Test,* Appendix IIIB
  Acceptance criteria: NMT 1 mg/kg, calculated on the anhydrous basis

Organic Impurities
- **REDUCING SUGARS**
  0.05 N Iodine VS: Dilute 0.1 N iodine VS with water (1:1).
  0.05 N Sodium thiosulfate VS: Dilute 0.1 N sodium thiosulfate VS with water (1:1).
  Sample: Amount equivalent to 3.3 g of sorbitol on the anhydrous basis
  Analysis: To the *Sample*, add 3 mL of water, 20.0 mL of alkaline cupric citrate TS and a few glass beads. Heat so that boiling begins after 4 min, and maintain the boiling for 3 min. Cool rapidly, and add 40 mL of diluted acetic acid TS, 60 mL of water, and 20.0 mL of *0.05 N Iodine VS*. With continuous shaking, add 25 mL of a mixture of 6 mL of hydrochloric acid and 94 mL of water. When the precipitate has dissolved, titrate the excess iodine with *0.05 N Sodium thiosulfate VS*. Use 2 mL of starch TS, added toward the end of the titration, as an indicator.
  Acceptance criteria: NLT 12.8 mL of *0.05 N Sodium thiosulfate VS* is required (NMT 0.3% reducing sugars, calculated on the anhydrous basis).

SPECIFIC TESTS
- **PH**, *pH Determination,* Appendix IIB
  Sample: 14% w/w solution of sample in carbon dioxide-free water
  Acceptance criteria: Between 5.0 and 7.5
- **RESIDUE ON IGNITION (SULFATED ASH)**, *Method II (for Liquids),* Appendix IIC
  Sample: 2 g
  Acceptance criteria: NMT 0.1%, calculated on the anhydrous basis
- **WATER**, *Water Determination,* Appendix IIB
  Acceptance criteria: Between 28.5% and 31.5%

Noncrystallizing Sorbitol Solution

First Published: First Supplement, FCC 6

INS: 420
UNII: 506T60A25R [sorbitol]

DESCRIPTION
Noncrystallizing Sorbitol Solution occurs as a clear, colorless, syrupy liquid. It is an aqueous solution of hydrogenated saccharides, consisting primarily of sorbitol and lesser amounts of hydrogenated mono-, di-, and polysaccharides. It is miscible with water, with ethanol, with glycerin, and with propylene glycol.
Function: Humectant; texturizing agent; nutritive sweetener
Packaging and Storage: Store in well-closed containers.

IDENTIFICATION
- **A. PROCEDURE**
  Sample solution: 1.4 g of sample in 75 mL of water
  Analysis: Transfer 3 mL of the *Sample solution* into a 15-cm test tube, add 3 mL of a freshly prepared 1:10 catechol solution, and mix. Add 6 mL of sulfuric acid, mix again, then gently heat the tube in a flame for about 30 s.
  Acceptance criteria: A deep pink or wine red color appears.
- **B. PROCEDURE**
  Acceptance criteria: The retention time of the major peak in the chromatogram of the *Sample solution* corresponds to that in the chromatogram of the *Standard solution* obtained in the *Assay* (below).

ASSAY
- **PROCEDURE**
  Mobile phase: Degassed water
  Standard solution: 4.8 mg/g USP Sorbitol RS
  System suitability solution: 4.8 mg/g each of USP Mannitol RS and USP Sorbitol RS
  Sample solution: 10 mg/g
  Chromatographic system, Appendix IIA
  Mode: High-performance liquid chromatography
  Detector: Refractive index
  Column: 10 cm × 7.8-mm, 9 µm with a lead ionic stationary phase on a sulfonated divinyl benzene–styrene copolymer[1]
  Column temperature: 50° ± 2°
  Detector temperature: 35°
  Flow rate: About 0.7 mL/min
  Injection size: About 10 µL

---
[1] Aminex Fast Carbohydrate Analytical Column (Bio-Rad Laboratories), or equivalent.

System suitability
Samples: *System suitability solution* and *Standard solution*
Suitability requirement 1: Resolution, R, between the sorbitol and mannitol in the *System suitability solution* is NLT 2.0
Suitability requirement 2: Relative standard deviation for three replicate injections of the *Standard solution* is NMT 2.0%
Analysis: Separately inject equal volumes of the *Standard solution* and *Sample solution* into the chromatograph and measure the responses for the major peaks on the resulting chromatograms. [NOTE—Approximate relative retention times for mannitol and sorbitol are 0.6 and 1.0, respectively.] Calculate the percentage of sorbitol, $C_6H_{14}O_6$, on the anhydrous basis in the portion of the sample taken by the formula:

$$\text{Result} = (C_S/C_U) \times (r_U/r_S) / (100 - W) \times F$$

C_S = concentration of USP Sorbitol RS in the *Standard solution* (mg/g)
C_U = concentration of sample in the *Sample solution* (mg/g)
r_U = peak response for sorbitol obtained with the *Sample solution*
r_S = peak response for sorbitol obtained with the *Standard solution*
W = percentage water determined separately in the test for *Water*, below
F = factor to convert to percentage, 10,000

Acceptance criteria: NLT 64.0% sorbitol ($C_6H_{14}O_6$) on the anhydrous basis

IMPURITIES
Inorganic Impurities
- **LEAD**
  [NOTE—Use deionized ultra-filtered water throughout this test procedure.]
  Digester solution (aqua regia): To 1200 mL of water add 360 mL of hydrochloric acid and 240 mL of nitric acid.
  Diluent: 20 mL/L nitric acid
  Internal standard solution: 2 µg/mL yttrium, prepared by diluting a commercially prepared yttrium reference standard solution with *Diluent*
  Standard stock solution: 10 µg/mL lead prepared by diluting a commercially prepared lead ICP standard with *Diluent*. [NOTE—Prepare this solution fresh every 2 months.]
  Standard solutions: 50, 100, and 200 ng/mL lead in *Diluent*: from *Standard stock solution*. [NOTE—Prepare these solutions fresh weekly.]
  Sample: 10.0 g, on the anhydrous basis
  Sample solution: Add the *Sample* into a 125-mL Erlenmeyer flask. Add 40 mL of *Digester solution* and place on a hotplate. Heat the solution for about 20 min, being careful to prevent the solution from boiling over. The solution will turn a dark caramel color. Transfer into a clean, dry, 50-mL volumetric flask with washings of *Diluent*. Dilute to volume with *Diluent*. Filter the sample into a 15-mL centrifuge tube, using a 10-mL B-D syringe, fitted with a 0.45-µm syringe filter.
  Apparatus: Use a suitable inductively coupled plasma-optical emission spectrometer (ICP-OES) configured in an axial optical alignment. This method was developed using a Perkin Elmer Optima 3100 ICP-OES unit. Instrument performance must be verified to conform to the manufacturer's specifications for resolution and sensitivity. Before analyzing samples, the instrument must pass a suitable performance check. The instrument parameters are as follows: Set the ultraviolet detector to scan lead at 220.353 nm and yttrium at 371.029 nm. Set the sample read time to 20 s minimum and 50 s maximum. Three replicate scans are taken with the integration set to one point per peak. Set the forward power from the RF generator to 1500 watts. Use an argon plasma feed gas flow of 15 L/min with the auxiliary gas (shear gas) set to flow at 0.5 L/min. Use a gem cone nebulizer with a nebulization gas flow rate of 0.55 L/min. The sample is delivered to the spray chamber by a multi-channel peristaltic pump set to deliver sample at a rate of 2.00 mL/min. The *Internal standard* is added in-line via a mixing block between the sample probe and spray chamber. Samples are flushed through the system for 45 s at a rate of 4.0 mL/min prior to analysis. A 45-second read delay is also programmed into the sampling routine to allow for fluid flow equilibration after the high-speed flush, prior to the first analytical read of the sample. Between samples the pumping system is washed by flushing the *Diluent* for 30 s at a rate of 4.0 mL/min.
  Analysis: Generate a calibration curve using *Diluent* as a *Blank* and the *Standard solutions* as follows: Scan the *Internal standard solution* while running the blank to measure the intensity of the yttrium emission. Hold this value constant throughout the remainder of the test. Separately scan the *Blank* and the *Standard solutions* for lead and yttrium. Normalize the yttrium intensity to the value of the *Internal standard solution*. [NOTE—The *Internal standard* is added in-line via a mixing block between the sample probe and spray chamber.] Also apply this normalization factor to the lead intensity, which is then referred to as the corrected lead intensity. A calibration curve is constructed by plotting the corrected lead intensity versus the known concentrations of the *Standard solutions*. The correlation coefficient for the best-fit line should not be less than 0.999.
  Similarly, analyze the *Sample solution* on the ICP. The intensity of the emission of the *Sample solution* is plotted on the calibration curve and the concentration is extrapolated against the x-axis. Calculate the anhydrous basis concentration (mg/kg) of lead in the *Sample* taken using the following equation:

$$\text{Result} = (C/W) \times (50/1000)$$

C = concentration (ng/mL) of lead in the *Sample solution* determined from the standard curve
W = weight (g) of *Sample* taken on the anhydrous basis
50 = *Sample* dilution factor
1000 = ng to µg conversion factor

Acceptance criteria: NMT 1 mg/kg, on the anhydrous basis

- **NICKEL**

[NOTE—Use deionized ultra-filtered water throughout this test procedure.]

Digester solution (aqua regia): To 1200 mL of water add 360 mL of hydrochloric acid and 240 mL of nitric acid.

Diluent: 20 mL/L nitric acid

Internal standard solution: 2 µg/mL yttrium, prepared by diluting a commercially prepared yttrium reference standard solution with *Diluent*

Standard stock solution: 10 µg/mL nickel prepared by diluting a commercially prepared nickel ICP standard with *Diluent*. [NOTE—Prepare this solution fresh every 2 months.]

Standard solutions: 50, 100, and 200 ng/mL lead in *Diluent*: from *Standard stock solution*. [NOTE—Prepare these solutions fresh weekly.]

Sample: 10.0 g, on the anhydrous basis

Sample solution: Add the *Sample* into a 125-mL Erlenmeyer flask. Add 40 mL of *Digester solution* and place on a hotplate. Heat the solution for about 20 min, being careful to prevent the solution from boiling over. The solution will turn a dark caramel color. Transfer into a clean, dry, 50-mL volumetric flask with washings of *Diluent*. Dilute to volume with *Diluent*. Filter the sample into a 15-mL centrifuge tube, using a 10-mL B-D syringe, fitted with a 0.45-µm syringe filter.

Apparatus: Use a suitable inductively coupled plasma-optical emission spectrometer (ICP-OES) configured in an axial optical alignment. This method was developed using a Perkin Elmer Optima 3100 ICP-OES unit. Instrument performance must be verified to conform to the manufacturer's specifications for resolution and sensitivity. Before analyzing samples, the instrument must pass a suitable performance check. The instrument parameters are as follows: Set the ultraviolet detector to scan nickel at 232.005 nm and yttrium at 371.029 nm. Set the sample read time to 10 s minimum and 50 s maximum. Three replicate scans are taken with the integration set to one point per peak. Set the forward power from the RF generator to 1500 watts. Use an argon plasma feed gas flow of 15 L/min with the auxiliary gas (shear gas) set to flow at 0.5 L/min. Use a gem cone nebulizer with a nebulization gas flow rate of 0.55 L/min. The sample is delivered to the spray chamber by a multi-channel peristaltic pump set to deliver sample at a rate of 1.00 mL/min. The *Internal standard* is added in-line via a mixing block between the sample probe and spray chamber. Samples are flushed through the system for 30 s at a rate of 4.0 mL/min prior to analysis. A 60-second read delay is also programmed into the sampling routine to allow for fluid flow equilibration after the high-speed flush, prior to the first analytical read of the sample. Between samples the pumping system is washed by flushing the *Diluent* for 30 s at a rate of 4.0 mL/min.

Analysis: Generate a calibration curve using *Diluent* as a *Blank* and the *Standard solutions* as follows: Scan the *Internal standard solution* while running the blank to measure the intensity of the yttrium emission. Hold this value constant throughout the remainder of the test. Separately scan the *Blank* and the *Standard solutions* for nickel and yttrium. Normalize the yttrium intensity to the value of the *Internal standard solution*. [NOTE—The *Internal standard solution* is added in-line via a mixing block between the sample probe and spray chamber.] Also apply this normalization factor to the nickel intensity, which is then referred to as the corrected nickel intensity. A calibration curve is constructed by plotting the corrected nickel intensity versus the known concentrations of the *Standard solutions*. The correlation coefficient for the best-fit line should not be less than 0.999.

Similarly, analyze the *Sample solution* on the ICP. The intensity of the emission of the *Sample solution* is plotted on the calibration curve and the concentration is extrapolated against the x-axis. Calculate the anhydrous basis concentration (mg/kg) of nickel in the *Sample* taken using the following equation:

$$\text{Result} = (C/W) \times (50/1000)$$

C = concentration (ng/mL) of nickel in the *Sample solution* determined from the standard curve
W = weight (g) of *Sample* taken on the anhydrous basis
50 = *Sample* dilution factor
1000 = ng to µg conversion factor

Acceptance criteria: NMT 1 mg/kg, on the anhydrous basis

Organic Impurities

- **REDUCING SUGARS**

0.05 N Iodine VS: Dilute 0.1 N iodine VS with water (1:1).

0.05 N Sodium thiosulfate VS: Dilute 0.1 N sodium thiosulfate VS with water (1:1).

Sample: Amount equivalent to 3.3 g, on the anhydrous basis

Analysis: To the *Sample*, add 3 mL of water, 20.0 mL of alkaline cupric citrate TS, and a few glass beads. Heat so that boiling begins after 4 min, and maintain the boiling for 3 min. Cool rapidly, and add 40 mL of diluted acetic acid TS, 60 mL of water, and 20.0 mL of *0.05 N Iodine VS*. With continuous shaking, add 25 mL of a mixture of 6 mL of hydrochloric acid and 94 mL of water. When the precipitate has dissolved, titrate the excess iodine with *0.05 N Sodium thiosulfate VS*. Use 2 mL of starch TS, added toward the end of the titration, as an indicator.

Acceptance criteria: NLT 12.8 mL of *0.05 N Sodium thiosulfate VS* is required (equivalent to NMT 0.3%

reducing sugars (as glucose), calculated on the anhydrous basis).

SPECIFIC TESTS
- **PH,** *pH Determination* Appendix IIB
  Sample: 14% w/w solution of sample in carbon dioxide-free water
  Acceptance criteria: Between 5.0 and 7.5
- **RESIDUE ON IGNITION (SULFATED ASH),** *Method II,* Appendix IIC
  Sample: 2 g
  Acceptance criteria: NMT 0.1%, calculated on the anhydrous basis
- **TOTAL SUGARS**
  Cupric sulfate–iodide solution: Dissolve 81 g of potassium citrate monohydrate, 92 g of potassium oxalate, and 74 g of potassium carbonate in hot water, and dilute with water to 600 mL (Solution A). Dissolve 25 g of cupric sulfate in hot water, and dilute with water to 200 mL. Combine this solution with *Solution A*, and mix for 30 min (Solution B). Dissolve 0.4 g of sodium hydroxide in about 100 mL of water. Dissolve 3.4 g of potassium iodate and 50 g of potassium iodide in this sodium hydroxide solution, and dilute with water to 200 mL (Solution C). Add *Solution C* to *Solution B*, and stir for at least 2 h.
  Sample: An amount equivalent to 0.25 g on the anhydrous basis
  Analysis: Transfer the *Sample* to a 300-mL conical flask. While swirling the solution, add 35 mL of 3 N sulfuric acid and a few glass beads. Connect a suitable condenser to the flask, bring to a boil on a hot plate within 3 min, and gently reflux the solution for 15 min. Remove the flask from the hot plate and cool it in a 20° water bath for at least 5 min. Add 5 drops of phenolphthalein TS and 20.0 mL of 5 N sodium hydroxide, and mix. Neutralize the solution with 1 N hydroxide (about 4.5 mL) to a pink endpoint. Adjust the volume of the solution with water to 50 mL, and add 50.0 mL of *Cupric sulfate–iodide solution*. Connect a suitable condenser to the flask, heat on a hot plate adjusted to bring the solution to boil within 3 min, and gently reflux the solution for 5 min. Remove the flask from the hot plate, and cool it in a water bath at 20° for 15 to 25 min. Do not overcool. Slowly add 25 mL of 5 N sulfuric acid, and swirl gently to mix. [NOTE—Foaming may occur when the 5 N sulfuric acid is added.] Titrate the liberated iodine with 0.1 N sodium thiosulfate VS to a pale green color. Add 1 mL of starch TS, mix, and continue the titration to a pale green-blue endpoint. Perform a blank determination. Calculate the titration difference, based on an anhydrous 0.5-g sample, by the formula:

  $$\text{Result} = (V_B - V_U)(0.5/W)(0.1/N_A)$$

  V_B = volume (mL) of sodium thiosulfate VS required for the blank
  V_U = volume (mL) of sodium thiosulfate VS required for the *Sample*
  0.5 = theoretical sample weight (g) on the anhydrous basis
  W = weight (g) of the *Sample* taken on the anhydrous basis
  0.1 = theoretical normality of the sodium thiosulfate VS
  N_A = actual normality of the sodium thiosulfate VS

  Acceptance criteria: The titration difference is NLT 5.8 mL, corresponding to NLT 7.0% total sugars (as glucose) on the anhydrous basis
- **WATER,** *Water Determination,* Appendix IIB
  Acceptance criteria: NMT 31.5%

Soy Protein Concentrate

First Published: Prior to FCC 6

CAS: [9010-10-0]

UNII: R44IWB3RN5 [soy protein]

DESCRIPTION
Soy Protein Concentrate occurs as a powder or as granules, textured flakes, or textured chunks, with color ranging from off-white to tan. It is derived from soybean (*Glycine max*) (Fam. Leguminosae) by specific processing steps employed to reduce or remove nonprotein constituents (water, oil, and carbohydrates) to achieve a 65% minimum protein content on the dry basis. Good manufacturing practices require that the pH during processing not exceed 9 to avoid formation of lysinoalanine.
Function: Protein supplement; water and fat binder; stabilizer and thickener; texturizing agent
Packaging and Storage: Store in tight containers protected from humidity.

IDENTIFICATION
- **PROCEDURE**
  Acceptance criteria: A sample exhibits the compositional profile specified below with respect to *Ash*, *Fat*, *Loss on Drying*, and *Protein*.

IMPURITIES
Inorganic Impurities
- **LEAD,** *Lead Limit Test, Atomic Absorption Spectrophotometric Graphite Furnace Method, Method I,* Appendix IIIB
  Acceptance criteria: NMT 1 mg/kg

SPECIFIC TESTS
- **ASH (TOTAL),** Appendix IIC
  Analysis: Proceed as directed to a final gray to white residue.
  Acceptance criteria: NMT 9.0%, calculated on the dried basis
- **FAT,** *Crude Fat,* Appendix X
  Acceptance criteria: NMT 4.0%, calculated on the dried basis
- **LOSS ON DRYING,** Appendix IIC: 65° at a pressure of less than 100 mm Hg for 16 h
  Sample: 2 g
  Acceptance criteria: NMT 10.0%

- **pH**, *pH Determination*, Appendix IIB
  Sample: 100 mg/mL suspension
  Acceptance criteria: Between 5.5 and 8.0
- **Protein**, *Nitrogen Determination*, Appendix IIIC
  Analysis: Calculate the percent protein (calculated to exclude added vitamins, minerals, amino acids, and food additives) by the formula:

  $$Result = 6.25 \times N$$

  N = percent nitrogen
  [Note—Alternatively, the protein content can be determined by the Protein Nitrogen Combustion Method, AOAC 992.23 or AOCS Ba 4e-93.]
  Acceptance criteria: NLT 65.0% and NMT 89.9%, calculated on the dried basis

Soybean Oil (Unhydrogenated)

First Published: Prior to FCC 6

CAS: [8001-22-7]

UNII: 241ATL177A [soybean oil]

DESCRIPTION
Soybean Oil (Unhydrogenated) occurs as a light amber colored oil. It is obtained from the seed of the legume *Glycine max* (Fam. Fabaceae), usually by solvent extraction. It is refined, bleached, and deodorized to substantially remove free fatty acids, phospholipids, color, odor and flavor components, and miscellaneous other non-oil materials. It is a liquid at 21° to 27° and remains so even at refrigerator temperatures (2° to 4°). It is free from visible foreign matter at 21° to 27°.
Function: Coating agent; texturizer
Packaging and Storage: Store in well-closed containers.

IDENTIFICATION
- **Fatty Acid Composition**, Appendix VII
  Acceptance criteria: A sample exhibits the following composition profile of fatty acids:

Fatty Acid	Weight % (Range)
<14	<0.1
14:0	<0.5
16:0	7.0–12
16:1	<0.5
18:0	2.0–5.5
18:1	19–30
18:2	48–65
18:3	5–10
20:0	<1.0
20:1	<1.0
22:0	<0.5
22:1	<0.1
24:0	<0.3

IMPURITIES
Inorganic Impurities
- **Lead**, *Lead Limit Test, Atomic Absorption Spectrophotometric Graphite Furnace Method, Method II*, Appendix IIIB
  Acceptance criteria: NMT 0.1 mg/kg

SPECIFIC TESTS
- **Cold Test**, Appendix VII
  Acceptance criteria: Passes test
- **Color (Fats and Related Substances)**, Appendix VII
  Acceptance criteria: NMT 20 yellow/2.0 red
- **Free Fatty Acids (as oleic acid)**, *Free Fatty Acids*, Appendix VII
  Analysis: Use the equivalence factor (e) in the formula given in the procedure: *Free Fatty Acids* as oleic acid, e = 28.2.
  Acceptance criteria: NMT 0.1%
- **Iodine Value**, Appendix VII
  Acceptance criteria: Between 120 and 143
- **Peroxide Value**, Appendix VII
  Acceptance criteria: NMT 10 mEq/kg
- **Stability**, Appendix VII
  Acceptance criteria: NLT 7 h
- **Unsaponifiable Matter**, Appendix VII
  Acceptance criteria: NMT 1.5%
- **Water**, *Water Determination*, Appendix IIB
  Analysis: In place of 35 to 40 mL of methanol, use 50 mL of chloroform to dissolve the sample.
  Acceptance criteria: NMT 0.1%

High Oleic Soybean Oil (Unhydrogenated)

First Published: FCC 7

CAS: [8001-22-7]

UNII: 241ATL177A [soybean oil]

DESCRIPTION
High Oleic Soybean Oil (Unhydrogenated) occurs as a light amber colored oil. It is obtained from the seed of the legume *Glycine max* (Fam. Fabaceae), usually by solvent extraction. It is refined, bleached, and deodorized to substantially remove free fatty acids, phospholipids, color, odor and flavor components, and miscellaneous other non-oil materials. It is a liquid at 21° to 27° and remains so even at refrigerator temperatures (2° to 4°). It is free from visible foreign matter at 21° to 27°. It is distinguished from *Soybean Oil (Unhydrogenated)* by its characteristic level of 18:1 (oleic acid). It is distinguished from hydrogenated soybean oils by its characteristic level of 18:0 (stearic acid). It is distinguished from other high oleic vegetable oils by its characteristic levels of γ- and δ-tocopherols.
Function: Coating agent; texturizer; source of oleic acid
Packaging and Storage: Store in well-closed containers.

IDENTIFICATION
- **Fatty Acid Composition**, Appendix VII
  Acceptance criteria: A sample exhibits the following composition profile of fatty acids:

Fatty Acid	Weight % (Range)
<14	<0.1
14:0	<0.5
16:0	4.0–8.0
16:1	<0.5
18:0	2.0–5.5
18:1	75–85
18:2	1.0–10
18:3	<6.0
20:0	<1.0
20:1	<1.0
22:0	<0.5
22:1	<0.1
24:0	<0.3

- **TOCOPHEROLS**, Appendix VII
  Acceptance criteria
  γ-tocopherol: NLT 100 mg/kg
  δ-tocopherol: NLT 150 mg/kg

ASSAY
- **OLEIC ACID CONTENT**, Fatty Acid Composition, Appendix VII
  Acceptance criteria: NLT 75% (w/w) 18:1 (oleic acid)

IMPURITIES
Inorganic Impurities
- **LEAD**, Lead Limit Test, Atomic Absorption Spectrophotometric Graphite Furnace Method, Method II, Appendix IIIB
  Acceptance criteria: NMT 0.1 mg/kg

SPECIFIC TESTS
- **COLD TEST**, Appendix VII
  Acceptance criteria: Passes test
- **COLOR (FATS AND RELATED SUBSTANCES)**, Appendix VII
  Acceptance criteria: NMT 20 yellow/2.0 red
- **FREE FATTY ACIDS (AS OLEIC ACID)**, Free Fatty Acids, Appendix VII
  Analysis: Use the equivalence factor (e) in the formula given in the procedure:

  Free fatty acids as oleic acid, e = 28.2

  Acceptance criteria: NMT 0.1%
- **IODINE VALUE**, Appendix VII
  Acceptance criteria: Between 75 and 95
- **PEROXIDE VALUE**, Appendix VII
  Acceptance criteria: NMT 10 mEq/kg
- **STABILITY**, Method II (Oil Stability Index), Appendix VII
  Analysis: Proceed as directed using a temperature of 110°.
  Acceptance criteria: NLT 15 h
- **UNSAPONIFIABLE MATTER**, Appendix VII
  Acceptance criteria: NMT 1.5%
- **WATER**, Water Determination, Appendix IIB
  Analysis: In place of 35–40 mL of methanol, use 50 mL of chloroform to dissolve the sample.
  Acceptance criteria: NMT 0.1%

Spearmint Oil
First Published: Prior to FCC 6

CAS: [8008-79-5]
UNII: C3M81465G5 [spearmint oil]

DESCRIPTION
Spearmint Oil occurs as a colorless, yellow, or green-yellow liquid having the characteristic odor and taste of spearmint. It is the volatile oil obtained by steam distillation from the fresh overground parts of the flowering plant *Mentha spicata* L. (Common Spearmint), or of *Mentha cardiaca* Gerard ex Baker (Scotch Spearmint) (Fam. Labiatae). It may be rectified by distillation.
Function: Flavoring agent
Packaging and Storage: Store in a cool place protected from light in full, tight containers.

IDENTIFICATION
- **INFRARED SPECTRA**, Spectrophotometric Identification Tests, Appendix IIIC
  Acceptance criteria: The spectrum of the sample exhibits relative maxima at the same wavelengths as those of the spectrum below.

ASSAY
- **PROCEDURE**
  Analysis: Determine as directed under *Aldehydes and Ketones, Neutral Sulfite Method*, Appendix VI.
  Acceptance criteria: NLT 55.0%, by volume, of ketones

SPECIFIC TESTS
- **ANGULAR ROTATION**, Optical (Specific) Rotation, Appendix IIB: Use a 100-mm tube.
  Acceptance criteria: Between −48° and −59°
- **REACTION**
  Sample solution: Recently prepared in 80% alcohol
  Analysis: Test the *Sample solution* with litmus paper.
  Acceptance criteria: The *Sample solution* is neutral or only slightly acid.
- **REFRACTIVE INDEX**, Appendix IIB
  [NOTE—Use an Abbé or other refractometer of equal or greater accuracy.]
  Acceptance criteria: Between 1.484 and 1.491 at 20°
- **SOLUBILITY IN ALCOHOL**, Appendix VI
  Acceptance criteria: One mL of the sample dissolves in 1 mL of 80% alcohol. On further dilution, the solution can become turbid.
- **SPECIFIC GRAVITY:** Determine by any reliable method (see *General Provisions*).
  Acceptance criteria: Between 0.917 and 0.934

OTHER REQUIREMENTS
- **LABELING:** Indicate whether the oil is natural or rectified.

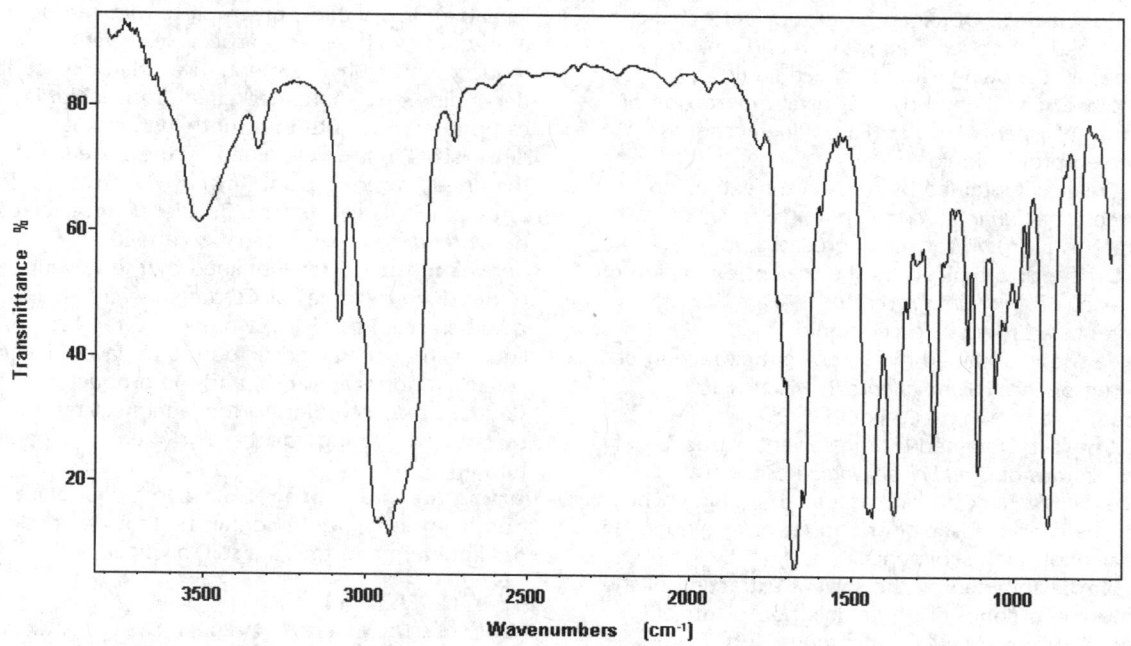

Spearmint Oil

Spice Oleoresins

First Published: Prior to FCC 6
Last Revision: Third Supplement, FCC 7

DESCRIPTION

Spice Oleoresins used in foods are derived from spices and contain the total sapid, odorous, and related characterizing principles normally associated with the respective spices. The oleoresins are produced by one of the following processes: (1) by extraction of the spice with any suitable solvent or solvents, in combination or sequence, followed by removal of the solvent or solvents in conformance with applicable residual solvent regulations (see *Identification* and *Residual Solvent* below); or (2) by removal of the volatile portion of the spice by distillation, followed by extraction of the nonvolatile portion, which after solvent removal, is combined with the total volatile portion.

Spice Oleoresins are frequently used in commerce with added suitable food-grade diluents, preservatives, antioxidants, and other substances consistent with good manufacturing practices, as provided for under *Added Substances* (see *General Provisions*). When added substances are used, they must be declared on the label in accordance with current U.S. regulations or with the regulations of other countries that recognize the *Food Chemicals Codex*.

Oleoresin Angelica Seed: Obtained by the solvent extraction of the dried seed of *Angelica archangelica* L. (Fam. Umbelliferae) as a dark brown or green liquid

Oleoresin Anise: Obtained by the solvent extraction of the dried ripe fruit of anise, *Pimpinella anisum* L., or star anise, *Illicium verum* Hooker (Fam. Umbelliferae) as a dark brown or green liquid

Oleoresin Basil: Obtained by the solvent extraction of the dried plant of *Ocimum basilicum* L. (Fam. Labiatae) as a dark brown or green semisolid

Oleoresin Black Pepper: Obtained by the solvent extraction of the dried fruit of *Piper nigrum* L. (Fam. Piperaceae) as a dark green, olive green, or olive drab extract usually consisting of an upper oily layer and a lower crystalline layer. It may appear as a homogeneous emulsion if examined shortly after the oleoresin has been homogenized, but the product separates on standing. It may be decolorized by partial removal of chlorophyll.

Oleoresin Capsicum: Obtained by the solvent extraction of dried pods of *Capsicum frutescens* L. or *Capsicum annum* L. (Fam. Solanaceae) as a clear red to dark red, somewhat viscous liquid of characteristic odor, flavor, and bite. It may be decolorized through good manufacturing practices. It is partly soluble in alcohol (with oily separation and/or sediment), and is soluble in most fixed oils. The bite is usually standardized according to the label declaration.

Oleoresin Caraway: Obtained by the solvent extraction of the dried seeds of *Carum carvi* L. (Fam. Umbelliferae) as a green-yellow to brown liquid

Oleoresin Cardamom: Obtained by the solvent extraction of the dried seeds of *Elettaria cardamomum* Maton (Fam. Zingiberaceae) as a dark brown or green liquid

Oleoresin Celery: Obtained by the solvent extraction of the dried ripe seed of *Apium graveolens* L. (Fam. Umbelliferae) as a dark green, somewhat viscous, non-homogeneous liquid with the characteristic odor and flavor of celery. It may be decolorized by the partial removal of chlorophyll. It is partly soluble in alcohol (with oily separation), and is soluble in most fixed oils.

Oleoresin Coriander: Obtained by the solvent extraction of the dried seeds of *Coriandrum sativum* L. (Fam. Umbelliferae) as a brown-yellow to green liquid

Oleoresin Cubeb: Obtained by the solvent extraction of the dried fruit of *Piper cubeba* L. (Fam. Piperaceae) as a green or green-brown liquid

Oleoresin Cumin: Obtained by the solvent extraction of the dried seeds of *Cuminum cyminum* L. (Fam. Umbelliferae) as a brown to yellow-green liquid

Oleoresin Dillseed: Obtained by the solvent extraction of the dried seeds of *Anethum graveolens* L. (Fam. Umbelliferae) as a brown or green liquid

Oleoresin Fennel: Obtained by the solvent extraction of the dried fruit of *Foeniculum vulgare* P. Miller (Fam. Umbelliferae) as a brown-green liquid

Oleoresin Ginger: Obtained by the solvent extraction of the dried rhizomes of *Zingiber officinale* Roscoe (Fam. Zingiberaceae) as a dark brown, viscous to highly viscous liquid with the characteristic odor and flavor of ginger. It is soluble in alcohol (with sediment).

Oleoresin Hop: Obtained by the solvent extraction of the dried membranous cones of the female hop plants of *Humulus lupulus* L. or *Humulus americanus* Nutt. (Fam. Moraceae), using a food-grade solvent such as liquid carbon dioxide. It occurs as a light golden to black liquid to semisolid with a characteristic odor. It is soluble in methanol and is slightly soluble in acidified water. It may be reduced with sodium borohydride or with hydrogen and palladium catalyst. It conforms to U.S. Food and Drug Administration regulations pertaining to the specifications for extraction solvents for modified hop extract.

Oleoresin Laurel Leaf: Obtained by the solvent extraction of the dried leaves of *Laurus nobilis* L. (Fam. Lauraceae) as a dark brown or green semisolid

Oleoresin Marjoram Sweet: Obtained by the solvent extraction of the dried herb of the marjoram shrub *Majorana hortensis* Moench (Fam. Labiatae) as a dark green to brown viscous liquid or semisolid

Oleoresin Origanum: Obtained by the solvent extraction of the dried flowering herb *Origanum spp.* (Fam. Labiatae) as a dark brown-green semisolid

Oleoresin Paprika: Obtained by the solvent extraction of the pods of *Capsicum annuum* L. (Fam. Solanaceae) as a deep red to deep purple-red, somewhat viscous liquid of characteristic odor and flavor. It frequently occurs as a two-phase mixture. The color is usually standardized according to the label declaration. It is partly soluble in alcohol (with oily separation), and is soluble in most fixed oils.

Oleoresin Parsley Leaf: Obtained by the solvent extraction of the dried herb of *Petroselinum crispum* (P. Miller) Nyman ex A.W. Hill (Fam. Umbelliferae) as a brown to green liquid

Oleoresin Parsley Seed: Obtained by the solvent extraction of the dried seeds of *Petroselinum crispum* (P. Miller) Nyman ex A.W. Hill (Fam. Umbelliferae) as a deep green, semiviscous liquid

Oleoresin Pimenta Berries: Obtained by the solvent extraction of the dried fruit of *Pimenta officinalis* Lindl (Fam. Myrtaceae) as a brown-green to dark green liquid

Oleoresin Rosemary: Obtained by the solvent extraction of the dried leaves of *Rosmarinus officinalis* L. (Fam. Labiatae). It is a thick, green paste that can be diluted with food-grade water- or oil-dispersible solvents. It may have a reduced chlorophyll content. The volatile oil content varies depending on its intended effect from a highly camphoraceous note to a subtle herbal note.

Oleoresin Thyme: Obtained by the solvent extraction of the dried flowering plant *Thymus vulgaris* L. or *Thymus zygis* L. and its var. *gracelis* Boissier (Fam. Labiatae) as a dark brown to green, viscous semisolid

Oleoresin Turmeric: Obtained by the solvent extraction of the dried rhizomes of *Curcuma longa* L. (Fam. Zingiberaceae) as a yellow-orange to red-brown, viscous liquid with a characteristic odor and flavor. The content of curcumin normally varies, and the product is generally standardized according to the label declaration.

Function: Flavoring agent; color (oleoresins paprika and turmeric only)

Packaging and Storage: Store in a cool place protected from light in full, tight containers that are made from steel or aluminum and that are suitably lined.

IDENTIFICATION
- **VOLATILE OIL CONTENT (OLEORESINS),** Appendix VIII
  Acceptance criteria: The volatile oil distilled from an oleoresin is similar in its physical and chemical properties, including its infrared spectrum, to that distilled from the spice of the same origin.

IMPURITIES
Inorganic Impurities
- **LEAD,** *Lead Limit Test,* Appendix IIIB
  Sample solution: Prepare as directed for organic compounds.
  Control: 5 µg Pb (5 mL of *Diluted Standard Lead Solution*)
  Acceptance criteria: NMT 5 mg/kg

Organic Impurities
- **RESIDUAL SOLVENT,** Appendix VIII
  Acceptance criteria
    Chlorinated hydrocarbons (total): NMT 0.003%
    Acetone: NMT 0.003%
    Isopropanol: NMT 0.003%
    Methanol: NMT 0.005%
    Hexane: NMT 0.0025%

SPECIFIC TESTS
- **COLOR VALUE,** Appendix VIII
  Acceptance criteria
    Oleoresin Paprika: 500–4500 units, as specified on the label (according to the method of analysis)
- **CURCUMIN,** *Curcumin Content,* Appendix VIII
  Acceptance criteria
    Oleoresin Turmeric: (or *Color Value* equivalent): 1%–45%, as specified on the label
- **PIPERINE,** *Piperine Content,* Appendix VIII
  Acceptance criteria
    Oleoresin Black Pepper: NLT 36%
- **TOTAL CAPSAICINOIDS CONTENT,** Appendix VIII
  Acceptance criteria

Oleoresin Capsicum: 6.7–133 mg/g, as specified on the label
Oleoresin Paprika (pungency): NMT 0.2 mg/g
- **VOLATILE OIL CONTENT (OLEORESINS)**, Appendix VIII
  Acceptance criteria
  Oleoresin Angelica Seed: 2–7 mL/100 g
  Oleoresin Anise: 9–22 mL/100 g
  Oleoresin Basil: 4–17 mL/100 g
  Oleoresin Black Pepper: 15–35 mL/100 g
  Oleoresin Caraway: 10–20 mL/100 g
  Oleoresin Cardamom: 50–80 mL/100 g
  Oleoresin Celery: 7–20 mL/100 g
  Oleoresin Coriander: 2–12 mL/100 g
  Oleoresin Cubeb: 50–80 mL/100 g
  Oleoresin Cumin: 10–30 mL/100 g
  Oleoresin Dillseed: 10–20 mL/100 g
  Oleoresin Fennel: 3–20 mL/100 g
  Oleoresin Ginger: 18–35 mL/100 g
  Oleoresin Hop: NMT 30 mL/100 g
  Oleoresin Laurel Leaf: 5–25 mL/100 g
  Oleoresin Marjoram Sweet: 8–20 mL/100 g
  Oleoresin Origanum: 20–45 mL/100 g
  Oleoresin Parsley Leaf: 2–10 mL/100 g
  Oleoresin Parsley Seed: 2–7 mL/100 g
  Oleoresin Pimenta Berries: 20–50 mL/100 g
  Oleoresin Rosemary: NMT 15 mL/100 g
  Oleoresin Thyme: 5–12 mL/100 g

Spike Lavender Oil

First Published: Prior to FCC 6

CAS: [84837-04-7]
UNII: 7S2HYV1VJQ [spike lavender oil]

DESCRIPTION
Spike Lavender Oil occurs as a pale yellow to yellow liquid with a camphoraceous, lavender odor. It is the volatile oil obtained by steam distillation from the flowers of *Lavandula latifolia,* Vill. *(Lavandula* spica, D.C.) (Fam. Labiatae). It is soluble in most fixed oils and in propylene glycol. It is slightly soluble in glycerin and in mineral oil.

Function: Flavoring agent

Packaging and Storage: Store in a cool place protected from light in full, tight containers that are made from steel or aluminum and that are suitably lined.

IDENTIFICATION
- **INFRARED SPECTRA,** *Spectrophotometric Identification Tests,* Appendix IIIC
  Acceptance criteria: The spectrum of the sample exhibits relative maxima at the same wavelengths as those of the spectrum below.

ASSAY
- **LINALOOL DETERMINATION,** Appendix VI
  Analysis: Proceed as directed using a 1.5 sample of the acetylated oil for the *Ester Determination,* Appendix VI.
  Acceptance criteria: NLT 40.0% and NMT 50.0% of total alcohols, calculated as linalool ($C_{10}H_{18}O$)

SPECIFIC TESTS
- **ANGULAR ROTATION,** *Optical (Specific) Rotation,* Appendix IIB: Use a 100-mm tube.
  Acceptance criteria: Between −5° and +5°
- **ESTERS,** *Ester Determination,* Appendix VI
  Sample: 10 g
  Analysis: Use 98.15 as the equivalence factor (e) in the formula given for the calculation.
  Acceptance criteria: NLT 1.5% and NMT 4.0% of esters, calculated as linalyl acetate ($C_{12}H_{20}O_2$)
- **REFRACTIVE INDEX,** Appendix IIB
  [NOTE—Use an Abbé or other refractometer of equal or greater accuracy.]
  Acceptance criteria: Between 1.463 and 1.468 at 20°
- **SOLUBILITY IN ALCOHOL,** Appendix VI
  Acceptance criteria: One mL of the sample dissolves in 3 mL of 70% alcohol. The solution frequently becomes hazy on further dilution.
- **SPECIFIC GRAVITY:** Determine by any reliable method (see *General Provisions*).
  Acceptance criteria: Between 0.893 and 0.909

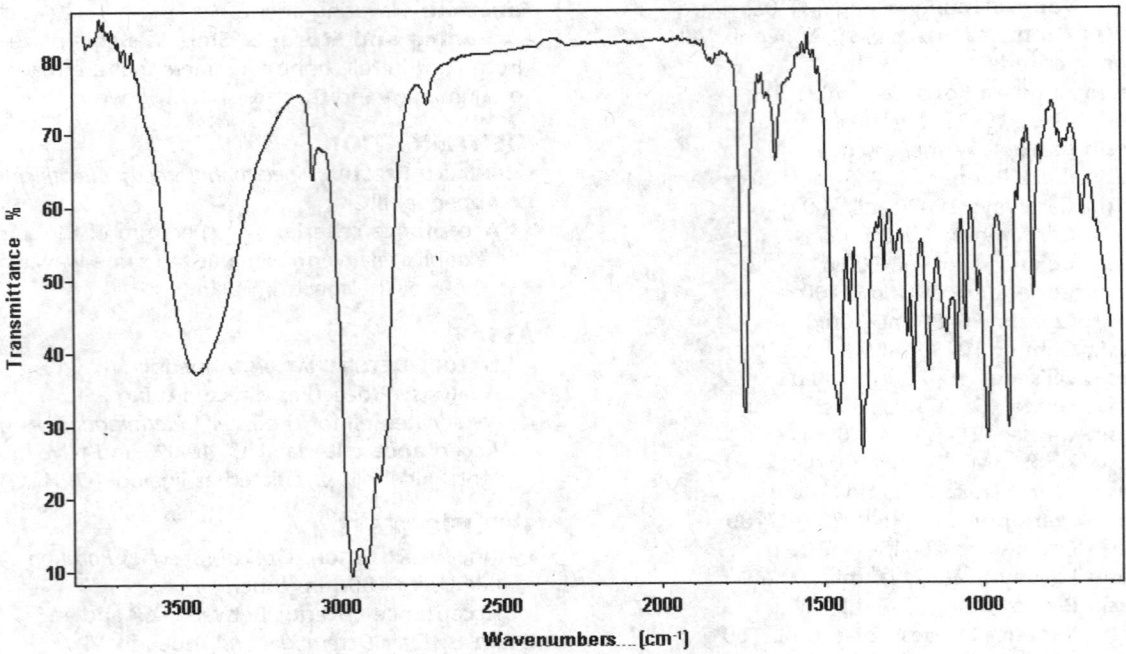

Spike Lavender Oil

Stannous Chloride

First Published: Prior to FCC 6
Last Revision: First Supplement, FCC 6

Tin Dichloride

SnCl₂	Formula wt, anhydrous 189.60
SnCl₂·2H₂O	Formula wt, dihydrate 225.63
INS: 521	CAS: anhydrous [7772-99-8]
	dihydrate [10025-69-1]

UNII: 1BQV3749L5 [stannous chloride]

DESCRIPTION
Stannous Chloride occurs as white or colorless crystals. It is anhydrous or contains two molecules of water of hydration. It is very soluble in water, and it is soluble in alcohol and in glacial acetic acid.
Function: Reducing agent; antioxidant
Packaging and Storage: Store in well-closed containers.

IDENTIFICATION
- **A. CHLORIDE,** Appendix IIIA
  Sample solution: 50 mg/mL
  Acceptance criteria: Passes test
- **B. PROCEDURE**
  Sample solution: 50 mg/mL in 2.7 N hydrochloric acid
  Analysis: Add mercuric chloride TS dropwise to the *Sample solution.*
  Acceptance criteria: A white or gray-white precipitate forms.

ASSAY
- **PROCEDURE**
  Sample: 2 g
  Analysis: Transfer the *Sample* into a 250-mL volumetric flask, dissolve it in 15 mL of hydrochloric acid, dilute with water to volume, and mix. Transfer 50.0 mL of this solution into a 500-mL flask, add 5 g of sodium potassium tartrate, and mix. Make the solution alkaline to litmus with a cold saturated solution of sodium bicarbonate and titrate at once with 0.1 N iodine, using starch TS as the indicator. Each mL of 0.1 N iodine is equivalent to 9.48 mg of SnCl₂ or 11.28 mg of SnCl₂·2H₂O.
  Acceptance criteria
  Anhydrous: NLT 99.0% and NMT 101.0% of SnCl₂
  Dihydrate: NLT 98.0% and NMT 102.2% of SnCl₂·2H₂O

IMPURITIES
Inorganic Impurities
- **IRON**
  Sample: Residue obtained in the test for *Substances Not Precipitated by Sulfide* (below)
  Sample solution: Add 3 mL of 1:2 hydrochloric acid to the *Sample*, cover the *Sample* with a watch glass, and digest on a steam bath for 15 min. Remove the cover, and evaporate to dryness on the steam bath. Dissolve the residue in a few mL of water and 8 mL of hydrochloric acid, dilute with water to 100 mL, and mix. Add 2 mL of hydrochloric acid, 46 mL of water, 40 mg of ammonium persulfate crystals, and 3 mL of ammonium thiocyanate TS to 2.0 mL of this solution.

Control solution: Combine 2.0 mL of *Iron Standard Solution* (20 μg iron; see *Standard Solutions for the Preparation of Controls and Standards*, Solutions and Indicators), with the same quantities of reagents used in the preparation of the *Sample solution*.
Acceptance criteria: Any red or pink color produced by the *Sample solution* does not exceed that of the *Control solution*. (NMT 0.005%)
- **LEAD,** *Lead Limit Test, APDC Extraction Method,* Appendix IIIB
  Acceptance criteria: NMT 4 mg/kg
- **SULFATE**
  Sample: 5 g
  Analysis: Dissolve the *Sample* in 5 mL of hydrochloric acid, and dilute with water to 50 mL. Filter if not clear, and heat the filtrate or clear solution to boiling. Add 5 mL of barium chloride TS, digest in a covered beaker on a steam bath for 2 h, and allow to stand overnight.
  Acceptance criteria: No precipitate forms.

SPECIFIC TESTS
- **SOLUBILITY IN HYDROCHLORIC ACID**
  Sample: 5 g
  Analysis: Dissolve the *Sample* in a mixture of 5 mL of hydrochloric acid and 5 mL of water. Heat to 40°, if necessary, to aid in dissolution.
  Acceptance criteria: The *Sample* dissolves completely, and the solution is clear.
- **SUBSTANCES NOT PRECIPITATED BY SULFIDE**
  Sample: 20 g
  Analysis: Transfer the *Sample* into a 250-mL beaker, and add 50 mL of a solution prepared by carefully adding 75 mL of bromine to 425 mL of 48% hydrobromic acid. Then, add 1 mL of sulfuric acid, and mix to aid in dissolution. Place the beaker on a hot plate, and volatilize the tin slowly, with gentle boiling, to fumes of sulfur trioxide. Cool, add 30 mL of water, and pass hydrogen sulfide gas through the solution for about 5 min. Pass through Whatman No. 42 filter paper, or equivalent, into a weighed platinum dish, and wash with three small portions of a 1% solution of sulfuric acid saturated with hydrogen sulfide. Carefully evaporate to dryness on a hot plate, and heat in a furnace at 800° ± 25° for 13 min. Cool in a desiccator for at least 30 min, and weigh. [NOTE—Retain the residue for the *Iron* test (above).] Calculate the percentage of substances not precipitated by sulfide by the formula:

  Result = 100A/B

  A = weight (g) of the residue
  B = weight (g) of the *Sample* taken
  Acceptance criteria: NMT 0.05%

Starter Distillate
First Published: Prior to FCC 6

Butter Starter Distillate

DESCRIPTION
Starter Distillate occurs as a clear, yellow, water-soluble liquid. It is the steam distillate of a culture of one or more species of *Lactococcus lactis* subsp. *diacetylactis* and/or *Leuconostoc cremoris* grown in a medium of skimmed milk that has been fortified with citric acid. It contains more than 97% water and a mixture of organic flavor compounds, principally diacetyl.
Function: Flavoring agent
Packaging and Storage: Store in a cool place in tight containers.

ASSAY
- **DIACETYL**
  Sample: Take a volume of sample equivalent to 25 mg of diacetyl.
  Osmic acid solution: 100 μg/mL osmium tetroxide. [**CAUTION**—Osmium tetroxide and its solutions are toxic. Use proper protective equipment, and avoid contact with the eyes, skin, and clothing.]
  Analysis: Transfer the *Sample* into a suitable flask and add 3 drops of phenolphthalein TS. Neutralize the acidity by titrating with 0.05 N sodium hydroxide to a faint pink endpoint. Add 0.25 mL of 30% hydrogen peroxide solution and 3 drops of *Osmic acid solution*. Mix, cover the flask, and allow it to stand in an incubator held at about 38° for not less than 4 h. Cool the flask to room temperature, and titrate with 0.05 N sodium hydroxide to a faint pink endpoint. Each mL of 0.05 N sodium hydroxide is equivalent to 8.6 mg of diacetyl.
  Acceptance criteria: NLT 90.0% and NMT 110.0% of the labeled amount of diacetyl

SPECIFIC TESTS
- **PH,** *pH Determination,* Appendix IIB
  Acceptance criteria: Between 2.8 and 3.8

OTHER REQUIREMENTS
- **LABELING:** Indicate the diacetyl content, in mg/mL.

Stearic Acid
First Published: Prior to FCC 6

Octadecanoic Acid

$C_{18}H_{36}O_2$ Formula wt 284.48
         CAS: [57-11-4]
UNII: 4ELV7Z65AP [stearic acid]

DESCRIPTION
Stearic Acid occurs as a hard, white or faintly yellow, somewhat glossy and crystalline solid or as a white or yellow-white powder. It is a mixture of solid organic acids

obtained from fats consisting chiefly of Stearic Acid ($C_{18}H_{36}O_2$) and palmitic acid ($C_{16}H_{32}O_2$). Stearic Acid is practically insoluble in water. One g dissolves in about 20 mL of alcohol, in 2 mL of chloroform, and in about 3 mL of ether.

Function: Component in the manufacture of other food-grade additives; lubricant; defoaming agent

Packaging and Storage: Store in well-closed containers.

IMPURITIES
Inorganic Impurities
- **LEAD,** *Lead Limit Test, Flame Atomic Absorption Spectrophotometric Method,* Appendix IIIB
  Sample: 5 g
  Acceptance criteria: NMT 2 mg/kg

SPECIFIC TESTS
- **ACID VALUE (FATS AND RELATED SUBSTANCES),** *Method I,* Appendix VII
  Acceptance criteria: Between 196 and 211
- **IODINE VALUE,** Appendix VII
  Acceptance criteria: NMT 7
- **RESIDUE ON IGNITION (SULFATED ASH),** Appendix IIC
  Sample: 2 g
  Acceptance criteria: NMT 0.1%
- **SAPONIFICATION VALUE,** Appendix VII
  Sample: 3 g
  Acceptance criteria: Between 197 and 212
- **TITER (SOLIDIFICATION POINT),** *Solidification Point,* Appendix IIB
  Acceptance criteria: Between 54.5° and 69°
- **UNSAPONIFIABLE MATTER,** Appendix VII
  Acceptance criteria: NMT 1.5%
- **WATER,** *Water Determination,* Appendix IIB
  Acceptance criteria: NMT 0.2%

Add the following:

▲Stearyl Alcohol

First Published: FCC 8

1-Octadecanol
Octadecyl Alcohol

$C_{18}H_{38}O$ Formula wt 270.5
                   CAS: [112-92-5]

UNII: 2KR89I4H1Y [stearyl alcohol]

DESCRIPTION
Stearyl Alcohol occurs as colorless to white granules or flakes. It is manufactured by the transesterification and distillation of unrefined coconut or palm oil using a zinc catalyst and in the presence of methanol. The resulting methyl esters are then hydrogenated in the presence of a copper catalyst. It is purified and catalysts are removed through fractional distillation. Stearyl Alcohol is soluble in alcohol, in ether, in benzene, and in acetone, and is insoluble in water.

Function: Texturizer

Packaging and Storage: Store in well-closed containers.

IDENTIFICATION
- **PROCEDURE**
  Acceptance criteria: The retention time of the major peak in the chromatogram of the *Sample solution* corresponds to that in the chromatogram of the *System suitability solution*, as obtained in the *Assay*.

ASSAY
- **PROCEDURE**
  System suitability solution: Prepare a solution containing 9 mg/mL of USP Stearyl Alcohol RS and 1 mg/mL of USP Cetyl Alcohol RS in dehydrated alcohol.
  Sample solution: 10 mg/mL in dehydrated alcohol
  Chromatographic system, Appendix IIA
    Mode: Gas chromatography
    Detector: Flame ionization
    Column: 2-m × 3-mm column packed with 10% liquid phase dimethylpolysiloxane gum on a support of silaceous earth for gas chromatography that has been flux-calcined by mixing diatomite Na_2CO_3 flux and calcining above 900°.[1] The silaceous earth may be silanized.
    Carrier gas: Helium
    Temperature
      Injection port: 275°
      Column: 205°
      Detector: 250°
    Injection volume: 2 µL
  System suitability
    Sample: *System suitability solution*
    Suitability requirement 1: The resolution, R, between cetyl alcohol and stearyl alcohol is NLT 4.0.
    Suitability requirement 2: The relative standard deviation for replicate injections, calculated with the area ratio of stearyl alcohol to cetyl alcohol, is NMT 1.5%.
  Analysis: Inject the *Sample solution* into the chromatograph, record the chromatogram, and measure the areas for the major peaks. Calculate the percentage of $C_{18}H_{38}O$ in the portion of the sample taken:

  $$\text{Result} = (r_U/r_S) \times 100$$

  r_U = peak area for stearyl alcohol obtained from the chromatogram of the *Sample solution*
  r_S = sum of the areas of all of the peaks (excluding the solvent peak) obtained from the chromatogram of the *Sample solution*
  Acceptance criteria: NLT 90.0%

IMPURITIES
Inorganic Impurities
- **COPPER,** *Elemental Impurities by ICP,* Appendix IIIC
  Acceptance criteria: NMT 1 mg/kg
- **LEAD,** *Elemental Impurities by ICP,* Appendix IIIC

---
[1] OV-1 on SUPELCOPORT (available at www.sigma-aldrich.com), or equivalent.

Acceptance criteria: NMT 1 mg/kg
- **Zinc**, *Elemental Impurities by ICP,* Appendix IIIC
  Acceptance criteria: NMT 1 mg/kg

SPECIFIC TESTS
- **Acid Value (Fats and Related Substances)**, Appendix VII
  Acceptance criteria: NMT 2
- **Hydroxyl Value**
  Sample: 2 g
  Analysis: Transfer the *Sample* to a dry, glass-stoppered, 250-mL flask, and add 2 mL of pyridine, followed by 10 mL of toluene. To the mixture add 10.0 mL of a solution of acetyl chloride in toluene (10:90 v/v). Insert the stopper into the flask, and immerse in a water bath heated at 60°–65° for 20 min. Add 25 mL of water, again insert the stopper into the flask, and shake vigorously for several minutes to decompose the excess acetyl chloride. Add 0.5 mL of phenolphthalein TS, and titrate to a permanent pink endpoint with 1 N sodium hydroxide, shaking the flask vigorously toward the end of the titration to maintain the contents in an emulsified condition. Perform a blank titration (see *General Provisions*). Calculate the hydroxyl value of the sample taken:

  $$\text{Result} = (V_B - V_S) \times 56.1 \times N \times 1/W$$

  V_B = volume of titrant consumed in the blank determination (mL)
  V_S = volume of titrant consumed in the *Sample* determination (mL)
  N = exact normality of the sodium hydroxide used in the titration (mol/L)
  W = weight of *Sample* used (g)
  Acceptance criteria: Between 195 and 220
- **Iodine Value**, Appendix VII
  Acceptance criteria: NMT 2
- **Melting Range or Temperature Determination**, Appendix IIB
  Acceptance criteria: 55°–60° ▲FCC8

Stearyl Citrate
First Published: Second Supplement, FCC 6

R_1, R_2, R_3 = stearyl or palmityl or H

INS: 484
UNII: YWW937R1QR [monostearyl citrate]

DESCRIPTION
Stearyl Citrate occurs as a cream-colored, unctuous substance. It is a mixture of the mono-, di-, and tri-stearyl esters of citric acid. Stearyl Citrate is prepared by esterifying citric acid with stearyl alcohol. It is soluble in hot ethanol and is insoluble in water and in cold ethanol. The article of commerce can be further specified by saponification value, total content, and composition of stearyl alcohol, iodine value, acid value, and citric acid content. Acids other than citric acid and alcohols other than those present in commercial stearyl alcohol should not be present.
Function: Antioxidant; emulsifier; sequestrant; surface-active agent
Packaging and Storage: Store in well-closed containers.

IDENTIFICATION
- **Test for Stearyl Alcohol**
  Sample: Hydrolyze 2 g by heating with 50 mL of sodium hydroxide TS under reflux for 1 h. Cool, and extract the aqueous solution with petroleum ether. Evaporate the petroleum ether in an evaporating dish. Use the residue so obtained as the *Sample*.
  Acceptance criteria: The *Sample* has a melting range of between 43° and 58°.
- **Test for Citrate**
  Sample: The aqueous solution obtained in the *Test for Stearyl Alcohol*
  Analysis 1: To 5 mL of the *Sample*, add 1 mL of calcium chloride TS and 3 drops of bromothymol blue TS, and slightly acidify with dilute hydrochloric acid TS. Add sodium hydroxide TS until the color changes to a clear blue, then boil the solution for 3 min, agitating it gently during the heating period.
  Acceptance criteria 1: A white crystalline precipitate appears, which is insoluble in sodium hydroxide TS, but is soluble in strong acetic acid TS.
  Analysis 2: To 10 mL of the *Sample*, add 1 mL of mercuric sulfate TS. Heat the mixture to boiling, and add a few drops of a 1.0% (w/v) solution of potassium permanganate.
  Acceptance criteria 2: A white precipitate of the acetone dicarboxylic acid salt of mercury is formed.

IMPURITIES
Inorganic Impurities
- **Lead**, *Lead Limit Test, Flame Atomic Absorption Spectrophotometric Method,* Appendix IIIB
  Sample: 10 g
  Acceptance criteria: NMT 2 mg/kg

SPECIFIC TESTS
- **Chloroform-Insoluble Matter**
  Sample: 50.0 g
  Analysis: Dissolve the *Sample* in 400 mL of chloroform. Pass the solution through a weighed sintered-glass filter of porosity 3. Keep the filter warm, and wash the residue in the filter with chloroform, dry at 100°, and weigh.
  Acceptance criteria: NMT 0.5%

Stearyl Monoglyceridyl Citrate

First Published: Prior to FCC 6

DESCRIPTION
Stearyl Monoglyceridyl Citrate occurs as a soft, off-white to tan, waxy solid having a lardlike consistency. It is prepared by a controlled chemical reaction from citric acid, monoglycerides of fatty acids (obtained by the glycerolysis of edible fats and oils or derived from fatty acids), and stearyl alcohol. It is insoluble in water, but is soluble in chloroform and in ethylene glycol.
Function: Emulsion stabilizer
Packaging and Storage: Store in well-closed containers.

IMPURITIES
Inorganic Impurities
- **LEAD,** Lead Limit Test, Flame Atomic Absorption Spectrophotometric Method, Appendix IIIB
  Sample: 10 g
  Acceptance criteria: NMT 2 mg/kg

SPECIFIC TESTS
- **ACID VALUE (FATS AND RELATED SUBSTANCES),** Method II, Appendix VII
  Acceptance criteria: Between 40 and 52
- **RESIDUE ON IGNITION (SULFATED ASH),** Appendix IIC
  Sample: 2 g
  Acceptance criteria: NMT 0.1%
- **SAPONIFICATION VALUE**
  Sample: 1 g
  Analysis: Transfer the Sample into a 250-mL Erlenmeyer flask, add 25 mL of ethylene glycol and 35.0 mL of 0.5 N alcoholic potassium hydroxide, and a few glass beads. Reflux for 1 h, using a water condenser, then rinse the condenser with water and cool. Add 1 mL of phenolphthalein TS, and titrate with 0.5 N hydrochloric acid. Perform a blank determination (see General Provisions), but do not reflux. The difference between the volumes, in mL, of 0.5 N hydrochloric acid consumed in the test and in the blank titration, multiplied by 28.05 and divided by the weight, in g, of the sample taken, is the saponification value.
  Acceptance criteria: Between 215 and 255
- **TOTAL CITRIC ACID**
  Brominating solution: 19.84 mg/mL of potassium bromide, 5.44 mg/mL of potassium bromate, and 12 mg/mL of sodium metavanadate (NaVO$_3$). [NOTE—Warm the solution before bringing it to volume in order to complete dissolution. Filter if necessary.]
  Ferrous sulfate solution: 440 mg/mL of ferrous sulfate heptahydrate in 1 N sulfuric acid. [NOTE—Use within 5 days of preparation.]
  Sulfide solution: Dissolve 4 g of thiourea in 100 mL of a 20 mg/mL solution of sodium borate decahydrate and add 2 mL of sodium sulfide TS. [NOTE—Prepare on the day of use and wait 30 min after addition of sodium sulfide TS before using.]
  Standard stock solution: Transfer 50 mg of sodium citrate dihydrate into a 500-mL volumetric flask, dissolve in and dilute to volume with water, and mix.
  Standard solution: Transfer 15 mL of Standard stock solution into a 100-mL volumetric flask, dilute to volume with water, and mix. Calculate the concentration (C), in µg/mL, of citric acid in the final solution by the formula:

  $$\text{Result} = (15 \times 1000 \times F \times W)/(100 \times 500)$$

  F = factor converting sodium citrate dihydrate to citric acid, 0.6533
  W = weight of the sodium citrate dihydrate (mg) taken to prepare the Standard stock solution

  Sample stock solution: Transfer 250 mg of sample into a 250-mL extraction flask, add 15 mL of 0.5 N sodium hydroxide, 5 mL of alcohol, and a few glass beads. Connect the flask to a water-cooled condenser, and reflux for 3 h. Immediately cool and neutralize to phenolphthalein TS with 0.5 N hydrochloric acid, then place the flask in an ice bath and add 5 mL of 95% sulfuric acid. Transfer the solution to a 125-mL separatory funnel, extract with three 40-mL portions of chloroform, and then extract the combined chloroform extracts in a 250-mL separatory funnel with three 10-mL portions of 0.5 N sulfuric acid, adding the acid extracts to a second 250-mL separatory funnel. Wash the combined acid extracts with two 60-mL portions of chloroform, and discard the chloroform washes. Filter the acid solution into a 500-mL volumetric flask, neutralize slowly with 6 N sodium carbonate, and dilute to volume with water.
  Sample solution: Transfer 10.0 mL of the Sample stock solution into a 100-mL volumetric flask, dilute to volume with water, and mix. This solution contains approximately 10 µg/mL citric acid.
  Analysis: Pipet 2 mL each of the Standard solution and of the Sample solution into separate, 40- or 45-mL glass-stoppered centrifuge tubes, and add 3 mL of water to each tube. Place 5 mL of water in a third tube for the reagent blank. Place the tubes in an ice bath, add 5 mL of 95% sulfuric acid, mix thoroughly, and allow to stand for exactly 5 min. Remove the tubes from the ice bath and allow them to come to room temperature during the next 5 min. Add 5 mL of the Brominating solution to each tube, insert the stoppers, invert the tubes once or twice, and heat in a water bath at 30° for 20 min. Remove the tubes, add 1.5 mL of Ferrous sulfate solution, invert again, and allow to stand for 5 min, shaking occasionally to ensure complete reduction of the excess free bromine in the tubes. Add 6.5 mL of petroleum ether, shake for 2 or 3 min, and remove the water layer with a syringe. Wash the ether solutions with 15 mL of water, then remove the water, and filter the ether extracts into the centrifuge tubes, which have been previously rinsed with the Sulfide solution. Filter each ether extract through a tight plug of glass wool containing a sufficient amount of anhydrous sodium sulfate to remove the last traces of water from the ether. Place 5.0 mL of each filtrate into separate clean,

dry centrifuge tubes, add 3 mL of *Sulfide solution*, shake vigorously for 1.5 min, and centrifuge. Decant about 0.5 mL of the supernatant ether layer from each tube, then carefully transfer the ether solutions into 1-cm cells, and determine the absorbance of the extracts obtained from the *Standard solution* and the *Sample solution* at 500 nm with a suitable spectrophotometer, using the reagent blank in the reference cell. Calculate the quantity, in mg, of citric acid in the sample taken by the formula:

$$Result = 5C \times A_U/A_S$$

C = concentration (mg/mL) of citric acid in the *Standard solution* calculated above under *Standard solution*.
A_U = absorbance of the solution from the *Sample solution*
A_S = absorbance of the solution from the *Standard solution*
Acceptance criteria: Between 15.0% and 18.0%
- **WATER,** *Water Determination,* Appendix IIB
Acceptance criteria: NMT 0.25%

Succinic Acid

First Published: Prior to FCC 6
Last Revision: Second Supplement, FCC 7

Butanedioic Acid

$C_4H_6O_4$ Formula wt 118.09
INS: 363   CAS: [110-15-6]
UNII: AB6MNQ6J6L [succinic acid]

DESCRIPTION
Succinic Acid occurs as colorless or white crystals. One g dissolves in 13 mL of water at 25°, in 1 mL of boiling water, in 18.5 mL of alcohol, and in 20 mL of glycerin.
Function: Buffer; neutralizing agent
Packaging and Storage: Store in well-closed containers.

IDENTIFICATION
- **INFRARED ABSORPTION**, *Spectrophotometric Identification Tests,* Appendix IIIC
  Reference standard: USP Succinic Acid RS
  Sample and standard preparation: K
  Acceptance criteria: The spectrum of the sample exhibits maxima at the same wavelengths as those in the spectrum of the *Reference standard.*

ASSAY
- **PROCEDURE**
  Sample: 250 mg
  Analysis: Dissolve the *Sample* in 25 mL of recently boiled and cooled water, add phenolphthalein TS, and titrate with 0.1 N sodium hydroxide to the first appearance of a faint pink color that persists for at least 30 seconds. Each mL of 0.1 N sodium hydroxide is equivalent to 5.905 mg of $C_4H_6O_4$.
  Acceptance criteria: 99.0%–100.5% of $C_4H_6O_4$

IMPURITIES
Inorganic Impurities
- **LEAD,** *Lead Limit Test, Flame Atomic Absorption Spectrophotometric Method,* Appendix IIIB
  Sample: 5 g
  Acceptance criteria: NMT 2 mg/kg

SPECIFIC TESTS
- **MELTING RANGE OR TEMPERATURE DETERMINATION,** Appendix IIB
  Acceptance criteria: 185.0°–190.0°
- **RESIDUE ON IGNITION (SULFATED ASH),** Appendix IIC
  Sample: 8 g
  Acceptance criteria: NMT 0.025%

Succinylated Monoglycerides

First Published: Prior to FCC 6

INS: 472g

DESCRIPTION
Succinylated Monoglycerides occur as waxy solids having an off white color. They are a mixture of succinic acid esters of mono- and diglycerides produced by the succinylation of a product obtained by the glycerolysis of edible fats and oils, or by the direct esterification of glycerol with edible fat-forming fatty acids. They melt at about 60°. They are soluble in warm methanol, in ethanol, and in *n*-propanol.
Function: Emulsifier; dough conditioner
Packaging and Storage: Store in well-closed containers.

IMPURITIES
Inorganic Impurities
- **LEAD,** *Lead Limit Test, Flame Atomic Absorption Spectrophotometric Method,* Appendix IIIB
  Sample: 10 g
  Acceptance criteria: NMT 2 mg/kg

SPECIFIC TESTS
- **ACID VALUE (FATS AND RELATED SUBSTANCES),** *Method I,* Appendix VII
  Acceptance criteria: Between 70 and 120

- **FREE SUCCINIC ACID**
  Titrant solution: 0.8 mg/mL sodium hydroxide in anhydrous methanol, made to 1000 mL. Standardize the solution against dried succinic acid, using phenolphthalein TS as the indicator. Nominal concentration is 0.02 N sodium hydroxide.
  Sample: 125 mg
  Analysis: Transfer the *Sample* into a 250-mL separatory funnel containing 100 mL of benzene and dissolve the *Sample* by heating the separatory funnel with warm water. Prepare a blank, by transferring 100 mL of benzene to another separatory funnel. Treat the *Sample* and blank as follows: Cool the contents of the separatory funnel, add 50 mL of water, and mix by inverting the funnel about 20 times. Allow to stand for about 15 min, and then transfer the aqueous layer into a 125-mL Erlenmeyer flask. Add 10 mL of water to the funnel, wash the benzene layer by inverting the funnel five times, and add the washings to the 125-mL flask. [NOTE—Reserve the benzene layer in the funnel for analysis of *Bound Succinic Acid*.] Add five drops of phenolphthalein TS to the flask, and titrate with the *Titrant solution*. Perform a blank determination (see *General Provisions*), make any necessary correction, and record the net volume (V) of titrant in mL.
  Calculate the percentage of *Free Succinic Acid* in the *Sample* by the formula:

  $$\text{Result} = 118.1 \times N/W \times V/2 \times 100\%$$

  N = normality of the sodium hydroxide solution
  W = weight of the sample taken (mg)
  Acceptance criteria: NMT 3%

- **BOUND SUCCINIC ACID**
  Titrant solution: As prepared for the determination of *Free Succinic Acid*
  Sample: Use the reserved benzene layer in the separatory funnel as noted in the analysis for *Free Succinic Acid*.
  Analysis: Transfer the *Sample* into a 500-mL round-bottom flask, and rinse the funnel with 10 mL of benzene. Add a few boiling chips to the flask, and evaporate the benzene, preferably on a thin-film evaporator, under partial vacuum at about 60°. Dissolve the residue in the flask in 10 mL of methanol, add 10 mL of water and 5 drops of phenolphthalein TS, and titrate with the *Titrant solution*. Perform a blank determination (see *General Provisions*), make any necessary correction, and record the net volume (V) of titrant in mL.
  Calculate the percentage of *Bound Succinic Acid* in the sample taken for determination of *Free Succinic Acid* by the formula:

  $$\text{Result} = 118.1 \times N/W \times V/2 \times 100\%$$

  N = normality of the sodium hydroxide solution
  W = weight of the sample taken (mg) for determination of *Free Succinic Acid*
  Acceptance criteria: NLT 14.8%

- **HYDROXYL VALUE,** *Method II*, Appendix VII
  Acceptance criteria: Between 138 and 152
- **IODINE VALUE,** Appendix VII
  Acceptance criteria: NMT 3
- **TOTAL SUCCINIC ACID**
  Analysis: Sum the percentages of *Free Succinic Acid* and *Bound Succinic Acid*.
  Acceptance criteria: Between 14.8% and 25.6%

Sucralose

First Published: Prior to FCC 6
Last Revision: FCC 7

1,6-Dichloro-1,6-dideoxy-β-D-fructofuranosyl-4-chloro-4-deoxy-α-D-galactopyranoside
4,1′,6′-Trichlorogalactosucrose

$C_{12}H_{19}Cl_3O_8$ Formula wt 397.64
INS: 955   CAS: [56038-13-2]
UNII: 96K6UQ3ZD4 [sucralose]

DESCRIPTION
Sucralose occurs as a white to off-white, crystalline powder. It is freely soluble in water, in methanol, and in alcohol, and slightly soluble in ethyl acetate.
Function: Non-nutritive sweetener; flavor enhancer
Packaging and Storage: Store in well-closed containers in a dry place protected from excessive heat.

IDENTIFICATION
- **A. INFRARED ABSORPTION,** *Spectrophotometric Identification Tests*, Appendix IIIC
  Reference standard: USP Sucralose RS
  Sample and standard preparation: K
  Acceptance criteria: The spectrum of the sample exhibits maxima at the same wavelengths as those in the spectrum of the *Reference standard*.
- **B. PROCEDURE**
  Acceptance criteria: The retention time of the major peak (excluding the solvent peak) in the liquid chromatogram of the *Sample solution* is the same as that of the *Standard solution* obtained in the *Assay* (below).
- **C. PROCEDURE**
  Acceptance criteria: The R_F value of the major spot in the thin-layer chromatogram of the *Sample solution* is the same as that of the *Standard solution* obtained in the test for *Related Substances*.

ASSAY
- **PROCEDURE**
  Mobile phase: 15:85 acetonitrile and water (v/v), passed through a 0.45-μm filter and degassed. Use glass-distilled (or equivalent) water.

Standard solution: 1 mg/mL of USP Sucralose RS in *Mobile phase*, passed through a 0.45-μm filter
Sample solution: 1 mg/mL of sample in *Mobile phase*, passed through a 0.45-μm filter
Chromatographic system, Appendix IIA
  Mode: High-performance liquid chromatography
  Detector: Refractive index
  Column: 8-mm × 10-cm, 5-μm RadPakC18 (or equivalent) reverse-phase column
  Temperature: Room temperature
  Flow rate: About 1.5 mL/min
  Injection volume: 20 μL
  System suitability
    Sample: *Standard solution*
    Suitability requirement: The relative standard deviation of the sucralose peak for duplicate injections does not exceed 2.0%. [NOTE—The retention time of sucralose is approximately 9 min. It may be necessary to adjust the *Mobile phase* composition to obtain the desired retention time.]
Analysis: Analyze duplicate injections of *Standard solution* and *Sample solution*, and calculate the mean peak areas. Calculate the percent of sucralose from the peak areas of the *Sample solution* and *Standard solution* according to the following formula:

$$\text{Result} = 100(A_U C_S)/(A_S C_U)$$

A_U = mean peak area in the chromatogram of the *Sample solution*
A_S = mean peak area in the chromatogram of the *Standard solution*
C_S = concentration of the *Standard solution* (mg/mL)
C_U = concentration of the *Sample solution* (mg/mL)

Acceptance criteria: 98.0%–102.0% of $C_{12}H_{19}Cl_3O_8$, on the anhydrous basis

IMPURITIES
Inorganic Impurities
- **LEAD,** Lead Limit Test, Atomic Absorption Spectrophotometric Graphite Furnace Method, Method I, Appendix IIIB
  Acceptance criteria: NMT 1 mg/kg

Organic Impurities
- **METHANOL**
  Standard stock solution: 1000 μg/mL of methanol
  Standard solution: 1000 μg of methanol per g of sucralose prepared as follows. Add 1.000 g of USP Sucralose RS to a 22-mL headspace vial. [NOTE—USP Sucralose RS does not contain measurable methanol, and is added here to make a matrix-matched *Standard solution*.] Add 4.0 mL of 10% (w/v) sodium chloride solution. Add 1.00 mL of *Standard stock solution*, crimp a cap with a teflon seal tightly onto the vial, and mix the solution well.
  Sample solution: Add 1.000 g of sample to a 22-mL headspace vial. Add 4.0 mL of a 10% (w/v) sodium chloride solution. Crimp a cap with a teflon seal tightly onto the vial, and mix the solution well.
  Chromatographic system, Appendix IIA
    Mode: Gas chromatography with balanced-pressure headspace sampler
    Detector: Flame ionization detector
    Column: 30-m × 0.32-mm capillary column with polyethylene glycol stationary phase and 1.0 μm film thickness[1] [NOTE— The capillary column is installed through the GC inlet and through the transfer line to give on-column injection.]
    Inlet temperature: 110°
    Column temperature: See the temperature program table below.

Temperature (°)	Rate (°/min)	Hold Time (min)
50	—	3
50→80	10	—
80→230	50	—
230	—	10

  Detector parameters
    Detector temperature: 250°
    Hydrogen flow rate: 40 mL/min
    Air flow rate: 400 mL/min
    Flow mode: Constant make up
    Make up/combo flow: 30 mL/min
  Headspace sampler parameters
    Transferline temperature: 110°
    Needle temperature: 100°
    Oven temperature: 90°
    Vial equilibration time: 10 min
    Cycle time: 25 min
    Vial pressurization time: 3 min
    Withdrawal time: 0.5 min
    Injection time: 0.15 min
    Sampler delivery system: Helium set at 90 psi (not to exceed 100 psi)
  System suitability
    Sample: *Standard solution*
    Suitability requirement: The relative standard deviation is NMT 10% for replicate injections.
  Analysis: Separately inject the *Standard solution* and the *Sample solution* into the chromatograph, and measure the areas of the peaks responses. [NOTE— The retention time for methanol is about 4.4 min.] Calculate the percentage of methanol in the portion of sample taken using the following formula:

$$\text{Result} = [(A_U \times C_S)/(A_S \times C_U)] \times F$$

A_U = methanol peak response from the *Sample solution*
C_S = weight of methanol in the *Standard solution* (μg)
A_S = methanol peak response from the *Standard solution*
C_U = weight of sample used to prepare the *Sample solution* (g)
F = conversion factor to convert from μg/g to g/g and to percent, 1/10,000

Acceptance criteria: NMT 0.1%

---
[1] Heliflex AT-Wax (Alltech Associates Inc., Deerfield, IL) or equivalent.

SPECIFIC TESTS
- **HYDROLYSIS PRODUCTS**
  Spray reagent: Dissolve 1.23 g of *p*-anisidine and 1.66 g of phthalic acid in 100 mL of methanol. [**CAUTION**—*p*-Anisidine is toxic if inhaled or absorbed through the skin and should be used with due caution.] [NOTE—Store the solution in darkness, and refrigerate to prevent discoloration. Discard if the solution becomes discolored.]
  Standard solution A: 100 mg/mL mannitol
  Standard solution B: 0.40 mg/mL fructose and 100 mg/mL mannitol
  Sample solution: 250 mg/mL in methanol
  Application volume: 5-µL portions separately applied in 1-µL increments, allowing the plate to dry between applications
  Analysis: [NOTE—This test does not require a developing solvent.] Spot *Standard solution A*, *Standard solution B*, and *Sample solution* onto a thin-layer chromatographic plate coated with a 0.25-mm layer of Merck-silica gel 60, or equivalent. The three spots should be of similar size. Spray the plate with the *Spray reagent*, and heat it at 100° ± 2° for 15 min. Immediately after heating, view the plate against a dark background. [NOTE—If the spot from *Standard solution A* darkens, this indicates that the plate has been held too long in the oven, and that a second plate should be prepared.]
  Acceptance criteria: The spot from the *Sample solution* is not more intense in color than the spot from *Standard solution B* (0.1% limit).
- **OPTICAL (SPECIFIC) ROTATION**, Appendix IIB
  Sample solution: 0.01 g/mL, calculated on the anhydrous basis
  Acceptance criteria: $[\alpha]_D^{20}$ between +84.0° and +87.5°, calculated on the anhydrous basis
- **RELATED SUBSTANCES**, Thin-Layer Chromatography, Appendix IIA
  Standard solution: 100.0 mg/mL of USP Sucralose RS in methanol
  Dilute standard solution: 0.5 mg/mL of USP Sucralose RS in methanol from the *Standard solution*
  Sample solution: 100 mg/mL in methanol
  Adsorbent: 0.20-mm layer of silica gel absorbent, or equivalent, coated on Whatman LKC18 thin-layer chromatographic plates, or equivalent
  Application volume: 5 µL
  Developing solvent system: Mix 70 volumes of 50-mg/mL sodium chloride solution and 30 volumes of acetonitrile. [NOTE—Prepare fresh before use.]
  Spray reagent: 15% (v/v) sulfuric acid in methanol
  Analysis: Apply *Standard solution*, *Dilute standard solution*, and *Sample solution* to the bottom of the chromatographic plate. Place the plate in a suitable chromatographic chamber containing *Developing solvent system*, and allow the solvent front to ascend approximately 15 cm. Remove the plate, allow it to dry, and spray it with the *Spray reagent*. Heat the plate in an oven at 125° for 10 min.
  Acceptance criteria: The main spot in the *Sample solution* is at the same R_F value as the main spot in the *Standard solution*, and any other single spot in the *Sample solution* is not more intense than the 0.5% spot in the *Dilute standard solution*.
- **RESIDUE ON IGNITION (SULFATED ASH)**, Appendix IIC
  Sample: 1 to 2 g
  Acceptance criteria: NMT 0.7%
- **WATER**, Water Determination, Appendix IIB
  Acceptance criteria: NMT 2.0%

Sucromalt
First Published: Third Supplement, FCC 7

Low Glycemic Carbohydrate

DESCRIPTION
Sucromalt occurs as a clear, colorless to light yellow, slightly cloudy liquid. It is the product of an enzyme-catalyzed reaction of sucrose and maltose, combined at a specific ratio. The reaction is pH- and temperature-controlled and utilizes a food-grade glucosyltransferase enzyme. The resulting syrup may be further treated to deactivate the enzyme, purified, and evaporated under vacuum to obtain an optimal dry solids content. Sucromalt is composed of 35%–45% fructose, 7%–15% leucrose, less than 5% other mono- and di-saccharides, and 40%–60% higher glucooligosaccharides of 12+ DP.
Function: Source of slowly digestible nutritive carbohydrate
Packaging and Storage: Store in well-closed containers.

IDENTIFICATION
- **¹H NMR SPECTROSCOPY**, Nuclear Magnetic Resonance Spectroscopy, Appendix IIC
  Solvent: Use deuterium oxide (D_2O, 99.999% atom D) that contains 0.01% (v/v) dimethylsulfoxide (DMSO) as an internal intensity standard and 0.01% (w/v) sodium 3,3,4,4,5,5-hexadeutero-2,2-dimethyl-2-silapentane-5-sulfonate (DSS-d_6) as an internal chemical shift standard.
  Standard solution: Prepare a solution in *Solvent* containing 5 mg/mL of USP Sucromalt RS. Vortex the mixture for 10 min at room temperature, then centrifuge at 7200 *g* for 10 min. Transfer 600-µL aliquots of the supernatant to 5-mm NMR tubes, and sonicate for 10 min to eliminate air bubbles.
  Sample solution: Prepare a solution in *Solvent* containing 5 mg/mL of Sucromalt. Vortex the mixture for 10 min at room temperature, then centrifuge at 7200 *g* for 10 min. Transfer 600-µL aliquots of the supernatant to 5-mm NMR tubes, and sonicate for 10 min to eliminate air bubbles.
  Analysis: Collect ¹H NMR spectra of the *Standard solution* and *Sample solution* at 25°. Compare the data collected between 4.80 ppm and 5.50 ppm within the anomeric region of the spectrum. For the spectrum obtained from the *Sample solution*, identify the signals due to α-(1,6) and α-(1,3) glycosidic linkages by comparison to the *Reference Spectrum* provided with the USP Sucromalt RS. Calculate the ratio of the intensities of the ¹H signals due to the α-(1,6) and α-(1,3)

glycosidic linkages in the spectrum obtained for the *Sample solution*.

Acceptance criteria: The spectrum obtained for the *Sample solution* exhibits a chemical shift pattern with signal locations and intensities that match those obtained from the *Standard solution* within the defined chemical shift range of 4.80–5.50 ppm. The α-(1,6)/α-(1,3) signal ratio for the *Sample solution* is within the range 1.4–1.9.

ASSAY
- **PROCEDURE**

    Mobile phase: Degassed, purified water passed through a 0.22-μm filter before use. The conductivity should be NMT 1 megaohm. [NOTE—Maintain the water at 85° during operation of the chromatograph.]

    Standard solution: Prepare a solution containing a total of about 10% solids, using sugars of known purity (e.g., USP Fructose RS, USP Dextrose RS, USP Maltose Monohydrate RS, or NIST Standard Reference Material; leucrose;[1] or equivalent) that approximates, on the dry basis, the composition of the sample to be analyzed. Dissolve each standard sugar in 20 mL of purified water contained in a 50-mL beaker. Heat on a steam bath until all sugars are dissolved, then cool, and transfer to a 100-mL volumetric flask. Dilute with water to volume, and mix. [NOTE—Freeze the solution if it is to be reused.]

    Sample solution: Dilute to approximately 7%–12% solids and filter through a syringe filter system.

    Chromatographic system, Appendix IIA
    [NOTE—Use a suitable high-performance liquid chromatography system.[2]]

    Mode: High-performance liquid chromatography
    Detector: Differential refractometer
    Column: 22- to 31-cm stainless steel column, or equivalent with a stationary phase of prepacked macroreticular polystyrene sulfonated divinylbenzene cation-exchange resin (2%–8% cross-linked, 8- to 25-μm particle size), preferably in the calcium or silver form. Examples of acceptable resins are Bio-Rad Aminex HPX-87C, or equivalent, for separating DP₁–DP₄ saccharides, and Aminex HPX-42C and HPX-42A, or equivalent, for separating DP₁–DP₇ saccharides. [NOTE—Condition the column before use by pumping solvent at 0.1 mL/min through the column while bringing it to operating temperature. Increase the flow rate to 0.5 mL/min, and allow to equilibrate for 45 min prior to use.]

    Temperature
    Column: 85°
    Detector: 45°
    Flow rate: 0.5–1.0 mL/min
    Injection volume: 10 μL
    Standardization: If a corn syrup or maltodextrin is used to supply a DP₄₊ fraction, take care to include all saccharides in the standard composition calculation.

Calculate the dry-basis concentration, as a percentage, of each individual component in the *Standard solution*:

$$\text{Result} = (W_C/\Sigma W_I) \times 100$$

W_C = weight of the sugar of interest
ΣW_I = sum of the weights of all sugar components

Standardize by injecting 10–20 μL (about 1.0–2.0 mg of solids) of the *Standard solution* into the chromatograph. Integrate the peaks and normalize. Sum the individual DP₄₊ responses from the normalized printout to obtain the total DP₄₊ normalized response.

Calculate the response factors:

$$R_I = \text{(known concentration, dry basis \%)/(measured concentration, normalized \%)}$$

R_I = response factor for component i

Compute the response factor for each component relative to glucose (R'_I):

$$R'_I = R_I/R_G$$

R'_I = response factor relative to glucose for component i
R_I = response factor for component i
R_G = response factor for glucose

The R'_I for DP₄₊ should be programmed as a default value (if automated equipment is used) and used to compute the concentration of higher saccharides.

Analysis: Inject a volume of the *Sample solution* into the chromatograph and record the resulting chromatogram.

Calculate the concentration of each component:

$$C_I = (A_I \times R_I \times 100)/(\Sigma A_N R_N)$$

C_I = concentration of component i
A_I = peak area recorded for component i
R_I = response factor for component i
$\Sigma A_N R_N$ = sum of the product of the areas (A) and response factors (R) for all components detected

Acceptance criteria
Fructose: 35%–45%, calculated on the dry basis
Leucrose: 7%–15%, calculated on the dry basis
Higher saccharides and polymer: NLT 40%, calculated on the dry basis
DP₂: NMT 5%, calculated on the dry basis

IMPURITIES
Inorganic Impurities
- **LEAD,** *Lead Limit Test, Atomic Absorption Spectrophotometric Graphite Furnace Method, Method I,* Appendix IIIB
    Sample: 5 g
    Acceptance criteria: NMT 0.1 mg/kg
- **SULFUR DIOXIDE,** *Sulfur Dioxide Determination,* Appendix X
    Sample: 50 g
    [NOTE—Alternately, the following method may be used.]
    Solution A: Dissolve 40 g of potassium iodide in 200 mL of water in a 1-L volumetric flask. Allow the solution to come to room temperature, add 12.7 g of

---
[1] Aldrich Chemical Company.
[2] Such as the one described in *Standard Analytical Methods of the Corn Refiners Association,* available from the Corn Refiners Association, Washington, DC.

crystalline iodine, and stir until the iodine is completely dissolved. Add 3 drops of concentrated hydrochloric acid, and dilute with water to volume. Mix the solution thoroughly, and store in an actinic glass bottle.

Solution B: Dilute 2 mL of *Solution A* with water to 100 mL (0.002 N iodine).

Indicator solution: Prepare a slurry of 10 g of soluble starch (Lintner) in 50 mL of cold water. Quantitatively transfer the slurry to 1 L of boiling water and stir, with boiling, until dissolved. Allow the solution to cool to room temperature before use.

Sample: 50 g

Analysis: Transfer the *Sample* to a 250-mL beaker, add 75 mL of water, and mix well. Transfer the solution to a 250-mL Erlenmeyer flask, and cool to 25°. Add 10 mL of cold 1.3 N potassium hydroxide to the flask, and stir, then immediately add 10 mL of cold 1.5 N sulfuric acid, and stir. Add a few drops of the *Indicator solution*, and titrate immediately with *Solution B* until the blue color remains for 30 s. Perform a blank titration (see *General Provisions*).

Calculate the sulfur dioxide content, in ppm, of the sample:

$$\text{Result} = (V_U - V_B) \times N_I \times F_1 \times (1/W_U) \times F_2$$

V_U = volume of titrant required for the sample titration (mL)
V_B = volume of titrant required for the blank titration (mL)
N_I = normality of the iodine solution, *Solution B*
F_1 = milliequivalent weight of sulfur dioxide $(64.071/2 \times 1000)$, 0.032
W_U = weight of the *Sample* (g)
F_2 = factor converting g to mg and g to kg, 1,000,000

Acceptance criteria: NMT 5 ppm

SPECIFIC TESTS

- **MOISTURE**

    Filter aid: Use a celite diatomite filter aid such as Hyflo Super-Cel,[3] or equivalent. [NOTE—Do not substitute an "acid-washed" diatomaceous earth filter aid.] Wash a large quantity of the filter aid by percolation on a Buchner funnel with water acidified with hydrochloric acid (1 mL of concentrated hydrochloric acid per L of water). Continue washing until the effluent is acid to litmus, then wash the filter aid with water until the effluent is pH 4 or above. Air dry the washed filter aid for storage. Before use, dry a quantity of the prepared filter aid overnight in an oven maintained at 105°, then store in a closed container.

    Sample: Amount of material equivalent to 4–7 g of dry substance

    Apparatus: Use a vacuum oven with uniform heat distribution and that is capable of maintaining the vacuum for several hours when the pump is shut off. The air inlet of the oven should be attached to a drying tower filled with a calcium sulfate desiccant with added moisture indicator.[4] The tower should be connected in series to a gas scrubber containing concentrated sulfuric acid.

    Stirrers: Use 100-mm × 13-mm borosilicate glass test tubes equipped with extensions. The extensions should be made from 8-mm × 180-mm stainless steel rods. Near one end of each rod, place two rubber rings (use appropriately-sized rubber o-rings or rings cut from rubber tubing) spaced such that when the rod is inserted into the test tube, it fits snugly at the top and bottom of the tube.

    Analysis: Transfer about 30 g of *Filter aid* to a 3-in diameter aluminum drying dish. Use dishes that are about 3.5-in high that are fitted with aluminum lids. Prepare two dishes: one for the sample analysis and one for a blank. Place one of the test tube *Stirrers* (without the stainless steel rod) in each sample dish. Dry the dishes uncovered in the vacuum oven described under *Apparatus* at 100° and NMT 25 torr while bleeding a small current of air through the oven and its drying tower. Continue drying for 5 h, then shut off the vacuum, and allow the oven to slowly fill with air drawn through the drying tower. Open the oven, quickly cover the dishes with their lids, then place the dishes in a desiccator, and allow them to cool to room temperature before weighing. Once the dishes are completely cooled, remove them from the desiccator, release the closure, and immediately weigh. Record all weights to the nearest mg.

    Weigh the *Sample* into a 45-mL weighing bottle equipped with a cap style ground glass stopper. Add 10 mL of warm water, and stir with a glass rod. Pour the diluted material onto the prepared *Filter aid* in one of the aluminum weighing dishes, using three 5-mL portions of warm water to assist the quantitative transfer. Insert the steel extension rod described in *Stirrers* into the sample dish, and stir until the mixture is homogenous and evenly dispersed. Remove the rod from the test tube, leaving the stirring tube in the dish. Place dishes for the blank and the sample, uncovered, in the vacuum oven. [NOTE—Set the oven at 70° for samples with a DE of over 58 (and for all samples containing fructose) and at 100° for samples with a DE of 58 and below.] Allow the materials to dry for 5 h in the vacuum oven, then remove the dishes from the oven. Re-insert the stainless steel rods into the test tube *Stirrers*, and stir the material in the dish until a fine powder free of lumps is obtained. Return the dishes to the oven, and continue heating for an additional 15–16 h. Once the heating period is over, shut off the vacuum line and allow the oven to slowly fill with air drawn through the drying tower. Open the oven, quickly cover the dishes with their lids, then place the dishes in a desiccator, and allow them to cool to room temperature before weighing. Once the dishes are completely cooled, remove them from the desiccator, release the closure, and immediately weigh. Record all weights to the nearest mg, and calculate the percent moisture in the *Sample*.

    Acceptance criteria: NMT 30.0%

- **pH,** *pH Determination,* Appendix IIB

    Sample solution: 10% (w/w)

---

[3] Available from Johns-Manville Products Corp., Lompoc, CA.
[4] Drierite®, or equivalent.

Analysis: Proceed as directed using pH 4.00 and 7.00 standard buffer solutions to calibrate the pH meter.
Acceptance criteria: 3.5–6.0

Sucrose

First Published: Prior to FCC 6

Sugar
Granulated Sugar
Cane Sugar
Beet Sugar
β-D-Fructofuranosyl-α-D-glucopyranoside

$C_{12}H_{22}O_{11}$ Formula wt 342.30
                                        CAS: [57-50-1]
UNII: C151H8M554 [sucrose]

DESCRIPTION
Sucrose, in its processed form, occurs as a white, crystalline solid. It is obtained for commercial use from sugar cane and sugar beets. It is very soluble in water, in formamide, and in dimethyl sulfoxide and is slightly soluble in ethanol.
Function: Nutritive sweetener; formulation and texturizing aid
Packaging and Storage: Store in tight containers in a dry place.
[NOTE—Consult ICUMSA[1] rules for further details applying to *Assay*, *Color*, and *Invert Sugar*.]

IDENTIFICATION
- **OPTICAL (SPECIFIC) ROTATION**
  Acceptance criteria: A sample meets the requirements under *Optical (Specific) Rotation* (below).

ASSAY
- **PROCEDURE**
  Apparatus: Use a saccharimeter calibrated with a certified quartz plate according to the directions of the instrument manufacturer and a 20-cm polarimeter tube with cover glasses. The tube and glasses should conform to ICUMSA specifications. Have ready 100-mL flasks accurate to within 0.01 mL. Maintain a water bath at 20° ± 0.1°.
  Sample solution: Quantitatively transfer 26.000 ± 0.002 g of sample to a 100-mL flask accurate to within 0.01 mL. Add 80 mL of water to the flask and, without heating, dissolve the sample by agitation, and add water to the flask to just below the calibration mark. Place the flask in the water bath to adjust the solution to 20° ± 0.1°. Dry the inside wall of the flask neck above the calibration mark with filter paper, and, using either a hypodermic syringe or a pipet with a drawn out point, adjust to the exact volume with water. Seal the flask with a clean, dry stopper, and mix the contents thoroughly by shaking.
  Analysis: Carefully rinse the polarimeter tube twice using two-thirds its volume of *Sample solution*, and fill it with *Sample solution* at 20° ± 0.1° in such a way that no air bubbles are trapped. Place the tube in the saccharimeter, and polarize it at 20°. Determine five values to 0.05 °Z, and record the average of these values.
  Acceptance criteria: NLT 99.8 and NMT 100.2 International Sugar Degrees (°Z)

IMPURITIES
Inorganic Impurities
- **ARSENIC**, *Arsenic Limit Test*, Appendix IIIB
  Sample: 1 g
  Standard solution: 1 μg of As (1 mL of *Standard Arsenic Solution*)
  Acceptance criteria: NMT 1 mg/kg
- **LEAD**, *Lead Limit Test, Atomic Absorption Spectrophotometric Graphite Furnace Method, Method I*, Appendix IIIB
  Sample: 10 g
  Acceptance criteria: NMT 0.1 mg/kg

Organic Impurities
- **INVERT SUGAR**
  Apparatus: Use a water bath with vigorously boiling water to ensure that the immersion of flasks does not interrupt the boiling. When instructed, place flasks in the water bath so that the water level is 2 cm above the liquid surface in the flasks.
  Muller's solution: Dissolve 35 g of cupric sulfate pentahydrate in 400 mL of boiling water. In a separate beaker, dissolve 173 g of potassium sodium tartrate tetrahydrate and 68 g of anhydrous sodium carbonate in 400 mL of boiling water. Cool both solutions and, while stirring, pour the sodium carbonate-potassium sodium tartrate solution into the cupric sulfate solution. Transfer the combined solutions into a 1000-mL volumetric flask, dilute to volume with water, and mix. Add 2 g of activated carbon, shake vigorously, and filter through hardened filter paper under vacuum. If cuprous oxide precipitates during storage, refilter the solution.
  Standardized iodine solution: Dissolve about 4.7 g of iodine in a solution of 6 g of iodate-free potassium iodide in 100 mL of water, add 3 drops of hydrochloric acid and dilute with water to 1000 mL. Standardize to 0.0333 N as directed for *0.1 N Iodine* in *Volumetric Solutions*, Solutions and Indicators. Adjust the normality repeatedly, if necessary.
  Standardized sodium thiosulfate solution: Dissolve about 8.7 g of sodium thiosulfate pentahydrate ($Na_2S_2O_3 \cdot 5H_2O$) and 67 mg of sodium carbonate in 1000 mL of freshly boiled and cooled water. Add 3 mL of 1.0 N sodium hydroxide. This solution contains 5.54 g of sodium thiosulfate ($Na_2S_2O_3$). Standardize to 0.0333 N as directed for *0.1 N Sodium Thiosulfate* in *Volumetric Solutions*, Solutions and Indicators. Adjust the normality repeatedly, if necessary.

---
[1] International Commission for Uniform Methods of Sugar Analysis (ICUMSA) (www.icumsa.org).

Starch indicator solution: Dissolve 1 g of soluble starch in 100 mL of saturated sodium chloride solution.
Sample: 25 g
Analysis: Transfer the *Sample* into a 250-mL Erlenmeyer flask and add 100 mL of water. Dissolve, add 10 mL of *Muller's solution*, and mix well. Place the flask in a boiling water bath for 10 min ± 5 s. Remove the flask, place a small beaker over its neck, and cool rapidly, without agitation, under cold running water. Without agitation (to avoid the oxidation of cuprous oxide with air), acidify the solution with 5 mL of 5 N acetic acid, and immediately add an excess (about 20 to 40 mL) of *Standardized iodine solution*. Mix well and, when the precipitate is completely dissolved, titrate the excess iodine with *Standardized sodium thiosulfate solution*, adding a few drops of *Starch indicator solution* as the endpoint is approached. Determine a *Water blank* as well as a *Cold blank* by the same procedure, but for the *Cold blank*, allow the flask containing the sample solution to stand at room temperature for 10 min rather than placing it in the boiling water bath. Calculate the percent of invert sugar by the formula:

$$Result = [(V_I - V_S - B_W - B_S - 0.2W) \times 100]/W$$

V_I = volume of the *Standardized iodine solution* (mL)
V_S = volume of the *Standardized sodium thiosulfate solution* (mL)
B_W = volume of the *Standardized iodine solution* in the *Water blank* (mL)
B_S = volume of the *Standardized iodine solution* in the *Cold blank* (mL)
0.2 = volume correction factor (mL) used to correct for the reducing value of sucrose
W = weight of sample (g) used in the original test

Acceptance criteria: NMT 0.1%

SPECIFIC TESTS

- **COLOR**
  Apparatus: Use a suitable variable wavelength spectrophotometer capable of measuring percent transmittance at 420 nm or a photometer with a 420- ± 10-nm band width filter. The instrument design should permit the use of a 10-cm cell. When using an instrument with a reference cell, the two cells should be identical with water within ±0.2% when the instrument is set at 100% transmittance on one of the cells.
  Sample solution: 50% (w/w) in water
  Analysis: Adjust the pH of the *Sample solution* to 7.0 ± 0.2 with 1% sodium hydroxide or 1% hydrochloric acid. Filter through a 0.45-μm pore-size membrane filter, using a vacuum and a diatomaceous earth filter aid (1% on solids) if necessary. Discard the first portion of the filtrate if it is cloudy. Determine the density and concentration of solids, in g/mL, refractometrically. Rinse the measuring cell three times with the filtered *Sample solution*, and then fill the cell. Measure absorbance (A_S) at 420 nm. Calculate the color in ICUMSA units (IU) as follows:

$$IU = (A_S/bc) \times 1000$$

A_S = absorbance of the filtered *Sample solution*
b = cell length (cm)
c = concentration of total solids (g/mL) determined refractometrically and calculated from density

  Acceptance criteria: NMT 75 IU
- **LOSS ON DRYING,** Appendix IIC: forced-draft air oven at 105° for 3 h
  Sample: 5 g
  Acceptance criteria: NMT 0.1%
- **OPTICAL (SPECIFIC) ROTATION,** Appendix IIB
  Sample solution: Dissolve 26 g of sample in water, diluting to 100 mL at 20°.
  Analysis: Test as directed using a 20-cm polarimeter tube to determine the specific rotation.
  Acceptance criteria: $[\alpha]_D^{20}$ between +65.9° and +66.7°
- **RESIDUE ON IGNITION (SULFATED ASH),** Appendix IIC
  Sample: 1 g
  Acceptance criteria: NMT 0.15%

Sucrose Acetate Isobutyrate

First Published: Prior to FCC 6

SAIB

$C_{40}H_{62}O_{19}$ Formula wt 846.9 (range 832–856)
INS: 444   CAS: [27216-37-1]
                              [123-13-6]

UNII: H5KI1C3YTV [sucrose acetate isobutyrate]

DESCRIPTION

Sucrose Acetate Isobutyrate occurs as a clear, pale yellow, viscous liquid. It consists of a mixture of sucrose esters of acetic and isobutyric acid, with sucrose diacetate hexaisobutyrate being the predominant sucrose ester. It is produced through the controlled esterification of sucrose with acetic anhydride and isobutyric anhydride. It is very soluble in essential oils such as orange oil, soluble in ethanol and in ethyl acetate, and very slightly soluble in water.
Function: Stabilizer
Packaging and Storage: Store in well-closed containers.

IDENTIFICATION
- **INFRARED SPECTRA,** *Spectrophotometric Identification Tests,* Appendix IIIC
  Acceptance criteria: The spectrum of the sample exhibits relative maxima at the same wavelengths as those of the spectrum below.

ASSAY
- **PROCEDURE**
  Calculate the percentage of Sucrose Acetate Isobutyrate by the formula:

  Result = $[(S_V \times 0.10586)/56.1] \times 100\%$

  S_V = saponification value

  Acceptance criteria: NLT 98.8% and NMT 101.9% of $C_{40}H_{62}O_{19}$

IMPURITIES
Inorganic Impurities
- **LEAD,** *Lead Limit Test, Atomic Absorption Spectrophotometric Graphite Furnace Method II,* Appendix IIIB
  Acceptance criteria: NMT 1 mg/kg

SPECIFIC TESTS
- **ACID VALUE (FATS AND RELATED SUBSTANCES),** Method I, Appendix VII
  Acceptance criteria: NMT 0.2
- **SAPONIFICATION VALUE,** Appendix VII
  Acceptance criteria: NLT 524 and NMT 540

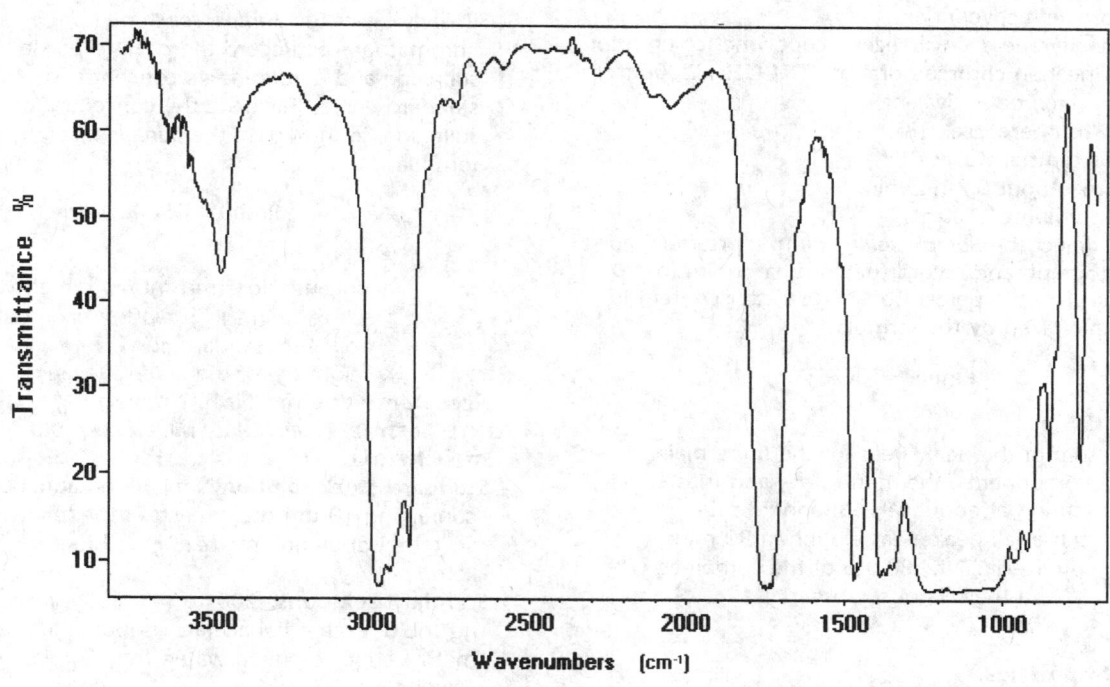

Sucrose Acetate Isobutyrate

Sucrose Fatty Acid Esters
First Published: Prior to FCC 6

Sucroesters
INS: 473

DESCRIPTION
Sucrose Fatty Acid Esters occur as stiff gels, soft solids, or white to slightly gray-white powders. They are the mono-, di-, and triesters of sucrose with edible fatty acids. They may be prepared from sucrose; the methyl and ethyl esters of edible fatty acids; or edible, naturally occurring vegetable oils in the presence of food-grade solvents such as ethyl acetate, methyl ethyl ketone, dimethylsulfoxide, or isobutanol. They are soluble in ethanol and, depending on the mono ester percentages, sparingly soluble in water.
Function: Emulsifier; stabilizer; texturizer
Packaging and Storage: Store in tight containers, and avoid high temperatures.

IDENTIFICATION
- **A. PROCEDURE**
  Sample: 0.1 g
  Analysis: To the *Sample*, add 1 mL of alcohol, dissolve by warming, add 5 mL of 2 N sulfuric acid, heat in a water bath for 30 min, and cool. [NOTE—Save a portion of the solution that is separated from the solid for *Identification* test *B* (below).]

Acceptance criteria: A yellow-white solid or oil forms that is soluble in 3 mL of ether.

- **B. Procedure**
  Sample: 2 mL of the solution separated from the solid in *Identification* test A
  Analysis: Transfer the *Sample* to a test tube and add 1 mL of anthrone TS carefully down the inside of the tube.
  Acceptance criteria: The boundary surface of the two layers turns to blue or green.

ASSAY
- **Procedure**
  Mobile phase: Tetrahydrofuran, HPLC-grade, degassed
  Sample solution: 5 mg/mL of sample in *Mobile phase*, filtered through a 0.5-μm membrane filter
  Chromatographic system, Appendix IIA
    Mode: High-performance liquid chromatography
    Detector: Refractive index
    Column: Styrene-divinylbenzene copolymer column for gel permeation chromatography (TSK-GEL G2000 from Supelco, Inc., or equivalent)
    Column temperature: 38°
    Detector temperature: 38°
    Flow rate: About 0.7 mL/min
    Injection volume: 100 μL
  Analysis: Inject the *Sample solution* into a prestabilized chromatograph and record the chromatogram for 90 min. Calculate the percent of sucrose ester content in the sample taken by the formula:

  $$Result = 100A/T$$

  A = sum of the peak areas for the three main components, the mono-, di-, and triesters eluting at about 65, 68, and 73 min
  T = sum of all peak areas eluting in 90 min
  Acceptance criteria: NLT 80.0% of the combined mono-, di-, and triesters of sucrose

IMPURITIES
Inorganic Impurities
- **Lead,** *Lead Limit Test, Flame Atomic Absorption Spectrophotometric Method,* Appendix IIIB
  Sample: 10 g
  Acceptance criteria: NMT 2 mg/kg

Organic Impurities
- **Dimethyl Sulfoxide**
  Standard stock solution: 0.25 mg/mL of dimethyl sulfoxide in tetrahydrofuran
  Standard solutions: 0.005 mg/mL, 0.001 mg/mL, and 0.0005 mg/mL of dimethyl sulfoxide in tetrahydrofuran: from *Standard stock solution*
  Sample: 5 g
  Sample solution: Transfer the *Sample* into a 25-mL volumetric flask, dilute with tetrahydrofuran to volume, and mix.
  Chromatographic system, Appendix IIA
    Mode: Gas chromatography
    Detector: Flame photometric detector with a 394-nm sulfur filter
    Column: 2-m × 3-mm (id) glass column packed with a 10% PEG 20M and 3% potassium hydroxide on Gas Chrom Z, or equivalent
    Column temperature: 160°
    Injection port temperature: 210°
    Carrier gas: Nitrogen
    Flow rate: 50 mL/min
    Injection volume: 3 μL
  Analysis: [Note—Condition the column before use by raising the column temperature to 180° at a rate of 1°/min and letting it stand for 24 to 48 h with nitrogen flowing at 30 to 40 mL/min.]
  Separately inject each of the *Standard solutions* into the gas chromatograph and record the resulting chromatograms. Prepare a calibration curve by plotting the concentration, in mg/mL, of each *Standard solution* versus its peak response, and draw the best straight line.
  Similarly inject the *Sample solution* into the chromatograph. Record the peak response for dimethyl sulfoxide and determine its concentration from the standard curve. Calculate the concentration of dimethyl sulfoxide, in mg/kg, in the *Sample* taken by the formula:

  $$Result = 2500C/W$$

  C = concentration (mg/mL) of dimethyl sulfoxide in the *Sample solution* determined from the standard curve
  W = weight (g) of the *Sample* taken
  Acceptance criteria: NMT 2 mg/kg

- **Ethyl Acetate, Isobutanol, Methanol, and Methyl Ethyl Ketone**
  Standard stock solution: Prepare an aqueous solution containing 10 mg/mL of each of the following: ethyl acetate, isobutanol, methanol, and methyl ethyl ketone.
  Standard solutions: 200 μg/mL, 300 μg/mL, and 400 μg/mL of each ethyl acetate, isobutanol, methanol, and methyl ethyl ketone in water: from *Standard stock solution*
  Sample solution: Transfer 1 g of powdered sample into a sample vial, add 5 μL of water, and seal the vial immediately with a septum.
  Chromatographic system, Appendix IIA
    Mode: Gas chromatography using an instrument equipped with a headspace sampler
    Detector: Flame ionization
    Column: 30-m × 0.53-mm (id) silica capillary column coated with 100% methylpolysiloxane (brand name, or equivalent)
    Temperature
      Column: 40°
      Injection port: 110°
      Detector: 110°
      Headspace sampler: 80°
      Syringe: 85°
    Carrier gas: Nitrogen
    Flow rate: 5 mL/min

Injection volume: 400 µL of the headspace volume from each solution

Analysis: [NOTE—Condition the column before use by heating it to 60° for 2 to 3 h with nitrogen flowing at approximately 10 mL/min.] Prepare a calibration curve by adding 5 µL of each of the *Standard solution*s to 1 g of sample in separate sample vials. Immediately seal each vial with a septum, and place them in the headspace sampler. Heat each vial at 80° for 40 min and introduce 400 µL of headspace into the gas chromatograph. Record the resulting detector responses and draw a calibration curve for each solvent by plotting the concentration, C_S, in mg/mL, of each solvent versus its corresponding detector response, r_S. Similarly place the vial containing the *Sample solution* in the headspace sampler, heat the vial at 80° for 40 min and introduce 400 µL of headspace into the gas chromatograph. Record the resulting detector responses and measure the detector response, r_U, for each solvent at retention times equivalent to those of the solvents in the *Standard solutions*. Using the detector responses of the *Sample solution* and the calibration curve for each solvent, calculate the concentration, in mg/kg, of each solvent in the sample by the formula:

$$Result = 1000C_S$$

C_S = concentration of each solvent in the *Sample solution* calculated from the solvent's respective calibration curve (mg/kg)

Acceptance criteria
  Ethyl acetate: NMT 350 mg/kg
  Isobutanol: NMT 10 mg/kg
  Methanol: NMT 10 mg/kg
  Methyl ethyl ketone: NMT 10 mg/kg

SPECIFIC TESTS
- **ACID VALUE,** Method I, Appendix VII
  Acceptance criteria: NMT 6
- **FREE SUCROSE**
  Mobile phase: Acetonitrile and water (85:15), degassed
  Standard solution: 10 mg/mL each of sucrose (reference standard material is available from NIST) and maltose (available from Sigma Chemical Co.) in water
  Sample solution: Transfer 5 g of sample into a 100-mL separatory funnel. Add 1.000 g of maltose and 50 mL of a warm mixture of chloroform:methanol:water (1:2:1) and shake gently to dissolve. Add 10 mL of chloroform and shake, then add 10 mL of water and 0.2 mL of 2 N hydrochloric acid and shake. Allow the layers to separate, then discard the bottom layer that contains fatty acids and sucrose esters. Quantitatively transfer the upper aqueous layer into a 100-mL volumetric flask that contains 0.3 mL of 2.5% ammonium hydroxide. Wash the separatory funnel with *Mobile phase*, adding the washings to the volumetric flask. Dilute to volume with the *Mobile phase,* and mix.
  Chromatographic system, Appendix IIA
    Mode: High-performance liquid chromatography
    Detector: Refractive index
    Column: 4.6-mm × 250-mm aminopropyl column (5 µm Spherisorb NH$_2$, or equivalent)
    Flow rate: 1.3 mL/min
    Injection volume: 20 µL
  Analysis: Separately inject the *Standard solution* and the *Sample solution* into the chromatograph and record the chromatograms. Note the retention times of the two major peaks exhibited by the *Standard solution*, and calculate the ratio of the response of sucrose to that of the internal standard maltose. Calculate the quantity, in mg, of sucrose in the portion of sample taken by the formula:

$$Result = 100C\,(R_U/R_S)$$

  C = concentration (mg/mL) of sucrose in the *Standard solution*
  R_U = peak response ratio of sucrose to maltose obtained from the *Sample solution*
  R_S = peak response ratio of sucrose to maltose obtained from the *Standard solution*
  Acceptance criteria: NMT 5.0%
- **RESIDUE ON IGNITION (SULFATED ASH),** Appendix IIC
  Sample: 1 g
  Acceptance criteria: NMT 2.0%

Sugar Beet Fiber

First Published: Prior to FCC 6
Last Revision: FCC 7

Beet Fiber
Dietary Fiber from Beets
Sugar Beet Pulp
UNII: 3CK0EOO6FA [beta vulgaris fiber]

DESCRIPTION
Sugar Beet Fiber occurs in various grades, from coarse fibrous flakes to fine, free-flowing powders. It is the natural, light brown colored fiber of sugar beets remaining after water extraction of the sugar from the mechanically sliced sugar beets.

Function: Anticaking agent; binding agent; bulking agent; dispersing agent; source of dietary fiber; stabilizing agent; texturizing agent; thickening agent

Packaging and Storage: Store in well-closed containers.

IDENTIFICATION
- **ABSENCE OF STARCH**
  Sample: 10 g
  Analysis: Boil the *Sample* in 90 mL of water for 5 min, filter while hot through No. 616 filter paper, and add 5 drops of iodine TS to the filtrate.
  Acceptance criteria: No change in color from the yellow-red to red-yellow is produced.
- **PRESENCE OF SOLUBLE FIBER**
  Sample: 5 g (Grind coarse grades so a major portion will pass through a 60-mesh screen.)

Analysis: Add 95 mL of water to the *Sample*, and mix. Heat to boiling and filter while hot. Add 1 mL of 1 N sodium hydroxide to 5 mL of cooled filtrate, mix, and allow it to stand at room temperature for 15 min. [NOTE—Retain filtrate for the test for *Presence of Residual Sucrose*.]

Acceptance criteria: A thick, yellow gel forms that dissolves upon the addition of a few drops of 6 N hydrochloric acid.

- **PRESENCE OF RESIDUAL SUCROSE**

  Sample solution: 5 mL of cooled filtrate from the test for *Presence of Soluble Fiber*

  α-Naphthol solution: Mix 1.25 g of α-naphthol with 25 mL of methanol.

  Analysis: Add a few drops of *α-Naphthol solution* to a test tube containing the *Sample solution*, and mix. Carefully layer sulfuric acid down the side of the test tube.

  Acceptance criteria: A purple color change occurs at the interface.

ASSAY

- **FIBER, TOTAL AND SOLUBLE**

  [NOTE—This method is taken from the *Official Methods of Analysis*, 16th edition, chapter 32, pp. 7–9, method number 991.43. 1995. AOAC INTERNATIONAL.]

  [NOTE—Verify that all enzymes used in this procedure exhibit not less than 95% of their declared activities using the tests given in *Enzyme Assays*, Appendix V.]

  Mixed 8.2 buffer solution: Mix equal volumes of 0.1 M 2-(*N*-morpholino) ethanesulfonic acid and 0.1 M tris-(hydroxymethyl) aminomethane (TRIS) and carefully adjust the pH to 8.2 at 24°, using 6 N sodium hydroxide as necessary. If the buffer temperature differs from 24°, adjust the pH by interpolation from a high of 8.3 at 20° to a low of 8.1 at 28°.

  Protease solution: 50 mg/mL of protease[1] in *Mixed 8.2 buffer solution*, freshly prepared

  Filtering crucibles: Prepare a set of 60-mL filtering crucibles, each with a coarse fritted disk,[2] as follows: Ignite the crucibles overnight at 525° in a muffle furnace. Allow the temperature to fall below 130° before removing them from the furnace. Treat each crucible as follows: Soak it for 1 h at room temperature in a 2% cleaning solution containing a liquid surfactant-type laboratory cleaner. At the end of the hour, rinse the crucible with water, deionized water, and 15 mL of acetone. Allow it to air dry and add about 1 g of diatomaceous earth,[3] packing it down firmly. Dry it at 130° to constant weight, cooling in a desiccator between weighings.

  Sample preparation: Transfer 1 g of sample into each of four 400-mL beakers and add 40 mL of *Mixed 8.2 buffer solution* to each beaker. To four additional beakers, add 40 mL of *Mixed 8.2 buffer solution* to serve as blanks. Treat each of the 8 beakers as follows: Stir the solution magnetically until the sample is totally dispersed. Add 50 μL of heat-stable α-amylase solution[4] to the beaker. Cover the beaker with aluminum foil, place it on a water bath and, while stirring, incubate at 95° to 100° for 15 min. (Start the timing when the temperature reaches 95°.) Remove the beaker from the bath and cool to 60°. Uncover the beaker. With a spatula, scrape any ring on the inside wall of the beaker and disperse any gels formed at the bottom of the beaker. Rinse the beaker walls and spatula with 10 mL of water. Add 100 μL of *Protease solution* to the beaker, cover with aluminum foil, and, while continuously stirring, incubate the mixture at 60° for 30 min. (Start the timing when the temperature of the solution reaches 60°.) Uncover the beaker, continue stirring, and immediately add 5 mL of 0.5 N hydrochloric acid. While maintaining the temperature at 60°, adjust the pH to between 4.0 and 4.7 using either 1 N hydrochloric acid or sodium hydroxide. [NOTE—Because the pH is temperature dependent, check and adjust the pH when the solution is at 60°.] Next, while stirring, add 300 μL of amyloglucosidase solution.[5] Cover, and incubate the mixture at 60° for 30 min with constant agitation. (Start the timing when the mixture reaches 60°.)

  Determination of total fiber: To each of two prepared samples and two blanks (prepared above under *Sample preparation*), add 225 mL of 78% ethanol, still maintained at 60°. [NOTE—One prepared sample will be used to determine nitrogen content and the other prepared sample to determine ash.] Remove the four beakers from the bath, cover them, and allow them to stand at room temperature for 1 h for complete precipitation. For each of the prepared samples and blanks: Wet and redistribute the Celite bed in a previously prepared and tared filtering crucible, using 15 mL of 78% ethanol to wash the sides of the crucible. Apply suction to draw the Celite onto the fritted disk as an even mat. Filter an alcohol-treated sample through the crucible, quantitatively transferring all particles to the crucible with the help of a spatula and a wash bottle containing 78% ethanol. If a gum forms, break the film with the spatula. Wash the residue in the filtering crucible successively with two 15-mL portions of 78% ethanol, 95% ethanol, and acetone, applying a vacuum after each wash. Dry the filtering crucible and its contents at 105° to constant weight. Use the residue from one prepared sample to determine the nitrogen content as directed under *Nitrogen Determination*, Appendix IIIC. The weight of nitrogen determined, multiplied by 6.25, gives the weight of protein. Use the residue from the second prepared sample for determination of ash (see *Ash (Total)*, below). The weight of each sample residue, corrected for the blank, protein, and ash, is equal to the weight of the total fiber (see *Calculations*, below).

  Determination of soluble fiber: Using about 3 mL of water, wet and redistribute the Celite bed in each of four filtering crucibles, applying suction to draw the Celite into an even mat. Treat the second set of

---

[1] Sigma Chemical Co. catalog number P 3910, or equivalent.
[2] Corning No. 36060-60C Pyrex Büchner funnel, 40- to 60-μm pore size, or equivalent.
[3] Celite 545 AW, or equivalent.
[4] Sigma Chemical Co. catalog number A 3306, or equivalent.
[5] Sigma Chemical Co., catalog number AMG A 9913, or equivalent.

duplicate prepared samples and blanks in the following manner: Filter each through a filtering crucible, collecting the filtrate and subsequent washings. Using water maintained at 70°, rinse the beaker, and wash the residue with two 10-mL portions of the hot water. Discard the residue and transfer the combined filtrate and all washings to a tared 600-mL beaker. Weigh the beaker to obtain an estimate of the volume of the contents. Add four volumes of 95% ethanol maintained at 60° and allow the beaker to stand at room temperature for 1 h for complete precipitation.

Wet and redistribute the Celite bed of another previously prepared and tared filtering crucible, using 15 mL of 78% ethanol to wash the sides of the crucible. Apply suction to draw the Celite onto the fritted disk as an even mat. Filter the contents of the beaker through the crucible, quantitatively transferring all particles to the crucible with the help of a spatula and a wash bottle containing 78% ethanol. If a gum forms, break the film with the spatula. Wash the residue in the crucible successively with two 15-mL portions of 78% ethanol, 95% ethanol, and acetone, applying a vacuum after each wash. Dry the crucible and its contents at 105° to constant weight.

Use the residue from one prepared sample to determine the nitrogen content as directed under *Nitrogen Determination*, Appendix IIIC. The weight of nitrogen determined, multiplied by 6.25, gives the weight of protein. Use the residue from the second prepared sample for determination of ash (see *Ash (Total)*, below). The weight of each sample residue, corrected for the blank, protein, and ash, is equal to the weight of soluble fiber (see *Calculations*, below).

Calculations: Determine the blank, B (mg) using the formula:

$$B = [(BR_1 + BR_2)/2] - P_S - A_S$$

BR_1 = residue weight of blank determination 1 (mg)
BR_2 = residue weight of blank determination 2 (mg)
P_S = weight of protein, determined in the first blank residue (mg)
A_S = weight of ash, determined in the second blank residue (mg)

Determine the percent of fiber (F), both total fiber and soluble fiber, using the formula:

$$F = \{[(R_1 + R_2)/2] - P - A - B\}/[(M_1 + M_2)/2] \times 100$$

R_1 = residue weight of sample 1 (mg)
R_2 = residue weight of sample 2 (mg)
P = weight of protein, determined for the first residue (mg)
A = weight of ash, determined for the second residue (mg)
B = weight of the blank (mg)
M_1 = weight of sample 1 corrected for *Loss on Drying* (mg)
M_2 = weight of sample 2 corrected for *Loss on Drying* (mg)

Acceptance criteria: NLT 62.0% total fiber, and NLT 20.0% soluble fiber, calculated on the dried basis

IMPURITIES
Inorganic Impurities
- **LEAD**, *Lead Limit Test, Atomic Absorption Spectrophotometric Graphite Furnace Method, Method I,* Appendix IIIB
  Acceptance criteria: NMT 1 mg/kg

SPECIFIC TESTS
- **ASH (TOTAL)**, Appendix IIC
  Sample: The residue obtained from one of the digested samples obtained under *Determination of Total Fiber* in the *Assay*
  Acceptance criteria: NMT 6.0%
- **LOSS ON DRYING**, Appendix IIC: 105° for 5 h
  Acceptance criteria: NMT 10.0%
- **PH**, *pH Determination*, Appendix IIB
  Sample dispersion: Mix 10 g of sample with 90 mL of water and allow to stand at room temperature for 2 h before testing.
  Acceptance criteria: Between 4.0 and 5.0

Sulfur Dioxide

First Published: Prior to FCC 6

SO_2
INS: 220
UNII: 0UZA3422Q4 [sulfur dioxide]

Formula wt 64.06
CAS: [7446-09-5]

DESCRIPTION
Sulfur Dioxide occurs as a colorless, nonflammable gas under normal conditions of temperature and pressure. It is shipped as a liquid under pressure in containers approved by the U.S. Department of Transportation. Its vapor density is 2.26 times that of air at atmospheric pressure and 0°. The specific gravity of the liquid is about 1.436 at 0°/4°. At 20° the solubility is about 10 g of Sulfur Dioxide per 100 g of solution.

[**CAUTION**—Sulfur dioxide gas is intensely irritating to the eyes, throat, and upper respiratory system. Liquid sulfur dioxide may cause skin burns, which result from the freezing effect of the liquid on tissue. Safety precautions to be observed in handling the material are specified in "Pamphlet G-3" published by the Compressed Gas Association, 4221 Walney Road, Fifth Floor, Chantilly, VA 20151-2923.]

Function: Antioxidant; bleaching agent; preservative
Packaging and Storage: Store in suitable pressure containers, observing applicable federal regulations pertaining to shipping containers.

[NOTE—Samples of sulfur dioxide may be safely withdrawn from a tank or from transfer lines, either of which should be equipped with a 3/8-in. nozzle and valve. Samples should be placed in sample cylinders constructed of 316 stainless steel, designed to withstand 1000 psig and equipped with 316 stainless-steel needle valves on both ends. To draw a sample, flush the sample cylinder with dry air to remove any sulfur dioxide remaining from previous sample drawings, and attach it to the tank or transfer lines with a solid pipe connection. Connect a hose to the other end of the sample cylinder, and submerge it in either a weak caustic solution or water. Discharge any gas in the sample cylinder into the caustic solution or water by first opening the valve at the pipe end, followed by slowly opening the valve at the hose end. When all of the gas is dispelled and liquid sulfur dioxide begins to emerge into the solution, block off the valve at the hose end. Tightly close the other valves, and detach the sample cylinder from the pipe connecting it to the tank or transfer line. Discharge approximately 15% of the liquid sulfur dioxide from the sample cylinder into the water or caustic solution. Cap the sample cylinder at its end, and transfer it to the laboratory for analysis.]

[CAUTION—Never store a sample cylinder containing an amount of gas equivalent to more than 85% of the total water capacity of the sample cylinder.]

IDENTIFICATION
- **SULFITE,** Appendix IIIA
  Sample solution: Saturated solution in water
  Acceptance criteria: Passes tests

ASSAY
- **PROCEDURE**
  Analysis: Subtract from 100 the percentages of *Nonvolatile Residue* and of *Water*, as determined below, to obtain the percentage of SO_2.
  Acceptance criteria: NLT 99.9% of SO_2 by weight

IMPURITIES
Inorganic Impurities
- **LEAD,** *Lead Limit Test,* Appendix IIIB
  Sample: 144 g, obtained by weighing the sample cylinder, transferring 100 mL of sample into a 125-mL Erlenmeyer flask, and reweighing the sample cylinder
  Sample stock solution: Evaporate the *Sample* contained in the flask to dryness on a steam bath, add 3 mL of nitric acid and 10 mL of water, and warm the solution gently on a hot plate for 15 min. Transfer the contents of the flask into a 100-mL volumetric flask, dilute to volume with water, and mix. Transfer a 10.0-mL aliquot into a second 100-mL volumetric flask, dilute to volume with water, and mix.
  Sample solution: Dilute 7.0 mL of the *Sample stock solution* to 40 mL
  Control: 2 µg Pb (2 mL of *Diluted Standard Lead Solution*)
  Acceptance criteria: NMT 2 mg/kg
- **SELENIUM,** *Selenium Limit Test, Method II,* Appendix IIIB
  Sample solution: 2 mL of the *Sample stock solution* prepared for the *Lead* analysis
  Acceptance criteria: NMT 0.002% by weight
- **WATER,** *Water Determination, Method I,* Appendix IIB
  Sample: 50 mL of liquid *Sulfur Dioxide*
  Analysis: Transfer the *Sample* into a Karl Fischer titration jar, determine the weight of the *Sample* taken, and proceed as directed.
  Acceptance criteria: NMT 0.05% by weight

SPECIFIC TESTS
- **NONVOLATILE RESIDUE**
  Sample: 288 g, obtained by weighing the sample cylinder, transferring 200 mL of sample into a tared 250-mL Erlenmeyer flask, and reweighing the sample cylinder
  Analysis: Evaporate the *Sample* contained in the flask to dryness on a steam bath, and displace the residual vapors with dry air. Wipe the flask dry, cool in a desiccator, and weigh.
  Acceptance criteria: NMT 0.05% by weight

Sulfuric Acid
First Published: Prior to FCC 6

H_2SO_4 Formula wt 98.07
INS: 513   CAS: [7664-93-9]
UNII: O40UQP6WCF [sulfuric acid]

DESCRIPTION
Sulfuric Acid occurs as a clear, colorless or slightly brown, oily liquid. It is very caustic and corrosive. It is miscible with water and with alcohol with the generation of much heat and contraction in volume. Sulfuric Acid should be added cautiously to the diluent when mixed with other liquids. Some commercially available concentrations of Sulfuric Acid are expressed in degrees Baumé (°Bé) and others (above 93.0%) as a percentage of H_2SO_4. The more common concentrations are 60 °Bé and 66 °Bé, equivalent to 77.67% and 93.19% of H_2SO_4, respectively, and 98.0% of H_2SO_4. Its specific gravity varies with the concentration of H_2SO_4 (see *Sulfuric Acid Table,* Appendix IIC).
Function: Acidifier
Packaging and Storage: Store in tight containers.

IDENTIFICATION
- **SULFATE,** Appendix IIIA
  Acceptance criteria: Passes tests

ASSAY
- **PROCEDURE**
  Sample: 1 mL
  Analysis: Transfer the *Sample* into a small, tared glass-stoppered Erlenmeyer flask; insert the stopper; accurately weigh; and cautiously add about 30 mL of water. Cool the mixture, add methyl orange TS, and titrate with 1 N sodium hydroxide. Each mL of 1 N sodium hydroxide is equivalent to 49.04 mg of H_2SO_4. [NOTE—For samples with concentrations below 93.0%, expressed in degrees Baumé, transfer about 200 mL of sample, previously cooled to a temperature below 15°, into a 250-mL hydrometer cylinder. Insert a suitable Baumé hydrometer graduated at 0.1 °Bé intervals, adjust the temperature of the sample to exactly 15.6°, and note the reading at the bottom of the meniscus, estimating it to the nearest 0.05 °Bé. Determine the equivalent percentage of H_2SO_4 from the *Sulfuric Acid Table,* Appendix IIC.]

Acceptance criteria: NLT the minimum or within the range of °Bé or the percentage of H₂SO₄ claimed or implied by the vendor

IMPURITIES
Inorganic Impurities
- **ARSENIC,** Arsenic Limit Test, Appendix IIIB
  Sample solution: 1 g of sample in 35 mL of water
  Control: 3 µg As (3 mL of Standard Arsenic Solution) mixed with 1 g of ACS reagent-grade sulfuric acid
  Acceptance criteria: NMT 3 mg/kg
- **CHLORIDE,** Chloride and Sulfate Limit Tests, Chloride Limit Test, Appendix IIIB
  Sample solution: Transfer an amount of sample equivalent to 5 g of sulfuric acid into a 50-mL volumetric flask and dissolve in and dilute to volume with water. [NOTE—Retain the unused portion for the tests for Iron and Lead (below).]
  Control: 20 µg chloride (2.0 mL of Standard Chloride Solution)
  Acceptance criteria: Any turbidity produced by 4 mL of the Sample solution does not exceed that shown in the Control. (NMT 0.005%)
- **IRON**
  Sample: 1 mL of the Sample solution prepared in the test for Chloride (above)
  Control: 20 µg of iron (2.0 mL of Iron Standard Solution, Solutions and Indicators)
  Analysis: Dilute the Sample to 40 mL with water and add about 30 mg of ammonium persulfate crystals and 10 mL of ammonium thiocyanate TS to the solution. Repeat the preceding using the Control and compare the colors of the resulting solutions.
  Acceptance criteria: Any resulting red color produced by the Sample does not exceed in intensity that produced by the Control. (NMT 0.02%)
- **LEAD,** Lead Limit Test, Appendix IIIB
  Sample: 10 mL of the Sample solution prepared in the test for Chloride (above), diluted to 40 mL with water.
  Control: 5 µg Pb (5 mL of Diluted Standard Lead Solution)
  Acceptance criteria: NMT 5 mg/kg
- **NITRATE**
  Standard stock solution: Transfer 8.022 g of potassium nitrate, previously dried at 105° for 1 h, into a 500-mL volumetric flask, dissolve in and dilute to volume with water, and mix well.
  Standard solution: Slowly add 5.0 mL of the Standard stock solution from a buret into 400 mL of ACS reagent-grade sulfuric acid, previously cooled to 5°, keeping the tip of the buret below the surface of the acid. After the solution has reached room temperature, transfer it into a 500-mL volumetric flask, and dilute to volume with ACS reagent-grade sulfuric acid. This solution contains 100 µg/mL of nitric acid.
  Sample: 10 mL, previously cooled to between 10° and 15°
  Analysis: Transfer 50 mL of ACS reagent-grade sulfuric acid into each of two 100-mL Nessler tubes, slowly add 5 mL of a freshly prepared 100 mg/mL solution of ferrous sulfate heptahydrate, mix with a glass rod, and cool in an ice bath to between 10° and 15°. Add the Sample to one tube of the cooled mixture and dilute to 100 mL with ACS reagent-grade sulfuric acid chilled to about 10° to 15°. Add the Standard solution, dropwise, from a microburet into the second (control) tube, mixing frequently, until the color of solution in the control tube nearly matches that of the solution prepared for the Sample. Dilute the control solution to 100 mL with ACS reagent-grade sulfuric acid, and continue adding Standard solution to as exact a match in color intensity as possible when compared with the solution prepared for the Sample by looking down through both solutions against a white background illuminated by diffused light. Calculate the weight of sulfuric acid in the sample from the specific gravity and the volume taken (see Sulfuric Acid Table, Appendix IIC).
  Acceptance criteria: NMT 0.1 mL of the Standard solution is required for each g of sulfuric acid. (NMT 10 mg/kg)
- **REDUCING SUBSTANCES (AS SO₂)**
  Sample: 8 g
  Analysis: Carefully dilute the Sample with about 50 mL of ice-cold water, keeping the solution cool during the addition. Add 0.1 mL of 0.1 N potassium permanganate.
  Acceptance criteria: The solution remains pink for NLT 5 min.
- **SELENIUM,** Selenium Limit Test, Method II, Appendix IIIB
  Sample: 300 mg
  Acceptance criteria: The absorbance of the extract from the solution containing the Sample is NMT that from the Standard Preparation. (NMT 0.002%)

Sunflower Oil (Unhydrogenated)
First Published: Prior to FCC 6

CAS: [8008-31-9]

UNII: 3W1JG795YI [sunflower oil]

DESCRIPTION
Sunflower Oil (Unhydrogenated) occurs as a light amber colored oil. It is obtained from the seed of the sunflower plant Helianthus annuus (Fam. Asteraceae) by mechanical expression or solvent extraction. It is refined, bleached, and deodorized to substantially remove free fatty acids, phospholipids, color, odor and flavor components, and miscellaneous other non-oil materials. It is a liquid at 21° to 27°, but traces of wax may cause the oil to cloud, unless removed by winterization.
Function: Coating agent; texturizer
Packaging and Storage: Store in well-closed containers.

Sunflower Oil (Unhydrogenated)

IDENTIFICATION
- **FATTY ACID COMPOSITION,** Appendix VII
  Acceptance criteria: Unhydrogenated Sunflower Oil exhibits the following composition profile of fatty acids:

Fatty Acid	Weight % (Range)
<14	<0.1
14:0	<0.5
16:0	3.0–10
16:1	<1.0
18:0	1.0–10
18:1	14–65
18:2	20–75
18:3	<0.5
20:0	<1.0
20:1	<0.5
22:0	<1.0
22:1	<0.1
24:0	<0.4

IMPURITIES
Inorganic Impurities
- **LEAD,** *Lead Limit Test, Atomic Absorption Spectrophotometric Graphite Furnace Method II,* Appendix IIIB
  Acceptance criteria: NMT 0.1 mg/kg

SPECIFIC TESTS
- **COLD TEST,** Appendix VII
  Acceptance criteria: Passes test
- **COLOR (FATS AND RELATED SUBSTANCES),** Appendix VII
  Acceptance criteria: NMT 1.3 red
- **FREE FATTY ACIDS (AS OLEIC ACID),** *Free Fatty Acids,* Appendix VII
  Analysis: Use the following equivalence factor (e) in the formula given in the procedure under *Free Fatty Acids*, e = 28.2
  Acceptance criteria: NMT 0.1%
- **IODINE VALUE,** Appendix VII
  Acceptance criteria: Between 110 and 143
- **LINOLENIC ACID,** *Fatty Acid Composition,* Appendix VII
  Acceptance criteria: NMT 1.5%
- **PEROXIDE VALUE,** Appendix VII
  Acceptance criteria: NMT 10 mEq/kg
- **UNSAPONIFIABLE MATTER,** Appendix VII
  Acceptance criteria: NMT 1.5%
- **WATER,** *Water Determination, Method I,* Appendix IIB: Use 50 mL of chloroform to dissolve the sample, instead of 35 to 40 mL of methanol.
  Acceptance criteria: NMT 0.1%

Sunset Yellow[1]

First Published: Prior to FCC 6

Sunset Yellow FCF
CI 15985
Class: Monoazo

$C_{16}H_{10}N_2O_7S_2Na_2$ Formula wt 452.38
INS: 110
UNII: H77VEI93A8 [fd&c yellow no. 6]   CAS: [2783-94-0]

DESCRIPTION
Sunset Yellow occurs as a brown-orange powder or granules. It is principally the disodium salt of 6-hydroxy-5-[(4-sulfophenyl)azo]-2-naphthalene-sulfonic acid. The trisodium salt of 3-hydroxy-4-[(4-sulfophenyl)azo]-2,7-naphthalenedisulfonic acid may be added in small amounts. It dissolves in water to give a solution yellow-orange at neutrality or in acid and red-brown in base. When dissolved in concentrated sulfuric acid, it yields an orange solution that turns yellow when diluted with water. It is insoluble in ethanol.
Function: Color
Packaging and Storage: Store in well-closed containers.

IDENTIFICATION
- **PROCEDURE**
  Sample solution: 18.5 µg/mL
  Analysis: Adjust the pH of two aliquots of the *Sample solution* to pH 1 and pH 13. Measure the absorbance intensities (A) and wavelength maxima of these solutions with a suitable UV-visible spectrophotometer.
  Acceptance criteria
  pH 1: A = 1.1 at 480 nm
  pH 13: A = 0.46 at 443 nm, with a shoulder at about 500 nm

ASSAY
- **TOTAL COLOR,** *Color Determination, Methods I and II,* Appendix IIIC: Both methods must be used.
  Method I: Spectrophotometric
  Sample: 200 to 225 mg
  Analysis: Transfer the *Sample* into a 1-L volumetric flask; dissolve in and dilute to volume with water. Determine as directed at 484 nm using 0.054 L/(mg·cm) for the absorptivity (a) for Sunset Yellow.
  Method II: TiCl$_3$ Titration
  Sample: 0.2 g

---

[1] To be used or sold for use to color food that is marketed in the United States, this color additive must be from a batch that has been certified by the U.S. Food and Drug Administration (FDA). If it is not from an FDA-certified batch, it is not a permitted color additive for food use in the United States, even if it is compositionally equivalent. The name FD&C Yellow No. 6 can be applied only to FDA-certified batches of this color additive. Sunset Yellow is a common name given to the uncertified colorant. See the monograph entitled *FD&C Yellow No. 6* for directions for producing an FDA-certified batch.

Analysis: Determine as directed using 8.84 as the stoichiometric factor (F_S) for Sunset Yellow.
Acceptance criteria: The average of results obtained from *Methods I and II* is NLT 87.0% total coloring matters.

IMPURITIES
Inorganic Impurities
- **ARSENIC,** *Arsenic Limit Test,* Appendix IIIB
  Sample: Prepare as directed for organic compounds.
  Acceptance criteria: NMT 3 mg/kg
- **LEAD,** *Lead Limit Test,* Appendix IIIB
  Sample solution: Prepare as directed for organic compounds.
  Control: 10 µg Pb (10 mL of *Diluted Standard Lead Solution*)
  Acceptance criteria: NMT 10 mg/kg
- **MERCURY,** *Color Determination,* Appendix IIIC
  Acceptance criteria: NMT 1 mg/kg

Organic Impurities
- **UNCOMBINED INTERMEDIATES AND PRODUCTS OF SIDE REACTIONS,** *Color Determination, Method II,* Appendix IIIC
  Sample solution: 2.5 mg/mL in 0.1 M disodium borate ($Na_2B_4O_7$)
  Analysis: Use an injection volume of 20 µL for the *Sample solution.*
  Acceptance criteria
    4-Aminoazobenzene: NMT 0.05 mg/kg
    4-Aminobiphenyl: NMT 0.015 mg/kg
    Aniline: NMT 0.25 mg/kg
    Azobenzene: NMT 0.2 mg/kg
    Benzidine: NMT 0.001 mg/kg
    1,3-Diphenyltriazene: NMT 0.04 mg/kg
    1-(Phenylazo)-2-naphthalenol: NMT 10 mg/kg
    4-Aminobenzenesulfonic acid, Sodium salt: NMT 0.2%
    6-Hydroxy-2-naphthalenesulfonic acid, Sodium salt: NMT 0.3%
    6,6'-Oxybis[2-naphthalenesulfonic acid], Disodium salt: NMT 1%
    4,4'-(1-Triazene-1,3-diyl)bis-[benzenesulfonic acid], Disodium salt: NMT 0.1%
    Sum of 6-Hydroxy-5-(phenylazo)-2-naphthalenesulfonic acid, Sodium salt and 4-[(2-Hydroxy-1-naphthyl-enyl)azo]-benzenesulfonic acid, Sodium salt: NMT 1%
    Sum of 3-Hydroxy-4-[(4-sulfophenyl)azo]-2,7-naphthalenedisulfonic acid, Trisodium salt and other, higher sulfonated subsidiaries: NMT 5%

SPECIFIC TESTS
- **COMBINED TESTS**
  Tests:
    - LOSS ON DRYING (VOLATILE MATTER), *Color Determination,* Appendix IIIC
    - CHLORIDE, *Sodium Chloride, Color Determination,* Appendix IIIC
    - SULFATES (AS SODIUM SALTS), *Sodium Sulfate, Color Determination,* Appendix IIIC
  Acceptance criteria: NMT 13.0% in combination
- **ETHER EXTRACTS,** *Color Determination,* Appendix IIIC
  Acceptance criteria: NMT 0.2%
- **WATER-INSOLUBLE MATTER,** *Color Determination,* Appendix IIIC
  Acceptance criteria: NMT 0.2%

Synthetic Iron Oxide

First Published: Second Supplement, FCC 6

Iron Oxide Yellow
Iron Oxide Red
Iron Oxide Black

Yellow: $FeO(OH) \cdot xH_2O$ Formula wt, anhydrous 88.85
Red: Fe_2O_3 Formula wt 159.70
Black: $FeO \cdot Fe_2O_3$ Formula wt 231.55
INS: INS,Yellow: 172(iii) CAS: [51274-00-1]
INS: INS,Red: 172(ii) CAS: [1309-37-1]
INS: INS,Black: 172(i) CAS: [1317-61-9]
UNII: 1K09F3G675 [ferric oxide red]
UNII: EX438O2MRT [ferric oxide yellow]
UNII: XM0M87F357 [ferrosoferric oxide]

DESCRIPTION
Synthetic Iron Oxide consists of any one or any combination of synthetically prepared iron oxides, including the hydrated forms. It is produced from ferrous sulfate by heat soaking, removal of water, decomposition, washing, filtration, drying, and grinding. It is produced in either anhydrous or hydrated forms. The range of hues for Synthetic Iron Oxide includes yellows, reds, browns and blacks. The food-quality iron oxides are primarily distinguished from technical grades by their comparatively low levels of contamination by other metals, which is achieved by the selection and control of the source of the iron or by the extent of chemical purification during the manufacturing process. Synthetic Iron Oxide is insoluble in water and organic solvents and soluble in concentrated mineral acids.

Function: Color
Packaging and Storage: Store in well-closed containers.

ASSAY
- **ASSAY FOR IRON (III)**
  Sample: 0.2 g
  Analysis: Place the *Sample* in a 200-mL conical flask, add 10 mL of 5 N hydrochloric acid to the flask, and heat cautiously to boiling until the *Sample* has dissolved. Allow to cool, add 6–7 drops of 30% hydrogen peroxide, and again heat cautiously to boiling until all the excess hydrogen peroxide has decomposed. [NOTE—This should take about 2–3 min.] Allow to cool, add 30 mL of water and 2 g of potassium iodide, and allow to stand for 5 min. Add 30 mL of water, and titrate with 0.1 N sodium thiosulfate, adding starch TS as the indicator towards the end of the titration. Each mL of 0.1 N sodium thiosulfate is equivalent to 5.585 mg of Fe(III).
  Acceptance criteria: NLT 60%

IMPURITIES
Inorganic Impurities
- **ARSENIC**

    Solution A: 30 mg/mL of sodium borohydride in 0.25 N sodium hydroxide. [NOTE—Store in a loosely covered container protected from direct sunlight.]

    Solution B: Dissolve 5 g of mercuric bromide in 100 mL of alcohol, using gentle heat to facilitate solution. [NOTE—Store in glass containers protected from light.]

    Mercuric bromide paper: Immerse several 15-mm diameter filter paper disks in *Solution B*, remove the disks from the solution, and allow to dry, protected from light. [NOTE—Store in glass containers protected from light.]

    Lead acetate cotton: Immerse absorbent cotton pledgets in a mixture of lead acetate TS and 2 N acetic acid (10:1). Remove excess liquid from the cotton pledgets by expression, and allow them to air-dry.

    Standard stock solution: Dissolve 132.0 mg of arsenic trioxide in 2.0 mL of 2 N sodium hydroxide, and dilute to 100 mL with water.

    Standard solution: Transfer 1.0 mL of the *Standard stock solution* to a 1000-mL volumetric flask, and dilute to volume with water. Dilute 1.5 mL of this solution with hydrochloric acid to 10.0 mL. The solution contains 0.15 µg/mL of arsenic.

    Sample solution: Dissolve 0.5 g of sample in several mL of hydrochloric acid with the aid of heat, and dilute to 10.0 mL with hydrochloric acid.

    Apparatus: Prepare a 300-mL side-arm conical flask containing a magnetic stirring bar. Attach to the conical flask a ground-glass stopper through which passes a 20-cm long glass tube with an internal diameter of 5 mm. The lower end of the tube is inside the conical flask and has been drawn to a tip with an internal diameter of 1 mm. About 15 mm from the tip and at least 3 mm below the lower surface of the stopper is an orifice about 2.5 mm in diameter. The upper end of the tube has a flat ground surface at a right angle to the axis of the tube. A second glass tube of the same internal diameter and 30 mm long, with a similar flat ground surface, is placed in contact with the ground surface of the first tube, and is held in position by a clamp and springs. Into the lower tube insert 55 mg of loosely packed *Lead acetate cotton*. Between the flat surfaces of the tubes, place a disk of *Mercuric bromide paper*.

    Analysis: Before placing the tube assembly into the flask, transfer the *Sample solution* to the flask, and add 5.0 mL of potassium iodide TS and 20 mL of water. Assemble the *Apparatus* immediately, and stir while slowly adding through the side-arm of the flask (over a period of about 20 min) 40 mL of *Solution A*. Examine the stain produced on the *Mercuric bromide paper*. Perform the same procedure using the *Standard solution*.

    Acceptance criteria: The stain produced on the *Mercuric bromide paper* from the *Sample solution* is not more intense than that from the *Standard solution*. (NMT 3 mg/kg)

- **CADMIUM,** Cadmium Limit Test, Appendix IIIB

    Sample solution: Transfer 20 g of sample to a 100-mL volumetric flask. Add a mixture of 8 mL of sulfuric acid and 10 mL of hydrochloric acid, and dilute to volume with water.

    Test solutions: Transfer 10.0 mL of the *Sample solution* to each of five separate 25-mL volumetric flasks. Proceed as directed, beginning with "Dilute the contents of *Flask 1* to volume..."

    Acceptance criteria: NMT 1 mg/kg

- **LEAD**

    Standard stock solution: 1.598 mg/mL of lead nitrate in 0.5 M nitric acid. [NOTE—Prepare and store this solution in glass containers free from soluble lead salts.]

    Standard solution: Transfer 5.0 mL of the *Standard stock solution* to a 100-mL volumetric flask, add 10 mL of 1 N hydrochloric acid, and dilute to volume with water. Transfer 1.0 mL of this solution to a second 100-mL volumetric flask, add 10 mL of 1 N hydrochloric acid, and dilute to volume with water. This solution contains 0.5 µg/mL of lead. [NOTE—Prepare this solution on the day of use.]

    Sample solution: Transfer 2.5 g of sample to a 100-mL glass-stoppered conical flask, add 35 mL of 0.1 N hydrochloric acid, and stir for 1 h. Filter, collect the filtrate in a 50-mL volumetric flask, and dilute to volume with 0.1 N hydrochloric acid.

    Analysis: Using a suitable atomic absorption spectrophotometer equipped with a lead hollow-cathode lamp, a flow spoiler, and an air–acetylene oxidizing flame, concomitantly determine the absorbance of the *Standard solution* and the *Sample solution* at the lead emission line of 217.0 nm.

    Acceptance criteria: The absorbance of the *Sample solution* does not exceed that of the *Standard solution*. (10 mg/kg)

- **MERCURY,** Mercury Limit Test, Method I, Appendix IIIB

    Sample solution: Dissolve 2 g of sample in 20 mL of water in a small beaker, and add 1 mL of sulfuric acid solution (1:5) and 1 mL of potassium permanganate solution (1:25). Cover the beaker with a watch glass, boil for a few seconds, and cool.

    Acceptance criteria: NMT 1 mg/kg

SPECIFIC TESTS
- **LOSS ON DRYING,** Appendix IIC: 105° for 4h
  Acceptance criteria
  Red iron oxide: NMT 1.0%
- **WATER-SOLUBLE MATTER**
  Sample: 5.0 g
  Analysis: Transfer the *Sample* to a 250-mL beaker, add 200 mL of water, and boil for 5 min. [NOTE—Stir to avoid bumping.] Cool the mixture, transfer the contents to a 250-mL volumetric flask, and rinse the beaker with 25 mL of water, adding the rinsings to the flask. Bring to volume with water. Allow the mixture to stand for 10 min, and filter the solution. Transfer 100 mL of the filtrate into a clean, dry, tared beaker, and carefully evaporate the solution to dryness on a boiling water bath. Dry the residue at between 105° and 110° for 2 h, cool the beaker with residue in a desiccator, weigh the beaker, and calculate the percentage of water-soluble matter using the formula:

$$\text{Result} = 250 \times (W_R/W_S)$$

W_R = weight of the residue (g)
W_S = weight of the sample taken (g)
Acceptance criteria: NMT 1.0%

D-Tagatose

First Published: FCC 6

D-Lyxo-Hexulose

$C_6H_{12}O_6$
UNII: T7A20Y888Y [tagatose, d-]

Formula wt 180.16
CAS: [87-81-0]

DESCRIPTION
D-Tagatose occurs as a white crystal or powder. It is a stereoisomer of D-fructose. D-Tagatose is manufactured from food-grade lactose by a two-step process involving enzymatic hydrolysis (immobilized *Aspergillus oryzae* lactase) to D-galactose, followed by chemical isomerization of D-galactose to D-tagatose (induced by calcium hydroxide) and crystallization. It is readily soluble in water and very slightly soluble in ethanol.

Function: Sweetener
Packaging and Storage: Store in tight containers in a dry place.

IDENTIFICATION
- **INFRARED ABSORPTION SPECTRA**
  Reference standard: Tagatose standard (Sigma-Aldrich Denmark A/S, DK-2665 Vallensbæk Strand, Denmark, or equivalent)
  Sample and standard preparation: Diamond ATR-crystal or potassium bromide dispersion
  Acceptance criteria: The spectrum of the sample exhibits maxima at the same wavelengths as those in the spectrum of the *Reference standard*.

ASSAY
- **PROCEDURE**
  Mobile phase: 50 µg/mL calcium acetate
  Standard solution: 5.0 mg/mL of D-tagatose, prepared using a previously dried tagatose standard (Sigma-Aldrich Denmark A/S, DK-2665 Vallensbæk Strand, Denmark, or equivalent)
  Sample: 50 mg, previously dried
  Sample solution: Transfer the *Sample* into a 10-mL volumetric flask, dissolve in and dilute to volume with water, and filter through a 0.2 µm filter
  Chromatographic system, Appendix IIA
  Mode: High-performance liquid chromatography
  Detector: Refractive index
  Column: 7.8 mm × 30-cm column packed with 9-µm Aminex HPX-87C (Biorad), or equivalent
  Column temperature: 85°
  Flow rate: 0.6 mL/min
  Injection volume: 20 µL
  Analysis: Separately inject the *Standard solution* and the *Sample solution* into the chromatograph. Record the chromatograms and measure the area responses. Determine the amount of D-Tagatose in the *Sample* taken by the formula:

  $$\text{Result} = 50 \times C \times (R_U/R_S)$$

  C = concentration (mg/mL) of D-tagatose in the *Standard solution*
  R_U = peak response of D-tagatose in the *Sample solution*
  R_S = peak response of D-tagatose in the *Standard solution*
  Acceptance criteria: NLT 98%, on the dried basis

IMPURITIES
Inorganic Impurities
- **LEAD,** Lead Limit Test, Atomic Absorption Spectrophotometric Graphite Furnace Method, Method I, Appendix IIIB
  Acceptance criteria: NMT 0.1 mg/kg

SPECIFIC TESTS
- **LOSS ON DRYING,** Appendix IIC: 87° for 6 h
  Acceptance criteria: NMT 0.5%
- **MELTING RANGE OR TEMPERATURE DETERMINATION,** Appendix IIB
  Acceptance criteria: Between 133° and 137°
- **OPTICAL (SPECIFIC) ROTATION,** Appendix IIB
  Sample solution: 10 mg/mL, made to 100 mL
  Acceptance criteria: $[\alpha]_D^{20}$ between −4° and −5.6°

Tagetes Extract

First Published: FCC 7

Xanthophylls

$C_{40}H_{56}O_2$
$C_{72}H_{116}O_4$
INS: 161b(ii)

Formula wt, lutein 568.88
Formula wt, helenien 1045.71
CAS: *Tagetes erecta*, ext. [90131-43-4]
lutein [127-40-2]
helenien [547-147-1]

UNII: UH5X33P33E [tagetes erecta flower]

DESCRIPTION
Tagetes Extract occurs as a dark yellow to brown liquid. The major coloring principles are lutein and helenien (dipalmitate of lutein) and they are obtained by the hexane extraction of dried petals of *Tagetes erecta* L., with subsequent solvent removal. Other hydroxy derivatives of carotenes may be present together with oxyderivatives such as epoxides. Tagetes Extract may contain fats, oils, and waxes naturally occurring in the plant material. Products of commerce are often further formulated in order to standardize the color content or to obtain water soluble or dispersible products. Tagetes Extract is insoluble in water and soluble in hexane.

Function: Color
Packaging and Storage: Store in tight, light-resistant containers in a cool place.

IDENTIFICATION
- **UV-VISIBLE ABSORPTION SPECTRUM**
  Acceptance criteria: A sample dissolved in acetone gives a spectrum exhibiting maximum absorption at about 444 nm.
- **TEST FOR CAROTENOIDS**
  Sample solution: Dissolve a sample in acetone.
  Analysis: Successively add to the *Sample solution* a 5% sodium nitrite solution and 0.5 M sulfuric acid.
  Acceptance criteria: The color of the *Sample solution* disappears.

ASSAY
- **PROCEDURE**
  Solution A: Cyclohexane and ethanol (1:1)
  Sample stock solution: 10–30 mg/mL in *Solution A* [NOTE—Dissolve the sample in a small amount of *Solution A* before bringing the solution to volume.]
  Sample solution: Transfer 0.200 mL of the *Sample stock solution* into a 25-mL volumetric flask, and dilute with *Solution A* to volume.
  Analysis: Using an appropriate spectrophotometer, measure the absorbance of the *Sample solution* at the wavelength of maxiumum absorption (about 444 nm) using *Solution A* as a blank. [NOTE—The absorbance should be 0.2–0.8, otherwise further dilution of the *Sample solution* is required.]
  Calculate the percentage of lutein in the sample taken:

  $$\text{Result} = A/(F \times C_U)$$

  A = absorbance of the solution containing the sample, corrected for the blank
  F = specific absorbance for lutein in cyclohexane/ethanol at 444 nm (2900)
  C_U = concentration of Tagetes Extract in the *Sample solution* (g/mL)

  Acceptance criteria: The content of total coloring matter, calculated as lutein, is NLT the amount declared on the label.

IMPURITIES
Inorganic Impurities
- **LEAD**, *Lead Limit Test, Flame Atomic Absorption Spectrophotometric Method*, Appendix IIIB
  Sample: 10 g
  Acceptance criteria: NMT 2 mg/kg

Organic Impurities
- **RESIDUAL SOLVENT**, Appendix VIII
  Acceptance criteria: NMT 50 ppm hexane

Talc
First Published: Prior to FCC 6

INS: 553(iii)   CAS: [14807-96-6]
UNII: 7SEV7J4R1U [talc]

DESCRIPTION
Talc occurs as a white to gray-white, unctuous powder. It is a naturally occurring form of hydrous magnesium silicate containing varying proportions of such associated minerals as alpha-quartz, calcite, chlorite, dolomite, kaolin, magnesite, and phlogopite. *Talc derived from deposits that are known to contain associated asbestos is not food grade*. It is insoluble in water and in solutions of alkali hydroxides, but is slightly soluble in dilute mineral acids.
Function: Anticaking agent; coating agent; lubricating and release agent; surface-finishing agent; texturizing agent
Packaging and Storage: Store in well-closed containers.

IDENTIFICATION
- **X-RAY DIFFRACTION PATTERN**
  Sample: Random powder sample
  Acceptance criteria: The *Sample* exhibits intense reflections at the following d values: 9.34 Å, 4.66 Å, and 3.12 Å.
- **INFRARED ABSORPTION SPECTRUM**
  Sample: A potassium bromide dispersion of the sample
  Acceptance criteria: The *Sample* exhibits major absorptions at approximately 1015 cm^{-1} and 450 cm^{-1}.

IMPURITIES
Inorganic Impurities
- **ARSENIC**, *Arsenic Limit Test*, Appendix IIIB
  Sample: 10.0 g
  Sample solution: Transfer the *Sample* into a 250-mL flask, and add 50 mL of 0.5 N hydrochloric acid. Attach a reflux condenser to the flask, heat on a steam bath for 30 min, cool, and let the undissolved material settle. Decant the supernatant liquid through Whatman No. 3 filter paper, or equivalent, into a 100-mL volumetric flask, retaining as much as possible of the insoluble material in the beaker. Wash the slurry and beaker with three 10-mL portions of hot water, decanting each washing through the filter into the flask. Finally wash the filter paper with 15 mL of hot water, cool the filtrate to room temperature, dilute to volume with water, and mix.
  Analysis: Use 10 mL of the *Sample solution*.
  Acceptance criteria: NMT 3 mg/kg
- **LEAD**, *Lead Limit Test*, Appendix IIIB
  Control: 5 µg Pb (5 mL of *Diluted Standard Lead Solution*)
  Sample: 10-mL portion of the *Sample solution* prepared for the *Arsenic* test (above)
  Acceptance criteria: NMT 5 mg/kg

SPECIFIC TESTS
- **ACID-SOLUBLE SUBSTANCES (AS SULFATE)**
  Sample: 1.00 g
  Analysis: Digest the *Sample* with 20 mL of 3 N hydrochloric acid at 50° for 15 min, add water to restore the original volume, mix, and filter. Add 1 mL of 2 N sulfuric acid to 10 mL of the filtrate, evaporate to dryness, and ignite to constant weight. Calculate the percent *Acid-Soluble Substances* by the formula:

  $$\text{Result} = (2R \times 100)/W$$

  R = weight of the ignited residue
  W = weight of *Sample*

Acceptance criteria: NMT 2.5%
- **FREE ALKALI (AS NaOH)**
  Analysis: Add 2 drops of phenolphthalein TS to 20 mL of the diluted filtrate prepared in the test for *Soluble Salts* (below), representing 1 g of sample.
  Acceptance criteria: NMT 2.5 mL of 0.1 N hydrochloric acid is required to discharge any pink color that appears. (NMT 1.0%)
- **LOSS ON DRYING**, Appendix IIC: 105° for 1 h
  Sample: 10.0 g
  Acceptance criteria: NMT 0.5%
- **LOSS ON IGNITION**
  Analysis: Weigh 1 g of sample into a tared platinum crucible provided with a cover. Initially apply heat gradually and then ignite to a constant weight.
  Acceptance criteria: NMT 6.0%
- **SOLUBLE SALTS**
  Sample: 10 g
  Analysis: Boil the *Sample* with 150 mL of water for 15 min. Cool to room temperature and add water to restore the original volume. Allow the mixture to stand for 15 min, and filter until clear. Add 25 mL of water to 75 mL of the clear filtrate. Evaporate to dryness 50 mL of this solution, representing 2.5 g of sample, in a tared platinum dish on a steam bath. Then ignite gently to constant weight.
  Acceptance criteria: The weight of the residue does not exceed 5 mg. (NMT 0.2%)

Tallow

First Published: Prior to FCC 6

UNII: 98HPY76U4W [beef tallow]

DESCRIPTION
Tallow occurs as an off-white fat. It is obtained by heat rendering of tissues (cuttings and trimmings) from beef and, to a lesser degree, mutton shortly after slaughter. Rendered Tallow may be alkali refined and bleached, or bleached and deodorized without prior refining. It is a firm fat containing a high proportion of saturated fatty acids and exhibiting greater flavor stability than lard or unhydrogenated vegetable oils.
Rendered, alkali-refined, and bleached-deodorized tallows are white to off-white solids at 21° to 27°. Alkali-refined and bleached-deodorized tallows, which are pale yellow to colorless and free of extraneous matter at 54°, differ from rendered Tallow, which is clear to hazy and may contain extraneous matter.
Function: Coating agent; texturizer
Packaging and Storage: Store in well-closed containers.

IDENTIFICATION
- **FATTY ACID COMPOSITION**, Appendix VII
  Acceptance criteria: Tallow exhibits the following composition profile:

Fatty Acid	Weight % (Range)
<14:0	<0.1
14:0	1.4–6.3
14:1	0.5–1.5
15:0	0.5–1.0
15:0 iso	<1.5
16:0	20–37
16:0 iso	<0.5
16:1	0.7–8.8
16:2	<1.0
17:0	0.5–2.0
17:1	<1.0
18:0	6–40
18:1	26–50
18:2	0.5–5.0
18:3	<2.5
20:0	<0.5
20:1	<0.5
20:4	<0.5

IMPURITIES
Inorganic Impurities
- **ARSENIC**, Appendix IIIB
  Sample: 2.0 g
  Analysis: Use 1.0 mL of the *Standard Arsenic Solution* (1 µg arsenic) for comparison to the absorbance of the *Sample Solution*.
  Acceptance criteria: NMT 0.5 mg/kg
- **LEAD**, *Lead Limit Test, Atomic Absorption Spectrophotometric Graphite Furnace Method, Method II*, Appendix IIIB
  Sample: 3 g
  Acceptance criteria: NMT 0.1 mg/kg

SPECIFIC TESTS
- **COLOR (FATS AND RELATED SUBSTANCES)**, Appendix VII
  Acceptance criteria
    Rendered tallow: NMT 3.0 red
    Alkali-refined tallow: NMT 1.5 red
    Bleached and deodorized tallow: NMT 1.5 red
- **FREE FATTY ACIDS (AS OLEIC ACID)**, Appendix VII
  Analysis: Use 28.2 as the equivalence factor (e).
  Acceptance criteria
    Rendered tallow: NMT 1.5%
    Alkali-refined tallow: NMT 0.5%
    Bleached and deodorized tallow: NMT 0.1%
- **HEXANE-INSOLUBLE MATTER**
  Sample: 100 g. [NOTE—If the material is plastic or semi-solid, soften a portion by warming it at a temperature not exceeding 60°, and then mix it thoroughly.]
  Analysis: Transfer the well-mixed *Sample* into a 1500-mL wide-mouth Erlenmeyer flask, add 1000 mL of hexane, and shake the flask until the sample is dissolved. Filter the resulting solution through a 600-mL Corning "C" porosity, or equivalent, filtering funnel that previously has been dried at 105° for 1 h, cooled in a desiccator, and weighed. Wash the flask with two successive 250-mL portions of hexane, and pass the washings through

the filter. Dry the funnel at 105° for 1 h, cool it to room temperature in a desiccator, and weigh. From the gain in weight of the funnel, calculate the percentage of the *Hexane-insoluble matter* in the *Sample*.
  Acceptance criteria
    Rendered tallow: NMT 0.1%
    Alkali-refined tallow: NMT 0.01%
    Bleached and deodorized tallow: NMT 0.01%
- **IODINE VALUE,** Appendix VII
    Acceptance criteria: Between 37 and 50
- **PEROXIDE VALUE**
    Sample: 10 g
    Analysis: Combine the *Sample* with 30 mL of a 3:2 glacial acetic acid:chloroform mixture, and mix. Add 1 mL of a saturated solution of potassium iodide, mix for 1 min, add 100 mL of water, and begin titrating with 0.05 N sodium thiosulfate, adding starch TS as the endpoint is approached. Continue the titration until the blue starch color has just disappeared. Perform a blank determination (see *General Provisions*), and make any necessary correction. Calculate the peroxide value (mEq/kg) of the *Sample*, by the formula:

    $$Result = S \times N \times 1000/W$$

    S = the net volume (mL), of sodium thiosulfate solution required for the *Sample*
    N = the exact normality of the sodium thiosulfate solution
    W = the weight of the *Sample* (g) taken
    Acceptance criteria: NMT 10 mEq/kg
- **UNSAPONIFIABLE MATTER,** Appendix VII
    Acceptance criteria: NMT 1.5%
- **WATER,** *Water determination,* Appendix IIB
    Analysis: In place of 35 to 40 mL of methanol, use 50 mL of chloroform to dissolve the sample.
    Acceptance criteria
      Rendered tallow: NMT 0.5%
      Alkali-refined tallow: NMT 0.2%
      Bleached and deodorized tallow: NMT 0.1%

Tangerine Oil, Coldpressed

First Published: Prior to FCC 6

Tangerine Oil, Expressed
FEMA: 3041
CAS: [8008-31-9]
UNII: NJO720F72R [mandarin oil]

DESCRIPTION
Tangerine Oil, Coldpressed occurs as a red-orange to brown-orange liquid with a pleasant, orange odor. Oils produced from the unripe fruit are often green. It is the oil obtained by expression from the peels of the ripe fruit of the Dancy tangerine, *Citrus nobilis* or *reticulata* (Fam. Rutaceae), and from some other closely related varieties. It is soluble in most fixed oils and in mineral oil, slightly soluble in propylene glycol, and relatively insoluble in glycerin. It may contain a suitable antioxidant.
Function: Flavoring agent
Packaging and Storage: Store in a cool place protected from light in full, tight containers that are made from steel or aluminum and that are suitably lined.

IDENTIFICATION
- **INFRARED SPECTRA,** *Spectrophotometric Identification Tests,* Appendix IIIC
    Acceptance criteria: The spectrum of the sample exhibits relative maxima at the same wavelengths as those of the spectrum below.

SPECIFIC TESTS
- **ALDEHYDES**
    Sample: 10 g
    Analysis: Determine as directed in Aldehydes and Ketones, *Hydroxylamine tert-Butyl Alcohol Method,* Appendix VI. Allow the *Sample* and the blank to stand at room temperature for 30 min after adding the hydroxylamine hydrochloride solution, and use 78.13 as the equivalence factor (e) in the calculation.
    Acceptance criteria: Between 0.8% and 1.9% of aldehydes, calculated as decyl aldehyde ($C_{10}H_{22}O$)
- **ANGULAR ROTATION,** *Optical (Specific) Rotation,* Appendix IIB: Use a 100-mm tube.
    Acceptance criteria: Between +88° and +96°
- **REFRACTIVE INDEX,** Appendix IIB
    [NOTE—Use an Abbé or other refractometer of equal or greater accuracy.]
    Acceptance criteria: Between 1.473 and 1.476 at 20°
- **RESIDUE ON EVAPORATION,** Appendix VI
    Sample: 5 g
    Analysis: Heat the *Sample* for 5 h.
    Acceptance criteria: Between 2.3% and 5.8%
- **SPECIFIC GRAVITY:** Determine by any reliable method (see *General Provisions*).
    Acceptance criteria: Between 0.844 and 0.854

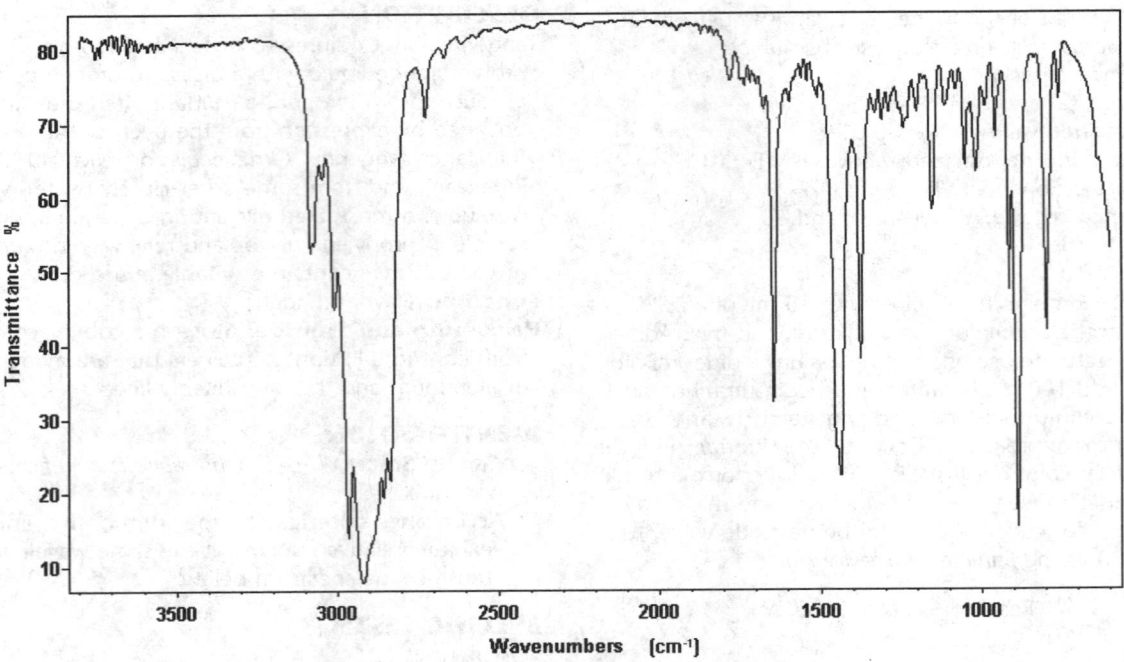

Tangerine Oil, Coldpressed

Tannic Acid

First Published: Prior to FCC 6
Last Revision: Second Supplement, FCC 6

Gallotannic Acid
Hydrolyzable Gallotannin
INS: 181   CAS: [1401-55-4]
FEMA: 3042
UNII: 28F9E0DJY6 [tannic acid, unspecified]

DESCRIPTION

Tannic Acid occurs as an amorphous powder, as glistening scales, or as spongy masses, varying in color from yellow-white to light brown. It is odorless or has a faint, characteristic odor and an astringent taste. It is a complex polyphenolic organic structure that yields gallic acid and either glucose or quinic acid as hydrolysis products. It is obtained by solvent extraction from the nutgalls or the excrescences that form on the young twigs of *Quercus infectoria* Olivier and allied species of *Quercus* L. (Fam. Fagaceae); from the seed pods of Tara (*Caesalpinia spinosa*) (Fam. Leguminosa); or from the nutgalls of various sumac species, including *Rhus semialata, R. coriaria, R. galabra*, and *R. typhia* (Fam. Anacardiaceae). Tannic acid is very soluble in water, in acetone, and in alcohol; slightly soluble in absolute alcohol; and practically insoluble in chloroform, in ether, and in solvent hexane. One g dissolves in about 1 mL of warm glycerin.

Function: Clarifying agent; flavoring agent; flavor enhancer; flavoring adjuvant

Packaging and Storage: Store in tight, light-resistant containers.

IDENTIFICATION

- **A. PROCEDURE**
  Sample solution: 100 mg/mL
  Analysis: Add a small quantity of ferric chloride TS to the *Sample solution*.
  Acceptance criteria: A blue-black color or precipitate forms.
- **B. PROCEDURE**
  Analysis: To a sample solution, add alkaloidal salt, albumin, or gelatin.
  Acceptance criteria: A precipitate is produced.

ASSAY

- **PROCEDURE**
  Sample solution: Transfer 2.0 g of previously dried sample into a 500-mL volumetric flask. Dissolve in and dilute with water to volume.
  Analysis: Transfer 100 mL of *Sample solution* into a 300-mL Erlenmeyer flask, and add 7.2 g of Hide Powder.[1] Shake the flask for 20 min, let it stand for 20 min, and pass through a Whatman grade 4 filter, or equivalent. The filtrate should be clear. Pipet 50 mL of the filtrate into a tared crystallizing dish. Evaporate to dryness on a steam bath, and heat the dish in an oven at 105° for 1 h. Cool it in a desiccator, and weigh the dry matter. Perform a blank test by transferring 7.2 g of Hide Powder EFT into a 300-mL Erlenmeyer flask containing 100 mL of water. Proceed as directed in the preceding

---
[1] L. H. Lincoln & Son, Inc., or equivalent.

paragraph, beginning with "Shake the flask for 20 min." Weigh the dry matter. [NOTE—This blank test should be performed on each lot of Hide Powder.]
Calculate the percent of Tannic Acid in the *Sample* taken by the formula:

$$\text{Result} = 100 \times [W - (A - B) \times 10]/W$$

W = weight of the sample taken (g)
A = the weight of the dry matter obtained from analysis of the *Sample solution* (g)
B = the weight of the dry matter obtained from analysis of the blank (g)
10 = factor representing dilution of the sample

Acceptance criteria: NLT 96.0% of Tannic Acid on the dried basis

IMPURITIES
Inorganic Impurities
- **LEAD**, *Lead Limit Test*, Appendix IIIB
  Sample solution: Prepare as directed for organic compounds.
  Control: 2 µg Pb (2 mL of *Diluted Standard Lead Solution*)
  Acceptance criteria: NMT 2 mg/kg

SPECIFIC TESTS
- **GUMS OR DEXTRIN**
  Sample: 1 g
  Analysis: Dissolve the *Sample* in 5 mL of water, and filter. Then add 10 mL of alcohol to the filtrate.
  Acceptance criteria: No turbidity forms within 15 min.
- **LOSS ON DRYING**, Appendix IIC: 105° for 2 h
  Acceptance criteria: NMT 7.0%
- **RESIDUE ON IGNITION (SULFATED ASH)**, Appendix IIC
  Sample: 1 g
  Acceptance criteria: NMT 1.0%
- **RESINOUS SUBSTANCES**
  Sample: 1 g
  Analysis: Dissolve the *Sample* in 5 mL of water, and filter. Then dilute the filtrate to 15 mL.
  Acceptance criteria: No turbidity forms.

Tara Gum

First Published: First Supplement, FCC 6

Peruvian carob
INS: 417   CAS: [39300-88-4]
UNII: WL3883U2PO [caesalpinia spinosa resin]

DESCRIPTION
Tara gum occurs as a white to tan, nearly odorless powder obtained by grinding the endosperm of the seeds of the tara tree, *Caesalpinia spinosa* (Fam. Leguminosae). The gum consists of polysaccharides of high molecular weight composed mainly of galactomannans. The principal component consists of a linear chain of (1→4)-β-D-mannopyranose (mannose) units with α-D-galactopyranose (galactose) units attached by (1→6) linkages. The ratio of mannose to galactose in tara gum is approximately 3:1. Tara gum is water-soluble, but insoluble in ethanol.
Function: Stabilizer; thickener
Packaging and Storage: Store in well-closed containers.

IDENTIFICATION
- **GEL TEST**
  Analysis: To an aqueous solution of the sample add small amounts of sodium borate.
  Acceptance criteria: A gel is formed.
- **MICROSCOPIC EXAMINATION**
  Analysis: Prepare an aqueous solution of 0.5% iodine and 1% potassium iodide. Add some ground sample to the solution and transfer a portion of this mixture onto a glass slide and examine under a microscope.
  Acceptance criteria: Tara gum contains groups of round to pear-shaped cells; their contents are yellow to brown. [NOTE—Guar gum cells are similar in form but markedly larger in size. Carob bean gum shows long, stretched tubiform cells, separate or slightly interspaced and can be easily distinguished from tara gum.]
- **VISCOSITY**
  Sample: 2 g
  Analysis: Transfer the *Sample* into a 400-mL beaker and moisten it thoroughly with about 4 mL of isopropanol. Add, with vigorous stirring, 200 mL of water and continue stirring until the gum is completely and uniformly dispersed and an opalescent, moderately viscous solution forms. [NOTE—This solution is more viscous than a carob bean gum solution when prepared in the same manner.] Transfer 100 mL of this solution into another 400-mL beaker, heat the mixture in a boiling water-bath for about 10 min, and cool to room temperature.
  Acceptance criteria: A marked increase in viscosity is observed.

IMPURITIES
Inorganic Impurities
- **ARSENIC**, *Arsenic Limit Test*, Appendix IIIB
  Sample solution: Prepare as directed for organic compounds.
  Acceptance criteria: NMT 3 mg/kg
- **LEAD**, *Lead Limit Test, Flame Atomic Absorption Spectrophotometric Method*, Appendix IIIB
  Sample solution: 10 g
  Acceptance criteria: NMT 2 mg/kg

Organic Impurities
- **PROTEIN**, *Nitrogen Determination, Method I*, Appendix IIIC
  Sample: 3.5 g
  Analysis: Transfer the *Sample* into a 500-mL Kjeldahl flask. The percentage of nitrogen determined multiplied by 5.7 gives the percentage of protein in the sample.
  Acceptance criteria: NMT 3.5%
- **STARCH**
  Sample solution: 100 mg/mL
  Analysis: Add a few drops of iodine TS.
  Acceptance criteria: No blue color develops.

SPECIFIC TESTS

- **ASH (TOTAL)**, Appendix IIC
  Analysis: Proceed as directed, but ignite at 675 ± 25°.
  Acceptance criteria: NMT 1.0%
- **ACID-INSOLUBLE MATTER**
  Sample: 2 g
  Analysis: Transfer the *Sample* into a 250-mL beaker containing 150 mL of water and 1.5 mL of sulfuric acid. Cover the beaker with a watch glass and heat the mixture on a steam bath for 6 h, rubbing down the wall of the beaker frequently with a rubber-tipped stirring rod and replacing any water lost by evaporation. Weigh 500 mg of a suitable acid-washed filter aid, pre-dried at 105° for 1 h, to the nearest 0.1 mg, add the filter aid to the sample solution, and filter it through a tared sintered-glass filter crucible. Wash the residue several times with hot water, dry the crucible and its contents at 105° for 3 h, cool in a desiccator, and weigh. The difference between the total weight and the weight of the filter aid plus crucible is the weight of the *Acid-insoluble matter*. Calculate as a percentage.
  Acceptance criteria: NMT 2.0%
- **GALACTOMANNANS**
  Analysis: Determine the difference between 100 and the sum of the percentages of *Acid-Insoluble Matter*, *Ash (Total)*, *Loss on Drying*, and *Protein*.
  Acceptance criteria: NLT 75%
- **LOSS ON DRYING**, Appendix IIC (105° for 5 h)
  Acceptance criteria: NMT 12.0%

Tarragon Oil

First Published: Prior to FCC 6

Estragon Oil
FEMA: 2412

CAS: [8016-88-4]

UNII: CQ9077P26M [tarragon oil]

DESCRIPTION

Tarragon Oil occurs as a pale yellow to amber liquid having a delicate, spicy odor similar to fennel and sweet basil but characteristic of Tarragon Oil. It is the volatile oil obtained by steam distillation from the leaves, stems, and flowers of the plant *Artemesia dracunculus* L. (Fam. Asteraceae). It is soluble in most fixed oils and in an equal volume of mineral oil, occasionally becoming hazy on further dilution. It is relatively insoluble in propylene glycol, and is insoluble in glycerin.

Function: Flavoring agent
Packaging and Storage: Store in a cool place protected from light in full, tight containers that are made from steel or aluminum and that are suitably lined.

IDENTIFICATION

- **INFRARED SPECTRA**, *Spectrophotometric Identification Tests*, Appendix IIIC
  Acceptance criteria: The spectrum of the sample exhibits relative maxima at the same wavelengths as those of the spectrum below.

SPECIFIC TESTS

- **ACID VALUE (ESSENTIAL OILS AND FLAVORS)**, Appendix VI
  Acceptance criteria: NMT 2.0
- **ANGULAR ROTATION**, *Optical (Specific) Rotation*, Appendix IIB: Use a 100-mm tube.
  Acceptance criteria: Between +1.5° and +6.5°
- **REFRACTIVE INDEX**, Appendix IIB
  [NOTE—Use an Abbé or other refractometer of equal or greater accuracy.]
  Acceptance criteria: Between 1.504 and 1.520 at 20°
- **SAPONIFICATION VALUE**, *Esters, Saponification Value*, Appendix VI
  Sample: 5 g
  Acceptance criteria: NMT 18
- **SOLUBILITY IN ALCOHOL**, Appendix VI
  Acceptance criteria: One mL of sample is soluble in 1 mL of 90% alcohol.
- **SPECIFIC GRAVITY:** Determine by any reliable method (see *General Provisions*).
  Acceptance criteria: Between 0.914 and 0.956

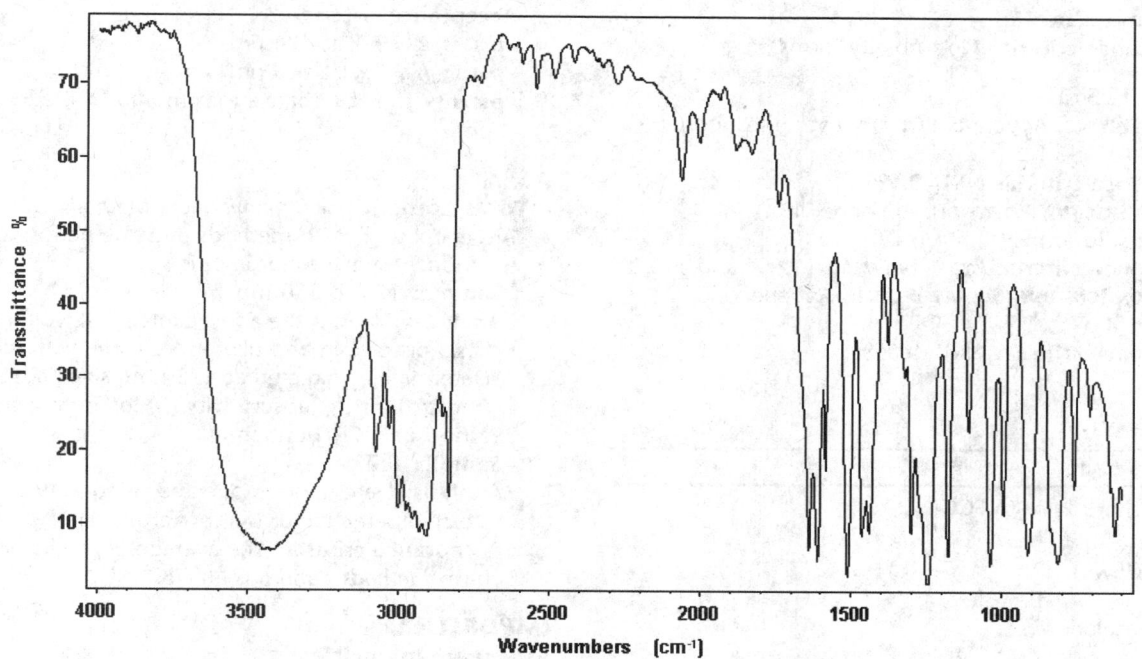

Tarragon Oil

Tartaric Acid

First Published: Prior to FCC 6
Last Revision: First Supplement, FCC 7

L(+)-Tartaric Acid

$C_4H_6O_6$
INS: 334
FEMA: 3044
UNII: W4888I119H [tartaric acid]

Formula wt 150.09
CAS: [87-69-4]

DESCRIPTION
Tartaric Acid occurs as colorless or translucent crystals or as a white, fine to granular, crystalline powder. It is stable in air. One g dissolves in 0.8 mL of water at 25°, in about 0.5 mL of boiling water, and in about 3 mL of alcohol. Its solutions are dextrorotatory.
Function: Acidifier; sequestrant; flavoring agent
Packaging and Storage: Store in well-closed containers.

IDENTIFICATION
- **INFRARED ABSORPTION**, *Spectrophotometric Identification Tests*, Appendix IIIC
  Reference standard: USP Tartaric Acid RS
  Sample and standard preparation: *K*
  Acceptance criteria: The spectrum of the sample exhibits maxima at the same wavelengths as those in the spectrum of the *Reference standard*.
- **TARTRATE**, Appendix IIIA
  Acceptance criteria: Passes test

ASSAY
- **PROCEDURE**
  Sample: 2 g, previously dried
  Analysis: Dissolve the *Sample*, in 40 mL of water, add phenolphthalein TS and titrate with 1 N sodium hydroxide. Each mL of 1 N sodium hydroxide is equivalent to 75.04 mg of $C_4H_6O_6$.
  Acceptance criteria: NLT 99.7% and NMT 100.5% of $C_4H_6O_6$, on the dried basis

IMPURITIES
Inorganic Impurities
- **LEAD,** *Lead Limit Test, Flame Atomic Absorption Spectrophotometric Method,* Appendix IIIB
  Sample: 5.0 g
  Acceptance criteria: NMT 2 mg/kg
- **SULFATE**
  Sample solution: 10 mg/mL
  Analysis: Add 3 drops of hydrochloric acid and 1 mL of barium chloride TS to 10 mL of the *Sample solution*.
  Acceptance criteria: No turbidity forms.

Organic Impurities
- **OXALATE**
  Sample solution: 100 mg/mL

Analysis: Nearly neutralize 10 mL of the *Sample solution* with 6 N ammonium hydroxide and add 10 mL of calcium sulfate TS.
Acceptance criteria: No turbidity forms.

SPECIFIC TESTS
- **LOSS ON DRYING**, Appendix IIC: Dry over phosphorus pentoxide for 3 h.
  Acceptance criteria: NMT 0.5%
- **OPTICAL (SPECIFIC) ROTATION**, Appendix IIB
  Sample solution: 200 mg/mL
  Acceptance criteria: $[\alpha]_D^{25}$ between +12.0° and +13.0°
- **RESIDUE ON IGNITION (SULFATED ASH)**, Appendix IIC
  Sample: 4 g
  Acceptance criteria: NMT 0.05%

Tartrazine[1]
First Published: Prior to FCC 6

CI Food Yellow 4
CI 19140
Class: Pyrazalone

$C_{16}H_9N_4O_9S_2Na_3$ Formula wt 534.37
INS: 102   CAS: [1934-21-0]
UNII: I753WB2F1M [fd&c yellow no. 5]

DESCRIPTION
Tartrazine occurs as a yellow-orange powder or granules. It is principally the trisodium salt of 4,5-dihydro-5-oxo-1-(4-sulfophenyl)-4-(4-sulfophenyl-azo)-1H-pyrazole-3-carboxylic acid. When dissolved in water, it yields a solution golden yellow at neutrality and in acid. When dissolved in concentrated sulfuric acid, it yields an orange-yellow solution that turns yellow when diluted with water. It is insoluble in ethanol.
Function: Color
Packaging and Storage: Store in well-closed containers.

IDENTIFICATION
- **PROCEDURE**
  Sample solution: 19.9 µg/mL
  Analysis: Adjust the pH of three aliquots of the *Sample solution* to pH 1, pH 7, and pH 13. Measure the absorbance intensities (A) and wavelength maxima of these solutions with a suitable UV-visible spectrophotometer.
  Acceptance criteria
  pH 1: A = 1.1 at 426 nm
  pH 7: A = 1.4 at 425 nm
  pH 13: The absorbance maximum is shifted below 400 nm

ASSAY
- **TOTAL COLOR**, *Color Determination, Methods I and II*, Appendix IIIC: Both methods must be performed.
  Method I: Spectrophotometric
  Sample: 175 to 250 mg
  Analysis: Transfer the *Sample* into a 1-L volumetric flask; dissolve in and dilute to volume with water. Determine as directed at 428 nm using 0.053 L/(mg·cm) for the absorptivity (a) for Tartrazine.
  Method II: TiCl$_3$ Titration
  Sample: 0.2 g
  Analysis: Determine as directed using 7.49 as the stoichiometric factor (F_s) for Tartrazine.
  Acceptance criteria: The average of results obtained from *Methods I and II* is NLT 87.0%.

IMPURITIES
Inorganic Impurities
- **ARSENIC**, *Arsenic Limit Test*, Appendix IIIB
  Sample solution: Prepare as directed for organic compounds.
  Acceptance criteria: NMT 3 mg/kg
- **LEAD**, *Lead Limit Test*, Appendix IIIB
  Sample solution: Prepare as directed for organic compounds.
  Control: 10 µg Pb (10 mL of *Diluted Standard Lead Solution*)
  Acceptance criteria: NMT 10 mg/kg

Organic Impurities
- **UNCOMBINED INTERMEDIATES AND PRODUCTS OF SIDE REACTIONS**, *Method II, Color Determination*, Appendix IIIC
  Sample solution: 1.5 mg/mL sample in 0.1 M disodium tetraborate (Na$_2$B$_4$O$_7$)
  Analysis: Use an Injection volume of 50 µL for the *Sample solution*.
  Acceptance criteria
  4,4'-[4,5-Dihydro-5-oxo-4-[(4-sulfophenyl)-hydrazono]-1H-pyrazol-1,3-diyl]bis(benzenesulfonic acid), Trisodium Salt: NMT 1%
  4-[(4',5-Disulfo[1,1'-biphenyl]-2-yl)hydrazono]-4,5-dihydro-5-oxo-1-(4-sulfophenyl)-1H-pyrazole-3-carboxylic acid, Tetrasodium Salt: NMT 1%
  Ethyl or Methyl 4,5-dihydro-5-oxo-1-(4-sulfophenyl)-4-[(4-sulfophenyl)hydrazono]-1H-pyrazole-3-carboxylate, Disodium Salt: NMT 1%
  Sum of 4,5-Dihydro-5-oxo-1-phenyl-4-[(4-sulfophenyl)-azo]-1H-pyrazole-3-carboxylic acid, Disodium Salt and 4,5-Dihydro-5-oxo-4-(phenylazo)-1-(4-sulfophenyl)-1H-pyrazole-3-carboxylic acid, Disodium Salt: NMT 0.5%
  4-Aminobenzenesulfonic acid, Sodium Salt: NMT 0.2%
  4,5-Dihydro-5-oxo-1-(4-sulfophenyl)-1H-pyrazole-3-carboxylic acid, Disodium Salt: NMT 0.2%

---

[1] To be used or sold for use to color food that is marketed in the United States, this color additive must be from a batch that has been certified by the U.S. Food and Drug Administration (FDA). If it is not from an FDA-certified batch, it is not a permitted color additive for food use in the United States, even if it is compositionally equivalent. The name FD&C Yellow No. 5 can be applied only to FDA-certified batches of this color additive. Tartrazine is a common name given to the uncertified colorant. See the monograph entitled *FD&C Yellow No. 5* for directions for producing an FDA-certified batch.

Ethyl or Methyl 4,5-dihydro-5-oxo-1-(4-sulfophenyl)-1H-pyrazole-3-carboxylate, Sodium Salt: NMT 0.1%
4,4'-(1-Triazene-1,3-diyl) bis(benzene sulfonic acid), Disodium Salt: NMT 0.05%
4-Aminoazobenzene: NMT 0.075 mg/kg
4-Aminobiphenyl: NMT 0.005 mg/kg
Aniline: NMT 0.1 mg/kg
Azobenzene: NMT 0.04 mg/kg
Benzidine: NMT 0.001 mg/kg
1,3-Diphenyltriazene: NMT 0.04 mg/kg

SPECIFIC TESTS
- **ETHER EXTRACTS (COMBINED)**, *Color Determination*, Appendix IIIC
  Acceptance criteria: NMT 0.2%
- **COMBINED TESTS**
  Tests
  - **LOSS ON DRYING (VOLATILE MATTER)**, *Color Determination*, Appendix IIIC
  - **CHLORIDE**, *Sodium Chloride, Color Determination*, Appendix IIIC
  - **SULFATE**, *Sodium Sulfate, Color Determination*, Appendix IIIC

  Acceptance criteria: NMT 13.0% in combination
- **WATER-INSOLUBLE MATTER**, *Color Determination*, Appendix IIIC
  Acceptance criteria: NMT 0.2%

TBHQ

First Published: Prior to FCC 6
Last Revision: First Supplement, FCC 6

tert-Butylhydroquinone
Mono-*tert*-butylhydroquinone

$C_{10}H_{14}O_2$ Formula wt 166.22
INS: 319   CAS: [1948-33-0]
UNII: C12674942B [tert-butylhydroquinone]

DESCRIPTION
TBHQ occurs as a white, crystalline solid. It is soluble in alcohol and in ether, and it is practically insoluble in water.
Function: Antioxidant
Packaging and Storage: Store in well-closed containers.

IDENTIFICATION
- **PROCEDURE**
  Analysis: Dissolve a few mg of sample in 1 mL of methanol, and add a few drops of a 25% solution of dimethylamine in water.
  Acceptance criteria: A pink to red color appears.

ASSAY
- **PROCEDURE**
  Sample: 170 mg, previously ground to a fine powder
  Analysis: Transfer *Sample*, into a 250-mL wide-mouth Erlenmeyer flask, and dissolve in 10 mL of methanol. To the flask, add 150 mL of water, 1 mL of 1 N sulfuric acid, and 4 drops of diphenylamine indicator (3 mg of *p*-diphenylaminesulfonic acid sodium salt per mL of 0.1 N sulfuric acid), and titrate with 0.1 N ceric sulfate to the first complete color change from yellow to red-violet. Record the volume, in mL, of 0.1 N ceric sulfate required as V. Calculate the percentage, A, of $C_{10}H_{14}O_2$ in the *Sample*, uncorrected for hydroquinone and 2,5-di-*tert*-butylhydroquinone, by the formula:

  $$\text{Result} = [F \times N \times (V - V_C)]/W$$

  F = factor, 8.311
  N = exact normality of the ceric sulfate solution
  V = volume of 0.1 N ceric sulfate required (mL)
  V_C = volume of ceric sulfate solution consumed by the primary oxidation products of TBHQ ordinarily present in the *Sample*, 0.1 mL
  W = weight of the sample taken (g)

  If hydroquinone (HQ) and 2,5-di-*tert*-butylhydroquinone (DTBHQ) are present in the *Sample*, they will be included in the titration. Calculate the corrected percentage of $C_{10}H_{14}O_2$ in the *Sample* by the formula:

  $$\text{Result} = A - (\%H \times F_1) - (\%DH \times F_2)$$

  A = percentage of $C_{10}H_{14}O_2$ in the *Sample*, determined above
  %H = percent hydroquinone (determined from the test for *2,5-Di-tert-butylhydroquinone and Hydroquinone*)
  F_1 = factor, 1.51
  %DH = percent 2,5-di-*tert*-butylhydroquinone (determined from the test for *2,5-Di-tert-butylhydroquinone and Hydroquinone*)
  F_2 = factor, 0.75
  Acceptance criteria: NLT 99.0% of $C_{10}H_{14}O_2$

IMPURITIES
Inorganic Impurities
- **LEAD**, *Lead Limit Test, Flame Atomic Absorption Spectrophotometric Method*, Appendix IIIB
  Sample: 10 g
  Acceptance criteria: NMT 2 mg/kg

Organic Impurities
- **TERT-BUTYL-P-BENZOQUINONE**
  Standard solution: Transfer 10 mg of monotertiary-butyl-*p*-benzoquinone into a 10-mL volumetric flask, dissolve in and dilute with chloroform to volume, and mix.
  Sample solution: Transfer 1 g of sample, previously reduced to a fine powder in a high-speed blender, into a 10-mL volumetric flask, dilute with chloroform to volume, and shake for 5 min to extract the *tert*-butyl-*p*-

benzoquinone. Pass through a Millipore filter (UHWP01300), or equivalent, before use.

Analysis: Use a suitable double-beam IR spectrophotometer and matched 0.4-mm liquid sample cells with calcium fluoride windows. Fill the reference cell with chloroform and the sample cell with *Standard solution*, place the cells in the respective reference and sample beams of the spectrophotometer, and record the spectrum from 1600 to 1775 cm^{-1}. Draw a background line on the spectrum from 1612 to 1750 cm^{-1}, and determine the net absorbance (A_S) of the *Standard solution* at 1659 cm^{-1}. Similarly, obtain the spectrum of the *Sample solution*, and determine its net absorbance (A_U) at 1659 cm^{-1}. Calculate the percentage of tert-butyl-p-benzoquinone in the sample taken by the formula:

$$\text{Result} = 100(A_U/A_S)(W_S/W_U)$$

W_S = weight of monotertiary-butyl-p-benzoquinone taken to prepare the *Standard solution* (mg)
W_U = weight of the sample taken to prepare the *Sample solution* (mg)

Acceptance criteria: NMT 0.2%

- **2,5-DI-TERT-BUTYLHYDROQUINONE AND HYDROQUINONE**
  HQ stock solution: 1 mg/mL hydroquinone in pyridine
  DTBHQ stock solution: 1 mg/mL 2,5-di-tert-butylhydroquinone in pyridine
  Methyl benzoate stock solution: 1 mg/mL methyl benzoate in pyridine
  Standard solutions: Prepare four *HQ standard solutions* as follows: Add 0.50, 1.00, 2.00, and 3.00 mL of *HQ stock solution* into separate 10-mL volumetric flasks, then add 2.00 mL of *Methyl benzoate stock solution* to each, dilute with pyridine to volume, and mix.
  Prepare four *DTBHQ Standard solutions* as follows: Add 0.50, 1.00, 2.00, and 3.00 mL of *DTBHQ stock solution* into separate 10-mL volumetric flasks, then add 2.00 mL of *Methyl benzoate stock solution* to each, dilute with pyridine to volume, and mix.
  Prepare the trimethylsilyl derivative of each standard solution as follows: Add 9 drops of standard solution to a 2-mL serum vial, cap the vial, evacuate with a 50-mL gas syringe, add 250 µL of *N,O*-bistrimethylsilylacetamide, and heat at about 80° for 10 min.
  Sample solution: Transfer 1 g of sample into a 10-mL volumetric flask, add 2.00 mL of *Methyl benzoate stock solution*, dilute with pyridine to volume, and mix. Add 9 drops of the resulting solution to a 2-mL serum vial, cap the vial, evacuate with a 50-mL gas syringe, add 250 µL of *N,O*-bistrimethylsilylacetamide, and heat at about 80° for 10 min.
  Chromatographic system, Appendix IIA
    Mode: Gas chromatography
    Detector: Thermal conductivity detector (F and M Model 810, or equivalent)
    Column: 0.61-m × 6.35-mm (od) stainless steel column (Perkin Elmer Instruments, or equivalent) packed with 20% Silicone SE-30, by weight, and 80% Diatoport S (60- to 80-mesh), or equivalent materials
    Column temperature: From 100° to 270°, heated at a rate of 15°/min
    Injection port temperature: 300°
    Carrier gas: Helium
    Flow rate: 100 mL/min
    Injection volume: 10 µL
  Analysis: [NOTE—Use bridge current of 140 mA, and sensitivity, 1× for the integrator (Infotronics CRS-100, or equivalent) and 2× for the recorder.]
  Chromatograph each *Standard solution* in duplicate, and plot the concentration ratio of *HQ standard solution* to *Methyl benzoate stock solution* (x-axis) against the response ratio of *HQ standard solution* to *Methyl benzoate stock solution* (y-axis). Plot the same relationships between *DTBHQ standard solution* and the *Methyl benzoate stock solution*.
  Chromatograph duplicate aliquots of *Sample solution*. The approximate peak times, in min, are methyl benzoate, 2.5; TMS derivative of HQ, 5.5; TMS derivative of tert-butylhydroquinone, 7.3; TMS derivative of DTBHQ, 8.4.
  Determine the peak areas (response) of interest by automatic integration or manual triangulation. Calculate the response ratio of *HQ standard solution* and *DTBHQ standard solution* to *Methyl benzoate stock solution*. From the calibration curves, determine the concentration ratio of *HQ standard solution* and *DTBHQ standard solution* to *Methyl benzoate stock solution*, and calculate the percentages of hydroquinone and of 2,5-di-tert-butylhydroquinone in the sample by the formula:

$$\text{Result} = Y \times I \times 10/S$$

  Y = concentration ratio (x-axis on calibration curve)
  I = percentage of *Methyl benzoate stock solution* in the *Sample solution* (w/v)
  S = weight of the sample taken to prepare the *Sample solution* (g)

  Acceptance criteria: NMT 0.2% 2,5-Di-tert-butylhydroquinone; NMT 0.1% Hydroquinone

- **TOLUENE**
  Standard solution: 50 µg/mL toluene in octyl alcohol
  Sample solution: 0.2 g/mL sample in octyl alcohol
  Chromatographic system, Appendix IIA
    Mode: Gas chromatography
    Detector: Flame ionization detector (F and M Model 810, or equivalent)
    Column: 3.66-m × 3.18-mm (od) stainless steel column, or equivalent, packed with 10% Silicone SE-30, by weight, and 90% Diatoport S (60- to 80-mesh), or equivalent materials
    Column temperature: From 70° to 280°, heated at a rate of 15°/min and held
    Injection port temperature: 275°
    Oven temperature: 300°
    Carrier gas: Helium
    Flow rate: 50 mL/min

Injection volume: 5 μL
Analysis: [NOTE—Use hydrogen and air settings of 20 psi for each.] Inject *Standard solution* into the chromatograph, and measure the height of the toluene peak (H_R) on the chromatogram. The toluene retention time is 3.3 min; other peaks are of no interest in this analysis. Similarly, obtain the chromatogram of *Sample solution*, and measure the height of the toluene peak (H_S). Calculate the percentage of toluene in the sample by the formula:

$$\text{Result} = 100(H_S/H_R)(C_R/C_S)$$

C_R = exact concentration of *Standard solution* in percent (w/v)
C_S = exact concentration of *Sample solution* in percent (w/v)

Acceptance criteria: NMT 0.0025%

SPECIFIC TESTS
- **MELTING RANGE OR TEMPERATURE DETERMINATION,** Appendix IIB
  Acceptance criteria: Between 126.5° and 128.5°
- **ULTRAVIOLET ABSORBANCE (POLYNUCLEAR HYDROCARBONS)**
  Sample preparation: Dissolve 1 g of L-ascorbic acid in 100 mL of ethanol and 100 mL of water contained in a 500-mL separator (*S-1*). Transfer about 50 g of sample into the separator, shake to dissolve, then add 50 mL of isooctane, and extract for 3 min. After the phases have separated, drain the lower, aqueous phase into a second 500-mL separator (*S-2*), then after 1 min of further separating, drain the lower phase into separator *S-2*. Add a second 50-mL portion of isooctane to the aqueous solution in *S-2*, and repeat the extraction procedure as previously described, drawing off the lower, aqueous phase into a third 500-mL separator (*S-3*). Add a third 50-mL portion of isooctane to the aqueous solution in *S-3*, and repeat the extraction procedure as previously described, drawing off and discarding the lower, aqueous phase.
  Extract the solutions in *S-1*, *S-2*, and *S-3* with two 100-mL portions of a 0.5% solution of 75 : 25 ethanol and water–ascorbic acid. Shake each mixture for 3 min, allow the phases to separate, and discard the lower, aqueous phases. Next, extract each isooctane solution with two 100-mL portions of a 5% solution of ethanol in water, and discard the lower, aqueous phases. Finally, wash each solution twice with 100 mL of water, and discard the washings.
  Lightly pack a standard-size chromatographic tube with 100 g of anhydrous sodium sulfate, and wash the packed column with 75 mL of isooctane, discarding the washings. Filter the isooctane solution from *S-1* through the column, and collect the filtrate in a 500-mL distillation flask. Wash *S-1* with the isooctane solution contained in *S-2*, then pour the solution onto the column, collecting the filtrate in the flask. Wash *S-2* and *S-1*, successively, with the isooctane solution in *S-3*, and filter the solution through the column as before. Wash *S-3*, *S-2*, and *S-1*, in that order and in tandem, with two successive 25-mL portions of isooctane, and pass the washings individually through the column and into the flask. Let the column drain completely.
  Add 2 mL of hexadecane and 2 boiling stones to the 500-mL distillation flask containing the combined isooctane extracts, and attach the flask to a suitable vacuum distillation assembly. Evacuate the assembly to about one-third atmosphere, then immerse the flask in a steam bath, and distill the solvent. When isooctane stops dripping into the receiver, turn off the vacuum, wash down the walls of the flask with 5 mL of isooctane added through the top of the distillation head, then replace the thermometer and again evacuate. The isooctane should distill over in about 1 min. At the end of this distillation, add another 5-mL portion of isooctane, and repeat the stripping procedure. Quantitatively wash the residue from the distillation flask into a 50-mL volumetric flask with isooctane, dilute with isooctane to volume, and mix.
  Analysis: Determine the ultraviolet absorption spectrum of the *Sample preparation* in a 5-cm silica cell from 400 nm to 250 nm with a suitable spectrophotometer, using isooctane as the blank. Determine the absorbance of a solvent control by following the above procedure in every detail, but with the sample omitted. From the sample spectrum determine the maximum absorbance per cm pathlength in each of the following wavelength intervals: (a) 280 to 289 nm; (b) 290 to 299 nm; (c) 300 to 359 nm; and (d) 360 to 400 nm. Calculate the maximum net absorbance/cm in each interval by subtracting from the sample absorbance the corresponding absorbance per cm of the solvent control.
  Acceptance criteria: The following net absorbance values are not exceeded at the indicated intervals: (a) 0.15; (b) 0.12; (c) 0.08; and (d) 0.02.

Terpene Resin, Natural
First Published: Prior to FCC 6

CAS: [9003-74-1]

DESCRIPTION
Terpene Resin, Natural, occurs as a pale yellow to yellow, solid, thermoplastic resin. It is a natural terpene occurring in some coal seams.
Function: Masticatory substance in chewing gum base
Packaging and Storage: Store in well-closed containers.

IMPURITIES
Inorganic Impurities
- **LEAD,** *Sample Solution for Lead Limit Test,* Appendix IV
  Control: 10 μg Pb (10 mL of *Diluted Standard Lead Solution*)
  Acceptance criteria: NMT 3 mg/kg

SPECIFIC TESTS
- **ACID VALUE**
  Sample: 3 g

1122 / Terpene Resin, Natural / *Monographs*

Analysis: Dissolve the *Sample* in 100 mL of a mixture of 75 mL of toluene and 36 mL of alcohol, previously neutralized to phenolphthalein TS with sodium hydroxide. Add 25 mL of a saturated sodium chloride solution, an additional 10 g of sodium chloride, and a few drops of phenolphthalein TS. Titrate with 0.1 N alcoholic potassium hydroxide to the first pink color that persists for at least 30 s.
Calculate the acid value by the formula:

$$\text{Result} = 56.1 \times V \times N/W$$

- V = volume (mL) of 0.1 N alcoholic potassium hydroxide
- N = normality of the alcoholic potassium hydroxide solution
- W = weight (g) of the sample taken

Acceptance criteria: Less than 8

- **MELTING RANGE OR TEMPERATURE DETERMINATION,** *Procedure for Class Ib,* Appendix IIB
  Acceptance criteria: NLT 155°

Terpene Resin, Synthetic

First Published: Prior to FCC 6

DESCRIPTION
Terpene Resin, Synthetic occurs as a pale yellow to yellow, solid, thermoplastic resin. It is composed essentially of α-pinene, β-pinene, and dipentene polymers. Its color is less than 4 on the Gardner scale (measured in 50% mineral spirit solution). It is insoluble in water.
Function: Masticatory substance in chewing gum base
Packaging and Storage: Store in well-closed containers.

IMPURITIES
Inorganic Impurities
- **LEAD,** *Sample Solution for Lead Limit Test,* Appendix IV
  Control: 10 μg Pb (10 mL of *Diluted Standard Lead Solution*)
  Acceptance criteria: NMT 3 mg/kg

SPECIFIC TESTS
- **ACID VALUE (FATS AND RELATED SUBSTANCES),** Appendix VII
  Acceptance criteria: Less than 5
- **SAPONIFICATION VALUE**
  Sample: 2 g
  Analysis: Transfer the *Sample* into a 250-mL Erlenmeyer flask. Add 25 mL of a 2:1 toluene:isopropyl alcohol mixture to dissolve the *Sample*. Then, using a volumetric pipet, add 50.0 mL of 0.1 N methanolic potassium hydroxide. Connect a condenser to the flask, and reflux gently until the sample is completely saponified (usually 30 min). Cool to room temperature, wash the condenser with water, add 2 to 3 drops of phenolphthalein TS, titrate the excess potassium hydroxide with 0.1 N hydrochloric acid, and record the total volume of acid required. Perform a blank determination (see *General Provisions*), and make any necessary correction.
  Calculate the saponification value by the formula:

$$\text{Result} = [(V_B - V_S) \times N \times F]/W$$

- V_B = volume of 0.1 N hydrochloric acid required for the blank
- V_S = volume of 0.1 N hydrochloric acid required for the *Sample*
- N = normality of hydrochloric acid
- F = factor, 56.1
- W = weight of the sample taken (g)

Acceptance criteria: NMT 5

Terpinen-4-ol

First Published: Prior to FCC 6

4-Carvomenthenol

$C_{10}H_{18}O$ Formula wt 154.25
FEMA: 2248
UNII: L65MV77ZG6 [4-carvomenthenol]

DESCRIPTION
Terpinen-4-ol occurs as a colorless to pale yellow liquid.
Odor: Piney
Solubility: Soluble in alcohol
Boiling Point: ~88° (6 mm Hg)
Solubility in Alcohol, Appendix VI: One mL dissolves in 1 mL of 95% ethanol.
Function: Flavoring agent

ASSAY
- **PROCEDURE:** Proceed as directed under *M-1b,* Appendix XI.
  Acceptance criteria: NLT 92.0% of $C_{10}H_{18}O$

SPECIFIC TESTS
- **REFRACTIVE INDEX,** Appendix II: At 20°
  Acceptance criteria: Between 1.476 and 1.480
- **SPECIFIC GRAVITY:** Determine at 25° by any reliable method (see *General Provisions*).
  Acceptance criteria: Between 0.928 and 0.934

α-Terpinene

First Published: Prior to FCC 6
Last Revision: First Supplement, FCC 6

1-Methyl-4-(1-methylethyl)-1,3-cyclohexadiene

$C_{10}H_{16}$ Formula wt 136.24
FEMA: 3558
UNII: I24X278AP1 [αterpinene]

DESCRIPTION
α-Terpinene occurs as a colorless liquid. It may contain a suitable antioxidant.
Odor: Lemon
Solubility: Soluble in alcohol, most fixed oils; insoluble or practically insoluble in water
Boiling Point: ~173°
Solubility in Alcohol, Appendix VI: One mL dissolves in 2 mL of 95% ethanol.
Function: Flavoring agent

ASSAY
- **PROCEDURE:** Proceed as directed under *M-1a,* Appendix XI.
  Acceptance criteria: NLT 89.0% of $C_{10}H_{16}$

SPECIFIC TESTS
- **REFRACTIVE INDEX,** Appendix II: At 20°
  Acceptance criteria: Between 1.475 and 1.480
- **SPECIFIC GRAVITY:** Determine at 25° by any reliable method (see *General Provisions*).
  Acceptance criteria: Between 0.833 and 0.838

γ-Terpinene

First Published: Prior to FCC 6
Last Revision: First Supplement, FCC 6

1-Methyl-4-(1-methylethyl)-1,4-cyclohexadiene

$C_{10}H_{16}$ Formula wt 136.24
FEMA: 3559
UNII: 4YGF4PQP49 [γ-terpinene]

DESCRIPTION
γ-Terpinene occurs as a colorless liquid. It may contain a suitable antioxidant.
Odor: Herbaceous, citrus
Solubility: Soluble in alcohol, most fixed oils; insoluble or practically insoluble in water
Boiling Point: ~182°
Solubility in Alcohol, Appendix VI: One mL dissolves in 3 mL of 95% ethanol.
Function: Flavoring agent

ASSAY
- **PROCEDURE:** Proceed as directed under *M-1a,* Appendix XI.
  Acceptance criteria: NLT 95.0% of $C_{10}H_{16}$

SPECIFIC TESTS
- **REFRACTIVE INDEX,** Appendix II: At 20°
  Acceptance criteria: Between 1.473 and 1.477
- **SPECIFIC GRAVITY:** Determine at 25° by any reliable method (see *General Provisions*).
  Acceptance criteria: Between 0.841 and 0.845

α-Terpineol

First Published: Prior to FCC 6

p-Menth-1-en-8-ol

$C_{10}H_{18}O$ Formula wt 154.25
FEMA: 3045
UNII: 21334LVV8W [α-terpineol]

DESCRIPTION
α-Terpineol occurs as a colorless, viscous liquid (high-purity material may solidify).
Odor: Lilac
Solubility: Soluble in propylene glycol, vegetable oils; slightly soluble in glycerin, water
Boiling Point: ~217°
Solubility in Alcohol, Appendix VI: One mL dissolves in 2 mL of 70% alcohol, in 4 mL of 60% alcohol, and in 8 mL of 50% alcohol.
Function: Flavoring agent

IDENTIFICATION
- **INFRARED SPECTRA,** *Spectrophotometric Identification Tests,* Appendix IIIC
  Acceptance criteria: The spectrum of the sample exhibits relative maxima at the same wavelengths as those of the spectrum below.

ASSAY
- **PROCEDURE:** Proceed as directed under *M-1a,* Appendix XI
  Acceptance criteria: NLT 96.0% of $C_{10}H_{18}O$ (sum of α-, (E)-β-, (Z)-β-, γ-, terpinen-4-ol, and terpinen-1-ol isomers)

SPECIFIC TESTS
- **REFRACTIVE INDEX,** Appendix II: At 20°
  Acceptance criteria: Between 1.482 and 1.485
- **SPECIFIC GRAVITY:** Determine at 25° by any reliable method (see *General Provisions*).
  Acceptance criteria: Between 0.930 and 0.936

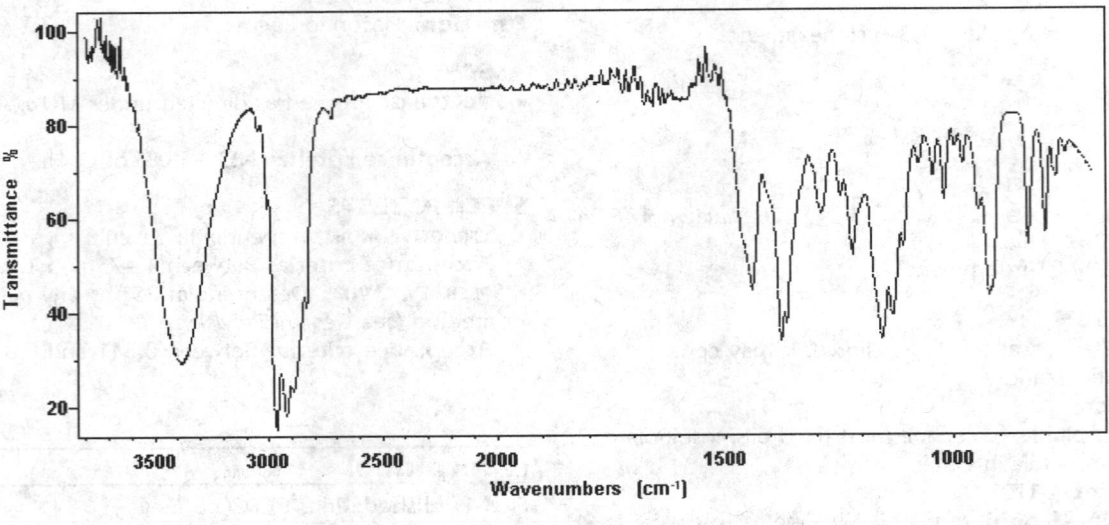

α-Terpineol

Terpinyl Acetate

First Published: Prior to FCC 6

Menthen-1-yl-8 Acetate

$C_{12}H_{20}O_2$ Formula wt 196.29
FEMA: 3047
UNII: NIT9SZT3D7 [terpinyl acetate]

DESCRIPTION
Terpinyl Acetate occurs as a colorless liquid.
Odor: Sweet, refreshing, herbaceous
Solubility: Soluble in alcohol, most fixed oils, mineral oil, propylene glycol; slightly soluble in glycerin; insoluble or practically insoluble in water
Boiling Point: ~220°
Solubility in Alcohol, Appendix VI: One mL dissolves in 5 mL of 70% alcohol and remains in solution upon dilution to 10 mL.

Function: Flavoring agent

IDENTIFICATION
- **INFRARED SPECTRA,** *Spectrophotometric Identification Tests,* Appendix IIIC
  Acceptance criteria: The spectrum of the sample exhibits relative maxima at the same wavelengths as those of the spectrum below.

ASSAY
- **PROCEDURE:** Proceed as directed under *M-1b,* Appendix XI
  Acceptance criteria: NLT 97.0% of $C_{12}H_{20}O_2$ (sum of α-, (E)-, β-, (Z)-β-, γ-, terpinen-4-ol, and terpinen-1-ol isomers)

SPECIFIC TESTS
- **REFRACTIVE INDEX,** Appendix II: At 20°
  Acceptance criteria: Between 1.464 and 1.467
- **SPECIFIC GRAVITY:** Determine at 25° by any reliable method (see *General Provisions*).
  Acceptance criteria: Between 0.953 and 0.962

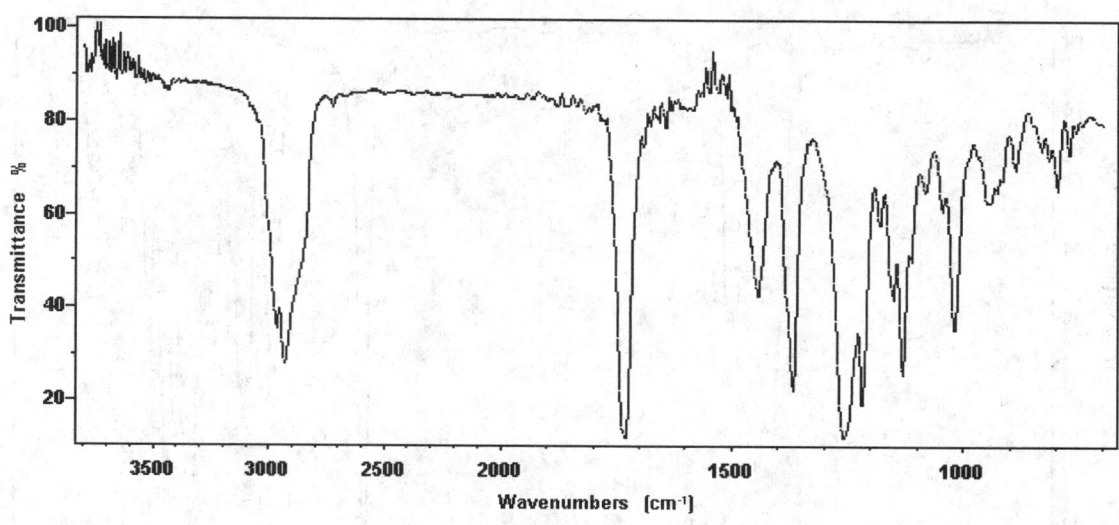

Terpinyl Acetate

Terpinyl Propionate

First Published: Prior to FCC 6

Menthen-1-yl-8 Propionate

$C_{13}H_{22}O_2$
FEMA: 3053

Formula wt 210.32

DESCRIPTION
Terpinyl Propionate occurs as a colorless to slightly yellow liquid.
Odor: Sweet, floral, herbaceous, lavender
Solubility: Soluble in glycerin; slightly soluble in propylene glycol; miscible in alcohol, chloroform, ether, most fixed oils; insoluble or practically insoluble in water
Boiling Point: ~240°
Solubility in Alcohol, Appendix VI: One mL dissolves in 2 mL of 80% alcohol to give a clear solution.

Function: Flavoring agent

IDENTIFICATION
- **INFRARED SPECTRA,** *Spectrophotometric Identification Tests,* Appendix IIIC
  Acceptance criteria: The spectrum of the sample exhibits relative maxima at the same wavelengths as those of the spectrum below.

ASSAY
- **PROCEDURE:** Proceed as directed under *M-1b,* Appendix XI
  Acceptance criteria: NLT 95.0% of $C_{13}H_{22}O_2$ (sum of α-, (E)-, β-, (Z)-β-, γ-, terpinen-4-ol, and terpinen-1-ol isomers)

SPECIFIC TESTS
- **ACID VALUE, FLAVOR CHEMICALS (OTHER THAN ESSENTIAL OILS),** *M-15,* Appendix XI
  Acceptance criteria: NMT 1.0
- **REFRACTIVE INDEX,** Appendix II: At 20°
  Acceptance criteria: Between 1.462 and 1.468
- **SPECIFIC GRAVITY:** Determine at 25° by any reliable method (see *General Provisions*).
  Acceptance criteria: Between 0.947 and 0.952

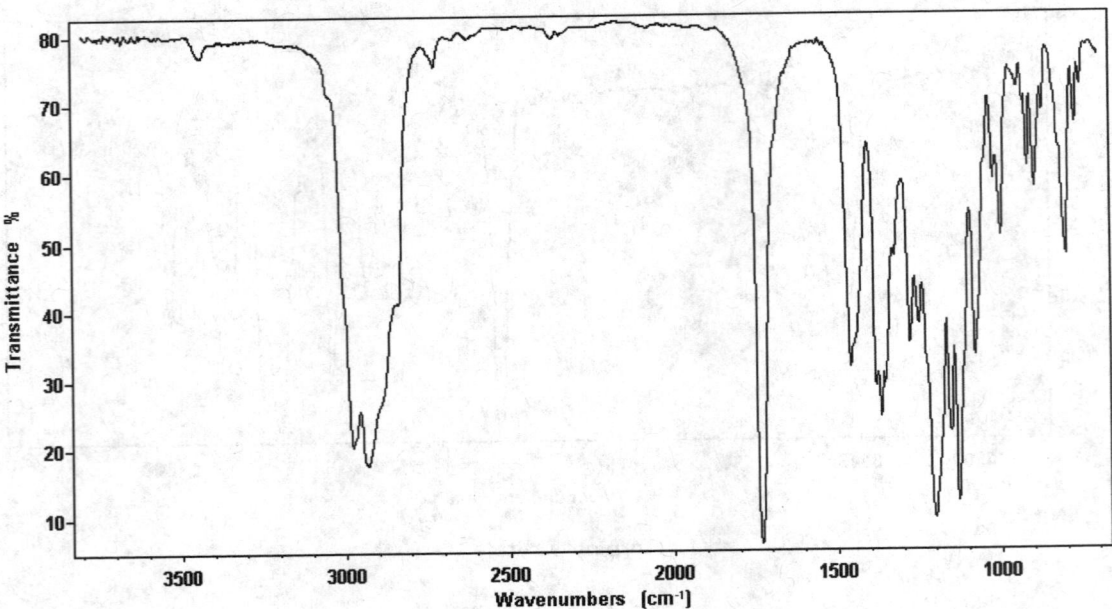

Terpinyl Propionate

δ-Tetradecalactone

First Published: Prior to FCC 6

C₁₄H₂₆O₂   Formula wt 226.36
FEMA: 3590
UNII: 46339AI51N [δ-tetradecalactone]

DESCRIPTION
δ-Tetradecalactone occurs as a colorless to pale yellow liquid.
Odor: Fruity
Solubility: Soluble in propylene glycol, vegetable oils; insoluble or practically insoluble in water
Boiling Point: ~130° (5 mm Hg)
Solubility in Alcohol, Appendix VI: One mL dissolves in 1 mL of 95% ethanol.
Function: Flavoring agent

IDENTIFICATION
- **INFRARED SPECTRA,** Spectrophotometric Identification Tests, Appendix IIIC
   Acceptance criteria: The spectrum of the sample exhibits relative maxima at the same wavelengths as those of the spectrum below.

ASSAY
- **PROCEDURE:** Proceed as directed under M-1b, Appendix XI.
   Acceptance criteria: NLT 98.0% of C₁₄H₂₆O₂

SPECIFIC TESTS
- **ACID VALUE, FLAVOR CHEMICALS (OTHER THAN ESSENTIAL OILS),** M-15, Appendix XI
   Acceptance criteria: NMT 5.0
- **REFRACTIVE INDEX,** Appendix II: At 20°
   Acceptance criteria: Between 1.459 and 1.465
- **SPECIFIC GRAVITY:** Determine at 25° by any reliable method (see General Provisions).
   Acceptance criteria: Between 0.931 and 0.937

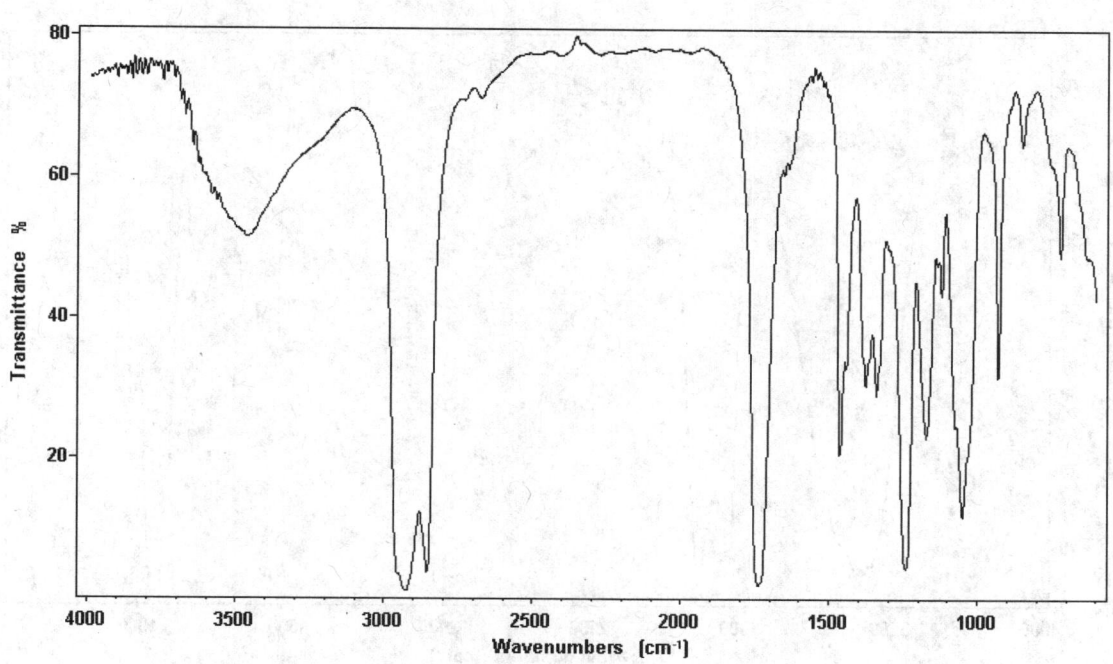

δ-Tetradecalactone

Tetrahydrofurfuryl Alcohol
First Published: Prior to FCC 6

$C_5H_{10}O_2$ Formula wt 102.13
FEMA: 3056
UNII: XD95821VF9 [tetrahydrofurfuryl alcohol]

DESCRIPTION
Tetrahydrofurfuryl alcohol occurs as a colorless liquid.
Odor: Mild, warm, oily, caramel
Boiling Point: ~178°
Function: Flavoring agent

IDENTIFICATION
- **INFRARED SPECTRA,** Spectrophotometric Identification Tests, Appendix IIIC

  Acceptance criteria: The spectrum of the sample exhibits relative maxima at the same wavelengths as those of the spectrum below.

ASSAY
- **PROCEDURE:** Proceed as directed under *M-1a,* Appendix XI.
  Acceptance criteria: NLT 99.0% of $C_5H_{10}O_2$

SPECIFIC TESTS
- **REFRACTIVE INDEX,** Appendix II: At 20°
  Acceptance criteria: Between 1.452 and 1.453
- **SPECIFIC GRAVITY:** Determine at 25° by any reliable method (see *General Provisions*).
  Acceptance criteria: Between 1.050 and 1.052

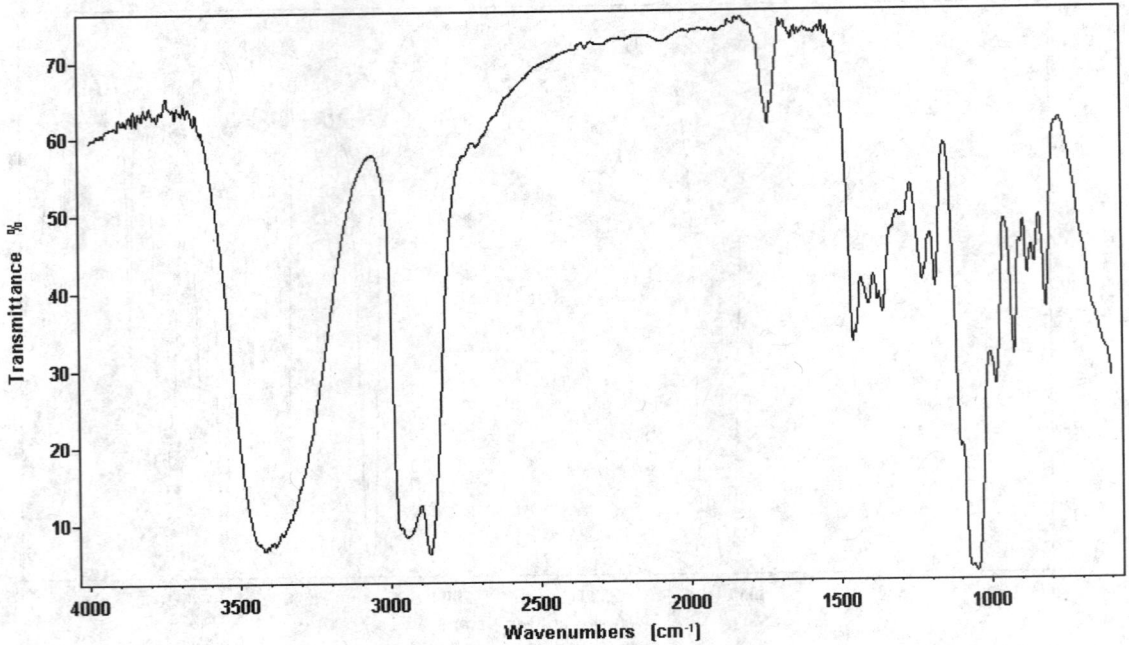
Tetrahydrofurfuryl Alcohol

Tetrahydrolinalool

First Published: Prior to FCC 6

3,7-Dimethyl-3-octanol

$C_{10}H_{22}O$ Formula wt 158.28
FEMA: 3060
UNII: UM4XS5M134 [tetrahydrolinalool]

DESCRIPTION
Tetrahydrolinalool occurs as a colorless liquid.
Odor: Distinct floral
Solubility: Soluble in alcohol, most fixed oils; insoluble or practically insoluble in water
Boiling Point: ~71° (6 mm Hg)
Function: Flavoring agent

ASSAY
- **PROCEDURE:** Proceed as directed under *M-1a*, Appendix XI.
  Acceptance criteria: NLT 95.0% of $C_{10}H_{22}O$

SPECIFIC TESTS
- **REFRACTIVE INDEX,** Appendix II: At 20°
  Acceptance criteria: Between 1.431 and 1.435
- **SPECIFIC GRAVITY:** Determine at 25° by any reliable method (see *General Provisions*).
  Acceptance criteria: Between 0.823 and 0.829

2,3,5,6-Tetramethylpyrazine

First Published: Prior to FCC 6

$C_8H_{12}N_2$ Formula wt 136.20
FEMA: 3237
UNII: V80F4IA5XG [tetramethylpyrazine]

DESCRIPTION
2,3,5,6-Tetramethylpyrazine occurs as a white crystalline solid or powder.
Odor: Fermented soybeans
Solubility: Soluble in alcohol, propylene glycol, most fixed oils; slightly soluble in water
Boiling Point: ~190°
Function: Flavoring agent

IDENTIFICATION
- **INFRARED SPECTRA,** *Spectrophotometric Identification Tests,* Appendix IIIC
  Acceptance criteria: The spectrum of the sample exhibits relative maxima at the same wavelengths as those of the spectrum below.

ASSAY
- **PROCEDURE:** Proceed as directed under *M-1a*, Appendix XI.
  Acceptance criteria: NLT 95.0% of $C_8H_{12}N_2$

OTHER REQUIREMENTS
- **MELTING RANGE OR TEMPERATURE DETERMINATION,** Appendix IIB
  Acceptance criteria: Between 85° and 90°
- **WATER,** *Water Determination, Method I,* Appendix IIB
  [NOTE—Use freshly distilled pyridine as the solvent.]
  Acceptance criteria: NMT 0.2%

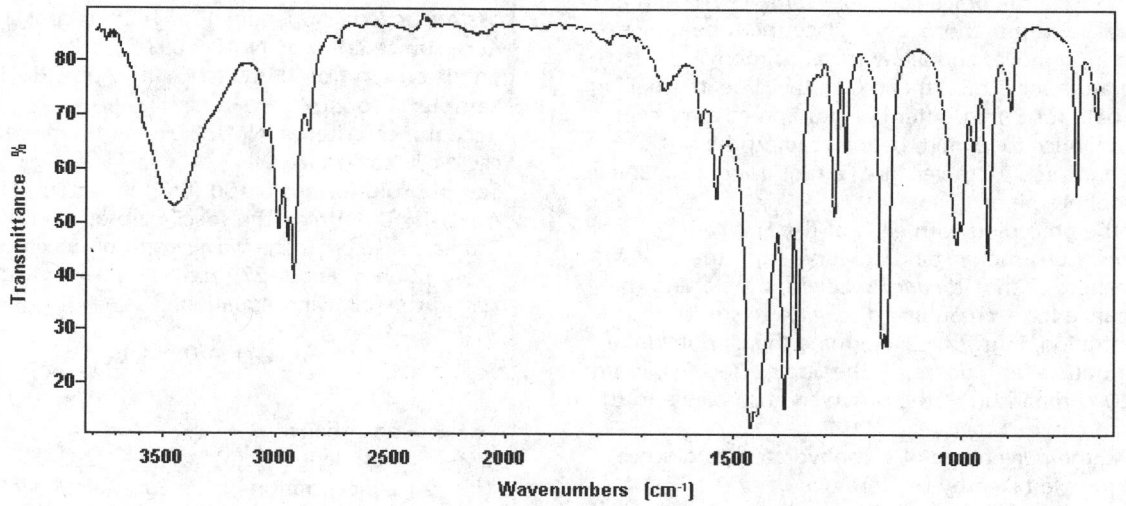

2,3,5,6-Tetramethylpyrazine

Thaumatin

First Published: Second Supplement, FCC 6

Thaumatin I
Thaumatin II

Formula wt, Thaumatin I 22,209
Formula wt, Thaumatin II 22,293
INS: 957   CAS: [53850-34-3]
FEMA: 3732
UNII: KNC9Q0EE6G [thaumatin]

DESCRIPTION
Thaumatin is an odorless, cream-colored powder. It is obtained by aqueous extraction of the arils of the fruit of *Thaumatococcus daniellii* (Benth), and consists essentially of the proteins Thaumatin I and Thaumatin II, together with minor amounts of plant constituents derived from the source material. It is very soluble in water and insoluble in acetone.
Function: Sweetener; flavor enhancer
Packaging and Storage: Store in well-closed containers.

IDENTIFICATION
- **NINHYDRIN TEST**
  Solution A: 2 mg/mL of triketohydrine hydrate in water
  Sample solution: 1 mg/mL
  Analysis: To 5 mL of the *Sample solution*, add 1 mL of freshly prepared *Solution A*.
  Acceptance criteria: A bluish color is produced.
- **INFRARED SPECTRA,** *Spectrophotometric Identification Tests,* Appendix IIIC
  Sample preparation: K
  Acceptance criteria: Characteristic maxima of absorption are shown at the following wavenumbers: 3300, 2960, 1650, 1529, 1452, 1395, 1237, 1103 and 612 cm^{-1}. The infrared spectrum of the *Sample preparation* corresponds to the infrared spectrum below.

ASSAY
- **PROTEIN,** *Nitrogen Determination, Method II,* Appendix IIIC
  Analysis: Calculate the percent protein with the formula:

  $$\text{Result} = 6.2 \times N$$

  N = percent nitrogen
  Acceptance criteria: NLT 93% determined on the dried basis

IMPURITIES
Inorganic Impurities
- **ALUMINUM,** *Aluminum Limit Test,* Appendix IIIB
  Sample: 10 g
  Acceptance criteria: NMT 0.01%
- **LEAD,** *Lead Limit Test, Flame Atomic Absorption Spectrophotometric Method,* Appendix IIIB
  Sample: 10 g
  Analysis: Proceed as directed using the *Diluted Standard Lead Solutions* corresponding to the *5 mg/kg Lead Limit.*
  Acceptance criteria: NMT 3 mg/kg

Organic Impurities
- **CARBOHYDRATES**
  Solution A: Combine 0.5 mL of a 3% (w/v) aqueous solution of L-cystine hydrochloride monohydrate with 25 mL of 86% (v/v) sulfuric acid, and cool on ice. [NOTE—Prepare immediately before use.]
  Sample solution: 2 mg/mL

Standard solutions: Prepare a series of at least four standard glucose solutions ranging in concentration from 10 µg/mL to 100 µg/mL.

Analysis: Place a 0.2-mL aliquot of the *Sample solution* in a very clean, dust-free glass tube, and cool in an ice bath. Add 1.2 mL of ice-cold *Solution A*, cover with a glass ball, and mix thoroughly. Place the tube on ice for 2 min, remove, and allow to set at room temperature for 3 min, then place the tube in a boiling water bath for 3 min. After boiling, immediately cool the tube in ice for 5 min, before reading the absorbance in a 1-cm cell at 412 nm, using a suitable spectrophotometer.

Repeat the preceding with each of the *Standard solutions*. Construct a standard curve from the absorbances of the *Standard solutions*, by plotting the absorbance for each *Standard solution* versus its concentration, in µg/mL. Determine the carbohydrate concentration (as glucose) in the *Sample solution*, in µg/mL, by comparison of the observed absorbance to the standard curve.

Calculate the percentage of carbohydrates (as glucose) in the sample taken by the formula:

$$\text{Result} = C_U/C_{SMP} \times F \times 100\%$$

C_U = concentration of carbohydrates in the *Sample solution* determined from the standard curve (µg/mL)

C_{SMP} = concentration of the sample in the *Sample solution* (mg/mL)

F = factor converting µg to mg (1/1000)

Acceptance criteria: NMT 3.0% on the dried basis

SPECIFIC TESTS

- **LOSS ON DRYING,** Appendix IIC: 105° to constant weight
  Acceptance criteria: NMT 9.0%
- **RESIDUE ON IGNITION (SULFATED ASH),** Appendix IIC
  Sample: 1 to 2 g
  Acceptance criteria: NMT 2.0% on the dried basis
- **SPECIFIC ABSORPTION**
  Sample solution: 1 in 100 (w/v) in water; pH 2.7
  Analysis: Determine the specific absorption of the *Sample solution* at the wavelength of maximum absorption of about 279 nm using a 1-cm cell and using the following equation:

$$A^{1\%}{}_{1cm} = A/(L \times C) \times 10$$

A = absorbance
L = path length (cm)
C = concentration of the *Sample solution* (g/100 mL)

Acceptance criteria: NLT 11.5 and NMT 13.0 on the dried basis

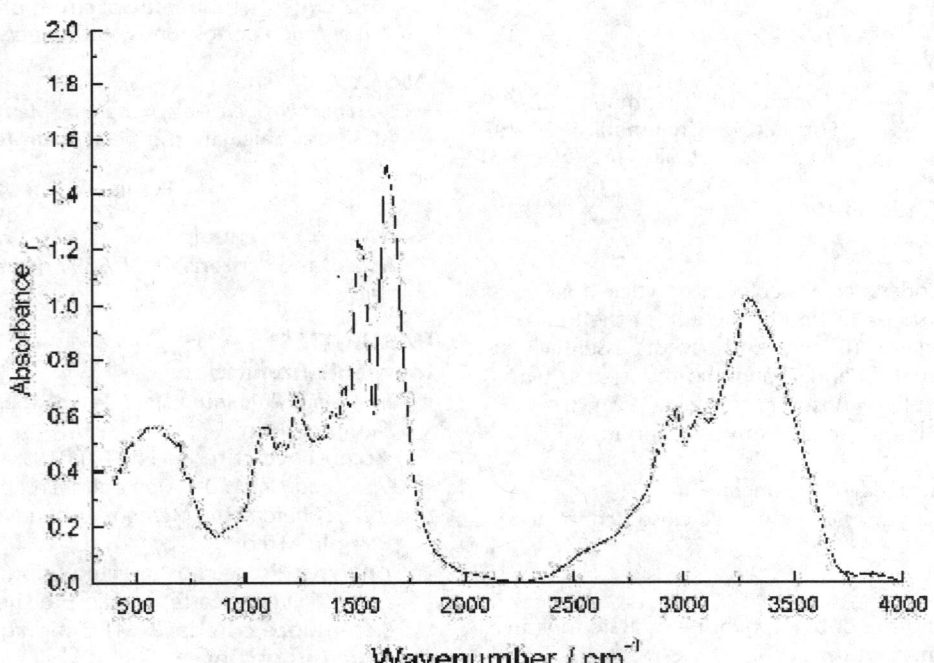

Thaumatin

L-Theanine

First Published: Third Supplement, FCC 7

5-N-Ethyl-L-glutamine
L-Glutamic acid-γ-monoethylamide
Gamma-glutamylethylamide

$C_7H_{14}N_2O_3$ Formula wt 174.20
CAS: [3081-61-6]

DESCRIPTION
L-Theanine occurs as a white, odorless, crystalline powder, with a slight sweet taste. L-Theanine is produced by enzymatic synthesis from L-glutamine and ethylamine, using glutaminase derived from either *Pseudomonas nitroreducens* or *Bacillus amyloliquefaciens*. The microorganisms are cultured, immobilized in a gel, and placed into reaction columns where the substrate and environmental conditions are controlled. The resultant mixture is cooled, purified, concentrated, and dried into the final product. It is soluble in water and forms a transparent, colorless solution. It is insoluble in ethanol.
Function: Nutrient
Packaging and Storage: Store in well-closed, light-resistant containers at room temperature.

IDENTIFICATION
- **A. INFRARED ABSORPTION,** *Spectrophotometric Identification Tests,* Appendix IIIC
  Reference standard: USP L-Theanine RS
  Sample and standard preparation: K
  Acceptance criteria: The spectrum of the sample exhibits maxima at the same wavelengths as those in the spectrum of the *Reference standard*.
- **B. PROCEDURE**
  Acceptance criteria: The retention time of the major peak (excluding the solvent peak) in the chromatogram of the *Sample solution* is the same as that observed in the *Standard solution*.

ASSAY
- **PROCEDURE**
  Mobile phase: 2% (v/v) methanol solution containing 0.1% trifluoroacetic acid
  Internal standard solution: 10 mg/mL of nicotinamide solution
  Standard solutions: 0.5 mg/mL, 1 mg/mL, and 2 mg/mL of USP L-Theanine RS in water. Add the *Internal standard solution* to the *Standard solutions* for a final *Internal standard* concentration of 1 mg/mL.
  Sample solution: 1 mg/mL in water. Add the *Internal standard solution* to the *Sample solution* for a final *Internal standard* concentration of 1 mg/mL.
  Chromatographic system, Appendix IIA
  Mode: High-performance liquid chromatography
  Detector: UV 210 nm
  Column: 4.0-mm (i.d.) × 150-mm C18 analytical column and 4.0-mm (i.d.) × 10-mm C18 precolumn[1]
  Column temperature: 30°
  Flow rate: 0.5 mL/min
  Injection volume: 11 µL
  System suitability
    Sample: 0.5 mg/mL of the *Standard solution*
    Suitability requirements
      Suitability requirement 1: The signal-to-noise ratio is NLT 10.
      Suitability requirement 2: The relative standard deviation is NMT 1.96% for the peak area and retention time from 0.5 mg/mL of the *Standard solution*.
      Suitability requirement 3: The retention time for the L-theanine peak from 0.5 mg/mL of the *Standard solution* is NMT 8.5 min.
  Analysis: Separately inject equal volumes of the *Standard solutions* and *Sample solution* into the chromatograph and measure the responses for the major peaks on the resulting chromatograms. Prepare a standard curve by plotting the ratio of the concentration of the *Standard solutions* and the *Internal standard* versus the ratio of the peak area of the *Standard solutions* and the *Internal standard*. From the regression of the standard curve, calculate the concentration of L-Theanine in the *Sample*. Calculate the percentage of L-Theanine in the *Sample* taken:

$$\text{Result} = C_O/C_{SMP} \times 100\%$$

C_O = concentration of L-Theanine in the sample, determined from the standard curve (mg/mL)
C_{SMP} = concentration of the sample in the *Sample solution* (mg/mL)
Acceptance criteria: 98%–102% on the dried basis

IMPURITIES
Inorganic Impurities
- **ARSENIC,** *Arsenic Limit Test,* Appendix IIIB
  Sample: 0.5 g
  Acceptance criteria: NMT 4 mg/kg
- **CHLORIDE,** *Chloride and Sulfate Limit Tests,* Appendix IIIB
  Sample: 1.0 g
  Control: 210 µg of chloride (21 mL of *Standard Chloride Solution*)
  Acceptance criteria: Any turbidity produced by the *Sample* does not exceed that shown in the *Control* (NMT 210 ppm).
- **LEAD,** *Lead Limit Test, Flame Atomic Absorption Spectrophotometric Method,* Appendix IIIB
  Acceptance criteria: NMT 1 mg/kg

SPECIFIC TESTS
- **LOSS ON DRYING,** Appendix IIC: 105°, 3h
  Sample: 1 g
  Acceptance criteria: NMT 1%
- **RESIDUE ON IGNITION (SULFATED ASH),** Appendix IIC
  Sample: 1 g
  Acceptance criteria: NMT 0.2%

---
[1] Develosil ODS-HG-50; Nomura Chemical Co. Ltd., or equivalent.

- **pH,** Appendix IIB
  Analysis: Analyze a 1% sample solution with a pH meter.
  Acceptance criteria: 5–6
- **Optical (Specific) Rotation,** Appendix IIB
  Sample: 50 mg/mL sample, previously dried
  Acceptance criteria: $[\alpha]_D^{20}$ between +7.7° and +8.5°, on the dry basis
- **Melting Range or Temperature Determination,** Appendix IIB
  Acceptance criteria: 214°–215°

Thiamine Hydrochloride

First Published: Prior to FCC 6

Aneurine Hydrochloride
Thiamine Chloride
Vitamin B₁
Vitamin B₁ Hydrochloride

$C_{12}H_{17}ClN_4OS \cdot HCl$ Formula wt 337.27
                                CAS: [67-03-8]
UNII: M572600E5P [thiamine hydrochloride]

DESCRIPTION
Thiamine Hydrochloride occurs as small, white to yellow-white crystals or crystalline powder. When exposed to air, the anhydrous product rapidly absorbs about 4% of water. It melts at about 248° with some decomposition. One g dissolves in about 1 mL of water and in about 100 mL of alcohol. It is soluble in glycerin, and is insoluble in ether.
Function: Nutrient
Packaging and Storage: Store in tight, light-resistant containers.

IDENTIFICATION
- **Chloride,** Appendix IIIA
  Sample solution: 20 mg/mL
  Acceptance criteria: Passes test
- **Infrared Absorption,** *Spectrophotometric Identification Tests,* Appendix IIIC
  Reference standard: USP Thiamine Hydrochloride RS.
  Sample and **Standard preparation:** K. [Note—Dry the sample at 105° for 2 h prior to dispersing in the potassium bromide.]
  Acceptance criteria: The spectrum of the sample exhibits maxima at the same wavelengths as those in the spectrum of the *Reference standard*.

ASSAY
- **Procedure**
  Solution A: 0.005 M sodium 1-octanesulfonate in 1:100 glacial acetic acid
  Solution B: Methanol and acetonitrile (3:2), (v/v)
  Mobile phase: *Solution A* and *Solution B* (60:40) (v/v), filtered and degassed. [Note—If necessary, adjust the relative quantities of the two solutions to obtain baseline separation of thiamine hydrochloride and methyl benzoate.]
  Internal standard solution: 20 µL/mL methyl benzoate in methanol, made to 100 mL
  Standard stock solution: 1 mg/mL USP Thiamine Hydrochloride RS in *Mobile phase*
  Standard solution: 400 µg/mL, made by transferring 20.0 mL of *Standard stock solution* into a 50-mL volumetric flask, adding 5.0 mL of *Internal standard solution*, diluting to volume with *Mobile phase*, and mixing
  Sample: 200 mg
  Sample stock solution: Transfer the *Sample* into a 100-mL volumetric flask, dissolve in and dilute to volume with *Mobile phase*, and mix.
  Sample solution: Transfer 10 mL of *Sample stock solution* into a 50 mL volumetric flask, add 5.0 mL of *Internal standard solution*, dilute to volume with *Mobile phase*, and mix.
  Chromatographic system, Appendix IIA
    Mode: High-performance liquid chromatography
    Detector: UV (254 nm)
    Column: 300-mm × 4-mm packed with 10-µm octadecylsilanized silica (µ Bondapak C 18, or equivalent)
    Flow rate: about 1 mL/min
    Injection volume: about 10 µL
  System suitability
    Sample: *Standard solution*
    Suitability requirements
      Resolution: NLT 4.0 between thiamine and methyl benzoate peaks
      Column efficiency: NLT 1500 theoretical plates determined from thiamine peak
      Tailing factor: NMT 2.0 for the thiamine peak
      Relative standard deviation: NMT 2.0% for three replicates of the *Standard solution*
  Analysis: Separately inject the *Standard solution* and the *Sample solution* into the chromatograph, record the chromatograms, and measure the peak area responses for the major peaks. Calculate the percent $C_{12}H_{17}ClN_{14}OS \cdot HCl$ in the *Sample* taken by the formula:

  $$\text{Result} = (C_S/C_U) \times (R_U/R_S) \times 100\%$$

  C_S = concentration of USP Thiamine Hydrochloride RS in the *Standard solution* (µg/mL)
  C_U = concentration of the sample in the *Sample solution* (µg/mL)
  R_U = ratio of the peak area of the sample to that of methyl benzoate for the *Sample solution*
  R_S = ratio of the peak area of thiamine to that of methyl benzoate for the *Standard solution*
  Acceptance criteria: NLT 98.0% and NMT 102.0% of $C_{12}H_{17}ClN_4OS \cdot HCl$, calculated on the anhydrous basis

IMPURITIES
Inorganic Impurities
- **LEAD**, *Lead Limit Test, Flame Atomic Absorption Spectrophotometric Method,* Appendix IIIB
  Sample: 10 g
  Acceptance criteria: NMT 2 mg/kg
- **NITRATE**
  Sample solution: 20 mg/mL
  Analysis: Add 2 mL of sulfuric acid to 2 mL of *Sample solution*, cool, and superimpose 2 mL of ferrous sulfate TS.
  Acceptance criteria: No brown ring forms at the junction of the two layers.

SPECIFIC TESTS
- **COLOR OF SOLUTION**
  Sample solution: 100 mg/mL
  Control: 1.5 mL of 0.1 N potassium dichromate diluted to 1000 mL
  Acceptance criteria: The *Sample solution* exhibits no more color than the *Control*.
- **PH**, *pH Determination,* Appendix IIB
  Sample solution: 10 mg/mL
  Acceptance criteria: Between 2.7 and 3.4
- **RESIDUE ON IGNITION (SULFATED ASH),** Appendix IIC
  Sample: 1 g
  Acceptance criteria: NMT 0.2%
- **WATER**, *Water Determination,* Appendix IIB
  Acceptance criteria: NMT 5.0%

Thiamine Mononitrate
First Published: Prior to FCC 6

Thiamine Nitrate
Vitamin B1
Vitamin B1 Mononitrate

$C_{12}H_{17}N_5O_4S$ Formula wt 327.36
                          CAS: [532-43-4]
UNII: 8K0I04919X [thiamine mononitrate]

DESCRIPTION
Thiamine Mononitrate occurs as white to yellow-white crystals or crystalline powder. One g dissolves in about 35 mL of water. It is slightly soluble in alcohol and in chloroform.
Function: Nutrient
Packaging and Storage: Store in tight, light-resistant containers.

IDENTIFICATION
- **A. PROCEDURE**
  Sample solution: 20 mg/mL
  Analysis: Add 2 mL of sulfuric acid to 2 mL of *Sample solution*, cool, and superimpose 2 mL of ferrous sulfate TS.
  Acceptance criteria: A brown ring forms at the junction of the two liquids.
- **B. PROCEDURE**
  Sample: 5 mg
  Analysis: Dissolve the *Sample* in a mixture of 1 mL of lead acetate TS and 1 mL of 100 mg/mL sodium hydroxide. [NOTE—A yellow color appears.] Heat the mixture for several minutes on a steam bath.
  Acceptance criteria: The color of the solution changes to brown and, on standing, a precipitate of lead sulfide forms.
- **C. PROCEDURE**
  Sample solution: 100 mg/mL
  Analysis: Treat aliquots of the *Sample solution* separately with each of the following solutions: mercuric chloride TS, iodine TS, mercuric-potassium iodide TS, and trinitrophenol TS.
  Acceptance criteria: A white precipitate results from treatment with mercuric chloride TS, and a red-brown precipitate results from treatment with iodine TS. Treatment with mercuric-potassium iodide TS and trinitrophenol TS also causes precipitates to form.
- **D. PROCEDURE**
  Sample: 5 mg
  Analysis: Dissolve the *Sample* in 5 mL of 0.5 N sodium hydroxide, add 0.5 mL of potassium ferrocyanide TS and 5 mL of isobutyl alcohol. Shake vigorously for 2 min, and allow the layers to separate. Illuminate the solution from above with a vertical beam of ultraviolet light and view at a right angle to this beam.
  Acceptance criteria: The air-liquid meniscus shows a vivid blue fluorescence which disappears when the mixture is slightly acidified and reappears when it is again made alkaline.

ASSAY
- **PROCEDURE**
  Solution A: 0.005 M sodium 1-octanesulfonate in 1:100 glacial acetic acid
  Solution B: Methanol and acetonitrile (3:2), (v/v)
  Mobile phase: Prepare a (60:40) (v/v) mixture of *Solution A* and *Solution B*, filter and degas. [NOTE—If necessary, adjust the relative quantities of the two solutions to obtain baseline separation of thiamine hydrochloride and methyl benzoate.]
  Internal standard solution: 20 µL/mL methyl benzoate in methanol
  Standard stock solution: 1 mg/mL USP Thiamine Hydrochloride RS in *Mobile phase*
  Standard solution: 400 µg/mL, made by transferring 20.0 mL of *Standard stock solution* into a 50-mL volumetric flask, adding 5.0 mL of *Internal standard solution*, diluting to volume with *Mobile phase*, and mixing.
  Sample: 200 mg
  Sample stock solution: Transfer the *Sample* into a 100-mL volumetric flask, dissolve in and dilute to volume with *Mobile phase*, and mix.

Sample solution: Transfer 10 mL of *Sample stock solution* into a 50 mL volumetric flask, add 5.0 mL of *Internal standard solution*, dilute to volume with *Mobile phase*, and mix.
Chromatographic system, Appendix IIA
  Mode: High-performance liquid chromatography
  Detector: UV (254 nm)
  Column: 300-mm × 4-mm packed with 10-μm octadecylsilanized silica (μ Bondapak C 18, or equivalent)
  Flow rate: About 1 mL/min
  Injection volume: About 10 μL
  System suitability
    Sample: *Standard solution*
    Suitability requirements
      Resolution: NLT 4.0 between thiamine and methyl benzoate peaks
      Column efficiency: NLT 1500 theoretical plates determined from thiamine peak
      Tailing factor: NMT 2.0 for the thiamine peak
      Relative standard deviation: NMT 2.0% for three replicates of the *Standard solution*
Analysis: Separately inject the *Standard solution* and the *Sample solution* into the chromatograph, record the chromatograms, and measure the peak area responses for the major peaks. Calculate the percent $C_{12}H_{17}N_5O_4S$ in the *Sample* taken by the formula:

$$\text{Result} = (R_U/R_S) \times 0.5C \times (M_{r1}/M_{r2})$$

R_U = ratio of the peak area of thiamine to that of methyl benzoate for the *Sample solution*
R_S = ratio of the peak area of thiamine to that of methyl benzoate for the *Standard solution*
C = concentration of USP Thiamine Hydrochloride RS in the *Standard solution* (μg/mL)
M_{r1} = formula weight of thiamine mononitrate, 327.36
M_{r2} = formula weight of thiamine hydrochloride, 337.27

Acceptance criteria: NLT 98.0% and NMT 102.0% of $C_{12}H_{17}N_5O_4S$, calculated on the anhydrous basis

IMPURITIES
Inorganic Impurities
- **CHLORIDE,** *Chloride and Sulfate Limit Tests*, *Chloride Limit Test*, Appendix IIIB
  Sample: 25 mg
  Control: 15 μg of chloride (1.5 mL of *Standard Chloride Solution*)
  Acceptance criteria: Any turbidity produced in the solution containing the *Sample* does not exceed that produced by the *Control*. (NMT 0.06%)
- **LEAD,** *Lead Limit Test, Flame Atomic Absorption Spectrophotometric Method*, Appendix IIIB
  Sample: 10 g
  Acceptance criteria: NMT 2 mg/kg

SPECIFIC TESTS
- **LOSS ON DRYING,** Appendix IIC: 105° for 2 h
  Sample: 500 mg
  Acceptance criteria: NMT 1.0%
- **PH,** *pH Determination*, Appendix IIB
  Sample solution: 20 mg/mL
  Acceptance criteria: Between 6.0 and 7.5
- **RESIDUE ON IGNITION (SULFATED ASH),** Appendix IIC
  Sample: 1 g
  Acceptance criteria: NMT 0.2%

L-Threonine

First Published: Prior to FCC 6
Last Revision: FCC 7

L-2-Amino-3-hydroxybutyric Acid

$C_4H_9NO_3$ Formula wt 119.12
 CAS: [72-19-5]
UNII: 2ZD004190S [threonine]

DESCRIPTION
L-Threonine occurs as a white, crystalline powder. It is freely soluble in water, and insoluble in alcohol, in ether, and in chloroform. It melts with decomposition at about 256°.
Function: Nutrient
Packaging and Storage: Store in well-closed containers.

IDENTIFICATION
- **INFRARED ABSORPTION,** *Spectrophotometric Identification Tests*, Appendix IIIC
  Reference standard: USP L-Threonine RS
  Sample and standard preparation: *M*
  Acceptance criteria: The spectrum of the sample exhibits maxima at the same wavelengths as those in the spectrum of the *Reference standard*.

ASSAY
- **PROCEDURE**
  Sample: 200 mg
  Analysis: Dissolve the *Sample* in 3 mL of formic acid and 50 mL of glacial acetic acid, add 2 drops of crystal violet TS, and titrate with 0.1 N perchloric acid to a green endpoint or until the blue color disappears completely. Perform a blank determination (see *General Provisions*), and make any necessary corrections. Each mL of 0.1 N perchloric acid is equivalent to 11.91 mg of $C_4H_9NO_3$. [**CAUTION**—Handle perchloric acid in an appropriate fume hood.]
  Acceptance criteria: 98.5%–101.5% of $C_4H_9NO_3$, calculated on the dried basis

IMPURITIES
Inorganic Impurities
- **LEAD,** *Lead Limit Test*, Appendix IIIB

Sample solution: Prepare as directed for organic compounds.
Control: 5 µg Pb (5 mL of *Diluted Standard Lead Solution*)
Acceptance criteria: NMT 5 mg/kg

SPECIFIC TESTS
- **LOSS ON DRYING**, Appendix IIC: 105° for 3 h
  Acceptance criteria: NMT 0.2%
- **OPTICAL (SPECIFIC) ROTATION**, Appendix IIB
  Sample: 6 g, previously dried
  Analysis: Dissolve the *Sample* in sufficient water to make 100 mL.
  Acceptance criteria
  $[\alpha]_D^{20}$ between −26.5° and −29.0°, on the dried basis; or
  $[\alpha]_D^{25}$ between −25.8° and −28.8°, on the dried basis
- **RESIDUE ON IGNITION (SULFATED ASH)**, Appendix IIC
  Sample: 1 g
  Acceptance criteria: NMT 0.1%

Thyme Oil

First Published: Prior to FCC 6

FEMA: 3064
UNII: 2UK410MY6B [thyme oil]
CAS: [8007-46-3]

DESCRIPTION
Thyme Oil occurs as a colorless, yellow, or red liquid with a characteristic, pleasant odor and a pungent, persistent taste. It is the volatile oil obtained by distillation from the flowering plant *Thymus vulgaris* L., or *Thymus zygis* L., and its var. *gracilis* Boissier (Fam. Labiatae). It is soluble in alcohol, in propylene glycol, and in most vegetable oils.
Function: Flavoring agent
Packaging and Storage: Store in a cool place in full, tight, light-resistant containers.

IDENTIFICATION
- **INFRARED SPECTRA,** *Spectrophotometric Identification Tests,* Appendix IIIC
  Acceptance criteria: The spectrum of the sample exhibits relative maxima at the same wavelengths as those of the spectrum below.

ASSAY
- **PHENOLS,** Appendix VI
  Analysis: Determine as directed, but allow the mixture to stand overnight rather than just 30 min. Then, add sufficient 1 N potassium hydroxide to raise the lower limit of the oily layer into the graduated portion of the neck of the flask. After the solution has become clear, adjust the temperature and read the volume of the residual liquid.
  Acceptance criteria: NLT 40%, by volume, of phenols

SPECIFIC TESTS
- **ANGULAR ROTATION,** *Optical (Specific) Rotation,* Appendix IIB: Use a 100-mm tube.
  Acceptance criteria: Between −3° and −0.1°
- **REFRACTIVE INDEX,** Appendix IIB
  [NOTE—Use an Abbé or other refractometer of equal or greater accuracy.]
  Acceptance criteria: Between 1.495 and 1.505 at 20°
- **SOLUBILITY IN ALCOHOL,** Appendix VI
  Acceptance criteria: One mL of the sample dissolves in 2 mL of 80% alcohol.
- **SPECIFIC GRAVITY:** Determine by any reliable method (see *General Provisions*).
  Acceptance criteria: Between 0.915 and 0.935
- **WATER-SOLUBLE PHENOLS**
  Sample: 1 mL
  Analysis: Shake the *Sample* with 10 mL of hot water and, after cooling, pass the water layer through a moistened filter. Add 1 drop of ferric chloride TS to the filtrate.
  Acceptance criteria: Not even a transient blue or violet color appears after addition of the ferric chloride TS.

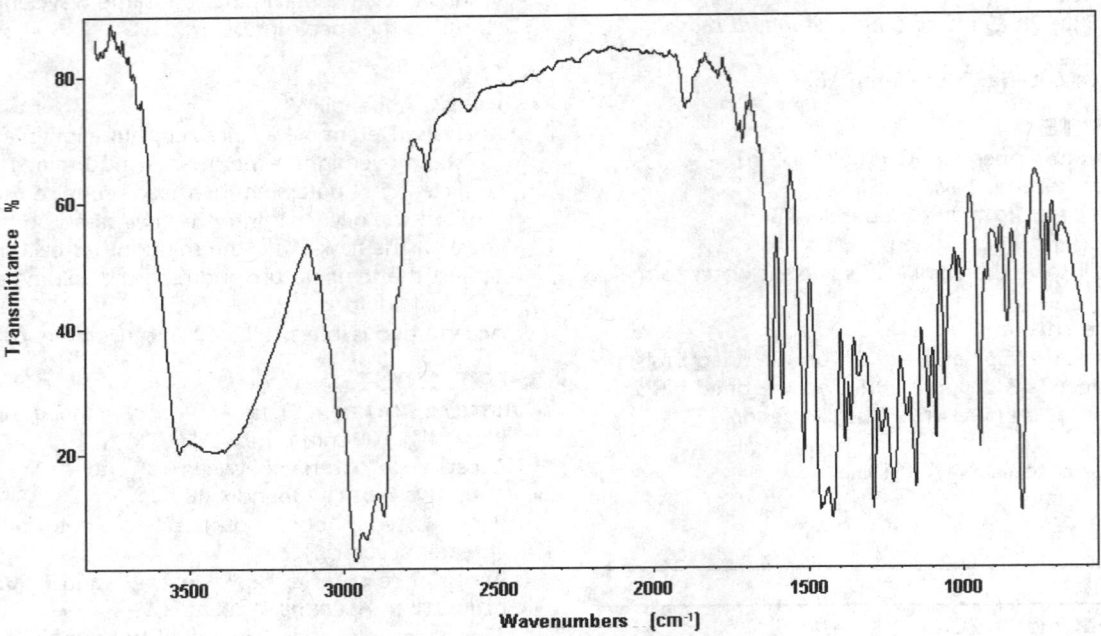

Thyme Oil

Thymol

First Published: Prior to FCC 6

C$_{10}$H$_{14}$O   Formula wt 150.22
FEMA: 3066
UNII: 3J50XA376E [thymol]

DESCRIPTION
Thymol occurs as white crystals.
Odor: Phenol
Solubility: Soluble in water, propylene glycol, vegetable oils
Boiling Point: ~232°
Solubility in Alcohol, Appendix VI: One g dissolves in 1 mL of 95% alcohol.
Function: Flavoring agent

IDENTIFICATION
- **INFRARED SPECTRA,** *Spectrophotometric Identification Tests,* Appendix IIIC
  Acceptance criteria: The spectrum of the sample exhibits relative maxima at the same wavelengths as those of the spectrum below.

ASSAY
- **PROCEDURE:** Proceed as directed under *M-1a,* Appendix XI.
  Acceptance criteria: NLT 99.0% of C$_{10}$H$_{14}$O

OTHER REQUIREMENTS
- **MELTING RANGE OR TEMPERATURE DETERMINATION,** Appendix IIB
  Acceptance criteria: Between 49° and 51°

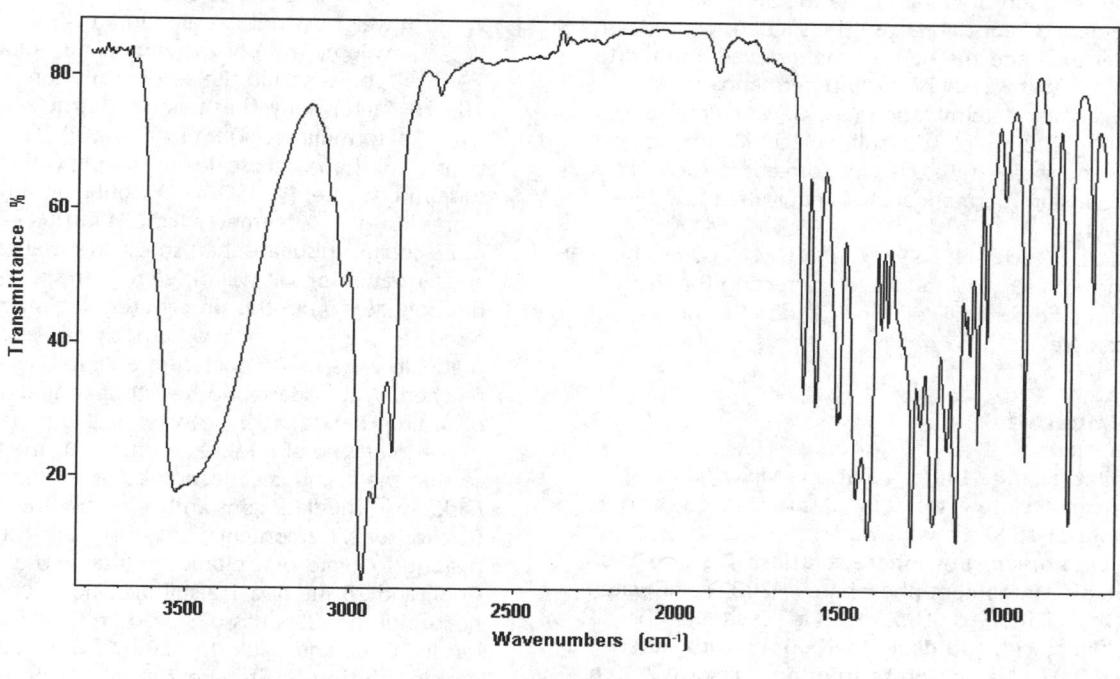

Thymol

Titanium Dioxide

First Published: Prior to FCC 6

TiO$_2$
INS: 171
UNII: 15FIX9V2JP [titanium dioxide]
Formula wt 79.90
CAS: [13463-67-7]

DESCRIPTION
Titanium Dioxide occurs as a white, amorphous powder. It is prepared synthetically. It is insoluble in water, in hydrochloric acid, in dilute sulfuric acid, and in alcohol and other organic solvents. It dissolves slowly in hydrofluoric acid and in hot sulfuric acid.
Function: Color
Packaging and Storage: Store in well-closed containers.

IDENTIFICATION
- **Procedure**
  Sample: 500 mg
  Analysis: Add 5 mL of sulfuric acid to the *Sample*, heat gently until fumes of sulfur trioxide evolve, continue heating for at least 10 s, and cool. Cautiously dilute to about 100 mL with water, and filter. Add a few drops of hydrogen peroxide TS to 5 mL of the clear filtrate.
  Acceptance criteria: A yellow-red to orange-red color appears immediately.

ASSAY
- **Procedure**
  Sample: 300 mg, previously dried at 105° for 3 h
  Sample solution: Transfer the *Sample* into a 250-mL beaker, add 20 mL of sulfuric acid and 7 to 8 g of ammonium sulfate, and mix. Heat on a hot plate until fumes of sulfur trioxide evolve, and continue heating over a strong flame until the sample dissolves or it is apparent that the undissolved residue is siliceous matter. Cool, cautiously dilute with 100 mL of water, and stir. While stirring, heat carefully to boiling, allow the insoluble matter to settle, and filter. Transfer the entire residue to the filter with the aid of cold 2 N sulfuric acid, and wash the residue thoroughly with the acid. Dilute the filtrate to 200 mL with water, and cautiously add about 10 mL of ammonium hydroxide to reduce the acid concentration to about 5%, by volume, of sulfuric acid.
  Zinc amalgam: Add 20- to 30-mesh zinc to a 2% mercuric chloride solution, using about 100 mL of the solution for each 100 g of zinc. After about 10 min, decant the solution from the zinc, then wash the zinc with water by decantation.
  Jones reductor: Place a pledget of glass wool in the bottom of a 25-cm Jones reductor apparatus, and fill the constricted portion of the column with the *Zinc amalgam*. Wash the column with 100-mL portions of 2 N sulfuric acid until 100 mL of the washing does not decolorize 1 drop of 0.1 N potassium permanganate.
  Analysis: Place 50 mL of ferric ammonium sulfate TS in a 500-mL suction flask, and add 0.1 N potassium permanganate until a faint pink color persists for 5 min. Attach the *Jones reductor* containing the *Zinc amalgam* to the neck of the flask, and pass 50 mL of 2 N sulfuric acid through the column at a rate of about 30 mL/min. Pass the *Sample solution* through the column at the same rate, followed by 100 mL each of 2 N sulfuric acid

and of water. During these operations, keep the column filled with solution or water above the upper level of the amalgam. Gradually release the suction, wash down the outlet tube and the sides of the receiver, and titrate immediately with 0.1 N potassium permanganate. Perform a blank determination (see *General Provisions*), substituting 200 mL of 1:20 sulfuric acid for the *Sample solution*, and make any necessary correction. Each mL of 0.1 N potassium permanganate is equivalent to 7.990 mg of TiO_2.

Acceptance criteria: NLT 99.0% and NMT 100.5% of TiO_2, on the dried basis and after correcting for any aluminum oxide and silicon dioxide found to be present in the sample

IMPURITIES
Inorganic Impurities
- **ALUMINUM OXIDE**

  Ammonium acetate buffer solution: Mix 77 g of ammonium acetate with 10 mL of glacial acetic acid and dilute to 1000 mL with water.

  Dibasic ammonium phosphate solution: Dissolve 150 g of dibasic ammonium phosphate in 700 mL of water. Adjust the solution to pH 5.5 with a 1:2 solution of hydrochloric acid, and dilute to 1000 mL with water.

  Standard 0.01 M zinc sulfate solution: Dissolve 2.90 g of zinc sulfate ($ZnSO_4 \cdot 7H_2O$) in sufficient water to make 1000 mL. Standardize the solution as follows: Dissolve 500 mg of high-purity (99.9%) aluminum wire in 20 mL of hydrochloric acid, heating gently to effect solution; transfer the solution into a 1000-mL volumetric flask, dilute to volume with water, and mix. Transfer a 10.0-mL aliquot of this solution into a 500-mL Erlenmeyer flask containing 90 mL of water and 3 mL of hydrochloric acid, add 1 drop of methyl orange TS and 25.0 mL of 0.02 M disodium EDTA, Add, dropwise, a 1:5 ammonium hydroxide solution to the Erlenmeyer flask until the color of the solution has just completely changed from red to orange-yellow. Then, add 10 mL of *Ammonium acetate buffer solution* and 10 mL of *Dibasic ammonium phosphate solution*. Boil the solution for 5 min, cool it quickly to room temperature in a stream of running water, add 3 drops of xylenol orange TS, and mix. Using the zinc sulfate solution as titrant, titrate the solution to the first yellow-brown or pink end-point color that persists for 5-10 s. [NOTE—Perform this titration quickly near the endpoint by rapidly adding 0.2-mL increments of the titrant until the first color change occurs; although the color will fade in 5 to 10 s, it is the true endpoint. Failure to observe the first color change will result in an incorrect titration. The fading end-point does not occur at the second end-point.] Add 2 g of sodium fluoride, boil the mixture for 2 to 5 min, and cool in a stream of running water. Titrate this solution, using the zinc sulfate solution as titrant, to the same transitory yellow-brown or pink endpoint as described above. Calculate the titer, T, of the zinc sulfate solution by the equation:

  $$T = (18.896 \times W)/V$$

  T = amount (mg) of aluminum oxide (Al_2O_3)/mL of zinc sulfate solution
  W = weight (g) of the aluminum wire
  V = volume (mL) of the zinc sulfate solution consumed in the second titration
  18.896 = factor derived as follows: (formula wt Al_2O_3/ formula wt Al) × (1000 mg/g) × (10 mL/2)

  Sample solution A: Fuse 1 g of sample with 10 g of sodium bisulfate, $NaHSO_4 \cdot H_2O$, contained in a 250-mL high-silica glass Erlenmeyer flask. [CAUTION—Do not use more sodium bisulfate than specified because an excess concentration of salt will interfere with the EDTA titration later on in this procedure.] Begin heating the fused sample at low heat on a hot plate, and then gradually raise the temperature until full heat is reached. When spattering has stopped and light fumes of sodium trioxide (SO_3) evolve, heat the fused sample in the full flame of a Meker burner with the flask tilted so that the fusion is concentrated at one end of the flask. Swirl the flask constantly until the melt is clear (except for silica content), but guard against prolonged heating to avoid precipitation of titanium dioxide. Cool, add 25 mL of a 1:2 sulfuric acid solution, and heat until the mass has dissolved and a clear solution results. Cool, and dilute to 120 mL with water.

  Sample solution B: Prepare 200 mL of approximately 6.25 M sodium hydroxide. Add 65 mL of it to *Sample solution A*, while stirring constantly with the magnetic stirrer; pour the remaining 135 mL of the alkali solution into a 500-mL volumetric flask. Slowly, with constant stirring, add the sample mixture to the alkali solution in the 500-mL volumetric flask, dilute to volume with water, and mix. [NOTE—If the procedure is delayed at this point for more than 2 h, store the contents of the volumetric flask in a polyethylene bottle.] Allow most of the precipitate to settle out (or centrifuge for 5 min) and filter the supernatant liquid through a very fine filter paper. The filtrate is *Sample solution B*.

  Sample solution C: Transfer 100.0 mL of *Sample solution B* into a 500-mL Erlenmeyer flask, add 1 drop of methyl orange TS, acidify with 1:2 hydrochloric acid solution, and add about 3 mL in excess. Add 25.0 mL of 0.02 M disodium EDTA, and mix. [NOTE—If the approximate aluminum oxide (Al_2O_3) content is known, calculate the optimum volume of EDTA solution to be added by the following formula.]

  $$\text{Result} = (4 \times \% Al_2O_3) + 5$$

  Add, dropwise, a 1:5 ammonium hydroxide solution to the flask until the color of the solution has just completely changed from red to orange-yellow. Then, add 10 mL of *Ammonium acetate buffer solution* and 10 mL of *Dibasic ammonium phosphate solution* and boil for 5 min. Cool quickly to room temperature in a stream of running water, add 3 drops of xylenol orange TS, and mix. If the solution is purple, yellow-brown, or pink, bring the pH to 5.3 to 5.7 by adding acetic acid; at the desired pH, a pink color indicates that not enough of the EDTA solution has been added. In this case, take another 100 mL of *Sample solution B*, and treat it as directed from the beginning of this paragraph, except use 50.0 mL, rather than 25.0 mL, of 0.02 M disodium EDTA.

Analysis: Titrate *Sample solution C* with *Standard 0.01 M zinc sulfate solution* to the first yellow-brown or pink endpoint color that persists for 5 to 10 s. [NOTE—Perform this titration quickly near the endpoint by rapidly adding 0.2-mL increments of the titrant until the first color change occurs; although the color will fade in 5 to 10 s, it is the true endpoint. Failure to observe the first color change will result in an incorrect titration. The fading end-point does not occur at the second end-point. The first titration should require more than 8 ml of titrant, but for more accurate work a titration of 10–15 mL is desirable.] Add 2 g of sodium fluoride to the titration flask, boil the mixture for 2 to 5 min, and cool in a stream of running water. Titrate this solution with the *Standard 0.01 M zinc sulfate solution* to the same transitory yellow-brown or pink endpoint as described above. Calculate the percent of aluminum oxide (Al_2O_3) in the sample taken by the formula:

$$Result = VT/2S$$

V = volume (mL) of *Standard 0.01 M zinc sulfate solution* consumed in the second titration
T = titer of the *Standard 0.01 M zinc sulfate solution*
S = weight (g) of the sample taken to prepare *Sample solution A*

Acceptance criteria: NMT 2.0%, either singly or combined with *Silicon Dioxide*

- **ANTIMONY**
  0.1 N Ceric sulfate solution: Dissolve 3.3 g of ceric sulfate [$Ce(SO_4)_2$] in 100 mL of water containing 3 mL of sulfuric acid.
  Stock standard solution: Transfer 274.28 mg of antimony potassium tartrate ($C_4H_4KO_7Sb \cdot 1/2H_2O$) into a 100 mL volumetric flask, dissolve in and dilute to volume with 6 N hydrochloric acid, and mix. (1mg Sb/mL)
  Diluted standard solution: Pipet 2.00 mL of *Stock standard solution* into a 100 mL volumetric flask, dilute to volume with 6 N hydrochloric acid, and mix. (20 µg Sb/mL)
  Standard solution: Transfer 1.00 mL of *Diluted standard solution* into a 250-mL separatory funnel. Add 25 mL of mercuric chloride solution (6% in hydrochloric acid) and 25 mL of hydrochloric acid.
  Sample solution: Transfer 10.00 g of sample into a 250-mL beaker, add 50 mL of hot 0.5 N hydrochloric acid, cover the beaker, and boil the slurry for 15 min, stirring occasionally. Remove the beaker from the heat, allow the slurry to settle for a few seconds, and decant through a double Whatman No. 42 filter paper plus a No. 12 fluted paper, or equivalent, all previously washed with 0.5 N hydrochloric acid. Evaporate the filtrate slowly on a hot plate until the volume is slightly less than 20 mL, then cool, and transfer it to a 25-mL graduate. Rinse the beaker with 5 mL of 0.5 N hydrochloric acid, and add this to the graduate. Dilute the solution to volume with 0.5 N hydrochloric acid and transfer it into a 250-mL separatory funnel. Rinse the beaker and graduate with a total of 25 mL of mercuric chloride solution (6% in hydrochloric acid) and with a total of 25 mL of hydrochloric acid, adding the washings to the funnel.
  Analysis: Add 1.0 mL of *0.1 N Ceric sulfate solution* to the *Sample solution* in the separatory funnel, and start a stopwatch at the moment of first addition. Mix the solutions together and pass a stream of clean air over the mixture. At exactly 1.0 min, add 75 mL of water, mix, and continue passing air over the solution. At 2.0 min, add 8 drops of a 1% solution of hydroxylamine hydrochloride, mix, and continue passing air over the solution. At 3.0 min, add 5.0 mL of a 0.2% solution of rhodamine B. Pipet 50.00 mL of benzene into the separatory funnel, shake the funnel for 1 min, and allow the layers to separate for 90 s. Discard the aqueous layer and a small portion of the organic phase. Transfer about 15 mL of the organic phase to a centrifuge tube and centrifuge at high speed for 1 min. Using a suitable spectrophotometer, measure the absorbance of the clarified solution in a 1-cm cell at 565 nm; use water as a blank (see *General Provisions*) after having compared benzene in the sample cell to water in the reference cell. As the color of the clarified solution is stable for several minutes, measure the absorbance within 15 to 20 min after starting the stopwatch. [NOTE—The colloidal antimony color complex may resist rinsing from the cell with benzene, in which case rinse the cell in succession with dilute nitric acid, hot water, acetone, and benzene. Check the absorbance of the cell with benzene against water contained in the reference cell.] Repeat the above procedure for the *Standard solution*.
  Acceptance criteria: The absorbance produced by the solution from the *Sample solution*, after correction for a reagent blank, is not greater than that produced by the solution from the *Standard solution*. (NMT 2 mg/kg)

- **ARSENIC**, *Arsenic Limit Test*, Appendix IIIB
  Sample solution: Transfer 10.00 g of sample into a 250-mL beaker, add 50 mL of 0.5 N hydrochloric acid, cover with a watch glass, and heat to boiling on a hot plate. Boil gently for 15 min, then pour the slurry into a 100- to 150-mL centrifuge bottle, and centrifuge for 10 to 15 min, or until undissolved material settles. Decant the supernatant extract through a Whatman No. 4 filter paper, or equivalent, collecting the filtrate in a 100-mL volumetric flask and retaining as much as possible of the undissolved material in the centrifuge bottle. Add 10 mL of hot water to the original beaker, washing off the watch glass with the water, and pour the slurry into the centrifuge bottle. Form a slurry, using a glass stirring rod, and centrifuge. Decant through the same filter paper, and collect the washings in the volumetric flask containing the initial extract. Repeat the entire washing process two more times. Finally, wash the filter paper with 10 to 15 mL of hot water. Cool the contents of the flask to room temperature, dilute to volume with water, and mix. [NOTE—This solution is also used for the test for *Lead*.]
  Analysis: Use a 30-mL aliquot of the *Sample solution*.

Acceptance criteria: NMT 1 mg/kg
- **LEAD**, *Lead Limit Test*, Appendix IIIB
  Sample: Use a 20-mL aliquot of the *Sample solution* from the test for *Arsenic* (above).
  Control: 20 μg Pb (20 mL of *Diluted Standard Lead Solution*)
  Acceptance criteria: NMT 10 mg/kg
- **MERCURY**
  Apparatus: Use an apparatus consisting of a source of nitrogen (supplied through a regulator or flowmeter capable of measuring a flow rate of 1 L/min) connected to a suitable quartz combustion tube contained in a hinged furnace (Type 70 T, Arthur H. Thomas Co., or equivalent) in which the sample can be pyrolyzed at 650°. Connect the exit end of the combustion tube to the optical cell of a suitable mercury vapor meter (Beckman Model K-23, or equivalent), the microammeter of which is connected in parallel through an attenuator to a 1-mV strip chart recorder. Fit a 48.3-cm × 18.3-mm (od) quartz combustion tube at each end with Pyrex ball-joint adapters, and pack the tube near the exit end with 40 g of copper oxide held in place by small wads of quartz wool. Use the inlet end to hold an 88- × 12- × 8-mm combustion boat for the sample.
  Standard stock solution: 1.353 mg/mL of mercuric chloride (This solution contains 1.0 mg of Hg per mL.)
  Standard working solution: 0.01 mg of Hg/mL
  Standardization of mercury vapor meter: Preheat the combustion tube furnace to 650° and adjust the nitrogen flow to 1 L/min. Standardize the meter in accordance with the manufacturer's instructions, using the internal standard with which the instrument is equipped. Adjust the attenuator so that the scale on the recorder is 200 mV. Under these conditions, a meter reading of 0.078 mg/m^3, obtained with the internal standard, is 50% of full scale on the strip-chart recorder. Check the standardization of the instrument periodically, and adjust as necessary.
  Calibration of mercury vapor meter: Prepare a set of mercury standards containing 0.01, 0.02, and 0.03 μg of mercury by pipetting the required amount of the *Standard working solution* onto 1- × 0.5- × 0.1-cm asbestos pads, previously ignited at 800° for 1 h, and contained in separate combustion boats. Cover each asbestos pad with 1 to 2 g of fine, granular, anhydrous sodium carbonate, previously checked for absence of mercury by the previous ignition procedure. Place a combustion boat containing a mercury standard in the tube furnace, and close the inlet with a ball joint sealed at one end and held in place by a clamp. After 1 min, start the gas flow by connecting the nitrogen supply tube to the inlet port of the combustion tube. Record the maximum response from either the observed meter deflection or the chart record for each mercury standard, and prepare a standard curve of the response versus the amount of mercury added. [NOTE—Calibrate the mercury vapor meter each time a series of samples is run, and check the calibration periodically by running a single mercury standard.]

Analysis: Place 25 mg of sample in a combustion boat, and cover it with 1 to 2 g of the fine, granular, anhydrous sodium carbonate prepared as previously described. Ignite the sample as described for the mercury standards, record the maximum response, and determine the amount of mercury in the sample by referring to the standard curve.
Acceptance criteria: NMT 1 mg/kg
- **SILICON DIOXIDE**
  Sample preparation: Fuse 1 g of sample with 10 g of sodium bisulfate, NaHSO$_4$·H$_2$O, contained in a 250-mL high-silica glass Erlenmeyer flask. While swirling the flask, heat it gently over a Meker burner until decomposition and fusion are complete and the melt is clear, except for the silica content, and then cool. [CAUTION—Do not overheat the contents of the flask at the beginning, and heat cautiously during fusion to avoid spattering.] Add 25 mL of a 1:2 sulfuric acid solution to the cold melt, and heat very carefully and very slowly until the melt is dissolved. Cool, and carefully add 150 mL of water, pouring very small portions down the sides of the flask, swirling frequently to avoid overheating and spattering. Allow the contents of the flask to cool, and filter them through fine ashless filter paper, using a 60° gravity funnel. Use a 1:10 sulfuric acid solution to wash out all of the silica from the flask onto the filter paper. Transfer the filter paper and its contents into a tared platinum crucible, dry in an oven at 120°, and then partly cover the crucible and heat it over a Bunsen burner. To prevent the filter paper from flaming, first heat the cover from above and then the crucible from below. When the filter paper is consumed, transfer the crucible to a muffle furnace, and ignite at 1000° for 30 min, cool the crucible in a desiccator.
  Analysis: Weigh the ignited, cooled crucible and its contents. Then, add 2 drops of 1:2 sulfuric acid and 5 mL of hydrofluoric acid (specific gravity: 1.15) to the contents, and carefully evaporate to dryness, first on a low-heat hot plate to remove the hydrofluoric acid, and then over a Bunsen burner to remove the sulfuric acid. Take precautions to avoid spattering, especially after removing the hydrofluoric acid. Ignite in a muffle furnace at 1000° for 10 min, cool in a desiccator, and weigh again. Record the difference between the two weights as the content of silicon dioxide, SiO$_2$, in the sample.
  Acceptance criteria: NMT 2.0%, either singly or combined with *Aluminum Oxide*

SPECIFIC TESTS
- **ACID-SOLUBLE SUBSTANCES**
  Sample preparation: Suspend 5.0 g of sample in 100 mL of 0.5 N hydrochloric acid, and heat on a steam bath for 30 min, stirring occasionally. Filter the suspension through a suitable tared, porous-bottom, porcelain filter crucible. Wash the residue with three 10-mL portions of 0.5 N hydrochloric acid, and evaporate the combined filtrate and washings to dryness.
  Analysis: Ignite the *Sample preparation* at 450° ± 25° to constant weight. [CAUTION—Avoid exposing the crucible

to sudden temperature changes.] Calculate the percent *Acid-Soluble Substances* by the formula:

$$\text{Result} = 100R/1000W$$

R = weight (mg) of the residue
W = starting weight (g) of the sample
100 = conversion factor to percent
1000 = conversion factor to mg
Acceptance criteria: NMT 0.5%

- **LOSS ON IGNITION**
  Sample: 2.0 g
  Analysis: Dry the *Sample* at 105° for 3 h and then ignite at 800° ± 25°, to constant weight.
  Acceptance criteria: NMT 0.5%, on the dried basis

- **WATER-SOLUBLE SUBSTANCES:**
  Sample preparation: Suspend 4.0 g of sample in 50 mL of water, mix, and allow to stand overnight. Transfer the suspension to a 200-mL volumetric flask, add 2 mL of ammonium chloride TS, and mix. If the sample does not settle, add another 2-mL portion of ammonium chloride TS, then allow the suspension to settle, dilute to volume with water, and mix. Filter the suspension through a double thickness of filter paper, discarding the first 10 mL of filtrate, and collect 100 mL of the subsequent clear filtrate. Transfer the filtrate into a tared platinum dish, and evaporate on a hot plate to dryness.
  Analysis: Ignite the *Sample preparation* at a dull red heat to constant weight. Calculate the percent water-soluble substances by the formula:

$$\text{Result} = 100AR/1000VW$$

A = volume (mL) of filtrate collected
R = weight (mg) of the residue
V = initial volume (mL) of the suspension
W = starting weight (g) of the sample
100 = conversion factor to percent
1000 = conversion to mg
Acceptance criteria: NMT 0.3%

RRR-α-Tocopherol Concentrate

First Published: Prior to FCC 6

D-α-Tocopherol Concentrate

$C_{29}H_{50}O_2$ Formula wt 430.71
INS: 307a CAS: [59-02-9]
UNII: N9PR3490H9 [α-tocopherol, d-]

DESCRIPTION

RRR-α-Tocopherol Concentrate occurs as a brown-red to light yellow, clear, viscous oil. It is a form of vitamin E obtained by the vacuum steam distillation of edible vegetable oil products, comprising a concentrated form of RRR-α-tocopherol. It oxidizes and darkens slowly in air and on exposure to light. It may contain an edible vegetable oil added to adjust the required amount of total tocopherols, and the content of RRR-α-tocopherol may be adjusted by suitable physical and chemical means. It is insoluble in water; soluble in alcohol; and miscible with acetone, with chloroform, with ether, and with vegetable oils.
Function: Nutrient; antioxidant
Packaging and Storage: Store in tight containers blanketed by inert gas and protected from heat and light.

[NOTE—Use low-actinic glassware for all solutions containing tocopherols.]

IDENTIFICATION

- **A. PROCEDURE**
  Sample: 50 mg
  Analysis: Dissolve the *Sample* in 10 mL of absolute alcohol. Add, with swirling, 2 mL of nitric acid and heat at about 75° for 15 min.
  Acceptance criteria: A bright-red to orange color develops.

- **B. CHROMATOGRAPHY**
  Acceptance criteria: The retention time of the major peak (excluding the solvent peak) in the chromatogram of the *Sample solution* is the same as that of the *Standard solution*, both relative to the *Internal standard solution*, as obtained in the *Assay* (below).

ASSAY

- **PROCEDURE**
  Internal standard solution: 3 mg/mL of hexadecyl hexadecanoate (Aldrich or equivalent) in *n*-hexane
  Standard solution: 3 mg/mL of USP α-Tocopherol RS in *Internal standard solution*
  Sample: 30 mg
  Sample solution: Dissolve the *Sample* in 10.0 mL of *Internal standard solution*.
  System suitability solution: 1 mg/mL each of USP α-Tocopheryl Acetate RS and USP α-Tocopherol RS in *n*-hexane
  Chromatographic system, Appendix IIA
  Mode: Gas chromatography
  Detector: Flame ionization
  Column: 2-m × 4-mm (id) borosilicate glass column, or equivalent, packed with 2% to 5% methylpolysiloxane gum on 80- to 100-mesh acid-washed, base-washed, silanized, chromatographic diatomaceous earth, or equivalent materials. [NOTE—The column should have a glass-lined sample introduction system or on-column injection. Cure and condition the column as necessary before use (see *Procedure* under *Gas Chromatography*, Appendix IIA).]
  Temperature
   Column: Isothermal between 240° and 260°
   Injection port: About 290°
   Detector block: About 300°
  Injection volume: 2–5 μL
  Carrier gas: Dry carrier gas
  Flow rate: Adjust to obtain a hexadecyl hexadecanoate peak approximately 18 to 20 min after sample introduction when using a 2% column, or 30 to 32 min when using a 5% column.
  System suitability
   Sample: *System suitability solution*

Suitability requirement: The resolution, R, between α-tocopheryl acetate and α-tocopherol is NLT 1.0.
Calibration: Chromatograph successive portions of the *Standard solution* until the relative response factor, F, is constant (i.e., within a range of approximately 2%) for three consecutive injections. If using graphic integration, adjust the instrument to obtain at least 70% maximum recorder response for the hexadecyl hexadecanoate peak. Measure the areas under the major peaks occurring at relative retention times of 0.51 (α-tocopherol) and 1.00 (hexadecyl hexadecanoate). Calculate F by the formula:

$$\text{Result} = (A_S/A_I) \times (C_I/C_S)$$

A_S = peak area of α-tocopherol
A_I = peak area of hexadecyl hexadecanoate
C_I = concentration of hexadecyl hexadecanoate in the *Standard solution* (mg/mL)
C_S = concentration of USP α-Tocopherol RS in the *Standard solution* (mg/mL)

Analysis: Chromatograph the *Sample solution* as described under *Calibration*. Measure the areas under the major peaks occurring at relative retention times of 0.51 (α-tocopherol) and 1.00 (hexadecyl hexadecanoate). Calculate the weight, in mg, of RRR-α-tocopherol concentrate in the *Sample* taken by the formula:

$$\text{Result} = (10C_I/F) \times (a_U/a_I)$$

C_I = concentration of hexadecyl hexadecanoate in the *Standard solution* (mg/mL)
F = relative response factor (see *Calibration*)
a_U = peak area for α-tocopherol from the *Sample solution*
a_I = peak area of hexadecyl hexadecanoate from the *Sample solution*

Acceptance criteria: NLT 40.0% of total tocopherols, of which NLT 95.0% consists of RRR-α-tocopherol ($C_{29}H_{50}O_2$)

IMPURITIES
Inorganic Impurities
- **LEAD,** *Lead Limit Test, Flame Atomic Absorption Spectrophotometric Method,* Appendix IIIB
  Sample: 10 g
  Acceptance criteria: NMT 2 mg/kg

SPECIFIC TESTS
- **ACIDITY**
  Sample solution: Dissolve 1.0 g of sample in 25 mL of a mixture of alcohol and ether (1:1) (v/v) that has been neutralized to phenolphthalein TS with 0.1 N sodium hydroxide.
  Analysis: Add 0.5 mL of phenolphthalein TS to the *Sample solution,* and titrate with 0.1 N sodium hydroxide until the solution remains faintly pink after shaking the flask for 30 s.
  Acceptance criteria: NMT 1.0 mL of titrant is required.

- **OPTICAL (SPECIFIC) ROTATION,** Appendix IIB
  Sample solution: Transfer an amount of sample equivalent to 100 mg of α-tocopherol to a separatory funnel and dissolve it in 50 mL of ether. Add 20 mL of a 10% solution of potassium ferricyanide in an 8 mg/mL sodium hydroxide solution and shake the solution for 3 min. Wash the ether solution with four 50-mL portions of water, discard the washings, and dry the solution over anhydrous sodium sulfate. Evaporate the dried ether solution on a water bath under reduced pressure or in an atmosphere of nitrogen until about 7 or 8 mL remains. Then, complete the evaporation, removing the last traces of ether without the application of heat. Immediately dissolve the residue in 5.0 mL of isooctane.
  Analysis: Determine the specific rotation of the *Sample solution* as directed, using as c in the equation, the concentration expressed in grams of α-tocopherol (as determined in the *Assay*) in 100 mL of the solution.
  Acceptance criteria: $[\alpha]_D^{25}$ NLT +24°

OTHER REQUIREMENTS
- **LABELING:** Indicate the milligrams per gram of RRR-α-tocopherol present. All label claims that are in terms of International Units (IU) should be based on the following: 1 mg of RRR-α-tocopherol = 1.49 IU.

All-rac-α-Tocopherol
First Published: Prior to FCC 6

DL-α-Tocopherol

$C_{29}H_{50}O_2$ Formula wt 430.71
INS: 307c   CAS: [10191-41-0]
UNII: 7QWA1RIO01 [α-tocopherol, dl-]

DESCRIPTION
All-rac-α-Tocopherol occurs as a yellow to amber, clear, viscous oil. It is a form of vitamin E. It oxidizes and darkens in air and on exposure to light. It is insoluble in water; freely soluble in alcohol; and miscible with acetone, with chloroform, with ether, with fats, and with vegetable oils.
Function: Nutrient; antioxidant
Packaging and Storage: Store in tight containers blanketed by inert gas and protected from heat and light.

[NOTE—Use low-actinic glassware for all solutions containing tocopherols.]

IDENTIFICATION
- **A. PROCEDURE**
  Sample: 10 mg
  Analysis: Dissolve the *Sample* in 10 mL of absolute alcohol. Add, with swirling, 2 mL of nitric acid and heat at about 75° for 15 min.

Acceptance criteria: A bright-red to orange color develops.
- **B. CHROMATOGRAPHY**
  Acceptance criteria: The retention time of the major peak (excluding the solvent peak) in the chromatogram of the Sample solution is the same as that of the Standard solution, both relative to the Internal standard solution, as obtained in the Assay (below).
- **C. OPTICAL (SPECIFIC) ROTATION, Appendix IIB**
  [NOTE—Only perform this test if the isomeric form is not otherwise known.]
  Sample solution: 1:10 solution in chloroform
  Acceptance criteria: $[\alpha]_D^{25}$ approximately ± 0.05°

ASSAY
- **PROCEDURE**
  Internal standard solution: 3 mg/mL of hexadecyl hexadecanoate (Aldrich or equivalent) in *n*-hexane
  Standard solution: 3 mg/mL of USP α-Tocopherol RS in Internal standard solution
  Sample: 30 mg
  Sample solution: Dissolve the Sample in 10.0 mL of Internal standard solution.
  System suitability solution: 1 mg/mL each of USP α-Tocopheryl Acetate RS and USP α-Tocopherol RS in *n*-hexane
  Chromatographic system, Appendix IIA
    Mode: Gas chromatography
    Detector: Flame ionization
    Column: 2-m × 4-mm (id) borosilicate glass column, or equivalent, packed with 2% to 5% methylpolysiloxane gum on 80- to 100-mesh acid-washed, base-washed, silanized, chromatographic diatomaceous earth, or equivalent materials. [NOTE—The column should have a glass-lined sample introduction system or on-column injection. Cure and condition the column as necessary before use (see Procedure under Gas Chromatography, Appendix IIA).]
    Temperature
      Column: Isothermal between 240° and 260°
      Injection port: About 290°
      Detector block: About 300°
    Injection volume: 2–5 μL
    Carrier gas: Dry carrier gas
    Flow rate: Adjust to obtain a hexadecyl hexadecanoate peak approximately 18 to 20 min after sample introduction when using a 2% column, or 30 to 32 min when using a 5% column.
  System suitability
    Sample: System suitability solution
    Suitability requirement: The resolution, R, between α-tocopheryl acetate and α-tocopherol is NLT 1.0.
  Calibration: Chromatograph successive portions of the Standard solution until the relative response factor, F, is constant (i.e., within a range of approximately 2%) for three consecutive injections. If using graphic integration, adjust the instrument to obtain at least 70% maximum recorder response for the hexadecyl hexadecanoate peak. Measure the areas under the major peaks occurring at relative retention times of 0.51 (α-tocopherol) and 1.00 (hexadecyl hexadecanoate). Calculate F by the formula:

  $$\text{Result} = (A_S/A_I) \times (C_I/C_S)$$

  A_S = peak area of α-tocopherol
  A_I = peak area of hexadecyl hexadecanoate
  C_I = concentration of hexadecyl hexadecanoate in the Standard solution (mg/mL)
  C_S = concentration of USP α-Tocopherol RS in the Standard solution (mg/mL)

  Analysis: Chromatograph the Sample solution as described under Calibration. Measure the areas under the major peaks occurring at relative retention times of 0.51 (α-tocopherol) and 1.00 (hexadecyl hexadecanoate). Calculate the weight (mg), of RRR-α-tocopherol concentrate in the Sample taken by the formula:

  $$\text{Result} = (10C_I/F) \times (a_U/a_I)$$

  C_I = concentration of hexadecyl hexadecanoate in the Standard solution (mg/mL)
  F = relative response factor (see Calibration)
  a_U = Peak area for α-tocopherol from the Sample solution
  a_I = peak area of hexadecyl hexadecanoate from the Sample solution

  Acceptance criteria: NLT 96.0% and NMT 102.0% of $C_{29}H_{50}O_2$

IMPURITIES
Inorganic Impurities
- **LEAD,** Lead Limit Test, Flame Atomic Absorption Spectrophotometric Method, Appendix IIIB
  Sample: 10 g
  Acceptance criteria: NMT 2 mg/kg

SPECIFIC TESTS
- **ACIDITY**
  Sample solution: Dissolve 1.0 g of sample in 25 mL of a mixture of alcohol and ether (1:1)(v/v) that has been neutralized to phenolphthalein TS with 0.1 N sodium hydroxide.
  Analysis: Add 0.5 mL of phenolphthalein TS to the Sample solution, and titrate with 0.1 N sodium hydroxide until the solution remains faintly pink after shaking the flask for 30 s.
  Acceptance criteria: NMT 1.0 mL of titrant is required.

OTHER REQUIREMENTS
Labeling: All label claims that are in terms of International Units (IU) should be based on the following: 1 mg of all-rac-α-tocopherol = 1.1 IU.

All-rac-α-Tocopheryl Acetate

First Published: Prior to FCC 6

DL-α-Tocopheryl Acetate
Vitamin E Acetate
DL-α-Tocopherol Acetate

$C_{31}H_{52}O_3$ Formula wt 472.75
                 CAS: [7695-91-2]
UNII: WR1WPI7EW8 [α-tocopherol acetate, dl-]

DESCRIPTION
All-rac-α-Tocopheryl Acetate occurs as a colorless to yellow or green-yellow, clear, viscous oil. It is a form of vitamin E. It is unstable in the presence of alkalies. It is insoluble in water; freely soluble in alcohol; and miscible with acetone, with chloroform, with ether, and with vegetable oils.

Function: Nutrient

Packaging and Storage: Store in tight, light-resistant containers.

[NOTE—Use low-actinic glassware for all solutions containing tocopherols.]

IDENTIFICATION
- **A. PROCEDURE**

  Sample solution: Transfer an amount of sample equivalent to 200 mg of α-tocopherol into a 150 mL round-bottom glass-stoppered flask and dissolve it in 25 mL of absolute alcohol. Add 20 mL of a 1:7 mixture of 2 N sulfuric acid in alcohol, and reflux in an all-glass apparatus for 3 h, protected from sunlight. Cool the mixture, transfer into a 200-mL volumetric flask, dilute to volume with a 1:72 mixture of 2 N sulfuric acid in alcohol, and mix.

  Analysis: Add, with swirling, 2 mL of nitric acid to 10 mL of the Sample solution and heat at about 75° for 15 min.

  Acceptance criteria: A bright red to orange color develops.

- **B. CHROMATOGRAPHY**

  Acceptance criteria: The retention time of the major peak (excluding the solvent peak) in the chromatogram of the Sample solution is the same as that of the Standard solution, both relative to the Internal standard solution, as obtained in the Assay (below).

- **C. OPTICAL (SPECIFIC) ROTATION,** Appendix IIB

  [NOTE—Only perform this test if the isomeric form is not otherwise known.]

  Sample solution: 1:10 solution in chloroform

  Acceptance criteria: $[\alpha]_D^{25}$ approximately ±0.05°

ASSAY
- **PROCEDURE**

  Internal standard solution: 3 mg/mL of hexadecyl hexadecanoate (Aldrich or equivalent) in n-hexane

  Standard solution: 3 mg/mL of USP α-Tocopheryl Acetate RS in the Internal standard solution

  Sample: Amount of sample equivalent to 30 mg of all-rac-α-tocopheryl acetate

  Sample solution: Dissolve the Sample in 10.0 mL of the Internal standard solution.

  System suitability solution: 1 mg/mL USP α-Tocopheryl Acetate RS and 1 mg/mL USP α-Tocopherol RS in n-hexane

  Chromatographic system, Appendix IIA
    Mode: Gas chromatography
    Detector: Flame ionization
    Column: 2-m × 4-mm (id) borosilicate glass column, or equivalent, packed with 2% to 5% methylpolysiloxane gum on 80- to 100-mesh acid-washed, base-washed, silanized, chromatographic diatomaceous earth, or equivalent materials. [NOTE—The column should have a glass-lined sample introduction system or on-column injection. Cure and condition the column as necessary before use (see Procedure under Gas Chromatography, Appendix IIA).]
    Temperature
      Column: Isothermal between 240° and 260°
      Injection port: About 290°
      Detector block: About 300°
    Injection volume: 2–5 µL
    Carrier gas: Dry carrier gas
    Flow rate: Adjust to obtain a hexadecyl hexadecanoate peak approximately 18 to 20 min after sample introduction when using a 2% column, or 30 to 32 min when using a 5% column.

  System suitability
    Sample: System suitability solution
    Suitability requirement: The resolution, R, between α-tocopheryl acetate and α-tocopherol is NLT 1.0.

  Calibration: Chromatograph successive portions of the Standard solution until the relative response factor, F, is constant (i.e., within a range of ~2%) for three consecutive injections. If using graphic integration, adjust the instrument to obtain at least 70% maximum recorder response for the hexadecyl hexadecanoate peak. Measure the areas under the major peaks occurring at relative retention times of 0.60 (α-tocopheryl acetate) and 1.00 (hexadecyl hexadecanoate). Calculate F by the formula:

  $$\text{Result} = (A_S/A_I) \times (C_I/C_S)$$

  A_S = peak area of α-tocopheryl acetate
  A_I = peak area of hexadecyl hexadecanoate
  C_I = concentration of hexadecyl hexadecanoate in the Standard solution (mg/mL)
  C_S = concentration of USP α-Tocopheryl Acetate RS in the Standard solution (mg/mL)

  Analysis: Chromatograph the Sample solution as described under Calibration. Measure the areas under the major peaks occurring at relative retention times of 0.60 (α-tocopheryl acetate) and 1.00 (hexadecyl hexadecanoate). Calculate the weight (mg) of all-rac-α-tocopheryl acetate in the Sample taken by the formula:

$$\text{Result} = (10C_I/F) \times (a_U/a_I)$$

C_I = concentration of hexadecyl hexadecanoate in the Standard solution (mg/mL)
F = relative response factor (see Calibration)
a_U = peak area for α-tocopheryl acetate from the Sample solution
a_I = peak area of hexadecyl hexadecanoate from the Sample solution

Acceptance criteria: NLT 96.0% and NMT 102.0% of $C_{31}H_{52}O_3$

IMPURITIES
Inorganic Impurities
- **LEAD,** Lead Limit Test, Flame Atomic Absorption Spectrophotometric Method, Appendix IIIB
  Sample: 10 g
  Acceptance criteria: NMT 2 mg/kg

SPECIFIC TESTS
- **ACIDITY**
  Sample solution: Dissolve 1.0 g of sample in 25 mL of a mixture of alcohol and ether (1:1) (v/v) that has been neutralized to phenolphthalein TS with 0.1 N sodium hydroxide.
  Analysis: Add 0.5 mL of phenolphthalein TS to the Sample solution, and titrate with 0.1 N sodium hydroxide until the solution remains faintly pink after shaking the flask for 30 s.
  Acceptance criteria: NMT 1.0 mL of titrant is required.

OTHER REQUIREMENTS
- **LABELING:** All label claims that are in terms of International Units (IU) should be based on the following: 1 mg of all-rac-α-tocopheryl acetate = 1 IU.

RRR-Tocopherols Concentrate, Mixed
First Published: Prior to FCC 6

Tocopherols Concentrate, Mixed
INS: 307b
UNII: R0ZB2556P8 [tocopherol]

DESCRIPTION
This monograph establishes specifications for two types of mixed tocopherols concentrate. Both types are obtained by the vacuum steam distillation of edible vegetable oil products, and both contain a specified minimum amount of total tocopherols, differing only in the levels of the RRR-tocopherol forms.
The High-alpha type contains a relatively high proportion of RRR-α-tocopherol and is recognized as a form of vitamin E and also as an antioxidant. The Low-alpha type contains a relatively high proportion of D-β-, D-γ-, and D-δ-tocopherols, with a minor level of RRR-α-tocopherol, and thus is not considered to be a form of vitamin E, but rather an antioxidant. Both types may contain an edible vegetable oil added to adjust the required amount of total tocopherols and the tocopherol forms may be adjusted by suitable physical or chemical means.
RRR-Tocopherols Concentrate, Mixed occurs as a brown-red to light yellow, clear, viscous oil. It may show a slight separation of wax-like constituents in microcrystalline form. It oxidizes and darkens slowly in air and on exposure to light, particularly when in alkaline media. It is insoluble in water; soluble in alcohol; and miscible with acetone, with chloroform, with ether, and with vegetable oils.

Function
High-alpha type: Nutrient; antioxidant
Low-alpha type: Antioxidant

Packaging and Storage: Store in tight containers blanketed by inert gas and protected from heat and light.

IDENTIFICATION
- **A. PROCEDURE**
  Sample: 50 mg
  Analysis: Dissolve the Sample in 10 mL of absolute alcohol. Add, with swirling, 2 mL of nitric acid and heat at about 75° for 15 min.
  Acceptance criteria: A bright-red to orange color develops.
- **B. CHROMATOGRAPHY**
  Acceptance criteria
  High-alpha type: The retention time of the major peak (excluding the solvent peak) in the chromatogram of the Sample solution is the same as that of the Standard solution, both relative to the Internal standard solution, as obtained in the Assay (below).
  Low-alpha type: The retention time of the third major peak (i.e., the peak occurring just before that of the Internal standard) in the chromatogram of the Sample solution is the same as that of the Standard solution, both relative to the Internal standard solution, as obtained in the Assay (below).

ASSAY
- **PROCEDURE**
  [NOTE—Use low-actinic glassware for all solutions containing tocopherols.]
  Internal standard solution: 3 mg/mL of hexadecyl hexadecanoate (Aldrich or equivalent) in a pyridine:propionic anhydride solution (2:1)
  Standard solutions: Transfer 12-, 25-, 37-, and 50-mg each of USP α-Tocopherol RS into separate 50-mL Erlenmeyer flasks having 19/38 standard-taper ground-glass necks. Pipet 25 mL of Internal standard solution into each flask, mix, and reflux for 10 min under water-cooled condensers.
  Sample: 60 mg
  Sample solution: Transfer the Sample into a 50 mL Erlenmeyer flask, pipet 10.0 mL of the Internal standard solution into the flask, mix, and reflux for 10 min under a water-cooled condenser.
  Chromatographic system, Appendix IIA
  Mode: Gas chromatography
  Detector: Flame ionization
  Column: 2-m × 4-mm (id) borosilicate glass column, or equivalent, packed with 2% to 5% methylpolysiloxane

gum on 80- to 100-mesh acid-washed, base-washed, silanized, chromatographic diatomaceous earth, or equivalent materials. [NOTE—The column should have a glass-lined sample introduction system or on-column injection. Cure and condition the column as necessary before use (see *Procedure* under *Gas Chromatography*, Appendix IIA).]

Temperature
 Column temperature: Isothermal between 240° and 260°
 Injection port: About 290°
 Detector block: About 300°
Injection volume: 2–5 µL
Carrier gas: Dry carrier gas
Flow rate: Adjust to obtain a hexadecyl hexadecanoate peak approximately 18 to 20 min after sample introduction when using a 2% column, or 30 to 32 min when using a 5% column.
System suitability
 Sample: *Sample solution*
 Suitability requirement: The resolution, R, between the major peaks occurring at retention times of approximately 0.50 (δ-tocopheryl propionate) and 0.63 (β- plus γ-tocopheryl propionate), relative to hexadecyl hexadecanoate at 1.00 is NLT 2.5.
Calibration: Chromatograph successive portions of each of the *Standard solutions* until the relative response factor, F, for each is constant (i.e., within a range of approximately 2%) for three consecutive injections. If using graphic integration, adjust the instrument to obtain at least 70% maximum recorder response for the hexadecyl hexadecanoate peak. Measure the areas under the first (α-tocopheryl propionate) and second (hexadecyl hexadecanoate) major peaks (excluding the solvent peak). Calculate F for the concentration of each of the *Standard solutions* by the formula:

$$\text{Result} = (A_S/A_I) \times (C_I/C_S)$$

A_S = peak area of α-tocopheryl propionate
A_I = peak area of hexadecyl hexadecanoate
C_I = concentration of hexadecyl hexadecanoate in the *Standard solutions* (mg/mL)
C_S = concentration of USP α-Tocopherol RS in a *Standard solution* (mg/mL)

Prepare a relative response factor curve by plotting the peak areas of α-tocopheryl propionate versus the response factor, F.
Analysis: Chromatograph the *Sample solution* as described under *Calibration*. Measure the areas under the four major peaks occurring at relative retention times of 0.50 (δ-tocopherol propionate), 0.63 (β- plus γ-tocopheryl propionates), 0.76 (α-tocopherol propionate), and 1.00 (hexadecyl hexadecanoate). Record the values as a_δ, $a_{\beta+\gamma}$, a_α, and a_I, respectively.

Calculate the weight (mg) of each tocopherol form in the sample by the formulas:

$$\delta\text{-tocopherol} = (10C_I/F) \times (a_\delta/a_I)$$

$$\beta\text{- plus }\gamma\text{-tocopherols} = (10C_I/F) \times (a_{\beta+\gamma}/a_I)$$

$$\alpha\text{-tocopherol} = (10C_I/F) \times (a_\alpha/a_I)$$

F = relative response factor obtained from the curve (see *Calibration*) for each of the corresponding areas under the δ-, β- plus γ-, and α-tocopheryl propionate peaks in the chromatogram of the *Sample solution*.

[NOTE—The relative response factor for δ-tocopheryl propionate and for β- plus γ-tocopheryl propionates has been determined empirically to be the same as that for α-tocopheryl propionate.]

Acceptance criteria
 High-alpha type: NLT 50.0% of total tocopherols, of which NLT 50.0% consists of RRR-α-tocopherol ($C_{29}H_{50}O_2$) and NLT 20.0% consists of D-β- plus D-γ- ($C_{28}H_{48}O_2$) plus D-δ-tocopherols ($C_{27}H_{46}O_2$)
 Low-alpha type: NLT 50.0% of total tocopherols, of which NLT 80.0% consists of D-β- plus D-γ- plus D-δ-tocopherols

IMPURITIES
Inorganic Impurities
- **LEAD,** *Lead Limit Test, Flame Atomic Absorption Spectrophotometric Method,* Appendix IIIB
 Sample: 10 g
 Acceptance criteria: NMT 2 mg/kg

SPECIFIC TESTS
- **ACIDITY**
 Sample solution: Dissolve 1.0 g of sample in 25 mL of a mixture of alcohol and ether (1:1)(v/v) that has been neutralized to phenolphthalein TS with 0.1 N sodium hydroxide.
 Analysis: Add 0.5 mL of phenolphthalein TS to the *Sample solution*, and titrate with 0.1 N sodium hydroxide until the solution remains faintly pink after shaking the flask for 30 s.
 Acceptance criteria: NMT 1.0 mL of titrant is required.
- **OPTICAL (SPECIFIC) ROTATION,** Appendix IIB
 [NOTE—Use low-actinic glassware for all solutions containing tocopherols.]
 Sample solution: Transfer an amount of sample equivalent to 100 mg of total tocopherols to a separatory funnel and dissolve it in 50 mL of ether. Add 20 mL of a 10% solution of potassium ferricyanide in an 8 mg/mL sodium hydroxide solution and shake the solution for 3 min. Wash the ether solution with four 50-mL portions of water, discard the washings, and dry the solution over anhydrous sodium sulfate. Evaporate the dried ether solution on a water bath under reduced pressure or in an atmosphere of nitrogen until about 7 or 8 mL remain. Then, complete the evaporation, removing the last traces of ether without the

application of heat. Immediately dissolve the residue in 5.0 mL of isooctane.
Analysis: Determine the specific rotation of the *Sample solution* as directed, using as *c* in the equation, the concentration expressed in grams of total tocopherols (as determined in the *Assay*) in 100 mL of the solution.
Acceptance criteria
High-alpha type: $[\alpha]_D^{25}$ NLT +24°
Low-alpha type: $[\alpha]_D^{25}$ NLT +20°

OTHER REQUIREMENTS
- **LABELING**
  High-alpha type: Indicate the milligrams per gram of total tocopherols and of RRR-α-tocopherol present. All label claims that are in terms of International Units (IU) should be based on the following: 1 mg of RRR-α-tocopherol = 1.49 IU.
  Low-alpha type: Indicate the milligrams per gram of total tocopherols and of D-β- plus D-γ- plus D-δ-tocopherols present.

RRR-α-Tocopheryl Acetate Concentrate
First Published: Prior to FCC 6

D-α-Tocopheryl Acetate Concentrate
D-α-Tocopheryl Acetate Preparation
UNII: A7E6112E4N [α-tocopherol acetate, d-]

DESCRIPTION
RRR-α-Tocopheryl Acetate Concentrate occurs as a light brown to light yellow, clear, viscous oil. It is a form of vitamin E obtained by the vacuum steam distillation and acetylation of edible vegetable oil products. The content of RRR-α-tocopheryl acetate may be adjusted by suitable physical or chemical means. It is unstable in the presence of alkalies. It is insoluble in water; soluble in alcohol; and miscible with acetone, with chloroform, with ether, and with vegetable oils.
Function: Nutrient
Packaging and Storage: Store in tight, light-resistant containers.

IDENTIFICATION
- **A. PROCEDURE**
  Sample: 10 mL of the *Sample solution* from *Optical (Specific) Rotation*, below
  Analysis: Add, with swirling, 2 mL of nitric acid to the *Sample* and heat at about 75° for 15 min.
  Acceptance criteria: A bright-red to orange color develops.
- **B. CHROMATOGRAPHY**
  Acceptance criteria: The retention time of the major peak (excluding the solvent peak) in the chromatogram of the *Sample solution* is the same as that of the *Standard solution*, both relative to the *Internal standard solution*, as obtained in the *Assay* (below).

ASSAY
- **PROCEDURE**
  [NOTE—Use low-actinic glassware for all solutions containing tocopherols.]
  Internal standard solution: 3 mg/mL of hexadecyl hexadecanoate (Aldrich or equivalent) in *n*-hexane
  Standard solution: 3 mg/mL of USP α-Tocopheryl Acetate RS in *Internal standard solution*.
  Sample: An amount of sample equivalent to 30 mg of RRR-α-tocopheryl acetate
  Sample solution: Dissolve the *Sample* in 10.0 mL of *Internal standard solution*.
  System suitability solution: 1 mg/mL USP α-Tocopheryl Acetate RS and 1 mg/mL USP α-Tocopherol RS in *n*-hexane
  Chromatographic system, Appendix IIA
    Mode: Gas chromatography
    Detector: Flame ionization
    Column: 2-m × 4-mm (id) borosilicate glass column, or equivalent, packed with 2% to 5% methylpolysiloxane gum on 80- to 100-mesh acid-washed, base-washed, silanized, chromatographic diatomaceous earth, or equivalent materials. [NOTE—The column should have a glass-lined sample introduction system or on-column injection. Cure and condition the column as necessary before use (see *Procedure* under *Gas Chromatography*, Appendix IIA).]
  Temperature
    Column: Isothermal between 240° and 260°
    Injection port: About 290°
    Detector block: About 300°
  Injection volume: 2–5 µL
  Carrier gas: Dry carrier gas
  Flow rate: Adjust to obtain a hexadecyl hexadecanoate peak approximately 18 to 20 min after sample introduction when using a 2% column, or 30 to 32 min when using a 5% column.
  System suitability
    Sample: *System suitability solution*
    Suitability requirement: The resolution, R, between α-tocopheryl acetate and α-tocopherol is NLT 1.0.
  Calibration: Chromatograph successive portions of the *Standard solution* until the relative response factor, F, is constant (i.e., within a range of approximately 2%) for three consecutive injections. If using graphic integration, adjust the instrument to obtain at least 70% maximum recorder response for the hexadecyl hexadecanoate peak. Measure the areas under the major peaks occurring at relative retention times of 0.60 (α-tocopheryl acetate) and 1.00 (hexadecyl hexadecanoate). Calculate F by the formula:

$$\text{Result} = (A_S/A_I) \times (C_I/C_S)$$

A_S = peak area of α-tocopheryl acetate
A_I = peak area of hexadecyl hexadecanoate
C_I = concentration of hexadecyl hexadecanoate in the *Standard solution* (mg/mL)
C_S = concentration of USP α-Tocopheryl Acetate RS in the *Standard solution* (mg/mL)

Analysis: Chromatograph the *Sample solution* as described under *Calibration*. Measure the areas under the major peaks occurring at relative retention times of 0.60 (α-tocopheryl acetate) and 1.00 (hexadecyl hexadecanoate). Calculate the weight (mg) of RRR-α-tocopheryl acetate in the *Sample* taken by the formula:

$$\text{Result} = (10C_I/F) \times (a_U/a_I)$$

C_I = concentration of hexadecyl hexadecanoate in the *Standard solution* (mg/mL)
F = relative response factor (see *Calibration*)
a_U = peak area for α-tocopheryl acetate from the *Sample solution*
a_I = peak area of hexadecyl hexadecanoate from the *Sample solution*

Acceptance criteria: NLT 40.0% of $C_{31}H_{52}O_3$

IMPURITIES
Inorganic Impurities
- **LEAD**, *Lead Limit Test, Flame Atomic Absorption Spectrophotometric Method*, Appendix IIIB
  Sample: 10 g
  Acceptance criteria: NMT 2 mg/kg

SPECIFIC TESTS
- **ACIDITY**
  Sample solution: Dissolve 1.0 g of sample in 25 mL of a mixture of alcohol and ether (1:1) (v/v) that has been neutralized to phenolphthalein TS with 0.1 N sodium hydroxide.
  Analysis: Add 0.5 mL of phenolphthalein TS to the *Sample solution*, and titrate with 0.1 N sodium hydroxide until the solution remains faintly pink after shaking the flask for 30 s.
  Acceptance criteria: NMT 1.0 mL of titrant is required.
- **OPTICAL (SPECIFIC) ROTATION,** Appendix IIB
  [NOTE—Use low-actinic glassware for all solutions containing tocopherols.]
  Sample solution: Transfer an amount of sample equivalent to 200 mg of α-tocopherol into a 150 mL round-bottom glass-stoppered flask and dissolve it in 25 mL of absolute alcohol. Add 20 mL of a 1:7 mixture of 2 N sulfuric acid in alcohol, and reflux in an all-glass apparatus for 3 h, protected from sunlight. Cool the mixture, transfer into a 200-mL volumetric flask, dilute to volume with a 1:72 mixture of 2 N sulfuric acid in alcohol, and mix. [NOTE—Retain 10 mL of this solution for *Identification* test A (above).]
  Analysis: Transfer a quantity of the *Sample solution* equivalent to 100 mg of α-tocopherol to a separatory funnel and add 200 mL of water. Extract first with 75 mL, then with two 25-mL portions of ether, and combine the ether extracts in another separatory funnel. Add 20 mL of a 10% solution of potassium ferricyanide in a 1:125 sodium hydroxide solution to the ether solution and shake the solution for 3 min. Wash the ether solution with four 50-mL portions of water, discard the washings, and dry the solution over anhydrous sodium sulfate. Evaporate the dried ether solution on a water bath under reduced pressure or in an atmosphere of nitrogen until about 7 or 8 mL remain. Then, complete the evaporation, removing the last traces of ether without the application of heat. Immediately dissolve the residue in 5.0 mL of isooctane. Determine the specific rotation of this solution using as c in the equation, the concentration expressed in grams of RRR-α-tocopheryl acetate (based on the *Assay* determination) per 100 mL of solution.
  Acceptance criteria: $[\alpha]_D^{25}$ NLT +24°

OTHER REQUIREMENTS
- **LABELING:** Indicate the milligrams per gram of RRR-α-tocopheryl acetate present. All label claims that are in terms of International Units (IU) should be based on the following: 1 mg of RRR-α-tocopheryl acetate = 1.36 IU.

RRR-α-Tocopheryl Acetate

First Published: Prior to FCC 6

D-α-Tocopheryl Acetate

$C_{31}H_{52}O_3$ Formula wt 472.75
                 CAS: [58-95-7]
UNII: A7E6112E4N [α-tocopherol acetate, d-]

DESCRIPTION
RRR-α-Tocopheryl Acetate occurs as a colorless to yellow, clear, viscous oil. It is a form of vitamin E obtained by the vacuum steam distillation and acetylation of edible vegetable oil products. It may solidify on standing, and melts at about 25°. It is unstable in the presence of alkalies. It is insoluble in water; freely soluble in alcohol; and miscible with acetone, with chloroform, with ether, and with vegetable oils.

Function: Nutrient
Packaging and Storage: Store in tight, light-resistant containers.

IDENTIFICATION
- **A. PROCEDURE**
  Sample solution: *Sample solution* from *Optical (Specific) Rotation* (below)
  Analysis: To 10 mL of the *Sample solution* add, with swirling, 2 mL of nitric acid and heat at about 75° for 15 min.
  Acceptance criteria: A bright-red to orange color develops.
- **B. PROCEDURE**
  Acceptance criteria: The retention time of the major peak (excluding the solvent peak) in the chromatogram of the *Sample solution* is the same as that of the *Standard solution*, both relative to the *Internal standard solution*, as obtained in the *Assay* (below).

ASSAY
- **PROCEDURE**
  [NOTE—Use low-actinic glassware for all solutions containing tocopherols.]
  Internal standard solution: 3 mg/mL hexadecyl hexadecanoate (Aldrich or equivalent) in *n*-hexane
  Standard solution: 3 mg/mL USP α-Tocopheryl Acetate RS in *Internal standard solution*
  Sample: 30 mg
  Sample solution: Dissolve the *Sample* in 10.0 mL of *Internal standard solution*.
  System suitability solution: 1 mg/mL USP α-Tocopheryl Acetate RS and 1 mg/mL USP α-Tocopherol RS in *n*-hexane
  Chromatographic system, Appendix IIA
    Mode: Gas chromatography
    Detector: Flame-ionization
    Column: 2-m × 4-mm (id) borosilicate glass column, or equivalent, packed with 2% to 5% methylpolysiloxane gum on 80- to 100-mesh acid-washed, base-washed, silanized, chromatographic diatomaceous earth, or equivalent materials. [NOTE—The column should have a glass-lined sample introduction system or on-column injection. Cure and condition the column as necessary before use.]
    Column temperature: Isothermal between 240° and 260°
    Injection port: About 290°
    Detector block: About 300°
    Injection volume: 2–5 μL
    Carrier gas: Dry carrier gas
    Flow rate: Adjust to obtain a hexadecyl hexadecanoate peak approximately 18 to 20 min after sample introduction when using a 2% column, or 30 to 32 min when using a 5% column.
  System suitability
    Sample: *System suitability solution*
    Suitability requirement: The resolution, R, between α-tocopheryl acetate and α-tocopherol is NLT 1.0.
  Calibration: Chromatograph successive portions of the *Standard solution* until the relative response factor, F, is constant (i.e., within a range of ~2%) for three consecutive injections. If using graphic integration, adjust the instrument to obtain at least 70% maximum recorder response for the hexadecyl hexadecanoate peak. Measure the areas under the major peaks occurring at relative retention times of 0.60 (α-tocopheryl acetate) and 1.00 (hexadecyl hexadecanoate). Calculate F by the formula:

  $$Result = (A_S/A_I) \times (C_I/C_S)$$

  A_S = peak area for α-tocopherol acetate
  A_I = peak area for hexadecyl hexadecanoate
  C_I = concentration of hexadecyl hexadecanoate in the *Standard solution* (mg/mL)
  C_S = concentration of USP α-Tocopherol Acetate RS in the *Standard solution* (mg/mL)

  Analysis: Chromatograph the *Sample solution* as described under *Calibration*. Measure the areas under the major peaks occurring at relative retention times of 0.60 (α-tocopheryl acetate) and 1.00 (hexadecyl hexadecanoate). Calculate the weight (mg), of RRR-α-Tocopheryl Acetate in the *Sample* taken by the formula:

  $$Result = (10C_I/F) \times (a_U/a_I)$$

  C_I = concentration of hexadecyl hexadecanoate in the *Standard solution* (mg/mL)
  F = relative response factor (see *Calibration*)
  a_U = peak area for α-tocopheryl acetate from the *Sample solution*
  a_I = peak area for hexadecyl hexadecanoate from the *Sample solution*

  Acceptance criteria: NLT 96.0% and NMT 102.0% of $C_{31}H_{52}O_3$

IMPURITIES
Inorganic Impurities
- **LEAD,** *Lead Limit Test, Flame Atomic Absorption Spectrophotometric Method,* Appendix IIIB
  Sample: 10 g
  Acceptance criteria: NMT 2 mg/kg

SPECIFIC TESTS
- **ACIDITY**
  Sample solution: Dissolve 1.0 g of sample in 25 mL of a mixture of alcohol and ether (1:1) (v/v) that has been neutralized to phenolphthalein TS with 0.1 N sodium hydroxide.
  Analysis: Add 0.5 mL of phenolphthalein TS to the *Sample solution*, and titrate with 0.1 N sodium hydroxide until the solution remains faintly pink after shaking the flask for 30 s.
  Acceptance criteria: NMT 1.0 mL of titrant is required
- **OPTICAL (SPECIFIC) ROTATION,** Appendix IIB
  [NOTE—Use low-actinic glassware for all solutions containing tocopherols.]
  Sample: An amount of sample equivalent to 200 mg of α-tocopherol
  Sample solution: Transfer the *Sample* into a 150 mL round-bottom glass-stoppered flask and dissolve it in 25 mL of absolute alcohol. Add 20 mL of a 1:7 mixture of 2 N sulfuric acid in alcohol, and reflux in an all-glass apparatus for 3 h, protected from sunlight. Cool the mixture, transfer into a 200-mL volumetric flask, dilute to volume with a 1:72 mixture of 2 N sulfuric acid in alcohol, and mix. [NOTE—Retain 10 mL of this solution for *Identification* test A (above).]
  Analysis: Transfer a volume of the *Sample solution*, equivalent to about 100 mg of α-tocopherol, into a separatory funnel, and add 200 mL of water. Extract first with 75 mL, then with two 25-mL portions of ether, and combine the ether extracts in another separatory funnel. Add 20 mL of a 10% solution of potassium ferricyanide in a 1:125 sodium hydroxide solution to the ether solution, and shake the funnel for 3 min. Wash the ether solution with four 50-mL portions of water, discard the washings, and dry over anhydrous sodium sulfate. Evaporate the dried ether solution on a water bath under reduced pressure or in

an atmosphere of nitrogen until about 7 or 8 mL remain; complete the evaporation, removing the last traces of ether without the application of heat. Immediately dissolve the residue in 5.0 mL of isooctane. Determine the specific rotation of this solution, using as c in the equation, the concentration expressed in grams of RRR-α-Tocopheryl Acetate (as determined in the *Assay*) in 100 mL of solution.
Acceptance criteria: $[\alpha]_D^{25}$ NLT +24°

OTHER REQUIREMENTS
- **LABELING** All label claims that are in terms of International Units (IU) should be based on the following: 1 mg of RRR-α-Tocopheryl Acetate = 1.36 IU

RRR-α-Tocopheryl Acid Succinate
First Published: Prior to FCC 6

D-α-Tocopheryl Acid Succinate

$C_{33}H_{54}O_5$ Formula wt 530.79
CAS: [4345-03-3]
UNII: LU4B53JYVE [α-tocopherol succinate, d-]

DESCRIPTION
RRR-α-Tocopheryl Acid Succinate occurs as a white to off-white, crystalline powder. It is a form of vitamin E obtained by the vacuum steam distillation and succinylation of edible vegetable oil products. It is stable in air, but is unstable to alkali and to heat. It is insoluble in water; soluble in acetone, in alcohol, in ether, and in vegetable oils; and very soluble in chloroform. It melts at about 75°.
Function: Nutrient
Packaging and Storage: Store in tight, light-resistant containers.

IDENTIFICATION
- **A. PROCEDURE**
  Sample: *Sample solution* from *Optical (Specific) Rotation* (below)
  Analysis: Add, with swirling, 2 mL of nitric acid to 10 mL of the *Sample* and heat at about 75° for 15 min.
  Acceptance criteria: A bright red to orange color develops.
- **B. CHROMATOGRAPHY**
  Acceptance criteria: The retention time of the major peak (excluding the solvent peak) in the chromatogram of the *Sample solution* is the same as that of the *Standard solution*, both relative to the *Internal standard solution*, as obtained in the *Assay* (below).

ASSAY
- **PROCEDURE**
  [NOTE—Use low-actinic glassware for all solutions containing tocopherols.]
  Internal standard solution: 3 mg/mL of hexadecyl hexadecanoate (Aldrich or equivalent) in *n*-hexane
  Standard solution: Transfer 30 mg of USP α-Tocopheryl Acid Succinate RS into a 4-dram (approximately 15-mL) screw-cap vial. Pipet 2.0 mL of absolute methanol, 1.0 mL of 2,2-dimethoxypropane, and 0.1 mL of concentrated hydrochloric acid into the vial, cap, mix well, and allow the vial to stand in the dark for 1 h. Evaporate the contents of the vial just to dryness on a steam bath with the aid of a stream of nitrogen. Pipet 10.0 mL of the *Internal standard solution* into the vial, cap and shake the vial vigorously.
  Sample solution: Prepare as directed for the *Standard solution* using an amount of sample equivalent to 30 mg of RRR-α-tocopheryl acid succinate.
  System suitability solution: 1 mg/mL each of USP α-Tocopherol RS and USP α-Tocopheryl Acetate RS in *n*-hexane
  Chromatographic system, Appendix IIA
    Mode: Gas chromatography
    Detector: Flame ionization
    Column: 2-m × 4-mm (id) borosilicate glass column, or equivalent, packed with 2% to 5% methylpolysiloxane gum on 80- to 100-mesh acid-washed, base-washed, silanized, chromatographic diatomaceous earth, or equivalent materials. [NOTE—The column should have a glass-lined sample introduction system or on-column injection. Cure and condition the column as necessary before use (see *Procedure* under *Gas Chromatography*, Appendix IIA).]
    Temperature
      Column: Isothermal between 260° and 280°
      Injection port: About 290°
      Detector block: About 300°
    Injection volume: 2–5 μL
    Carrier gas: Dry carrier gas
    Flow rate: Adjust to obtain a hexadecyl hexadecanoate peak approximately 12 to 14 min after sample introduction.
  System suitability
    Sample: *System suitability solution*
    Suitability requirement: The resolution, R, between α-tocopheryl acetate and α-tocopherol is NLT 1.0.
  Calibration: Chromatograph successive portions of the *Standard solution* until the relative response factor, F, is constant (i.e., within a range of approximately 2%) for three consecutive injections. If using graphic integration, adjust the instrument to obtain at least 70% maximum recorder response for the hexadecyl hexadecanoate peak. Measure the areas under the major peaks occurring at relative retention times of approximately 1.00 (hexadecyl hexadecanoate) and 1.99 (methyl α-tocopheryl succinate). Calculate F by the formula:

  $$\text{Result} = (A_S/A_I) \times (C_I/C_S)$$

  A_S = peak area for methyl α-tocopheryl succinate
  A_I = peak area for hexadecyl hexadecanoate
  C_I = concentration of hexadecyl hexadecanoate in the *Standard solution* (mg/mL)

C_S = concentration of USP α-Tocopheryl Acid Succinate RS in the Standard solution (mg/mL)

Analysis: Chromatograph the Sample solution as described under Calibration. Measure the areas under the major peaks occurring at relative retention times of approximately 1.00 (hexadecyl hexadecanoate) and 1.99 (methyl α-tocopheryl succinate). Calculate the weight, in mg, of RRR-α-tocopheryl acid succinate in the sample taken by the following formula:

$$\text{Result} = (10C_I/F) \times (a_U/a_I)$$

C_I = concentration of hexadecyl hexadecanoate in the Standard solution (mg/mL)
F = relative response factor (see Calibration)
a_U = peak area for methyl α-tocopheryl succinate from the Sample solution
a_I = peak area of hexadecyl hexadecanoate from the Sample solution

Acceptance criteria: NLT 96.0% and NMT 102.0% of $C_{33}H_{54}O_5$

IMPURITIES
Inorganic Impurities
- **LEAD,** Lead Limit Test, Flame Atomic Absorption Spectrophotometric Method, Appendix IIIB
  Sample: 10 g
  Acceptance criteria: NMT 2 mg/kg

SPECIFIC TESTS
- **ACIDITY**
  Sample solution: Dissolve 1.0 g of sample in 25 mL of a mixture of alcohol and ether (1:1) (v/v) that has been neutralized to phenolphthalein TS with 0.1 N sodium hydroxide.
  Analysis: Add 0.5 mL of phenolphthalein TS to the Sample solution and titrate with 0.1 N sodium hydroxide until the solution remains faintly pink after shaking the flask for 30 s.
  Acceptance criteria: Between 18.0 mL and 19.3 mL of titrant are required.

- **OPTICAL (SPECIFIC) ROTATION,** Appendix IIB
  [NOTE—Use low-actinic glassware for all solutions containing tocopherols.]
  Sample solution: Transfer an amount of sample equivalent to 200 mg of α-tocopherol into a 250 mL round-bottom glass-stoppered flask, dissolve it in 50 mL of absolute alcohol, and reflux the solution for 1 min. While the solution is boiling, add through the condenser 1 g of potassium hydroxide pellets, one at a time to avoid overheating. [CAUTION—Use appropriate eye protection.] Continue refluxing for 20 min and, then, without cooling, add 2 mL of hydrochloric acid, dropwise, through the condenser. [NOTE—This technique is essential to prevent oxidative action by air while the sample is in an alkaline medium.] Cool, and transfer the contents of the flask into a 500-mL separatory funnel, rinsing the flask with 100 mL each of water and of ether and adding the rinsings to the funnel. Shake the funnel vigorously, allow the layers to separate, and collect each of the two layers in separate funnels. Extract the aqueous layer with two 50-mL portions of ether and add these extracts to the main ether extract. Wash the combined ether extracts with four 100-mL portions of water. Then evaporate the solutions on a water bath under reduced pressure or in an atmosphere of nitrogen until about 7 or 8 mL remain. Complete the evaporation, removing the last traces of ether without the application of heat. Immediately dissolve the residue in a 1:72 solution of 2 N sulfuric acid in alcohol, transfer to a 200-mL volumetric flask, dilute to volume with the same, and mix. [NOTE—Retain 10 mL of this solution for Identification test A (above).]
  Analysis: Transfer a volume of Sample solution, equivalent to about 100 mg of α-tocopherol into a separatory funnel and add 200 mL of water. Extract first with 75 mL, then with two 25-mL portions of ether, and combine the ether extracts in another separatory funnel. Add 20 mL of a 10% solution of potassium ferricyanide in a 1:125 sodium hydroxide solution to the ether solution and shake the solution for 3 min. Wash the ether solution with four 50-mL portions of water, discard the washings, and dry over anhydrous sodium sulfate. Evaporate the dried ether solution on a water bath under reduced pressure or in an atmosphere of nitrogen until about 7 or 8 mL remain. Then, complete the evaporation, removing the last traces of ether without the application of heat. Immediately dissolve the residue in 5.0 mL of isooctane. Determine the specific rotation of this solution using as c in the equation, the concentration expressed in grams of RRR-α-tocopheryl acid succinate (based on the Assay determination) per 100 mL of solution.
  Acceptance criteria: $[\alpha]_D^{25}$ NLT +24°

OTHER REQUIREMENTS
- **LABELING:** All label claims that are in terms of International Units (IU) should be based on the following: 1 mg of RRR-α-Tocopheryl Acid Succinate = 1.21 IU.

p-Tolualdehyde

First Published: Prior to FCC 6
Last Revision: First Supplement, FCC 6

p-Tolyl Aldehyde
p-Methylbenzaldehyde

C_8H_8O Formula wt 120.15
FEMA: 3068
UNII: GAX22QZ28Q [p-tolualdehyde]

DESCRIPTION
p-Tolualdehyde occurs as a colorless liquid. It may contain a suitable antioxidant.

1152 / p-Tolualdehyde / Monographs

Odor: Cherry
Boiling Point: ~83° to 85° (11 mm Hg)
Solubility in Alcohol, Appendix VI: One mL dissolves in 1 mL of 95% alcohol.
Function: Flavoring agent

ASSAY
- **PROCEDURE:** Proceed as directed under *M-1b,* Appendix XI.
  Acceptance criteria: NLT 97.0% of C_8H_8O

SPECIFIC TESTS
- **ACID VALUE, FLAVOR CHEMICALS (OTHER THAN ESSENTIAL OILS),** *M-15,* Appendix XI
  Acceptance criteria: NMT 5.0
- **REFRACTIVE INDEX,** Appendix II: At 20°
  Acceptance criteria: Between 1.542 and 1.548
- **SPECIFIC GRAVITY:** Determine at 25° by any reliable method (see *General Provisions*).
  Acceptance criteria: Between 1.012 and 1.018

Tolualdehyde, Mixed Isomers

First Published: Prior to FCC 6
Last Revision: First Supplement, FCC 6

Tolyl Aldehyde, mixed isomers
Methylbenzaldehyde

C_8H_8O Formula wt 120.15
FEMA: 3068
UNII: ALC105UA3K [tolualdehyde, mixed isomers]

DESCRIPTION
Tolualdehyde, Mixed Isomers occurs as a colorless liquid. It may contain a suitable antioxidant.
Odor: Cherry
Boiling Point: ~198°
Solubility in Alcohol, Appendix VI: One mL dissolves in 1 mL of 95% alcohol.
Function: Flavoring agent

IDENTIFICATION
- **INFRARED SPECTRA,** *Spectrophotometric Identification Tests,* Appendix IIIC
  Acceptance criteria: The spectrum of the sample exhibits relative maxima at the same wavelengths as those of the spectrum below.

ASSAY
- **PROCEDURE:** Proceed as directed under *M-1b,* Appendix XI
  Acceptance criteria: NLT 94.0% of C_8H_8O (sum of three isomers)

SPECIFIC TESTS
- **ACID VALUE, FLAVOR CHEMICALS (OTHER THAN ESSENTIAL OILS),** *M-15,* Appendix XI
  Acceptance criteria: NMT 5.0
- **REFRACTIVE INDEX,** Appendix II: At 20°
  Acceptance criteria: Between 1.540 and 1.548
- **SPECIFIC GRAVITY:** Determine at 25° by any reliable method (see *General Provisions*).
  Acceptance criteria: Between 1.019 and 1.029

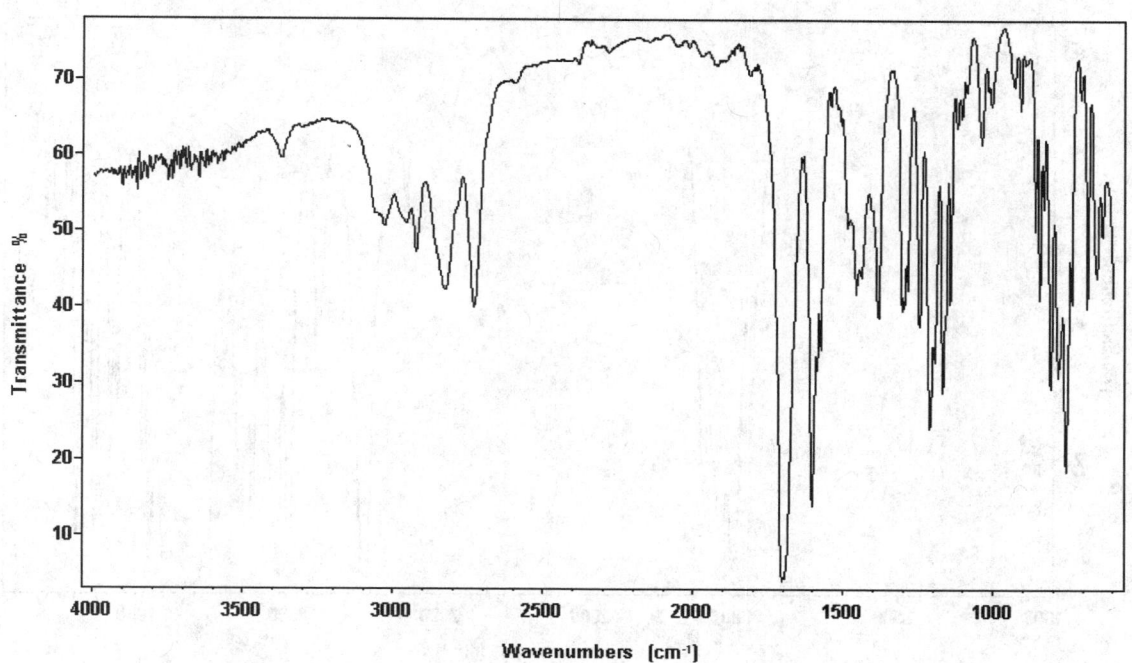

Tolualdehyde, Mixed Isomers

p-Tolyl Isobutyrate

First Published: Prior to FCC 6

p-Cresyl Isobutyrate

$C_{11}H_{14}O_2$
FEMA: 3075
UNII: 8H719PT14T [p-cresyl isobutyrate]

Formula wt 178.23

DESCRIPTION
p-Tolyl Isobutyrate occurs as a colorless liquid.
Odor: Fruity
Solubility: Soluble in alcohol; insoluble or practically insoluble in water
Boiling Point: ~237°
Solubility in Alcohol, Appendix VI: One mL dissolves in 7 mL of 70% alcohol to give a clear solution.

Function: Flavoring agent

IDENTIFICATION
- **INFRARED SPECTRA,** Spectrophotometric Identification Tests, Appendix IIIC
  Acceptance criteria: The spectrum of the sample exhibits relative maxima at the same wavelengths as those of the spectrum below.

ASSAY
- **PROCEDURE:** Proceed as directed under M-1b, Appendix XI.
  Acceptance criteria: NLT 95.0% of $C_{11}H_{14}O_2$

SPECIFIC TESTS
- **ACID VALUE, FLAVOR CHEMICALS (OTHER THAN ESSENTIAL OILS),** M-15, Appendix XI
  Acceptance criteria: NMT 1.0
- **REFRACTIVE INDEX,** Appendix II: At 20°
  Acceptance criteria: Between 1.485 and 1.489
- **SPECIFIC GRAVITY:** Determine at 25° by any reliable method (see General Provisions).
  Acceptance criteria: Between 0.990 and 0.996

1154 / *p*-Tolyl Isobutyrate / *Monographs*

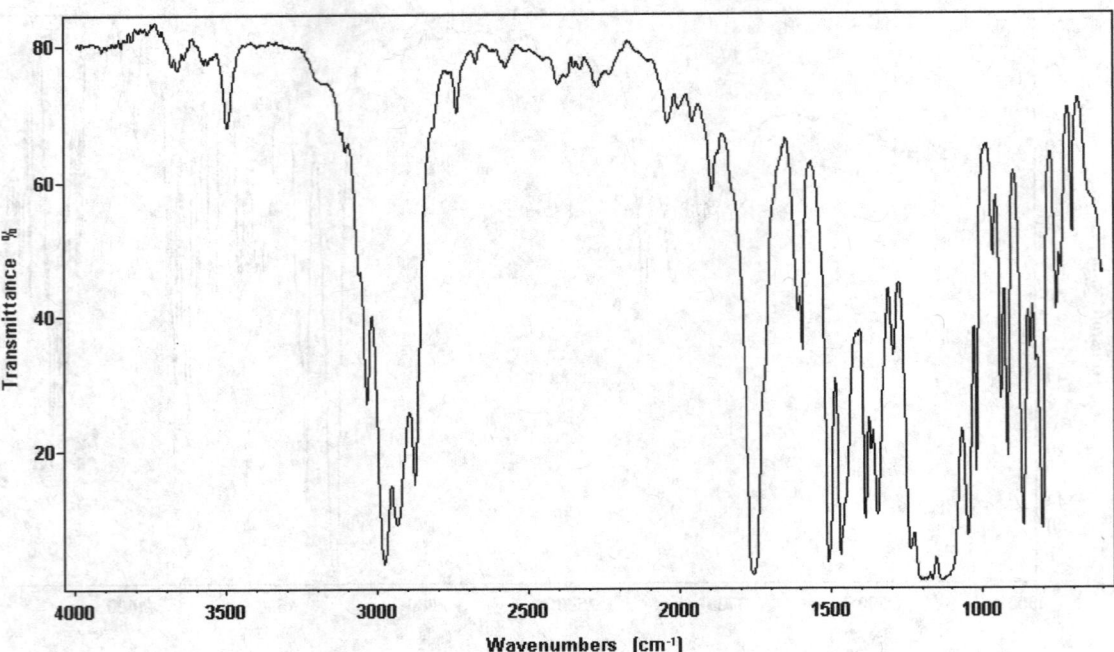

p-Tolyl Isobutyrate

Tragacanth

First Published: Prior to FCC 6

Gum Tragacanth
Tragacanth Gum
INS: 413
UNII: 2944357O2O [tragacanth]
CAS: [9000-65-1]

DESCRIPTION
Tragacanth is a dried, gummy exudation obtained from the stems and branches of *Astragalus gummifer* Labillardiere, or other Asiatic species of *Astragalus* (Fam. Leguminosae). It consists mainly of high-molecular-weight polysaccharides (arabinogalactans and acidic polysaccharides) that, on hydrolysis, yield galacturonic acid, galactose, arabinose, xylose, and fucose; small amounts of rhamnose and of glucose (derived from traces of starch and/or cellulose) may also be present. Unground tragacanth occurs as flattened, lamellated, frequently curved fragments or straight or spirally twisted linear pieces from 0.5 to 2.5 mm in thickness. It is white to weak yellow (although some pieces may have a red tinge) and translucent, with a horny texture and a short fracture. It is easier to pulverize if heated to 50°. Powdered tragacanth is white to yellow-white or pink-brown.
Function: Stabilizer; thickener; emulsifier
Packaging and Storage: Store in well-closed containers.

[NOTE—For tests under *Impurities* and *Specific Tests*, prepare unground samples for analysis by powdering them to pass through a Number 45 sieve and mix well.]

IDENTIFICATION
- **A. PROCEDURE**
  Analysis: Examine unground sample under microscope in water mounts.
  Acceptance criteria: Examination reveals numerous angular fragments with circular or irregular lamellae, and starch grains up to 25 μm in diameter. There should be very few or no fragments of lignified vegetable tissue.
- **B. PROCEDURE**
  Analysis: Add iodinated zinc chloride solution to a representative sample.
  Acceptance criteria: Cellular membranes turn violet.
- **C. PROCEDURE**
  Sample: 1 g
  Analysis: Mix the *Sample* with 50 mL of water. Observe the results and compare to the same amount of sample in 60% (w/v) aqueous ethanol.
  Acceptance criteria: The sample swells to form a smooth, stiff, opalescent mucilage free from cellular fragments when mixed with the water. The sample does not swell in the ethanol.

IMPURITIES
Inorganic Impurities
- **LEAD,** *Lead Limit Test, Flame Atomic Absorption Spectrophotometric Method,* Appendix IIIB
  Sample: 10 g
  Acceptance criteria: NMT 2 mg/kg

SPECIFIC TESTS
- **ASH (ACID-INSOLUBLE)**, Appendix IIC
  Acceptance criteria: NMT 0.5%
- **ASH (TOTAL)**, Appendix IIC
  Acceptance criteria: NMT 3.0%
- **KARAYA GUM**
  Sample: 1 g
  Analysis: Boil the *Sample* with 20 mL of water until it forms a mucilage, add 5 mL of hydrochloric acid, and boil the mixture for 5 min.
  Acceptance criteria: No permanent pink or red color appears.
- **VISCOSITY DETERMINATION**, *Viscosity of Cellulose Gum*, Appendix IIB
  Sample preparation: Transfer 4.0 g of finely powdered sample into the container of a stirring apparatus equipped with blades capable of revolving at 10,000 rpm. Add 10 mL of alcohol, swirl to wet the gum uniformly, and then add 390 mL of water, avoiding the formation of lumps. Immediately stir the mixture for 7 min, pour the resulting dispersion into a 500-mL bottle, insert a stopper, and allow it to stand for about 24 h in a water bath at 25°.
  Analysis: Determine the apparent viscosity of the resulting *Sample preparation* at 25° with a Model LVF Brookfield, or equivalent, viscometer using Spindle No. 2 at 30 rpm and a factor of 10.
  Acceptance criteria: NLT 250 cp

Trehalose

First Published: Prior to FCC 6
Last Revision: Third Supplement, FCC 7

α-D-Glucopyranosyl-α-D-glucopyranoside, dihydrate

$C_{12}H_{22}O_{11} \cdot 2H_2O$ Formula wt 378.33
                                CAS: dihydrate [6138-23-4]
UNII: B8WCK70T7I [trehalose]

DESCRIPTION
Trehalose occurs as a nonhygroscopic, white, crystalline powder. It is obtained through enzymatic conversion of food-grade starch into a stable, nonreducing disaccharide with two glucose molecules linked in an α,α-1,1 configuration. The powder is freely soluble or readily dispersible in water. Viewed under a light microscope at 50× magnification Trehalose appears as colorless, rectangular crystals with a prismatic structure. Trehalose is typically used in its dihydrate form.
Function: Humectant; nutritive sweetener, stabilizer; thickener; texturizer
Packaging and Storage: Store in tight containers in a dry place.

IDENTIFICATION
- **INFRARED ABSORPTION**, *Spectrophotometric Identification Tests,* Appendix IIIC
  Reference standard: USP Trehalose RS
  Sample and standard preparations: M
  Acceptance criteria: The spectrum of the sample exhibits maxima at the same wavelengths as those in the spectrum of the *Reference standard*.

ASSAY
- **PROCEDURE**
  Mobile phase: Water
  Standard solution: 10 mg/mL of USP Trehalose RS, calculated on the basis of the USP RS label claim
  Sample solution: 10 mg/mL, calculated on the anhydrous basis
  Chromatographic system, Appendix IIA
  Mode: High-performance liquid chromatography
  Detector: Refractive index
  Column: 8-mm × 30-cm[1]
  Temperature
    Detector: 40°
    Column: 80°
  Flow rate: Adjust so that the retention time of trehalose is about 15 min.
  Injection size: 20 μL
  System suitability
    Sample: *Standard solution*
    Suitability requirement: The relative standard deviation of the trehalose area responses from replicate injections is NMT 2.0%.
  Analysis: Separately inject equal volumes of the *Standard solution* and *Sample solution* into the chromatograph, and measure the responses for the major peaks on the resulting chromatograms. Calculate the percentage of trehalose in the portion of the sample taken:

  $$\text{Result} = (r_U/r_S) \times (C_S/C_U) \times 100$$

  r_U = peak response from the *Sample solution*
  r_S = peak response from the *Standard solution*
  C_S = concentration of the *Standard solution*, calculated based on the USP Trehalose RS label claim (mg/mL)
  C_U = concentration of the *Sample solution* (mg/mL)

  Acceptance criteria: NLT 98.0%, calculated on the anhydrous basis

IMPURITIES
Inorganic Impurities
- **LEAD**, *Lead Limit Test, Atomic Absorption Spectrophotometric Graphite Furnace Method, Method I,* Appendix IIIB
  Sample: 5 g
  Acceptance criteria: NMT 0.1 mg/kg

SPECIFIC TESTS
- **COLOR IN SOLUTION**
  Sample solution: Dissolve 33 g of the sample in 67 g of recently boiled water.

---
[1] Shodex SUGAR KS-801, or equivalent.

Analysis: Determine the absorbance of the *Sample solution* at 420 nm and 720 nm using a 10-cm cuvette. Calculate *Color in Solution*:

$$\text{Result} = A_{420} - A_{720}$$

A_{420} = absorbance at 420 nm
A_{720} = absorbance at 720 nm
Acceptance criteria: NMT 0.100
- **WATER**, *Water Determination*, Appendix IIB
  Acceptance criteria: NMT 11.0%
- **PH**, *pH Determination*, Appendix IIB
  Sample solution: Dissolve 33 g of the sample in 67 g of recently boiled water.
  Acceptance criteria: 4.5–6.5
- **RESIDUE ON IGNITION (SULFATED ASH)**, Appendix IIC
  Sample: 5 g
  Acceptance criteria: NMT 0.05%
- **TURBIDITY OF A 30% SOLUTION**
  Sample solution: Dissolve 33 g of the sample in 67 g of recently boiled water.
  Analysis: Using a suitable spectrophotometer, determine the absorbance of the *Sample solution* at 720 nm using a 10-cm cuvette.
  Acceptance criteria: NMT 0.050

2-Tridecanone

First Published: Prior to FCC 6

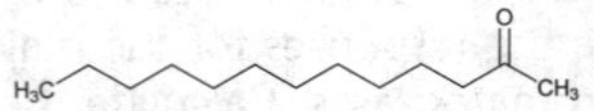

$C_{13}H_{26}O_6$
FEMA: 3388

Formula wt 198.35

UNII: 5Q35VHX26K [2-tridecanone]

DESCRIPTION
2-Tridecanone occurs as a white to pale yellow solid.
Odor: Herbal
Solubility: Soluble in propylene glycol, vegetable oils; insoluble or practically insoluble in water
Boiling Point: ~134° (10 mm Hg)
Solubility in Alcohol, Appendix VI: One g dissolves in 1 mL of 95% ethanol.
Function: Flavoring agent

IDENTIFICATION
- **INFRARED SPECTRA**, *Spectrophotometric Identification Tests*, Appendix IIIC
  Acceptance criteria: The spectrum of the sample exhibits relative maxima at the same wavelengths as those of the spectrum below.

ASSAY
- **PROCEDURE:** Proceed as directed under *M-1b*, Appendix XI.
  Acceptance criteria: NLT 95.0% of $C_{13}H_{26}O$

OTHER REQUIREMENTS
- **MELTING RANGE OR TEMPERATURE DETERMINATION**, Appendix IIB
  Acceptance criteria: NLT 27.0°

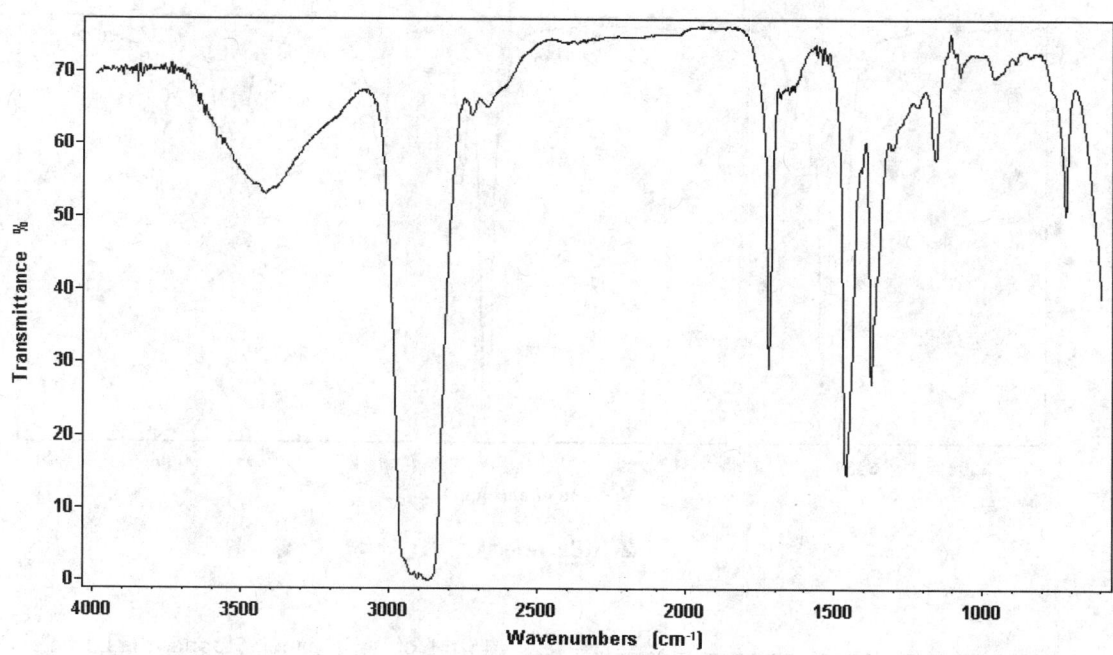

2-Tridecanone

2-Tridecenal

First Published: Prior to FCC 6
Last Revision: Third Supplement, FCC 7

$C_{13}H_{24}O$ Formula wt 196.33
FEMA: 3082
UNII: C950P0MYML [2-tridecenal]

DESCRIPTION
2-Tridecenal occurs as a white or slightly yellow liquid. It may contain a suitable antioxidant.
Odor: Oily, citrus
Solubility: Soluble in alcohol, most fixed oils; insoluble or practically insoluble in water
Solubility in Alcohol, Appendix VI: One mL dissolves in 1 mL of 95% ethanol.

Function: Flavoring agent

IDENTIFICATION
- **INFRARED SPECTRA,** Spectrophotometric Identification Tests, Appendix IIIC
  Acceptance criteria: The spectrum of the sample exhibits relative maxima at the same wavelengths as those of the spectrum below.

ASSAY
- **PROCEDURE:** Proceed as directed under M-1a, Appendix XI.
  Acceptance criteria: NLT 92.0% of $C_{13}H_{24}O$

SPECIFIC TESTS
- **REFRACTIVE INDEX,** Appendix II: At 20°
  Acceptance criteria: 1.457–1.462
- **SPECIFIC GRAVITY:** Determine at 25° by any reliable method (see General Provisions).
  Acceptance criteria: 0.842–0.862

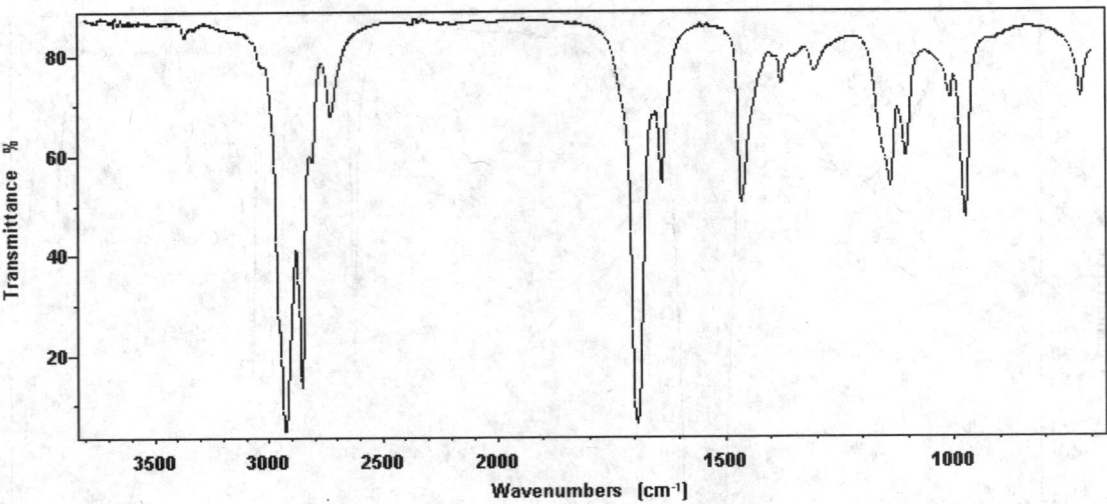

2-Tridecenal

Triacetin

First Published: Prior to FCC 6

Glyceryl Triacetate

$C_9H_{14}O_6$
INS: 1518
UNII: XHX3C3X673 [triacetin]
Formula wt 218.21
CAS: [102-76-1]

DESCRIPTION
Triacetin occurs as a colorless, somewhat oily liquid. It is soluble in 14 parts water, and is miscible with alcohol, with ether, and with chloroform. It distills between 258° and 270°.

Function: Humectant; solvent
Packaging and Storage: Store in well-closed containers.

IDENTIFICATION
- **A. PROCEDURE**
  Analysis: Heat a few drops of sample in a test tube with about 500 mg of potassium bisulfate.
  Acceptance criteria: Pungent vapors of acrolein evolve.
- **B. ACETATE,** Appendix IIIA
  Sample solution: Use the solution resulting from the *Assay* (below).
  Acceptance criteria: Passes tests

ASSAY
- **PROCEDURE**
  Sample: 1 g
  Analysis: Transfer the *Sample* into a suitable pressure bottle and add 25 mL of 1 N potassium hydroxide and 15 mL of isopropanol. Stopper the bottle and wrap it securely in a canvas bag. Place it in a water bath maintained at 98° ± 2° for 1 h, allowing the water in the bath to just cover the liquid in the bottle. Remove the bottle from the bath, cool in air to room temperature, then loosen the wrapper, uncap the bottle to release any pressure, and remove the wrapper. Add 6-8 drops of phenolphthalein TS, and titrate the excess alkali with 0.5 N sulfuric acid until the disappearance of the pink color. Perform a blank determination, and make any necessary correction (see *General Provisions*). Each mL of 0.5 N sulfuric acid is equivalent to 36.37 mg of $C_9H_{14}O_6$.
  Acceptance criteria: NLT 98.5% of $C_9H_{14}O_6$

IMPURITIES
Inorganic Impurities
- **LEAD,** *Lead Limit Test, Atomic Absorption Spectrophotometric Graphite Furnace Method, Method I,* Appendix IIIB
  Acceptance criteria: NMT 1 mg/kg

SPECIFIC TESTS
- **ACIDITY**
  Sample: 25 g
  Analysis: Transfer the *Sample* into a 125-mL conical flask. Add 50 mL of toluene and 2 drops of thymol blue TS and titrate rapidly with 0.02 M sodium methoxide in toluene until the yellow color changes to a dark color; continue the titration without stopping but slowing the addition of titrant until a single drop changes the solution to a clear blue color.
  [NOTE—The endpoint is stable for about 8 to 15 seconds.]
  Acceptance criteria: NMT 1.0 mL of titrant is used
- **REFRACTIVE INDEX,** Appendix IIB
  [NOTE—Use an Abbé or other refractometer of equal or greater accuracy.]
  Acceptance criteria: Between 1.429 and 1.431 at 25°

- **SPECIFIC GRAVITY:** Determine by any reliable method (see *General Provisions*)
  Acceptance criteria: Between 1.154 and 1.158
- **UNSATURATED COMPOUNDS**
  Sample: 10 mL
  Analysis: Add dropwise, bromine in carbon tetrachloride (1:100) to the *Sample* contained in a glass-stoppered tube until a permanent yellow color appears. Allow the tube to stand in a dark place for 18 h.
  Acceptance criteria: No turbidity or precipitate forms.
- **WATER,** *Water Determination,* Appendix IIB
  Acceptance criteria: NMT 0.2%

Tributyrin

First Published: Prior to FCC 6

Glyceryl Tributyrate
Butyrin

$C_{15}H_{26}O_6$ Formula wt 302.37
FEMA: 2223

UNII: S05LZ624MF [tributyrin]

DESCRIPTION
Tributyrin occurs as a colorless, somewhat oily liquid.
Odor: Almost odorless, slightly fatty
Solubility: Soluble in alcohol, chloroform, ether; insoluble or practically insoluble in water
Boiling Point: ~308°
Function: Flavoring agent

IDENTIFICATION
- **INFRARED SPECTRA,** *Spectrophotometric Identification Tests,* Appendix IIIC
  Acceptance criteria: The spectrum of the sample exhibits relative maxima at the same wavelengths as those of the spectrum below.

ASSAY
- **PROCEDURE:** Proceed as directed under *M-1b,* Appendix XI.
  Acceptance criteria: NLT 99.0% of $C_{15}H_{26}O_6$

SPECIFIC TESTS
- **ACID VALUE, FLAVOR CHEMICALS (OTHER THAN ESSENTIAL OILS),** *M-15,* Appendix XI
  Acceptance criteria: NMT 5.0
- **REFRACTIVE INDEX,** Appendix II: At 20°
  Acceptance criteria: Between 1.431 and 1.441
- **SPECIFIC GRAVITY:** Determine at 25° by any reliable method (see *General Provisions*).
  Acceptance criteria: Between 1.034 and 1.037

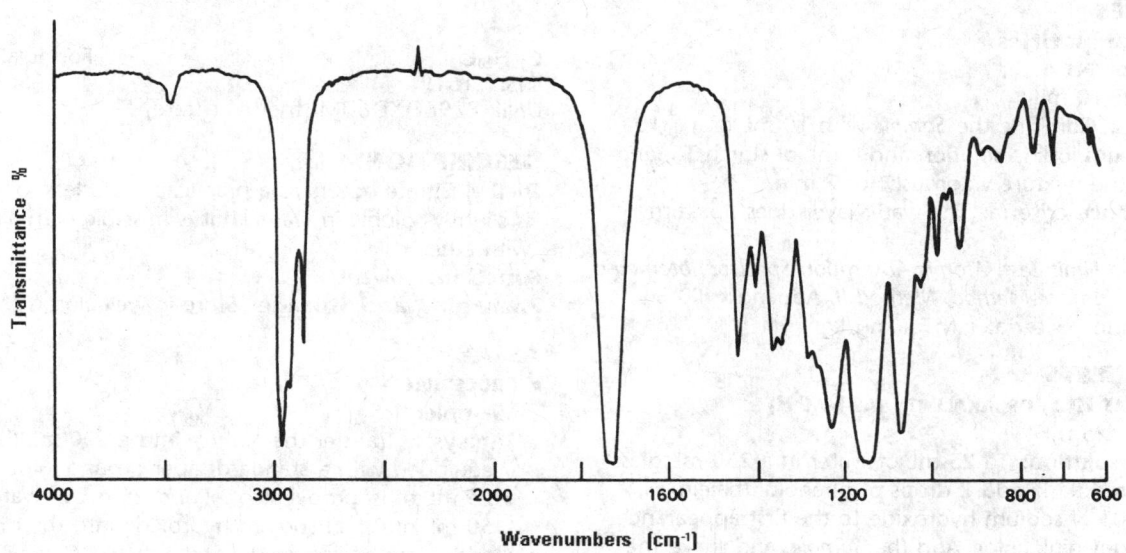

Tributyrin

Trichloroethylene

First Published: Prior to FCC 6

Ethylene Trichloride
Trichloroethene
1,1,2-Trichloroethylene

C_2HCl_3
UNII: 290YE8AR51 [trichloroethylene]

Formula wt 131.39
CAS: [79-01-6]

DESCRIPTION
Trichloroethylene occurs as a clear, colorless liquid free from sediment and suspended matter. It is immiscible with water, but is miscible with alcohol, with ether, and with acetone. Its refractive index at 20° is about 1.477. It may contain a suitable stabilizer.

Function: Extraction solvent
Packaging and Storage: Store in tight containers.

IDENTIFICATION
- **PROCEDURE**
  Sample: 5 mL
  Analysis: Transfer the Sample into a glass-stoppered test tube, add 5 mL of bromine TS, and shake the test tube vigorously every 15 min for 1 h.
  Acceptance criteria: The color of the bromine fades, and a white turbidity forms in the lower layer.

IMPURITIES
Inorganic Impurities
- **FREE HALOGENS**
  Sample: 10 mL
  Analysis: Combine the Sample with 10 mL of a 1:10 potassium iodide solution and 1 mL of starch TS, and shake the mixture vigorously for 2 min.
  Acceptance criteria: The water layer does not turn blue.
- **LEAD,** Lead Limit Test, Atomic Absorption Spectrophotometric Graphite Furnace Method, Method II, Appendix IIIB
  Acceptance criteria: NMT 1 mg/kg

SPECIFIC TESTS
- **ACIDITY (AS HCL) OR AKALINITY (AS NAOH)**
  Sample: 25 mL
  Sample solution: To 25 mL of water in a 250-mL glass-stoppered flask, add 2 drops of phenolphthalein TS. Add 0.01 N sodium hydroxide to the first appearance of a slight pink color. Add the Sample, and shake the flask for 30 s. The pink color will either persist or discharge.
  Analysis: If the pink color persists in the Sample solution, titrate with 0.01 N hydrochloric acid, shaking the flask repeatedly, until the pink color just disappears. However, if the pink color discharges in the Sample solution, titrate with 0.01 N sodium hydroxide until the faint pink color is restored.
  Acceptance criteria: If the pink color persists in the Sample solution, not more than 0.9 mL of 0.01 N hydrochloric acid is required to discharge it (NMT 10 mg/kg). But, if the pink color discharges in the Sample solution, not more than 1.0 mL of 0.01 N sodium hydroxide is required to restore it. (NMT 10 mg/kg)
- **DISTILLATION RANGE,** Appendix IIB
  Acceptance criteria: Between 86° and 88°
- **NONVOLATILE RESIDUE**
  Analysis: Evaporate 69 mL (about 100 g) of sample to dryness in a tared dish on a steam bath, dry the residue at 105° for 30 min, cool, and weigh.
  [**CAUTION**—Carry out this procedure in a fume hood.]
  Acceptance criteria: NMT 10 mg/kg
- **SPECIFIC GRAVITY:** Determine by any reliable method (see General Provisions).
  Acceptance criteria: Between 1.454 and 1.458
- **WATER,** Water Determination, Appendix IIB
  Acceptance criteria: 0.05%

Triethyl Citrate

First Published: Prior to FCC 6

Ethyl Citrate

$C_{12}H_{20}O_7$
INS: 1519
UNII: 8Z96QXD6UM [triethyl citrate]

Formula wt 276.29
CAS: [77-93-0]

DESCRIPTION
Triethyl Citrate occurs as a practically colorless, oily liquid. It is slightly soluble in water, but is miscible with alcohol and with ether.

Function: Solvent
Packaging and Storage: Store in well-closed containers.

ASSAY
- **PROCEDURE**
  Sample: 1.5 g
  Analysis: Transfer the Sample into a 500-mL flask equipped with a standard-taper ground joint, and add 25 mL of isopropyl alcohol and 25 mL of water. Pipet 50 mL of 0.5 N sodium hydroxide into the mixture, add a few boiling chips, and attach a suitable water-cooled condenser to the flask. Reflux for 1.5 h, then cool, wash down the condenser with about 20 mL of water, add 5 drops of phenolphthalein TS, and titrate the excess alkali with 0.5 N sulfuric acid. Perform a blank determination (see General Provisions) and make any necessary correction. Each mL of 0.5 N sulfuric acid is equivalent to 46.05 mg of $C_{12}H_{20}O_7$.

Acceptance criteria: NLT 99.0% and NMT 100.5% of $C_{12}H_{20}O_7$, calculated on the anhydrous basis

IMPURITIES
- **LEAD,** *Lead Limit Test, Flame Atomic Absorption Spectrophotometric Method,* Appendix IIIB
  Sample: 10 g
  Acceptance criteria: NMT 2 mg/kg

SPECIFIC TESTS
- **ACIDITY (AS CITRIC ACID)**
  Sample: 32 g
  Analysis: Dissolve the *Sample* in 30 mL of alcohol neutralized to bromothymol blue, and titrate with 0.1 N sodium hydroxide.
  Acceptance criteria: Not more than 1.0 mL of titrant is required. (NMT 0.02%)
- **REFRACTIVE INDEX,** Appendix IIB
  [NOTE—Use an Abbé or other refractometer of equal or greater accuracy.]
  Acceptance criteria: Between 1.439 and 1.443 at 25°; or between 1.440 and 1.444 at 20°
- **SPECIFIC GRAVITY:** Determine by any reliable method (see *General Provisions*).
  Acceptance criteria: Between 1.135 and 1.139 at 25°
- **WATER,** *Water Determination,* Appendix IIB
  Acceptance criteria: NMT 0.25%

2,4,5-Trimethyl δ-3-Oxazoline

First Published: Prior to FCC 6

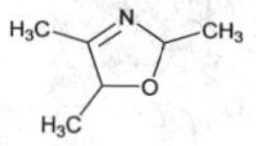

$C_6H_{11}NO$
FEMA: 3525

Formula wt 113.16

UNII: KHQ1Z14L8P [2,4,5-trimethyl-3-oxazoline]

DESCRIPTION
2,4,5-Trimethyl δ-3-Oxazoline occurs as a yellow-orange liquid.
Odor: Powerful, musty, slight green, wood, nut
Solubility: Soluble in alcohol, propylene glycol, water; insoluble or practically insoluble in most fixed oils
Function: Flavoring agent

IDENTIFICATION
- **INFRARED SPECTRA,** *Spectrophotometric Identification Tests,* Appendix IIIC
  Acceptance criteria: The spectrum of the sample exhibits relative maxima at the same wavelengths as those of the spectrum below.

ASSAY
- **PROCEDURE:** Proceed as directed under *M-1a,* Appendix XI.
  Acceptance criteria: NLT 94.0% of $C_6H_{11}NO$

SPECIFIC TESTS
- **REFRACTIVE INDEX,** Appendix II: At 20°
  Acceptance criteria: Between 1.414 and 1.435
- **SPECIFIC GRAVITY:** Determine at 25° by any reliable method (see *General Provisions*).
  Acceptance criteria: Between 0.911 and 0.932

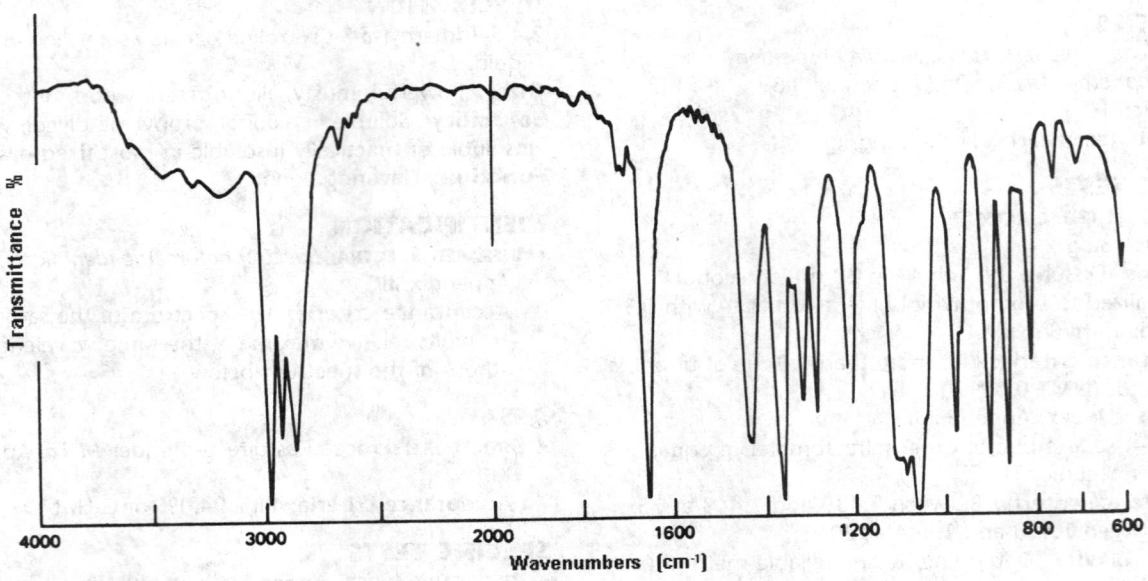

2,4,5-Trimethyl δ-3-Oxazoline

3,5,5-Trimethyl Hexanal

First Published: Prior to FCC 6
Last Revision: First Supplement, FCC 6

$C_9H_{18}O$ Formula wt 142.24
FEMA: 3524
UNII: U62H30BXPJ [3,5,5-trimethylhexanal]

DESCRIPTION
3,5,5-Trimethyl Hexanal occurs as a colorless to pale yellow liquid. It may contain a suitable antioxidant.
Odor: Melon, green
Boiling Point: ~67° (2.5 mm Hg)
Function: Flavoring agent

ASSAY
- **PROCEDURE:** Proceed as directed under *M-1b*, Appendix XI.
  Acceptance criteria: NLT 97.0%

SPECIFIC TESTS
- **ACID VALUE, FLAVOR CHEMICALS (OTHER THAN ESSENTIAL OILS),** *M-15*, Appendix XI
  Acceptance criteria: NMT 5.0
- **REFRACTIVE INDEX,** Appendix II: At 20°
  Acceptance criteria: Between 1.419 and 1.424
- **SPECIFIC GRAVITY:** Determine at 25° by any reliable method (see *General Provisions*).
  Acceptance criteria: Between 0.817 and 0.823

Trimethylamine

First Published: Prior to FCC 6

C_3H_9N Formula wt 59.11
FEMA: 3241
UNII: LHH7G8O305 [trimethylamine]

DESCRIPTION
Trimethylamine occurs as a gas.
Odor: Pungent, fishy, ammoniacal
Boiling Point: ~2.9°
Function: Flavoring agent

ASSAY
- **PROCEDURE:** Proceed as directed under *M-1a*, Appendix XI [NOTE—Use a suitable solvent in which to dissolve the gas.]
  Acceptance criteria: NLT 98.0% of C_3H_9N

2,3,5-Trimethylpyrazine

First Published: Prior to FCC 6

$C_7H_{10}N_2$ Formula wt 122.17
FEMA: 3244
UNII: Q8PR0W8TIT [2,3,5-trimethylpyrazine]

DESCRIPTION
2,3,5-Trimethylpyrazine occurs as a colorless to slightly yellow liquid.
Odor: Baked potato, peanut
Solubility: Soluble in organic solvents, water
Boiling Point: ~171°
Solubility in Alcohol, Appendix VI: One mL dissolves in 1 mL of 95% ethanol.
Function: Flavoring agent

IDENTIFICATION
- **INFRARED SPECTRA,** Spectrophotometric Identification Tests, Appendix IIIC
  Acceptance criteria: The spectrum of the sample exhibits relative maxima at the same wavelengths as those of the spectrum below.

ASSAY
- **PROCEDURE:** Proceed as directed under M-1a, Appendix XI.
  Acceptance criteria: NLT 98.0% of $C_7H_{10}N_2$

SPECIFIC TESTS
- **REFRACTIVE INDEX,** Appendix II: At 20°
  Acceptance criteria: Between 1.503 and 1.507
- **SPECIFIC GRAVITY:** Determine at 25° by any reliable method (see General Provisions).
  Acceptance criteria: Between 0.970 and 0.980

OTHER REQUIREMENTS
- **WATER,** Method I (Karl Fischer Titrimetric Method), Appendix IIB
  [NOTE—Use freshly distilled pyridine as solvent.]
  Acceptance criteria: NMT 0.2%

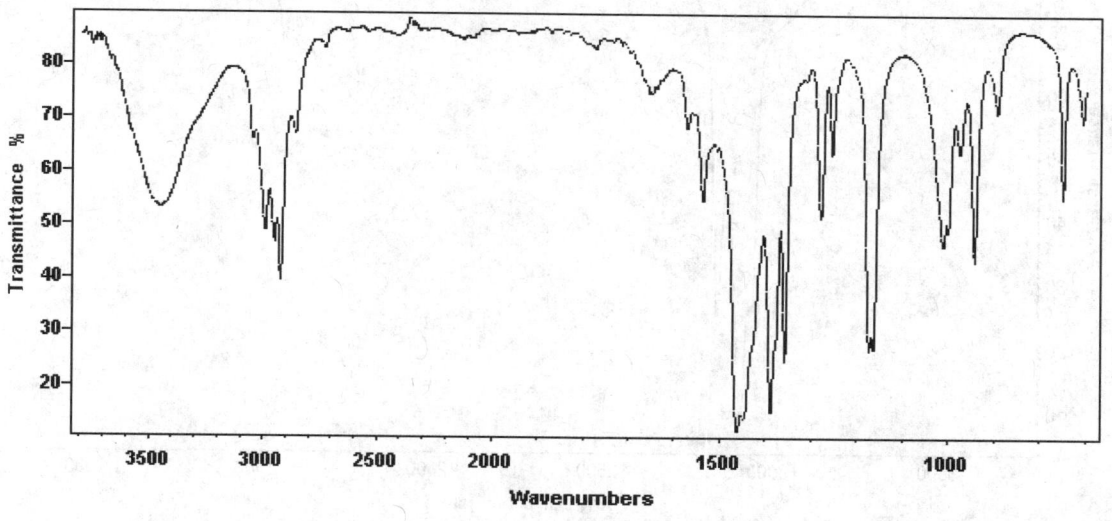

2,3,5-Trimethylpyrazine

DL-Tryptophan

First Published: Prior to FCC 6

DL-α-Amino-3-indolepropionic Acid

$C_{11}H_{12}N_2O_2$ Formula wt 204.22
  CAS: [54-12-6]
UNII: X9U7434L7A [tryptophan, dl-]

DESCRIPTION
DL-Tryptophan occurs as white crystals or as a crystalline powder. It is soluble in water and in dilute acids and alkalies. It is sparingly soluble in alcohol. It is optically inactive.
Function: Nutrient
Packaging and Storage: Store in well-closed containers.

IDENTIFICATION
- **INFRARED SPECTRA,** Spectrophotometric Identification Tests, Appendix IIIC
  Sample preparation: Mineral oil mull

1164 / DL-Tryptophan / Monographs

Acceptance criteria: The spectrum of the sample exhibits relative maxima at the same wavelengths as those of the spectrum below.

ASSAY
- **PROCEDURE**
  Sample: 300 mg, previously dried
  Analysis: Dissolve the *Sample* in 3 mL of formic acid and 50 mL of glacial acetic acid. Add 2 drops of crystal violet TS and titrate with 0.1 N perchloric acid to a green endpoint or until the blue color disappears completely. Perform a blank determination (see *General Provisions*), and make any necessary correction. Each mL of 0.1 N perchloric acid is equivalent to 20.42 mg of $C_{11}H_{12}N_2O_2$. [**CAUTION**—Handle perchloric acid in an appropriate fume hood.]
  Acceptance criteria: NLT 98.5% and NMT 101.5% of $C_{11}H_{12}N_2O_2$, on the dried basis

IMPURITIES
Inorganic Impurities
- **LEAD,** *Lead Limit Test,* Appendix IIIB
  Sample solution: Prepare as directed for organic compounds.
  Control: 5 µg Pb (5 mL of *Diluted Standard Lead Solution*)
  Acceptance criteria: NMT 5 mg/kg

SPECIFIC TESTS
- **LOSS ON DRYING,** Appendix IIC: 105° for 3 h
  Acceptance criteria: NMT 0.3%
- **RESIDUE ON IGNITION (SULFATED ASH),** Appendix IIC
  Sample: 2 g
  Acceptance criteria: NMT 0.1%

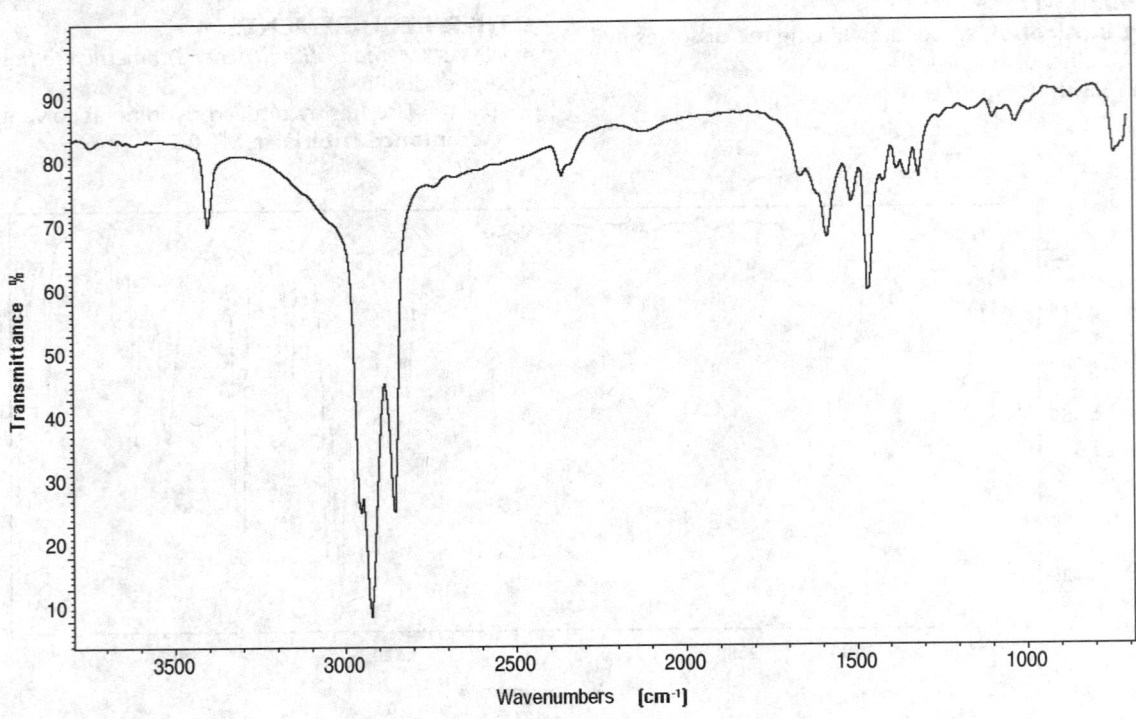

DL-Tryptophan (Mineral Oil Mull)

L-Tryptophan

First Published: Prior to FCC 6
Last Revision: FCC 7

L-α-Amino-3-indolepropionic Acid

$C_{11}H_{12}N_2O_2$

Formula wt 204.22
CAS: [73-22-3]

UNII: 8DUH1N11BX [tryptophan]

DESCRIPTION
L-Tryptophan occurs as white to yellow-white crystals or as a crystalline powder. One g dissolves in about 100 mL of water. It is soluble in hot alcohol, in dilute hydrochloric acid, and in alkali hydroxide solutions.
Function: Nutrient
Packaging and Storage: Store in well-closed, light-resistant containers.

IDENTIFICATION
- **INFRARED ABSORPTION,** *Spectrophotometric Identification Tests,* Appendix IIIC

Reference standard: USP L-Tryptophan RS
Sample and standard preparation: M
Acceptance criteria: The spectrum of the sample exhibits maxima at the same wavelengths as those in the spectrum of the Reference standard.

ASSAY
- **PROCEDURE**
  Sample: 300 mg
  Analysis: Dissolve the Sample in 3 mL of formic acid and 50 mL of glacial acetic acid. Add 2 drops of crystal violet TS and titrate with 0.1 N perchloric acid to a green endpoint or until the blue color disappears completely. Perform a blank determination (see General Provisions), and make any necessary correction. Each mL of 0.1 N perchloric acid is equivalent to 20.42 mg of $C_{11}H_{12}N_2O_2$. [CAUTION—Handle perchloric acid in an appropriate fume hood.]
  Acceptance criteria: 98.5%–101.5% of $C_{11}H_{12}N_2O_2$, calculated on the dried basis

IMPURITIES
Inorganic Impurities
- **LEAD**, Lead Limit Test, Appendix IIIB
  Sample solution: Prepare as directed for organic compounds.
  Control: 5 µg Pb (5 mL of Diluted Standard Lead Solution)
  Acceptance criteria: NMT 5 mg/kg

SPECIFIC TESTS
- **LOSS ON DRYING**, Appendix IIC: 105° for 3 h
  Acceptance criteria: NMT 0.3%
- **OPTICAL (SPECIFIC) ROTATION**, Appendix IIB
  Sample solution: 1 g of previously dried sample in sufficient water to make 100 mL
  Acceptance criteria
  $[\alpha]_D^{20}$ between –30.0° and –33.0°, on the dried basis; or
  $[\alpha]_D^{25}$ between –29.7° and –32.7°, on the dried basis
- **RESIDUE ON IGNITION (SULFATED ASH)**, Appendix IIC
  Sample: 1 g
  Acceptance criteria: NMT 0.1%

L-Tyrosine

First Published: Prior to FCC 6
Last Revision: FCC 7

L-β-(p-Hydroxyphenyl)alanine

$C_9H_{11}NO_3$ Formula wt 181.19
        CAS: [60-18-4]
UNII: 42HK56048U [tyrosine]

DESCRIPTION
L-Tyrosine occurs as colorless, silky needles or as a white, crystalline powder. One g is soluble in about 230 mL of water. It is soluble in dilute mineral acids and in alkaline solutions. It is very slightly soluble in alcohol.
Function: Nutrient
Packaging and Storage: Store in well-closed containers.

IDENTIFICATION
- **INFRARED ABSORPTION**, Spectrophotometric Identification Tests, Appendix IIIC
  Reference standard: USP L-Tyrosine RS
  Sample and standard preparation: M
  Acceptance criteria: The spectrum of the sample exhibits maxima at the same wavelengths as those in the spectrum of the Reference standard.

ASSAY
- **PROCEDURE**
  Sample: 400 mg, previously dried
  Analysis: Transfer the Sample into a 250-mL flask. Dissolve the Sample in about 50 mL of glacial acetic acid. Add 2 drops of crystal violet TS and titrate with 0.1 N perchloric acid to a blue-green endpoint. Perform a blank determination (see General Provisions), and make any necessary correction. Each mL of 0.1 N perchloric acid is equivalent to 18.12 mg of $C_9H_{11}NO_3$. [CAUTION—Handle perchloric acid in an appropriate fume hood.]
  Acceptance criteria: 98.5%–101.5% of $C_9H_{11}NO_3$, on the dried basis

IMPURITIES
Inorganic Impurities
- **LEAD**, Lead Limit Test, Appendix IIIB
  Sample solution: Prepare as directed for organic compounds.
  Control: 5 µg Pb (5 mL of Diluted Standard Lead Solution)
  Acceptance criteria: NMT 5 mg/kg

SPECIFIC TESTS
- **LOSS ON DRYING**, Appendix IIC: 105° for 3 h
  Acceptance criteria: NMT 0.3%
- **OPTICAL (SPECIFIC) ROTATION**, Appendix IIB
  Sample solution: 5 g of previously dried sample in sufficient 1 N hydrochloric acid to make 100 mL
  Acceptance criteria: $[\alpha]_D^{20}$ between –11.3° and –12.3°, on the dried basis; or $[\alpha]_D^{25}$ between –10.0° and –11.0°, on the dried basis
- **RESIDUE ON IGNITION (SULFATED ASH)**, Appendix IIC
  Sample: 2 g
  Acceptance criteria: NMT 0.1%

δ-Undecalactone

First Published: Prior to FCC 6

5-Hydroxyundecanoic Acid Lactone

$C_{11}H_{20}O_2$ Formula wt 184.28
FEMA: 3294
UNII: ERL32M2M38 [δ-undecalactone]

DESCRIPTION
δ-Undecalactone occurs as a colorless to pale yellow liquid.
Odor: Creamy, peach
Boiling Point: ~152° to 155° (10.5 mm Hg)
Solubility in Alcohol, Appendix VI: One mL dissolves in 1 mL of 95% alcohol.
Function: Flavoring agent

IDENTIFICATION
- **INFRARED SPECTRA,** Spectrophotometric Identification Tests, Appendix IIIC
  Acceptance criteria: The spectrum of the sample exhibits relative maxima at the same wavelengths as those of the spectrum below.

ASSAY
- **PROCEDURE:** Proceed as directed under *M-1a*, Appendix XI
  Acceptance criteria: NLT 98.0% of $C_{11}H_{20}O_2$ (sum of two isomers) and NLT 96.0% of the δ isomer.

SPECIFIC TESTS
- **REFRACTIVE INDEX,** Appendix II: At 20°
  Acceptance criteria: Between 1.457 and 1.461
- **SPECIFIC GRAVITY:** Determine at 25° by any reliable method (see *General Provisions*).
  Acceptance criteria: Between 0.956 and 0.961

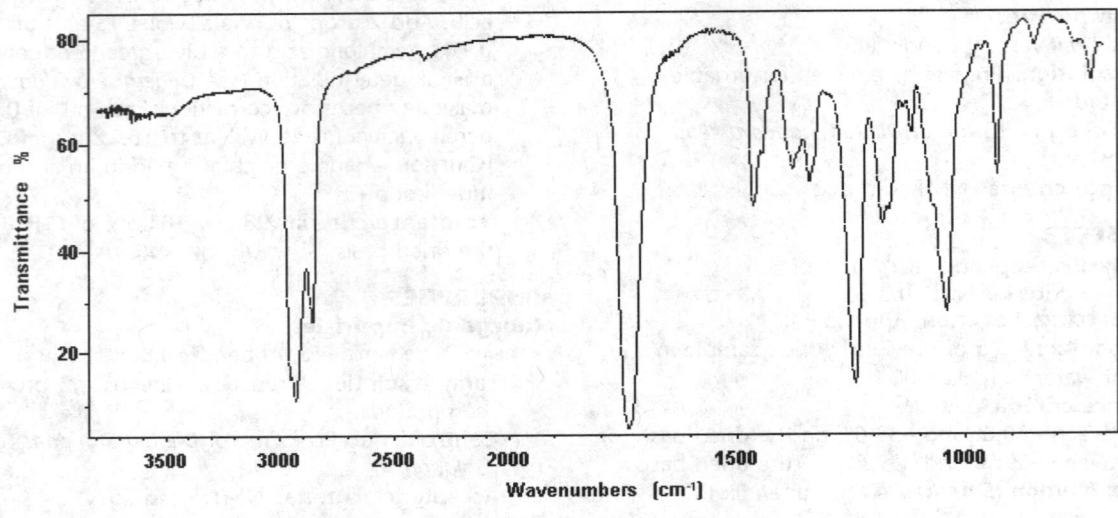

δ-Undecalactone

γ-Undecalactone

First Published: Prior to FCC 6

Aldehyde C-14 Pure, So-Called
Peach Aldehyde

$C_{11}H_{20}O_2$ Formula wt 184.28
FEMA: 3091
UNII: QB1T0AG2YL [γ-undecalactone]

DESCRIPTION
γ-Undecalactone occurs as a colorless to slightly yellow liquid.
Odor: Fruity, peach
Solubility: Soluble in alcohol, most fixed oils, propylene glycol; insoluble or practically insoluble in glycerin, water
Boiling Point: ~297°
Solubility in Alcohol, Appendix VI: One mL dissolves in 5 mL of 60% alcohol.
Function: Flavoring agent

IDENTIFICATION
- **INFRARED SPECTRA,** Spectrophotometric Identification Tests, Appendix IIIC
  Acceptance criteria: The spectrum of the sample exhibits relative maxima at the same wavelengths as those of the spectrum below.

ASSAY
- **PROCEDURE:** Proceed as directed under *M-1b*, Appendix XI.

Acceptance criteria
 Sum of two isomers: NLT 98.0% of $C_{11}H_{20}O_2$
 γ isomer: NLT 96.0% of $C_{11}H_{20}O_2$

SPECIFIC TESTS
- **ACID VALUE, FLAVOR CHEMICALS (OTHER THAN ESSENTIAL OILS),** *M-15*, Appendix XI
 Acceptance criteria: NMT 5.0
- **REFRACTIVE INDEX,** Appendix II: At 20°
 Acceptance criteria: Between 1.448 and 1.453
- **SPECIFIC GRAVITY:** Determine at 25° by any reliable method (see *General Provisions*).
 Acceptance criteria: Between 0.942 and 0.945

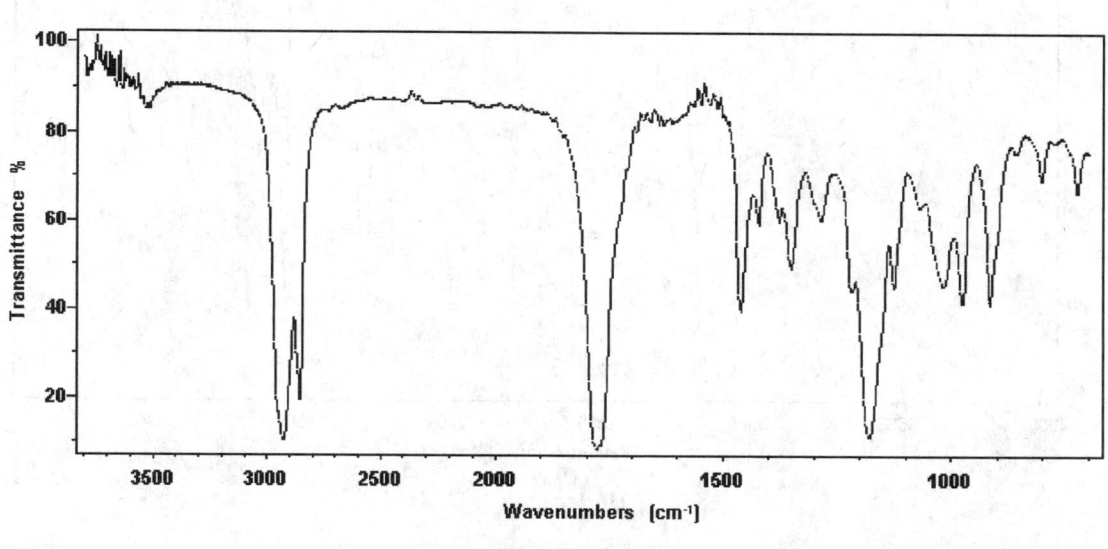

γ-Undecalactone

Undecanal

First Published: Prior to FCC 6
Last Revision: First Supplement, FCC 6

Aldehyde C-11 Undecyclic
n-Undecyl Aldehyde

$C_{11}H_{22}O$ Formula wt 170.30
FEMA: 3092
UNII: B6P0A9PSHN [undecanal]

DESCRIPTION
Undecanal occurs as a colorless to slightly yellow liquid. It may contain a suitable antioxidant.
Odor: Sweet, fatty, floral
Solubility: Soluble in most fixed oils, propylene glycol; insoluble or practically insoluble in glycerin, water
Boiling Point: ~223°

Function: Flavoring agent

IDENTIFICATION
- **INFRARED SPECTRA,** *Spectrophotometric Identification Tests*, Appendix IIIC
 Acceptance criteria: The spectrum of the sample exhibits relative maxima at the same wavelengths as those of the spectrum below.

ASSAY
- **PROCEDURE:** Proceed as directed under *M-1b*, Appendix XI.
 Acceptance criteria: NLT 92.0% of $C_{11}H_{22}O$

SPECIFIC TESTS
- **ACID VALUE, FLAVOR CHEMICALS (OTHER THAN ESSENTIAL OILS),** *M-15*, Appendix XI
 Acceptance criteria: NMT 10.0
- **REFRACTIVE INDEX,** Appendix II: At 20°
 Acceptance criteria: Between 1.430 and 1.435
- **SPECIFIC GRAVITY:** Determine at 25° by any reliable method (see *General Provisions*).
 Acceptance criteria: Between 0.825 and 0.832

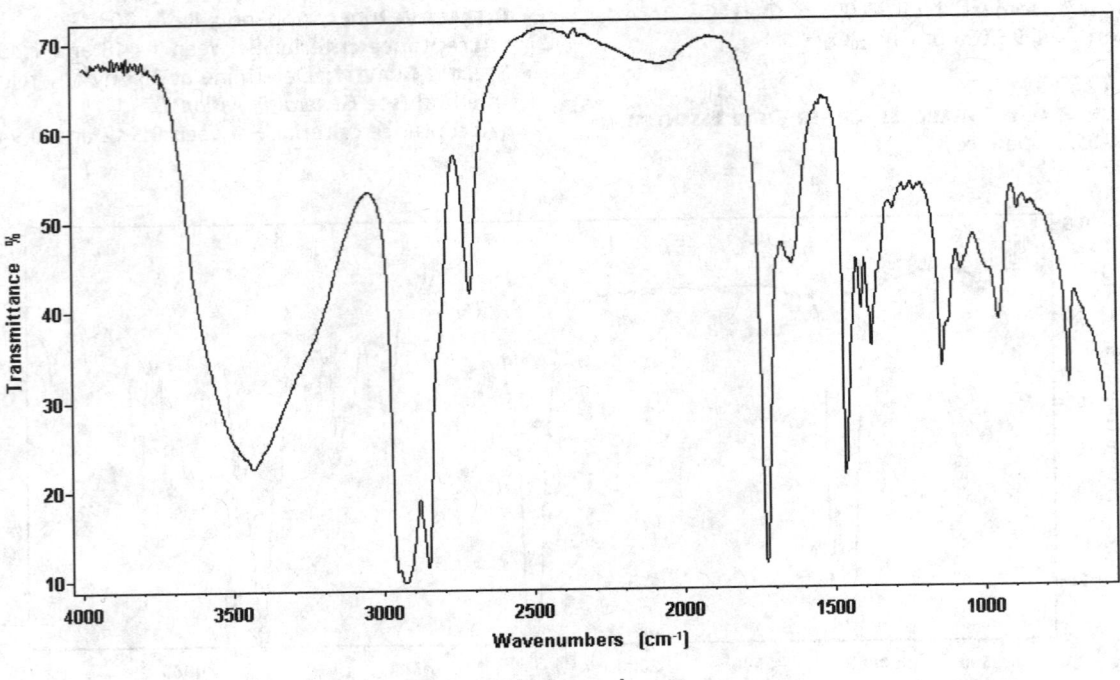

Undecanal

1,3,5-Undecatriene

First Published: Prior to FCC 6
Last Revision: First Supplement, FCC 6

$C_{11}H_{18}$
FEMA: 3795
UNII: PWB1EM60KN [1,3,5-undecatriene]

Formula wt 150.26

DESCRIPTION
1,3,5-Undecatriene occurs as a clear, colorless to pale yellow liquid. It may contain a suitable antioxidant.
Odor: Oily, waxy, peppery
Boiling Point: ~88° (1 mm Hg)
Solubility in Alcohol, Appendix VI: One mL dissolves in 25 mL of 95% alcohol.

Function: Flavoring agent

IDENTIFICATION
- **INFRARED SPECTRA,** *Spectrophotometric Identification Tests,* Appendix IIIC
  Acceptance criteria: The spectrum of the sample exhibits relative maxima at the same wavelengths as those of the spectrum below.

ASSAY
- **PROCEDURE:** Proceed as directed under *M-1b,* Appendix XI
  Acceptance criteria: NLT 90% of $C_{11}H_{18}$ (sum of isomers)

SPECIFIC TESTS
- **REFRACTIVE INDEX,** Appendix II: At 20°
  Acceptance criteria: Between 1.508 and 1.517
- **SPECIFIC GRAVITY:** Determine at 25° by any reliable method (see *General Provisions*).
  Acceptance criteria: Between 0.787 and 0.793

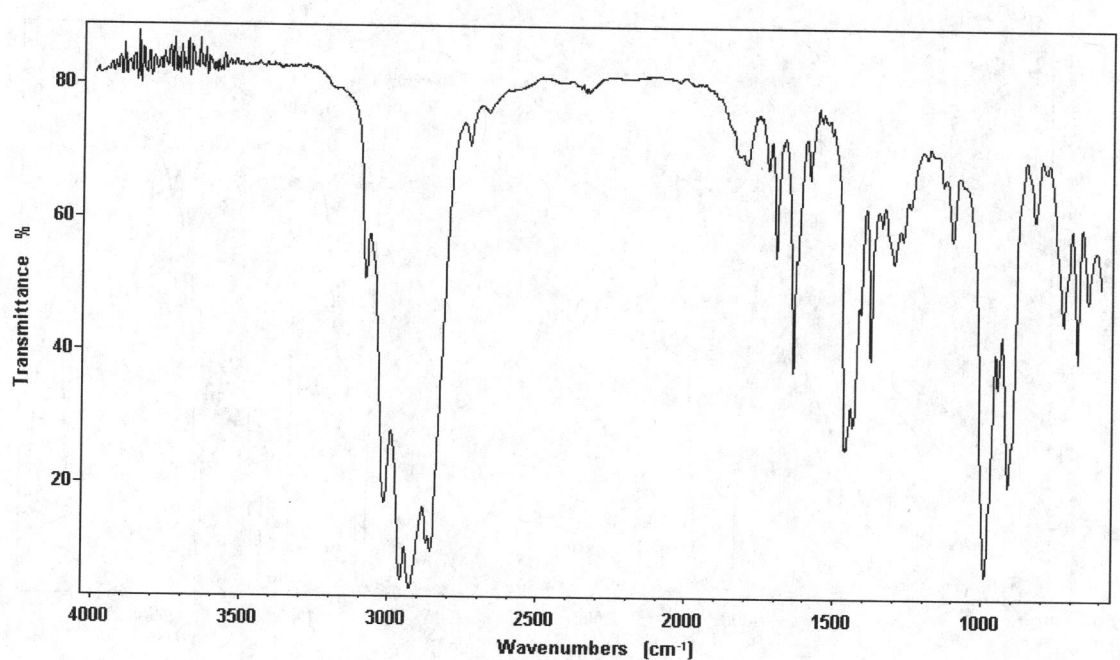

1,3,5-Undecatriene

2-Undecanone

First Published: Prior to FCC 6

Methyl Nonyl Ketone

$C_{11}H_{22}O$ Formula wt 170.30
FEMA: 3093
UNII: YV5DSO8CY9 [2-undecanone]

DESCRIPTION
2-Undecanone occurs as a colorless to pale yellow liquid.
Odor: Citrus, fatty, rue
Boiling Point: ~231° to 232°
Solubility in Alcohol, Appendix VI: One mL dissolves in 1 mL of 95% alcohol.
Function: Flavoring agent

IDENTIFICATION
- **INFRARED SPECTRA,** *Spectrophotometric Identification Tests,* Appendix IIIC
  Acceptance criteria: The spectrum of the sample exhibits relative maxima at the same wavelengths as those of the spectrum below.

ASSAY
- **PROCEDURE:** Proceed as directed under *M-1a,* Appendix XI.
  Acceptance criteria: NLT 96.0% of $C_{11}H_{22}O$

SPECIFIC TESTS
- **ACID VALUE, FLAVOR CHEMICALS (OTHER THAN ESSENTIAL OILS),** *M-15,* Appendix XI
  Acceptance criteria: NMT 5.0
- **REFRACTIVE INDEX,** Appendix II: At 20°
  Acceptance criteria: Between 1.428 and 1.432
- **SPECIFIC GRAVITY:** Determine at 25° by any reliable method (see *General Provisions*).
  Acceptance criteria: Between 0.822 and 0.826

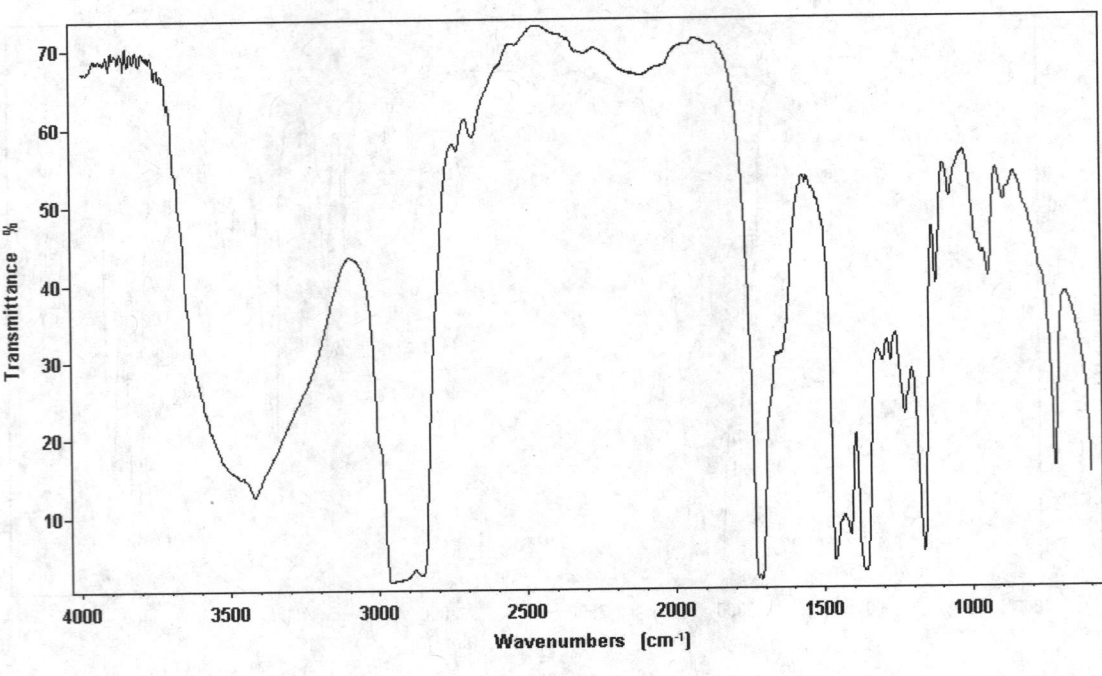
2-Undecanone

10-Undecenal

First Published: Prior to FCC 6
Last Revision: First Supplement, FCC 6

Aldehyde C-11 Undecylenic
Undecen-10-al

$C_{11}H_{20}O$
FEMA: 3095
UNII: DU1OTA08RY [10-undecenal]

Formula wt 168.28

DESCRIPTION
10-Undecenal occurs as a colorless to light yellow liquid. It may contain a suitable antioxidant.
Odor: Fatty; rose on dilution
Solubility: Soluble in most fixed oils, propylene glycol; insoluble or practically insoluble in glycerin, water
Boiling Point: ~235°

Function: Flavoring agent

IDENTIFICATION
- **INFRARED SPECTRA,** *Spectrophotometric Identification Tests,* Appendix IIIC
  Acceptance criteria: The spectrum of the sample exhibits relative maxima at the same wavelengths as those of the spectrum below.

ASSAY
- **PROCEDURE:** Proceed as directed under *M-1b,* Appendix XI.
  Acceptance criteria: NLT 90.0% of $C_{11}H_{20}O$

SPECIFIC TESTS
- **ACID VALUE, FLAVOR CHEMICALS (OTHER THAN ESSENTIAL OILS),** *M-15,* Appendix XI
  Acceptance criteria: NMT 6.0
- **REFRACTIVE INDEX,** Appendix II: At 20°
  Acceptance criteria: Between 1.441 and 1.447
- **SPECIFIC GRAVITY:** Determine at 25° by any reliable method (see *General Provisions*).
  Acceptance criteria: Between 0.840 and 0.850

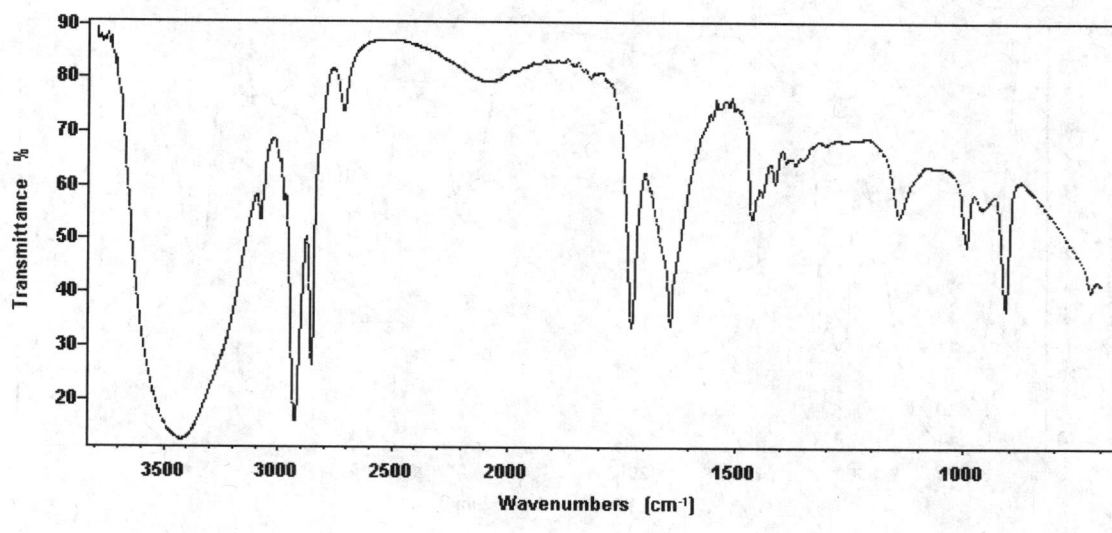

10-Undecenal

(E)-2-Undecenol

First Published: Prior to FCC 6

C$_{11}$H$_{22}$O Formula wt 170.30
FEMA: 4068
UNII: NTG184UJN9 [2-undecen-1-ol, (2e)-]

DESCRIPTION
(E)-2-Undecenol occurs as a white to slightly yellow liquid.
Odor: Oily, sweet, floral
Solubility: Insoluble or practically insoluble in water
Solubility in Alcohol, Appendix VI: One mL dissolves in 1 mL of 95% ethanol.
Function: Flavoring agent

IDENTIFICATION
- **INFRARED SPECTRA,** *Spectrophotometric Identification Tests,* Appendix IIIC
  Acceptance criteria: The spectrum of the sample exhibits relative maxima at the same wavelengths as those of the spectrum below.

ASSAY
- **PROCEDURE:** Proceed as directed under *M-1a,* Appendix XI.
  Acceptance criteria: NLT 92.0% of C$_{11}$H$_{22}$O

SPECIFIC TESTS
- **REFRACTIVE INDEX,** Appendix II: At 20°
  Acceptance criteria: Between 1.448 and 1.453
- **SPECIFIC GRAVITY:** Determine at 25° by any reliable method (see *General Provisions*).
  Acceptance criteria: Between 0.840 and 0.846

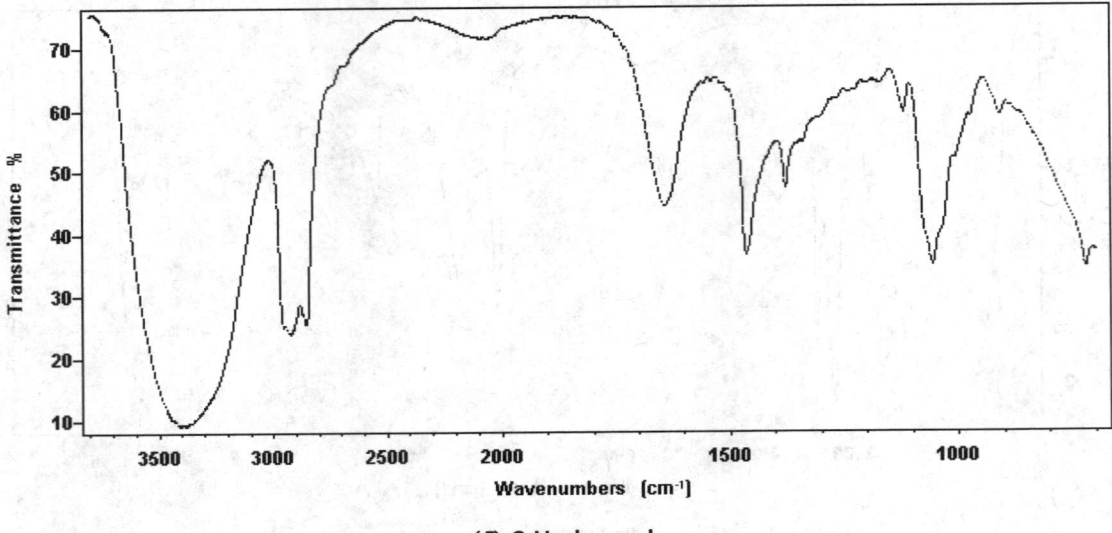

(E)-2-Undecenol

Undecyl Alcohol

First Published: Prior to FCC 6

Alcohol C-11

$C_{11}H_{24}O$
FEMA: 3097
UNII: 06MJ0P28T3 [undecyl alcohol]

Formula wt 172.31

DESCRIPTION
Undecyl Alcohol occurs as a colorless liquid.
Odor: Fatty-floral
Solubility: Soluble in most fixed oils; insoluble or practically insoluble in water
Boiling Point: ~146° (30 mm Hg)
Function: Flavoring agent

IDENTIFICATION
- **INFRARED SPECTRA,** *Spectrophotometric Identification Tests,* Appendix IIIC
  Acceptance criteria: The spectrum of the sample exhibits relative maxima at the same wavelengths as those of the spectrum below.

ASSAY
- **PROCEDURE:** Proceed as directed under *M-1a,* Appendix XI.
  Acceptance criteria: NLT 97.0% of $C_{11}H_{24}O$

SPECIFIC TESTS
- **REFRACTIVE INDEX,** Appendix II: At 20°
  Acceptance criteria: Between 1.437 and 1.443
- **SPECIFIC GRAVITY:** Determine at 25° by any reliable method (see *General Provisions*).
  Acceptance criteria: Between 0.820 and 0.840

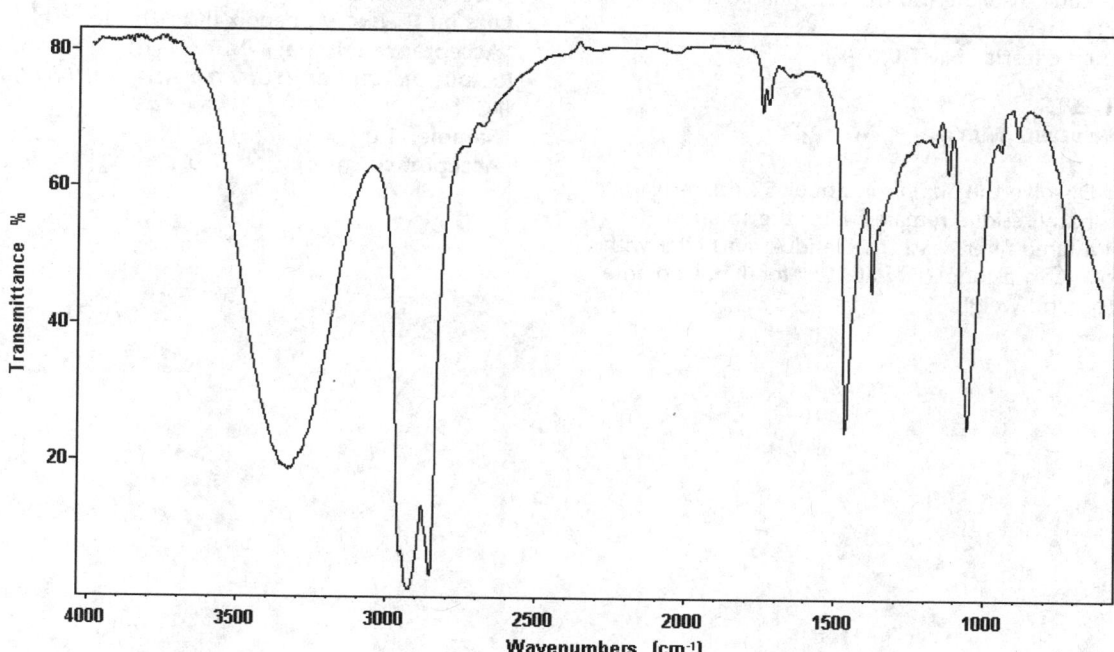
Undecyl Alcohol

Urea

First Published: Prior to FCC 6

Carbamide

CH_4N_2O
UNII: 8W8T17847W [urea]

Formula wt 60.06
CAS: [57-13-6]

DESCRIPTION
Urea occurs as a colorless to white, prismatic, crystalline powder or as small, white pellets. It is commonly produced from CO_2 by ammonolysis or from cyanamide by hydrolysis. It is freely soluble in water and in boiling alcohol, but practically insoluble in chloroform and in ether. It melts at a range of 132° to 135°.

Function: Fermentation aid

Packaging and Storage: Store in a well-closed container.

IDENTIFICATION
- **A. Procedure**
  Sample: 500 mg
  Analysis: Heat the *Sample* in a test tube until it liquefies. Ammonia vapor is produced. Continue heating until the liquid becomes turbid, and then cool. Dissolve the fused mass in a 1:10 sodium hydroxide solution:water mixture. Add 1 drop of cupric sulfate TS.
  Acceptance criteria: A red-violet colored solution develops.

- **B. Procedure**
  Sample: 100 mg
  Analysis: Dissolve the *Sample* in 1 mL of water and add 1 mL of nitric acid.
  Acceptance criteria: A white precipitate of urea nitrate forms.

ASSAY
- **Nitrogen,** *Nitrogen Determination, Method II,* Appendix IIIC
  Sample: 2 mL of a 2.5 mg/mL aqueous sample solution
  Analysis: During the sample heating step, heat the sample until it begins to fume, and then heat for 1 additional hour. Each mL of 0.01 N acid is equivalent to 0.3003 mg of CH_4N_2O.
  Acceptance criteria: NLT 99.0% and NMT 100.5% of CH_4N_2O

IMPURITIES
Inorganic Impurities
- **Chloride,** *Chloride Limit Test,* Appendix IIIB
  Sample: 200 mg
  Control: 14 µg chloride (1.4 mL of *Standard Chloride Solution*)
  Acceptance criteria: NMT 0.007%
- **Lead,** *Lead Limit Test,* Appendix IIIB
  Sample: 2 g
  Control: 10 µg Pb (10 mL of *Diluted Standard Lead Solution*)
  Acceptance criteria: NMT 5 mg/kg
- **Sulfate,** *Chloride and Sulfate Limit Tests, Chloride Limit Test,* Appendix IIIB
  Sample: 2 g

Control: 200 µg sulfate (20 mL of *Standard Sulfate Solution*)
Acceptance criteria: NMT 0.01%

SPECIFIC TESTS
- **ALCOHOL-INSOLUBLE MATTER**
  Sample: 5 g
  Analysis: Dissolve the *Sample* in about 50 mL of warm alcohol. If any residue remains, filter the solution through a tared filter, wash the residue, and filter with 20 mL of warm alcohol. Dry at 105° for 1 h. Cool in a desiccator, and weigh.
  Acceptance criteria: NMT 0.04%
- **LOSS ON DRYING,** Appendix IIC: 105° for 3 h
  Acceptance criteria: NMT 1.0%
- **RESIDUE ON IGNITION (SULFATED ASH),** *Method I,* Appendix IIC
  Sample: 1 g
  Acceptance criteria: NMT 0.1%

Valeraldehyde

First Published: Prior to FCC 6
Last Revision: First Supplement, FCC 6

$C_5H_{10}O$
FEMA: 3098
UNII: B975S3014W [valeraldehyde]

Formula wt 86.13

DESCRIPTION
Valeraldehyde occurs as a colorless to pale yellow liquid. It may contain a suitable antioxidant.
Odor: Chocolate
Boiling Point: ~103°
Solubility in Alcohol, Appendix VI: One mL dissolves in 1 mL of 95% alcohol.
Function: Flavoring agent

IDENTIFICATION
- **INFRARED SPECTRA,** *Spectrophotometric Identification Tests,* Appendix IIIC
  Acceptance criteria: The spectrum of the sample exhibits relative maxima at the same wavelengths as those of the spectrum below.

ASSAY
- **PROCEDURE:** Proceed as directed under *M-2a,* Appendix XI.
  Acceptance criteria: NLT 97.0% of $C_5H_{10}O$

SPECIFIC TESTS
- **ACID VALUE, FLAVOR CHEMICALS (OTHER THAN ESSENTIAL OILS),** *M-15,* Appendix XI
  Acceptance criteria: NMT 5.0
- **REFRACTIVE INDEX,** Appendix II: At 20°
  Acceptance criteria: Between 1.390 and 1.395
- **SPECIFIC GRAVITY:** Determine at 25° by any reliable method (see *General Provisions*).
  Acceptance criteria: Between 0.805 and 0.809

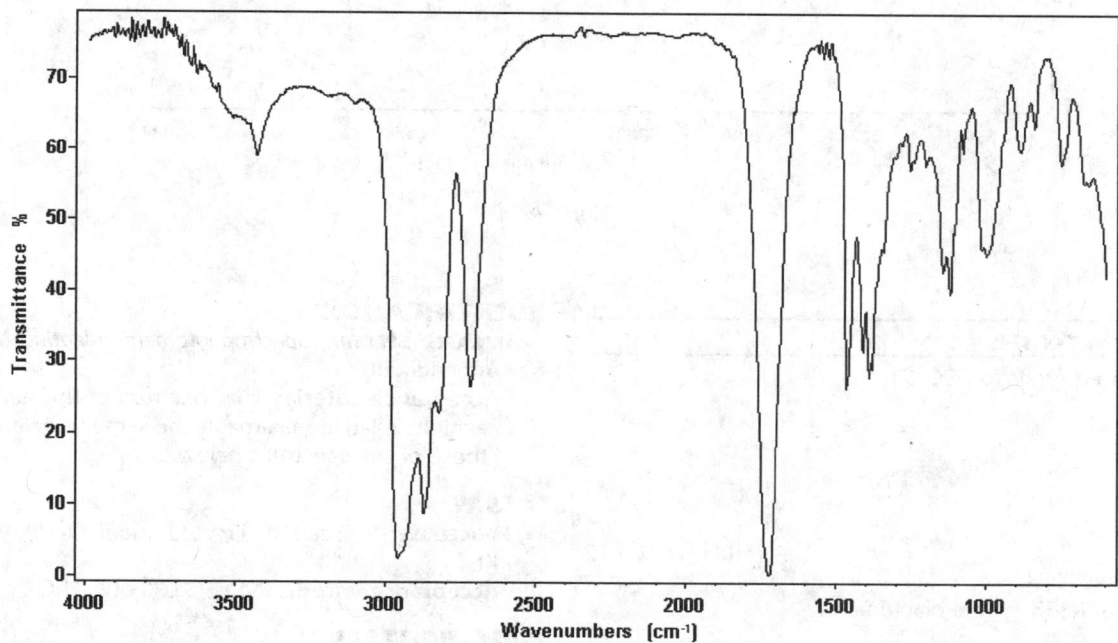

Valeraldehyde

Valeric Acid

First Published: Prior to FCC 6

Pentanoic Acid

$C_5H_{10}O_2$
FEMA: 3101

Formula wt 102.13

UNII: GZK92PJM7B [valeric acid]

DESCRIPTION
Valeric Acid occurs as a colorless to pale yellow, mobile liquid.
Odor: Unpleasant, penetrating, rancid
Solubility: Miscible in alcohol, ether; 1 mL dissolves in 40 mL water
Boiling Point: ~186°
Function: Flavoring agent

IDENTIFICATION
- **INFRARED SPECTRA,** *Spectrophotometric Identification Tests,* Appendix IIIC
  Acceptance criteria: The spectrum of the sample exhibits relative maxima at the same wavelengths as those of the spectrum below.

ASSAY
- **PROCEDURE:** Proceed as directed under *M-3b,* Appendix XI.
  Acceptance criteria: NLT 99.0% of $C_5H_{10}O_2$

SPECIFIC TESTS
- **REFRACTIVE INDEX,** Appendix II: At 20°
  Acceptance criteria: Between 1.405 and 1.412
- **SPECIFIC GRAVITY:** Determine at 25° by any reliable method (see *General Provisions*).
  Acceptance criteria: Between 0.935 and 0.940

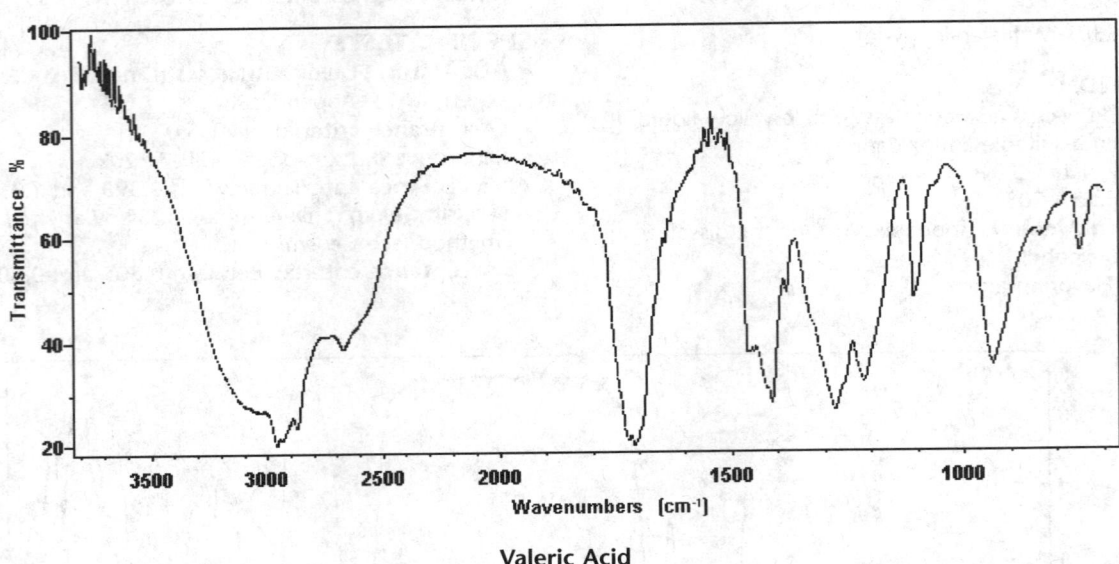

Valeric Acid

γ-Valerolactone

First Published: Prior to FCC 6

$C_5H_8O_2$ Formula wt 100.12
FEMA: 3103
UNII: O7056XK37X [γ-valerolactone]

DESCRIPTION
γ-Valerolactone occurs as a colorless to slightly yellow liquid.
Odor: Warm, sweet, herbaceous
Solubility: Miscible in alcohol, most fixed oils, water
Boiling Point: ~207°
Function: Flavoring agent

IDENTIFICATION
- **INFRARED SPECTRA,** *Spectrophotometric Identification Tests,* Appendix IIIC
  Acceptance criteria: The spectrum of the sample exhibits relative maxima at the same wavelengths as those of the spectrum below.

ASSAY
- **PROCEDURE:** Proceed as directed under *M-1b,* Appendix XI.
  Acceptance criteria: NLT 95.0% of $C_5H_8O_2$

SPECIFIC TESTS
- **REFRACTIVE INDEX,** Appendix II: At 20°
  Acceptance criteria: Between 1.431 and 1.434
- **SPECIFIC GRAVITY:** Determine at 25° by any reliable method (see *General Provisions*).
  Acceptance criteria: Between 1.047 and 1.054

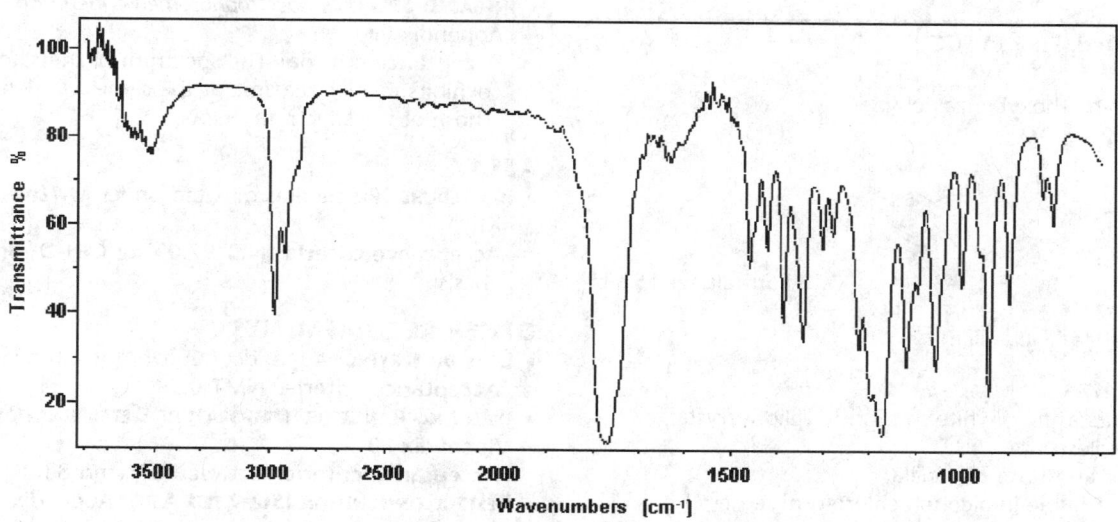
γ-Valerolactone

L-Valine

First Published: Prior to FCC 6
Last Revision: FCC 7

L-2-Amino-3-methylbutyric Acid

$C_5H_{11}NO_2$ Formula wt 117.15
                                CAS: [72-18-4]

UNII: HG18B9YRS7 [valine]

DESCRIPTION
L-Valine occurs as a white, crystalline powder. It is freely soluble in water, and practically insoluble in alcohol and in ether. The pH of a 1:20 aqueous solution is between 5.5 and 7.0. In a closed capillary tube, it melts at about 315°.
Function: Nutrient
Packaging and Storage: Store in well-closed containers.

IDENTIFICATION
- **INFRARED ABSORPTION**, Spectrophotometric Identification Tests, Appendix IIIC
  Reference standard: USP L-Valine RS
  Sample and standard preparation: M
  Acceptance criteria: The spectrum of the sample exhibits maxima at the same wavelengths as those in the spectrum of the Reference standard.

ASSAY
- **PROCEDURE**
  Sample: 200 mg
  Analysis: Dissolve the Sample in 3 mL of formic acid and 50 mL of glacial acetic acid. Add 2 drops of crystal violet TS and titrate with 0.1 N perchloric acid to a green endpoint or until the blue color disappears completely. Perform a blank determination (see General Provisions), and make any necessary correction. Each mL of 0.1 N perchloric acid is equivalent to 11.72 mg of $C_5H_{11}NO_2$. [**CAUTION**—Handle perchloric acid in an appropriate fume hood.]
  Acceptance criteria: 98.5%–101.5% of $C_5H_{11}NO_2$, calculated on the dried basis

IMPURITIES
Inorganic Impurities
- **LEAD**, Lead Limit Test, Appendix IIIB
  Sample solution: Prepare as directed for organic compounds.
  Control: 5 μg Pb (5 mL of Diluted Standard Lead Solution)
  Acceptance criteria: NMT 5 mg/kg

SPECIFIC TESTS
- **LOSS ON DRYING**, Appendix IIC: 105° for 3 h
  Acceptance criteria: NMT 0.3%
- **OPTICAL (SPECIFIC) ROTATION**, Appendix IIB
  Sample solution: 8 g of previously dried sample in sufficient 6 N hydrochloric acid to make 100 mL
  Acceptance criteria
  $[α]_D^{20}$ between +26.7° and +29.0° on the dried basis; or $[α]_D^{25}$ between +26.6° and +28.9° on the dried basis
- **RESIDUE ON IGNITION (SULFATED ASH)**, Appendix IIC
  Sample: 1 g
  Acceptance criteria: NMT 0.1%

Vanillin

First Published: Prior to FCC 6

4-Hydroxy-3-methoxybenzaldehyde

$C_8H_8O_3$
FEMA: 3107
UNII: CHI530446X [vanillin]

Formula wt 152.15

DESCRIPTION
Vanillin occurs as fine, white to slightly yellow crystals, usually needles.
Odor: Odor and taste of vanilla
Solubility: Soluble in alcohol, chloroform, ether; 1 g dissolves in 100 mL water at 25°, in 20 mL glycerin, and in 20 mL water at 80°
Function: Flavoring agent

IDENTIFICATION
- **INFRARED SPECTRA,** *Spectrophotometric Identification Tests,* Appendix IIIC
  Acceptance criteria: The spectrum of the sample exhibits relative maxima at the same wavelengths as those of the spectrum below.

ASSAY
- **PROCEDURE:** Proceed as directed under *M-1b,* Appendix XI.
  Acceptance criteria: NLT 97.0% of $C_8H_8O_3$ on the dried basis

OTHER REQUIREMENTS
- **LOSS ON DRYING,** Appendix IIC: Dry for 4 h over silica gel.
  Acceptance criteria: NMT 0.5%
- **MELTING RANGE OR TEMPERATURE DETERMINATION,** Appendix IIB
  Acceptance criteria: Between 81° and 83°
- **RESIDUE ON IGNITION (SULFATED ASH),** Appendix IIC
  Sample: 2 g
  Acceptance criteria: NMT 0.05%

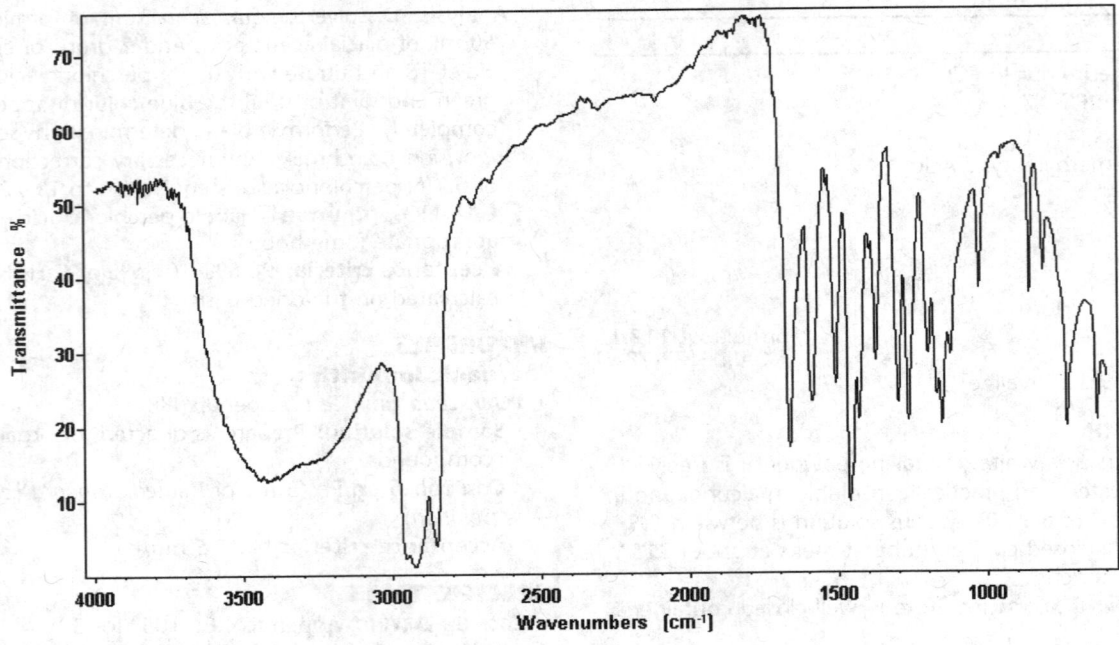

Vanillin

Vegetable Oil Phytosterol Esters

First Published: Prior to FCC 6

R_1 = H, Δ^5 (Cholesterol)
R_1 = CH3, Δ^5, Δ^{22} (Brassicasterol)
R_1 = CH3, Δ^5 or = CH3 (Campesterol)
R_1 = C_2H_5, Δ^5, Δ^{22} (Stigmasterol)
R_1 = C_2H_5, Δ^5 or = C_2H_5 (α-Sitosterol)
R_1 = C_2H_5, Δ^5, Δ^{25} (Δ^5-Avenasterol)
R_1 = C_2H_5, Δ^7 (Δ^7-Stigmastenol = Δ^7-β-Sitosterol)
R_1 = C_2H_5, Δ^7, Δ^{25} (Δ^7-Avenasterol)
R_2 = Vegetable oil derived fatty acid
Δ^5 = double C bond at 5,6 position
Δ^7 = double C bond at 7,8 position
Δ^{22} = double C bond at 22,23 position
Δ^{25} = double C bond at 25,26 position

DESCRIPTION

Vegetable Oil Phytosterol Esters occur as a light yellow, thick liquid to waxy solid at room temperature and become fully liquid at elevated temperatures. Liquid Vegetable Oil Phytosterol Esters are more viscous than vegetable oils. They are obtained by esterification of free vegetable oil sterols with fatty acids obtained from vegetable oils or fats. (Vegetable oil sterols are commercially obtained by various processes, including vacuum distillation of vegetable oils or fats such as those recovered from deodorizer distillates.) They are freely soluble in edible oils, in chloroform, and in methylene chloride; partly soluble in alcohol, in acetone, in ethyl acetate, and in hexane; and insoluble in water.

Function: Source of phytosterols

Packaging and Storage: Store in well-closed, light-resistant containers.

IDENTIFICATION

- **A. Procedure**
  Acceptance criteria: The retention times of the major peaks in the chromatogram of the *Sample preparation* obtained in the *Assay* for *Sterol Content* (below) are the same as that of the *Standard solution*, both relative to the *Internal standard*.
- **B. Infrared Spectra,** *Spectrophotometric Identification Tests,* Appendix IIIC
  Acceptance criteria: The spectrum of the sample exhibits relative maxima at the same wavelengths as those of the spectrum below.

ASSAY

- **Total Level of Des-methyl-sterols**
  Internal standard solution: 100 mg/mL of β-cholestanol (5α-cholestan-3β-ol) in methyl-tertiary butyl ether
  Saponification solution: Dissolve 14 g of potassium hydroxide in 10 mL of boiled water in a 100-mL volumetric flask. Dilute to volume with ethanol.
  Standard stock solution: 2.5 mg/mL commercially available soybean sterol mix in heptane
  Standard solution: 62.5 µg/mL soybean sterol mix in heptane obtained by diluting *Standard stock solution* 1:40 with heptane
  Sample preparation: Melt a sample in an oven to obtain a clear and homogenous liquid. Transfer 50 mg of melted sample into a 10-mL reaction vial with screw cap and add 200 µL of *Internal standard solution* and 1 mL of the *Saponification solution*. Hydrolyze the sample by heating for 50 min at 70°, shaking at regular intervals to ensure proper mixing. Add 1 mL of water, and extract the free vegetable oil sterols and the *Internal standard solution* with 5 mL of heptane. Repeat the extraction three more times using 3 mL of heptane each time. Combine the heptane layers and use anhydrous sodium sulfate to remove any traces of water. Dilute a suitable portion of the combined dried heptane layers 1:40 with heptane. This dilution is the *Sample preparation*.
  Chromatographic system, Appendix IIA
  Mode: Gas chromatography, equipped with a cold-on-column injector
  Detector: Flame-ionization detector
  Column system: A suitable deactivated precolumn and a 10-m × 0.32-mm (id) capillary column coated with an apolar stationary phase 0.12-µm film thickness
  Temperature
   Column: Heat to 60°, hold for 1 min, heat to 300° at 20°/min, and hold for 3 min
   Detector: 320°
  System suitability
   Sample: *Standard solution*
   Suitability requirement 1: The relative standard deviation for each peak, obtained from five replicate injections, should be below 2%.
   Suitability requirement 2: The peaks for brassicasterol and campesterol should be baseline resolved (R_S > 1.0) and show no tailing.
  Analysis: Measure the response of the *Internal standard solution* and all the individual sterols eluting in the relative retention window of 0.98 to 1.13.
  [Note—Retention times of components, relative to the *Internal standard solution*, are as follows.]

Substance	Relative Retention Time
Cholesterol	0.98
Internal standard solution	1.00
Brassicasterol	1.01
Campesterol, Campestanol	1.03
Stigmasterol	1.04
Δ^7-Campesterol, Clerosterol, β-Sitosterol, Sitostanol	1.06
Δ^5-Avenasterol, 7-Stigmasterol	1.08
Δ^7-Avenasterol	1.11

Calculation: Calculate the individual and total percentages of vegetable sterol esters in the sample by the formula:

Result = $[(C_{IS} \times V_{IS} \times A_{sterol})/(A_{IS} \times W_S \times 10)] \times (P_{IS}/100)$

- C_{IS} = concentration of the *Internal standard solution* (mg/mL)
- V_{IS} = volume of the *Internal standard solution* (μL)
- A_{sterol} = peak response of the sterol(s)
- A_{IS} = peak response of the *Internal standard solution*
- W_S = weight of the sample taken for the *Sample preparation* (mg)
- P_{IS} = purity, in percent, of the *Internal standard solution*

Acceptance criteria: NLT 59% of des-methyl-sterols

- **RELATIVE LEVELS OF VEGETABLE OIL PHYTOSTEROL ESTERS AND VEGETABLE OIL STEROLS**

  Standard solution: Use the *Standard solution* prepared under *Total Level of Des-methyl-sterols* (above).

  Sample solution: Melt a sample in an oven to obtain a clear and homogeneous liquid. Transfer about 50 mg of melted sample, accurately weighed, into a 10-mL reaction vial with screw cap, and successively add 200 μL of N,O-Bis(trimethylsilyl)trifluoroacetamide (BSTFA, 99%, silylation reagent) and 800 μL of pyridine (catalyst). Homogenize by means of a vortex, and silylate for 30 min at room temperature. Dilute with 9 mL of hexane.

  Chromatographic system, Appendix IIA
  Mode: Gas chromatography, equipped with a cold-on-column injector
  Detector: Flame-ionization detector
  Column system: A suitable deactivated precolumn and a 10-m × 0.32-mm (id) capillary column coated with an apolar stationary phase 0.12-μm film thickness
  Temperature
  Column: Heat to 80°, hold for 2 min, heat to 360° at 10°/min, and hold for 15 min.
  Detector: 370°
  System suitability
  Sample: *Standard solution*
  Suitability requirement 1: The relative standard deviation for each peak, obtained from five replicate injections, should be below 2%.
  Suitability requirement 2: The peaks for stigmasterol and campesterol should be baseline resolved ($R_S > 1.0$) and show no tailing.
  Analysis: Measure the response of sterols (sum) and the sterol esters (sum). Inspect the chromatogram for the presence of partial acyl-glycerides and tri-acyl-glycerides. Derive the relative vegetable oil phytosterol esters and vegetable oil sterols content of the sample from the areas for each component group relative to the total area of the chromatogram, assuming uniform response.

  Acceptance criteria
  Vegetable oil phytosterol esters: NLT 86.0%
  Free vegetable oil sterols: NMT 9.0%
  Sum of vegetable oil phytosterol esters and free vegetable oil sterols: NLT 95.0%
  Acyl-glycerides: NMT 5.0%
  The vegetable oil sterols in vegetable oil phytosterol esters show the following typical distribution:

Sterol	Min (%)	Max (%)
Cholesterol	0.0	2.0
Brassicasterol	0.0	12.0
Campesterol plus Campestanol	10.0	40.0
Stigmasterol	0.0	30.0
β-Sitosterol plus Sitostanol	30.0	65.0
Δ^5-Avenasterol plus Δ^7-Stigmastenol	0.0	6.0
Δ^7-Avenasterol plus others	0.0	7.0

IMPURITIES
Inorganic Impurities
- **LEAD,** *Lead Limit Test, Atomic Absorption Spectrophotometric Graphite Furnace Method, Method II,* Appendix IIIB
  Acceptance criteria: NMT 0.1 mg/kg

SPECIFIC TESTS
- **ACIDITY,** *Acid value (Fats and Related Substances),* Appendix VII
  Acceptance criteria: NMT 0.2 expressed as g of potassium hydroxide (KOH) per kg of vegetable oil phytosterol esters
- **LOSS ON DRYING,** Appendix IIC
  Acceptance criteria: NMT 0.1%

OTHER REQUIREMENTS
- **LABELING:** Label as Vegetable Oil (Plant) Sterol Esters to indicate that the vegetable oil sterols and the fatty acids originate from vegetable oils. Declare the presence of any preservative, antioxidant, or other added substance.

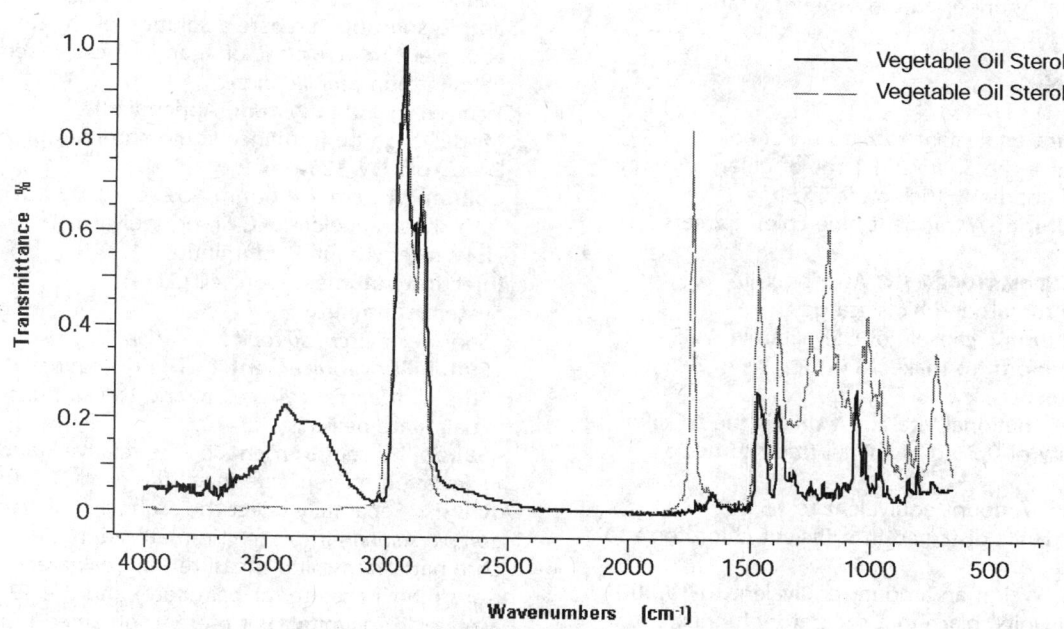

Vegetable Oil Phytosterol Esters

Veratraldehyde

First Published: Prior to FCC 6

Methyl Vanillin
Veratryl Aldehyde
3,4-Dimethoxybenzaldehyde

$C_9H_{10}O_3$ Formula wt 166.18
FEMA: 3109
UNII: UI88P68JZD [veratraldehyde]

DESCRIPTION
Veratraldehyde occurs as white to tan or blue-gray flakes or as a solid.
Odor: Sweet, vanilla
Boiling Point: ~281°
Solubility in Alcohol, Appendix VI: One g dissolves in 1 mL of 95% alcohol.
Function: Flavoring agent

ASSAY
- **PROCEDURE:** Proceed as directed under *M-1b,* Appendix XI.
  Acceptance criteria: NLT 95.0% of $C_9H_{10}O_3$

OTHER REQUIREMENTS
- **SOLIDIFICATION POINT,** Appendix IIB
  Acceptance criteria: NLT 40°

Vitamin A

First Published: Prior to FCC 6

All-*trans*-Retinol

CAS: [68-26-8]
UNII: 81G40H8B0T [vitamin a, unspecified]

DESCRIPTION
Vitamin A occurs as a light yellow to red oil that may solidify on refrigeration (liquid form). In solid form, it may have the appearance of the diluent that has been added to it. It is a suitable form or derivative of retinol ($C_{20}H_{30}O$; vitamin A alcohol). It usually consists of retinol or esters of retinol formed from edible fatty acids, principally acetic and palmitic acids, or mixtures of these. It may be diluted with edible oils, or it may be incorporated in solid edible carriers, extenders, or excipients. It may contain suitable preservatives, dispersants, and antioxidants, providing it is not to be used in foods in which such substances are prohibited. In liquid form it is very soluble in chloroform and in ether, it is soluble in absolute alcohol and in vegetable oils, but it is insoluble in glycerin and in water. In solid form, it may be dispersible in water. It is unstable in air and light.
Function: Nutrient

Packaging and Storage: Store in a cool place in tight containers, preferably under an atmosphere of an inert gas, protected from light.

IDENTIFICATION

- **A. PROCEDURE**
  Sample: Amount equivalent to 6 μg of retinol
  Analysis: Dissolve the *Sample* in 1 mL of chloroform and add 10 mL of antimony trichloride TS.
  Acceptance criteria: A transient blue color appears immediately.

- **B. THIN-LAYER CHROMATOGRAPHY,** Appendix IIA
  Adsorbent: Chromatographic silica gel
  Standard solution: 1 capsule of USP Vitamin A RS in sufficient chloroform to make 25.0 mL
  Sample solution
  [NOTE—One International Vitamin A Unit is the specific biologic activity of 0.3 μg of the all-*trans* isomer of retinol.]
  Liquid sample: Amount equivalent to 15,000 International Units dissolved in sufficient chloroform to make 10 mL
  Solid sample: Weigh an amount equivalent to 15,000 International Units, place in a separatory funnel, add 75 mL of water, heat, if necessary, to dissolve the carrier, and cool. Shake vigorously for 1 min, extract with 10 mL of chloroform by shaking for 1 min, and centrifuge to clarify the chloroform extract. Use this extract as the *Sample solution*.
  Application volume: 0.015 mL of the *Standard solution* and 0.01 mL of the *Sample solution*
  Developing solvent system: Cyclohexane: ether (4:1)
  Spray reagent: Antimony trichloride TS
  Analysis: Proceed as directed, with filter paper dipping into the solvent mixture during development. [NOTE—The blue spot formed is indicative of the presence of retinol.]
  Acceptance criteria: The approximate R_f values of the predominant spots, corresponding to the different forms of retinol, are 0.1 for the alcohol, 0.45 for the acetate, and 0.7 for the palmitate.

ASSAY

[NOTE—Choose the appropriate *Assay* below for the form of vitamin A being tested. The first method is for samples in the ester form (acetate or palmitate); the second method is for other forms of vitamin A.]

- **ASSAY FOR VITAMIN A ESTER (ACETATE OR PALMITATE)**
  [NOTE—Use low-actinic glassware throughout this procedure.]
  Mobile phase: *n*-Hexane
  Standard solution: 40 μg/mL of USP Vitamin A RS (all-*trans* retinyl acetate) in *Mobile Phase*
  Retinyl palmitate solution: 40 μg/mL of retinyl palmitate[1] in *Mobile phase*
  System suitability solution: 20 μg/mL each of USP Vitamin A RS and retinyl palmitate; obtained by mixing equal volumes of *Retinyl palmitate solution* and *Standard solution*
  Sample solution: Prepare a solution of the sample equivalent to 40 μg/mL of vitamin A ester (acetate or palmitate) in *Mobile phase*.
  Chromatographic system, Appendix IIA
    Mode: High-performance liquid chromatography
    Detector: UV 325-nm
    Column: 15-cm × 4.6-mm (id) column that contains 3-μm silica (Supelcosil LC-Si, or equivalent)
    Flow rate: About 1 mL/minute
    Injection volume: About 40 μL
  System suitability
    Sample: *System suitability solution*
    Suitability requirement 1: The resolution, *R*, between the all-*trans* retinyl acetate and the all-*trans* retinyl palmitate peaks is NLT 10.
    Suitability requirement 2: The relative standard deviation for replicate injections is NMT 3.0%.
  Analysis: Separately inject the *Standard solution* and the *Sample solution* into the chromatograph. Record the chromatograms, and measure the peak areas for the all-*trans* retinyl acetate (or palmitate) and the 13-*cis* retinyl acetate (or palmitate), if present, obtained from the *Standard solution* and *Sample solution*. [NOTE—The relative retention times are about 0.7 for 13-*cis* retinyl acetate and 1.0 for all-*trans* retinyl acetate; or the relative retention times are about 0.8 for 13-*cis* retinyl palmitate and 1.0 for all-*trans* retinyl palmitate.]
  If the sample is in the form of the acetate, calculate the quantity, in mg/g, of vitamin A acetate in the sample taken by the formula:

  $$\text{Result} = (C/D)(r_U/r_S)$$

  C = concentration of all-*trans* retinyl acetate in the *Standard solution* (mg/mL)
  D = concentration of sample in the *Sample solution* (mg/mL)
  r_U = summed peak areas of the 13-*cis* and all-*trans* retinyl acetate obtained from the chromatogram of the *Sample solution*
  r_S = summed peak areas of the 13-*cis* and all-*trans* retinyl acetate obtained from the chromatogram of the *Standard solution*

  If the sample is in the form of the palmitate, calculate the quantity, in mg/g, of vitamin A palmitate in the sample taken by the formula:

  $$\text{Result} = (r_U/r_S) \times (C/D) \times (M_{r1}/M_{r2})$$

  r_U = summed peak areas of the 13-*cis* and all-*trans* retinyl acetate from the chromatogram of the *Sample solution*
  r_S = summed peak areas of the 13-*cis* and all-*trans* retinyl acetate from the chromatogram of the *Standard solution*
  C = concentration of all-*trans* retinyl acetate in the *Standard solution* (mg/mL)

---
[1] A suitable grade of retinyl palmitate may be obtained from Sigma-Aldrich Company.

D = concentration of the *Sample solution* (mg/mL)
M_{r1} = formula weight of vitamin A palmitate, 524.96
M_{r2} = formula weight of vitamin A acetate, 328.54

Acceptance criteria: NLT 95.0% and NMT 100.5% of the vitamin A activity declared on the label

- **ASSAY FOR OTHER FORMS OF VITAMIN A**
  [NOTE—Complete the *Assay* promptly and exercise care throughout the procedure to keep to a minimum exposure to atmospheric oxygen and other oxidizing agents and to actinic light, preferably by using an atmosphere of an inert gas and nonactinic glassware.]

  Isopropyl alcohol: Use reagent-grade isopropyl alcohol. Redistill, if necessary, to meet the following requirements for spectral purity: When measured in a 1-cm quartz cell against water, it shows an absorbance NMT 0.05 at 300 nm and NMT 0.01 between 320 and 350 nm.

  Ether: Use freshly redistilled reagent-grade ether, discarding the first and last 10% portions.

  Sample preparation: Transfer a portion of sample containing the equivalent of 0.15 mg of retinol (but containing NMT 1 g of fat) into a saponification flask. If the sample is in solid form, heat the portion taken in 10 mL of water on a steam bath for about 10 min, crush the remaining solid with a blunt glass rod, and warm for about 5 min.

  Add 30 mL of alcohol if the sample is liquid, or 23 mL of alcohol and 7 mL of glycerin if the sample is solid, followed by 3 mL of a 9:10 potassium hydroxide solution. Reflux under an all-glass condenser for 30 min. Cool the solution, add 30 mL of water, and transfer into a separatory funnel. Add 2 g of finely powdered sodium sulfate. Extract by shaking for 2 min with one 150-mL portion of *Ether* and, if an emulsion forms, with three additional 25-mL portions of *Ether*. Combine the ether extracts, if necessary, and wash by swirling gently with 50 mL of water. Wash more vigorously with three additional 50-mL portions of water. Transfer the washed ether extract into a 250-mL volumetric flask, and add *Ether* to volume. This diluted ether extract is the *Sample preparation*.

  Analysis: Evaporate a 25.0-mL portion of the *Sample preparation* to about 5 mL. Without applying heat and with the aid of a stream of inert gas or vacuum, continue the evaporation to about 3 mL. Dissolve the residue in sufficient *Isopropyl alcohol* to give an expected concentration of the equivalent of 3 to 5 µg/mL of retinol or such that it will give an absorbance in the range of 0.5 to 0.8 at 325 nm. Using a suitable spectrophotometer fitted with matched quartz cells, determine the absorbances of the resulting solution at the wavelengths of 310, 325, and 334 nm.

Calculate the corrected absorbance at 325 nm by the equation:

$$[A_{325}] = (6.815\, A_{325}) - (2.555\, A_{310}) - (4.260\, A_{334})$$

$[A_{325}]$ = corrected absorbance at 325 nm
A_{325} = measured absorbance at 325 nm
A_{310} = absorbance at 310 nm
A_{334} = absorbance at 334 nm

If A_{325} has a value NLT $[A_{325}]/1.030$ and NMT $[A_{325}]/0.970$, calculate the retinol content (mg) as follows:

$$\text{Result} = 0.549\, A_{325}/LC$$

L = length of the absorption cell (cm)
C = amount of sample in each 100 mL of the final isopropyl alcohol solution (g)

If $[A_{325}]$ has a value less than $A_{325}/1.030$, apply the calculate the retinol content (mg) as follows:

$$\text{Result} = 0.549\, [A_{325}]/LC$$

L = length of the absorption cell (cm)
C = amount of sample in each 100 mL of the final isopropyl alcohol solution (g)

[NOTE—The range of the limits of error (confidence interval), indicating the extent of discrepancy to be expected in the results of different laboratories at P = 0.05, is approximately ±8%.]

Acceptance criteria: NLT 95.0% and NMT 100.5% of the vitamin A activity declared on the label

IMPURITIES
Inorganic Impurities
- **LEAD,** *Lead Limit Test, Flame Atomic Absorption Spectrophotometric Method,* Appendix IIIB
  Sample: 10 g
  Acceptance criteria: NMT 2 mg/kg

SPECIFIC TESTS
- **ABSORBANCE RATIO**
  [NOTE—The *Absorbance ratio* is the ratio of absorbances corrected/observed at 325 nm.]
  Analysis: Determine the *Absorbance ratio* by the following formula using data obtained in the *Assay* (above):

$$\text{Result} = [A_{325}]/A_{325}$$

$[A_{325}]$ = corrected absorbance at 325 nm
A_{325} = measured absorbance at 325 nm

Acceptance criteria: NLT 0.85

Vitamin B₁₂

First Published: Prior to FCC 6

Cyanocobalamin

C₆₃H₈₈CoN₁₄O₁₄P

Formula wt 1355.38
CAS: [68-19-9]

UNII: P6YC3EG2O4 [cyanocobalamin]

DESCRIPTION
Vitamin B₁₂ occurs as dark red crystals or as an amorphous or crystalline powder. In the anhydrous form, it is very hygroscopic, and when exposed to air, it may absorb about 12% of water. It is sparingly soluble in water; soluble in alcohol; and insoluble in acetone, in chloroform, and in ether.

Function: Nutrient
Packaging and Storage: Store in tight containers.

IDENTIFICATION
- **A. UV-Visible Absorption Spectrum**
  Sample solution: 30 µg/mL (same as the *Sample solution* used to measure absorbance in the *Assay* below)
  Acceptance criteria
  Maxima (±1 nm) at: 278 nm, 361 nm, 550 nm
  Ratio A_{361}/A_{278}: Between 1.70 and 1.90
  Ratio A_{361}/A_{550}: Between 3.15 and 3.40
- **B. Cobalt**
  Sample: 1 mg
  Analysis: Fuse the *Sample* with about 50 mg of potassium pyrosulfate in a porcelain crucible, cool, and break up the mass with a glass rod. Add 3 mL of water, and dissolve by boiling. Add 1 drop of phenolphthalein TS, mix, and then add drops of a 1:10 solution of sodium hydroxide until just pink. Add 500 mg of sodium acetate, 0.5 mL of 1 N acetic acid, and 0.5 mL of a 1:500 solution of Nitroso-R-salt (i.e., 3-hydroxy-4-nitroso-2,7-naphthalenedisulfonic acid, disodium salt).
  Acceptance criteria: A red or orange-red color appears immediately, and persists following the addition of 0.5 mL of hydrochloric acid and boiling for 1 min.

- **C. Procedure**
  Sample: 5 mg
  Analysis: Introduce 5 mL of water into a 50-mL distilling flask connected to a short water-cooled vertical condenser. The tip of the condenser dips into a test tube containing 1 mL of a 1:50 solution of sodium hydroxide. Transfer the *Sample* to the flask and dissolve it in the water. Add 2.5 mL of hypophosphorous acid to the flask, then close the flask, heat at simmering for 10 min, and distill 1 mL into the test tube. Add 4 drops of cold, saturated ferrous ammonium sulfate solution to the tube, shake gently, then add about 30 mg of sodium fluoride, and bring the contents to a boil. Immediately add drops of 1:7 sulfuric acid until a clear solution results, and then add 3 to 5 drops more of the acid.
  Acceptance criteria: A blue or blue-green color appears within a few minutes.

ASSAY
- **Procedure**
  Sample solution: 30 µg/mL
  Standard solution: 30 µg/mL USP Cyanocobalamin RS
  Analysis: Determine the absorbances of the *Sample solution* and the *Standard solution* at 361 nm, using 1-cm cells and water as the blank. Calculate the percentage of Vitamin B₁₂ in the sample taken with the formula:

  $$\text{Result} = (A_U/A_S) \times (C_S/C_U) \times 100\%$$

  A_U = absorbance obtained from the *Sample solution*
  A_S = peak response obtained from the *Standard solution*
  C_S = concentration of *Standard solution* (µg/mL)
  C_U = concentration of *Sample solution* (µg/mL)

  Acceptance criteria: NLT 96.0% and NMT 100.5% of Vitamin B₁₂, calculated on the dried basis

SPECIFIC TESTS
- **Loss on Drying**, Appendix IIC
  Sample: 25 mg
  Analysis: 105° for 2 h in a vacuum of NMT 5 mm Hg
  Acceptance criteria: NMT 12.0%
- **Pseudo Cyanocobalamin**
  Sample: 1.0 mg
  Control solution: 0.15 mL of 0.1 N potassium permanganate in 250 mL of water
  Analysis: Dissolve the *Sample* in 20 mL of water contained in a small separatory funnel. Add 5 mL of a (1:1) mixture of carbon tetrachloride and cresol, and shake well for about 1 min. Allow the layers to separate, and draw off the lower layer into a second small separatory funnel. Add 5 mL of 1:7 sulfuric acid, shake well, and allow the solution to separate completely, centrifuging if necessary.
  Acceptance criteria: The separated upper layer from the *Analysis* is colorless or has no more color than the *Control solution*.

Vitamin D₂

First Published: Prior to FCC 6

Ergocalciferol
Vitamin D

$C_{28}H_{44}O$ Formula wt 396.66
CAS: [50-14-6]
UNII: VS041H42XC [ergocalciferol]

DESCRIPTION
Vitamin D₂ occurs as white crystals. It is affected by air and by light. It is insoluble in water, but is soluble in alcohol, in chloroform, in ether, and in fatty oils.
Function: Nutrient
Packaging and Storage: Store in hermetically sealed containers under nitrogen in a cool place protected from light.

IDENTIFICATION
- **THIN-LAYER CHROMATOGRAPHY,** Appendix IIA
  Adsorbent: 0.25-mm layer of chromatographic silica gel containing a suitable fluorescing substance
  [NOTE—Prepare the following three solutions without heating and handle without delay. Perform the development and subsequent operations in the dark.]
  Sample solution: 50 mg/mL of sample in squalane and chloroform (1:100)
  Ergocalciferol standard solution: 50 mg/mL of USP Ergocalciferol RS in squalane and chloroform (1:100)
  Ergosterol standard solution: 100 µg/mL of USP Ergosterol RS in squalane and chloroform (1:100)
  Application volume: 10 µL
  Developing solvent system: cyclohexane and ether (1:1)
  Analysis: Spray the plate with a solution of acetyl chloride and antimony trichloride TS (1:50).
  Acceptance criteria: The chromatogram obtained with the Sample solution shows a yellow-orange area (ergocalciferol) having the same R_F value as the area of the spot from the Ergocalciferol standard solution, which may show a violet area underneath. [NOTE—Reserve the chromatogram for the Ergosterol test below.]
- **INFRARED ABSORPTION,** Spectrophotometric Identification Tests, Appendix IIIC
  Reference standard: USP Ergocalciferol RS
  Sample and **Standard preparation:** K
  Acceptance criteria: The spectrum of the sample exhibits maxima at the same wavelengths as those in the spectrum of the Reference standard.
- **ULTRAVIOLET ABSORPTION,** Spectrophotometric Identification Tests, Appendix IIIC
  Standard solution: USP Ergocalciferol RS in ethanol
  Sample solution: Dissolve in ethanol.
  Acceptance criteria: The spectrum of the Sample solution exhibits inflections at the same wavelengths as those in the spectrum of the Standard solution and the respective absorptivities at the point of maximum absorbance (about 265 nm) do not differ by more than 3.0%.

ASSAY
- **PROCEDURE**
  Mobile phase: ACS Reagent-Grade Hexanes and n-amyl alcohol (1000:3). [NOTE—The hexanes must be suitable for use in ultraviolet spectrophotometry and be dried by passing through a 60-cm × 8-cm column containing 500 g of 50-µm to 250-µm chromatographic siliceous earth. The ratio of components and the flow rate may be varied to meet the requirements under System suitability.]
  System suitability solution: 25 mg/mL USP Vitamin D Assay System Suitability RS in toluene and Mobile phase (1:1) made to 10 mL. Reflux this solution at 90° for 45 min, and cool. This solution contains cholecalciferol, pre-cholecalciferol, and trans-cholecalciferol.
  [NOTE—Prepare the following solutions fresh daily using low-actinic glassware. Do not use heat to aid dissolution of solutes.]
  Standard stock solution: 0.6 mg/mL USP Ergocalciferol RS in toluene, made to 50 mL
  Standard solution: 0.12 mg/mL USP Ergocalciferol RS: made from Standard stock solution diluted to 50 mL with Mobile phase
  Sample stock solution: 0.6 mg/mL in toluene, made to 50 mL
  Sample solution: 0.12 mg/mL: made from Sample stock solution diluted to 50 mL with Mobile phase
  Chromatographic system, Appendix IIA
    Mode: liquid chromatography
    Detector: UV, 254 nm
    Column: 25-cm × 4.6-mm stainless steel column, or equivalent, packed with porous silica (5 to 10 µm in particle diameter) or equivalent
    Injection volume: 5–10 µL
  System suitability
    Sample: System suitability solution
    Suitability requirements
      Resolution: Between trans-cholecalciferol and pre-cholecalciferol NLT 1.0
      Relative standard deviation: NMT 2.0%
      Relative retention times: Pre-cholecalciferol, trans-cholecalciferol, and cholecalciferol are 0.4, 0.5, and 1.0, respectively.
  Analysis: Separately inject equal volumes of the Standard solution and Sample solution into the chromatograph, record the chromatograms, and measure the responses of the major peaks.
  Calculate the percentage of $C_{28}H_{44}O$ in the sample taken by the equation:

  $$\% \ C_{28}H_{44}O = (r_U/r_S) \times (C_S/C_U) \times 100\%$$

  r_U = peak response obtained from the Sample solution

r_S = peak response obtained from the *Standard solution*
C_S = concentration of the *Standard solution* (mg/mL)
C_U = concentration of the *Sample solution* (mg/mL)

Acceptance criteria: NLT 97.0% and NMT 103.0% of $C_{28}H_{44}O$

SPECIFIC TESTS

- **ERGOSTEROL**
  Acceptance criteria: The color of any violet area apparent under the red-orange spot in the chromatogram of the *Sample solution*, obtained as directed under *Thin Layer Chromatography, Identification*, is not more intense than that of the violet area in the chromatogram of *Ergosterol standard solution*, obtained as directed under *Thin Layer Chromatography, Identification*.
- **MELTING RANGE OR TEMPERATURE DETERMINATION,** *Procedure for Class Ib*, Appendix IIB
  Acceptance criteria: Between 115° and 119°
- **OPTICAL (SPECIFIC) ROTATION,** Appendix IIB
  Sample: 5 mg/mL in alcohol. [NOTE—Prepare the solution without delay, using a sample from a container opened not longer than 30 min, and determine the rotation within 30 min after the solution has been prepared.]
  Acceptance criteria: $[\alpha]_D^{25}$ between +103° and +106°
- **REDUCING SUBSTANCES**
  Solution A: 5 mg/mL blue tetrazolium in absolute alcohol
  Solution B: One volume of a 10% tetramethylammonium hydroxide solution diluted with nine volumes of absolute alcohol
  Sample stock solution: 10 mg/mL in absolute alcohol
  Sample solution: Add 0.5 mL of *Solution A* to 10 mL of *Sample stock solution* and mix. Add 0.5 mL of *Solution B* and allow the mixture to stand for 5 min, then add 1 mL of glacial acetic acid and mix.
  Blank solution: Prepare as directed for *Sample solution*, but using 10 mL absolute alcohol in place of the 10 mL *Sample stock solution*.
  Control solution: 0.2 µg/mL of hydroquinone in absolute alcohol
  Analysis: Measure the absorbencies of the *Sample solution* and *Control solution* at 525 nm against the *Blank solution*.
  Acceptance criteria: The absorbance of the *Sample solution* is not greater than that of the *Control solution*.

Vitamin D₃

First Published: Prior to FCC 6

Cholecalciferol
Vitamin D

$C_{27}H_{44}O$ Formula wt 384.65
               CAS: [67-97-0]
UNII: 1C6V77QF41 [cholecalciferol]

DESCRIPTION
Vitamin D₃ occurs as white crystals. It is affected by air and by light. It is insoluble in water. It is soluble in alcohol, in chloroform, and in fatty oils.
Function: Nutrient
Packaging and Storage: Store in hermetically sealed containers under nitrogen in a cool place protected from light.

IDENTIFICATION
- **THIN-LAYER CHROMATOGRAPHY,** Appendix IIA
  Adsorbent: 0.25-mm layer of chromatographic silica gel containing a suitable fluorescing substance
  [NOTE—Prepare the following two solutions without heating and handle without delay. Perform the development and subsequent operations in the dark.]
  Sample solution: 50 mg/mL sample in squalane and chloroform (1:100)
  Standard solution: 50 mg/mL of USP Cholecalciferol RS in squalane and chloroform (1:100)
  Application volume: 10 µL
  Developing solvent system: Cyclohexane and ether (1:1)
  Analysis: Spray the plate with a solution of acetyl chloride and antimony trichloride TS (1:50).
  Acceptance criteria: The chromatogram obtained with the *Sample solution* shows a yellow-orange area (cholecalciferol) having the same R_F value as the area of the *Standard solution* and may show a violet area, attributed to 7-dehydrocholesterol, below the cholecalciferol area.
- **INFRARED ABSORPTION,** *Spectrophotometric Identification Tests*, Appendix IIIC
  Reference standard: USP Cholecalciferol RS
  Sample and Standard preparation: *K*
  Acceptance criteria: The spectrum of the sample exhibits maxima at the same wavelengths as those in the spectrum of the *Reference standard*.
- **ULTRAVIOLET ABSORPTION,** *Spectrophotometric Identification Tests*, Appendix IIIC
  Standard solution: USP Cholecalciferol RS in ethanol (1:100,000)
  Sample solution: 1:100,000 in ethanol

Acceptance criteria: The spectrum of the *Sample solution* exhibits inflections at the same wavelengths as those in the spectrum of the *Standard solution* and the respective absorptivities at the point of maximum absorbance (about 265 nm) do not differ by more than 3.0%.

ASSAY
- **PROCEDURE**
  Mobile phase: ACS Reagent-Grade Hexanes and n-amyl alcohol (1000:3). [NOTE—The hexanes must be suitable for use in ultraviolet spectrophotometry and be dried by passing through a 60-cm × 8-cm column containing 500 g of 50-μm to 250-μm chromatographic siliceous earth.]
  System suitability solution: 25 mg/mL USP Vitamin D Assay System Suitability RS in toluene and *Mobile phase* (1:1) made to 10 mL. Reflux this solution at 90° for 45 min, and cool. This solution contains cholecalciferol, pre-cholecalciferol, and trans-cholecalciferol.
  [NOTE—Prepare the following solutions fresh daily using low-actinic glassware. Do not use heat to aid dissolution of solutes.]
  Standard stock solution: 0.6 mg/mL USP Cholecalciferol RS in toluene, made to 50 mL
  Standard solution: 0.12 mg/mL USP Cholecalciferol RS: made from *Standard stock solution* diluted to 50 mL with *Mobile phase*
  Sample stock solution: 0.6 mg/mL in toluene, made to 50 mL
  Sample solution: 0.12 mg/mL: made from *Sample stock solution* diluted to 50 mL with *Mobile phase*
  Chromatographic system, Appendix IIA
    Mode: High-performance liquid chromatography
    Detector: UV, 254 nm
    Column: 25-cm × 4.6-mm stainless steel column, or equivalent, packed with porous silica (5 to 10 μm in particle diameter) or equivalent
    Injection volume: 5-10 μL
  System suitability
    Sample: *System suitability solution*
    Suitability requirements
      Resolution: Between trans-cholecalciferol and pre-cholecalciferol NLT 1.0
      Relative standard deviation: NMT 2.0%
      Relative retention times: Pre-cholecalciferol, trans-cholecalciferol, and cholecalciferol are 0.4, 0.5, and 1.0, respectively.
  Analysis: Separately inject equal volumes of the *Standard solution* and *Sample solution* into the chromatograph, record the chromatograms, and measure the responses of the major peaks.
  Calculate the percentage of $C_{27}H_{44}O$ in the sample taken by the equation:

  $$\%C_{27}H_{44}O = (r_U/r_S) \times (C_S/C_U) \times 100\%$$

  r_U = peak response obtained from the *Sample solution*
  r_S = peak response obtained from the *Standard solution*
  C_S = concentration of *Standard solution* (mg/mL)
  C_U = concentration of *Sample solution* (mg/mL)
  Acceptance criteria: NLT 97.0% and NMT 103.0% of $C_{27}H_{44}O$

SPECIFIC TESTS
- **MELTING RANGE OR TEMPERATURE DETERMINATION,** *Procedure for Class Ib,* Appendix IIB
  Acceptance criteria: 84°-89°
- **OPTICAL (SPECIFIC) ROTATION,** Appendix IIB
  Sample solution: 5 mg/mL in alcohol. [NOTE—Prepare the solution without delay, using a sample from a container opened not longer than 30 min, and determine the rotation within 30 min after the solution has been prepared.]
  Acceptance criteria: $[\alpha]_D^{25}$ between +105° and +112°

Vitamin K

First Published: Prior to FCC 6

1,4-Naphthalenedione
2-Methyl-3-(3,7,11,15-tetramethyl-2-hexadecenyl)
Phylloquinone
Phytonadione

$C_{31}H_{46}O_2$ Formula wt 450.71
                             CAS: [84-80-0]
UNII: S5Z3U87QHF [phytonadione, (e)-]

DESCRIPTION
Vitamin K occurs as a clear, yellow to amber, very viscous liquid. It has a specific gravity of about 0.967. It is stable in air, but decomposes on exposure to sunlight. It is insoluble in water; soluble in dehydrated alcohol, in chloroform, in ether, and in vegetable oils; and slightly soluble in alcohol.
Function: Nutrient
Packaging and Storage: Store in tight, light-resistant containers.

[NOTE—Protect solutions containing Vitamin K from exposure to light.]

IDENTIFICATION
- **INFRARED ABSORPTION,** *Spectrophotometric Identification Tests,* Appendix IIIC
  Reference standard: USP Phytonadione RS
  Sample and Standard preparation: E
  Acceptance criteria: The spectrum of the sample exhibits maxima at the same wavelengths as those in the spectrum of the *Reference standard*.
- **ULTRAVIOLET ABSORPTION,** *Spectrophotometric Identification Tests,* Appendix IIIC
  Standard solution: 10 μg/mL USP Phytonadione RS in n-hexane
  Sample solution: 10 μg/mL in n-hexane

Acceptance criteria: The spectrum of the *Sample solution* exhibits maxima and minima at the same wavelengths as those in the spectrum of the *Standard solution* and the respective absorptivities at 248 nm do not differ by more than 3.0%.

ASSAY
- **PROCEDURE**
  [NOTE—Protect solutions containing vitamin K from exposure to light.]
  Mobile phase: *n*-hexane:*n*-amyl alcohol (2000:1.5), filtered and degassed
  Internal standard: 2.5 mg/mL cholesteryl benzoate in *Mobile phase*
  Standard stock solution: 0.096 mg/mL USP Phytonadione RS in *Mobile phase*
  Standard solution: 10 mL of *Standard stock solution* mixed with 7 mL of *Internal standard solution*, diluted to 25 mL with *Mobile phase*
  Sample stock solution: 0.096 mg/mL in *Mobile phase*
  Sample solution: 10 mL of *Sample stock solution* mixed with 7 mL of *Internal standard solution*, diluted to 25 mL with *Mobile phase*
  Chromatographic system, Appendix IIA
   Mode: High-performance liquid chromatography
   Detector: UV 254 nm
   Column: 25-cm × 4.6-mm (id) column that contains 5- to 10-µm porous silica microparticles (µPorasil, or equivalent)
   Flow rate: About 1 mL/min
   Injection volume: About 50 µL
  System suitability
   Sample: *Standard solution*
   Suitability requirement 1: The relative standard deviation for replicate injections is NMT 2.0%.
   Suitability requirement 2: The resolution, R, between (Z)-phytonadione and (E)-phytonadione is NLT 1.5.
  Analysis: Separately inject the *Standard solution* and *Sample solution* into the chromatograph, record the chromatograms, and measure the responses for the major peaks. [NOTE—The relative retention times are about 0.7 for the *Internal standard*, 0.9 for (Z)-phytonadione, and 1.0 for (E)-phytonadione.]
  Calculate the quantity, in mg, of $C_{31}H_{46}O_2$ in the portion of sample taken by the formula:

  $$\text{Result} = 1.56\ C\ (R_U/R_S)$$

  C = concentration of *Standard solution* (µg/mL)
  R_U = relative peak response ratio obtained from the chromatogram of the *Sample solution*
  R_S = relative peak response ratio obtained from the chromatogram of the *Standard solution*
  Calculate R_U and R_S by the formula:

  $$\text{Result} = (r_Z + r_E)/r_I$$

  r_Z = peak response of (Z)-phytonadione
  r_E = peak response of (E)-phytonadione
  r_I = peak response of cholesteryl benzoate in the *Internal standard* peak
  Acceptance criteria: NLT 97.0% and NMT 103.0% of $C_{31}H_{46}O_2$

IMPURITIES
Inorganic Impurities
- **LEAD,** *Lead Limit Test, Flame Atomic Absorption Spectrophotometric Method,* Appendix IIIB
  Sample: 10 g
  Acceptance criteria: NMT 2 mg/kg

SPECIFIC TESTS
- **MENADIONE**
  Sample: 20 mg
  Analysis: Mix the *Sample* with 0.5 mL of a 1:1 (v/v) mixture of 6 N ammonium hydroxide: alcohol. Add 1 drop of ethyl cyanoacetate and shake gently.
  Acceptance criteria: No purple or blue color appears.
- **REFRACTIVE INDEX,** Appendix IIB
  [NOTE—Use an Abbé or other refractometer of equal or greater accuracy.]
  Acceptance criteria: Between 1.523 and 1.526
- **(Z) ISOMER CONTENT**
  Analysis: Determine as directed in the *Assay* (above) using the *Mobile phase, Internal standard solution, Sample solution,* and *Chromatographic system* described therein, but modify the calculation as follows: Calculate the percentage of (Z) isomer taken by the formula:

  $$\text{Result} = 100 \times r_Z/(r_Z + r_E)$$

  r_Z = peak area of the (Z)-phytonadione isomer peak obtained from the chromatogram of the *Sample solution*
  r_E = peak area of the (E)-phytonadione isomer peak obtained from the chromatogram of the *Sample solution*
  Acceptance criteria: NMT 21.0%

Wheat Gluten

First Published: Prior to FCC 6

Vital Wheat Gluten
Devitalized Wheat Gluten

CAS: [8002-80-0]

UNII: 1534K8653J [wheat gluten]

DESCRIPTION
Wheat Gluten occurs as a cream to light tan, free-flowing powder. It is the water-insoluble complex protein obtained by water extraction of wheat or wheat flour. It is soluble in alkalies, and partly soluble in alcohol and dilute acids. *Vital Wheat Gluten* is characterized by high viscoelasticity when hydrated, while *Devitalized Wheat Gluten* has lost this character because of denaturation by heat.

Function: Dough strengthener; nutrient; stabilizer and thickener; surface-finishing agent; and texturizing agent

Packaging and Storage: Store in well-closed containers.

IDENTIFICATION
- **PROCEDURE**
  Sample: 20 g
  Analysis: Add 40 mL of room-temperature water to the sample and stir.
  Acceptance criteria: *Vital Wheat Gluten* forms a cohesive, viscoelastic mass, which can be lifted with the stirring rod without breaking apart. *Devitalized Wheat Gluten* does not form such a mass.

ASSAY
- **PROTEIN,** *Nitrogen Determination,* Appendix IIIC
  Analysis: Calculate the percent protein with the formula:

  $$\text{Result} = 5.7 \times N$$

  N = percent nitrogen
  Acceptance criteria: NLT 71.0% calculated on the dried basis

IMPURITIES
Inorganic Impurities
- **LEAD,** *Lead Limit Test, Atomic Absorption Spectrophotometric Graphite Furnace Method, Method I,* Appendix IIIB
  Sample: 1 g
  Acceptance criteria: NMT 1 mg/kg

SPECIFIC TESTS
- **ASH (TOTAL),** Appendix IIC
  Acceptance criteria: NMT 2.0% calculated on the dried basis
- **CRUDE FAT,** Appendix X
  Acceptance criteria: NMT 2.0%
- **STARCH**
  Analysis: The remainder, after subtracting from 100.0% the sum of the percents of *Ash (Total), Loss on Drying,* and *Protein,* represents the percent of starch in the sample.
  Acceptance criteria: NMT 21.0%
- **LOSS ON DRYING,** Appendix IIC: 105° for 2 h
  Sample: 2 g
  Acceptance criteria: NMT 10.0%

Wheat Protein Isolate

First Published: Prior to FCC 6

DESCRIPTION
Wheat Protein Isolate occurs as a powder. It is produced by acidic deamidation of gluten that converts glutamine and asparagine to their nonamidated derivatives, glutamic acid and aspartic acid, followed by several purification measures. Alternatively, gluten can be solubilized in an acidic or alkaline medium, and the dissolved protein is then separated and purified by filtration or centrifugation.

Function: Texturizer; nutrient; emulsifier; water-binding aid; gelling agent; foaming agent

Packaging and Storage: Store in tight containers protected from humidity.

IDENTIFICATION
- **PROCEDURE**
  Acceptance criteria: A sample exhibits the compositional profile specified below with respect to *Ash (Total), Fat, Loss on Drying,* and *Protein.*

ASSAY
- **PROTEIN,** *Nitrogen Determination,* Appendix IIIC
  Analysis: Determine the percent nitrogen as directed or alternatively using the Protein Nitrogen Combustion Method, AOAC 992.23 or AOCS Ba 4e-93 methods. Calculate the percent protein (calculated to exclude added vitamins, minerals, amino acids, and food additives) using the equation:

  $$\%\text{Protein} = N \times 5.7$$

  N = percent nitrogen
  5.7 = nitrogen to protein conversion factor
  Acceptance criteria: NLT 75% protein, calculated on the dried basis, drying to constant weight at 130°

IMPURITIES
Inorganic Impurities
- **LEAD,** *Lead Limit Test, Atomic Absorption Spectrophotometric Graphite Furnace Method, Method I,* Appendix IIIB
  Acceptance criteria: NMT 0.5 mg/kg, calculated on the dried basis, drying to constant weight at 130°

SPECIFIC TESTS
- **ASH (TOTAL),** Appendix IIC
  [NOTE—Final residue is gray to white.]
  Acceptance criteria: NMT 8%, calculated on the dried basis, drying to constant weight at 130°
- **FAT,** *Crude Fat,* Appendix X
  Acceptance criteria: NMT 6%, calculated on the dried basis, drying to constant weight at 130°
- **LOSS ON DRYING,** Appendix IIC: 65° at less than 100 mm Hg for 16 h
  Sample: 2 g
  Acceptance criteria: NMT 10%
- **PH,** *pH Determination,* Appendix IIB
  Sample solution: 100 mg/mL

Acceptance criteria: Between 4.3 and 7.5

OTHER REQUIREMENTS
- LABELING: Indicate the protein content.

Whey

First Published: Prior to FCC 6

UNII: 8617Z5FMF6 [whey]

DESCRIPTION
Whey is the liquid obtained by separating the coagulum from milk, cream, and/or skim milk in cheese making. Whey obtained from the process in which a significant amount of lactose is converted to lactic acid or obtained from the curd formed by direct acidification of milk is known as *Acid-Type Whey*. Whey obtained from the process in which there is insignificant conversion of lactose to lactic acid is known as *Sweet-Type Whey*. The acidity of Whey may be adjusted by the addition of safe and suitable pH-adjusting ingredients. The final product is pasteurized and is available as a liquid or dry product.

Function: Texturizer; nutrient
Packaging and Storage: Store in tight containers protected from humidity.

IDENTIFICATION
- PROCEDURE: A sample exhibits the compositional profile specified below with respect to *Ash, Fat, Lactose, Loss on Drying,* and *Protein*.

IMPURITIES
Inorganic Impurities
- LEAD, *Lead Limit Test, Atomic Absorption Spectrophotometric Graphite Furnace Method, Method II,* Appendix IIIB
   Acceptance criteria: NMT 0.5 mg/kg calculated on the dried basis

SPECIFIC TESTS
- ASH (TOTAL), Appendix IIC
   [NOTE—Final residue is gray to white.]
   Acceptance criteria: 7.0%–14.0% calculated on the dried basis
- FAT
   Sample: 1 g
   Analysis: Transfer the *Sample* to a fat-extraction flask, add 10 mL of water, and shake until homogeneous (warm if necessary). Add approximately 1 mL of ammonium hydroxide and heat in a water bath for 15 min at 60° to 70°, shaking occasionally. Add 10 mL of alcohol, and mix well. Add 25 mL of peroxide-free ether, stopper, and shake vigorously for 1 min. Allow to cool if necessary, add 25 mL of petroleum ether; and shake vigorously. Allow the layers to separate and clarify, or centrifuge at 600 rpm to expedite the process. Decant the organic layer into a suitable flask or dish, and repeat the extraction twice with 15 mL each of ether and petroleum ether for each extraction. Evaporate the combined ether extractions on a steam bath, and dry the residue to a constant weight at 102°, or 70° to 75° at less than 50 mm Hg.
   Calculate the percent of fat in the sample taken with the equation:

   $$\%Fat = R/S \times 100\%$$

   R = weight (mg) of the residue
   S = weight (mg) of the sample taken
   Acceptance criteria: 0.2%–2.0% calculated on the dried basis
- LACTOSE
   Mobile phase: Acetonitrile and water (80:20), filtered and degassed
   Internal standard solution: 100 mg/mL USP Fructose RS
   Standard stock solution: 20 mg/mL USP Lactose RS
   Standard solution: 18 mg/mL of USP Lactose RS prepared by mixing *Internal standard solution* with *Standard stock solution* (1:9). Prepare fresh daily.
   Sample solution: Transfer an accurately weighed quantity of sample containing about 180 mg of lactose into a 10-mL volumetric flask, add 1 mL of the *Internal standard solution*, dilute with water to volume, and mix.
   Chromatographic system, Appendix IIA
    Mode: High-performance liquid chromatography
    Detector: Differential refractometer
    Column: 250-mm × 4.6-mm (id) microparticle silica gel with siloxane-bonded cyanoamino moieties (Whatman P-10 carbohydrate, or equivalent)
    Flow rate: 2 mL/min
    Injection volume: 25 µL
   System suitability
    Sample: *Standard solution*
   Suitability requirements
    Relative standard deviation: NMT 2.0% for the ratio of the lactose response to that of the internal standard, for replicate injections
   Analysis: Separately inject equal volumes of the *Standard solution* and *Sample solution* into the chromatograph, record the chromatograms, and measure the responses. Calculate the percent lactose in the sample taken from the equation:

   $$\%Lactose = (R_U/R_S) \times (C_S/C_U) \times 100\%$$

   R_U = response ratio of lactose to internal standard for the *Sample solution*
   R_S = response ratio of lactose to internal standard for the *Standard solution*
   C_S = concentration of *USP Lactose RS* in the *Standard solution* (mg/mL)
   C_U = concentration of sample in the *Sample solution* (mg/mL)
   Acceptance criteria: 61.0%–75.0% calculated on the dried basis
- LOSS ON DRYING, Appendix IIC
   Dry product
    Sample: 2 g

Conditions: 65°, below 100 mm Hg, 16 h
Acceptance criteria: NMT 5.0%
Liquid product
Conditions: Evaporate a sample to dryness on a steam bath, and continue as directed for the *Dry product*.
Acceptance criteria: NMT 95.0%
- **PROTEIN**, *Nitrogen Determination*, Appendix IIIC
  Analysis: Calculate the percent protein using the equation:

  $$\%\text{Protein} = N \times 6.38$$

  N = %Nitrogen
  Acceptance criteria: Between 10.0% and 15.0%, calculated on the dried basis
- **TITRATABLE ACIDITY (AS LACTIC ACID)**
  Sample: For dry or liquid sample, the equivalent of 10.0 g of total solids based on the value obtained under *Loss on Drying*
  Analysis: Transfer the *Sample* into a 500-mL conical flask, add 100 mL of carbon dioxide-free water, and stir for 1 min. Allow to stand for 1 h at room temperature. Add 0.5 mL of phenolphthalein TS, and titrate with 0.1 N sodium hydroxide to a pink endpoint that persists for 30 s. Each mL of 0.1 N sodium hydroxide is equivalent to 9.008 mg of lactic acid.
  Acceptance criteria
  Sweet-type whey: NMT 0.16%, calculated on the dried basis
  Acid-type whey: NLT 0.35%, calculated on the dried basis

OTHER REQUIREMENTS
- **LABELING:** State whether the product is sweet or acid, if the product is liquid, and the concentration, as total solids based on the value obtained under *Loss on Drying*.

Whey, Reduced Lactose

First Published: Prior to FCC 6

DESCRIPTION
Whey, Reduced Lactose, occurs as either a liquid or a dry product. It is the substance obtained by the selective removal of lactose from whey. Removal of lactose is accomplished by physical separation techniques such as precipitation, filtration, or dialysis. The acidity of Reduced Lactose Whey may be adjusted by the addition of safe and suitable pH-adjusting ingredients. The final product is pasteurized.
Function: Texturizer; nutrient; emulsifier
Packaging and Storage: Store in tight containers protected from humidity.

IDENTIFICATION
- **PROCEDURE**
  Acceptance criteria: A sample exhibits the compositional profile specified below with respect to *Ash (Total), Fat, Lactose, Loss on Drying,* and *Protein*.

IMPURITIES
Inorganic Impurities
- **LEAD**, *Lead Limit Test, Atomic Absorption Spectrophotometric Graphite Furnace Method, Method II*, Appendix IIIB
  Acceptance criteria: NMT 0.5 mg/kg, on the dried basis

SPECIFIC TESTS
- **ASH (TOTAL)**, Appendix IIC
  [NOTE—Final residue is gray to white.]
  Acceptance criteria: Between 11.0% and 27.0%, on the dried basis
- **FAT**
  Sample: 1 g
  Analysis: Transfer the *Sample* to a fat-extraction flask, add 10 mL of water, and shake until homogeneous (warm if necessary). Add approximately 1 mL of ammonium hydroxide and heat in a water bath for 15 min at 60° to 70°, shaking occasionally. Add 10 mL of alcohol, and mix well. Add 25 mL of peroxide-free ether, stopper, and shake vigorously for 1 min. Allow to cool if necessary, add 25 mL of petroleum ether; and shake vigorously. Allow the layers to separate and clarify, or centrifuge at 600 rpm to expedite the process. Decant the organic layer into a suitable flask or dish, and repeat the extraction twice with 15 mL each of ether and petroleum ether for each extraction. Evaporate the combined ether extractions on a steam bath, and dry the residue to a constant weight at 102°, or 70° to 75° at less than 50 mm Hg.
  Calculate the percent of fat in the sample taken with the equation:

  $$\%\text{Fat} = R/S \times 100\%$$

  R = weight (mg) of the residue
  S = weight (mg) of the sample taken
  Acceptance criteria: Between 0.2% and 4.0%, on the dried basis
- **LACTOSE**
  Mobile phase: Acetonitrile and water (80:20), filtered and degassed
  Internal standard solution: 100 mg/mL USP Fructose RS
  Standard stock solution: 20 mg/mL USP Lactose RS
  Standard solution: 18 mg/mL of USP Lactose RS prepared by mixing *Internal standard solution* with a 20 mg/mL solution of USP Lactose RS (1:9). Prepare fresh daily.
  Sample solution: Transfer an accurately weighed quantity of sample containing about 180 mg of lactose into a 10-mL volumetric flask, add 1 mL of the *Internal standard solution*, dilute with water to volume, and mix.
  Chromatographic system, Appendix IIA
  Mode: Liquid chromatography
  Detector: Differential refractometer
  Column: 250-mm × 4.6-mm (id) microparticle silica gel with siloxane-bonded cyanoamino moieties (Whatman P-10 carbohydrate, or equivalent)
  Flow rate: 2 mL/min
  Injection volume: 25 µL

System suitability
Sample: Standard solution
Suitability requirement: The relative standard deviation of the ratio of the lactose response to that of the Internal standard is NMT 2.0% for replicate injections.
Analysis: Separately inject equal volumes of the Standard solution and Sample solution into the chromatograph, record the chromatograms, and measure the responses. Calculate the percent lactose in the sample taken from the equation:

$$\%\text{Lactose} = (R_U/R_S) \times (C_S/C_U) \times 100\%$$

R_U = response ratio of lactose to internal standard for the Sample solution
R_S = response ratio of lactose to internal standard for the Standard solution
C_S = concentration of USP Lactose RS in the Standard solution (mg/mL)
C_U = concentration of sample in the Sample solution (mg/mL)

Acceptance criteria: NMT 60.0%, on the dried basis

- **LOSS ON DRYING,** Appendix IIC
  Sample: 2 g
  Conditions: 65°, below 100 mm Hg, to constant weight
  Acceptance criteria (dry product): NMT 4.0%

- **PH,** pH Determination, Appendix IIB
  Sample: 100 mg/mL if the product is in the dry form, or as-is if the product is in the liquid form
  Acceptance criteria: Between 5.5 and 7.2, on the dried basis

- **PROTEIN,** Nitrogen Determination, Appendix IIIC
  Analysis: Calculate the percent protein using the equation:

$$\%\text{Protein} = N \times 6.38$$

N = percent nitrogen
6.38 = nitrogen to protein conversion factor

Acceptance criteria: Between 16.0% and 24.0%, on the dried basis

OTHER REQUIREMENTS

- **LABELING:** If the product is liquid, indicate the concentration, as total solids, based on the value obtained under Loss on Drying (above).

Whey, Reduced Minerals

First Published: Prior to FCC 6

DESCRIPTION

Whey, Reduced Minerals, occurs as either a liquid or a dry product. It is the substance obtained by the removal of a portion of the minerals from whey. Reduced Minerals Whey is produced by physical separation techniques such as precipitation, filtration, ion exchange, or dialysis. The acidity of the Reduced Minerals Whey may be adjusted by the addition of safe and suitable pH-adjusting ingredients. The final product is pasteurized.

Function: Texturizer; nutrient
Packaging and Storage: Store in tight containers protected from humidity.

IDENTIFICATION

- **PROCEDURE**
  Acceptance criteria: A sample exhibits the compositional profile specified below with respect to Ash (Total), Fat, Lactose, Loss on Drying, and Protein.

IMPURITIES

Inorganic Impurities

- **LEAD,** Lead Limit Test, Atomic Absorption Spectrophotometric Graphite Furnace Method, Method II, Appendix IIIB
  Acceptance criteria: NMT 0.5 mg/kg, on the dried basis

SPECIFIC TESTS

- **ASH (TOTAL),** Appendix IIC
  [NOTE—Final residue is gray to white.]
  Acceptance criteria: NMT 7.0%, on the dried basis

- **FAT**
  Sample: 1 g
  Analysis: Transfer the Sample to a fat-extraction flask, add 10 mL of water, and shake until homogeneous (warm if necessary). Add approximately 1 mL of ammonium hydroxide and heat in a water bath for 15 min at 60° to 70°, shaking occasionally. Add 10 mL of alcohol, and mix well. Add 25 mL of peroxide-free ether, stopper, and shake vigorously for 1 min. Allow to cool if necessary, add 25 mL of petroleum ether; and shake vigorously. Allow the layers to separate and clarify, or centrifuge at 600 rpm to expedite the process. Decant the organic layer into a suitable flask or dish, and repeat the extraction twice with 15 mL each of ether and petroleum ether for each extraction. Evaporate the combined ether extractions on a steam bath, and dry the residue to a constant weight at 102°, or 70° to 75° at less than 50 mm Hg.
  Calculate the percent of fat in the sample taken with the equation:

$$\%\text{Fat} = R/S \times 100\%$$

R = weight (mg) of the residue
S = weight (mg) of the sample taken

Acceptance criteria: Between 0.2% and 4.0%, on the dried basis

- **LACTOSE**
  Mobile phase: Acetonitrile and water (80:20), filtered and degassed
  Internal standard solution: 100 mg/mL USP Fructose RS
  Standard stock solution: 20 mg/mL USP Lactose RS
  Standard solution: 18 mg/mL of USP Lactose RS prepared by mixing Internal standard solution with a 20 mg/mL solution of USP Lactose RS (1:9). Prepare fresh daily.

Whey Protein Concentrate

First Published: Prior to FCC 6

DESCRIPTION

Whey Protein Concentrate occurs as either a liquid or a dry product. It is the substance obtained by the removal of sufficient nonprotein constituents from whey so that the finished dry product contains not less than 25.0% protein. Whey Protein Concentrate is produced by physical separation techniques such as precipitation, filtration, or dialysis. The acidity of the Whey Protein Concentrate may be adjusted by the addition of safe and suitable pH-adjusting ingredients. The final product is pasteurized.

Function: Texturizer; nutrient; emulsifier; water-binding aid; gelling agent

Packaging and Storage: Store in tight containers protected from humidity.

IDENTIFICATION
- **PROCEDURE**
  Acceptance criteria: A sample exhibits the compositional profile specified below with respect to *Ash (Total), Fat, Lactose, Loss on Drying,* and *Protein.*

IMPURITIES

Inorganic Impurities
- **LEAD,** *Lead Limit Test, Atomic Absorption Spectrophotometric Graphite Furnace Method, Method II, Appendix IIIB*
  Acceptance criteria: NMT 0.5 mg/kg, calculated on the dried basis

SPECIFIC TESTS
- **ASH (TOTAL),** Appendix IIC
  [NOTE—Final residue is gray to white.]
  Acceptance criteria: Between 2.0% and 15.0%, calculated on the dried basis
- **FAT**
  Sample: 1 g
  Analysis: Transfer the *Sample* to a fat-extraction flask, add 10 mL of water, and shake until homogeneous (warm if necessary). Add approximately 1 mL of ammonium hydroxide and heat in a water bath for 15 min at 60° to 70°, shaking occasionally. Add 10 mL of alcohol, and mix well. Add 25 mL of peroxide-free ether, stopper, and shake vigorously for 1 min. Allow to cool if necessary, add 25 mL of petroleum ether; and shake vigorously. Allow the layers to separate and clarify, or centrifuge at 600 rpm to expedite the process. Decant the organic layer into a suitable flask or dish, and repeat the extraction twice with 15 mL each of ether and petroleum ether for each extraction. Evaporate the combined ether extractions on a steam bath, and dry the residue to a constant weight at 102°, or 70° to 75° at less than 50 mm Hg.
  Calculate the percent of fat in the sample taken with the equation:

  $$\%\text{Fat} = R/S \times 100\%$$

  Sample solution: Transfer an accurately weighed quantity of sample containing about 180 mg of lactose into a 10-mL volumetric flask, add 1 mL of the *Internal standard solution,* dilute with water to volume, and mix.
  Chromatographic system, Appendix IIA
    Mode: Liquid chromatography
    Detector: Differential refractometer
    Column: 250-mm × 4.6-mm (id) microparticle silica gel with siloxane-bonded cyanoamino moieties (Whatman P-10 carbohydrate, or equivalent)
    Flow rate: 2 mL/min
    Injection volume: 25 µL
    System suitability
      Sample: *Standard solution*
      Suitability requirement: The relative standard deviation of the ratio of the lactose response to that of the *Internal standard* is NMT 2.0% for replicate injections.
  Analysis: Separately inject equal volumes of the *Standard solution* and *Sample solution* into the chromatograph, record the chromatograms, and measure the responses. Calculate the percent lactose in the sample taken from the equation:

  $$\%\text{Lactose} = (R_U/R_S) \times (C_S/C_U) \times 100\%$$

  R_U = response ratio of lactose to internal standard for the *Sample solution*
  R_S = response ratio of lactose to internal standard for the *Standard solution*
  C_S = concentration of USP Lactose RS in the *Standard solution* (mg/mL)
  C_U = concentration of sample in the *Sample solution* (mg/mL)
  Acceptance criteria: NMT 85.0%, on the dried basis
- **LOSS ON DRYING,** Appendix IIC
  Sample: 2 g
  Conditions: 65°, below 100 mm Hg, to constant weight
  Acceptance criteria (dry product): NMT 4.0%
- **pH,** *pH Determination,* Appendix IIB
  Sample: 100 mg/mL if the product is in the dry form, or as-is if the product is in the liquid form
  Acceptance criteria: Between 6.2 and 7.2, on the dried basis
- **PROTEIN,** *Nitrogen Determination,* Appendix IIIC
  Analysis: Calculate the percent protein using the equation:

  $$\%\text{Protein} = N \times 6.38$$

  N = percent nitrogen
  6.38 = nitrogen to protein conversion factor
  Acceptance criteria: Between 10.0% and 24.0%, on the dried basis

OTHER REQUIREMENTS
- **LABELING:** If the product is liquid, indicate the concentration as total solids based on the value obtained under *Loss on Drying* (above).

R = weight (mg) of the residue
S = weight (mg) of the sample taken
Acceptance criteria: Between 0.2% and 10.0%, calculated on the dried basis

- **LACTOSE**
  Mobile phase: Acetonitrile and water (80:20), filtered and degassed
  Internal standard solution: 100 mg/mL USP Fructose RS
  Standard stock solution: 20 mg/mL USP Lactose RS
  Standard solution: 18 mg/mL of USP Lactose RS prepared by mixing *Internal standard solution* with a 20 mg/mL solution of USP Lactose RS (1:9) respectively. Prepare fresh daily.
  Sample solution: Transfer an accurately weighed quantity of sample containing about 180 mg of lactose into a 10-mL volumetric flask, add 1 mL of the *Internal standard solution*, dilute with water to volume, and mix.
  Chromatographic system, Appendix IIA
    Mode: Liquid chromatography
    Detector: Differential refractometer
    Column: 250-mm × 4.6-mm (id) microparticle silica gel with siloxane-bonded cyano-amino moieties (Whatman P-10 carbohydrate, or equivalent)
    Flow rate: 2 mL/min
    Injection volume: 25 μL
    System suitability
      Sample: *Standard solution*
      Suitability requirement: The relative standard deviation of the ratio of the lactose response to that of the *Internal standard* is NMT 2.0% for replicate injections.
  Analysis: Separately inject equal volumes of the *Standard solution* and *Sample solution* into the chromatograph, record the chromatograms, and measure the responses. Calculate the percent lactose in the sample taken from the equation:

$$\%\text{Lactose} = (R_U/R_S) \times (C_S/C_U) \times 100\%$$

  R_U = response ratio of lactose to internal standard for the *Sample solution*
  R_S = response ratio of lactose to internal standard for the *Standard solution*
  C_S = concentration of USP Lactose RS in the *Standard solution* (mg/mL)
  C_U = concentration of sample in the *Sample solution* (mg/mL)
  Acceptance criteria: NMT 60.0%, calculated on the dried basis

- **LOSS ON DRYING,** Appendix IIC
  Sample: 2 g
  Conditions: 65°, below 100 mm Hg, to constant weight
  Acceptance criteria (dry product): NMT 6.0%

- **PH,** *pH Determination,* Appendix IIB
  Sample: 100 mg/mL, if the product is in the dry form, or as-is if the product is in the liquid form
  Acceptance criteria: Between 6.0 and 7.2

- **PROTEIN,** *Nitrogen Determination,* Appendix IIIC
  Analysis: Calculate the percent protein using the equation:

$$\%\text{Protein} = N \times 6.38$$

  N = percent nitrogen
  6.38 = nitrogen to protein conversion factor
  Acceptance criteria: NLT 25.0% and NMT 89.9%, calculated on the dried basis

OTHER REQUIREMENTS

- **LABELING:** Indicate the concentration of protein and, if the product is liquid, state the concentration, as total solids, based on the value obtained under *Loss on Drying* (above).

Whey Protein Isolate

First Published: Prior to FCC 6

DESCRIPTION

Whey Protein Isolate occurs either as a liquid or as a dry product. It is the substance obtained by the removal of sufficient nonprotein constituents from whey so that the finished dry product contains not less than 90% protein. Removal of nonprotein constituents is accomplished by separation techniques such as precipitation, membrane filtration, and/or ion exchange. The acidity of Whey Protein Isolate may be adjusted by the addition of safe and suitable pH-adjusting ingredients. The final product is pasteurized.
Function: Source of high-quality protein; gelling agent; water-binding aid; foaming or whipping aid; emulsifier; edible coating used as a moisture barrier
Packaging and Storage: Store in tight containers protected from humidity.

IDENTIFICATION

- **PROCEDURE**
  Acceptance criteria: A sample exhibits the compositional profile specified below with respect to *Ash (Total), Fat, Lactose, Loss on Drying,* and *Protein*.

IMPURITIES

Inorganic Impurities

- **LEAD,** *Lead Limit Test, Atomic Absorption Spectrophotometric Graphite Furnace Method, Method II,* Appendix IIIB
  Acceptance criteria: NMT 0.5 mg/kg, on the dried basis

SPECIFIC TESTS

- **ASH (TOTAL),** Appendix IIC
  [NOTE—Final residue is gray to white.]
  Acceptance criteria: Less than 6.0%, on the dried basis

- **FAT**
  Sample: 1 g
  Analysis: Transfer the *Sample* to a fat-extraction flask, add 10 mL of water, and shake until homogeneous

(warm if necessary). Add approximately 1 mL of ammonium hydroxide and heat in a water bath for 15 min at 60° to 70°, shaking occasionally. Add 10 mL of alcohol, and mix well. Add 25 mL of peroxide-free ether, stopper, and shake vigorously for 1 min. Allow to cool if necessary, add 25 mL of petroleum ether; and shake vigorously. Allow the layers to separate and clarify, or centrifuge at 600 rpm to expedite the process. Decant the organic layer into a suitable flask or dish, and repeat the extraction twice with 15 mL each of ether and petroleum ether for each extraction. Evaporate the combined ether extractions on a steam bath, and dry the residue to a constant weight at 102°, or 70° to 75° at less than 50 mm Hg.
Calculate the percent of fat in the sample taken with the equation:

$$\%Fat = R/S \times 100\%$$

R = weight (mg) of the residue
S = weight (mg) of the sample taken
Acceptance criteria: Less than 6.0%, on the dried basis

- **LACTOSE**
  Mobile phase: Acetonitrile and water (80:20), filtered and degassed
  Internal standard solution: 100 mg/mL USP Fructose RS
  Standard stock solution: 20 mg/mL USP Lactose RS
  Standard solution: 18 mg/mL of USP Lactose RS prepared by mixing *Internal standard solution* with a 20 mg/mL solution of USP Lactose RS (1:9). Prepare fresh daily.
  Sample solution: Transfer an accurately weighed quantity of sample containing about 180 mg of lactose into a 10-mL volumetric flask, add 1 mL of the *Internal standard solution*, dilute with water to volume, and mix.
  Chromatographic system, Appendix IIA
    Mode: Liquid chromatography
    Detector: Differential refractometer
    Column: 250-mm × 4.6-mm (id) microparticle silica gel with siloxane-bonded cyanoamino moieties (Whatman P-10 carbohydrate, or equivalent)
    Flow rate: 2 mL/min
    Injection volume: 25 µL
  System suitability
    Sample: *Standard solution*
    Suitability requirement: The relative standard deviation of the ratio of the lactose response to that of the *Internal standard* is NMT 2.0% for replicate injections.
  Analysis: Separately inject equal volumes of the *Standard solution* and *Sample solution* into the chromatograph, record the chromatograms, and measure the responses. Calculate the percent lactose in the sample taken from the equation:

$$\%Lactose = (R_U/R_S) \times (C_S/C_U) \times 100\%$$

R_U = response ratio of lactose to internal standard for the *Sample solution*
R_S = response ratio of lactose to internal standard for the *Standard solution*
C_S = concentration of USP Lactose RS in the *Standard solution* (mg/mL)
C_U = concentration of sample in the *Sample solution* (mg/mL)
Acceptance criteria: NMT 6.0%, on the dried basis

- **LOSS ON DRYING,** Appendix IIC
  Sample: 2 g
  Conditions: 65°, below 100 mm Hg, to constant weight
  Acceptance criteria (dry product): NMT 6.0%
- **PH,** *pH Determination,* Appendix IIB
  Sample solution: 100 mg/mL if the product is in the dry form, or as-is if the product is in the liquid form
  Acceptance criteria: Between 6.0 and 7.2
- **PROTEIN,** *Nitrogen Determination,* Appendix IIIC
  Analysis: Calculate the percent protein using the equation:

$$\%Protein = N \times 6.38$$

N = percent nitrogen
6.38 = nitrogen to protein conversion factor
Acceptance criteria: NLT 90.0%, on the dried basis

OTHER REQUIREMENTS
- **LABELING:** Indicate the concentration of protein and, if the product is liquid, state the concentration, as total solids, based on the value obtained under *Loss on Drying* (above).

Wintergreen Oil

First Published: Prior to FCC 6

Gaultheria Oil

CAS: [68917-75-9]
UNII: LAV5U5022Y [methyl salicylate]

DESCRIPTION
Wintergreen Oil occurs as a colorless to yellow liquid with the characteristic odor and taste of wintergreen. It is obtained by maceration and subsequent distillation with steam from the leaves of *Gualtheria procumbens* L. (Fam. Ericaceae) or from the bark of *Betula lenta* L. (Fam. Betulaceae). It boils, with decomposition, between 219° and 224°. It is soluble in alcohol and in glacial acetic acid, and it is very slightly soluble in water.
Function: Flavoring agent
Packaging and Storage: Store in a cool place protected from light in full, tight containers.

IDENTIFICATION
- **A. PROCEDURE**
  Analysis: Shake 1 drop of sample with about 5 mL of water, and add 1 drop of ferric chloride TS.
  Acceptance criteria: A deep violet color appears.
- **B. INFRARED SPECTRA,** *Spectrophotometric Identification Tests,* Appendix IIIC

Acceptance criteria: The spectrum of the sample exhibits relative maxima at the same wavelengths as those of the spectrum below.

ASSAY
- **ESTERS,** *Ester Determination,* Appendix VI
  Sample: 2 g
  Analysis: Modify the procedure by using 50.0 mL of 0.5 N alcoholic potassium hydroxide and by refluxing on the steam bath for 2 h. Use 76.08 as the equivalence factor (e) in the calculation.
  Acceptance criteria: NLT 98.0% and NMT 100.5% of methyl salicylate ($C_8H_8O_3$)

SPECIFIC TESTS
- **ACID VALUE (ESSENTIAL OILS AND FLAVORS),** Appendix VI
  Analysis: Use bromocresol purple TS as the indicator instead of phenolphthalein TS.
  Acceptance criteria: NMT 1.0
- **ANGULAR ROTATION,** *Optical (Specific) Rotation,* Appendix IIB: Use a 100-mm tube.
  Acceptance criteria: Levorotatory (not more levorotatory than −1.5°)
- **REFRACTIVE INDEX,** Appendix IIB
  [NOTE—Use an Abbé or other refractometer of equal or greater accuracy.]
  Acceptance criteria: Between 1.535 and 1.538 at 20°
- **SOLUBILITY IN ALCOHOL,** Appendix VI
  Acceptance criteria: One mL of sample dissolves in 7 mL of 70% alcohol. The solution should not have more than a slight cloudiness.
- **SPECIFIC GRAVITY:** Determine by any reliable method (see *General Provisions*).
  Acceptance criteria: Between 1.176 and 1.182

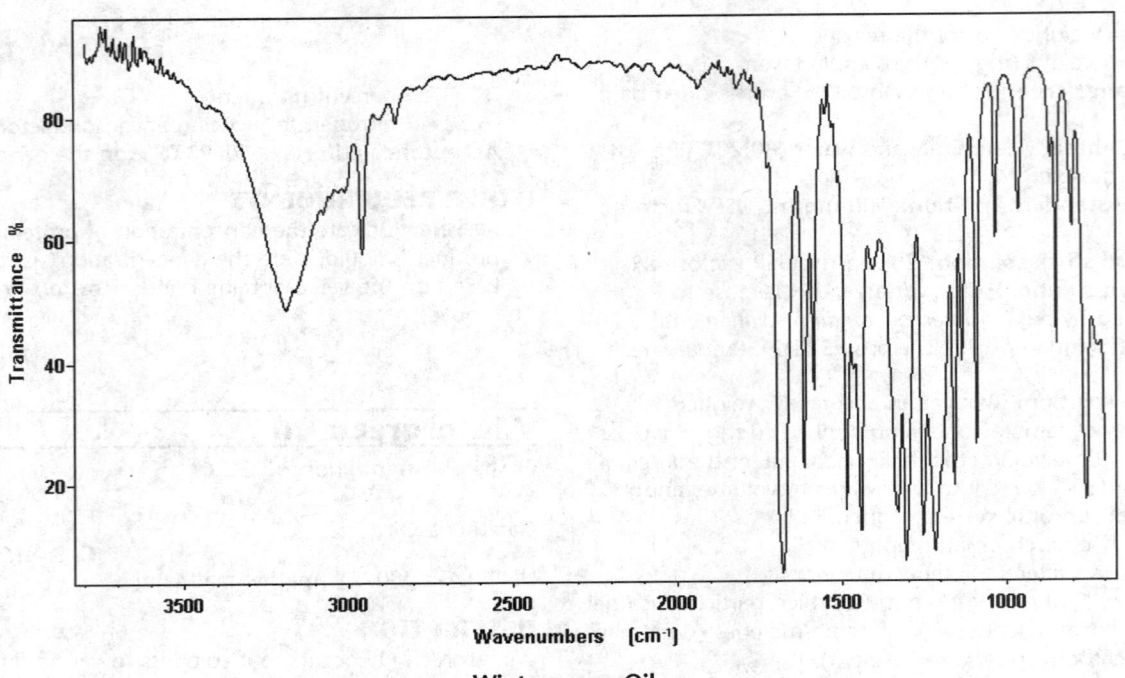

Wintergreen Oil

Xanthan Gum

First Published: Prior to FCC 6
Last Revision: FCC 8

INS: 415
UNII: TTV12P4NEE [xanthan gum]
CAS: [11138-66-2]

DESCRIPTION

Change to read:

Xanthan Gum occurs as a cream-colored powder. It is a high-molecular-weight polysaccharide gum produced by a pure culture fermentation of a carbohydrate with *Xanthomonas campestris*, purified by recovery with isopropyl alcohol or ethanol, dried, and milled. It contains D-glucose and D-mannose as the dominant hexose units, along with D-glucuronic acid and pyruvic acid, and it is prepared as the sodium, potassium, or calcium salt. ▲The pyruvic acid content of this ingredient is variable depending on the fermentation process used, and in the case of "reduced-pyruvate" materials may be less than 1.5%.▲FCC8 It is readily soluble in hot or cold water, but it is insoluble in alcohol. Its solutions are neutral.

Function: Stabilizer; thickener; emulsifier; suspending agent; bodying agent; foam enhancer
Packaging and Storage: Store in well-closed containers.

IDENTIFICATION

- **PROCEDURE**
  Sample solution: Transfer 300 mL of water, previously heated to 80°, into a 400-mL beaker and stir rapidly with a mechanical stirrer. At the point of maximum agitation, add a dry blend of 1.5 g of sample and 1.5 g of locust bean gum. Stir until the gums dissolve, and then continue stirring for 30 min longer. Do not allow the water temperature to drop below 60°. Discontinue stirring, and allow the solution to cool at room temperature for at least 2 h.
  Control solution: Prepare as described above for the *Sample solution*, but using a 1% solution of sample and omitting the locust bean gum.
  Acceptance criteria: For the *Sample solution*, a firm, rubbery gel forms after the temperature of the mixture drops below 40°. No such gel forms in the *Control solution*.

ASSAY

- **ALGINATES ASSAY**, Appendix IIIC
  Sample: 1.2 g
  Acceptance criteria: 4.2%–5.4% of carbon dioxide (corresponds to 91.0%–117.0% of xanthan gum), calculated on the dried basis

IMPURITIES

Inorganic Impurities
- **LEAD**, *Lead Limit Test, Flame Atomic Absorption Spectrophotometric Method*, Appendix IIIB
  Sample: 10 g
  Acceptance criteria: NMT 2 mg/kg

Change to read:

Organic Impurities
- **ETHANOL AND ISOPROPYL ALCOHOL**
  EtOH standard solution: 1 mg/mL of ethanol (chromatography grade) in water
  IPA standard solution: 1 mg/mL of isopropyl alcohol (chromatography grade) in water
  TBA standard solution: 1 mg/mL of *tert*-butyl alcohol (chromatography grade) in water
  Mixed standard solution: Pipet 4 mL each of the *EtOH standard solution*, the *IPA standard solution*, and the *TBA standard solution* into a 125-mL graduated conical flask, dilute to about 100 mL with water, and mix. The solution contains about 40 µg/mL each of ethanol, isopropyl alcohol, and *tert*-butyl alcohol.
  Sample: 5 g
  Sample solution: Disperse 1 mL of a suitable antifoam emulsion, such as Dow-Corning G-10, or equivalent, in 200 mL of water contained in a 1000-mL 24/40 round-bottom distilling flask. Add the *Sample* and shake for 1 h on a wrist-action mechanical shaker. Connect the flask to a fractionating column, and distill about 100 mL, adjusting the heat so that foam does not enter the column. Add 4.0 mL of *TBA standard solution* to the distillate to obtain the *Sample solution*.
  Chromatographic system, Appendix IIA
   Mode: Gas chromatography
   Detector type: Flame-ionization
   Column: 1.8-m × 3.2-mm (id) stainless steel, or equivalent, packed with 80- to 100-mesh Porapak QS, or equivalent
   Temperature
    Column: 165°
    Injection port: 200°
    Detector: 200°
   Carrier gas: Helium
   Flow rate: 80 mL/min
   Injection volume: About 5 µL
  Analysis: Inject the *Mixed standard solution* and separately inject the *Sample solution*. From the chromatogram of the *Mixed standard solution*, calculate the response factors for ethanol and isopropyl alcohol:

  $$R_{EtOH} = A_{EtOH}/A_{TBA}$$

  $$R_{IPA} = A_{IPA}/A_{TBA}$$

  A_{EtOH} = area of the ethanol peak
  A_{IPA} = area of the isopropyl alcohol peak
  A_{TBA} = area of the *tert*-butyl alcohol peak
  R_{EtOH} = response factor for ethanol
  R_{IPA} = response factor for isopropyl alcohol

From the chromatogram of the *Sample solution*, calculate the concentrations of ethanol and isopropyl alcohol in the *Sample* taken:

$$\text{EtOH (mg/kg)} = (S_{EtOH} \times 4000)/(R_{EtOH} \times S_{TBA} \times W)$$

$$\text{IPA (mg/kg)} = (S_{IPA} \times 4000)/(R_{IPA} \times S_{TBA} \times W)$$

S_{EtOH} = area of the ethanol peak
S_{IPA} = area of the isopropyl alcohol peak
S_{TBA} = area of the *tert*-butyl alcohol peak
W = weight of sample taken (g)

Acceptance criteria: NMT 0.075% ethanol and isopropyl alcohol, singly or combined

▲▲FCC8

SPECIFIC TESTS

- **LOSS ON DRYING,** Appendix IIC: 105° for 2.5 h
  Acceptance criteria: NMT 15.0%
- **VISCOSITY DETERMINATION,** *Viscosity of Cellulose Gum,* Appendix IIB
  Sample solution: 10 mg/mL of xanthan gum and 10 mg/mL of potassium chloride
  Analysis: Prepare a pair of identical *Sample solutions* and stir each for 2 h. Determine the viscosity (V_1) of one solution at 23.9°, using a No. 3 spindle rotating at 60 rpm (Brookfield, or equivalent). Determine the viscosity (V_2) of the other solution in the same manner, but maintain the temperature at 65.6°.
  Acceptance criteria
  V_1: NLT 600 cp
  (V_1/V_2): 1.02–1.45

Xylitol

First Published: Prior to FCC 6

1,2,3,4,5-Pentahydroxypentane

$C_5H_{12}O_5$ Formula wt 152.15
INS: 967   CAS: [87-99-0]
UNII: VCQ006KQ1E [xylitol]

DESCRIPTION

Xylitol occurs as white crystals or as a crystalline powder. One g dissolves in about 0.65 mL of water. It is sparingly soluble in ethanol.

Function: Nutritive sweetener
Packaging and Storage: Store in well-closed containers in a dry place.

IDENTIFICATION

- **INFRARED ABSORPTION,** *Spectrophotometric Identification Tests,* Appendix IIIC
  Reference standard: USP Xylitol RS
  Sample and standard preparation: K
  Acceptance criteria: The spectrum of the sample exhibits maxima at the same wavelengths as those in the spectrum of the *Reference standard*. [NOTE—If a difference appears, dissolve portions of both the sample and the *Reference standard* in a suitable solvent, evaporate the solutions to dryness, and repeat the test on the residues.]

ASSAY

- **PROCEDURE**
  Internal standard solution: 20 mg/mL erythritol
  Standard solution: 49 mg/mL USP Xylitol RS and 0.25 mg/mL each of L-arabinitol, galactitol, mannitol, and sorbitol
  Sample solution: 50 mg/mL
  Chromatographic system, Appendix IIA
    Mode: Gas chromatography
    Detector: Flame-ionization
    Column: 2-mm (id) × 2-m glass column, or equivalent, packed with 3% liquid phase of 25% phenyl-25% cyanopropylmethylsilicone; (OV-225, or equivalent) on silanized, siliceous earth support (Chromosorb W-HP, or equivalent)
    Temperature
      Column: 200°
      Injector port: 250°
      Detector: 250°
    Carrier gas: Nitrogen
    Flow rate: About 30 mL/minute
    Injection volume: 1 µL
  System suitability
    Sample: *Standard solution* (derivatized as directed under *Analysis*)
    Suitability requirement: The relative standard deviation of the response ratios of the derivatized xylitol to the derivatized erythritol from three replicate injections is NMT 2.0%.
  Analysis: Pipet 1-mL portions of the *Standard solution* and the *Sample solution* into separate 100-mL, round bottom boiling flasks. Add 1.0 mL of *Internal standard solution* to each flask, and evaporate each mixture to dryness on a water bath at 60° with the aid of a rotary evaporator. Dissolve each dry residue in 1 mL of pyridine, and add 1 mL of acetic anhydride to each flask. Boil each solution under reflux for 1 h to complete the acetylation. Inject the derivatized solutions into the chromatograph and measure the peak responses. [NOTE—The relative retention times corresponding to erythritol, L-arabinitol, xylitol, galactitol, mannitol, and sorbitol are usually about 1.0, 2.77, 3.90, 6.96, 7.63, and 8.43, respectively.]

  Calculate the percent of xylitol, on the as-is basis, by the formula:

  $$\text{Result} = 100\ (C_S/C_U)\ (r_U/r_S)$$

  C_S = concentration (mg/mL) of xylitol in the *Standard solution*
  C_U = concentration (mg/mL) of the *Sample solution*

r_U = peak response ratio of the derivatized analyte to the derivatized erythritol in the *Internal standard solution*, obtained from the chromatogram of the *Sample solution*

r_S = peak response ratio of the derivatized analyte to the derivatized erythritol in the *Internal standard solution*, obtained from the chromatogram of the *Standard solution*

Acceptance criteria: NLT 98.5% and NMT 101.0% of $C_5H_{12}O_5$, calculated on the anhydrous basis

IMPURITIES

Inorganic Impurities

- **LEAD,** *Lead Limit Test, Atomic Absorption Spectrophotometer Graphite Furnace Method, Method I,* Appendix IIIB
  Acceptance criteria: NMT 1 mg/kg
- **NICKEL,** *Nickel Limit Test,* Appendix IIIB
  Sample: 20.0 g
  Acceptance criteria: NMT 1 mg/kg

Organic Impurities

- **OTHER POLYOLS**
  Analysis: Determine as directed in the *Assay* (above) using the *Internal standard solution*, *Standard solution*, *Sample solution*, and *Chromatographic system* described therein. Modify the calculation under *Analysis* as follows. Calculate the percentage of each polyol (L-arabinitol, galactitol, mannitol, and sorbitol) by the formula:

  $$\text{Result} = 100\,(C_S/C_U)\,(r_U/r_S)$$

  C_S = concentration of the respective polyol (mg/mL) in the *Standard solution*
  C_U = concentration (mg/mL) of the *Sample solution*
  r_U = peak response ratio of the corresponding polyol obtained from the *Sample solution*
  r_S = peak response ratio of the corresponding polyol obtained from the *Standard solution*

  Add the four individual polyol percentages to obtain the total.
  Acceptance criteria: NMT 1.0%, combined

- **REDUCING SUGARS (AS GLUCOSE)**
  Sample solution: 500 mg in 2 mL of water
  Control: 2 mL of a 0.75 mg/mL dextrose solution
  Analysis: Transfer the *Sample solution* to a conical flask. Add 1 mL each of *The Copper Solution A* and *The Alkaline Tartrate Solution B* (see *cupric tartrate TS, alkaline,* Solutions and Indicators) to the flask, heat to boiling, and cool. Repeat the preceding using 2 mL of the *Control* in place of the *Sample solution*.
  Acceptance criteria: The *Sample solution* produces less turbidity than the *Control*, which forms a red-brown precipitate. (NMT 0.3%)

SPECIFIC TESTS

- **RESIDUE ON IGNITION (SULFATED ASH),** Appendix IIC
  Sample: 2 g
  Acceptance criteria: NMT 0.1%
- **WATER,** *Water Determination,* Appendix IIB
  Acceptance criteria: NMT 0.5%

Yeast, Autolyzed

First Published: Prior to FCC 6
Last Revision: Second Supplement, FCC 7

Autolyzed Yeast

DESCRIPTION
Yeast, Autolyzed, occurs in granular, powdered, flake, or paste form. It is the concentrated, nonextracted, partially soluble digest obtained from food-grade yeasts. Solubilization is accomplished by enzyme hydrolysis or autolysis of yeast cells. Food-grade salts and enzymes may be added. Yeast, Autolyzed, contains both soluble and insoluble components derived from the whole yeast cell. It is composed primarily of amino acids, peptides, proteins, carbohydrates, fats, and salts.
Function: Flavoring agent; flavor enhancer; protein source; binder
Packaging and Storage: Store in well-closed containers.

[NOTE—Perform all analyses using a sample previously dried as follows: Liquid and paste samples should be evaporated to dryness on a steam bath, then, as for the powdered and granular forms, dried to constant weight at 65° (see *General Provisions*).]

ASSAY
- **PROTEIN,** *Nitrogen Determination,* Appendix IIIC
  Analysis: Calculate the percentage of protein:

  Result = N × F

  N = percentage of nitrogen
  F = nitrogen-to-protein conversion factor, 6.25
  Acceptance criteria: NLT 38.1% protein (NLT 6.1% nitrogen), calculated on the sodium chloride-free basis

IMPURITIES
Inorganic Impurities
- **LEAD,** *Lead Limit Test, Flame Atomic Absorption Spectrophotometric Method,* Appendix IIIB
  Sample: 10 g
  Acceptance criteria: NMT 2 mg/kg
- **MERCURY,** *Mercury Limit Test,* Appendix IIIB
  Acceptance criteria: NMT 3 mg/kg

SPECIFIC TESTS
- **α-AMINO NITROGEN/TOTAL NITROGEN (AN/TN) PERCENT RATIO,** α-*Amino Nitrogen (AN) Determination,* Appendix IIIC and *Total Nitrogen (TN), Nitrogen Determination,* Appendix IIIC
  Analysis: Calculate the AN/TN percent ratio, as corrected for *Ammonia Nitrogen*:

  Result = [(AN − AmN)/(TN − AmN)] × 100

  AN = percentage of α-*Amino Nitrogen*
  AmN = percentage of *Ammonia Nitrogen* determined below
  TN = percentage of *Total Nitrogen*

  Acceptance criteria: NLT 5.0%
- **AMMONIA NITROGEN,** *Ammonia Nitrogen (NH$_3$-N) Determination,* Appendix IIIC
  Acceptance criteria: NMT 1.0%, calculated on the sodium chloride-free basis
- **GLUTAMIC ACID,** Appendix IIIC
  Acceptance criteria: NMT 13.0% as C$_5$H$_9$NO$_4$ calculated on the sodium chloride-free basis, and NMT 24.0% of the total protein
- **INSOLUBLE MATTER**
  Sample: 5 g
  Analysis: Transfer the *Sample* into a 250-mL Erlenmeyer flask, add 75 mL of water, cover the flask with a watch glass, and boil gently for 2 min. Filter the solution through a tared filtering crucible, dry the crucible at 105° for 1 h, cool, and weigh.
  Acceptance criteria: 20.0%–60.0%
- **MICROBIAL LIMITS**
  [NOTE—Current methods for the following tests may be found in the Food and Drug Administration's Bacteriological Analytical Manual online at www.cfsan.fda.gov.]
  Acceptance criteria
   Aerobic plate count: NMT 50,000 CFU/g
   Coliforms: NMT 10 CFU/g
   Salmonella: Negative in 25 g
   Yeasts and Molds: NMT 50 CFU/g
- **POTASSIUM**
  Standard stock solution: 200 µg/mL potassium in deionized water prepared as follows: Transfer 38.20 mg of reagent-grade potassium chloride into a 100-mL volumetric flask, add deionized water to dissolve the salt, dilute with deionized water to volume, and mix.
  Standard solution: 1.0 µg/mL potassium in deionized water from the *Standard stock solution*
  Sample stock solution: Transfer 2.33 g of sample into a silica or porcelain dish. Ash it in a muffle furnace at 550° for 2–4 h. Allow the ash to cool and add 5 mL of 20% hydrochloric acid. If necessary, warm the mixture to completely dissolve the residue. Filter the solution through acid-washed filter paper into a 1000-mL volumetric flask. Wash the filter paper with hot water, dilute the solution to volume, and mix.
  Sample solution: 1:300 dilution of the *Sample stock solution*
  Analysis: Using a suitable spectrophotometer, measure the absorbance of the *Sample solution* and the *Standard solution* at 766.5 nm.
  Acceptance criteria: The absorbance of the *Sample solution* does not exceed that of the *Standard solution*. (NMT 13.0%)
- **SODIUM CHLORIDE**
  Standard stock solution: 430 µg/mL sodium chloride in deionized water
  Standard solution: 4.3 µg/mL sodium chloride in deionized water from the *Standard stock solution*
  Sample stock solution: Transfer 1.0 ± 0.05 g of sample into a silica or porcelain dish. Ash in a muffle furnace at 550° for 2–4 h. Allow the ash to cool and add 5 mL of 20% hydrochloric acid. If necessary, warm the mixture to completely dissolve the residue. Filter the solution

through acid-washed filter paper into a 100-mL volumetric flask. Wash the filter paper with hot water, dilute the solution to volume, and mix.
Sample solution: 1:100 dilution of the *Sample stock solution*
Analysis: Using a suitable spectrophotometer, measure the absorbance of the *Sample solution* and the *Standard solution* at 589.0 nm.
Acceptance criteria: The absorbance of the *Sample solution* does not exceed that of the *Standard solution*. (NMT 50.0%)

Yeast, Dried
First Published: Prior to FCC 6

Brewer's Yeast
Dried Yeast
Torula Yeast
UNII: 3NY3SM6B8U [yeast]

DESCRIPTION
Yeast, Dried, occurs as a light brown to buff powder, granules, or flakes. It is the comminuted, washed, dried, and pasteurized cell walls from *Saccharomyces cerevisiae*, *Saccharomyces fragilis*, or *Torula utilis*. It contains no added substances.
Function: Carrier; flavor-enhancer
Packaging and Storage: Store in tight containers in a cool, dry place.

IDENTIFICATION
- **MICROSCOPY**
  Acceptance criteria: A sample exhibits numerous irregular masses and isolated yeast cells—the latter ovate, elliptical, spheroidal, or elliptic-elongate in shape, some with one or more attached buds—up to 12 μm in length and up to 7.5 μm in width. Each has a wall of cellulose surrounding a protoplast containing refractile glycogen vacuoles and oil globules.

ASSAY
- **PROTEIN,** *Nitrogen Determination,* Appendix IIIC
  Analysis: Calculate the percent protein by the formula:

  $$Result = N \times F$$

  N = percent nitrogen
  F = nitrogen-to-protein conversion factor, 6.25
  Acceptance criteria: NLT 45.0% protein

IMPURITIES
Inorganic Impurities
- **LEAD,** *Lead Limit Test, Atomic Absorption Spectrophotometric Graphite Furnace Method, Method II,* Appendix IIIB
  Acceptance criteria: NMT 1 mg/kg

SPECIFIC TESTS
- **ASH (TOTAL),** Appendix IIC
  Acceptance criteria: NMT 8.0%

- **FOLIC ACID**
  [NOTE—In the microbiological assay of folic acid, the microorganism is highly sensitive to minute amounts of growth factors and to many cleansing agents. Meticulously clean 20- × 150-mm test tubes and other necessary glassware with a suitable detergent, sodium lauryl sulfate, or an equivalent substitute. Follow cleaning by heating for 1 to 2 h at approximately 250°. The following method is based on AOAC method 960.46.]
  Vitamin-free, acid-hydrolyzed casein solution: Mix 400 g of vitamin-free casein with 2 L of boiling 5 N hydrochloric acid. Autoclave for 10 h at 121°. Concentrate the mixture by distillation under reduced pressure until a thick paste remains. Redissolve the paste in water, adjust the solution to pH 3.5 ± 0.1 with a 10% solution of sodium hydroxide, and dilute with water to a final volume of 4 L. Add 80 g of activated charcoal, stir for 1 h, and filter. Repeat the treatment with activated charcoal. Filter the solution if a precipitate forms on storage.
  Adenine–guanine–uracil solution: Dissolve 1.0 g each of adenine sulfate, guanine hydrochloride, and uracil in 50 mL of warm 1:2 hydrochloric acid, cool, and dilute with water to 1 L.
  Asparagine solution: 10 mg/mL of L-asparagine monohydrate
  Manganese sulfate solution: 10 mg/mL of manganese sulfate monohydrate
  Polysorbate 80 solution: 100 mg/mL in ethyl alcohol
  Salt solution: Dissolve 20 g of magnesium sulfate heptahydrate, 1 g of sodium chloride, 1 g of ferrous sulfate heptahydrate, and 1 g of manganese sulfate monohydrate in water, dilute with water to 1 L, add 10 drops of hydrochloric acid, and mix.
  Tryptophan solution: Suspend 2.0 g of L-tryptophan in 800 mL of water, heat to 80°, and add, dropwise and while stirring, 1:2 hydrochloric acid until the suspension dissolves. Cool, and dilute with water to 1 L.
  Vitamin solution: Dissolve 10 mg of p-aminobenzoic acid, 8 mg of calcium pantothenate, 40 mg of pyridoxine hydrochloride, 4 mg of thiamine hydrochloride, 8 mg of niacin, and 0.2 mg of biotin in approximately 300 mL of water. Add 10 mg of riboflavin dissolved in approximately 200 mL of 0.02 N acetic acid. Add a solution containing 1.9 g of anhydrous sodium acetate and 1.6 mL of glacial acetic acid in approximately 40 mL of water. Dilute the solution with water to a final volume of 2 L.
  Xanthine solution: Suspend 1.0 g of xanthine in 200 mL of water, heat to approximately 70°, add 30 mL of 2:5 ammonium hydroxide, and stir until the suspension dissolves. Cool the solution and dilute with water to 1 L.
  Basal medium stock solution: Add, with mixing, in the following order: 25 mL of the *Vitamin-free, acid-hydrolyzed casein solution,* 25 mL of the *Tryptophan solution,* 2.5 mL of the *Adenine–guanine–uracil solution,* 5 mL of the *Xanthine solution,* 15 mL of the *Asparagine solution,* 50 mL of the *Vitamin solution,* and 5 mL of the *Salt solution.* Add approximately 50 mL of water, and

add, with mixing, 0.19 g of L-cysteine monohydrochloride monohydrate, 10 g of anhydrous glucose, 13 g of sodium citrate dihydrate, 1.6 g of anhydrous dipotassium hydrogen phosphate, and 0.0013 g of glutathione. When solution is complete, adjust to pH 6.8 with 10% sodium hydroxide solution, and add, with mixing, 0.25 mL of the *Polysorbate 80 solution* and 5 mL of the *Manganese sulfate solution*. Dilute to a final volume of 250 mL with water.

Liquid culture medium: Dissolve 15 g of peptonized milk, 5 g of water-soluble yeast extract, 10 g of anhydrous glucose, and 2 g of anhydrous potassium dihydrogen phosphate in about 600 mL of water. Add 100 mL of filtered tomato juice (use Whatman No. 1 filter paper, or equivalent), and adjust to pH 6.5 by the dropwise addition of 1.0 N sodium hydroxide. Add, with mixing, 10 mL of the *Polysorbate 80 solution*. Dilute with water to a final volume of 1000 mL. Add 10-mL portions of this solution to test tubes, cover the tubes to prevent contamination, and sterilize them by heating in an autoclave at 121° for 15 min. Cool the tubes rapidly to keep color formation to a minimum, and store at 10° in the dark.

Agar culture medium: Add 6.0 g of agar to 500 mL of *Liquid culture medium*, and heat with stirring on a steam bath until the agar dissolves. Add approximately 10-mL portions of the hot solution to test tubes, cover them to prevent contamination, and sterilize them by heating in an autoclave at 121° for 15 min. Then, cool the tubes in an upright position to keep color formation to a minimum. Store them at 10° in the dark.

Suspension medium: Dilute an appropriate volume of the *Basal medium stock solution* with an equal volume of water. Distribute 10-mL portions of this solution to test tubes, cover the tubes to prevent contamination, sterilize them by heating in an autoclave at 121° for 15 min, and cool them rapidly to keep color formation to a minimum. Store them at 10° in the dark.

Test organism: Maintain *Enterococcus (Streptococcus) faecalis* ATCC 8043 by subculturing in stab cultures of *Agar culture medium* and incubating at 37° for 24 h. [NOTE—Stab cultures may be stored in the dark at 10° for a maximum of 7 days until use and should be prepared fresh at least on a weekly basis.]

Inoculum: Before using a new culture in the test, make several successive transfers of the culture over a 1- to 2-week period. Transfer cells from the stab culture of the *Test organism* to a sterile tube containing 10 mL of *Liquid culture medium*. Incubate the tube for 18 h at 37°. Under aseptic conditions, centrifuge the culture, and decant the supernatant. Wash the cells with three 10-mL portions of sterile *Suspension medium* and resuspend them in 10 mL of sterile *Suspension medium*—these cells serve as the *Inoculum*.

Folic acid stock solution: Weigh, in a closed system, 50 to 60 mg of USP Folic Acid RS that has been dried to constant weight and stored in the dark over phosphorus pentoxide in a desiccator. Dissolve in approximately 30 mL of 0.01 N sodium hydroxide, add approximately 300 mL of water, adjust to pH 7.5 with 1:2 hydrochloric acid, and dilute with additional water to a final folic acid concentration of exactly 100 µg/mL. Store under toluene in the dark at 10°.

Intermediate folic acid stock solution: 1 µg/mL, prepared by placing 10 mL of the *Folic acid stock solution* in a flask, adding approximately 500 mL of water, adjusting to pH 7.5 with dilute hydrochloric acid or sodium hydroxide as necessary, and diluting with additional water to a final volume of 1 L. Store under toluene in the dark at 10°.

Final folic acid stock solution: 100 ng/mL, prepared by taking 100 mL of the *Intermediate folic acid stock solution*, adding approximately 500 mL of water, adjusting to pH 7.5 with dilute hydrochloric acid or sodium hydroxide as necessary, and diluting with additional water to a final volume of 1 L. Store under toluene in the dark at 10°.

Folic acid standard solution: Dilute the *Final folic acid stock solution* with water to a measured volume such that after incubation, as described below, response at the 5.0-mL level of this solution is equivalent to a titration volume of 8 to 12 mL. This concentration is usually 1–4 ng/mL of folic acid, but it can vary with the culture used in the assay.

Standard curve: To duplicate test tubes, add 0.0 (for uninoculated blanks), 0.0 (for inoculated blanks), 1.0, 2.0, 3.0, 4.0, and 5.0 mL, respectively, of the *Folic acid standard solution*. Add water to each tube to make a final volume of 5.0 mL. Add 5.0 mL of the *Basal medium stock solution* to each tube, and mix. Cover the tubes suitably to prevent bacterial contamination and sterilize them by heating them in an autoclave at 121° for 10 min. Cool the tubes rapidly to keep color formation to a minimum. [NOTE—Sterilizing and cooling conditions must be kept uniform to obtain reproducible results.] Aseptically inoculate each tube with 1 drop of the *Inoculum*, except for one set of duplicate tubes containing 0.0 mL of the *Folic acid standard solution*, which serve as the uninoculated blanks. Incubate the tubes for 72 h at 37°. [NOTE—Contamination of assay tubes with any foreign organism invalidates the test.] Titrate the contents of each tube with 0.1 N sodium hydroxide, using bromothymol blue as the indicator. Disregard the results of the test if the titration volume for the inoculated blank is more than 1.5 mL greater than that for the uninoculated blank. The titration volume for the 5.0-mL level of the *Folic acid standard solution* should be approximately 8 to 12 mL. Plot the titration values (mL of 0.1 N sodium hydroxide) for each level of the *Folic acid standard solution* used against the amount of folic acid contained in that tube.

Sample solution: Weigh and suspend 1.0 g of sample in 100 mL of water. Add 2 mL of 2:5 ammonium hydroxide. If the sample is not readily soluble, comminute it so that it disperses evenly in the liquid, then agitate the mixture vigorously and wash down the sides of the flask with 0.1 N ammonium hydroxide. Heat the mixture in an autoclave at 121° for 15 min. If lumping occurs, agitate the sample until the particles are evenly dispersed. Dilute the mixture with water to 200 mL. Filter through Whatman No. 1 filter paper, or equivalent, if necessary, to remove any undissolved particles. Adjust the filtered mixture to pH 6.8 and dilute to 1000 mL with water. Take 1.0 mL of this solution and dilute with water to a final volume of 50.0 mL.

Analysis: To duplicate test tubes, add 0.0 (for uninoculated blanks), 0.0 (for inoculated blanks), 1.0, 2.0, 3.0, 4.0, and 5.0 mL, respectively, of the *Sample solution*. Add water to each tube to make a final volume of 5.0 mL. Add 5.0 mL of the *Basal medium stock solution* to each tube, and mix. Cover the tubes suitably to prevent bacterial contamination and sterilize them by heating them in an autoclave at 121° for 10 min. Cool the tubes rapidly to keep color formation to a minimum. [NOTE—Sterilizing and cooling conditions must be kept uniform to obtain reproducible results.] Aseptically inoculate each tube with 1 drop of the *Inoculum*. Incubate the tubes for 72 h at 37°. [NOTE—Contamination of assay tubes with any foreign organism invalidates the test.] Titrate the contents of each tube with 0.1 N sodium hydroxide, using bromothymol blue as the indicator. Determine the amount of folic acid for each level of the *Sample solution* by interpolation from the *Standard curve*. Discard any observed titration values equivalent to less than 0.5 mL or more than 4.5 mL of the *Folic acid standard solution*. If necessary, the *Sample solution* can be diluted to achieve the ideal concentration range of folic acid. For each level of *Sample solution* used, calculate the vitamin content per mL of *Sample solution*. Calculate the average vitamin content of values obtained from tubes that do not vary by greater than 10% from this average. More than two-thirds of the original number of tubes must be within 10% of the average folic acid value or the data cannot be used to calculate the folic acid concentration in the sample. If the data are acceptable, determine the folic acid concentration in the sample by multiplying the average folic acid concentration (ng/mL) of the *Sample solution* by 0.025 to give the concentration (mg/g) of folic acid in the sample.

Acceptance criteria: NMT 0.04 mg/g

- **LOSS ON DRYING,** Appendix IIC: 105° for 4 h
  Sample: 1 g
  Acceptance criteria: NMT 7.0%
- **MICROBIAL LIMITS**
  [NOTE—Current methods for the following tests may be found in the Food and Drug Administration's Bacteriological Analytical Manual online at www.cfsan.fda.gov.]
  Acceptance criteria
  Aerobic plate count: NMT 7500 CFU/g
  Coliforms: NMT 10 CFU/g
  Salmonella: Negative in 25 g

Yeast Extract

First Published: Prior to FCC 6
Last Revision: Third Supplement, FCC 7

Autolyzed Yeast Extract
UNII: 3NY3SM6B8U [yeast]

DESCRIPTION
Yeast Extract occurs as a liquid, paste, powder, or granular substance. It comprises the water-soluble components of the yeast cell, the composition of which is primarily amino acids, peptides, carbohydrates, and salts. Yeast Extract is produced through the hydrolysis of peptide bonds by the naturally occurring enzymes present in edible yeasts or by the addition of food-grade enzymes. Food-grade salts may be added during processing.
Function: Flavoring agent; flavor enhancer
Packaging and Storage: Store in well-closed containers.

[NOTE—Perform all calculations on the dried basis. In a suitable tared container, evaporate liquid and paste samples to dryness on a steam bath, then, as for the powdered and granular forms, dry to constant weight at 105° (see *General Provisions*).]

ASSAY
- **PROTEIN,** *Nitrogen Determination,* Appendix IIIC
  Analysis: Calculate the percentage of protein:

  $$\text{Result} = N \times 6.25$$

  N = percentage of nitrogen
  6.25 = nitrogen-to-protein conversion factor
  Acceptance criteria: NLT 42.0% protein

IMPURITIES
Inorganic Impurities
- **LEAD,** *Lead Limit Test, Flame Atomic Absorption Spectrophotometric Method,* Appendix IIIB
  Sample: 10 g
  Acceptance criteria: NMT 2 mg/kg
- **MERCURY,** *Mercury Limit Test,* Appendix IIIB
  Acceptance criteria: NMT 3 mg/kg

SPECIFIC TESTS
- **α-AMINO NITROGEN/TOTAL NITROGEN (AN/TN) PERCENT RATIO,** *α-Amino Nitrogen (AN) Determination,* Appendix IIIC and *Nitrogen Determination,* Appendix IIIC
  Analysis: Calculate the AN/TN percent ratio, where AN is the percentage of α-Amino Nitrogen and TN is the percentage of total nitrogen determined from the *Nitrogen Determination* test.
  Acceptance criteria: 15.0%–55.0%
- **AMMONIA NITROGEN,** *Ammonia Nitrogen (NH$_3$-N) Determination,* Appendix IIIC
  Acceptance criteria: NMT 2.0%, calculated on the sodium chloride-free basis
- **INSOLUBLE MATTER**
  Sample: 5 g
  Analysis: Transfer the *Sample* into a 250-mL Erlenmeyer flask, add 75 mL of water, cover the flask with a watch

glass, and boil gently for 2 min. Filter the solution through a tared filtering crucible, dry the crucible at 105° for 1 h, cool, and weigh.
Acceptance criteria: NMT 2%

- **MICROBIAL LIMITS**
  [NOTE—Current methods for the following tests may be found in the Food and Drug Administration's Bacteriological Analytical Manual online at www.cfsan.fda.gov.]
  Acceptance criteria
  Aerobic plate count: NMT 50,000 cfu/g
  Coliforms: NMT 10 cfu/g
  Salmonella: Negative in 25 g
  Yeasts and Molds: NMT 50 cfu/g

- **POTASSIUM**
  Standard stock solution: 200 µg/mL of potassium in deionized water prepared as follows. Transfer 38.20 mg of reagent-grade potassium chloride into a 100-mL volumetric flask, add deionized water to dissolve the salt, dilute with deionized water to volume, and mix.
  Standard solution: 1.0 µg/mL of potassium in deionized water from the *Standard stock solution*
  Sample stock solution: Transfer 2.33 g of sample into a silica or porcelain dish. Ash it in a muffle furnace at 550° for 2–4 h. Allow the ash to cool, and add 5 mL of 20% hydrochloric acid. If necessary, warm the mixture to completely dissolve the residue. Filter the solution through acid-washed filter paper into a 1000-mL volumetric flask. Wash the filter paper with hot water, dilute the solution to volume, and mix.
  Sample solution: 1:300 dilution of the *Sample stock solution*
  Analysis: Using a suitable spectrophotometer, measure the absorbance of the *Sample solution* and the *Standard solution* at 766.5 nm.
  Acceptance criteria: The absorbance of the *Sample solution* does not exceed that of the *Standard solution*. (NMT 13.0%)

- **SODIUM CHLORIDE**
  Standard stock solution: 500 µg/mL of sodium chloride in deionized water
  Standard solution: 5.0 µg/mL of sodium chloride in deionized water from the *Standard stock solution*
  Sample stock solution: Transfer 1.0 ± 0.05 g of sample into a silica or porcelain dish. Ash in a muffle furnace at 550° for 2–4 h. Allow the ash to cool, and add 5 mL of 20% hydrochloric acid. If necessary, warm the mixture to completely dissolve the residue. Filter the solution through acid-washed filter paper into a 100-mL volumetric flask. Wash the filter paper with hot water, dilute the solution to volume, and mix.
  Sample solution: 1:100 dilution of the *Sample stock solution*
  Analysis: Using a suitable spectrophotometer, measure the absorbance of the *Sample solution* and the *Standard solution* at 589.0 nm.
  Acceptance criteria: The absorbance of the *Sample solution* does not exceed that of the *Standard solution*. (NMT 50.0%)

Zein

First Published: Prior to FCC 6

CAS: [9010-66-6]

UNII: 80N308T1NN [zein]

DESCRIPTION
Zein occurs as a very light yellow to tan colored, granular or fine powder. It comprises the prolamine protein component of corn (*Zea mays* Linné). It is produced commercially by extraction from corn gluten with alkaline aqueous isopropyl alcohol. The extract is then cooled, which causes the Zein to precipitate. It is insoluble in water.

Function: Surface-finishing agent; texturizing agent
Packaging and Storage: Store in well-closed containers.

IDENTIFICATION
- **A. Procedure**
  Sample: 0.1 g
  Analysis: Dissolve the *Sample* in 10 mL of 0.1 N sodium hydroxide, add a few drops of cupric sulfate TS, and warm the solution in a water bath.
  Acceptance criteria: A purple color appears.
- **B. Procedure**
  Sample: 25 mg
  Analysis: Add 1 mL of nitric acid to a test tube containing the *Sample*. Agitate the tube vigorously until the solution turns light yellow. Add about 10 mL of 6 N ammonium hydroxide.
  Acceptance criteria: An orange color is produced.

ASSAY
- **Protein,** *Nitrogen Determination,* Appendix IIIC
  Analysis: Calculate the percent protein by the formula:

  $$Result = N \times F$$

  N = percent nitrogen
  F = nitrogen-to-protein conversion factor, 6.25
  Acceptance criteria: NLT 88.0% and NMT 96.0% protein, calculated on the dried basis

IMPURITIES
Inorganic Impurities
- **Lead,** *Lead Limit Test, Flame Atomic Absorption Spectrophotometric Method,* Appendix IIIB
  Sample: 10 g
  Acceptance criteria: NMT 2 mg/kg

SPECIFIC TESTS
- **Loss on Drying,** Appendix IIC: 105° for 2 h in an air oven
  Sample: 2 g
  Acceptance criteria: NMT 8.0%
- **Loss on Ignition, Ash (Total),** Appendix IIC
  Sample: 2 g
  Acceptance criteria: NMT 2%

Zinc Gluconate

First Published: Prior to FCC 6

$C_{12}H_{22}O_{14}Zn$ Formula wt 455.68
                                          CAS: [4468-02-4]
UNII: U6WSN5SQ1Z [zinc gluconate]

DESCRIPTION
Zinc Gluconate occurs as a white or nearly white, granular or crystalline powder and as a mixture of various states of hydration, up to the trihydrate, depending on the method of isolation. It is freely soluble in water and very slightly soluble in alcohol.

Function: Nutrient
Packaging and Storage: Store in well-closed containers.

IDENTIFICATION
- **Zinc,** Appendix IIIA
  Sample: 100 mg/mL
  Acceptance criteria: Passes test
- **Thin-Layer Chromatography,** Appendix IIA
  Sample solution: 10 mg/mL in water
  Standard solution: 10 mg/mL of USP Potassium Gluconate RS in water
  [Note—*Sample solution* and *Standard solution* (above), if necessary, can be heated in a water bath at 60° to aid dissolution.]
  Adsorbent: 0.25-mm layer of chromatographic silica gel
  Application volume: 5 µL
  Developing solvent system: Alcohol, water, ammonium hydroxide, and ethyl acetate, [5:3:1:1]
  Analysis: Following development, dry the plate at 110° for 20 min, and allow to cool. Spray the cooled plate with a solution of 25 mg/mL of ammonium molybdate and 10 mg/mL of ceric sulfate in 2 N sulfuric acid. After spraying, heat the plate at 110° for about 10 minutes.
  Acceptance criteria: The principal spot obtained from the *Sample solution* corresponds in color, size, and R_f value to that obtained from the *Standard solution*.

ASSAY
- **Procedure**
  Sample: 700 mg
  Analysis: Dissolve the sample in 100 mL of water, warming if necessary to aid dissolution. Add 5 mL of ammonia–ammonium chloride buffer TS and 0.1 mL of eriochrome black TS. Titrate with 0.05 M disodium EDTA until the solution turns blue. Each mL of 0.05 M disodium EDTA is equivalent to 22.78 mg of $C_{12}H_{22}O_{14}Zn$.
  Acceptance criteria: NLT 97.0% and NMT 102.0% of $C_{12}H_{22}O_{14}Zn$, calculated on the anhydrous basis

1206 / Zinc Gluconate / Monographs

IMPURITIES
Inorganic Impurities
- **CADMIUM,** *Cadmium Limit Test,* Appendix IIIB
  Acceptance criteria: NMT 2 mg/kg
- **CHLORIDE,** *Chloride Limit Test,* Appendix IIIB
  Sample: 40 mg
  Control: 20 µg chloride (2 mL of *Standard Chloride Solution*)
  Acceptance criteria: Any turbidity produced by the *Sample* does not exceed that shown in the *Control* (NMT 0.05%).
- **LEAD,** *Lead limit Test, Flame Atomic Absorption Spectrophotometric Method,* Appendix IIIB
  Sample: 5 g
  Acceptance criteria: NMT 2 mg/kg
- **SULFATE,** *Chloride and Sulfate Limit Tests, Chloride Limit Test,* Appendix IIIB
  Sample: 500 mg
  Control: 250 µg sulfate (25 mL of *Standard Sulfate Solution*)
  Acceptance criteria: Any turbidity produced by the *Sample* does not exceed that shown in the *Control* (NMT 0.05%).

SPECIFIC TESTS
- **REDUCING SUBSTANCES**
  Sample: 1 g
  Analysis: Transfer the *Sample* to a 250-mL Erlenmeyer flask and dissolve it in 10 mL of water. Add 25 mL of alkaline cupric citrate TS. Cover the flask with a small beaker, boil gently for exactly 5 min, and cool rapidly to room temperature. Add 25 mL of a 1:10 acetic acid solution, 10.0 mL of 0.1 N iodine, 10 mL of 2.7 N hydrochloric acid, and 3 mL of starch TS. Titrate with 0.1 N sodium thiosulfate until the blue color disappears.
  Calculate the weight (mg) of reducing substances (as D-glucose) in the *Sample* taken, from the formula:

  $$Result = (V_1N_1 - V_2N_2) \times 27$$

  V_1 = volume (mL) of the iodine solution
  V_2 = volume (mL) of the sodium thiosulfate solution
  N_1 = normality of the iodine solution
  N_2 = normality of the sodium thiosulfate solution
  [NOTE—27 is an empirically determined equivalence factor for D-glucose.]
  Acceptance criteria: NMT 1.0%
- **WATER,** *Water Determination, Method Ib (Residual Titration),* Appendix IIB
  Acceptance criteria: NMT 11.6%

OTHER REQUIREMENTS
- **LABELING:** Indicate the powder or granular form of the product.

Zinc Oxide
First Published: Prior to FCC 6
Last Revision: First Supplement, FCC 6

ZnO   Formula wt 81.38
       CAS: [1314-13-2]
UNII: SOI2LOH54Z [zinc oxide]

DESCRIPTION
Zinc Oxide occurs as a fine, white, amorphous powder. It gradually absorbs carbon dioxide from the air. It is insoluble in water and in alcohol, and is soluble in dilute acids and in strong bases.
Function: Nutrient
Packaging and Storage: Store in well-closed containers.

IDENTIFICATION
- **A. ZINC,** Appendix IIIA
  Sample solution: Dissolve a sample in a slight excess of 3 N hydrochloric acid.
  Acceptance criteria: Passes tests
- **B. PROCEDURE**
  Analysis: Strongly heat a sample.
  Acceptance criteria: A yellow color forms that disappears on cooling.

ASSAY
- **PROCEDURE**
  Sample: 1.5 g, freshly ignited
  Analysis: Dissolve the *Sample* and 2.5 g of ammonium chloride in 50 mL of 1 N sulfuric acid with the aid of gentle heat, if necessary. When solution is complete, add methyl orange TS and titrate the excess sulfuric acid with 1 N sodium hydroxide. Each mL of 1 N sulfuric acid is equivalent to 40.69 mg of ZnO.
  Acceptance criteria: NLT 99.0% of ZnO, on the ignited basis

IMPURITIES
Inorganic Impurities
- **CADMIUM,** *Cadmium Limit Test,* Appendix IIIB
  Sample solution: Transfer 5 g of sample into a 50-mL volumetric flask, dissolve the sample in a minimum volume of 2:3 hydrochloric acid, dilute with water to volume, and mix.
  Acceptance criteria: NMT 3 mg/kg
- **LEAD,** *Lead Limit Test, APDC Extraction Method,* Appendix IIIB
  Acceptance criteria: NMT 10 mg/kg
- **SUBSTANCES NOT PRECIPITATED BY SULFIDE**
  Sample: 2 g
  Analysis: Transfer the *Sample* into a 200-mL flask and dissolve it in 20 mL of 1:4 acetic acid. Dilute with water to about 150 mL, and mix. Precipitate the zinc completely with ammonium sulfide TS, dilute with water to volume, and mix. Pass through a dry filter, discarding the first portion of filtrate, and collect 100 mL of the subsequent filtrate. Add a few drops of sulfuric acid to the collected filtrate, and evaporate to dryness on a steam bath in a tared dish. Ignite cautiously until the ammonium salts are volatilized,

ignite to constant weight at 800° ± 25°, cool, and weigh.
Acceptance criteria: The weight of the residue does not exceed 5 mg. (NMT 0.5%)

SPECIFIC TESTS
- **ALKALINITY**
  Sample: 2 g
  Analysis: Suspend the *Sample* in 20 mL of water, boil for 1 min, filter, and add 0.1 mL of phenolphthalein TS to the filtrate.
  Acceptance criteria: No red color appears.
- **LOSS ON IGNITION**
  Sample: 2 g
  Analysis: Ignite at 800° ± 25° to constant weight.
  Acceptance criteria: NMT 1.0%

Zinc Sulfate

First Published: Prior to FCC 6
Last Revision: First Supplement, FCC 6

$ZnSO_4 \cdot H_2O$ Formula wt, monohydrate 179.45
$ZnSO_4 \cdot 7H_2O$ Formula wt, heptahydrate 287.54
CAS: monohydrate [7446-19-7]
heptahydrate [7446-20-0]
UNII: N57JI2K7WP [zinc sulfate heptahydrate]
UNII: PTX099XSF1 [zinc sulfate monohydrate]

DESCRIPTION
Zinc Sulfate occurs as colorless, transparent prisms or small needles, or as a granular, crystalline powder. It contains one or seven molecules of water of hydration. The monohydrate loses water at temperatures above 238°; the heptahydrate effloresces in dry air at room temperature. Its solutions are acid to litmus. The monohydrate is soluble in water and practically insoluble in alcohol. One g of the heptahydrate dissolves in about 0.6 mL of water and in about 2.5 mL of glycerin; it is insoluble in alcohol.
Function: Nutrient
Packaging and Storage: Store in tight containers.

IDENTIFICATION
- **SULFATE,** Appendix IIIA
  Sample solution: 50 mg/mL
  Acceptance criteria: Passes tests
- **ZINC,** Appendix IIIA
  Sample solution: 50 mg/mL
  Acceptance criteria: Passes tests

ASSAY
- **PROCEDURE**
  Sample: 175 mg of the monohydrate, or 300 mg of the heptahydrate
  Analysis: Dissolve the *Sample* in 100 mL of water, and add 5 mL of ammonia–ammonium chloride buffer TS and 0.1 mL of eriochrome black TS. Titrate with 0.05 M disodium EDTA until the solution turns deep blue. Each mL of 0.05 M disodium EDTA is equivalent to 8.973 mg of $ZnSO_4 \cdot H_2O$, or 14.38 mg of $ZnSO_4 \cdot 7H_2O$.
  Acceptance criteria
    Monohydrate: NLT 98.0% and NMT 100.5% of $ZnSO_4 \cdot H_2O$
    Heptahydrate: NLT 99.0% and NMT 108.7% of $ZnSO_4 \cdot 7H_2O$

IMPURITIES
- **ALKALIES AND ALKALINE EARTHS**
  Sample: 2 g
  Analysis: Transfer the *Sample* into a 200-mL volumetric flask, dissolve the sample in about 150 mL of water, and precipitate the zinc completely with ammonium sulfide TS. Dilute with water to volume, and mix. Filter the contents of the flask through a dry filter, rejecting the first portion of the filtrate, and add a few drops of sulfuric acid to 100 mL of the subsequent filtrate. Evaporate to dryness in a tared dish, ignite to constant weight, cool, and weigh.
  Acceptance criteria: The weight of the residue does not exceed 5 mg. (NMT 0.5%)
- **CADMIUM,** *Cadmium Limit Test,* Appendix IIIB
  Acceptance criteria: NMT 2 mg/kg
- **LEAD,** *Lead Limit Test, APDC Extraction Method,* Appendix IIIB
  Acceptance criteria: NMT 4 mg/kg
- **MERCURY,** *Mercury Limit Test,* Appendix IIIB
  Sample preparation: Dissolve 400 mg of sample in 10 mL of water in a small beaker, add 1 mL of 1:5 sulfuric acid solution, and 1 mL of 1:25 potassium permanganate solution. Cover the beaker, boil for a few seconds, and cool.
  Acceptance criteria: NMT 5 mg/kg
- **SELENIUM,** *Selenium Limit Test, Method I,* Appendix IIIB
  Sample: 200 mg
  Acceptance criteria: NMT 0.003%

SPECIFIC TESTS
- **ACIDITY**
  Sample solution: 50 mg/mL
  Analysis: Add methyl orange TS to the *Sample solution*.
  Acceptance criteria: No pink color appears.

Zingerone

First Published: Prior to FCC 6
Last Revision: Second Supplement, FCC 7

$C_{11}H_{14}O_3$ Formula wt 194.23
FEMA: 3124
UNII: 4MMW850892 [zingerone]

DESCRIPTION
Zingerone occurs as a yellow to yellow-brown fused mass or crystals.
Odor: Spicy

1208 / Zingerone / Monographs

Boiling Point: ~290°
Function: Flavoring agent

IDENTIFICATION
- **INFRARED SPECTRA,** *Spectrophotometric Identification Tests,* Appendix IIIC
  Acceptance criteria: The spectrum of the sample exhibits relative maxima at the same wavelengths as those of the spectrum below.

ASSAY
- **PROCEDURE:** Proceed as directed under *M-1b*, Appendix XI.
  Acceptance criteria: NLT 95.0% of $C_{11}H_{14}O_3$

OTHER REQUIREMENTS
- **MELTING RANGE OR TEMPERATURE DETERMINATION,** Appendix IIB
  Acceptance criteria: 39°–43°

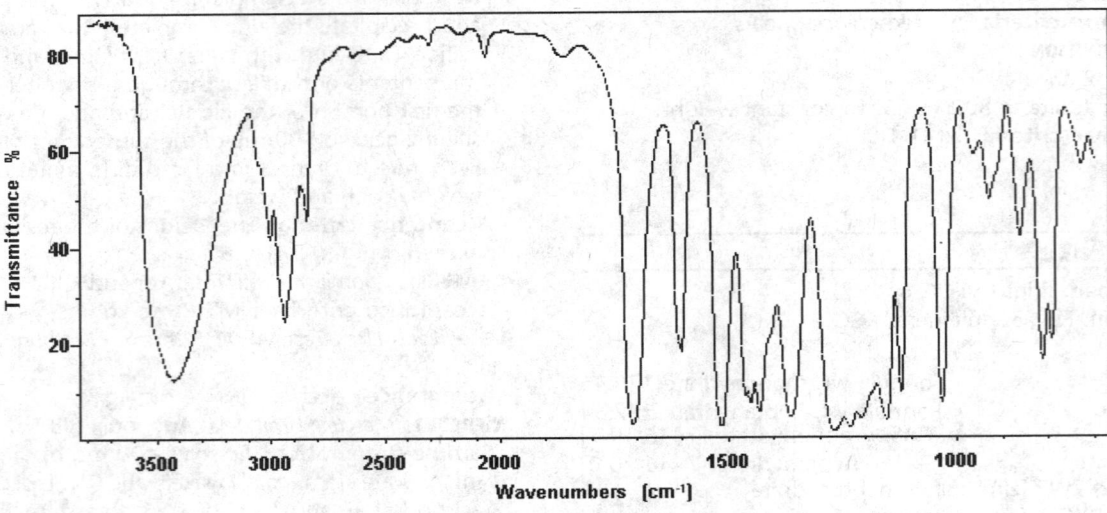

Zingerone

Provisional Monographs

Meso-Zeaxanthin

First Published: First Supplement, FCC 7
Last Revision: Third Supplement, FCC 7

β-β-Carotene-3,3'-diol, (3R,3'S)-
(3R,3'S-meso)-Zeaxanthin

$C_{40}H_{56}O_2$

Formula wt 568.88
CAS: [31272-50-1]

UNII: CV0IB81ORO [zeaxanthin]

DESCRIPTION
Meso-Zeaxanthin occurs as a free-flowing, orange to pale-yellow powder. It is the purified fraction obtained from isomerization of lutein from *Tagetes erecta* L., which contains both the (3R,3S'-meso)-zeaxanthin and the (3R,3'R)-zeaxanthin isomers with approximate concentrations of 94% and 6% (of total zeaxanthin), respectively.

Function: Source of meso-zeaxanthin; color
Packaging and Storage: Store in tight, light-resistant containers in a cool place.

IDENTIFICATION
- **A. ULTRAVIOLET ABSORPTION**
  Acceptance criteria: The *Sample solution* from the test for *Total Carotenoids* shows an absorption maximum at about 453 nm.
- **B. PROCEDURE**
  Acceptance criteria: The retention time of the major peak in the chromatogram of the *Sample solution* corresponds to that in the chromatogram of the *Standard solution* as obtained in the *Assay* for *Zeaxanthin*.
- **C. STEREOISOMERIC COMPOSITION**
  Mobile phase: Hexane, alcohol, and isopropanol (80:5:5)
  Sample solution: Transfer 10 mg of sample to a 100-mL volumetric flask, add 50 mL of alcohol, and place the flask in an ultrasonic bath at 60° for 2–5 min to dissolve the sample. Remove the flask from the bath, cool to room temperature, and dilute with hexane to volume. Filter the solution through a 0.45-μm filter membrane.
  Standard solution: Prepare a solution containing 0.1 mg/mL of USP Meso-Zeaxanthin RS as follows: dissolve an amount of Reference Standard in an amount of ethanol equal to 50% of the final volume of the solution. Heat in an ultrasonic bath at 60° for 2–5 min to dissolve the Reference Standard. Remove the flask from the bath, cool to room temperature, and dilute with hexane to the desired volume (the volume of hexane used in the solution should equal the volume of ethanol used to dissolve the standard). Filter the solution through a 0.45-μm filter membrane.
  Chromatographic system, Appendix IIA
  Mode: High-performance liquid chromatography
  Detector: 453 nm
  Column: 4.6-mm × 25-cm column containing amylose tris-3,5-dimethylphenylcarbamate-coated, porous, spherical silica particles, 5-μm in diameter[1]
  Column temperature: 35°
  Flow rate: 0.5 mL/min
  Injection size: 20 μL
  System suitability
  Sample: *Standard solution*
  [NOTE—The approximate relative retention times for (3S,3'S)-zeaxanthin, (3R,3'S, meso)-zeaxanthin, (3R,3'R)-zeaxanthin, and (3R,3'R,6'R)-lutein are 0.94, 1.00, 1.06, and 1.11, respectively. The chromatogram from the *Standard solution* should be similar to the Reference Chromatogram provided with the USP Meso-Zeaxanthin RS being used.]
  Suitability requirement: The resolution between each pair peak due to (3S,3'S)-zeaxanthin, (3R,3'S, meso)-zeaxanthin, (3R,3'R)-zeaxanthin, and (3R,3'R,6'R)-lutein is NLT 1.5.
  Analysis: Separately inject the *Sample solution* and the *Standard solution* into the chromatograph, record the chromatograms, and compare them to the Reference Chromatogram provided with the USP Meso-Zeaxanthin RS being used in order to identify the relevant analyte peaks. Measure the peak areas and calculate the percentage of (3S,3'S)-zeaxanthin, (3R,3'S, meso)-zeaxanthin, and (3R,3'R)-zeaxanthin:

  $$\text{Result} = (r_U/r_T) \times 100$$

  r_U = peak area of the analyte of interest
  r_T = total peak area of the chromatogram
  Acceptance criteria
  (3S,3'S)-Zeaxanthin: NMT 1.0%
  (3R,3'S, meso)-Zeaxanthin: NLT 85.0%
  (3R,3'R)-Zeaxanthin: NMT 15.0%

ASSAY
- **ZEAXANTHIN**
  [NOTE—Use low-actinic glassware.]
  Mobile phase: Hexane and ethyl acetate (75:25); filtered and degassed. Make adjustments if necessary.
  Standard solution: 150 μg/mL of USP Meso-Zeaxanthin RS prepared as follows: dissolve 15.0 mg of USP Meso-Zeaxanthin RS in 10 mL of chloroform, swirling briefly, and dilute with *Mobile phase* to 100 mL.
  Sample solution: Transfer 15.0 mg of sample to a 100-mL volumetric flask, add 10 mL of chloroform, and place the flask in an ultrasonic bath at 30° for 2–5 min to obtain a clear solution. Dilute with *Mobile phase* to volume.

---
[1] Chiralpak AD-H from Chiral Technologies, or equivalent.

Chromatographic system, Appendix IIA
  Mode: High-performance liquid chromatography
  Detector: 453 nm
  Column: 4.6-mm × 25-cm column that contains 5- to 10-μm porous silica packing[2]
  Flow rate: 1.5 mL/min
  Injection size: 10 μL
  System suitability
  Sample: *Standard solution*
  [NOTE—The approximate relative retention times for lutein and zeaxanthin are about 0.95 and 1.0, respectively.]
  Suitability requirement 1: The resolution between zeaxanthin and lutein is NLT 1.0.
  Suitability requirement 2: The tailing factor is NMT 2.
  Suitability requirement 3: The relative standard deviation for replicate injections is NMT 2.0%.
  Analysis: Inject the *Sample solution* into the chromatograph, record the chromatogram, and measure the peak area responses. [NOTE—The peak area of zeaxanthin is NLT 90.0% of the total detected area of peaks in the chromatogram.]
  Calculate the percentage of zeaxanthin in the sample taken:

$$Result = T \times (r_U/r_T)$$

  T = percentage of *Total Carotenoids* determined below
  r_U = peak response of zeaxanthin
  r_T = sum of the responses of all of the peaks
  Acceptance criteria: NLT 74.0%

- **TOTAL CAROTENOIDS**
  [NOTE—Use low-actinic glassware.]
  Sample stock solution: Transfer 25.0 mg of the sample to a 100-mL volumetric flask, add 20 mL of chloroform, and place the flask in an ultrasonic bath at 30° for 2–5 min to obtain a clear solution. Dilute with cyclohexane to volume to obtain a solution containing 250 μg/mL.
  Sample solution: 2.5 μg/mL in cyclohexane from the *Sample stock solution*
  Blank: Cyclohexane
  Analysis: Determine the absorbance of the *Sample solution* against that of the *Blank* at the wavelength of maximum absorbance at about 453 nm, with a suitable spectrophotometer.
  Calculate the percentage of total carotenoids as zeaxanthin ($C_{40}H_{56}O_2$):

$$Result = A/(C \times F)$$

  A = absorbance of the *Sample solution*
  C = concentration of the *Sample solution* (g/mL)
  F = absorptivity of zeaxanthin in cyclohexane (2540 mL·g^{-1}·cm^{-1})
  Acceptance criteria: NLT 80.0%

---
[2] Agilent Zorbax Rx-SIL, or equivalent.

IMPURITIES
Inorganic Impurities
- **LEAD,** *Lead Limit Test, Flame Atomic Absorption Spectrophotometric Method,* Appendix IIIB
  Sample: 10 g
  Acceptance criteria: NMT 1 mg/kg

Organic Impurities
- **LUTEIN AND OTHER RELATED COMPOUNDS**
  [NOTE—Use low-actinic glassware.]
  Mobile phase: Hexane and ethyl acetate (75:25); filtered and degassed. Make adjustments if necessary.
  Standard solution: 150 μg/mL of USP Meso-Zeaxanthin RS prepared as follows: dissolve 15.0 mg of USP Meso-Zeaxanthin RS in 10 mL of chloroform, swirling briefly, and dilute with *Mobile phase* to 100 mL.
  Sample solution: Transfer 15.0 mg of sample to a 100-mL volumetric flask, add 10 mL of chloroform, and place the flask in an ultrasonic bath at 30° for 2–5 min to obtain a clear solution. Dilute with *Mobile phase* to volume.
  Chromatographic system, Appendix IIA
  Mode: High-performance liquid chromatography
  Detector: 453 nm
  Column: 4.6-mm × 25-cm column that contains 5- to 10-μm porous silica packing[2]
  Flow rate: 1.5 mL/min
  Injection size: 10 μL
  System suitability
  Sample: *Standard solution*
  [NOTE—The approximate relative retention times for lutein and zeaxanthin are about 0.95 and 1.0, respectively.]
  Suitability requirement 1: The resolution between zeaxanthin and lutein is NLT 1.0.
  Suitability requirement 2: The tailing factor is NMT 2.
  Suitability requirement 3: The relative standard deviation for replicate injections is NMT 2.0%.
  Analysis: Inject the *Sample solution* into the chromatograph, record the chromatogram, and measure the peak area responses. [NOTE—The peak area of lutein is NMT 9.0% of the total detected area of peaks in the chromatogram of the *Sample solution*.]
  Calculate the percentage of lutein in the sample taken:

$$Result = T \times (r_U/r_T)$$

  T = percentage of *Total Carotenoids* determined above
  r_U = peak response of lutein
  r_T = sum of the responses of all of the peaks
  Calculate the percentage of other related compounds in the portion of the sample taken:

$$Result = 100 \times (r_O/r_T)$$

  r_O = individual peak response of any other peak in the chromatogram, excluding zeaxanthin and lutein
  r_T = sum of the responses of all of the peaks

Acceptance criteria
Lutein: NMT 8.5%
Other related compounds: NMT 1.0% of any other single related compound

SPECIFIC TESTS
- **RESIDUE ON IGNITION (SULFATED ASH)**, Appendix IIC
Analysis: Proceed as directed, but igniting at 600 ± 50°.
Acceptance criteria: NMT 1.0%
- **WATER**, *Water Determination*, Appendix IIB
Acceptance criteria: NMT 1.0%

Provisional Monographs

General Tests and Assays

CONTENTS

APPENDIX I: APPARATUS FOR TESTS AND ASSAYS ... 1217
    Oxygen Flask Combustion ... 1217
    Thermometers ... 1217
    Volumetric Apparatus ... 1218
    Weights And Balances ... 1219

APPENDIX II: PHYSICAL TESTS AND DETERMINATIONS ... 1221
  A. **Chromatography** ... 1221
    Column Chromatography ... 1222
    Paper Chromatography ... 1222
    Thin-Layer Chromatography ... 1223
    Gas Chromatography ... 1224
    High-Performance Liquid Chromatography ... 1226
  B. **Physicochemical Properties** ... 1230
    Distillation Range ... 1230
    Melting Range or Temperature Determination ... 1231
    Optical (Specific) Rotation ... 1232
    pH Determination ... 1233
    Readily Carbonizable Substances ... 1233
    Refractive Index ... 1234
    Solidification Point ... 1234
    Viscosity Determination ... 1236
    Water Determination ... 1239
  C. **Others** ... 1242
    Ash (Acid-Insoluble) ... 1242
    Ash (Total) ... 1242
    Hydrochloric Acid Table ... 1242
    Loss on Drying ... 1243
    Nuclear Magnetic Resonance ... 1244
    Oil Content of Synthetic Paraffin ... 1251
    Plasma Spectrochemistry ... 1253
    Residue on Ignition (Sulfated Ash) ... 1259
    Sieve Analysis of Granular Metal Powders ... 1259
    Sulfuric Acid Table ... 1260
    Water-Insoluble Matter ... 1261

APPENDIX III: CHEMICAL TESTS AND DETERMINATIONS ... 1262
  A. **Identification Tests** ... 1262
  B. **Limit Tests** ... 1264
    Aluminum Limit Test ... 1264
    Arsenic Limit Test ... 1264
    Cadmium Limit Test ... 1266
    Chloride and Sulfate Limit Tests ... 1266
    1,4-Dioxane Limit Test ... 1267
    Fluoride Limit Test ... 1268
    Lead Limit Test ... 1270
    Manganese Limit Test ... 1275
    Mercury Limit Test ... 1275
    Nickel Limit Test ... 1276
    Phosphorus Limit Test ... 1277
    Selenium Limit Test ... 1278
  C. **Others** ... 1279
    Alginates Assay ... 1279
    α-Amino Nitrogen (AN) Determination ... 1280
    Ammonia Nitrogen (NH_3-N) Determination ... 1280
    Benzene ... 1280
    Color Determination ... 1283
    Elemental Impurities by ICP ... 1289
    Glutamic Acid ... 1291
    Hydroxypropoxyl Determination ... 1291
    Methoxyl Determination ... 1292
    Nitrogen Determination ... 1293
    Spectrophotometric Identification Tests ... 1294
    Sulfur ... 1295

APPENDIX IV: CHEWING GUM BASE POLYMERS ... 1298
    Bound Styrene ... 1298
    Molecular Weight ... 1299
    Quinones ... 1299
    Residual Styrene ... 1300
    Sample Solution for Arsenic Limit Test ... 1301
    Sample Solution for Lead Limit Test ... 1301
    Total Unsaturation ... 1301

APPENDIX V: ENZYME ASSAYS ... 1303
    Enzyme Preparations Used in Food Processing ... 1303
    Acid Phosphatase Activity ... 1306
    Aminopeptidase (Leucine) Activity ... 1307
    α-Amylase Activity (Nonbacterial) ... 1308
    α-Amylase Activity (Bacterial) ... 1309
    Catalase Activity ... 1309
    Cellulase Activity ... 1310
    Chymotrypsin Activity ... 1311
    Diastase Activity (Diastatic Power) ... 1312
    α-Galactosidase Activity ... 1313
    β-Glucanase Activity ... 1313
    Glucoamylase Activity (Amyloglucosidase Activity) ... 1314
    Glucose Isomerase Activity ... 1315

Glucose Oxidase Activity	1316
Hemicellulase Activity	1317
Invertase Sumner Unit Activity	1318
Lactase (Neutral) (β-Galactosidase) Activity	1319
Lactase (Acid) (β-Galactosidase) Activity	1320
Lipase Activity	1321
Lipase (Microbial) Activity for Medium- and Long-Chain Fatty Acids	1322
Lysozyme Activity	1323
Maltogenic Amylase Activity	1324
Milk-Clotting Activity	1324
Pancreatin Activity	1325
Pepsin Activity	1327
Phospholipase A$_2$ Activity	1328
Phytase Activity	1328
Plant Proteolytic Activity	1330
Proteolytic Activity, Bacterial (PC)	1331
Proteolytic Activity, Fungal (HUT)	1331
Proteolytic Activity, Fungal (SAP)	1332
Pullulanase Activity	1333
Transglutaminase Activity	1334
Trypsin Activity	1335

APPENDIX VI: ESSENTIAL OILS AND FLAVORS ... 1336

Acetals	1336
Acid Value (Essential Oils and Flavors)	1336
Aldehydes	1336
Aldehydes and Ketones	1336
Chlorinated Compounds	1337
Esters	1337
Linalool Determination	1338
Percentage of Cineole	1338
Phenols	1338
Phenols, Free	1339
Residue on Evaporation	1339
Solubility in Alcohol	1339
Total Alcohols	1339
Ultraviolet Absorbance of Citrus Oils	1339
Volatile Oil Content (Essential Oils and Flavors)	1340

APPENDIX VII: FATS AND RELATED SUBSTANCES ... 1341

Acetyl Value	1341
Acid Value (Fats and Related Substances)	1341
Anisidine Value	1341
Chlorophyll	1342
Cold Test	1342
Color (Fats and Related Substances)	1342
Lovibond Color	1342
Fatty Acid Composition	1343
Fatty Acid Composition (Saturated, cis-Monounsaturated, and cis-Polyunsaturated) in Oils Containing Long Chain Polyunsaturated Fatty Acids	1344
Free Fatty Acids	1346
Free Glycerin or Propylene Glycol	1347
Hexane-Insoluble Matter	1347
Hydroxyl Value	1347
Iodine Value	1348
Melting Range (Fats and Related Substances)	1348
1-Monoglycerides	1348
Total Monoglycerides	1349
Oxyethylene Determination	1350
Peroxide Value	1351
Reichert-Meissl Value	1352
Saponification Value	1352
Soap	1353
Specific Gravity	1353
Stability (Fats and Related Substances)	1353
Tocopherols	1354
Unsaponifiable Matter	1355
Volatile Acidity	1356

APPENDIX VIII: OLEORESINS ... 1357

Color Value (Oleoresins)	1357
Curcumin Content	1357
Piperine Content	1357
Residual Solvent (Oleoresins)	1358
Total Capsaicinoids Content	1359
Volatile Oil Content (Oleoresins)	1359

APPENDIX IX: ROSINS AND RELATED SUBSTANCES ... 1360

Acid Number (Rosins and Related Substances)	1360
Softening Point	1360
Viscosity (Rosins and Related Substances)	1363

APPENDIX X: CARBOHYDRATES (STARCHES, SUGARS, AND RELATED SUBSTANCES) ... 1364

Acetyl Groups	1364
Crude Fat	1364
Invert Sugar Determination	1364
Lactose Determination	1366
Propylene Chlorohydrin Determination	1366
Reducing Sugars Assay	1367
Sulfur Dioxide Determination	1368
Total Solids	1370

APPENDIX XI: FLAVOR CHEMICALS (OTHER THAN ESSENTIAL OILS) ... 1375
- M-1 Assay by Gas Chromatography ... 1375
  - GC Conditions for Analysis ... 1375
  - Calculations and Methods ... 1375
  - GC System Suitability Test Sample ... 1376
- M-2 Assays for Certain Aldehydes and Ketones ... 1376
- M-3 Assay by Titrimetric Procedures ... 1377
- M-4 Alcohol Content of Ethyl Oxyhydrate ... 1378
- M-5 Acidity Determination by Iodometric Method ... 1378
- M-6 Limit Test for Antioxidants in Ethyl Acrylate ... 1378
- M-7 Limit Test for Hydrocarbons in Eugenol ... 1379
- M-8 Limit Test for Hydrocyanic Acid in Benzaldehyde ... 1379
- M-9 Limit Test for Lead ... 1379
- M-10 Limit Test for Methyl Compounds in Ethyl Acetate ... 1379
- M-11 Limit Test for Peroxide Value ... 1379
- M-12 Limit Test for Readily Carbonizable Substances in Ethyl Acetate ... 1379
- M-13 Limit Test for Readily Oxidizable Substances in dl-Menthol ... 1380
- M-14 Limit Test for Reducing Substances ... 1380
- M-15 Acid Value, Flavor Chemicals (Other than Essential Oils) ... 1380
- M-16 Residue On Evaporation ... 1380
- M-17 Qualitative Test for Phenols Using Ferric Chloride ... 1380

APPENDIX XII: MICROBIOLIGICAL TESTS ... 1381
- Media and Reagents ... 1381
- Microbiological Enumeration Tests ... 1382
- Total Aerobic Microbial Count ... 1382
- Total Yeasts and Molds Count ... 1382
- Tests for Absence of Specific Microorganisms ... 1382
- Bile-Tolerant Gram-Negative Bacteria ... 1383
- *Enterobacter sakazakii* (Cronobacter Spp.) ... 1383
- *Salmonella Spp.* ... 1383

APPENDIX XIII: ADULTERANTS AND CONTAMINANTS IN FOOD INGREDIENTS ... 1384
- Diethylene Glycol and Ethylene Glycol in Glycerin ... 1384
- Pesticide Residues ... 1384

APPENDIX XIV: MARKERS FOR AUTHENTICITY TESTING ... 1388
- Biobased Content of 1,3-Propanediol ... 1388

SOLUTIONS AND INDICATORS ... 1393
- Colormetric Solutions ... 1393
- Standard Buffer Solutions ... 1393
- Standard Solutions for the Preparation of Controls and Standards ... 1394
- Test Solutions (TS) and Other Reagents ... 1394
- Volumetric Solutions ... 1400
- Indicators ... 1404
- Indicator Papers and Test Papers ... 1406
- Detector Tubes ... 1406

General Tests and Assays

APPENDIX I: APPARATUS FOR TESTS AND ASSAYS

OXYGEN FLASK COMBUSTION

Apparatus The apparatus consists of a heavy-walled, deeply lipped or cupped, conical flask of a volume suitable for the complete combustion of the sample in which the particular element is being determined (e.g., see *Selenium Limit Test*, Appendix IIIB). The flask is fitted with a ground-glass stopper to which is fused a sample carrier consisting of heavy-gauge platinum wire and a piece of welded platinum gauze measuring about 1.5 × 2 cm. A suitable apparatus may be obtained as Catalog Nos. 6513-C20 (500-mL capacity) and 6513-C30 (1000-mL capacity) from the Arthur H. Thomas Co., P.O. Box 779, Philadelphia, PA 19105. Equivalent apparatus available from other sources, or other suitable apparatus embodying the principles described herein, may also be used.

Procedure [CAUTION—Analysts should wear safety glasses and should use a suitable safety shield between themselves and the apparatus. Further safety measures should be observed as necessary to ensure maximum protection of the analysts. Furthermore, the flask must be scrupulously clean and free from even traces of organic solvents. Samples containing water of hydration or more than 1% of moisture should be dried at 140° for 2 h before combustion, unless otherwise directed.] Accurately weigh the amount of sample specified in the monograph or general test. Solids should be weighed on a 4-cm square piece of halide-free paper, which should be folded around the sample. Liquid samples not exceeding 0.2 mL in volume should be weighed in tared cellulose acetate capsules [available as Catalog Nos. 6513-C80 (100 capsules) and 6513-C82 (1000 capsules) from the Arthur H. Thomas Co.]; gelatin capsules are satisfactory for liquid samples exceeding 0.2 mL in volume.

[NOTE—Gelatin capsules may contain significant amounts of combined halide or sulfur, in which case a blank determination should be made as necessary.]

Place the sample, together with a filter paper fuse-strip, in the platinum gauze sample holder. Place the absorbing liquid, as specified in the individual monograph or general test, into the flask, moisten the joint of the stopper with water, and flush the air from the flask with a stream of rapidly flowing oxygen, swirling the liquid to facilitate its taking up oxygen.

[NOTE—Saturation of the liquid with oxygen is essential for successful performance of this procedure.]

Ignite the fuse-strip by suitable means. If the strip is ignited outside the flask, immediately plunge the sample holder into the flask, invert the flask so that the absorption solution makes a seal around the stopper, and hold the stopper firmly in place. If the ignition is carried out in a closed system, the inversion of the flask may be omitted. After combustion is complete, shake the flask vigorously, and allow it to stand for not less than 10 min with intermittent shaking. Continue as directed in the individual monograph or general test chapter.

THERMOMETERS

Thermometers suitable for *Food Chemicals Codex* use conform to the specifications of the American Society for Testing and Materials, ASTM Standards E 1, and are standardized in accordance with ASTM Method E 77.

The thermometers are of the mercury in glass type, and the column above the liquid is filled with nitrogen. They may be standardized for "total immersion" or for "partial immersion" and should be used as near as practicable under the same condition of immersion.

Total immersion means standardization with the thermometer immersed to the top of the mercury column, with the remainder of the stem and the upper expansion chamber exposed to the ambient temperature. Partial immersion means standardization with the thermometer immersed to the indicated immersion line etched on the front of the thermometer, with the remainder of the stem exposed to the ambient temperature. If used under any other condition of immersion, an emergent-stem correction is necessary to obtain correct temperature readings.

Thermometer Specifications

ASTM No. E1	Range °C	Range °F	Subdivision °C	Subdivision °F	Immersion (mm)
For General Use					
1 C	−20 to +150	—	1	—	76
1 F	—	0 to 302	—	2	76

[a] For determination of melting range of Class III solids.
[b] For determination of the titer of fatty acids.
[c] For determination of Saybolt viscosity.
[e] For determination of Engler viscosity.
[e] For determination of congealing point.
[f] For determination of oil in wax.

Thermometer Specifications (continued)

ASTM No. E1	Range °C	Range °F	Subdivision °C	Subdivision °F	Immersion (mm)
2 C	−5 to +300	—	1	—	76
2 F	—	20 to 580	—	2	76
3 C	−5 to +400	—	1	—	76
3 F	—	20 to 760	—	2	76
For Determination of Softening Point					
15 C	−2 to +80	—	0.2	—	total
15 F	—	30 to 180	—	0.5	total
16 C	30 to 200	—	0.5	—	total
16 F	—	85 to 392	—	1	total
For Determination of Kinematic Viscosity					
44 F	—	66.5 to 71.5	—	0.1	total
45 F	—	74.5 to 79.5	—	0.1	total
28 F	—	97.5 to 102.5	—	0.1	total
46 F	—	119.5 to 124.5	—	0.1	total
29 F	—	127.5 to 132.5	—	0.1	total
47 F	—	137.5 to 142.5	—	0.1	total
48 F	—	177.5 to 182.5	—	0.1	total
30 F	—	207.5 to 212.5	—	0.1	total
For Determination of Distillation Range					
37 C	−2 to +52	—	0.2	—	100
38 C	24 to 78	—	0.2	—	100
39 C	48 to 102	—	0.2	—	100
40 C	72 to 126	—	0.2	—	100
41 C	98 to 152	—	0.2	—	100
102 C	123 to 177	—	0.2	—	100
103 C	148 to 202	—	0.2	—	100
104 C	173 to 227	—	0.2	—	100
105 C	198 to 252	—	0.2	—	100
106 C	223 to 277	—	0.2	—	100
107 C	248 to 302	—	0.2	—	100
For Determination of Solidification Point					
89 C	−20 to +10	—	0.1	—	76
90 C	0 to 30	—	0.1	—	76
91 C	20 to 50	—	0.1	—	76
92 C	40 to 70	—	0.1	—	76
93 C	60 to 90	—	0.1	—	76
94 C	80 to 110	—	0.1	—	76

[a] For determination of melting range of Class III solids.
[b] For determination of the titer of fatty acids.
[c] For determination of Saybolt viscosity.
[d] For determination of Engler viscosity.
[e] For determination of congealing point.
[f] For determination of oil in wax.

Thermometer Specifications (continued)

ASTM No. E1	Range °C	Range °F	Subdivision °C	Subdivision °F	Immersion (mm)
95 C	100 to 130	—	0.1	—	76
96 C	120 to 150	—	0.1	—	76
100 C	145 to 205	—	0.2	—	76
101 C	195 to 305	—	0.5	—	76
For Special Use					
14 C [a]	38 to 82	—	0.1	—	79
38 C [b]	−2 to +68	—	0.2	—	45
18 C [c]	34 to 42	—	0.1	—	total
18 F [c]	—	94 to 108	—	0.2	total
22 C [c]	95 to 103	—	0.1	—	total
22 F [c]	—	204 to 218	—	0.2	total
23 C [d]	18 to 28	—	0.2	—	90
24 C [d]	30 to 54	—	0.2	—	90
54 F [e]	—	68 to 213	—	0.5	total
71 F [f]	—	−35 to +70	—	1	76

[a] For determination of melting range of Class III solids.
[b] For determination of the titer of fatty acids.
[c] For determination of Saybolt viscosity.
[d] For determination of Engler viscosity.
[e] For determination of congealing point.
[f] For determination of oil in wax.

In selecting a thermometer, careful consideration should be given to the conditions under which it is to be used. The preceding table lists several ASTM thermometers, together with their usual conditions of use, which may be required in *Food Chemicals Codex* tests. Complete specifications for these thermometers are given in "ASTM Standards on Thermometers."

VOLUMETRIC APPARATUS

Most of the volumetric apparatus available in the United States is calibrated at 20°, although the temperatures generally prevailing in laboratories more nearly approach 25°, which is the temperature specified generally for tests and assays. This discrepancy is inconsequential provided the room temperature is reasonably constant and the apparatus has been calibrated accurately prior to and under the conditions of its intended use.

Before use, all volumetric ware must be cleaned in such a manner that when rinsed with water, no droplet of water can be seen on the inside walls. Many kinds of "degreasing" solutions are available, and the user should consult the manufacturer's literature for the system of choice.

Use To attain the degree of precision required in many assays involving volumetric measurements and directing that a quantity be "accurately measured" (see *Tests and Assays* under *General Provisions*), the apparatus must be chosen and used with exceptional care. Where less than 10 mL of titrant is to be measured, a 10-mL buret or microburet generally is required.

The design of volumetric apparatus is an important factor in ensuring accuracy. For example, the length of the graduated portions of graduated cylinders should be not less than five times the inside diameter, and the tips of burets should permit an outflow of not more than 0.5 mL/s.

Pipets and burets must be allowed to drain properly in use. Usually, transfer pipets for dilute aqueous solutions should drain for the time specified by the manufacturer before the tip is touched to the wall of the vessel. Buret volumes should not be read immediately upon delivery of the titrant. A suitable length of time should elapse to allow the titrant retained on the walls to drain down. A time interval of 5 to 10 s is usually sufficient.

Standards of Accuracy The capacity tolerances for volumetric flasks, transfer pipets, and burets are those accepted by the National Institute of Standards and Technology (Class A),[1] as indicated in the accompanying tables. Use Class A volumetric apparatus unless otherwise specified in the individual monograph. For plastic volumetric apparatus, the accepted capacity tolerances are Class B.[2]

Volumetric Flasks

	Designated Volume (mL)						
	10	25	50	100	250	500	1000
Limit of error (mL)	0.02	0.03	0.05	0.08	0.12	0.15	0.30
Limit of error (%)	0.20	0.12	0.10	0.08	0.05	0.03	0.03

Transfer Pipets

	Designated Volume (mL)						
	1	2	5	10	25	50	100
Limit of error (mL)	0.006	0.006	0.01	0.02	0.03	0.05	0.08
Limit of error (%)	0.6	0.30	0.20	0.20	0.12	0.10	0.08

Burets

	Designated Volume (mL)		
	10 ("micro" type)	25	50
Subdivisions (mL)	0.02	0.10	0.10
Limit of error (mL)	0.02	0.03	0.05

The capacity tolerances for measuring (i.e., "graduated") pipets of up to and including 10-mL capacity are somewhat larger than those for the corresponding sizes of transfer pipets, namely, 0.01, 0.02, and 0.03 mL for the 2-, 5-, and 10-mL sizes, respectively.

Transfer and measuring pipets calibrated "to deliver" should be drained in a vertical position and then touched against the wall of the receiving vessel to drain the tips.

---

[1] See "Testing of Glass Volumetric Apparatus," NBS Circ. 602, April 1, 1959. Apparatus meeting the specifications of NB SIR 74–461 ("The Calibration of Small Volumetric Laboratory Glassware"), as well as of ANSI/ASTM E 694–79 ("Specifications for Volumetric Ware"), is also acceptable.

[2] See ASTM E 288, Fed. Spec. NNN-F-289, and ISO Standard 284.

Volume readings on burets should be estimated to the nearest 0.01 mL for 25- and 50-mL burets, and to the nearest 0.005 mL for 5- and 10-mL burets. Pipets calibrated "to contain" may be called for in special cases, generally for measuring viscous fluids. In such cases, the pipet should be washed clean, after draining, and the washings added to the measured portion.

WEIGHTS AND BALANCES

Food Chemicals Codex tests and assays are designed for use with three types of analytical balances, known as micro-, semimicro-, and macro-.

By custom, microbalances weigh objects with a sensitivity down to the microgram range (or lower); semimicrobalances down to the 0.01-mg range; and analytical macrobalances down to the 0.1-mg range.

Tolerances The analytical weights meet the tolerances of the American National Standard ANSI/ASTM E617, "Laboratory Weights and Precision Mass Standards." This standard is incorporated by reference and should be consulted for full descriptions and information on the tolerances and construction of weights.[3] Where quantities of 25 mg or less are to be "accurately weighed" (see *Tests and Assays* under *General Provisions*), any applicable corrections for weights should be used.

Class 1.1 weights are used for calibration of low-capacity, high-sensitivity balances. They are available in various denominations from 1 to 500 mg. The tolerance for any denomination in this class is 5 µg. They are recommended for calibration of balances using optical or electrical methods for accurately weighing quantities below 20 mg.

Class 1 weights are designated as high-precision standards for calibration. They may be used for accurately weighing quantities below 20 mg.

Class 2 weights are used as working standards for calibration, built-in weights for analytical balances, and laboratory weights for routine analytical work.

Class 3 and Class 4 weights are used with moderate-precision laboratory balances.

Use Where substances are to be "accurately weighed" (see *Tests and Assays* under *General Provisions*), in an assay or a test, the weighing is to be performed in such manner as to limit the error to 0.1% or less. For example, a quantity of 50 mg is to be weighed to the nearest 0.05 mg; a quantity of 0.1 g is to be weighed to the nearest 0.1 mg; and a quantity of 10 g is to be weighed to the nearest 10 mg.

Calibration All precision balances and weights should be calibrated periodically (preferably at least once a year) and a record kept of the calibration date and results. The user may have a set of weights calibrated by the nearest Department of Weights and Measurements (or its equivalent). This is usually done for little or no charge. Alternatively, an independent, outside company may be retained for the purpose of performing such calibrations.

Buoyancy Effect When a weighing is to be performed with an accuracy of 0.1% or better, the buoyancy effect

---

[3] Copies of ASTM Standard E 617-81 (Reapproved 1985) may be obtained from the American Society for Testing and Materials, 1916 Race Street, Philadelphia, PA 19103.

should not be neglected. The equation to be used in correcting for this effect is:

$$M_V = M_A[1 + 0.0012(1/D_O + D_W)]$$

in which M_V is the mass in vacuum; M_A is the mass in air; 0.0012 is the density of air; D_O is the density of the weighed object; and D_W is the density of the calibrated weights.

APPENDIX II: PHYSICAL TESTS AND DETERMINATIONS

A. CHROMATOGRAPHY

[NOTE—Chromatographic separations may also be characterized according to the type of instrumentations or apparatus used. The types of chromatography that may be used in the *Food Chemicals Codex* (*FCC*) are column, thin-layer, gas, and high-pressure or high-performance liquid chromatography.

The Committee on *Food Chemicals Codex* recognizes that the field of chromatography continues to advance. Accordingly, the use of equivalent or improved systems is acceptable with appropriate validation.]

For the purposes of the *FCC*, chromatography is defined as an analytical technique whereby a mixture of chemicals may be separated by virtue of their differential affinities for two immiscible phases. One of these, the stationary phase, consists of a fixed bed of small particles with a large surface area, while the other, the mobile phase, is a gas or liquid that moves constantly through, or over the surface of, the fixed phase. Chromatographic systems achieve their ability to separate mixtures by selectively retarding the passage of some compounds through the stationary phase while permitting others to move more freely. Therefore, the chromatogram may be evaluated qualitatively by determining the R_F, or retardation factor, for each of the eluted substances. The R_F is a measure of that fraction of its total elution time that any compound spends in the mobile phase. Because this fraction is directly related to the fraction of the total amount of the solute that is in the mobile phase, the R_F can be expressed as:

$$R_F = V_m C_m / (V_m C_m + V_s C_s)$$

in which V_m and V_s are the volumes of the mobile and stationary phase, respectively, and C_m and C_s are the concentrations of the solute in either phase at any time. This can be simplified to:

$$R_F = V_m / (V_m + K V_s)$$

in which $K = C_s / C_m$ and is an equilibrium constant that indicates this differential affinity of the solute for the phases. Alternatively, a new constant, k, the capacity factor, may be introduced, giving another form of the expression:

$$R_F = 1/(1 + k)$$

in which $k = K V_s / V_m$. The capacity factor, k, which is normally constant for small samples, is a parameter that expresses the ability of a particular chromatographic system to interact with a solute. The larger the k value, the more the sample is retarded.

Both the retardation factor and the capacity factor may be used for qualitative identification of a solute or for developing strategies for improving separation. In terms of parameters easily obtainable from the chromatogram, the R_F is defined as the ratio of the distance traveled by the solute band to the distance traveled by the mobile solvent in a particular time. The capacity factor, k, can be evaluated by the expression:

$$k = (t_r - t_o)/t_o$$

in which t_r, the retention time, is the elapsed time from the start of the chromatogram to the elution maximum of the solute, and t_o is the retention time of a solute that is not retained by the chromatographic system.

Retardation of the solutes by the stationary phase may be achieved by one or a combination of mechanisms. Certain substances, such as alumina or silica gel, interact with the solutes primarily by *adsorption*, either *physical adsorption*, in which the binding forces are weak and easily reversible, or *chemisorption*, in which strong bonding to the surface can occur. Another important mechanism of retardation is *partition*, which occurs when the solute dissolves in the stationary phase, usually a liquid coated as a thin layer on the surface of an inert particle or chemically bonded to it. If the liquid phase is a polar substance (e.g., polyethylene glycol) and the mobile phase is nonpolar, the process is termed *normal-phase chromatography*. When the stationary phase is nonpolar (e.g., octadecylsilane) and the mobile phase is polar, the process is *reversed-phase chromatography*. For the separation of mixtures of ionic species, insoluble polymers called *ion exchangers* are used as the stationary phase. Ions of the solutes contained in the mobile phase are adsorbed onto the surface of the ion exchanger while at the same time displacing an electrically equivalent amount of less strongly bound ions to maintain the electroneutrality of both phases. The chromatographic separation of mixtures of large molecules such as proteins may be accomplished by a mechanism called *size exclusion chromatography*. The stationary phases used are highly cross-linked polymers that have imbibed a sufficient amount of solvent to form a gel. The separation is based on the physical size of the solvated solutes; those that are too large to fit within the interstices of the gel are eluted rapidly, while the smaller molecules permeate into the pores of the gel and are eluted later. In any chromatographic separation, more than one of the above mechanisms may be occurring simultaneously.

Chromatographic separations may also be characterized according to the type of instrumentation or apparatus used. The types of chromatography that may be used in the *FCC* are column, thin-layer, gas, and high-performance liquid chromatography.

COLUMN CHROMATOGRAPHY

Apparatus The equipment needed for column chromatography is not elaborate, consisting only of a cylindrical glass or Teflon tube that has a restricted outflow orifice. The dimensions of the tube are not critical and may vary from 10 to 40 mm in inside diameter and from 100 to 600 mm in length. For a given separation, greater efficiency may be obtained with a long narrow column, but the resultant flow rate will be lower. A fritted-glass disk may be seated in the end of the tube to act as a support for the packing material. The column is fitted at the end with a stopcock or other flow-restriction device to control the rate of delivery of the eluant.

Procedure The stationary phase is introduced into the column either as a dry powder or as a slurry in the mobile phase. Because a homogeneous bed free of void spaces is necessary to achieve maximum separation efficiency, the packing material is introduced in small portions and allowed to settle before further additions are made. Settling may be accomplished by allowing the mobile phase to flow through the bed, by tapping or vibrating the column if a dry powder is used, or by compressing each added portion using a tamping rod. The rod can be a solid glass, plastic, or metal cylinder whose diameter is slightly smaller than that of the column, or it can be a thinner rod onto the end of which has been attached a disk of suitable diameter. Ion-exchange resins and exclusion polymers are never packed as dry powders because after introduction of the mobile phase, they will swell and create sufficient pressure to shatter the column. When the packing has been completed, the sample is introduced onto the top of the column. If the sample is soluble, it is dissolved in a minimum amount of the mobile phase, pipetted onto the column, and allowed to percolate into the top of the bed. If it is not soluble or if the volume of solution is too large, it may be mixed with a small amount of the column packing. This material is then transferred to the chromatographic tube to form the top of the bed.

The chromatogram is then developed by adding the mobile phase to the column in small portions and allowing it to percolate through the packed bed either by gravity or under the influence of pressure or vacuum. Development of the chromatogram takes place by selective retardation of the components of the mixture as a result of their interaction with the stationary phase. In column chromatography, the stationary phase may act by adsorption, partition, ion exchange, exclusion of the solutes, or a combination of these effects.

When the development is complete, the components of the sample mixture may be detected and isolated by either of two procedures. The entire column may be extruded carefully from the tube, and if the compounds are colored or fluorescent under ultraviolet light, the appropriate segments may be cut from the column using a razor blade. If the components are colorless, they may be visualized by painting or spraying a thin longitudinal section of the surface of the chromatogram with color-developing reagents. The chemical may then be separated from the stationary phase by extraction with a strong solvent such as methanol and subsequently quantitated by suitable methods.

In the second procedure, the mobile phase may be allowed to flow through the column until the components of the mixture successively appear in the effluent. This eluate may be collected in fractions and the mobile phase evaporated if desired. The chemicals present in each fraction may then be determined by suitable analytical techniques.

PAPER CHROMATOGRAPHY

In this type of chromatography, the stationary phase ordinarily consists of a sheet of paper of suitable texture and thickness. The paper used is made from highly purified cellulose, which has a great affinity for water and other polar solvents since it has many hydroxyl functional groups. The tightly bound water acts as the stationary phase, and therefore the mechanism that predominates is liquid–liquid or partition chromatography. Adsorption of solutes to the cellulose surface may also occur, but this is of lesser importance. Papers especially impregnated to permit ion-exchange or reverse-phase chromatography are also available.

Apparatus The essential equipment for paper chromatography consists of the following:

Vapor-Tight Chamber: The chamber is constructed preferably of glass, stainless steel, or porcelain. It is provided with inlets for the addition of solvent or for releasing internal pressure, and it is designed to permit observation of the progress of the chromatographic run without being opened. Tall glass cylinders are convenient if they are made vapor-tight with suitable covers and a sealing compound.

Supporting Rack: The rack serves as a support for the solvent troughs and antisiphoning rods. It is constructed of a corrosion-resistant material about 5 cm shorter than the inside height of the chamber.

Solvent Troughs: The troughs, made of glass, are designed to be longer than the width of the chromatographic sheets and to contain a volume of solvent greater than that required for one chromatographic run.

Antisiphoning Rods: Constructed of heavy glass, the rods are placed on the rack and arranged to run outside of, parallel to, and slightly above the edge of the glass trough.

Chromatographic Sheets: Special chromatographic filter paper is cut to length approximately equal to the height of the chamber. The sheet is a least 2.5 cm wide but not wider than the length of the trough. A fine pencil line is drawn horizontally across the filter paper at a distance from one end such that when the sheet is suspended from the antisiphoning rods with the upper end of the paper resting in the trough and the lower portion hanging free into the chamber, the line is located a few cm below the rods. Care is necessary to avoid contaminating the paper by excessive handling or by contact with dirty surfaces.

Procedure for Descending Chromatography Separation of substances by descending chromatography is accomplished by allowing the mobile phase to flow downward on the chromatographic sheet.

The substance or substances to be analyzed are dissolved in a suitable solvent. Convenient volumes of the resulting solution, normally containing 1–20 µg of the compound, are placed in 6–10-mm spots along the pencil line not less than 3 cm apart. If the total volume to be applied would produce spots of a diameter greater than 6–10 mm, it is applied in separate portions to the same spot, each portion being allowed to dry before the next is added.

The spotted chromatographic sheet is suspended in the chamber by use of the antisiphoning rod and an additional heavy glass rod that holds the upper end of the sheet in the solvent trough. The bottom of the chamber is covered with a mixture containing both phases of the prescribed solvent system. It is important to ensure that the portion of the sheet hanging below the rods is freely suspended in the chamber without touching the rack or the chamber walls. The chamber is sealed to allow equilibration (saturation) of the chamber and the paper with solvent vapor. Any excess pressure is released as necessary. For large chambers, equilibration overnight may be necessary.

A volume of the mobile phase in excess of the volume required for complete development of the chromatogram is saturated with the immobile phase. After equilibration of the chamber, the prepared mobile solvent is introduced into the trough through the inlet. The inlet is closed, and the mobile phase is allowed to travel down the paper the desired distance. Precautions must be taken against allowing the solvent to run down the sheet when opening the chamber and removing the chromatogram. The location of the solvent front is quickly marked, and the sheets are dried.

The chromatogram is observed and measured directly or after suitable development to reveal the location of the spots of the isolated components of the mixture.

Procedure for Ascending Chromatography   In ascending chromatography, the lower edge of the sheet (or strip) is dipped into the mobile phase to permit the mobile phase to rise on the chromatographic sheet.

The test materials are applied to the chromatographic sheet as directed under *Procedure for Descending Chromatography*. Enough of both phases of the solvent mixture to cover the bottom of the chamber is added. Empty solvent troughs are placed on the bottom of the chamber, and the chromatographic sheet is suspended so that the end near which the spots have been added hangs free inside the empty trough.

The chamber is sealed, and equilibration is allowed to proceed as described under *Procedure for Descending Chromatography*. Then the solvent is added through the inlet to the trough in excess of the quantity of solvent required for complete moistening of the chromatographic sheet. The chamber is resealed. When the solvent front has reached the desired height, the chamber is opened and the sheet is removed, the location of the solvent front is quickly marked, and the sheet is dried.

Small cylinders may be used without troughs so that only the mobile phase is placed on the bottom. The chromatographic sheet is suspended during equilibration with the lower end just above the solvent, and chromatography is started by lowering the sheet so that it touches the solvent.

Detection of Chromatographic Bands   After the chromatogram has been fully developed, the bands corresponding to the various solutes may be detected by means similar to those described in *Column Chromatography*. If the compounds are colored or fluorescent under ultraviolet light, they may be visualized directly. Colorless compounds may be detected by spraying the paper with color-developing reagents. The bands corresponding to the individual components can be cut from the paper, and the chemical substances eluted from the cellulose by the use of a strong solvent such as methanol.

Identification of Solutes   Since the chromatographic mobilities of the solutes may change from run to run due to varying experimental conditions, presumptive identification of a substance should be based on comparison with a reference standard. The R_F values of the unknown substance and the standard on the same chromatogram must be identical. Alternatively, the ratio between the distances traveled by a given compound and a reference substance, the R_r value, must be 1.0. Identification may also be made by mixing a small amount of the reference substance with the unknown and chromatographing. The resulting chromatogram should contain only one spot. Definitive identification of solutes may be achieved by eluting them from the paper and subjecting them to IR, NMR, or mass spectrometry.

THIN-LAYER CHROMATOGRAPHY

In thin-layer chromatography (TLC), the stationary phase is a uniform layer of a finely divided powder that has been coated on the surface of a glass or plastic sheet and that is held in place by a binder. The capacity of the system is dependent on the thickness of the layer, which may range from 0.1–2.0 mm. The thinner layers are used primarily for analytical separations, while the thicker layers, because of their greater sample-handling ability, are useful for preparative work.

Substances that are used as coatings in TLC include silica gel, alumina, cellulose, and reversed-phase packings. Separations occur because of adsorption of the solutes from the mobile phase onto the surface of the thin layer. However, adsorption of water from the air or solvent components from the mobile phase can give rise to partition or liquid–liquid chromatography. Specially coated plates are available that permit ion-exchange or reversed-phase separations.

Apparatus   Acceptable apparatus and materials for thin-layer chromatography consist of the following:

Glass Plates: Flat glass plates of uniform thickness throughout their areas. The most common sizes are 20 cm, 10 cm, and 5 cm × 20 cm. (Aluminum plates also are commonly used.)

Aligning Tray: An aligning tray or other suitable flat surface is used to align and hold plates during application of the adsorbent.

Adsorbent: The adsorbent may consist of finely divided adsorbent materials for chromatography. It can be applied directly to the glass plate, or it can be bonded to the plate by means of plaster of Paris or with starch paste. Pretreated chromatographic plates are available commercially.

Spreader: A suitable spreading device that, when moved over the glass plate, applies a uniform layer of adsorbent of the desired thickness over the entire surface of the plate.

Storage Rack: A rack of convenient size to hold the prepared plates during drying and transportation.

Developing Chamber: A glass chamber that can accommodate one or more plates and can be properly closed and sealed. It is fitted with a plate-support rack that can support the plates when the lid of the chamber is in place.

[NOTE—Preformed TLC plates available commercially may also be used.]

Procedure Clean the plates scrupulously, as by immersion in a chromic acid cleansing mixture, rinse them with copious quantities of water until the water runs off the plates without leaving any visible water or oily spots, and dry.

Arrange the plate or plates on the aligning tray, and secure them so that they will not slip during the application of the adsorbent. Mix an appropriate quantity of adsorbent and liquid, usually water, which when shaken for 30 s gives a smooth slurry that will spread evenly with the aid of a spreader. Transfer the slurry to the spreader, and apply the coating at once before the binder begins to harden. Move the spreader smoothly over the plates from one end of the tray to the other. Remove the spreader, and wipe away excess slurry. Allow the plates to set for 10 min, and then place them in the storage rack and dry at 105° for 30 min or as directed in the individual monograph. Store the finished plates in a desiccator.

Equilibrate the atmosphere in the *Developing Chamber* by placing in it a volume of the mobile phase in excess of that required for complete development of the chromatogram, cover the chamber with its lid, and allow it to stand for at least 30 min.

Apply the *Sample Solution* and the *Standard Solution* at points about 1.5 cm apart and about 2 cm from the lower edge of the plate (the lower edge is the first part over which the spreader moves in the application of the adsorbent layer), and allow to dry. A template will aid in determining the spot points and the 10-cm to 15-cm distance through which the solvent front should move.

Arrange the plate on the supporting rack (sample spots on the bottom), and introduce the rack into the developing chamber. The solvent in the chamber must be deep enough to reach the lower edge of the adsorbent, but must not touch the spot points. Seal the cover in place, and maintain the system until the solvent ascends to a point 10–15 cm above the initial spots; this usually requires 15 min to 1 h. Remove the plates, and dry them in air. Measure and record the distance of each spot from the point of origin. If so directed, spray the spots with the reagent specified, observe, and compare the sample with the standard chromatogram.

Detection and Identification Detection and identification of solute bands is done by methods essentially the same as those described in *Column Chromatography*. However, in TLC an additional method called *fluorescence quenching* is also used. In this procedure, an inorganic phosphor is mixed with the adsorbent before it is coated on the plate. When the developed chromatogram is irradiated with ultraviolet light, the surface of the plate fluoresces with a characteristic color, except in those places where ultraviolet-absorbing solutes are situated. These quench the fluorescence and are detectable as dark spots.

Detection with an ultraviolet light source suitable for observations with short (254-nm) and long (360-nm) ultraviolet wavelengths may be called for in some cases.

Quantitative Analysis Two methods are available if quantitation of the solute is necessary. In the first, the bands are detected and their positions marked. Those areas of adsorbent containing the compounds of interest are scraped from the surface of the plate into a centrifuge tube. The chemicals are extracted from the adsorbent with the aid of a suitable strong solvent, the suspension is centrifuged, and the supernatant layer is subjected to appropriate methods of quantitative analysis.

The second method involves the use of a scanning densitometer. This is a spectrophotometric device that directs a beam of monochromatic radiation across the surface of the plate. After interaction with the solutes in the adsorbent layer, the radiation is detected as transmitted or reflected light and a recording of light intensity versus distance traveled is produced. The concentration of a particular species is proportional to the area under its peak and can be determined accurately by comparison with standards.

GAS CHROMATOGRAPHY

The distinguishing features of gas chromatography are a gaseous mobile phase and a solid or immobilized liquid stationary phase. Liquid stationary phases are available in packed or capillary columns. In the packed columns, the liquid phase is deposited on a finely divided, inert solid support, such as diatomaceous earth or porous polymer, which is packed into a column that typically has a 2-mm to 4-mm id and is 1–3 m long. In capillary columns, which contain no particles, the liquid phase is deposited on the inner surface of the fused silica column and may be chemically bonded to it. In gas–solid chromatography, the solid phase is an active adsorbent, such as alumina, silica, or carbon, packed into a column. Polyaromatic porous resins, which are sometimes used in packed columns, are not coated with a liquid phase.

When a volatile compound is introduced into the carrier gas and carried into the column, it is partitioned between the gas and stationary phases by a dynamic countercurrent distribution process. The compound is carried down the column by the carrier gas, retarded to a greater or lesser extent by sorption and desorption in the stationary phase. The elution of the compound is characterized by the partition ratio, k, a dimensionless quantity also called the capacity factor. It is equivalent to the ratio of the time required for the compound to flow through the column (the retention time) to the retention time of a nonretarded compound. The value of the capacity factor depends on the chemical nature of the compound; the nature, amount, and surface area of the liquid phase; and the column temperature. Under a specified set of experimental conditions, a characteristic capacity factor exists for every compound. Separation by gas chromatography occurs only if the compounds concerned have different capacity factors.

Apparatus A gas chromatograph consists of a carrier gas source, an injection port, column, detector, and recording device. The injection port, column, and detector are carefully temperature controlled. The typical carrier gas is helium or nitrogen, depending on the column and detector in use. The gas is supplied from a high-pressure cylinder and passes through suitable pressure-reducing valves to the injection port and column. Compounds to be chromatographed, either in solution or as gases, are injected into the gas stream at the injection port. Depending on the configuration of the apparatus, the test mixture may be injected directly into the column or be vaporized in the injection port and mixed into the flowing carrier gas before entering the column.

Once in the column, compounds in the test mixture are separated by virtue of differences in their capacity factors, which in turn depend on their vapor pressure and degree of interaction with the stationary phase. The capacity factor, which governs resolution and retention times of components of the test mixture, is also temperature dependent. The use of temperature-programmable column ovens takes advantage of this dependence to achieve efficient separation of compounds differing widely in vapor pressure.

As resolved compounds emerge from the column, they pass through a detector, which responds to the amount of each compound present. The type of detector to be used depends on the nature of the compounds to be analyzed, and is specified in the individual monograph. Detectors are heated above the maximum column operating temperature to prevent condensation of the eluting compounds.

Detector output is recorded as a function of time, producing a chromatogram, which consists of a series of peaks on a time axis. Each peak represents a compound in the vaporized test mixture, although some peaks may overlap. The elution time is characteristic of the individual compounds (qualitative analysis), and the peak area is a function of the amount present (quantitative analysis).

Injectors: Sample injection devices range from simple syringes to fully programmable automatic injectors. The amount of sample that can be injected into a capillary column without overloading is small compared with the amount that can be injected into a packed column, and may be less than the smallest amount that can be manipulated satisfactorily by syringe. Capillary columns are therefore used with injectors able to split samples into two fractions, a small one that enters the column and a large one that goes to waste (split injector). Such injectors may also be used in a splitless mode for analyses of trace or minor components.

Purge and trap injectors are equipped with a sparging device by which volatile compounds in solution are carried into a low-temperature trap. When sparging is complete, trapped compounds are thermally desorbed into the carrier gas by rapid heating of the temperature-programmable trap.

Headspace injectors are equipped with a thermostatically controlled sample-heating chamber. Solid or liquid samples in tightly closed containers are heated in the chamber for a fixed period of time, allowing the volatile components in the sample to reach an equilibrium between the non-gaseous phase and the gaseous or headspace phase.

After this equilibrium has been established, the injector automatically introduces a fixed amount of the headspace in the sample container into the gas chromatograph.

Columns: Capillary columns, which are usually made of fused silica, have a 0.2-mm to 0.53-mm id and are 5–30 m long. The liquid or stationary phase is 0.1–1.0 μm thick, although nonpolar stationary phases may be up to 5 μm thick.

Packed columns, made of glass or metal, are 1–3 m long, with a 2-mm to 4-mm id. Those used for analysis typically have liquid phase loadings of about 5% (w/w) on a solid support.

Supports for analysis of polar compounds on low-capacity, low-polarity liquid phase columns must be inert to avoid peak tailing. The reactivity of support materials can be reduced by silanizing before coating with liquid phase. Acid-washed, flux-calcined diatomaceous earth is often used for drug analysis. Support materials are available in various mesh sizes, with 80- to 100-mesh and 100- to 120-mesh being more commonly used with 2-mm to 4-mm columns. Because of the absence of a solid support, capillary compounds are much more inert than packed columns.

Retention time and the peak efficiency depend on the carrier gas flow rate; retention time is also directly proportional to column length, while resolution is proportional to the square root of the column length. For packed columns, the carrier gas flow rate is usually expressed in mL/min at atmospheric pressure and room temperature. It is measured at the detector outlet with a soap film flow meter while the column is at operating temperature. Unless otherwise specified in the individual monograph, flow rates for packed columns are 60–75 mL/min for 4-mm id columns and ~30 mL/min for 2-mm id columns.

For capillary columns, linear flow velocity is often used instead of flow rate. This is conveniently determined from the length of the column and the retention time of a dilute methane sample, provided a flame-ionization detector is in use. Typical linear velocities are 20–60 cm/s for helium. At high operating temperatures there is sufficient vapor pressure to result in a gradual loss of liquid phase, a process called "bleeding."

Detectors: Flame-ionization detectors are used for most analyses, with lesser use made of thermal conductivity, electron-capture, nitrogen–phosphorus, and mass spectrometric detectors. For quantitative analyses, detectors must have a wide linear dynamic range: the response must be directly proportional to the amount of compound present in the detector over a wide range of concentrations. Flame-ionization detectors have a wide linear range (~10^6) and are sensitive to organic compounds. Unless otherwise specified in individual monographs, flame-ionization detectors with either helium or nitrogen carrier gas are to be used for packed columns, and helium is used for capillary columns.

The thermal conductivity detector detects changes in the thermal conductivity of the gas stream as solutes are eluted. Although its linear dynamic range is smaller than that of the flame-ionization detector, it is quite rugged and occasionally used with packed columns, especially for compounds that do not respond to flame-ionization detectors.

The alkali flame-ionization detector, sometimes called an NP or nitrogen–phosphorus detector, contains a thermionic source, such as an alkali-metal salt or a glass element containing rubidium or other metal, that results in the efficient ionization of organic nitrogen and phosphorus compounds. It is a selective detector that shows little response to hydrocarbons.

The electron-capture detector contains a radioactive source (usually ^{63}Ni) of ionizing radiation. It exhibits an extremely high response to compounds containing halogens and nitro groups but little response to hydrocarbons. The sensitivity increases with the number and atomic weight of the halogen atoms.

Data Collection Devices: Modern data stations receive the detector output, calculate peak areas, and print chromatograms, complete with run parameters and peak data. Chromatographic data may be stored and reprocessed, with integration and other calculation variables being changed as required. Data stations are used also to program the chromatograph, controlling most operational variables and providing for long periods of unattended operation.

Data can also be collected for manual measurement on simple recorders or on integrators whose capabilities range from those providing a printout of peak areas to those providing chromatograms with peak areas and peak heights calculated and data stored for possible reprocessing.

Procedure Capillary columns must be tested to ensure that they comply with the manufacturers' specifications before they are used. These tests consist of the following injections: a dilute methane sample to determine the linear flow velocity; a mixture of alkanes (e.g., C_{14}, C_{15}, and C_{16}) to determine resolution; and a polarity test mixture to check for active sites on the column. The latter mixture may include a methyl ester, an unsaturated compound, a phenol, an aromatic amine, a diol, a free carboxylic acid, and a polycyclic aromatic compound, depending on the samples to be analyzed.

Packed columns must be conditioned before use until the baseline and other characteristics are stable. This may be done by operation at a temperature above that called for by the method or by repeated injections of the compound or mixture to be chromatographed. A suitable test for support inertness should be done. Very polar molecules (like free fatty acids) may require a derivatization step.

Before any column is used for assay purposes, a calibration curve should be constructed to verify that the instrumental response is linear over the required range and that the curve passes through the origin. If the compound to be analyzed is adsorbed within the system, the calibration curve will intersect the abscissa at a nonzero value. This may result in error, particularly for compounds at low concentrations determined by a procedure based on a single reference point. At high concentrations, the liquid phase may be overloaded, leading to loss of peak height and symmetry.

Assays require quantitative comparison of one chromatogram with another. A major source of error is irreproducibility in the amount of sample injected, notably when manual injections are made with a syringe. The effects of variability can be minimized by addition of an internal standard, a noninterfering compound present at the same concentration as in the sample and standard solutions. The ratio of peak response of the analyte to that of the internal standard is compared from one chromatogram to another. Where the internal standard is chemically similar to the substance being determined, there is also compensation for minor variations in column and detector characteristics. In some cases, the internal standard may be carried through the sample preparation procedure before gas chromatography to control other quantitative aspects of the assay. Automatic injectors greatly improve the reproducibility of sample injections and reduce the need for internal standards.

Many monographs require that system suitability requirements be met before samples are analyzed, see *System Suitability* below.

HIGH-PERFORMANCE LIQUID CHROMATOGRAPHY

High-performance liquid chromatography (HPLC) is a separation technique based on a solid stationary phase and a liquid mobile phase. Separations are achieved by partition, adsorption, exclusion, or ion-exchange processes, depending on the type of stationary phase used. HPLC has distinct advantages over gas chromatography for the analysis of nonvolatile organic compounds. Compounds to be analyzed are dissolved in a liquid, and most separations take place at room temperature.

As in gas chromatography, the elution time of a compound can be described by the capacity factor, k, which depends on the chemical nature of the composition and flow rate of the mobile phase, and the composition and surface area of the stationary phase. Column length is an important determinant of resolution. Only compounds having different capacity factors can be separated by HPLC.

Apparatus A liquid chromatograph consists of one, two, or more reservoirs containing the mobile phase, a pump to force the mobile phase through the system at high pressure, an injector to introduce the sample into the mobile phase, a chromatographic column, a detector, and a data collection device such as a computer, integrator, or recorder. Short, 3-cm, 5-cm, 10-cm, and 25-cm small-bore columns containing densely packed particles of stationary phase provide for the rapid exchange of compounds between the mobile and stationary phases. In addition to receiving and reporting detector output, computers are used to control chromatographic settings and operations, thus providing for long periods of unattended operation.

Pumping Systems: HPLC pumping systems deliver metered amounts of mobile phase from the solvent reservoirs to the column through high-pressure tubing and fittings. Modern systems consist of one or more computer-controlled metering pumps that can be programmed to vary the ratio of mobile phase components, as is required for gradient chromatography, or to mix isocratic mobile phases (i.e., mobile phases having a fixed ratio of solvents). However, the proportion of ingredients in premixed isocratic mobile phases can be more accurately controlled than in those delivered by most pumping systems. Operating pressures up to 5000 psi with delivery rates up to about 10 mL/min are typical. Pumps used for quantitative analysis should be constructed of materials inert to corrosive mobile phase components and be capable of delivering the mobile phase at a constant rate with minimal fluctuations over extended periods of time.

Injectors: After dissolution in mobile phase or other suitable solution, compounds to be chromatographed are injected into the mobile phase, either manually by syringe or loop injectors, or automatically by autosamplers. The latter consist of a carousel or rack to hold sample vials with tops that have a pierceable septum or stopper and an injection device to transfer sample from the vials to a calibrated, fixed-volume loop from which it is loaded into the chromatograph. Some autosamplers can be programmed to control sample volume, the number of injections and loop rinse cycles, the interval between injections, and other operating variables.

Some valve systems incorporate a calibrated sample loop that is filled with test solution for transfer to the column in the mobile phase. In other systems, test solution is transferred to a cavity by syringe and then switched into the mobile phase.

Columns: For most analyses, separation is achieved by partition of compounds in the test solution between the mobile and stationary phases. Systems consisting of polar stationary phases and nonpolar mobile phases are described as normal phase, while the opposite arrangement, polar mobile phases and nonpolar stationary phases, is called reversed-phase chromatography. Partition chromatography is almost always used for hydrocarbon-soluble compounds of a molecular weight that is less than 1000. The affinity of a compound for the stationary phase, and thus its retention time on the column, is controlled by making the mobile phase more or less polar. Mobile phase polarity can be varied by the addition of a second, and sometimes a third or even a fourth, component.

Stationary phases for modern, reversed-phase liquid chromatography typically consist of an organic phase chemically bound to silica or other materials. Particles are usually 3 μm, 5 μm, or 10 μm in diameter, but sizes may range up to 50 μm for preparative columns. Small particles thinly coated with organic phase allow fast mass transfer and, hence, rapid transfer of compounds between the stationary and mobile phases. Column polarity depends on the polarity of the bound functional groups, which range from relatively nonpolar octadecyl silane to very polar nitrile groups.

Columns used for analytical separations usually have internal diameters of 2–4.6 mm; larger diameter columns are used for preparative chromatography. Columns may be heated to give more efficient separations, but only rarely are they used at temperatures above 60° because of potential stationary phase degradation or mobile phase volatility. Unless otherwise specified in the individual monograph, columns are used at an ambient temperature.

Ion-exchange chromatography is used to separate water-soluble, ionizable compounds of molecular weights that are less than 2000. The stationary phases are usually synthetic organic resins; cation-exchange resins contain negatively charged active sites and are used to separate basic substances such as amines; while anion-exchange resins have positively charged active sites for separation of compounds with negatively charged groups such as phosphate, sulfonate, or carboxylate groups. Water-soluble ionic or ionizable compounds are attracted to the resins, and differences in affinity bring about the chromatographic separation. The pH of the mobile phase, temperature, ion type, ionic concentration, and organic modifiers affect the equilibrium, and these variables can be adjusted to obtain the desired degree of separation.

In size-exclusion chromatography, columns are packed with a porous stationary phase. Molecules of the compounds being chromatographed are filtered according to size. Those too large to enter the pores pass unretained through the column (total exclusion). Smaller molecules enter the pores and are increasingly retained as molecular size decreases. These columns are typically used to remove high molecular weight matrices or to characterize the molecular weight distribution of a polymer.

Detectors: Many compendial HPLC methods require the use of spectrophotometric detectors. Such a detector consists of a flow-through cell mounted at the end of the column. A beam of ultraviolet radiation passes through the flow cell and into the detector. As compounds elute from the column, they pass through the cell and absorb the radiation, resulting in measurable energy level changes.

Fixed, variable, and photodiode array (PDA) detectors are widely available. Fixed wavelength detectors operate at a single wavelength, typically 254 nm, emitted by a low-pressure mercury lamp. Variable wavelength detectors contain a continuous source, such as a deuterium or high-pressure xenon lamp, and a monochromator or an interference filter to generate monochromatic radiation at a wavelength selected by the operator. Modern variable wavelength detectors can be programmed to change wavelength while an analysis is in progress. Multi-wavelength detectors measure absorbance at two or more wavelengths simultaneously. In diode array multi-wavelength detectors, continuous radiation is passed through the sample cell, then resolved into its constituent wavelengths, which are individually detected by the photodiode array. These detectors acquire absorbance data over the entire UV-visible range, thus providing the analyst with chromatograms at multiple, selectable wavelengths and spectra of the eluting peaks. Diode array detectors usually have lower signal-to-noise ratios than fixed or variable wavelength detectors, and thus are less suitable for analysis of compounds present at low concentrations.

Differential refractometer detectors measure the difference between the refractive index of the mobile phase alone and that of the mobile phase containing chromatographed compounds as it emerges from the column. Refractive index detectors are used to detect non-UV absorbing compounds, but they are less sensitive than UV detectors. They are sensitive to small changes in solvent composition, flow rate, and temperature, so that a reference column may be required to obtain a satisfactory baseline.

Fluorometric detectors are sensitive to compounds that are inherently fluorescent or that can be converted to fluorescent derivatives either by chemical transformation of the compound or by coupling with fluorescent reagents at specific functional groups. If derivatization is required, it can be done before chromatographic separation or, alternatively, the reagent can be introduced into the mobile phase just before its entering the detector.

Potentiometric, voltammetric, or polarographic electrochemical detectors are useful for the quantitation of species that can be oxidized or reduced at a working electrode. These detectors are selective, sensitive, and reliable, but require conducting mobile phases free of dissolved oxygen and reducible metal ions. A pulseless pump must be used, and care must be taken to ensure that the pH, ionic strength, and temperature of the mobile phase remain constant. Working electrodes are prone to contamination by reaction products with consequent variable responses.

Electrochemical detectors with carbon-paste electrodes may be used advantageously to measure nanogram quantities of easily oxidized compounds, notably phenols and catechols.

Data Collection Devices: Modern data stations receive and store detector output and print out chromatograms complete with peak heights, peak areas, sample identification, and method variables. They are also used to program the liquid chromatograph, controlling most variables and providing for long periods of unattended operation.

Data also may be collected on simple recorders for manual measurement or on stand-alone integrators, which range in complexity, from those providing a printout of peak areas to those providing a printout of peak areas and peak heights calculated and data stored for possible subsequent reprocessing.

Procedure   The mobile phase composition significantly influences chromatographic performance and the resolution of compounds in the mixture being chromatographed. Composition has a much greater effect than temperature on the capacity factor, k.

In partition chromatography, the partition coefficient, and hence the separation, can be changed by addition of another component to the mobile phase. In ion-exchange chromatography, pH and ionic strength as well as changes in the composition of the mobile phase affect capacity factors. The technique of continuously increasing mobile phase strength during the chromatographic run is called gradient elution or solvent programming. It is sometimes used to chromatograph complex mixtures of components differing greatly in their capacity factors. Detectors that are sensitive to change in solvent composition, such as the differential refractometer, are more difficult to use with the gradient elution technique.

For accurate quantitative work, high-purity, "HPLC-grade" solvents and reagents must be used. The detector must have a broad linear dynamic range, and compounds to be measured must be resolved from any interfering substances. The linear dynamic range of a compound is the range over which the detector signal response is directly proportional to the amount of the compound. For maximum flexibility in quantitative work, this range should be about three orders of magnitude. HPLC systems are calibrated by plotting peak responses in comparison with known concentrations of a reference standard, using either an external or an internal standardization procedure.

Reliable quantitative results are obtained by external calibration if automatic injectors or autosamplers are used. This method involves direct comparison of the peak responses obtained by separately chromatographing the test and reference standard solutions. If syringe injection, which is irreproducible at the high pressures involved, must be used, better quantitative results are obtained by the internal calibration procedure where a known amount of a noninterfering compound, the internal standard, is added to the test and reference standard solutions, and the ratios of peak responses of the analyte and internal standard are compared.

Because of normal variations in equipment, supplies, and techniques, a system suitability test is required to ensure that a given operating system may be generally applicable. The main features of *System Suitability* tests are described below.

For information on the interpretation of results, see the section *Interpretation of Chromatograms.*

Interpretation of Chromatograms   *Figure 1* represents a typical chromatographic separation of two substances, 1 and 2, in which $t_{R(1)}$ and $t_{R(2)}$ are the respective retention times; h, h/2, and $W_{h/2}$ are the height, the half-height, and the width at half-height, respectively, for peak 1; and W_1 and W_2 are the respective widths of peaks 1 and 2 at the baseline. Air peaks are a feature of gas chromatograms and correspond to the solvent front in liquid chromatography.

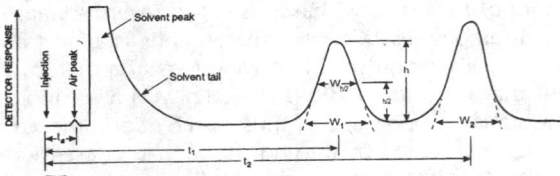

Figure 1. Chromatographic Separation of Two Substances

Chromatographic retention times are characteristic of the compounds they represent but are not unique. Coincidence of retention times of a test and a reference substance can be used as a feature in construction of an identity profile but is insufficient on its own to establish identity. Absolute retention times of a given compound vary from one chromatogram to the next. Comparisons are normally made in terms of relative retention, which is calculated by the equation:

$$\alpha = (t_{R(2)} - t_{R(0)})/(t_{R(1)} - t_0)$$

in which $t_{R(2)}$ and $t_{R(1)}$ are the retention times, measured from the point of injection, of the test and reference substances, respectively, determined under identical experimental conditions on the same column, and t_0 is the retention time of a nonretained substance, such as methane in this case, of gas chromatography.

In this and the following expressions, the corresponding retention volumes or linear separations on the chromatogram, both of which are directly proportional to retention time, may be substituted in the equations. Where the value of t_0 is small, R_r may be estimated from the retention times measured from the point of injection ($t_{R(2)}/t_{R(1)}$).

The number of theoretical plates, N, is a measure of column efficiency. For Gaussian peaks, it is calculated by the equations:

$$N = 16(t_R/W)^2 \text{ or } N = 5.54(t_R/W_{1/2})^2$$

in which t_R is the retention time of the substance and W is the width of the peak at its base, obtained by extrapolating the relatively straight sides of the peak to the baseline. $W_{1/2}$ is the peak width at half-height, obtained directly by electronic integrators. The value of N depends on the substance being chromatographed as well as the operating conditions such as mobile phase or carrier gas flow rates and temperature, the quality of the packing, the uniformity of the packing within the column, and for capillary columns, the thickness of the stationary phase film and the internal diameter and length of the column.

The separation of two components in a mixture, the resolution, R, is determined by the equation:

$$R = 2(t_{R(2)} - t_{R(1)})/(W_2 + W_1)$$

in which $t_{R(2)}$ and $t_{R(1)}$ are the retention times of the two components, and W_2 and W_1 are the corresponding widths at the bases of the peaks obtained by extrapolating the relatively straight sides of the peaks to the baseline.

Peak areas and peak heights are usually proportional to the quantity of compound eluting. These are commonly measured by electronic integrators but may be determined by more classical approaches. Peak areas are generally used but may be less accurate if peak interference occurs. For manual measurements, the chart should be run faster than usual, or a comparator should be used to measure the width at half-height and the width at the base of the peak, to minimize error in these measurements. For accurate quantitative work, the components to be measured should be separated from any interfering components. Peak tailing and fronting and the measurement of peaks on solvent tails are to be avoided (see *Figure 2*). The relative standard deviation is expressed by the equation:

$$S_R(\%) = (100/\bar{X})\left\{\left[\sum_{i=1}^{N}(X_i - \bar{X})^2\right]/(N-1)\right\}^{1/2}$$

in which S_R is the relative standard deviation in percent, $\bar{X}$ is the mean of the set of N measurements, and X_i is an individual measurement. When an internal standard is used, the measurement X_i usually refers to the measurement of relative area, A_s:

$$X_i = A_s = a_r/a_i$$

in which a_r is the area of the peak corresponding to the standard substance and a_i is the area of the peak corresponding to the internal standard. When peak heights are used, the measurement X_i refers to the measurement of relative heights, H_s:

$$X_i = H_s = h_r/h_i$$

in which h_r is the height of the peak corresponding to the standard substance and h_i is the height of the peak corresponding to the internal standard.

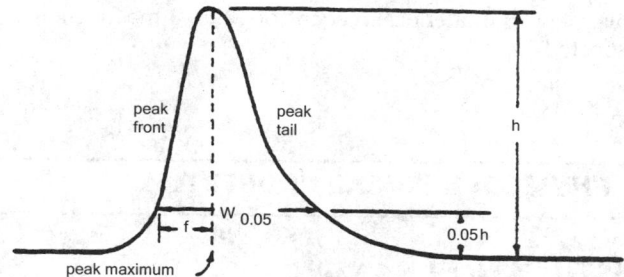

Figure 2. Asymmetrical Chromatographic Peak

System Suitability Such tests are an integral part of gas and liquid chromatographic methods. They are used to verify that the resolution and reproducibility of the chromatographic system are adequate for the analysis to be done. The tests are based on the concept that the equipment, electronics, analytical operations, and samples to be analyzed constitute an integral system that can be evaluated as such.

The resolution, R, is a function of column efficiency, N, and is specified to ensure that closely eluting compounds are resolved from each other, to establish the general resolving power of the system, and to ensure that internal standards are resolved from the analyte. Column efficiency may be specified also as a system suitability requirement, especially if there is only one peak of interest in the chromatogram; however, it is a less reliable means to ensure resolution than direct measurement. Column efficiency is a measure of peak sharpness, which is important for the detection of trace components.

Replicate injections of a standard preparation used in the assay or other standard solution are compared to ascertain whether requirements for precision are met. Unless otherwise specified in the individual monograph, data from five replicate injections of the analyte are used to calculate the relative standard deviation if the requirement is 2.0% or less; data from six replicate injections are used if the relative standard deviation requirement is more than 2.0%.

The tailing factor, T, a measure of peak symmetry, is unity for perfectly symmetrical peaks, and its value increases as tailing becomes more pronounced. In some cases, values less than unity may be observed. As peak asymmetry increases, integration, and hence precision, becomes less reliable. The calculation is expressed by the equation:

$$\text{tailing factor} = T = W_{0.05}/2f$$

These tests are performed by collecting data from replicate injections of standard or other solutions as specified in the individual monograph. The specification of definitive parameters in a monograph does not preclude the use of other suitable operating conditions (see *Procedures* under *Tests and Assays* in *General Provisions*). Adjustments of operating conditions to meet system suitability requirements may be necessary.

Unless otherwise directed in the monograph, system suitability parameters are determined from the analyte peak.

To ascertain the effectiveness of the final operating system, it should be subjected to a suitability test before use and during testing whenever there is a significant change in equipment or in a critical reagent or when a malfunction is suspected.

B. PHYSICOCHEMICAL PROPERTIES

DISTILLATION RANGE

Scope This method is to be used for determining the distillation range of pure or nearly pure compounds or mixtures having a relatively narrow distillation range of about 40° or less. The result so determined is an indication of purity, not necessarily of identity. Products having a distillation range of greater than 40° may be determined by this method if a wide-range thermometer, such as ASTM E1, 1C, 2C, or 3C, is specified in the individual monograph.

Definitions

Distillation Range The difference between the temperature observed at the start of a distillation and that observed at which a specified volume has distilled, or at which the dry point is reached.

Initial Boiling Point The temperature indicated by the distillation thermometer at the instant the first drop of condensate leaves the end of the condenser tube.

Dry Point The temperature indicated at the instant the last drop of liquid evaporates from the lowest point in the distillation flask, disregarding any liquid on the side of the flask.

Apparatus

Distillation Flask: A 200-mL round-bottom distilling flask of heat-resistant glass is preferred when sufficient sample (in excess of 100 mL) is available for the test. If a sample of less than 100 mL must be used, a smaller flask having a capacity of at least double the volume of the liquid taken may be employed. The 200-mL flask has a total length of 17–19 cm, and the inside diameter of the neck is 20–22 mm. Attached about midway on the neck, approximately 12 cm from the bottom of the flask, is a side arm 10–12.7 cm long and 5 mm in internal diameter, which forms an angle of 70°–75° with the lower portion of the neck.

Condenser: Use a straight glass condenser of heat-resistant tubing, 56–60 cm long and equipped with a water jacket so that about 40 cm of the tubing is in contact with the cooling medium. The lower end of the condenser may be bent to provide a delivery tube or it may be connected to a bent adapter that serves as the delivery tube.

[NOTE—All-glass apparatus with standard-taper ground joints may be used alternatively if the assembly employed provides results equal to those obtained with the flask and condenser described above.]

Receiver: The receiver is a 100-mL cylinder that is graduated in 1-mL subdivisions and calibrated "to contain." It is used for measuring the sample as well as for receiving the distillate.

Thermometer: An accurately standardized partial-immersion thermometer having the smallest practical subdivisions (not greater than 0.2°) is recommended to avoid the necessity for an emergent stem correction. Suitable thermometers are available as the ASTM E1 Series 37C through 41C, and 102C through 107C, or as the MCA types R-1 through R-4 (see *Thermometers*, Appendix I).

Source of Heat: A Bunsen burner is the preferred source of heat. An electric heater may be used, however, if it is shown to give results comparable to those obtained with the gas burner.

Shield: The entire burner and flask assembly should be protected from external air currents. Any efficient shield may be employed for this purpose.

Flask Support: A heat-resistant board, 5–7 mm in thickness and having a 10-cm circular hole, is placed on a suitable ring or platform support and fitted loosely inside the shield to ensure that hot gases from the source of heat do not come in contact with the sides or neck of the flask. A second 5–7-mm thick heat-resistant board, 14–16-cm square and provided with a 30–40-mm circular hole, is placed on top of the first board. This board is used to hold the 200-mL distillation flask, which should be fitted firmly on the board so that direct heat is applied to the flask only through the opening in the board.

Procedure [NOTE—For materials boiling below 50°, cool the liquid to below 10° before sampling, receive the distillate in a water bath cooled to below 10°, and use water cooled to below 10° in the condenser.]

Measure 100 ± 0.5 mL of the liquid in the 100-mL graduate, and transfer the sample, together with an efficient antibumping device, into the distilling flask. Do not use a funnel in the transfer or allow any of the sample to enter the side arm of the flask. Place the flask on the heat-resistant boards, which are supported on a ring or platform, and position the shield for the flask and burner. Connect the flask and condenser, place the graduate under the outlet of the condenser tube, and insert the thermometer. The thermometer should be located in the center of the neck so that the top of the contraction chamber (or bulb, if 37C or 38C is used) is level with the bottom of the outlet to the side arm. Regulate the heating so that the first drop of liquid is collected within 5–10 min. Read the thermometer at the instant the first drop of distillate falls from the end of the condenser tube, and record as the initial boiling point. Continue the distillation at the rate of 4 or 5 mL/min of distillate, noting the temperature as soon as the last drop of liquid evaporates from the bottom of the flask (dry point) or when the specified percentage has distilled over. Correct the observed temperature readings for any variation in the barometric pressure from the normal (760 mm) by allowing 0.1° for each 2.7 mm of variation, adding the correction if the pressure is lower, or subtracting if higher, than 760 mm.

When a total-immersion thermometer is used, correct for the temperature of the emergent stem:

$$\text{Result} = 0.00015 \times N(T - t)$$

in which N represents the number of degrees of emergent stem from the bottom of the stopper, T represents the observed temperatures of the distillation, and t represents the temperature registered by an auxiliary thermometer, the bulb of which is placed midway of the emergent stem, adding the correction to the observed readings of the main thermometer.

MELTING RANGE OR TEMPERATURE DETERMINATION

For purposes of the FCC, the melting range or temperature of a solid is defined as those points of temperature within which or the point at which the solid coalesces and is completely melted when determined as directed below. Any apparatus or method capable of equal accuracy may be used. The accuracy should be checked frequently by the use of one or more of the six USP Melting Point Reference Standards, preferably the one that melts nearest the melting temperature of the compound to be tested.

Five procedures for the determination of melting range or temperature are given herein, varying in accordance with the nature of the substance. When no class is designated in the monograph, use the procedure for *Class I*.

The procedure known as the mixed melting point determination, whereby the melting range of a solid under test is compared with that of an intimate mixture of equal parts of the solid and an authentic specimen of it, may be used as a confirmatory identification test. Agreement of the observations on the original and the mixture usually constitutes reliable evidence of chemical identity.

Apparatus The melting range apparatus consists of a glass container for a bath of colorless fluid, a suitable stirring device, an accurate thermometer (see Appendix I), and a controlled source of heat. The bath fluid is selected consistent with the temperature required, but light paraffin is used generally, and certain liquid silicones are well adapted to the higher temperature ranges. The fluid is deep enough to permit immersion of the thermometer to its specified immersion depth so that the bulb is still about 2 cm above the bottom of the bath. The heat may be supplied electrically or by an open flame. The capillary tube is about 10 cm long, with an internal diameter of 0.8–1.2 mm, and with walls 0.2–0.3 mm thick.

The thermometer is preferably one that conforms to the specifications provided under *Thermometers*, Appendix I, selected for the desired accuracy and range of temperature.

Procedure for Class I Reduce the sample to a very fine powder, and unless otherwise directed, render it anhydrous when it contains water of hydration by drying it at the temperature specified in the monograph, or when the substance contains no water of hydration, dry it over a suitable desiccant for 16–24 h.

Charge a capillary glass tube, one end of which is sealed, with a sufficient amount of the dry powder to form a column in the bottom of the tube 2.5–3.5 mm high when packed down as closely as possible by moderate tapping on a solid surface.

Heat the bath until a temperature approximately 30° below the expected melting point is reached, attach the capillary tube to the thermometer, and adjust its height so that the material in the capillary is level with the thermometer bulb. Return the thermometer to the bath, continue the heating, with constant stirring, at a rate of rise of approximately 3°/min until a temperature 3° below the expected melting point is attained, then carefully regulate the rate to about 1°–2°/min until melting is complete.

The temperature at which the column of the sample is observed to collapse definitely against the side of the tube at any point is defined as the beginning of melting, and the temperature at which the sample becomes liquid throughout is defined as the end of melting. The two temperatures fall within the limits of the melting range.

Procedure for Class Ia Prepare the sample and charge the capillary glass tube as directed for *Class I*. Heat the bath until a temperature 10 ± 1° below the expected melting range is reached, then introduce the charged tube, and heat at a rate of rise of 3 ± 0.5°/min until melting is complete. Record the melting range as for *Class I*.

Procedure for Class Ib Place the sample in a closed container, and cool to 10° or lower for at least 2 h. Without previous powdering, charge the cooled material into the capillary tube as directed for *Class I*, immediately place the charged tube in a vacuum desiccator, and dry at a pressure not exceeding 20 mm Hg for 3 h. Immediately upon removal from the desiccator, fire-seal the open end of the tube. As soon as is practicable, proceed with the determination of the melting range as follows: Heat the bath until a temperature of 10 ± 1° below the expected melting range is reached, then introduce the charged tube, and heat at a rate of rise of 3 ± 0.5°/min until melting is complete. Record the melting range as directed in *Class I*.

If the particle size of the material is too large for the capillary, precool the sample as directed above, then with as little pressure as possible, gently crush the particles to fit the capillary, and immediately charge the tube.

Procedure for Class II Carefully melt the material to be tested at as low a temperature as possible, and draw it into a capillary tube that is left open at both ends to a depth of about 10 mm. Cool the charged tube at 10°, or lower, for 24 h, or in contact with ice for at least 2 h. Then attach the tube to the thermometer by means of a rubber band, adjust it in a water bath so that the upper edge of the material is 10 mm below the water level, and heat as directed for *Class I*, except within 5° of the expected melting temperature, regulate the rate of rise of temperature to 0.5°–1.0°/min. The temperature at which the material is observed to rise in the capillary tube is the melting temperature.

Procedure for Class III Melt a quantity of the substance slowly, while stirring, until it reaches a temperature of 90°–92°. Remove the source of heat, and allow the molten substance to cool to a temperature of 8°–10° above the expected melting point. Chill the bulb of an ASTM 14C thermometer (see Appendix I) to 5°, wipe it dry, and while it is still cold, dip it into the molten substance so that approximately the lower half of the bulb is submerged. Withdraw it immediately, and hold it vertically away from the heat until the wax surface dulls, then dip it for 5 min into a water bath having a temperature not higher than 16°.

Fix the thermometer securely in a test tube so that the lower point is 15 mm above the bottom of the test tube. Suspend the test tube in a water bath adjusted to about 16°, and raise the temperature of the bath at the rate of

2°/min to 30°, then change to a rate of 1°/min, and note the temperature at which the first drop of melted substance leaves the thermometer. Repeat the determination twice on a freshly melted portion of the sample. If the variation of three determinations is less than 1°, take the average of the three as the melting point. If the variation of three determinations is greater than 1°, make two additional determinations and take the average of the five.

OPTICAL (SPECIFIC) ROTATION

Many chemicals in a pure state or in solution are optically active in the sense that they cause incident polarized light to emerge in a plane forming a measurable angle with the plane of the incident light. When this effect is large enough for precise measurement, it may serve as the basis for an assay or an identity test. In this connection, the optical rotation is expressed in degrees, as either *angular rotation* (observed) or *specific rotation* (calculated with reference to the specific concentration of 1 g of solute in 1 mL of solution, measured under stated conditions).

Specific rotation of a liquid substance usually is expressed by the equation $[\alpha]_x^t = a/ld$, and for solutions of solid substances, expressed by the equation $[\alpha]_x^t = 100a/lpd = 100a/lc$, in which a is the corrected observed rotation, in degrees, at temperature t; x is the wavelength of the light used; l is the length of the polarimeter cell, in dm; d is the specific gravity of the liquid or solution at the temperature of observation; p is the concentration of the solution expressed as the number of grams of substance in 100 g of solution; and c is the concentration of the solution expressed as the number of grams of substance in 100 mL of solution. The concentrations p and c should be calculated on the dried or anhydrous basis, unless otherwise specified. Spectral lines most frequently employed are the D line of sodium (doublet at 589.0 nm and 589.6 nm) and the yellow-green line of mercury at 546.1 nm. The specific gravity and the rotatory power vary appreciably with the temperature.

The accuracy and precision of optical rotatory measurements will be increased if they are carried out with due regard for the following general considerations.

Supplement the source of illumination with a filtering system capable of transmitting light of a sufficiently monochromatic nature. Precision polarimeters generally are designed to accommodate interchangeable disks to isolate the D line from sodium light or the 546.1-nm line from the mercury spectrum. With polarimeters not thus designed, cells containing suitably colored liquids may be employed as filters (see also A. Weissberger and B. W. Rossiter, *Techniques of Chemistry*, Vol. I: *Physical Methods of Chemistry*, Part 3, Wiley-Interscience, New York, 1972).

Pay special attention to temperature control of the solution and of the polarimeter. Make accurate and reproducible observations to the extent that differences between replicates, or between observed and true values of rotation (the latter value having been established by calibration of the polarimeter scale with suitable standards), calculated in terms of either specific rotation or angular rotation, whichever is appropriate, do not exceed one-fourth of the range given in the individual monograph for the rotation of the article being tested. Generally, a polarimeter accurate to 0.05° of angular rotation, and capable of being read with the same precision, suffices for *FCC* purposes; in some cases, a polarimeter accurate to 0.01°, or less, of angular rotation, and read with comparable precision, may be required.

Fill polarimeter tubes in such a way as to avoid creating or leaving air bubbles, which interfere with the passage of the beam of light. Interference from bubbles is minimized with tubes in which the bore is expanded at one end. However, tubes of uniform bore, such as semimicro- or microtubes, require care for proper filling. At the time of filling, the tubes and the liquid or solution should be at a temperature not higher than that specified for the determination to guard against the formation of a bubble upon cooling and contraction of the contents.

In closing tubes having removable end plates fitted with gaskets and caps, the latter should be tightened only enough to ensure a leak-proof seal between the end plate and the body of the tube. Excessive pressure on the end plate may set up strains that result in interference with the measurements. In determining the specific rotation of a substance of low rotatory power, loosen the caps and tighten them again between successive readings in the measurement of both the rotation and the zero point. Differences arising from end plate strain thus generally will be revealed and appropriate adjustments to eliminate the cause may be made.

Procedure In the case of a solid, dissolve the substance in a suitable solvent, reserving a separate portion of the latter for a blank determination. Make at least five readings of the rotation of the solution, or of the substance itself if liquid, at 25° or the temperature specified in the individual monograph. Replace the solution with the reserved portion of the solvent (or, in the case of a liquid, use the empty tube), make the same number of readings, and use the average as the zero point value. Subtract the zero point value from the average observed rotation if the two figures are of the same sign, or add if opposite in sign, to obtain the corrected observed rotation.

Calculation Calculate the specific rotation of a liquid substance, or of a solid in solution, by application of one of the following formulas:

1. for liquid substances,

$$[\alpha]_x^t = a/ld$$

2. for solutions of solids,

$$[\alpha]_x^t = 100a/lpd = 100a/lc$$

in which a is the corrected observed rotation, in degrees, at temperature t; x is the wavelength of the light used; l is the length, in dm, of the polarimeter cell; d is the specific gravity of the liquid or solution at the temperature of observation; p is the concentration of the solution expressed as the number of grams of substance in 100 g of solution; and c is the concentration of the solution expressed as the number of grams of substance in 100 mL of solution. The concentrations p and c should be calculated on the dried or anhydrous basis, unless otherwise specified.

pH DETERMINATION

Principle The definition of pH is the negative log of the hydrogen ion concentration in moles per liter of aqueous solutions. Measure pH potentiometrically by using a pH meter or colorimetrically by using pH indicator paper.

Scope This method is suitable to determine the pH of aqueous solutions. While pH meters, calibrated with aqueous solutions, are sometimes used to make measurements in semiaqueous solutions or in nonaqueous polar solutions, the value obtained is the apparent pH value only and should not be compared with the pH of aqueous solutions. For nonpolar solutions, pH has no meaning, and pH electrodes may be damaged by direct contact with these solutions. References to the pH of nonpolar solutions or liquids usually indicate the pH of a water extract of the nonpolar liquid or the apparent pH of a mixture of the nonpolar liquid in a polar liquid such as alcohol or alcohol–water mixtures.

Procedure [Potentiometric Method (pH Meter)]

Calibration: Select two standard buffers to bracket, if possible, the anticipated pH of the unknown substances. These commercially available standards and the sample should be at the same temperature, within 2°. Set the temperature compensator of the pH meter to the temperature of the samples and standards. Follow the manufacturer's instructions for setting temperature compensation and for adjusting the output during calibration. Rinse the electrodes with distilled or deionized water, and blot them dry with clean, absorbent laboratory tissue. Place the electrode(s) in the first standard buffer solution, and adjust the standardization control so that the pH reading matches the stated pH of the standard buffer. Repeat this procedure with fresh portions of the first buffer solution until two successive readings are within ±0.02 pH units with no further adjustment. Rinse the electrodes, blot them dry, and place them in a portion of the second standard buffer solution. Following the manufacturer's instructions, adjust the slope control (not the standardization control) until the output displays the pH of the second standard buffer.

Repeat the sequence of standardization with both buffers until pH readings are within ± 0.02 pH units for both buffers without adjustments to either the slope or standardization controls. The pH of the unknown may then be measured, using either a pH electrode in combination with a reference electrode or a single combination electrode. Select electrodes made of chemically resistant glass when measuring samples of either low or high pH.

pH Indicator Paper: Test papers impregnated with acid–base indicators, although less accurate than pH meters, offer a convenient way to determine the pH of an aqueous solution. They may be purchased in rolls or strips covering all or part of the pH range; papers covering a narrow part of the pH range can be sensitive to differences of 0.2 pH units. Some test papers comprise a plastic strip with small squares of test paper attached. The different squares are sensitive to different pH ranges. When using this type of test paper, wet all of the squares with the test sample to ensure a correct pH reading.

Test paper can contaminate the sample being tested; therefore, do not dip it into the sample. Either use a clean glass rod to remove a drop of the test solution and place it on the test paper, or transfer a small amount of the sample to a small container, dip the test paper into this portion, and compare the developed color with the color comparison chart provided with the test paper to determine the pH of the sample.

READILY CARBONIZABLE SUBSTANCES

Reagents

Sulfuric Acid, 95%: Add a quantity of sulfuric acid of known concentration to sufficient water to adjust the final concentration to 94.5%–95.5% of H_2SO_4. Because the acid concentration may change upon standing or upon intermittent use, check the concentration frequently and either adjust solutions assaying more than 95.5% or less than 94.5% by adding either diluted or fuming sulfuric acid, as required, or discard them.

Cobaltous Chloride CS: Dissolve about 65 g of cobaltous chloride ($CoCl_2 \cdot 6H_2O$) in enough of a mixture of 25 mL of hydrochloric acid and 975 mL of water to make 1000 mL. Pipet 5 mL of this solution into a 250-mL iodine flask, add 5 mL of hydrogen peroxide TS (3%) and 15 mL of a solution of sodium hydroxide (1:5), boil for 10 min, cool, and add 2 g of potassium iodide and 20 mL of sulfuric acid (1:4). When the precipitate has dissolved, titrate the liberated iodine with 0.1 N sodium thiosulfate. The titration is sensitive to air oxidation and should be blanketed with carbon dioxide. Each mL of 0.1 N sodium thiosulfate is equivalent to 23.79 mg of $CoCl_2 \cdot 6H_2O$. Adjust the final volume of the solution by adding enough of the mixture of hydrochloric acid and water so that each mL contains 59.5 mg of $CoCl_2 \cdot 6H_2O$.

Cupric Sulfate CS: Dissolve about 65 g of cupric sulfate ($CuSO_4 \cdot 5H_2O$) in enough of a mixture of 25 mL of hydrochloric acid and 975 mL of water to make 1000 mL. Pipet 10 mL of this solution into a 250-mL iodine flask; add 40 mL of water, 4 mL of acetic acid, and 3 g of potassium iodide; and titrate the liberated iodine with 0.1 N sodium thiosulfate, adding starch TS as the indicator. Each mL of 0.1 N sodium thiosulfate is equivalent to 24.97 mg of $CuSO_4 \cdot 5H_2O$. Adjust the final volume of the solution by adding enough of the mixture of hydrochloric acid and water so that each mL contains 62.4 mg of $CuSO_4 \cdot 5H_2O$.

Ferric Chloride CS: Dissolve about 55 g of ferric chloride ($FeCl_3 \cdot 6H_2O$) in enough of a mixture of 25 mL of hydrochloric acid and 975 mL of water to make 1000 mL. Pipet 10 mL of this solution into a 250-mL iodine flask; add 15 mL of water, 5 mL of hydrochloric acid, and 3 g of potassium iodide; and allow the mixture to stand for 15 min. Dilute with 100 mL of water, and titrate the liberated iodine with 0.1 N sodium thiosulfate, adding starch TS as the indicator. Perform a blank determination with the same quantities of the same reagents and in the same manner, and make any necessary correction. Each mL of 0.1 N sodium thiosulfate is equivalent to 27.03 mg of $FeCl_3 \cdot 6H_2O$. Adjust the final volume of the solution by adding the mixture of hydrochloric acid and water so that each mL contains 45.0 mg of $FeCl_3 \cdot 6H_2O$.

Platinum–Cobalt CS: Transfer 1.246 g of potassium chloroplatinate (K_2PtCl_6) and 1.00 g of crystallized cobaltous chloride ($CoCl_2 \cdot 6H_2O$) into a 1000-mL volumetric flask, dissolve in about 200 mL of water and 100 mL of hydrochloric acid, dilute with water to volume, and mix. This solution has a color of 500 APHA units.

[NOTE—Use this solution only when specified in an individual monograph.]

Procedure Unless otherwise directed, add the specified quantity of the substance, finely powdered if in solid form, in small portions to the comparison container, which is made of colorless glass resistant to the action of sulfuric acid and contains the specified volume of *95% Sulfuric Acid*.

Stir the mixture with a glass rod until solution is complete, allow the solution to stand for 15 min, unless otherwise directed, and compare the color of the solution with that of the specified matching fluid in a comparison container that also is of colorless glass and has the same internal and cross-section dimensions, viewing the fluids transversely against a background of white porcelain or white glass.

When heat is directed to effect solution of the substance in the *95% Sulfuric Acid*, mix the sample and the acid in a test tube, heat as directed, cool, and transfer the solution to the comparison container for matching.

Matching Fluids For purposes of comparison, a series of 20 matching fluids, each designated by a letter of the alphabet, is provided, the composition of each being as indicated in the accompanying table. To prepare the matching fluid specified, pipet the prescribed volumes of the colorimetric test solutions (CS) and water into one of the matching containers, and mix the solutions in the container.

Matching Fluids[a]

Matching Fluid	Parts of Cobaltous Chloride CS	Parts of Ferric Chloride CS	Parts of Cupric Sulfate CS	Parts of Water
A	0.1	0.4	0.1	4.4
B	0.3	0.9	0.3	8.5
C	0.1	0.6	0.1	4.2
D	0.3	0.6	0.4	3.7
E	0.4	1.2	0.3	3.1
F	0.3	1.2	0.0	3.5
G	0.5	1.2	0.2	3.1
H	0.2	1.5	0.0	3.3
I	0.4	2.2	0.1	2.3
J	0.4	3.5	0.1	1.0
K	0.5	4.5	0.0	0.0
L	0.8	3.8	0.1	0.3
M	0.1	2.0	0.1	2.8
N	0.0	4.9	0.1	0.0

[a] Solutions A–D, very light brown-yellow. Solutions E–L, yellow through red-yellow. Solutions M–O, green-yellow. Solutions P–T, light pink.

Matching Fluids[a] (continued)

Matching Fluid	Parts of Cobaltous Chloride CS	Parts of Ferric Chloride CS	Parts of Cupric Sulfate CS	Parts of Water
O	0.1	4.8	0.1	0.0
P	0.2	0.4	0.1	4.3
Q	0.2	0.3	0.1	4.4
R	0.3	0.4	0.2	4.1
S	0.2	0.1	0.0	4.7
T	0.5	0.5	0.4	3.6

[a] Solutions A–D, very light brown-yellow. Solutions E–L, yellow through red-yellow. Solutions M–O, green-yellow. Solutions P–T, light pink.

REFRACTIVE INDEX

The refractive index of a transparent substance is the ratio of the velocity of light in air to its velocity in that material under like conditions. It is equal to the ratio of the sine of the angle of incidence made by a ray in air to the sine of the angle of refraction made by the ray in the material being tested. The refractive index values specified in this Codex are for the D line of sodium (589 nm) unless otherwise specified. The determination should be made at the temperature specified in the individual monograph, or at 25° if no temperature is specified. This physical constant is used as a means for identification of, and detection of impurities in, volatile oils and other liquid substances. The Abbé refractometer, or other refractometers of equal or greater accuracy, may be employed at the discretion of the operator.

SOLIDIFICATION POINT

Scope This method is designed to determine the solidification point of food-grade chemicals having appreciable heats of fusion. It is applicable to chemicals having solidification points between −20° and +150°. Necessary modifications will be noted in individual monographs.

Definition Solidification Point is an empirical constant defined as the temperature at which the liquid phase of a substance is in approximate equilibrium with a relatively small portion of the solid phase. It is measured by noting the maximum temperature reached during a controlled cooling cycle after the appearance of a solid phase.

The solidification point is distinguished from the freezing point in that the latter term applies to the temperature of equilibrium between the solid and liquid state of pure compounds.

Some chemical compounds have more than one temperature at which there may be an equilibrium between the solid and liquid state depending on the crystal form of the solid that is present.

Apparatus The apparatus illustrated in *Figures 3* and *4* consists of the components described in the following paragraphs.

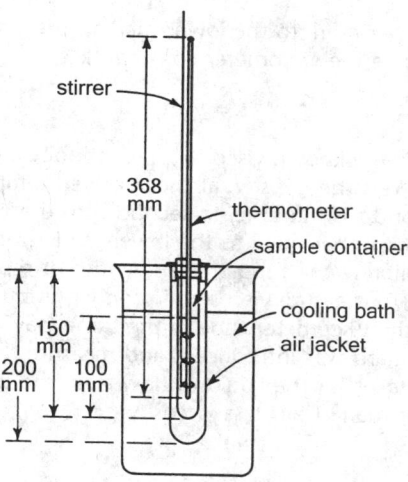

Figure 3. Apparatus for Determination of Solidification Point

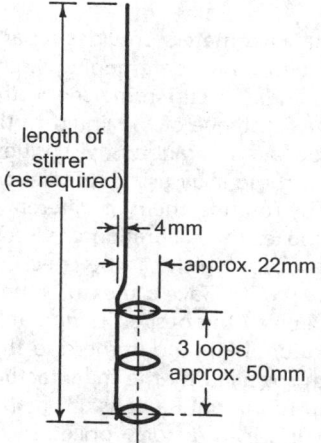

Figure 4. Stirrer for Solidification Point Determination

Thermometer: A thermometer having a range not exceeding 30°, graduated in 0.1° divisions, and calibrated for 76-mm immersion should be employed. A satisfactory series of thermometers, covering a range from −20° to +150°, is available as ASTM-E1 89C through 96C (see *Thermometers*, Appendix I). A thermometer should be chosen such that the solidification point is not obscured by the cork stopper of the sample container.

Sample Container: Use a standard glass 25-mm × 150-mm test tube with a lip, fitted with a two-hole cork stopper to hold the thermometer in place and to allow adequate stirring with a stirrer.

Air Jacket: For the air jacket, use a standard glass 38-mm × 200-mm test tube with a lip and fitted with a cork or rubber stopper bored with a hole into which the sample container can easily be inserted up to the lip.

Cooling Bath: Use a 2000-mL beaker or a similar, suitable container as a cooling bath. Fill it with an appropriate cooling medium such as glycerin, mineral oil, water, water and ice, or alcohol–dry ice.

Stirrer: The stirrer (*Figure 4*) consists of a 1-mm in diameter (B & S gauge 18), corrosion-resistant wire bent into a series of three loops about 25 mm apart. It should be made so that it will move freely in the space between the thermometer and the inner wall of the sample container. The shaft of the stirrer should be of a convenient length designed to pass loosely through a hole in the cork holding the thermometer. Stirring may be hand operated or mechanically activated at 20–30 strokes/min.

Assembly: Assemble the apparatus in such a way that the cooling bath can be heated or cooled to control the desired temperature ranges. Clamp the air jacket so that it is held rigidly just below the lip, and immerse it in the cooling bath to a depth of 160 mm.

Sample Preparation   The solidification point of chemicals is usually determined as they are received. Some may be hygroscopic, however, and will require special drying. If this is necessary, it will be noted in the individual monographs.

Products that are normally solid at room temperature must be carefully melted at a temperature about 10° above the expected solidification point. Care should be observed to avoid heating in such a way as to decompose or distill any portion of a sample.

Procedure   Adjust the temperature of the cooling bath to about 5° below the expected solidification point. Fit the thermometer and stirrer with a cork stopper so that the thermometer is centered and the bulb is about 20 mm from the bottom of the sample container. Transfer a sufficient amount of the sample, previously melted if necessary, into the sample container to fill it to a depth of about 90 mm when in the molten state. Place the thermometer and stirrer in the sample container, and adjust the thermometer so that the immersion line will be at the surface of the liquid and so that the end of the bulb is 20 ± 4 mm from the bottom of the sample container. When the temperature of the sample is about 5° above the expected solidification point, place the assembled sample tube in the air jacket.

Allow the sample to cool while stirring, at the rate of 20–30 strokes/min, in such a manner that the stirrer does not touch the thermometer. Stir the sample continuously during the remainder of the test.

The temperature at first will gradually fall, then will become constant as crystallization starts and continues under equilibrium conditions, and finally will start to drop again. Some chemicals may supercool slightly below (0.5°) the solidification point; as crystallization begins, the temperature will rise and remain constant as equilibrium conditions are established. Other products may cool more than 0.5° and cause deviation from the normal pattern of temperature change. If the temperature rise exceeds 0.5° after the initial crystallization begins, repeat the test, and seed the melted compound with small crystals of the sample at 0.5° intervals as the temperature approaches the expected solidification point. Crystals for seeding may be obtained by freezing a small sample in a test tube directly in the cooling bath. It is preferable that seed of the stable phase be used from a previous determination.

Observe and record the temperature readings at regular intervals until the temperature rises from a minimum, due to supercooling, to a maximum and then finally drops. The maximum temperature reading is the solidification point. Readings 10 s apart should be taken to establish that the temperature is at the maximum level and should continue until the drop in temperature is established.

VISCOSITY DETERMINATION

Viscosity is a fluid's measured internal resistance to flow. Thick, slow-moving fluids have higher viscosities than thin, free-flowing fluids. The basic unit of measure for viscosity is the poise or Pascal second, Pa·s, in SI units. The relationship between poise and Pa·s is 1 poise = 0.1 Pa·s. Since commonly encountered viscosities are often fractions of 1 poise, viscosities are commonly expressed as centipoises (one centipoise = 0.01 poise). Poise or centipoise is the unit of measure for absolute viscosity. Kinematic viscosity also is commonly used and is determined by dividing the absolute viscosity of the test liquid by the density of the test liquid at the same temperature as the viscosity measurement and is expressed as stokes or centistokes (poise/density = stokes). The specified temperature is important: viscosity varies greatly with temperature, generally decreasing with increasing temperature.

Absolute viscosity can be determined directly if accurate dimensions of the measuring instruments are known. It is common practice to calibrate an instrument with a fluid of known viscosity and to determine the unknown viscosity of another fluid by comparison with that of the known viscosity.

Many substances, such as gums, have a variable viscosity, and most of them are less resistant to flow at higher flow (more correctly, shear) rates. In such cases, select a given set of conditions for measurement, and consider the measurement obtained to be an apparent viscosity. Since a change in the conditions of measurement would yield a different value for the apparent viscosity of such substances, the operator must closely adhere to the instrument dimensions and conditions for measurement.

Measuring Viscosity Several common methods are available for measuring viscosity. Two very common ones are the use of capillary tubes such as Ubbelohde, Ostwald, or Cannon-Fenske viscometer tubes and the use of a rotating spindle such as the Brookfield viscometer.

Determine the viscosity in capillary tubes by measuring the amount of time it takes for a given volume of liquid to flow through a calibrated capillary tube. Calibrate the capillary tube by using liquids of known viscosity. The calibration may be supplied with the viscometer tube when purchased along with specific instructions for its use. Many types of capillary viscometer tubes are available, and exact procedures will vary with the type of tube chosen. Examples of procedures are in the following sections: *Viscosity of Dimethylpolysiloxane* and *Viscosity of Methylcellulose*. In general, calibrate capillary viscometers by filling the viscometers per the manufacturer's instructions and allowing the filled tube to equilibrate to the given temperature in a constant-temperature bath. Draw the liquid to the top graduation line, and measure the time, in seconds, it takes for the liquid to flow from the upper mark to the lower mark in the capillary tube. Calculate the viscometer constant, k:

$$k = v/dt$$

in which v is the known viscosity, in centipoises, of the standard liquid; d is the density, at the specified temperature, of the liquid; and t is the time, in seconds, for the liquid to pass from the upper mark to the lower mark. It is not necessary to recalibrate the tube unless changes or repairs are made to it. To measure viscosity, introduce the unknown liquid into the viscometer tube in the same way as the calibration standard was introduced, and measure the time, in seconds, it takes for the liquid to flow from the upper mark to the lower mark. Calculate viscosity:

$$v = kdt$$

in which v is the viscosity to be determined, k is the viscometer constant, and d is the density of the liquid being measured.

Using rotational viscometers provides a particularly rapid and convenient method for determining viscosity. They employ a rotating spindle or cup immersed in the liquid, and they measure the resistance of the liquid to the rotation of the spindle or cup. A wide range of viscosities can be measured with one instrument by using spindles or cups of different sizes and by rotating them at different speeds. The manufacturer supplies the calibration of viscosity versus the spindle size and speed, which can be checked by using fluids of known viscosity. Take a measurement by allowing the sample to come to the desired temperature in a constant-temperature bath and immersing the spindle or cup to the depth specified by the manufacturer. Allow the spindle or cup to rotate until a constant reading is obtained. Multiply the reading by a factor supplied by the manufacturer for a given spindle or cup and given rotational speed to obtain the viscosity. The exact procedures will vary with the particular instrument. An example is given in the section on *Viscosity of Cellulose Gum*.

Another method to determine viscosity uses the falling-ball viscometer. Determine viscosity by noting the time it takes for a ball to fall through the distance between two marks on a tube filled with the unknown liquid (the tube is generally in a constant-temperature bath). Use balls of different weights to measure a wide range of viscosities. Calculate the viscosity by using manufacturer-supplied constants for the ball used. These instruments can be quite precise for Newtonian liquids, that is, liquids that do not have viscosities that vary with flow (more correctly, shear) rate.

Three specific methods are described below:

Viscosity of Dimethylpolysiloxane

Apparatus The Ubbelohde suspended level viscometer, shown in *Figure 5* is preferred to determine the viscosity of dimethylpolysiloxane. Alternatively, a Cannon-Ubbelohde viscometer may be used.

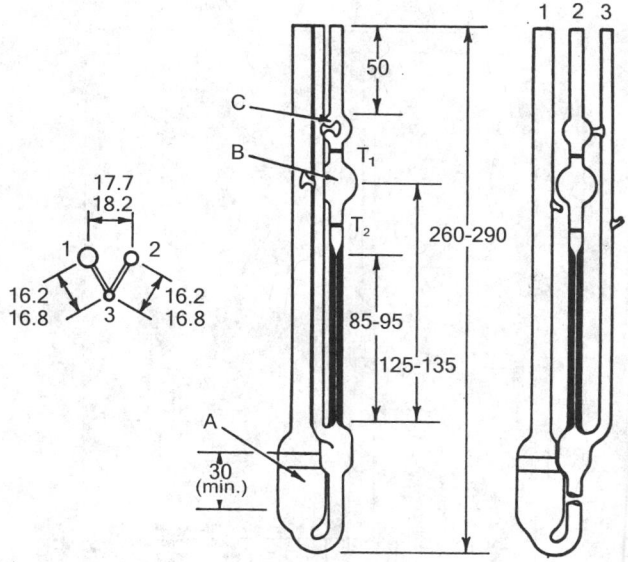

Figure 5. Ubbelohde Viscometer for Dimethylpolysiloxane
(all dimensions are in mm)

Select a viscometer having a minimum flow time of at least 200 s. Use a No. 3 size Ubbelohde, or a No. 400 size Cannon-Ubbelohde, viscometer for the range of 300–600 centistokes. The viscometer should be fitted with holders that satisfy the dimensional positions of the separate tubes as shown in the diagram and that hold the viscometer vertically. Filling lines in bulb A indicate the minimum and maximum volumes of liquid to be used for convenient operation. The volume of bulb B is approximately 5 mL.

Calibration of the Viscometer Determine the viscosity constant, C, for each viscometer by using an oil of known viscosity.[1] Charge the viscometer by tilting the instrument about 30 degrees from the vertical, with bulb A below the capillary, and then introduce enough of the sample into tube I to bring the level up to the lower filling line. The level should not be above the upper filling line when the viscometer is returned to the vertical position and the sample has drained from tube I. Charge the viscometer in such a manner that the U-tube at the bottom fills completely without trapping air.

After the viscometer has been in a constant-temperature bath (25 ± 0.2°) long enough for the sample to reach temperature equilibrium, place a finger over tube 3, and apply suction to tube 2 until the liquid reaches the center of bulb C. Remove suction from tube 2, then remove the finger from tube 3, and place it over tube 2 until the sample drops away from the lower end of the capillary. Remove the finger from tube 2, and measure the time, to the nearest 0.1 s, required for the meniscus to pass from the first timing mark (T_1) to the second (T_2).

Calculate the viscometer constant, C:

$$C = cs/t_1$$

in which cs is the viscosity, in centistokes, and t_1 is the efflux time, in seconds, for the standard liquid.

Determination of the Viscosity of Dimethylpolysiloxane Charge the viscometer with the sample in the same manner as described for the calibration procedure; determine the efflux time, t_2; and calculate the viscosity of the dimethylpolysiloxane:

$$V = C \times t_2$$

Viscosity of Methylcellulose

Apparatus Viscometers used to determine the viscosity of methylcellulose and some related compounds are illustrated in *Figure 6* and consist of three parts: a large filling tube, A; an orifice tube, B; and an air vent to the reservoir, C.

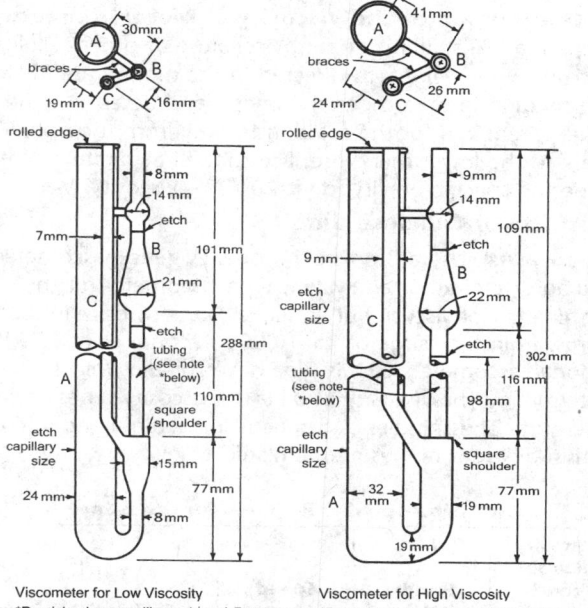

Viscometer for Low Viscosity
*Precision bore capillary tubing 1.5 mm id for 15 cps, 1.8 mm id for 25 cps, 2.4 mm id for 100 cps, and 3.2 mm id for 400 cps viscosities.

Viscometer for High Viscosity
*Precision bore capillary tubing 5.0 mm id for 1500 cps and 6.0 mm id for 4000 cps viscosities.

Figure 6. Methylcellulose Viscometers

There are two basic types of methylcellulose viscometers—one for cellulose derivatives of a range between 1500 and 4000 centipoises, and the other for less viscous ones. Each type of viscometer is modified slightly for the different viscosities.

Calibration of the Viscometer Determine the viscometer constant, K, for each viscometer by using an oil of known viscosity.[2] Place an excess of the liquid that is to be tested (adjusted to 20 ± 0.1°) in the filling tube, A, and transfer it to the orifice tube, B, by gentle suction, taking care to keep the liquid free from air bubbles by closing the air vent tube, C. Adjust the column of liquid in tube B so it is even with the top graduation line. Open both tubes B and C to permit the liquid to flow into the reservoir against atmospheric pressure.

---

[1] Oils of known viscosities may be obtained from the Cannon Instrument Co., P.O. Box 812, State College, PA 16801. For determining the viscosity of dimethylpolysiloxane, choose an oil with a viscosity as close as possible to that of the type of sample to be tested.

[2] Oils of known viscosities may be obtained from the Cannon Instrument Co., P.O. Box 812, State College, PA 16801. For determining the viscosity of methylcellulose, choose an oil that has a viscosity as close as possible to that of the type of sample to be tested.

[Note—Failure to open air vent tube C before determining the viscosity will yield false values.]

Record the time, in seconds, for the liquid to flow from the upper mark to the lower mark in tube B.

Calculate the viscometer constant, K:

$$K = V/dt$$

in which V is the viscosity, in centipoises, of the liquid; K is the viscometer constant; d is the specific gravity of the liquid tested at 20°/20°; and t is the time, in seconds, for the liquid to pass from the upper to the lower mark.

For the calibration, all values in the equation are known or can be determined except K, which must be solved. If a tube is repaired, it must be recalibrated to avoid obtaining significant changes in the value of K.

Determination of the Viscosity of Methylcellulose

Prepare a 2% solution of methylcellulose or other cellulose derivative, by weight, as directed in the monograph. Place the solution in the proper viscometer and determine the time, t, required for the solution to flow from the upper mark to the lower mark in orifice tube B. Separately determine the specific gravity, d, at 20°/20°. Viscosity, V = Kdt.

Viscosity of Cellulose Gum

Apparatus Use a Brookfield Model LV series viscometer, analog or digital, or equivalent type viscometer for the determination of viscosity of aqueous solutions of cellulose gum within the range of 25–10,000 centipoises at 25°. Rotational viscometers of this type have spindles for use in determining the viscosity of different viscosity types of cellulose gum. The spindles and speeds for determining viscosity within different ranges are tabulated below.

Viscometer Spindles Required for Given Speeds

Viscosity Range (centipoises)	Spindle No.	Speed (rpm)	Scale	Factor
10–100	1	60	100	1
100–200	1	30	100	2
200–1000	2	30	100	10
1000–4000	3	30	100	40
4000–10,000	4	30	100	200

Mechanical Stirrer: Use an agitator, essentially as shown in *Figure 7*, that can be attached to a variable-speed motor capable of operating at 900 ± 100 rpm under varying load conditions.

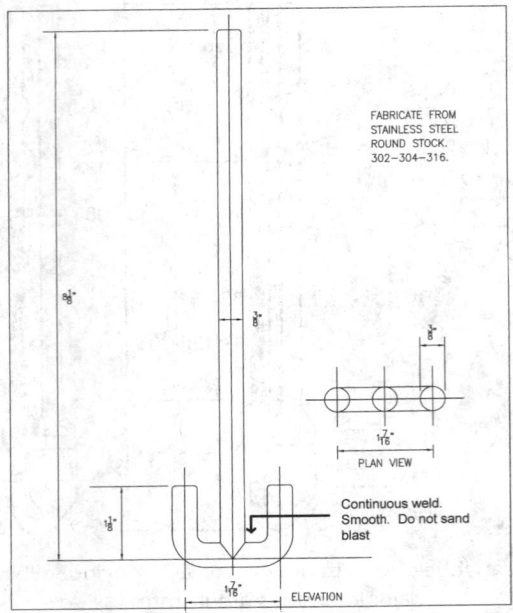

Figure 7. Agitator for Viscosity of Cellulose Gum

[Note—The agitator may be fabricated from stainless steel (Hercules, Inc., Wilmington, Delaware, or equivalent.) or glass as shown in *Figure 7*. Where this procedure is specified for viscosity measurements by reference in other monographs, equivalent three-blade agitators may be used.]

Sample Container: Use a glass jar about 152 mm deep having an od of approximately 64 mm and a capacity of about 340 g.

Water Bath: Use a water bath capable of maintaining a constant temperature. Set the temperature to 25°, and maintain it within ±0.2°.

Thermometer: Use an ASTM Saybolt Viscosity Thermometer having a range from 19° to 27° and conforming to the requirements for Thermometer 17C as described in ASTM Specification E1.

Sample Preparation Accurately weigh an amount of sample equivalent to 4.8 g of cellulose gum on the dried basis, and record the actual quantity required, in grams, as S. Transfer an accurately measured volume of water equivalent to 240 − S g into the sample container. Position the stirrer in the sample container, allowing minimal clearance between the stirrer and the bottom of the container. Begin stirring, and slowly add the sample. Adjust the stirring speed to approximately 900 ± 100 rpm. Mix for exactly 2 h. Do not allow the stirring speed to exceed 1200 rpm. Remove the stirrer, cap the sample container, and transfer the sample container into a constant-temperature water bath, maintained at 25 ± 0.2°, for 1 h. Check the sample temperature with a thermometer at the end of 1 h to ensure that the test temperature has been reached.

Procedure Remove the sample container from the water bath, shake vigorously for 10 s, and measure the viscosity with the Brookfield viscometer, using the proper spindle and speed indicated in the accompanying table. Be sure to use the viscometer guard, and allow the spindle to rotate for 3 min before taking the reading. Calculate the viscosity, in centipoises, by multiplying the reading observed by the appropriate factor from the table.

WATER DETERMINATION

Method I (Karl Fischer Titrimetric Method) Determine the water by *Method Ia*, unless otherwise specified in the individual monograph.

Method Ia (Direct Titration)

Principle The titrimetric determination of water is based on the quantitative reaction of water with an anhydrous solution of sulfur dioxide and iodine in the presence of a buffer that reacts with hydrogen ions.

In the original titrimetric solution, known as *Karl Fischer Reagent*, the sulfur dioxide and iodine are dissolved in pyridine and methanol. Pyridine-free reagents are more commonly used now. The test specimen may be titrated with the *Karl Fischer Reagent* directly, or the analysis may be carried out by a residual titration procedure. The stoichiometry of the reaction is not exact, and the reproducibility of the determination depends on such factors as the relative concentrations of the *Karl Fischer Reagent* ingredients, the nature of the inert solvent used to dissolve the test specimen, the apparent pH of the final mixture, and the technique used in the particular determination. Therefore, an empirically standardized technique is used to achieve the desired accuracy. Precision in the method is governed largely by the extent to which atmospheric moisture is excluded from the system. The titration of water is usually carried out with the use of anhydrous methanol as the solvent for the test specimen; however, other suitable solvents may be used for special or unusual test specimens.

Substances that may interfere with the test results are ferric ion, chlorine, and similar oxidizing agents, as well as significant amounts of strong acids or bases, phosgene, or anything that will reduce iodide to iodine, poison the reagent, and show the sample to be bone dry when water may be present (false negative). 8-Hydroxyquinoline may be added to the vessel to eliminate interference from ferric ion. Chlorine interference can be eliminated with sulfur dioxide or unsaturated hydrocarbon. Excess pyridine or other amines may be added to the vessel to eliminate the interference of strong acids. Excess acetic acid or other carboxylic acid can be added to reduce the interference of strong bases. Aldehydes and ketones may react with the solution, showing the sample to be wet while the detector never reaches an endpoint (false positive).

Apparatus Any apparatus may be used that provides for adequate exclusion of atmospheric moisture and for determination of the endpoint. In the case of a colorless solution that is titrated directly, the endpoint may be observed visually as a change in color from canary yellow to amber. The reverse is observed in the case of a test specimen that is titrated residually. More commonly, however, the endpoint is determined electrometrically with an apparatus employing a simple electrical circuit that serves to impress about 200 mV of applied potential between a pair of platinum electrodes (about 5 mm^2 in area and about 2.5 cm apart) immersed in the solution to be titrated. At the endpoint of the titration, a slight excess of the reagent increases the flow of current to 50–150 microamperes for 30 s to 30 min, depending on the solution being titrated. The time is shortest for substances that dissolve in the reagent. The longer times are required for solid materials that do not readily go into solution in the *Karl Fischer Reagent*. With some automatic titrators, the abrupt change in current or potential at the endpoint serves to close a solenoid-operated valve that controls the buret delivering the titrant. A commercially available apparatus generally comprises a closed system consisting of one or two automatic burets and a tightly covered titration vessel fitted with the necessary electrodes and a magnetic stirrer. The air in the system is kept dry with a suitable desiccant such as phosphorus pentoxide, and the titration vessel may be purged by means of a stream of dry nitrogen or a current of dry air.

Reagent The *Karl Fischer Reagent* may be prepared as follows: Add 125 g of iodine to a solution containing 670 mL of methanol and 170 mL of pyridine, and cool. Place 100 mL of pyridine in a 250-mL graduated cylinder, and keeping the pyridine cold in an ice bath, pass in dry sulfur dioxide until the volume reaches 200 mL. Slowly add this solution, with shaking, to the cooled iodine mixture. Shake to dissolve the iodine, transfer the solution to the apparatus, and allow the solution to stand overnight before standardizing. One mL of this solution, when freshly prepared, is equivalent to approximately 5 mg of water, but it deteriorates gradually; therefore, standardize it within 1 h before use, or daily in continual use. Protect the solution from light while in use. Store any bulk stock of the solution in a suitably sealed, glass-stoppered container, fully protected from light and under refrigeration.

A commercially available, stabilized solution of a Karl Fischer-type reagent may be used. Commercially available reagents containing solvents or bases other than pyridine and/or alcohols other than methanol also may be used. These may be single solutions or reagents formed in situ by combining the components of the reagents present in two discrete solutions. The diluted *Karl Fischer Reagent* called for in some monographs should be diluted as directed by the manufacturer. Either methanol, or another suitable solvent such as ethylene glycol monomethyl ether, may be used as the diluent.

Test Preparation Unless otherwise specified in the individual monograph, use an accurately weighed or measured amount of the specimen under test estimated to contain 10–250 mg of water.

Where the monograph specifies that the specimen under test is hygroscopic, accurately weigh a sample of the specimen into a suitable container. Use a dry syringe to inject an appropriate volume of methanol, or other suitable solvent, accurately measured, into the container and shake to dissolve the specimen. Dry the syringe, and use it to remove the solution from the container and transfer it to a titration vessel prepared as directed under *Procedure*. Repeat the procedure with a second portion of methanol, or other suitable solvent, accurately measured; add this washing to the titration vessel; and immediately titrate. Determine the water content, in milligrams, of a portion of solvent of the same total volume as that used to dissolve the specimen and to wash the container and syringe, as directed under *Standardization of Water Solution for Residual Titration*, and subtract this value from the water content, in mg, obtained in the titration of the specimen under test.

Standardization of the Reagent Place enough methanol or other suitable solvent in the titration vessel to cover the electrodes, and add sufficient *Karl Fischer Reagent* to give the characteristic color or 100 ± 50 microamperes of direct current at about 200 mV of applied potential. Pure methanol can make the detector overly sensitive, particularly at low ppm levels of water, causing it to deflect to dryness and slowly recover with each addition of reagent. This slows down the titration and may allow the system to actually pick up ambient moisture during the resulting long titration. Adding chloroform or a similar nonconducting solvent will retard this sensitivity and can improve the analysis.

For determination of trace amounts of water (less than 1%), quickly add 25 µL (25 mg) of pure water, using a 25- or 50-µL syringe, and titrate to the endpoint. The water equivalence factor F, in mg of water per mL of reagent, is given below:

$$Result = 25/V$$

in which V is the volume, in mL, of the *Karl Fischer Reagent* consumed in the second titration.

For the precise determination of significant amounts of water (more than 1%), quickly add 25–250 mg (25–250 µL) of pure water, accurately weighed by difference from a weighing pipet or from a precalibrated syringe or micropipet, the amount of water used being governed by the reagent strength and the buret size, as referred to under *Volumetric Apparatus*. Titrate to the endpoint. Calculate the water equivalence factor, F, in mg of water per mL of reagent:

$$Result = W/V$$

in which W is the weight, in mg, of the water, and V is the volume, in mL, of the *Karl Fischer Reagent* required.

Procedure Unless otherwise specified, transfer 35–40 mL of methanol or other suitable solvent to the titration vessel, and titrate with the *Karl Fischer Reagent* to the electrometric or visual endpoint to consume any moisture that may be present. (Disregard the volume consumed because it does not enter into the calculations.) Quickly add the *Test Preparation*, mix, and again titrate with the *Karl Fischer Reagent* to the electrometric or visual endpoint. Calculate the water content of the specimen, in mg:

$$Result = SF$$

in which S is the volume, in mL, of the *Karl Fischer Reagent* consumed in the second titration, and F is the water equivalence factor of the *Karl Fischer Reagent*.

Method Ib (Residual Titration)

Principle See the information in the section entitled *Principle* under *Method Ia*. In the residual titration, add excess *Karl Fischer Reagent* to the test specimen, allow sufficient time for the reaction to reach completion, and titrate the unconsumed *Karl Fischer Reagent* with a standard solution of water in a solvent such as methanol. The residual titration procedure is generally applicable and avoids the difficulties that may be encountered in the direct titration of substances from which the bound water is released slowly.

Apparatus, Reagent, and **Test Preparation** Use those in *Method Ia*.

Standardization of Water Solution for Residual Titration Prepare a *Water Solution* by diluting 2 mL of pure water to 1000 mL with methanol or another suitable solvent. Standardize this solution by titrating 25.0 mL with the *Karl Fischer Reagent*, previously standardized as directed under *Standardization of the Reagent*. Calculate the water content, in mg/mL, of the *Water Solution*:

$$Result = VF/25$$

in which V is the volume of the *Karl Fischer Reagent* consumed, and F is the water equivalence factor of the *Karl Fischer Reagent*. Determine the water content of the *Water Solution* weekly, and standardize the *Karl Fischer Reagent* against it periodically as needed. Store the *Water Solution* in a tightly capped container.

Procedure Where the individual monograph specifies the water content is to be determined by *Method Ib*, transfer 35–40 mL of methanol or other suitable solvent into the titration vessel, and titrate with the *Karl Fischer Reagent* to the electrometric or visual endpoint. Quickly add the *Test Preparation*, mix, and add an accurately measured excess of the *Karl Fischer Reagent*. Allow sufficient time for the reaction to reach completion, and titrate the unconsumed *Karl Fischer Reagent* with standardized *Water Solution* to the electrometric or visual endpoint. Calculate the water content of the specimen, in mg:

$$Result = F(X' - XR)$$

in which F is the water equivalence factor of the *Karl Fischer Reagent*; X' is the volume, in mL, of the *Karl Fischer Reagent* added after introduction of the specimen; X is the volume, in mL, of standardized *Water Solution* required to neutralize the unconsumed *Karl Fischer Reagent*; and R is the ratio V/25 (mL of *Karl Fischer Reagent*/mL of *Water Solution*), determined from the *Standardization of Water Solution for Residual Titration*.

Method Ic (Coulometric Titration)

Principle Use the Karl Fischer reaction in the coulometric determination of water. In this determination, iodine is not added in the form of a volumetric solution, but is produced in an iodide-containing solution by anodic oxidation. The reaction cell usually consists of a large anode compartment and a small cathode compartment that are separated by a diaphragm. Other suitable types of reaction cells (e.g., without diaphragms) may be used. Each compartment has a platinum electrode that conducts current through the cell. Iodine, which is produced at the anode electrode, immediately reacts with the water present in the compartment. When all the water has been consumed, an excess of iodine occurs, which can be detected potentiometrically, thus indicating the endpoint. Pre-electrolysis, which can take several hours, eliminates moisture from the system. Therefore, changing the *Karl Fischer Reagent* after each determination is not practical. Individual determinations may be carried out in succession in the same reagent solution. A requirement for this method is that each component of the test specimen be compatible with the other components and that no side reactions take place. Samples may be transferred into the vessel as solids or as solutions by means of injection through a septum. Gases can be introduced into the cell by means of a suitable gas inlet tube. For the water determination of solids, another common technique is to dissolve the solid in a suitable solvent and then inject a portion of this solution into the cell. In the case of insoluble solids, water may be extracted using suitable solvents, and then the extracts injected into the coulometric cell. Alternatively, an evaporation technique may be used in which the sample is heated in a tube and the water is evaporated and carried into the cell by means of a stream of dry, inert gas. Precision in the method is predominantly governed by the extent to which atmospheric moisture is excluded from the system. Control of the system may be monitored by measuring the amount of baseline drift. The titration of water in solid test specimens is usually carried out with the use of anhydrous methanol as the solvent. Other suitable solvents may be used for special or unusual test specimens. This method is particularly suited to chemically inert substances such as hydrocarbons, alcohols, and ethers. In comparison with the volumetric Karl Fischer titration, coulometry is a micro-method. The method uses extremely small amounts of current. It is predominantly used for substances with a very low water content (0.1%–0.0001%).

Apparatus Any commercially available apparatus consisting of an absolutely tight system fitted with the necessary electrodes and a magnetic stirrer is appropriate. The instrument's microprocessor controls the analytical procedure and displays the results. Calibration of the instrument is not necessary as the current consumed can be measured absolutely. Proper operation of the instrument can be confirmed by injecting 1 µL of water into the vessel. The instrument should read 1000 µg of water on reaching the endpoint.

Reagent See *Reagent* under *Method Ia*.

Test Preparation Using a dry syringe, inject an appropriate volume of test specimen estimated to contain 0.5–5 mg of water, accurately measured, into the anolyte solution. The sample may also be introduced as a solid, accurately weighed, into the anolyte solution. Perform coulometric titration, and determine the water content of the specimen under test.

Alternatively, when the specimen is a suitable solid, dissolve an appropriate quantity, accurately weighed, in anhydrous methanol or another suitable solvent, and inject a suitable portion into the anolyte solution.

When the specimen is an insoluble solid, extract the water by using a suitable anhydrous solvent from which an appropriate quantity, accurately weighed, may be injected into the anolyte solution. Alternatively use an evaporation technique.

Procedure Quickly inject the *Test Preparation*, or transfer the solid sample, into the anolyte, mix, and perform the coulometric titration to the electrometric endpoint. Read the water content of the *Test Preparation* directly from the instrument's display, and calculate the percent that is present in the substance.

Method II (Toluene Distillation Method)

Principle This method determines water by distillation of a sample with an immiscible solvent, usually toluene.

Apparatus Use a glass distillation apparatus (see *Figure 8*) provided with 24/40 ground-glass connections. The components consist of a 500-mL short-neck, round-bottom flask connected by means of a trap to a 400-mm water-cooled condenser. The lower tip of the condenser should be about 7 mm above the surface of the liquid in the trap after distillation conditions have been established (see *Procedure*).

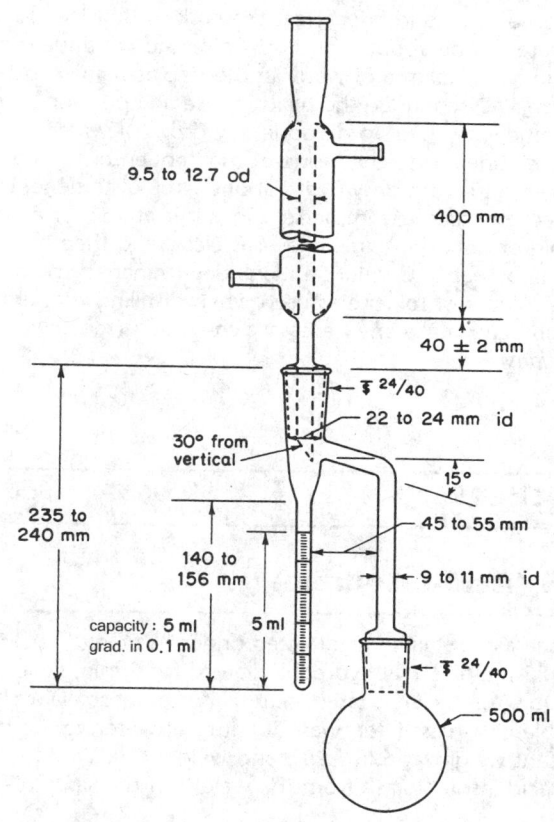

Figure 8. Moisture Distillation Apparatus

The trap should be constructed of well-annealed glass, the receiving end of which is graduated to contain 5 mL and subdivided into 0.1-mL divisions, with each 1-mL line numbered from 5 mL beginning at the top. Calibrate the receiver by adding 1 mL of water, accurately measured, to 100 mL of toluene contained in the distillation flask. Conduct the distillation, and calculate the volume of water obtained as directed in the *Procedure*. Add another mL of water to the cooled apparatus, and repeat the distillation. Continue in this manner until five 1-mL portions of water have been added. The error at any indicated capacity should not exceed 0.05 mL. The source of heat is either an oil bath or an electric heater provided with a suitable means of temperature control. The distillation may be better controlled by insulating the tube leading from the flask to the receiver. It is also advantageous to protect the flask from drafts. Clean the entire apparatus with potassium dichromate-sulfuric acid cleaning solution, rinse thoroughly, and dry completely before using.

Procedure Place in the previously cleaned and dried flask a quantity of the substance, weighed accurately to the nearest 0.01 g, that is expected to yield 1.5–4 mL of water. If the substance is of a pastelike consistency, weigh it in a boat of metal foil that will pass through the neck of the flask. If the substance is likely to cause bumping, take suitable precautions to prevent it. Transfer about 200 mL of ACS reagent-grade toluene into the flask, and swirl to mix it with the sample. Assemble the apparatus, fill the receiver with toluene by pouring it through the condenser until it begins to overflow into the flask, and insert a loose cotton plug in the top of the condenser. Heat the flask so that the distillation rate will be about 200 drops/min, and continue distilling until the volume of water in the trap remains constant for 5 min. Discontinue the heating, use a copper or nichrome wire spiral to dislodge any drops of water that may be adhering to the inside of the condenser tube or receiver, and wash down with about 5 mL of toluene. Disconnect the receiver, immerse it in water at 25° for at least 15 min or until the toluene layer is clear, and then read the volume of water. Conduct a blank determination using the same volume of toluene as used when distilling the sample mixture, and make any necessary correction (see *General Provisions*).

C. OTHERS

ASH (Acid-Insoluble)

Boil the ash obtained as directed under *Ash (Total)*, below, with 25 mL of 2.7 N hydrochloric acid for 5 min, collect the insoluble matter on a tared, porous-bottom porcelain filter crucible or ashless filter, wash it with hot water, ignite to constant weight at 675 ± 25°, and weigh. Calculate the percent acid-insoluble ash from the weight of the sample taken.

[NOTE—Avoid exposing the crucible to sudden temperature changes.]

ASH (Total)

Unless otherwise directed, accurately weigh about 3 g of the sample in a tared crucible, ignite it at a low temperature (about 550°), not to exceed a very dull redness, until it is free from carbon, cool it in a desiccator, and weigh. If a carbon-free ash is not obtained, wet the charred mass with hot water, collect the insoluble residue on an ashless filter paper, and ignite the residue and filter paper until the ash is white or nearly so. Finally, add the filtrate, evaporate it to dryness, and heat the whole to a dull redness. If a carbon-free ash is still not obtained, cool the crucible, add 15 mL of ethanol, break up the ash with a glass rod, then burn off the ethanol, again heat the whole to a dull redness, cool it in a desiccator, and weigh.

HYDROCHLORIC ACID TABLE

°Bé	Sp. Gr.	Percent HCl
1.00	1.0069	1.40
2.00	1.0140	2.82
3.00	1.0211	4.25
4.00	1.0284	5.69
5.00	1.0357	7.15
5.25	1.0375	7.52
5.50	1.0394	7.89
5.75	1.0413	8.26
6.00	1.0432	8.64
6.25	1.0450	9.02
6.50	1.0469	9.40
6.75	1.0488	9.78
7.00	1.0507	10.17
7.25	1.0526	10.55
7.50	1.0545	10.94
7.75	1.0564	11.32
8.00	1.0584	11.71
8.25	1.0603	12.09
8.50	1.0623	12.48
8.75	1.0642	12.87
9.00	1.0662	13.26
9.25	1.0681	13.65
9.50	1.0701	14.04
9.75	1.0721	14.43
10.00	1.0741	14.83
10.25	1.0761	15.22
10.50	1.0781	15.62
10.75	1.0801	16.01
11.00	1.0821	16.41
11.25	1.0841	16.81
11.50	1.0861	17.21
11.75	1.0881	17.61
12.00	1.0902	18.01
12.25	1.0922	18.41
12.50	1.0943	18.82
12.75	1.0964	19.22
13.00	1.0985	19.63
13.25	1.1006	20.04
13.50	1.1027	20.44
13.75	1.1048	20.86
19.2	1.1526	30.00
19.3	1.1535	30.18
19.4	1.1544	30.35

°Bé	Sp. Gr.	Percent HCl
19.5	1.1554	30.53
19.6	1.1563	30.71
19.7	1.1572	30.90
19.8	1.1581	31.08
19.9	1.1590	31.27
20.0	1.1600	31.45
20.1	1.1609	31.64
20.2	1.1619	31.82
20.3	1.1628	32.01
20.4	1.1637	32.19
20.5	1.1647	32.38
20.6	1.1656	32.56
20.7	1.1666	32.75
20.8	1.1675	32.93
20.9	1.1684	33.12
21.0	1.1694	33.31
21.1	1.1703	33.50
21.2	1.1713	33.69
21.3	1.1722	33.88
21.4	1.1732	34.07
21.5	1.1741	34.26
21.6	1.1751	34.45
21.7	1.1760	34.64
21.8	1.1770	34.83
21.9	1.1779	35.02
22.0	1.1789	35.21
22.1	1.1798	35.40
22.2	1.1808	35.59
22.3	1.1817	35.78
22.4	1.1827	35.97
22.5	1.1836	36.16
22.6	1.1846	36.35
22.7	1.1856	36.54
22.8	1.1866	36.73
22.9	1.1875	36.93
23.0	1.1885	37.14
23.1	1.1895	37.36
23.2	1.1904	37.58
23.3	1.1914	37.80
23.4	1.1924	38.03
23.5	1.1934	38.26
23.6	1.1944	38.49
23.7	1.1953	38.72
23.8	1.1963	38.95
23.9	1.1973	39.18
24.0	1.1983	39.41
24.1	1.1993	39.64
24.2	1.2003	39.86
24.3	1.2013	40.09
24.4	1.2023	40.32
24.5	1.2033	40.55

°Bé	Sp. Gr.	Percent HCl
24.6	1.2043	40.78
24.7	1.2053	41.01
24.8	1.2063	41.24
24.9	1.2073	41.48
25.0	1.2083	41.72
25.1	1.2093	41.99
25.2	1.2103	42.30
25.3	1.2114	42.64
25.4	1.2124	43.01
25.5	1.2134	43.40

Specific gravity determinations were made at 60°F, compared with water at 60°F.

From the specific gravities, the corresponding degrees Baumé were calculated by the following formula:

$$\text{degrees Baumé} = 145 - (145/\text{sp. gr.})$$

Baumé hydrometers for use with this table must be graduated by the above formula, which should always be printed on the scale.

Allowance for Temperature
10°–15°Bé: 1/40 °Bé or 0.0002 sp. gr. for 1°F
15°–22°Bé: 1/30 °Bé or 0.0003 sp. gr. for 1°F
22°–25°Bé: 1/28 °Bé or 0.00035 sp. gr. for 1°F

LOSS ON DRYING

This procedure is used to determine the amount of volatile matter expelled under the conditions specified in the monograph. Because the volatile matter may include material other than adsorbed moisture, this test is designed for compounds in which the loss on drying may not definitely be attributable to water alone. For substances appearing to contain water as the only volatile constituent, the *Direct (Karl Fischer) Titration Method*, provided under *Water*, Appendix IIB, is usually appropriate.

Procedure Unless otherwise directed in the monograph, conduct the determination on 1–2 g of the substance, previously mixed and accurately weighed. If the sample is in the form of large crystals, reduce the particle size to about 2 mm, quickly crushing the sample to avoid absorption or loss of moisture. Tare a glass-stoppered, shallow weighing bottle that has been dried for 30 min under the same conditions to be used in the determination. Transfer the sample to the bottle, replace the cover, and weigh the bottle and its contents. By gentle sideways shaking, distribute the sample as evenly as possible to a depth of about 5 mm for most substances and not over 10 mm in the case of bulky materials. Place the loaded bottle in the drying chamber, removing the stopper and leaving it also in the chamber, and dry at the temperature and for the length of time specified in the monograph. Upon opening the chamber, close the bottle promptly and allow it to come to room temperature, preferably in a desiccator, before weighing.

Where drying in vacuum is specified in the monograph, use a pressure as low as that obtainable by an aspirating water pump (NMT 20 mm Hg).

If the test substance melts at a temperature lower than that specified for the determination, preheat the bottle and its contents for 1–2 h at a temperature 5°–10° below the melting range, then continue drying at the specified temperature for the determination. When drying the sample in a desiccator, ensure that the desiccant is kept fully effective by replacing it frequently.

NUCLEAR MAGNETIC RESONANCE

Nuclear magnetic resonance (NMR) spectroscopy is an analytical procedure based on the magnetic properties of certain atomic nuclei. It is similar to other types of spectroscopy in that absorption or emission of electromagnetic energy at characteristic frequencies provides analytical information. NMR differs in that the discrete energy levels between which the transitions take place are created artificially by placing the nuclei in a magnetic field.

Atomic nuclei are charged and behave as if they were spinning on the nuclear axis, thus creating a magnetic dipole of moment μ along this axis. The angular momentum of the spinning nucleus is characterized by a spin quantum number (I). If the mass number is odd, I is $1/2$ or an integer plus $1/2$; otherwise, it has a value of 0 or a whole number.

Nuclei having a spin quantum number $I \neq 0$, when placed in an external uniform static magnetic field of strength, H_0, align with respect to the field in $(2I + 1)$ possible orientations. Thus, for nuclei with $I = 1/2$, which include most isotopes of analytical significance, as shown in the table below, there are two possible orientations, corresponding to two different energy states. A nuclear resonance is the transition between these states, by absorption or emission of the corresponding amount of energy. In a static magnetic field the nuclear magnetic axis precesses (Larmor precession) about the external field axis. The precessional angular velocity, ω_0, is related to the external magnetic field strength through the equation:

$$\omega_0 = \gamma H_0$$

in which γ is the magnetogyric ratio and is a constant for all nuclei of a given isotope. If energy from an oscillating radio-frequency field is introduced, the absorption of radiation takes place according to the relationship:

$$\Delta E = h\nu = \mu H_0/I$$

where h is Planck's constant, and

$$\nu = \omega_0/2\pi = \gamma H_0/2\pi$$

Thus, when the frequency (ν_0) of the external energy field ($E = h\nu$) is the same as the precessional angular velocity, resonance is achieved.

The energy difference between the two levels corresponds to electromagnetic radiation in the radio-frequency range. It is a function of γ, which is a property of the nucleus, and H_0, the external field strength. As shown in the table below, the resonance frequency of a nucleus increases with the increase of the magnetic field strength.

NMR is a technique of high specificity but relatively low sensitivity. The basic reason for the low sensitivity is the comparatively small difference in energy between the excited and the ground states (0.02 calories at 15–20 kilogauss field strength), which results in a population difference between the two levels of only a few ppm. Another important aspect of the NMR phenomenon, with negative effects on the sensitivity, is the long lifetime of most nuclei in the excited state, which affects the design of the NMR analytical test, especially in pulsed repetitive experiments. Simultaneous acquisition of the entire spectrum instead of frequency-swept spectra can give sensitivity enhancement.

Properties of Some Nuclei Amenable to NMR Study

Nucleus	I	Natural Abundance, %	Sensitivity	Resonance Frequency (MHZ) at 1.4093 T*	2.3488 T	4.6975 T
^{1}H	$1/2$	99.980	1.000	60.000	100.000	200.000
^{13}C	$1/2$	1.108	0.0159	15.087	25.144	50.288
^{19}F	$1/2$	100.000	0.830	56.446	94.077	188.154
^{31}P	$1/2$	100.000	0.0663	24.289	40.481	80.961
^{11}B	$(3/2)$	80.420	0.170	19.250	32.084	64.167

* T = tesla, 1 T = 10,000 Gauss.

Apparatus The distinctive components of an NMR spectrometer are a magnet and a source of radio frequency. The instruments are described by the approximate resonance frequency of the analytical nucleus, e.g., ^{1}H NMR. More recently, instruments are being referred to by their field strengths. Some spectrometers are dedicated to the analysis of one type of nucleus; others are designed to obtain spectra of different nuclei.

There are two types of commercial NMR spectrometers: the classical continuous wave (CW) instruments and the more modern pulse Fourier-transform (FT) instruments. The CW spectrometers use a technique similar to that of classical optical spectrometers: a slow scan of the radio frequency (at fixed magnetic field) or the magnetic field (at fixed radio frequency) over a domain corresponding to the resonance of the nuclei being studied. The signal generated by the absorption of energy is detected, amplified, and recorded.

Various instrument configurations are possible. The arrangement of a typical double-coil spectrometer, as one might see in the lower resolution 60-MHz and 100-MHz CW instruments, is illustrated in *Figure 9*.

The limitations of the CW spectrometers are low sensitivity and long analysis time. In pulsed NMR spectrometers, a single pulse of radio frequency energy is used to simultaneously activate all nuclei. The excited nuclei returning to the

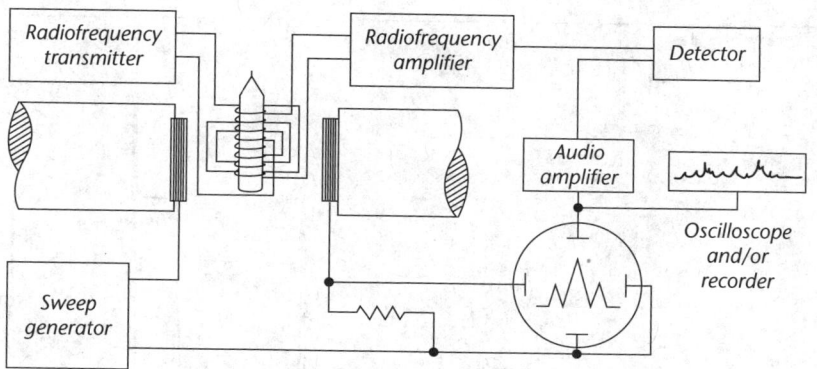

Figure 9. Block Diagram of a Typical NMR Spectrometer

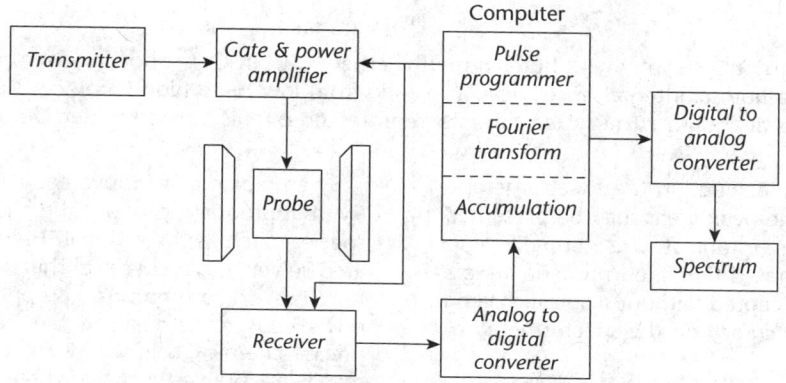

Figure 10. Block Diagram of a Typical Pulsed FT-NMR Spectrometer

lower energy level generate a free induction decay (FID) signal that contains in a time domain all the information obtained in a frequency domain with a CW spectrometer. The time domain and the frequency domain responses form a pair of FTs; the mathematical operation is performed by a computer after analog-to-digital conversion. After a delay allowing for relaxation of the excited nuclei, the pulse experiment (transient) may be repeated and the response coherently added in the computer memory, with random noise being averaged out. (A similar signal-to-noise increase can be obtained by combining CW spectrometers with computers that average transients.)

The block diagram of a typical high-resolution pulsed spectrometer is shown in *Figure 10*.

It is a typical configuration of the high-resolution spectrometer that uses a superconducting (cryogenic) solenoid as the source of the magnetic field. Introduction of the pulsed NMR spectrometer has made the acquisition of spectra of many nuclei, other than protons, routine. It has also allowed proton spectra to be obtained in much less time, and with smaller amounts of specimen, as compared to CW techniques.

NMR spectrometers have strict stability and homogeneity requirements. Stability is often achieved by a field-frequency locking system that "locks" the magnetic field to the resonance frequency of a reference signal. The lock signal can be homonuclear or heteronuclear. In the latter case, the reference resonance is usually a deuterium signal from a deuterated solvent. On older spectrometers, using deuterium as a locking nucleus permits noise decoupling of protons to be carried out while studying nuclei like ^{13}C. While internal homonuclear locks are still used in CW proton spectrometers (where tetramethylsilane at about 0.5% provides a convenient lock), they are hardly ever used in pulsed FT spectrometers.

No type of magnet is capable of producing a homogeneous field over the space occupied by the specimen. Two techniques are usually employed to compensate for this lack of homogeneity: specimen spinning and the use of additional (shim) coils. Because of design, particularly probe design, the spinning in the case of the electromagnet or permanent magnet is perpendicular to the basic field. In the superconducting magnet, the axis of rotation can only be parallel to the basic magnetic field. The spin rate should be sufficient to produce averaging of the field, but not fast enough to produce an extended vortex in the specimen tube. A vortex extended near the region exposed to the radio-frequency coils decreases resolution. The shim coils are adjusted by the operator until instrumental contributions to the observed line width are minimized.

An electronic integrator is a feature of most NMR spectrometers. On a CW instrument (^1H and ^{19}F) the integrator, connected to the spectrometer output stage, determines the relative areas of the resonance peaks and presents these areas as a series of stepped horizontal lines when a sweep is made in the integration mode. On FT-NMR spectrometers,

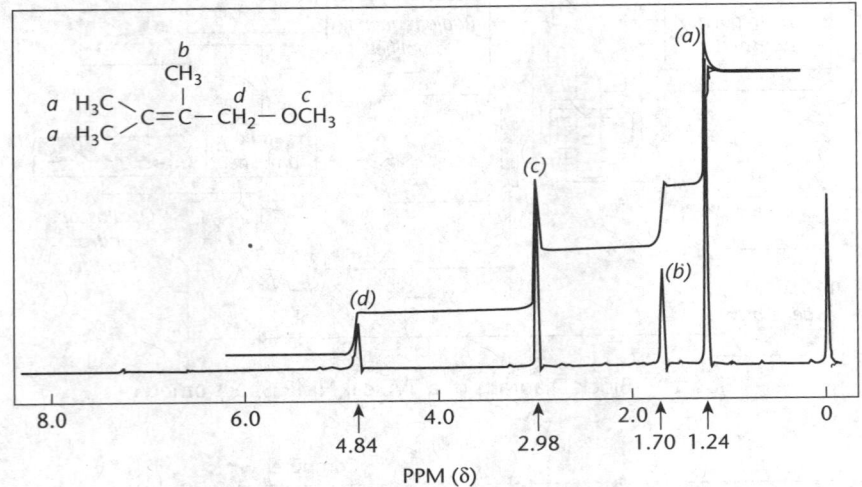

Figure 11. NMR Spectrum of 2,3-Dimethyl-2-butenyl methyl ether (15% in CCl$_4$) showing four nonequivalent, apparently uncoupled protons with a normal integral trace (peak area ratio from low H$_0$ to high H$_0$ of 2:3:3:6). (Tetramethylsilane, the NMR Reference, appears at 0 ppm.) The system of units represented by δ is defined under *The Spectrum*, in this section.

an integration algorithm is included in the spectrometer software, and the resonance peak areas may be presented graphically as stepped lines or tabulated as numeric values. The use of computer-generated tabulated/numeric integration data should not be accepted without a specific demonstration of precision and accuracy on the spectrometer in question.

The Spectrum The signals (peaks) in an NMR spectrum are characterized by four attributes: resonance frequency, multiplicity, line width, and relative intensity. The analytical usefulness of the NMR technique resides in the fact that the same types of nuclei, when located in different molecular environments, exhibit different resonance frequencies. The reason for this difference is that the effective field experienced by a particular nucleus is a composite of the external field provided by the instrument and the field generated by the circulation of the surrounding electrons. (The latter is generally opposed to the external field and the phenomenon is called "shielding.") In contrast with other spectroscopic methods, it is not possible to measure accurately the absolute values of transition frequencies. However, it is possible to measure accurately the difference in frequencies between two resonance signals. The position of a signal in an NMR spectrum is described by its separation from another resonance signal arbitrarily taken as standard. This separation is called chemical shift.

The chemical shift, being the difference between two resonance frequencies, is directly proportional to the magnetic field strength (or to the frequency of the oscillator). However, the ratio between the chemical shift, in frequency units, and the instrument frequency is constant. This allows definition of a dimensionless chemical shift parameter (δ) that is independent of the instrument frequency:

$$\delta = (\nu_s - \nu_r)/\nu_o + \delta_r$$

in which ν_s is the test substance line frequency, ν_r is the reference line frequency, ν_o is the instrument frequency, in mHz, and δ_r is the chemical shift of the reference.

By employing the above equation, it is possible to use (with appropriate caution) the chemical shift of any known species (such as the residual ^{1}H-containing species in deuterated solvent) as a chemical shift reference. The above equation, now in common use, is applicable to nearly all methods except in the relatively rare cases where extremely precise chemical shift values must be determined, and is readily adaptable to nuclei where non-zero reference standards are the only practical method of chemical shift determinations.

For CW instruments, tetramethylsilane (TMS) is the most widely used chemical shift reference for proton and carbon spectra. It is chemically inert, exhibits only one line, which is at a higher field than most signals, and is volatile, thus allowing for ready specimen recovery. Sodium 3-(trimethylsilyl)propionate (TSP) or sodium 2,2-dimethyl-2-silapentane-5-sulfonate (DSS) are used as NMR references for aqueous solutions. The resonance frequency of the TSP or DSS methyl groups closely approximate that of the TMS signal; however, DSS has the disadvantage of showing a number of methylene multiplets that may interfere with signals from the test substance. Where the use of an internal NMR reference material is not desirable, an external reference may be used.

Conventional NMR spectra are shown with the magnetic field strength increasing from left to right. Nuclei that resonate at high magnetic field strengths (to the right) are said to be more shielded (greater electron density) than those that resonate at lower magnetic field strengths: these are said to be de-shielded (lower electron density).

Figure 11 shows the proton NMR spectrum of 2,3-dimethyl-2-butenyl methyl ether. This compound contains protons in a methylene group (marked *d* in the graphic formula) and in four methyl groups (*a, a, b,* and *c*). Methyl groups *b* and *c* are situated in distinctly different molecular environments than the two *a* methyl groups. Three different methyl proton resonances are observed as spectral peaks in addition to the peak corresponding to methylene proton resonance. The two *a* methyl groups, being in very similar environments, have the same chemical shift. Interaction between magnetically active nuclei situated within a few bond lengths of each other leads to coupling, which results in a mutual splitting of the respective signals into sets of peaks or multiplets.

The coupling between two nuclei may be described in terms of the spin-spin coupling constant, J, which is the separation (in hertz) between the individual peaks of the multiplet. Where two nuclei interact and cause reciprocal splitting, the measured coupling constants in the two resulting mutiplets are equal. Furthermore, J is independent of magnetic field strength.

In a first-order, comparatively noncomplex spin system, the number of individual peaks that are expected to be present in a multiplet and the relative peak intensities are predictable. The number of peaks is determined by 2 nI + 1, where n is the number of nuclei on adjacent groups that are active in splitting. For protons this becomes (n + 1) peaks. In general, the relative intensity of each peak in the multiplet follows the coefficient of the binomial expansion (a + b)^n. These coefficients may conveniently be found by use of Pascal's triangle, which produces the following relative areas for the specified multiplets: doublet, 1:1; triplet, 1:2:1; quartet, 1:3:3:1; quintet, 1:4:6:4:1; sextet, 1:5:10:10:5:1; and septet, 1:6:15:20:15:6:1. This orderly arrangement, generally referred to as first-order behavior, may be expected when the ratio of Dv to J is greater than about 10; Dv is the chemical shift difference between two nuclei or two groups of equivalent nuclei. Two examples of idealized spectra arising from first-order coupling are shown in *Figure 12*.

Figure 13 shows a spectrum displaying triplet signals resulting from the mutual splitting of two adjacent methylene groups.

Coupling may occur between ^{1}H and other nuclei, such as ^{19}F, ^{13}C, and ^{31}P. In some cases, e.g., in the CW mode, the coupling constants may be large enough so that part of the multiplet is off scale at either the upfield or downfield end. This type of coupling may occur over the normal "three-bond distance," as for ^{1}H-^{1}H coupling.

Magnetically active nuclei with I ≥ 1, such as ^{14}N, possess an electrical quadrupole moment, which produces line-broadening of the signal due to neighboring nuclei.

Another characteristic of the signal, its relative intensity, has wide analytical applications. In carefully designed experiments (see *General Method*, below), the area or intensity of a signal is directly proportional to the number of protons giving rise to the signal. As a result, it is possible to determine the relative ratio of the different kinds of protons or other nuclei in a specimen or to perform NMR assays with the aid of an internal standard.

The NMR spectra may contain extraneous signals due to the inhomogeneity of the magnetic field throughout the specimen. These artifacts, called spinning side bands, appear as minor lines symmetrically located around each signal. The presence of large spinning side bands indicates that the non-spinning shims require adjustment. The separation is equal to the frequency of the specimen tube spin rate or some integral multiple of that frequency. Thus, spinning side bands are readily identifiable.

General Method Inadequate specimen preparation or incorrect instrumental adjustments and parameters may lead to poor resolution, decreased sensitivity, spectral artifacts, and erroneous data. It is preferable that the operator be familiar with the basic theory of NMR, the properties of the specimen, and the operating principles of the instruments. Strict adherence to the instruction manuals provided by the manufacturer and frequent checks of the performance of the instrument are essential.

The method and procedures discussed here refer specifically to ^{1}H (proton) and ^{19}F NMR. They are applicable, with modification, to other nuclei. The discussion presumes that the NMR spectra are obtained from liquid test substances or solutions in suitable solvents.

Selection of Solvent In addition to having good solubility properties, suitable solvents do not exhibit resonance peaks that obscure resonance peaks of the specimen being analyzed. The most commonly used solvents for proton and carbon NMR are listed in the table below. Deuterated solvents also provide the signal for the heteronuclear system lock. If solvent peaks might interfere with any signals from the specimen, then the isotopic purity of the solvent should be as high as possible. Deuterium (I = 1) does not exhibit resonance under ^{1}H conditions but may cause J-coupling to

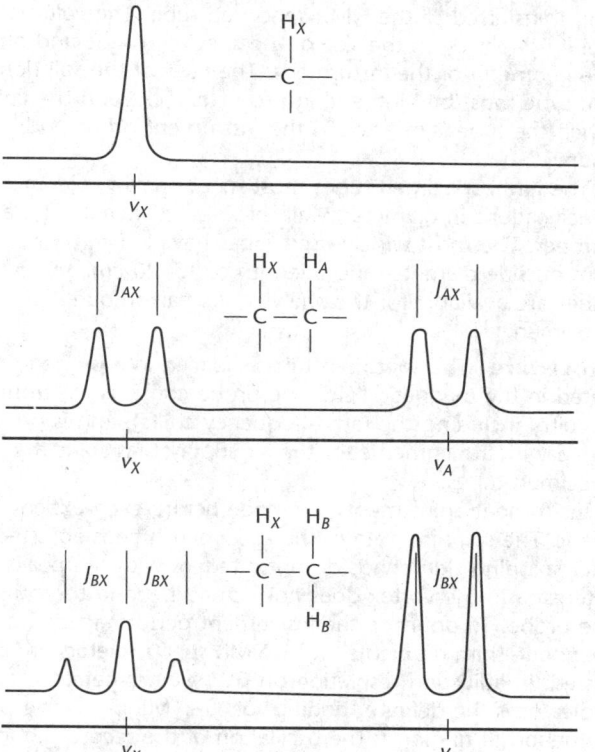

Figure 12. Diagrammatic Representation of Simple First-Order Coupling of Adjacent Protons

1248 / Appendix II / General Tests and Assays

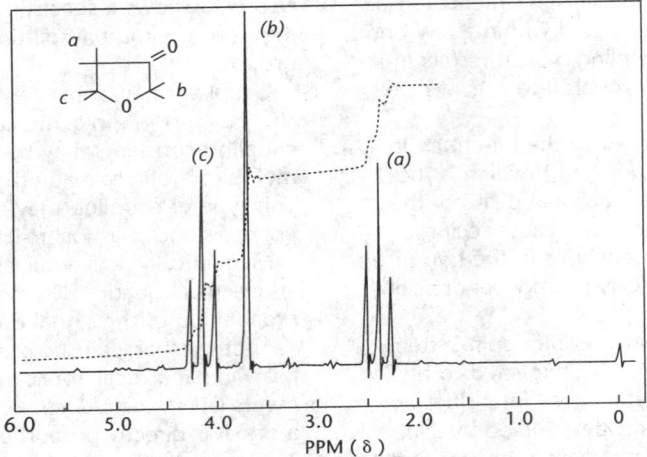

Figure 13. NMR Spectrum of 3-Keto-tetrahydrofuran (10% in CCl$_4$) showing three nonequivalent protons, with a normal integral trace (peak area ratio from low H$_0$ to high H$_0$ of 1:1:1). Note two sets of methylene groups coupled to each other at 4.2 and 2.4 ppm. (Tetramethylsilane, the NMR Reference, appears at 0 ppm.)

be observed. The residual protons generate solvent peaks whose chemical shifts are shown in the table below.

Solvents Commonly Used for Proton NMR

Solvent	Residual Proton Signal, δ^a
CCl$_4$[b]	—
CS$_2$[b]	—
SO$_2$ (liquid)	—
(CF$_3$)$_2$CO	—
CDCl$_3$	7.27
CD$_3$OD	3.35, 4.8[c]
(CD$_3$)$_2$CO	2.05
D$_2$O	4.7[c]
DMSO-d$_6$[d]	2.50
C$_6$D$_6$	7.20
p-Dioxane-d$_8$	3.55
CD$_3$CO$_2$D	2.05, 8.5[c]
DMF-d$_7$[e]	2.77, 2.93, 8.05

[a] δ in ppm relative to tetramethylsilane arbitrarily taken as 0δ or 0 ppm.
[b] Spectrophotometric grade.
[c] Highly variable; depends on solute and temperature.
[d] Dimethyl sulfoxide-d$_6$.
[e] N,N-Dimethylformamide-d$_7$ per Aldrich, Alfa, Fluka, and Sigma catalogs.

Some solvents (e.g., D$_2$O or CD$_3$OD) enter into fast exchange reactions with protons and may eliminate resonance signals from –COOH, –OH, and –NH$_2$ structural groups. The protons in alcohols and amines do not take part in rapid exchange unless catalyzed by small concentrations of acid or base, except in the presence of D$_2$O and some other solvents (e.g., CD$_3$OD).

For ^{19}F NMR, most solvents used in proton NMR may be employed, the most common ones being CHCl$_3$, CCl$_4$, H$_2$O, CS$_2$, aqueous acids and bases, and dimethylacetamide. In general, any nonfluorinated solvent may be used, provided that it is of spectral quality. Obviously, there is no interference from the protonated functional groups of the solvent. However, unless they are decoupled, protonated functional groups on the ^{19}F-containing specimen will provide J-coupling.

Specimen Preparation Directions are usually given in individual monographs. The solute concentration depends on the objective of the experiment and on the type of instrument. Detection of minor contaminants may require higher concentrations. The solutions are prepared in separate vials and transferred to the NMR specimen tube. The volume required depends on the size of the specimen tube and on the geometry of the instrument. The level of the solution in the tube must be high enough to extend beyond the coils when the tube is inserted in the instrument probe and spun.

The NMR specimen tubes must meet narrow tolerance specifications in diameter, wall thickness, concentricity, and camber. The most widely used tubes have a 5-mm or 10-mm outside diameter and a length of 15–20 cm. Microtubes are available for the analysis of small amounts of specimen.

Procedure The specimen tube is placed in a probe located in the magnetic field. The probe contains electronic circuitry including the radio-frequency coil(s), and is provided with attachments for the air supply that spins the specimen tubes.

Instrument adjustments are made before each experiment. The spinning rate of the specimen tube is adjusted so that spinning side bands do not interfere with the peaks of interest and the vortex does not extend beyond the coils in the probe. To optimize the instrument performance, the magnetic shim gradients on FT-NMR spectrometers are adjusted. In adjusting resolution on CW spectrometers, a good indicator is the definite "ringing" of the TMS peak. The phenomenon of ringing is the oscillation of the recorder trace after the magnetic field has passed through a resonance frequency. Ringing, evident on a number of the peaks in Figures 13 and 14, arises during rapid scans and decays exponentially to the baseline value.

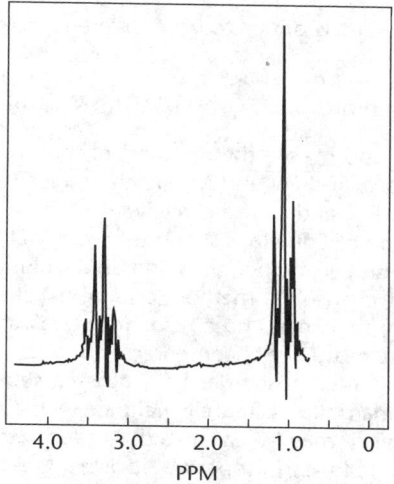

Figure 14. Continuous Wave Proton Spectrum of Ethyl Ether

Figure 15 clearly indicates the absence, in an FT experiment, of the ringing phenomenon. Ringing will not appear because the spectrum obtained is the result of analysis of the FID by Fourier transformation and not a magnetic field or frequency sweep through the individual resonance positions.

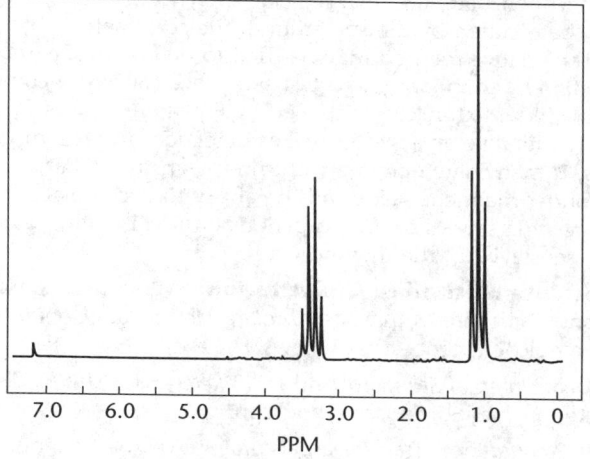

Figure 15. Proton NMR Spectrum of Ethyl Ether in Deuterated Chloroform

With proton CW instruments the spectrum is scanned from 0 ppm to about 10 ppm with a scan time of about 1–5 min. The amplification is adjusted so that all peaks remain on scale. If the response is low at reasonable amplitude, the radio-frequency power is increased to obtain the highest possible peak response without peak broadening. After the initial scan, the presence of peaks downfield of 10 ppm is quickly checked by off-setting the instrument response by about 5 ppm. With CW instrumentation, it is common for the TMS peak to shift slightly during an extended scan. The extent of the shift is usually obtained by comparing the relative positions of another peak in the initial scan with the same peak in the offset scan.

The operation of an FT-NMR spectrometer is a much more elaborate experiment. The computer serves to control the spectrometer, to program the experiment, and to store and process the data. Programming the experiment involves setting values for a large number of variables including the spectral width to be examined, the duration ("width") of the excitation pulse, the time interval over which data will be acquired, the number of transients to be accumulated, and the delay between one acquisition and the next. The analysis time for one transient is in the order of seconds. The number of transients is a function of the specimen concentration, the type of nucleus, and the objective of the experiment. At the end of the experiment, the FID signal is stored in digitized form in the computer memory and is displayed on the video screen. The signal can be processed mathematically to enhance either the resolution or the sensitivity, and it can be Fourier-transformed into a frequency-domain spectrum. The instrument provides a plot of the spectrum. The integration routine, accessed through keyboard commands, results in a stepped-line plot. Considerably more accurate integrals are obtained if the signals or regions of interest are separately integrated.

FT-NMR spectrometers may yield qualitative and quantitative data from the same experiment, but this is seldom done in practice. In quantitative FT experiments, special precautions must be taken for the signal areas to be proportional to the number of protons. The delays between pulses must be long enough to allow complete relaxation of all excited nuclei. This results in a considerable increase in analysis time and in some loss of resolution. Qualitative analysis is usually performed in nonquantitative conditions, with the design of the experiment directed to fast analysis with maximum resolution or sensitivity.

Qualitative and Quantitative Analysis NMR spectroscopy has been used for a wide range of applications such as structure elucidation; thermodynamic, kinetic, and mechanistic studies; and quantitative analysis. Some of these applications are beyond the scope of compendial methods.

All five characteristics of the signal (chemical shift, multiplicity, line width, coupling constants, and relative intensity) contribute analytical information.

Qualitative Applications Comparison of a spectrum from the literature or from an authentic specimen with that of a test specimen may be used to confirm the identity of a compound and to detect the presence of impurities that generate extraneous signals. The NMR spectra of simple structures can be adequately described by the numeric value of the chemical shifts and coupling constants, and by the number of protons under each signal. (The software of modern instruments includes programs that generate simulated spectra using these data.) Experimental details, such as the solvent used, the specimen concentration, and the chemical shift reference, must also be provided.

For unknown specimens, NMR analysis, usually coupled with other analytical techniques, is a powerful tool for structure elucidation. Chemical shifts provide information on the chemical environment of the nuclei. Extensive literature is available with correlation charts and rules for predicting chemical shifts. The multiplicity of the signals provides important stereochemical information. Mutual signal splitting of functional groups indicates close proximity. The magnitude of the coupling constant, J, between residual protons on substituted aromatic, olefinic, or cycloalkyl structures is used to identify the relative position of the substituents.

Several special techniques (double resonance, chemical exchange, use of shift reagents, two-dimensional analysis, etc.) are available to simplify some of the more complex spectra, to identify certain functional groups, and to determine coupling correlations.

Double resonance, or spin decoupling, is a technique that removes the coupling between nuclei and thus simplifies the spectrum and identifies the components in a coupling relationship. For example, in a simple two-proton system, generally designated an AX system (see *Figure 12*), each proton appears as a doublet. If a strong radio-frequency field is introduced at the frequency of X, while the normal radio-frequency field is maintained at the frequency that causes A to resonate, the coupling between A and X is removed (homonuclear decoupling). A is no longer split, but instead appears as a singlet. Routine ^{13}C spectra are obtained under proton decoupling conditions that remove all heteronuclear ^{13}C-^{1}H couplings. As a result of this decoupling, the carbon signals appear as singlets, unless other nuclei that are not decoupled are present (e.g., ^{19}F, ^{31}P).

Functional groups containing exchangeable protons bound to hetero-atoms such as –OH, –NH$_2$, or –COOH groups may be identified by taking advantage of the rapid exchange of these protons with D$_2$O. To determine the presence and position of these groups, scan the test substance in CDCl$_3$ or DMSO-d_6, then add a few drops of D$_2$O to the specimen tube, shake, and scan again. The resonance peaks from these groups collapse in the second scan and are replaced by the HDO singlet between 4.7 and 5.0 ppm.

This chemical exchange is an example of the effect of intermolecular and intramolecular rate processes on NMR spectra. If a proton can experience different environments by virtue of such a process (tautomerism, rotation about a bond, exchange equilibria, ring inversion, etc.), the appearance of the spectrum will be a function of the rate of the process. Slow processes (on an NMR time scale) result in more than one signal, fast processes average these signals to one line, and intermediate processes produce broad signals.

The software of modern FT-NMR spectrometers allows for sequences of pulses much more complex than the repetitive accumulation of transients described above. Such experiments include homonuclear or heteronuclear two-dimensional analysis, which determines the correlation of couplings and may simplify the interpretation of otherwise complex spectra.

Quantitative Applications If appropriate instrument settings for quantitative analysis have been made, the areas (or intensities) of two signals are proportional to the total number of protons generating the signals.

$$A_1/A_2 = N_1/N_2 \quad (1)$$

If the two signals originate from two functional groups of the same molecule, the equation can be simplified to:

$$A_1/A_2 = n_1/n_2 \quad (2)$$

in which n_1 and n_2 are the number of protons in the respective functional groups.

If the two signals originate from different molecular species,

$$A_1/A_2 = n_1 m_1 / n_2 m_2 = (n_1 W_1/M_1)/(n_2 W_2/M_2) \quad (3)$$

in which m_1 and m_2 are the numbers of moles; W_1 and W_2 are the masses; and M_1 and M_2 are the molecular weights of compounds 1 and 2, respectively.

Examination of Equations 2 and 3 shows that NMR quantitative analysis can be performed in an absolute or relative manner. In the absolute method, an internal standard is added to the specimen and a resonance peak area arising from the test substance is compared with a resonance peak area from the internal standard. If both test substance and internal standard are accurately weighed, the absolute purity of the substance may be calculated. A good internal standard has the following properties: it presents a reference resonance peak, preferably a singlet, at a field position removed from all specimen peaks; it is soluble in the analytical solvent; its proton equivalent weight, i.e., the molecular weight divided by the number of protons giving rise to the reference peak, is low; and it does not interact with the compound being tested. Typical examples of useful standards are 1,2,4,5-tetrachlorobenzene, 1,4-dinitrobenzene, benzyl benzoate, and maleic acid. The choice of a standard will be dictated by the spectrum of the specimen.

The relative method may be used to determine the molar fraction of an impurity in a test substance (or of the components in a mixture) as calculated by Equation 3.

Quantitative analysis, as well as detection of trace impurities, is markedly improved with modern instrumentation. Stronger magnetic fields and the ability to accumulate and/or average signals over long periods of time greatly enhance the sensitivity of the method.

Absolute Method of Quantitation Where the individual monograph directs that the *Absolute Method of Quantitation* be employed, proceed as follows.

Solvent, Internal Standard, and *NMR Reference:* Use as directed in the individual monograph.

Test Preparation: Transfer an accurately weighed quantity of the test substance, containing about 4.5 proton mEq, to a glass-stoppered, graduated centrifuge tube. Add about 4.5 proton mEq of *Internal Standard*, accurately weighed, and 3.0 mL of *Solvent*, insert the stopper, and shake. When dissolution is complete, add about 30 µL (30 mg if a solid) of *NMR Reference*, provided that it does not interfere with subsequent measurements, and shake.

Procedure: Transfer an appropriate amount (0.4–0.8 mL) of *Test Preparation* to a standard 5-mm NMR spinning tube, and record the spectrum, adjusting the spin rate so that no spinning side bands interfere with the peaks of interest. Measure the area under each of the peaks specified in the individual monograph by integrating not fewer than five times. Record the average area of the *Internal Standard* peak as A_S and that of the *Test Preparation* peak as A_U.

Calculate the quantity, in mg, of the analyte in the *Test Preparation*:

$$W_S(A_U/A_S)(E_U/E_S)$$

in which W_S is the weight, in mg, of *Internal Standard* taken; and E_U and E_S are the proton equivalent weights (i.e., the molecular weights divided by the number of protons giving rise to the reference peak) of the analyte and the *Internal Standard*, respectively.

Relative Method of Quantitation Where the individual monograph directs that the *Relative Method of Quantitation* be employed, proceed as follows.

Solvent, *NMR Reference*, and *Test Preparation:* Use as directed under *Absolute Method of Quantitation*.

Procedure: Transfer an appropriate amount (0.4–0.8 mL) of *Test Preparation* to a standard 5-mm NMR spinning tube, and record the spectrum, adjusting the spin rate so that no spinning side bands interfere with the peaks of interest. Measure the area or intensity under each of the peaks specified in the individual monograph by integrating not fewer than five times. Record the average area or intensity resulting from the resonances of the groups designated in the individual monograph as A_1 and A_2.

Calculate the quantity, in mole percent, of the analyte in the *Test Preparation*:

$$(100 \times (A_1/n_1)/[(A_1/n_1) + (A_2/n_2)]$$

in which n_1 and n_2 are, respectively, the numbers of protons in the designated groups.

OIL CONTENT OF SYNTHETIC PARAFFIN

Apparatus

Filter Stick: Use either a 10-mm diameter sintered-glass filter stick of 10–15-μm maximum pore diameter, or a filter stick made of stainless steel and having a 0.5-in. disk of 10–15-μm maximum pore diameter. Determine conformance with the pore diameter specified as follows: Clean sintered-glass filter sticks by soaking in hydrochloric acid, or stainless steel sticks by soaking in nitric acid, wash with water, rinse with acetone, and dry in air followed by drying in an oven at 105° for 30 min.

Thoroughly wet the clean filter stick by soaking in water, and then connect it with an apparatus (see *Figure 16*) consisting of a mercury-filled manometer, readable to 0.5 mm; a clean and filtered air supply; a drying bulb filled with silica gel; and a needle-valve type air pressure regulator. Apply pressure slowly from the air source, and immerse the filter just below the surface of water contained in a beaker.

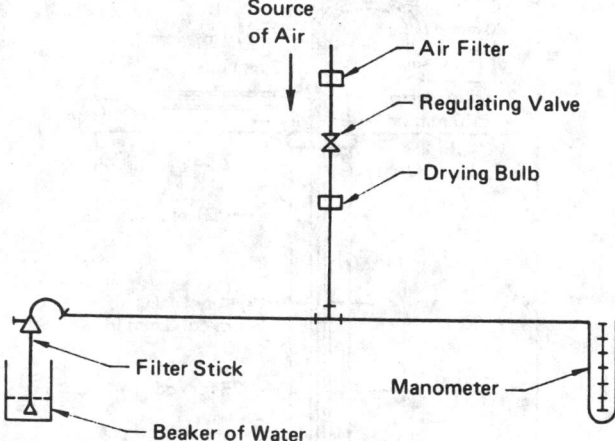

Figure 16. Assembly for Checking Pore Diameter of Filter Sticks

[NOTE—If a head of liquid is noted above the surface of the filter after it is inserted into the water, the back pressure thus produced should be subtracted from the observed pressure when the pore diameter is calculated as directed below.]

Increase the air pressure to 10 mm below the acceptable pressure limit, and then increase the pressure at a slow, uniform rate of about 3 mm Hg per minute until the first bubble passes through the filter. This can be conveniently observed by placing the beaker over a mirror. Read the manometer when the first bubble passes off the underside of the filter. Calculate the pore diameter, in μm:

$$\text{Result} = 2180/p$$

in which p is the observed pressure, in mm, corrected for any back pressure as mentioned above.

Filtration Assembly: Connect the *Filter Stick* with an air pressure inlet tube and delivery nozzle and ground-glass joint to fit a 25-mm × 170-mm test tube as shown in *Figure 17*. If a stainless steel *Filter Stick* is used, make the connection to the test tube by means of a cork.

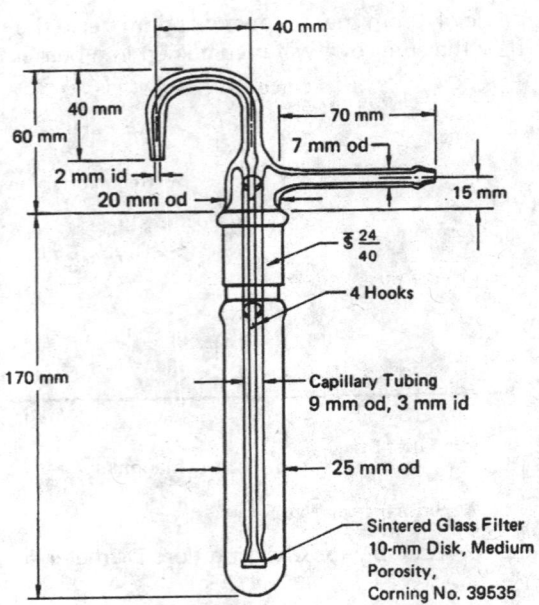

Figure 17. Filtration Assembly for Determination of Oil Content

Cooling Bath: Use a suitable insulated box having 1-in. holes in the center to accommodate any desired number of test tubes. The bath may be filled with a suitable medium such as kerosene and may be cooled by circulating a refrigerant through coils, or by using solid carbon dioxide, to produce a temperature of 30 ± 2°F.

Air Pressure Regulator: Use a suitable pressure-reduction valve, or other suitable regulator, that will supply air to the *Filtration Assembly* at the volume and pressure required to give an even flow of filtrate (see *Procedure*). Connect the regulator with rubber tubing to the end of the *Filter Stick* in the *Filtration Assembly*.

Thermometer: Use an ASTM Oil in Wax Thermometer having the range of −35° to +70°F and conforming to the requirements for an ASTM 71F thermometer (see *Thermometers*, Appendix I).

Weighing Bottles: Use glass-stoppered conical bottles having a capacity of 15 mL. The bottles are used as evaporating flasks in the *Procedure*.

Evaporation Assembly: The assembly consists of an evaporating cabinet capable of maintaining a temperature of 95 ± 2°F around the evaporation flasks, and air jets (4 ± 0.2 mm id) for delivering a stream of clean, dry air vertically downward into the flasks. In the *Procedure* below, support each jet so that the tip is 15 ± 5 mm above the surface of the liquid at the start of the evaporation. Supply the air (purified by passage through a tube of 1-cm bore packed loosely to a height of 20 cm with absorbent cotton) at the rate of 2 to 3 L/min per jet. The cleanliness of the air should be checked periodically to ensure that NMT 0.1 mg of residue is obtained when 4 mL of methyl ethyl ketone is evaporated as directed in the *Procedure*.

Wire Stirrer Use a 250-mm length of stiff iron or nichrome wire of about No. 20 B & S gauge. Form a 10-mm diameter loop at each end, and bend the loop at the bottom end so that the plane of the loop is perpendicular to the length of the wire.

Sample Selection If the sample weighs about 1 kg or less, obtain a representative portion by melting the entire sample and stirring thoroughly. For samples heavier than about 1 kg, exercise special care to ensure that a truly representative portion is obtained, noting that the oil may not be distributed uniformly throughout the sample and that mechanical operations may have expressed some of the oil.

Procedure Melt a representative portion of the sample in a beaker, using a water bath or oven maintained at 160°–210°F. As soon as the sample is completely melted, thoroughly mix it by stirring. Preheat a dropper pipet, provided with a rubber bulb and calibrated to deliver 1 ± 0.05 g of molten sample, and withdraw a 1-g portion of the sample as soon as possible after it has melted. Hold the pipet in a vertical position, and carefully transfer its contents into a clean, dry test tube previously weighed to the nearest milligram. Evenly coat the bottom of the tube by swirling, allow the tube to cool, and weigh to the nearest milligram. Calculate the sample weight, in grams, and record it as B (see *Calculation*). Pipet 15 mL of methyl ethyl ketone (ASTM Specification D 740, or equivalent) into the tube, and immerse the tube up to the top of the liquid in a hot water or steam bath. Stir with an up-and-down motion with the wire stirrer, and continue heating and stirring until a homogeneous solution is obtained, exercising care to avoid loss of solvent by prolonged boiling.

[NOTE—If it appears that a clear solution will not be obtained, stir until any undissolved material is well dispersed so as to produce a slightly cloudy solution.]

After the sample solution is prepared, plunge the test tube into an 800-mL beaker of ice water, and continue to stir until the contents are cold. Remove the stirrer, then remove the test tube from the bath, dry the outside of the tube with a cloth, and weigh to the nearest 100 mg. Calculate the weight, in grams, of solvent in the test tube, and record it as C (see *Calculation*). Place the tube in the cooling bath, maintained at −30 ± 2°F, and stir continuously with the thermometer until the temperature reaches −25 ± 0.5°F, maintaining the slurry at a uniform consistency and taking precautions to prevent the sample from setting up on the walls of the tube or forming crystals.

Place the filter stick in a test tube and cool at −30 ± 2°F in the cooling bath for a minimum of 10 min. Immerse the cooled filter stick in the sample, then connect the filtration assembly, seating the ground-glass joint of the filter so as to make an airtight seal. Place an unstoppered weighing bottle, previously weighed together with the glass stopper to the nearest 0.1 mg, under the delivery nozzle of the filtration assembly.

[NOTE—Suitable precautions and proper analytical technique should be applied to ensure the accuracy of the weight of the bottle. Before determining its weight, the bottle and its stopper should have been cleaned and dried, then rinsed with methyl ethyl ketone, wiped dry on the outside, dried in the evaporation assembly for about 5 min, and cooled. Then allow it to stand for about 10 min near the balance before weighing.]

Apply air pressure to the filtration assembly, immediately collect about 4 mL of filtrate in the weighing bottle, and release the air pressure to permit the liquid to drain back slowly from the delivery nozzle. Stopper the bottle, and weigh it to the nearest 10 mg without waiting for it to come to room temperature. Remove the stopper, transfer the bottle to the evaporation assembly maintained at 95 ± 2°F, and place it under an air jet centered inside the neck, with the tip 15 ± 5 mm above the surface of the liquid. After the solvent has evaporated (usually less than 30 min), stopper the bottle, and allow it to stand near the balance for about 10 min before it is weighed to the nearest 0.1 mg. Repeat the evaporation procedure for 5-min periods until the loss between successive weighings is NMT 0.2 mg. Determine the weight of the oil residue, in grams, by subtracting the weight of the empty stoppered bottle from the weight of the stoppered bottle plus the oil residue after the evaporation procedure, and record the results as A (see *Calculation*). Determine the weight of solvent evaporated, in grams, by subtracting the weight of the bottle plus oil residue from the weight of the bottle plus filtrate, and record the result as D (see *Calculation*).

Calculation Calculate the percent, by weight, of oil in the sample:

$$\text{Result} = (100\ AC/BD) - 0.15$$

in which 0.15 is a factor to correct for solubility of the sample in the solvent at −25°F.

PLASMA SPECTROCHEMISTRY

Plasma-based instrumental techniques that are useful for food ingredient analyses fall into two major categories: those based on the inductively coupled plasma, and those where a plasma is generated at or near the surface of the sample. An inductively coupled plasma (ICP) is a high-temperature excitation source that desolvates, vaporizes, and atomizes aerosol samples and ionizes the resulting atoms. The excited analyte ions and atoms can then subsequently be detected by observing their emission lines, a method termed inductively coupled plasma–atomic emission spectroscopy (ICP–AES), also known as inductively coupled plasma–optical emission spectroscopy (ICP–OES); or the excited or ground state ions can be determined by a technique known as inductively coupled plasma–mass spectrometry (ICP–MS). ICP–AES and ICP–MS may be used for either single- or multi-element analysis, and they provide good general-purpose procedures for either sequential or simultaneous analyses over an extended linear range with good sensitivity.

An emerging technique in plasma spectrochemistry is laser-induced breakdown spectroscopy (LIBS). In LIBS, a solid, liquid, or gaseous sample is heated directly by a pulsed laser, or indirectly by a plasma generated by the laser. As a result, the sample is volatilized at the laser beam contact point, and the volatilized constituents are reduced to atoms, molecular fragments, and larger clusters in the plasma that forms at or just above the surface of the sample. Emission from the atoms and ions in the sample is collected, typically using fiber optics or a remote viewing system, and is measured using an array detector such as a charge-coupled device (CCD). LIBS can be used for qualitative analysis or against a working standard curve for quantitative analysis. Although LIBS is not currently in wide use, it might be suited for at-line or on-line measurements in a production setting, as well as in the laboratory. Because of its potential, it should be considered a viable technique for plasma spectrochemistry in the laboratory. However, because LIBS is still an emerging technique, details will not be further discussed here.[3]

Sample Preparation Sample preparation is critical to the success of plasma-based analysis and is the first step in performing any analysis via ICP–AES or ICP–MS. Plasma-based techniques are heavily dependent on sample transport into the plasma, and because ICP–AES and ICP–MS share the same sample introduction system, the means by which samples are prepared may be applicable to either technique. The most conventional means by which samples are introduced into the plasma is via solution nebulization. If solution nebulization is employed, solid samples must be dissolved in order to be presented into the plasma for analysis. Samples may be dissolved in any appropriate solvent. There is a strong preference for the use of aqueous or dilute nitric acid solutions, because there are minimal interferences with these solvents compared to other solvent choices. Hydrogen peroxide, hydrochloric acid, sulfuric acid, perchloric acid, combinations of acids, or various concentrations of acids can all be used to dissolve the sample for analysis. Dilute hydrofluoric acid may also be used, but great care must be taken to ensure the safety of the analyst, as well as to protect the quartz sample introduction equipment when using this acid; specifically, the nebulizer, spray chamber, and inner torch tube should be manufactured from hydrofluoric acid-tolerant materials. Additionally, alternative means of dissolving the sample can be employed. These include, but are not limited to, the use of dilute bases, straight or diluted organic solvents, combinations of acids or bases, and combinations of organic solvents.

When samples are introduced into the plasma via solution nebulization, it is important to consider the potential matrix effects and interferences that might arise from the solvent. The use of an appropriate internal standard and/or matching the standard matrix with samples should be applied for ICP–AES and ICP–MS analyses in cases where accuracy and precision are not adequate. In either event, the selection of an appropriate internal standard should consider the analyte in question, ionization energy, wavelengths or masses, and the nature of the sample matrix.

Where a sample is found not to be soluble in any acceptable solvent, a variety of digestion techniques can be employed. These include hot-plate digestion and microwave-

---

[3] Yueh F-Y, Singh JP, Zhang H. Laser-induced breakdown spectroscopy, elemental analysis. In: *Encyclopedia of Analytical Chemistry: Instrumentation and Applications.* New York: Wiley; 2000:2066–2087.

assisted digestions, including open- and closed-vessel approaches. The decision regarding the type of digestion technique to use depends on the nature of the sample being digested, as well as on the analytes of interest.

Open-vessel digestion is generally not recommended for the analysis of volatile metals, e.g., selenium and mercury. The suitability of a digestion technique, whether open- or closed-vessel, should be supported by spike recovery experiments in order to verify that, within an acceptable tolerance, volatile metals have not been lost during sample preparation. Use acids, bases, and hydrogen peroxide of ultra-high purity, especially when ICP–MS is employed. Deionized water must be at least 18 megaohm. Check diluents for interferences before they are used in an analysis. Because it is not always possible to obtain organic solvents that are free of metals, use organic solvents of the highest quality possible with regard to metal contaminants.

It is important to consider the selection of the type, material of construction, pretreatment, and cleaning of analytical labware used in ICP–AES and ICP–MS analyses. The material must be inert and, depending on the specific application, resistant to caustics, acids, and/or organic solvents. For some analyses, diligence must be exercised to prevent the adsorption of analytes onto the surface of a vessel, particularly in ultra-trace analyses. Contamination of the sample solutions from metal and ions present in the container can also lead to inaccurate results.

The use of labware that is not certified to meet Class A tolerances for volumetric flasks is acceptable if the linearity, accuracy, and precision of the method have been experimentally demonstrated to be suitable for the purpose at hand.

Sample Introduction   There are two ways to introduce the sample into the nebulizer: by a peristaltic pump and by self-aspiration. The peristaltic pump is preferred, and serves to ensure that the flow rate of sample and standard solution to the nebulizer is the same, irrespective of sample viscosity. In some cases, where a peristaltic pump is not required, self-aspiration can be used.

A wide variety of nebulizer types is available, including pneumatic (concentric and cross-flow), grid, and ultrasonic nebulizers. Micronebulizers, high-efficiency nebulizers, direct-injection high-efficiency nebulizers, and flow-injection nebulizers are also available. The selection of the nebulizer for a given analysis should consider the sample matrix, analyte, and desired sensitivity. Some nebulizers are better suited for use with viscous solutions or those containing a high concentration of dissolved solids, whereas others are better suited for use with organic solutions.

Note that the self-aspiration of a fluid is due to the Bernoulli or Venturi effect. Not all types of nebulizers will support self-aspiration. The use of a concentric nebulizer, for example, is required for self-aspiration of a solution.

Once a sample leaves the nebulizer as an aerosol, it enters the spray chamber, which is designed to permit only the smallest droplets of sample solution into the plasma; as a result, typically only 1%–2% of the sample aerosol reaches the ICP, although some special-purpose nebulizers have been designed that permit virtually all of the sample aerosol to enter the ICP. As with nebulizers, there is more than one type of spray chamber available for use with ICP–AES or ICP–MS. Examples include the Scott double-pass spray chamber, as well as cyclonic spray chambers of various configurations. The spray chamber must be compatible with the sample and solvent, and must equilibrate and wash out in as short a time as possible. When a spray chamber is selected, the nature of the sample matrix, the nebulizer, the desired sensitivity, and the analyte should all be considered.

Gas and liquid chromatography systems can be interfaced with ICP–AES and ICP–MS for molecular speciation, ionic speciation, or other modes of separation chemistry, based on elemental emission or mass spectrometry.

Ultimately, the selection of sample introduction hardware should be demonstrated experimentally to provide sufficient specificity, sensitivity, linearity, accuracy, and precision of the analysis at hand.

In addition to solution nebulization, it is possible to analyze solid samples directly via laser ablation (LA). In such instances, the sample enters the torch as a solid aerosol. LA–ICP–AES and LA–ICP–MS are better suited for qualitative analyses of compounds, because of the difficulty in obtaining appropriate standards. Nonetheless, quantitative analyses can be performed if it can be demonstrated through appropriate method validation that the available standards are adequate.[4]

Standard Preparation   Single- or multi-element standard solutions, which have concentrations traceable to primary reference standards, such as those of the National Institute of Standards and Technology (NIST), can be purchased for use in the preparation of working standard solutions. Alternatively, standard solutions of elements can be accurately prepared from standard materials and their concentrations, determined independently, as appropriate. Working standard solutions, especially those used for ultra-trace analyses, may have limited shelf life. As a general rule, working standard solutions should be retained for no more than 24 h, unless stability is demonstrated experimentally. The selection of the standard matrix is of fundamental importance in the preparation of element standard solutions. Spike recovery experiments should be conducted with specific sample matrices in order to determine the accuracy of the method. If sample matrix effects cause excessive inaccuracies, standards, blanks, and sample solutions should be matrix matched, if possible, in order to minimize matrix interferences.

In cases where matrix matching is not possible, an appropriate internal standard or the method of standard additions should be used for ICP–AES or ICP–MS. Internal standards can also be introduced through a T connector into the sample uptake tubing. In any event, the selection of an appropriate internal standard should consider the analytes in question, their ionization and excitation energies, their chemical behavior, their wavelengths or masses, and the nature of the sample matrix. Ultimately, the selection of an internal standard should be demonstrated experimentally to provide sufficient specificity, sensitivity, linearity, accuracy, and precision of the analysis at hand.

The method of standard additions involves adding a known concentration of the analyte element to the sample

---

[4] For additional information on laser ablation, see Russo R, Mao X, Borisov O, Liu H. Laser ablation in atomic spectrometry. In: *Encyclopedia of Analytical Chemistry: Instrumentation and Applications.* New York: Wiley; 2000.

at no fewer than two concentration levels plus an unspiked sample preparation. The instrument response is plotted against the concentration of the added analyte element, and a linear regression line is drawn through the data points. The absolute value of the x-intercept multiplied by any dilution factor is the concentration of the analyte in the sample.

The presence of dissolved carbon at concentrations of a small percentage in aqueous solutions enhances ionization of selenium and arsenic in an inductively coupled argon plasma. This phenomenon frequently results in a positive bias for ICP–AES and ICP–MS selenium and arsenic quantification measurements, which can be remedied by using the method of standard additions or by adding a small percentage of carbon, such as analytically pure glacial acetic acid, to the linearity standards.

ICP The components that make up the ICP excitation source include the argon gas supply, torch, radio frequency (RF) induction coil, impedance-matching unit, and RF generator. Argon gas is almost universally used in an ICP. The plasma torch consists of three concentric tubes designated as the inner, the intermediate, and the outer tube. The intermediate and outer tubes are almost universally made of quartz. The inner tube can be made of quartz or alumina if the analysis is conducted with solutions containing hydrofluoric acid. The nebulizer gas flow carries the aerosol of the sample solution into and through the inner tube of the torch and into the plasma. The intermediate tube carries the intermediate (sometimes referred to as the auxiliary) gas. The intermediate gas flow helps to lift the plasma off the inner and intermediate tubes to prevent their melting and the deposition of carbon and salts on the inner tube. The outer tube carries the outer (sometimes referred to as the plasma or coolant) gas, which is used to form and sustain the toroidal plasma. The tangential flow of the coolant gas through the torch constricts the plasma and prevents the ICP from expanding to fill the outer tube, keeping the torch from melting. An RF induction coil, also called the load coil, surrounds the torch and produces an oscillating magnetic field, which in turn sets up an oscillating current in the ions and electrons produced from the argon. The impedance-matching unit serves to efficiently couple the RF energy from the generator to the load coil. The unit can be of either the active or passive type. An active matching unit adjusts the impedance of the RF power by means of a capacitive network, whereas the passive type adjusts the impedance directly through the generator circuitry. Within the load coil of the RF generator, the energy transfer between the coil and the argon creates a self-sustaining plasma. Collisions of the ions and electrons liberated from the argon ionize and excite the analyte atoms in the high-temperature plasma. The plasma operates at temperatures of 6,000 to 10,000 K, so most covalent bonds and analyte-to-analyte interactions have been eliminated.

ICP–AES An inductively coupled plasma can use either an optical or a mass spectral detection system. In the former case, ICP–AES, analyte detection is achieved at an emission wavelength of the analyte in question. Because of differences in technology, a wide variety of ICP–AES systems are available, each with different capabilities, as well as different advantages and disadvantages. Simultaneous-detection systems are capable of analyzing multiple elements at the same time, thereby shortening analysis time and improving background detection and correction. Sequential systems move from one wavelength to the next to perform analyses, and often provide a larger number of analytical lines from which to choose. Array detectors, including charge-coupled devices and charge-injection devices, with detectors on a chip, make it possible to combine the advantages of both simultaneous and sequential systems. These types of detection devices are used in the most powerful spectrometers, providing rapid analysis and a wide selection of analytical lines.

The ICP can be viewed in either axial or radial (also called lateral) mode. The torch is usually positioned horizontally in axially viewed plasmas and is viewed end on, whereas it is positioned vertically in radially viewed plasmas and is viewed from the side. Axial viewing of the plasma can provide higher signal-to-noise ratios (better detection limits and precision); however, it also incurs greater matrix and spectral interferences. Methods validated on an instrument with a radial configuration will probably not be completely transferable to an instrument with an axial configuration, and vice versa.

Additionally, dual-view instrument systems are available, making it possible for the analyst to take advantage of either torch configuration. The selection of the optimal torch configuration will depend on the sample matrix, analyte in question, analytical wavelength(s) used, cost of instrumentation, required sensitivity, and type of instrumentation available in a given laboratory.

Regardless of torch configuration or detector technology, ICP–AES is a technique that provides a qualitative and/or quantitative measurement of the optical emission from excited atoms or ions at specific wavelengths. These measurements are then used to determine the analyte concentration in a given sample. Upon excitation, an atom or atomic ion emits an array of different frequencies of light that are characteristic of the distinct energy transition allowed for that element. The intensity of the light is generally proportional to the analyte concentration. It is necessary to correct for the background emission from the plasma. Sample concentration measurements are usually determined from a working curve of known standards over the concentration range of interest. It is, however, also possible to perform a single-point calibration under certain circumstances, such as with limit tests, if the methodology has been validated for sufficient specificity, sensitivity, linearity, accuracy, precision, ruggedness, and robustness.

Because there are distinct transitions between atomic energy levels, and because the atoms in an ICP are rather dilute, emission lines have narrow bandwidths. However, because the emission spectra from the ICP contain many lines, and because "wings" of these lines overlap to produce a nearly continuous background on top of the continuum that arises from the recombination of argon ions with electrons, a high-resolution spectrometer is required in ICP–AES. The decision regarding which spectral line to measure should include an evaluation of potential spectral interferences. All atoms in a sample are excited simultaneously; however, the presence of multiple elements in some samples can lead to spectral overlap. Spectral interference can also be caused by background emission from the sample or plasma. Modern ICPs usually have background correction available, and a number of background correction techniques can be applied. Simple background correction typically involves measuring the background emission intensity at some point away from the main peak and subtracting this value from the total signal being measured. Mathematical modeling to subtract the interfering signal as a background correction can also be performed with certain types of ICP–AES spectrometers.

The selection of the analytical spectral line is critical to the success of an ICP–AES analysis, regardless of torch configuration or detector type. Though some wavelengths are preferred, the final choice must be made in the context of the sample matrix, the type of instrument being used, and the sensitivity required. Analysts might choose to start with the wavelengths recommended by the manufacturer of their particular instrument, and select alternative wavelengths based on manufacturer recommendations or published wavelength tables.[5,6,7,8,9] Ultimately, the selection of analytical wavelengths should be demonstrated experimentally to provide sufficient specificity, sensitivity, linearity, accuracy, and precision of the analysis at hand.

Forward power, gas flow rates, viewing height, and torch position can all be optimized to provide the best signal. However, it must also be kept in mind that these same variables can influence matrix and spectral interferences.

In general, it is desirable to operate the ICP under robust conditions, which can be gauged on the basis of the MgII/MgI line pair at (280.270 nm/285.213 nm). If that ratio of intensities is above 6.0 in an aqueous solution, the ICP is said to be *robust*, and is less susceptible to matrix interferences. A ratio of about 10.0 is generally what is sought. Note that the term *robust conditions* is unrelated to *robustness* as applied to analytical method validation. Operation of an instrument with an MgII/MgI ratio greater than 6.0 is not mandated, but is being suggested as a means of optimizing instrument parameters in many circumstances.

The analysis of the Group I elements can be an exception to this strategy. When atomic ions are formed from elements in this group, they assume a noble gas electron configuration, with correspondingly high excitation energy. Because the first excited state of these ions is extremely high, few are excited, so emission intensity is correspondingly low. This situation can be improved by reducing the fractional ionization, which can in turn be achieved by using lower forward power settings in combination with adjusted viewing height or nebulizer gas flow, or by adding an ionization suppression agent to the samples and standards.

When organic solvents are used, it is often necessary to use a higher forward power setting, higher intermediate and outer gas flows, and a lower nebulizer gas flow than would be employed for aqueous solutions, as well as a reduction in the nebulizer gas flow. When using organic solvents, it may also be necessary to bleed small amounts of oxygen into the torch to prevent carbon buildup in the torch.

Calibration The wavelength accuracy for ICP–AES detection must comply with the manufacturer's applicable operating procedures. Because of the inherent differences among the types of instruments available, there is no general system suitability procedure that can be employed. Calibration routines recommended by the instrument manufacturer for a given ICP–AES instrument should be followed. These might include, but are not limited to, use of a multielement wavelength calibration with a reference solution, internal mercury (Hg) wavelength calibration, and peak search. The analyst should perform system checks in accordance with the manufacturer's recommendations.

Standardization The instrument must be standardized for quantification at time of use. However, because ICP–AES is a technique generally considered to be linear over a range of 6–8 orders of magnitude, it is not always necessary to continually demonstrate linearity by the use of a standard curve composed of multiple standards. Once a method has been developed and is in routine use, it is possible to calibrate with a blank and a single standard. One-point standardizations are suitable for conducting limit tests on production materials and final products if the methodology has been rigorously validated for sufficient specificity, sensitivity, linearity, accuracy, precision, ruggedness, and robustness. The use of a single-point standardization is also acceptable for qualitative ICP–AES analyses, where the purpose of the experiment is to confirm the presence or absence of elements without the requirement of an accurate quantification.

An appropriate blank solution and standards that bracket the expected range of the sample concentrations should be assayed and the detector response plotted as a function of analyte concentration, as in the case where the concentration of a known component is being determined within a specified tolerance. However, it is not always possible to employ a bracketing standard when an analysis is performed at or near the detection limit. This lack of use of a bracketing standard is acceptable for analyses conducted to demonstrate the absence or removal of elements below a specified limit. The number and concentrations of standard solutions used should be based on the purpose of the quantification, the analyte in question, the desired sensitivity, and the sample matrix. Regression analysis of the standard plot should be employed to evaluate the linearity of detector response, and individual monographs may set criteria for the residual error of the regression line. Optimally, a correlation coefficient of NLT 0.99, or as indicated in the individual monograph, should be demonstrated for the working curve. Here, too, however, the nature of the sample matrix, the analyte(s), the desired sensitivity, and the type of instrumentation available may dictate a correlation coefficient lower than 0.99. The analyst should use caution when proceeding with such an analysis, and should employ additional working standards.

To demonstrate the stability of the system's initial standardization, a solution used in the initial standard curve

---

[5] Payling R, Larkins P. *Optical Emission Lines of the Elements.* New York: Wiley; 2000.
[6] Harrison GR. *Massachusetts Institute of Technology Wavelength Tables* [also referred to as *MIT Wavelength Tables*]. Cambridge, MA: MIT Press; 1969.
[7] Winge RK, Fassel VA, Peterson VJ, Floyd MA. *Inductively Coupled Plasma Atomic Emission Spectroscopy: An Atlas of Spectral Information.* New York: Elsevier; 1985.
[8] Boumans PWJM. *Spectrochim Acta A.* 1981;36B:169.
[9] Boumans PWJM. *Line Coincidence Tables for Inductively Coupled Plasma Atomic Emission Spectrometry.* 2nd ed.; Oxford, UK: Pergamon; 1984.

must be reassayed as a check standard at appropriate intervals throughout the analysis of the sample set. The reassayed standard should agree with its expected value to within ±10%, or as specified in an individual monograph, for single-element analyses when analytical wavelengths are 200–500 nm, or concentrations are >1 µg/mL. The reassayed standard should agree with its theoretical value to within ±20%, or as specified in an individual monograph, for multi-element analyses, when analytical wavelengths are <200 nm or >500 nm, or at concentrations of <1 µg/mL. In cases where an individual monograph provides different guidance regarding the reassayed check standard, the requirements of the monograph take precedence.

Procedure Follow the procedure as directed in the individual monograph for the instrumental parameters. Because of differences in manufacturers' equipment configurations, the manufacturer's suggested default conditions may be used and modified as needed. The specification of definitive parameters in a monograph does not preclude the use of other suitable operating conditions, and adjustments of operating conditions may be necessary. Alternative conditions must be supported by suitable validation data, and the conditions in the monograph will take precedence for official purposes. Data collected from a single sample introduction are treated as a single result. This result might be the average of data collected from replicate sequential readings from a single solution introduction of the appropriate standard or sample solution. Sample concentrations are calculated versus the working curve generated by plotting the detector response versus the concentration of the analyte in the standard solutions. This calculation is often performed directly by the instrument.

ICP–MS When an inductively coupled plasma uses a mass spectral detection system, the technique is referred to as inductively coupled plasma–mass spectrometry (ICP–MS). In this technique, analytes are detected directly at their atomic masses. Because these masses must be charged to be detected in ICP–MS, the method relies on the ability of the plasma source to both atomize and ionize sample constituents. As is the case with ICP–AES, a wide variety of ICP–MS instrumentation systems are available.

The systems most commonly in use are quadrupole-based systems. Gaining in interest is time-of-flight ICP–MS. Although still not in widespread use, this approach may see greater use in the future. Additionally, high-resolution sector field instruments are available.

Regardless of instrument design or configuration, ICP–MS provides both a qualitative and a quantitative measurement of the components of the sample. Ions are generated from the analyte atoms by the plasma. The analyte ions are then extracted from the atmospheric-pressure plasma through a sampling cone into a lower-pressure zone, ordinarily held at a pressure near 1 Torr. In this extraction process, the sampled plasma gases, including the analyte species, form a supersonic beam, which dictates many of the properties of the resulting analyte ions. A skimmer cone, located behind the sampling cone, "skims" the supersonic beam of ions as they emerge from the sampling cone. Behind the skimmer cone is a lower-pressure zone, often held near a milliTorr. Lastly, the skimmed ions pass a third-stage orifice to enter a zone held near a microTorr, where they encounter ion optics and are passed into the mass spectrometer. The mass spectrometer separates the ions according to their mass-to-charge (m/z) ratios. The ICP–MS has a mass range up to 240 atomic mass units (amu). Depending on the equipment configuration, analyte adducts can form with diluents, with argon, or with their decomposition products. Also formed are oxides and multiply-charged analyte ions, which can increase the complexity of the resulting mass spectra. Interferences can be minimized by appropriate optimization of operational parameters, including gas flows (central, intermediate, and outer gas flow rates), sample-solution flow, RF power, extraction-lens voltage, etc., or by the use of collision or reaction cells, or cool plasma operation, if available on a given instrument. Unless a laboratory is generating or examining isotopes that do not naturally occur, a list of naturally occurring isotopes will provide the analyst with acceptable isotopes for analytical purposes. Isotopic patterns also serve as an aid to element identification and confirmation. Additionally, tables of commonly found interferences and polyatomic isobaric interferences and correction factors can be used.

ICP–MS generally offers considerably lower (better) detection limits than ICP–AES, largely because of the extremely low background that it generates. This ability is a major advantage of ICP–MS for determination of very low analyte concentrations or when elimination of matrix interferences is required. In the latter case, some interferences can be avoided simply by additional dilution of the sample solution. In some applications, analytes can be detected below the parts per trillion (ppt) level using ICP–MS. As a general rule, ICP–MS as a technique requires that samples contain significantly less total dissolved solids than does ICP–AES.

The selection of the analytical mass to use is critical to the success of an ICP–MS analysis, regardless of instrument design. Though some masses are often considered to be the primary ones, because of their high natural abundance, an alternative mass for a given element is often used to avoid spectral overlaps (isobaric interferences). Selection of an analytical mass must always be considered in the context of the sample matrix, the type of instrument being used, and the concentrations to be measured. Analysts might choose to start with masses recommended by the manufacturer of their particular instrument, and select alternate masses based on manufacturer's recommendations or published tables of naturally occurring isotopes.[10]

Optimization of an ICP–MS method is also highly dependent on the plasma parameters and means of sample introduction. Forward power, gas flow rates, and torch position may all be optimized to provide the best signal. When organic solvents are used, it is often necessary to use a higher forward power setting and a lower nebulizer flow rate than would be used for aqueous solutions. Additionally, when organic solvents are used, it might be necessary to introduce small amounts of oxygen into the central or intermediate gas to prevent carbon buildup in the torch or on the sampler cone orifice. The use of a platinum-tipped sampling or skimmer cone may also be required in order to reduce cone degradation with some organic solvents.

---

[10] Horlick G, Montaser A. Analytical characteristics of ICPMS. In: Montaser A, Editor. *Inductively Coupled Plasma Mass Spectrometry.* New York: Wiley-VCH; 1998:516–518.

Calibration The mass spectral accuracy for ICP–MS detection must be in accordance with the applicable operating procedures. Because of the inherent differences between the types of instruments available, there is no general system suitability procedure that can be employed. Analysts should refer to the tests recommended by the instrument manufacturer for a given ICP–MS instrument. These may include, but are not limited to, tuning on a reference mass or masses, peak search, and mass calibration. The analyst should perform system checks recommended by the instrument manufacturer.

Standardization The instrument must be standardized for quantification at the time of use. Because the response (signal vs. concentration) of ICP–MS is generally considered to be linear over a range of 6–8 orders of magnitude, it is not always necessary to continually demonstrate linearity by the use of a working curve. Once a method has been developed and is in routine use, it is common practice to calibrate with a blank and a single standard. One-point standardizations are suitable for conducting limit tests on production materials and final products, provided that the methodology has been rigorously validated for sufficient specificity, sensitivity, linearity, accuracy, precision, ruggedness, and robustness. An appropriate blank solution and standards that bracket the expected range of the sample concentrations should be assayed and the detector response plotted as a function of analyte concentration. The number and concentration of standard solutions used should be based on the analyte in question, the expected concentrations, and the sample matrix, and should be left to the discretion of the analyst. Optimally, a correlation coefficient of NLT 0.99, or as indicated in the individual monograph, should be demonstrated for the working standard curve. Here, too, however, the nature of the sample matrix, the analyte, the desired sensitivity, and the type of instrumentation available might dictate a correlation coefficient lower than 0.99. The analyst should use caution when proceeding with such an analysis and should employ additional working standards.

To demonstrate the stability of the system since initial standardization, a solution used in the initial standard curve must be reassayed as a check standard at appropriate intervals throughout the analysis of the sample set. Appropriate intervals may be established as occurring after every fifth or tenth sample, or as deemed adequate by the analyst, on the basis of the analysis being performed. The reassayed standard should agree with its expected value to within ±10% for single-element analyses when analytical masses are free of interferences and when concentrations are >1 ng/mL. The reassayed standard should agree with its expected value to within ±20% for multi-element analyses, or when concentrations are <1 ng/mL. In cases where an individual monograph provides different guidance regarding the reassayed check standard, the requirements of the monograph take precedence.

The method of standard additions should be employed in situations where matrix interferences are expected or suspected. This method involves adding a known concentration of the analyte element to the sample solution at no fewer than two concentration levels. The instrument response is plotted against the concentration of the added analyte element, and a linear regression line is drawn through the data points. The absolute value of the x-intercept multiplied by any dilution factor is the concentration of the analyte in the sample.

Procedure Follow the procedure as directed in the individual monograph for the detection mode and instrument parameters. The specification of definitive parameters in a monograph does not preclude the use of other suitable operating conditions, and adjustments of operating conditions may be necessary. Alternative conditions must be supported by suitable validation data, and the conditions in the monograph will take precedence for official purposes. Because of differences in manufacturers' equipment configurations, the analyst may wish to begin with the manufacturer's suggested default conditions and modify them as needed. Data collected from a single sample introduction are treated as a single result. Data collected from replicate sequential readings from a single introduction of the appropriate standard or sample solutions are averaged as a single result. Sample concentrations are calculated versus the working curve generated by plotting the detector response versus the concentration of the analyte in the standard solutions. With modern instruments, this calculation is often performed by the instrument.

Glossary

AUXILIARY GAS See *Intermediate (or Auxiliary) Gas*.

AXIAL VIEWING A configuration of the plasma for AES in which the plasma is directed toward the spectrometer optical path, also called "end-on viewing."

CENTRAL (OR NEBULIZER) GAS One of three argon gas flows in an ICP torch. The central gas is used to help create a fine mist of the sample solution when solution nebulization is employed. This fine mist is then directed through the central tube of the torch and into the plasma.

COLLISION CELL A design feature of some ICP–MS instruments. Collision cells are used to reduce interferences from argon species or polyatomic ions and to facilitate the analysis of elements that might be affected by those interferences.

COOL PLASMA Plasma conditions used for ICP–MS that result in a plasma that is cooler than that normally used for an analysis. This condition is achieved by using a lower forward power setting and higher central-gas flow rate, and is used to help reduce isotopic interferences caused by argon and some polyatomic ions.

COOLANT GAS See *Outer (or Coolant or Plasma) Gas*.

FORWARD POWER The number of watts used to ignite and sustain the plasma during an analysis. Forward power requirements may vary, depending on sample matrix and analyte.

INTERMEDIATE (OR AUXILIARY) GAS Gas used to "lift" the plasma off the surface of the torch, thereby preventing melting of the intermediate tube and the formation of carbon and salt deposits on the inner tube.

INTERNAL STANDARD An element added to or present in the same concentration in blanks, standards, and samples to act as an intensity reference for the analysis. An internal standard should be used for ICP–AES work and must always be used for quantitative ICP–MS analyses.

LATERAL VIEWING   See *Radial Viewing.*

m   The ion mass of interest.

MULTIPLY-CHARGED IONS   Atoms that, when subjected to the high-ionization temperature of the ICP, can form doubly or triply charged ions (X^{++}, X^{+++}, etc.). When detected by MS, the apparent mass of these ions will be half or one-third that of the atomic mass.

NEBULIZER   Used to form a consistent sample aerosol that mixes with the argon gas, which is subsequently sent into the ICP.

OUTER (OR COOLANT OR PLASMA) GAS   The main gas supply for the plasma.

PLASMA GAS   See *Outer (or Coolant or Plasma) Gas.*

RADIAL VIEWING   A configuration of the plasma for AES in which the plasma is viewed orthogonal to the spectrometer optic path. Also called "side-on viewing." See also *Lateral Viewing.*

REACTION CELL   Similar to *Collision Cell,* but operating on a different principle. Designed to reduce or eliminate spectral interferences.

SAMPLING CONE   A metal cone (usually nickel-, aluminum-, or platinum-tipped) with a small opening, through which ionized sample material flows after leaving the plasma.

SEQUENTIAL   A type of detector configuration for AES or MS in which discrete emission lines or isotopic peaks are observed by scanning or hopping across the spectral range by means of a monochromator or scanning mass spectrometer.

SIMULTANEOUS   A type of detector configuration for AES or MS in which all selected emission lines or isotopic peaks are observed at the same time by using a polychromator or simultaneous mass spectrometer, offering increased analysis speed for analyses of multi-element samples.

SKIMMER CONE   A metal cone through which ionized sample flows after leaving the sampling cone and before entering the high-vacuum region of an ICP–MS.

STANDARD ADDITIONS   A method used to determine the actual analyte concentration in a sample when viscosity or matrix effects might cause erroneous results.

TORCH   A series of three concentric tubes, usually manufactured from quartz, in which the ICP is formed.

RESIDUE ON IGNITION (Sulfated Ash)

Method I (for Solids)

Transfer the quantity of the sample directed in the individual monograph onto a tared 50-mL to 100-mL platinum dish or other suitable container, and add sufficient 2 N sulfuric acid to moisten the entire sample. Heat gently, using a hot plate, an Argand burner, or an infrared heat lamp, until the sample is dry and thoroughly charred, then continue heating until all of the sample has been volatilized or nearly all of the carbon has been oxidized, and cool. Moisten the residue with 0.1 mL of sulfuric acid, and heat in the same manner until the remainder of the sample and any excess sulfuric acid have been volatilized. To promote volitilization of sulfuric acid, add a few pieces of ammonium carbonate just before completing ignition. Finally, ignite to constant weight in a muffle furnace at 800 ± 25° for 15 min, or longer if necessary to complete ignition, cool in a desiccator, and weigh.

Method II (for Liquids)

Unless otherwise directed, transfer the required weight of the sample onto a tared 75-mL to 100-mL platinum dish. Heat gently, using an Argand or Meker burner, until the sample ignites, then allow the sample to burn until it self-extinguishes. Cool, then wet the residue with 2 mL of concentrated sulfuric acid, and heat the sample over a low flame until dry. Ignite to constant weight in a muffle furnace at 800 ± 25° for 30 min, or longer if necessary for complete ignition, cool in a desiccator, and weigh.

SIEVE ANALYSIS OF GRANULAR METAL POWDERS (Based on ASTM Designation: B 214)[11]

Apparatus

Sieves: Use a set of standard sieves, ranging from 80-mesh to 325-mesh, conforming to the specifications in ASTM Designation: E 11 (Sieves for Testing Purposes).

Sieve Shaker: Use a mechanically operated sieve shaker that imparts to the set of sieves a horizontal rotary motion of 270–300 rotations/min and a tapping action of 140–160 taps/min. The sieve shaker is fitted with a plug to receive the impact of the tapping device. The entire apparatus is rigidly mounted—bolted to a solid foundation, preferably of concrete. Preferably a time switch is provided to ensure the accuracy of test duration.

Procedure   Assemble the sieves in consecutive order by opening size, with the coarsest sieve (80-mesh) at the top, and place a solid-collecting pan below the bottom sieve (325-mesh). Place 100.0 g of the test sample, W, on the top sieve, and close the sieve with a solid cover. Securely fasten the assembly to the sieve shaker, and operate the shaker for 15 min. Remove the most coarse sieve from the nest, gently tap its contents to one side, and pour the contents onto a tared, glazed paper. Using a soft brush, transfer onto the next finer sieve any material adhering to the bottom of the sieve and frame. Place the sieve just removed upside down on the paper containing the retained portion, and tap the sieve. Accurately weigh the paper and its contents, and record the net weight of the fraction, F, obtained. Repeat this process for each sieve in the nest and for the portion of the sample that has been collected in the bottom pan. Record the total of the fractions retained on the sieves as T and that portion collected in the pan as t.

---

[11] Adapted from ASTM B214 Standard Test Method for Sieve Analysis of Metal Powders. The original ASTM method is available in its entirety from ASTM International, 100 Barr Harbor Drive, West Conshohocken, PA 19428. Phone: 610-832-9585, Fax: 610-832-9555, Email: service@astm.org, Website: www.astm.org.

The combined total, S, of T + t is the amount of the sample, W, recovered in the test. Calculate the percent recovery:

$$\text{Result} = S/W \times 100$$

If the percent recovery is less than 99.0%, check the condition of the sieves and for possible errors in weighing, and repeat the test. If the percent recovery is NLT 99.0%, calculate the percent retained on each sieve:

$$\text{Result} = F/W \times 100$$

Calculate the percent through the smallest mesh sieve from the portion collected in the pan:

$$\text{Result} = [(100 - t)/W] \times 100$$

SULFURIC ACID TABLE

°Bé	Sp. Gr.	Percent H_2SO_4
0	1.0000	0.00
1	1.0069	1.02
2	1.0140	2.08
3	1.0211	3.13
4	1.0284	4.21
5	1.0357	5.28
6	1.0432	6.37
7	1.0507	7.45
8	1.0584	8.55
9	1.0662	9.66
10	1.0741	10.77
11	1.0821	11.89
12	1.0902	13.01
13	1.0985	14.13
14	1.1069	15.25
15	1.1154	16.38
16	1.1240	17.53
17	1.1328	18.71
18	1.1417	19.89
19	1.1508	21.07
20	1.1600	22.25
21	1.1694	23.43
22	1.1789	24.61
23	1.1885	25.81
24	1.1983	27.03
25	1.2083	28.28
26	1.2185	29.53
27	1.2288	30.79
28	1.2393	32.05
29	1.2500	33.33
30	1.2609	34.63
31	1.2719	35.93
32	1.2832	37.26

°Bé	Sp. Gr.	Percent H_2SO_4
33	1.2946	38.58
34	1.3063	39.92
35	1.3182	41.27
36	1.3303	42.63
37	1.3426	43.99
38	1.3551	45.35
39	1.3679	46.72
40	1.3810	48.10
41	1.3942	49.47
42	1.4078	50.87
43	1.4216	52.26
44	1.4356	53.66
45	1.4500	55.07
46	1.4646	56.48
47	1.4796	57.90
48	1.4948	59.32
49	1.5104	60.75
50	1.5263	62.18
51	1.5426	63.66
52	1.5591	65.13
53	1.5761	66.63
54	1.5934	68.13
55	1.6111	69.65
56	1.6292	71.17
57	1.6477	72.75
58	1.6667	74.36
59	1.6860	75.99
60	1.7059	77.67
61	1.7262	79.43
62	1.7470	81.30
63	1.7683	83.34
64	1.7901	85.66
64.25	1.7957	86.33
64.50	1.8012	87.04
64.75	1.8068	87.81
65	1.8125	88.65
65.25	1.8182	89.55
65.50	1.8239	90.60
66	1.8354	93.19

Specific gravity determinations were made at 60°F, compared with water at 60°F. The values given above for aqueous sulfuric acid solutions were adopted as standard in 1904 by the Manufacturing Chemists' Association of the United States.

From the specific gravities, the corresponding degrees Baumé were calculated by the following equation:

$$°\text{Baumé} = 145 - (145/\text{sp. gr.})$$

Baumé hydrometers for use with this table must be graduated by the above formula, which should always be printed on the scale. Acids stronger than 66°Bé should have their percentage compositions determined by chemical analysis.

WATER-INSOLUBLE MATTER

Sample Preparation Add 5 g of sample (if a different amount of sample is specified in the individual monograph, use that amount) to 100 mL of water, and stir until the sample is dissolved.

Procedure Dry a membrane filter (cellulose nitrate, 0.45-μm porosity) at 110°C for 1 h, allow to cool in a desiccator, and weigh to the nearest 0.1 mg. Pass the *Sample Preparation* through the dried membrane filter and wash with three successive 10-mL portions of water. Dry the membrane filter at 110°C for 1 h. Cool in a desiccator, and weigh the membrane filter to the nearest 0.1 mg. Calculate the insoluble matter as percentage.

APPENDIX III: CHEMICAL TESTS AND DETERMINATIONS

A. IDENTIFICATION TESTS

The identification tests described in section A of this Appendix are frequently referred to in the *Food Chemicals Codex* for the presumptive identification of FCC-grade chemicals taken from labeled containers. These tests are not intended to be applied to mixtures unless so specified.

Acetate
Acetic acid or acetates, when warmed with sulfuric acid and alcohol, form ethyl acetate, recognizable by its characteristic odor. With neutral solutions of acetates, ferric chloride TS produces a deep red color that is destroyed by the addition of a mineral acid.

Aluminum
Solutions of aluminum salts yield with 6 N ammonia a white, gelatinous precipitate that is insoluble in an excess of the 6 N ammonia. The same precipitate is produced by 1 N sodium hydroxide, but it dissolves in an excess of this reagent.

Ammonium
Ammonium salts are decomposed by 1 N sodium hydroxide with the evolution of ammonia, recognizable by its alkaline effect on moistened red litmus paper. The decomposition is accelerated by warming.

Benzoate
Neutral solutions of benzoates yield a salmon colored precipitate with ferric chloride TS. From moderately concentrated solutions of benzoate, 2 N sulfuric acid precipitates free benzoic acid, which is readily soluble in ether.

Bicarbonate
See *Carbonate*.

Bisulfite
See *Sulfite*.

Bromide
Free bromine is liberated from solutions of bromides upon the dropwise addition of chlorine TS. When shaken with chloroform, the bromine dissolves, coloring the chloroform red to red-brown. A yellow-white precipitate, which is insoluble in nitric acid and slightly soluble in 6 N ammonia, is produced when solutions of bromides are treated with silver nitrate TS.

Calcium
Insoluble oxalate salts are formed when solutions of calcium salts are treated in the following manner: using 2 drops of methyl red TS as the indicator, neutralize a 1:20 solution of a calcium salt with 6 N ammonia, then add 2.7 N hydrochloric acid, dropwise, until the solution is acid. A white precipitate of calcium oxalate forms upon the addition of ammonium oxalate TS. This precipitate is insoluble in acetic acid but dissolves in hydrochloric acid.

Calcium salts moistened with hydrochloric acid impart a transient yellow-red color to a nonluminous flame.

Carbonate
Carbonates and bicarbonates effervesce with acids, yielding a colorless gas that produces a white precipitate immediately when passed into calcium hydroxide TS. Cold solutions of soluble carbonates are colored red by phenolphthalein TS, whereas solutions of bicarbonates remain unchanged or are slightly changed.

Chloride
Solutions of chlorides yield with silver nitrate TS a white, curdy precipitate that is insoluble in nitric acid but soluble in a slight excess of 6 N ammonia.

Citrate
To 15 mL of pyridine add a few mg of a citrate salt, dissolved or suspended in 1 mL of water, and shake. Add 5 mL of acetic anhydride to this mixture, and shake. A light red color appears.

Cobalt
Solutions of cobalt salts (1:20) in 2.7 N hydrochloric acid yield a red precipitate when heated on a steam bath with an equal volume of a hot, freshly prepared 1:10 solution of 1-nitroso-2-naphthol in 9 N acetic acid. Solutions of cobalt salts yield a yellow precipitate when saturated with potassium chloride and treated with potassium nitrite and acetic acid.

Copper
When solutions of cupric compounds are acidified with hydrochloric acid, a red film of metallic copper is deposited on a bright untarnished surface of metallic iron. An excess of 6 N ammonia, added to a solution of a cupric salt, produces first a blue precipitate and then a deep blue colored solution. Solutions of cupric salts yield with potassium ferrocyanide TS a red-brown precipitate, insoluble in diluted acids.

Hypophosphite
Hypophosphites evolve spontaneously flammable phosphine when strongly heated. Solutions of hypophosphites yield a white precipitate with mercuric chloride TS. This precipitate becomes gray when an excess of hypophosphite is present. Hypophosphite solutions, acidified with sulfuric acid and warmed with copper sulfate TS, yield a red precipitate.

Iodide
Solutions of iodides, upon the dropwise addition of chlorine TS, liberate iodine, which colors the solution yellow to red. Chloroform is colored violet when shaken with this solution. The iodine thus liberated gives a blue color with starch TS. In solutions of iodides, silver nitrate TS produces a yellow, curdy precipitate that is insoluble in nitric acid and in 6 N ammonia.

Iron
Solutions of ferrous and ferric compounds yield a black precipitate with ammonium sulfide TS. This precipitate is dissolved by cold 2.7 N hydrochloric acid with the evolution of hydrogen sulfide.

Ferric Salts: Potassium ferrocyanide TS (10%) produces a dark blue precipitate in acid solutions of ferric salts. With an excess of 1 N sodium hydroxide, a red-brown precipitate is formed. Solutions of ferric salts produce with ammonium thiocyanate TS (1.0 N) a deep red color that is not destroyed by diluted mineral acids.

Ferrous Salts: Potassium ferricyanide TS (10%) produces a dark blue precipitate in solutions of ferrous salts. This precipitate, which is insoluble in dilute hydrochloric acid, is decomposed by 1 N sodium hydroxide. Solutions of ferrous salts yield with 1 N sodium hydroxide a green-white precipitate, the color rapidly changing to green and then to brown when shaken.

Lactate
When solutions of lactates are acidified with sulfuric acid, potassium permanganate TS (0.1 N) is added, and the mixture is heated, acetaldehyde is evolved. This can be detected by allowing the vapor to come into contact with a filter paper that has been moistened with a freshly prepared mixture of equal volumes of 20% aqueous morpholine and sodium nitroferricyanide TS. A blue color is produced.

Magnesium
Solutions of magnesium salts in the presence of ammonium chloride yield no precipitate with ammonium carbonate TS, but a white crystalline precipitate, which is insoluble in 6 N ammonium hydroxide, is formed on the subsequent addition of sodium phosphate TS (6%).

Manganese
Solutions of manganous salts yield with ammonium sulfide TS a salmon colored precipitate that dissolves in acetic acid.

Nitrate
When a solution of a nitrate is mixed with an equal volume of sulfuric acid, the mixture cooled, and a solution of ferrous sulfate superimposed, a brown color is produced at the junction of the two liquids. Brown-red fumes are evolved when a nitrate is heated with sulfuric acid and metallic copper. Nitrates do not decolorize acidified potassium permanganate TS (0.1 N) (distinction from nitrites).

Nitrite
Nitrites yield brown-red fumes when treated with diluted mineral acids or acetic acid. A few drops of potassium iodide TS (15%) and a few drops of 2 N sulfuric acid added to a solution of nitrite liberate iodine, which colors starch TS blue.

Peroxide
Solutions of peroxides slightly acidified with sulfuric acid yield a deep blue color on the addition of potassium dichromate TS. On shaking the mixture with an equal volume of diethyl ether and allowing the liquids to separate, the blue color is transferred to the ether layer.

Phosphate
Neutral solutions of orthophosphates yield with silver nitrate TS (0.1 N) a yellow precipitate, which is soluble in 1.7 N nitric acid or in 6 N ammonium hydroxide. With ammonium molybdate TS, a yellow precipitate, which is soluble in 6 N ammonium hydroxide, is formed.

Potassium
Potassium compounds impart a violet color to a nonluminous flame if not masked by the presence of small quantities of sodium. In neutral, concentrated or moderately concentrated solutions of potassium salts, sodium bitartrate TS (10%) slowly produces a white, crystalline precipitate that is soluble in 6 N ammonium hydroxide and in solutions of alkali hydroxides or carbonates. The precipitation may be accelerated by stirring or rubbing the inside of the test tube with a glass rod or by the addition of a small amount of glacial acetic acid or alcohol.

Sodium
Dissolve 0.1 g of the sodium compound in 2 mL of water. Add 2 mL of 15% potassium carbonate, and heat to boiling. No precipitate is formed. Add 4 mL of potassium pyroantimonate TS, and heat to boiling. Allow to cool in ice water, and if necessary, rub the inside of the test tube with a glass rod. A dense precipitate is formed. Sodium compounds impart an intense yellow color to a nonluminous flame.

Sulfate
Solutions of sulfates yield with barium chloride TS a white precipitate that is insoluble in hydrochloric and nitric acids. Sulfates yield with lead acetate TS a white precipitate that is soluble in ammonium acetate solution. Hydrochloric acid produces no precipitate when added to solutions of sulfates (distinction from thiosulfates).

Sulfite
When treated with 2.7 N hydrochloric acid, sulfites and bisulfites yield sulfur dioxide, recognizable by its characteristic odor. This gas blackens filter paper moistened with mercurous nitrate TS.

Tartrate
When a few mg of a tartrate are added to a mixture of 15 mL of pyridine and 5 mL of acetic anhydride, an emerald green color is produced.

Thiosulfate
With hydrochloric acid, solutions of thiosulfates yield a white precipitate that soon turns yellow, liberating sulfur dioxide, recognizable by its odor. The addition of ferric chloride TS to solutions of thiosulfates produces a dark violet color that quickly disappears.

Zinc
Zinc salts, in the presence of sodium acetate, yield a white precipitate with hydrogen sulfide. This precipitate, which is insoluble in acetic acid, is dissolved by 2.7 N hydrochloric acid. A similar precipitate is produced by ammonium sulfide TS in neutral or alkaline solutions. Solutions of zinc salts yield with potassium ferrocyanide TS (10%) a white precipitate that is insoluble in 2.7 N hydrochloric acid.

B. LIMIT TESTS

ALUMINUM LIMIT TEST

[NOTE—The *Standard Solutions* and *Sample Solution* may be modified, if necessary, to obtain solutions of suitable concentrations adaptable to the linear or working range of the instrument.]

Nitric Acid Diluent   Dilute 40 mL of nitric acid with water to 1000 mL.

Standard Aluminum Solutions   Treat a quantity of aluminum wire with 6 N hydrochloric acid at 80° for a few min. Dissolve 100 mg of the treated wire in a mixture consisting of 10 mL of hydrochloric acid and 2 mL of nitric acid, by heating at 80° for about 30 min. Continue heating until the volume is reduced to about 4 mL. Cool to room temperature, and add 4 mL of water. Evaporate to about 2 mL by heating. Cool, and transfer this solution, with the aid of water, to a 100-mL volumetric flask, and dilute with water to volume (1 mg/mL aluminum). Transfer 10.0 mL of this solution to a second 100-mL volumetric flask, and dilute with water to volume (100 µg/mL aluminum). Transfer 1.0 mL of this solution to a third 100-mL volumetric flask, and dilute with water to volume (1 µg/mL aluminum).   [NOTE—If more diluted *Standard Aluminum Solutions* are required, transfer 1.0-mL, 2.0-mL, and 4.0-mL portions of the 1 µg/mL *Standard Aluminum Solution* to separate 100-mL volumetric flasks, dilute with *Nitric Acid Diluent* to volume, and mix. These solutions contain 0.01 µg/mL, 0.02 µg/mL, and 0.04 µg/mL of aluminum, respectively.]

Sample Solution   Transfer the amount of sample specified in the monograph to a plastic 100-mL volumetric flask. Add 50 mL of water, and sonicate for 30 min. Add 4 mL of nitric acid, and dilute with water to volume.

Procedure   Determine the absorbances of the *Standard Aluminum Solutions* and the *Sample Solution* at the aluminum emission line at 309.3 nm with a suitable atomic absorption spectrophotometer equipped with an aluminum hollow-cathode lamp and a flameless electrically heated furnace, using the *Nitric Acid Diluent* as the blank. Plot the absorbances of the *Standard Solutions* versus the concentration of aluminum, in µg/mL, drawing a straight line best fitting the three points. From the graph so obtained, determine the concentration, in µg/mL, of aluminum in the *Sample Solution*.

Calculate the amount of aluminum in the sample taken, in µg/g:

$$\text{Result} = C_A/C_S$$

in which C_A is the concentration of aluminum in the *Sample Solution*, in µg/mL, obtained from the standard curve; and C_S is the concentration of the *Sample Solution*, in g/mL.

ARSENIC LIMIT TEST

Silver Diethyldithiocarbamate Colorimetric Method

[NOTE—All reagents used in this test should be very low in arsenic content.]

Apparatus   Use the general apparatus shown in *Figure 1* unless otherwise specified in an individual monograph. It consists of a 125-mL arsine generator flask (*a*) fitted with a scrubber unit (*c*) and an absorber tube (*e*), with a 24/40 standard-taper joint (*b*) and a ball-and-socket joint (*d*), secured with a No. 12 clamp, connecting the units. The tubing between *d* and *e* and between *d* and *c* is a capillary having an id of 2 mm and an od of 8 mm. Alternatively, an apparatus embodying the principle of the general assembly described and illustrated may be used.

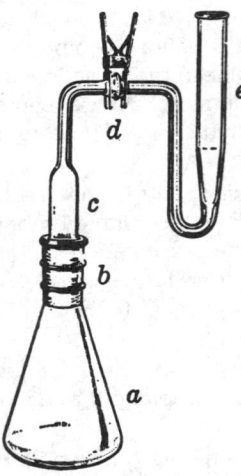

Figure 1. General Apparatus for Arsenic Limit Test (Courtesy of the Fisher Scientific Co., Pittsburgh, PA.)

[NOTE—The special assemblies shown in *Figures 2, 3,* and *4* are to be used only when specified in certain monographs.]

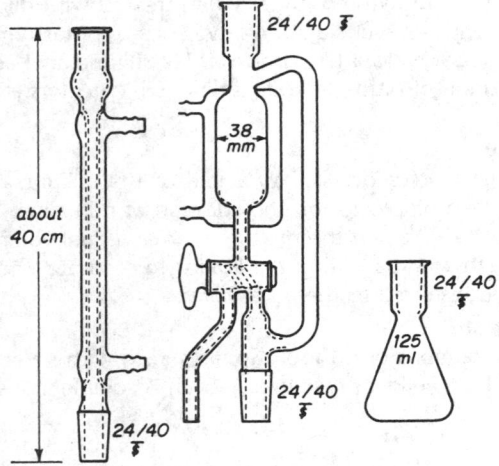

Figure 2. Modified Bethge Apparatus for the Distillation of Arsenic Tribromide

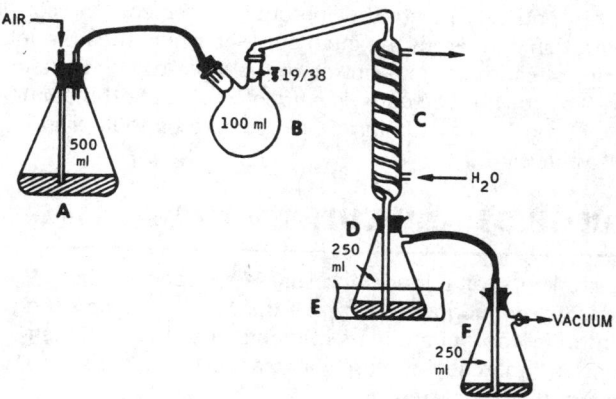

Figure 3. Special Apparatus for the Distillation of Arsenic Trichloride (Flask *A* contains 150 mL of hydrochloric acid; flasks *D* and *F* contain 20 mL of water. Flask *D* is placed in an ice water bath, *E*.)

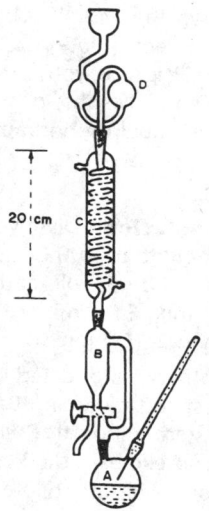

Figure 4. Special Apparatus for the Determination of Inorganic Arsenic (*A*, 250-mL distillation flask; *B*, receiver chamber, approximately 50-mL capacity; *C*, reflux condenser; *D*, splash head.)

Standard Arsenic Solution Accurately weigh 132.0 mg of arsenic trioxide that has been previously dried at 105° for 1 h, and dissolve it in 5 mL of a 1:5 sodium hydroxide solution. Neutralize the solution with 2 N sulfuric acid, add 10 mL in excess, and dilute with recently boiled water to 1000.0 mL. Transfer 10.0 mL of this solution into a 1000-mL volumetric flask, add 10 mL of 2 N sulfuric acid, dilute with recently boiled water to volume, and mix. Use this final solution, which contains 1 μg of arsenic in each mL, within 3 days.

Silver Diethyldithiocarbamate Solution Dissolve 1 g of ACS reagent-grade silver diethyldithiocarbamate in 200 mL of recently distilled pyridine. Store this solution in a light-resistant container and use within 1 month.

Stannous Chloride Solution Dissolve 40 g of stannous chloride dihydrate ($SnCl_2 \cdot 2H_2O$) in 100 mL of hydrochloric acid. Store the solution in glass containers and use within 3 months.

Lead Acetate-Impregnated Cotton Soak cotton in a saturated solution of lead acetate trihydrate, squeeze out the excess solution, and dry in a vacuum at room temperature.

Sample Solution Use directly as the *Sample Solution* in the *Procedure* the solution obtained by treating the sample as directed in an individual monograph. Prepare sample solutions of organic compounds in the generator flask (*a*), unless otherwise directed, according to the following general procedure:

[**CAUTION**—Some substances may react unexpectedly with explosive violence when digested with hydrogen peroxide. Use appropriate safety precautions at all times.]

[NOTE—If halogen-containing compounds are present, use a lower temperature while heating the sample with sulfuric acid; do not boil the mixture; and add the peroxide, with caution, before charring begins to prevent loss of trivalent arsenic.]

Transfer 1.0 g of the sample into the generator flask, add 5 mL of sulfuric acid and a few glass beads, and digest at a temperature not exceeding 120° until charring begins, preferably using a hot plate in a fume hood. (Additional sulfuric acid may be necessary to completely wet some samples, but the total volume added should not exceed about 10 mL.) After the acid has initially decomposed the sample, cautiously add, dropwise, hydrogen peroxide (30%), allowing the reaction to subside and reheating the sample between drops. Add the first few drops very slowly with sufficient mixing to prevent a rapid reaction, and discontinue heating if foaming becomes excessive. Swirl the solution in the flask to prevent unreacted substance from caking on the walls or bottom of the flask during digestion.

[NOTE—Maintain oxidizing conditions at all times during the digestion by adding small quantities of the peroxide whenever the mixture turns brown or darkens.]

Continue the digestion until the organic matter is destroyed, gradually raising the temperature of the hot plate to 250° to 300° until fumes of sulfur trioxide are copiously evolved and the solution becomes colorless or retains only a light straw color. Cool, cautiously add 10 mL of water, heat again to strong fuming, and cool. Cautiously add 10 mL of water, mix, wash the sides of the flask with a few mL of water, and dilute to 35 mL.

Procedure If the *Sample Solution* was not prepared in the generator flask, transfer to the flask a volume of the solution, prepared as directed, equivalent to 1.0 g of the substance being tested, and add water to make 35 mL. Add 20 mL of 1:5 sulfuric acid, 2 mL of potassium iodide TS, 0.5 mL of *Stannous Chloride Solution*, and 1 mL of isopropyl alcohol, and mix. Allow the mixture to stand for 30 min at room temperature. Pack the scrubber unit (*c*) with two plugs of *Lead Acetate-Impregnated Cotton*, leaving a small air space between the two plugs, lubricate joints *b* and *d* with stopcock grease, if necessary, and connect the scrubber unit with the absorber tube (*e*). Transfer 3.0 mL of *Silver Diethyldithiocarbamate Solution* to the absorber tube, add

3.0 g of granular zinc (20-mesh) to the mixture in the flask, and immediately insert the standard-taper joint (*b*) into the flask. Allow the evolution of hydrogen and color development to proceed at room temperature (25 ± 3°) for 45 min, swirling the flask gently at 10-min intervals. Disconnect the absorber tube from the generator and scrubber units, and transfer the *Silver Diethyldithiocarbamate Solution* to a 1-cm absorption cell. Determine the absorbance at the wavelength of maximum absorption between 535 nm and 540 nm, with a suitable spectrophotometer or colorimeter, using *Silver Diethyldithiocarbamate Solution* as the blank. The absorbance due to any red color from the solution of the sample does not exceed that produced by 3.0 mL of *Standard Arsenic Solution* (3 μg As) when treated in the same manner and under the same conditions as the sample. The room temperature during the generation of arsine from the standard should be held to within ±2° of that observed during the determination of the sample.

Interferences Metals or salts of metals such as chromium, cobalt, copper, mercury, molybdenum, nickel, palladium, and silver may interfere with the evolution of arsine. Antimony, which forms stibine, is the only metal likely to produce a positive interference in the color development with the silver diethyldithiocarbamate. Stibine forms a red color with silver diethyldithiocarbamate that has a maximum absorbance at 510 nm, but at 535–540 nm, the absorbance of the antimony complex is so diminished that the results of the determination would not be altered significantly.

CADMIUM LIMIT TEST

Spectrophotometer Use any suitable atomic absorption spectrophotometer equipped with a Boling-type burner, an air–acetylene flame, and a hollow-cathode cadmium lamp. The instrument should be capable of operating within the sensitivity necessary for the determination.

Standard Solution Transfer 100 mg of cadmium chloride crystals ($CdCl_2 \cdot 2\frac{1}{2}H_2O$), accurately weighed, into a 1000-mL volumetric flask, dissolve in and dilute with water to volume, and mix. Pipet 25 mL of this solution into a 100-mL volumetric flask, add 1 mL of hydrochloric acid, dilute with water to volume, and mix. Each mL contains 12.5 μg of cadmium.

Sample Solution Transfer 10 g of sample, accurately weighed, into a 50-mL volumetric flask, dissolve in and dilute with water to volume, and mix.

Test Solutions Transfer 5.0 mL of the *Sample Solution* into each of five separate 25-mL volumetric flasks. Dilute the contents of *Flask 1* with water to volume, and mix. Add 1.00 mL, 2.00 mL, 3.00 mL, and 4.00 mL of *Standard Solution* to *Flasks 2, 3, 4*, and *5*, respectively; then dilute each flask with water to volume; and mix. The *Test Solutions* contain, respectively, 0 μg/mL, 0.5 μg/mL, 1.0 μg/mL, 1.5 μg/mL, and 2.0 μg/mL of cadmium.

Procedure Determine the absorbance of each *Test Solution* at 228.8 nm, setting the instrument to previously established optimum conditions, using water as a blank. Plot the absorbance of the *Test Solutions* versus their contents of cadmium, in μg/mL. Draw the straight line best fitting the five points, and extrapolate the line until it intercepts the concentration axis. From the intercept, determine the amount, in μg, of cadmium in each mL of the *Test Solution* containing 0 mL of the *Standard Preparation*. Calculate the quantity, in mg/kg, of cadmium in the sample by multiplying this value by 25.

CHLORIDE AND SULFATE LIMIT TESTS

Where limits for chloride and sulfate are specified in the individual monograph, compare the *Sample Solution* and control in appropriate glass cylinders of the same dimensions and matched as closely as practicable with respect to their optical characteristics.

If the solution is not perfectly clear after acidification, pass it through filter paper that has been washed free of chloride and sulfate. Add identical quantities of the precipitant (silver nitrate TS or barium chloride TS) in rapid succession to both the *Sample Solution* and the control solution.

Experience has shown that visual turbidimetric comparisons are best made between solutions containing from 10 to 20 μg of chloride (Cl) ion or from 200 to 400 μg of sulfate (SO_4) ion in 50 mL. Weights of samples are specified on this basis in the individual monographs in which these limits are included.

Chloride Limit Test

Standard Chloride Solution Dissolve 165 mg of sodium chloride in water and dilute to 100.0 mL. Transfer 10.0 mL of this solution into a 1000-mL volumetric flask, dilute with water to volume, and mix. Each mL of the final solution contains 10 μg of chloride (Cl) ion.

Procedure Unless otherwise directed, dissolve the specified amount of the test substance in 30–40 mL of water; neutralize to litmus external indicator with nitric acid, if necessary; and add 1 mL in excess. Add 1 mL of silver nitrate TS to the clear solution or filtrate, dilute with water to 50 mL, mix, and allow to stand for 5 min protected from direct sunlight. Compare the turbidity, if any, with that produced similarly in a control solution containing the required volume of *Standard Chloride Solution* and the quantities of the reagents used for the sample.

Sulfate Limit Test

Standard Sulfate Solution Dissolve 148 mg of anhydrous sodium sulfate in water, and dilute to 100.0 mL. Transfer 10.0 mL of this solution to a 1000-mL volumetric flask, dilute with water to volume, and mix. Each mL of the final solution contains 10 μg of sulfate (SO_4).

Procedure Unless otherwise directed, dissolve the specified amount of the test substance in 30–40 mL of water; neutralize to litmus external indicator with hydrochloric acid, if necessary; then add 1 mL of 2.7 N hydrochloric acid. Add 3 mL of barium chloride TS to the clear solution or filtrate, dilute with water to 50 mL, and mix. After 10 min compare the turbidity, if any, with that produced in a solution containing the required volume of *Standard Sulfate Solution* and the quantities of the reagents used for the sample.

1,4-DIOXANE LIMIT TEST

Vacuum Distillation Apparatus   Assemble a closed-system vacuum distillation apparatus employing glass vacuum stopcocks (A, B, and C), as shown in *Figure 5*.

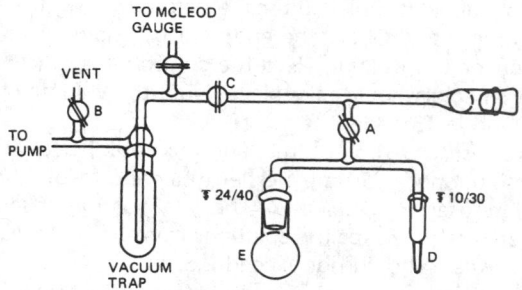

Figure 5. Closed-System Vacuum Distillation Apparatus for 1,4-Dioxane

The concentrator tube (D) is made of borosilicate or quartz (not flint) glass, graduated precisely enough to measure the 0.9 mL or more of distillate and marked so that the analyst can accurately dilute to 2.0 mL (available as Chromaflex concentrator tube, Kontes Glass Co., Vineland, NJ, Catalog No. K42560-0000).

Standard Preparation   Prepare a solution of 1,4-dioxane in water containing 100 µg/mL. Keep the solution refrigerated, and prepare fresh weekly.

Sample Preparation   Transfer 20 g of the sample, accurately weighed, into a 50-mL round-bottom flask (E) having a 24/40 ground-glass neck. Semisolid or waxy samples should be liquefied by heating on a steam bath before making the transfer. Add 2.0 mL of water to the flask for crystalline samples, and 1.0 mL for liquid, semisolid, or waxy samples. Place a small Teflon-covered stirring bar in the flask, stopper, and stir to mix. Immerse the flask in an ice bath, and chill for about 1 min.

Wrap heating tape around the tube connecting the Chromaflex tube (D) and the round-bottom flask (E), and apply about 10 V to the tape. Apply a light coating of high-vacuum silicone grease to the ground-glass joints, and connect the Chromaflex tube to the 10/30 joint and the round-bottom flask to the 24/40 joint. Immerse the vacuum trap in a Dewar flask filled with liquid nitrogen, close stopcocks A and B, open stopcock C, and begin evacuating the system with a vacuum pump. Prepare a slush bath from powdered dry ice and methanol, and raise the bath to the neck of the round-bottom flask. After freezing the contents of the flask for about 10 min, and when the vacuum system is operating at 0.05 mm pressure or lower, open stopcock A for 20 s, and then close it. Remove the slush bath, and allow the flask to warm in air for about 1 min. Immerse the flask in a water bath at 20°–25°, and after about 5 min warm the water in the bath to 35°–40° (sufficient to liquefy most samples) while stirring slowly but constantly with the magnetic bar. Cool the water in the bath by adding ice, and chill for about 2 min. Replace the water bath with the slush bath, freeze the contents of the flask for about 10 min, then open stopcock A for 20 s, and close it. Remove the slush bath, and repeat the heating steps as before, this time reaching a final temperature of 45°–50° or a temperature necessary to melt the sample completely. If there is any condensation in the tube connecting the round-bottom flask to the Chromaflex tube, slowly increase the voltage to the heating tape and heat until condensation disappears.

Stir with the magnetic stirrer throughout the following steps: very slowly immerse the Chromaflex tube in the Dewar flask containing liquid nitrogen. [**CAUTION**—When there is liquid distillate in the Chromaflex tube, the tube must be immersed in the nitrogen very slowly, or the tube will break.]

Water will begin to distill into the tube. As ice forms in the tube, raise the Dewar flask to keep the liquid nitrogen level only slightly below the level of ice in the tube. When water begins to freeze in the neck of the 10/30 joint, or when liquid nitrogen reaches the 2.0-mL graduation mark on the Chromaflex tube, remove the Dewar flask and let the ice melt without heating. After the ice has melted, check the volume of water that has distilled, and repeat the sequence of chilling and thawing until at least 0.9 mL of water has been collected. Freeze the tube once again for about 2 min, and release the vacuum first by opening stopcock B, followed by stopcock A. Remove the Chromaflex tube from the apparatus, close it with a greased stopper, and let the ice melt without heating. Mix the contents of the tube by swirling, note the volume of distillate, and dilute with water to 2.0 mL, if necessary. Use this *Sample Preparation* as directed under *Chromatography*.

Chromatography   (See *Chromatography*, Appendix IIA.) Use a gas chromatograph equipped with a flame-ionization detector. Under typical conditions, the instrument contains a 4-mm (id) × 6-ft glass column, or equivalent, packed with 80-/100- or 100-/120-mesh Chromosorb 104, or equivalent. The column is maintained isothermally at about 140°, the injection port at 200°, and the detector at 250°. Nitrogen is the carrier gas, flowing at a rate of about 35 mL/min. Install an oxygen scrubber between the carrier gas line and the column. The column should be conditioned for about 72 h at 250° with 30–40 mL/min carrier flow.

[NOTE—Chromosorb 104 is oxygen sensitive. Both new and used columns should be flushed with carrier gas for 30–60 min before heating each time they are installed in the gas chromatograph.]

Inject a volume of the *Standard Preparation*, accurately measured, to give about 20% of maximum recorder response. Where possible, keep the injection volume in the range of 2–4 µL, and use the solvent-flush technique to minimize errors associated with injection volumes. In the same manner, inject an identical volume of the *Sample Preparation*. The height of the peak produced by the *Sample Preparation* does not exceed that produced by the *Standard Preparation*.[1]

---

[1] If the sample fails the test because of known or suspected interference, another aliquot may be run on a 6-ft × 2-mm (id) column, or equivalent, of 0.2% Carbowax 1500 on Carbopak C, operating at 100° isothermal, with 20 mL/min of helium carrier flow. Under these conditions, the 1,4-dioxane elutes in about 4 min.

FLUORIDE LIMIT TEST

Method I (Thorium Nitrate Colorimetric Method)
Use this method unless otherwise directed in the individual monograph.

[CAUTION—When applying this test to organic compounds, rigidly control at all times the temperature at which the distillation is conducted to the recommended range of 135°–140° to avoid the possibility of explosion.]

[NOTE—To minimize the distillation blank resulting from fluoride leached from the glassware, treat the distillation apparatus as follows: treat the glassware with hot 10% sodium hydroxide solution, followed by flushing with tap water and rinsing with distilled water. At least once daily, treat in addition by boiling down 15–20 mL of 1:2 sulfuric acid until the still is filled with fumes; cool, pour off the acid, treat again with 10% sodium hydroxide solution, and rinse thoroughly. For further details, see AOAC method 944.08.]

Unless otherwise directed, place a 5.0-g sample and 30 mL of water in a 125-mL Pyrex distillation flask having a side arm and trap. The flask is connected with a condenser and carries a thermometer and a capillary tube, both of which must extend into the liquid. Slowly add, with continuous stirring, 10 mL of 70% perchloric acid, and then add 2 or 3 drops of a 1:2 solution of silver nitrate and a few glass beads. Connect a small dropping funnel or a steam generator to the capillary tube. Support the flask on a flame-resistant mat or shielding board, with a hole that exposes about one-third of the flask to the low, "clean" flame of a Bunsen burner.

[NOTE—The shielding is essential to prevent the walls of the flask from overheating above the level of its liquid contents.]

Distill until the temperature reaches 135°. Add water from the funnel or introduce steam through the capillary, maintaining the temperature between 135° and 140° at all times. Continue the distillation until 100 mL of distillate has been collected. After the 100-mL portion (*Distillate A*) is collected, collect an additional 50-mL portion of distillate (*Distillate B*) to ensure that all of the fluorine has been volatilized.

Place 50 mL of *Distillate A* in a 50-mL Nessler tube. In another, similar Nessler tube, place 50 mL of water distilled through the apparatus as a control. Add to each tube 0.1 mL of a filtered 1:1000 solution of sodium alizarinsulfonate and 1 mL of a freshly prepared 1:4000 solution of hydroxylamine hydrochloride, and mix well. Add, dropwise and with stirring, either 1 N or 0.05 N sodium hydroxide, depending on the expected volume of volatile acid distilling over, to the tube containing the distillate until its color just matches that of the control, which is faintly pink. Then add to each tube 1.0 mL of 0.1 N hydrochloric acid, and mix well. From a buret, graduated in 0.05 mL, add slowly to the tube containing the distillate enough of a 1:4000 solution of thorium nitrate so that, after mixing, the color of the liquid just changes to a faint pink. Note the volume of the solution added, then add exactly the same volume to the control, and mix. Now add to the control solution sodium fluoride TS (10 µg F/mL) from a buret to make the colors of the two tubes match after dilution to the same volume. Mix well, and allow all air bubbles to escape before making the final color comparison. Check the endpoint by adding 1 or 2 drops of sodium fluoride TS to the control. A distinct change in color should take place. Note the volume of sodium fluoride TS added.

Dilute *Distillate B* to 100 mL, and mix well. Place 50 mL of this solution in a 50-mL Nessler tube, and follow the procedure used for *Distillate A*. The total volume of sodium fluoride TS required for the solutions from both *Distillate A* and *Distillate B* should not exceed 2.5 mL.

Method II (Ion-Selective Electrode Method A)

Buffer Solution   Dissolve 36 g of cyclohexylenedinitrilotetraacetic acid (CDTA) in sufficient 1 N sodium hydroxide to make 200 mL. Transfer 20 mL of this solution (equivalent to 4 g of disodium CDTA) into a 1000-mL beaker containing 500 mL of water, 57 mL of glacial acetic acid, and 58 g of sodium chloride, and stir to dissolve. Adjust the pH of the solution to 5.0–5.5 by the addition of 5 N sodium hydroxide, then cool to room temperature, dilute with water to 1000 mL, and mix.

Procedure   Unless otherwise directed in the individual monograph, transfer 8.0 g of sample and 20 mL of water into a 250-mL distilling flask, cautiously add 20 mL of perchloric acid, and then add 2 or 3 drops of a 1:2 solution of silver nitrate and a few glass beads.

[CAUTION—Handle perchloric acid in an appropriate fume hood.]

Following the directions, and observing the *Caution* and *Notes*, as given under *Method I*, distill the solution until 200 mL of distillate has been collected.

Transfer a 25.0-mL aliquot of the distillate into a 250-mL plastic beaker, and dilute with the *Buffer Solution* to 100 mL. Place the fluoride ion and reference electrodes (or a combination fluoride electrode) of a suitable ion-selective electrode apparatus in the solution. Adjust the calibration control until the indicator needle points to the center on the logarithmic concentration scale, allowing sufficient time for equilibration (about 20 min), and stirring constantly during the equilibration period and throughout the remainder of the procedure. Pipet 1.0 mL of a solution containing 100 µg of fluoride (F) ion per mL (prepared by dissolving 22.2 mg of sodium fluoride, previously dried at 200° for 4 h, in sufficient water to make 100.0 mL) into the beaker, allow the electrode to come to equilibrium, and record the final reading on the logarithmic concentration scale.

[NOTE—Follow the instrument manufacturer's instructions regarding precautions and interferences, electrode filling and check, temperature compensation, and calibration.]

Calculations   Calculate the fluoride content, in mg/kg, of the sample taken:

$$\text{Result} = [IA/(R - I)] \times 100 \times (200/25W)$$

in which I is the initial scale reading before the addition of the sodium fluoride solution; A is the concentration, in µg/mL, of fluoride in the sodium fluoride solution added to the sample solution; R is the final scale reading after addition of the sodium fluoride solution; and W is the original weight, in grams, of the sample.

Method III (Ion-Selective Electrode Method B)

Sodium Fluoride Solution (5 µg F/mL) Transfer 2.210 g of sodium fluoride, previously dried at 200° for 4 h and accurately weighed, into a 400-mL plastic beaker, add 200 mL of water, and stir until dissolved. Quantitatively transfer this solution into a 1000-mL volumetric flask with the aid of water, dilute with water to volume, and mix. Store this stock solution in a plastic bottle. On the day of use, transfer 5.0 mL of the stock solution into a 1000-mL volumetric flask, dilute with water to volume, and mix.

Calibration Curve Transfer 1.0 mL, 2.0 mL, 3.0 mL, 5.0 mL, 10.0 mL, and 15.0 mL of the *Sodium Fluoride Solution* into separate 250-mL plastic beakers; add 50 mL of water, 5 mL of 1 N hydrochloric acid, 10 mL of 1 M sodium citrate, and 10 mL of 0.2 M disodium EDTA to each beaker; and mix. Transfer each solution into separate 100-mL volumetric flasks, dilute with water to volume, and mix. Transfer a 50-mL portion of each solution into separate 125-mL plastic beakers, and measure the potential of each solution with a suitable ion-selective electrode apparatus (such as the Orion Model No. 94-09, with solid-state membrane), using a suitable reference electrode (such as the Orion Model No. 90-01, with single junction). Plot the calibration curve on two-cycle semilogarithmic paper (such as K & E No. 465130) or with the use of a suitable graphing calculator or spreadsheet program, with µg of F per 100 mL solution on the logarithmic scale.

Procedure Transfer 1.00 g of sample into a 150-mL glass beaker, add 10 mL of water, and, while stirring continuously, slowly add 20 mL of 1 N hydrochloric acid to dissolve the sample. Boil rapidly for 1 min, then transfer into a 250-mL plastic beaker, and cool rapidly in ice water. Add 15 mL of 1 M sodium citrate and 10 mL of 0.2 M disodium EDTA, and mix. Adjust the pH to 5.5 ± 0.1 with 1 N hydrochloric acid or 1 N sodium hydroxide, if necessary; transfer into a 100-mL volumetric flask; dilute with water to volume; and mix. Transfer a 50-mL portion of this solution into a 125-mL plastic beaker, and measure the potential of the solution with the apparatus described under *Calibration Curve*. Determine the fluoride content, in µg, of the sample from the *Calibration Curve*. Determine the percentage of fluoride in the sample taken:

$$\text{Result} = (C/W_S) \times 0.000001 \times 100\%$$

in which C is the content of fluoride, in µg, in the sample, determined from the *Calibration Curve*; W_S is the sample weight, in g; and 0.000001 is a factor converting µg to grams.

Method IV (Ion-Selective Electrode Method C)

[NOTE—Unless directed otherwise by the individual monograph, use *Buffer Solution A* for samples with a neutral to higher pH, and use *Buffer Solution B* for samples with a neutral to lower pH.]

Buffer Solution A Add 2 volumes of 6 N acetic acid to 1 volume of water, and adjust the pH to 5.0 with 50% potassium hydroxide solution.

Buffer Solution B Dissolve 150 g of sodium citrate dihydrate and 10.3 g of disodium EDTA dihydrate in 800 mL of water, adjust the pH to 8.0 with 50% sodium hydroxide solution, and dilute with water to 1000 mL.

Fluoride Standard Solutions

1000 mg/kg Fluoride Standard: Transfer 2.2108 g of sodium fluoride, previously dried at 200° for 4 h, into a 1000-mL volumetric flask, and dissolve in and dilute with water to volume. The resulting solution contains 1000 µg of fluoride per mL.

50 mg/kg Fluoride Standard: Pipet 50 mL of the *1000 mg/kg Fluoride Standard* into a 1000-mL volumetric flask. Dilute with water to volume.

10 mg/kg Fluoride Standard: Pipet 100 mL of the *50 mg/kg Fluoride Standard* into a 500-mL volumetric flask. Dilute with water to volume.

Fluoride Limit Solutions (for a 1-g sample)

50 mg/kg Fluoride Limit Solution (1 mg/kg fluoride standard): Pipet 50 mL of the *10 mg/kg Fluoride Standard* into a 500-mL volumetric flask, and dilute with water to volume.

10 mg/kg Fluoride Limit Solution (0.2 mg/kg fluoride standard): Pipet 10 mL of the *10 mg/kg Fluoride Standard* into a 500-mL volumetric flask, and dilute with water to volume.

Fluoride Limit Solutions (for a 2-g sample)

50 mg/kg Fluoride Limit Solution (2 mg/kg fluoride standard): Pipet 100 mL of the *10 mg/kg Fluoride Standard* into a 500-mL volumetric flask, and dilute with water to volume.

10 mg/kg Fluoride Limit Solution (0.4 mg/kg fluoride standard): Pipet 20 mL of the *10 mg/kg Fluoride Standard* into a 500-mL volumetric flask, and dilute with water to volume.

[NOTE—Store all standard and limit solutions in plastic containers.]

Sample Preparation Accurately weigh the amount of sample specified in the monograph, transfer it into a 100-mL volumetric flask, and dissolve it in a minimal amount of water. Add 50.0 mL of the appropriate *Buffer Solution*, dilute with water to volume, and mix.

Electrode Calibration Pipet 50 mL of the appropriate *Buffer Solution* into a plastic beaker. Place the fluoride ion and reference electrodes (or a combination fluoride electrode) into the plastic beaker and stir. At 5-min intervals, add 100 µL and 1000 µL of the *1000 mg/kg Fluoride Standard* and read the potential, in mV, after each addition. The difference between the two readings is the slope of the fluoride electrode and should typically be in the range of 63–70 mV at 25° for *Buffer Solution A* and in the range of 54–60 mV at 25° for *Buffer Solution B*. If the difference in potential is not within this range, check, and, if necessary, replace the electrode, instrument, or solutions.

Alternatively, the electrode calibration should be performed according to the manufacturer's instructions and should comply with the manufacturer's calibration range at 25°. If the difference in potential is not within this range, evaluate the system and equipment as necessary.

1270 / Appendix III / General Tests and Assays

Procedure Transfer the entire sample into a plastic beaker. Place the electrode into the beaker, allow the solution to equilibrate for 5 min with stirring, and read the potential, in mV. Remove and rinse the electrode(s) with water. In another beaker, using a pipet, add 50 mL of the appropriate *Buffer Solution* followed by 50 mL of the *Fluoride Limit Solution* that best reflects the fluoride limit of the sample. Place the electrode in the beaker, equilibrate for 3 min, and read the potential in mV. If the potential of the *Fluoride Limit Solution* is less than that of the sample, the sample passes the test criteria for maximum acceptable fluoride level limit.

Method V

Lime Suspension Carefully shake about 56 g of low-fluorine calcium oxide (about 2 mg/kg of F) with 250 mL of water, and while stirring, slowly add 250 mL of 60% perchloric acid. Add a few glass beads, and boil until copious fumes of perchloric acid evolve, then cool, add 200 mL of water, and boil again.

[CAUTION—Handle perchloric acid in an appropriate fume hood.]

Repeat the dilution and boiling once more, cool, dilute considerably, and if precipitated silicon dioxide forms, pass through a fritted-glass filter. While stirring, pour the clear solution into 1000 mL of a 1:10 solution of sodium hydroxide, allow the precipitate to settle, and siphon off the supernatant liquid. Remove the sodium salts from the precipitate by washing five times with water in large centrifuge bottles, shaking the mass thoroughly each time. Finally, shake the precipitate into a suspension, and dilute with water to 2000 mL. Store in paraffin-lined bottles, and shake well before use.

[NOTE—100 mL of this suspension should give no appreciable fluoride blank when evaporated, distilled, and titrated as directed under *Method I*.]

Procedure Assemble the distilling apparatus as described under *Method I*, and add 1.67 g of sample, accurately weighed, and 25 mL of 1:2 sulfuric acid to the distilling flask. Distill until the temperature reaches 160°, then maintain at 160°–165° by adding water from the funnel, collecting 300 mL of distillate. Oxidize the distillate by cautiously adding 2 or 3 mL of fluorine-free 30% hydrogen peroxide (to remove sulfates), allow to stand for a few minutes, and evaporate in a platinum dish with an excess of *Lime Suspension*. Ignite briefly at 600°, then cool and wet the ash with about 10 mL of water. Cover the dish with a watch glass, and cautiously introduce under the watch glass just sufficient 60% perchloric acid to dissolve the ash. Add the contents of the dish through the dropping funnel of a freshly prepared distilling apparatus (the distilling flask should contain a few glass beads), using a total of 20 mL of the 60% perchloric acid to dissolve the ash and transfer the solution. Add 10 mL of water and a few drops of a 1:2 solution of silver perchlorate through the dropping funnel, and continue as directed under *Method I*, beginning with "Distill until the temperature reaches 135°...".

LEAD LIMIT TEST

[NOTE—Unless otherwise specified in the monograph, use the *Dithizone Method* to determine lead levels.]

Dithizone Method

Special Reagents Select reagents having as low a lead content as practicable, and store all solutions in containers of borosilicate glass. Rinse all glassware thoroughly with warm, 1:2 nitric acid followed by water.

Ammonia–Cyanide Solution Dissolve 2 g of potassium cyanide in 15 mL of ammonium hydroxide, and dilute with water to 100 mL.

Ammonium Citrate Solution Dissolve 40 g of citric acid in 90 mL of water, add 2 or 3 drops of phenol red TS, then cautiously add ammonium hydroxide until the solution acquires a red color. Extract it with 20-mL portions of *Dithizone Extraction Solution* until the dithizone solution retains its green color or remains unchanged.

Diluted Standard Lead Solution (1 µg Pb in 1 mL)

Lead Nitrate Stock Solution: Dissolve 159.8 mg of ACS Reagent-Grade Lead Nitrate [$Pb(NO_3)_2$] in 100 mL of water containing 1 mL of nitric acid, dilute with water to 1000.0 mL, and mix. Prepare and store this solution in glass containers that are free from lead salts.

Standard Lead Solution: On the day of use, dilute 10.0 mL of *Lead Nitrate Stock Solution* with water to 100.0 mL. Each mL of *Standard Lead Solution* contains the equivalent of 10 µg of lead (Pb) ion.

Diluted Standard Lead Solution: Immediately before use, transfer 10.0 mL of *Standard Lead Solution* into a 100-mL volumetric flask, dilute with 1:100 nitric acid to volume, and mix.

Dithizone Extraction Solution Dissolve 30 mg of dithizone in 1000 mL of chloroform, add 5 mL of alcohol, and mix. Store in a refrigerator. Before use, shake a suitable volume of the solution with about half its volume of 1:100 nitric acid, discarding the nitric acid.

Hydroxylamine Hydrochloride Solution Dissolve 20 g of hydroxylamine hydrochloride in sufficient water to make about 65 mL, transfer the solution into a separator, add a few drops of thymol blue TS, then add ammonium hydroxide until the solution assumes a yellow color. Add 10 mL of a 1:25 solution of sodium diethyldithiocarbamate, mix, and allow to stand for 5 min. Extract the solution with successive 10- to 15-mL portions of chloroform until a 5-mL test portion of the chloroform extract does not assume a yellow color when shaken with cupric sulfate TS. Add 2.7 N hydrochloric acid until the extracted solution is pink, adding 1 or 2 drops more of thymol blue TS if necessary, then dilute with water to 100 mL, and mix.

Potassium Cyanide Solution Dissolve 50 g of potassium cyanide in sufficient water to make 100 mL. Remove the lead from the solution by extraction with successive portions of *Dithizone Extraction Solution* as described under *Ammonium Citrate Solution*, then extract any dithizone remaining in the cyanide solution by shaking with chloroform. Finally, dilute the cyanide solution with sufficient water so that each 100 mL contains 10 g of potassium cyanide.

Standard Dithizone Solution Dissolve 10 mg of dithizone in 1000 mL of chloroform, keeping the solution in a glass-stoppered, lead-free bottle suitably wrapped to protect it from light and stored in a refrigerator.

Sample Solution Use the solution obtained by treating the sample as directed in an individual monograph as the *Sample Solution* in the *Procedure*. Sample solutions of organic compounds are prepared, unless otherwise directed, according to the following general method: [**CAUTION**—Some substances may react unexpectedly with explosive violence when digested with hydrogen peroxide. Use appropriate safety precautions at all times.]

Transfer 1.0 g of sample into a suitable flask, add 5 mL of sulfuric acid and a few glass beads, and digest at a temperature not exceeding 120° until charring begins, using preferably a hot plate in a fume hood. (Additional sulfuric acid may be necessary to completely wet some samples, but the total volume added should not exceed about 10 mL.) After the sample has initially been decomposed by the acid, add with caution, dropwise, hydrogen peroxide (30%), allowing the reaction to subside and reheating between drops. The first few drops must be added very slowly with sufficient mixing to prevent a rapid reaction, and heating should be discontinued if foaming becomes excessive. Swirl the solution in the flask to prevent unreacted substance from caking on the walls or bottom of the flask during the digestion.

[NOTE—Add small quantities of the peroxide when the solution begins to darken.]

Continue the digestion until the organic matter is destroyed, gradually raising the temperature of the hot plate to 250°–300° until fumes of sulfur trioxide are copiously evolved and the solution becomes colorless or retains only a light straw color. Cool, cautiously add 10 mL of water, again evaporate to strong fuming, and cool. Quantitatively transfer the solution into a separator with the aid of small quantities of water.

Procedure Transfer the *Sample Solution*, prepared as directed in the individual monograph, into a separator, and unless otherwise directed, add 6 mL of *Ammonium Citrate Solution* and 2 mL of *Hydroxylamine Hydrochloride Solution*. (Use 10 mL of the citrate solution when determining lead in iron salts.) Add 2 drops of phenol red TS to the separator, and make the solution just alkaline (red in color) by the addition of ammonium hydroxide. Cool the solution, if necessary, under a stream of tap water, then add 2 mL of *Potassium Cyanide Solution*. Immediately extract the solution with 5-mL portions of *Dithizone Extraction Solution*, draining each extract into another separator, until the dithizone solution retains its green color. Shake the combined dithizone solutions for 30 s with 20 mL of 1:100 nitric acid, discard the chloroform layer, add 5.0 mL of *Standard Dithizone Solution* and 4 mL of *Ammonia–Cyanide Solution* to the acid solution, and shake for 30 s. The purple hue in the chloroform solution of the sample caused by any lead dithizonate present does not exceed that in a control, containing the volume of *Diluted Standard Lead Solution* equivalent to the amount of lead specified in the monograph, when treated in the same manner as the sample.

Flame Atomic Absorption Spectrophotometric Method
Select reagents having as low a lead content as practicable, and store all solutions in high-density polyethylene containers. Rinse all plastic and glassware thoroughly with warm, 1:2 nitric acid followed by water.

Lead Nitrate Stock Solution (100 µg/mL) Dissolve 159.8 mg of reagent-grade lead nitrate [$Pb(NO_3)_2$] in 100 mL of water containing 1 mL of nitric acid in a 1000-mL volumetric flask, and dilute with water to volume.

Standard Lead Solution (10 µg/mL) On the day of use, transfer 10 mL of *Lead Nitrate Stock Solution* into a 100-mL volumetric flask, and dilute with water to volume.

Diluted Standard Lead Solutions On the day of use, prepare a set of standard lead solutions that corresponds to the lead limit specified in the monograph:

1 mg/kg Lead Limit (0.5 µg/mL, 1.0 µg/mL, and 1.5 µg/mL standards): On the day of use, transfer 5.0 mL, 10.0 mL, and 15.0 mL of *Standard Lead Solution* into three separate 100-mL volumetric flasks, add 10 mL of 3 N hydrochloric acid to each, and dilute with water to volume.

5 mg/kg Lead Limit (1.0 µg/mL, 5.0 µg/mL, and 10.0 µg/mL standards): On the day of use, transfer 10.0 mL and 50.0 mL of *Standard Lead Solution* into two separate 100-mL volumetric flasks, add 10 mL of 3 N hydrochloric acid to each, and dilute with water to volume. The final standard, 10.0 µg/mL, is taken directly from the *Standard Lead Solution*.

10 mg/kg Lead Limit (5.0 µg/mL, 10.0 µg/mL, and 15.0 µg/mL standards): On the day of use, transfer 5.0 mL, 10.0 mL, and 15.0 mL of *Lead Nitrate Stock Solution* into three separate 100-mL volumetric flasks, add 10 mL of 3 N hydrochloric acid to each, and dilute with water to volume.

25% Sulfuric Acid Solution (by volume) Cautiously add 100 mL of sulfuric acid to 300 mL of water with constant stirring while cooling in an ice bath.

Sample Preparation Transfer the sample weight as specified in the monograph, weighed to the nearest 0.1 mg, into an evaporating dish. Add a sufficient amount of *25% Sulfuric Acid Solution*, and distribute the sulfuric acid uniformly through the sample. Within a hood, place the dish on a steam bath to evaporate most of the water. Place the dish on a burner, and slowly pre-ash the sample by expelling most of the sulfuric acid. Place the dish in a muffle furnace that has been set at 525°, and ash the sample until the residue appears free from carbon. Prepare a *Sample Blank* by ashing 5 mL of 25% sulfuric acid. Cool and cautiously wash down the inside of each evaporation dish with water.

Add 5 mL of 1 N hydrochloric acid. Place the dish on a steam bath, and evaporate to dryness. Add 1.0 mL of 3 N hydrochloric acid and approximately 5 mL of water, and heat briefly on a steam bath to dissolve any residue. Transfer each solution quantitatively to a 10-mL volumetric flask, dilute to volume, and mix.

Procedure Concomitantly determine the absorbances of the *Sample Blank*, the *Diluted Standard Lead Solutions*, and the *Sample Preparation* at the lead emission line of 283.3 nm, using a slit-width of 0.7 nm. Use a suitable atomic absorption spectrophotometer equipped with a lead electrodeless discharge lamp (EDL), an air–acetylene flame, and a 4-in burner head. Use water as the blank.

Calculations Determine the corrected absorbance values by subtracting the *Sample Blank* absorbance from each of the *Diluted Standard Lead Solutions* and from the *Sample Preparation* absorbances. Prepare a standard curve by plotting the corrected *Diluted Standard Lead Solutions* absorbance values versus their corresponding concentrations expressed as µg/mL. Determine the lead concentration in the *Sample Preparation* by reference to the calibration curve. Calculate the quantity of lead, in mg/kg, in the sample taken:

$$\text{Result} = 10C/W_S$$

in which C is the concentration, in µg/mL, of lead from the standard curve; and W_S is the weight, in grams, of the sample taken.

Change to read:
Atomic Absorption Spectrophotometric Graphite Furnace Method

The following methods are primarily intended for the analysis of applicable substances containing less than 1 mg/kg of lead.

Method I

This method is intended for the quantitation of lead in substances that are soluble in water, such as sugars and sugar syrups, at levels as low as 0.03 mg/kg. The method detection limit is approximately 5 ng/kg.

Apparatus Use a suitable graphite furnace atomic absorption spectrophotometer set at 283.3 nm and equipped with an autosampler, pyrolytically coated graphite tubes, solid pyrolytic graphite platforms, and an adequate means of background correction. Zeeman effect or Smith-Hieftje background correction is preferred, but deuterium arc background correction should be acceptable. (This method was developed on a Perkin-Elmer Model Z5100, 0.7-nm slit, HGA-600 furnace, AS-60 autosampler with Zeeman background correction.) If the instrument does not have a well-defined calibration function, a separate calculator or computer is required for linear least squares, nonlinear, or quadratic calibrations. Use either a hollow-cathode lamp or an electrode-less discharge lamp as the source, and use argon as the purge gas and breathing-quality air (for oxygen ashing to avoid residue build up during the char step) as the alternate gas. Set up the instrument according to the manufacturer's specifications with consideration of current good GFAAS practices—addressing such factors as line voltage, cooling water temperature, graphite part specifications, and furnace temperature. If an optical pyrometer or thermocouple is not available to check the furnace controller temperature calibration, dim the room lights, and observe the furnace emission through the sample introduction port while increasing the furnace temperature. A characteristic cherry red glow should begin to appear at 800°. If it glows at a lower temperature, then the furnace is hotter, and temperatures must be adjusted downward accordingly.

Use acid-cleaned [in a mixture of 5% sub-boiling, distilled nitric acid and 5% sub-boiling, distilled hydrochloric acid made up in deionized, distilled water (18 megohm), and thoroughly rinsed with deionized, distilled water (18 megohm)] autosampler cups (PE B008-7600 Teflon, or equivalent) to avoid contamination. Use micropipets with disposable tips free of lead contamination for dilution. Ensure accuracy and precision of micropipets and tips by dispensing and weighing 5–10 replicate portions of water onto a microbalance. Use acid-cleaned volumetric glassware to prepare standards and dilute samples to a final volume. For digestion, use acid-cleaned, high-density polyethylene tubes, polypropylene tubes, Teflon tubes, or quartz tubes. Store final diluted samples in plastic tubes.

Standard Solutions Prepare all lead solutions in 5% sub-boiling distilled nitric acid. Use a single-element 1000- or 10,000-µg/mL lead stock to prepare (weekly) an intermediate 10-µg/mL standard in 5% nitric acid. Prepare (daily) a *Lead Standard Solution* (1 µg/mL) by diluting the intermediate 10-µg/mL stock solution 1:10. Prepare *Working Calibration Standards* of 100.0 ng/mL, 50.0 ng/mL, 25.0 ng/mL, and 10.0 ng/mL from this, using appropriate dilutions. Store standards in acid-cleaned polyethylene test tubes or bottles. If the GFAAS autosampler is used to automatically dilute standards, ensure calibration accuracy by pipetting volumes of 3 µL or greater.

Modifier Stock Solution Weigh 20 g of ultrapure magnesium nitrate hexahydrate, and dilute to 100 mL. Just before use, prepare a *Modifier Working Solution* by diluting stock solution 1:10. A volume of 5 µL will provide 0.06 mg of magnesium nitrate.

Sample Digestion [CAUTION—Perform the procedure in a fume hood, and wear safety glasses.] Obtain a representative subsample to be analyzed. For liquid samples such as sugar syrups, ultrasonicate and/or vortex mix before weighing. For solid samples such as crystalline sucrose, make a sugar solution using equal weights of sample (5-g minimum) and deionized, distilled (18 megohm) water. Mix samples until completely dissolved. Transfer approximately 1.5 g (record to nearest mg) of sample (or 3.0 g of sugar solution), accurately weighed, into a digestion tube. Run a *Sample Preparation Blank* of 1.5 g of deionized, distilled (18 megohm) water through the entire procedure with each batch of samples. Add 0.75 mL of sub-boiling, distilled nitric acid. Heat plastic tubes in a water bath, quartz tubes in a water bath or heating block, warming slowly to 90°–95° to avoid spattering. Monitor the temperature by using a "dummy" sample. Heat until all brown vapors have dissipated and any rust-colored tint is gone (20–30 min). Cool. Add 0.5 mL of 50% hydrogen peroxide dropwise, heat at 90°–95° for 5 min, and cool. Add a second 0.5-mL portion of 50% hydrogen peroxide, dropwise, and heat at 90°–100° for 5–10 min until clear. Cool, and dilute ▲with water▲FCC8 to a final volume of 10 mL.

Procedure The furnace program is as follows: (1) Dry at 200°, using a 20-s ramp and a 30-s hold and a 300-mL/min argon flow; (2) char the sample at 750°, using a 40-s ramp and a 40-s hold and a 300-mL/min air flow; (3) cool down, and purge the air from the furnace for 60 s, using a 20° set temperature and a 300-mL/min argon flow; (4) atomize at

1800°, using a 0-s ramp and a 10-s hold with the argon flow stopped; (5) clean out at 2600°, with a 1-s ramp and a 7-s hold; (6) cool down the furnace (if necessary) at 20°, with a 1-s ramp and a 5-s hold with a 300-mL/min argon flow.

Use the autosampler to inject 20 µL each of blanks, calibration standards, and sample solutions and 5 µL of *Modifier Working Solution*. Inject each respective solution in triplicate, and average results. Use peak area measurements for all quantitation. After ensuring that the furnace is clean by running a 5% nitric acid blank, check the instrument sensitivity ▲according to manufacturer's specifications▲*FCC8* by running the 25-ng/mL calibration standard. ▲▲*FCC8* Calculate the characteristic mass (m_o) (mass of Pb pg necessary to produce an integrated absorbance of 0.0044 abs-sec) as follows:

$$m_o = \frac{(0.0044 \text{ abs-sec})(25 \text{ pg/µL})(20 \text{ µL})}{\text{(measured 25 pg/µL abs-sec)}}$$

Record and track the integrated absorbance and m_o for reference and quality assurance.

Standard Curve: Inject each calibration standard in triplicate ▲and determine the instrument linearity according to manufacturer's instructions.▲*FCC8* Use the calibration algorithms provided in the instrument software. Recheck calibration periodically (≤15 samples) by running a 25- or 50-ng/mL calibration standard interspersed with samples. If recheck differs from calibration by >10%, recalibrate the instrument. The instrumental detection limit (DL) and quantitation limit (QL), in picograms, may be based on 7–10 replicates of the *Sample Preparation Blank* and calculated as follows:

$$DL = \frac{(3)(\text{s.d. blank abs-sec})(10 \text{ pg/µL})(20 \text{µL})}{(\text{abs-sec 10 ng/mL std})}$$

$$QL = \frac{(10)(\text{s.d. blank abs-sec})(10 \text{ pg/µL})(20 \text{ µL})}{(\text{abs-sec 10 ng/mL std})}$$

During method development, detection limits were typically 10–14 pg, corresponding to 0.5–0.7 ng/mL for 20 µL. This corresponds to a method detection limit of 3.3–4.7 ng/g of sugar.

Sample Analyses: Inject each sample digest in triplicate, and record the integrated absorbance. If instrument response exceeds that of the calibration curve, dilute with 5% nitric acid to bring the sample response into working range, and note the dilution factor (DF). Sample solutions having a final concentration ▲beyond the linearity range▲*FCC8* should be diluted 1:10 to facilitate analysis in the linear range for systems not equipped with nonlinear calibration. All sample analyses should be blank corrected using the sample preparation blank. This can typically be done automatically by the software after identifying and running a representative sample preparation blank. Use the calibration algorithm provided in the instrument software to calculate a blank-corrected, digest lead concentration (in ng/mL).

Calculation of Lead Content: Calculate the lead level in the original sample as follows:

$$Pb \text{ (ng/g)} = \frac{(\text{blank-corrected Pb ng/mL})(DF)[\text{sample vol (10 mL)}]}{[\text{sample wt (approx. 1.5 g)}]}[2]$$

Quality Assurance To ensure analytical accuracy, National Institute of Standards and Technology (NIST) SRM 1643c acidified water or a similar material should be analyzed before the unknown samples are. The certified content of SRM 1643c is 35.3 ± 0.9 ng/mL. If the concentration determined is not within 10% of the mean reference value (31.8–38.8 ng/mL), the reason for inaccuracy should be evaluated, and unknown samples should not be analyzed until acceptable accuracy is achieved. Also prepare an in-house control solution made from uncontaminated table sugar or reagent-grade sucrose (or other appropriate substance with a Pb content <5 ng/g as received) mixed with an equal volume of water. Spike this solution with Pb to produce a concentration of 100 ng/g. Analyze with each batch of samples. Recoveries should be 100 ± 20%, and the precision for complete replicate digestions should be <5% RSD. Periodically, a sample digest should be checked using the method of standard additions to ensure that there are no multiplicative or chemical interferences. Spiking samples and checking recoveries is always a good practice.

Method II

This method is primarily intended for the determination of lead at levels of less than 1 mg/kg in substances immiscible with water, such as edible oils.

Apparatus Use a suitable atomic absorption spectrophotometer (Perkin-Elmer Model 3100 or equivalent) fitted with a graphite furnace (Perkin-Elmer HGA 600 or equivalent). Use a lead hollow-cathode lamp (Perkin-Elmer or equivalent) with argon as the carrier gas. Follow the manufacturers' directions for setting the appropriate instrument parameters for lead determination.

[NOTE—For this test, use reagent-grade chemicals with as low a lead content as is practicable, as well as high-purity water and gases. Before use in this analysis, rinse all glassware and plasticware twice with 10% nitric acid and twice with 10% hydrochloric acid, and then rinse them thoroughly with high-purity water, preferably obtained from a mixed-bed strong-acid, strong-base ion-exchange cartridge capable of producing water with an electrical resistivity of 12–15 megohms.]

Hydrogen Peroxide–Nitric Acid Solution Dissolve equal volumes of 10% hydrogen peroxide and 10% nitric acid.

[NOTE—Use caution.]

Lead Nitrate Stock Solution Dissolve 159.8 mg of ACS Reagent-Grade Lead Nitrate (alternatively, use NIST Standard Reference Material, containing 10 mg of lead per kg, or equivalent) in 100 mL of *Hydrogen Peroxide–Nitric Acid Solution*. Dilute with *Hydrogen Peroxide–Nitric Acid Solution* to 1000.0 mL, and mix. Prepare and store this solution in glass containers that are free from lead salts. Each mL of this solution contains the equivalent of 100 µg of lead (Pb) ion.

---

[2] If a sample solution was prepared initially to ensure sample homogeneity, this is the weight of the original sugar digested (not the weight of the solution).

Standard Lead Solution On the day of use, dilute 10.0 mL of *Lead Nitrate Stock Solution* with *Hydrogen Peroxide–Nitric Acid Solution* to 100.0 mL, and mix. Each mL of *Standard Lead Solution* contains the equivalent of 10 µg of lead (Pb) ion.

Butanol–Nitric Acid Solution Slowly add 50 mL of nitric acid to approximately 500 mL of butanol contained in a 1000-mL volumetric flask. Dilute with butanol to volume, and mix.

Standard Solutions Prepare a series of lead standard solutions serially diluted from the *Standard Lead Solution* in *Butanol–Nitric Acid Solution*. Pipet into separate 100-mL volumetric flasks 0.2 mL, 0.5 mL, 1 mL, and 2 mL, respectively, of *Standard Lead Solution*, dilute with *Butanol–Nitric Acid Solution* to volume, and mix. The *Standard Solutions* contain, respectively, 0.02 µg, 0.05 µg, 0.1 µg, and 0.2 µg of lead per mL. (For lead limits greater than 1 mg/kg, prepare a series of standard solutions in a range encompassing the expected lead concentration in the sample.)

Sample Solution [CAUTION—Perform this procedure in a fume hood, and wear safety glasses.] Transfer 1 g of sample, accurately weighed, into a large test tube. Add 1 mL of nitric acid. Place the test tube in a rack in a boiling water bath. As soon as the rusty tint is gone, add 1 mL of 30% hydrogen peroxide dropwise to avoid a vigorous reaction, and wait for bubbles to form. Stir with an acid-washed plastic spatula if necessary. Remove the test tube from the water bath, and let it cool. Transfer the solution into a 10-mL volumetric flask, and dilute with *Butanol–Nitric Acid Solution* to volume, and mix. Use this solution for analysis.

Procedure

Tungsten Solution: Transfer 0.1 g of tungstic acid (H_2WO_4) and 5 g of sodium hydroxide pellets into a 50-mL plastic bottle. Add 5.0 mL of high-purity water, and mix. Heat the mixture in a hot water bath until complete solution is achieved. Cool, and store at room temperature.

Procedure: Place the graphite tube in the furnace. Inject a 20-µL aliquot of the *Tungsten Solution* into the graphite tube, using a 300-mL/min argon flow and the following sequence of conditions: dry at 110° for 20 s, char at 700°–900° for 20 s, and with the argon flow stopped, atomize at 2700° for 10 s; repeat this procedure once more using a second 20-µL aliquot of the *Tungsten Solution*. Clean the quartz windows.

Standard Curve: [NOTE—The sample injection technique is the most crucial step in controlling the precision of the analysis; the volume of the sample must remain constant. Rinse the µL pipet tip (Eppendorf or equivalent) three times with either the *Standard Solutions* or *Sample Solution* before injection. Use a fresh pipet tip for each injection, and start the atomization process immediately after injecting the sample. Between injections, flush the graphite tube of any residual lead by purging at a high temperature as recommended by the manufacturer.]

With the hollow-cathode lamp properly aligned for maximum absorbance and the wavelength set at 283.3 nm, atomize 20-µL aliquots of the four *Standard Solutions*, using a 300-mL/min argon flow and the following sequence of conditions: dry at 110° for 30 s, with a 20-s ramp period and a 10-s hold time; then char at 700° for 42 s, with a 20-s ramp period and a 22-s hold time; and then, with the argon flow stopped, atomize at 2300° for 7 s.

Plot a standard curve using the concentration, in µg/mL, of each *Standard Solution* versus its maximum absorbance value compensated for background correction as directed for the particular instrument, and draw the best straight line.

Atomize 20 µL of the *Sample Solution* under identical conditions, and measure its corrected maximum absorbance. From the *Standard Curve*, determine the concentration, C, in µg/mL, of the *Sample Solution*. Calculate the quantity, in mg/kg, of lead in the sample:

$$\text{Result} = 10C/W$$

in which W is the weight, in grams, of the sample taken.

APDC Extraction Method

Select reagents having as low a lead content as practicable, and store all solutions in high-density polyethylene containers. Rinse all plastic and glassware thoroughly with warm, 1:2 nitric acid followed by water.

2% APDC Solution Dissolve 2.0 g of ammonium pyrrolidinedithiocarbamate (APDC) in 100 mL of water. Filter any slight residue of insoluble APDC from the solution before use.

Lead Nitrate Stock Solution (100 µg/mL) Dissolve 159.8 mg of reagent-grade lead nitrate [$Pb(NO_3)_2$] in 100 mL of water containing 1 mL of nitric acid in a 1000-mL volumetric flask, and dilute with water to volume.

Standard Lead Solutions

2 mg/kg Lead Standard: On the day of use, transfer 2.0 mL of *Lead Nitrate Stock Solution* into a 100-mL volumetric flask, and dilute with water to volume. The resulting solution contains 2 µg of lead per mL.

3 mg/kg Lead Standard: On the day of use, transfer 3.0 mL of *Lead Nitrate Stock Solution* into a 100-mL volumetric flask, and dilute with water to volume. The resulting solution contains 3 µg of lead per mL.

4 mg/kg Lead Standard: On the day of use, transfer 4.0 mL of *Lead Nitrate Stock Solution* into a 100-mL volumetric flask, and dilute with water to volume. The resulting solution contains 4 µg of lead per mL.

10 mg/kg Lead Standard: On the day of use, transfer 10.0 mL of *Lead Nitrate Stock Solution* into a 100-mL volumetric flask, and dilute with water to volume. The resulting solution contains 10 µg of lead per mL.

Sample Preparation Transfer a 10.0-g sample to a clean 150-mL beaker, and 10 mL of water to a second 150-mL beaker to serve as the blank. Add to each 30 mL of water and the minimum amount of hydrochloric acid needed to dissolve the sample, plus an additional 1 mL of hydrochloric acid to ensure the dissolution of any lead present. Heat to boiling, and boil for several minutes. Allow to cool, and dilute with deionized water to about 100 mL. Adjust the pH of the resulting solution to 1.0–1.5 with 25% NaOH. Quantitatively transfer the pH-adjusted solution to a clean 250-mL separatory funnel, and dilute with water to about 200 mL. Add 2 mL of *2% APDC Solution*, and mix. Extract with two 20-mL portions of chloroform, collecting the extracts in a clean 50-mL beaker. Evaporate to dryness on a steam bath. Add 3 mL of nitric acid to the residue, and heat to near dryness. Then add 0.5 mL of nitric acid and 10 mL of deionized water to the beaker, and heat until the volume is reduced to about 3–5 mL. Transfer the digested extract to a clean 10-mL volumetric flask, and dilute with water to volume.

Procedure Concomitantly determine the absorbances of the appropriate *Standard Lead Solution* and the *Sample Preparation* against the blank at the lead emission line of 283.3 nm, using a slit-width of 0.7 nm. Use a suitable atomic absorption spectrophotometer equipped with a lead electrodeless discharge lamp (EDL), or equivalent; an air–acetylene flame; and a 4-in burner head. Use water as the blank. The absorbance of the *Sample Preparation* is not greater than that of the *Standard Lead Solution*.

MANGANESE LIMIT TEST

Manganese Detection Instrument Use any suitable atomic absorption spectrophotometer equipped with a fast-response recorder or other readout device and capable of measuring the radiation absorbed by manganese atoms at the manganese resonance line of 279.5 nm.

Standard Preparations Transfer 1000 mg, accurately weighed, of manganese metal powder into a 1000-mL volumetric flask, dissolve by warming in a mixture of 10 mL of water and 10 mL of 0.5 N hydrochloric acid, cool, dilute with water to volume, and mix. Pipet 5.0 mL of this solution into a 50-mL volumetric flask, dilute with water to volume, and mix. Finally, pipet 5.0 mL, 10.0 mL, 15.0 mL, and 25.0 mL of this solution into separate 1000-mL volumetric flasks, dilute each flask with water to volume, and mix. The final solutions contain 0.5 mg/kg, 1.0 mg/kg, 1.5 mg/kg, and 2.5 mg/kg of Mn, respectively.

Sample Preparation Transfer 10.000 g of the sample into a 200-mL Kohlrausch volumetric flask, previously rinsed with 0.5 N hydrochloric acid, add 140 mL of 0.5 N hydrochloric acid, and shake vigorously for 15 min, preferably with a mechanical shaker. Dilute with 0.5 N hydrochloric acid to volume, and shake. Centrifuge approximately 100 mL of the sample mixture in a heavy-walled centrifuge tube at 2000 rpm for 5 min, and use the clear supernatant liquid in the following *Procedure*.

Procedure Aspirate 0.5 N hydrochloric acid through the air–acetylene burner for 5 min, and obtain a baseline reading at 279.5 nm, following the manufacturer's instructions for operating the atomic absorption spectrophotometer being used for the analysis. Aspirate a portion of each *Standard Preparation* in the same manner, note the readings, then aspirate a portion of the *Sample Preparation*, and note the reading. Prepare a standard curve by plotting the mg/kg of Mn in each *Standard Preparation* against the respective readings. From the graph determine the mg/kg of Mn in the *Sample Preparation*, and multiply this value by 20 to obtain the mg/kg of Mn in the original sample taken for analysis.

MERCURY LIMIT TEST

Method I

Mercury Detection Instrument Use any suitable atomic absorption spectrophotometer equipped with a fast-response recorder and capable of measuring the radiation absorbed by mercury vapors at the mercury resonance line of 253.6 nm. A simple mercury vapor meter or detector equipped with a variable span recorder also is satisfactory.

[NOTE—Wash all glassware associated with the test with nitric acid, and rinse thoroughly with water before use.]

Aeration Apparatus The apparatus, shown in *Figure 6*, consists of a flowmeter (*a*), capable of measuring flow rates from 500 to 1000 mL/min, connected via a three-way stopcock (*b*), with a Teflon plug, to 125-mL gas washing bottles (*c* and *d*), followed by a drying tube (*e*), and finally a suitable quartz liquid absorption cell (*f*), terminating with a vent (*g*) to a fume hood.

[NOTE—The absorption cell will vary in optical pathlength depending on the type of mercury detection instrument used.]

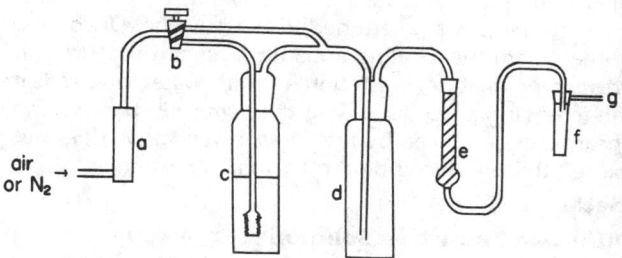

Figure 6. Aeration Apparatus for Mercury Limit Test

Bottle *c* is fitted with an extra-coarse fritted bubbler (Corning 31770 125 EC, or equivalent), and the bottle is marked with a 60-mL calibration line. The drying tube *e* is lightly packed with magnesium perchlorate. Bottle *c* is used for the test solution, and bottle *d*, which remains empty throughout the procedure, is used to collect water droplets.

Alternatively, an apparatus embodying the principle of the assembly described and illustrated may be used. The aerating medium may be either compressed air or compressed nitrogen.

Standard Preparation Transfer 1.71 g of mercuric nitrate [$Hg(NO_3)·H_2O$] into a 1000-mL volumetric flask, dissolve in a mixture of 100 mL of water and 2 mL of nitric acid, dilute with water to volume, and mix. Discard after 1 month. Transfer 10.0 mL of this solution into a second 1000-mL volumetric flask, acidify with 5 mL of a 1:5 sulfuric acid solution, dilute with water to volume, and mix. Discard after 1 week. On the day of use, transfer 10.0 mL of the second solution into a 100-mL volumetric flask, acidify with 5 mL of 1:5 sulfuric acid, dilute with water to volume, and mix. Each mL of this solution contains 1 µg of mercury. Transfer 2.0 mL of this solution (2 µg Hg) into a 50-mL beaker, and add 20 mL of water, 1 mL of a 1:5 sulfuric acid solution, and 1 mL of a 1:25 solution of potassium permanganate. Cover the beaker with a watch glass, boil for a few seconds, and cool.

Sample Preparation Prepare as directed in the individual monograph.

Procedure Assemble the aerating apparatus as shown in *Figure 16*, with bottles *c* and *d* empty and stopcock *b* in the bypass position. Connect the apparatus to the absorption cell (*f*) in the instrument, and adjust the air or nitrogen flow rate so that in the following procedure, maximum absorption and reproducibility are obtained without excessive foaming in the test solution. Obtain a baseline reading at 253.6 nm, following the manufacturer's instructions for operating the instrument.

Treat the *Standard Preparation* as follows: destroy the excess permanganate by adding a 1:10 solution of hydroxylamine hydrochloride, dropwise, until the solution is colorless. Immediately wash the solution into bottle *c* with water, and dilute with water to the 60-mL mark. Add 2 mL of 10% stannous chloride solution (prepared fresh each week by dissolving 10 g of $SnCl_2 \cdot 2H_2O$ in 20 mL of warm hydrochloric acid and diluting with 80 mL of water), and immediately reconnect bottle *c* to the aerating apparatus. Turn stopcock *b* from the bypass to the aerating position, and continue the aeration until the absorption peak has been passed and the recorder pen has returned to the baseline. Disconnect bottle *c* from the aerating apparatus, discard the *Standard Preparation* mixture, wash bottle *c* with water, and repeat the foregoing procedure using the *Sample Preparation*; any absorbance produced by the *Sample Preparation* does not exceed that produced by the *Standard Preparation*.

Method II

Dithizone Extraction Solution Dissolve 30 mg of dithizone in 1000 mL of chloroform, add 5 mL of alcohol, and mix. Store in a refrigerator. Before use, shake a suitable volume of the solution with about half its volume of 1:100 nitric acid, discarding the nitric acid. Discard the solution after 1 month.

Diluted Dithizone Extraction Solution Just before use, dilute 5 mL of *Dithizone Extraction Solution* with 25 mL of chloroform.

Hydroxylamine Hydrochloride Solution Dissolve 20 g of hydroxylamine hydrochloride in sufficient water to make about 65 mL, transfer the solution into a separator, add a few drops of thymol blue TS, and then add ammonium hydroxide until a yellow color develops. Add 10 mL of a 1:25 solution of sodium diethyldithiocarbamate, mix, and allow to stand for 5 min. Extract the solution with successive 10- to 15-mL portions of chloroform until a 5-mL test portion of the chloroform extract does not develop a yellow color when shaken with a dilute solution of cupric sulfate. Add 2.7 N hydrochloric acid until the extracted solution is pink, adding one or two more drops of thymol blue TS, if necessary, then dilute with water to 100 mL, and mix.

Mercury Stock Solution Transfer 135.4 mg of mercuric chloride, accurately weighed, into a 100-mL volumetric flask, dissolve in and dilute with 1 N sulfuric acid to volume, and mix. Dilute 5.0 mL of this solution with 1 N sulfuric acid to 500.0 mL. Each mL contains the equivalent of 10 μg of mercury.

Diluted Standard Mercury Solution On the day of use, transfer 10.0 mL of *Mercury Stock Solution* into a 100-mL volumetric flask, dilute with 1 N sulfuric acid to volume, and mix. Each mL contains the equivalent of 1 μg of mercury.

Sodium Citrate Solution Dissolve 250 g of sodium citrate dihydrate in 1000 mL of water.

Sample Solution Dissolve 1 g of sample in 30 mL of 1.7 N nitric acid by heating on a steam bath. Cool to room temperature in an ice bath, stir, and pass through S and S No. 589, or equivalent, filter paper that has been previously washed with 1.7 N nitric acid, followed by water. Add 20 mL of *Sodium Citrate Solution* and 1 mL of *Hydroxylamine Hydrochloride Solution* to the filtrate.

Procedure [NOTE—Because mercuric dithizonate is light sensitive, perform this procedure in subdued light.] Prepare a control containing 3.0 mL of *Diluted Standard Mercury Solution* (3 μg Hg), 30 mL of 1.7 N nitric acid, 5 mL of *Sodium Citrate Solution*, and 1 mL of *Hydroxylamine Hydrochloride Solution*. Treat the control and the *Sample Solution* as follows: using a pH meter, adjust the pH of each solution to 1.8 with ammonium hydroxide, and transfer the solutions into different separators. Extract each with two 5-mL portions of *Dithizone Extraction Solution*, and then extract again with 5 mL of chloroform, discarding the aqueous solutions. Transfer the combined extracts from each separator into different separators, add 10 mL of 1:2 hydrochloric acid to each, shake well, and discard the chloroform layers. Extract the acid solutions with about 3 mL of chloroform, shake well, and discard the chloroform layers. Add 0.1 mL of 0.05 M disodium EDTA and 2 mL of 6 N acetic acid to each separator, mix, and then slowly add 5 mL of ammonium hydroxide. Stopper the separators, cool under a stream of cold water, and dry the outside of the separators. To avoid loss, carefully pour the solutions through the tops of the separators into separate beakers, and using a pH meter, adjust the pH of both solutions to 1.8 with 6 N ammonium hydroxide. Return the sample and control solutions to their original separators, add 5.0 mL of *Diluted Dithizone Extraction Solution*, and shake vigorously. Any color developed in the *Sample Solution* does not exceed that in the control.

NICKEL LIMIT TEST

[NOTE—Unless otherwise specified in the individual monograph, use *Method I*.]

Method I

Atomic Absorption System Apparatus Use a suitable atomic absorption spectrometer equipped with a nickel hollow-cathode lamp and an air–acetylene flame to measure the absorbance of the *Blank Preparation*, the *Standard Preparations*, and the *Test Preparation* as directed under *Procedure*.

Test Preparation Dissolve 20.0 g of sample in dilute acetic acid TS, and dilute with the same solvent to 150.0 mL. Add 2.0 mL of a saturated solution of ammonium pyrrolidinedithiocarbamate (about 10 g/L of water) and 10.0 mL of methyl isobutyl ketone, and shake for 30 s. Protect from bright light. Allow the two layers to separate, and use the methyl isobutyl ketone layer.

Blank Preparation Prepare in the same manner as in the *Test Preparation*, but omit the sample.

Standard Preparations Prepare three *Standard Preparations* in the same manner as in the *Test Preparation*, but add 0.5 mL, 1.0 mL, and 1.5 mL, respectively, of 10 mg/kg nickel standard solution TS in addition to 20.0 g of sample.

Procedure Zero the instrument with the *Blank Preparation*. Concomitantly determine the absorbances of each of the *Standard Preparations* and of the *Test Preparation* at least three times each, and record the average of the steady readings for each. Between each measurement, aspirate the *Blank Preparation*, and ascertain that the reading returns to its initial blank value.

Calculation Calculate the linear equation of the graph using a least-squares fit, and derive from it the concentration of nickel in the *Test Preparation*. Alternatively, plot on a graph the mean of the readings against the added quantity of nickel. Extrapolate the line joining the points on the graph until it meets the concentration axis. The distance between this point and the intersection of the axes represents the concentration of nickel in the *Test Preparation*.

Method II

[NOTE—All glassware used must be soaked in *1% Nitric Acid* for at least 2 h, and then rinsed with water.]

1% Nitric Acid Cautiously add 10 mL of nitric acid to a 1000-mL volumetric flask containing about 500 mL of water. Mix, and dilute with water to volume.

Blank Solution Use *1% Nitric Acid*.

Nickel Stock Standard Solution Immediately before use, dilute an appropriate amount of nickel standard[3] with *1% Nitric Acid* to prepare a solution containing the equivalent of 10 µg of nickel per mL.

Standard Solutions Into three identical 100-mL volumetric flasks, introduce respectively 2.0 mL, 5.0 mL, and 10.0 mL of *Nickel Stock Standard solution*. Dilute with *1% Nitric Acid* to volume, and mix. These standards contain 0.2 µg, 0.5 µg, and 1.0 µg of nickel per mL.

Test Solution Weigh accurately a quantity of test specimen containing about 5 g of solids into a 100-mL volumetric flask. Dissolve in and dilute with *1% Nitric Acid* to volume, and mix.

Procedure Concomitantly determine the absorbances of the *Standard Solutions* and the *Test Solution* at least three times each, at the wavelength of maximum absorbance at 232.0 nm, with a suitable atomic absorption spectrophotometer equipped with an air–acetylene flame and a nickel hollow-cathode lamp using the *Blank Solution* to zero the instrument. Record the average of the steady readings for each of the *Standard Solutions* and the *Test Solution*. Clear the nebulizer using the *Blank Solution* and aspirate each of the *Standard Solutions* and the *Test Solution* in turn. The standard chosen for reslope should be run every 4 to 5 samples. If there is a significant change in its response, reslope and repeat the previous samples. The standard deviation for the *Standard Solution* of 0.2 µg of nickel per mL must be less than 20%. Plot the absorbances of the *Standard Solutions* versus the concentration, in µg/mL, of nickel, and draw the straight line best fitting the three plotted points. From the graph so obtained, determine the concentration, C, in µg/mL, of nickel in the *Test Solution*. Calculate the quantity, in µg, of nickel in each g of test specimen taken:

Result = 100C/W

in which W is the weight, in g, of test specimen taken to prepare the *Test Solution*.

PHOSPHORUS LIMIT TEST

Reagents

Ammonium Molybdate Solution (5%): Dissolve 50 g of ammonium molybdate tetrahydrate, $(NH_4)_6Mo_7O_{24} \cdot 4H_2O$, in 900 mL of warm water, cool to room temperature, dilute with water to 1000 mL, and mix.

Ammonium Vanadate Solution (0.25%): Dissolve 2.5 g of ammonium metavanadate, NH_4VO_3, in 600 mL of boiling water, cool to 60°–70°, and add 20 mL of nitric acid. Cool to room temperature, dilute with water to 1000 mL, and mix.

Zinc Acetate Solution (10%): Dissolve 120 g of zinc acetate dihydrate, $Zn(C_2H_3O_2)_2 \cdot 2H_2O$, in 880 mL of water, and pass through Whatman No. 2V or equivalent filter paper before use.

Nitric Acid Solution (29%): Add 300 mL of nitric acid (sp. gr. 1.42) to 600 mL of water, and mix.

Standard Phosphorus Solution (100 µg P in 1 mL): Dissolve 438.7 mg of monobasic potassium phosphate, KH_2PO_4, in water in a 1000-mL volumetric flask, dilute with water to volume, and mix.

Standard Curve Pipet 5.0 mL, 10.0 mL, and 15.0 mL of the *Standard Phosphorus Solution* into separate 100-mL volumetric flasks. To each of these flasks, and to a fourth, blank flask, add in the order stated 10 mL of *Nitric Acid Solution*, 10 mL of *Ammonium Vanadate Solution*, and 10 mL of *Ammonium Molybdate Solution*, mixing thoroughly after each addition. Dilute with water to volume, mix, and allow to stand for 10 min. Determine the absorbance of each standard solution in a 1-cm cell at 460 nm, with a suitable spectrophotometer, using the blank to set the instrument to zero. Prepare a standard curve by plotting the absorbance of each solution versus its concentration, in mg of phosphorus (P) per 100 mL.

Treated Sample Place 20–25 g of the starch sample in a 250-mL beaker, add 200 mL of a 7:3 mixture of methanol and water, disperse the sample, and agitate mechanically for 15 min. Recover the starch by vacuum filtration in a 150-mL medium-porosity fritted-glass or Büchner funnel, and wash the wet cake with 200 mL of the methanol and water mixture. Reslurry the wet cake in the solvent, and wash it a second time in the same manner. Dry the filter cake in an air oven at a temperature below 50°, then grind the sample to 20-mesh or finer, and blend thoroughly. Determine the

---

[3] Suitable nickel standards are available from e.g. Fisher Scientific, Fair Lawn, NJ (nickel, reference standard solution, 1000 ppm ± 1%, certified, application: for atomic absorption) or RICCA Chemical Company, Arlington, TX (nickel standard, 1000 ppm Ni, for atomic absorption).

amount of dry substance by drying a 5-g portion in a vacuum oven, not exceeding 100 mm Hg, at 120° for 5 h.

[NOTE—The treatment outlined above is satisfactory for starch products that are insoluble in cold water. For pregelatinized starch and other water-soluble starches, prepare a 1%–2% aqueous paste, place it in a cellophane tube, and dialyze against running distilled water for 30–40 h. Precipitate the starch by pouring the solution into 4 volumes of acetone per volume of paste while stirring. Recover the starch by vacuum filtration in a medium-porosity fritted-glass or Büchner funnel, and wash the filter cake with absolute ethanol. Dry the filter cake, and determine the amount of dry substance as directed for water-insoluble starches.]

Sample Preparation Transfer about 10 g of the *Treated Sample*, calculated on the dry-substance basis and accurately weighed, into a Vycor dish, and add 10 mL of *Zinc Acetate Solution* in a fine stream, distributing the solution uniformly in the sample. Carefully evaporate to dryness on a hot plate, then increase the heat, and carbonize the sample on the hot plate or over a gas flame. Ignite in a muffle furnace at 550° until the ash is free from carbon (about 1–2 h), and cool. Wet the ash with 15 mL of water, and slowly wash down the sides of the dish with 5 mL of *Nitric Acid Solution*. Heat to boiling, cool, and quantitatively transfer the mixture into a 200-mL volumetric flask, rinsing the dish with three 20-mL portions of water and adding the rinsings to the flask. Dilute with water to volume, and mix. Transfer an accurately measured aliquot (V, in mL) of this solution, containing not more than 1.5 mg of phosphorus, into a 100-mL volumetric flask, and add 50 mL of water to a second flask to serve as a blank. To each flask add in the order stated 10 mL of *Nitric Acid Solution*, 10 mL of *Ammonium Vanadate Solution*, and 10 mL of *Ammonium Molybdate Solution*, mixing thoroughly after each addition. Dilute with water to volume, mix, and allow to stand for 10 min.

Procedure Determine the absorbance of the *Sample Preparation* in a 1-cm cell at 460 nm, with a suitable spectrophotometer, using the blank to set the instrument at zero. From the *Standard Curve*, determine the mg of phosphorus in the aliquot taken, recording this value as a. Calculate the amount, in mg/kg, of phosphorus (P) in the original sample:

$$\text{mg/kg P} = (a \times 200 \times 1000)/(V \times W)$$

in which W is the weight, in grams, of the sample taken.

SELENIUM LIMIT TEST

Change to read:
Reagents and Solutions

2,3-Diaminonaphthalene Solution: On the day of use, dissolve 100 mg of 2,3-diaminonaphthalene ($C_{10}H_{10}N_2$) and 500 mg of hydroxylamine hydrochloride ($NH_2OH \cdot HCl$) in sufficient 0.1 N hydrochloric acid to make 100 mL.

Selenium Stock Solution: Transfer 40.0 mg of powdered metallic selenium into a 1000-mL volumetric flask, and dissolve in 100 mL of 1:2 nitric acid, warming gently on a steam bath to effect solution. Cool, dilute with water to volume, and mix.

Selenium Standard Solution: Pipet 5.0 mL of *Selenium Stock Solution* into a 200-mL volumetric flask, dilute with water to volume, and mix. Each mL of this solution contains the equivalent of 1 µg of selenium (Se). ▲Alternatively, the solution may be prepared using a commercially available stock solution diluted to 1 µg/mL.▲FCC8

Method I

Standard Preparation Pipet 6.0 mL of *Selenium Standard Solution* into a 150-mL beaker, add 50 mL of 0.25 N nitric acid, and mix.

Sample Preparation Using a 1000-mL combustion flask and 25 mL of 0.5 N nitric acid as the absorbing liquid, proceed as directed under *Oxygen Flask Combustion*, Appendix I, using the amount of sample specified in the individual monograph (and the magnesium oxide or other reagent, where specified).

[NOTE—If the sample contains water of hydration or more than 1% of moisture, dry it at 140° for 2 h before combustion, unless otherwise directed.]

Upon completion of combustion, place a few mL of water in the cup or lip of the combustion flask, loosen the stopper of the flask, and rinse the stopper, sample holder, and sides of the flask with about 10 mL of water. Transfer the solution, with the aid of about 20 mL of water, into a 150-mL beaker, heat gently to boiling, boil for 10 min, and cool.

Procedure Treat the *Sample Preparation*, the *Standard Preparation*, and 50 mL of 0.25 N nitric acid, to serve as the blank, similarly and in parallel as follows: add a 1:2 solution of ammonium hydroxide to adjust the pH of the solution to 2.0 ± 0.2. Dilute with water to 60.0 mL, and transfer to a low-actinic separator with the aid of 10.0 mL of water, adding the 10.0 mL of rinsings to the separator. Add 200 mg of hydroxylamine hydrochloride, swirl to dissolve, immediately add 5.0 mL of *2,3-Diaminonaphthalene Solution*, insert the stopper, and swirl to mix. Allow the solution to stand at room temperature for 100 min. Add 5.0 mL of cyclohexane, shake vigorously for 2 min, and allow the layers to separate. Discard the aqueous phases, and centrifuge the cyclohexane extracts to remove any traces of water. Determine the absorbance of each extract in a 1-cm cell at the maximum at about 380 nm with a suitable spectrophotometer, using the extract from the blank to set the instrument. The absorbance of the extract from the *Sample Preparation* is not greater than that from the *Standard Preparation* when a 200-mg sample is tested, or not greater than one-half the absorbance of the extract from the *Standard Preparation* when a 100-mg sample is tested.

Method II

Standard Preparation Pipet 6.0 mL of *Selenium Standard Solution* into a 150-mL beaker, add 50 mL of 2 N hydrochloric acid, and mix.

Sample Preparation Transfer the amount of the sample specified in the individual monograph into a 150-mL beaker, dissolve in 25 mL of 4 N hydrochloric acid, swirling if necessary to effect solution, heat gently to boiling, and digest on a steam bath for 15 min. Remove from heat, add 25 mL of water, and allow to cool to room temperature.

Procedure Place the beakers containing the *Standard Preparation* and the *Sample Preparation* in a fume hood, and to a third beaker add 50 mL of 2 N hydrochloric acid to serve as the blank. Cautiously add 5 mL of ammonium hydroxide to each beaker, mix, and allow the solution to cool. Treat each solution, similarly and in parallel, as directed under *Procedure* in *Method I*, beginning with "Add a 1:2 solution of ammonium hydroxide...".

C. OTHERS

ALGINATES ASSAY

In a suitable closed system, liberate the carbon dioxide from the uronic acid groups of about 250 mg of the test sample by heating with hydrochloric acid, and sweep the carbon dioxide, by means of an inert gas, into a titration vessel containing excess standardized sodium hydroxide. Any suitable system may be used as long as it provides precautions against leakage and overheating of the reaction mixture, adequate sweeping time, avoidance of entrainment of hydrochloric acid, and meets the requirements of the *System Suitability Test*. One suitable system, with accompanying procedure, is given below.

Apparatus The apparatus is shown in *Figure 7*. It consists essentially of a soda lime column, *A*, a mercury valve, *B*, connected through a side arm, *C*, to a reaction flask, *D*, by means of a rubber connection. Flask *D* is a 100-mL round-bottom, long-neck boiling flask, resting in a suitable heating mantle, *E*.

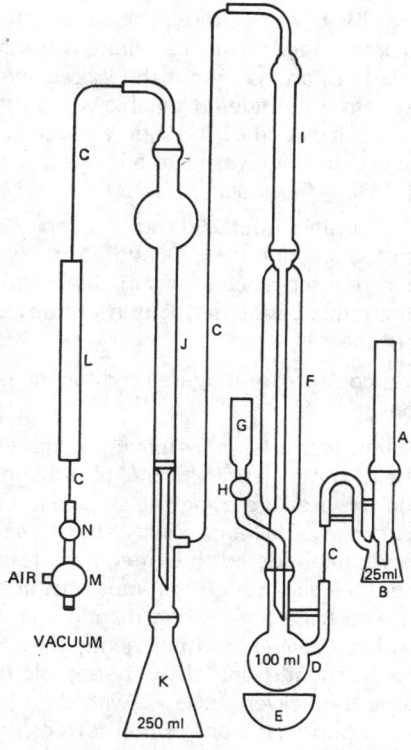

Figure 7. Apparatus for Alginates Assay

The reaction flask is provided with a reflux condenser, *F*, to which is fitted a delivery tube, *G*, of 40-mL capacity, having a stopcock, *H*. The reflux condenser terminates in a trap, *I*, containing 25 g of 20-mesh zinc or tin, which can be connected with an absorption tower, *J*.

The absorption tower consists of a 45-cm tube fitted with a medium-porosity fritted glass disk sealed to the inner part above the side arm and having a delivery tube sealed to it extending down to the end of the tube. A trap, consisting of a bulb of approximately 100-mL capacity, is blown above the fritted disk and the outer portion of a ground spherical joint is sealed on above the bulb. A 250-mL Erlenmeyer flask, *K*, is connected to the bottom of the absorption tower. The top of the tower is connected to a soda lime tower, *L*, which is connected to a suitable pump to provide vacuum and air supply, the choice of which is made by a three-way stopcock, *M*. The volume of air or vacuum is controlled by a capillary-tube regulator or needle valve, *N*.

All joints are a size 35/25 ground spherical type.

Standard D-Glucurono-6,3-lactone This chemical ($C_6H_8O_6$) is available as a reference standard with an assay of 100.0 ± 1.0% (24.99 ± 0.25% CO_2) from Aldrich Chemical Co.

System Suitability Test Transfer about 250.0 mg of Standard D-*Glucurono-6,3-lactone*, accurately weighed, into the reaction flask, *D*, and carry out the *Procedure* described below. The system is considered suitable when the net titration results in a calculation of %CO$_2$ in a range of 24.73–25.26, which is equivalent to a range of 98.95%–101.06% D-*Glucurono-6,3-lactone*.

Procedure Transfer about 250 mg of sample, accurately weighed, into the reaction flask, *D*, add 25 mL of 0.1 N hydrochloric acid, insert several boiling chips, and connect the flask to the reflux condenser, *F*, using syrupy phosphoric acid as a lubricant.

[NOTE—Stopcock grease may be used for the other connections.]

Check the system for air leaks by forcing mercury up into the inner tube of the mercury valve, *B*, to a height of about 5 cm. Turn off the pressure using the stopcock, *M*. If the mercury level does not fall appreciably after 1–2 min, the apparatus may be considered to be free from leaks. Draw carbon dioxide-free air through the apparatus at a rate of 3000–6000 mL/h. Raise the heating mantle, *E*, to the flask, heat the sample to boiling, and boil gently for 2 min. Turn off and lower the mantle, and allow the sample to cool for 15 min. Charge the delivery tube, *G*, with 23 mL of hydrochloric acid. Disconnect the absorption tower, *J*, rapidly transfer 25.0 mL of 0.25 N sodium hydroxide into the tower, add 5 drops of *n*-butanol, and reconnect the absorption tower. Draw carbon dioxide-free air through the apparatus at the rate of about 2000 mL/h, add the hydrochloric acid to the reaction flask through the delivery tube, raise the heating mantle, and heat the reaction mixture to boiling. After 2 h, discontinue the current of air and heating. Force the sodium hydroxide solution down into the flask, *K*, using gentle air pressure, and then rinse down the absorption tower with three 15-mL portions of water, forcing each washing into the flask with air pressure. Remove the flask, and add to it 10 mL of a 10% solution of barium chloride (BaCl$_2$·2H$_2$O). Stopper the flask, shake gently for about 2 min, add phenolphthalein TS, and titrate with 0.1 N hydrochloric acid. Perform a blank determination (see *General Provisions*). Each mL of 0.25 N sodium hydroxide consumed is equivalent to 5.5 mg of carbon dioxide (CO$_2$). Calculate the results on the dried basis.

α-AMINO NITROGEN (AN) DETERMINATION

Transfer 7–25 g of sample, accurately weighed, into a 500-mL volumetric flask with the aid of several 50-mL portions of warm, ammonia-free water, dilute with water to volume, and mix. Neutralize 20.0 mL of the solution with 0.2 N barium hydroxide or 0.2 N sodium hydroxide, using phenolphthalein TS as the indicator, and add 10 mL of freshly prepared phenolphthalein–formol solution (50 mL of 40% formaldehyde containing 1 mL of 0.05% phenolphthalein in 50% alcohol neutralized exactly to pH 7 with 0.2 N barium hydroxide or 0.2 N sodium hydroxide). Titrate with 0.2 N barium hydroxide or 0.2 N sodium hydroxide to a distinct red color, add a small, but accurately measured, volume of 0.2 N barium hydroxide or 0.2 N sodium hydroxide in excess, and back titrate to neutrality with 0.2 N hydrochloric acid. Conduct a blank titration using the same reagents, with 20 mL of water in place of the test solution. Each mL of 0.2 N barium hydroxide or 0.2 N sodium hydroxide is equivalent to 2.8 mg of α-amino nitrogen.

AMMONIA NITROGEN (NH$_3$-N) DETERMINATION

[CAUTION—Provide adequate ventilation.]

[NOTE—Use nitrogen-free reagents, where available, or reagents very low in nitrogen content.]

Transfer between 700 mg and 2.2 g of sample into a 500- to 800-mL Kjeldahl digestion flask of hard, moderately thick, well-annealed glass. If desired, wrap the sample, if solid or semisolid, in nitrogen-free filter paper to facilitate the transfer.

Add about 200 mL of water, and mix. Add a few granules of zinc to prevent bumping, tilt the flask, and cautiously pour sodium hydroxide pellets, or a 2:5 sodium hydroxide solution, down the inside of the flask so that it forms a layer under the solution, using a sufficient amount (usually about 25 g of solid sodium hydroxide) to make the mixture strongly alkaline. Immediately connect the flask to a distillation apparatus consisting of a Kjeldahl connecting bulb and a condenser that has a delivery tube extending well beneath the surface of a measured excess of 0.5 N hydrochloric or sulfuric acid contained in a 500-mL flask. Add 5 to 7 drops of methyl red indicator (1 g of methyl red in 200 mL of alcohol) to the receiver flask. Rotate the Kjeldahl flask to mix its contents thoroughly, and heat until all of the ammonia has distilled, collecting at least 150 mL of distillate. Wash the tip of the delivery tube, collecting the washings in the receiving flask, and titrate the excess acid with 0.5 N sodium hydroxide. Perform a blank determination (see *General Provisions*), substituting 2 g of sucrose for the sample, and make any necessary correction. Each mL of 0.5 N acid consumed is equivalent to 7.003 mg of ammonia nitrogen.

[NOTE—If it is known that the substance to be determined has a low nitrogen content, 0.1 N acid and alkali may be used, in which case each mL of 0.1 N acid consumed is equivalent to 1.401 mg of nitrogen.]

Calculate the percent ammonia nitrogen:

$$\text{Result} = (NH_3\text{-}N/S) \times 100$$

in which NH$_3$-N is the weight, in mg, of ammonia nitrogen, and S is the weight, in mg, of the sample.

BENZENE (in Paraffinic Hydrocarbon Solvents)

Apparatus (See *Chromatography*, Appendix IIA.) Use a suitable gas chromatograph, equipped with a column, or equivalent, that will elute *n*-decane before benzene under the conditions of the System Suitability Test. Column materials and conditions that have been found suitable for this method are listed in the accompanying tables. See Figure 8 for a typical chromatogram obtained with column No. 5.

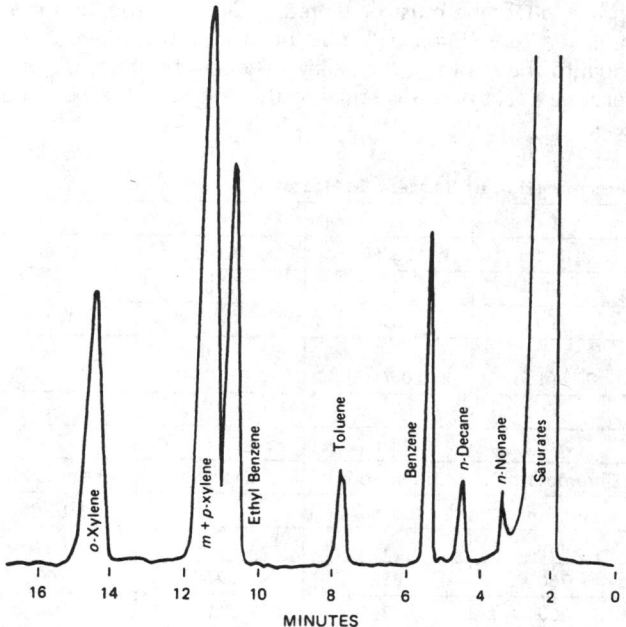

Figure 8. Typical Chromatogram for the Determination of Benzene in Hexanes Using Column No. 5

Reagents

Isooctane: 99 mole percent minimum containing less than 0.05 mole percent aromatic material

Benzene: 99.5 mole percent minimum

Internal Standard: n-Decane and either n-undecane or n-dodecane according to the requirement of the System Suitability Test

Reference Solution A: Prepare a standard solution containing 0.5% by weight each of the Internal Standard and of benzene in isooctane.

Reference Solution B: Prepare a standard solution containing about 0.5% by weight each of n-decane, of Internal Standard, and of benzene in isooctane.

Calibration Select the instrument conditions necessary to give the desired sensitivity. Inject a known volume of Reference Solution A, and change the attenuation, if necessary, so that the benzene peak is measured with a chart deflection of not less than 25% or more than 95% of full scale. When choosing the attenuation, consider all unresolved peaks to represent a single compound. There may be tailing of the nonaromatic peak, but do not use any conditions that lead to a depth of the valley ahead of the benzene peak (A) less than 50% of the weight of the benzene peak (B) as depicted in Figure 9.

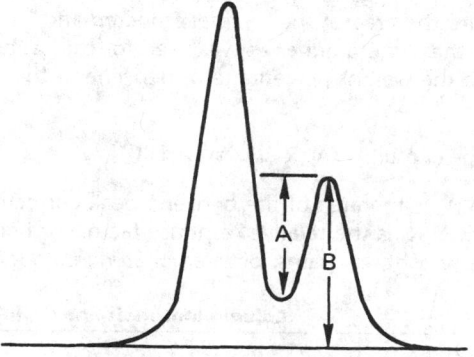

Figure 9. Illustration of A/B Ratio

If there is tailing of the nonaromatic material, construct a baseline by drawing a line from the bottom of the valley ahead of the benzene peak to the point of tangency after the peak (see Figure 10). Measure the areas of the benzene peak and the internal standard peak by any of the following means: triangulation, planimeter, paper cutout, or mechanical or electronic integrator. Do not use integrators on peaks without a constant baseline, unless the integrator has provision for making baseline corrections with accuracy at least as good as that of manual methods.

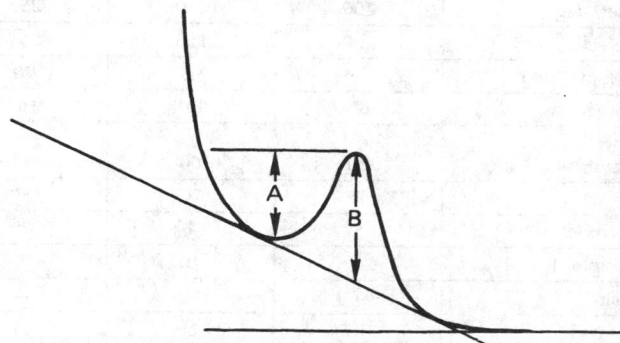

Figure 10. Illustration of A/B Ratio for a Small Component Peak on the Tail of a Large Peak

Calculate a response factor for benzene (R_b) relative to the Internal Standard:

$$\text{Result} = A_i/W_i \times W_b/A_b$$

in which A_i is the area of the Internal Standard peak in arbitrary units corrected for attenuation; W_i is the weight percent of Internal Standard in Reference Solution A; W_b is the weight percent of benzene in Reference Solution A; and A_b is the area of the benzene peak in arbitrary units corrected for attenuation.

Procedure Place approximately 0.1 mL of Internal Standard into a tared 25-mL volumetric flask, weigh on an analytical balance, and dissolve in and dilute with the sample to be analyzed to volume.

Using the exact instrumental conditions that were used in the calibration, inject the same volume of sample containing the Internal Standard. Before measuring the area of the Internal Standard and benzene peaks, change the attenuation to ensure at least 25% chart deflection.

1282 / Appendix III / General Tests and Assays

Measure the area of the *Internal Standard* and benzene peaks in the same manner as was used for the calibration. Calculate the weight percentage of benzene in the sample (W_B):

$$\text{Result} = (A_b \times R_b \times W_i \times 100)/(A_i \times S)$$

in which A_b is the area of the benzene peak corrected for attenuation; R_b is the relative response factor for benzene; W_i is the weight, in grams, of *Internal Standard* added; A_i is the area of the *Internal Standard* peak corrected for attenuation; and S is the weight, in grams, of the sample taken.

System Suitability Test Inject the same volume of *Reference Solution B* as in the *Calibration* and record the chromatogram. *n*-Decane must be eluted before benzene, and the ratio of A to B (*Figure 19*) must be at least 0.5 where A is equal to the depth of the valley between the *n*-decane and benzene peaks and B is equal to the height of the benzene peak.

Column Materials and Conditions for the Determination of Benzene in Hexanes

Column No.	1	2	3	4	5	6	7
Liquid phase	CEF	PEF 200	CEF	DEGS	TCEPE	TCEPE	DEGS
Length, ft	15	6	16	10	15	100	12
m	—	4.5	2	5	3.1	—	313.7
Diameter, in (mm) Inside	0.07(1.8)	—	0.07	0.18(4.5)	0.06(1.5)	0.01(.254)	
Outside	1/8(3.2)	1/4(6.4)	1/8	—	—	—	1/8
Weight, percent	17	30	20	20	10	—	20
Solid support	Chromosorb P	Chromosorb P	Chromosorb P	Chromosorb P	Chromosorb P	Capillary	Chromosorb P
Mesh	60–80	60–80	60–80	80–100	60–80	—	80–100
Treatment	AW	AW	AW	none	AW	none	AW Sil
Inlet, deg	200	210	250	260	250	275	260
Detector, deg	200	155	250	200	175	250	240
Column, deg	115	95	90	100	115	95	65
Carrier gas	N_2	He	He	He	N_2	N_2	He
Flow rate, cm³/min	30	60	60	60	1	3	52
Detector	FI	TC	FI	FI	FI	FI	FI
Recorder, mV	5	1	1	1	10	1	1
Sample, 1	5	10	1	2	5	0.8	5
Split	9 + 1	—	—	—	100 + 1	100 − 1	—
Area	Tri	EI	DI	Tri Plan	EI	EI	Tri

Abbreviations Used in Table: AW—Acid washed; CEF—*N,N*-Bis(2-cyanoethyl)formamide; DEGS—Diethylene Glycol Succinate; DI—Disk integrator; EI—Electronic integrator; FI—Flame ionization; Sil—Silanized; TC—Thermal conductivity; TCEPE—Tetracyanoethylated Pentaerythritrol; Tri—Triangulation.

Retention Times in Minutes for Selected Hydrocarbons under the Conditions for the Determination of Benzene in Hexanes

Column No.	1	2	3	4	5	6	7
Benzene	3.4	2.0	6.5	6.7	5.4	6.1	6.7
Toluene	4.4	3.2	9.0	10.3	7.8	7.0	10.3
Ethylbenzene	5.4	5.2	11.5	14.8	10.8	8.0	14.8
p-m-Xylenes	5.8	—	12.5	—	11.4	8.5	—
o-Xylene	7.5	6.8	17.0	16.1	14.5	10.0	—
n-Undecane	3.0	2.8	3.5	—	—	—	—
n-Dodecane	—	—	—	12.8	8.5	6.5	—

Color Determination

Chromium

Standards

Standard Chromium Solution (1000 mg/kg): Transfer 2.829 g of $K_2Cr_2O_7$, accurately weighed (NIST No. 136) into a 1-L volumetric flask; dissolve in and dilute with water to volume.

Standard Colorant Solution: Transfer 62.5 g of colorant previously shown to be free of chromium to a 1-L volumetric flask; dissolve in and dilute with water to volume.

Apparatus Use any suitable atomic absorption spectrophotometer equipped with a fast response recorder and capable of measuring the radiation absorbed at 357.9 nm.

Instrument Parameters *Wavelength setting*: 357.9 nm; *optical passes*: 5; *lamp current*: 8 mA; *lamp voltage*: 500 v; *fuel*: hydrogen; *oxidant*: air; *recorder*: l mv with a scale expansion of 5 or 10. Alternatively, follow the instructions supplied with the instrument.

Procedure Set the instrument at the optimum conditions for measuring chromium as directed by the manufacturer's instructions. Prepare a series of seven standard chromium solutions containing Cr at approximately 5 mg/kg, 10 mg/kg, 15 mg/kg, 20 mg/kg, 40 mg/kg, 50 mg/kg, and 60 mg/kg by appropriate dilutions of the *Standard Chromium Solution* into 100-mL volumetric flasks; add 80 mL of the *Standard Colorant Solution*, and dilute each flask with water to volume.

Transfer 5 g of the colorant to be analyzed to a 100-mL volumetric flask; dissolve in and dilute with water to volume. Prepare a calibration curve using the series of standards, and using this curve, determine the chromium content of the colorant samples.

Ether Extracts

[CAUTION—Isopropyl ether forms explosive peroxides. To ensure the absence of peroxides, perform the following test: prepare a colorless solution of ferrous thiocyanate by mixing equal volumes of 0.1 N ferrous sulfate and 0.1 N ammonium thiocyanate. Using titanous chloride, carefully discharge any red coloration due to ferric ions. Add 10 mL of ether to 50 mL of the solution, and shake vigorously for 2–3 min. A red color indicates the presence of peroxides. If redistillation is necessary, the usual precautions against peroxide detonation should be observed. Immediately before use, pass the ether through a 30-cm column of chromatography-grade aluminum oxide to remove peroxides and inhibitors.]

Apparatus Use an upward displacement-type liquid–liquid extractor, as shown in *Figure 11*, with a sintered-glass diffuser and a working capacity of 200 mL. Suspend a piece of bright copper wire through the condenser, and place a small coil of copper wire (about 0.5 g) in the distillation flask.

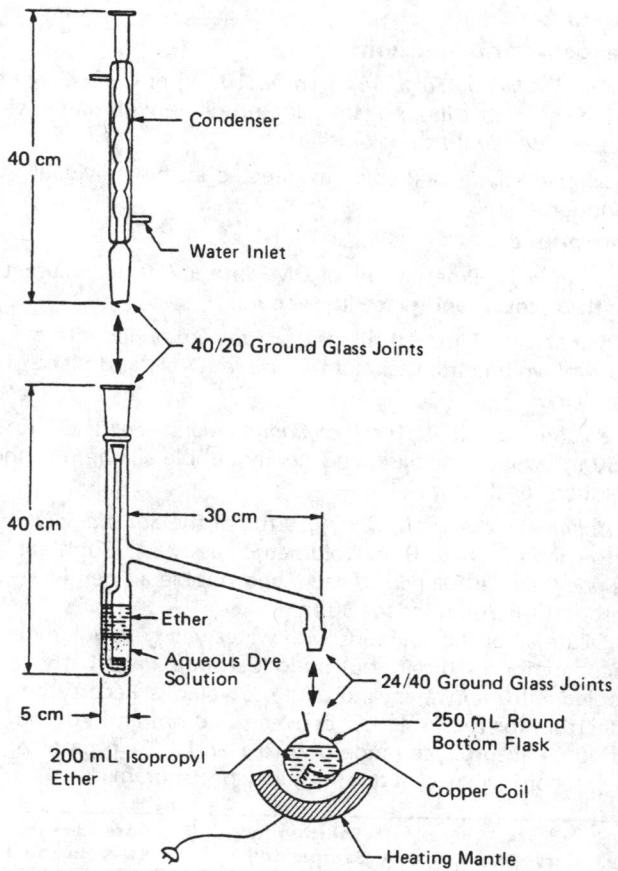

Figure 11. Upward Displacement-Type Liquid–Liquid Extractor with Sintered-Glass Diffuser

Alkaline Ether Extract Transfer 5 g of the colorant to a beaker, and dissolve in 150 mL of water. Add 2 mL of 2.5 N NaOH solution, transfer the solution into the extractor, and dilute with water to approximately 200 mL. Add 200 mL of ether to the distillation flask, and extract for 2 h with a reflux rate of about 15 mL/min. Set the extracted colorant solution aside. Transfer the ether extract into a separatory funnel, and wash with two 25-mL portions of 0.1 N NaOH followed by two 25-mL portions of water. Reduce the volume of the ether extract to about 5 mL by distillation (in portions) from a tared flask containing a small piece of clean copper coil.

Acid Ether Extract Add 5 mL of 3 N hydrochloric acid to the extracted colorant solution set aside in the alkaline ether extract procedure above, mix, and extract with ether as directed above. Wash the ether extract with two 25-mL portions of 0.1 N hydrochloric acid and water. Transfer the washed ether in portions to the flask containing the evaporated alkaline extract, and carefully remove all the ether by distillation. Dry the residue in an oven at 85° for 20 min. Then allow the flask to cool in a desiccator for 30 min, and weigh. Repeat drying and cooling until a constant weight is

---

[4] To be used or sold for use to color food that is marketed in the United States, color additives must be from batches that have been certified by the U.S. Food and Drug Administration (FDA). If color additives are not from FDA-certified batches, they are not permitted color additives for food use in the United States, even if they are compositionally equivalent. The FD&C names can be applied only to FDA-certified batches of these color additives.

obtained. The increase in weight of the tared flask, expressed as a percentage of the sample weight, is the combined ether extract.

Leuco Base

Reagents and Solutions

Cupric Chloride Solution: Transfer 10.0 g of $CuCl_2 \cdot 2H_2O$ to a 1-L volumetric flask; dissolve in and dilute with dimethylformamide (DMF) to volume.

Sample Solution: Prepare as directed in the individual monograph.

Procedure

Solution 1: Pipet 50 mL of DMF into a 250-mL volumetric flask, cover, and place in the dark.

Solution 2: Pipet 10 mL of the *Sample Solution* into a 250-mL volumetric flask, add 50 mL of DMF, and place in the dark.

Solution 3: Pipet 50 mL of *Cupric Chloride Solution* into a 250-mL volumetric flask, and gently bubble air through the solution for 30 min.

Solutions 4a and 4b: Pipet 10 mL of the *Sample Solution* into each of two 250-mL volumetric flasks, add 50 mL of *Cupric Chloride Solution* to each, and bubble air gently through the solutions for 30 min.

Dilute all of the solutions with water nearly to volume; incubate for 5–10 min, but no longer, in a water bath cooled with tap water; and dilute to volume. Record the spectrum for each solution between 500 nm and 700 nm using an absorbance range of 0 to 1 and a 1-cm pathlength cell; record all spectra on the same spectrogram.

Curve No.	Solution in Sample Cell	Solution in Reference Cell
I	1	1
II	1	2
III	3	3
IVa	3	4a
IVb	3	4b

Calculation

$$\% \text{Leuco Base} = \frac{[(IV - III) - (II - I)] \times 2500}{a \times W \times r}$$

in which the Roman numerals I through IV represent the absorbance readings for solutions of the corresponding Arabic numerals (above) at the wavelength maximum; a is the absorptivity (for Fast Green, a = 0.156 at 625 nm; for Brillant Blue, a = 0.164 at 630 nm); W is the weight, in grams, of the sample taken; and r is the ratio of the molecular weights of colorant and leuco base (for Fast Green, r = 0.9712; for Brillant Blue, r = 0.9706).

Mercury

Apparatus The apparatus used for the direct microdetermination of mercury is shown in *Figure 12*. It consists of a quartz combustion tube designed to hold a porcelain combustion boat (60 × 10 × 8 mm) and a small piece of copper oxide wire. The combustion tube is placed in a heavy-duty hinged combustion tube furnace (Lindburg Type 70T, or equivalent), and it is connected by clamped ball-joints at one end to a source of nitrogen and connected to a series of three traps at the other. The traps are constructed of a linear array of 18- × 2-mm Pyrex tubes connected by clamped ball-joints and extend from the connection at the combustion tube. Trap I contains anhydrous calcium sulfate packed between quartz-wool plugs, trap II contains ascarite packed between cotton plugs, and trap III contains aluminum oxide packed between cotton plugs. The nitrogen flow forces the mercury through the combustion tube, the three traps, and a section of Tygon tube to a mercury vapor meter (Beckman model K-23, or equivalent). The mercury released from a sample during combustion is quantitated by comparing the recorder response with that given by a series of mercury standards.

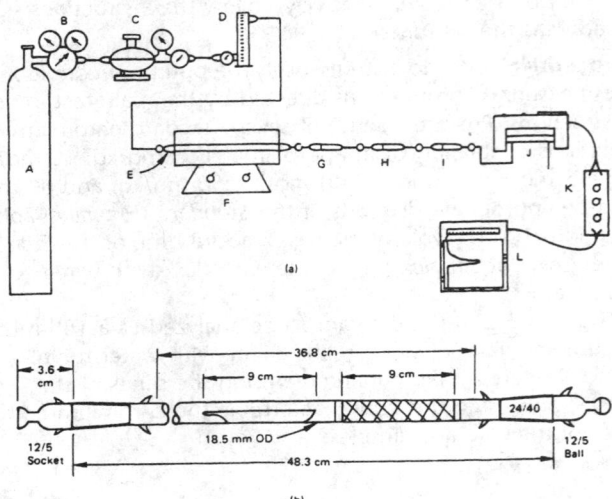

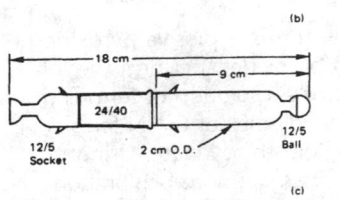

Figure 12. (a) Schematic Diagram of Apparatus for Photometric Mercury Vapor M Method:

A. Tank of nitrogen	G. Dehydrite trap
B. Two-stage pressure regulator	H. Ascarite trap
C. Low-pressure regulator	I. Aluminum oxide trap
D. Flowmeter	J. Mercury vapor meter
E. Combustion tube	K. Atenuator
F. Combustion-tube furnace	L. Recorder
(b) Quartz Combustion Tube with Boat and Copper Oxide Packing;	
(c) Schematic Diagram of Trap Used to Contain Ascarite, Dehydrite, and Aluminum Oxide.	

Reagents and Equipment

Absorbent Cotton

Aluminum Oxide: Anhydrous

Calcium Sulfate: Anhydrous, dehydrate, or equivalent

Asbestos Pads: (1 × 0.5 × 1 cm) Preheated at 800° for 1 h

Ascarite: 20- to 30-mesh

Copper Oxide Wire: Preheated at 850° for 2 h

Nitrogen: Purified grade

Quartz Wool

Sodium Carbonate: Anhydrous, fine granular

Standard Solution: Transfer approximately 1.35 g of reagent-grade mercurous chloride, accurately weighed, into a 1-L volumetric flask. Dissolve in and dilute with water to volume. When diluted 100-fold, the solution contains 0.01 µg Hg per microliter (*Diluted Standard Solution*).

Procedure Preheat the furnace to 650°, and adjust the nitrogen flow to 1 L/min.

Blank Analysis: Place a square piece of preheated asbestos pad in the combustion boat, and cover it with sodium carbonate. Stop the nitrogen flow, disconnect the ball-joint, quickly insert the boat into the combustion tube with large forceps, and reconnect the joint. Note the time, allow the boat to sit in the tube with no nitrogen flow for exactly 1 min, and then restart the flow of nitrogen. Mercury elutes almost immediately with the reinstated nitrogen flow; note the recorder response. Allow about 30 s between runs.

Calibration: Determine the recorder response after the application to the asbestos pad of 1 µL, 2 µL, and 3 µL of the *Diluted Standard Solution*.

Sample Analysis: Transfer 25 mg of colorant, accurately weighed, to the combustion boat, and cover the sample completely with sodium carbonate. Follow the procedure used for the *Blank Analysis*, and calculate the mercury content using the standard curve.

Trap Problems

1. Some colorants (e.g., Brillant Blue and Fast Green) may give a response that is symmetrically dissimilar to the Hg peak. If such a response "carries over" to the next sample, then the aluminum oxide trap may need to be changed.
2. If the recorder response is of inadequate sensitivity (peak height induced by 0.01 µg less than 0.5 cm), then the traps are packed too tightly. Remove or redistribute packing first in the aluminum oxide trap, then try the other traps.
3. The traps will need changing periodically as indicated by a change in the physical appearance of the trap material or by chart responses of different retention times or different symmetry from that of mercury standards.
4. If two or more standards are run in succession, a later sample might give an erroneous mercury response. Run blanks and then repeat the sample analysis to confirm the validity of the response.

Sodium Chloride

Dissolve approximately 2 g of colorant, accurately weighed, in 100 mL of water, and add 10 g of activated carbon that is free of chloride and sulfate. Boil gently for 2–3 min. Cool to room temperature, add 1 mL of 6 N nitric acid, and stir. Dilute with water to volume in a 200-mL volumetric flask, and then filter through dry paper. Repeat the treatment with 2-g portions of carbon until no color is adsorbed onto filter paper dipped into the filtrate.

Transfer 50 mL of filtrate to a 250-mL flask. Add 2 mL of 6 N nitric acid, 5 mL of nitrobenzene, and 10 mL of standardized 0.1 N silver nitrate solution. Shake the flask until the silver chloride coagulates. Prepare a saturated solution of ferric ammonium sulfate, and add just enough concentrated nitric acid to discharge the red color; add 1 mL of this solution to the 250-mL flask to serve as the indicator. Titrate with 0.1 N ammonium thiocyanate solution that has been standardized against the silver nitrate solution until the color persists after shaking for 1 min. Calculate the weight percent of sodium chloride, P:

$$P = [(V \times N)/W] \times 22.79$$

in which V is the net volume, in mL, of silver nitrate solution required; N is the normality of the silver nitrate solution; and W is the weight, in grams, of the sample taken. The factor 22.79 incorporates a total volume of 195 mL because 10 g of activated carbon occupies 5 mL.

Sodium Sulfate

Place 25 mL of the decolorized filtrate obtained from the *Sodium Chloride* test into a 125-mL Erlenmeyer flask, and add 1 drop of a 0.5% phenolphthalein solution in 50% ethanol. Add 0.05 N sodium hydroxide, dropwise, until the solution is alkaline to pH paper, and then add 0.002 N hydrochloric acid until the indicator is decolorized. Add 25 mL of ethanol and about 0.2 g of tetrahydroquinone sulfate indicator. Titrate with 0.03 N barium chloride solution to a red endpoint. Make a blank determination.

Calculate the weight percent, P, of sodium sulfate:

$$P = [(V - B) \times N/W] \times 55.4$$

in which V is the volume, in mL, of barium chloride solution required to titrate the sample; B is the volume, in mL, of barium chloride solution required for the blank; N is the normality of the barium chloride solution; and W is the weight, in grams, of the sample taken. The factor 55.4 incorporates a total volume of 195 mL because 10 g of activated carbon occupies 5 mL.

Total Color

Method I (Spectrophotometric)

Pipet 10.0 mL of the dissolved colorant into a 250-mL Erlenmeyer flask containing 90 mL of 0.04 N ammonium acetate, and mix well. Determine the net absorbance of the solution relative to water at the wavelength maximum given for each color. Calculate the percentage of colorant present:

$$\%\text{total color} = A/(a \times C \times b) \times 100$$

in which A is the absorbance; a is the absorptivity specified in the individual monograph (L/(mg·cm); C is the concentration of sample in the final test solution (mg/L); and b is the cell pathlength (cm).

Method II (Titration with Titanium Chloride)

Apparatus The apparatus for determining total color by titration with titanium chloride ($TiCl_3$) is shown in *Figure 13*. It consists of a storage bottle, A, of 0.1 N titanium chloride titrant maintained under hydrogen produced by a Kipp generator; an Erlenmeyer flask, B, equipped with a source of CO_2 or N_2 to maintain an inert atmosphere in which the reaction takes place; a stirrer; and the buret, C.

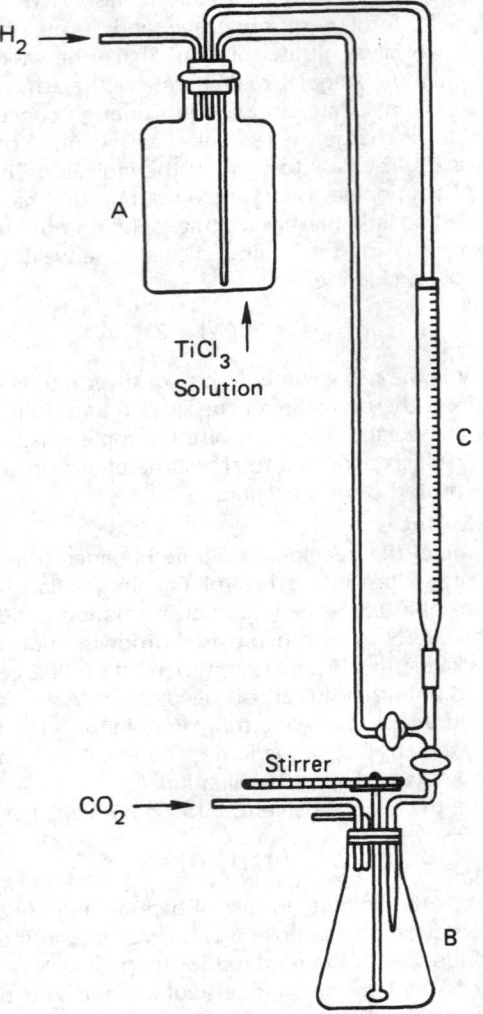

Figure 13. Titanous Chloride Titration Apparatus

Reagents and Solutions

Titanium Chloride Solution (0.1 N): Transfer 73 mL of commercially prepared 20% $TiCl_3$ solution into a storage bottle, and carefully add 82 mL of concentrated HCl per L of final solution. Mix well, and bubble CO_2 or N_2 through the solution for 1 h. Before standardizing, maintain the solution under a hydrogen atmosphere for at least 16 h using a Kipp generator.

Potassium Dichromate Solution (0.1 N, primary standard): Transfer 4.9032 g of $K_2Cr_2O_7$ (NIST No. 136) to a 1-L volumetric flask; dissolve in and dilute with water to volume.

Ammonium Thiocyanate (50%): Transfer 500 g of NH_4SCN, ACS certified, to a 1-L volumetric flask; dissolve in about 600 mL of water, warming if necessary; and dilute to volume.

Ferrous Ammonium Sulfate: $Fe(NH_4)_2(SO_4)_2 \cdot 6H_2O$, ACS certified

Sodium Bitartrate

Standardization of the Titanium Chloride Solution
Drain any standing titanium chloride ($TiCl_3$) from the feed lines and buret, and refill with fresh solution. Add 3.0 g of *Ferrous Ammonium Sulfate* to a wide-mouth Erlenmeyer flask followed by 200 mL of water, 25 mL of 50% sulfuric acid, 25 mL of 0.1 N *Potassium Dichromate Solution* (by pipet), and 2 or 3 boiling chips. Boil the solution vigorously on a hot plate for 30 s to remove dissolved air, then quickly transfer the flask to the titration apparatus, securely connect the stopper assembly, and start the carbon dioxide flow and stirrer. Pass carbon dioxide over the solution for 1 min before beginning the titration.

Add the 0.1 N *Titanium Chloride Solution* at a fast, steady drip to within 1 mL of the estimated endpoint (about 20 mL). Reduce the carbon dioxide flow, remove the solid-glass rod from the stopper assembly, pipet 10 mL of *Ammonium Thiocyanate* (50%) into the flask, insert the glass rod, and increase the carbon dioxide flow. Continue titrating slowly until the endpoint: a color change from brown-red to light green is observed. Perform a blank determination using the same reagents and quantities, and calculate the normality, N, of the 0.1 N *Titanium Chloride Solution* on the basis of three titrations:

$$N = (V_r \times N_r/V_t - V_b)$$

in which V_r is the volume, in mL, of 0.1 N *Potassium Dichromate* used; N_r is the normality of the 0.1 N *Potassium Dichromate*; V_t is the volume, in mL, of 0.1 N *Titanium Chloride Solution* used; and V_b is the volume, in mL, of titanium dichloride used in the blank titration.

Procedure Transfer the quantity of colorant prescribed in the individual monograph into a 500-mL wide-mouth Erlenmeyer flask and add 21–22 g of *Sodium Bitartrate* (sodium citrate for Sunset Yellow), 275 mL of water, and two or three boiling chips. Boil the solution vigorously on a hot plate for 30 s to remove dissolved air, then quickly transfer the flask to the titration apparatus, securely connect the stopper assembly, and start the carbon dioxide flow and stirrer. Pass carbon dioxide over the solution for 1 min before beginning the titration.

Titrate the sample until the color lightens, wait 20 s, and then continue the addition with about 2 s between drops. When the color is almost completely bleached, wait 20 s, and then continue the addition with 5 s between drops. A complete color change indicates the endpoint. Perform a blank determination using the same reagents and quantities, and calculate the total color, T, in percent and on the basis of three titrations:

$$T = [(V_t - V_b)/(W \times F_s)] \times 100 \times N$$

in which V_t is the volume of titrant used; V_b is the volume of titrant required to produce the endpoint in a blank; W is the weight, in grams, of the sample taken; F_s is a factor derived from the stoichiometry of the reaction characteristics of each colorant and is given in the individual monograph; and N is the normality of the titrant.

Method III (Gravimetric)
Transfer approximately 0.5 g of colorant, accurately weighed, to a 400-mL beaker, add 100 mL of water, and

heat to boiling. Add 25 mL of 1:50 hydrochloric acid, and bring to a boil. Wash down the sides of the beaker with water, cover, and keep on a steam bath for several hours or overnight. Cool to room temperature, and quantitatively transfer the precipitate into a tared filtering crucible with 1:100 hydrochloric acid. Wash the precipitate with two 15-mL portions of water, and dry the crucible for 3 h at 135°. Cool in a desiccator, and weigh. Calculate the total color, P, in weight percent:

$$P = [(W_p \times F)/W_s] \times 100$$

in which W_p is the weight, in grams, of the precipitate; F is the gravimetric conversion factor given in the individual monograph; and W_s is the original weight, in grams, of the sample taken.

Uncombined Intermediates and Products of Side Reactions

Method I

Sample Solution Transfer approximately 2 g of colorant to a 100-mL volumetric flask; dissolve in and dilute with water to volume.

Apparatus Pack a 2.5-cm × 45-cm glass column with approximately 20 g of cellulose (Whatman CF-11 grade, or equivalent) that has been slurried in the eluant and from which the fines have been removed by decantation. Equilibrate the column thoroughly with the eluant, 35% ammonium sulfate.

Procedure Pipet 5 mL of the *Sample Solution* into a beaker containing 5 g of cellulose that has been slurried in eluant and from which the fines have been removed by decantation. Stir the mixture thoroughly, add 10 g of ammonium sulfate, and stir until uniformly mixed. Mix the slurry with 15 mL of eluant, and apply it to the column. Allow the fluid to enter the column, and wash the beaker with eluant until the sample is quantitatively transferred. Elute the column with approximately 500 mL of 35% ammonium sulfate, and collect a total of eight 60-mL fractions. Divide each collected fraction in half and add 0.5 mL of NH_4OH to one half and 0.5 mL of HCl to the other.

Calculation After identifying each intermediate and side product by comparing spectra of the fractions with commercial standards, calculate the concentration, C, of each:

$$C = A/(a \times b)$$

in which A is the absorbance at the wavelength of maximal absorption; a is the absorptivity given in the individual monograph; and b is the cell pathlength, in cm.

Method II

Apparatus Use a suitable high-performance liquid chromatography system (see *Chromatography*, Appendix IIA) equipped with a dual wavelength detector system such that the effluent can be monitored serially at 254 nm and 325–385 nm (wide-band pass). Use a 1-m × 2.1-mm (id) column, or equivalent, packed with a strong anion-exchange resin (Dupont No. 830950405, or equivalent).

Operating Conditions The operating conditions required may vary depending on the system used. The following conditions have been shown to give suitable results for Allura Red, Tartrazine, and Sunset Yellow.

Allura Red
 Primary Eluant: 0.01 M aqueous $Na_2B_4O_7$
 Secondary Eluant: 0.20 M $NaClO_4$ in aqueous 0.01 M $Na_2B_4O_7$
 Sample Size: 20 µL of a 0.25% solution
 Flow Rate: 0.60 mL/min
 Gradient: Linear, in two phases: 0%–18% in 40 min, 18%–62% in 8 min more, then hold for 18 min more at 62%
 Temperature: 50°
 Pressure: 1000 psi
 Order of Elution: (1) Cresidinesulfonic acid (CSA); (2) unknown; (3) Schaeffer's salt (SS); (4) unknown; (5) 4,4'-diazoaminobis(5-methoxy-2-methylbenzenesulfonic acid) (DMMA); (6) unknown; (7) Allura Red; (8) 6,6'-oxybis(2-naphthalenesulfonic acid) (DONS)

Tartrazine
 Primary Eluant: 0.01 M aqueous $Na_2B_4O_7$
 Secondary Eluant: 0.10 M $NaClO_4$ in aqueous 0.01 M $Na_2B_4O_7$
 Sample Size: 50 µL of a 0.15% solution, prepared within 13 min of injection
 Flow Rate: 1.00 mL/min
 Gradient: Exponential at 4%/min: 0.95%
 Temperature: 50°
 Pressure: 1000 psi
 Order of Elution: (1) Phenylhydrazine-p-sulfonic acid (PHSA); (2) sulfanilic acid (SA); (3) 1-(4-sulfophenyl)-3-ethylcarboxy-5-hydroxypyrazolone (PY-T); (4) 1-(4-sulfophenyl)-3-carboxy-5-hydroxypyrazolone (EEPT); (5) 4,4'-(diazoamino)-dibenzenesulfonic acid (DAADBSA)

Sunset Yellow
 Primary Eluant: 0.01 M aqueous $Na_2B_4O_7$
 Secondary Eluant: 0.20 M $NaClO_4$ in aqueous 0.01 M $Na_2B_4O_7$
 Sample Size: 5 µL of a 1% solution
 Flow Rate: 0.50 mL/min
 Gradient: Linear in four phases: 0%–11% in 10 min; hold 25 min; 11%–38% in 10 min; 38%–42% in 10 min; 42%–98% in 20 min; hold 20 min
 Temperature: 50°
 Pressure: 1000 psi
 Order of Elution: (1) Sulfanilic acid (SA); (2) Schaeffer's salt (SS); (3) 4,4'-(diazoamino)-dibenzenesulfonic acid (DAADBSA); (4) R-salt dye; (5) Sunset Yellow; (6) 6,6'-oxybis(2-naphthalenesulfonic acid) (DONS)

Standard Solutions

Allura Red: Prepare a solution containing 0.25 g of colorant, 0.5 mg of CSA, 0.75 mg of SS, 0.25 mg of DMMA, and 1.25 mg of DONS in a 100-mL volumetric flask. Dissolve in and dilute with 0.1 M $Na_2B_4O_7$ to volume.

Tartrazine: Prepare a solution containing 0.15 g of colorant and 0.3 mg each of PHSA, SA, PY-T, EEPT, and DAADBSA in a 100-mL volumetric flask. Dissolve in and dilute with 0.1 M $Na_2B_4O_7$ to volume.

Sunset Yellow: Prepare a solution containing 0.25 g of colorant, 0.5 mg of SA, 0.75 mg of SS, 0.25 mg of

DAADBSA, and 1.25 mg of DONS in a 100-mL volumetric flask. Dissolve in and dilute with 0.1 M Na$_2$B$_4$O$_7$ to volume.

Test Solutions Prepare at least four test solutions, each containing the colorant, and one impurity, accurately weighed, dissolved in 0.1 M Na$_2$B$_4$O$_7$, and diluted to volume in a 100-mL volumetric flask. The solutions should encompass the range of concentrations, evenly spaced, given below for each constituent:

Allura Red (250 mg): CSA (0.05–0.5 mg); SS (0.05–0.75 mg); DONS (0.5–2.5 mg); DMMA (0.025–0.25 mg). Inject 20 µL of each solution.

Tartrazine (150 mg): SA (7.5 to 300 µg); PY-T (7.5–300 µg); EEPT (7.5–300 µg); DAADBSA (7.5–300 µg). Inject 50 µL of each solution.

Sunset Yellow (250 mg): SA (0.05–0.5 mg); SS (0.05–0.75 mg); DONS (0.5–2.5 mg); DAADBSA (0.05–0.25 mg). Inject 20 µL of each solution.

System Suitability

Resolution: Elute the column, or equivalent, with the gradient specified under *Operating Conditions* until a smooth baseline is obtained. Inject an aliquot of the *Standard Solution*. The resolution of the eluted components matches or exceeds that shown for the corresponding colorant (see *Figures 14, 15,* and *16*). After determining that the column, or equivalent, will give the required resolution, allow it to rest for 2 weeks before use.

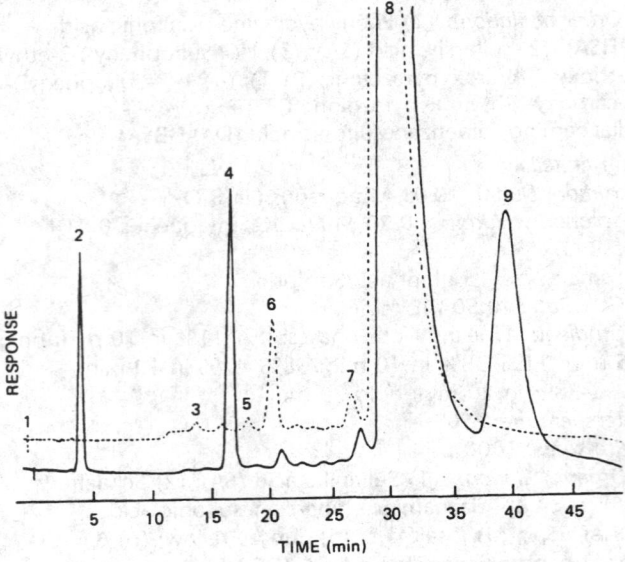

Figure 14. Allura Red—Top Trace: Eluant Monitored at 254 nm; Bottom Trace: Eluant Monitored at 375–385 nm

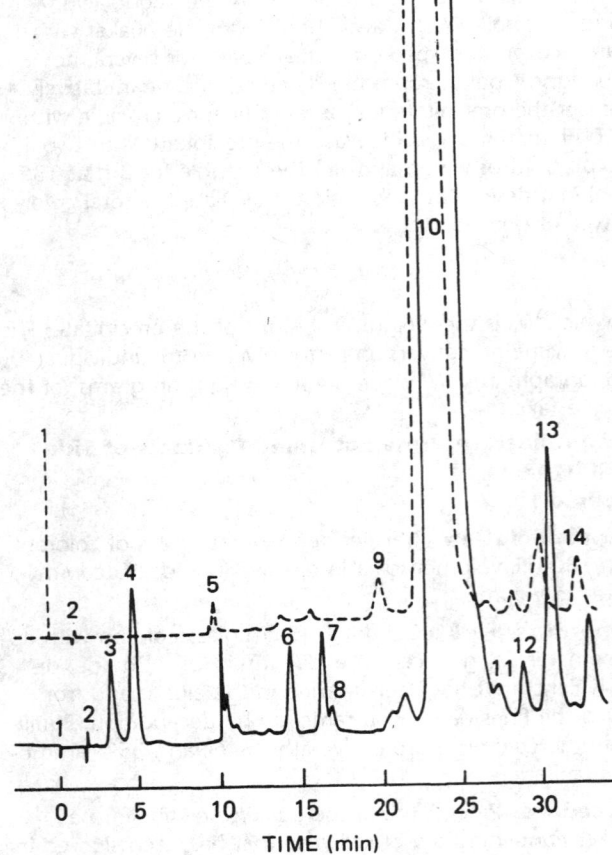

Figure 15. Tartrazine—Top Trace: Eluant Monitored at 254 nm; Bottom Trace: Eluant Monitored at 375–385 nm

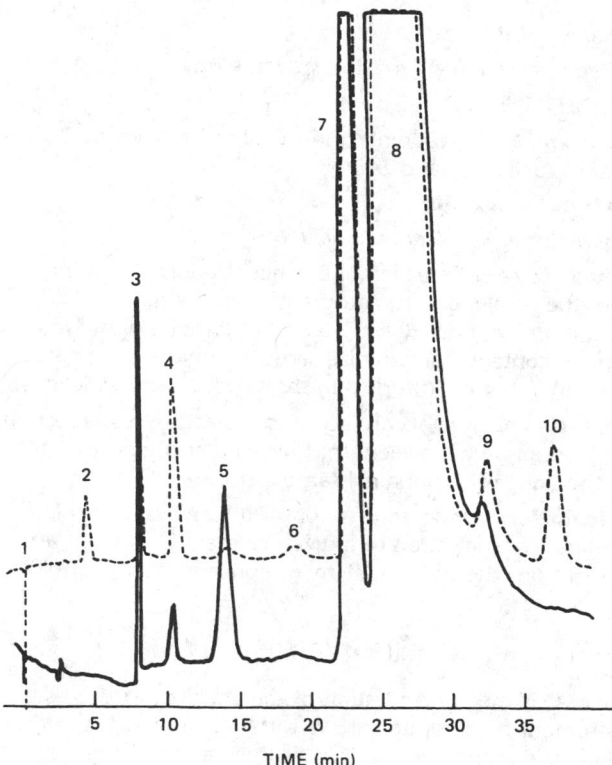

Figure 16. Sunset Yellow–Top Trace: Eluant Monitored at 254 nm; Bottom Trace: Eluant Monitored at 375–385 nm

Calibration Inject the designated volume of each *Test Solution* onto a conditioned column, and prepare a standard curve corresponding to each unreacted intermediate and side reaction product. Determine the area, A, for each peak from the integrator if an automated system is used or by multiplying the peak height by the width at one-half the height. The peak height alone may be used for EEPT, PY-T, and DAADBSA. Calculate the concentration, C_i, of each intermediate or side product:

$$C_i = mA_i + b$$

in which A_i is the area of its corresponding chromatographic peak. Calculate the slope, m, and intercept, b, using the following linear regression equations:

$$m = [N\Sigma C_i A_i - \Sigma C_i \Sigma A_i]/[N\Sigma A_i^2 - (\Sigma A_i)^2]$$

$$b = [\overline{A}]_i - m[\overline{C}]_i$$

in which $\overline{A}$ and $\overline{C}$ are the calculated averages of the peak areas and concentrations, respectively, used to construct the standard curve for one intermediate or side reaction product. Calculate the correlation coefficient, r:

$$r = [\Sigma(C_i - \overline{C})(A_i - \overline{A})]/[\Sigma(C_i - \overline{C})^2 \times \Sigma(A_i - \overline{A})^2]$$

Each time the system is calibrated, add the new data to those accumulated from previous analyses. The correlation coefficient must be 0.95–1.00 for any single experiment or from accumulated data.

Recalibrate the system after every 10 determinations or 2 days, whichever occurs first.

Sample Preparation Prepare as directed in the individual monograph.

Procedure Inject the volume of *Sample Preparation* as designated in the monograph into the column. Determine the concentration of intermediates and side reaction products from the peak areas using the slope, m, and intercept, b, calculated under *Calibration*:

$$C_s = mA_s + b$$

in which C_s is the concentration of the unknown in the *Sample Preparation* and A_s its corresponding peak area.

Loss on Drying (Volatile Matter)
Transfer 1.5–2.5 g of colorant, accurately weighed, to a tared crucible. Heat in a vacuum oven at 135° for 12–15 h. Lower the pressure in the oven to −125 mm Hg, and continue heating for an additional 2 h. Cover the crucible, and allow to cool in a desiccator. Reweigh the crucible when cool. The loss of weight is defined as the volatile matter.

Water-Insoluble Matter
Transfer about 1 g of colorant, accurately weighed, to a 250-mL beaker, and add 200 mL of boiling water. Stir to facilitate dissolution of the color.

Tare a filtering crucible equipped with a glass fiber filter (Reeve Angel, No. 5270, or equivalent). Filter the solution with the aid of suction when it has cooled to ambient temperature. Rinse the beaker three times, pouring the rinsings through the crucible. Wash the filter with water until the filtrate is colorless.

Dry the crucible and filter in an oven at 135° for at least 3 h, cool them in a desiccator, and reweigh to the nearest 0.1 mg. Calculate the percent water-insoluble matter, I:

$$I = (W_c/W_s) \times 100$$

in which W_c is the difference in crucible weight and W_s is the sample weight.

ELEMENTAL IMPURITIES BY ICP

Before the initial use of either of the procedures below, the analyst should ensure that the procedure is appropriate for the instrument and sample used. *Method I* can be used for elemental impurities generally amenable to detection by inductively coupled plasma–atomic (optical) emission spectroscopy (ICP–OES). *Method II* can be used for elemental impurities generally amenable to detection by inductively coupled plasma–mass spectrometry (ICP–MS). If no method is specified in the individual monograph, analysts are instructed to use *Method II* (ICP–MS).

Method I: ICP–OES

Reagents All reagents used for the preparation of the sample and standard solutions should be free of elemental impurities. Reagents should be commercial elemental stock standards that are NIST-traceable, or equivalent, at a recommended concentration of 100 µg/mL or greater; or appropriate USP Reference Standards, as either single element or multielement.

Aqua Regia: Ultra pure nitric acid/hydrochloric acid (1:3) prepared as needed. (A 1%–5% solution of aqua regia is used as a rinsing solution between analyses and as calibration blanks.)

Sample Preparation   Use this sample preparation procedure unless otherwise specified in the individual monograph.   [NOTE—Weights and volumes provided may be adjusted to meet the requirements of the microwave digestion apparatus used, if proportions remain constant.] Dehydrate and predigest 0.5 g of sample in 5 mL of freshly prepared *Aqua Regia*. Sulfuric acid may also be used as a last resort. [NOTE—Sulfuric acid should be used only when absolutely needed because addition of sulfuric acid may cause an extreme exothermic reaction and result in elements being lost and because the viscosity of sulfuric acid is higher than that of other acids, which affects the overall flow of solution.] Allow the sample to sit loosely covered for 30 min in a fume hood. Add an additional 10 mL of *Aqua Regia* and digest, using a closed vessel microwave technique. Microwave until digestion or extraction is complete. Repeat if necessary by adding an additional 5 mL of *Aqua Regia*. [NOTE—Follow the recommended procedures provided by the manufacturer of the closed vessel microwave digestion apparatus to ensure safe usage. In closed vessel microwave digestion, the use of concentrated hydrofluoric acid (HF) is not recommended; however, when its use is necessary, practice the utmost caution in the preparation of test articles, and review or establish local procedures for safe handling, safe disposal, and HF-tolerant instrumental configurations.]

Sample Solution   Allow the digestion vessel containing the *Sample Preparation* to cool (for mercury measurements, add an appropriate stabilizer, such as gold at about 0.1 ppm), and dilute with water to 50.0 mL.

Calibration Solution 1   2J of the element of interest in a matched matrix (acid concentrations similar to that of the *Sample Solution*), where J is the limit for the specific elemental impurity.   [NOTE—Multiple elements of interest may be included in this solution at the same concentration ratio. For mercury analysis, add an appropriate stabilizer, such as gold at about 0.1 ppm.]

Calibration Solution 2   0.1J of the element of interest in a matched matrix (acid concentrations similar to that of the *Sample Solution*), where J is the limit for the specific elemental impurity.   [NOTE—Multiple elements of interest may be included in this solution at the same concentration ratio. For mercury analysis, add an appropriate stabilizer, such as gold at about 0.1 ppm.]

Check Standard Solution   1 ppm of the element of interest in a matched matrix (acid concentrations similar to that of the *Sample Solution*).   [NOTE—Multiple elements of interest may be included in this solution at the same concentration ratio. For mercury analysis, add an appropriate stabilizer, such as gold at about 0.1 ppm.]

Blank   Matched matrix (acid concentrations similar to that of the *Sample Solution*)

Elemental Spectrometric System (see *Plasma Spectrochemistry*, Appendix IIC)

Mode: ICP

Detector: Optical emission spectroscopy

Rinse: 5% *Aqua Regia*

Calibration: Two-point, using *Calibration Solution 1*, *Calibration Solution 2*, and *Blank*

System Suitability

Sample: *Check Standard Solution*

Suitability requirement: The concentration determined from the resulting chromatogram differs from actual concentration by NMT 20%.   [NOTE—If samples are high in mineral content, to minimize sample carryover, rinse system well (60 s) before introducing the *Check Standard Solution*.]

Analysis   Analyze according to manufacturer's suggestions for program and wavelength. Calculate and report results on the basis of the original sample size.

Calculation   Upon completion of the analysis, calculate the final concentration of a given element in the test article (µg/g) from the solution element concentration (µg/mL) as follows:

$$C = [(A \times V_1)/W] \times (V_2/V_3)$$

where C is the concentration of the analyte, µg/g; A is the instrument reading, µg/mL; V_1 is the volume of the initial test article preparation, mL; W is the weight of the test article preparation, g; V_2 is the total volume of any dilution performed, mL; and V_3 is the volume of the aliquot of initial test article preparation used in any dilution performed, mL.

Similarly, calculate the final concentration of a given element in the test article (µg/g) from the solution element concentration (ng/mL) as follows:

$$C = [(A \times V_1)/W] \times (1\ \mu g/1000\ ng)(V_2/V_3)$$

where A is the instrument reading, ng/mL; and the other factors are as defined above.

Method II: ICP–MS

Reagents   All reagents used for the preparation of sample and standard solutions should be free of elemental impurities. Reagents should be commercial elemental stock standards that are NIST-traceable, or equivalent, at a recommended concentration of 100 µg/mL or greater; or appropriate USP Reference Standards, as either single element or multielement.

Aqua Regia: Ultra pure nitric acid/hydrochloric acid (1:3) prepared as needed. (A 1%–5% solution of aqua regia is used as a rinsing solution between analyses and as calibration blanks.)

Sample Preparation   Proceed as directed under *Method I*.

Sample Solution   Allow the digestion vessel containing the *Sample Preparation* to cool, and add appropriate internal standards at appropriate concentrations (for mercury measurements, gold should be one of the internal standards). Dilute with water to 50.0 mL.

Calibration Solution 1   Proceed as directed under *Method I*.

Calibration Solution 2   Proceed as directed under *Method I*.

Blank   Matched matrix (acid concentrations similar to that of the *Sample Solution*)

Elemental Spectrometric System (see *Plasma Spectrochemistry*, Appendix IIC)

   Mode: ICP.   [NOTE—An instrument with a cooled spray chamber is recommended.]

   Detector: Mass spectrometer

   Rinse: 5% Aqua Regia

   Calibration: Calibration Solution 1, Calibration Solution 2, and *Blank*

System Suitability

   Sample: Calibration Solution 1

   Suitability requirement: The concentration determined from the resulting chromatogram differs from actual concentration by NMT 20%.   [NOTE—If samples are high in mineral content, to minimize sample carryover, rinse system well (60 s) before introducing the *Check Standard Solution*.]

Analysis   Analyze according to the manufacturer's suggestions for the program and m/z. Calculate and report results based on the original sample size.   [NOTE—Arsenic is subject to interference from argon chloride. Appropriate measures, including a sample preparation without *Aqua Regia*, must be taken to correct for the interference, depending on instrumental capabilities.]

Calculation   Upon completion of the analysis, calculate the final concentration of a given element in the test article (µg/g) from the solution element concentration (µg/mL) as follows:

$$C = [(A \times V_1)/W] \times (V_2/V_3)$$

where C is the concentration of the analyte, µg/g; A is the instrument reading, µg/mL; V_1 is the volume of the initial test article preparation, mL; W is the weight of the test article preparation, g; V_2 is the total volume of any dilution performed, mL; and V_3 is the volume of the aliquot of initial test article preparation used in any dilution performed, mL.

Similarly, calculate the final concentration of a given element in the test article (µg/g) from the solution element concentration (ng/mL) as follows:

$$C = [(A \times V_1)/W] \times (1 \text{ µg}/1000 \text{ ng})(V_2/V_3)$$

where A is the instrument reading, ng/mL; and the other factors are as defined above.

GLUTAMIC ACID

Apparatus   Use an ion-exchange amino acid analyzer, equipped with sulfonated polystyrene columns, in which the effluent from the sample is mixed with ninhydrin reagent and the absorbance of the resultant color is measured continuously and automatically at 570 nm and 440 nm by a recording photometer.

Standard Solution   Transfer 1250 ± 2 mg of reagent-grade glutamic acid, accurately weighed, into a 500-mL volumetric flask. Fill the flask half-full with water, add 5 mL of hydrochloric acid to help dissolve the amino acid, dilute with water to volume, and mix. Prepare the standard for analysis by diluting 1 mL of this solution with 4 mL of 0.2 N sodium citrate, pH 2.2, buffer. This *Standard Solution* contains 0.5 mg of glutamic acid per mL (C_S).

Sample Preparation   Dilute 5 mg of sample, accurately weighed, to exactly 5 mL with 0.2 N sodium citrate, pH 2.2, buffer. Remove any insoluble material by centrifugation or filtration.

Procedure   Using 2-mL aliquots of the *Standard Solution* and *Sample Preparation*, proceed according to the apparatus manufacturer's instructions. From the chromatograms thus obtained, match the retention times produced by the *Standard Preparation* with those produced by the *Sample Solution*, and identify the peak produced by glutamic acid. Record the area of the glutamic acid peak from the sample as A_U, and that from the standards as A_S.

Calculations   Calculate the concentration, C_A, in mg/mL, of glutamic acid in the *Sample Preparation*:

$$\text{Result} = A_U \times C_S/A_S$$

in which C_S is the concentration, in mg/mL, of glutamic acid in the *Standard Solution*.

Calculate the percent glutamic acid, on the basis of total protein:

$$\text{Result} = (100 \times C_A)/(6.25 \times N_T)$$

in which 6.25 is the conversion factor for protein and amino acids, and N_T is the percent total nitrogen determined in the monograph *Assay*.

Calculate the percent glutamic acid in the sample:

$$\text{Result} = 100 \times C_A/S_W$$

in which S_W is the weight, in mg, of the sample taken.

HYDROXYPROPOXYL DETERMINATION

Apparatus   The apparatus for hydroxypropoxyl group determination is shown in *Figure 17*.

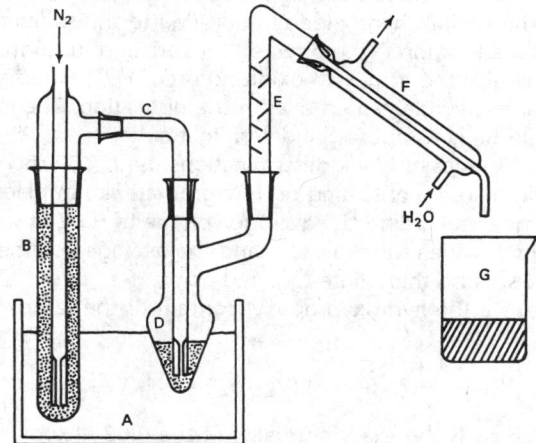

Figure 17. Apparatus for Hydroxypropoxyl Determination

The boiling flask, *D*, is fitted with an aluminum foil-covered Vigreaux column, *E*, on the side arm and with a bleeder tube through the neck and to the bottom of the flask for the introduction of steam and nitrogen. A steam generator, B, is attached to the bleeder tube through tube C, and a condenser, F, is attached to the Vigreaux column. The boiling flask and steam generator are immersed in an oil bath, A, equipped with a thermoregulator such that a temperature of 155° and the desired heating rate may be maintained. The distillate is collected in a 150-mL beaker, G, or other suitable container.

Procedure Unless otherwise directed, transfer about 100 mg of the sample, previously dried at 105° for 2 h and accurately weighed, into the boiling flask, and add 10 mL of chromium trioxide solution (60 g in 140 mL of water). Immerse the steam generator and the boiling flask in the oil bath (at room temperature) to the level of the top of the chromium trioxide solution. Start cooling water through the condenser, and pass nitrogen gas through the boiling flask at the rate of one bubble per second. Starting at room temperature, raise the temperature of the oil bath to 155° over a period of not less than 30 min, and maintain this temperature until the end of the determination. Distill until 50 mL of distillate is collected. Detach the condenser from the Vigreaux column, and wash it with water, collecting the washings in the distillate container. Titrate the combined washings and distillate with 0.02 N sodium hydroxide to a pH of 7.0, using a pH meter set at the expanded scale.

[NOTE—Phenolphthalein TS may be used for this titration if it is also used for all standards and blanks.]

Record the volume, V_a, of the 0.02 N sodium hydroxide used. Add 500 mg of sodium bicarbonate and 10 mL of 2 N sulfuric acid, and then after evolution of carbon dioxide has ceased, add 1 g of potassium iodide. Stopper the flask, shake the mixture, and allow it to stand in the dark for 5 min. Titrate the liberated iodine with 0.02 N sodium thiosulfate to the sharp disappearance of the yellow color, confirming the endpoint by the addition of a few drops of starch TS. Record the volume of 0.02 N sodium thiosulfate required as Y_a.

Make several reagent blank determinations, using only the chromium trioxide solution in the above procedure. The ratio of the sodium hydroxide titration (V_b) to the sodium thiosulfate titration (Y_b), corrected for variation in normalities, will give the acidity-to-oxidizing ratio, $V_b/Y_b = K$, for the chromium trioxide carried over in the distillation. The factor K should be constant for all determinations.

Make a series of blank determinations using 100 mg of methylcellulose (containing no foreign material) in place of the sample, recording the average volume of 0.02 N sodium hydroxide required as V_m and the average volume of 0.02 N sodium thiosulfate required as Y_m.

Calculate the hydroxypropoxyl content of the sample, in mg:

$$\text{Result} = 75.0 \times [N_1(V_a - V_m) - kN_2(Y_a - Y_m)]$$

in which N_1 is the exact normality of the 0.02 N sodium hydroxide solution, $k = V_bN_1/Y_bN_2$, and N_2 is the exact normality of the 0.02 N sodium thiosulfate solution.

The percentage of substitution, by weight, of hydroxypropoxyl groups, determined as directed above, may be converted to molecular substitution per glucose unit by reference to *Figure 18*.

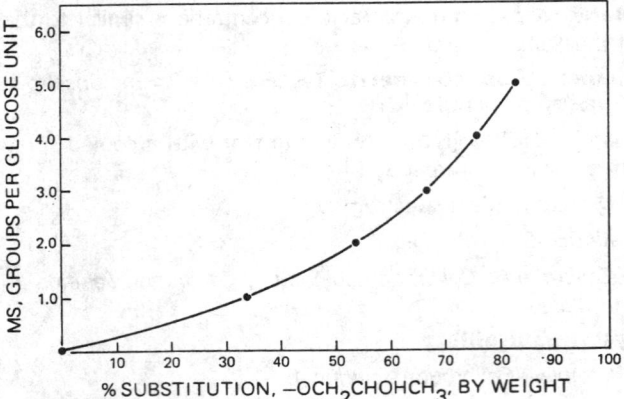

Figure 18. Chart for Converting Percentage of Substitution, by Weight, of Hydroxypropoxyl Groups to Molecular Substitution per Glucose Unit

METHOXYL DETERMINATION

Apparatus The apparatus for methoxyl determination, as shown in *Figure 19*, consists of a boiling flask, A, fitted with a capillary side arm to provide an inlet for carbon dioxide and connected to a column, B, which separates aqueous hydriodic acid from the more volatile methyl iodide. After the methyl iodide passes through a suspension of aqueous red phosphorus in the scrubber trap, C, it is absorbed in the bromine–acetic acid absorption tube, D. The carbon dioxide is introduced from a device arranged to minimize pressure fluctuations and connected to the apparatus by a small capillary containing a small plug of cotton.

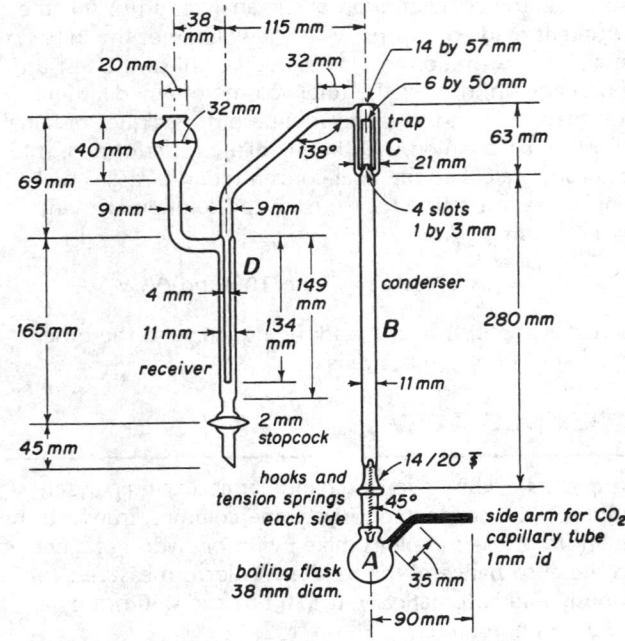

Figure 19. Distillation Apparatus for Methoxyl Determination

Reagents

Acetic Potassium Acetate: Dissolve 100 g of potassium acetate in 1000 mL of a mixture consisting of 900 mL of glacial acetic acid and 100 mL of acetic anhydride.

Bromine–Acetic Acid Solution: On the day of use, dissolve 5 mL of bromine in 145 mL of the *Acetic Potassium Acetate* solution.

Hydriodic Acid: Use special-grade hydriodic acid suitable for alkoxyl determinations, or purify reagent grade as follows: distill over red phosphorus in an all-glass apparatus, passing a slow stream of carbon dioxide through the apparatus until the distillation is terminated and the receiving flask has completely cooled.

[CAUTION—Use a safety shield, and conduct the distillation in a fume hood.]

Collect the colorless, or almost colorless, constant-boiling acid distilling between 126°–127°. Store the acid in a cool, dark place in small, brown, glass-stoppered bottles previously flushed with carbon dioxide and finally sealed with paraffin.

Procedure Fill trap C half-full with a suspension of about 60 mg of red phosphorus in 100 mL of water, introduced through the funnel on tube D and the side arm that connects with the trap at C. Rinse tube D and the side arm with water, collecting the rinsings in trap C, then charge absorption tube D with 7 mL of *Bromine–Acetic Acid Solution*. Place the sample, previously accurately weighed in a tared gelatin capsule, into the boiling flask A, along with a few glass beads or boiling stones, then add 6 mL of *Hydriodic Acid*. Connect the flask to the condenser, using a few drops of the acid to seal the junction, and begin passing the carbon dioxide through the apparatus at the rate of about two bubbles per second. Heat the flask in an oil bath at 150°, continue the reaction for 40 min, and drain the contents of absorption tube D into a 500-mL Erlenmeyer flask containing 10 mL of a 1:4 solution of sodium acetate. Rinse tube D with water, collecting the rinsings in the flask, and dilute with water to about 125 mL. Discharge the red-brown color of bromine by adding formic acid, dropwise with swirling, then add 3 drops in excess. Usually a total of 12 to 15 drops of formic acid is required. Allow the flask to stand for 3 min, add 15 mL of 2 N sulfuric acid and 3 g of potassium iodide, and titrate immediately with 0.1 N sodium thiosulfate, adding starch TS near the endpoint. Perform a blank determination with the same quantities of the same reagents, including the gelatin capsule, and in the same manner, and make any necessary correction. Each mL of 0.1 N sodium thiosulfate is equivalent to 0.517 mg (517 µg) of methoxyl groups (–OCH$_3$).

NITROGEN DETERMINATION (Kjeldahl Method)

[NOTE—All reagents should be nitrogen free, where available, or otherwise very low in nitrogen content.]

Method I

Use this method unless otherwise directed in the individual monograph. It is not applicable to certain nitrogen-containing compounds that do not yield their entire nitrogen upon digestion with sulfuric acid.

Nitrites and Nitrates Absent

Unless otherwise directed, transfer 1 g of sample into a 500-mL to 800-mL Kjeldahl digestion flask of hard borosilicate, moderately thick, well-annealed glass, wrapping the sample, if solid or semisolid, in nitrogen-free filter paper to facilitate the transfer if desired. Add 10 g of powdered potassium sulfate or anhydrous sodium sulfate, 500 mg of powdered cupric sulfate, and 20 mL of sulfuric acid. Place the flask in an inclined position (about 45°), and heat gently keeping the temperature below the boiling point until frothing ceases, adding a small amount of paraffin, if necessary, to reduce frothing.

[CAUTION—The digestion should be conducted in a fume hood, or the digestion apparatus should be equipped with a fume exhaust system.]

Increase the heat until the acid boils briskly and continue the heating process until the solution clears, and then continue boiling for 30 min longer (or for 2 h for samples containing organic material). Cool, add about 150 mL of water, mix, and then cool to below 25°. Add cautiously 100 mL of a 2:5 sodium hydroxide solution, in such a manner as to cause the solution to flow down the inner side of the flask to form a layer under the acid solution, to make the mixture strongly alkaline. Add a few granules of zinc to prevent bumping, and immediately connect the flask to a distillation apparatus consisting of a Kjeldahl connecting bulb and a condenser, the delivery tube of which extends well beneath the surface of 100 mL of a 1:25 boric acid solution contained in a conical flask or a wide-mouth bottle of about 500-mL capacity. Gently, rotate the Kjeldahl flask to mix its contents thoroughly, and then heat until all of the ammonia has distilled, collecting at least 150 mL of distillate (about 80% of the contents of the flask). Wash the tip of the delivery tube, collecting the washings in the receiving flask, and titrate with 0.5 N sulfuric acid, determining the endpoint potentiometrically. Perform a blank determination, substituting 2 g of sucrose for the sample, and make any necessary correction (see *General Provisions*). Each mL of 0.5 N acid is equivalent to 7.003 mg of nitrogen.

[NOTE—An indicator solution can also be used to determine the titration endpoint. For example, dissolve 0.2 g of methyl red in 100 mL of 95% ethanol, 1 g of bromocresol green in 500 mL of 95% ethanol, then combine 1 part of the methyl red solution and 5 parts of the bromocresol green solution. Add 3 mL of methyl red/bromocresol green indicator solution per L of boric acid solution. Then, titrate the sample to the first trace of pink. Also, a bromocresol green–methyl red solution can be used as an alternative. To make the solution, dissolve 0.15 g of bromocresol green and 0.1 g of methyl red in 180 mL of alcohol, and dilute with water to a final volume of 200 mL.]

[NOTE—If the substance to be determined is known to have a low nitrogen content, 0.1 N acid and alkali may be used, in which case each mL of 0.1 N acid consumed is equivalent to 1.401 mg of nitrogen.]

[NOTE—Nitrogen recovery verification can be run to check for accuracy of the procedure and the equipment.
1. *Nitrogen loss:* Use 0.12 g of ammonium sulfate and 0.85 g of sucrose. Add all other reagents, digest, and distill under the same conditions as for the sample. Recoveries should be NLT 99%.
2. *Digestion efficiency:* Use 0.16 g of lysine hydrochloride or 0.18 g of tryptophan, with 0.67 g of sucrose per flask. Add all other reagents, digest, and distill under the same conditions as for the sample. Recoveries should be NLT 98%.]

Nitrites and Nitrates Present

[NOTE—This procedure is not applicable to liquids or to materials having a high chlorine-to-nitrate ratio.]

Unless otherwise directed, transfer a quantity of sample, accurately weighed, corresponding to about 150 mg of nitrogen into a Kjeldahl flask, and add 25 mL of 93%–98% sulfuric acid containing 1 g of salicylic acid. Mix thoroughly by shaking, and then allow to stand for 30 min or more, with frequent shaking. Add 5 g of $Na_2S_2O_3 \cdot 5H_2O$ (as an impalpable powder, not granules or filings), mix, then add 500 mg of powdered cupric sulfate, and proceed as directed under *Nitrates and Nitrites Absent*, beginning with "Incline the flask at an angle of about 45°". When the nitrogen content of the substance is known to exceed 10%, 500 mg to 1 g of benzoic acid may be added, prior to digestion, to facilitate the decomposition of the substance.

Method II (Semimicro)

[NOTE—Automated instruments may be used in place of this manual method, provided the automated equipment has been properly calibrated.]

Transfer an accurately weighed or measured quantity of the sample, equivalent to about 2 or 3 mg of nitrogen, into the digestion flask of a semimicro Kjeldahl apparatus. Add 1 g of a 10:1 powdered mixture of potassium sulfate and cupric sulfate, using a fine jet of water to wash down any material adhering to the neck of the flask, and then pour 7 mL of sulfuric acid down the inside wall of the flask to rinse it. Cautiously add down the inside of the flask 1 mL of 30% hydrogen peroxide, swirling the flask during the addition.

[CAUTION—Do not add any peroxide during the digestion.]

Heat over a free flame or an electric heater until the solution has attained a clear blue color and the walls of the flask are free from carbonized material. Cautiously add 20 mL of water, cool, then add through a funnel 30 mL of a 2:5 solution of sodium hydroxide, and rinse the funnel with 10 mL of water. Connect the flask to a steam distillation apparatus, and immediately begin the distillation with steam. Collect the distillate in 15 mL of a 1:25 solution of boric acid to which has been added 3 drops of methyl red–methylene blue TS and enough water to cover the end of the condensing tube. Continue passing the steam until 80–100 mL of distillate has been collected, then remove the absorption flask, rinse the end of the condenser tube with a small quantity of water, and titrate with 0.01 N sulfuric acid. Each mL of 0.01 N acid is equivalent to 140 µg of nitrogen.

When more than 2 or 3 mg of nitrogen is present in the measured quantity of the substance to be determined, 0.02 or 0.1 N sulfuric acid may be used in the titration if at least 15 mL of titrant is required. If the total dry weight of the material taken is greater than 100 mg, increase proportionately the quantities of sulfuric acid and sodium hydroxide added before distillation.

SPECTROPHOTOMETRIC IDENTIFICATION TESTS

Spectrophotometric tests contribute meaningfully toward the identification of many compendial chemical substances. The test procedures that follow are applicable to substances that absorb IR and/or UV radiation. The IR absorption spectrum of a substance, compared with that obtained concomitantly for the corresponding USP Reference Standard, provides perhaps the most conclusive evidence of the identity of the substance that can be realized from any single test. The UV absorption spectrum, on the other hand, does not exhibit a high degree of specificity. Conformance with both IR absorption and UV absorption test specifications leaves little doubt, if any, regarding the identity of the specimen under examination.

Infrared Spectra   This test is used for comparison of an IR spectrum for a sample specimen with a reference spectrum provided in the individual monograph.

Sample specimens should be prepared using the same technique as that used for the provided spectra. Unless otherwise noted in the individual monograph or spectrum caption, the spectra for liquid substances were obtained on neat liquids contained in fixed-volume sodium chloride cells or between salt plates. Spectra for solid substances were obtained on a potassium bromide pellet or a mineral oil (Nujol or equivalent) dispersion, as indicated in individual monographs or spectrum caption.

Infrared Absorption   This test is used for comparison of the IR spectrum of a sample specimen with that of a physical USP Reference Standard.

Sample and USP Reference Standard specimens should both be prepared for analysis using the same technique, as directed in the individual monographs, which use the below letter designations. Sample and USP Reference Standard specimens should be used as either dried or undried specimens as directed on the Reference Standard Label.

Record the spectra of the sample and USP Reference Standard specimens over the range of about 2.6–15 µm (3800 cm^{-1} to 650 cm^{-1}) unless otherwise specified in the individual monograph.

Designation	Specimen Preparation Technique
A	Intimately in contact with an internal reflection element for attenuated total reflectance (ATR) analysis
E	Pressed as a thin sample against a suitable plate for IR microscopic analysis
F	Suspended neat between suitable (for example sodium chloride or potassium bromide) plates

Designation	Specimen Preparation Technique
K	Mixed intimately with potassium bromide and compressed into a translucent pellet
M	Finely ground and dispersed in mineral oil
S	A solution of designated concentration, prepared as directed in the individual monograph, and examined in 0.1-mm cells (unless otherwise specified in the individual monograph)

[NOTE—A and E techniques can be used as alternative methods for K, M, F, and S where testing is performed qualitatively and the Reference Standard spectra are similarly obtained.]

Ultraviolet Absorption The test is used for comparison of the UV spectrum of a sample specimen with that of a physical USP Reference Standard.

Sample and USP Reference Standard specimens should be prepared using the solvents and concentrations specified in the individual monograph.

Record the spectra of the sample and USP Reference Standard solutions concomitantly using 1-cm cells over the spectral range of 200–400 nm, unless otherwise indicated in the individual monograph. Calculate absorptivities and/or absorbance ratios where these criteria are included in an individual monograph. Unless otherwise specified, absorbances indicated for these calculations are those measured at the maximum absorbance at the wavelength specified in the individual monograph. Where the absorbance is to be measured at a wavelength other than that of maximum absorbance, the abbreviations (min) and (sh) are used to indicate a minimum and shoulder, respectively, in an absorbance spectrum.

SULFUR (by Oxidative Microcoulometry) (Based on ASTM D3120)[5]

[NOTE—All reagents used in this test should be reagent grade; water should be of high purity, and gases must be high-purity grade.]

Apparatus Use the Dohrmann Microcoulometric Titrating System (MCTS-30), or equivalent (shown in *Figure 20*), unless otherwise specified in an individual monograph. It consists of a constant rate injector, A, a pyrolysis furnace, B, a quartz pyrolysis tube, C, a granular-tin scrubber, D, a titration cell, E, and a microcoulometer with a digital readout, F.

Granular-Tin Scrubber: Place 5 g of 20- to 30-mesh granular reagent-grade tin between quartz-wool plugs in an elongated 18/9–12/5 standard-taper adaptor that connects the pyrolysis tube and the titration cell.

Microcoulometer: Must have variable attenuation; gain control; and be capable of measuring the potential of the sensing-reference electrode pair, and comparing this potential with a bias potential, amplifying the potential difference, and applying the amplified difference to the working-auxiliary electrode pair to generate a titrant. The microcoulometer output voltage signal must also be proportional to the generating current.

Pyrolysis Furnace: The sample should be pyrolyzed in an electric furnace having at least two separate and independently controlled temperature zones, the first being an inlet section that can maintain a temperature sufficient to volatilize all the organic sample. The second zone is a pyrolysis section that can maintain a temperature sufficient to pyrolyze the organic matrix and oxidize all the organically bound sulfur. A third outlet temperature zone is optional.

Pyrolysis Tube: Must be fabricated from quartz and constructed in such a way that a sample, which is vaporized completely in the inlet section, is swept into the pyrolysis zone by an inert gas where it mixes with oxygen and is burned. The inlet end of the tube shall hold a septum for syringe entry of the sample and side arms for the introduction of oxygen and inert gases. The center or pyrolysis section should be of sufficient volume to ensure complete pyrolysis of the sample.

Sampling Syringe: A microlitre syringe of 10-µL capacity capable of accurately delivering 1–10 µL of sample into the pyrolysis tube. Three-in × 24-gauge needles are recommended to reach the inlet zone of the pyroloysis furnace.

Titration Cell: Must contain a sensor-reference pair of electrodes to detect changes in triiodide ion concentration and a generator anode–cathode pair of electrodes to maintain constant triiodide ion concentration and an inlet for a gaseous sample from the pyrolysis tube. The sensor electrode shall be platinum foil and the reference electrode platinum wire in saturated triiodide half-cell. The generator anode and cathode half-cell shall also be platinum. The titration cell shall be placed on a suitable magnetic stirrer.

Preparation of Apparatus: Carefully insert the quartz pyrolysis tube into the furnace, attach the tin scrubber, and connect the reactant and carrier-gas lines. Add the *Cell Electrolyte Solution* (see below) to the titration cell, and flush the cell several times. Maintain an electrolyte level of 3.2–6.6 mm above the platinum electrodes. Place the titration cell on a magnetic stirrer, and connect the cell inlet to the tin scrubber outlet. Position the platinum-foil electrodes (mounted on the movable cell head) so that the gas-inlet flow is parallel to the electrodes with the generator anode adjacent to the generator cathode. Assemble and connect the coulometer in accordance with the manufacturer's instructions. Double-wrap the adaptor containing the tin scrubber with heating tape and turn the heating tape on. Adjust the flow of the gases, the pyrolysis furnace temperature, the titration cell, and the coulometer to the desired operating conditions. Typical operating conditions are as follows:

Reactant gas flow (oxygen), cm³/min	200
Carrier-gas flow (Ar, He), cm³/min	40
Furnace temperature, °C Inlet zone	700 (maximum)
Pyrolysis zone	800–1000

---

[5] Adapted from ASTM D3120 Standard Test Method for Trace Quantities of Sulfur in Light Liquid Petroleum Hydrocarbons by Oxidative Microcoulometry. The original ASTM method is available in its entirety from ASTM International, 100 Barr Harbor Drive, West Conshohocken, PA 19428. Phone: 610-832-9585, Fax: 610-832-9555, Email: service@astm.org, Website: www.astm.org.

Outlet zone	800 (maximum)
Tin-scrubber temperature, °C	200
Titration cell	Stirrer speed set to produce slight vortex
Coulometer	
Bias voltage, mV	160
Gain	50
Constant Rate Injector, µL/s	0.25

The tin scrubber must be conditioned to sulfur, nitrogen, and chlorine before quantitative analysis can be achieved. A solution containing 10 mg/kg of butyl sulfide, 100 mg/kg of pyridine, and 200 mg/kg of chlorobenzene in isooctane has proven an effective conditioning agent. With a fresh scrubber installed and heated, two 30-µL samples of this conditioning agent injected at a flow rate of 0.5 µL/s produce a steadily increasing response, with final conditioning indicated by a constant reading from the offset during the second injection.

Reagents

Argon or Helium (argon preferred): High-purity grade, used as the carrier gas. Two-stage gas regulators must be used.

Cell Electrolyte Solution: Dissolve 0.5 g of potassium iodide and 0.6 g of sodium azide in 500 mL of high-purity water, add 5 mL of glacial acetic acid, and dilute to 1 L. Store in a dark bottle or in a dark place and prepare fresh at least every 3 months.

Oxygen: High-purity grade, used as the reactant gas.

Iodine: Resublimed, 20-mesh or less, for saturated reference electrode

Sulfur Standard (approximately 100 mg/kg): Transfer 0.1569 g of *n*-butyl sulfide, accurately weighed, into a tared 500-mL volumetric flask. Dilute to the mark with isooctane, and reweigh. Calculate the sulfur concentration (S), as a percentage:

$$S = W_b/W_s \times 2.192 \times 10^5$$

in which W_b is the weight of *n*-butyl sulfide and W_s is the weight of the solution.

Calibration Prepare a calibration standard (approximately 5 mg/kg) by pipetting 5 mL of *Sulfur Standard* into a 10-mL volumetric flask and diluting with isooctane to volume. Fill and clamp the syringe onto the constant-rate injector, push the sliding carriage forward to penetrate the septum with the needle, and zero the meter in case of long-term drift in the automatic baseline zero circuitry. Switch S_1 automatically starts the stepper-motor syringe drive and initiates the analysis cycle. At 2.5 min (before the 3-min meter hold point) set the digital meter with the scan potentiometer to correspond to the sulfur content of the known standard to the nearest 0.01 mg/kg. At the 3-min point, the number displayed on the meter stops, the plunger drive block is retracted to its original position, as preset by switch S_2, and a baseline re-equilibration period equal to the injection period elapses before a ready light and a beeper indicate that a new sample may be injected. Repeat the *Calibration* step a total of at least four times.

Procedure Rinse the syringe several times with sample; then fill it, clamp it onto the constant-rate injector, push the sliding carriage forward to penetrate the septum with the needle, and zero the meter. Turn on switch S_1 to start the stepper-motor syringe drive automatically and initiate the analysis cycle. After the 3-min hold point, the number displayed on the meter corresponds to the sulfur content of the injected sample.

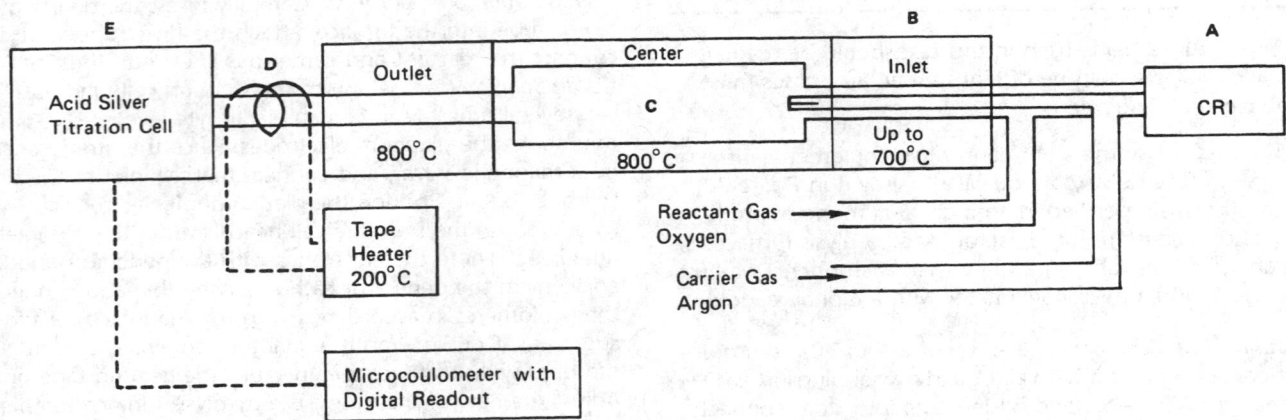

Figure 20. Microcoulometric Titrating System for the Determination of Sulfur in Hexanes

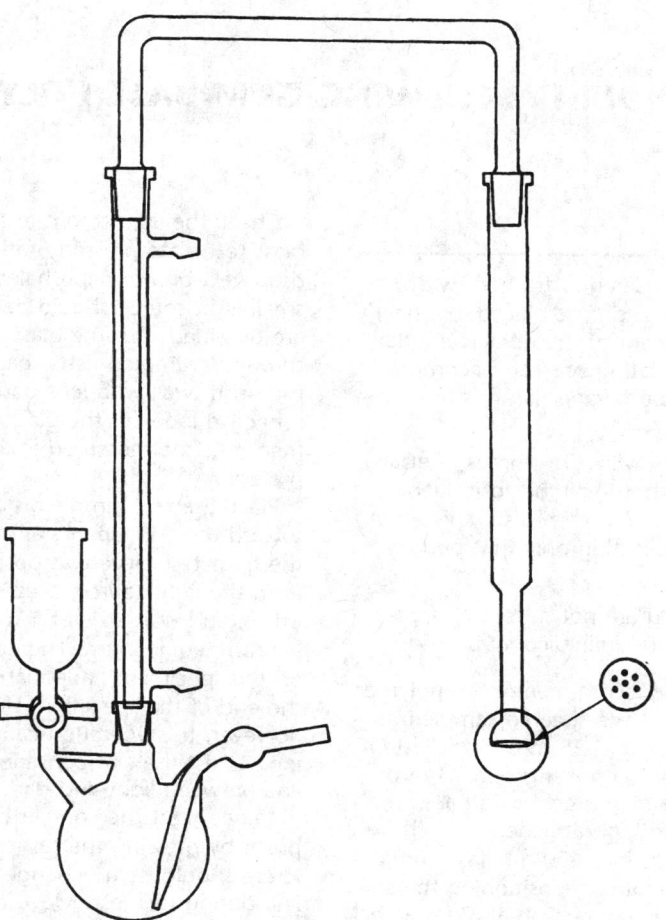

Figure 21. Raney Nickel Reduction Apparatus

APPENDIX IV: CHEWING GUM BASE POLYMERS

BOUND STYRENE

Abbé-Type Refractometer Use an instrument with fourth decimal place accuracy that can be placed in a nearly horizontal position for measurement of the refractive index of solids. An Amici-type compensating prism for achromatization is necessary unless a sodium vapor lamp is used as a light source.

Ethanol–Toluene Azeotrope Mix 70 volumes of ethanol or of formula 2B ethanol with 30 volumes of toluene, reflux for 4 h over calcium oxide, and then distill, discarding the first and last portions and collecting only that portion distilling within a range of 1°.

[NOTE—Refluxing and distilling are not necessary if anhydrous 2B ethanol or absolute grain alcohol is used.]

Sample Preparation Sheet out a sample of the polymer to a thickness of 0.5 mm, and cut the sheeted sample into strips approximately 13 mm wide and 25 mm long. Fasten one strip to each leg of a "spider," consisting of a 13-mm square of sheet aluminum or stainless steel having a Nichrome wire leg about 38 mm long attached to each corner. Place the spider and strips in a 400-mL flask containing 60 mL of *Ethanol–Toluene Azeotrope*, positioning the spider so that each sample strip is in contact on all sides with the solvent. Extract for 1 h at a temperature at which the solvent boils gently, then replace the solvent with another 60-mL portion of *Ethanol–Toluene Azeotrope*, and extract for an additional hour. Remove the spider and sample strips from the flask, and dry them at 100° to constant weight in a vacuum oven at a pressure of about 10 mm Hg.

[CAUTION—The samples must be extracted and dried thoroughly, but avoid overheating, which would cause plasticization.]

Remove the extracted and dried strips from the spider, and press the strips between aluminum foil (0.025 to 0.08 mm thick, having good tear strength) at 100° for 3 to 10 min (preferably not more than 5 min), using any suitable apparatus to produce a uniform thickness not exceeding 0.5 mm. If the pressing is done between flat platens without a cavity, use a force between about 500 and 1500 lb, increasing the applied force proportionally if several strips are pressed at one time. If cavity pressing plates are used, close the platens without applying pressure and preheat for 1 min, then apply a force of about 11 tons for 3 min, remove the specimens from the press, and allow them to cool.

Procedure Cut the pressed sample in half with sharp scissors, and peel off one piece of the foil. Cut off a strip about 6 mm wide and 12 mm long with the scissors so that one of the narrower ends is freshly cut.

Check the adjustment of the refractometer by means of a glass test plate pressed firmly against the prism, using a drop of α-bromo-naphthalene as the contact liquid. The small light source should be collimated. The best readings are obtained with the glass test piece if the light is diffused through crumpled tissue paper. After this adjustment, clean the prism well with lens paper moistened with alcohol. The refractive index of the glass test piece and of the test specimen must be measured at a known constant temperature, preferably 25°.

Place the test sample on the prism with the cut edge toward the light source approximately where the edge of the glass test piece was positioned. Remove the tissue paper from the light source, press the specimen firmly on the prism, and wait at least 1 min for the sample to attain temperature equilibrium. The upper prism may be closed lightly on the specimen if adequate light can still be focused on the end of the specimen. Unless the specimen is very thin, however, this operation can damage the prism or its mounting. Adjust the compensating prism until a sharp dividing line between light and dark fields with minimum color is obtained. Test the contact between the specimen and the prism by pressing the test specimen against the prism: There should be no change in the position of the boundary line during this test. Move the hand control from the light into the dark field until the boundary line just reaches the cross hairs, and make at least three readings. If the readings differ by more than 0.0001 refractive index unit, make further readings. Repeat the process of obtaining readings with another portion of the sample having a freshly cut edge, and average the mean values of the two sets of readings thus obtained. If the two mean values do not differ by more than 0.0002 refractive index unit, report the average as the results of the calculations. If necessary, correct the refractive index measurements to 25° using the equation

$$n_{25} = n_t + 0.00037(t - 25),$$

in which n_{25} is the refractive index at 25°, and n_t is the refractive index at the temperature, t, of measurement.

Calculate the percentage of bound styrene in emulsion-polymerized samples by the formula

$$\text{Result} = 23.50 + 1164(n_{25} - 1.53456) - 3497(n_{25} - 1.53456)^2.$$

Calculate the percentage of bound styrene in solution-polymerized samples by the formula

$$\text{Result} = (1212.1212)(n_{25}) - 1838.3636.$$

Alternatively, the percentage of bound styrene may be determined by reference to suitable tables.

MOLECULAR WEIGHT

Polyethylene

Sample Solutions Dissolve 1 g of sample, accurately weighed, in 95 mL of tetrahydronaphthalene, filter into a 100-mL volumetric flask, dilute to volume with the solvent, and mix (*Solution 1*). Transfer 50.0 mL of *Solution 1* into a tared dish, evaporate on a steam bath for about 1 h, and then evaporate to dryness by heating in a vacuum oven at 70° for 2 h or to constant weight. Calculate the concentration, C_1, in grams per 100 mL, of *Solution 1*. Prepare *Solutions 2* and *3*, respectively, by diluting 5.0-mL and 10.0-mL portions of *Solution 1* to 50.0 mL with the solvent, and then calculate the concentration of each (C_2 and C_3, respectively).

Procedure Determine the flow time, in seconds, of the solvent (t_0) and of the three *Sample Solutions* (t_1, t_2, and t_3, respectively) in a Cannon-Fenske viscometer immersed in a constant-temperature bath maintained at 130°. Calculate the specific viscosity, η_{sp}, of each *Sample Solution* by the formula

$$\text{Result} = (t/t_0) - 1,$$

and then calculate the reduced viscosity of each by the formula

$$\text{Result} = \eta_{sp}/C.$$

Plot the reduced viscosity of each solution against concentration, and extrapolate to zero concentration to obtain the intrinsic viscosity, $[\eta]$. Finally, calculate the molecular weight of the polyethylene by the formula

$$\text{Result} = ([\eta]/K)^{1/a},$$

in which K is 5.1×10^{-4}, and a is 0.725.

Polyisobutylene (Flory Method)

Sample Solutions Dissolve 1 g of sample, accurately weighed, in 95 mL of diisobutylene, filter into a 100-mL volumetric flask, dilute to volume with solvent, and mix (*Solution 1*). Transfer 50.0 mL of *Solution 1* into a tared dish, evaporate on a steam bath for about 1 h, and then evaporate to dryness by heating in a vacuum oven at 70° for 2 h or to constant weight. Calculate the concentration, C_1, in grams per 100 mL, of *Solution 1*. Prepare *Solutions 2* and *3*, respectively, by diluting 5.0-mL and 10.0-mL portions of *Solution 1* to 50.0 mL with solvent, and then calculate the concentration of each (C_2 and C_3, respectively).

Procedure Determine the flow time, in seconds, of the solvent (t_0) and of the three *Sample Solutions* (t_1, t_2, and t_3, respectively) in a Cannon-Fenske viscometer immersed in a constant-temperature bath maintained at 20°. Calculate the specific viscosity, η_{sp}, of each *Sample Solution* by the formula

$$\text{Result} = (t/t_0) - 1,$$

and then calculate the reduced viscosity of each by the formula

$$\text{Result} = \eta_{sp}/C.$$

Plot the reduced viscosity of each solution against concentration, and extrapolate to zero concentration to obtain the intrinsic viscosity, $[\eta]$. Finally, calculate the molecular weight of the polyisobutylene by the formula

$$\text{Result} = ([\eta]/K)^{1/a},$$

in which K is 3.60×10^{-4}, and a is 0.64.

Polyvinyl Acetate

Sample Solutions Dissolve 1 g of sample, accurately weighed, in 95 mL of acetone, filter into a 100-mL volumetric flask, dilute to volume with the solvent, and mix (*Solution 1*). Transfer 50.0 mL of *Solution 1* into a tared dish, evaporate on a steam bath for about 1 h, and then evaporate to dryness by heating in a vacuum oven at 70° for 2 h or to constant weight. Calculate the concentration, C_1, in grams per 100 mL, of *Solution 1*. Prepare *Solutions 2* and *3*, respectively, by diluting 5.0-mL and 10.0-mL portions of *Solution 1* to 50.0 mL with solvent, and then calculate the concentration of each (C_2 and C_3, respectively).

Procedure Determine the flow time, in seconds, of the solvent (t_0) and of the three *Sample Solutions* (t_1, t_2, and t_3, respectively) in a Cannon-Fenske viscometer immersed in a constant-temperature bath maintained at 25°. Calculate the specific viscosity, η_{sp}, of each *Sample Solution* by the formula

$$\text{Result} = (t/t_0) - 1,$$

and then calculate the reduced viscosity of each by the formula

$$\text{Result} = \eta_{sp}/C.$$

Plot the reduced viscosity of each solution against concentration, and extrapolate to zero concentration to obtain the intrinsic viscosity, $[\eta]$. Finally, calculate the molecular weight of the polyvinyl acetate by the formula

$$\text{Result} = ([\eta]/K)^{1/a},$$

in which K is 1.88×10^{-4}, and a is 0.69.

QUINONES

Standard Preparations Transfer 25.0 mg of hydroquinone into a 100-mL volumetric flask, dissolve in and dilute to volume with water, and mix. Transfer 1.0-, 2.0-, 3.0-, 4.0-, and 6.0-mL aliquots of this solution into a series of 100-mL volumetric flasks, dilute each to volume with water, and mix. Transfer 2.0 mL of each of these solutions and 3.0 mL of water into a series of 25-mL graduates, add 0.5 mL of 0.1 N sodium carbonate to each, and continue as directed under *Sample Preparations* (below), beginning with "… shake immediately, then add 1.0 mL of 15% sulfuric acid…."

Sample Preparations Place 30 g of freshly coagulated and washed sample into a 250-mL two-necked flask, add 100 mL of water, and heat at 66° for 2 h.

[CAUTION—Do not boil.]

Cool to room temperature, and transfer 5.0 mL of the extract into a 25-mL glass-stoppered graduate. Transfer 5.0 mL of water into a second graduate to serve as the blank. To each graduate add 1.0 mL of 15% sulfuric acid. To the graduate containing the sample extract add 0.5 mL of 0.1 N sodium carbonate, shake immediately, and then add 1.0 mL of 15% sulfuric acid.

[NOTE—The elapsed time for this operation should not exceed 15 s.]

Add to each graduate 1.0 mL of 2,4-dinitrophenylhydrazine solution (dissolve 100 mg of 2,4-dinitrophenylhydrazine in 50 mL of carbonyl-free methanol, add 4 mL of hydrochloric acid, and dilute to 100 mL with water), stopper, and heat at 70° in a water bath for 1 h. Cool to room temperature, then add to each graduate 13 mL of water and 5.0 mL of benzene, stopper, and shake vigorously. Allow the phases to separate, and pipet 2.0 mL of the benzene layer from each graduate into corresponding test tubes containing 10 mL of a 1:100 solution of diethanolamine in pyridine. Shake each tube, and allow the color to develop for 10 min.

Procedure Determine the absorbance of the *Sample Preparation* in a 1-cm cell at 620 nm, with a suitable spectrophotometer, against the reagent blank. Determine the absorbance of each *Standard Preparation* in the same manner. Prepare a *Standard Curve* by plotting absorbance of each *Standard Preparation* against micrograms of quinone. From the *Standard Curve*, read the quantity, in micrograms, of quinones (as benzoquinone) in the *Sample Preparation*, and record the value thus obtained as Q. Calculate the quantity of quinones (as benzoquinone), in parts per million, in the sample by the formula

Result = 20Q/W,

in which W is the weight, in grams, of the sample taken.

RESIDUAL STYRENE

Standard Preparation Place 25 mL of carbon disulfide in a 100-mL volumetric flask, cap with a serum stopper, and tare the flask to the nearest 0.1 mg. Using 50-μg syringes, inject 15 μL each of styrene and of alpha-methylstyrene (AMS), reweighing after each addition to obtain the weight of each solution injected. Record the weight, in milligrams, of styrene as w_1 and that of AMS as w_2. Dilute to volume with carbon disulfide, and mix. Pipet 2 mL of this solution into a second 100-mL volumetric flask, dilute to volume with carbon disulfide, and mix. Finally, pipet 25 mL of the diluted solution into a third 100-mL volumetric flask, dilute to volume with carbon disulfide, and mix.

AMS–Solvent Solution Place 25 mL of carbon disulfide into a 100-mL volumetric flask, cap with a serum stopper, and tare the flask to the nearest 0.1 mg. Using a 50-μL syringe, inject 15 μL of AMS, and reweigh to obtain the weight of AMS injected. Dilute to volume with carbon disulfide, and mix. Pipet 2 mL of this solution into a second 100-mL volumetric flask, dilute to volume with carbon disulfide, and mix. Finally, pipet 25 mL of the diluted solution into a third 100-mL volumetric flask, dilute to volume, and mix. Calculate the weight, in grams, of AMS in each milliliter of the final solution, and record the result as w' (approximately 7.5×10^{-7}).

Sample Preparation

Latex Samples Add, with agitation, 100 mL of the latex to a mixture consisting of 15 mL of glacial acetic acid and 10 g of sodium chloride in 500 mL of hot water. Coagulation starts almost immediately. When coagulation is complete, collect the coagulum on a coarse filter or cheesecloth, and wash with 1000 mL of a hot solution prepared with 5.6 g of sodium hydroxide and 1000 mL of water. Wash with hot water until the wash water is free of alkali, then cut the coagulum into small pieces, and dry at 105° for 4 h. Continue as directed under *Solid Samples* (below), beginning with "Transfer 1.5 g, accurately weighed...."

Solid Samples Cut a piece approximately 2 in. × 3 in. × 5 in. from the corner of a polymer bale, and pass it through a cold mill, set at least 1/4 in. open, four times, reversing the sample on each pass. Cut the sample into two pieces at least 1 in. from the edge to expose clean polymer, and then dice approximately 2 g of the clean polymer or cut into small strips. Transfer 1.5 g, accurately weighed, into a 4-oz bottle fitted with a polyethylene cap, add 25.0 mL of the *AMS–Solvent Solution*, cap tightly, and agitate on a mechanical shaker until the polymer dissolves.

[NOTE—Some polymers tend to swell and form viscous cements instead of dissolving cleanly. If this occurs, add 5- to 10-mL increments of carbon disulfide to obtain a mobile slurry, and in the next step increase the volume of methanol by a proportional amount.]

Add 25 mL of methanol, cap the bottle, and shake vigorously on the shaker for 30 min. After the contents have settled, decant 10 mL of the coagulant serum into a 1-oz bottle, add 10 mL of water, and stopper with a serum cap. Shake vigorously for 1 min, then turn the bottle upside down, and allow the layers to separate. Withdraw by syringe 1 to 2 mL of the lower (carbon disulfide) layer, and transfer it into a 10-dram vial filled with 1/4 in. of anhydrous sodium sulfate. Seal with a polyethylene cap, shake to mix, and allow to settle.

Procedure (See *Chromatography*, Appendix IIA.) Inject a 10-μL portion of the *Sample Preparation* into a suitable gas chromatograph in which the detector is the hydrogen flame-ionization type and the column is 10-ft × 3/16-in. stainless steel tubing, or equivalent, packed with 25% Ucon 50 HB 2000 on 60- to 80-mesh acid-washed DMCS Chromosorb W, or with equivalent packing materials. Use nitrogen or helium as the carrier gas, flowing at 40 mL/min. The injection port temperature is 240°; the column temperature, 170° isothermal; and the detector temperature, 250°. Adjust the sensitivity of the instrument to give as large a signal as possible for styrene and AMS as is consistent with an acceptable background level. Measure the styrene and AMS peaks by any convenient method, recording the area of the styrene peak as A_1 and that of the AMS peak as A_2.

In the same manner, inject a 10-μL portion of the *Standard Preparation* into the chromatograph, obtain the chromatogram, and record the area of the styrene peak as a_1 and that of the AMS peak as a_2. Calculate the styrene factor, F, by the formula

$$\text{Result} = (w_1/w_2) \times (a_2/a_1).$$

Calculate the content of residual styrene in the sample taken, in parts per million, by the formula

$$\text{Result} = (A_1/A_2) \times F \times 25 \times (w'/W) \times 10^6,$$

in which W is the weight, in grams, of the sample taken.

SAMPLE SOLUTION FOR ARSENIC LIMIT TEST

Transfer 1 g of sample, accurately weighed, into a Kjeldahl flask, rest the open end of the flask in a Kjeldahl fume bulb attached to a water aspirator, add 5 mL of sulfuric acid and 4 mL of 30% hydrogen peroxide, and digest over a small flame. (See *Caution* statement under *Arsenic Limit Test*, Appendix IIIB.) Continue adding the peroxide in 2-mL portions, allowing the reaction to subside between additions, until all organic matter is destroyed, fumes of sulfuric acid are copiously evolved, and the solution becomes colorless. Maintain oxidizing conditions at all times during the digestion by adding peroxide whenever the mixture turns brown or darkens. (The amount of peroxide required to completely digest the samples will vary, but as much as 200 mL may be required in some cases, depending on the nature of the material.) Cool, cautiously add 10 mL of water, again evaporate to strong fuming, and cool. Transfer the solution into an arsine generator flask, wash the Kjeldahl flask and bulb with water, adding the washings to the generator flask, and dilute to 35 mL with water.

SAMPLE SOLUTION FOR LEAD LIMIT TEST

Transfer 3.3 g of sample, accurately weighed, into a porcelain dish or casserole, heat on a hot plate until completely charred, then heat in a muffle furnace at 480° for 8 h or overnight, and cool. Cautiously add 5 mL of nitric acid, evaporate to dryness on a hot plate, then heat again in the muffle furnace at 480° for exactly 15 min, and cool. Extract the ash with two 10-mL portions of water, filtering each extract into a separator. Leach any insoluble material on the filter with 6 mL of *Ammonium Citrate Solution*, 2 mL of *Hydroxylamine Hydrochloride Solution*, and 5 mL of water (see *Lead Limit Test*, Appendix IIIB, for preparation of these solutions), adding the filtered washings to the separator. Continue as directed under *Procedure* in the *Lead Limit Test*, Appendix IIIB, beginning with "Add 2 drops of phenol red TS to the separator...."

TOTAL UNSATURATION

This method measures total unsaturation in a sample by the multivariate analysis of Fourier transform infrared spectra. It correlates the absorbance in the spectral regions corresponding to two major types of unsaturation with their concentrations. This is an extension of univariate least squares analysis that correlates a single band absorbance height or area with concentration.

Apparatus Use a Fourier transform infrared spectrometer (FTIR), with its associated computer and peripherals, capable of measuring from 4500 to 500 cm^{-1} and of acquiring data with a resolution of at least 2 cm^{-1}. The optics of the instrument must be sealed and desiccated, or, like the sample chamber, must be under continuous dry air or nitrogen gas purge. The spectrometer is equipped with software capable of multicomponent analysis using the partial least squares method (PLS-1, or equivalent). This software is commercially available as an accessory to the spectrometer or as an external software package.

Laboratory Press Use a Carver-type press capable of pressing polymer films.

Sample Preparation Compression-mold a thin film of the sample to roughly a 500-μm thickness at 10 tons and 90° for 30 to 60 s. Do not exceed this time or temperature, as structural changes in unsaturation can occur.

Operating Conditions Collect not less than 64 FTIR spectral scans of the standards and sample in the absorbance mode. Boxcar apodization and 2 cm^{-1} resolution are recommended parameters. Spectral normalization should be done on the 4333 cm^{-1} peak to account for varying sample thicknesses. Use identical operating conditions for the standards and for the sample.

Calibration Assemble a set of at least ten calibration standards available from the given supplier of food-grade butyl rubber (such as Exxon Chemical Co.) that covers the entire unsaturation range expected. Identify characteristic FTIR spectral regions corresponding to the unsaturation components by proton magnetic resonance spectroscopy. These spectral regions may include 1700 to 1600 cm^{-1} C=C stretching, 900 to 600 cm^{-1} vinylic H deformations, and 2200 to 1800 cm^{-1} overtone regions.

Collect not less than 64 spectral scans of the standards. Construct a calibration matrix containing infrared absorbance values for unsaturation types in the standards and their known concentrations. Confirm the validity of the calibration matrix model as recommended in the software manual. A recommended method is cross-validation for all standards by sequentially excluding one of the standards from the calibration matrix, then using the remaining standards to predict the concentrations. After validation, determine the optimum number of factors, or loading vectors, needed to minimize the deviation between actual and predicted concentrations. This determination is automated in most multicomponent analysis packages. For the highest possible precision, a calibration for each rubber grade for each manufacturer is recommended.

Procedure Obtain the FTIR spectra of the sample under identical sample preparation and operating conditions as described above. Determine the amount of unsaturation in the sample using the same multivariate analysis parameters and optimal number of factors that were obtained from the calibration matrix. Sum the different unsaturation amounts to obtain the total unsaturation in the sample.

APPENDIX V: ENZYME ASSAYS

A list of the enzymes covered by the general monograph on *Enzyme Preparations* is shown in the accompanying *table*. Also incorporated in the table are the trivial names by which each is commonly known, as well as the systematic names of the major components or of the enzyme for which the preparation is standardized, in accordance with the *Recommendations (1992) of the Nomenclature Committee of the International Union of Biochemistry and Molecular Biology on the Nomenclature and Classification of Enzymes*.

Enzyme Preparations Used in Food Processing

TRIVIAL NAME	CLASSIFICATION	SOURCE	NAMES (IUB)[a]	NO.[a]
α-Acetolactate-decarboxylase	lyase	*Bacillus subtilis** (d-*Bacillus brevis*)	(2S)-2-hydroxy-2-methyl-3-oxobutanoate carboxy-lyase[(3R)-3-hydroxybutan-2-one-forming]	4.1.1.5
Aminopeptidase, Leucine	protease	(1) *Aspergillus niger*	none	3.4.11.1
		(2) *Aspergillus oryzae*		
		(3) *Rhizopus oryzae*		
		(4) *Rhizopus arrhizus*		
		(5) *Lactococcus lactis*		
		(6) *Trichoderma reesei*		
		(7) *Trichoderma longibrachiatum*		
		(8) *Aeromonas caviae*		
		(9) *Lactobacillus casei*		
α-Amylase	carbohydrase	(1) *Aspergillus niger* var.	1,4-α-D-glucan glucanohydrolase	3.2.1.1
		(2) *Aspergillus oryzae* var.		
		(3) *Rhizopus oryzae* var.		
		(4) *Bacillus subtilis* var.		
		(5) barley malt		
		(6) *Bacillus licheniformis* var.		
		(7) *Bacillus stearothermophilus*		
		(8) *Bacillus subtilis** (d-*Bacillus megaterium*)		
		(9) *Bacillus subtilis** (d-*Bacillus stearothermophilus*)		
		(10) *Bacillus licheniformis** (d-*Bacillus stearothermophilus*)		
β-Amylase	carbohydrase	(1) barley malt	1,4-α-D-glucan maltohydrolase	3.2.1.2
		(2) barley		
Bromelain	protease	pineapples: *Ananas comosus Ananas bracteatus* (L)	none	3.4.22.32
				3.4.22.33
Catalase	oxidoreductase	(1) *Aspergillus niger* var.	hydrogen peroxide: hydrogen peroxide oxidoreductase	1.11.1.6

[a] *Enzyme Nomenclature: Recommendations (1992) of the Nomenclature Committee of the International Union of Biochemistry and Molecular Biology*, Academic Press, New York, 1992.
[b] Usually a mixture of pectin depolymerase, pectin methylesterase, pectin lyase, and pectate lyase.
* The asterisk indicates a genetically modified organism. The donor organism is listed after "d-."

Enzyme Preparations Used in Food Processing (continued)

TRIVIAL NAME	CLASSIFICATION	SOURCE	NAMES (IUB)[a]	NO.[a]
		(2) bovine liver		
		(3) *Micrococcus lysodeikticus*		
Cellulase	carbohydrase	(1) *Aspergillus niger* var.	endo-1,4-(1,3;1,4)-β-D-glucan 4-glucanohydrolase	3.2.1.4
		(2) *Trichoderma longibrachiatum* (formerly *reesei*)		
Chymosin	protease	(1) *Aspergillus niger* var. *awamori*[*] (d-calf prochymosin gene)		3.4.23.4
		(2) *Escherichia coli* K-12[*] (d-calf prochymosin gene)		
		(3) *Kluyveromyces marxianus* var. *lactis*[*] (d-calf prochymosin gene)		
Chymotrypsin	protease	bovine or porcine pancreatic extract	none	3.4.21.1
Ficin	protease	figs: *Ficus* sp.	none	3.4.22.3
α-Galactosidase	carbohydrase	(1) *Mortierella vinacea* var. *raffinoseutilizer*	α-D-galactoside galactohydrolase	3.2.1.22
		(2) *Aspergillus niger*		
β-Glucanase	carbohydrase	(1) *Aspergillus niger* var.	1,3-(1,3;1,4)-β-D-glucan 3(4)-glucanohydrolase	3.2.1.6
		(2) *Bacillus subtilis* var.		
		(3) *Trichoderma longibrachiatum*		
Glucoamylase (Amyloglucosidase)	carbohydrase	(1) *Aspergillus niger* var.	1,4-α-D-glucan glucohydrolase	3.2.1.3
		(2) *Aspergillus oryzae* var.		
		(3) *Rhizopus oryzae* var.		
		(4) *Rhizopus niveus*		
Glucose Isomerase	isomerase	(1) *Actinoplanes missouriensis*	D-xylose ketoisomerase	5.3.1.5
		(2) *Bacillus coagulans*		
		(3) *Streptomyces olivaceus*		
		(4) *Streptomyces olivochromogenus*		
		(5) *Streptomyces rubiginosus*		
		(6) *Streptomyces murinus*		
		(7) *Microbacterium arborescens*		
Glucose Oxidase	oxidoreductase	*Aspergillus niger* var.	β-D-glucose: oxygen 1-oxidoreductase	1.1.3.4
β-D-Glucosidase	carbohydrase	(1) *Aspergillus niger* var.	β-D-glucoside glucohydrolase	3.2.1.21
		(2) *Trichoderma longibrachiatum*		

[a] Enzyme Nomenclature: Recommendations (1992) of the Nomenclature Committee of the International Union of Biochemistry and Molecular Biology, Academic Press, New York, 1992.
[b] Usually a mixture of pectin depolymerase, pectin methylesterase, pectin lyase, and pectate lyase.
[*] The asterisk indicates a genetically modified organism. The donor organism is listed after "d-."

Enzyme Preparations Used in Food Processing (continued)

TRIVIAL NAME	CLASSIFICATION	SOURCE	NAMES (IUB)[a]	NO.[a]
Hemicellulase	carbohydrase	(1) *Aspergillus niger* var.	(1) α-L-arabinofuranoside arabinofuranohydrolase	3.2.1.55
		(2) *Trichoderma longibrachiatum*	(2) 1,4-β-D-mannan mannanohydrolase	3.2.1.78
			(3) 1,3-β-D-xylan xylanohydrolase	3.2.1.32
			(4) 1,5-α-L-arabinan arabinanohydrolase	3.2.1.99
Invertase	carbohydrase	*Saccharomyces* sp. (*Kluyveromyces*) and *Saccharomyces* sp (*cerevisiae*)	β-D-fructofuranoside fructohydrolase	3.2.1.26
Lactase	carbohydrase	(1) *Aspergillus niger* var.	β-D-galactoside galactohydrolase	3.2.1.23
		(2) *Aspergillus oryzae* var.		
		(3) *Saccharomyces* sp.		
		(4) *Candida pseudotropicalis*		
		(5) *Kluyveromyces marxianus* var. *lactis*		
Lipase	lipase	(1) edible forestomach tissue of calves, kids, and lambs	(1) carboxylic-ester hydrolase	3.1.1.1
		(2) animal pancreatic tissues	(2) triacylglycerol acylhydrolase	3.1.1.3
		(3) *Aspergillus oryzae* var.		
		(4) *Aspergillus niger* var.		
		(5) *Rhizomucor miehei*		
		(6) *Candida rugosa*		
Lysozyme	lysozyme	egg white	peptidoglycan N-acetylmuramoylhydrolase	3.2.1.17
Maltogenic Amylase	carbohydrase	*Bacillus subtilis*[*] (d-*Bacillus stearothermophilus*)	1,4-α-D-glucan α-maltohydrolase	3.2.1.133
Pancreatin	mixed carbohydrase, protease, and lipase	bovine and porcine pancreatic tissue	(1) 1,4-α-D-glucan glucanohydrolase	3.2.1.1
			(2) triacylglycerol acylhydrolase	3.1.1.3
			(3) protease	3.4.21.4
Papain	protease	papaya: *Carica papaya* (L)	none	3.4.22.2
				3.4.22.6
Pectinase[b]	carbohydrase	(1) *Aspergillus niger* var.	(1) poly(1,4-α-D-galacturonide) glycanohydrolase	3.2.1.15
		(2) *Rhizopus oryzae* var.	(2) pectin pectylhydrolase	3.1.1.11
			(3) poly(1,4-α-D-glacturonide) lyase	4.2.2.2
			(4) poly(methoxyl-L-galacturonide) lyase	4.2.2.10

[a] Enzyme Nomenclature: Recommendations (1992) of the Nomenclature Committee of the International Union of Biochemistry and Molecular Biology, Academic Press, New York, 1992.
[b] Usually a mixture of pectin depolymerase, pectin methylesterase, pectin lyase, and pectate lyase.
[*] The asterisk indicates a genetically modified organism. The donor organism is listed after "d-."

Enzyme Preparations Used in Food Processing (continued)

TRIVIAL NAME	CLASSIFICATION	SOURCE	NAMES (IUB)[a]	NO.[a]
Pepsin	protease	porcine or other animal stomach tissue	none	3.4.23.1 3.4.23.2
Phospholipase A$_2$	lipase	animal pancreatic tissue	phosphatidylcholine 2-acylhydrolase	3.1.1.4
Phytase	phosphatase	*Aspergillus niger* var.	(1) *myo*-inositol-hexakisphosphate-3-phosphohydrolase	3.1.3.8
			(2) orthophosphoric-mono ester phosphohydrolase	3.1.3.2
Protease (general)	protease	(1) *Aspergillus niger* var.	none	3.4.23.18
		(2) *Aspergillus oryzae* var		
		(3) *Bacillus subtilis* var.		3.4.24.28
		(4) *Bacillus licheniformis* var.		3.4.21.62
Pullulanase	carbohydrase	*Bacillus acidopullulyticus*	α-dextrin-6-glucanohydrolase	3.2.1.41
Rennet	protease	(1) fourth stomach of ruminant animals	none	3.4.23.1
		(2) *Endothia parasitica*		3.4.23.4
		(3) *Rhizomucor miehei*		3.4.23.22
		(4) *Rhizomucor pusillus* (Lindt)		3.4.23.23
		(5) *Bacillus cereus*		
Trypsin	protease	animal pancreas	none	3.4.21.4

[a] Enzyme Nomenclature: Recommendations (1992) of the Nomenclature Committee of the International Union of Biochemistry and Molecular Biology, Academic Press, New York, 1992.
[b] Usually a mixture of pectin depolymerase, pectin methylesterase, pectin lyase, and pectate lyase.
* The asterisk indicates a genetically modified organism. The donor organism is listed after "d-."

The following procedures are provided for application as necessary in determining compliance with the vendor's declared representations for enzyme activity. For all of the procedures use filtered, ultra-high purity water with a resistivity of 16 to 18 megohms.

ACID PHOSPHATASE ACTIVITY

Application and Principle This procedure is used to determine acid phosphatase activity in preparations derived from *Aspergillus niger* var. The test is based on the enzymatic hydrolysis of *p*-nitrophenyl phosphate, followed by the measurement of the released inorganic phosphate.

Reagents and Solutions

Glycine Buffer (0.2 M, pH 2.5) Dissolve 15.014 g of glycine (Merck, Catalog No. 4201) in about 800 mL of water. Adjust the pH to 2.5 with 1 M hydrochloric acid (consumption should be about 80 mL), and dilute to 1000 mL with water.

Substrate (30 mM) Dissolve 1.114 g of *p*-nitrophenyl phosphate (Boehringer, Catalog No. 738 352) in *Glycine Buffer*, and adjust the volume to 100 mL with the buffer. Prepare a fresh substrate solution daily.

TCA Solution Dissolve 15 g of trichloroacetic acid in water, and dilute to 100 mL.

Ascorbic Acid Solution Dissolve 10 g of ascorbic acid in water, and dilute to 100 mL. Store under refrigeration. The solution is stable for 7 days.

Ammonium Molybdate Solution Dissolve 2.5 g of ammonium molybdate [(NH$_4$)$_6$MoO$_{24}$·4H$_2$O] (Merck, Catalog No. 1182) in water, and dilute to 100 mL.

1 M Sulfuric Acid Stir 55.6 mL of concentrated sulfuric acid (H$_2$SO$_4$) (Merck, Catalog No. 731) into about 800 mL of water. Allow to cool, and make up to 1000 mL with water.

Reagent C Mix 3 volumes of *1 M Sulfuric Acid* with 1 volume of *Ammonium Molybdate Solution*, then add 1 volume of *Ascorbic Acid Solution*, and mix well. Prepare fresh daily.

Standard Phosphate Solution Prepare a 9.0-mM phosphate stock solution. Dissolve and dilute 612.4 mg of potassium dihydrogen phosphate (KH$_2$PO$_4$) (dried in desiccator with silica) to 500 mL with water in a volumetric flask. Make the following dilutions in water from the stock solution, and use these as standards.

Dilution	Phosphorus Concentration (nmol/mL)	Acid Phosphatase Activity (HFU/mL)
1:100	90	2400
1:200	45	1200
1:400	22.5	600

Pipet 4.0 mL of each dilution into two test tubes. Also pipet 4.0 mL of water into one tube (reagent blank). Add 4.0 mL of *Reagent C*, and mix. Incubate at 500 for 20 min, and cool to room temperature. Measure the absorbances at 820 nm against that of the reagent blank. Prepare a standard curve by plotting the absorbances against acid phosphatase activity [HFU (acid phosphatase unit)/mL]. Construct a new standard curve with each series of assays.

Test Preparation Prepare a solution of the enzyme preparation in the *Glycine Buffer* so that 1 mL will contain between 600 and 2400 HFU/mL.

Procedure Pipet 1.9 mL of *Substrate* in two test tubes. Add 2.0 mL of *TCA Solution* to one of the tubes (blank), and mix. Put the tubes without *TCA Solution* in a water bath at 37° and let them equilibrate for 5 min. While using a stopwatch, start the hydrolysis by adding sequentially at proper intervals 0.1 mL of *Test Preparation* to each tube, and mix. After exactly 15 min of incubation, stop the reaction by adding 2.0 mL of *TCA Solution* to each tube. Mix, and cool to room temperature. Add 0.1 mL of *Test Preparation* to the reagent blank tube (kept at room temperature), and mix. If precipitate occurs, separate it by centrifugation for 10 min at 2000 g.

Pipet 0.4 mL of each sample after hydrolysis into separate test tubes. Add 3.6 mL of water to each tube. Add 4.0 mL of *Reagent C*, and mix. Incubate at 50° for 20 min, and cool to room temperature. Determine the absorbance against that of reagent blank at 820 nm.

Calculation One acid phosphatase unit (HFU) is the amount of enzyme that liberates, under the conditions of the assay, inorganic phosphate from *p*-nitrophenyl phosphate at the rate of 1 nmol/min.

Subtract the blank absorbance from the sample absorbance (the difference should be between 0.100 and 1.000). Determine the acid phosphatase activity (HFU/mL) from the standard curve, and multiply by the dilution factor. For the activity of solid samples, use the following equation:

$$HFU/g = (HFU/mL \times f)/g$$

in which f is the dilution factor and g is the weight, in grams, of the sample.

AMINOPEPTIDASE (LEUCINE) ACTIVITY

Application and Principle This procedure is used to determine leucine aminopeptidase activity in enzyme preparations derived from *Lactococcus lactis*. The assay is based on the rate of absorbance change over 5 min at 30°; the change in absorbance is due to liberated *p*-nitroaniline from the hydrolysis of leucine *p*-nitroanilide.

Apparatus

Spectrophotometer Use a spectrophotometer with temperature control, suitable for measuring absorbancies at 410 nm.

Cuvette Use a 10-mm light path, quartz.

Thermometer Use a partial immersion thermometer with a suitable range.

Vortex Mixer Use a standard, variable-speed mixer.

Reagents and Solutions

pH 7.0 Phosphate Buffer (100 mM) Dissolve 13.6 g of anhydrous potassium dihydrogen orthophosphate in water, and dilute to 1 L (*Solution A*). Dissolve 22.8 g of dipotassium hydrogen orthophosphate trihydrate in water, and dilute to 1 L (*Solution B*). Slowly add approximately 550 mL of *Solution B* to approximately 400 mL of *Solution A* until the pH of the buffer stabilizes at 7 ± 0.02.

Substrate Solution Dissolve 0.0200 g of leucine *p*-nitroanilide hydrochloride (Sigma Chemical Co., Catalog No. L2158) in 100 mL of *pH 7.0 Phosphate Buffer*.

p-Nitroaniline Stock Solution Transfer 156.9 mg of *p*-nitroaniline (Aldrich Chemical Co., Catalog No. 18,531-0) to a 1-L volumetric flask, and dilute to volume with water. This solution is 1.1136 mM.

[**CAUTION**—*p*-Nitroaniline is highly toxic. Avoid breathing its dust; avoid contact with skin, eyes, and clothing. Wash the affected area with water; for eyes seek medical attention.]

Standard p-Nitroaniline Solutions Prepare the following dilutions of *p-Nitroaniline Stock Solution*: dilute 1 mL of *p-Nitroaniline Stock Solution* to 100 mL with *pH 7.0 Phosphate Buffer* (*Solution 1*, 0.01136 mM); dilute 9 mL of *Solution 1* with 3 mL of *pH 7.0 Phosphate Buffer* (*Solution 2*, 0.00852 mM); and dilute 5 mL of *Solution 1* with 5 mL of *pH 7.0 Phosphate Buffer* (*Solution 3*, 0.00568 mM).

Sample Solution Prepare a solution in *pH 7.0 Phosphate Buffer* that contains between 0.025 and 0.1 unit of aminopeptidase activity per mL.

Procedure Determine the absorbance of each of the three standard *p*-nitroaniline dilutions (solutions *1*, *2*, and *3*) at 410 nm using *pH 7.0 Phosphate Buffer* as the blank.

Pipet 3 mL of *Substrate Solution* into a cuvette, insert a thermometer in each to ensure that the temperature of the solution is correct, and equilibrate in the spectrophotometer to 30° ± 0.2°. Add 150 µL of *Sample Solution* to the equilibrated *Substrate Solution*. Mix, and start recording the absorbance. Continue recording the absorbance for approximately 5 min; it should increase linearly with time. To determine the rate of change of absorbance, ignore the initial 0.5 min of the assay line, and use a period of at least 4 min to estimate the rate of change.

Calculation One aminopeptidase activity unit (AP) is defined as the quantity of aminopeptidase required to liberate 1 µmol/min of leucine from leucine *p*-nitroanilide under the conditions of the assay at pH 7.0 and 30°.

For each of the diluted *Standard Solutions*—*1*, *2*, and *3*— plot absorbance against *p*-nitroaniline mM concentration.

The result is a straight line that passes through the origin. Calculate the millimolar extinction coefficient (ε) of each *Standard p-Nitroaniline Solution* using the following formula:

$$\varepsilon = A_N/C$$

in which A_N is the absorbance of the *Standard p-Nitroaniline Solution* at 410 nm and C is the millimolar concentration of *p*-nitroaniline of that solution. Average the three calculated values; this should result in a value of approximately 8.8. Calculate the activity of each sample taken by the equation:

$$AP/g = (\Delta A \times TCV \times 1000)/(\varepsilon \times SV \times C)$$

in which ΔA is the rate of change of absorbance per minute; TCV is the total cuvette volume (3.150 mL); SV is the sample volume (0.150 mL); and C is the concentration, in milligrams per milliliter, of the sample.

α-AMYLASE ACTIVITY (NONBACTERIAL)

Application and Principle This procedure is used to determine the α-amylase activity of enzyme preparations derived from *Aspergillus niger* var.; *Aspergillus oryzae* var.; *Rhizopus oryzae* var.; and barley malt. The assay is based on the time required to obtain a standard degree of hydrolysis of a starch solution at 30° ± 0.1°. The degree of hydrolysis is determined by comparing the iodine color of the hydrolysate with that of a standard.

Apparatus

Reference Color Standard Use a special Alpha-Amylase Color Disk (Orbeco Analytical Systems, 185 Marine Street, Farmingdale, NY 11735, Catalog No. 620-S5). Alternatively, prepare a color standard by dissolving 25.0 g of cobaltous chloride ($CoCl_2 \cdot 6H_2O$) and 3.84 g of potassium dichromate in 100 mL of 0.01 N hydrochloric acid. This standard is stable indefinitely when stored in a stoppered bottle or comparator tube.

Comparator Use either the standard Hellige comparator (Orbeco, Catalog No. 607) or the pocket comparator with prism attachment (Orbeco, Catalog No. 605AHT). The comparator should be illuminated with a 100-W frosted lamp placed 6 in. from the rear opal glass of the comparator and mounted so that direct rays from the lamp do not shine into the operator's eyes.

Comparator Tubes Use the precision-bored square tubes with a 13-mm viewing depth that are supplied with the Hellige comparator. Suitable tubes are also available from other apparatus suppliers (e.g., Thomas Scientific).

Reagents and Solutions

Buffer Solution (pH 4.8) Dissolve 164 g of anhydrous sodium acetate in about 500 mL of water, add 120 mL of glacial acetic acid, and adjust the pH to 4.8 with glacial acetic acid. Dilute to 1000 mL with water, and mix.

β-Amylase Solution Dissolve into 5 mL of water a quantity of β-amylase, free from α-amylase activity (Sigma Chemical Co., Catalog No. A7005), equivalent to 250 mg of β-amylase with 2000° diastatic power.

Special Starch Use starch designated as "Starch (Lintner) Soluble" (Baker Analyzed Reagent, Catalog No. 4010).

Before using new batches, test them in parallel with previous lots known to be satisfactory. Variations of more than ±3° diastatic power in the averages of a series of parallel tests indicate an unsuitable batch.

Buffered Substrate Solution Disperse 10.0 g (dry-weight basis) of *Special Starch* in 100 mL of cold water, and slowly pour the mixture into 300 mL of boiling water. Boil and stir for 1 to 2 min, then cool, and add 25 mL of *Buffer Solution*, followed by all of the *β-Amylase Solution*. Quantitatively transfer the mixture into a 500-mL volumetric flask with the aid of water saturated with toluene, dilute to volume with the same solvent, and mix. Store the solution at 30° ± 2° for not less than 18 h nor more than 72 h before use. (This solution is also known as "buffered limit dextrin substrate.")

Stock Iodine Solution Dissolve 5.5 g of iodine and 11.0 g of potassium iodide in about 200 mL of water, dilute to 250 mL with water, and mix. Store in a dark bottle, and make a fresh solution every 30 days.

Dilute Iodine Solution Dissolve 20 g of potassium iodide in 300 mL of water, and add 2.0 mL of *Stock Iodine Solution*. Quantitatively transfer the mixture into a 500-mL volumetric flask, dilute to volume with water, and mix. Prepare daily.

Sample Preparation Prepare a solution of the sample so that 5 mL of the final dilution will give an endpoint between 10 and 30 min under the conditions of the assay.

For barley malt, finely grind 25 g of the sample in a Miag-Seck mill (Buhler-Miag, Inc., P.O. Box 9497, Minneapolis, MN 55440). Quantitatively transfer the powder into a 1000-mL Erlenmeyer flask, add 500 mL of a 0.5% solution of sodium chloride, and allow the infusion to stand for 2.5 h at 30° ± 0.2°, agitating the contents by gently rotating the flask at 20-min intervals.

> [CAUTION—Do not mix the infusion by inverting the flask. The quantity of the grist left adhering to the inner walls of the flask as a result of agitation must be as small as possible.]

Filter the infusion through a 32-cm fluted filter of Whatman No. 1, or equivalent, paper on a 20-cm funnel, returning the first 50 mL of filtrate to the filter. Collect the filtrate until 3 h have elapsed from the time the sodium chloride solution and the sample were first mixed. Pipet 20.0 mL of the filtered infusion into a 100-mL volumetric flask, dilute to volume with the 0.5% sodium chloride solution, and mix.

Procedure Pipet 5.0 mL of *Dilute Iodine Solution* into a series of 13- × 100-mm test tubes, and place them in a water bath maintained at 30° ± 0.1°, allowing 20 tubes for each assay.

Pipet 20.0 mL of the *Buffered Substrate Solution*, previously heated in the water bath for 20 min, into a 50-mL Erlenmeyer flask, and add 5.0 mL of 0.5% sodium chloride solution, also previously heated in the water bath for 20 min. Place the flask in the water bath.

At zero time, rapidly pipet 5.0 mL of the *Sample Preparation* into the equilibrated substrate, mix immediately by swirling, stopper the flask, and place it back in the water bath. After 10 min, transfer 1.0 mL of the reaction mixture from the 50-mL flask into one of the test tubes containing the *Dilute Iodine Solution*, shake the tube, then pour its contents into a *Comparator Tube*, and immediately compare with the *Reference Color Standard* in the *Comparator*, using a tube of water behind the color disk.

[NOTE—Be certain that the pipet tip does not touch the iodine solution; carryback of iodine to the hydrolyzing mixture will interfere with enzyme action and will affect the results of the determination.]

In the same manner, repeat the transfer and comparison procedure at accurately timed intervals until the α-amylase color is reached, at which time record the elapsed time. In cases where two comparisons 30 s apart show that one is darker and the other lighter than the *Reference Color Standard*, record the endpoint to the nearest quarter min. Shake out the 13-mm *Comparator Tube* between successive readings. Minimize slight differences in color discrimination between operators by using a prism attachment and by maintaining a 6- to 10-in. distance between the *Comparator* and the operator's eye.

Calculation One α-amylase dextrinizing unit (DU) is defined as the quantity of α-amylase that will dextrinize soluble starch in the presence of an excess of β-amylase at the rate of 1 g/h at 30°.

Calculate the α-amylase dextrinizing units in the sample as follows:

$$DU\ (solution) = 24/(W \times T)$$

and

$$DU\ (dry\ basis) = DU\ (solution) \times 100/(100 - M)$$

in which W is the weight, in grams, of the enzyme sample added to the incubation mixture in the 5-mL aliquot of the *Sample Preparation* used; T is the elapsed dextrinizing time, in minutes; 24 is the product of the weight of the starch substrate (0.4 g) and 60 min; and M is the percent moisture in the sample, determined by suitable means.

α-AMYLASE ACTIVITY (BACTERIAL)

Application and Principle This procedure is used to determine the α-amylase activity, expressed as bacterial amylase units (BAU), of enzyme preparations derived from *Bacillus subtilis* var., *Bacillus licheniformis* var., and *Bacillus stearothermophilus*. It is not applicable to products that contain β-amylase. The assay is based on the time required to obtain a standard degree of hydrolysis of a starch solution at 30° ± 0.1°. The degree of hydrolysis is determined by comparing the iodine color of the hydrolysate with that of a standard.

Apparatus Use the *Reference Color Standard*, the *Comparator*, and the *Comparator Tubes* as described under α-Amylase Activity (Nonbacterial), described in this Appendix, but use either daylight or daylight-type fluorescent lamps as the light source for the *Comparator*. (Incandescent lamps give slightly lower results.)

Reagents and Solutions

pH 6.6 Buffer Dissolve 9.1 g of potassium dihydrogen phosphate (KH_2PO_4) in sufficient water to make 1000 mL (*Solution A*). Dissolve 9.5 g of dibasic sodium phosphate (Na_2HPO_4) in sufficient water to make 1000 mL (*Solution B*). Add 400 mL of *Solution A* to 600 mL of *Solution B*, mix, and adjust the pH to 6.6, if necessary, by the addition of *Solution A* or *Solution B* as required.

Dilute Iodine Solution Prepare as directed under α-Amylase Activity (Nonbacterial).

Special Starch Use the material described under α-Amylase Activity (Nonbacterial).

Starch Substrate Solution Disperse 10.0 g (dry-weight basis) of *Special Starch* in 100 mL of cold water, and slowly pour the mixture into 300 mL of boiling water. Boil and stir for 1 to 2 min, and then cool while continuously stirring. Quantitatively transfer the mixture into a 500-mL volumetric flask with the aid of water, add 10 mL of *pH 6.6 Buffer*, dilute to volume with water, and mix.

Sample Preparation Prepare a solution of the sample so that 10 mL of the final dilution will give an endpoint between 15 and 35 min under the conditions of the assay.

Procedure Pipet 5.0 mL of *Dilute Iodine Solution* into a series of 13- × 100-mm test tubes, and place them in a water bath maintained at 30° ± 0.1°, allowing 20 tubes for each assay.

Pipet 20.0 mL of the *Starch Substrate Solution* into a 50-mL Erlenmeyer flask, stopper, and allow to equilibrate for 20 min in the water bath at 30°.

At zero time, rapidly pipet 10.0 mL of the *Sample Preparation* into the equilibrated mixture, and continue as directed in the *Procedure* under α-Amylase Activity (Nonbacterial), beginning with ". . . mix immediately by swirling, stopper the flask. . . ."

Calculation One bacterial amylase unit (BAU) is defined as that quantity of enzyme that will dextrinize starch at the rate of 1 mg/min under the specified test conditions.

Calculate the α-amylase activity of the sample, expressed as BAU, by the formula

$$BAU/g = 40F/T$$

in which 40 is a factor (400/10) derived from the 400 mg of starch (20 mL of a 2% solution) and the 10-mL aliquot of *Sample Preparation* used; F is the dilution factor (total dilution volume/sample weight, in grams); and T is the dextrinizing time, in minutes.

CATALASE ACTIVITY

Application and Principle This procedure is used to determine the catalase activity, expressed as Baker Units, of preparations derived from *Aspergillus niger* var., bovine liver, or *Micrococcus lysodeikticus*. The assay is an exhaustion method based on the breakdown of hydrogen peroxide by catalase and the simultaneous breakdown of the catalase by the peroxide under controlled conditions.

Reagents and Solutions

Ammonium Molybdate Solution (1%) Dissolve 1.0 g of ammonium molybdate [$(NH_4)_6MoO_{24} \cdot 4H_2O$] (Merck, Catalog No. 1182) in water, and dilute to 100 mL.

0.250 N Sodium Thiosulfate Dissolve 62.5 g of sodium thiosulfate ($Na_2S_2O_3 \cdot 5H_2O$) in 750 mL of recently boiled and cooled water, add 3.0 mL of 0.2 N sodium hydroxide as a stabilizer, dilute to 1000 mL with water, and mix. Standardize as directed for *0.1 N Sodium Thiosulfate* (see *Solutions and Indicators*), and, if necessary, adjust to exactly 0.250 N.

Peroxide Substrate Solution Dissolve 25.0 g of anhydrous dibasic sodium phosphate (Na_2HPO_4), or 70.8 g of $Na_2HPO_4 \cdot 12H_2O$, in about 1500 mL of water, and adjust to pH 7.0 ± 0.1 with 85% phosphoric acid. Cautiously add 100 mL of 30% hydrogen peroxide, dilute to 2000 mL in a graduate, and mix. Store in a clean amber bottle, loosely stoppered. The solution is stable for more than 1 week if kept at 5° in a full container. (With freshly prepared substrate, the blank will require about 16 mL of *0.250 N Sodium Thiosulfate*. If the blank requires less than 14 mL, the substrate solution is unsuitable and should be prepared fresh again. The sample titration must be between 50% and 80% of that required for the blank.)

Procedure Pipet an aliquot of not more than 1.0 mL of the sample, previously diluted to contain approximately 3.5 Baker Units of catalase, into a 200-mL beaker. Rapidly add 100 mL of *Peroxide Substrate Solution*, previously adjusted to 25°, and stir immediately for 5 to 10 s. Cover the beaker, and incubate at $25° \pm 1°$ until the reaction is completed. Stir vigorously for 5 s, and then pipet 4.0 mL from the beaker into a 50-mL Erlenmeyer flask. Add 5 mL of 2 N sulfuric acid to the flask, mix, then add 5.0 mL of 40% potassium iodide solution, freshly prepared, and 1 drop of *Ammonium Molybdate Solution* (1%), and mix. While continuing to mix, titrate rapidly to a colorless endpoint with *0.250 N Sodium Thiosulfate*, recording the volume, in milliliters, required as S. Perform a blank determination with 4.0 mL of *Peroxide Substrate Solution*, and record the volume required, in milliliters, as B.

[NOTE—When preparations derived from beef liver are tested, the reaction is complete within 30 min. Preparations derived from *Aspergillus* and other sources may require up to 1 h. In assaying an enzyme of unknown origin, run a titration after 30 min and then at 10-min intervals thereafter. The reaction is complete when two consecutive titrations are the same.]

Calculation One Baker Unit is defined as the amount of catalase that will decompose 264 mg of hydrogen peroxide under the conditions of the assay.

Calculate the activity of the sample by the equation

$$\text{Baker Units/g or mL} = 0.4(B - S) \times (1/C)$$

in which C is the milliliters of aliquot of original enzyme preparation added to each 100 mL of *Peroxide Substrate Solution*, or when 1 mL of diluted enzyme is used, C is the dilution factor; B is the volume, in milliliters, as defined above; and S is the milliliters of *0.250 N Sodium Thiosulfate*, as defined above.

CELLULASE ACTIVITY

Application and Principle This assay is based on the enzymatic hydrolysis of the interior β-1,4-glucosidic bonds of a defined carboxymethyl cellulose substrate at pH 4.5 and at 40°. The corresponding reduction in substrate viscosity is determined with a calibrated viscometer.

Apparatus

Calibrated Viscometer Use a size 100 Calibrated Cannon-Fenske Type Viscometer, or its equivalent (Scientific Products, Catalog No. P2885-100).

Constant-Temperature Glass Water Bath ($40° \pm 0.1°$) Use a constant-temperature glass water bath, or its equivalent (Scientific Products, Catalog No. W3520-10).

Stopwatches Use two stopwatches, *Stopwatch No. 1*, calibrated in $1/10$ min for determining the reaction time (T_r), and *Stopwatch No. 2*, calibrated in $1/5$ s for determining the efflux time (T_t).

Waring Blender Use a two-speed Waring blender, or its equivalent (Scientific Products, Catalog No. 58350-1).

Reagents and Solutions

Acetic Acid Solution (2 N) While agitating a 1-L beaker containing 800 mL of water, carefully add 116 mL of glacial acetic acid. Cool to room temperature. Quantitatively transfer the solution to a 1-L volumetric flask, and dilute to volume with water.

Sodium Acetate Solution (2 N) Dissolve 272.16 g of sodium acetate trihydrate in approximately 800 mL of water contained in a 1-L beaker. Quantitatively transfer to a 1-L volumetric flask, and dilute to volume with water.

Acetic Acid Solution (0.4 N) Transfer 200 mL of *Acetic Acid Solution (2 N)* into a 1-L volumetric flask, and dilute to volume with water.

Sodium Acetate Solution (0.4 N) Transfer 200 mL of *Sodium Acetate Solution (2 N)* into a 1-L volumetric flask, and dilute to volume with water.

Acetate Buffer (pH 4.5) Using a standardized pH meter, add *Sodium Acetate Solution (0.4 N)* with continuous agitation to 400 mL of *Acetic Acid Solution (0.4 N)* in a suitable flask until the pH is 4.5 ± 0.05.

Sodium Carboxymethylcellulose Use sodium carboxymethylcellulose (Hercules, Inc., CMC Type 7HF).

Sodium Carboxymethylcellulose Substrate (0.2% w/v) Transfer 200 mL of water into the bowl of the Waring blender. With the blender on low speed, slowly disperse 1.0 g (moisture-free basis) of the *Sodium Carboxymethylcellulose* into the bowl, being careful not to splash out any of the liquid. Using a rubber policeman, wash down the sides of the glass bowl with water. Place the top on the bowl and blend at high speed for 1 min. Quantitatively transfer to a 500-mL volumetric flask, and dilute to volume with water. Filter the substrate through gauze before use.

Sample Preparation Prepare an enzyme solution so that 1 mL of the final dilution will produce a relative fluidity change between 0.18 and 0.22 in 5 min under the conditions of the assay. Weigh the enzyme, and quantitatively transfer it to a glass mortar. Triturate with water and quantitatively transfer the mixture to an appropriate volumetric flask. Dilute to volume with water, and filter the enzyme solution through Whatman No. 1 filter paper before use.

Procedure Place the *Calibrated Viscometer* in the 40° ± 0.1° water bath in an exactly vertical position. Use only a scrupulously clean viscometer. (To clean the viscometer, draw a large volume of detergent solution followed by water through the viscometer by using an aspirator with a rubber tube connected to the narrow arm of the viscometer.)

Pipet 20 mL of filtered *Sodium Carboxymethylcellulose Substrate* and 4 mL of *Acetate Buffer* into a 50-mL Erlenmeyer flask. Allow at least two flasks for each enzyme sample and one flask for a substrate blank. Stopper the flasks, and equilibrate them in the water bath for 15 min.

At zero time, pipet 1 mL of the enzyme solution into the equilibrated substrate. Start stopwatch no. 1, and mix the solution thoroughly. Immediately pipet 10 mL of the reaction mixture into the wide arm of the viscometer.

After approximately 2 min, apply suction with a rubber tube connected to the narrow arm of the viscometer, drawing the reaction mixture above the upper mark into the driving fluid head. Measure the efflux time by allowing the reaction mixture to freely flow down past the upper mark. As the meniscus of the reaction mixture falls past the upper mark, start stopwatch no. 2. At the same time, record the reaction time, in minutes, from stopwatch no. 1 (T_r). As the meniscus of the reaction mixture falls past the lower mark, record the time, in seconds, from stopwatch no. 2 (T_t).

Repeat the final step until a total of four determinations is obtained over a reaction time (T_r) of not more than 15 min.

Prepare a substrate blank by pipetting 1 mL of water into 24 mL of buffered substrate. Pipet 10 mL of the reaction mixture into the wide arm of the viscometer. Determine the time (T_s) in seconds required for the meniscus to fall between the two marks. Use an average of five determinations for (T_s).

Prepare a water blank by pipetting 10 mL of equilibrated water into the wide arm of the viscometer. Determine the time (T_w) in seconds required for the meniscus to fall between the two marks. Use an average of five determinations for (T_w).

Calculations One Cellulase Unit (CU) is defined as the amount of activity that will produce a relative fluidity change of 1 in 5 min in a defined carboxymethyl cellulose substrate under the conditions of the assay.

Calculate the relative fluidities (F_r) and the (T_n) values for each of the four efflux times (T_t) and reaction times (T_r) as follows:

$$F_r = (T_s - T_w)/(T_t - T_w)$$

$$T_n = \tfrac{1}{2}(T_t/60 \text{ s/min}) + T_r = (T_t/120) + T_r,$$

in which F_r is the relative fluidity for each reaction time; T_s is the average efflux time, in seconds, for the substrate blank; T_w is the average efflux time, in seconds, for the water blank; T_t is the efflux time, in seconds, of reaction mixture; T_r is the elapsed time, in minutes, from zero time, that is, the time from addition of the enzyme solution to the buffered substrate until the beginning of the measurement of efflux time (T_t); and T_n is the reaction time, in minutes (T_r), plus one-half of the efflux time (T_t), converted to minutes.

Plot the four relative fluidities (F_r) as the ordinate against the four reaction times (T_n) as the abscissa. A straight line should be obtained. The slope of this line corresponds to the relative fluidity change per minute and is proportional to the enzyme concentration. The slope of the best line through a series of experimental points is a better criterion of enzyme activity than is a single relative fluidity value. From the graph, determine the F_r values at 10 and 5 min. They should have a difference in fluidity of not more than 0.22 or less than 0.18. Calculate the activity of the enzyme unknown as follows:

$$CU/g = [1000(F_{r10} - F_{r5})]/W$$

in which F_{r5} is the relative fluidity at 5 min of reaction time; F_{r10} is the relative fluidity at 10 min of reaction time; 1000 is the milligrams per gram; and W is the weight, in milligrams, of enzyme added to the reaction mixture in a 1-mL aliquot of enzyme solution.

CHYMOTRYPSIN ACTIVITY

Application and Principle This procedure is used to determine chymotrypsin activity in chymotrypsin preparations derived from purified extracts of porcine or bovine pancreas.

Reagents and Solutions

0.15 M Phosphate Buffer (pH 7.0) Dissolve 4.54 g of monobasic potassium phosphate in water, and dilute to 500 mL. Dissolve 4.73 g of anhydrous dibasic sodium phosphate in water, and dilute to 500 mL. Mix 38.0 mL of the monobasic potassium phosphate solution with 61.1 mL of the dibasic sodium phosphate solution. Adjust the pH of the mixture to 7.0 by the dropwise addition of the dibasic sodium phosphate solution, if necessary.

Substrate Solution Dissolve 23.7 mg of *N*-acetyl-*L*-tyrosine ethyl ester in about 50 mL of the *0.15 M Phosphate Buffer* with warming. When the solution has cooled, dilute to 100.0 mL with the *0.15 M Phosphate Buffer*.

Sample Preparation Dissolve a sufficient amount of sample, accurately weighed, in 0.001 N hydrochloric acid to produce a solution containing between 12 and 16 USP Chymotrypsin Units per milliliter. This solution should cause a change in absorbance between 0.008 and 0.012 in a 30-s interval.

Procedure Conduct the assay in a suitable spectrophotometer equipped to maintain a temperature of 24° ± 0.1° in the cell compartment. Determine the temperature before and after measuring the absorbance to ensure that the temperature does not change more than 0.5° during the assay. Pipet 0.2 mL of the 0.001 N hydrochloric acid and 3.0 mL of the *Substrate Solution* into a 1-cm cell. Place the cell in the spectrophotometer, and adjust the instrument so that the absorbance will read 0.200 at 237 nm. Pipet 0.2 mL of the *Sample Preparation* into a second cell, add 3.0 mL of the *Substrate Solution*, and place the cell in the spectrophotometer. Begin timing the reaction from the addition of the *Substrate Solution*. Read the absorbance at 30-s intervals for at least 5 min. Repeat the procedure at least once. If the rate of change fails to remain constant for at least 3 min, repeat the test, and if necessary, use a lower sample concentration. The duplicate determinations at the same sample concentration should match the first determination in rate of absorbance change.

Calculations One USP Chymotrypsin Unit is defined as the activity causing a change in absorbance at the rate 0.0075/min under the conditions of the assay. Determine the average absorbance change per min using only those values within the 3-min portion of the curve where the rate of change is constant. Plot a curve of absorbance against time.

Calculate the number of Chymotrypsin Units per milligram by the formula

$$\text{Result} = (A_2 - A_1)/(0.0075TW)$$

in which A_2 is the straight-line initial absorbance reading; A_1 is the straight-line final absorbance reading; T is the elapsed time, in minutes; and W is the weight, in milligrams, of the sample in the volume of solution used to determine the absorbance.

DIASTASE ACTIVITY (DIASTATIC POWER)

Application and Principle This procedure is used to determine the amylase activity of barley malt and other enzyme preparations. The assay is based on a 30-min hydrolysis of a starch substrate at pH 4.6 and 20°. The reducing sugar groups produced on hydrolysis are measured in a titrimetric procedure using alkaline ferricyanide.

Apparatus

Mill Use a laboratory mill of the type Miag-Seck, for fine grinding of malt (Buhler Miag, Inc.).

Reagents and Solutions

Acetate Buffer Solution Dissolve 68 g of sodium acetate ($NaC_2H_3O_2 \cdot 3H_2O$) in 500 mL of 1 N acetic acid in a 1000-mL volumetric flask, dilute to volume with water, and mix.

Special Starch Use the material described under α-Amylase Activity (Nonbacterial).

Starch Substrate Solution Disperse 20.0 g (dry-weight basis) of *Special Starch* in 50 mL of water, mix to a fine paste, and pour slowly into 750 mL of boiling water. Boil and stir for 2 min, cool, add 20 mL of *Acetate Buffer Solution*, and mix. Quantitatively transfer into a 1000-mL volumetric flask, dilute to volume with water, and mix.

Acetic Acid–Potassium Chloride–Zinc Sulfate Solution (A-P-Z) Dissolve 70 g of potassium chloride and 20 g of zinc sulfate ($ZnSO_4 \cdot 7H_2O$) in 700 mL of water in a 1000-mL volumetric flask, add 200 mL of glacial acetic acid, dilute to volume with water, and mix.

Alkaline Ferricyanide Solution (0.05 N) Dissolve 16.5 g of potassium ferricyanide [$K_3Fe(CN)_6$] and 22 g of anhydrous sodium carbonate in 800 mL of water in a 1000-mL volumetric flask, dilute to volume with water, and mix.

Potassium Iodide Solution Dissolve 50 g of potassium iodide in 50 mL of water in a 100-mL volumetric flask, dilute to volume with water, and mix. Add 2 drops of 50% sodium hydroxide solution, and mix. The solution should be colorless.

Sample Preparation

Malt Samples Grind 30 g of the sample to a fine powder in a Maig-Seck mill. Accurately weigh 25 g of the powder, and transfer it into a 1000-mL Erlenmeyer flask. Add 500 mL of a 0.5% sodium chloride solution, and allow the infusion to stand for 2.5 h at 20° ± 0.2°, agitating the contents by gently rotating the flask at 20-min intervals.

[NOTE—Do not mix the infusion by inverting the flask. The quantity of grist left adhering to the inner walls of the flask as a result of agitation must be as small as possible. Gently swirl the contents of the flask without splashing them against the walls to mix sufficiently.]

Filter the infusion through a 32-cm fluted filter of Whatman No. 1, or equivalent, paper on a 20-cm funnel, returning the first 50 mL of filtrate to the filter. Place a watch glass over the funnel, and use a suitable cover around the stem and over the receiver to reduce evaporation losses during filtration. Collect the filtrate until 30 min of filtration time have elapsed. Pipet 20.0 mL of the filtrate into a 100-mL volumetric flask, dilute to volume with 0.5% sodium chloride solution, and mix.

Other Enzyme Preparations Prepare a solution so that 10 mL of the final dilution will give a diastatic power (DP) value between 2° and 150°.

Procedure Pipet 10.0 mL of the *Sample Preparation* into a 250-mL volumetric flask, and at zero time, add 200 mL of *Starch Substrate Solution*, previously equilibrated for 30 min in a water bath maintained at 20° ± 0.2°. Start the stopwatch at zero time.

Place the mixture in the water bath at 20°, and allow it to cool for exactly 30 min, then add 20.0 mL of 0.5 N sodium hydroxide, dilute to volume with water, and mix.

Prepare a blank by adding 20.0 mL of 0.5 N sodium hydroxide to a 250-mL volumetric flask, followed by 10.0 mL of the *Sample Preparation*. Swirl to mix, add 200 mL of *Starch Substrate Solution*, dilute to volume with water, and mix.

Pipet 5.0 mL of the sample digestion mixture into a 125-mL Erlenmeyer flask, add 10.0 mL of *Alkaline Ferricyanide Solution*, and swirl to mix. Heat the flask for exactly 20 min in a boiling water bath, and then cool to room temperature. Add 25 mL of *A-P-Z Solution*, followed by 1 mL of *Potassium Iodide Solution*, and swirl to mix. Titrate with 0.05 N sodium thiosulfate to the complete disappearance of the blue color, recording the volume, in milliliters, of 0.05 N sodium thiosulfate required as S.

Treat the blank solution in the same manner as described for the sample, recording the volume, in milliliters, of 0.05 N sodium thiosulfate required as B.

Calculation One unit of diastase activity, expressed as degrees diastatic power (DP°), is defined as that amount of enzyme contained in 0.1 mL of a 5% solution of the sample enzyme preparation that will produce sufficient reducing sugars to reduce 5 mL of Fehling's solution when the sample is incubated with 100 mL of the substrate for 1 h at 20°.

[NOTE—The definition of the unit does not correspond to the method of the determination.]

Calculate the diastase activity, expressed as DP°, of the sample by the formulas

$$DP°, \text{ as-is basis} = (B - S) \times 23$$

and

$$DP°, \text{ dry basis} = DP°, \text{ as-is basis} \times 100/(100 - M)$$

in which 23 is a factor, determined by collaborative study, required to convert to the units of the definition, and M is the percent moisture of the sample, determined by suitable means.

α-GALACTOSIDASE ACTIVITY

Application and Principle Use this procedure to determine α-galactosidase activity in enzyme preparations derived from *Aspergillus niger* var. The assay is based on a 15-min hydrolysis of *p*-nitrophenyl-α-D-galactopyranoside followed by spectrophotometric measurement of the liberated *p*-nitrophenol.

Reagents and Solutions

Acetate Buffer Dissolve 11.55 mL of glacial acetic acid in water, and dilute to 1 L (*Solution A*). Dissolve 16.4 g of sodium acetate in water, and dilute to 1 L (*Solution B*). Mix 7.5 mL of *Solution A* and 42.5 mL of *Solution B*, and dilute to 200 mL with water. Adjust the pH of this solution to 5.5 with either *Solution A* or *Solution B* as necessary.

Substrate Solution Dissolve 0.210 g of *p*-nitrophenyl-α-D-galactopyranoside (Sigma Chemical Co., Catalog No. 877, or equivalent) in and dilute to 100 mL with *Acetate Buffer*.

Borax Buffer Dissolve 47.63 g of sodium borate decahydrate in warm water. Cool to room temperature. Add 20 mL of 4 N sodium hydroxide solution, adjust the pH of the solution to 9.7 with 4 N sodium hydroxide, and dilute to 2 L with water.

p-Nitrophenol Stock Solution Dissolve 0.0334 g of *p*-nitrophenol (Aldrich Chemical Co., Catalog No. 24,132-6, or equivalent) in and dilute to 1 L with water. This solution contains 0.24 µmol of *p*-nitrophenol per milliliter of water.

Preparation of Standards and Samples

Standards Prepare the following dilutions of p-*Nitrophenol Stock Solution* with water: 100:50 (v/v) (0.16 µmol/mL); 50:100 (v/v) (0.08 µmol/mL); and 25:125 (v/v) (0.04 µmol/mL). Transfer 2.0 mL of the *Substrate Solution* to each of five separate test tubes. Add 1 mL of the p-*Nitrophenol Stock Solution* to the first tube, 1.0 mL of each dilution to the next three tubes, and 1.0 mL of water to the fifth tube. Add 5.0 mL of *Borax Buffer* to each tube, and mix.

Samples Prepare a solution of α-galactosidase sample in *Acetate Buffer* that contains between 0.008 and 0.024 galactosidase units of activity per milliliter.

Procedure Equilibrate the *Substrate Solution* in a water bath at 37° ± 0.2° for at least 15 min. For active samples, transfer 1.0 mL of each sample to separate test tubes and equilibrate in the 37° ± 0.2° water bath. At zero time, add 2.0 mL of *Substrate Solution*, mix, and return to the water bath. After exactly 15.0 min, add 5.0 mL of *Borax Buffer* to each tube, mix, and remove from the water bath.

For sample blanks, transfer, in sequence, 1.0 mL of each sample to separate test tubes, add 5.0 mL of *Borax Buffer*, and mix. Add 2.0 mL of *Substrate Solution* to each tube, and mix.

Measure the absorbance of each standard sample and blank at 405 nm versus that of water. Determine the absorbances of all solutions within 30 min of completing the tests.

Calculations One galactosidase activity unit (GalU) is defined as the quantity of the enzyme that will liberate *p*-nitrophenol at the rate of 1 µmol/min under the conditions of the assay.

Calculate the factor ε for the *p*-nitrophenol standards using the following equation:

$$\text{Result} = \varepsilon = A_N/C$$

in which A_N is the absorbance of the *p*-nitrophenol standards at 405 nm, and C is the concentration, in millimoles per milliliter, of *p*-nitrophenol.

Because the averaged millimolar extinction coefficient of *p*-nitrophenol at 405 nm is 18.3, ε should be approximately 2.29 [or (18.3)/8].

$$\text{GalU/g} = [(A_S - A_B) \times F]/(\varepsilon \times T \times M)$$

in which A_S is the sample absorbance; A_B is the blank absorbance; F is the appropriate dilution factor; T is the reaction time, in minutes; M is the weight, in grams, of the sample; and ε is a factor calculated above for the *p*-nitrophenol standards (proportional to the millimolar extinction coefficient for *p*-nitrophenol).

β-GLUCANASE ACTIVITY

Application and Principle This procedure is used to determine β-glucanase activity of enzyme preparations derived from *Aspergillus niger* var. and *Bacillus subtilis* var. The assay is based on a 15-min hydrolysis of lichenin substrate at 40° and at pH 6.5. The increase in reducing power due to liberated reducing groups is measured by the neocuproine method.

Reagents and Solutions

Phosphate Buffer Dissolve 13.6 g of monobasic potassium phosphate in about 1900 mL of water, add 70% sodium hydroxide solution until the pH is 6.5 ± 0.05, then transfer the solution into a 2000-mL volumetric flask, dilute to volume with water, and mix.

Neocuproine Solution A Dissolve 40.0 g of anhydrous sodium carbonate, 16.0 g of glycine, and 450 mg of cupric sulfate pentahydrate in about 600 mL of water. Transfer the solution into a 1000-mL volumetric flask, dilute to volume with water, and mix.

Neocuproine Solution B Dissolve 600 mg of neocuproine hydrochloride in about 400 mL of water, transfer the solution into a 500-mL volumetric flask, dilute to volume with water, and mix. Discard when a yellow color develops.

Lichenin Substrate Grind 150 mg of lichenin (Sigma Chemical Co., Catalog No. L-6133, or equivalent) to a fine powder in a mortar, and dissolve it in about 50 mL of water at about 85°. After solution is complete (20 to 30 min), add 90 mg of sodium borohydride and continue heating below the boiling point for 1 h. Add 15 g of Amberlite MB-3, or an equivalent ion-exchange resin, and stir continuously for 30 min. Filter with the aid of a vacuum through Whatman No. 1 filter paper, or equivalent, in a Büchner funnel, and wash the paper with about 20 mL of water. Add 680 mg of monobasic potassium phosphate to the filtrate, and refilter through a 0.22-μm Millipore filter pad, or equivalent. Wash the pad with 10 mL of water, and adjust the pH of the filtrate to 6.5 ± 0.05 with 1 N sodium hydroxide or 1 N hydrochloric acid. Transfer the filtrate into a 100-mL volumetric flask, dilute to volume with water, and mix. Store at 2° to 4° for not more than 3 days.

Glucose Standard Solution Dissolve 36.0 mg of anhydrous dextrose in *Phosphate Buffer* in a 1000-mL volumetric flask, dilute to volume with water, and mix.

Test Preparation Prepare a solution from the enzyme preparation sample so that 1 mL of the final dilution will contain between 0.01 and 0.02 β-glucanase units. Weigh the sample, transfer it into a volumetric flask of appropriate size, dilute to volume with *Phosphate Buffer*, and mix.

Procedure Pipet 2 mL of *Lichenin Substrate* into each of four separate test tubes graduated at 25 mL, and heat the tubes in a water bath at 40° for 10 to 15 min to equilibrate.

After equilibration, add 1 mL of *Phosphate Buffer* to tube 1 (substrate blank), 1 mL of *Glucose Standard Solution* to tube 2 (glucose standard), 4 mL of *Neocuproine Solution A* and 1 mL of the *Test Preparation* to tube 3 (enzyme blank), and 1 mL of the *Test Preparation* to tube 4 (sample). Prepare a fifth tube for the buffer blank, and add 3 mL of *Phosphate Buffer*.

Incubate the five tubes at 40° for exactly 15 min, and then add 4 mL of *Neocuproine Solution A* to tubes 1, 2, 4, and 5. Add 4 mL of *Neocuproine Solution B* to all five tubes, and cap each with a suitably sized glass marble.

[**Caution**—Do not use rubber stoppers.]

Heat the tubes in a vigorously boiling water bath for exactly 12 min to develop color, then cool to room temperature in cold water, and adjust the volume of each to 25 mL with water. Cap the tubes with Parafilm, or other suitable closure, and mix by inverting several times.

Determine the absorbance of each solution at 450 nm in 1-cm cells, with a suitable spectrophotometer, against the buffer blank in tube 5.

Calculation One β-glucanase unit (BGU) is defined as that quantity of enzyme that will liberate reducing sugar (as glucose equivalence) at a rate of 1 μmol/min under the conditions of the assay.

Calculate the activity of the enzyme preparation taken for analysis as follows:

$$BGU = [(A_4 - A_3) \times 36 \times 10^6] / [(A_2 - A_1) \times 180 \times 15 \times \mu g \text{ sample}]$$

in which A_4 is the absorbance of the sample (tube 4), A_3 is the absorbance of the enzyme blank (tube 3), A_2 is the absorbance of the glucose standard (tube 2), A_1 is the absorbance of the substrate blank (tube 1), 36 is the micrograms of glucose in the *Glucose Standard Solution*, 10^6 is the factor converting micrograms to grams, 180 is the weight of 1 μmol of glucose, and 15 is the reaction time, in minutes.

GLUCOAMYLASE ACTIVITY (AMYLOGLUCOSIDASE ACTIVITY)

Application and Principle This procedure is used to determine the glucoamylase activity of preparations derived from *Aspergillus niger* var., but it may be modified to determine preparations derived from *Aspergillus oryzae* var. and *Rhizopus oryzae* var. (as indicated by the variations in the text below). The sample hydrolyzes p-nitrophenyl-α-D-glucopyranoside (PNPG) to p-nitrophenol (PNP) and glucose at pH 4.3 and 50°.

Use the quantity of PNP liberated per unit of time to calculate the enzyme activity. Measure the PNP liberated against a quantity of a standard preparation of PNP by measuring the absorbance of the solutions at 400 nm after adjusting the pH of the reaction mixture to pH 8.0.

[NOTE—Use a pH of 5.0 when testing preparations derived from *Aspergillus oryzae* var. or *Rhizopus oryzae* var.]

Apparatus

Water Bath Use an open, circulating water bath with control accuracy of at least ±0.1°.

Spectrophotometer Use a spectrophotometer suitable for measuring absorbances at 400 nm.

Cuvettes Use 10-mm light-path fused quartz.

Thermometer Use a partial immersion thermometer with a suitable range, graduated in 1/10°.

Timer Use a solid-state timer, model 69240 (GCS Corporation, Precision Scientific Group), or equivalent, accurate to ±0.01 min in 240 min.

Vortex Mixer Use a standard variable-speed mixer.

Reagents and Solutions

p-Nitrophenol Stock Solution (PNP) (0.001 M) Dissolve 139.11 mg of p-nitrophenol previously dried (60°, maximum 4 h) into water, and dilute to 1000 mL.

[**Caution**—Avoid contact with skin. If contact occurs, wash the affected area with water. Work in a well-ventilated area.]

Acetate Buffer Solution (0.1 M) Dissolve 4.4 g of sodium acetate trihydrate ($NaC_2H_3O_2 \cdot 3H_2O$) in approximately 800 mL of water, add 4.5 mL of acetic acid ($C_2H_4O_2$). Adjust to pH 4.5 ± .05 by adding either sodium acetate or glacial acetic acid as required. Dilute to 1 L.

[NOTE—Use a pH of 5.0 when testing preparations derived from *Aspergillus oryzae* var. or *Rhizopus oryzae* var.]

The pH optimum is 5.0 for *Aspergillus oryzae* var.—or *Rhizopus oryzae* var.—derived preparations.

Sodium Carbonate Solution (0.3 M) Dissolve 15.9 g of sodium carbonate (Na_2CO_3) in water, and dilute to 500 mL.

p-Nitrophenyl-α-D-glucopyranoside Solution (PNPG) Dissolve 100.0 mg of PNPG (Sigma Chemical Co., Catalog No. N1377) in acetate buffer, and dilute to 100 mL.

Preparation of Standards and Samples

Standards Dilute three portions of *PNP Stock Solution* to produce standards for the standard curve. Add 3 mL of the *PNP Stock Solution* to 125 mL of *Sodium Carbonate Solution*, and dilute to 500 mL with water to produce the first standard, containing 0.006 µmol/mL. Add 2 mL of *PNP Stock Solution* to 25 mL of *Sodium Carbonate Solution*, and dilute to 100 mL with water to produce the second standard, containing 0.02 µmol/mL. Add 5 mL of *PNP Stock Solutions* to 25 mL of *Sodium Carbonate Solution*, and dilute to 100 mL with water to produce the third standard, containing 0.05 µmol/mL.

Sample Solution Dilute 1.00 ± 0.01 g of sample in sufficient *Acetate Buffer Solution* to produce a solution that contains between 0.1 and 0.3 glucoamylase units of activity per milliliter.

Procedure Measure absorbances of each of the three *PNP Standard Solutions* to calculate the molar extinction coefficient. Equilibrate the *PNPG Solution* in a 50° water bath for at least 15 min. For active samples, transfer 2.0 mL of the *Sample Solution* to a test tube. Loosely stopper, and place the tube in the water bath to equilibrate for 5 min. At zero time, add 2.0 mL of *PNPG Solution*, and mix at moderate speed on a vortex mixer. Return the mixture to the water bath. Exactly 10.0 min later, add 3.0 mL of the *Sodium Carbonate Solution*, mix on the vortex, and remove from the water bath.

For sample blanks, transfer 2.0 mL of the *Sample Solution* and 3.0 mL of the *Sodium Carbonate Solution* into a test tube, and mix. Add 2.0 mL of *PNPG Solution*, and mix. Measure the absorbance of each sample and the blank versus water in a 10-mm cell.

[NOTE—Determine the absorbance of the sample and blank solutions not more than 20 min after adding *Sodium Carbonate Solution*.]

Calculations One unit of glucoamylase activity is defined as the amount of glucoamylase that will liberate 0.1 µmol/min of *p*-nitrophenol from the *PNPG Solution* under the conditions of the assay.

Calculate the millimolar extinction of the PNP standards using the following equation:

$$\varepsilon = A_n/C$$

in which A_n is the absorbance of the *p*-nitrophenol standard, at 400 nm, and C is concentration, in µmol/mL, of *p*-nitrophenol.

The averaged millimolar extinction coefficient, M, should be approximately 18.2.

$$\text{Glucoamylase } \mu/g = [(A_S - A_B) \times 7 \times F]/\varepsilon \times 10 \times 0.10 \times W \times 2,$$

in which A_S is the sample absorbance; A_B is the blank absorbance; F is the appropriate dilution factor; W is the weight of sample, in grams; 7 is the final volume of the test solutions; 10 is the reaction time, in minutes; 0.10 is the amount of PNP liberated, in µmol/min/unit of enzyme; 2 is the sample aliquot, in milliliters, and M is the millimolar extinction coefficient.

GLUCOSE ISOMERASE ACTIVITY

[NOTE—Glucose isomerase activity of the commercial enzyme is usually determined on the enzyme that has been immobilized by binding with a polymer matrix or other suitable material. The following method is designed for use with such preparations.]

Application and Principle Use this procedure to determine glucose isomerase preparations derived from *Actinoplanes missouriensis*, *Bacillus coagulans*, *Microbacterium arborescens*, *Streptomyces murinus*, *Streptomyces olivaceus*, *Streptomyces olivochromogenes*, and *Streptomyces rubiginosus*. It is based on measurement of the rate of conversion of glucose to fructose in a packed-bed reactor. The procedure as outlined approximates an initial velocity assay method. Specific conditions are glucose concentration, 45% w/w; pH (inlet), measured at room temperature in the 7.0 to 8.5 range, as specified; temperature, 60.0°; and magnesium concentration, 4×10^{-3} M.

The optimum conditions for enzymes from different microbial sources and methods of preparation may vary; therefore, if the manufacturer recommends different pH conditions, buffering systems, or methods of sample preparation, use such variations in the instructions given in the text.

Apparatus

Column Assembly and Apparatus

[NOTE—Make all connections with inert tubing, glass, or plastic as appropriate.]

The column assembly is shown in Fig. 1. Use a 2.5- × 40-cm glass column provided with a coarse, sintered-glass bottom and a water jacket connected to a constant-temperature water bath, maintained at 60.0°, by means of a circulating pump. Connect the top of the column to a variable-speed peristaltic pump having a maximum flow rate of 800 mL/h. The diameter of the tubing with which the peristaltic pump is fitted should permit variation of the pumping volume from 60 to 150 mL/h. Connect the outlet of the column with a collecting vessel.

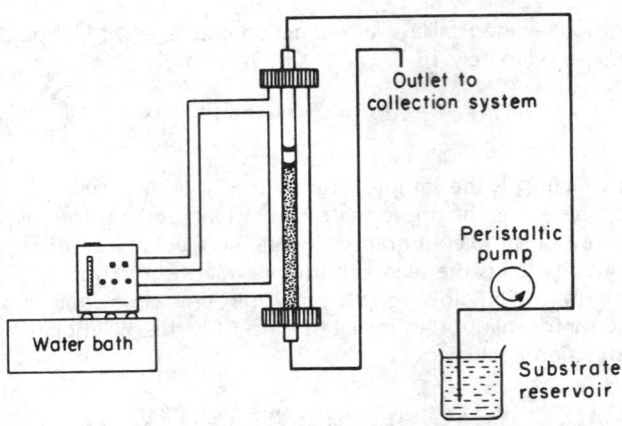

Figure 1 Column Assembly for Assay of Immobilized Glucose Isomerase.

Reagents and Solutions

Glucose Substrate Dissolve 539 g of anhydrous glucose and 1.0 g of magnesium sulfate (MgSO$_4$·7H$_2$O) in 700 mL of water or the manufacturer's recommended buffer, previously heated to 50° to 60°. Cool the solution to room temperature, and adjust the pH as specified by the enzyme manufacturer. Transfer the solution to a 1000-mL volumetric flask, dilute to volume with water or the specified buffer, and mix. Transfer to a vacuum flask, and de-aerate for 30 min.

Magnesium Sulfate Solution Dissolve 1.0 g of magnesium sulfate (MgSO$_4$·7H$_2$O) in 700 mL of water. Adjust the pH to 7.5 to 8.0 as specified by the manufacturer, using 1 N sodium hydroxide, dilute to 1000 mL with water, and mix.

Sample Preparation Transfer to a 500-mL vacuum flask an amount of the sample, accurately weighed in grams or measured in milliliters, as appropriate, sufficient to obtain 2000 to 8000 glucose isomerase units (Gl$_c$U). Add 200 mL of *Glucose Substrate*, stir gently for 15 s, and repeat the stirring every 5 min for 40 min. De-aerate by vacuum for 30 min.

Column Preparation

Quantitatively transfer the *Sample Preparation* to the column with the aid of *Magnesium Sulfate Solution* as necessary. Allow the enzyme granules to settle, and then place a porous disk so that it is even with, and in contact with, the top of the enzyme bed. Displace all of the air from the disk. Place a cotton plug about 1 or 2 cm above the disk. (This plug acts as a filter. It ensures proper heating of the solution and traps dissolved gases that may be present in the *Glucose Substrate*.) Connect the tubing from the peristaltic pump with the top of the column, and seal the connection by suitable means to protect the column contents from the atmosphere. Place the inlet tube of the peristaltic pump into the *Glucose Substrate* solution, and begin a downward flow of the *Glucose Substrate* into the column at a rate of at least 80 mL/h. Maintain the flow rate for 1 h at room temperature.

Assay Adjust the flow of the *Glucose Substrate* to such a rate that a fractional conversion of 0.2 to 0.3 will be produced, based on the estimated activity of the sample. Calculate the fractional conversion from optical rotation values obtained on the starting *Glucose Substrate* and the sample effluent, as specified under *Calculations*, below. After establishing the correct flow rate, run the column overnight (16 h minimum), then check the pH of the *Glucose Substrate*, and readjust if necessary to the specified pH. Measure the flow rate, and collect a sample of the column effluent. Cover the effluent sample, allow it to stand for 30 min at room temperature, and then determine the fractional conversion of glucose to fructose (see *Calculations*, below). If the conversion is less than 0.2 or more than 0.3, adjust the flow rate to bring the conversion into this range. If a flow rate adjustment is required, collect an additional effluent sample after allowing the column to re-equilibrate for at least 2 h, and then determine the fractional conversion. Measure the flow rate, and collect an effluent sample. Cover the sample, let it stand at room temperature for 30 min, and determine the fractional conversion.

Calculations

Specific Rotation Measure the optical rotation of the effluent sample and of the starting *Glucose Substrate* at 25.0°, and calculate their specific rotations [see *Optical (Specific) Rotation*, Appendix IIB] by the equation

$$[\alpha] = 100a/lpd$$

in which a is the corrected observed rotation, in degrees; l is the length of the polarimeter tube, in decimeters; p is the concentration of the test solution, expressed as grams of solute per 100 g of solution; and d is the specific gravity of the solution at 25°.

Fractional Conversion Calculate the fractional conversion, X, by the equation

$$X = (\alpha_E - \alpha_S)/(\alpha_F - \alpha_S)$$

in which α_E is the specific rotation of the column effluent, α_S is the specific rotation of the *Glucose Substrate*, and α_F is the specific rotation of fructose (which, in this case, has been calculated to be −94.54).

Activity The enzyme activity is expressed in glucose isomerase units (Gl$_c$U, the subscript c signifying column process). One Gl$_c$U is defined as the amount of enzyme that converts glucose to fructose at an initial rate of 1 μmol/min, under the conditions specified.

Calculate the glucose isomerase activity by the equation:

$$Gl_cU/g \text{ or } mL = (FS/W) \times X_E \times \ln[X_E/(X_E - X)]$$

in which F is the flow rate, in milliliters per minute; S is the concentration of the *Glucose Substrate*, in micromoles per milliliter; X is the fractional conversion, as determined above; X_E is the fractional conversion at equilibrium, or 0.51; and W is the weight or volume of the sample taken, in grams or milliliters, respectively.

GLUCOSE OXIDASE ACTIVITY

Application and Principle This procedure is used to determine glucose oxidase activity in preparations derived from *Aspergillus niger* var. The assay is based on the titrimetric measurement of gluconic acid produced in the presence of excess substrate and excess air.

Reagents and Solutions

Chloride–Acetate Buffer Solution Dissolve 2.92 g of sodium chloride and 4.10 g of sodium acetate in about 900 mL of water. Adjust the pH to 5.1 with either dilute acetic acid or dilute sodium hydroxide solution and dilute to 1000.0 mL.

Sodium Hydroxide Solution (0.1 N)

Hydrochloric Acid Solution (0.05 N) Standardized.

Phenolphthalein Solution (2% w/v) Solution in methanol.

Octadecanol Solution Saturated solution in methanol.

Substrate Solution Dissolve 30.00 g of anhydrous glucose in 1000 mL of the *Chloride–Acetate Buffer Solution*.

Sample Preparation Dissolve an accurately weighed amount of enzyme preparation in the *Chloride–Acetate Buffer Solution*, and dilute in the buffer solution to obtain an enzyme activity of 5 to 7 activity units per milliliter.

Procedure Transfer 25.0 mL of the *Substrate Solution* to a 32- × 200-mm test tube. To a second 32- × 200-mm test tube transfer 25.0 mL of the *Chloride–Acetate Buffer Solution* (blank). Equilibrate both tubes in a 35° ± 0.1° water bath for 20 min. Add 3.0 mL of the *Sample Preparation* to each test tube, mix, and insert a glass sparger into each tube with a preadjusted air flow of 700 to 750 mL/min. If excessive foaming occurs, add 3 drops of the *Octadecanol Solution* to each tube. After exactly 15 min, remove the sparge and rinse any adhering reaction mixture back into the tube with water. Immediately add 10 mL of the *Sodium Hydroxide Solution* and 3 drops of the *Phenolphthalein Solution* to each tube. Insert a small magnetic stirrer bar, stir, and titrate to the phenolphthalein endpoint with the standardized 0.05 N *Hydrochloric Acid Solution*.

Calculation One Glucose Oxidase Titrimetric unit of activity (GOTu) is the quantity of enzyme that will oxidize 3 mg of glucose to gluconic acid under the conditions of the assay. Determine the enzyme activity using the following equation:

$$GOTu/g = [(B - T) \times N \times 180 \times F]/[3 \times W]$$

in which B is the titration volume, in milliliters, of the blank; T is the titration volume, in milliliters, of the sample; N is the normality of the titrant; 180 is the molecular weight of glucose; F is the sample dilution factor; 3 is from the unit definition; and W is the weight, in grams, of the enzyme preparation contained in each milliliter of the sample solution.

HEMICELLULASE ACTIVITY

Application and Principle This procedure is used to determine hemicellulase activity of preparations derived from *Aspergillus niger* var. The test is based on the enzymatic hydrolysis of the interior glucosidic bonds of a defined locust (carob) bean gum substrate at 40° and pH 4.5. Determine the corresponding reduction in substrate viscosity with a calibrated viscometer.

Apparatus

Viscometer Use a size 100 calibrated Cannon-Fenske Type Viscometer, or equivalent (Scientific Products, Catalog No. 2885-100).

Glass Water Bath Use a constant-temperature glass water bath, maintained at 40° ± 0.1° (Scientific Products, Catalog No. W3520-10).

Stopwatches Use two stopwatches—*Stopwatch No. 1*, calibrated in $1/10$ min for determining the reaction time (T_r), and *Stopwatch No. 2*, calibrated in $1/5$ s for determining the efflux time (T_t).

Reagents and Solutions

Acetate Buffer (pH 4.5) Add 0.2 N sodium acetate, with continuous agitation, to 400 mL of 0.2 N acetic acid until the pH is 4.5 ± 0.05, as determined by a pH meter.

Locust Bean Gum Use Powdered Type D-200 locust bean gum, or its equivalent (Meer Corp.). Because the substrate may vary from lot to lot, test each lot in parallel with a previous lot known to be satisfactory. Variations of more than ±5% viscosity in the average of a series of parallel tests indicate an unsuitable lot.

Substrate Solution Place 12.5 mL of 0.2 N hydrochloric acid and 250 mL of warm water (72° to 75°) in the bowl of a power blender (Waring two-speed, or equivalent, Scientific Products, Catalog No. 58350-1), and set the blender on low speed. Slowly disperse 2.0 g of *Locust Bean Gum*, on a moisture-free basis, into the bowl, taking care not to splash out any of the liquid in the bowl. Wash down the sides of the bowl with warm water, using a rubber policeman, cover the bowl, and blend at high speed for 5 min. Quantitatively transfer the mixture to a 1000-mL beaker, and cool to room temperature. Using a pH meter, adjust the mixture to pH 6.0 with 0.2 N sodium hydroxide. Quantitatively transfer the mixture to a 1000-mL volumetric flask, dilute to volume with water, and mix. Filter the substrate through gauze before use.

Sample Preparation Prepare a solution of the sample in water so that 1 mL of the final dilution will produce a change in relative fluidity between 0.18 and 0.22 in 5 min under the conditions specified in the *Procedure*.

Weigh the enzyme preparation, quantitatively transfer it to a glass mortar, and triturate with water. Quantitatively transfer the mixture to an appropriately sized volumetric flask, dilute to volume with water, and mix. Filter through Whatman No. 1 filter paper, or equivalent, before use.

Procedure Scrupulously clean the viscometer by drawing a large volume of detergent solution, followed by water, through the instrument, and place the viscometer, previously calibrated, in the glass water bath in an exactly vertical position. Pipet 20.0 mL of *Substrate Solution* and 4.0 mL of *Acetate Buffer* into a 50-mL Erlenmeyer flask, allowing at least two flasks for each enzyme sample and one flask for a substrate blank. Stopper the flasks, and equilibrate them in the water bath for 15 min. At zero time, pipet 1.0 mL of the *Sample Preparation* into the equilibrated substrate, start timing with stopwatch no. 1, and mix thoroughly. Immediately pipet 10.0 mL of this mixture into the wide arm of the viscometer. After about 2 min, draw the reaction mixture above the upper mark into the driving fluid head by applying suction with a rubber tube connected to the narrow arm of the instrument. Measure the efflux time by allowing the reaction mixture to flow freely down past the upper mark. As the meniscus falls past the upper mark, start stopwatch no. 2, and at the same time, record the reaction time (T_R), in minutes, from stopwatch no. 1. As the meniscus of the reaction mixture falls past the lower mark, record the time (T_T), in seconds, from stopwatch no. 2. Immediately re-draw the reaction mixture above the upper mark and into the driving fluid head. As the meniscus falls freely past the upper mark, restart stopwatch no. 2, and at the same time record the reaction time (T_R), in minutes, from stopwatch no. 1. As the meniscus falls past the lower mark, record the time (T_T), in seconds, from stopwatch no. 2.

Repeat the latter operation, beginning with "Immediately re-draw the reaction mixture. . . ," until a total of four determinations is obtained over a reaction time (T_R) of not more than 15 min.

Prepare a substrate blank by pipetting 1.0 mL of water into a mixture of 20.0 mL of *Substrate Solution* and 4.0 mL of *Acetate Buffer*, and then immediately pipet 10.0 mL of this mixture into the wide arm of the viscometer. Determine the time (T_S), in seconds, required for the meniscus to fall between the two marks. Use an average of five determinations as T_S.

Prepare a water blank by pipetting 10.0 mL of water, previously equilibrated to 40° ± 0.1°, into the wide arm of the viscometer. Determine the time (T_W), in seconds, required for the meniscus to fall between the two marks. Use an average of five determinations as T_W.

Calculation One hemicellulase unit (HCU) is defined as that activity that will produce a relative fluidity change of 1 over a period of 5 min in a locust bean gum substrate under the conditions specified. Calculate the relative fluidities (F_R) and T_N values (see definition below) for each of the four efflux times (T_T) and reaction times (T_R) as follows:

$$F_R = (T_S - T_W)/(T_T - T_W)$$

and

$$T_N = \tfrac{1}{2}(T_T/60 \text{ s/min}) + T_R = (T_T/120) + T_R,$$

in which F_R is the relative fluidity for each reaction time; T_S is the average efflux time, in seconds, for the substrate blank; T_W is the average efflux time, in seconds, for the water blank; T_T is the efflux time, in seconds, of the sample reaction mixture; T_R is the elapsed time, in minutes, from zero time, that is, the time from addition of the enzyme solution to the buffered substrate until the beginning of the measurement of the efflux time (T_T); and T_N is the reaction time (T_R), in minutes, plus one-half of the efflux time (T_T) converted to minutes.

Plot the four relative fluidities (F_R) as the ordinate against the four reaction times (T_N) as the abscissa. This should result in a straight line. The slope of the line corresponds to the relative fluidity change per minute and is proportional to the enzyme concentration. The slope of the best line through a series of experimental points is a better criterion of enzyme activity than a single relative fluidity value. From the curve, determine the F_R values at 10 and 5 min.

They should have a difference in fluidity of not more than 0.22 and not less than 0.18. Calculate the activity of the enzyme sample as follows:

$$\text{HCU/g} = 1000(F_{R10} - F_{R5}/W)$$

in which F_{R10} is the relative fluidity at 10 min reaction time; F_{R5} is the relative fluidity at 5 min reaction time; 1000 is milligrams per gram; and W is the weight, in milligrams, of the enzyme sample contained in the 1.0-mL aliquot of *Sample Preparation* added to the equilibrated substrate in the *Procedure*.

INVERTASE SUMNER UNIT ACTIVITY

Application and Principle This procedure is used to measure the strength of invertase (sucrase) enzyme preparations from yeast *Saccharomyces* sp *(Kluyveromyces)* and *Saccharomyces* sp *(cerevisiae)*. This assay is based on a 30-min hydrolysis of a 5.4% (w/v) solution of sucrose at pH 4.5 and 20°. The amount of monosaccharides produced is measured spectrophotometrically using a 3,5-Dinitrosalicylic Acid (DNS) acid–phenol reagent correlated to a glucose standard.

Reagents and Solutions

3,5-DNS Acid Stock Solutions Weigh 308 g of sodium potassium tartrate tetrahydrate and 19.4 g of sodium hydroxide into a 1000-mL volumetric flask. Dissolve in and dilute with deionized water to volume. In a second 1000-mL volumetric flask, transfer 10.7 g of 3,5-dinitrosalicylic acid. Dissolve in and dilute with deionized water to volume. In a third vessel (100-mL volumetric flask), transfer 8.33 g of phenol, 1.83 g of sodium hydroxide, and 8.33 g of sodium metabisulfite. Dissolve in and dilute with deionized water to volume.

3,5-DNS Acid Working Solution Combine the three solutions prepared for the *3,5-DNS Acid Stock Solutions,* and set aside for at least 48 h. Pass the solution through a glass fiber filter. The final solution should be stored in a dark location in a plastic bottle. Re-filter the solution through a glass fiber filter when it becomes turbid.

pH 4.5 Acetate Buffer Dissolve 29.25 g sodium acetate trihydrate in 300 mL of deionized water. Add 17.1 g of glacial acetic acid and mix. Adjust the pH to 4.50 with dilute sodium hydroxide or hydrochloric acid solutions as necessary. Quantitatively transfer the solution to a 500-mL volumetric flask and dilute with deionized water to volume.

Sucrose Substrate Solution (6.5% w/v) Dissolve 16.25 g (dry wt basis) of sucrose in 200 mL deionized water and add 25.0 mL of *pH 4.5 Acetate Buffer*. Transfer the solution to a 250-mL volumetric flask and dilute with deionized water to volume. After the enzyme is added this will give a 5.4% solution. Prepare fresh daily.

Standard Glucose Solution (0.300%) Dissolve 0.1500 g (dry wt basis) of D-(+)-glucose anhydrous in 40 mL of deionized water. Quantitatively transfer the solution to a 50-mL volumetric flask and dilute with deionized water to volume.

3,5-DNS Working Solution Immediately prior to use, add 3.00 mL of the *Standard Glucose Solution (0.300%)* into 200 mL of the *3,5-DNS Acid Working Solution*. This is enough to assay three enzyme samples.

Enzyme Sample Preparation   Quantitatively dilute the enzyme in deionized water such that the final solution will contain 0.5 SU/mL. Solid samples that do not dissolve easily should be triturated with deionized water prior to transfer to an appropriate volumetric flask. Samples should be assayed within 30 min of dilution.

Analysis   Pipet 5 mL of the *Sucrose Substrate Solution* into a series of test tubes, allowing 6 test tubes for each enzyme sample (3 for the enzyme reaction and 3 for the enzyme blank). Also prepare 3 test tubes for the *Standard Glucose Solution* and 3 test tubes for the substrate blank, each containing 5 mL of the *Sucrose Substrate Solution*. Equilibrate these test tubes in a 20.0 ± 0.1° water bath for 10 min. At the same time, equilibrate 10 mL of each *Enzyme Sample Preparation* in a 20.0 ± 0.1° water bath for 10 min.

To start the enzyme reaction vessels, using a stopwatch beginning at time zero, in the order of the series and within regular time intervals, add 1 mL of the equilibrated *Enzyme Sample Preparation* into each of the three equilibrated *Sucrose Substrate Solution* test tubes and mix thoroughly.

Prepare enzyme blanks by placing an amount of the *Enzyme Sample Preparation* in a boiling water bath for 10 min and cooling in an ice bath for 5 min. Add 1 mL of this deactivated enzyme solution to each of the three appropriate *Sucrose Substrate Solution* test tubes, and mix thoroughly.

To prepare the glucose standards, add 1 mL of the *Standard Sucrose Solution* to each of the 3 appropriate *Sucrose Substrate Solution* test tubes.

To prepare the substrate blanks, add 1 mL of deionized water to each of the 3 appropriate *Sucrose Substrate Solution* test tubes.

At time equals exactly 30 min, in the order of the series and within the regular time intervals, stop the reaction by pipetting 3 mL of the appropriate enzyme reaction mixture into a test tube (>50 mL capacity) containing 7 mL of the *3, 5-DNS Working Solution* and mix thoroughly. Likewise, transfer 3 mL of each glucose standard solution, 3 mL of each substrate blank solution, and 3 mL of each of enzyme blank solution into the appropriate test tubes (>50 ml capacity) containing 7 mL of 3,5-DNS Working Solution, and mix thoroughly.

Place all test tubes into a boiling water bath for exactly 10 min. At the end of 10 min, place all test tubes in an ice water bath for 5 min. To each test tube, add 40 mL deionized water and mix thoroughly. Allow the test tubes to set at room temperature for at least 10 min and then measure the absorbance at 515 nm against a water blank in a 1-cm cuvette.

Calculation   One Sumner Unit (SU) is the quantity of enzyme which, under the conditions of the assay, will convert 1 mg of sucrose to glucose and fructose in 5 min. Calculate the activity of the enzyme preparation as follows:

$$SU/g = [(A_U - A_B)/(A_S - A_W)] \times (0.5/C)$$

in which A_U is the average absorbance of the enzyme sample; A_B is the average absorbance of the enzyme blank; A_S is the average absorbance of the glucose standard; A_W is the average absorbance of the substrate blank; C is the concentration (in g/mL) of the *Enzyme Sample Preparation*; and 0.5 = [(3 mg glucose × 5 min unit definition)/30 min reaction].

LACTASE (NEUTRAL) (β-GALACTOSIDASE) ACTIVITY

Application and Principle   This procedure is used to determine the neutral lactase activity of enzyme preparations derived from *Kluyveromyces marxianus* var. *lactis* and *Saccharomyces* sp. The assay is based on a 10-min hydrolysis of an o-nitrophenyl-β-D-galactopyranoside (ONPG) substrate at 30.0° ± 0.1° and at pH 6.50.

Reagents and Solutions

Magnesium Solution   Dilute 24.65 g of magnesium sulfate heptahydrate (MgSO$_4$·7H$_2$O) in about 950 mL of water. Transfer the solution into a 1000-mL volumetric flask, dilute to volume with water, and mix.

EDTA Solution   Dissolve 1.86 g of disodium EDTA dihydrate (C$_{10}$H$_{14}$N$_2$Na$_2$O$_8$·2H$_2$O) in about 950 mL of water. Transfer the solution into a 1000-mL volumetric flask, dilute to volume with water, and mix.

P-E-M Buffer   Dissolve 8.8 g of potassium dihydrogen phosphate (KH$_2$PO$_4$) and 8.0 g of dipotassium hydrogen phosphate trihydrate (K$_2$HPO$_4$·3H$_2$O) in about 900 mL of water. Add 10.0 mL of *Magnesium Solution* and 10.0 mL of *EDTA Solution*. Transfer the solution into a 1000-mL volumetric flask, dilute to volume with water, and mix. The pH should be 6.50 ± 0.05.

Lactase Reference Preparation   (Highly concentrated lactase preparation) This preparation can be obtained from Gist-Brocades, Delft, The Netherlands.

ONPG (o-nitrophenyl-β-D-galactopyranoside) is validated according to the following procedure:

Validation of New ONPG   Transfer 150, 250, and 375 mg of the new ONPG into separate 100-mL volumetric flasks, dilute to volume with *P-E-M Buffer*, and mix. Prepare solutions of the *Lactase Reference Preparation* by weighing an amount of *Lactase Reference Preparation* corresponding to 5000 ± 250 Neutral Lactase Units (NLU) accurately to within 1 mg in duplicate in 50-mL volumetric flasks, dissolve in *P-E-M Buffer*, dilute to volume with the same, and mix. Prepare dilutions of this initial solution with *P-E-M Buffer* so that 1 mL of the final dilution will contain 0.0375, 0.0750, and 0.1125 NLU of activity. In duplicate, determine the enzyme activity of the three enzyme concentrations using each of the new *ONPG Substrate* solutions corresponding to 150, 250, and 375 mg and the old *ONPG Substrate* at 250 mg by following the steps in the *Procedure*, below.

Calculation   Calculate the enzyme activity following the steps indicated under *Calculation for NLU Activity*, below. Determine the average of the duplicates for each enzyme concentration at each level of *ONPG Substrate* (the maximum allowable difference between these duplicates is 6.5%). Determine the overall average for the three enzyme concentrations (0.0375, 0.0750, and 0.1125) for each *ONPG Substrate* level (150, 250, and 375 mg of *ONPG*).

To determine the overall average of three enzyme concentrations at 150 mg of *ONPG*:

$$X = (A + B + C)/3,$$

in which A is the average result of 0.0375 at 150 mg of *ONPG*, B is the average result of 0.0750 at 150 mg of *ONPG*, and C is the average result of 0.1125 at 150 mg of *ONPG*.

To determine the overall average of three enzyme concentrations at 250 mg of *ONPG*:

$$Y = (D + E + F)/3,$$

in which D is the average result of 0.0375 at 250 mg of *ONPG*, E is the average result of 0.0750 at 250 mg of *ONPG*, and F is the average result of 0.1125 at 250 mg of *ONPG*.

To determine the overall average of three enzyme concentrations at 375 mg of *ONPG*:

$$Z = (G + H + I)/3,$$

in which G is the average result of 0.0375 at 375 mg of *ONPG*, H is the average result of 0.0750 at 375 mg of *ONPG*, and I is the average result of 0.1125 at 375 mg of *ONPG*.

The *ONPG* analyzed is suitable for use when the following specifications are met for each *ONPG* concentration:

1. The average result of each enzyme concentration for each *ONPG* level does not deviate more than 3% from the overall average of the three enzyme concentrations for that level of *ONPG*. For example, A or B or C should not deviate more than 3% from X; D or E or F should not deviate more than 3% from Y; G or H or I should not deviate more than 3% from Z.

2. The overall average of the three enzyme concentrations found for 150 mg of *ONPG* (X) should not vary more than 81% to 99% of the overall average of the three enzymes concentrations found for 250 mg of *ONPG* (Y). The overall average of the three enzyme concentrations found for 375 mg of *ONPG* (Z) should not vary more than 96% to 114% of the overall average of the three enzyme concentrations of 250 mg of *ONPG* (Y).

3. The absorbance of each blank is less than 0.050.

4. For each new lot of *ONPG*, the overall average of the three enzyme concentrations found for 250 mg of *ONPG* (Y) per 100 mL should be within 5% of the overall average of the three enzyme concentrations found for 250 mg of *ONPG* of the lot in use at that moment.

ONPG Substrate   Dissolve 250.0 mg *ONPG* (use lot currently in use) in about 80 mL of *P-E-M Buffer*. Transfer the solution to a 100-mL volumetric flask, dilute to volume with *P-E-M Buffer*, and mix. Prepare, at most, 2 h before incubation.

Sodium Carbonate Solution   Dissolve 50.0 g of sodium carbonate anhydrous (Na_2CO_3) and 37.2 g of disodium EDTA dihydrate ($C_{10}H_{14}N_2Na_2O_8 \cdot 2H_2O$) in about 900 mL of water. Transfer the solution into a 1000-mL volumetric flask, dilute to volume with water, and mix.

Standard o-Nitrophenol Solution   Transfer 139.0 mg of o-nitrophenol into a 1000-mL volumetric flask, dissolve in 10 mL of 96% ethanol, dilute to volume with water, and mix. Pipet 2-, 4-, 6-, 8-, 10-, 12-, and 14-mL portions of this solution into a series of 100-mL volumetric flasks, add 25 mL of *Sodium Carbonate Solution* to each, dilute each to volume with *P-E-M Buffer*, and mix. The dilutions contain, respectively, 0.02, 0.04, 0.06, 0.08, 0.10, 0.12 and 0.14 µmol/mL of o-nitrophenol.

Determine the absorbance of each dilution at 420 nm in a 1-cm path-length cell, with a suitable spectrophotometer, using water as the blank. For each dilution, plot absorbance against µmol of o-nitrophenol (this must result in a straight line through the origin). Divide the absorbance of each dilution by µmol of o-nitrophenol to obtain the extinction coefficient (M) at that dilution (the slope of the line is the extinction coefficient). Average the seven values thus calculated (this should result in a value of 4.60 ± 0.05).

Test Preparation   Using a volumetric flask, prepare a test solution from the starting enzyme preparation by accurately weighing out a minimum of 1 g of sample to the nearest milligram. Dissolve in *P-E-M Buffer* so that 1 mL of the final dilution will contain between 0.027 and 0.095 NLU. Transfer 1 mL of this final dilution to a 15- × 150-mm test tube as the *Test Preparation*. Perform in duplicate.

Procedure   Equilibrate the test tubes containing each *Test Preparation* in a water bath maintained at 30.0° ± 0.1° for at least 5 but not more than 15 min. At zero time, in the order of the series and at regular time intervals, rapidly pipet 5.00 mL of *ONPG Substrate*, equilibrated at 30.0° ± 0.1°, into the test tubes, and mix by shaking. After a 10.0-min incubation (reaction) time, in the same order and with the same regular intervals, pipet 2.00 mL of *Sodium Carbonate Solution* into each, mix by shaking, and hold at room temperature. Determine the absorbance of each solution within 30 min at 420 nm in a 1-cm cell with a suitable spectrophotometer, using as the blank a solution prepared in the same manner as for the sample except adding *ONPG Substrate* and *Sodium Carbonate Solution* in reverse order.

Calculation for NLU Activity   One Neutral Lactase Unit (NLU) is defined as that quantity of enzyme that will liberate 1.30 µmol/min of o-nitrophenol under the conditions of the assay. Calculate the activity of the enzyme preparation taken for the analysis as follows:

$$NLU/g = [(A \times 8 \times f)/(M \times 10 \times W)]/1.30$$

in which A is the average of the absorbance readings for the sample, corrected for the sample blank; 8 is the volume, in milliliters, of the incubation mixture after termination; f is the total dilution factor of the sample; M is the extinction coefficient, determined as directed under *Standard o-Nitrophenol Solution*; 10 is the incubation time, in minutes; W is the sample weight, in grams; and 1.30 is the factor used in the unit definition.

LACTASE (ACID) (β-GALACTOSIDASE) ACTIVITY

Application and Principle   This procedure is used to determine lactase activity of enzyme preparations derived from *Aspergillus oryzae* var. The assay is based on a 15-min hydrolysis of an o-nitrophenyl-β-D-galactopyranoside substrate at 37° and pH 4.5.

Reagents and Solutions

2.0 N Acetic Acid Dilute 57.5 mL of glacial acetic acid to 500 mL with water. Mix well, and store in a refrigerator.

4.0 N Sodium Hydroxide Dissolve 40.0 g of sodium hydroxide in sufficient water to make 250 mL.

Acetate Buffer Combine 50 mL of *2.0 N Acetic Acid* and 11.3 mL of *4.0 N Sodium Hydroxide* in a 1000-mL volumetric flask, and dilute to volume with water. Verify that the pH is 4.50 ± 0.05, using a pH meter, and adjust, if necessary, with *2.0 N Acetic Acid* or *4.0 N Sodium Hydroxide*.

2.0 mM o-Nitrophenol Stock Transfer 139.0 mg of o-nitrophenol to a 500-mL volumetric flask, dissolve in 10 mL of USP alcohol (95% ethanol) by swirling, and dilute to volume with 1% sodium carbonate.

o-Nitrophenol Standards

0.10 mM Standard Solution Pipet 5.0 mL of the *2.0 mM o-Nitrophenol Stock* solution into a 100-mL volumetric flask, and dilute to volume with 1% sodium carbonate solution.

0.14 mM Standard Solution Pipet 7.0 mL of the *2.0 mM o-Nitrophenol Stock* solution into a 100-mL volumetric flask, and dilute to volume with 1% sodium carbonate solution.

0.18 mM Standard Solution Pipet 9.0 mL of the *2.0 mM o-Nitrophenol Stock* solution into a 100-mL volumetric flask, and dilute to volume with 1% sodium carbonate solution.

Substrate Transfer 370.0 mg of o-nitrophenyl-β-D-galactopyranoside to a 100-mL volumetric flask, and add 50 mL of *Acetate Buffer*. Swirl to dissolve, and dilute to volume with *Acetate Buffer*.

[NOTE—Perform the assay procedure within 2 h of *Substrate* preparation.]

Test Preparation Prepare a solution from the test sample preparation such that 1 mL of the final dilution will contain between 0.15 and 0.65 lactase unit. Weigh, and quantitatively transfer the enzyme to a volumetric flask of appropriate size. Dissolve the enzyme in water, swirling gently, and dilute with water if necessary.

[NOTE—Perform the assay procedure within 2 h of dissolution of the *Test Preparation*.]

System Suitability Determine the absorbance of the three *o-Nitrophenol Standards* at 420 nm in a 1-cm cell, using a suitable spectrophotometer. Use water to zero the instrument. Calculate the millimolar extinction, M, for each of the *o-Nitrophenol Standards* (0.10, 0.14, and 0.18 mM) by the equation

$$\varepsilon = A_n/C$$

in which A_n is the absorbance of each *o-Nitrophenol Standard* at 420 nm and C is the corresponding concentration of o-nitrophenol in the standard. M for each standard should be approximately 4.60/mM. Perform a linear regression analysis of the absorbance readings of the three *o-Nitrophenol Standards* versus the o-nitrophenol concentration in each (0.10, 0.14, and 0.18 mM). The r^2 should not be less than 0.99. Determine the mean M of the three *o-Nitrophenol Standards* for use in the calculations below.

Procedure For each sample or blank, pipet 2.0 mL of the *Substrate* solution into a 25- × 150-mm test tube, and equilibrate in a water bath maintained at 37.0° ± 0.1° for approximately 10 min. At zero time, rapidly pipet 0.5 mL of the *Test Preparation* (or 0.5 mL of water as a blank) into the equilibrated substrate, mix by brief (1 s) vortex, and immediately return the tubes to the water bath. After exactly 15 min of incubation, rapidly add 2.5 mL of 10% sodium carbonate solution, and vortex the tube to stop the enzyme reaction. Dilute the samples and blanks to 25.0 mL by adding 20.0 mL of water, and thoroughly mix. Determine the absorbance of the diluted samples and blanks at 420 nm in a 1-cm cell, using a suitable spectrophotometer. Use water to zero the instrument.

Calculation One lactase unit (ALU) is defined as that quantity of enzyme that will liberate o-nitrophenol at a rate of 1 μmol/min under the conditions of the assay.

Calculate the activity (lactase activity per gram) of the enzyme preparation taken for analysis as follows:

$$\text{ALU/g} = [(A_S - B)(25)]/[(\varepsilon)(15)(W)]$$

in which A_S is the average of absorbance readings for the *Test Preparation*; B is the average of absorbance readings for the blank; 25 is the final volume, in milliliters, of the diluted incubation mixture; ε is the mean absorptivity of the *o-Nitrophenol Standards* per micromole, 15 is the incubation time, in minutes, and W is the weight, in grams, of original enzyme preparation contained in the 0.5-mL aliquot of *Test Preparation* used in the incubation.

LIPASE ACTIVITY

Application and Principle This procedure is used to determine the lipase activity in preparations derived from microbial sources and animal pancreatic tissues. The assay is based on the potentiometric measurement of the rate at which the preparations will catalyze the hydrolysis of tributyrin.

Apparatus

Automatic Recording Titrimeter Use an instrument operating in the pH stat mode and equipped with a jacketed titration cell (Radiometer Titralab, or equivalent).

Constant Temperature Bath Operated at 30° ± 0.1°.

Blender

Reagents and Solutions

0.05 N Sodium Hydroxide Dissolve 2.0 g of sodium hydroxide in water, and dilute to 100 mL. Standardize with NIST grade potassium hydrogen phthalate.

Emulsification Reagent Dissolve 17.9 g of sodium chloride and 0.41 g of monobasic potassium phosphate in about 400 mL of water. Add 540 mL of glycerol and, with vigorous stirring, add 6.0 g of gum arabic (Sigma, Catalog No. G 9752). Stir until dissolved. Dilute to 1000 mL.

Glycine Buffer (0.1 M) Dissolve 7.50 g of glycine (Sigma, Catalog No. G 126) and 3.8 g of sodium hydroxide in about 900 mL water. Adjust the pH to 10.8, and dilute to 1000 mL.

[NOTE—Instead of the *Glycine Buffer*, some enzyme preparations may require the use of 0.01 M pH 8.0 *Tris Buffer* prepared as directed for *Tris Buffer* under *Proteolytic Activity, Bacterial (PC)*, except to titrate with 1 N hydrochloric acid to pH 8.0.]

Substrate Emulsion Transfer 15.9 mL of tributyrin (Sigma, Catalog No. T 8626) to a blender, add 50 mL *Emulsification Reagent* and 235 mL water. Blend for 15 min at maximum speed. Equilibrate in the 30° constant temperature bath for at least 15 min before use. Use within 4 h.

Sample Preparation Dissolve an accurately weighed amount of the enzyme preparation in *Glycine Buffer* (or pH 8.0 *Tris Buffer* if specified) so that each milliliter contains between 2000 and 5000 lipase units per milliliter. Accurately dilute a portion of this solution with water to obtain a final solution containing between 0.5 and 1.5 lipase units per milliliter.

Procedure Fill the titrator buret with the *0.05 N Sodium Hydroxide* solution, and following the manufacturer's instructions, set the temperature to 30° and the pH set point to 7.0. Transfer 15.0 mL of the *Substrate Emulsion* to the titration cell, and add a small stirrer bar. Add 1.0 mL of the diluted *Sample Preparation*, and actuate the titrator. Record the rate of *0.05 N Sodium Hydroxide* addition. Stop the titration after a constant (linear) rate of addition has been observed for 5 min. Determine the addition rate, in milliliters per minute, from the linear portion of the recording and record this value as R.

Calculation One lipase unit (LU) is defined as the quantity of enzyme that will liberate 1 μmol of butyric acid per min under the conditions of the test.

Calculate the activity of the enzyme preparation by the formula

$$LU/g = R \times N \times 1000/W$$

in which R is the addition rate, in milliliters per minute; N is the normality of the *Sodium Hydroxide* solution; 1000 converts mM to μM; and W is the weight, in grams, of the enzyme preparation contained in 1 mL of the diluted *Sample Preparation*.

LIPASE (MICROBIAL) ACTIVITY FOR MEDIUM- AND LONG-CHAIN FATTY ACIDS

Application and Principle

This procedure is used to determine the lipase activity in preparations derived from microbial sources. The assay is based on the measurement of the amount of free fatty acids formed from an olive oil emulsion in the presence of sodium taurocholate over a fixed time interval. This assay is particularly used for measuring lipase activity in foods.

Reagents and Solutions

Gum Arabic Solution Dissolve 110 g of gum arabic (acacia) (Sigma, Catalog No. G-9752, or equivalent) and 12.5 g of analytical-grade calcium chloride ($CaCl_2 \cdot 2H_2O$) in 800 mL of water in a 1000-mL volumetric flask, and dilute to volume with water. Shake or stir for 30 min at room temperature to dissolve completely. Centrifuge at $4000 \times g$ for 20 min or filter through a Büchner funnel using Celite as a filter aid. Store the supernatant or filtrate at 4°. Divide into single-use, 24-mL aliquots. The solution is stable for 6 months at −20°.

Substrate Emulsion Place 130 mL of olive oil (Sigma, Catalog No. O-1500, or equivalent) and 400 mL of *Gum Arabic Solution* in a mixer bowl, and cool the mixture to 5° to 10° on ice. Emulsify the mixture with a Waring Blender, or equivalent, operated at high speed for 30 min, keeping the temperature below 30° by repeatedly mixing at high speed for 5 min and turning the blender off for 1 min. Check the quality of the emulsion microscopically: 90% of the droplets should have a diameter equal to or less than 3 μm, and the remaining 10% should not exceed 10 μm. The emulsion is stable for 3 days at 4°.

Reference Standard Solution Dissolve an aliquot of Fungi Lipase-International FIP Standard (International Commission on Pharmaceutical Enzymes F.I.P., Center for Standards of the Federation Internationale Pharmaceutique, Harelbekestraat 72, B-9000 Gent, Belgium) in a 1% sodium chloride solution and dilute it to obtain a solution of 2.4 to 3.6 FIP microbial lipase units per milliliter. Prepare this solution fresh.

0.02 N Sodium Hydroxide Solution Prepare daily by diluting 10 mL of analytical-grade 1 N sodium hydroxide to 500 mL with recently boiled water.

0.5% Sodium Taurocholate Solution Dissolve 0.5 g of sodium taurocholate (DIFCO, Catalog No. 0278-15-8) in 100 mL of water. Prepare this solution fresh.

Sample Preparation Dissolve an accurately weighed amount of the enzyme preparation in a 1% sodium chloride solution, and dilute to obtain a solution of 2.4 to 3.6 FIP microbial lipase units per milliliter. Prepare this solution fresh.

Procedure

[NOTE—Assay the Fungi Lipase-International FIP Standard as an internal standard each time.]

Automatic Titration Use an automatic titration device with a 25 mL ± 0.02 mL buret, a pH meter giving a resolution to 0.01, and a reaction vessel with a capacity of 100 mL. Add 24 mL of *Substrate Emulsion*, 9 mL of water, and 2 mL of *0.5% Sodium Taurocholate Solution* to the reaction vessel. Place the reaction vessel in a water bath preheated to 37° ± 0.5° over a hot plate provided with magnetic stirring, and add a magnet to the reaction vessel. Pre-incubate the reaction vessel at 37° ± 0.5° for 10 to 15 min while stirring at about 300 rpm. Immerse a pH-electrode and the tip of the buret into the solution. If desired, gently blow nitrogen gas onto the solution. Adjust the pH of the solution to 7.0 with *0.02 N Sodium Hydroxide Solution*. Set the automatic buret to zero. Add 5.0 mL of the enzyme solution while simultaneously starting a timer. Maintain the pH at 7.0 by automatic titration. After 10.0 min, abruptly (within 30 s) bring the pH to 9.0 by manually adding additional *0.02 N Sodium*

Hydroxide Solution. Record the volume of *0.02 N Sodium Hydroxide Solution* consumed as N_1. Run the test with a blank by setting up the titration in the same manner, except after adjusting the pH to 7.0 with *0.02 N Sodium Hydroxide Solution*, set the automatic buret to zero, and maintain the pH at 7.0 by automatic titration. After 10.0 min, abruptly (within 30 s) bring the pH to 9.0 as before, and then add 5.0 mL of enzyme solution. Because the enzyme lowers the pH, return the pH to 9.0 by adding *0.02 N Sodium Hydroxide Solution*. Record the volume of *0.02 N Sodium Hydroxide Solution* consumed as N_2.

Manual Titration Follow the same procedure as with *Automatic Titration*, but keep the pH at 7.0 with *0.02 N Sodium Hydroxide Solution* from a 25-mL buret, demarked in 0.02-mL units.

Calculation One unit of enzyme activity (FIP Unit) is defined as that quantity of a standard lipase preparation (Fungi Lipase-International FIP Standard) that liberates the equivalent of 1 µmol of fatty acid per minute from the *Substrate Emulsion* under the described assay conditions. The specific activity is expressed in international FIP units per milligram of the *Sample Preparation*.

The use of an enzyme reference standard of known activity, controlled by the Center for Standards of the Commission, eliminates difficulties from interlaboratory differences in quality of reagents such as the *Gum Arabic Solution*, olive oil, or *Substrate Emulsion* or in the set-up of the experiment. The activity (FIP U/mg) using an enzyme reference standard is calculated by the formula

$$\text{Result} = (A \times C)/B$$

in which A is the specific activity, in units/mg, of the test sample (measured); B is the specific activity, in units/mg, of Fungi Lipase-International FIP Standard (measured); and C is the number of FIP units/mg of Fungi Lipase-International FIP Standard as indicated on the container.

One milliliter of the *0.02 N Sodium Hydroxide Solution* corresponds with the neutralization of 20 µmol of fatty acids. Five milliliters of enzyme solution liberates $(N_1 - N_2)$ mL × 20 µmol of fatty acids over a 10-min time interval. If the enzyme solution contains W mg of enzyme preparation per milliliter, the specific activity, in units/mg, is calculated as follows:

$$\text{Result} = [(N_1 - N_2) \times 20]/(10 \times 5 \times W)$$

in which $(N_1 - N_2)$ is the volume, in milliliters, of the *0.02 N Sodium Hydroxide Solution* used for the titration.

LYSOZYME ACTIVITY[1]

Application and Principle The purpose of this procedure is to determine the lysozyme activity in purified lysozyme preparations derived from animal or microbial sources. The assay is based on the rate of decrease in absorbance at 450 nm, attributed to the lysis of *Micrococcus lysodeikticus* by lysozyme. The decrease in absorbance is measured using a UV/V spectrophotometer equipped to control the sample temperature at 25°.

[NOTE—Ensure that all glassware and supplies are heat sterilized. The work area should be aseptically clean. Any residual lysozyme contamination will adversely affect the results of the assay.]

Reagents and Solutions

Sodium Phosphate Buffer Solution Dissolve 10.4 g of monobasic sodium phosphate ($NaH_2PO_4 \cdot H_2O$) in 500 mL of sterile, deionized water in a 1000-mL volumetric flask, and dilute to volume. Similarly, dissolve 9.465 g of anhydrous dibasic sodium phosphate (Na_2HPO_4) in sterile, deionized water, and dilute to 1000 mL. Mix 815 mL of the monobasic sodium phosphate solution with 185 mL of the dibasic sodium phosphate solution. Adjust the pH of the buffer to 6.2; when checking the pH, use an aliquot of the buffer to prevent contamination of the solution. Adjust the pH by adding more monobasic or dibasic sodium phosphate solution as needed. The buffer solution may be stored under refrigeration for up to 1 month.

Substrate Solution Add 30 to 40 mg of *Micrococcus lysodeikticus* (Sigma M-3770, or equivalent) to 100 mL of *Sodium Phosphate Buffer Solution* in a 250-mL Erlenmeyer flask, tilt gently to mix, and do not shake. Allow the substrate to incubate at 37° for 30 min before using it. The substrate solution is stable for 2 h at room temperature. Zero a spectrophotometer against air, then measure the absorbance of the substrate solution, which should give a reading of 1.7 ± 0.1 at 450 nm.

[NOTE—If the absorbance is significantly lower than 1.7, do not adjust the concentration. Run the analysis, and check the rate of the reaction. The rate of the decrease in absorbance should range between 0.03 and 0.06 units per min.]

Standard Preparation Use a commercial reference standard lysozyme of a specified strength from an animal or microbial source in accordance with the origin of the preparation being measured. Measure 50 mg of the reference standard lysozyme into a 50-mL volumetric flask, and dissolve, with stirring, in approximately 25-mL of *Sodium Phosphate Buffer Solution*. Dilute to volume with *Sodium Phosphate Buffer Solution*, and mix thoroughly. If desired, freeze aliquots of this *Standard Preparation* for subsequent assays. Quantitatively transfer 3 mL of the *Standard Preparation* to a 100-mL volumetric flask, and dilute to volume with *Sodium Phosphate Buffer Solution*.

Sample Preparation Measure 50 mg of sample into a 50-mL volumetric flask. Dissolve the sample, with stirring, in approximately 25 mL of *Sodium Phosphate Buffer Solution*. Dilute to volume with *Sodium Phosphate Buffer Solution*, and mix the solution thoroughly. Quantitatively transfer 3 mL of the solution to a 100-mL volumetric flask, and dilute to volume with *Sodium Phosphate Buffer Solution*.

Procedure Conduct the test in a spectrophotometer equipped to maintain a temperature of 25° in the cell compartment. Perform the test in triplicate for the *Standard Preparation* and for the *Sample Preparation*.

---

[1] Shugar, D. 1952. The measurement of lysozyme activity and the ultraviolet inactivation of lysozyme. Biochimica et Biophysica Acta. 8:302–309.

Place a 1-cm cell into the spectrophotometer, and adjust the absorbance to zero. Pipet 2.9 mL of *Substrate Solution* into the cell; the initial absorbance of the solution should be 1.7 ± 0.1 at 450 nm (see *Note* above). Pipet 0.1 mL of the *Standard Preparation* into the substrate, and mix well. Record the decrease in absorbance over 3 min, recording the absorbance value approximately every 15 s. The rate of the decrease in absorbance should be linear, and range between 0.03 and 0.06 per min. Repeat the procedure with the *Sample Preparation*.

Calculation One lysozyme unit is defined as the amount of lysozyme that causes a decrease in absorbance of 0.001 per min at 450 nm, 25°, and pH 6.2, using a suspension of *Micrococcus lysodeikticus* as the substrate.

The assay stabilizes over the first min; disregard the first min of readings in the calculation. Determine the average absorbance change per min using only the linear portion of the curve where the rate of change is constant, usually the final 2 min.

Calculate the number of lysozyme units per mg by the equation

$$\text{lysozyme units} = (A_1 - A_2)/(T \times W \times 0.001)$$

in which A_1 is the initial absorbance reading in the straight-line portion of the curve; A_2 is the final absorbance reading in the straight-line portion of the curve; T is the elapsed time, in min, between the initial and final absorbance readings; W is the weight, in mg, of the lysozyme in the volume of *Sample Preparation* used in the *Assay*; and 0.001 is the decrease in absorbance caused by one unit of lysozyme per min.

MALTOGENIC AMYLASE ACTIVITY

Application and Principle This procedure is used to determine maltogenic amylase activity in preparations derived from *Bacillus subtilis* containing a *Bacillus stearothermophilus* amylase gene. The test is based on a 30-min hydrolysis of maltotriose under controlled conditions and measurement of the glucose formed by high-performance liquid chromatography (HPLC).

Reagents and Solutions

Citrate Buffer, 0.1 M Dissolve 5.255 g of citric acid ($C_6H_8O_7 \cdot H_2O$) in about 150 mL of water. Adjust the pH to 5.0 with 1 N sodium hydroxide, and dilute to 250 mL.

Substrate Solution Dissolve 1.00 g of maltotriose (Sigma Chemical Co., Catalog No. M 8378) in *Citrate Buffer* in a 50-mL volumetric flask, and dilute to volume with *Citrate Buffer*.

Sodium Chloride Solution, 1 M Dissolve 29.22 g of sodium chloride in water, and dilute to 500 mL.

Amberlite MB-1 Ion Exchange Resin Air dry at room temperature for about 1 week. Protect from contamination.

Glucose Standards Dissolve 1.80 g of anhydrous glucose in water, and dilute to 1000 mL. Transfer 20.0, 50.0, 75.0, and 100.0 mL to separate 100-mL volumetric flasks, and dilute to volume with water. These solutions contain 0.36, 0.9, 1.35, and 1.80 mg of glucose per mL. Using filtered, degassed water as the mobile phase, equilibrate an HPX 87C column, or equivalent, in a high-performance liquid chromatography equipped with a differential refractometer. Chromatograph 5-μL portions of the glucose standards, and record the chromatograms. Prepare a standard curve of the glucose concentration versus the peak height.

Sample Preparation Prepare a solution of each sample to contain approximately 7.5 Maltogenic Amylase Units (MANU) per mL. Further dilute an aliquot of each sample so that the final dilution contains 1% by volume of the *Sodium Chloride Solution, 1 M* and contains between 0.150 and 0.600 MANU per mL.

Procedure Transfer 2.00 mL of each sample to separate test tubes, and equilibrate in the 37° water bath for at least 10 min. At the same time, equilibrate the *Substrate Solution* in the same water bath. At zero time, transfer 2.0 mL of the equilibrated *Substrate Solution* to the first sample tube, mix thoroughly, and return the tube to the 37° bath. Repeat the process for each sample. After exactly 30.0 min, transfer the test tube to a boiling water bath for 15 min, then remove and cool to room temperature. Add approximately 100 mg of *Amberlite MB-1 Ion Exchange Resin* to each tube, place the tubes on the shaker, and mix for at least 15 min. Pass the treated solution through a 0.45-μm filter. Use a separate filter for each sample. Inject a 5-μL portion of each filtered sample into a previously equilibrated high-performance liquid chromatograph equipped with an HPX 87C column (Biorad, or equivalent) and a differential refractometer. Filtered, degassed water is the mobile phase. Record the elution curve.

Calculation One Maltogenic Amylase Unit (MANU) is defined as the amount of enzyme that will cleave maltotriose at a rate of 1 μmol/min under the conditions of the test. From the elution curve of each sample, determine the glucose concentration (G) in the sample from the previously prepared standard curve. Calculate the MANU/g by the equation

$$\text{MANU/g} = G \times 4 \times F/180.1 \times 30 \times W$$

in which G is the glucose concentration in the test solution; 4 is the total test solution volume; 30 is the reaction time, in min; F is the dilution factor; and W is the sample weight, in g.

MILK-CLOTTING ACTIVITY

Application and Principle This procedure is to be applied to enzyme preparations derived from either animal or microbial sources.

Apparatus

Bottle-Rotating Apparatus Use a suitable assembly, designed to rotate at a rate of 16 to 18 rpm.

Sample Bottles Use 125-mL, squat, round, wide-mouth bottles (such as Scientific Products, Catalog No. B-7545-125).

Substrate Solution Dissolve 60 g of low-heat, nonfat dry milk (such as Galloway West, Peake Grade A) in 500 mL of a solution, adjusted to pH 6.3 if necessary, containing in each mL 2.05 mg of sodium acetate (NaC$_2$H$_3$O$_2$) and 1.11 mg of calcium chloride (CaCl$_2$).

Standard Preparation Use a standard-strength rennet, bovine rennet, microbial rennet (*Endothia parasitica*), or microbial rennet (*Mucor* species), as appropriate for the preparation to be assayed. Such standards, which are available from commercial coagulant manufacturers, should be of known activity. Dilute the standard-strength material 1 to 200 with water, and mix. Equilibrate to 300 before use, and prepare no more than 2 h before use.

Sample Preparation Prepare aqueous solutions or dilutions of the sample to produce a final concentration such that the clotting time, as determined in the *Procedure* below, will be within 1 min of that of the *Standard Preparation*. Prepare no more than 1 h before use.

Procedure Transfer 50.0 mL of the *Substrate Solution* into each of four 125-mL *Sample Bottles*. Place the bottles on the *Bottle-Rotating Apparatus*, and suspend the apparatus in a water bath, maintained at 30° ± 0.5°, so that the bottles are at an angle of approximately 20° to 30° to the horizontal. Immerse the bottles so that the water level in the bath is about equal to the substrate level in the bottles. Begin rotating the apparatus at 16 to 18 rpm, then add 1.0 mL of the *Sample Preparation* to each of two bottles, and record the exact time of addition. Add 1.0 mL of the *Standard Preparation* to each of the other two bottles, recording the exact time.

Observe the rotating bottles, and record the exact time of the first evidence of clotting (i.e., when fine granules or flecks adhere to the sides of the bottle). Variations in the response of different lots of the substrate may cause variations in clotting time; therefore, measure the test samples and standards simultaneously on the same substrate. Average the clotting time, in s, of the duplicate samples, recording the time for the *Standard Preparation* as T_S and that for the *Sample Preparation* as T_U.

Calculation Calculate the activity of the enzyme preparation by the equation

$$\text{Milk-clotting units/mL} = 100 \times (T_S/T_U) \times (D_S/D_U)$$

in which 100 is the activity assigned to the *Standard Preparation*, D_S is the dilution factor for the *Standard Preparation*, and D_U is the dilution factor for the *Sample Preparation*.

[NOTE—The dilution factors should be expressed as fractions; for example, a dilution of 1 to 200 would be expressed as $1/200$.]

PANCREATIN ACTIVITY

Application and Principle These procedures are used to determine the primary enzyme activities in pancreatin preparations.

Reference Standards

USP Sodium Taurocholate Reference Standard [CAUTION—Avoid inhaling airborne particles.] Keep container tightly closed. Dry at 105° for 4 h before using.

USP Pancreatin Reference Standard Keep container tightly closed, and store in a refrigerator. Do not open while cold, and do not dry before using.

Amylase Activity

pH 6.8 Phosphate Buffer On the day of use, dissolve 13.6 g of monobasic potassium phosphate in water to make 500 mL of solution. Dissolve 14.2 g of anhydrous dibasic sodium phosphate in water to make 500 mL of solution. Mix 51 mL of the monobasic potassium phosphate solution with 49 mL of the dibasic sodium phosphate solution. If necessary, adjust by the dropwise addition of the appropriate solution to a pH of 6.8.

Substrate Solution On the day of use, stir a portion of purified soluble starch equivalent to 2.0 g of dried substance with 10 mL of water, and add this mixture to 160 mL of water, add it to the hot solution, and heat to boiling, with continuous mixing. Cool to room temperature, and add water to make 200 mL.

Standard Preparation Weigh accurately about 20 mg of USP Pancreatin Reference Standard into a suitable mortar. Add about 30 mL of *pH 6.8 Phosphate Buffer*, and triturate for 5 to 10 min. Transfer the mixture with the aid of *pH 6.8 Phosphate Buffer* to a 50-mL volumetric flask, dilute with *pH 6.8 Phosphate Buffer* to volume, and mix. Calculate the activity, in USP Units of amylase activity per mL, of the resulting solution from the declared potency on the label of the Reference Standard.

Assay Preparation For Pancreatin having about the same amylase activity as the USP Pancreatin Reference Standard, weigh accurately about 40 mg of Pancreatin into a suitable mortar.

[NOTE—For Pancreatin having a different amylase activity, weigh accurately the amount necessary to obtain an *Assay Preparation* having amylase activity per mL corresponding approximately to that of the *Standard Preparation*.]

Add about 3 mL of *pH 6.8 Phosphate Buffer*, and triturate for 5 to 10 min. Transfer the mixture with the aid of *pH 6.8 Phosphate Buffer* to a 100-mL volumetric flask, dilute with *pH 6.8 Phosphate Buffer* to volume, and mix.

Procedure Prepare four stoppered, 250-mL conical flasks, and mark them S, U, BS, and BU. Pipet into each flask 25 mL of *Substrate Solution*, 10 mL of *pH 6.8 Phosphate Buffer*, and 1 mL of sodium chloride solution (11.7 in 1000), insert the stoppers, and mix. Place the flasks in a water bath maintained at 25° ± 0.1°, and allow them to equilibrate. To flasks BU and BS add 2 mL of 1 N hydrochloric acid, mix, and return the flasks to the water bath. To flasks U and BU add 1.0-mL portions of the *Assay Preparation*, and to flasks S and BS add 1.0 mL of the *Standard Preparation*. Mix each, and return the flasks to the water bath. After 10 min, accurately timed from the addition of the enzyme, add 2-mL portions of 1 N hydrochloric acid to flasks S and U, and mix. To each flask, with continuous stirring, add 10.0 mL of 1 N iodine VS, and immediately add 45 mL of 0.1 N sodium hydroxide. Place the flasks in the dark at a temperature between 15° and 25° for 15 min. To each flask add 4 mL of 2 N sulfuric acid, and titrate with 0.1 N sodium thiosulfate VS to the disappearance of the blue color. Calculate the amylase activity, in USP Units per mg, taken by the formula

$$\text{Result} = 100(C_S/W_U)(V_{BU} - V_U)/(V_{BS} - V_S)$$

in which C_S is the amylase activity of the *Standard Preparation*, in USP Units per mL; W_U is the amount, in mg, of Pancreatin taken; and V_U, V_S, V_{BU} and V_{BS} are the volumes, in mL, of 0.1 N sodium thiosulfate consumed in the titration of the solutions in flasks, *U*, *S*, *BU*, and *BS*, respectively.

Lipase Activity

Gum Arabic Solution Centrifuge a 1:10 solution of gum arabic until clear. Use only the clear solution.

Olive Oil Substrate Combine 165 mL of the *Gum Arabic Solution*, 20 mL of olive oil, and 15 g of crushed ice in the cup of an electric blender. Cool the mixture in an ice bath to 5°, and homogenize at high speed for 15 min, intermittently cooling in an ice bath to prevent the temperature from exceeding 30°. Test for suitability of mixing as follows: Place a drop of the homogenate on a microscope slide and gently press a cover slide in place to spread the liquid. Examine the entire field under high power (43 × magnification objective lens and 5 × magnification ocular), using an eyepiece equipped with a calibrated micrometer. The substrate is satisfactory if 90% of the particles do not exceed 2 µm in diameter and none exceeds 10 µm in diameter.

Buffer Solution Dissolve 60 mg of tris(hydroxymethyl)-aminomethane and 234 mg of sodium chloride in water to make 100 mL.

Sodium Taurocholate Solution Prepare a solution to contain 80.0 mg of USP Sodium Taurocholate Reference Standard in each mL.

Standard Test Dilution Suspend about 200 mg of USP Pancreatin Reference Standard, accurately weighed, in about 3 mL of cold water in a mortar, triturate for 10 min, and add cold water to a volume necessary to produce a concentration of 8 to 16 USP Units of lipase activity per mL, based on the declared potency on the label of the Reference Standard. Maintain the suspension at 4°, and mix before using. For each determination, withdraw 5 to 10 mL of the cold suspension, and allow the temperature to rise to 20° before pipeting the exact volume.

Assay Test Dilution Suspend about 200 mg of the Pancreatin sample, accurately weighed, in about 3 mL of cold water in a mortar, triturate for 10 min, and add cold water to a volume necessary to produce a concentration of 8 to 16 USP Units of lipase activity per mL, based on the estimated potency of the test material. Maintain the suspension at 4°, and mix before using. For each determination, withdraw 5 to 10 mL of the cold suspension, and allow the temperature to rise to 20° before pipeting the exact volume.

Procedure Mix 10.0 mL of *Olive Oil Substrate*, 8.0 mL of *Buffer Solution*, 2.0 mL of *Sodium Taurocholate Solution*, and 9.0 mL of water in a jacketed glass vessel of about 50-mL capacity, the outer chamber of which is connected to a thermostatically controlled water bath. Cover the mixture, and stir continuously with a mechanical stirring device. With the mixture maintained at a temperature of 37° ± 0.1°, add 0.1 N sodium hydroxide, from a microburet inserted through an opening in the cover, to adjust potentiometrically the pH to 9.20, using a calomel-glass electrode system. Add 1.0 mL of *Assay Test Dilution*, and then continue adding the 0.1 N sodium hydroxide for 5 min to maintain the pH at 9.0. Determine the volume of 0.1 N sodium hydroxide added after each min.

In the same manner, titrate 1.0 mL of *Standard Test Dilution*.

Calculation From the *Standard Test Dilution*, plot the volume of 0.1 N sodium hydroxide titrated against time. Using only the points that fall on the straight-line segment of the curve, calculate the mean acidity released per min by the *Assay Test Dilution*. Taking into consideration dilution factors, calculate the lipase activity of the *Standard Test Dilution*, using the lipase activity of the USP Pancreatin Reference Standard stated on the label.

Protease Activity

Casein Substrate Place 1.25 g of finely powdered casein in a 100-mL conical flask containing 5 mL of water, shake to form a suspension, add 10 mL of 0.1 N sodium hydroxide, shake for 1 min, add 50 mL of water, and shake for about 1 h to dissolve the casein. Adjust the pH to about 8.0 ± 0.1, using 1 N sodium hydroxide or 1 N hydrochloric acid. Transfer the solution to a 100-mL volumetric flask, dilute with water to volume, and mix. Use this substrate on the day it is prepared.

Buffer Solution Dissolve 6.8 g of monobasic potassium phosphate and 1.8 g of sodium hydroxide in 950 mL of water in a 1000-mL volumetric flask, adjust to a pH of 7.5 ± 0.2, using 0.2 N sodium hydroxide, dilute with water to volume, and mix. Store this solution in a refrigerator.

Trichloroacetic Acid Solution Dissolve 50 g of trichloroacetic acid in 1000 mL of water. Store this solution at room temperature.

Filter Paper Determine the suitability of the filter paper by filtering a 5-mL portion of *Trichloroacetic Acid Solution* through the paper and measuring the absorbance of the filtrate at 280 nm, using an unfiltered portion of the same *Trichloroacetic Acid Solution* as the blank. The absorbance is not more than 0.04. If the absorbance is more than 0.04, the filter paper may be washed repeatedly with *Trichloroacetic Acid Solution* until the absorbance of the filtrate, determined as above, is not more than 0.04.

Standard Test Dilution Add about 100 mg of USP Pancreatin Reference Standard, accurately weighed, to 100.0 mL of *Buffer Solution*, and mix by shaking intermittently at room temperature for about 25 min. Dilute quantitatively with *Buffer Solution* to produce a concentration of about 2.5 USP Units of protease activity per mL, based on the potency declared on the label of the Reference Standard.

Assay Test Dilution Add an amount of pancreatin sample equivalent to about 100 mg of USP Pancreatin Reference Standard, accurately weighed, to 100.0 mL of *Buffer Solution*, and mix by shaking intermittently at room temperature for 25 min. Dilute quantitatively with *Buffer Solution* to obtain a dilution that corresponds in activity to the *Standard Test Dilution*.

Procedure Label test tubes in duplicate S_1, S_2, and S_3 for the standard series, and U for the sample. Pipet into tubes S_1 2.0 mL, into S_2 and U 1.5 mL, and into S_3 1.0 mL of *Buffer Solution*. Pipet into tubes S_1 1.0 mL, into S_2 1.5 mL, and into S_3 2.0 mL of the *Standard Test Dilution*. Pipet into tubes U 1.5 mL of the *Assay Test Dilution*. Pipet into one tube each of S_1, S_2, S_3, and U 5.0 mL of *Trichloroacetic Acid Solution*, and mix. Designate these tubes as S_{1B}, S_{2B}, S_{3B}, and U_B, respectively. Prepare a blank by mixing 3 mL of *Buffer Solution* and 5 mL of *Trichloroacetic Acid Solution* in a separate test tube marked B. Place all the tubes in a 40° water bath, insert a glass stirring rod into each tube, and allow temperature equilibration. At zero time, add to each tube, at timed intervals, 2.0 mL of the *Casein Substrate*, preheated to the bath temperature, and mix. Accurately timed, 60 min after the addition of the *Casein Substrate*, stop the reaction in tubes S_1, S_2, S_3, and U by adding 5.0 mL of *Trichloroacetic Acid Solution* at the corresponding time intervals, stir, and remove all the tubes from the bath. Allow to stand for 10 min at room temperature to complete protein precipitation, and filter. The filtrates must be free from haze. Determine the absorbances of each filtrate, in a 1-cm cell, at 280 nm, with a suitable spectrophotometer, using the intake from the blank (tube B) to set the instrument.

Calculation Correct the absorbance values for the filtrates from tubes S_1, S_2, and S_3 by subtracting the absorbance values for the filtrates from tubes S_{1B}, S_{2B}, and S_{3B}, respectively, and plot the corrected absorbance values against the corresponding volumes of the *Standard Test Dilution* used. From the curve, using the corrected absorbance value ($U - U_B$ for the USP Pancreatin Reference Standard taken), and taking into consideration the dilution factors, calculate the protease activity, in USP Units, of the USP Pancreatin Reference Standard taken by comparison with that of the standard, using the protease activity stated on the label of USP Pancreatin Reference Standard.

PEPSIN ACTIVITY

Application This procedure is to be applied to preparations derived from porcine or other animal stomachs.

Apparatus

Measuring Vessels Use 100-mL conically shaped measuring vessels complying with the following descriptions: (1) diameters not exceeding 1 cm at the bottom; (2) comply in other respects with the water and sediment tube ASTM Standard Method D96-68; (3) graduated from 0 to 0.5 mL in 0.05-mL graduations, from 2 to 3 mL in 0.1-mL graduations, from 3 to 5 mL in 0.2-mL graduations, from 5 to 10 mL in 1-mL graduations, from 10 to 25 mL in 5-mL graduations, and with graduation marks at 50, 75, and 100 mL.

[NOTE—Measuring vessels other than the type described herein may be used if they are of such design and graduation to permit measurement of the residue with equivalent accuracy.]

Reagents and Solutions

Hydrochloric Acid Solution Mix 35 mL of 1.0 N hydrochloric acid with 385 mL of water.

Substrate Boil one or more hen eggs for 15 min to provide coagulated albumen (Miles, Inc.), and cool rapidly by immersion in cold water. Remove the shell and pellicle and all of the yolk, and at once rub the albumen through a clean, dry No. 40 sieve, rejecting the first portion that passes through the sieve.

Substrate Preparation Place 10 g of the *Substrate* in each of as many 100-mL wide-mouth bottles as needed for the test, and immediately add 35 mL of *Hydrochloric Acid Solution* (all at one time or in portions). By suitable means, thoroughly disintegrate the particles of albumen. Equilibrate to 52° before use in the *Procedure*, below.

Standard Preparation Dissolve 100 mg of USP Pepsin Reference Standard in 150 mL of *Hydrochloric Acid Solution*. Use this solution within 1 h.

Sample Preparation Dissolve 100 mg of the pepsin sample, or an amount of the enzyme preparation that will provide a solution similar to or slightly stronger than the *Standard Preparation*, in 150 mL of *Hydrochloric Acid Solution*. Use this solution within 1 h.

Procedure Pipet 5.0 mL of the *Standard Preparation* into each of two bottles containing the *Substrate Preparation*. To two or more additional substrate bottles add graduated aliquots of the *Sample Preparation* so that one bottle will contain approximately the same amount, and the others will contain successively lesser amounts, of pepsin as is contained in the 5.0 mL of the *Standard Preparation*, using, for example, 5.0, 4.9, and 4.8 mL. When less than 5.0 mL of the *Sample Preparation* is used, add sufficient *Hydrochloric Acid Solution* to make 5.0 mL of combined *Sample Preparation* plus acid added. At once stopper the bottles securely, invert them three times, and heat in a water bath, maintained at 52° ± 0.5°, for 2.5 h, agitating the contents equally every 10 min by inverting the bottles once. Remove the bottles from the bath, and pour the contents of each into separate measuring vessels.

Transfer the undigested albumen that adheres to the sides of the bottles into the respective measuring vessel with the aid of small portions of water until 50 mL has been used for each. Mix the contents of each vessel, allow them to stand for 30 min, and then read for each the volume of undigested albumen. Average the sediment volumes in the two standard vessels, and note which of the sample vessels contains undigested albumen closest to the average for the standards. Finally, record as v the volume, in mL, of *Sample Preparation* that produced the undigested albumen closest to the average produced by the *Standard Preparations*.

Calculation One pepsin unit is defined as that quantity of enzyme that digests 3000 times its weight of coagulated egg albumen under the conditions of the assay.

Calculate the activity of the enzyme preparation by the equation

$$\text{Pepsin units/mg} = 3000 \times (S/u) \times (5.0/v)$$

in which S is the weight, in mg, of USP Pepsin Reference Standard used to make the *Standard Preparation*; u is the weight, in mg, of enzyme preparation taken for analysis; and v is as defined in the *Procedure*.

PHOSPHOLIPASE A₂ ACTIVITY

Application and Principle   This procedure is used to determine the phospholipase A₂ activity from extracts of porcine pancreatic tissue. The analysis is performed by potentiometric titration.

Apparatus

Automatic Titrator   Use a suitable automatic recording titrator equipped with a stirred, thermostated, controlled-atmosphere titration cell (e.g., Radiometer Autotitrator).

Homogenizer   Use a suitable homogenizer (e.g., Biomixer; Fisher Scientific, Catalog No. 11-504-2-4, or equivalent).

Constant-Temperature Water Bath   Set at 40° ± 0.1°.

Reagents and Solutions

Calcium Chloride Solution (0.3 M)   Transfer 4.41 g of calcium chloride dihydrate to a 100-mL volumetric flask, dissolve in, and dilute to volume with water.

Sodium Deoxycholate Solution (0.016 M)   Dissolve 0.67 g of sodium deoxycholate (Sigma Chemical Co., Catalog No. D6750) in 100 mL of water.

Sodium Hydroxide Solution (0.1 N)   Use a standardized solution.

Substrate Solution   Add the yolk of one fresh egg to 100 mL of deionized water and homogenize until a stable emulsion is obtained. Add 5 mL of the *Calcium Chloride Solution*, and mix.

Sample Preparation   Dissolve an accurately weighed amount of enzyme preparation in 0.001 N hydrochloric acid, and dilute to obtain an enzyme activity of 10 to 80 units of activity per mL.

Procedure   Pre-equilibrate the *Substrate Solution*, the *Sodium Deoxycholate Solution*, and about 50 mL of water to 40° in the water bath. Transfer 10 mL of the *Substrate Solution* to the thermostated titration vessel. Add 5 mL of the *Sodium Deoxycholate Solution* and 10 mL of deionized water. Blanket the cell with nitrogen and equilibrate for approximately 5 min. Using the *Automatic Titrator* filled with *0.1 N Sodium Hydroxide Solution*, adjust the pH of the solution to 8.0 ± 0.05. Monitor the consumption (if any) of sodium hydroxide for 5 min as a blank. Refill the *Automatic Titrator*. Add 0.1 mL of *Sample Solution* containing between 1 and 8 units of activity and start the *Automatic Titrator*. Record the sodium hydroxide consumption for at least 5 min.

Calculation   One phospholipase unit is defined as the quantity of enzyme that produces 1 microequivalent of free fatty acid per min under the conditions of the test. Determine the rate, R, of titrant consumption during 0 to 3 min of the reaction.

[NOTE—The recorder trace must be linear during the first 3 min of the reaction.]

Determine the rate of titrant consumption (if any) during equilibration (blank) (R_B):

$$\text{Units/g} = (R \times N) - (R_B \times N)/W,$$

in which R and R_B are the rates of titrant consumption of the sample and blank, respectively, in µL/min; N is the normality of the titrant; and W is the weight, in g, contained in 0.1 mL of the *Sample Preparation* taken for the test.

PHYTASE ACTIVITY

Application and Principle   This procedure is used to determine the activity of enzymes releasing phosphate from phytate. The assay is based on enzymatic hydrolysis of sodium phytate under controlled conditions by measurement of the amount of ortho phosphate released.

Reagents and Solutions

[NOTE—All glassware must be acid washed, rinsed, and scrupulously cleaned to ensure the absence of phosphate.]

Acetate Buffer (pH 5.5)   Dissolve 1.76 g of 100% acetic acid ($C_2H_4O_2$), 30.02 g of sodium acetate trihydrate ($C_2H_3O_2Na\cdot3H_2O$), and 0.147 g of calcium chloride dihydrate in about 900 mL of water. Transfer the solution into a 1000-mL volumetric flask, dilute to volume with water, and mix. The pH should be 5.50 ± 0.05.

Substrate Solution   Dissolve 8.40 g of sodium phytate decahydrate ($C_6H_6O_{24}P_6Na_{12}\cdot10H_2O$) (Sigma Chemical Co.) in 900 mL of *Acetate Buffer*. Adjust the pH to 5.50 ± 0.05 at 37.0° ± 0.1° by adding 4 M acetic acid. Cool to ambient temperature. Quantitatively transfer the mixture to a 1000-mL volumetric flask, dilute to volume with *Acetate Buffer*, and mix. Prepare fresh daily.

Nitric Acid Solution (27%)   While stirring, slowly add 70 mL of 65% nitric acid to 130 mL of water.

Ammonium Heptamolybdate Solution   Dissolve 100 g of ammonium heptamolybdate tetrahydrate [$(NH_4)_6Mo_7O_{24}\cdot4H_2O$] in 900 mL of water in a 1000-mL volumetric flask. Add 10 mL of 25% ammonia solution, dilute to volume with water, and mix. This solution is stable for 4 weeks when stored at ambient temperature and shielded from light.

Ammonium Vanadate Solution   Dissolve 2.35 g of ammonium monovanadate (NH_4VO_3) in 400 mL of warm (60°) water. While stirring, slowly add 20 mL of *Nitric Acid Solution (27%)*. Cool to ambient temperature. Quantitatively transfer the mixture to a 1000-mL volumetric flask, dilute to volume with water, and mix. This solution is stable for 4 weeks when stored at ambient temperature and shielded from light.

Color/Stop Solution   While stirring, add 250 mL of *Ammonium Vanadate Solution* to 250 mL of *Ammonium Heptamolybdate Solution*. Slowly add 165 mL of 65% nitric acid. Cool to ambient temperature. Quantitatively transfer the mixture to a 1000-mL volumetric flask, dilute to volume with water, and mix. Prepare fresh daily.

Potassium Dihydrogen Phosphate Solution   Dry a sufficient amount of potassium dihydrogen phosphate (KH_2PO_4) in a vacuum oven at 100° to 104° for 2 h. Cool to ambient temperature in a desiccator over dried silica gel.

In duplicate (solutions A and B), weigh approximately 0.245 g of dried potassium dihydrogen phosphate accurately to within 1 mg and dilute with *Acetate Buffer* to 1 L to obtain solutions containing 1.80 mmol/L of potassium dihydrogen phosphate.

Phytase Reference Preparation (Highly concentrated phytase preparation) This preparation can be obtained from Gist-Brocades, Delft, The Netherlands, with an assigned activity (by collaborative assay), or the activity of the reference preparation can be determined according to *Procedure 2*.

Phytase Reference Solutions, Procedure 1 Weigh an amount of *Phytase Reference Preparation* corresponding with 20,000 phytase units accurately to within 1 mg in duplicate in 200-mL volumetric flasks. Dissolve in and dilute to volume with *Acetate Buffer*, and mix. Dilute with *Acetate Buffer* to obtain dilutions containing approximately 0.01, 0.02, 0.04, 0.06, and 0.08 phytase units per 2.0 mL of the final dilution.

Sample Preparation, Procedure 1 Suspend or dissolve and dilute accurately weighed amounts of sample in *Acetate Buffer* so that 2.0 mL of the final dilution will contain between 0.02 and 0.08 phytase units.

Sample Preparation, Procedure 2 In duplicate, accurately weigh amounts of *Phytase Reference Preparation* and dissolve and dilute in *Acetate Buffer* to obtain dilutions containing 0.06 ± 0.006 phytase units per 2.0 mL of the final dilution.

Procedures

Procedure 1 (Determination of the phytase activity) Transfer 2.00 mL of the *Sample Preparation, Procedure 1*, and the *Phytase Reference Solutions, Procedure 1*, into separate 20- × 150-mm glass test tubes. Using a stopwatch and starting at time equals zero, in the order of the series and within regular time intervals, place the tubes into a 37.0° ± 0.1° water bath and allow their contents to equilibrate for 5 min. At time equals 5 min, in the same order of the series and with the same time intervals, add 4.0 mL of *Substrate Solution* (previously equilibrated to 37.00 ± 0.10) to each test tube. Mix, and replace in the 37.0° ± 0.1° water bath. At time equals 65 min, in the same order and within the same time intervals, terminate the incubation by adding 4.0 mL of *Color/Stop Solution*. Mix, and cool to ambient temperature.

Prepare blanks by transferring 2.00 mL of the *Sample Preparation, Procedure 1*, and the *Phytase Reference Solutions, Procedure 1*, into separate 20- × 150-mm glass test tubes. Using a stopwatch and starting at time equals zero, in the order of the series and within regular time intervals, place the tubes into a 37.0° ± 0.1° water bath and allow them to equilibrate for 5 min. At time equal 5 min, in the same order of the series and within the same time intervals, add 4.0 mL of *Color/Stop Solution*. Mix, and cool to ambient temperature. Next add 4.00 mL of *Substrate Solution* to the blank tubes, and mix.

Centrifuge all test tubes for 5 min at 3000 × g. Determine the absorbance of each solution at 415 nm in a 1-cm path-length cell with a suitable spectrophotometer, using water to zero the instrument.

Procedure 2 (Determination of the phytase activity of the *Phytase Reference Preparation*) Transfer 2.00 mL of *Sample Preparation, Procedure 2*, and 2.00 mL (three times from *Potassium Dihydrogen Phosphate Solution A* and two times from B) of *Potassium Dihydrogen Phosphate Solutions* into separate 20- × 150-mm glass test tubes. Using a stopwatch and starting at time equals zero, in the order of the series and within regular time intervals, place the tubes into a 37.0° ± 0.1° water bath and allow their contents to equilibrate for 5 min. At time equals 5 min, in the same order of the series and within the same time intervals, add 4.0 mL of *Substrate Solution* (previously equilibrated to 37.0° ± 0.1°) to the test tubes. Mix, and replace in the 37.0° ± 0.1° water bath. At time equals 35 min, in the same order and within the same time intervals, terminate the incubation by adding 4.0 mL of *Color/Stop Solution*. Mix, and cool to ambient temperature.

Prepare blanks by transferring 2.00 mL of *Sample Preparation, Procedure 2*, into separate 20- × 150-mm glass test tubes. Prepare *Reagent Blanks* by transferring 2.00 mL of water into a series of five separate 20- × 150-mm glass test tubes. Add 4.0 mL of *Color/Stop Solution* to all blank tubes and mix. Next add 4.0 mL of *Substrate Solution*, and mix. Determine the absorbance of each solution at 415 nm in a 1-cm path-length cell with a suitable spectrophotometer, using water to zero the instrument.

Calculations

Calculation, Procedure 1 One Phytase (fytase) unit (FTU) is the amount of enzyme that liberates inorganic phosphate at 1 µmol/min from sodium phytate 0.0051 mol/L at 37.00 at pH 5.50 under the conditions of the test. Calculate the corrected absorbance (sample minus blank) for each *Sample Preparation* and *Phytase Reference Solution*. Plot the accurately calculated phytase activity (FTU per 2 mL) of each *Phytase Reference Solution* against the corresponding absorbance. From the curve, determine the phytase activity in each *Sample Preparation* (FTU per 2 mL):

Activity (FTU/g) = (FTU per 2 mL × dilution)/sample weight (g).

Calculation, Procedure 2 Calculate the corrected absorbances A_R for each *Sample Preparation* (absorbance *Phytase Reference Solution* minus corresponding absorbance blank) and for each *Potassium Dihydrogen Phosphate Solution*, A_p (absorbance *Potassium Dihydrogen Phosphate Solution* minus average absorbance reagent blank). Calculate C, the phosphate concentration of each *Potassium Dihydrogen Phosphate Solution*:

(W × 1000 × 2)/MW = C (mmol/2 mL).

Calculate the absorbances D for each *Potassium Dihydrogen Phosphate Solution* after correction for the amount of potassium dihydrogen phosphate weighed:

A_p/C = D(absorbance units/mmol of phosphate per 2 mL).

Calculate the average of results D, giving E (maximum allowable difference, 5%).

Calculate the activity for each *Phytase Reference Preparation*:

$$(A_R \times f)/(30 \times R \times E) = FTU/g,$$

in which A_R equals the corrected absorbance of the *Phytase Standard Solution*; f equals the total dilution factor of the reference preparation; 30 equals the incubation time, in min; R equals sample weight, in g; E equals average of D factors; W equals the weight of potassium dihydrogen phosphate, in g; and MW equals the molecular weight of potassium dihydrogen phosphate, 136.09 (g/mol).

PLANT PROTEOLYTIC ACTIVITY

Application and Principle This procedure is used to determine the proteolytic activity of papain, ficin, and bromelain. The assay is based on a 60-min proteolytic hydrolysis of a casein substrate at pH 6.0 and 40°. Unhydrolyzed substrate is precipitated with trichloroacetic acid and removed by filtration; solubilized casein is then measured spectrophotometrically.

Reagents and Solutions

Sodium Phosphate Solution (0.05 M) Transfer 7.1 g of anhydrous dibasic sodium phosphate into a 1000-mL volumetric flask, dissolve in about 500 mL of water, dilute to volume with water, and mix. Add 1 drop of toluene as a preservative.

Citric Acid Solution (0.05 M) Transfer 10.5 g of citric acid monohydrate into a 1000-mL volumetric flask, dissolve in about 500 mL of water, dilute to volume with water, and mix. Add 1 drop of toluene as a preservative.

Phosphate–Cysteine–EDTA Buffer Solution Dissolve 7.1 g of anhydrous dibasic sodium phosphate in about 800 mL of water, and then dissolve in this solution 14.0 g of disodium EDTA dihydrate and 6.1 g of cysteine hydrochloride monohydrate.

Adjust to pH 6.0 ± 0.1 with 1 N hydrochloric acid or 1 N sodium hydroxide, then transfer into a 1000-mL volumetric flask, dilute to volume with water, and mix.

Trichloroacetic Acid Solution Dissolve 30 g of trichloroacetic acid in 100 mL of water.

Casein Substrate Solution Disperse 1 g (moisture-free basis) of Hammarsten-grade casein (United States Biochemical Corp., Catalog No. 12840, or equivalent) in 50 mL of *Sodium Phosphate Solution*, and heat for 30 min in a boiling water bath, with occasional agitation. Cool to room temperature, and with rapid and continuous agitation, adjust to pH 6.0 ± 0.1 by the addition of *Citric Acid Solution*.

[NOTE—Rapid and continuous agitation during the addition prevents casein precipitation.]

Quantitatively transfer the mixture into a 100-mL volumetric flask, dilute to volume with water, and mix.

Stock Standard Solution Transfer 100.0 mg of USP Papain Reference Standard into a 100-mL volumetric flask, dissolve, and dilute to volume with *Phosphate–Cysteine–EDTA Buffer Solution*, and mix.

Diluted Standard Solutions Pipet 2, 3, 4, 5, 6, and 7 mL of *Stock Standard Solution* into a series of 100-mL volumetric flasks, dilute each to volume with *Phosphate–Cysteine–EDTA Buffer Solution*, and mix by inversion.

Test Solution Prepare a solution from the enzyme preparation so that 2 mL of the final dilution will give a ΔA in the *Procedure* between 0.2 and 0.5. Weigh the sample accurately, transfer it quantitatively to a glass mortar, and triturate with *Phosphate–Cysteine–EDTA Buffer Solution*. Transfer the mixture quantitatively into a volumetric flask of appropriate size, dilute to volume with *Phosphate–Cysteine–EDTA Buffer Solution*, and mix.

Procedure Pipet 5 mL of *Casein Substrate Solution* into each of a series of 25- × 150-mm test tubes, allowing three tubes for the enzyme unknown, six for a papain standard curve, and nine for enzyme blanks. Equilibrate the tubes for 15 min in a water bath maintained at $40° \pm 0.1°$. Starting the stopwatch at zero time, rapidly pipet 2 mL of each of the *Diluted Standard Solutions*, and 2-mL portions of the *Test Solution*, into the equilibrated substrate. Mix each by swirling, stopper, and place the tubes back in the water bath. After 60.0 min, add 3 mL of *Trichloroacetic Acid Solution* to each tube. Immediately mix each tube by swirling.

Prepare enzyme blanks containing 5.0 mL of *Casein Substrate Solution*, 3.0 mL of *Trichloroacetic Acid Solution*, and 2.0 mL of one of the appropriate *Diluted Standard Solutions* or the *Test Solution*.

Return all tubes to the water bath, and heat for 30.0 min, allowing the precipitated protein to coagulate completely. Filter each mixture through Whatman No. 42, or equivalent, filter paper, discarding the first 3 mL of filtrate. The subsequent filtrate must be perfectly clear. Determine the absorbance of each filtrate in a 1-cm cell at 280 nm, with a suitable spectrophotometer, against its respective blank.

Calculation One papain unit (PU) is defined in this assay as that quantity of enzyme that liberates the equivalent of 1 µg of tyrosine per h under the conditions of the assay.

Prepare a standard curve by plotting the absorbances of filtrates from the *Diluted Standard Solutions* against the corresponding enzyme concentrations, in mg/mL. By interpolation from the standard curve, obtain the equivalent concentration of the filtrate from the *Test Solution*.

Calculate the activity of the enzyme preparation taken for analysis as follows:

$$PU/mg = (A \times C \times 10)/W$$

in which A is the activity of USP Papain Reference Standard, in PU per mg; C is the concentration, in mg/mL, of Reference Standard from the standard curve, equivalent to the enzyme unknown; 10 is the total volume, in mL, of the final incubation mixture; and W is the weight, in mg, of original enzyme preparation in the 2-mL aliquot of *Test Solution* added to the incubation mixture.

PROTEOLYTIC ACTIVITY, BACTERIAL (PC)

Application and Principle This procedure is used to determine protease activity, expressed as PC units, of preparations derived from *Bacillus subtilis* var. and *Bacillus licheniformis* var. The assay is based on a 30-min proteolytic hydrolysis of casein at 37° and pH 7.0. Unhydrolyzed casein is removed by filtration, and the solubilized casein is determined spectrophotometrically.

Reagents and Solutions

Casein Use Hammarsten-grade casein (United States Biochemical Corp., Catalog No. 12840, or equivalent).

Tris Buffer (pH 7.0) Dissolve 12.1 g of enzyme-grade (or equivalent) tris(hydroxymethyl)aminomethane in 800 mL of water, and titrate with 1 N hydrochloric acid to pH 7.0. Transfer into a 1000-mL volumetric flask, dilute to volume with water, and mix.

TCA Solution Dissolve 18 g of trichloroacetic acid and 19 g of sodium acetate trihydrate in 800 mL of water in a 1000-mL volumetric flask, add 20 mL of glacial acetic acid, dilute to volume with water, and mix.

Substrate Solution Dissolve 6.05 g of enzyme-grade tris(hydroxymethyl)aminomethane in 500 mL of water, add 8 mL of 1 N hydrochloric acid, and mix. Dissolve 7 g of *Casein* in this solution, and heat for 30 min in a boiling water bath, stirring occasionally.

Cool to room temperature, and adjust to pH 7.0 with 0.2 N hydrochloric acid, adding the acid slowly, with vigorous stirring, to prevent precipitation of the casein. Transfer the mixture into a 1000-mL volumetric flask, dilute to volume with water, and mix.

Sample Preparation Using *Tris Buffer*, prepare a solution of the sample enzyme preparation so that 2 mL of the final dilution will contain between 10 and 44 bacterial protease units.

Procedure Pipet 10.0 mL of the *Substrate Solution* into each of a series of 25- × 150-mm test tubes, allowing one tube for each enzyme test, one tube for each enzyme blank, and one tube for a substrate blank. Equilibrate the tubes for 15 min in a water bath maintained at 37° ± 0.1°.

Starting the stopwatch at zero time, rapidly pipet 2.0 mL of the *Sample Preparation* into the equilibrated substrate. Mix, and replace the tubes in the water bath. Add 2 mL of *Tris Buffer* (instead of the *Sample Preparation*) to the substrate blank. After exactly 30 min, add 10 mL of *TCA Solution* to each enzyme incubation and to the substrate blank to stop the reaction. Heat the tubes in the water bath for an additional 30 min to allow the protein to coagulate completely.

At the end of the second heating period, shake each tube vigorously, and filter through 11-cm Whatman No. 42, or equivalent, filter paper, discarding the first 3 mL of filtrate.

[NOTE—The filtrate must be perfectly clear.]

Determine the absorbance of each sample filtrate in a 1-cm cell, at 275 nm, with a suitable spectrophotometer, using the filtrate from the substrate blank to set the instrument at zero. Correct each reading by subtracting the appropriate enzyme blank reading, and record the value so obtained as A_U.

Standard Curve Transfer 100.0 mg of L-tyrosine, chromatographic-grade or equivalent (Aldrich Chemical Co.), previously dried to constant weight, to a 1000-mL volumetric flask. Dissolve in 60 mL of 0.1 N hydrochloric acid. When completely dissolved, dilute the solution to volume with water, and mix thoroughly. This solution contains 100 μg of tyrosine in 1.0 mL. Prepare three more dilutions from this stock solution to contain 75.0, 50.0, and 25.0 μg of tyrosine per mL. Determine the absorbance of the four solutions at 275 nm in a 1-cm cell on a suitable spectrophotometer versus 0.006 N hydrochloric acid. Prepare a plot of absorbance versus tyrosine concentration.

Calculation One bacterial protease unit (PC) is defined as that quantity of enzyme that produces the equivalent of 1.5 μg/mL of L-tyrosine per min under the conditions of the assay.

From the *Standard Curve*, and by interpolation, determine the absorbance of a solution having a tyrosine concentration of 60 μg/mL. A figure close to 0.0115 should be obtained. Divide the interpolated value by 40 to obtain the absorbance equivalent to that of a solution having a tyrosine concentration of 1.5 μg/mL, and record the value thus derived as A_S.

Calculate the activity of the sample enzyme preparation by the equation

$$PC/g = (A_U/A_S) \times (22/30W)$$

in which 22 is the final volume, in mL, of the reaction mixture; 30 is the time, in min, of the reaction; and W is the weight, in g, of the original sample taken.

PROTEOLYTIC ACTIVITY, FUNGAL (HUT)

Application and Principle This procedure is used to determine the proteolytic activity, expressed as hemoglobin units on the tyrosine basis (HUT), of preparations derived from *Aspergillus oryzae* var. and *Aspergillus niger* var., and it may be used to determine the activity of other proteases at pH 4.7. The test is based on the 30-min enzymatic hydrolysis of a hemoglobin substrate at pH 4.7 and 40°. Unhydrolyzed substrate is precipitated with trichloroacetic acid and removed by filtration. The quantity of solubilized hemoglobin in the filtrate is determined spectrophotometrically.

Reagents and Solutions

Hemoglobin Use Hemoglobin Substrate Powder (Sigma Chemical Co., Catalog No. H2625) or a similar high-grade material that is completely soluble in water.

Acetate Buffer Solution Dissolve 136 g of sodium acetate ($NaC_2H_3O_2 \cdot 3H_2O$) in sufficient water to make 500 mL. Mix 25.0 mL of this solution with 50.0 mL of 1 M acetic acid, dilute to 1000 mL with water, and mix. The pH of this solution should be 4.7 ± 0.02.

Substrate Solution Transfer 4.0 g of the *Hemoglobin* into a 250-mL beaker, add 100 mL of water, and stir for 10 min to dissolve. Immerse the electrodes of a pH meter in the solution, and while stirring continuously, adjust the pH to 1.7 by adding 0.3 N hydrochloric acid. After 10 min, adjust the pH to 4.7 by adding 0.5 M sodium acetate. Transfer the solution into a 200-mL volumetric flask, dilute to volume with water, and mix. This solution is stable for about 5 days when refrigerated.

Trichloroacetic Acid Solution Dissolve 140 g of trichloroacetic acid in about 750 mL of water. Transfer the solution to a 1000-mL volumetric flask, dilute to volume with water, and mix thoroughly.

Sample Preparation Dissolve an amount of the sample in the *Acetate Buffer Solution* to produce a solution containing, in each mL, between 9 and 22 HUT. (Such a concentration will produce an absorbance reading, in the procedure below, within the preferred range of 0.2 to 0.5.)

Procedure Pipet 10.0 mL of the *Substrate Solution* into each of a series of 25- × 150-mm test tubes: one for each enzyme test and one for the substrate blank. Heat the tubes in a water bath at 40° for about 5 min. To each tube, except the substrate blank, add 2.0 mL of the *Sample Preparation*, and begin timing the reaction at the moment the solution is added; add 2.0 mL of the *Acetate Buffer Solution* to the substrate blank tube. Close the tubes with No. 4 rubber stoppers, and tap each tube gently for 30 s against the palm of the hand to mix. Heat each tube in a water bath at 40° for exactly 30 min, and then rapidly pipet 10.0 mL of the *Trichloroacetic Acid Solution* into each tube. Shake each tube vigorously against the stopper for about 40 s, and then allow to cool to room temperature for 1 h, shaking each tube against the stopper at 10- to 12-min intervals during this period. Prepare enzyme blanks as follows: Heat, in separate tubes, 10.0 mL of the *Substrate Solution* and about 5 mL of the *Sample Preparation* in the water bath for 30 min, then add 10.0 mL of the *Trichloroacetic Acid Solution* to the *Substrate Solution*, shake well for 40 s, and to this mixture add 2.0 mL of the preheated *Sample Preparation*. Shake again, and cool at room temperature for 1 h, shaking at 10- to 12-min intervals.

At the end of 1 h, shake each tube vigorously, and filter through 11-cm Whatman No. 42, or equivalent, filter paper, refiltering the first half of the filtrate through the same paper. Determine the absorbance of each filtrate in a 1-cm cell, at 275 nm, with a suitable spectrophotometer, using the filtrate from the substrate blank to set the instrument to zero. Correct each reading by subtracting the appropriate enzyme blank reading, and record the value so obtained as A_U.

[NOTE—If a corrected absorbance reading between 0.2 and 0.5 is not obtained, repeat the test using more or less of the enzyme preparation as necessary.]

Standard Curve Transfer 100.0 mg of L-tyrosine, chromatographic-grade, or equivalent (Aldrich Chemical Co.), previously dried to constant weight, to a 1000-mL volumetric flask. Dissolve in 60 mL of 0.1 N hydrochloric acid. When the L-tyrosene is completely dissolved, dilute the solution to volume with water, and mix thoroughly. This solution contains 100 µg of tyrosine in 1.0 mL. Prepare three more dilutions from this stock solution to contain 75.0, 50.0, and 25.0 µg of tyrosine per mL. Determine the absorbance of the four solutions at 275 nm in a 1-cm cell on a suitable spectrophotometer versus 0.006 N hydrochloric acid. Prepare a plot of absorbance versus tyrosine concentration. Determine the slope of the curve in terms of absorbance per µg of tyrosine. Multiply this value by 1.10, and record it as A_S. A value of approximately 0.0084 should be obtained.

Calculation One HUT unit of proteolytic (protease) activity is defined as that amount of enzyme that produces, in 1 min under the specified conditions, a hydrolysate whose absorbance at 275 nm is the same as that of a solution containing 1.10 µg/mL of tyrosine in 0.006 N hydrochloric acid.

Calculate the HUT per g of the original enzyme preparation by the equation

$$\text{HUT/g} = (A_U/A_S) \times (22/30W)$$

in which 22 is the final volume of the test solution; 30 is the reaction time, in min; and W is the weight, in g, of the original sample taken.

[NOTE—The value for A_S, under carefully controlled and standardized conditions, is 0.0084; this value may be used for routine work in lieu of the value obtained from the standard curve, but the exact value calculated from the standard curve should be used for more accurate results and in cases of doubt.]

PROTEOLYTIC ACTIVITY, FUNGAL (SAP)

Application and Principle This procedure is used to determine proteolytic activity, expressed in spectrophotometric acid protease units (SAP), of preparations derived from *Aspergillus niger* var. and *Aspergillus oryzae* var. The test is based on a 30-min enzymatic hydrolysis of a Hammarsten Casein Substrate at pH 3.0 and at 37°. Unhydrolyzed substrate is precipitated with trichloroacetic acid and removed by filtration. The quantity of solubilized casein in the filtrate is determined spectrophotometrically.

Reagents and Solutions

Casein Use Hammarsten-grade casein (United States Biochemical Corp., Catalog No. 12840, or equivalent).

Glycine–Hydrochloric Acid Buffer (0.05 M) Dissolve 3.75 g of glycine in about 800 mL of water. Add 1 N hydrochloric acid until the solution is pH 3.0, determined with a pH meter. Quantitatively transfer the solution to a 1000-mL volumetric flask, dilute to volume with water, and mix.

TCA Solution Dissolve 18.0 g of trichloroacetic acid and 11.45 g of anhydrous sodium acetate in about 800 mL of water, and add 21.0 mL of glacial acetic acid. Quantitatively transfer the solution to a 1000-mL volumetric flask, dilute to volume with water, and mix.

Substrate Solution Pipet 8 mL of 1 N hydrochloric acid into about 500 mL of water, and with continuous agitation, disperse 7.0 g (moisture-free basis) of *Casein* into this solution. Heat for 30 min in a boiling water bath, stirring occasionally, and cool to room temperature. Dissolve 3.75 g of glycine in the solution, and using a pH meter, adjust to pH 3.0 with 0.1 N hydrochloric acid. Quantitatively transfer the solution to a 1000-mL volumetric flask, dilute to volume with water, and mix.

Sample Preparation Using *Glycine–Hydrochloric Acid Buffer*, prepare a solution of the sample enzyme preparation so that 2 mL of the final dilution will give a corrected absorbance of enzyme incubation filtrate at 275 nm (ΔA, as defined in the *Procedure*) between 0.200 and 0.500. Weigh the enzyme preparation, quantitatively transfer it to a glass mortar, and triturate with *Glycine–Hydrochloric Acid Buffer*. Quantitatively transfer the mixture to an appropriately sized volumetric flask, dilute to volume with *Glycine–Hydrochloric Acid Buffer*, and mix.

Procedure Pipet 10.0 mL of *Substrate Solution* into each of a series of 25- × 150-mm test tubes, allowing at least two tubes for each sample, one for each enzyme blank, and one for a substrate blank. Stopper the tubes, and equilibrate them for 15 min in a water bath maintained at 37° ± 0.1°.

At zero time, start the stopwatch, and rapidly pipet 2.0 mL of the *Sample Preparation* into the equilibrated substrate. Mix by swirling, and replace the tubes in the water bath.

[NOTE—Keep the tubes stoppered during incubation.]

Add 2 mL of *Glycine–Hydrochloric Acid Buffer* (instead of the *Sample Preparation*) to the substrate blank. After exactly 30 min, add 10 mL of *TCA Solution* to each enzyme incubation and to the substrate blank to stop the reaction. In the following order, prepare an enzyme blank containing 10 mL of *Substrate Solution*, 10 mL of *TCA Solution*, and 2 mL of the *Sample Preparation*. Heat all tubes in the water bath for 30 min, allowing the precipitated protein to coagulate completely.

At the end of the second heating period, cool the tubes in an ice bath for 5 min, and filter through Whatman No. 42 filter paper, or equivalent. The filtrates must be perfectly clear. Determine the absorbance of each filtrate in a 1-cm cell at 275 nm with a suitable spectrophotometer, against the substrate blank. Correct each absorbance by subtracting the absorbance of the respective enzyme blank.

Standard Curve Transfer 181.2 mg of L-tyrosine, chromatographic-grade or equivalent (Sigma Chemical Co.), previously dried to constant weight, to a 1000-mL volumetric flask. Dissolve in 60 mL of 0.1 N hydrochloric acid. When the L-tyrosine is completely dissolved, dilute the solution to volume with water, and mix thoroughly. This solution contains 1.00 µmol of tyrosine per 1.0 mL. Prepare dilutions from this stock solution to contain 0.10, 0.20, 0.30, 0.40, and 0.50 µmol/mL. Determine against a water blank the absorbance of each dilution in a 1-cm cell at 275 nm. Prepare a plot of absorbance versus µmol of tyrosine per mL. A straight line must be obtained. Determine the slope and intercept for use in the *Calculation* below. A value close to 1.38 should be obtained. The slope and intercept may be calculated by the least squares method as follows:

$$\text{Slope} = [n\Sigma (MA) - \Sigma (M) \Sigma(A)]/[n\Sigma (M^2) - (\Sigma M)^2]$$

$$\text{Intercept} = [\Sigma(A) \Sigma(M^2) - \Sigma (M) \Sigma(MA)]/[n\Sigma (M^2) - (\Sigma M)^2],$$

in which n is the number of points on the standard curve, M is the µmol of tyrosine per mL for each point on the standard curve, and A is the absorbance of the sample.

Calculation One spectrophotometric acid protease unit is that activity that will liberate 1 µmol of tyrosine per min under the conditions specified. The activity is expressed as follows:

$$\text{SAP/g} = (\Delta A - I) \times 22/(S \times 30 \times W)$$

in which ΔA is the corrected absorbance of the enzyme incubation filtrate; I is the intercept of the *Standard Curve*; 22 is the final volume of the incubation mixture, in mL; S is the slope of the *Standard Curve*; 30 is the incubation time, in min; and W is the weight, in g, of the enzyme sample contained in the 2.0-mL aliquot of *Sample Preparation* added to the incubation mixture in the *Procedure*.

PULLULANASE ACTIVITY

Application and Principle

This procedure is used to determine the pullulanase activity of pullulanase preparations and pullulanase preparations blended with glucoamylase. Acarbose is used in this method to inhibit the glucoamylase enzyme. The method is based on measuring the increase in reducing sugars formed by a 30-min hydrolysis of pullulan at 40° and pH 5.0. The increase in reducing sugars is measured spectrophotometrically at 520 nm using a modified Nelson-Somogyi procedure.

Reagents and Solutions

Citrate Buffer (with 0.1 g/L acarbose, pH 5.0) Dissolve 10.5 g of citric acid monohydrate in 950 mL of water, adjust the pH to 5.0 ± 0.005 using 5 N sodium hydroxide, and dilute to 1000 mL. Dissolve 0.1 g of acarbose (Bayer HealthCare) into 1000 mL of *Citrate Buffer* at pH 5.0.

Nelson's Color Reagent Dissolve 25.0 g of ammonium molybdate tetrahydrate in 300 mL of water, and carefully add 20.0 mL of concentrated sulfuric acid while stirring. Dissolve 3.0 g of sodium arsenate heptahydrate in 25 mL of water. Slowly add this solution to the ammonium molybdate solution with stirring. Dilute this solution to 500 mL with water.

Somogyi's Copper Reagent Dissolve 14.0 g of anhydrous dibasic sodium phosphate and 20.0 g of potassium sodium tartrate tetrahydrate into 250 mL of water. Add 60.0 g of 1 M sodium hydroxide solution. Dissolve 4.0 g of cupric sulfate pentahydrate into 25 mL of water. Add this solution to the tartrate solution. Add 90.0 g of anhydrous sodium sulfate while stirring. Dilute the final solution to 500 mL.

Glucose Standards Dissolve 800 mg of previously dried anhydrous D-glucose in 100 mL of the *Citrate Buffer*. Prepare glucose standards containing 80, 120, 160, and 250 µg/mL of glucose.

Pullulan Substrate Dissolve 150 mg of pullulan (Sigma Chemical Co, Catalog No. P-4516, or equivalent) in 49.80 g of the *Citrate Buffer*. Prepare daily.

Sample Preparation Dissolve an accurately weighed amount of the enzyme preparation in *Citrate Buffer* and dilute in *Citrate Buffer* to obtain an enzyme activity of 0.015 to 0.040 activity units per mL.

Procedure

Transfer 1.0 mL aliquots of *Pullulan Substrate* to separate 15- × 150-mm test tubes and equilibrate for 15 min in a 40° ±

0.1° water bath. At time equals zero and at 30 s intervals, add 1.0 mL of the respective samples, and mix. Exactly 30.0 min after addition of the samples, add 2.0 mL of *Somogyi's Copper Reagent* to each tube to terminate the reaction. Mix thoroughly, and allow the tubes to come to room temperature.

Run sample blanks by adding 2.0 mL of *Somogyi's Copper Reagent* to 1.0 mL of sample, then add 1.0 mL of substrate. The sample blanks should not be incubated at 40°.

Prepare a standard curve by adding 2.0 mL of each *Glucose Standard* and 2.0 mL of *Somogyi's Copper Reagent* to a test tube, and mix. Run a buffer blank to subtract from the *Glucose Standards* by adding 2.0 mL of buffer and 2.0 mL *Somogyi's Copper Reagent* to a test tube, and mix. The *Glucose Standards* should not be incubated at 40°. Loosely stopper samples, blanks, and *Glucose Standards* containing *Somogyi's Copper Reagent*, and place them in a vigorously boiling water bath for exactly 25.0 min. Cool in an ice bath for 5 min. Add 2.0 mL of *Nelson's Color Reagent* to each tube, and mix thoroughly to dissolve any red precipitate that might be present. Let the solutions stand for 5 min. Add 2.0 mL of water to each tube, and mix. Measure the absorbance of all solutions at 520 nm, using water as the reference. Mix the contents of each tube before transferring them to the cuvette.

Calculations

One pullulanase unit (PUN) is the amount of activity that, under the conditions of the test, will liberate reducing sugars equivalent to 1 μmol of glucose per min. Determine the linear regression line for absorbance versus 2 times the glucose concentration (μg/mL) in the standards. Use the slope, α, in the following equation to determine the activity in the enzyme preparation:

$$PUN/g = (A_S - A_B) / (\alpha \times W \times 180 \times 30)$$

in which A_S is the absorbance of the sample; A_B is the absorbance of the blank; W is the weight, in g, of the enzyme preparation contained in the 1.0 mL of *Sample Preparation* taken for analysis; 180 is the molecular weight of glucose; and 30 is the incubation time in min.

TRANSGLUTAMINASE ACTIVITY (Glutaminyl-peptide γ-Glutaminyltransferase)

Application and Principle This procedure is used to determine transglutaminase activity in preparations derived from *Streptoverticillium mobaraense* var. The assay is based on the enzymatic formation of a glutamic acid γ-hydroxamate in a glutaminyl residue in the substrate peptide with another substrate, hydroxylamine. The amount of the glutamic acid γ-hydroxamate formed as a red complex with ferric ion in acidic conditions at 37° is measured spectrophotometrically.

Reagents and Solutions

Substrate Solution Transfer 12.110 g of Tris [tri(hydroxymethyl)aminomethane], 3.475 g of hydroxylamine hydrochloride, 1.624 g of glutathione, and 5.060 g of carbobenzyloxy-glutaminylglycine into a 500-mL beaker. Add 350 mL of water, and using a magnetic stirrer, mix well. Adjust the pH to 6.0 with appropriate concentrations (usually 1 N and 6 N) of hydrochloric acid. Quantitatively transfer this mixture into a 500-mL volumetric flask, and dilute to volume with water.

Stopping Solution Prepare a 3 N hydrochloric acid solution by diluting concentrated hydrochloric acid (ca. 36%) four-fold with water. Make a 12% trichloroacetic acid (TCA) solution by transferring 12.0 g of TCA into a 100-mL volumetric flask, adding water to dissolve the TCA, and diluting to volume with water. Prepare a 5% solution of ferric chloride ($FeCl_3$) in 0.1 N hydrochloric acid by transferring 5.0 g of ferric chloride hexahydrate ($FeCl_3 \cdot 6H_2O$) into a 100-mL volumetric flask, adding 0.1 N hydrochloric acid to dissolve the ferric chloride, and diluting to volume with 0.1 N hydrochloric acid. On the day of use, combine all three solutions (3 N hydrochloric acid, 12% TCA, and 5% ferric chloride) in equal volumes in a beaker, and using a magnetic stirrer, mix well.

0.2 M Tris-HCl Buffer (pH 6.0) Transfer 18.11 g of Tris [tri(hydroxymethyl)aminomethane] into a 500-mL beaker. Add 350 mL of water, and using a magnetic stirrer, mix well. Adjust the pH to 6.0 with appropriate concentrations (usually 1 N and 6 N) of hydrochloric acid. Quantitatively transfer this mixture into a 500-mL volumetric flask, and dilute to volume with water.

Sample Solution Place 100 mg of sample, accurately weighed, into a 100-mL beaker, and add about 45 mL of *0.2 M Tris-HCl Buffer*. Using a magnetic stirrer, mix well at room temperature for 30 min. Quantitatively transfer the mixture into a 50-mL volumetric flask, and dilute to volume with *0.2 M Tris-HCl Buffer*.

Procedure

Calibration Curve Transfer 64.8 mg of L-glutamic acid γ-monohydroxamate standard, accurately weighed, into a suitable flask, and add 10 mL of *0.2 M Tris-HCl Buffer*. Dilute this solution sequentially in five steps each by a geometric factor of 2 with *0.2 M Tris-HCl Buffer*. Transfer 200 μL of each dilution by pipet into individual test tubes, and incubate at 37° for 1 min. Add 2 mL of *Substrate Solution*, previously incubated at 37° for 10 min, to each tube, and mix vigorously with a vortex mixer. Further incubate the mixtures for exactly 10 min, add 2 mL of *Stopping Solution* to each tube, and start a stopwatch. Mix vigorously with the vortex mixture, and separate any insoluble material by centrifugation at $1500 \times g$ for 10 min at about 25°. Measure the absorbance of the supernatant in each tube at 525 nm exactly 30 min after the addition of the *Stopping Solution*. Plot the absorbance against the amount of L-glutamic acid γ-monohydroxamate, and obtain a standard calibration curve used to calculate the amount of glutamic acid γ-monohydroxamate in carbobenzyloxy-glutaminylglycine from the absorbance obtained in the analysis of the samples.

Analysis of Samples Transfer 200 μL of *Sample Solution* by pipet into a test tube, and incubate at 37° for 1 min. Add 2 mL of *Substrate Solution*, previously incubated at 37° for 10 min, and mix vigorously using a vortex mixer. Further incubate the mixture for exactly 10 min, add 2 mL of *Stopping*

Solution, and start a stopwatch. Mix vigorously using a vortex mixer, and separate any insoluble material by centrifugation at 1500 × g for 10 min at about 25°. Measure the absorbance of the supernatant at 525 nm exactly 30 min after adding the *Stopping Solution*.

For the blank, place 200 µL of *Sample Solution* into a test tube, and incubate at 37° for 1 min. Add 2 mL of *Stopping Solution*, and mix vigorously using a vortex mixer. Further incubate for exactly 10 min, and add 2 mL of *Substrate Solution*, previously incubated at 37° for 10 min, and start a stopwatch. Mix vigorously using a vortex mixer. Separate any insoluble material by centrifugation at 1500 × g for 10 min. Measure the absorbance of the supernatant at 525 nm exactly 30 min after adding the *Substrate Solution*.

Calculation   One unit of enzyme activity is defined as the amount of enzyme that catalyzes the transglutamination of 1 µmol of substrate into product in 1 min under the conditions of the assay. The specific activity of Transglutaminase is defined as

$$\text{Transglutaminase activity (U/g)} = C \times T_S \times 1/S \times 1/10,$$

in which C is the concentration, in micromoles per milliliter, of hydroxamate in the *Sample Solution* (obtained from the standard calibration curve); T_S is the total volume, in milliliters, of *Sample Solution*; S is the mass, in grams, of the sample taken; and 10 is the reaction time in min.

Transglutaminase   Transfer of acyl groups between the γ-carboxyamide group of peptide-bound glutamine residues and various amines, including the ε-amino group of peptide-bound lysine, to form intra- and inter-molecular ε-(γ-glutamyl)lysine crosslinks.

Trivial Name	Classification	Source	Systematic Name (IUB)	IUB No.
Transglutaminase	Acyltransferase or aminotransferase	*Streptoverticillium mobaraense* var.	R-glutaminyl-peptide: amine γ-glutamyl-transferase	2.3.2.13

TRYPSIN ACTIVITY

Application and Principle   This procedure is used to determine the trypsin activity of trypsin preparations derived from purified extracts of porcine or bovine pancreas.

Reagents and Solutions

Fifteenth Molar Phosphate Buffer (pH 7.6)   Dissolve 4.54 g of monobasic potassium phosphate in sufficient water to make 500 mL of solution. Dissolve 4.73 g of anhydrous dibasic sodium phosphate in sufficient water to make 500 mL of solution.

Mix 13 mL of the monobasic potassium phosphate solution with 87 mL of the anhydrous dibasic sodium phosphate solution.

Substrate Solution   Dissolve 85.7 mg of N-benzoyl-l-arginine ethyl ester hydrochloride, suitable for use in assaying trypsin, in sufficient water to make 100 mL.

[NOTE—Determine the suitability of the substrate and check the adjustment of the spectrophotometer by performing the assay using USP Trypsin Reference Standard.]

Dilute 10.0 mL of this solution to 100.0 mL with *Fifteenth Molar Phosphate Buffer*. Determine the absorbance of this solution at 253 nm in a 1-cm cell, with a suitable spectrophotometer, using water as the blank and maintaining the cell temperature at 25° ± 0.1°. Adjust the absorbance of the solution, if necessary, by the addition of *Fifteenth Molar Phosphate Buffer* so that it measures not less than 0.575 and not more than 0.585. Use this solution within a period of 2 h.

Sample Preparations   Dissolve a sufficient amount of sample, accurately weighed, in 0.001 N hydrochloric acid to produce a solution containing about 3000 USP trypsin units in each mL. Prepare three dilutions using 0.001 N hydrochloric acid so that the final solutions will contain 12, 18, and 24 USP trypsin units in each 0.2 mL. Use these concentrations in the *Procedure* below.

Procedure   Conduct the test in a spectrophotometer equipped to maintain a temperature of 25° ± 0.1° in the cell compartment.

Determine the temperature in the reaction cell before and after the measurement of absorbance to ensure that the temperature does not change by more than 0.5°.

Pipet 0.2 mL of 0.001 N hydrochloric acid and 3.0 mL of *Substrate Solution* into a 1-cm cell. Place this cell in the spectrophotometer, and adjust the instrument so that the absorbance will read 0.050 at 253 nm. Pipet 0.2 mL of the *Sample Preparation* containing 12 USP units into another 1-cm cell. Add 3.0 mL of *Substrate Solution*, and place the cell in the spectrophotometer. At the same time the *Substrate Solution* is added, start a stopwatch, and read the absorbance at 30-s intervals for 5 min. Repeat the procedure with the *Sample Preparations* containing 18 and 24 USP units. Plot curves of absorbance versus time for each concentration, and use only those values that form a straight line to determine the activity of the trypsin. Discard the values on the plateau, and take the average of the results from the three concentration levels as the actual activity of the trypsin.

Calculations   One USP trypsin unit is the activity causing a change in the absorbance of 0.003/min under the conditions specified in this assay.

Calculate the number of USP trypsin units per mg at each level by the equation

$$\text{USP trypsin units} = (A_1 - A_2)/(T \times W \times 0.003)$$

in which A_1 is the absorbance straight-line final reading; A_2 is the absorbance straight-line initial reading; T is the elapsed time, in min, between the initial and final readings; and W is the weight, in mg, of trypsin in the volume of solution used in determining the absorbance.

APPENDIX VI: ESSENTIAL OILS AND FLAVORS

ACETALS

Hydroxylamine Hydrochloride Solution Prepare as directed under *Aldehydes*, this Appendix.

Procedure Weigh accurately the quantity of the sample specified in the monograph, and transfer it into a 125-mL Erlenmeyer flask. Add 30 mL of *Hydroxylamine Hydrochloride Solution*, and reflux on a steam bath for exactly 60 min. Allow the condenser to drain into the flask for 5 min after removing the flask from the steam bath. Detach, and rapidly cool the flask to room temperature. Add bromophenol blue TS as the indicator, and titrate with 0.5 N alcoholic potassium hydroxide to pH 3.4, or to the same light color as produced in the original hydroxylamine hydrochloride solution on adding the indicator. Calculate the mL of 0.5 N alcoholic potassium hydroxide consumed per g of sample (A).

Using a separate portion of the sample, proceed as directed under *Aldehydes*, this Appendix. Calculate the mL of 0.5 N alcoholic potassium hydroxide consumed per g of sample (B).

Calculate the percentage of acetals by the formula

$$\text{Result} = (A - B) \times f,$$

in which f is the equivalence factor given in the monograph.

ACID VALUE (Essential Oils and Flavors)

Dissolve about 10 g of the sample, accurately weighed, in 50 mL of alcohol, previously neutralized to phenolphthalein with 0.1 N sodium hydroxide. (Add 50 g of ice when testing cinnamyl formate, citronellyl formate, geranyl formate, isoamyl formate, or linalyl formate.) Add 1 mL of phenolphthalein TS, and titrate with 0.1 N sodium hydroxide until the solution remains faintly pink after shaking for 10 s, unless otherwise directed in the individual monograph. Calculate the acid value (AV) by the formula

$$AV = (5.61 \times S)/W,$$

in which S is the number of mL of 0.1 N sodium hydroxide consumed in the titration of the sample, and W is the weight, in g, of the sample.

ALDEHYDES

Hydroxylamine Hydrochloride Solution Dissolve 50 g of hydroxylamine hydrochloride (preferably reagent grade or freshly recrystallized before using) in 90 mL of water, and dilute to 1000 mL with aldehyde-free alcohol. Adjust the solution to a pH of 3.4 with 0.5 N alcoholic potassium hydroxide.

Procedure Weigh accurately the quantity of sample specified in the monograph, and transfer it into a 125-mL Erlenmeyer flask. Add 30 mL of *Hydroxylamine Hydrochloride Solution*, mix thoroughly, and allow to stand at room temperature for 10 min, unless otherwise specified in the monograph. Titrate with 0.5 N alcoholic potassium hydroxide to a greenish yellow endpoint that matches the color of 30 mL of *Hydroxylamine Hydrochloride Solution* in a 125-mL flask when the same volume of bromophenol blue TS has been added to each flask, or preferably titrate to a pH of 3.4 using a suitable pH meter. Calculate the percentage of aldehyde (A) by the equation

$$A = (S - b)(100e)/W,$$

in which S is the number of mL of 0.5 N alcoholic potassium hydroxide consumed in the titration of the sample, b is the number of mL of 0.5 N alcoholic potassium hydroxide consumed in the titration of the blank, e is the equivalence factor given in the monograph, and W is the weight, in mg, of the sample.

ALDEHYDES AND KETONES

Hydroxylamine Method

Hydroxylamine Solution Dissolve 20 g of hydroxylamine hydrochloride (reagent grade or, preferably, freshly crystallized) in 40 mL of water, and dilute to 400 mL with alcohol. Add, with stirring, 300 mL of 0.5 N alcoholic potassium hydroxide, and filter. Use this solution within 2 days.

Procedure Weigh accurately the quantity of the sample specified in the individual monograph, and transfer it into a 250-mL glass-stoppered flask. Add 75.0 mL of *Hydroxylamine Solution* to this flask and to a similar flask for a residual blank titration (see *General Provisions*). If the component to be determined is an *aldehyde*, stopper the flasks and allow them to stand at room temperature for 1 h unless otherwise stated in the monograph. If the component to be determined is a *ketone*, attach the flask to a suitable condenser, and reflux the mixture for 1 h unless otherwise stated in the monograph, and then cool to room temperature. Titrate both flasks to the same greenish yellow endpoint using bromophenol blue TS as the indicator or, preferably, to a pH of 3.4 using a pH meter. (If the indicator is used, the endpoint color must be the same as that produced when the blank is titrated to a pH of 3.4.) Calculate the percentage of aldehyde or ketone by the equation

$$AK = (b - S)(100e)/W,$$

in which AK is the percentage of aldehyde or ketone, b is the number of mL of 0.5 N hydrochloric acid consumed in the residual blank titration, S is the number of mL of 0.5 N hydrochloric acid consumed in the titration of the sample, e is the equivalence factor given in the monograph, and W is the weight, in mg, of the sample.

Hydroxylamine *tert*-Butyl Alcohol Method

Hydroxylamine Solution Dissolve 45 g of reagent-grade hydroxylamine hydrochloride in 130 mL of water, add 850 mL of *tert*-butyl alcohol, mix, and using a pH meter, neutralize to a pH of 3.0 to 3.5 with sodium hydroxide.

[**Caution**—Do not heat the solution.]

Procedure Weigh accurately the quantity of the sample specified in the individual monograph, and transfer it into a 250-mL glass-stoppered flask. Add 50 mL of the *Hydroxylamine Solution*, or the volume specified in the monograph, mix thoroughly, and allow to stand at room temperature for the time specified in the monograph. Titrate with 0.5 N sodium hydroxide to the same pH as the *Hydroxylamine Solution* used. Calculate the percentage of aldehyde or ketone by the equation

$$AK = (S)(100e)/W,$$

in which AK is the percentage of aldehyde or ketone, S is the number of mL of 0.5 N sodium hydroxide consumed in the titration of the sample, e is the equivalence factor given in the monograph, and W is the weight, in mg, of the sample.

Neutral Sulfite Method

Pipet a 10-mL sample into a 100-mL cassia flask fitted with a stopper, and add 50 mL of a freshly prepared 30 in 100 solution of sodium sulfite. Add 2 drops of phenolphthalein TS, and neutralize with 50% (by volume) acetic acid solution. Heat the mixture in a boiling water bath, and shake the flask repeatedly, neutralizing the mixture from time to time by the addition of a few drops of the 50% acetic acid solution, stoppering the flask to prevent loss of volatile material. After no coloration appears upon the addition of a few more drops of phenolphthalein TS and heating for 15 min, cool to room temperature. When the liquids have separated completely, add sufficient sodium sulfite solution to raise the lower level of the oily layer within the graduated portion of the neck of the flask. Calculate the percentage, by volume, of the aldehyde or ketone by the equation

$$AK = 100 - (V \times 10),$$

in which AK is the percentage, by volume, of the aldehyde or ketone in the sample, and V is the number of mL of separated oil in the graduated neck of the flask.

CHLORINATED COMPOUNDS

Wind a 1.5- × 5-cm strip of 20-mesh copper gauze around the end of a copper wire. Heat the gauze in a nonluminous flame of a Bunsen burner until it glows without coloring the flame green. Permit the gauze to cool, and re-ignite it several times until a good coat of oxide has formed. With a medicine dropper, apply 2 drops of the sample to the cooled gauze, ignite, and permit it to burn freely in the air. Again cool the gauze, add 2 more drops, and burn as before. Continue this process until a total of 6 drops have been added and ignited. Then hold the gauze in the outer edge of a Bunsen flame adjusted to a height of 4 cm. Not even a transient green color is imparted to the flame. If at any of the additions the sample appears to be instantly vaporized, the test must be repeated from the beginning.

ESTERS

Ester Determination Weigh accurately the quantity of the sample specified in the monograph, and transfer it into a 125-mL Erlenmeyer flask containing a few boiling stones. Add to this flask and, simultaneously, to a similar flask for a residual blank titration (see *General Provisions*) 25.0 mL of 0.5 N alcoholic potassium hydroxide. Connect each flask to a reflux condenser, and reflux the mixtures on a steam bath for exactly 1 h, unless otherwise directed in the monograph. Allow the mixtures to cool, add 10 drops of phenolphthalein TS to each flask, and titrate the excess alkali in each flask with 0.5 N hydrochloric acid. Calculate the percentage of esters (E) in the sample by the equation

$$E = (b - S)(100e)/W,$$

in which b is the number of mL of 0.5 N hydrochloric acid consumed in the residual blank titration, S is the number of mL of 0.5 N hydrochloric acid consumed in the titration of the sample, e is the equivalence factor given in the monograph, and W is the weight, in mg, of the sample.

Ester Determination (High-Boiling Solvent)

0.5 N Potassium Hydroxide Solution Dissolve about 35 g of potassium hydroxide in 75 mL of water, add 1000 mL of a suitable grade of monoethyl ether of diethylene glycol, and mix.

Procedure Weigh accurately the quantity of the sample specified in the monograph, and transfer it into a 200-mL Erlenmeyer flask having a standard-taper joint. To this flask and to a similar flask for a residual blank titration (see *General Provisions*) add two glass beads and 25.0 mL of *0.5 N Potassium Hydroxide Solution*, allowing exactly 1 min for drainage from the buret or pipet. Attach an air condenser to each flask, reflux gently for 1 h, and cool. Rinse down the condensers with about 50 mL of water, then add phenolphthalein TS to each flask, and titrate the excess alkali with 0.5 N sulfuric acid to the disappearance of the pink color. Calculate the percentage of esters (E) in the sample by the equation

$$E = (b - S)(100e)/W,$$

in which b is the number of mL of 0.5 N sulfuric acid consumed in the blank determination, S is the number of mL of 0.5 N sulfuric acid required in the titration of the sample, e is the equivalence factor given in the monograph, and W is the weight, in mg, of the sample.

Saponification Value Proceed as directed for *Ester Determination* or *Ester Determination (High-Boiling Solvent)*, as specified in the monograph. Calculate the saponification value (SV) by the equation

$$SV = (b - S)(28.05)/W,$$

in which b and S are as defined under *Ester Determination*, and W is the weight, in g, of the sample.

Ester Value If the sample contains no free acids, the saponification value and the ester value are identical. If a determination of the *Acid Value* (AV) is specified in the monograph, calculate the ester value (EV) by the equation

$$EV = SV - AV,$$

in which SV is the saponification value.

LINALOOL DETERMINATION

Transfer a 10-mL sample, previously dried with sodium sulfate, into a 125-mL glass-stoppered Erlenmeyer flask previously cooled in an ice bath. Add to the cooled oil 20 mL of dimethyl aniline (monomethyl-free), and mix thoroughly. To the mixture add 8 mL of acetyl chloride and 5 mL of acetic anhydride, cool for several min, permit to stand at room temperature for another 30 min, then immerse the flask in a water bath maintained at 40° ± 1° for 16 h. Wash the acetylated oil with three 75-mL portions of ice water, followed by successive washes with 25-mL portions of 5% sulfuric acid, until the separated acid layer no longer becomes cloudy or emits an odor of dimethyl aniline when made alkaline. After removal of the dimethyl aniline, wash the acetylated oil first with 10 mL of sodium carbonate TS and then with successive portions of water until the washings are neutral to litmus. Finally, dry the acetylated oil with anhydrous sodium sulfate, and proceed as directed for *Ester Determination* under *Esters*, this Appendix. Calculate the percentage of linalool ($C_{10}H_{18}O$) by the equation

$$L = [7.707(b - S)]/[W - 0.021(b - S)],$$

in which L is the percentage of linalool, b is the number of mL of 0.5 N hydrochloric acid consumed in the residual blank titration, S is the number of mL of 0.5 N hydrochloric acid consumed in the titration of the sample, and W is the weight, in g, of the sample.

[NOTE—When this method is applied to essential oils containing appreciable amounts of esters, perform an *Ester Determination*, this appendix, on a sample of the *original oil* and calculate the percentage of total linalool by the equation

$$L = [7.707(b - S)(1 - 0.0021E)]/[W - 0.21(b - S)],$$

in which L is the percentage of linalool, E is the percentage of esters, calculated as linalyl acetate ($C_{12}H_{20}O_2$) in the sample of the original oil, and b, S, and W are as defined in the preceding paragraph.]

[NOTE—This entire procedure is applicable only to linalool and linalool-containing oils. It is not intended for the determination of other tertiary alcohols.]

PERCENTAGE OF CINEOLE

Temperature	0.0	0.1	0.2	0.3	0.4	0.5	0.6	0.7	0.8	0.9
24	45.6	45.7	45.9	46.0	46.1	46.3	46.4	46.5	46.6	46.8
25	46.9	47.0	47.2	47.3	47.4	47.6	47.7	47.8	47.9	48.1
26	48.2	48.3	48.5	48.6	48.7	48.9	49.0	49.1	49.2	49.4
27	49.5	49.6	49.8	49.9	50.0	50.2	50.3	50.4	50.5	50.7
28	50.8	50.9	51.1	51.2	51.3	51.5	51.6	51.7	51.8	52.0
29	52.1	52.2	52.4	52.5	52.6	52.8	52.9	53.0	53.1	53.3
30	53.4	53.5	53.7	53.8	53.9	54.1	54.2	54.3	54.4	54.6
31	54.7	54.8	55.0	55.1	55.2	55.4	55.5	55.6	55.7	55.9
32	56.0	56.1	56.3	56.4	56.5	56.7	56.8	56.9	57.0	57.2
33	57.3	57.4	57.6	57.7	57.8	58.0	58.1	58.2	58.3	58.5
34	58.6	58.7	58.9	59.0	59.1	59.3	59.4	59.5	59.6	59.8
35	59.9	60.0	60.2	60.3	60.4	60.6	60.7	60.8	60.9	61.1
36	61.2	61.3	61.5	61.6	61.7	61.9	62.0	62.1	62.2	62.4
37	62.5	62.6	62.8	62.9	63.0	63.2	63.3	63.4	63.5	63.7
38	63.8	63.9	64.1	64.2	64.4	64.5	64.6	64.8	64.9	65.1
39	65.2	65.4	65.5	65.7	65.8	66.0	66.2	66.3	66.5	66.6
40	66.8	67.0	67.2	67.3	67.5	67.7	67.9	68.1	68.2	68.4
41	68.6	68.8	69.0	69.2	69.4	69.6	69.7	69.9	70.1	70.3
42	70.5	70.7	70.9	71.0	71.2	71.4	71.6	71.8	71.9	72.1
43	72.3	72.5	72.7	72.9	73.1	73.3	73.4	73.6	73.8	74.0
44	74.2	74.4	74.6	74.8	75.0	75.2	75.3	75.5	75.7	75.9
45	76.1	76.3	76.5	76.7	76.9	77.1	77.2	77.4	77.6	77.8
46	78.0	78.2	78.4	78.6	78.8	79.0	79.2	79.4	79.6	79.8
47	80.0	80.2	80.4	80.6	80.8	81.1	81.3	81.5	81.7	81.9
48	82.1	82.3	82.5	82.7	82.9	83.2	83.4	83.6	83.8	84.0
49	84.2	84.4	84.6	84.8	85.0	85.3	85.5	85.7	85.9	86.1
50	86.3	86.6	86.8	87.1	87.3	87.6	87.8	88.1	88.3	88.6
51	88.8	89.1	89.3	89.6	89.8	90.1	90.3	90.6	90.8	91.1
52	91.3	91.6	91.8	92.1	92.3	92.6	92.8	93.1	93.3	93.6
53	93.8	94.1	94.3	94.6	94.8	95.1	95.3	95.6	95.8	96.1
54	96.3	96.6	96.9	97.2	97.5	97.8	98.1	98.4	98.7	99.0
55	99.3	99.7	100.0							

PHENOLS

Pipet 10 mL of the oil, which has been subjected to any treatment specified in the monograph, into a 100-mL cassia flask, add 75 mL of 1 N potassium hydroxide, and shake vigorously for 5 min to ensure complete extraction of the phenol by the alkali solution. Allow the mixture to stand for about 30 min, then add sufficient 1 N potassium hydroxide to raise the oily layer into the graduated portion of the flask, stopper the flask, and allow it to stand overnight. Read the volume of insoluble oil to 0.05 mL. Calculate the percentage, by volume, of phenols by the equation

$$P = (10 - V) \times 10,$$

in which P is the percentage, by volume, of phenols, and V is the observed volume, in mL, of insoluble oil.

PHENOLS, FREE

Transfer about 5 g, accurately weighed, of the sample into a 150-mL flask having a standard-taper neck. Pipet exactly 10 mL of a 1:10 solution of acetic anhydride in anhydrous pyridine into the flask, and pipet exactly 10 mL of this solution, preferably measured with the same pipet, into a second 150-mL flask for the residual blank titration (see *General Provisions*). Connect the flasks to condensers, reflux for 1 h, and cool to a temperature below 100°. Add 25 mL of water to each flask through the condensers, and reflux again for 10 min. Cool the flasks, add phenolphthalein TS, and titrate with 0.5 N potassium hydroxide. Calculate the percentage of free phenols by the equation

$$\text{Percentage of Free Phenols} = (b - S) \times 100f/W,$$

in which b is the number of mL of 0.5 N potassium hydroxide consumed in the residual blank titration, s is the number of mL of 0.5 N potassium hydroxide consumed in the titration of the sample, f is the equivalence factor given in the monograph, and W is the weight, in mg, of the sample.

RESIDUE ON EVAPORATION

Weigh accurately the quantity of sample specified in the monograph, and transfer it into a suitable evaporating dish that has previously been heated on a steam bath, cooled to room temperature in a desiccator, and accurately weighed. Weigh the sample in the dish. Heat the evaporating dish containing the sample on the steam bath for the period of time specified in the monograph. Cool the dish and its contents to room temperature in a desiccator, and weigh accurately. Calculate the residue as percentage of the sample used.

SOLUBILITY IN ALCOHOL

Transfer a 1.0-mL sample into a calibrated 10-mL glass-stoppered cylinder graduated in 0.1-mL subdivisions, and add slowly, in small portions, alcohol of the concentration specified in the monograph. Maintain the temperature at 25°, and shake the cylinder thoroughly after each addition of alcohol. When a clear solution is first obtained, record the number of mL of alcohol required. Continue the addition of the alcohol until a total of 10 mL has been added. If opalescence or cloudiness occurs during these subsequent additions of alcohol, record the number of mL of alcohol at which the phenomenon occurs.

TOTAL ALCOHOLS

Unless otherwise stated in the monograph, transfer 10 g of a solid sample, or 10 mL of a liquid sample, accurately weighed, into a 100-mL flask having a standard-taper neck. Add 10 mL of acetic anhydride and 1 g of anhydrous sodium acetate, mix these materials, attach a reflux condenser to the flask, and reflux the mixture for 1 h. Cool, and through the condenser, add 50 mL of water at a temperature between 50° and 60°. Shake intermittently for 15 min, cool to room temperature, transfer the mixture completely to a separator, allow the layers to separate, and then remove and reject the lower, aqueous layer. Wash the oil layer successively with 50 mL of a saturated sodium chloride solution, 50 mL of a 10% sodium carbonate solution, and 50 mL of saturated sodium chloride solution. If the oil is still acid to moistened litmus paper, wash it with additional portions of sodium chloride solution until it is free from acid. Drain off the oil, dry it with anhydrous sodium sulfate, and then filter it.

Transfer the quantity of acetylated oil specified in the monograph, and accurately weighed, into a tared 125-mL Erlenmeyer flask, and add 10 mL of neutral alcohol, 10 drops of phenolphthalein TS, and 0.1 N alcoholic potassium hydroxide, dropwise, until a pink endpoint is obtained. If more than 0.20 mL is needed, reject the sample, and wash and test the remaining acetylated oil until its acid content is below this level. Prepare a blank for residual titration (see *General Provisions*), using the same volume of alcohol and indicator, and add 1 drop of 0.1 N alkali to produce a pink endpoint. Transfer 25.0 mL of 0.5 N alcoholic potassium hydroxide into each of the flasks, reflux them simultaneously for 1 h, cool, and titrate the contents of each flask with 0.5 N hydrochloric acid to the disappearance of the pink color. Calculate the percentage of *Total Alcohols* (A) by the equation

$$A = [(b - S)(100e)]/[W - 21(b - S)],$$

in which b is he number of milliliters of 0.5 N hydrochloric acid consumed in the residual blank titration; S is the number of milliliters of 0.5 N hydrochloric acid consumed in the titration of the sample; e is the equivalence factor given in the monograph; and W is the weight, in milligrams, of the sample of the acetylated oil.

ULTRAVIOLET ABSORBANCE OF CITRUS OILS

Transfer the quantity of the sample specified in the monograph into a 100-mL volumetric flask, add alcohol to volume, and mix. Determine the ultraviolet absorption spectrum of the solution in the range of 260 to 400 nm in a 1-cm cell with a suitable recording or manual spectrophotometer, using alcohol as the blank. If a manual instrument is used, read absorbances at 5-nm intervals from 260 nm to a point about 12 nm from the expected maximum absorbance, then at 3-nm intervals for three readings, and at 1-nm intervals to a point about 5 nm beyond the maximum, and then at 10-nm intervals to 400 nm. From these data, plot the absorbances as ordinates against wavelength on the abscissa, and draw the spectrogram. Draw a baseline tangent to the areas of minimum absorbance, as shown in Fig. 1 (which is typical of lemon oil), joining point A in the region of 280 to 300 nm and a second point, B, in the region of 355 to 380 nm. Locate the point of maximum absorbance, C, and from it drop a vertical line, perpendicular to the abscissa, that intersects line AB at D. Read from the ordinate the absorbances corresponding to points C and D, subtract the latter from the former, and correct the difference for the actual weight of oil taken, calculating on the basis of the sample weight specified in the monograph.

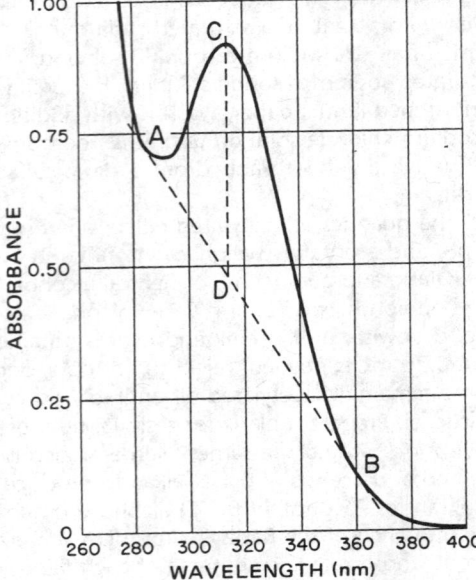

Figure 1. Typical Spectrogram of Lemon Oil

VOLATILE OIL CONTENT (Essential Oils and Flavors)

This procedure is used, when specified in the individual monograph, for determining the volatile oil content of gums, resins, and essential oils.

Apparatus The apparatus is shown in *Fig. 2*. It consists of a 1000-mL boiling flask, A, attached through a trap, D, to a Liebig condenser, C, which is connected to a 25-mL collector tube, B, graduated in 0.10-mL units.

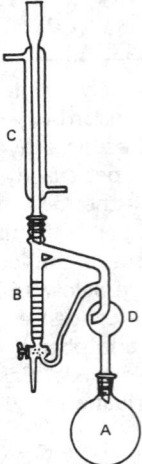

Figure 2. Apparatus for Determination of Volatile Oil Content

Procedure Place 750 mL of water in the boiling flask, boil for 10 min, and cool to 50°. Transfer the specified volume of the sample, prepared as directed in the monograph, into the flask, then immediately attach the remainder of the apparatus to the flask, and boil until the volume of distilled oil collected in the graduated collector tube remains constant. Avoid splashing the contents of the flask in order to prevent contamination of the distillate with nonvolatile material, and do not continue distillation for an extended time after the volume of distillate becomes constant. If the distilled oil is heavier than water, set the stopcock in the closed position to prevent return of the heavy distillate to the flask.

When distillation is complete, allow the contents of the collection tube to settle until the oil and water layers are separated completely. Allow the distillate to cool to room temperature, read its volume, and calculate therefrom the percentage of volatile oil.

[NOTE—When the volatile oil thus collected is to be used in additional tests, as may be specified in the monograph, the oil should be drained off, dried, and filtered before use.]

APPENDIX VII: FATS AND RELATED SUBSTANCES

ACETYL VALUE
(Based on AOCS Method Cd 4-40[1])

The acetyl value is defined as the number of mg of potassium hydroxide required to neutralize the acetic acid obtained by saponifying 1 g of the acetylated sample.

Acetylation Boil 50 mL of the oil or melted fat with 50 mL of freshly distilled acetic anhydride for 2 h under a reflux condenser. Pour the mixture into a beaker containing 500 mL of water, and boil for 15 min, bubbling a stream of nitrogen or carbon dioxide through the mixture to prevent bumping. Cool slightly, remove the water, add another 500 mL of water, and boil again. Repeat for a third time with another 500-mL portion of water, and remove the wash water, which should be neutral to litmus. Transfer the acetylated fat to a separator, and wash with two 200-mL portions of warm water, separating as much as possible of the wash water each time. Transfer the washed sample to a beaker, add 5 g of anhydrous sodium sulfate, and let stand for 1 h, agitating occasionally to assist drying. Filter the oil through a dry filter paper, preferably in an oven at 100°–110°, and keep the filtered oil in the oven until it is completely dry. The acetylated product should be a clear, brilliant oil.

Saponification Weigh accurately from 2–2.5 g each of the acetylated oil and of the original, untreated sample into separate 250-mL Erlenmeyer flasks. Add to each flask 25.0 mL of 0.5 N alcoholic potassium hydroxide, and continue as directed in the *Procedure* under *Saponification Value*, in this Appendix, beginning with "Connect an air condenser. . . ." Record the saponification value of the untreated sample as S, and that of the acetylized oil as S′, then calculate the acetyl value of the sample:

$$\text{Result} = (S' - S)/(1.000 - 0.00075S)$$

ACID VALUE (Fats and Related Substances)
(Based on AOCS Methods Te 1a-64[1] and Cd 3d-63[1])

The acid value is defined as the number of mg of potassium hydroxide required to neutralize the fatty acids in 1 g of the test substance.

Method I (Commercial Fatty Acids)
Unless otherwise directed, weigh accurately about 5 g of the sample into a 500-mL Erlenmeyer flask, and dissolve it in 75–100 mL of hot alcohol, previously boiled and neutralized to phenolphthalein TS with sodium hydroxide. Agitation and further heating may be necessary to effect complete solution of the sample. Add 0.5 mL of phenolphthalein TS, and titrate immediately, while shaking, with 0.5 N sodium hydroxide to the first pink color that persists for at least 30 s. Calculate the acid value:

$$\text{Result} = 56.1V \times N/W$$

in which V is the volume, in mL, and N is the normality, respectively, of the sodium hydroxide solution; and W is the weight, in grams, of the sample taken.

Method II (Animal Fats and Vegetable and Marine Oils)
Prepare a solvent mixture consisting of equal parts, by volume, of isopropyl alcohol and toluene. Add 2 mL of a 1% solution of phenolphthalein in isopropyl alcohol to 125 mL of the mixture, and neutralize with alkali to a faint but permanent pink color. Weigh accurately the appropriate amount of well-mixed liquid sample indicated in the table below, dissolve it in the neutralized solvent mixture, warming if necessary, and shake vigorously while titrating with 0.1 N potassium hydroxide to the first permanent pink color of the same intensity as that of the neutralized solvent before mixing with the sample. Calculate the acid value:

$$\text{Result} = 56.1V \times N/W$$

in which V is the volume, in mL, and N is the normality, respectively, of the potassium hydroxide solution; and W is the weight, in grams, of the sample taken.

Acid Value	Sample Weight (g)
0–1	20
1–4	10
4–15	2.5
15–75	0.5
75 and over	0.1

ANISIDINE VALUE

The Anisidine Value is defined as 100 times the optical density measured in a 1-cm cell of a solution containing 1 g of the substance to be examined in 100 mL of a mixture of solvents and reagents according to the method below. [NOTE—Carry out the operations as rapidly as possible, avoiding exposure to actinic light.]

Reagents and Solutions

Test Solution A: Dissolve 0.500 g of the substance to be examined in isooctane, and dilute with isooctane to 25.0 mL.

Test Solution B: To 5.0 mL of *Test Solution A* add 1.0 mL of a 2.5 g/L solution of *p*-anisidine in glacial acetic acid, shake, and store protected from light.

---
[1] Full text of method available from the American Oil Chemists' Society (AOCS) at www.aocs.org.

Standard Solution: To 5.0 mL of isooctane add 1.0 mL of a 2.5 g/L solution of *p*-anisidine in glacial acetic acid, shake, and store protected from light.

Procedure Measure the absorbance of *Test Solution A* at 350 nm using isooctane as the blank. Measure the absorbance of *Test Solution B* at 350 nm exactly 10 min after its preparation, using the *Standard Solution* as the compensation liquid. Calculate the *Anisidine Value*:

$$\text{Result} = 25 \times (1.2A_S - A_B)/m$$

where A_S is the absorbance of *Test Solution B* at 350 nm; A_B is the absorbance of *Test Solution A* at 350 nm; and m is the weight, in g, of the substance to be examined in *Test Solution A*.

CHLOROPHYLL
(Based on AOCS Method Cc 13d-55[1])

Use a reliable spectrophotometer with a sample holder equilibrated at $44 \pm 3°$ to obtain absorbance values at 630 nm, 670 nm, and 710 nm. Calculate the concentration of chlorophyll (C):

$$C = [A_{670} - (A_{630}/2) - (A_{710}/2)]/(K \times b)$$

in which C is the concentration of chlorophyll, in mg/kg; A is the absorbance at the wavelength indicated by the subscript; K is the constant for the specific spectrophotometer being used and is equal to 0.1016 for the Beckman Model DU; and b is the optical pathlength through the sample, in cm.

COLD TEST
(Based on AOCS Method Cc 11-53[1])

Filter a sample (200–300 mL), and transfer to a clean, dry bottle. Fill the bottle completely, and insert a cork stopper. Seal with paraffin, and equilibrate at 25° in a water bath so that it is completely covered. Next, immerse the bottle in an ice and water bath so it is completely covered. Monitor the bath during the test and replenish the ice frequently to keep the bath at 0°.

After 5.5 h remove the bottle from the bath. The sample must be clear; fat crystals or cloudiness must be totally absent.

COLOR (Fats and Related Substances)
(AOCS-Wesson) (Based on AOCS Method Cc 13b-45[1])

Apparatus Use a Lovibond tintometer or the equivalent and a set of color comparison glasses that conform to the AOCS-Wesson Tintometer Color Scale (available from the National Institute of Standards and Technology). A minimum set of glasses consists of the following:

Red	0.1	0.2	0.3	0.4	0.5	0.6	0.8	0.9
	1.0	2.0	2.5	3.0	3.5	4.0	5.0	6.0
	7.0	7.6	8.0	9.0	10.0	11.0	12.0	16.0
	20.0							
Yellow	1.0	2.0	3.0	5.0	10.0	15.0	20.0	35.0
	50.0	70.0						

For making color comparisons, use color tubes of clear, colorless glass with a smooth, flat, polished bottom (length 154 mm; id 19 mm; od 22 mm), and marked to indicate liquid columns of 25.4 mm and 133.35 mm.

Procedure Add 0.1 g of diatomaceous earth to a 60-g sample, agitate for 2.5 min at room temperature (or 10°–15° above the melting point if the sample is not liquid), and filter. Adjust the temperature to 25°–35° (or not more than 100 above the melting point), and fill the color tube to the desired mark. Place the tube in the tintometer (in a dark booth or cabinet), and match the sample color as closely as possible with a standard glass.

LOVIBOND COLOR
(Based on AOCS method Cc 13e-92[1])

Apparatus

Colorimeter: A colorimeter such as the universal Lovibond Tintometer Model F/C and Model F (BS684)[2], or equivalent. The Lovibond Schofield Tintometer Wesson Colorimeter, and the AOCS Tintometer have been found not suitable for use in this method.

Color racks: Use red, yellow, blue, and neutral racks with color readings as follows, and fitted with colorless compensating slides:

Red	0.1–0.9
	1.0–9.0
	10.0
	70.0
Yellow	0.1–0.9
	1.0–9.0
	10.0–70.0
Blue	0.1–0.9
	1.0–9.0
	10.0–40.0
Neutral	0.1–0.9
	1.0–3.0

Lighting cabinet: Should consist of two 60-watt pearl (not coated) lamps, operated at the correct main voltage and each illuminating the sample and white reference field at 45°. The lamps shall be positioned at either side of the viewing tube (Tintometer AF 905/E, AF 900/C, Model E, or equivalent[2]). [NOTE—Lamps shall not be used for longer than 100 h. Change lamps in pairs.]

The viewing tube shall have a field of view subtending 2° at the eye, and it shall contain a daylight correction filter.

[2] Available from The Tintometer Limited, Waterloo Road, Salisbury, Wiltshire, SPI 2JY, UK. Tel: +44 1722 327242; Fax: +44 1722 412322.

The lighting cabinet shall enable the samples and white reference field to be viewed at 90° to normal. Inspect at frequent intervals for dirt particles and aging of the paint. Repaint, when necessary, with a matte white paint when the color becomes darker than Munsell Notation 5Y 9/1 (also obtainable from Tintometer Ltd.[2]), or equivalent reference.

Spillage tray: Use where required.

Glass cells: Use cells made of optical glass with optical path lengths as follows: 1.6 mm (1/16 in), 3.2 mm (1/8 in), 6.4 mm (1/4 in), 12.7 mm (1/2 in), 25.4 mm (1 in), 76.2 mm (3 in), 133.4 mm (5 1/4 in).

Sample Use a sample that is completely liquid, clear, and bright. If the sample is not liquid at room temperature, heat it to a temperature of about 10° above the melting point. Avoid heating if it is likely to cause a color change.

Procedure Carry out all determinations in subdued ambient light (i.e., not facing a window or in direct sunlight). Pour the prepared *Sample* into an appropriate *Glass cell* of sufficient optical path length to give color readings within the ranges required. The *Glass cell* should be thoroughly cleaned and dried before use and prewarmed, if necessary, to prevent solid matter from separating from the *Sample* during the determination.

Place the cell containing the sample in the *Lighting cabinet* and close the viewing tube. Immediately determine the color of the *Sample*, initially by using the color racks in the ratio of 10 yellow to 1 red and using the minimum number of blue or neutral units to obtain the match. Do not use more than 9.0 blue or 3.0 neutral. To ensure that the number of glass surfaces in both the *Sample* and color filter fields are the same, the racks holding the color filters should be fitted with compensating slides. Record the size of the cell used and the red, yellow, blue, or neutral readings forming the color match.

The test must be carried out by two trained operators. Because the onset of eye fatigue is rapid, operators should rest their eyes after each 30-s period of matching. If the requirements under *Repeatability* (r) in *Table 1* are not satisfied, a third trained operator must carry out the test. The mean of the two closest readings (of three) should be taken.

Results Compare the mean of the results obtained by the two trained operators with the requirements in *Table 1*. If the requirements of *Repeatability* are not met, the mean of the two closest readings (of three) should be taken. Express the results in terms of the number of red, yellow, and blue or neutral readings needed to obtain the match and the length of the cell used. Color measurements taken in one cell length should not be used to calculate the color values for another cell length.

Repeatability The difference between two test results on the same material, in the same laboratory under the same conditions, should not exceed the repeatability value, r.

Reproducibility The difference between two test results on the same material, under the same conditions in different laboratories, should not exceed the reproducibility value, R.

Table 1: Repeatability and Reproducibility Limits

Color Scale	Level	r	R
Red: 133.4-mm cell (5 1/4 in)	2	0.2	0.8
	5	0.7	2
Yellow: 133.4-mm cell (5 1/4 in)	20	3	5
	50	6	12

FATTY ACID COMPOSITION
(Based on AOCS Methods Ce 1-62[1] and Ce 1b-89[1])

Apparatus Use a suitable gas chromatograph (see *Chromatography*, Appendix IIA) equipped with a flame ionization detector (FID) and containing either a 3.05-m × 2-mm or 4-mm id glass column packed with preconditioned 10%, by weight, DEGS-PS on 100- to 120-mesh diatomaceous earth (Chromosorb WHP, or equivalent) or a 30-m × 0.20-mm to 0.35-mm id capillary fused silica column, or equivalent, containing a suitable stationary phase.

Operating Conditions The operating conditions may vary with the instrument used, but a suitable chromatogram may be obtained using a temperature program 180°–215°; inlet temperature (injector), 300°; detector, 300°; and a suitable carrier gas flow.

Standard Solutions Run through the chromatograph a commercially available standard containing a mixture of fatty-acid methyl esters. Fatty acids and methyl esters with a wide range of carbon numbers and double-bond configurations can be purchased. The calculated concentration should compare to that claimed within ±2 σ, where σ is the standard deviation calculated from at least 10 replicate determinations, preferably made over a period of several days.

Determine that the system is functioning properly: inject into the chromatograph a suitable number of samples of the standard to ensure that the resolution factor, R, defining the efficiency of the separation between methyl stearate and methyl oleate is 0.9 or greater. Calculate R:

$$R = 2 \times (t_2 - t_1)/(w_2 + w_1)$$

in which t_2 and t_1 are the retention times of peak 2 and peak 1, respectively, and w_2 and w_1 are the corresponding widths of the bases of the peaks obtained by extrapolating relatively straight sides of the peaks to the baseline. Baseline separation of the various components in both the standard and the sample preparations is desirable.

Sample Preparation (for fats and oils) (Based on AOCS Method Ce 2-66[1]) Introduce 100–1000 mg of the fat into a 50-mL or 125-mL reaction flask. Add 4–10 mL of 0.5 N methanolic sodium hydroxide, and add a boiling chip. Attach a condenser, and heat the mixture on a steam bath until the fat globules go into solution. This step should take 5–10 min. Add 5–12 mL of 12.5% boron fluoride–methanol reagent (this reagent contains 125 g of boron fluoride per liter of methanol and is available commercially) through the condenser, and boil for 2 min. Add 2–5 mL of heptane through the condenser, and boil for 1 min longer. Remove from heat, remove condenser, and add about 15 mL of saturated sodium chloride solution. Stopper the flask, and shake vigorously for 15 s. Transfer about 1 mL of the heptane solution into a test tube and add a small amount of anhydrous sodium sulfate. The dry heptane solution may then be injected directly into a gas chromatograph.

The methyl esters should be analyzed as soon as possible. They may be kept in an atmosphere of nitrogen in a screw-cap vial at 2° for 24 h. For longer storage, they should be sealed in a glass ampule, subjected first to a vacuum and then backfilled with nitrogen and stored at −20° (freezer).

Procedure Inject an appropriate volume (0.1–1.0 µL) of the sample into the chromatograph. If an automated system is used, follow the manufacturer's instructions; if calculations are to be done manually, proceed as follows:

Calculate the area percentage of each component (C_N):

$$C_N = [A_N/T_S] \times 100$$

in which A_N is the area of the peak corresponding to component C_N, and T_S is the total area for all detected components [$T_S = \Sigma A_N$].

FATTY ACID COMPOSITION (SATURATED, cis-MONOUNSATURATED, and cis-POLYUNSATURATED) IN OILS CONTAINING LONG CHAIN POLYUNSATURATED FATTY ACIDS
(Based on AOCS Methods Ce 1i-07 and Ce 2-66[1])

Apparatus Use a gas chromatograph (see *Chromatography*, Appendix IIA) suitable for use with capillary columns, a temperature-controlled split/splitless injector operated in split mode, and a flame-ionization detector (FID). The capillary GC column should be of fused silica, 30-m × 0.25-mm, with a 0.25-µm coating of polyethylene glycol (PEG)[3].

Operating Conditions The carrier gas should be gas chromatography-grade hydrogen or helium (99.99% or better purity) that has been dried, and from which the oxygen has been removed using suitable filters. Do not use nitrogen as a carrier gas for this method. The flame gases should be gas chromatography-grade hydrogen and air, and the make-up gas should be gas chromatography-grade nitrogen or helium. Use a 78.5-mm × 4-mm (i.d.) × 6.3-mm (o.d.) base deactivated precision injection port split liner with glass wool[4]. The injection port should be operated at 235°. The detector should be operated at 325°. The column (oven) temperature should be held at 170° initially, with a 1°/min ramp and a final temperature of 225°. When a hydrogen carrier gas is used, the column head pressure is 77.9 kPa (11.3 psi) with a constant flow rate of 1.2 mL/min, a linear velocity of 43 cm/s, and a split ratio of 100:1. When helium is used as the carrier gas, the column head pressure is 226 kPa (32.77 psi) with a constant flow rate of 2.4 mL/min, a linear velocity of 53 cm/s, and a split ratio of 100:1. [NOTE—These conditions may not be appropriate for the determination of very long chain fatty acids (25:0 and greater).]

Reagents and Solutions

Internal Standard Solution: 2.0 mg/mL of USP Tritricosanoin RS in chloroform. [NOTE—Care must be taken to prevent the loss of chloroform during use and storage. This solution is stable indefinitely if precautions are taken to eliminate the loss of chloroform and, therefore, a change in the concentration of the solution. Store the solution in a refrigerator in a well-sealed amber bottle when not in use.]

System Suitability Preparation: USP Menhaden Oil RS

Standard Solution: Prepare a 20 mg/mL solution of USP FAME Standard Mixture RS in either *n*-heptane or *n*-hexanes as follows: Dilute 100 mg of USP FAME Standard Mixture RS in 5 mL of solvent, rinsing the ampule containing the Standard with the solvent to ensure complete and homogeneous transfer of the mixture.

Sample Preparation (for fats and oils) Transfer sufficient *Internal Standard Solution* into a 50-mL or 125-mL reaction flask so that the concentration in the final solution, after the oil is added, is 0.05–0.10 mg of internal standard per 1 mg of oil. Evaporate the chloroform (from the *Internal Standard Solution*) from the flask, then introduce 100–1000 mg of the oil to the reaction flask. Add 4–10 mL of 0.5 N methanolic sodium hydroxide, and add a boiling chip. Attach a condenser, and heat the mixture on a steam bath until the fat globules go into solution. This step should take 5–10 min. Add 5–12 mL of 12.5% boron fluoride–methanol reagent (this reagent contains 125 g of boron fluoride per liter of methanol and is available commercially) through the condenser, and boil for 2 min. [NOTE—The addition of antioxidants such as pyrogallol or BHT at a level of 1 mg/mg of the sample may help protect highly unsaturated fatty acids from oxidation during methylation.]

Add 2–5 mL of heptane through the condenser, and boil for 1 min longer. Remove from heat, remove condenser, and add about 15 mL of saturated sodium chloride solution. Stopper the flask, and shake vigorously for 15 s. Dilute the fatty acid methyl ester (FAME) so obtained in *n*-heptane or *n*-hexanes to a concentration of approximately 15–20 mg/mL of FAME in solvent.

System Suitability Proceed as directed under *Sample Preparation* using the *System Suitability Preparation* in place of the sample oil. Using a microsyringe suitable for gas chromatography (10-µL), inject 1 µL of the fatty acid methyl esters obtained from the preparation into the chromatograph, and record the resulting chromatogram. Compare the chromatogram to the one obtained using commercially-available authentic standards of fatty acid methyl esters, if needed, to identify the peaks. Baseline separation should be obtained between 23:0 (the internal standard) and 6*c*, 9*c*, 12*c*, 15*c*, 18*c*-21:5 (21:5n-3). Baseline separation should also be obtained between 24:0 and 4*c*, 7*c*, 10*c*, 13*c*, 16*c*, 19*c*-22:6 (DHA or 22:6n-3), which should be almost baseline resolved from the 24:1 isomers.

---

[3] Supelco SUPELCOWAX®-10, Restek FAMEWAX™, Agilent HP-INNOwax™, Varian CP-WAX™ 52 CB, Agilent Carbowax™-20M, Supelco Omegawax™ 320, or equivalent.
[4] Restek part no. 21022-211.5, SGE part no. 092002, or equivalent.

Theoretical and Empirical Correction Factors Theoretical correction factors may be calculated as directed below or may be available from several reference sources. Empirical correction factors are determined from the analysis of the *Standard Solution*. Using the microsyringe described under *System Suitability*, inject 1 µL of the *Standard Solution* into the chromatograph, and record the resulting chromatogram. Calculate the theoretical correction factors (TCF) for each fatty acid:

$$TCF_X = MW_X/(N_X - 1) \times (AWC) \times (1.3344)$$

in which TCF_X is the theoretical flame ionization detector response factor for fatty acid X (as the methyl ester) with respect to 23:0 FAME internal standard; MW_X is the molecular weight of component X; N_X is the number of carbon atoms in the fatty acid methyl ester of component X; AWC is the atomic weight of carbon (12.011); and 1.3344 is the TCF for 23:0 FAME.

Empirical correction factors are required for long chain polyunsaturated fatty acid methyl esters of 20 carbons or more and three or more double bonds for which standards are readily available. Using the certificate of analysis for USP FAME Standard Mixture RS, which should list both the purity (P) and amount (Amt_{FAMEx}) of each fatty acid methyl ester used to make up the standard, calculate the actual amount ($AAmt_{FAMEx}$) of each fatty acid methyl ester:

$$AAmt_{FAMEx} = P \times Amt_{FAMEx}$$

The response factor (RF) for each peak is determined using the equation:

$$RF_{FAMEx} = Area_{FAMEx}/AAmt_{FAMEx}$$

in which $Area_{FAMEx}$ is the peak area of the fatty acid methyl ester obtained from the chromatogram.

Each RF is then made relative to the 23:0 RF using the equation:

$$RRF_{FAMEx} = RF_{FAMEx}/RF_{23:0}$$

The empirical correction factor (ECF) for each FAME is then calculated by taking the inverse of the RRF using the equation:

$$ECF_{FAMEx} = 1/RRF_{FAMEx}$$

Procedure Using the microsyringe described under *System Suitability*, inject 1 µL of the *Sample Preparation* into the chromatograph, and record the resulting chromatogram.

Calculate the amount, in grams, of individual fatty acids, expressed as FAME (W_{FAMEx}) and triacylglycerol (W_{TAGx}) equivalents:

$$W_{FAMEx} = (A_X \times W_{TAG-IS} \times F \times R_X)/A_{IS}$$

$$W_{TAGx} = W_{FAMEx} \times F_{TAGx}$$

in which A_X is the peak area count for fatty acid X from the chromatogram obtained; W_{TAG-IS} is the weight of 23:0 internal standard (in grams) added to the oil; F is a factor for converting the weight of the internal standard (which is 23:0 triacylglycerol) from the triacylglycerol form to its corresponding weight of the fatty acid methyl ester form (1.0037); R_X is the theoretical correction factor (TCF) or empirical correction factor (ECF) for the fatty acid methyl esters relative to 23:0 methyl ester internal standard determined; A_{IS} is the peak area count for the internal standard; and F_{TAGx} is the conversion factor for fatty acid methyl esters to triacyl glycerols for individual fatty acids (from the table below). The TCF should be applied to the analytical data for optimum accuracy and to minimize variation between laboratories because of differences in calculating response factors. TCFs are also used for fatty acids where standards are not available. ECFs are needed because of the large deviation from TCFs for long chain polyunsaturated fatty acids of 20 carbons or more and three or more double bonds.

Calculation of Total Fat Calculate the amount of total fat in the sample tested (sum of all fatty acids; expressed as triacylglycerols):

$$\text{Total fat (g/100-g portion of test sample)} = (\Sigma W_{TAG}/W_{TS}) \times 100$$

in which W_{TS} is the weight of the sample, in grams.

Calculation of Individual Fatty Acids Calculate the weight, in g, of each individual fatty acid (W_X):

$$W_X \text{ (per gram of sample)} = W_{FAMEx} \times F_{FAx}$$

where F_{FAx} is the factor for conversion of the fatty acid methyl ester to its corresponding fatty acid (from the table below).

Calculation of Saturated Fats Calculate the weight of saturated fats (sum of all saturated fatty acids):

$$\text{Saturated fat (g/100-g portion of test sample)} = (\Sigma \text{ Saturated } W_X/W_{TS}) \times 100$$

where Σ Saturated W_X is the sum of all saturated fatty acids (4:0; 5:0; 6:0; 7:0; 8:0; 9:0; 10:0; *iso* 10:0; 11:0; 12:0; *anteiso* and *iso* 12:0; 13:0; *anteiso* and *iso* 13:0; 14:0; *anteiso* and *iso* 14:0; 15:0; *anteiso* and *iso* 15:0; 2,6,10,14-tetramethyl 15:0; 16:0; *anteiso* and *iso* 16:0; 3,7,11,15-tetramethyl 16:0; 17:0; *anteiso* and *iso* 17:0; 18:0; *anteiso* and *iso* 18:0; 19:0; *anteiso* 19:0; 20:0; *iso* 20:0; 21:0; *iso* 21:0; 22:0; 24:0; 25:0; 26:0; 27:0; 28:0; 29:0; and 31:0).

Calculation of *cis*-Monounsaturated Fat Calculate the weight of *cis*-monounsaturated fat (fatty acids containing one double bond):

$$\textit{cis}\text{-Monounsaturated fat (g/100-g portion of test sample)} = (\Sigma \textit{ cis}\text{-monounsaturated } W_X/W_{TS}) \times 100$$

where Σ *cis*-monounsaturated W_X is the sum of all *cis*-monounsaturated fatty acids.

Calculation of *cis*-Polyunsaturated Fat Calculate the weight of *cis*-polyunsaturated fat (fatty acids containing two or more double bonds):

$$\textit{cis}\text{-Monounsaturated fat (g/100-g portion of test sample)} = (\Sigma \textit{ cis}\text{-polyunsaturated } W_X/W_{TS}) \times 100$$

where Σ cis-polyunsaturated W_x is the sum of all cis-polyunsaturated fatty acids.

Calculation of EPA and DHA Calculate the weight of EPA and DHA:

EPA or DHA (g/100-g portion of test sample) = (ΣEPA or DHA W_x/W_{TS}) × 100

Factors for Converting FAME to FA and TAG Equivalents

Fatty Acid[a]	F_{FAx}	F_{TAGx}	Fatty Acid[a]	F_{FAx}	F_{TAGx}
4:0	0.8626	0.9868	20:0	0.9570	0.9959
5:0	0.8792	0.9884	20:1	0.9568	0.9959
6:0	0.8922	0.9897	20:2	0.9565	0.9958
7:0	0.9027	0.9907	20:3	0.9562	0.9958
8:0	0.9114	0.9915	20:4	0.9560	0.9958
9:0	0.9186	0.9922	20:5	0.9557	0.9958
10:0	0.9247	0.9928	21:0	0.9588	0.9961
10:1	0.9239	0.9927	21:5	0.9576	0.9959
11:0	0.9300	0.9933	22:0	0.9604	0.9962
11:1	0.9293	0.9932	22:1	0.9602	0.9962
12:0	0.9346	0.9937	22:2	0.9600	0.9962
12:1	0.9339	0.9937	22:3	0.9598	0.9961
13:0	0.9386	0.9941	22:4	0.9595	0.9961
13:1	0.9380	0.9941	22:5	0.9593	0.9961
14:0	0.9421	0.9945	22:6	0.9590	0.9961
14:1	0.9416	0.9944	23:0 (IS)	0.9619	0.9964
15:0[b]	0.9453	0.9948	23:5	0.9609	0.9963
Tetra Methyl 15:0	0.9551	0.9957	24:0	0.9633	0.9965
15:1	0.9449	0.9947	24:1	0.9631	0.9965
16:0[c]	0.9481	0.9950	24:3	0.9628	0.9964
Tetra Methyl 16:0	0.9570	0.9959	24:4	0.9626	0.9964
16:1	0.9477	0.9950	24:5	0.9624	0.9964
16:2	0.9473	0.9950	24:6	0.9621	0.9964
16:3	0.9469	0.9949	25:0	0.9646	0.9966
16:4	0.9465	0.9949	26:0	0.9658	0.9967
17:0	0.9507	0.9953	26:5	0.9650	0.9966
17:1	0.9503	0.9952	26:6	0.9648	0.9966
18:0	0.9530	0.9955	27:0	0.9670	0.9968
18:1	0.9527	0.9955	28:0	0.9680	0.9969
18:2	0.9524	0.9954	28:7	0.9670	0.9968
18:3	0.9520	0.9954	28:8	0.9668	0.9968
18:4	0.9517	0.9954	29:0	0.9690	0.9970
18:5	0.9514	0.9953	30:0	0.9700	0.9971
19:0	0.9551	0.9957	31:0	0.9708	0.9972
19:1	0.9548	0.9957			

[a] Only one factor is given for all positional and geometric isomers and for branched-chain FAME, as the factors are dependent only on the content of carbon to which hydrogen is bonded.
[b] 3,7,11-Trimethyldodecanoic acid (TMDD) has equivalent F_{FAx} and F_{TAGx} to 15:0.
[c] 4,8,12-Trimethyltridecanoic acid (TMTD) has equivalent F_{FAx} and F_{TAGx} to 16:0.

FREE FATTY ACIDS
(Based on AOCS Method Ca 5a-40[1])

Unless otherwise directed, accurately weigh the appropriate amount of the sample, indicated in the table below, into a 250-mL Erlenmeyer flask or other suitable container. Add 2 mL of phenolphthalein TS to the specified amount of hot alcohol, neutralize with alkali to the first faint, but permanent, pink color, and then add the hot, neutralized alcohol to the sample container. Titrate with the appropriate normality of sodium hydroxide, shaking vigorously, to the first permanent pink color of the same intensity as that of the neutralized alcohol. The color must persist for at least 30 s. Calculate the percentage of free fatty acids (FFA) in the sample:

$$\text{Result} = VNe/W$$

in which V is the volume and N is the normality of the sodium hydroxide used; e is the equivalence factor given in the monograph; and W is the weight of the sample, in grams.

FFA Range (%)	Grams of Sample	mL of Alcohol	Strength of NaOH
0.00–0.2	56.4 ± 0.2	50	0.1 N
0.2–1.0	28.2 ± 0.2	50	0.1 N
1.0–30.0	7.05 ± 0.05	75	0.25 N
30.0–50.0	7.05 ± 0.05	100	0.25–1.0 N
50.0–100	3.525 ± 0.001	100	1.0 N

FREE GLYCERIN OR PROPYLENE GLYCOL
(Based on AOCS Method Ca 14-56[1])

Reagents and Solutions Use the *Periodic Acid Solution* and *Chloroform* as described under *1-Monoglycerides*, in this Appendix.

Procedure To the combined aqueous extracts obtained as directed under *1-Monoglycerides*, add 50.0 mL of *Periodic Acid Solution*. Run two blanks by adding 50.0 mL of this reagent solution to two 500-mL glass-stoppered Erlenmeyer flasks, each containing 75 mL of water. Continue as directed in the *Procedure* under *1-Monoglycerides*, beginning with ". . . and allow to stand for at least 30 min but no longer than 90 min."

Calculation Calculate the percentage of free glycerin in the original sample:

$$\text{Result} = (b - S) \times N \times 2.30/W$$

or calculate the percentage of free propylene glycol:

$$\text{Result} = (b - S) \times N \times 3.81/W$$

in which b is the number of mL of sodium thiosulfate consumed in the blank determination; S is the number of mL required in the titration of the aqueous extracts from the sample; N is the exact normality of the sodium thiosulfate; W is the weight, in grams, of the original sample taken; 2.30 is the molecular weight of glycerin divided by 40; and 3.81 is the molecular weight of propylene glycol divided by 20.

[NOTE—If the aqueous extract contains more than 20 mg of glycerin or more than 30 mg of propylene glycol, dilute the extract in a volumetric flask and transfer a suitable aliquot into a 500-mL glass-stoppered Erlenmeyer flask before proceeding with the test. The weight of the sample should be corrected in the calculation.]

HEXANE-INSOLUBLE MATTER

If the sample is plastic or semisolid, soften a portion by warming it at a temperature not exceeding 60°, and then mix it thoroughly. Transfer 100 g of well-mixed sample into a 1500-mL wide-mouth Erlenmeyer flask, add 1000 mL of solvent hexane, and shake until the sample is dissolved. Pass the resulting solution through a 600-mL Corning "C" porosity, or equivalent, filtering funnel that previously has been dried at 105° for 1 h, cooled in a desiccator, and weighed. Wash the flask with two successive 250-mL portions of solvent hexane, and pass the washings through the filter. Dry the funnel at 105° for 1 h, cool to room temperature in a desiccator, and weigh. From the gain in weight of the funnel, calculate the percentage of the hexane-insoluble matter in the sample.

HYDROXYL VALUE
(Based on AOCS Methods Cd 4-40[1] and Cd 13-60[1])

The hydroxyl value is defined as the number of mg of potassium hydroxide equivalent to the hydroxyl content of 1 g of the unacetylated sample.

Method I
Proceed as directed under *Acetyl Value*, in this Appendix, but calculate the hydroxyl value:

$$\text{Result} = (S' - S)/(1.000 - 0.00075S')$$

Method II
Unless otherwise directed, accurately weigh the appropriate amount of the sample indicated in the table below, transfer it into a 250-mL glass-stoppered Erlenmeyer flask, and add 5.0 mL of pyridine–acetic anhydride reagent (mix 3 volumes of freshly distilled pyridine with 1 volume of freshly distilled acetic anhydride).

Hydroxyl Value	Sample Weight (g)
0–20	10
20–50	5
50–100	3
100–150	2
150–200	1.50
200–250	1.25
250–300	1
300–350	0.75

Pipet 5 mL of the pyridine–acetic anhydride reagent into a second 250-mL flask for the reagent blank. Heat the flasks for 1 h on a steam bath under reflux condensers, then add 10 mL of water through each condenser, heat for 10 min longer, and allow the flasks to cool to room temperature. Add 15 mL of *n*-butyl alcohol, previously neutralized to phenolphthalein TS with 0.5 N alcoholic potassium hydroxide, through the condenser, then remove the condensers, and wash the sides of the flasks with 10 mL of *n*-butyl alcohol. To each flask add 1 mL of phenolphthalein TS, and titrate to a faint pink endpoint with 0.5 N alcoholic potassium hydroxide, recording the mL required for the sample as S and that for the blank as B. To correct for free acid, mix about 10 g of the sample, accurately weighed, with 10 mL of freshly distilled pyridine, previously neutralized to phenolphthalein, add 1 mL of phenolphthalein TS, and titrate to a faint endpoint with 0.5 N alcoholic potassium hydroxide, recording the mL required as A. Calculate the hydroxyl value:

$$\text{Result} = [B + (WA/C) - S] \times 56.1 N/W$$

in which W and C are the weights, in grams, of the samples taken for acetylation and for the free acid determination, respectively; and N is the exact normality of the alcoholic potassium hydroxide.

IODINE VALUE
(Based on AOCS Method Cd 1d-92[1])

The iodine value is a measure of unsaturation and is expressed as the number of grams of iodine absorbed, under the prescribed conditions, by 100 g of the test substance.

Modified Wijs Method (Acetic Acid/Cyclohexane Method)

Wijs Solution Dissolve 13 g of resublimed iodine in 1000 mL of glacial acetic acid. Pipet 10.0 mL of this solution into a 250-mL flask, add 20 mL of potassium iodide TS and 100 mL of water, and titrate with 0.1 N sodium thiosulfate, adding starch TS near the endpoint. Record the volume required as A. Set aside about 100 mL of the iodine–acetic acid solution for future use. Pass chlorine gas, washed and dried with sulfuric acid, through the remainder of the solution until a 10.0-mL portion requires not quite twice the volume of 0.1 N sodium thiosulfate consumed in the titration of the original iodine solution. A characteristic color change occurs when the desired amount of chlorine has been added. Alternatively, *Wijs Solution* may be prepared by dissolving 16.5 g of iodine monochloride, ICl, in 1000 mL of glacial acetic acid. Store the solution in amber bottles sealed with paraffin until ready for use, and use within 30 days.

Total Halogen Content: Pipet 10.0 mL of *Wijs Solution* into a 500-mL Erlenmeyer flask containing 150 mL of recently boiled and cooled water and 15 mL of potassium iodide TS. Titrate immediately with 0.1 N sodium thiosulfate, recording the volume required as B.

Halogen Ratio: Calculate the I/Cl ratio:

$$\text{Result} = A/(B - A)$$

The halogen ratio must be between 1.0 and 1.2. If the ratio is not within this range, the halogen content can be adjusted by adding the original solution or by passing more chlorine through the solution.

[NOTE—*Wijs Solution* is commercially available.]

Procedure The appropriate weight of the sample, in grams, is calculated by dividing the number 25 by the expected iodine value. Melt the sample, if necessary, and pass it through a dry filter paper. Transfer the accurately weighed quantity of sample into a clean, dry, 500-mL glass-stoppered bottle or flask containing 20 mL of glacial acetic acid/cyclohexane, 1:1, v/v, and pipet 25.0 mL of *Wijs Solution* into the flask. The excess of iodine should be 50%–60% of the quantity added, that is, 100%–150% of the quantity absorbed. Swirl, and let stand in the dark for 1.0 h where the iodine value is <150 and for 2.0 h where the iodine value is ≥150. Add 20 mL of potassium iodide TS and 100 mL of recently boiled and cooled water, and titrate the excess iodine with 0.1 N sodium thiosulfate, adding the titrant gradually and shaking constantly until the yellow color of the solution almost disappears. Add starch TS, and continue the titration until the blue color disappears entirely. Toward the end of the titration, stopper the container and shake it violently so that any iodine remaining in solution in the glacial acetic acid/cyclohexane, 1:1, solution may be taken up by the potassium iodide solution. Concomitantly, conduct two determinations on blanks in the same manner and at the same temperature. Calculate the iodine value:

$$\text{Result} = (B - S) \times 12.69 N/W$$

in which B − S represents the difference between the volumes of sodium thiosulfate required for the blank and for the sample, respectively; N is the normality of the sodium thiosulfate; and W is the weight, in grams, of the sample taken.

MELTING RANGE (Fats and Related Substances)

Fats of animal and vegetable origin do not exhibit a sharp melting point. For the purpose of this test, melting range is defined as the range of temperature in which the sample becomes a perfectly clear liquid after first passing through a stage of gradual softening, during which it may become opalescent.

Apparatus Use any suitable commercial or other apparatus. Use melting-point capillary tubes—id, 1 mm; od, 2 mm; length, 50–80 mm; and open at both ends.

Procedure

Capillary Method (Based on AOCS Method Cc 1-25[1]): Melt the sample and pass it through filter paper; the sample must be absolutely dry. Dip three capillary tubes in the liquid sample so that the oil stands approximately 10 mm high in the tubes, and fuse the end of the tube containing the sample without burning it. Place the tubes containing the liquid sample in a beaker, and equilibrate them at least 16 h at 4°–10° in a refrigerator. Determine the melting range, using a temperature increase of 0.5° per min when within 10° of the anticipated melting point. The melting ranges of the three samples should be no more than 0.5° apart.

1-MONOGLYCERIDES
(Based on AOCS Method Cd 11-57[1])

Reagents and Solutions

Periodic Acid Solution: Dissolve 5.4 g of periodic acid, H_5IO_6, in 100 mL of water, add 1900 mL of glacial acetic acid, and mix. Store in a light-resistant, glass-stoppered bottle or in a clear, glass-stoppered bottle protected from light.

Chloroform: Use chloroform meeting the following test: To each of three 500-mL flasks add 50.0 mL of *Periodic Acid Solution*, then add 50 mL of chloroform and 10 mL of water to two of the flasks and 50 mL of water to the third. To each flask add 20 mL of potassium iodide TS, mix gently, and continue as directed in the *Procedure*, beginning with "... allow to stand at least 1 min...." The difference between the volume of 0.1 N sodium thiosulfate required in the titrations with and without the chloroform is not greater than 0.5 mL.

Procedure Melt the sample, if not liquid, at a temperature not higher than 10° above its melting point, and mix thoroughly. Transfer an accurately weighed portion of the sample, equivalent to about 150 mg of 1-monoglycerides, into a 100-mL beaker (or weigh a sample equivalent to 20 mg of glycerin or 30 mg of propylene glycol if only *Free Glycerin or Propylene Glycol* is to be determined), and dissolve in 25 mL of chloroform. Transfer the solution, with the aid of an additional 25 mL of chloroform, into a separator, wash the beaker with 25 mL of water, and add the washing to the separator. Stopper the separator tightly, shake vigorously for 30–60 s, and allow the layers to separate. (Add 1–2 mL of glacial acetic acid to break emulsions formed due to the presence of soap.) Collect the aqueous layer in a 500-mL glass-stoppered Erlenmeyer flask, and extract the chloroform solution again using two 25-mL portions of water. Retain the combined aqueous extracts for the determination of *Free Glycerin or Propylene Glycol* (in this Appendix). Transfer the chloroform to a 500-mL glass-stoppered Erlenmeyer flask, and add 50.0 mL of *Periodic Acid Solution* to this flask and to each of two blank flasks containing 50 mL of chloroform and 10 mL of water. Swirl the flasks during the addition of the reagent, and allow to stand for at least 30 min, but no longer than 90 min. To each flask, add 20 mL of potassium iodide TS, and allow to stand at least 1 min, but no longer than 5 min, before titrating. Add 100 mL of water, and titrate with 0.1 N sodium thiosulfate, using a magnetic stirrer to keep the solution thoroughly mixed, to the disappearance of the brown iodine color. Then add 2 mL of starch TS, and continue the titration to the disappearance of the blue color. Calculate the percentage of 1-monoglycerides[5] in the sample:

$$\text{Result} = (B - S) \times N \times 17.927/W$$

in which B is the number of mL of sodium thiosulfate consumed in the blank determination; S is the number of mL required in the titration of the sample; N is the exact normality of the sodium thiosulfate; W is the weight, in grams, of the sample taken; and 17.927 is the molecular weight of glyceryl monostearate divided by 20.

TOTAL MONOGLYCERIDES

Preparation of Silica Gel Place about 10 g of 100- to 200-mesh silica gel of a grade suitable for chromatographic work in a tared weighing bottle, cap immediately, and weigh accurately. Remove the cap, dry at 200° for 2 h, cap immediately, and cool for 30 min. Raise the cap momentarily to equalize the pressure, then weigh again, reheat for 5 min at 200°, cool, and reweigh. Repeat this 5-min drying cycle until two consecutive weights agree within 10 mg. Calculate the percentage of water in the original silica gel (A):

$$\text{Result} = (\text{loss in wt/sample wt}) \times 100$$

then calculate the amount of water required to adjust the water content to 5%:

$$\text{Result} = W \times (5 - A)/95$$

in which W is the weight, in grams, of the undried sample to be used.

Accurately weigh the appropriate amount of the undried silica gel to be used in the determination, transfer to a suitable blender or mixer, and add the calculated amount of water to give a final water content of $5 \pm 0.1\%$. Blend for 1 h to ensure complete water distribution, and store in a sealed container. Determine the water content of the adjusted silica gel as directed above, and readjust if necessary.

[NOTE—Each new lot of silica gel should be checked for suitability by the analysis of a monoglyceride of known composition.]

Sample Preparation [CAUTION—To avoid rearrangement of partial glycerides, use extreme caution in applying heat to the samples, and do not heat above 50°.]

Samples Melting Below 50°: Melt the sample, if necessary, by warming for short periods below 50°, not exceeding a total of 30 min.

Samples Melting Above 50°: Grind about 10 g in a mortar and pestle, chilling solid samples, if necessary, in carbon dioxide.

Weigh accurately about 1 g of the prepared sample into a 100-mL beaker, add 15 mL of chloroform, and warm, if necessary, to effect solution. Use only minimal heat, and do not heat above 40°.

Preparation of Chromatographic Column Connect a 19-mm × 290-mm chromatographic tube, equipped with an outer 19/22 standard-taper joint at the top and a coarse, fritted-glass disk and inner 19/22 standard-taper joint at the bottom, with an adapter consisting of an outer 19/22 joint connected to a Teflon stopcock. Do not grease the joints. Weigh 30 g of the prepared silica gel into a 150-mL beaker, add 50–60 mL of petroleum ether, and stir slowly with a glass rod until all air bubbles are expelled. Transfer the slurry to the column through a powder funnel, and open the stopcock, allowing the liquid level to drop to about 2 cm above the silica gel. Transfer any silica gel slurry remaining in the beaker into the column with a minimum amount of petroleum ether, then rinse the funnel and sides of the column. Drain the solvent through the stopcock until the level drops to 2 cm above the silica gel, and remove the powder funnel.

Procedure Carefully add the *Sample Preparation* to the prepared column. Open the stopcock, and adjust the flow rate to about 2 mL/min, discarding the eluate. Rinse the

---

[5] The monoglyceride may be calculated to some monoester other than glyceryl monostearate by dividing the molecular weight of the monoglyceride by 20 and substituting the value so obtained for 17.927 in the formula, using 17.80, for example, in calculating to the monooleate.

sample beaker with 5 mL of chloroform, and add the rinsing to the column when the level drops to 2 cm above the silica gel. Never allow the column to become dry on top, and maintain a flow rate of 2 mL/min throughout the elution. Avoid interruptions during elution as they may cause pressure buildup and result in leakage through the stopcock or cracks in the silica gel packing.

Attach a 250-mL reservoir separator, provided with a Teflon stopcock and a 19/22 standard-taper drip tip inner joint, to the column. Add 200 mL of benzene, elute, and discard the eluate, which contains the triglycerides fraction. When the level of benzene drops to 2 cm above the silica gel, add 200 mL of a mixture of ether in benzene (1:10), elute, and discard the eluate, which contains the diglycerides and the free fatty acid fraction. When all of the ether–benzene solvent has been added from the separator and the level in the column drops to 2 cm above the silica gel, add from 250–300 mL of ether, and collect the monoglyceride fraction in a tared flask. Rinse the tip of the column into the flask with a few mL of ether, and evaporate to dryness on a steam bath under a stream of nitrogen or dry air. Cool for at least 15 min, weigh, then reheat on the steam bath for 5 min in the same manner. Cool, reweigh, and repeat the 5-min evaporation, cooling, and reweighing procedures until two consecutive weights agree within 2 mg. The weight of the residue represents the total monoglycerides in the sample taken.

OXYETHYLENE DETERMINATION

Apparatus The apparatus for oxyethylene group determination is shown in *Figure 1*. It consists of a boiling flask, *A*, fitted with a capillary side tube to provide an inlet for carbon dioxide and connected by a condenser with trap *B*, which contains an aqueous suspension of red phosphorus. The first absorption tube, *C*, contains a silver nitrate solution to absorb ethyl iodide. Absorption tube *D* is fitted with a 1.75-mm spiral rod (23 turns, 8.5-mm rise per turn), which is required to provide a longer contact of the evolved ethylene with the bromine solution. A standard-taper adapter and stopcock are connected to tube *D* to permit the transfer of the bromine solution into a titration flask without loss. A final trap, *E*, containing a potassium iodide solution, collects any bromine swept out by the flow of carbon dioxide.

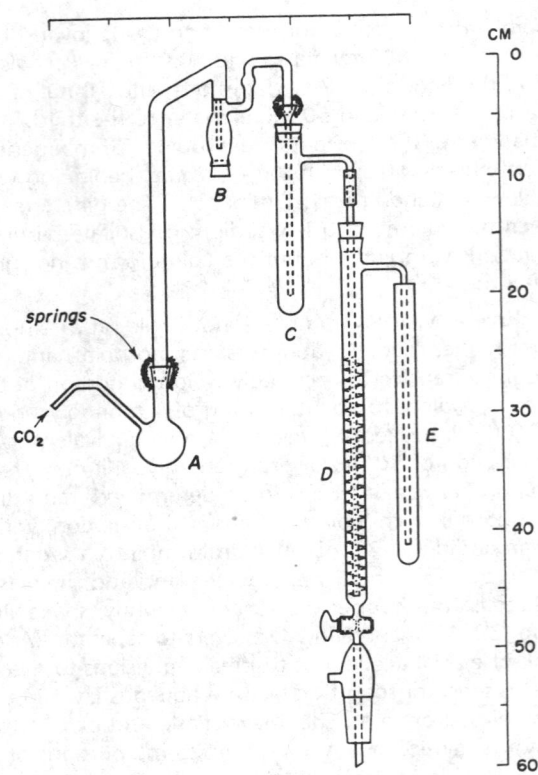

Figure 1. Apparatus for Oxyethylene Determination

Dimensions of the apparatus not readily determined from *Figure 1* are as follows: carbon dioxide inlet capillary, 1-mm id; flask *A*, 28-mm diameter, 12/18 standard-taper joint; condenser, 9-mm id; inlet to trap *B*, 2-mm id; inlet to trap *C*, 7/15 standard-taper joint, 2-mm id; trap *C*, 14-mm id; trap *D*, inner tube, 8-mm od, 2-mm opening at bottom of spiral; outer tube, approximately 12.5-mm id; side arm 7 cm from top of inserted spiral, 3.5-mm id, 2-mm opening at bottom.

Reagents

Hydriodic Acid: Use special-grade hydriodic acid suitable for alkoxyl determinations, or purify reagent-grade as follows: Distill over red phosphorus in an all-glass apparatus, passing a slow stream of carbon dioxide through the apparatus until the distillation is terminated and the receiving flask has completely cooled. [**CAUTION**—Use a safety shield, and conduct the distillation in a hood.]

Silver Nitrate Solution: Dissolve 15 g of silver nitrate in 50 mL of water, mix with 400 mL of alcohol, and add a few drops of nitric acid.

Bromine–Bromide Solution: Add 1 mL of bromine to 300 mL of glacial acetic acid saturated with dry potassium iodide (about 5 g). Fifteen mL of this solution requires about 40 mL of 0.05 N sodium thiosulfate. Store in a brown bottle in a dark place, and standardize at least once a day during use.

Procedure Fill trap *B* with enough of a suspension of 60 mg of red phosphorus in 100 mL of water to cover the inlet tube. Pipet 10 mL of the *Silver Nitrate Solution* into tube *C* and 15 mL of the *Bromine–Bromide Solution* into tube *D*, and place 10 mL of a 1:10 solution of potassium iodide in trap

E. Transfer an accurately weighed quantity of the sample specified in the monograph into the reaction flask, A, and add 10 mL of *Hydriodic Acid* along with a few glass beads or boiling stones. Connect the flask to the condenser, and begin passing carbon dioxide through the apparatus at the rate of about one bubble per s. Heat the flask in an oil bath at 140°–145°, and continue the reaction at this temperature for at least 40 min. Heating should be continued until the cloudy reflux in the condenser becomes clear and until the supernatant liquid in the silver nitrate tube, C, is almost completely clarified. Five min before the reaction is terminated, heat the *Silver Nitrate Solution* in tube C in a hot water bath at 50°–60° to expel any dissolved olefin. At the completion of the decomposition, cautiously disconnect tubes D and C in the order named, then disconnect the carbon dioxide source and remove the oil bath. Connect tube D to a 500-mL iodine flask containing 150 mL of water and 10 mL of a 1:10 solution of potassium iodide, run the *Bromine–Bromide Solution* into the flask, and rinse the tube and spiral with water. Add the potassium iodide solution from trap E to the flask, rinsing the side arm and tube with a few mL of water, stopper the flask, and allow to stand for 5 min. Add 5 mL of 2 N sulfuric acid, and titrate immediately with 0.05 N sodium thiosulfate, using 2 mL of starch TS for the endpoint. Transfer the silver nitrate solution from tube C into a flask, rinsing the tube with water, dilute to 150 mL with water, and heat to boiling. Cool, and titrate with 0.05 N ammonium thiocyanate, using 3 mL of ferric ammonium sulfate TS as the indicator. Perform a blank determination. Calculate the percentage of oxyethylene groups (—CH$_2$CH$_2$O—), as ethylene:

$$\text{Result} = (B - S) \times N \times 2.203/W$$

in which B − S represents the difference between the volumes of sodium thiosulfate required for the blank and the sample solution, respectively; N is the normality of the sodium thiosulfate; W is the weight, in grams, of the sample taken; and 2.203 is an equivalence factor for oxyethylene. Calculate the percentage of oxyethylene groups, as ethyl iodide:

$$\text{Result} = (B' - S') \times N' \times 4.405/W$$

in which B′ − S′ represents the difference between the volumes of ammonium thiocyanate required for the blank and the sample solution, respectively; N′ is the normality of the ammonium thiocyanate; and 4.405 is an equivalence factor for oxyethylene. The sum of the values so obtained represents the percentage of oxyethylene groups in the sample taken.

PEROXIDE VALUE

Unless otherwise indicated in the monograph, use *Method I: Acetic Acid–Isooctane Method*.

The peroxide value is defined as the number of mEq of peroxde per 1000 g of sample that oxidizes potassium iodide under the given test conditions.

Method 1: Acetic Acid–Isooctane Method (Based on AOCS Method Cd 8b-90[1])

Solutions

Acetic Acid–Isooctane Solution: Mix 3 volumes of glacial acetic acid with 2 volumes of isooctane. [NOTE—Use a fume hood at all times, and avoid inhalation, injection, and skin contact.]

Saturated Potassium Iodide Solution: Dissolve an excess of potassium iodide in recently boiled water. Prepare fresh daily, and make certain the solution remains saturated during use.

Starch Indicator Solution: Make a paste with 1 g of starch and a small amount of cold water, and add it, while stirring to 200 mL of boiling water. Remove from heat within a few seconds, and cool. If desired, add salicylic acid (1.25 g/L) as a preservative. The solution may be kept refrigerated at 4°–10° for not more than 3 weeks. Test the solution for sensitivity before use by placing 5 mL of the solution in 100 mL of water and adding 0.05 mL of 0.1 N potassium iodide solution. The deep blue color produced must be discharged by 0.05 mL of 0.1 N sodium thiosulfate. If the solution fails the test, prepare a fresh starch solution.

Procedure Transfer 5.00 ± 0.05 g of sample, accurately weighed, into a 250-mL Erlenmeyer flask fitted with a glass stopper, and add 50 mL of *Acetic Acid–Isooctane Solution*. Swirl to dissolve the sample, and add 0.5 mL of *Saturated Potassium Iodide Solution*. Allow the sample solution to stand, agitating it occasionally, for exactly 1 min, and immediately add 30 mL of water. Titrate with 0.1 N sodium thiosulfate solution, adding the solution gradually while constantly agitating until the yellow iodine color has almost disappeared. Add 0.5 mL of a 10% sodium lauryl sulfate solution, and then add approximately 0.5 mL of *Starch Indicator Solution*. Continue the titration while constantly agitating, especially near the endpoint, to liberate all of the iodine from the solvent layer. Add 0.1 N thiosulfate solution dropwise until the blue color just disappears. If the titration is less than 0.5 mL using 0.1 N sodium thiosulfate, repeat the determination using 0.01 N sodium thiosulfate. Conduct a blank determination (see *General Provisions*), and make any necessary correction. Calculate the peroxide value:

$$\text{Result} = [(S - B) \times N \times 1000]/W$$

in which S is the volume, in mL, of 0.1 N sodium thiosulfate consumed by the sample; B is the volume, in mL, of 0.1 N sodium thiosulfate consumed by the blank; N is the normality of the sodium thiosulfate solution; and W is the weight, in grams, of the sample taken.

Method II (Alternatively, follow the AOCS Method Cd 8-53[1])

Accurately weigh about 10 g of sample, add 30 mL of a mixture of glacial acetic acid and chloroform (3:2), and mix. Add 1 mL of a saturated solution of potassium iodide, mix, and allow it to stand for 10 min. Add 100 mL of water, begin titrating with 0.05 N sodium thiosulfate, adding starch TS as the endpoint is approached, and continue the titration until the blue starch color has just disappeared. Perform a blank determination (see *General Provisions*), and make any necessary correction. Calculate the peroxide value, as mEq of peroxide per kg of the sample:

$$\text{Result} = S \times N \times 1000/W$$

in which S is the net volume, in mL, of sodium thiosulfate solution required for the sample; N is the exact normality of the sodium thiosulfate solution; and W is the weight, in grams, of the sample taken.

REICHERT-MEISSL VALUE
(Based on AOCS Method Cd 5-40[1])

The Reichert-Meissl value is a measure of soluble volatile fatty acids (chiefly butyric and caproic). It is expressed in terms of the number of mL of 0.1 N sodium hydroxide required to neutralize the fatty acids obtained from a 5-g sample under the specified conditions of the method.

Apparatus Use a glass distillation apparatus of the same dimensions and construction as that shown in *Figure 2*.

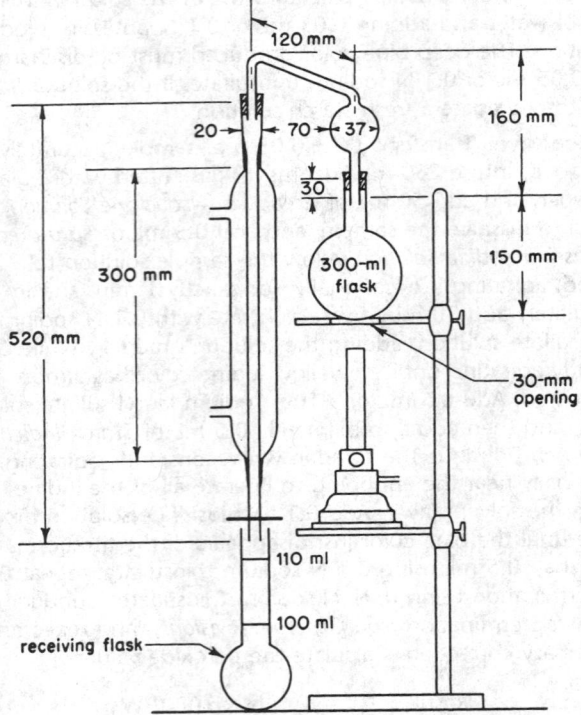

Figure 2. Reichert-Meissl Distillation Apparatus [NOTE—A suitable heating mantle may be substituted for the burner.]

Reagents

Sodium Hydroxide Solution: Prepare a solution containing 50.0% by weight of NaOH, and protect from contact with carbon dioxide. Allow the solution to settle, and use only the clear liquid.

Glycerin–Sodium Hydroxide Mixture: Add 20 mL of the *Sodium Hydroxide Solution* to 180 mL of glycerin.

Procedure Unless otherwise directed, accurately weigh about 5 g of the sample, previously melted if necessary, into the 300-mL distillation flask. Add 20.0 mL of the *Glycerin–Sodium Hydroxide Mixture*, and heat until the sample is completely saponified, as indicated by the mixture becoming perfectly clear. Shake the flask gently if any foaming occurs. Add 135 mL of recently boiled and cooled water, dropwise at first to prevent foaming, then add 6 mL of 1:5 sulfuric acid and a few pieces of pumice stone or silicon carbide. Rest the flask on a piece of heat-proof board having a center hole 5 cm in diameter, and begin the distillation, regulating the flame so as to collect 110 mL of distillate in 30 ± 2 min (measure time from the passage of the first drop of distillate from the condenser to the receiving flask), letting the distillate drip into the flask at a temperature not higher than 20°.

When 110 mL has distilled, disconnect the receiving flask, and remove the flame. Mix the contents of the flask with gentle shaking, and immerse almost completely for 15 min in water cooled to 15°. Filter the distillate through dry, 9-cm, moderately retentive paper (S & S No. 589 White Ribbon, or equivalent), add phenolphthalein TS, and titrate 100 mL of the filtrate with 0.1 N sodium hydroxide to the first pink color that remains unchanged for 2–3 min. Perform a blank determination using the same quantities of the same reagents, and calculate the Reichert-Meissl value:

$$\text{Result} = 1.1 \times (S - B)$$

in which S is the volume of 0.1 N sodium hydroxide required for the sample, and B is the volume required for the blank.

SAPONIFICATION VALUE
(Based on AOCS Methods Tl 1a-64[1] and Cd 3-25[1])

The saponification value is defined as the number of mg of potassium hydroxide required to neutralize the free acids and saponify the esters in 1 g of the test substance.

Procedure Melt the sample, if necessary, and pass it through a dry filter paper to remove any traces of moisture. Unless otherwise directed, weigh accurately into a 250-mL flask a sample of such size that the titration of the sample solution after saponification will require between 45% and 55% of the volume of 0.5 N hydrochloric acid required for the blank, and add to the flask 50.0 mL of 0.5 N alcoholic potassium hydroxide. Connect an air condenser, at least 65 cm in length, to the flask, and reflux gently until the sample is completely saponified (usually 30 min to 1 h). Cool slightly, wash the condenser with a few mL of water, add 1 mL of phenolphthalein TS, and titrate the excess potassium hydroxide with 0.5 N hydrochloric acid. Heat the contents of the flask to boiling, again titrate to the disappearance of any pink color that may have developed, and record the total volume of acid required. Perform a blank determination using the same amount of 0.5 N alcoholic potassium hydroxide. Calculate the saponification value:

$$\text{Result} = 56.1(B - S) \times N/W$$

in which $B - S$ represents the difference between the volumes of 0.5 N hydrochloric acid required for the blank and the sample, respectively; N is the normality of the hydrochloric acid; and W is the weight, in grams, of the sample taken.

[NOTE—A "masked phenolphthalein indicator" may be used with off-color materials. Prepare the indicator by dissolving 1.6 g of phenolphthalein and 2.7 g of methylene blue in 500 mL of alcohol, and adjust the pH with alcoholic alkali solution so that the greenish blue color is faintly tinged with purple. The color change, when going from acid to alkali, is from green to purple.]

SOAP

Prepare a solvent mixture consisting of equal parts, by volume, of benzene and methanol, add bromophenol blue TS, and neutralize with 0.5 N hydrochloric acid, or use neutralized acetone as the solvent. Accurately weigh the amount of sample specified in the individual monograph, dissolve it in 100 mL of the neutralized solvent mixture, and titrate with 0.5 N hydrochloric acid to a definite yellow endpoint. Calculate the percentage of soap in the sample:

$$Result = VNe/W$$

in which V and N are the volume and normality, respectively, of the hydrochloric acid; e is the equivalence factor given in the monograph; and W is the weight of the sample, in grams.

SPECIFIC GRAVITY

The specific gravity of a fat or oil is determined at 25°, except when the substance is a solid at that temperature, in which case the specific gravity is determined at the temperature specified in the monograph, and is referred to water at 25°.

Clean a suitable pycnometer by filling it with a saturated solution of chromic acid (CrO_3) in sulfuric acid and allowing it to stand for at least 4 h. Empty the pycnometer, rinse it thoroughly, then fill it with recently boiled water, previously cooled to about 20°, and place in a constant-temperature bath at 25°. After 30 min, adjust the level of water to the proper point on the pycnometer, and stopper. Remove the pycnometer from the bath, wipe dry with a clean cloth free from lint, and weigh. Empty the pycnometer, rinse several times with alcohol and then with ether, allow to dry completely, remove any ether vapor, and weigh. Determine the weight of the contained water at 25° by subtracting the weight of the pycnometer from its weight when full.

Pass the oil or melted sample through filter paper to remove any impurities and the last traces of moisture, and cool to a few degrees below the temperature at which the determination is to be made. Fill the clean, dry pycnometer with the sample, and place it in the constant-temperature bath at the specified temperature. After 30 min, adjust the level of the oil to the mark on the pycnometer, insert the stopper, wipe dry, and weigh. Subtract the weight of the empty pycnometer from its weight when filled with the sample, and divide the difference by the weight of the water contained at 25°. The quotient is the specific gravity at the temperature of observation, referred to water at 25°.

STABILITY (Fats and Related Substances)

Unless otherwise indicated in the monograph, use *Method I: Active Oxygen Method*.

Method I: Active Oxygen Method (Based on AOCS Method Cd 12-57[1])

Fat stability is the time, in hours, required for a sample of fat or oil to attain a peroxide value of 100. This period of time is determined by interpolation between two measurements and is assumed to be an index of resistance to rancidity. [CAUTION—All equipment must be scrupulously clean. Do not use chromic acid or other acidic cleaning agents. All receptacles in the heater must be calibrated for temperature under the exact conditions of the test. During the test, the temperature must be monitored in a sample tube containing the recommended quantity of oil.]

Apparatus Use a suitable heating block and aeration apparatus, such as shown in JAOCS 33 (1956), pp. 628–630.

Sampling Remove the samples from large containers or processing equipment with sampling devices only of stainless steel, aluminum, nickel, or glass. Solid fat samples should be taken at least 5 cm from the walls of large containers and 2.5 cm from the walls of small containers. If liquid oil is to be poured from a container, clean the spout or lip with an acetone-moistened cloth. Under no circumstances should samples be taken from containers equipped with plastic or enameled tops or paper or wax liners.

Procedure Unless already completely liquid, the sample should be melted at a temperature not more than 10° above its melting point. Pour 20 mL into each of two or more sample tubes ensuring that the sample does not contact the tube where the stopper will later fit. Insert the aeration tube assembly so that the end of the air delivery tube is 5 cm below the surface of the sample. Place the sample tube in a container of vigorously boiling water for 5 min (during this time adjust the air flow rate from the manifold). Remove the tube, wipe dry, and transfer immediately to the constant-temperature heater, maintained at 97.8 ± 0.2°, and connect the aeration tube to the manifold. Determine to the nearest hour the time required for the sample to attain a *Peroxide Value* (in this Appendix) of 100 mEq as follows: With 1-g samples determine when the peroxide value is approximately 75 mEq and 125 mEq, then perform the test on four 5-g samples determining the peroxide value in duplicate at the times corresponding to 75 mEq and 125 mEq. Make a second determination on two 5-g samples exactly 1 h after the first pair. Plot these values against aeration time; the AOM stability value in hours is given where the line crosses 100 mEq.

Method II: Oil Stability Index (Based on AOCS Method Cd 12b-92[1])

The oil stability index (OSI) is an indication of the resistance of a fat or oil to oxidation. It is measured as the length of time required, under specific accelerated oxidation conditions, before a rapid acceleration of oxidation occurs for a test oil or fat, also called the "induction period".

Apparatus The Oxidative Stability Instrument,[6] Rancimat Model 617,[7] or equivalent[8]

Sampling The samples should be kept cool and in the dark. Remove samples from large containers with clean sampling devices only of stainless steel, aluminum, nickel, or glass. Solid fat samples should be taken at least 5 cm from the walls of large containers and 2.5 cm from the walls of small containers. If liquid oil is to be poured, clean the spout with a clean, acetone-moistened cloth. Samples should be protected from heat, light, and air before analysis.

Procedure Fill the conductivity tubes with 50 mL of water (deionized or distilled with conductivity <5 $\mu S \cdot cm^{-1}$) and attach the probes. Verify that the water conductivity in the tube is 25 $\mu S \cdot cm^{-1}$ or less and that the conductivity is constant. Unless already completely liquid, the sample should be melted at a temperature not more than 10° above its melting point. Carefully place a 5.0 ± 0.2-g sample (Oxidative Stability and Rancimat instruments without an insert), or 2.5 ± 0.2-g sample (Rancimat instruments fitted with disposable inserts) into the bottom of the reaction tube, avoiding coating the sides of the tubes and contamination of the samples. Connect tubing from the air manifold to the conductivity measurement tube, adjusting aeration tubes to within 5 mm of the bottom of both the reaction and the conductivity tubes. Adjust the airflow to 2.5 ± 0.2 mL/s unless otherwise indicated in the individual monograph. Set the instrument to the temperature indicated in the individual monograph.

Use a computer or multichannel strip chart recorder to monitor the conductivity of each probe. Plot water conductivity versus time in hours. Calculate the OSI value of the sample as the time in hours that corresponds to the inflection point of the conductivity versus time curve. This time-based end point can be determined either by a microprocessor-computed slope/change algorithm or a maximum of the second derivative, or by the tangential method. [NOTE—Improper temperature control is the most likely source of error for this procedure. Temperature calibration of the instrument should be performed before sample analysis by checking the actual temperature of the sample in the bath. Temperatures during analysis should be maintained within at least ±0.1°. For temperature calibration of the Rancimat instrument, an NIST traceable calibrated platinum resistance (RTD) digital thermometer can be used.[9]]

[NOTE—Water in the effluent trap must not exceed 25° to minimize loss of formic acid.]

[NOTE—Trace-metal contamination of glassware will cause accelerated oxidation; rinse water should be tested; chromate cleaning solutions should not be used; only detergents without surface-active agents should be used for cleaning.]

[NOTE—Reaction tube cleaning procedures for instruments that do not utilize disposable glassware, or for precautionary cleaning of disposable glassware are described elsewhere[8].]

TOCOPHEROLS
(Based on AOCS Method Ce 8-89[1])

[NOTE—All solutions containing tocopherols should be stored in low-actinic glassware, or suitably protected from light.]

Standard Stock Solutions Prepare individual standard stock solutions of α-, β-, γ-, and δ-tocopherol, unless otherwise directed in the monograph, according to the following general procedure.

Transfer 10 mg of suitable tocopherol standard into a 100-mL volumetric flask, and dilute with hexane to volume. Pipet 10 mL of this solution into an amber glass round-bottom flask, and remove all hexane using a suitable rotary evaporator at a temperature not higher than 40°. Restore atmospheric pressure with nitrogen and remove the flask from the evaporator as soon as all solvent has been removed. Dissolve remaining tocopherol residue with 10 mL of methanol. Measure the absorbance (A) of this solution using a suitable spectrophotometer at the wavelength specified in the table below for the individual tocopherol being measured. Calculate the concentration (μg/mL) of the individual tocopherol in the solution:

$$Result = A/(a \times b)$$

in which A is the absorbance of the solution at the measured wavelength; a is the absorptivity of the individual tocopherol from the table below; b is the cell path length (cm).

Tocopherol	Measurement Wavelength (nm)	Absorptivity (mL · μg^{-1} · cm^{-1})
α-tocopherol	292	0.0076
β-tocopherol	296	0.0089
γ-tocopherol	298	0.0091
δ-tocopherol	298	0.0087

[NOTE—The *Standard Stock Solutions* can be stored for up to one week under refrigerated conditions in low-actinic glassware or suitably protected from light.]

Standard Solution Prepare a mixed tocopherol standard solution, unless otherwise directed in the monograph, as follows. Mix appropriate volumes of the individual tocopherol *Standard Stock Solutions*, and dilute with hexane to obtain a solution containing 1–5 μg/mL of each tocopherol.

[NOTE—A more concentrated *Standard Solution* may be necessary if UV detection is used.]

[NOTE—The *Standard Solution* should be prepared fresh daily and stored under refrigerated conditions in low-actinic glassware or suitably protected from light.]

---

[6] Omnion Inc., Rockland, MA, USA (manufactured under license from Archer Daniel Midland Co., Decatur, IL, USA).
[7] Brinkmann Instruments, Inc., Westbury NY, USA (subsidiary of Sybron Corporation).
[8] Suitable alternative equipment is described in AOCS Official Method Cd 12b-92. Official Methods and Recommended Practices of the American Oil Chemists' Society. American Oil Chemists' Society, 5th Edn, Champaign, IL.
[9] Omega Engineering, Inc. (Stanford, CT) provides such a thermometer. A custom 3 wire 2-mm × 7-mm sensor probe is required for calibration of sample temperature with air flowing through the sample.

Test Solution Accurately weigh 2 g of the sample into a 25-mL volumetric flask. Add hexane to dissolve the sample, and dilute with hexane to volume. [NOTE—If a fluorescence detector is used, it may be necessary to further dilute this test solution before analysis.]

[NOTE—The *Test Solution* should be prepared and analyzed on the same day, and stored in low-actinic glassware or suitably protected from light.]

Apparatus Use a suitable high-performance liquid chromatography system (see *Chromatography*, Appendix IIA) equipped with either a UV (292 nm) or fluorescence (290 nm excitation and 330 nm emission) detector, or as directed in the monograph. Use a 250-mm × 4-mm analytical column packed with a 5-μm microparticulate silica[10].

Operating Conditions [NOTE—New columns should be washed and conditioned for 10 min with methanol, then dicholormethane, followed by hexane at 1 mL/min. All columns should be equilibrated, if necessary with mobile phase for 30 min before analysis.]

Mobile phase Isopropanol in hexane (0.5:99.5, v/v)

Flow rate About 1 mL/min

Injection volume About 20 μL

System Suitability Inject the *Standard Solution* into the chromatograph, and measure the peak responses on the resulting chromatograms. The retention time for α-tocopherol is NLT 5 min. The resolution, R, between β- and γ-tocopherol is NLT 1.0. The relative standard deviation for the α-tocopherol peak area for replicate injections is NMT 5%.

Procedure Inject the *Test Solution* into the chromatograph, and measure the peak responses on the resulting chromatograms. The relative retention times for α-, β-, γ-, and δ-tocopherol are approximately 1.0, 1.6, 3.0, and 1.7, respectively. Separately calculate the concentration, in mg/kg, of each tocopherol in the portion of the sample taken:

$$\text{Result} = (r_U/r_S) \times (C_S/C_U)$$

in which r_U is the peak response for tocopherol from the *Test Solution*; r_S is the peak response for tocopherol from the *Standard Solution*; C_S is the concentration of tocopherol in the *Standard Solution* (μg/mL); and C_U is the concentration of sample in the *Test Solution* (g/mL).

UNSAPONIFIABLE MATTER
(Based on AOCS Methods Ca 6a-40 and Ca 6b-53[1], respectively)

Unless indicated otherwise in the individual monograph, use *Method I*.

Method I
This procedure determines those substances frequently found dissolved in fatty materials that cannot be saponified by alkali hydroxides but that are soluble in the ordinary fat solvents.

Procedure Accurately weigh 5.0 g of the sample into a 250-mL flask, add a solution of 2 g of potassium hydroxide in 40 mL of alcohol, and boil gently under a reflux condenser for 1 h or until saponification is complete. Transfer the contents of the flask to a glass-stoppered extraction cylinder (approximately 30 cm in length, 3.5 cm in diameter, and graduated at 40 mL, 80 mL, and 130 mL). Wash the flask with sufficient alcohol to make a volume of 40 mL in the cylinder, and complete the transfer with warm and then cold water until the total volume is 80 mL. Finally, wash the flask with a few mL of petroleum ether, add the washings to the cylinder, cool the contents of the cylinder to room temperature, and add 50 mL of petroleum ether.

Insert the stopper, shake the cylinder vigorously for at least 1 min, and allow both layers to become clear. Siphon the upper layer as completely as possible without removing any of the lower layer, collecting the ether fraction in a 500-mL separator. Repeat the extraction and siphoning at least six times with 50-mL portions of petroleum ether, shaking vigorously each time. Wash the combined extracts, with vigorous shaking, with 25-mL portions of 10% alcohol until the wash water is neutral to phenolphthalein, and discard the washings. Transfer the ether extract to a tared beaker, and rinse the separator with 10 mL of ether, adding the rinsings to the beaker. Evaporate the ether on a steam bath just to dryness, and dry the residue to constant weight, preferably at 75°–80° under a vacuum of not more than 200 mm Hg, or at 100° for 30 min. Cool in a desiccator, and weigh to obtain the uncorrected weight of unsaponifiable matter.

Determine the quantity of fatty acids in the residue as follows: Dissolve the residue in 50 mL of warm alcohol (containing phenolphthalein TS and previously neutralized with sodium hydroxide to a faint pink color), and titrate with 0.02 N sodium hydroxide to the same color. Each mL of 0.02 N sodium hydroxide is equivalent to 5.659 mg of fatty acids, calculated as oleic acid.

Subtract the calculated weight of fatty acids from the weight of the residue to obtain the corrected weight of unsaponifiable matter in the sample.

Method II
This procedure determines those substances frequently found dissolved in fats and oils that cannot be saponified by the usual caustic treatment, but are soluble in ordinary fat and oil solvents. Included in this group of compounds are higher aliphatic alcohols, sterols, pigments, and hydrocarbons. This method is applicable to fats and oils containing higher levels of unsaponifiable matter than usually found in normal tallows and greases. It is especially suited for marine oils.

Procedure Accurately weigh 2.0–2.5 g of the well-mixed sample into a 250-mL conical flask with a ground-glass joint. Add 25 mL of alcohol and 1.5 mL of a 50% (w/w) aqueous solution of potassium hydroxide. Boil the contents of the flask gently but steadily under reflux with occasional swirling for 30 min or until saponification is complete. The material must be completely saponified before proceeding. No loss of alcohol should occur during saponification. Transfer the warm solution to a graduated, glass-stoppered extraction cylinder with a capacity of about 200 mL, using a total of 50 mL of water. [CAUTION—Alcohol is flammable.] Wash the conical flask with 50 mL of diethyl ether, and add the washing to the extraction cylinder. Cool the contents of the cylinder to room temperature.

---
[10] LiChrosorb SI 60, Spherisorb S5W, or equivalent.

Insert the stopper into the extraction cylinder, and shake vigorously for at least 1 min. Allow the contents to settle until both layers are clear. Use a glass siphon to remove the upper layer as completely as possible without including any of the lower portion. [NOTE—A 500-mL separatory funnel may be used in place of the extraction cylinder and siphon. If this substitution is made, draw off the lower aqueous layer into a second separatory funnel, retaining the diethyl ether extract in the first funnel. Repeat the diethyl ether extraction of the aqueous phase, as noted above, combining all of the diethyl ether extracts in the first separatory funnel.] Transfer the diethyl ether layer to a 250-mL separatory funnel. Repeat this extraction two more times, using 50-mL portions of diethyl ether each time and shaking vigorously with each extraction. If necessary, continue extracting with diethyl ether until no more unsaponifiable material remains. Rotate the combined diethyl ether extracts gently with 20 mL of water. Violent agitation at this step may result in emulsions that are difficult to break. Allow the layers to separate completely, and draw off the lower aqueous layer. Wash the diethyl ether layer two more times, using 20 mL of water each time and shaking gently each time, discarding the lower aqueous layer after separation.

Wash the combined extracts in the separatory funnel three times, using 20-mL portions of 0.5 N potassium hydroxide, and shaking vigorously. Follow each alkali washing by washing with 20 mL of water. If an emulsion forms during this washing procedure, allow to separate as much as possible, discard the clear aqueous layer, and proceed with the next step, leaving any emulsion in the separatory funnel with the diethyl ether layer. After the third washing with 0.5 N potassium hydroxide, wash the diethyl ether with successive 20-mL portions of water until the washings are no longer alkaline to phenolphthalein.

Transfer the diethyl ether extract to a tared beaker, rinsing the separatory funnel and its pouring edge with diethyl ether and adding the rinsings to the solution in the beaker. Evaporate to dryness in a water bath, using a gentle stream of clean, dry nitrogen. When almost all of the diethyl ether has been evaporated, add 2–3 mL of acetone, and remove all traces of solvent with the aid of a stream of nitrogen. Complete the drying to constant weight in a vacuum oven at 75°–80° and an internal pressure of NMT 200 mm of mercury. Cool in a desiccator, and weigh to obtain the mass of the residue, A, in grams.

After weighing the residue, add to it 2 mL of diethyl ether and then 10 mL of alcohol that contains phenolphthalein indicator. The alcohol used should be previously neutralized to the phenolphthalein endpoint. Titrate the solution with 0.02 N sodium hydroxide to the same final color. Correct the weight of the residue for free fatty acid content, B, in grams, using the following relationship: 1 mL of 0.02 N sodium hydroxide is equivalent to 0.0056 g of oleic acid. A reagent blank correction should also be determined as, C, in grams.

Calculate the percent of unsaponifiable matter in the sample:

$$Result = [A - (B + C)]/W \times 100$$

in which W is the mass, in grams, of the sample used.

VOLATILE ACIDITY

Modified Hortvet-Sellier Method

Apparatus Assemble a modified Hortvet-Sellier distillation apparatus as shown in *Figure 3*, using a sufficiently large (approximately 38-mm × 203-mm) inner Sellier tube and large distillation trap.

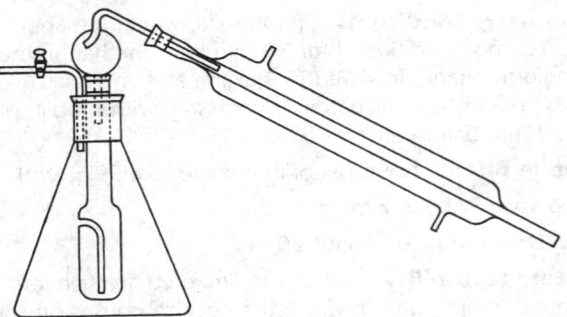

Figure 3. Modified Hortvet-Sellier Distillation Apparatus

Procedure Transfer the amount of sample, accurately weighed and as specified in the monograph, into the inner tube of the assembly, and insert the tube in the outer flask containing about 300 mL of recently boiled hot water. To the sample add 10 mL of approximately 4 N perchloric acid [35 mL (60 g) of 70% perchloric acid in 100 mL of water], and connect the inner tube to a water-cooled condenser through the distillation trap. Distill by heating the outer flask so that 100 mL of distillate is collected within 20–25 min. Collect the distillate in 100-mL portions, add phenolphthalein TS to each portion, and titrate with 0.5 N sodium hydroxide. Continue the distillation until a 100-mL portion of the distillate requires no more than 0.5 mL of 0.5 N sodium hydroxide for neutralization.

[**CAUTION**—Do not distill to dryness.]

Calculate the weight, in mg, of volatile acids in the sample taken:

$$Result = V \times e$$

in which V is the total volume, in mL, of 0.5 N sodium hydroxide consumed in the series of titrations, and e is the equivalence factor given in the monograph.

APPENDIX VIII: OLEORESINS

COLOR VALUE (Oleoresins)

Sample Preparation Transfer 70–100 mg of the sample, previously mixed well by shaking and accurately weighed, into a 100-mL volumetric flask, dissolve in acetone, dilute with acetone to volume, and mix. Allow the solution to stand for 2 min, then pipet 10 mL into a second 100-mL volumetric flask, dilute to volume with acetone, and mix.

Procedure Determine the absorbance of the *Sample Preparation* with a suitable spectrophotometer in a 1-cm cell at 460 nm, using acetone as the blank. Record the value obtained as A_S. In the same manner, determine the absorbance of a National Institute of Standards and Technology Standard Glass Filter 930, and record the value obtained as A_F.

[NOTE—The recommended range for absorbance values is 0.30–0.70. Solutions having absorbances greater than 0.70 should be diluted with acetone to one-half the original concentration, and those having absorbances less than 0.30 should be discarded and the *Sample Preparation* prepared with a larger sample. Appropriate adjustments should be made in the sample weight (W) used in the *Calculation* below.]

Calculation Determine the instrument correction factor, F:

$$\text{Result} = A_N/A_F$$

in which A_N is the absorbance of the filter as stated by the National Institute of Standards and Technology. Calculate the color value of the sample:

$$\text{Result} = (A_S \times 164 \times F)/W$$

in which W is the weight, in g, of the sample taken.

CURCUMIN CONTENT

Sample Preparation Transfer about 500 mg of the sample, accurately weighed, into a 100-mL volumetric flask, and record the weight, in mg, as W. Dissolve the sample in about 75 mL of acetone, dilute with acetone to volume, and mix. Pipet a 5-mL portion of this solution into a second 100-mL volumetric flask, dilute with acetone to volume, and mix. Finally, pipet a 1-mL portion of the last solution into a 50-mL volumetric flask, dilute with acetone to volume, and mix.

[NOTE—Protect all solutions from light by using active glassware or by covering the glassware with aluminum foil. Make the absorbance readings as soon as possible after the solutions are prepared.]

Procedure Determine the absorbance of the *Sample Preparation* in a 1-cm cell at the wavelength of maximum absorption 420–425 nm with a suitable spectrophotometer, using acetone as the blank. Calculate the percent curcumin in the sample:

$$\text{Result} = (A \times 100)(165 \times b \times c)$$

in which A is the absorbance of the *Sample Preparation*; 100 is the conversion to percent; 165 is the absorptivity factor, in liters per gram-centimeter, for curcumin; b is the path length of the cell; and c is the concentration, in grams per liter, of the solution presented to the spectrophotometer. Calculate c:

$$\text{Result} = W \times 5 \times 10^6$$

in which W is the starting weight, in mg, of the sample, and 5×10^6 is the conversion factor for the dilution schedule.

PIPERINE CONTENT

Stock Standard Solution Purify piperine by repeated crystallization from isopropanol until a product having a melting range of 129°–130° is obtained. Transfer 100.0 mg of the crystals, accurately weighed, into a 100-mL volumetric flask, dissolve in ethylene dichloride, dilute with ethylene dichloride to volume, and mix. Pipet 10.0 mL of this solution into a second 100-mL volumetric flask, dilute with ethylene dichloride to volume, and mix.

Standard Dilutions Pipet 1.0 mL, 3.0 mL, 5.0 mL, and 10.0 mL of the *Stock Standard Solution* (corresponding to 0.1 mg, 0.3 mg, 0.5 mg, and 1.0 mg of piperine, respectively) into separate 100-mL volumetric flasks, dilute each flask with ethylene dichloride to volume, and mix. Determine the absorbance of each dilution at once, as directed in the *Procedure*.

Sample Preparation Heat a portion of the sample to 100° on a steam bath or in an oven (but not on a hot plate), mix with a glass stirring rod, and transfer 100 mg, accurately weighed, into a 100-mL volumetric flask. Dissolve in ethylene dichloride, dilute with ethylene dichloride to volume, and mix. Pipet 1.0 mL of this solution into a second 100-mL volumetric flask, dilute with ethylene dichloride to volume, and mix. Determine the absorbance of the solution at once, as directed in the *Procedure*.

Procedure Determine the absorbance of the *Sample Preparation* and of each of the *Standard Dilutions* in 1-cm cells at the wavelength of maximum absorption at about 342 nm with a suitable spectrophotometer, using ethylene dichloride as the blank. Prepare a standard curve of concentration, in mg per 100 mL, versus absorbance for the four *Standard Dilutions*, including the absorbance at zero concentration obtained with the blank. From the standard curve, determine the concentration of piperine in the *Sample Preparation*, and record the value as C, in mg per 100 mL. Calculate the percentage of piperine in the sample:

$$\text{Result} = 100 \times (100C/W)$$

in which W is the weight, in mg, of the sample taken.

RESIDUAL SOLVENT (Oleoresins)

This procedure is for the determination of acetone, ethylene dichloride, hexane, isopropanol, methanol, methylene chloride, and trichloroethylene residues.

Distilling Head Use a Clevenger trap designed for use with oils heavier than water. A suitable design is shown in *Figure 1a*.

Toluene The toluene used for this analysis should not contain any of the solvents determined by this method. The purity may be determined by gas chromatographic analysis, using one of the following columns or their equivalent: (1) 17% by weight of Ucon 75-H-90,000 on 35/80-mesh Chromosorb W; (2) 20% Ucon LB-135 on 35/80-mesh Chromosorb W; (3) 15% Ucon LB-1715 on 60/80-mesh Chromosorb W; or (4) Porapak Q 50/60 mesh. Follow the conditions described under *Procedure*, and inject the same amount of toluene as will be injected in the analysis of the solvents. If impurities interfering with the test are present, they will appear as peaks occurring before the toluene peak and should be removed by fractional distillation.

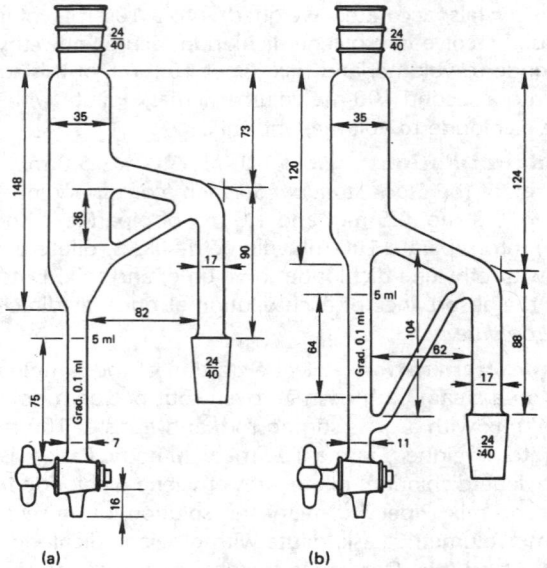

Figure 1. Clevenger Traps (all measurements are in mm) (a) Oils Heavier Than Water; (b) Oils Lighter Than Water

Benzene The benzene used for this analysis should be free from interfering impurities. The purity may be determined as described under *Toluene*.

Detergent and Antifoam Any such products that are free from volatile compounds may be used. If volatile compounds are present, they may be removed by prolonged boiling of the aqueous solutions of the products.

Reference Solution A Prepare a solution in *Toluene* containing 2500 ppm of benzene. If the toluene available contains benzene as the only impurity, the benzene level can be determined by gas chromatography and sufficient benzene added to bring the level to 2500 ppm.

Reference Solution B Prepare a solution containing 0.63% v/w of acetone in water.

Sample Preparation A (all solvents except methanol) Place 50.0 g of the sample, 1.00 mL of *Reference Solution A*, 10 g of anhydrous sodium sulfate, 50 mL of water, and a small amount each of *Detergent* and *Antifoam* in a 250-mL round-bottom flask with a 24/40 ground-glass neck. Attach the *Distilling Head*, a 400-mm water-cooled condenser, and a receiver, and collect approximately 15 mL of distillate. Add 15 g of anhydrous potassium carbonate to the distillate, cool while shaking, and allow the phases to separate. All of the solvents except methanol will be present in the toluene layer, which is used in the *Procedure*. Draw off the aqueous layer for use in *Sample Preparation B*.

Sample Preparation B (methanol only) Place the aqueous layer obtained from *Sample Preparation A* in a 50-mL round-bottom distilling flask with a 24/40 ground-glass neck, add a few boiling chips and 1.00 mL of *Reference Solution B*, and collect approximately 1 mL of distillate, which will contain any methanol from the sample, together with acetone as the internal standard. The distillate is used in the *Procedure*.

Procedure Use a gas chromatograph equipped with a hot-wire detector and a suitable sample-injection system or on-column injection. Under typical conditions, the instrument contains a 1/4-in. (od) × 6- to 8-ft column, or equivalent, maintained isothermally at 70°–80°. The flow rate of dry carrier gas is 50–80 mL/min, and the sample size is 15–20 µL (for the hot-wire detector). The column selected for use in the chromatograph depends on the components to be analyzed and, to a certain extent, on the preference of the analyst. The columns 1, 2, 3, and 4, as described under *Toluene*, may be used as follows: (1) This column separates acetone and methanol from their aqueous solution. It may be used for the separation and analysis of hexane, acetone, and trichloroethylene in the toluene layer from *Sample Preparation A*. The elution order is acetone, methanol, and water, or hexane, acetone, isopropanol plus methylene chloride, benzene, trichloroethylene, and ethylene dichloride plus toluene. (2) This column separates methylene chloride and isopropanol, and ethylene dichloride. The elution order is hexane plus acetone, methylene chloride, isopropanol, benzene, ethylene dichloride, trichloroethylene, and toluene. (3) This is the best general-purpose column, except for the determination of methanol. The elution order is hexane, acetone, benzene, ethylene dichloride, and toluene. (4) This column is used for the determination of methanol, which elutes just after the large water peak.

Calibration Determine the response of the detector for known ratios of solvents by injecting known mixtures of solvents and benzene in toluene. The levels of the solvents and benzene in toluene should be of the same magnitude as they will be present in the sample under analysis.

Calculate the areas of the solvents with respect to benzene, and then calculate the calibration factor, F, as follows:

F (solvent) = (wt % solvent/wt % benzene) × (area of benzene/area of solvent)

The recovery of the various solvents from the oleoresin sample, with respect to the recovery of benzene, is as follows: hexane, 52%; acetone, 85%; isopropanol, 100%; methylene chloride, 87.5%; trichloroethylene, 113%; ethylene dichloride, 102%; and methanol, 87%.

Calculation Calculate the ppm of residual solvent (except methanol):

Residual solvent = {[43.4 × F (solvent) × 100]/[% recovery of solvent]} × (area of solvent/area of benzene)

in which 43.4 is the ppm of benzene internal standard, related to the 50-g oleoresin sample taken for analysis. Calculate the ppm of residual methanol:

Methanol = {[100 × F (methanol)]/0.87} × (area of methanol/area of benzene)

in which 100 is the ppm of acetone internal standard, related to the 50-g oleoresin sample taken for analysis.

TOTAL CAPSAICINOIDS CONTENT

Standard Solution 0.5 mg/mL of USP Capsaicin RS in methanol

Test Solution Transfer the equivalent to about 1000 mg of capsicum oleoresin, accurately weighed, to a 100-mL volumetric flask, dissolve in and dilute with methanol to volume, and mix.

Apparatus Use a suitable high-performance liquid chromatographic system (see *Chromatography*, Appendix IIA) equipped with a UV detector (280 nm). Use an online 0.45-μm filter, and a 30-cm × 3.9-cm (id) stainless steel column or equivalent, packed with octadecylsilane (C18) chemically bonded to porous silica or ceramic micro-particles of 1.5–10 μm particle size.[1]

Mobile Phase Mixture of methanol and 2% acetic acid (56:44, v/v), filtered through a 0.5-μm or finer porosity filter, and degassed

Suitability Requirements Allow the chromatographic system to equilibrate at a flow rate of 2 mL/min, then inject 10 μL of the *Standard Solution*. The relative retention times for nordihydrocapsaicin, capsaicin, and dihydrocapsaicin are about 0.9, 1.0, and 1.6, respectively. The resolution between the norhydrocapsaicin peak and the capsaicin peak is NLT 1.2. The tailing factor is NMT 2.0, and the relative standard deviation for replicate injections is NMT 2.0%.

Procedure Separately inject equal volumes (about 10 μL) of the *Standard Solution* and *Test Solution* into the chromatograph, record the chromatograms, and measure the responses for the three major peaks. Use peak areas where responses are indicated. Calculate the percentage of total capsaicins in the portion of capsicum oleoresin taken:

Result = (C/W) × (r_U/r_S)

in which C is the concentration of USP Capsaicin RS in the *Standard Solution* corrected for purity based on the USP label claim (mg/mL); W is the weight of capsicum oleoresin in the sample used to prepare the *Test Solution* (mg); r_U is the sum of the peak responses for nordihydrocapsaicin, capsaicin, and dihydrocapsaicin obtained from the sample; and r_S is the peak response obtained from the capsaicin in the *Standard Solution*.

[NOTE—1.0 μg total capsaicinoids/g = ca 15 Scoville Heat Units (SHU)]

VOLATILE OIL CONTENT (Oleoresins)

Weigh accurately an amount of the sample sufficient to yield 2–5 mL of volatile oil, and transfer with the aid of water into a 1000- or 2000-mL round-bottom shortneck flask with a 24/40 ground-glass neck. Add a magnetic stirring bar and about 500 mL of water, and connect a Clevenger trap of the proper type (see *Figures 1a* and *1b*) and a 400-mm water-cooled condenser. Heat the flask with stirring, and distill at a rate of 1–1.5 drops per s until two consecutive readings taken at 1-h intervals show no change of oil volume in the trap. Cool to room temperature, allow to stand until the oil layer is clear, and read the volume of oil collected, estimating to the nearest 0.02 mL. Calculate the percentage (v/w) of volatile oil in the sample:

Result = 100(V/W)

in which V is the volume, in mL, of oil collected, and W is the weight, in g, of the sample taken.

---

[1] μBondapack C18, Waters Corp., or equivalent.

APPENDIX IX: ROSINS AND RELATED SUBSTANCES

ACID NUMBER (Rosins and Related Substances)

The acid number is the number of mg of potassium hydroxide required to neutralize the free acids in 1 g of the test substance.

Procedure Unless otherwise directed in the individual monograph, transfer about 4 g of the sample, previously crushed into small lumps and accurately weighed, into a 250-mL Erlenmeyer flask, and add 100 mL of a 1:3 mixture of toluene–isopropyl alcohol, previously neutralized to phenolphthalein TS with sodium hydroxide. Dissolve the sample by shaking or heating gently, if necessary, then add about 0.5 mL of phenolphthalein TS, and titrate with 0.5 N or 0.1 N alcoholic potassium hydroxide to the first pink color that persists for 30 s. Calculate the acid number by the formula

$$\text{Result} = 56.1V \times N/W,$$

in which V is the exact volume, in mL, and N is the exact normality, respectively, of the potassium hydroxide solution, and W is the weight, in g, of the sample.

SOFTENING POINT

Drop Method

The *drop softening point* is that temperature at which a given weight of rosin or rosin derivative begins to drop from the bulb of a special thermometer mounted in a test tube that is immersed in a constant-temperature bath.

Apparatus The apparatus illustrated in *Fig. 1* consists of the components described in the following paragraphs.

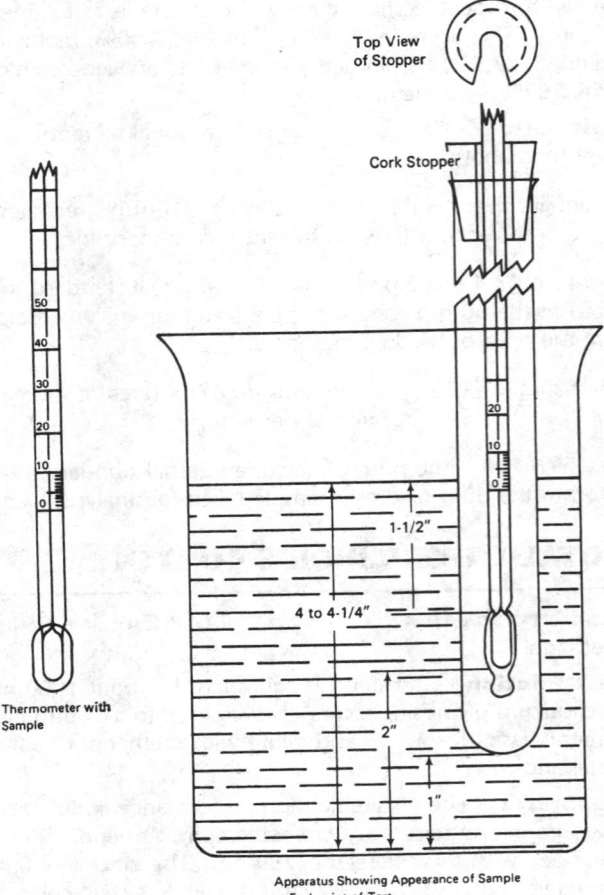

Figure 1. Apparatus for Drop Softening Point Determination

Thermometer Use a special total-immersion softening point thermometer,[1] covering the range from 0° to 250° and graduated in 10 divisions. The bulb should be 15.9 ± 0.8 mm in length and 6.35 ± 0.4 mm in diameter.

Heating Bath Use an 800- to 2000-mL beaker containing a suitable heating medium. For rosins having a softening point below 80°, use water; for those having softening points above 80°, use glycerin or silicone oil, depending upon the temperature range required. Maintain the temperature of the heating medium within ±1° of the temperature specified in the individual monograph. Stir the bath medium constantly during the test with a suitable mechanical stirrer to ensure uniform heating of the medium.

Test Tube Use a standard 22-mm od × 200- to 250-mm test tube with a rim, fitted with a cork stopper as shown in *Fig. 1*.

---

[1] Available from the Walter K. Kessler Co., Inc.

Sample Preparation Place about 20 g of the sample in a 50-mL beaker, and heat it in an oven, on a sand bath or hot plate, or in an oil bath until the sample becomes soft enough to mold on the thermometer bulb. Tare the softening point thermometer, and cautiously warm the bulb over a hot plate until it registers 15° to 20° above the expected softening point of the sample. Immediately dip the thermometer bulb into the melted sample, withdraw, and rotate it to deposit a uniform film of the molten sample over the surface of the bulb, taking care not to extend the film higher than the top of the bulb. Quickly place the thermometer on a balance, and weigh. The weight of the sample on the thermometer bulb should be between 0.5 and 0.55 g. If the weight is low, again dip the bulb in the molten sample; if the weight is high, pull off some of the sample with the fingers. When the correct sample weight has been obtained, mold the sample uniformly around the bulb by rolling it on the palm of the hand or between the fingers. The sample must be of uniform thickness over the bulb, and it must not extend up onto the thermometer stem (see *Fig. 1*). (If the film of the sample is not uniform when cooled, remove it completely from the bulb and apply a new one. Do not reheat the film and try to remold it.) Allow the film and thermometer to cool to approximately 35° or lower, allowing about 15 min for cooling.

[NOTE—If samples having high softening points crack or "check" on the thermometer bulb upon cooling to room temperature, prepare another sample film and cool only to about 50° below the expected softening point.]

Procedure Fill the glass beaker to a depth of not less than 101.6 mm or more than 108 mm with a suitable heating medium; support the beaker over a Bunsen burner, hot plate, or other suitable source of heat; and insert the bath stirrer and a bath temperature thermometer. Place the stirrer to one side so that the impeller clears the side of the beaker and is about 12.7 mm above the bottom of the beaker. Start the stirrer, heat the bath to the temperature specified in the individual monograph, and maintain this temperature within ±1° throughout the test.

Insert the prepared sample thermometer in the test tube, supporting it with a notched cork stopper so that the lower end of the bulb is 25.4 mm from the bottom of the test tube. Place the test tube in the bath so that the bottom of the thermometer bulb is 50.8 mm from the bottom of the beaker; the top of the bulb should be about 25.4 to 38.1 mm below the liquid level of the bath. Stir the bath to keep its temperature uniform throughout. Observe the sample thermometer, and record as the softening point the reading at which the elongated drop of sample on the end of the bulb first becomes constricted (see *Fig. 1*). Report the softening point to the nearest 1.0°.

[CAUTION—If the rosin crystallizes, thus making it difficult to obtain the correct softening point, prepare a new sample by heating the rosin rapidly, yet cautiously, over a flame to a temperature of 160° to 170° to destroy all crystal nuclei. Dip the thermometer bulb into the molten resin, remove it momentarily, and rotate the thermometer to provide a uniform resin film on the bulb as it partially cools in the air. Dip the bulb in the melted sample repeatedly until the proper amount of resin is deposited on the bulb. Do not report results if a crystal-free sample cannot be obtained.]

Ring-and-Ball Method
The *ring-and-ball softening point* is the temperature at which a disk of the sample held within a horizontal ring is forced downward a distance of 25.4 mm under the weight of a steel ball as the sample is heated at a prescribed rate in a water, glycerin, or silicone oil (Dow Corning 200 fluid 50 cs or an equivalent is suitable) bath.

Apparatus Ring-and-ball softening point may be determined manually using the apparatus described below. Automated apparatus may be used provided equivalent results are obtained. The calibration of any automated apparatus should be monitored on a regular basis because accurate temperature control is required. The apparatus illustrated in *Figs. 2* and *Figs. 3* consists of the components described in the following paragraphs.

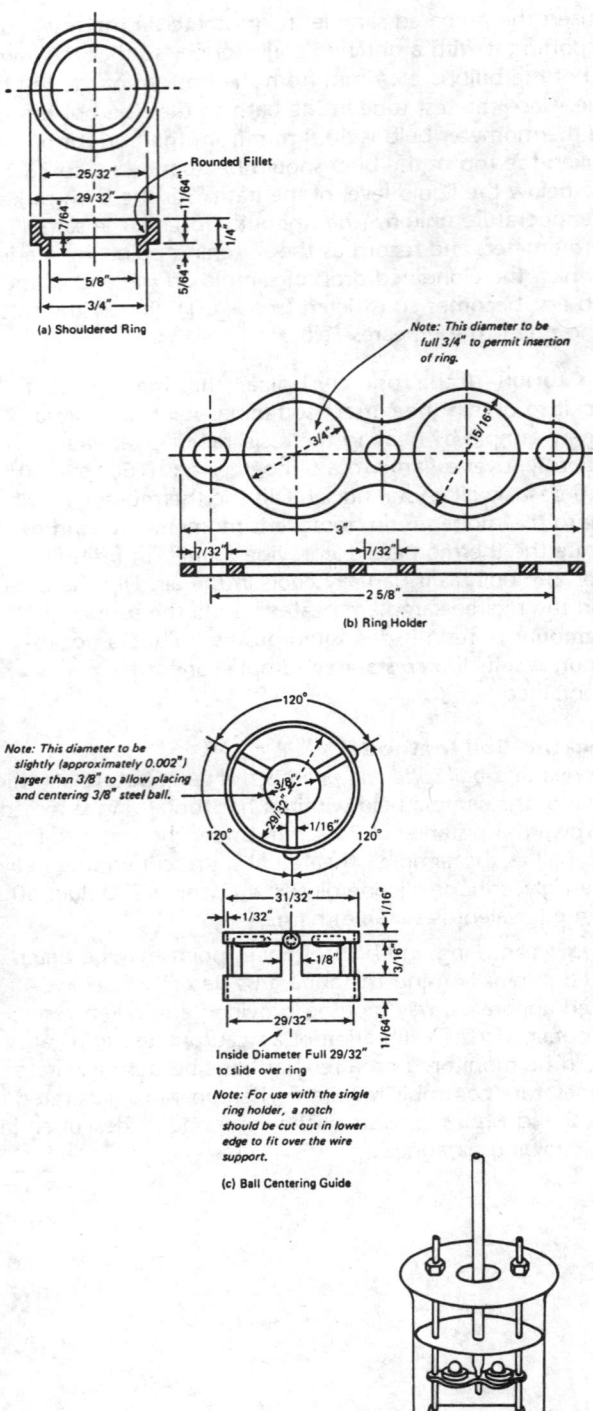

Figure 2. Shouldered Ring, Ring Holder, Ball-Centering Guide, and Assembly of Apparatus Showing Two Rings

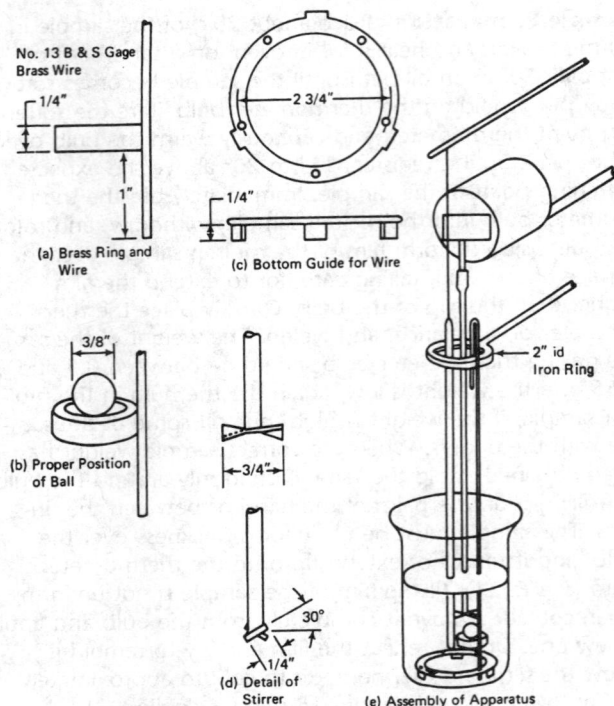

Figure 3. Assembly of Apparatus Showing Stirrer and Single-Shouldered Ring

Ring Use a brass-shouldered ring conforming to the dimensions shown in *Fig. 2a*. If desired, the ring may be attached by brazing or other convenient manner to a brass wire of about 13 B & S gauge (1.52 to 2.03 mm in diameter) as shown in *Fig. 3a*.

Ball Use a steel ball, 9.53 mm in diameter, weighing between 3.45 and 3.55 g.

Ball-Centering Guide If desired, center the ball by using a guide constructed of brass and having the general shape and dimensions illustrated in *Fig. 2c*.

Container Use a heat-resistant glass vessel, such as an 800-mL low-form Griffin beaker, not less than 85 mm in diameter and not less than 127 mm in depth from the bottom of the flare.

Support for Ring and Thermometer Use any convenient device for supporting the ring and thermometer, provided that it meets the following requirements: (1) the ring is supported in a substantially horizontal position; (2) when the apparatus shown in *Fig. 2d* is used, the bottom of the ring is 25.4 mm above the horizontal plate below it, the bottom surface of the horizontal plate is 12.7 to 19 mm above the bottom of the container, and the depth of the liquid in the container is not less than 101.6 mm; (3) if the apparatus shown in *Fig. 3e* is used, the bottom of the ring is 25.4 mm above the bottom of the container, with the bottom end of the rod resting on the bottom of the container, and the depth of the liquid in the container is not less than 101.6 mm, as shown in *Figs. 3a, b,* and *c*; and (4) in both assemblies, the thermometer is suspended so that the bottom of the bulb is level with the bottom of the ring and within 12.7 mm of, but not touching, the ring.

Thermometers Depending on the expected softening point of the sample, use either an ASTM 15C or 15F low-softening-point thermometer (−2° to 80°) or an ASTM 16C or 16F high-softening-point thermometer (30° to 200°), as described under *Thermometers*, Appendix I.

Stirrer Use a suitable mechanical stirrer rotating between 500 and 700 rpm. To ensure uniform heat distribution in the heating medium, the direction of the shaft rotation should move the liquid upward. (See *Fig. 3d* for recommended dimensions.)

Sample Preparation Select a representative sample of the material under test consisting of freshly broken lumps free of oxidized surfaces. Immediately before use, scrape off the surface layer of samples received as lumps, avoiding inclusion of finely divided material or dust. The amount of sample taken should be at least twice that necessary to fill the desired number of rings, but in no case less than 40 g. Immediately melt the sample in a clean container, using an oven, hot plate, or sand or oil bath to prevent local overheating. Avoid incorporating air bubbles in the melting sample, which must not be heated above the temperature necessary to pour the material readily without inclusion of air bubbles. The time from the beginning of heating to the pouring of the sample shall not exceed 15 min. Immediately before filling the rings, preheat them to approximately the same temperature at which the sample is to be poured. While being filled, the rings should rest on an aluminum or steel plate. Pour a sufficient amount of the sample into the rings to leave an excess on cooling. Cool for at least 30 min, and then cut the excess material off cleanly with a slightly heated knife or spatula. Use a clean container and a fresh sample if the test is repeated.

Procedure

Materials Having Softening Points above 80° Fill the glass vessel with glycerin to a depth of not less than 101.6 mm and not more than 107.95 mm. The starting temperature of the bath shall be 32°. For resins (including rosin), cool the bath liquid to not less than 27° below the anticipated softening point, but in no case lower than 35°. Position the axis of the stirrer shaft near the back wall of the container, with the blades clearing the wall and with the bottom of the blades 19 mm above the top of the ring. Unless the ball-centering guide is used, make a slight indentation in the center of the sample by pressing the ball or a rounded rod, slightly heated for hard materials, into the sample at this point. Suspend the ring containing the sample in the bath so that the lower surface of the filled ring is 25.4 mm above the upper surface of the lower horizontal plate (see *Fig. 2d*), which is at least 12.7 mm and not more than 19 mm above the bottom of the glass vessel, or 25.4 mm above the bottom of the container (see *Fig. 3e*). Place the ball in the bath but not on the test specimen. Suspend an ASTM high-softening-point thermometer (16C or 16F) in the bath so that the bottom of its bulb is level with the bottom of the ring and within 12.7 mm of, but not touching, the ring. Maintain the initial temperature of the bath for 15 min. Begin stirring, and continue stirring at 500 to 700 rpm until the determination is complete. Apply heat in such a manner that the temperature of the bath liquid is raised 5° per min, avoiding the effects of drafts by using shields if necessary.

[NOTE—The rate of rise of the temperature should be uniform and should not be averaged over the test period. Reject all tests in which the rate of rise exceeds ±0.5° for any min period after the first three.]

Record as the softening point the temperature of the thermometer at the instant the sample touches the lower horizontal plate (see *Fig. 2d*) or the bottom of the container (see *Fig. 3e*). Make no correction for the emergent stem of the thermometer.

Materials Having Softening Points of 80° or Below Follow the above procedure, except use an ASTM low-softening-point thermometer (15C or 15F) and use freshly boiled water cooled to 5° as the heating medium. For resins (including rosins), use water cooled to not less than 27° below the anticipated softening point, but in no case lower than 5°. Report the softening point to the nearest 1.0°.

VISCOSITY (Rosins and Related Substances)

Unless otherwise directed in the individual monograph, transfer the prepared sample into a 8-oz wide-mouth glass jar, 10.8 cm high and 7 cm in inside diameter, equipped with a screw lid. Condition the sample in a water bath at 25 ± 0.2° for 30 min (±5 min), taking care to prevent water from coming into contact with the sample. Insert a No. 4 spindle in a Bookfield Model RVF viscometer,[2] or equivalent, and move the jar into place under the spindle, adjusting the elevation of the jar so tha the upper surface of the sample is in the center of the shaft indentation and the spindle is in the center of the jar.

[NOTE—Keep the viscometer level at all times during the test procedure.]

Set the viscometer to rotate at 20 rpm, and allow the spindle to rotate until a constant dial reading is obtained. The viscosity, in centipoise, is the dial reading on the 0 to 100 scale multiplied by the appropriate factor (for a Brookfield RVF, spindle No. 4, 20 rpm, the factor is 100).

---

[2] Available from Bookfield Engineering Laboratories, Inc., Stoughton, MA.

APPENDIX X: CARBOHYDRATES (STARCHES, SUGARS, AND RELATED SUBSTANCES)

ACETYL GROUPS

Transfer about 5 g of the sample, accurately weighed, into a 250-mL Erlenmeyer flask, suspend in 50 mL of water, add a few drops of phenolphthalein TS, and titrate with 0.1 N sodium hydroxide to a permanent pink endpoint. Add 25.0 mL of 0.45 N sodium hydroxide, stopper the flask, and shake vigorously for 30 min, preferably with a mechanical shaker. Remove the stopper, wash the stopper and sides of the flask with a few mL of water, and titrate the excess alkali with 0.2 N hydrochloric acid to the disappearance of the pink color, recording the volume, in mL, of 0.2 N hydrochloric acid required as S. Perform a blank titration of 25.0 mL of 0.45 N sodium hydroxide, and record the volume, in mL, of 0.2 N hydrochloric acid required as B. Calculate the percentage of acetyl groups by the formula

$$\text{Acetyl Groups} = (B - S) \times N \times 0.043 \times 100/W,$$

in which N is the exact normality of the hydrochloric acid solution, and W is the weight, in g, of the sample.

CRUDE FAT

Apparatus The apparatus consists of a Butt-type extractor,[1] as shown in Fig. 1, having a standard-taper 34/45 female joint at the upper end, to which is attached a Friedrichs- or Hopkins-type condenser, and a 24/40 male joint at the lower end, to which is attached a 125-mL Erlenmeyer flask.

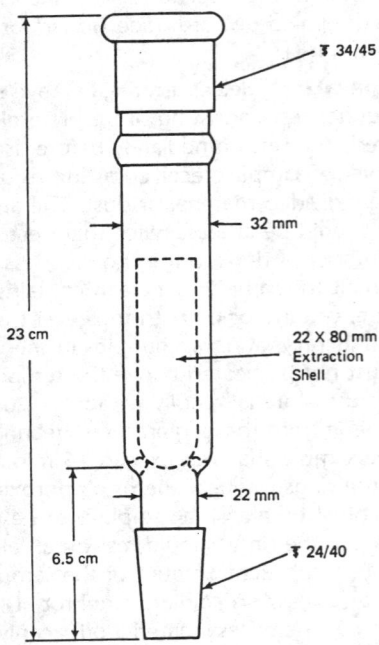

Figure 1. Butt-Type Extractor for Crude Fat Determination.

Procedure Transfer about 10 g of the sample, previously ground to 20-mesh or finer and accurately weighed, to a 15-cm filter paper, roll the paper tightly around the sample, and place it in a suitable extraction shell. Plug the top of the shell with cotton previously extracted with hexane, and place the shell in the extractor. Attach the extractor to a dry 125-mL Erlenmeyer flask containing about 50 mL of hexane and to a water-cooled condenser, apply heat to the flask to produce 150 to 200 drops of condensed solvent per min, and extract for 16 h. Disconnect the flask, and filter the extract to remove any insoluble residue. Rinse the flask and filter with a few mL of hexane, combine the washings and filtrate in a tared flask, and evaporate on a steam bath until no odor of solvent remains. Dry in a vacuum for 1 h at 100°, cool in a desiccator, and weigh.

INVERT SUGAR DETERMINATION[2]

Assay

Apparatus Mount a ring support on a ringstand 1 to 2 in. above a gas burner, and mount a second ring 6 to 7 in. above the first. Place a 6-in. open-wire gauze on the lower ring to support a 400-mL Erlenmeyer flask, and place a 4-in. watch glass with a center hole on the upper ring to deflect heat. Attach a 50-mL buret to the ringstand so that the tip just passes through the watch glass centered above the

---

[1] Available from H.S. Martin & Co., Evanston, IL.

[2] Based on ICUMSA Method GS 4/3-3 (2007).

flask. Alternatively, a buret with an offset tip may be used in place of a buret with a straight tip extending through the hole in the watch glass. Place an indirectly lighted white surface behind the assembly for observing the endpoint. Alternatively, use a hot titrator/illuminator.[3]

Mixed Fehling's Solution

Copper Sulfate Solution Dissolve 34.639 g of $CuSO_4 \cdot 5H_2O$ in water; dilute to 500 mL, and filter.

Alkaline Tartrate Solution Dissolve 173 g of potassium sodium tartrate ($KNaC_4H_4O_6 \cdot 4H_2O$) and 50 g of NaOH in water, and dilute to 500 mL; allow to stand 2 days, and filter before use.

Just before use, prepare the *Mixed Fehling's Solution* by mixing equal volumes of *Copper Sulfate Solution* and *Alkaline Tartrate Solution*.

Stock Standard Solution Transfer approximately 9.5 g of NF-grade sucrose, accurately weighed, to a 1000-mL volumetric flask; dissolve in 100 mL of water, add 5 mL of hydrochloric acid, and store 3 days at 20° to 25°. Dilute to volume with water. This solution is stable for several months.

Sample Solution Transfer 10 g or a suitable weight of sample, accurately weighed, to a 1-L volumetric flask; dissolve in and dilute to volume with water so that the final *Sample Solution* contains between 250 and 400 mg of Invert Sugar per 100 mL.

Invert Sugar Solution (0.25 g per 100 mL) Immediately before use in standardizing the *Mixed Fehling's Solution*, pipet 25 mL of *Stock Standard Solution* into a 100-mL volumetric flask, dilute to volume with water, and mix.

Standardized Fehling's Solution To 20 mL of *Mixed Fehling's Solution* in a 400-mL flask containing a few boiling chips add 15 mL of water and 39 mL of *Invert Sugar Solution*. Mix by swirling, heat, and titrate with the *Invert Sugar Solution* as directed under *Procedure*. Adjust the *Mixed Fehling's Solution* for the correct amount of copper (equivalent to 100 mg of invert sugar), and restandardize if the total volume of *Invert Sugar Solution* is more or less than 40 mL.

Procedure

Invert Sugar Conduct a preliminary test to ascertain the volume of water to be added to the 20 mL of *Standardized Fehling's Solution* to obtain a final total volume of 75 mL when the endpoint of the titration is reached. The invert sugar content of the *Sample Solution* should be between 250 and 400 mg per 100 mL so that a titer between 25 and 40 mL is needed to achieve the endpoint. Calculate the amount of water to be added to the *Mixed Fehling's Solution* as the difference

Result = 75 − [20 (mL of Mixed Fehling's Solution) + (number of mL of preliminary titer)].

Pipet 20 mL of *Mixed Fehling's Solution* in a 400-mL flask containing a few glass beads or boiling chips, add the required amount of water and mix. Rinse a 50-mL buret, and fill with *Sample Solution*. Rapidly add the *Sample Solution* within 0.5 mL of the endpoint, mix by swirling at room temperature. Immediately place the flask on the wire gauze, adjust the burner flame so that the boiling point of the solution is reached in 2 min. Boil gently but steadily for 2 min. As boiling continues, add 3 to 4 drops of 1% aqueous methylene blue indicator. Complete the titration within 1 min by adding the *Sample Solution* dropwise or in small increments until the blue color disappears. Allow a 5-s reaction time between drops at the end of the titration. Calculate the percent of invert sugar, P_I, in the sample by using the following equation:

$$P_I = f \times 10000/C_S V,$$

in which f is the correction factor for the apparent reducing power of sucrose as seen from the table immediately following this *Assay* (f = 1 if no sucrose is present), C_S is the concentration (dry basis), in mg/mL, of the *Sample Solution*, and V is the volume, in mL, of the *Sample Solution* used in the titration.

Sucrose Pipet 100 mL of *Sample Solution* into a 200-mL volumetric flask, and add slowly 10 mL of 2.7 N hydrochloric acid, diluted 1:1, while gently swirling the solution; place in a constant-temperature bath maintained at 60°; agitate continuously for 3 min; and allow to sit in the bath for an additional 7 min. Remove the flask from the bath, and cool to 20° as rapidly as possible; dilute to volume with water, and mix well. Continue as directed in the *Procedure* (above) under *Invert Sugar*. Calculate the percent invert sugar present after hydrolysis (P_H) using the equation

$$P_H = 20000/C_S V_H,$$

in which C_S is the concentration, in mg/mL, of sample in the *Sample Solution*, as defined above, and V_H is the volume, in mL, of the hydrolyzed *Sample Solution* used in the titration. If V_H falls outside the limits of 25 to 40 mL, repeat the hydrolysis with a different volume of *Sample Solution*. Calculate the percent sucrose by using the following equation:

$$P_S = 0.95(P_H − P_I),$$

in which P_H and P_I are the percentages of invert sugar determined after and before hydrolysis, respectively.

ICUMSA Table: Sucrose Correction to Be Applied in Lane & Eynon Constant Volume Method

Sucrose in Boiling Mixture, g	Correction Factor (f)	Sucrose in Boiling Mixture, g	Correction Factor (f)
0.5	0.988	5.5	0.900
1.0	0.975	6.0	0.894
1.5	0.962	6.5	0.889
2.0	0.950	7.0	0.884
2.5	0.942	7.5	0.879
3.0	0.934	8.0	0.874
3.5	0.925	8.5	0.870
4.0	0.917	9.0	0.865
4.5	0.912	9.5	0.861
5.0	0.906	10.0	0.856

---

[3] Available from Clive Shelton Associates, Provident House, Burrell Row, Beckenham, Kent BR3 IAR, England.

LACTOSE DETERMINATION

Assay

Apparatus Use a suitable high-performance liquid chromatographic system (see *Chromatography*, Appendix IIA) equipped with a differential refractometer detector, a precolumn, an online 0.45-μm filter, and a 250-mm × 4.6-mm (id) stainless steel column, or equivalent.

Solid Phase Microparticle silica gel with siloxane bonded cyano-amino moieties (Whatman P-10 carbohydrate, or equivalent) equilibrated and operated at room temperature.

Mobile Phase Acetonitrile–water (80:20) at a flow rate of 2 mL/min.

Reagents

Acetonitrile An appropriate grade for liquid chromatography.

Fructose Internal Standard Solution Prepare a solution of fructose to be used as an internal standard by transferring 50 g of commercial grade β-D(−)fructose powder to a 500-mL volumetric flask, and dissolve in and dilute to volume with water.

Standard Solution Transfer about 2 g of NF-grade anhydrous lactose, accurately weighed, to a 100-mL volumetric flask, add 10 mL of *Fructose Internal Standard Solution*, and dilute to volume with water. Prepare fresh daily.

Water An appropriate grade for liquid chromatography.

System Suitability (See *Chromatography*, Appendix IIA.)

Repeatability Allow the chromatographic system to equilibrate at a flow rate of 2 mL/min, then inject 25-μL aliquots of the *Standard Solution*. The chromatogram should show baseline resolution and a retention time for water of 1 to 2 min; fructose, 2 to 3 min; and lactose, 5 to 6 min. The coefficient of variation for the relative peak heights (lactose peak height/fructose peak height) for ten injections should be ≤0.6% when column equilibration is complete.

Linearity of Detector Response On a monthly basis (or when changes in the system are made), monitor the linearity of detector response by injecting standard lactose solutions containing 1.4%, 1.8%, 2.0%, 2.2%, and 2.6% lactose. Linear regression of the curve generated by plotting peak height versus concentration should give a correlation coefficient of at least 0.999.

Sample Preparation Prepare the sample as directed in the individual monograph. Analysis must be performed within 24 h.

Procedure Inject triplicate 25-μL aliquots of sample and standard solutions. If more than one sample is to be analyzed, inject the standard solution after every third sample. Calculate results using average standard response factors bracketing every three samples (see *Chromatography*, Appendix IIA).

Calculation Calculate the % Lactose (dry basis) by the formula

$$\text{Result} = (R_L/R_F) \times (W_L/W_S) \times (100 - M_L/100 - M_S) \times P,$$

in which R_L and R_F are the response factors for lactose and fructose; W_S and W_L are the weights, in g, of the sample and lactose standard in their respective solutions; M_S and M_L are the percentages of moisture in the sample and lactose standard; and P is the purity, in percent, of the lactose standard. Determine the moisture content by drying at 120° for 16 h.

PROPYLENE CHLOROHYDRIN DETERMINATION
(2-Chloro-1-propanol)

Special Apparatus

Gas Chromatograph (See *Chromatography*, Appendix IIA.) Use a suitable gas chromatograph. A dual-column, or equivalent, instrument equipped with a flame-ionization detector and an integrator is preferred.

Concentrator Use a Kuderna-Danish concentrator having a 500-mL flask, available from Kontes Glass Co., Vineland, NJ (Catalog No. K-57000), or equivalent.

Pressure Bottles Use 200-mL pressure bottles, with a Neoprene washer, glass stopper, and attached wire clamp, available from Fisher Scientific Co. (Vitro 400, Catalog No. 3-100), or equivalent.

Gas Chromatography Column Use a stainless steel column, or equivalent, 3 m × 3.2 mm (od), packed with 10% Carbowax 20 M on 80/100-mesh Gas Chrom 2, or equivalent. After packing and before use, condition the column overnight at 200°, using a helium flow of 25 mL/min.

Reagents

Diethyl Ether Use anhydrous, analytical reagent-grade diethyl ether, available from Fisher Scientific Co. or J. T. Baker Co., or other suitable sources.

[NOTE—Some lots of diethyl ether contain foreign residues that interfere with the analysis and/or the interpretation of the chromatograms. If the ether quality is unknown or suspect, concentrate 50 mL to a volume of about 1 mL in the concentrator, and then chromatograph a 2.0-μL portion using the conditions outlined under the *Procedure*. If the chromatogram is excessively noisy and contains signal peaks that overlap or interfere in the measurement of the peaks produced by the propylene chlorohydrin isomers, the ether should be redistilled.]

Florisil PR Use 60/100-mesh material, available from Floridin Co., 3 Penn Center, Pittsburgh, PA 15235, or an equivalent product available from Supelco, Bellefonte, PA 16823.

Propylene Chlorohydrins Use 1-Chloro-2-propanol Practical Grade, containing 25% 2-Chloro-1-propanol, available from Aldrich Chemical Company, Milwaukee, WI 53233.

Standard Preparation Draw 25 μL of *Propylene Chlorohydrins* into a 50-μL syringe, weigh accurately, and discharge the contents into a 500-mL volumetric flask partially filled with water. Reweigh the syringe, and record the weight of the chlorohydrins taken. Dilute to volume with water, and mix. This solution contains about 27.5 mg of mixed chlorohydrins, or about 55 μg/mL. Prepare this solution fresh daily.

Sample Preparation Transfer a blended representative 50.0-g sample into a pressure bottle, and add 125 mL of 2 N sulfuric acid. Clamp the top in place, and swirl the contents until the sample is completely dispersed. Place the bottle in a boiling water bath, heat for 10 min, then swirl the bottle to mix the contents, and heat in the bath for an additional 15 min. Cool in air to room temperature, then neutralize the hydrolyzed sample to pH 7 with 25% sodium hydroxide solution, and filter through Whatman No. 1 paper, or equivalent, in a Büchner funnel, using suction. Wash the bottle and filter paper with 25 mL of water, and combine the washings with the filtrate. Add 30 g of anhydrous sodium sulfate, and stir with a magnetic stirring bar for 5 to 10 min, or until the sodium sulfate is completely dissolved. Transfer the solution into a 500-mL separator equipped with a Teflon plug, rinse the flask with 25 mL of water, and combine the washings with the sample solution. Extract with five 50-mL portions of *Diethyl Ether*, allowing at least 5 min in each extraction for adequate phase separation. Transfer the combined ether extracts in a concentrator, place the graduated receiver of the concentrator in a water bath maintained at 50° to 55°, and concentrate the extract to a volume of 4 mL.

[NOTE—Ether extracts of samples may contain foreign residues that interfere with the analysis and/or interpretation of the chromatograms. These residues are believed to be degradation products arising during the hydrolysis treatment. Analytical problems created by their presence can be avoided through application of a cleanup treatment performed as follows: Concentrate the ether extract to about 8 mL, instead of 4 mL specified above. Add 10 g of *Florisil PR*, previously heated to 130° for 16 h just before use, to a chromatographic tube of suitable size, then tap gently, and add 1 g of anhydrous sodium sulfate to the top of the column. Wet the column with 25 mL of *Diethyl Ether*, and quantitatively transfer the concentrated extract to the column with the aid of small portions of the ether. Elute with three 25-mL portions of the ether, collect all of the eluate, transfer it to a concentrator, and concentrate to a volume of 4 mL.]

Cool the extract to room temperature, transfer it quantitatively to a 5.0-mL volumetric flask with the aid of small portions of *Diethyl Ether*, dilute to volume with the ether, and mix.

Control Preparations Transfer 50.0-g portions of unmodified (underivatized) waxy corn starch into five separate pressure bottles, and add 125 mL of 2 N sulfuric acid to each bottle. Add 0.0, 0.5, 1.0, 2.0, and 5.0 mL of the *Standard Preparation* to the bottles, respectively, giving propylene chlorohydrin concentrations, on the starch basis, of 0, 0.5, 1, 2, and 5 mg/kg, respectively. Calculate the exact concentration in each bottle from the weight of *Propylene Chlorohydrins* used in making the *Standard Preparation*. Clamp the tops in place, swirl until the contents of each bottle are completely dissolved, and proceed with the hydrolysis, neutralization, filtration, extraction, extract concentration, and final dilution as directed under *Sample Preparation*.

Procedure Perform the analysis by gas chromatography with the gas chromatograph and gas chromatography column previously described. The operating conditions may be varied, depending on the column and instrument used. A suitable chromatogram was obtained using a column oven temperature of 110°, isothermal; injection port temperature of 210°; detector temperature of 240°; and hydrogen (30 mL/min), air (350 mL/min), or helium (25 mL/min), as the carrier gas.

Inject 2.0-µL aliquots of each of the concentrated extracts, prepared as directed under *Control Preparations*, allowing sufficient time between injections for signal peaks corresponding to the two chlorohydrin isomers to be recorded (and integrated) and for the column to be purged. Record and sum the signal areas (integrator outputs) from the two chlorohydrin isomers for each of the controls.

Using identical operating conditions, inject a 2.0-µL aliquot of the concentrated extract prepared as directed under *Sample Preparation*, and record and sum the signal areas (integrator outputs) from the sample.

Calculation Prepare a standard curve for the summed signal areas for each of the controls against the calculated propylene chlorohydrin concentrations, in mg/kg, derived from the actual weight of chlorohydrin isomers used. Using the summed signal areas corresponding to the 1-chloro-2-propanol and 2-chloro-1-propanol from the sample, determine the concentration of mixed propylene chlorohydrins, in mg/kg, in the sample by reference to the calibration plot.

[NOTE—After gaining experience with the procedure and demonstrating that the calibration plot derived from the control samples is linear and reproducible, the number of controls can be reduced to one containing about 5 mg/kg of mixed propylene chlorohydrin isomers. The propylene chlorohydrin level in the sample can then be calculated as follows:

Propylene chlorohydrins, mg/kg = $(C \times a)/A$,

in which C is the concentration, in mg/kg, of propylene chlorohydrins (sum of isomers) in the control; a is the sum of the signal areas produced by the propylene chlorohydrin isomers in the sample; and A is the sum of the signal areas produced by the propylene chlorohydrin isomers in the control.]

REDUCING SUGARS ASSAY

Apparatus Mount a ring support on a ringstand 1 to 2 in. above a gas burner, and mount a second ring 6 to 7 in. above the first. Place a 6-in. open-wire gauze on the lower ring to support a 250-mL Erlenmeyer flask, and place a 4-in. watch glass with a center hole on the upper ring to deflect heat. Attach a 25-mL buret to the ringstand so that the tip just passes through the watch glass centered above the flask. Place an indirectly lighted white surface behind the assembly for observing the endpoint.

Standardized Fehling's Solution Measure a quantity of *Fehling's Solution A*, add an equal quantity of *Fehling's Solution B*, and mix (see *Cupric Tartrate TS, Alkaline* in the section on *Solutions and Indicators*). Immediately before use, standardize as follows: Transfer 3.000 g of primary standard dextrose (NIST Standard Reference Material, or equivalent), previously dried in vacuum at 100° for 2 h, into a 500-mL volumetric flask, dissolve in and dilute to volume with water, and mix. Pipet 25 mL of the mixed Fehling's solution into a 200-mL Erlenmeyer flask containing a few glass beads, and titrate with the standard dextrose solution as directed under *Procedure*. Adjust the concentration of *Fehling's Solution A* by dilution or the addition of copper sulfate, so that the titration requires 20.0 mL of the standard dextrose solution.

Procedure Transfer about 3 g of the sample, accurately weighed, into a 500-mL volumetric flask, dissolve in and dilute to volume with water, and mix. Pipet 25.0 mL of *Standardized Fehling's Solution* into a 200-mL Erlenmeyer flask containing a few glass beads, and add the sample solution from a buret to within 0.5 mL of the anticipated endpoint (determined by preliminary titration). Immediately place the flask on the wire gauze of the *Apparatus*, and adjust the burner so that the boiling point will be reached in about 2 min. Bring to a boil, and boil gently for 2 min. As boiling continues, add 2 drops of a 1% aqueous solution of methylene blue, and complete the titration within 1 min by adding the sample solution dropwise or in small increments until the blue color disappears. Record the volume, in mL, of sample solution required as V. Calculate the percentage of reducing sugars, as D-glucose on the dried basis, by the equation

$$\% \text{ Reducing Sugars} = (500 \times 0.12 \times 100)/(V \times W),$$

in which W is the weight, in g, of the sample of dry substance.

SULFUR DIOXIDE DETERMINATION
(Based on AOAC Method 962.16)

Reagents

3% Hydrogen Peroxide Solution Dilute 30% hydrogen peroxide to 3% with water. Just before use, add 3 drops of methyl red TS, and titrate to a yellow endpoint using 0.01 N sodium hydroxide. If the endpoint is exceeded, discard the solution and prepare another 3% hydrogen peroxide solution.

Standardized Titrant Prepare a solution of 0.01 N sodium hydroxide.

Nitrogen A source of high-purity nitrogen is required with a flow regulator that will maintain a flow of 200 ± 10 mL/min. To guard against the presence of oxygen in the nitrogen, an oxygen scrubbing apparatus or solution such as an alkaline pyrogallol trap may be used. Prepare the pyrogallol trap as follows: Add 4.5 g of pyrogallol to the trap, purge the trap with nitrogen for 2 to 3 min, and add potassium hydroxide solution (65 g of potassium hydroxide added to 85 mL of water) to the trap while maintaining an atmosphere of nitrogen in the trap.

[**Caution**—Exothermic reaction.]

Sample Preparation (for solids) Transfer 50 g of the sample, or a quantity of the sample with a known quantity of sulfur dioxide (500 to 1500 µg of SO₂), to a food processor or blender, if necessary. Add 50 mL of 5% ethanol in water, and briefly grind the mixture, reserving another 50 mL of 5% ethanol in water to rinse the blender jar. Grinding or blending should be continued only until the food is chopped into pieces small enough to pass through the 24/40 joint of a flask (see Fig. 2).

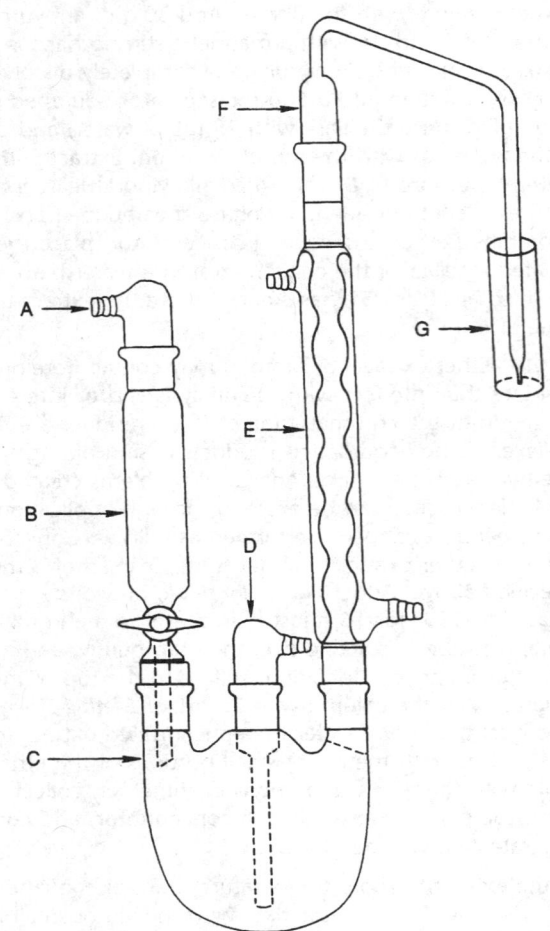

Figure 2. The Optimized Monier-Williams Apparatus; Component Identification Is Given in Text (component F is depicted in Figure 3).

Sample Preparation (for liquids) Mix 50 g of the sample, or a quantity with a known amount of sulfur dioxide (500 to 1500 µg of SO₂), with 100 mL of 5% ethanol in water.

Apparatus The apparatus shown diagrammatically (Fig. 2) is designed to accomplish the selective transfer of sulfur dioxide from the sample in boiling aqueous hydrochloric acid to the *3% Hydrogen Peroxide Solution*. This apparatus is easier to assemble than the official apparatus, and the back-pressure inside the apparatus is limited to the unavoidable pressure due to the height of the *3% Hydrogen Peroxide Solution* above the tip of the bubbler, F. Keeping the back-pressure as low as possible reduces the likelihood that sulfur dioxide will be lost through leaks.

[NOTE—Tygon and silicon tubing should be preboiled before use in this procedure.]

The apparatus should be assembled as shown in Fig. 2 with a thin film of stopcock grease on the sealing surfaces of all the joints except the joint between the separatory funnel and the flask. Each joint should be clamped together to ensure a complete seal throughout the analysis. The separatory funnel, B, should have a capacity of 100 mL or greater. An inlet adapter, A, with a hose connector (Kontes K-183000, or equivalent) is required to provide a means of applying a head of pressure above the solution. (A pressure-equalizing dropping funnel is not recommended because condensate, perhaps with sulfur dioxide, is deposited in the funnel and the side arm.) The round-bottom flask, C, is a 1000-mL flask with three 24/40 tapered joints. The gas inlet tube, D (Kontes K-179000, or equivalent), should be of sufficient length to permit introduction of the nitrogen within 2.5 cm of the bottom of the flask. The Allihn condenser, E (Kontes K-431000-2430, or equivalent), has a jacket length of 300 mm. The bubbler, F, is fabricated from glass according to the dimensions given in Fig. 3, and it has the same dimensions as a 50-mL graduated cylinder (see Fig. 3). The *3% Hydrogen Peroxide Solution* can be contained in a receiving vessel, G, with an id of about 2.5 cm and a depth of 18 cm.

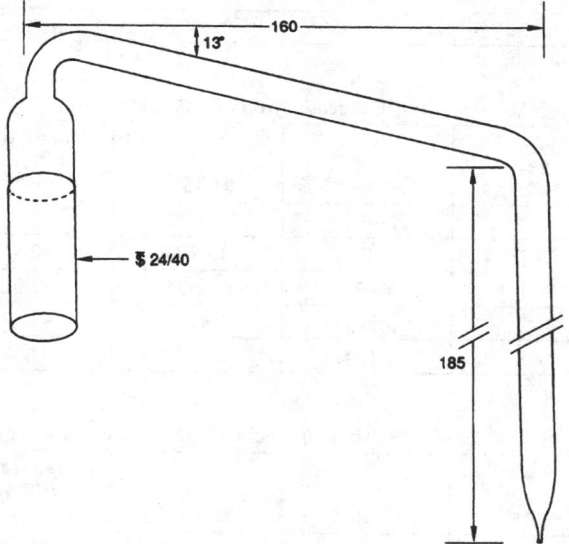

Figure 3. Diagram of Bubbler (F in Figure 2) (lengths are given in mm).

Buret Use a 10-mL buret with overflow tube and hose connections for an Ascarite tube or equivalent air-scrubbing apparatus. This will permit the maintenance of a carbon dioxide-free atmosphere over the *Standardized Titrant*.

Chilled Water Circulator The condenser must be chilled with a coolant, such as 20% methanol–water, at a flow rate so that the condenser outlet temperature is maintained at 5°. A circulating pump equivalent to the Neslab Coolflow 33 is suitable.

Determination Assemble the apparatus as shown in Fig. 2. The flask must be positioned in a heating mantle that is controlled by a power-regulating device such as Variac, or equivalent. Add 400 mL of distilled water to the flask. Close the stopcock of the separatory funnel, and add 90 mL of 4 N hydrochloric acid to the separatory funnel. Begin the flow of nitrogen at a rate of 200 ± 10 mL/min. The condenser coolant flow must be initiated at this time. Add 30 mL of *3% Hydrogen Peroxide Solution*, which has been titrated to a yellow endpoint with the *Standardized Titrant*, to the receiving vessel, G. After 15 min, the apparatus and the water will be thoroughly deoxygenated, and the apparatus will be ready for sample introduction.

Sample Introduction and Distillation Remove the separatory funnel, and quantitatively transfer the sample in aqueous ethanol to the flask. Wipe the tapered joint clean with a laboratory tissue, apply stopcock grease to the outer joint of the separatory funnel, and return the separatory funnel to the tapered joint flask. The nitrogen flow through the *3% Hydrogen Peroxide Solution* should resume as soon as the funnel is reinserted into the appropriate joint in the flask. Examine each joint to ensure that it is sealed.

Apply a head pressure above the hydrochloric acid solution in the separatory funnel with a rubber bulb equipped with a valve. Open the stopcock in the separatory funnel, and permit the hydrochloric acid solution to flow into the flask. Continue to maintain sufficient pressure above the acid solution to force the solution into the flask. The stopcock may temporarily be closed, if necessary, to pump up the pressure above the acid. To guard against the escape of sulfur dioxide into the separatory funnel, close the stopcock before the last few mL drain out of the separatory funnel.

Apply the power to the heating mantle. Use a power setting that will cause 80 to 90 drops of condensate to return to the flask from the condenser per min. After 1.75 h of boiling, cool the contents of the 1000-mL flask at the condensation rate stated above, and remove the contents of the receiving vessel, G.

Titration Add 3 drops of *Methyl Red Indicator*, and titrate the above-mentioned contents with the *Standardized Titrant* to a yellow endpoint that persists for at least 20 s. Calculate the sulfur dioxide content, expressed as µg of sulfur dioxide per g of sample (µg/g or mg/kg) as follows:

$$mg/kg = (32.03 \times V_B \times N \times 1000)/Wt,$$

in which 32.03 is the milliequivalent weight, in mg, of sulfur dioxide; V_B is the volume, in mL, of sodium hydroxide titrant of normality, N, required to reach the endpoint; the factor 1000 converts mg to µg; and Wt is the weight, in g, of sample introduced into the 1000-mL flask.

TOTAL SOLIDS

[NOTE—The refractive index, RI, of solutions of various carbohydrates at specific temperatures is directly correlated with the solutions' concentrations (in g/100 g or percent dried solids). The following tables, as required in some monographs in this edition, are provided for the user's convenience.]

Apparatus Use a suitable refractometer (see *Refractive Index*, Appendix IIB) equipped with a jacket for water circulation or some other mechanism for maintaining the sample at 20.0° ± 0.1° or some other fixed temperature. Before proceeding with measurements, ensure that the prism has reached the equilibrium temperature.

Standardization To achieve the theoretical accuracy of ±0.0001, calibrate the instrument daily by determining the refractive index of distilled water, which is 1.3330 at 20°, and 1.3325 at 25°.

Procedure Determine the refractive index after ensuring that the sample and prism have reached the equilibrium temperature.

For *Corn Syrups*, *High-Fructose Corn Syrups*, *Liquid Fructose*, and *Maltodextrin*, convert the refractive index to approximate percent solids using the accompanying tables.

[NOTE—These tables cover the approximate total solids levels of these products in commerce. If the ash or dextrose equivalent of the sample differs from the product in the table, use the accompanying ash and dextrose equivalent correction table.]

Glucose Syrup (Corn Syrup)

28 DE[a] Glucose Syrup—0.3% Ash

%aDS[b]	RI[c] 20°C	RI 45°C	°Baumé at 140°F (60°C) + 1
76.0	1.4888	1.4837	40.98
77.0	1.4915	1.4864	41.49
78.0	1.4943	1.4892	42.00
79.0	1.4971	1.4919	42.51
80.0	1.4999	1.4947	43.01

[a] Dextrose Equivalent
[b] Dry Substance
[c] Refractive Index

36 DE Glucose Syrup—0.3% Ash

%DS	RI 20°C	RI 45°C	°Baumé at 140°F (60°C) + 1
78.4	1.4938	1.4887	42.01
79.4	1.4965	1.4914	42.52
80.4	1.4993	1.4941	43.02

36 DE Glucose Syrup—0.3% Ash (continued)

%DS	RI 20°C	RI 45°C	°Baumé at 140°F (60°C) + 1
81.4	1.5021	1.4969	43.52
82.4	1.5049	1.4997	44.02

34 DE High-Maltose Glucose Syrup—0.3% Ash

%DS	RI 20°C	RI 45°C	°Baumé at 140°F (60°C) + 1
78.6	1.4933	1.4882	41.99
79.6	1.4960	1.4909	42.49
80.6	1.4988	1.4936	42.99
81.6	1.5015	1.4964	43.49
82.6	1.5043	1.4992	43.99

43 DE High-Maltose Glucose Syrup—0.3% Ash

%DS	RI 20°C	RI 45°C	°Baumé at 140°F (60°C) + 1
78.9	1.4934	1.4883	42.00
79.9	1.4961	1.4910	42.51
80.9	1.4988	1.4937	43.01
81.9	1.5016	1.4964	43.51
82.9	1.5044	1.4992	44.01

43 DE Glucose Syrup—0.3% Ash

%DS	RI 20°C	RI 45°C	°Baumé at 140°F (60°C) + 1
78.7	1.4933	1.4882	42.01
79.7	1.4960	1.4909	42.51
80.7	1.4988	1.4936	43.02
81.7	1.5015	1.4964	43.52
82.7	1.5043	1.4992	44.01

43 DE (Ion-Exchanged) Glucose Syrup—0.03% Ash

%DS	RI 20°C	RI 45°C	°Baumé at 140°F (60°C) + 1
78.8	1.4935	1.4884	41.99
79.8	1.4962	1.4911	42.50
80.8	1.4990	1.4938	43.00
81.8	1.5018	1.4966	43.50
82.8	1.5045	1.4994	43.99

53 DE Glucose Syrup—0.3% Ash

%DS	RI 20°C	RI 45°C	°Baumé at 140°F (60°C) + 1
80.5	1.4962	1.4911	42.64
81.5	1.4989	1.4938	43.14

53 DE Glucose Syrup—0.3% Ash (continued)

%DS	Ri 20°C	RI 45°C	°Baumé at 140°F (60°C) + 1
82.5	1.5016	1.4965	43.64
83.5	1.5044	1.4992	44.13
84.5	1.5072	1.5020	44.63

63 DE Glucose Syrup—0.3% Ash

%DS	Ri 20°C	RI 45°C	°Baumé at 140°F (60°C) + 1
81.0	1.4955	1.4904	42.53
82.0	1.4982	1.4931	43.02
83.0	1.5009	1.4958	43.52
84.0	1.5037	1.4985	44.01
85.0	1.5064	1.5012	44.50

63 DE (Ion-Exchanged) Glucose Syrup—0.03% Ash

%DS	Ri 20°C	RI 45°C	°Baumé at 140°F (60°C) + 1
81.3	1.4963	1.4912	42.60
82.3	1.4990	1.4939	43.10
83.3	1.5017	1.4965	43.59
84.3	1.5044	1.4993	44.09
85.3	1.5072	1.5020	44.58

66 DE Glucose Syrup—0.3% Ash

%DS	Ri 20°C	RI 45°C	°Baumé at 140°F (60°C) + 1
81.0	1.4949	1.4898	42.36
82.0	1.4975	1.4924	42.86
83.0	1.5002	1.4951	43.36
84.0	1.5029	1.4978	43.85
85.0	1.5056	1.5005	44.35

95 DE Glucose Syrup—0.3% Ash

%DS	Ri 20°C	RI 45°C	°Baumé at 140°F (60°C) + 1
69.0	1.4598	1.4550	35.46
70.0	1.4621	1.4573	35.96
71.0	1.4644	1.4596	36.46

95 DE Glucose Syrup—0.3% Ash (continued)

%DS	Ri 20°C	RI 45°C	°Baumé at 140°F (60°C) + 1
72.0	1.4668	1.4619	36.96
73.0	1.4692	1.4643	37.45

95 DE (Ion-Exchanged) Glucose Syrup—0.03% Ash

%DS	Ri 20°C	RI 45°C	°Baumé at 140°F (60°C) + 1
69.0	1.4597	1.4549	35.39
70.0	1.4620	1.4572	35.89
71.0	1.4644	1.4595	36.39
72.0	1.4667	1.4619	36.89
73.0	1.4691	1.4642	37.38

High-Fructose Corn Syrup Solids

42% High-Fructose Corn Syrup—0.03% Ash

%DS[a]	RI[b] 20°C	RI 45°C
69.0	1.4597	1.4543
70.0	1.4620	1.4565
71.0	1.4643	1.4589
72.0	1.4667	1.4612
73.0	1.4691	1.4635

[a] Dry Substance
[b] Refractive Index

55% High-Fructose Corn Syrup—0.05% Ash

%DS[a]	RI[b] 20°C	RI 45°C
75.0	1.4738	1.4680
76.0	1.4762	1.4704
77.0	1.4786	1.4728
78.0	1.4811	1.4752
79.0	1.4835	1.4776

Liquid Fructose

%DS[a]	RI[b] 20°C	RI 45°C
75.0	1.4732	1.4667
76.0	1.4756	1.4691
77.0	1.4780	1.4715

[a] Dry Substance
[b] Refractive Index

Liquid Fructose (continued)

%DS[a]	RI[b] 20°C	RI 45°C
78.0	1.4805	1.4739
79.0	1.4829	1.4763

[a] Dry Substance
[b] Refractive Index

Maltodextrin

12 DE[a] Maltodextrin—0.3% Ash

%DS[b]	RI[c] 20°C	RI 45°C	Commercial °Baumé 140°F (60°C) + 1
45.0	1.4149	1.4105	24.57
46.0	1.4171	1.4126	25.13
47.0	1.4193	1.4148	25.68
48.0	1.4215	1.4170	26.24
49.0	1.4237	1.4192	26.79
50.0	1.4260	1.4214	27.34
51.0	1.4282	1.4237	27.89
52.0	1.4305	1.4259	28.44
53.0	1.4328	1.4282	28.99
54.0	1.4351	1.4305	29.53
55.0	1.4375	1.4328	30.08
56.0	1.4398	1.4351	30.62
57.0	1.4422	1.4375	31.16
58.0	1.4446	1.4399	31.71
59.0	1.4470	1.4422	32.24
60.0	1.4494	1.4446	32.78
61.0	1.4519	1.4471	33.32
62.0	1.4544	1.4495	33.85
63.0	1.4569	1.4520	34.39
64.0	1.4594	1.4545	34.92
65.0	1.4619	1.4570	35.45
66.0	1.4644	1.4595	35.98
67.0	1.4670	1.4621	36.51
68.0	1.4696	1.4646	37.04
69.0	1.4722	1.4672	37.56
70.0	1.4748	1.4698	38.08
71.0	1.4775	1.4724	38.61
72.0	1.4801	1.4751	39.13
73.0	1.4828	1.4778	39.65
74.0	1.4855	1.4805	40.16
75.0	1.4883	1.4832	40.68
76.0	1.4910	1.4859	41.19
77.0	1.4938	1.4887	41.71
78.0	1.4966	1.4915	42.22
79.0	1.4994	1.4943	42.73
80.0	1.5023	1.4971	43.24

[a] Dextrose Equivalent
[b] Dry Substance
[c] Refractive Index

12 DE[a] Maltodextrin—0.3% Ash (continued)

%DS[b]	RI[c] 20°C	RI 45°C	Commercial °Baumé 140°F (60°C) + 1
81.0	1.5051	1.4999	43.74
82.0	1.5080	1.5028	44.25
83.0	1.5110	1.5057	44.75
84.0	1.5139	1.5086	45.26
85.0	1.5168	1.5116	45.76
86.0	1.5198	1.5145	46.26
87.0	1.5228	1.5175	46.76
88.0	1.5259	1.5206	47.25
89.0	1.5289	1.5236	47.75
90.0	1.5320	1.5267	48.24
91.0	1.5351	1.5298	48.73
92.0	1.5382	1.5329	49.23
93.0	1.5414	1.5360	49.72
94.0	1.5446	1.5392	50.21
95.0	1.5478	1.5424	50.69

[a] Dextrose Equivalent
[b] Dry Substance
[c] Refractive Index

Ash and DE[a] Corrections for Corn Syrup and Maltodextrin:[b] Changes in Refractive Index for an increase of...

%DS[c]	1% Ash	1 DE
2	0.000000	−0.000001
4	0.000000	−0.000003
6	0.000001	−0.000005
8	0.000002	−0.000007
10	0.000003	−0.000010
12	0.000004	−0.000012
14	0.000006	−0.000015
16	0.000008	−0.000017
18	0.000010	−0.000020
20	0.000013	−0.000023
22	0.000016	−0.000026
24	0.000019	−0.000029
26	0.000022	−0.000033
28	0.000026	−0.000036
30	0.000030	−0.000040
32	0.000034	−0.000044
34	0.000039	−0.000048
36	0.000044	−0.000052
38	0.000049	−0.000057
40	0.000055	−0.000061
42	0.000061	−0.000066
44	0.000068	−0.000071
46	0.000074	−0.000076

[a] Dextrose Equivalent
[b] Wartman, A. M., et al. J. Chemical and Engineering Data 21:467, 1976.
[c] Dry Substance

Ash and DE[a] Corrections for Corn Syrup and Maltodextrin:[b] Changes in Refractive Index for an increase of... (continued)

%DS[c]	1% Ash	1 DE
48	0.000082	−0.000081
50	0.000089	−0.000087
52	0.000097	−0.000093
54	0.000105	−0.000099
56	0.000114	−0.000105
58	0.000123	−0.000112
60	0.000133	−0.000118
62	0.000143	−0.000125
64	0.000153	−0.000132
66	0.000164	−0.000140
68	0.000175	−0.000147
70	0.000187	−0.000155
72	0.000199	−0.000163
74	0.000212	−0.000172
76	0.000225	−0.000181
78	0.000239	−0.000190

[a] Dextrose Equivalent
[b] Wartman, A. M., et al. J. Chemical and Engineering Data 21:467, 1976.
[c] Dry Substance

Ash and DE[a] Corrections for Corn Syrup and Maltodextrin:[b] Changes in Refractive Index for an increase of... (continued)

%DS[c]	1% Ash	1 DE
80	0.000253	−0.000199
82	0.000268	−0.000208
84	0.000283	−0.000218

[a] Dextrose Equivalent
[b] Wartman, A. M., et al. J. Chemical and Engineering Data 21:467, 1976.
[c] Dry Substance

Invert Sugar

For invert sugar, convert the refractive index to approximate percent solids (uncorrected for invert sugar) using the accompanying sucrose table. Correct for invert sugar by using the following formula:

$$D = (S + C) + (P_1 \times 0.022),$$

in which S is the approximate percent solids determined from the refractive index table for sucrose, C is the temperature correction derived from the accompanying temperature correction table if the refractometer was operated at other than 20°, and P_1 is the percent invert sugar determined as directed under *Assay* for *Invert Sugar* in this Appendix.

Sucrose

International Refractive Index Scale of ICUMSA[a] (1974) for Pure Sucrose Solutions at 20°C and 589 nm[b]

Sucrose g/100 g	0.0	0.1	0.2	0.3	0.4	0.5	0.6	0.7	0.8	0.9
56	1.4329	4332	4334	4336	4338	4340	4343	4345	4347	4349
57	1.4352	4354	4356	4358	4360	4363	4365	4367	4369	4372
58	1.4374	4376	4378	4380	4383	4385	4387	4389	4392	4394
59	1.4396	4398	4401	4403	4405	4407	4410	4412	4414	4417
60	1.4419	4421	4423	4426	4428	4430	4432	4435	4437	4439
61	1.4442	4444	4446	4448	4451	4453	4455	4458	4460	4462
62	1.4464	4467	4469	4471	4474	4476	4478	4481	4483	4485
63	1.4488	4490	4492	4495	4497	4499	4502	4504	4506	4509
64	1.4511	4513	4516	4518	4520	4523	4525	4527	4530	4532
65	1.4534	4537	4539	4541	4544	4546	4548	4551	4553	4556
66	1.4558	4560	4563	4565	4567	4570	4572	4575	4577	4579
67	1.4582	4584	4586	4589	4591	4594	4596	4598	4601	4603
68	1.4606	4608	4610	4613	4615	4618	4620	4623	4625	4627
69	1.4630	4632	4635	4637	4639	4642	4644	4647	4649	4652
70	1.4654	4657	4659	4661	4664	4666	4669	4671	4674	4676
71	1.4679	4681	4683	4686	4688	4691	4693	4696	4698	4701
72	1.4703	4706	4708	4711	4713	4716	4718	4721	4723	4726
73	1.4728	4730	4733	4735	4738	4740	4743	4745	4748	4750
74	1.4753	4756	4758	4761	4763	4766	4768	4771	4773	4776
75	1.4778	4781	4783	4786	4788	4791	4793	4796	4798	4801
76	1.4804	4806	4809	4811	4814	4816	4819	4821	4824	4826

[a] Adapted from "Refractometry and Tables—Official" (ICUMSA SPS-3 2000), International Commission for Uniform Methods of Sugar Analysis (ICUMSA).
[b] No rounding has been carried out; therefore, values given may be too low by a maximum of 1×10^{-4}.

International Refractive Index Scale of ICUMSA[a] (1974) for Pure Sucrose Solutions at 20°C and 589 nm[b] (continued)

Sucrose g/100 g	0.0	0.1	0.2	0.3	0.4	0.5	0.6	0.7	0.8	0.9
77	1.4829	4832	4834	4837	4839	4842	4844	4847	4850	4852
78	1.4855	4857	4860	4862	4865	4868	4870	4873	4875	4878
79	1.4881	4883	4886	4888	4891	4894	4896	4899	4901	4904
80	1.4907	4909	4912	4914	4917	4920	4922	4925	4928	4930
81	1.4933	4935	4938	4941	4943	4946	4949	4951	4954	4957
82	1.4959	4962	4964	4967	4970	4972	4975	4978	4980	4983
83	1.4986	4988	4991	4994	4996	4999	5002	5004	5007	5010
84	1.5012	5015	5018	5020	5023	5026	5029	5031	5034	5037
85	1.5039									

[a] Adapted from "Refractometry and Tables—Official" (ICUMSA SPS-3 2000), International Commission for Uniform Methods of Sugar Analysis (ICUMSA).
[b] No rounding has been carried out; therefore, values given may be too low by a maximum of 1×10^{-4}.

Temperature Corrections for Refractometric Sucrose Solutions with Measurements at 20° and 589 nm

Measured Sucrose (% solids)

Temperature (°C)	0	5	10	15	20	25	30	35	40	45	50	55	60	65	70	75	80	85
						Subtract from the measured value												
15	0.29	0.30	0.32	0.33	0.34	0.35	0.36	0.37	0.37	0.38	0.38	0.38	0.38	0.38	0.38	0.38	0.37	0.37
16	0.24	0.25	0.26	0.27	0.28	0.28	0.29	0.30	0.30	0.30	0.31	0.31	0.31	0.31	0.31	0.30	0.30	0.30
17	0.18	0.19	0.20	0.20	0.21	0.21	0.22	0.22	0.23	0.23	0.23	0.23	0.23	0.23	0.23	0.23	0.23	0.22
18	0.12	0.13	0.13	0.14	0.14	0.14	0.15	0.15	0.15	0.15	0.15	0.15	0.15	0.15	0.15	0.15	0.15	0.15
19	0.06	0.06	0.07	0.07	0.07	0.07	0.07	0.08	0.08	0.08	0.08	0.08	0.08	0.08	0.08	0.08	0.08	0.07
						Add to the measured value												
21	0.06	0.07	0.07	0.07	0.07	0.07	0.08	0.08	0.08	0.08	0.08	0.08	0.08	0.08	0.08	0.08	0.08	0.07
22	0.13	0.14	0.14	0.14	0.15	0.15	0.15	0.15	0.16	0.16	0.16	0.16	0.16	0.16	0.15	0.15	0.15	0.15
23	0.20	0.21	0.21	0.22	0.22	0.23	0.23	0.23	0.23	0.24	0.24	0.24	0.24	0.23	0.23	0.23	0.23	0.22
24	0.27	0.28	0.29	0.29	0.30	0.30	0.31	0.31	0.31	0.32	0.32	0.32	0.32	0.31	0.31	0.31	0.30	0.30
25	0.34	0.35	0.36	0.37	0.38	0.38	0.39	0.39	0.40	0.40	0.40	0.40	0.40	0.39	0.39	0.38	0.38	0.37
26	0.42	0.43	0.44	0.45	0.46	0.46	0.47	0.47	0.48	0.48	0.48	0.48	0.48	0.47	0.47	0.46	0.46	0.45
27	0.50	0.51	0.52	0.53	0.54	0.55	0.55	0.56	0.56	0.56	0.56	0.56	0.56	0.55	0.55	0.54	0.53	0.52
28	0.58	0.59	0.60	0.61	0.62	0.63	0.64	0.64	0.64	0.65	0.65	0.64	0.64	0.63	0.63	0.62	0.61	0.60
29	0.66	0.67	0.68	0.70	0.71	0.71	0.72	0.73	0.73	0.73	0.73	0.73	0.72	0.72	0.71	0.70	0.69	0.67
30	0.74	0.76	0.77	0.78	0.79	0.80	0.81	0.81	0.82	0.82	0.81	0.81	0.80	0.80	0.79	0.78	0.76	0.75
31	0.83	0.84	0.85	0.87	0.88	0.89	0.89	0.90	0.90	0.90	0.90	0.89	0.89	0.88	0.87	0.86	0.84	0.82
32	0.92	0.93	0.94	0.96	0.97	0.98	0.98	0.99	0.99	0.99	0.99	0.98	0.97	0.96	0.95	0.93	0.92	0.90
33	1.01	1.02	1.03	1.05	1.06	1.07	1.07	1.08	1.08	1.08	1.07	1.07	1.06	1.04	1.03	1.01	1.00	0.98
34	1.10	1.11	1.13	1.14	1.15	1.16	1.16	1.17	1.17	1.16	1.16	1.15	1.14	1.13	1.11	1.09	1.07	1.05
35	1.19	1.21	1.22	1.23	1.24	1.25	1.25	1.26	1.26	1.25	1.25	1.24	1.23	1.21	1.19	1.17	1.15	1.13
36	1.29	1.30	1.31	1.33	1.34	1.34	1.35	1.35	1.35	1.34	1.34	1.33	1.31	1.29	1.28	1.25	1.23	1.20
37	1.39	1.40	1.41	1.42	1.43	1.44	1.44	1.44	1.44	1.43	1.43	1.41	1.40	1.38	1.36	1.33	1.31	1.28
38	1.49	1.50	1.51	1.52	1.53	1.53	1.54	1.54	1.53	1.53	1.52	1.50	1.48	1.46	1.44	1.42	1.39	1.36
39	1.59	1.60	1.61	1.62	1.63	1.63	1.63	1.63	1.63	1.62	1.61	1.59	1.57	1.55	1.52	1.50	1.47	1.43
40	1.69	1.70	1.71	1.72	1.73	1.73	1.73	1.73	1.72	1.71	1.70	1.68	1.66	1.63	1.61	1.58	1.54	1.51

SOURCE: Adapted from "Refractometry and Tables—Official" (ICUMSA SPS-3 2000), International Commission for Uniform Methods of Sugar Analysis (ICUMSA).

APPENDIX XI: FLAVOR CHEMICAL (OTHER THAN ESSENTIAL OILS)

M-1 ASSAY BY GAS CHROMATOGRAPHY

M-1a General Method, Polar Column
Proceed as directed below using a polar column.

M-1b General Method, Nonpolar Column
Proceed as directed below using a nonpolar column.

[NOTE—Column composition and the conditions of analysis (as described below) may be varied at the discretion of the analyst, provided that such changes would result in equal or improved separations and/or quantification as would be obtained by use of the particular column material and test conditions specified therein.]

This procedure applies both to the assay of flavor chemicals and to the quantitation of minor components in flavor chemicals. Analysts following this procedure and performing the test should obtain sufficient resolution of major and even trace components of a mixture to calculate accurately the concentration of the desired component; should be familiar with the general principles, usual techniques, and instrumental variables normally met in gas chromatographic analysis; and should pay particular attention to the following:

1. Stability of baseline, return to baseline before and after each peak of interest, and minimum use of recorder attenuation.
2. Any incompatibility between a sensitive sample component and column support, liquid substrate, or construction material.
3. The response to different components of the same or different detectors. Because sizable errors may be encountered in correlating area percent directly to weight percent, analysts must know the methods for calculating response factors.
4. Where limits for minor components are specified under *Other Requirements* in flavor chemical monographs, analysts should use authentic materials to confirm the retention times of minor components. Determine the quantity of components following the instructions below under *Calculations and Methods*.

GC CONDITIONS FOR ANALYSIS
Column: Open tubular capillary column of fused silica 30 m × 0.25 to 0.53 mm (id), or equivalent.

Stationary phase:
1. For a **nonpolar column** (or equivalent): methyl silicone gum, or equivalent (preferably a bonded and cross-linked dimethyl polysiloxane);
2. For a **polar column** (or equivalent): polyethylene glycol, or equivalent (preferably a bonded and cross-linked polyethylene glycol);
3. The stationary phase coating should have a thickness of 0.25 to 3 μm.

Carrier gas: Helium flowing at a linear velocity of 20 to 40 cm/s

Sample size: 0.1 to 1.0 μL

Split ratio: [for 0.25-mm to 0.35-mm (id) columns only] 50:1 to 200:1, typically, making sure that no one component exceeds the capacity of the column. Peak fronting is indicative of an overloaded column.

Inlet temperature: 225° to 275°

Detector temperature: 250° to 300°

Detectors: Use a thermal conductivity detector or a flame ionization detector or a mass spectrometer, operating all as recommended by the manufacturer.

Oven program: 50° to 240°, increasing the temperature by 5°/min; and holding at 240° for 5 min.

Analysts may also use any GC conditions providing separations equal to (or better than) those obtained with the above method, but in the case of a dispute, the above method must stand.

CALCULATIONS AND METHODS

A. Peak area integration with total area detected normalized to 100%, using electronic integrators: Use an electronic peak integrator in accordance with the manufacturer's recommendations, ensuring that the integration parameters permit proper integration of the peaks of a variety of shapes and magnitudes and do not interpret baseline shifts and noise spikes as area contributed by the sample. Use internal or external standards as needed to confirm that the total GC peak area corresponds to 100% of the components present in the sample.

B. Results obtained as described above are based on the assumption that the entire sample has eluted and the peaks of all of the components have been included in the calculation. They will be incorrect if any part of the sample does not elute or if not all of the peaks are measured. In such cases, and in all methods described above, the internal standard method may be used to determine percentages based on the total sample. For this method, measurements are required of the peaks of the component(s) being assayed and of the internal standard.

An accurately weighed or pipetted mixture of the internal standard and the sample is prepared and chromatographed, the area ratio(s) of the component(s) to the standard is computed, and the percentage(s) of the component(s) is calculated.

If this calculation is to be applied, the substance used as the standard should be one that meets the following criteria:

a. Its detector response is similar to that of the component(s) to be determined. In general, the more nearly the chemical structure of the component resembles that of the standard, the closer the response will be.

b. Its retention time is close to, but not identical to, that of the component(s).

c. The internal standard is never a natural component found in the sample.

The weight ratio of the internal standard to the sample should be such that the internal standard and the component sought produce approximately equal peaks. This is, of course, not possible if several components of interest are at different levels of concentration.

If the internal standard method is applied properly, it may be assumed that the ratio of the weight of component to the weight of internal standard is exactly proportional to the peak area ratio, and under these conditions no correction factor is needed. The sample is first run by itself to determine whether the internal standard would mask any component by peak superposition. If there is no interference, a mixture is prepared of the sample and of the internal standard in the specified weight ratio, and the percentages of the internal standard and of the sample in the mixture are calculated. The mixture is chromatographed, and the areas of the component peak and the internal standard peak are calculated by one of the methods described above.

The calculations are as follows:

1a. % Component in Mixture / % Internal Standard in Mixture = Component Area / Internal Standard Area

or

1b. % Component in Mixture = % Internal Standard in Mixture × (Component Area / Internal Standard Area)

2. % Component in Sample = (% Component in Mixture × 100) / % Sample in Mixture

If calibration is necessary, mixtures should be prepared of the internal standard and component, either of 100% or of known purity. The number of mixtures and the weight ratios to be used depend on the component being analyzed. Usually, a minimum of three mixtures will be required. The weight ratio of one is chosen so that the heights of component and standard are equal. The ratios of the other two may be two-thirds and four-thirds of this value. Each mixture should be chromatographed at least three times, and the areas calculated. The factor for each chromatograph should be calculated as specified below, and the averages taken for each mixture. An overall average factor is calculated from them. The calibration should be performed periodically.

1. Factor = [(Weight Component × % Purity) / (Weight of Internal Standard × % Purity)] × [Internal Standard Area / Component Area]

2. % Component in Sample Mixture = (Component Area × Factor × % Internal Standard in Sample Mixture) / Internal Standard Area

3. % Component in Sample = (% Component in Sample Mixture × 100) / % Sample in Sample Mixture

GC SYSTEM SUITABILITY TEST SAMPLE

The GC system suitability test sample consists of an equal-weight mixture of FCC-quality acetophenone, benzyl alcohol, benzyl acetate, linalool, and hydroxycitronellal.

Using the test sample described below, periodically test the performance of and resolution provided by the gas chromatograph employed. The test sample must display results comparable in quantitative composition, peak shape, and elution order to those specified herein. The quantitative composition should not deviate from the results listed below by more than ±10%. Analyze the GC test sample using the *GC Conditions for Analysis* given above.

Component in Test Sample	Order of Elution Nonpolar	Order of Elution Polar	Normalized % Area (FID) Nonpolar	Normalized % Area (FID) Polar
Benzyl Alcohol	1	4	22.0	21.3
Acetophenone	2	2	21.1	21.4
Linalool	3	1	20.8	21.0
Benzyl Acetate	4	3	18.6	19.1
Hydroxycitronellal	5	5	16.7	16.7

M-2 ASSAYS FOR CERTAIN ALDEHYDES AND KETONES

M-2a Aldehydes—Hydroxylamine *tert*-Butyl Alcohol Method

Hydroxylamine Solution Dissolve 45 g of reagent-grade hydroxylamine hydrochloride in 130 mL of water, add 850 mL of *tert*-butyl alcohol, mix, and using a pH meter, neutralize to a pH of 3.0 to 3.5 with sodium hydroxide. [**Caution**—Do not heat the solution.]

Procedure Transfer an accurately weighed quantity of sample, as specified below, into a 250-mL glass-stoppered flask. Add 50 mL of the *Hydroxylamine Solution*, mix thoroughly, and allow to stand at room temperature for the time specified. Titrate with 0.5 N sodium hydroxide to the same pH as that of the *Hydroxylamine Solution* used. Calculate the percent aldehyde or ketone by the equation

$$AK = (S)(100e)/W,$$

in which AK is the percent aldehyde or ketone; S is the number of milliliters of 0.5 N sodium hydroxide consumed in the titration of the sample; e is the equivalence factor given below; and W is the weight, in milligrams, of the sample taken.

Substance	Sample Weight (g)	Reaction Time (min)	1 mL of 0.5 N NaOH Equivalent to
Cuminic Aldehyde	1	60	74.11 mg of $C_{10}H_{12}O$
Myristaldehyde	1.5	60	106.18 mg of $C_{14}H_{28}O$
Valeraldehyde	1	60	43.07 mg of $C_5H_{10}O$

M-2b Procedure Requiring the Use of Sealed Glass Vials or Ampules

Transfer 65 mL of 0.5 N hydroxylamine hydrochloride and 50.0 mL of 0.5 N triethanolamine into a suitable heat-resistant pressure bottle provided with a tight closure that can be fastened securely. Replace the air in the bottle by passing a gentle stream of nitrogen for 2 min through a glass tube positioned so that the end is just above the surface of the liquid. Add the quantity of sample specified below, contained in a sealed glass ampule, to the mixture in the pressure bottle. Introduce several pieces of 8-mm glass rod, cap the bottle, and shake vigorously to break the ampule. Allow the bottle to stand at room temperature for the time specified, swirling occasionally. Cool, if necessary, and uncap the bottle cautiously to prevent any loss of the contents. Titrate with 0.5 N sulfuric acid to pH 3.4, using a suitable pH meter. Perform a residual blank titration (see *General Provisions*). Each milliliter of 0.5 N sulfuric acid is equivalent to the amount specified below.

Substance	Sample Weight (mg)	Reaction Time (min)	1 mL of 0.5 N H$_2$SO$_4$ Equivalent to
Acetaldehyde	600	30	22.03 mg of C$_2$H$_4$O

M-2c Aldehydes—Hydroxylamine Method

Hydroxylamine Hydrochloride Solution   Dissolve 50 g of hydroxylamine hydrochloride (preferably reagent grade or freshly recrystallized before using) in 90 mL of water, and dilute to 1000 mL with aldehyde-free alcohol. Adjust the solution to a pH of 3.4 with 0.5 N alcoholic potassium hydroxide.

Procedure   Transfer an accurately weighed quantity of sample, as specified in the table below, into a 125-mL Erlenmeyer flask. Add 30 mL of *Hydroxylamine Hydrochloride Solution*, mix thoroughly, and allow to stand at room temperature for the time specified below. Titrate with 0.5 N alcoholic potassium hydroxide to a green-yellow endpoint that matches the color of 30 mL of *Hydroxylamine Hydrochloride Solution* in a 125-mL flask when the same volume of bromophenol blue TS has been added to each flask, or preferably, using a suitable pH meter, titrate to a pH of 3.4. Calculate the percent aldehyde (A) by the equation

$$A = (S - b)(100e)/W,$$

in which S is the number of milliliters of 0.5 N alcoholic potassium hydroxide consumed in the titration of the sample; b is the number of milliliters of 0.5 N alcoholic potassium hydroxide consumed in the titration of the blank; e is the equivalence factor given below; and W is the weight, in milligrams, of the sample taken.

Substance	Sample Weight (mg)	Reaction Time (min)	1 mL of 0.5 N KOH Equivalent to
Butyraldehyde	900	60	36.06 mg of C$_4$H$_8$O
Isobutyraldehyde	900	60	36.06 mg of C$_4$H$_8$O
Propionaldehyde	750	30	29.04 mg of C$_3$H$_6$O

M-2d Ketones—Hydroxylamine Method

Hydroxylamine Solution   Dissolve 20 g of hydroxylamine hydrochloride (reagent grade or, preferably, freshly crystallized) in 40 mL of water, and dilute to 400 mL with alcohol. While stirring, add 300 mL of 0.5 N alcoholic potassium hydroxide, and filter. Use this solution within 2 days.

Procedure   Transfer an accurately weighed quantity of sample, as specified below, into a 250-mL glass-stoppered flask. Add 75.0 mL of *Hydroxylamine Solution* to this flask and to a similar flask for a residual blank titration (see *General Provisions*). Attach the flask to a suitable condenser, reflux the mixture for the time specified, and then cool to room temperature. Titrate both flasks with 0.5 N hydrochloric acid to the same green-yellow endpoint using bromophenol blue TS as the indicator or, preferably, using a pH meter, to a pH of 3.4. (If the indicator is used, the endpoint color must be the same as that produced when the blank is titrated to a pH of 3.4.) Calculate the percent ketone by the equation

$$K = (b - S)(100e)/W,$$

in which K is the percent ketone; b is the number of milliliters of 0.5 N hydrochloric acid consumed in the residual blank titration; S is the number of milliliters of 0.5 N hydrochloric acid consumed in the titration of the sample; e is the equivalence factor given below; and W is the weight, in milligrams, of the sample taken.

Substance	Sample Weight (mg)	Reaction Time (min)	1 mL of 0.5 N HCl Equivalent to
4-Methyl-2-pentanone	1200	60	50.08 mg of C$_6$H$_{12}$O

M-3 ASSAY BY TITRIMETRIC PROCEDURES

M-3a Direct Aqueous Acid Base Titrations

Transfer an accurately weighed amount of sample, as specified below, into a 250-mL Erlenmeyer flask containing 75 to 100 mL of water, add phenolphthalein TS, and titrate with 0.5 N sodium hydroxide to the first pink color that persists for 15 s. Each milliliter of 0.5 N sodium hydroxide is equivalent to the amount of substance as specified below.

Substance	Sample Weight (g)	1 mL of 0.5 N NaOH Equivalent to
Butyric Acid	1.5	44.06 mg of C$_4$H$_8$O$_2$
Hexanoic Acid	2.0	58.08 mg of C$_6$H$_{12}$O$_2$
Isobutyric Acid	1.5	44.06 mg of C$_4$H$_8$O$_2$
Isovaleric Acid	1.5	51.07 mg of C$_5$H$_{10}$O$_2$
Levulinic Acid	1.0	58.06 mg of C$_5$H$_8$O$_3$
2-Mercaptopropionic Acid	1.0	53.08 mg of C$_3$H$_6$O$_2$S
2-Methyl-2-pentenoic Acid	2.0	57.02 mg of C$_6$H$_{10}$O$_2$
2-Methylbutyric Acid	1.0	51.07 mg of C$_5$H$_{10}$O$_2$
4-Methylpentanoic Acid	2.0	58.08 mg of C$_6$H$_{12}$O$_2$
2-Methylpentanoic Acid	2.0	58.08 mg of C$_6$H$_{12}$O$_2$
Nonanoic Acid	1.0	79.12 mg of C$_9$H$_{18}$O$_2$

M-3b Direct Aqueous Alcoholic Acid Base Titrations

Dissolve 1 g of sample, accurately weighed, in 50% ethanol/water that previously has been neutralized to phenolphthalein TS with 0.1 N sodium hydroxide. Titrate with 0.5 N sodium hydroxide to a pink color. Each mL of titrant is equivalent to the amount of substance specified below.

Conditions for Direct Aqueous Alcoholic Acid Base Titrations

Substance	1 mL of 0.5 N NaOH Equivalent to
Cinnamic Acid (dried in desiccator 3 h over silica gel)	74.08 mg of $C_9H_8O_2$
2-Ethylbutyric Acid	58.08 mg of $C_6H_{12}O_2$
Phenylacetic Acid (dried 3 h over H_2SO_4)	68.08 mg of $C_8H_8O_2$
Valeric Acid	51.07 mg of $C_5H_{10}O_2$

M-4 ALCOHOL CONTENT OF ETHYL OXYHYDRATE

Mix 25.0 mL of sample with an equal volume of water in a separator, saturate with sodium chloride, and extract with three 25-mL portions of solvent hexane. Extract the combined solvent hexane extracts with three 10-mL portions of a saturated solution of sodium chloride, and then discard the solvent hexane solutions. Combine the saline solutions in a suitable distillation flask, and distill, collecting 25 mL of distillate. The specific gravity of the distillate is not greater than 0.9814, indicating an alcohol content of not less than 14.0% by volume.

M-5 ACIDITY DETERMINATION BY IODOMETRIC METHOD

Ethyl Formate (Acidity as Formic Acid)   Transfer about 5 g of sample, accurately weighed, into a glass-stoppered flask containing a solution of 500 mg of potassium iodate and 2 g of potassium iodide in 50 mL of water. Titrate the liberated iodine with 0.1 N sodium thiosulfate, using starch TS as the indicator. Each mL of 0.1 N sodium thiosulfate is equivalent to 4.603 mg of CH_2O_2.

M-6 LIMIT TEST FOR ANTIOXIDANTS IN ETHYL ACRYLATE

Preliminary Examination of the Sample   Wash a 25-mL portion of the sample with 25 mL of a 1:10 solution of sodium hydroxide. Any yellow or brown coloration in the extract indicates the presence of hydroquinone, in which case both of the procedures below (A and B) must be followed to determine the antioxidant content. If the sodium hydroxide extract remains colorless, the first procedure (A) need not be run, and the antioxidant content is determined by the second procedure (B) alone.

A. Determination of Hydroquinone

Carbonyl-Free Methanol   Add 5 g of 2,4-dinitrophenylhydrazine to 500 mL of anhydrous methanol, heat the mixture under a reflux condenser for 2 h, and then recover the methanol by distillation. Store the carbonyl-free methanol in tight containers.

2,4-Dinitrophenylhydrazine Solution   Dissolve 100 mg of 2,4-dinitrophenylhydrazine in 50 mL of *Carbonyl-Free Methanol*, add 4 mL of hydrochloric acid, and dilute to 100 mL with water.

Sodium Carbonate Solution   Dissolve 530 mg of sodium carbonate in sufficient water to make 100 mL.

Pyridine–Diethanolamine Solution   Mix 5 mL of diethanolamine with 500 mL of freshly distilled pyridine.

Calibration Curve   Transfer 25 mg of hydroquinone, accurately weighed, into a 100-mL volumetric flask, add sufficient butyl acetate to volume, and mix thoroughly (250 µg/mL). Prepare a series of standards by transferring 1.0-, 2.0-, 3.0-, 4.0-, and 6.0-mL portions of this solution into separate 50-mL volumetric flasks, and diluting each aliquot to 50.0 mL with butyl acetate. One milliliter of each of these standards contains 5, 10, 15, 20, and 30 µg, respectively, of hydroquinone. Transfer 1.0 mL of each solution into separate 25-mL glass-stoppered graduates, and continue as directed in the *Procedure*, beginning with "...add 2.0 mL of water..." Plot a calibration curve of absorbance versus micrograms of hydroquinone. Fifteen micrograms of hydroquinone should be equivalent to approximately 0.30 units of absorbance, and the curve should intersect the origin.

Procedure   Using a hypodermic syringe, transfer 0.2 mL of sample, accurately weighed, into a 25-mL glass-stoppered graduate, add 2.0 mL of water, stopper the graduate, and mix the contents well without allowing contact between the liquid and the stopper. Add 0.5 mL of *Sodium Carbonate Solution* to the mixture, and immediately shake gently for 5 s, avoiding contact between the solution and the stopper. Immediately add 1.0 mL of a 15% (v/v) solution of sulfuric acid, shake as previously directed, and add 1 mL of *2,4-Dinitrophenylhydrazine Solution*. Stopper the graduate and place it in a water bath, maintained at a temperature between 70° and 72°, for 1 h. Shake samples three times during the heating period. Cool the graduate to room temperature, dilute the contents to 15 mL with water, add 5.8 mL of benzene, stopper, shake vigorously, and then allow the phases to separate. Using a suitable pipet, transfer 2.0 mL of the benzene layer into a test tube, add 10.0 mL of *Pyridine–Diethanolamine Solution*, and mix. Transfer a portion of this solution into a 2-cm cell, and determine the absorbance at 620 nm with a suitable spectrophotometer, using as a blank 1.0 mL of butyl acetate treated in the same manner as the sample except that 5.0 mL of benzene is used for the extraction instead of 5.8 mL. From the previously prepared *Calibration Curve*, read the micrograms of hydroquinone and/or benzoquinone corresponding to the absorbance of the solution from the sample, and record this value as w. Calculate the milligrams per kilogram of hydroquinone (mg/kg HQ) in the sample by the formula

$$\text{Result} = 1000w/W,$$

in which W is the weight (mg) of the sample taken.

B. Determination of Hydroquinone Monomethyl Ether

Antioxidant-Free Ethyl Acrylate Wash a suitable volume of the sample with three separate, similar-sized volumes of a 1:10 sodium hydroxide solution. After the last washing, add a small amount of sodium chloride, if necessary, to remove any turbidity that may be present.

Calibration Curve Transfer 25.0 mg of hydroquinone monomethyl ether, accurately weighed, into a 100-mL volumetric flask, add *Antioxidant-Free Ethyl Acrylate* to volume, and shake to effect complete solution (250 µg/mL). Prepare a series of standards by transferring 1.0-, 5.0-, 10.0-, and 20.0-mL portions of this solution into separate 25-mL volumetric flasks, diluting each to volume with *Antioxidant-Free Ethyl Acrylate*, and mixing. One milliliter of each of the standards contains 10, 50, 100, and 200 µg, respectively, of hydroquinone monomethyl ether. Transfer 5.0 mL of each solution into separate 50-mL volumetric flasks, dilute each to volume with isooctane, and mix. Determine the absorbance of each solution in a 1-cm silica cell at 292 nm with a suitable spectrophotometer, using a 1:10 dilution of *Antioxidant-Free Ethyl Acrylate* as the blank. Plot a calibration curve of absorbance versus micrograms of hydroquinone monomethyl ether. The curve should be linear and should intersect the origin.

Procedure Transfer 5.0 mL of sample, accurately weighed, into a 50-mL volumetric flask, dilute to volume with isooctane, and mix. Determine the absorbance of this solution in a 1-cm silica cell at 292 nm with a suitable spectrophotometer, using a 1:10 dilution of *Antioxidant-Free Ethyl Acrylate* in isooctane as the blank. From the previously prepared *Calibration Curve* read the micrograms of hydroquinone monomethyl ether corresponding to the absorbance of the sample solution, and record this value as w. Calculate the milligrams per kilogram of hydroquinone monomethyl ether (mg/kg HMME) in the sample by the formula

$$\text{Result} = w/W,$$

in which W is the weight, in grams, of the sample taken.

[NOTE—If the first sodium hydroxide extract obtained under *Preliminary Examination of the Sample* (or under *Antioxidant-Free Ethyl Acrylate*) showed a yellow coloration, the true mg/kg HMME is obtained by subtracting the mg/kg HQ, obtained under section *A*, from the apparent mg/kg HMME.]

M-7 LIMIT TEST FOR HYDROCARBONS IN EUGENOL

Dissolve 1 mL of sample in 20 mL of 0.5 N sodium hydroxide contained in a stoppered 50-mL tube, add 18 mL of water, and mix. A clear mixture results immediately, but it may become turbid when exposed to air.

M-8 LIMIT TEST FOR HYDROCYANIC ACID IN BENZALDEHYDE

Shake 0.5 mL of sample with 5 mL of water, add 0.5 mL of 1 N sodium hydroxide and 0.1 mL of ferrous sulfate TS, and warm the mixture gently. Upon the addition of a slight excess of hydrochloric acid, no green-blue color or blue precipitate evolves within 15 min.

M-9 LIMIT TEST FOR LEAD

A *Sample Solution* containing a 1-g sample and prepared as directed for organic compounds meets the requirements of the *Lead Limit Test*, Appendix IIIB, using 10 µg Pb (10 mL of *Diluted Standard Lead Solution*) in the control.

M-10 LIMIT TEST FOR METHYL COMPOUNDS IN ETHYL ACETATE

Transfer 20 mL of sample into a 500-mL separatory funnel, add a solution of 20 g of sodium hydroxide in 50 mL of water, stopper the separatory funnel, and wrap it securely in a towel for protection against the heat of the reaction. Shake the mixture vigorously for about 5 min, cautiously opening the stopcock from time to time to permit the escape of air. Continue shaking the mixture vigorously until a homogeneous liquid results, then distill, and collect about 25 mL of the distillate. Add 1 drop of dilute phosphoric acid (1:20) and 1 drop of a 1:20 solution of potassium permanganate to 1 drop of the distillate. Mix, allow to stand for 1 min, and add, dropwise, a 1:20 solution of sodium bisulfite until the color disappears. If a brown color remains, add 1 drop of the dilute phosphoric acid. Add to the colorless solution 5 mL of a freshly prepared 1:2000 solution of chromotropic acid in 75% sulfuric acid, and heat on a steam bath for 10 min at 60°. No violet color appears.

M-11 LIMIT TEST FOR PEROXIDE VALUE

Add 10 mL of sample to 50 mL of a 3:2 (v/v) mixture of glacial acetic acid and chloroform. Add 1 mL of a saturated solution of potassium iodide to this solution, allow to stand for exactly 1 min with gentle shaking, and then introduce 100 mL of water and a few drops of starch TS. Titrate immediately with 0.1 N sodium thiosulfate. Each mL of 0.1 N sodium thiosulfate, multiplied by 5, equals the peroxide value, expressed in millimoles of peroxide per liter of the sample.

M-12 LIMIT TEST FOR READILY CARBONIZABLE SUBSTANCES IN ETHYL ACETATE

Carefully pour 2 mL of sample onto 10 mL of 95% sulfuric acid to form separate layers. No discoloration appears within 15 min.

M-13 LIMIT TEST FOR READILY OXIDIZABLE SUBSTANCES IN dl-MENTHOL

Transfer 500 mg of dl-menthol into a clean, dry test tube, and add 10 mL of potassium permanganate solution (prepared by diluting 3 mL of 0.1 N potassium permanganate to 100 mL with water). Place the test tube in a beaker of water maintained between 45° and 50°. At 30-s intervals, quickly remove the test tube from the bath and shake. The color of potassium permanganate is still apparent after 5 min.

M-14 LIMIT TEST FOR REDUCING SUBSTANCES

Dilute 2 mL of sample in a glass-stoppered flask with 50 mL of water and 5 mL of sulfuric acid, shaking the flask during the addition. While the solution is still warm, titrate with 0.1 N potassium permanganate. Not more than 1 mL is required to produce a pink color that persists for 30 min.

M-15 ACID VALUE, FLAVOR CHEMICALS (OTHER THAN ESSENTIAL OILS)

Dissolve about 10 g of sample, accurately weighed, in 50 mL of alcohol, previously neutralized to phenolphthalein with 0.1 N sodium hydroxide. (Add 50 g of ice when testing cinnamyl formate, citronellyl formate, geranyl formate, isoamyl formate, or linalyl formate.) Add 1 mL of phenolphthalein TS, and titrate with 0.1 N sodium hydroxide until the solution remains faintly pink after shaking for 10 s, unless otherwise directed in the individual monograph. Calculate the acid value (AV) by the equation

$$AV = (5.61 \times S)/W,$$

in which S is the number of milliliters of 0.1 N sodium hydroxide consumed in the titration of the sample, and W is the weight (g) of the sample.

When phenol red TS is specified as the indicator in the individual monograph, proceed as directed above, and titrate with 0.1 N sodium hydroxide to the appearance of the first endpoint, a yellow-orange color.

M-16 RESIDUE ON EVAPORATION

Transfer the quantity of sample specified in the monograph, accurately weighed, into a suitable evaporating dish that has previously been heated on a steam bath, cooled to room temperature in a desiccator, and accurately weighed. Weigh the sample in the dish. Heat the evaporating dish containing the sample on the steam bath for 1 h. Cool the dish and its contents to room temperature in a desiccator, and accurately weigh. Calculate the residue as percent of the sample used.

M-17 QUALITATIVE TEST FOR PHENOLS USING FERRIC CHLORIDE

Allyl Isothiocyanate Dilute 1 mL of the sample with 5 mL of alcohol, and add 1 drop of ferric chloride TS. A blue color does not immediately appear.

Anethole Shake 1 mL of sample with 20 mL of water, and allow the liquids to separate. Filter the water layer through a filter paper previously moistened with water, and add 3 drops of ferric chloride TS to 10 mL of the filtrate. No purple color appears.

Anisole Shake 1 mL of sample with about 20 mL of water, allow the layers to separate, collect the water layer in a test tube, and add a few drops of ferric chloride TS. No green, blue, or purple color appears.

Cresyl Acetate (Test for Free Cresol)

Ferric Chloride Solution Add 1.5 g of anhydrous ferric chloride to 850 mL of chloroform contained in a 2-L beaker. Add 100 mL of ethylene glycol monobutyl ether. When the ferric chloride has dissolved, add 50 mL of pyridine, mix, and filter through a Büchner funnel.

Procedure Transfer 5 mL of sample into a 15-mm test tube, and add 10 mL of the *Ferric Chloride Solution*. The color of the solution is not a darker green than is a solution of 5 mL of a 1% solution of cresol in cresol-free methyl p-cresol mixed with 10 mL of the *Ferric Chloride Solution*.

APPENDIX XII: MICROBIOLOGICAL TESTS

A. MEDIA AND REAGENTS

The following solutions and culture media have been found satisfactory for the purposes for which they are prescribed in the tests for microbial contamination in this appendix. Other media may be used provided that their suitability can be demonstrated.

Stock Buffer Solution Transfer 34 g of potassium dihydrogen phosphate to a 1000-mL volumetric flask, dissolve in 500 mL of water, adjust with sodium hydroxide to a pH of 7.2 ± 0.2, add water to volume, and mix. Dispense in containers, and sterilize. Store at a temperature of 2°–8°.

Phosphate Buffer Solution pH 7.2 Prepare a mixture of water and Stock Buffer Solution (800:1 v/v), and sterilize.

Buffered Sodium Chloride-Peptone Solution pH 7.0

Potassium dihydrogen phosphate	3.6 g
Disodium hydrogen phosphate dihydrate	7.2 g (equivalent to 0.067 M phosphate)
Sodium chloride	4.3 g
Peptone (meat or casein)	1.0 g
Water	1000 mL

Sterilize in an autoclave using a validated cycle.

Enterobacteria Enrichment Broth Mossel

Pancreatic digest of gelatin	10.0 g
Glucose monohydrate	5.0 g
Dehydrated ox bile	20.0 g
Potassium dihydrogen phosphate	2.0 g
Disodium hydrogen phosphate dihydrate	8.0 g
Brilliant green	15 mg
Water	1000 mL

Adjust the pH so that after heating it is 7.2 ± 0.2 at 25°. Heat at 100° for 30 min, and cool immediately.

Rappaport Vassiliadis Salmonella Enrichment Broth

Soya peptone	4.5 g
Magnesium chloride hexahydrate	29.0 g
Sodium chloride	8.0 g
Dipotassium phosphate	0.4 g
Potassium dihydrogen phosphate	0.6 g
Malachite green	0.036 g
Water	1000 mL

Dissolve, warming slightly. Sterilize in an autoclave using a validated cycle, at a temperature not exceeding 115°. The pH is to be 5.2 ± 0.2 at 25° after heating and autoclaving.

Sabouraud Dextrose Agar

Dextrose	40.0 g
Mixture of peptic digest of animal tissue and pancreatic digest of casein (1:1)	10.0 g
Agar	15.0 g
Water	1000 mL

Adjust the pH so that after sterilization it is 5.6 ± 0.2 at 25°. Sterilize in an autoclave using a validated cycle.

Soybean-Casein Digest Agar

Pancreatic digest of casein	15.0 g
Papaic digest of soybean	5.0 g
Sodium chloride	5.0 g
Agar	15.0 g
Water	1000 mL

Adjust the pH so that after sterilization it is 7.3 ± 0.2 at 25°. Sterilize in an autoclave using a validated cycle.

Soybean-Casein Digest Broth

Pancreatic digest of casein	17.0 g
Papaic digest of soybean	3.0 g
Sodium chloride	5.0 g
Dibasic hydrogen phosphate	2.5 g
Glucose monohydrate	2.5 g
Water	1000 mL

Adjust the pH so that after sterilization it is 7.3 ± 0.2 at 25°. Sterilize in an autoclave using a validated cycle.

Violet Red Bile Glucose Agar

Yeast extract	3.0 g
Pancreatic digest of gelatin	7.0 g
Bile salts	1.5 g
Sodium chloride	5.0 g
Glucose monohydrate	10.0 g
Agar	15.0 g
Neutral red	30 mg
Crystal violet	2 mg
Water	1000 mL

Adjust the pH so that after heating it is 7.4 ± 0.2 at 25°. Heat to boiling; do not heat in an autoclave.

Xylose Lysine Deoxycholate Agar

Xylose	3.5 g
L-Lysine	5.0 g
Lactose monohydrate	7.5 g
Sucrose	7.5 g
Sodium chloride	5.0 g
Yeast extract	3.0 g
Phenol red	80 mg
Agar	13.5 g
Sodium deoxycholate	2.5 g
Sodium thiosulfate	6.8 g
Ferric ammonium citrate	0.8 g
Water	1000 mL

Adjust the pH so that after heating it is 7.4 ± 0.2 at 25°. Heat to boiling, cool to 50°, and pour into Petri dishes. Do not heat in an autoclave.

B. MICROBIOLOGICAL ENUMERATION TESTS

The tests described in section B of this appendix are used for quantitative enumeration of mesophilic bacteria and fungi that may grow under aerobic conditions in food ingredients.

The tests are designed primarily to determine whether a food ingredient complies with an established specification for microbiological quality. When used for such purposes, follow the instructions given below, including the number of samples to be taken, and interpret the results as stated.

The methods are not applicable to products containing viable microorganisms as active ingredients. Alternative microbiological procedures, including automated methods, may be used, provided that their equivalence to the FCC method has been demonstrated. [NOTE—In preparing for and in applying the tests, observe aseptic precautions in handling the specimens.]

TOTAL AEROBIC MICROBIAL COUNT

Method I (Plate Count Method)
Sample Preparation
Unless otherwise directed in the monograph, dissolve or dilute 10 g or 10 mL of sample to be examined in 100 mL of *Buffered Sodium Chloride-Peptone Solution pH 7.0*, *Phosphate Buffer Solution pH 7.2*, or *Soybean-Casein Digest Broth*. If necessary, adjust to a pH of 6–8. Further dilutions, where necessary, are prepared with the same diluent.

Procedure

Negative Control To verify testing conditions, a negative control is performed using the chosen diluent in place of the test preparation. There must be no growth of microorganisms.

Analysis To 9-cm Petri dishes add 1 mL of the *Sample Preparation* and 15–20 mL of *Soybean-Casein Digest Agar* which is not more than 45°. Prepare at least 2 Petri dishes for each level of dilution. Incubate the plates at 30°–35° for 3–5 days.

Interpretation of Results
Select the plates corresponding to a given dilution and showing the highest number of colonies less than 250. The total aerobic microbial count (TAMC) is considered to be equal to the number of cfu found. If colonies of fungi are detected, they are counted as part of the TAMC. Take the arithmetic mean of the counts and calculate the number of cfu per g or per mL of product.

TOTAL YEASTS AND MOLDS COUNT

Method I (Plate Count Method)
Sample Preparation
Unless otherwise directed in the monograph, dissolve or dilute 10 g or 10 mL of sample to be examined in 100 mL of *Buffered Sodium Chloride-Peptone Solution pH 7.0*, *Phosphate Buffer Solution pH 7.2*, or *Soybean-Casein Digest Broth*. If necessary, adjust to a pH of 6–8. Further dilutions, where necessary, are prepared with the same diluent.

Procedure

Negative Control To verify testing conditions, a negative control is performed using the chosen diluent in place of the test preparation. There must be no growth of microorganisms.

Analysis To 9-cm Petri dishes add 1 mL of the *Sample Preparation* and 15–20 mL of *Sabouraud Dextrose Agar*, which is not more than 45°. Prepare at least two Petri dishes for each level of dilution. Incubate the plates at 20°–25° for 5–7 days.

Interpretation of Results
Select the plates corresponding to a given dilution and showing the highest number of colonies less than 50. The total combined yeasts and molds count (TYMC) is considered to be equal to the number of cfu found. If colonies of bacteria are detected, they are counted as part of the TYMC. Take the arithmetic mean of the counts and calculate the number of cfu per g or per mL of sample.

C. TESTS FOR ABSENCE OF SPECIFIC MICROORGANISMS

The tests described in section C of this appendix are used for determining the absence of objectionable microorganisms in food ingredients. [NOTE—In preparing for and in applying the tests, observe aseptic precautions in handling the specimens.]

BILE-TOLERANT GRAM-NEGATIVE BACTERIA

Sample Preparation Unless otherwise directed in the monograph, dissolve a sample of not less than 1 g in *Soybean-Casein Digest Broth* at a sample/broth ratio of 1:10, mix, and incubate at 20°–25° for a time sufficient to resuscitate the bacteria but not sufficient to encourage multiplication of the organisms (usually 2 h but not more than 5 h).

Procedure Unless otherwise directed in the monograph, inoculate *Enterobacteria Enrichment Broth Mossel* with a volume of *Sample Preparation* corresponding to 1 g of sample. Incubate at 30°–35° for 24–48 h. Subculture on plates of *Violet Red Bile Glucose Agar*. Incubate at 30°–35° for 18–24 h.

Interpretation of Results The product complies with the test if there is no growth of colonies.

ENTEROBACTER SAKAZAKII (CRONOBACTER SPP.)

Sample Preparation Proceed as directed in the test for *Bile-Tolerant Gram-Negative Bacteria* above.

Procedure Proceed as directed in the test for *Bile-Tolerant Gram-Negative Bacteria* above. Growth of yellow-pigmented colonies indicates the possible presence of *E. sakazakii*. This is confirmed by a negative oxidase test in conjunction with other commercially available identification tests[1].

[1] API ID 32 E (bioMérieux, Durham, NC), or equivalent.

Interpretation of Results If the identification of a colony identified on *Violet Red Bile Glucose Agar* leads to *E. sakazakii*, then the test is considered as positive. If the identification leads to other bacteria than *E. sakazakii*, then the test is considered as negative. If there is no growth on the *Violet Red Bile Glucose Agar* plate, then the test is considered as negative.

SALMONELLA SPP.

Sample Preparation Dissolve the quantity of sample, as directed in the monograph, in a volume of *Soybean-Casein Digest Broth*, as directed in the monograph, mix, and incubate at 30°–35° for 18–24 h.

Procedure Transfer 0.1 mL of the *Sample Preparation* to 10 mL of *Rappaport Vassiliadis Salmonella Enrichment Broth*, and incubate at 30°–35° for 18–24 h. Subculture on plates of *Xylose Lysine Deoxycholate Agar*. Incubate at 30°–35° for 18–48 h. The possible presence of *Salmonella* is indicated by the growth of well-developed, red colonies, with or without black centers. This is confirmed by commercially available identification tests.

Interpretation of Results The product complies with the test if colonies of the types described are not present or if the confirmatory identification tests are negative.

APPENDIX XIII: ADULTERANTS AND CONTAMINANTS IN FOOD INGREDIENTS

Tests contained within this Appendix are not monograph requirements, but rather are provided as informational methods for FCC users.

DIETHYLENE GLYCOL AND ETHYLENE GLYCOL IN GLYCERIN[1]

This method was developed for the identification and quantification of low levels of ethylene glycol and diethylene glycol in glycerin.

Standard solution: 0.025 mg/mL of USP Ethylene Glycol RS, 0.025 mg/mL of USP Diethylene Glycol RS, 50 mg/mL of USP Glycerin RS, and 0.05 mg/mL of 2,2,2-trichloroethanol (internal standard) in methanol

Sample solution: 50 mg/mL of sample and 0.05 mg/mL of 2,2,2-trichloroethanol (internal standard) in methanol

Chromatographic system, *Appendix IIA*
 Mode: GC
 Detector: Flame ionization
 Column: 0.53-mm × 30-m fused-silica analytical column coated with 3.0-μm 6% cyanopropylphenyl–94% dimethylpolysiloxane stationary phase[2]
 Temperature
  Injector: 220°
  Detector: 250°
  Column: See the temperature program table below.

Initial Temperature (°)	Temperature Ramp (°/min)	Final Temperature (°)	Hold Time at Final Temperature (min)
100	—	100	4
100	50	120	10
120	50	220	6

 Carrier gas: Helium
 Injection size: 1.0 μL
 Flow rate: 4.5 mL/min
 Injection type: Split flow ratio is about 10:1
 System suitability requirement: The resolution, R, between diethylene glycol and glycerin from the *Standard solution* is NLT 1.5.

Analysis: Separately inject equal volumes of the *Standard solution* and *Sample solution* into the chromatograph, and measure the responses for the major peaks on the resulting chromatograms. Diethylene glycol and ethylene glycol can be identified in the *Sample solution* on the basis of peak retention times compared to those in the *Standard solution*. [NOTE—The relative retention times for ethylene glycol, 2,2,2-trichloroethanol, diethylene glycol, and glycerin are about 0.3, 0.6, 0.8, and 1.0, respectively. See *Figure 1* for example chromatograms.] The percentages of diethylene glycol and ethylene glycol in the portion of sample taken are calculated using the following formula:

$$\text{Result} = (R_U/R_S) \times (C_S/C_U) \times 100$$

in which R_U is the analyte relative response (analyte peak response/2,2,2-trichloroethanol peak response) from the *Sample solution*; R_S is the analyte relative response (analyte peak response/2,2,2-trichloroethanol peak response) from the *Standard solution*; C_S is the concentration of analyte in the *Standard solution* (mg/mL); and C_U is the concentration of sample in the *Sample solution* (mg/mL).

Performance characteristics
 Limit of quantitation: 0.025% (w/w) for ethylene glycol and diethylene glycol
 Range: 0.013–0.031 mg/mL for ethylene glycol and 0.012–0.030 mg/mL for diethylene glycol. [NOTE—Wider linear ranges may be achievable but were not investigated when developing this method.]
 Accuracy: 99%–107% recovery from samples spiked with diethylene glycol and ethylene glycol at levels of 50%–120%
 Precision: Instrument precision: Less than 3.0% RSD; repeatability less than 4.0% RSD for analysis in the 50%–120% range

PESTICIDE RESIDUES

The methods and information contained in this section were designed to measure pesticide residues in food ingredients of botanical origin.

General Method for Pesticide Residues Analysis

DEFINITION

Where used in this compendium, the designation *pesticide* applies to any substance or mixture of substances intended to prevent, destroy, or control any unwanted species of plants or animals causing harm during or otherwise interfering with the production, processing, storage, transport, or marketing of pure articles. The designation includes substances intended for use as growth regulators, defoliants, or desiccants, and any substance applied to crops before or after harvest to protect the product from deterioration during storage and transport.

LIMITS

Limits for pesticides for foods are determined by the Environmental Protection Agency (EPA), and where no limit is set, the limit is zero. The limits contained in *Table 1*, therefore, may not be applicable in the United States and are provided for guidance purposes only, and not for the purpose of meeting a regulatory requirement in the United States. The limits may be applicable in other countries where the presence of pesticide residues is permitted. Unless otherwise specified in the individual monograph, the article under test contains NMT the amount of any pesticide indicated in *Table 1*.

Table 1

Substance	Limit (mg/kg)
Alachlor	0.02
Aldrin and Dieldrin (sum of)	0.05
Azinphos-methyl	1.0

---
[1] Based on the following published method: Holloway G., Maheswaran R., Bradby, S., and Wahab, S. 2010. Screening method for ethylene glycol and diethylene glycol in glycerin-containing products. *J Pharm Biomed Anal.* 51:507-511.
[2] DB-624 (J & W Scientific), or equivalent.

Table 1 (Continued)

Substance	Limit (mg/kg)
Bromopropylate	3.0
Chlordane (sum of cis- and trans- isomers and oxychlordane)	0.05
Chlorfenvinphos	0.5
Chlorpyrifos	0.2
Chlorpyrifos-methyl	0.1
Cypermethrin (and isomers)	1.0
DDT (sum of p,p'-DDT, o,p'-DDT, p,p'-DDE, and p,p'-TDE)	1.0
Deltamethrin	0.5
Diazinon	0.5
Dichlorvos	1.0
Dithiocarbamates (as CS_2)	2.0
Endosulfan (sum of endosulfan isomers and endosulfan sulfate)	3.0
Endrin	0.05
Ethion	2.0
Fenitrothion	0.5
Fenvalerate	1.5
Fonofos	0.05
Heptachlor (sum of heptachlor and heptachlor epoxide)	0.05
Hexachlorobenzene	0.1
Hexachlorocyclohexane isomers (other than γ)	0.3
Lindane (γ-hexachlorocyclohexane)	0.6
Malathion	1.0
Methidathion	0.2
Parathion	0.5
Parathion-methyl	0.2
Permethrin	1.0
Phosalone	0.1
Piperonyl butoxide	3.0
Pirimiphos-methyl	4.0
Pyrethrins (sum of)	3.0
Quintozene (sum of quintozene, pentachloroaniline and methyl pentachlorophenyl sulfide)	1.0

SAMPLING

For articles in containers holding less than 1 kg, mix the contents, and withdraw a quantity sufficient for the tests. For articles in containers holding between 1 and 5 kg, withdraw equal portions from the upper, middle, and lower parts of the container, each of the samples being sufficient to carry out the tests. Thoroughly mix the samples, and withdraw an amount sufficient to carry out the tests. For containers holding more than 5 kg, withdraw three samples, each weighing NLT 250 g, from the upper, middle, and lower parts of the container. Thoroughly mix the samples, and withdraw a portion sufficient to carry out the tests.

If the number of the containers, n, is three or fewer, withdraw samples from each container as indicated above. If the number of containers is more than three, take samples from

$$\sqrt{n} + 1$$

containers, rounding up to the nearest whole number if necessary.

[NOTE—Conduct tests without delay to avoid possible degradation of the residues. If this is not possible, store the samples in hermetic containers suitable for food contact, at a temperature below 0°, and protected from light.]

REAGENTS

Use reagents and solvents that are free from any contaminants, especially pesticides, that might interfere with the analysis. It is often necessary to use special grade solvents suitable for pesticide residue analysis or solvents that have recently been redistilled in an apparatus made entirely of glass. In any case, suitable blank tests must be performed.

PREPARATION OF APPARATUS

Clean all equipment, especially glassware, to ensure that it is free from pesticides. Soak all glassware for a minimum of 16 hours in a solution of phosphate-free detergent, rinse with copious quantities of distilled water, and then wash with acetone, followed by hexane or heptane.

QUALITATIVE AND QUANTITATIVE ANALYSIS OF PESTICIDE RESIDUES

Use validated analytical procedures that satisfy the following criteria. The method, especially with respect to its purification steps, is suitable for the combination of pesticide residue and substance under test, and is not susceptible to interference from co-extractives. Measure the limits of detection and quantification for each pesticide matrix combination to be analyzed: the method is shown to recover between 70% and 110% of each pesticide; the repeatability and reproducibility of the method are NLT the appropriate values indicated in *Table 2*; and the concentrations of test and reference solutions and the setting of the apparatus are such that a linear response is obtained from the analytical detector.

Table 2

Concentration of Pesticide (mg/kg)	Repeatability (difference, ± mg/kg)	Reproducibility (difference, ± mg/kg)
0.010	0.005	0.01
0.100	0.025	0.05
1.000	0.125	0.25

Test for Pesticides

Depending on the substance being examined, it may be necessary to modify, sometimes extensively, the procedure described hereafter. Additionally, it may be necessary to perform another method with another column having a different polarity, another detection method (e.g., mass spectrometry), or a different method (e.g., immunochemical method) to confirm the results.

EXTRACTION

[NOTE—Use the following procedure for the analysis of samples and articles having a water content of less than 15%. Samples having a higher water content may be dried, provided that the drying procedure does not significantly affect the pesticide content.]

To 10 g of the coarsely powdered substance under test, add 100 mL of acetone, and allow to stand for 20 min. Add 1 mL of a solution in toluene containing 1.8 µg/mL of carbophenothion. Mix in a high-speed blender for 3 min. Filter this solution, and wash the residue with two 25-mL portions of acetone. Combine the filtrate and the washings, and heat, in a rotary evaporator, maintaining the temperature of the bath below 40° until the solvent has almost completely evaporated. To the residue add a few mL of toluene, and heat again until the acetone is completely re-

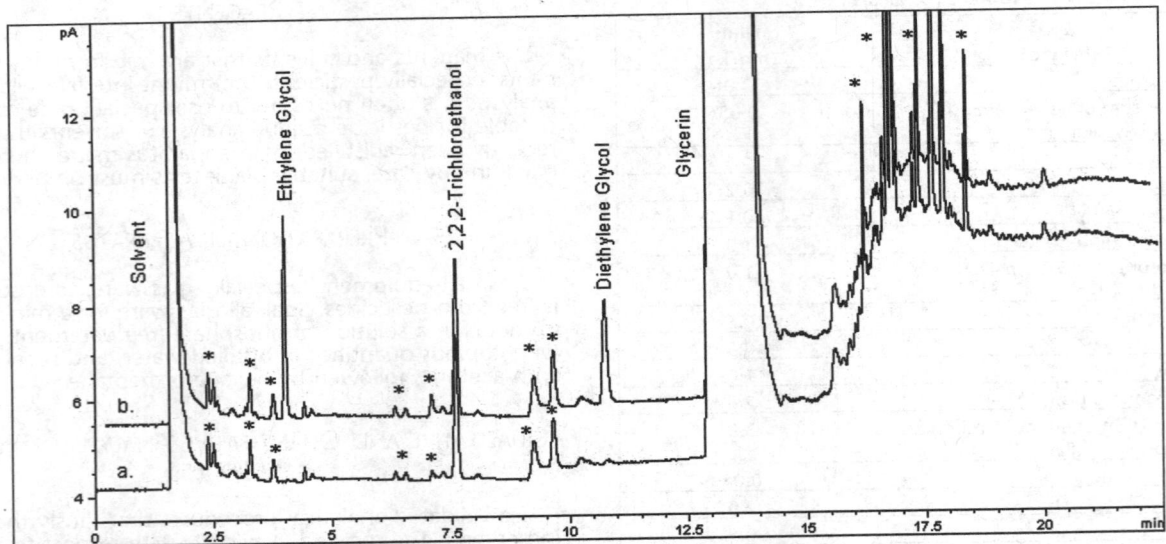

Figure 1. Overlay chromatogram of (a) *Sample solution* and (b) *Standard solution*. *Peaks from solvent and glycerin.

moved. Dissolve the residue in 8 mL of toluene. Pass through a membrane filter having a 45-µm porosity, rinse the flask and the filter with toluene, and dilute with toluene to 10.0 mL. This is *Solution A*.

PURIFICATION

Organochlorine, organophosphorus, and pyrethroid insecticides: The size-exclusion chromatograph is equipped with a 7.8-mm × 30-cm stainless steel column containing 5-µm packing of styrene-divinylbenzene copolymer. Toluene is used as the mobile phase at a flow rate of 1 mL/min.

Performance of the column: Inject 100 µL of a solution in toluene containing, in each mL, 0.5 mg of methyl red and 0.5 mg of oracet blue. The column is not suitable unless the color of the eluate changes from orange to blue at an elution volume of about 10.3 mL. If necessary, calibrate the column, using a solution in toluene containing suitable concentrations of the pesticide of interest having the lowest molecular weight (for example, dichlorvos) and that having the highest molecular weight (for example, deltamethrin). Determine which fraction of the eluate contains both pesticides.

Purification of the sample solution: Inject a suitable volume (100 to 500 µL) of *Solution A* into the chromatograph. Collect the fraction (*Solution B*) as determined above under *Performance of the column*. Organophosphorus pesticides elute between 8.8 and 10.9 mL. Organochlorine and pyrethroid pesticides elute between 8.5 and 10.3 mL.

Organochlorine and pyrethroid insecticides: Into a 5-mm × 10-cm chromatographic column, introduce a piece of fat-free cotton and 0.5 g of silica gel treated as follows. Heat chromatographic silica gel in an oven at 150° for NLT 4 hours. Allow to cool, and add dropwise a quantity of water corresponding to 1.5% of the weight of the silica gel used. Shake vigorously until agglomerates have disappeared, and continue shaking by mechanical means for 2 hours. Condition the column with 1.5 mL of hexane. [NOTE—Prepacked columns containing about 0.50 g of a suitable silica gel may also be used, provided they have been previously validated.] Concentrate *Solution B* almost to dryness, with the aid of a stream of helium or oxygen-free nitrogen, and dilute with toluene to a suitable volume (200 µL to 1 mL, according to the volume injected in the preparation of *Solution B*). Quantitatively transfer this solution to the column, and proceed with the chromatography, using 1.8 mL of toluene as the mobile phase. Collect the eluate (*Solution C*).

QUANTITATIVE ANALYSIS OF ORGANOPHOSPHORUS INSECTICIDES

Sample solution: Concentrate *Solution B* almost to dryness, with the aid of a stream of helium, and dilute with toluene to 100 µL.

Standard solution: Prepare at least three solutions in toluene containing each of the pesticides of interest and carbophenothion at concentrations suitable for plotting a calibration curve.

Chromatographic system, Appendix IIA
  Mode: GC
  Detector: Flame-ionization detector (alkali) or flame-photometric detector
  Column: 0.32-mm × 30-m fused silica column coated with a 0.25-µm layer of dimethylpolysiloxane
  Carrier gas: Hydrogen (may also use helium or nitrogen)
  Temperature
    Injector: 250°
    Detector: 275°
    Column: See the temperature program table below.

Initial Temperature (°)	Temperature Ramp (°/min)	Final Temperature (°)	Hold Time at Final Temperature (min)
80	—	80	1
80	30	150	3
150	4	280	1

Analysis: Use carbophenothion as the internal standard. [NOTE—If necessary, use a second internal standard to identify any possible interference with the peak corresponding to carbophenothion.] Inject the chosen volume of each solution, record the chromatograms, and measure the peak responses. [NOTE—The approximate relative retention times are listed in *Table 3*.] Calculate the content of each pesticide from the peak areas and the concentrations of the solution.

Table 3

Substance	Relative Retention Time
Dichlorvos	0.20
Fonofos	0.50
Diazinon	0.52
Parathion-methyl	0.59
Chlorpyrifos-methyl	0.60
Pirimiphos-methyl	0.66
Malathion	0.67
Parathion	0.69
Chlorpyrifos	0.70
Methidathion	0.78
Ethion	0.96
Carbophenothion	1.00
Azinphos-methyl	1.17
Phosalone	1.18

QUANTITATIVE ANALYSIS OF ORGANOCHLORINE AND PYRETHROID INSECTICIDES

Sample solution: Concentrate *Solution C* almost to dryness, with the aid of a stream of helium or oxygen-free nitrogen, and dilute with toluene to 500 µL.
Standard solution: Prepare at least three solutions in toluene containing each of the pesticides of interest and carbophenothion at concentrations suitable for plotting a calibration curve.
Chromatographic system, Appendix IIA
 Mode: GC
 Detector: Electron capture
 Column: 0.32-mm × 30-m fused silica column coated with a 0.25-µm layer of dimethylpolysiloxane
 Carrier gas: Hydrogen (may also use helium or nitrogen)
 Temperature
  Injector: 275°
  Detector: 300°
  Column: See the temperature program table below.

Initial Temperature (°)	Temperature Ramp (°/min)	Final Temperature (°)	Hold Time at Final Temperature (min)
80	—	80	1
80	30	150	3
150	4	280	1

Analysis: Use carbophenothion as the internal standard. [NOTE—If necessary, use a second internal standard to identify any possible interference with the peak corresponding to carbophenothion.] Inject the chosen volume of each solution, record the chromatograms, and measure the peak responses. [NOTE—The approximate relative retention times are listed in *Table 4*.] Calculate the content of each pesticide from the peak areas and the concentrations of the solution.

Table 4

Substance	Relative Retention Time
α-Hexachlorocyclohexane	0.44
Hexachlorobenzene	0.45
β-Hexachlorocyclohexane	0.49
Lindane	0.49
δ-Hexachlorocyclohexane	0.54
ε-Hexachlorocyclohexane	0.56
Heptachlor	0.61
Aldrin	0.68
cis-Heptachlor epoxide	0.76
o,p'-DDE	0.81
α-Endosulfan	0.82
Dieldrin	0.87
p,p'-DDE	0.87
o,p'-DDD	0.89
Endrin	0.91
β-Endosulfan	0.92
o,p'-DDT	0.95
Carbophenothion	1.00
p,p'-DDT	1.02
cis-Permethrin	1.29
trans-Permethrin	1.31
Cypermethrin*	1.40
Fenvalerate*	1.47
	1.49
Deltamethrin	1.54

*The substance shows several peaks.

APPENDIX XIV: MARKERS FOR AUTHENTICITY TESTING

Tests contained within this Appendix are not monograph requirements, but rather are provided as informational methods for FCC users.

BIOBASED CONTENT OF 1,3-PROPANEDIOL (BASED ON ASTM D6866 METHOD B)[1]

Principle: Biobased content is the amount of biobased carbon (renewable organic carbon such as that derived from recent plant and animal sources) in the material or sample as a percent of the weight (mass) of the total organic carbon in the sample. It is measured by comparing the radiocarbon signature of a sample to that of a modern reference standard derived from plant sources of a known age. Radiocarbon signatures of samples and modern reference standards are analyzed by combustion to convert carbon to carbon dioxide and using accelerator mass spectrometry to relate the signatures between the two. A biobased content value of 100% indicates that all carbon originated from modern plants or animals. A value of 0% indicates all carbon originated from petrochemicals. A value between 0% and 100% indicates the relative amount of carbon derived from recent plants and animals versus petrochemicals.

The basic principle behind using radiocarbon as a biosource-marker lies in the nature of its formation and decay. Radiocarbon is formed continually in the atmosphere from nitrogen-14 in the air reacting with thermal neutrons from cosmic radiation. Radiocarbon undergoes radioactive beta-decay to form nitrogen-14, with a half-life of 5730 years. Living plant and animal feedstocks will have radiocarbon in them in an amount defined as 100%. Petrochemicals will not have any radiocarbon (i.e., 0%) because it has long since decayed away. By comparing the radiocarbon content of 1,3-propanediol to modern plants, the sample can be assigned a biobased value representing the amount of plant carbon versus petrochemically sourced carbon in the material.

Vacuum and Gas Transfer Manifold System: The vacuum manifold system should be capable of air and noncondensable gas evacuation, sample introduction, water distillation, cryogenic gas transfer, and temperature and pressure monitoring. Required equipment includes the following:

- Manifold tubing that is composed of clean stainless steel;
- Vacuum pump(s) capable of achieving a vacuum of 101 Pa or less within the vacuum region;
- Calibrated pressure transducer with coupled or integrated signal response controllers;
- Calibrated sample collection volume with associated temperature readout; and
- Clean quartz tubing for sample combustion and subsequent gas transfer, quantification, and storage.

See Figure 1 for a picture of an example setup. Adapt a "tube cracker" to the system. The "tube cracker" is comprised of parts made from stainless steel and compression fittings with appropriate welds. Pictures and descriptions of suitable configurations for this "tube cracker" are shown in Figure 2 and Figure 3.

Combustion and Trapping System: A temperature-controlled furnace or suitable alternative equipment (e.g., continuous flow interfaces and associated carbon dioxide trapping system) capable of quantitative carbon dioxide recovery.

System Suitability: Setup conditions should be effective in combusting all organic carbon-bearing species to carbon dioxide. A suitable procedure for determining recovery is to combust a material of known organic carbon content, and use calibrated pressure and volume variables to calculate percent recovery. Available standardized materials are NIST SRM 8541 (USGS graphite, pure carbon) or NIST SRM 8542 (ANU Sucrose, $C_{12}H_{22}O_{11}$). The system should be tested with a broad range of materials including those with very high water content and with highly volatile components.

Accelerator Mass Spectrometry (AMS) System: AMS facilities are equipped to make direct measurement of isotopes with mass separation of only one neutron. Although methods of analysis are published, they are not standardized, and each facility will have its own standard operating procedures. As such, it is recommended to obtain quality assurance methods, staffing expertise, and any accreditations (e.g., ISO-17025); and to validate reference standard results with sample results. AMS facilities will typically validate reliability in detection by measuring known radiocarbon content standards such as TIRI-wood (known radiocarbon content 0.571 ± 0.3 percent modern carbon (pMC) available through the Department of Statistics, University of Glasgow (Scotland); NIST SRM 4990c (known radiocarbon content 1.341 ± 0.6 pMC); or the ratio of NIST SRM 4990c to 4990b (1.2993 non-normalized; 1.3407 normalized).

---

[1] Reprinted, with permission, from ASTM D6866-10 Standard Test Methods for Determining the Biobased Content of Solid, Liquid, and Gaseous Samples Using Radiocarbon Analysis, copyright ASTM International, 100 Barr Harbor Dr., West Conshohocken, PA 19428. A copy of the complete standard may be obtained from ASTM International, www.astm.org.

Figure 1. Vacuum and Gas Transfer Manifold System.[1]

Isotope Ratio Mass Spectrometry (IRMS) System: Stable carbon isotopic ratios ($^{13}C/^{12}C$) are utilized by the AMS facility to ensure systematic isotopic fractionation between reference materials and unknowns. Some AMS facilities are capable of measuring the ratio directly in the AMS and making a total fractionation correction, some AMS facilities make assumptions as to systematic fraction between all reference standards and samples, and some AMS facilities will make a separate $^{13}C/^{12}C$ in an IRMS. AMS facilities do not generally report the ratio because it is one of many variables used in the calculation of final radiocarbon results. However, because it is a commonly used variable in the food industry, if a $^{13}C/^{12}C$ is obtained from the AMS laboratory, it is important to obtain the methodology from which it was derived. Values reported by IRMS measurement on the sample material will include natural and any manufacturing-induced fractionation effects. Values reported from within an AMS detector will include the same, plus laboratory- and AMS-induced fractionation effects, which can be large. Because confusion is possible, it is recommended to use only IRMS values directly on the sample material for interpretation of $^{13}C/^{12}C$ within the sample.

Sample: Use a sample size with mass proportional to generate approximately 1–4 cm³ of carbon dioxide (0.5–2 mg of carbon) for the AMS facility, and suitable for volume capacity of the combustion and trapping system.

^{14}C Standard: Any one of the following ^{14}C standards is suitable for use. Use enough standard to generate approximately 1–4 cm³ of carbon dioxide (0.5–2 mg of carbon) for the AMS facility, and enough suitable for volume capacity of the combustion and trapping system.
- NIST SRM 4990c, Oxalic Acid, $C_2H_2O_4$, 27% carbon;
- NIST SRM 4990b, Oxalic Acid, $C_2H_2O_4$, 27% carbon; or
- NIST SRM 8542, Sucrose, $C_{12}H_{22}O_{11}$, 42% carbon

Analysis: Analyze the *Sample* and *^{14}C Standard* as follows:

[NOTE—This standard applies specifically to organic carbon components; inorganic carbon components are factored out of the final result (per the definition of "biobased"). The correction is made by (1) isolating the organic component and measuring it independent of inorganic components; (2) factoring out the carbonate radiocarbon contribution using mass-fraction determinations and radiocarbon content analysis on total carbon versus inorganic carbon; or (3) in extreme cases, measuring the components individually rather than combined in the final sample.]

Preparation: Place an approximately 2-cm length of cupric oxide (CuO) into a suitable quartz sample tube (9.5-mm OD and ~20 cm long) that has been previously cleaned, furnace-baked at 200° for NLT 2 h, and torch-sealed at the bottom end. Fill the tube with nitrogen gas. Place liquid nitrogen around the tube to a level slightly above the cupric oxide, and allow to equilibrate. Insert a tiny drop of *Sample* or a glass rod piece wetted with the

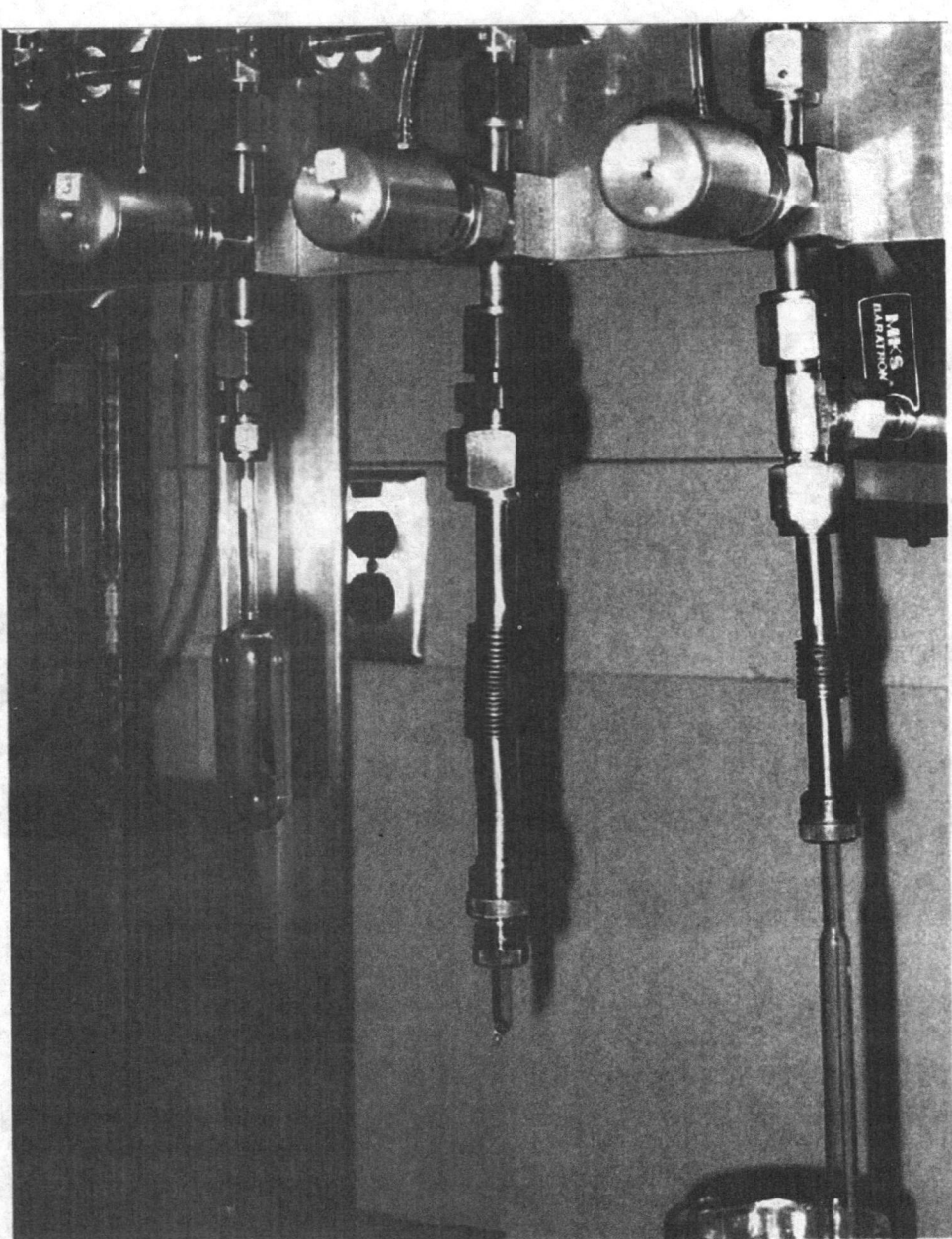

Figure 2. Flexible Glass Tube Cracker.[1] Close up of a portion of the manifold in *Figure 1*, showing hardware and glassware used in transferring carbon dioxide from combustion tubes to a manifold suitable to "scrub" the gas free of non-carbon-dioxide gaseous species. Visible are ports, valves, pressure transducer, glass storage vessels, and a flexible (and expandable) stainless steel "tube cracker" suitable for cracking open sealed quartz or pyrex tubes of less than 9.5-mm diameter.

Sample or ^{14}C *Standard* into the tube.   [NOTE—1,3-Propanediol will freeze upon contact with the cupric oxide.] With the tube adapted to the *Vacuum Manifold System*, evacuate the nitrogen to a pressure of NMT 101 Pa. Flame-seal the glass tube at the top end, and remove the liquid nitrogen.

Combustion: Combust the evacuated sample tube at 900° for 2–4 h using the *Combustion and Trapping System*. [NOTE—Combustion is indicated by the appearance of elemental copper in the tube upon cooling. The remaining presence of cupric oxide will indicate that excess was available and complete combustion was achieved. If all of the cupric oxide has been reduced to elemental copper, incomplete combustion occurred and recombustion should be performed using a larger quantity of cupric oxide.] [NOTE—"Sealed tube" combustion can lead to pressure explosion either during or after heating if too much 1,3-propanediol is used.] After combustion, score the quartz sample tube to facilitate a clean break within the flexible hose portion of the "tube cracker" assembly adapted to the manifold. With the manifold closed to the vacuum pump, crack the quartz tubing and immediately cryogenically transfer the liberated sample of carbon dioxide to a transfer manifold, and distill the gas to remove residual water, using a slurry of dry ice and alcohol maintained at −76°. Simultaneously release the sample carbon dioxde gas, and immediately condense in a calibrated volume. Close the calibrated volume, and allow the carbon dioxide to equilibrate to room temperature. Record the volume (cm³) of carbon dioxide recovered from the combustion.

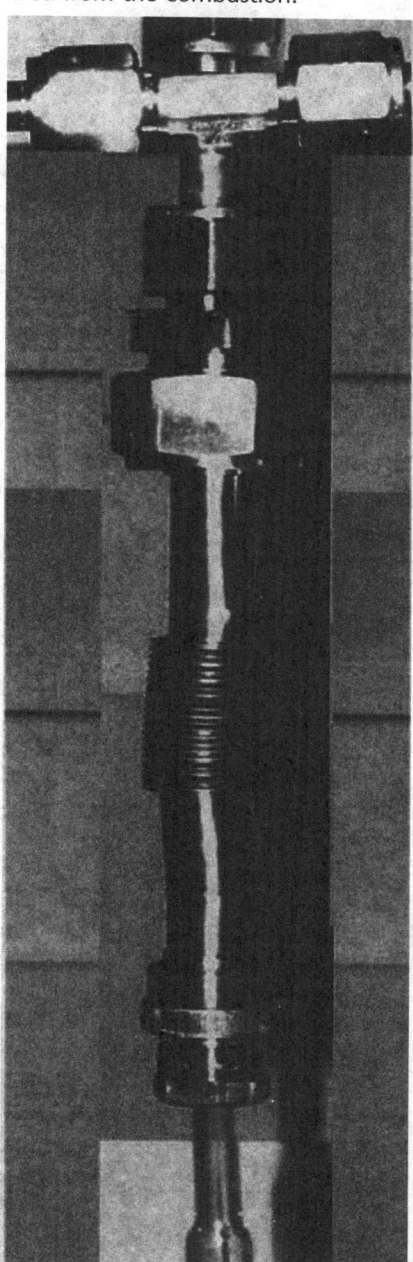

Figure 3. Flexible Glass Tube Cracker with Three-Way Valve.[1] Close-up of the "tube cracker" assembly in *Figure 2*, showing the standard Swagelock fittings typically used in a line configuration.

Carbon Isotope Analysis: Transfer the *Sample* and ^{14}C *Standard* preparations to borosilicate break seal tubes for analysis of $^{14}C/^{13}C$ (or $^{14}C/^{12}C$) using the *AMS System* and, if appropriate, for analysis of $^{13}C/^{12}C$ using the *IRMS System*.

[NOTE—AMS analysis can be done using either $^{14}C/^{13}C$ or $^{14}C/^{12}C$ ratios, but the same ratio must be determined for both the *Sample* and ^{14}C *Standard*.]

Calculate the pMC in the *Sample* taken:

$$\text{Result} = (A/A_O) \times 100$$

in which A is the $^{14}C/^{13}C$ (or $^{14}C/^{12}C$) ratio of the *Sample* preparation, and A_O is the $^{14}C/^{13}C$ (or $^{14}C/^{12}C$) ratio of the ^{14}C *Standard* preparation.

Calculate the pMC, corrected for anthopogenic effects, in the *Sample* taken:

$$\text{Result} = (\text{pMC} \times C)$$

in which pMC is the percent modern carbon relative to NIST SRM 4990c, NIST SRM 4990b, or NIST SRM 8542, calculated above; and C is the correction factor for anthropogenic effects associated with thermonuclear weapons testing, 0.95, as of ASTM-D6866-10, August 6, 2010. [NOTE—The most up-to-date factor should be used here, and can be obtained from review of the latest publication revision of ASTM-D6866.]

Explanation of Calculation and Assumptions: The analysis is performed by comparing the $^{14}C/^{13}C$ (or $^{14}C/^{12}C$) ratio within the *Sample* to the NIST standard. The analytical result from the comparison is termed "percent modern carbon (pMC)". A value of 100 pMC would indicate the ratio of the *Sample* was identical to the NIST standard. A value of 0 pMC would indicate there is no statistically identifiable ^{14}C in the *Sample*.

The percent biobased content is calculated from the pMC value by multiplying the pMC value by a constant. This constant represents an assumed correction factor for anthropogenic effects associated with thermonuclear weapons testing. As mentioned previously, radiocarbon is naturally created in the atmosphere by reactions of nitrogen-14 with neutrons produced by cosmic rays. This same reaction occurred on a very large scale when thermonuclear weapons were tested in the atmosphere in the 1950s–1960s. The explosions created "excess" radiocarbon in the atmosphere of non-natural origin, leading to a factor of 1.93 times "natural" by 1963 when the atmospheric nuclear weapons testing was halted with the signing of the joint nonproliferation treaty. Since that time, the excess has been fixed within the biosphere, taken up by oceans, and diluted with combustion of fossil fuels. As of the writing of this Appendix, ASTM-D6866-10 cites the correction factor to be 0.95 (1/1.053 factor). This indicates that the atmosphere still contains 5.3% excess radiocarbon. As a consequence, the analytical pMC measure is mulitiplied by 0.95 to derive the percent biobased equivalent. This correction factor predictably will continue to change at a rate of 0.3%–0.5% per year and will be accounted for appropriately within future revisions to the ASTM-D6866 standard.

Two important assumptions are made in the calculation of the final biobased content result:
1. All the organic carbon within the *Sample* was derived from plant bodies (or animal) that were actively respiring carbon dioxide either within the last 10 years or more than 40,000 years ago. With this criteria met, a biobased content value of 100% indicates that the *Sample*

is entirely from recent biomass (or animal), a value of 0% means the sample is entirely from petrochemicals (or other fossil source), and a value in between represents the percentage carbon from each.
2. The organic carbon component within the *Sample* can be effectively and precisely isolated from inorganic carbon components.

Performance Characteristics: Typical precision is ±0.1%–0.5% RSD on the analytical measure. Uncertainties exist within the reported result beyond the analytical errors. Absolute error on the biobased content result is ±3%. Typical indeterminant errors are local variation in the atmospheric correction factor, heterogeneity in the *Sample*, and the effectiveness in the laboratory of extracting all carbon species as carbon dioxode.

SOLUTIONS AND INDICATORS

The directions given for the preparation of solutions and indicators are for guidance; the use of commercially available ones is acceptable.

COLORIMETRIC SOLUTIONS (CS)

Colorimetric solutions are used in the preparation of colorimetric standards for certain chemicals and for the carbonization tests with sulfuric acid that are specified in several monographs. Directions for the preparation of the primary colorimetric solutions and *Matching Fluids* are given under the test for *Readily Carbonizable Substances*, Appendix IIB. Store the solutions in suitably resistant, tight containers.

Comparison of colors as directed in the *Food Chemicals Codex* tests is preferably made in matched color-comparison tubes or in a suitable colorimeter under conditions that ensure that the colorimetric reference solution and that of the specimen under test are treated alike in all respects.

STANDARD BUFFER SOLUTIONS

Reagent Solutions Before mixing, dry the crystalline reagents, except the boric acid, at 110° to 120°, and use water that has been previously boiled and cooled in preparing the solutions. Store the prepared reagent solutions in chemically resistant glass or polyethylene bottles, and use within 3 months. Discard if molding is evident.

Potassium Chloride, 0.2 M Dissolve 14.91 g of potassium chloride (KCl) in sufficient water to make 1000.0 mL.

Potassium Biphthalate, 0.2 M Dissolve 40.84 g of potassium biphthalate [$KHC_6H_4(COO)_2$] in sufficient water to make 1000.0 mL.

Potassium Phosphate, Monobasic, 0.2 M Dissolve 27.22 g of monobasic potassium phosphate (KH_2PO_4) in sufficient water to make 1000.0 mL.

Boric Acid–Potassium Chloride, 0.2 M Dissolve 12.37 g of boric acid (H_3BO_3) and 14.91 g of potassium chloride (KCl) in sufficient water to make 1000.0 mL.

Hydrochloric Acid, 0.2 M, and **Sodium Hydroxide, 0.2 M** Prepare and standardize as directed under *Volumetric Solutions* in this section.

Procedure To prepare 200 mL of a standard buffer solution having a pH within the range 1.2 to 10.0, place 50.0 mL of the appropriate 0.2 M salt solution, prepared as above, in a 200-mL volumetric flask, add the volume of 0.2 M hydrochloric acid or of sodium hydroxide specified for the desired pH in the accompanying table, dilute with water to volume, and mix.

Composition of Standard Buffer Solutions

Hydrochloric Acid Buffer		Acid Phthalate Buffer		Neutralized Phthalate Buffer		Phosphate Buffer		Alkaline Borate Buffer	
To 50.0 mL of 0.2 M KCl add the mL of HCl specified		To 50.0 mL of 0.2 M $KHC_6H_4(COO)_2$ add the mL of HCl specified		To 50.0 mL of 0.2 M $KHC_6H_4(COO)_2$ add the mL of NaOH specified		To 50.0 mL of 0.2 M KH_2PO_4 add the mL of NaOH specified		To 50.0 mL of 0.2 M H_3BO_3-KCl add the mL of NaOH specified	
pH	0.2 M HCl (mL)	pH	0.2 M HCl (mL)	pH	0.2 M NaOH (mL)	pH	0.2 M NaOH (mL)	pH	0.2 M NaOH (mL)
1.2	85.0	2.2	49.5	4.2	3.0	5.8	3.6	8.0	3.9
1.3	67.2	2.4	42.2	4.4	6.6	6.0	5.6	8.2	6.0
1.4	53.2	2.6	35.4	4.6	11.1	6.2	8.1	8.4	8.6
1.5	41.4	2.8	28.9	4.8	16.5	6.4	11.6	8.6	11.8
1.6	32.4	3.0	22.3	5.0	22.6	6.6	16.4	8.8	15.8
1.7	26.0	3.2	15.7	5.2	28.8	6.8	22.4	9.0	20.8
1.8	20.4	3.4	10.4	5.4	34.1	7.0	29.1	9.2	26.4
1.9	16.2	3.6	6.3	5.6	38.8	7.2	34.7	9.4	32.1
2.0	13.0	3.8	2.9	5.8	42.3	7.4	39.1	9.6	36.9
2.1	10.2	4.0	0.1	—	—	7.6	42.4	9.8	40.6
2.2	7.8	—	—	—	—	7.8	44.5	10.0	43.7
						8.0	46.1	—	—

Dilute all final solutions to 200.0 mL (see *Procedure*). The standard pH values given in this table are considered to be reproducible to within ±0.02 of the pH unit specified at 25°.

STANDARD SOLUTIONS FOR THE PREPARATION OF CONTROLS AND STANDARDS

The following solutions are used in tests for impurities that require the comparison of the color or turbidity produced in a solution of the test substance with that produced by a known amount of the impurity in a control. Directions for the preparation of other standard solutions are given in the monographs or under the general tests in which they are required (see also *Index*).

Ammonium Standard Solution (10 μg NH$_4$ in 1 mL) Dissolve 296.0 mg of ammonium chloride (NH$_4$Cl) in sufficient water to make 100.0 mL, and mix. Transfer 10.0 mL of this solution into a 1000-mL volumetric flask, dilute with water to volume, and mix.

Barium Standard Solution (100 μg Ba in 1 mL) Dissolve 177.9 mg of barium chloride (BaCl$_2$·2H$_2$O) in water in a 1000-mL volumetric flask, dilute with water to volume, and mix.

Iron Standard Solution (10 μg Fe in 1 mL) Dissolve 702.2 mg of ferrous ammonium sulfate [Fe(NH$_4$)$_2$(SO$_4$)$_2$·6H$_2$O] in 10 mL of 2 N sulfuric acid in a 100-mL volumetric flask, dilute with water to volume, and mix. Transfer 10.0 mL of this solution into a 1000-mL volumetric flask, add 10 mL of 2 N sulfuric acid, dilute with water to volume, and mix.

Magnesium Standard Solution (50 μg Mg in 1 mL) Dissolve 50.0 mg of magnesium metal (Mg) in 1 mL of hydrochloric acid in a 1000-mL volumetric flask, dilute with water to volume, and mix.

Phosphate Standard Solution (10 μg PO$_4$ in 1 mL) Dissolve 143.3 mg of monobasic potassium phosphate (KH$_2$PO$_4$) in water in a 100-mL volumetric flask, dilute with water to volume, and mix. Transfer 10.0 mL of this solution into a 1000-mL volumetric flask, dilute with water to volume, and mix.

TEST SOLUTIONS (TS) AND OTHER REAGENTS

Certain of the following test solutions are intended for use as acid–base indicators in volumetric analyses. Such solutions should be adjusted so that when 0.15 mL of the indicator solution is added to 25 mL of carbon dioxide-free water, 0.25 mL of 0.02 N acid or alkali, respectively, will produce the characteristic color change.

In general, the directive to prepare a solution "fresh" indicates that the solution is of limited stability and must be prepared on the day of use.

Acetic Acid TS, Diluted (1 N) A solution containing about 6% (w/v) of CH$_3$COOH. Prepare by diluting 60.0 mL of glacial acetic acid, or 166.6 mL of 36% acetic acid (6 N), with sufficient water to make 1000 mL.

Acetic Acid TS, Strong (5 N) A solution containing 30% (v/v) of CH$_3$COOH. Prepare by diluting 300.0 mL of glacial acetic acid with sufficient water to make 1000 mL.

Acetic Periodic Acid TS Dissolve 2.7 g of periodic acid (H$_5$IO$_6$) in 50 mL of water, add 950 mL of glacial acetic acid, and mix thoroughly. [**Caution**—This solution is an oxidizing agent and is dangerous in contact with organic materials. Do not use cork or rubber stoppers on storage bottles.]

[Note—Store this solution protected from light.]

Alcohol (*Ethanol; Ethyl Alcohol;* C$_2$H$_5$OH) Use ACS reagent-grade *Ethyl Alcohol* (NLT 95.0%, by volume, of C$_2$H$_5$OH).

[Note—For use in assays and tests involving ultraviolet spectrophotometry, use ACS reagent-grade *Ethyl Alcohol Suitable for Use in Ultraviolet Spectrophotometry*.]

Alcohol, Absolute (*Anhydrous Alcohol; Dehydrated Alcohol*) Use ACS reagent-grade *Ethyl Alcohol, Absolute* (NLT 99.5%, by volume, of C$_2$H$_5$OH).

Alcohol, Diluted A solution containing 41.0%–42.0%, by weight, corresponding to 48.4%–49.5%, by volume, at 15.56°, of C$_2$H$_5$OH.

Alcohol, 70% (at 15.56°) A 38.6:15 mixture (v/v) of 95% alcohol and water, having a specific gravity of 0.884 at 25°. To prepare 100 mL, dilute 73.7 mL of alcohol to 100 mL with water at 25°.

Alcohol, 80% (at 15.56°) A 45.5:9.5 mixture (v/v) of 95% alcohol and water, having a specific gravity of 0.857 at 25°. To prepare 100 mL, dilute 84.3 mL of alcohol to 100 mL with water at 25°.

Alcohol, 90% (at 15.56°) A 51:3 mixture (v/v) of 95% alcohol and water, having a specific gravity of 0.827 at 25°. To prepare 100 mL, dilute 94.8 mL of alcohol to 100 mL with water at 25°.

Alcohol, Aldehyde-Free Dissolve 2.5 g of lead acetate in 5 mL of water, add the solution to 1000 mL of alcohol contained in a glass-stoppered bottle, and mix. Dissolve 5 g of potassium hydroxide in 25 mL of warm alcohol, cool, and add slowly, without stirring, to the alcoholic solution of lead acetate. Allow to stand for 1 h, then shake the mixture vigorously, allow to stand overnight, decant the clear liquid, and recover the alcohol by distillation. *Ethyl Alcohol FCC, Alcohol USP*, or *USSD #3A* or *#30* may be used. If the titration of a 250-mL sample of the alcohol by *Hydroxylamine Hydrochloride TS* does not exceed 0.25 mL of 0.5 N alcoholic potassium hydroxide, the above treatment may be omitted.

Alcoholic Potassium Hydroxide TS See *Potassium Hydroxide TS, Alcoholic*.

Alkaline Cupric Tartrate TS (*Fehling's Solution*) See *Cupric Tartrate TS, Alkaline*.

Alkaline Mercuric Potassium Iodide TS (*Nessler's Reagent*) See *Mercuric Potassium Iodide TS, Alkaline*.

Ammonia–Ammonium Chloride Buffer TS (approximately pH 10) Dissolve 67.5 g of ammonium chloride (NH$_4$Cl) in water, add 570 mL of ammonium hydroxide (28%), and dilute with water to 1000 mL.

Ammonia TS (6 N in NH$_3$) A solution containing 9.5%–10.5% of NH$_3$. Prepare by diluting 400 mL of ammonium hydroxide (28%) with sufficient water to make 1000 mL.

Ammonia TS, Stronger (15.2 N in NH₃) (*Ammonium Hydroxide; Stronger Ammonia Water*) Use ACS reagent-grade *Ammonium Hydroxide*, which is a practically saturated solution of ammonia in water, containing 28%–30% of NH₃.

Ammoniacal Silver Nitrate TS Add 6 N ammonium hydroxide, dropwise, to a 1:20 solution of silver nitrate until the precipitate that first forms is almost, but not entirely, dissolved. Filter the solution, and place in a dark bottle. [CAUTION—*Ammoniacal Silver Nitrate TS* forms explosive compounds on standing. Do not store this solution, but prepare a fresh quantity for each series of determinations. Neutralize the excess reagent and rinse all glassware with hydrochloric acid immediately after completing a test.]

Ammonium Acetate TS Dissolve 10 g of ammonium acetate (NH₄C₂H₃O₂) in sufficient water to make 100 mL.

Ammonium Carbonate TS Dissolve 20 g of ammonium carbonate and 20 mL of *Ammonia TS* in sufficient water to make 100 mL.

Ammonium Chloride TS Dissolve 10.5 g of ammonium chloride (NH₄Cl) in sufficient water to make 100 mL.

Ammonium Molybdate TS Dissolve 6.5 g of finely powdered molybdic acid (85%) in a mixture of 14 mL of water and 14.5 mL of ammonium hydroxide. Cool the solution, and add it slowly, with stirring, to a well-cooled mixture of 32 mL of nitric acid and 40 mL of water. Allow to stand for 48 h, and pass through a fine-porosity, sintered-glass crucible lined at the bottom with a layer of glass wool. This solution deteriorates upon standing and is unsuitable for use if, upon the addition of 2 mL of *Sodium Phosphate TS* to 5 mL of the solution, an abundant yellow precipitate does not form at once or after slight warming. Store it in the dark. If a precipitate forms during storage, use only the clear, supernatant solution.

Ammonium Oxalate TS Dissolve 3.5 g of ammonium oxalate [(NH₄)₂C₂O₄·H₂O] in sufficient water to make 100 mL.

Ammonium Sulfanilate TS To 2.5 g of sulfanilic acid add 15 mL of water and 3 mL of 6 N ammonium hydroxide, and mix. Add, with stirring, more 6 N ammonium hydroxide, if necessary, until the acid dissolves, adjust the pH of the solution to about 4.5 with 2.7 N hydrochloric acid, using *Bromocresol Green TS* as an outside indicator, and dilute to 25 mL.

Ammonium Sulfide TS Saturate 6 N ammonium hydroxide with hydrogen sulfide (H₂S), and add two-thirds of its volume of 6 N ammonium hydroxide. Residue upon ignition: NMT 0.05%. The solution is not rendered turbid either by *Magnesium Sulfate TS* or by *Calcium Chloride TS* (carbonate). This solution is unsuitable for use if an abundant precipitate of sulfur is present. Store it in small, well-filled, dark amber-colored bottles in a cold, dark place.

Ammonium Thiocyanate TS (1 N) Dissolve 8 g of ammonium thiocyanate (NH₄SCN) in sufficient water to make 100 mL.

Anthrone TS Carefully dissolve about 0.1 g of anthrone in 100 g of sulfuric acid. Use a freshly prepared solution.

Antimony Trichloride TS Dissolve 20 g of antimony trichloride (SbCl₃) in chloroform to make 100 mL. Filter if necessary.

Barium Chloride TS Dissolve 12 g of barium chloride (BaCl₂·2H₂O) in sufficient water to make 100 mL.

Barium Diphenylamine Sulfonate TS Dissolve 300 mg of *p*-diphenylamine sulfonic acid barium salt in 100 mL of water.

Barium Hydroxide TS Use a saturated solution of barium hydroxide in recently boiled water. Use a freshly prepared solution.

Benedict's Qualitative Reagent See *Cupric Citrate TS, Alkaline*.

Benzidine TS Dissolve 50 mg of benzidine in 10 mL of glacial acetic acid, dilute with water to 100 mL, and mix.

Bismuth Nitrate TS Reflux 5 g of bismuth nitrate [Bi(NO₃)₃·5H₂O] with 7.5 mL of nitric acid and 10 mL of water until dissolved, cool, filter, and dilute with water to 250 mL.

Bromine TS (*Bromine Water*) Prepare a saturated solution of bromine by agitating 2–3 mL of bromine (Br₂) with 100 mL of cold water in a glass-stoppered bottle, the stopper of which should be lubricated with petrolatum. Store it in a cold place protected from light.

Bromocresol Blue TS Use *Bromocresol Green TS*.

Bromocresol Green TS Dissolve 50 mg of bromocresol green in 100 mL of alcohol, and filter if necessary.

Bromocresol Purple TS Dissolve 250 mg of bromocresol purple in 20 mL of 0.05 N sodium hydroxide, and dilute with water to 250 mL.

Bromophenol Blue TS Dissolve 100 mg of bromophenol blue in 100 mL of 1:2 alcohol, and filter if necessary.

Bromothymol Blue TS Dissolve 100 mg of bromothymol blue in 100 mL of 1:2 alcohol, and filter if necessary.

Calcium Chloride TS Dissolve 7.5 g of calcium chloride (CaCl₂·2H₂O) in sufficient water to make 100 mL.

Calcium Hydroxide TS A solution containing approximately 140 mg of Ca(OH)₂ in each 100 mL. To prepare, add 3 g of calcium hydroxide [Ca(OH)₂] to 1000 mL of water, and agitate the mixture vigorously and repeatedly for 1 h. Allow the excess calcium hydroxide to settle, and decant or draw off the clear, supernatant liquid.

Calcium Sulfate TS A saturated solution of calcium sulfate in water.

Carr-Price Reagent See *Antimony Trichloride TS*.

Ceric Ammonium Nitrate TS Dissolve 6.25 g of ceric ammonium nitrate [(NH₄)₂Ce(NO₃)₆] in 100 mL of 0.25 N nitric acid. Prepare the solution fresh every third day.

Chlorine TS (*Chlorine Water*) A saturated solution of chlorine in water. Place the solution in small, completely filled, light-resistant containers. *Chlorine TS*, even when kept from light and air, is apt to deteriorate. Store it in a cold, dark place. For full strength, prepare this solution fresh.

Chromotropic Acid TS Dissolve 50 mg of chromotropic acid or its sodium salt in 100 mL of 75% sulfuric acid (made by cautiously adding 75 mL of 95%–98% sulfuric acid to 33.3 mL of water).

Cobaltous Chloride TS Dissolve 2 g of cobaltous chloride ($CoCl_2 \cdot 6H_2O$) in 1 mL of hydrochloric acid and sufficient water to make 100 mL.

Cobalt–Uranyl Acetate TS Dissolve, with warming, 40 g of uranyl acetate [$UO_2(C_2H_3O_2)_2 \cdot 2H_2O$] in a mixture of 30 g of glacial acetic acid and sufficient water to make 500 mL. Similarly, prepare a solution containing 200 g of cobaltous acetate [$Co(C_2H_3O_2)_2 \cdot 4H_2O$] in a mixture of 30 g of glacial acetic acid and sufficient water to make 500 mL. Mix the two solutions while still warm, and cool to 20°. Maintain the temperature at 20° for about 2 h to separate the excess salts from solution, and then pass through a dry filter.

Congo Red TS Dissolve 500 mg of congo red in a mixture of 10 mL of alcohol and 90 mL of water.

Copper Sulfate TS Dissolve 12.5 g of cupric sulfate in sufficient water to make 100 mL.

Cresol Red TS Triturate 100 mg of cresol red in a mortar with 26.2 mL of 0.01 N sodium hydroxide until solution is complete, then dilute the solution with water to 250 mL.

Cresol Red–Thymol Blue TS Add 15 mL of *Thymol Blue TS* to 5 mL of *Cresol Red TS*, and mix.

Crystal Violet TS Dissolve 100 mg of crystal violet in 10 mL of glacial acetic acid.

Cupric Citrate TS, Alkaline (*Benedict's Qualitative Reagent*) With the aid of heat, dissolve 173 g of sodium citrate ($C_6H_5Na_3O_7 \cdot 2H_2O$) and 117 g of sodium carbonate ($Na_2CO_3 \cdot H_2O$) in about 700 mL of water, and filter through paper, if necessary. In a separate container, dissolve 17.3 g of cupric sulfate ($CuSO_4 \cdot 5H_2O$) in about 100 mL of water, and slowly add this solution, with constant stirring, to the first solution. Cool the mixture, dilute to 1000 mL, and mix.

Cupric Nitrate TS Dissolve 2.4 g of cupric nitrate [$Cu(NO_3)_2 \cdot 3H_2O$] in sufficient water to make 100 mL.

Cupric Sulfate TS Dissolve 12.5 g of cupric sulfate ($CuSO_4 \cdot 5H_2O$) in sufficient water to make 100 mL, and mix.

Cupric Tartrate TS, Alkaline (*Fehling's Solution*) *The Copper Solution* (A): Dissolve 34.66 g of carefully selected, small crystals of cupric sulfate, $CuSO_4 \cdot 5H_2O$, showing no trace of efflorescence or of adhering moisture, in sufficient water to make 500 mL. Store this solution in small, tight containers. *The Alkaline Tartrate Solution* (B): Dissolve 173 g of crystallized potassium sodium tartrate ($KNaC_4H_4O_6 \cdot 4H_2O$) and 50 g of sodium hydroxide (NaOH) in sufficient water to make 500 mL. Store this solution in small, alkali-resistant containers. For use, mix exactly equal volumes of solutions A and B at the time required.

Cyanogen Bromide TS Dissolve 5 g of cyanogen bromide in water to make 50 mL.

[**Caution**—Prepare this solution in a hood, as cyanogen bromide volatilizes at room temperature, and the vapor is highly irritating and poisonous.]

Denigès' Reagent See *Mercuric Sulfate TS*.

Dichlorophenol–Indophenol TS Warm 100 mg of 2,6-dichlorophenol–indophenol sodium with 100 mL of water. Filter and use within 3 days.

2,7-Dihydroxynaphthalene TS Dissolve 100 mg of 2,7-dihydroxynaphthalene in 1000 mL of sulfuric acid, and allow the solution to stand until the initial color disappears. If the solution is very dark, discard it and prepare a new solution from a different supply of sulfuric acid. This solution is stable for approximately 1 month if stored in a dark bottle.

Diphenylamine TS Dissolve 1 g of diphenylamine in 100 mL of sulfuric acid. The solution should be colorless.

Diphenylcarbazone TS Dissolve about 1 g of diphenylcarbazone ($C_{13}H_{12}N_4O$) in sufficient alcohol to make 100 mL. Store this solution in a brown bottle.

α,α-Dipyridyl TS Dissolve 100 mg of α,α-dipyridyl ($C_{10}H_8N_2$) in 50 mL of absolute alcohol.

Dithizone TS Dissolve 25.6 mg of dithizone in 100 mL of alcohol.

Eosin Y TS (adsorption indicator) Dissolve 50 mg of eosin Y in 10 mL of water.

Eriochrome Black TS Dissolve 200 mg of eriochrome black T and 2 g of hydroxylamine hydrochloride ($NH_2OH \cdot HCl$) in sufficient methanol to make 50 mL, and filter. Store the solution in a light-resistant container and use within 2 weeks.

p-Ethoxychrysoidin TS Dissolve 50 mg of *p*-ethoxychrysoidin monohydrochloride in a mixture of 25 mL of water and 25 mL of alcohol, add 3 drops of hydrochloric acid, stir vigorously, and filter if necessary to obtain a clear solution.

Fehling's Solution See *Cupric Tartrate TS, Alkaline*.

Ferric Ammonium Sulfate TS Dissolve 8 g of ferric ammonium sulfate [$FeNH_4(SO_4)_2 \cdot 12H_2O$] in sufficient water to make 100 mL.

Ferric Chloride TS Dissolve 9 g of ferric chloride ($FeCl_3 \cdot 6H_2O$) in sufficient water to make 100 mL.

Ferric Chloride TS, Alcoholic Dissolve 100 mg of ferric chloride ($FeCl_3 \cdot 6H_2O$) in 50 mL of absolute alcohol. Prepare this solution fresh.

Ferric Sulfate TS, Acid Add 7.5 mL of sulfuric acid to 100 mL of water, and dissolve 80 g of ferrous sulfate in the mixture with the aid of heat. Mix 7.5 mL of nitric acid and 20 mL of water, warm, and add to this the ferrous sulfate solution. Concentrate the mixture until, upon the sudden disengagement of ruddy vapors, the black color of the liquid changes to red. Test for the absence of ferrous iron, and, if necessary, add a few drops of nitric acid and heat again. When the solution is cold, add sufficient water to make 110 mL.

Ferroin TS Dissolve 0.7 g of ferrous sulfate and 1.76 g of phenanthroline hydrochloride in 70 mL of water. Transfer the solution to a 100-mL volumetric flask, and dilute with water to volume. Test the sensitivity of *Ferroin TS* by adding 0.1 mL of *Ferroin TS* and 0.15 mL of osmium tetroxide solution (2.5 g/L of osmium tetroxide in 0.05 M sulfuric acid) to

50 mL of 1 M sulfuric acid. Add 0.1 mL of a 0.1 M ammonium cerium (IV) nitrate solution; a color change from red to light blue should be observed.

Ferrous Sulfate TS Dissolve 8 g of clear crystals of ferrous sulfate (FeSO$_4$·7H$_2$O) in about 100 mL of recently boiled and thoroughly cooled water. Prepare this solution fresh.

Formaldehyde TS A solution containing approximately 37.0% (w/v) of HCHO. It may contain methanol to prevent polymerization.

Fuchsin–Sulfurous Acid TS Dissolve 200 mg of basic fuchsin in 120 mL of hot water, and allow the solution to cool. Add a solution of 2 g of anhydrous sodium sulfite in 20 mL of water, and then add 2 mL of hydrochloric acid. Dilute the solution with water to 200 mL, and allow to stand for at least 1 h. Prepare this solution fresh.

Hydrochloric Acid (approximately 12 N) Use ACS reagent-grade *Hydrochloric Acid* (36.5%–38.0% of HCl).

Hydrochloric Acid TS, Diluted (2.7 N) A solution containing 10% (w/v) of HCl. Prepare by diluting 226 mL of hydrochloric acid (36%) with sufficient water to make 1000 mL.

Hydrogen Peroxide TS A solution containing 2.5–3.5 g of H$_2$O$_2$ in each 100 mL. It may contain suitable preservatives, totaling not more than 0.05%.

Hydrogen Sulfide TS A saturated solution of hydrogen sulfide made by passing H$_2$S into cold water. Store it in small, dark, amber-colored bottles, filled nearly to the top. It is unsuitable unless it possesses a strong odor of H$_2$S, and unless it produces at once a copious precipitate of sulfur when added to an equal volume of *Ferric Chloride TS*. Store in a cold, dark place.

Hydroxylamine Hydrochloride TS Dissolve 3.5 g of hydroxylamine hydrochloride (NH$_2$OH·HCl) in 95 mL of 60% alcohol, and add 0.5 mL of a 1:1000 solution of bromophenol blue and 0.5 N alcoholic potassium hydroxide until a green tint develops in the solution. Then add sufficient 60% alcohol to make 100 mL.

8-Hydroxyquinoline TS Dissolve 5 g of 8-hydroxyquinoline (oxine) in sufficient alcohol to make 100 mL.

Indigo Carmine TS (*Sodium Indigotindisulfonate TS*) Dissolve a quantity of sodium indigotindisulfonate, equivalent to 180 mg of C$_{16}$H$_8$N$_2$O$_2$(SO$_3$Na)$_2$, in sufficient water to make 100 mL. Use within 60 days.

Iodine TS Dissolve 14 g of iodine (I$_2$) in a solution of 36 g of potassium iodide (KI) in 100 mL of water, add 3 drops of hydrochloric acid, dilute with water to 1000 mL, and mix.

Iodinated Zinc Chloride Dissolve 10 g of potassium iodide, KI, and 0.15 g of iodine, I, in 10 mL of water. Add this solution to 100 mL of a 60% solution of zinc chloride, ZnCl$_2$, in water (sp. gr. 1.8). Keep a few crystals of iodine in the solution.

Isopropanol [*Isopropyl Alcohol*; *2-Propanol*; (CH$_3$)$_2$CHOH] Use ACS reagent-grade *Isopropyl Alcohol*.

[NOTE—For use in assays and tests involving ultraviolet spectrophotometry, use ACS reagent-grade *Isopropyl Alcohol Suitable for Use in Ultraviolet Spectrophotometry*.]

Isopropanol, Anhydrous (*Dehydrated Isopropanol*) Use isopropanol that has been previously dried by shaking with anhydrous calcium chloride, followed by filtering.

Lead Acetate TS Dissolve 9.5 g of clear, transparent crystals of lead acetate [Pb(C$_2$H$_3$O$_2$)$_2$·3H$_2$O] in sufficient recently boiled water to make 100 mL. Store in well-stoppered bottles.

Lead Subacetate TS Triturate 14 g of lead monoxide (PbO) to a smooth paste with 10 mL of water, and transfer the mixture to a bottle, using an additional 10 mL of water for rinsing. Dissolve 22 g of lead acetate [Pb(C$_2$H$_3$O$_2$)$_2$·3H$_2$O] in 70 mL of water, and add the solution to the lead oxide mixture. Shake it vigorously for 5 min, then set it aside, shaking it frequently during 7 days. Finally, filter, and add enough recently boiled water through the filter to make 100 mL.

Lead Subacetate TS, Diluted Dilute 3.25 mL of *Lead Subacetate TS* with sufficient water, recently boiled and cooled, to make 100 mL. Store in small, well-fitted, tight containers.

Litmus TS Digest 25 g of powdered litmus with three successive 100-mL portions of boiling alcohol, continuing each extraction for about 1 h. Filter, wash with alcohol, and discard the alcohol filtrate. Macerate the residue with about 25 mL of cold water for 4 h, filter, and discard the filtrate. Finally, digest the residue with 125 mL of boiling water for 1 h, cool, and filter.

Magnesia Mixture TS Dissolve 5.5 g of magnesium chloride (MgCl$_2$·6H$_2$O) and 7 g of ammonium chloride (NH$_4$Cl) in 65 mL of water, add 35 mL of 6 N ammonium hydroxide, set the mixture aside for a few days in a well-stoppered bottle, and filter. If the solution is not perfectly clear, filter it before using.

Magnesium Sulfate TS Dissolve 12 g of crystals of magnesium sulfate (MgSO$_4$·7H$_2$O), selected for freedom from efflorescence, in water to make 100 mL.

Malachite Green TS Dissolve 1 g of malachite green oxalate in 100 mL of glacial acetic acid.

Mayer's Reagent See *Mercuric–Potassium Iodide TS*.

Mercuric Acetate TS Dissolve 6 g of mercuric acetate [Hg(C$_2$H$_3$O$_2$)$_2$] in sufficient glacial acetic acid to make 100 mL. Store in tight containers protected from direct sunlight.

Mercuric Chloride TS Dissolve 6.5 g of mercuric chloride (HgCl$_2$) in water to make 100 mL.

Mercuric–Potassium Iodide TS (*Mayer's Reagent*) Dissolve 1.358 g of mercuric chloride (HgCl$_2$) in 60 mL of water. Dissolve 5 g of potassium iodide (KI) in 10 mL of water. Mix the two solutions, and add water to make 100 mL.

Mercuric–Potassium Iodide TS, Alkaline (*Nessler's Reagent*) Dissolve 10 g of potassium iodide (KI) in 10 mL of water, and add slowly, with stirring, a saturated solution of mercuric chloride until a slight red precipitate remains undissolved. To this mixture add an ice-cold solution of 30 g of potassium hydroxide (KOH) in 60 mL of water, then add 1 mL more of the saturated solution of mercuric chloride. Dilute with water to 200 mL. Allow the precipitate to settle, and draw off the clear liquid. A 2-mL portion of this reagent, when added to 100 mL of a 1:300,000 solution of ammonium chloride in ammonia-free water, instantly produces a yellow-brown color.

Mercuric Sulfate TS (*Denigès' Reagent*) Mix 5 g of yellow mercuric oxide (HgO) with 40 mL of water, and while stirring, slowly add 20 mL of sulfuric acid, then add another 40 mL of water, and stir until completely dissolved.

Mercurous Nitrate TS Dissolve 15 g of mercurous nitrate in a mixture of 90 mL of water and 10 mL of 2 N nitric acid. Store in dark, amber-colored bottles in which a small globule of mercury has been placed.

Methanol (*Methyl Alcohol*) Use ACS reagent-grade *Methanol*.

Methanol, Anhydrous (*Dehydrated Methanol*) Use *Methanol*.

p-Methylaminophenol Sulfate TS Dissolve 2 g of p-methylaminophenol sulfate [(HOC$_6$H$_4$NHCH$_3$)$_2$·H$_2$SO$_4$] in 100 mL of water. To 10 mL of this solution add 90 mL of water and 20 g of sodium bisulfite. Confirm the suitability of this solution by the following test: Add 1 mL of the solution to each of four tubes containing 25 mL of 0.5 N sulfuric acid and 1 mL of *Ammonium Molybdate TS*. Add 5 µg of phosphate (PO$_4$) to one tube, 10 µg to a second, and 20 µg to a third, using 0.5 mL, 1.0 mL, and 2.0 mL, respectively, of *Phosphate Standard Solution*, and allow to stand for 2 h. The solutions in the three tubes should show readily perceptible differences in blue color corresponding to the relative amounts of phosphate added, and the one to which 5 µg of phosphate was added should be perceptibly bluer than the blank.

Methylene Blue TS Dissolve 125 mg of methylene blue in 100 mL of alcohol, and dilute with alcohol to 250 mL.

Methyl Orange TS Dissolve 100 mg of methyl orange in 100 mL of water, and filter if necessary.

Methyl Red TS Dissolve 100 mg of methyl red in 100 mL of alcohol, and filter if necessary.

Methyl Red–Methylene Blue TS Add 10 mL of *Methyl Red TS* to 10 mL of *Methylene Blue TS*, and mix.

Methylrosaniline Chloride TS See *Crystal Violet TS*.

Methyl Violet TS See *Crystal Violet TS*.

Millon's Reagent To 2 mL of mercury in an Erlenmeyer flask add 20 mL of nitric acid. Shake the flask in a hood to break the mercury into small globules. After about 10 min add 35 mL of water, and if a precipitate or crystals appear, add sufficient 1:5 nitric acid (prepared from nitric acid from which the oxides have been removed by blowing air through it until it is colorless) to dissolve the separated solid. Add a 1:10 solution of sodium hydroxide, dropwise, with thorough mixing, until the curdy precipitate that forms after the addition of each drop no longer redissolves but is dispersed to form a suspension. Add 5 mL more of the dilute nitric acid, and mix well. Prepare this solution fresh.

α-Naphtholbenzein TS Dissolve 0.2 g of α-naphtholbenzein in glacial acetic acid to make 100 mL. *Sensitivity*: Add 100 mL of freshly boiled and cooled water to 0.2 mL of a 1:1000 solution of α-naphtholbenzein in ethanol, and add 0.1 mL of 0.1 N sodium hydroxide: a green color develops. Add subsequently 0.2 mL of 0.1 N hydrochloric acid: the color of the solution changes to yellow-red.

Naphthol Green TS Dissolve 500 mg of naphthol green B in water to make 1000 mL.

Nessler's Reagent See *Alkaline Mercuric–Potassium Iodide TS*.

Neutral Red TS Dissolve 100 mg of neutral red in 100 mL of 50% alcohol.

Nickel Standard Solution TS (10 mg/kg) Prepare a 0.40% (w/v) solution of analytical reagent-grade nickel chloride (NiCl$_2$·6H$_2$O) with water. Pipet 1.0 mL of the solution into a 100-mL volumetric flask, and dilute with water to volume.

Ninhydrin TS See *Triketohydrindene Hydrate TS*.

Nitric Acid (approximately 15.7 N) Use ACS reagent-grade *Nitric Acid* (69.0%–71.0% of HNO$_3$).

Nitric Acid TS, Diluted (1.7 N) A solution containing about 10% (w/v) of HNO$_3$. Prepare by diluting 105 mL of nitric acid (70%) with water to make 1000 mL.

Orthophenanthroline TS Dissolve 150 mg of orthophenanthroline (C$_{12}$H$_8$N$_2$·H$_2$O) in 10 mL of a solution of ferrous sulfate, prepared by dissolving 700 mg of clear crystals of ferrous sulfate (FeSO$_4$·7H$_2$O) in 100 mL of water. The ferrous sulfate solution must be prepared immediately before dissolving the orthophenanthroline. Store the solution in well-closed containers.

Oxalic Acid TS Dissolve 6.3 g of oxalic acid (H$_2$C$_2$O$_4$·2H$_2$O) in water to make 100 mL.

Phenol Red TS (*Phenolsulfonphthalein TS*) Dissolve 100 mg of phenolsulfonphthalein in 100 mL of alcohol, and filter if necessary.

Phenolphthalein TS Dissolve 1 g of phenolphthalein in 100 mL of alcohol.

Phenolsulfonphthalein TS See *Phenol Red TS*.

p-Phenylphenol TS On the day of use, dissolve 750 mg of p-phenylphenol in 50 mL of *Sodium Hydroxide TS*.

Phosphoric Acid Use ACS reagent-grade *Phosphoric Acid* (NLT 85.0% of H$_3$PO$_4$).

Phosphotungstic Acid TS Dissolve 1 g of phosphotungstic acid (approximately 24WO$_3$·2H$_3$PO$_4$·48H$_2$O) in water to make 100 mL.

Picric Acid TS See *Trinitrophenol TS*.

Potassium Acetate TS Dissolve 10 g of potassium acetate (KC$_2$H$_3$O$_2$) in water to make 100 mL.

Potassium Chromate TS Dissolve 10 g of potassium chromate (K$_2$CrO$_4$) in water to make 100 mL.

Potassium Dichromate TS Dissolve 7.5 g of potassium dichromate (K$_2$Cr$_2$O$_7$) in water to make 100 mL.

Potassium Ferricyanide TS (10%) Dissolve 1 g of potassium ferricyanide [K$_3$Fe(CN)$_6$] in 10 mL of water. Prepare this solution fresh.

Potassium Ferrocyanide TS Dissolve 1 g of potassium ferrocyanide [K$_4$Fe(CN)$_6$·3H$_2$O] in 10 mL of water. Prepare this solution fresh.

Potassium Hydroxide TS (1 N) Dissolve 6.5 g of potassium hydroxide (KOH) in water to make 100 mL.

Potassium Hydroxide TS, Alcoholic Use *0.5 N Alcoholic Potassium Hydroxide* (see *Volumetric Solutions* in this section).

Potassium Iodide TS Dissolve 16.5 g of potassium iodide (KI) in water to make 100 mL. Store in light-resistant containers.

Potassium Permanganate TS Use *0.1 N Potassium Permanganate* (see *Volumetric Solutions* in this section).

Potassium Pyroantimonate TS Dissolve 2 g of potassium pyroantimonate in 95 mL of hot water. Cool quickly, and add a solution containing 2.5 g of potassium hydroxide in 50 mL of water and 1 mL of an 8.5:100 solution of sodium hydroxide. Allow to stand for 24 h, filter, and dilute with water to 150 mL.

Potassium Sulfate TS Dissolve 1 g of potassium sulfate (K_2SO_4) in sufficient water to make 100 mL.

Quimociac TS Dissolve 70 g of sodium molybdate ($Na_2MoO_4 \cdot 2H_2O$) in 150 mL of water (*Solution A*). Dissolve 60 g of citric acid in a mixture of 85 mL of nitric acid and 150 mL of water, and cool (*Solution B*). Gradually add *Solution A* to *Solution B*, with stirring, to produce *Solution C*. Dissolve 5.0 mL of natural or synthetic quinoline in a mixture of 35 mL of nitric acid and 100 mL of water (*Solution D*). Gradually add *Solution D* to *Solution C*, mix well, and allow to stand overnight. Filter the mixture, add 280 mL of acetone to the filtrate, dilute with water to 1000 mL, and mix. Store in a polyethylene bottle.

[**Caution**—This reagent contains acetone. Do not use it near an open flame. Operations involving heating or boiling should be conducted in a well-ventilated hood.]

Quinaldine Red TS Dissolve 100 mg of quinaldine red in 100 mL of glacial acetic acid.

Schiff's Reagent, Modified Dissolve 200 mg of rosaniline hydrochloride ($C_{20}H_{20}ClN_3$) in 120 mL of hot water. Cool, add 2 g of sodium bisulfite ($NaHSO_3$) followed by 2 mL of hydrochloric acid, and dilute with water to 200 mL. Store in a brown bottle at 15° or lower.

Silver Nitrate TS Use *0.1 N Silver Nitrate* (see *Volumetric Solutions* in this section).

Sodium Bisulfite TS Dissolve 10 g of sodium bisulfite ($NaHSO_3$) in water to make 30 mL. Prepare this solution fresh.

Sodium Bitartrate TS Dissolve 1 g of sodium bitartrate ($NaHC_4H_4O_6 \cdot H_2O$) in water to make 10 mL. Prepare this solution fresh.

Sodium Borate TS Dissolve 2 g of sodium borate ($Na_2B_4O_7 \cdot 10H_2O$) in water to make 100 mL.

Sodium Carbonate TS Dissolve 10.6 g of anhydrous sodium carbonate (Na_2CO_3) in water to make 100 mL.

Sodium Cobaltinitrite TS Dissolve 10 g of sodium cobaltinitrite [$Na_3Co(NO_2)_6$] in water to make 50 mL, and filter if necessary.

Sodium Fluoride TS Dry about 500 mg of sodium fluoride (NaF) at 200° for 4 h. Weigh accurately 222 mg of the dried sodium fluoride, and dissolve it in sufficient water to make exactly 100 mL. Transfer 10.0 mL of this solution into a 1000-mL volumetric flask, dilute with water to volume, and mix. Each mL of this final solution corresponds to 10 µg of fluorine (F).

Sodium Hydroxide TS (1 N) Dissolve 4.3 g of sodium hydroxide (NaOH) in water to make 100 mL.

Sodium Indigotindisulfonate TS See *Indigo Carmine TS*.

Sodium Nitroferricyanide TS Dissolve 1 g of sodium nitroferricyanide [$Na_2Fe(NO)(CN)_5 \cdot 2H_2O$] in water to make 20 mL. Prepare this solution fresh.

Sodium Phosphate TS Dissolve 12 g of clear crystals of dibasic sodium phosphate ($Na_2HPO_4 \cdot 7H_2O$) in water to make 100 mL.

Sodium Sulfide TS Dissolve 1 g of sodium sulfide ($Na_2S \cdot 9H_2O$) in water to make 10 mL. Prepare this solution fresh.

Sodium Tetraphenylborate TS Dissolve 1.2 g of sodium tetraphenylborate in water to make 200 mL. If necessary, stir for 5 min with 1 g of freshly prepared hydrous aluminum oxide, and filter to clarify.

Sodium Thiosulfate TS Use *0.1 N Sodium Thiosulfate* (see *Volumetric Solutions* in this section).

Stannous Chloride TS Dissolve 40 g of reagent-grade stannous chloride dihydrate ($SnCl_2 \cdot 2H_2O$) in 100 mL of hydrochloric acid.

Starch TS Mix 1 g of a suitable starch and sufficient cold water to make a thin paste. Add 20 mL of boiling water, boil for 1 min with continuous stirring, and cool. Use only the clear solution. Test the sensitivity of the *Starch TS* as follows: Prepare a solution of 50 mg/kg chlorine by diluting 1 mL of a commercial 5% sodium hypochlorite (NaOCl) solution in 1000 mL of water. Combine 5 mL of *Starch TS* with 100 mL of water and add 0.5 mL of 0.1 N potassium iodide. Addition of one drop of the 50 mg/kg chlorine solution should give a swirl of color where the drop hits. Addition of 1 mL of 50 mg/kg chlorine solution should give a deep blue color throughout the solution. The deep blue color produced is discharged by addition of 0.05 mL of 0.1 N sodium thiosulfate. Prepare fresh solution when *Starch TS* no longer passes the sensitivity test.

Starch Iodide Paste TS Heat 100 mL of water in a 250-mL beaker to boiling, add a solution of 750 mg of potassium iodide (KI) in 5 mL of water, then add 2 g of zinc chloride ($ZnCl_2$) dissolved in 10 mL of water, and while the solution is boiling, add with stirring a smooth suspension of 5 g of potato starch in 30 mL of cold water. Continue to boil for 2 min, then cool. Store in well-closed containers in a cool place. This mixture must show a definite blue streak when a glass rod dipped in a mixture of 1 mL of 0.1 M sodium nitrite, 500 mL of water, and 10 mL of hydrochloric acid is streaked on a smear of the paste.

Sulfanilic Acid TS Dissolve 800 mg of sulfanilic acid (*p*-$NH_2C_6H_4SO_3H \cdot H_2O$) in 100 mL of acetic acid. Store in tight containers.

Sulfuric Acid (approximately 36 N) Use ACS reagent-grade *Sulfuric Acid* (95.0%–98.0% of H_2SO_4).

Sulfuric Acid TS (95%) Add a quantity of sulfuric acid of known concentration to sufficient water to adjust the final concentration to 94.5%–95.5% of H_2SO_4. Because the acid concentration may change upon standing or upon intermittent use, the concentration should be checked frequently and solutions assaying more than 95.5% or less than 94.5% discarded or adjusted by adding either diluted or fuming sulfuric acid, as required.

Sulfuric Acid TS, Diluted (2 N) A solution containing 10% (w/v) of H_2SO_4. Prepare by cautiously adding 57 mL of sulfuric acid (95%–98%) or *Sulfuric Acid TS* to about 100 mL of water, then cool to room temperature, and dilute with water to 1000 mL.

Tannic Acid TS Dissolve 1 g of tannic acid (tannin) in 1 mL of alcohol, and add water to make 10 mL. Prepare this solution fresh.

Thymol Blue TS Dissolve 100 mg of thymol blue in 100 mL of alcohol, and filter if necessary.

Thymolphthalein TS Dissolve 100 mg of thymolphthalein in 100 mL of alcohol, and filter if necessary.

Triketohydrindene Hydrate TS (*Ninhydrin TS*) Dissolve 200 mg of triketohydrindene hydrate ($C_9H_4O_3 \cdot H_2O$) in water to make 100 mL. Prepare this solution fresh.

Trinitrophenol TS (*Picric Acid TS*) Dissolve the equivalent of 1 g of anhydrous trinitrophenol in 100 mL of hot water. Cool the solution, and filter if necessary.

Xylenol Orange TS Dissolve 100 mg of xylenol orange in 100 mL of alcohol.

VOLUMETRIC SOLUTIONS

Normal Solutions A normal solution contains 1 g equivalent weight of the solute per L of solution. The normalities of solutions used in volumetric determinations are designated as 1 N, 0.1 N, 0.05 N, etc., in *FCC*.

Molar Solutions A molar solution contains 1 g molecular weight of the solute per L of solution. The molarities of such solutions are designated as 1 M, 0.1 M, 0.05 M, etc., in *FCC*.

Preparation and Methods of Standardization The details for the preparation and standardization of solutions used in several normalities are usually given only for the one most frequently required. Solutions of other normalities are prepared and standardized in the same general manner as described. Solutions of lower normalities may be prepared accurately by making an exact dilution of a stronger solution, but solutions prepared in this way should be restandardized before use.

Dilute solutions that are not stable, such as 0.01 N potassium permanganate and sodium thiosulfate, are preferably prepared by diluting exactly the higher normality with thoroughly boiled and cooled water on the same day they are to be used.

All volumetric solutions should be prepared, standardized, and used at the standard temperature of 25°, if practicable. When a titration must be carried out at a markedly different temperature, the volumetric solution should be standardized at that same temperature, or a suitable temperature correction should be made. Because the strength of a standard solution may change upon standing, the normality or molarity factor should be redetermined frequently.

Although the directions provide only one method of standardization, other methods of equal or greater accuracy may be used. For substances available as certified primary standards, or of comparable quality, the final standard solution may be prepared by weighing accurately a suitable quantity of the substance and dissolving it to produce a specific volume solution of known concentration. Hydrochloric and sulfuric acids may be standardized against a certified primary standard.

In volumetric assays described in *FCC*, the number of mg of the test substance equivalent to 1 mL of the primary volumetric solution is given. In general, these equivalents may be derived by simple calculation (see also *Solutions*, in the *General Provisions*).

Ammonium Thiocyanate, 0.1 N (7.612 g NH_4SCN per 1000 mL): Dissolve about 8 g of ammonium thiocyanate (NH_4SCN) in 1000 mL of water, and standardize by titrating the solution against *0.1 N Silver Nitrate* as follows: transfer about 30 mL of *0.1 N Silver Nitrate*, accurately measured, into a glass-stoppered flask. Dilute with 50 mL of water, then add 2 mL of *Ferric Ammonium Sulfate TS* and 2 mL of nitric acid, and titrate with the ammonium thiocyanate solution to the first appearance of a red-brown color. Calculate the normality, and, if desired, adjust the solution to exactly 0.1 N. If desired, *0.1 N Ammonium Thiocyanate* may be replaced by 0.1 N potassium thiocyanate where the former is directed in various tests and assays.

Barium Hydroxide, 0.2 N [17.14 g $Ba(OH)_2$ per 1000 mL]: Dissolve about 36 g of barium hydroxide [$Ba(OH)_2 \cdot 8H_2O$] in 1 L of recently boiled and cooled water, and quickly filter the solution. Keep this solution in bottles with well-fitted rubber stoppers with a soda–lime tube attached to each bottle to protect the solution from carbon dioxide in the air. Standardize as follows: transfer quantitatively about 60 mL of 0.1 N hydrochloric acid, accurately measured, to a flask; add 2 drops of *Phenolphthalein TS*; and slowly titrate with the barium hydroxide solution, with constant stirring, until a permanent pink color is produced. Calculate the normality of the barium hydroxide solution and, if desired, adjust to exactly 0.2 N with freshly boiled and cooled water.

> [NOTE—Solutions of alkali hydroxides absorb carbon dioxide when exposed to air. Connect the buret used for titrations with barium hydroxide solution directly to the storage bottle, and provide the bottle with a soda–lime tube so that air entering must pass through this tube, which will absorb carbon dioxide. Frequently restandardize standard solutions of barium hydroxide.]

Bromine, 0.1 N (7.990 g Br per 1000 mL): Dissolve 3 g of potassium bromate ($KBrO_3$) and 15 g of potassium bromide (KBr) in sufficient water to make 1000 mL, and standardize the solution as follows: transfer about 25 mL of the solution, accurately measured, into a 500-mL iodine flask, and dilute with 120 mL of water. Add 5 mL of hydrochloric acid, stopper the flask, and shake it gently. Then add 5 mL of *Potassium Iodide TS*, restopper, shake the mixture, allow it to stand for 5 min, and titrate the liberated iodine with *0.1 N Sodium Thiosulfate*, adding *Starch TS* near the end of the titration. Calculate the normality. Store this solution in dark, amber-colored, glass-stoppered bottles.

Ceric Sulfate, 0.1 N [33.22 g Ce(SO$_4$)$_2$ per 1000 mL]: Transfer 59 g of ceric ammonium nitrate [Ce(NO$_3$)$_4$·2NH$_4$NO$_3$·2H$_2$O] to a beaker, add 31 mL of sulfuric acid, mix, and cautiously add water, in 20-mL portions, until solution is complete. Cover the beaker, let stand overnight, pass through a sintered-glass crucible of fine porosity, add water to make 1000 mL, and mix. Alternatively, use the commercially available volumetric standard solution.

Standardize *Ceric Sulfate, 0.1 N* as follows: weigh 0.2 g of sodium oxalate, primary standard, dried according to the instructions on its label, and dissolve in 75 mL of water. Add, with stirring, 2 mL of sulfuric acid that has previously been mixed with 5 mL of water, mix well, add 10 mL of hydrochloric acid, and heat to 70°–75°. Titrate with *Ceric Sulfate, 0.1 N* to a permanent slight yellow color. Each 6.700 mg of sodium oxalate is equivalent to 1 mL of 0.1 N ceric sulfate.

$$N = (mg\ Na_2C_2O_4)/[67.00 \times mL\ Ce(SO_4)_2\ solution]$$

Ceric Sulfate, 0.01 N [3.322 g Ce(SO$_4$)$_2$ per 1000 mL]: Dissolve 4.2 g of ceric sulfate [Ce(SO$_4$)$_2$·4H$_2$O] or 5.5 g of the acid sulfate [Ce(HSO$_4$)$_4$] in about 500 mL of water containing 28 mL of sulfuric acid, and dilute to 1000 mL. Allow the solution to stand overnight, and filter. Standardize this solution daily as follows: weigh accurately about 275 mg of hydroquinone (C$_6$H$_6$O$_2$), dissolve it in sufficient *0.5 N Alcoholic Sulfuric Acid* to make 500.0 mL, and mix. To 25.0 mL of this solution add 75 mL of 0.5 N sulfuric acid, 20 mL of water, and 2 drops of *Diphenylamine TS*. Titrate with the ceric sulfate solution at a rate of about 25 drops per 10 s until an endpoint is reached that persists for 10 s. Perform a blank determination using 100 mL of *0.5 N Alcoholic Sulfuric Acid*, 20 mL of water, and 2 drops of *Diphenylamine TS*, and make any necessary correction. Calculate the normality of the ceric sulfate solution by the formula

$$Result = 0.05W/55.057V,$$

in which W is the weight, in mg, of the hydroquinone sample taken, and V is the volume, in mL, of the ceric sulfate solution consumed in the titration.

Disodium EDTA, 0.05 M (16.81 g C$_{10}$H$_{14}$N$_2$Na$_2$O$_8$ per 1000 mL): Dissolve 18.6 g of disodium ethylenediaminetetraacetate (C$_{10}$H$_{14}$N$_2$Na$_2$O$_8$·2H$_2$O) in sufficient water to make 1000 mL, and standardize the solution as follows: weigh accurately about 200 mg of chelometric standard calcium carbonate (CaCO$_3$), transfer to a 400-mL beaker, add 10 mL of water, and swirl to form a slurry. Cover the beaker with a watch glass, and introduce 2 mL of 2.7 N hydrochloric acid from a pipet inserted between the lip of the beaker and the edge of the watch glass. Swirl the contents of the beaker to dissolve the calcium carbonate. Wash down the sides of the beaker, the outer surface of the pipet, and the watch glass, and dilute with water to about 100 mL. While stirring, preferably with a magnetic stirrer, add about 30 mL of the disodium EDTA solution from a 50-mL buret, then add 15 mL of *1 N Sodium Hydroxide* and 300 mg of Hydroxy Naphthol Blue Indicator, and continue the titration to a blue endpoint. Calculate the molarity by the formula

$$Result = W/100.09V,$$

in which W is the weight, in mg, of CaCO$_3$ in the sample of calcium carbonate taken, and V is the volume, in mL, of disodium EDTA solution consumed. Each 5.004 mg of CaCO$_3$ is equivalent to 1 mL of *0.05 M Disodium EDTA*.

For the determination of aluminum in its salts, use *0.05 M Disodium EDTA* standardized as follows: transfer 2 g, accurately weighed, of aluminum wire to a 1000-mL volumetric flask, and add 50 mL of a 1:1 mixture of hydrochloric acid and water. Swirl the flask to ensure complete wetting of the wire, and allow the reaction to proceed. When dissolution is complete, dilute with water to volume, and mix. Transfer 10.0 mL of this solution to a 250-mL beaker, add 25.0 mL of the disodium EDTA solution, boil gently for 5 min, and cool. Add in the order given, and with continuous stirring, 20 mL of pH 4.5 buffer solution (77.1 g of ammonium acetate and 57 mL of glacial acetic acid in 1000 mL of solution), 50 mL of alcohol, and 2 mL of *Dithizone TS*. Titrate with *0.05 M Zinc Sulfate* to a bright rose pink color, and perform a blank determination, substituting 10 mL of water for the 10.0 mL of aluminum solution. Each mL of disodium EDTA solution is equivalent to 1.349 mg of aluminum (Al).

Ferrous Ammonium Sulfate, 0.1 N [39.21 g Fe(NH$_4$)$_2$(SO$_4$)$_2$·6H$_2$O per 1000 mL]: Dissolve 40 g of ferrous ammonium sulfate hexahydrate in a previously cooled mixture of 40 mL of sulfuric acid and 200 mL of water, dilute with water to 1000 mL, and mix. On the day of use, standardize the solution as follows: transfer from 25 to 30 mL of the solution, accurately measured, into a flask, add 2 drops of *Orthophenanthroline TS*, and titrate with *0.1 N Ceric Sulfate* until the red color is changed to pale blue. From the volume of *0.1 N Ceric Sulfate* consumed, calculate the normality.

Hydrochloric Acid, 1 N (36.46 g HCl per 1000 mL): Dilute 85 mL of hydrochloric acid with water to make 1000 mL, and standardize the solution as follows: accurately weigh about 1.5 g of primary standard anhydrous sodium carbonate (Na$_2$CO$_3$) that has been heated at a temperature of about 270° for 1 h. Dissolve it in 100 mL of water, and add 2 drops of *Methyl Red TS*. Add the acid slowly from a buret, with constant stirring, until the solution becomes faintly pink. Heat the solution to boiling, and continue the titration until the faint pink color is no longer affected by continued boiling. Calculate the normality. Each 52.99 mg of Na$_2$CO$_3$ is equivalent to 1 mL of *1 N Hydrochloric Acid*.

Hydroxylamine Hydrochloride, 0.5 N (35 g NH$_2$OH·HCl per 1000 mL): Dissolve 35 g of hydroxylamine hydrochloride in 150 mL of water, and dilute with anhydrous methanol to 1000 mL. To 500 mL of this solution add 15 mL of a 0.04% solution of bromophenol blue in alcohol, and titrate with *0.5 N Triethanolamine* until the solution appears green-blue by transmitted light. Prepare this solution fresh before each series of analyses.

Iodine, 0.1 N (12.69 g I per 1000 mL): Dissolve about 14 g of iodine (I) in a solution of 36 g of potassium iodide (KI) in 100 mL of water, add 3 drops of hydrochloric acid, dilute with water to 1000 mL, and standardize as follows: weigh accurately about 150 mg of primary standard arsenic trioxide (As_2O_3) previously dried at 105° for 1 h, and dissolve it in 20 mL of *1 N Sodium Hydroxide* by warming if necessary. Dilute with 40 mL of water, add 2 drops of *Methyl Orange TS*, and follow with 2.7 N hydrochloric acid until the yellow color is changed to pink. Then add 2 g of sodium bicarbonate ($NaHCO_3$), dilute with 50 mL of water, add 3 mL of *Starch TS*, and slowly add the iodine solution from a buret until a permanent blue color is produced. Calculate the normality. Each 4.946 mg of As_2O_3 is equivalent to 1 mL of *0.1 N Iodine*. Store this solution in glass-stoppered bottles.

Lithium Methoxide, 0.1 N (3.797 g CH_3OLi per 1000 mL): Dissolve 600 mg of freshly cut lithium metal in a mixture of 150 mL of anhydrous methanol and 850 mL of benzene. Filter the resulting solution if it is cloudy, and standardize it as follows: dissolve about 80 mg of benzoic acid (National Institute of Standards and Technology primary standard), accurately weighed, in 35 mL of dimethylformamide, add 5 drops of *Thymol Blue TS*, and titrate with the lithium methoxide solution to a dark blue endpoint.

[**Caution**—Protect the solution from absorption of carbon dioxide and moisture by covering the titration vessel with aluminum foil while dissolving the benzoic acid sample and during the titration.]

Each mL of *0.1 N Lithium Methoxide* is equivalent to 12.21 mg of benzoic acid.

Mercuric Nitrate, 0.1 M [32.46 g $Hg(NO_3)_2$ per 1000 mL]: Dissolve about 35 g of mercuric nitrate [$Hg(NO_3)_2 \cdot H_2O$] in a mixture of 5 mL of nitric acid and 500 mL of water, and dilute with water to 1000 mL. Standardize the solution as follows: transfer an accurately measured volume of about 20 mL of the solution into an Erlenmeyer flask, and add 2 mL of nitric acid and 2 mL of *Ferric Ammonium Sulfate TS*. Cool to below 20°, and titrate with *0.1 N Ammonium Thiocyanate* to the first appearance of a permanent brown color. Calculate the molarity.

Oxalic Acid, 0.1 N (4.502 g $H_2C_2O_4$ per 1000 mL): Dissolve 6.45 g of oxalic acid ($H_2C_2O_4 \cdot 2H_2O$) in sufficient water to make 1000 mL. Standardize by titration against freshly standardized *0.1 N Potassium Permanganate* as directed under *Potassium Permanganate, 0.1 N*. Store this solution in glass-stoppered bottles, protected from light.

Perchloric Acid, 0.1 N (10.046 g $HClO_4$ per 1000 mL): Mix 8.5 mL of perchloric acid (70%) with 500 mL of glacial acetic acid and 30 mL of acetic anhydride.

[**Caution**—Handle perchloric acid in an appropriate fume hood.]

Cool, and add glacial acetic acid to make 1000 mL. Allow the prepared solution to stand for 1 day for the excess acetic anhydride to be combined, and determine the water content by the *Karl Fischer Titrimetric Method*, Appendix IIB. If the water content exceeds 0.05%, add more acetic anhydride, but if the solution contains no titratable water, add sufficient water to make the content between 0.02% and 0.05%. Allow to stand for 1 day, and again determine the water content by titration. Standardize the solution as follows: weigh accurately about 700 mg of primary standard potassium biphthalate [$KHC_6H_4(COO)_2$], previously dried at 120° for 2 h, and dissolve it in 50 mL of glacial acetic acid in a 250-mL flask. Add 2 drops of *Crystal Violet TS*, and titrate with the perchloric acid solution until the violet color changes to emerald green. Deduct the volume of the perchloric acid consumed by 50 mL of the glacial acetic acid, and calculate the normality. Each 20.42 mg of $KHC_6H_4(COO)_2$ is equivalent to 1 mL of *0.1 N Perchloric Acid*.

Perchloric Acid, 0.1 N, in Dioxane Mix 8.5 mL of perchloric acid (70%) with sufficient dioxane, which has been especially purified by adsorption, to make 1000 mL.

[**Caution**—Handle perchloric acid in an appropriate fume hood.]

Standardize the solution as follows: weigh accurately about 700 mg of primary standard potassium biphthalate [$KHC_6H_4(COO)_2$], previously dried at 105° for 2 h, and dissolve in 50 mL of glacial acetic acid in a 250-mL flask. Add 2 drops of *Crystal Violet TS*, and titrate with the perchloric acid solution until the violet color changes to blue-green. Deduct the volume of the perchloric acid consumed by 50 mL of the glacial acetic acid, and calculate the normality. Each 20.42 mg of $KHC_6H_4(COO)_2$ is equivalent to 1 mL of *0.1 N Perchloric Acid*.

Potassium Acid Phthalate, 0.1 N [20.42 g $KHC_6H_4(COO)_2$ per 1000 mL]: Dissolve 20.42 g of primary standard potassium biphthalate [$KHC_6H_4(COO)_2$], previously dried at 105° for 2 h, in glacial acetic acid in a 1000-mL volumetric flask, warming on a steam bath if necessary to effect solution and protecting the solution from contamination by moisture. Cool to room temperature, dilute with glacial acetic acid to volume, and mix.

Potassium Dichromate, 0.1 N (4.903 g $K_2Cr_2O_7$ per 1000 mL): Dissolve about 5 g of potassium dichromate ($K_2Cr_2O_7$) in 1000 mL of water, transfer quantitatively 25 mL of this solution to a 500-mL glass-stoppered flask, add 2 g of potassium iodide (free from iodate) (KI), dilute with 200 mL of water, add 5 mL of hydrochloric acid, and mix. Allow to stand for 10 min in a dark place, and titrate the liberated iodine with *0.1 N Sodium Thiosulfate*, adding *Starch TS* as the endpoint is approached. Correct for a blank run on the same quantities of the same reagents, and calculate the normality.

Potassium Hydroxide, 1 N (56.11 g KOH per 1000 mL): Prepare and standardize 1 N potassium hydroxide by the procedure set forth for *1 N Sodium Hydroxide*, using 74 g of the potassium hydroxide (KOH) to prepare the solution. Each 204.2 mg of $KHC_6H_4(COO)_2$ is equivalent to 1 mL of *1 N Potassium Hydroxide*.

Potassium Hydroxide, 0.5 N, Alcoholic

[CAUTION—The solution may become very hot. Allow it to cool before adding the aldehyde-free alcohol.]

Dissolve about 35 g of potassium hydroxide (KOH) in 20 mL of water, and add sufficient aldehyde-free alcohol to make 1000 mL. Allow the solution to stand in a tightly stoppered bottle for 24 h. Then quickly decant the clear supernatant liquid into a suitable, tight container, and standardize as follows: transfer quantitatively 25 mL of 0.5 N hydrochloric acid into a flask, dilute with 50 mL of water, add 2 drops of *Phenolphthalein TS*, and titrate with the alcoholic potassium hydroxide solution until a permanent, pale pink color is produced. Calculate the normality. Store this solution in tightly stoppered bottles protected from light.

Potassium Iodate, 0.05 M (10.70 g KIO_3 per 1000 mL): Dissolve 10.700 g of potassium iodate of primary standard quality (KIO_3), previously dried at 110° to constant weight, in sufficient water to make 1000.0 mL.

Potassium Permanganate, 0.1 N (3.161 g $KMnO_4$ per 1000 mL): Dissolve about 3.3 g of potassium permanganate ($KMnO_4$) in 1000 mL of water in a flask, and boil the solution for about 15 min. Stopper the flask, allow it to stand for at least 2 days, and pass through a fine-porosity, sintered-glass crucible. If necessary, the bottom of the crucible may be lined with a pledget of glass wool. Standardize the solution as follows: weigh accurately about 200 mg of sodium oxalate of primary standard quality ($Na_2C_2O_4$), previously dried at 100° to constant weight, and dissolve it in 250 mL of water. Add 7 mL of sulfuric acid, heat to about 70°, and then slowly add the permanganate solution from a buret, with constant stirring, until a pale pink color that persists for 15 s is produced. The temperature at the conclusion of the titration should be not less than 60°. Calculate the normality. Each 6.700 mg of $Na_2C_2O_4$ is equivalent to 1 mL of *0.1 N Potassium Permanganate*. Potassium permanganate is reduced on contact with organic substances such as rubber; therefore, the solution must be handled in an apparatus made entirely of glass or other suitably inert material. Store it in glass-stoppered, amber-colored bottles, and restandardize frequently.

Silver Nitrate, 0.1 N (16.99 g $AgNO_3$ per 1000 mL): Dissolve about 17.5 g of silver nitrate ($AgNO_3$) in 1000 mL of water, and standardize the solution as follows: weigh accurately 100 mg of primary standard sodium chloride, previously dried at 120° for 16 h, into a 150-mL beaker, and dissolve it in 5 mL of water. Add 5 mL of 6 N acetic acid, 50 mL of methanol, and 2 or 3 drops of *Eosin Y TS*, and titrate with the silver nitrate solution to the endpoint. Calculate the normality.

Sodium Acetate, 0.1 N (8.203 g CH_3COONa per 1000 mL): Dissolve 8.20 g of anhydrous sodium acetate in glacial acetic acid to make 1000 mL, and standardize the solution as follows: to 25.0 mL of the prepared sodium acetate solution add 50 mL of glacial acetic acid and 1 mL of α-*Naphtholbenzein TS*. Titrate with *0.1 N Perchloric Acid* until a yellow-brown color changes through yellow to green.

[CAUTION—Handle perchloric acid in an appropriate fume hood.]

Perform a blank determination, and make any necessary correction. Calculate the normality factor.

Sodium Arsenite, 0.05 N (3.248 g $NaAsO_2$ per 1000 mL): Transfer 2.4725 g of arsenic trioxide, which has been pulverized and dried at 100° to constant weight, to a 1000-mL volumetric flask, dissolve it in 20 mL of *1 N Sodium Hydroxide*, and add *1 N Sulfuric Acid* or *1 N Hydrochloric Acid* until the solution is neutral or only slightly acid to litmus. Add 15 g of sodium bicarbonate, dilute with water to volume, and mix.

Sodium Hydroxide, 1 N (40.00 g NaOH per 1000 mL): Dissolve about 40 g of sodium hydroxide (NaOH) in about 1000 mL of carbon dioxide-free water. Shake the mixture thoroughly, and allow it to stand overnight in a stoppered bottle. Standardize the clear liquid as follows: transfer about 5 g of primary standard potassium biphthalate [$KHC_6H_4(COO)_2$], previously dried at 105° for 2 h and accurately weighed, to a flask, and dissolve it in 75 mL of carbon dioxide-free water. If the potassium biphthalate is in the form of large crystals, crush it before drying. To the flask add 2 drops of *Phenolphthalein TS*, and titrate with the sodium hydroxide solution to a permanent pink color. Calculate the normality. Each 204.2 mg of potassium biphthalate is equivalent to 1 mL of *1 N Sodium Hydroxide*.

[NOTE—Solutions of alkali hydroxides absorb carbon dioxide when exposed to air. Therefore, store them in bottles with well-fitted, suitable stoppers provided with a tube filled with a mixture of sodium hydroxide and lime so that air entering the container must pass through this tube, which will absorb the carbon dioxide. Frequently restandardize standard solutions of sodium hydroxide.]

Sodium Hydroxide, 0.5 N, Alcoholic (22.5 g NaOH per 1000 mL)

[CAUTION—The following solution may become very hot. Allow it to cool before adding the aldehyde-free alcohol.)]

Dissolve about 22.5 g of sodium hydroxide (NaOH) in 20 mL of water, and add sufficient aldehyde-free alcohol to make 1000 mL. Allow the solution to stand in a tightly stoppered bottle for 24 h. Then quickly decant the clear supernatant liquid into a suitable, tight container, and standardize as follows: Quantitatively transfer 25 mL of 0.5 N hydrochloric acid into a flask, dilute with 50 mL of water, add 2 drops of *Phenolphthalein TS*, and titrate with the alcoholic sodium hydroxide solution until a permanent, pale pink color appears. Calculate the normality. Store this solution in tightly stoppered bottles protected from light.

Sodium Methoxide, 0.1 N, in Pyridine (5.40 g CH_3ONa per 1000 mL): Weigh 14 g of freshly cut sodium metal, and cut into small cubes. Place about 0.5 mL of anhydrous methanol in a round-bottom 120-mL flask equipped with a ground-glass joint, add 1 cube of the sodium metal, and when the reaction subsides, add the remaining sodium metal to the flask. Connect a water-cooled condenser to the flask, and slowly add 100 mL of anhydrous methanol, in small portions, through the top of the condenser. Regulate the addition of the methanol so that the vapors are condensed and do not escape through the top of the condenser. After addition of the methanol is complete, connect a drying tube to the top of the condenser, and allow the solution to cool. Transfer 17.5 mL of this solution (approximately 6 N) into a 1000-mL volumetric flask containing 70 mL of anhydrous methanol, and dilute with freshly distilled pyridine to volume. Store preferably in the reservoir of an automatic buret suitably protected from carbon dioxide and moisture. Standardize the solution as follows: weigh accurately about 400 mg of primary standard benzoic acid, transfer it into a 250-mL wide-mouth Erlenmeyer flask, and dissolve it in 50 mL of freshly distilled pyridine. Add a few drops of *Thymolphthalein TS*, and titrate immediately with the sodium methoxide solution to a blue endpoint. During the titration, direct a gentle stream of nitrogen into the flask through a short piece of 6-mm glass tubing fastened near the tip of the buret. Perform a blank determination (see the *General Provisions*), correct for the volume of sodium methoxide solution consumed by the blank, and calculate the normality. Each 12.21 mg of benzoic acid is equivalent to 1 mL of *0.1 N Sodium Methoxide in Pyridine*.

Sodium Methoxide, 0.02 N, in Toluene (1.08 g CH_3ONa per 1000 mL): Weigh 2.5 g of freshly cut sodium metal, and cut into small cubes. Place about 200 mL of anhydrous methanol in a 1000-mL volumetric flask, chill in an ice bath, and add the cubes one at a time to the methanol. When the last cube is dissolved, dilute with toluene to the mark, and mix. Dilute 100 mL of this solution to 500 mL with toluene, adding small amounts of methanol if cloudiness results. Standardize the solution as follows: weigh accurately about 20 mg of primary standard benzoic acid, transfer it into a 50-mL conical flask, and dissolve it in 25 mL of dimethylformamide. Add 2 drops of a solution of 100 mg of thymol blue in 10 mL of dimethylformamide, and titrate immediately with the sodium methoxide solution to a blue endpoint. Titrate a blank solution of dimethylformamide in the same manner, correct the volume of sodium methoxide solution consumed by the blank, and calculate the normality. Each 2.442 mg of benzoic acid is equivalent to 1 mL of *0.02 N Sodium Methoxide in Toluene*.

Sodium Thiosulfate, 0.1 N (15.81 g $Na_2S_2O_3$ per 1000 mL): Dissolve about 26 g of sodium thiosulfate ($Na_2S_2O_3 \cdot 5H_2O$) and 200 mg of sodium carbonate (Na_2CO_3) in 1000 mL of recently boiled and cooled water. Standardize the solution as follows: weigh accurately about 210 mg of primary standard potassium dichromate, previously pulverized and dried at 120° for 4 h, and dissolve in 100 mL of water in a 500-mL glass-stoppered flask. Swirl to dissolve the sample, remove the stopper, and quickly add 2 g of sodium bicarbonate, 3 g of potassium iodide, and 5 mL of hydrochloric acid. Stopper the flask, swirl to mix, and let stand in the dark for 10 min. Rinse the stopper and inner walls of the flask with water, and titrate the liberated iodine with the sodium thiosulfate solution until the solution is only faint yellow. Add *Starch TS*, and continue the titration to the discharge of the blue color. Calculate the normality.

Sulfuric Acid, 1 N (49.04 g H_2SO_4 per 1000 mL): Add slowly, with stirring, 30 mL of sulfuric acid to about 1020 mL of water, allow to cool to 25°, and standardize by titration against primary standard sodium carbonate (Na_2CO_3) as directed under *1 N Hydrochloric Acid*. Each 52.99 mg of Na_2CO_3 is equivalent to 1 mL of *1 N Sulfuric Acid*.

Sulfuric Acid, Alcoholic, 5 N (245.2 g H_2SO_4 per 1000 mL): Add cautiously, with stirring, 139 mL of sulfuric acid to a sufficient quantity of absolute alcohol to make 1000.0 mL.

Sulfuric Acid, Alcoholic, 0.5 N Add cautiously, with stirring, 13.9 mL of sulfuric acid to a sufficient quantity of absolute alcohol to make 1000.0 mL. Alternatively, prepare this solution by diluting 100.0 mL of *5 N Sulfuric Acid* with absolute alcohol to make 1000.0 mL.

Thorium Nitrate, 0.1 M [48.01 g $Th(NO_3)_4$ per 1000 mL]: Weigh accurately 55.21 g of thorium nitrate [$Th(NO_3)_4 \cdot 4H_2O$], dissolve it in water, dilute to 1000.0 mL, and mix. Standardize the solution as follows: transfer 50.0 mL into a 500-mL volumetric flask, dilute with water to volume, and mix. Transfer 50.0 mL of the diluted solution into a 400-mL beaker, add 150 mL of water and 5 mL of hydrochloric acid, and heat to boiling. While stirring, add 25 mL of a saturated solution of oxalic acid, then digest the mixture for 1 h just below the boiling point, and allow to stand overnight. Decant through Whatman No. 42, or equivalent, filter paper, and transfer the precipitate to the filter using about 100 mL of a wash solution consisting of 70 mL of the saturated oxalic acid solution, 430 mL of water, and 5 mL of hydrochloric acid. Transfer the precipitate and filter paper to a tared tall-form porcelain crucible, dry, char the paper, and ignite at 950° for 1.5 h or to constant weight. Cool in a desiccator, weigh, and calculate the molarity of the solution by the formula

$$\text{Result} = 200W/264.04,$$

in which W is the weight, in g, of thorium oxide obtained.

Triethanolamine, 0.5 N [74 g $N(CH_2CH_2OH)_3$ per 1000 mL]: Transfer 65 mL (74 g) of 98% triethanolamine into a 1000-mL volumetric flask, dilute with water to volume, stopper the flask, and mix thoroughly.

Zinc Sulfate, 0.05 M (8.072 g $ZnSO_4$ per 1000 mL): Dissolve about 15 g of zinc sulfate ($ZnSO_4 \cdot 7H_2O$) in sufficient water to make 1000 mL, and standardize the solution as follows: dilute about 35 mL, accurately measured, with 75 mL of water, add 5 mL of *Ammonia–Ammonium Chloride Buffer TS* and 0.1 mL of *Eriochrome Black TS*, and titrate with *0.05 M Disodium EDTA* until the solution is deep blue. Calculate the molarity.

INDICATORS

The necessary solutions of indicators may be prepared as directed under *Test Solutions (TS) and Other Reagents*. The sodium salts of many indicators are commercially available and may be used interchangeably in water solutions with the alcohol solutions specified for the free indicators.

Useful pH indicators, listed in ascending order of the lower limit of their range, are methyl yellow (pH 2.9 to 4.0), bromophenol blue (pH 3.0 to 4.6), bromocresol green (pH 4.0 to 5.4), methyl red (pH 4.2 to 6.2), bromocresol purple (pH 5.2 to 6.8), bromothymol blue (pH 6.0 to 7.6), phenol red (pH 6.8 to 8.2), thymol blue (pH 8.0 to 9.2), and thymolphthalein (pH 9.3 to 10.5).

Alphazurine 2G Use a suitable grade.

Azo Violet [4-(p-Nitrophenylazo) Resorcinol] A red powder, melting at about 193° with decomposition.

Bromocresol Blue Use *Bromocresol Green*.

Bromocresol Green (*Bromocresol Blue; Tetrabromo-m-cresolsulfonphthalein*) A white or pale buff-colored powder; slightly soluble in water; soluble in alcohol and in solutions of alkali hydroxides. Transition interval: from pH 3.8 (yellow) to 5.4 (blue).

Bromocresol Purple (*Dibromo-o-cresolsulfonphthalein*) A white to pink, crystalline powder; insoluble in water; soluble in alcohol and in solutions of alkali hydroxides. Transition interval: from pH 5.2 (yellow) to 6.8 (purple).

Bromophenol Blue (*Tetrabromophenolsulfonphthalein*) Pink crystals, soluble in alcohol. Insoluble in water; soluble in solutions of alkali hydroxides. Transition interval: from pH 3.0 (yellow) to 4.6 (blue).

Bromothymol Blue (*Dibromothymolsulfonphthalein*) A rose red powder. Insoluble in water; soluble in alcohol and in solutions of alkali hydroxides. Transition interval: from pH 6.0 (yellow) to 7.6 (blue).

Cresol Red (*o-Cresolsulfonphthalein*) A red-brown powder. Slightly soluble in water; soluble in alcohol and in dilute solutions of alkali hydroxides. Transition interval: from pH 7.2 (yellow) to 8.8 (blue).

Crystal Violet (*Hexamethyl-p-rosaniline Chloride*) Dark green crystals. Slightly soluble in water; sparingly soluble in alcohol and in glacial acetic acid. Its solutions are deep violet.

Sensitiveness Dissolve 100 mg in 100 mL of glacial acetic acid, and mix. Pipet 1 mL of the solution into a 100-mL volumetric flask, and dilute with glacial acetic acid to volume. The solution is violet-blue and does not show a red tint. Pipet 20 mL of the diluted solution into a beaker, and titrate with *0.1 N Perchloric Acid*, adding the perchloric acid slowly from a microburet. Not more than 0.1 mL of *0.1 N Perchloric Acid* is required to produce an emerald green color.

[**Caution**—Handle perchloric acid in an appropriate fume hood.]

Dithizone (*Diphenylthiocarbazone*) A blue-black powder. Insoluble in water; soluble in alcohol and in chloroform, yielding intensely green solutions even in high dilutions.

Eriochrome Black T [*Sodium 1-(1-Hydroxy-2-naphthylazo)-5-nitro-2-naphthol-4-sulfonate*] A brown-black powder having a faint metallic sheen. Soluble in alcohol, in methanol, and in hot water.

Sensitiveness To 10 mL of a 1:200,000 solution in a mixture of equal parts (v/v) of methanol and water add a 1:100 solution of sodium hydroxide until the pH is 10. The solution is pure blue and free from cloudiness. Add 0.2 mL of *Magnesium Standard Solution* (10 µg Mg ion). The color of the solution changes to red-violet, and with the continued addition of magnesium ion, it becomes wine red.

***p*-Ethoxychrysoidin Monohydrochloride** [4-(p-Ethoxyphenylazo)-m-phenylenediamine Monohydrochloride; 4'-Ethoxy-2,4-diaminoazobenzene Monohydrochloride] A red powder, insoluble in water. Transition interval: from pH 3.5 (red) to 5.5 (yellow).

Hydroxy Naphthol Blue The disodium salt of 1-(2-naphtholazo-3,6-disulfonic acid)-2-naphthol-4-sulfonic acid deposited on crystals of sodium chloride. Small blue crystals, freely soluble in water. In the pH range between 12 and 13, its solution is red-pink in the presence of calcium ion and deep blue in the presence of excess disodium EDTA.

Suitability for Calcium Determinations Dissolve 300 mg in 100 mL of water, add 10 mL of *1 N Sodium Hydroxide* and 1.0 mL of a 1:200 calcium chloride solution, and dilute with water to 165 mL. The solution is red-pink. Add 1.0 mL of *0.05 M Disodium EDTA*. The solution becomes deep blue.

Litmus A blue powder, cubes, or pieces. Partly soluble in water and in alcohol. Transition interval: from approximately pH 4.5 (red) to 8 (blue). Litmus is unsuitable for determining the pH of solutions of carbonates or bicarbonates.

Methylene Blue [*3,7-Bis(dimethylamino)phenazathionium Chloride*] Dark green crystals or a crystalline powder having a bronzelike luster. Soluble in water and in chloroform; sparingly soluble in alcohol.

Methyl Orange (*Helianthin; Tropaeolin D; 4'-Dimethylaminoazobenzene-4-sodium Sulfonate*) An orange-yellow powder or crystalline scales. Slightly soluble in cold water; readily soluble in hot water; insoluble in alcohol. Transition interval: from pH 3.2 (pink) to 4.4 (yellow).

Methyl Red (*o-Carboxybenzeneazodimethylaniline Hydrochloride*) A dark red powder or violet crystals. Sparingly soluble in water; soluble in alcohol. Transition interval: from pH 4.2 (red) to 6.2 (yellow).

Methyl Red Sodium The sodium salt of o-carboxybenzeneazo-dimethylaniline. An orange-brown powder. Freely soluble in cold water and in alcohol. Transition interval: from pH 4.2 (red) to 6.2 (yellow).

Methyl Yellow (*p-Dimethylaminoazobenzene*) Yellow crystals, melting between 114° and 117°. Insoluble in water; soluble in alcohol, in benzene, in chloroform, in ether, in dilute mineral acids, and in oils. Transition interval: from pH 2.9 (red) to 4.0 (yellow).

Murexide Indicator Preparation Add 400 mg of murexide to 40 g of powdered potassium sulfate (K_2SO_4), and grind in a glass mortar to a homogeneous mixture. Alternatively, use tablets containing 0.4 mg of murexide admixed with potassium sulfate or potassium chloride, available commercially.

Naphthol Green B The ferric salt of 6-sodium sulfo-1-isonitroso-1,2-naphthoquinone. A dark green powder, insoluble in water.

Neutral Red (*3-Amino-7-dimethylamino-2-methylphenazine Chloride*) A coarse, red to olive green powder. Sparingly soluble in water and in alcohol. Transition interval: from pH 6.8 (red) to 8.0 (orange).

Phenol Red (*Phenolsulfonphthalein*) A bright to dark red, crystalline powder. Very slightly soluble in water; sparingly soluble in alcohol; soluble in solutions of alkali hydroxides. Transition interval: from pH 6.8 (yellow) to 8.2 (red).

Phenolphthalein White or yellow-white crystals. Practically insoluble in water; soluble in alcohol and in solutions of alkali hydroxides. Transition interval: from pH 8.0 (colorless) to 10.0 (red).

Quinaldine Red (*5-Dimethylamino-2-strylethylquinolinium Iodide*) A dark, blue-black powder, melting at about 260° with decomposition. Sparingly soluble in water; freely soluble in alcohol. Transition interval: from pH 1.4 (colorless) to 3.2 (red).

Thymol Blue (*Thymolsulfonphthalein*) A dark, brown-green, crystalline powder. Slightly soluble in water; soluble in alcohol and in dilute alkali solutions. Acid transition interval: from pH 1.2 (red) to 2.8 (yellow). Alkaline transition interval: from pH 8.0 (yellow) to 9.2 (blue).

Thymolphthalein A white to slightly yellow, crystalline powder. Insoluble in water; soluble in alcohol and in solutions of alkali hydroxides. Transition interval: from pH 9.3 (colorless) to 10.5 (blue).

Xylenol Orange [*3,3'-Bis-di(carboxymethyl)aminomethyl-o-cresolsulfonphthalein*] An orange powder. Soluble in water and in alcohol. In acid solution it is lemon yellow, and its metal complexes are intensely red. It gives a distinct endpoint in the direct EDTA titration of metals such as bismuth, thorium, scandium, lead, zinc, lanthanum, cadmium, and mercury.

INDICATOR PAPERS AND TEST PAPERS

Indicator papers and test papers are strips of paper of suitable dimension and grade (usually Swedish O filter paper or other makes of like surface, quality, and ash) impregnated with a sufficiently stable indicator solution or reagent.

Treat strong, white filter paper with hydrochloric acid, and wash with water until the last washing shows no acid reaction to *Methyl Red TS*. Then treat with 6 N ammonium hydroxide, wash again with water until the last washing is not alkaline toward *Phenolphthalein TS*, and dry thoroughly. Saturate the dry paper with the appropriate indicator solution prepared as directed below, and dry carefully by suspending from glass rods or other inert material in still air free from acid, alkali, and other fumes. Cut the paper into strips of convenient size, and store in well-closed containers protected from light and moisture.

Indicator papers and test papers that are available commercially may be used, if desired.

Acetaldehyde Test Paper Use a solution prepared by mixing equal volumes of a 20% solution of morpholine and a 5% solution of sodium nitroferricyanide. Saturate the prepared filter paper in the mixture, and use the moistened paper without drying.

Cupric Sulfate Test Paper Use *Cupric Sulfate TS*.

Lead Acetate Test Paper Usually about 6 × 80 mm in size. Use *Lead Acetate TS*, and dry the paper at 100°, avoiding contact with metal.

Litmus Paper, Blue Usually about 6 × 50 mm in size. It meets the requirements of the following tests.

Phosphate Place 10 strips in 10 mL of water to which have been added 1 mL of nitric acid and 0.5 mL of 6 N ammonium hydroxide. Allow to stand for 10 min, then decant the solution, warm, and add 5 mL of *Ammonium Molybdate TS*. Shake at about 40° for 5 min. No precipitate of phosphomolybdate is formed.

Residue on Ignition Ignite carefully 10 strips of the paper to constant weight. The weight of the residue corresponds to not more than 400 µg per strip of about 3 cm^2.

Rosins, Acids, etc. Immerse a strip of the blue paper in a solution of 100 mg of silver nitrate (AgNO$_3$) in 50 mL of water. The color of the paper does not change in 30 s.

Sensitiveness Drop a 10- to 12-mm strip in 100 mL of 0.0005 N hydrochloric acid contained in a beaker, and stir continuously. The color of the paper is changed within 45 s.

Litmus Paper, Red Usually about 6 × 50 mm in size. Red litmus meets the requirements for *Phosphate*, *Residue on Ignition*, and *Rosins, Acids, etc.*, under *Litmus Paper, Blue*.

Sensitiveness Drop a 10- × 12-mm strip into 100 mL of 0.0005 N sodium hydroxide contained in a beaker, and stir continuously. The color of the paper changes within 30 s.

Phenolphthalein Paper Use a 1:1000 solution of phenolphthalein in 1:2 alcohol.

Starch Iodate Paper Use a mixture of equal volumes of *Starch TS* and potassium iodate solution (1:20).

Starch Iodide Paper Use a solution of 500 mg of potassium iodide (KI) in 100 mL of freshly prepared *Starch TS*.

DETECTOR TUBES

Ammonia Detector Tube A fuse-sealed glass tube (Draeger or equivalent) that is designed to allow gas to be passed through it and that contains suitable absorbing filters and support media for the indicator bromophenol blue. The Draeger Reference Number is CH 20501; the measuring range is 5 to 70 ppm.

[NOTE—Suitable detector tubes are available from National Draeger, Inc., P.O. Box 120, Pittsburgh, PA 15205-0120. Tubes other than those specified in the monograph may be used in accordance with the section entitled *Alternative Analytical Procedures* under *FCC Specifications* in the *General Provisions*.]

Carbon Dioxide Detector Tube A fuse-sealed glass tube (Draeger or equivalent) that is designed to allow gas to be passed through it and that contains suitable absorbing filters and support media for the indicators hydrazine and crystal violet. The Draeger Reference Number is CH 30801; the measuring range is 0.01% to 0.30%.

Carbon Monoxide Detector Tube A fuse-sealed glass tube (Draeger or equivalent) that is designed to allow gas to be passed through it and that contains suitable absorbing filters and support media for the indicators iodine pentoxide, selenium dioxide, and fuming sulfuric acid. The Draeger Reference Number is CH 25601; the measuring range is 5 to 150 ppm.

Chlorine Detector Tube A fuse-sealed glass tube (Draeger or equivalent) that is designed to allow gas to be passed through it and that contains suitable absorbing filters and support media for the indicator o-toluidine. The Draeger Reference Number is CH 24301; the measuring range is 0.2 to 3 ppm.

Hydrogen Sulfide Detector Tube A fuse-sealed glass tube (Draeger or equivalent) that is designed to allow gas to be passed through it and that contains suitable absorbing filters and support media for the indicator, which is a suitable lead salt. The Draeger Reference Number is 6719001; the measuring range is 1 to 20 ppm.

Nitric Oxide–Nitrogen Dioxide Detector Tube A fuse-sealed glass tube (Draeger or equivalent) that is designed to allow gas to be passed through it and that contains suitable absorbing filters and support media for an oxidizing layer and the indicator diphenylbenzidine. The Draeger Reference Number is CH 29401; the measuring range is 0.5 to 10 ppm.

Sulfur Dioxide Detector Tube A fuse-sealed glass tube (Draeger or equivalent) that is designed to allow gas to be passed through it and that contains suitable absorbing filters and support media for an iodine–starch indicator. The Draeger Reference Number is CH 31701; the measuring range is 1 to 25 ppm.

Water Vapor Detector Tube A fuse-sealed glass tube (Draeger or equivalent) that is designed to allow gas to be passed through it and that contains suitable absorbing filters and support media for the indicator, which consists of a selenium sol in suspension in sulfuric acid. The Draeger Reference Number is CH 67 28531; the measuring range is 5 to 200 mg/m^3.

General Information

CONTENTS

Validation of Food Chemicals Codex Methods	1411
Guidelines for Collaborative Study Procedures to Validate Characteristics of a Method of Analysis	1414
USP Reference Standards for Food Ingredients	1427
General Information Analytical Techniques	1434
Electrophoresis	1434
Capillary Electrophoresis	1437
Mass Spectrometry	1441
Nuclear Magnetic Resonance	1445
Radioactivity	1452
Spectrophotometry and Light-Scattering	1459
Ion Chromatography	1465
Near-Infrared Spectroscopy	1467
Raman Spectroscopy	1472
Scoville Heat Units	1478
Infrared Spectra	1479
General Information Tables	1501
Alcoholometric Table	1501
Atomic Weights	1504
Relative Atomic Mass and Half-Lives of Selected Radionuclides	1507
Thermometric Equivalents	1509
General Good Manufacturing Practices Guidelines for Food Chemicals	1511
Food Ingredients: Pharmaceutical Applications and Use of Appropriate GMPs	1513
FCC in the U.S. Code of Federal Regulations	1522
Food Ingredients Fraud Database	1530

General Information

VALIDATION OF FOOD CHEMICALS CODEX METHODS

Submissions to the Food Chemicals Codex

Submissions for new or revised specifications and analytical methods must contain sufficient information to enable the Expert Committee to evaluate the proposals. In most cases, evaluations involve assessing the clarity and completeness of the analytical methods' description, determining the need for the methods, and reviewing documentation that the methods have been appropriately validated. Information may vary depending on the type of test method involved. However, in most cases a submission will consist of the following sections:

Rationale

Use this section to identify the need for the analytical method and describe the capability of the specific method proposed and why it is preferred over other types of determinations. For revised analytical methods, provide a comparison of limitations of the existing FCC analytical method and advantages offered by the suggested method.

Suggested Analytical Method

Use this section to present a complete description of the analytical method sufficiently detailed to enable persons "skilled in the art" to replicate it. Include all important operational parameters and specific instructions such as reagent preparation, systems suitability tests performance, description of blanks used, precautions, and explicit formulas for calculating test results.

Data Elements

Use this section to provide thorough and complete documentation of the validation of the analytical method. Include summaries of experimental data and calculations substantiating each of the applicable analytical performance parameters.

These parameters are described in the following section.

Validation

Validation of an analytical method is the process of establishing, by laboratory studies, that the performance characteristics of the method meet the requirements for the intended analytical applications. Express performance characteristics in terms of analytical parameters. Each of the recommended parameters is defined in the next section of this chapter, along with a delineation of a typical method by which it may be measured.

Typical analytical parameters used in assay validation are accuracy, precision, specificity, limit of detection, limit of quantitation, linearity, range, and ruggedness.

Accuracy

Definition

The accuracy of an analytical method is the closeness of test results obtained by that method to the true value. Accuracy may often be expressed as percent recovery by the assay of known, added amounts of analyte.

Determination

Determine the accuracy of an analytical method by applying that method to samples to which known amounts of analyte have been added both above and below the normal levels expected in the samples. Calculate the accuracy from the test results as the percentage of analyte recovered by the assay.

Precision

Definition

The precision of an analytical method is the degree of agreement among individual test results when the procedure is applied repeatedly to multiple samplings of a homogeneous sample. The precision of an analytical method is usually expressed as the standard deviation or relative standard deviation (coefficient of variation). Precision may be a measure of the degree of either reproducibility or repeatability of the analytical method under normal operating conditions. In this context, reproducibility refers to the use of the analytical procedure in different laboratories. Intermediate precision expresses within-laboratory variation, as on different days, or with different analysts or equipment within the same laboratory. Repeatability refers to the use of the analytical procedure within a laboratory over a short time, using the same analyst with the same equipment.

Determination

Determine the precision of an analytical method by assaying a sufficient number of aliquots of a homogeneous sample to be able to calculate statistically valid estimates of standard deviation or relative standard deviation (coefficient of variation). Assays in this context are independent analyses of samples that have been carried through the complete analytical procedure from sample preparation to final test result.

Specificity

Definition

The specificity of an analytical method is its ability to measure, both accurately and specifically, the analyte in the presence of components that may be expected to be present in the sample matrix. Specificity may often be expressed as the degree of bias of test results obtained by analysis of samples containing added impurities, degradation products, or related chemical compounds when compared with test results from samples without added substances. The bias may be expressed as the difference in assay results between the two groups of samples. Specificity is a measure of the degree of interference (or absence thereof) in the analysis of complex sample mixtures.

Determination

Determine the specificity of an analytical method by comparing test results obtained from the analysis of samples containing impurities, degradation products, or related chemical compounds with those obtained from the analysis of samples without these elements. The bias of the assay, if any, is the difference in test results between the two groups of samples. When impurities or degradation products are unidentified, demonstrate specificity by analyzing samples (with the method in question) containing impurities or degradation products and by comparing the results to those from additional purity assays (e.g., chromatographic assay). The degree of agreement of test results is a measure of the specificity.

Limit of Detection

Definition

The limit of detection is a parameter of limit tests. It is the lowest concentration of analyte in a sample that can be detected, but not necessarily quantitated, under the stated experimental conditions. Thus, limit tests merely substantiate that the analyte concentration is above or below a certain level. The limit of detection is usually expressed as the concentration of analyte (e.g., percentage, milligrams per gram, parts per billion) in the sample.

Determination

Determining the limit of detection of an analytical method will vary depending on whether it is an instrumental or noninstrumental procedure. For instrumental procedures, different techniques may be used. Some investigators determine the signal-to-noise ratio by comparing test results from samples containing known concentrations of analyte with those of blank samples and establish the minimum level at which the analyte can be reliably detected. A signal-to-noise ratio of 2:1 or 3:1 is generally accepted. Other investigators measure the magnitude of analytical background response by analyzing a number of blank samples and calculating the standard deviation of this response. The standard deviation, multiplied by a factor, usually 2 or 3, provides an estimate of the limit of detection. This limit is subsequently validated by the analysis of a suitable number of samples known to be close to or at the limit of detection.

For noninstrumental methods, determine the limit of detection by analyzing samples with known concentrations of analyte and by establishing the minimum level at which the analyte can reliably be detected.

Limit of Quantitation

Definition

Limit of quantitation is a parameter of quantitative assays for low levels of compounds in sample matrices, such as impurities and degradation products in food additives and processing aids. It is the lowest concentration of analyte in a sample that can be determined with acceptable precision and accuracy under the stated experimental conditions. The limit of quantitation is expressed as the concentration of analyte (e.g., percentage, milligrams per kilogram, parts per billion) in the sample.

Determination

Determining the limit of quantitation of an analytical method may vary depending on whether it is an instrumental or a noninstrumental procedure. For instrumental procedures, a common approach is to measure the magnitude of analytical background response by analyzing a number of blank samples and calculating the standard deviation of this response. Multiplying the standard deviation by a factor, usually 10, provides an estimate of the limit of quantitation. This limit is subsequently validated by the analysis of a suitable number of samples known to be close to or at the limit of quantitation.

For noninstrumental methods, determine the limit of quantitation by analyzing samples having known concentrations of analyte and by establishing the minimum level at which the analyte can be detected with acceptable accuracy and precision.

Linearity and Range

Definition of Linearity

The linearity of an analytical method is its ability (within a given range) to elicit test results that are directly, or by a well-defined mathematical transformation, proportional to the concentration of analyte in samples within a given range. Linearity is usually expressed in terms of the variance around the slope of the regression line (correlation coefficient), calculated according to an established mathematical relationship from test results obtained by the analysis of samples with varying concentrations of analyte.

Definition of Range

The range of an analytical method is the interval between and including the upper and lower levels of analyte that have been demonstrated to be determined with precision, accuracy, and linearity using the method as written. The range is normally expressed in the same units as test results (e.g., percentage, milligrams per kilogram, parts per billion) obtained by the analytical method.

Determination of Linearity and Range

Determine the linearity of an analytical method by mathematically treating test results obtained from analysis of samples with analyte concentrations across the claimed range of the method. The treatment is normally a calculation of a regression line by the method of least squares of test results versus analyte concentrations. In some cases, to obtain proportionality between assays and sample concentrations, the test data may have to be subjected to a mathematical transformation before the regression analysis. The slope of the regression line and its variance (correlation coefficient) provide a mathematical measure of linearity; the y-intercept is a measure of the potential assay bias.

Validate the range of the method by verifying that the analytical method provides acceptable precision, accuracy, and linearity when applied to samples containing analyte at the extremes of the range as well as within the range.

Ruggedness

Definition

The ruggedness of an analytical method is the degree of reproducibility of test results obtained by the analysis of the same samples under a variety of normal test conditions, such as different laboratories, analysts, instruments, lots of reagents, elapsed assay times, assay temperatures, and days. Ruggedness is normally expressed as the lack of influence on test results of operational and environmental variables of the analytical method. Ruggedness is a measure of reproducibility of test results under normal, expected operational conditions from laboratory to laboratory and from analyst to analyst.

Determination

Determine the ruggedness of an analytical method by analyzing aliquots from homogeneous lots in different laboratories, by different analysts, using operational and environmental conditions that may differ but still are within the specified parameters of the assay. Determine the degree of reproducibility of test results as a function of the assay variables. This reproducibility may be compared to the precision of the assay under normal conditions to obtain a measure of the ruggedness of the analytical method.

Robustness

The robustness of an analytical method is a measure of the method's capacity to remain unaffected by small, but deliberate, variations in method parameters, and it provides an indication of the method's reliability during normal use.

Data Elements Required for Assay Validation

FCC assay procedures vary from highly exacting analytical determinations to subjective evaluation of attributes. Considering this variety of assays, it is only logical that different test methods require different validation schemes. This section covers only the most common categories of assays for which validation data should be required.

These categories are as follows:

- *Category I:* Analytical methods for quantitation of major components of food additives or processing aids (including preservatives).
- *Category II:* Analytical methods for determination of impurities in food additives or processing aids. These methods include quantitative assays and limit tests.
- *Category III:* Analytical methods for determination of performance characteristics (e.g., solubility, melting point).

For each assay category, different analytical information is needed. In the following table, data elements that are normally required for each assay category are listed.

Already-established general assays and tests (e.g., titrimetric method of water determination, identification test) should also be validated to verify their accuracy (and absence of possible interference) when used for a new product or raw material.

The validity of an analytical method can be verified only by laboratory studies. Therefore, documentation of the successful completion of such studies is a basic requirement for determining whether a method is suitable for its intended applications.

Appropriate documentation should accompany any proposal for new or revised compendial analytical procedures.

Data Elements Required for Assay Validation

Analytical Performance Parameter	Assay Category I	Assay Category II Quantitative	Assay Category II Limit Tests	Assay Category III
Accuracy	Yes	Yes	*	*
Precision	Yes	Yes	No	Yes
Specificity	No	Yes	No	*
Limit of Detection	Yes	Yes	Yes	*
Limit of Quantitation	No	No	Yes	*
Linearity	Yes	Yes	No	*
Range	Yes	Yes	*	*
Ruggedness	Yes	Yes	Yes	Yes

*May be required, depending on the nature of the specific test.

Guidelines for Collaborative Study Procedures To Validate Characteristics of a Method of Analysis

COPYRIGHT © 2005 BY AOAC INTERNATIONAL. REPRINTED WITH PERMISSION.

{NOTE—These guidelines incorporate symbols, terminology, and recommendations accepted by consensus by the participants at the IUPAC Workshop on Harmonization of Collaborative Analytical Studies, Geneva, Switzerland, May 4–5, 1987 [*Pure Appl. Chem.* **60**, 855–864(1988); published as "Guidelines for Collaborative Study of Procedure to Validate Characteristics of a Method of Analysis," *J. Assoc. Off. Anal. Chem.* **72**, 694–704(1989)]. The original guidelines were revised at Lisbon, Portugal, August 4, 1993, and at Delft, The Netherlands, May 9, 1994, *Pure Appl. Chem.* **67**, 331–343(1995). These revised, harmonized guidelines have been adopted by AOAC INTERNATIONAL as the guidelines for the AOAC Official Methods Program, *J. AOAC Int.* **78**(5), 143A–160A(1995). Although the directions were developed for chemical studies, some parts may be applicable to all types of collaborative studies.}

Summary Statement of AOAC Recommendation for Design of a Collaborative Study

Minimum Criteria for Quantitative Study

Minimum number of materials (see Note 1).—Five (only when a single level specification is involved for a single matrix may this minimum be reduced to 3).

Minimum number of laboratories.—Eight reporting valid data for each material (only in special cases involving very expensive equipment or specialized laboratories may the study be conducted with a minimum of 5 laboratories, with the resulting expansion in the confidence interval for the statistical estimates of the method characteristics).

Minimum number of replicates.—One, if within-laboratory repeatability parameters are not desired; 2, if these parameters are required. Replication should ordinarily be attained by blind replicates or split levels (Youden pairs).

Minimum Criteria for Qualitative Analyses

Ten laboratories reporting on 2 analyte levels per matrix, 6 test samples per level, and 6 negative controls per matrix. (NOTE—AOAC criteria for qualitative analyses are not part of the harmonized guidelines.)

1. Preliminary Work (Within One Laboratory)

1.1 Determine Purpose and Scope of the Study and Method

Determine purpose of the study (e.g., to determine attributes of a method, proficiency of analysts, reference values of a material, or to compare methods), the type of method (empirical, screening, practical, reference, definitive), and the probable use of the method (enforcement, surveillance, monitoring, acceptance testing, quality control, research). Also, on the basis of the relative importance of the various method attributes (bias, precision, specificity, limit of determination), select the design of the collaborative study. The directions in this document pertain primarily to determining the precision characteristics of a method, although many sections are also appropriate for other types of studies.

Alternatives for Method Selection
(1) Sometimes obvious (only method available).
(2) Critical literature review (reported within-laboratory attributes are often optimistic).
(3) Survey of laboratories to obtain candidate methods; comparison of within-laboratory attributes of candidate methods (sometimes choice may still not be objective).
(4) Selection by expert [AOAC-preferred procedure (selection by Study Director with concurrence of General Referee)].
(5) Selection by Committee (ISO-preferred procedure; often time-consuming).
(6) Development of new method or modification of existing method when an appropriate method is not available. (Proceed as a research project.) (This alternative is time-consuming and resource-intensive; use only as a last resort.)

1.2 Optimize Either New or Available Method

Practical Principles
(1) Do not conduct collaborative study with an unoptimized method. An unsuccessful study wastes a tremendous amount of collaborators' time and creates ill will. This applies especially to methods that are formulated by committees and have not been tried in practice.
(2) Conduct as much experimentation within a single laboratory as possible with respect to optimization, ruggedness, and interferences. Analysis of the same material on different days provides considerable information on variability that may be expected in practice.

Alternative Approaches to Optimization
(1) Conduct trials by changing one variable at a time.
(2) Conduct formal ruggedness testing for identification and control of critical variables. *See* Youden and Steiner (pp 33–36, 50–55). The actual procedure is even simpler than it appears. (This is an extremely efficient way for optimizing a method.)
(3) Use Deming simplex optimization to identify critical steps. *See* Dols and Armbrecht. The simplex concept can be used in the optimization of instrument performance and in application to analytical chemical method development.

1.3 Develop Within-Laboratory Attributes of Optimized Method

(Some items can be omitted; others can be combined depending on whether study is qualitative or quantitative.)

Determine calibration function (response vs concentration in pure or defined solvent) to determine useful measurement range of method. For some techniques, e.g., immunoassay, linearity is not a prerequisite. Indicate any mathematical transformations needed.

Determine analytical function (response vs concentration in matrix, including blank) to determine applicability to commodity(ies) of interest.

Test for interferences (specificity): (1) Test effects of impurities, ubiquitous contaminants, flavors, additives, and other components expected to be present and at usual concentrations. (2) Test nonspecific effects of matrices. (3) Test effects of transformation products, if method is to indicate stability, and metabolic products, if tissue residues are involved.

Conduct bias (systematic error) testing by measuring recoveries of analyte added to matrices of interest and to extracts, digests, or other treated solutions thereof. (Not necessary when method defines property or component.)

Develop performance specifications for instruments and suitability tests for systems (which utilize columns or adsorbents) to ensure satisfactory performance of critical steps (columns, instruments, etc.) in method.

Conduct precision testing at the concentration levels of interest, including variation in experimental conditions expected in routine analysis (ruggedness). In addition to estimating the "classical" repeatability standard deviation, s_r, the initiating laboratory may estimate the total within-laboratory standard deviation (s_e) whereby s_e is the variability at different days and with different calibration curves, by the same or different analysts within a single laboratory. This total within-laboratory estimate reflects both between-run (between-batch) and within-run (within-batch) variability.

Delineate the range of applicability to the matrices or commodities of interest.

Compare the results of the application of the method with existing, studied methods intended for the same purposes, if other methods are available.

If any of the preliminary estimates of the relevant performance of these characteristics are unacceptable, revise the method to improve them, and re-study as necessary.

Have method tried by analysts not involved in its development.

Revise method to handle questions raised and problems encountered.

1.4 Prepare Description of Method

NOTE—A collaborative study of a method involves practical testing of the written version of the method, in its specific style and format, by a number of laboratories on identical materials.

Prepare method description as closely as possible to format and style that will be used for eventual publication.

Always express reagent concentrations in terms of mass (or volume) per volume (or mass); never in terms requiring the analyst to recalculate or look up formula weights, e.g., moles. Moles may be used, particularly with volumetric standards, but only in addition to mass and volume. Many errors are caused by incorrect recalculation of formula weights.

Clearly specify requirements for chromatographic materials, enzymes, antibodies, and other performance-related reagents.

Clearly describe and explain every step in the analytical method so as to discourage deviations. Use imperative directions; avoid subjunctive and conditional expressions as options as far as possible.

Clearly describe any safety precautions needed.

Edit method for completeness, credibility (e.g., buffer pH consistent with specified chemicals, volumes not greater than capacity of container), continuity, and clarity.

Check for inclusion of performance specifications and system suitability tests, defined critical points, and convenient stopping points. Incorporate physical or chemical constants of working standards solutions, e.g., absorptivities, half-scale deflections, recoveries, etc., or properties of operating solutions and chromatographic materials, e.g., pH, volumes, resolution, etc., and any other indicators (e.g., sum equals 100%) that suggest analysis is proceeding properly.

If time and resources are available, conduct pilot study involving 2–3 laboratories.

1.5 Invite Participation

Selection of Collaborators/Candidate Laboratories

Laboratories invited to participate should have personnel experienced in the basic techniques employed; experience with the method itself is not a prerequisite for selection. Lists of possible participants can be developed through personal contacts, technical societies, trade associations, or literature search, and advertisements in the Referee section of AOAC's magazine, *Inside Laboratory Management*. Collaborators are chosen by the organizers of the collaborative study from a diversity of laboratories with interest in the method, including regulatory agencies, industry, and universities.

Letter of Invitation

Address a formal letter to the individual responsible for assignment of laboratory effort. State reason for selecting that laboratory (e.g., as a volunteer or has responsibility or familiarity with the problem or method), estimated number of person-hours required for performance, number of test samples to be sent, number of analyses to be required, expected date for test sample distribution, and target date for completion of the study. *Emphasize the importance of management support in assigning the necessary time for the project.* Enclose a copy of the method and a return form or card (with postage affixed, if appropriate), requiring only a check mark for acceptance or refusal of the invitation, a signature, space for address corrections, telephone and fax numbers, e-mail, and date.

Laboratory Coordinator

With large studies, involving several analysts per laboratory, several familiarization samples, receipt of items at different times, or similar recurrent situations, acceptance of the invitation should be followed by a letter suggesting that a Laboratory Coordinator be appointed. The

Laboratory Coordinator should be responsible for receiving and storing the study materials, assigning the work, dispensing study materials and information related to the study, seeing that the method is followed as written, accumulating the data, assuring that the data are correctly reported, and submitting the collaborative study manuscript within the deadline.

1.6 Instructions and Report Forms

Carefully design and prepare instructions and forms, and scrutinize them before distribution. A pilot study is also useful for uncovering problems in these documents.

Send instructions and report forms immediately on receipt of acceptance, independent of study materials, if selection of laboratories is not to be based on performance in pilot or training studies. The instructions should include in bold face or capital letters a statement:

THIS IS A STUDY OF THE METHOD, NOT OF THE LABORATORY. THE METHOD MUST BE FOLLOWED AS CLOSELY AS PRACTICABLE, AND ANY DEVIATIONS FROM THE METHOD AS DESCRIBED, NO MATTER HOW TRIVIAL THEY MAY SEEM, MUST BE NOTED ON THE REPORT FORM.

Include instructions on storage and handling, markings, and identifications to be noted, any special preparation for analysis, and criteria for use of practice or familiarization samples, if included. Pre-code the form for each laboratory and provide sufficient space for as much sequential data as may be required for proper evaluation of the results, including a check of the calculations.

The initiating laboratory should indicate the number of significant figures to be reported, usually based on the output of the measuring instrument.

NOTE—In making statistical calculations from the reported data, the full power of the calculator or computer is to be used with no rounding or truncating until the final reported mean and standard deviations are achieved. At this point the standard deviations are rounded to 2 significant figures and the means and relative standard deviations are rounded to accommodate the significant figures of the standard deviation. For example, if the reproducibility standard deviation $s_R = 0.012$, the mean is reported as 0.147, not as 0.1473 or 0.15, and RSD_R, relative reproducibility standard deviation, is reported as 8.2%. If standard deviation calculations must be conducted manually in steps, with the transfer of intermediate results, the number of significant figures to be retained for squared numbers should be at least 2 times the number of figures in the data plus 1.

When recorder tracing reproductions are required to evaluate method performance, request their submission both in the instructions and as a check item on the form. Provide instructions with regard to labeling of recorder tracings, such as identification with respect to item analyzed, axes, date, submitter, experimental conditions, and instrument settings.

Include in the report form a signature line for the analyst and lines for a printed or typed version of the name and address for correct acknowledgement.

Provide for a review by the laboratory supervisor. An example of a completed form is helpful. A questionnaire may be included or sent after completion of the analyses in which the questions can be designed to reveal if modifications have been made at critical steps in the method.

Request a copy of the calibration curve or other relationship between response and concentration or amount of analyte so that if discrepancies become apparent after examining all of the data, it can be determined whether the problem is in the calibration or in the analysis.

1.7 Familiarization or Practice Samples

If deemed necessary, supply as far ahead as practicable, familiarization samples, with instructions, before actual materials are sent. When familiarization samples have been submitted, supply forms for reporting progress toward satisfactory performance.

2. Design of the Collaborative Study

2.1 General Principles

The purpose of a collaborative study is to determine estimates of the attributes of a method, particularly the "precision" of the method that may be expected when the method is used in actual practice. The AOACI uses 2 terms to define the precision of a method under 2 circumstances of replication: repeatability and reproducibility. Repeatability is a measure of the variation, s_r^2, between replicate determinations by the same analyst. It defines how well an analyst can check himself using the same method on blind replicates of the same material or split levels (Youden pairs), under the same conditions (e.g., same laboratory, same apparatus, and same time). Reproducibility is a composite measure of variation, s_R^2, which includes the between-laboratory and within-laboratory variations. It measures how well an analyst in a given laboratory can check the results of another analyst in another laboratory using the same method to analyze the same test material under different conditions (e.g., different apparatus and different time). The between-laboratory variation represents a systematic error that reflects variation arising from environmental conditions (e.g., condition of reagent and instruments, variation in calibration factors, and interpretations of the steps of the method) associated with the laboratories used in the study. Therefore, it is important to identify the causes of the differences among laboratories so that they may be controlled. Otherwise they will be summed into s_R^2.

Present test samples sent for analysis as unknowns (blind) and coded in a random pattern. If necessary to conserve analyst time, an indication of the potential range of concentration or amount of analyte may be provided. If spiking solutions are used, provide one coded solution for each material. All spiking solutions should be identical in appearance and volume. Do not provide a single solution from which aliquots are to be removed for spiking. Any information with regard to concentration (e.g., utilizing factorial aliquots or serial dilutions of the same spiking solutions) or known replication is likely to lead to an underestimate of the variability.

The study must be extensive enough to assure sufficient data surviving in the face of possible loss of materials during shipment, inability of collaborators to participate after acceptance, and a maximum outlier rate of 2/9 and still maintain valid data from a minimum of 8 laboratories.

Improper preparation of reference standards and standard solutions can cause a significant portion of the analytical error. A decision must be made whether such error is to be considered separately or as part of the method, i.e., will the analysts procure their own standard solutions or will standards be provided by the Study Director. The decision depends primarily on the availability of the standard. If the standard is readily available, the analysts should prepare their own. If the standard is not readily available, the standard may be supplied, but physical constants, e.g., absorptivity of working standard solutions, should be incorporated into the description as a check on proper preparation of the solution.

Obtain the necessary administrative and operational approvals. Review by potential users of the method is also desirable.

2.2 Laboratories

Laboratories must realize the importance of the study. A large investment is being made in studying the method and this probably will be only collaborative study of the method that will performed. Therefore, it is important to have a fair and thorough evaluation of the method.

Type

The most appropriate laboratory is one with a responsibility related to the analytical problem. Laboratory types may be representative (selection of laboratories that will be using the method in practice), reference (assumed to be "best"), or the entire population of laboratories (usually certified or accredited) that will be using the method. Final selection of participants should be based on a review with the General Referee and others of each laboratory's capabilities and past performance in collaborative studies, followed up, if possible, by telephone conversations or by personal visits. Selection may also be based on performance with familiarization samples. Sometimes only laboratories with dedicated or very specialized instruments must be used. If the study is intended for international consideration, laboratories from different countries should be invited to participate.

Number of Laboratories

Minimum of 8 laboratories submitting valid data (to avoid unduly large confidence bands about the estimated parameters). Only in special cases of very expensive equipment or specialized laboratories may the study be conducted with a minimum of 5 laboratories. Fewer laboratories widen the confidence limits of the mean and of the variance components (see design considerations). The optimum number of laboratories, balancing logistics and costs against information obtained, often is 8–10. However, larger studies are not discouraged.

For qualitative analyses, a minimum of 10 laboratories is needed; collaborative study must be designed to include 2 analyte levels per matrix, 6 test samples per level, and 6 negative controls per matrix. (NOTE 1—AOAC criteria for qualitative analyses are not part of the harmonized guidelines.)

Analysts

Most designs require only 1 analyst per laboratory. If analyst–within-laboratory variability is a desired variance component, multiple analysts should be requested from all participating laboratories. Ordinarily 2 analysts from the same laboratory cannot be substituted for different laboratories, unless standard solutions, reagents, chromatographic columns and/or materials, instrument calibrations, standard curves, etc., are prepared independently, and no consultation is permitted during the work. Different laboratories from the same organization may be used as separate laboratories if they operate independently with their own instruments, standards, reagents, and supervision.

2.3 Test Materials

Homogeneous Materials

Materials must be homogeneous; this is critical. Establish homogeneity by testing a representative number of laboratory samples taken at random before shipment. (A collaborator who reports an outlying value will frequently claim receipt of a defective laboratory sample.) The penalty for inhomogeneity is an increased variance in the analytical results that is not due to the intrinsic method variability.

Test Sample Coding

Code test samples at random so that there is no preselection from order of presentation.

Concentration Range

Choose analyte levels to cover concentration range of interest. If concentration range of interest is a tolerance limit or a specification level, bracket it and include it with materials of appropriate concentration. If design includes the determination of absence of analyte, include blank (not detectable) materials as part of range of interest.

Number of Materials

A minimum of 5 materials must be used in the collaborative study. Three materials are allowed but only when a single specification is involved for a single matrix.

NOTE 1—A material is an analyte (or test component)/matrix/concentration combination to which the method-performance parameters apply. This parameter determines the applicability of the method.

NOTE 2—The 2 test samples of blind or open duplicates are a single material (they are not independent).

The 2 test samples constituting a matched pair (called X and Y) are considered Youden matched pairs only if they are sufficiently close in composition. "Sufficiently close" would be considered as ≤5% difference in composition between X and Y. That is, given that the concentration of analyte in X (x_c) is higher than the concentration of the analyte in Y (y_c) then:

$$(x_c - y_c)/x_c \leq 0.05$$

or:

$$y_c \geq (x_c - 0.05 x_c)$$

NOTE 3—The blank or negative control may or may not be a material, depending on the usual purpose of the analysis. For example, in trace analysis, where very low levels (near the limit of quantitation) are often sought, the blanks are considered as materials, and are necessary to determine certain statistical "limits of measurement;" however, if the blank is merely a procedural control, in macro-level analysis (e.g., fat in cheese), it would not be considered a material.

Nature of Materials

Materials should be representative of commodities usually analyzed, with customary and extreme values for the analyte.

Size of Test Samples

Furnish only enough test sample to provide the number of test portions specified in the instructions. If additional test portions are required, the collaborator must request them, with an explanation.

Interferences

If pertinent, some materials, but not all, should contain contaminants and interferences in concentrations likely to be encountered, unless they have been shown to be unimportant through within-laboratory study. The success of the method in handling interference on an intralaboratory basis will be demonstrated by passing systems suitability tests.

Familiarization Samples

With new, complex, or unfamiliar techniques, provide material(s) of stated composition for practice, on different days, if possible. The valuable collaborative materials should not be used until the analyst can reproduce the stated value of the familiarization samples within a given range. However, it should be pointed out that one of the assumptions of analysis of variance is that the underlying distribution of results is independent of time (i.e., there is no drift). The Study Director must be satisfied that this assumption is met.

2.4 Replication

When within-laboratory variability is also of interest, as is usually the case, independent replication can be ensured by applying at least one of the following procedures (listed in suggested order of desirability; the nature of the design should not be announced beforehand):

(1) *Split levels (Youden pairs)*—The 2 test materials, nearly identical but of slightly different composition (e.g., ≤5% difference in composition, see 2.3 Number of Materials, Note 2) are obtained either naturally or by diluting (or by fortifying) one portion of the material with a small amount of diluent (or of analyte). Both portions are supplied to the participating laboratories as test samples, each under a random code number, and each test sample should be analyzed only once; replication defeats the purpose of the design.

(2) *Split levels for some materials and blind duplicates for other materials in the same study*—Obtain only single values from each test sample supplied.

(3) *Blind duplicate test samples, randomly coded*—NOTE—Triplicate and higher replication are relatively inefficient when compared with duplicate test samples because replication provides additional information only on individual within-laboratory variability, which is usually the less important component of error. It is more effective to utilize resources for the analysis of more levels and/or materials rather than for increasing the number of replicates for the individual materials.

PRACTICAL PRINCIPLE: With respect to replication, the greatest net marginal gain is always obtained in going from 2 to 3 as compared to going from 3 to 4, 4 to 5, etc.

(4) *Independent materials*—(NOTE—Unrelated independent materials may be used as a split level in the calculations of the precision parameters or for plotting. There should be ≤5% difference in composition for such materials (see 2.3 Number of Materials, Note 2). The more they differ in concentration, the less reliable the information they provide on within-laboratory variability.)

(5) *Known replicates—Use of known replicates is a common practice.*—It is much preferable to use the same resources on blind replicates or split levels.

(6) *Quality control materials*—Instead of obtaining repeatability parameters through the collaborative study, information can be obtained from use of quality control materials in each laboratory individually, for its own use, independent of the collaborative study, for a separate calculation of s_r, using 2 (or more) replicates from each quality control test, according to the pattern developed for each product.

2.5 Other Design Considerations

The design can be reduced in the direction of less work and less cost, but at the sacrifice of reduced confidence in the reliability of the developed information.

More work (values) is required if more confidence is needed, e.g., greater confidence is required to enforce a tolerance at 1.00 mg/kg than at 1.0 mg/kg. (The distinction is a precision requirement of the order of 1% rather than 10%.)

The estimate of the standard deviation or the corresponding relative standard deviation obtained from a collaborative study is a random variable that varies about its corresponding true value. For example, the standard deviation, s_r, which measures within laboratory or repeatability precision has associated with it a standard deviation (STD = s_r) describing its scatter about the true value σ_r. Therefore, s_r, whose STD (s_r) is a function of s_r^2, number of laboratories, and number of analyses per laboratory, will vary about σ_r from occasion-to-occasion even for the same test conditions and material. The STD s_R, which measures among laboratory or reproducibility precision, has a STD (s_R) that is a function of the random variables s_r^2 and s_L^2, number of laboratories, and number of analyses per laboratory. s_R will vary about its true value σ_R from occasion-to-occasion for the same test material.

The validity of extrapolating the use of a method beyond concentrations and components tested can be estimated only on the basis of the slope of the calibration curve (sensitivity) observed as a function of the nature and concentration of the matrix and contaminant components. If the signal is more or less independent of these variables, a reasonable amount of extrapolation may be utilized. The extrapolator assumes the burden of proof as to what is reasonable.

3. Preparation of Materials for Collaborative Studies

3.1 General Principles

Heterogeneity between test samples from a single test material must be negligible compared to analytical variability, as measured within the Study Director's laboratory.

The containers must not contribute extraneous analytes to the contents, and they must not adsorb or absorb analytes or other components from the matrix, e.g., water.

If necessary, the materials may be stabilized, preferably by physical means (freezing, dehydrating), or by chemical means (preservatives, antioxidants) which do not affect the performance of the method.

Composition changes must be avoided, where necessary, by the use of vapor-tight containers, refrigeration, flushing with an inert gas, or other protective packaging.

3.2 Materials Suitable for Collaborative Studies

Material and analyte stability: Ensure analyte and matrix stability over projected transport time and projected length of study.

Single batch of homogenous, stable product such as milk powder, peanut butter, vegetable oil, starch, etc., is the best type of material.

Reference materials supplied by standards organizations such as National Institute of Standards and Technology (NIST, Gaithersburg, MD) and EC's Joint Research Center and Institute on Reference Materials and Methods (IRMM, Belgium) are excellent, unless they have easily recognizable characteristics (e.g., odor and color of NIST Orchard Leaves). However, they are of limited availability, composition, and analyte level. If available, they are expensive. Sometimes the certification organization may be interested in making reference materials available for the analyte under study, in which case it may assist in providing the material for the study.

Synthetic materials may be especially formulated with known amounts of analytes by actual preparation for the study. This procedure is best used for macro-constituents such as drugs or pesticide formulations.

Spiked materials consisting of normal or blank materials to which a known amount of analyte has been added may be used. The amount of analyte added should not be excessive in relation to the amount present (e.g., about 2×), and the analyte added should be in the same chemical form as present in the commodities to be analyzed subsequently.

In drug and pesticide residue-type problems, it is often necessary to use spiked materials in order to assess recovery. However, because incurred residues are likely to present different problems from those of spiked residues, collaborative studies should include some test samples with incurred residues to ensure that the method is applicable under these conditions as well.

(1) *Preparation in bulk*—This requires thorough and uniform incorporation of analyte, often by serial dilution of solids. The danger of segregation due to differences in densities always exists. Fluid materials susceptible to segregation should be prepared under constant agitation. Uniformity should be checked by direct analysis, with an internal standard, or by a marker compound (dye or radioactive label).

(2) *Test samples, individually prepared*—A known amount of analyte is either weighed directly or added as an aliquot of a prepared solution to pre-measured portions of the matrix in individual containers. The collaborator is instructed to use each entire portion for the analysis, transferring the contents of the container quantitatively or a substantial weighed fraction of the portion. (This is the preferred alternative to spiked solid materials at trace [mg/kg] levels, at the expense of considerably more work.)

(3) *Concentrated unknown solutions for direct addition by collaborators to their own commodities*—Should be used only as a last resort when instability of the analyte precludes distribution from a central point. To preclude direct analysis of the spiking solution, supply individual coded solutions to be added in their entirety to portions of the matrix for single analyses by each laboratory. All solutions should have the same volume and appearance. This type of material is analogous to that of test samples except for the source of matrix. This case should be used only for perishable commodities that are altered by all available preservation techniques.

Materials analyzed by another, presumably accurate, method, if available, in the Study Director's laboratory or by some or all the collaborators.

Only as an absolutely last resort (usually with unstable materials and preparation of material studies) should the collaborators be permitted to prepare their own materials for analysis. Since it is impossible to avoid the personal bias introduced by knowledge of the composition of the material, the materials should be prepared in each laboratory by an individual who will not be involved in the analyses.

3.3 Blanks

When the absence of a component is as important as its presence, when determinations must be corrected for the amount of the component or the presence of background in the matrix, or when recovery data are required, provision must be made for the inclusion of blank materials containing "none" (not detected) of the analyte. It is also important to know the variability of the blank and the tendency of the method to produce false positives. There are 2 types of blanks: matrix blanks and reagent blanks. Since laboratories often will utilize reagents from different sources, each laboratory should perform reagent blanks. Matrix blanks, when required, are an intrinsic part of the method, and the number of blanks needed depends on the combined variance of the material (s_M) and of the blank (s_B). Standard deviation reflecting the total variability of a blank corrected value will be $s = (s_M^2 + s_B^2)^{1/2}$.

3.4 Limit of Detection/Quantitation

If the limit of detection/quantitation is important, it is necessary to provide a design which gives special attention to the number of blanks, and to the necessity for interpreting false positives and false negatives. In all cases, the definition of limit of detection/quantitation used in the study must be given by the Study Director.

3.5 Controls

When separation from interferences is critical to the analysis, appropriate materials incorporating these interferences must be included.

PRACTICAL ADVICE: Always allow for contingencies and prepare more sets (e.g., 25% more) of laboratory samples than there are collaborators. Some packages may never arrive, some materials may spoil, and some may be lost or the container broken. New laboratories may have to be substituted for those which are unable to complete the promised work. Some sets may have to be analyzed at a later time for different purposes, such as to verify stability on storage.

4. Submission of Test Samples

4.1 Sending Collaborative Study Material

Notify collaborators of shipping arrangements, including waybill numbers, arrival time, and required storage conditions.

Label test samples legibly and without ambiguity.

Pack shipping cartons well and label properly to avoid transportation delays. If the containers are breakable, pack well to minimize possibility of breakage. If material is perishable, ship frozen with solid CO_2, sufficient to last several days longer than anticipated travel time. Use special transportation services, if necessary. For international delivery, mark as "Laboratory samples—no commercial value" or other designation as required by customs regulations of the country to which the package is being sent. Hazardous materials must be packed and labeled as required by transportation regulations. Animal and plant products sent across international borders may require special certification from health authorities.

Include a return slip, to confirm safe receipt, with each package. If not sent previously, include copy of method, instructions, and report forms.

Provide instructions for proper storage of test samples between unpacking and analysis. Note that analysts should not use thawed or decomposed test samples without consulting the Study Director.

When it is important to have instruments calibrated with the same reference material, supply reference material to collaborators. Provision for supplying reference standards is particularly important when commercial sources of standards have not yet been developed. The inclusion of a working standard solution as an unknown is useful to establish a consensus value for standardization of quality control parameters, such as absorptivity, retention time, and sensitivity (change in signal intensity divided by the change in concentration).

4.2 Obligations of Collaborators

Analyze test samples at times indicated, according to submitted protocol. With unstable materials (e.g., with microbial or decomposition problems), analyses must be started at specified times.

FOLLOW METHOD EXACTLY (*this is critical*). If method is unclear, contact Study Director. Any deviation, such as the necessity to substitute reagents, columns, apparatus, or instruments, must be recorded at the time and reported. If the collaborator has no intention of following the submitted method, he or she should not participate in the study. If the collaborator wishes to check another method on the same materials, additional test samples should be requested for that purpose, to be analyzed separately.

Conduct exactly the number of determinations stated in the instructions. Any other number complicates the statistical analysis. Too few determinations may require discarding the results from that laboratory for that material or inserting "missing values"; too many values may require discarding the contribution of that laboratory or at least some of the values. If a laboratory cannot follow instructions as to number of analyses to perform, it raises a question as to its ability to follow the method.

Report individual values, including blanks. Do not average or do other data manipulations unless required by the instructions. Undisclosed averaging distorts statistical measures. If blank is larger than determination, report the negative value; do not equate negative values to zero. Follow or request instructions with regard to reporting "traces" or "less than." Descriptive (i.e., nonquantitative) terms are not amenable to statistical analysis and should be avoided. When results are below the limit of determination, report actual calculated result, regardless of its value.

Supply raw data, graphs, recorder tracings, photographs, or other documentation as requested in the instructions.

Since collaborators may have no basis for judging whether a value is an outlier, the results should be communicated to the Study Director as soon as the protocol is complete and before time and equipment are reassigned, so that repeat assays may be performed at once, if necessary and if permitted by the protocol.

NOTE—The sooner an apparent outlier is investigated, the greater the likelihood of finding a reason for its occurrence.

The most frequent causes of correctable outliers are:
- Incorrect calculations and arithmetic errors.
- Errors in reporting, such as transposition of numbers, misplacement of the decimal point, or use of the wrong units.
- Incorrect standards due to weighing or volumetric errors (check physical constants or compare against freshly prepared standard solutions).
- Contamination of reagents, equipment, or test samples.

5. Statistical Analysis

5.1 Initial Review of Data (Data Audit)

The Study Director may first plot the collaborative study results, material by material (or one value against the other for a split level [Youden pair]), value vs laboratory, preferably in ascending or descending order of reported average concentration. Usually major discrepancies will be apparent: displaced means, unduly spread replicates, outlying values, differences between methods, consistently high or low laboratory rankings, etc.

Only valid data should be included in the statistical analysis. Valid data are values that the Study Director has no reason to suspect as being wrong. Invalid data may result when: (1) the method is not followed; (2) a nonlinear calibration curve is found although a linear curve is expected; (3) system suitability specifications were not met; (4) resolution is inadequate; (5) distorted absorption curves arise; (6) unexpected reactions occur; or (7) other atypical phenomena materialize. Other potential causes of invalid data are noted previously.

5.2 Outliers

Collaborative studies seem to have an inherent level of outliers, the number depending on the definition of outliers and the basis for calculation (analytes, materials, laboratories, or determinations). Rejection of more than 2/9 of the data from each material in a study, without an explanation (e.g., failure to follow the method), is ordinarily considered excessive. Study must maintain valid data from a minimum of 8 labs. For larger studies, a smaller acceptable percentage of rejections may be more appropriate. Determine the probability that the apparent aberrant value(s) is part of the main group of values considered as a normal population by applying the following tests in order:

(1) *Cochran test* for removal of laboratories (or indirectly for removal of extreme individual values from a set of laboratory values) showing significantly greater variability among replicate (within-laboratory) analyses than the other laboratories for a given material. Apply as a 1-tail test at a probability value of 2.5%.

To calculate the Cochran test statistic: Compute the within-laboratory variance for each laboratory and divide the largest of these by the sum of all of these variances. The resulting quotient is the Cochran statistic which indicates the presence of a removable outlier if this quotient exceeds the critical value listed in the Cochran table for P = 2.5% (1-tail) and L (number of laboratories), **Appendix 1**.

(2) Grubbs tests for removal of laboratories with extreme averages. Apply in the following order: single value test (2-tail; P = 2.5%); then if no outlier is found, apply pair value test (2 values at the highest end, 2 values at the lowest end, and 2 values, one at each end, at an overall P = 2.5%).

To calculate the single Grubbs test statistic: Compute the average for each laboratory and then calculate the standard deviation (SD) of these L averages (designate as the original s). Calculate the SD of the set of averages with the highest average removed (s_H); calculate the SD of the set averages with the lowest average removed (s_L). Then calculate the percentage decrease in SD as follows:

$$100 \times [1 - (s_L/s)] \text{ and } 100 \times [1 - (s_H/s)]$$

The higher of these 2 percentage decreases is the single Grubbs statistic, which signals the presence of an outlier to be omitted if it *exceeds* the critical value listed in the single Grubbs tables at the P = 2.5% level, 2-tail, for L laboratories, **Appendix 2**.

To calculate the Grubbs pair statistic, proceed in an analogous fashion, except calculate the standard deviations s_{2L}, s_{2H}, and s_{HL}, following removal of the 2 lowest, the 2 highest, and the highest and the lowest averages, respectively, from the original set of averages. Take the smallest of these 3 SD values and calculate the corresponding percentage decrease in SD from the original s. A Grubbs outlier pair is present if the selected value for the percentage decrease from the original s *exceeds* the critical value listed in the Grubbs pair value table at the P = 2.5% level, for L laboratories, **Appendix 2**.

(3) If the single value Grubbs test signals the need for outlier removal, remove the single Grubbs outlier and recycle back to the Cochran test as shown in the flow chart, **Appendix 3**.

If the single value Grubbs test is negative, check for masking by performing the pair value Grubbs test. If this second test is positive, remove the 2 values responsible for activating the test and recycle back to the Cochran test as shown in the flow chart, **Appendix 3**, and repeat the sequence of Cochran, single value Grubbs, and pair value Grubbs. Note, however, that outlier removal should stop before more than 2/9 laboratories are removed.

(4) If no outliers are removed for a given cycle (Cochran, single Grubbs, pair Grubbs), outlier removal is complete. Also, stop outlier removal whenever more than 2/9 of the laboratories are flagged for removal. With a higher removal rate, either the precision parameters must be taken without removal of all outliers or the method must be considered as suspect.

NOTE—The decision as to whether a value(s) should be removed as an outlier ultimately is not statistical in nature. The decision must be made by the Study Director on the basis of the indicated probability given by the outlier test and any other information that is pertinent. (However, for consistency with other organizations adhering to the harmonized outlier removal procedure, the estimate resulting from rigid adherence to the prescribed procedure should be reported.)

5.3 Bias (Systematic Deviation) of Individual Results

Bias is defined as follows:

$$(\text{Estimated) bias} = \text{mean amount found} - \text{amount added (or known or assigned value)}$$

Single-value error and recovery are defined as follows:

$$\text{Error of a single value} = \text{the single value} - \text{amount added (true value)}$$

There are 2 methods for defining percent recovery: marginal and total. The formulas used to estimate these percent recoveries are provided in the following:

$$\text{Marginal \%Rec} = 100 R_M = 100((C_f - C_u)/C_A)$$

$$\text{Total \%Rec} = 100 R_T = 100(C_f)/(C_u + C_A)$$

where C_f is the amount found for the fortified concentration, C_u is the amount present originally for the unfortified concentration, and C_A is the amount added for the added concentration. The amount added is known or fixed and should be a substantial fraction of, or more than, the amount present in the unfortified material; all other quantities are measured and are usually reported as means, all of which have variations or uncertainties. The variation associated with the marginal percent recovery is $var(100R_M) = (100^2/C_A^2)[var(C_f) + var(C_u)]$ is larger than the variation associated with the total percent recovery. The variation associated with total percent recovery is $var(100R_T) = [100^2/(C_u + C_A)^2][var(C_f) + (R_T^2)var(C_u)]$. In each formula var means variance and refers to the concentration variation for the defined concentrations.

A true or assigned value is known only in cases of spiked or fortified materials, certified reference materials, or by analysis by another (presumably unbiased) method. Concentration in the unfortified material is obtained by direct analysis by the method of additions. In other cases, there is no direct measure of bias, and consensus values derived from the collaborative study itself often must be used for the reference point.

NOTES—(1) Youden equates "true" or "pure" between-laboratory variability (not including the within-laboratory variability) to the variability in bias (or variability in systematic error) of the individual laboratories. Technically, this definition refers to the average squared difference between individual laboratory biases and the mean bias of the assay.

(2) The presence of random error limits the ability to estimate the systematic error. To detect the systematic error of a single laboratory when the magnitude of such error is comparable to that laboratory's random error, at least 15 values are needed, under reasonable confidence limit assumptions.

5.4 Precision

The precision of analytical methods is usually characterized for 2 circumstances of replication: within laboratory or repeatability and among laboratories or reproducibility. Repeatability is a measure of how well an analyst in a given laboratory can check himself using the same analytical method to analyze the same test sample at the same time. Reproducibility is a measure of how well an analyst in one laboratory can check the results of another analyst in another laboratory using the same analytical method to analyze the same test sample at the same or different time. Given that test samples meet the criteria for a single material, the repeatability standard deviation (s_r) is:

$$s_r = (\Sigma d_i^2/2L)^{1/2}$$

where d_i is the difference between the individual values for the pair in laboratory i and L is the number of laboratories or number of pairs.

The reproducibility standard deviation (s_R) is computed as:

$$s_R = (1/2(s_d^2 + s_r^2))^{1/2}$$

where $s_d^2 = \Sigma(T_i - T)^2/(2(L-1))$, T_i is the sum of the individual values for the pair in laboratory i, T is the mean of the T_i across all laboratories or pairs, L is the number of laboratories or pairs, and s_r^2 is the square of $s_r = (\Sigma d_i^2/2L)^{1/2}$.

When the pairs of test samples meet the criteria for Youden matched pairs, i.e., when:

$$[(x_c - y_c)/x_c] \leq 0.05$$

or

$$y_c \geq (x_c - 0.05x_c),$$

s_r, a practical approximation for repeatability standard deviation, is calculated as:

$$s_r = [\Sigma(d_i - d)^2/(2(L-1))]^{1/2}$$

where d_i is the difference between the individual values for the pair in laboratory i, d is the mean of the d_i across all laboratories or pairs, and L is the number of laboratories or pairs. The reproducibility standard deviation, s_R, which reflects the square root of the average of the reproducibility variances for the individual materials (i.e., $s_R = [1/2(s_{Rx}^2 + s_{Ry}^2)]^{1/2}$), previously called X and Y, should be determined only if the individual variances are not significantly different from each other. To compare s_{Rx}^2 and s_{Ry}^2, the following formula may be used.

$$t = [(s_{Rx}^2 - s_{Ry}^2)(L-2)^{1/2}]/2[(s_{Rx}^2)(s_{Ry}^2) - (cov_{xy})^2]^{1/2}$$

where $s_{Rx}^2 = [1/(L-1)][\Sigma x_i^2 - (\Sigma x_i)^2/L]$, $s_{Ry}^2 = [1/(L-1)][\Sigma y_i^2 - (\Sigma y_i)^2/L]$, and $cov_{xy} = [1/(L-1)][\Sigma x_i y_i - (\Sigma x_i \Sigma y_i)/L]$. If t is greater than or equal to the tabular t-value for L – 2 degrees of freedom for a significance level of $\alpha = 0.05$, this may be taken to indicate that s_{Rx}^2 and s_{Ry}^2 are not equivalent and should not be pooled for a single estimate of s_R^2. That is, s_{Rx}^2 and s_{Ry}^2 should be taken as the reproducibility variance estimates for the individual test materials X and Y, respectively. This means that there is no rigorous basis for calculating s_r^2 because the within laboratory variability cannot be estimated directly.

Though s_r and s_R are the most important types of precision, it is the relative standard deviations ($RSD_r\% = 100s_r/$mean and $RSD_R\% = 100s_R/$mean) that are the most useful measures of precision in chemical analytical work because the RSD values are usually independent of concentration. Therefore, the use of the RSD values facilitates comparison of variabilities at different concentrations. When the RSD increases rapidly with decreasing concentration or amount, the rise delineates the limit of usefulness of the method (limit of reliable measurement).

5.5 HorRat

HorRat value is the ratio of the reproducibility relative standard deviation, expressed as a percent (RSD_R, %) to the predicted reproducibility relative standard deviation, expressed as a percent ($PRSD_R$, %), i.e.,

$$HorRat = RSD_R, \% / PRSD_R, \%$$

where $PRSD_R$, % = $2C^{-0.1505}$ and C = the estimated mean concentration expressed as a decimal fraction (i.e., 100% = 1; 1% = 0.01; 1 ppm = 0.000001). HorRat values between 0.5 to 1.5 may be taken to indicate that the performance value for the method corresponds to historical performance. The limits for performance acceptability are 0.5–2.

The precision of a method must be presented in the collaborative study manuscript. The HorRat will be used as a guide to determine the acceptability of the precision of a method.

The HorRat is applicable to most chemical methods. HorRat is not applicable to physical properties (viscosity, RI, density, pH, absorbance, etc.) and empirical methods [e.g., fiber, enzymes, moisture, methods with indefinite analytes (e.g., polymers) and "quality" measurements, e.g., drained weight]. Deviations may also occur at both extremes of the concentration scale (near 100% and ≤10^{-8}). In areas where there is a question if the HorRat is applicable, the General Referee will be the determining judge.

The following guidelines should be used to evaluate the assay precision:
- HorRat ≤ 0.5—Method reproducibility may be in question due to lack of study independence, unreported averaging, or consultations.
- 0.5 < HorRat ≤ 1.5—Method reproducibility as normally would be expected.
- HorRat > 1.5—Method reproducibility higher than normally expected: the Study Director should critically look into possible reasons for a "high" HorRat (e.g., were test samples sufficiently homogeneous, indefinite analyte or property?), and discuss this in the collaborative study report.
- HorRat > 2.0—Method reproducibility is problematic. A high HorRat may result in rejection of a method because it may indicate unacceptable weaknesses in the method or the study. Some organizations may use information about the HorRat as a criterion not to accept the method for official purposes (e.g., this is currently the case in the EU for aflatoxin methods for food analysis, where only methods officially allowed are those with HorRats ≤ 2).

5.6 Incorrect, Improper, or Illusory Values (False Positive and False Negative Values)

These results are not necessarily outliers (no *a priori* basis for decision), since there is a basis for determining their incorrectness (a positive value on a blank material, or a zero (not found) or negative value on a spiked material). There is a statistical basis for the presence of false negative values: In a series of materials with decreasing analyte concentration, as the RSD increases, the percent false negatives increases from an expected 2% at an RSD = 50% to 17% at an RSD = 100%, merely from normal distribution statistics alone.

When false positives and/or false negatives exceed about 10% of all values, analyses become uninterpretable from lack of confidence in the presence or absence of the analyte, unless all positive laboratory samples are re-analyzed by a more reliable (confirmatory) method with a lower limit of determination than the method under study. When the proportion of zeros (not necessarily false negatives) becomes greater than approximately 30%, the distribution can become bimodal and even more uninterpretable (is the analyte present or absent?).

5.7 Final Collaborative Study Manuscript

The final manuscript should contain a description of the materials used, their preparation, any unusual features in their distribution, and a table of all *valid* data, including outliers. When replication is performed, the individual values, not just averages, must be given, unless the method requires averages (e.g., microbiological methods). Values not used for specified reasons, such as decomposition, failure to follow method, or contamination, should not be included in the table since they may be included erroneously in subsequent recalculations. AOAC INTERNATIONAL requires the calculation and reporting of mean, percent recovery (% Rec), HorRat, repeatability (within-laboratory, s_r) and reproducibility (interlaboratory, s_R) standard deviations, and repeatability and reproducibility relative standard deviations (RSD_r and RSD_R, respectively). The accuracy (bias, trueness) of a method measuring a specific, identifiable analyte should be presented in the collaborative study manuscript as a recovery of added (spiked) analyte, as the results of analysis of a reference material, or by comparison with results by a reference method. Methods that are unable to report accuracy because of the unavailability of an accepted "true" value, or because of the nature of the method (empirical, microbiological, quality factors) should mention the reason in the manuscript. Proofread tables very carefully since many errors are of typographical origin. Give the names of the participants and their organizations, including complete contact information (name, preliminary address, telephone and fax numbers, and e-mail address).

The final manuscript should be published in a generally accessible publication, or availability of the report from the organization sponsoring the method should be indicated in the published method. Without public documentation, the significance of the study is very limited.

The manuscript should be sent to all participants, preferably at the preliminary stage, so that clerical and typographical errors may be corrected before publication. If changes in values from the original submission are offered, they must be accompanied by an explanation.

Example of Table of Interlaboratory Study Results: See **Table 1**.

The summary table as it will appear in the *Official Methods of Analysis of AOAC INTERNATIONAL* is given in **Table 2**.

6. References

(1) W.J. Youden & E.H. Steiner (1975) *Statistical Manual of the AOAC*, AOAC INTERNATIONAL, 481 N. Frederick Ave, Suite 500, Gaithersburg, MD 20877-7077, USA. The fifth printing (1987) contains several explanatory footnotes.
(2) G.T. Wernimont (1985) *Use of Statistics to Develop and Evaluate Analytical Methods*, W. Spendley (Ed.) AOAC INTERNATIONAL, 481 N. Frederick Ave, Suite 500, Gaithersburg, MD 20877-7077, USA.
(3) T. Dols & B. Armbrecht (1976) *J. Assoc. Off. Anal. Chem.* **59**, 1204–1207.
(4) International Organization for Standardization Guide 18, ISO, Case Postale 56, CH-1211 Geneva,

Switzerland, and other national standards organizations.

(5) International Organization for Standardization ISO 5725, ISO, Case Postale 56, CH-1211 Geneva, Switzerland, and other national standards organizations.

Appendix 1. Critical values for the Cochran maximum variance ratio at the 2.5% (1-tail) rejection level, expressed as the percentage the highest variance is of the total variance

L = number of laboratories at a given level (concentration)
r = number of replicates per laboratory

L	r = 2	r = 3	r = 4	r = 5	r = 6
4	94.3	81.0	72.5	65.4	62.5
5	88.6	72.6	64.6	58.1	53.9
6	83.2	65.8	58.3	52.2	47.3
7	78.2	60.2	52.2	47.3	42.3
8	73.6	55.6	47.4	43.0	38.5
9	69.3	51.8	43.3	39.3	35.3
10	65.5	48.6	39.9	36.2	32.6
11	62.2	45.8	37.2	33.6	30.3
12	59.2	43.1	35.0	31.3	28.3
13	56.4	40.5	33.2	29.2	26.5
14	53.8	38.3	31.5	27.3	25.0
15	51.5	36.4	29.9	25.7	23.7
16	49.5	34.7	28.4	24.4	22.0
17	47.8	33.2	27.1	23.3	21.2
18	46.0	31.8	25.9	22.4	20.4
19	44.3	30.5	24.8	21.5	19.5
20	42.8	29.3	23.8	20.7	18.7
21	41.5	28.2	22.9	19.9	18.0
22	40.3	27.2	22.0	19.2	17.3
23	39.1	26.3	21.2	18.5	16.6
24	37.9	25.5	20.5	17.8	16.0
25	36.7	24.8	19.9	17.2	15.5
26	35.5	24.1	19.3	16.6	15.0
27	34.5	23.4	18.7	16.1	14.5
28	33.7	22.7	18.1	15.7	14.1
29	33.1	22.1	17.5	15.3	13.7
30	32.5	21.6	16.9	14.9	13.3
35	29.3	19.5	15.3	12.9	11.6
40	26.0	17.0	13.5	11.6	10.2
50	21.6	14.3	11.4	9.7	8.6

Cochran statistic = (largest individual within-laboratory variance)/(sum of all the within-laboratory variances).

Appendix 2. Critical values for the Grubbs extreme deviation outlier tests at the 2.5% (2-tail), 1.25% (1-tail) rejection level, expressed as the percent reduction in the standard deviations caused by removal of the suspect value(s) (see text for calculating the Grubbs statistics)

L = number of laboratories at a given level (concentration)

L	One highest or lowest	Two highest or two lowest	One highest and one lowest
4	86.1	98.9	99.1
5	73.5	90.3	92.7
6	64.0	81.3	84.0
7	57.0	73.1	76.2
8	51.4	66.5	69.6
9	46.8	61.0	64.1
10	42.8	56.4	59.5
11	39.3	52.5	55.5
12	36.1	48.5	51.6
13	33.8	46.1	49.1
14	31.7	43.5	46.5
15	29.9	41.2	44.1
16	28.3	39.2	42.0
17	26.9	37.4	40.1
18	25.7	35.9	38.4
19	24.6	34.5	36.9
20	23.6	33.2	35.4
21	22.7	31.9	34.0
22	21.9	30.7	32.8
23	21.2	29.7	31.8
24	20.5	28.8	30.8
25	19.8	28.0	29.8
26	19.1	27.1	28.9
27	18.4	26.2	28.1
28	17.8	25.4	27.3
29	17.4	24.7	26.6
30	17.1	24.1	26.0
40	13.3	19.1	20.5
50	11.1	16.2	17.3

Source: Both tables were calculated by R. Albert (October 1993) by computer simulation involving several runs of approximately 7000 cycles each for each value, and then smoothed. Although the table of **Appendix 1** is strictly applicable only to a balanced design (same number of replicates from all laboratories), it can be applied to an unbalanced design without too much error, if there are only a few deviations.

Table 1. [x] Collaborative tests carried out at the international level in [year(s)] by [organization(s)] in which [y and z] laboratories participated, each performing [k] replicates, gave the following statistical results [results expressed in (units)]:

Material [description and listed across the top in increasing order of magnitude of means]
Number of laboratories retained after eliminating outliers
Number of outlying laboratories removed
Mean ($\bar{x}$)
True or accepted value, if known
Repeatability standard deviation (s_r)
Repeatability relative standard deviation (RSD_r)
Repeatability value, r ($2.8 \times s_r$)
Total within laboratory standard deviation (s_e)—optional if s_r is not valid.

Table 1. [x] Collaborative tests carried out at the international level in [year(s)] by [organization(s)] in which [y and z] laboratories participated, each performing [k] replicates, gave the following statistical results [results expressed in (units)]: *(continued)*

Material [description and listed across the top in increasing order of magnitude of means]
Reproducibility standard deviation (s_R)
Reproducibility relative standard deviation (RSD_R)
HorRat
Reproducibility value, R ($2.8 \times s_R$)
Percent recovery (% Rec), if applicable
The repeatability and reproducibility values may also be expressed as a relative value (as a percentage of the determined mean value), when the results so suggest.
If the recovery and precision values are more or less constant for all materials or for group of materials, an overall average value may be presented. Although such averaging may not have statistical validity, it does have practical value.

Table 2. Model table for presentation of chemistry results from AOAC Official Methods

Table 200X.XX Interlaboratory results for [analyte] by [technique]

Material					Repeatabiltiy	Reproducibility	
Matrix	Level (units)	No. of labs[a(b)]	Mean (units)	Recovery, %	RSD_r, %	RSD_R, %	HorRat

[a(b)] a = Number of laboratories remaining after removal of the number of outliers indicated by (b).

1426 / Collaborative Study Procedures / *General Information*

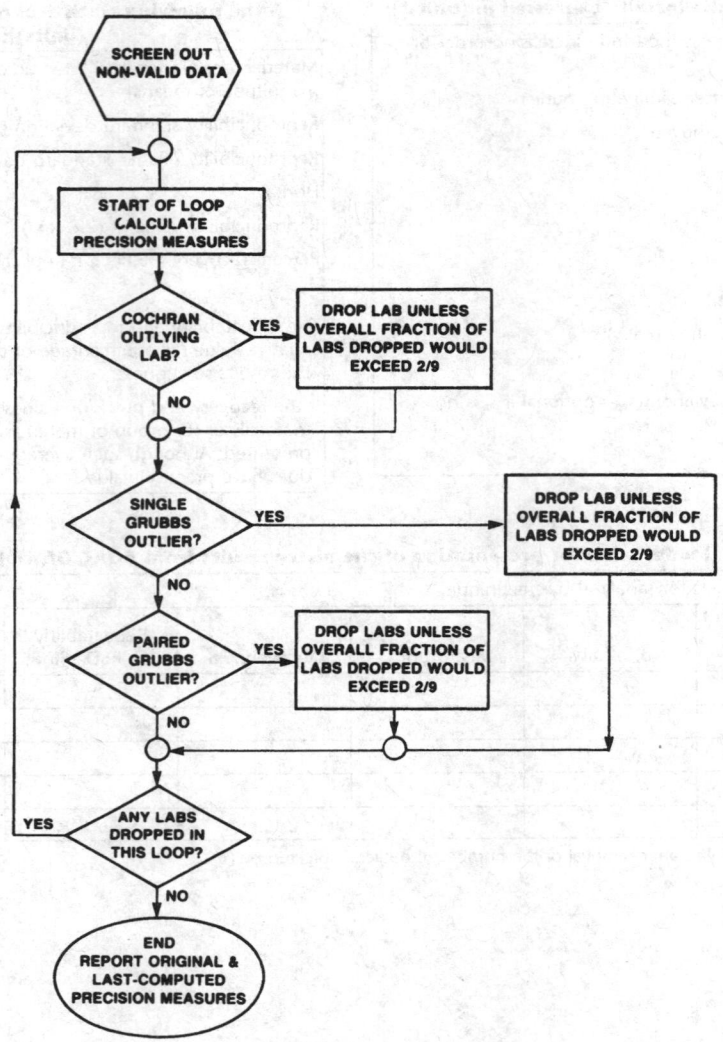

Appendix 3. Flowchart.

USP Reference Standards for Food Ingredients

As of January 1, 2012, please check the USP website at www.usp.org for any updates and newly added reference materials.

FCC Monograph	Supporting USP Reference Standard(s)	CAS Number	Catalog Number
Acesulfame Potassium	Acesulfame Potassium (200 mg)	[55589-62-3]	1002505
5′-Adenylic Acid	5′-Adenylic Acid (500 mg)	[61-19-8]	1012178
5′-Adenylic Acid	5′-Cytidylic Acid (500 mg)	[63-37-6]	1162126
5′-Adenylic Acid	Disodium Guanylate (350 mg)	[5550-12-9]	1221000
5′-Adenylic Acid	Disodium Inosinate (500 mg)	[4691-65-0]	1222002
5′-Adenylic Acid	Disodium 5′-Uridylate (500 mg)	[3387-36-8]	1222400
Adipic Acid	Adipic Acid (100 mg)	[124-04-9]	1012190
L-Alanine	L-Alanine (200 mg)	[56-41-7]	1012509
Alitame	Alitame (250 mg)	[99016-42-9]	1012848
Anethole	Anethole (2 mL) (AS)	[4180-23-8]	1035005
L-Arginine	L-Arginine (200 mg)	[74-79-3]	1042500
L-Arginine Monohydrochloride	Arginine Hydrochloride (125 mg)	[1119-34-2]	1042601
Ascorbic Acid	Ascorbic Acid (1 g) (Vitamin C)	[50-81-7]	1043003
Ascorbyl Palmitate	Ascorbyl Palmitate (2 g)	[137-66-6]	1043105
Aspartame	Aspartame (200 mg)	[22839-47-0]	1043706
Aspartame	Aspartame Related Compound A (25 mg) (5-Benzyl-3,6-dioxo-2-piperazineacetic Acid)	[5262-10-2]	1043728
Aspartame–Acesulfame Salt	Aspartame Acesulfame (200 mg)	[106372-55-8]	1043750
L-Aspartic Acid	Aspartic Acid (100 mg)	[56-84-8]	1043819
Benzaldehyde	Benzaldehyde (2 × 1 mL) (List Chemical)	[100-52-7]	1050905
Benzyl Alcohol	Benzyl Alcohol (500 mg/ampule)	[100-51-6]	1061901
Benzyl Benzoate	Benzyl Benzoate (5 g)	[120-51-4]	1062008
Beta Glucan from Baker's Yeast (Saccharomyces cerevisiae)	Beta Glucan (1 g) Beta Glucan from Baker's Yeast (Saccharomyces cerevisiae)	[9041-22-9]	1048288
Betaine	Betaine (1 g)	[107-43-7]	1065695
BHA	2-*tert*-Butyl-4-hydroxyanisole (200 mg)	[88-32-4]	1083008
BHA	3-*tert*-Butyl-4-hydroxyanisole (200 mg)	[121-00-6]	1083100
Biotin	Biotin (200 mg)	[58-85-5]	1071508
Butyl Acetate	Butyl Acetate (1.2 mL/ampule; 3 ampules)	[123-86-4]	1082606
Caffeine	Caffeine (200 mg)	[58-08-2]	1085003
Calcium Benzoate	Benzoic Acid (300 mg)	[65-85-0]	1055002
Calcium Benzoate	Calcium Benzoate (200 mg)	[5743-30-6]	1086378
Calcium Cyclamate	Calcium Cyclamate (200 mg)	[5897-16-5]	1086447
Calcium Disodium EDTA	Edetate Calcium Disodium (200 mg)	[23411-34-9]	1232006
Calcium Gluconate	Potassium Gluconate (200 mg)	[299-27-4]	1550001
Calcium Lactobionate	Calcium Lactobionate (200 mg)	[110638-68-1]	1086902
Calcium Pantothenate	Calcium Pantothenate (200 mg) (Vitamin B5)	[137-08-6]	1087009
Calcium Pantothenate, Calcium Chloride Double Salt	Calcium Pantothenate (200 mg) (Vitamin B5)	[137-08-6]	1087009
Calcium Pantothenate, Racemic	Calcium Pantothenate (200 mg) (Vitamin B5)	[137-08-6]	1087009
Calcium Phosphate, Dibasic	Sodium Fluoride (1 g) (Internationally Restricted Sales Item)	[7681-49-4]	1614002
Calcium Phosphate, Monobasic	Sodium Fluoride (1 g) (Internationally Restricted Sales Item)	[7681-49-4]	1614002
Calcium Phosphate, Tribasic	Sodium Fluoride (1 g) (Internationally Restricted Sales Item)	[7681-49-4]	1614002
(+)-Camphor	Camphor (1 g)	[464-49-3]	1087508
L-Carnitine	Levocarnitine (400 mg)	[541-15-1]	1359903

FCC Monograph	Supporting USP Reference Standard(s)	CAS Number	Catalog Number
β-Carotene	Beta Carotene	[7235-40-7]	1065480
β-Carotene	Beta Carotene System Suitability (200 mg)	[Mixture]	1065491
Cholic Acid	Cholic Acid (2 g)	[81-25-4]	1133503
Choline Bitartrate	Choline Bitartrate (200 mg)	[87-67-2]	1133536
Choline Chloride	Choline Chloride (200 mg)	[67-48-1]	1133547
Copovidone	Copovidone (100 mg)	[Mixture]	1148500
Copper Gluconate	Potassium Gluconate (200 mg)	[299-27-4]	1550001
Crospovidone	Crospovidone (100 mg)	[9003-39-8]	1150706
α-Cyclodextrin	Alpha Cyclodextrin (500 mg)	[10016-20-3]	1154558
β-Cyclodextrin	Alpha Cyclodextrin (500 mg)	[10016-20-3]	1154558
β-Cyclodextrin	Beta Cyclodextrin (250 mg)	[7585-39-9]	1154569
L-Cysteine Monohydrochloride	L-Cysteine Hydrochloride (200 mg)	[7048-04-6]	1161509
5′-Cytidylic Acid	5′-Adenylic Acid (500 mg)	[61-19-8]	1012178
5′-Cytidylic Acid	5′-Cytidylic Acid (500 mg)	[63-37-6]	1162126
5′-Cytidylic Acid	Disodium Guanylate (350 mg)	[5550-12-9]	1221000
5′-Cytidylic Acid	Disodium Inosinate (500 mg)	[4691-65-0]	1222002
5′-Cytidylic Acid	Disodium 5′-Uridylate (500 mg)	[3387-36-8]	1222400
Dehydroacetic Acid	Dehydroacetic Acid (200 mg)	[520-45-6]	1166309
Dexpanthenol	Dexpanthenol (500 mg)	[81-13-0]	1179504
Diethyl Sebacate	Diethyl Sebacate (1 mL)	[110-40-7]	1194803
Dimethylpolysiloxane	Polydimethylsiloxane (500 mg)	[9016-00-6]	1546300
Dioctyl Sodium Sulfosuccinate	Bis(2-ethylhexyl)maleate (2 g)	[142-16-5]	1075203
Dioctyl Sodium Sulfosuccinate	Docusate Sodium (500 mg)	[577-11-7]	1224802
Dioctyl Sodium Sulfosuccinate	Docusate Sodium Related Compound B (40 mg) (Disodium mono (2-ethylhexyl) sulfosuccinate)		1224824
Disodium EDTA	Edetate Disodium (200 mg)	[6381-92-6]	1233009
Disodium Guanylate	Disodium Guanylate (350 mg)	[5550-12-9]	1221000
Disodium Inosinate	Disodium Inosinate (500 mg)	[4691-65-0]	1222002
Disodium 5′-Uridylate	5′-Adenylic Acid (500 mg)	[61-19-8]	1012178
Disodium 5′-Uridylate	5′-Cytidylic Acid (500 mg)	[63-37-6]	1162126
Disodium 5′-Uridylate	Disodium Guanylate (350 mg)	[5550-12-9]	1221000
Disodium 5′-Uridylate	Disodium Inosinate (500 mg)	[4691-65-0]	1222002
Disodium 5′-Uridylate	Disodium 5′-Uridylate (500 mg)	[3387-36-8]	1222400
Erythritol	Erythritol (200 mg)	[149-32-6]	1241903
Erythritol	Glycerin (2 mL)	[56-81-5]	1295607
Ethyl Acetate	Ethyl Acetate (1.2 mL/ampule; 3 ampules)	[141-78-6]	1265402
Ethyl Formate	Ethyl Formate (1.2 mL/ampule; 3 ampules)	[109-94-4]	1265606
Ethyl Laurate	Ethyl Laurate (500 mg)	[106-33-2]	1265752
Ethyl Lauroyl Arginate	Arginine Ethyl Ester Dihydrochloride (250 mg)	[36589-29-4]	1042554
Ethyl Lauroyl Arginate	Arginine Hydrochloride (125 mg)	[1119-34-2]	1042601
Ethyl Lauroyl Arginate	Ethyl Laurate (500 mg)	[106-33-2]	1265752
Ethyl Lauroyl Arginate	Ethyl Lauroyl Arginate	[60372-77-2]	1265800
Ethyl Lauroyl Arginate	Lauroyl Arginine (100 mg) ((S)-2-Dodecanamido-5-guanidinopentanoic acid hydrochloride)	[181434-85-5]	1356945
Ethyl Lauroyl Arginate	Lauric Acid (500 mg)	[143-07-7]	1356949
Ethyl Maltol	Ethyl Maltol (1 g)	[4940-11-8]	1266008
Ethyl Vanillin	Ethyl Vanillin (200 mg)	[121-32-4]	1267500
Eucalyptol	Eucalyptol (200 mg)	[470-82-6]	1268900
Eugenol	Eugenol (500 mg)	[97-53-0]	1268965
Folic Acid	Folic Acid (500 mg) (Vitamin M or Vitamin Bc)	[59-30-3]	1286005

FCC Monograph	Supporting USP Reference Standard(s)	CAS Number	Catalog Number
Folic Acid	Folic Acid Related Compound A (50 mg) (Calcium formyltetrahydrofolate)	[1492-18-8]	1286027
Fructose	Dextrose (500 mg)	[50-99-7]	1181302
Fructose	Fructose (125 mg)	[57-48-7]	1286504
Fumaric Acid	Fumaric Acid (200 mg)	[110-17-8]	1286708
Fumaric Acid	Maleic Acid (300 mg)	[110-16-7]	1374500
Glucono delta-Lactone	Potassium Gluconate (200 mg)	[299-27-4]	1550001
L-Glutamic Acid	Glutamic Acid (200 mg)	[56-86-0]	1294976
L-Glutamine	Glutamine (100 mg)	[56-85-9]	1294808
Glutathione	Glutathione (300 mg)	[70-18-8]	1294820
Glycerin	Diethylene Glycol (0.5 mL)	[111-46-6]	1193265
Glycerin	Glycerin (2 mL)	[56-81-5]	1295607
Glyceryl Behenate	Glyceryl Behenate (200 mg)	[18641-57-1]	1295709
Glyceryl Monooleate	Glycerin (2 mL)	[56-81-5]	1295607
Glyceryl Monooleate	Glyceryl Monooleate 90% (250 mg)	[25496-72-4]	1295742
Glyceryl Monooleate	Monoglycerides (125 mg)	[68990-53-4]	1446000
Glyceryl Monostearate	Monoglycerides (125 mg)	[68990-53-4]	1446000
Glyceryl Palmitostearate	Palmitic Acid (500 mg)	[57-10-3]	1492007
Glyceryl Palmitostearate	Stearic Acid (500 mg)	[57-11-4]	1621008
Glycine	Glycine (200 mg)	[56-40-6]	1295800
High-Fructose Corn Syrup	Dextrose (500 mg)	[50-99-7]	1181302
High-Fructose Corn Syrup	Fructose (125 mg)	[57-48-7]	1286504
L-Histidine	L-Histidine (200 mg)	[71-00-1]	1308505
4-(p-Hydroxyphenyl)-2-Butanone	Raspberry Ketone (100 mg) (4-(4-Hydroxyphenyl)-2-butanone)	[5471-51-2]	1598813
Isobutyl acetate	Isobutyl acetate (1.2 mL/ampule; 3 ampules)	[110-19-0]	1347802
L-Isoleucine	L-Isoleucine (200 mg)	[73-32-5]	1349502
Isomaltulose	Fructose (125 mg)	[57-48-7]	1286504
Isomaltulose	Isomaltulose (5 g)	[343336-76-5]	1349637
Isomaltulose	Sucrose (100 mg)	[57-50-1]	1623637
Isopropyl Alcohol	2-Propanol System Suitability (3 × 1 mL)	[Mixture]	1570439
Isopropyl Acetate	Isopropyl Acetate (1.2 mL/ampule; 3 ampules)	[108-21-4]	1350104
Alpha-Lactalbumin	Alpha-Lactalbumin (400 mg) (COLD SHIPMENT REQUIRED)	[9051-29-0]	1013909
Lactitol	Lactitol (500 mg)	[81025-04-9]	1356687
L-Leucine	L-Leucine (200 mg)	[61-90-5]	1357001
Lutein	Lutein (1 mL)	[Mixture]	1370804
Lycopene Extract From Tomato	Lycopene (500 mg)	[Mixture]	1370860
Lycopene Extract From Tomato	Tomato Extract Containing Lycopene (1 g)		1672100
Lycopene From Blakeslea Trispora	Lycopene (500 mg)	[Mixture]	1370860
L-Lysine Monohydrochloride	L-Lysine Hydrochloride (200 mg)	[657-27-2]	1372005
Magnesium Gluconate	Potassium Gluconate (200 mg)	[299-27-4]	1550001
Malic Acid	Fumaric Acid (200 mg)	[110-17-8]	1286708
Malic Acid	Maleic Acid (300 mg)	[110-16-7]	1374500
Malic Acid	Malic Acid (500 mg)	[6915-15-7]	1374601
Maltitol	Maltitol (200 mg)	[585-88-6]	1374907
Maltitol Syrup	Maltitol (200 mg)	[585-88-6]	1374907
Maltitol Syrup	Sorbitol (125 mg)	[50-70-4]	1617000
Maltol	Maltol (4 g)	[118-71-8]	1375003
Manganese Gluconate	Potassium Gluconate (200 mg)	[299-27-4]	1550001
Mannitol	Mannitol (200 mg)	[69-65-8]	1375105

1430 / USP Reference Standards for Food Ingredients / General Information

FCC Monograph	Supporting USP Reference Standard(s)	CAS Number	Catalog Number
Maritime Pine Extract	Ferulic Acid (25 mg) (trans-4-Hydroxy-3-methoxy-cinnamic acid)	[1135-24-6]	1270311
Maritime Pine Extract	Maritime Pine Extract (2 g)	[90082-75-0]	1539803
Maritime Pine Extract	Protocatechuic Acid (25 mg) (3,4-Dihydroxy-benzoic acid)	[99-50-3]	1579310
L-Methionine	L-Methionine (200 mg)	[63-68-3]	1411504
Methylparaben	Methylparaben (125 mg)	[99-76-3]	1432005
Methyl Salicylate	Methyl Salicylate (2 mL) (AS)	[119-36-8]	1437450
Monk Fruit Extract	Mogroside V	[88901-36-4]	1445448
Monk Fruit Extract	Monk Fruit Extract		1445492
Natamycin	Natamycin (200 mg)	[7681-93-8]	1457505
Neotame	Neotame (200 mg)	[165450-17-9]	1460204
Neotame	Neotame Related Compound A (15 mg) (N-[N-(3,3-Dimethylbutyl)-L-alpha-aspartyl]-L-phenylalanine)		1460215
Neotame	Sucrose (100 mg)	[57-50-1]	1623637
Niacin	Niacin (200 mg)	[59-67-6]	1461003
Niacinamide	Niacinamide (500 mg) (Vitamin B$_3$)	[98-92-0]	1462006
Niacinamide Ascorbate	Ascorbic Acid (1 g) (Vitamin C)	[50-81-7]	1043003
Niacinamide Ascorbate	Niacinamide (500 mg) (Vitamin B$_3$)	[98-92-0]	1462006
Ox Bile Extract	Cholic Acid (2 g)	[81-25-4]	1133503
DL-Panthenol	Dexpanthenol (500 mg)	[81-13-0]	1179504
L-Phenylalanine	L-Phenylalanine (200 mg)	[63-91-2]	1530503
Polyvinyl Alcohol	Acetone (1.5 mL/ampule; 3 ampules)	[67-64-1]	1006801
Polyvinyl Alcohol	Methyl Acetate (1.2 mL/ampule; 3 ampules)	[79-20-9]	1424051
Polyvinyl Alcohol	Methyl Alcohol (3 × 1.5 mL)	[67-56-1]	1424109
Polyvinyl Alcohol	Polyvinyl Alcohol (100 mg)	[9002-89-5]	1548065
Polyvinyl Acetate	Polyvinyl Acetate (1 g)	[9003-20-7]	1548032
Potassium Benzoate	Benzoic Acid (300 mg)	[65-85-0]	1055002
Potassium Benzoate	Potassium Benzoate (1 g) (AS)	[582-25-2]	1548101
Potassium Gibberellate	Gibberellic Acid (200 mg)	[77-06-5]	1291005
Potassium Gluconate	Potassium Gluconate (200 mg)	[299-27-4]	1550001
L-Proline	L-Proline (200 mg)	[147-85-3]	1568506
1,3-Propanediol	1,3-Propanediol (1 mL)	[504-63-2]	1570483
1,3-Propanediol	Propylene Glycol (1 mL)	[57-55-6]	1576708
Propyl Acetate	Propyl Acetate (1.2 mL/ampule; 3 ampules)	[109-60-4]	1576402
Propylene Glycol	Propylene Glycol (1 mL)	[57-55-6]	1576708
Propylene Oxide	Propylene Oxide (5 × 0.1 mL)	[75-56-9]	1576945
Propylparaben	Propylparaben (200 mg)	[94-13-3]	1577008
Rebaudioside A	Rebaudioside A (300 mg)	[58543-16-1]	1600121
Rebaudioside A	Stevioside (30 mg)	[57817-89-7]	1622408
Riboflavin	Riboflavin (500 mg) (Vitamin B$_2$)	[83-88-5]	1603006
Riboflavin 5′-Phosphate Sodium	Phosphated Riboflavin (100 mg)	[6184-17-4]	1535700
Riboflavin 5′-Phosphate Sodium	Riboflavin (500 mg) (Vitamin B$_2$)	[83-88-5]	1603006
L-Selenomethionine	L-Methionine (200 mg)	[63-68-3]	1411504
L-Selenomethionine	Selenomethionine (100 mg)	[3211-76-5]	1611955
L-Serine	L-Serine (200 mg)	[56-45-1]	1612506
Sodium Iron EDTA	Nitrilotriacetic Acid (50 mg)	[139-13-9]	1463950
Sodium Iron EDTA	Sodium Iron EDTA (200 mg)	[15708-41-5]	1614239
Sodium Stearyl Fumarate	Sodium Stearyl Fumarate (200 mg)	[4070-80-8]	1614705
Sodium Stearyl Fumarate	Stearyl Alcohol (125 mg)	[112-92-5]	1622000
Sodium Benzoate	Benzoic Acid (300 mg)	[65-85-0]	1055002

FCC Monograph	Supporting USP Reference Standard(s)	CAS Number	Catalog Number
Sodium Benzoate	Sodium Benzoate (1 g)	[532-32-1]	1613564
Sodium Cyclamate	Sodium Cyclamate (200 mg)	[139-05-9]	1613860
Sodium Fumarate	Maleic Acid (300 mg)	[110-16-7]	1374500
Sodium Gluconate	Potassium Gluconate (200 mg)	[299-27-4]	1550001
Sodium Pyrophosphate	Sodium Fluoride (1 g) (Internationally Restricted Sales Item)	[7681-49-4]	1614002
Sorbitan Monopalmitate	Isosorbide (75% solution, 1 g)	[652-67-5]	1352008
Sorbitan Monopalmitate	1,4-Sorbitan (300 mg)	[27299-12-3]	1616008
Sorbitan Monopalmitate	Sorbitol (125 mg)	[50-70-4]	1617000
Sorbitan Monolaurate	Isosorbide (75% solution, 1 g)	[652-67-5]	1352008
Sorbitan Monolaurate	1,4-Sorbitan (300 mg)	[27299-12-3]	1616008
Sorbitan Monolaurate	Sorbitol (125 mg)	[50-70-4]	1617000
Sorbitan Monooleate	Isosorbide (75% solution, 1 g)	[652-67-5]	1352008
Sorbitan Monooleate	1,4-Sorbitan (300 mg)	[27299-12-3]	1616008
Sorbitan Monooleate	Sorbitol (125 mg)	[50-70-4]	1617000
Sorbitan Monostearate	Isomalt (200 mg)	[64519-82-0]	1349626
Sorbitan Monostearate	Isosorbide (75% solution, 1 g)	[652-67-5]	1352008
Sorbitan Monostearate	1,4-Sorbitan (300 mg)	[27299-12-3]	1616008
Sorbitan Tristearate	Isosorbide (75% solution, 1 g)	[652-67-5]	1352008
Sorbitan Tristearate	1,4-Sorbitan (300 mg)	[27299-12-3]	1616008
Sorbitan Tristearate	Sorbitol (125 mg)	[50-70-4]	1617000
Sorbitol	Mannitol (200 mg)	[69-65-8]	1375105
Sorbitol	Sorbitol (125 mg)	[50-70-4]	1617000
Sorbitol Solution	Mannitol (200 mg)	[69-65-8]	1375105
Sorbitol Solution	Sorbitol (125 mg)	[50-70-4]	1617000
Hydrogenated Starch Hydrolysate	Dextrose (500 mg)	[50-99-7]	1181302
Hydrogenated Starch Hydrolysate	Maltitol (200 mg)	[585-88-6]	1374907
Hydrogenated Starch Hydrolysate	Sorbitol (125 mg)	[50-70-4]	1617000
Stearyl Alcohol	Cetyl Alcohol (100 mg)	[36653-82-4]	1103003
Stearyl Alcohol	Stearyl Alcohol (125 mg)	[112-92-5]	1622000
Succinic Acid	Succinic Acid (100 mg)	[110-15-6]	1623411
Sucralose	Sucralose (400 mg)	[56038-13-2]	1623626
Sucromalt	Sucromalt (200 mg)	[911432-63-8]	1623659
Tartaric Acid	Tartaric Acid (1 g)	[87-69-4]	1643340
L-Theanine	L-Theanine (200 mg)	[3081-61-6]	1652704
Thiamine Hydrochloride	Thiamine Hydrochloride (500 mg) (Vitamin B_1 Hydrochloride)	[67-03-8]	1656002
Thiamine Mononitrate	Thiamine Hydrochloride (500 mg) (Vitamin B_1 Hydrochloride)	[67-03-8]	1656002
L-Threonine	L-Threonine (200 mg)	[72-19-5]	1667202
All-rac-α-Tocopherol	Alpha Tocopherol (250 mg) (Vitamin E Alcohol)	[59-02-9]	1667600
All-rac-α-Tocopherol	Alpha Tocopheryl Acetate (250 mg) (Vitamin E Acetate)	[7695-91-2]	1667701
RRR-α-Tocopherol Concentrate	Alpha Tocopherol (250 mg) (Vitamin E Alcohol)	[59-02-9]	1667600
RRR-α-Tocopherol Concentrate	Alpha Tocopheryl Acetate (250 mg) (Vitamin E Acetate)	[7695-91-2]	1667701
RRR-Tocopherol Concentrate, Mixed	Alpha Tocopherol (250 mg) (Vitamin E Alcohol)	[59-02-9]	1667600
All-rac-α-Tocopherol Acetate	Alpha Tocopherol (250 mg) (Vitamin E Alcohol)	[59-02-9]	1667600
All-rac-α-Tocopherol Acetate	Alpha Tocopheryl Acetate (250 mg) (Vitamin E Acetate)	[7695-91-2]	1667701
RRR-α-Tocopherol Acetate	Alpha Tocopherol (250 mg) (Vitamin E Alcohol)	[59-02-9]	1667600
RRR-α-Tocopherol Acetate	Alpha Tocopheryl Acetate (250 mg) (Vitamin E Acetate)	[7695-91-2]	1667701

FCC Monograph	Supporting USP Reference Standard(s)	CAS Number	Catalog Number
RRR-α-Tocopherol Concentrate	Alpha Tocopherol (250 mg) (Vitamin E Alcohol)	[59-02-9]	1667600
RRR-α-Tocopherol Concentrate	Alpha Tocopheryl Acetate (250 mg) (Vitamin E Acetate)	[7695-91-2]	1667701
RRR-α-Tocopherol Acid Succinate	Alpha Tocopherol (250 mg) (Vitamin E Alcohol)	[59-02-9]	1667600
RRR-α-Tocopherol Acid Succinate	Alpha Tocopheryl Acetate (250 mg) (Vitamin E Acetate)	[7695-91-2]	1667701
RRR-α-Tocopherol Acid Succinate	Alpha Tocopheryl Acid Succinate (250 mg) (Vitamin E Succinate)	[4345-03-3]	1667803
Trehalose	Trehalose (400 mg)	[6138-23-4]	1673715
L-Tryptophan	L-Tryptophan (200 mg)	[73-22-3]	1700501
L-Tyrosine	L-Tyrosine (500 mg)	[60-18-4]	1705006
L-Valine	L-Valine (200 mg)	[72-18-4]	1708503
Vitamin A	Retinyl Acetate (Vitamin A) (10 ampules × 0.5 g)	[Mixture]	1716002
Vitamin B_{12}	Cyanocobalamin (1.5 g of mixture with mannitol) (Vitamin B_{12})	[Mixture]	1152009
Vitamin D_2	Ergocalciferol (30 mg/ampule; 5 ampules) (Vitamin D_2)	[50-14-6]	1239005
Vitamin D_2	Ergosterol (50 mg)	[57-87-4]	1241007
Vitamin D_2	Vitamin D Assay System Suitability (1.5 g)	[Mixture]	1717504
Vitamin D_3	Cholecalciferol (30 mg/ampule; 5 ampules) (Vitamin D_3)	[67-97-0]	1131009
Vitamin D_3	Vitamin D Assay System Suitability (1.5 g)	[Mixture]	1717504
Vitamin K	Phytonadione (500 mg) (Vitamin K_1)	[84-80-0]	1538006
Whey	Fructose (125 mg)	[57-48-7]	1286504
Whey	Lactose Monohydrate (500 mg)	[5989-81-1]	1356701
Whey Protein Concentrate	Fructose (125 mg)	[57-48-7]	1286504
Whey Protein Concentrate	Lactose Monohydrate (500 mg)	[5989-81-1]	1356701
Whey Protein Isolate	Fructose (125 mg)	[57-48-7]	1286504
Whey Protein Isolate	Lactose Monohydrate (500 mg)	[5989-81-1]	1356701
Whey, Reduced Lactose	Fructose (125 mg)	[57-48-7]	1286504
Whey, Reduced Lactose	Lactose Monohydrate (500 mg)	[5989-81-1]	1356701
Xylitol	Xylitol (1 g)	[87-99-0]	1720600
Yeast, Dried	Folic Acid (500 mg) (Vitamin M or Vitamin Bc)	[59-30-3]	1286005
Zinc Gluconate	Potassium Gluconate (200 mg)	[299-27-4]	1550001
Zinc Gluconate	Trypsin Crystallized (300 mg)	[9002-07-7]	1700002
Appendix IIB—Melting Range or Temperature Determination	Caffeine Melting Point Standard (1 g) (Approximately 236°)	[58-08-2]	1086006
Appendix IIB—Melting Range or Temperature Determination	Phenacetin Melting Point Standard (500 mg) (Approximately 135°)	[62-44-2]	1514008
Appendix IIB—Melting Range or Temperature Determination	Acetanilide Melting Point Standard (500 mg) (Approximately 114°)	[103-84-4]	1004001
Appendix IIB—Melting Range or Temperature Determination	Vanillin Melting Point Standard (1 g) (Approximately 82°)	[121-33-5]	1711009
Appendix IIB—Melting Range or Temperature Determination	Sulfanilamide Melting Point Standard (500 mg) (Approximately 165°)	[63-74-1]	1633007
Appendix IIB—Melting Range or Temperature Determination	Sulfapyridine Melting Point Standard (1 g) (Approximately 191°)	[144-83-2]	1635002
Appendix IIIC—Glutamic Acid	Glutamic Acid (200 mg)	[56-86-0]	1294976
Appendix V—Enzyme Assays	Bile Salts (Sodium taurocholate) (10 g)	[145-42-6]	1071304
Appendix V—Enzyme Assays	Pancreatin Amylase and Protease (2 g)	[8049-47-6]	1494057
Appendix V—Enzyme Assays	Pancreatin Lipase (2 g)	[8049-47-6]	1494079
Appendix V—Enzyme Assays	Papain (1 g)	[9001-73-4]	1495005
Appendix V—Enzyme Assays	Trypsin Crystallized (300 mg)	[9002-07-7]	1700002
Appendix VII—Fats And Related Substances	FAME Standard Mixture (100 mg)	[71076-49-8]	1269119

FCC Monograph	Supporting USP Reference Standard(s)	CAS Number	Catalog Number
Appendix VII—Fats And Related Substances	Menhaden Oil	[8002-50-4]	1381200
Appendix VII—Fats And Related Substances	Tritricosanoin (50 mg)	[86850-72-8]	1696153
Appendix VIII—Oleoresins	Capsaicin (100 mg)	[404-86-4]	1091108
Appendix XIII—Adulterants and Contaminants in Food Ingredients	Diethylene Glycol (0.5 mL)	[111-46-6]	1193265
Appendix XIII—Adulterants and Contaminants in Food Ingredients	Ethylene Glycol (0.5 mL)	[107-21-1]	1265515
Appendix XIII—Adulterants and Contaminants in Food Ingredients	Glycerin (2 mL)	[56-81-5]	1295607

General Information Analytical Techniques

ELECTROPHORESIS*

Electrophoresis refers to the migration of electrically charged proteins, colloids, molecules, or other particles when dissolved or suspended in an electrolyte through which an electric current is passed.

Based upon the type of apparatus used, electrophoretic methods may be divided into two categories, one called *free solution* or moving boundary electrophoresis and the other called *zone electrophoresis*.

In the *free solution* method, a buffered solution of proteins in a U-shaped cell is subjected to an electric current which causes the proteins to form a series of layers in order of decreasing mobility, which are separated by boundaries. Only a part of the fastest moving protein is physically separated from the other proteins, but examination of the moving boundaries using a schlieren optical system provides data for calculation of mobilities and information on the qualitative and quantitative composition of the protein mixture.

In *zone electrophoresis*, the sample is introduced as a narrow zone or spot in a column, slab, or film of buffer. Migration of the components as narrow zones permits their complete separation. Remixing of the separated zones by thermal convection is prevented by stabilizing the electrolyte in a porous matrix such as a powdered solid, or a fibrous material such as paper, or a gel such as starch, agar, or polyacrylamide.

Various methods of zone electrophoresis are widely employed. *Gel electrophoresis*, particularly the variant called *disk electrophoresis*, is especially useful for protein separation because of its high resolving power.

Gel electrophoresis, which is employed by the compendium, is discussed in more detail following the presentation of some theoretical principles and methodological practices, which are shared in varying degrees by all electrophoretic methods.

The electrophoretic migration observed for particles of a particular substance depends on characteristics of the particle, primarily its electrical charge, its size or molecular weight, and its shape, as well as characteristics and operating parameters of the system. These latter include the pH, ionic strength, viscosity and temperature of the electrolyte, density or cross-linking of any stabilizing matrix such as gel, and the voltage gradient employed.

Effect of Charge, Particle Size, Electrolyte Viscosity, and Voltage Gradient—Electrically charged particles migrate toward the electrode of opposite charge, and molecules with both positive and negative charges move in a direction dependent on the net charge. The rate of migration is directly related to the magnitude of the net charge on the particle and is inversely related to the size of the particle, which in turn is directly related to its molecular weight.

Very large spherical particles, for which Stokes' law is valid, exhibit an electrophoretic mobility, u_0, which is inversely related to the first power of the radius as depicted in the equation:

$$u_0 = v/E = Q/6\pi r\eta$$

where v is the velocity of the particle, E is the voltage gradient imposed on the electrolyte, Q is the charge on the particle, r is the particle radius, and η is the viscosity of the electrolyte. This idealized expression is strictly valid only at infinite dilution and in the absence of a stabilizing matrix such as paper or a gel.

Ions, and peptides up to molecular weights of at least 5000, particularly in the presence of stabilizing media, do not obey Stokes' law, and their electrophoretic behavior is best described by an equation of the type:

$$u_0 = Q/A6\pi r^2\eta$$

where A is a shape factor generally in the range of 4 to 6, which shows an inverse dependence of the mobility on the square of the radius. In terms of molecular weight, this implies an inverse dependence of mobility on the $2/3$ power of the molecular weight.

Effect of pH—The direction and rate of migration of molecules containing a variety of ionizable functional groups, such as amino acids and proteins, depends upon the pH of the electrolyte. For instance, the mobility of a simple amino acid such as glycine varies with pH approximately as shown in *Figure 1*. The pK_a values of 2.2 and 9.9 coincide with the inflection points of the sigmoid portions of the plot. Since the respective functional groups are 50% ionized at the pH values where $pH = pK_a$, the electrophoretic mobilities at these points are half of the value observed for the fully ionized cation and anion obtained at very low and very high pH, respectively. The zwitterion that exists at the intermediate pH range is electrically neutral and has zero mobility.

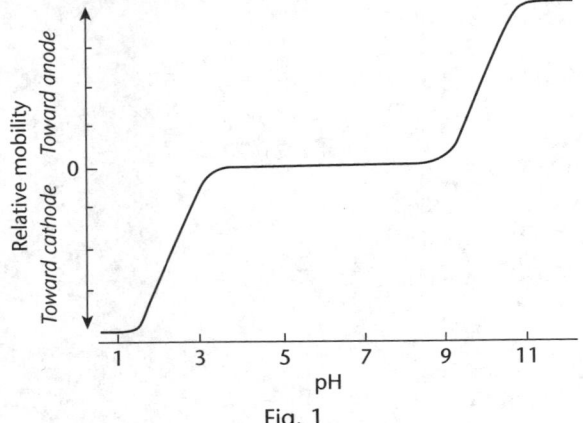

Fig. 1

---

* This text is adapted from General Chapter ⟨726⟩ of the *United States Pharmacopeia and National Formulary* (USP–NF) as published in USP 32–NF 27. This text is provided for informational purposes only and is intended as a resource for the FCC user. Note that because the USP–NF is in continuous revision, this General Chapter is subject to change and the text printed here may not continue to represent the current version.

Effect of Ionic Strength and Temperature—Electrophoretic mobility decreases with increasing ionic strength of the supporting electrolyte. Ionic strength, μ, is defined as:

$$\mu = 0.5\Sigma C_i Z_i^2$$

where C_i is the concentration of an ion in moles per L and Z_i is its valence, and the sum is calculated for all ions in the solution. For buffers in which both the anion and cation are univalent, ionic strength is identical with molarity.

Ionic strengths of electrolytes employed in electrophoresis commonly range from about 0.01 to 0.10. A suitable strength is somewhat dependent on the sample composition, since the buffer capacity must be great enough to maintain a constant pH over the area of the component zones. Zones become sharper or more compact as ionic strength is increased.

Temperature affects mobility indirectly, since the viscosity, η, of the supporting electrolyte is temperature-dependent. The viscosity of water decreases at a rate of about 3% per °C in the range of 0° to 5° and at a slightly lower rate in the vicinity of room temperature. Mobility, therefore, increases with increasing electrolyte temperature.

Considerable heat is evolved as a result of current passing through the supporting electrolyte. This heat increases with the applied voltage and with increasing ionic strength. Particularly in larger apparatus, despite the circulation of a coolant, this heat produces a temperature gradient across the bed which may lead to distortion of the separated zones. Therefore, practical considerations and the design of the particular apparatus dictate the choice of ionic strength and operating voltage.

Effect of a Stabilizing Medium, Electroosmosis—When an electrical current is passed through an electrolyte contained in a glass tube or contained between plates of glass or plastic, a bulk flow of the electrolyte toward one of the electrodes is observed. This flow is called electroosmosis. It results from the surface charge on the walls of the apparatus, which arises either from ionizable functional groups inherent in the structural material or from ions adsorbed on the cell walls from the electrolyte contacting them. The effect is usually increased when the cell is filled with a bed of porous substance, such as a gel, used to stabilize the supporting electrolyte and prevent remixing of separated zones by thermal convection or diffusion. The solution immediately adjacent to the surface builds up an electrical charge, equal but opposite to the surface charge, and the electrical field traversing the cell produces a movement of solution toward the electrode of opposite charge.

The substances commonly used as stabilizing media in zone electrophoresis develop a negative surface charge, and therefore electroosmotic flow of the electrolyte is toward the cathode. As a result, all zones, including neutral substances, are carried toward the cathode during the electrophoretic run.

The degree of electroosmosis observed varies with the stabilizing substance. It is appreciable with agar gel, while it is negligibly small with polyacrylamide gel.

Molecular Sieving—In the absence of a stabilizing medium or in cases where the medium is very porous, electrophoretic separation of molecules results from differences in the ratio of their electrical charge to their size. In the presence of a stabilizing medium, differences in adsorptive or other affinity of molecules for the medium introduces a chromatographic effect that may enhance the separation.

If the stabilizing medium is a highly cross-linked gel such that the size of the resultant pores is of the order of the dimensions of the molecules being separated, a molecular sieving effect is obtained. This effect is analogous to that obtained in separations based on gel permeation or molecular exclusion chromatography, but in gel electrophoresis the effect is superimposed on the electrophoretic separation. Molecular sieving may be visualized to result from a steric barrier to the passage of larger molecules. Small molecules pass through pores of a wide size range, and therefore their electrophoretic passage through the gel will not be impeded. As size increases, fewer pores will permit passage of the molecules, causing a retardation of the migration of substances of large molecular weight.

Gel Electrophoresis

Processes employing a gel such as agar, starch, or polyacrylamide as a stabilizing medium are broadly termed gel electrophoresis. The method is particularly advantageous for protein separations. The separation obtained depends upon the electrical charge to size ratio coupled with a molecular sieving effect dependent primarily on the molecular weight.

Polyacrylamide gel has several advantages that account for its extensive use. It has minimal adsorptive properties and produces a negligible electroosmotic effect. Gels of a wide range of pore size can be reproducibly prepared by varying the total gel concentration (based on monomer plus cross-linking agent) and the percentage of cross-linking agent used to form the gel. These quantities are conveniently expressed as

$$T(\%) = (a + b/V) \times 100$$

$$T(\%) = (b/a + b) \times 100$$

where T is the total gel concentration in %; C is the percentage of cross-linking agent used to prepare the gel; V is the volume, in mL, of buffer used in preparing the gel; and a and b are the weights, in g, of monomer (acrylamide) and cross-linking agent (usually N,N'-methylenebisacrylamide) used to prepare the gel. Satisfactory gels ranging in concentration (T) from about 3% to 30% have been prepared. The amount of cross-linking agent is usually about one-tenth to one-twentieth of the quantity of monomer (C = 10% to 5%), a smaller percentage being used for higher values of T.

In the preparation of the gel, the bed of the electrophoresis apparatus is filled with an aqueous solution of monomer and cross-linking agent, usually buffered to the pH desired in the later run, and polymerized in place by a free radical process. Polymerization may be initiated by a chemical process, frequently using ammonium persulfate plus N,N,N',N'-tetramethylenediamine or photochemically using a mixture of riboflavin and N,N,N',N'-tetramethylenediamine. Polymerization is inhibited by molecular oxygen and by acidic conditions. The gel composition and polymerization conditions chosen must be adhered to rigorously to ensure reproducible qualities of the gel.

Apparatus for Gel Electrophoresis—In general, the bed or medium in which electrophoresis is carried out may be supported horizontally or vertically, depending upon the design of the apparatus. A series of separations to be compared may also be carried out in several individual tubes or by placing different samples in adjacent wells, cast or cut into a single slab of gel. A vertical slab assembly such as that depicted schematically in *Figure 2* is convenient for direct comparison of several samples. A particular advantage derives from the comparison of the samples in a single bed of gel which is likely to be more uniform in composition than gels cast in a series of chambers.

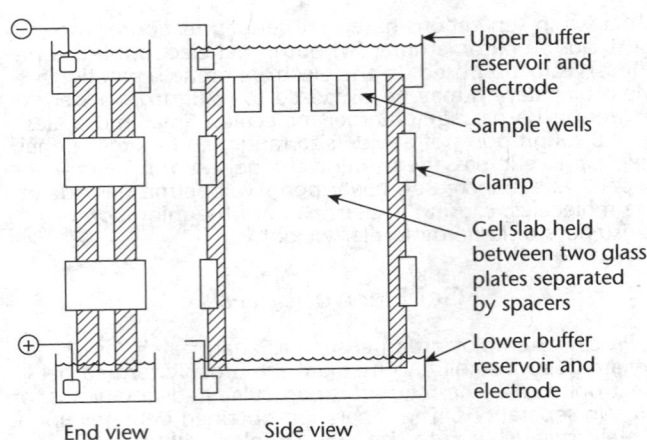

Fig. 2. Vertical Slab Gel Electrophoresis Apparatus.

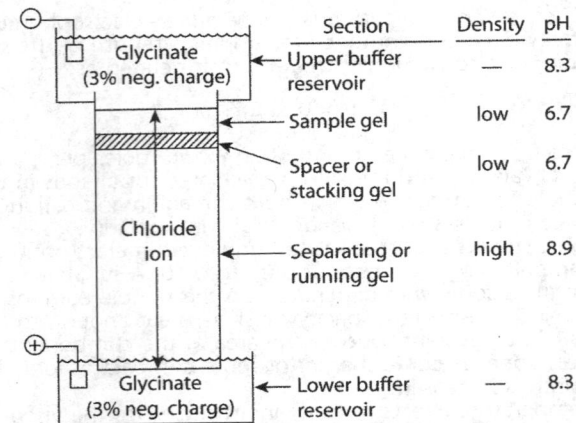

Fig. 3. Terminology, Buffer pH, and Buffer Composition for Acrylamide Gel Disk Electrophoresis.

A feature of many types of apparatus, not illustrated in the schematic view, seals the lower buffer chamber to the base of the bed and allows the level of the buffer in the lower chamber to be made equal to that in the upper chamber, thereby eliminating hydrostatic pressure on the gel. In addition, some units provide for the circulation of coolant on one or both sides of the gel bed.

In the preparation of the gel, the base of the gel chamber is closed with a suitable device and the unit is filled with the solution of monomer, cross-linking agent, and catalyst. A comb, having teeth of an appropriate size, is inserted in the top, and polymerization is allowed to proceed to completion. Removal of the comb leaves a series of sample wells in the polymerized gel.

In simple gel electrophoresis, an identical buffer is used to fill the upper and lower buffer chambers as well as in the solution used to prepare the gel. After filling the chambers, the samples, dissolved in sucrose or other dense and somewhat viscous solution to prevent diffusion, are introduced with a syringe or micropipet into the bottoms of the sample wells, and the electrophoresis is begun immediately thereafter.

DISK ELECTROPHORESIS

An important variant of polyacrylamide gel electrophoresis, which employs a discontinuous series of buffers and often also a discontinuous series of gel layers, is called disk electrophoresis. The name is derived from the discoid shape of the very narrow zones that result from the technique. As a result of the narrow zones produced, this technique exhibits an extremely high resolving power and is to be recommended for the characterization of protein mixtures and for the detection of contaminants that may have mobilities close to that of the major component.

The basis of disk electrophoresis is outlined in the following paragraphs with reference to an anionic system suitable for separating proteins bearing a net negative charge. To understand disk electrophoresis, it is essential to have a knowledge of the general aspects of electrophoresis and the apparatus already described.

Basis of Disk Electrophoresis—The high resolution obtained in disk electrophoresis depends on the use of a buffer system that is discontinuous with respect to both pH and composition. This is usually combined with a discontinuous series of two or three gels that differ in density.

A typical system is illustrated schematically in Figure 3.

A high density (T = 10% to 30%) separating gel several centimeters high is polymerized in a tris-chloride buffer in the bed of the apparatus. During polymerization the buffer is overlayered with a thin layer of water to prevent fixation of a meniscus in the top of the gel. The overlayer of water is then removed and a thin layer, 3 mm to 10 mm thick, of low density (T = 3%) gel, called the spacer or stacking gel, is polymerized in a tris-chloride buffer on top of the separating gel. An overlayer of water is again used to ensure a flat surface. The sample is mixed with a small amount of the spacer gel monomer solution which is applied on top of the spacer gel and allowed to polymerize. The pH of the separating gel is typically 8.9, while that of the spacer and sample gels is 6.7. All three gels are prepared using chloride as the anion.

The upper and lower buffer reservoirs are filled with a pH 8.3 buffer prepared from tris and glycine. At this pH about 3% of the glycine molecules bear a net negative charge.

When a voltage is applied across the system, the glycinate-chloride interface moves downward toward the anode. It was initially positioned at the junction of the buffer in the upper reservoir and the top of the sample gel layer. The chloride anion, by virtue of its small size, migrates faster than any of the proteins present in the sample. The pH of the sample and spacer layers was chosen to be about 3 units below the higher pK_a of glycine. Therefore, in traversing these layers, only about 0.1% of the glycine molecules bear a net negative charge. Consequently, glycine migrates more slowly than chloride. The tendency for the faster-moving chloride to move away from glycinate lowers the concentration at the interface, producing a greater voltage drop at the interface, which in turn causes the glycinate to catch up to the chloride. Under these conditions, a very sharp interface is maintained, and as it moves through the sample and spacer layers, the proteins in the sample tend to stack themselves at the interface in very thin layers in order of mobility. The process is called stacking and is the source of the disks which are separated.

When the stacked proteins reach the high-density separating gel, they are slowed down by a molecular sieving process. The higher pH encountered in the running gel also causes the glycinate to migrate faster, so that the discontinuous buffer interface overtakes the proteins and eventually reaches the bottom of the separating gel. During this period, the disks of protein continue to separate by electrophoresis and molecular sieving in the separating gel. At the end of the run, the pH of the separating gel will have risen above its original value of 8.9 to a value of about pH 9.5.

Relative Mobility—Bromophenol blue is often used as a standard for calculating the relative mobility of separated zones and to judge visually the progress of a run. It may be added to one of the sample wells, or mixed with the sample itself, or simply added to the buffer in the upper sample reservoir.

Relative mobility, M_B, is calculated as:

M_B = distance from origin to sample zone/distance from origin to bromophenol blue zone

Visualization of Zones—Since polyacrylamide is transparent, protein bands may be located by scanning in a densitometer with UV light. The zones may be fixed by immersing in protein precipitants such as phosphotungstic acid or 10% trichloroacetic acid. A variety of staining reagents including naphthalene black (amido black) and Coomassie brilliant blue R250 may be used. The fixed or stained zones may be conveniently viewed and photographed with transmitted light from an X-ray film illuminator.

SAFETY PRECAUTIONS

Voltages used in electrophoresis can readily deliver a lethal shock. The hazard is increased by the use of aqueous buffer solutions and the possibility of working in damp environments.

The equipment, with the possible exception of the power supply, should be enclosed in either a grounded metal case or a case made of insulating material. The case should have an interlock that deenergizes the power supply when the case is opened, after which reactivation should be prevented until activation of a reset switch is carried out.

High-voltage cables from the power supply to the apparatus should preferably be a type in which a braided metal shield completely encloses the insulated central conductor, and the shield should be grounded. The base of the apparatus should be grounded metal or contain a grounded metal rim which is constructed in such a way that any leakage of electrolyte will produce a short which will deenergize the power supply before the electrolyte can flow beyond the protective enclosure.

If the power supply contains capacitors as part of a filter circuit, it should also contain a bleeder resistor to ensure discharge of the capacitors before the protective case is opened. A shorting bar that is activated by opening the case may be considered as an added precaution.

Because of the potential hazard associated with electrophoresis, laboratory personnel should be completely familiar with electrophoresis equipment before using it.

CAPILLARY ELECTROPHORESIS*

Electrophoresis refers to the migration of charged electrical species when dissolved or suspended in an electrolyte through which an electric current is passed. Cations migrate toward the negatively charged electrode (cathode), while anions are attracted toward the positively charged electrode (anode). Neutral particles are not attracted toward either electrode.

The use of capillaries as a migration channel in electrophoresis has enabled analysts to perform electrophoretic separations on an instrumental level comparable to that of high-performance liquid chromatography (HPLC), albeit with some distinct operational differences, advantages, and disadvantages relative to HPLC. This method of analysis is commonly known as capillary electrophoresis (CE). During typical CE operation with an uncoated capillary filled with a buffer, referred to as the "operating buffer," silanol groups present on the inner wall of the glass capillary release hydrogen ions to the buffer and the wall surface becomes negatively charged, even at a fairly low pH. Cations, or solutes having partial positive charges in the medium, are electrostatically attracted to the negatively charged wall, forming an electrical double layer. The initiation of electrophoresis by applying voltage across the length of the capillary causes the solution portion of the electrical double layer to move toward the cathode end of the capillary, drawing the bulk solution. This movement of the bulk solution under the force of the electrical field is called the electroosmotic flow (EOF). The degree of ionization of the inner-wall capillary silanol groups depends mainly on the pH of the operating buffer and on the modifiers that may have been added to the electrolyte. At low pH, the silanol groups generally have a low ionization and the EOF is low. At higher pH, silanol groups become more ionized and the EOF increases. In some cases organic solvents, such as methanol or acetonitrile, are added to the aqueous buffer to increase the solubility of the solute and other additives or to affect the degree of ionization of the sample. The addition of such organic modifiers generally causes a decrease in the EOF. The detector is located toward the cathode end of the capillary. The EOF is usually greater than the electrophoretic mobility; thus, even anions are swept toward the cathode and the detector. When an uncoated capillary containing pH 7.0 phosphate buffer is used, the usual order of appearance of solutes in an electropherogram is cationic species, neutral solutes, and anionic species.

Currently, there are five major modes of operation of CE: capillary zone electrophoresis (CZE), also referred to as free solution or free flow capillary electrophoresis; micellar electrokinetic chromatography (MEKC); capillary gel electrophoresis (CGE); capillary isoelectric focusing (CIEF); and capillary isotachophoresis (CITP).

In CZE, separations are controlled by differences in the relative electrophoretic mobilities of the individual components in the sample or test solution. The mobility differences are functions of analyte charge and size under specific method conditions. They are optimized by appropriate control of the composition of the buffer, its pH, and its ionic strength.

In MEKC, ionic surfactants are added to the operating buffer at a concentration above their critical micelle concentration. The micelles provide a pseudostationary phase with which analytes can partition. This technique is useful for the separation of neutral and ionic species.

CGE, which is analogous to gel filtration, uses gel-filled capillaries to separate molecules on the basis of relative differences in their respective molecular weight or molecular size. It was first used for the separation of proteins, peptides, and oligomers. Gels may have the advantage of decreasing the EOF and also significantly reducing protein adsorption onto the inner wall of the capillary, which can significantly reduce analyte peak tailing effects.

In CIEF, substances are separated on the basis of their relative differences in isoelectric points. This is accomplished by achieving steady-state sample zones within a buffer pH gradient, where the pH is low at the anode and high at the cathode. The gradient is established by applying a voltage across a capillary filled with a mixture of carrier components consisting of amphoteric substances having different pI values.

CITP employs two buffers that enclose the analyte zones between them. Either anions or cations can be analyzed in sharply separated zones. In addition, the analyte concentrations are the same in each zone; thus, the length of each zone is proportional to the amount of the particular analyte.

The most commonly utilized capillary electrophoresis techniques are CZE and MEKC. These are briefly discussed in the following sections. Pertinent general principles and

---

* This text is adapted from General Chapter ⟨727⟩ of the *United States Pharmacopeia and National Formulary (USP–NF)* as published in *USP 32–NF 27*. This text is provided for informational purposes only and is intended as a resource for the FCC user. Note that because the *USP–NF* is in continuous revision, this General Chapter is subject to change and the text printed here may not continue to represent the current version.

theory, instrumental considerations, analysis, and operational considerations and parameters are discussed as well.

PRINCIPLES OF CAPILLARY ZONE ELECTROPHORESIS

CZE makes use of the principles of electrophoresis and electroosmosis to achieve separation of charged species.

(1) The electrophoretic mobility of an ion, μ_{EP}, is described by the equation:

$$\mu_{EP} = q/(6\pi\eta r)$$

in which q is the charge of the ion, η is the solution viscosity, and r is the radius of the hydrated ion. This relationship infers that small, highly charged analytes have high mobilities and large, slightly charged analytes have low mobilities.

(2) The velocity of migration, v_{EP}, in cm per second, is represented by the equation:

$$v_{EP} = \mu_{EP}(V/L)$$

in which μ_{EP} is the electrophoretic mobility; V is the applied voltage; and L, in cm, is the total capillary length.

(3) The velocity of the EOF, v_{EO}, in cm per second, is described by the equation:

$$v_{EO} = \mu_{EO}(V/L)$$

in which μ_{EO} is the EOF mobility (the coefficient of electroosmotic flow), and the other terms are as defined above.

(4) The time, t, in seconds, necessary for a solute to migrate the entire effective length of the capillary (from the inlet to the detector), l, is represented by the relationship:

$$t = l/E(\mu_{EP} + \mu_{EO}) = lL/V(\mu_{EP} + \mu_{EO})$$

in which E is the strength of the applied electrical field, and the other terms are as defined above.

(5) Efficiency of an electrophoretic system can be related to mobility and EOF and expressed in terms of the number of theoretical plates, N, by the equation:

$$N = (\mu_{EP} + \mu_{EO})V/2D$$

in which D is the diffusion coefficient of the solute, and the other terms are as defined above.

(6) The resolution, R, of two consecutively eluting solutes can be defined by the equation:

$$R = 0.18(\mu_{EP1} - \mu_{EP2})[V/D(\overline{\mu_{EP}} + \mu_{EO})]^{1/2}$$

where μ_{EP1} and μ_{EP2} are the mobilities of the two solutes,

$$\overline{\mu_{EP}}$$

is their average, and the other terms are as defined above.

PRINCIPLES OF MICELLAR ELECTROKINETIC CHROMATOGRAPHY

In MEKC, the supporting electrolyte medium contains a surfactant at a concentration above its critical micelle concentration (CMC). In this aqueous medium, the surfactant self-aggregates and forms micelles whose hydrophilic head groups form an outer shell and whose hydrophobic tail groups form a nonpolar core into which the solutes can partition. Generally, the micelles are anionic on their surface, and, under the applied voltage, they migrate in the opposite direction to the EOF. This type of partitioning is analogous to that in solvent extraction or reverse-phase HPLC. The differential partitioning of neutral molecules between the buffered aqueous mobile phase and the micellar pseudostationary phase is the sole basis for separation. The buffer and micelles form a two-phase system, and the analyte can partition between these two phases.

A micellar system suitable for MEKC meets the following criteria: the surfactant is highly soluble in the buffer, and the micellar solution is homogeneous and transparent when UV detection is employed. The most common surfactant for MEKC is sodium dodecyl sulfate (anionic surfactant). Others include cetyltrimethylammonium bromide (cationic surfactant) and bile salts (chiral surfactant). The selectivity of an MEKC system is mainly dependent on the nature of the surfactant. Organic solvents are often added to the MEKC buffer to adjust the capacity factors, just as in reverse-phase HPLC separations. MEKC may be used for the separation of enantiomers. For such separations, a chiral additive is added to the buffer or a chiral surfactant, such as a bile salt, is used.

A general knowledge of conventional column chromatographic principles aids in understanding MEKC principles. However, in MEKC the micelles are not truly stationary; therefore, the column chromatographic theory needs to be modified. The major modification introduced to MEKC principles is the finite nature of the separation window for neutral molecules.

(7) The migration time, t_R, for a neutral species is expressed with the following equation:

$$t_R = (1 + k')t_0/[1 + (t_0/t_{MC})]$$

in which t_0 is the time required for an unretained substance to travel the effective length of the capillary; t_{MC} is the time required for a micelle to traverse the capillary; k' is the capacity factor; and t_R is always between t_0 and t_{MC}.

(8) The capacity factor, k', for a neutral species, is calculated by the equation:

$$k' = (t_R/t_0 - 1)/(1 - t_R/t_{MC})$$

in which the terms are as defined above.

(9) For practical purposes, k' is calculated by the equation:

$$k' = t_R/t_0 - 1$$

in which t_R is the time measured from the point of voltage application (or injection) to the peak maximum; and t_0 is measured from the point of voltage application (or injection) to the leading edge of the solvent front or of an unretained substance. In contrast with CZE, k' in MEKC is significant and is a characteristic of a given solute in a given MEKC system. Further discussion of k' appears later in the *System Suitability* section under *Operational Parameters*.

(10) The resolution, R_S, for neutral species is calculated by the equation:

$$R_S = [(\sqrt{N})/4][(\alpha - 1)/\alpha][k'_2/(1 + k'_2)] \\ [(1 - (t_0/t_{MC}))/(1 + (t_0/t_{MC})k'_1)]$$

in which α is the selectivity, defined as the ratio of k'_2 to k'_1, of the operating conditions for separating two solutes. If the two solutes elute close together ($\alpha \leq 1.1$), either k' may be used. The equation shows that, just as with conventional chromatography, resolution in MEKC can be improved through controlling efficiency, selectivity, retention, and the chemical nature of the resolving surfactant-medium system. The last term of the equation is due to the limited elution range. Although MEKC is particularly useful in the separation of neutral species, this technique may also be used for the separation of charged solutes. The latter procedure involves a combination of chromatographic and electrophoretic separation mechanisms. The additional interaction between charged solutes and micelle can be used to optimize a separation. Ion-pairs may form if the charges borne on the surfactant and solute are opposite; otherwise, surfactant and

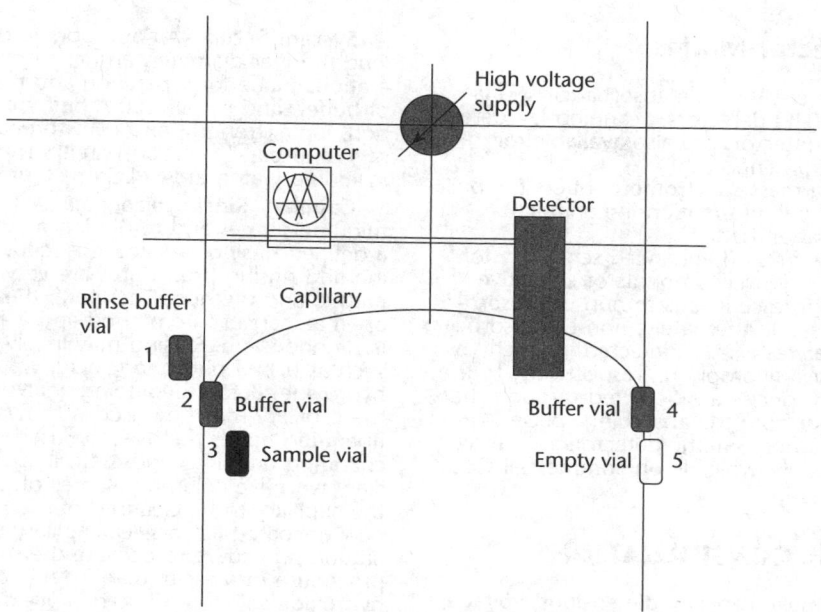

Fig. 1. Typical CE Instrument Configuration.

solute repel each other. These differences can significantly influence the separation of charged molecules.

INSTRUMENTAL CONSIDERATIONS

A typical CE system (see *Figure 1*) contains a fused-silica capillary having an internal diameter of 50 to 100 µm and a length of 20 to 100 cm. The ends of the capillary are placed in separate electrolyte reservoirs. The direct-current power supply is capable of furnishing high voltages, typically ranging from 0 to 30 kV. A detector and autosampler with some form of data-recording device complete the system. An automatic buffer replenishment system and a computer-based control and data acquisition system may also be found on the standard commercial systems. Temperature controls for both the capillary and the autosampler are also available on commercial instruments.

The primary considerations of instrumentation include capillary type and configuration, modes of sampling, power supply and detector modes.

Capillary Type and Configuration

Capillaries used in CZE are usually made of fused silica and with no internal coating. Some instruments are configured with a "free-swinging" style of capillary; that is, the capillary is not encased within an enclosure. In most commercial instruments, the capillary is housed in a cartridge. Both configurations offer specific advantages and disadvantages. The ability of the instrument to accommodate different types of capillaries and capillaries of various diameters and lengths is an important consideration. Capillaries with a variety of internal coatings are also available; therefore, the ability of the instrument to accommodate different capillaries is important. Internal capillary coatings may be employed to alter the magnitude or direction of EOF or to reduce sample absorption. If an internally coated capillary is to be used, then sufficient details and the indication of the supplier must be included in the method. Capillaries from an alternate supplier can be used if it is demonstrated that they are suitable.

Sample Introduction and Injector Technology

Modes of sample introduction onto the capillary include electromigration (electrokinetic mode) and negative- and positive-pressure injection (hydrostatic mode).

For injection via electromigration, the sample solution is electrophoresed into the capillary by inserting the capillary and electrode into the sample vials and applying a brief, high voltage. The sample enters the capillary by a combination of electrophoresis and EOF. Therefore, analytes with different mobilities are loaded into the capillary to different extents. The conductivities of the sample and standard solutes also affect the EOF and the volume injected.

Negative-pressure injectors place negative pressure at the detector end of the capillary and draw the sample solution into the injection end of the capillary. Positive-pressure injectors pressurize the sample vial, forcing the sample into the capillary. Pressure injection loads all sample components into the capillary to the same extent, and it is generally the most reproducible and the most frequently applied injection mode. The sample volume injected depends on the capillary length and internal diameter and the voltage or pressure applied. The typical sample volumes injected into the capillary are between 1 and 20 nL.

Each injection method offers specific advantages and disadvantages, depending on the sample composition, the separation mode, and the application of the method. None of the above injection modes is as reproducible as commercially available HPLC injectors. Based on the circumstances, it may be necessary to use internal standards for specific methods where high injection precision is required.

Power Supply

Most commercially available CE units have direct-current power supplies that are capable of furnishing power on a ramp-up or step-function mode to achieve and maintain the desired operational voltage in a smooth manner. This will help to ensure a relatively smooth baseline.

Another essential feature of the power supply is its utility in introducing a sample at the cathodic or the anodic end of the capillary. Because it is impractical to relocate the on-line detector from one end of the instrument to the other, it is beneficial to be able to specify whether the sample injection end is at the cathode or the anode.

Detector Modes

CE systems generally offer UV-visible absorbance and laser-induced fluorescence (LIF) detectors. Scanning UV detectors or photodiode-array detectors are also available for many commercial CE instruments.

The coupling of CE to a mass spectrometer offers the possibility of obtaining structural information in conjunction with electrophoretic migration data.

Fluorescence detection offers an enhanced sensitivity for samples containing only very small amounts of UV-active analytes. Application of fluorescent tags to non-UV-absorbing compounds can be useful. Alternately, non-UV-absorbing or nonfluorescent analytes can be detected indirectly by adding a chromophore or a fluorophore, respectively, to the buffer: the non-absorbing species are detected through the absence of expected signal from the absorbing species. Conductivity and pulsed amperometric detectors can also be used but are not generally available on commercial CE instruments.

ANALYTICAL CONSIDERATIONS

Several parameters, namely, capillary dimensions, voltage, ionic strength, and pH, are optimized to give adequate resolution and separation. Care should be taken to avoid changes in temperature that will affect the viscosity of the buffer and, in turn, influence both the EOF and the solute mobilities.

Capillary Dimensions—Variation of the capillary diameter and length can affect the electrophoretic resolution. Increasing the capillary length results in longer migration times, usually increasing resolution and generating a lower current. Increasing the capillary diameter will usually increase current and associated internal temperature gradients that decrease resolution. Conversely, a reduction in capillary diameter will result in lower heat and better resolution. However, larger capillary diameters have advantages of better mass loading and improved signal-to-noise ratio.

Voltage Effects—When higher voltages are applied, additional internal heating of the operating buffer occurs because of the current flow through the buffer. This heating effect, known as Joule heating, must be controlled because resistance, dielectric constant, and viscosity are temperature-dependent and alter the velocity of the EOF and solute mobilities.

In general, increasing the voltage will result in increased efficiency and resolution (up to the point where Joule heat cannot be adequately dissipated). Maximum resolution is obtained by maintaining the voltage below the level at which Joule heating and diffusion become limiting factors.

Ionic Strength Effects—Control of ionic strength and its manipulation allow adjustment of resolution, efficiency, and sensitivity. Increasing ionic strength will generally improve resolution, peak efficiency, and peak shape. Sensitivity may be improved because better focusing is achieved. However, because the current generated is directly proportional to the buffer concentration, more heat is produced when ionic strength of the buffer is increased, hence limiting the ionic strengths that can be utilized.

pH Effects—Resolution, selectivity, and peak shape can be dramatically altered by changes in pH as this parameter affects the extent of solute ionization and the level of EOF. The EOF is high at high pH and low at low pH in uncoated fused-silica capillaries.

OPERATIONAL PARAMETERS

The major steps in operating a CE system are system setup, capillary rinsing procedure, running a sample, system suitability testing, sample analysis, data handling, and system shutdown.

System Setup—An appropriate capillary of specific length, inner diameter, and coating is selected, with considerations made for separation and resolution, ionic strength of buffer, and pH effects. A buffer of appropriate composition, ionic strength, and pH is prepared, degassed, if necessary, and passed through an appropriate filter. All solvents, including water, are HPLC or CE grade.

Capillary Rinsing Procedure—Improved consistency of migration times and resolution may generally be obtained if a defined rinsing procedure is followed. Capillary conditioning and rinsing procedures are very specific to the analyte, matrix, and method. Therefore, these procedures are developed as part of the method and are specified in the individual monograph. Rinsing may involve the use of solutions such as 0.1 M phosphoric acid, water, and 0.1 M sodium hydroxide. Before beginning analysis of the test specimen, the capillary may be rinsed with five column volumes of the operating buffer that is to be used for the test. When changing buffer composition, it is advisable to rinse the capillary with five column volumes of each new buffer to allow the capillary to be cleansed of the previous buffer. Use of a new uncoated fused-silica capillary usually requires a regeneration procedure to activate the surface silanol groups. This procedure may include an extended rinse with a sodium hydroxide solution. Coated capillaries are rinsed according to the manufacturer's guidelines because inappropriate rinsing can remove or damage the coating. Columns may be dedicated to particular methods or buffer types to prevent cross-contamination.

Running a Sample—An appropriate capillary, electrolyte, and injection procedure are selected to achieve adequate resolution, sensitivity, and separation, with well-shaped and well-defined peaks. The required injection precision for a specific method may require use of an internal standard. The internal standard is selected with consideration of its ability to adequately separate from the analyte. The performance of the system may be improved by rinsing the capillary between injections and supplying fresh buffer to the source and destination vials used during voltage application, namely, vials 2 and 4 in *Figure 1*. Replicate injections from the same sample vial may be performed provided that no cross-contamination occurs. If cross-contamination occurs, the capillary tip may be rinsed by briefly inserting it into a vial containing the buffer prior to inserting the capillary into the electrolyte or sample vial.

The operational parameters are specified in each individual monograph so as to minimize voltage effects, ionic strength effects, and pH effects. The instrument is set up to run with the appropriate capillary configuration and injection conditions, within the established linear dynamic range of the detector; and acceptable migration precision is ensured by appropriate choice of sample diluent, separation electrolyte, electrolyte additives, and capillary pretreatment conditions. Exercise caution to avoid overloading the capillary with sample, as this decreases efficiency and reproducibility.

System Suitability—Parameters measured may include injector reproducibility, system selectivity, system efficiency, and tailing. Resolution between the analytes and other compounds may be determined by using test mixture standards.

Parameters typically used to determine system suitability include relative standard deviation (RSD), capacity factor (k'), the number of theoretical plates (N), sensitivity (limit of detection or quantitation), number of theoretical plates per meter (TPM), tailing factor (T), and resolution (R).

The peak shape is closely examined; ideally, the peak is symmetrical, with no shoulders and no excessive tailing. If these conditions are not met, corrective actions are taken before proceeding with the analysis. Peak integration is also closely examined to ensure that the peak response is correctly quantitated.

Replicate injections of a Standard preparation of known concentration can be used to determine the reproducibility of the CE system. Data from five or more replicate injections are used to calculate RSD. Unless otherwise specified in the individual monograph, the relative standard deviation for replicate injections is not more than 3.0%. Minimum injection precision values may be specified in specific CE methods, especially when determining trace-level components. Calculation of electrophoretic parameters in MEKC, as in other forms of CE, may involve a combination of chromatographic and electrophoretic relationships. Hence, capacity factor, k', for neutral analyte migration in MEKC can be calculated by the equation:

$$k' = t_R - t_0(1 - t_R/t_{MC})$$

in which t_R, t_0, and t_{MC} are the migration times of the analyte, the bulk solution (EOF), and the micelle, respectively.

The number of theoretical plates, N, is a measure of the efficiency of the system and is calculated by the equation:

$$N = 16(t_R/W)^2 \text{ or } N = 5.54(t_R/W_{1/2})^2$$

in which W is the analyte peak width at baseline, $W_{1/2}$ is the analyte peak width at half-height, and t_R is the analyte migration time.

The number of theoretical plates per meter, TPM, is a measure of the efficiency of the capillary as a function of peak width at baseline and can be calculated by the equation:

$$TPM = 1600(t_R/W)^2/L$$

in which L, in cm, is the total capillary length; and the other terms are as defined above. The tailing factor, T, of the analyte peak is a measure of peak symmetry, and it represents the degree of deviation of the symmetry of the peak from an ideally symmetrical Gaussian peak. This factor can be calculated by the equation:

$$T = W_{0.05}/2f$$

in which $W_{0.05}$ is the length of a line constructed parallel to the peak base from the leading edge to the tailing edge of the peak at 5% of peak height; and f is the distance along the same line from the leading edge of the peak, appearing to the left of the peak maximum in the electropherogram, to the intercept of a perpendicular line dropped from the peak maximum to the base. A ratio of 1.0 indicates a perfectly symmetrical peak. If electrodispersive effects occur, they can generate highly asymmetrical peaks. This can occur when high sample concentrations are used, such as those for testing of impurities. Use of highly asymmetrical peaks is acceptable provided that they are reproducible and that they do not compromise separation selectivity.

The resolution factor, R, is a measure of the ability of the capillary system to separate consecutively migrating analytes. Resolution is determined for all sample analytes of interest, with the pH of the buffer adjusted as necessary to meet system suitability requirements. It can be calculated by the equation:

$$R = 2(t_2 - t_1)/(W_1 + W_2)$$

in which t_2 and t_1 are the migration times, measured at peak maxima, for the slower migrating peak and the faster migrating peak, respectively; and W_2 and W_1 are the corresponding widths of these two peaks measured at their bases.

Sample Analysis—Once the suitability of the CE system has been established, aliquots of both the Standard preparation and the test preparation are injected. Standards are injected before or after the samples and intermittently throughout the run.

Data Handling—Time-normalized peak areas are often used in quantitative calculations. These are determined by dividing the observed integrated peak area by the migration time of the analyte. This compensates for the fact that in CE, unlike HPLC, each analyte travels through the detector at a different velocity. Unless this normalization is performed, slowly moving (later-migrating) analytes will have disproportionately large peak areas compared with those for early migrating components.

System Shutdown—After analysis, the capillary is rinsed according to the directions specified in each monograph or as recommended by the manufacturer. For example, the capillary might be rinsed with distilled water to remove buffer components and then filled with air or nitrogen by performing a rinse from an empty vial. Naturally, the destination and source vials, namely, vials 4 and 2 in *Figure 1*, are emptied of buffer and rinsed thoroughly with deionized water.

MASS SPECTROMETRY*

A mass spectrometer produces ions from the substance under investigation, separates them according to their mass-to-charge ratio (m/z), and records the relative abundance of each ionic species present. The instrument consists of three major components (see *Figure 1*):

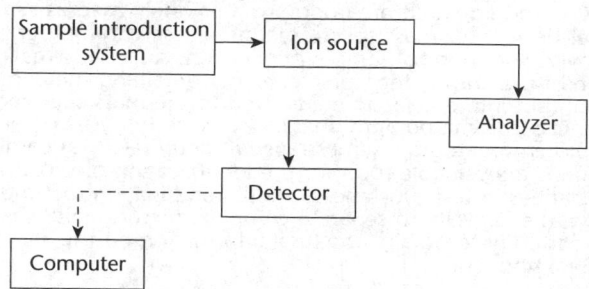

Fig. 1. Major components of a mass spectrometer.

an ion source for producing gaseous ions from the substance being studied, an analyzer for resolving the ions into their characteristic mass components according to their mass-to-charge ratios, and a detector system for detecting the ions and recording the relative abundance of each of the resolved ionic species. In addition, a sample introduction system is necessary to admit the samples to be studied to the ion source while maintaining the high vacuum requirements ($\sim 10^{-6}$ to 10^{-8} mm of mercury) of the technique; and a computer is required to control the instrument, acquire and manipulate data, and compare spectra to reference libraries.

This chapter gives an overview of the theory, construction, and use of mass spectrometers. The discussion is limited to those instruments and measurements with actual or potential application to compendial requirements: generally, the identification and quantitation of specific compounds.

SAMPLE INTRODUCTION

Samples are introduced either as a gas to be ionized in the ion source, or by ejection of charged molecular species from a solid surface or solution. In some cases sample intro-

---

* This text is adapted from General Chapter ⟨736⟩ of the *United States Pharmacopeia and National Formulary* (*USP–NF*) as published in *USP 32–NF 27*. This text is provided for informational purposes only and is intended as a resource for the FCC user. Note that because the *USP–NF* is in continuous revision, this General Chapter is subject to change and the text printed here may not continue to represent the current version.

duction and ionization take place in a single process, making a distinction between them somewhat artificial.

Substances that are gases or liquids at room temperature and atmospheric pressure can be admitted to the source as a neutral beam via a controllable leak system. Volatilizable compounds dissolved or adsorbed in solids or liquids can be removed and concentrated with a headspace analyzer. Vapors are flushed from the solid or liquid matrix with a stream of carrier gas and trapped on an adsorbing column. The trapped vapors are subsequently desorbed by programmed heating of the trap and introduced into the mass spectrometer by a capillary connection.

For volatilizable solids, the most frequently used method of sample introduction is the direct insertion probe. Here, the sample is placed in a small crucible at the tip of the probe, which is heated under high vacuum in close proximity to the ion source. A variation of this technique involves desorption of samples inside the ionization chamber from a rapidly heated wire or with the aid of a laser beam. Such desorption techniques, in combination with electron, chemical, or field ionization, are preferred for the analysis of heat sensitive or poorly volatile samples.

Sample introduction techniques that involve the ejection of charged molecules from the surface of solid samples include the field desorption method and various sputtering techniques, where the samples are bombarded by high energy photons, by a primary ion beam, or by a neutral particle beam. Similarly, ions can be ejected from solutions either by bombardment with a primary beam, or by one of the various spray techniques described below.

Gas and liquid chromatographs are widely used as sample inlet devices for mass spectrometers. These chromatographs provide for an initial sample purification, since only that portion of the chromatographic effluent containing the compound of interest need be admitted to the mass spectrometer. Gas chromatography/mass spectrometry (GC/MS) and liquid chromatography/mass spectrometry (LC/MS) combinations are valuable tools for the identification of unknown impurities in test substances. These combination methods have the capacity to separate complex mixtures with the opportunity to obtain structural information on the individual components.

Gas Chromatography/Mass Spectrometry

Gas chromatographic effluents are already in the vapor state and can be admitted directly into the mass spectrometer. Bridging the several orders of magnitude difference in the operating pressures of the two systems was initially accomplished with the use of various carrier gas separators. However, with the advent of capillary gas chromatographic columns and high capacity vacuum pumps for mass spectrometers, the gas chromatographic effluents are now fed directly into the ion source.

Liquid Chromatography/Mass Spectrometry

This technique is particularly useful for analyzing materials that cannot be analyzed by GC/MS, either because of thermal instability, high polarity, or high molecular weight. Compounds of biological interest such as polar endogenous substances, and macromolecules—including peptides, proteins, nucleic acids, and oligosaccharides—often fall into one of these categories.

Currently available LC/MS interfaces encompass a number of approaches to separating the compound of interest from the liquid chromatographic mobile phase and transforming it into an ionized species suitable for mass spectrometry. These include transport devices such as the particle beam; various spray techniques including thermospray, electrospray, and ionspray; and particle-induced desorption such as continuous-flow fast atom bombardment (CF-FAB).

PARTICLE BEAM INTERFACE

The solvent is removed from an aerosol of the liquid chromatographic effluent, and the resulting neutral analyte molecules are introduced into the ion source of the mass spectrometer where they are ionized by electron ionization (EI) or chemical ionization (CI). The resulting spectra are thus classical EI or CI spectra, the former with a wealth of structural information. There are limitations with respect to polarity, thermal lability, and molecular weight, so this technique is best suited for small organic molecules with molecular weights of less than 1000 daltons.

THERMOSPRAY

The compound of interest in a volatile buffer mobile phase, such as ammonium acetate, is passed through heated, narrow bore tubing directly into the ion source of a mass spectrometer. The solution is vaporized in the tubing, and analyte ions desorb into the gas phase and pass into the mass analyzer. Neutral analyte molecules in the gas phase may undergo chemical ionization by reaction with gas phase buffer ions such as NH_4^+. Thermospray is compatible with relatively high flow rates of 1 to 2 mL per minute, solvents containing a high percentage of water, and many types of polar analytes. Thermal degradation may occur, since the analytes are exposed to relatively high temperatures during the volatilization process.

ELECTROSPRAY

The mobile phase is sprayed through a small opening (needle tip) held at a potential of several kilovolts. The charged droplets so produced are desolvated by passing through a drying gas, and the resulting ions are injected directly into the high vacuum of the analyzer through an orifice or glass capillary. Classical electrospray is limited to flow rates of 1 to 5 µL per minute, and is therefore compatible with either microbore HPLC or post-column stream splitting techniques.

The ions may carry multiple charges, so that the m/z value of high molecular weight substances will fall into the usable range for most quadrupole or magnetic sector mass analyzers (m/z < 4000). Analytes of up to 150,000 daltons can thus be successfully analyzed.

IONSPRAY

A variant of electrospray in which nebulization with a gas flow is used to assist the formation of microdroplets of mobile phase. The technique can extend the upper limit of usable flow rates to 0.1 mL per minute. Volatile buffers must be used with both techniques.

DESORPTION TECHNIQUES

Microflow liquid chromatography can also be interfaced to particle induced desorption techniques such as fast atom bombardment (FAB) and liquid secondary ion mass spectroscopy (LSIMS), described in the following section on ionization techniques. Typically, column effluent flowing at a rate of 1 to 10 µL per minute is mixed with a small percentage of nonvolatile liquid such as glycerol. The mixture is introduced via a capillary inlet onto a target within the ion source where it is bombarded with high energy (5 to 20 keV) atoms or ions. The resulting spectra are similar to FAB or LSIMS spectra but with the background from the sample matrix greatly reduced. Frit-FAB is a variant of continuous flow FAB where the sample is introduced through a porous frit target.

IONIZATION TECHNIQUES

Electron Impact

Molecules of the sample under analysis enter the ionization chamber in the vapor state. Positive ions are produced by passing a beam of electrons, obtained from tungsten or rhenium filaments, through the vapor, which is maintained at a pressure of 10^{-4} to 10^{-6} mm of mercury. Provided the energy of the electron beam is greater than the ionization potential of the sample, the sample is ionized and/or fragmented, as represented by the following equation:

$$e^- + M \rightarrow M^+ \cdot + 2e^-$$

Chemical Ionization (CI)

In this process, a reagent gas at a pressure between 0.1 to 10 mm of mercury is admitted to the source and ionized by a high energy electron beam or discharge. At these pressures, ion-molecule reactions occur and the primary reagent gas ions react further. The most commonly used reagent gases are methane, isobutane, and ammonia. Typical reactions for methane are shown in the following equations:

$$CH_4 + e^- \rightarrow CH_4^+ \cdot + 2e^-$$

$$CH_4^+ + CH_4 \rightarrow CH_5^+ + CH_3 \cdot$$

$$CH_3^+ + CH_4 \rightarrow C_2H_5^+ + H_2$$

The CH_5^+ species is a strong Bronsted acid and readily transfers a proton to most organic compounds

$$CH_5^+ + M \rightarrow MH^+ + CH_4$$

In the case of methane, the protonated ion $(MH)^+$ initially formed may be sufficiently energetic to dissociate further.

Fast Atom Bombardment (FAB)

The sample is ionized by bombardment with a beam of high speed xenon atoms, produced by exchange with highly accelerated xenon ions in a collision cell. The process is summarized as follows:

$$Xe \rightarrow Xe^+ + e^-$$

$$\underrightarrow{Xe^+} + Xe \rightarrow \underrightarrow{Xe} + Xe^+,$$

where the subscript arrows indicate the fast-moving particles.

FAB is a surface analysis technique, and care must be taken during sample preparation to optimize the condition of the surface. When the sample is coated on a probe by evaporation of a solution, the sample ion beam obtained is often transitory. Molecular adducts with alkali metals, such as (M + Na) and (M + K), favor ion formation. This phenomenon is used to assist in the ionization of biological molecules. Thus, treatment of the sample surface with sodium chloride solution may enhance the yield of adduct ions. Heating the sample during analysis may also increase the ion yield.

The declining yield of sample ions during analysis is probably due to destruction of the sample surface. The surface can, in effect, be continuously replaced by dissolving the sample in a suitable nonvolatile liquid and by coating the mixture onto the top of the probe. Using this approach, the lifetime of samples in the source has been extended to more than 1 hour and the range of compounds amenable to FAB analysis expanded dramatically. The long sample lifetimes and higher sensitivities so achieved make FAB an important mass spectral technique for biochemical analysis, providing the elemental formula of the sample through accurate mass determination. A further advantage of FAB, unlike CI, is the presence of fragment ions within the spectra, which aid in structural elucidation.

Recently, neutral atom bombardment has been replaced by cesium ion bombardment. Although this technique is still referred to as FAB, it is more correctly described as liquid secondary ion mass spectrometry (LSIMS).

Negative and positive ions are formed in the various ionization processes described above, and both are readily analyzed by modern mass spectrometers. Samples with a high electron capture cross section, notably those containing halide atoms, yield an abundance of negative ions. For this reason, halide derivatives of compounds to be studied are often prepared. Negative ion mass spectrometry has been successfully applied to the analysis of pesticide residues, since the structures of these compounds are well suited to the technique.

ANALYZERS

Mass analyzers separate the charged species in the ionized sample according to their m/z ratios, thus permitting the mass and abundance of each species to be determined. Four commonly used analyzers are the magnetic sector, the quadrupole, the time-of-flight, and the Fourier transform analyzers.

Magnetic Sector Analyzers

Ions generated in the ion source are collimated into a beam through the focusing action of a magnetic field and a slit assembly. After exiting the source, ions are subjected to a magnetic field perpendicular to the direction of the beam. Each ion experiences a force at right angles to both its direction of travel and the direction of the magnetic field, thereby deflecting the beam. The motion of each ion is given by

$$m/z = H^2 r^2 / 2V$$

where m is the mass in atomic mass units, z is the number of electronic charges, H is the magnetic field strength in gauss, r is the radius of the ion trajectory in centimeters, and V is the accelerating voltage. The mass spectrum is scanned by varying the strength of the magnetic field and detecting those ions passing through an exit slit as they come into "focus." The magnetic sector mass spectrometer affords spatial resolution of ions, giving a unique trajectory at a given field strength for each value of m/z.

Quadrupole Analyzers

The instrument is based on four parallel rods in a square array. The ion beam is focused down the axis of the array and an electrical potential of fixed (DC) and radio frequency (RF) components is applied to diagonally opposed rods. For a given combination of DC and RF components, ions of one specific m/z ratio have a stable path down the axis. All others are deflected to the sides and lost. Mass scanning is achieved by changing the DC and RF components of the voltage, while maintaining a fixed ratio. The quadrupole analyzer is a mass filter because it separates ions on the basis of their m/z ratio.

Ion-trap Analyzer

This quadrupole-type device is composed of a ring electrode placed between two end cap electrodes. Depending upon the commercial version employed, the end caps are either held at ground potential or have an RF voltage applied to them, while an RF voltage is placed on the ring electrode. As a result of these potentials, the hyperbolic surfaces of the three elements form a three-dimensional quadrupole analyzer.

Both ionization and mass analysis take place within the three-dimensional quadrupole field. In the ionization step, the RF voltage on the ring electrode is set low enough so that the ions within the mass range of interest are trapped within the device. Following ionization, mass analysis is accomplished through use of the "mass selective instability" mode of operation. That is, by raising the RF voltage on the ring electrode, ions of successively higher mass are ejected from the ion trap into an electron multiplier detector. In its most common application, the ion-trap analyzer is used in conjunction with a gas chromatograph and covers the mass range of 10 to 560 daltons. However, recent advances in ion-trap technology have extended the workable mass range to many thousands of daltons.

Time-of-flight Analyzers

Ion separation is based on the principle that ions of different masses, possessing equal kinetic energy, have different velocities. If there is a fixed distance for the ions to travel, the time of travel will vary with their mass, the lighter ions traveling faster and reaching the detector in a shorter period of time. The time-of-flight is given by

$$t_f = k \sqrt{m/z}$$

where t_f is the time-of-flight in seconds. Thus, the time-of-flight of the various ions is simply proportional to the square root of the mass-to-charge ratio of the ions. To measure the time-of-flight, ions are introduced into the mass spectrometer in discrete packets so that a starting point for the timing process can be established. Ion packets are generated either through a pulsed ionization process or through a gating system in which ions are produced continuously, but are introduced only at given times into the flight tube.

Fourier Transform Analyzers

In a magnetic field of flux density B, ions move in circular orbits. The angular frequency, ω, of the orbital motion is given by

$$\omega = (z/m)B$$

In this type of mass spectrometer, the orbits are varied by subjecting the ions to a resonant alternating electric field. When the frequency of the alternating field matches the orbital frequency, the ions are steadily accelerated to larger and larger orbits in coherent motion, developing a high level of kinetic energy. After the alternating electric field is turned off, the orbiting ions give rise to an alternating image current on the electrodes. A frequency analysis of this signal yields the mass of the ions involved. Thus, the Fourier transform of the time domain transient signal yields the corresponding frequency spectrum from which the mass spectrum is computed. This is a high resolution technique, yielding m/z ratios accurate to about one thousandth of a dalton.

TANDEM MASS SPECTROMETRY

Two mass spectrometers connected in series (MS/MS), tandem mass spectrometry, refers to the use of two or more sequential mass analysis steps. In its simplest form MS/MS (*Figure 2*) consists of two mass spectrometers linked in such a way that ions preselected by the first mass analyzer (MS1) are chemically or energetically modified and the results analyzed by the second mass analyzer (MS2).

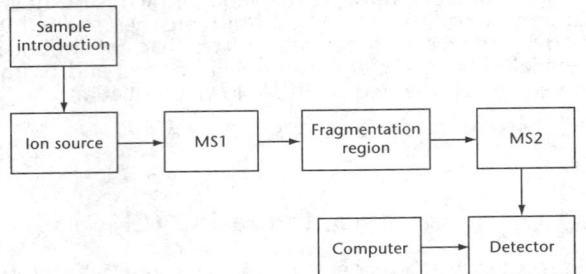

Fig. 2. Tandem Mass Spectrometry.

The basic concept of MS/MS involves the ability to determine the mass relationship between a precursor ion in MS1 and a product ion in MS2. Different mass relationships can be probed depending on how MS1 and MS2 are scanned. These include fragmentation of a precursor and measurement of all its fragments (a product scan), selection of multiple precursors and testing for a common fragment (a precursor scan), or scanning to see if a number of precursors all lose the same neutral species (a constant neutral loss scan).

Fragmentation of the precursor ion can be induced by momentum transfer through collision with gas molecules and/or solid surfaces or by electronic excitation using lasers. These techniques are known as collision-induced dissociation, surface-induced dissociation, or laser-induced dissociation, respectively. Allowing the ion to fragment without additional activation is known as metastable decomposition.

There are many applications of MS/MS. Product scans can be used to obtain qualitative information from precursor ions of test substances, impurities, and contaminants. This can aid in the identification of unknowns. The method can also be used to determine the amino acid sequence of peptides and protein fragments.

MS/MS has advantages for mixture analysis. Even when the mass spectrometer is coupled to a separation device such as a liquid or gas chromatograph, the resulting signals may be a result of overlapping or unresolved components. MS/MS can be employed to select the precursor ion from one component and obtain structural information without interference from the others.

Selected reaction monitoring is used to reduce the interference encountered during quantitative analysis for low levels of the analyte. Signals from other compounds in the matrix can mask the desired signal. Interference is reduced if a analyte-specific fragment is selected with MS1 and a structure-specific fragment with MS2. The odds of another molecule producing the same mass relationship are diminishingly small.

MS/MS can also be used in metabolism studies to search for molecules with common structural features. All of the metabolites might contain the same functional group that is lost as a neutral fragment. In this case a constant-neutral-loss scan will show all of these species. For instance, carboxylic acids will all lose neutral carbon dioxide. If the common functionality is lost as an ionic fragment, then a precursor scan will show all of the molecules that produce that fragment ion.

DATA ANALYSIS AND INTERPRETATION

The mass spectral experiment yields information on the molecular weight of ions derived from the sample and the relative abundance of each of these ions. Spectra are often complex, and not all of the ions may be separated by the mass spectrometer. The ability of the instrument to separate ions is called the resolving power, commonly described by the "10% valley" definition. This states that the resolving power is the highest mass number at which two peaks differing by one molecular weight unit and of equal height have a valley between them that is equal to 10% of the peak height. For low, medium, and high resolution mass spectrometers, this value is between 100 and 2000, 2000 and 10,000, and greater than 10,000, respectively.

If one electron is removed or added to a neutral molecule, a molecular ion of essentially the same molecular weight as the parent molecule results. It is often possible to determine the mass of this ion with sufficient precision to enable the empirical formula of the compound to be calculated. Molecular masses may be determined accurately by using high resolution instruments or by peak-matching measurements using reference compounds.

Fragment ions are those produced from the molecular ion by various bond cleavage processes. Numerous papers in the literature relate bond cleavage patterns (fragmentation patterns) to molecular structure.

In addition to measurement of the mass of a molecular ion and its associated fragment ions, mass spectrometers are also used to quantitate compounds with a high degree of selectivity, precision, and accuracy. Compounds are introduced into the mass spectrometer either via direct insertion probe, gas inlet, or, as is more common, via gas or liquid chromatographic interfaces, which provide sample purification. Ionization may be by EI, CI, FAB, thermospray, or electrospray and mass separation by magnetic sector, quadrupole, or quadrupole ion-trap mass spectrometers. Quantitative mass spectrometry involves measuring the abundance of a specific ion, or set of ions, and relating the response to a known standard. External or internal standards may be used, but the latter are preferred for greater accuracy.

For mass spectrometry, internal standards may be either structural or stable isotope analogs. The former have the advantage of lower cost and availability while precision and accuracy are typically achieved by use of a stable isotope (^2H, ^{13}C, ^{15}N) labeled analog of the analyte. The only requirements for labeling the analyte are that the ion monitored for the internal standard must retain an isotopic label after ionization and the label must not be exchangeable under the sampling, separation, or ionization conditions. Stable isotope internal standards are often required for acceptable quantitation, particularly with FAB and LC/MS techniques such as thermospray and electrospray.

Relative abundances of the analyte and internal standard ions are typically determined by selected ion monitoring, by which only specific ions due to the analyte and the internal standard are monitored. This technique has the advantage over scanning the full mass range in that more time is spent integrating the ion current at a selected mass-to-charge ratio, thereby increasing sensitivity. Chromatographic peak area or amount of analyte in a sample is calculated from the ratio of analyte to internal standard peak area (or height) and the regression parameters as determined by a calibration curve, using standard techniques.

NUCLEAR MAGNETIC RESONANCE*

Nuclear magnetic resonance (NMR) spectroscopy is an analytical procedure based on the magnetic properties of certain atomic nuclei. It is similar to other types of spectroscopy in that absorption or emission of electromagnetic energy at characteristic frequencies provides analytical information. NMR differs in that the discrete energy levels between which the transitions take place are created artificially by placing the nuclei in a magnetic field.

Atomic nuclei are charged and behave as if they were spinning on the nuclear axis, thus creating a magnetic dipole of moment μ along this axis. The angular momentum of the spinning nucleus is characterized by a spin quantum number (I). If the mass number is odd, I is $1/2$ or an integer plus $1/2$; otherwise, it has a value of 0 or a whole number.

Nuclei having a spin quantum number, $I \neq 0$, when placed in an external uniform static magnetic field of strength, H_0, align with respect to the field in $(2I + 1)$ possible orientations. Thus, for nuclei with $I = 1/2$, which include most isotopes of analytical significance (*Table 1*), there are two possible orientations, corresponding to two different energy states. A nuclear resonance is the transition between these states, by absorption or emission of the corresponding amount of energy. In a static magnetic field the nuclear magnetic axis precesses (Larmor precession) about the external field axis. The precessional angular velocity, ω_0, is related to the external magnetic field strength through the equation:

$$\omega_0 = \gamma H_0$$

in which γ is the magnetogyric ratio and is a constant for all nuclei of a given isotope. If energy from an oscillating radio-frequency field is introduced, the absorption of radiation takes place according to the relationship:

$$\Delta E = h\nu = \mu H_0 / I$$

where h is Planck's constant, and

$$\nu = \omega_0 / 2\pi = \gamma H_0 / 2\pi$$

Thus, when the frequency (ν_0) of the external energy field ($E = h\nu$) is the same as the precessional angular velocity, resonance is achieved.

---
* This text is adapted from General Chapter ⟨761⟩ of the *United States Pharmacopeia and National Formulary* (*USP–NF*) as published in *USP 32–NF 27*. This text is provided for informational purposes only and is intended as a resource for the FCC user. Note that because the *USP–NF* is in continuous revision, this General Chapter is subject to change and the text printed here may not continue to represent the current version.

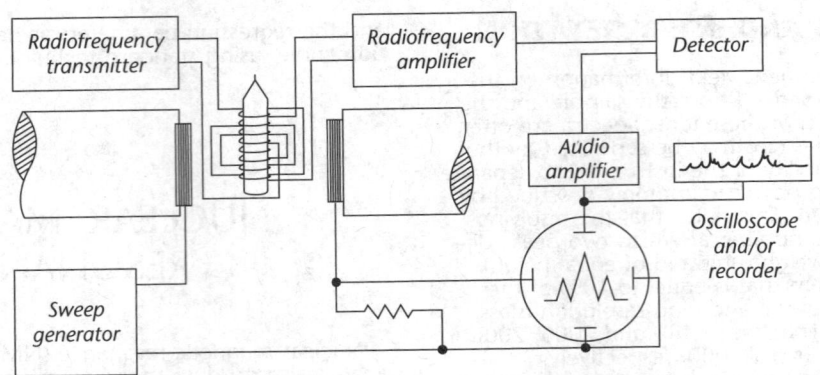

Fig. 1. Block diagram of a typical NMR spectrometer.

The energy difference between the two levels corresponds to electromagnetic radiation in the radio-frequency range. It is a function of γ, which is a property of the nucleus, and H_0, the external field strength. As shown in Table 1, the resonance frequency of a nucleus increases with the increase of the magnetic field strength.

NMR is a technique of high specificity but relatively low sensitivity. The basic reason for the low sensitivity is the comparatively small difference in energy between the excited and the ground states (0.02 calories at 15 to 20 kilogauss field strength), which results in a population difference between the two levels of only a few parts per million. Another important aspect of the NMR phenomenon, with negative effects on the sensitivity, is the long lifetime of most nuclei in the excited state, which affects the design of the NMR analytical test, especially in pulsed repetitive experiments. Simultaneous acquisition of the entire spectrum instead of frequency-swept spectra can give sensitivity enhancement.

Apparatus

The distinctive components of an NMR spectrometer are a magnet and a source of radio frequency. The instruments are described by the approximate resonance frequency of the analytical nucleus, e.g., ^1H NMR. More recently, instruments are being referred to by their field strengths. Some spectrometers are dedicated to the analysis of one type of nucleus; others are designed to obtain spectra of different nuclei.

There are two types of commercial NMR spectrometers: the classical continuous wave (CW) instruments and the more modern pulse Fourier-transform (FT) instruments. The CW spectrometers use a technique similar to that of classical optical spectrometers: a slow scan of radio frequency (at fixed magnetic field) or of the magnetic field (at fixed radio frequency) over a domain corresponding to the resonance of the nuclei being studied. The signal generated by the absorption of energy is detected, amplified, and recorded.

Various instrument configurations are possible. The arrangement of a typical double-coil spectrometer, as one might see in the lower resolution 60-MHz and 100-MHz CW instruments, is illustrated in Figure 1.

The limitations of the CW spectrometers are low sensitivity and long analysis time. In pulsed NMR spectrometers, a single pulse of radio frequency energy is used to simultaneously activate all nuclei. The excited nuclei returning to the lower energy level generate a free induction decay (FID) signal that contains in a time domain all the information obtained in a frequency domain with a CW spectrometer. The time domain and the frequency domain responses form a pair of FTs; the mathematical operation is performed by a computer after analog-to-digital conversion. After a delay allowing for relaxation of the excited nuclei, the pulse experiment (transient) may be repeated and the response coherently added in the computer memory, with random noise being averaged out. (A similar signal-to-noise increase can be obtained by combining CW spectrometers with computers that average transients.)

The block diagram of a typical high-resolution pulsed spectrometer is shown in Figure 2. It is a typical configuration of the high-resolution spectrometer that uses a superconducting (cryogenic) solenoid as the source of the magnetic field. Introduction of the pulsed NMR spectrometer has made the acquisition of spectra of many nuclei, other than protons, routine. It has also allowed proton spectra to be obtained in much less time, and with smaller amounts of specimen, as compared to CW techniques.

NMR spectrometers have strict stability and homogeneity requirements. Stability is often achieved by a field-frequency locking system that "locks" the magnetic field to the resonance frequency of a reference signal. The lock signal can be homonuclear or heteronuclear. In the latter case, the reference resonance is usually a deuterium signal from a deuterated solvent. On older spectrometers, using deuterium as a locking nucleus permits noise decoupling of protons to be carried out while studying nuclei like ^{13}C. While internal homonuclear locks are still used in CW proton spectrometers (where tetramethylsilane at about 0.5% provides a convenient lock), they are hardly ever used in pulsed FT spectrometers.

No type of magnet is capable of producing a homogeneous field over the space occupied by the specimen. Two techniques are usually employed to compensate for this lack

Table 1. Properties of Some Nuclei Amenable to NMR Study

Nucleus	I	Natural Abundance, %	Sensitivity	Resonance Frequency (MHZ) at 1.4093 T*	2.3488 T	4.6975 T
^1H	$^1/_2$	99.98	1.00	60.000	100.000	200.000
^{13}C	$^1/_2$	1.108	0.0159	15.087	25.144	50.288
^{19}F	$^1/_2$	100	0.83	56.446	94.077	188.154
^{31}P	$^1/_2$	100	0.0663	24.289	40.481	80.961
^{11}B	($^3/_2$)	80.42	0.17	19.250	32.084	64.167

* T = tesla: 1.4093 T = 14.093 kilogauss.

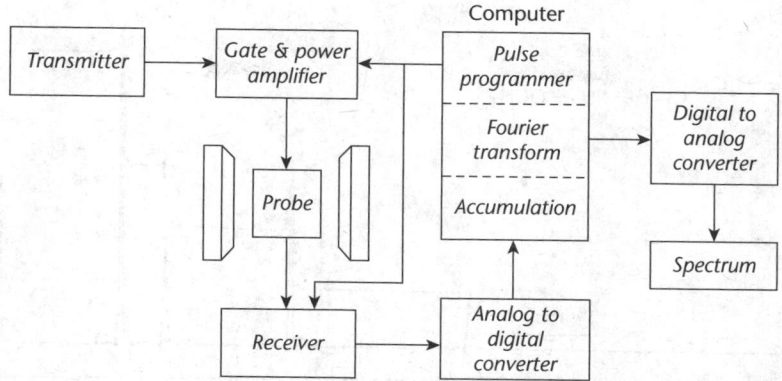

Fig. 2. Block diagram of a typical pulsed FT-NMR spectrometer.

of homogeneity: specimen spinning and the use of additional (shim) coils. Because of design, particularly probe design, the spinning in the case of the electromagnet or permanent magnet is perpendicular to the basic field. In the superconducting magnet, the axis of rotation can only be parallel to the basic magnetic field. The spin rate should be sufficient to produce averaging of the field, but not fast enough to produce an extended vortex in the specimen tube. A vortex extended near the region exposed to the radio-frequency coils decreases resolution. The shim coils are adjusted by the operator until instrumental contributions to the observed line width are minimized.

An electronic integrator is a feature of most NMR spectrometers. On a CW instrument (^{1}H and ^{19}F) the integrator, connected to the spectrometer output stage, determines the relative areas of the resonance peaks and presents these areas as a series of stepped horizontal lines when a sweep is made in the integration mode. On FT-NMR spectrometers, an integration algorithm is included in the spectrometer software, and the resonance peak areas may be presented graphically as stepped lines or tabulated as numeric values. The use of computer-generated tabulated/numeric integration data should not be accepted without a specific demonstration of precision and accuracy on the spectrometer in question.

The Spectrum

The signals (peaks) in an NMR spectrum are characterized by four attributes: resonance frequency, multiplicity, line width, and relative intensity. The analytical usefulness of the NMR technique resides in the fact that the same types of nuclei, when located in different molecular environments, exhibit different resonance frequencies. The reason for this difference is that the effective field experienced by a particular nucleus is a composite of the external field provided by the instrument and the field generated by the circulation of the surrounding electrons. (The latter is generally opposed to the external field and the phenomenon is called "shielding.") In contrast with other spectroscopic methods, it is not possible to measure accurately the absolute values of transition frequencies. However, it is possible to measure accurately the difference in frequencies between two resonance signals. The position of a signal in an NMR spectrum is described by its separation from another resonance signal arbitrarily taken as standard. This separation is called chemical shift.

The chemical shift, being the difference between two resonance frequencies, is directly proportional to the magnetic field strength (or to the frequency of the oscillator). However, the ratio between the chemical shift, in frequency units, and the instrument frequency is constant. This allows definition of a dimensionless chemical shift parameter (δ) that is independent of the instrument frequency:

$$\delta = (\nu_s - \nu_r)/\nu_o + \delta_r$$

in which ν_s is the test substance line frequency, ν_r is the reference line frequency, ν_o is the instrument frequency, in mHz, and δ_r is the chemical shift of the reference.

By employing the above equation, it is possible to use (with appropriate caution) the chemical shift of any known species (such as the residual ^{1}H-containing species in deuterated solvent) as a chemical shift reference. The above equation, now in common use, is applicable to nearly all methods except in the relatively rare cases where extremely precise chemical shift values must be determined, and is readily adaptable to nuclei where non-zero reference standards are the only practical method of chemical shift determinations.

For CW instruments, tetramethylsilane (TMS) is the most widely used chemical shift reference for proton and carbon spectra. It is chemically inert, exhibits only one line, which is at a higher field than most signals, and is volatile, thus allowing for ready specimen recovery. Sodium 3-(trimethylsilyl)propionate (TSP) or sodium 2,2-dimethyl-2-silapentane-5-sulfonate (DSS) are used as NMR references for aqueous solutions. The resonance frequency of the TSP or DSS methyl groups closely approximate that of the TMS signal; however, DSS has the disadvantage of showing a number of methylene multiplets that may interfere with signals from the test substance. Where the use of an internal NMR reference material is not desirable, an external reference may be used.

Conventional NMR spectra are shown with the magnetic field strength increasing from left to right. Nuclei that resonate at high magnetic field strengths (to the right) are said to be more shielded (greater electron density) than those that resonate at lower magnetic field strengths: these are said to be de-shielded (lower electron density).

Figure 3 shows the proton NMR spectrum of 2,3-dimethyl-2-butenyl methyl ether. This compound contains protons in a methylene group (marked *d* in the graphic formula) and in four methyl groups (*a*, *a*, *b*, and *c*). Methyl groups *b* and *c* are situated in distinctly different molecular environments than the two *a* methyl groups. Three different methyl proton resonances are observed as spectral peaks in addition to the peak corresponding to methylene proton resonance.

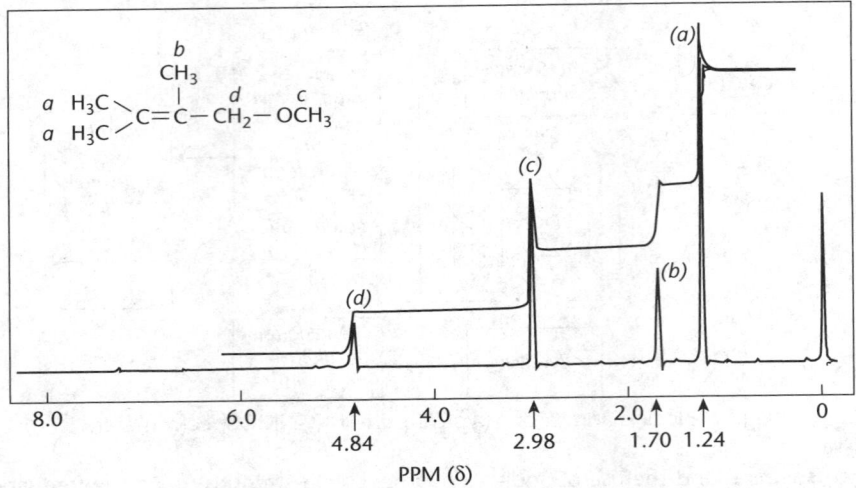

Fig. 3. NMR spectrum of 2,3-dimethyl-2-butenyl methyl ether (15% in CCl₄) showing four nonequivalent, apparently uncoupled protons with a normal integral trace (peak area ratio from low H₀ to high H₀ of 2:3:3:6). (Tetramethylsilane, the NMR Reference, appears at 0 ppm.) The system of units represented by δ is defined under *The Spectrum*, in this chapter.

The two *a* methyl groups, being in very similar environments, have the same chemical shift. Interaction between magnetically active nuclei situated within a few bond lengths of each other leads to coupling, which results in a mutual splitting of the respective signals into sets of peaks or multiplets.

The coupling between two nuclei may be described in terms of the spin-spin coupling constant, J, which is the separation (in hertz) between the individual peaks of the multiplet. Where two nuclei interact and cause reciprocal splitting, the measured coupling constants in the two resulting mutiplets are equal. Furthermore, J is independent of magnetic field strength.

In a first-order, comparatively noncomplex spin system, the number of individual peaks that are expected to be present in a multiplet and the relative peak intensities are predictable. The number of peaks is determined by $2nI + 1$, where n is the number of nuclei on adjacent groups that are active in splitting. For protons this becomes $(n + 1)$ peaks. In general, the relative intensity of each peak in the multiplet follows the coefficient of the binomial expansion $(a + b)^n$. These coefficients may conveniently be found by use of Pascal's triangle, which produces the following relative areas for the specified multiplets: doublet, 1:1; triplet, 1:2:1; quartet, 1:3:3:1; quintet, 1:4:6:4:1; sextet, 1:5:10:10:5:1; and septet, 1:6:15:20:15:6:1. This orderly arrangement, generally referred to as first-order behavior, may be expected when the ratio of Dv to J is greater than about 10; Dv is the chemical shift difference between two nuclei or two groups of equivalent nuclei. Two examples of idealized spectra arising from first-order coupling are shown in *Figure 4*.

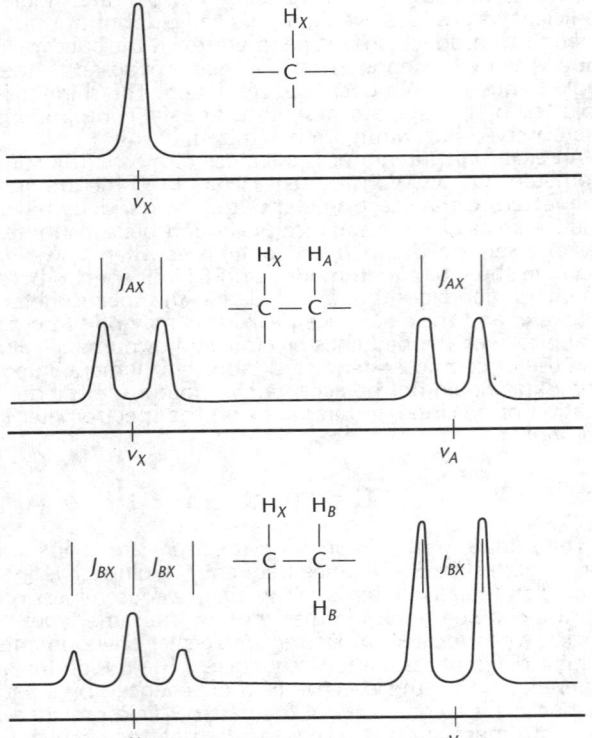

Fig. 4. Diagrammatic representation of simple first-order coupling of adjacent protons.

Figure 5 shows a spectrum displaying triplet signals resulting from the mutual splitting of two adjacent methylene groups.

Coupling may occur between ¹H and other nuclei, such as ¹⁹F, ¹³C, and ³¹P. In some cases, e.g., in the CW mode, the coupling constants may be large enough so that part of the multiplet is off scale at either the upfield or downfield end. This type of coupling may occur over the normal "three-bond distance," as for ¹H-¹H coupling.

Magnetically active nuclei with $I \geq 1$, such as ¹⁴N, possess an electrical quadrupole moment, which produces line-broadening of the signal due to neighboring nuclei.

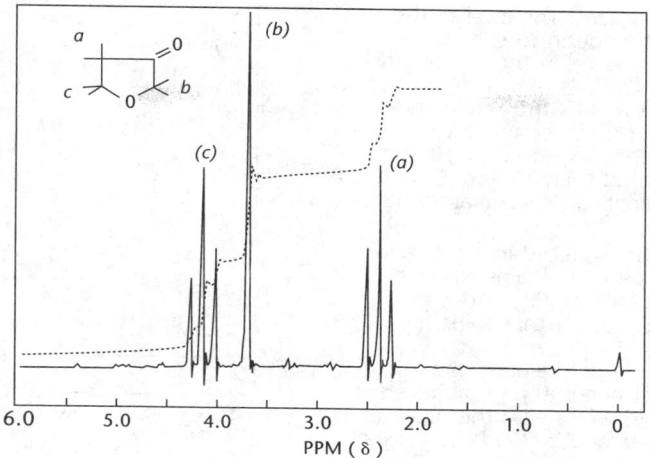

Fig. 5. NMR spectrum of 3-keto-tetrahydrofuran (10% in CCl$_4$) showing three nonequivalent protons, with a normal integral trace (peak area ratio from low H$_0$ to high H$_0$ of 1:1:1). Note two sets of methylene groups coupled to each other at 4.2 and 2.4 ppm. (Tetramethylsilane, the NMR Reference, appears at 0 ppm.)

Another characteristic of the signal, its relative intensity, has wide analytical applications. In carefully designed experiments (see the section *General Method*), the area or intensity of a signal is directly proportional to the number of protons giving rise to the signal. As a result, it is possible to determine the relative ratio of the different kinds of protons or other nuclei in a specimen or to perform NMR assays with the aid of an internal standard.

The NMR spectra may contain extraneous signals due to the inhomogeneity of the magnetic field throughout the specimen. These artifacts, called spinning side bands, appear as minor lines symmetrically located around each signal. The presence of large spinning side bands indicates that the non-spinning shims require adjustment. The separation is equal to the frequency of the specimen tube spin rate or some integral multiple of that frequency. Thus, spinning side bands are readily identifiable.

General Method

Inadequate specimen preparation or incorrect instrumental adjustments and parameters may lead to poor resolution, decreased sensitivity, spectral artifacts, and erroneous data. It is preferable that the operator be familiar with the basic theory of NMR, the properties of the specimen, and the operating principles of the instruments. Strict adherence to the instruction manuals provided by the manufacturer and frequent checks of the performance of the instrument are essential.

The method and procedures discussed here refer specifically to ^{1}H (proton) and ^{19}F NMR. They are applicable, with modification, to other nuclei. The discussion presumes that the NMR spectra are obtained from liquid test substances or solutions in suitable solvents.

Selection of Solvent—In addition to having good solubility properties, suitable solvents do not exhibit resonance peaks that obscure resonance peaks of the specimen being analyzed. The most commonly used solvents for proton and carbon NMR are listed in *Table 2*. Deuterated solvents also provide the signal for the heteronuclear system lock. If solvent peaks might interfere with any signals from the specimen, then the isotopic purity of the solvent should be as high as possible. Deuterium (I = 1) does not exhibit resonance under ^{1}H conditions but may cause J-coupling to be observed. The residual protons generate solvent peaks whose chemical shifts are shown in *Table 2*.

Table 2. Solvents Commonly Used for Proton NMR

Solvent	Residual Proton Signal, δ^a
CCl$_4^b$	—
CS$_2^b$	—
SO$_2$ (liquid)	—
(CF$_3$)$_2$CO	—
CDCl$_3$	7.27
CD$_3$OD	3.35, 4.8^c
(CD$_3$)$_2$CO	2.05
D$_2$O	4.7^c
DMSO-d_6^d	2.50
C$_6$D$_6$	7.20
p-Dioxane-d_8	3.55
CD$_3$CO$_2$D	2.05, 8.5^c
DMF-d_7^e	2.77, 2.93, 8.05

^{a} δ in ppm relative to tetramethylsilane arbitrarily taken as 0δ or 0 ppm.
^{b} Spectrophotometric grade.
^{c} Highly variable; depends on solute and temperature.
^{d} Dimethyl sulfoxide-d_6.
^{e} N,N-Dimethylformamide-d_7 per Aldrich, Alfa, Fluka, and Sigma catalogs.

Some solvents (e.g., D$_2$O or CD$_3$OD) enter into fast exchange reactions with protons and may eliminate resonance signals from –COOH, –OH, and –NH$_2$ structural groups. The protons in alcohols and amines do not take part in rapid exchange unless catalyzed by small concentrations of acid or base, except in the presence of D$_2$O and some other solvents (e.g., CD$_3$OD).

For ^{19}F NMR, most solvents used in proton NMR may be employed, the most common ones being CHCl$_3$, CCl$_4$, H$_2$O, CS$_2$, aqueous acids and bases, and dimethylacetamide. In general, any nonfluorinated solvent may be used, provided that it is of spectral quality. Obviously, there is no interference from the protonated functional groups of the solvent. However, unless they are decoupled, protonated functional groups on the ^{19}F-containing specimen will provide J-coupling.

Specimen Preparation—Directions are usually given in individual monographs. The solute concentration depends on the objective of the experiment and on the type of instrument. Detection of minor contaminants may require higher concentrations. The solutions are prepared in separate vials and transferred to the NMR specimen tube. The volume required depends on the size of the specimen tube and on the geometry of the instrument. The level of the solution in the tube must be high enough to extend beyond the coils when the tube is inserted in the instrument probe and spun.

The NMR specimen tubes must meet narrow tolerance specifications in diameter, wall thickness, concentricity, and camber. The most widely used tubes have a 5- or 10-mm outside diameter and a length of between 15 and 20 cm. Microtubes are available for the analysis of small amounts of specimen.

Procedure—The specimen tube is placed in a probe located in the magnetic field. The probe contains electronic circuitry including the radio-frequency coil(s), and is provided with attachments for the air supply that spins the specimen tubes.

Instrument adjustments are made before each experiment. The spinning rate of the specimen tube is adjusted so that spinning side bands do not interfere with the peaks of interest and the vortex does not extend beyond the coils in the probe. To optimize the instrument performance, the magnetic shim gradients on FT-NMR spectrometers are adjusted. In adjusting resolution on CW spectrometers, a good indicator is the definite "ringing" of the TMS peak. The phenomenon of ringing is the oscillation of the recorder trace after the magnetic field has passed through a resonance frequency. Ringing, evident on a number of the peaks in *Figures 5* and *6*, arises during rapid scans and decays exponentially to the baseline value.

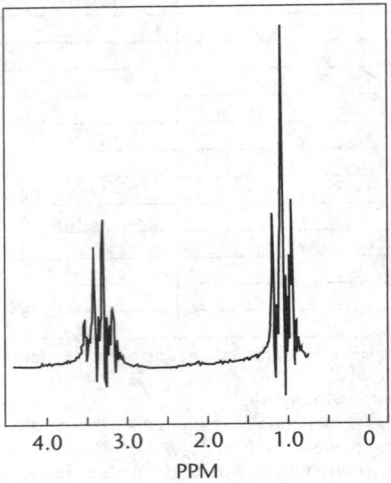

Fig. 6. Continuous wave proton spectrum of ethyl ether.

Figure 7 clearly indicates the absence, in an FT experiment, of the ringing phenomenon. Ringing will not appear because the spectrum obtained is the result of analysis of the FID by Fourier transformation and not a magnetic field or frequency sweep through the individual resonance positions.

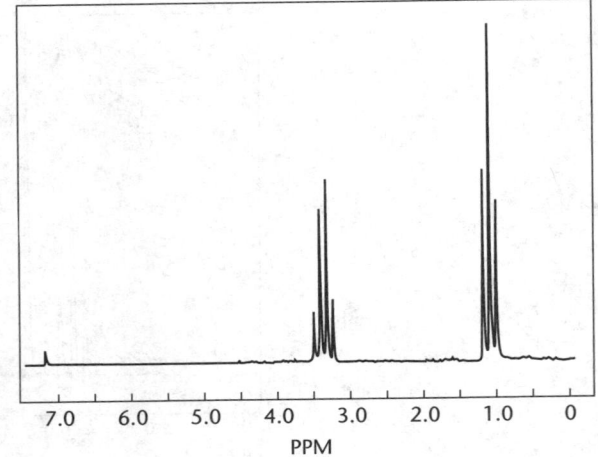

Fig. 7. Proton NMR spectrum of ethyl ether in deuterated chloroform.

With proton CW instruments the spectrum is scanned from 0 ppm to about 10 ppm with a scan time of about 1 to 5 minutes. The amplification is adjusted so that all peaks remain on scale. If the response is low at reasonable amplitude, the radio-frequency power is increased to obtain the highest possible peak response without peak broadening. After the initial scan, the presence of peaks downfield of 10 ppm is quickly checked by off-setting the instrument response by about 5 ppm. With CW instrumentation, it is common for the TMS peak to shift slightly during an extended scan. The extent of the shift is usually obtained by comparing the relative positions of another peak in the initial scan with the same peak in the offset scan.

The operation of an FT-NMR spectrometer is a much more elaborate experiment. The computer serves to control the spectrometer, to program the experiment, and to store and process the data. Programming the experiment involves setting values for a large number of variables including the spectral width to be examined, the duration ("width") of the excitation pulse, the time interval over which data will be acquired, the number of transients to be accumulated, and the delay between one acquisition and the next. The analysis time for one transient is in the order of seconds. The number of transients is a function of the specimen concentration, the type of nucleus, and the objective of the experiment. At the end of the experiment, the FID signal is stored in digitized form in the computer memory and is displayed on the video screen. The signal can be processed mathematically to enhance either the resolution or the sensitivity, and it can be Fourier-transformed into a frequency-domain spectrum. The instrument provides a plot of the spectrum. The integration routine, accessed through keyboard commands, results in a stepped-line plot. Considerably more accurate integrals are obtained if the signals or regions of interest are separately integrated.

FT-NMR spectrometers may yield qualitative and quantitative data from the same experiment, but this is seldom done in practice. In quantitative FT experiments, special precautions must be taken for the signal areas to be proportional to the number of protons. The delays between pulses must be long enough to allow complete relaxation of all excited nuclei. This results in a considerable increase in analysis time and in some loss of resolution. Qualitative analysis is usually performed in nonquantitative conditions, with the design of the experiment directed to fast analysis with maximum resolution or sensitivity.

Qualitative and Quantitative Analysis

NMR spectroscopy has been used for a wide range of applications such as structure elucidation; thermodynamic, kinetic, and mechanistic studies; and quantitative analysis. Some of these applications are beyond the scope of compendial methods.

All five characteristics of the signal—chemical shift, multiplicity, line width, coupling constants, and relative intensity—contribute analytical information.

Qualitative Applications—Comparison of a spectrum from the literature or from an authentic specimen with that of a test specimen may be used to confirm the identity of a compound and to detect the presence of impurities that generate extraneous signals. The NMR spectra of simple structures can be adequately described by the numeric value of the chemical shifts and coupling constants, and by the number of protons under each signal. (The software of modern instruments includes programs that generate simulated spectra using these data.) Experimental details, such as the solvent used, the specimen concentration, and the chemical shift reference, must also be provided.

For unknown specimens, NMR analysis, usually coupled with other analytical techniques, is a powerful tool for structure elucidation. Chemical shifts provide information on the chemical environment of the nuclei. Extensive literature is available with correlation charts and rules for predicting chemical shifts. The multiplicity of the signals provides important stereochemical information. Mutual signal splitting of functional groups indicates close proximity. The magnitude of the coupling constant, J, between residual protons on substituted aromatic, olefinic, or cycloalkyl structures is used to identify the relative position of the substituents.

Several special techniques (double resonance, chemical exchange, use of shift reagents, two-dimensional analysis, etc.) are available to simplify some of the more complex spectra, to identify certain functional groups, and to determine coupling correlations.

Double resonance, or spin decoupling, is a technique that removes the coupling between nuclei and thus simplifies the spectrum and identifies the components in a coupling relationship. For example, in a simple two-proton system, generally designated an AX system (see *Figure 4*), each proton appears as a doublet. If a strong radio-frequency field is introduced at the frequency of X, while the normal radio-frequency field is maintained at the frequency that causes A to resonate, the coupling between A and X is removed (homonuclear decoupling). A is no longer split, but instead appears as a singlet. Routine ^{13}C spectra are obtained under proton decoupling conditions that remove all heteronuclear ^{13}C-^{1}H couplings. As a result of this decoupling, the carbon signals appear as singlets, unless other nuclei that are not decoupled are present (e.g., ^{19}F, ^{31}P).

Functional groups containing exchangeable protons bound to hetero-atoms such as –OH, –NH$_2$, or –COOH groups may be identified by taking advantage of the rapid exchange of these protons with D$_2$O. To determine the presence and position of these groups, scan the test substance in CDCl$_3$ or DMSO-d_6, then add a few drops of D$_2$O to the specimen tube, shake, and scan again. The resonance peaks from these groups collapse in the second scan and are replaced by the HDO singlet between 4.7 and 5.0 ppm.

This *chemical exchange* is an example of the effect of intermolecular and intramolecular rate processes on NMR spectra. If a proton can experience different environments by virtue of such a process (tautomerism, rotation about a bond, exchange equilibria, ring inversion, etc.), the appearance of the spectrum will be a function of the rate of the process. Slow processes (on an NMR time scale) result in more than one signal, fast processes average these signals to one line, and intermediate processes produce broad signals.

The software of modern FT-NMR spectrometers allows for sequences of pulses much more complex than the repetitive accumulation of transients described above. Such experiments include homonuclear or heteronuclear *two-dimensional analysis*, which determines the correlation of couplings and may simplify the interpretation of otherwise complex spectra.

Quantitative Applications—If appropriate instrument settings for quantitative analysis have been made, the areas (or intensities) of two signals are proportional to the total number of protons generating the signals.

$$A_1/A_2 = N_1/N_2 \quad (1)$$

If the two signals originate from two functional groups of the same molecule, the equation can be simplified to

$$A_1/A_2 = n_1/n_2 \quad (2)$$

in which n_1 and n_2 are the number of protons in the respective functional groups.

If the two signals originate from different molecular species,

$$A_1/A_2 = n_1 m_1 / n_2 m_2 = (n_1 W_1/M_1)/(n_2 W_2/M_2) \quad (3)$$

where m_1 and m_2 are the numbers of moles; W_1 and W_2 are the masses; and M_1 and M_2 are the molecular weights of compounds 1 and 2, respectively.

Examination of *Equations 2* and *3* shows that NMR quantitative analysis can be performed in an absolute or relative manner. In the absolute method, an internal standard is added to the specimen and a resonance peak area arising from the test substance is compared with a resonance peak area from the internal standard. If both test substance and internal standard are accurately weighed, the absolute purity of the substance may be calculated. A good internal standard has the following properties: it presents a reference resonance peak, preferably a singlet, at a field position removed from all specimen peaks; it is soluble in the analytical solvent; its proton equivalent weight, i.e., the molecular weight divided by the number of protons giving rise to the reference peak, is low; and it does not interact with the compound being tested. Typical examples of useful standards are 1,2,4,5-tetrachlorobenzene, 1,4-dinitrobenzene, benzyl benzoate, and maleic acid. The choice of a standard will be dictated by the spectrum of the specimen.

The relative method may be used to determine the molar fraction of an impurity in a test substance (or of the components in a mixture) as calculated by *Equation 3*.

Quantitative analysis, as well as detection of trace impurities, is markedly improved with modern instrumentation. Stronger magnetic fields and the ability to accumulate and/or average signals over long periods of time greatly enhance the sensitivity of the method.

Absolute Method of Quantitation—Where the individual monograph directs that the *Absolute Method of Quantitation* be employed, proceed as follows.

Solvent, Internal Standard, and *NMR Reference*—Use as directed in the individual monograph.

Test Preparation—Transfer an accurately weighed quantity of the test substance, containing about 4.5 proton mEq, to a glass-stoppered, graduated centrifuge tube. Add about 4.5 proton mEq of *Internal Standard*, accurately weighed, and 3.0 mL of *Solvent*, insert the stopper, and shake. When dissolution is complete, add about 30 µL (30 mg if a solid) of *NMR Reference*, provided that it does not interfere with subsequent measurements, and shake.

Procedure—Transfer an appropriate amount (0.4 to 0.8 mL) of *Test Preparation* to a standard 5-mm NMR spinning tube, and record the spectrum, adjusting the spin rate so that no spinning side bands interfere with the peaks of interest. Measure the area under each of the peaks specified in the individual monograph by integrating not fewer than five times. Record the average area of the *Internal Standard* peak as A_S and that of the *Test Preparation* peak as A_U.

Calculate the quantity, in mg, of the analyte in the *Test Preparation* by the formula:

$$W_S(A_U/A_S)(E_U/E_S)$$

in which W_S is the weight, in mg, of *Internal Standard* taken; and E_U and E_S are the proton equivalent weights (i.e., the molecular weights divided by the number of protons giving rise to the reference peak) of the analyte and the *Internal Standard*, respectively.

Relative Method of Quantitation—Where the individual monograph directs that the *Relative Method of Quantitation* be employed, proceed as follows.

Solvent, NMR Reference, and *Test Preparation*—Use as directed under *Absolute Method of Quantitation*.

Procedure—Transfer an appropriate amount (0.4 to 0.8 mL) of *Test Preparation* to a standard 5-mm NMR spinning tube, and record the spectrum, adjusting the spin rate so that no spinning side bands interfere with the peaks of interest. Measure the area or intensity under each of the peaks specified in the individual monograph by integrating not fewer than five times. Record the average area or intensity resulting from the resonances of the groups designated in the individual monograph as A_1 and A_2.

Calculate the quantity, in mole percent, of the analyte in the *Test Preparation* by the formula:

$$(100 \times (A_1/n_1)/((A_1/n_1) + (A_2/n_2))$$

in which n_1 and n_2 are, respectively, the numbers of protons in the designated groups.

RADIOACTIVITY*

GENERAL CONSIDERATIONS

Fundamental Decay Law

The decay of a radioactive source is described by the equation:

$$N_t = N_0 e^{-\lambda t}$$

in which N_t is the number of atoms of a radioactive substance at elapsed time t, N_0 is the number of those atoms when t = 0, and λ is the transformation or decay constant, which has a characteristic value for each radionuclide. The *half-life*, $T_{1/2}$, is the time interval required for a given activity of a radionuclide to decay to one-half of its initial value, and is related to the decay constant by the equation:

$$T_{1/2} = 0.69315/\lambda$$

The activity of a radioactive source (A) is related to the number of radioactive atoms present by the equation:

$$A = \lambda N$$

from which the number of radioactive atoms at time t can be computed, and hence the mass of the radioactive material can be determined.

The activity of a pure radioactive substance as a function of time can be obtained from the exponential equation or from decay tables, or by graphical means based on the half-life (see *Normalized Decay Chart, Figure 1*).

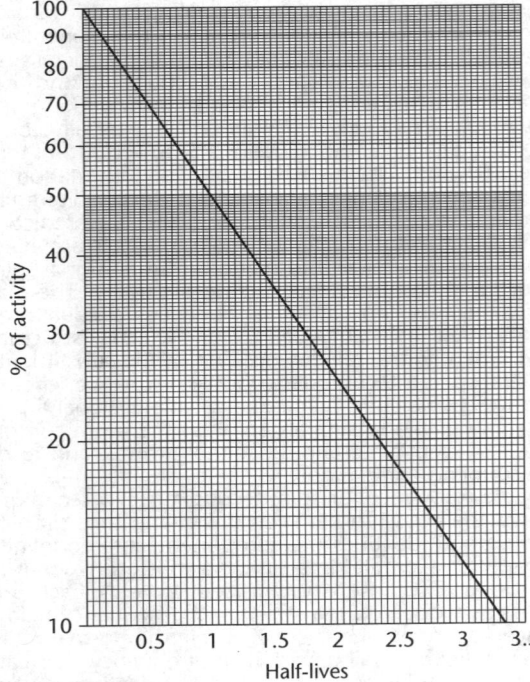

Fig. 1. Normalized Decay Chart.

The activity of a radioactive material is expressed as the number of nuclear transformations per unit time. The fundamental unit of radioactivity, the *curie* (Ci), is defined as 3.700×10^{10} nuclear transformations per second. The *millicurie* (mCi) and *microcurie* (μCi) are commonly used subunits. The "number of nuclear transformations per unit time" is the sum of rates of decay from all competing modes of disintegration of the parent nuclide. Before the activity of any given radionuclide in a measured specimen can be expressed in curies, it is often necessary to know the abundance(s) of the emitted radiation(s) measured.

Geometry

The validity of relative calibration and measurement of radionuclides is dependent upon the reproducibility of the relationship of the source to the detector and its surroundings. Appropriate allowance must be made for source configuration.

---

* This text is adapted from General Chapter ⟨821⟩ of the *United States Pharmacopeia and National Formulary* (*USP–NF*) as published in *USP 32–NF 27*. This text is provided for informational purposes only and is intended as a resource for the FCC user. Note that because the *USP–NF* is in continuous revision, this General Chapter is subject to change and the text printed here may not continue to represent the current version.

Background

Cosmic rays, radioactivity present in the detector and shielding materials, and radiation from nearby radioactive sources not properly shielded from the measuring equipment, all contribute to the background count rate. All radioactivity measurements must be corrected by subtracting the background count rate from the gross count rate in the test specimen.

Statistics of Counting

Since the process of radioactive decay is a random phenomenon, the events being counted form a random sequence in time. Therefore, counting for any finite time can yield only an estimate of the true counting rate. The precision of this estimate, being subject to statistical fluctuations, is dependent upon the number of counts accumulated in a given measurement and can be expressed in terms of the standard deviation σ. An *estimate* for σ is

$$\sqrt{n}$$

where n is the number of counts accumulated in a given measurement. The probability of a single measurement falling within

$$\pm 100/\sqrt{n}\%$$

of the mean of a great many measurements is 0.68. That is, if many measurements of n counts each were to be made, approximately two-thirds of the observations would lie within

$$\pm 100/\sqrt{n}\%$$

of the mean, and the remainder outside.

Because of the statistical nature of radioactive decay, repeated counting of an undisturbed source in a counting assembly will yield count-rate values in accordance with the frequency of a normal distribution. Deviations in these values from the normal distribution conform to the χ^2 test. For this reason, the χ^2 test is frequently applied to determine the performance and correct operation of a counting assembly. In the selection of instruments and conditions for assay of radioactive sources, the figure of merit ϵ^2/B should be maximized (where ϵ = counter efficiency = observed count rate/sample disintegration rate, and B = background count rate).

Counting Losses

The minimum time interval that is required for the counter to resolve two consecutive signal pulses is known as the dead time. The dead time varies typically from the order of microseconds for proportional and scintillation counters, to hundreds of microseconds for Geiger-Müller counters. Nuclear events occurring within the dead time of the counter will not be registered. To obtain the corrected count rate, R, from the observed count rate, r, it is necessary to use the formula:

$$R = r/(1 - r\tau)$$

in which τ is the dead time. The foregoing correction formula assumes a nonextendable dead time. Thus, for general validity, the value of $r\tau$ should not exceed 0.1. The observed count rate, r, refers to the gross specimen count rate and is not to be corrected for background before use in the foregoing equation.

Calibration Standards

Perform all radioactivity assays using measurement systems calibrated with appropriately certified radioactivity standards. Such calibration standards may be purchased either direct from the National Institute of Standards and Technology or from other sources that have established traceability to the National Institute of Standards and Technology through participation in a program of inter-comparative measurements. These data, as well as half-life values, are obtained from the Evaluated Nuclear Structure Data File of the Oak Ridge Nuclear Data Project, and reflect the most recent values at the time of publication.

IDENTIFICATION AND ASSAY OF RADIONUCLIDES

Instrumentation

IONIZATION CHAMBERS

An ionization chamber is an instrument in which an electric field is applied across a volume of gas for the purpose of collecting ions produced by a radiation field. The positive ions and negative electrons drift along the lines of force of the electric field, and are collected on electrodes, producing an ionization current. In a properly designed well-type ionization chamber, the ionization current should not be too dependent on the position of the radioactive specimen, and the value of the current per unit activity, known as the calibration factor, is characteristic of each gamma-ray-emitting radionuclide.

The ionization current produced in an ionization chamber is related to the mean energy of the emitted radiation and is proportional to the intensity of the radiation. If standard sources of known disintegration rates are used for efficiency calibration, the ionization chamber may then be used for activity determinations between several microcuries and several hundred millicuries or more. The upper limit of activity that may be measured in an ionization chamber usually is not sharply defined and may be limited by saturation considerations, range of the amplifier, and design of the chamber itself. The data supplied with or obtained from a particular instrument should be reviewed to ascertain the useful ranges of energies and intensities of the device.

Reproducibility within approximately 5% or less can be readily obtained in about 10 seconds, with a deep re-entrant well-type chamber. One of the most commonly used form of ionization chamber is known as a dose calibrator.

Although the calibration factor for a radionuclide may be interpolated from an ionization chamber energy-response curve, there are a number of sources of error possible in such a procedure. It is therefore recommended that all ionization chamber calibrations be performed with the use of authentic reference sources of the individual radionuclides, as described hereinafter.

The calibration of a dose calibrator should be maintained by relating the measured response of a standard to that of a long-lived performance standard, such as radium 226 in equilibrium with its daughters. The instrument must be checked daily with the ^{226}Ra or other source to ascertain the stability over a long period of time. This check should include performance standard readings at all radionuclide settings employed. To obtain the activity (A_x) of the radionuclide being measured, use the relationship:

$$A_x = R_x R/R_n$$

in which R_n is the new reading for the radium or other source, R_c is the reading for the same source obtained during the initial calibration procedure, and R is the observed reading for the radionuclide specimen. Obviously, any necessary corrections for radioactive decay of the reference source must first be applied. Use of this procedure should minimize any effects due to drift in the response of the instrument. The recommended activity of the ^{226}Ra or other monitor used in the procedure described above is 75 to 150 µCi. It is recommended also that the reproducibility and/or stability of multirange instruments be checked for all ranges with the use of appropriate standards.

The size and shape of a radioactive source may affect the response of a dose calibrator, and it is often necessary to apply a small correction when measuring a bulky specimen.

SCINTILLATION and SEMICONDUCTOR DETECTORS

When all or part of the energy of beta or gamma radiation is dissipated within scintillators, photons of intensity proportional to the amount of dissipated energy are produced. These pulses are detected by an electron multiplier phototube and converted to electrical pulses, which are subsequently analyzed with a pulse-height analyzer to yield a pulse-height spectrum related to the energy spectrum of the radiation emitted by the source. In general, a beta-particle scintillation pulse-height spectrum approximates the true beta-energy spectrum, provided that the beta-particle source is prepared in such a manner that self-absorption is minimized. Beta-ray spectra may be obtained by using calcium fluoride or anthracene as the scintillator, whereas gamma-ray spectra are usually obtained with a thallium-activated sodium iodide crystal or a large-volume lithium-drifted germanium semiconductor detector. The spectra of charged particles also may be obtained using silicon semiconductor detectors and/or gas proportional counters. Semiconductor detectors are in essence solid-state ionization chambers, but the energy required to create an electron-hole pair or to promote an electron from the valence band to the conduction band in the semiconductor is about one-tenth the energy required for creation of an ion-pair in a gas-filled ionization chamber or proportional counter and is far less than the energy needed to produce a photon in a NaI(Tl) scintillation crystal. In gamma-ray spectrometry, a Ge(Li) detector can yield an energy resolution of 0.33% for 1.33 MeV gamma-rays from ^{60}Co, while a 3- × 3-inch NaI(Tl) crystal can give a value of 5.9% for the same gamma-ray energy. The energy resolution is a measure of the ability to distinguish the presence of two gamma rays closely spaced in energy and is defined by convention as the full width of the photopeak at its half maximum (FWHM), expressed in percentage of the photopeak energy.

Gamma-ray spectra exhibit one or more sharp, characteristic photopeaks, or full-energy peaks, as a result of total absorption in the detector of the full energy of gamma radiations from the source; these photopeaks are useful for identification purposes. Other secondary peaks are observed as a consequence of backscatter, annihilation radiation, coincidence summing, fluorescent X-rays, etc., accompanied by a broad band known as the Compton continuum arising from scattering of the photons in the detector and from surrounding materials. Since the photopeak response varies with gamma-ray energy, calibration of a gamma-ray spectrometer should be achieved with radionuclide standards having well-known gamma-ray energies and emission rates. The shape of the gamma-ray spectrum is dependent upon the shape and size of the detector and the types of shielding materials used.

When confirming the identity of a radionuclide by gamma-ray spectrometry, it is necessary to make a comparison of the specimen spectrum with that of a specimen of known purity of the same radionuclide obtained under *identical instrument parameters and specimen geometry*. Where the radionuclides emit coincident X- or gamma-radiations, the character of the pulse-height distribution often changes quite dramatically because of the summing effect of these coincident radiations in the detector as the efficiency of detection is increased (e.g., by bringing the source closer to the detector). Such an effect is particularly evident in the case of iodine 125. Among the more useful applications of gamma-ray spectrometry are those for the identification of radionuclides and the determination of radionuclidic impurities.

Where confirmation of the identity of a given radionuclide by means of a direct comparison with the spectrum of a specimen of the same radionuclide of known purity is not possible, the identity of the radionuclide in question must then be established by the following method. Two or more of the following nuclear decay scheme parameters of the radionuclide specimen to be identified shall be measured, and agreement shall be within ±10%: (1) half-life, (2) energy of each gamma- or X-ray emitted, (3) the abundance of each emission, and (4) E_{max} for those radionuclides that decay with beta-particle emissions. Such measurements are to be performed as directed in the *Identification* and *Assay* sections of this chapter. Agreement of two or more of the measured parameters with the corresponding published nuclear decay scheme data constitutes confirmation of the identity of the radionuclide.

LIQUID-SCINTILLATION COUNTERS

Alpha- and beta-emitting radionuclides may be assayed with the use of a liquid-scintillation detector system. In the liquid scintillator, the radiation energy is ultimately converted into light quanta that are usually detected by two multiplier phototubes so arranged as to count only coincidence radiation. The liquid scintillator is a solution consisting of a solvent, primary and secondary solutes, and additives. The charged particle dissipates its energy in the solvent, and a fraction of this energy is converted into fluorescence in the primary soluté. The function of the secondary solute is to shift the fluorescence radiation to longer wavelengths that are more efficiently detected by the multiplier phototubes. Frequently used solvents are toluene and p-xylene; primary solutes are 2,5-diphenyloxazole (PPO) and 2-(4'-tert-butylphenyl)-5-(4-biphenylyl)-1,3,4-oxadiazole (butyl-PBD); and secondary solutes are 2,2'-p-phenylenebis[4-methyl-5-phenyloxazole] (dimethyl-POPOP) and p-bis(o-methylstrylyl)benzene (bis-MSB). As a means of attaining compatibility and miscibility with aqueous specimens to be assayed, many additives, such as surfactants and solubilizing agents, are also incorporated into the scintillator. For an accurate determination of radioactivity of the specimen, care must be exercised to prepare a specimen that is truly homogeneous. The presence of impurities or color in solution causes a decrease in photon output of the scintillator; such a decrease is known as quenching. Accurate radioactivity measurement requires correcting for count-rate loss due to quenching.

The disintegration rate of a beta-particle source may be determined by a procedure in which the integral count rate of the specimen is measured as a function of the pulse-height discriminator bias, and the emission rate is then obtained by extrapolation to zero bias. Energetic alpha-particle emitters may be similarly measured by this method.

Identification

A radionuclide can be identified by its mode of decay, its half-life, and the energies of its nuclear emissions.

The radioactive half-life is readily determined by successive counting of a given source of the radionuclide over a period of time that is long compared to its half-life. The response of the counting assembly when employed for the decay measurement of long-lived radionuclides should be monitored with an even longer-lived reference source to assess and compensate for errors arising from electronic drift. In the case of short-lived radionuclides, when the counting period constitutes a significant fraction of the half-life of the radionuclide, the recorded count rate must be corrected to the time when the count is initiated, as follows:

$$R_t = r\lambda t/(1 - e^{-\lambda t})$$

in which R_t is the count rate at the beginning of a counting period, r is the count rate observed over the entire counting period, t is the duration of the counting period, λ is the decay constant of the radionuclide, and e is the base of the natural logarithm. When t is small compared to the half-life of the radionuclide under study so that $\lambda t < 0.05$, then $(1 - e^{-\lambda t})$ approaches λt, and no such correction is necessary.

The energy of nuclear emissions is often determined by the maximum range of penetration of the radiation in matter (in the case of alpha- and beta-particles) and by the full-energy peak or photopeak in the gamma-ray spectrum (in the case of X- and gamma-rays). Since beta-particles are emitted with a continuous energy spectrum, the maximum beta-energy, E_{max}, is a unique index for each beta-emitting radionuclide. In addition to the maximum range and energy spectrum of the beta-particles, the absorption coefficient, when obtained under reproducible counting conditions, can serve as a reliable index for identification of a beta-emitter. Fortuitously, beta-particles are absorbed in matter in an approximately exponential manner, and a plot of the logarithm of the beta-particle count rate as a function of the absorber thickness is known as the absorption curve. The initial portion of the absorption curve shows linearity from which the absorption coefficient can be obtained. The maximum range is determined by the use of absorbers of varying thickness, and the energy spectrum is measured by beta-ray scintillation spectrometry.

The absorption of gamma-rays in matter is strictly exponential, but the half-value layers of attenuation have not been very useful for the purpose of radionuclide characterization. Gamma-rays from each isomeric transition are monoenergetic; their energy can be directly measured by gamma-ray spectrometry. Because of their high energy resolution, solid-state detectors [Ge(Li)] are vastly superior to scintillation detectors [NaI(Tl)] in gamma-ray spectrometry.

BETA-EMITTING RADIONUCLIDES

Mass Absorption Coefficient Procedure—Deposit and dry an aliquot of the radioactive phosphorus 32 solution on a thin plastic film to minimize backscattering, and place it under a suitable counter. Determine the counting rates successively, using not less than six different "thicknesses" of aluminum each between 20 and 50 mg/cm² and a single absorber thicker than 800 mg/cm², which is used to measure the background. (The absorbers are inserted between the test specimen and the counter but are placed nearer the counter window to minimize scattering.) Net beta-particle count rates are obtained after subtraction of the count rate found with the absorber having a thickness of 800 mg/cm² or greater. Plot the logarithm of the net beta-particle count rate as a function of the total absorber "thickness." The total absorber "thickness" is the "thickness" of the aluminum absorbers plus the "thickness" of the counter window (as stated by the manufacturer) plus the air-equivalent "thickness" (the distance in centimeters of the specimen from the counter window multiplied by 1.205 mg/cm³ at 20° and 76 cm of mercury), all expressed in mg/cm². An approximately straight line results.

Choose two total absorber "thicknesses" that differ by 20 mg/cm² or more and that fall on the linear plot, and calculate the mass absorption coefficient, μ, by the equation:

$$\mu = 1/(t_2 - t_1) \cdot \ln(N_{t_1}/N_{t_2}) = (2.303/(t_2 - t_1)) \times (\log N_{t_1} - \log N_{t_2})$$

in which t_1 and t_2 represent the total absorber "thicknesses," in mg/cm², t_2 being the thicker absorber, and N_{t_1} and N_{t_2} being the net beta-particle rates with the t_1 and t_2 absorbers, respectively.

For characterization of the radionuclide, the mass absorption coefficient should be within ±5% of the value found for a pure specimen of the same radionuclide when determined under identical counting conditions and geometry.

Other Methods of Identification—Other methods for determining the identity of a beta emitter also rely upon the determination of E_{max}. This may be accomplished in several ways. For example, (1) utilization of the range energy relationships of beta particles in an absorber, or (2) determination of E_{max} from a beta-particle spectrum obtained on an energy-calibrated beta-spectrometer using a thin source of the radionuclide (see *Scintillation and Semiconductor Detectors* in this chapter).

GAMMA-EMITTING RADIONUCLIDES

The gamma-ray spectrum of a radionuclide is a valuable tool for the qualitative identification of gamma-ray emitting radionuclides. The full-energy peak, or the photopeak, is identified with the gamma-ray transition energy that is given in the decay scheme of the radionuclide.

In determining radionuclidic identity and purity, the gamma-ray spectrum of a radioactive substance is obtained with either a NaI(Tl) crystal or a semiconductor Ge(Li) detector. The latter has an energy resolution more than an order of magnitude better than the former and is highly preferred for analytical purposes. The spectrum obtained shall be identical in shape to that of a specimen of the pure radionuclide, measured with the same detection system and in the same geometry. For low geometrical efficiencies, the areas under the photopeaks, after correction for the measured detector efficiency, shall be proportional to the abundances or emission rates of the respective gamma-rays in the radionuclide.

RADIONUCLIDIC IMPURITIES

Procedures for identifying beta- and gamma-active radionuclides as given in the foregoing text are applicable to the detection of gamma and usually beta contaminants.

The gross alpha-particle activity can be measured by the use of a windowless proportional counter or a scintillation detector employing a silver-activated zinc-sulfide phosphor or by the techniques of liquid-scintillation counting.

The heavy ionization caused by alpha particles allows the measurement of alpha-emitting radionuclides in the presence of large quantities of beta- and gamma-active nuclides by the use of appropriate techniques for discriminating the amplitudes of signal pulses. In proportional counting, the operating voltage region for counting alpha particles, referred to as the "alpha plateau," is considerably lower than the "beta plateau" for counting beta and gamma radiations. Typical "alpha plateau" and "beta plateau" voltage settings with P-10 counting gas are 900 to 1300 and 1600 to 2000 volts, respectively.

When silver-activated zinc-sulfide phosphor is employed for alpha-particle detection, the alpha particles can be distinguished from other interfering radiation by pulse-height discrimination. Care must be exercised to minimize self-absorption at the source whenever specimens are prepared for alpha-particle counting.

Assay

BETA-EMITTING RADIONUCLIDES

Procedure—The disintegration rate (A) of a beta-particle-emitting specimen is obtained by counting a quantitatively deposited aliquot in a fixed geometry according to the formula:

$$A = R/(\varepsilon \times f_r \times f_b \times f_s)$$

in which ε is the counting efficiency of the counter; f_r is the correction factor for counter dead time; f_b is the correction factor for backscatter; and f_s is the correction factor for self-absorption. The count rate for zero absorber is obtained by extrapolation of the initial linear portion of the absorption curve to zero absorber "thickness," taking into consideration the mg/cm^2 "thickness" of specimen coverings, counter window, and the intervening air space between specimen and the counter window. The counter efficiency, ε, is determined by use of a long-lived secondary standard with similar spectral characteristics. RaD + E has frequently been used for efficiency calibration of counters for phosphorus 32. By the use of identical measurement conditions for the specimen and the standard (and extrapolation to zero absorber), the ratio of the values of f_r, f_b, and f_s for the standard and the specimen approaches unity.

The previous relationship is valid also when the counter has been calibrated with a standard of the radionuclide to be assayed. In this case, however, the extrapolations to zero absorber "thickness" for the specimen and standard are not required, as the two absorption corrections cancel for a given geometry.

Another useful and frequently employed method for the determination of the disintegration rate of beta-emitting radionuclides is liquid-scintillation counting, which also utilizes an extrapolation of the specimen count rate to zero pulse-height discriminator bias.

GAMMA-EMITTING RADIONUCLIDES

For the assay of gamma-emitting radionuclides, three methods are provided. The selection of the preferred method is dictated by the availability of a calibration standard of the radionuclide to be assayed and the radionuclidic purity of the article itself.

Direct comparison with a calibration standard is required if a calibration standard of the radionuclide to be assayed is available and if the upper limit of conceivable error in the activity determination arising from the presence of radionuclidic impurities has been determined to be less than 3%. If the required calibration standard is not routinely available, as would probably be the case for a short-lived radionuclide, but was available at some time prior to the performance of the assay for determination of efficiency of the counting system for the radionuclide to be assayed, use a calibrated counting system, provided the radionuclidic impurity content of the specimen meets the requirements stated for the direct comparison method. If the requirements for either of the first two methods cannot be met, use the method for determination of activity from a calibration curve.

With the exception of the first method, the counting systems used are monitored for stability. This requirement is met by daily checks with a long-lived performance check source and weekly checks with at least three sources covering a broad range of gamma-ray emission energies (e.g., ^{57}Co, ^{137}Cs, and ^{60}Co). If a discrepancy for any of the aforementioned measurements is found, either completely recalibrate or repair and recalibrate the system prior to further use.

Assay by Direct Comparison with a Calibration Standard—An energy selective measurement system (e.g., pulse-height analyzer) is not required for this procedure. Use either an ionization chamber or an integral counting system with a NaI(Tl) detector. A consistently reproducible geometrical factor from specimen to specimen is essential for accurate results. With proper precautions, the accuracy of this method approaches the accuracy with which the disintegration rate of the calibration standard is known.

Determine the counting rate of the detector system for a calibration standard of the radionuclide to be assayed (e.g., active enough to give good measurement statistics in a reasonable time, but not so active as to cause serious dead-time problems), selecting such a standard as to provide optimum accuracy with the particular assembly used. Place an accurately measured aliquot of the unknown assay specimen (diluted, if necessary) in a container identical to that used for the standard, and measure this specimen at approximately the same time and under the same geometrical conditions as for the standard. If the elapsed time between the measurements of the calibration standard and the specimen exceeds 12 hours, check the stability of the measurement system within 8 hours of the specimen measurement time with a long-lived performance check source. Record the system response with respect to the same check source at the time of calibration, and if subsequent checks exceed the original recorded response by more than ±3%, recalibration is required. Correct both activity determinations for background, and calculate the activity, in µCi per mL, by the formula:

$$SD(g/b)$$

in which S is the µCi strength of the standard, D is the dilution factor, and g and b are the measured values of counting rate for the specimen and the standard, respectively.

Assay with a Calibrated Integral Counting System—The procedure and precautions given for the preceding direct-comparison method apply, except that the efficiency of the detector system is determined and recorded for each radionuclide to be assayed, rather than simply recording the counting rate of the standard. Thus, the efficiency for a given radionuclide, x, is determined by $\varepsilon_x = b_x/s_x$, in which b_x is the counting rate, corrected for background and dead-time, for the calibration standard of the radionuclide, x, and s_x is the corresponding activity of the certified calibration standard in nuclear transformations per second. For subsequent specimen assays, the activity is given by the formula:

$$A_x = Dg_x/\varepsilon_x$$

in which D is the dilution factor, g_x is the specimen counting rate (corrected for background and dead-time), and ε_x is the corresponding efficiency for the radionuclide.

Determination of Activity from a Calibration Curve—Versatility in absolute gamma-ray intensity measurements can be achieved by employing multi-channel pulse-height analysis. The photopeak efficiency of a detector system can be determined as a function of gamma-ray energy by means of a series of gamma-ray emission rate standard specimens, and the gamma-ray emission rate of any radionuclide for which no standard is available can be determined by interpolation from this efficiency curve. However, exercise care to ensure that the efficiency curve for the detector system is adequately defined over the entire region of interest by using a sufficient number of calibration points along the photopeak-energy axis.

Procedure—Minimal requirements for the maintenance of instrument calibrations shall consist of weekly performance checks with a suitable reference source and a complete recalibration semi-annually. Should the weekly performance check deviate from the value determined at the time of calibration by more than 4.0%, a complete recalibration of the instrument is required at that time.

This method involves three basic steps, namely photopeak integration, determination of the photopeak efficiency curve, and calculation of the activity of the specimen.

PHOTOPEAK INTEGRATION—The method for the determination of the required photopeak area utilizes a Gaussian approximation for fitting the photopeak. A fixed fraction of the total number of photopeak counts can be obtained by taking the peak width, a, at some fraction of the maximum, where the shape has been experimentally found to be very close to Gaussian, and multiplying by the counting rate of the peak channel, P, after correction for any Compton and background contributions to the peak channel count rate. This background usually can be adequately determined by linear interpolation. This is illustrated in *Figure 2*.

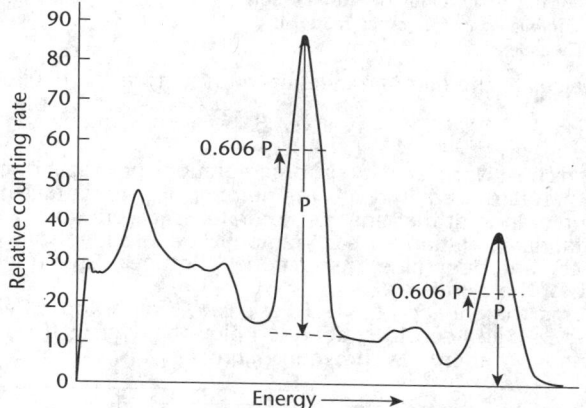

Fig. 2 Typical Gamma-ray Spectrum Showing the Selection of the Peak Channel Counting Rate, P, after the Correction for Compton and Background Contributions.

The photopeak-curve shape is closest to a straight line at 0.606P, and the contribution of the fractional channels to a can be accurately estimated by interpolation. Calculate a by the equation:

$$a = D' - D + (d - 0.606P)/(d - c) + (d' - 0.606P)/(d' - c')$$

in which c and d and also c' and d' are the single *channel counting* rates on either side of 0.606P, and D and D' are the channel *numbers* (locations) of d and d', respectively. The location of the required variables on the photopeak is illustrated in *Figure 3*.

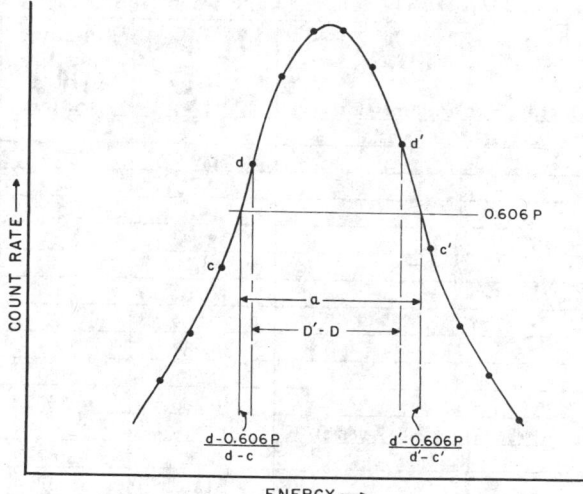

Fig. 3. Location of the Variables Required for the Determination of the Peak Width, a, at 0.606P.

From the known values for the counting rate in the peak channel of the photopeak, P, and the width of the peak at 0.606P, a, a calibrated fraction of the photopeak area is then obtained from the product, (aP).

To summarize the procedures involved in obtaining a calibrated fraction of a photopeak area using this method, the necessary steps or calculations are presented below in a stepwise manner:

(1) Subtract any Compton and background contributions from the photopeak to be measured.

(2) Determine the counting rate of the peak channel (maximum channel counting rate after subtracting Compton and background), P.

(3) Multiply P by 0.606, and locate the horizontal line corresponding to the peak width, a.

(4) Obtain the peak width, a, by inserting the values of variables (obtained as shown in the preceding figure) into the equation defining a.

(5) The desired calibrated fraction of the peak area is then equal to the product of a times P or F = aP, where F is a fractional area of the peak proportional to the emission rate of the source.

This method provides a quick and accurate means of determining the gamma-ray emission rate of sources while avoiding, to a large extent, subjective estimates of the detailed shape of the tails of the peaks. The error due to using the maximum channel counting rate, rather than the theoretical maximum or peak channel rate, is of the order of 1.0% if a is 6 or greater.

PHOTOPEAK EFFICIENCY CALIBRATION—Radionuclides such as those listed in the accompanying table together with some of their nuclear decay data are available as certified reference standards.* A sufficient number of radioactive standard reference sources should be selected in order to obtain the calibration curve over the desired range. Where possible, standard sources of those radionuclides that are to be assayed should be included.

---
* These certified reference standards are obtainable from the National Institute of Standards and Technology, Washington, DC 20234.

Nuclear Properties of Selected Calibration Standards[1,2]

Principal Photon Emissions	Energy (keV)	Photons per 100 Disintegrations
^{133}Ba ($T_{1/2}$ = 10.5 years)		
$K_{\alpha 1}$	30.97	63.4
$K_{\alpha 2}$	30.62	34.2
K_{β}	35.0	22.8
γ_1	53.15	2.14
γ_2	79.62	2.55
γ_3	80.99	33.0
γ_6	276.39	6.9
γ_7	302.83	17.8
γ_8	356.0	60.0
γ_9	383.85	8.7
^{137}Cs–^{137m}Ba ($T_{1/2}$ = 30.17 years)		
$K_{\alpha 1}$	32.19	3.82
$K_{\alpha 2}$	31.82	2.07
K_{β}	36.4	1.39
Weighted Mean[4]	(32.9)	(7.28)
γ_1	661.6	89.98
^{22}Na ($T_{1/2}$ = 2.60 years)		
$h\nu$	511	179.80[5]
γ_1	1274.54	99.94
^{60}Co ($T_{1/2}$ = 5.27 years)		
γ_1	1173.2[6]	100.0
γ_2	1332.5[6]	100.0
^{57}Co ($T_{1/2}$ = 270.9 days)		
ΣX_K	7.0	56.0
γ_1	14.4	9.5
γ_2	122.06	85.51
γ_3	136.47	10.60
Weighted Mean ($\gamma_2 + \gamma_3$)[4]	(125.0)	(96.11)
^{54}Mn ($T_{1/2}$ = 312.7 days)		
ΣX_K	6.0	25.0
γ_1	834.83	99.98
^{109}Cd–^{109}Ag ($T_{1/2}$ = 464 days)		
$K_{\alpha 1}$	22.16	35.3
$K_{\alpha 2}$	21.99	18.6
K_{β}	24.9	11.4
Weighted Mean[4]		63.5
γ_1	88.0	3.72
^{129}I ($T_{1/2}$ = 1.57 × 10^7 years)		
$K_{\alpha 1}$[3]	29.78	37.0
$K_{\alpha 2}$	29.46	20.0
K_{β}	13.2	37.0

Nuclear Properties of Selected Calibration Standards[1,2] (Continued)

Principal Photon Emissions	Energy (keV)	Photons per 100 Disintegrations
γ_1	39.58	7.52
Weighted Mean[4]	(31.3)	(77.80)

(1) In measurements for gamma- (or X-)ray assay purposes, fluorescent radiation from lead shielding (specifically, lead K X-rays ~76 keV) may interfere with quantitative results. Allowance must be made for these effects, or the radiation suppressed; a satisfactory means of absorbing this radiation is covering the exposed lead with cadmium sheet 0.06 to 0.08 inch thick, and then covering the cadmium with copper 0.02 to 0.04 inch thick.
(2) Only those photon emissions having an abundance ≥1% are normally included.
(3) The K notation refers to X-ray emissions.
(4) The weighted mean energies and total intensities are given for groups of photons that would not be resolved by a NaI(Tl) detector.
(5) For this photon intensity to be usable, all emitted positrons must be annihilated in the source material.
(6) Cascade.

Calculate the gamma-ray emission rate from the equation:

$$\Gamma = A_s b$$

in which A_s is the activity, in disintegrations per second, of the standard used, and b is the number of gamma rays per disintegration at that energy. Accurately measure quantities of standard solutions of each radionuclide into identical containers, and determine the fractional photopeak area (F) for each of the standards.

Using the equation $\varepsilon_p = F/\Gamma$, calculate the photopeak efficiency, ε_p, and construct a log-log plot of ε_p versus the gamma-ray energy as shown in *Figure 4*.

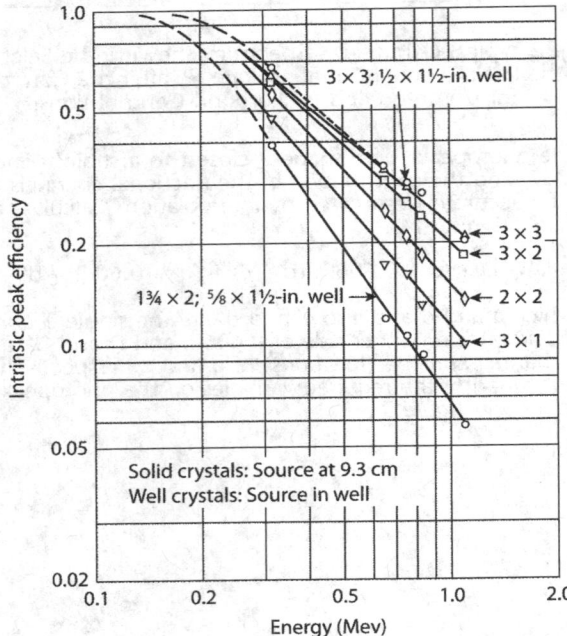

Fig. 4. Typical Photopeak Efficiency Calibration Curves for Various NaI(Tl) Detectors.

DETERMINATION OF SPECIMEN ACTIVITY—In the same manner as in the preparation of the calibration curve, determine the fractional area (F) of the principal photopeak of the specimen under assay or an accurately measured aliquot adjusted to the same volume in an identical container as used for the standards. From the calibration curve, find the value of ε_p for this radionuclide. Using the equation $\Gamma = F/\varepsilon_p$, calculate the gamma-ray emission rate (Γ). Calculate the activity (A), in disintegrations per second, of the specimen using the equation $A = (\Gamma/b)(D)$, in which b is the number of gamma rays per disintegration and D is the dilution factor. To obtain the activity, in μCi or mCi, divide A by 3.7×10^4 or 3.7×10^7, respectively. The above relationship is equally valid for obtaining the activity of an undiluted specimen or capsule; in this case, the dilution factor, D, is unity.

SPECTROPHOTOMETRY AND LIGHT-SCATTERING*

ULTRAVIOLET, VISIBLE, INFRARED, ATOMIC ABSORPTION, FLUORESCENCE, TURBIDIMETRY, NEPHELOMETRY, AND RAMAN MEASUREMENT

Absorption spectrophotometry is the measurement of an interaction between electromagnetic radiation and the molecules, or atoms, of a chemical substance. Techniques frequently employed in pharmaceutical analysis include UV, visible, IR, and atomic absorption spectroscopy. Spectrophotometric measurement in the visible region was formerly referred to as *colorimetry*; however, it is more precise to use the term "colorimetry" only when considering human perception of color.

Fluorescence spectrophotometry is the measurement of the emission of light from a chemical substance while it is being exposed to UV, visible, or other electromagnetic radiation. In general, the light emitted by a fluorescent solution is of maximum intensity at a wavelength longer than that of the exciting radiation, usually by some 20 to 30 nm.

Light-Scattering involves measurement of the light scattered because of submicroscopic optical density inhomogeneities of solutions and is useful in the determination of weight-average molecular weights of polydisperse systems in the molecular weight range from 1000 to several hundred million. Two such techniques utilized in pharmaceutical analysis are *turbidimetry* and *nephelometry*.

Raman spectroscopy (inelastic light-scattering) is a light-scattering process in which the specimen under examination is irradiated with intense monochromatic light (usually laser light) and the light scattered from the specimen is analyzed for frequency shifts.

The wavelength range available for these measurements extends from the short wavelengths of the UV through the IR. For convenience of reference, this spectral range is roughly divided into the UV (190 to 380 nm), the visible (380 to 780 nm), the near-IR (780 to 3000 nm), and the IR (2.5 to 40 μm or 4000 to 250 cm^{-1}).

---

* This text is adapted from General Chapter ⟨851⟩ of the *United States Pharmacopeia and National Formulary* (*USP–NF*) as published in USP 32–NF 27. This text is provided for informational purposes only and is intended as a resource for the FCC user. Note that because the *USP–NF* is in continuous revision, this General Chapter is subject to change and the text printed here may not continue to represent the current version.

COMPARATIVE UTILITY OF SPECTRAL RANGES

For many pharmaceutical substances, measurements can be made in the UV and visible regions of the spectrum with greater accuracy and sensitivity than in the near-IR and IR. When solutions are observed in 1-cm cells, concentrations of about 10 μg of the specimen per mL often will produce absorbances of 0.2 to 0.8 in the UV or the visible region. In the IR and near-IR, concentrations of 1 to 10 mg per mL and up to 100 mg per mL, respectively, may be needed to produce sufficient absorption; for these spectral ranges, cell lengths of from 0.01 mm to upwards of 3 mm are commonly used.

The UV and visible spectra of substances generally do not have a high degree of specificity. Nevertheless, they are highly suitable for quantitative assays, and for many substances they are useful as additional means of identification.

There has been increasing interest in the use of near-IR spectroscopy in pharmaceutical analysis, especially for rapid identification of large numbers of samples, and also for water determination.

The near-IR region is especially suitable for the determination of –OH and –NH groups, such as water in alcohol, –OH in the presence of amines, alcohols in hydrocarbons, and primary and secondary amines in the presence of tertiary amines.

The IR spectrum is unique for any given chemical compound with the exception of optical isomers, which have identical spectra. However, polymorphism may occasionally be responsible for a difference in the IR spectrum of a given compound in the solid state. Frequently, small differences in structure result in significant differences in the spectra. Because of the large number of maxima in an IR absorption spectrum, it is sometimes possible to quantitatively measure the individual components of a mixture of known qualitative composition without prior separation.

The Raman spectrum and the IR spectrum provide similar data, although the intensities of the spectra are governed by different molecular properties. Raman and IR spectroscopy exhibit different relative sensitivities for different functional groups, e.g., Raman spectroscopy is particularly sensitive to C–S and C–C multiple bonds, and some aromatic compounds are more easily identified by means of their Raman spectra. Water has a highly intense IR absorption spectrum, but a particularly weak Raman spectrum. Therefore, water has only limited IR "windows" that can be used to examine aqueous solutes, while its Raman spectrum is almost completely transparent and useful for solute identification. The two major limitations of Raman spectroscopy are that the minimum detectable concentration of specimen is typically 10^{-1} M to 10^{-2} M and that the impurities in many substances fluoresce and interfere with the detection of the Raman scattered signal.

Optical reflectance measurements provide spectral information similar to that obtained by transmission measurements. Since reflectance measurements probe only the surface composition of the specimen, difficulties associated with the optical thickness and the light-scattering properties of the substance are eliminated. Thus, reflectance measurements are frequently more simple to perform on intensely absorbing materials. A particularly common technique used for IR reflectance measurements is termed attenuated total reflectance (ATR), also known as multiple internal reflectance (MIR). In the ATR technique, the beam of the IR spectrometer is passed through an appropriate IR window material (e.g., KRS-5, a TlBr-TlI eutectic mixture), which is cut at such an angle that the IR beam enters the first (front) surface of the window, but is totally reflected when it impinges on the second (back) surface (i.e., the angle of incidence of the radiation upon the second surface of the window exceeds the critical angle for that material). By appropriate window construction, it is possible to have many internal reflections of the IR beam before it is transmitted out of the window. If a specimen is placed in close contact with the window along the sides that totally reflect the IR beam, the intensity of reflected radiation is reduced at each wavelength (frequency) that the specimen absorbs. Thus, the ATR technique provides a reflectance spectrum that has been increased in intensity, when compared to a simple reflectance measurement, by the number of times that the IR beam is reflected within the window. The ATR technique provides excellent sensitivity, but it yields poor reproducibility, and is not a reliable quantitative technique unless an internal standard is intimately mixed with each test specimen.

Fluorescence spectrophotometry is often more sensitive than absorption spectrophotometry. In absorption measurements, the specimen transmittance is compared to that of a blank; and at low concentrations, both solutions give high signals. Conversely, in fluorescence spectrophotometry, the solvent blank has low rather than high output, so that the background radiation that may interfere with determinations at low concentrations is much less. Whereas few compounds can be determined conveniently at concentrations below 10^{-5} M by light absorption, it is not unusual to employ concentrations of 10^{-7} M to 10^{-8} M in fluorescence spectrophotometry.

THEORY AND TERMS

The power of a radiant beam decreases in relation to the distance that it travels through an absorbing medium. It also decreases in relation to the concentration of absorbing molecules or ions encountered in that medium. These two factors determine the proportion of the total incident energy that emerge. The decrease in power of monochromatic radiation passing through a homogeneous absorbing medium is stated quantitatively by Beer's law, $\log_{10}(1/T) = A = abc$, in which the terms are as defined below.

Absorbance [Symbol: A]—The logarithm, to the base 10, of the reciprocal of the transmittance (T). [NOTE—Descriptive terms used formerly include optical density, absorbancy, and extinction.]

Absorptivity [Symbol: a]—The quotient of the absorbance (A) divided by the product of the concentration of the substance (c), expressed in g per L, and the absorption path length (b) in cm. [NOTE—It is not to be confused with absorbancy index; specific extinction; or extinction coefficient.]

Molar Absorptivity [Symbol: ε]—The quotient of the absorbance (A) divided by the product of the concentration, expressed in *moles* per L, of the substance and the absorption path length in cm. It is also the product of the absorptivity (a) and the molecular weight of the substance. [NOTE—Terms formerly used include molar absorbancy index; molar extinction coefficient; and molar absorption coefficient.]

For most systems used in absorption spectrophotometry, the absorptivity of a substance is a constant independent of the intensity of the incident radiation, the internal cell length, and the concentration, with the result that concentration may be determined photometrically.

Beer's law gives no indication of the effect of temperature, wavelength, or the type of solvent. For most analytical work the effects of normal variation in temperature are negligible.

Deviations from Beer's law may be caused by either chemical or instrumental variables. Apparent failure of Beer's law may result from a concentration change in solute molecules because of association between solute molecules or between solute and solvent molecules, or dissociation or ionization. Other deviations might be caused by instrumental effects such as polychromatic radiation, slit-width effects, or stray light.

Even at a fixed temperature in a given solvent, the absorptivity may not be truly constant. However, in the case of specimens having only one absorbing component, it is not necessary that the absorbing system conform to Beer's law for use in quantitative analysis. The concentration of an unknown may be found by comparison with an experimentally determined standard curve.

Although, in the strictest sense, Beer's law does not hold in atomic absorption spectrophotometry because of the lack of quantitative properties of the cell length and the concentration, the absorption processes taking place in the flame under conditions of reproducible aspiration do follow the Beer relationship in principle. Specifically, the negative log of the transmittance, or the absorbance, is directly proportional to the absorption coefficient, and, consequently, is proportional to the number of absorbing atoms. On this basis, calibration curves may be constructed to permit evaluation of unknown absorption values in terms of concentration of the element in solution.

Absorption Spectrum—A graphic representation of absorbance, or any function of absorbance, plotted against wavelength or function of wavelength.

Transmittance [Symbol: T]—The quotient of the radiant power transmitted by a specimen divided by the radiant power incident upon the specimen. [NOTE—Terms formerly used include transmittancy and transmission.]

Fluorescence Intensity [Symbol: I]—An empirical expression of fluorescence activity, commonly given in terms of arbitrary units proportional to detector response. The *fluorescence emission spectrum* is a graphical presentation of the spectral distribution of radiation emitted by an activated substance, showing intensity of emitted radiation as ordinate, and wavelength as abscissa. The *fluorescence excitation spectrum* is a graphical presentation of the activation spectrum, showing intensity of radiation emitted by an activated substance as ordinate, and wavelength of the incident (activating) radiation as abscissa. As in absorption spectrophotometry, the important regions of the electromagnetic spectrum encompassed by the fluorescence of organic compounds are the UV, visible, and near-IR, i.e., the region from 250 to 800 nm. After a molecule has absorbed radiation, the energy can be lost as heat or released in the form of radiation of the same or longer wavelength as the absorbed radiation. Both absorption and emission of radiation are due to the transitions of electrons between different energy levels, or orbitals, of the molecule. There is a time delay between the absorption and emission of light; this interval, the duration of the excited state, has been measured to be about 10^{-9} second to 10^{-8} second for most organic fluorescent solutions. The short lifetime of fluorescence distinguishes this type of luminescence from phosphorescence, which is a long-lived afterglow having a lifetime of 10^{-3} second up to several minutes.

Turbidance [Symbol: S]—The light-scattering effect of suspended particles. The amount of suspended matter may be measured by observation of either the transmitted light (turbidimetry) or the scattered light (nephelometry).

Turbidity [Symbol: τ]—In light-scattering measurements, the turbidity is the measure of the decrease in incident beam intensity per unit length of a given suspension.

Raman Scattering Activity—The molecular property (in units of cm^4 per g) governing the intensity of an observed Raman band for a randomly oriented specimen. The scattering activity is determined from the derivative of the molecular polarizability with respect to the molecular motion giving rise to the Raman shifted band. In general, the Raman band intensity is linearly proportional to the concentration of the analyte.

USE OF REFERENCE STANDARDS

With few exceptions, the Pharmacopeial spectrophotometric tests and assays call for comparison against a USP Reference Standard. This is to ensure measurement under conditions identical for the test specimen and the reference substance. These conditions include wavelength setting, slit-width adjustment, cell placement and correction, and transmittance levels. It should be noted that cells exhibiting identical transmittance at a given wavelength may differ considerably in transmittance at other wavelengths. Appropriate cell corrections should be established and used where required.

The expressions, "similar preparation" and "similar solution," as used in tests and assays involving spectrophotometry, indicate that the reference specimen, generally a USP Reference Standard, is to be prepared and observed in a manner identical for all practical purposes to that used for the test specimen. Usually in making up the solution of the specified Reference Standard, a solution of about (i.e., within 10%) the desired concentration is prepared and the absorptivity is calculated on the basis of the exact amount weighed out; if a previously dried specimen of the Reference Standard has not been used, the absorptivity is calculated on the anhydrous basis.

The expressions, "concomitantly determine" and "concomitantly measured," as used in tests and assays involving spectrophotometry, indicate that the absorbances of both the solution containing the test specimen and the solution containing the reference specimen, relative to the specified test blank, are to be measured in immediate succession.

APPARATUS

Many types of spectrophotometers are available. Fundamentally, most types, except those used for IR spectrophotometry, provide for passing essentially monochromatic radiant energy through a specimen in suitable form, and measuring the intensity of the fraction that is transmitted. Fourier transform IR spectrophotometers use an interferometric technique whereby polychromatic radiation passes through the analyte and onto a detector on an intensity and time basis. UV, visible, and dispersive IR spectrophotometers comprise an energy source, a dispersing device (e.g., a prism or grating), slits for selecting the wavelength band, a cell or holder for the test specimen, a detector of radiant energy, and associated amplifiers and measuring devices. In *diode array* spectrophotometers, the energy from the source is passed through the test specimen and then dispersed via a grating onto several hundred light-sensitive diodes, each of which in turn develops a signal proportional to the number of photons at its small wavelength interval; these signals then may be computed at rapid chosen intervals to represent a complete spectrum. Fourier transform IR systems utilize an interferometer instead of a dispersing device and a digital computer to process the spectral data. Some instruments are manually operated, whereas others are equipped for automatic and continuous recording. Instruments that are interfaced to a digital computer have the capabilities also of co-adding and storing spectra, performing spectral comparisons, and performing difference spectroscopy (accomplished with the use of a digital absorbance subtraction method).

Instruments are available for use in the visible; in the visible and UV; in the visible, UV, and near-IR; and in the IR regions of the spectrum. Choice of the type of spectrophotometric analysis and of the instrument to be used depends upon factors such as the composition and amount of available test specimen, the degree of accuracy, sensitivity, and selectivity desired, and the manner in which the specimen is handled.

The apparatus used in atomic absorption spectrophotometry has several unique features. For each element to be determined, a specific source that emits the spectral line to be absorbed should be selected. The source is usually a hollow-cathode lamp, the cathode of which is designed to emit the desired radiation when excited. Since the radiation to be absorbed by the test specimen element is usually of the same wavelength as that of its emission line, the element in the hollow-cathode lamp is the same as the element to be determined. The apparatus is equipped with an aspirator for introducing the test specimen into a flame, which is usually provided by air–acetylene, air–hydrogen, or, for refractory cases, nitrous oxide–acetylene. The flame, in effect, is a heated specimen chamber. A detector is used to read the signal from the chamber. Interfering radiation produced by the flame during combustion may be negated by the use of a chopped source lamp signal of a definite frequency. The detector should be tuned to this alternating current frequency so that the direct current signal arising from the flame is ignored. The detecting system, therefore, reads only the change in signal from the hollow-cathode source, which is directly proportional to the number of atoms to be determined in the test specimen. For Pharmacopeial purposes, apparatus that provides the readings directly in absorbance units is usually required. However, instruments providing readings in percent transmission, percent absorption, or concentration may be used if the calculation formulas provided in the individual monographs are revised as necessary to yield the required quantitative results. Percent absorption or percent transmittance may be converted to absorbance, A, by the following two equations:

$$A = 2 - \log_{10}(100 - \% \text{ absorption})$$

or:

$$A = 2 - \log_{10}(\% \text{ transmittance})$$

Depending upon the type of apparatus used, the readout device may be a meter, digital counter, recorder, or printer. Both single-beam and double-beam instruments are commercially available, and either type is suitable.

Measurement of fluorescence intensity can be made with a simple *filter fluorometer*. Such an instrument consists of a radiation source, a primary filter, a specimen chamber, a secondary filter, and a fluorescence detection system. In most such fluorometers, the detector is placed on an axis at 90° from that of the exciting beam. This right-angle geometry permits the exciting radiation to pass through the test specimen and not contaminate the output signal received by the fluorescence detector. However, the detector unavoidably receives some of the exciting radiation as a result of the inherent scattering properties of the solutions themselves, or if dust or other solids are present. Filters are used to eliminate this residual scatter. The primary filter selects short-wavelength radiation capable of exciting the test specimen, while the secondary filter is normally a sharp cut-off filter that allows the longer-wavelength fluorescence to be transmitted but blocks the scattered excitation.

Most fluorometers use photomultiplier tubes as detectors, many types of which are available, each having special characteristics with respect to spectral region of maximum sensitivity, gain, and electrical noise. The photocurrent is amplified and read out on a meter or recorder.

A *spectrofluorometer* differs from a filter fluorometer in that filters are replaced by monochromators, of either the prism or the grating type. For analytical purposes, the spectrofluorometer is superior to the filter fluorometer in wavelength selectivity, flexibility, and convenience, in the same way in which a spectrophotometer is superior to a filter photometer.

Many radiation sources are available. Mercury lamps are relatively stable and emit energy mainly at discrete wavelengths. Tungsten lamps provide an energy continuum in the visible region. The high-pressure xenon arc lamp is often used in spectrofluorometers because it is a high-intensity source that emits an energy continuum extending from the UV into the IR.

In spectrofluorometers, the monochromators are equipped with slits. A narrow slit provides high resolution and spectral purity, while a large slit sacrifices these for high sensitivity. Choice of slit size is determined by the separation between exciting and emitting wavelengths as well as the degree of sensitivity needed.

Specimen cells used in fluorescence measurements may be round tubes or rectangular cells similar to those used in absorption spectrophotometry, except that they are polished on all four vertical sides. A convenient test specimen size is 2 to 3 mL, but some instruments can be fitted with small cells holding 100 to 300 µL, or with a capillary holder requiring an even smaller amount of specimen.

Light-scattering instruments are available and consist in general of a mercury lamp, with filters for the strong green or blue lines, a shutter, a set of neutral filters with known transmittance, and a sensitive photomultiplier to be mounted on an arm that can be rotated around the solution cell and set at any angle from −135° to 0° to +135° by a dial outside the light-tight housing. Solution cells are of various shapes, such as square for measuring 90° scattering; semioctagonal for 45°, 90°, and 135° scattering; and cylindrical for scattering at all angles. Since the determination of molecular weight requires a precise measure of the difference in refractive index between the solution and solvent, $[(n - n_0)/c]$, a second instrument, a differential refractometer, is needed to measure this small difference.

Raman spectrometers include the following major components: a source of intense monochromatic radiation (invariably a laser); optics to collect the light scattered by the test specimen; a (double) monochromator to disperse the scattered light and reject the intense incident frequency; and a suitable light-detection and amplification system. Raman measurement is simple in that most specimens are examined directly in melting-point capillaries. Because the laser source can be focused sharply, only a few microliters of the specimen is required.

PROCEDURE

Absorption Spectrophotometry

Detailed instructions for operating spectrophotometers are supplied by the manufacturers. To achieve significant and valid results, the operator of a spectrophotometer should be aware of its limitations and of potential sources of error and variation. The instruction manual should be followed closely on such matters as care, cleaning, and calibration of the instrument, and techniques of handling absorption cells, as well as instructions for operation. The following points require special emphasis.

Check the instrument for accuracy of calibration. Where a continuous source of radiant energy is used, attention should be paid to both the wavelength and photometric scales; where a spectral line source is used, only the photometric scale need be checked. A number of sources of radiant energy have spectral lines of suitable intensity, adequately spaced throughout the spectral range selected. The best single source of UV and visible calibration spectra is the quartz-mercury arc, of which the lines at 253.7, 302.25, 313.16, 334.15, 365.48, 404.66, and 435.83 nm may be used. The glass-mercury arc is equally useful above 300 nm. The 486.13-nm and 656.28-nm lines of a hydrogen discharge lamp may be used also. The wavelength scale may be calibrated also by means of suitable glass filters, which have useful absorption bands through the visible and UV regions. Standard glasses containing didymium (a mixture of praseodymium and neodymium) have been used widely, although glasses containing holmium were found to be superior. Standard holmium oxide solution has superseded the use of holmium glass.[1] The wavelength scales of near-IR and IR spectrophotometers are readily checked by the use of absorption bands provided by polystyrene films, carbon dioxide, water vapor, or ammonia gas.

[1] National Institute of Standards and Technology (NIST), Gaithersburg, MD 20899: "Spectral Transmittance Characteristics of Holmium Oxide in Perchloric Acid," *J. Res. Natl. Bur. Stds.* **90**, No. 2, 115 (1985). The performance of an uncertified filter should be checked against a certified standard.

For checking the photometric scale, a number of standard inorganic glass filters as well as standard solutions of known transmittances such as potassium dichromate are available.[2]

Quantitative absorbance measurements usually are made on solutions of the substance in liquid-holding cells. Since both the solvent and the cell window absorb light, compensation must be made for their contribution to the measured absorbance. Matched cells are available commercially for UV and visible spectrophotometry for which no cell correction is necessary. In IR spectrophotometry, however, corrections for cell differences usually must be made. In such cases, pairs of cells are filled with the selected solvent and the difference in their absorbances at the chosen wavelength is determined. The cell exhibiting the greater absorbance is used for the solution of the test specimen and the measured absorbance is corrected by subtraction of the cell difference.

With the use of a computerized Fourier transform IR system, this correction need not be made, since the same cell can be used for both the solvent blank and the test solution. However, it must be ascertained that the transmission properties of the cell are constant.

Comparisons of a test specimen with a Reference Standard are best made at a peak of spectral absorption for the compound concerned. Assays prescribing spectrophotometry give the commonly accepted wavelength for peak spectral absorption of the substance in question. It is known that different spectrophotometers may show minor variation in the apparent wavelength of this peak. Good practice demands that comparisons be made at the wavelength at which peak absorption occurs. Should this differ by more than ±1 nm from the wavelength specified in the individual monograph, recalibration of the instrument may be indicated.

TEST PREPARATION

For determinations utilizing UV or visible spectrophotometry, the specimen generally is dissolved in a solvent. Unless otherwise directed in the monograph, determinations are made at room temperature using a path length of 1 cm. Many solvents are suitable for these ranges, including water, alcohols, chloroform, lower hydrocarbons, ethers, and dilute solutions of strong acids and alkalies. Precautions should be taken to utilize solvents free from contaminants absorbing in the spectral region being used. It is usually advisable to use water-free methanol or alcohol, or alcohol denatured by the addition of methanol but not containing benzene or other interfering impurities, as the solvent. Solvents of special spectrophotometric quality, guaranteed to be free from contaminants, are available commercially from several sources. Some other analytical reagent-grade organic solvents may contain traces of impurities that absorb strongly in the UV region. New lots of these solvents should be checked for their transparency, and care should be taken to use the same lot of solvent for preparation of the test solution and the standard solution and for the blank.

No solvent in appreciable thickness is completely transparent throughout the near-IR and IR spectrum. Carbon tetrachloride (up to 5 mm in thickness) is practically transparent to 6 µm (1666 cm^{-1}). Carbon disulfide (1 mm in thickness) is suitable as a solvent to 40 µm (250 cm^{-1}) with the exception of the 4.2-µm to 5.0-µm (2381-cm^{-1} to 2000-cm^{-1}) and the 5.5-µm to 7.5-µm (1819-cm^{-1} to 1333-cm^{-1}) regions, where it has strong absorption. Other solvents have relatively narrow regions of transparency. For IR spectrophotometry, an additional qualification for a suitable solvent is that it must not affect the material, usually sodium chloride, of which the cell is made. The test specimen may also be prepared by dispersing the finely ground solid specimen in

[2] For further detail regarding checks on photometric scale of a spectrophotometer, reference may be made to the following NIST publications: *J. Res. Nalt. Bur. Stds.* **76A**, 469 (1972) [re: SRM 93l, "Liquid Absorbance Standards for Ultraviolet and Visible Spectrophotometry" as well as potassium chromate and potassium dichromate]; *NIST Spec. Publ.* 260–116 (1994) [re: SRM 930 and SRM 1930, "Glass Filters for Spectrophotometry."]

mineral oil or by mixing it intimately with previously dried alkali halide salt (usually potassium bromide). Mixtures with alkali halide salts may be examined directly or as transparent disks or pellets obtained by pressing the mixture in a die. Typical drying conditions for potassium bromide are 105° in vacuum for 12 hours, although grades are commercially available that require no drying. Infrared microscopy or a mineral oil dispersion is preferable where disproportionation between the alkali halide and the test specimen is encountered. For suitable materials the test specimen may be prepared neat as a thin sample for IR microscopy or suspended neat as a thin film for mineral oil dispersion. For Raman spectrometry, most common solvents are suitable, and ordinary (nonfluorescing) glass specimen cells can be used. The IR region of the electromagnetic spectrum extends from 0.8 to 400 µm. From 800 to 2500 nm (0.8 to 2.5 µm) is generally considered to be the near-IR (NIR) region; from 2.5 to 25 µm (4000 to 400 cm^{-1}) is generally considered to be the mid-range (mid-IR) region; and from 25 to 400 µm is generally considered to be the far-IR (FIR) region. Unless otherwise specified in the individual monograph, the region from 3800 to 650 cm^{-1} (2.6 to 15 µm) should be used to ascertain compliance with monograph specifications for IR absorption.

Where values for IR line spectra are given in an individual monograph, the letters s, m, and w signify strong, medium, and weak absorption, respectively; sh signifies a shoulder, bd signifies a band, and v means very. The values may vary as much as 0.1 µm or 10 cm^{-1}, depending upon the particular instrument used. Polymorphism gives rise to variations in the IR spectra of many compounds in the solid state. Therefore, when conducting IR absorption tests, if a difference appears in the IR spectra of the analyte and the standard, dissolve equal portions of the test substance and the standard in equal volumes of a suitable solvent, evaporate the solutions to dryness in similar containers under identical conditions, and repeat the test on the residues.

In NIR spectroscopy much of the current interest centers around the ease of analysis. Samples can be analyzed in powder form or by means of reflectance techniques, with little or no preparation. Compliance with in-house specifications can be determined by computerized comparison of spectra with spectra previously obtained from reference materials. Many pharmaceutical materials exhibit low absorptivity in this spectral region, which allows incident near-IR radiation to penetrate samples more deeply than UV, visible, or IR radiation. NIR spectrophotometry may be used to observe matrix modifications and, with proper calibration, may be used in quantitative analysis.

In atomic absorption spectrophotometry, the nature of the solvent and the concentration of solids must be given special consideration. An ideal solvent is one that interferes to a minimal extent in the absorption or emission processes and one that produces neutral atoms in the flame. If there is a significant difference between the surface tension or viscosity of the test solution and standard solution, the solutions are aspirated or atomized at a different rate, causing significant differences in the signals generated. The acid concentration of the solutions also affects the absorption processes. Thus, the solvents used in preparing the test specimen and the standard should be the same or as much alike in these respects as possible, and should yield solutions that are easily aspirated via the specimen tube of the burner-aspirator. Since undissolved solids present in the solutions may give rise to matrix or bulk interferences, the total undissolved solids content in all solutions should be kept below 2% wherever possible.

CALCULATIONS

The application of absorption spectrophotometry in an assay or a test generally requires the use of a Reference Standard. Where such a measurement is specified in an assay, a formula is provided in order to permit calculation of the desired result. A numerical constant is frequently included in the formula. The following derivation is provided to introduce a logical approach to the deduction of the constants appearing in formulas in the assays in many monographs.

The Beer's law relationship is valid for the solutions of both the Reference Standard (S) and the test specimen (U):

$$A_S = abC_S \quad (1)$$

$$A_U = abC_U \quad (2)$$

in which A_S is the absorbance of the Standard solution of concentration C_S; and A_U is the absorbance of the test specimen solution of concentration C_U. If C_S and C_U are expressed in the same units and the absorbances of both solutions are measured in matching cells having the same dimensions, the absorptivity, a, and the cell thickness, b, are the same; consequently, the two equations may be combined and rewritten to solve for C_U:

$$C_U = C_S(A_U/A_S) \quad (3)$$

Quantities of solid test specimens to be taken for analysis are generally specified in mg. Instructions for dilution are given in the assay and, since dilute solutions are used for absorbance measurements, concentrations are usually expressed for convenience in units of µg per mL. Taking a quantity, in mg, of a test specimen of a drug substance or solid dosage form for analysis, it therefore follows that a volume (V_U), in L, of solution of concentration C_U may be prepared from the amount of test specimen that contains a quantity W_U, in mg, of the drug substance [NOTE—C_U is numerically the same whether expressed as µg per mL or mg per L], such that:

$$W_U = V_U C_U \quad (4)$$

The form in which the formula appears in the assay in a monograph for a solid article may be derived by substituting C_U of equation (3) into equation (4). In summary, the use of equation (4), with due consideration for any unit conversions necessary to achieve equality in equation (5), permits the calculation of the constant factor (V_U) occurring in the final formula:

$$W_U = V_U C_S(A_U/A_S) \quad (5)$$

The same derivation is applicable to formulas that appear in monographs for liquid articles that are assayed by absorption spectrophotometry. For liquid dosage forms, results of calculations are generally expressed in terms of the quantity, in mg, of drug substance in each mL of the article. Thus it is necessary to include in the denominator an additional term, the volume (V), in mL, of the test preparation taken.

Assays in the visible region usually call for comparing concomitantly the absorbance produced by the *Assay preparation* with that produced by a *Standard preparation* containing approximately an equal quantity of a USP Reference Standard. In some situations, it is permissible to omit the use of a Reference Standard. This is true where spectrophotometric assays are made with routine frequency, and where a suitable standard curve is available, prepared with the respective USP Reference Standard, and where the substance assayed conforms to Beer's law within the range of about 75% to 125% of the final concentration used in the assay. Under these circumstances, the absorbance found in the assay may be interpolated on the standard curve, and the assay result calculated therefrom.

Such standard curves should be confirmed frequently, and always when a new spectrophotometer or new lots of reagents are put into use.

In spectrophotometric assays that direct the preparation and use of a standard curve, it is permissible and preferable, when the assay is employed infrequently, not to use the standard curve but to make the comparison directly against a quantity of the Reference Standard approximately equal to that taken of the specimen, and similarly treated.

Fluorescence Spectrophotometry

The measurement of fluorescence is a useful analytical technique. *Fluorescence* is light emitted from a substance in an excited state that has been reached by the absorption of radiant energy. A substance is said to be *fluorescent* if it can be made to fluoresce. Many compounds can be assayed by procedures utilizing either their inherent fluorescence or the fluorescence of suitable derivatives.

Test specimens prepared for fluorescence spectrophotometry are usually one-tenth to one-hundredth as concentrated as those used in absorption spectrophotometry, for the following reason. In analytical applications, it is preferable that the fluorescence signal be linearly related to the concentration; but if a test specimen is too concentrated, a significant part of the incoming light is absorbed by the specimen near the cell surface, and the light reaching the center is reduced. That is, the specimen itself acts as an "inner filter." However, fluorescence spectrophotometry is inherently a highly sensitive technique, and concentrations of 10^{-5} M to 10^{-7} M frequently are used. It is necessary in any analytical procedure to make a working curve of fluorescence intensity versus concentration in order to establish a linear relationship. All readings should be corrected for a solvent blank.

Fluorescence measurements are sensitive to the presence of dust and other solid particles in the test specimen. Such impurities may reduce the intensity of the exciting beam or give misleading high readings because of multiple reflections in the specimen cell. It is, therefore, wise to eliminate solid particles by centrifugation; filtration also may be used, but some filter papers contain fluorescent impurities.

Temperature regulation is often important in fluorescence spectrophotometry. For some substances, fluorescence efficiency may be reduced by as much as 1% to 2% per degree of temperature rise. In such cases, if maximum precision is desired, temperature-controlled specimen cells are useful. For routine analysis, it may be sufficient to make measurements rapidly enough so that the specimen does not heat up appreciably from exposure to the intense light source. Many fluorescent compounds are light-sensitive. Exposed in a fluorometer, they may be photo-degraded into more or less fluorescent products. Such effects may be detected by observing the detector response in relationship to time, and may be reduced by attenuating the light source with filters or screens.

Change of solvent may markedly affect the intensity and spectral distribution of fluorescence. It is inadvisable, therefore, to alter the solvent specified in established methods without careful preliminary investigation. Many compounds are fluorescent in organic solvents but virtually nonfluorescent in water; thus, a number of solvents should be tried before it is decided whether or not a compound is fluorescent. In many organic solvents, the intensity of fluorescence is increased by elimination of dissolved oxygen, which has a strong quenching effect. Oxygen may be removed by bubbling an inert gas such as nitrogen or helium through the test specimen.

A semiquantitative measure of the strength of fluorescence is given by the ratio of the fluorescence intensity of a test specimen and that of a standard obtained with the same instrumental settings. Frequently, a solution of stated concentration of quinine in 0.1 N sulfuric acid or fluorescein in 0.1 N sodium hydroxide is used as a reference standard.

Light-Scattering

Turbidity can be measured with a standard photoelectric filter photometer or spectrophotometer, preferably with illumination in the blue portion of the spectrum. Nephelometric measurements require an instrument with a photocell placed so as to receive scattered rather than transmitted light; this geometry applies also to fluorometers, so that, in general, fluorometers can be used as nephelometers, by proper selection of filters. A ratio turbidimeter combines the technology of 90° nephelometry and turbidimetry: it contains photocells that receive and measure scattered light at a 90° angle from the sample as well as receiving and measuring the forward scatter in front of the sample; it also measures light transmitted directly through the sample. Linearity is attained by calculating the ratio of the 90° angle scattered light measurement to the sum of the forward scattered light measurement and the transmitted light measurement. The benefit of using a ratio turbidimetry system is that the measurement of stray light becomes negligible.

In practice, it is advisable to ensure that settling of the particles being measured is negligible. This is usually accomplished by including a protective colloid in the liquid suspending medium. It is important that results be interpreted by comparison of readings with those representing known concentrations of suspended matter, produced under precisely the same conditions.

Turbidimetry or nephelometry may be useful for the measurement of precipitates formed by the interaction of highly dilute solutions of reagents, or other particulate matter, such as suspensions of bacterial cells. In order that consistent results may be achieved, all variables must be carefully controlled. Where such control is possible, extremely dilute suspensions may be measured.

The specimen solute is dissolved in the solvent at several different accurately known concentrations, the choice of concentrations being dependent on the molecular weight of the solute and ranging from 1% for $M_w = 10,000$ to 0.01% for $M_w = 1,000,000$. Each solution must be very carefully cleaned before measurement by repeated filtration through fine filters. A dust particle in the solution vitiates the intensity of the scattered light measured. A criterion for a clear solution is that the dissymmetry, 45°/135° scattered intensity ratio, has attained a minimum.

The turbidity and refractive index of the solutions are measured. From the general 90° light-scattering equation, a plot of HC/τ versus C is made and extrapolated to infinite dilution, and the weight-average molecular weight, M, is calculated from the intercept, $1/M$.

Visual Comparison

Where a color or a turbidity comparison is directed, color-comparison tubes that are matched as closely as possible in internal diameter and in all other respects should be used. For color comparison, the tubes should be viewed downward, against a white background, with the aid of a light source directed from beneath the bottoms of the tubes, while for turbidity comparison the tubes should be viewed horizontally, against a dark background, with the aid of a light source directed from the sides of the tubes.

In conducting limit tests that involve a comparison of colors in two like containers (e.g., matched color-comparison tubes), a suitable instrument, rather than the unaided eye, may be used.

ION CHROMATOGRAPHY*

INTRODUCTION

Ion chromatography (IC) is a high-performance liquid chromatography (HPLC) instrumental technique used in USP test procedures such as identification tests and assays to measure inorganic anions and cations, organic acids, carbohydrates, sugar alcohols, aminoglycosides, amino acids, proteins, glycoproteins, and potentially other analytes.

As dictated by the nature of the analyte, IC has been applied to all aspects of the manufacturing and disposition of pharmaceutical products, including characterization of active ingredients, excipients, degradation products, impurities, and process streams. The following sample types are among those that have been analyzed: raw materials, intermediates (including media and culture broths), bulk active ingredients, diluents, formulated products, production equipment cleaning solutions, and waste streams. The technique is especially valuable for ionic or ionizable (in the mobile phase) analytes that have little or no native UV absorbance. The ability to couple the ion-exchange separation with numerous detection strategies, e.g., pulsed amperometric detection (PAD), expands IC applications to instances where analyte-specific detection strategies can provide the required degree of sensitivity or specificity. Utilization of such strategies allows IC applications to be implemented on appropriately configured HPLC systems. Additionally, ion-exclusion separations and pulsed amperometric detection expand the range of application of IC to aliphatic organic acids as well as to nonionic analytes of significant pharmaceutical interest including alcohols, alditols, carbohydrates, and amino acids. The wide dynamic range of the methodology makes it applicable for the quantification of trace contaminants as well as major product components.

Because IC typically uses dilute acids, alkalis, or salt solutions as the mobile phase, and does not use an organic solvent, IC does not require the purchase of costly organic solvents and hazardous disposal of the waste effluent. The effluent can be disposed of after appropriate neutralization (to ~pH 7) and, when necessary, after dilution with water.

IC allows separation using ion exchange, ion exclusion, or ion-pair approaches. IC separations are based on differences in charge density of the analyte species, which in turn depend on the valence and size of the individual ionic species to be measured. Separations are also performed on the basis of differences in the hydrophobic character of the ionic species. IC is typically performed at ambient temperature. As with other forms of HPLC, IC separations are based on varying capacity factors and typically follow the Knox equation. Ion chromatography is a technique complimentary to the more commonly used reversed-phase and normal-phase HPLC and to atomic absorption and ion-coupled plasma (plasma spectrochemistry) techniques in pharmaceutical analysis.

APPARATUS

IC instruments closely resemble conventional HPLC instruments. Typical components include an autosampler, a high-pressure pump, an injection valve with a sample loop of suitable size (typically 10 to 250 µL), a guard column, an analytical column, an optional suppressor or other forms of a post-column reaction system, a flow-through detector, and a data system ranging in complexity from an integrator to a computerized data system (Figure 1). Because mobile phases generally consist of dilute acids, alkalis, or salt solutions, the components in contact with the mobile phase and the sample are typically made from inert materials, such as polyetheretherketone. Conventional HPLC systems also may be used provided that their components are compatible with the mobile phase and injected sample solutions. A metal-free system should be used for trace metal analysis. Following suitable preparation, the sample is introduced via the injection valve. After the optional chemical suppression or other post-column reaction on the column effluent, the analyte species are detected using conductivity, amperometry, UV/VIS, or other detection modes. Because IC uses a predominantly ionic mobile phase, a suppressor is often necessary prior to conductometric detection, although non-suppressed conductometric detection has been successfully used in pharmaceutical analysis.

Stationary and Mobile Phases

As IC has developed and matured as an instrumental technique, the number of ion-exchange materials developed for IC has increased, facilitated by the understanding of the processes taking place at the surface of the stationary phase. In contrast to the silica-based column packing prevalent in classical HPLC, organic polymers are predominately used as support materials for IC. Such materials have a higher stability with respect to extremes in pH and in many cases are compatible with organic solvents. Typically, separation of anions requires the use of polymer-based anion exchangers and dilute bases as mobile phases. However, for cation separations, the stability over the entire pH range that is typical of organic polymers is not necessary, because dilute acids serve as mobile phases. Therefore, silica-based cation exchangers that exhibit a significantly higher chromatographic efficiency are commonly used for the separation of cations.

Depending on the separation mode (ion exchange, ion exclusion, or ion-pair), different types of stationary phases are used. For ion exchange, the stationary phase is either an anion or a cation exchanger. Typically, a strong cation exchanger is used for the ion-exclusion separation of organic acids, and a reversed-phase stationary phase is used when ion-pair is the separation mode. The ion-exchange capacity of a resin is defined as the number of ion-exchange sites per weight equivalent of the column packing and is typically expressed in terms of mEq per g of resin. With ion exchange, the retention times for the analyte ions increase with increasing ion-exchange capacity of the resin. This effect can be partly compensated for by using mobile phases of higher ionic strength. Styrene/divinylbenzene copolymers, polymethacrylate, and polyvinyl resins are the substrate materials used in the manufacturing process of the polymer-based ion exchangers. Organic polymers are functionalized directly at their surface, with the exception of latex-based ion exchangers, where the totally porous latex particle acts as an ion-exchange material. Surface-functionalized, "pellicular" substrates show a much higher chromatographic efficiency compared with the fully functionalized resins.

With ion exchange, a mobile phase consisting of mono- or divalent ionic species, alone or mixed at an optimum ratio, is used to accomplish the separation. In ion-exclusion methods, particularly for organic acids, the mobile phase consists of mineral acids to maintain organic acids in their undissociated forms. Often, the nature of the analyte dictates the mobile phase and the detection mode used. Typical mobile phases used in IC are described below in the section on detectors.

Detectors

Conductivity detection is by far the most commonly employed mode of detection in IC. Although the original IC development work included the use of low-capacity ion-ex-

---
* This text is adapted from General Chapter ⟨1065⟩ of the *United States Pharmacopeia and National Formulary* (USP–NF) as published in USP 32–NF 27. This text is provided for informational purposes only and is intended as a resource for the FCC user. Note that because the USP–NF is in continuous revision, this General Chapter is subject to change and the text printed here may not continue to represent the current version.

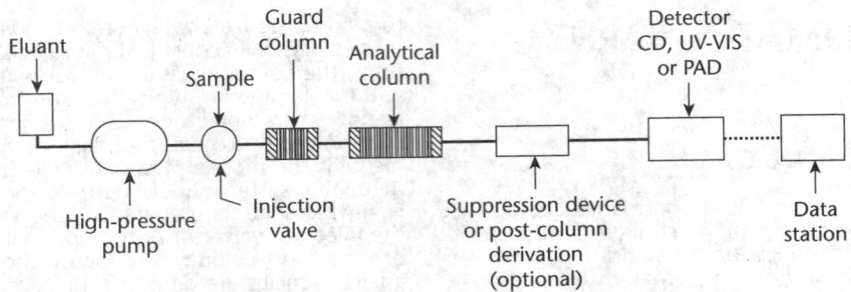

Figure 1. Components of a typical IC system illustrated schematically; CD = conductivity detector and PAD = pulsed amperometric detector.

change resins for efficient chromatographic separation and conductometric detection of ions in a chemically suppressed mobile phase, the advances in column technologies as well as instrumentation development allow the use of high-capacity ion exchange today.

In suppressed IC, the background conductance of the ionic mobile phase is significantly reduced as it flows through the suppression device. For example, dilute NaOH, about 10 to 50 mM, used as the mobile phase in IC of anions is converted to H_2O (poor conductivity) when the column effluent containing NaOH flows through a suppressor device present in an acidic form. The analyte ionic species in the column effluent are converted from their sodium or other metal salt forms to highly conducting acid forms (due to higher equivalent conductance of hydrogen ions compared to other cations). Analogous reactions occur in the hydroxide form suppressor in IC of cations, wherein the acidic mobile phase is converted to water, and the analyte cations are converted to highly conducting hydroxide forms (due to higher equivalent conductance of hydroxide ions compared to other anions).

The reduced background conductance and the enhanced signal due to the ionic species result in an enhanced signal-to-noise ratio for the conductometric detection of ions in suppressed IC. This results in reduced background noise and increasing sensitivity and reproducibility of the analysis. The commonly used chemical suppression devices fall into three broad categories. In the first type, the reactions occur across an ion-exchange membrane with the regenerant ions furnished by either a chemical or as products of electrolysis of water. In the second type, the suppression reactions occur in a packed bed of high-exchange capacity resin material, with regeneration either by a chemical or by electrolysis of water. In the third type, although not commonly used, the suppression reactions occur as the eluant stream mixes with the flowing stream of high-capacity resin material.

For pharmaceutical analyses, suppressed conductometric detection may be used for detection of trace ions in high purity waters. The commonly used mobile phases for the separation of anions by suppressed IC include hydroxide ions or a mixture of bicarbonate and carbonate ions. The common mobile phases for separation of cations usually consist of mineral acids or methanesulfonic acid.

Ion-chromatographic analyses also can be performed without chemical suppression, in which case the analytical column effluent flows directly to a conductivity detector. The typical eluants used in nonsuppressed IC are phthalic acid and p-hydroxybenzoic acid for the determination of anions and methanesulfonic acid for the determination of cations. The equivalent conductance values of chloride, sulfate, and other common anions are significantly greater than that of the eluant anion, and therefore, a positive peak is detected as the anions are carried through the detector. The equivalent conductance values of sodium, potassium, calcium, magnesium, and other common cations are significantly lower than that of the cation (H+) in the eluant. In this instance, a negative peak is detected as the cations are carried through the detector.

Nonsuppressed IC is easier to perform, and it is a useful technique for determining ions of weak acids such as cyanide and sulfide, which are nonconductive after chemical suppression but show a higher baseline noise. Pharmaceutical analyses can be performed in the nonsuppressed mode because the quantification limits are usually in the upper mg per L to low percentage levels. While suppressor-based methodologies must often be implemented on the instrument systems specifically designed for this purpose, IC may be performed without the suppressor on an existing HPLC. This is possible because the commonly used eluants in IC include dilute bases or acids that are compatible for use on existing HPLC instruments. When this approach is considered, analysts are encouraged to consult the instrument manufacturer for applicability of the instrument for the IC analysis.

OTHER DETECTORS

Other commonly used detection modes in IC include pulsed amperometry, direct UV detection, or post-column derivatization followed by UV/VIS detection.

Pulsed Amperometric Detection Mode (PAD)—PAD uses a specialized mode of the conventional amperometric technique. This type of detector is commonly used for the detection of electroactive species, e.g., organic compounds such as carbohydrates, sugar alcohols, amino acids, and organic sulfur species. In PAD, analytes are detected by an oxidative desorption process at the surface of an electrode located in the column effluent stream. Following the detection process, a series of potentials are applied for fixed time periods to clean the electrode surface. Unlike conventional amperometry that suffers from electrode surface fouling, a rapidly repeating sequence of different working potentials, referred to as waveform, helps the removal of the products of redox reactions from the electrode surface.

Direct and Indirect UV Detection—Direct UV Detection is used for inorganic and organic ions that possess a UV chromophore. These include organic acids, bromide, iodide, nitrate, nitrite, thiosulfate, and cyano-metal complexes. Analogous to the inverse conductometric detection of cations, UV detection may also be performed indirectly. This method is called indirect photometric chromatography (IPC).

Photometric Detection—Photometric detection involves chelation of the metal ions in column effluent with a color-forming reagent prior to detection with a visible wavelength. A classic example is the separation of metal ions in which the column effluent is chelated with 4-(2-pyridylazo)-resorcinol followed by detection at 510 to 530 nm.

SAMPLE PREPARATION

Typically sample preparation for IC includes dilution or filtering through a 0.45-μm filter, or both. Under certain circumstances, samples may require removal of undesirable species through solid-phase extraction (SPE) techniques. For example, a highly alkaline sample can be neutralized by having it pass through an SPE cartridge packed with cation-exchange material in the acidic form.

PROCEDURE

Conductometric detection requires high purity water (generally, resistivity greater than 18 megohm-cm) and high-purity chemicals for the preparation of the mobile phase. For ion-pair separation with UV detection, water and mobile phase components of low UV absorbance should be used.

For ion exchange, the retention time of ions increases with a decrease in the ionic strength and valency (charge) of the mobile phase components. For example, at equimolar concentrations of sodium hydroxide or sodium carbonate mobile phase, capacity factors (k') for anions are smaller with sodium hydroxide as the mobile phase than with sodium carbonate as the mobile phase. Some mobile phases, such as sodium hydroxide, can absorb ambient carbon dioxide, resulting in its composition change and often in baseline artifacts. In this instance, care should be taken to prevent absorption of carbon dioxide by the sodium hydroxide mobile phase.

For ion exclusion, capacity factors of organic acids increase with an increase in ionic strength or concentration of mineral acids but decrease with the increase of the column temperature. Because permeation volume remains constant, these effects are usually small. Addition of a solvent such as acetonitrile shortens the retention of organic acids.

Like other HPLC techniques, IC systems are calibrated by plotting peak responses in comparison with known concentrations of a reference standard, using either an external or internal standardization procedure.

NEAR-INFRARED SPECTROSCOPY*

INTRODUCTION

Near-infrared (NIR) spectroscopy is a branch of vibrational spectroscopy that shares many of the principles that apply to other spectroscopic measurements. The NIR spectral region comprises two subranges associated with detectors used in the initial development of NIR instrumentation. The short-wavelength (Herschel or silicon region) extends from approximately 780 to 1100 nm (12,821–9000 cm^{-1}); and longer wavelengths, between 1100 and 2500 nm, compose the traditional (lead sulfide) NIR region. Applications of NIR spectroscopy use spectra displayed in either wavelength or wavenumber units. As is the case with other spectroscopy measurements, interactions between NIR radiation and matter provide information that can be for both qualitative and quantitative assessment of the chemical composition of samples. In addition, qualitative and quantitative characterization of a sample's physical properties can be made because of the sample's influence on NIR spectra. Measurements can be made directly on samples in situ in addition to applications during standard sampling and testing procedures.

*This text is adapted from General Chapter ⟨1119⟩ of the *United States Pharmacopeia and National Formulary* (*USP–NF*) as published in *USP 32–NF 27*. This text is provided for informational purposes only and is intended as a resource for the FCC user. Note that because the *USP–NF* is in continuous revision, this General Chapter is subject to change and the text printed here may not continue to represent the current version.

Applications of qualitative analysis include identification of raw material, in-process sample, or finished product. These applications often involve comparing an NIR spectrum from a sample to reference spectra and assessing similarities against acceptance criteria developed and validated for a specific application. In contrast, applications of quantitative analysis involve the development of a predictive relationship between NIR spectral attributes and sample properties. These applications typically use numerical models to quantitatively predict chemical and/or physical properties of the sample on the basis of NIR spectral attributes.

Vibrational spectroscopy in the NIR region is dominated by overtones and combinations that are much weaker than the fundamental mid-IR vibrations from which they originate. Because molar absorptivities in the NIR range are low, radiation can penetrate several millimeters into materials, including solids. Many materials, such as glass, are relatively transparent in this region. Fiber-optic technology is readily implemented in the NIR range, which allows monitoring of processes in environments that might otherwise be inaccessible.

The instrument qualification tests and acceptance criteria provided in this chapter may not be appropriate for all instrument configurations. In such cases, alternative instrument qualification and performance checks should be scientifically justified and documented. In addition, validation parameters discussed in this chapter may not be applicable for all applications of NIR spectroscopy. Validation parameters characterized for a specific NIR application should demonstrate suitability of the NIR application for its intended use.

Transmission and Reflection

The most common measurements performed in the NIR spectral range are transmission and reflection spectroscopy. Incident NIR radiation is absorbed or scattered by the sample and is measured as transmittance or reflectance, respectively. Transflection spectrometry is a hybrid of transmission and reflection wherein a reflector is placed behind the sample so that the optical path through the sample and back to the detector is doubled compared to a transmission measurement of a sample of the same thickness. Transflection is used to describe any double-pass transmission technique. The light may be reflected from a diffuse or specular (mirror) reflector placed behind the sample. This configuration can be adapted to share instrument geometry with certain reflection or fiber-optic probe systems in which the source and the detector are on the same side of the sample.

TRANSMITTANCE, T, is a measure of the decrease in radiation intensity as a function of wavelength when radiation is passed through a sample. The sample is placed in the optical beam between the source and the detector. The results of both transmission and transflection measurements are usually presented directly in terms of absorbance, i.e., $\log_{10}(1/T)$.

REFLECTANCE, R, is a measure of the ratio of the intensity of light reflected from the sample, I, to that reflected from a background or reference reflective surface, I_R. Most reflection measurements in the NIR are made of scattering samples such as powders and slurries. For such materials NIR radiation can penetrate a substantial distance into the sample, where it can be absorbed when the wavelength of the radiation corresponds to a transition between the ground vibrational state of the analyte and either a harmonic of a given vibrational mode (an *overtone*) or the sum of two or more different modes (a *combination band*). Nonabsorbed radiation is scattered back from the sample to the detector. NIR reflection spectra are accessed by calculating and plotting $\log(1/R)$ versus wavelength. This logarithmic form is the pseudo-absorbance of the material and is commonly called absorbance.

Factors That Affect NIR Spectra

The following list is not exhaustive, but it includes many of the major factors that affect NIR spectra.

Sample Temperature—Sample temperature influences spectra obtained from aqueous solutions and other hydrogen-bonded liquids, and a difference of a few degrees may result in significant spectral changes. Temperature may also affect spectra obtained from less polar liquids, as well as solids that contain solvents and/or water.

Moisture and Solvent—Moisture and solvent present in the sample material and analytical system may change the spectrum of the sample. Both absorption by moisture and solvent and their influence on hydrogen bonding of the APIs and excipients can change the NIR spectrum.

Sample Thickness—Sample thickness is a known source of spectral variability and must be understood and/or controlled. The sample thickness in transmission mode is typically controlled by using a fixed optical path length for the sample. In diffuse reflection mode, the sample thickness is typically controlled by using samples that are "infinitely thick" relative to the detectable penetration depth of NIR light into a solid material. Here "infinite thickness" implies that the reflection spectrum does not change if the thickness of the sample is increased.

Sample Optical Properties—In solids, both surface and bulk scattering properties of calibration standards and analytical samples must be taken into account. Surface morphology and refractive index properties affect the scattering properties of solid materials. For powder materials, particle size and bulk density influence scattering properties and the NIR spectrum.

Polymorphism—Variation in crystalline structure (polymorphism) from materials with the same chemical composition can influence NIR spectral response. Different polymorphs and amorphous forms of solid material may be distinguished from one another on the basis of their NIR spectral properties. Similarly, different crystalline hydration or solvation states of the same material can display different NIR spectral properties.

Age of Samples—Samples may exhibit changes in their chemical, physical, or optical properties over time. Care must be taken to ensure that both samples and standards used for NIR analysis are suitable for the intended application.

INSTRUMENTATION

Apparatus

All NIR measurements are based on exposing material to incident NIR light radiation and measuring the attenuation of the emerging (transmitted, scattered, or reflected) light. Several spectrophotometers are available; they are based on different operating principles—for example: filters, grating-based dispersive, acousto-optical tunable filter (AOTF), Fourier–transform NIR (FT–NIR), and liquid crystal tunable filter (LCTF). Silicon, lead sulfide, indium gallium arsenide, and deuterated triglycine sulphate are common detector materials. Conventional cuvette sample holders, fiber-optic probes, transmission dip cells, and spinning or traversing sample holders are common examples of sample interfaces for introducing the sample to the optical train of a spectrometer.

The selection of specific NIR instrumentation and sampling accessories should be based on the intended application, and particular attention should be paid to the suitability of the sampling interface for the type of sample that will be analyzed.

Near-Infrared Reference Spectra

NIR references, by providing known stable measurements to which other measurements can be compared, are used to minimize instrumental variations that would affect the measurement.

Transmittance—The measurement of transmittance requires a background reference spectrum for determining the absorption by the sample relative to the background. Suitable transmittance reference materials depend on the specific NIR application and include air, an empty cell, a solvent blank, or a reference sample.

Reflectance—The measurement of reflectance requires the measurement of a reference reflection spectrum to determine the attenuation of reflected light relative to the unattenuated incident beam. The reflectance spectrum is calculated as the ratio of the single-beam spectrum of the sample to that of the reference material. Suitable reflectance reference materials depend on the specific NIR application and include ceramic, perfluorinated polymers, gold, and other suitable materials.

Qualification of NIR Instruments

Qualification—Qualification of an NIR instrument can be divided into three elements: Installation Qualification (IQ); Operational Qualification (OQ); and Performance Qualification (PQ).

Installation Qualification—The IQ requirements help ensure that the hardware and software are installed to accommodate safe and effective use of the instrument at the desired location.

Operational Qualification—In operational qualification, an instrument's performance is characterized using standards to verify that the system operates within target specifications. The purpose of operational qualification is to demonstrate that instrument performance is suitable. Because there are so many different approaches for measuring NIR spectra, operational qualification using standards with known spectral properties is recommended. Using external traceable reference standard materials does not justify omitting the instrument's internal quality control procedures. As is the case with any spectroscopic device, wavelength uncertainty, photometric linearity, and noise characteristics of NIR instruments should be qualified against target specifications for the intended application.

Performance Qualification—Performance qualification demonstrates that the NIR measurement consistently operates within target specifications defined by the user for a specific application; it is often referred to as *system suitability*. Performance qualification for NIR measurements can include comparing a sample or standard spectrum to previously recorded spectra. Comparisons of spectra taken over time from identical and stable samples or reference standard materials can form the basis for evaluating the long-term stability of an NIR measurement system. The objective is to demonstrate that no abnormal wavelength shift or change in detector sensitivity has occurred during ongoing analysis.

Characterizing Instrument Performance—Specific procedures, acceptance criteria, and time intervals for characterizing NIR instrument performance depend on the instrument and intended application. Many NIR applications use previously validated models that relate NIR spectral response to a physical or chemical property of interest. Demonstrating stable instrument performance over extended periods of time provides some assurance that reliable measurements can be taken from sample spectra using previously validated NIR models.

Wavelength Uncertainty—NIR spectra from sample and/or reference standard materials can be used to demonstrate an instrument's suitable wavelength dispersion performance against target specifications. The USP Near IR System Suitability Reference Standard or the National Institute of Standards and Technology (NIST) Standard Reference Material (SRM) 2036 for reflectance measurement and NIST SRM 2035 for transmittance measurement can be used for wavelength verification. Suitable materials for demonstrating wavelength dispersion performance include polystyrene, mixtures of rare earth oxides, and absorption by water vapor for instruments that use an interferometer for wavelength dispersion. With appropriate justification, alternative standards may be used. Wavelength uncertainty typically is characterized from a single spectrum (collected with the same spectral resolution to obtain the standard value) using a minimum of three peaks that cover a suitable spectral range of the instrument. Typical tolerances for agreement with standard values are ±1.0 nm from approximately 700 to 2000 nm and ±1.5 nm above 2000 nm to approximately 2500 nm (±8 cm^{-1} below 5000 cm^{-1} and ±4 cm^{-1} from 5000 cm^{-1} to approximately 14,000 cm^{-1}). Alternative tolerances may be used when justified for specific applications.

Photometric Linearity and Response Stability—NIR spectra from samples and/or reference standard materials with known relative transmittance or reflectance can be used to demonstrate a suitable relationship between NIR light attenuation (due to absorption) and instrument response. For reflectance measurements, commercially-available reflectance standards with known reflectance properties are often used. Spectra obtained from reflection standards are subject to variability as a result of the difference between the experimental conditions under which they were factory calibrated and those under which they are subsequently put to use. Hence, the reflectance values supplied with a set of calibration standards may not be useful in the attempt to establish an "absolute" calibration for a given instrument. Provided that (1) the standards do not change chemically or physically, (2) the same reference background is also used to obtain the standard values, and (3) the instrument measures each standard under identical conditions (including precise sample positioning), the reproducibility of the photometric scale will be established over the range of standards. Subsequent measurements on the identical set of standards give information on long-term stability. Photometric linearity is typically characterized using a minimum of four reference standards in the range from 10% to 90% reflection (or transmission). NIR applications based on measuring an absorbance larger than 1.0 may require standards with reflectivity properties between 2% and 5% reflection (or transmission) for characterizing instrument performance at low reflectance. The purpose is to demonstrate a linear relationship between NIR reflectance and/or transmittance and instrument response over the scanning range of the instrument. Typical tolerances for a linear relationship are 1.00 ± 0.05 for the slope and 0.00 ± 0.05 for the intercept of a plot of the measured photometric response versus standard photometric response. Alternative tolerances may occur when justified for specific applications.

Spectroscopic Noise—NIR instrument software may include built-in procedures to automatically determine system noise and to provide a statistical report of noise or S/N over the instrument's operating range. In addition, it may be desirable to supplement such checks with measurements that do not rely directly on manufacturer-supplied procedures. Typical procedures involve measuring spectra of traceable reference materials with high and low reflectance. Tolerances for these procedures should demonstrate suitable S/N for the intended application.

HIGH-FLUX NOISE—Instrument noise is evaluated at high-light flux by measuring reflectance or transmittance of the reference standard, with the reference material (e.g., 99% reflection standard) acting as both the sample and the background reference.

LOW-FLUX NOISE—The same procedure may be used with a lower-reflectivity reference material (e.g., 10% reflectance standard) to determine system noise at reduced light flux.

The source, optics, detector, and electronics make significant contributions to the noise under these conditions.

METHOD VALIDATION

Introduction

The objective of NIR method validation, as is the case with the validation of any analytical procedure, is to demonstrate that the measurement is suitable for its intended purpose. NIR spectroscopy is somewhat different from conventional analytical techniques because validation of the former generally is achieved by the assessment of chemometric parameters, but these parameters can still be related to the fundamental validation characteristics required for any analytical method.

Data pretreatment is often a vital step in the chemometric analysis of NIR spectral data. Data pretreatment can be defined as the mathematical transformation of NIR spectral data to enhance spectral features and/or remove or reduce unwanted sources of variation prior to using the spectrum. *Calibration* is the process of developing a mathematical relationship between NIR spectral response and properties of samples. Many suitable chemometric algorithms for data pretreatment and calibration exist; the selection should be based on sound scientific judgment and suitability for the intended application.

Validation Parameters

Performance characteristics that demonstrate the suitability of NIR methods are similar to those required for any analytical procedure. A discussion of the applicable general principles is found elsewhere in the Food Chemicals Codex. These principles should be considered typical for NIR procedures, but exceptions should be dealt with on a case-by-case basis. Specific acceptance criteria for each validation parameter must be consistent with the intended use of the method. The samples for validation should be independent of the calibration set.

Specificity—The extent of specificity testing depends on the intended application. Demonstration of specificity in NIR methods is typically accomplished by using the following approaches:

Qualitative—Identification testing is a common application of qualitative NIR spectroscopy. Identification is achieved by comparing a sample spectrum to a reference spectrum or a library of reference spectra. The specificity of the NIR identification method is demonstrated by obtaining positive identification from samples coupled with negative results from materials that should not meet criteria for positive identification. Materials to demonstrate specificity should be based on sound scientific judgment and can include materials similar in visual appearance, chemical structure, or name.

Quantitative—Quantitative applications of NIR spectroscopy typically involve establishing a mathematical relationship between NIR spectral response and a physical or chemical property of interest. Demonstrating specificity against a physical or chemical property of interest is based on interpreting both NIR spectral attributes and chemometric parameters in terms of the intended application and may include the following:
- Spectral regions in the calibration model can be correlated to a known NIR spectral response associated with the property of interest.
- Wavelengths used by regression analysis for the calibration (e.g., for multiple linear regression [MLR] models) or the loading vector for each factor (e.g., for partial least squares [PLS] or principal component regression [PCR] models) can be examined to verify relevant spec-

troscopic information that is used for the mathematical model.
- Variation in spectra from samples for calibration can be examined and interpreted as expected spectral observations.
- Variation in material composition and sample matrix may be shown to have no significant effect on quantification of the property of interest within the specified method range.

Linearity—Quantitative NIR methods generally attempt to demonstrate a linear relationship between NIR spectral response and the property of interest. Although demonstrating a linear response is not required for all NIR applications, the model chosen, whether linear or not, should properly represent the relationship.

Validation of linearity in NIR methods may be accomplished by examining a plot of NIR spectral response versus actual or accepted values for the property of interest. Many statistical methods are available for evaluation of the goodness of fit of the linear relationship. Other applicable statistics and graphical methods may be as appropriate.

The correlation coefficient, r, may not be an informative measure of linearity. The square of the (Pearson) correlation coefficient is a measure of the fraction of the data's variation that is adequately modeled by the equation. Linearity depends on the standard error of the calibration equation (and hence the reference method) and on the range of the calibration data. Thus, although values very near 1.00, such as 0.99 or greater, typically indicate a linear relationship, lower values do not distinguish between nonlinearity and variability around the line.

Range—The specified range of an NIR method depends on the specific application. The range typically is established by confirming that the NIR method provides suitable measurement capability (accuracy and precision) when applied to samples within extreme limits of the NIR measurement. Controls must be used to ensure that results outside the validated range are not accepted. In certain circumstances, it may not be possible or desirable to extend the validated range to include sample variability outside the validated range. Extending the range of an NIR method requires demonstration of suitable measurement capability within the limits of the expanded range. Examples of situations in which only a limited sample range may be available are samples from a controlled manufacturing process and in-process samples. A limited method range does not preclude the use of an NIR method.

Accuracy—Accuracy in NIR methods is demonstrated by showing the closeness of agreement between the value that is accepted as either a conventional true value or an accepted reference value. Accuracy can be determined by direct comparison between NIR validation results and actual or accepted reference values. Suitable agreement between NIR and reference values is based on required measurement capability for a specific application. The purpose is to demonstrate a linear relationship between NIR results and actual values. Accuracy can be determined by agreement between the standard error of prediction (SEP) and the standard error of the reference method for validation. The error of the reference method may be known on the basis of historical data, through validation results specific to the reference method, or by calculating the standard error of the laboratory (SEL). Suitable agreement between SEP and SEL is based on required measurement capability for a specific application.

Precision—The precision of an NIR method expresses the closeness of agreement between a series of measurements under prescribed conditions. Two levels of precision should be considered: repeatability and intermediate precision. The precision of an NIR method typically is expressed as the relative standard deviation of a series of NIR method results and should be suitable for the intended application. Demonstration of precision in NIR methods may be accomplished using the following approaches:

Repeatability—Repeatability can be demonstrated by the following:
- Statistical evaluation of a number of replicate measurements of the sample without repositioning the sample between each individual spectral acquisition, or
- Statistical evaluation of multiple NIR method results, each result from a replicate analysis of a sample subsequent to re-positioning between spectral acquisitions

Intermediate Precision—Intermediate precision can be shown by the following:
- Statistical evaluation of a number of replicate NIR measurements of the same or similar samples in the *Repeatability* study by different analysts on different days.

Robustness—NIR measurement parameters selected to demonstrate robustness will vary depending on the application and the sample's interface with the NIR instrument. Critical measurement parameters associated with robustness often are identified and characterized during method development. Typical measurement parameters include the following:
- Effect of environmental conditions (e.g., temperature, humidity, and vibration)
- Effect of sample temperature
- Sample handling (e.g., probe depth, compression of material, sample depth/thickness, sample presentation)
- Influence of instrument changes (e.g., lamp change, warm-up time)

Ongoing Method Evaluation

Validated NIR methods should be subject to ongoing performance evaluation, which may include monitoring accuracy, precision, and other suitable method parameters. If performance is unacceptable, corrective action is necessary. It involves conducting an investigation to identify the cause of change in method performance and may indicate that the NIR method is not suitable for continued use. Improving the NIR method to meet measurement suitability criteria may require additional method development and documentation of validation experiments demonstrating that the improved method is suitable for the intended application. The extent of revalidation required depends on the cause of change in method performance and the nature of corrective action required in order to establish suitable method performance. Appropriate change controls should be implemented to document ongoing method improvement activities.

Revalidation of a qualitative model may be necessary as a result of the following:
- Addition of a new material to the spectral reference library
- Changes in the physical properties of the material
- Changes in the source of material supply
- Identification of previously unknown critical attribute(s) of material(s)

Revalidation of a quantitative model may be necessary as a result of the following:
- Changes in the composition of the test sample or finished product
- Changes in the manufacturing process
- Changes in the sources or grades of raw materials
- Changes in the reference analytical method
- Major changes in instrument hardware

Outliers—Sample spectra that produce an NIR response that differs from the qualitative or quantitative calibration model may produce an outlier. This does not necessarily indicate an out-of-specification result; but rather an outlier indicates that further testing of the sample may be required and is dependent on the particular NIR method. If subsequent testing of the sample by an appropriate method indicates that the property of interest is within specifications, then the sample meets its specifications. Outlier samples may be incorporated into an updated calibration model subsequent to execution and documentation of suitable validation studies.

Method Transfer

Controls and measures for demonstrating the suitability of NIR method performance following method transfer are similar to those required for any analytical procedure. Exceptions to general principles for conducting method transfer for NIR methods should be justified on a case-by-case basis. The transfer of an NIR method is often performed by using an NIR calibration model on a second instrument that is similar to the primary instrument used to develop and validate the method. When a calibration model is transferred to another instrument, procedures and criteria must be applied to demonstrate that the calibration model meets suitable measurement criteria on the second instrument. The selection of an appropriate calibration model transfer procedure should be based on sound scientific judgment.

GLOSSARY

ABSORBANCE, A, is represented by the equation:

$$A = -\log T = \log (1/T)$$

where T is the transmittance of the sample. Absorbance is also frequently given as:

$$A = \log (1/R)$$

where R is the reflectance of the sample.

BACKGROUND SPECTRUM is used for generating a sample spectrum with minimal contributions from instrument response. It is also referred to as a *reference spectrum* or *background reference*. The ratio of the sample spectrum to the background spectrum produces a transmittance or reflectance spectrum dominated by NIR spectral response associated with the sample. In reflection measurements, a highly reflective diffuse standard reference material is for the measurement of the background spectrum. For transmission measurement, the background spectrum may be measured with no sample present in the spectrometer or using a cell with the solvent blank or a cell filled with appropriate reference material.

CALIBRATION MODEL is a mathematical expression to relate the response from an analytical instrument to the properties of samples.

DIFFUSE REFLECTANCE is the ratio of the spectrum of radiated light penetrating the sample surface, interacting with the sample, passing back through the sample's surface, and reaching the detector to the background spectrum. This is the component of the overall reflectance that produces the absorption spectrum of the sample.

FIBER-OPTIC PROBES consist of two components: optical fibers that may vary in length and in the number of fibers and a terminus, which contains specially designed optics for examination of the sample matrix.

INSTALLATION QUALIFICATION is the documented collection of activities necessary to establish that an instrument is delivered as designed and specified, is properly installed in the selected environment, and that this environment is suitable for the instrument's intended purpose.

INSTRUMENT BANDWIDTH OR RESOLUTON is a measure of the ability of a spectrometer to separate radiation of similar wavelengths.

MULTIPLE LINEAR REGRESSION is a calibration algorithm to relate the response from an analytical instrument to the properties of samples. The distinguishing feature of this algorithm is the use of a limited number of independent variables. Linear-least-squares calculations are performed to establish a relationship between these independent variables and the properties of the samples.

OPERATIONAL QUALIFICATION is the process by which it is demonstrated and documented that an instrument performs according to specifications and that it can perform the intended task. This process is required following any significant change such as instrument installation, relocation, or major repair.

OVERALL REFLECTANCE is the sum of diffuse and specular reflectance.

PARTIAL LEAST SQUARES (PLS) is a calibration algorithm to relate instrument responses to the properties of samples. The distinguishing feature of this algorithm is that data concerning the properties of the samples for calibration are used in the calculation of the factors to describe instrument responses.

PERFORMANCE QUALIFICATION is the process of using one or more well-characterized and stable reference materials to verify consistent instrument performance. Performance qualification may employ the same or different standards for different performance characteristics.

PHOTOMETRIC LINEARITY, also referred to as *photometric verification*, is the process of verifying the response of the photometric scale of an instrument.

PRINCIPAL COMPONENT REGRESSION (PCR) is a calibration algorithm to relate the response from an analytical instrument to the properties of samples. This algorithm, which expresses a set of independent variables as a linear combination of factors, is a method of relating these factors to the properties of the samples for which the independent variables were obtained.

PSEUDO-ABSORBANCE, A, is represented by the equation:

$$A = -\log R = \log (1/R)$$

where R is the diffuse reflectance of the sample.

REFERENCE SPECTRUM—See *Background Spectrum*.

REFLECTANCE is described by the equation:

$$R = I/I_R$$

in which I is the intensity of radiation reflected from the surface of the sample and I_R is the intensity of radiation reflected from a background reference material and its incorporated losses due to solvent absorption, refraction, and scattering.

ROOT-MEAN-SQUARE (RMS) NOISE is calculated by the equation:

$$RMS = \sqrt{\frac{1}{N} \times \sum_{i}^{N} \left(A_i - \overline{A} \right)^2}$$

in which A_i is the absorbance for each data point; $\overline{A}$ is the mean absorbance over the spectral segment; and N is the number of points per segment.

SPECTRAL REFERENCE LIBRARY is a collection of spectra of known materials for comparison with unknown materials. The term is commonly used in connection with qualitative methods of spectral analysis (e.g., identification of materials).

SPECULAR (SURFACE) REFLECTANCE is the reflectance of the front surface of the sample.

STANDARD ERROR OF CALIBRATION (SEC) is a measure of the capability of a model to fit reference data. SEC is the standard deviation of the residuals obtained from comparing the known values for each of the calibration samples to the values that are calculated from the calibration. SEC should not be used as an assessment tool for the expected method accuracy (trueness and precision of prediction) of the predicted value of future samples. The method accuracy should generally be verified by calculating the standard error of prediction (SEP), using an independent validation set of samples. An accepted method is to mark a part of the calibration set as the validation set. This set is not fully independent but can be used as an alternative for the determination of the accuracy.

STANDARD ERROR OF CROSS-VALIDATION (SECV) is the standard deviation calculated using the leave-one-out method. In this method, one calibration sample is omitted from the calibration, and the difference is found between the value for this sample calculated from its reference value and the value obtained from the calibration calculated from all the other samples in the set. This process is repeated for all samples in the set, and the SECV is the standard deviation of the differences calculated for all the calibration samples. This procedure can also be performed with a group of samples. Instead of leaving the sample out, a group of samples is left out. The SECV is a measure of the model accuracy that one can expect when measuring future samples if not enough samples are available for the SEP to be calculated from a completely independent validation set.

STANDARD ERROR OF THE LABORATORY (SEL) is a calculation based on repeated readings of one or more samples to estimate the precision and/or accuracy of the reference laboratory method, depending on how the data were collected.

STANDARD ERROR OF PREDICTION (SEP) is a measure of model accuracy of an analytical method based on applying a given calibration model to the spectral data from a set of samples different from but similar to those used to calculate the calibration model. SEP is the standard deviation of the residuals obtained from comparing the values from the reference laboratory to those from the method under test for the specified samples. SEP provides a measure of the model accuracy expected when one measures future samples.

SURFACE REFLECTANCE, also known as *specular reflection*, is that portion of the radiation not interacting with the sample but simply reflecting back from the sample surface layer (sample–air interface).

TRANSFLECTION is a transmittance measurement technique in which the radiation traverses the sample twice. The second time occurs after the radiation is reflected from a surface behind the sample.

TRANSMITTANCE is represented by the equation:

$$T = I/I_0 \text{ or } T = 10^A$$

in which I is the intensity of the radiation transmitted through the sample; I_0 is the intensity of the radiant energy incident on the sample and includes losses due to solvent absorption, refraction, and scattering; and A is the absorbance.

RAMAN SPECTROSCOPY*

INTRODUCTION

Raman spectroscopy shares many of the principles that apply to other spectroscopic measurements discussed in *Spectrophotometry and Light-Scattering*. Raman is a vibrational spectroscopic technique and is therefore related to infrared (IR) and near-infrared (NIR) spectroscopy. The Raman effect itself arises as a result of a change in the polarizability of molecular bonds during a given vibrational mode and is measured as inelastically scattered radiation.

---

* This text is adapted from General Chapter ⟨1120⟩ of the *United States Pharmacopeia and National Formulary* (*USP–NF*) as published in *USP 32–NF 27*. This text is provided for informational purposes only and is intended as a resource for the FCC user. Note that because the *USP–NF* is in continuous revision, this General Chapter is subject to change and the text printed here may not continue to represent the current version.

A Raman spectrum is generated by exciting the sample of interest to a virtual state with a monochromatic source, typically a laser. Light elastically scattered (no change in wavelength) is known as Rayleigh scatter and is not of interest in Raman spectrometry, except for marking the laser wavelength. However, if the sample relaxes to a vibrational energy level that differs from the initial state, the scattered radiation is shifted in energy. This shift is commensurate with the energy difference between the initial and final vibrational states. This "inelastically scattered" light is referred to as Raman scatter. Only about one in 10^6–10^8 photons incident on the sample undergoes Raman scattering. Thus lasers are employed in Raman spectrometers. If the Raman-scattered photon is of lower energy, it is referred to as Stokes scattering. If it is of higher energy, it is referred to as anti-Stokes scattering. In practice, nearly all analytically useful Raman measurements make use of Stokes-shifted Raman scatter.

The appearance of a Raman spectrum is much like an infrared spectrum plotted linearly in absorbance. The intensities, or the number of Raman photons counted, are plotted against the shifted energies. The x-axis is generally labeled "Raman Shift/cm^{-1}" or "Wavenumber/cm^{-1}". The Raman shift is usually expressed in wavenumber and represents the difference in the absolute wavenumber of the peak and the laser wavenumber. The spectrum is interpreted in the same manner as the corresponding mid-infrared spectrum. The positions of the (Raman shifted) wavenumbers for a given vibrational mode are identical to the wavenumbers of the corresponding bands in an IR absorption spectrum. However, the stronger peaks in a Raman spectrum are often weak in an IR spectrum, and vice versa. Thus the two spectroscopic techniques are often said to be complementary.

Raman spectroscopy is advantageous because quick and accurate measurements can often be made without destroying the sample (solid, semisolid, liquid or, less frequently, gas) and with minimal or no sample preparation. The Raman spectrum contains information on fundamental vibrational modes of the sample that can yield both sample and process understanding. The signal is typically in the visible or NIR range, allowing efficient coupling to fiber optics. This also means that a signal can be obtained from any medium transparent to the laser light; examples are glass, plastics, or samples in aqueous media. In addition, because Raman spectra are ordinarily excited with visible or NIR radiation, standard glass/quartz optics may be used. From an instrumental point of view, modern systems are easy to use, provide fast analysis times (seconds to several minutes), and are reliable. However, the danger of using high-powered lasers must be recognized, especially when their wavelengths are in the NIR and, therefore, not visible to the eye. Fiber-optic probes should be used with caution and with reference to appropriate government regulations regarding lasers and laser classes.

In addition to "normal" Raman spectroscopy, there are several more specialized Raman techniques. These include resonance Raman (RR), surface-enhanced Raman spectroscopy (SERS), Raman optical activity (ROA), coherent anti-Stokes Raman spectroscopy (CARS), Raman gain or loss spectroscopy, and hyper-Raman spectroscopy; however, these techniques are not discussed in this general information chapter.

QUALITATIVE AND QUANTITATIVE RAMAN MEASUREMENTS

There are two general classes of measurements that are commonly performed by Raman spectrometry: qualitative and quantitative.

Qualitative Raman Measurements

Qualitative Raman measurements yield spectral information about the functional groups that are present in a sample. Because the Raman spectrum is specific for a given compound, qualitative Raman measurements can be used as a compendial ID test, as well as for structural elucidation.

Quantitative Raman Measurements

For instruments equipped with a detector that measures optical power (such as Fourier transform [FT]-Raman spectrometers), quantitative Raman measurements utilize the following relationship between signal, S_v, at a given wavenumber, v, and the concentration of an analyte, C:

$$S_v = K\sigma_v(v_L - v_\beta)^4 P_0 C$$

in which K is a constant that depends on laser beam diameter, collection optics, sample volume, and temperature; σ_v is the Raman cross section of the particular vibrational mode; v_L is the laser wavenumber; v_β is the wavenumber of the vibrational mode; and P_0 is the laser power. The Raman cross section, σ_v, is characteristic of the nature of the particular vibrational mode. The sample volume is defined by size of the focus of the laser beam at the sample, the optic being used for focusing, and the optical properties of the sample itself. Spot sizes at the sample can range from less than 1 µm for a microprobe to 6 mm for a large area sample system. For Raman spectrometers that measure the number of photons per second (such as change-coupled device [CCD]-Raman spectrometers) the corresponding equation is:

$$S_v = K\sigma_v v_L (v_L - v_\beta)^3 P_0 C$$

From the above equations, it is apparent that peak signal is directly proportional to concentration. It is this relationship that is the basis for the majority of quantitative Raman applications.

FACTORS AFFECTING QUANTIFICATION

Sample-Based Factors

The most important sample-based factors that deleteriously affect quantitative Raman spectrometry are fluorescence, sample heating, absorption by the matrix or the sample itself, and the effect of polarization. If the sample matrix includes fluorescent compounds, the measured signal will usually contain a contribution from fluorescence. Fluorescence will be observed only if the laser excitation wavelength overlaps with an absorption band of a fluorescent compound. Fluorescence is typically observed as a broad sloping background underlying the Raman spectrum. Fluorescence can cause both a baseline offset and reduced signal-to-noise ratio. The wavelength range and intensity of the fluorescence is dependent on the chemical composition of the fluorescent material. Because fluorescence is generally a much more efficient process than Raman scattering, even very minor amounts of fluorescent impurities can lead to significant degradation of the Raman signal. Fluorescence can be reduced by using longer wavelength excitation sources such as 785 nm or 1064 nm. However, it should be remembered that the strength of the Raman signal is proportional to $(v_L - v_\beta)^4$, so the advantage of using a long-wavelength excitation laser to minimize fluorescence is at least partially offset by the reduced strength of the Raman signal. The greatest signal-to-noise ratio will be obtained by balancing fluorescence rejection, signal strength, and detector response.

Fluorescence in solids can sometimes be mitigated by exposing the sample to the laser radiation for a period of time before measurement. This process is called photobleaching, and operates by degrading the highly absorbing species. Photobleaching is less effective in liquids, where the sample is mobile, or if the amount of fluorescent material is more than a trace.

Sample heating by the laser source can cause a variety of effects, such as physical form change (melting), polymorph conversion, or sample burning. The chance for sample heating is greatest when the spot size at the sample is the smallest, i.e., when a microprobe is being used. This is usually an issue for colored, highly absorbing species, or very small particles that have low heat transfer. The effects of sample heating are usually observable either as changes in the Raman spectrum over time or by visual inspection of the sample. Besides decreasing the laser flux, a variety of methods can be employed to diminish laser-induced heating, such as moving the sample or laser during the measurement or improving the heat transfer from the sample with thermal contact or liquid immersion.

Absorption of the Raman signal by the matrix or the sample itself can also occur. This problem is more prevalent with long-wavelength FT-Raman systems where the Raman signal can overlap with an NIR overtone absorption. This effect will be dependent on the optics of the system as well as on the sample presentation. Associated with this effect is variability from scattering in solids as a result of packing and particle-size differences. The magnitude of all of these effects, however, is typically less severe than in NIR because of the limited depth of penetration and the relatively narrower wavelength region sampled in Raman spectroscopy.

Finally, it should be recognized that laser radiation is polarized and the Raman spectra of crystalline materials and other oriented samples can differ significantly depending on the way that the sample is mounted. If the Raman spectrometer is capable of producing linearly polarized radiation at the sample then a polarization scrambler is recommended for routine sample analysis.

Sampling Factors

Raman spectroscopy is a zero-background technique, in that the signal at the detector is expected to be zero in the absence of a sample. This situation can be contrasted with absorption spectrometry, where the signal at the detector is at a maximum in the absence of a sample. Zero-background techniques are inherently sensitive because small changes in sample concentration lead to proportionate changes in the signal level. The instrument will also be sensitive to other sources of light that can cause sample-to-sample variations in the measured signal level. In addition, a large background signal caused by fluorescence will lead to an increased noise level (photon shot noise). Thus it may be very difficult to use the absolute Raman signal for direct determination of an analyte. Other potential sources of variation are changes in the sample opacity and heterogeneity, changes in the laser power at the sample, and changes in optical collection geometry or sample position. These effects can be minimized by sampling in a reproducible, representative manner. Careful design of the instrumentation can reduce these effects but they cannot be eliminated entirely.

Use of an internal reference standard is the most common and robust method of eliminating variations caused by absolute intensity fluctuations. There are several choices for this approach. An internal standard can be deliberately added, and isolated peaks from this standard can be employed; or a band due to a moiety such as an aromatic ring, the Raman cross-section of which does not change with the way the sample is prepared, can also be used. For solution spectra, an isolated solvent band can be employed because the solvent will remain relatively unchanged from sample to sample. Also, in a formulation, an excipient peak can be used if it is in substantial excess compared to the analyte.

The entire spectrum can also be used as a reference, with the assumption that laser and sample-orientation changes will affect the entire spectrum equally.

A second important sampling-based factor to consider is spectral contamination. Raman scattering is a weak effect that can be masked by a number of external sources. Common contamination sources include sample-holder artifacts (container or substrate) and ambient light. Typically, these issues can be identified and resolved by careful experimentation.

APPARATUS

Components

All modern Raman measurements involve irradiating a sample with a laser, collecting the scattered radiation, rejecting the Rayleigh-scattered light, differentiating the Raman photons by wavelength, and detecting the resulting Raman spectrum. All commercial Raman instruments therefore share the following common features to perform these functions:

1. Excitation source (laser)
2. Sampling device
3. Device to filter/reject light scattered at the laser wavelength
4. Wavelength processing unit
5. Detector and electronics

EXCITATION SOURCE (LASER)

Table 1 identifies several common lasers used for Raman spectrometry. UV lasers have also been used for specialized applications but have various drawbacks that limit their utility for general analytical measurements. As more applications for UV lasers are described, it is likely that they may become more common for Raman spectrometry.

SAMPLING DEVICE

Several sampling arrangements are possible, including direct optical interfaces, microscopes, fiber optic-based probes (either noncontact or immersion optics), and sample chambers (including specialty sample holders and automated sample changers). The sampling optics can also be designed to obtain the polarization-dependent Raman spectrum, which often contains additional information. Selection of the sampling device will often be dictated by the analyte and sample. However, considerations such as sampling volume, speed of the measurement, laser safety, and reproducibility of sample presentation should be evaluated to optimize the sampling device for any given application.

FILTERING DEVICE

The intensity of scattered light at the laser wavelength (Rayleigh) is many orders of magnitude greater than the Raman signal and must be rejected prior to the detector. Notch filters are almost universally used for this purpose and provide excellent rejection and stability combined with small size. The traditional use of multistage monochromators for this purpose, although still viable, is now rare. In addition, various filters or physical barriers to shield the sample from external radiation sources (e.g., room lights, laser plasma lines) may be required depending on the collection geometry of the instrument.

WAVELENGTH PROCESSING UNIT

The wavelength scale may be encoded by either a scanning monochromator, a grating polychromator (in CCD-Raman spectrometers) or a two-beam interferometer (in FT-Raman spectrometers). A discussion of the specific benefits and drawbacks of each of the dispersive designs compared to the FT instrument is beyond the scope of this chapter. Any properly qualified instruments should be suitable for qualitative measurements. However, care must be taken when selecting an instrument for quantitative measurements, as dispersion and response linearity might not be uniform across the full spectral range.

DETECTOR

The silicon-based CCD array is the most common detector for dispersive instruments. The cooled array detector allows measurements over the spectral range from 4500 to 100 cm^{-1} Raman shift with low noise when most visible lasers, such as frequency-doubled neodymium-doped yttrium–aluminum–garnet (Nd:YAG) (532 nm) or helium–neon (632.8 nm) lasers, are used. When a 785-nm diode laser is used, the wavelength range is reduced to about 3100 to 100 cm^{-1}. The most commonly used CCD has its peak wavelength responsivity when matched to the commonly used 632.8-nm He–Ne gas laser or 785-nm diode laser. FT instruments typically use single-channel germanium or indium–gallium–arsenide (InGaAs) detectors responsive in the NIR to match the 1064-nm excitation of a Nd:YAG laser.

Table 1. Lasers Used Commonly for Raman Spectroscopy

Laser λ, nm (nearest whole number)	Type	Typical Power at Laser	Wavelength Range, nm (Stokes Region, 100 cm^{-1} to 3000 cm^{-1} shift)	Comments
NIR Lasers				
1064	Solid state (Nd:YAG)	Up to 3 W	1075–1563	Commonly used in Fourier transform instruments
830	Diode	Up to 300 mW	827–980	Typically limited to 2000 cm^{-1}; Raman shift because of CCD spectral response; less common than the other lasers
785	Diode	Up to 500 mW	791–1027	Most widely used dispersive Raman laser
Visible Lasers				
632.8	He–Ne	Up to 500 mW	637–781	Relatively small fluorescence risk
532	Doubled (Nd:YAG)	Up to 1 W	535–632.8	High fluorescence risk
514.5	Ar+	Up to 1 W	517–608	High fluorescence risk
488–632.8	Ar+	Up to 1 W	490–572	High fluorescence risk

Calibration

Raman instrument calibration involves three components: primary wavelength (x-axis), laser wavelength, and intensity (y-axis).

PRIMARY WAVELENGTH (X-AXIS)

In the case of FT-Raman instruments, primary wavelength-axis calibration is maintained, at least to a first approximation, with an internal He–Ne laser. Most dispersive instruments utilize atomic emission lamps for primary wavelength-axis calibration. In all instruments suitable for analytical Raman measurements, the vendor will offer a procedure of x-axis calibration that can be performed by the user. For dispersive Raman instruments, a calibration based on multiple atomic emission lines is preferred. The validity of this calibration approach can be verified subsequent to laser wavelength calibration by using a suitable Raman shift standard. For scanning dispersive instruments, calibration might need to be performed more frequently, and precision in both a scanning and static operation mode may need to be verified.[1]

LASER WAVELENGTH

Laser wavelength variation can impact both the wavelength precision and the photometric (signal) precision of a given instrument. Even the most stable current lasers can vary slightly in their measured wavelength output. The laser wavelength must therefore be confirmed to ensure that the Raman shift positions are accurate for both FT-Raman or dispersive Raman instruments. A reference Raman shift standard material such as those outlined in ASTM E1840-96 (2002)[1] or other suitably verified materials can be utilized for this purpose. [NOTE—Reliable Raman shift standard values for frequently used liquid and solid reagents, required for wavenumber calibration of Raman spectrometers, are provided in the ASTM Standard Guide cited. These values can be used in addition to the highly accurate and precise low-pressure arc lamp emission lines that are also available for use in Raman instrument calibration.] Spectrometric grade material can be purchased from appropriate suppliers for this use. Certain instruments may use an internal Raman standard separate from the primary optical path. External calibration devices exactly reproduce the optical path taken by the scattered radiation. [NOTE—When chemical standards are used, care must be taken to avoid contamination and to confirm standard stability.]

Unless the instrument is of a continuous calibration type, the primary wavelength axis calibration should be performed, as per vendor procedures, just prior to measuring the laser wavelength. For external calibration, the Raman shift standard should be placed at the sample location and measured using appropriate acquisition parameters. The peak center of a strong, well-resolved band in the spectral region of interest should be evaluated. The position can be assessed manually or with a suitable, valid peak-picking algorithm. The software provided by the vendor might measure the laser wavelength and adjust the laser wavelength appropriately so that this peak is at the proper position. If the vendor does not provide this functionality, the laser wavelength should be adjusted manually. Depending on the type of laser, the laser wavelength can vary with temperature, current, and voltage. Wavelength tolerances can vary depending on the specific application.

SIGNAL LEVEL (Y-AXIS)

Calibration of the photometric axis can be critical for successful quantification by using certain analytical methods (chemometrics) and method transfer between instruments. Both FT-Raman and dispersive Raman spectrometers should undergo similar calibration procedures. The tolerance of photometric precision acceptable for a given measurement should be assessed during the method development stage.

To calibrate the photometric response of a Raman instrument, a broad-band emission source should be used. There are two accepted methods. *Method A* utilizes a tungsten white light source.[2] The output power of such sources is traceable to the National Metrology Institute (NMI). In the United Kingdom, the National Physical Laboratory also provides calibrated light bulbs. Several other vendors also provide NIST-traceable irradiance calibration standards. This method is applicable to all common laser excitation wavelengths listed in *Table 1*. In *Method B,* NIST standard reference materials (SRMs) are utilized.[3] Several doped-glass fluorescence standards are currently available.

Method A—The source should be placed at the sample location with the laser off and the response of the detector measured (using parameters appropriate for the instrument). The output for the source used for calibration should be known. The ratio of the measured response to the true response should be determined and a correction file generated. This correction should be applied to all spectra acquired with the instrument. Most manufacturers will provide both appropriate calibration sources and software for this approach. If the manufacturer does not provide a procedure or method, the user can accomplish the task using a source obtained from NIST and appropriate software. If a manufacturer's method is used, attention must be paid to the calibration procedure and source validity. The user should obtain appropriate documentation from the manufacturer to ensure a qualified approach.

Method B—The fluorescence standard should be placed at the sample location. With the laser on, a spectrum of the SRM should be obtained (using parameters appropriate for the instrument). The output of the source used for calibration should be known. The ratio of the measured response to the true response should be determined and a correction file generated. This correction should be applied to all spectra acquired with the instrument. Most manufacturers will provide both appropriate calibration sources and software for this approach. If the manufacturer does not provide a procedure or method, the user can accomplish the task using a source obtained from NIST and appropriate software. If a manufacturer's method is used, attention must be paid to the calibration procedure and source validity. The user should obtain appropriate documentation from the manufacturer to ensure a qualified approach. [NOTE—*Method B* is currently appropriate for systems with 785-nm (SRM 2241), 532-nm (SRM 2242), and both 514.5-nm and 488-nm (SRM 2243) laser excitation. NIST is currently developing other SRMs that will be wavelength-specific for 1064-nm (SRM 2244) and 632.8-nm excitation (expected to be available in 2006).]

EXTERNAL CALIBRATION

Detailed functional validation employing external reference standards is recommended to demonstrate instrumental suitability for laboratory instruments, even for instruments that possess an internal calibration approach. The use

---

[1] ASTM E1840-96 (2002) *Standard Guide for Raman Shift Standards for Spectrometer Calibration,* ASTM International, 100 Barr Harbor Drive, PO Box C700, West Conshohocken, PA, USA 19428-2959.

[2] NIST-traceable tungsten white light source statement: While the calibration of the Raman frequency (or Raman shift, cm^{-1}) axis using pure materials and an existing ASTM standard is well accepted, techniques for calibration of the Raman intensity axis are not. Intensity calibrations of Raman spectra can be accomplished with certified white light sources.
[3] NIST SRM 2241: Ray KG, McCreery RL. Raman intensity correction standard for systems operating with 785-nm excitation. *Appl. Spectrosc.* 1997, 51, 108–116.

of external reference standards does not obviate the need for internal quality control procedures; rather, it provides independent documentation of the fitness of the instrument to perform the specific analysis or purpose. For instruments installed in a process location or in a reactor where positioning of an external standard routinely is not possible, including those instruments that employ an internal calibration approach, the relative performance of an internal versus an external calibration approach should be periodically checked. The purpose of this test is to check for changes in components that might not be included in the internal calibration method (process lens, fiber-optic probe, etc.), e.g., photometric calibration of the optical system.

QUALIFICATION AND VERIFICATION OF RAMAN SPECTROMETERS

The suitability of a specific instrument for a given method is ensured by a thorough technology-suitability evaluation for the application; a routine, periodic instrument operational qualification; and the more frequent performance verification (see *Definition of Terms and Symbols*). The purpose of the technology-suitability evaluation is to ensure that the technology proposed is suitable for the intended application. The purpose of the instrument qualification is to ensure that the instrument to be used is suitable for its intended application and, when requalified periodically, continues to function properly over extended time periods. When the device is used for a specific qualitative or quantitative analysis, regular performance verifications are made. Because there are many different approaches to measuring Raman spectra, instrument operational qualification and performance verification often employ external standards that can be used on any instrument. As with any spectrometric device, a Raman instrument needs to be qualified for both wavenumber (x-axis and shift from the excitation source) and photometric (signal axis) precision.

In performance verification, a quality-of-fit to an initial scan or group of scans (often referred to in nonscanning instruments as an accumulation) included in the instrumental qualification can be employed. In such an analysis, it is assumed that reference standard spectra collected on a new or a newly repaired, properly operating instrument represent the best available spectra. Comparison of spectra taken over time on identical reference standards (either the original standard or identical new standards, if stability of the reference standards is a concern) forms the basis for evaluating the long-term stability of a Raman measurement system.

Frequency of Testing

Instrumental qualification is performed at designated intervals or following a repair or significant optical reconfiguration, such as the replacement of the laser, the detector or the notch or edge filters. Full instrument requalification might not be necessary when changing between sampling accessories such as a microprobe, a sample compartment, or a fixed fiber-optic probe. Performance verification tests may be sufficient in these cases; instrument-specific guidance from the vendor on qualification requirements should be followed. Tests include wavelength (x-axis and shift from the excitation source) and photometric (signal axis) precision. Instrument qualification tests require that specific application-dependent tolerances be met.

Performance verification is carried out on the instrument configured for the analytical measurements and is performed more frequently than instrument qualification. Performance verification includes measurement of the wavelength uncertainty and intensity-scale precision. Wavelength precision and intensity-scale precision tests may be needed prior to any data collection on a given day. Performance is verified by matching the current spectra to those collected during the previous instrument qualification.

Instrument Operational Qualification

It is important to note that the acceptance specifications given in both the *Instrument Operational Qualification* and *Performance Qualification* sections are applicable for general use; specifications for particular instruments and applications can vary depending on the analysis method used and the desired accuracy of the final result. ASTM standard reference materials are also specified, with the understanding that under some circumstances (specifically remote on-line applications) calibration using one of these materials may be impractical, and other suitably verified materials can be employed. At this juncture it is important to note that specific parameters such as spectrometer noise, limits of detection (LOD), limits of quantification (LOQ), and acceptable spectral bandwidth for any given application should be included as part of the analytical method development. Specific values for tests such as spectrometer noise and bandwidth will be dependent on the instrument chosen and the purpose required. As a result, specific instrument tests for these parameters are not dictated in this information chapter.

WAVELENGTH (X-AXIS) ACCURACY

It is important to ensure the accuracy of the wavelength axis via calibration to maintain the integrity of Raman peak positions. Wavelength calibration of a Raman spectrometer consists of two parts: primary wavelength axis and laser wavelength calibration. After both the primary wavelength axis and the laser wavelength are calibrated, instrument wavelength uncertainty can be determined. This can be accomplished using a Raman shift standard such as the ASTM shift standards or other suitably verified material. Selection of a standard with bands present across the full Raman spectral range is recommended so that instrument wavelength uncertainty can be evaluated at multiple locations within the spectrum. The tolerance of wavelength precision that is required for a given measurement should be assessed during the method-development stage. [NOTE—For scanning dispersive instruments, calibration might need to be performed more frequently, and precision in both a scanning and static operation mode may need to be verified.]

PHOTOMETRIC PRECISION

Laser variation in terms of the total emitted photons occurring between two measurements can give rise to changes in the photometric precision of the instrument. Unfortunately, it is very difficult to separate changes in the photometric response associated with variations in the total emitted laser photons from the sample- and sampling-induced perturbations. This is one of the reasons why absolute Raman measurements are strongly discouraged and why the photometric precision specification is set relatively loosely. The tolerance of photometric precision required for a given measurement should be assessed during the method-development stage.

PERFORMANCE QUALIFICATION

The objective of performance qualification is to ensure that the instrument is performing within specified limits with respect to wavelength precision, photometric axis precision, and sensitivity. In certain cases when the instrument has been set up for a specific measurement (for example, installed in a process reactor), it might no longer be possible or desirable to measure the wavelength and photometric (signal) qualification reference standards identified above. Provided instrument operational qualification has shown that the equipment is fit for use, a single external performance verification standard can be used to reverify function on a continuing basis (for example, a routinely used process solvent signal, for both wavelength and photometric precision, following reactor cleaning). The performance verification standard should match the format of the samples in the current analysis as closely as possible and use similar spectral acquisition parameters. Quantitative measurements of an external performance verification standard spectrum check both the wavelength (x-axis and laser wavelength) and the photometric (signal) precision. Favorable comparison of a series of performance verification spectra demonstrates proper continued operation of the instrument.

WAVELENGTH PRECISION

The wavelength precision should be measured by collecting data for a single spectrum of the selected Raman shift standard for a period equal to that used in the photometric consistency test. When appropriate, powdered samples should be repacked between each set of measurements. Peak positions across the spectral range of interest are used to calculate precision. Performance is verified by matching the current peak positions to those collected during the previous instrument qualification and should not vary with a standard deviation of more than ± 0.3 cm^{-1}, although this specification can be adjusted according to the required accuracy of the measurement.

PHOTOMETRIC PRECISION

The photometric precision should be measured by collecting data for a single spectrum of a suitably verified reference standard material for a specified time. After suitable baseline correction, the areas of a number of bands across the spectral range of interest should be calculated by means of an appropriate algorithm. The area of the strongest band is set to 1, and all other envelopes are normalized to this band. Performance is verified by matching the current band areas to the respective areas collected during the previous instrument qualification. The areas should vary by no more than 10%, although this specification can be adjusted according to the required accuracy of the measurement.

LASER POWER OUTPUT PRECISION AND ACCURACY

This test is applicable only to Raman instruments with automatic, internal laser power meters. Instruments without laser power measurement should utilize a calibrated laser power meter from a reputable supplier. The laser output should be set to a representative output, dictated by the requirements of the analytical measurement and the laser power measured. The output should be measured and checked against the output measured at instrument qualification. The power (in milliwatts or watts) should vary by no more than 25% compared to the qualified level. If the power varies by more than this amount, the instrument should be serviced (as this variation might indicate, among other things, a gross misalignment of the system or the onset of failure of the laser).

For instruments with an automatic, internal laser power meter, the accuracy of the values generated from the internal power meter should be compared to a calibrated external laser power meter at an interval of not more than 12 months. The internally calculated value should be compared to that generated by the external power meter. Performance is verified by matching the current value to that generated during the previous instrument qualification. The manufacturer might provide software to facilitate this analysis. If the instrument design prevents the use of an external power meter, then the supplier should produce documentation to ensure the quality of the instrument and provide a recommended procedure for the above analysis to be accomplished during a scheduled service visit.

METHOD VALIDATION

Validation of Raman methods will follow the same protocols as for other instrumental analytical methods in terms of accuracy, precision, etc. However, several of these criteria are affected by variables specific to Raman spectrometry.

Fluorescence is the primary variable that can affect the suitability of a method. The presence of fluorescent impurities in samples can be quite variable and have little effect on the acceptability of a material. The method must be flexible enough to accommodate different sampling regimes that may be necessary to minimize the effects of these impurities.

Detector linearity must be confirmed over the range of possible signal levels. Fluorescence might drive both the signal baseline and the noise higher than that used in the validation, in which case the fluorescence must be decreased, or the method modified to accommodate the higher fluorescence levels. This is also true for the precision, limit of detection, and limit of quantification of the method, as increased baseline noise will negatively impact all of these values. Because fluorescence can also affect quantification caused by baseline shifts, acceptable quantification at different levels of photobleaching, when used, should also be confirmed.

The impact of the laser on the sample must be determined. Visual inspection of the sample and qualitative inspection of the Raman spectrum for measurements with differing laser powers and exposure times will confirm that the sample is not being altered (other than by photobleaching). Specific variables to confirm in the spectrum are shifts in peak position, changes in peak height and band width, and unexpected changes in background intensity.

Method precision must also encompass sample position. The sample presentation is a critical factor for both solids and liquids, and must be either tightly controlled or accounted for in the calibration model. Sample-position sensitivity can often be minimized by appropriate sample preparation or sample holder geometry, but will vary from instrument to instrument based on excitation and collection optical configuration.

DEFINITION OF TERMS AND SYMBOLS

CALIBRATION MODEL is a mathematical expression that relates the response from an analytical instrument to the properties of samples.

INSTRUMENT BANDPASS (OR RESOLUTION) is a measure of the capability of a spectrometer to separate radiation of similar wavelengths.

OPERATIONAL QUALIFICATION is the process by which it is demonstrated and documented that the instrument performs according to specifications, and that it can perform the intended task. This process is required following any significant change such as instrument installation, relocation, major repair, etc.

PERFORMANCE QUALIFICATION is the process of using one or more well-characterized and stable reference materials to verify consistent instrument performance. Qualification may employ the same or different standards for different performance characteristics.

RAMAN SPECTRA[4] are plots of the radiant energy, or number of photons, scattered by the sample through the indirect interaction between the molecular vibrations in the sample and monochromatic radiation of frequency much higher than that of the vibrations. The abscissa is usually the difference in wavenumber between the incident and scattered radiation.

(NORMAL) RAMAN SCATTERING[4] is the inelastic scattering of radiation that occurs because of changes in the polarizability, of the relevant bonds during a molecular vibration. Normal

---
[4] Chalmers, J., Griffiths, P., Eds. *Handbook of Vibrational Spectroscopy;* John Wiley & Sons, Ltd: New York, 2002.

Raman spectra are excited by radiation that is not in resonance with electronic transitions in the sample.

RAMAN WAVENUMBER SHIFT[4],

$$\Delta \tilde{\nu}$$

is the wavenumber of the exciting line minus the wavenumber of the scattered radiation. SI unit: m^{-1}. Common unit: $cm^{-1} = 100\ m^{-1}$.

$$\beta \Delta \tilde{\nu}$$

where β is the differential Raman cross section, is positive for Stokes scattering and negative for anti-Stokes scattering.

SCOVILLE HEAT UNITS

Sample Preparation Transfer 200 mg of the sample into a 50-mL volumetric flask, dilute with alcohol to volume, and mix thoroughly by shaking. Allow the insolubles to settle before use.

Sucrose Solution Prepare a suitable volume of a 10% (w/v) solution of sucrose in water.

Standard Solution Add 0.15 mL of the *Sample Preparation* to 140 mL of the *Sucrose Solution*, and mix. This solution contains the equivalent of 240,000 Scoville Heat Units.

Test Solutions If the oleoresin sample is claimed to contain more than 240,000 Scoville Heat Units, prepare one or more dilutions according to the following table:

Scoville Heat Units	Standard Solution (mL)	Sucrose Solution (mL)
360,000	20	10
480,000	20	20
600,000	20	30
720,000	20	40
840,000	20	50
960,000	20	60
1,080,000	20	70
1,200,000	20	80
1,320,000	20	90
1,440,000	20	100
1,560,000	20	110
1,680,000	20	120
1,800,000	20	130
1,920,000	20	140
2,040,000	20	150

If the oleoresin sample is claimed to contain less than 240,000 Scoville Heat Units, prepare one or more dilutions according to the following table:

Scoville Heat Units	Sample Preparation (mL)	Sucrose Solution (mL)
100,000	0.15	60
117,500	0.15	70
170,000	0.15	100
205,000	0.15	120

Procedure Select five panel members who are thoroughly experienced with this method. Instruct the panelists to swallow 5 mL of the solution corresponding to the claimed content of Scoville Heat Units. The sample passes the test if three of the five panel members perceive a pungent or stinging sensation in the throat.

Acceptance criteria

Capsicum: Between 100,000 and 2,000,000, as specified on the label

Paprika (pungency): NMT 3000

Infrared Spectra

Notice to Users

The spectra included in this section have been published in previous versions of the *Food Chemicals Codex* as part of individual monographs. Comparison of samples to the spectra in this section does not satisfy monograph requirements for any of the samples represented by these images. These spectra are included for general information only, and users are required to comply with all of the tests in individual monographs in order to meet monograph specifications. As such, in cases where a monograph requires comparison of a sample IR spectrum to that of a Reference Standard, users may not substitute comparison to images in this section to meet monograph requirements.

Sample Preparation

Most of the substances for which spectra are provided are liquids at or near room temperature. Unless otherwise noted in the caption for an individual spectrum, the spectra for essential oils and flavor chemicals were obtained on the neat liquids contained in fixed-volume sodium chloride cells or between salt plates. For solids, the sample was prepared as a potassium bromide pellet or a mineral oil (Nujol or equivalent) dispersion, as indicated in the individual spectrum captions.

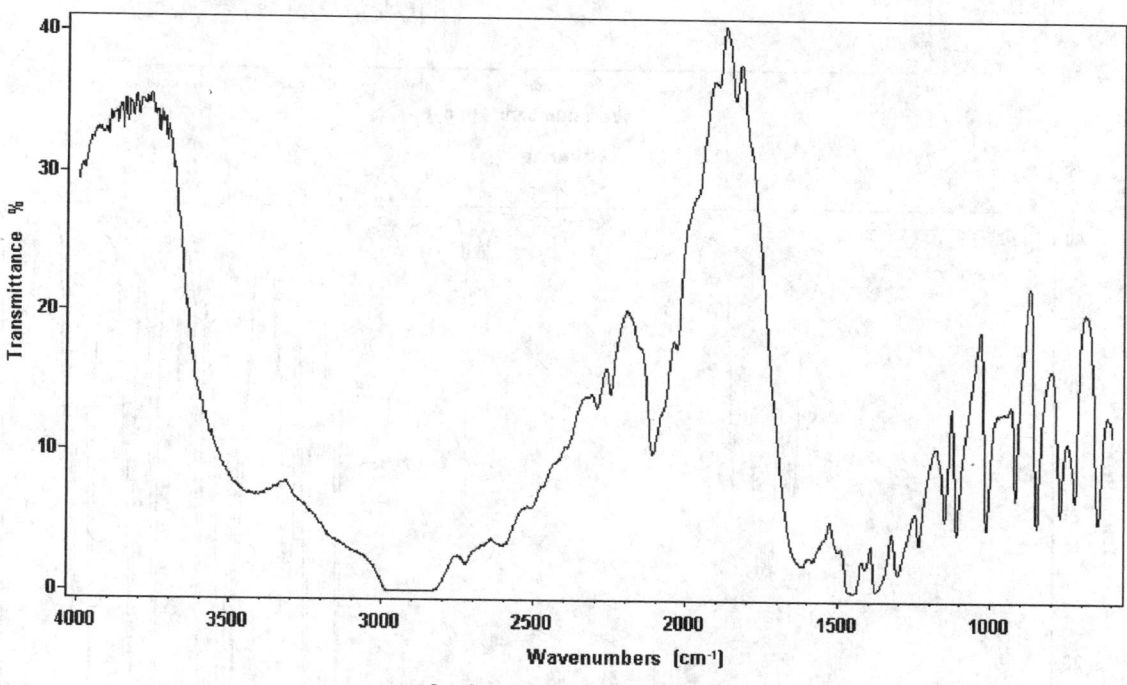

L-Alanine (Mineral Oil Mull)

1480 / Infrared Spectra / *General Information*

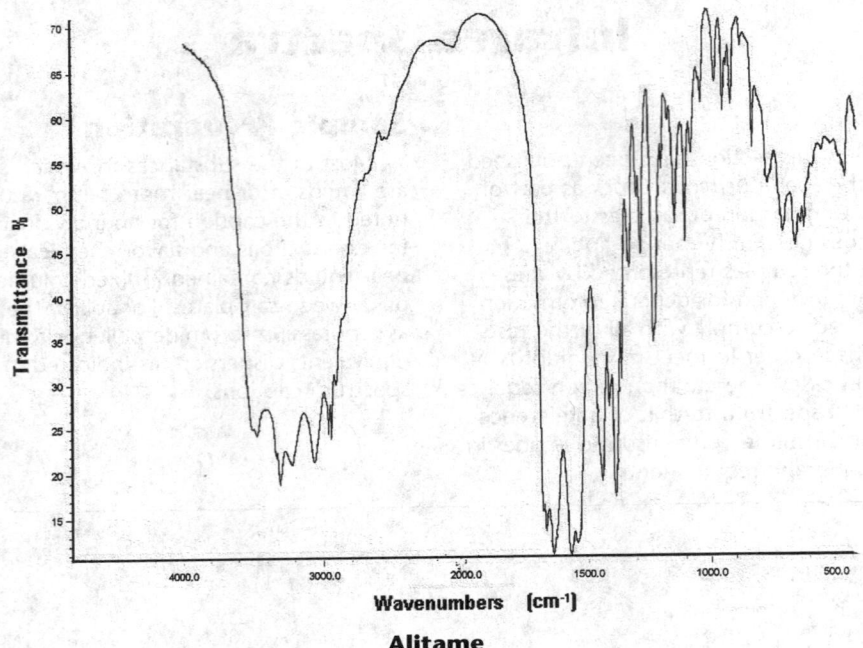

Alitame

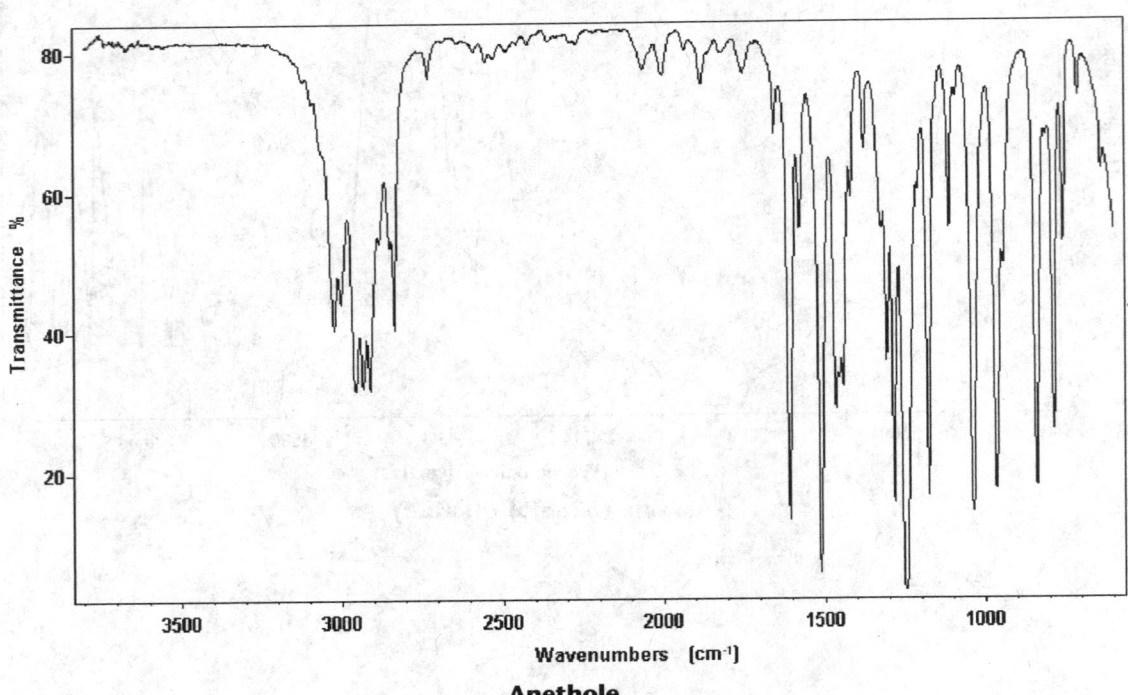

Anethole

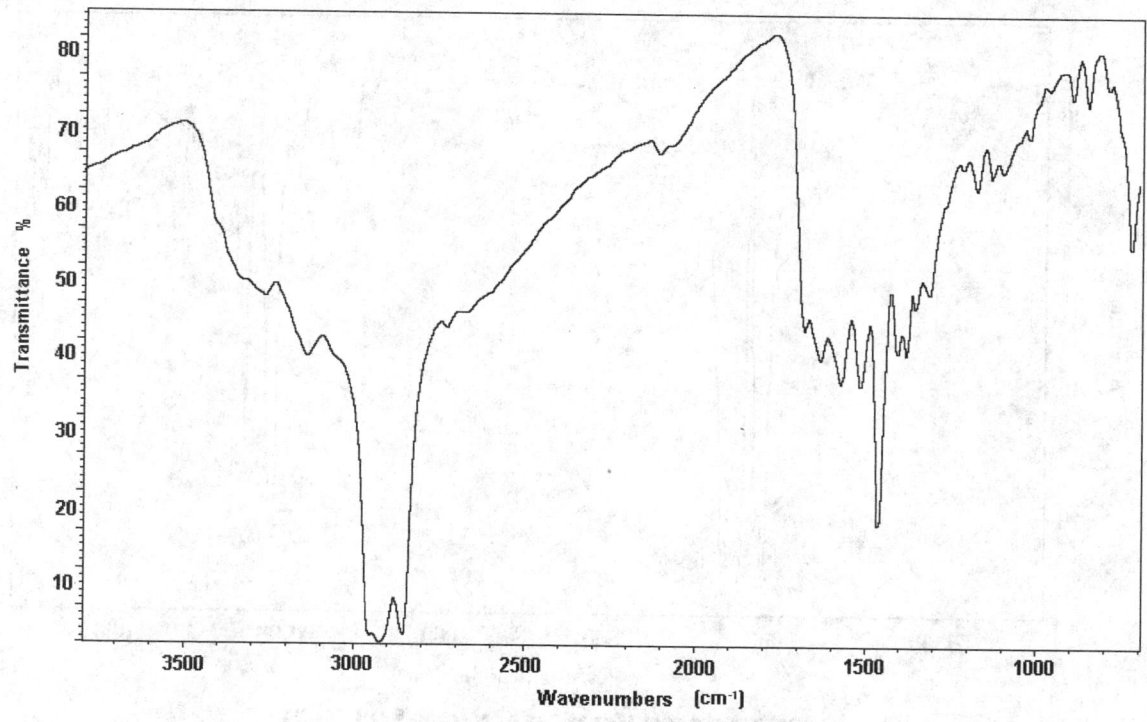

L-Arginine (Mineral Oil Mull)

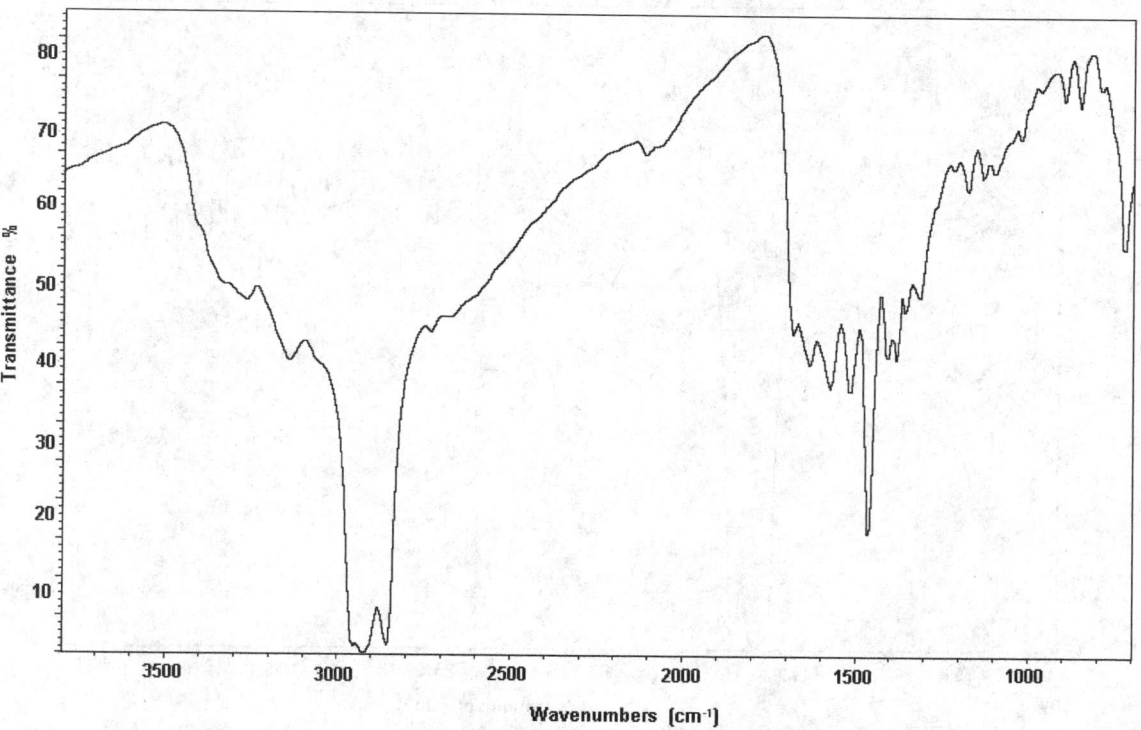

L-Arginine Monohydrochloride (Mineral Oil Mull)

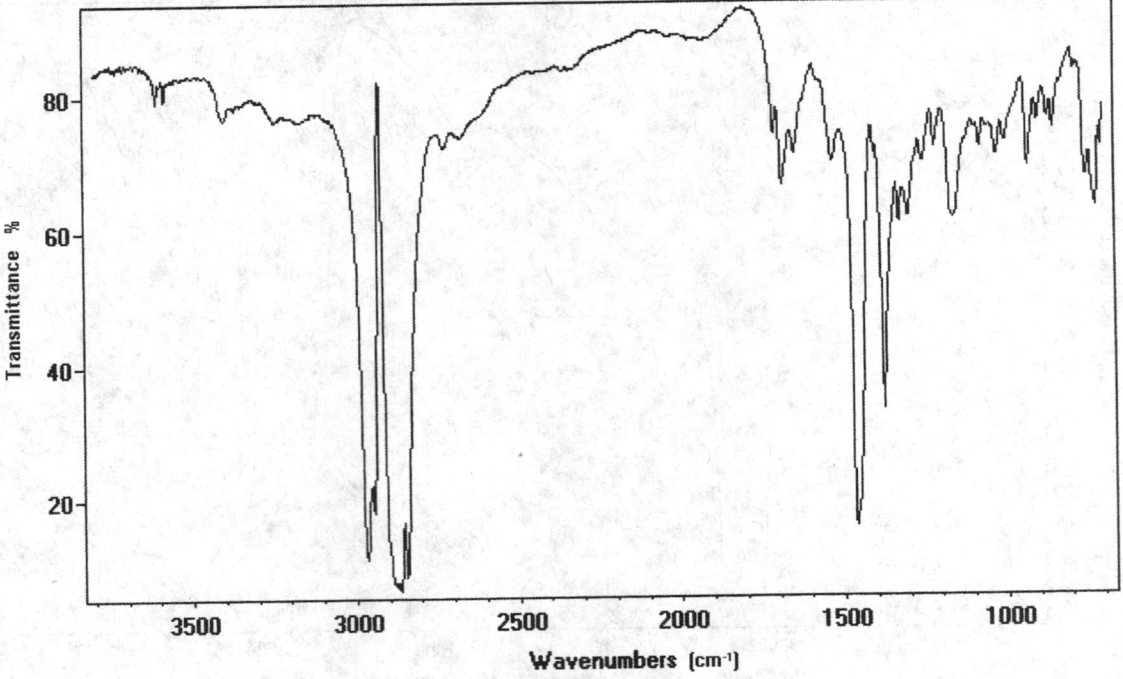

Aspartame-Acesulfame Salt (Mineral Oil Mull)

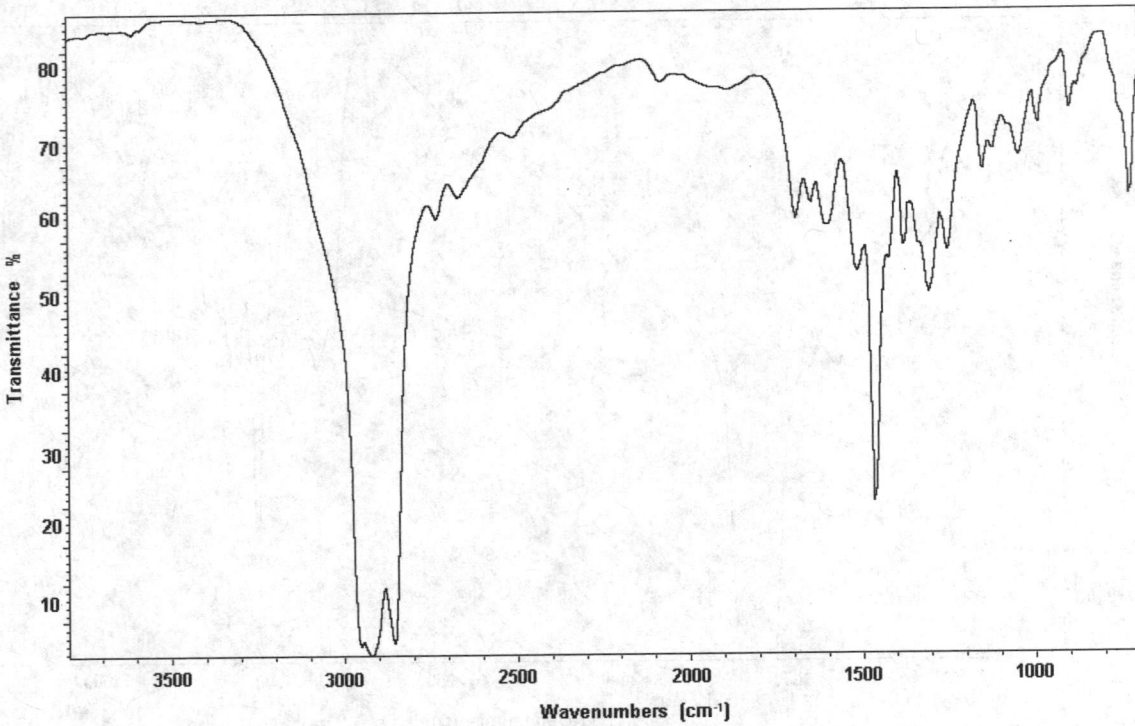

L-Aspartic Acid (Mineral Oil Mull)

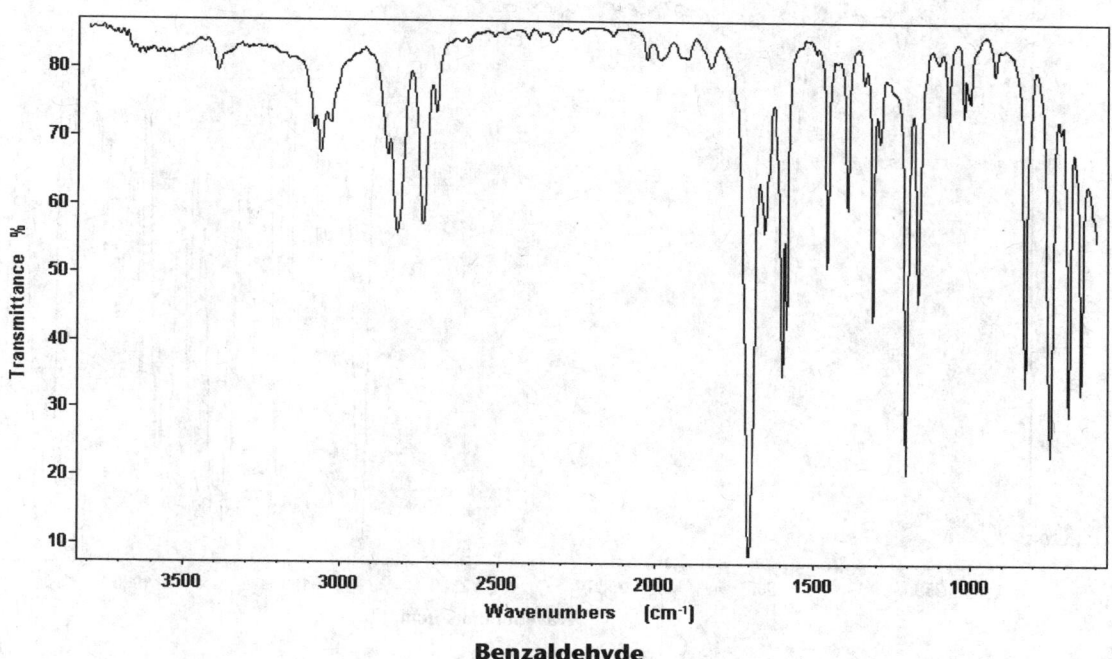
Benzaldehyde

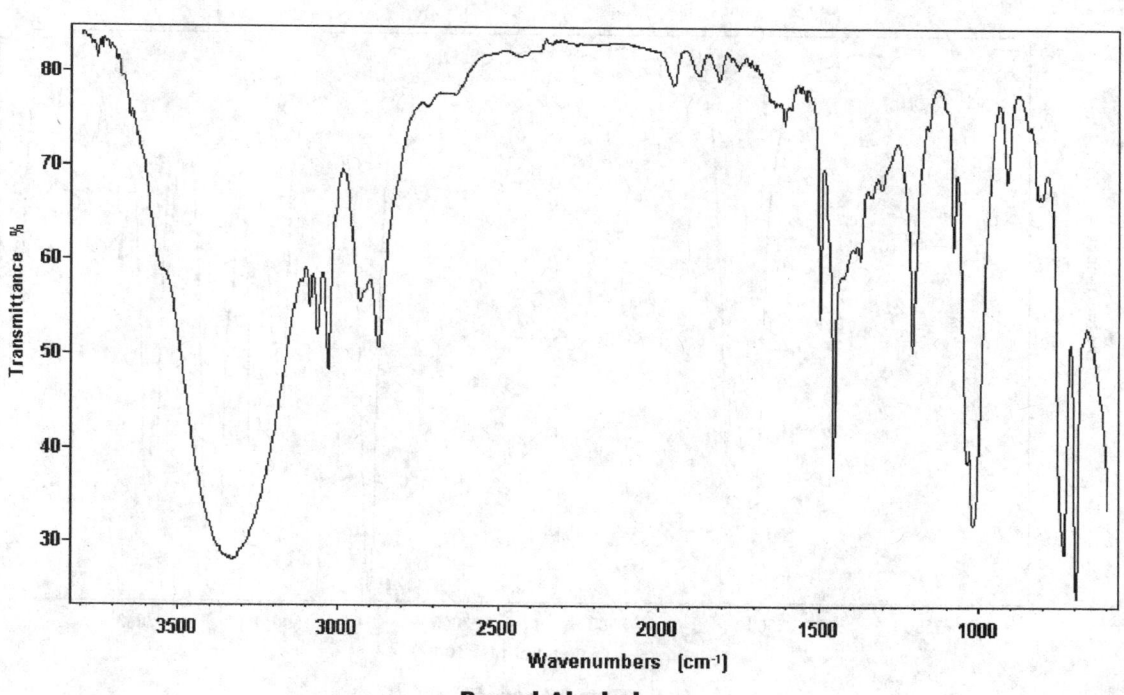
Benzyl Alcohol

1484 / Infrared Spectra / *General Information*

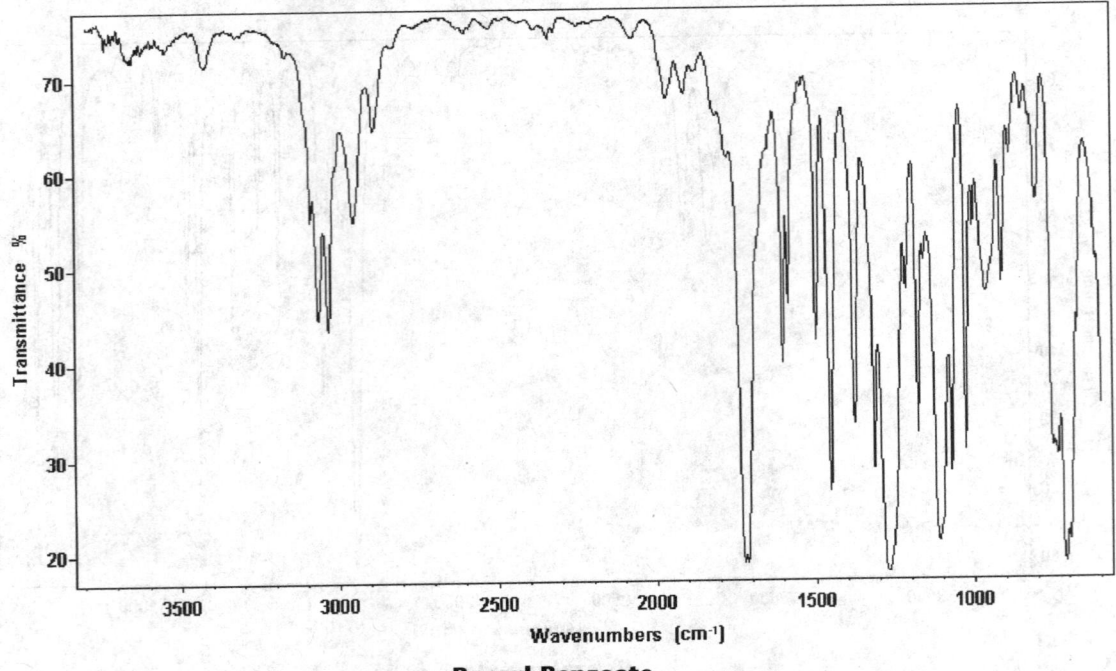

Benzyl Benzoate

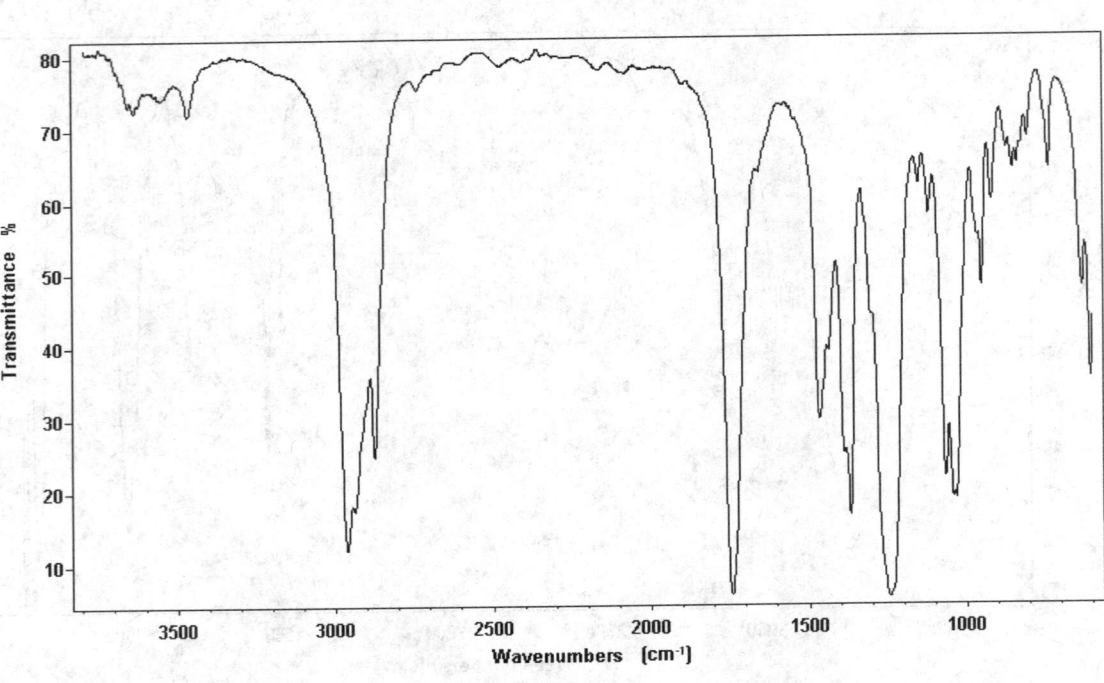

Butyl Acetate

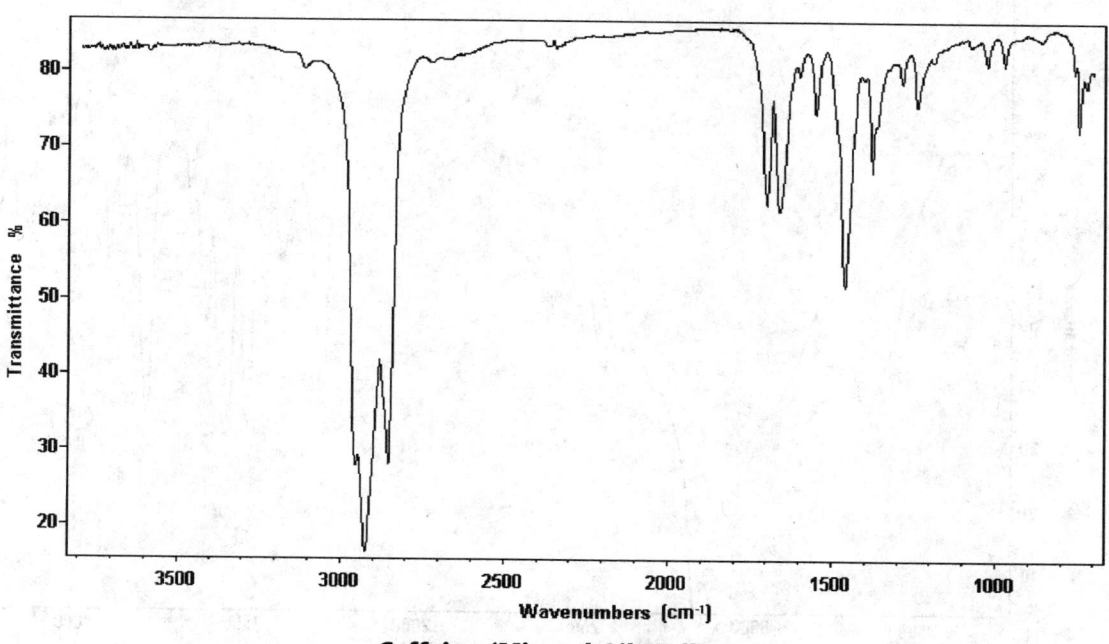
Caffeine (Mineral Oil Mull)

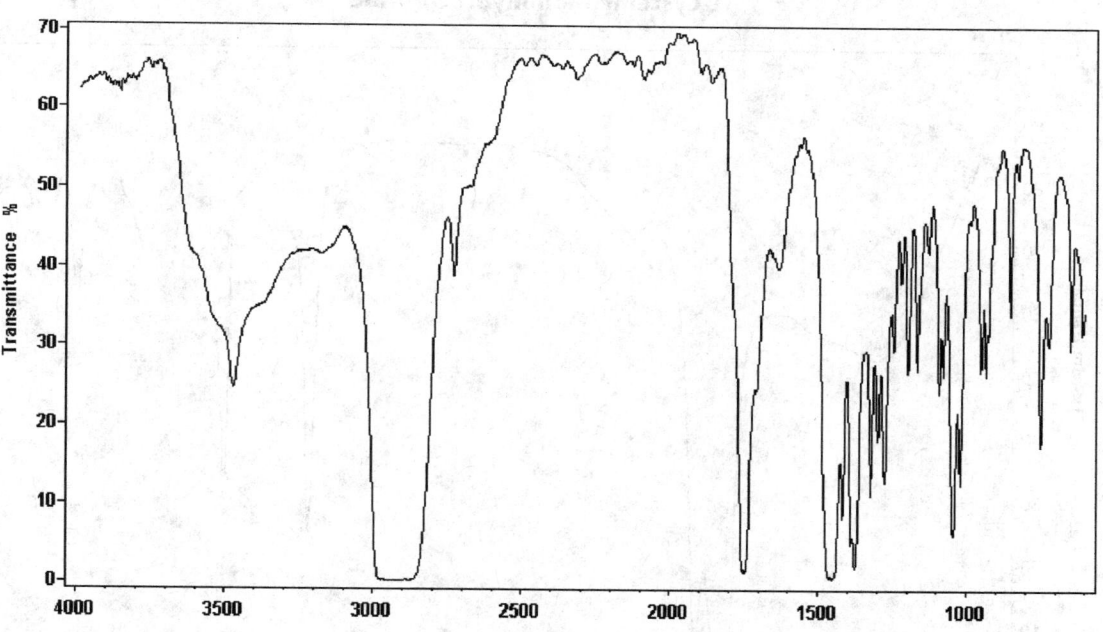
***d*-Camphor**

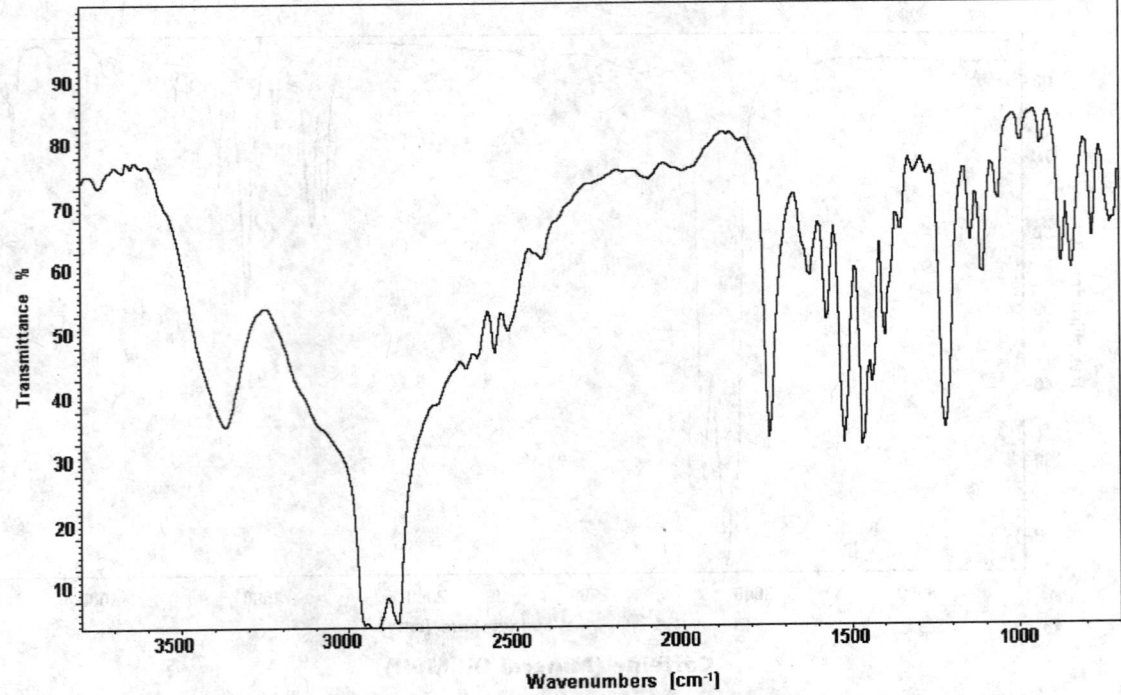

L-Cysteine Monohydrochloride

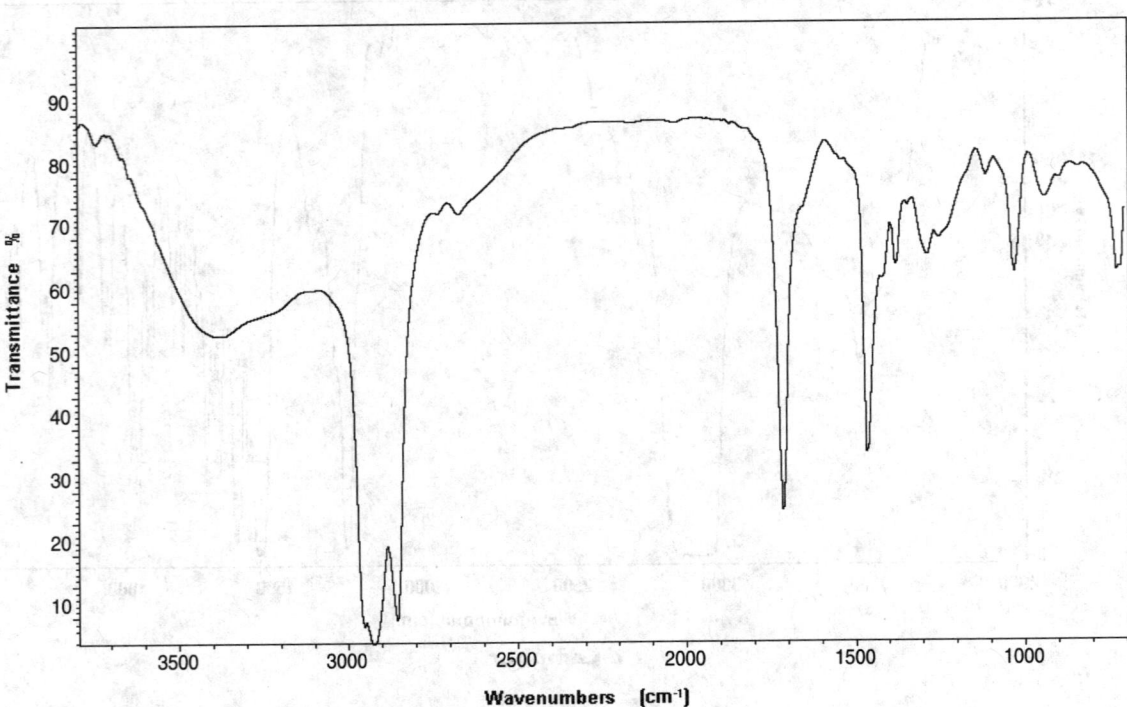

Decanoic Acid (Nujol Mull)

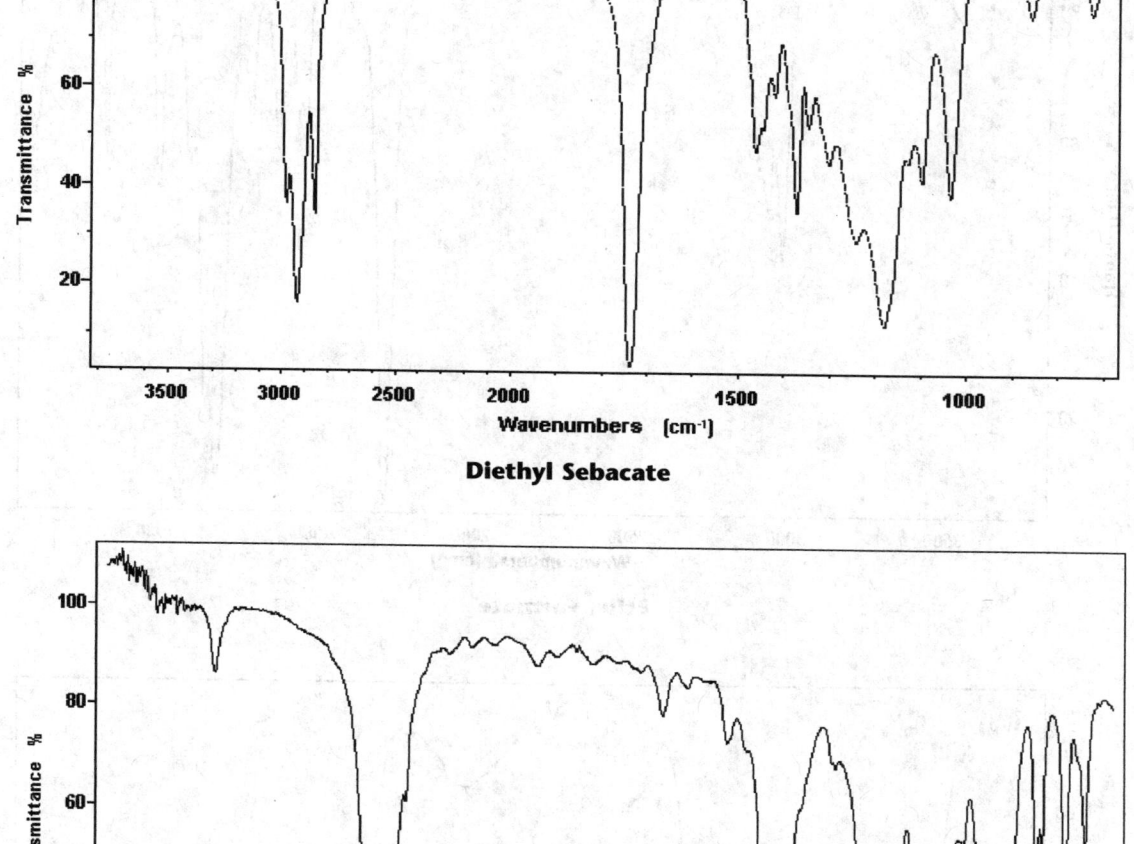

Diethyl Sebacate

Ethyl Acetate

1488 / Infrared Spectra / *General Information*

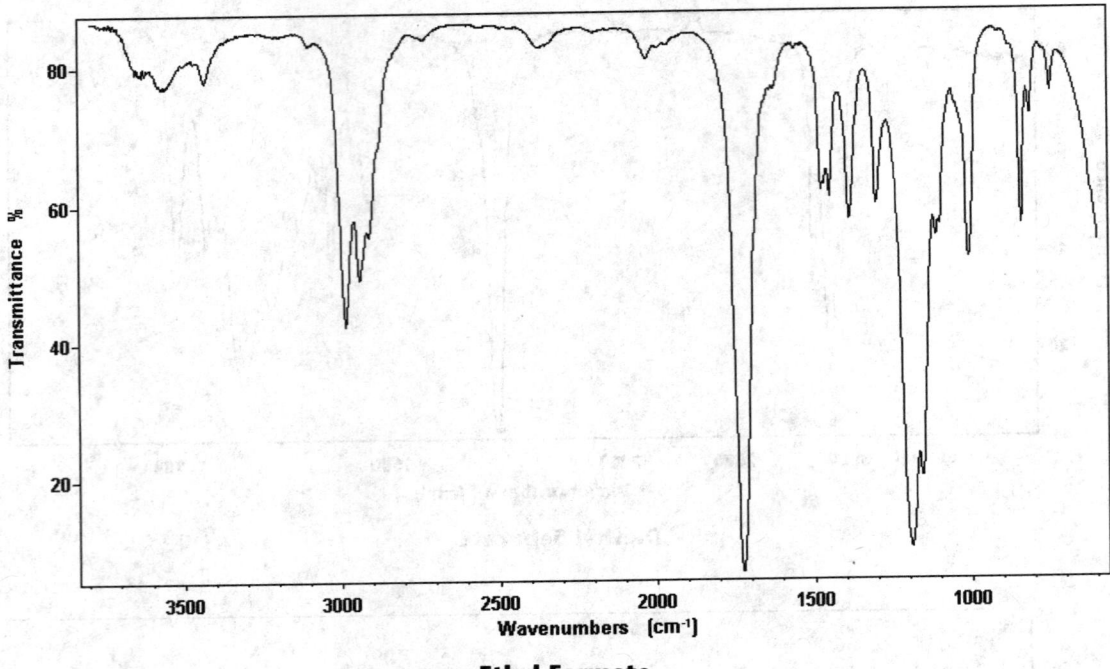

Ethyl Formate

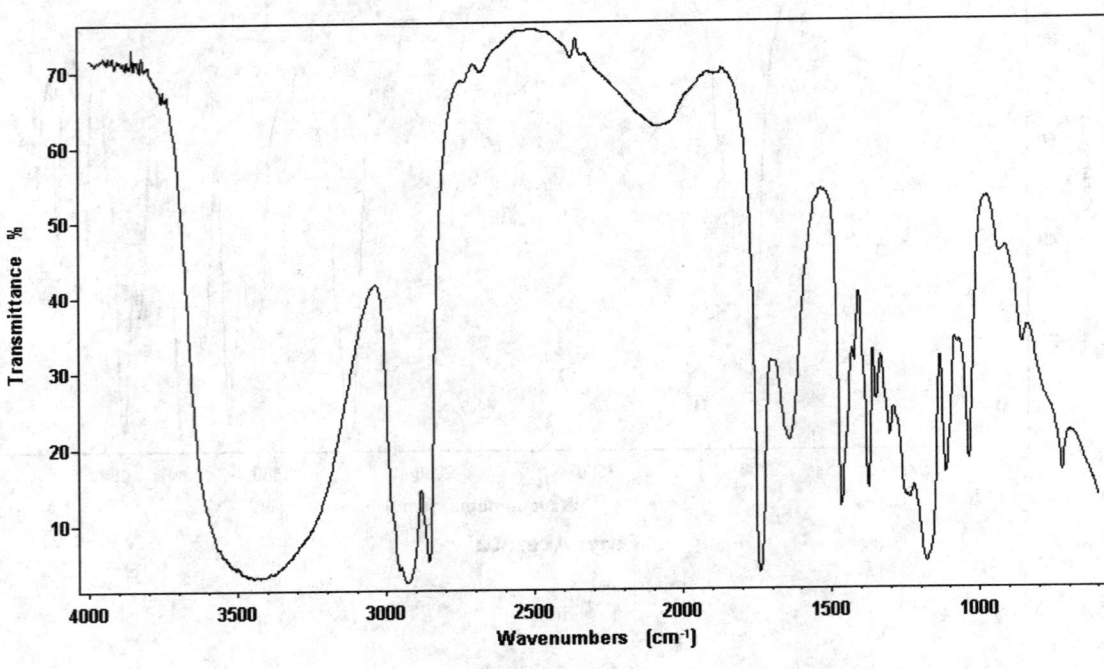

Ethyl Laurate

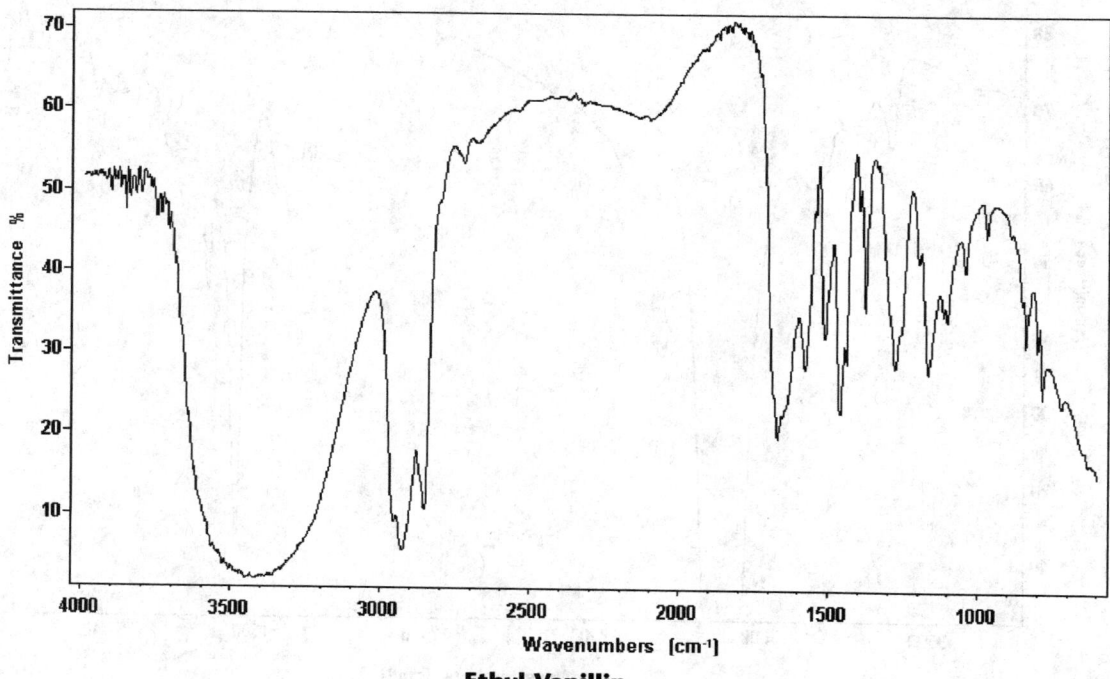
Ethyl Vanillin

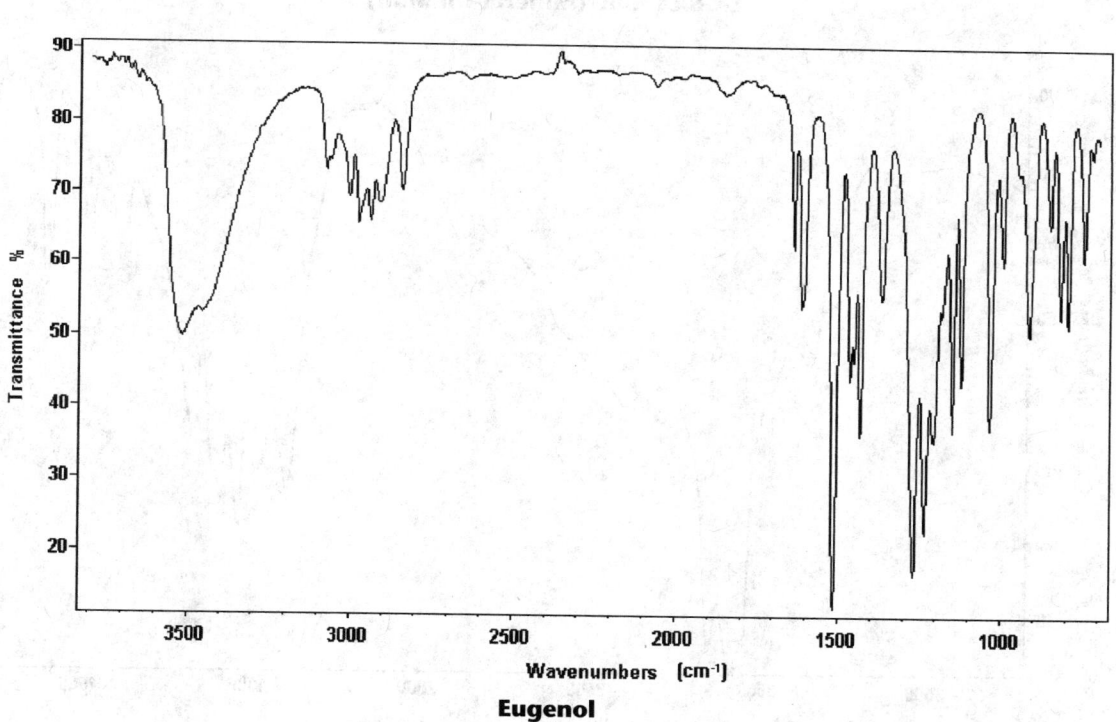
Eugenol

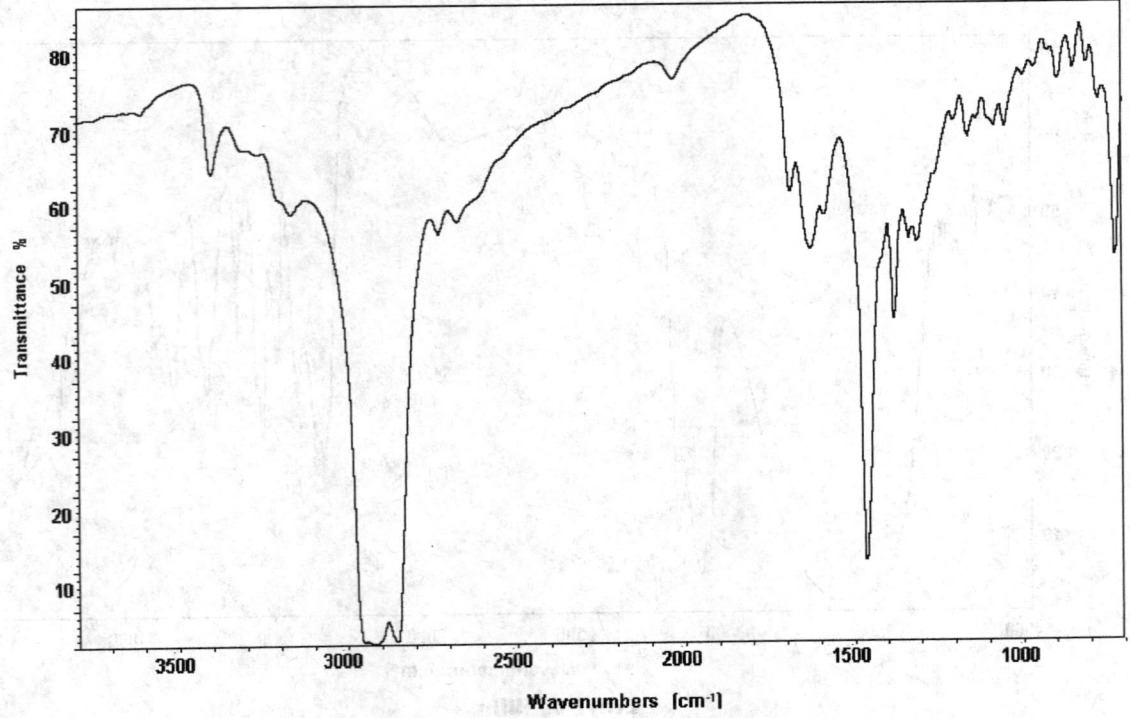

L-Glutamine (Mineral Oil Mull)

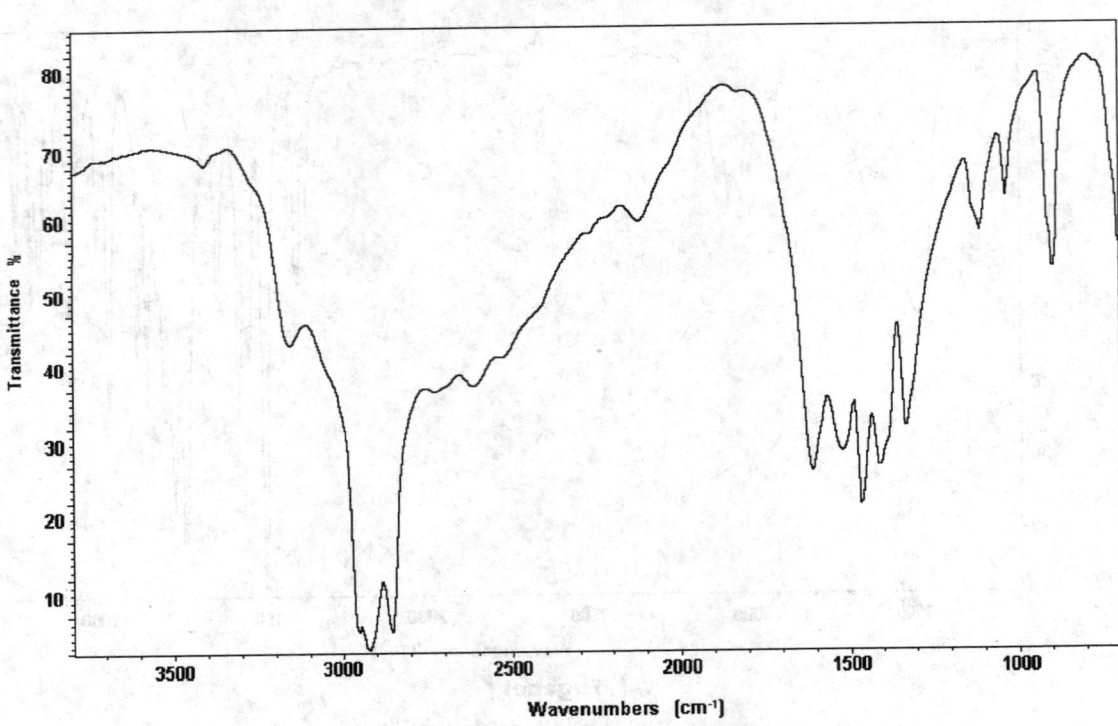

Glycine (Mineral Oil Mull)

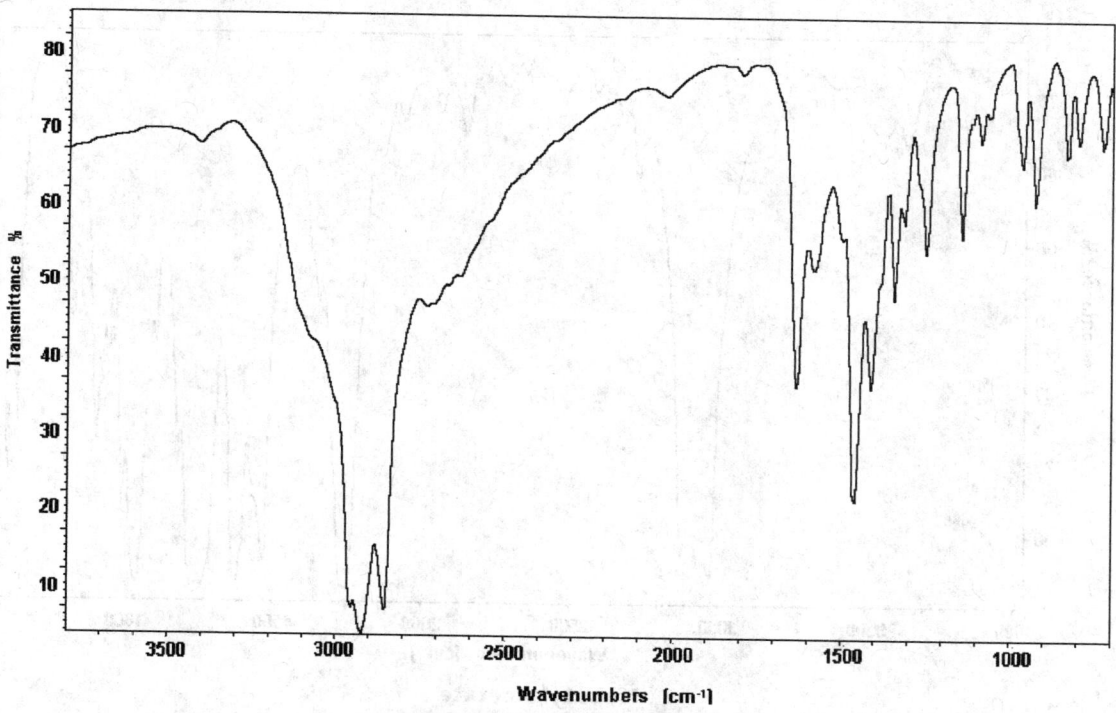
L-Histidine (Mineral Oil Mull)

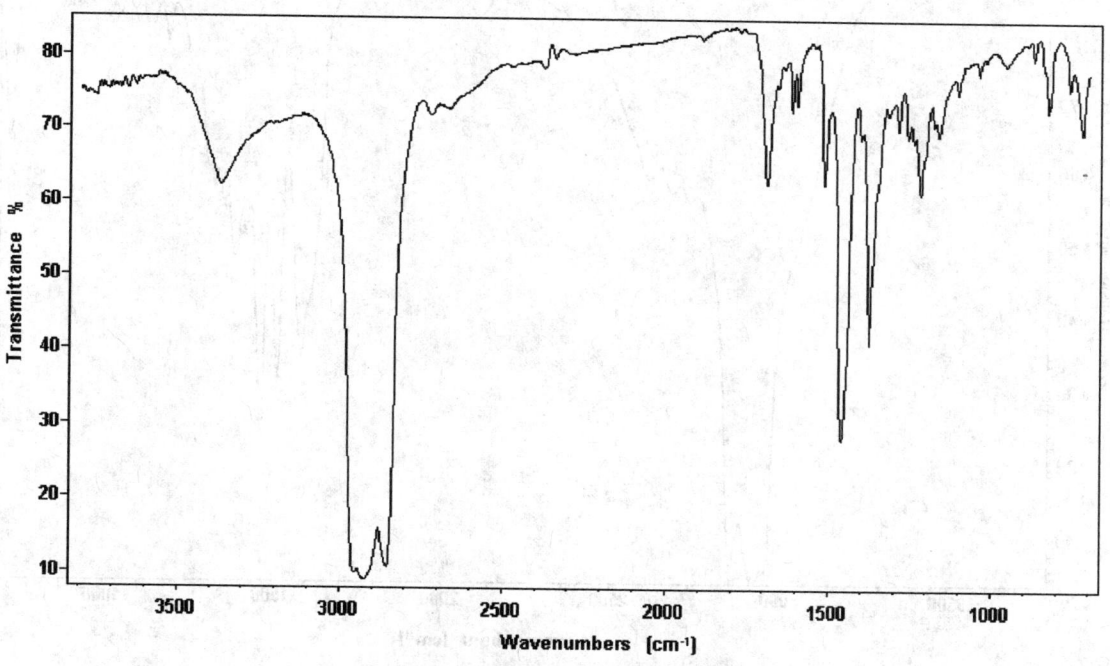
4-(*p*-Hydroxyphenyl)-2-butanone

1492 / Infrared Spectra / *General Information*

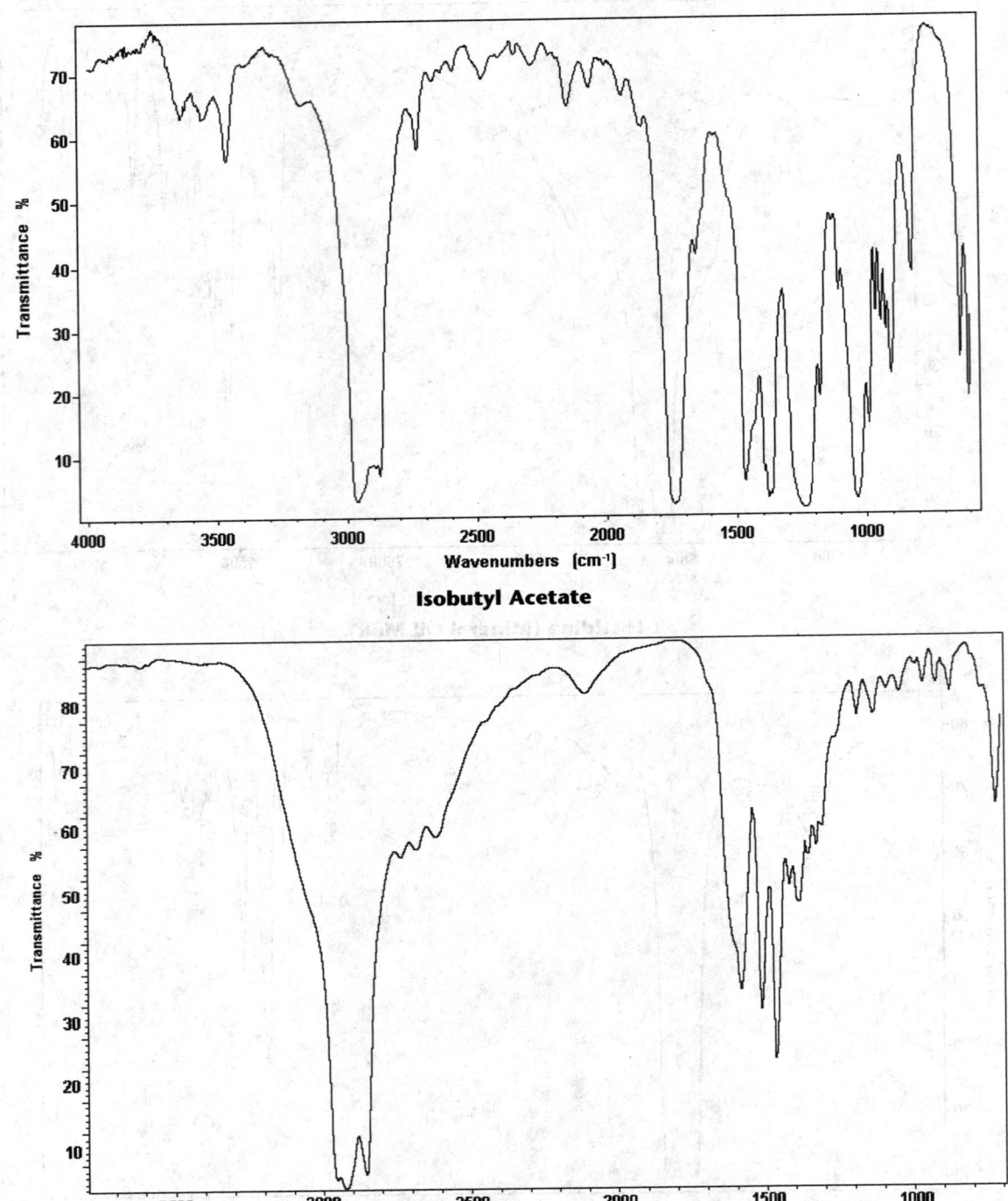

Isobutyl Acetate

L-Isoleucine (Mineral Oil Mull)

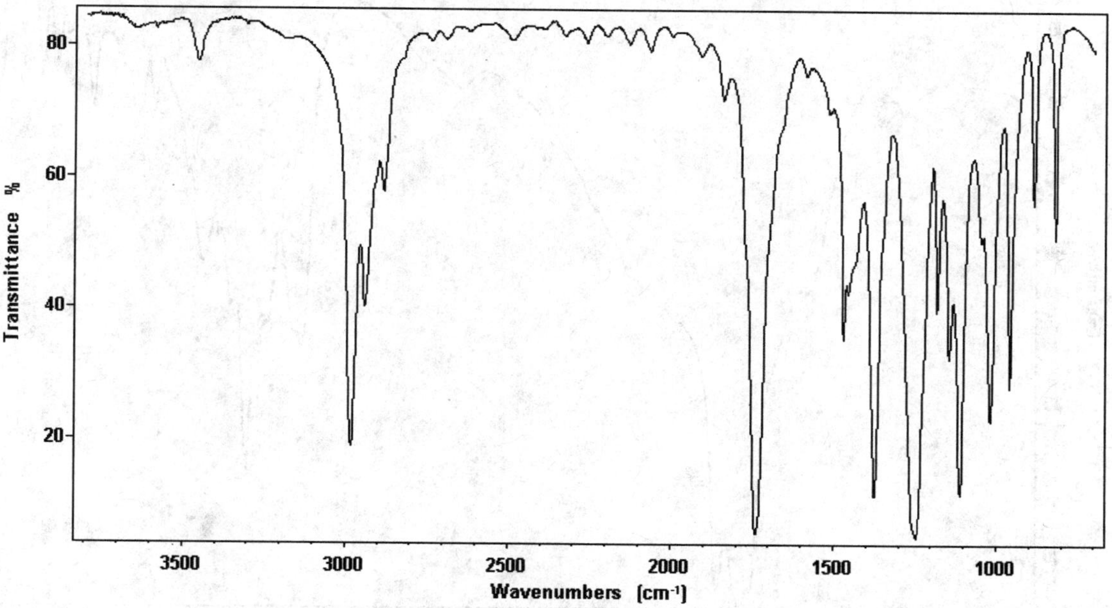

Isopropyl Acetate

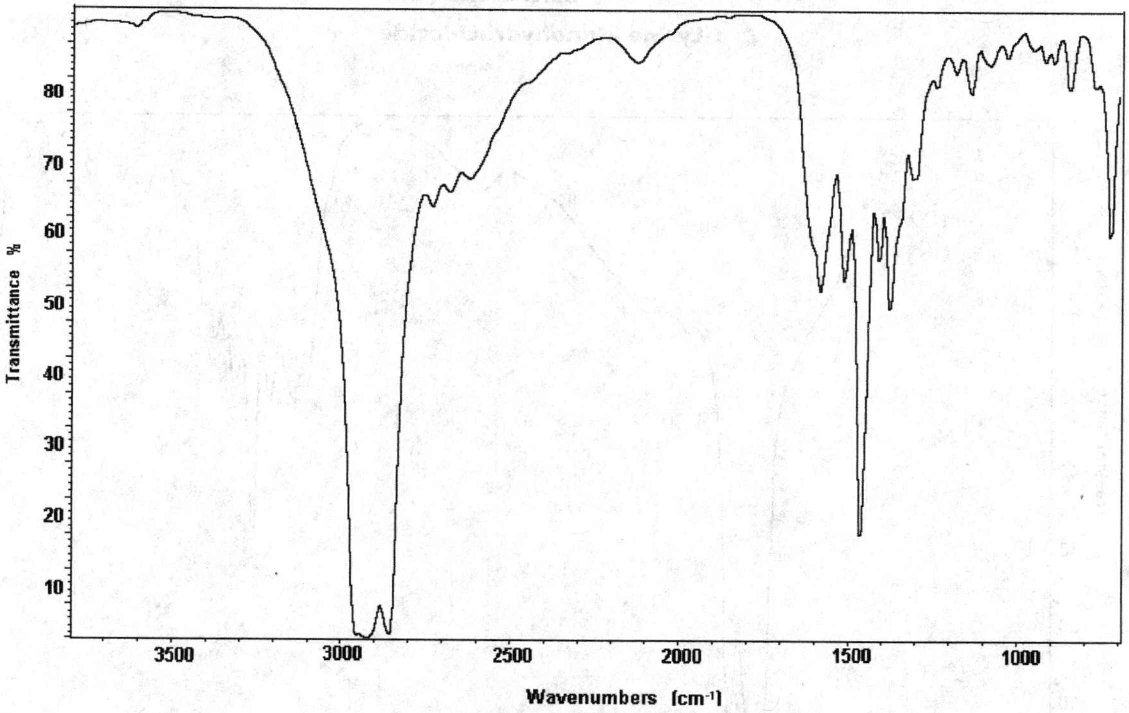

L-Leucine (Mineral Oil Mull)

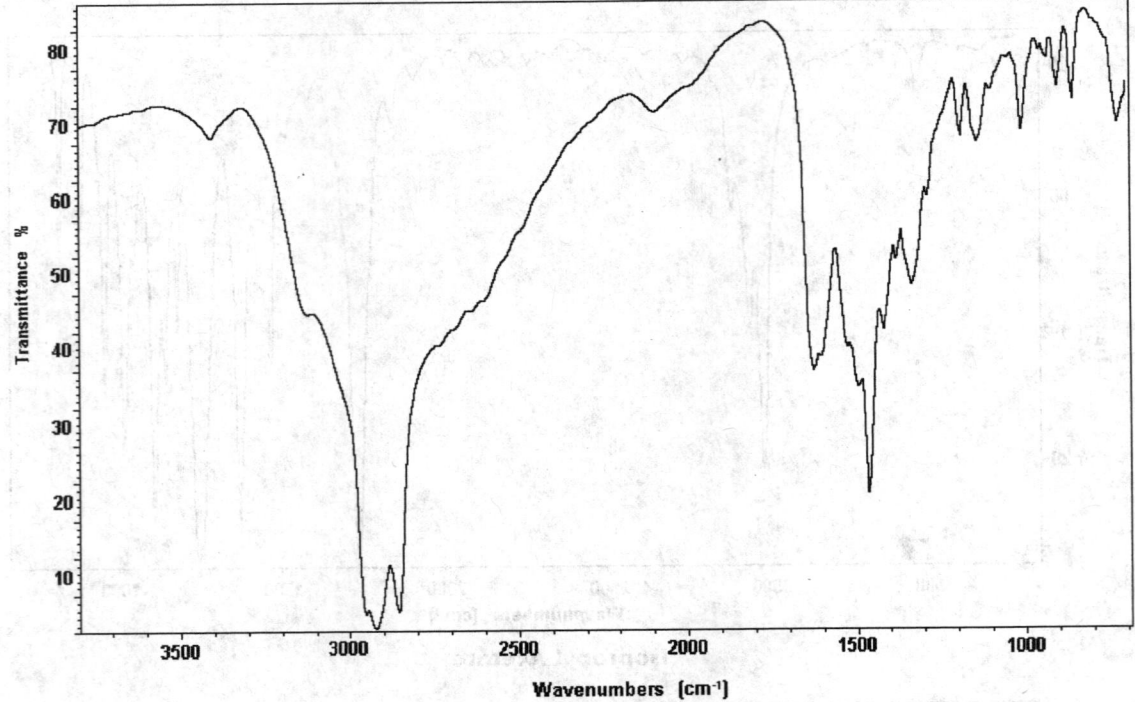

L-Lysine Monohydrochloride

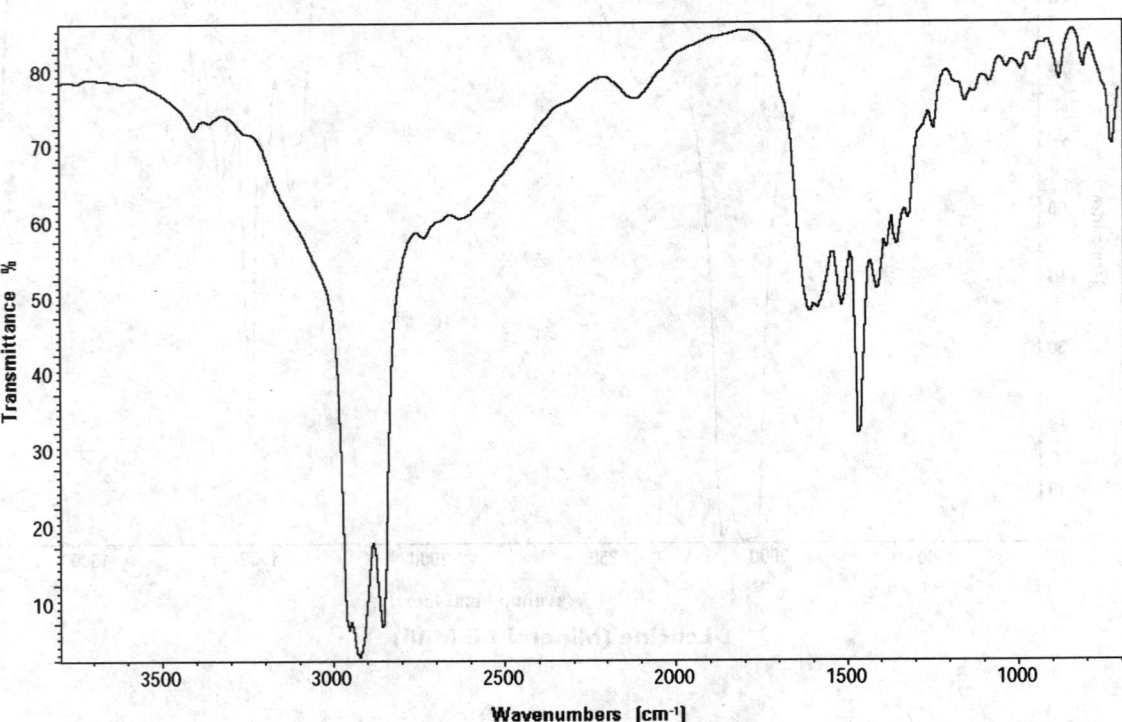

L-Methionine (Mineral Oil Mull)

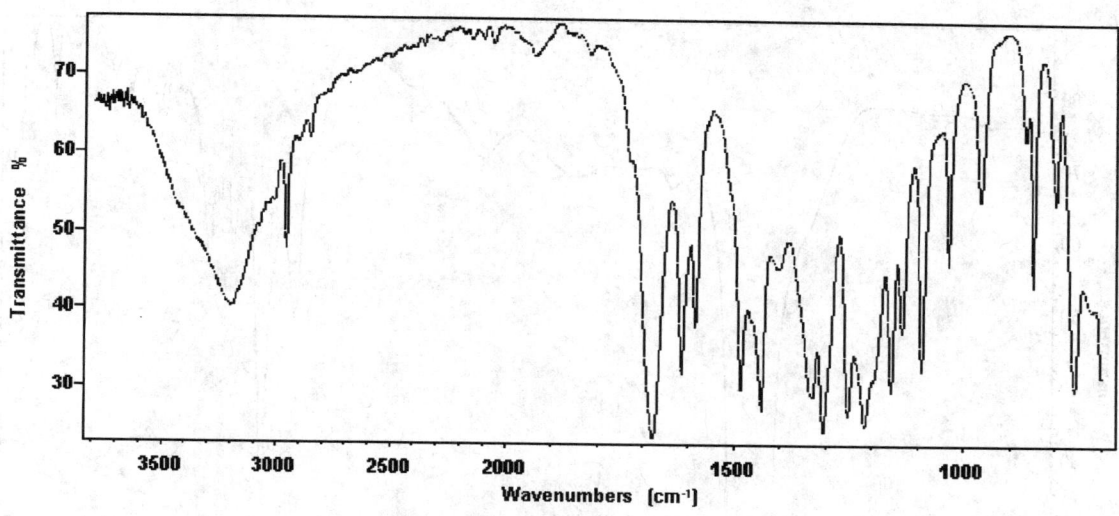

Methyl Salicylate

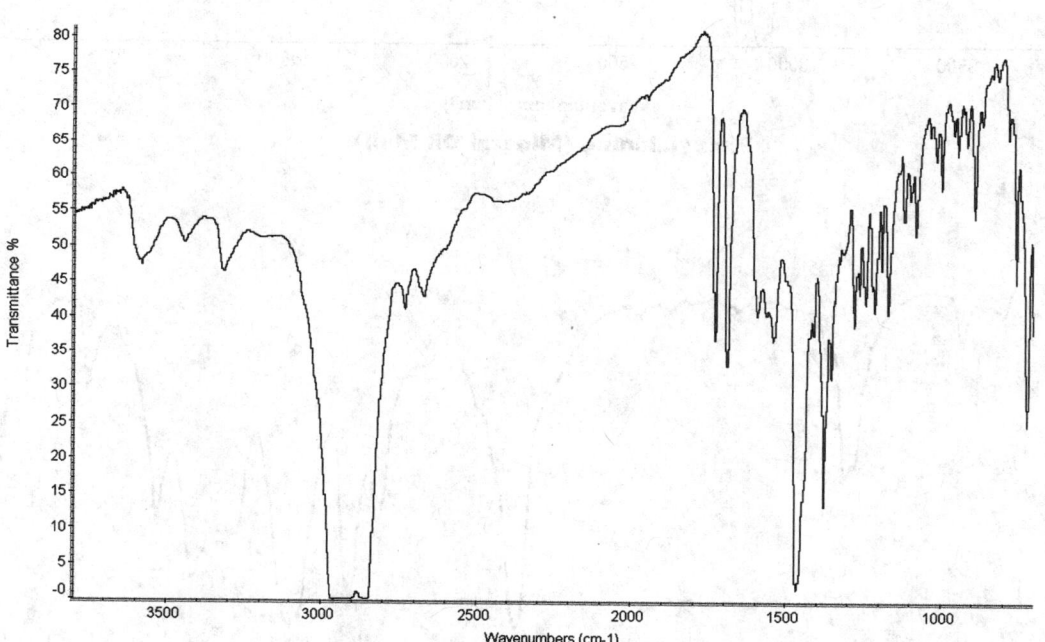

Neotame (Potassium Bromide Pellet)

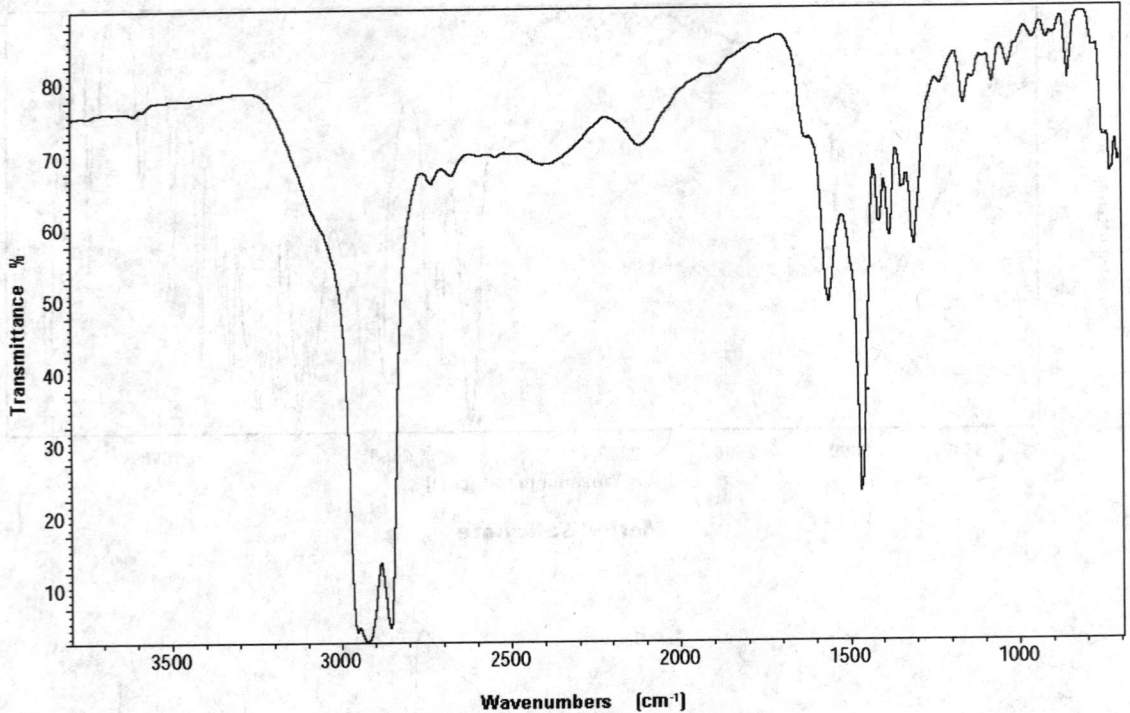

L-Phenylalanine (Mineral Oil Mull)

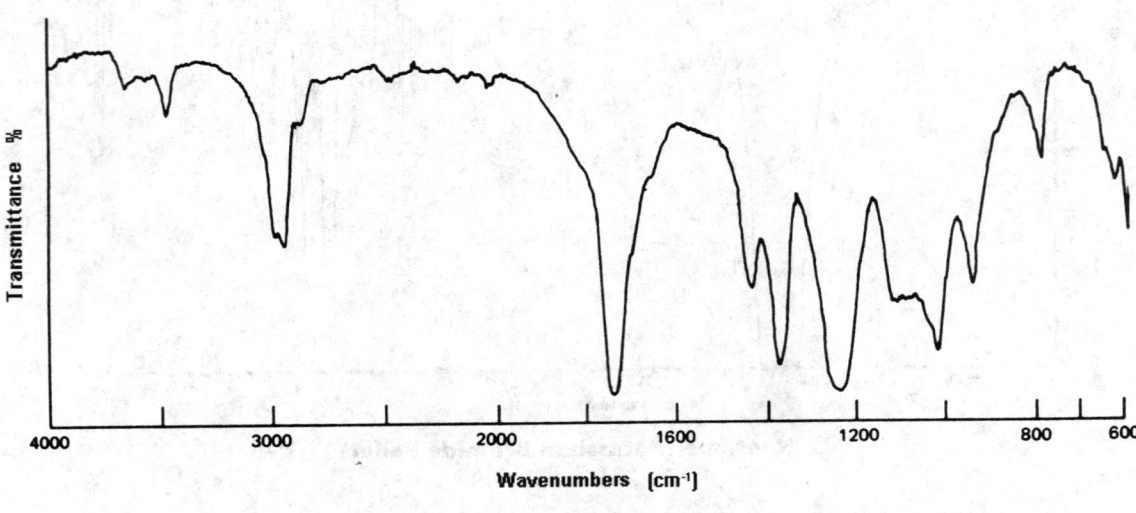

Polyvinyl Acetate

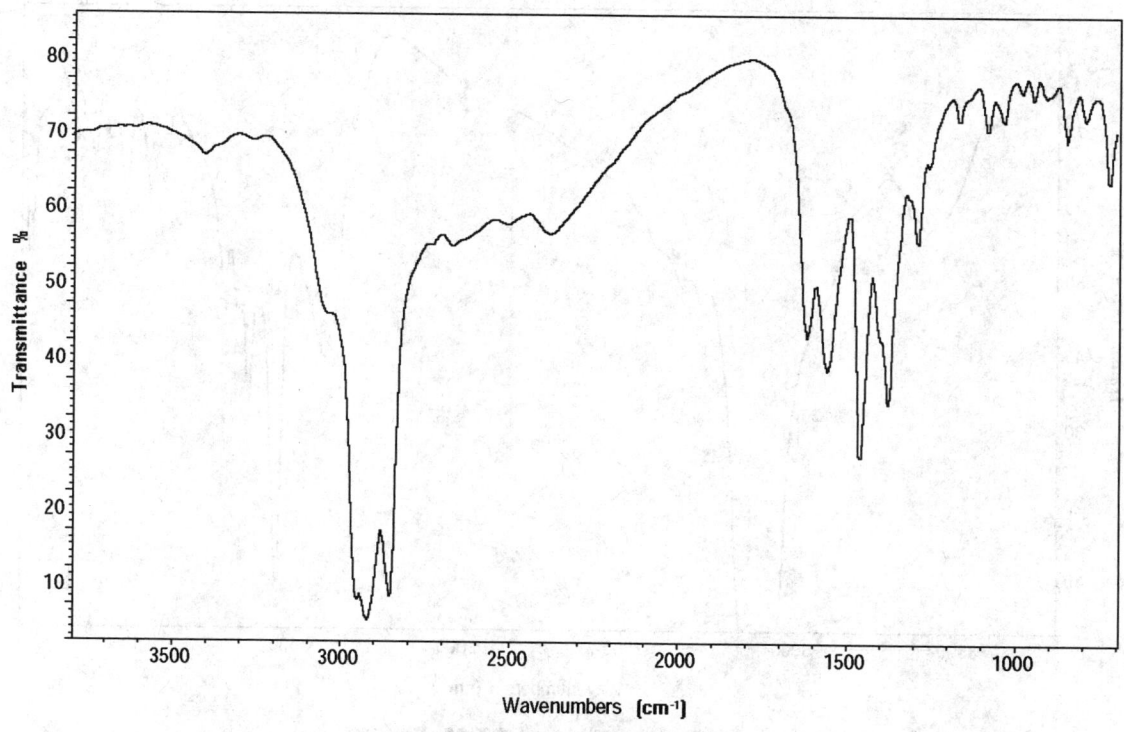

L-Proline (Mineral Oil Mull)

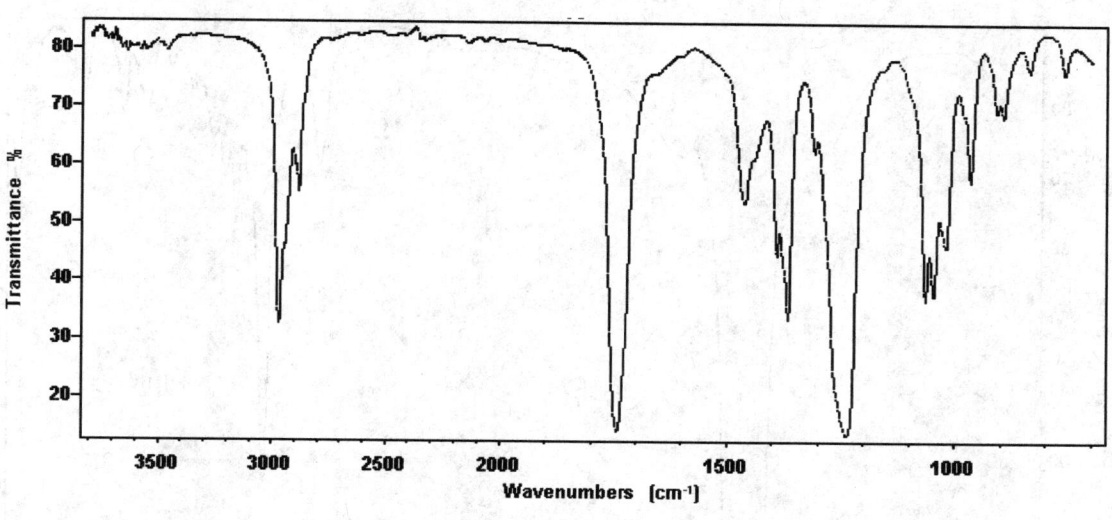

Propyl Acetate

1498 / Infrared Spectra / *General Information*

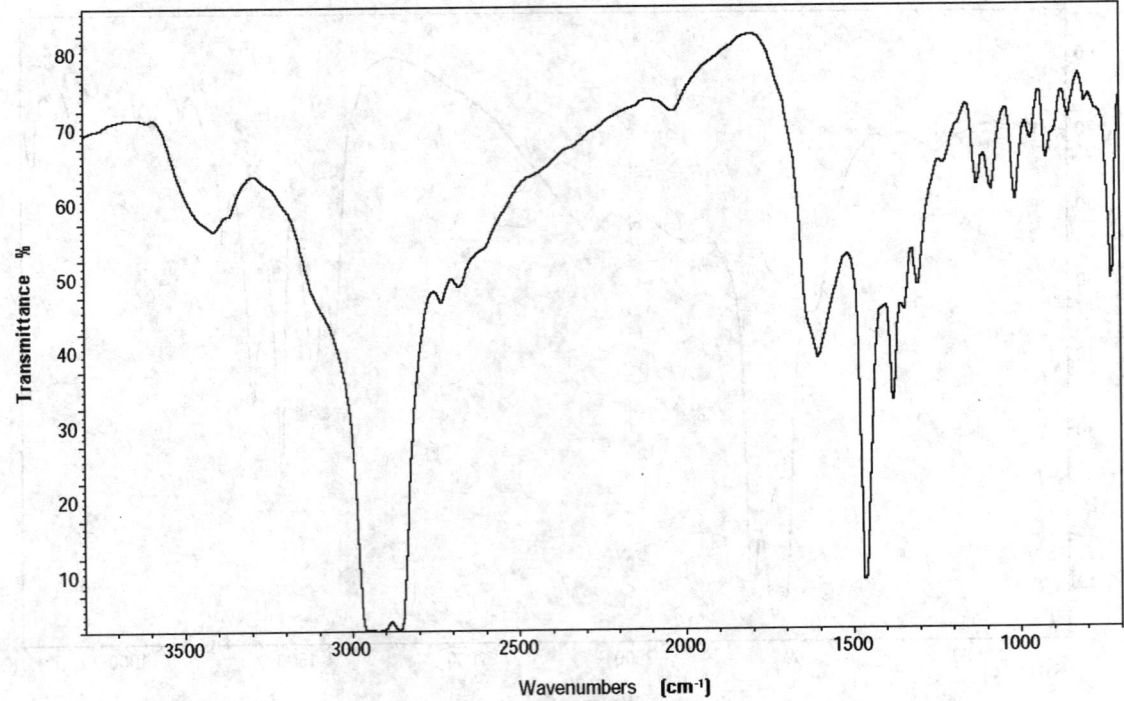

L-Serine (Mineral Oil Mull)

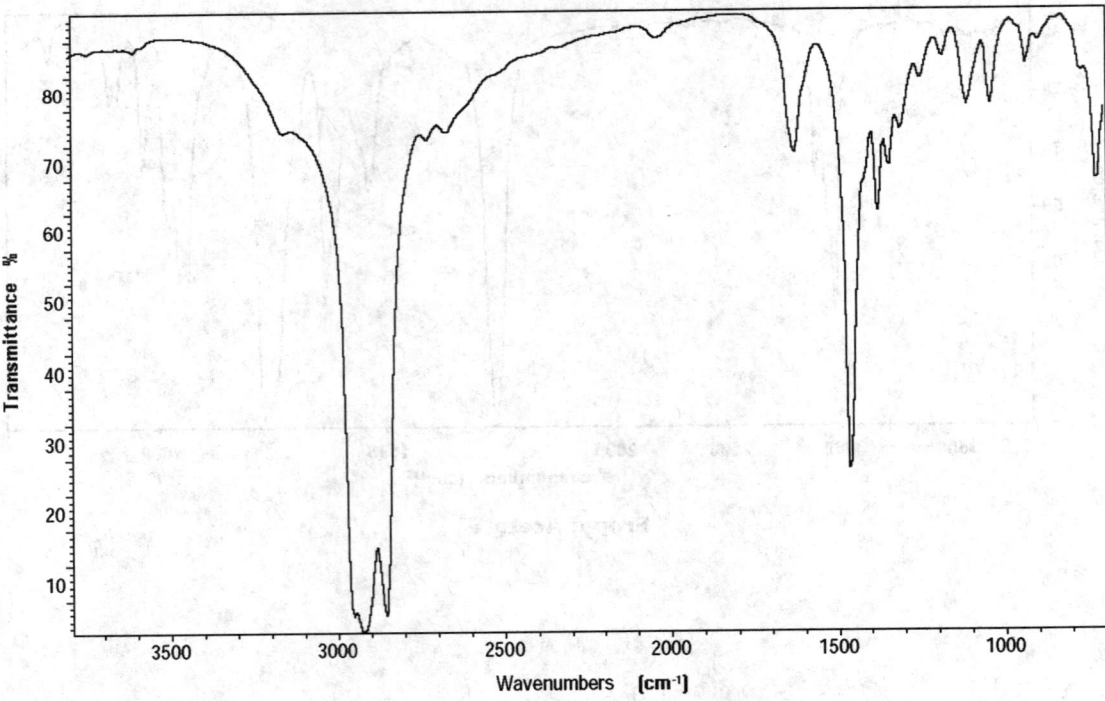

L-Threonine (Mineral Oil Mull)

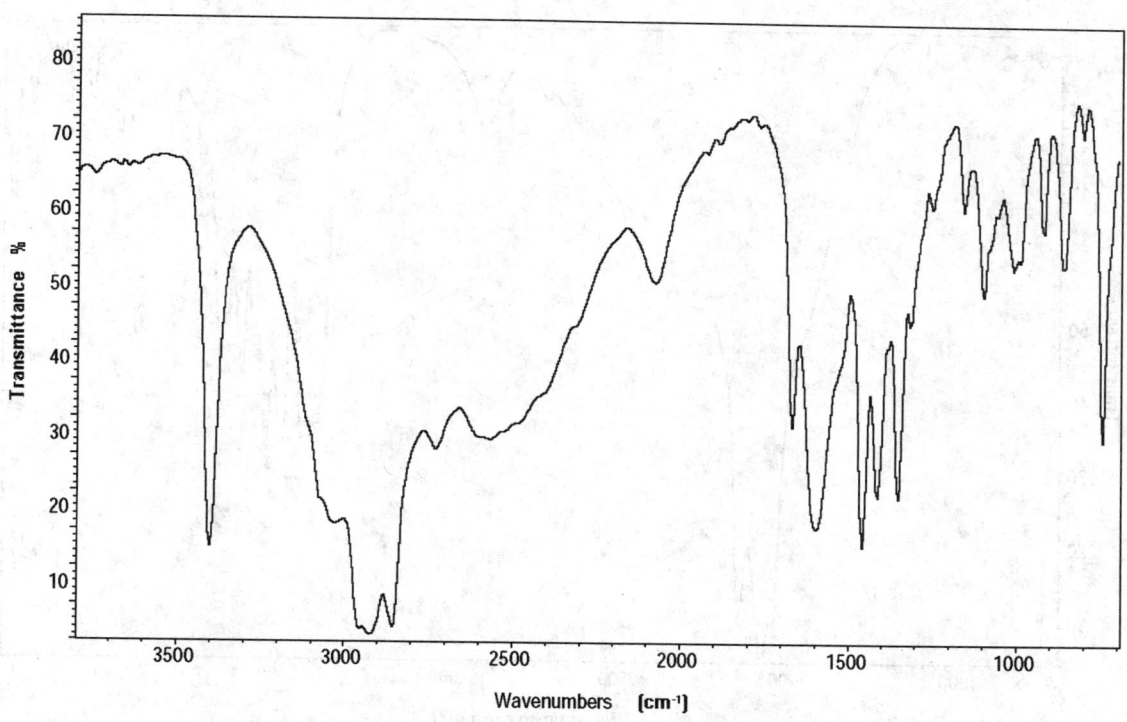

L-Tryptophan (Mineral Oil Mull)

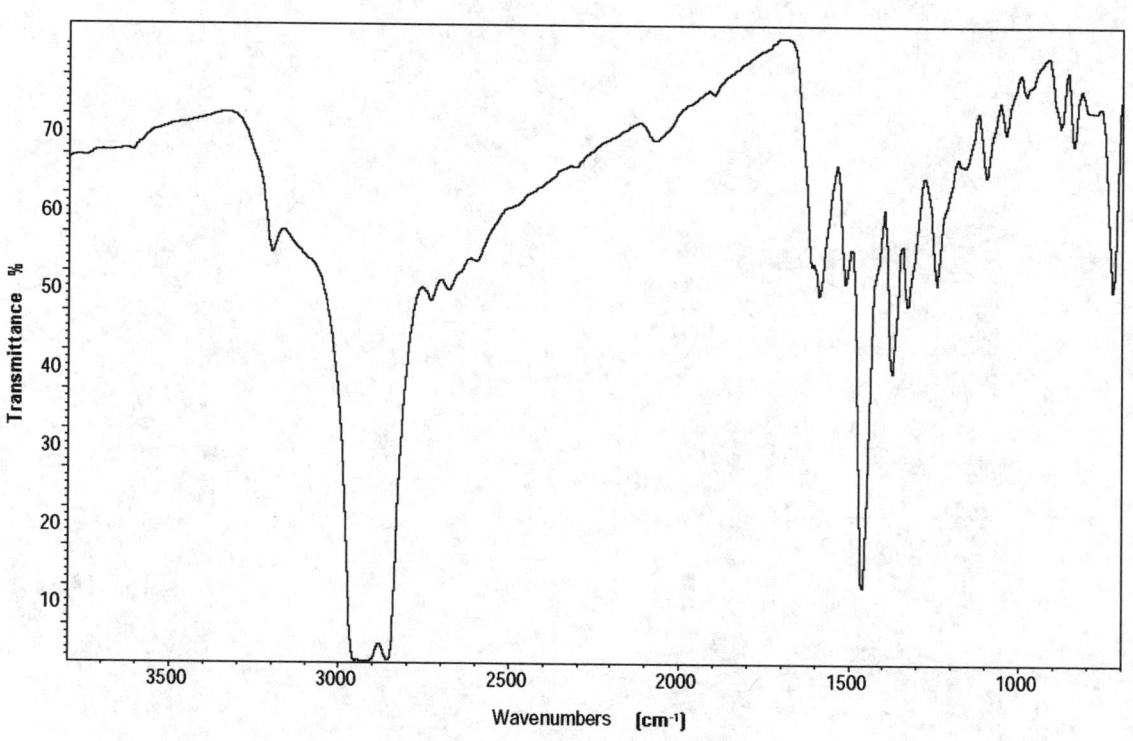

L-Tyrosine (Mineral Oil Mull)

1500 / Infrared Spectra / *General Information*

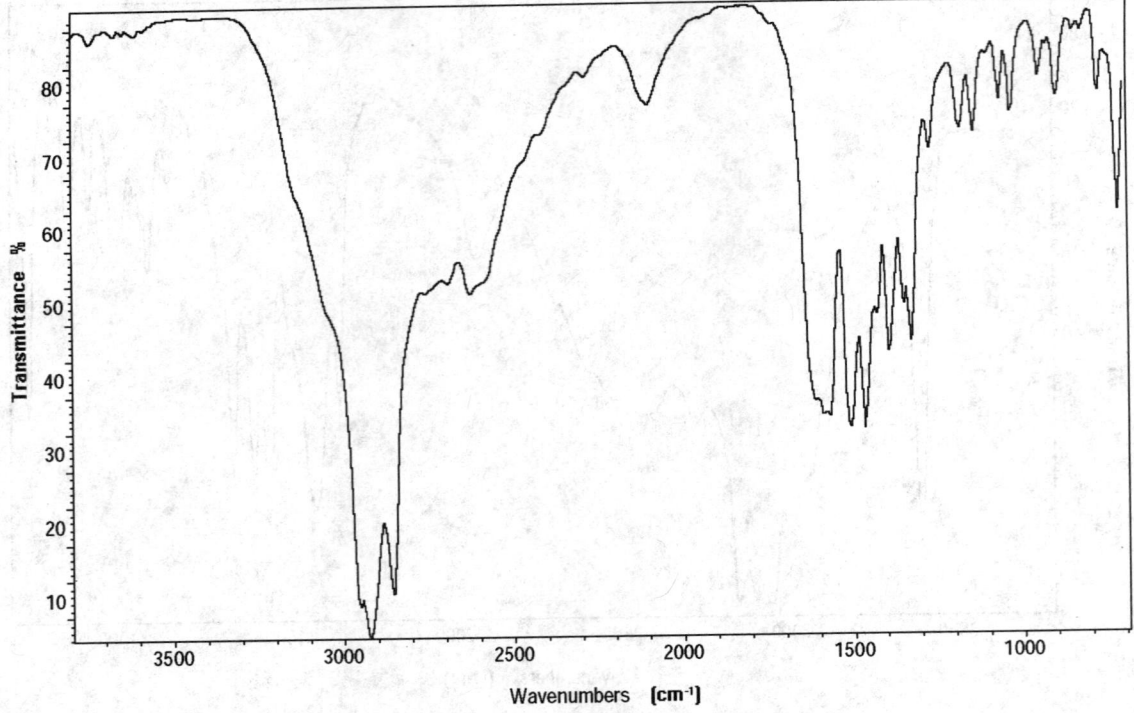

L-Valine (Mineral Oil Mull)

General Information Tables

ALCOHOLOMETRIC TABLE*

Based on data appearing in the National Bureau of Standards Bulletin, vol. 9, pp. 424–425 (publication of the National Institute of Standards and Technology).

(1) Percentage of C_2H_5OH By volume at 15.56°C	(2) By weight	(3) Specific gravity in air At 25°/25°	(4) At 15.56°/15.56°	(5) Percentage of C_2H_5OH By weight	(6) By volume at 15.56°C	(7) Specific gravity in air At 25°/25°	(8) At 15.56°/15.56°
0	0.00	1.0000	1.0000	0	0.00	1.0000	1.0000
1	0.80	0.9985	0.9985	1	1.26	0.9981	0.9981
2	1.59	0.9970	0.9970	2	2.51	0.9963	0.9963
3	2.39	0.9956	0.9956	3	3.76	0.9945	0.9945
4	3.19	0.9941	0.9942	4	5.00	0.9927	0.9928
5	4.00	0.9927	0.9928	5	6.24	0.9911	0.9912
6	4.80	0.9914	0.9915	6	7.48	0.9894	0.9896
7	5.61	0.9901	0.9902	7	8.71	0.9879	0.9881
8	6.42	0.9888	0.9890	8	9.94	0.9863	0.9867
9	7.23	0.9875	0.9878	9	11.17	0.9848	0.9852
10	8.05	0.9862	0.9866	10	12.39	0.9833	0.9839
11	8.86	0.9850	0.9854	11	13.61	0.9818	0.9825
12	9.68	0.9838	0.9843	12	14.83	0.9804	0.9812
13	10.50	0.9826	0.9832	13	16.05	0.9789	0.9799
14	11.32	0.9814	0.9821	14	17.26	0.9776	0.9787
15	12.14	0.9802	0.9810	15	18.47	0.9762	0.9774
16	12.96	0.9790	0.9800	16	19.68	0.9748	0.9763
17	13.79	0.9778	0.9789	17	20.88	0.9734	0.9751
18	14.61	0.9767	0.9779	18	22.08	0.9720	0.9738
19	15.44	0.9756	0.9769	19	23.28	0.9706	0.9726
20	16.27	0.9744	0.9759	20	24.47	0.9692	0.9714
21	17.10	0.9733	0.9749	21	25.66	0.9677	0.9701
22	17.93	0.9721	0.9739	22	26.85	0.9663	0.9688
23	18.77	0.9710	0.9729	23	28.03	0.9648	0.9675
24	19.60	0.9698	0.9719	24	29.21	0.9633	0.9662
25	20.44	0.9685	0.9708	25	30.39	0.9617	0.9648
26	21.29	0.9673	0.9697	26	31.56	0.9601	0.9635
27	22.13	0.9661	0.9687	27	32.72	0.9585	0.9620
28	22.97	0.9648	0.9676	28	33.88	0.9568	0.9605
29	23.82	0.9635	0.9664	29	35.03	0.9551	0.9590
30	24.67	0.9622	0.9653	30	36.18	0.9534	0.9574
31	25.52	0.9609	0.9641	31	37.32	0.9516	0.9558
32	26.38	0.9595	0.9629	32	38.46	0.9498	0.9541
33	27.24	0.9581	0.9617	33	39.59	0.9480	0.9524
34	28.10	0.9567	0.9604	34	40.72	0.9461	0.9506
35	28.97	0.9552	0.9590	35	41.83	0.9442	0.9488
36	29.84	0.9537	0.9576	36	42.94	0.9422	0.9470

*This table is reproduced from the *United States Pharmacopeia and National Formulary (USP–NF)* as published in *USP 32–NF 27*. It is provided for informational purposes only and is intended as a resource for the FCC user. Note that because the *USP–NF* is in continuous revision, this table is subject to change and the information printed here may not continue to represent the current version.

Alcoholometric Table / General Information

(1) Percentage of C_2H_5OH By volume at 15.56°C	(2) By weight	(3) Specific gravity in air At 25°/25°	(4) At 15.56°/15.56°	(5) Percentage of C_2H_5OH By weight	(6) By volume at 15.56°C	(7) Specific gravity in air At 25°/25°	(8) At 15.56°/15.56°
37	30.72	0.9521	0.9562	37	44.05	0.9402	0.9451
38	31.60	0.9506	0.9548	38	45.15	0.9382	0.9432
39	32.48	0.9489	0.9533	39	46.24	0.9362	0.9412
40	33.36	0.9473	0.9517	40	47.33	0.9341	0.9392
41	34.25	0.9456	0.9501	41	48.41	0.9320	0.9372
42	35.15	0.9439	0.9485	42	49.48	0.9299	0.9352
43	36.05	0.9421	0.9469	43	50.55	0.9278	0.9331
44	36.96	0.9403	0.9452	44	51.61	0.9256	0.9310
45	37.87	0.9385	0.9434	45	52.66	0.9235	0.9289
46	38.78	0.9366	0.9417	46	53.71	0.9213	0.9268
47	39.70	0.9348	0.9399	47	54.75	0.9191	0.9246
48	40.62	0.9328	0.9380	48	55.78	0.9169	0.9225
49	41.55	0.9309	0.9361	49	56.81	0.9147	0.9203
50	42.49	0.9289	0.9342	50	57.83	0.9124	0.9181
51	43.43	0.9269	0.9322	51	58.84	0.9102	0.9159
52	44.37	0.9248	0.9302	52	59.85	0.9079	0.9137
53	45.33	0.9228	0.9282	53	60.85	0.9056	0.9114
54	46.28	0.9207	0.9262	54	61.85	0.9033	0.9092
55	47.25	0.9185	0.9241	55	62.84	0.9010	0.9069
56	48.21	0.9164	0.9220	56	63.82	0.8987	0.9046
57	49.19	0.9142	0.9199	57	64.80	0.8964	0.9024
58	50.17	0.9120	0.9177	58	65.77	0.8941	0.9001
59	51.15	0.9098	0.9155	59	66.73	0.8918	0.8978
60	52.15	0.9076	0.9133	60	67.79	0.8895	0.8955
61	53.15	0.9053	0.9111	61	68.64	0.8871	0.8932
62	54.15	0.9030	0.9088	62	69.59	0.8848	0.8909
63	55.17	0.9006	0.9065	63	70.52	0.8824	0.8886
64	56.18	0.8983	0.9042	64	71.46	0.8801	0.8862
65	57.21	0.8959	0.9019	65	72.38	0.8777	0.8839
66	58.24	0.8936	0.8995	66	73.30	0.8753	0.8815
67	59.28	0.8911	0.8972	67	74.21	0.8729	0.8792
68	60.33	0.8887	0.8948	68	75.12	0.8706	0.8768
69	61.38	0.8862	0.8923	69	76.02	0.8682	0.8745
70	62.44	0.8837	0.8899	70	76.91	0.8658	0.8721
71	63.51	0.8812	0.8874	71	77.79	0.8634	0.8697
72	64.59	0.8787	0.8848	72	78.67	0.8609	0.8673
73	65.67	0.8761	0.8823	73	79.54	0.8585	0.8649
74	66.77	0.8735	0.8797	74	80.41	0.8561	0.8625
75	67.87	0.8709	0.8771	75	81.27	0.8537	0.8601
76	68.98	0.8682	0.8745	76	82.12	0.8512	0.8576
77	70.10	0.8655	0.8718	77	82.97	0.8488	0.8552
78	71.23	0.8628	0.8691	78	83.81	0.8463	0.8528
79	72.38	0.8600	0.8664	79	84.64	0.8439	0.8503
80	73.53	0.8572	0.8636	80	85.46	0.8414	0.8479
81	74.69	0.8544	0.8608	81	86.28	0.8389	0.8454
82	75.86	0.8516	0.8580	82	87.08	0.8364	0.8429
83	77.04	0.8487	0.8551	83	87.89	0.8339	0.8404
84	78.23	0.8458	0.8522	84	88.68	0.8314	0.8379
85	79.44	0.8428	0.8493	85	89.46	0.8288	0.8354
86	80.66	0.8397	0.8462	86	90.24	0.8263	0.8328
87	81.90	0.8367	0.8432	87	91.01	0.8237	0.8303
88	83.14	0.8335	0.8401	88	91.77	0.8211	0.8276
89	84.41	0.8303	0.8369	89	92.52	0.8184	0.8250
90	85.69	0.8271	0.8336	90	93.25	0.8158	0.8224
91	86.99	0.8237	0.8303	91	93.98	0.8131	0.8197
92	88.31	0.8202	0.8268	92	94.70	0.8104	0.8170
93	89.65	0.8167	0.8233	93	95.41	0.8076	0.8142
94	91.03	0.8130	0.8196	94	96.10	0.8048	0.8114
95	92.42	0.8092	0.8158	95	96.79	0.8020	0.8086

(1)	(2)	(3)	(4)	(5)	(6)	(7)	(8)
Percentage of C_2H_5OH		Specific gravity in air		Percentage of C_2H_5OH		Specific gravity in air	
By volume at 15.56°C	By weight	At 25°/25°	At 15.56°/15.56°	By weight	By volume at 15.56°C	At 25°/25°	At 15.56°/15.56°
96	93.85	0.8053	0.8118	96	97.46	0.7992	0.8057
97	95.32	0.8011	0.8077	97	98.12	0.7962	0.8028
98	96.82	0.7968	0.8033	98	98.76	0.7932	0.7998
99	98.38	0.7921	0.7986	99	99.39	0.7902	0.7967
100	100.00	0.7871	0.7936	100	100.00	0.7871	0.7936

ATOMIC WEIGHTS*

Standard Atomic Weights of the Elements, Recommended by the Commission on Atomic Weights and Isotopic Abundances of the International Union of Pure and Applied Chemistry (2007) (©2008 IUPAC)
Standard atomic weights 2007 [In alphabetical order: scaled to $A_r(^{12}C) = 12$, where ^{12}C is a neutral atom in its nuclear and electronic ground state.]

The atomic weights of many elements are not invariant but depend on the origin and treatment of the material. The standard values of $A_r(E)$ and the uncertainties (in parentheses, following the last significant figure to which they are attributed) apply to elements of natural terrestrial origin. The footnotes to this Table elaborate the types of variation which may occur for individual elements and which may be larger than the listed uncertainties of values of $A_r(E)$. Names of elements with atomic numbers 112, 113, 114, 115, 116, and 118 are temporary.

Name	Atomic Symbol	Atomic Number	Atomic Weight	Footnotes
Actinium*	Ac	89		
Aluminum	Al	13	26.9815386(8)	
Americium*	Am	95		
Antimony (Stibium)	Sb	51	121.760(1)	g
Argon	Ar	18	39.948(1)	g, r
Arsenic	As	33	74.92160(2)	
Astatine*	At	85		
Barium	Ba	56	137.327(7)	
Berkelium*	Bk	97		
Beryllium	Be	4	9.012182(3)	
Bismuth	Bi	83	208.98040(1)	
Bohrium*	Bh	107		
Boron	B	5	10.811(7)	g, m, r
Bromine	Br	35	79.904(1)	
Cadmium	Cd	48	112.411(8)	g
Caesium (Cesium)	Cs	55	132.9054519(2)	
Calcium	Ca	20	40.078(4)	g
Californium*	Cf	98		
Carbon	C	6	12.0107(8)	g, r
Cerium	Ce	58	140.116(1)	g
Chlorine	Cl	17	35.453(2)	m
Chromium	Cr	24	51.9961(6)	
Cobalt	Co	27	58.933195(5)	
Copper	Cu	29	63.546(3)	r
Curium*	Cm	96		
Darmstadtium*	Ds	110		
Dubnium*	Db	105		
Dysprosium	Dy	66	162.500(1)	g

*Element has no stable nuclides. One or more well-known isotopes are given in the accompanying table with the appropriate relative atomic mass and half-life. However, three such elements (Th, Pa, and U) do have a characteristic terrestrial isotopic composition, and for these an atomic weight is tabulated.

†Commercially available Li materials have atomic weights that are known to range between 6.939 and 6.996; if a more accurate value is required, it must be determined for the specific material.

gGeological specimens are known in which the element has an isotopic composition outside the limits for normal material. The difference between the atomic weight of the element in such specimens and that given in the *Table* may exceed the stated uncertainty.

mModified isotopic compositions may be found in commercially available material because it has been subjected to an undisclosed or inadvertent isotopic fractionation. Substantial deviations in atomic weight of the element from that given in the *Table* can occur.

rRange in isotopic composition of normal terrestrial material prevents a more precise Ar(E) being given; the tabulated Ar(E) value should be applicable to any normal material.

---

*This table is reproduced from the *United States Pharmacopeia and National Formulary (USP–NF)* as published in *USP 32–NF 27*. It is provided for informational purposes only and is intended as a resource for the FCC user. Note that because the *USP–NF* is in continuous revision, this table is subject to change and the information printed here may not continue to represent the current version.

Name	Atomic Symbol	Atomic Number	Atomic Weight	Footnotes
Einsteinium*	Es	99		
Erbium	Er	68	167.259(3)	g
Europium	Eu	63	151.964(1)	g
Fermium*	Fm	100		
Fluorine	F	9	18.9984032(5)	
Francium*	Fr	87		
Gadolinium	Gd	64	157.25(3)	g
Gallium	Ga	31	69.723(1)	
Germanium	Ge	32	72.64(1)	
Gold	Au	79	196.966569(4)	
Hafnium	Hf	72	178.49(2)	
Hassium*	Hs	108		
Helium	He	2	4.002602(2)	g, r
Holmium	Ho	67	164.93032(2)	
Hydrogen	H	1	1.00794(7)	g, m, r
Indium	In	49	114.818(3)	
Iodine	I	53	126.90447(3)	
Iridium	Ir	77	192.217(3)	
Iron	Fe	26	55.845(2)	
Krypton	Kr	36	83.798(2)	g, m
Lanthanum	La	57	138.90547(7)	g
Lawrencium*	Lr	103		
Lead	Pb	82	207.2(1)	g, r
Lithium	Li	3	6.941(2)†	g, m, r
Lutetium	Lu	71	174.9668(1)	g
Magnesium	Mg	12	24.3050(6)	
Manganese	Mn	25	54.938045(5)	
Meitnerium*	Mt	109		
Mendelevium*	Md	101		
Mercury	Hg	80	200.59(2)	
Molybdenum	Mo	42	95.96(2)	g
Neodymium	Nd	60	144.242(3)	g
Neon	Ne	10	20.1797(6)	g, m
Neptunium*	Np	93		
Nickel	Ni	28	58.6934(4)	
Niobium	Nb	41	92.90638(2)	
Nitrogen	N	7	14.0067(2)	g, r
Nobelium*	No	102		
Osmium	Os	76	190.23(3)	g
Oxygen	O	8	15.9994(3)	g, r
Palladium	Pd	46	106.42(1)	g
Phosphorus	P	15	30.973762(2)	
Platinum	Pt	78	195.084(9)	
Plutonium*	Pu	94		
Polonium*	Po	84		
Potassium (Kalium)	K	19	39.0983(1)	
Praseodymium	Pr	59	140.90765(2)	
Promethium*	Pm	61		
Protactinium*	Pa	91	231.03588(2)	
Radium*	Ra	88		
Radon*	Rn	86		

*Element has no stable nuclides. One or more well-known isotopes are given in the accompanying table with the appropriate relative atomic mass and half-life. However, three such elements (Th, Pa, and U) do have a characteristic terrestrial isotopic composition, and for these an atomic weight is tabulated.
†Commercially available Li materials have atomic weights that are known to range between 6.939 and 6.996; if a more accurate value is required, it must be determined for the specific material.
gGeological specimens are known in which the element has an isotopic composition outside the limits for normal material. The difference between the atomic weight of the element in such specimens and that given in the Table may exceed the stated uncertainty.
mModified isotopic compositions may be found in commercially available material because it has been subjected to an undisclosed or inadvertent isotopic fractionation. Substantial deviations in atomic weight of the element from that given in the Table can occur.
rRange in isotopic composition of normal terrestrial material prevents a more precise Ar(E) being given; the tabulated Ar(E) value should be applicable to any normal material.

Name	Atomic Symbol	Atomic Number	Atomic Weight	Footnotes
Rhenium	Re	75	186.207(1)	
Rhodium	Rh	45	102.90550(2)	
Roentgenium*	Rg	111		
Rubidium	Rb	37	85.4678(3)	g
Ruthenium	Ru	44	101.07(2)	g
Rutherfordium*	Rf	104		
Samarium	Sm	62	150.36(2)	g
Scandium	Sc	21	44.955912(6)	
Seaborgium*	Sg	106		
Selenium	Se	34	78.96(3)	
Silicon	Si	14	28.0855(3)	r
Silver	Ag	47	107.8682(2)	g
Sodium (Natrium)	Na	11	22.98976928(2)	
Strontium	Sr	38	87.62(1)	g, r
Sulfur	S	16	32.065(5)	g, r
Tantalum	Ta	73	180.94788(2)	
Technetium*	Tc	43		
Tellurium	Te	52	127.60(3)	g
Terbium	Tb	65	158.92535(2)	
Thallium	Tl	81	204.3833(2)	
Thorium*	Th	90	232.03806(2)	g
Thulium	Tm	69	168.93421(2)	
Tin	Sn	50	118.710(7)	g
Titanium	Ti	22	47.867(1)	
Tungsten (Wolfram)	W	74	183.84(1)	
Ununbium*	Uub	112		
Ununhexium*	Uuh	116		
Ununoctium*	Uuo	118		
Ununpentium*	Uup	115		
Ununquadium*	Uuq	114		
Ununtrium*	Uut	113		
Uranium*	U	92	238.02891(3)	g, m
Vanadium	V	23	50.9415(1)	
Xenon	Xe	54	131.293(6)	g, m
Ytterbium	Yb	70	173.054(5)	g
Yttrium	Y	39	88.90585(2)	
Zinc	Zn	30	65.38(2)	
Zirconium	Zr	40	91.224(2)	g

*Element has no stable nuclides. One or more well-known isotopes are given in the accompanying table with the appropriate relative atomic mass and half-life. However, three such elements (Th, Pa, and U) do have a characteristic terrestrial isotopic composition, and for these an atomic weight is tabulated.
†Commercially available Li materials have atomic weights that are known to range between 6.939 and 6.996; if a more accurate value is required, it must be determined for the specific material.
gGeological specimens are known in which the element has an isotopic composition outside the limits for normal material. The difference between the atomic weight of the element in such specimens and that given in the Table may exceed the stated uncertainty.
mModified isotopic compositions may be found in commercially available material because it has been subjected to an undisclosed or inadvertent isotopic fractionation. Substantial deviations in atomic weight of the element from that given in the Table can occur.
rRange in isotopic composition of normal terrestrial material prevents a more precise Ar(E) being given; the tabulated Ar(E) value should be applicable to any normal material.

Relative Atomic Masses and Half-Lives of Selected Radionuclides (© 1998 IUPAC).*

[Abbreviations for units are: a = year; d = day; h = hour; min = minute; s = second; ms = millisecond. Names of elements with atomic numbers 110, 111, and 112 are temporary.]

Atomic Number	Name	Symbol	Mass Number	Relative Atomic Mass	Half-Life and Uncertainty	Unit
43	Technetium	Tc	97	96.9064	$2.6 \pm 0.4 \times 10^6$	a
			98	97.9072	$4.2 \pm 0.3 \times 10^6$	a
			99	98.9063	$2.1 \pm 0.3 \times 10^5$	a
61	Promethium	Pm	145	144.9127	17.7 ± 0.4	a
			147	146.9151	2.623 ± 0.003	a
84	Polonium	Po	209	208.9824	102 ± 5	a
			210	209.9828	138.4 ± 0.1	d
85	Astatine	At	210	209.9871	8.1 ± 0.4	h
			211	210.9875	7.21 ± 0.01	h
86	Radon	Rn	211	210.9906	14.6 ± 0.2	h
			220	220.0114	55.6 ± 0.1	s
			222	222.0176	3.823 ± 0.004	d
87	Francium	Fr	223	223.0197	22.0 ± 0.1	min
88	Radium	Ra	223	223.0185	11.43 ± 0.01	d
			224	224.0202	3.66 ± 0.02	d
			226	226.0254	1599 ± 4	a
			228	228.0311	5.75 ± 0.03	a
89	Actinium	Ac	227	227.0277	21.77 ± 0.02	a
90	Thorium	Th	230	230.0331	$7.54 \pm 0.03 \times 10^4$	a
			232	232.0380	$1.40 \pm 0.01 \times 10^{10}$	a
91	Protactinium	Pa	231	231.0359	$3.25 \pm 0.01 \times 10^4$	a
92	Uranium	U	233	233.0396	$1.592 \pm 0.002 \times 10^5$	a
			234	234.0409	$2.455 \pm 0.006 \times 10^5$	a
			235	235.0439	$7.04 \pm 0.01 \times 10^8$	a
			236	236.0456	$2.342 \pm 0.004 \times 10^7$	a
			238	238.0508	$4.47 \pm 0.02 \times 10^9$	a
93	Neptunium	Np	237	237.0482	$2.14 \pm 0.01 \times 10^6$	a
			239	239.0529	2.355 ± 0.006	d
94	Plutonium	Pu	238	238.0496	87.7 ± 0.1	a
			239	239.0522	$2.410 \pm 0.003 \times 10^4$	a
			240	240.0538	$6.56 \pm 0.01 \times 10^3$	a
			241	241.0568	14.4 ± 0.1	a
			242	242.0587	$3.75 \pm 0.02 \times 10^5$	a
			244	244.0642	$8.00 \pm 0.09 \times 10^7$	a
95	Americium	Am	241	241.0568	432.7 ± 0.6	a
			243	243.0614	$7.37 \pm 0.02 \times 10^3$	a
96	Curium	Cm	243	243.0614	29.1 ± 0.1	a
			244	244.0627	18.1 ± 0.1	a
			245	245.0655	$8.48 \pm 0.06 \times 10^3$	a
			246	246.0672	$4.76 \pm 0.04 \times 10^3$	a
			247	247.0703	$1.56 \pm 0.05 \times 10^7$	a
			248	248.0723	$3.48 \pm 0.06 \times 10^5$	a

[a] The uncertainties of these elements are asymmetric.
[b] The value given is determined from only a few decays.

*This table is reproduced from the *United States Pharmacopeia and National Formulary* (*USP–NF*) as published in *USP 32–NF 27*. It is provided for informational purposes only and is intended as a resource for the FCC user. Note that because the *USP–NF* is in continuous revision, this table is subject to change and the information printed here may not continue to represent the current version.

Atomic Number	Name	Symbol	Mass Number	Relative Atomic Mass	Half-Life and Uncertainty	Unit
97	Berkelium	Bk	247	247.0703	$1.4 \pm 0.3 \times 10^3$	a
			249	249.0750	$3.20 \pm 0.06 \times 10^2$	d
98	Californium	Cf	249	249.0748	351 ± 2	a
			250	250.0764	13.1 ± 0.1	a
			251	251.0796	$9.0 \pm 0.5 \times 10^2$	a
			252	252.0816	2.64 ± 0.01	a
99	Einsteinium	Es	252	252.0830	472 ± 2	d
100	Fermium	Fm	257	257.0951	100.5 ± 0.2	d
101	Mendelevium	Md	256	256.0941	78 ± 2	min
			258	258.0984	51.5 ± 0.3	d
102	Nobelium	No	259	259.1011	58 ± 5	min
103	Lawrencium	Lr	262	262.110	3.6 ± 0.3	min
104	Rutherfordium	Rf	261	261.1088	1.3[a]	min
105	Dubnium	Db	262	262.1141	34 ± 5	s
106	Seaborgium	Sg	266	266.1219	21[a]	s
107	Bohrium	Bh	264	264.1247	0.44[a]	s
108	Hassium	Hs	269	269.1341	9.35[a,b]	s
109	Meitnerium	Mt	268	268.1388	70[a,b]	ms
110	Ununnilium	Uun	271	271.1461	1.1[a,b]	ms
111	Unununium	Uuu	272	272.1535	1.5[a,b]	ms
112	Ununbium	Uub	277		0.24[a,b]	ms

[a] The uncertainties of these elements are asymmetric.
[b] The value given is determined from only a few decays.

THERMOMETRIC EQUIVALENTS*

Fahrenheit to Centigrade (Celsius) Scale

(°F − 32) (5 / 9) = °C

°F	°C	°F	°C	°F	°C	°F	°C	°F	°C
0	−17.78	51	10.56	101	38.33	151	66.11	201	93.89
1	−17.22	52	11.11	102	38.89	152	66.67	202	94.44
2	−16.67	53	11.67	103	39.44	153	67.22	203	95.
3	−16.11	54	12.22	104	40.	154	67.78	204	95.56
4	−15.56	55	12.78	105	40.56	155	68.33	205	96.11
5	−15.	56	13.33	106	41.11	156	68.89	206	96.67
6	−14.44	57	13.89	107	41.67	157	69.44	207	97.22
7	−13.89	58	14.44	108	42.22	158	70.	208	97.78
8	−13.33	59	15.	109	42.78	159	70.56	209	98.33
9	−12.78	60	15.56	110	43.33	160	71.11	210	98.89
10	−12.22	61	16.11	111	43.89	161	71.67	211	99.44
11	−11.67	62	16.67	112	44.44	162	72.22	212	100.
12	−11.11	63	17.22	113	45.	163	72.78	213	100.56
13	−10.56	64	17.78	114	45.56	164	73.33	214	101.11
14	−10.	65	18.33	115	46.11	165	73.89	215	101.67
15	−9.44	66	18.89	116	46.67	166	74.44	216	102.22
16	−8.89	67	19.44	117	47.22	167	75.	217	102.78
17	−8.33	68	20.	118	47.78	168	75.56	218	103.33
18	−7.78	69	20.56	119	48.33	169	76.11	219	103.89
19	−7.22	70	21.11	120	48.89	170	76.67	220	104.44
20	−6.67	71	21.67	121	49.44	171	77.22	221	105.
21	−6.11	72	22.22	122	50.	172	77.78	222	105.56
22	−5.56	73	22.78	123	50.56	173	78.33	223	106.11
23	−5.	74	23.33	124	51.11	174	78.89	224	106.67
24	−4.44	75	23.89	125	51.67	175	79.44	225	107.22
25	−3.89	76	24.44	126	52.22	176	80.	226	107.78
26	−3.33	77	25.	127	52.78	177	80.56	227	108.33
27	−2.78	78	25.56	128	53.33	178	81.11	228	108.89
28	−2.22	79	26.11	129	53.89	179	81.67	229	109.44
29	−1.67	80	26.67	130	54.44	180	82.22	230	110.
30	−1.11	81	27.22	131	55.	181	82.78	231	110.56
31	−0.56	82	27.78	132	55.56	182	83.33	232	111.11
32	0.	83	28.33	133	56.11	183	83.89	233	111.67
33	0.56	84	28.89	134	56.67	184	84.44	234	112.22
34	1.11	85	29.44	135	57.22	185	85.	235	112.78
35	1.67	86	30.	136	57.78	186	85.56	236	113.33
36	2.22	87	30.56	137	58.33	187	86.11	237	113.89
37	2.78	88	31.11	138	58.89	188	86.67	238	114.44
38	3.33	89	31.67	139	59.44	189	87.22	239	115.
39	3.89	90	32.22	140	60.	190	87.78	240	115.56
40	4.44	91	32.78	141	60.56	191	88.33	241	116.11
41	5.	92	33.33	142	61.11	192	88.89	242	116.67
42	5.56	93	33.89	143	61.67	193	89.44	243	117.22
43	6.11	94	34.44	144	62.22	194	90.	244	117.78
44	6.67	95	35.	145	62.78	195	90.56	245	118.33

*This table is reproduced from the *United States Pharmacopeia and National Formulary* (*USP–NF*) as published in *USP 32–NF 27*. It is provided for informational purposes only and is intended as a resource for the FCC user. Note that because the *USP–NF* is in continuous revision, this table is subject to change and the information printed here may not continue to represent the current version.

Thermometric Equivalents

Fahrenheit to Centigrade (Celsius) Scale

$$(°F - 32)(5/9) = °C$$

°F	°C	°F	°C	°F	°C	°F	°C	°F	°C
45	7.22	96	35.56	146	63.33	196	91.11	246	118.89
46	7.78	97	36.11	147	63.89	197	91.67	247	119.44
47	8.33	98	36.67	148	64.44	198	92.22	248	120.
48	8.89	99	37.22	149	65.	199	92.78	249	120.56
49	9.44	100	37.78	150	65.56	200	93.33	250	121.11
50	10.								

Centigrade (Celsius) to Fahrenheit Scale

$$(9/5)°C + 32 = °F$$

°C	°F	°C	°F	°C	°F	°C	°F	°C	°F
−20	−4.0	21	69.8	61	141.8	101	213.8	141	285.8
−19	−2.2	22	71.6	62	143.6	102	215.6	142	287.6
−18	−0.4	23	73.4	63	145.4	103	217.4	143	289.4
−17	1.4	24	75.2	64	147.2	104	219.2	144	291.2
−16	3.2	25	77.	65	149.	105	221.	145	293.
−15	5.	26	78.8	66	150.8	106	222.8	146	294.8
−14	6.8	27	80.6	67	152.6	107	224.6	147	296.6
−13	8.6	28	82.4	68	154.4	108	226.4	148	298.4
−12	10.4	29	84.2	69	156.2	109	228.2	149	300.2
−11	12.2	30	86.	70	158.	110	230.	150	302.
−10	14.	31	87.8	71	159.8	111	231.8	151	303.8
−9	15.8	32	89.6	72	161.6	112	233.6	152	305.6
−8	17.6	33	91.4	73	163.4	113	235.4	153	307.4
−7	19.4	34	93.2	74	165.2	114	237.2	154	309.2
−6	21.2	35	95.	75	167.	115	239.	155	311.
−5	23.	36	96.8	76	168.8	116	240.8	156	312.8
−4	24.8	37	98.6	77	170.6	117	242.6	157	314.6
−3	26.6	38	100.4	78	172.4	118	244.4	158	316.4
−2	28.4	39	102.2	79	174.2	119	246.2	159	318.2
−1	30.2	40	104.	80	176.	120	248.	160	320.
0	32.	41	105.8	81	177.8	121	249.8	161	321.8
1	33.8	42	107.6	82	179.6	122	251.6	162	323.6
2	35.6	43	109.4	83	181.4	123	253.4	163	325.4
3	37.4	44	111.2	84	183.2	124	255.2	164	327.2
4	39.2	45	113.	85	185.	125	257.	165	329.
5	41.	46	114.8	86	186.8	126	258.8	166	330.8
6	42.8	47	116.6	87	188.6	127	260.6	167	332.6
7	44.6	48	118.4	88	190.4	128	262.4	168	334.4
8	46.4	49	120.2	89	192.2	129	264.2	169	336.2
9	48.2	50	122.	90	194.	130	266.	170	338.
10	50.	51	123.8	91	195.8	131	267.8	171	339.8
11	51.8	52	125.6	92	197.6	132	269.6	172	341.6
12	53.6	53	127.4	93	199.4	133	271.4	173	343.4
13	55.4	54	129.2	94	201.2	134	273.2	174	345.2
14	57.2	55	131.	95	203.	135	275.	175	347.
15	59.	56	132.8	96	204.8	136	276.8	176	348.8
16	60.8	57	134.6	97	206.6	137	278.6	177	350.6
17	62.6	58	136.4	98	208.4	138	280.4	178	352.4
18	64.4	59	138.2	99	210.2	139	282.2	179	354.2
19	66.2	60	140.	100	212.	140	284.	180	356.
20	68.								

GENERAL GOOD MANUFACTURING PRACTICES GUIDELINES FOR FOOD CHEMICALS[1]

Food chemicals and other substances employed as adjuncts in foods and as aids in food processing must meet recognized standards of performance and quality for their intended uses and applications. The requirements contained in the monographs of the *FCC* pertain to the characteristics of food chemicals at the time of their use.

It is not sufficient, however, for an end product merely to meet the *FCC* requirements.

Production of food-grade chemicals is best achieved by implementing procedures that place primary emphasis on preventing defects and deficiencies. Thus, a product must be made and handled in a sanitary manner, in a way designed either to preclude the formation of undesirable by-products, or to ensure their adequate removal, as well as to prevent contamination, deterioration, mix-up and mislabeling, and the introduction of unusual or unexpected impurities.

Food chemicals are subject to applicable regulations promulgated by the responsible government agencies in countries in which *FCC* specifications are recognized. In the United States, for example, the pertinent regulations that deal primarily with sanitation are the "Current Good Manufacturing Practices in Manufacturing, Packing, or Holding Human Food."[2]

Beyond requirements related to sanitation, however, manufacturers, processors, packers, and distributors should establish and exercise other appropriate systems of controls throughout their operations, including food safety assurance systems such as Hazard Analysis and Critical Control Points (HACCP), where applicable, to ensure that *FCC* substances are safe and otherwise suitable for their intended use. These controls, together with the regulations cited above, constitute "good manufacturing practices." While the details of the application of the principles of good manufacturing practices to the manufacturing, processing, packing, and distribution of food chemical substances will vary, the fundamental relevance of such principles at all stages of an operation should be recognized.

The principles of good manufacturing practices encompass such considerations as

- Systems of quality control and assurance, including self-auditing procedures;
- Clearly defined responsibilities of supervisory and other personnel, all of whom must be qualified and adequately trained;
- Design, operation and maintenance of buildings and equipment, with attention to housekeeping, sanitation, pest control, prevention of contamination of product, cleaning of equipment, a calibration program for all instruments and gauges, and environmentally satisfactory methods of waste disposal;
- Documentation of validation studies pertaining to the manufacturing process, laboratory test methods, and equipment and computer applications, when any such studies are appropriate;
- Written operational instructions that should include such items as
    - General instructions and hazards
    - Master manufacturing instructions
    - Master packaging instructions
    - Master specifications for raw materials, in-process materials, packaging materials, labels, and finished products
    - Laboratory test methods
    - Control instrumentation and computer applications
    - Labeling, holding, and distribution instructions;
- Handling and control, including the testing and approval, of raw materials, process aids, intermediates, and finished products;
- Product containers, closures, and labeling (including the control of labels and labeling);
- Laboratory and inspection controls and records (including the effect of process changes);
- Reserve samples of raw materials and products;
- Written records that contain essential operational data for each individual lot of food chemical and that permit tracing the lot history from the raw materials through manufacturing, packaging, holding, and distributing the product;
- Product stability and lifespan;
- Systems for holding, evaluating, and disposing of rejected products and returned materials;
- Procedures for investigating complaints and taking appropriate corrective action.

Some food chemicals have uses other than as food chemicals—in fact, the food-grade material may be only a small part of production for industrial or other uses. In such situations, the principles of good manufacturing practices must apply, and particular attention must be paid to the suitability of the raw materials used; the prevention of cross-contamination; and the segregation of food chemicals from nonfood chemicals, including material in process, final product, and product in storage. The necessary controls to ensure the above must be developed and implemented.

[NOTE—Depending on the processes used, it frequently is possible to divert the food-grade product from the main product stream as the final steps in producing a food-grade product are approached, and to complete the processing under conditions suitable for food-grade substances. In such cases, if the diverted material can be adequately characterized by a

---

[1] These guidelines are presented for information only and are not intended to be mandatory in any sense in regards to compliance with *FCC* specifications.
[2] *Code of Federal Regulations*, Title 21, Part 110, which may be obtained from the Superintendent of Documents, U.S. Government Printing Office, Washington, D.C. 20402. Also, Parts 113 and 114 are of interest, particularly with regard to record keeping.

knowledge of its history, and/or by appropriate analytical testing, it may be considered to be the raw material for the food-grade product.]

Biotechnology (processes involving the use of biological systems) is an important source of chemicals, enzymes, and other substances used in foods and in food processing.

Some food ingredients have long been made by fermentation and by enzymatic processes, but now processes involving genetically modified organisms have become a prominent emerging source of such substances.

The manufacture of food chemicals, whether it involves chemical or biological synthesis and purification, or recovery from natural materials, has a number of characteristics that must be taken into account in establishing a system of good manufacturing practice. For example, in the production of many chemicals, recycling of process liquors and recovery from waste streams are necessary for reasons of quality, economics, and environmental protection. In addition, the production of some food chemicals involves processes in which chemical and biochemical mechanisms have not been fully elucidated, and thus the methods and procedures for materials accountability usually will differ from those applicable to the manufacture of other classes of materials.

Another aspect of good manufacturing practices for food chemicals relates to the possible presence of objectionable impurities. While the limits and tests provided in the FCC are consistent with the information available to the committee regarding current methods of manufacture and common impurities that may be present, it obviously is impossible to provide limits and tests in each FCC monograph for the detection of all possible impurities because these may vary with the raw materials and the method of processing used in making the chemical. Thus, to evaluate whether other undesirable impurities may be present, the manufacturer should understand, to the best degree possible for the process at hand, the factors that contribute to the presence of impurities. Solvents as well as impurities in the raw materials and processing aids, all of which might carry into the final product, must be considered. In synthetic processes, it is necessary similarly to consider intermediates and the products of side reactions, as well as the possible formation of isomeric compounds, including epimers and enantiomorphs.

The same general considerations apply to biological processes, be they traditional or based on newer biotechnology. For products of biotechnology, a review that includes adequate characterization and documentation of the genetic origins of the starting materials and the characteristics of the process provides the necessary guidance for identifying and setting levels of undesirable impurities, which need to be controlled to suitable levels or to be absent altogether. Therefore, the active genetic components in the process (e.g., culture, recombinant DNA) should be known, well characterized, and free from any potential for introducing biologically significant levels of undesirable constituents (e.g., toxins, antibiotics, antinutrients, allergens) that cannot be kept out of the final product by preliminary processing. As in the production of all food chemicals, testing is appropriate when possible and particularly to demonstrate the absence of certain toxins and certain specific DNA sequences.

Because of the necessity to maintain the purity and integrity of the genetic materials associated with the biotechnological process, containment[3] is a particularly important consideration in preventing cross-contamination as well as the inadvertent release of biologically active materials.

Exposure of all products used in foods and food processing to foreign material contamination must be prevented. If objectionable impurities from any source, other than those covered by FCC requirements, are suspected to be present, good manufacturing practice requires the manufacturer to ensure that the substance is suitable for its intended applications as a food chemical by applying additional tests and limits. Current analytical technology should be applied wherever possible.

---

[3] See NIH Guidelines for Research Involving Recombinant DNA Molecules, Federal Register, Vol. 51, No. 88, pages 16957–16985, May 7, 1986. Copies, which include later revisions of the Guidelines, may be obtained from the Office of Recombinant DNA Activities, National Institutes of Health, Building 31, Room 4B11, Bethesda, MD 20892.

Food Ingredients: Pharmaceutical Applications and Use of Appropriate GMPs[*]

1. Introduction

Many food ingredients have potential application as pharmaceutical excipients. However, the expectations from pharmaceutical customers for current Good Manufacturing Practices (cGMPs) are rather different from those of the food industry. This *FCC* informational article compares and contrasts pharmaceutical excipient and food ingredient cGMPs, identifies and highlights key differences in the requirements, and shows how cGMPs may influence the use of a food ingredient as a pharmaceutical ingredient. This article is not intended as a definitive legal or procedural guide. The focus here is on GMPs, which are enforceable by the Food and Drug Administration under Food Drug and Cosmetic Act 501(a)(2)(B), not compendial standards applicable to excipients in drugs and enforceable by FDA under 501(b). The purpose of this article is to help food ingredient suppliers understand the needs of potential pharmaceutical customers and, in turn, allow those customers to better understand the food ingredients industry.

Food ingredients—food chemicals and other substances used in foods or as processing aids—must meet recognized standards of safety, quality, and performance for their intended use and application in foods. They range from naturally sourced products to specialized synthetic chemicals manufactured for food applications. Fermentation, enzymatic preparations, and manipulation of genetically modified organisms are some of the ways used to produce food ingredients. Food ingredients vary widely in origin and in their extent and history of use in both the food and pharmaceutical industries. Examples as to variation of origin include sodium chloride (common table salt), talc, and titanium dioxide which are mined; sugars and starches are plant derived; and gelatin and lactose are animal derived. The pharmaceutical industry refers to food ingredients used in drug products as pharmaceutical inactive ingredients or *excipients*.

Excipients used in pharmaceutical products are substances, other than the active drug substance or finished dosage form, that have been appropriately evaluated for safety and are included in drug delivery systems 1) to aid in the processing of the drug delivery system during its manufacture; 2) to protect, support, or enhance stability, bioavailability, or patient acceptability; 3) to assist in product identification; or 4) to enhance any other attribute of the overall safety, effectiveness, or delivery of the drug during storage or use.[1]

Excipient manufacturers mainly are food chemical or fine chemical manufacturers who may be less familiar with drug-related safety and cGMPs/regulatory requirements for excipients used in pharmaceutical products, than with food-related requirements with which they more routinely deal. In broad summary:

- Food and drug manufacturers have a legal responsibility to determine the suitability of an ingredient for its intended use. A drug product manufacturer must also determine the suitability of the excipient in terms of quality and safety for its intended use in the particular drug product or dosage form, [e.g., FDA evaluates excipients used in drug products in terms of amount used (daily dose), duration of intended use, and route of administration].
- For example, mannitol,[2] a food ingredient, functions both as a nutritive sweetener and texturizing agent in foods. Mannitol[3] is also used as both an active pharmaceutical ingredient (API) and inactive ingredient (excipient) in many drug products.
- Major deficiencies in the current drug cGMPs for excipients may lead to confusion for the food industry supplier and the pharmaceutical industry mainly because drug cGMPs focus on the finished dosage form and not on the excipient.
- Global sourcing of excipients creates an even greater challenge for the pharmaceutical industry.

---

[*] This information, in part, was originally presented at the June 2009 Institute of Food Technology (IFT) annual meeting. The poster title was: "Food Ingredients: Pharmaceutical Applications and Use of Appropriate GMPs" by Catherine M. Sheehan, MS, US Pharmacopeia, Rockville, MD; James C. Griffiths, PhD, US Pharmacopeia, Rockville, MD; Richard C. Moreton, PhD, FinnBrit Consulting, Waltham, MA.

[1] USP. *USP 32–NF 27*, General Information Chapter, *Good Manufacturing Practices for Bulk Pharmaceutical Excipients* ⟨1078⟩. Rockville, MD; 2008.
[2] USP. *Food Chemicals Codex FCC, Mannitol*. 6th ed. Baltimore; United Book Press; 2009.
[3] USP. *USP 32–NF 27, Mannitol*. Rockville, MD; 2009.

2. Comparison and Contrast of Food and Drug Regulations

Food Regulations	Drug Regulations[4]
• US food ingredient manufacturers are subject to regulations dealing with sanitation, the cGMPs in Manufacturing, Packing, or Holding Human Food, 21 CFR Part 110[5] to ensure compliance with sections 402 (a)(3) and (4) of the Federal Food Drug & Cosmetic Act (FFDCA). • Food cGMPs describe the methods, equipment, facilities, and controls for producing processed food (*Table 1, Table 1a*). • Food cGMPs focus on sanitation, i.e., control of food safety hazards such as microbiological, chemical, or physical hazards, prevention of spoilage, and contamination with filth. • Under a contract with the FDA,[6] Eastern Research Group, Inc. (ERG) undertook a study of current food safety problems and the range of preventive controls needed to address them. • The ERG report suggested that in addition to food cGMPs sanitation requirements, manufacturers, processors, packers, and distributors, where applicable, may better control physical hazards by establishing appropriate systems to monitor food safety assurance systems such as Hazard Analysis Critical Control Points (HACCP) practices[7], where appropriate, to ensure that the foods are suitable for their intended use and application (*Table 2*). • HACCP has 7 principles established by the National Advisory Committee for Microbiological Criteria for Foods[8] that control product safety (*Table 3*). • Manufacturers who produce food additives or food ingredients under food cGMPs are not required to test to the analytical specifications of food ingredients because food cGMPs focus on the sanitation and contamination aspects of inspection.	• US Drug cGMPs *Requirements for Finished Pharmaceutical Products* are found in Section 501(a)(2)(B) of the FFDCA to ensure that quality is built into—and not tested into—the drug product. [9, 10, 11] • Two parts: 21 CFR Part 210 deals with definitions and terms, and 21 CFR Part 211 deals with manufacture, processing, packing, or holding of the drug product (*Table 1, Table 1b*). • An excipient used in a drug product approved and marketed in the US, must, at minimum, be manufactured to appropriate cGMPs and must have validated analytical specifications.[12] • Drug cGMPs, in contrast to food cGMPs, require testing of each component to ensure the identity, strength, quality, and purity of the finished dosage form (i.e., the drug product must be safe and must provide the intended benefit to the patient). • If a *USP* or *NF* monograph exits, the excipient, if labeled as such, must meet those specifications. If it does not, this must be detailed in the marketing application and justified. • *USP–NF* also includes a General Information Chapter on cGMP requirements for excipient manufacture.[13] • In 2002, the FDA launched a new initiative, *Pharmaceutical cGMPs for the 21st Century*, to integrate quality systems and risk management approaches into its existing programs. The goal is to encourage industry to adopt modern and innovative manufacturing technologies. • In 2006, the FDA issued guidance for industry to help manufacturers implement modern quality systems and risk management approaches to meet cGMPs regulations.[14] The guidance describes a comprehensive quality systems model, which allows manufacturers to support modern quality systems that are consistent with cGMP regulations and aligns with other widely used quality management systems, including ISO 9000, non-U.S. pharmaceutical quality management requirements, and FDA's own medical device quality system regulations. • The guidance elaborates key concepts integral to the quality systems approach that includes quality, quality by design (QbD), and product development, quality risk management, corrective and preventive action (CAPA), change control, the quality unit, and the six-sigma inspection model. • Excipient selection and control require a greater understanding of the critical process parameters. Excipient specifications must ensure product performance with the desired quality attributes (e.g., control of source, lot-to-lot, and batch-to-batch variations). Meaningful tests must provide knowledge and understanding of how excipient performance influences the formula, process, and product.

[4] While the focus of this article is on GMPs, it is important to note that drugs (including any excipients) are subject to standards of identity, and strength, quality, and purity, contained in *USP–NF*, and that these compendial standards apply whether USP is referenced on the drug label or not. See 21 Code of Federal Regulations (CFR) 299.5, and FDCA Section 501(b); see also *USP General Notices*, including with particular regard to excipients, *General Notices* §3.10.10, 5.20, 5.20.10, and 5.20.20. Furthermore, unlike foods, drugs are subject to premarket review for safety and efficacy by the FDA, and are subject to the requirements in a given product's New Drug Application (NDA), Abbreviated NDA, or Biologic License Application, which will include detailed product and manufacturing specifications, for both active and inactive ingredients (including excipients). See, e.g., 21 CFR 314.50.

[5] Title 21 Code of Federal Regulations (CFR), Part 110. *cGMP in Manufacturing, Packing, or Holding Human Food.* http://www.access.gpo.gov/nara/cfr/waisidx_08/21cfr110_08.html. Accessed on September 4, 2009.

[6] ERG. *Comparison of Food GMPs to Quality Systems and Other GMPs, Appendix E.* http://www.fda.gov/Food/GuidanceComplianceRegulatoryInformation/CurrentGoodManufacturingPracticeCGMPs/ucm110977.htm. Accessed on September 11, 2009.

[7] 21 CFR Part 120. *HACCP Systems.* http://www.access.gpo.gov/nara/cfr/waisidx_08/21cfr120_08.html. Accessed on March 25, 2009.

[8] FDA. *HACCP: A State-of-the-Art Approach to Food Safety.* http://www.cfsan.fda.gov/~lrd/bghaccp.html. Accessed on September 4, 2009.

[9] Center for Drug and Evaluation Research (CDER), Grace E. McNally. *Forum for International Drug Regulatory Authorities. Ensuring Conformance with Requirements Using Risk Management Strategies.* http://www.fda.gov/downloads/Drugs/NewsEvents/UCM167319.pdf. Accessed on September 15, 2009.

[10] 21 CFR, Part 211. GMPs. http://www.accessdata.fda.gov/scripts/cdrh/cfdocs/cfcfr/CFRSearch.cfm?CFRPart=211, http://www.fda.gov/downloads/AboutFDA/CentersOffices/CDER/UCM095852.txt. Accessed on September 14, 2009.

[11] FD&C Act. *Chapter II—Definitions.* http://www.fda.gov/opacom/laws/fdcact/fdcact1.htm. Accessed on September 4, 2009.

[12] USP. *USP 32–NF 27*, General Information Chapter, *Validation of Compendial Methods* ⟨1225⟩. Rockville, MD; 2008.

[13] USP. *USP 32–NF 27*, General Information Chapter *Good Manufacturing Practices for Bulk Pharmaceutical Excipients* ⟨1078⟩. Rockville, MD; 2008.

[14] FDA. *Guidance for Industry: Quality Systems Approach to Pharmaceutical cGMP Regulations.* http://www.fda.gov/downloads/Drugs/GuidanceComplianceRegulatoryInformation/Guidances/UCM070337.pdf. Accessed on September 14, 2009.

Table 1
Title 21 Code of Federal Regulations (CFR) part 110 Current Good Manufacturing Practices in Manufacturing, Packing, or Holding Human Food
Title 21 CFR part 211 Current Good Manufacturing Practices for Finished Pharmaceuticals

Title 21 CFR part 110		Title 21 CFR part 211	
Subpart A	General provisions	Subpart A	General provisions
Subpart B	Buildings and Facilities	Subpart B	Organization and personnel
Subpart C	Equipment	Subpart C	Buildings and Facilities
Subpart D	Reserved	Subpart D	Equipment
Subpart E	Production and process controls	Subpart E	Control of components, drug product containers, and closures
Subpart F	Reserved	Subpart F	Production and process controls
Subpart G	Defect action levels	Subpart G	Packaging and labeling control
		Subpart H	Holding and distribution
		Subpart I	Laboratory controls
		Subpart J	Records and reports
		Subpart K	Returned and salvaged drug products

TABLE 1a
Title 21—Food and Drugs
Chapter I—Food and Drug Administration
Department of Health and Human Services
Subchapter B—Food for Human Consumption

Part 110, Current Good Manufacturing Practice in Manufacturing, Packing, or Holding Human Food

Subpart A—General Provisions
§110.3–Definitions.
§110.5–Current good manufacturing practice.
§110.10–Personnel.
§110.19–Exclusions.

Subpart B—Buildings and Facilities
§110.20–Plant and grounds.
§110.35–Sanitary operations.
§110.37–Sanitary facilities and controls.

Subpart C—Equipment
§110.40–Equipment and utensils.

Subpart D [Reserved]

Subpart E—Production and Process Controls
§110.80–Processes and controls.
§110.93–Warehousing and distribution.

Subpart F [Reserved]

Subpart G—Defect Action Levels
§110.110–Natural or unavoidable defects in food for human use that present no health hazard.

Authority: 21 U.S.C. 342, 371, 374; 42 U.S.C. 264.

Source: 51 FR 24475, June 19, 1986, unless otherwise noted.

TABLE 1b
Title 21—Food and Drugs
Chapter I—Food and Drug Administration
Department of Health and Human Services
Subchapter C—Drugs: General

Part 211, Current Good Manufacturing Practice For Finished Pharmaceuticals

Subpart A—General Provisions
§211.1–Scope.
§211.3–Definitions.

Subpart B—Organization and Personnel
§211.22–Responsibilities of quality control unit.
§211.25–Personnel qualifications.
§211.28–Personnel responsibilities.
§211.34–Consultants.

TABLE 1b
Title 21—Food and Drugs
Chapter I—Food and Drug Administration
Department of Health and Human Services
Subchapter C—Drugs: General (continued)

Part 211, Current Good Manufacturing Practice For Finished Pharmaceuticals

Subpart C—Buildings and Facilities
§211.42–Design and construction features.
§211.44–Lighting.
§211.46–Ventilation, air filtration, air heating and cooling.
§211.48–Plumbing.
§211.50–Sewage and refuse.
§211.52–Washing and toilet facilities.
§211.56–Sanitation.
§211.58–Maintenance.

Subpart D—Equipment
§211.63–Equipment design, size, and location.
§211.65–Equipment construction.
§211.67–Equipment cleaning and maintenance.
§211.68–Automatic, mechanical, and electronic equipment.
§211.72–Filters.

Subpart E—Control of Components and Drug Product Containers and Closures
§211.80–General requirements.
§211.82–Receipt and storage of untested components, drug product containers, and closures.
§211.84–Testing and approval or rejection of components, drug product containers, and closures.
§211.86–Use of approved components, drug product containers, and closures.
§211.87–Retesting of approved components, drug product containers, and closures.
§211.89–Rejected components, drug product containers, and closures.
§211.94–Drug product containers and closures.

Subpart F—Production and Process Controls
§211.100–Written procedures; deviations.
§211.101–Charge-in of components.
§211.103–Calculation of yield.
§211.105–Equipment identification.
§211.110–Sampling and testing of in-process materials and drug products.
§211.111–Time limitations on production.
§211.113–Control of microbiological contamination.
§211.115–Reprocessing.

Subpart G—Packaging and Labeling Control
§211.122–Materials examination and usage criteria.
§211.125–Labeling issuance.
§211.130–Packaging and labeling operations.
§211.132–Tamper-evident packaging requirements for over-the-counter (OTC) human drug products.
§211.134–Drug product inspection.
§211.137–Expiration dating.

Subpart H—Holding and Distribution
§211.142–Warehousing procedures.
§211.150–Distribution procedures.

Subpart I—Laboratory Controls
§211.160–General requirements.
§211.165–Testing and release for distribution.
§211.166–Stability testing.
§211.167–Special testing requirements.
§211.170–Reserve samples.
§211.173–Laboratory animals.
§211.176–Penicillin contamination.

Subpart J—Records and Reports
§211.180–General requirements.
§211.182–Equipment cleaning and use log.
§211.184–Component, drug product container, closure, and labeling records.
§211.186–Master production and control records.
§211.188–Batch production and control records.
§211.192–Production record review.
§211.194–Laboratory records.
§211.196–Distribution records.
§211.198–Complaint files.

Subpart K—Returned and Salvaged Drug Products

Authority: 21 U.S.C. 321, 351, 352, 355, 360b, 371, 374; 42 U.S.C. 216, 262, 263a, 264.

Source: 43 FR 45077, Sept. 29, 1978, unless otherwise noted.

Table 2
Title 21 CFR part 120 Hazard Analysis Critical Control Points (HACCP) systems

Title 21 CFR Part 120			
120.1	Applicability	120.11	Verification and validation
120.3	Definitions	120.12	Records
120.5	Current good manufacturing practice	120.13	Training
120.6	Sanitation standard operating procedures	120.14	Application of requirements to imported products
120.7	Hazard analysis	120.20	General
120.8	Hazard Analysis and Critical Control Point (HACCP) plan	120.24	Process controls
120.9	Legal basis	120.25	Process verification for certain processors
120.10	Corrective actions		

Table 3
Seven Principles of HACCP

HACCP involves seven principles:

- **Analyze hazards.** Potential hazards associated with a food and measures to control those hazards are identified. The hazard could be biological, such as a microbe; chemical, such as a toxin; or physical, such as ground glass or metal fragments.
- **Identify critical control points.** These are points in a food's production—from its raw state through processing and shipping to consumption by the consumer—at which the potential hazard can be controlled or eliminated. Examples are cooking, cooling, packaging, and metal detection.
- **Establish preventive measures with critical limits for each control point.** For a cooked food, for example, this might include setting the minimum cooking temperature and time required to ensure the elimination of any harmful microbes.
- **Establish procedures to monitor the critical control points.** Such procedures might include determining how and by whom cooking time and temperature should be monitored.
- **Establish corrective actions to be taken when monitoring shows that a critical limit has not been met**—For example, reprocessing or disposing of food if the minimum cooking temperature is not met.
- **Establish procedures to verify that the system is working properly**—For example, testing time-and-temperature recording devices to verify that a cooking unit is working properly.
- **Establish effective recordkeeping to document the HACCP system.** This would include records of hazards and their control methods, the monitoring of safety requirements and action taken to correct potential problems. Each of these principles must be backed by sound scientific knowledge: for example, published microbiological studies on time and temperature factors for controlling foodborne pathogens. http://www.cfsan.fda.gov/~lrd/bghaccp.html.

3. Compare and Contrast Shared Subparts

Title 21 CFR Part 110, Food GMPs	Title 21 CFR Part 211, Drug cGMPs[15]
General Provisions	General Provisions/Organization and Personnel
Subpart A §110.3, §110.5, §110.10, and §110.19	Subpart A §211.1, §211.3; Subpart B §211.22, §211.25, §211.28, and §211.34
<ul><li>Both regulations require that personnel should be qualified and have relevant education and experience to meet the job description/position requirements, §110.10.</li><li>Both regulations require on-going training programs. The personnel who provide the training must be qualified to do so, §211.25, §211.28, and §211.34.</li><li>In general, both require personnel hygiene, disease control, and cleanliness practices and wearing of suitable protective clothing, §110.10 and §211.28.</li></ul>	

---

[15] All citations in this section refer to 21 CFR.
[16] The FDA Web site has several validation guidance documents, including: Q2B: *Validation of Analytical Procedures*: http://www.fda.gov/downloads/RegulatoryInformation/Guidances/UCM128049.pdf; Q3A: *Impurities in New Drug Substances*: http://www.fda.gov/downloads/Drugs/GuidanceComplianceRegulatoryInformation/Guidances/ucm073385.pdf; Q3C: *Impurities—Residual Solvents*: http://www.fda.gov/downloads/RegulatoryInformation/Guidances/ucm128317.pdf; Q6A: *Specifications: Test Procedures and Acceptance Criteria for New Drug Substances and New Drug Products: Chemical Substances*: http://www.ich.org/cache/compo/363-272-1.html#Q6A; Q7A: *Good Manufacturing Practice Guidance for Active Pharmaceutical Ingredients*. http://www.fda.gov/downloads/RegulatoryInformation/Guidances/ucm129098.pdf. All accessed September 11, 2009.
[17] Sharp J. *Good Pharmaceutical Manufacturing Practice, Chapter 15, Validation—General Principles*. Boca Raton, FL: CRC Press; 2005.
[18] USP. *USP 32–NF 27*, Supplement 1, General Information Chapter, *Significant Change Guide for Bulk Pharmaceutical Excipients* ⟨1195⟩. Rockville, MD; 2009.

Title 21 CFR Part 110, Food GMPs	Title 21 CFR Part 211, Drug cGMPs[15]
• Food GMPs focus on awareness of dangers of poor personal hygiene and unsanitary practices, §110.10.	• Drug cGMPs focus on maintaining the safety, identity, strength, quality, and purity of the drug product, §211.25. • Drug cGMPs also include under Organization and Personnel, §211.22, responsibilities of the Quality Control Unit. A typical Quality Control Unit is comprised of Quality Assurance (QA) and Quality Control (QC) release testing. • QA is responsible for reviewing and approving all procedures related to production, quality control, and QA that deal with sampling, specifications, and testing, as well as their documentation to ensure that procedures are adequate for their intended use and materials are not released until their quality is satisfactory. • QC focuses on individual testing units within the manufacturing process to ensure drug products meet required specifications for identity, strength, quality, and purity.
Buildings and Facilities	
CFR Subpart B §110.20, §110.35, §110.37	CFR Subpart C §211.42, §211.44, §211.46, §211.48, §211.50, §211.52, §211.56, and §211.58
• Food cGMPs provide general requirements for plant design and construction in terms of walls, floors, and ceilings, and appropriate working conditions in terms of lighting, temperature, humidity, and ventilation to prevent contamination from external sources. Also covered are sanitation and pest control operations, maintenance workshops, toilet facilities, and hand-washing facilities, §110.20 and §110.35. • Focuses on the sanitary operations (physical facilities, equipment, and utensils must be sanitized in a way that protects against food contamination) and describes the requirements for adequate sanitary facilities and controls, including water supply, plumbing, toilet, and hand-washing, §110.37.	• Drug cGMPs require adequate space, defined areas, adequate materials of construction, areas that are easily cleaned and maintained, efficient material flow patterns, and personnel traffic, §211.46. • Focuses on prevention of contamination (§211.56) or mix-ups during "Receipt, identification, storage, and withholding from use of components, drug product containers, closures, and labeling, pending the appropriate sampling, testing, or examination by the quality control unit before release for manufacturing or packaging," §211.42.
Equipment	
CFR Subpart C §110.40	CFR Subpart D §211.63, §211.65, §211.67, §211.68, and §211.72
• Food cGMPs describe the requirements and expectations for the design, construction, and maintenance of equipment and utensils to ensure sanitary conditions. They are fairly general and are intended to prevent contamination from any source, §110.40.	• Drug cGMPs are similar in their general requirements (design, construction, location, cleaning, and maintenance) but also include requirements for equipment surfaces, §211.65, computers and related systems, and filters, §211.72, relating to their calibration and inspection against written procedures that must be recorded and maintained, §211.68.

[15] All citations in this section refer to 21 CFR.
[16] The FDA Web site has several validation guidance documents, including: Q2B: *Validation of Analytical Procedures*: http://www.fda.gov/downloads/RegulatoryInformation/Guidances/UCM128049.pdf; Q3A: *Impurities in New Drug Substances*: http://www.fda.gov/downloads/Drugs/GuidanceComplianceRegulatoryInformation/Guidances/ucm073385.pdf; Q3C: *Impurities—Residual Solvents*: http://www.fda.gov/downloads/RegulatoryInformation/Guidances/ucm128317.pdf; Q6A: *Specifications: Test Procedures and Acceptance Criteria for New Drug Substances and New Drug Products: Chemical Substances*: http://www.ich.org/cache/compo/363-272-1.html#Q6A; Q7A: *Good Manufacturing Practice Guidance for Active Pharmaceutical Ingredients*. http://www.fda.gov/downloads/RegulatoryInformation/Guidances/ucm129098.pdf. All accessed September 11, 2009.
[17] Sharp J. *Good Pharmaceutical Manufacturing Practice, Chapter 15, Validation—General Principles*. Boca Raton, FL: CRC Press; 2005.
[18] USP. *USP 32–NF 27*, Supplement 1, General Information Chapter, *Significant Change Guide for Bulk Pharmaceutical Excipients* ⟨1195⟩. Rockville, MD; 2009.

Title 21 CFR Part 110, Food GMPs	Title 21 CFR Part 211, Drug cGMPs[15]
\multicolumn{2}{c}{**Production and Process Controls**}	
CFR Subpart E §110.80 and §110.93	CFR Subpart F §211.100, §211.101, §211.103, §211.105, §211.110, §211.111, §211.113, and §211.115

• Food cGMPs list general sanitation processes and controls necessary to ensure that food is suitable for human consumption. They also delineate processes and controls for raw materials and other ingredients, as well as manufacturing operations, §110.80.
• The cGMPs do not require evaluation/validation to determine whether an activity is accomplishing its goal. The manufacturing facility may "verify" compliance with microbial levels for raw materials and other ingredients by any effective means including using a supplier certification or by testing.
• HACCP can be employed to determine the critical operations within the production process of the food product from beginning to end in terms of potential risk to quality and the health of the consumer. HACCP establishes CAPAs, but these are not addressed under food GMPs.
• Change Control is not a formal requirement for food cGMPs.
	• Drug cGMPs make four specific references to validation,[16] computer systems, supplier test results, sampling and testing in-process materials, and sterilization processes §211.68, §211.84, §211.110, and §211.113.[17]
	• Drug cGMPs require written procedures, qualified and calibrated equipment/instruments, validation programs, change control, and a materials management system (forward and backward traceability), §211.100.
	• Change control and notification are critical to the successful use of an excipient in a drug product. Regulatory authorities often require notification of significant changes involving the manufacture of excipients:
	  • Evaluating the effect of a change in the manufacture of an excipient is difficult because the pharmaceutical excipient is often used with a broad range of active ingredients in a diverse range of finished dosage forms, and a significant change can lead to increased risks to both the drug product and for the patient.
	  • The manufacturer has an obligation to notify its customers of a significant change so that the customer can evaluate the effect of the change on the customer's products.
	  • Several types of change must be considered, as listed below:[18]
	    • Site
	    • Scale
	    • Equipment
	    • Process
	    • Packaging
	    • Specifications

[15] All citations in this section refer to 21 CFR.
[16] The FDA Web site has several validation guidance documents, including: Q2B: *Validation of Analytical Procedures*: http://www.fda.gov/downloads/RegulatoryInformation/Guidances/UCM128049.pdf; Q3A: *Impurities in New Drug Substances*: http://www.fda.gov/downloads/Drugs/GuidanceComplianceRegulatoryInformation/Guidances/ucm073385.pdf; Q3C: *Impurities—Residual Solvents*: http://www.fda.gov/downloads/RegulatoryInformation/Guidances/ucm128317.pdf; Q6A: *Specifications: Test Procedures and Acceptance Criteria for New Drug Substances and New Drug Products: Chemical Substances*: http://www.ich.org/cache/compo/363-272-1.html#Q6A; Q7A: *Good Manufacturing Practice Guidance for Active Pharmaceutical Ingredients*. http://www.fda.gov/downloads/RegulatoryInformation/Guidances/ucm129098.pdf. All accessed September 11, 2009.
[17] Sharp J. *Good Pharmaceutical Manufacturing Practice, Chapter 15, Validation—General Principles*. Boca Raton, FL: CRC Press; 2005.
[18] USP. *USP 32–NF 27*, Supplement 1, General Information Chapter, *Significant Change Guide for Bulk Pharmaceutical Excipients* ⟨1195⟩. Rockville, MD; 2009.

1520 / Food Ingredients: Pharmaceutical Applications / *General Information*

Title 21 CFR 211 Drug cGMPs—Additional Subparts

Control of Components and Drug Product Containers and Closures
Subpart E §211.80, §211.82, §211.84, §211.86, §211.87, §211.89, and §211.94

- Drug cGMPs refer to ingredients as components, §211.80.
- The pharmaceutical manufacturer can qualify an excipient from an excipient supplier (manufacturer or distributor) by: a) conducting at least one identity test to verify identity of the excipient, and b) testing the excipient for conformity with all appropriate written specifications for purity, strength, and quality, §211.84.
- In lieu of such testing, the manufacturer may accept a Certificate of Analysis (CoA) from the supplier of the excipient, provided that at least one specific identity test is conducted on the excipient by the manufacturer and provided that the manufacturer establishes the reliability of the supplier's analyses through appropriate validation of the supplier's test results at appropriate intervals, §211.84.
- If the drug manufacturer procures an excipient from multiple manufacturers, all claiming to be of a similar grade (e.g., *USP–NF*), the excipient manufacturers must ensure equivalence of the excipient by demonstrating that each batch of excipient complies with the requirements of the tests specified in the approved drug product application (or the specifications in a compendial monograph, if it exists) before its approval, release, and use in a drug product batch. Drug manufacturers must confirm the excipient manufacturer's validated process parameters for each source of excipient.
- Many drug product manufacturers perform additional testing that is related to the specific use of the excipient in the drug product that may or may not be included in the CoA[19] because excipients function in different ways in different drug products. These functionality-related tests, performance tests, or functionality related characteristics (FRCs) test critical performance criteria of the excipient.
- When an excipient is procured from multiple sources (manufacturers and vendors), the excipient may display differences in physical properties (e.g., particle size) that may have an effect on the dosage form (e.g., dose uniformity and dissolution). Identification and control of these critical properties are needed to ensure consistent performance of the dosage form.
- Internal company audits or self-inspections and external audits are expected as part of the drug cGMPs QA program or quality systems approach, §211.84.

- Food ingredient manufacturers may believe that compliance with *USP–NF* compendial specification is all that is required to qualify the food ingredient for use in a drug product.
- Testing into compliance is not sufficient because of the requirement that the manufacture of *USP–NF* materials be performed in accordance with an appropriate level of cGMPs.
- As a result, food ingredient manufacturers who supply excipient-grade material to the drug manufacturer often experience difficulties in conforming to drug cGMPs expectations and requirements because of the additional costs associated with conformance to testing requirements—in some cases an excipient vendor's supply to the drug industry is a very low percentage of the total production.
- Manufacturers who produce food additives or food ingredients under food cGMPs are not required to test to the analytical specifications of food ingredients because food cGMPs focus on the sanitation and contamination aspects of inspection.
- The extent of cGMPs requirements for excipient manufacture should be based on an assessment of potential risk in terms of identifying and controlling critical attributes, knowledge of intended use, and requirements of the end user.
- Good communication between the food ingredient/excipient supplier and the drug manufacturer via quality agreements is essential.
- Internal audits or inspections are not explicitly specified within the food cGMPs.

Laboratory controls
CFR Subpart I §211.160, §211.165, §211.166, §211.167, §211.170, §211.173, and §211.176

- Requires that appropriate laboratory testing be carried out for each batch of drug product, and the results must be in conformance with final approved specifications for the drug product. These specifications include the identity and strength of each active ingredient, and drug products must be free of objectionable microorganisms before release for distribution. Requires the calibration of instruments at suitable intervals in accordance with an established written program. Also requires written sampling and testing procedures conducted by the QC Unit and validation and documentation of analytical tests.
- Compendial methods are validated for the pharmacopeial materials or products. All results (product, intermediate, raw material, and environmental and water samples) that fall outside the specification or acceptance criteria established by the NDA or official compendium or by the manufacturer are considered out of specification (OOS) and must have an official investigation, root cause analysis, conclusion, and documentation.

Records and Reports
CFR Subpart J §211.180, §211.182, §211.184, §211.186, §211.188, §211.192, §211.194, §211.196, and §211.198

- Requires that written procedures must be established and followed for every step of the manufacturing process to ensure a state of control. Procedures must be documented and records must be readily available to FDA inspectors.
- Documentation requirements are not explicitly specified for food cGMPs except for supplier certification for cleaning compounds and raw materials.
- CAPAs are part of the risk-based approach to drug cGMPs compliance. This is not a requirement under food cGMPs.

Packaging and Labeling Control
CFR Subpart G §211.122, §211.125, §211.130, §211.132, §211.134, and §211.137

- Requires that all packaging and labeling operations be conducted in accordance with written procedures and records to prevent mix-ups and to ensure identification with a correct label and lot or control number for batches and an expiration date before release.
- This is not a requirement under food cGMPs.

Holding and Distribution
CFR Subpart H §211.142 and §211.150

- Requires written procedures for warehousing and distribution to ensure that the identity, strength, quality, and purity of the drug products are not compromised. QA plays a critical role at this point via the implementation of good distribution and handling practices in the delivery of the finished drug to the patient.
- This is not a requirement under food cGMPs.

Title 21 CFR 211 Drug cGMPs—Additional Subparts (continued)

Returned and Salvaged Drug Products
CFR Subpart K
• Describes handling of returned drug products subject to improper storage conditions and conditions under which salvaging operations may be conducted. • This is not a requirement under food cGMPs.

[19] USP. *USP 32–NF 27*, General Information Chapter, *Bulk Pharmaceutical Excipients Certificate of Analysis* ⟨1080⟩. Rockville, MD; 2009.

21 CFR Part 110 Food cGMPs—Additional Subparts

Defect Action Levels
Subpart G §110.110 Natural or unavoidable defects in food for human use that present no health hazard.
• Allows FDA to define maximum defect action levels (DALs) for a defect that is natural or unavoidable even when foods are produced under cGMPs as set out in the other subparts of the regulations. • Those exceeding maximum DALs will be considered in violation of §402(3)(a) of the Federal Food Drug and Cosmetic Act (FFDCA). Such an approach may not be acceptable to pharmaceutical industry.

4. Conclusions

The FFDCA requires that food ingredients and excipients be manufactured in conformance with cGMP. Any ingredient used in the manufacture of a pharmaceutical drug product must be manufactured according to appropriate cGMPs. Pharmaceutical customers often represent a small portion of the total sales for food ingredient manufacturers, and this may make it more difficult to justify the additional expense to comply with excipient cGMP testing requirements. Regulations and guidance do not provide the specific details for control of the excipient. The exact level of cGMP requirements depends on the type of ingredient (API), inactive ingredient (excipient), packaging component, state or local legislation, and the intended use. Both the supplier and the user of the food ingredient should know the target market and route of administration in determining the product's suitability as a pharmaceutical excipient. Therefore, supplier–user communications are critical for both food ingredient and drug manufacturers when challenged with meeting the drug cGMPs requirements. cGMP compliance ensures quality, consistency, and control of the excipient specifications for the ingredient's intended use. Overall, food ingredients require less testing of final food ingredients to the specifications of a CoA compared to pharmaceutical manufacturing. The Quality Control Unit operates independently of manufacturing under drug cGMPs. Compendial excipients must meet compendial standards.

The *Drug GMPs for the 21st Century* initiative emphasizes the Quality Management Systems approach ensuring the use of appropriate cGMPs based on risk analysis and management and a thorough knowledge of the manufacturing process. The extent of cGMP controls applied to the manufacture of pharmaceutical excipients is based on risk assessment relating to the function of the excipient in the finished dosage form. Some key areas of cGMP control include having thorough procedures for change control, controlled manufacturing processes, testing to verify conformance with critical control attributes in each lot, and preventing the use of contaminated excipients.[20] The intended uses of pharmaceutical excipients in drug applications directly relates to their qualification for their target market, intended use, and appropriate level of cGMPs requirements. The use of food cGMPs for the manufacture of pharmaceutical excipients may not be sufficient unless the food cGMPs are augmented by specific agreements for a documented quality system, including procedures, test methods, results, validation, and change control notification.

[20] Rothman B. Excipient Testing and Control, A Regulatory Perspective. Presented at: IPEC Regulatory Affairs Conference, VA, 2007.

FCC in the U.S. Code of Federal Regulations

The following table is provided for informational purposes only and is to be used at the sole risk of the reader. While USP strives to provide accurate information, it does not guarantee the accuracy of this document and does not accept any liability for the content.

Food Chemicals Codex (FCC) Editions Incorporated by Reference in Title 21 Code of Federal Regulations Parts 170–184 (as of October 2009)[1]

21 CFR	FCC Edition Referenced	Name	FCC Reference	FCC Page Number
170.30(h)(1)	2nd Ed. (1972) and 3rd Ed. (1981)	Eligibility for classification as generally recognized as safe (GRAS)	Meets any applicable food grade specifications of FCC	15
172.170(b)	6th Ed. (2008)	Hydrogen peroxide	Meets FCC specifications	463–464
172.320(b)(1)	3rd Ed. (1981)	Amino acids	Meets FCC specifications	13, 26, 92-93, 135, 140, 154, 171, 176,193, 202, 244, 254, 270, 326, 340–341
172.345(b)	4th Ed. (1996)	Folic acid (folacin)	Meets FCC specifications	157–158
172.379(b)	6th Ed. (2008)	Vitamin D_2	Meets FCC specifications	1013–1014
172.380(b)	5th Ed. (2004)	Vitamin D_3	Meets FCC specifications	498–499
172.665(d)(2)	4th Ed. (1996)	Gellan gum	Residual isopropyl alcohol limit not to exceed 0.075%	437–438
172.712(b)	4th Ed. (1996)	1,3-Butylene glycol	Conform to FCC identity and specifications	52
172.723(b)(3)	4th Ed. (1996)	Epoxidized soybean oil	Heavy metals (as Pb) content cannot be more than 10 ppm as determined by Heavy Metals test	760–761
172.736(b)(2)	5th Ed. (2004)	Glycerides and polyglycerides of hydrogenated vegetable oils	Acid value not greater than 2, and hydroxyl value, not greater than 56 as determined by Acid Value and Hydroxyl Value methods	934–936
172.780	5th Ed. (2004)	Acacia (gum arabic)	Meets FCC specifications	210–211
172.800(b)(2)	3rd Ed. (1981)	Acesulfame potassium	*Fluoride Limit Test, Method III, Appendix IIIB*	511
172.804(b)	3rd Ed. 1st Supp.	Aspartame	Meets FCC specifications	28–29
172.810	3rd Ed. (1981)	Dioctyl sodium sulfosuccinate	Meets FCC specifications	102–104
172.812(a)	3rd Ed. (1981)	Glycine	Meets FCC specifications	140
172.831(b)	4th Ed. (1996)	Sucralose	Meets FCC specifications	398–400
172.833(b)(4)	4th Ed. (1996)	Sucrose acetate isobutyrate (SAIB)	Lead not to exceed 1.0 mg/kg determined by the *Lead Limit Test, Atomic Absorption Spectrophotometric Graphite Furnace Method, Method I*, Appendix IIIB, with an attached modification to sample digestion section	763–764
172.841(b)	5th Ed. (2004) and 1st Supp. (2006)	Polydextrose	Meets FCC specifications	336–339
172.846(b)	3rd Ed. (1981)	Sodium stearoyl lactylate	Meets FCC specifications	300–301

[1] Most of the incorporation by reference sections are also listed in the Material Approved for Incorporation by Reference Finding Aids of Title 21 CFR Parts 170–199 (Revised as of April 1, 2008) and the Standards Incorporated by Reference (SIBR) Database accessed on September 29, 2009 and available at http://standards.gov/sibr/query/index.cfm?fuseaction=rsibr.regulatory_sibr_all&startRow=1701. The CFR sections listed in this table are provided only as a resource for illustrative purposes to facilitate the identification of FCC-related incorporations by reference that need updating. The accuracy and completeness of the listings should be checked and confirmed independently.

Food Chemicals Codex (FCC) Editions Incorporated by Reference in Title 21 Code of Federal Regulations Parts 170–184 (as of October 2009)[1] *(continued)*

21 CFR	FCC Edition Referenced	Name	FCC Reference	FCC Page Number
172.858(a)	3rd Ed. (1981)	Propylene glycol alginate	Meets FCC specifications	256
172.862(b)(1)	3rd Ed. (1981)	Oleic acid derived from tall oil fatty acids	Except that titer (solidification point) shall not exceed 13.5° and unsaponifiable matter shall not exceed 0.5%	207–208
172.867(b)	4th Ed. 1st Supp (1997)	Olestra	Meets FCC specifications	33–35
172.869(b)(6)	4th Ed. (1996)	Sucrose oligoesters	Acid value not more than 4.0, *Acid Value, Method I (Commercial Fatty Acids),* Appendix VII	820
172.869(b)(7)	4th Ed. (1996)	Sucrose oligoesters	Residue on ignition not more than 0.7% *Residue on Ignition,* Appendix IIC, Method I (using a 1-g sample)	751–752
172.869(b)(8)	4th Ed. 1st Supp (1997)	Sucrose oligoesters	Residual methanol not more than 10 mg/kg *Sucrose Fatty Acid Esters*	44–45
172.869(b)(11)	4th Ed. (1996)	Sucrose oligoesters	Lead not more than 1.0 mg/kg, *Lead Limit Test, Atomic Absorption Spectrophotometric Graphite Furnace Method, Method I,* Appendix IIIB	763–765
173.115(b)(3)	4th Ed. (1996)	Alpha-acetolactate decarboxylase (*a*-ALDC) enzyme preparation derived from a recombinant Bacillus subtilis	Enzyme preparation must meet general and additional requirements for enzyme preparations in FCC	133–134
173.160(d)	3rd Ed. (1981)	*Candida gulliermondii*	Citric acid produced must conform to FCC specifications under *Citric Acid*	86–87
173.165(d)	3rd Ed. (1981)	*Candida lipolytica*	Citric acid produced must conform to FCC specifications under *Citric Acid*	86–87
173.228(a)	4th Ed. (1996)	Ethyl acetate	Meets FCC specifications	136
173.280(c)	3rd Ed. (1981)	Solvent extraction process for citric acid	Meets FCC specifications	86–87
173.310(c)	4th Ed. (1996)	Boiler water additives	Contains not less than 95% sodium carboxymethylcellulose on a dry-weight basis, with maximum substitution of 0.9 carboxymethylcellulose groups per anhydroglucose unit, and with a minimum viscosity of 15 centipoises for 2% by weight aqueous	744–745

[1] Most of the incorporation by reference sections are also listed in the Material Approved for Incorporation by Reference Finding Aids of Title 21 CFR Parts 170–199 (Revised as of April 1, 2008) and the Standards Incorporated by Reference (SIBR) Database accessed on September 29, 2009 and available at http://standards.gov/sibr/query/index.cfm?fuseaction=rsibr.regulatory_sibr_all&startRow=1701. The CFR sections listed in this table are provided only as a resource for illustrative purposes to facilitate the identification of FCC-related incorporations by reference that need updating. The accuracy and completeness of the listings should be checked and confirmed independently.

Food Chemicals Codex (FCC) Editions Incorporated by Reference in Title 21 Code of Federal Regulations Parts 170–184 (as of October 2009)[1] *(continued)*

21 CFR	FCC Edition Referenced	Name	FCC Reference	FCC Page Number
173.310(c)	4th Ed. (1996)	Boiler water additives: list of substances and limitations	Sorbitol anhydride esters: a mixture consisting of sorbitan monostearate as defined in §172.842 of this chapter; polysorbate 60 ((polyoxyethylene (20) sorbitan monostearate)) as defined in §172.836 of this chapter; and polysorbate 20 ((polyoxyethylene (20) sorbitan monolaurate))	306–307
173.368(c)	4th Ed. (1996)	Ozone	Meets FCC specifications	277
178.1005(c)	3rd Ed. (1981)	Hydrogen peroxide solution	Meets FCC specifications	146–147
180.25(b)	3rd Ed. (1981)	Mannitol	Meets FCC specifications	188–190
180.30(a)	3rd Ed. (1981)	Brominated vegetable oil	Meets FCC specifications	40–41
180.37(b)	3rd Ed. (1981)	Saccharin, ammonium saccharin, calcium saccharin, and sodium saccharin	Meets FCC specifications	22, 62, 266–267, 297–299
184.1005(b)	3rd Ed. (1981)	Acetic acid	Meets FCC specifications	8
184.1007(b)(1)	4th Ed. (1996)	Aconitic acid: assay	Not less than 98.0% of acetic acid	102–103
184.1007(b)(6)	4th Ed. (1996)	Aconitic acid: readily carbonizable substances	Passes the test for citric acid	102–103
184.1007(b)(7)	4th Ed. (1996)	Aconitic acid: residue on ignition	Not more than 0.1% as determined by the FCC	102–103
184.1009(b)	3rd Ed. (1981)	Adipic acid	Meets FCC specifications	11
184.1011(b)	3rd Ed. (1981)	Alginic acid	Meets FCC specifications	13
184.1012(b)	3rd Ed. (1981)	alpha-Amylase enzyme preparation from *Bacillus stearothermophilus*	Meets general and additional requirements for enzyme preparations	107–110
184.1021(b)	3rd Ed. (1981)	Benzoic acid	Meets FCC specifications	35
184.1024(b)	3rd Ed. (1981)	Bromelain	Meets general and additional requirements for enzyme preparations	110
184.1025(b)	3rd Ed. (1981)	Caprylic acid	Meets FCC specifications	207
184.1027(b)	3rd Ed. (1981)	Mixed carbohydrase and protease enzyme product	Meets general and additional requirements for enzyme preparations	107
184.1033(b)	3rd Ed. (1981) and 3rd Supp. (1992)	Citric acid	Meets FCC specifications	86–87
184.1034(b)	3rd Ed. (1981)	Catalase (bovine liver)	Meets general and additional requirements for enzyme preparations	110
184.1061(b)	3rd Ed. (1981)	Lactic acid	Meets FCC specifications	159
184.1063(b)	4th Ed. (1996)	Enzyme-modified lecithin	Unless otherwise noted, compliance with (b)(1) through (b)(8) specifications listed in the section is determined according to the methods set forth for lecithin in *FCC*.	220–221
184.1069(b)	3rd Ed. (1981)	Malic acid	Meets FCC specifications	183–184

[1] Most of the incorporation by reference sections are also listed in the Material Approved for Incorporation by Reference Finding Aids of Title 21 CFR Parts 170–199 (Revised as of April 1, 2008) and the Standards Incorporated by Reference (SIBR) Database accessed on September 29, 2009 and available at http://standards.gov/sibr/query/index.cfm?fuseaction=rsibr.regulatory_sibr_all&startRow=1701. The CFR sections listed in this table are provided only as a resource for illustrative purposes to facilitate the identification of FCC-related incorporations by reference that need updating. The accuracy and completeness of the listings should be checked and confirmed independently.

Food Chemicals Codex (FCC) Editions Incorporated by Reference in Title 21 Code of Federal Regulations Parts 170–184 (as of October 2009)[1] *(continued)*

21 CFR	FCC Edition Referenced	Name	FCC Reference	FCC Page Number
184.1077(b)	3rd Ed. (1981)	Potassium acid tartrate	Meets FCC specifications	238
184.1081(b)	3rd Ed. (1981)	Propionic acid	Meets FCC specifications	254
184.1090(b)	3rd Ed. (1981)	Stearic acid	Meets FCC specifications	313
184.1091(b)	3rd Ed. (1981)	Succinic acid	Meets FCC specifications	314–315
184.1095(b)	3rd Ed. (1981)	Sulfuric acid	Meets FCC specifications	317–318
184.1097(b)	3rd Ed. (1981)	Tannic acid	Meets FCC specifications	319
184.1099(b)	3rd Ed. (1981)	Tartaric acid	Meets FCC specifications	320
184.1101(b)	3rd Ed. (1981)	Diacetyl tartaric acid esters of mono- and diglycerides	Meets FCC specifications	98–99
184.1115(b)	3rd Ed. (1981)	Agar-agar	Meets FCC specifications	11
184.1120(b)	3rd Ed. (1981)	Brown algae	Meets FCC specifications	157
184.1121(b)	3rd Ed. (1981)	Red algae	Meets FCC specifications	157
184.1133(b)	3rd Ed. (1981)	Ammonium alginate	Meets FCC specifications	18
184.1135(b)	3rd Ed. (1981)	Ammonium bicarbonate	Meets FCC specifications	19
184.1137(b)	3rd Ed. (1981)	Ammonium carbonate	Meets FCC specifications	19
184.1138(b)	3rd Ed. (1981)	Ammonium chloride	Meets FCC specifications	20
184.1139(b)	3rd Ed. (1981)	Ammonium hydroxide	Meets FCC specifications	20
184.1141a(b)	3rd Ed. (1981)	Ammonium phosphate, monobasic	Meets FCC specifications	21
184.1141b(b)	3rd Ed. (1981)	Ammonium phosphate, dibasic	Meets FCC specifications	21
184.1143(b)	3rd Ed. (1981)	Ammonium sulfate	Meets FCC specifications	22–23
184.1148(b)	4th Ed. (1996)	Bacterially-derived carbohydrase enzyme preparation	Meets general and additional requirements for enzyme preparations	128–135
184.1150(b)	4th Ed. (1996)	Bacterially-derived protease enzyme preparation	Meets general and additional requirements for enzyme preparations	128–135
184.1157(b)	3rd Ed. (1981)	Benzoyl peroxide	Meets FCC specifications	35
184.1185(b)	3rd Ed. (1981)	Calcium acetate	Meets FCC specifications	44
184.1187(b)	3rd Ed. (1981)	Calcium alginate	Meets FCC specifications	45
184.1191(b)	3rd Ed. (1981)	Calcium carbonate	Meets FCC specifications	46
184.1193(b)	3rd Ed. (1981)	Calcium chloride	Meets FCC specifications	47
184.1195(b)	3rd Ed. (1981)	Calcium citrate	Meets FCC specifications	49–50
184.1199(b)	3rd Ed. (1981)	Calcium gluconate	Meets FCC specifications	51
184.1201(b)	3rd Ed. (1981)	Calcium glycerophosphate	Meets FCC specifications	51–52
184.1205(b)	3rd Ed. (1981)	Calcium hydroxide	Meets FCC specifications	52
184.1206(b)	3rd Ed. (1981)	Calcium iodate	Meets FCC specifications	53
184.1207(b)	3rd Ed. (1981)	Calcium lactate	Meets FCC specifications	53
184.1210(b)	3rd Ed. (1981)	Calcium oxide	Meets FCC specifications	55
184.1212(b)	3rd Ed. (1981)	Calcium pantothenate	Meets FCC specifications	56
184.1221(b)	3rd Ed. (1981)	Calcium propionate	Meets FCC specifications	60
184.1229(b)	3rd Ed. (1981)	Calcium stearate	Meets FCC specifications	64
184.1230(b)	3rd Ed. (1981)	Calcium sulfate	Meets FCC specifications	66
184.1245(b)	3rd Ed. (1981)	Beta-carotene	Meets FCC specifications	73

[1] Most of the incorporation by reference sections are also listed in the Material Approved for Incorporation by Reference Finding Aids of Title 21 CFR Parts 170–199 (Revised as of April 1, 2008) and the Standards Incorporated by Reference (SIBR) Database accessed on September 29, 2009 and available at http://standards.gov/sibr/query/index.cfm?fuseaction=rsibr.regulatory_sibr_all&startRow=1701. The CFR sections listed in this table are provided only as a resource for illustrative purposes to facilitate the identification of FCC-related incorporations by reference that need updating. The accuracy and completeness of the listings should be checked and confirmed independently.

Food Chemicals Codex (FCC) Editions Incorporated by Reference in Title 21 Code of Federal Regulations Parts 170–184 (as of October 2009)[1] *(continued)*

21 CFR	FCC Edition Referenced	Name	FCC Reference	FCC Page Number
184.1250(b)	4th Ed. (1996)	Cellulase enzyme preparation derived from Trichoderma longibrachiatum	Meets general and additional requirements for enzyme preparations	129–134
184.1257(b)	4th Ed. (1996)	Clove and its derivatives	Clove bud oil, clove leaf oil, clove stem oil and eugenol meet FCC specifications	104–105
184.1257(b)(1)	4th Ed. (1996)	Clove and its derivatives	Meets the assay for phenols, as eugenol	104–105
184.1259(b)(3)	4th Ed. (1996)	Cocoa butter substitute: heavy metals limit	Heavy metals (as lead), not more than 10 milligrams per kilogram, as determined by the FCC Heavy Metals Test	760–761
184.1260(b)	3rd Ed. (1981)	Copper gluconate	Meets FCC specifications	90
184.1271(b)	3rd Ed. (1981)	L-Cysteine	Meets FCC specifications	92–93
184.1272(b)	3rd Ed. (1981)	L-Cysteine monohydrochloride	Meets FCC specifications	92–93
184.1277(b)	3rd Ed. (1981)	Dextrin	Meets FCC specifications	96
184.1278(b)	3rd Ed. (1981)	Diacetyl	Meets FCC specifications	368
184.1282(b)	4th Ed. (1996)	Dill and its derivatives	Meets FCC specifications	122–123
184.1293(b)	4th Ed. (1996)	Ethyl alcohol	Meets FCC specifications	136
184.1295(b)	3rd Ed. (1981)	Ethyl formate	Meets FCC specifications	376
184.1296(b)	3rd Ed. (1981)	Ferric ammonium citrate	Meets FCC specifications	116–117
184.1301(b)	3rd Ed. (1981)	Ferric phosphate	Meets FCC specifications	118–120
184.1304(b)	3rd Ed. (1981)	Ferric pyrophosphate	Meets FCC specifications	120
184.1307d	3rd Ed. (1981)	Ferrous fumarate	Meets FCC specifications	120–122
184.1308(b)	3rd Ed. (1981)	Ferrous gluconate	Meets FCC specifications	122–123
184.1311(b)	4th Ed. (1996)	Ferrous lactate	Meets FCC specifications	154–155
184.1315(b)	3rd Ed. (1981)	Ferrous sulfate	Meets FCC specifications for ferrous sulfate heptahydrate and ferrous sulfate, dried	123–124
184.1316(b)	3rd Ed. (1981)	Ficin	Meets general and additional requirements for enzyme preparations	110
184.1317(b)	3rd Ed. (1981)	Garlic and its derivatives	Garlic oil meets FCC specifications	132
184.1318(b)	3rd Ed. (1981)	Glucono delta-lactone	Meets FCC specifications	134
184.1330(b)	3rd Ed. (1981)	Acacia (gum arabic)	Meets FCC specifications	7
184.1339(b)	3rd Ed. (1981)	Guar gum	Meets FCC specifications	141
184.1343(b)	3rd Ed. (1981)	Locust (carob) bean gum	Meets FCC specifications	174–175
184.1349(b)	3rd Ed. (1981)	Karaya gum (sterculia gum)	Meets FCC specifications	157
184.1351(b)	3rd Ed. (1981)	Gum tragacanth	Meets FCC specifications	337
184.1366(b)	3rd Ed. (1981)	Hydrogen peroxide	Meets FCC specifications	146–147
184.1370(b)	3rd Ed. (1981)	Inositol	Meets FCC specifications	150
184.1372(b)	3rd Ed. (1981)	Insoluble glucose isomerase enzyme preparations	Meets general and additional requirements for enzyme preparations	107

[1] Most of the incorporation by reference sections are also listed in the Material Approved for Incorporation by Reference Finding Aids of Title 21 CFR Parts 170–199 (Revised as of April 1, 2008) and the Standards Incorporated by Reference (SIBR) Database accessed on September 29, 2009 and available at http://standards.gov/sibr/query/index.cfm?fuseaction=rsibr.regulatory_sibr_all&startRow=1701. The CFR sections listed in this table are provided only as a resource for illustrative purposes to facilitate the identification of FCC-related incorporations by reference that need updating. The accuracy and completeness of the listings should be checked and confirmed independently.

Food Chemicals Codex (FCC) Editions Incorporated by Reference in Title 21 Code of Federal Regulations Parts 170–184 (as of October 2009)[1] *(continued)*

21 CFR	FCC Edition Referenced	Name	FCC Reference	FCC Page Number
184.1375(b)	3rd Ed. (1981)	Iron, elemental (carbonyl)	Meets FCC specifications	151
184.1375(b)	3rd Ed. (1981)	Iron, elemental (electrolytic)	Meets FCC specifications	151–152
184.1375(b)	3rd Ed. (1981)	Iron, elemental (reduced)	Meets FCC specifications	152–153
184.1387(b)	3rd Ed. (1981)	Lactase enzyme preparation from *Candida pseudotropicalis*	Meets general and additional requirements for enzyme preparations	107–110
184.1388(b)	3rd Ed. (1981)	Lactase enzyme preparation from *Kluyveromyces lactis*	Meets general and additional requirements for enzyme preparations	107–110
184.1400(b)	3rd Ed. (1981)	Lecithin	Meets FCC specifications	166–167
184.1408(b)(2)	3rd Ed. (1981)	Licorice and licorice derivatives	Ash. Not more than 9.5 percent for licorice, 2.5 percent for ammoniated glycyrrhizin, and 0.5 percent for monoammonium glycyrrhizinate on an anhydrous basis	466
184.1409(b)	3rd Ed. (1981)	Ground limestone	Meets FCC specifications	173
184.1415(b)	3rd Ed. (1981)	Animal lipase	Meets general and additional requirements for enzyme preparations	110
184.1420(b)	4th Ed. (1996)	Lipase enzyme preparation derived from *Rhizopus niveus*	Meets general and additional requirements for enzyme preparations	133–134
184.1425(b)	3rd Ed. (1981)	Magnesium carbonate	Meets FCC specifications	177
184.1426(b)	3rd Ed. (1981)	Magnesium chloride	Meets FCC specifications	177
184.1428(b)	3rd Ed. (1981)	Magnesium hydroxide	Meets FCC specifications	178
184.1431(b)	3rd Ed. (1981)	Magnesium oxide	Meets FCC specifications	178
184.1434(b)	3rd Ed. (1981)	Magnesium phosphate	Meets FCC specifications	179
184.1440(b)	3rd Ed. (1981)	Magnesium stearate	Meets FCC specifications	182
184.1443(b)	3rd Ed. (1981)	Magnesium sulfate	Meets FCC specifications	183
184.1443a(b)	3rd Ed. (1981)	Malt	Meets general and additional requirements for enzyme preparations	110
184.1444(b)(2)	3rd Ed. 3rd Supp. (1992)	Maltodextrin from potato starch	Meets FCC specifications	125
184.1444(b)(3)	4th Ed. (1996)	Maltodextrin from rice starch	Meets FCC specifications	239–240
184.1446(b)	3rd Ed. (1981)	Manganese chloride	Meets FCC specifications	186
184.1452(b)	3rd Ed. (1981)	Manganese gluconate	Meets FCC specifications	186
184.1461(b)	3rd Ed. (1981)	Manganese sulfate	Meets FCC specifications	188
184.1490(b)	3rd Ed. (1981)	Methylparaben	Meets FCC specifications	199
184.1505(b)	3rd Ed. (1981)	Mono- and diglycerides	Meets FCC specifications	201
184.1530(b)	4th Ed. (1996)	Niacin	Meets FCC specifications	264
184.1535(b)	3rd Ed. (1981)	Niacinamide	Meets FCC specifications	205
184.1555(b)(2)	3rd Ed. (1981)	Rapeseed oil	Meets FCC specifications relating to mono- and diglycerides	201
184.1583(b)	3rd Ed. (1981)	Pancreatin	Meets general and additional requirements for enzyme preparations	110

[1] Most of the incorporation by reference sections are also listed in the Material Approved for Incorporation by Reference Finding Aids of Title 21 CFR Parts 170–199 (Revised as of April 1, 2008) and the Standards Incorporated by Reference (SIBR) Database accessed on September 29, 2009 and available at http://standards.gov/sibr/query/index.cfm?fuseaction=rsibr.regulatory_sibr_all&startRow=1701. The CFR sections listed in this table are provided only as a resource for illustrative purposes to facilitate the identification of FCC-related incorporations by reference that need updating. The accuracy and completeness of the listings should be checked and confirmed independently.

Food Chemicals Codex (FCC) Editions Incorporated by Reference in Title 21 Code of Federal Regulations Parts 170–184 (as of October 2009)[1] *(continued)*

21 CFR	FCC Edition Referenced	Name	FCC Reference	FCC Page Number
184.1585(b)	3rd Ed. (1981)	Papain	Meets FCC specifications	107–110
184.1588(b)	3rd Ed. (1981)	Pectins	Meets FCC specifications	215
184.1595(b)	3rd Ed. (1981)	Pepsin	Meets general and additional requirements for enzyme preparations	110
184.1610(b)	3rd Ed. (1981)	Potassium alginate	Meets FCC specifications	239
184.1613(b)	3rd Ed. (1981)	Potassium bicarbonate	Meets FCC specifications	239
184.1619(b)	3rd Ed. (1981)	Potassium carbonate	Meets FCC specifications	240
184.1622(b)	3rd Ed. (1981)	Potassium chloride	Meets FCC specifications	241
184.1625(b)	3rd Ed. (1981)	Potassium citrate	Meets FCC specifications	242
184.1631(b)	3rd Ed. (1981)	Potassium hydroxide	Meets FCC specifications	244
184.1634(b)	3rd Ed. (1981)	Potassium iodide	Meets FCC specifications	246–247
184.1635(b)	3rd Ed. (1981)	Potassium iodate	Meets FCC specifications	245–246
184.1643	3rd Ed. (1981)	Potassium sulfate	Meets FCC specifications	252
184.1660(b)	3rd Ed. (1981)	Propyl gallate	Meets FCC specifications	257–258
184.1666(b)	3rd Ed. (1981)	Propylene glycol	Meets FCC specifications	255
184.1670(b)	3rd Ed. (1981)	Propylparaben	Meets FCC specifications	258
184.1676(b)	3rd Ed. (1981)	Pyridoxine hydrochloride	Meets FCC specifications	260
184.1685(b)	3rd Ed. (1981)	Rennet (animal-derived) and chymosin preparation (fermentation-derived)	Meets general and additional requirements for enzyme preparations	107–110
184.1695(b)	3rd Ed. (1981)	Riboflavin	Meets FCC specifications	262
184.1697(b)	3rd Ed. (1981)	Riboflavin-5'-phosphate (sodium)	Meets FCC specifications	263
184.1699(b)	4th Ed. (1996)	Oil of rue	Meets FCC specifications	342–343
184.1721(b)	3rd Ed. (1981)	Sodium acetate	Meets FCC specifications	272–273
184.1724(b)	3rd Ed. (1981)	Sodium alginate	Meets FCC specifications	274
184.1733(b)	3rd Ed. (1981)	Sodium benzoate	Meets FCC specifications	278
184.1736(b)	3rd Ed. (1981)	Sodium bicarbonate	Meets FCC specifications	278
184.1742(b)	3rd Ed. (1981)	Sodium carbonate	Meets FCC specifications	280
184.1751(b)	3rd Ed. (1981)	Sodium citrate	Meets FCC specifications	283–284
184.1754(b)	3rd Ed. (1981)	Sodium diacetate	Meets FCC specifications	284
184.1763(b)	3rd Ed. (1981)	Sodium hydroxide	Meets FCC specifications	287
184.1784(b)	3rd Ed. (1981)	Sodium propionate	Meets FCC specifications	296
184.1792(b)	3rd Ed. (1981)	Sodium sesquicarbonate	Meets FCC specifications	299
184.1801(b)	3rd Ed. (1981)	Sodium tartrate	Meets FCC specifications	303
184.1804(b)	3rd Ed. (1981)	Sodium potassium tartrate	Meets FCC specifications	296
184.1807(b)	3rd Ed. (1981)	Sodium thiosulfate	Meets FCC specifications	304
184.1835(b)	3rd Ed. (1981)	Sorbitol	Meets FCC specifications	308
184.1845(b)	3rd Ed. (1981)	Stannous chloride (anhydrous and dihydrated)	Meets FCC specifications	312
184.1857(b)	3rd Ed. (1981)	Corn sugar (under Dextrose)	Meets FCC specifications	97–98
184.1866(b)	4th Ed. (1996)	High fructose corn syrup	Must conform to FCC identity and specifications	191–192
184.1875(b)	3rd Ed. (1981)	Thiamine hydrochloride	Meets FCC specifications	324

[1] Most of the incorporation by reference sections are also listed in the Material Approved for Incorporation by Reference Finding Aids of Title 21 CFR Parts 170–199 (Revised as of April 1, 2008) and the Standards Incorporated by Reference (SIBR) Database accessed on September 29, 2009 and available at http://standards.gov/sibr/query/index.cfm?fuseaction=rsibr.regulatory_sibr_all&startRow=1701. The CFR sections listed in this table are provided only as a resource for illustrative purposes to facilitate the identification of FCC-related incorporations by reference that need updating. The accuracy and completeness of the listings should be checked and confirmed independently.

Food Chemicals Codex (FCC) Editions Incorporated by Reference in Title 21 Code of Federal Regulations Parts 170–184 (as of October 2009)[1] *(continued)*

21 CFR	FCC Edition Referenced	Name	FCC Reference	FCC Page Number
184.1878(b)	3rd Ed. (1981)	Thiamine mononitrate	Meets FCC specifications	325
184.1890(b)	3rd Ed. (1981)	alpha-Tocopherols	Meets FCC specifications	330–331
184.1901(b)	3rd Ed. (1981)	Triacetin	Meets FCC specifications	337–338
184.1903(b)	3rd Ed. (1981)	Tributyrin	Meets FCC specifications	416
184.1911(b)	3rd Ed. (1981)	Triethyl citrate	Meets FCC specifications	339
184.1924(b)	3rd Ed. (1981)	Urease enzyme preparation from Lactobacillus fermentum	Meets general and additional requirements for enzyme preparations	107–110
184.1930(b)	3rd Ed. (1981)	Vitamin A	Meets FCC specifications	342
184.1945(b)	3rd Ed. (1981)	Vitamin B	Meets FCC specifications	343
184.1950(b)	3rd Ed. (1981)	Vitamin D	Meets FCC specifications	344–345
184.1973(b)	3rd Ed. (1981)	Beeswax (yellow and white)	Meets FCC specifications	34–35
184.1976(b)	3rd Ed. (1981)	Candelilla wax	Meets FCC specifications	67
184.1978(b)	3rd Ed. (1981)	Carnauba wax	Meets FCC specifications	73
184.1979(b)(2)	4th Ed. (1996)	Whey	Limits of impurities are: Heavy metals (as Pb). Not more than 10 ppm (0.001%)	760–761
184.1979a(b)(2)	4th Ed. (1996)	Reduced lactose whey	Limits of impurities are: Heavy metals (as Pb). Not more than 10 ppm (0.001%)	760–761
184.1979b(b)(2)	4th Ed. (1996)	Reduced minerals whey	Limits of impurities are: Heavy metals (as Pb). Not more than 10 ppm (0.001%)	760–761
184.1979c(b)(2)	4th Ed. (1996)	Whey protein concentrate	Limits of impurities are: Heavy metals (as lead). Not more than 10 parts per million (0.001 percent)	760–761
184.1985(b)	3rd Ed. (1981)	Aminopeptidase enzyme preparation derived from lactococcus lactis	Meets general and additional requirements for enzyme preparations	107–110

[1] Most of the incorporation by reference sections are also listed in the Material Approved for Incorporation by Reference Finding Aids of Title 21 CFR Parts 170–199 (Revised as of April 1, 2008) and the Standards Incorporated by Reference (SIBR) Database accessed on September 29, 2009 and available at http://standards.gov/sibr/query/index.cfm?fuseaction=rsibr.regulatory_sibr_all&startRow=1701. The CFR sections listed in this table are provided only as a resource for illustrative purposes to facilitate the identification of FCC-related incorporations by reference that need updating. The accuracy and completeness of the listings should be checked and confirmed independently.

FOOD INGREDIENTS FRAUD DATABASE

Introduction

A database on food ingredient fraud has been developed by USP as a repository for reported types of fraud for specific food ingredients and associated analytical methods for detection. Such information can be useful to *FCC* users responsible for assessing existing and emerging risks and trends for economically motivated adulteration, authenticity, fraud, or counterfeiting issues for food ingredients. In addition, it can be useful for those managing the risk of food fraud by providing a library of detection methods reported in peer-reviewed scientific journals.

The database will be available mid-2012 in a searchable format on USP's website at: www.usp.org. This chapter presents the information currently available in the database in tabular format, divided into two sections. *Table 1* contains information from scholarly literature (e.g., scientific journal articles) and includes information on analytical methods of detection. *Table 2* contains information from media-based articles reporting on food fraud collected by USP and does not include analytical methods of detection. Each entry in these two tables represents a unique food ingredient/adulterant/report combination. Entries are organized using the following food ingredient categories:

  Cereals, grains, and pulses
  Colors
  Dairy products and milk derivatives
  Flavor chemicals
  Fruit juices, concentrates, jams, purees, and preserves
  Functional food ingredients
  Gums
  Meats
  Milk
  Natural flavoring complexes
  Oils
  Other
  Protein-based ingredients
  Seafood
  Spices
  Sweeteners
  Wines, musts, spirits, liquors, and vinegars

Three terms are used to categorize the type or nature of food fraud reported; "Replacement", "Addition of", or "Removal of…".

"**Replacement**" is used to describe incidents resulting in the complete or partial replacement of a food ingredient or valuable authentic constituent with a less expensive substitute. This is typically achieved through the dilution or extension of an authentic ingredient by adding an adulterant or mixture of adulterants with the intention of circumventing standard measures for quality control. One example is the addition of melamine to milk to artificially increase apparent protein contents measured by total nitrogen methods. Other examples are the addition of water and citric acid to lemon juice to fraudulently increase the titratable acidity of the final juice product and overtreating frozen fish with extra water (ice) to increase the apparent weight of the product. This category also includes false claims and non-declarations including:

- False declaration of geographic, species, botanical, or varietal origin. Examples include the substitution of less expensive cow's milk for sheep's or goat's milk. It can also include false declaration of origin to evade taxes or tariffs, for example the import of catfish into the USA from Vietnam labeled as grouper to avoid anti-dumping duties or transshipment of Chinese shrimp through Indonesia to avoid anti-dumping duties.
- False declaration of production process such as the fraudulent labeling of a synthetically derived flavor chemical as being "naturally" derived

"**Addition**" is used to describe incidents resulting in the addition of small amounts of a non-authentic substance to mask inferior quality ingredient. An example is the addition of a color additive to paprika to enhance the color of poor quality materials.

"**Removal**" is used to describe incidents resulting in the removal of an authentic and valuable constituent without the purchasers' knowledge. For example, the removal of non-polar constituents from paprika (e.g. lipids and flavor compounds) is done to produce paprika-derived flavoring extracts. The sale of the resulting "defatted" paprika which lacks valuable flavoring compounds as normal paprika is a fraudulent practice.

[NOTE—* Indicates that a monograph for this ingredient is available in the *Food Chemicals Codex*.]

Table 1: Scholarly Reports on Food Ingredient Fraud and Analytical Methods for Detection

Ingredient Category	Ingredient	Adulterant	Type of Fraud	Publication Year	Reported Detection Method and Reference
Cereals, grains, and pulses	Bajara flour	Chalk powder	Replacement	2009	Wet-chemical tests for adulterant (Gupti and Panchal 2009)
Cereals, grains, and pulses	Cereal grains	Melamine	Replacement	2010	HPLC-UV for adulterant (Sharma and Paradakar 2010)
Cereals, grains, and pulses	Corn flour	Melamine and related compounds	Replacement	2007	HPLC-PDA for adulterants (Ehling and others 2007)
Cereals, grains, and pulses	Rajagara flour	Chalk powder	Replacement	2009	Wet-chemical tests for adulterant (Gupti and Panchal 2009)

Table 1: Scholarly Reports on Food Ingredient Fraud and Analytical Methods for Detection (continued)

Ingredient Category	Ingredient	Adulterant	Type of Fraud	Publication Year	Reported Detection Method and Reference
Cereals, grains, and pulses	Red lentils (Lens culinaris)	Red vetch [Blanche fleur (V. sativa)]	Replacement	1992	NR (Tate and Enneking 1992)
Cereals, grains, and pulses	Red lentils (Lens culinaris)	Red vetch [Blanche fleur (V. sativa)]	Replacement	2005	CE for adulterant marker proteins (Piergiovanni and Taranto 2005)
Cereals, grains, and pulses	Rice	Rice from non-authentic botanical origin	Replacement	2008	Review of methods combined with chemometrics: PCR–DNA-based methods, digital imaging, NIR (Vlachos and Arvanitoyannis 2008)
Cereals, grains, and pulses	Rice	Rice from non-authentic botanical origin	Replacement	2008	Review of methods for volatiles analysis: GC-FID, head space or SPME GC-MS, electronic nose (Vlachos and Arvanitoyannis 2008)
Cereals, grains, and pulses	Rice	Rice from non-authentic botanical origin	Replacement	2008	Review of methods for starchy or non-starchy polysaccharides analysis by GC-FID, CE-ED, or colorimetric methods (Vlachos and Arvanitoyannis 2008)
Cereals, grains, and pulses	Rice	Rice from non-authentic botanical origin	Replacement	2009	ICP-MS for elemental analysis combined with chemometrics (Laursen and others 2009)
Cereals, grains, and pulses	Rice	Rice from non-authentic geographic origin	Replacement	2008	Review of methods for trace elements analysis combined with chemometrics: ICP-AES, ICP-MS (Vlachos and Arvanitoyannis 2008)
Cereals, grains, and pulses	Rice	Rice from non-authentic geographic origin	Replacement	2008	SDS-PAGE for proteins fingerprinting (Vlachos and Arvanitoyannis 2008)
Cereals, grains, and pulses	Rice (Basmati)	Rice from non-authentic botanical origin	Replacement	2007	DNA-based PCR with CE microsatellite marker analysis (Vemireddy and others 2007)
Cereals, grains, and pulses	Rice (Basmati)	Rice from non-authentic botanical origin	Replacement	2007	DNA-based PCR with CE microsatellite marker analysis (Archak and others 2007)
Cereals, grains, and pulses	Rice (Basmati)	Rice from non-authentic botanical origin	Replacement	2008	PCR based method (Lopez 2008)
Cereals, grains, and pulses	Rice (Basmati)	Rice from non-authentic botanical origin	Replacement	2008	PCR based microsatellite marker analysis (Colyer and others 2008)
Cereals, grains, and pulses	Rice (Basmati)	Rice from non-authentic botanical origin	Replacement	2000	DNA-based method using fluorescent simple sequence length polymorphisms between authentic rice and adulterant rice cultivars (Bligh 2000)
Cereals, grains, and pulses	Rice (Basmati)	Rice from non-authentic botanical origin	Replacement	2010	Review: PCR by lab-on-chip (Primrose and others 2010)
Cereals, grains, and pulses	Rice (Basmati)	U.S. long grain rice	Replacement	2006	Digital imaging with chemometrics (Carter and others 2006)
Cereals, grains, and pulses	Rice (Thai)	U.S. long grain rice	Replacement	2006	Digital imaging with chemometrics (Carter and others 2006)
Cereals, grains, and pulses	Rice flour	Melamine and related compounds	Replacement	2007	HPLC-PDA for adulterants (Ehling and others 2007)
Cereals, grains, and pulses	Soy flour	Melamine and related compounds	Replacement	2007	HPLC-PDA for adulterants (Ehling and others 2007)
Cereals, grains, and pulses	Spelt flour	Wheat flour	Replacement	2001	PCR for adulterant DNA (von Büren and others 2001)
Cereals, grains, and pulses	Wheat (durum)	Soft wheat	Replacement	2007	DNA microsatellites for adulterants (Pasqualone and others 2007)
Cereals, grains, and pulses	Wheat (durum)	Soft wheat	Replacement	2009	Real-time PCR for adulterant DNA markers (Sonnante and others 2009)

Table 1: Scholarly Reports on Food Ingredient Fraud and Analytical Methods for Detection (continued)

Ingredient Category	Ingredient	Adulterant	Type of Fraud	Publication Year	Reported Detection Method and Reference
Cereals, grains, and pulses	Wheat flour	Chalk powder	Replacement	2009	Wet-chemical tests for adulterant (Gupti and Panchal 2009)
Cereals, grains, and pulses	Wheat flour	Melamine and related compounds	Replacement	2010	Review of methods: HPLC-PDA (Tittlemier 2010)
Cereals, grains, and pulses	Wheat flour	Melamine and related compounds	Replacement	2010	Micellar electrokinetic chromatography for melamine (Hsu and others 2010)
Cereals, grains, and pulses	Wheat flour	Melamine and related compounds	Replacement	2007	HPLC-PDA for adulterants (Ehling and others 2007)
Cereals, grains, and pulses	Wheat flour (common, Triticum aestivum)	Melamine	Replacement	2010	ELISA for adulterant (Garber and Brewer 2010)
Cereals, grains, and pulses	Wheat flour (durum, Triticum durum)	Melamine	Replacement	2010	ELISA for adulterant (Garber and Brewer 2010)
Cereals, grains, and pulses	Wheat pasta (durum, Triticum durum)	Common wheat (Triticum aestivum)	Replacement	2002	Common wheat content determined as a ratio of common wheat DNA to total wheat DNA using real-time duplex PCR (Alary and others 2002)
Cereals, grains, and pulses	Wheat pasta (durum, Triticum durum)	Common wheat (Triticum aestivum)	Replacement	2006	NIR with chemometrics (Cocchi and others 2006)
Cereals, grains, and pulses	Wheat pasta (durum, Triticum durum)	Common wheat (Triticum aestivum)	Replacement	2004	HPLC or free zone CE on extract proteins combined with chemometrics (Bonetti and others 2004)
Cereals, grains, and pulses	Wheat pasta (durum, Triticum durum)	Common wheat (Triticum aestivum)	Replacement	1994	HPLC for gamma- and beta-gliadin (adulterant protein markers) (Barnwell and others 1994)
Cereals, grains, and pulses	Wheat pasta (durum, Triticum durum)	Common wheat (Triticum aestivum)	Replacement	2010	HPLC for C17:0 to C21:0 alkylresorcinol homologue ratios (Knödler and others 2010)
Cereals, grains, and pulses	Wheat pasta (durum, Triticum durum)	Common wheat (Triticum aestivum)	Replacement	2010	Review: PCR by lab-on-chip (Primrose and others 2010)
Cereals, grains, and pulses	Wheat pasta (durum, Triticum durum)	Common wheat (Triticum aestivum)	Replacement	1990	HPLC for gliadins fingerprinting (McCarthy and others 1990)
Cereals, grains, and pulses	Wheat pasta (durum, Triticum durum)	Farina wheat	Replacement	1993	HPLC for campesterol and beta-sitosterol (adulterant markers) (Sarwar and McDonald 1993)
Colors	Betalain pigments derived from purple pitaya fruit	Betalain pigments derived from red beets	Replacement	2006	IRMS ($^{13}C/^{12}C$) and ($^{2}H/^{1}H$) on isolated betanin and isobetanin (Herbach and others 2006)
Colors	Cochineal derived colors*	Cochineal color from non-authentic geographic origin	Replacement	2004	Chromatic attributes, spectrophotometric determination of carminic acid, and HLPC for pigments analysis, all combined with chemometrics (Méndez and others 2004)
Dairy products and milk derivatives	Butter	Butter of non-authentic geographic origin	Replacement	2007	Review: IRMS ($^{13}C/^{12}C$), ($^{18}O/^{16}O$), ($^{32}S/^{34}S$), ($^{14}N/^{15}N$) (Karoui and De Baerdemaeker 2007)
Dairy products and milk derivatives	Butter	Hydrogenated vegetable oil	Replacement	2010	ATR-MIR with chemometrics (Koca and others 2010)
Dairy products and milk derivatives	Butter	Margarine	Replacement	1990	NIR for specific absorption bands (Sato and others 1990)
Dairy products and milk derivatives	Butter	Non-authentic fat	Replacement	1996	GC for triglyceride composition combined with chemometrics (Lipp 1996)
Dairy products and milk derivatives	Casein coprecipitate*	Whey	Replacement	2006	HPLC with fluorescence detection for cysteine (Ballin 2006)
Dairy products and milk derivatives	Cheese	Soy protein	Replacement	2006	Reversed-phase perfusion HPLC for adulterant proteins (Garcia and Marina 2006)
Dairy products and milk derivatives	Cheese (caprine)	Non-authentic milk (bovine)	Replacement	2006	PCR for adulterant marker DNA (Maskova and Paulickova 2006)

Table 1: Scholarly Reports on Food Ingredient Fraud and Analytical Methods for Detection (continued)

Ingredient Category	Ingredient	Adulterant	Type of Fraud	Publication Year	Reported Detection Method and Reference
Dairy products and milk derivatives	Cheese (caprine)	Non-authentic milk (bovine)	Replacement	2005	Isoelectric focusing electrophoresis for gamma-caseins fingerprinting or use of PCR (Mayer 2005)
Dairy products and milk derivatives	Cheese (Emmental)	Cheese of non-authentic geographic origin	Replacement	2007	Review: MIR with chemometrics (Karoui and De Baerdemaeker 2007)
Dairy products and milk derivatives	Cheese (non-bovine animal origin)	Non-authentic milk (bovine)	Replacement	2000	CE for fingerprinting of whey proteins (Herrero-Martínez and others 2000)
Dairy products and milk derivatives	Cheese (ovine)	Non-authentic milk (bovine)	Replacement	2005	Isoelectric focusing electrophoresis for gamma-caseins fingerprinting or use of PCR (Mayer 2005)
Dairy products and milk derivatives	Cheese (ovine)	Non-authentic milk (bovine)	Replacement	2004	Urea–polyacrylamide gel electrophoresis and HPLC for protein analysis (Veloso and others 2004)
Dairy products and milk derivatives	Cheese (ovine)	Non-authentic milk (bovine)	Replacement	2006	Immunochemistry test for bovine immunoglobulin G (adulterant marker) (Colak and others 2006)
Dairy products and milk derivatives	Cheese (ovine)	Non-authentic milk (bovine)	Replacement	2008	HPLC-MS for proteolytic oligopeptides (adulterant markers) (Sforza and others 2008)
Dairy products and milk derivatives	Cheese (ovine)	Non-authentic milk (bovine)	Replacement	2006	Sandwich ELISA for immunoglobulin (adulterant marker) (Hurley and others 2006)
Dairy products and milk derivatives	Cheese (ovine)	Non-authentic milk (bovine)	Replacement	2006	Sandwich ELISA for immunoglobulin (adulterant marker) (Hurley and others 2006)
Dairy products and milk derivatives	Cheese (ovine)	Non-authentic milk (bovine)	Replacement	2006	PCR for adulterant marker DNA (Maskova and Paulickova 2006)
Dairy products and milk derivatives	Cheese (water buffalo)	Non-authentic milk (bovine)	Replacement	2006	Sandwich ELISA for immunoglobulin (adulterant marker) (Hurley and others 2006)
Dairy products and milk derivatives	Cheese (water buffalo)	Non-authentic milk (bovine)	Replacement	2005	PCR for adulterant DNA (López-Calleja and others 2005a)
Dairy products and milk derivatives	Milk and milk derived ingredients	Milk of non-authentic geographic origin	Replacement	2005	Review of authenticity methods using microbiological parameters, physico-chemical parameters, IRMS (de la Fuente and Juarez 2005)
Dairy products and milk derivatives	Milk fat	Non-authentic fat	Replacement	1995	Review of methods: Triglycerides profile by HPLC or GC (Lipp 1995)
Dairy products and milk derivatives	Milk fat	Non-authentic fat	Replacement	2009	GC-FID for triacylglycerols fingerprinting combined with chemometrics (Gutierrez and others 2009)
Dairy products and milk derivatives	Milk fat	Non-authentic fats	Replacement	2005	Review of methods including scanning calorimetry, triglycerides profile, fatty acid composition, pyrogram fingerprints by pyrolysis GC-FID, headspace GC, and minor (non-dairy origin) lipid constituents in unsaponifiable fraction by GC (de la Fuente and Juarez 2005)
Dairy products and milk derivatives	Milk fat	Non-authentic fats	Replacement	1995	GC FAMEs fatty acid fingerprinting combined with chemometrics (Ulberth 1995)
Dairy products and milk derivatives	Milk fat	Refined beef tallow	Replacement	1994	GC-FID for 3,5-cholestadiene (adulterant marker) (Mariani and others 1994)
Dairy products and milk derivatives	Milk fat	Vegetable oil	Replacement	1994	GC-FID for fatty acid fingerprinting with chemometrics (Ulberth 1994)
Dairy products and milk derivatives	Milk fat	Vegetable oil	Replacement	1994	GC-FID for dehydroxylated phytosterols (adulterant markers) (Mariani and others 1994)

Table 1: Scholarly Reports on Food Ingredient Fraud and Analytical Methods for Detection (continued)

Ingredient Category	Ingredient	Adulterant	Type of Fraud	Publication Year	Reported Detection Method and Reference
Dairy products and milk derivatives	Milk fat (bovine)	Goat fat	Replacement	2009	Apparent solidification time measurement (Kumar and others 2009)
Dairy products and milk derivatives	Milk fat (bovine)	Hydrogenated vegetable oil	Replacement	2009	Apparent solidification time measurement (Kumar and others 2009)
Dairy products and milk derivatives	Milk fat (bovine)	Pig fat	Replacement	2009	Apparent solidification time measurement (Kumar and others 2009)
Dairy products and milk derivatives	Milk fat (water buffalo)	Goat fat	Replacement	2009	Apparent solidification time measurement (Kumar and others 2009)
Dairy products and milk derivatives	Milk fat (water buffalo)	Hydrogenated vegetable oil	Replacement	2009	Apparent solidification time measurement (Kumar and others 2009)
Dairy products and milk derivatives	Milk fat (water buffalo)	Pig fat	Replacement	2009	Apparent solidification time measurement (Kumar and others 2009)
Dairy products and milk derivatives	Milk-derived formula	Melamine	Replacement	2009	Detection of melamine by NIR and MIR (Mauer and others 2009)
Dairy products and milk derivatives	Milk-derived formula	Melamine	Replacement	2010	ELISA for adulterant (Garber and Brewer 2010)
Dairy products and milk derivatives	Powdered milk product	Melamine	Replacement	2009	Non-targeted H-NMR (Lachenmeier and others 2009)
Dairy products and milk derivatives	Raw milk derived ingredients	Heat-processed milk	Replacement	2005	Review of methods for measuring beta-casein to alpha-lactalbumin ratio by CE (de la Fuente and Juarez 2005)
Dairy products and milk derivatives	Raw milk derived ingredients	Heat-processed milk	Replacement	2005	Review of methods for measuring markers of heat processing (e.g., Maillard reaction products) by visual spectrometry; HPLC (de la Fuente and Juarez 2005)
Dairy products and milk derivatives	Yogurt (ovine)	Milk (bovine)	Replacement	2002	Polyacrylamide gel electrophoresis on para-kappa-casein (adulterant marker) (Kaminarides and Koukiassa 2002)
Flavor chemicals	(E)-alpha-Ionone (natural)	Synthetic or semi-synthetic (E)-alpha-ionone	Replacement	2005	Constant flow multidimensional GC-combustion/pyrolysis-IRMS ($^{13}C/^{12}C$) and ($^{2}H/^{1}H$) (Sewenig and others 2005)
Flavor chemicals	(E)-beta-Ionone (natural)	Synthetic or semi-synthetic (E)-beta-ionone	Replacement	2005	Constant flow multidimensional GC-combustion/pyrolysis-IRMS ($^{13}C/^{12}C$) and ($^{2}H/^{1}H$) (Sewenig and others 2005)
Flavor chemicals	Decanal (natural)	Synthetic decanal	Replacement	2000	GC-pyrolysis-IRMS ($^{2}H/^{1}H$) (Hör and others 2000)
Flavor chemicals	E-2-Hexenal (natural)	Synthetic E-2-hexanal	Replacement	2000	GC-pyrolysis-IRMS ($^{2}H/^{1}H$) (Hör and others 2000)
Flavor chemicals	E-2-Hexenol (natural)	Synthetic E-2-hexenol	Replacement	2000	GC-pyrolysis-IRMS ($^{2}H/^{1}H$) (Hör and others 2000)
Flavor chemicals	Estragole (natural)	Synthetic estragole	Replacement	2002	GC-pyrolysis-IRMS($^{2}H/^{1}H$), ($^{13}C/^{12}C$), ($^{18}O/^{16}O$) (Ruff and others 2002)
Flavor chemicals	Ethyl butyrate (natural)	Synthetic ethyl butyrate	Replacement	1986	Radiocarbon (^{14}C) analysis (Byrne and others 1986)
Flavor chemicals	Linalool (natural)	Synthetic linalool	Replacement	2000	GC-pyrolysis-IRMS ($^{2}H/^{1}H$) (Hör and others 2000)
Flavor chemicals	Linalyl acetate (natural)	Synthetic linalyl acetate	Replacement	2000	GC-pyrolysis-IRMS ($^{2}H/^{1}H$) (Hör and others 2000)
Flavor chemicals	Methyl eugenol (natural)	Synthetic eugenol	Replacement	2002	GC-pyrolysis-IRMS ($^{2}H/^{1}H$), ($^{13}C/^{12}C$), ($^{18}O/^{16}O$) (Ruff and others 2002)
Flavor chemicals	Methyl salicylate (natural)	Synthetic or semi-synthetic methyl salicylate	Replacement	2005	SNIF-NMR ($^{2}H/^{1}H$) (Le Grand and others 2005)
Flavor chemicals	Raspberry ketone (natural)	Synthetic or semi-synthetic raspberry ketone	Replacement	1998	SNIF-NMR ($^{2}H/^{1}H$) (Fronza and others 1998)
Flavor chemicals	Vanillin (natural)	Synthetic vanillin	Replacement	2010	GC-combustion-IRMS for ($^{13}C/^{12}C$) and GC-P-IRMS for ($^{2}H/^{1}H$) (Greule and others 2010)

Table 1: Scholarly Reports on Food Ingredient Fraud and Analytical Methods for Detection (continued)

Ingredient Category	Ingredient	Adulterant	Type of Fraud	Publication Year	Reported Detection Method and Reference
Flavor chemicals	alpha-Ionone (natural)	Synthetic or semi-synthetic alpha-ionone	Replacement	2007	GC-combustion/pyrolysis IRMS ($^{13}C/^{12}C$) and ($^{2}H/^{1}H$) (Caja Mdel and others 2007)
Flavor chemicals	beta-Ionone (natural)	Synthetic or semi-synthetic beta-ionone	Replacement	2007	GC-combustion/pyrolysis IRMS ($^{13}C/^{12}C$) and ($^{2}H/^{1}H$) (Caja Mdel and others 2007)
Flavor chemicals	gamma- or delta-decalactone (natural)	Synthetic gamma- or delta-decalactone	Replacement	2005	GC-combustion/pyrolysis-IRMS (Tamura and others 2005)
Fruit juices, concentrates, jams, purees, and preserves	Apple juice	DL-malic acid	Replacement	1994	L-malic/total malic acid ratio (Elkins and Heuser 1994)
Fruit juices, concentrates, jams, purees, and preserves	Apple juice	DL-malic acid	Replacement	2008	HPLC with optical rotation detector for L-malate (authentic marker) determination (Yamamoto and others 2008)
Fruit juices, concentrates, jams, purees, and preserves	Apple juice	D-malic acid	Replacement	1996	HPLC-UV for adulterant (Eisele 1996)
Fruit juices, concentrates, jams, purees, and preserves	Apple juice	Fig juice	Replacement	1992	HPLC for citric acid (adulterant marker) (Pilando and Wrolstad 1992)
Fruit juices, concentrates, jams, purees, and preserves	Apple juice	Fructose, glucose, and sucrose	Replacement	2005	NIR with chemometrics (Leon and others 2005)
Fruit juices, concentrates, jams, purees, and preserves	Apple juice	Grape juice	Replacement	1992	HPLC for tartaric acid (adulterant marker) (Pilando and Wrolstad 1992)
Fruit juices, concentrates, jams, purees, and preserves	Apple juice	High-fructose corn syrup	Replacement	2001	GC-FID for adulterant markers (Low and others 2001)
Fruit juices, concentrates, jams, purees, and preserves	Apple juice	High-fructose corn syrup	Replacement	1992	IRMS ($^{13}C/^{12}C$) (Pilando and Wrolstad 1992)
Fruit juices, concentrates, jams, purees, and preserves	Apple juice	High-fructose corn syrup	Replacement	2005	NIR with chemometrics (Leon and others 2005)
Fruit juices, concentrates, jams, purees, and preserves	Apple juice	Hydrolyzed inulin	Replacement	2001	GC-FID for adulterant markers (Low and others 2001)
Fruit juices, concentrates, jams, purees, and preserves	Apple juice	Invert sugar syrup	Replacement	1999	GC-FID for oligosaccharide adulterant markers (Low and others 1999)
Fruit juices, concentrates, jams, purees, and preserves	Apple juice	Inverted beet syrup	Replacement	2000	MIR with chemometrics (Sivakesava and others 2000)
Fruit juices, concentrates, jams, purees, and preserves	Apple juice	Inverted cane syrup	Replacement	2005	Non-target FTIR with chemometrics (Kelly and Downey 2005)

Table 1: Scholarly Reports on Food Ingredient Fraud and Analytical Methods for Detection (continued)

Ingredient Category	Ingredient	Adulterant	Type of Fraud	Publication Year	Reported Detection Method and Reference
Fruit juices, concentrates, jams, purees, and preserves	Apple juice	Inverted cane syrup	Replacement	2000	MIR with chemometrics (Sivakesava and others 2000)
Fruit juices, concentrates, jams, purees, and preserves	Apple juice	Pear juice	Replacement	2006	HPLC-RI for sorbitol content, proline content, and arbutin (adulterant marker) analysis by HPLC-PDA (Thavarajah and Low 2006)
Fruit juices, concentrates, jams, purees, and preserves	Apple juice	Pear juice	Replacement	1992	HPLC for citric acid (adulterant marker) (Pilando and Wrolstad 1992)
Fruit juices, concentrates, jams, purees, and preserves	Apple juice	Pineapple juice	Replacement	1992	HPLC for citric acid (adulterant marker) (Pilando and Wrolstad 1992)
Fruit juices, concentrates, jams, purees, and preserves	Apple juice	Pineapple juice	Replacement	1992	IRMS ($^{13}C/^{12}C$) (Pilando and Wrolstad 1992)
Fruit juices, concentrates, jams, purees, and preserves	Apple juice	Raisin sweetener	Replacement	1992	HPLC for tartaric acid (adulterant marker) (Pilando and Wrolstad 1992)
Fruit juices, concentrates, jams, purees, and preserves	Apple juice	Synthetic malic acid with beet sugar	Replacement	1992	Enzymatic and HPLC assays for L-malic and total malic acids (Pilando and Wrolstad 1992)
Fruit juices, concentrates, jams, purees, and preserves	Apple or orange juice	Corn derived sweeteners	Replacement	2010	IRMS ($^{13}C/^{12}C$) (Primrose and others 2010)
Fruit juices, concentrates, jams, purees, and preserves	Apple or orange juice	Corn syrup and beet or cane invert syrup	Replacement	1996	GC-FID for oligosaccharides adulterant markers (Low 1996)
Fruit juices, concentrates, jams, purees, and preserves	Apple puree	Fruit from non-authentic botanical origin	Replacement	1995	Non-targeted FTIR combined with chemometrics (Defernez and others 1995)
Fruit juices, concentrates, jams, purees, and preserves	Apricot puree	Pumpkin puree	Replacement	2008	HPLC-PDA or HPLC-MS for carotenoid and carotenoid esters fingerprinting (Kurz and others 2008b)
Fruit juices, concentrates, jams, purees, and preserves	Apricot puree	Pumpkin puree	Replacement	2005	HPLC-PDA for syringic acid (adulterant marker compound) (Dragovic-Uzelac and others 2005)
Fruit juices, concentrates, jams, purees, and preserves	Bayberry juice	Water	Replacement	2008	NIR with chemometrics (Xie and others 2008)
Fruit juices, concentrates, jams, purees, and preserves	Black currant juice	Strawberry juice	Replacement	2006	HPLC for free amino acid fingerprinting (Stoj and Targonski 2006)
Fruit juices, concentrates, jams, purees, and preserves	Blackberry juice concentrate	Plum juice	Replacement	1982	HPLC and GC for sugars and organic acids fingerprinting (Wrolstad and others 1982)

Table 1: Scholarly Reports on Food Ingredient Fraud and Analytical Methods for Detection (continued)

Ingredient Category	Ingredient	Adulterant	Type of Fraud	Publication Year	Reported Detection Method and Reference
Fruit juices, concentrates, jams, purees, and preserves	Blood orange juice	Orange juice from non-authentic botanical origin	Replacement	1997	HPLC fingerprinting of narirutin, hesperidin, didymin, and cinnamic acids (authentication markers) (Mouly and others 1997)
Fruit juices, concentrates, jams, purees, and preserves	Citrus juice	Cane sucrose	Replacement	1991	IRMS ($^{13}C/^{12}C$) and SNIF-NMR ($^{2}H/^{1}H$) on ethanol derived from fermented sugars, and IRMS ($^{2}H/^{1}H$), ($^{18}O/^{16}O$) on water, all combined with chemometrics (Martin and others 1991)
Fruit juices, concentrates, jams, purees, and preserves	Fruit juice	Citric acid from non-authentic source	Replacement	2005	IRMS ($^{2}H/^{1}H$) on isolated citric acid (Jamin and others 2005)
Fruit juices, concentrates, jams, purees, and preserves	Fruit juice	Juice from non-authentic botanical origin	Replacement	2001	HPLC-PAD or GC-FID fingerprinting of sugars (Hammond 2001)
Fruit juices, concentrates, jams, purees, and preserves	Fruit juice	Juice from non-authentic botanical origin	Replacement	2000	CE for organic acids fingerprinting (Saavedra and others 2000)
Fruit juices, concentrates, jams, purees, and preserves	Fruit juice	Juice from non-authentic botanical origin	Replacement	1998	IRMS ($^{13}C/^{12}C$) on sugars, malic acid, and citric acid isolated by preparative HPLC (Jamin and others 1998b)
Fruit juices, concentrates, jams, purees, and preserves	Fruit juice	Non-authentic sugars	Replacement	2003	Review of methods: NMR and MS (Ogrinc and others 2003)
Fruit juices, concentrates, jams, purees, and preserves	Fruit juice	Sugar syrup	Replacement	2001	HPLC-PAD and GC-FID for saccharides fingerprinting analysis (Hammond 2001)
Fruit juices, concentrates, jams, purees, and preserves	Fruit juices (general)	High-fructose syrup	Replacement	2000	Spectrophotometric automatic flow analysis for mono- and disaccharides (Cáceres and others 2000)
Fruit juices, concentrates, jams, purees, and preserves	Fruit puree	Fruit from non-authentic botanical origin	Replacement	2005	Review of methods: Polyphenolics fingerprinting, anthocyanins fingerprinting, IR, PCR, MS, and NMR (Fügel and others 2005)
Fruit juices, concentrates, jams, purees, and preserves	Fruit purees and preparations	Fruit from non-authentic botanical origin	Replacement	2004	Neutral sugars analysis by CE on alcohol-insoluble residue fractions (water-, oxalate-, acid-, and alkali-soluble pectins; hemicellulose and cellulose fractions) (Fügel and others 2004)
Fruit juices, concentrates, jams, purees, and preserves	Fruit purees and products	Fruit from non-authentic botanical origin	Replacement	2008	Neutral sugars analysis by GF-FID on alcohol-insoluble residue fractions (water-, oxalate-, acid-, and alkali-soluble pectins; hemicellulose and cellulose fractions) (Kurz and others 2008a)
Fruit juices, concentrates, jams, purees, and preserves	Grapefruit juice	Juice from non-authentic botanical origin	Replacement	1998	IRMS ($^{13}C/^{12}C$) on isolated protein (Gonzalez and others 1998)
Fruit juices, concentrates, jams, purees, and preserves	Lemon juice	Bergamot juice (Citrus bergamia Risso and Poit.)	Replacement	2008	HPLC detection of naringin, neohesperidin, and neoeriocitrin (adulterant markers) (Cautela and others 2008)
Fruit juices, concentrates, jams, purees, and preserves	Lemon juice	Citric acid	Replacement	1998	SNIF-NMR ($^{2}H/^{1}H$) on triethyl citrate (citric acid isolated from juice and transformed into triethyl citrate) (Gonzalez and others 1998)

Table 1: Scholarly Reports on Food Ingredient Fraud and Analytical Methods for Detection (continued)

Ingredient Category	Ingredient	Adulterant	Type of Fraud	Publication Year	Reported Detection Method and Reference
Fruit juices, concentrates, jams, purees, and preserves	Lemon juice	Citric acid (C_4 or paraffin derived)	Replacement	1985	IRMS ($^{13}C/^{12}C$) on citric acid isolated from juice (Doner 1985)
Fruit juices, concentrates, jams, purees, and preserves	Lemon juice	Juice from non-authentic botanical origin	Replacement	1998	IRMS ($^{13}C/^{12}C$) on isolated protein (Gonzalez and others 1998)
Fruit juices, concentrates, jams, purees, and preserves	Lemon juice	Mixture of sugars (C_4 derived)	Replacement	1985	IRMS ($^{13}C/^{12}C$) on sugars isolated from juice (Doner 1985)
Fruit juices, concentrates, jams, purees, and preserves	Mango juice	Sucrose	Replacement or addition to mask poor quality	2010	FTIR with chemometrics (Jha and Gunasekaran 2010)
Fruit juices, concentrates, jams, purees, and preserves	Mei (*Prunus mume*) preserves	Plum fruit (*Prunus salicina*)	Replacement	2005	PCR-based method using ribosomal internal transcribed spacer target (authentic marker) (Ng and others 2005)
Fruit juices, concentrates, jams, purees, and preserves	Orange juice	Beet medium invert sugar	Replacement	1991	HPLC-PAD for oligosaccharides adulterant markers (Swallow and others 1991)
Fruit juices, concentrates, jams, purees, and preserves	Orange juice	Beet medium invert sugar	Replacement	1992	HPLC-PAD for oligosaccharide adulterant marker (White and Cancalon 1992)
Fruit juices, concentrates, jams, purees, and preserves	Orange juice	Beet sugar	Replacement	1992	IRMS ($^{18}O/^{16}O$) (Doner and others 1992)
Fruit juices, concentrates, jams, purees, and preserves	Orange juice	Beta-apo-8'-carotenal	Replacement	1989	Carotenoids fingerprinting by HPLC (Philip and others 1989)
Fruit juices, concentrates, jams, purees, and preserves	Orange juice	Beta-carotene	Replacement	1989	Carotenoids fingerprinting by HPLC (Philip and others 1989)
Fruit juices, concentrates, jams, purees, and preserves	Orange juice	Citrus peel extract	Replacement	1989	Carotenoids fingerprinting by HPLC (Philip and others 1989)
Fruit juices, concentrates, jams, purees, and preserves	Orange juice	Grapefruit juice	Replacement	2009	Quantitative PCR by laboratory-on-a-chip capillary electrophoresis for adulterant (Scott and Knight 2009)
Fruit juices, concentrates, jams, purees, and preserves	Orange juice	Grapefruit juice	Replacement	2008	H-NMR with chemometrics (Cuny and others 2008)
Fruit juices, concentrates, jams, purees, and preserves	Orange juice	Grapefruit juice	Replacement	1988	HPLC fingerprinting with chemometrics for 32 authentic carotenoid and flavone constituents (Perfetti and others 1988)
Fruit juices, concentrates, jams, purees, and preserves	Orange juice	Grapefruit juice	Replacement	1995	NIR with chemometrics (Twomey and others 1995)

Table 1: Scholarly Reports on Food Ingredient Fraud and Analytical Methods for Detection (continued)

Ingredient Category	Ingredient	Adulterant	Type of Fraud	Publication Year	Reported Detection Method and Reference
Fruit juices, concentrates, jams, purees, and preserves	Orange juice	Grapefruit juice plus synthetic sugar/acid mixture	Replacement	1995	NIR with chemometrics (Twomey and others 1995)
Fruit juices, concentrates, jams, purees, and preserves	Orange juice	High-fructose corn syrup, cane sugar hydrolysates, or beet sugar hydrolysates	Replacement	1993	HPLC-PAD for adulterant markers (Wudrich and others 1993)
Fruit juices, concentrates, jams, purees, and preserves	Orange juice	Juice from non-authentic botanical origin	Replacement	1998	IRMS ($^{13}C/^{12}C$) on isolated protein (Jamin and others 1998a)
Fruit juices, concentrates, jams, purees, and preserves	Orange juice	Juice from non-authentic geographic origin	Replacement	2010	IRMS ($^{2}H/^{1}H$), ($^{13}C/^{12}C$), ($^{18}O/^{16}O$), ($^{34}S/^{32}S$), and ($^{87}Sr/^{86}Sr$) on isolate pulp, protein, amino acids, and sugars, all combined with chemometrics (Rummel and others 2010)
Fruit juices, concentrates, jams, purees, and preserves	Orange juice	Lemon juice	Replacement	2007	HPLC for organic acids, sugars, amino acids, and flavonoids contents compared against standards from the Association of the Industry of Juices and Nectars from Fruits and Vegetables of the European Union (Kirit and Ozdemir 2007)
Fruit juices, concentrates, jams, purees, and preserves	Orange juice	Mandarin juice	Replacement	2009	Quantitative PCR by laboratory-on-a-chip capillary electrophoresis for adulterant (Scott and Knight 2009)
Fruit juices, concentrates, jams, purees, and preserves	Orange juice	Mandarin juice	Replacement	2006	PCR (Mooney and others 2006)
Fruit juices, concentrates, jams, purees, and preserves	Orange juice	Marigold flower extract (Tagetes erecta)	Addition to mask poor quality	1989	Carotenoids fingerprinting by HPLC (Philip and others 1989)
Fruit juices, concentrates, jams, purees, and preserves	Orange juice	Mixture of high-fructose corn syrup and water	Replacement	1982	IRMS ($^{13}C/^{12}C$) (Doner and others 1982)
Fruit juices, concentrates, jams, purees, and preserves	Orange juice	Mixture of sugar (cane or corn) and water	Replacement	2001	IRMS ($^{13}C/^{12}C$) on sugars isolated from juice (Antolovich and others 2001)
Fruit juices, concentrates, jams, purees, and preserves	Orange juice	Mixture of sugar (corn, beet, or cane) and water	Replacement	1987	IRMS ($^{13}C/^{12}C$) and ($^{2}H/^{1}H$) on sugars isolated from juice (Bricout and Koziet 1987)
Fruit juices, concentrates, jams, purees, and preserves	Orange juice	Mixture of sugar (corn, beet, or cane) and water	Replacement	1995	IRMS ($^{2}H/^{1}H$) and ($^{18}O/^{16}O$) of water from juice (Yunianta and others 1995)
Fruit juices, concentrates, jams, purees, and preserves	Orange juice	Mixture of sugar (corn, beet, or cane) and water	Replacement	1998	SNIF-NMR ($^{2}H/^{1}H$) and IRMS ($^{13}C/^{12}C$) on isolated ethanol, IRMS ($^{18}O/^{16}O$) of water (Pupin and others 1998)
Fruit juices, concentrates, jams, purees, and preserves	Orange juice	Mixture of sugar (corn, beet, or cane) and water	Replacement	1996	Non-targeted ^{1}HNMR on freeze-dried samples combined with chemometrics (Vogels and others 1996)

Table 1: Scholarly Reports on Food Ingredient Fraud and Analytical Methods for Detection (continued)

Ingredient Category	Ingredient	Adulterant	Type of Fraud	Publication Year	Reported Detection Method and Reference
Fruit juices, concentrates, jams, purees, and preserves	Orange juice	Non-authentic aroma compounds	Addition to mask poor quality	2003	SPME-GC for enantiomeric compositions of chiral terpenes (Ruiz del Castillo and others 2003)
Fruit juices, concentrates, jams, purees, and preserves	Orange juice	Non-authentic juice	Replacement	2009	HPLC x HPLC-PDA- and ToF-MS for carotenoids fingerprinting (Dugo and others 2009)
Fruit juices, concentrates, jams, purees, and preserves	Orange juice	Non-authentic juices (e.g., grapefruit juice)	Replacement	1998	CE-UV for fingerprinting organic acids markers (Pupin and others 1998)
Fruit juices, concentrates, jams, purees, and preserves	Orange juice	Non-authentic sugars	Replacement	1996	HPLC-PAD for oligosaccharide fingerprinting (Luliano 1996)
Fruit juices, concentrates, jams, purees, and preserves	Orange juice	Non-authentic sweeteners	Replacement	1996	HPLC-PAD for adulterant oligosaccharides markers (Iuliano 1996)
Fruit juices, concentrates, jams, purees, and preserves	Orange juice	Orange juice of non-authentic geographic origin	Replacement	2001	Electronic nose/sensor array (Steine and others 2001)
Fruit juices, concentrates, jams, purees, and preserves	Orange juice	Orange juice of non-authentic geographic origin	Replacement	2000	Non-targeted pyrolysis MS combined with chemometrics (Garcia-Wass and others 2000)
Fruit juices, concentrates, jams, purees, and preserves	Orange juice	Orange pulpwash	Replacement	1983	Analysis of nitrate, sulfate, phenolics, carbohydrates, protein, pectin, UV-Vis absorption characteristics, minerals, and carotenes (Park and others 1983)
Fruit juices, concentrates, jams, purees, and preserves	Orange juice	Orange pulpwash	Replacement	1980	UV-Vis absorption and fluorescence excitation and emission analysis (Petrus and Attaway 1980)
Fruit juices, concentrates, jams, purees, and preserves	Orange juice	Orange pulpwash	Replacement	1995	NIR with chemometrics (Twomey and others 1995)
Fruit juices, concentrates, jams, purees, and preserves	Orange juice	Orange pulpwash plus synthetic sugar/acid mixture	Replacement	1995	NIR with chemometrics (Twomey and others 1995)
Fruit juices, concentrates, jams, purees, and preserves	Orange juice	Paprika extract (color)	Addition to mask poor quality	1999	HPLC for carotenoid analysis for adulterant markers (Mouly and others 1999)
Fruit juices, concentrates, jams, purees, and preserves	Orange juice	Sodium benzoate fortified orange pulpwash	Replacement	1983	HPLC for detection of sodium benzoate (tracer added to pulpwash) (Fisher 1983)
Fruit juices, concentrates, jams, purees, and preserves	Orange juice	Sodium benzoate fortified orange pulpwash	Replacement	1996	Non-targeted ^{1}H-NMR on freeze-dried samples combined with chemometrics (Vogels and others 1996)
Fruit juices, concentrates, jams, purees, and preserves	Orange juice	Sodium benzoate fortified orange pulpwash	Replacement	1988	HPLC fingerprinting with chemometrics for 32 authentic carotenoid and flavone constituents (Perfetti and others 1988)

Table 1: Scholarly Reports on Food Ingredient Fraud and Analytical Methods for Detection (continued)

Ingredient Category	Ingredient	Adulterant	Type of Fraud	Publication Year	Reported Detection Method and Reference
Fruit juices, concentrates, jams, purees, and preserves	Orange juice	Sucrose	Replacement or addition to mask poor quality	2000	Non-targeted pyrolysis MS combined with chemometrics (Garcia-Wass and others 2000)
Fruit juices, concentrates, jams, purees, and preserves	Orange juice	Tangelo juice	Replacement	2002	HPLC for polymethoxylated flavones and carotenoids fingerprinting, combined with chemometrics (Pan and others 2002)
Fruit juices, concentrates, jams, purees, and preserves	Orange juice	Tangerine or mandarin juice	Replacement	1989	Carotenoids fingerprinting by HPLC (Philip and others 1989)
Fruit juices, concentrates, jams, purees, and preserves	Orange juice (fresh-squeezed)	Reconstituted orange juice	Replacement	2005	HPLC-MS/MS for amino acids fingerprinting (Gómez-Ariza and others 2005)
Fruit juices, concentrates, jams, purees, and preserves	Pineapple juice	Added sugars	Replacement	1999	IRMS ($^{13}C/^{12}C$) on fructose, glucose, and sucrose (Gonzalez and others 1999)
Fruit juices, concentrates, jams, purees, and preserves	Pineapple juice	Juice from non-authentic botanical origin	Replacement	1998	IRMS ($^{13}C/^{12}C$) on isolated protein (Jamin and others 1998a)
Fruit juices, concentrates, jams, purees, and preserves	Pomegranate juice	Grape juice	Replacement or addition to mask poor quality	2008	FTIR combined with chemometrics (Vardin and others 2008)
Fruit juices, concentrates, jams, purees, and preserves	Pomegranate juice	Grape juice and grape skin color	Replacement or addition to mask poor quality	2009	HPLC-PDA for amino acids and organic acids analysis to detect elevated levels of malic acid, proline, and tartaric acid; HPLC-PDA to detect grape anthocyanins or other non-pomegranate anthocyanins (Zhang and others 2009b)
Fruit juices, concentrates, jams, purees, and preserves	Pomegranate juice	Non-pomegranate anthocyanins from aronia, grape skin, elderberry, black currant, or black carrot	Addition to mask the color of poor quality juice	2009	HPLC-PDA for polyphenols fingerprinting (authentic and adulterant markers) and HPLC-PDA for organic acids analysis (authentic and adulterant markers) (Zhang and others 2009b)
Fruit juices, concentrates, jams, purees, and preserves	Pomegranate juice	Sorbitol-containing fruit juices (e.g., apple, pear, cherry, or aronia	Replacement	2009	HPLC-PDA fingerprinting for non-pomegranate; HPLC to detect elevated levels of sorbitol, malic acid, or sucrose (Zhang and others 2009b)
Fruit juices, concentrates, jams, purees, and preserves	Pomegranate juice	Sugars (corn- or cane-derived)	Addition to mask poor-quality juice	2009	IRMS ($^{13}C/^{12}C$) on sugars isolated from juice; HPLC-RI for adulterant marker compounds (sucrose or maltose) (Zhang and others 2009b)
Fruit juices, concentrates, jams, purees, and preserves	Quince jam	Apple or pear puree	Replacement	2000	HPLC-PDA for phenolics (authentic and adulterant markers) fingerprinting (Silva and others 2000a)
Fruit juices, concentrates, jams, purees, and preserves	Quince jelly	Apple or pear puree	Replacement	2000	HPLC-PDA for phenolics (authentic and adulterant markers) fingerprinting (Silva and others 2000b)
Fruit juices, concentrates, jams, purees, and preserves	Raspberry juice	Red currant juice	Replacement	2006	HPLC for free amino acid fingerprinting (Stoj and Targonski 2006)

Table 1: Scholarly Reports on Food Ingredient Fraud and Analytical Methods for Detection (continued)

Ingredient Category	Ingredient	Adulterant	Type of Fraud	Publication Year	Reported Detection Method and Reference
Fruit juices, concentrates, jams, purees, and preserves	Raspberry juice	Strawberry juice	Replacement	2006	HPLC for free amino acid fingerprinting (Stoj and Targonski 2006)
Fruit juices, concentrates, jams, purees, and preserves	Raspberry puree	Apple puree	Replacement	1996	FTIR combined with chemometrics (Kemsley and others 1996)
Fruit juices, concentrates, jams, purees, and preserves	Raspberry puree	Apple puree	Replacement	2004	Non-targeted visible and NIR spectroscopy combined with chemometrics (Downey and Kelly 2004)
Fruit juices, concentrates, jams, purees, and preserves	Raspberry puree	Fruit puree from non-authentic botanical origin	Replacement	1995	Non-targeted FTIR combined with chemometrics (Defernez and others 1995)
Fruit juices, concentrates, jams, purees, and preserves	Raspberry puree	Plum puree	Replacement	1996	FTIR with chemometrics (Kemsley and others 1996)
Fruit juices, concentrates, jams, purees, and preserves	Raspberry puree	Sucrose	Addition to mask poor quality	1996	FTIR with chemometrics (Kemsley and others 1996)
Fruit juices, concentrates, jams, purees, and preserves	Red raspberry juice	Juice from non-authentic botanical origin	Replacement	1995	Analysis of sugars and nonvolatile acids ($^{13}C/^{12}C$) of juice and minerals (Durst and others 1995)
Fruit juices, concentrates, jams, purees, and preserves	Royal jelly	Non-authentic sugars	Replacement	2006	IRMS ($^{13}C/^{12}C$) and ($^{15}N/^{14}N$) (Stocker and others 2006)
Fruit juices, concentrates, jams, purees, and preserves	Royal jelly	Yeast powder	Replacement	2006	IRMS ($^{13}C/^{12}C$) and ($^{15}N/^{14}N$) (Stocker and others 2006)
Fruit juices, concentrates, jams, purees, and preserves	Strawberry juice	Juice from non-authentic botanical origin	Replacement	1998	IRMS ($^{13}C/^{12}C$) on isolated protein (Jamin and others 1998a)
Fruit juices, concentrates, jams, purees, and preserves	Strawberry puree	Apple puree	Replacement	1998	FTIR with chemometrics (Holland and others 1998)
Fruit juices, concentrates, jams, purees, and preserves	Strawberry puree	Apple puree	Replacement	2004	Non-targeted visible and NIR spectroscopy combined with chemometrics (Downey and Kelly 2004)
Fruit juices, concentrates, jams, purees, and preserves	Strawberry puree	Apple puree	Replacement	2004	SPME-GC for volatile aroma compounds fingerprinting combined with chemometrics (Reid and others 2004)
Fruit juices, concentrates, jams, purees, and preserves	Strawberry puree	Apple, plum, sugar solutions, red grape juice, and rhubarb compote	Replacement	1998	FTIR with chemometrics (Holland and others 1998)
Fruit juices, concentrates, jams, purees, and preserves	Strawberry puree	Fruit puree from non-authentic botanical origin	Replacement	1995	Non-targeted FTIR combined with chemometrics (Defernez and others 1995)

Table 1: Scholarly Reports on Food Ingredient Fraud and Analytical Methods for Detection (continued)

Ingredient Category	Ingredient	Adulterant	Type of Fraud	Publication Year	Reported Detection Method and Reference
Fruit juices, concentrates, jams, purees, and preserves	Strawberry puree	Plum puree	Replacement	1998	FTIR with chemometrics (Holland and others 1998)
Fruit juices, concentrates, jams, purees, and preserves	Strawberry puree	Red grape juice	Replacement	1998	FTIR with chemometrics (Holland and others 1998)
Fruit juices, concentrates, jams, purees, and preserves	Strawberry puree	Rhubarb compote	Replacement	1998	FTIR with chemometrics (Holland and others 1998)
Fruit juices, concentrates, jams, purees, and preserves	Strawberry puree	Sugar solution	Replacement	1998	FTIR with chemometrics (Holland and others 1998)
Fruit juices, concentrates, jams, purees, and preserves	Sweet cherries (Cereza del Jerte) fruit preparation	Fruit from non-authentic botanical origin	Replacement	2008	Free-zone CE for fingerprinting methanol soluble proteins (Serradilla and others 2008)
Functional food ingredients	Aloe vera gel powder	Glucose	Replacement	2007	NR (Bozzi and others 2007)
Functional food ingredients	Aloe vera gel powder	Glycerine	Replacement	2007	NR (Bozzi and others 2007)
Functional food ingredients	Aloe vera gel powder	Malic acid	Replacement	2007	NR (Bozzi and others 2007)
Functional food ingredients	Aloe vera gel powder	Maltodextrin	Replacement	1998	TLC and HPLC for adulterant (Kim and others 1998)
Functional food ingredients	Aloe vera gel powder	Non-authentic substances	Replacement	2007	^{1}H-NMR for authentic markers (acemannan, malic acid, and glucose); HPLC-UV for hydroxyanthracene derivatives (adulterant markers) (Bozzi and others 2007)
Functional food ingredients	Bilberry	Amaranth color additive	Replacement	2006	NR (Penman and others 2006)
Functional food ingredients	Black cohosh (Actaea racemosa L.)	Asian Actaea species	Replacement	2006	HPLC-MS for cimifugin (adulterant marker) and cimiracemoside C (authentic marker) (Jiang and others 2006)
Functional food ingredients	Ginseng	Ginseng of non-authentic botanical origin	Replacement	2008	DNA microarray based on 18S rRNA gene sequence (Zhu and others 2008)
Functional food ingredients	Ginseng, American (Panax quinquefolius)	Ginseng, Chinese (Panax ginseng)	Replacement	2002	DNA analysis using amplified fragment length polymorphism and directed amplification of minisatellite region (Ha and others 2002)
Functional food ingredients	Ginseng, Chinese (Panax ginseng)	Ginseng, American (Panax quinquefolius)	Replacement	2008	IR with chemometrics (Yap and others 2008)
Functional food ingredients	Ginseng, notoginseng (Panax notoginseng)	Ginseng of non-authentic botanical origin	Replacement	2009	HPLC-PDA for marker saponins (Wang and others 2009a)
Functional food ingredients	Mushroom polysaccharide extract	Carboxymethyl cellulose	Replacement	2009	SEM, XRD, IR, and optical rotation (Qian and others 2009)
Functional food ingredients	Mushroom polysaccharide extract	Guar gum	Replacement	2009	SEM, XRD, IR, and optical rotation (Qian and others 2009)
Functional food ingredients	Mushroom polysaccharide extract	Maltodextrin	Replacement	2009	SEM, XRD, IR, and optical rotation (Qian and others 2009)
Functional food ingredients	Mushroom polysaccharide extract	Water-soluble corn starch	Replacement	2009	SEM, XRD, IR, and optical rotation (Qian and others 2009)

Table 1: Scholarly Reports on Food Ingredient Fraud and Analytical Methods for Detection (continued)

Ingredient Category	Ingredient	Adulterant	Type of Fraud	Publication Year	Reported Detection Method and Reference
Functional food ingredients	Radix astragali	Root of non-authentic botanical origin	Replacement	2005	DNA method using PCR with internal transcribed spacer method (Chen and others 2005)
Functional food ingredients	Radix astragali	Root of non-authentic botanical origin	Replacement	2002	HPLC fingerprinting for isoflavonoids and astragalosides (Ma and others 2002)
Gums	Carrageenan*	Konjac gum	Replacement	2010	ELISA for adulterant galactomannan (Hurley and others 2010)
Gums	Guar gum*	Carboxymethyl-cellulose	Replacement	2005	FTIR with chemometrics (Prado and others 2005)
Gums	Guar gum*	Fenugreek gum	Replacement	2005	FTIR with chemometrics (Prado and others 2005)
Gums	Guar gum*	Konjac gum	Replacement	2010	ELISA for adulterant galactomannan (Hurley and others 2010)
Gums	Guar gum*	Locust bean gum	Replacement	2001	PCR and restriction fragment length polymorphism analysis (Meyer and others 2001)
Gums	Guar gum*	Locust bean gum	Replacement	2005	FTIR with chemometrics (Prado and others 2005)
Gums	Guar gum*	Locust bean gum	Replacement	2005	DNA PCR analysis (Urdiain and others 2005)
Gums	Guar gum*	Tara gum	Replacement	2005	FTIR with chemometrics (Prado and others 2005)
Gums	Gum arabic* (Acacia senegal)	Gum from Acacia seyal	Replacement	2004	ELISA for adulterant markers (Ireland and others 2004)
Gums	Gum arabic* (Acacia senegal)	Gum from Combretum erythrophyllum	Replacement	2004	ELISA for adulterant markers (Ireland and others 2004)
Gums	Gum arabic* (Acacia senegal)	Gum from non-authentic botanical origin	Replacement	1991	^{13}C-NMR (Anderson and others 1991)
Gums	Gum arabic* (Acacia senegal)	Gum from non-authentic botanical origin	Replacement	1998	Specific optical rotation, intrinsic viscosity, content of nitrogen, arabinose, rhamnose, galactose and uronic acids, all combined with chemometrics (Mocak and others 1998)
Gums	Gum arabic* (Acacia senegal)	Gum talha (Acacia seyal)	Replacement	1998	Review of methods: Analysis of physical properties and chemical constituents including monosaccharides analysis, all combined with chemometrics (Prodolliet and Hischenhuber 1998)
Gums	Gum arabic* (Acacia senegal)	Gum talha (Acacia seyal)	Replacement	1998	Review of methods: Immunochemical test for adulterant markers using antiAGP/AG monoclonal antibody (Prodolliet and Hischenhuber 1998)
Gums	Locust bean gum*	Guar gum	Replacement	2000	CE for adulterant marker proteins and polarized light microscopy with selective staining techniques for authentic and adulterant markers (cellular components) (Flurer and others 2000)
Gums	Locust bean gum*	Guar gum	Replacement	2005	DNA PCR analysis (Urdiain and others 2005)
Gums	Locust bean gum*	Guar gum	Replacement	1998	Review of methods: HPLC for mannose and galactose (Prodolliet and Hischenhuber 1998)
Gums	Locust bean gum*	Guar gum	Replacement	2005	Diffuse reflectance FI-IR with chemometrics (Prado and others 2005)
Gums	Locust bean gum*	Konjac gum	Replacement	2010	ELISA for adulterant galactomannan (Hurley and others 2010)

Table 1: Scholarly Reports on Food Ingredient Fraud and Analytical Methods for Detection (continued)

Ingredient Category	Ingredient	Adulterant	Type of Fraud	Publication Year	Reported Detection Method and Reference
Gums	Locust bean gum*	Tara gum	Replacement	2000	CE for adulterant marker proteins and polarized light microscopy with selective staining techniques for authentic and adulterant markers (cellular components) (Flurer and others 2000)
Gums	Xanthan gum*	Konjac gum	Replacement	2010	ELISA for adulterant galactomannan (Hurley and others 2010)
Meats	Chicken meat (corn-fed)	Chicken meat from non-corn-fed chickens	Replacement	2010	IRMS ($^{13}C/^{12}C$) on extracted protein and lipid fractions of meat (Rhodes and others 2010)
Meats	Meat products	Chickpea flour	Replacement	2009	HPLC for isoflavones, phytic acid, and galactooligosaccharides (adulterant markers) (Vanha and others 2009)
Meats	Meat products	Pea flour	Replacement	2009	HPLC for isoflavones, phytic acid, and galactooligosaccharides (adulterant markers) (Vanha and others 2009)
Meats	Meat products	Rice flour	Replacement	2009	HPLC for isoflavones, phytic acid, and galactooligosaccharides (adulterant markers) (Vanha and others 2009)
Meats	Meat products	Soy flour	Replacement	2009	HPLC for isoflavones, phytic acid, and galactooligosaccharides (adulterant markers) (Vanha and others 2009)
Meats	Meat products	Soy flour	Replacement	2009	HPLC for isoflavones, phytic acid, and galactooligosaccharides (adulterant markers) (Vanha and others 2009)
Meats	Minced meat (beef)	Ox offal tissue (kidney or liver)	Replacement	1999	MIR with chemometrics (Al-Jowder and others 1999)
Meats	Minced meat (chicken, pork, or turkey)	Meat from non-authentic species	Replacement	1997	MIR with chemometrics (Al-Jowder and others 1997)
Meats	Processed meat product	Soybean protein	Replacement	2005	Perfusion reversed phase chromatography with UV detection on extracted protein for adulterant marker detection (Castro-Rubio and others 2005)
Milk	Milk (fluid)	Cyanuric acid	Replacement	2010	HPLC-MS/MS for adulterant (ISO-IDF 2010)
Milk	Milk (fluid)	Cyanuric acid	Replacement	2009	HPLC-MS/MS for adulterant (Desmarchelier and others 2009)
Milk	Milk (fluid)	Dextrin	Replacement	2008	Isolation of dextrins and photometric determination (Wang and others 2008b)
Milk	Milk (fluid)	Fake milk	Replacement	2001	Rheological evaluation (Haake rheometer) (Paradkar and others 2001b)
Milk	Milk (fluid)	Fake milk	Replacement	2006	Conductance measurements (Sadat and others 2006)
Milk	Milk (fluid)	Fake milk (oil, urea, detergent, caustic soda, sugar, salt, and skim milk powder)	Replacement	2004	NIR with chemometrics (Jha and Matsuoka 2004)
Milk	Milk (fluid)	Fake milk containing sodium bicarbonate	Replacement	2001	Rosolic acid test for sodium bicarbonate adulterant (Paradkar and others 2001a)
Milk	Milk (fluid)	Fake milk with anionic detergents	Replacement	2008	Colorimetric determination of a detergent-methylene blue complex (Paradkar and others 2000b)
Milk	Milk (fluid)	Melamine	Replacement	2009	Detection of melamine by chemiluminescence (Wang and others 2009d)
Milk	Milk (fluid)	Melamine	Replacement	2009	Ultrasound-assisted extractive electrospray ionization-MS for adulterant detection (Zhu and others 2009)

Table 1: Scholarly Reports on Food Ingredient Fraud and Analytical Methods for Detection (continued)

Ingredient Category	Ingredient	Adulterant	Type of Fraud	Publication Year	Reported Detection Method and Reference
Milk	Milk (fluid)	Melamine	Replacement	2009	Detection of melamine using ambient ionization by low-temperature plasma probe combined with MS/MS (Huang and others 2009)
Milk	Milk (fluid)	Melamine	Replacement	2010	Colorimetric reaction with gold nanoparticle to detect melamine (Guo and others 2010b)
Milk	Milk (fluid)	Melamine	Replacement	2009	HPLC-MS/MS or GC-MS for melamine (Chan and others 2009)
Milk	Milk (fluid)	Melamine	Replacement	2009	Ultrasonic analysis (Elvira and others 2009)
Milk	Milk (fluid)	Melamine	Replacement	2010	NR (Sharma and Paradakar 2010)
Milk	Milk (fluid)	Melamine	Replacement	2010	HPLC-MS/MS for adulterant (ISO-IDF 2010)
Milk	Milk (fluid)	Melamine	Replacement	2010	HPLC-MS/MS for adulterant (ISO-IDF 2010)
Milk	Milk (fluid)	Melamine	Replacement	2010	ELISA screening method for melamine (ISO-IDF 2010)
Milk	Milk (fluid)	Melamine	Replacement	2010	HPLC-UV screening method for melamine (ISO-IDF 2010)
Milk	Milk (fluid)	Melamine	Replacement	2010	GC-MS confirmatory method for melamine (ISO-IDF 2010)
Milk	Milk (fluid)	Melamine	Replacement	2010	HPLC-MS/MS confirmatory method for melamine (ISO-IDF 2010)
Milk	Milk (fluid)	Melamine and related compounds	Replacement	2010	Review of methods: HPLC-MS/MS, ELISA, extractive electrospray ionization time-of-flight MS, and low temperature plasma-MS/MS (Tittlemier 2010)
Milk	Milk (fluid)	Milk (non-authentic species)	Replacement	2010	FTIR with chemometrics (Nicolaou and others 2010)
Milk	Milk (fluid)	Milk from non-authentic geographic origin	Replacement	2007	GC-IRMS ($^{18}O/^{16}O$) and chromatographic analysis of terpenes, fatty acids, carotenoids, and vitamins combined with chemometrics (Engel and others 2007)
Milk	Milk (fluid)	Milk from non-authentic geographic origin	Replacement	2007	Review: IRMS ($^{2}H/^{1}H$); ($^{18}O/^{16}O$) (Karoui and De Baerdemaeker 2007)
Milk	Milk (fluid)	Milk from non-authentic geographic origin	Replacement	2007	Review: Dynamic head space-GC-MS with chemometrics (Karoui and De Baerdemaeker 2007)
Milk	Milk (fluid)	Milk from non-authentic heat process	Replacement	2006	HPLC for furosine, lactulose, and beta-lactoglobulin; lab-on-chip for native and denatured alpha-lactalbumin ratio; all combined with chemometrics (Feinberg and others 2006)
Milk	Milk (fluid)	Milk from non-authentic species	Replacement	2005	Review of methods for adulterant marker protein detection by electrophoretic methods (IEF, PAGE, CE, and CZE), chromatographic methods (RP-HPLC), and immunological (ELISA) methods (de la Fuente and Juarez 2005)
Milk	Milk (fluid)	Milk from non-authentic species	Replacement	2005	Review of methods for adulterant marker DNA detection by PCR (de la Fuente and Juarez 2005)
Milk	Milk (fluid)	Milk from non-authentic species	Replacement	2004	Review of methods for adulterant marker DNA detection by PCR (Hurley and others 2004b)

Table 1: Scholarly Reports on Food Ingredient Fraud and Analytical Methods for Detection (continued)

Ingredient Category	Ingredient	Adulterant	Type of Fraud	Publication Year	Reported Detection Method and Reference
Milk	Milk (fluid)	Milk from non-authentic species	Replacement	2004	Review of methods for adulterant marker protein detection by immunological (ELISA) methods (Hurley and others 2004b)
Milk	Milk (fluid)	Milk from non-authentic species	Replacement	2005	Review of methods for adulterant marker fatty acid detection by GC and adulterant marker triglycerides by NMR (de la Fuente and Juarez 2005)
Milk	Milk (fluid)	Non-authentic diluent	Replacement	2010	Quantitative PCR for microRNAs (authentic markers) (Chen and others 2010)
Milk	Milk (fluid)	Non-authentic milk species (ovine, bovine, caprine, and water buffalo)	Replacement	2010	MALDI-MS for adulterant marker peptides from tryptic digest of sample (Cuollo and others 2010)
Milk	Milk (fluid)	Pea protein	Replacement	2007	HPLC-MS/MS on peptides resulting from tryptic digests of protein isolate from sample (Luykx and others 2007a)
Milk	Milk (fluid)	Pea protein	Replacement	2002	SDS-GE for adulterant proteins on sample pre-treated to remove authentic proteins (Manso and others 2002)
Milk	Milk (fluid)	Pea protein	Replacement	2002	ELISA for adulterant proteins (Sanchez and others 2002)
Milk	Milk (fluid)	Pea protein	Replacement	1989	1D GE on proteins (Schoonderwoerd and Misra 1989)
Milk	Milk (fluid)	Plant proteins	Replacement	2005	Review of methods for detecting adulterant proteins by chromatographic methods (RP-HPLC), electrophoretic methods (CE, IEF, and SDS-PAGE), and immunological biosensor methods (de la Fuente and Juarez 2005)
Milk	Milk (fluid)	Reconstituted milk powder	Replacement	2000	Spectrophotometric determination of hydroxymethylfurfural (adulterant marker) (Rehman and others 2000)
Milk	Milk (fluid)	Reconstituted milk powder	Replacement	2002	HPLC for furosine (adulterant marker) (Ohta and others 2002)
Milk	Milk (fluid)	Reconstituted milk powder	Replacement	2005	Fluorescence spectroscopy for advanced Maillard products and soluble tryptophan (adulterant markers) (Guan and others 2005)
Milk	Milk (fluid)	Reconstituted milk powder	Replacement	1998	CE for protein fingerprinting with chemometrics (Vallejo-Cordoba 1998)
Milk	Milk (fluid)	Rennet whey proteins	Replacement	2008	Fourth derivative absorption spectrometry for whey to total protein ratio (Ayala and others 2008)
Milk	Milk (fluid)	Soy milk	Replacement	1990	ELISA immunoassay for adulterant protein marker (Hewedy and Smith 1990)
Milk	Milk (fluid)	Soy milk	Replacement	2009	HPLC for stachyose (adulterant marker) (Sharma and others 2009)
Milk	Milk (fluid)	Soy protein	Replacement	2007	HPLC-MS/MS on peptides resulting from tryptic digests protein isolate from sample (Luykx and others 2007a)
Milk	Milk (fluid)	Soy protein	Replacement	2002	SDS-GE for adulterant proteins on sample pre-treated to remove authentic proteins (Manso and others 2002)
Milk	Milk (fluid)	Soy protein	Replacement	2002	ELISA for adulterant (Sanchez and others 2002)
Milk	Milk (fluid)	Soy protein	Replacement	1989	1D GE on proteins (Schoonderwoerd and Misra 1989)
Milk	Milk (fluid)	Soybean protein	Replacement	1997	HPLC-FID protein fingerprinting (García and others 1997)

Table 1: Scholarly Reports on Food Ingredient Fraud and Analytical Methods for Detection (continued)

Ingredient Category	Ingredient	Adulterant	Type of Fraud	Publication Year	Reported Detection Method and Reference
Milk	Milk (fluid)	Soymilk	Replacement	2010	Polarimetric method for optical activity of sugars; isoelectric precipitation of proteins; protein fingerprinting by SDS-PAGE (Sharma and others 2010)
Milk	Milk (fluid)	Urea	Replacement (as component of "synthetic milk")	2000	Enzymatic determination of urea (Paradkar and others 2000a)
Milk	Milk (fluid)	Vegetable oil	Replacement (as component of "synthetic milk")	2001	HP-TLC for adulterant marker detection (Paradkar and others 2001a)
Milk	Milk (fluid)	Water	Replacement	2007	NIR and chemometrics (Kasemsumran and others 2007)
Milk	Milk (fluid)	Wheat protein	Replacement	2002	ELISA for adulterant proteins (Sanchez and others 2002)
Milk	Milk (fluid)	Whey	Replacement	1989	Wolfschoon-Pombo phosphomolybdate method for casein-bound phorphorus; TCA-Kjeldahl for protein nitrogen content (Wolfschoon-Pombo and Furtado 1989)
Milk	Milk (fluid)	Whey	Replacement	2007	NIR and chemometrics (Kasemsumran and others 2007)
Milk	Milk (fluid)	Whey protein	Replacement	2005	Review of methods for caseinomacropeptide (adulterant marker) detection by electrophoretic (CE and IEF), chromatographic (HPLC), and immunological (ELISA) methods (de la Fuente and Juarez 2005)
Milk	Milk (fluid)	Whey protein	Replacement	2005	Review of methods for determining ratio of whey proteins to total proteins by SDS-PAGE, polarographic evaluation, pyrolysis-mass spectrometry, FTIR spectroscopy, photoacoustic spectroscopy, CE, and UV spectroscopy (de la Fuente and Juarez 2005)
Milk	Milk (fluid)	Whey protein	Replacement	2009	Immunochromatographic determination of glycomacropeptide (adulterant marker) (Oancea 2009)
Milk	Milk (fluid)	Whey proteins	Replacement	2003	CE for whey protein to total protein ratio determination (Miralles and others 2003)
Milk	Milk (fluid, bubaline)	Milk (bovine)	Replacement	2008	DNA analysis by PCR with restriction fragment length polymorphism for adulterant (Otaviano and others 2008)
Milk	Milk (fluid, caprine)	Milk (bovine)	Replacement	2008	CE-MS for whey proteins (Muller and others 2008)
Milk	Milk (fluid, caprine)	Milk (bovine)	Replacement	2002	HPLC for major milk proteins (Veloso and others 2002)
Milk	Milk (fluid, caprine)	Milk (bovine)	Replacement	1996	Immunostick ELISA for beta-casein (adulterant marker) (Anguita and others 1996)
Milk	Milk (fluid, caprine)	Milk (bovine)	Replacement	1993	ELISA for bovine caseins (adulterant markers) (Rodríguez and others 1993)
Milk	Milk (fluid, caprine)	Milk (bovine)	Replacement	2006	Sandwich ELISA for immunoglobulin (adulterant marker) (Hurley and others 2006)
Milk	Milk (fluid, caprine)	Milk (bovine)	Replacement	2004	Sandwich ELISA for immunoglobulin (adulterant marker) (Hurley and others 2004a)
Milk	Milk (fluid, caprine)	Milk (bovine)	Replacement	2001	Indirect and sandwich ELISA for adulterant markers (Hu and others 2001)

Table 1: Scholarly Reports on Food Ingredient Fraud and Analytical Methods for Detection (continued)

Ingredient Category	Ingredient	Adulterant	Type of Fraud	Publication Year	Reported Detection Method and Reference
Milk	Milk (fluid, caprine)	Milk (bovine)	Replacement	1999	CE for bovine whey proteins (adulterant markers) (Cartoni and others 1999)
Milk	Milk (fluid, caprine)	Milk (bovine)	Replacement	2008	DNA-based analysis of kappa-casein gene (Reale and others 2008)
Milk	Milk (fluid, caprine)	Milk (bovine)	Replacement	2004	Biosensor immunoassay for bovine kappa-casein (adulterant marker) (Haasnoot and others 2004)
Milk	Milk (fluid, caprine)	Milk (bovine)	Replacement	2010	Immunochromatographic method for bovine immunoglobulin G (adulterant marker) (Stanciuc and Rapeanu 2010)
Milk	Milk (fluid, caprine)	Milk (bovine)	Replacement	2010	HPLC-PDA for protein fingerprinting combined with chemometrics (Rodriguez and others 2010)
Milk	Milk (fluid, caprine)	Milk (bovine)	Replacement	2007	Review of ELISA methods (Song and Han 2007)
Milk	Milk (fluid, caprine)	Milk (bovine)	Replacement	1999	CE for casein fraction fingerprinting (Molina and others 1999)
Milk	Milk (fluid, caprine)	Milk (ovine)	Replacement	2008	DNA-based analysis of kappa-casein gene (Reale and others 2008)
Milk	Milk (fluid, caprine)	Milk (ovine)	Replacement	2010	HPLC-PDA for protein fingerprinting combined with chemometrics (Rodriguez and others 2010)
Milk	Milk (fluid, caprine)	Milk (ovine)	Replacement	2007	Review of ELISA methods (Song and Han 2007)
Milk	Milk (fluid, caprine)	Milk (water buffalo)	Replacement	2008	DNA-based analysis of kappa-casein gene (Reale and others 2008)
Milk	Milk (fluid, ewe)	Milk (bovine)	Replacement	2006	Biosensor inhibition immunoassay for bovine kappa-casein (Haasnoot and others 2006)
Milk	Milk (fluid, ewe)	Milk (bovine)	Replacement	2001	MALDI-MS for protein fingerprinting (Cozzolino and others 2001)
Milk	Milk (fluid, ovine)	Milk (bovine)	Replacement	2004	Biosensor immunoassay for bovine kappa-casein (adulterant marker) (Haasnoot and others 2004)
Milk	Milk (fluid, ovine)	Milk (bovine)	Replacement	2008	CE-MS for whey proteins (Muller and others 2008)
Milk	Milk (fluid, ovine)	Milk (bovine)	Replacement	1999	CE for casein fraction fingerprinting (Molina and others 1999)
Milk	Milk (fluid, ovine)	Milk (bovine)	Replacement	2006	Sandwich ELISA for immunoglobulin (adulterant marker) (Hurley and others 2006)
Milk	Milk (fluid, ovine)	Milk (bovine)	Replacement	2004	HPLC-MS for adulterant protein markers (Chen and others 2004)
Milk	Milk (fluid, ovine)	Milk (bovine)	Replacement	2004	Sandwich ELISA for immunoglobulin (adulterant marker) (Hurley and others 2004a)
Milk	Milk (fluid, ovine)	Milk (bovine)	Replacement	2008	DNA-based analysis of kappa-casein gene (Reale and others 2008)
Milk	Milk (fluid, ovine)	Milk (bovine)	Replacement	2010	Immunochromatographic method for bovine immunoglobulin G (adulterant marker) (Stanciuc and Rapeanu 2010)
Milk	Milk (fluid, ovine)	Milk (bovine)	Replacement	2001	PCR DNA-based analysis of bovine cytochrome b (adulterant marker) (Bania and others 2001)
Milk	Milk (fluid, ovine)	Milk (bovine)	Replacement	1990	ELISA for bovine whey proteins (adulterant markers) (García and others 1990)
Milk	Milk (fluid, ovine)	Milk (bovine)	Replacement	2010	HPLC-PDA for protein fingerprinting combined with chemometrics (Rodriguez and others 2010)

Table 1: Scholarly Reports on Food Ingredient Fraud and Analytical Methods for Detection (continued)

Ingredient Category	Ingredient	Adulterant	Type of Fraud	Publication Year	Reported Detection Method and Reference
Milk	Milk (fluid, ovine)	Milk (bovine)	Replacement	2011	Polyacrylamide gel electrophoresis for beta-lactoglobulins (Pesic and others 2011)
Milk	Milk (fluid, ovine)	Milk (caprine)	Replacement	2011	Polyacrylamide gel electrophoresis for beta-lactoglobulins (Pesic and others 2011)
Milk	Milk (fluid, ovine)	Milk (caprine)	Replacement	2007	PCR for adulterant DNA (Díaz and others 2007)
Milk	Milk (fluid, ovine)	Milk (caprine)	Replacement	2005	PCR for adulterant DNA (López-Calleja and others 2005b)
Milk	Milk (fluid, ovine)	Milk (caprine)	Replacement	2007	Real-time PCR for adulterant DNA (López-Calleja and others 2007)
Milk	Milk (fluid, ovine)	Milk (caprine)	Replacement	2008	DNA-based analysis of kappa-casein gene (Reale and others 2008)
Milk	Milk (fluid, ovine)	Milk (caprine)	Replacement	2010	HPLC-PDA for protein fingerprinting combined with chemometrics (Rodriguez and others 2010)
Milk	Milk (fluid, ovine)	Milk (caprine)	Replacement	1997	ELISA for caprine alpha-S2-casein (adulterant marker protein) (Haza and others 1997)
Milk	Milk (fluid, ovine)	Milk (water buffalo)	Replacement	2008	DNA-based analysis of kappa-casein gene (Reale and others 2008)
Milk	Milk (fluid, water buffalo)	Milk (bovine)	Replacement	2011	PCR for adulterant DNA (Dalmasso and others 2011)
Milk	Milk (fluid, water buffalo)	Milk (bovine)	Replacement	2011	PCR for adulterant DNA (De and others 2011)
Milk	Milk (fluid, water buffalo)	Milk (bovine)	Replacement	2001	MALDI-MS for protein fingerprinting (Cozzolino and others 2001)
Milk	Milk (fluid, water buffalo)	Milk (bovine)	Replacement	2010	HPLC-MS for beta-lactoglobulin (adulterant marker) (Czerwenka and others 2010)
Milk	Milk (fluid, water buffalo)	Milk (bovine)	Replacement	2007	Review: NMR and chemometrics (Karoui and De Baerdemaeker 2007)
Milk	Milk (fluid, water buffalo)	Milk (bovine)	Replacement	2006	Sandwich ELISA for immunoglobulin (adulterant marker) (Hurley and others 2006)
Milk	Milk (fluid, water buffalo)	Milk (bovine)	Replacement	2004	Sandwich ELISA for immunoglobulin (adulterant marker) (Hurley and others 2004a)
Milk	Milk (fluid, water buffalo)	Milk (bovine)	Replacement	2005	PCR for adulterant DNA (López-Calleja and others 2005a)
Milk	Milk (fluid, water buffalo)	Milk (bovine)	Replacement	2008	DNA-based analysis of kappa-casein gene (Reale and others 2008)
Milk	Milk (fluid, water buffalo)	Milk (caprine)	Replacement	2008	DNA-based analysis of kappa-casein gene (Reale and others 2008)
Milk	Milk (fluid, water buffalo)	Milk (ovine)	Replacement	2008	DNA-based analysis of kappa-casein gene (Reale and others 2008)
Milk	Milk (fluid, yak)	Milk (bovine)	Replacement	2009	PCR for adulterant DNA (Bai and others 2009)
Milk	Milk (non-UHT)	UHT milk	Replacement	1998	HPLC or GC for lactulose (adulterant marker) (Prodolliet and Hischenhuber 1998)
Milk	Milk (organic)	Non-organic milk	Replacement	2009	IRMS ($^{13}C/^{12}C$) on milk fat, and GC-FID for alpha-linolenic acid (authenticity marker) (Molkentin 2009)
Milk	Milk (organic)	Non-organic milk	Replacement	2010	IRMS ($^{13}C/^{12}C$) on milk fat or milk protein, and GC-FID for alpha-linolenic acid (Molkentin and Giesemann 2010)
Milk	Milk (powder)	Cane sugar	Replacement	2009	FTIR with chemometrics (Zhou and others 2009)

Table 1: Scholarly Reports on Food Ingredient Fraud and Analytical Methods for Detection (continued)

Ingredient Category	Ingredient	Adulterant	Type of Fraud	Publication Year	Reported Detection Method and Reference
Milk	Milk (powder)	Cyanuric acid	Replacement	2010	Decreased protein content when measured by Bradford or Ninhydrin methods (Field and Field 2010)
Milk	Milk (powder)	Dextrin	Replacement	2008	Isolation of dextrins and photometric determination (Wang and others 2008b)
Milk	Milk (powder)	Lactose	Replacement	2009	FTIR with chemometrics (Zhou and others 2009)
Milk	Milk (powder)	Maltodextrin	Replacement	2010	HPLC-MS for adulterant marker saccharides (Sanvido and others 2010)
Milk	Milk (powder)	Melamine	Replacement	2010	Decreased protein content when measured by Bradford or Ninhydrin methods (Field and Field 2010)
Milk	Milk (powder)	Melamine	Replacement	2010	Raman for adulterant (Cheng and others 2010)
Milk	Milk (powder)	Melamine	Replacement	2009	Raman for adulterant (Okazaki and others 2009)
Milk	Milk (powder)	Pea protein	Replacement	2002	NIR with chemometrics (Adele Maraboli 2002)
Milk	Milk (powder)	Raman	Replacement	2011	FT-Raman with chemometrics (Almeida and others 2011)
Milk	Milk (powder)	Soy protein	Replacement	2005	CE for casein to total protein and SDS-GE (Zhang and others 2005)
Milk	Milk (powder)	Soy protein	Replacement	2002	NIR with chemometrics (Adele Maraboli 2002)
Milk	Milk (powder)	Soy protein	Replacement	1999	CE for adulterant proteins (López-Tapia and others 1999)
Milk	Milk (powder)	Soy protein	Replacement	2007	HPLC-MS/MS on tryptic digest of isolated plant proteins (Luykx and others 2007b)
Milk	Milk (powder)	Starch	Replacement	2006	NIR with chemometrics (Borin and others 2006)
Milk	Milk (powder)	Sucrose	Replacement	2006	NIR with chemometrics (Borin and others 2006)
Milk	Milk (powder)	Wheat protein	Replacement	2002	NIR with chemometrics (Adele Maraboli 2002)
Milk	Milk (powder)	Whey	Replacement	2006	NIR with chemometrics (Borin and others 2006)
Milk	Milk (powder)	Whey	Replacement	2006	HPLC with fluorescence detection for cysteine (Ballin 2006)
Milk	Milk (powder)	Whey	Replacement	1985	GE on proteins (Basch and others 1985)
Milk	Milk (skim milk powder)	Pea protein	Replacement	2009	Non-targeted HPLC-ToF-MS with chemometrics (Cordewener and others 2009)
Milk	Milk (skim milk powder)	Soy protein	Replacement	2009	Non-targeted HPLC-ToF-MS with chemometrics (Cordewener and others 2009)
Milk	Soy milk	Milk (bovine)	Replacement	1998	SDS-PAGE for alpha-lactalbumin and beta-lactoglobulin (adulterant marker proteins) (Molina and others 1998)
Natural flavoring complexes	Almond oil*	Oil from non-authentic botanical origin	Replacement	2003	FTIR with chemometrics (Ozen and others 2003)
Natural flavoring complexes	Almond oil, bitter*	Synthetic benzaldehyde	Replacement	1992	NMR on benzaldehyde (Hagedorn 1992)
Natural flavoring complexes	Almond oil, bitter*	Synthetic or semi-synthetic benzaldehyde	Replacement	1997	SNIF-NMR (^{2}H/^{1}H) on four sites of isolated benzaldehyde (Remaud and others 1997a)
Natural flavoring complexes	Balm oil (Melissa ofjcinalis)	Citronella oil (Java type, Cymbopogon winterianus)	Replacement	1997	IRMS (^{13}C/^{12}C) (König and others 1997)

Table 1: Scholarly Reports on Food Ingredient Fraud and Analytical Methods for Detection (continued)

Ingredient Category	Ingredient	Adulterant	Type of Fraud	Publication Year	Reported Detection Method and Reference
Natural flavoring complexes	Balm oil (Melissa ofjcinalis)	Eucalyptus citriodora	Replacement	1997	Enantioselective GC for enantiomeric composition of citronellal (König and others 1997)
Natural flavoring complexes	Bergamot oil* (Citrus aurantium L. subsp. bevgamia (Risso et Poit.)	Non-authentic linalool and linalyl acetate	Replacement	1997	Enantioselective GC for enantiomeric composition of linalool and linalyl acetate (König and others 1997)
Natural flavoring complexes	Bois de rose essential oil*	Synthetic or semi-synthetic linalool	Replacement	1992	SNIF-NMR ($^2H/^1H$) on ten sites of isolated linalool and IRMS ($^{13}C/^{12}C$) combined with chemometrics (Hanneguelle and others 1992)
Natural flavoring complexes	Cassia oil*	Oil from non-authentic species	Replacement	2005	HPLC-PDA fingerprinting for five authentic marker compounds (He and others 2005)
Natural flavoring complexes	Cassia oil*	Synthetic benzaldehyde	Replacement	1992	^1H-NMR on benzaldehyde (Hagedorn 1992)
Natural flavoring complexes	Cinnamon oil*	Synthetic or semi-synthetic cinnamaldehyde	Replacement	1997	SNIF-NMR ($^2H/^1H$) on four sites of benzaldehyde (transformed from extracted cinnamaldehyde) (Remaud and others 1997a)
Natural flavoring complexes	Coriander oil* (Coriandrum sativum L.)	Synthetic or semi-synthetic linalool	Replacement	1992	SNIF-NMR ($^2H/^1H$) on 10 sites of isolated linalool and IRMS ($^{13}C/^{12}C$) combined with chemometrics (Hanneguelle and others 1992)
Natural flavoring complexes	Coriander oil* (Coriandrum sativum L.)	Non-authentic oils	Replacement	1995	Enantioselective GC as well as enantio-GC-IRMS ($^{13}C/^{12}C$) (Frank and others 1995)
Natural flavoring complexes	Essential oils (general)	Oil from non-authentic botanical/varietal origin	Replacement	2006	NIR with chemometrics (Juliani and others 2006)
Natural flavoring complexes	Grapefruit oil*	Non-authentic citrus oil	Replacement	2001	NIR with chemometrics (Steuer and others 2001)
Natural flavoring complexes	Ho-leaf oil	Synthetic or semi-synthetic linalool	Replacement	1992	SNIF-NMR ($^2H/^1H$) on 10 sites of isolated linalool and IRMS ($^{13}C/^{12}C$) combined with chemometrics (Hanneguelle and others 1992)
Natural flavoring complexes	Lemon oil*	Non-authentic citrus oil	Replacement	2001	NIR with chemometrics (Steuer and others 2001)
Natural flavoring complexes	Lime oil*	Non-authentic citrus oil	Replacement	2001	NIR with chemometrics (Steuer and others 2001)
Natural flavoring complexes	Mandarin oil*	Non-authentic citrus oil	Replacement	2001	NIR with chemometrics (Steuer and others 2001)
Natural flavoring complexes	Mandarin oil*	Non-authentic essential oil	Replacement	2010	GC-combustion-IRMS ($^{13}C/^{12}C$) j5095 (Schipilliti and others 2010)
Natural flavoring complexes	May Chang berry oil (Litsea cubeba)	Industrial alcohol	Replacement	1994	GC-MS fingerprinting and physicochemical methods (Shen and others 1994)
Natural flavoring complexes	Mustard oil*	Synthetic allyl isothiocyanate	Replacement	1997	SNIF-NMR ($^2H/^1H$) at multiple allyl isothiocyanate sites (Remaud and others 1997c)
Natural flavoring complexes	Orange oil*	Non-authentic citrus oil	Replacement	2001	NIR with chemometrics (Steuer and others 2001)
Natural flavoring complexes	Orange oil, bitter* (Citrus aurantium L.)	Grapefruit oil	Replacement	1996	HPLC fingerprinting of coumarins, psoralens, and polymethoxyflavones for adulterant compounds (Dugo and others 1996)
Natural flavoring complexes	Orange oil, bitter* (Citrus aurantium L.)	Lemon oil	Replacement	1996	HPLC fingerprinting of coumarins, psoralens, and polymethoxyflavones for adulterant compounds (Dugo and others 1996)

Table 1: Scholarly Reports on Food Ingredient Fraud and Analytical Methods for Detection (continued)

Ingredient Category	Ingredient	Adulterant	Type of Fraud	Publication Year	Reported Detection Method and Reference
Natural flavoring complexes	Orange oil, bitter* (Citrus aurantium L.)	Lime oil	Replacement	1996	HPLC fingerprinting of coumarins, psoralens, and polymethoxyflavones for adulterant compounds (Dugo and others 1996)
Natural flavoring complexes	Orange oil, bitter* (Citrus aurantium L.)	Sweet orange oil	Replacement	1996	HPLC fingerprinting of coumarins, psoralens, and polymethoxyflavones for authentic compounds (Dugo and others 1996)
Natural flavoring complexes	Peppermint oil* (Mentha piperita)	Cornmint oil (Mentha antensis)	Replacement	1997	Enantioselective GC for fingerprinting of chiral compounds (König and others 1997)
Natural flavoring complexes	Rose oil*	beta-Phenylethanol	Addition	1997	Enantioselective GC for enantiomeric composition of citronellol heptakis and beta-phenylethanol (König and others 1997)
Natural flavoring complexes	Vanilla extract	Ethyl maltol	Replacement	2007	CE-ED microchip for adulterant (Ávila and others 2007)
Natural flavoring complexes	Vanilla extract	Ethyl vanillin	Replacement	2007	CE-ED microchip for adulterant (Ávila and others 2007)
Natural flavoring complexes	Vanilla extract	Maltol	Replacement	2007	CE-ED microchip for adulterant (Ávila and others 2007)
Natural flavoring complexes	Vanilla extract	Synthetic or semi-synthetic or p-hydroxybenzaldehyde	Replacement	1997	SNIF-NMR (^{2}H/^{1}H) on isolated vanillin or p-hydroxybenzaldehyde (Remaud and others 1997b)
Natural flavoring complexes	Vanilla extract	Synthetic or semi-synthetic or p-hydroxybenzaldehyde	Replacement	1997	SNIF-NMR (^{2}H/^{1}H) and IRMS (^{13}C/^{12}C) on isolated authentic constituents (vanillin, p-hydroxybenzaldehyde, etc.) (Kaunzinger and others 1997)
Natural flavoring complexes	Vanilla extract	Synthetic or semi-synthetic or p-hydroxybenzaldehyde	Replacement	2004	SNIF-NMR (^{2}H/^{1}H) and IRMS (^{13}C/^{12}C) on isolated authentic constituents (vanillin, p-hydroxybenzaldehyde, etc.) (John and Jamin 2004)
Natural flavoring complexes	Vanilla extract	Synthetic or semi-synthetic vanillin	Replacement	1997	SNIF-NMR (^{2}H/^{1}H) on isolated vanillin or p-hydroxybenzaldehyde (Remaud and others 1997b)
Natural flavoring complexes	Vanilla extract	Synthetic or semi-synthetic vanillin	Replacement	1997	SNIF-NMR (^{2}H/^{1}H) and IRMS (^{13}C/^{12}C) on isolated authentic constituents (vanillin, p-hydroxybenzaldehyde, etc.) (Kaunzinger and others 1997)
Natural flavoring complexes	Vanilla extract	Synthetic or semi-synthetic vanillin	Replacement	2002	IRMS (^{13}C/^{12}C) and (^{18}O/^{16}O) on guaiacol converted from isolated vanillin (Bensaid and others 2002)
Natural flavoring complexes	Vanilla extract	Synthetic or semi-synthetic vanillin	Replacement	2004	SNIF-NMR (^{2}H/^{1}H) and IRMS (^{13}C/^{12}C) on isolated authentic constituents (vanillin, p-hydroxybenzaldehyde, etc.) (John and Jamin 2004)
Natural flavoring complexes	Vanilla extract	Synthetic or semi-synthetic vanillin	Replacement	2004	SNIF-NMR (^{13}C/^{12}C) on isolated vanillin (Tenailleau and others 2004)
Natural flavoring complexes	Vanilla extract	Synthetic or semi-synthetic vanillin	Replacement	1993	SNIF-NMR (^{13}C/^{12}C) on isolated vanillin (Martin and others 1993)
Natural flavoring complexes	Vanilla extract	Vanillic alcohol	Replacement	2007	CE-ED microchip for adulterant (Ávila and others 2007)
Natural flavoring complexes	Vanilla extract	Vanillin	Replacement	2007	CE-ED microchip for adulterant (Ávila and others 2007)
Natural flavoring complexes	Vanilla extract (natural)	Synthetic or semi-synthetic vanillin	Replacement	1994	IRMS (^{13}C/^{12}C) on isolated vanillin (Lamprecht and others 1994)
Natural flavoring complexes	Vanilla extract (natural)	Synthetic or semi-synthetic vanillin	Replacement	1994	HPLC fingerprinting for authentic marker components (Lamprecht and others 1994)

Table 1: Scholarly Reports on Food Ingredient Fraud and Analytical Methods for Detection (continued)

Ingredient Category	Ingredient	Adulterant	Type of Fraud	Publication Year	Reported Detection Method and Reference
Oils	Amazonian oils and fats (e.g., brazil nut oil)	Oil from non-authentic botanical origin	Replacement	2009	MALDI-MS for triglycerides with chemometrics (Saraiva and others 2009)
Oils	Apricot kernel oil	Oil from non-authentic botanical origin	Replacement	2003	FTIR with chemometrics (Ozen and others 2003)
Oils	Argan oil	Oil from non-authentic botanical origin	Replacement	2010	ICP-OES trace elements fingerprinting with chemometrics (Gonzálvez and others 2010)
Oils	Argan oil	Oil from non-authentic botanical origin	Replacement	2007	GC-FID for campesterol (adulterant marker) (Hilali and others 2007)
Oils	Black currant oil	Oil from non-authentic botanical origin	Replacement	2003	FTIR with chemometrics (Ozen and others 2003)
Oils	Borage oil	Oil from non-authentic botanical origin	Replacement	2003	FTIR with chemometrics (Ozen and others 2003)
Oils	Camelina sativa oil	Oil from non-authentic botanical origin	Replacement	2009	GC-combustion-IRMS ($^{13}C/^{12}C$) on authentic fatty acids (Hrastar and others 2009)
Oils	Camellia seed oil	Corn oil	Replacement	2010	GC-IRMS on individual fatty acids, combustion-IRMS on oils, and GC-MS for fatty acids fingerprinting (Guo and others 2010a)
Oils	Camellia seed oil	Maize oil	Replacement	2006	Electronic nose with chemometrics (Hai and Wang 2006)
Oils	Camellia seed oil	Soybean oil	Replacement	2006	Attenuated total reflectance MIR or fiber optic diffuse reflectance NIR with chemometrics (Wang and others 2006)
Oils	Camellia seed oil	Soybean oil	Replacement	2010	GC-IRMS on individual fatty acids, combustion-IRMS on oils, and GC-MS for fatty acids fingerprinting (Guo and others 2010a)
Oils	Canola oil*	Animal fat (lard, beef tallow, or chicken fat)	Replacement	2005	HPLC with triacylglycerol fingerprinting with chemometrics (Marikkar and others 2005a)
Oils	Canola oil*	Animal fat (lard, beef tallow, or chicken fat)	Replacement	2005	GC-FID fatty acid fingerprinting chemometrics analysis (Marikkar and others 2005b)
Oils	Canola oil*	Beef tallow	Replacement	2002	DSC for cooling and heating thermograms (Marikkar and others 2002a)
Oils	Canola oil*	Chicken fat	Replacement	2002	DSC for cooling and heating thermograms (Marikkar and others 2002a)
Oils	Canola oil*	Lard	Replacement	2002	DSC for cooling and heating thermograms (Marikkar and others 2002a)
Oils	Cocoa butter	Cocoa butter replacer	Replacement	2004	GC-FID for triglycerols analysis (Buchgraber and others 2004)
Oils	Coconut oil (virgin)	Palm kernel oil	Replacement	2010	Electronic nose with chemometrics (Marina and others 2010)
Oils	Coconut oil (virgin)	Palm oil	Replacement	2009	FTIR with chemometrics (Rohman and Che Man 2009b)
Oils	Coconut oil*	Caster oil	Replacement	1993	^{13}C-NMR for C9, C10, C11, C12, and C13 carbons of ricinoleic acid (adulterant markers) (Husain and others 1993)
Oils	Cod liver oil	Beef fat	Replacement	2009	FTIR with chemometrics (Rohman and Che Man 2009a)
Oils	Cod liver oil	Chicken fat	Replacement	2009	FTIR with chemometrics (Rohman and Che Man, 2009a)
Oils	Cod liver oil	Lard	Replacement	2009	FTIR with chemometrics (Rohman and Che Man, 2009a)
Oils	Cod liver oil	Mutton fat	Replacement	2009	FTIR with chemometrics (Rohman and Che Man, 2009a)

Table 1: Scholarly Reports on Food Ingredient Fraud and Analytical Methods for Detection (continued)

Ingredient Category	Ingredient	Adulterant	Type of Fraud	Publication Year	Reported Detection Method and Reference
Oils	Cod liver oil	Oil from non-authentic origin	Replacement	2003	FTIR with chemometrics (Ozen and others 2003)
Oils	Cooking oil	Argemone oil (*Argemone Mexicana*)	Replacement	2008	NR (Babu and others 2008)
Oils	Corn germ oil	Sunflower oil	Replacement	2009	FTIR (Alexa and others 2009)
Oils	Corn oil*	Canola oil	Replacement	2010	IRMS ($^{13}C/^{12}C$) (Primrose and others 2010)
Oils	Corn oil*	Non-authentic oil	Replacement	2003	IRMS ($^{13}C/^{12}C$) on major and minor constituents combined with chemometrics (Mottram and others 2003)
Oils	Edible oil	Non-authentic oils	Replacement	1994	LC-GC-FID for sterol fraction constituents (Grob and others 1994d)
Oils	Edible oil	Non-authentic oils	Replacement	1994	NR (Grob and others 1994a)
Oils	Edible oil	Non-authentic oils	Replacement	1994	LC-GC-FID for olefinic degradation products of sterols (adulterant makers) (Grob and others 1994c)
Oils	Edible oil (cold-pressed, extra virgin, or non-refined)	Refined edible oil	Replacement	1995	HPLC for stigmastadiene (Biedermann and others 1995a)
Oils	Evening primrose oil	Oil from non-authentic botanical origin	Replacement	2003	FTIR with chemometrics (Ozen and others 2003)
Oils	Flax seed oil	Corn oil	Replacement	2010	GC-IRMS on individual fatty acids, combustion-IRMS on oils, and GC-MS for fatty acids fingerprinting (Guo and others 2010a)
Oils	Flax seed oil	Oil from non-authentic botanical origin	Replacement	2003	FTIR with chemometrics (Ozen and others 2003)
Oils	Flax seed oil	Soybean oil	Replacement	2010	GC-IRMS on individual fatty acids, combustion-IRMS on oils, and GC-MS for fatty acids fingerprinting (Guo and others 2010a)
Oils	Grapeseed oil	Oil from non-authentic botanical origin	Replacement	2006	Multi-authentic constituent analysis (Crews and others 2006b)
Oils	Grapeseed oil	Oil from non-authentic botanical origin	Replacement	2003	FTIR with chemometrics (Ozen and others 2003)
Oils	Groundnut oil	Caster oil	Replacement	1993	^{13}C-NMR for C9, C10, C11, C12, and C13 carbons of ricinoleic acid (adulterant markers) (Husain and others 1993)
Oils	Hazelnut oil	Oil from non-authentic botanical origin	Replacement	2002	FTIR with chemometrics (Ozen and Mauer 2002)
Oils	Hazelnut oil	Oil from non-authentic botanical origin	Replacement	2003	FTIR with chemometrics (Ozen and others 2003)
Oils	Hempseed oil	Oil from non-authentic botanical origin	Replacement	2003	FTIR with chemometrics (Ozen and others, 2003)
Oils	Macadamia nut oil	Oil from non-authentic botanical origin	Replacement	2003	FTIR with chemometrics Ozen and others, 2003)
Oils	Mustard oil	Caster oil	Replacement	1993	^{13}C-NMR for C9, C10, C11, C12, and C13 carbons of ricinoleic acid (adulterant markers) (Husain and others 1993)
Oils	Mustard oil (*Brassica compestris*)	Argemone oil (*Argemone mexicana*)	Replacement	2005	HP-TLC for sanguinarine (adulterant marker) (Ghosh and others 2005b)
Oils	Mustard oil (*Brassica compestris*)	Argemone oil (*Argemone mexicana*)	Replacement	2005	HP-TLC for sanguinarine (adulterant marker) (Ghosh and others 2005b)
Oils	Mustard oil (*Brassica compestris*)	Argemone oil (*Argemone mexicana*)	Replacement	1999	HPLC for sanguinarine (adulterant marker) (Husain and others 1999)

Table 1: Scholarly Reports on Food Ingredient Fraud and Analytical Methods for Detection (continued)

Ingredient Category	Ingredient	Adulterant	Type of Fraud	Publication Year	Reported Detection Method and Reference
Oils	Olive oil	Canola oil	Replacement	1996	NIR with chemometrics (Wesley and others 1996)
Oils	Olive oil	Canola oil	Replacement	2010	Dielectric spectroscopy with chemometrics (Lizhi and others 2010)
Oils	Olive oil	Chlorophylls (copper complexes of)	Addition to mask poor quality	2010	HPLC-PDA for adulterant (Roca and others 2010)
Oils	Olive oil	Corn oil	Replacement	1995	NIR with chemometrics (Wesley and others 1995)
Oils	Olive oil	Corn oil	Replacement	1993	Bellier test (Amr and Abu-Al-Rub 1993)
Oils	Olive oil	Corn oil	Replacement	2001	GC-FID for trilinolein and tripalmitin (adulterant marker triglycerides) (Andrikopoulos and others 2001)
Oils	Olive oil	Corn oil	Replacement	2010	GC for campesterol and stigmasterol (Al-Ismail and others 2010)
Oils	Olive oil	Corn oil	Replacement	2004	NIR with chemometrics (Christy and others 2004)
Oils	Olive oil	Corn oil	Replacement	2010	Silver ion TLC for triacylglycerols (Marekov and others 2010)
Oils	Olive oil	Corn oil	Replacement	2010	Dielectric spectroscopy with chemometrics (Lizhi and others 2010)
Oils	Olive oil	Cottonseed oil	Replacement	1993	Bellier test (Amr and Abu-Al-Rub 1993)
Oils	Olive oil	Cottonseed oil	Replacement	2001	GC-FID for trilinolein and tripalmitin (adulterant marker triglycerides) (Andrikopoulos and others 2001)
Oils	Olive oil	Cottonseed oil	Replacement	2010	Silver ion TLC for triacylglycerols (Marekov and others 2010)
Oils	Olive oil	Grapeseed oil	Replacement	1995	HPLC with ampoheric detection for tocotrienols (adulterant markers) (Dionisi and others 1995)
Oils	Olive oil	Grapeseed oil (desterolilzed)	Replacement	1994	LC-GC-FID for degradation products of sitosterol and campesterol (Grob and others 1994c)
Oils	Olive oil	Hazelnut oil	Replacement	1998	HPLC coupled with GC for the enantiomeric composition determination of filbertone (adulterant marker) (Ruiz del Castillo and others 1998)
Oils	Olive oil	Hazelnut oil	Replacement	1998	HPLC coupled with GC for detection of filbertone (adulterant marker) (Blanch and others 1998)
Oils	Olive oil	Hazelnut oil	Replacement	2001	HPLC-PDA fingerprinting on isolated polar fraction (Gordon and others 2001)
Oils	Olive oil	Hazelnut oil	Replacement	2010	SDS-PAGE for adulterant protein markers (Arlorio and others 2010)
Oils	Olive oil	Hazelnut oil	Replacement	2007	HPLC for triglycerides analysis with chemometrics (Garcia-Gonzalez and others 2007)
Oils	Olive oil	Hazelnut oil	Replacement	2005	FT-Raman and FT-MIR on oil and unsaponifiable fraction, with chemometrics (Baeten and others 2005)
Oils	Olive oil	Hazelnut oil	Replacement	2010	^{1}H-NMR for fatty acids and acid value and ^{31}P-NMR for minor compounds including phenolic compounds, diacylglycerols, sterols, and free fatty acids, all combined with chemometrics (Agiomyrgianaki and others 2010)
Oils	Olive oil	Hazelnut oil	Replacement	1999	GC-FID for R- and S-enantiomers filbertone (adulterant marker) (Caja and others 1999)

Table 1: Scholarly Reports on Food Ingredient Fraud and Analytical Methods for Detection (continued)

Ingredient Category	Ingredient	Adulterant	Type of Fraud	Publication Year	Reported Detection Method and Reference
Oils	Olive oil	Hazelnut oil	Replacement	2009	DART-ToF-MS fingerprinting of triacylglycerols and/or polar compounds with chemometrics (Vaclavik and others 2009)
Oils	Olive oil	Hazelnut oil	Replacement	2006	GC analysis for campesterol and delta-7-stigmastenol (adulterant markers) in the apolar fraction (Mariani and others 2006)
Oils	Olive oil	Hazelnut oil	Replacement	2006	SPME–multi-dimensional-GC-FID for detection of filbertone (adulterant marker) (Flores and others 2006a)
Oils	Olive oil	Hazelnut oil	Replacement	2005	Headspace coupled directly to MS (Peña and others 2005)
Oils	Olive oil	Hazelnut oil	Replacement	2006	HPLC coupled with GC for detection of filbertone (adulterant marker) (Flores and others 2006b)
Oils	Olive oil	Hazelnut oil	Replacement	2008	SPME-GC-FID or SPME-GC-MS/MS for volatile compounds fingerprinting with chemometrics (Mildner-Szkudlarz and Jelen 2008)
Oils	Olive oil	Hazelnut oil	Replacement	2009	NMR with chemometrics (Mannina and others 2009)
Oils	Olive oil	Hazelnut oil	Replacement	2004	NIR with chemometrics (Christy and others 2004)
Oils	Olive oil	Hazelnut oil	Replacement	2000	HPLC-MS for triacylglycerol, tocopherol and sterols fingerprinting using chemometrics (Parcerisa and others 2000)
Oils	Olive oil	Hazelnut oil	Replacement	2004	Non-targeted H-NMR and C-NMR with chemometrics (Garcia-Gonzalez and others 2004)
Oils	Olive oil	Hazelnut oil	Replacement	2004	Spectrofluorimetric analysis with multivariate analysis (Sayago and others 2004)
Oils	Olive oil	Hazelnut oil	Replacement	2000	GC-FID for filbertone (Blanch and others 2000)
Oils	Olive oil	Hazelnut oil	Replacement	1999	Chiral-GC enantiomeric analysis of filbertone (Blanch and others 1999)
Oils	Olive oil	Lampante or refined olive oil	Replacement	2005	GC-MS/MS for methyl 9(E),11(E)-octadecadienoate (adulterant marker) (Saba and others 2005)
Oils	Olive oil	Linseed oil	Replacement	1993	Bellier test (Amr and Abu-Al-Rub 1993)
Oils	Olive oil	Oil from non-authentic botanical origin	Replacement	1995	LC-GC-FID for delta-7- and delta-8(14)-stigmastenol (adulterant marker) (Biedermann and others 1995b)
Oils	Olive oil	Oil from non-authentic botanical origin	Replacement	2004	GC-FID for fatty acid analysis and HPLC for triglycerides analysis (Christopoulou and others 2004)
Oils	Olive oil	Oil from non-authentic botanical origin	Replacement	2003	GC-FID analysis of total fatty acids and their regiospecific distribution in positions 1 and 3 in triacylglycerols, combined with chemometrics (Dourtoglou and others 2003)
Oils	Olive oil	Oil from non-authentic botanical origin	Replacement	1998	GC-combustion-IRMS ($^{13}C/^{12}C$) of fatty acids (Spangenberg and others 1998)
Oils	Olive oil	Oil from non-authentic botanical origin	Replacement	2003	H-NMR and P-NMR with chemometrics (Vigli and others 2003)
Oils	Olive oil	Oil from non-authentic botanical origin	Replacement	2001	GC-combustion-IRMS ($^{13}C/^{12}C$) on FAMEs (Spangenberg and Ogrinc 2001)

Table 1: Scholarly Reports on Food Ingredient Fraud and Analytical Methods for Detection *(continued)*

Ingredient Category	Ingredient	Adulterant	Type of Fraud	Publication Year	Reported Detection Method and Reference
Oils	Olive oil	Oil from non-authentic botanical origin	Replacement	2009	Raman intensity ratio for specific bands combined with chemometrics (Zou and others 2009)
Oils	Olive oil	Oil from non-authentic botanical origin	Replacement	1993	Review of methods (Grob and Romann 1993)
Oils	Olive oil	Oil from non-authentic botanical origin	Replacement	2007	Review of methods combined with chemometrics: HPLC-MS, GC-combustion-IRMS, distortionless enhanced by polarization transfer, NMR, FTIR, FT-Raman, and NIR (Arvanitoyannis and Vlachos 2007)
Oils	Olive oil	Oil from non-authentic botanical origin	Replacement	2003	FTIR with chemometrics (Ozen and others 2003)
Oils	Olive oil	Oil from non-authentic botanical origin rich in linoleic acid	Replacement	1986	HPLC for triglycerides fingerprinting (Kapoulas and Andrikopoulos 1986)
Oils	Olive oil	Oil from non-authentic botanical origin rich in linoleic acid	Replacement	1995	HPLC for triacylglycerols fingerprinting (El-Hamdy and El-Fizga 1995)
Oils	Olive oil	Olive oil from non-authentic botanical origin	Replacement	1999	^{13}C-NMR with chemometrics (Vlahov and others 1999)
Oils	Olive oil	Olive pomace oil	Replacement	1997	High-resolution GC and IRMS (^{13}C/^{12}C) of aliphatic alcoholic fraction (Angerosa and others 1997)
Oils	Olive oil	Olive pomace oil	Replacement	1986	Wax esters (adulterant markers) by GC (Mariani and Fedeli 1986)
Oils	Olive oil	Olive pomace oil	Replacement	2001	FT-Raman with chemometrics (Yang and Irudayaraj 2001)
Oils	Olive oil	Olive pomace oil	Replacement	2010	UV-Vis spectrometry with chemometrics (Torrecilla and others 2010)
Oils	Olive oil	Olive pomace oil	Replacement	1993	Bellier test (Amr and Abu-Al-Rub 1993)
Oils	Olive oil	Olive pomace oil	Replacement	2002	Headspace coupled directly to MS (Marcos Lorenzo and others 2002)
Oils	Olive oil	Palm oil	Replacement	1995	HPLC with ampopheric detection for tocotrienols (adulterant markers) (Dionisi and others 1995)
Oils	Olive oil	Palm oil	Replacement	1993	Bellier test (Amr and Abu-Al-Rub 1993)
Oils	Olive oil	Palm oil	Replacement	2001	GC-FID for trilinolein and tripalmitin (adulterant marker triglycerides) (Andrikopoulos and others 2001)
Oils	Olive oil	Palm oil (desterolilzed)	Replacement	1994	LC-GC-FID for degradation products of sitosterol and campesterol (Grob and others 1994c)
Oils	Olive oil	Perilla oil	Replacement	2010	Dielectric spectroscopy with chemometrics (Lizhi and others 2010)
Oils	Olive oil	Sesame oil	Replacement	1993	Bellier test (Amr and Abu-Al-Rub 1993)
Oils	Olive oil	Sesame oil	Replacement	2010	Dielectric spectroscopy with chemometrics (Lizhi and others 2010)
Oils	Olive oil	Soy oil	Replacement	2010	Dielectric spectroscopy with chemometrics (Lizhi and others 2010)
Oils	Olive oil	Soybean oil	Replacement	1996	NIR with chemometrics (Wesley and others 1996)
Oils	Olive oil	Soybean oil	Replacement	1993	Bellier test (Amr and Abu-Al-Rub 1993)
Oils	Olive oil	Soybean oil	Replacement	2001	GC-FID for trilinolein and tripalmitin (adulterant marker triglycerides) (Andrikopoulos and others 2001)
Oils	Olive oil	Soybean oil	Replacement	1993	GC-FID for trilinolein (adulterant marker) (Antoniosi Filho and others 1993)

Table 1: Scholarly Reports on Food Ingredient Fraud and Analytical Methods for Detection (continued)

Ingredient Category	Ingredient	Adulterant	Type of Fraud	Publication Year	Reported Detection Method and Reference
Oils	Olive oil	Soybean oil	Replacement	2004	NIR with chemometrics (Christy and others 2004)
Oils	Olive oil	Soybean oil	Replacement	2010	Silver ion TLC for triacylglycerols (Marekov and others 2010)
Oils	Olive oil	Soybean oil	Replacement	2010	HPLC-APCI-MS-MS for triacylglycerols fingerprinting combined with chemometrics (Fasciotti and Pereira Netto 2010)
Oils	Olive oil	Soybean oil (desterolilzed)	Replacement	1994	LC-GC-FID for degradation products of sitosterol and campesterol (Grob and others 1994c)
Oils	Olive oil	Sunflower oil	Replacement	2000	FT-Raman with chemometrics (Davies and others 2000)
Oils	Olive oil	Sunflower oil	Replacement	1996	NIR with chemometrics (Wesley and others 1996)
Oils	Olive oil	Sunflower oil	Replacement	1995	NIR with chemometrics (Wesley and others 1995)
Oils	Olive oil	Sunflower oil	Replacement	2002	FTIR with chemometrics (Tay and others 2002)
Oils	Olive oil	Sunflower oil	Replacement	1993	Bellier test (Amr and Abu-Al-Rub 1993)
Oils	Olive oil	Sunflower oil	Replacement	2010	Microwave dielectric spectroscopy using Cole–Cole dielectric parameters (Cataldo and others 2010)
Oils	Olive oil	Sunflower oil	Replacement	2001	GC-FID for trilinolein and tripalmitin (adulterant marker triglycerides) (Andrikopoulos and others 2001)
Oils	Olive oil	Sunflower oil	Replacement	2002	Headspace coupled directly to MS (Marcos Lorenzo and others 2002)
Oils	Olive oil	Sunflower oil	Replacement	2004	NIR with chemometrics (Christy and others 2004)
Oils	Olive oil	Sunflower oil	Replacement	2010	Silver ion TLC for triacylglycerols (Marekov and others 2010)
Oils	Olive oil	Sunflower oil	Replacement	2009	FTIR (Alexa and others 2009)
Oils	Olive oil	Sunflower oil (desteroled)	Replacement	1995	GC for delta-8(14) and delta-14 sterols (Mariani and others 1995)
Oils	Olive oil	Sunflower oil (desterolilzed)	Replacement	1994	LC-GC-FID for degradation products of sitosterol and campesterol (Grob and others 1994c)
Oils	Olive oil	Walnut oil	Replacement	2004	NIR with chemometrics (Christy and others 2004)
Oils	Olive oil (extra virgin)	Olive oil from non-authentic botanical origin	Replacement	2002	Chemical analysis with chemometrics (Bucci and others 2002)
Oils	Olive oil (extra virgin)	Canola oil	Replacement	2010	FTIR with chemometrics (Maggio and others 2010)
Oils	Olive oil (extra virgin)	Coconut oil	Replacement	2007	GC-MS on lipids with chemometrics (Capote and others 2007)
Oils	Olive oil (extra virgin)	Corn oil	Replacement	2002	Chemiluminescence emission (Papadopoulos and others 2002)
Oils	Olive oil (extra virgin)	Corn oil	Replacement	2010	FTIR with chemometrics (Lerma-García and others 2010)
Oils	Olive oil (extra virgin)	Corn oil	Replacement	2009	MIR with chemometrics (Gurdeniz and Ozen 2009)
Oils	Olive oil (extra virgin)	Corn oil	Replacement	2007	GC-MS on lipids with chemometrics (Capote and others 2007)
Oils	Olive oil (extra virgin)	Cottonseed oil	Replacement	2009	MIR with chemometrics (Gurdeniz and Ozen 2009)

Table 1: Scholarly Reports on Food Ingredient Fraud and Analytical Methods for Detection (continued)

Ingredient Category	Ingredient	Adulterant	Type of Fraud	Publication Year	Reported Detection Method and Reference
Oils	Olive oil (extra virgin)	Extra virgin olive oil from non-authentic botanical origin or geographic region	Replacement	1997	C-NMR with chemometrics (Shaw and others 1997)
Oils	Olive oil (extra virgin)	Grapeseed oil	Replacement	2010	Review: HPLC for tocotrienols (Frankel 2010)
Oils	Olive oil (extra virgin)	Hazelnut oil	Replacement	2010	NMR with chemometrics (Smejkalová and Piccolo 2010)
Oils	Olive oil (extra virgin)	Hazelnut oil	Replacement	2010	FTIR with chemometrics (Lerma-García and others 2010)
Oils	Olive oil (extra virgin)	Hazelnut oil	Replacement	2010	MALDI-ToF-MS analysis of isolated polar compounds (Calvano and others 2010)
Oils	Olive oil (extra virgin)	Hazelnut oil	Replacement	2008	DSC (Chiavaro and others 2008)
Oils	Olive oil (extra virgin)	Hazelnut oil	Replacement	2009	^{13}C-NMR (Vlahov 2009)
Oils	Olive oil (extra virgin)	Hazelnut oil	Replacement	2002	FTIR with chemometrics (Ozen and Mauer 2002)
Oils	Olive oil (extra virgin)	Hazelnut oil	Replacement	2010	FTIR with chemometrics (Maggio and others 2010)
Oils	Olive oil (extra virgin)	Hazelnut oil	Replacement	2010	Review: HPLC-MS for tocopherol, sterols, and fingerprinting of triacylglycerols, all with chemometrics (Frankel 2010)
Oils	Olive oil (extra virgin)	Hazelnut oil	Replacement	2010	Review: SPE-HPLC on polar fraction (Frankel 2010)
Oils	Olive oil (extra virgin)	Hazelnut oil	Replacement	2010	Review: GC-MS for sterols (Frankel 2010)
Oils	Olive oil (extra virgin)	Hazelnut oil	Replacement	2010	Review: GC-MS for filbertone (Frankel 2010)
Oils	Olive oil (extra virgin)	Hazelnut oil	Replacement	2010	Review: GC-MS for filbertone (Frankel 2010)
Oils	Olive oil (extra virgin)	High linoleic/oleic sunflower oil	Replacement	2010	FTIR with chemometrics (Maggio and others 2010)
Oils	Olive oil (extra virgin)	Lampante or refined olive oil	Replacement	2005	P-NMR and chemometrics (Fragaki and others 2005)
Oils	Olive oil (extra virgin)	Non-authentic cultivar	Replacement	2010	Review: GC for sterols and fingerprinting of triacylglycerols with chemometrics (Frankel 2010)
Oils	Olive oil (extra virgin)	Non-authentic oils	Replacement	2010	Review: FTIR with chemometrics (Frankel 2010)
Oils	Olive oil (extra virgin)	Non-authentic oils	Replacement	1994	NR (Grob and others 1994b)
Oils	Olive oil (extra virgin)	Non-authentic oils	Replacement	2010	Review: ^{1}H-NMR for unsaturated and acyl groups (Frankel 2010)
Oils	Olive oil (extra virgin)	Non-authentic oils	Replacement	2010	Review: HPLC-MS for sterols and fingerprinting of triacylglycerols and diacylglycerols, all combined with chemometrics (Frankel 2010)
Oils	Olive oil (extra virgin)	Non-authentic oils	Replacement	2010	Review: HPLC-MS on polar phenolics and fatty acids with chemometrics (Frankel 2010)
Oils	Olive oil (extra virgin)	Non-authentic oils	Replacement	2010	Review: GC-MS for FAMEs with chemometrics (Frankel 2010)
Oils	Olive oil (extra virgin)	Non-authentic oils	Replacement	2010	Review: CE for tocoppherols and tocotrienols with chemometrics (Frankel 2010)
Oils	Olive oil (extra virgin)	Non-authentic oils	Replacement	2010	Review: HPLC-MS fingerprinting of triacylglycerols with chemometrics (Frankel 2010)
Oils	Olive oil (extra virgin)	Non-authentic oils	Replacement	2010	Review: FTIR with chemometrics (Frankel 2010)
Oils	Olive oil (extra virgin)	Non-authentic oils	Replacement	2010	Review: NMR for triacylglycerols with chemometrics (Frankel 2010)

Table 1: Scholarly Reports on Food Ingredient Fraud and Analytical Methods for Detection (continued)

Ingredient Category	Ingredient	Adulterant	Type of Fraud	Publication Year	Reported Detection Method and Reference
Oils	Olive oil (extra virgin)	Non-authentic olive oils	Replacement	2010	Review: HPLC-MS with chemometrics (Frankel 2010)
Oils	Olive oil (extra virgin)	Olive oil	Replacement	2009	Synchronous fluorescence spectroscopy (Dankowska and Malecka 2009)
Oils	Olive oil (extra virgin)	Olive oil from non-authentic geographic origin	Replacement	2010	IRMS ($^{13}C/^{12}C$), ($^{2}H/^{1}H$), ($^{18}O/^{16}O$), and ICP-MS for trace minerals (Camin and others 2010)
Oils	Olive oil (extra virgin)	Olive oil from non-authentic geographic origin	Replacement	2008	NIR with chemometrics (Woodcock and others 2008)
Oils	Olive oil (extra virgin)	Olive oil from non-authentic geographic origin	Replacement	2006	Electronic nose with chemometrics (Cosio and others 2006)
Oils	Olive oil (extra virgin)	Olive oil from non-authentic geographic origin	Replacement	2010	Review: ^{1}H-NMR and ^{31}P-NMR with chemometrics (Frankel 2010)
Oils	Olive oil (extra virgin)	Olive oil or olive pomace oil	Replacement	2009	DART-ToF-MS fingerprinting of triacylglycerols and/or polar compounds with chemometrics (Vaclavik and others 2009)
Oils	Olive oil (extra virgin)	Olive pomace oil	Replacement	2010	FTIR with chemometrics (Maggio and others 2010)
Oils	Olive oil (extra virgin)	Olive pomace oil	Replacement	2005	Excitation–emission fluorescence spectroscopy with chemometrics (Guimet and others 2005)
Oils	Olive oil (extra virgin)	Olive pomace oil	Replacement	2010	Review: ^{13}C NMR on polar fraction with chemometrics (Frankel 2010)
Oils	Olive oil (extra virgin)	Palm oil	Replacement	2010	Review: HPLC for tocopherols (Frankel 2010)
Oils	Olive oil (extra virgin)	Peanut oil	Replacement	2010	NMR with chemometrics (Smejkalová and Piccolo 2010)
Oils	Olive oil (extra virgin)	Peanut oil	Replacement	2007	GC-MS on lipids with chemometrics (Capote and others 2007)
Oils	Olive oil (extra virgin)	Rapeseed oil	Replacement	2009	MIR with chemometrics (Gurdeniz and Ozen 2009)
Oils	Olive oil (extra virgin)	Seed oils	Replacement	2010	Review: ^{13}C-NMR for unsaturated fatty acids with chemometrics (Frankel 2010)
Oils	Olive oil (extra virgin)	Soybean oil	Replacement	2010	NMR with chemometrics (Smejkalová and Piccolo 2010)
Oils	Olive oil (extra virgin)	Soybean oil	Replacement	2010	FTIR with chemometrics (Lerma-García and others 2010)
Oils	Olive oil (extra virgin)	Sunflower oil	Replacement	2002	Chemiluminescence emission (Papadopoulos and others 2002)
Oils	Olive oil (extra virgin)	Sunflower oil	Replacement	2001	IR with chemometrics (Küpper and others 2001)
Oils	Olive oil (extra virgin)	Sunflower oil	Replacement	2002	UV-Visible and NIR with chemometrics (Downey and others 2002)
Oils	Olive oil (extra virgin)	Sunflower oil	Replacement	2010	NMR with chemometrics (Smejkalová and Piccolo 2010)
Oils	Olive oil (extra virgin)	Sunflower oil	Replacement	2010	FTIR with chemometrics (Lerma-García and others 2010)
Oils	Olive oil (extra virgin)	Sunflower oil	Replacement	2009	MIR with chemometrics (Gurdeniz and Ozen 2009)
Oils	Olive oil (extra virgin)	Sunflower oil	Replacement	2007	GC-MS on lipids combined with (Capote and others 2007)
Oils	Olive oil (extra virgin)	Sunflower oil	Replacement	2005	FT-Raman with chemometrics (Heise and others 2005)

Table 1: Scholarly Reports on Food Ingredient Fraud and Analytical Methods for Detection (continued)

Ingredient Category	Ingredient	Adulterant	Type of Fraud	Publication Year	Reported Detection Method and Reference
Oils	Olive oil (extra virgin)	Sunflower oil	Replacement	2010	Review: UV-Visible and NIR with chemometrics (Frankel 2010)
Oils	Olive oil (extra virgin)	Sunflower oil	Replacement	2010	Review: synchronous fluorescence with chemometrics (Frankel 2010)
Oils	Olive oil (extra virgin)	Vegetable oils	Replacement	2010	Review: HPLC-ELSD fingerprinting of triacylglycerols with chemometrics (Frankel 2010)
Oils	Olive oil (extra virgin)	Vegetable oils	Replacement	2010	Review: Raman (Frankel 2010)
Oils	Olive oil (extra virgin)	Vegetable oils	Replacement	2010	Review: GC and HLPC for fatty acid alkyl esters and triacylglycerols (Frankel 2010)
Oils	Olive oil (extra virgin)	Vegetable oils rich in linoleic acid	Replacement	2010	Review: HPLC-RI fingerprinting of triacylglycerols (Frankel 2010)
Oils	Olive oil (extra virgin)	Virgin olive oil and other vegetable oils	Replacement	2010	Review: ^{1}H-NMR on unsaponifiable matter with chemometrics (Frankel 2010)
Oils	Olive oil (virgin)	Corn oil	Replacement	1993	Pyrolysis-MS with chemometrics (Goodacre and others 1993)
Oils	Olive oil (virgin)	Corn oil	Replacement	2007	Total synchronous fluorescence with chemometrics (Poulli and others 2007)
Oils	Olive oil (virgin)	Corn oil	Replacement	1996	FTIR with chemometrics (Baeten and others 1996)
Oils	Olive oil (virgin)	Hazelnut oil	Replacement	2001	GC-FID for free sterols and HPLC-RI for triglycerols (Vichi and others 2001)
Oils	Olive oil (virgin)	Hazelnut oil	Replacement	2003	Raman and chemometrics (Lopez-Diez and others 2003)
Oils	Olive oil (virgin)	Hazelnut oil	Replacement	2005	GC-MS on adulterant sterol markers isolated by TLC (Damirchi and others 2005)
Oils	Olive oil (virgin)	Oil from non-authentic botanical origin	Replacement	1997	Triterpenic alcohols (markers of authenticity) isolated by TLC and analyzed by GC-FID (Aparicio and others 1997)
Oils	Olive oil (virgin)	Oil from non-authentic botanical origin	Replacement	1995	NR (Grob and others 1995)
Oils	Olive oil (virgin)	Olive oil from non-authentic geographic origin	Replacement	1995	^{1}H-NMR on the unsaponifiable fraction of the oil combined with chemometrics (Lai and others 1995)
Oils	Olive oil (Virgin)	Olive oil from non-authentic geographic origin	Replacement	2010	^{1}H-NMR and IRMS (^{13}C/^{12}C), (^{2}H/^{1}H) data with chemometrics (Alonso-Salces and others 2010)
Oils	Olive oil (virgin)	Olive oil from non-authentic geographic origin	Replacement	2007	NIR with chemometrics (Galtier and others 2007)
Oils	Olive oil (virgin)	Olive pomace oil	Replacement	2007	Total synchronous fluorescence with chemometrics (Poulli and others 2007)
Oils	Olive oil (virgin)	Olive pomace oil	Replacement	1996	FTIR with chemometrics (Baeten and others 1996)
Oils	Olive oil (virgin)	Peanut oil	Replacement	1993	Pyrolysis-MS with chemometrics (Goodacre and others 1993)
Oils	Olive oil (virgin)	Rapeseed oil	Replacement	2007	Total synchronous fluorescence with chemometrics (Poulli and others 2007)
Oils	Olive oil (virgin)	Soybean oil	Replacement	1993	Pyrolysis-MS with chemometrics (Goodacre and others 1993)
Oils	Olive oil (virgin)	Soybean oil	Replacement	2000	^{13}C-NMR on 12 peaks between 127.5 and 130.0 ppm, combined with chemometrics (Mavromoustakos and others 2000)
Oils	Olive oil (virgin)	Soybean oil	Replacement	2007	Total synchronous fluorescence with chemometrics (Poulli and others 2007)

Table 1: Scholarly Reports on Food Ingredient Fraud and Analytical Methods for Detection (continued)

Ingredient Category	Ingredient	Adulterant	Type of Fraud	Publication Year	Reported Detection Method and Reference
Oils	Olive oil (virgin)	Soybean oil	Replacement	1996	FTIR with chemometrics (Baeten and others 1996)
Oils	Olive oil (virgin)	Sunflower oil	Replacement	1993	Pyrolysis-MS with chemometrics (Goodacre and others 1993)
Oils	Olive oil (virgin)	Walnut oil	Replacement	2007	Total synchronous fluorescence with chemometrics (Poulli and others 2007)
Oils	Palm kernel oil*	Animal fat (lard, beef tallow, or chicken fat)	Replacement	2005	HPLC with triacylglycerol fingerprinting combined with chemometrics (Marikkar and others 2005a)
Oils	Palm kernel oil*	Animal fat (lard, beef tallow, or chicken fat)	Replacement	2005	GC-FID fatty acid fingerprinting combined multivariate analysis (Marikkar and others 2005b)
Oils	Palm oil*	Animal fat (lard, beef tallow, or chicken fat)	Replacement	2005	HPLC with triacylglycerol fingerprinting combined with chemometrics (Marikkar and others 2005a)
Oils	Palm oil*	Animal fat (lard, beef tallow, or chicken fat)	Replacement	2005	GC-FID fatty acid fingerprinting combined multivariate analysis (Marikkar and others 2005b)
Oils	Palm oil*	Argemone oil (*Argemone Mexicana*)	Replacement	1999	HPLC for sanguinarine (adulterant marker compound) (Husain and others 1999)
Oils	Palm oil*	Caster oil	Replacement	1993	^{13}C-NMR for C9, C10, C11, C12, and C13 carbons of ricinoleic acid (adulterant markers) (Husain and others 1993)
Oils	Palm oil*	Lard	Replacement	2005	Surface acoustic wave and sensing electronic nose (Man and others 2005)
Oils	Palm oil*	Lard	Replacement	2001	DSC thermal profiling (Marikkar and others 2001)
Oils	Palm oil*	Lipase-catalyzed interesterified lard	Replacement	2002	DSC (Marikkar and others 2002b)
Oils	Peanut oil	Sunflower oil	Replacement	2009	FTIR (Alexa and others 2009)
Oils	Perilla seed oil	Corn oil	Replacement	2010	GC-IRMS on individual fatty acids, combustion-IRMS on oils, and GC-MS for fatty acids fingerprinting (Guo and others 2010a)
Oils	Perilla seed oil	Soybean oil	Replacement	2010	GC-IRMS on individual fatty acids, combustion-IRMS on oils, and GC-MS for fatty acids fingerprinting (Guo and others 2010a)
Oils	Poppy seed oil	Sunflower oil	Replacement	2006	SPME-GC-MS for alpha-pinene (adulterant marker) and MALDI-MS for triglycerides analysis (Krist and others 2006)
Oils	Pumpkin seed oil	Oil from non-authentic botanical origin	Replacement	1999	GC fingerprinting analysis of delta-7-phytosterols in the unsaponifiable fraction (Mandl and others 1999)
Oils	Pumpkin seed oil	Oil from non-authentic botanical origin	Replacement	2001	GC-combustion-IRMS (^{13}C/^{12}C) on FAMEs (Spangenberg and Ogrinc 2001)
Oils	Pumpkin seed oil	Oil from non-authentic botanical origin	Replacement	2010	HPLC for authentic triglycerides (Butinar and others 2010)
Oils	Pumpkin seed oil	Oil from non-authentic botanical origin	Replacement	2002	GC-FID for beta-sitosterol (adulterant marker) (Wenzl and others 2002)
Oils	Pumpkin seed oil	Oil from non-authentic botanical origin	Replacement	2003	FTIR with chemometrics (Ozen and others 2003)
Oils	Pumpkin seed oil	Sunflower oil	Replacement	2009	FTIR (Alexa and others 2009)
Oils	Rice bran oil	Argemone oil (*Argemone Mexicana*)	Replacement	1999	HPLC for sanguinarine (adulterant marker compound) (Husain and others 1999)

Table 1: Scholarly Reports on Food Ingredient Fraud and Analytical Methods for Detection (continued)

Ingredient Category	Ingredient	Adulterant	Type of Fraud	Publication Year	Reported Detection Method and Reference
Oils	Sesame oil	Argemone oil (Argemone Mexicana)	Replacement	1999	HPLC for sanguinarine (adulterant marker compound) (Husain and others 1999)
Oils	Sesame oil	Maize oil	Replacement	2006	Electronic nose with chemometrics (Hai and Wang 2006)
Oils	Sesame oil	Oil from non-authentic botanical origin	Replacement	2008	GC-MS for fatty acid fingerprinting (Wang and others 2008a)
Oils	Sesame oil	Oil from non-authentic botanical origin	Replacement	2000	UV spectroscopy (Zhu and others 2000)
Oils	Sesame oil	Oil from non-authentic botanical origin	Replacement	2000	GC for FAMEs fingerprinting and use of specifications (Xiao and others 2000)
Oils	Sesame oil	Sesame oil of non-authentic geographic origin	Replacement	2006	Compositional analysis for fatty acids, fatty acids in the triglyceride 2-position, tocopherols and tocotrienols, triglycerides, sterols, steradienes, and iodine value (Crews and others 2006a)
Oils	Sesame oil	Soybean oil	Replacement	2010	HPLC-ELSD for triacylglycerols fingerprinting and GC-FID for fatty acids fingerprinting (Park and others 2010)
Oils	Sesame oil	Soybean oil	Replacement	1993	GC for FAMEs fingerprinting and use of specifications (Lee and others 1993)
Oils	Sesame oil	Vegetable oil	Replacement	2008	GC-MS for fatty acid fingerprinting combined with the Chinese national standard for sesame oil (Wang and others 2008a)
Oils	Vegetable oil	Oil from non-authentic botanical origin	Replacement	1994	FTIR with chemometrics (Lai and others 1994)
Oils	Vegetable oil	Oil from non-authentic botanical origin	Replacement	2003	GC for FAMEs fingerprinting (Wei and others 2003)
Oils	Vegetable oil	Oil from non-authentic botanical origin	Replacement	2003	GC for FAMEs fingerprinting (Wei and others 2003)
Oils	Vegetable oil (species specific)	Palm oil	Replacement	2009	Real-time PCR for adulterant marker gene (Zhang and others 2009a)
Oils	Vegetable oil (species specific)	Palm oil	Replacement	2000	Review of methods HPLC and GC for analyzing composition (authentic or adulterant marker) for fatty acids composition, triglycerols, waxes, sterols, hydrocarbons, alcohols, tocopherols, and volatiles (Aparicio and Aparicio-Ruíz 2000)
Oils	Vegetable oils	Vegetable oil from non-authentic botanical origin	Replacement	1998	MIR with chemometrics (Marigheto and others 1998)
Oils	Vegetable oils (single seed)	Oil from non-authentic botanical origin	Replacement	1997	GC-combustion-IRMS ($^{13}C/^{12}C$) on FAMEs (Kelly and others 1997)
Oils	Vegetable oils (single seed)	Oil from non-authentic botanical origin	Replacement	2009	Palmitic acid, stearic acids, oleic acid, and linoleic acid (Torrecilla and others 2009)
Oils	Vegetable oils (single seed)	Oil from non-authentic botanical origin	Replacement	2009	HPLC-MS for triglycerides with chemometrics (Lisa and others 2009)
Oils	Vegetable oils (single seed)	Oil from non-authentic botanical origin	Replacement	2008	PCR and CE with lab-on-chip for DNA analysis (Spaniolas and others 2008a)
Oils	Walnut oil	Grapeseed oil (desterolilzed)	Replacement	1994	LC-GC-FID for degradation products of sitosterol and campesterol (Grob and others 1994c)
Oils	Walnut oil	Palm oil (desterolilzed)	Replacement	1994	LC-GC-FID for degradation products of sitosterol and campesterol (Grob and others 1994c)
Oils	Walnut oil	Soybean oil (desterolilzed)	Replacement	1994	LC-GC-FID for degradation products of sitosterol and campesterol (Grob and others 1994c)

Table 1: Scholarly Reports on Food Ingredient Fraud and Analytical Methods for Detection (continued)

Ingredient Category	Ingredient	Adulterant	Type of Fraud	Publication Year	Reported Detection Method and Reference
Oils	Walnut oil	Sunflower oil (desterolilzed)	Replacement	1994	LC-GC-FID for degredation products of sitosterol and campesterol (Grob and others 1994c)
Oils	Wheat germ oil	Oil from non-authentic botanical origin	Replacement	2003	FTIR with chemometrics (Ozen and others 2003)
Other	Beeswax*	Carnuba wax	Replacement	2005	Physicochemical parameters including density, acid, saponification, ester, ratio number, iodine, peroxide, melting point, and ash content values (Bernal and others 2005)
Other	Beeswax*	Gypsum	Replacement	1999	Solubility in benzene (Li and Zhao 1999)
Other	Beeswax*	Paraffin wax	Replacement	2005	Physicochemical parameters including density, acid, saponification, ester, ratio number, iodine, peroxide, melting point, and ash content values (Bernal and others 2005)
Other	Beeswax*	Paraffin wax	Replacement	1999	Carbonization determination (Li and Zhao 1999)
Other	Beeswax*	Starch	Replacement	1999	Solubility in benzene (Li and Zhao 1999)
Other	Beeswax*	Stearic acid	Replacement	2005	Physicochemical parameters including density, acid, saponification, ester, ratio number, iodine, peroxide, melting point, and ash content values (Bernal and others 2005)
Other	Beeswax*	Stearic acid	Replacement	1998	Carbonification method (Zhao and others 1998)
Other	Beeswax*	Tallow	Replacement	2005	Physicochemical parameters including density, acid, saponification, ester, ratio number, iodine, peroxide, melting point, and ash content values (Bernal and others 2005)
Other	Chanterelle mushroom (*Cantharellus cibarius*)	Mushroom of non-authentic botanical origin (*Hygrophoropsis aurantiaca*)	Replacement	1998	HP-TLC for sugar alcohol fingerprinting (Prodolliet and Hischenhuber 1998)
Other	Chestnut	Grains or legumes (wheat, barley, kidney bean, etc.)	Replacement	2007	PCR for adulterant DNA (Alary and others 2007)
Other	Chestnut puree (*Castanea sativa*)	*Phaseolus vulgaris* beans	Replacement	2003	PCR for adulterant DNA (Krahulcová and others 2003)
Other	Chili tomato sauce	Sudan I dye	Addition to mask poor quality	2004	HPLC-MS for adulterant dyes (Calbiani and others 2004)
Other	Chili tomato sauce	Sudan II dye	Addition to mask poor quality	2004	HPLC-MS for adulterant dyes (Calbiani and others 2004)
Other	Chili tomato sauce	Sudan III dye	Addition to mask poor quality	2004	HPLC-MS for adulterant dyes (Calbiani and others 2004)
Other	Chili tomato sauce	Sudan IV dye	Addition to mask poor quality	2004	HPLC-MS for adulterant dyes Calbiani and others, 2004)
Other	Chocolate	Cocoa butter substitute	Replacement	2004	GC-FID for triglycerols analysis (Buchgraber and others 2004)
Other	Chocolate	Lard	Replacement	2005	FTIR with chemometrics (Che Man and others 2005)
Other	Cocoa powder	Carob powder	Replacement	1986	GC for pinitol (adulterant marker) (Baumgartner and others 1986)
Other	Cocoa powder	Chestnut shell	Replacement	2008	PCR for adulterants (Youngsheng and others 2008)
Other	Cocoa powder	Non-authentic material	Replacement	2006	NIR with chemometrics (Trilcova and others 2006)
Other	Cocoa powder	Non-authentic material	Replacement	2004	NIR with chemometrics (Trilcova and others 2004)

Table 1: Scholarly Reports on Food Ingredient Fraud and Analytical Methods for Detection (continued)

Ingredient Category	Ingredient	Adulterant	Type of Fraud	Publication Year	Reported Detection Method and Reference
Other	Cocoa powder	Peanut shell	Replacement	2008	PCR for adulterants (Youngsheng and others 2008)
Other	Cocoa powder	Sesame meal	Replacement	2008	PCR for adulterants (Youngsheng and others 2008)
Other	Cocoa powder	Soybean flour	Replacement	1988	Protein determination (Tomris and Meral 1988)
Other	Cocoa powder	Soybean meal	Replacement	1988	Protein determination (Altug and Gonul 1988)
Other	Cocoa powder	Soybean meal	Replacement	2008	PCR for adulterants (Youngsheng and others 2008)
Other	Coffee	Cereals	Replacement	2009	CE for xylose and glucose on acid hydrolyzed samples (Nogueira and do Lago 2009)
Other	Coffee	Coffee husk	Replacement	2009	HPAEC-PAD for carbohydrates fingerprinting combined with chemometrics (Garcia and others 2009)
Other	Coffee	Coffee of non-authentic botanical origin	Replacement	1997	MIR and NIR combined with chemometrics (Downey and others 1997)
Other	Coffee	Coffee of non-authentic botanical origin	Replacement	2007	NIR with chemometrics (Pizarro and others 2007)
Other	Coffee	Coffee of non-authentic botanical origin	Replacement	2006	PCR-restriction fragment length polymorphism analyzed with lab-on-chip CE to monitor a single nucleotide polymorphism (Spaniolas and others 2006)
Other	Coffee	Coffee of non-authentic botanical origin	Replacement	2001	HPLC-RI for triglycerides fingerprinting and HPLC-F tocopherols combined with chemometrics (González and others 2001)
Other	Coffee	Coffee twigs	Replacement	2007	NR (Jham and others 2007)
Other	Coffee	Corn	Replacement	2009	HPAEC-PAD for carbohydrates fingerprinting combined with chemometrics (Garcia and others 2009)
Other	Coffee	Roasted corn	Replacement	2007	HPLC-F for gamma-tocopherol (adulterant marker) (Jham and others 2007)
Other	Coffee	Roasted, ground barley	Replacement	1984	Photoacoustic spectroscopy (Cesar and others 1984)
Other	Coffee	Roasted, ground barley	Replacement	2009	SPME-GC-MS for headspace analysis combined with chemometrics (Oliveira and others 2009)
Other	Coffee	Roasted, ground corn	Replacement	1984	Photoacoustic spectroscopy (Cesar and others 1984)
Other	Coffee	Roasted, ground parchment	Replacement	1984	Photoacoustic spectroscopy (Cesar and others 1984)
Other	Coffee (instant)	Caramel	Replacement	1991	Enzymatic determination of fructose and glucose on hydrolyzed samples (Berger and others 1991)
Other	Coffee (instant)	Caramelized sugar	Replacement	2006	HPAEC-PAD for total xylose and total glucose determination (adulterant markers) (Girard and others 2006)
Other	Coffee (instant)	Cereals	Replacement	2006	HPAEC-PAD for total xylose and total glucose determination (adulterant markers) (Girard and others 2006)
Other	Coffee (instant)	Chicory	Replacement	2006	HPAEC-PAD for total xylose and total glucose determination (adulterant markers) (Girard and others 2006)
Other	Coffee (instant)	Chicory	Replacement	1996	IR and chemometrics (Briandet and others 1996)

Table 1: Scholarly Reports on Food Ingredient Fraud and Analytical Methods for Detection (continued)

Ingredient Category	Ingredient	Adulterant	Type of Fraud	Publication Year	Reported Detection Method and Reference
Other	Coffee (instant)	Chicory	Replacement	1991	Enzymatic determination of fructose and glucose on hydrolyzed samples (Berger and others 1991)
Other	Coffee (instant)	Coffee husk or parchment	Replacement	1995	Xylose detection as adulterant marker (Prodolliet and others 1995)
Other	Coffee (instant)	Coffee husks/parchment	Replacement	1991	Enzymatic determination of fructose and glucose on hydrolyzed samples (Berger and others 1991)
Other	Coffee (instant)	Coffee husks/parchments	Replacement	2006	HPAEC-PAD for total xylose and total glucose determination (adulterant markers) (Girard and others 2006)
Other	Coffee (instant)	Figs	Replacement	1991	Enzymatic determination of fructose and glucose on hydrolyzed samples (Berger and others 1991)
Other	Coffee (instant)	Glucose	Replacement	1996	IR and chemometrics (Briandet and others 1996)
Other	Coffee (instant)	Glucose syrup	Replacement	1991	Enzymatic determination of fructose and glucose on hydrolyzed samples (Berger and others 1991)
Other	Coffee (instant)	Leguminous plants	Replacement	2006	HPAEC-PAD for total xylose and total glucose determination (adulterant markers) (Girard and others 2006)
Other	Coffee (instant)	Malt	Replacement	2006	HPAEC-PAD for total xylose and total glucose determination (adulterant markers) (Girard and others 2006)
Other	Coffee (instant)	Maltodextrins	Replacement	2006	HPAEC-PAD for total xylose and total glucose determination (adulterant markers) (Girard and others 2006)
Other	Coffee (instant)	Maltodextrins	Replacement	1991	Enzymatic determination of fructose and glucose on hydrolyzed samples (Berger and others 1991)
Other	Coffee (instant)	Non-authentic manufacturer	Replacement	2002	^{1}H-NMR with chemometrics (Charlton and others 2002)
Other	Coffee (instant)	Starch	Replacement	1996	IR and chemometrics (Briandet and others 1996)
Other	Coffee (instant)	Starch	Replacement	1991	Enzymatic determination of fructose and glucose on hydrolyzed samples (Berger and others 1991)
Other	Coffee (Kona)	Coffee of non-authentic geographic origin	Replacement	2009	FTIR with chemometrics (Wang and others 2009b)
Other	Glycerin	Diethylene glycol	Replacement	2009	Review of historically reported cases (Schier and others 2009)
Other	Glycerin	Diethylene glycol	Replacement	2010	GC-FID for diethylene glycol (Holloway and others 2010)
Other	Glycerin	Diethylene glycol	Replacement	2011	Identity and purity determination for glycerin by IR, GC-FID, and sodium periodiate titrimetric method (USP 2011)
Other	Hazelnut paste	Corn oil	Replacement	2009	GC FAMEs for fatty acids fingerprinting, HPLC for triacylglycerols fingerprinting, and HPLC for tocopherols and tocotrienols fingerprinting (Bonvehi and Coll 2009)
Other	Hazelnut paste	High oleic-acid sunflower oil	Replacement	2009	GC FAMEs for fatty acids fingerprinting, HPLC for triacylglycerols fingerprinting, and HPLC for tocopherols and tocotrienols fingerprinting (Bonvehi and Coll 2009)

Table 1: Scholarly Reports on Food Ingredient Fraud and Analytical Methods for Detection (continued)

Ingredient Category	Ingredient	Adulterant	Type of Fraud	Publication Year	Reported Detection Method and Reference
Other	Hazelnut paste	Peanut oil	Replacement	2009	GC FAMEs for fatty acids fingerprinting, HPLC for triacylglycerols fingerprinting, and HPLC for tocopherols and tocotrienols fingerprinting (Bonvehi and Coll 2009)
Other	Hazelnut paste	Soybean oil	Replacement	2009	GC FAMEs for fatty acids fingerprinting, HPLC for triacylglycerols fingerprinting, and HPLC for tocopherols and tocotrienols fingerprinting (Bonvehi and Coll 2009)
Other	King boletus mushroom (*Boletus edulis*)	Mushroom of non-authentic botanical origin (*Suillus luteus*)	Replacement	1998	HP-TLC for sugar alcohol fingerprinting (Prodolliet and Hischenhuber 1998)
Other	Malt extract	Corn syrup	Replacement	2001	IRMS ($^{13}C/^{12}C$) (Peterson and others 2001)
Other	Phenylalanine (natural)	Synthetic phenylalanine	Replacement	2003	^{1}H-NMR ($^2H/^1H$) and IRMS ($^{13}C/^{12}C$) (Brenna and others 2003)
Other	Raisin concentrate	Glucose	Replacement	2004	Total and invert sugar analysis using the Lane–Eynon method, and AAS for minerals analysis (Simsek and others 2004)
Other	Raisin concentrate	Non-authentic fruit juice concentrates such as mulberry, fig, and carob bean	Replacement	2004	NR (Simsek and others 2004)
Other	Sodium chloride	Chalk powder	Replacement	2009	Wet-chemical tests for adulterant (Gupti and Panchal 2009)
Other	Soy sauce (soy fermentation)	Soy sauce derived from acid hydrolyzed vegetable protein	Replacement	2010	HPLC for tryptophan (authentic marker) (Zhu and others 2010b)
Other	Soy sauce (soy fermentation)	Soy sauce derived from acid hydrolyzed vegetable protein	Replacement	2007	HPLC-MS for levulinic acid (adulterant marker) (Sano and others 2007)
Other	Sucrose*	Powdered stone	Replacement	2009	Wet-chemical tests for adulterant (Gupti and Panchal 2009)
Other	Tea (partially fermented)	Tea of non-authentic botanical origin	Replacement	2010	NIR with chemometrics (Liu and others 2010)
Other	Tea (partially fermented)	Tea of non-authentic geographic origin	Replacement	2010	NIR with chemometrics (Liu and others 2010)
Other	Tomato sauce	Sudan I dye	Addition to mask inferior quality (color enhancement)	2010	ELISA for adulterant (Xu and others 2010)
Other	Tyrosine (natural)	Synthetic tyrosine	Replacement	2003	^{1}H-NMR ($^2H/^1H$) and IRMS ($^{13}C/^{12}C$) (Brenna and others 2003)
Other	Tyrosine (plant-derived)	Animal-derived tyrosine	Replacement	2002	IRMS ($^{18}O/^{16}O$) (Fronza and others 2002)
Protein-based ingredients	Corn gluten	Melamine and related compounds	Replacement	2010	Review of methods: GC-MS (Tittlemier 2010)
Protein-based ingredients	Eggs	Melamine and related compounds	Replacement	2010	Review of methods: HPLC-UV (Tittlemier 2010)
Protein-based ingredients	Rice protein isolate	Melamine and related compounds	Replacement	2010	Review of methods: GC-MS and HPLC-PDA (Tittlemier 2010)
Protein-based ingredients	Soy protein isolate	Milk proteins	Replacement	2004	Enzymatic hydrolysis of proteins followed by HPLC and chemometrics analysis (Dziuba and others 2004b)
Protein-based ingredients	Soy protein isolate	Milk proteins	Replacement	2004	HPLC-PDA peptide fingerprinting on tryptic digest (Dziuba and others 2004b)

Table 1: Scholarly Reports on Food Ingredient Fraud and Analytical Methods for Detection (continued)

Ingredient Category	Ingredient	Adulterant	Type of Fraud	Publication Year	Reported Detection Method and Reference
Protein-based ingredients	Soy protein isolate	Milk proteins	Replacement	2004	HPLC-PDA peptide fingerprinting on tryptic digest (Dziuba and others 2004a)
Protein-based ingredients	Soybean meal	Fish meal	Replacement	2009	NIR with chemometrics (Cozzolino and others 2009)
Protein-based ingredients	Soybean meal	Meat meal	Replacement	2009	NIR with chemometrics (Cozzolino and others 2009)
Protein-based ingredients	Soybeans	Non-authentic material	Replacement	2009	UV-Vis, FTIR, HPLC-PDA, and GC-FID for authentication and phytochemical fingerprinting (Socaci and others 2009)
Protein-based ingredients	Soy milk	Bovine milk proteins	Replacement	1997	HPLC-FID protein fingerprinting (García and others 1997)
Protein-based ingredients	Wheat gluten*	Melamine	Replacement	2008	Surface enhanced Raman spectroscopy for melamine (Lin and others 2008)
Protein-based ingredients	Wheat gluten*	Melamine and related compounds	Replacement	2010	Review of methods: HPLC-MS/MS, ELISA, extractive electrospray ionization time-of-flight MS, and GC-MS (Tittlemier 2010)
Seafood	Anglerfish	Anglerfish of non-authentic species	Replacement	2008	PCR-based methods [restriction fragment length polymorphism or phylogenetic analysis of DNA sequences (forensically informative nucleotide sequencing)] (Espineira and others 2008)
Seafood	Canned tuna	Bonito (Euthynnus affinis)	Replacement	1996	Sequence and restriction site analysis of PCR mitochondrial DNA (Ram and others 1996)
Seafood	Canned tuna	Frigate mackerel (Auxis thazard)	Replacement	1996	Sequence and restriction site analysis of PCR mitochondrial DNA (Ram and others 1996)
Seafood	Crab (species specific)	Crustacean of non-authentic species	Replacement	2007	UV-Vis spectrometry with chemometrics (Gayo and Hale 2007)
Seafood	Crab meat	Surimi-based artificial crab meat	Replacement	2006	UV-Vis spectrometry with chemometrics (Gayo and others 2006)
Seafood	Eel	Fish of non-authentic species	Replacement	2008	DNA based method using fluorogenic ribonuclease protection assay to detect single nucleotide polymorphisms (Kitaoka and others 2008)
Seafood	Fish	Melamine	Replacement	1982	Wet-chemical method with UV detection (Cattaneo and Cantoni 1982)
Seafood	Fish	Melamine	Replacement	1982	Wet-chemical method with UV detection (Cattaneo and Cantoni 1982)
Seafood	Fish	Non-authentic species	Replacement	2001	Isoelectric focusing electrophoresis for protein fingerprinting (Etienne and others 2001)
Seafood	Grouper (Epinephelus guaza)	Wreck fish (Polyprion americanus) or Nile perch (Lates niloticus)	Replacement	2001	DNA analysis using mitochondrial 12S rRNA gene by PCR followed by single strand conformational polymorphism analysis (Asensio and others 2001)
Seafood	Prawns	Crustacean of non-authentic species	Replacement	2008	PCR (Pascoal and others 2008)
Seafood	Scampi (Neplirops norvegicus)	Crustacean of non-authentic species	Replacement	1995	SDS electrophoresis on protein extract (Craig and others 1995)
Seafood	Shrimp (species specific)	Crustacean of non-authentic species	Replacement	2008	PCR (Pascoal and others 2008)
Seafood	Tuna	Fish of non-authentic species	Replacement	2008	DNA based method using fluorogenic ribonuclease protection assay to detect single nucleotide polymorphisms (Kitaoka and others 2008)
Seafood	Tuna	Fish of non-authentic species	Replacement	2007	Triplex-PRC DNA analysis (Michelini and others 2007)

Table 1: Scholarly Reports on Food Ingredient Fraud and Analytical Methods for Detection (continued)

Ingredient Category	Ingredient	Adulterant	Type of Fraud	Publication Year	Reported Detection Method and Reference
Seafood	Tuna (*Auxis thazard* and *Auxis rochei*)	Fish of non-authentic species	Replacement	2004	Multiplex-PCR DNA analysis (Infante and others 2004)
Spices	Asafoetida	Resin	Replacement	2009	Wet-chemical tests for adulterant (Gupti and Panchal 2009)
Spices	Black pepper	Buckwheat flour	Replacement	2011	NIR hyperspectral imaging with chemometrics (September 2011)
Spices	Black pepper	Millet	Replacement	2011	NIR hyperspectral imaging with chemometrics (September 2011)
Spices	Black pepper	Papaya seed	Replacement	2009	PCR-DNA analysis using sequence characterized amplified region of adulterant (Dhanyaa and others 2009)
Spices	Black pepper	Papaya seed	Replacement	2003	TLC for adulterant markers detection of super critical fluid extracts (Bhattacharjee and others 2003)
Spices	Black pepper	Papaya seed	Replacement	2001	TLC for adulterant markers (Paradkar and others 2001c)
Spices	Chili powder	Color additives	Addition to mask poor quality	2007	Paper chromatography and Vis-spectrophotometry (Tripathi and others 2007)
Spices	Chili powder	Curcumin	Addition to mask poor quality	2008	2-dimensional HPTLC for adulterants (Dixit and others 2008)
Spices	Chili powder	Metanil yellow	Addition to mask poor quality	2008	2-dimensional HPTLC for adulterants (Dixit and others 2008)
Spices	Chili powder	Sudan dyes	Addition to mask poor quality	2008	2-dimensional HPTLC for adulterants (Dixit and others 2008)
Spices	Chili powder	Sudan dyes	Addition to mask poor quality	2006	HPLC with on-line electrogenerated BrO-luminol chemiluminescence detection for adulterant (Zhang and others 2006)
Spices	Chili powder	Sudan I dye	Addition to mask poor quality	2004	HPLC-MS for adulterant (Tateo and Bononi 2004)
Spices	Chili powder	Sudan I dye	Addition to mask inferior quality (color enhancement)	2007	SPE-HPLC for Sudan I (Wang and others 2007)
Spices	Chili powder	Sudan I dye	Addition to mask inferior quality (color enhancement)	2009	HP-TLC for Sudan I (Kandler and others 2009)
Spices	Chili powder	Sudan I dye	Addition to mask inferior quality (color enhancement)	2010	ELISA for adulterant (Xu and others 2010)
Spices	Chili powder	Sudan I, II, III, or IV dyes	Addition to mask inferior quality (color enhancement)	2007	CE with amperometric detection for adulterants (Liu and others 2007)
Spices	Chinese star anise (*Illicium verum* Hook. f.)	Japanese star anise (*Illicium anisatum* Linn)	Replacement	2006	TLC flavonoid pattern combined with HPLC-MS/MS for lactone anisatin (an adulterant marker compound) (Lederer and others 2006)
Spices	Chinese star anise (*Illicium verum* Hook. f.)	Japanese star anise (*Illicium anisatum* Linn)	Replacement	2005	Microscopy for endocarp cell morphology combined with GC-FID for detection of adulterant marker compounds (methoxyeugenol, eugenol, and 2,6-dimethoxy-4-allylphenol) (Joshi and others 2005)

Table 1: Scholarly Reports on Food Ingredient Fraud and Analytical Methods for Detection (continued)

Ingredient Category	Ingredient	Adulterant	Type of Fraud	Publication Year	Reported Detection Method and Reference
Spices	Chinese star anise (Illicium verum Hook. f.)	Japanese star anise (Illicium anisatum Linn)	Replacement	2005	Fluorescent microscopy for epicarp morphology, and GC-FID for methoxyeugenol, eugenol, and 2, 6-dimethoxy-4-allylphenol (adulterant markers) (Joshi and others 2005)
Spices	Chinese star anise (Illicium verum Hook. f.)	Japanese star anise (Illicium anisatum Linn)	Replacement	2009	DNA analysis using PCR and use of fragment length polymorphisms (Techen and others 2009)
Spices	Chinese star anise (Illicium verum Hook. f.)	Japanese star anise (Illicium anisatum Linn)	Replacement	2004	NR (Ize-Ludlow and others 2004)
Spices	Chinese star anise (Illicium verum Hook. f.)	Non-authentic species	Replacement	2009	GC-MS for quantification of E-anethole (authentic marker compound) and detection of adulterant marker compounds (asaricin; methoxyeugenol) (Howes and others 2009)
Spices	Chinese star anise (Illicium verum Hook. f.)	Non-authentic species	Replacement	2006	TLC for flavonoid fingerprinting, HPLC/ESI-MS/MS for sesquiterpene lactone anisatin (adulterant marker) (Lederer and others 2006)
Spices	Chinese star anise (Illicium verum Hook. f.)	Non-authentic species	Replacement	2009	Thermal desorption-GC-MS for authentic and adulterant marker volatile compounds (Howes and others 2009)
Spices	Coriander powder	Dung	Replacement	2009	Wet-chemical tests for adulterant (Gupti and Panchal 2009)
Spices	Curry powder	Curcumin	Addition to mask poor quality	2008	2-dimensional HPTLC for adulterants (Dixit and others 2008)
Spices	Curry powder	Metanil yellow	Addition to mask poor quality	2008	2-dimensional HPTLC for adulterants (Dixit and others 2008)
Spices	Curry powder	Sudan dyes	Addition to mask poor quality	2008	2-dimensional HPTLC for adulterants (Dixit and others 2008)
Spices	Curry powder	Sudan I dye	Addition to mask inferior quality (color enhancement)	2009	HP-TLC for Sudan I (Kandler and others 2009)
Spices	Curry powder	Sudan I, II, III, or IV dyes	Addition to mask inferior quality (color enhancement)	2009	UV-Vis spectrometry combined with chemometrics (Di Anibal and others 2009)
Spices	Curry powder	Sudan I, II, III, or IV dyes	Addition to mask inferior quality (color enhancement)	2011	^{1}H-NMR for chemometrics (Di Anibal and others 2011)
Spices	Oregano (Mediterranean)	Leaves from non-authentic botanical origin (Rhus coriaria L., Cistus spp., or Rubus spp.)	Replacement	2010	PCR-DNA analysis using sequence characterized amplified region (Marieschi and others 2010)
Spices	Paprika	Lead tetroxide	Replacement or addition to mask poor quality	1998	Photoacoustic spectroscropy for adulterant (Doka and others 1998)
Spices	Paprika	Paprika of non-authentic geographic origin	Replacement	2010	ICP-MS for (^{86}Sr/^{87}Sr) and trace elements fingerprinting combined with chemometrics (Brunner and others 2010)
Spices	Paprika	Sudan I dye	Addition to mask inferior quality (color enhancement)	2009	HP-TLC for Sudan I (Kandler and others 2009)

Table 1: Scholarly Reports on Food Ingredient Fraud and Analytical Methods for Detection (continued)

Ingredient Category	Ingredient	Adulterant	Type of Fraud	Publication Year	Reported Detection Method and Reference
Spices	Paprika	Sudan I, II, III, or IV dyes	Addition to mask inferior quality (color enhancement)	2009	UV-Vis spectrometry combined with chemometrics (Di Anibal and others 2009)
Spices	Paprika	Sudan I, II, III, or IV dyes	Addition to mask inferior quality (color enhancement)	2011	1H-NMR for chemometrics (Di Anibal and others 2011)
Spices	Paprika	Sudan I, II, III, or IV dyes	Addition to mask inferior quality (color enhancement)	2009	UV-Vis spectrometry combined with chemometrics (Di Anibal and others 2009)
Spices	Paprika	Sudan I, II, III, or IV dyes	Addition to mask inferior quality (color enhancement)	2011	1H-NMR for chemometrics (Di Anibal and others 2011)
Spices	Saffron (Crocus sativus L.)	Allura red	Replacement or addition to mask poor quality	2004	UV-Vis spectroscopy (Carmona and others 2004)
Spices	Saffron (Crocus sativus L.)	Allura red	Addition to mask poor quality	2005	UV-Vis spectrometry for adulterants (Zalacain and others 2005)
Spices	Saffron (Crocus sativus L.)	Amaranth	Addition to mask poor quality	2005	UV-Vis spectrometry for adulterants (Zalacain and others 2005)
Spices	Saffron (Crocus sativus L.)	Amaranth dye	Replacement or addition to mask poor quality	2004	UV-Vis spectroscopy (Carmona and others 2004)
Spices	Saffron (Crocus sativus L.)	Amaranth dye	Replacement or addition to mask poor quality	2004	UV-Vis spectroscopy (Carmona and others 2004)
Spices	Saffron (Crocus sativus L.)	Azorubine	Addition to mask poor quality	2005	UV-Vis spectrometry for adulterants (Zalacain and others 2005)
Spices	Saffron (Crocus sativus L.)	Azorubine dye	Replacement or addition to mask poor quality	2004	UV-Vis spectroscopy (Carmona and others 2004)
Spices	Saffron (Crocus sativus L.)	Barium sulfate	Replacement	1998	NR (Alonso and others 1998)
Spices	Saffron (Crocus sativus L.)	Betanine dye	Replacement or addition to mask poor quality	2004	UV-Vis spectroscopy (Carmona and others 2004)
Spices	Saffron (Crocus sativus L.)	Borax	Replacement	1998	NR (Alonso and others 1998)
Spices	Saffron (Crocus sativus L.)	Calcium carbonate	Replacement	1998	NR (Alonso and others 1998)
Spices	Saffron (Crocus sativus L.)	Cochinela dye	Replacement or addition to mask poor quality	2004	UV-Vis spectroscopy (Carmona and others 2004)
Spices	Saffron (Crocus sativus L.)	Color additives	Addition to mask poor quality (color enhancement)	2005	Second derivative spectroscopy on isolated crocetin to detect adulterants (Zalacain and others 2005)
Spices	Saffron (Crocus sativus L.)	Curcuma (Curcuma longa L.)	Replacement	1998	NR (Alonso and others 1998)

Table 1: Scholarly Reports on Food Ingredient Fraud and Analytical Methods for Detection (continued)

Ingredient Category	Ingredient	Adulterant	Type of Fraud	Publication Year	Reported Detection Method and Reference
Spices	Saffron (*Crocus sativus* L.)	Curcumin dye	Replacement or addition to mask poor quality	2004	UV-Vis spectroscopy (Carmona and others 2004)
Spices	Saffron (*Crocus sativus* L.)	Dyed strips of other parts of the saffron plant (stamens or perigonia)	Replacement	1998	NR (Alonso and others 1998)
Spices	Saffron (*Crocus sativus* L.)	Erythrosine	Replacement or addition to mask poor quality	2004	UV-Vis spectroscopy (Carmona and others 2004)
Spices	Saffron (*Crocus sativus* L.)	Fibers of dried animal meats	Replacement	1998	NR (Alonso and others 1998)
Spices	Saffron (*Crocus sativus* L.)	Flowers from non-authentic botanical origin cut into strips (*Papaver rhoeas* L., *Punica granatum* L., *Arinica montana* L., or *Scolymus hispanicus* L.)	Replacement	1998	NR (Alonso and others 1998)
Spices	Saffron (*Crocus sativus* L.)	Fuchsin color	Replacement or addition to mask poor quality	1998	NR (Alonso and others 1998)
Spices	Saffron (*Crocus sativus* L.)	Glauber's salt	Replacement	1998	NR (Alonso and others 1998)
Spices	Saffron (*Crocus sativus* L.)	Glucose	Replacement	1998	NR (Alonso and others 1998)
Spices	Saffron (*Crocus sativus* L.)	Ground red pepper (*Capsicum annuum* L.)	Replacement	1998	NR (Alonso and others 1998)
Spices	Saffron (*Crocus sativus* L.)	Gypsum	Replacement	1998	NR (Alonso and others 1998)
Spices	Saffron (*Crocus sativus* L.)	Herbaceous plants cut into strips and dyed with azo or cochineal dye	Replacement	1998	NR (Alonso and others 1998)
Spices	Saffron (*Crocus sativus* L.)	Lactose	Replacement	1998	NR (Alonso and others 1998)
Spices	Saffron (*Crocus sativus* L.)	Logwood particles	Replacement	1998	NR (Alonso and others 1998)
Spices	Saffron (*Crocus sativus* L.)	Martius yellow color	Replacement or addition to mask poor quality	1998	NR (Alonso and others 1998)
Spices	Saffron (*Crocus sativus* L.)	Naphthol yellow	Addition to mask poor quality	2005	UV-Vis spectrometry for adulterants (Zalacain and others 2005)
Spices	Saffron (*Crocus sativus* L.)	Naphtol yellow	Replacement or addition to mask poor quality	2004	UV-Vis spectroscopy (Carmona and others 2004)
Spices	Saffron (*Crocus sativus* L.)	Norbixin	Replacement or addition to mask poor quality	2004	HPLC-PDA (Carmona and others 2004)
Spices	Saffron (*Crocus sativus* L.)	Petals of *Carthamus tinctorius* L. or *Calendula officinalis* L.	Replacement	1998	Thermal desorption GC-MS for safranal and fingerprinting (Alonso and others 1998)

Table 1: Scholarly Reports on Food Ingredient Fraud and Analytical Methods for Detection (continued)

Ingredient Category	Ingredient	Adulterant	Type of Fraud	Publication Year	Reported Detection Method and Reference
Spices	Saffron (Crocus sativus L.)	Picric acid color	Replacement or addition to mask poor quality	1998	NR (Alonso and others 1998)
Spices	Saffron (Crocus sativus L.)	Ponceau 4R	Replacement or addition to mask poor quality	2004	UV-Vis spectroscopy (Carmona and others 2004)
Spices	Saffron (Crocus sativus L.)	Ponceau 4R	Addition to mask poor quality	2005	UV-Vis spectrometry for adulterants (Zalacain and others 2005)
Spices	Saffron (Crocus sativus L.)	Potassium hydroxide	Replacement	1998	NR (Alonso and others 1998)
Spices	Saffron (Crocus sativus L.)	Quinoline dye	Replacement or addition to mask poor quality	2004	UV-Vis spectroscopy (Carmona and others 2004)
Spices	Saffron (Crocus sativus L.)	Quinoline yellow	Addition to mask poor quality	2005	UV-Vis spectrometry for adulterants (Zalacain and others 2005)
Spices	Saffron (Crocus sativus L.)	Red 2G	Replacement or addition to mask poor quality	2004	UV-Vis spectroscopy (Carmona and others 2004)
Spices	Saffron (Crocus sativus L.)	Red 2G	Addition to mask poor quality	2005	UV-Vis spectrometry for adulterants (Zalacain and others 2005)
Spices	Saffron (Crocus sativus L.)	Roots of Allium porrum L.	Replacement	1998	NR (Alonso and others 1998)
Spices	Saffron (Crocus sativus L.)	Saffron impregnated with syrups, glycerin, or oils	Replacement	1998	NR (Alonso and others 1998)
Spices	Saffron (Crocus sativus L.)	Saffron of non-authentic geographic origin	Replacement	1998	NR (Alonso and others 1998)
Spices	Saffron (Crocus sativus L.)	Saffron with artificially increased water content	Replacement	1998	NR (Alonso and others 1998)
Spices	Saffron (Crocus sativus L.)	Saltpeter	Replacement	1998	NR (Alonso and others 1998)
Spices	Saffron (Crocus sativus L.)	Sandlewood dust	Replacement	1998	NR (Alonso and others 1998)
Spices	Saffron (Crocus sativus L.)	Seignette's salt	Replacement	1998	NR (Alonso and others 1998)
Spices	Saffron (Crocus sativus L.)	Stamens of carnation species	Replacement	1998	NR (Alonso and others 1998)
Spices	Saffron (Crocus sativus L.)	Starch	Replacement	1998	NR (Alonso and others 1998)
Spices	Saffron (Crocus sativus L.)	Stigmas from non-authentic crocus botanical origin (Crocus vernus L.; Crocus especiousus L.)	Replacement	1998	NR (Alonso and others 1998)
Spices	Saffron (Crocus sativus L.)	Sunset yellow	Addition to mask poor quality	2005	UV-Vis spectrometry for adulterants (Zalacain and others 2005)
Spices	Saffron (Crocus sativus L.)	Sunset yellow dye	Replacement or addition to mask poor quality	2004	UV-Vis spectroscopy (Carmona and others 2004)
Spices	Saffron (Crocus sativus L.)	Synthetic safranal	Replacement	1998	Thermal desorption GC-MS for safranal and fingerprinting (Alonso and others 1998)

Table 1: Scholarly Reports on Food Ingredient Fraud and Analytical Methods for Detection (continued)

Ingredient Category	Ingredient	Adulterant	Type of Fraud	Publication Year	Reported Detection Method and Reference
Spices	Saffron (Crocus sativus L.)	Tartrazine	Replacement or addition to mask poor quality	2004	HPLC-PDA (Carmona and others 2004)
Spices	Saffron (Crocus sativus L.)	Tartrazine	Addition to mask poor quality	2005	UV-Vis spectrometry for adulterants (Zalacain and others 2005)
Spices	Saffron (Crocus sativus L.)	Threads of gelatin	Replacement	1998	NR (Alonso and others 1998)
Spices	Saffron (Crocus sativus L.)	Tropeolin color	Replacement or addition to mask poor quality	1998	NR (Alonso and others 1998)
Spices	Salt (sindhav, rock salt)	Powdered stone	Replacement	2009	Wet-chemical tests for adulterant (Gupti and Panchal 2009)
Spices	Sanchal	Earth material/powdered stone	Replacement	2009	Wet-chemical tests for adulterant (Gupti and Panchal 2009)
Spices	Smoked paprika from "La Vera" region	Smoked paprika from non-authentic geographic origin	Replacement	2006	Free zone CE fingerprinting for methanol soluble proteins (Hernandez and others 2006)
Spices	Smoked paprika from "La Vera" region	Smoked paprika from non-authentic geographic origin	Replacement	2010	PCR for adulterant DNA (Hernandez and others 2010)
Spices	Smoked paprika from "La Vera" region	Smoked paprika from non-authentic geographic origin	Replacement	2007	Free zone CE fingerprinting of proteins isolated by temperature-induced phase partition (Hernandez and others 2007)
Spices	Turmeric	Chalk powder	Replacement	2009	Wet-chemical tests for adulterant (Gupti and Panchal 2009)
Spices	Turmeric	Color additives	Addition to mask poor quality	2007	Paper chromatography and Vis-spectrophotometry (Tripathi and others 2007)
Spices	Turmeric	Curcuma zedoaria	Replacement	2004	DNA analysis (Sasikumar and others 2004)
Spices	Turmeric	Curcumin	Addition to mask poor quality	2008	2-dimensional HP-TLC for adulterants (Dixit and others 2008)
Spices	Turmeric	Food starches	Replacement	2004	Curcumin content determination (Sasikumar and others 2004)
Spices	Turmeric	Food starches	Replacement	2009	2-dimensional HP-TLC for curcumin contents (Dixit and others 2009)
Spices	Turmeric	Metanil yellow	Addition to mask poor quality	2008	2-dimensional HP-TLC for adulterants (Dixit and others 2008)
Spices	Turmeric	Metanil yellow (color additive)	Replacement	2009	2-dimensional HP-TLC for adulterant (Dixit and others 2009)
Spices	Turmeric	Spice powder from non-authentic botanical/varietal origin	Replacement	2009	2-dimensional HP-TLC for curcumin contents (Dixit and others 2009)
Spices	Turmeric	Sudan dyes	Addition to mask poor quality	2008	2-dimensional HP-TLC for adulterants (Dixit and others 2008)
Spices	Turmeric	Sudan I, II, III, or IV dyes	Addition to mask inferior quality (color enhancement)	2009	UV-Vis spectrometry combined with chemometrics (Di Anibal and others 2009)
Spices	Turmeric	Sudan I, II, III, or IV dyes	Addition to mask inferior quality (color enhancement)	2011	^{1}H-NMR for chemometrics (Di Anibal and others 2011)
Sweeteners	Honey	Beet medium invert sugar	Replacement	2001	FTIR with chemometrics (Sivakesava and Irudayaraj 2001a)
Sweeteners	Honey	Beet sugar	Replacement	2006	FT-MIR with chemometrics (Kelly and others 2006)

1576 / Food Ingredients Fraud Database / *General Information*

Table 1: Scholarly Reports on Food Ingredient Fraud and Analytical Methods for Detection (continued)

Ingredient Category	Ingredient	Adulterant	Type of Fraud	Publication Year	Reported Detection Method and Reference
Sweeteners	Honey	Beet sugar	Replacement	2006	IRMS ($^{13}C/^{12}C$) on carbohydrate fraction (Cabanero and others 2006)
Sweeteners	Honey	Beet sugar	Replacement	1998	IRMS ($^{13}C/^{12}C$) on carbohydrate fraction (González Martín and others 1998)
Sweeteners	Honey	C_4 sugars	Replacement	2007	IRMS ($^{13}C/^{12}C$) on honey and isolated proteins, SNIF-NMR ($^2H/^1H$) on ethanol from sample fermentation (Cotte and others 2007)
Sweeteners	Honey	C_4 sugars	Replacement	1989	IRMS ($^{13}C/^{12}C$) on isolated proteins (White and Winters 1989)
Sweeteners	Honey	Cane or corn sugars	Replacement	2006	IRMS ($^{13}C/^{12}C$) on carbohydrate and protein fractions (Pang and others 2006)
Sweeteners	Honey	Cane sugar	Replacement	2006	IRMS ($^{13}C/^{12}C$) on carbohydrate fraction (Cabanero and others 2006)
Sweeteners	Honey	Cane sugar	Replacement	2010	NIR with chemometrics (Mishra and others 2010)
Sweeteners	Honey	Cane sugar syrup	Replacement	2005	Fluorescence spectroscopy (Ghosh and others 2005a)
Sweeteners	Honey	Corn syrup	Replacement	1980	Multiple methods including IRMS ($^{13}C/^{12}C$) on carbohydrate fraction, TLC sugars, and determination of hydroxymethylfurfural (White 1980)
Sweeteners	Honey	Corn syrup	Replacement	1991	IRMS ($^{13}C/^{12}C$) (Brookes and others 1991)
Sweeteners	Honey	Corn syrup	Replacement	2001	FTIR with chemometrics (Sivakesava and Irudayaraj 2001c)
Sweeteners	Honey	Corn syrup	Replacement	2008	HPLC-PAD for oligosaccharides fingerprinting (Morales and others 2008)
Sweeteners	Honey	Corn syrup	Replacement	2009	SPE plus HPLC-PAD for adulterant marker polysaccharides (Megherbi and others 2009)
Sweeteners	Honey	Corn syrup	Replacement	2010	FTIR for glucose, sucrose, fructose, and maltose fingerprinting with chemometrics (Wang and others 2010)
Sweeteners	Honey	Corn syrup	Replacement	2009	FTIR with chemometrics (Gallardo-Velázquez and others 2009)
Sweeteners	Honey	Dextrose syrup	Replacement	2006	FT-MIR with chemometrics (Kelly and others 2006)
Sweeteners	Honey	Essential oils	Replacement	2010	NR (Alissandrakis and others 2010)
Sweeteners	Honey	Fructose	Replacement	2002	MIR with chemometrics (Sivakesava and Irudayaraj 2002)
Sweeteners	Honey	Fructose and glucose mixture	Replacement	2010	NIR with chemometrics (Zhu and others 2010a)
Sweeteners	Honey	Glucose	Replacement	2002	MIR with chemometrics (Sivakesava and Irudayaraj 2002)
Sweeteners	Honey	Glucose and fructose	Replacement	2003	IR and chemometrics (Downey and others 2003)
Sweeteners	Honey	High-fructose corn syrup	Replacement	2009	FTIR with chemometrics (Gallardo-Velázquez and others 2009)
Sweeteners	Honey	High-fructose corn syrup	Replacement	2006	IRMS ($^{13}C/^{12}C$) on carbohydrate fraction (Cabanero and others 2006)
Sweeteners	Honey	High-fructose corn syrup	Replacement	1993	Multi component analysis for dry matter, apparent viscosity, sodium, potassium, proline, nitrogen, ash, calcium, HMF, and moisture (Abdel-Aal and others 1993)
Sweeteners	Honey	High-fructose corn syrup	Replacement	2003	IRMS ($^{13}C/^{12}C$) on carbohydrate and protein fractions (Padovan and others 2003)

Table 1: Scholarly Reports on Food Ingredient Fraud and Analytical Methods for Detection (continued)

Ingredient Category	Ingredient	Adulterant	Type of Fraud	Publication Year	Reported Detection Method and Reference
Sweeteners	Honey	High-fructose inulin syrup	Replacement	2010	GC-MS for inulotriose (adulterant marker) (Ruiz-Matute and others 2010)
Sweeteners	Honey	Honey from non-authentic botanical or geographic origin	Replacement	2007	SNIF-NMR (^{2}H/^{1}H) on ethanol from sample fermentation (Cotte and others 2007)
Sweeteners	Honey	Honey from non-authentic botanical origin	Replacement	2009	HPAEC-PAD for monosacchardies and oligosaccharides fingerprinting (Korosec and others 2009)
Sweeteners	Honey	Honey from non-authentic botanical origin	Replacement	2006	FT-NIR with chemometrics (Ruoff and others 2006b)
Sweeteners	Honey	Honey from non-authentic botanical origin	Replacement	2006	FT-MIR with chemometrics (Ruoff and others 2006c)
Sweeteners	Honey	Honey from non-authentic botanical origin	Replacement	2005	Front-face fluorescence spectroscopy with chemometrics (Ruoff and others 2005)
Sweeteners	Honey	Honey from non-authentic botanical origin	Replacement	2003	HPLC-PAD for major and minor sugars fingerprinting (Cordella and others 2003)
Sweeteners	Honey	Honey from non-authentic botanical origin	Replacement	2008	FTIR with chemometrics (Etzold and Lichtenberg-Kraag 2008)
Sweeteners	Honey	Honey from non-authentic botanical origin	Replacement	2008	MADLI-ToF-MS fingerprinting of proteins (Won and others 2008)
Sweeteners	Honey	Honey from non-authentic botanical origin	Replacement	2001	GC-MS for aroma compound fingerprinting (Radovic and others 2001)
Sweeteners	Honey	Honey from non-authentic botanical origin	Replacement	2009	SPME-GC for volatiles analysis, HPLC-MS for free aminio acids, and HPLC-RI for sugars analysis, all combined with chemometrics (Senyuva and others 2009)
Sweeteners	Honey	Honey from non-authentic botanical origin	Replacement	2006	FT-MIR for 20 quantitative measurements (Ruoff and others 2006a)
Sweeteners	Honey	Honey from non-authentic botanical origin	Replacement	2004	HPLC-PDA for phenolic acids fingerprinting (Yao and others 2004)
Sweeteners	Honey	Honey from non-authentic geographic origin	Replacement	2005	AAS for trace mineral and elements analysis combined with chemometrics (Arvanitoyannis and others 2005)
Sweeteners	Honey	Honey from non-authentic geographic origin	Replacement	2009	MALDI-MS on extracted proteins, combined with chemometrics (Wang and others 2009c)
Sweeteners	Honey	Honey from non-authentic geographic region	Replacement	2001	GC-MS for aroma compound fingerprinting (Radovic and others 2001)
Sweeteners	Honey	Industrial sugar syrups	Replacement	2003	HPLC and GC for saccharides analysis, both combined with chemometrics (Cotte and others 2003)
Sweeteners	Honey	Invert beet sugar	Replacement	1995	GC-FID for adulterant oligosaccharides (Low and South 1995a)
Sweeteners	Honey	Invert beet sugar	Replacement	2002	MIR with chemometrics (Sivakesava and Irudayaraj 2002)
Sweeteners	Honey	Invert cane sugar	Replacement	2002	MIR with chemometrics (Sivakesava and Irudayaraj 2002)

Table 1: Scholarly Reports on Food Ingredient Fraud and Analytical Methods for Detection (continued)

Ingredient Category	Ingredient	Adulterant	Type of Fraud	Publication Year	Reported Detection Method and Reference
Sweeteners	Honey	Invert sugar syrups	Replacement	1980	Multiple methods including IRMS ($^{13}C/^{12}C$) on carbohydrate fraction, TLC sugars, and determination of hydroxymethylfurfural (White 1980)
Sweeteners	Honey	Invert syrups (beet or cane)	Replacement	1995	GC for oligosaccharides fingerprinting (adulterant markers) (Low and South 1995b)
Sweeteners	Honey	Invert syrups (beet or cane)	Replacement	1994	HPLC-PAD oligosaccharides fingerprinting (adulterant markers) (Swallow and Low 1994)
Sweeteners	Honey	Inverted cane sugar	Replacement	2001	FTIR with chemometrics (Sivakesava and Irudayaraj 2001b)
Sweeteners	Honey	Inverted cane syrup	Replacement	2003	FTIR with chemometrics (Irudayaraj and others 2003)
Sweeteners	Honey	Inverted sugar	Replacement	2009	FTIR with chemometrics (Gallardo-Velázquez and others 2009)
Sweeteners	Honey	Inverted syrup	Replacement	2007	GC-FID for difructose anhydrides (adulterant markers) on samples pre-treated with fermentation step to enhance difructose anhydrides concentration (Ruiz-Matute and others 2007)
Sweeteners	Honey	Isoglucose syrup	Replacement	2006	IRMS ($^{13}C/^{12}C$) on carbohydrate fraction (Cabanero and others 2006)
Sweeteners	Honey	Mixture of glucose and fructose	Replacement	2003	NIR with chemometrics (Gerard Downey 2003)
Sweeteners	Honey	Non-authentic sugars	Replacement	2008	NIR with chemometrics (Chen and others 2008)
Sweeteners	Honey	Non-authentic sugars	Replacement	2006	FT-MIR for 20 quantitative measurements (Ruoff and others 2006a)
Sweeteners	Honey	Non-authentic sugars	Replacement	2004	Amylase activity and total protein content (Li and others 2004)
Sweeteners	Honey	Non-authentic sweeteners	Replacement	2010	NMR (1D and 2D) and chemometrics (Bertelli and others 2010)
Sweeteners	Honey	Non-authentic sweeteners	Replacement	2005	HPLC-PAD and chemometrics (Cordella and others 2005)
Sweeteners	Honey	Non-authentic sweeteners	Replacement	1998	IRMS ($^{13}C/^{12}C$) on carbohydrate and protein fractions (White and others 1998)
Sweeteners	Honey	Non-authentic sweeteners	Replacement	2005	Review of physical and physicochemical tests: color, electrical conductivity, DSC, and rheological properties (Arvanitoyannis and others 2005)
Sweeteners	Honey	Non-authentic sweeteners	Replacement	2005	Review of instrumental methods for sugars analysis in combination with chemometrics: HPLC, GC-MS, TLC, HPLC-PAD, HPLC-MS, NMR, FT-Raman, and NIR (Arvanitoyannis and others 2005)
Sweeteners	Honey	Partial invert cane syrup	Replacement	2006	FT-MIR with chemometrics (Kelly and others 2006)
Sweeteners	Honey	Solution of D-fructose and D-glucose	Replacement	2004	MIR with chemometrics (Kelly and others 2004)
Sweeteners	Honey	Sucrose	Replacement	2002	MIR with chemometrics (Sivakesava and Irudayaraj 2002)
Sweeteners	Honey	Sucrose solution	Replacement	2003	IRMS ($^{13}C/^{12}C$) on carbohydrate and protein fractions (Padovan and others 2003)
Sweeteners	Honey	Sugar syrup	Replacement	2004	HPLC for amino acid fingerprinting with chemometrics (Cotte and others 2004)

Table 1: Scholarly Reports on Food Ingredient Fraud and Analytical Methods for Detection (continued)

Ingredient Category	Ingredient	Adulterant	Type of Fraud	Publication Year	Reported Detection Method and Reference
Sweeteners	Honey	Sugar syrups	Replacement	2001	DSC for the second enthalpy of fusion and the glass transition temperature (Cordella and others 2001)
Sweeteners	Honey	Sugar syrups	Replacement	2004	Immunochemical detection of Apalbumin-1 (authenticity marker) (Simuth and others 2004)
Sweeteners	Maple syrup	Beet invert syrup	Replacement	2003	FTIR with chemometrics (Paradkar and others 2003)
Sweeteners	Maple syrup	Beet medium invert syrup	Replacement	1995	HPLC-PAD oligosaccharides analysis for adulterant markers (Stuckel and Low 1995)
Sweeteners	Maple syrup	Beet sugar	Replacement	2006	IRMS ($^{13}C/^{12}C$) on sample and on isolated malic acid (Tremblay and Paquin 2006)
Sweeteners	Maple syrup	Beet sugar	Replacement	2001	SNIF-NMR ($^{2}H/^{1}H$) on ethanol from sample (Martin 2001)
Sweeteners	Maple syrup	Beet sugar	Replacement	1996	SNIF-NMR ($^{2}H/^{1}H$) and IRMS ($^{13}C/^{12}C$) on ethanol from sample fermentation (Martin and others 1996)
Sweeteners	Maple syrup	Beet sugar	Replacement	2003	FTIR with chemometrics (Paradkar and others 2003)
Sweeteners	Maple syrup	Cane invert syrup	Replacement	2003	FTIR with chemometrics (Paradkar and others 2003)
Sweeteners	Maple syrup	Cane sugar	Replacement	2006	IRMS ($^{13}C/^{12}C$) on sample and on isolated malic acid (Tremblay and Paquin 2006)
Sweeteners	Maple syrup	Cane sugar	Replacement	2001	SNIF-NMR ($^{2}H/^{1}H$) on ethanol from sample fermentation (Martin 2001)
Sweeteners	Maple syrup	Cane sugar	Replacement	1996	SNIF-NMR ($^{2}H/^{1}H$) and IRMS ($^{13}C/^{12}C$) on ethanol from sample fermentation (Martin and others 1996)
Sweeteners	Maple syrup	Cane sugar	Replacement	2002	FTIR with chemometrics (Paradkar and others 2003)
Sweeteners	Maple syrup	Corn sugar	Replacement	2001	SNIF-NMR ($^{2}H/^{1}H$) and IRMS ($^{13}C/^{12}C$) on ethanol from sample fermentation (Martin and others 1996)
Sweeteners	Maple syrup	Corn syrup	Replacement	2003	NIR combined with chemometrics (Paradkar and others 2002)
Sweeteners	Maple syrup	Corn syrup	Replacement	2002	FTIR combined with chemometrics (Paradkar and others 2002)
Sweeteners	Maple syrup	Corn syrup	Replacement	2002	FT-Raman combined with chemometrics (Paradkar and others 2002)
Sweeteners	Maple syrup	High-fructose corn syrup	Replacement	1995	HPLC-PAD oligosaccharides analysis for adulterant markers (Stuckel and Low 1995)
Sweeteners	Palm sugar	Cane sugar	Replacement	2010	Review: IRMS ($^{13}C/^{12}C$) (Primrose and others 2010)
Wines, musts, spirits, liquors, and vinegars	Agiorgitiko monovarietal grape wine	Cabernet Sauvignon wine	Replacement	2008	DNA-based assay using cleaved amplified polymorphic sequence and analysis with standard agarose gel or lab-on-a-chip capillary electrophoresis (Spaniolas and others 2008b)
Wines, musts, spirits, liquors, and vinegars	Falanghina monovarietal grape wine	Grape wine from non-authentic botanical origin	Replacement	2008	GC/MS, HPLC/ESIMS, and MALDI-ToF-MS for a characterization of varietal volatile and precursor non-aroma compounds (Nasi and others 2008)
Wines, musts, spirits, liquors, and vinegars	Grape musts (concentrated rectified)	Sugars	Replacement	1996	Chemometrics analysis of data from SNIF-NMR ($^{2}H/^{1}H$) on isolated ethanol, IRMS ($^{13}C/^{12}C$), and determination of *myo*- and *scyllo*-inositol contents by GC (Monetti and others 1996)

Table 1: Scholarly Reports on Food Ingredient Fraud and Analytical Methods for Detection *(continued)*

Ingredient Category	Ingredient	Adulterant	Type of Fraud	Publication Year	Reported Detection Method and Reference
Wines, musts, spirits, liquors, and vinegars	Grape musts (*Vitis vinifera*)	Grape wine from non-authentic botanical origin	Replacement	1994	Trace element analysis for Zn, Ca, Sr, and Mg used in combination with SNIF-NMR (Day and others 1994)
Wines, musts, spirits, liquors, and vinegars	Grape musts (*Vitis vinifera*)	Grape wine from non-authentic botanical origin	Replacement	2000	Microsatellite DNA analysis (Faria and others 2000)
Wines, musts, spirits, liquors, and vinegars	Grape wine (*Vitis vinifera*)	Apple juice	Replacement	1991	HPLC for chlorogenic acid (adulterant marker) (Burda and Collins 1991)
Wines, musts, spirits, liquors, and vinegars	Grape wine (*Vitis vinifera*)	Black rice pigment	Replacement	2007	HPLC for anthocyanins adulterant marker pigments (Zhang 2007)
Wines, musts, spirits, liquors, and vinegars	Grape wine (*Vitis vinifera*)	Elderberry pigments	Addition to mask poor quality	1996	HPLC-PDA for adulterant marker anthocyanins (Bridle and García-Viguera 1996)
Wines, musts, spirits, liquors, and vinegars	Grape wine (*Vitis vinifera*)	Grape wine from non-authentic botanical origin	Replacement	1989	GC for free amino acid fingerprinting (authentic and adulterant markers) (Vasconcelos and Chaves das Neves 1989)
Wines, musts, spirits, liquors, and vinegars	Grape wine (*Vitis vinifera*)	Grape wine from non-authentic botanical origin	Replacement	2000	Residual DNA analysis using microsatellite markers (Siret and others 2000)
Wines, musts, spirits, liquors, and vinegars	Grape wine (*Vitis vinifera*)	Grape wine from non-authentic botanical origin	Replacement	2006	Non-targeted analysis using MIR combined with chemometrics (Bevin and others 2006)
Wines, musts, spirits, liquors, and vinegars	Grape wine (*Vitis vinifera*)	Grape wine from non-authentic botanical origin	Replacement	2003	Visible and NIR combined with chemometrics (Cozzolino and others 2003)
Wines, musts, spirits, liquors, and vinegars	Grape wine (*Vitis vinifera*)	Grape wine from non-authentic botanical origin	Replacement	1999	Review of methods coupled with chemometrics: SNIF-NMR ($^2H/^1H$) on isolated ethanol; trace elements analysis; phenolics profiling by HPLC; Volatiles analysis by GC; tri-stimulus color parameters L*, a* and b*; amino acids fingerprinting (Arvanitoyannis and others 1999)
Wines, musts, spirits, liquors, and vinegars	Grape wine (*Vitis vinifera*)	Grape wine from non-authentic geographic origin	Replacement	2001	SNIF-NMR and IRMS combined with chemometrics (Ogrinc and others 2001)
Wines, musts, spirits, liquors, and vinegars	Grape wine (*Vitis vinifera*)	Grape wine from non-authentic geographic origin	Replacement	1997	ICP-MS for trace elements analysis combined with chemometrics (J. Baxter and others 1997)
Wines, musts, spirits, liquors, and vinegars	Grape wine (*Vitis vinifera*)	Must concentration	Addition to mask poor quality	1995	IRMS ($^2H/^1H$) and ($^{18}O/^{16}O$) of water from wine (Yunianta and others 1995)
Wines, musts, spirits, liquors, and vinegars	Grape wine (*Vitis vinifera*)	Sorbitol	Replacement	1991	GC-FID for sorbitol (Burda and Collins 1991)
Wines, musts, spirits, liquors, and vinegars	Grape wine (*Vitis vinifera*)	Sugars	Addition to mask poor quality	1995	IRMS ($^2H/^1H$) and ($^{18}O/^{16}O$) of water from wine (Yunianta and others 1995)
Wines, musts, spirits, liquors, and vinegars	Grape wine (*Vitis vinifera*)	Sugars	Addition to mask poor quality	2003	Review and NMR and MS methods (Ogrinc and others 2003)
Wines, musts, spirits, liquors, and vinegars	Grape wine (*Vitis vinifera*)	Sugars	Addition to mask poor quality	2006	IRMS ($^{13}C/^{12}C$) (Versini and others 2006)
Wines, musts, spirits, liquors, and vinegars	Mezcal	Mezcal of non-authentic age/grade	Replacement	2009	ICP-MS for sodium, potassium, calcium, sulfur, magnesium, iron, strontium, copper, and zinc, combined with chemometrics (Ceballos-Magana and others 2009)

Table 1: Scholarly Reports on Food Ingredient Fraud and Analytical Methods for Detection (continued)

Ingredient Category	Ingredient	Adulterant	Type of Fraud	Publication Year	Reported Detection Method and Reference
Wines, musts, spirits, liquors, and vinegars	Scotch whiskey (brand specific)	Non-authentic brand	Replacement	1998	GC-combustion IRMS ($^{13}C/^{12}C$) on acetaldehyde, ethyl acetate, n-propanol, isobutanol, and amyl alcohol (Parker and others 1998)
Wines, musts, spirits, liquors, and vinegars	Tequila	Non-authentic spirit or geographic origin	Replacement	2002	SPME and GC-pyrolysis/combustion IRMS ($^{18}O/^{16}O$) on ethanol (Aguilar-Cisneros and others 2002)
Wines, musts, spirits, liquors, and vinegars	Tequila	Tequila (derived from non-agave fermentable sugars)	Replacement	2003	GC for methanol and 2-/3-methyl-1-butanol ratio and SNIF-NMR ($^{13}C/^{12}C$) on ethanol (Bauer-Christoph and others 2003)
Wines, musts, spirits, liquors, and vinegars	Tequila	Tequila from non-authentic geographic origin	Replacement	2005	FTIR and chemometrics (Lachenmeier and others 2005)
Wines, musts, spirits, liquors, and vinegars	Tequila	Tequila of non-authentic age (grade)	Replacement	2009	ICP-MS for sodium, potassium, calcium, sulfur, magnesium, iron, strontium, copper, and zinc, combined with chemometrics (Ceballos-Magana and others 2009)
Wines, musts, spirits, liquors, and vinegars	Vinegar	Synthetically derived acetic acid	Replacement	1992	SNIF-NMR ($^2H/^1H$) and ($^{13}C/^{12}C$) (Remaud and others 1992)
Wines, musts, spirits, liquors, and vinegars	Vinegar	Vinegar from non-authentic fermentable sugar source	Replacement	2010	GC-combustion-IRMS ($^{13}C/^{12}C$) on acetic acid isolated by head space solid-phase microextraction (Hattori and others 2010)
Wines, musts, spirits, liquors, and vinegars	Vinegar	Vinegar from non-authentic fermentable sugar source	Replacement	2005	NIR with chemometrics (Saiz-Abajo and others 2005)
Wines, musts, spirits, liquors, and vinegars	Vinegar (apple cider)	Corn-derived vinegar	Replacement	1992	IRMS ($^{13}C/^{12}C$) on acetic acid (Krueger 1992)
Wines, musts, spirits, liquors, and vinegars	Vinegar (wine)	Alcohol-derived vinegar	Replacement	2004	NIR with chemometrics (Saiz-Abajo and others 2004)
Wines, musts, spirits, liquors, and vinegars	Zivania	Non-authentic spirits	Replacement	2003	ICP-MS for trace metals analysis with chemometrics (Kokkinofta and others 2003)
Wines, musts, spirits, liquors, and vinegars	Zivania	Non-authentic spirits	Replacement	2005	H-NMR with chemometrics (Petrakis and others 2005)

Table 2: Media and Other Reports of Food Ingredient Fraud

Ingredient Category	Ingredient	Adulterant	Type of Fraud and Reference	Publication Year
Cereals, grains, and pulses	Grains	Sand, marble, or stones	Replacement (Jaiswal 2008)	2008
Cereals, grains, and pulses	Pulses	Khesari dal or lathyrus sativus	Replacement (Mishra 2010)	2010
Cereals, grains, and pulses	Pulses	Khesari dal or lathyrus sativus	Replacement (Jaiswal 2008)	2008
Cereals, grains, and pulses	Pulses	Lead chromate	Addition to mask poor quality (Jaiswal 2008)	2008
Cereals, grains, and pulses	Pulses	Yellow dye	Addition to mask poor quality (Jaiswal 2008)	2008
Cereals, grains, and pulses	Rice	Mixture of potato and plastic resin	Replacement (Anonymous 2011a)	2011
Cereals, grains, and pulses	Rice (Basmati)	Non-authentic varietal	Replacement (Rovner 2010)	2010
Cereals, grains, and pulses	Rice (Basmati)	Non-authentic varietal	Replacement (Kermack 2008)	2008
Cereals, grains, and pulses	Rice (Basmati)	Non-authentic varietal	Replacement (FSA 2004)	2004
Cereals, grains, and pulses	Rice (Basmati)	Non-authentic varietal	Replacement (FSA 2004)	2004
Cereals, grains, and pulses	Rice protein concentrate	Melamine	Replacement (FDA 2007b)	2007

Table 2: Media and Other Reports of Food Ingredient Fraud (continued)

Ingredient Category	Ingredient	Adulterant	Type of Fraud and Reference	Publication Year
Cereals, grains, and pulses	Wheat	Nitrogen containing fertilizers (urea, ammonia, or ammonia salts)	Replacement (McDonald and Bruns 1988)	1988
Cereals, grains, and pulses	Wheat	Urea	Replacement (Folkenberg 1990)	1990
Cereals, grains, and pulses	Wheat flour	Chalk	Replacement (Jaiswal 2008)	2008
Cereals, grains, and pulses	Wheat flour	Melamine	Replacement (Weise and Schmit 2008)	2008
Cereals, grains, and pulses	Wheat flour	Pulverized lime	Replacement (Harrington 2010)	2010
Cereals, grains, and pulses	Wheat gluten*	Melamine	Replacement (FDA 2007b)	2007
Cereals, grains, and pulses	Wheat gluten*	Melamine	Replacement (Barboza and Barrionuevo 2007)	2007
Cereals, grains, and pulses	Wheat gluten*	Melamine	Replacement (FDA 2007a)	2007
Dairy products and milk derivatives	Ghee	Mash potato	Replacement (Jaiswal 2008)	2008
Dairy products and milk derivatives	Ghee	Synthetic colors	Addition to mask poor quality (Jaiswal 2008)	2008
Dairy products and milk derivatives	Ghee	Vanaspati (hydrogenated vegetable fat)	Replacement (Jaiswal 2008)	2008
Dairy products and milk derivatives	Goat's cheese	Cow's cheese	Replacement (Anonymous 2010b)	2010
Fruit juices, concentrates, jams, purees, and preserves	Apple juice	Mixture of water, sweeteners, flavorings, and colors	Replacement (Buder 1988)	1988
Fruit juices, concentrates, jams, purees, and preserves	Apple juice	Mixture of water, sweeteners, flavorings, and colors	Replacement (Traub 1988)	1988
Fruit juices, concentrates, jams, purees, and preserves	Apple juice	Mixture of water, sweeteners, flavorings, and colors	Replacement (Modeland 1988)	1988
Fruit juices, concentrates, jams, purees, and preserves	Juice	Colorants	Addition to mask poor quality (Rovner 2010)	2010
Fruit juices, concentrates, jams, purees, and preserves	Juice	Mixture of water and sweeteners	Replacement (GAO 1995)	1995
Fruit juices, concentrates, jams, purees, and preserves	Juice	Mixture of water, sweeteners, and preservatives	Replacement (Henriques 1993)	1993
Fruit juices, concentrates, jams, purees, and preserves	Orange juice	Mixture of beet sugar, corn sugar, monosodium glutamate, ascorbic acid, potassium sulfate, orange pulp wash, grapefruit solids, and a byproduct from a water distillation system	Replacement (Blumenthal and Holland 1989)	1989
Fruit juices, concentrates, jams, purees, and preserves	Orange juice	Mixture of beet sugar, pulp wash, amino and citric acids, and natamycin	Replacement (Ropp 1994)	1994
Fruit juices, concentrates, jams, purees, and preserves	Pomegranate juice	High-fructose corn syrup	Replacement (Hein 2008)	2008
Functional food ingredients	Bilberry	Amaranth dye or non-authentic source of anthocyanins	Replacement (Dentali 2007)	2007
Functional food ingredients	Black cohosh (*Actaea racemosa*)	Other *Actea* and *Cimicifuga* species	Replacement (Starling 2010)	2010
Functional food ingredients	Ginko	Non-authentic botanical ingredients with flavanoids	Replacement (Starling 2008)	2008
Functional food ingredients	Inulin	Free glucose or sucrose	Replacement (Anonymous 2009c)	2009
Meats	Chicken breasts	Protein powder	Addition to mask poor quality or undeclared addition (FSA 2009)	2009
Meats	Chicken meat	Beef and pork gristle and bones	Replacement (Hickman 2009)	2009
Meats	Chicken meat	Condemned/contaminated chicken meat	Replacement (Kermack 2008)	2008
Milk	Milk (fluid)	Hydrolyzed leather	Replacement (Rovner 2009)	2009

Table 2: Media and Other Reports of Food Ingredient Fraud (continued)

Ingredient Category	Ingredient	Adulterant	Type of Fraud and Reference	Publication Year
Milk	Milk (fluid)	Hydrolyzed leather	Replacement (Anonymous 2009d)	2009
Milk	Milk (fluid)	Melamine	Replacement (Rovner 2009)	2009
Milk	Milk (fluid)	Melamine	Replacement (Toy 2008)	2008
Milk	Milk (fluid)	Melamine	Replacement (Branigan 2008)	2008
Milk	Milk (fluid)	Melamine	Replacement (Wines 2010)	2010
Milk	Milk (powder)	Gardenia yellow dye	Addition to enhance color (Anonymous 2009a)	2009
Natural flavoring complexes	Almond oil, bitter* (*Prunus amygdalus* var. *dulcis*)	Benzaldehyde, as the oil	Replacement (Burfield 2003)	2003
Natural flavoring complexes	Anise oil* (*Pimpinella* spp.)	Star anise oil (*Illicium verum*)	Replacement (Burfield 2003)	2003
Natural flavoring complexes	Anise oil* (*Pimpinella* spp.)	Technical grade anethol	Replacement (Burfield 2003)	2003
Natural flavoring complexes	Basil oil exotic (*Ocimum* spp.)	Methyl chavicol and linalol	Replacement (Burfield 2003)	2003
Natural flavoring complexes	Benzoin resinoid (*Styrax* spp.)	Vanillin, benzyl benzoate, ethyl and benzyl cinnamates, and benzoic acid to enhance odor (or to pass off cheaper "Sumatra" grades as "Siam")	Replacement (Burfield 2003)	2003
Natural flavoring complexes	Bergamot oil* (*Citrus bergamia*)	Lemon oil, rectified ho oil (*Cinnamomum* spp.), acetylated ho oil, or Bitter orange oil (*Citrus aurantium* subsp. *aurantium*)	Replacement (Burfield 2003)	2003
Natural flavoring complexes	Bergamot oil* (*Citrus bergamia*)	Linalol and linalyl acetate	Replacement (Burfield 2003)	2003
Natural flavoring complexes	Bergamot oil* (*Citrus bergamia*)	Sweet orange oil (*Citrus sinensis*) and orange terpenes, plus trace amounts of character compounds	Replacement (Burfield 2003)	2003
Natural flavoring complexes	Buchu leaf oil (*Barosma betulina* and *B. crenulata*)	Monoterpene sulphide fractions synthesised from the hydrogen sulphide treatment of pulegone, including *p*-menthan-8- thiol-3-one	Replacement (Burfield 2003)	2003
Natural flavoring complexes	Caraway oil* (*Carum carvii*)	Limonene and (+)-carvone	Replacement (Burfield 2003)	2003
Natural flavoring complexes	Cardamom oil* (*Elletaria cardamomum*)	Linalyl acetate, 1,8-cineole, and alpha-terpinyl acetate	Replacement (Burfield 2003)	2003
Natural flavoring complexes	Cassia oil* (*Cinnamomum aromaticum*)	Synthetic cinnamic aldehyde, methyl cinnamic aldehyde, and coumarin	Replacement (Burfield 2003)	2003
Natural flavoring complexes	Cedarwood oil Virginia (*Juniperus virginiana*)	Cedarwood oil Chinese (*Cupressus funebris*)	Replacement (Burfield 2003)	2003
Natural flavoring complexes	Celery seed oil* (*Petroselenium crispum*)	Limonene and touches of alkyl phthalides	Replacement (Burfield 2003)	2003
Natural flavoring complexes	Chamomile oil* (*Anthemis nobilis*)	Isobutyl angelate and bisabolols	Replacement (Burfield 2003)	2003
Natural flavoring complexes	Cinnamon bark oil* (*Cinnamomum zeylanicum*)	Cinnamon leaf oil	Replacement (Burfield 2003)	2003
Natural flavoring complexes	Cinnamon bark oil* (*Cinnamomum zeylanicum*)	Synthetic benzaldehde, eugenol, and cinnamic aldehyde	Replacement (Burfield 2003)	2003
Natural flavoring complexes	Cinnamon leaf oil* (*Cinnamomum zeylanicum*)	Clove fractions, eugenol, and cinnamic aldehyde	Replacement (Burfield 2003)	2003
Natural flavoring complexes	Citrus oils	Fatty aldehydes and monoterpene alcohols and esters to terpeneless and folded citrus oils	Replacement (Burfield 2003)	2003
Natural flavoring complexes	Clove oil* (*Syzygium aromaticum*)	Clove stem oil and isolates (eugenol) and eugenyl acetate	Replacement (Burfield 2003)	2003

Table 2: Media and Other Reports of Food Ingredient Fraud (continued)

Ingredient Category	Ingredient	Adulterant	Type of Fraud and Reference	Publication Year
Natural flavoring complexes	Cognac oil*	Ethyl esters of aliphatic acids (e.g., ethyl oenanthate)	Replacement (Burfield 2003)	2003
Natural flavoring complexes	Coriander oil* (Coriandrum sativum)	Linalol and trace amounts of certain pyrazines	Replacement (Burfield 2003)	2003
Natural flavoring complexes	Cumin oil* (Cuminum cyminum)	Cuminaldehyde	Replacement (Burfield 2003)	2003
Natural flavoring complexes	Cypress oil (Cupressus sempervirens)	alpha-Pinene, d-3-carene, myrcene	Replacement (Burfield 2003)	2003
Natural flavoring complexes	Dill seed oil* (Anethum graveolens)	alpha-Phellandrene and limonene	Replacement (Burfield 2003)	2003
Natural flavoring complexes	Elemi oil (Canarium luzonicum)	alpha-Phellandrene and limonene	Replacement (Burfield 2003)	2003
Natural flavoring complexes	Essential oils (general)	Diluent solvents including: Abitol, benzyl alcohol, benzyl benzoate, carbitol (diethylene glycol monoethyl ether), diacetone alcohol, dipropylene glycol, dipropylene glycol methyl ether and tripropylene glycol methyl ether, hydrogenated methyl ester of rosin, isoparä (odorless kerosene fractions often used as a candle perfume diluent), isopropyl myristate (IPM), phthalate esters such as dibutylphthalate or diethyl phthalate, or triacetin (glycerol triacetate, 3,3,5-trimethyl-hexan-1-ol, isotridecyl acetate)	Replacement (Burfield 2003)	2003
Natural flavoring complexes	Eucalyptus oil*	Cinnamomum camphora (var. cineole type) fractions (1,8-cineole rich)	Replacement (Burfield 2003)	2003
Natural flavoring complexes	Galbanum resinoid (Ferula galbaniflua)	beta-Pinene, undecatrienes	Replacement (Burfield 2003)	2003
Natural flavoring complexes	Garlic oil* (Allium sativa)	Aliphatic sulphide mixtures containing 2-propenyl disulphide, and 1-propenyl disulphide	Replacement (Burfield 2003)	2003
Natural flavoring complexes	Geranium oil, Chinese (Pelargonium hybrids)	Indian geranium oil	Replacement (Burfield 2003)	2003
Natural flavoring complexes	Grapefruit oil* (Citrus paradisi)	Orange terpenes or sweet orange oil distilled and minor amounts of (+)-nootkatone	Replacement (Burfield 2003)	2003
Natural flavoring complexes	Juniper berries oil* (Juniperus communis var. erecta)	Terpene hydrocarbon mixtures containing a-pinene and d-3-carene, also Juniper branch oil and second grade oils from spoiled Juniper berries	Replacement (Burfield 2003)	2003
Natural flavoring complexes	Labdanum oil* (Cistus landiferus)	Abitol with small amounts of ambroxan and p-methyl acetophenone to enhance odour	Replacement (Burfield 2003)	2003
Natural flavoring complexes	Lavender oil* (Lavandula angustifolia)	Spike lavender oil (Lavandula latifolia)	Replacement (Burfield 2003)	2003
Natural flavoring complexes	Lavender oil* (Lavandula angustifolia)	Ho oil rectified (Cinnamomum spp.) and acetylated ho or acetylated lavandin oils	Replacement (Burfield 2003)	2003
Natural flavoring complexes	Lavender oil* (Lavandula angustifolia)	Lavandin (Lavandula x intermedia) oil varieties	Replacement (Burfield 2003)	2003
Natural flavoring complexes	Lemon oil* (Citrus limon)	Expressed lime or grapefruit oil	Replacement (Burfield 2003)	2003
Natural flavoring complexes	Lemon oil* (Citrus limon)	Orange terpenes, lemon terpenes, and by-products (e.g., steam-stripped lemon oil)	Replacement (Burfield 2003)	2003

Table 2: Media and Other Reports of Food Ingredient Fraud (continued)

Ingredient Category	Ingredient	Adulterant	Type of Fraud and Reference	Publication Year
Natural flavoring complexes	Lemongrass oil* (Cympogon spp.)	Citral	Replacement (Burfield 2003)	2003
Natural flavoring complexes	Mentha citrata oil	Linalol and linalyl acetate	Replacement (Burfield 2003)	2003
Natural flavoring complexes	Mustard oil* (Brassica nigra and B. juncea)	Allyl isothiocyanate	Replacement (Burfield 2003)	2003
Natural flavoring complexes	Mustard oil* (Brassica nigra and B. juncea)	Neroli oil (Citrus aurantium subsp. aurantium)	Replacement (Burfield 2003)	2003
Natural flavoring complexes	Nutmeg oil* (Myristica fragrans)	Nutmeg terpenes, a-pinene, limonene, and turpentine fractions	Replacement (Burfield 2003)	2003
Natural flavoring complexes	Onion oil* (Allium cepa)	Aliphatic sulphide mixtures	Replacement (Burfield 2003)	2003
Natural flavoring complexes	Orange oil, Sweet, Florida type	Sweet orange oil Brazil	Replacement (Burfield 2003)	2003
Natural flavoring complexes	Origanum oil* (Origanum spp.)	para-Cymene and carvacrol	Replacement (Burfield 2003)	2003
Natural flavoring complexes	Palmarosa oil* (Cymbopogon martinii var. motia)	Geraniol	Replacement (Burfield 2003)	2003
Natural flavoring complexes	Patchouli oil (Pogostemon cablin)	Gurjun balsam (Dipterocarpus spp.)	Replacement (Burfield 2003)	2003
Natural flavoring complexes	Patchouli oil (Pogostemon cablin)	Patchouli and vetiver distillation residues	Replacement (Burfield 2003)	2003
Natural flavoring complexes	Patchouli oil (Pogostemon cablin)	Indonesian patchouli oil blended with the cheaper Chinese oil	Replacement (Burfield 2003)	2003
Natural flavoring complexes	Patchouli oil (Pogostemon cablin)	Vegetable oils, Hercolyn D	Replacement (Burfield 2003)	2003
Natural flavoring complexes	Peppermint oil* (Mentha x piperita)	Cornmint oil (Mentha arvensis)	Replacement (Burfield 2003)	2003
Natural flavoring complexes	Peppermint oil* (Mentha x piperita)	Cornmint oil from Mentha arvensis var. piperascens	Replacement (Burfield 2003)	2003
Natural flavoring complexes	Petitgrain oil, Paraguay type* (Citrus aurantia subsp. aurantium)	Admixture of linalol, linalyl acetate, alpha-terpineol, geranyl, and neryl acetates with trace amounts of pyrazines	Replacement (Burfield 2003)	2003
Natural flavoring complexes	Petitgrain oils (Citrus spp)	Other citrus leaf oils and fractions, fatty aldehydes, linalyl acetate, and orange terpenes	Replacement (Burfield 2003)	2003
Natural flavoring complexes	Pine needle oil* (Pinus spp.)	(−)-Bornyl acetate, isobornyl acetate, (−)-limonene, alpha-pinene, and camphene	Replacement (Burfield 2003)	2003
Natural flavoring complexes	Rose oil*	beta-Phenylethyl alcohol, rhodinol fractions, and cheaper rose oils (Morocco, Crimea, etc.)	Replacement (Burfield 2003)	2003
Natural flavoring complexes	Rose oil*	Reconstructions using damascones, beta-ionone plus (−)-citronellol and other rose alcohols, plus rose steroptenes	Replacement (Burfield 2003)	2003
Natural flavoring complexes	Rosemary oil* (Rosmarinus officinalis)	Camphor, isobornyl acetate (+ Eucalyptus and turpentine oil fractions)	Replacement (Burfield 2003)	2003
Natural flavoring complexes	Rosemary oil* (Rosmarinus officinalis)	Eucalyptus oil (Eucalyptus globulus) and camphor oil white (Cinnamomum camphora)	Replacement (Burfield 2003)	2003
Natural flavoring complexes	Rosewood oil (Aniba spp.)	Linalol, plus trace amounts of methyl heptenone, methyl heptenol, 3-octanol, and para-methyl acetophenone	Replacement (Burfield 2003)	2003
Natural flavoring complexes	Rosewood oil (Aniba spp.)	Petitgrain oil terpeneless (Citrus aurantium subsp. aurantium)	Replacement (Burfield 2003)	2003
Natural flavoring complexes	Sandalwood oil* EI (Santalum album)	Sandalwood terpenes and sandalwood fragrance chemicals	Replacement (Burfield 2003)	2003

Table 2: Media and Other Reports of Food Ingredient Fraud (continued)

Ingredient Category	Ingredient	Adulterant	Type of Fraud and Reference	Publication Year
Natural flavoring complexes	Spearmint oil* (*Mentha spicata*)	(–)-Carvone	Replacement (Burfield 2003)	2003
Natural flavoring complexes	Spike lavender oil* (*Lavandula latifolia*)	Eucalyptus and white camphor oil fractions, spanish sage oil	Replacement (Burfield 2003)	2003
Natural flavoring complexes	Tangerine oil* (*Citrus reticula* var. *tangerine*)	gamma-Terpinene, dimethyl anthranilate, alpha-sinesal, and perilla aldehyde to convert to Mandarin oil (*Citrus reticulata* var. *mandarin*)	Replacement (Burfield 2003)	2003
Natural flavoring complexes	Tea tree oil (*Melaleuca altenaria*)	Patchouli oil, vetiver oil, and to some extent ginger oil	Replacement (Burfield 2003)	2003
Natural flavoring complexes	Tea tree oil (*Melaleuca altenaria*)	Terpinen-4-ol and alpha- and gamma-terpinenes	Replacement (Burfield 2003)	2003
Natural flavoring complexes	Thyme oil* (*Thymus spp.*)	para-Cymene and thymol	Replacement (Burfield 2003)	2003
Natural flavoring complexes	Vanilla extract	Vanillin	Replacement (Weise 2009)	2009
Natural flavoring complexes	Verbena oil (*Lippia citriodora*)	*L. citriodora* herb distilled over lemon oil	Replacement (Burfield 2003)	2003
Natural flavoring complexes	Violet leaf absolute (*Viola odorata*)	Spinach absolute (*Spinacia oleracea*)	Replacement (Burfield 2003)	2003
Natural flavoring complexes	Ylang ylang oil (*Cananga odorata* var. *genuina*)	Benzyl acetate, methyl benzoate, para-cresyl methyl ether, geranyl acetate, benzyl benzoate, benzyl cinnamate, cedarwood oil, and others or complete reconstitutions/bases	Replacement (Burfield 2003)	2003
Natural flavoring complexes	Ylang ylang oil qualities (*Cananga odorata* subsp. *genuina*)	Cananga oil (*Cananga odorata*), ylang ylang oil tails, and ylang ylang oil reconstitutions	Replacement (Burfield 2003)	2003
Oils	Cooking oil	Argemone oil	Replacement (Jaiswal 2008)	2008
Oils	Cooking oil	Mineral oil	Replacement (Jaiswal 2008)	2008
Oils	Cooking oil	Rancid cooking oil	Replacement (Jaiswal 2008)	2008
Oils	Cooking oil	Waste or recycled oil	Replacement (Rui and Yan 2010)	2010
Oils	Cooking oil	Waste or recycled oil	Replacement (Zhiling 2010)	2010
Oils	Olive oil	Canola oil	Replacement (Henkel 1994)	1994
Oils	Olive oil	Mixture of sunflower oil, chlorophyll, and beta-carotene	Replacement (Anonymous 2008)	2008
Oils	Olive oil	Olive oil from non-authentic geographic origin	Replacement (Moore 2007)	2007
Oils	Olive oil	Soybean oil	Replacement (Anonymous 2006)	2006
Oils	Olive oil	Sunflower oil	Replacement (Gombu 1998)	1998
Oils	Olive oil	Vegetable oil	Replacement (Anonymous 2005a)	2005
Oils	Olive oil	Vegetable oil	Replacement (Gombu 1998)	1998
Oils	Olive oil (extra virgin)	Non-authentic oil	Replacement (Frankel and others 2010)	2010
Oils	Olive oil (extra virgin)	Soybean oil	Replacement (Weise 2009)	2009
Oils	Olive oil (pomace)	Soybean oil	Replacement (Anonymous 2006)	2006
Oils	Palm oil*	Agric white oil and red color additive	Replacement (Mosadoni 2009)	2009
Oils	Palm oil*	Sudan IV dye	Addition to mask poor quality (Anonymous 2009a)	2009
Other	Coffee	Coffee husk or cereals	Replacement (Rovner 2010)	2010
Other	Coffee (Arabica)	Coffee (Robusta)	Replacement (Rovner 2010)	2010
Other	Duck eggs	Sudan red dyes	Addition to mask poor quality (Yan 2006)	2006
Other	Fresh fruits	Carbide	Addition to enhance ripeness and mask poor quality (Rahman 2010)	2010

Table 2: Media and Other Reports of Food Ingredient Fraud (continued)

Ingredient Category	Ingredient	Adulterant	Type of Fraud and Reference	Publication Year
Other	Fresh fruits	Oxytocin	Addition to enhance ripeness and mask poor quality (Anonymous 2010a)	2010
Other	Pinenuts	Non-authentic species	Replacement (Gray 2010)	2010
Other	Salt*	Industrial salt	Replacement (Anonymous 2009b)	2009
Other	Salt*	Industrial salt	Replacement (Tian 2009)	2009
Other	Tea	Non-authentic variety	Replacement (Rovner 2010)	2010
Other	Tea leaves	Colored saw dust	Replacement (Jaiswal 2008)	2008
Other	Tea leaves	Non-authentic leaves	Replacement (Jaiswal 2008)	2008
Seafood	Belacan (shrimp paste)	Fake shrimp paste	Replacement (Shah 2010)	2010
Seafood	Caviar (beluga or sevruga)	Paddlefish roe	Replacement (Frantz 1999)	1999
Seafood	Caviar (beluga or sevruga)	Paddlefish roe	Replacement (Frantz 1999)	1999
Seafood	Caviar (beluga)	Catfish roe	Replacement (Burros 1992a)	1992
Seafood	Caviar (beluga)	Lumpfish roe	Replacement (Burros 1992a)	1992
Seafood	Caviar (beluga)	Salmon roe	Replacement (Burros 1992a)	1992
Seafood	Fish	Non-authentic fish species	Replacement (Burros 1992b)	1992
Seafood	Fish (Bluefish)	Herring	Replacement (Sampson 2009)	2009
Seafood	Fish (Catfish)	Asian basa	Replacement (Sampson 2009)	2009
Seafood	Fish (Cod)	Alaskan pollack	Replacement (Burros 1992a)	1992
Seafood	Fish (Grouper)	Catfish	Replacement (to avoid anti-dumping tariffs) (GAO 2009)	2009
Seafood	Fish (Grouper, wild)	Catfish	Replacement (Reed 2006)	2006
Seafood	Fish (Grouper, wild)	Grouper (farm-raised)	Replacement (Burros 1992b)	1992
Seafood	Fish (Halibut)	Sea bass	Replacement (Burros 1992a)	1992
Seafood	Fish (Mahi-mahi)	Yellowtail fish	Replacement (Burros 1992a)	1992
Seafood	Fish (Monkfish)	Puffer fish	Replacement (Sampson 2009)	2009
Seafood	Fish (Monkfish)	Puffer fish	Replacement (GAO 2009)	2009
Seafood	Fish (Orange roughy)	John Dory	Replacement (Burros 1992a)	1992
Seafood	Fish (Red snapper)	Non-authentic fish species	Replacement (Sampson 2009)	2009
Seafood	Fish (Red snapper)	Pacific rockfish	Replacement (Burros 1992a)	1992
Seafood	Fish (Red snapper)	Tilapia or white bass	Replacement (Zavitsanos 2010)	2010
Seafood	Fish (Salmon, Atlantic, wild)	Salmon (farm-raised)	Replacement (Weise 2009)	2009
Seafood	Fish (Salmon, Pacific, wild)	Salmon (Atlantic, farm-raised)	Replacement (Sampson 2009)	2009
Seafood	Fish (Sea bass, Chilean)	Patagonian toothfish	Replacement (Sampson 2009)	2009
Seafood	Fish (Swordfish)	Mako shark	Replacement (Burros 1992a)	1992
Seafood	Fish (Tilapia, USA)	Tilapia (Chinese)	Replacement (Sampson 2009)	2009
Seafood	Fish (Tuna, white)	Tilapia	Replacement (Sampson 2009)	2009
Seafood	Fish (Red snapper)	Tilapia	Replacement (Sampson 2009)	2009
Seafood	Fish (Tuna, sushi-grade)	Skipjack	Replacement (Sampson 2009)	2009
Seafood	Scallops	Water (use of water retention agents or overglazing)	Replacement (over-treating with water) (Burros 1992a)	1992
Seafood	Shrimp (Indonesian)	Shrimp (Chinese)	Replacement (to avoid anti-dumping tariffs) (GAO 2009)	2009
Spices	Asafoetida	Chalk	Replacement (Jaiswal 2008)	2008
Spices	Asafoetida	Soap stone	Replacement (Jaiswal 2008)	2008
Spices	Black cardamom (Badi Elaichi)	Choti Elaichi seeds	Replacement (Jaiswal 2008)	2008

Table 2: Media and Other Reports of Food Ingredient Fraud (continued)

Ingredient Category	Ingredient	Adulterant	Type of Fraud and Reference	Publication Year
Spices	Black pepper	Artificially colored non-authentic seed	Replacement (Jaiswal 2008)	2008
Spices	Black pepper	Buckwheat	Replacement (Anonymous 2004)	2004
Spices	Black pepper	Juniper berry	Replacement (Anonymous 2004)	2004
Spices	Black pepper	Millet seeds	Replacement (Anonymous 2004)	2004
Spices	Black pepper	Papaya or other non-authentic plant seeds	Replacement (Jaiswal 2008)	2008
Spices	Black pepper	Spent black pepper meal	Replacement (Anonymous 2004)	2004
Spices	Capsicum spices	Dextrose or disaccahrides	Replacement (Anonymous 2004)	2004
Spices	Chili powder	Brick powder, sand, or dirt	Replacement (Jaiswal 2008)	2008
Spices	Chili powder	Sudan red I dyes	Replacement (Anonymous 2004)	2004
Spices	Chili powder	Sudan red I dyes	Replacement (Ramesh and others 2005)	2005
Spices	Chili powder	Sudan red I dyes	Replacement (Meikle 2005)	2005
Spices	Chili powder	Sudan red I dyes	Replacement (Lawrence 2005)	2005
Spices	Chili powder	Sudan red I dyes	Replacement (Anonymous 2005b)	2005
Spices	Chili powder	Sudan red I dyes	Replacement (Commission 2003)	2003
Spices	Chili powder	Sudan red I dyes	Replacement (Derbyshire 2005)	2005
Spices	Cinnamon	Coffee husks	Replacement (Anonymous 2004)	2004
Spices	Coriander powder	Dung	Replacement (Jaiswal 2008)	2008
Spices	Coriander powder	Salt	Replacement (Jaiswal 2008)	2008
Spices	Cumin seeds	Artificially colored non-authentic seed	Replacement (Jaiswal 2008)	2008
Spices	Cumin seeds	Grass seeds colored with charcoal dust	Replacement (Jaiswal 2008)	2008
Spices	Mustard seeds	Argemone seeds	Replacement (Jaiswal 2008)	2008
Spices	Nutmeg	Coffee husks	Replacement (Anonymous 2004)	2004
Spices	Oregano	Non-authentic herbs (e.g., savory, thyme)	Replacement (Anonymous 2004)	2004
Spices	Oregano	Non-authentic leaves (e.g., sumac, cistus)	Replacement (Anonymous 2004)	2004
Spices	Paprika	Color additives	Replacement (Anonymous 2004)	2004
Spices	Paprika	Defatted paprika	Removal of valuable constituent (Anonymous 2004)	2004
Spices	Paprika	Lead oxide	Replacement (Anonymous 2004)	2004
Spices	Paprika	Sudan 1 and 4 dyes	Addition to enhance color (Anonymous 2009a)	2009
Spices	Paprika	Turmeric	Replacement (Anonymous 2004)	2004
Spices	Poppy seeds	Artificially colored non-authentic seed	Replacement (Jaiswal 2008)	2008
Spices	Saffron	Artificial colors	Addition to mask poor quality (Rovner 2010)	2010
Spices	Saffron	Color additives	Replacement (Anonymous 2004)	2004
Spices	Saffron	Crocus's yellow stamen	Replacement (Herbert 2000)	2000
Spices	Saffron	Floral waste	Replacement (Anonymous 2004)	2004
Spices	Saffron	Saffron stamens or styles, or stigmas from other Crocus species such as marigolds	Replacement (Rovner 2010)	2010
Spices	Spice mixtures	Lead chromate	Replacement (Jaiswal 2008)	2008
Spices	Spices, general	Artificial colors	Addition to mask poor quality (Rovner 2010)	2010
Spices	Spices, general	Bran or saw dust	Replacement (Jaiswal 2008)	2008
Spices	Turmeric	Lead	Replacement (Anonymous 2011c)	2011

Table 2: Media and Other Reports of Food Ingredient Fraud (continued)

Ingredient Category	Ingredient	Adulterant	Type of Fraud and Reference	Publication Year
Spices	Turmeric	Lead chromate	Replacement (Jaiswal 2008)	2008
Spices	Turmeric	Lead chromate	Replacement with lead chromate (Mishra 2010)	2010
Spices	Turmeric	Maize starch	Replacement (Jaiswal 2008)	2008
Spices	Turmeric	Metanil yellow dye	Replacement (Jaiswal 2008)	2008
Sweetener	Stevia-based sweetener	Artificial sweeteners	Replacement (Halliday 2009)	2009
Sweeteners	Honey	Beet sugar	Replacement (Weise 2009)	2009
Sweeteners	Honey	Corn syrup	Replacement (Kurtzweil 1997)	1997
Sweeteners	Honey	Corn syrup	Replacement (Anonymous 1995)	1995
Sweeteners	Honey	Corn syrup	Replacement (Nichols 1996)	1996
Sweeteners	Honey	Corn syrup	Replacement (Breen 2010)	2010
Sweeteners	Honey	Corn syrup, inverted syrups, or high-fructose corn syrup	Replacement (Stones 2009)	2009
Sweeteners	Honey	High-fructose corn syrup	Replacement (Weise 2009)	2009
Sweeteners	Honey	Honey of non-authentic geographic origin	Replacement (to evade US anti-dumping duties) (Anonymous 2009e)	2009
Sweeteners	Honey	Honey of non-authentic geographic origin)	Replacement (Schneider 2008)	2008
Sweeteners	Honey	Honey with chloramphenicol	Replacement (Lumpkin 2003)	2003
Sweeteners	Honey	Invert sugar	Replacement (Jaiswal 2008)	2008
Sweeteners	Honey	Non-authentic country origin	Replacement (Anonymous 2010c)	2010
Sweeteners	Honey	Non-authentic country origin	Replacement (Scott-Thomas 2010)	2010
Sweeteners	Honey	Sugar syrups from corn, sugar cane, sugar beet, and maple syrup	Replacement (Pilizota 2009)	2009
Sweeteners	Maple syrup	Sugar and water	Replacement (Weise 2009)	2009
Sweeteners	Sugar	Sugar of non-authentic geographic origin	Replacement (to qualify for subsidized pricing) (Castle and Carvajal 2009)	2009
Wines, musts, spirits, liquors, and vinegars	Liquor	Methyl alcohol	Replacement (Anonymous 1992)	1992
Wines, musts, spirits, liquors, and vinegars	Liquors	Methanol	Replacement (Jaiswal 2008)	2008
Wines, musts, spirits, liquors, and vinegars	Wine	Diethylene glycol	Addition to mask poor quality (Molotsky 1985)	1985
Wines, musts, spirits, liquors, and vinegars	Wine	Non-authentic brand of wine	Replacement (Anonymous 2011b)	2011
Wines, musts, spirits, liquors, and vinegars	Wine (Pinot Noir)	Merlot and Syrah wine	Replacement (Rovner 2010)	2010

Abbreviations and Terms Used

APCI-MS: Mass spectrometry using an atmospheric pressure chemical ionization
ATR-MIR: Attenuated total reflectance mid-infrared spectroscopy
Caprine: Indicates goat origin
CE: Capillary electrophoresis
DART-ToF-MS: Direct analysis in real time time of flight mass spectrometry
DNA: Deoxyribonucleic acid
DSC: Differential scanning calorimetry
ED: Electrochemical detection
ELISA: Enzyme linked immunosorbent assay
ELSD: Evaporative light scattering detector
Ewe milk: Indicates sheep origin

FAMEs: Fatty acid methyl esters
FID: Flame ionization detection
FT: Fourier trasform
FTIR: Fourier transform infrared spectroscopy
GC: Gas chromatography
HPLC: High-performance liquid chromatography
HP-TLC: High-performance thin layer chromatography interface
IR: Infrared spectroscopy
IRMS: Isotope ratio mass spectrometry
MALDI: Matrix-assisted laser desorption/ionization
MIR: Mid-infrared spectroscopy
MS: Mass spectrometer
NIR: Near-infrared spectroscopy
NMR: Nuclear magnetic resonance spectroscopy

NR: None reported
Ovine milk: Indicates sheep origin
PAD: Pulsed amperometric detection
PCR: Polymerase chain reaction
PDA: Photodiode array detector
SEM: Scanning electron microscopy
SNIF: Site-specific natural isotope fractionation
SPE: Solid phase extraction
SPME: Solid phase micro-extraction
TCA: Trichloroacetic acid
TLC: Thin-layer chromatography
UV: Ultraviolet detection
Vis: Visible absorption detection
XRD: X-ray diffractometry

References

1. Abdel-Aal ESM, Ziena HM & Youssef MM. 1993. Adulteration of honey with high-fructose corn syrup: Detection by different methods. Food Chem 48(2):209–212.
2. Adele Maraboli TMPC, Roberto Giangiacomo. 2002. Detection of vegetable proteins from soy, pea and wheat isolates in milk powder by near infrared spectroscopy. Near Infrared Spec 10(1):63–69.
3. FSA. 2009. Study into injection powders used as water retaining agents in frozen chicken breast products. Food Standards Agency. http://www.food.gov.uk/news/newsarchive/2009/jun/chicken. Accessed May 15, 2011.
4. Agiomyrgianaki A, Petrakis PV & Dais P. 2010. Detection of refined olive oil adulteration with refined hazelnut oil by employing NMR spectroscopy and multivariate statistical analysis. Talanta 80(5):2165–2171.
5. Aguilar-Cisneros BO, Lopez MG, Richling E, Heckel F & Schreier P. 2002. Tequila authenticity assessment by headspace SPME-HRGC-IRMS analysis of $^{13}C/^{12}C$ and $^{18}O/^{16}O$ ratios of ethanol. J Agric Food Chem 50(26):7520–7523.
6. Al-Ismail KM, Alsaed AK, Ahmad R & Al-Dabbas M. 2010. Detection of olive oil adulteration with some plant oils by GLC analysis of sterols using polar colurnn. Food Chem 121(4):1255–1259.
7. Al-Jowder O, Defernez M, Kemsley EK & Wilson RH. 1999. Mid-infrared spectroscopy and chemometrics for the authentication of meat products. J Agric Food Chem 47(8):3210–3218.
8. Al-Jowder O, Kemsley EK & Wilson RH. 1997. Mid-infrared spectroscopy and authenticity problems in selected meats: A feasibility study. Food Chem 59(2):195–201.
9. Alary R, Buissonade C, Joudrier P & Gautier M-F. 2007. Detection and discrimination of cereal and leguminous species in chestnut flour by duplex PCR. Eur Food Res Technol 225(3):427–434.
10. Alary R, Serin A, Duviau M-P, Jourdrier P & Gautier M-F. 2002. Quantification of common wheat adulteration of durum wheat pasta using real-time quantitative polymerase chain reaction (PCR). Anglais 79(4):553–558.
11. Alexa E, Dragomirescu A, Pop G, Jianu C & Dragos D 2009. The use of FT-IR spectroscopy in the identification of vegetable oils adulteration. J Food Agri Environ 7(2):20–24.
12. Alissandrakis E, Mantziaras E, Tarantilis P, Harizanis P & Polissiou M. 2010. Generation of linalool derivatives in an artificial honey produced from bees fed with linalool-enriched sugar syrup. Eur Food Res Technol 231(1):21–25.
13. Almeida MR, Oliveira KdS, Stephani R & de Oliveira LFC. 2011. Fourier-transform Raman analysis of milk powder: A potential method for rapid quality screening. Raman Spectrosc 42(7):1548–1552.
14. Alonso-Salces RM, Moreno-Rojas JM, Holland MV, Reniero F, Guillou C & Heberger K. 2010. Virgin olive oil authentication by multivariate analyses of ^1H NMR fingerprints and delta^{13}C and delta^2H data. J Agric Food Chem 58(9):5586–5596.
15. Alonso GL, Salinas MR & Garijo J. 1998. Method to determine the authenticity of aroma of saffron (Crocus sativus L.). J Food Protect 61(11):1525–1528.
16. Altug T & Gonul M. 1988. The detection of soybean flour in cocoa powder. Food Quality 10(5):295–298.
17. Amr AS & Abu-Al-Rub AAI. 1993. Evaluation of the bellier test in the detection of olive oil adulteration with vegetable oils. J Sci Food Agr 61(4):435–437.
18. Anderson DM, Millar JR & Weiping W. 1991. Gum arabic (Acacia senegal): Unambiguous identification by ^{13}C-NMR spectroscopy as an adjunct to the Revised JECFA Specification, and the application of ^{13}C-NMR spectra for regulatory/legislative purposes. Food Addit Contam 8(4):405–421.
19. Andrikopoulos NK, Giannakis IG & Tzamtzis V. 2001. Analysis of olive oil and seed oil triglycerides by capillary gas chromatography as a tool for the detection of the adulteration of olive oil. J Chromatogr Sci 39:137–145.
20. Angerosa F, Camera L, Cumitini S, Gleixner G & Reniero F. 1997. Carbon stable isotopes and olive oil adulteration with pomace oil. J Agric Food Chem 45(8):3044–3048.
21. Anguita G, Martín R, García L, Morales P, Haza AI, González I, Sanz B & Hernández PE. 1996. Immunostick ELISA for detection of cow's milk in ewe's milk and cheese using a monoclonal antibody against bovine-casein. J Food Protect 59(4):436–437.
22. Anonymous. 1992. 200 Die from contaminated liquor in India. New York Times.
23. Anonymous. 1995. Five persons indicted in honey adulteration conspiracy. The US Department of Justice. http://www.justice.gov/opa/pr/Pre_96/January95/47.txt.html. Accessed May 15, 2011.
24. Anonymous. 2004. Spice adulteration, White Paper. American Spice Trade Association. www.astaspice.org/files/public/SpiceAdulteration.pdf. Accessed May 15, 2011.
25. Anonymous. 2005a. Not-so-extra-virgin olive oil. ABC News. http://abcnews.go.com/GMA/AmericanFamily/story?id=988980&page=1. Accessed May 15, 2011.
26. Anonymous. 2005b. Tracking down the rogue powder. Telegraph.
27. Anonymous. 2006. Feds seize more than 22,000 gallons of adulterated "olive oil". US Fed News Service.

28. Anonymous. 2008. Italy confiscates fake olive oil. BBC News. http://news.bbc.co.uk/go/pr/fr/-/2/hi/europe/7360434.stm. Accessed May 15, 2011.
29. Anonymous. 2009a. Rapid alert system for food and feed. June 30, 2009 ed.: Directorate General Communication.
30. Anonymous. 2009b. Industrial salt kills 1, sickens 25 at food shop. China Daily. Chinadaily.com. http://www.chinadaily.com.cn/cndy/2009-10/19/content_8808283.htm.
31. Anonymous. 2009c. New inulin test to beat counterfeiters. NUTRA ingredients-USA.com. http://www.nutraingredients-usa.com/content/view/print/248562. Accessed May 15, 2011.
32. Anonymous. 2009d. Possible carcinogenic protein found in Chinese dairy products. Epoch Times. http://www.theepochtimes.com/n2/index2.php?option=com_content&task=view&id=1605. Accessed May 15, 2011.
33. Anonymous. 2009e. United States of America v. Shu Bei Yuan. http://www.justice.gov/usao/iln/pr/chicago/2011/pr0217_02a.pdf. Accessed May 15, 2011.
34. Anonymous. 2010a. Centre for strict action against food adulterators. Times of India. http://timesofindia.indiatimes.com/india/Centre-for-strict-action-against-food-adulterators/articleshow/6263104.cms. Accessed May 15, 2011.
35. Anonymous. 2010b. Cheating cheese. SeparationsNOW.com.
36. Anonymous. 2010c. So honey, where ya from? Scientists work to track down mislabeled honey. Food Quality June/July 2010.
37. Anonymous. 2011a. China, plastic rice distribution. Weekly Hong Kong. http://www.weeklyhk.com/news.php?code=&mode=view&num=10793. Accessed May 15, 2011.
38. Anonymous. 2011b. Fake Jacob's Creek wine seized in off licences. BBC News, England.
39. Anonymous. 2011c. Turmeric recalled due to lead levels. Food Safety News. http://www.foodsafetynews.com/2011/04/turmeric-recalled-due-to-excessive-lead-levels/. Accessed May 15, 2011.
40. Antolovich M, Li X & Robards K. 2001. Detection of adulteration in Australian orange juices by stable carbon isotope ratio analysis (SCIRA). J Agric Food Chem 49(5):2623–2626.
41. Antoniosi Filho N, Carrilho E & Lanças F. 1993. Fast quantitative analysis of soybean oil in olive oil by high-temperature capillary gas chromatography. J Am Oil Chem Soc 70(10):1051–1053.
42. Aparicio R & Aparicio-Ruíz R. 2000. Authentication of vegetable oils by chromatographic techniques. J Chromatogr A 881(1-2):93–104.
43. Aparicio R, Morales MT & Alonso V. 1997. Authentication of European virgin olive oils by their chemical compounds, sensory attributes, and consumers' attitudes. J Agric Food Chem 45(4):1076–1083.
44. Archak S, Lakshminarayanareddy V & Nagaraju J. 2007. High-throughput multiplex microsatellite marker assay for detection and quantification of adulteration in basmati rice (Oryza sativa). Electrophoresis 28(14):2396–2405.
45. Arlorio M, Coisson JD, Bordiga M, Travaglia F, Garino C, Zuidmeer L, Van Ree R, Giuffrida MG, Conti A & Martelli A. 2010. Olive oil adulterated with hazelnut oils: Simulation to identify possible risks to allergic consumers. Food Addit Contam Part A Chem Anal Control Expo Risk Assess 27(1):11–18.
46. Arvanitoyannis IS, Chalhoub C, Gotsiou P, Lydakis-Simantiris N & Kefalas P. 2005. Novel quality control methods in conjunction with chemometrics (multivariate analysis) for detecting honey authenticity. Crit Rev Food Sci Nutr 45(3):193–203.
47. Arvanitoyannis IS, Katsota MN, Psarra EP, Soufleros EH & Kallithraka S. 1999. Application of quality control methods for assessing wine authenticity: Use of multivariate analysis (chemometrics). Trends Food Sci Tech 10(10):321–336.
48. Arvanitoyannis IS & Vlachos A. 2007. Implementation of physicochemical and sensory analysis in conjunction with multivariate analysis towards assessing olive oil authentication/adulteration. Crit Rev Food Sci Nutr 47(5):441–498.
49. Asensio L, Gonzalez I, Fernandez A, Rodriguez MA, Hernandez PE, Garcia T & Martin R. 2001. PCR-SSCP: A simple method for the authentication of grouper (Epinephelus guaza), wreck fish (Polyprion americanus), and Nile perch (Lates niloticus) fillets. J Agric Food Chem 49(4):1720–1723.
50. Ávila M, González MC, Zougagh M, Escarpa A & Ríos Á. 2007. Rapid sample screening method for authenticity controlling vanilla flavors using a CE microchip approach with electrochemical detection. Electrophoresis 28(22):4233–4239.
51. Ayala RA, Leon SV, Flores GP & Gutierrez R. 2008. Rennet whey solids detection in Mexican ultrapasteurized milk using fourth derivative absorption. Veterinaria Mexico 39(1):17–27.
52. Babu CK, Khanna SK & Das M. 2008. Antioxidant status of erythrocytes and their response to oxidative challenge in humans with argemone oil poisoning. Toxicol Appl Pharm 230(3):304–311.
53. Baeten V, Fernandez Pierna JA, Dardenne P, Meurens M, Garcia-Gonzalez DL & Aparicio-Ruiz R. 2005. Detection of the presence of hazelnut oil in olive oil by FT-Raman and FT-MIR spectroscopy. J Agric Food Chem 53(16):6201–6206.
54. Baeten V, Meurens M, Morales MT & Aparicio R. 1996. Detection of virgin olive oil adulteration by Fourier transform Raman spectroscopy. J Agric Food Chem 44(8):2225–2230.
55. Bai WL, Yin RH, Zhao SJ, Dou QL, Yang JC, Jiang WQ, Zhao ZH & Luo GB. 2009. Rapid detection of bovine milk in yak milk using a polymerase chain reaction technique. J Dairy Sci 92(4):1354–1360.
56. Ballin NZ. 2006. Estimation of whey protein in casein coprecipitate and milk powder by high-performance liquid chromatography quantification of cysteine. J Agric Food Chem 54(12):4131–4135.
57. Bania J, Ugorski M, Polanowski A & Adamczyk E. 2001. Application of polymerase chain reaction for detection

of goats' milk adulteration by milk of cow. J Dairy Res 68(02):333–336.
58. Barboza D & Barrionuevo A. 2007. Filler in animal feed is open secret in China. New York Times.
59. Barnwell P, McCarthy PK, Lumley ID & Griffin M. 1994. The use of reversed-phase high-performance liquid chromatography to detect common wheat (Triticum aestivum) adulteration of durum wheat (Triticum durum) pasta products dried at low and high temperatures. Cereal Sci 20(3):245–252.
60. Basch JJ, Douglas Jr FW, Procino LG, Holsinger VH & Farrell Jr HM. 1985. Quantitation of caseins and whey proteins of processed milks and whey protein concentrates, application of gel electrophoresis, and comparison with Harland-Ashworth procedure. J Dairy Sci 68(1):23–31.
61. Bauer-Christoph C, Christoph N, Aguilar-Cisneros BO, López MG, Richling E, Rossmann A & Schreier P. 2003. Authentication of tequila by gas chromatography and stable isotope ratio analyses. Eur Food Res Technol 217(5):438–443.
62. Baumgartner S, Genner-Ritzmann R, Haas J, Amado R & Neukom H. 1986. Isolation and identification of cyclitols in carob pods (Ceratonia siliqua L.). J Agric Food Chem 34(5):827–829.
63. Bensaid FF, Wietzerbin K & Martin GJ. 2002. Authentication of natural vanilla flavorings: Isotopic characterization using degradation of vanillin into guaiacol. J Agric Food Chem 50(22):6271–6275.
64. Berger A, Brulhart M & Prodolliet J. 1991. Detection of adulteration in pure soluble coffee by enzymatic sugar determination. Lebensmittel-Wissenschaft and Technologie 24(1):59–62.
65. Bernal JL, Jiménez JJ, del Nozal MJ, Toribio L & Martín MT. 2005. Physico-chemical parameters for the characterization of pure beeswax and detection of adulterations. Eur Lipid Sci Tech 107(3):158–166.
66. Bertelli D, Lolli M, Papotti G, Bortolotti L, Serra G & Plessi M. 2010. Detection of honey adulteration by sugar syrups using one-dimensional and two-dimensional high-resolution nuclear magnetic resonance. J Agric Food Chem 58(15):8495–8501.
67. Bevin CJ, Fergusson AJ, Perry WB, Janik LJ & Cozzolino D. 2006. Development of a rapid 'fingerprinting' system for wine authenticity by mid-infrared spectroscopy. J Agric Food Chem 54(26):9713–9718.
68. Bhattacharjee P, Singhal RS & Gholap AS. 2003. Supercritical carbon dioxide extraction for identification of adulteration of black pepper with papaya seeds. J Sci Food Agr 83(8):783–786.
69. Biedermann M, Grob K & Bronz M. 1995a. Determination of stigmastadiene in edible oils by HPLC-HPLC-UV. Riv Ital Sostanze Grasse 72:397–401.
70. Biedermann M, Grob K & Mariani C. 1995b. Online LC-UV-GC-FID for the determination of Delta7- and Delta8(14)-sterols and its application for the detection of adulterated olive oils. Riv Ital Sostanze Grasse 72:339–344.
71. Blanch GP, Caja Md, Ruiz del Castillo ML & Herraiz M. 1998. Comparison of different methods for the evaluation of the authenticity of olive oil and hazelnut oil. J Agric Food Chem 46(8):3153–3157.
72. Blanch GP, Caja MM, del Castillo MLR & Herraiz M. 1999. A contribution to the study of the enantiomeric composition of a chiral constituent in hazelnut oil used in the detection of adulterated olive oil. Eur Food Res Technol 210(2):139–143.
73. Blanch GP, Caja MM, León M & Herraiz M. 2000. Determination of (E)-5-methylhept-2-en-4-one in deodorised hazelnut oil. Application to the detection of adulterated olive oils. J Sci Food Agr 80(1):140–144.
74. Bligh HFJ. 2000. Detection of adulteration of basmati rice with non-premium long-grain rice. Int J Food Sci Tech 35(3):257–265.
75. Blumenthal D & Holland L. 1989. Orange juice: Pure or adulterated? Bodine Inc. FDA Consum (Dec.–Jan.).
76. Bonetti A, Marotti I, Catizone P, Dinelli G, Maietti A, Tedeschi P & Brandolini V. 2004. Compared use of HPLC and FZCE for cluster analysis of Triticum spp and for the identification of T. durum adulteration. J Agric Food Chem 52(13):4080–4089.
77. Bonvehi JS & Coll FV. 2009. Detecting vegetable oil adulteration in hazelnut paste (Corylus avellana L.). Int J Food Sci Tech 44(3):456–466.
78. Borin A, Ferrão MF, Mello C, Maretto DA & Poppi RJ. 2006. Least-squares support vector machines and near infrared spectroscopy for quantification of common adulterants in powdered milk. Analytica Chimica Acta 579(1):25–32.
79. Bozzi A, Perrin C, Austin S & Arce Vera F. 2007. Quality and authenticity of commercial aloe vera gel powders. Food Chem 103(1):22–30.
80. Branigan T. 2008. Head of watchdog resigns as number of babies in hospital from tainted milk rises to 13,000. Guardian.
81. Breen T. 2010. States expand efforts to combat 'funny honey' that isn't pure. USA Today. http://www.usatoday.com/money/industries/food/2010-09-25-honey-producers_N.htm. Accessed May 15, 2011.
82. Brenna E, Fronza G, Fuganti C & Pinciroli M. 2003. Differentiation of natural and synthetic phenylalanine and tyrosine through natural abundance ^{2}H nuclear magnetic resonance. J Agric Food Chem 51(17):4866–4872.
83. Briandet R, Kemsley EK & Wilson RH. 1996. Approaches to adulteration detection in instant coffees using infrared spectroscopy and chemometrics. J Sci Food Agr 71(3):359–366.
84. Bricout J & Koziet J. 1987. Control of the authenticity of orange juice by isotopic analysis. J Agric Food Chem 35(5):758–760.
85. Bridle P & García-Viguera C. 1996. A simple technique for the detection of red wine adulteration with elderberry pigments. Food Chem 55(2):111–113.
86. Brookes ST, Barrie A & Davies JE. 1991. A rapid ^{13}C/^{12}C test for determination of corn syrups in honey. J Assoc Off Ana Chem 74(4):627–629.
87. Brunner M, Katona R, Stefánka Z & Prohaska T. 2010. Determination of the geographical origin of processed spice using multielement and isotopic pattern on the

example of Szegedi paprika. Eur Food Res Technol 231(4):623–634.
88. Bucci R, Magrí AD, Magrí AL, Marini D & Marini F. 2002. Chemical authentication of extra virgin olive oil varieties by supervised chemometric procedures. J Agric Food Chem 50(3):413–418.
89. Buchgraber M, Senaldi C, Ulberth F & Anklam E. 2004. Detection and quantification of cocoa butter equivalents in cocoa butter and plain chocolate by gas liquid chromatography of triacylglycerols. J AOAC Int 87(5):1153–1163.
90. Buder L. 1988. 2 former executives of Beech-Nut guilty in phony juice case. New York Times.
91. Burda K & Collins M. 1991. Adulteration of wine with sorbitol and apple juice. J Food Protect 54(5):381–382.
92. Burfield T. 2003. The adulteration of essential oils and the consequences to aromatherapy & natural perfumery practice. p. 17. http://www.users.globalnet.co.uk/~nodice/new/magazine/october/october.htm. Accessed May 15, 2011.
93. Burros M. 1992a. Eating Well; Pollack or cod? Fish or foul? F.D.A. takes a closer look. New York Times.
94. Burros M. 1992b. Study of retail fish markets finds wide contamination and mislabeling. New York Times.
95. Butinar B, Bucar-Miklavcic M, Valencic V & Raspor P. 2010. Stereospecific analysis of triacylglycerols as a useful means to evaluate genuineness of pumpkin seed oils: Lesson from virgin olive oil analyses. J Agric Food Chem 58(9):5227–5234.
96. Byrne B, Wengenroth KJ & Kruger DA. 1986. Determination of adulterated natural ethyl butyrate by carbon isotopes. J Agric Food Chem 34(4):736–738.
97. Cabanero AI, Recio JL & Ruperez M. 2006. Liquid chromatography coupled to isotope ratio mass spectrometry: A new perspective on honey adulteration detection. J Agric Food Chem 54(26):9719–9727.
98. Cáceres A, Cárdenas S, Gallego M & Valcárcel M. 2000. A continuous spectrophotometric system for the discrimination/determination of monosaccharides and oligosaccharides in foods. Analytica Chimica Acta 404(1):121–129.
99. Caja M, Ruiz del Castillo M, Herraiz M & Blanch G. 1999. Study of the enantiomeric composition of chiral constituents in edible oils by simultaneous distillation-extraction. Detection of adulterated olive oils. J Am Oil Chem Soc 76(9):1027–1030.
100. Caja Mdel M, Preston C, Kempf M & Schreier P. 2007. Flavor authentication studies of alpha-ionone, beta-ionone, and alpha-ionol from various sources. J Agric Food Chem 55(16):6700–6704.
101. Calbiani F, Careri M, Elviri L, Mangia A, Pistara L & Zagnoni I. 2004. Development and in-house validation of a liquid chromatography-electrospray-tandem mass spectrometry method for the simultaneous determination of Sudan I, Sudan II, Sudan III and Sudan IV in hot chilli products. J Chromatogr A 1042(1-2):123–130.
102. Calvano CD, Aresta A & Zambonin CG. 2010. Detection of hazelnut oil in extra-virgin olive oil by analysis of polar components by micro-solid phase extraction based on hydrophilic liquid chromatography and MALDI-ToF mass spectrometry. J Mass Spectrom 45(9):981–988.
103. Camin F, Larcher R, Perini M, Bontempo L, Bertoldi D, Gagliano G, Nicolini G & Versini G. 2010. Characterisation of authentic Italian extra-virgin olive oils by stable isotope ratios of C, O and H and mineral composition. Food Chem 118(4):901–909.
104. Capote F, Jiménez J & de Castro M. 2007. Sequential (step-by-step) detection, identification and quantitation of extra virgin olive oil adulteration by chemometric treatment of chromatographic profiles. Anal Bioanal Chem 388(8):1859–1865.
105. Carmona M, Carrion ME, Zalacain A & Alonso GL. 2004. Detection of adulterated saffron through UV-Vis spectral analysis. J Food Sci Technol 41(4):451–455.
106. Carter RM, Yan Y & Tomlins K. 2006. Digital imaging based classification and authentication of granular food products. Meas Sci Technol 17(2):235–240.
107. Cartoni G, Coccioli F, Jasionowska R & Masci M. 1999. Determination of cows' milk in goats' milk and cheese by capillary electrophoresis of the whey protein fractions. J Chromatogr A 846(1-2):135–141.
108. Castle S & Carvajal D. 2009. Subsidies spur fraud in European sugar. New York Times.
109. Castro-Rubio F, Garcia MC, Rodriguez R & Marina ML. 2005. Simple and inexpensive method for the reliable determination of additions of soybean proteins in heat-processed meat products: An alternative to the AOAC official method. J Agric Food Chem 53(2):220–226.
110. Cataldo A, Piuzzi E, Cannazza G, De Benedetto E & Tarricone L. 2010. Quality and anti-adulteration control of vegetable oils through microwave dielectric spectroscopy. Measurement 43(8):1031–1039.
111. Cattaneo P & Cantoni C. 1982. On the presence of melamine in fish meals. Tecnica Molitoria 33(1):17–18.
112. Cautela D, Laratta B, Santelli F, Trifiro A, Servillo L & Castaldo D. 2008. Estimating bergamot juice adulteration of lemon juice by high-performance liquid chromatography (HPLC) analysis of flavanone glycosides. J Agric Food Chem 56(13):5407–5414.
113. Ceballos-Magana SG, Jurado JM, Martin MJ & Pablos F. 2009. Quantitation of twelve metals in tequila and mezcal spirits as authenticity parameters. J Agric Food Chem 57(4):1372–1376.
114. Cesar CL, Vargas H, Lima CAS, Mendes Filho J & Miranda LCM. 1984. On the use of photoacoustic spectroscopy for investigating adulterated or altered powdered coffee samples. J Agric Food Chem 32(6):1355–1358.
115. Chan M, Lo CK, Cheng LS, Cheung TC & Wong YC. 2009. Evaluation of testing capabilities for the determination of melamine in milk through an interlaboratory proficiency test programme during the melamine crisis. Food Addit Contam Part A Chem Anal Control Expo Risk Assess 26(11):1450–1458.
116. Charlton AJ, Farrington WH & Brereton P. 2002. Application of ^{1}H NMR and multivariate statistics for screening complex mixtures: Quality control and authenticity of instant coffee. J Agric Food Chem 50(11):3098–3103.
117. Che Man YB, Syahariza ZA, Mirghani MES, Jinap S &

Bakar J. 2005. Analysis of potential lard adulteration in chocolate and chocolate products using Fourier transform infrared spectroscopy. Food Chem 90(4):815–819.

118. Chen G, Wang XL, Wong WS, Liu XD, Xia B & Li N. 2005. Application of 3′ untranslated region (UTR) sequence-based amplified polymorphism analysis in the rapid authentication of Radix astragali. J Agric Food Chem 53(22):8551–8556.

119. Chen LZ, Zhao J, Ye ZH & Zhong YP. 2008. Determination of adulteration in honey using near-infrared spectroscopy. Guang Pu Xue Yu Guang Pu Fen Xi 28(11):2565–2568.

120. Chen R-K, Chang L-W, Chung Y-Y, Lee M-H & Ling Y-C. 2004. Quantification of cow milk adulteration in goat milk using high-performance liquid chromatography with electrospray ionization mass spectrometry. Rapid Commun Mass Sp 18(10):1167–1171.

121. Chen X, Gao C, Li H, Huang L, Sun Q, Dong Y, Tian C, Gao S, Dong H, Guan D, Hu X, Zhao S, Li L, Zhu L, Yan Q, Zhang J, Zen K & Zhang CY. 2010. Identification and characterization of microRNAs in raw milk during different periods of lactation, commercial fluid, and powdered milk products. Cell Res 20(10):1128–1137.

122. Cheng Y, Dong Y, Wu J, Yang X, Bai H, Zheng H, Ren D, Zou Y & Li M. 2010. Screening melamine adulterant in milk powder with laser Raman spectrometry. J Food Compos Anal 23(2):199–202.

123. Chiavaro E, Vittadini E, Rodriguez-Estrada MT, Cerretani L & Bendini A. 2008. Differential scanning calorimeter application to the detection of refined hazelnut oil in extra virgin olive oil. Food Chem 110(1):248–256.

124. Christopoulou E, Lazaraki M, Komaitis M & Kaselimis K. 2004. Effectiveness of determinations of fatty acids and triglycerides for the detection of adulteration of olive oils with vegetable oils. Food Chem 84(3):463–474.

125. Christy AA, Kasemsumran S, Du Y & Ozaki Y. 2004. The detection and quantification of adulteration in olive oil by near-infrared spectroscopy and chemometrics. Anal Sci 20:6.

126. Cocchi M, Durante C, Foca G, Marchetti A, Tassi L & Ulrici A. 2006. Durum wheat adulteration detection by NIR spectroscopy multivariate calibration. Talanta 68(5):1505–1511.

127. Colak H, Aydin A, Nazli B & Ergun O. 2006. Detection of presence of cow's milk in sheep's cheeses by immunochromatography. Food Control 17(11):905–908.

128. Colyer A, Macarthur R, Lloyd J & Hird H. 2008. Comparison of calibration methods for the quantification of basmati and non-basmati rice using microsatellite analysis. Food Addit Contam Part A Chem Anal Control Expo Risk Assess 25(10):1189–1194.

129. Commission E. 2003. Commission decision of 20 June 2003 on emergency measures regarding hot chilli and hot chilli products. Official Journal of the European Union.

130. Cordella C, Antinelli J-F, Aurieres C, Faucon J-P, Cabrol-Bass D & Sbirrazzuoli N. 2001. Use of differential scanning calorimetry (DSC) as a new technique for detection of adulteration in honeys. 1. Study of adulteration effect on honey thermal behavior. J Agric Food Chem 50(1):203–208.

131. Cordella C, Militão JSLT, Clément M-C, Drajnudel P & Cabrol-Bass D. 2005. Detection and quantification of honey adulteration via direct incorporation of sugar syrups or bee-feeding: Preliminary study using high-performance anion exchange chromatography with pulsed amperometric detection (HPAEC-PAD) and chemometrics. Analytica Chimica Acta 531(2):239–248.

132. Cordella CB, Militao JS, Clement MC & Cabrol-Bass D. 2003. Honey characterization and adulteration detection by pattern recognition applied on HPAEC-PAD profiles. 1. Honey floral species characterization. J Agric Food Chem 51(11):3234–3242.

133. Cordewener JH, Luykx DM, Frankhuizen R, Bremer MG, Hooijerink H & America AH. 2009. Untargeted LC-Q-TOF mass spectrometry method for the detection of adulterations in skimmed-milk powder. J Sep Sci 32(8):1216–1223.

134. Cosio MS, Ballabio D, Benedetti S & Gigliotti C. 2006. Geographical origin and authentication of extra virgin olive oils by an electronic nose in combination with artificial neural networks. Analytica Chimica Acta 567(2):202–210.

135. Cotte JF, Casabianca H, Chardon S, Lhéritier J & Grenier-Loustalot MF. 2003. Application of carbohydrate analysis to verify honey authenticity. J Chromatogr A 1021(1–2):145–155.

136. Cotte JF, Casabianca H, Giroud B, Albert M, Lhéritier J & Grenier-Loustalot MF. 2004. Characterization of honey amino acid profiles using high-pressure liquid chromatography to control authenticity. Anal Bioanal Chem 378(5):1342–1350.

137. Cotte JF, Casabianca H, Lhéritier J, Perrucchietti C, Sanglar C, Waton H & Grenier-Loustalot MF. 2007. Study and validity of ^{13}C stable carbon isotopic ratio analysis by mass spectrometry and ^{2}H site-specific natural isotopic fractionation by nuclear magnetic resonance isotopic measurements to characterize and control the authenticity of honey. Analytica Chimica Acta 582(1):125–136.

138. Cozzolino D, Restaino E, La Manna A, Fernandez E & Fassio A. 2009. Usefulness of near infrared reflectance (NIR) spectroscopy and chemometrics to discriminate between fishmeal, meat meal and soya meal samples. Ciencia e investigación agraria 36(2):209–214.

139. Cozzolino D, Smyth HE & Gishen M. 2003. Feasibility study on the use of visible and near-infrared spectroscopy together with chemometrics to discriminate between commercial white wines of different varietal origins. J Agric Food Chem 51(26):7703–7708.

140. Cozzolino R, Passalacqua S, Salemi S, Malvagna P, Spina E & Garozzo D. 2001. Identification of adulteration in milk by matrix-assisted laser desorption/ionization time-of-flight mass spectrometry. Mass Spectrom 36(9):1031–1037.

141. Craig A, Ritchie AH & Mackie IM. 1995. Determining the authenticity of raw reformed breaded scampi (Nephrops norvegicus) by electrophoretic techniques. Food Chem 52(4):451–454.
142. Crews C, Hough P, Brereton P, Godward J, Lees M, Guiet S & Winkelmann W. 2006a. Quantitation of the main constituents of some authentic sesame seed oils of different origin. J Agric Food Chem 54(17):6266–6270.
143. Crews C, Hough P, Godward J, Brereton P, Lees M, Guiet S & Winkelmann W. 2006b. Quantitation of the main constituents of some authentic grape-seed oils of different origin. J Agric Food Chem 54(17):6261–6265.
144. Cuny M, Vigneau E, Le Gall G, Colquhoun I, Lees M & Rutledge D. 2008. Fruit juice authentication by ^{1}H NMR spectroscopy in combination with different chemometrics tools. Anal Bioanal Chem 390(1):419–427.
145. Cuollo M, Caira S, Fierro O, Pinto G, Picariello G & Addeo F. 2010. Toward milk speciation through the monitoring of casein proteotypic peptides. Rapid Commun Mass Sp 24(11):1687–1696.
146. Czerwenka C, Muller L & Lindner W. 2010. Detection of the adulteration of water buffalo milk and mozzarella with cow's milk by liquid chromatography-mass spectrometry analysis of [beta]-lactoglobulin variants. Food Chem 122(3):901–908.
147. Dalmasso A, Civera T, La Neve F & Bottero MT. 2011. Simultaneous detection of cow and buffalo milk in mozzarella cheese by Real-Time PCR assay. Food Chem 124(1):362–366.
148. Damirchi S, Savage G & Dutta P. 2005. Sterol fractions in hazelnut and virgin olive oils and 4,4'-dimethylsterols as possible markers for detection of adulteration of virgin olive oil. J Am Oil Chem Soc 82(10):717–725.
149. Dankowska A & Malecka M. 2009. Application of synchronous fluorescence spectroscopy for determination of extra virgin olive oil adulteration. Eur Lipid Sci Tech 111(12):1233–1239.
150. Davies AN, McIntyre P & Morgan E. 2000. Study of the use of molecular spectroscopy for the authentication of extra virgin olive oils. Part I: Fourier transform Raman spectroscopy. Appl Spectrosc 54(12):1864–1867.
151. Day MP, Zhang B-L & Martin GJ. 1994. The use of trace element data to complement stable isotope methods in the characterization of grape musts. Am J Enol Vitic 45(1):79–85.
152. de la Fuente MA & Juarez M. 2005. Authenticity assessment of dairy products. Crit Rev Food Sci Nutr 45(7-8):563–585.
153. De S, Brahma B, Polley S, Mukherjee A, Banerjee D, Gohaina M, Singh KP, Singh R, Datta TK & Goswami SL. 2011. Simplex and duplex PCR assays for species specific identification of cattle and buffalo milk and cheese. Food Control 22(5):690–696.
154. Defernez M, Kemsley EK & Wilson RH. 1995. Use of infrared spectroscopy and chemometrics for the authentication of fruit purees. Agric Food Chem 43(1):109–113.
155. Dentali S. 2007. Adulteration: Spotlight on bilberry. Nutraceuticals World July/August:72–75.
156. Derbyshire D. 2005. How did banned dye get in food? Telegraph.
157. Desmarchelier A, Guillamon Cuadra M, Delatour T & Mottier P. 2009. Simultaneous quantitative determination of melamine and cyanuric acid in cow's milk and milk-based infant formula by liquid chromatography-electrospray ionization tandem mass spectrometry. J Agric Food Chem 57(16):7186–7193.
158. Dhanyaa K, Syamkumara S & Sasikumara B. 2009. Development and application of SCAR marker for the detection of papaya seed adulteration in traded black pepper powder. Food Biotechnol 23(2):97–106.
159. Di Anibal CV, Odena M, Ruisanchez I & Callao MP. 2009. Determining the adulteration of spices with Sudan I-II-II-IV dyes by UV-visible spectroscopy and multivariate classification techniques. Talanta 79(3):887–892.
160. Di Anibal CV, Ruisánchez I & Callao MP. 2011. High-resolution ^{1}H nuclear magnetic resonance spectrometry combined with chemometric treatment to identify adulteration of culinary spices with Sudan dyes. Food Chem 124(3):1139–1145.
161. Díaz I, Alonso I, Fajardo V, Martín I, Hernández P, Lacarra T & de Santos R. 2007. Application of a polymerase chain reaction to detect adulteration of ovine cheeses with caprine milk. Eur Food Res Technol 225(3):345–349.
162. Dionisi F, Prodolliet J & Tagliaferri E. 1995. Assessment of olive oil adulteration by reversed-phase high-performance liquid chromatography/amperometric detection of tocopherols and tocotrienols. J Am Oil Chem Soc 72(12):1505–1511.
163. Dixit S, Khanna SK & Das M. 2008. A simple 2-directional high-performance thin-layer chromatographic method for the simultaneous determination of curcumin, metanil yellow, and Sudan dyes in turmeric, chili, and curry powders. J AOAC Int 91(6):1387–1396.
164. Dixit S, Purshottam SK, Khanna SK & Das M. 2009. Surveillance of the quality of turmeric powders from city markets of India on the basis of curcumin content and the presence of extraneous colours. Food Addit Contam: Part A 26(9):1227–1231.
165. Doka O, Bicanic D & Szollosy L. 1998. Rapid and gross screening for Pb3O4 adulterant in ground sweet red paprika by means of photoacoustic spectroscopy. Instrum Sci Technol 26(2&3):203–208.
166. Doner LW. 1985. Carbon isotope ratios in natural and synthetic citric acid as indicators of lemon juice adulteration. J Agric Food Chem 33(4):770–772.
167. Doner LW, Bills DD, Carro O, Drimmie R, Fritz P, Gearing JN, Hillaire-Marcel C, Parker PL, Reeseman FM, Smith BN & Ziegler H. 1982. Mass spectrometric ^{13}C/^{12}C determinations to detect high fructose corn syrup in orange juice: Collaborative study. J Assoc Off Anal Chem 65(3):608–610.
168. Doner LW, Brause AR & Petrus DR. 1992. Delta-O-18 measurements in water for detection of sugar beet-

168. ...derived syrups in frozen concentrated orange juice: Collaborative study. J AOAC Int 75(6):1107–1111.
169. Dourtoglou V, Dourtoglou T, Antonopoulos A, Stefanou E, Lalas S & Poulos C. 2003. Detection of olive oil adulteration using principal component analysis applied on total and regio FA content. J Am Oil Chem Soc 80(3):203–208.
170. Downey G, Briandet R, Wilson RH & Kemsley EK. 1997. Near- and mid-infrared spectroscopies in food authentication: Coffee varietal identification. J Agric Food Chem 45(11):4357–4361.
171. Downey G, Fouratier V & Kelly JD. 2003. Detection of honey adulteration by addition of fructose and glucose using near infrared transflectance spectroscopy. J Near Infrared Spec 11:447–456.
172. Downey G & Kelly JD. 2004. Detection and quantification of apple adulteration in diluted and sulfited strawberry and raspberry purees using visible and near-infrared spectroscopy. J Agric Food Chem 52(2):204–209.
173. Downey G, McIntyre P & Davies AN. 2002. Detecting and quantifying sunflower oil adulteration in extra virgin olive oils from the eastern mediterranean by visible and near-infrared spectroscopy. J Agric Food Chem 50(20):5520–5525.
174. Dragovic-Uzelac V, Delonga K, Levaj B, Djakovic S & Pospisil J. 2005. Phenolic profiles of raw apricots, pumpkins, and their purees in the evaluation of apricot nectar and jam authenticity. J Agric Food Chem 53(12):4836–4842.
175. Dugo P, Giuffrida D, Herrero M, Donato P & Mondello L. 2009. Epoxycarotenoids esters analysis in intact orange juices using two-dimensional comprehensive liquid chromatography. J Sep Sci 32(7):973–980.
176. Dugo P, Mondello L, Cogliandro E, Verzera A & Dugo G. 1996. On the genuineness of citrus essential oils. 51. Oxygen heterocyclic compounds of bitter orange oil (Citrus aurantium L.). J Agric Food Chem 44(2):544–549.
177. Durst RW, Wrolstad RE & Krueger DA. 1995. Sugar, nonvolatile acid, $^{13}C/^{12}C$ ratio, and mineral analysis for determination of the authenticity and quality of red raspberry juice composition. J AOAC Int 78(5):1195–1204.
178. Dziuba J, Nalecz D & Minkiewicz P. 2004a. Chromatographic identification and determination of commercial milk protein preparations in mixtures with soybean protein isolate. Milchwissenschaft 59(7–8):366–369.
179. Dziuba J, Nalecz D, Minkiewicz P & Dziuba B. 2004b. Identification and determination of milk and soybean protein preparations using enzymatic hydrolysis followed by chromatography and chemometrical data analysis. Analytica Chimica Acta 521(1):17–24.
180. Ehling S, Tefera S & Ho IP. 2007. High-performance liquid chromatographic method for the simultaneous detection of the adulteration of cereal flours with melamine and related triazine by-products ammeline, ammelide, and cyanuric acid. Food Addit Contam 24(12):1319–1325.
181. Eisele TA. 1996. Determination of D-malic acid in apple juice by liquid chromatography: Collaborative study. J AOAC Int 79(1):50–54.
182. El-Hamdy AH & El-Fizga NK. 1995. Detection of olive oil adulteration by measuring its authenticity factor using reversed-phase high-performance liquid chromatography. J Chromatogr A 708(2):351–355.
183. Elkins ER & Heuser JR. 1994. Detection of adulteration in apple juice by L-malic/total malic acid ratio: collaborative study. J AOAC Int 77(2):411–415.
184. Elvira L, Rodriguez J & Lynnworth LC. 2009. Sound speed and density characterization of milk adulterated with melamine. J Acoust Soc Am 125(5):EL177–EL182.
185. Engel E, Ferlay A, Cornu A, Chilliard Y, Agabriel C, Bielicki G & Martin B. 2007. Relevance of isotopic and molecular biomarkers for the authentication of milk according to production zone and type of feeding of the cow. J Agric Food Chem 55(22):9099–9108.
186. Espineira M, Gonzalez-Lavin N, Vieites JM & Santaclara FJ. 2008. Authentication of anglerfish species (Lophius spp) by means of polymerase chain reaction-restriction fragment length polymorphism (PCR-RFLP) and forensically informative nucleotide sequencing (FINS) methodologies. J Agric Food Chem 56(22):10594–10599.
187. Etienne M, Jérôme M, Fleurence J, Rehbein H, Kündiger R, Mendes R, Costa H & Martínez I. 2001. Species identification of formed fishery products and high pressure-treated fish by electrophoresis: A collaborative study. Food Chem 72(1):105–112.
188. Etzold E & Lichtenberg-Kraag B. 2008. Determination of the botanical origin of honey by Fourier-transformed infrared spectroscopy: An approach for routine analysis. Eur Food Res Technol 227(2):579–586.
189. Faria MA, Magalhaes R, Ferreira MA, Meredith CP & Monteiro FF. 2000. Vitis vinifera must varietal authentication using microsatellite DNA analysis (SSR). J Agric Food Chem 48(4):1096–1100.
190. Fasciotti M & Pereira Netto AD. 2010. Optimization and application of methods of triacylglycerol evaluation for characterization of olive oil adulteration by soybean oil with HPLC-APCI-MS-MS. Talanta 81(3):1116–1125.
191. FDA. 2007a. FDA update and synopsis on the pet food outbreak. US Food and Drug Administration. http://www.fda.gov/oc/opacom/hottopics/petfood_update.html. Accessed July 16, 2007.
192. FDA. 2007b. Import Alert #99–29. Detention without physical examination of all vegetable protein products from China for animal or human food use due the presence of melamine and/or melamine analogs. US Food and Drug Administration. http://www.accessdata.fda.gov/cms_ia/importalert_267.html. Accessed May 15, 2011.
193. Feinberg M, Dupont D, Efstathiou T, Louâpre V & Guyonnet J-P. 2006. Evaluation of tracers for the authentication of thermal treatments of milks. Food Chem 98(1):188–194.
194. Field A & Field J. 2010. Melamine and cyanuric acid do not interfere with Bradford and Ninhydrin assays for protein determination. Food Chem 121(3):912–917.
195. Fisher JF. 1983. High-performance liquid chromatographic determination of sodium benzoate

when used as a tracer to detect pulpwash adulteration of orange juice. J Agric Food Chem 31(1):66–68.
196. Flores G, Ruiz del Castillo ML, Blanch GP & Herraiz M. 2006a. Detection of the adulteration of olive oils by solid phase microextraction and multidimensional gas chromatography. Food Chem 97(2):336–342.
197. Flores G, Ruiz del Castillo ML, Herraiz M & Blanch GP. 2006b. Study of the adulteration of olive oil with hazelnut oil by on-line coupled high performance liquid chromatographic and gas chromatographic analysis of filbertone. Food Chem 97(4):742–749.
198. Flurer CL, Crowe JB & Wolnik KA. 2000. Detection of adulteration of locust bean gum with guar gum by capillary electrophoresis and polarized light microscopy. Food Addit Contam 17(1):3–15.
199. Folkenberg J. 1990. Spiked wheat - Schuler Grain Co. uses additive to artificially boost the protein content of its wheat. FDA Consum (December).
200. Fragaki G, Spyros A, Siragakis G, Salivaras E & Dais P. 2005. Detection of extra virgin olive oil adulteration with lampante olive oil and refined olive oil using nuclear magnetic resonance spectroscopy and multivariate statistical analysis. J Agric Food Chem 53(8):2810–2816.
201. Frank C, Dietrich A, Kremer U & Mosandl A. 1995. GC-IRMS in the authenticity control of the essential oil of coriandrum sativum L. J Agric Food Chem 43(6):1634–1637.
202. Frankel EN. 2010. Chemistry of extra virgin olive oil: Adulteration, oxidative stability, and antioxidants. J Agric Food Chem 58(10):5991–6006.
203. Frankel EN, Mailer RJ, Shoemaker CF, Wang SC & Flynn JD. 2010. Tests indicate that imported "extra virgin" olive oil often fails international and USDA standards. http://olivecenter.ucdavis.edu/news-events/news/files/oliveoilappendix071510.pdf. Accessed May 15, 2011.
204. Frantz D. 1999. An inquiry finds roe impersonating caviar. New York Times.
205. Fronza G, Fuganti C, Guillou C, Reniero F & Joulain D. 1998. Natural abundance ^{2}H nuclear magnetic resonance study of the origin of raspberry ketone. J Agric Food Chem 46(1):248–254.
206. Fronza G, Fuganti C, Schmidt H-L & Werner R. 2002. The delta^{18}O-value of the p-OH group of L-tyrosine permits the assignment of its origin to plant or animal sources. Eur Food Res Technol 215(1):55–58.
207. FSA. 2004. Survey on basmati rice. Food Standards Agency. http://www.food.gov.uk/multimedia/pdfs/fsis4704basmati.pdf. Accessed May 15, 2011.
208. Fügel R, Carle R & Schieber A. 2004. A novel approach to quality and authenticity control of fruit products using fractionation and characterisation of cell wall polysaccharides. Food Chem 87(1):141–150.
209. Fügel R, Carle R & Schieber A. 2005. Quality and authenticity control of fruit purées, fruit preparations and jams—A review. Trends Food Sci Tech 16(10):433–441.
210. Gallardo-Velázquez T, Osorio-Revilla G, Loa MZ & Rivera-Espinoza Y. 2009. Application of FTIR-HATR spectroscopy and multivariate analysis to the quantification of adulterants in Mexican honeys. Food Res Int 42(3):313–318.
211. Galtier O, Dupuy N, Le Dréau Y, Ollivier D, Pinatel C, Kister J & Artaud J. 2007. Geographic origins and compositions of virgin olive oils determined by chemometric analysis of NIR spectra. Analytica Chimica Acta 595(1–2):136–144.
212. GAO. 1995. Fruit juice adulteration. Detection is difficult, and enhanced efforts would be costly. GAO/RCED-96-18. In: Resources, C., and Economic Development Division, editor. United States General Accountability Office. http://www.gpo.gov/fdsys/pkg/GAOREPORTS-RCED-96-18/pdf/GAOREPORTS-RCED-96-18.pdf. Accessed May 15, 2011.
213. GAO. 2009. Seafood fraud: FDA program changes and better collaboration among key federal agencies could improve detection and prevention. GAO-09-258. United States Government Accountability Office. http://www.gao.gov/new.items/d09258.pdf. Accessed May 15, 2011.
214. Garber EAE & Brewer V. 2010. Enzyme-linked immunosorbent assay detection of melamine in infant formula and wheat food products. J Food Protect 73(4):701–707.
215. Garcia-Gonzalez D, Mannina L, D'Imperio M, Segre AL & Aparicio R. 2004. Using ^{1}H and ^{13}C NMR techniques and artificial neural networks to detect the adulteration of olive oil with hazelnut oil. Eur Food Res Technol 219:545–548.
216. Garcia-Gonzalez DL, Viera-Macias M, Aparicio-Ruiz R, Morales MT & Aparicio R. 2007. Validation of a method based on triglycerides for the detection of low percentages of hazelnut oil in olive oil by column liquid chromatography. J AOAC Int 90(5):1346–1353.
217. Garcia-Wass F, Hammond D, Mottram DS & Gutteridge CS. 2000. Detection of fruit juice authenticity using pyrolysis mass spectroscopy. Food Chem 69(2):215–220.
218. Garcia LMZ, Pauli ED, Cristiano V, da Camara CAP, Scarminio S & Nixdorf SL. 2009. Chemometric evaluation of adulteration profile in coffee due to corn and husk by determining carbohydrates using HPAECPAD. J Chromatogr Sci 47:825–832.
219. Garcia MC & Marina ML. 2006. Rapid detection of the addition of soybean proteins to cheese and other dairy products by reversed-phase perfusion chromatography. Food Addit Contam 23(4):339–347.
220. García MC, Marina ML & Torre M. 1997. Simultaneous separation of soya bean and animal whey proteins by reversed-phase high-performance liquid chromatography. Quantitative analysis in edible samples. Anal Chem 69(11):2217–2220.
221. García T, Martín R, Rodríguez E, Morales P, Hernández PE & Sanz B. 1990. Detection of bovine milk in ovine milk by an indirect enzyme-linked immunosorbent assay. J Dairy Sci 73(6):1489–1493.
222. Gayo J & Hale SA. 2007. Detection and quantification of species authenticity and adulteration in crabmeat using visible and near-infrared spectroscopy. J Agric Food Chem 55(3):585–592.
223. Gayo J, Hale SA & Blanchard SM. 2006. Quantitative

analysis and detection of adulteration in crab meat using visible and near-infrared spectroscopy. J Agric Food Chem 54(4):1130–1136.
224. Gerard Downey VF, & Daniel Kelly J. 2003. Detection of honey adulteration by addition of fructose and glucose using near infrared transflectance spectroscopy. Near Infrared Spec 11(6):447–456.
225. Ghosh N, Verma Y, Majumder SK & Gupta PK. 2005a. A Fluorescence spectroscopic study of honey and cane sugar syrup. Food Sci Technol Res 11(1):59–62.
226. Ghosh P, Krishna Reddy MM & Sashidhar RB. 2005b. Quantitative evaluation of sanguinarine as an index of argemone oil adulteration in edible mustard oil by high performance thin layer chromatography. Food Chem 91(4):757–764.
227. Girard P, Stober P, Blanc M & Prodolliet J. 2006. Carbohydrate specification limits for the authenticity assessment of soluble (instant) coffee: Statistical approach. J AOAC Int 89(4):999–1003.
228. Gombu P. 1998. Seven firms fined, 'Olive' oil seized in crackdown: Investigators find $1 million in adulterated oil. Toronto Star.
229. Gómez-Ariza JL, Villegas-Portero MJ & Bernal-Daza V. 2005. Characterization and analysis of amino acids in orange juice by HPLC-MS/MS for authenticity assessment. Analytica Chimica Acta 540(1):221–230.
230. González AG, Pablos F, Martín MJ, León-Camacho M & Valdenebro MS. 2001. HPLC analysis of tocopherols and triglycerides in coffee and their use as authentication parameters. Food Chem 73(1):93–101.
231. Gonzalez J, Jamin E, Remaud G, Martin Y-L, Martin GG & Martin ML. 1998. Authentication of lemon juices and concentrates by a combined multi-isotope approach using SNIF-NMR and IRMS. J Agric Food Chem 46(6):2200–2205.
232. Gonzalez J, Remaud G, Jamin E, Naulet N & Martin GG. 1999. Specific natural isotope profile studied by isotope ratio mass spectrometry (SNIP-IRMS): $^{13}C/^{12}C$ ratios of fructose, glucose, and sucrose for improved detection of sugar addition to pineapple juices and concentrates. J Agric Food Chem 47(6):2316–2321.
233. González Martín I, Marqués Macías E, Sánchez Sánchez J & González Rivera B. 1998. Detection of honey adulteration with beet sugar using stable isotope methodology. Food Chem 61(3):281–286.
234. Gonzálvez A, Armenta S & de la Guardia M. 2010. Adulteration detection of argan oil by inductively coupled plasma optical emission spectrometry. Food Chem 121(3):878–886.
235. Goodacre R, Kell DB & Bianchi G. 1993. Rapid assessment of the adulteration of virgin olive oils by other seed oils using pyrolysis mass spectrometry and artificial neural networks. J Sci Food Agr 63(3):297–307.
236. Gordon M, Covell C & Kirsch N. 2001. Detection of pressed hazelnut oil in admixtures with virgin olive oil by analysis of polar components. J Am Oil Chem Soc 78(6):621–624.
237. Gray N. 2010. Metallic tasting pine nuts are from illegitimate Chinese sources. Food Navigator-US.com.
238. Greule M, Tumino L, Kronewald T, Hener U, Schleucher J, Mosandl A & Keppler F. 2010. Improved rapid authentication of vanillin using delta^{13}C and delta^{2}H values. Eur Food Res Technol 231(6):933–941.
239. Grob K, Biedermann M & Bronz M. 1994a. Monitoring of edible oils: Adulteration and contamination. Mitt Geb Lebensmittelunters Hyg 85:351–365.
240. Grob K, Bronz M, Biedermann M, Etter R & Romann E. 1994b. Cold pressed oils. On many frauds and an unsettled market. Mitt Geb Lebensmittelunters Hyg 85:630–640.
241. Grob K, Bronz M, Biedermann M, Grolimund B, Boderius U, Neukom HP, Brunner M & Etter R. 1995. Adulterated olive oils from the Swiss market 1993-1995. Riv Ital Sostanze Grasse 72:525–528.
242. Grob K, Giuffre AM, Biedermann M & Bronz M. 1994c. The detection of adulteration with desterolized oils. Fett Wiss Technol 96:341–345.
243. Grob K, Giuffre AM, Leuzzi U & Mincione B. 1994d. Recognition of adulterated oils by direct analysis of the minor components. Fett Wiss Technol 96:286–290.
244. Grob K & Romann E. 1993. The detection of adulterated olive oils and consequences thereof for food control. Mitt Geb Lebensmittelunters Hyg 84:99–111.
245. Guan RF, Liu DH, Ye XQ & Yang K. 2005. Use of fluorometry for determination of skim milk powder adulteration in fresh milk. J Zhejiang Univ Sci B. 6(11):1101–1106.
246. Guimet F, Ferré J & Boqué R. 2005. Rapid detection of olive-pomace oil adulteration in extra virgin olive oils from the protected denomination of origin 'Siurana' using excitation-emission fluorescence spectroscopy and three-way methods of analysis. Analytica Chimica Acta 544(1–2):143–152.
247. Guo L-X, Xu X-M, Yuan J-P, Wu C-F & Wang J-H. 2010a. Characterization and authentication of significant Chinese edible oilseed oils by stable carbon isotope analysis. J Am Oil Chem Soc 87(8):839–848.
248. Guo L, Zhong J, Wu J, Fu F, Chen G, Zheng X & Lin S. 2010b. Visual detection of melamine in milk products by label-free gold nanoparticles. Talanta 82(5):1654–1658.
249. Gupti N & Panchal P. 2009. Extent of awareness and food adulteration detection in selected food items purchased by home makers. Pakistan Journal of Nutrition 8(5):660–667.
250. Gurdeniz G & Ozen B. 2009. Detection of adulteration of extra-virgin olive oil by chemometric analysis of mid-infrared spectral data. Food Chem 116(2):519–525.
251. Gutierrez R, Vega S, Diaz G, Sanchez J, Coronado M, Ramirez A, Perez J, Gonzalez M & Schettino B. 2009. Detection of non-milk fat in milk fat by gas chromatography and linear discriminant analysis. J Dairy Sci 92(5):1846–1855.
252. Ha WY, Shaw PC, Liu J, Yau FC & Wang J. 2002. Authentication of Panax ginseng and Panax quinquefolius using amplified fragment length polymorphism (AFLP) and directed amplification of minisatellite region DNA (DAMD). J Agric Food Chem 50(7):1871–1875.

253. Haasnoot W, Marchesini GR & Koopal K. 2006. Spreeta-based biosensor immunoassays to detect fraudulent adulteration in milk and milk powder. J AOAC Int 89(3):849–855.
254. Haasnoot W, Smits NG, Kemmers-Voncken AE & Bremer MG. 2004. Fast biosensor immunoassays for the detection of cows' milk in the milk of ewes and goats. J Dairy Res 71(03):322–329.
255. Hagedorn ML. 1992. Differentiation of natural and synthetic benzaldehydes by ^{2}H nuclear magnetic resonance. J Agric Food Chem 40(4):634–637.
256. Hai Z & Wang J. 2006. Detection of adulteration in camellia seed oil and sesame oil using an electronic nose. Eur Lipid Sci Tech 108(2):116–124.
257. Halliday J. 2009. Early harmonisation urged for stevia standards, methods. Food Navigator. http://www.foodnavigator-usa.com/Financial-Industry/Early-harmonisation-urged-for-stevia-standards-methods. Accessed May 15, 2011.
258. Hammond DA. 2001. Synergy between liquid chromatographic-pulsed amperometric detection and capillary-gas chromatographic methods for the detection of juice adulteration. J AOAC Int 84(3):964–975.
259. Hanneguelle S, Thibault JN, Naulet N & Martin GJ. 1992. Authentication of essential oils containing linalool and linalyl acetate by isotopic methods. J Agric Food Chem 40(1):81–87.
260. Harrington R. 2010. Chinese flour adulterated with pulverised lime - reports. Food Navigator.com. http://www.foodnavigator.com/content/view/print/285451. Accessed May 15, 2011.
261. Hattori R, Yamada K, Shibata H, Hirano S, Tajima O & Yoshida N. 2010. Measurement of the isotope ratio of acetic acid in vinegar by HS-SPME-GC-TC/C-IRMS. J Agric Food Chem 58(12):7115–7118.
262. Haza AI, Morales P, Martin R, Garcia T, Anguita G, Gonzalez I, Sanz B & Hernandez PE. 1997. Use of a monoclonal antibody and two enzyme-linked immunosorbent assay formats for detection and quantification of the substitution of caprine milk for ovine milk. J Food Protect 60(8):973–977.
263. He ZD, Qiao CF, Han QB, Cheng CL, Xu HX, Jiang RW, But PP & Shaw PC. 2005. Authentication and quantitative analysis on the chemical profile of cassia bark (cortex cinnamomi) by high-pressure liquid chromatography. J Agric Food Chem 53(7):2424–2428.
264. Hein K. 2008. Pure juice found guilty of false advertising. Adweek. http://www.adweek.com/news/advertising-branding/purely-juice-found-guilty-false-advertising-96450. Accessed May 15, 2011.
265. Heise HM, Damm U, Lampen P, Davies AN & McIntyre PS. 2005. Spectral variable selection for partial least squares calibration applied to authentication and quantification of extra virgin olive oils using Fourier transform Raman spectroscopy. Appl Spectrosc 59(10):1286–1294.
266. Henkel J. 1994. Olive oil distributor sentenced. FDA Consum 28.
267. Henriques DB. 1993. 10% of Fruit juice sold in U.S. is not all juice, regulators say. New York Times. http://www.nytimes.com/1993/10/31/us/10-of-fruit-juice-sold-in-us-is-not-all-juice-regulators-say.html. Accessed May 15, 2011.
268. Herbach KM, Stintzing FC, Elss S, Preston C, Schreier P & Carle R. 2006. Isotope ratio mass spectrometrical analysis of betanin and isobetanin isolates for authenticity evaluation of purple pitaya-based products. Food Chem 99(1):204–209.
269. Herbert I. 2000. Gangs make a fortune from the ancient art of adulterating saffron. Independent.
270. Hernandez A, Aranda E, Martin A, Benito MJ, Bartolome T & de Gua Cordoba M. 2010. Efficiency of DNA typing methods for detection of smoked paprika "pimenton de la vera" adulteration used in the elaboration of dry-cured Iberian pork sausages. J Agric Food Chem 58(22):11688–11694.
271. Hernandez A, Martin A, Aranda E, Bartolome T & Cordoba Mde G. 2006. Detection of smoked paprika "Pimenton de La Vera" adulteration by free zone capillary electrophoresis (FZCE). J Agric Food Chem 54(12):4141–4147.
272. Hernandez A, Martin A, Aranda E, Bartolome T & Cordoba MdG. 2007. Application of temperature-induced phase partition of proteins for the detection of smoked paprika adulteration by free zone capillary electrophoresis (FZCE). Food Chem 105:1219–1227.
273. Herrero-Martínez JM, Simó-Alfonso EF, Ramis-Ramos G, Gelfi C & Righetti PG. 2000. Determination of cow's milk in non-bovine and mixed cheeses by capillary electrophoresis of whey proteins in acidic isoelectric buffers. J Chromatogr A 878(2):261–271.
274. Hewedy MM & Smith CJ. 1990. Modified immunoassay for the detection of soy milk in pasteurized skimmed bovine milk. Food Hydrocolloid 3(6):485–490.
275. Hickman M. 2009. Chicken injected with beef waste sold in UK. Independent. p. 4. http://www.independent.co.uk/life-style/food-and-drink/news/chicken-injected-with-beef-w. Accessed May 15, 2011.
276. Hilali M, Charrouf Z, Soulhi A, Hachimi L & Guillaume D. 2007. Detection of argan oil adulteration using quantitative campesterol GC-analysis. J Am Oil Chem Soc 84(8):761–764.
277. Holland JK, Kemsley EK & Wilson RH. 1998. Use of Fourier transform infrared spectroscopy and partial least squares regression for the detection of adulteration of strawberry purées. J Sci Food Agr 76(2):263–269.
278. Holloway G, Maheswaran R, Leeks A, Bradby S & Wahab S. 2010. Screening method for ethylene glycol and diethylene glycol in glycerin-containing products. J Pharm Biomed Anal 51(3):507–511.
279. Hör K, Ruff C, Weckerle B, König T & Schreier P. 2000. Flavor authenticity studies by ^{2}H/^{1}H ratio determination using on-line gas ghromatography pyrolysis isotope ratio mass spectrometry. J Agric Food Chem 49(1):21–25.
280. Howes MJ, Kite GC & Simmonds MS. 2009. Distinguishing Chinese star anise from Japanese star anise using thermal desorption-gas chromatography-

280. mass spectrometry. J Agric Food Chem 57(13):5783–5789.
281. Hrastar R, Petrisic MG, Ogrinc N & Kosir IJ. 2009. Fatty acid and stable carbon isotope characterization of Camelina sativa oil: Implications for authentication. J Agric Food Chem 57(2):579–585.
282. Hsu YF, Chen KT, Liu YW, Hsieh SH & Huang HY. 2010. Determination of melamine and related triazine by-products ammeline, ammelide, and cyanuric acid by micellar electrokinetic chromatography. Anal Chim Acta 673(2):206–211.
283. Hu CB, Ding HC & Chen S. 2001. Rapid detection of bovine milk adulteration in caprine milk. Taiwan Nongye Huaxue Yu Shipin Kexue 39(6):405–414.
284. Huang G, Ouyang Z & Cooks RG. 2009. High-throughput trace melamine analysis in complex mixtures. Chem Commun (Camb) (5):556–558.
285. Hurley IP, Coleman RC, Ireland HE & Williams JHH. 2004a. Measurement of bovine IgG by indirect competitive ELISA as a means of detecting milk adulteration. Dairy Sci 87(3):543–549.
286. Hurley IP, Coleman RC, Ireland HE & Williams JHH. 2006. Use of sandwich IgG ELISA for the detection and quantification of adulteration of milk and soft cheese. Int Dairy 16(7):805–812.
287. Hurley IP, Elyse Ireland H, Coleman RC & Williams JHH. 2004b. Application of immunological methods for the detection of species adulteration in dairy products. Int J Food Sci Tech 39(8):873–878.
288. Hurley IP, Pickles NA, Qin H, Elyse Ireland H, Coleman RC, Tosun BN, Buyuktuncer Z & Williams JHH. 2010. Detection of Konjac glucomannan by immunoassay. Int J Food Sci Tech 45(7):1410–1416.
289. Husain S, Kifayatullah M, Sastry G & Raju N. 1993. Quantitative determination of castor oil in edible and heat abused oils by C-13 nuclear magnetic resonance spectroscopy. J Am Oil Chem Soc 70(12):1251–1254.
290. Husain S, Narsimha R & Rao RN. 1999. Separation, identification and determination of sanguinarine in argemone and other adulterated edible oils by reversed-phase high-performance liquid chromatography. J Chromatogr A 863(1):123–126.
291. Infante C, Catanese G, Ponce M & Manchado M. 2004. Novel method for the authentication of frigate tunas (Auxis thazard and Auxis rochei) in commercial canned products. J Agric Food Chem 52(25):7435–7443.
292. Ireland HE, Clutterbuck A, Cloquet JP, Thurston MI, Williams PA, Cronk QC, Dewey FM & Williams JH. 2004. The development of immunoassays to identify and quantify species source of gum arabic. J Agric Food Chem 52(26):7804–7808.
293. Irudayaraj J, Xu R & Tewari J. 2003. Rapid determination of invert cane sugar adulteration in honey using FTIR spectroscopy and multivariate analysis. Food Sci 68(6):2040–2045.
294. ISO-IDF. 2010. Milk, milk products and infant formulae—Guidelines for the quantitative determination of melamine and cyanuric acid by LC-MS/MS, 1st ed. ISO/TS 15495 IDF/RM 230.
295. Iuliano TA. 1996. A simplified method for determining undeclared sweeteners added to pure orange juice. J AOAC Int 79(6):1381–1387.
296. Ize-Ludlow D, Ragone S, Bruck IS, Bernstein JN, Duchowny M & Pena BMG. 2004. Neurotoxicities in infants seen with the consumption of star anise tea. Pediatrics.
297. J. Baxter M, M. Crews H, John Dennis M, Goodall I & Anderson D. 1997. The determination of the authenticity of wine from its trace element composition. Food Chem 60(3):443–450.
298. Jaiswal PK. 2008. Common adulterants/contaminants in food and simple screening tests for their detection. Central Agmark Laboratory. p. 11. http://www.agmarknet.nic.in/adulterants.htm. Accessed May 15, 2011.
299. Jamin E, Gonzalez J, Bengoechea I, Kerneur G, Remaud G, Iriondo C & Martin GG. 1998a. Proteins as intermolecular isotope reference for detection of adulteration of fruit juices. J Agric Food Chem 46(12):5118–5123.
300. Jamin E, Gonzalez J, Bengoechfa I, Kerneur G, Remaud G, Naulet N & Martin GG. 1998b. Measurement of $^{13}C/^{12}C$ ratios of sugars, malic acid, and citric acid as authenticity probes of citrus juices and concentrates. J AOAC Int 81(3):604–609.
301. Jamin E, Martin F, Santamaria-Fernandez R & Lees M. 2005. Detection of exogenous citric acid in fruit juices by stable isotope ratio analysis. J Agric Food Chem 53(13):5130–5133.
302. Jha SN & Gunasekaran S. 2010. Authentication of sweetness of mango juice using Fourier transform infrared-attenuated total reflection spectroscopy. Food Eng 101(3):337–342.
303. Jha SN & Matsuoka T. 2004. Detection of adulterants in milk using near infrared spectroscopy. J Food Sci Technol. 41(3):313–316.
304. Jham GN, Winkler JK, Berhow MA & Vaughn SF. 2007. Gamma-tocopherol as a marker of Brazilian coffee (Coffea arabica L.) adulteration by corn. J Agric Food Chem 55(15):5995–5999.
305. Jiang B, Kronenberg F, Nuntanakorn P, Qiu MH & Kennelly EJ. 2006. Evaluation of the botanical authenticity and phytochemical profile of black cohosh products by high-performance liquid chromatography with selected ion monitoring liquid chromatography-mass spectrometry. J Agric Food Chem 54(9):3242–3253.
306. John TV & Jamin E. 2004. Chemical investigation and authenticity of Indian vanilla beans. J Agric Food Chem 52(25):7644–7650.
307. Joshi VC, Srinivas PV & Khan IA. 2005. Rapid and easy identification of Illicium verum Hook. f. and its adulterant Illicium anisatum Linn. by fluorescent microscopy and gas chromatography. J AOAC Int 88(3):703–706.
308. Juliani HR, Kapteyn J, Jones D, Koroch AR, Wang M, Charles D & Simon JE. 2006. Application of near-infrared spectroscopy in quality control and determination of adulteration of African essential oils. Phytochem Anal 17(2):121–128.
309. Kaminarides SE & Koukiassa P. 2002. Detection of

bovine milk in ovine yoghurt by electrophoresis of para-[kappa]-casein. Food Chem 78(1):53–55.
310. Kandler H, Bleisch M, Widmer V & Reich E. 2009. A validated HPTLC method for the determination of illegal dyes in spices and spice mixtures. J Liq Chromatogr 32(9):1273–1288.
311. Kapoulas VM & Andrikopoulos NK. 1986. Detection of olive oil adulteration with linoleic acid-rich oils by reversed-phase high-performance liquid chromatography. J Chromatogr A 366:311–320.
312. Karoui R & De Baerdemaeker J. 2007. A review of the analytical methods coupled with chemometric tools for the determination of the quality and identity of dairy products. Food Chem 102(3):621–640.
313. Kasemsumran S, Thanapase W & Kiatsoonthon A. 2007. Feasibility of near-infrared spectroscopy to detect and to quantify adulterants in cow milk. Anal Sci 23(7):907–910.
314. Kaunzinger A, Juchelka D & Mosandl A. 1997. Progress in the authenticity assessment of vanilla. 1. Initiation of authenticity profiles. J Agric Food Chem 45(5):1752–1757.
315. Kelly JD, Petisco C & Downey G. 2006. Application of Fourier transform midinfrared spectroscopy to the discrimination between Irish artisanal honey and such honey adulterated with various sugar syrups. J Agric Food Chem 54(17):6166–6171.
316. Kelly JF & Downey G. 2005. Detection of sugar adulterants in apple juice using Fourier transform infrared spectroscopy and chemometrics. J Agric Food Chem 53(9):3281–3286.
317. Kelly JF, Downey G & Fouratier V. 2004. Initial study of honey adulteration by sugar solutions using midinfrared (MIR) spectroscopy and chemometrics. J Agric Food Chem 52(1):33–39.
318. Kelly S, Parker I, Sharman M, Dennis J & Goodall I. 1997. Assessing the authenticity of single seed vegetable oils using fatty acid stable carbon isotope ratios ($^{13}C/^{12}C$). Food Chem 59(2):181–186.
319. Kemsley EK, Holland JK, Defernez M & Wilson RH. 1996. Detection of adulteration of raspberry purees using infrared spectroscopy and chemometrics. Agric Food Chem 44(12):3864–3870.
320. Kermack G. 2008. FSA launches food fraud hotline. FoodNavigator.com. p. 2. http://www.foodnavigator.com/content/view/print/226888. Accessed May 15, 2011.
321. Kim KH, Lee JG, Kim DG, Kim MK, Park JH, Shin YG, Lee SK, Jo TH & Oh ST. 1998. The development of a new method to detect the adulteration of commercial aloe gel powders. Arch Pharm Res 21(5):514–520.
322. Kirit AB & Ozdemir Y. 2007. Organic acids, sugars, amino acids and flavonoids in turkish orange juices and characterization for adulteration. Adv Food Sci 29(1):35–41.
323. Kitaoka M, Okamura N, Ichinose H & Goto M. 2008. Detection of SNPs in fish DNA: Application of the fluorogenic ribonuclease protection (FRIP) assay for the authentication of food contents. J Agric Food Chem 56(15):6246–6251.
324. Knödler M, Most M, Schieber A & Carle R. 2010. A novel approach to authenticity control of whole grain durum wheat (Triticum durum Desf.) flour and pasta, based on analysis of alkylresorcinol composition. Food Chem 118(1):177–181.
325. Koca N, Kocaoglu-Vurma NA, Harper WJ & Rodriguez-Saona LE. 2010. Application of temperature-controlled attenuated total reflectance-mid-infrared (ATR-MIR) spectroscopy for rapid estimation of butter adulteration. Food Chem 121(3):778–782.
326. Kokkinofta R, Petrakis PV, Mavromoustakos T & Theocharis CR. 2003. Authenticity of the traditional cypriot spirit "zivania" on the basis of metal content using a combination of coupled plasma spectroscopy and statistical analysis. J Agric Food Chem 51(21):6233–6239.
327. König WA, Fricke C, Saritas Y, Momeni B & Hohenfeld G. 1997. Adulteration or natural variability? Enantioselective gas chromatography in purity control of essential oils. J High Res Chromatog 20(2):55–61.
328. Korosec M, Bertoncel J, Pereyra Gonzales A, Kropf U & Golob T. 2009. Monosaccharides and oligosaccharides in four types of Slovenian honey. Acta Alimentaria 38(4):459–469.
329. Krahulcová J, Pangallo D, Piknová L, Siekel P & Kuchta T. 2003. Polymerase chain reaction for the detection of Phaseolus vulgaris beans in chestnut purée. Eur Food Res Technol 217(1):80–82.
330. Krist S, Stuebiger G, Bail S & Unterweger H. 2006. Detection of adulteration of poppy seed oil with sunflower oil based on volatiles and triacylglycerol composition. J Agric Food Chem 54(17):6385–6389.
331. Krueger DA. 1992. Stable carbon isotope ratio method for detection of corn-derived acetic acid in apple cider vinegar: Collaborative study. J AOAC Int 75(4):725–728.
332. Kumar A, Ghai DL, Seth R & Sharma V. 2009. Apparent solidification time test for detection of foreign oils and fats adulterated in clarified milk fat, as affected by season and storage. Int J Dairy Technol 62(1):33–38.
333. Küpper L, Heise HM, Lampen P, Davies AN & McIntyre P. 2001. Authentication and quantification of extra virgin olive oils by attenuated total reflectance infrared spectroscopy using silver halide fiber probes and partial least-squares calibration. Appl Spectrosc 55(5):563–570.
334. Kurtzweil P. 1997. Sticking public with impure products puts syrup makers in prison. FDA Consum (April).
335. Kurz C, Carle R & Schieber A. 2008a. Characterisation of cell wall polysaccharide profiles of apricots (Prunus armeniaca L.), peaches (Prunus persica L.), and pumpkins (Cucurbita sp.) for the evaluation of fruit product authenticity. Food Chem 106(1):421–430.
336. Kurz C, Carle R & Schieber A. 2008b. HPLC-DAD-MS characterisation of carotenoids from apricots and pumpkins for the evaluation of fruit product authenticity. Food Chem 110(2):522–530.
337. Lachenmeier DW, Humpfer E, Fang F, Schütz B, Dvortsak P, Sproll C & Spraul M. 2009. NMR-spectroscopy for nontargeted screening and

simultaneous quantification of health-relevant compounds in foods: The example of melamine. J Agric Food Chem 57(16):7194–7199.
338. Lachenmeier DW, Richling E, Lopez MG, Frank W & Schreier P. 2005. Multivariate analysis of FTIR and ion chromatographic data for the quality control of tequila. J Agric Food Chem 53(6):2151–2157.
339. Lai YW, Kemsley EK & Wilson RH. 1994. Potential of Fourier transform infrared spectroscopy for the authentication of vegetable oils. J Agric Food Chem 42(5):1154–1159.
340. Lai YW, Kemsley EK & Wilson RH. 1995. Quantitative analysis of potential adulterants of extra virgin olive oil using infrared spectroscopy. Food Chem 53(1):95–98.
341. Lamprecht G, Pichlmayer F & Schmid ER. 1994. Determination of the authenticity of vanilla extracts by stable isotope ratio analysis and component analysis by HPLC. J Agric Food Chem 42(8):1722–1727.
342. Laursen KH, Hansen TH, Persson DP, Schjoerring JK & Husted S. 2009. Multi-elemental fingerprinting of plant tissue by semi-quantitative ICP-MS and chemometrics. J Anal Atom Spectrom 24(9):1198–1207.
343. Lawrence F. 2005. Watchdog under fire as cancer-dye foods top 400. Guardian.
344. Le Grand F, George G & Akoka S. 2005. Natural abundance 2H-ERETIC-NMR authentication of the origin of methyl salicylate. J Agric Food Chem 53(13):5125–5129.
345. Lederer I, Schulzki G, Gross J & Steffen JP. 2006. Combination of TLC and HPLC-MS/MS methods. Approach to a rational quality control of Chinese star anise. J Agric Food Chem 54(6):1970–1974.
346. Lee YL, Ku KL & Huang HY. 1993. Adulteration detection of commercial sesame oils. Zhongguo Nongye Huaxue Huizhi 31(5):697–701.
347. Leon L, Kelly JD & Downey G. 2005. Detection of apple juice adulteration using near-infrared transflectance spectroscopy. Appl Spectrosc 59(5):593–599.
348. Lerma-García MJ, Ramis-Ramos G, Herrero-Martínez JM & Simó-Alfonso EF. 2010. Authentication of extra virgin olive oils by Fourier-transform infrared spectroscopy. Food Chem 118(1):78–83.
349. Li F & Zhao T. 1999. Determination of the adulteration in beeswax. Shiyou Huagong Gaodeng Xuexiao Xuebao 12(4):36–39.
350. Li J, He R, Jiang Q, Wei J & Yan L. 2004. Amylase activity of honey was used as new target for detecting honey adulteration. Shipin Kexue 25(10):59–62.
351. Lin M, He L, Awika J, Yang L, Ledoux DR, Li H & Mustapha A. 2008. Detection of melamine in gluten, chicken feed, and processed foods using surface enhanced Raman spectroscopy and HPLC. J Food Sci 73(8):T129–T134.
352. Lipp M. 1995. Review of methods for the analysis of triglycerides in milk fat: Application for studies of milk quality and adulteration. Food Chem 54(2):213–221.
353. Lipp M. 1996. Determination of the adulteration of butter fat by its triglyceride composition obtained by GC. A comparison of the suitability of PLS and neural networks. Food Chem 55(4):389–395.
354. Lisa M, Holcapek M & Bohac M. 2009. Statistical evaluation of triacylglycerol composition in plant oils based on high-performance liquid chromatography-atmospheric pressure chemical ionization mass spectrometry data. J Agric Food Chem 57(15):6888–6898.
355. Liu S, Zhang X, Lin X, Wu X, Fu F & Xie Z. 2007. Development of a new method for analysis of Sudan dyes by pressurized CEC with amperometric detection. Electrophoresis 28(11):1696–1703.
356. Liu SL, Tsai YS & Ou AS. 2010. Classifying the variety, production area and season of Taiwan partially fermented tea by near infrared spectroscopy. J Food Drug Anal 18(1):34–43.
357. Lizhi H, Toyoda K & Ihara I. 2010. Discrimination of olive oil adulterated with vegetable oils using dielectric spectroscopy. J Food Eng 96(2):167–171.
358. López-Calleja I, Alonso IG, Fajardo V, Rodríguez MA, Hernández PE, García T & Martín R. 2005a. PCR detection of cows' milk in water buffalo milk and mozzarella cheese. Int Dairy J 15(11):1122–1129.
359. López-Calleja I, González I, Fajardo V, Martín I, Hernández PE, García T & Martín R. 2005b. Application of polymerase chain reaction to detect adulteration of sheep's milk with goats' milk. J Dairy Sci 88(9):3115–3120.
360. López-Calleja I, González I, Fajardo V, Martín I, Hernández PE, García T & Martín R. 2007. Quantitative detection of goats' milk in sheep's milk by real-time PCR. Food Control 18(11):1466–1473.
361. Lopez-Diez EC, Bianchi G & Goodacre R. 2003. Rapid quantitative assessment of the adulteration of virgin olive oils with hazelnut oils using Raman spectroscopy and chemometrics. J Agric Food Chem 51(21):6145–6150.
362. López-Tapia J, García-Risco MR, Manso MA & López-Fandiño R. 1999. Detection of the presence of soya protein in milk powder by sodium dodecyl sulfate capillary electrophoresis. J Chromatogr A 836(1):153–160.
363. Lopez S. 2008. TaqMan based real time PCR method for quantitative detection of basmati rice adulteration with non-basmati rice. Eur Food Res Technol 227(2):619–622.
364. Low NH. 1996. Determination of fruit juice authenticity by capillary gas chromatography with flame ionization detection. J AOAC Int 79(3):724–737.
365. Low NH, McLaughlin M, Hofsommer HJ & Hammond DA. 1999. Capillary gas chromatographic detection of invert sugar in heated, adulterated, and adulterated and heated apple juice concentrates employing the equilibrium method. J Agric Food Chem 47(10):4261–4266.
366. Low NH, McLaughlin MA, Page SW, Canas BJ & Brause AR. 2001. Identification of hydrolyzed inulin syrup and high-fructose corn syrup in apple juice by capillary gas chromatography: PVM 4:1999. J AOAC Int 84(2):486–492.
367. Low NH & South W. 1995a. Determination of honey authenticity by capillary gas chromatography. J AOAC Int 78(5).

368. Low NH & South W. 1995b. Determination of honey authenticity by capillary gas chromatography. J AOAC Int 78(5):1210–1218.
369. Luliano TA. 1996. A simplified method for determining undeclared sweeteners added to pure orange juice. J AOAC Int 79(6):1381–1387.
370. Lumpkin D. 2003. Contaminated chinese honey puts Sara Lee, Smuckers in sticky situation. Albion Monitor.
371. Luykx DM, Cordewener JH, Ferranti P, Frankhuizen R, Bremer MG, Hooijerink H & America AH. 2007a. Identification of plant proteins in adulterated skimmed milk powder by high-performance liquid chromatography–mass spectrometry. J Chromatogr A 1164(1–2):189–197.
372. Luykx DMAM, Cordewener JHG, Ferranti P, Frankhuizen R, Bremer MGEG, Hooijerink H & America AHP. 2007b. Identification of plant proteins in adulterated skimmed milk powder by high-performance liquid chromatography–mass spectrometry. J Chromatogr A 1164(1–2):189–197.
373. Ma XQ, Shi Q, Duan JA, Dong TT & Tsim KW. 2002. Chemical analysis of Radix Astragali (Huangqi) in China: A comparison with its adulterants and seasonal variations. J Agric Food Chem 50(17):4861–4866.
374. Maggio RM, Cerretani L, Chiavaro E, Kaufman TS & Bendini A. 2010. A novel chemometric strategy for the estimation of extra virgin olive oil adulteration with edible oils. Food Control 21(6):890–895.
375. Man YBC, Gan HL, NorAini I, Nazimah SAH & Tan CP. 2005. Detection of lard adulteration in RBD palm olein using an electronic nose. Food Chem 90(4):829–835.
376. Mandl A, Reich G & Lindner W. 1999. Detection of adulteration of pumpkin seed oil by analysis of content and composition of specific Delta7-phytosterols. Eur Food Res Technol 209(6):400–406.
377. Mannina L, D'Imperio M, Capitani D, Rezzi S, Guillou C, Mavromoustakos T, Vilchez MD, Fernandez AH, Thomas F & Aparicio R. 2009. ^{1}H NMR-based protocol for the detection of adulterations of refined olive oil with refined hazelnut oil. J Agric Food Chem 57(24):11550–11556.
378. Manso MA, Cattaneo TM, Barzaghi S, Olieman C & Lopez-Fandino R. 2002. Determination of vegetal proteins in milk powder by sodium dodecyl sulfate-capillary gel electrophoresis: Interlaboratory study. J AOAC Int 85(5):1090–1095.
379. Marcos Lorenzo I, Pérez Pavón JL, Fernández Laespada ME, García Pinto C & Moreno Cordero B. 2002. Detection of adulterants in olive oil by headspace-mass spectrometry. J Chromatogr A 945(1–2):221–230.
380. Marekov I, Panayotova S & Tarandjiiskay R. 2010. Silver ION TLC of minor triacylglycerol components for unambiguous detection of adulteration of olive oil with vegetable oils. J Liq Chromatogr RT 33:1013–1027.
381. Mariani C, Bellan G, Lestini E & Aparicio R. 2006. The detection of the presence of hazelnut oil in olive oil by free and esterified sterols. Eur Food Res Technol 223(5):655–661.
382. Mariani C & Fedeli E. 1986. Detection of extraction oils in pressed oils. Note 1. Rivista Italiana delle Sostanze Grasse 63(1):3–17.
383. Mariani C, Venturini S, Fedeli E & Contarini G. 1994. Detection of refined animal and vegetable fats in adulteration of pure milkfat. J Am Oil Chem Soc 71(12):1381–1384.
384. Mariani C, Venturini S & Grob K. 1995. Identification of desteroled high oleic sunflower oil in olive oil. Riv Ital Sostanze Grasse 72:473–482.
385. Marieschi M, Torelli A, Poli F, Bianchi A & Bruni R. 2010. Quality control of commercial Mediterranean oregano: Development of SCAR markers for the detection of the adulterants Cistus incanus L., Rubus caesius L. and Rhus coriaria L. Food Control 21(7):998–1003.
386. Marigheto N, Kemsley E, Defernez M & Wilson R. 1998. A comparison of mid-infrared and Raman spectroscopies for the authentication of edible oils. J Am Oil Chem Soc 75(8):987–992.
387. Marikkar J, Lai O, Ghazali H & Che Man Y. 2001. Detection of lard and randomized lard as adulterants in refined-bleached-deodorized palm oil by differential scanning calorimetry. J Am Oil Chem Soc 78(11):1113–1119.
388. Marikkar JMN, Ghazali HM, Che Man YB & Lai OM. 2002a. The use of cooling and heating thermograms for monitoring of tallow, lard and chicken fat adulterations in canola oil. Food Res Int 35(10):1007–1014.
389. Marikkar JMN, Ghazali HM, Che Man YB, Peiris TSG & Lai OM. 2005a. Distinguishing lard from other animal fats in admixtures of some vegetable oils using liquid chromatographic data coupled with multivariate data analysis. Food Chem 91(1):5–14.
390. Marikkar JMN, Ghazali HM, Man YBC, Peiris TSG & Lai OM. 2005b. Use of gas liquid chromatography in combination with pancreatic lipolysis and multivariate data analysis techniques for identification of lard contamination in some vegetable oils. Food Chem 90(1–2):23–30.
391. Marikkar JMN, Lai OM, Ghazali HM & Che Man YB. 2002b. Compositional and thermal analysis of RBD palm oil adulterated with lipase-catalyzed interesterified lard. Food Chem 76(2):249–258.
392. Marina A, Che Man Y & Amin I. 2010. Use of the SAW sensor electronic nose for detecting the adulteration of virgin coconut oil with RBD palm kernel olein. J Am Oil Chem Soc 87(3):263–270.
393. Martin GG, Martin Y-L, Naulet N & McManus HJD. 1996. Application of ^{2}H SNIF-NMR and ^{13}C SIRA-MS analyses to maple syrup: Detection of added sugars. J Agric Food Chem 44(10):3206–3213.
394. Martin GJ, Danho D & Vallet C. 1991. Natural isotope fractionation in the discrimination of sugar origins. J Sci Food Agr 56(4):419–434.
395. Martin GJ, Hanneguelle S & Remaud G. 1993. Application of site-specific natural isotope fractionation studied by nuclear magnetic resonance (SNIF-NMR) to the detection of flavour and fragrance adulteration. Ital J Food Sci 5(3):191–213.
396. Martin YL. 2001. Detection of added beet or cane

sugar in maple syrup by the site-specific deuterium nuclear magnetic resonance (SNIF-NMR) method: collaborative study. J AOAC Int 84(5):1509–1521.

397. Maskova E & Paulickova I. 2006. PCR-based detection of cow's milk in goat and sheep cheeses marketed in the Czech Republic. Czech J. Food Sci 24 (3):127–132.

398. Mauer LJ, Chernyshova AA, Hiatt A, Deering A & Davis R. 2009. Melamine detection in infant formula powder using near- and mid-infrared spectroscopy. J Agric Food Chem.

399. Mavromoustakos T, Zervou M, Bonas G, Kolocouris A & Petrakis P. 2000. A novel analytical method to detect adulteration of virgin olive oil by other oils. J Am Oil Chem Soc 77(4):405–411.

400. Mayer HK. 2005. Milk species identification in cheese varieties using electrophoretic, chromatographic and PCR techniques. Int Dairy J 15(6–9):595–604.

401. McCarthy PK, Scanlon BF, Lumley ID & Griffin M. 1990. Detection and quantification of adulteration of durum wheat flour by flour from common wheat using reverse phase HPLC. J Sci Food Agr 50(2):211–226.

402. McDonald CE & Bruns CJ. 1988. Error in near infrared and Kjeldahl protein results from treatment of wheat grain with compounds used as nitrogen fertilizers. Cereal Food World 33(4):367–369.

403. Megherbi M, Herbreteau B, Faure R & Salvador A. 2009. Polysaccharides as a marker for detection of corn sugar syrup addition in honey. J Agric Food Chem 57(6):2105–2111.

404. Meikle J. 2005. Carcinogenic dye in hundreds of food products. Guardian.

405. Méndez J, González M, Lobo MG & Carnero A. 2004. Color quality of pigments in cochineals (Dactylopius coccus Costa). Geographical origin characterization using multivariate statistical analysis. J Agric Food Chem 52(5):1331–1337.

406. Meyer K, Rosa C, Hischenhuber C & Meyer R. 2001. Determination of locust bean gum and guar gum by polymerase chain reaction and restriction fragment length polymorphism analysis. J AOAC Int 84(1):89–99.

407. Michelini E, Cevenini L, Mezzanotte L, Simoni P, Baraldini M, De Laude L & Roda A. 2007. One-step triplex-polymerase chain reaction assay for the authentication of yellowfin (Thunnus albacares), bigeye (Thunnus obesus), and skipjack (Katsuwonus pelamis) tuna DNA from fresh, frozen, and canned tuna samples. J Agric Food Chem 55(19):7638–7647.

408. Mildner-Szkudlarz S & Jelen HH. 2008. The potential of different techniques for volatile compounds analysis coupled with PCA for the detection of the adulteration of olive oil with hazelnut oil. Food Chem 110(3):751–761.

409. Miralles B, Ramos M & Amigo L. 2003. Influence of proteolysis of milk on the whey protein to total protein ratio as determined by capillary electrophoresis. J Dairy Sci 86(9):2813–2817.

410. Mishra A. 2010. This food could be injurious to health. Times of India.

411. Mishra S, Kamboj U, Kaur H & Kapur P. 2010. Detection of jaggery syrup in honey using near-infrared spectroscopy. Int J Food Sci Nutr 61(3):306–315.

412. Mocak J, Jurasek P, Phillips GO, Varga S, Casadei E & Chikemai BN. 1998. The classification of natural gums. X. Chemometric characterization of exudate gums that conform to the revised specification of the gum arabic for food use, and the identification of adulterants. Food Hydrocolloid 12(2):141–150.

413. Modeland V. 1988. Juiceless baby juice leads to full-length justice. FDA Consum (June).

414. Molina E, Amigo L & Ramos M. 1998. Detection of bovine milk proteins in soymilk by western blotting. J Food Protect 61(12):1691–1694.

415. Molina E, Jesús Martín-Álvarez P & Ramos M. 1999. Analysis of cows', ewes' and goats' milk mixtures by capillary electrophoresis: Quantification by multivariate regression analysis. Int Dairy J 9(2):99–105.

416. Molkentin J. 2009. Authentication of organic milk using delta^{13}C and the alpha-linolenic acid content of milk fat. J Agric Food Chem 57(3):785–790.

417. Molkentin J & Giesemann A. 2010. Follow-up of stable isotope analysis of organic versus conventional milk. Anal Bioanal Chem 398(3):1493–1500.

418. Molotsky I. 1985. Popular windes found to hold toxic chemical. New York Times. http://www.nytimes.com/1985/11/01/us/popular-wines-found-to-hold-toxic-chemical.html. Accessed May 1, 2011.

419. Monetti A, Versini G, Dalpiaz G & Reniero F. 1996. Sugar adulterations control in concentrated rectified grape musts by finite mixture distribution analysis of the myo- and scyllo-inositol content and the D/H methyl ratio of fermentative ethanol. J Agric Food Chem 44(8):2194–2201.

420. Mooney R, Chappell L & Knight AI. 2006. Evaluation of a polymerase chain reaction-based heteroduplex assay for detecting the adulteration of processed orange juice with mandarin juice. J AOAC Int 89(4):1052–1060.

421. Moore M. 2007. Murky Italian olive oil to be pored over. Telegraph.

422. Morales V, Corzo N & Sanz ML. 2008. HPAEC-PAD oligosaccharide analysis to detect adulterations of honey with sugar syrups. Food Chem 107(2):922–928.

423. Mosadoni W. 2009. Police swoop on palm oil adulterators. Vanguard.

424. Mottram HR, Woodbury SE, Rossell JB & Evershed RP. 2003. High-resolution detection of adulteration of maize oil using multi-component compound-specific delta^{13}C values of major and minor components and discriminant analysis. Rapid Commun Mass Sp 17(7):706–712.

425. Mouly PP, Gaydou EM & Corsetti J. 1999. Characterization of paprika (Capsicum annuum) extract in orange juices by liquid chromatography of carotenoid profiles. J Agric Food Chem 47(3):968–976.

426. Mouly PP, Gaydou EM, Faure R & Estienne JM. 1997. Blood orange juice authentication using cinnamic acid derivatives. Variety differentiations associated with flavanone glycoside content. J Agric Food Chem 45(2):373–377.

427. Muller L, Bartak P, Bednar P, Frysova I, Sevcik J & Lemr K. 2008. Capillary electrophoresis-mass spectrometry—

A fast and reliable tool for the monitoring of milk adulteration. Electrophoresis 29(10):2088–2093.
428. Nasi A, Ferranti P, Amato S & Chianese L. 2008. Identification of free and bound volatile compounds as typicalness and authenticity markers of non-aromatic grapes and wines through a combined use of mass spectrometric techniques. Food Chem 110(3):762–768.
429. Ng C-C, Lin C-Y, Tzeng W-S, Chang C-C & Shyu Y-T. 2005. Establishment of an internal transcribed spacer (ITS) sequence-based differentiation identification procedure for mei (Prunus mume) and plum (Prunus salicina) and its use to detect adulteration in preserved fruits. Food Res Int 38(1):95–101.
430. Nichols R. 1996. In the honey trade, sweet times turning sticky with supplies off, a buzz over price, purity. Inquirer. Philadelphia.
431. Nicolaou N, Xu Y & Goodacre R. 2010. Fourier transform infrared spectroscopy and multivariate analysis for the detection and quantification of different milk species. J Dairy Sci 93(12):5651–5660.
432. Nogueira T & do Lago CL. 2009. Detection of adulterations in processed coffee with cereals and coffee husks using capillary zone electrophoresis. J Sep Sci 32(20):3507–3511.
433. Oancea S. 2009. Identification of glycomacropeptide as indicator of milk and dairy drinks adulteration with whey by immunochromatographic assay. Rom Biotech Lett 14(1):4146–4151.
434. Ogrinc N, Košir I, Spangenberg J & Kidrič J. 2003. The application of NMR and MS methods for detection of adulteration of wine, fruit juices, and olive oil. A review. Anal Bioanal Chem 376(4):424–430.
435. Ogrinc N, Košir IJ, Kocjančič M & Kidrič J. 2001. Determination of authenticy, regional origin, and vintage of slovenian wines using a combination of IRMS and SNIF-NMR analyses. J Agric Food Chem 49(3):1432–1440.
436. Ohta T, Yoshida KB, Hosono A & Suyama K. 2002. Quantitative determination of furosine in cow's milk containing reconstituted skim milk. Milchwissenschaft-Milk Science International 57(2):70–73.
437. Okazaki S, Hiramatsu M, Gonmori K, Suzuki O & Tu A. 2009. Rapid nondestructive screening for melamine in dried milk by Raman spectroscopy. Forensic Toxicol 27(2):94–97.
438. Oliveira RCS, Oliveira LS, Franca AS & Augusti R. 2009. Evaluation of the potential of SPME-GC-MS and chemometrics to detect adulteration of ground roasted coffee with roasted barley. J Food Compos Anal 22(3):257–261.
439. Otaviano AR, Lima ALF, Laureano MMM, Sena JAD, Albuquerque LcGd & Tonhati H. 2008. Beta-casein gene polymorphism permits identification of bovine milk mixed with bubaline milk in mozzarella cheese. Genet Mol Biol 31:902–905.
440. Ozen BF & Mauer LJ. 2002. Detection of hazelnut oil adulteration using FT-IR spectroscopy. J Agric Food Chem 50(14):3898–3901.
441. Ozen BF, Weiss I & Mauer LJ. 2003. Dietary supplement oil classification and detection of adulteration using Fourier transform infrared spectroscopy. J Agric Food Chem 51(20):5871–5876.
442. Padovan GJ, De Jong D, Rodrigues LP & Marchini JS. 2003. Detection of adulteration of commercial honey samples by the $^{13}C/^{12}C$ isotopic ratio. Food Chem 82(4):633–636.
443. Pan GG, Kilmartin PA, Smith BG & Melton LD. 2002. Detection of orange juice adulteration by tangelo juice using multivariate analysis of polymethoxylated flavones and carotenoids. J Sci Food Agr 82(4):421–427.
444. Pang G-F, Fan C-L, Cao Y-Z, Zhang J-J, Li X-M, Li Z-Y & Jia G-Q. 2006. Study on distribution pattern of stable carbon isotope ratio of Chinese honeys by isotope ratio mass spectrometry. J Sci Food Agr 86(2):315–319.
445. Papadopoulos K, Triantis T, Tzikis CH, Nikokavoura A & Dimotikali D. 2002. Investigations of the adulteration of extra virgin olive oils with seed oils using their weak chemiluminescence. Anal Chim Acta 464(1):135–140.
446. Paradkar MM, Sakhamuri S & Irudayaraj J. 2002. Comparison of FTIR, FT-Raman, and NIR spectroscopy in a maple syrup adulteration study. J Food Sci 67(6):2009–2015.
447. Paradkar MM, Singhal RS & Kulkarni PR. 2000a. An approach to the detection of synthetic milk in dairy milk: 1. Detection of urea. Int J Dairy Technol 53(3):87–91.
448. Paradkar MM, Singhal RS & Kulkarni PR. 2000b. An approach to the detection of synthetic milk in dairy milk: 2. Detection of detergents. Int J Dairy Technol 53(3):92–95.
449. Paradkar MM, Singhal RS & Kulkarni PR. 2001a. An approach to the detection of synthetic milk in dairy milk: 3. Detection of vegetable oil and sodium bicarbonate. Int J Dairy Technol 54(1):34–35.
450. Paradkar MM, Singhal RS & Kulkarni PR. 2001b. An approach to the detection of synthetic milk in dairy milk: 4. Effect of the addition of synthetic milk on the flow behaviour of pure cow milk. Int J Dairy Technol 54(1):36–37.
451. Paradkar MM, Singhal RS & Kulkarni PR. 2001c. A new TLC method to detect the presence of ground papaya seed in ground black pepper. J Sci Food Agr 81(14):1322–1325.
452. Paradkar MM, Sivakesava S & Irudayaraj J. 2003. Discrimination and classification of adulterants in maple syrup with the use of infrared spectroscopic techniques. J Sci Food Agr 83(7):714–721.
453. Parcerisa J, Casals I, Boatella J, Codony R & Rafecas M. 2000. Analysis of olive and hazelnut oil mixtures by high-performance liquid chromatography-atmospheric pressure chemical ionisation mass spectrometry of triacylglycerols and gas-liquid chromatography of non-saponifiable compounds (tocopherols and sterols). J Chromatogr A 881(1–2):149–158.
454. Park GL, Byers JL, Pritz CM, Nelson DB, Navarro JL, Smolensky DC & Vandercook CE. 1983. Characteristics of California navel orange juice and pulpwasn. Food Sci 48(2):627–632.
455. Park YW, Chang P-S & Lee J. 2010. Application of

456. Parker IG, Kelly SD, Sharman M, Dennis MJ & Howie D. 1998. Investigation into the use of carbon isotope ratios ($^{13}C/^{12}C$) of Scotch whisky congeners to establish brand authenticity using gas chromatography-combustion-isotope ratio mass spectrometry. Food Chem 63(3):423–428.

457. Pascoal A, Barros-Velázquez J, Cepeda A, Gallardo JM & Calo-Mata P. 2008. Survey of the authenticity of prawn and shrimp species in commercial food products by PCR-RFLP analysis of a 16S rRNA/tRNAVal mitochondrial region. Food Chem 109(3):638–646.

458. Pasqualone A, Montemurro C, Grinn-Gofron A, Sonnante G & Blanco A. 2007. Detection of soft wheat in semolina and durum wheat bread by analysis of DNA microsatellites. J Agric Food Chem 55(9):3312–3318.

459. Peña F, Cárdenas S, Gallego M & Valcárcel M. 2005. Direct olive oil authentication: Detection of adulteration of olive oil with hazelnut oil by direct coupling of headspace and mass spectrometry, and multivariate regression techniques. J Chromatogr A 1074(1–2):215–221.

460. Penman KG, Halstead CW, Matthias A, De Voss JJ, Stuthe JM, Bone KM & Lehmann RP. 2006. Bilberry adulteration using the food dye amaranth. J Agric Food Chem 54(19):7378–7382.

461. Perfetti GA, Joe FL, Jr., Fazio T & Page SW. 1988. Liquid chromatographic methodology for the characterization of orange juice. J Assoc Off Anal Chem 71(3):469–473.

462. Pesic M, Barac M, Vrvic M, Ristic N, Macej O & Stanojevic S. 2011. Qualitative and quantitative analysis of bovine milk adulteration in caprine and ovine milks using native-PAGE. Food Chem 125(4):1443–1449.

463. Peterson DM, Budde AD, Henson CA & Jones BL. 2001. Detecting corn syrup in barley malt extracts. Anglais 78(3):349–353.

464. Petrakis P, Touris I, Liouni M, Zervou M, Kyrikou I, Kokkinofta R, Theocharis CR & Mavromoustakos TM. 2005. Authenticity of the traditional cypriot spirit 'zivania' on the basis of ^{1}H NMR spectroscopy diagnostic parameters and statistical analysis. J Agric Food Chem 53(13):5293–5303.

465. Petrus DR & Attaway JA. 1980. Visible and ultraviolet absorption and fluorescence excitation and emission characteristics of Florida orange juice and orange pulpwash: Detection of adulteration. J Assoc Off Anal Chem 63(6):1317–1331.

466. Philip T, Chen TS & Nelson DB. 1989. Detection of adulteration of California orange juice concentrates with externally added carotenoids by liquid chromatography. J Agric Food Chem 37(1):90–95.

467. Piergiovanni AR & Taranto G. 2005. Simple and rapid method for the differentiation of Lens culinaris Medik. from false lentil species. J Agric Food Chem 53(17):6593–6597.

468. Pilando LS & Wrolstad RE. 1992. The effectiveness of pattern recognition, sugar, nonvolatile acid, and ^{13}C/^{12}C analyses for detecting adulteration in apple juice. J Food Compos Anal 5(1).

469. Pilizota VT, N. N. 2009. Advances in honey adulteration detection. Food Safety Magazine (August/September).

470. Pizarro C, Esteban-Diez I & Gonzalez-Saiz JM. 2007. Mixture resolution according to the percentage of robusta variety in order to detect adulteration in roasted coffee by near infrared spectroscopy. Anal Chim Acta 585(2):266–276.

471. Poulli KI, Mousdis GA & Georgiou CA. 2007. Rapid synchronous fluorescence method for virgin olive oil adulteration assessment. Food Chem 105(1):369–375.

472. Prado BM, Kim S, Ozen BF & Mauer LJ. 2005. Differentiation of carbohydrate gums and mixtures using Fourier transform infrared spectroscopy and chemometrics. J Agric Food Chem 53(8):2823–2829.

473. Primrose S, Woolfe M & Rollinson S. 2010. Food forensics: Methods for determining the authenticity of foodstuffs. Trends Food Sci Tech 21(12):582–590.

474. Prodolliet J, Bruelhart M, Blanc MB, Leloup V, Cherix G, Donnelly CM & Viani R. 1995. Adulteration of soluble coffee with coffee husks and parchments. J AOAC Int 78(3):761–767.

475. Prodolliet J & Hischenhuber C. 1998. Food authentication by carbohydrate chromatography. Zeitschrift fur Lebensmitteluntersuchung und-Forschung A 207(1):1–12.

476. Pupin AM, Dennis MJ, Parker I, Kelly S, Bigwood T & Toledo MCF. 1998. Use of isotopic analyses To determine the authenticity of Brazilian orange juice (Citrus sinensis). J Agric Food Chem 46(4):1369–1373.

477. Qian J-Y, Chen W, Zhang W-M & Zhang H. 2009. Adulteration identification of some fungal polysaccharides with SEM, XRD, IR and optical rotation: A primary approach. Carbohyd Poly 78(3):620–625.

478. Radovic BS, Careri M, Mangia A, Musci M, Gerboles M & Anklam E. 2001. Contribution of dynamic headspace GC-MS analysis of aroma compounds to authenticity testing of honey. Food Chem 72(4):511–520.

479. Rahman K. 2010. Drive against adulterated food. Financial Express. http://www.thefinancialexpress-bd.com/more.php?news_id=109106&date=2010-08-15. Accessed May 15, 2011.

480. Ram JL, Ram ML & Baidoun FF. 1996. Authentication of canned tuna and bonito by sequence and restriction site analysis of polymerase chain reaction products of mitochondrial DNA. J Agric Food Chem 44(8):2460–2467.

481. Ramesh R, Jha S, Lawrence F & Dodd V. 2005. From Mumbai to your supermarket: On the murky trail of Britain's biggest food scandal. Guardian.

482. Reale S, Campanella A, Merigioli A & Pilla F. 2008. A novel method for species identification in milk and milk-based products. J Dairy Res 75(01):107–112.

483. Reed M. 2006. Florida restaurants fight off fake grouper. USA Today.

484. Rehman ZU, Saeed A & Zafar SI. 2000. Hydroxymethylfurfural as an indicator for the detection

of dried powder in liquid milk. Milchwissenschaft 55(5):256–257

485. Reid LM, O'Donnell CP & Downey G. 2004. Potential of SPME-GC and chemometrics to detect adulteration of soft fruit purees. J Agric Food Chem 52(3):421–427.

486. Remaud G, Debon AA, Martin Y-I, Martin GG & Martin GJ. 1997a. Authentication of bitter almond oil and cinnamon oil: Application of the SNIF-NMR method to benzaldehyde. J Agric Food Chem 45(10):4042–4048.

487. Remaud G, Guillou C, Vallet C & Martin GJ. 1992. A coupled NMR and MS isotopic method for the authentication of natural vinegars. Fresen J Anal Chem 342(4):457–461.

488. Remaud GS, Martin Y-L, Martin GG & Martin GJ. 1997b. Detection of sophisticated adulterations of natural vanilla flavors and extracts: Application of the SNIF-NMR method to vanillin and p-hydroxybenzaldehyde. J Agric Food Chem 45(3):859–866.

489. Remaud GS, Martin Y-L, Martin GG, Naulet N & Martin GJ. 1997c. Authentication of mustard oils by combined stable isotope analysis (SNIF-NMR and IRMS). J Agric Food Chem 45(5):1844–1848.

490. Rhodes CN, Lofthouse JH, Hird S, Rose P, Reece P, Christy J, Macarthur R & Brereton PA. 2010. The use of stable carbon isotopes to authenticate claims that poultry have been corn-fed. Food Chem 118(4):927–932.

491. Roca M, Gallardo-Guerrero L, Minguez-Mosquera MI & Gandul Rojas B. 2010. Control of olive oil adulteration with copper-chlorophyll derivatives. J Agric Food Chem 58(1):51v56.

492. Rodríguez E, Martín R, García T, González I, Morales P, Sanz B & Hernández PE. 1993. Detection of cows' milk in ewes' milk and cheese by a sandwich enzyme-linked immunosorbent assay (ELISA). J J Sci Food Agr 61(2):175–180.

493. Rodriguez N, Ortiz MC, Sarabia L & Gredilla E. 2010. Analysis of protein chromatographic profiles joint to partial least squares to detect adulterations in milk mixtures and cheeses. Talanta 81(1-2):255–264.

494. Rohman A & Che Man Y. 2009a. Analysis of cod-liver oil adulteration using Fourier transform infrared (FTIR) spectroscopy. J Am Oil Chem Soc 86(12):1149–1153.

495. Rohman A & Che Man YB. 2009b. Monitoring of virgin coconut oil (VCO) adulteration with palm oil using Fourier transform infrared spectscropy. J Food Lipids 16(4):618–628.

496. Ropp K, L. 1994. Juice maker cheats consumers of $40 million—Flavor fresh foods corp. FDA Consum (Jan–Feb).

497. Rovner S. 2009. Silverlining in melamine case. Chemical & Engineering News. p.3. www.cen-online.org. Accessed May 15, 2011.

498. Rovner SL. 2010. Food Detectives. Chem Eng News 88(14):36–37.

499. Ruff C, Hor K, Weckerle B, Konig T & Schreier P. 2002. Authenticity assessment of estragole and methyl eugenol by on-line gas chromatography-isotope ratio mass spectrometry. J Agric Food Chem 50(5):1028–1031.

500. Rui G & Yan W. 2010. Illegal oil a 'hot' business. China Daily. http://www.chinadaily.com.cn/cndy/2010-03/22/content_9619784.htm. Accessed May 15, 2011.

501. Ruiz-Matute AI, Rodríguez-Sánchez S, Sanz ML & Martínez-Castro I. 2010. Detection of adulterations of honey with high fructose syrups from inulin by GC analysis. J Food Compos Anal 23(3):273–276.

502. Ruiz-Matute AI, Soria AC, Martinez-Castro I & Sanz ML. 2007. A new methodology based on GC-MS to detect honey adulteration with commercial syrups. J Agric Food Chem 55(18):7264–7269.

503. Ruiz del Castillo ML, Caja MdM, Herraiz M & Blanch GP. 1998. Rapid recognition of olive oil adulterated with hazelnut oil by direct analysis of the enantiomeric composition of filbertone. J Agric Food Chem 46(12):5128–5131.

504. Ruiz del Castillo ML, Caja MM & Herraiz M. 2003. Use of the enantiomeric composition for the assessment of the authenticity of fruit beverages. J Agric Food Chem 51(5):1284–1288.

505. Rummel S, Hoelzl S, Horn P, Rossmann A & Schlicht C. 2010. The combination of stable isotope abundance ratios of H, C, N and S with 87Sr/86Sr for geographical origin assignment of orange juices. Food Chem 118:890–900.

506. Ruoff K, Iglesias M, Luginbühl W, Bosset J-O, Bogdanov S & Amadó R. 2006a. Quantitative analysis of physical and chemical measurands in honey by mid-infrared spectrometry. Eur Food Res Technol 223(1):22–29.

507. Ruoff K, Karoui R, Dufour E, Luginbuhl W, Bosset JO, Bogdanov S & Amado R. 2005. Authentication of the botanical origin of honey by front-face fluorescence spectroscopy. A preliminary study. J Agric Food Chem 53(5):1343–1347.

508. Ruoff K, Luginbuhl W, Bogdanov S, Bosset JO, Estermann B, Ziolko T & Amado R. 2006b. Authentication of the botanical origin of honey by near-infrared spectroscopy. J Agric Food Chem 54(18):6867–6872.

509. Ruoff K, Luginbuhl W, Kunzli R, Iglesias MT, Bogdanov S, Bosset JO, von der Ohe K, von der Ohe W & Amado R. 2006c. Authentication of the botanical and geographical origin of honey by mid-infrared spectroscopy. J Agric Food Chem 54(18):6873–6880.

510. Saavedra L, García A & Barbas C. 2000. Development and validation of a capillary electrophoresis method for direct measurement of isocitric, citric, tartaric and malic acids as adulteration markers in orange juice. J Chromatogr A 881(1-2):395–401.

511. Saba A, Mazzini F, Raffaelli A, Mattei A & Salvadori P. 2005. Identification of 9(E),11(E)-18:2 fatty acid methyl ester at trace level in thermal stressed olive oils by GC coupled to acetonitrile CI-MS and CI-MS/MS, a possible marker for adulteration by addition of deodorized olive oil. J Agric Food Chem 53(12):4867–4872.

512. Sadat A, Mustajab P & Khan IA. 2006. Determining the adulteration of natural milk with synthetic milk using ac conductance measurement. Food Eng 77(3):472–477.

513. Saiz-Abajo MJ, Gonzales-Saiz JM & Pizarro C. 2004.

Classification of wine and alcohol vinegar samples based on near-infrared spectroscopy. Feasibility study on the detection of adulterated vinegar samples. J Agric Food Chem 52(25):7711–7719.

514. Saiz-Abajo MJ, Gonzalez-Saiz JM & Pizarro C. 2005. Orthogonal signal correction applied to the classification of wine and molasses vinegar samples by near-infrared spectroscopy. Feasibility study for the detection and quantification of adulterated vinegar samples. Anal Bioanal Chem 382(2):412–420.

515. Sampson S. 2009. At the fish counter you may not get what you pay for. The Star.com.

516. Sanchez L, Perez MD, Puyol P, Calvo M & Brett G. 2002. Determination of vegetal proteins in milk powder by enzyme-linked immunosorbent assay: interlaboratory study. J AOAC Int 85(6):1390–1397.

517. Sano A, Satoh T, Oguma T, Nakatoh A, Satoh J-i & Ohgawara T. 2007. Determination of levulinic acid in soy sauce by liquid chromatography with mass spectrometric detection. Food Chem 105(3):1242–1247.

518. Sanvido GB, Garcia JS, Corilo YE, Vaz BG, Zacca JJ, Cosso RG, Eberlin MN & Peter MG. 2010. Fast screening and secure confirmation of milk powder adulteration with maltodextrin via electrospray ionization-mass spectrometry [ESI(+)-MS] and selective enzymatic hydrolysis. J Agric Food Chem 58(17):9407–9412.

519. Saraiva SrA, Cabral EC, Eberlin MN & Catharino RR. 2009. Amazonian vegetable oils and fats: Fast typification and quality control via triacylglycerol (TAG) profiles from dry matrix-assisted laser desorption/ionization time-of-flight (MALDI-TOF) mass spectrometry fingerprinting. J Agric Food Chem 57(10):4030–4034.

520. Sarwar M & McDonald CE. 1993. Detection of bread wheat farina adulterant in durum wheat semolina and pasta dried at low, high, and ultra-high temperatures. Anglais 70(4):405–411.

521. Sasikumar B, Syamkumar S, Remya R & Zachariah TJ. 2004. PCR based detection of adulteration in the market samples of turmeric powder. Food Biotechnol 18(3):299–306.

522. Sato T, Kawano S & Iwamoto M. 1990. Detection of foreign fat adulteration of milk fat by near infrared spectroscopic method. J Dairy Sci 73(12):3408–3413.

523. Sayago A, Morales MT & Aparicio R. 2004. Detection of hazelnut oil in virgin olive oil by a spectrofluorimetric method. Eur Food Res Technol 218(5):480–483.

524. Schier JG, Rubin CS, Miller D, Barr D & McGeehin MA. 2009. Medication-associated diethylene glycol mass poisoning: A review and discussion on the origin of contamination. J Public Health Pol 30(17):127–143.

525. Schipilliti L, Tranchida PQ, Sciarrone D, Russo M, Dugo P, Dugo G & Mondello L. 2010. Genuineness assessment of mandarin essential oils employing gas chromatography-combustion-isotope ratio MS (GC-C-IRMS). J Sep Sci 33(4-5):617–625.

526. Schneider A. 2008. Experts call for better U.S. standards for honey. Seattle Pi.

527. Schoonderwoerd M & Misra V. 1989. Detection and quantitation of pea and soy-derived proteins in calf milk replacers. J Dairy Sci 72(1):157–161.

528. Scott-Thomas C. 2010. US officials crack down on alleged international honey smuggling conspiracy. Food Navigator-USA.

529. Scott M & Knight A. 2009. Quantitative PCR analysis for fruit juice authentication using PCR and laboratory-on-a-chip capillary electrophoresis according to the Hardy-Weinberg Law. J Agric Food Chem 57(11):4545–4551.

530. Senyuva HZ, Gilbert J, Silici S, Charlton A, Dal C, Gurel N & Cimen D. 2009. Profiling Turkish honeys to determine authenticity using physical and chemical characteristics. J Agric Food Chem 57(9):3911–3919.

531. September DJF. 2011. Detection and quantification of spice adulteration by near infrared hyperspectral imaging. Department of Food Science. Stellenbosch University.

532. Serradilla MJ, Martín A, Aranda E, Hernández A, Benito MJ, Lopez-Corrales M & Córdoba MdG. 2008. Authentication of "Cereza del Jerte" sweet cherry varieties by free zone capillary electrophoresis (FZCE). Food Chem 111(2):457–461.

533. Sewenig S, Bullinger D, Hener U & Mosandl A. 2005. Comprehensive authentication of (E)-alpha(beta)-ionone from raspberries, using constant flow MDGC-C/P-IRMS and enantio-MDGC-MS. J Agric Food Chem 53(4):838–844.

534. Sforza S, Aquino G, Cavatorta V, Galaverna G, Mucchetti G, Dossena A & Marchelli R. 2008. Proteolytic oligopeptides as molecular markers for the presence of cows' milk in fresh cheeses derived from sheep milk. Int Dairy 18(10–11):1072–1076.

535. Shah AH. 2010. An overview of food adulteration issues: Focus on Malaysia. Food Safety Magazine (May).

536. Sharma K & Paradakar M. 2010. The melamine adulteration scandal. Food Security 2(1):97–107.

537. Sharma R, Poonam & Rajput YS. 2010. Methods for detection of soymilk adulteration in milk. Milchwissenschaft-Milk Science International 65(2):157–160

538. Sharma R, Rajput YS, Poonam, Dogra G & Tomar SK. 2009. Estimation of sugars in milk by HPLC and its application in detection of adulteration of milk with soymilk. Int J Dairy Technol 62(4):514–519.

539. Shaw AD, di Camillo A, Vlahov G, Jones A, Bianchi G, Rowland J & Kell DB. 1997. Discrimination of the variety and region of origin of extra virgin olive oils using ^{13}C NMR and multivariate calibration with variable reduction. Analytica Chimica Acta 348(1-3):357–374.

540. Shen Z, Wan D, Yan Y & Chen M. 1994. Study on the method for detection of adulteration in Litsea cubeba oil. Huaxue Shijie 35(12):649–653.

541. Silva BM, Andrade PB, Mendes GC, Valentao P, Seabra RM & Ferreira MA. 2000a. Analysis of phenolic compounds in the evaluation of commercial quince jam authenticity. J Agric Food Chem 48(7):2853–2857.

542. Silva BM, Andrade PB, Valentão P, Mendes GC, Seabra

RM & Ferreira MA. 2000b. Phenolic profile in the evaluation of commercial quince jellies authenticity. Food Chem 71(2):281-285.
543. Simsek A, Artlk N & Baspinar E. 2004. Detection of raisin concentrate (Pekmez) adulteration by regression analysis method. J Food Compos Anal 17(2):155-163.
544. Simuth J, Bilikova K, Kovacova E, Kuzmova Z & Schroder W. 2004. Immunochemical approach to detection of adulteration in honey: Physiologically active royal jelly protein stimulating TNF-alpha release is a regular component of honey. J Agric Food Chem 52(8):2154-2158.
545. Siret R, Boursiquot JM, Merle MH, Cabanis JC & This P. 2000. Toward the authentication of varietal wines by the analysis of grape (Vitis vinifera L.) residual DNA in must and wine using microsatellite markers. J Agric Food Chem 48(10):5035-5040.
546. Sivakesava S & Irudayaraj J. 2001a. Detection of inverted beet sugar adulteration of honey by FTIR spectroscopy. J J Sci Food Agr 81(8):683-690.
547. Sivakesava S & Irudayaraj J. 2001b. Prediction of inverted cane sugar adulteration of honey by Fourier transform infrared spectroscopy. J Food Sci 66(7):972-978.
548. Sivakesava S & Irudayaraj J. 2001c. A rapid spectroscopic technique for determining honey adulteration with corn syrup. J Food Sci 66(6):787-791.
549. Sivakesava S & Irudayaraj J. 2002. Classification of simple and complex sugar adulterants in honey by mid-infrared spectroscopy. Int J Food Sci Tech 37(4):351-360.
550. Sivakesava S, Irudayaraj JMK & Korach RL. 2000. Dectection of adulteration in apple juice using mid infrared spectroscopy. Applied Eng Agric 17(6):815-820.
551. Smejkalová D & Piccolo A. 2010. High-power gradient diffusion NMR spectroscopy for the rapid assessment of extra-virgin olive oil adulteration. Food Chem 118(1):153-158.
552. Socaci C, Ranga F, Fetea F, Leopold L, Dulf F & Parlog R. 2009. Complementary advanced techniques applied for plant and food authentication. Czech J Food Sci 27.
553. Song H-x & Han Y. 2007. Immunological detection of adulteration of cow's milk in goat's milk. Zhongguo Rupin Gongye 35(10):43-46.
554. Sonnante G, Montemurro C, Morgese A, Sabetta W, Blanco A & Pasqualone A. 2009. DNA microsatellite region for a reliable quantification of soft wheat adulteration in durum wheat-based foodstuffs by real-time PCR. J Agric Food Chem 57(21):10199-10204.
555. Spangenberg JE, Macko SA & Hunziker J. 1998. Characterization of olive oil by carbon isotope analysis of individual fatty acids: Implications for authentication. J Agric Food Chem 46(10):4179-4184.
556. Spangenberg JE & Ogrinc N. 2001. Authentication of vegetable oils by bulk and molecular carbon isotope analyses with emphasis on olive oil and pumpkin seed oil. J Agric Food Chem 49(3):1534-1540.
557. Spaniolas S, Bazakos C, Awad M & Kalaitzis P. 2008a. Exploitation of the chloroplast trnL (UAA) intron polymorphisms for the authentication of plant oils by means of a lab-on-a-chip capillary electrophoresis system. J Agric Food Chem 56(16):6886-6891.
558. Spaniolas S, May ST, Bennett MJ & Tucker GA. 2006. Authentication of coffee by means of PCR-RFLP analysis and lab-on-a-chip capillary electrophoresis. J Agric Food Chem 54(20):7466-7470.
559. Spaniolas S, Tsachaki M, Bennett MJ & Tucker GA. 2008b. Toward the authentication of wines of Nemea denomination of origin through cleaved amplified polymorphic sequence (CAPS)-based assay. J Agric Food Chem 56(17):7667-7671.
560. Stanciuc N & Rapeanu G. 2010. Identification of adulterated sheep and goat cheeses marketed in Romania by immunocromatographic assay. Food Agr Immunol 21(2):157-164.
561. Starling S. 2008. Fenchem fights fake ginkgo. Nutra ingredients-USA.com. p.3. http://www.nutraingredients.com/Industry/Fenchem-fights-fake-ginkgo. Accessed May 15, 2011.
562. Starling S. 2010. Counterfeit to blame for Danish black cohosh warning? Nutra Ingredients.com. http://www.nutraingredients.com/content/view/print/315479. Accessed May 15, 2011.
563. Steine C, Beaucousin F, Siv C & Peiffer G. 2001. Potential of semiconductor sensor arrays for the origin authentication of pure Valencia orange juices. J Agric Food Chem 49(7):3151-3160.
564. Steuer B, Schulz H & Läger E. 2001. Classification and analysis of citrus oils by NIR spectroscopy. Food Chem 72(1):113-117.
565. Stocker A, Rossmann A, Kettrup A & Bengsch E. 2006. Detection of royal jelly adulteration using carbon and nitrogen stable isotope ratio analysis. Rapid Commun Mass Sp 20(2):181-184.
566. Stoj A & Targonski Z. 2006. Use of amino acid analysis for estimation of berry juice authenticity. ACTA Scientiarum Polonorum 5(1):61-72.
567. Stones M. 2009. Sweet solution to honey fraud. Food Production Daily.com. http://www.foodproductiondaily.com/content/view/print/246481.
568. Stuckel JG & Low NH. 1995. Maple syrup authenticity analysis by anion-exchange liquid chromatography with pulsed amperometric detection. J Agric Food Chem 43(12):3046-3051.
569. Swallow KW & Low NH. 1994. Determination of honey authenticity by anion-exchange liquid chromatography. J AOAC Int 77(3):695-702.
570. Swallow KW, Low NH & Petrus DR. 1991. Detection of orange juice adulteration with beet medium invert sugar using anion-exchange liquid chromatography with pulsed amperometric detection. J Assoc Off Anal Chem 74(2):341-345.
571. Tamura H, Appel M, Richling E & Schreier P. 2005. Authenticity assessment of gamma- and delta-decalactone from prunus fruits by gas chromatography combustion/pyrolysis isotope ratio mass spectrometry (GC-C/P-IRMS). J Agric Food Chem 53(13):5397-5401.
572. Tate ME & Enneking D. 1992. A mess of red pottage. Nature 359(6394):357-358.
573. Tateo F & Bononi M. 2004. Fast determination of

Sudan I by HPLC/APCI-MS in hot chilli, spices, and oven-baked foods. J Agric Food Chem 52(4):655–658.

574. Tay A, Singh RK, Krishnan SS & Gore JP. 2002. Authentication of olive oil adulterated with vegetable oils using Fourier transform infrared spectroscopy. Lebensmittel Wissenschaft und-Technologie 35(1):99–103.

575. Techen N, Pan Z, Scheffler BE & Khan IA. 2009. Detection of Illicium anisatum as adulterant of Illicium verum. Planta Med 75(4):392–395.

576. Tenailleau EJ, Lancelin P, Robins RJ & Akoka S. 2004. Authentication of the origin of vanillin using quantitative natural abundance ^{13}C NMR. J Agric Food Chem 52(26):7782–7787.

577. Thavarajah P & Low NH. 2006. Adulteration of apple with pear juice: Emphasis on major carbohydrates, proline, and arbutin. J Agric Food Chem 54(13):4861–4867.

578. Tian L. 2009. Fake salt bust hints at bribery in sector. China Daily. Chinadaily.com. http://www.chinadaily.com.cn/china/2009-12/02/content_9099576.htm. Accessed May 15, 2011.

579. Tittlemier SA. 2010. Methods for the analysis of melamine and related compounds in foods: A review. Food Addit Contam Part A Chem Anal Control Expo Risk Assess 27(2):129–145.

580. Tomris A & Meral G. 1988. The detection of soybean flour in cocoa powder. J Food Quality 10(5):295–298.

581. Torrecilla JS, Rojo E, Dominguez JC & Rodriguez F. 2010. A novel method to quantify the adulteration of extra virgin olive oil with low-grade olive oils by UV-vis. J Agric Food Chem 58(3):1679–1684.

582. Torrecilla JS, Rojo E, Oliet M, Domínguez JC & Rodríguez F. 2009. Self-organizing maps and learning vector quantization networks as tools to identify vegetable oils. J Agric Food Chem 57(7):2763–2769.

583. Toy MA. 2008. Milk sickens 50,000 children. Sydney Morning Herald.

584. Traub J. 1988. Into the mouths of babes. New York Times.

585. Tremblay P & Paquin R. 2006. Improved detection of sugar addition to maple syrup using malic icid as internal standard and in ^{13}C isotope ratio mass spectrometry (IRMS). J Agric Food Chem 55(2):197–203.

586. Trilcova A, Copikova J, Coimbra MA, Barros AS, Egert L, Synytsya A & Kristkova H. 2004. Application of NIR analysis to verify cocoa powder authenticity. Czech Food Scis 22:329–332.

587. Trilcova A, Copikova J, Coimbra MA, Barros AS, Kristkova H, Egert L & Synytsya A. 2006. Application of infrared spectroscopy in cocoa powder quality monitoring. Chemicke Listy 99(11):821–824.

588. Tripathi M, Khanna SK & Das M. 2007. Surveillance on use of synthetic colours in eatables vis a vis prevention of food adulteration act of India. Food Control 18(3):211–219.

589. Twomey M, Downey G & McNulty PB. 1995. The potential of NIR spectroscopy for the detection of the adulteration of orange juice. J Sci Food Agr 67(1):77–84.

590. Ulberth F. 1994. Detection of milk fat adulteration by linear discriminant analysis of fatty acid data. J AOAC Int 77(5):1326–1334.

591. Ulberth F. 1995. Quantitation of foreign fat in foreign fat/milkfat mixtures by multivariate regression analysis of fatty acid data. J Agric Food Chem 43(6):1556–1560.

592. Urdiain M, Domenech-Sanchez A, Alberti S, Benedi VJ & Rossello JA. 2005. New method of DNA isolation from two food additives suitable for authentication in polymerase chain reaction assays. J Agric Food Chem 53(9):3345–3347.

593. USP. 2011. Glycerin monograph in: The Food Chemicals Codex, 3rd Supplement to the 7th Edition ed. Rockville, MD: The United States Pharmacopeial Convention.

594. Vaclavik L, Cajka T, Hrbek V & Hajslova J. 2009. Ambient mass spectrometry employing direct analysis in real time (DART) ion source for olive oil quality and authenticity assessment. Analytica Chimica Acta 645(1-2):56–63.

595. Vallejo-Cordoba B. 1998. A chemometric approach to the detection of milk adulteration based on protein profiles determined by capillary electrophoresis. J Capillary Electrophor 5(3-4):133–137.

596. Vanha J, Hinkova A, Slukova M & Kvasnicka F. 2009. Detection of plant raw materials in meat products by HPLC. Czech J Food Sci 27(4):234–239.

597. Vardin H, Tay A, Ozen B & Mauer L. 2008. Authentication of pomegranate juice concentrate using FTIR spectroscopy and chemometrics. Food Chem 108(2):742–748.

598. Vasconcelos AMP & Chaves das Neves HJ. 1989. Characterization of elementary wines of Vitis vinifera varieties by pattern recognition of free amino acid profiles. J Agric Food Chem 37(4):931–937.

599. Veloso ACA, Teixeira N & Ferreira IMPLVO. 2002. Separation and quantification of the major casein fractions by reverse-phase high-performance liquid chromatography and urea-polyacrylamide gel electrophoresis: Detection of milk adulterations. J Chromatogr A 967(2):209–218.

600. Veloso ACA, Teixeira N, Peres AM, Mendonça Á & Ferreira IMPLVO. 2004. Evaluation of cheese authenticity and proteolysis by HPLC and urea-polyacrylamide gel electrophoresis. Food Chem 87(2):289–295.

601. Vemireddy LR, Archak S & Nagaraju J. 2007. Capillary electrophoresis is essential for microsatellite marker based detection and quantification of adulteration of basmati rice (Oryza sativa). J Agric Food Chem 55(20):8112–8117.

602. Versini G, Camin F, Ramponi M & Dellacassa E. 2006. Stable isotope analysis in grape products: ^{13}C-based internal standardisation methods to improve the detection of some types of adulterations. Analytica Chimica Acta 563(1-2):325–330.

603. Vichi S, Pizzale L, Toffano E, Bortolomeazzi R & Conte L. 2001. Detection of hazelnut oil in virgin olive oil by assessment of free sterols and triacylglycerols. J AOAC Int 84(5):1534–1541.

604. Vigli G, Philippidis A, Spyros A & Dais P. 2003. Classification of edible oils by employing ^{31}P and ^{1}H NMR spectroscopy in combination with multivariate statistical analysis. A proposal for the detection of seed oil adulteration in virgin olive oils. J Agric Food Chem 51(19):5715–5722.

605. Vlachos A & Arvanitoyannis IS. 2008. A review of rice authenticity/adulteration methods and results. Crit Rev Food Sci Nutr 48(6):553–598.

606. Vlahov G. 2009. ^{13}C nuclear magnetic resonance spectroscopic detection of the adulteration of extra virgin olive oils extracted from different cultivars with cold-pressed hazelnut oil. J AOAC Int 92(6):1747–1754.

607. Vlahov G, Shaw A & Kell D. 1999. Use of ^{13}C nuclear magnetic resonance distortionless enhancement by polarization transfer pulse sequence and multivariate analysis to discriminate olive oil cultivars. J Am Oil Chem Soc 76(10):1223–1231.

608. Vogels JTWE, Terwel L, Tas AC, van den Berg F, Dukel F & van der Greef J. 1996. Detection of adulteration in orange juices by a new screening method using proton NMR spectroscopy in combination with pattern recognition techniques. J Agric Food Chem 44(1):175–180.

609. von Büren M, Stadler M & Lüthy J. 2001. Detection of wheat adulteration of spelt flour and products by PCR. Eur Food Res Technol 212(2):234–239.

610. Wang C, Lu L & Li J. 2008a. Identification of adulteration in sesame oil by GC-MS and national standard method. Zhongguo Weisheng Gongchengxue 7(6):363–364.

611. Wang CZ, Ni M, Sun S, Li XL, He H, Mehendale SR & Yuan CS. 2009a. Detection of adulteration of notoginseng root extract with other panax species by quantitative HPLC coupled with PCA. J Agric Food Chem 57(6):2363–2367.

612. Wang D, Wang C, Li M & Liu W. 2008b. Test methods for dextrin adulteration in raw milk and milk powder. Zhongguo Rupin Gongye 36(4):62–64.

613. Wang J, Jun S, Bittenbender HC, Gautz L & Li QX. 2009b. Fourier transform infrared spectroscopy for kona coffee authentication. J Food Sci 74(5):C385–C391.

614. Wang J, Kliks MM, Jun S, Jackson M & Li QX. 2010. Rapid analysis of glucose, fructose, sucrose, and maltose in honeys from different geographic regions using Fourier transform infrared spectroscopy and multivariate analysis. J Food Sci 75(2):C208–214.

615. Wang J, Kliks MM, Qu W, Jun S, Shi G & Li QX. 2009c. Rapid determination of the geographical origin of honey based on protein fingerprinting and barcoding using MALDI TOF MS. J Agric Food Chem 57(21):10081–10088.

616. Wang L, Lee FSC, Wang X & He Y. 2006. Feasibility study of quantifying and discriminating soybean oil adulteration in camellia oils by attenuated total reflectance MIR and fiber optic diffuse reflectance NIR. Food Chem 95(3):529–536.

617. Wang S, Xu Z, Fang G, Duan Z, Zhang Y & Chen S. 2007. Synthesis and characterization of a molecularly imprinted silica gel sorbent for the on-line determination of trace Sudan I in chilli powder through high-performance liquid chromatography. J Agric Food Chem 55(10):3869–3876.

618. Wang Z, Chen D, Gao X & Song Z. 2009d. Subpicogram determination of melamine in milk products using a luminol-myoglobin chemiluminescence system. J Agric Food Chem 57(9):3464–3469.

619. Wei M, Cao X-z & Liao C-h. 2003. Gas chromatography detection of adulteration of edible vegetable oils. Shipin Kexue 24(12):103–106.

620. Weise E. 2009. Something fishy? Counterfeit foods enter the U.S. market. USA Today. p. 3. http://www.usatoday.com/news/health/2009-01-19-fake-foods_N.htm. Accessed May 15, 2011.

621. Weise E & Schmit J. 2008. Pet food scare in USA had a precursor. USA Today.

622. Wenzl T, Prettner E, Schweiger K & Wagner FS. 2002. An improved method to discover adulteration of Styrian pumpkin seed oil. J Biochem Bioph Meth 53(1–3):193–202.

623. Wesley I, Barnes R & McGill A. 1995. Measurement of adulteration of olive oils by near-infrared spectroscopy. J Am Oil Chem Soc 72(3):289–292.

624. Wesley I, Pacheco F & McGill A. 1996. Identification of adulterants in olive oils. J Am Oil Chem Soc 73(4):515–518.

625. White JW. 1980. Detection of honey adulteration by carbohydrate analysis. J Assoc Off Ana Chem 63(1):11–18.

626. White JW & Winters K. 1989. Honey protein as internal standard for stable carbon isotope ratio detection of adulteration of honey. J Assoc Off Ana Chem 72(6):907–911.

627. White JW, Winters K, Marin P & Rossman A. 1998. Stable carbon isotope ratio analysis of honey: Validation of internal standard procedure for worldwide application. J AOAC Int 81(3):610–619.

628. White RD & Cancalon PF. 1992. Detection of beet sugar adulteration of orange juice by liquid chromatography/pulsed amperometric detection with column switching. J AOAC Int 75(3):584–587.

629. Wines M. 2010. More tainted dairy products are found in chinese stores. New York Times.

630. Wolfschoon-Pombo AF & Furtado MAM. 1989. Detection of adulteration of pasteurised milk with whey by determination of the casein-bound phosphorus and protein nitrogen content. Zeitschrift fur Lebensmitteluntersuchung und-Forschung A 188(1):16–21.

631. Won S-R, Lee D-C, Ko SH, Kim J-W & Rhee H-I. 2008. Honey major protein characterization and its application to adulteration detection. Food Res Int 41(10):952–956.

632. Woodcock T, Downey G & O'Donnell CP. 2008. Confirmation of declared provenance of European extra virgin olive oil samples by NIR spectroscopy. J Agric Food Chem 56(23):11520–11525.

633. Wrolstad RE, Culbertson JD, Cornwell CJ & Mattick LR. 1982. Detection of adulteration in blackberry juice

633. concentrates and wines. J Assoc Off Ana Chem 65(6):1417–1423.
634. Wudrich GG, McSheffrey S & Low NH. 1993. Liquid chromatographic detection of a variety of inexpensive sweeteners added to pure orange juice. J AOAC Int 76(2):342–354.
635. Xiao D, Liu S, Yu H & Li Y. 2000. Method of judging adulteration of vegetable oil in production. Zhongguo Youzhi 25(3):43–46.
636. Xie LJ, Ye XQ, Liu DH & Ying YB. 2008. Application of principal component-radial basis function neural networks (PC-RBFNN) for the detection of water-adulterated bayberry juice by near-infrared spectroscopy. J Zhejiang Univ Sci B 9(12):982–989.
637. Xu T, Wei KY, Wang J, Eremin SA, Liu SZ, Li QX & Li J. 2010. Development of an enzyme-linked immunosorbent assay specific to Sudan red I. Anal Biochem 405(1):41–49.
638. Yamamoto A, Kawai M, Miwa T, Tsukamoto T, Kodama S & Hayakawa K. 2008. Determination of adulteration in apple juice by HPLC with novel optical rotation detector. J Agric Food Chem 56(16):7302–7304.
639. Yan Y. 2006. Ministry orders inspections for harmful duck eggs. China View.
640. Yang H & Irudayaraj J. 2001. Comparison of near-infrared, Fourier transform-infrared, and Fourier transform-Raman methods for determining olive pomace oil adulteration in extra virgin olive oil. J Am Oil Chem Soc 78(9):889–895.
641. Yao L, Jiang Y, Singanusong R, Datta N & Raymont K. 2004. Phenolic acids and abscisic acid in Australian Eucalyptus honeys and their potential for floral authentication. Food Chem 86(2):169–177.
642. Yap KY-L, Chan SY & Lim CS. 2008. The reliability of traditional authentication—A case of ginseng misfit. Food Chem 107(1):570–575.
643. Youngsheng J, Weijuan Z & Xiangru L. 2008. PCR Detection of Exogenous Vegetative Components in Cocoa Powder. Biotechnology Bulletin 05.
644. Yunianta, Zhang B-L, Lees M & Martin GJ. 1995. Stable isotope fractionation in fruit juice concentrates: Application to the authentication of grape and orange products. J Agric Food Chem 43(9):2411–2417.
645. Zalacain A, Ordoudi SA, Blazquez I, Diaz-Plaza EM, Carmona M, Tsimidou MZ & Alonso GL. 2005. Screening method for the detection of artificial colours in saffron using derivative UV-Vis spectrometry after precipitation of crocetin. Food Addit Contam 22(7):607–615.
646. Zavitsanos P. 2010. Fish and chips. Lab-on-a-chip technology is one tool for fighting seafood substitution. Food Quality June/July 2010.
647. Zhang D, Pang G, Gao F, Zhang T, Chen Q & Hu Z. 2005. Application of capillary electrophoresis in determination of casein quantity and detection of adulteration in milk. Shipin Yu Fajiao Gongye 31(1):130–132.
648. Zhang J. 2007. A method for the detection of red wine adulteration with blackrice pigment. Keji Daobao 25(14):46–48.
649. Zhang L, Wu G, Wu Y, Cao Y, Xiao L & Lu C. 2009a. The gene MT3-B can differentiate palm oil from other oil samples. J Agric Food Chem 57(16):7227–7232.
650. Zhang Y, Krueger D, Durst R, Lee R, Wang D, Seeram N & Heber D. 2009b. International multidimensional authenticity specification (IMAS) algorithm for detection of commercial pomegranate juice adulteration. J Agric Food Chem 57(6):2550–2557.
651. Zhang Y, Zhang Z & Sun Y. 2006. Development and optimization of an analytical method for the determination of Sudan dyes in hot chilli pepper by high-performance liquid chromatography with on-line electrogenerated BrO- luminol chemiluminescence detection. J Chromatogr A 1129(1):34–40.
652. Zhao T, Li F, Xu F & Zhao Y. 1998. Analysis of the beeswax purity and examination of the adulteration in it improvement of the determination method of the carbonification. Jingxi Huagong 15(5):39–42.
653. Zhiling H. 2010. Storm in a hot pot brews over swill oil. ChinaDaily. http://www.chinadaily.com.cn/china/2010-03/31/content_9665682.htm. Accessed May 15, 2011.
654. Zhou J, Sun SQ, Li YJ & Zhou Q. 2009. FTIR and classification study on the powdered milk with different assist material. Spectrosc Spect Anal 29(1):110–113.
655. Zhu L, Gamez G, Chen H, Chingin K & Zenobi R. 2009. Rapid detection of melamine in untreated milk and wheat gluten by ultrasound-assisted extractive electrospray ionization mass spectrometry (EESI-MS). Chem Commun (5):559–561.
656. Zhu S, Fushimi H & Komatsu K. 2008. Development of a DNA microarray for authentication of ginseng drugs based on 18S rRNA gene sequence. J Agric Food Chem 56(11):3953–3959.
657. Zhu X, Li S, Shan Y, Zhang Z, Li G, Su D & Liu F. 2010a. Detection of adulterants such as sweeteners materials in honey using near-infrared spectroscopy and chemometrics. J Food Eng 101(1):92–97.
658. Zhu X, Wang K, Zang R, Jiang X & Qiu L. 2000. Study on ultraviolet spectrometry method for detecting adulteration of sesame oil. Zhongguo Youzhi 25(1):50–51.
659. Zhu Y, Yang Y, Zhou Z, Li G, Jiang M, Zhang C & Chen S. 2010b. Direct determination of free tryptophan contents in soy sauces and its application as an index of soy sauce adulteration. Food Chem 118(1):159–162.
660. Zou MQ, Zhang XF, Qi XH, Ma HL, Dong Y, Liu CW, Guo X & Wang H. 2009. Rapid authentication of olive oil adulteration by Raman spectrometry. J Agric Food Chem 57(14):6001–6006.

Index

Titles of monographs are shown in the boldface type.

A

Abbreviations, 6
Absolute Alcohol (Reagent), 5
Acacia, 516
"Accuracy", Defined, 1411
Acesulfame K, 9
Acesulfame Potassium, 9
Acetal, 10
Acetaldehyde, 10
Acetaldehyde Diethyl Acetal, 10
Acetaldehyde Test Paper, 1406
Acetals (Essential Oils and Flavors), 1336
Acetanisole, 11
Acetate Identification Test, 1262
Aceteugenol, 430
Acetic Acid, Glacial, 12
Acetic Acid TS, Diluted, 1394
Acetic Acid TS, Strong, 1394
Acetic Aldehyde, 10
Acetic and Fatty Acid Esters of Glycerol, 20
Acetic Periodic Acid TS, 1394
Acetoacetic Ester, 397
Acetoglycerides, 20
Acetoin (Dimer), 13
Acetoin (Monomer), 13
α-Acetolactatedecarboxylase, 376
2-Acetonaphthone, 733
Acetone, 14
Acetone Peroxides, 15
Acetophenone, 16
N-Acetyl-L-2-amino-4-(methylthio)butyric Acid, 18
3-Acetyl-6-methyl-1,2-pyran-2,4(3H)-dione, 321
4-Acetylanisole, 11
Acetylated Mono- and Diglycerides, 20
Acetylated Monoglycerides, 20
Acetylbenzene, 16
3-Acetyl-2,5-Dimethyl Furan, 17
Acetyl Eugenol, 430
Acetyl Groups, 1364
N-Acetyl-L-Methionine, 18
Acetyl Methyl Carbinol, 13
Acetyl Propionyl, 858
2-Acetylpyrazine, 22
3-Acetylpyridine, 21
2-Acetylpyrrole, 21
2-Acetyl Thiazole, 19
Acetyl Valeryl, 522
Acetyl Value, 1341
Achilleic Acid, 25
Acid (Reagent), 5
Acid Calcium Phosphate, 186
Acid Hydrolysates of Proteins, 23

Acid-Hydrolyzed Milk Protein, 23
Acid-Hydrolyzed Proteins, 23
Acidic Sodium Aluminum Phosphate, 1017
Acidified Sodium Chlorite Solutions, 25
Acidity Determination by Iodometric Method, 1378
Acid Magnesium Phosphate, 679
Acid Number (Rosins and Related Substances), 1360
Acid Phosphatase Activity, 1306
Acid Phthalate Buffer, 1393
Acid Sodium Pyrophosphate, 1014
Acid Value
 Fats and Related Substances, 1341
 Flavor Chemicals (Other than Essential Oils), 1380
Acid Value (Essential Oils and Flavors), 1336
Aconitic Acid, 25
Activated Carbon, 209
Active Oxygen Method, 1353
Added Substances, 2
Adenosine 5'-monophosphate, 26
Adenosine 5'-phosphoric acid, 26
Adenylic acid, 26
5'-Adenylic Acid, 26
Adipic Acid, 29
Admissions, xviii
Adulterants and Contaminants in Food Ingredients, 1384
 Diethylene Glycol and Ethylene Glycol in Glycerin, 1384
 Pesticide Residues, 1384
Agar, 30
DL-Alanine, 31
L-Alanine, 32
Alcohol, 399, 1394
Alcohol (Reagent), 5
Alcohol, 70%, 1394
Alcohol, 80%, 1394
Alcohol, 90%, 1394
Alcohol, Absolute, 1394
Alcohol, Aldehyde-Free, 1394
Alcohol C-10, 320
Alcohol C-11, 1172
Alcohol C-12, 630
Alcohol C-6, 538
Alcohol C-8, 823
Alcohol C-9, 812
Alcohol Content of Ethyl Oxyhydrate Flavor Chemicals (Other than Essential Oils), 1378
Alcohol, Diluted, 1394
Alcoholic Potassium Hydroxide TS, 1394

Alcoholometric Table, 1501
Aldehyde C-10, 317
Aldehyde C-11 Undecyclic, 1167
Aldehyde C-11 Undecylenic, 1170
Aldehyde C-12, 631
Aldehyde C-12 MNA, 766
Aldehyde C-14 Pure, So-Called, 1166
Aldehyde C-16, 415
Aldehyde C-18, So-Called, 805
Aldehyde C-6, 529
Aldehyde C-7, 521
Aldehyde C-8, 816
Aldehyde C-9, 806
Aldehydes (Essential Oils and Flavors), 1336
Aldehydes and Ketones
 Flavor Chemicals (Other than Essential Oils), 1376
 Hydroxylamine Method, 1377
 Hydroxylamine tert-Butyl Alcohol Method, 1376
Aldehydes and Ketones (Essential Oils and Flavors), 1336
Algin, 54, 162, 928, 1014
Alginates Assay, 1279
Algin Derivative, 964
Alginic Acid, 33
Alitame, 33
Alkaline Borate Buffer, 1393
Alkaline Cupric Tartrate TS, 1394
Alkaline Mercuric Potassium Iodide TS, 1394, 1397
All-trans-Retinol, 1181
Allspice Oil, 889
All-trans-lycopene, 660, 662
Allura Red, 35
Allura Red AC, 35, 436
4-Allyl-1,2-dimethoxy Benzene, 748
4-Allyl-2-methoxyphenol, 429
4-Allyl-2-methoxy-phenyl Acetate, 430
Allyl-3-cyclohexanepropionate, 37
p-Allylanisole, 384
Allyl Caproate, 39
Allyl Cyclohexanepropionate, 37
4-Allylguaiacol, 429
Allyl Heptanoate, 38
Allyl Heptoate, 38
Allyl Hexanoate, 39
Allyl Ionone, 36
Allyl α-Ionone, 36
Allyl Isopentanoate, 41
Allyl Isothiocyanate, 40, 1380
Allyl Isovalerate, 41
Allyl Phenoxy Acetate, 42
Allyl Propionate, 43
Almond Oil, Bitter, FFPA, 44
Alphazurine 2G, 1405

Alternative Analytical Procedures, 2
Aluminum Ammonium Sulfate, 45
Aluminum Identification Test, 1262
Aluminum Limit Test, 1264
Aluminum Potassium Sulfate, 46
Aluminum Silicate, 105
Aluminum Sodium Sulfate, 46
Aluminum Sulfate, 47
Amaranth, 48
Ambrette Seed Liquid, 52
Ambrette Seed Oil, 52
N-[4-[[(2-Amino-1,4-dihydro-4-oxo-6-pteridinyl) methyl]amino]benzoyl]-L-glutamic Acid, 461
L-α-Amino-β-phenylpropionic Acid, 882
DL-α-Amino-β-phenylpropionic Acid, 881
L-2-Amino-3-hydroxybutyric Acid, 1134
4-Amino-3-hydroxybutyric Acid Trimethylbetaine, 217
DL-2-Amino-3-hydroxypropanoic Acid, 1008
L-2-Amino-3-hydroxypropanoic Acid, 1009
DL-α-Amino-3-indolepropionic Acid, 1163
L-α-Amino-3-indolepropionic Acid, 1164
L-2-Amino-3-mercaptopropanoic Acid Monohydrochloride, 308
L-2-Amino-3-methylbutyric Acid, 1177
DL-2-Amino-3-methylvaleric Acid, 601
L-2-Amino-3-methylvaleric Acid, 602
DL-2-Amino-4-(methylthio)butyric Acid, 716
L-2-Amino-4-(methylthio)butyric Acid, 717
L-α-Amino-4(or 5)-imidazolepropionic Acid, 547
L-α-Amino-4(or 5)-imidazolepropionic Acid Monohydrochloride, 547
N-[p-[[(2-Amino-4-hydroxy-6-pteridinyl)methyl]amino]benzoyl] glutamic Acid, 461
DL-2-Amino-4-methylvaleric Acid, 640
L-2-Amino-4-methylvaleric Acid, 641
L-2-Amino-5-guanidinovaleric Acid, 80
L-2-Amino-5-guanidinovaleric Acid Monohydrochloride, 81
Aminoacetic Acid, 514
L-2-Aminoglutaramic Acid, 497
α-Amino Nitrogen Determination, 1280
L-2-Aminopentanedioic Acid, 495
2-Aminopentanedioic Acid Hydrochloride, 496
Aminopeptidase Activity, 1307
Aminopeptidase, Leucine, 376
DL-2-Aminopropanoic Acid, 31
L-2-Aminopropanoic Acid, 32
L-α-Aminosuccinamic Acid, 83
DL-Aminosuccinic Acid, 87
L-Aminosuccinic Acid, 88
Ammonia-Ammonium Chloride Buffer TS, 1394

Ammoniacal Silver Nitrate TS, 1395
Ammonia Detector Tube, 1406
Ammonia Nitrogen Determination, 1280
Ammonia Solution, 53
Ammoniated Glycyrrhizin, 54
Ammonia TS, 1394
Ammonia TS, Stronger, 1395
Ammonium Acetate TS, 1395
Ammonium Alginate, 54
Ammonium Alum, 45
Ammonium Bicarbonate, 55
Ammonium Carbonate, 56
Ammonium Carbonate TS, 1395
Ammonium Chloride, 56
Ammonium Chloride TS, 1395
Ammonium Citrate, Dibasic, 57
Ammonium Citrate, Tribasic, 57
Ammonium Dihydrogen Phosphate, 59
Ammonium Glutamate, 773
Ammonium Glycyrrhizinate, 775
Ammonium Glycyrrhizinate, Pentahydrate, 775
Ammonium Hydroxide, 53
Ammonium Hydroxide (Reagent), 5
Ammonium Identification Test, 1262
Ammonium Iron (II) Phosphate, 450
Ammonium Magnesium Potassium Chloride, Hydrate, 670
Ammonium Molybdate TS, 1395
Ammonium Oxalate TS, 1395
Ammonium Phosphate, Dibasic, 58
Ammonium Phosphate, Monobasic, 59
Ammonium Saccharin, 59
Ammonium Standard Solution, 1394
Ammonium Sulfanilate TS, 1395
Ammonium Sulfate, 61
Ammonium Sulfide TS, 1395
Ammonium Thiocyanate, 0.1 N, 1400
Ammonium Thiocyanate TS, 1395
AMP, 26
Amyl Acetate, 576
1-Amyl Alcohol, 61
Amylase, 375
α-Amylase Activity (Bacterial), 1309
α-Amylase Activity (Nonbacterial), 1308
α-Amylase, 1308
β-Amylase, 378
Amyl Butyrate, 61, 578
Amyl Caprylate, 62
Amylcinnamaldehyde, 64
α-Amylcinnamaldehyde, 64
Amyl Formate, 62, 580
Amyl Heptanoate, 62
Amyl Hexanoate, 581
Amyl Isovalerate, 583
Amyl Octanoate, 62
Amyloglucosidase, 1304
Amyloglucosidase Activity, 1314
Amyl Propionate, 63
Amyl Salicylate, 584
Amyl Valerate, 583
Amyl Vinyl Carbinol, 819

Amyris Oil, West Indian Type, 65
Analytical Samples, 4
Anethole, 66, 1380
trans-Anethole, 66
Aneurine Hydrochloride, 1132
Angelica Root Oil, 67
Angelica Seed Oil, 68
Angelica Seed Oleoresin, 1083
Angular Rotation, 1232
Anhydrous Alcohol (Reagent), 5
p-Anisaldehyde, 719
Anise Oil, 69
Anise Oleoresin, 1083
Anisic Alcohol, 71
Anisic Aldehyde, 719
Anisidine Value, 1341
Anisole, 70, 1380
Anisyl Acetate, 71
Anisyl Acetone, 767
Anisyl Alcohol, 71
Anisyl Formate, 72
Annatto Extracts, 73
Annotations, xix
Anthrone TS, 1395
Antimony Trichloride TS, 1395
APDC Extraction Method (for Lead), 1274
APM, 84
APM-Ace, 86
APO, 74
Apocarotenal, 74
β-**Apo-8'-Carotenal**, 74
Apparatus for Tests and Assays, 4, 1217
Arabinogalactan, 80
D-Araboascorbic Acid, 380
Arachidonic Acid-Rich Oil, 75
ARA from Fungal (Mortierella alpina) Oil, 75
ARA Fungal Oil, 75
ARA-Rich Oil, 75
ARA-Rich Single Cell Oil, 75
L-**Arginine**, 80
L-**Arginine Monohydrochloride**, 81
Arsenic Limit Test, 1264
Arsenic Limit Test (Chewing Gum Base Polymers), 1301
Ascorbic Acid, 81
L-Ascorbic Acid, 81
Ascorbyl Palmitate, 82
Ash (Acid-Insoluble), 1242
Ash (Total), 1242
L-**Asparagine**, 83
Aspartame, 84
Aspartame-Acesulfame Salt, 86
DL-**Aspartic Acid**, 87
L-**Aspartic Acid**, 88
N-L-α-Aspartyl-L-phenylalanine 1-Methyl Ester, 84
L-α-Aspartyl-N-(2,2,4,4-tetramethyl-3-thietanyl)-D-alaninamide, hydrated, 33
Aspergillus niger, 1303
Aspergillus niger var., 1303
Astaxanthin, 89
Astaxanthin Esters, 89

Astaxanthin Esters from *Haematococcus pluvialis*, 89
Astaxanthin Fatty Acid Esters, 89
Atomic Absorption Spectrophotometric Graphite Furnace Method (for Lead), 1272
Atomic Weights, 4, 1504
Autolyzed Yeast, 1200
Autolyzed Yeast Extract, 1203
Azodicarbonamide, 94
Azodicarboxylic Acid Diamide, 94
Azorubine, 95
Azo Violet, 1405

B

Baker's Yeast Beta Glucan, 121
Baking Soda, 1019
Balsam Fir Oil, 459
Balsam Peru Oil, 100
Barium Chloride TS, 1395
Barium Diphenylamine Sulfonate TS, 1395
Barium Hydroxide, 0.2 N, 1400
Barium Hydroxide TS, 1395
Barium Standard Solution, 1394
Barley, 1303
Barley Malt, 1303
Basic Sodium Aluminum Phosphate, 1018
Basil Oil, Comoros Type, 100
Basil Oil, European Type, 101
Basil Oil Exotic, 100
Basil Oil, Italian Type, 101
Basil Oil, Réunion Type, 100
Basil Oleoresin, 1083
Bay Leaf Oil, 628
Bay Oil, 102
BCD, 298
Beeswax, White, 103
Beeswax, Yellow, 104
Beet Fiber, 1101
Beet Sugar, 1097
1,3-Behenic-2-oleic Glyceride, 129
Benedict's Qualitative Reagent, 1395
Bentonite, 105
Benzaldehyde, 106
Benzaldehyde Glyceryl Acetal, 107
Benzene (in Paraffinic Hydrocarbon Solvents), 1280
Benzidine TS, 1395
1,2-Benzisothiazole-3(2H)-one-1,1-Dioxide, 990
1,2-Benzisothiazole-3(2H)-one 1,1-Dioxide Sodium Salt, 1059
1,2-Benzisothiazolin-3-one 1,1-Dioxide Ammonium Salt, 59
1,2-Benzisothiazolin-3-one-1,1-Dioxide, Calcium Salt, 190
Benzoate Identification Test, 1262
1,2-Benzodihydropyrone, 108
Benzoic Acid, 108
Benzophenone, 109
o-Benzosulfimide, 990
Benzoylbenzene, 109
Benzoyl Peroxide, 110

Benzyl Acetate, 111
Benzyl Alcohol, 112
Benzyl Benzoate, 112
Benzyl Butyrate, 113
Benzyl n-Butyrate, 113
Benzyl Cinnamate, 113
Benzyl Formate, 114
Benzyl Isobutyrate, 115
Benzyl Isovalerate, 116
Benzyl 3-Methyl Butyrate, 116
Benzyl 2-Methyl Propionate, 115
Benzyl Phenylacetate, 117
Benzyl Propanoate, 118
Benzyl Propionate, 118
Benzyl Salicylate, 119
Bergamot Oil, Coldpressed, 120
Beta-1,3-glucan, 293
Beta Glucan from Baker's Yeast (*Saccharomyces cerevisiae*), 121
Betaine, 124
BHA, 125
BHT, 126
Bicarbonate Identification Test, 1262
Bile-Tolerant Gram-Negative Bacteria, 1383
Biobased Content of 1,3-Propanediol, 1388
Biotin, 127
d-Biotin, 127
Birch Tar Oil, Rectified, 127
Bismuth Nitrate TS, 1395
Bisulfite Identification Test, 1262
Bitter Almond Oil Free from Prussic Acid, 44
Black Pepper Oil, 128
Black Pepper Oleoresin, 1083
Blank Tests, 4
Bohenin, 129
Bois de Rose Oil, 130
Boric Acid-Potassium Chloride, 0.2 M, 1393
Borneol, 131
Bornyl Acetate, 132
L-Bornyl Acetate, 132
Bound Styrene (Chewing Gum Base Polymers), 1298
Brewer's Yeast, 1201
Brilliant Blue, 133
Brilliant Blue FCF, 133, 433
Bromelain, 375, 1303
Bromide Identification Test, 1262
Brominated Vegetable Oil, 134
Bromine, 0.1 N, 1400
Bromine TS, 1395
Bromocresol Blue, 1405
Bromocresol Blue TS, 1395
Bromocresol Green, 1405
Bromocresol Green TS, 1395
Bromocresol Purple, 1405
Bromocresol Purple TS, 1395
Bromophenol Blue, 1405
Bromophenol Blue TS, 1395
Bromothymol Blue, 1405
Bromothymol Blue TS, 1395
Brown HT, 135
Buffer Solutions
  Acid Phthalate, 1393

  Alkaline Borate, 1393
  Hydrochloric Acid, 1393
  Neutralized Phthalate, 1393
  Phosphate, 1393
  Phosphate, pH 7.2, 1381
  Standard, 1393
  Stock, 1381
Butadiene-Styrene Rubber, 139
Butane, 145
n-Butane, 145
Butane-1,3-diol, 156
1,4-Butanedicarboxylic Acid, 29
Butanedioic Acid, 1091
2,3-Butanedione, 335
Butanoic Acid, 2-amino-4-(methylseleno)-, (S)-, 1006
1-Butanol, 149
2-Butanone, 146
Butan-3-one-2-yl Butanoate, 144
(E)-Butenedioic Acid, 469
Butter Starter Distillate, 1087
Butyl Acetate, 149
n-Butyl Acetate, 149
Butyl Alcohol, 149
Butyl Aldehyde, 156
Butylated Hydroxyanisole, 125
Butylated Hydroxymethylphenol, 155
Butylated Hydroxytoluene, 126
Butyl Butyrate, 151
n-Butyl n-Butyrate, 151
Butyl Butyryllactate, 151
2-sec-Butyl Cyclohexanone, 147
1,3-Butylene Glycol, 156
Butyl Ester, 151
tert-Butylhydroquinone, 1119
Butyl Isobutyrate, 152
Butyl Isovalerate, 153
Butyl 2-Methyl Butyrate, 148
Butyl Octadecanoate, 155
Butyl Phenylacetate, 154
Butyl Rubber, 596
Butyl Stearate, 155
Butyraldehyde, 156
Butyrate, 151
Butyric Acid, 157
Butyrin, 1159
γ-**Butyrolactone**, 158
Butyryllactic Acid, 151

C

Cadmium Limit Test, 1266
Caffeine, 160
Calcium Acetate, 160
Calcium Acid Pyrophosphate, 161
Calcium Alginate, 162
Calcium Ascorbate, 162
Calcium Benzoate, 163
Calcium Biphosphate, 186
Calcium Bromate, 164
Calcium Carbonate, 164
Calcium Chloride, 165
Calcium Chloride Double Salt of DL- or D-Calcium Pantothenate, 182
Calcium Chloride Solution, 166

Calcium Chloride TS, 1395
Calcium Citrate, 167
Calcium Cyclamate, 167
Calcium Cyclohexanesulfamate, 167
Calcium Cyclohexylsulfamate, 167
Calcium Disodium Edetate, 168
Calcium Disodium EDTA, 168
Calcium Disodium Ethylenediaminetetraacetate, 168
Calcium Disodium (Ethylenedinitrilo)tetraacetate, 168
Calcium Gluconate, 170
Calcium Glycerophosphate, 170
Calcium Hydroxide, 171
Calcium Hydroxide TS, 1395
Calcium Hydroxyapatite, 187
Calcium Identification Test, 1262
Calcium Iodate, 172
Calcium Lactate, 172
Calcium Lactobionate, 173
Calcium Lignosulfonate, 174
Calcium Lignosulfonate (40-65), 176
Calcium Oxide, 180
Calcium Pantothenate, 181
D-Calcium Pantothenate, 181
Calcium Pantothenate, Calcium Chloride Double Salt, 182
Calcium Pantothenate, Racemic, 183
Calcium Peroxide, 184
Calcium Phosphate, Dibasic, 185
Calcium Phosphate, Monobasic, 186
Calcium Phosphate, Tribasic, 187
Calcium Propanoate, 188
Calcium Propionate, 188
Calcium Pyrophosphate, 189
Calcium Saccharin, 190
Calcium, Seaweed-Derived, 1004
Calcium Silicate, 191
Calcium Sorbate, 193
Calcium Stearate, 193
Calcium Stearoyl Lactate, 194
Calcium Stearoyl Lactylate, 194
Calcium Stearoyl-2-Lactylate, 194
Calcium Sulfate, 196
Calcium Sulfate TS, 1395
Camphene, 196
d-Camphor, 197
(+)-Camphor, 197
Cananga Oil, 197
Candelilla Wax, 198
Cane Sugar, 1097
Canola Oil, 199
Cantha, 201
Canthaxanthin, 201
Capillary Electrophoresis, 1437
Capraldehyde, 317
Capric Acid, 318
Caproic Acid, 529
Caproic Aldehyde, 529
Capryl Alcohol, 823
Caprylic Acid, 817
Caprylic Aldehyde, 816
Capsicum Oleoresin, 1083
Caramel, 202

Caramel Color, 202
Caraway Oil, 208
Caraway Oleoresin, 1083
Carbamide, 1173
Carbohydrase, 376, 1304
   Aspergillus niger var., 1303, 1304, 1305
   Aspergillus oryzae var., 1303, 1304, 1305
   Bacillus acidopullulyticus, 1306
   Bacillus licheniformis (Containing a *Bacillus stearothermophilus* Gene), 1303
   Bacillus licheniformis var., 1303
   Bacillus stearothermophilus, 1303
   Bacillus subtilis (Containing a *Bacillus megaterium* Gene), 1303
   Bacillus subtilis (Containing a *Bacillus stearothermophilus Gene*), 1303, 1305
   Bacillus subtilis var., 1303, 1304
   Barley, 1303
   Barley Malt, 1303
   Candida pseudotropicalis, 1305
   Kluyveromyces marxianus var. *lactis*, 1305
   Mortierella vinacea var. raffinoseutilizer, 1304
   Rhizopus niveus, 1304
   Rhizopus oryzae var., 1304
   Saccharomyces sp., 1305
   Saccharomyces sp. (*cerevesiae*), 1305
   Saccharomyces sp. (*Kluyveromyces*), 1305
   Trichoderma longibrachiatum, 1304, 1305
   Trichoderma longibrachiatum (Formerly *reesei*), 1304
Carbohydrase and Protease, Mixed, 377
Carbohydrates and Related Substances, Tests and Assays, 1364
   Acetyl Groups, 1364
   Crude Fat, 1364
   Invert Sugar Determination, 1364
   Lactose Determination, 1366
   Propylene Chlorohydrin Determination, 1366
   Reducing Sugars Assay, 1367
   Sulfur Dioxide Determination, 1368
   Total Solids, 1370
Carbon, Activated, 209
Carbonate Identification Test, 1262
Carbon Dioxide, 212
Carbon Dioxide Detector Tube, 1406
Carbon Dioxide-Free Water, 5
Carbon Monoxide Detector Tube, 1406
(*R*)-3-Carboxy-2-hydroxy-*N,N,N*-trimethyl-1-propanaminium Hydroxide, Inner Salt, 217
[2-Carboxy-β-(*N*-(*b*-methoxycarbonyl-2 phenyl)ethylcarbamoyl)] ethanaminium 6-methyl-4-oxo-1,2, 3-oxathiazin-3-ide-2,2-dioxide, 86
Cardamom Oil, 214
Cardamom Oleoresin, 1083

Carmine, 215
Carminic Acid, 215
Carnauba Wax, 216
L-**Carnitine**, 217
Carob Bean Gum, 657
Carotene, 218
β-β-Carotene-3,3'-diol, (3*R*,3'*S*)-(3*R*, 3'*S*-meso)-Zeaxanthin, 1209
β-Carotene-4,4'-dione, 201
β-**Carotene**, 218
Carrageenan, 219
Carrot Seed Oil, 228
Carr-Price Reagent, 1395
Carvacrol, 229
(×)-**Carveol**, 229
L-Carveol, 229
4-Carvomenthol, 1122
(×)-**Carvone**, 231
(+)-**Carvone**, 230
d-Carvone, 230
dextro-Carvone, 230
L-Carvone, 231
levo-Carvone, 231
(×)-**Carvyl Acetate**, 232
L-Carvyl Acetate, 232
β-**Caryophyllene**, 233
Cascarilla Oil, 234
Casein and Caseinate Salts, 235
CAS number, 2
Cassia Oil, 236
Castor Oil, 237
Catalase, 0000, 377
Catalase Activity, 1309
Catalase, Bovine Liver, 375
Caustic Potash, 937
Caustic Soda, 1036
Caustic Soda Solutions, 1035
gamma-CD, 300
Cedar Leaf Oil, 238
Celery Oleoresin, 1083
Celery Seed Oil, 239
Cellulase Activity, 1310
Cellulose, Ethyl, 403
Cellulose Gel, 240
Cellulose Gum, 241
Cellulose Gum Viscosity, 1238
Cellulose, Hydroxypropyl, 560
Cellulose, Methyl Ethyl, 742
Cellulose, Microcrystalline, 240
Cellulose, Powdered, 243
Centrifuge, 5
Ceric Ammonium Nitrate TS, 1395
Ceric Sulfate, 0.01 N, 1401
Ceric Sulfate, 0.1 N, 1400
Chamomile Oil, English Type, 244
Chamomile Oil, German Type, 245
Chamomile Oil, Hungarian Type, 245
Chemical Formulas, 2
Chemical Tests and Determinations, 1262
Chewing Gum Base Polymers, 1298
   Arsenic Limit Test, 1301
   Bound Styrene, 1298
   Lead Limit Test, 1301
   Molecular Weight, 1299
   Quinones, 1299
   Residual Styrene, 1300

Total Unsaturation, 1301
Chicle, 702
Chilte, 703
China Clay, 611
Chiquibul, 702
Chloride and Sulfate Limit Tests, 1266
Chloride Identification Test, 1262
Chloride Limit Test, 1266
Chlorinated Compounds (Essential Oils and Flavors), 1337
Chlorine, 246
Chlorine Detector Tube, 1406
Chlorine TS, 1395
Chlorophyll, 1342
Chocolate Brown HT, 135
Cholalic Acid, 247
Cholecalciferol, 1186
Cholic Acid, 247
Choline Bitartrate, 248
Choline Chloride, 248
Chromatography, 1221
    Column, 1222
    Gas, 1224
    High-Performance Liquid, 1226
    Paper, 1222
    Thin-Layer, 1223
Chromium (Color Additive Assays), 1283
Chromotropic Acid TS, 1395
Chymosin, 377, 1304
Chymotrypsin, 375, 1311
Chymotrypsin Activity, 1311
Cinene, 647
1,8-Cineol, 427
Cineole, Percentage of (Essential Oils and Flavors), 1338
Cinnamal, 249
Cinnamaldehyde, 249
Cinnamic Acid, 250
Cinnamic Alcohol, 254
Cinnamic Aldehyde, 249
Cinnamon Bark Oil, Ceylon Type, 251
Cinnamon Leaf Oil, 252
Cinnamon Oil, 236
Cinnamyl Acetate, 253
Cinnamyl Alcohol, 254
Cinnamyl Butyrate, 255
Cinnamyl Cinnamate, 256
Cinnamyl Formate, 257
Cinnamyl Isobutyrate, 258
Cinnamyl Isovalerate, 259
Cinnamyl Propionate, 260
Citral, 261
Citrate Identification Test, 1262
CITREM, 263
Citric Acid, 262
Citric Acid Esters of Mono- and Diglycerides, 263
Citric and Fatty Acid Esters of Glycerol, 263
Citridic Acid, 25
Citroglycerides, 263
Citronellal, 265
Citronellol, 266
Citronellyl Acetate, 267
Citronellyl Butyrate, 268

Citronellyl Formate, 269
Citronellyl Isobutyrate, 270
Citronellyl Propanoate, 271
Citronellyl Propionate, 271
Citrus Oils, Ultraviolet Absorbance (Essential Oils and Flavors), 1339
Clary Oil, 272
Clary Sage Oil, 272
Class: Bis-azo, 135
CI Food Blue 1, 563
CI Food Brown 3, 135
CI Food Red 14, 382
CI Food Yellow 4, 1118
CI No. 20285, 135
Clove Bud Oil, 274
Clove Leaf Oil, 273
Clove Oil, 274
Clove Stem Oil, 275
CMC, 241
Coagulated or Concentrated Latices of Vegetable Origin, 702
CMP, 310
Cobalt Identification Test, 1262
Cobaltous Chloride TS, 1396
Cobalt-Uranyl Acetate TS, 1396
Cocoa Butter Substitute, 276
Coconut Oil (Unhydrogenated), 278
Cognac Oil, Green, 278
Cold Test, 1342
Color (AOCS-Wesson), 1342
Color Additive Assays
    Chromium, 1283
    Ether Extracts, 1283
    Leuco Base, 1284
    Loss on Drying, 1289
    Mercury, 1284
    Sodium Chloride, 1285
    Sodium Sulfate, 1285
    Total Color, 1285
    Uncombined Intermediates and Products of Side Reactions, 1287
    Water-Insoluble Matter, 1289
Color Determination, 1283
Colorimetric Solutions, 1393
Color Value (Oleoresins), 1357
Column Chromatography, 1222
Congo Red TS, 1396
"Constant Weight", Defined, 6
Containers, 3
    "Light-Resistant Container", Defined, 3
    "Tight Container", Defined, 3
    "Well-Closed Container", Defined, 3
Copaiba Oil, 279
Copovidone, 280
Copper Gluconate, 283
Copper Identification Test, 1262
Copper Sulfate, 284
Copper Sulfate TS, 1396
Coriander Oil, 285
Coriander Oleoresin, 1084
Cornmint Oil, Partially Dementholized, 712
Corn Oil (Unhydrogenated), 285
Corn Sugar, 325
Corn Syrup, 494

Costus Root Oil, 286
Cottonseed Oil (Unhydrogenated), 287
Coulometric Titration (for water), 1240
Cream of Tartar, 928
Cresol Red, 1405
Cresol Red-Thymol Blue TS, 1396
Cresol Red TS, 1396
Cresyl Acetate (Test for Free Cresol), 1380
p-**Cresyl Acetate**, 288
p-Cresyl Isobutyrate, 1153
p-Cresyl Methyl Ether, 723
Crospovidone, 289
Crown gum, 702
Crude Fat, 1364
Crypthecodinium cohnii Oil, 326
Crystal Violet, 1405
Crystal Violet TS, 1396
Cubeb Oil, 290
Cubeb Oleoresin, 1084
Cuminal, 292
Cuminaldehyde, 292
Cuminic Aldehyde, 292
p-Cuminic Aldehyde, 292
Cumin Oil, 291
Cumin Oleoresin, 1084
Cupric Citrate TS, Alkaline, 1395, 1396
Cupric Nitrate TS, 1396
Cupric Sulfate, 284
Cupric Sulfate Test Paper, 1406
Cupric Sulfate TS, 1396
Cupric Tartrate TS, Alkaline, 1396
Curcumin Content, 1357
Curdlan, 293
Cyanocobalamin, 1184
Cyanogen Bromide TS, 1396
Cyclamen Aldehyde, 294
Cyclamic Acid, 295
alpha-Cyclodextrin, 296
β-Cyclodextrin, 298
γ-Cyclodextrin, 300
beta-Cyclodextrin, 298
gamma-Cyclodextrin, 300
Cyclohexane, 303
1,2,3,5/4,6-Cyclohexanehexol, 565
Cyclohexyl Acetate, 307
Cyclomaltooctaose, 300
Cyclooctaamylose, 300
Cyclopentadecanolide, 856
p-**Cymene**, 307
L-**Cysteine Monohydrochloride**, 308
L-**Cystine**, 309
Cytidine 5′-monophosphate, 310
Cytidine 5′-phosphoric acid, 310
Cytidylic acid, 310
5′-Cytidylic Acid, 310

D

D.E., 340
DAG Oil, 338
Damar Gum, 314
Damar Resin, 314

Dammar, 314
Dammar Gum, 314
Dammar Resin, 314
Danish Agar, 470
Data Elements Required for Assay Validation, 1413
DATEM, 336, 336
"Deaerated water", Defined, 5
(E),(E)-2,4-Decadienal, 314
trans,trans-2,4-Decadienal, 314
δ-**Decalactone**, 315
γ-**Decalactone**, 316
Decanal, 317
Decanoic Acid, 318
1-Decanol, 320
(E)-2-Decenal, 318
(Z)-4-Decenal, 319
cis-4-Decenal, 319
trans-2-Decenal, 318
Decyl Alcohol, 320
"Degassed Water", Defined, 5
Dehydrated Alcohol (Reagent), 5
Dehydroacetic Acid, 321
Denigès' Reagent, 1396
Deoxycholic Acid, 322
Description, Statement of, 3
　Function, Statement of, 3
　"Odorless", Defined, 3
Desiccators and Desiccants, 5
Desoxycholic Acid, 322
Detector Tubes, 1406
　Ammonia Detector Tube, 1406
　Carbon Dioxide Detector Tube, 1406
　Carbon Monoxide Detector Tube, 1406
　Chlorine Detector Tube, 1406
　Hydrogen Sulfide Detector Tube, 1406
　Nitric Oxide-Nitrogen Dioxide Detector Tube, 1406
　Sulfur Dioxide Detector Tube, 1406
　Water Vapor Detector Tube, 1406
Devitalized Wheat Gluten, 1189
Dexpanthenol, 322
Dextrin, 323
Dextro Calcium Pantothenate, 181
Dextrose, 325
DHA from Algal (*Crypthecodinium*) Oil, 326
DHA from Algal (*Schizochytrium*) Oil, 330
DHA from Algal (*Ulkenia*) Oil, 334
Diacetyl, 335
Diacetyl Tartaric Acid Esters of Mono- and Diglycerides, 336
Diacylglycerol Oil, 338
2,6-Diaminohexanoic Acid Hydrochloride, 668
Diammonium Hydrogen Citrate, 57
Diammonium Hydrogen Phosphate, 58
Diammonium Phosphate, 58
Diaquo bis(glycinato) iron (II), 454
Diastase Activity, 1312
Diatomaceous Earth, 340
Diatomaceous Silica, 340

Diatomite, 340
Dibenzyl Ether, 341
2,6-Di-*tert*-butyl-*p*-cresol, 126
Dicalcium Phosphate, 185
Dicarbonic Acid, 355
1,6-Dichloro-1,6-dideoxy-β-D-fructofuranosyl-4-chloro-4-deoxy-α-D-galactopyranoside, 1092
1,2-Dichloroethane, 426
Dichloromethane, 761
Dichlorophenol-Indophenol TS, 1396
Dietary Fiber from Beets, 1101
1,2-Di[(1'-ethoxy)ethoxy]propane, 342
Diethylene Glycol and Ethylene Glycol in Glycerin, 1384
Diethylene Imidoxide, 779
Diethylene Oximide, 779
Diethyl Malonate, 342
Diethyl Sebacate, 343
Diethyl Succinate, 343
Dihydroanethole, 959
Dihydrocarveol, 344
(+)-Dihydrocarvone, 345
d-Dihydrocarvone, 345
Dihydrocoumarin, 108
(3S,3'S)-3,3'-Dihydroxy-β,β-carotene-4,4'-dione, 89
3α,12α-Dihydroxycholanic Acid, 322
2,7-Dihydroxynaphthalene TS, 1396
1,2-Dihydroxypropane, 963
1,3-Dihydroxypropane, 954
4,4'-Diketo-β-carotene, 201
Dilauryl Thiodipropionate, 346
Dill Herb Oil, American Type, 348
Dill Oil, 348
Dill Oil, Indian Type, 347
Dill Seed Oil, European Type, 346
Dill Seed Oil, Indian, 347
Dill Seed Oil, Indian Type, 347
Dillseed Oleoresin, 1084
Dillweed Oil, American Type, 348
Dimagnesium Phosphate, 678
1,2-Dimethoxy-4-allylbenzene, 743
3,4-Dimethoxybenzaldehyde, 1181
2,6-Dimethoxy Phenol, 358
2,5-Dimethyl-3-acetylfuran, 17
6,6-Dimethyl-2-methylenebicyclo[3.1.1]heptane, 893
3,7-Dimethyl-1,6-octadien-3-ol, 649
cis-3,7-Dimethyl-2,6-octadien-1-ol, 790
E-3,7-Dimethyl-2,6-octadien-1-ol, 482
trans-3,7-Dimethyl-2,6-octadien-1-ol, 482
3,7-Dimethyl-1,6-octadien-3-yl Acetate, 484, 651
cis-3,7-Dimethyl-2,6-octadien-1-yl Acetate, 792
3,7-Dimethyl-1,6-octadien-3-yl Benzoate, 485, 652
3,7-Dimethyl-2,6-octadien-1-yl Butyrate, 486
3,7-Dimethyl-2,6-octadien-1-yl Formate, 487, 653
3,7-Dimethyl-6-octadien-3-yl Isobutyrate, 654

3,7-Dimethyl-2,6-octadien-1-yl Phenylacetate, 489
3,7-Dimethyl-2,6-octadien-1-yl Propionate, 490
3,7-Dimethyl-6-octadien-3-yl Propionate, 655
3,7-Dimethyl-3-octanol, 1128
3,7-Dimethyl-6-octen-1-al, 265
3,7-Dimethyl-6-octen-1-ol, 266
3,7-Dimethyl-6-octen-1-yl Acetate, 267
3,7-Dimethyl-6-octen-1-yl Butyrate, 268
3,7-Dimethyl-6-octen-1-yl Formate, 269
3,7-Dimethyl-6-octen-1-yl Isobutyrate, 270
3,7-Dimethyl-6-octen-1-yl Propionate, 271
Dimethyl Anthranilate, 352
Dimethyl Benzyl Carbinol, 352
Dimethyl Benzyl Carbinyl Acetate, 353
Dimethyl Benzyl Carbinyl Butyrate, 354
N-[N-(3,3-Dimethylbutyl)-L-α-aspartyl]-L-phenylalanine 1-Methyl Ester, 788
3,4-Dimethyl 1,2-Cyclopentandione, 350
Dimethyl Dicarbonate, 355
Dimethyldiketone, 335
Dimethyl Ester, 355
Dimethylglyoxal, 335
2,6-Dimethyl-5-heptenal, 349
Dimethylketol, 13
Dimethyl Ketone, 14
Dimethyl Octanol, 351
3,7-Dimethyl-1-octanol, 351
α,α-Dimethylphenethyl Acetate, 353
α,α-Dimethylphenethyl Alcohol, 352
α,α-Dimethylphenethyl Butyrate, 354
Dimethylpolysiloxane, 358
Dimethylpolysiloxane Viscosity, 1236
2,3-Dimethylpyrazine, 359
2,5-Dimethylpyrazine, 360
2,6-Dimethylpyrazine, 361
Dimethyl Pyrocarbonate, 355
2,5-Dimethylpyrrole, 362
Dimethyl Silicone, 358
Dimethyl Succinate, 356
Dimethyl Sulfide, 357
Dioctyl Sodium Sulfosuccinate, 363
1,4-Dioxane Limit Test, 1267
Diphenylamine TS, 1396
Diphenylcarbazone TS, 1396
Diphenyl Ether, 365
Diphenyl Ketone, 109
Diphenyl Oxide, 365
Dipotassium Monophosphate, 943
Dipotassium Phosphate, 943
α,α-Dipyridyl TS, 1396
Direct Aqueous Acid Base Titrations (Flavor Chemicals Other Than Essential Oils), 1377
Direct Aqueous Alcoholic Acid Base Titrations (Flavor Chemicals Other Than Essential Oils), 1378

Direct Titration (for Water), 1239
Disodium (Ethylenedinitrilo)tetraacetate, 366
Disodium 5'-Guanylate, 367
Disodium 5'-Inosinate, 368
Disodium 5'-Uridylate, 369
Disodium Dihydrogen Diphosphate, 1014
Disodium Dihydrogen Pyrophosphate, 1014
Disodium 4,4'-(2,4-dihydroxy-5-hydroxymethyl-1,3-phenylene-bisazo) di-1-naphthalene-sulfonate, 135
Disodium Edetate, 366
Disodium EDTA, 366
Disodium EDTA, 0.05 M, 1401
Disodium Ethylenediaminetetraacetate, 366
Disodium Guanosine-5'-monophosphate, 367
Disodium Guanylate, 367
Disodium Inosinate, 368
Disodium Inosine-5'-monophosphate, 368
Disodium Monohydrogen Phosphate, 1052
Disodium Phosphate, 1052
Disodium Pyrophosphate, 1014
Disodium Tartrate, 1066
Disodium L-Tartrate, 1066
Disodium uridine 5'-monophosphate, 369
Distillation Range, 1230
3,3'-Dithiobis(2-aminopropanoic acid), 309
Dithizone, 1405
Dithizone Method (for Lead), 1270
Dithizone TS, 1396
DMDC, 355
Docusate Sodium, 363
δ-Dodecalactone, 372
γ-Dodecalactone, 373
Dodecanal, 631
Dodecanoic Acid, 630
1-Dodecanol, 630
(E)-2-Dodecen-1-al, 374
trans-2-Dodecen-1-al, 374
Dried Glucose Syrup, 494
Dried Yeast, 1201
DSS, 363

E

Edible Gelatin, 478
Electrolytic Iron, 572
Electrophoresis, 1434
Elemental Impurities by ICP, 1289
Enanthic Alcohol, 526
Enocianina, 514
Enterobacteria Enrichment Broth Mossel, 1381
Enterobacter Sakazakii (Cronobacter SPP.), 1383
Enzyme Assays, 1303
    Acid Phosphatase Activity, 1306
    Aminopeptidase Activity, 1307
    α-Amylase Activity (Bacterial), 1309
    α-Amylase Activity (Nonbacterial), 1308
    Amyloglucosidase Activity, 1314
    Catalase Activity, 1309
    Cellulase Activity, 1310
    Chymotrypsin Activity, 1311
    Diastase Activity, 1312
    α-Galactosidase Activity, 1313
    β-Glucanase Activity, 1313
    Glucoamylase Activity, 1314
    Glucose Isomerase Activity, 1315
    Glucose Oxidase Activity, 1316
    Hemicellulase Activity, 1317
    Invertase Sumner Unit Activity, 1318
    Lactase (Acid) Activity, 1320
    Lactase (Neutral) Activity, 1319
    Lipase (Microbial) Activity for Medium- and Long-Chain Fatty Acids, 1322
    Lipase Activity, 1321
    Lysozyme Activity, 1323
    Maltogenic Amylase Activity, 1324
    Milk-Clotting Activity, 1324
    Pancreatin Activity, 1325
    Pepsin Activity, 1327
    Phospholipase A_2 Activity, 1328
    Phytase Activity, 1328
    Plant Proteolytic Activity, 1330
    Proteolytic Activity, Bacterial (PC), 1331
    Proteolytic Activity, Fungal (HUT), 1331
    Proteolytic Activity, Fungal (SAP), 1332
    Pullulanase Activity, 1333
    Transglutaminase Activity, 1334
    Trypsin Activity, 1335
Enzyme-Hydrolyzed (Source) Protein, 845
Enzyme-Modified Fats, 380
Enzyme-Modified (Source) Protein, 845
Enzyme Preparations, 375
Enzyme Preparations Used in Food Processing, 1303
Eosin Y TS, 1396
1,8 Epoxy-p-menthane, 427
Epoxypropane, 966
Epsom Salt, 683
Equisetic Acid, 25
Ergocalciferol, 1185
Eriochrome Black T, 1405
Eriochrome Black TS, 1396
Erythorbic Acid, 380
Erythritol, 381
meso-Erythritol, 381
Erythrosine, 382, 435
Essential Oils and Flavors, Tests and Assays, 1336
    Acetals, 1336
    Acid Value, 1336
    Aldehydes, 1336
    Aldehydes and Ketones, 1336
    Chlorinated Compounds, 1337
    Esters, 1337
    Linalool Determination, 1338
    Percentage of Cineole, 1338
    Phenols, 1338
    Phenols, Free, 1339
    Residue on Evaporation, 1339
    Solubility in Alcohol, 1339
    Total Alcohols, 1339
    Ultraviolet Absorbance of Citrus Oils, 1339
    Volatile Oil Content, 1340
Ester Determination (Essential Oils and Flavors), 1337
Ester Gum, 500, 506
Esters (Essential Oils and Flavors), 1337
Ester Value (Essential Oils and Flavors), 1338
Estragole, 384
Estragon Oil, 1116
Ethanal, 10
Ethanol, 399
Ethanol (Reagent), 5
Ether Extracts (Color Additive Assays), 1283
Ethone, 385
6-Ethoxy-1,2-dihydro-2,2,4-trimethylquinoline, 386
1-Ethoxy-2-hydroxy-4-propenylbenzene, 955
3-Ethoxy-4-hydroxybenzaldehyde, 422
p-Ethoxychrysoidin TS, 1396
p-Ethoxychrysoidin Monohydrochloride, 1405
Ethoxylated Mono- and Diglycerides, 385
Ethoxyquin, 386
Ethyl Acetate, 396
Ethyl Acetoacetate, 397
Ethyl Acrylate, 398
Ethyl Alcohol, 399
Ethyl Alcohol (Reagent), 5
Ethyl o-Aminobenzoate, 400
Ethyl p-Anisate, 393
Ethyl Anthranilate, 400
Ethyl Benzoate, 401
Ethyl Benzoyl Acetate, 402
Ethyl-(E)-2-Butenoate, 423
Ethyl-trans-2-butenoate, 423
Ethyl Butyl Ketone, 524
2-Ethylbutyraldehyde, 425
Ethyl Butyrate, 402
2-Ethylbutyric Acid, 425
Ethyl Caprate, 405
Ethyl Caproate, 407
Ethyl Capronate, 407
Ethyl Caprylate, 417
Ethyl Cellulose, 403
Ethyl Cinnamate, 404
Ethyl Citrate, 1160
Ethyl Crotonate, 423
Ethyl Decanoate, 405
2-Ethyl-3,5(6)-dimethylpyrazine, 388
Ethyl Dodecanoate, 411
Ethylene Brassylate, 424
trans-1,2-Ethylenedicarboxylic Acid, 469

1620 / Ethylene Dichloride / Index

Ethylene Dichloride, 426
Ethylene Trichloride, 1160
2-Ethyl Fenchol, 387
Ethyl Formate, 406
5-N-Ethyl-L-glutamine, 1131
4-Ethyl Guaiacol, 391
Ethyl Heptanoate, 406
Ethyl Heptoate, 406
Ethyl Hexanoate, 407
2-Ethyl Hexanol, 388
2-Ethyl-1-hexanol, 388
2-Ethyl-3-hydroxy-4-pyrone, 414
5-Ethyl 3-Hydroxy 4-Methyl 2(5H)-Furanone, 392
Ethyl 2-Hydroxypropionate, 410
Ethyl Isobutyrate, 408
Ethyl Isovalerate, 409
Ethyl Lactate, 410
Ethyl Laurate, 411
Ethyl Lauroyl Arginate, 411
Ethyl Levulinate, 413
Ethyl Malonate, 342
Ethyl Maltol, 414
Ethyl p-Methoxybenzoate, 393
Ethyl 3-Methylbutyrate, 409
Ethyl 2-Methylbutyrate, 394
Ethyl 2-Methylpentanoate, 395
Ethyl Methylphenylglycidate, 415
2-Ethyl-3-Methylpyrazine, 389
Ethyl 3-Methylthiopropionate, 396
Ethyl Myristate, 416
Ethyl Nonanoate, 416
Ethyl-N$^\alpha$-Dodecanoyl-L-Arginate · HCl, 411
Ethyl-N$^\alpha$-Lauroyl-L-Arginate · HCl, 411
Ethyl 9-Octadecenoate, 418
Ethyl Octanoate, 417
Ethyl Octoate, 417
Ethyl Oleate, 418
Ethyl 3-Oxybutanoate, 397
Ethyl Oxyhydrate (So-Called), 418
Ethyl Pelargonate, 416
Ethyl n-Pentanoate, 422
Ethyl Phenylacetate, 419
Ethyl Phenylglycidate, 420
Ethyl 3-Phenylpropenate, 404
Ethyl Propionate, 420
3-Ethyl Pyridine, 390
Ethyl Salicylate, 421
Ethyl Sebacate, 343
Ethyl Succinate, 343
Ethyl 10-Undecenoate, 394
Ethyl Valerate, 422
Ethyl Vanillin, 422
Eucalyptol, 427
Eucalyptus Oil, 428
Eugenic Acid, 429
Eugenol, 429
Eugenol Acetate, 430
Eugenyl Acetate, 430
Eugenyl Methyl Ether, 743
Exaltolide, 856
Expanded Perlite, 861

F

Farnesol, 431
Fast Green, 432
Fast Green FCF, 432, 435
Fats and Related Substances, 1341
  Acetyl Value, 1341
  Acid Value, 1341
  Anisidine Value, 1341
  Chlorophyll, 1342
  Cold Test, 1342
  Color (AOCS-Wesson), 1342
  Fatty Acid Composition, 1343
  Fatty Acid Composition (Saturated, cis-Monosaturated, and cis-Polyunsaturated) in Oils Containing Long Chain Polyunsaturated Fatty Acids, 1344
  Free Fatty Acids, 1346
  Free Glycerin or Propylene Glycol, 1347
  Hexane-Insoluble Matter, 1347
  Hydroxyl Value, 1347
  Iodine Value, 1348
  Lovibond Color, 1342
  Melting Range, 1348
  1-Monoglycerides, 1348
  Oxyethylene Determination, 1350
  Peroxide Value, 1351
  Reichert-Meissl Value, 1352
  Saponification Value, 1352
  Soap, 1353
  Specific Gravity, 1353
  Stability, 1353
  Tocopherols, 1354
  Total Monoglycerides, 1349
  Unsaponifiable Matter, 1355
  Volatile Acidity, 1356
Fatty Acid Composition, 1343
Fatty Acid Composition (Saturated, cis-Monosaturated, and cis-Polyunsaturated) in Oils Containing Long Chain Polyunsaturated Fatty Acids, 1344
Fatty Acids, Free, 1346
FCC in the U.S. Code of Federal Regulations, 1522
FCC Specifications, 1
FD&C Blue No. 1, 433
FD&C Blue No. 2, 434
FD&C Green No. 3, 435
FD&C Red No. 3, 435
FD&C Red No. 40, 436
FD&C Yellow No. 5, 437
FD&C Yellow No. 6, 438
Federal Regulations
  FCC in the U.S. Code of, 1522
Fehling's Solution, 1396
FEMA number, 2
(+)-Fenchone, 439
d-Fenchone, 439
Fenchyl Alcohol, 440
Fennel Oil, 440
Fennel Oleoresin, 1084
Ferric Ammonium Citrate, Brown, 441
Ferric Ammonium Citrate, Green, 443

Ferric Ammonium Sulfate TS, 1396
Ferric Chloride TS, 1396
Ferric Chloride TS, Alcoholic, 1396
Ferric Citrate, 444
Ferric Orthophosphate, 445
Ferric Phosphate, 445
Ferric Pyrophosphate, 447
Ferric Sulfate TS, Acid, 1396
Ferroin TS, 0000
Ferrous Ammonium Phosphate, 450
Ferrous Ammonium Sulfate, 0.1 N, 1401
Ferrous Bisglycinate, 454
Ferrous Citrate, 450
Ferrous Fumarate, 451
Ferrous Gluconate, 453
Ferrous Glycinate, 454
Ferrous Lactate, 455
Ferrous Sulfate, 457
Ferrous Sulfate, Dried, 458
Ferrous Sulfate TS, 1397
FHMO, 703
Ficin, 376, 1304
"Filtration", Defined, 5
Fir Needle Oil, Canadian Type, 459
Fir Needle Oil, Siberian Type, 460
Fischer-Tropsch Paraffin, 841
Flame Atomic Absorption Spectrophotometric Method (for Lead), 1271
Flavin Mononucleotide, Sodium Salt, 983
Flavor Chemicals, Tests and Assays, 1375
  Acidity Determination by Iodometric Method (M-5), 1378
  Alcohol Content of Ethyl Oxyhydrate (M-4), 1378
  Assay by Gas Chromatography (M-1), 1375
  Assay by Titrimetric Procedures (M-3), 1377
  Aldehydes and Ketones (M-2), 1376
  Limit Test for Antioxidants in Ethyl Acrylate (M-6), 1378
  Limit Test for Hydrocarbons in Eugenol (M-7), 1379
  Limit Test for Hydrocyanic Acid in Benzaldehyde (M-8), 1379
  Limit Test for Lead (M-9), 1379
  Limit Test for Methyl Compounds in Ethyl Acetate (M-10), 1379
  Limit Test for Peroxide Value (M-11), 1379
  Limit Test for Readily Carbonizable Substances in Ethyl Acetate (M-12), 1379
  Limit Test for Readily Oxidizable Substances in dl-Menthol (M-13), 1380
  Limit Test for Reducing Substances (M-14), 1380
  Acid Value (M-15), 1380
  Residue on Evaporation (M-16), 1380

Qualitative Test for Phenols Using Ferric Chloride (M-17), 1380

Flavoring Agents
Acetaldehyde, 10
Acetaldehyde Diethyl Acetal, 10
Acetanisole, 11
Acetoin Dimer, 13
Acetoin Monomer, 13
Acetophenone, 16
3-Acetyl-2,5-dimethyl Furan, 17
2-Acetylpyrazine, 22
3-Acetylpyridine, 21
2-Acetylpyrrole, 21
2-Acetyl Thiazole, 19
Allyl Cyclohexanepropionate, 37
Allyl Heptanoate, 38
Allyl Hexanoate, 39
Allyl α-Ionone, 36
Allyl Isothiocyanate, 40
Allyl Isovalerate, 41
Allyl Phenoxy Acetate, 42
Allyl Propionate, 43
Almond Oil, Bitter, FFPA, 44
Ambrette Seed Oil, 52
Ammoniated Glycyrrhizin, 54
1-Amyl Alcohol, 61
Amyl Butyrate, 61
α-Amylcinnamaldehyde, 64
Amyl Formate, 62
Amyl Heptanoate, 62
Amyl Octanoate, 62
Amyl Propionate, 63
Amyris Oil, West Indian Type, 65
Anethole, 66
Angelica Root Oil, 67
Angelica Seed Oil, 68
Anise Oil, 69
Anisole, 70
Anisyl Acetate, 71
Anisyl Alcohol, 71
Anisyl Formate, 72
Balsam Peru Oil, 100
Basil Oil, Comoros Type, 100
Basil Oil, European Type, 101
Bay Oil, 102
Benzaldehyde, 106
Benzaldehyde Glyceryl Acetal, 107
1,2-Benzodihydropyrone, 108
Benzophenone, 109
Benzyl Acetate, 111
Benzyl Alcohol, 112
Benzyl Benzoate, 112
Benzyl Butyrate, 113
Benzyl Cinnamate, 113
Benzyl Formate, 114
Benzyl Isobutyrate, 115
Benzyl Isovalerate, 116
Benzyl Phenylacetate, 117
Benzyl Propionate, 118
Benzyl Salicylate, 119
Bergamot Oil, Coldpressed, 120
Birch Tar Oil, Rectified, 127
Black Pepper Oil, 128
Bois de Rose Oil, 130
Borneol, 131
Bornyl Acetate, 132
2-Butanone, 146

Butan-3-one-2-yl Butanoate, 144
Butyl 2-Methyl Butyrate, 148
Butyl Acetate, 149
Butyl Alcohol, 149
Butyl Butyrate, 151
Butyl Butyryllactate, 151
2-sec-Butyl Cyclohexanone, 147
Butyl Isobutyrate, 152
Butyl Isovalerate, 153
Butyl Phenylacetate, 154
Butyl Stearate, 155
Butyraldehyde, 156
Butyric Acid, 157
γ-Butyrolactone, 158
Caffeine, 160
Camphene, 196
(+)-Camphor, 197
Cananga Oil, 197
Caraway Oil, 208
Cardamom Oil, 214
Carrot Seed Oil, 228
Carvacrol, 229
(−)-Carveol, 229
(−)-Carvone, 231
(+)-Carvone, 230
(−)-Carvyl Acetate, 232
β-Caryophyllene, 233
Cascarilla Oil, 234
Cassia Oil, 236
Cedar Leaf Oil, 238
Celery Seed Oil, 239
Chamomile Oil, English Type, 244
Chamomile Oil, German Type, 245
Cinnamaldehyde, 249
Cinnamic Acid, 250
Cinnamon Bark Oil, Ceylon Type, 251
Cinnamon Leaf Oil, 252
Cinnamyl Acetate, 253
Cinnamyl Alcohol, 254
Cinnamyl Butyrate, 255
Cinnamyl Cinnamate, 256
Cinnamyl Formate, 257
Cinnamyl Isobutyrate, 258
Cinnamyl Isovalerate, 259
Cinnamyl Propionate, 260
Citral, 261
Citronellal, 265
Citronellol, 266
Citronellyl Acetate, 267
Citronellyl Butyrate, 268
Citronellyl Formate, 269
Citronellyl Isobutyrate, 270
Citronellyl Propionate, 271
Clary Oil, 272
Clove Leaf Oil, 273
Clove Oil, 274
Clove Stem Oil, 275
Cognac Oil, Green, 278
Copaiba Oil, 279
Coriander Oil, 285
Costus Root Oil, 286
p-Cresyl Acetate, 288
Cubeb Oil, 290
Cuminic Aldehyde, 292
Cumin Oil, 291
Cyclamen Aldehyde, 294

Cyclohexyl Acetate, 307
p-Cymene, 307
(E),(E)-2,4-Decadienal, 314
δ-Decalactone, 315
γ-Decalactone, 316
Decanal, 317
(E)-2-Decenal, 318
(Z)-4-Decenal, 319
Decyl Alcohol, 320
1,2-Di[(1′-ethoxy)ethoxy]propane, 108
Diacetyl, 335
Dibenzyl Ether, 341
Diethyl Malonate, 342
Diethyl Sebacate, 343
Diethyl Succinate, 343
Dihydrocarveol, 344
(+)-Dihydrocarvone, 345
Dill Seed Oil, European Type, 346
Dill Seed Oil, Indian Type, 347
Dillweed Oil, American Type, 348
2,6-Dimethoxy Phenol, 358
3,4-Dimethyl 1,2-Cyclopentandione, 350
3,7-Dimethyl-1-octanol, 351
2,6-Dimethyl-5-heptenal, 349
Dimethyl Anthranilate, 352
Dimethyl Benzyl Carbinol, 352
Dimethyl Benzyl Carbinyl Acetate, 353
Dimethyl Benzyl Carbinyl Butyrate, 354
2,3-Dimethylpyrazine, 359
2,5-Dimethylpyrazine, 360
2,6-Dimethylpyrazine, 361
2-Ethyl-3,5(6)-dimethylpyrazine, 388
2,5-Dimethylpyrrole, 362
Dimethyl Succinate, 356
Dimethyl Sulfide, 357
Diphenyl Ether, 365
δ-Dodecalactone, 372
γ-Dodecalactone, 373
(E)-2-Dodecen-1-al, 374
Enzyme-Modified Fats, 380
Estragole, 384
Ethone, 385
Ethyl Acetate, 396, 397
Ethyl Acrylate, 398
Ethyl p-Anisate, 393
Ethyl Anthranilate, 400
Ethyl Benzoate, 401
Ethyl Benzoyl Acetate, 402
Ethyl-(E)-2-butenoate, 423
2-Ethylbutyraldehyde, 425
Ethyl Butyrate, 402
2-Ethylbutyric Acid, 425
Ethyl Cinnamate, 404
Ethyl Decanoate, 405
Ethylene Brassylate, 424
2-Ethyl Fenchol, 387
Ethyl Formate, 406
4-Ethyl Guaiacol, 391
Ethyl Heptanoate, 406
Ethyl Hexanoate, 407
2-Ethyl Hexanol, 388
5-Ethyl 3-Hydroxy 4-Methyl 2(5H)-Furanone, 392

Ethyl Isobutyrate, 408
Ethyl Isovalerate, 409
Ethyl Lactate, 410
Ethyl Laurate, 411
Ethyl Levulinate, 413
Ethyl 2-Methylbutyrate, 394
Ethyl 2-Methylpentanoate, 395
Ethyl Methylphenylglycidate, 415
2-Ethyl-3-methylpyrazine, 389
Ethyl 3-Methylthiopropionate, 396
Ethyl Myristate, 416
Ethyl Nonanoate, 416
Ethyl Octanoate, 417
Ethyl Oleate, 418
Ethyl Oxyhydrate (so-called), 418
Ethyl Phenylacetate, 419
Ethyl Phenylglycidate, 420
Ethyl Propionate, 420
3-Ethyl Pyridine, 390
Ethyl Salicylate, 421
Ethyl 10-Undecenoate, 394
Ethyl Valerate, 422
Ethyl Vanillin, 422
Eucalyptol, 427
Eucalyptus Oil, 428
Eugenol, 429
Eugenyl Acetate, 430
Farnesol, 431
(+)-Fenchone, 439
Fenchyl Alcohol, 440
Fennel Oil, 440
Fir Needle Oil, Canadian Type, 459
Fir Needle Oil, Siberian Type, 460
Furfural, 472
Furfuryl Alcohol, 473
Furfuryl Mercaptan, 474
2-Furyl Methyl Ketone, 475
Fusel Oil, Refined, 476
Garlic Oil, 478
Geraniol, 482
Geranium Oil, Algerian Type, 483
Geranyl Acetate, 484
Geranyl Benzoate, 485
Geranyl Butyrate, 486
Geranyl Formate, 487
Geranyl Isovalerate, 488
Geranyl Phenylacetate, 489
Geranyl Propionate, 490
Ginger Oil, 492
Glyceryl Tripropanoate, 512
Grapefruit Oil, Coldpressed, 515
(E),(E)-2,4-Heptadienal, 519
γ-Heptalactone, 520
Heptanal, 521
2,3-Heptanedione, 522
2-Heptanone, 523
3-Heptanone, 524
(Z)-4-Hepten-1-al, 525
Heptyl Alcohol, 526
γ-Hexalactone, 528
Hexanal, 529
Hexanoic Acid, 529
(E)-2-Hexen-1-al, 530
(E)-2-Hexen-1-ol, 531
(Z)-3-Hexenol, 531
(E)-2-Hexenyl Acetate, 532
(Z)-3-Hexenyl Acetate, 533

(Z)-3-Hexenyl Butyrate, 534
(Z)-3-Hexenyl Formate, 535
(Z)-3-Hexenyl Isovalerate, 536
(Z)-3-Hexenyl 2-Methylbutyrate, 536
Hexyl-2-butenoate, 541
Hexyl Acetate, 537
Hexyl Alcohol, 538
Hexyl Butyrate, 539
α-Hexylcinnamaldehyde, 542
Hexyl Hexanoate, 540
Hexyl Isovalerate, 541
Hexyl 2-Methylbutyrate, 537
Hops Oil, 548
Hydroxycitronellal, 555
Hydroxycitronellal Dimethyl Acetal, 556
4-Hydroxy-2,5-dimethyl-3(2H)-furanone, 557
6-Hydroxy-3,7-dimethyloctanoic Acid Lactone, 558
4-(p-Hydroxyphenyl)-2-butanone, 560
Indole, 564
α-Ionone, 568
β-Ionone, 569
Isoamyl Acetate, 576
Isoamyl Alcohol, 577
Isoamyl Benzoate, 577
Isoamyl Butyrate, 578
Isoamyl Cinnamate, 579
Isoamyl Formate, 580
Isoamyl Hexanoate, 581
Isoamyl Isobutyrate, 582
Isoamyl Isovalerate, 583
Isoamyl Phenyl Acetate, 583
Isoamyl Salicylate, 584
Isoborneol, 585
Isobornyl Acetate, 586
Isobutyl Acetate, 588
Isobutyl Alcohol, 589
Isobutyl-2-butenoate, 595
Isobutyl Butyrate, 590
Isobutyl Cinnamate, 591
Isobutyl Formate, 592
Isobutyl Hexanoate, 592
Isobutyl Phenylacetate, 593
Isobutyl Salicylate, 594
Isobutyraldehyde, 597
Isobutyric Acid, 598
Isoeugenol, 599
Isoeugenyl Acetate, 600
Isopropyl Acetate, 606
Isopulegol, 608
Isovaleric Acid, 609
Juniper Berries Oil, 610
Labdanum Oil, 615
Laurel Leaf Oil, 628
Lauryl Alcohol, 630
Lauryl Aldehyde, 631
Lavandin Oil, Abrial Type, 632
Lavender Oil, 633
Lemongrass Oil, 639
Lemon Oil, Coldpressed, 636
Lemon Oil, Desert Type, Coldpressed, 637
Lemon Oil, Distilled, 638
Levulinic Acid, 642

Lime Oil, Coldpressed, 643
Lime Oil, Distilled, 645
(+)-Limonene, 647
(−)-Limonene, 648
Linaloe Wood Oil, 648
Linalool, 649
Linalool Oxide, 650
Linalyl Acetate, 651
Linalyl Benzoate, 652
Linalyl Formate, 653
Linalyl Isobutyrate, 654
Linalyl Propionate, 655
Lovage Oil, 657
Mace Oil, 669
Maltol, 691
Maltol Isobutyrate, 691
Mandarin Oil, Coldpressed, 692
Marjoram Oil, Spanish Type, 700
Marjoram Oil, Sweet, 701
Mentha Arvensis Oil, Partially Dementholized, 712
Menthol, 713
(−)-Menthone, 714
(−)-Menthyl Acetate, 715
l-Menthyl Acetate, 715
Menthyl Acetate, Racemic, 714
2-Mercaptopropionic Acid, 715
2-Methoxy-3(5)-methylpyrazine, 719
2-Methoxy 3-(or 5- or 6-) Isopropyl Pyrazine, 718
p-Methoxybenzaldehyde, 719
4-p-Methoxyphenyl-2-butanone, 767
2-Methoxypyrazine, 720
Methyl Acetate, 735
4-Methyl Acetophenone, 727
p-Methyl Anisole, 723
Methyl Anthranilate, 737
Methyl Benzoate, 738
Methylbenzyl Acetate, 755
α-Methylbenzyl Alcohol, 756
2-Methyl Butanal, 724
3-Methyl Butanal, 726
2-Methylbutyl Acetate, 758
2-Methylbutyl Isovalerate, 758
Methyl Butyrate, 739
2-Methylbutyric Acid, 757
α-Methylcinnamaldehyde, 760
Methyl Cinnamate, 739
6-Methylcoumarin, 721
Methyl Cyclopentenolone, 740
5H-5-Methyl-6,7-dihydrocyclopenta[6]pyrazine, 729
Methyl Eugenol, 743
5-Methyl Furfural, 730
Methyl Furoate, 744
6-Methyl-5-hepten-2-one, 732
Methyl Hexanoate, 745
Methyl Hexyl Ketone, 746
Methyl Ionones, 747
Methyl Isobutyrate, 747
Methyl Isoeugenol, 748
5-Methyl-2-isopropyl-2-hexenal, 731
Methyl Isovalerate, 749
Methyl 2-Methylbutyrate, 734
Methyl-3-methylthiopropionate, 754
Methyl β-Naphthyl Ketone, 733

Methyl 2-Octynoate, 734
2-Methylpentanoic Acid, 763
4-Methylpentanoic Acid, 722
4-Methyl-2-pentanone, 728
2-Methyl-2-pentenoic Acid, 725
Methyl Phenylacetate, 750
Methyl Phenylcarbinyl Acetate, 751
5-Methyl 2-Phenyl 2-Hexenal, 730
2-Methyl Propyl 3-Methyl Butyrate, 724
2-Methylpyrazine, 764
Methyl Salicylate, 752
Methyl Thiobutyrate, 752
3-Methylthiopropionaldehyde, 765
2-Methylundecanal, 766
Methyl Valerate, 753
Monoammonium Glycyrrhizinate, 775
Mustard Oil, 780
Myrcene, 780
Myristaldehyde, 781
Myristyl Alcohol, 782
Myrrh Oil, 782
β-Naphthyl Ethyl Ether, 784
Nerol, 790
Nerolidol, 791
Neryl Acetate, 792
(E),(E)-2,4-Nonadienal, 801
(E),(Z)-2,6-Nonadienal, 802
(E),(Z)-2,6-Nonadienol, 803
δ-Nonalactone, 804
γ-Nonalactone, 805
Nonanal, 806
Nonanoic Acid, 808
2-Nonanone, 807
(E)-2-Nonen-1-ol, 808
(Z)-6-Nonen-1-ol, 809
(E)-2-Nonenal, 810
Nonyl Acetate, 811
Nonyl Alcohol, 812
Nutmeg Oil, 813
δ-Octalactone, 815
γ-Octalactone, 815
Octanal, 816
3-Octanol, 817
(E)-2-Octen-1-al, 818
(Z)-3-Octen-1-ol, 818
1-Octen-3-ol, 819
1-Octen-3-yl Acetate, 820
1-Octen-3-yl Butyrate, 821
Octyl Acetate, 822
3-Octyl Acetate, 822
Octyl Alcohol, 823
Octyl Formate, 824
Octyl Isobutyrate, 825
Olibanum Oil, 828
Onion Oil, 829
Orange Oil, Bitter, Coldpressed, 830
Orange Oil, Coldpressed, 831
Orange Oil, Distilled, 832
Origanum Oil, Spanish Type, 833
Orris Root Oil, 834
Palmarosa Oil, 839
Parsley Herb Oil, 843
Parsley Seed Oil, 844
Pennyroyal Oil, 855
ω-Pentadecalactone, 856

2,3-Pentanedione, 858
2-Pentanone, 859
Peppermint Oil, 860
Petitgrain Oil, Paraguay Type, 862
α-Phellandrene, 867
2-Phenethyl 2-Methylbutyrate, 874
Phenethyl Acetate, 868
Phenethyl Alcohol, 869
Phenethyl Isobutyrate, 870
Phenethyl Isovalerate, 871
Phenethyl Phenylacetate, 872
Phenethyl Salicylate, 873
Phenoxyethyl Isobutyrate, 874
3-Phenyl-1-propanol, 877
Phenylacetaldehyde, 879
Phenylacetaldehyde Dimethyl Acetal, 878
Phenylacetic Acid, 880
Phenylethyl Anthranilate, 883
Phenylethyl Butyrate, 884
Phenyl Ethyl Cinnamate, 875
Phenyl Ethyl Propionate, 876
2-Phenylpropionaldehyde, 885
3-Phenylpropionaldehyde, 886
2-Phenylpropionaldehyde Dimethyl Acetal, 867
3-Phenylpropyl Acetate, 884
Pimenta Leaf Oil, 890
Pimenta Oil, 889
α-Pinene, 893
β-Pinene, 893
Pine Needle Oil, Dwarf, 891
Pine Needle Oil, Scotch Type, 892
Piperidine, 894
Piperonal, 895
Propenylguaethol, 955
Propionaldehyde, 956
Propyl Acetate, 958
Propyl Alcohol, 958
p-Propyl Anisole, 959
Propyl Formate, 960
Propyl Mercaptan, 962
Propyl Propionate, 963
Pyrrole, 971
Quinine Hydrochloride, 972
Quinine Sulfate, 973
Rhodinol, 979
Rhodinyl Acetate, 980
Rhodinyl Formate, 981
Rosemary Oil, 987
Rose Oil, 986
Rue Oil, 988
Sage Oil, Dalmatian Type, 992
Sage Oil, Spanish Type, 993
Salicylaldehyde, 999
Sandalwood Oil, East Indian Type, 1000
Santalol, 1001
Santalyl Acetate, 1002
Savory Oil (Summer Variety), 1003
Spearmint Oil, 1082
Spice Oleoresins, 1083
Spike Lavender Oil, 1085
Starter Distillate, 1087
Tangerine Oil, Coldpressed, 1113
Tarragon Oil, 1116
Terpinen-4-ol, 1122

α-Terpinene, 1123
γ-Terpinene, 1123
α-Terpineol, 1123
Terpinyl Acetate, 1124
Terpinyl Propionate, 1125
δ-Tetradecalactone, 1126
Tetrahydrofurfuryl Alcohol, 1127
Tetrahydrolinalool, 1128
2,3,5,6-Tetramethylpyrazine, 1128
4-Methyl-5-thiazole Ethanol, 728
Thyme Oil, 1135
Thymol, 1136
Tolualdehyde, Mixed Isomers, 1152
p-Tolualdehyde, 1151
p-Tolyl Isobutyrate, 1153
Tributyrin, 1159
2-Tridecanone, 1156
2-Tridecenal, 1157
Trimethylamine, 1162
2,4,5-Trimethyl δ-3-Oxazoline, 1161
3,5,5-Trimethyl Hexanal, 1162
2,3,5-Trimethylpyrazine, 1163
δ-Undecalactone, 1166
γ-Undecalactone, 1166
Undecanal, 1167
2-Undecanone, 1169
1,3,5-Undecatriene, 1168
10-Undecenal, 1170
(E)-2-Undecenol, 1171
Undecyl Alcohol, 1172
Valeraldehyde, 1175
Valeric Acid, 1175
γ-Valerolactone, 1176
Vanillin, 1178
Veratraldehyde, 1181
Wintergreen Oil, 1195
Zingerone, 1207
Fluoride Limit Test, 1268
Folic Acid, 461
Food-Grade Gelatin, 478
Food Ingredients Fraud Database, 1530
Food Ingredients: Pharmaceutical Applications and Use of Appropriate GMPs, 1513
Food Starch–Modified, 462
Food Starch, Modified, 462
Food Starch, Unmodified, 465
Formaldehyde TS, 1397
Formic Acid, 466
Free Cresol (Cresyl Acetate in Flavor Chemicals Other Than Essential Oils), 1380
Free Fatty Acids, 1346
Free Glycerin or Propylene Glycol, 1347
Free Phenols (Essential Oils and Flavors), 1339
Freskomenthe, 147
β-D-Fructofuranosyl-α-D-glucopyranoside, 1097
Fructooligosaccharides, Short Chain, 467
Fructose, 468
D-Fructose, 468
Fruit Sugar, 468
Fuchsin–Sulfurous Acid TS, 1397

Fully Hydrogenated Rapeseed Oil, 974
Fumaric Acid, 469
Function, Statement of, 3
2-Furaldehyde, 472
Furcelleran, 470
Furfural, 472
Furfuryl Alcohol, 473
Furfuryl Mercaptan, 474
2-Furyl Methyl Ketone, 475
Fusel Oil, Refined, 476

G

β-D-Galactopyranosyl-D-glucitol, 621
4-O-β-Galactopyranosyl-D-glucose, 622
α-Galactosidase Activity, 1313
α-Galactosidase, 1313
Galam, 1010
Gallic Acid Propyl Ester, 961
Gallotannic Acid, 1114
Gamma-glutamylethylamide, 1131
Garlic Oil, 478
Gas Chromatography, 1224
  Flavor Chemicals (Other than Essential Oils), 1375
Gaultheria Oil, 1195
Gelatin, 478
Gellan Gum, 481
General Information Analytical Techniques, 1434
  Capillary Electrophoresis, 1437
  Electrophoresis, 1434
  Ion Chromatography, 1465
  Mass Spectrometry, 1441
  Near-Infrared Spectroscopy, 1467
  Nuclear Magnetic Resonance, 1445
  Radioactivity, 1452
  Raman Spectroscopy, 1472
  Scoville Heat Units, 1478
  Spectrophotometry and Light-Scattering, 1459
General Information Tables, 1501
  Alcoholometric, 1501
  Atomic Weights, 1504
  Relative Atomic Mass and Half-Lives of Selected Radionuclides, 1507
  Thermometric Equivalents, 1509
General Provisions and Requirements, 1
General Specifications and Statements, 2
Geraniol, 482
Geranium Oil, Algerian Type, 483
Geranium Oil, East Indian Type, 839
Geranium Oil, Turkish Type, 839
Geranyl Acetate, 484
Geranyl Benzoate, 485
Geranyl Butyrate, 486
Geranyl Formate, 487
Geranyl Isovalerate, 488
Geranyl Phenylacetate, 489
Geranyl Propionate, 490
Gibberellic Acid, 491
Ginger Oil, 492
Ginger Oleoresin, 1084

Glacial Acetic Acid, 12
Glassy Sodium Polyphosphates, 1055
(1-3), (1-6)-β-d-glucan, Poly-(1-6)-β-d-glucopyranosyl-(1,3)-β-d glucopyranose, 121
β-Glucanase Activity, 1313
β-Glucanase, 1313
D-Glucitol, 1075
Glucoamylase, 1314
Glucoamylase Activity, 1314
D-Gluconic Acid, Monopotassium Salt, 935
Glucono delta-Lactone, 493
α-D-Glucopyranosyl-1,4-D-glucitol, 688
α-D-Glucopyranosyl-α-D-glucopyranoside, dihydrate, 1155
Glucose, 325
D-Glucose, 325
Glucose Isomerase, 377, 1315
Glucose Isomerase Activity, 1315
Glucose Oxidase, 377, 1316
Glucose Oxidase Activity, 1316
Glucose Syrup, 494
Glucose Syrup (Corn Syrup), 1370
Glucose Syrup, Dried, 494
Glucose Syrup Solids, 494
β-D-Glucosidase, 1304
Gluside, 990
Glutamic Acid, 495, 1291
L-Glutamic Acid Hydrochloride, 496
L-Glutamic Acid, 495
L-Glutamic acid-γ-monoethylamide, 1131
L-Glutamine, 497
Glutaral, 498
Glutaraldehyde, 498
Gluten, Wheat, 1189
Glycerin, 499
Glycerin or Propylene Glycol, Free, 1347
Glycerol, 499
Glycerol Ester of Gum Rosin, 500
Glycerol Ester of Partially Dimerized Rosin, 501
Glycerol Ester of Partially Hydrogenated Gum Rosin, 502
Glycerol Ester of Partially Hydrogenated Wood Rosin, 503
Glycerol Ester of Polymerized Rosin, 504
Glycerol Ester of Tall Oil Rosin, 505
Glycerol Ester of Wood Rosin, 506
Glycerol Esters of Condensed Castor Oil Fatty Acids, 910
Glyceryl Behenate, 507
Glyceryl-Lacto Esters of Fatty Acids, 513
Glyceryl Monooleate, 508
Glyceryl Monostearate, 509
Glyceryl Palmitostearate, 511
Glyceryl Triacetate, 1158
Glyceryl Tribehenate, 507
Glyceryl Tributyrate, 1159
Glyceryl Tridocosanoate, 507
Glyceryl Tripropanoate, 512

Glyceryl Tristearate, 512
Glycine, 514
Glycine betaine, 124
Glycocoll, 514
Good Manufacturing Practices
  Food Ingredients: Pharmaceutical Applications and Use of, 1513
  General Guidelines for Food Chemicals, 1511
Good Manufacturing Practices, General Guidelines for Food Chemicals, 1511
Graham's Salt, 1055
Granulated Sugar, 1097
Grapefruit Oil, Coldpressed, 515
Grapefruit Oil, Expressed, 515
Grape Skin Extract, 514
Ground Limestone, 646
Guaiac Resin, 518
Guar Gum, 516
Guidelines for Collaborative Study Procedures To Validate Characteristics of a Method of Analysis, 1414
Gum Arabic, 516
Gum Ghatti, 517
Gum Guaiac, 518
Gum Tragacanth, 1154
Gutta hang kang, 702
Gutta Katiau, 702

H

Heliotropine, 895
Helium, 519
Hemicellulase, 1317
Hemicellulase Activity, 1317
(E),(E)-2,4-Heptadienal, 519
trans,trans-2,4-Heptadienal, 519
γ-**Heptalactone**, 520
Heptaldehyde, 521
Heptanal, 521
2,3-Heptanedione, 522
2-Heptanone, 523
3-Heptanone, 524
cis-4-Hepten-1-al, 525
(Z)-4-Hepten-1-al, 525
Heptyl Alcohol, 526
n-Heptyl-p-hydroxybenzoate, 527
Heptylparaben, 527
Hexadecanoic Acid, 840
2,4-Hexadienoic Acid, 1069
2,4-Hexadienoic Acid, Calcium Salt, 193
2,4-Hexadienoic Acid, Potassium Salt, 947
cis-Hexahydro-2-oxo-1H-thieno[3,4]imidazole-4-valeric Acid, 127
Hexahydropyridine, 894
γ-**Hexalactone**, 528
Hexaldehyde, 529
Hexanal, 529
Hexanedioic Acid, 29
1,2,3,4,5,6-Hexanehexol, 697, 1075
Hexane-Insoluble Matter, 1347

Hexanes, 529
Hexanoic Acid, 529
1-Hexanol, 538
(E)-2-Hexen-1-al, 530
trans-2-Hexen-1-al, 530
(E)-2-Hexen-1-ol, 531
cis-3-Hexen-1-ol, 531
trans-2-Hexen-1-ol, 531
(Z)-3-Hexenol, 531
(E)-2-Hexenyl Acetate, 532
(Z)-3-Hexenyl Acetate, 533
cis-3-Hexen-1-yl Acetate, 533
trans-2-Hexen-1-yl Acetate, 532
(Z)-3-Hexenyl Butyrate, 534
(Z)-3-Hexenyl Formate, 535
(Z)-3-Hexenyl Isovalerate, 536
cis-3-Hexen-1-yl Isovalerate, 536
(Z)-3-Hexenyl 2-Methylbutyrate, 536
cis-3-Hexenyl 2-Methylbutyrate, 536
Hexyl Acetate, 537
Hexyl Alcohol, 538
4-Hexyl-1,3-benzenediol, 543
Hexyl-2-butenoate, 541
Hexyl Butyrate, 539
α-Hexylcinnamaldehyde, 542
Hexyl Hexanoate, 540
Hexyl Isovalerate, 541
Hexyl 2-methylbutyrate, 537
Hexylresorcinol, 543
4-Hexylresorcinol, 543
High-Fructose Corn Syrup, 545, 1371
High Oleic Soybean Oil (Unhydrogenated), 1081
High-Performance Liquid Chromatography, 1226
L-Histidine, 547
L-Histidine Monohydrochloride, 547
HMO, 703
Hop Oleoresin, 1084
Hops Oil, 548
HPMC, 561
Hydratropic Aldehyde, 885
Hydratropic Aldehyde Dimethyl Acetal, 867
Hydrocarbons in Eugenol, Limit Test, 1379
Hydrochloric Acid, 549, 1397
Hydrochloric Acid, 0.2 M, 1393, 1393
Hydrochloric Acid, 1 N, 1401
Hydrochloric Acid Buffer, 1393
Hydrochloric Acid Table, 1242
Hydrochloric Acid TS, Diluted, 1397
Hydrocinnamaldehyde, 886
Hydrocinnamyl Alcohol, 877
Hydrocyanic Acid in Benzaldehyde, Limit Test, 1379
Hydrogenated Glucose Syrup, 689
Hydrogenated Lactose, 621
Hydrogenated Maltose, 688
Hydrogenated Starch Hydrolysate, 554
Hydrogen Peroxide, 553
Hydrogen Peroxide TS, 1397
Hydrogen Sulfide Detector Tube, 1406

Hydrogen Sulfide TS, 1397
α-Hydro-omega-hydroxy-poly(oxyethylene)-poly(oxypropylene)(51-57 moles)poly(oxyethylene) Block Copolymer, 895
α-Hydro-omega-hydroxy-poly(oxyethylene)-poly(oxypropylene)(63-71 moles)poly(oxyethylene) Block Copolymer, 897
Hydrolyzable Gallotannin, 1114
Hydrolyzed Plant Protein (HPP), 23
Hydrolyzed (Source) Protein Extract, 23
Hydrolyzed Vegetable Protein (HVP), 23
Hydroquinone Determination, 1378
Hydroquinone Monomethyl Ether Determination, 1379
2-Hydroxybutanedioic Acid, 683
3-Hydroxy-2-butanone, 13
Hydroxycitronellal, 555
Hydroxycitronellal Dimethyl Acetal, 556
4-Hydroxydecanoic Acid Lactone, 316
4-Hydroxy-2,5-Dimethyl-3(2H)-furanone, 557
7-Hydroxy-3,7-dimethyl Octanal, 555
7-Hydroxy-3,7-dimethyl Octanal Dimethyl Acetal, 556
6-Hydroxy-3,7-dimethyloctanoic Acid Lactone, 558
4-Hydroxydodecanoic Acid Lactone, 373
(2-Hydroxyethyl)trimethylammonium Chloride, 248
(2-Hydroxyethyl)trimethylammonium-L-(+)-tartrate Salt, 248
4-Hydroxyhexanoic Acid Lactone, 528
Hydroxylamine Hydrochloride, 0.5 N, 1401
Hydroxylamine Hydrochloride TS, 1397
Hydroxylamine Method, 1377
Flavor Chemicals (Other than Essential Oils), 1377
Hydroxylamine tert-Butyl Alcohol Method, 1376
Flavor Chemicals (Other than Essential Oils), 1376
Hydroxylated Lecithin, 558
Hydroxyl Value, 1347
4-Hydroxy-3-methoxybenzaldehyde, 1178
5-Hydroxy-6-methyl-3,4-pyridinedimethanol Hydrochloride, 970
3-Hydroxy-2-methyl-4-pyrone, 691
4-Hydroxy-3-methylethylbenzene, 391
Hydroxy Naphthol Blue, 1405
5-Hydroxynonanoic Acid, Lactone, 804
5-Hydroxyoctanoic Acid Lactone, 815
L-β-(p-Hydroxyphenyl)alanine, 1165
4-(4-Hydroxyphenyl)-2-butanone, 560
4-(p-Hydroxyphenyl)-2-butanone, 560

2-Hydroxypropanoic Acid, Calcium Salt, 172
2-Hydroxypropanoic Acid, Monopotassium Salt, 939
2-Hydroxypropanoic Acid, Monosodium Salt, 1040
2-Hydroxypropionic Acid, 620
α-Hydroxypropionic Acid, 620
Hydroxypropyl Alginate, 964
Hydroxypropyl Cellulose, 560
Hydroxypropyl Determination, 1291
Hydroxypropyl Methylcellulose, 561
8-Hydroxyquinoline TS, 1397
Hydroxysuccinic Acid, 683
5-Hydroxyundecanoic Acid Lactone, 1166
Hypophosphite Identification Test, 1262

I

Identification Tests, 5, 1262
   Acetate, 1262
   Aluminum, 1262
   Ammonium, 1262
   Benzoate, 1262
   Bicarbonate, 1262
   Bisulfite, 1262
   Bromide, 1262
   Calcium, 1262
   Carbonate, 1262
   Chloride, 1262
   Citrate, 1262
   Cobalt, 1262
   Copper, 1262
   Hypophosphite, 1262
   Iodide, 1262
   Iron, 1262
   Lactate, 1263
   Magnesium, 1263
   Manganese, 1263
   Nitrate, 1263
   Nitrite, 1263
   Peroxide, 1263
   Phosphate, 1263
   Potassium, 1263
   Sodium, 1263
   Sulfate, 1263
   Sulfite, 1263
   Tartrate, 1263
   Thiosulfate, 1263
   Zinc, 1263
IMP, 1047
Indian Gum, 517
Indicator Papers And Test Papers, 1406
   Acetaldehyde Test Paper, 1406
   Cupric Sulfate Test Paper, 1406
   Lead Acetate Test Paper, 1406
   Litmus Paper, Blue, 1406
   Litmus Paper, Red, 1406
   Phenolphthalein Paper, 1406
   Starch Iodate Paper, 1406
   Starch Iodide Paper, 1406
Indicators, 1404
   Alphazurine 2G, 1405

1626 / Indicators / Index

Azo Violet, 1405
Bromocresol Blue, 1405
Bromocresol Green, 1405
Bromocresol Purple, 1405
Bromophenol Blue, 1405
Bromothymol Blue, 1405
Cresol Red, 1405
Crystal Violet, 1405
Dithizone, 1405
Eriochrome Black T, 1405
p-Ethoxychrysoidin Monohydrochloride, 1405
Hydroxy Naphthol Blue, 1405
Litmus, 1405
Methylene Blue, 1405
Methyl Orange, 1405
Methyl Red, 1405
Methyl Red Sodium, 1405
Methyl Yellow, 1405
Murexide Indicator Preparation, 1405
Naphthol Green B, 1405
Neutral Red, 1405
Phenolphthalein, 1406
Phenol Red, 1406
Quantity Used, 5
Quinaldine Red, 1406
Thymol Blue, 1406
Thymolphthalein, 1406
Xylenol Orange, 1406
Indigo Carmine, 434, 563
Indigo Carmine TS, 1397
Indigotine, 434, 563
Indigotine Disulfonate, 563
Indole, 564
Infrared Absorption, 1294
Infrared Spectra, 1294, 1479
Inositol, 565
i-Inositol, 565
meso-Inositol, 565
myo-Inositol, 565
INS number, 2
Insoluble Sodium Polyphosphate, 1047
Inulin, 566
Invertase, 1318
Invertase Sumner Unit Activity, 1318
Invert Sugar, 567, 1373
Invert Sugar Determination, 1364
Invert Sugar Syrup, 567
Iodide Identification Test, 1262
Iodinated Zinc Chloride, 1397
Iodine, 0.1 N, 1402
Iodine TS, 1397
Iodine Value, 1348
Ion Chromatography, 1465
α-**Ionone**, 568
β-**Ionone**, 569
Iron Ammonium Citrate, 441, 443
Iron, Carbonyl, 570
Iron, Electrolytic, 572
Iron (II) Fumarate, 451
Iron (II) Gluconate, 453
Iron (II) 2-Hydroxypropionate, 455
Iron Identification Test, 1262
Iron (II) Lactate, 455
Iron Phosphate, 445
Iron Pyrophosphate, 447

Iron, Reduced, 574
Iron Standard Solution, 1394
Isoamyl Acetate, 576
Isoamyl Alcohol, 577
Isoamyl Benzoate, 577
Isoamyl Butyrate, 578
Isoamyl Caproate, 581
Isoamyl Caprylate, 62
Isoamyl Cinnamate, 579
Isoamyl Formate, 580
Isoamyl Hexanoate, 581
Isoamyl Isobutyrate, 582
Isoamyl Isovalerate, 583
Isoamyl Octanoate, 62
Isoamyl Phenyl Acetate, 583
Isoamyl 3-Phenyl Propenate, 579
Isoamyl Propionate, 63
Isoamyl Salicylate, 584
Isoborneol, 585
Isobornyl Acetate, 586
Isobutane, 587
Isobutyl Acetate, 588
Isobutyl Alcohol, 589
Isobutyl-2-butenoate, 595
Isobutyl Butyrate, 590
Isobutyl Cinnamate, 591
Isobutylene-Isoprene Copolymer, 596
Isobutyl Formate, 592
Isobutyl Hexanoate, 592
Isobutyl Isovalerate, 724
Isobutyl Phenylacetate, 593
Isobutyl Salicylate, 594
Isobutyraldehyde, 597
Isobutyric Acid, 598
Isodihydrolavandulal, 731
Isoestragole, 66
Isoeugenol, 599
Isoeugenyl Acetate, 600
Isoeugenyl Methyl Ether, 748
DL-Isoleucine, 601
L-Isoleucine, 602
Isomalt, 603
Isomaltulose, 604
Isomerase
  Actinoplanes missouriensis, 1304
  Bacillus coagulans, 1304
  Microbacterium arborescens, 1304
  Streptomyces murinus, 1304
  Streptomyces olivaceus, 1304
  Streptomyces olivochromgenus, 1304
  Streptomyces rubiginosus, 1304
Isopropanol, 606, 1397
Isopropanol, Anhydrous, 1397
Isopropyl Acetate, 606
Isopropylacetic Acid, 609
Isopropyl Alcohol, 606
p-Isopropylbenzaldehyde, 292
Isopropylformic Acid, 598
Isopulegol, 608
Isovaleraldehyde, 726
Isovaleric Acid, 609

J

Jelutong, 702

Juniper Berries Oil, 610

K

Kaolin, 611
Karaya Gum, 611
Karite, 1010
Karl Fischer Titrimetric Method (for Water), 1239
KASAL, 1018
Kelp, 612
Kjeldahl Nitrogen Determination, 1293
Konjac, 613
Konjac Flour, 613
Konjac Gum, 613
Konnyaku, 613

L

Labdanum Oil, 615
Labeling, Statements for, 2
Alpha-Lactalbumin, 615
Lactase, 1319
Lactase (Acid) Activity, 1320
Lactase (Neutral) Activity, 1319
Lactated Mono-Diglycerides, 513
Lactate Identification Test, 1263
Lactic Acid, 151, 620
Lactic and Fatty Acid Esters of Glycerol, 513
Lactitol, 621
D-Lactitol, 621
Lactose, 622
Lactose Determination, 1366
Lactylated Fatty Acid Esters of Glycerol and Propylene Glycol, 623
Lactylic Esters of Fatty Acids, 625
LAE, 411
Lanolin, Anhydrous, 627
Larch Fiber, 80
Larch Gum, 80
Lard (Unhydrogenated), 627
Lauramide Arginine Ethyl Ester, 411
Laurel Leaf Oil, 628
Laurel Leaf Oleoresin, 1084
Lauric Acid, 630
Lauric Arginate Ethyl Ester, 411
Lauryl Alcohol, 630
Lauryl Aldehyde, 631
Lavandin Oil, Abrial Type, 632
Lavender Oil, 633
Lead Acetate Test Paper, 1406
Lead Acetate TS, 1397
Lead Limit Test, 1270
  APDC Extraction Method, 1274
  Atomic Absorption Spectrophotometric Graphite Furnace Method, 1272
  Chewing Gum Base Polymers, 1301
  Dithizone Method, 1270
  Flame Atomic Absorption Spectrophotometric Method, 1271

Flavor Chemicals Other Than
  Essential Oils, 1379
Lead Subacetate TS, 1397
Lead Subacetate TS, Diluted, 1397
LEAR Oil, 199
Leche caspi (sorva), 702
Leche de vaca, 703
Lecithin, 634
Lemongrass Oil, 639
Lemon Oil Arizona, 637
Lemon Oil, Cold-pressed, 636
Lemon Oil, Desert Type, Coldpressed, 637
Lemon Oil, Distilled, 638
Lemon Oil, Expressed, 636
DL-Leucine, 640
L-Leucine, 641
Leuco Base (Color Additive Assays), 1284
Levocarnitine, 217
Levulinic Acid, 642
Levulose, 468
"Light-Resistant Container", Defined, 3
Lignosulfonic Acid, Calcium Salt (40×65), 176
Lime, 180
Lime Oil, Cold-pressed, 643
Lime Oil, Distilled, 645
Lime Oil, Expressed, 643
Limestone, Ground, 646
"Limit of Detection", Defined, 1412
"Limit of Quantitation", Defined, 1412
Limit Tests, 1264
  Aluminum, 1264
  Antioxidants in Ethyl Acrylate, 1378
  Arsenic, 1264
  Cadmium, 1266
  Chloride, 1266
  1,4-Dioxane, 1267
  Fluoride, 1268
  Hydrocarbons in Eugenol, 1379
  Hydrocyanic Acid in Benzaldehyde, 1379
  Hydroquinone in Ethyl Acrylate, 1378
  Hydroquinone Monomethyl Ether in Ethyl Acrylate, 1379
  Lead, 1270
  Lead (Flavor Chemicals Other Than Essential Oils), 1379
  Manganese, 1275
  Mercury, 1275
  Methyl Compounds in Ethyl Acetate, 1379
  Nickel, 1276
  Peroxide Value (Flavor Chemicals Other Than Essential Oils), 1379
  Phosphorus, 1277
  Readily Carbonizable Substances in Ethyl Acetate, 1379
  Readily Oxidizable Substances in dl-Menthol, 1380
  Reducing Substances (Flavor Chemicals Other Than Essential Oils), 1380
  Selenium, 1278
  Sulfate, 1266

(−)-Limonene, 648
(+)-Limonene, 647
d-Limonene, 647
l-Limonene, 648
Linaloe Wood Oil, 648
Linalool, 649
Linalool Determination (Essential Oils and Flavors), 1338
Linalool Oxide, 650
Linalyl Acetate, 651
Linalyl Benzoate, 652
Linalyl Formate, 653
Linalyl Isobutyrate, 654
Linalyl Propionate, 655
"Linearity and Range", Defined, 1412
Linoleic Acid, 656
Lipase, 378, 1321
  Animal Pancreatic Tissue; 2-Acylhydrolase, 1305
  Animal Pancreatic Tissues, 1305
  Aspergillus niger var., 1305
  Aspergillus oryzae var., 1305
  Candida rugosa, 1305
  Edible Forestomach Tissue of Calves, Kids, and Lambs, 1305
  Rhizomucor meihei, 1306
Lipase (Microbial) Activity for Medium- and Long-Chain Fatty Acids, 1322
Lipase Activity, 1321
Lipase, Animal, 375
Liquid Paraffin, 768, 770
Liquid Petrolatum, 768, 770
Lithium Methoxide, 0.1 N, 1402
Litmus, 1405
Litmus Paper, Blue, 1406
Litmus Paper, Red, 1406
Litmus TS, 1397
Locust Bean Gum, 657
Locust (Carob) Bean Gum, 657
Loss on Drying, 1243
  Color Additives, 1289
Lovage Oil, 657
Lovibond Color, 1342
Low Erucic Acid Rapeseed Oil, 199
Low Glycemic Carbohydrate, 1094
Low Linolenic Acid Flaxseed Oil (Unhydrogenated), 1069
Low Linolenic Acid Linseed Oil, 1069
Luo Han Fruit Concentrate, 772
Luo Han Guo Concentrate, 772
Luo Han Guo Extract, 772
Lutein, 658
Lycopene Extract from Tomato, 662
Lycopene from Blakeslea trispora, 660
Lycopene, Synthetic, 665
Lycopene (Tomato), 662
Lycopene, Tomato Extract, 662
Lye, 1036
Lye Solutions, 1035
L-Lysine Monohydrochloride, 668
Lysozyme, 375
Lysozyme Activity, 1323
D-Lyxo-Hexulose, 1110

M

Mace Oil, 669
Maddrell's Salt, 1047
Magadi Soda, 1061
Magnesal, 670
Magnesia Mixture TS, 1397
Magnesium Ammonium Potassium Carnallite, 670
Magnesium Ammonium Potassium Chloride, Hydrate, 670
Magnesium Ammonium Potassium Chloride, Triple Salt, 670
Magnesium Biphosphate, 679
Magnesium Carbonate, 672
Magnesium Chloride, 672
Magnesium Dihydrogen Phosphate, 679
Magnesium Gluconate, 673
Magnesium Hydroxide, 674
Magnesium Identification Test, 1263
Magnesium Lactate, 675
Magnesium Oxide, 676
Magnesium Phosphate, Dibasic, Mixed Hydrates, 677
Magnesium Phosphate, Dibasic, Trihydrate, 678
Magnesium Phosphate, Monobasic, 679
Magnesium Phosphate, Tribasic, 680
Magnesium Silicate, 680
Magnesium Standard Solution, 1394
Magnesium Stearate, 682
Magnesium Sulfate, 683
Magnesium Sulfate TS, 1397
Malachite Green TS, 1397
Malic Acid, 683
DL-Malic Acid, 683
Malonic Ester, 342
Malt, 376
Malt Extract, 684
Maltitol, 688
D-Maltitol, 688
Maltitol Syrup, 689
Maltodextrin, 690, 1372
Maltogenic Amylase, 1324
Maltogenic Amylase Activity, 1324
Maltol, 691
Maltol Isobutyrate, 691
Malt Syrup, 684
Mandarin Oil, Cold-pressed, 692
Mandarin Oil, Expressed, 692
Manganese Chloride, 693
Manganese Citrate, 694
Manganese Gluconate, 695
Manganese Glycerophosphate, 695
Manganese Hypophosphite, 696
Manganese Identification Test, 1263
Manganese Limit Test, 1275
Manganese Sulfate, 697
Mannite, 697
Mannitol, 697
D-Mannitol, 697
Maple Furanone, 392
Maritime Pine Extract, 698

1628 / Marjoram Oil, Spanish Type / Index

Marjoram Oil, Spanish Type, 700
Marjoram Oil, Sweet, 701
Marjoram Sweet Oleoresin, 1084
Markers for Authenticity Testing, 1388
  Biobased Content of 1,3-Propanediol, 1388
Massaranduba balata, 702
Massaranduba chocolate, 702
Mass Spectrometry, 1441
Masticatory Substances, Natural, 702
Mayer's Reagent, 1397
MC, 759
Media and Reagents (Microbiological Tests), 1381
Melting Range
  Fats and Related Substances, 1348
Melting Range or Temperature Determination, 1231
Menhaden Oil, Hydrogenated, 703
Menhaden Oil, Refined, 708
Mentha Arvensis Oil, Partially Dementholized, 712
d-p-Mentha-1,8-diene, 647
l-p-Mentha-1,8-diene, 648
p-Mentha-1,5-diene, 867
p-Mentha-6,8-dien-2-ol, 229
p-Mentha-6,8-dien-2-yl Acetate, 232
3-p-Menthanol, 713
l-p-Menthan-3-one, 714
dl-p-Menthan-3-yl Acetate, 714
l-p-Menthan-3-yl Acetate, 715
p-Menth-4-en-3-ol, 608
p-Menth-1-en-8-ol, 1123
Menthen-1-yl-8 Acetate, 1124
Menthen-1-yl-8 Propionate, 1125
Menthol, 713
(−)-Menthone, 714
L-Menthone, 714
(−)-Menthyl Acetate, 715
DL-Menthyl Acetate, 714
l-Menthyl Acetate, 715
Menthyl Acetate, Racemic, 714
2-Mercaptopropionic Acid, 715
Mercuric Acetate TS, 1397
Mercuric Chloride TS, 1397
Mercuric Nitrate, 0.1 M, 1402
Mercuric-Potassium Iodide TS, 1397
Mercuric-Potassium Iodide TS, Alkaline, 1394, 1397
Mercuric Sulfate TS, 1398
Mercurous Nitrate TS, 1398
Mercury (Color Additive Assays), 1284
Mercury Limit Test, 1275
Meso-Zeaxanthin, 1209
Methanol, 736, 1398
Methanol, Anhydrous, 1398
Methional, 765
DL-Methionine, 716
L-Methionine, 717
p-Methoxyacetophenone, 11
p-Methoxybenzaldehyde, 719
p-Methoxybenzyl Acetate, 71
p-Methoxybenzyl Alcohol, 71
p-Methoxybenzyl Formate, 72
2-Methoxy 3- (or 5- or 6-) Isopropyl Pyrazine, 718

Methoxyl Determination, 1292
2-Methoxy-3(5)-Methylpyrazine, 719
4-p-Methoxyphenyl-2-butanone, 767
1-(p-Methoxyphenyl)-1-penten-3-one, 385
2-Methoxy-4-propenylphenol, 599
2-Methoxy-4-propenyl Phenyl Acetate, 600
2-Methoxypyrazine, 720
Methyl Acetate, 735
4-Methyl Acetophenone, 727
Methylacetopyronone, 321
Methyl Alcohol, 736
p-Methylaminophenol Sulfate TS, 1398
Methyl Amyl Ketone, 523
p-Methyl Anisole, 723
Methyl Anthranilate, 737
Methylbenzaldehyde, 1152
p-Methylbenzaldehyde, 1151
Methyl Benzoate, 738
Methylbenzyl Acetate, 755
α-Methylbenzyl Alcohol, 756
2-Methyl Butanal, 724
3-Methyl Butanal, 726
2-Methylbutyl Acetate, 758
β-Methyl Butyl Acetate, 576
2-Methylbutyl Isovalerate, 758
2-Methylbutyl-3-methylbutanoate, 758
Methyl Butyrate, 739
2-Methylbutyric Acid, 757
Methylcellulose, 759
Methylcellulose, Hydroxypropyl, 561
Methylcellulose Viscosity, 1237
Methyl Chavicol, 384
α-Methylcinnamaldehyde, 760
Methyl Cinnamate, 739
Methyl Compounds in Ethyl Acetate, Limit Test, 1379
6-Methylcoumarin, 721
Methyl p-Cresol, 723
3-Methylcyclopentane-1,2-dione, 740
Methyl Cyclopentenolone, 740
5H-5-Methyl-6,7-dihydrocyclopenta[b]pyrazine, 729
Methylene Blue, 1405
Methylene Blue TS, 1398
Methylene Chloride, 761
Methylene Dichloride, 761
3,4-(Methylenedioxy)-benzaldehyde, 895
Methyl Ester of Rosin, Partially Hydrogenated, 741
Methyl Ethyl Cellulose, 742
Methyl Ethylene Oxide, 966
Methyl Ethyl Ketone, 146
Methyl Eugenol, 743
5-Methyl Furfural, 730
Methyl Furoate, 744
Methyl Glycol, 963
Methyl Heptenone, 732
6-Methyl-5-hepten-2-one, 732
Methyl Heptine Carbonate, 734
Methyl Heptyl Ketone, 807
Methyl Hexanoate, 745

Methyl Hexyl Ketone, 746
Methyl p-Hydroxybenzoate, 762
Methyl Ionones, 747
Methyl Isobutyl Ketone, 728
Methyl Isobutyrate, 747
Methyl Isoeugenol, 748
d-1-Methyl-4-isopropenyl-6-cyclohexen-2-one, 230
l-1-Methyl-4-isopropenyl-6-cyclohexen-2-one, 231
5-Methyl-2-isopropyl-2-hexenal, 731
2-Methyl-3-(p-isopropylphenyl)propionaldehyde, 294
Methyl Isovalerate, 749
Methyl N-Methyl Anthranilate, 352
Methyl 2-Methylbutanoate, 734
Methyl 2-Methylbutyrate, 734
7-Methyl-3-methylene-1,6-octadiene, 780
d-2-Methyl-5-(1-methylethenyl)-cyclohexanone, 345
1-Methyl-4-(1-methylethyl)-1,3-cyclohexadiene, 1123
1-Methyl-4-(1-methylethyl)-1,4-cyclohexadiene, 1123
Methyl-3-methylthiopropionate, 754
Methyl β-Naphthyl Ketone, 733
Methyl n-Nonyl Acetaldehyde, 766
Methyl Nonyl Ketone, 1169
Methyl 2-Octynoate, 734
Methyl Orange, 1405
Methyl Orange TS, 1398
6-Methyl-1,2,3-oxathiazine-4(3H)-one-2,2 Dioxide Potassium Salt, 9
Methyl Oxirane, 966
Methylparaben, 762
2-Methylpentanoic Acid, 763
4-Methylpentanoic Acid, 722
4-Methyl-2-pentanone, 728
2-Methyl-2-pentenoic acid, 725
α-Methyl Phenylacetaldehyde, 885
Methyl Phenylacetate, 750
p-Methylphenyl Acetate, 288
Methyl Phenylcarbinol, 756
Methyl Phenylcarbinyl Acetate, 751
Methylphenyl Ether, 70
5-Methyl 2-Phenyl 2-Hexenal, 730
Methyl Phenyl Ketone, 16
2-Methyl Propanoic Acid, 598
2-Methyl Propanyl Butyrate, 590
Methyl Propyl Ketone, 859
2-Methyl Propyl 3-Methyl Butyrate, 724
2-Methylpyrazine, 764
Methyl Pyrazinyl Ketone, 22
Methyl Pyridyl Ketone, 21
Methyl 2-Pyrrolyl Ketone, 21
Methyl Red, 1405
Methyl Red-Methylene Blue TS, 1398
Methyl Red Sodium, 1405
Methyl Red TS, 1398
Methylrosaniline Chloride TS, 1398
Methyl Salicylate, 752

Methyl Sulfide, 357
2-Methyl-3-(3,7,11,15-tetramethyl-2-hexadecenyl), 1187
4-Methyl-5-thiazole Ethanol, 728
Methyl Thiobutyrate, 752
3-Methylthiopropionaldehyde, 765
Methyl *p*-Tolyl Ketone, 727
2-Methylundecanal, 766
Methyl Valerate, 753
Methyl Vanillin, 1181
Methyl Violet TS, 1398
Methyl Yellow, 1405
mg/kg and Percent, 5
Microbial Limit Tests, 5
Microbiological Enumeration Tests, 1382
Microbiological Tests, 1381
    Bile-Tolerant Gram-Negative Bacteria, 1383
    Enterobacteria Enrichment Broth Mossel, 1381
    Enterobacter Sakazakii (Cronobacter SPP.), 1383
    Media and Reagents, 1381
    Microbiological Enumeration Tests, 1382
    Phosphate Buffer Solution pH 7.2, 1381
    Rappaport Vassiliadis Salmonella Enrichment Broth, 1381
    Sabouraud Dextrose Agar, 1381
    Salmonella SPP., 1383
    Buffered Sodium Chloride-Peptone Solution pH 7.0, 1381
    Soybean-Casein Digest Agar, 1381
    Soybean-Casein Digest Broth, 1381
    Stock Buffer Solution, 1381
    Tests for Absence of Specific Microorganisms, 1382
    Total Aerobic Microbial Count, 1382
    Total Yeasts and Molds Count, 1382
    Violet Red Bile Glucose Agar, 1381
    Xylose Lysine Deoxycholate Agar, 1382
Milk-Clotting Activity, 1324
Millon's Reagent, 1398
Mineral Oil, High Viscosity, 768
Mineral Oil, Medium and Low Viscosity, 770
Mineral Oil, White, 770
Mixed Paraffinic Hydrocarbons, 529
Mixture of 1,2- and 1,3-Benzaldehyde Cyclic Acetals of Glycerin, 107
Mixture of α-, β-, γ- or α-iso, and δ-isomers, 747
Mixture of Geranial [(E)-3,7-dimethyl-2,6-octadien-1-al] and Neral [the (Z) isomer], 261
Modified Cellulose, 241, 560, 561, 742, 759
Modified Cellulose, EC, 403
Modified Food Starch, 462
Molar Solutions, 1400
Molecular Structure and Chemical Formulas, 2

Molecular Weight (Chewing Gum Base Polymers), 1299
Monk Fruit Concentrate, 772
Monk Fruit Extract, 772
Monoammonium L-Glutamate, 773
Monoammonium Glutamate Monohydrate, 773
Monoammonium Glycyrrhizinate, 775
Monoammonium Phosphate, 59
Mono- and Diglycerides, 773
Mono- And Diglycerides, Ethoxylated, 385
Mono-*tert*-butylhydroquinone, 1119
Monocalcium Benzoate, 163
Monocalcium Phosphate, 186
Monoglyceride Citrate, 775
Monoglycerides
    Total in Fats and Related Substances, 1349
1-Monoglycerides (Fats and Related Substances), 1348
Monomagnesium Dihydrogen Phosphate, 679
Monomagnesium Orthophosphate, 679
Monomagnesium Phosphate, 679
Monoolein, 508
Monopotassium D-Gluconate, 935
Monopotassium L-Glutamate, 776
Monopotassium Glutamate Monohydrate, 776
Monopotassium Phosphate, 944
Monosodium Dihydrogen Phosphate, 1053
Monosodium Glutamate, 777
Monosodium L-Glutamate, 777
Monosodium Glutamate Monohydrate, 777
Monosodium Phosphate, 1053
Monostearin, 509
Morpholine, 779
Mortierella alpina Oil, 75
MPG, 776
MSG, 777
Murexide Indicator Preparation, 1405
Mustard Oil, 780
Myrcene, 780
Myrcia Oil, 102
Myristaldehyde, 781
Myristic Acid, 781
Myristica Oil, 813
Myristyl Alcohol, 782
Myrrh Oil, 782

N

1,4-Naphthalenedione, 1187
α-Naphtholbenzein TS, 1398
Naphthol Green B, 1405
Naphthol Green TS, 1398
β-Naphthyl Ethyl Ether, 784
Natamycin, 785
Natural rubber (latex solids), 703
Natural Terpene Resin, 1121

Near-Infrared Spectroscopy, 1467
"Negligible", Defined, 5
Neohesperidine Dihydrochalcone, 786
Neotame, 788
Nerol, 790
Nerolidol, 791
Nerolin II, 784
Nerolin Bromelia, 784
Neryl Acetate, 792
Nessler's Reagent, 1398
Neutralized Phthalate Buffer, 1393
Neutral Red, 1405
Neutral Red TS, 1398
Neutral Sulfite Method (Essential Oils and Flavors), 1337
Niacin, 793
Niacinamide, 794
Niacinamide Ascorbate, 795
Nickel, 795
Nickel Catalysts, 795
Nickel Limit Test, 1276
Nickel Standard Solution TS, 1398
Nicotinamide, 794
Nicotinamide Ascorbate, 795
Nicotinic Acid, 793
Niger Gutta, 703
Ninhydrin TS, 1398
Nisin A Preparation, 797
Nispero, 702
Nitrate Identification Test, 1263
Nitre Cake, 1020
Nitric Acid, 1398
Nitric Acid, TS, Diluted, 1398
Nitric Oxide-Nitrogen Dioxide Detector Tube, 1406
Nitrite Identification Test, 1263
Nitrogen, 798
Nitrogen Determination
    α-Amino, 1280
    Ammonia, 1280
    Kjeldahl Method, 1293
Nitrogen Enriched Air, 799
Nitrogen Oxide, 800
Nitrous Oxide, 800
(*E*),(*E*)-2,4-Nonadienal, 801
trans,cis-2,6-Nonadienal, 802
(*E*),(*Z*)-2,6-Nonadienal, 802
trans,trans-2,4-Nonadienal, 801
(*E*),(*Z*)-2,6-Nonadienol, 803
trans,cis-2,6-Nonadienol, 803
δ-Nonalactone, 804
γ-Nonalactone, 805
Nonanal, 806
Nonanoic Acid, 808
1-Nonanol, 812
2-Nonanone, 807
Noncrystallizing Sorbitol Solution, 1077
(*E*)-2-Nonenal, 810
trans-2-Nonenal, 810
(*E*)-2-Nonen-1-ol, 808
(*Z*)-6-Nonen-1-ol, 809
cis-6-Nonen-1-ol, 809
trans-2-Nonenol, 808
Nonyl Acetate, 811
Nonyl Alcohol, 812

Normal Solutions, 1400
Nuclear Magnetic Resonance, 1244, 1445
Nutmeg Oil, 813

O

(Z);(Z)-9,12-Octadecadienoic Acid, 656
Octadecanoic Acid, 512, 1087
(Z)-9-Octadecenoic Acid, 825
δ-Octalactone, 815
γ-Octalactone, 815
Octanal, 816
Octanoic Acid, 817
1-Octanol, 823
3-Octanol, 817
2-Octanone, 746
(E)-2-Octen-1-al, 818
trans-2-Octen-1-al, 818
(Z)-3-Octen-1-ol, 818
1-Octen-3-ol, 819
cis-3-Octen-1-ol, 818
1-Octen-3-yl Acetate, 820
1-Octen-3-yl Butyrate, 821
Octyl Acetate, 822
3-Octyl Acetate, 822
Octyl Alcohol, 823
Octyl Formate, 824
Octyl Isobutyrate, 825
Octyl 2-Methylpropanoate, 825
"Odorless", Defined, 3
Oil Content of Synthetic Paraffin, 1251
Oil of Frankincense, 828
Oil of Shaddock, 515
Oleic Acid, 825
Oleoresin Angelica Seed, 1083
Oleoresin Anise, 1083
Oleoresin Basil, 1083
Oleoresin Black Pepper, 1083
Oleoresin Capsicum, 1083
Oleoresin Caraway, 1083
Oleoresin Cardamom, 1083
Oleoresin Celery, 1083
Oleoresin Coriander, 1084
Oleoresin Cubeb, 1084
Oleoresin Cumin, 1084
Oleoresin Dillseed, 1084
Oleoresin Fennel, 1084
Oleoresin Ginger, 1084
Oleoresin Hop, 1084
Oleoresin Laurel Leaf, 1084
Oleoresin Marjoram Sweet, 1084
Oleoresin Origanum, 1084
Oleoresin Paprika, 1084
Oleoresin Parsley Leaf, 1084
Oleoresin Parsley Seed, 1084
Oleoresin Pimenta Berries, 1084
Oleoresin Rosemary, 1084
Oleoresins, 1357
    Color Value, 1357
    Curcumin Content, 1357
    Piperine Content, 1357
    Residual Solvent, 1358
    Total Capsaicinoids Content, 1359
    Volatile Oil Content, 1359

Oleoresin Thyme, 1084
Oleoresin Turmeric, 1084
Olestra, 826
Olibanum Oil, 828
Onion Oil, 829
Optical (Specific) Rotation, 1232
Orange Oil, Bitter, Cold-pressed, 830
Orange Oil, Cold-pressed, 831
Orange Oil, Distilled, 832
Origanum Oil, Spanish Type, 833
Origanum Oleoresin, 1084
Orris Root Oil, 834
Orthophenanthroline TS, 1398
Orthophosphoric Acid, 888
Oxalic Acid, 0.1 N, 1402
Oxalic Acid TS, 1398
Ox Bile Extract, 835
1:8 Oxido-p-menthane, 427
Oxidoreductase
    Aspergillus niger var., 1303, 1304
    Bovine Liver, 1304
    Micrococcus lysodeikticus, 1304
Oxyethylene Determination, 1350
Oxygen Flask Combustion, 1217
Oxystearin, 836
Ozone, 836

P

Packaging and Storage
    Containers, 3
    "Cool Place", Defined, 3
    "Excessive Heat", Defined, 3
    "Light-Resistant Container", Defined, 3
    Product Security, 3
    Storage Under Nonspecific Conditions, 3
    "Tight Container", Defined, 3
    "Well-Closed Container", Defined, 3
Palmarosa Oil, 839
Palmitic Acid, 840
Palmitoyl L-Ascorbic Acid, 82
Palm Kernel Oil (Unhydrogenated), 838
Palm Oil (Unhydrogenated), 838
Pancreatin, 375, 1325
Pancreatin Activity, 1325
Panthenol, 322
DL-Panthenol, 840
D(+)-Pantothenyl Alcohol, 322
DL-Pantothenyl Alcohol, 840
Papain, 376, 1305
Paper Chromatography, 1222
Paprika Oleoresin, 1084
Paraffin, Synthetic, 841
Parsley Herb Oil, 843
Parsley Leaf Oleoresin, 1084
Parsley Seed Oil, 844
Parsley Seed Oleoresin, 1084
Partial Acid Digest of (Source) Protein, 845
Partial Enzymatic Digest of (Source) Protein, 845

Partially Dementholized Mentha Arvensis Oil, 712
Partially Hydrolyzed (Source) Protein, 845
Partially Hydrolyzed Proteins, 845
Patent Blue 5, 847
Patent Blue V, 847
Peach Aldehyde, 1166
Peanut Oil (Unhydrogenated), 851
Pectinase, 1305
Pectins, 851
PEG, 906
Pelargonic Aldehyde, 806
Pendare, 702
Pennyroyal Oil, 855
ω-Pentadecalactone, 856
Pentaerythritol Ester of Partially Hydrogenated Wood Rosin, 857
Pentaerythritol Ester of Wood Rosin, 857
1,2,3,4,5-Pentahydroxypentane, 1198
1,5-Pentanedial, 498
2,3-Pentanedione, 858
Pentanoic Acid, 1175
1-Pentanol, 61
2-Pentanone, 859
Pentapotassium Triphosphate, 948
Pentasodium Triphosphate, 1067
1-Pentyl Butyrate, 61
1-Pentyl Formate, 62
Pentyl Heptanoate, 62
Pentyl Hexanoate, 581
People
    2010–2015, xi
Peppermint Oil, 860
Pepsin, 375, 1327
Pepsin Activity, 1327
Peptone (Source), 845
Percentage of Cineole (Essential Oils and Flavors), 1338
Perchloric Acid, 0.1 N, 1402
Perchloric Acid, 0.1 N, in Dioxane, 1402
Perillo, 702
Perlite, 861
Peroxide Identification Test, 1263
Peroxide Value
    Fats and Related Substances, 1351
    Flavor Chemicals Other Than Essential Oils, 1379
Pesticide Residues, 1384
Petitgrain Oil, Paraguay Type, 862
Petrolatum, 863
Petroleum Jelly, 863
Petroleum Wax, 864
Petroleum Wax, Synthetic, 866
pH Determination, 1233
α-**Phellandrene**, 867
Phenethyl Acetate, 868
2-Phenethyl Acetate, 868
Phenethyl Alcohol, 869
α-Phenethyl Alcohol, 756
Phenethyl Isobutyrate, 870
Phenethyl Isovalerate, 871
2-Phenethyl 2-Methylbutyrate, 874
Phenethyl Phenylacetate, 872

Phenethyl Salicylate, 873
Phenolphthalein, 1406
Phenolphthalein Paper, 1406
Phenolphthalein TS, 1398
Phenol Red, 1406
Phenol Red TS, 1398
Phenols (Essential Oils and Flavors), 1338
Phenols, Free (Essential Oils and Flavors), 1339
Phenolsulfonphthalein TS, 1398
Phenoxyethyl Isobutyrate, 874
Phenylacetaldehyde, 879
Phenylacetaldehyde Dimethyl Acetal, 878
Phenylacetic Acid, 880
DL-**Phenylalanine**, 881
L-**Phenylalanine**, 882
L-Phenylalanine, L-α-aspartyl-2-methyl ester compound with 6-methyl-1,2,3-oxathiazin-4(3H)-one 2,2-dioxide (1:1), 86
Phenyl Carbinol, 112
α-Phenyl Ethyl Acetate, 751
2-Phenylethyl Alcohol, 869
Phenylethyl Anthranilate, 883
Phenylethyl Butyrate, 884
Phenyl Ethyl Cinnamate, 875
Phenyl Ethyl Propionate, 876
p-Phenylphenol TS, 1398
3-Phenyl-1-propanol, 877
3-Phenylpropenoic Acid, 250
2-Phenylpropionaldehyde, 885
3-Phenylpropionaldehyde, 886
2-Phenylpropionaldehyde Dimethyl Acetal, 867
3-Phenylpropyl Acetate, 884
Phenylpropyl Alcohol, 877
Phenylpropyl Aldehyde, 886
PHMO, 703
Phosphatase
  Aspergillus niger var., 1305
Phosphate Buffer, 1393
Phosphate Buffer Solution pH 7.2, 1381
Phosphate Identification Test, 1263
Phosphate Standard Solution, 1394
Phospholipase A₂, 375, 1328
Phospholipase A₂ Activity, 1328
Phosphoric Acid, 888, 1398
Phosphoric acid, ammonium iron (II) salt, 450
Phosphorus Limit Test, 1277
Phosphotungstic Acid TS, 1398
Phylloquinone, 1187
Physical Tests and Determinations, 1221
Physiochemical Properties, 1230
Phytase, 378, 1328
Phytase Activity, 1328
Phytonadione, 1187
Picric Acid TS, 1398
Pimaricin, 785
Pimenta Berries Oil, 889
Pimenta Berries Oleoresin, 1084
Pimenta Leaf Oil, 890
Pimenta Oil, 889

Pimento Leaf Oil, 890
Pimento Oil, 889
Pineapples: *Ananas comosus Ananas bracteatus* (L), 1303
1-α-Pinene, 893
2-Pinene, 893
α-Pinene, 893
β-Pinene, 893
Pine Needle Oil, 460, 891
Pine Needle Oil, Dwarf, 891
Pine Needle Oil, Scotch Type, 892
Pinus pinaster Extract, 698
Piperidine, 894
Piperine Content, 1357
Piperonal, 895
Piperonyl Aldehyde, 895
Plant Proteolytic Activity, 1330
Plasma Spectrochemistry, 1253
Poloxamer 331, 895
Poloxamer 407, 897
Polydextrose, 899
Polydextrose Solution, 902
Polydimethylsiloxane, 358
Polyethylene, 905
Polyethylene Glycols, 906
Polyglucitol, 554
Polyglycerate (60), 385
Polyglycerol Esters of Fatty Acids, 909
Polyglycerol Esters of Interesterified Ricinoleic Acid, 910
Polyglycerol Polyricinoleate, 910
Polyglycerol Polyricinoleic Acid, 910
Polyisobutylene, 911
Poly[1-(2-oxo-1-pyrrolidinyl)ethylene], 950
Poly(oxy-1,2-ethanediyl) Derivative, 913, 915, 918
Polyoxyethylene (20) Mono- and Diglycerides of Fatty Acids, 385
Polyoxyethylene (20) Sorbitan Monolaurate, 913
Polyoxyethylene (20) Sorbitan Monooleate, 918
Polyoxyethylene (20) Sorbitan Monostearate, 915
Polyoxyethylene (20) Sorbitan Tristearate, 917
Polypropylene Glycol, 912
Polysorbate 20, 913
Polysorbate 40, 915
Polysorbate 60, 915
Polysorbate 65, 917
Polysorbate 80, 918
Polyvinyl Acetate, 919
Poly(vinyl acetate), 919
Polyvinyl Alcohol, 920
Poly(vinyl alcohol), 920
Polyvinylpolypyrrolidone, 289
Polyvinylpyrrolidone, 950
Ponceau 4R, 922
Pork Collagen, 926
Potassium Acetate TS, 1398
Potassium Acid Phthalate, 0.1 N, 1402
Potassium Acid Tartrate, 928
Potassium Alginate, 928

Potassium Alum, 46
Potassium Benzoate, 929
Potassium Bicarbonate, 929
Potassium Biphosphate, 944
Potassium Biphthalate, 0.2 M, 1393
Potassium Bitartrate, 928
Potassium Bromate, 930
Potassium Carbonate, 931
Potassium Carbonate Solution, 931
Potassium Chloride, 931
Potassium Chloride, 0.2 M, 1393
Potassium Chromate TS, 1398
Potassium Citrate, 934
Potassium Dichromate, 0.1 N, 1402
Potassium Dichromate TS, 1398
Potassium Dihydrogen Phosphate, 944
Potassium Ferricyanide TS, 1398
Potassium Ferrocyanide TS, 1398
Potassium Gibberellate, 934
Potassium Gluconate, 935
Potassium Glutamate, 776
Potassium Glycerophosphate, 936
Potassium Hydroxide, 937
Potassium Hydroxide, 0.5 N, Alcoholic, 1403
Potassium Hydroxide, 1 N, 1402
Potassium Hydroxide Solution, 937
Potassium Hydroxide TS, 1399
Potassium Hydroxide TS, Alcoholic, 1399
Potassium Identification Test, 1263
Potassium Iodate, 938
Potassium Iodate, 0.05 M, 1403
Potassium Iodide, 939
Potassium Iodide TS, 1399
Potassium Kurrol's Salt, 945
Potassium Lactate Solution, 939
Potassium Metabisulfite, 941
Potassium Metaphosphate, 945
Potassium Nitrate, 942
Potassium Nitrite, 943
Potassium Permanganate, 0.1 N, 1403
Potassium Permanganate TS, 1399
Potassium Phosphate, Dibasic, 943
Potassium Phosphate, Monobasic, 944
Potassium Phosphate, Monobasic, 0.2 M, 1393
Potassium Phosphate, Tribasic, 944
Potassium Polymetaphosphate, 945
Potassium Polyphosphates, 945
Potassium Pyroantimonate TS, 1399
Potassium Pyrophosphate, 946
Potassium Pyrosulfite, 941
Potassium Salt, 947
Potassium Sodium Tartrate, 1055
Potassium Sorbate, 947
Potassium Sulfate, 948
Potassium Sulfate TS, 1399
Potassium Sulfite, 948
Potassium Triphosphate, 948

1632 / Potassium Tripolyphosphate / Index

Potassium Tripolyphosphate, 948
Povidone, 950
Powdered Cellulose, 243
Precipitated Calcium Phosphate, 187
"Precision", Defined, 1411
Preface, v
Pressure Measurements, 5
L-Proline, 952
Propane, 953
Propane, 1-3-diol, 954
1,2-Propanediol, 963
1,3-Propanediol, 954
   Biobased Content of, 1388
1,2,3-Propanetriol Octadecanoate, 509
1,2,3-Propane Tristearoyl Ester, 512
2-Propanol, 606
n-Propanol, 958
2-Propanone, 14
1-Propene-1,2,3-tricarboxylic Acid, 25
Propene Oxide, 966
p-Propenylanisole, 66
Propenylguaethol, 955
4-Propenyl Veratrole, 748
Propionaldehyde, 956
Propionic Acid, 957
Propyl Acetate, 958
n-Propyl Acetate, 958
Propyl Alcohol, 958
p-Propyl Anisole, 959
Propylene Chlorohydrin
   Determination, 1366
Propylene Glycol, 963
Propylene Glycol Alginate, 964
Propylene Glycol Ether of
   Methylcellulose, 561
Propylene Glycol Lactostearate, 623
Propylene Glycol Mono- and Diesters, 965
Propylene Glycol Mono- and Diesters
   of Fatty Acids, 965
Propylene Glycol Monostearate, 965
Propylene Oxide, 966
1,2-Propylene Oxide, 966
Propyl Formate, 960
Propyl Gallate, 961
Propyl p-Hydroxybenzoate, 968
Propyl Mercaptan, 962
Propylparaben, 968
Propyl Propionate, 963
n-Propyl Propionate, 963
Protease, 378
   Animal Pancreas, 1306
   Aspergillus niger, 1303
   Aspergillus niger var., 1303
   Aspergillus niger var. *awamori*
     (Containing a *Calf Prochymosin*
     Gene), 1304
   Aspergillus oryzae var., 1303
   Bacillus cereus, 1306
   Bacillus licheniformis var., 1306
   Bacillus subtilis var., 1306
   Endothia parasitica, 1306
   Escherichia coli K-12 (Containing a
     Calf Prochymosin Gene), 1304
   Figs (*Ficus*) sp., 1304
   Kluyveromyces marxianus, 1304

Pancreatic Extract, Bovine or
   Porcine, 1304
Papaya (*Carica papaya* (L)), 1305
Pineapples: *Ananas comosus Ananas bracteatus* (L), 1303
Porcine or Other Animal Stomach
   Tissue, 1306
   Rhizomucor meihei, 1306
   Rhizomucor pusillus (Lindt), 1306
   Ruminant Animal Stomach, 1306
Proteins, Partially Hydrolyzed, 845
Proteolytic Activity, Bacterial (PC), 1331
Proteolytic Activity, Fungal (HUT), 1331
Proteolytic Activity, Fungal (SAP), 1332
Pteroylglutamic Acid, 461
Pullalanase, 1333
Pullulan, 969
Pullulanase Activity, 1333
Purified Oxgall, 835
PVOH, 920
PVP, 950
PVPP, 289
3-Pyridinecarboxylic Acid, 793
Pyridoxine Hydrochloride, 970
Pyridoxol Hydrochloride, 970
Pyromucic Aldehyde, 472
Pyrrole, 971
L-2-Pyrrolidinecarboxylic Acid, 952

Q

Qualitative Test for Phenols Using
   Ferric Chloride (Flavor Chemicals
   Other Than Essential Oils), 1380
Quimociac TS, 1399
Quinaldine Red, 1406
Quinaldine Red TS, 1399
Quinine Hydrochloride, 972
Quinine Sulfate, 973
Quinones (Chewing Gum Base
   Polymers), 1299

R

Racemic Pantothenyl Alcohol, 840
Radioactivity, 1452
Raman Spectroscopy, 1472
Rapeseed Oil, Fully Hydrogenated, 974
Rapeseed Oil, Superglycerinated, 974
Rappaport Vassiliadis Salmonella
   Enrichment Broth, 1381
Raspberry Ketone, 560
Readily Carbonizable Substances, 1233
Readily Carbonizable Substances in
   Ethyl Acetate, Limit Test, 1379
Readily Oxidizable Substances in *dl*-
   Menthol, 1380
Reagents, Specifications, 5
Reb A, 975
Rebaudioside A, 975
Rebiana, 975

Reduced Iron, 574
Reducing Substances (Flavor Chemicals
   Other Than Essential Oils), 1380
Reducing Sugars Assay, 1367
Reference Standards, 5
Refined Arachidonic Acid-Rich Oil
   (RAO), 75
Refined Bleached Shellac, 1011
Refined Microcrystalline Wax, 864
Refined Paraffin Wax, 864
Refractive Index, 1234
Regular Bleached Shellac, 1010
Reichert-Meissl Value, 1352
Relative Atomic Mass and Half-Lives of
   Selected Radionucleotides, 1507
Rennet, 1306
Rennet, Bovine, 375
Rennet, Calf, 375
Rennet, Microbial, 378
Requirements for Listing Substances in
   FCC, 2
Residual Solvent (Oleoresins), 1358
Residual Styrene (Chewing Gum Base
   Polymers), 1300
Residual Titration (for Water), 1240
Residue on Evaporation
   Essential Oils and Flavors, 1339
   Flavor Chemicals (Other than
     Essential Oils), 1380
Residue on Ignition (Sulfated Ash), 1259
Rhodinol, 979
Rhodinyl Acetate, 980
Rhodinyl Formate, 981
Riboflavin, 982
Riboflavin 5'-Phosphate Ester
   Monosodium Salt, 983
Riboflavin 5'-Phosphate Ester
   Monosodium Salt, Dihydrate, 983
Riboflavin 5'-Phosphate Sodium, 983
Rice Bran Wax, 985
Ricinus Oil, 237
"Robustness", Defined, 1413
Rochelle Salt, 1055
Rose Geranium Oil, Algerian Type, 483
Rosemary Oil, 987
Rosemary Oleoresin, 1084
Rose Oil, 986
Rosidinha (rosadinha), 702
Rosins and Related Substances
   Acid Number, 1360
   Softening Point, 1360
   Viscosity, 1363
Rosins and Related Substances, Tests
   and Assays, 1360
Rue Oil, 988
"Ruggedness", Defined, 1412
Rum Ether, So-Called, 418

S

(S)-2-Amino-4-(methylselenyl)butyric
   Acid, 1006
Sabouraud Dextrose Agar, 1381
Saccharin, 990

Safflower Oil (Unhydrogenated), 991
Sage Oil, Dalmatian Type, 992
Sage Oil, Spanish Type, 993
SAIB, 1098
Salatrim, 994
Salicylaldehyde, 999
Salmonella SPP., 1383
SALP, 1017
Salt, 1023
Sandalwood Oil, East Indian Type, 1000
Sandalwood Oil, West Indian Type, 65
Santalol, 1001
Santalyl Acetate, 1002
Saponification Value
  Essential Oils and Flavors, 1337
  Fats and Related Substances, 1352
Savory Oil (Summer Variety), 1003
Schiff's Reagent, Modified, 1399
Schizochytrium Oil, 330
Scoville Heat Units, 1478
Seaweed-Derived Calcium, 1004
Seignette Salt, 1055
Selenium Limit Test, 1278
L-Selenomethoinine, 1006
DL-Serine, 1008
L-Serine, 1009
Shea Butter, 1010
Sheanut Oil, Refined, 1010
Shellac, Bleached, 1010
Shellac, Bleached, Wax-Free, 1011
Short- and Long-Chain Acyl Triglyceride Molecules, 994
Short Chain Fructooligosaccharides, 467
Sieve Analysis of Granular Metal Powders, 1259
Significant Figures, 6
Silicon Dioxide, 1012
Silver Nitrate, 0.1 N, 1403
Silver Nitrate TS, 1399
Siraitia grosvenorii Extract, 772
Slaked Lime, 171
Smectite, 105
Soap, 1353
Soda Alum, 46
Soda Ash, 1021
Sodium Acetate, 1013
Sodium Acetate, 0.1 N, 1403
Sodium Acid Pyrophosphate, 1014
Sodium Acid Sulfate, 1020
Sodium Acid Sulfite, 1020
Sodium Alginate, 1014
Sodium Alum, 46
Sodium Aluminosilicate, 1015
Sodium Aluminum Phosphate, Acidic, 1017
Sodium Aluminum Phosphate, Basic, 1018
Sodium Arsenite, 0.05 N, 1403
Sodium Ascorbate, 1018
Sodium L-Ascorbate, 1018
Sodium Benzoate, 1019
Sodium o-Benzosulfimide, 1059
Sodium Bicarbonate, 1019
Sodium Biphosphate, 1053

Sodium Bisulfate, 1020
Sodium Bisulfite, 1020
Sodium Bisulfite TS, 1399
Sodium Bitartrate TS, 1399
Sodium Borate TS, 1399
Sodium Carbonate, 1021
Sodium Carbonate TS, 1399
Sodium Carboxymethylcellulose, 241
Sodium Carboxymethyl Cellulose, Enzymatically Hydrolyzed, 1021
Sodium Chloride, 1023
Sodium Chloride (Color Additive Assays), 1285
Buffered Sodium Chloride-Peptone Solution pH 7.0, 1381
Sodium Chlorite Solutions, Acidified, 25
Sodium Choleate, 835
Sodium Citrate, 1027
Sodium Cobaltinitrite TS, 1399
Sodium Cyclamate, 1028
Sodium Cyclohexanesulfamate, 1028
Sodium Cyclohexylsulfamate, 1028
Sodium Dehydroacetate, 1029
Sodium Diacetate, 1029
Sodium Dodecyl Sulfate, 1041
Sodium Erythorbate, 1030
Sodium Ferric Pyrophosphate, 1030
Sodium Ferrocyanide, 1032
Sodium Fluoride TS, 1399
Sodium Fumarate, 1033
Sodium Gluconate, 1034
Sodium D-Gluconate, 1034
Sodium Glutamate, 777
Sodium Hexametaphosphate, 1055
Sodium Hydrogen Carbonate, 1019
Sodium Hydrogen Diacetate, 1029
Sodium Hydrogen Sulfite, 1020
Sodium Hydroxide, 1036
Sodium Hydroxide, 0.2 M, 1393, 1393
Sodium Hydroxide, 0.5 N, Alcoholic, 1403
Sodium Hydroxide, 1 N, 1403
Sodium Hydroxide Solutions, 1035
Sodium Hydroxide TS, 1399
Sodium 3-(1-Hydroxyethylidene)-6-methyl-1,2-pyran-2,4(3H)-dione, 1029
Sodium Hypophosphite, 1037
Sodium Hyposulfite, 1066
Sodium Identification Test, 1263
Sodium Indigotindisulfonate TS, 1399, 1399
Sodium Iron EDTA, 1037
Sodium Iron Pyrophosphate, 1030
Sodium Lactate Solution, 1040
Sodium Lauryl Sulfate, 1041
Sodium Lignosulfonate, 1042
Sodium Magnesium Aluminosilicate, 1044
Sodium Metabisulfite, 1046
Sodium Metaphosphate, Insoluble, 1047
Sodium Metasilicate, 1047
Sodium Methoxide, 1048

Sodium Methoxide, 0.1 N, in Pyridine, 1403
Sodium Methoxide, 0.02 N, in Toluene, 1404
Sodium Methylate, 1048
Sodium Molybdate Dihydrate, 1049
Sodium Monohydrogendicarbonate, 1061
Sodium Nitrate, 1050
Sodium Nitrite, 1051
Sodium Nitroferricyanide TS, 1399
Sodium Phosphate, Dibasic, 1052
Sodium Phosphate, Monobasic, 1053
Sodium Phosphate, Tribasic, 1054
Sodium Phosphate TS, 1399
Sodium Polyphosphates, Glassy, 1055
Sodium Potassium Tartrate, 1055
Sodium Potassium Tripolyphosphate, 1056
Sodium Propanoate, 1057
Sodium Propionate, 1057
Sodium Pyrophosphate, 1058
Sodium Pyrosulfite, 1046
Sodium Saccharin, 1059
Sodium Sesquicarbonate, 1061
Sodium Silicoaluminate, 1015
Sodium Stearoyl Lactylate, 1062
Sodium Stearyl Fumarate, 1063
Sodium Sulfate, 1065
Sodium Sulfate (Color Additive Assays), 1285
Sodium Sulfide TS, 1399
Sodium Sulfite, 1065
Sodium Tartrate, 1066
Sodium Tetraphenylborate TS, 1399
Sodium Tetrapolyphosphate, 1055
Sodium Thiosulfate, 1066
Sodium Thiosulfate, 0.1 N, 1404
Sodium Thiosulfate TS, 1399
Sodium Trimetaphosphate, 1067
Sodium Triphosphate, 1067
Sodium Tripolyphosphate, 1067
Softening Point (Rosins and Related Substances), 1360
  Drop Method, 1360
  Ring-And-Ball Method, 1361
Solidification Point, 1234
Solin Oil, 1069
Solubility in Alcohol (Essential Oils and Flavors), 1339
Solubility Specifications and Statements, 3
Soluble Saccharin, 1059
Solutions
  Colorimetric, 1393
  Preparation of, 6
  Standard Buffer, 1393
  Water for, 6
Solutions and Indicators, 1393
Sorbic Acid, 1069
Sorbitan Monododecanoate, 913
Sorbitan Monolaurate, 1070
Sorbitan Monooctadecanoate, 915
Sorbitan Mono-9-octadecenoate, 918

Sorbitan Monooleate, 1071
Sorbitan Monopalmitate, 1072
Sorbitan Monostearate, 1073
Sorbitan Tristearate, 1074
D-Sorbite, 1075
Sorbitol, 1075
D-Sorbitol, 1075
Sorbitol Solution, 1076
  Noncrystallizing, 1077
Soybean-Casein Digest Agar, 1381
Soybean-Casein Digest Broth, 1381
Soybean Oil (Unhydrogenated), 1081
  High oleic, 1081
Soy Protein Concentrate, 1080
Spearmint Oil, 1082
Specific Gravity, 6
  Fats and Related Substances, 1353
"Specificity", Defined, 1411
Specific Rotation, 1232
Spectrophotometric Identification Tests, 1294
  Infrared Absorption, 1294
  Infrared Spectra, 1294
  Ultraviolet Absorption, 1295
Spectrophotometry and Light-Scattering, 1459
Spice Oleoresins, 1083
  Angelica seed, 1083
  Anise, 1083
  Basil, 1083
  Black pepper, 1083
  Capsicum, 1083
  Caraway, 1083
  Cardamom, 1083
  Celery, 1083
  Coriander, 1084
  Cubeb, 1084
  Cumin, 1084
  Dillseed, 1084
  Fennel, 1084
  Ginger, 1084
  Hop, 1084
  Laurel leaf, 1084
  Marjoram sweet, 1084
  Origanum, 1084
  Paprika, 1084
  Parsley leaf, 1084
  Parsley seed, 1084
  Pimenta berries, 1084
  Rosemary, 1084
  Thyme, 1084
  Turmeric, 1084
Spike Lavender Oil, 1085
Stability (Fats and Related Substances), 1353
  Active Oxygen Method, 1353
Standard Buffer Solutions, 1393
Standard Solutions
  Ammonium, 1394
  Barium, 1394
  Iron, 1394
  Magnesium, 1394
  Phosphate, 1394
Standard Solutions for the Preparation of Controls and Standards, 1394
Stannous Chloride, 1086

Stannous Chloride TS, 1399
Starch Hydrolysate, Hydrogenated, 554
Starch Iodate Paper, 1406
Starch Iodide Paper, 1406
Starch Iodide Paste TS, 1399
Starch TS, 1399
Starter Distillate, 1087
Stearic Acid, 1087
Stearin, 512
Stearyl Alcohol, 1088
Stearyl Citrate, 1089
Stearyl Monoglyceridyl Citrate, 1090
Sterculia Gum, 611
Stock Buffer Solution, 1381
Strawberry Aldehyde, 415
Stronger Ammonia Water, 53
Submissions to the Food Chemicals Codex, 1411
Succinic Acid, 1091
Succinylated Monoglycerides, 1091
Sucralose, 1092
Sucroesters, 1099
Sucromalt, 1094
Sucrose, 1097
Sucrose Acetate Isobutyrate, 1098
Sucrose Fatty Acid Esters, 1099
Sucrose (Refractive Index Scale), 1373
Sugar, 1097
Sugar Beet Fiber, 1101
Sugar Beet Pulp, 1101
Sulfanilic Acid TS, 1399
Sulfated Ash (Residue on Ignition), 1259
Sulfate Identification Test, 1263
Sulfate Limit Test, 1266
Sulfite Identification Test, 1263
Sulfiting Agents, Labeling, 2
Sulfur, 1295
Sulfur Dioxide, 1103
Sulfur Dioxide Detector Tube, 1406
Sulfur Dioxide Determination, 1368
Sulfuric Acid, 1104, 1400
Sulfuric Acid, 1 N, 1404
Sulfuric Acid, Alcoholic, 0.5 N, 1404
Sulfuric Acid, Alcoholic, 5 N, 1404
Sulfuric Acid Table, 1260
Sulfuric Acid TS, 1400
Sulfuric Acid TS, Diluted, 1400
Sulfurol, 728
Summer Savory Oil, 1003
Sunflower Oil (Unhydrogenated), 1105
Sunset Yellow, 1106
Sunset Yellow FCF, 438, 1106
Superglycerinated Fully Hydrogenated Rapeseed Oil, 974
Sweet Basil Oil, 101
Sweet Orange Oil, 831
Sweetwood Bark Oil, 234
Symbols, 6
Synthetic Amorphous Silica, 1012
Synthetic Iron Oxide, 1107
Synthetic Lycopene, 665
Synthetic Magnesium Silicate, 680

Synthetic Paraffin, 841
  Oil Content, 1251
Synthetic Petroleum Wax, 866
Synthetic Terpene Resin, 1122
Synthetic Wax (Ethylene Polymer or Ethylene Copolymer with Alpha-Olefins), 866

T

D-Tagatose, 1110
Tagetes Extract, 1110
Talc, 1111
Tallow, 1112
Tangerine Oil, Coldpressed, 1113
Tangerine Oil, Expressed, 1113
Tannic Acid, 1114
Tannic Acid TS, 1400
Tara Gum, 1115
"Tared Container", Defined, 6
Tarragon Oil, 1116
Tartaric Acid, 1117
L(+)-Tartaric Acid, 1117
Tartrate Identification Test, 1263
Tartrazine, 437, 1118
TBHQ, 1119
Temperatures, 6
Terpene Resin, Natural, 1121
Terpene Resin, Synthetic, 1122
α-**Terpinene**, 1123
γ-**Terpinene**, 1123
Terpinen-4-ol, 1122
α-**Terpineol**, 1123
Terpinyl Acetate, 1124
Terpinyl Propionate, 1125
Tests and Assays, 4
Tests for Absence of Specific Microorganisms, 1382
Test Solutions (TS) and Other Reagents, 1394
δ-**Tetradecalactone**, 1126
Tetradecanal, 781
Tetradecanoic Acid, 781
1-Tetradecanol, 782
Tetradecyl Alcohol, 782
Tetrahydrofurfuryl Alcohol, 1127
Tetrahydrogeraniol, 351
Tetrahydrolinalool, 1128
Tetrahydro-2H-1,4-oxazine, 779
2,3,5,6-Tetramethylpyrazine, 1128
Tetrapotassium Pyrophosphate, 946
Tetrasodium Diphosphate, 1058
Tetrasodium Pyrophosphate, 1058
Thaumatin, 1129
L-**Theanine**, 1131
Thermometers, 1217
Thermometric Equivalents, 1509
Thiamine Chloride, 1132
Thiamine Hydrochloride, 1132
Thiamine Mononitrate, 1133
Thiamine Nitrate, 1133
Thibetolide, 856
Thin-Layer Chromatography, 1223
Thiobismethane, 357
Thiosulfate Identification Test, 1263
Thorium Nitrate 0.1 M, 1404

L-**Threonine**, 1134
Thuja Oil, 238
Thyme Oil, 1135
Thyme Oleoresin, 1084
Thymol, 1136
Thymol Blue, 1406
Thymol Blue TS, 1400
Thymolphthalein, 1406
Thymolphthalein TS, 1400
"Tight Container", Defined, 3
Time Limits, 6
Tin Dichloride, 1086
Titanium Dioxide, 1137
Title of Monograph
  CAS number, 2
  FEMA number, 2
  INS number, 2
  Molecular Structure and Chemical Formulas, 2
Titrimetric Assays (Flavor Chemicals Other Than Essential Oils), 1377
  Direct Aqueous Acid Base Titrations, 1377
  Direct Aqueous Alcoholic Acid Base Titrations, 1378
TMG, 124
All-rac-α-**Tocopherol**, 1142
DL-α-Tocopherol, 1142
DL-α-Tocopherol Acetate, 1144
D-α-Tocopherol Concentrate, 1141
RRR-α-Tocopherol Concentrate, 1141
Tocopherols, 1354
Tocopherols Concentrate, Mixed, 1145
RRR-Tocopherols Concentrate, Mixed, 1145
All-rac-α-**Tocopheryl Acetate**, 1144
D-α-Tocopheryl Acetate, 1148
DL-α-Tocopheryl Acetate, 1144
RRR-α-Tocopheryl Acetate, 1148
D-α-Tocopheryl Acetate Concentrate, 1147
RRR-α-Tocopheryl Acetate Concentrate, 1147
D-α-Tocopheryl Acetate Preparation, 1147
D-α-Tocopheryl Acid Succinate, 1150
RRR-α-Tocopheryl Acid Succinate, 1150
Tolerances, 6
p-**Tolualdehyde**, 1151
Tolualdehyde, Mixed Isomers, 1152
Toluene Distillation Method (for Water), 1241
α-Toluic Acid, 880
α-Toluic Aldehyde, 879
o-Tolyl Acetate, 755
p-Tolyl Acetate, 288
Tolyl Aldehyde, Mixed Isomers, 1152
p-Tolyl Aldehyde, 1151
p-**Tolyl Isobutyrate**, 1153
Tomato Oleoresin Extract, 662
Torula Yeast, 1201
Total Aerobic Microbial Count, 1382
Total Alcohols (Essential Oils and Flavors), 1339

Total Capsaicinoids Content, 1359
Total Color (Color Additive Assays), 1285
Total Monoglycerides, 1349
Total Solids, 1370
  Glucose Syrup (Corn Syrup), 1370
  High-Fructose Corn Syrup, 1371
  Invert Sugar, 1373
  Maltodextrin, 1372
Total Unsaturation (Chewing Gum Base Polymers), 1301
Total Yeasts and Molds Count, 1382
Trace Impurities, 6
Tragacanth, 1154
Tragacanth Gum, 1154
Transglutaminase, 378
Transglutaminase Activity, 1334
Trehalose, 1155
Triacetin, 1158
Triatomic Oxygen, 836
Tribehenoyl-sn-glycerol, 507
Tributyrin, 1159
Tricalcium Citrate, 167
Tricalcium Phosphate, 187
Trichloroethene, 1160
Trichloroethylene, 1160
1,1,2-Trichloroethylene, 1160
4,1',6'-Trichlorogalactosucrose, 1092
2-**Tridecanone**, 1156
2-**Tridecenal**, 1157
Tridocosanoyl-sn-glycerol, 507
Triethanolamine, 0.5 N, 1404
Triethyl Citrate, 1160
3,7,12-Trihydroxycholanic Acid, 247
2,4α,7-Trihydroxy-1-methyl-8-methylenegibb-3-ene-1,10-dicarboxylic Acid 1,4-Lactone, 491
Triketohydrindene Hydrate TS, 1400
Trimagnesium Phosphate, 680
Trimethylamine, 1162
4-Trimethylamino-3-hydroxybutyrate, 217
2-Trimethylammonioacetate, 124
2,6,6-Trimethylbicyclo(3.1.1)hept-2-ene, 893
4-(2,6,6-Trimethyl-1-cyclohexenyl)-3-butene-2-one, 568, 569
3,7,11-Trimethyl-1,6,10-dodecatrien-3-ol, 791
3,7,11-Trimethyl-2,6,10-dodecatrien-1-ol, 431
Trimethylene Glycol, 954
Trimethylglycine, 124
3,5,5-**Trimethyl Hexanal**, 1162
2,4,5-**Trimethyl δ-3-Oxazoline**, 1161
2,3,5-**Trimethylpyrazine**, 1163
1,3,7-Trimethylxanthine, 160
Trinitrophenol TS, 1400
Triphosphate, 1067
Tripotassium Citrate, 934
Tripotassium Phosphate, 944
Tripropionin, 512
Trisodium Citrate, 1027
Trisodium Dipotassium Tripolyphosphate, 1056
Trisodium Phosphate, 1054

Tristearin, 512
Trypsin, 375, 1335
Trypsin Activity, 1335
DL-**Tryptophan**, 1163
L-**Tryptophan**, 1164
Tunu (tuno), 703
Turmeric Oleoresin, 1084
L-**Tyrosine**, 1165

U

Ultraviolet Absorbance of Citrus Oils (Essential Oils and Flavors), 1339
Ultraviolet Absorption, 1295
UMP disodium salt, 369
Uncombined Intermediates and Products of Side Reactions, 1287
δ-**Undecalactone**, 1166
γ-**Undecalactone**, 1166
Undecanal, 1167
2-**Undecanone**, 1169
1,3,5-Undecatriene, 1168
Undecen-10-al, 1170
10-Undecenal, 1170
(E)-2-**Undecenol**, 1171
Undecyl Alcohol, 1172
n-Undecyl Aldehyde, 1167
UNII Code, 2
Unmodified Food Starch, 465
Unsaponifiable Matter, 1355
Urea, 1173
Uridine 5'-monophosphate disodium salt, 369
USP Reference Standards for Food Ingredients, 1427

V

"Vacuum", Defined, 6
Valeraldehyde, 1175
Valeric Acid, 1175
γ-**Valerolactone**, 1176
"Validation", Defined, 1411
Validation of Food Chemicals Codex Methods, 1411
L-**Valine**, 1177
Vanillin, 1178
Vegetable Oil, Brominated, 134
Vegetable Oil Phytosterol Esters, 1179
Venezuelan chicle, 702
Veratraldehyde, 1181
Veratryl Aldehyde, 1181
Vinyl alcohol polymer, 920
1-Vinyl-2-pyrrolidone Crosslinked Insoluble Polymer, 289
Violet Red Bile Glucose Agar, 1381
Viscosity (Rosins and Related Substances), 1363
Viscosity Determination, 1236
  Cellulose Gum, 1238
  Dimethylpolysiloxane, 1236
  Methylcellulose, 1237
Vital Wheat Gluten, 1189
Vitamin A, 1181

Vitamin B$_1$, 1132, 1133
Vitamin B$_1$ Hydrochloride, 1132
Vitamin B$_1$ Mononitrate, 1133
Vitamin B$_2$, 982
Vitamin B$_6$, 970
Vitamin B$_6$ Hydrochloride, 970
Vitamin B$_{12}$, 1184
Vitamin C, 81
Vitamin C Sodium, 1018
Vitamin D, 1185, 1186
Vitamin D$_2$, 1185
Vitamin D$_3$, 1186
Vitamin E Acetate, 1144
Vitamin K, 1187
Volatile Acidity, 1356
Volatile Oil Content Oleoresins, 1359
Volatile Oil Content (Essential Oils and Flavors), 1340
Volumetric Apparatus, 1218
Volumetric Solutions, 1400

W

Water (Reagent), 5
  Carbon Dioxide-Free, 5
  Deaerated water, 5
  Degassed Water, 5
Water and Loss on Drying, 6
Water Determination, 1239
  Coulometric Titration, 1240
  Direct Titration, 1239
  Karl Fischer Titrimetric Method, 1239
  Residual Titration, 1240
  Toluene Distillation, 1241
Water for Solutions, 6
Water-Insoluble Matter, 1261
Water-Insoluble Matter (Color Additive Assays), 1289
Water Vapor Detector Tube, 1406
Weighing Practices
  "Constant Weight", Defined, 6
  "Tared Container", Defined, 6
Weights and Balances, 1219
Weights and Measures, 6
"Well-Closed Container", Defined, 3
Wheat Gluten, 1189
Wheat Protein Isolate, 1189
Whey, 1190
Whey Protein Concentrate, 1193
Whey Protein Isolate, 1194
Whey, Reduced Lactose, 1191
Whey, Reduced Minerals, 1192
White Cedar Leaf Oil, 238
White Petrolatum, 863
White Shellac, 1010
White Wax, 103
Wine Yeast Oil, 278
Wintergreen Oil, 1195
Wool Fat, 627

X

Xanthan Gum, 1197
Xylenol Orange, 1406
Xylenol Orange TS, 1400
Xylitol, 1198
Xylose Lysine Deoxycholate Agar, 1382

Y

Yam Flour, 613
Yeast, Autolyzed, 1200
Yeast, Dried, 1201
Yeast Extract, 1203
Yellow Petrolatum, 863
Yellow Prussiate of Soda, 1032
Yellow Wax, 104

Z

Zein, 1205
Zinc Gluconate, 1205
Zinc Identification Test, 1263
Zinc Oxide, 1206
Zinc Sulfate, 1207
Zinc Sulfate, 0.05 M, 1404
Zingerone, 1207